2001

BASEBALL CARD

PRICE GUIDE

•15TH EDITION•

PRICE GUIDE
EDITORS OF

Sports
Collectors
Digest Voice for the Hobby

Published by

700 E. State Street • Iola, WI 54990-0001
Telephone: 715/445-2214

Please call or write for our free catalog of sports publications.
Our toll-free number to place an order or obtain a free catalog is 800-258-0929
or please use our regular business telephone 715-445-2214
for editorial comment and further information.

Library of Congress Catalog Number: 87-80033
ISBN: 0-87349-238-2

Printed in the United States of America

TABLE OF CONTENTS

B

C

D

E

F

L

M

P

S

T

U

Z

HOW TO USE THIS CATALOG

This catalog has been uniquely designed to serve the needs of collectors and dealers at all levels from beginning to advanced. It provides a comprehensive guide to more than 20 years of baseball card issues, arranged so that even the most novice hobbyist can consult it with confidence and ease.

The following explanations summarize the general practices used in preparing this catalog's listings. However, because of specialized requirements which may vary from card set to card set, these must not be considered ironclad. Where these standards have been set aside, appropriate notations are usually incorporated.

ARRANGEMENT

The most important feature in identifying and pricing a baseball card is its set of origin. Therefore, the main body of this catalog, covering cards issued from 1981-date, has been alphabetically arranged within specific eras of issue according to the name by which the set is most popularly known to collectors, or by which it can be most easily identified by a person examining a card.

Among those card issuers who produced sets for more than a single year, their sets are then listed chronologically, from earliest to most recent, again within specific eras.

Within each set, the cards are listed by their designated card number, or in the absence of card numbers, alphabetically according to the last name of the player pictured. Listing numbers found in parentheses indicate the number does not appear on the card. Certain cards which fall outside the parameters of the normal card numbering for a specific set may be found at the beginning or end of the listings for that set.

VINTAGE-MODERN ISSUES

The main body of the book details modern major league baseball card issues from 1981-2000, as produced by the major national card companies. In general, prior to about 1990, this will include issues which picture one or more baseball players, usually contemporary with their playing days, printed on paper or cardboard in a variety of shapes and sizes and given away as a premium with the purchase of another product or service. After 1990 or so the definition is broadened to remove the restriction of the card as an ancillary product and to include those printed on plastic, wood, metal, etc.

Following the modern section is a vintage card section which details a range of Topps issues from 1980 and prior.

IDENTIFICATION

While most modern baseball cards are well identified on front, back or both, as to date and issue, such has not always been the case. In general, the back of the card is more useful in identifying the set of origin than the front. The issuer or sponsor's name will usually appear on the back since, after all, baseball cards were first produced as a promotional item to stimulate sales of other products. As often as not, that issuer's name is the name by which the set is known to collectors and under which it will be found listed in this catalog.

In some difficult cases, identifying a baseball card's general age, if not specific year of issue, can usually be accomplished by studying the biological or statistical information on the back of the card. The last year mentioned in either the biography or stats is usually the year which preceded the year of issue.

PHOTOGRAPHS

A photograph of the front and (prior to 1981) back of at least one representative card from virtually every set listed in this catalog has been incorporated into the listings to aid in identification.

Photographs have been printed in reduced size. The actual size of cards in each set is given in the introductory text preceding its listing, unless the card is the standard size (2.5" by 3.5").

DATING

The dating of baseball cards by year of issue on the front or back of the card itself is a relatively new phenomenon. In most cases, to accurately determine a date of issue for an unidentified card, it must be studied for clues. As mentioned, the biography, career summary or statistics on the back of the card are the best way to pinpoint a year of issue. In most cases, the year of issue will be the year after the last season mentioned on the card.

In some cases, particular card sets were issued over a period of more than one calendar year, but since they are collected together as a single set, their specific year of issue is not important. Such sets will be listed with their complete known range of issue years.

NUMBERING

While many baseball card issues as far back as the 1880s have contained card numbers assigned by the issuer to facilitate the collecting of a complete set, the practice has by no means been universal. Even today, not every set bears card numbers.

Logically, those baseball cards which were numbered by their manufacturer are presented in that numerical order within the listings of this catalog whenever possible. In a few cases, complete player checklists were obtained from earlier published sources which did not note card numbers, and so numbers have been arbitrarily assigned. Many other unnumbered issues have been assigned catalog numbers to facilitate their universal identification within the hobby, especially when buying and selling by mail.

In all cases, numbers which have been assigned, or which otherwise do not appear on the card through error or by design, are shown in this catalog within parentheses. In virtually all cases, unless a more natural system suggested itself by the unique matter of a particular set, the assignment of numbers by the cataloging staff has been done by alphabetical arrangement of the players' last names or the card's principal title.

Significant collectible variations for any particular card are noted within the listings by the application of a suffix letter. In instances of variations, the suffix "a" is assigned to the variation which was created first, when it can be so identified.

NAMES

The identification of a player by full name on the front of his baseball card has been a common practice only since the 1920s. Prior to that, the player's last name and team were the usual information found on the card front.

As a general -- though not universally applied -- practice, the listings in this volume present the player's name exactly as it appears on the front of the card. If the player's full name only appears on the back, rather than on the front of the card, the listing may correspond to that designation.

A player's name checklisted in italic type indicates a rookie card.

Cards which contain misspelled first or last names, or even wrong initials, will have included in their listings the incorrect information, with a correction accompanying in parentheses. This extends, also, to cases where the name on the card does not correspond to the player actually pictured.

In some cases, to facilitate efficient presentations, to maintain ease of use for the reader, or to allow for proper computer sorting of data, a player's name or card title may be listed other than as it appears on the card.

GRADING

It is necessary that some sort of card grading standard be used so that buyer and seller (especially when dealing by mail) may reach an informed agreement on the value of a card.

Modern issues, which have been preserved in top condition in considerable number, are listed only in grade of Mint (MT), reflective of the fact that there exists in the current market little or no demand for cards of the recent past in lower grades.

Values for lower-grade cards from 1981-date may be generally figured by using a figure of 75% of the Mint price for Near Mint specimens, and 40% of the Mint price for Excellent cards.

For the benefit of the reader, we present herewith the grading guide which was originally formulated in 1981 by Baseball Cards magazine (now SportsCards magazine) and Sports Collectors Digest, and has been continually refined since that time.

These grading definitions have been used in the pricing of cards in this book, but they are by no means a universally-accepted grading standard.

The potential buyer of a baseball card should keep that in mind when encountering cards of nominally the same grade, but at a price which differs widely from that quoted in this book.

Ultimately, the collector himself must formulate his own personal grading standards in deciding whether cards available for purchase meet the needs of his own collection.

Mint (MT): A perfect card. Well-centered, with parallel borders which appear equal to the naked eye. Four sharp, square corners. No creases, edge dents, surface scratches, paper flaws, loss of luster, yellowing or fading, regardless of age. No imperfectly printed card -- out of register, badly cut or ink flawed -- or card stained by contact with gum, wax or other substances can be considered truly Mint, even if new out of the pack. Generally, to be considered in Mint condition, a card's borders must exist in a ratio of 60/40 side to side and top to bottom.

Near Mint (NR MT): A nearly perfectly card. At first glance, a Near Mint card appears perfect; upon closer examination, however, a minor flaw will be discovered. On well-centered cards, three of the four corners must be perfectly sharp; only one corner shows a minor imperfection upon close inspection. A slightly off-center card with one or more borders being noticeably unequal -- but no worse than in a ratio of 70/30 S/S or T/B -- would also fit this grade.

Excellent (EX): Corners are still fairly sharp with only moderate wear. Card borders may be off center as much as 80/20. No creases. May have very minor gum, wax or product stains, front or back. Surfaces may show slight loss of luster from rubbing across other cards.

Very Good (VG): Show obvious handling. Corners rounded and/or perhaps showing minor creases. Other minor creases may be visible. Surfaces may exhibit loss of luster, but all printing is intact. May show major gum, wax or other packaging stains. No major creases, tape marks or extraneous markings or writing. All four borders visible, though the ratio may be as poor as 95/5. Exhibits honest wear.

Good (G): A well-worn card, but exhibits no intentional damage or abuse. May have major or multiple creases. Corners rounded well beyond the border. A good card will generally sell for about 50% the value of a card in Very Good condition.

Fair (F or Fr.): Shows excessive wear, along with damage or abuse. Will show all the wear characteristics of a Good card, along with such damage as thumb tack holes in or near margins, evidence of having been taped or pasted, perhaps small tears around the edges, or creases so heavy as to break the cardboard. Backs may show minor added pen or pencil writing, or be missing small bits of paper. Still, basically a complete card. A Fair card will generally for 50% the value of a Good specimen.

Poor (P): A card that has been tortured to death. Corners or other areas may be torn off. Card may have been trimmed, show holes from a paper punch or have been used for BB gun practice. Front may have extraneous pen or pencil writing, or other defacement. Major portions of front or back design may be missing. Not a pretty sight.

In addition to these terms, collectors may encounter intermediate grades, such as NM-MT or EX-MT. These cards usually have characteristics of both the lower and higher grades, and are generally priced midway between those two values.

Grading and pricing reflected in this book are for cards which have not been authenticated, graded and encapsulated by one of the third-party certification services. Cards which have been "slabbed" by these services generally sell for a premium above the price which a "raw" card will bring.

ROOKIE CARDS

While the status (and automatic premium value) which a player's rookie card carries has fallen and risen in recent years, and though the hobby still has not reached a universal definition of a rookie card, many significant rookie cards are noted in this catalog's listings by the use of italic type. For purposes of this catalog, a player's rookie card is considered to be any card in a licensed set from a major manufacturer in the first year in which that player appears on a card.

VALUATIONS

Values quoted in this book represent the current retail market at the time of compilation (January, 2001). The quoted values are the result of a unique system of evaluation and verification created by the catalog's editors. Utilizing specialized computer analysis and drawing upon recommendations provided through their daily involvement in the publication of the hobby's leading sports collectors' periodicals, as well as the input of consultants, dealers and collectors, each listing is, in the final analysis, the interpretation of that data by one or more of the editors.

It should be stressed, however, that this book is intended to serve only as an aid in evaluating cards; actual market conditions are constantly changing. This is especially true of the cards of current players, whose on-field performance during the course of a season can greatly affect the value of their cards -- upwards or downwards. Because of the extremely volatile nature of new card prices, especially high-end issues, we have chosen not to include the very latest releases such as premium-price brands from the major companies, feeling it is better to have no listings at all for those cards than to have inaccurate values in print.

Because this volume is intended to reflect the national market, users will find regional price variances caused by demand differences. Cards of Astros slugger Jeff Bagwell will, for instance, often sell at prices greater than quoted herein at shops and shows in the Houston area. Conversely, his cards may be acquired at a discount from these valuations when purchased on the East or West Coast.

Publication of this book is not intended as a solicitation to buy or sell the listed cards by the editors, publishers or contributors.

Again, the values here are retail prices -- what a collector can expect to pay when buying a card from a dealer. The wholesale price, that which a collector can expect to receive from a dealer when selling cards, will be significantly lower.

Most dealers operate on a 100 percent mark-up, generally paying about 50 percent of a card's retail value for cards which they are purchasing for inventory. On some high-demand cards, dealers will pay up to 75 percent or even 100 percent or more of retail value, anticipating continued price increases. Conversely, for many low-demand cards, such as common players' cards, dealers may pay as little as 10 percent or even less of retail with many base-brand cards of recent years having no resale value at all.

SETS

Collectors may note that the complete set prices for newer issues quoted in these listings are usually significantly lower than the total of the value of the individual cards which comprise the set. This reflects two factors in the baseball card market. First, a seller is often willing to take a lower composite price for a complete set as a "volume discount" and to avoid carrying in inventory a large number of common player or other lower-demand cards.

Second, to a degree, the value of common cards can be said to be inflated as a result of having a built-in overhead charge to justify the dealer's time in sorting cards, carrying them in stock and filling orders. This accounts for the fact that even brand new base-brand baseball cards, which cost the dealer around one cent each when bought in bulk, carry individual price tags of five cents or higher.

Some set prices shown, especially for old cards in top condition, are merely theoretical in that it is unlikely that a complete set exists in that condition. In general among older cards the range of conditions found in even the most painstakingly assembled complete set make the set values quoted useful only as a starting point for price negotiations.

ERRORS/VARIATIONS

It is often hard for the beginning collector to understand that an error on a baseball card, in and of itself, does not usually add premium value to that card. It is usually only when the correcting of an error in the subsequent printing creates a variation that premium value attaches to an error.

Minor errors, such as wrong stats or personal data, misspellings, inconsistencies, etc. -- usually affecting the back of the card -- are very common, especially in recent years. Unless a corrected variation was also printed, these errors are not noted in the listings of this book because they are not generally perceived by collectors to have premium value.

On the other hand, major effort has been expended to include the most complete listings ever for collectible variation cards. Many scarce and valuable variations are included in these listings because they are widely collected and often have significant premium value.

Beginning in the early 1990s, some card companies began production of their basic sets at more than one printing facility. This frequently resulted in numerous minor variations in photo cropping and back data presentation. Combined with a general decline in quality control from the mid-1980s through the early 1990s, which allowed unprecedented numbers of uncorrected error cards to be released, this caused a general softening of collector interest in errors and variations. Despite the fact most of these modern variations have no premium value, they are listed here as a matter of record.

COUNTERFEITS/REPRINTS

As the value of baseball cards has risen, certain cards and sets have become too expensive for the average collector to obtain. This, along with changes in the technology of color printing, has given rise to increasing numbers of counterfeit and reprint cards.

While both terms describe essentially the same thing -- a modern day copy which attempts to duplicate as closely as possible an original baseball card -- there are differences which are important to the collector.

Generally, a counterfeit is made with the intention of deceiving somebody into believing it is genuine, and thus paying large amounts of money for it. The counterfeiter takes every pain to try to make his fakes look as authentic as possible. In recent years, the 1963 Pete Rose, 1984 Donruss Don Mattingly and more than 100 superstar cards of the late 1960s-early 1990s have been counterfeited - many of which were quickly detected because of the differences in quality of cardboard on which they were printed.

A reprint, on the other hand, while it may have been made to look as close as possible to an original card, is made with the intention of allowing collectors to buy them as substitutes for cards they may never be otherwise able to afford. The big difference is that a reprint is generally marked as such, usually on the back of the card.

In other cases, like the Topps 1952 reprint set and 1953-54 Archives issues, the replicas are printed in a size markedly different from the originals. Collectors should be aware, however, that unscrupulous persons will sometimes cut off or otherwise obliterate the distinguishing word -- "Reprint," "Copy," -- or modern copyright date on the back of a reprint card in an attempt to pass it as genuine.

A collector's best defense against reprints and counterfeits is to acquire a knowledge of the look and feel of genuine baseball cards of various eras and issues.

MODERN MAJOR LEAGUE CARDS (1981-2000)

The vast majority of cards listed in this section were issued between 1981 and late-2000 and feature major league players only. The term "card" is used rather loosely as in this context it is construed to include virtually any series of cardboard or paper product, of whatever size and/or shape, depicting baseball players. Further, "cards" printed on wood, metal, plastic and other materials are either by their association with other issues or by their compatibility in size with the current 2-1/2" x 3-1/2" card standard also listed here.

Because modern cards are generally not popularly collected in lower grades, cards in this section carry only a Mint (MT) value quote. In general, post-1980 cards which grade Near Mint (NM) will retail at about 75% of the Mint price, while Excellent (EX) condition cards bring 40%.

B

1988 Bazooka

This 22-card set from Topps marks the first Bazooka issue since 1971. Full-color player photos are bordered in white, with the player name printed on a red, white and blue bubble gum box in the lower right corner. Flip sides are also red, white and blue, printed vertically. A large, but faint, Bazooka logo backs the Topps baseball logo team name, card number, player's name and position, followed by batting records, personal information and brief career highlights. Cards were sold inside specially marked 59Û and 79Û Bazooka gum and candy boxes, one card per box.

		MT
Complete Set (22):		6.00
Common Player:		.20
1	George Bell	.20
2	Wade Boggs	.60
3	Jose Canseco	.60
4	Roger Clemens	.60
5	Vince Coleman	.20
6	Eric Davis	.25
7	Tony Fernandez	.20
8	Dwight Gooden	.25
9	Tony Gwynn	.60
10	Wally Joyner	.25
11	Don Mattingly	.75
12	Willie McGee	.20
13	Mark McGwire	2.00
14	Kirby Puckett	.75
15	Tim Raines	.20
16	Dave Righetti	.20
17	Cal Ripken, Jr.	2.00
18	Juan Samuel	.20
19	Ryne Sandberg	.50
20	Benny Santiago	.20
21	Darryl Strawberry	.25
22	Todd Worrell	.20

1989 Bazooka

Topps produced this 22-card set in 1989 to be included (one card per box) in specially-marked boxes of its Bazooka brand bubblegum. The player photos have the words "Shining Star" along the top, while the player's name appears along the bottom of the card, along with the Topps Bazooka logo in the lower right corner. The cards are numbered alphabetically.

		MT
Complete Set (22):		5.00
Common Player:		.15
1	Tim Belcher	.15
2	Damon Berryhill	.15
3	Wade Boggs	.60
4	Jay Buhner	.20
5	Jose Canseco	.60
6	Vince Coleman	.15
7	Cecil Espy	.15
8	Dave Gallagher	.15
9	Ron Gant	.20
10	Kirk Gibson	.15
11	Paul Gibson	.15
12	Mark Grace	.50
13	Tony Gwynn	.75
14	Rickey Henderson	.35
15	Orel Hershiser	.20
16	Gregg Jefferies	.20
17	Ricky Jordan	.15
18	Chris Sabo	.15
19	Gary Sheffield	.30
20	Darryl Strawberry	.20
21	Frank Viola	.15
22	Walt Weiss	.15

1990 Bazooka

For the second consecutive year, Bazooka entitled its set "Shining Stars." Full color action and posed player shots are featured on the card fronts. The flip sides feature player statistics in a style much like the cards from the previous two Bazooka issues. Unlike the past two releases, the cards are not numbered alphabetically. The cards measure 2-1/2" x 3-1/2" in size and 22 cards complete the set.

		MT
Complete Set (22):		5.00
Common Player:		.15
1	Kevin Mitchell	.15
2	Robin Yount	.35
3	Mark Davis	.15
4	Bret Saberhagen	.20
5	Fred McGriff	.25
6	Tony Gwynn	.50
7	Kirby Puckett	.50
8	Vince Coleman	.15
9	Rickey Henderson	.30
10	Ben McDonald	.15
11	Gregg Olson	.15
12	Todd Zeile	.15
13	Carlos Martinez	.15
14	Gregg Jefferies	.20
15	Craig Worthington	.15
16	Gary Sheffield	.25
17	Greg Briley	.15
18	Ken Griffey, Jr.	2.50
19	Jerome Walton	.15
20	Bob Geren	.15
21	Tom Gordon	.15
22	Jim Abbott	.20

1991 Bazooka

For the third consecutive year Bazooka entitled its set "Shining Stars." The cards are styled like the 1990 issue, but include the Topps "40th Anniversary" logo. The 1991 issue is considered much scarcer than the previous releases. The cards measure 2-1/2" x 3-1/2" in size and 22 cards complete the set.

		MT
Complete Set (22):		10.00
Common Player:		.30
1	Barry Bonds	1.50
2	Rickey Henderson	.35
3	Bob Welch	.30
4	Doug Drabek	.30
5	Alex Fernandez	.30
6	Jose Offerman	.30
7	Frank Thomas	1.50
8	Cecil Fielder	.30
9	Ryne Sandberg	.75
10	George Brett	.90
11	Willie McGee	.30
12	Vince Coleman	.30
13	Hal Morris	.30
14	Delino DeShields	.30
15	Robin Ventura	.35
16	Jeff Huson	.30
17	Felix Jose	.30
18	Dave Justice	.35
19	Larry Walker	.50
20	Sandy Alomar, Jr.	.35
21	Kevin Appier	.30
22	Scott Radinsky	.30

1992 Bazooka

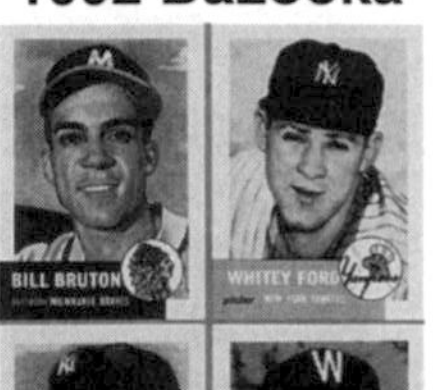

This set of 22 cards features miniature versions of the 1953 Topps Archives issue. The mini-cards are set against a blue background on front and back. Besides reproductions of issued 1953 Topps cards, these "Quadracards" include miniature versions of many of the special cards created for the Archives set. Cards feature the Bazooka logo on back, and were distributed in boxes of that bubble gum. They are readily available in complete set form.

		MT
Complete Set (22):		10.00
Common Player:		.50
1	Joe Adcock, Bob Lemon, Willie Mays, Vic Wertz	2.00
2	Carl Furillo, Don Newcombe, Phil Rizzuto, Hank Sauer	.50
3	Ferris Fain, John Logan, Ed Mathews, Bobby Shantz	.50
4	Yogi Berra, Del Crandall, Howie Pollett, Gene Woodling	.50
5	Richie Ashburn, Leo Durocher, Allie Reynolds, Early Wynn	.50
6	Hank Aaron, Ray Boone, Luke Easter, Dick Williams	2.00
7	Ralph Branca, Bob Feller, Rogers Hornsby, Bobby Thomson	.50
8	Jim Gilliam, Billy Martin, Orestes Minoso, Hal Newhouser	.50
9	Smoky Burgess, John Mize, Preacher Roe, Warren Spahn	.50
10	Monte Irvin, Bobo Newsom, Duke Snider, Wes Westrum	.50
11	Carl Erskine, Jackie Jensen, George Kell, Al Schoendienst	.50
12	Bill Bruton, Whitey Ford, Ed Lopat, Mickey Vernon	.50
13	Joe Black, Lew Burdette, Johnny Pesky, Enos Slaughter	.50
14	Gus Bell, Mike Garcia, Mel Parnell, Jackie Robinson	1.50
15	Alvin Dark, Dick Groat, Pee Wee Reese, John Sain	.50
16	Gil Hodges, Sal Maglie, Wilmer Mizell, Billy Pierce	.50
17	Nellie Fox, Ralph Kiner, Ted Kluszewski, Eddie Stanky	.50
18	Ewell Blackwell, Vern Law, Satchell Paige, Jim Wilson	.75
19	Lou Boudreau, Roy Face, Harvey Haddix, Bill Rigney	.50
20	Roy Campanella, Walt Dropo, Harvey Kuenn, Al Rosen	.50
21	Joe Garagiola, Robin Roberts, Casey Stengel, Hoyt Wilhelm	.50
22	John Antonelli, Bob Friend, Dixie Walker, Ted Williams	1.50

1993 Bazooka Team USA

The members of Team USA are featured on this boxed set. The 2-1/2" x 3-1/2" cards feature the same basic design as 1993 Topps baseball, except for a Bazooka gum logo in one of the upper corners. Both front and back feature posed player photos. Backs have a design simulating the U.S. flag and include amateur stats, biographical details and career highlights. The cards are virtually identical to the same players' cards in the 1993 Topps Traded set, with the addition of the Bazooka logo on front and the differences in card numbers.

		MT
Complete Set (22):		12.00
Common Player:		.25
1	Terry Harvey	.25
2	Dante Powell	.90
3	Andy Barkett	.25
4	Steve Reich	.25
5	Charlie Nelson	.25
6	Todd Walker	1.50
7	Dustin Hermanson	1.00
8	Pat Clougherty	.25
9	Danny Graves	.25
10	Paul Wilson	.75
11	Todd Helton	2.00
12	Russ Johnson	.75
13	Darren Grass	.25
14	A.J. Hinch	.35
15	Mark Merila	.25
16	John Powell	.25
17	Bob Scafa	.25
18	Matt Beaumont	.40
19	Todd Dunn	.35
20	Mike Martin	.25
21	Carlton Loewer	.25
22	Bret Wagner	.25

1995 Bazooka

Topps returned to the beginner's level baseball card niche in 1995 by resurrecting its Bazooka brand name. The set was unabashedly aimed at the younger collector, offering five cards and a Bazooka Joe cartoon-wrapped chunk of bubble-gum for 50 cents. Cards feature on their backs a "roulette" wheel design based on the player's 1994 stats, to be used to play a game of spinner baseball. A game instruction card and cardboard spinner was included in each pack. Limiting the set to 132 cards allowed for a concentration of established stars and hot rookies. A 22-card Red Hot insert set is found at the rate of one card per six packs, on average.

		MT
Complete Set (132):		10.00
Common Player:		.05
Pack (5):		.50
Wax Box (36):		15.00
1	Greg Maddux	.75
2	Cal Ripken Jr.	1.50
3	Lee Smith	.05
4	Sammy Sosa	1.00
5	Jason Bere	.05
6	Dave Justice	.10
7	Kevin Mitchell	.05
8	Ozzie Guillen	.05
9	Roger Clemens	.50
10	Mike Mussina	.30
11	Sandy Alomar	.10
12	Cecil Fielder	.10
13	Dennis Martinez	.05
14	Randy Myers	.05
15	Jay Buhner	.05
16	Ivan Rodriguez	.35
17	Mo Vaughn	.35
18	Ryan Klesko	.15
19	Chuck Finley	.05
20	Barry Bonds	.60
21	Dennis Eckersley	.05
22	Kenny Lofton	.30
23	Rafael Palmeiro	.15
24	Mike Stanley	.05
25	Gregg Jefferies	.05
26	Robin Ventura	.10
27	Mark McGwire	1.50
28	Ozzie Smith	.40
29	Troy Neel	.05
30	Tony Gwynn	.75
31	Ken Griffey Jr.	2.00
32	Will Clark	.25
33	Craig Biggio	.10
34	Shawon Dunston	.05
35	Wilson Alvarez	.05
36	Bobby Bonilla	.05
37	Marquis Grissom	.05
38	Ben McDonald	.05
39	Delino DeShields	.05
40	Barry Larkin	.15
41	John Olerud	.10
42	Jose Canseco	.35
43	Greg Vaughn	.10
44	Gary Sheffield	.20
45	Paul O'Neill	.10
46	Bob Hamelin	.05
47	Don Mattingly	.60
48	John Franco	.05
49	Bret Boone	.05
50	Rick Aguilera	.05
51	Tim Wallach	.05
52	Roberto Kelly	.05
53	Danny Tartabull	.05
54	Randy Johnson	.25
55	Greg McMichael	.05
56	Bip Roberts	.05
57	David Cone	.10
58	Raul Mondesi	.25
59	Travis Fryman	.05
60	Jeff Conine	.05
61	Jeff Bagwell	.50
62	Rickey Henderson	.20
63	Fred McGriff	.25
64	Matt Williams	.25
65	Rick Wilkins	.05
66	Eric Karros	.05
67	Mel Rojas	.05
68	Juan Gonzalez	.50
69	Chuck Carr	.05
70	Moises Alou	.10
71	Mark Grace	.20
72	Alex Fernandez	.05
73	Rod Beck	.05
74	Ray Lankford	.05
75	Dean Palmer	.05
76	Joe Carter	.08

77	Mike Piazza	.75
78	Eddie Murray	.40
79	Dave Nilsson	.05
80	Brett Butler	.05
81	Roberto Alomar	.35
82	Jeff Kent	.05
83	Andres Galarraga	.15
84	Brady Anderson	.05
85	Jimmy Key	.05
86	Bret Saberhagen	.08
87	Chili Davis	.05
88	Jose Rijo	.05
89	Wade Boggs	.35
90	Len Dykstra	.05
91	Steve Howe	.05
92	Hal Morris	.05
93	Larry Walker	.35
94	Jeff Montgomery	.05
95	Wil Cordero	.05
96	Jay Bell	.05
97	Tom Glavine	.15
98	Chris Hoiles	.05
99	Steve Avery	.05
100	Ruben Sierra	.05
101	Mickey Tettleton	.05
102	Paul Molitor	.40
103	Carlos Baerga	.05
104	Walt Weiss	.05
105	Darren Daulton	.05
106	Jack McDowell	.05
107	Doug Drabek	.05
108	Mark Langston	.05
109	Manny Ramirez	.40
110	Kevin Appier	.05
111	Andy Benes	.05
112	Chuck Knoblauch	.10
113	Kirby Puckett	.60
114	Dante Bichette	.15
115	Deion Sanders	.20
116	Albert Belle	.40
117	Todd Zeile	.05
118	Devon White	.05
119	Tim Salmon	.15
120	Frank Thomas	.75
121	John Wetteland	.05
122	James Mouton	.05
123	Javy Lopez	.10
124	Carlos Delgado	.25
125	Cliff Floyd	.05
126	Alex Gonzalez	.05
127	Billy Ashley	.05
128	Rondell White	.05
129	Rico Brogna	.05
130	Melvin Nieves	.05
131	Jose Oliva	.05
132	J.R. Phillips	.05

1995 Bazooka Red Hot Inserts

Twenty-two of the game's biggest stars were chosen for inclusion in 1995 Bazooka's only insert set - Red Hots. The chase cards are found at an average rate of one per six packs. Red Hots are identical to the players' cards in the regular set except that the background has been rendered in shades of red, and the player name printed in gold foil. Card numbers have an "RH" prefix.

		MT
Complete Set (22):		16.00
Common Player:		.25
1	Greg Maddux	2.00
2	Cal Ripken Jr.	3.00
3	Barry Bonds	1.50
4	Kenny Lofton	.60
5	Mike Stanley	.25
6	Tony Gwynn	1.50
7	Ken Griffey Jr.	4.00
8	Barry Larkin	.30
9	Jose Canseco	.75
10	Paul O'Neill	.25
11	Randy Johnson	.75
12	David Cone	.35
13	Jeff Bagwell	1.50
14	Matt Williams	.75
15	Mike Piazza	2.00
16	Roberto Alomar	1.00
17	Jimmy Key	.25
18	Wade Boggs	.75
19	Paul Molitor	.75
20	Carlos Baerga	.25
21	Albert Belle	1.00
22	Frank Thomas	1.00

1996 Bazooka

Using a simple, yet nostalgic design, Topps' 1996 Bazooka set offers collectors a source of fun with its cards geared for a flipping game. Each front has a full-color action photo of the player. The back contains one of five different Bazooka Joe characters, along with the Bazooka Ball game, the player's biographical data, and 1995 and career stats. Each card also contains a Funny Fortune, which predicts the fate of a player on a particular date. Cards were available five per pack for 50 cents. The complete set of all 132 cards is also offered in a factory set, packaged in an attractive gift box. All the top veterans, rookies and rising stars are included, as well as a Bazooka Ball info card containing all the rules to play the flipping game. As an exclusive bonus, one 1959 Bazooka Mickey Mantle reprint card can be found in every factory set. This card was originally found on boxes of Bazooka gum sold that year. Ten pieces of Mega Bazooka Gum are also included with the set.

		MT
Complete Set (132):		12.00
Common Player:		.05
Pack (5):		.50
Wax Box (36):		15.00
1	Ken Griffey Jr.	2.00
2	J.T. Snow	.05
3	Rondell White	.10
4	Reggie Sanders	.05
5	Jeff Montgomery	.05
6	Mike Stanley	.05
7	Bernie Williams	.25
8	Mike Piazza	1.00
9	Brian Hunter	.05
10	Len Dykstra	.05
11	Ray Lankford	.05
12	Kenny Lofton	.45
13	Robin Ventura	.10
14	Devon White	.05
15	Cal Ripken Jr.	1.50
16	Heathcliff Slocumb	.05
17	Ryan Klesko	.20
18	Terry Steinbach	.05
19	Travis Fryman	.05
20	Sammy Sosa	1.00
21	Jim Thome	.10
22	Kenny Rogers	.05
23	Don Mattingly	.75
24	Kirby Puckett	.75
25	Matt Williams	.25
26	Larry Walker	.25
27	Tim Wakefield	.05
28	Greg Vaughn	.10
29	Denny Neagle	.05
30	Ken Caminiti	.10
31	Garret Anderson	.10
32	Brady Anderson	.05
33	Carlos Baerga	.05
34	Wade Boggs	.35
35	Roberto Alomar	.50
36	Eric Karros	.05
37	Jay Buhner	.05
38	Dante Bichette	.15
39	Darren Daulton	.05
40	Jeff Bagwell	.75
41	Jay Bell	.05
42	Dennis Eckersley	.05
43	Will Clark	.25
44	Tom Glavine	.15
45	Rick Aguilera	.05
46	Kevin Seitzer	.05
47	Bret Boone	.05
48	Mark Grace	.35
49	Ray Durham	.05
50	Rico Brogna	.05
51	Kevin Appier	.05
52	Moises Alou	.10
53	Jeff Conine	.05
54	Marty Cordova	.05
55	Jose Mesa	.05
56	Rod Beck	.05
57	Marquis Grissom	.05
58	David Cone	.10
59	Albert Belle	.50
60	Lee Smith	.05
61	Frank Thomas	.75
62	Roger Clemens	.65
63	Bobby Bonilla	.05
64	Paul Molitor	.35
65	Chuck Knoblauch	.10
66	Steve Finley	.05
67	Craig Biggio	.10
68	Ramon Martinez	.05
69	Jason Isringhausen	.05
70	Mark Wohlers	.05
71	Vinny Castilla	.05
72	Ron Gant	.10
73	Juan Gonzalez	.50
74	Mark McGwire	1.50
75	Jeff King	.05
76	Pedro Martinez	.35
77	Chad Curtis	.05
78	John Olerud	.15
79	Greg Maddux	1.00
80	Derek Jeter	1.00
81	Mike Mussina	.30
82	Gregg Jefferies	.05
83	Jim Edmonds	.05
84	Carlos Perez	.05
85	Mo Vaughn	.35
86	Todd Hundley	.05
87	Roberto Hernandez	.05
88	Derek Bell	.05
89	Andres Galarraga	.10
90	Brian McRae	.05
91	Joe Carter	.10
92	Orlando Merced	.05
93	Cecil Fielder	.10
94	Dean Palmer	.05
95	Randy Johnson	.35
96	Chipper Jones	1.00
97	Barry Larkin	.20
98	Hideo Nomo	.35
99	Gary Gaetti	.05
100	Edgar Martinez	.05
101	John Wetteland	.05
102	Rafael Palmeiro	.15
103	Chuck Finley	.05
104	Ivan Rodriguez	.15
105	Shawn Green	.25
106	Manny Ramirez	.75
107	Lance Johnson	.05
108	Jose Canseco	.25
109	Fred McGriff	.30
110	David Segui	.05
111	Tim Salmon	.25
112	Hal Morris	.05
113	Tino Martinez	.15
114	Bret Saberhagen	.08
115	Brian Jordan	.05
116	David Justice	.25
117	Jack McDowell	.05
118	Barry Bonds	.65
119	Mark Langston	.05
120	John Valentin	.05
121	Raul Mondesi	.20
122	Quilvio Veras	.05
123	Randy Myers	.05
124	Tony Gwynn	.75
125	Johnny Damon	.15
126	Doug Drabek	.05
127	Bill Pulsipher	.05
128	Paul O'Neill	.10
129	Rickey Henderson	.25
130	Deion Sanders	.15
131	Orel Hershiser	.05
132	Gary Sheffield	.15

1996 Bazooka Mickey Mantle 1959 Reprint

Continuing its tribute to the late Mickey Mantle across all of its product lines, Topps produced a special reprint of the 1959 Bazooka Mantle card exclusively for inclusion in factory sets of its 1996 Bazooka cards. While the original '59 Mantle was printed in nearly 3" x 5" size on the bottom of gum boxes, the reprint is in the current 2-1/2" x 3-1/2" size.

	MT
Mickey Mantle	6.00

1989 Bowman

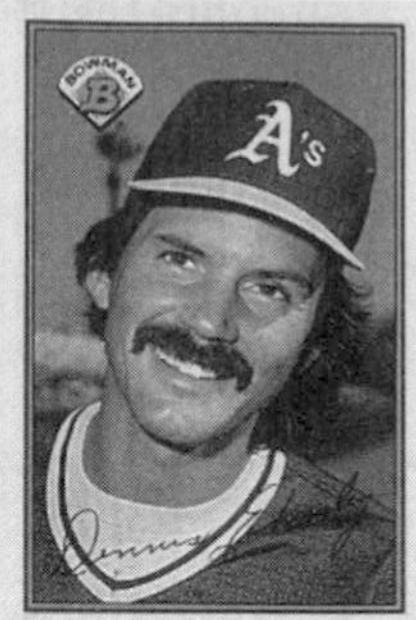

Topps, which purchased Bowman in 1955, revived the brand name in 1989, issuing a 484-card set. The 2-1/2" x 3-3/4" cards are slightly taller than current standard. Fronts contain a full-color player photo, with facsimile autograph and the Bowman logo in an upper corner. Backs include a breakdown of the player's stats against each team in his league. A series of "Hot Rookie Stars" highlights the set. The cards were distributed in both wax packs and rack packs. Each pack included a special reproduction of a classic Bowman card with a sweepstakes on the back.

		MT
Complete Set (484):		30.00
Common Player:		.05
Pack (12+1):		2.25
Wax Box (36):		53.00
1	Oswald Peraza	.05
2	Brian Holton	.05
3	Jose Bautista	.05
4	*Pete Harnisch*	.20
5	Dave Schmidt	.05
6	Gregg Olson	.05
7	Jeff Ballard	.05
8	Bob Melvin	.05
9	Cal Ripken, Jr.	.75
10	Randy Milligan	.05
11	*Juan Bell*	.05
12	Billy Ripken	.05
13	Jim Traber	.05
14	Pete Stanicek	.05
15	*Steve Finley*	.25
16	Larry Sheets	.05
17	Phil Bradley	.05
18	Brady Anderson	.40
19	Lee Smith	.08
20	Tom Fischer	.05
21	Mike Boddicker	.05
22	Rob Murphy	.05
23	Wes Gardner	.05
24	John Dopson	.05
25	Bob Stanley	.05
26	Roger Clemens	.50
27	Rich Gedman	.05
28	Marty Barrett	.05
29	Luis Rivera	.05
30	Jody Reed	.05
31	Nick Esasky	.05
32	Wade Boggs	.40
33	Jim Rice	.10
34	Mike Greenwell	.05
35	Dwight Evans	.08
36	Ellis Burks	.12
37	Chuck Finley	.05
38	Kirk McCaskill	.05
39	Jim Abbott	.10
40	*Bryan Harvey*	.05
41	Bert Blyleven	.08
42	Mike Witt	.05
43	Bob McClure	.05
44	Bill Schroeder	.05
45	Lance Parrish	.08
46	Dick Schofield	.05
47	Wally Joyner	.10
48	Jack Howell	.05
49	Johnny Ray	.05
50	Chili Davis	.08
51	Tony Armas	.05
52	Claudell Washington	.05
53	Brian Downing	.05
54	Devon White	.08
55	Bobby Thigpen	.05
56	Bill Long	.05
57	Jerry Reuss	.05
58	Shawn Hillegas	.05
59	Melido Perez	.05
60	Jeff Bittiger	.05
61	Jack McDowell	.08
62	Carlton Fisk	.15
63	Steve Lyons	.05
64	Ozzie Guillen	.05
65	Robin Ventura	.20
66	Fred Manrique	.05
67	Dan Pasqua	.05
68	Ivan Calderon	.05
69	Ron Kittle	.05
70	Daryl Boston	.05
71	Dave Gallagher	.05
72	Harold Baines	.08
73	*Charles Nagy*	.25
74	John Farrell	.05
75	Kevin Wickander	.05
76	Greg Swindell	.05
77	Mike Walker	.05
78	Doug Jones	.05
79	Rich Yett	.05
80	Tom Candiotti	.05
81	Jesse Orosco	.05
82	Bud Black	.05
83	Andy Allanson	.05
84	Pete O'Brien	.05
85	Jerry Browne	.05
86	Brook Jacoby	.05
87	*Mark Lewis*	.10
88	Luis Aguayo	.05
89	Cory Snyder	.05
90	Oddibe McDowell	.05
91	Joe Carter	.08
92	Frank Tanana	.05
93	Jack Morris	.08
94	Doyle Alexander	.05
95	Steve Searcy	.05
96	Randy Bockus	.05
97	Jeff Robinson	.05
98	Mike Henneman	.05
99	Paul Gibson	.05
100	Frank Williams	.05
101	Matt Nokes	.05
102	Rico Brogna	.05
103	Lou Whitaker	.08
104	Al Pedrique	.05
105	Alan Trammell	.10
106	Chris Brown	.05
107	Pat Sheridan	.05
108	Gary Pettis	.05
109	Keith Moreland	.05
110	Mel Stottlemyre, Jr.	.05
111	Bret Saberhagen	.08
112	Floyd Bannister	.05
113	Jeff Montgomery	.05
114	Steve Farr	.05
115	Tom Gordon	.05
116	Charlie Leibrandt	.05
117	Mark Gubicza	.05
118	Mike MacFarlane	.05
119	Bob Boone	.05
120	Kurt Stillwell	.05
121	George Brett	.40
122	Frank White	.05
123	Kevin Seitzer	.05
124	Willie Wilson	.08
125	Pat Tabler	.05
126	Bo Jackson	.20
127	Hugh Walker	.05
128	Danny Tartabull	.05
129	Teddy Higuera	.05
130	Don August	.05
131	Juan Nieves	.05
132	Mike Birkbeck	.05
133	Dan Plesac	.05
134	Chris Bosio	.05
135	Bill Wegman	.05
136	Chuck Crim	.05
137	B.J. Surhoff	.08
138	Joey Meyer	.05
139	Dale Sveum	.05
140	Paul Molitor	.40
141	Jim Gantner	.05
142	*Gary Sheffield*	1.50
143	Greg Brock	.05
144	Robin Yount	.40
145	Glenn Braggs	.05
146	Rob Deer	.05
147	Fred Toliver	.05
148	Jeff Reardon	.05
149	Allan Anderson	.05
150	Frank Viola	.05
151	Shane Rawley	.05
152	Juan Berenguer	.05
153	Johnny Ard	.05
154	Tim Laudner	.05
155	Brian Harper	.05
156	Al Newman	.05
157	Kent Hrbek	.08
158	Gary Gaetti	.08
159	Wally Backman	.05
160	Gene Larkin	.05
161	Greg Gagne	.05
162	Kirby Puckett	.50
163	Danny Gladden	.05
164	Randy Bush	.05
165	Dave LaPoint	.05
166	Andy Hawkins	.05
167	Dave Righetti	.05
168	Lance McCullers	.05
169	Jimmy Jones	.05
170	Al Leiter	.08
171	John Candelaria	.05
172	Don Slaught	.05
173	Jamie Quirk	.05
174	Rafael Santana	.05
175	Mike Pagliarulo	.05
176	Don Mattingly	.40
177	Ken Phelps	.05
178	Steve Sax	.05
179	Dave Winfield	.20
180	Stan Jefferson	.05
181	Rickey Henderson	.20
182	Bob Brower	.05
183	Roberto Kelly	.05
184	Curt Young	.05
185	Gene Nelson	.05
186	Bob Welch	.05
187	Rick Honeycutt	.05
188	Dave Stewart	.05
189	Mike Moore	.05
190	Dennis Eckersley	.08
191	Eric Plunk	.05
192	Storm Davis	.05
193	Terry Steinbach	.05
194	Ron Hassey	.05
195	Stan Royer	.05
196	Walt Weiss	.05
197	Mark McGwire	1.50
198	Carney Lansford	.05
199	Glenn Hubbard	.05
200	Dave Henderson	.05
201	Jose Canseco	.30
202	Dave Parker	.08
203	Scott Bankhead	.05
204	Tom Niedenfuer	.05
205	Mark Langston	.08
206	*Erik Hanson*	.08
207	Mike Jackson	.05
208	Dave Valle	.05
209	Scott Bradley	.05
210	Harold Reynolds	.08
211	Tino Martinez	.25
212	Rich Renteria	.05
213	Rey Quinones	.05
214	Jim Presley	.05
215	Alvin Davis	.05
216	Edgar Martinez	.05
217	Darnell Coles	.05
218	Jeffrey Leonard	.05
219	Jay Buhner	.08
220	*Ken Griffey, Jr.*	20.00
221	Drew Hall	.05
222	Bobby Witt	.05
223	Jamie Moyer	.05
224	Charlie Hough	.05
225	Nolan Ryan	.75
226	Jeff Russell	.05
227	Jim Sundberg	.05
228	Julio Franco	.08
229	Buddy Bell	.05
230	Scott Fletcher	.05
231	Jeff Kunkel	.05
232	Steve Buechele	.05
233	Monty Fariss	.05
234	Rick Leach	.05
235	Ruben Sierra	.05
236	Cecil Espy	.05
237	Rafael Palmeiro	.15
238	Pete Incaviglia	.05
239	Dave Steib	.05
240	Jeff Musselman	.05
241	Mike Flanagan	.05
242	Todd Stottlemyre	.08
243	Jimmy Key	.05
244	Tony Castillo	.05
245	Alex Sanchez	.05
246	Tom Henke	.05
247	John Cerutti	.05
248	Ernie Whitt	.05
249	Bob Brenly	.05
250	Rance Mulliniks	.05
251	Kelly Gruber	.05
252	Ed Sprague	.10
253	Fred McGriff	.15
254	Tony Fernandez	.08
255	Tom Lawless	.05
256	George Bell	.08
257	Jesse Barfield	.05
258	Sandy Alomar, Sr.	.05
259	Ken Griffey (with Ken Griffey, Jr.)	1.00
260	Cal Ripken, Sr.	.15
261	Mel Stottlemyre, Sr.	.05
262	Zane Smith	.05
263	Charlie Puleo	.05
264	Derek Lilliquist	.05
265	Paul Assenmacher	.05
266	John Smoltz	.25
267	Tom Glavine	.15
268	*Steve Avery*	.10
269	*Pete Smith*	.05
270	Jody Davis	.05
271	Bruce Benedict	.05
272	Andres Thomas	.05
273	Gerald Perry	.05
274	Ron Gant	.15
275	Darrell Evans	.08
276	Dale Murphy	.20
277	Dion James	.05
278	Lonnie Smith	.05
279	Geronimo Berroa	.05
280	Steve Wilson	.05
281	Rick Sutcliffe	.05
282	Kevin Coffman	.05
283	Mitch Williams	.05
284	Greg Maddux	.60
285	Paul Kilgus	.05
286	Mike Harkey	.05
287	Lloyd McClendon	.05
288	Damon Berryhill	.05
289	Ty Griffin	.05
290	Ryne Sandberg	.50
291	Mark Grace	.35
292	Curt Wilkerson	.05
293	Vance Law	.05
294	Shawon Dunston	.12
295	Jerome Walton	.05
296	Mitch Webster	.05
297	Dwight Smith	.05
298	Andre Dawson	.15
299	Jeff Sellers	.05
300	Jose Rijo	.05
301	John Franco	.05
302	Rick Mahler	.05
303	Ron Robinson	.05
304	Danny Jackson	.05
305	Rob Dibble	.05
306	Tom Browning	.05
307	Bo Diaz	.05
308	Manny Trillo	.05
309	Chris Sabo	.05
310	Ron Oester	.05
311	Barry Larkin	.15
312	Todd Benzinger	.05
313	Paul O'Neill	.10
314	Kal Daniels	.05
315	Joel Youngblood	.05
316	Eric Davis	.10
317	Dave Smith	.05
318	Mark Portugal	.05
319	Brian Meyer	.05
320	Jim Deshaies	.05
321	Juan Agosto	.05
322	Mike Scott	.05
323	Rick Rhoden	.05
324	Jim Clancy	.05
325	Larry Andersen	.05
326	Alex Trevino	.05
327	Alan Ashby	.05

328	Craig Reynolds	.05
329	Bill Doran	.05
330	Rafael Ramirez	.05
331	Glenn Davis	.05
332	*Willie Ansley*	.05
333	Gerald Young	.05
334	Cameron Drew	.05
335	Jay Howell	.05
336	Tim Belcher	.05
337	Fernando Valenzuela	.08
338	Ricky Horton	.05
339	Tim Leary	.05
340	Bill Bene	.05
341	Orel Hershiser	.08
342	Mike Scioscia	.05
343	Rick Dempsey	.05
344	Willie Randolph	.05
345	Alfredo Griffin	.05
346	Eddie Murray	.35
347	Mickey Hatcher	.05
348	Mike Sharperson	.05
349	John Shelby	.05
350	Mike Marshall	.05
351	Kirk Gibson	.05
352	Mike Davis	.05
353	Bryn Smith	.05
354	Pascual Perez	.05
355	Kevin Gross	.05
356	Andy McGaffigan	.05
357	Brian Holman	.05
358	Dave Wainhouse	.05
359	Denny Martinez	.08
360	Tim Burke	.05
361	Nelson Santovenia	.05
362	Tim Wallach	.05
363	Spike Owen	.05
364	Rex Hudler	.05
365	Andres Galarraga	.15
366	Otis Nixon	.05
367	Hubie Brooks	.05
368	Mike Aldrete	.05
369	Rock Raines	.08
370	Dave Martinez	.05
371	Bob Ojeda	.05
372	Ron Darling	.05
373	Wally Whitehurst	.05
374	Randy Myers	.05
375	David Cone	.15
376	Dwight Gooden	.10
377	Sid Fernandez	.05
378	Dave Proctor	.05
379	Gary Carter	.10
380	Keith Miller	.05
381	Gregg Jefferies	.10
382	Tim Teufel	.05
383	Kevin Elster	.05
384	Dave Magadan	.05
385	Keith Hernandez	.08
386	Mookie Wilson	.05
387	Darryl Strawberry	.10
388	Kevin McReynolds	.05
389	Mark Carreon	.05
390	Jeff Parrett	.05
391	Mike Maddux	.05
392	Don Carman	.05
393	Bruce Ruffin	.05
394	Ken Howell	.05
395	Steve Bedrosian	.05
396	Floyd Youmans	.05
397	Larry McWilliams	.05
398	Pat Combs	.05
399	Steve Lake	.05
400	Dickie Thon	.05
401	Ricky Jordan	.05
402	Mike Schmidt	.40
403	Tom Herr	.05
404	Chris James	.05
405	Juan Samuel	.05
406	Von Hayes	.05
407	Ron Jones	.05
408	Curt Ford	.05
409	Bob Walk	.05
410	Jeff Robinson	.05
411	Jim Gott	.05
412	Scott Medvin	.05
413	John Smiley	.05
414	Bob Kipper	.05
415	Brian Fisher	.05
416	Doug Drabek	.05
417	Mike Lavalliere	.05
418	Ken Oberkfell	.05
419	Sid Bream	.05
420	Austin Manahan	.05
421	Jose Lind	.05
422	Bobby Bonilla	.10
423	Glenn Wilson	.05
424	Andy Van Slyke	.05
425	Gary Redus	.05
426	Barry Bonds	.50
427	Don Heinkel	.05
428	Ken Dayley	.05
429	Todd Worrell	.05
430	Brad DuVall	.05
431	Jose DeLeon	.05
432	Joe Magrane	.05
433	John Ericks	.05
434	Frank DiPino	.05
435	Tony Pena	.05
436	Ozzie Smith	.40
437	Terry Pendleton	.05
438	Jose Oquendo	.05
439	Tim Jones	.05
440	Pedro Guerrero	.05
441	Milt Thompson	.05
442	Willie McGee	.08
443	Vince Coleman	.05
444	Tom Brunansky	.05
445	Walt Terrell	.05
446	Eric Show	.05
447	Mark Davis	.05
448	*Andy Benes*	.25
449	Eddie Whitson	.05
450	Dennis Rasmussen	.05
451	Bruce Hurst	.05
452	Pat Clements	.05
453	Benito Santiago	.08
454	Sandy Alomar, Jr.	.15
455	Garry Templeton	.05
456	Jack Clark	.05
457	Tim Flannery	.05
458	Roberto Alomar	.30
459	Camelo Martinez	.05
460	John Kruk	.05
461	Tony Gwynn	.50
462	Jerald Clark	.05
463	Don Robinson	.05
464	Craig Lefferts	.05
465	Kelly Downs	.05
466	Rick Rueschel	.05
467	Scott Garrelts	.05
468	Wil Tejada	.05
469	Kirt Manwaring	.05
470	Terry Kennedy	.05
471	Jose Uribe	.05
472	*Royce Clayton*	.10
473	Robby Thompson	.05
474	Kevin Mitchell	.05
475	Ernie Riles	.05
476	Will Clark	.20
477	Donnell Nixon	.05
478	Candy Maldonado	.05
479	Tracy Jones	.05
480	Brett Butler	.08
481	Checklist 1-121	.05
482	Checklist 122-242	.05
483	Checklist 243-363	.05
484	Checklist 364-484	.05

1989 Bowman Inserts

Bowman inserted sweepstakes cards in its 1989 packs. Each sweepstakes card reproduces a classic Bowman card on the front, with a prominent "REPRINT" notice. With one card in each pack, they are by no means scarce. A "Tiffany" version of the reprints was produced for inclusion in the factory set of 1989 Bowman cards. The glossy-front inserts are valued at 10X the standard version.

		MT
Complete Set (11):		10.00
Common Player:		.20
(1)	Richie Ashburn	.20
(2)	Yogi Berra	.30
(3)	Whitey Ford	.20
(4)	Gil Hodges	.20
(5)	Mickey Mantle (1951)	4.00
(6)	Mickey Mantle (1953)	2.00
(7)	Willie Mays	1.00
(8)	Satchel Paige	.50
(9)	Jackie Robinson	1.50
(10)	Duke Snider	.30
(11)	Ted Williams	1.50

1989 Bowman Tiffany

A special collectors' version of the revitalized Bowman cards was produced in 1989, differing from the regular-issue cards in the application of a high-gloss finish to the front and the use of a white cardboard stock. The "Tiffany" version (as the glossies are known to collectors), was sold only in complete boxed sets, with an estimated production of 6,000 sets.

	MT
Complete (Sealed) Set (495):	800.00
Complete (Opened) Set (495):	150.00
Common Player:	.25

(Star/rookie cards valued at 4-5X regular-issue 1989 Bowman.)

1990 Bowman

Bowman followed its 1989 rebirth with a 528-card set in 1990. The 1990 cards follow the classic Bowman style featuring a full-color photo bordered in white. The Bowman logo appears in the upper-left corner. The player's team nickname and name appear on the bottom border of the card photo. Unlike the 1989 set, the 1990 cards are standard 2-1/2" x 3-1/2". Backs are horizontal and display the player's statistics against the teams in his league. Included in the set are special insert cards featuring a painted image of a modern-day superstar done in the style of the 1951 Bowman cards. The paintings were produced for Bowman by artist Craig Pursley. Insert backs contain a sweepstakes offer with a chance to win a complete set of 11 lithographs made from these paintings.

		MT
Complete Set (528):		25.00
Common Player:		.05
Wax Pack (14+1):		2.00
Wax Box (36):		43.00
1	*Tommy Greene*	.20
2	Tom Glavine	.15
3	Andy Nezelek	.05
4	Mike Stanton	.05
5	Rick Lueken	.05
6	Kent Mercker	.05
7	Derek Lilliquist	.05
8	Charlie Liebrandt	.05
9	Steve Avery	.10
10	John Smoltz	.15
11	Mark Lemke	.05
12	Lonnie Smith	.05
13	Oddibe McDowell	.05
14	*Tyler Houston*	.10
15	Jeff Blauser	.05
16	Ernie Whitt	.05
17	Alexis Infante	.05
18	Jim Presley	.05
19	Dale Murphy	.15
20	Nick Esasky	.05
21	Rick Sutcliffe	.05
22	Mike Bielecki	.05
23	Steve Wilson	.05
24	Kevin Blankenship	.05
25	Mitch Williams	.05
26	Dean Wilkins	.05
27	Greg Maddux	.75
28	Mike Harkey	.05
29	Mark Grace	.30
30	Ryne Sandberg	.40
31	Greg Smith	.05
32	Dwight Smith	.05
33	Damon Berryhill	.05
34	Earl Cunningham	.05
35	Jerome Walton	.05
36	Lloyd McClendon	.05
37	Ty Griffin	.05
38	Shawon Dunston	.10
39	Andre Dawson	.15
40	Luis Salazar	.05
41	Tim Layana	.05
42	Rob Dibble	.05
43	Tom Browning	.05
44	Danny Jackson	.05
45	Jose Rijo	.05
46	Scott Scudder	.05
47	Randy Myers	.08
48	Brian Lane	.05
49	Paul O'Neill	.08
50	Barry Larkin	.10
51	Reggie Jefferson	.10
52	Jeff Branson	.05
53	Chris Sabo	.05
54	Joe Oliver	.05
55	Todd Benzinger	.05
56	Rolando Roomes	.05
57	Hal Morris	.05
58	Eric Davis	.12
59	Scott Bryant	.05
60	Ken Griffey	.08
61	*Darryl Kile*	.30
62	Dave Smith	.05

No.	Player	Price
63	Mark Portugal	.05
64	*Jeff Juden*	.20
65	Bill Gullickson	.05
66	Danny Darwin	.05
67	Larry Andersen	.05
68	Jose Cano	.05
69	Dan Schatzeder	.05
70	Jim Deshaies	.05
71	Mike Scott	.05
72	Gerald Young	.05
73	Ken Caminiti	.10
74	Ken Oberkfell	.05
75	Dave Rhode	.05
76	Bill Doran	.05
77	Andujar Cedeno	.05
78	Craig Biggio	.08
79	Karl Rhodes	.05
80	Glenn Davis	.05
81	*Eric Anthony*	.15
82	John Wetteland	.15
83	Jay Howell	.05
84	Orel Hershiser	.10
85	Tim Belcher	.05
86	Kiki Jones	.05
87	Mike Hartley	.05
88	Ramon Martinez	.08
89	Mike Scioscia	.05
90	Willie Randolph	.05
91	Juan Samuel	.05
92	*Jose Offerman*	.15
93	Dave Hansen	.05
94	Jeff Hamilton	.05
95	Alfredo Griffin	.05
96	Tom Goodwin	.05
97	Kirk Gibson	.05
98	Jose Vizcaino	.05
99	Kal Daniels	.05
100	Hubie Brooks	.05
101	Eddie Murray	.30
102	Dennis Boyd	.05
103	Tim Burke	.05
104	Bill Sampen	.05
105	Brett Gideon	.05
106	Mark Gardner	.05
107	Howard Farmer	.05
108	Mel Rojas	.05
109	Kevin Gross	.05
110	Dave Schmidt	.05
111	Denny Martinez	.08
112	Jerry Goff	.05
113	Andres Galarraga	.10
114	Tim Welch	.05
115	*Marquis Grissom*	.50
116	Spike Owen	.05
117	*Larry Walker*	1.50
118	Rock Raines	.08
119	*Delino DeShields*	.20
120	Tom Foley	.05
121	Dave Martinez	.05
122	Frank Viola	.05
123	Julio Valera	.05
124	Alejandro Pena	.05
125	David Cone	.08
126	Dwight Gooden	.10
127	Kevin Brown	.20
128	John Franco	.05
129	Terry Bross	.05
130	Blaine Beatty	.05
131	Sid Fernandez	.05
132	Mike Marshall	.05
133	Howard Johnson	.05
134	Jaime Roseboro	.05
135	Alan Zinter	.05
136	Keith Miller	.05
137	Kevin Elster	.05
138	Kevin McReynolds	.05
139	Barry Lyons	.05
140	Gregg Jefferies	.15
141	Darryl Strawberry	.12
142	*Todd Hundley*	.25
143	Scott Service	.05
144	Chuck Malone	.05
145	Steve Ontiveros	.05
146	Roger McDowell	.05
147	Ken Howell	.05
148	Pat Combs	.10
149	Jeff Parrett	.05
150	Chuck McElroy	.05
151	Jason Grimsley	.10
152	Len Dykstra	.05
153	Mickey Morandini	.05
154	John Kruk	.05
155	Dickie Thon	.05
156	Ricky Jordan	.05
157	Jeff Jackson	.05
158	Darren Daulton	.05
159	Tom Herr	.05
160	Von Hayes	.05
161	*Dave Hollins*	.20
162	Carmelo Martinez	.05
163	Bob Walk	.05
164	Doug Drabek	.05
165	Walt Terrell	.05
166	Bill Landrum	.05
167	Scott Ruskin	.05
168	Bob Patterson	.05
169	Bobby Bonilla	.10
170	Jose Lind	.05
171	Andy Van Slyke	.05
172	Mike LaValliere	.05
173	*Willie Greene*	.15
174	Jay Bell	.08
175	Sid Bream	.05
176	Tom Prince	.05
177	Wally Backman	.05
178	*Moises Alou*	.25
179	Steve Carter	.05
180	Gary Redus	.05
181	Barry Bonds	.50
182	Don Slaught	.05
183	Joe Magrane	.05
184	Bryn Smith	.05
185	Todd Worrell	.05
186	Jose Deleon	.05
187	Frank DiPino	.05
188	John Tudor	.05
189	Howard Hilton	.05
190	John Ericks	.05
191	Ken Dayley	.05
192	*Ray Lankford*	.40
193	Todd Zeile	.10
194	Willie McGee	.08
195	Ozzie Smith	.40
196	Milt Thompson	.05
197	Terry Pendleton	.05
198	Vince Coleman	.05
199	Paul Coleman	.05
200	Jose Oquendo	.05
201	Pedro Guerrero	.05
202	Tom Brunansky	.05
203	Roger Smithberg	.05
204	Eddie Whitson	.05
205	Dennis Rasmussen	.05
206	Craig Lefferts	.05
207	Andy Benes	.10
208	Bruce Hurst	.05
209	Eric Show	.05
210	Rafael Valdez	.05
211	Joey Cora	.05
212	Thomas Howard	.10
213	Rob Nelson	.05
214	Jack Clark	.05
215	Garry Templeton	.05
216	Fred Lynn	.08
217	Tony Gwynn	.50
218	Benny Santiago	.05
219	Mike Pagliarulo	.05
220	Joe Carter	.15
221	Roberto Alomar	.30
222	Bip Roberts	.05
223	Rick Reuschel	.05
224	Russ Swan	.05
225	Eric Gunderson	.05
226	Steve Bedrosian	.05
227	Mike Remlinger	.05
228	Scott Garrelts	.05
229	Ernie Camacho	.05
230	Andres Santana	.05
231	Will Clark	.20
232	Kevin Mitchell	.05
233	Robby Thompson	.05
234	Bill Bathe	.05
235	Tony Perezchica	.05
236	Gary Carter	.10
237	Brett Butler	.10
238	Matt Williams	.20
239	Ernie Riles	.05
240	Kevin Bass	.05
241	Terry Kennedy	.05
242	*Steve Hosey*	.10
243	*Ben McDonald*	.15
244	Jeff Ballard	.05
245	Joe Price	.05
246	Curt Schilling	.08
247	Pete Harnisch	.05
248	Mark Williamson	.05
249	Gregg Olson	.05
250	Chris Myers	.05
251	David Segui	.08
252	Joe Orsulak	.05
253	Craig Worthington	.05
254	Mickey Tettleton	.05
255	Cal Ripken, Jr.	1.00
256	Billy Ripken	.05
257	Randy Milligan	.05
258	Brady Anderson	.10
259	*Chris Hoiles*	.20
260	Mike Devereaux	.05
261	Phil Bradley	.05
262	*Leo Gomez*	.10
263	Lee Smith	.08
264	Mike Rochford	.05
265	Jeff Reardon	.05
266	Wes Gardner	.05
267	Mike Boddicker	.05
268	Roger Clemens	.75
269	Rob Murphy	.05
270	Mickey Pina	.05
271	Tony Pena	.05
272	Jody Reed	.05
273	Kevin Romine	.05
274	Mike Greenwell	.05
275	*Mo Vaughn*	2.00
276	Danny Heep	.05
277	Scott Cooper	.05
278	*Greg Blosser*	.10
279	Dwight Evans	.05
280	Ellis Burks	.10
281	Wade Boggs	.40
282	Marty Barrett	.05
283	Kirk McCaskill	.05
284	Mark Langston	.05
285	Bert Blyleven	.08
286	Mike Fetters	.05
287	Kyle Abbott	.05
288	Jim Abbott	.12
289	Chuck Finley	.05
290	Gary DiSarcina	.05
291	Dick Schofield	.05
292	Devon White	.08
293	Bobby Rose	.05
294	Brian Downing	.05
295	Lance Parrish	.08
296	Jack Howell	.05
297	Claudell Washington	.05
298	John Orton	.05
299	Wally Joyner	.08
300	Lee Stevens	.05
301	Chili Davis	.08
302	Johnny Ray	.05
303	Greg Hibbard	.05
304	Eric King	.05
305	Jack McDowell	.10
306	Bobby Thigpen	.05
307	Adam Peterson	.05
308	*Scott Radinsky*	.10
309	Wayne Edwards	.05
310	Melido Perez	.05
311	Robin Ventura	.25
312	*Sammy Sosa*	6.00
313	Dan Pasqua	.05
314	Carlton Fisk	.25
315	Ozzie Guillen	.05
316	Ivan Calderon	.05
317	Daryl Boston	.05
318	Craig Grebeck	.05
319	Scott Fletcher	.05
320	*Frank Thomas*	4.00
321	Steve Lyons	.05
322	Carlos Martinez	.05
323	Joe Skalski	.05
324	Tom Candiotti	.05
325	Greg Swindell	.05
326	Steve Olin	.05
327	Kevin Wickander	.05
328	Doug Jones	.05
329	Jeff Shaw	.05
330	Kevin Bearse	.05
331	Dion James	.05
332	Jerry Browne	.05
333	Albert Belle	.75
334	Felix Fermin	.05
335	Candy Maldonado	.05
336	Cory Snyder	.05
337	Sandy Alomar	.12
338	Mark Lewis	.05
339	*Carlos Baerga*	.15
340	Chris James	.05
341	Brook Jacoby	.05
342	Keith Hernandez	.08
343	Frank Tanana	.05
344	Scott Aldred	.05
345	Mike Henneman	.05
346	Steve Wapnick	.05
347	Greg Gohr	.05
348	Eric Stone	.05
349	Brian DuBois	.05
350	Kevin Ritz	.05
351	Rico Brogna	.05
352	Mike Heath	.05
353	Alan Trammell	.10
354	Chet Lemon	.05
355	Dave Bergman	.05
356	Lou Whitaker	.08
357	Cecil Fielder	.10
358	Milt Cuyler	.05
359	Tony Phillips	.05
360	*Travis Fryman*	.40
361	Ed Romero	.05
362	Lloyd Moseby	.05
363	Mark Gubicza	.05
364	Bret Saberhagen	.08
365	Tom Gordon	.05
366	Steve Farr	.05
367	Kevin Appier	.08
368	Storm Davis	.05
369	Mark Davis	.05
370	Jeff Montgomery	.05
371	Frank White	.05
372	Brent Mayne	.05
373	Bob Boone	.05
374	Jim Eisenreich	.05
375	Danny Tartabull	.05
376	Kurt Stillwell	.05
377	Bill Pecota	.05
378	Bo Jackson	.15
379	*Bob Hamelin*	.15
380	Kevin Seitzer	.05
381	Rey Palacios	.05
382	George Brett	.50
383	Gerald Perry	.05
384	Teddy Higuera	.05
385	Tom Filer	.05
386	Dan Plesac	.05
387	*Cal Eldred*	.15
388	Jaime Navarro	.05
389	Chris Bosio	.05
390	Randy Veres	.05
391	Gary Sheffield	.12
392	George Canale	.05
393	B.J. Surhoff	.08
394	Tim McIntosh	.05
395	Greg Brock	.05
396	Greg Vaughn	.12
397	Darryl Hamilton	.05
398	Dave Parker	.10
399	Paul Molitor	.40
400	Jim Gantner	.05
401	Rob Deer	.05
402	Billy Spiers	.05
403	Glenn Braggs	.05
404	Robin Yount	.40
405	Rick Aguilera	.05
406	Johnny Ard	.05
407	*Kevin Tapani*	.15
408	Park Pittman	.05
409	Allan Anderson	.05
410	Juan Berenguer	.05
411	Willie Banks	.05
412	Rich Yett	.05
413	Dave West	.05
414	Greg Gagne	.05
415	*Chuck Knoblauch*	.75
416	Randy Bush	.05
417	Gary Gaetti	.08
418	Kent Hrbek	.08
419	Al Newman	.05
420	Danny Gladden	.05
421	Paul Sorrento	.05
422	Derek Parks	.05
423	Scott Leius	.08
424	Kirby Puckett	.60
425	Willie Smith	.05
426	Dave Righetti	.05
427	Jeff Robinson	.05
428	Alan Mills	.05
429	Tim Leary	.05
430	Pascual Perez	.05
431	Alvaro Espinoza	.05
432	Dave Winfield	.20
433	Jesse Barfield	.05
434	Randy Velarde	.05
435	Rick Cerone	.05
436	Steve Balboni	.05
437	Mel Hall	.05
438	Bob Geren	.05
439	*Bernie Williams*	2.00
440	Kevin Maas	.05
441	Mike Blowers	.05
442	Steve Sax	.05
443	Don Mattingly	.60
444	Roberto Kelly	.05
445	Mike Moore	.05
446	Reggie Harris	.05

447	Scott Sanderson	.05
448	Dave Otto	.05
449	Dave Stewart	.08
450	Rick Honeycutt	.05
451	Dennis Eckersley	.10
452	Carney Lansford	.05
453	Scott Hemond	.05
454	Mark McGwire	1.50
455	Felix Jose	.05
456	Terry Steinbach	.05
457	Rickey Henderson	.20
458	Dave Henderson	.05
459	Mike Gallego	.05
460	Jose Canseco	.30
461	Walt Weiss	.05
462	Ken Phelps	.05
463	*Darren Lewis*	.20
464	Ron Hassey	.05
465	*Roger Salkeld*	.10
466	Scott Bankhead	.05
467	Keith Comstock	.05
468	Randy Johnson	.35
469	Erik Hanson	.05
470	Mike Schooler	.05
471	Gary Eave	.05
472	Jeffrey Leonard	.05
473	Dave Valle	.05
474	Omar Vizquel	.08
475	Pete O'Brien	.05
476	Henry Cotto	.05
477	Jay Buhner	.10
478	Harold Reynolds	.08
479	Alvin Davis	.05
480	Darnell Coles	.05
481	Ken Griffey, Jr.	2.50
482	Greg Briley	.05
483	Scott Bradley	.05
484	Tino Martinez	.20
485	Jeff Russell	.05
486	Nolan Ryan	.75
487	Robb Nen	.05
488	Kevin Brown	.08
489	Brian Bohanon	.05
490	Ruben Sierra	.05
491	Pete Incaviglia	.05
492	*Juan Gonzalez*	2.00
493	Steve Buechele	.05
494	Scott Coolbaugh	.05
495	Geno Petralli	.05
496	Rafael Palmeiro	.12
497	Julio Franco	.08
498	Gary Pettis	.05
499	Donald Harris	.05
500	Monty Fariss	.05
501	Harold Baines	.08
502	Cecil Espy	.05
503	Jack Daugherty	.05
504	Willie Blair	.05
505	Dave Steib	.05
506	Tom Henke	.05
507	John Cerutti	.05
508	Paul Kilgus	.05
509	Jimmy Key	.08
510	*John Olerud*	.50
511	Ed Sprague	.05
512	Manny Lee	.05
513	Fred McGriff	.15
514	Glenallen Hill	.08
515	George Bell	.05
516	Mookie Wilson	.05
517	Luis Sojo	.05
518	Nelson Liriano	.05
519	Kelly Gruber	.05
520	Greg Myers	.05
521	Pat Borders	.05
522	Junior Felix	.05
523	Eddie Zosky	.12
524	Tony Fernandez	.08
525	Checklist	.05
526	Checklist	.05
527	Checklist	.05
528	Checklist	.05

1990 Bowman Inserts

Bowman inserted sweepstakes cards in its 1990 packs, much like in 1989. This 11-card set features current players displayed in drawings by Craig Pursley.

		MT
Complete Set (11):		1.25
Common Player:		.05
(1)	Will Clark	.10
(2)	Mark Davis	.05
(3)	Dwight Gooden	.10
(4)	Bo Jackson	.10
(5)	Don Mattingly	.25
(6)	Kevin Mitchell	.05
(7)	Gregg Olson	.05
(8)	Nolan Ryan	.50
(9)	Bret Saberhagen	.05
(10)	Jerome Walton	.05
(11)	Robin Yount	.15

1990 Bowman Tiffany

Reported production of fewer than 10,000 sets has created a significant premium for these glossy "Tiffany" versions of Bowman's 1990 baseball card set. The use of white cardboard stock and high-gloss front finish distinguishes these cards from regular-issue Bowmans.

	MT
Complete (Sealed) Set (539):	600.00
Complete (Opened) Set (539):	150.00
Common Player:	.25

(Star/rookie cards valued about 4-5X regular-issue 1990 Bowman.)

1991 Bowman

The 1991 Bowman set features 704 cards compared to 528 cards in the 1990 issue. The cards imitate the 1953 Bowman style. Special Rod Carew cards and gold foil-stamped cards are included. The set is numbered by teams. Like the 1989 and 1990 issues, the card backs feature a breakdown of performance against each other team in the league.

		MT
Complete Set (704):		40.00
Factory Set (704):		50.00
Common Player:		.05
Green Cello Pack (14):		2.75
Green Cello Wax Box (36):		69.00
1	Rod Carew-I	.10
2	Rod Carew-II	.10
3	Rod Carew-III	.10
4	Rod Carew-IV	.10
5	Rod Carew-V	.10
6	Willie Fraser	.05
7	John Olerud	.15
8	William Suero	.05
9	Roberto Alomar	.30
10	Todd Stottlemyre	.08
11	Joe Carter	.10
12	*Steve Karsay*	.15
13	Mark Whiten	.05
14	Pat Borders	.05
15	Mike Timlin	.05
16	Tom Henke	.05
17	Eddie Zosky	.05
18	Kelly Gruber	.05
19	Jimmy Key	.08
20	Jerry Schunk	.05
21	Manny Lee	.05
22	Dave Steib	.05
23	Pat Hentgen	.08
24	Glenallen Hill	.05
25	Rene Gonzales	.05
26	Ed Sprague	.05
27	Ken Dayley	.05
28	Pat Tabler	.05
29	*Denis Boucher*	.08
30	Devon White	.08
31	Dante Bichette	.15
32	Paul Molitor	.35
33	Greg Vaughn	.08
34	Dan Plesac	.05
35	Chris George	.05
36	Tim McIntosh	.05
37	Franklin Stubbs	.05
38	Bo Dodson	.05
39	Ron Robinson	.05
40	Ed Nunez	.05
41	Greg Brock	.05
42	Jaime Navarro	.05
43	Chris Bosio	.05
44	B.J. Surhoff	.08
45	Chris Johnson	.05
46	Willie Randolph	.05
47	Narciso Elvira	.05
48	Jim Gantner	.05
49	Kevin Brown	.05
50	Julio Machado	.05
51	Chuck Crim	.05
52	Gary Sheffield	.20
53	Angel Miranda	.05
54	Teddy Higuera	.05
55	Robin Yount	.35
56	Cal Eldred	.05
57	Sandy Alomar	.15
58	Greg Swindell	.05
59	Brook Jacoby	.05
60	Efrain Valdez	.05
61	Ever Magallanes	.05
62	Tom Candiotti	.05
63	Eric King	.05
64	Alex Cole	.05
65	Charles Nagy	.08
66	Mitch Webster	.05
67	Chris James	.05
68	*Jim Thome*	1.50
69	Carlos Baerga	.08
70	Mark Lewis	.05
71	Jerry Browne	.05
72	Jesse Orosco	.05
73	Mike Huff	.05
74	Jose Escobar	.05
75	Jeff Manto	.05
76	*Turner Ward*	.10
77	Doug Jones	.05
78	*Bruce Egloff*	.05
79	Tim Costo	.05
80	Beau Allred	.05
81	Albert Belle	.40
82	John Farrell	.05
83	Glenn Davis	.05
84	Joe Orsulak	.05
85	Mark Williamson	.05
86	Ben McDonald	.08
87	Billy Ripken	.05
88	Leo Gomez	.05
89	Bob Melvin	.05
90	Jeff Robinson	.05
91	Jose Mesa	.05
92	Gregg Olson	.05
93	Mike Devereaux	.05
94	Luis Mercedes	.05
95	*Arthur Rhodes*	.20
96	Juan Bell	.05
97	*Mike Mussina*	2.00
98	Jeff Ballard	.05
99	Chris Hoiles	.05
100	Brady Anderson	.10
101	Bob Milacki	.05
102	David Segui	.05
103	Dwight Evans	.08
104	Cal Ripken, Jr.	1.00
105	Mike Linskey	.05
106	*Jeff Tackett*	.05
107	Jeff Reardon	.05
108	Dana Kiecker	.05
109	Ellis Burks	.08
110	Dave Owen	.05
111	Danny Darwin	.05
112	Mo Vaughn	.40
113	Jeff McNeely	.05
114	Tom Bolton	.05
115	Greg Blosser	.05
116	Mike Greenwell	.05
117	*Phil Plantier*	.15
118	Roger Clemens	.50
119	John Marzano	.05
120	Jody Reed	.05
121	Scott Taylor	.05
122	Jack Clark	.05
123	Derek Livernois	.05
124	Tony Pena	.05
125	Tom Brunansky	.05
126	Carlos Quintana	.05
127	Tim Naehring	.05
128	Matt Young	.05
129	Wade Boggs	.35
130	Kevin Morton	.05
131	Pete Incaviglia	.05
132	Rob Deer	.05
133	Bill Gullickson	.05
134	Rico Brogna	.05
135	Lloyd Moseby	.05
136	Cecil Fielder	.10
137	Tony Phillips	.05
138	Mark Leiter	.05
139	John Cerutti	.05
140	Mickey Tettleton	.05
141	Milt Cuyler	.05
142	Greg Gohr	.05
143	Tony Bernazard	.05
144	Dan Gakeler	.05
145	Travis Fryman	.10
146	Dan Petry	.05
147	Scott Aldred	.05
148	John DeSilva	.05
149	Rusty Meacham	.05
150	Lou Whitaker	.08
151	Dave Haas	.05
152	Luis de los Santos	.05
153	Ivan Cruz	.05
154	Alan Trammell	.12
155	Pat Kelly	.05
156	*Carl Everett*	1.50
157	Greg Cadaret	.05
158	Kevin Maas	.05
159	Jeff Johnson	.05
160	Willie Smith	.05
161	Gerald Williams	.08
162	Mike Humphreys	.05
163	Alvaro Espinoza	.05
164	Matt Nokes	.05
165	Wade Taylor	.05
166	Roberto Kelly	.05
167	John Habyan	.05
168	Steve Farr	.05
169	Jesse Barfield	.05
170	Steve Sax	.05
171	Jim Leyritz	.08
172	Robert Eenhoorn	.05

173	Bernie Williams	.30
174	Scott Lusader	.05
175	Torey Lovullo	.05
176	Chuck Cary	.05
177	Scott Sanderson	.05
178	Don Mattingly	.50
179	Mel Hall	.05
180	Juan Gonzalez	.40
181	Hensley Meulens	.05
182	Jose Offerman	.05
183	*Jeff Bagwell*	4.00
184	*Jeff Conine*	.25
185	*Henry Rodriguez*	.50
186	Jimmie Reese	.10
187	Kyle Abbott	.05
188	Lance Parrish	.08
189	Rafael Montalvo	.05
190	Floyd Bannister	.05
191	Dick Schofield	.05
192	Scott Lewis	.05
193	Jeff Robinson	.05
194	Kent Anderson	.05
195	Wally Joyner	.08
196	Chuck Finley	.05
197	Luis Sojo	.05
198	Jeff Richardson	.05
199	Dave Parker	.10
200	Jim Abbott	.12
201	Junior Felix	.05
202	Mark Langston	.08
203	*Tim Salmon*	1.00
204	Cliff Young	.05
205	Scott Bailes	.05
206	Bobby Rose	.05
207	Gary Gaetti	.08
208	Ruben Amaro	.05
209	Luis Polonia	.05
210	Dave Winfield	.25
211	Bryan Harvey	.05
212	Mike Moore	.05
213	Rickey Henderson	.20
214	Steve Chitren	.05
215	Bob Welch	.05
216	Terry Steinbach	.05
217	Ernie Riles	.05
218	*Todd Van Poppel*	.10
219	Mike Gallego	.05
220	Curt Young	.05
221	Todd Burns	.05
222	Vance Law	.05
223	Eric Show	.05
224	*Don Peters*	.05
225	Dave Stewart	.08
226	Dave Henderson	.05
227	Jose Canseco	.35
228	Walt Weiss	.05
229	Dann Howitt	.05
230	Willie Wilson	.05
231	Harold Baines	.08
232	Scott Hemond	.05
233	Joe Slusarski	.05
234	Mark McGwire	1.50
235	*Kirk Dressendorfer*	.12
236	*Craig Paquette*	.08
237	Dennis Eckersley	.10
238	Dana Allison	.05
239	Scott Bradley	.05
240	Brian Holman	.05
241	Mike Schooler	.05
242	Rich Delucia	.05
243	Edgar Martinez	.05
244	Henry Cotto	.05
245	Omar Vizquel	.08
246a	Ken Griffey, Jr.	1.50
246b	Ken Griffey Sr. (should be #255)	.10
247	Jay Buhner	.08
248	Bill Krueger	.05
249	*Dave Fleming*	.15
250	*Patrick Lennon*	.10
251	Dave Valle	.05
252	Harold Reynolds	.08
253	Randy Johnson	.20
254	Scott Bankhead	.05
255	(Not issued, see #246b)	
256	Greg Briley	.05
257	Tino Martinez	.10
258	Alvin Davis	.05
259	Pete O'Brien	.05
260	Erik Hanson	.05
261	*Bret Boone*	.25
262	Roger Salkeld	.05
263	Dave Burba	.05
264	*Kerry Woodson*	.10
265	Julio Franco	.05
266	Dan Peltier	.05
267	Jeff Russell	.05
268	Steve Buechele	.05
269	Donald Harris	.05
270	Robb Nen	.08
271	Rich Gossage	.08
272	*Ivan Rodriguez*	4.00
273	Jeff Huson	.05
274	Kevin Brown	.10
275	*Dan Smith*	.10
276	Gary Pettis	.05
277	Jack Daugherty	.05
278	Mike Jeffcoat	.05
279	Brad Arnsberg	.05
280	Nolan Ryan	.75
281	Eric McCray	.05
282	Scott Chiamparino	.05
283	Ruben Sierra	.05
284	Geno Petralli	.05
285	Monty Fariss	.05
286	Rafael Palmeiro	.20
287	Bobby Witt	.05
288	Dean Palmer	.10
289	Tony Scruggs	.05
290	Kenny Rogers	.08
291	Bret Saberhagen	.08
292	*Brian McRae*	.20
293	Storm Davis	.05
294	Danny Tartabull	.05
295	David Howard	.05
296	Mike Boddicker	.05
297	Joel Johnston	.05
298	Tim Spehr	.05
299	Hector Wagner	.05
300	George Brett	.40
301	Mike Macfarlane	.05
302	Kirk Gibson	.05
303	Harvey Pulliam	.05
304	Jim Eisenreich	.05
305	Kevin Seitzer	.05
306	Mark Davis	.05
307	Kurt Stillwell	.05
308	Jeff Montgomery	.05
309	Kevin Appier	.05
310	Bob Hamelin	.08
311	Tom Gordon	.05
312	*Kerwin Moore*	.05
313	Hugh Walker	.05
314	Terry Shumpert	.05
315	Warren Cromartie	.05
316	Gary Thurman	.05
317	Steve Bedrosian	.05
318	Danny Gladden	.05
319	Jack Morris	.08
320	Kirby Puckett	.45
321	Kent Hrbek	.08
322	Kevin Tapani	.08
323	Denny Neagle	.05
324	Rich Garces	.05
325	Larry Casian	.05
326	Shane Mack	.05
327	Allan Anderson	.05
328	Junior Ortiz	.05
329	*Paul Abbott*	.08
330	Chuck Knoblauch	.20
331	Chili Davis	.08
332	*Todd Ritchie*	.05
333	Brian Harper	.05
334	Rick Aguilera	.05
335	Scott Erickson	.08
336	Pedro Munoz	.05
337	Scott Leuis	.05
338	Greg Gagne	.05
339	Mike Pagliarulo	.05
340	Terry Leach	.05
341	Willie Banks	.05
342	Bobby Thigpen	.05
343	*Roberto Hernandez*	.20
344	Melido Perez	.05
345	Carlton Fisk	.20
346	*Norberto Martin*	.08
347	*Johnny Ruffin*	.05
348	*Jeff Carter*	.05
349	Lance Johnson	.05
350	Sammy Sosa	1.00
351	Alex Fernandez	.15
352	Jack McDowell	.08
353	Bob Wickman	.05
354	Wilson Alvarez	.05
355	Charlie Hough	.05
356	Ozzie Guillen	.05
357	Cory Snyder	.05
358	Robin Ventura	.15
359	Scott Fletcher	.05
360	Cesar Bernhardt	.05
361	Dan Pasqua	.05
362	Tim Raines	.08
363	Brian Drahman	.05
364	Wayne Edwards	.05
365	Scott Radinsky	.05
366	Frank Thomas	.75
367	Cecil Fielder	.10
368	Julio Franco	.08
369	Kelly Gruber	.05
370	Alan Trammell	.12
371	Rickey Henderson	.25
372	Jose Canseco	.25
373	Ellis Burks	.10
374	Lance Parrish	.08
375	Dave Parker	.08
376	Eddie Murray	.25
377	Ryne Sandberg	.25
378	Matt Williams	.15
379	Barry Larkin	.08
380	Barry Bonds	.40
381	Bobby Bonilla	.08
382	Darryl Strawberry	.08
383	Benny Santiago	.05
384	Don Robinson	.05
385	Paul Coleman	.05
386	Milt Thompson	.05
387	Lee Smith	.08
388	Ray Lankford	.15
389	Tom Pagnozzi	.05
390	Ken Hill	.05
391	Jamie Moyer	.05
392	*Greg Carmona*	.05
393	John Ericks	.05
394	Bob Tewksbury	.05
395	Jose Oquendo	.05
396	Rheal Cormier	.05
397	*Mike Milchin*	.05
398	Ozzie Smith	.40
399	*Aaron Holbert*	.08
400	Jose DeLeon	.05
401	Felix Jose	.05
402	Juan Agosto	.05
403	Pedro Guerrero	.05
404	Todd Zeile	.08
405	Gerald Perry	.05
406	Not issued	
407	Bryn Smith	.05
408	Bernard Gilkey	.08
409	Rex Hudler	.05
410a	Ralph Branca, Bobby Thomson	.10
410b	Donovan Osborne	.08
411	Lance Dickson	.05
412	Danny Jackson	.05
413	Jerome Walton	.05
414	Sean Cheetham	.05
415	Joe Girardi	.05
416	Ryne Sandberg	.25
417	Mike Harkey	.05
418	George Bell	.05
419	*Rick Wilkins*	.25
420	Earl Cunningham	.05
421	Heathcliff Slocumb	.05
422	Mike Bielecki	.05
423	*Jessie Hollins*	.08
424	Shawon Dunston	.08
425	Dave Smith	.05
426	Greg Maddux	.60
427	Jose Vizcaino	.05
428	Luis Salazar	.05
429	Andre Dawson	.10
430	Rick Sutcliffe	.05
431	Paul Assenmacher	.05
432	Erik Pappas	.05
433	Mark Grace	.25
434	Denny Martinez	.08
435	Marquis Grissom	.12
436	*Wil Cordero*	.20
437	Tim Wallach	.05
438	*Brian Barnes*	.05
439	Barry Jones	.05
440	Ivan Calderon	.05
441	*Stan Spencer*	.05
442	Larry Walker	.25
443	*Chris Haney*	.08
444	Hector Rivera	.05
445	Delino DeShields	.08
446	Andres Galarraga	.10
447	Gilberto Reyes	.05
448	Willie Greene	.05
449	Greg Colbrunn	.05
450	*Rondell White*	.50
451	Steve Frey	.05
452	*Shane Andrews*	.12
453	Mike Fitzgerald	.05
454	Spike Owen	.05
455	Dave Martinez	.05
456	Dennis Boyd	.05
457	Eric Bullock	.05
458	*Reid Cornelius*	.10
459	Chris Nabholz	.05
460	David Cone	.08
461	Hubie Brooks	.05
462	Sid Fernandez	.05
463	*Doug Simons*	.08
464	Howard Johnson	.05
465	Chris Donnels	.05
466	Anthony Young	.10
467	Todd Hundley	.10
468	Rick Cerone	.05
469	Kevin Elster	.05
470	Wally Whitehurst	.05
471	Vince Coleman	.05
472	Dwight Gooden	.10
473	Charlie O'Brien	.05
474	*Jeromy Burnitz*	1.00
475	John Franco	.05
476	Daryl Boston	.05
477	Frank Viola	.05
478	D.J. Dozier	.05
479	Kevin McReynolds	.05
480	Tom Herr	.05
481	Gregg Jefferies	.08
482	Pete Schourek	.05
483	Ron Darling	.05
484	Dave Magadan	.05
485	*Andy Ashby*	.10
486	Dale Murphy	.12
487	Von Hayes	.05
488	*Kim Batiste*	.08
489	*Tony Longmire*	.10
490	Wally Backman	.05
491	Jeff Jackson	.05
492	Mickey Morandini	.05
493	Darrel Akerfelds	.05
494	Ricky Jordan	.05
495	Randy Ready	.05
496	Darrin Fletcher	.05
497	Chuck Malone	.05
498	Pat Combs	.05
499	Dickie Thon	.05
500	Roger McDowell	.05
501	Len Dykstra	.05
502	Joe Boever	.05
503	John Kruk	.05
504	Terry Mulholland	.08
505	Wes Chamberlain	.05
506	*Mike Lieberthal*	.75
507	Darren Daulton	.05
508	Charlie Hayes	.05
509	John Smiley	.05
510	Gary Varsho	.05
511	Curt Wilkerson	.05
512	*Orlando Merced*	.20
513	Barry Bonds	.40
514	Mike Lavalliere	.05
515	Doug Drabek	.05
516	Gary Redus	.05
517	*William Pennyfeather*	.05
518	Randy Tomlin	.05
519	*Mike Zimmerman*	.05
520	Jeff King	.05
521	*Kurt Miller*	.10
522	Jay Bell	.08
523	Bill Landrum	.05
524	Zane Smith	.05
525	Bobby Bonilla	.10
526	Bob Walk	.05
527	Austin Manahan	.05
528	*Joe Ausanio*	.05
529	Andy Van Slyke	.05
530	Jose Lind	.05
531	*Carlos Garcia*	.15
532	Don Slaught	.05
533	Colin Powell	.25
534	*Frank Bolick*	.05
535	*Gary Scott*	.05
536	Nikco Riesgo	.05
537	*Reggie Sanders*	.40
538	*Tim Howard*	.05
539	*Ryan Bowen*	.10
540	Eric Anthony	.05
541	Jim Deshaies	.05
542	Tom Nevers	.05
543	Ken Caminiti	.10
544	Karl Rhodes	.05
545	Xavier Hernandez	.05
546	Mike Scott	.05
547	Jeff Juden	.08
548	Darryl Kile	.05
549	Willie Ansley	.05
550	*Luis Gonzalez*	.75
551	*Mike Simms*	.08
552	Mark Portugal	.05

553	Jimmy Jones	.05
554	Jim Clancy	.05
555	Pete Harnisch	.05
556	Craig Biggio	.10
557	Eric Yelding	.05
558	Dave Rohde	.05
559	Casey Candaele	.05
560	Curt Schilling	.08
561	Steve Finley	.05
562	Javier Ortiz	.05
563	Andujar Cedeno	.05
564	Rafael Ramirez	.05
565	*Kenny Lofton*	1.00
566	Steve Avery	.05
567	Lonnie Smith	.05
568	Kent Mercker	.05
569	*Chipper Jones*	8.00
570	Terry Pendleton	.05
571	Otis Nixon	.05
572	Juan Berenguer	.05
573	Charlie Leibrandt	.05
574	Dave Justice	.20
575	Keith Mitchell	.05
576	Tom Glavine	.15
577	Greg Olson	.05
578	Rafael Belliard	.05
579	Ben Rivera	.05
580	John Smoltz	.10
581	Tyler Houston	.05
582	*Mark Wohlers*	.15
583	Ron Gant	.10
584	Ramon Caraballo	.05
585	Sid Bream	.05
586	Jeff Treadway	.05
587	*Javier Lopez*	1.00
588	Deion Sanders	.15
589	Mike Heath	.05
590	*Ryan Klesko*	.75
591	Bob Ojeda	.05
592	Alfredo Griffin	.05
593	*Raul Mondesi*	1.50
594	Greg Smith	.05
595	Orel Hershiser	.08
596	Juan Samuel	.05
597	Brett Butler	.08
598	Gary Carter	.10
599	Stan Javier	.05
600	Kal Daniels	.05
601	*Jamie McAndrew*	.10
602	Mike Sharperson	.05
603	Jay Howell	.05
604	*Eric Karros*	.75
605	Tim Belcher	.05
606	Dan Opperman	.05
607	Lenny Harris	.05
608	Tom Goodwin	.08
609	Darryl Strawberry	.10
610	Ramon Martinez	.08
611	Kevin Gross	.05
612	Zakary Shinall	.05
613	Mike Scioscia	.05
614	Eddie Murray	.20
615	Ronnie Walden	.05
616	Will Clark	.25
617	Adam Hyzdu	.05
618	Matt Williams	.20
619	Don Robinson	.05
620	Jeff Brantley	.05
621	Greg Litton	.05
622	Steve Decker	.05
623	Robby Thompson	.05
624	*Mark Leonard*	.08
625	Kevin Bass	.05
626	Scott Garrelts	.05
627	Jose Uribe	.05
628	Eric Gunderson	.05
629	Steve Hosey	.05
630	Trevor Wilson	.05
631	Terry Kennedy	.05
632	Dave Righetti	.05
633	Kelly Downs	.05
634	Johnny Ard	.05
635	*Eric Christopherson*	.10
636	Kevin Mitchell	.05
637	John Burkett	.05
638	*Kevin Rogers*	.10
639	Bud Black	.05
640	Willie McGee	.08
641	Royce Clayton	.05
642	Tony Fernandez	.08
643	Ricky Bones	.05
644	Thomas Howard	.05
645	Dave Staton	.05
646	Jim Presley	.05
647	Tony Gwynn	.50
648	Marty Barrett	.05
649	Scott Coolbaugh	.05
650	Craig Lefferts	.05
651	Eddie Whitson	.05
652	Oscar Azocar	.05
653	Wes Gardner	.05
654	Bip Roberts	.05
655	*Robbie Beckett*	.08
656	Benny Santiago	.05
657	Greg W. Harris	.05
658	Jerald Clark	.05
659	Fred McGriff	.20
660	Larry Andersen	.05
661	Bruce Hurst	.05
662	Steve Martin	.05
663	Rafael Valdez	.05
664	*Paul Faries*	.05
665	Andy Benes	.08
666	Randy Myers	.08
667	Rob Dibble	.05
668	Glenn Sutko	.05
669	Glenn Braggs	.05
670	Billy Hatcher	.05
671	Joe Oliver	.05
672	Freddie Benavides	.05
673	Barry Larkin	.10
674	Chris Sabo	.05
675	Mariano Duncan	.05
676	*Chris Jones*	.10
677	*Gino Minutelli*	.05
678	Reggie Jefferson	.05
679	Jack Armstrong	.05
680	Chris Hammond	.05
681	Jose Rijo	.05
682	Bill Doran	.05
683	Terry Lee	.05
684	Tom Browning	.05
685	Paul O'Neill	.10
686	Eric Davis	.12
687	*Dan Wilson*	.15
688	Ted Power	.05
689	Tim Layana	.05
690	Norm Charlton	.05
691	Hal Morris	.05
692	Rickey Henderson	.20
693	*Sam Militello*	.08
694	*Matt Mieske*	.10
695	*Paul Russo*	.05
696	*Domingo Mota*	.05
697	*Todd Guggiana*	.05
698	Marc Newfield	.05
699	Checklist	.05
700	Checklist	.05
701	Checklist	.05
702	Checklist	.05
703	Checklist	.05
704	Checklist	.05

1992 Bowman

Topps introduced several changes with the release of its 1992 Bowman set. The 705-card set features 45 special insert cards stamped with gold foil. The cards are printed with a premium UV coated glossy card stock. Several players without major league experience are featured in the set. Included in this group are 1991 MVP's of the minor leagues and first round draft choices. Eighteen of the gold-foil enchanced cards have been identified as shortprints (designated SP in the listings), printed in quantities one-half the other foils.

		MT
Complete Set (705):		300.00
Common Player:		.20
Pack (15):		9.00
Wax Box (36):		250.00
1	Ivan Rodriguez	3.00
2	Kirk McCaskill	.20
3	Scott Livingstone	.25
4	*Salomon Torres*	.20
5	Carlos Hernandez	.20
6	Dave Hollins	.30
7	Scott Fletcher	.20
8	Jorge Fabregas	.25
9	Andujar Cedeno	.20
10	Howard Johnson	.25
11	*Trevor Hoffman*	2.00
12	Roberto Kelly	.20
13	Gregg Jefferies	.35
14	Marquis Grissom	.20
15	Mike Ignasiak	.20
16	Jack Morris	.25
17	William Pennyfeather	.20
18	Todd Stottlemyre	.25
19	Chito Martinez	.20
20	Roberto Alomar	2.00
21	Sam Militello	.20
22	Hector Fajardo	.20
23	*Paul Quantrill*	.40
24	Chuck Knoblauch	.40
25	Reggie Jefferson	.25
26	Jeremy McGarity	.20
27	Jerome Walton	.20
28	Chipper Jones	30.00
29	*Brian Barber*	.40
30	Ron Darling	.20
31	*Roberto Petagine*	.20
32	Chuck Finley	.20
33	Edgar Martinez	.30
34	Napolean Robinson	.20
35	Andy Van Slyke	.20
36	Bobby Thigpen	.20
37	Travis Fryman	.30
38	Eric Christopherson	.20
39	Terry Mulholland	.25
40	Darryl Strawberry	.35
41	*Manny Alexander*	.50
42	*Tracey Sanders*	.25
43	Pete Incaviglia	.20
44	Kim Batiste	.20
45	Frank Rodriguez	.25
46	Greg Swindell	.20
47	Delino DeShields	.20
48	John Ericks	.20
49	Franklin Stubbs	.20
50	Tony Gwynn	3.00
51	*Clifton Garrett*	.25
52	Mike Gardella	.20
53	Scott Erickson	.25
54	Gary Caballo	.20
55	*Jose Oliva*	.30
56	Brook Fordyce	.20
57	Mark Whiten	.20
58	Joe Slusarski	.20
59	*J.R. Phillips*	.50
60	Barry Bonds	3.00
61	Bob Milacki	.20
62	Keith Mitchell	.20
63	Angel Miranda	.20
64	Raul Mondesi	6.00
65	Brian Koelling	.20
66	Brian McRae	.30
67	John Patterson	.20
68	John Wetteland	.25
69	Wilson Alvarez	.25
70	Wade Boggs	1.00
71	Darryl Ratliff	.20
72	Jeff Jackson	.20
73	Jeremy Hernandez	.25
74	Darryl Hamilton	.25
75	Rafael Belliard	.20
76	Ricky Trilcek	.20
77	*Felipe Crespo*	.40
78	Carney Lansford	.20
79	Ryan Long	.20
80	Kirby Puckett	2.50
81	Earl Cunningham	.20
82	Pedro Martinez	30.00
83	Scott Hatteberg	.25
84	Juan Gonzalez	2.00
85	Robert Nutting	.20
86	*Calvin Reese*	3.00
87	Dave Silvestri	.20
88	*Scott Ruffcorn*	.50
89	Rick Aguilera	.20
90	Cecil Fielder	.30
91	Kirk Dressendorfer	.20
92	Jerry DiPoto	.20
93	Mike Felder	.20
94	Craig Paquette	.25
95	Elvin Paulino	.20
96	Donovan Osborne	.20
97	Hubie Brooks	.20
98	*Derek Lowe*	.25
99	David Zancanaro	.20
100	Ken Griffey, Jr.	8.00
101	Todd Hundley	.75
102	Mike Trombley	.25
103	*Ricky Gutierrez*	.50
104	Braulio Castillo	.20
105	Craig Lefferts	.20
106	Rick Sutcliffe	.20
107	Dean Palmer	.40
108	Henry Rodriguez	.50
109	*Mark Clark*	.50
110	Kenny Lofton	.75
111	Mark Carreon	.20
112	*J.T. Bruett*	.20
113	Gerald Williams	.25
114	Frank Thomas	4.00
115	Kevin Reimer	.20
116	Sammy Sosa	5.00
117	Mickey Tettleton	.20
118	Reggie Sanders	.30
119	Trevor Wilson	.20
120	Cliff Brantley	.20
121	Spike Owen	.20
122	Jeff Montgomery	.20
123	Alex Sutherland	.20
124	*Brien Taylor*	.35
125	Brian Williams	.25
126	Kevin Seitzer	.20
127	*Carlos Delgado*	35.00
128	Gary Scott	.20
129	Scott Cooper	.20
130	*Domingo Jean*	.20
131	*Pat Mahomes*	.50
132	Mike Boddicker	.20
133	Roberto Hernandez	.35
134	Dave Valle	.20
135	Kurt Stillwell	.20
136	*Brad Pennington*	.50
137	Jermaine Swifton	.20
138	Ryan Hawblitzel	.20
139	Tito Navarro	.20
140	Sandy Alomar	.35
141	Todd Benzinger	.20
142	Danny Jackson	.20
143	*Melvin Nieves*	.75
144	Jim Campanis	.20
145	Luis Gonzalez	.25
146	Dave Doorneweerd	.20
147	Charlie Hayes	.20
148	Greg Maddux	4.00
149	Brian Harper	.20
150	Brent Miller	.20
151	*Shawn Estes*	3.00
152	Mike Williams	.20
153	Charlie Hough	.20
154	Randy Myers	.25
155	*Kevin Young*	2.00
156	Rick Wilkins	.20
157	Terry Schumpert	.20
158	Steve Karsay	.30
159	Gary DiSarcina	.20
160	Deion Sanders	.75
161	Tom Browning	.20
162	Dickie Thon	.20
163	Luis Mercedes	.20
164	Ricardo Ingram	.20
165	*Tavo Alavarez*	.50
166	Rickey Henderson	.50
167	Jaime Navarro	.20
168	*Billy Ashley*	.50
169	Phil Dauphin	.20
170	Ivan Cruz	.20
171	Harold Baines	.25
172	Bryan Harvey	.20
173	Alex Cole	.20
174	Curtis Shaw	.20
175	Matt Williams	.75

No.	Player	Value
176	Felix Jose	.20
177	Sam Horn	.20
178	Randy Johnson	1.50
179	Ivan Calderon	.20
180	Steve Avery	.25
181	William Suero	.20
182	Bill Swift	.20
183	*Howard Battle*	.50
184	Ruben Amaro	.20
185	Jim Abbott	.35
186	Mike Fitzgerald	.20
187	Bruce Hurst	.20
188	Jeff Juden	.50
189	Jeromy Burnitz	3.00
190	Dave Burba	.20
191	Kevin Brown	.20
192	Patrick Lennon	.20
193	Jeffrey McNeely	.20
194	Wil Cordero	.25
195	Chili Davis	.25
196	Milt Cuyler	.20
197	Von Hayes	.20
198	Todd Revening	.20
199	Joel Johnson	.20
200	Jeff Bagwell	3.00
201	Alex Fernandez	.50
202	Todd Jones	.20
203	Charles Nagy	.30
204	Tim Raines	.30
205	Kevin Maas	.20
206	Julio Franco	.25
207	Randy Velarde	.20
208	Lance Johnson	.20
209	Scott Leius	.20
210	Derek Lee	.30
211	Joe Sondrini	.20
212	Royce Clayton	.25
213	Chris George	.20
214	Gary Sheffield	1.00
215	Mark Gubicza	.20
216	Mike Moore	.20
217	Rick Huisman	.20
218	Jeff Russell	.20
219	D.J. Dozier	.20
220	Dave Martinez	.20
221	Al Newman	.20
222	Nolan Ryan	8.00
223	Teddy Higuera	.20
224	*Damon Buford*	.40
225	Ruben Sierra	.20
226	Tom Nevers	.20
227	Tommy Greene	.30
228	*Nigel Wilson*	.40
229	John DeSilva	.20
230	Bobby Witt	.20
231	Greg Cadaret	.20
232	John VanderWal	.20
233	Jack Clark	.20
234	Bill Doran	.20
235	Bobby Bonilla	.35
236	Steve Olin	.20
237	Derek Bell	.35
238	David Cone	.25
239	Victor Cole	.20
240	Rod Bolton	.20
241	Tom Pagnozzi	.20
242	Rob Dibble	.20
243	Michael Carter	.20
244	Don Peters	.20
245	Mike LaValliere	.20
246	Joe Perona	.20
247	Mitch Williams	.20
248	Jay Buhner	.35
249	Andy Benes	.30
250	*Alex Ochoa*	1.00
251	Greg Blosser	.20
252	Jack Armstrong	.20
253	Juan Samuel	.20
254	Terry Pendleton	.20
255	Ramon Martinez	.25
256	Rico Brogna	.25
257	John Smiley	.20
258	Carl Everett	.30
259	Tim Salmon	1.00
260	Will Clark	.75
261	*Ugueth Urbina*	1.00
262	Jason Wood	.20
263	Dave Magadan	.20
264	Dante Bichette	.50
265	Jose DeLeon	.20
266	*Mike Neill*	.30
267	Paul O'Neill	.50
268	Anthony Young	.25
269	Greg Harris	.20
270	Todd Van Poppel	.25
271	Pete Castellano	.20
272	Tony Phillips	.25
273	Mike Gallego	.20
274	*Steve Cooke*	.25
275	Robin Ventura	.25
276	Kevin Mitchell	.20
277	Doug Linton	.20
278	Robert Eenhorn	.20
279	*Gabe White*	.50
280	Dave Stewart	.30
281	Mo Sanford	.20
282	Greg Perschke	.20
283	Kevin Flora	.20
284	Jeff Williams	.20
285	Keith Miller	.20
286	Andy Ashby	.20
287	Doug Dascenzo	.20
288	Eric Karros	.50
289	*Glenn Murray*	.25
290	*Troy Percival*	1.00
291	Orlando Merced	.20
292	Peter Hoy	.20
293	Tony Fernandez	.25
294	Juan Guzman	.20
295	Jesse Barfield	.20
296	Sid Fernandez	.20
297	Scott Cepicky	.20
298	*Garret Anderson*	6.00
299	Cal Eldred	.20
300	Ryne Sandberg	1.50
301	Jim Gantner	.20
302	*Mariano Rivera*	10.00
303	Ron Lockett	.20
304	Jose Offerman	.20
305	Denny Martinez	.25
306	*Luis Ortiz*	.25
307	David Howard	.20
308	Russ Springer	.40
309	Chris Howard	.20
310	Kyle Abbott	.25
311	*Aaron Sele*	2.00
312	Dave Justice	.50
313	Pete O'Brien	.20
314	Greg Hansell	.20
315	Dave Winfield	.50
316	Lance Dickson	.20
317	Eric King	.20
318	Vaughn Eshelman	.20
319	Tim Belcher	.20
320	Andres Galarraga	.60
321	Scott Bullett	.20
322	Doug Strange	.20
323	Jerald Clark	.20
324	Dave Righetti	.20
325	Greg Hibbard	.20
326	Eric Dillman	.20
327	*Shane Reynolds*	1.00
328	Chris Hammond	.20
329	Albert Belle	1.00
330	*Rich Becker*	.50
331	Eddie Williams	.20
332	Donald Harris	.20
333	Dave Smith	.20
334	Steve Fireovid	.20
335	Steve Buechele	.20
336	Mike Schooler	.20
337	Kevin McReynolds	.20
338	Hensley Meulens	.20
339	*Benji Gil*	.50
340	Don Mattingly	2.50
341	Alvin Davis	.20
342	Alan Mills	.20
343	Kelly Downs	.20
344	Leo Gomez	.20
345	*Tarrik Brock*	.20
346	Ryan Turner	.50
347	John Smoltz	.50
348	Bill Sampen	.20
349	Paul Byrd	.20
350	Mike Bordick	.20
351	Jose Lind	.20
352	David Wells	.25
353	Barry Larkin	.40
354	Bruce Ruffin	.20
355	Luis Rivera	.20
356	Sid Bream	.20
357	Julian Vasquez	.20
358	*Jason Bere*	.50
359	Ben McDonald	.25
360	Scott Stahoviak	.20
361	Kirt Manwaring	.20
362	Jeff Johnson	.20
363	Rob Deer	.20
364	Tony Pena	.20
365	Melido Perez	.20
366	Clay Parker	.20
367	Dale Sveum	.20
368	Mike Scioscia	.20
369	Roger Salkeld	.25
370	Mike Stanley	.20
371	Jack McDowell	.25
372	Tim Wallach	.20
373	Billy Ripken	.20
374	Mike Christopher	.20
375	Paul Molitor	1.00
376	Dave Stieb	.20
377	Pedro Guerrero	.20
378	Russ Swan	.20
379	Bob Ojeda	.20
380	Donn Pall	.20
381	Eddie Zosky	.30
382	Darnell Coles	.20
383	Tom Smith	.20
384	Mark McGwire	8.00
385	Gary Carter	.25
386	Rich Amaral	.20
387	Alan Embree	.20
388	Jonathan Hurst	.20
389	*Bobby Jones*	1.00
390	Rico Rossy	.20
391	Dan Smith	.25
392	Terry Steinbach	.20
393	Jon Farrell	.20
394	Dave Anderson	.20
395	Benito Santiago	.30
396	Mark Wohlers	.20
397	Mo Vaughn	1.00
398	Randy Kramer	.20
399	*John Jaha*	1.00
400	Cal Ripken, Jr.	7.50
401	Ryan Bowen	.40
402	Tim McIntosh	.20
403	Bernard Gilkey	.30
404	Junior Felix	.20
405	Cris Colon	.20
406	Marc Newfield	.50
407	Bernie Williams	1.50
408	Jay Howell	.20
409	Zane Smith	.20
410	Jeff Shaw	.20
411	Kerry Woodson	.20
412	Wes Chamberlain	.20
413	Dave Mlicki	.20
414	Benny Distefano	.20
415	Kevin Rogers	.20
416	Tim Naehring	.20
417	Clemente Nunez	.30
418	Luis Sojo	.20
419	Kevin Ritz	.20
420	Omar Oliveras	.20
421	Manuel Lee	.20
422	Julio Valera	.20
423	Omar Vizquel	.30
424	Darren Burton	.20
425	Mel Hall	.20
426	Dennis Powell	.20
427	Lee Stevens	.20
428	Glenn Davis	.20
429	Willie Greene	.30
430	Kevin Wickander	.20
431	Dennis Eckersley	.30
432	Joe Orsulak	.20
433	Eddie Murray	.75
434	*Matt Stairs*	1.00
435	Wally Joyner	.30
436	Rondell White	2.00
437	Rob Mauer	.20
438	Joe Redfield	.20
439	Mark Lewis	.20
440	Darren Daulton	.20
441	Mike Henneman	.20
442	John Cangelosi	.20
443	*Vince Moore*	.25
444	John Wehner	.20
445	Kent Hrbek	.30
446	Mark McLemore	.20
447	Bill Wegman	.20
448	Robby Thompson	.20
449	Mark Anthony	.20
450	Archi Cianfrocco	.20
451	Johnny Ruffin	.20
452	Javier Lopez	4.00
453	Greg Gohr	.20
454	Tim Scott	.20
455	Stan Belinda	.20
456	Darrin Jackson	.20
457	Chris Gardner	.20
458	Esteban Beltre	.20
459	Phil Plantier	.20
460	Jim Thome	8.00
461	*Mike Piazza*	60.00
462	Matt Sinatro	.20
463	Scott Servais	.30
464	*Brian Jordan*	4.00
465	Doug Drabek	.20
466	Carl Willis	.20
467	Bret Barbarie	.20
468	Hal Morris	.25
469	Steve Sax	.20
470	Jerry Willard	.20
471	Dan Wilson	.25
472	Chris Hoiles	.20
473	Rheal Cormier	.20
474	John Morris	.20
475	Jeff Reardon	.20
476	Mark Leiter	.20
477	Tom Gordon	.20
478	*Kent Bottenfield*	1.50
479	Gene Larkin	.20
480	Dwight Gooden	.40
481	B.J. Surhoff	.25
482	Andy Stankiewicz	.20
483	Tino Martinez	.50
484	Craig Biggio	.50
485	Denny Neagle	.25
486	Rusty Meacham	.20
487	Kal Daniels	.20
488	Dave Henderson	.20
489	Tim Costo	.20
490	Doug Davis	.20
491	Frank Viola	.20
492	Cory Snyder	.20
493	Chris Martin	.20
494	Dion James	.20
495	Randy Tomlin	.20
496	Greg Vaughn	.25
497	Dennis Cook	.20
498	Rosario Rodriguez	.20
499	Dave Staton	.20
500	George Brett	3.00
501	Brian Barnes	.20
502	Butch Henry	.20
503	Harold Reynolds	.25
504	*David Nied*	.25
505	Lee Smith	.30
506	Steve Chitren	.20
507	Ken Hill	.20
508	Robbie Beckett	.20
509	Troy Afenir	.20
510	Kelly Gruber	.20
511	Bret Boone	.30
512	Jeff Branson	.25
513	Mike Jackson	.20
514	Pete Harnisch	.20
515	Chad Kreuter	.20
516	Joe Vitko	.20
517	Orel Hershiser	.25
518	*John Doherty*	.30
519	Jay Bell	.30
520	Mark Langston	.25
521	Dann Howitt	.20
522	Bobby Reed	.20
523	Roberto Munoz	.20
524	Todd Ritchie	.20
525	Bip Roberts	.20
526	*Pat Listach*	.40
527	*Scott Brosius*	2.50
528	*John Roper*	.25
529	*Phil Hiatt*	.40
530	Denny Walling	.20
531	Carlos Baerga	.25
532	*Manny Ramirez*	50.00
533	Pat Clements	.20
534	Ron Gant	.30
535	Pat Kelly	.20
536	Billy Spiers	.20
537	Darren Reed	.30
538	Ken Caminiti	.40
539	*Butch Huskey*	1.00
540	Matt Nokes	.20
541	John Kruk	.20
542	John Jaha (Foil, SP)	1.00
543	*Justin Thompson*	1.00
544	Steve Hosey	.35
545	Joe Kmak	.20
546	John Franco	.20
547	Devon White	.30
548	Elston Hansen (Foil, SP)	.25
549	Ryan Klesko	3.00
550	Danny Tartabull	.20
551	Frank Thomas (Foil, SP)	4.00
552	Kevin Tapani	.20
553a	Willie Banks	.20
553b	Pat Clements	.20
554	*B.J. Wallace* (Foil, SP)	.50
555	*Orlando Miller*	.35

556 *Mark Smith* .25
557 Tim Wallach (Foil) .30
558 Bill Gullickson .20
559 Derek Bell (Foil) .50
560 Joe Randa (Foil) .50
561 Frank Seminara .20
562 Mark Gardner .20
563 Rick Greene (Foil) .40
564 Gary Gaetti .25
565 Ozzie Guillen .20
566 Charles Nagy (Foil) .40
567 Mike Milchin .20
568 Ben Shelton (Foil) .40
569 Chris Roberts (Foil) .50
570 Ellis Burks .25
571 Scott Scudder .20
572 Jim Abbott (Foil) .40
573 Joe Carter .30
574 Steve Finley .20
575 Jim Olander (Foil) .25
576 Carlos Garcia .20
577 Greg Olson .20
578 Greg Swindell (Foil) .25
579 Matt Williams (Foil) .75
580 Mark Grace .40
581 Howard House (Foil) .20
582 Luis Polonia .20
583 Erik Hanson .20
584 Salomon Torres (Foil) .25
585 Carlton Fisk .40
586 Bret Saberhagen .25
587 *Chad McDonnell* (Foil) .30
588 Jimmy Key .25
589 Mike MacFarlane .20
590 Barry Bonds (Foil) 3.00
591 Jamie McAndrew .40
592 Shane Mack .20
593 Kerwin Moore .20
594 Joe Oliver .20
595 Chris Sabo .20
596 *Alex Gonzalez* 1.00
597 Brett Butler .30
598 Mark Hutton .20
599 Andy Benes (Foil) .50
600 Jose Canseco 1.50
601 Darryl Kile .50
602 Matt Stairs (Foil, SP) .30
603 Rob Butler (Foil) .25
604 Willie McGee .25
605 Jack McDowell .25
606 Tom Candiotti .20
607 Ed Martel .20
608 Matt Mieske (Foil) .50
609 Darrin Fletcher .20
610 Rafael Palmeiro .60
611 Bill Swift (Foil) .30
612 Mike Mussina 2.50
613 Vince Coleman .20
614 Scott Cepicky (Foil) .30
615 Mike Greenwell .20
616 Kevin McGehee .20
617 Jeffrey Hammonds (Foil) 2.00
618 Scott Taylor .30
619 Dave Otto .20
620 Mark McGwire (Foil) 8.00
621 Kevin Tatar .20
622 Steve Farr .20
623 Ryan Klesko (Foil) 1.50
625 Andre Dawson .50
626 Tino Martinez (Foil, SP) 1.00
627 *Chad Curtis* .75
628 Mickey Morandini .20
629 Gregg Olson (Foil, SP) .50
630 Lou Whitaker .25
631 Arthur Rhodes .25
632 Brandon Wilson .20
633 *Lance Jennings* .30
634 *Allen Watson* .35
635 Len Dykstra .25
636 Joe Girardi .20
637 Kiki Hernandez (Foil, SP) .30
638 *Mike Hampton* 8.00
639 Al Osuna .20
640 Kevin Appier .25
641 Rick Helling (Foil, SP) .30
642 Jody Reed .20
643 Ray Lankford .35
644 John Olerud .50
645 Paul Molitor (Foil, SP) 1.50
646 Pat Borders .20
647 Mike Morgan .20
648 Larry Walker .75
649 Pete Castellano (Foil, SP) .30
650 Fred McGriff .50
651 Walt Weiss .20
652 *Calvin Murray* (Foil, SP) .50
653 Dave Nilsson .20
654 Greg Pirkl .20
655 Robin Ventura (Foil, SP) .50
656 Mark Portugal .20
657 Roger McDowell .20
658 Rick Hirtensteiner (Foil, SP) .30
659 Glenallen Hill .20
660 Greg Gagne .20
661 Charles Johnson (Foil, SP) 2.00
662 Brian Hunter .40
663 Mark Lemke .20
664 Tim Belcher (Foil, SP) .40
665 Rich DeLucia .20
666 Bob Walk .20
667 Joe Carter (Foil, SP) .50
668 Jose Guzman .20
669 Otis Nixon .20
670 Phil Nevin (Foil) .40
671 Eric Davis .30
672 *Damion Easley* 1.00
673 Will Clark (Foil) .75
674 Mark Kiefer .20
675 Ozzie Smith 1.25
676 Manny Ramirez (Foil) 8.00
677 Gregg Olson .20
678 *Cliff Floyd* 3.00
679 Duane Singleton .25
680 Jose Rijo .20
681 Willie Randolph .20
682 *Michael Tucker* (Foil) 1.00
683 Darren Lewis .20
684 Dale Murphy .35
685 Mike Pagliarulo .20
686 Paul Miller .20
687 Mike Robertson .20
688 Mike Devereaux .20
689 Pedro Astacio .50
690 Alan Trammell .40
691 Roger Clemens 4.00
692 Bud Black .20
693 Turk Wendell .30
694 Barry Larkin (Foil, SP) 1.50
695 Todd Zeile .20
696 Pat Hentgen .25
697 *Eddie Taubensee* .40
698 Guillermo Vasquez .20
699 Tom Glavine .35
700 Robin Yount 1.00
701 Checklist .20
702 Checklist .20
703 Checklist .20
704 Checklist .20
705 Checklist .20

1993 Bowman

Bowman's 708-card 1993 set once again features a premium UV-coated glossy stock. There are also 48 special insert cards, with gold foil stamping, randomly inserted one per pack or two per jumbo pack. The foil cards, numbered 339-374 and 693-704, feature top prospects and rookie-of-the-year candidates, as do several regular cards in the set. Cards are standard size.

	MT
Complete Set (708):	80.00
Common Player:	.10
Pack (15):	2.50
Wax Box (24):	50.00

1 Glenn Davis .10
2 *Hector Roa* .15
3 *Ken Ryan* .25
4 *Derek Wallace* .20
5 Jorge Fabregas .10
6 Joe Oliver .10
7 Brandon Wilson .15
8 *Mark Thompson* .40
9 Tracy Sanders .10
10 Rich Renteria .10
11 Lou Whitaker .15
12 *Brian Hunter* .75
13 Joe Vitiello .20
14 Eric Karros .25
15 Joe Kmak .10
16 Tavo Alvarez .10
17 *Steve Dunn* .30
18 Tony Fernandez .12
19 Melido Perez .10
20 Mike Lieberthal .20
21 Terry Steinbach .10
22 Stan Belinda .10
23 Jay Buhner .15
24 Allen Watson .10
25 *Daryl Henderson* .25
26 *Ray McDavid* .30
27 Shawn Green 1.50
28 Bud Black .10
29 *Sherman Obando* .25
30 *Mike Hostetler* .10
31 *Nate Hinchey* .20
32 Randy Myers .10
33 *Brian Grebeck* .20
34 John Roper .10
35 Larry Thomas .10
36 Alex Cole .10
37 *Tom Kramer* .15
38 *Matt Whisenant* .25
39 *Chris Gomez* .40
40 Luis Gonzalez .12
41 Kevin Appier .12
42 *Omar Daal* .75
43 Duane Singleton .10
44 Bill Risley .10
45 *Pat Meares* .25
46 Butch Huskey .15
47 Bobby Munoz .10
48 Juan Bell .10
49 *Scott Lydy* .25
50 Dennis Moeller .10
51 Marc Newfield .10
52 *Tripp Cromer* .20
53 Kurt Miller .10
54 Jim Pena .10
55 Juan Guzman .10
56 Matt Williams .45
57 Harold Reynolds .12
58 *Donnie Elliott* .15
59 *Jon Shave* .25
60 *Kevin Roberson* .20
61 *Hilly Hathaway* .15
62 Jose Rijo .10
63 *Kerry Taylor* .20
64 Ryan Hawblitzel .10
65 Glenallen Hill .10
66 *Ramon D. Martinez* .20
67 Travis Fryman .15
68 Tom Nevers .10
69 Phil Hiatt .12
70 Tim Wallach .10
71 B.J. Surhoff .12
72 Rondell White .65
73 *Denny Hocking* .20
74 *Mike Oquist* .25
75 Paul O'Neill .20
76 Willie Banks .10
77 Bob Welch .10
78 *Jose Sandoval* .20
79 Bill Haselman .10
80 Rheal Cormier .10
81 Dean Palmer .15
82 *Pat Gomez* .25
83 Steve Karsay .15
84 *Carl Hanselman* .20
85 *T.R. Lewis* .25
86 Chipper Jones 4.00
87 Scott Hatteberg .20
88 Greg Hibbard .10
89 *Lance Painter* .20
90 *Chad Mottola* .40
91 Jason Bere .25
92 Dante Bichette .35
93 Sandy Alomar .15
94 Carl Everett .15
95 *Danny Bautista* .25
96 Steve Finley .10
97 David Cone .20
98 Todd Hollandsworth .50
99 Matt Mieske .10
100 Larry Walker .75
101 Shane Mack .10
102 *Aaron Ledesma* .20
103 *Andy Pettitte* 4.00
104 Kevin Stocker .10
105 Mike Mobler .10
106 Tony Menedez .10
107 Derek Lowe .10
108 Basil Shabazz .10
109 Dan Smith .10
110 *Scott Sanders* .25
111 Todd Stottlemyre .10
112 *Benji Sikonton* .25
113 Rick Sutcliffe .10
114 *Lee Heath* .15
115 Jeff Russell .10
116 *Dave Stevens* .20
117 *Mark Holzemer* .20
118 Tim Belcher .10
119 Bobby Thigpen .10
120 *Roger Bailey* .20
121 *Tony Mitchell* .25
122 Junior Felix .10
123 *Rich Robertson* .20
124 *Andy Cook* .20
125 *Brian Bevil* .25
126 Darryl Strawberry .25
127 Cal Eldred .10
128 Cliff Floyd .20
129 Alan Newman .10
130 Howard Johnson .10
131 Jim Abbott .15
132 Chad McConnell .10
133 *Miguel Jimenez* .20
134 *Brett Backlund* .20
135 *John Cummings* .30
136 Brian Barber .10
137 Rafael Palmeiro .20
138 *Tim Worrell* .20
139 *Jose Pett* .20
140 Barry Bonds 1.00
141 Damon Buford .10
142 Jeff Blauser .10
143 Frankie Rodriguez .15
144 Mike Morgan .10
145 Gary DeSarcina .10
146 Calvin Reese .10
147 Johnny Ruffin .10
148 David Nied .10
149 Charles Nagy .12
150 *Mike Myers* .20
151 *Kenny Carlyle* .20
152 Eric Anthony .10
153 Jose Lind .10
154 Pedro Martinez 3.00
155 Mark Kiefer .10
156 *Tim Laker* .20
157 Pat Mahomes .10
158 Bobby Bonilla .15
159 Domingo Jean .10
160 Darren Daulton .10
161 Mark McGwire 5.00
162 *Jason Kendall* 4.00
163 Desi Relaford .25
164 Ozzie Canseco .10
165 Rick Helling .10
166 *Steve Pegues* .20
167 Paul Molitor .40
168 *Larry Carter* .20
169 Arthur Rhodes .10
170 *Damon Hollins* .40
171 Frank Viola .10
172 *Steve Trachsel* .40

173 *J.T. Snow* 1.50
174 *Keith Gordon* .20
175 Carlton Fisk .15
176 *Jason Bates* .20
177 *Mike Crosby* .20
178 Benny Santiago .10
179 Mike Moore .10
180 Jeff Juden .20
181 Darren Burton .10
182 *Todd Williams* .20
183 John Jaha .10
184 *Mike Lansing* .75
185 *Pedro Grifol* .20
186 Vince Coleman .10
187 Pat Kelly .10
188 *Clemente Alvarez* .20
189 Ron Darling .10
190 Orlando Merced .10
191 Chris Bosio .10
192 *Steve Dixon* .20
193 Doug Dascenzo .10
194 *Ray Holbert* .25
195 Howard Battle .10
196 Willie McGee .12
197 *John O'Donoghue* .20
198 Steve Avery .10
199 Greg Blosser .10
200 Ryne Sandberg .75
201 Joe Grahe .10
202 Dan Wilson .10
203 *Domingo Martinez* .20
204 Andres Galarraga .20
205 *Jamie Taylor* .20
206 *Darrell Whitmore* .25
207 *Ben Blomdahl* .20
208 Doug Drabek .10
209 Keith Miller .10
210 Billy Ashley .10
211 *Mike Farrell* .20
212 John Wetteland .10
213 Randy Tomlin .10
214 Sid Fernandez .10
215 *Quilvio Veras* .25
216 Dave Hollins .15
217 Mike Neill .10
218 Andy Van Slyke .10
219 Bret Boone .20
220 Tom Pagnozzi .10
221 *Mike Welch* .20
222 Frank Seminara .10
223 Ron Villone .10
224 *D.J. Thielen* .25
225 Cal Ripken, Jr. 4.00
226 *Pedro Borbon* .20
227 Carlos Quintana .10
228 *Tommy Shields* .20
229 Tim Salmon .60
230 John Smiley .10
231 Ellis Burks .15
232 Pedro Castellano .10
233 Paul Byrd .10
234 Bryan Harvey .10
235 Scott Livingstone .10
236 *James Mouton* .35
237 Joe Randa .15
238 Pedro Astacio .15
239 Darryl Hamilton .10
240 *Joey Eischen* .40
241 *Edgar Herrera* .20
242 Dwight Gooden .15
243 Sam Militello .10
244 *Ron Blazier* .20
245 Ruben Sierra .10
246 Al Martin .10
247 Mike Felder .10
248 Bob Tewksbury .10
249 Craig Lefferts .10
250 Luis Lopez .10
251 Devon White .12
252 Will Clark .35
253 Mark Smith .15
254 Terry Pendleton .10
255 Aaron Sele .25
256 *Jose Viera* .15
257 Damion Easley .15
258 *Rod Lofton* .20
259 *Chris Snopek* .40
260 *Quinton McCracken* .50
261 *Mike Matthews* .25
262 *Hector Carrasco* .40
263 Rick Greene .10
264 *Chris Bolt* .25
265 George Brett 1.00
266 *Rick Gorecki* .25
267 *Francisco Gamez* .15
268 Marquis Grissom .15
269 Kevin Tapani .10
270 Ryan Thompson .15
271 Gerald Williams .12
272 *Paul Fletcher* .20
273 Lance Blankenship .10
274 *Marty Heff* .20
275 Shawn Estes .50
276 *Rene Arocha* .25
277 *Scott Evre* .25
278 Phil Plantier .10
279 *Paul Spoljaric* .30
280 Chris Gahbs .10
281 Harold Baines .12
282 *Jose Oliva* .15
283 Matt Whiteside .15
284 *Brant Brown* .75
285 Russ Springer .10
286 Chris Sabo .10
287 Ozzie Guillen .10
288 *Marcus Moore* .20
289 Chad Ogea .25
290 Walt Weiss .10
291 Brian Edmondson .10
292 Jimmy Gonzalez .10
293 *Danny Miceli* .30
294 Jose Offerman .10
295 Greg Vaughn .15
296 Frank Bolick .10
297 *Mike Maksudian* .25
298 John Franco .10
299 Danny Tartabull .10
300 Len Dykstra .10
301 Bobby Witt .10
302 *Trey Beamon* .50
303 Tino Martinez .25
304 Aaron Holbert .10
305 Juan Gonzalez 1.00
306 *Billy Hall* .25
307 Duane Ward .10
308 Rod Beck .10
309 *Jose Mercedes* .25
310 Otis Nixon .10
311 *Gettys Glaze* .25
312 Candy Maldonado .10
313 Chad Curtis .15
314 Tim Costo .10
315 Mike Robertson .10
316 Nigel Wilson .10
317 *Greg McMichael* .25
318 *Scott Pose* .20
319 Ivan Cruz .10
320 Greg Swindell .10
321 Kevin McReynolds .10
322 Tom Candiotti .10
323 *Bob Wishnevski* .20
324 Ken Hill .10
325 Kirby Puckett 1.00
326 *Tim Bogar* .20
327 Mariano Rivera .45
328 Mitch Williams .10
329 Craig Paquette .10
330 Jay Bell .15
331 *Jose Martinez* .35
332 Rob Deer .10
333 Brook Fordyce .10
334 Matt Nokes .10
335 Derek Lee .15
336 *Paul Ellis* .20
337 *Desi Wilson* .15
338 Roberto Alomar .75
339 Jim Tatum (Foil) .20
340 J.T. Snow (Foil) .30
341 Tim Salmon (Foil) .75
342 *Russ Davis* (Foil) 1.00
343 Javier Lopez (Foil) .60
344 *Troy O'Leary* (Foil) 1.00
345 *Marty Cordova* (Foil) .50
346 *Bubba Smith* (Foil) .25
347 Chipper Jones (Foil) 4.00
348 Jessie Hollins (Foil) .20
349 Willie Greene (Foil) .25
350 Mark Thompson (Foil) .30
351 Nigel Wilson (Foil) .25
352 Todd Jones (Foil) .20
353 Raul Mondesi (Foil) .50
354 Cliff Floyd (Foil) .40
355 Bobby Jones (Foil) .30
356 Kevin Stocker (Foil) .20
357 Midre Cummings (Foil) .35
358 Allen Watson (Foil) .20
359 Ray McDavid (Foil) .30
360 Steve Hosey (Foil) .25
361 Brad Pennington (Foil) .25
362 Frankie Rodriguez (Foil) .25
363 Troy Percival (Foil) .25
364 Jason Bere (Foil) .25
365 Manny Ramirez (Foil) 3.00
366 Justin Thompson (Foil) .25
367 Joe Vitello (Foil) .25
368 Tyrone Hill (Foil) .20
369 David McCarty (Foil) .15
370 Brien Taylor (Foil) .20
371 Todd Van Poppel (Foil) .15
372 Marc Newfield (Foil) .25
373 *Terrell Lowery* (Foil) .40
374 Alex Gonzalez (Foil) .40
375 Ken Griffey, Jr. 4.00
376 Donovan Osborne .10
377 *Ritchie Moody* .15
378 Shane Andrews .30
379 Carlos Delgado 1.50
380 Bill Swift .10
381 Leo Gomez .10
382 Ron Gant .15
383 Scott Fletcher .10
384 *Matt Walbeck* .15
385 Chuck Finley .10
386 Kevin Mitchell .10
387 Wilson Alvarez .10
388 *John Burke* .25
389 Alan Embree .10
390 Trevor Hoffman .20
391 Alan Trammell .15
392 Todd Jones .10
393 Felix Jose .10
394 Orel Hershiser .15
395 Pat Listach .10
396 Gabe White .10
397 *Dan Serafini* .30
398 Todd Hundley .15
399 Wade Boggs .50
400 Tyler Green .10
401 Mike Bordick .10
402 Scott Bullett .10
403 *Lagrande Russell* .20
404 Ray Lankford .15
405 Nolan Ryan 3.00
406 Robbie Beckett .10
407 *Brent Bowers* .20
408 *Adell Davenport* .20
409 Brady Anderson .25
410 Tom Glavine .15
411 *Doug Hecker* .25
412 Jose Guzman .10
413 Luis Polonia .10
414 Brian Williams .10
415 Bo Jackson .20
416 Eric Young .15
417 Kenny Lofton .50
418 Orestes Destrade .10
419 Tony Phillips .10
420 Jeff Bagwell 1.00
421 Hark Gardner .10
422 Brett Butler .15
423 *Graeme Lloyd* .15
424 Delino DeShields .10
425 Scott Erickson .10
426 Jeff Kent .10
427 Jimmy Key .10
428 Mickey Morandini .10
429 *Marcos Arkas* .25
430 Don Slaught .10
431 Randy Johnson .45
432 Omar Olivares .10
433 Charlie Leibrandt .10
434 Kurt Stillwell .10
435 *Scott Brow* .15
436 Robby Thompson .10
437 Ben McDonald .15
438 Deion Sanders .50
439 Tony Pena .10
440 Mark Grace .35
441 Eduardo Perez .10
442 *Tim Pugh* .30
443 Scott Ruffcorn .10
444 *Jay Gainer* .20
445 Albert Belle .75
446 Bret Barberie .10
447 Justin Mashore .10
448 Pete Harnisch .10
449 Greg Gagne .10
450 Eric Davis .15
451 Dave Mlicki .10
452 Moises Alou .15
453 Rick Aguilera .10
454 Eddie Murray .50
455 Bob Wickman .10
456 Wes Chamberlain .10
457 Brent Gates .10
458 Paul Weber .10
459 Mike Hampton .10
460 Ozzie Smith .50
461 Tom Henke .10
462 Ricky Gutuerrez .10
463 Jack Morris .12
464 *Joel Chimelis* .20
465 Gregg Olson .10
466 Javier Lopez .40
467 Scott Cooper .10
468 Willie Wilson .12
469 Mark Langston .10
470 Barry Larkin .20
471 Rod Bolton .10
472 Freddie Benavides .10
473 *Ken Ramos* .20
474 Chuck Carr .10
475 Cecil Fielder .25
476 Eddie Taubensee .10
477 *Chris Eddy* .25
478 Greg Hansell .10
479 Kevin Reimer .10
480 Denny Martinez .12
481 Chuck Knoblauch .25
482 Mike Draper .10
483 Spike Owen .10
484 Terry Mulholland .10
485 Dennis Eckersley .12
486 Blas Minor .10
487 Dave Fleming .10
488 Dan Cholonsky .10
489 Ivan Rodriguez .75
490 Gary Sheffield .25
491 Ed Sprague .10
492 Steve Hosey .10
493 *Jimmy Haynes* .50
494 John Smoltz .25
495 Andre Dawson .25
496 Rey Sanchez .10
497 *Ty Van Burkleo* .20
498 *Bobby Ayala* .40
499 Tim Raines .15
500 Charlie Hayes .10
501 Paul Sorrento .10
502 *Richie Lewis* .30
503 *Jason Pfaff* .15
504 Ken Caminiti .25
505 Mike Macfarlane .10
506 Jody Reed .10
507 *Bobby Hughes* .75
508 Wil Cordero .10
509 *George Tsanis* .20
510 Bret Saberhagen .12
511 *Derek Jeter* 35.00
512 Gene Schall .30
513 Curtis Shaw .10
514 Steve Cooke .10
515 Edgar Martinez .15
516 Mike Milchin .10
517 Billy Ripken .10
518 Andy Benes .12
519 *Juan de la Rosa* .20
520 John Burkett .10
521 Alex Ochoa .20
522 *Tony Tarasco* .25
523 Luis Ortiz .10
524 Rick Williams .10
525 *Chris Turner* .20
526 Rob Dibble .10
527 Jack McDowell .12
528 Daryl Boston .10
529 *Bill Wertz* .20
530 Charlie Hough .10
531 Sean Bergman .15
532 Doug Jones .10
533 Jeff Montgomery .10
534 *Roger Cedeno* 2.00
535 Robin Yount .50
536 Mo Vaughn .75
537 Brian Harper .10
538 Juan Castillo .10
539 Steve Farr .10
540 John Kruk .10
541 Troy Neel .15
542 *Danny Clyburn* .30
543 *Jim Converse* .25
544 Gregg Jefferies .15
545 Jose Canseco .40
546 *Julio Bruno* .25
547 Rob Butler .10

548	Royce Clayton	.10
549	Chris Hoiles	.10
550	Greg Maddux	1.50
551	*Joe Ciccarella*	.25
552	Ozzie Timmons	.10
553	Chili Davis	.12
554	Brian Koelling	.10
555	Frank Thomas	2.00
556	Vinny Castilla	.50
557	Reggie Jefferson	.10
558	Rob Natal	.10
559	Mike Henneman	.10
560	Craig Biggio	.20
561	*Billy Brewer*	.20
562	Dan Melendez	.10
563	*Kenny Felder*	.40
564	*Miguel Batista*	.25
565	Dave Winfield	.30
566	Al Shirley	.10
567	Robert Eenhoorn	.10
568	Mike Williams	.10
569	*Tanyon Sturtze*	.25
570	Tim Wakefield	.10
571	Greg Pirkl	.10
572	*Sean Lowe*	.40
573	*Terry Burows*	.15
574	*Kevin Higgins*	.25
575	Joe Carter	.20
576	Kevin Rogers	.10
577	Manny Alexander	.10
578	Dave Justice	.35
579	*Brian Conroy*	.15
580	*Jessie Hollins*	.20
581	*Ron Watson*	.20
582	Bip Roberts	.10
583	*Tom Urbani*	.15
584	*Jason Hutchins*	.25
585	Carlos Baerga	.20
586	Jeff Mutis	.10
587	Justin Thompson	.30
588	Orlando Miller	.15
589	Brian McRae	.15
590	Ramon Martinez	.12
591	Dave Nilsson	.10
592	*Jose Vidro*	6.00
593	Rich Becker	.10
594	*Preston Wilson*	3.00
595	Don Mattingly	1.25
596	Tony Longmire	.10
597	Kevin Seitzer	.10
598	*Midre Cummings*	.45
599	Omar Vizquel	.15
600	Lee Smith	.12
601	*David Hulse*	.15
602	*Darrell Sherman*	.20
603	Alex Gonzalez	.25
604	Geronimo Pena	.10
605	Mike Devereaux	.10
606	*Sterling Hitchcock*	.50
607	Mike Greenwell	.10
608	Steve Buechele	.10
609	Troy Percival	.10
610	Bobby Kelly	.10
611	*James Baldwin*	3.00
612	Jerald Clark	.10
613	*Albie Lopez*	.25
614	Dave Magadan	.10
615	Mickey Tettleton	.10
616	*Sean Runyan*	.25
617	Bob Hamelin	.10
618	Raul Mondesi	.75
619	Tyrone Hill	.20
620	Darrin Fletcher	.10
621	Mike Trombley	.10
622	Jeromy Burnitz	.15
623	Bernie Williams	.60
624	*Mike Farmer*	.20
625	Rickey Henderson	.45
626	Carlos Garcia	.10
627	*Jeff Darwin*	.25
628	Todd Zeile	.15
629	Benji Gil	.10
630	Tony Gwynn	2.00
631	*Aaron Small*	.25
632	*Joe Rosselli*	.25
633	Mike Mussina	.50
634	Ryan Klesko	.50
635	Roger Clemens	2.00
636	Sammy Sosa	3.00
637	*Orlando Palmeiro*	.20
638	Willie Greene	.10
639	George Bell	.10
640	*Garvin Alston*	.30
641	*Pete Janicki*	.25
642	*Chris Sheff*	.25
643	*Felipe Lira*	.40
644	Roberto Petagine	.10
645	Wally Joyner	.12
646	Mike Piazza	3.00
647	Jaime Navarro	.10
648	*Jeff Hartsock*	.25
649	David McCarty	.15
650	Bobby Jones	.20
651	Mark Hutton	.10
652	Kyle Abbott	.10
653	*Steve Cox*	.50
654	Jeff King	.10
655	Norm Charlton	.10
656	*Mike Gulan*	.25
657	Julio Franco	.10
658	*Cameron Cairncross*	.25
659	John Olerud	.35
660	Salomon Torres	.10
661	Brad Pennington	.10
662	Melvin Nieves	.10
663	Ivan Calderon	.10
664	Turk Wendell	.10
665	Chris Pritchett	.10
666	Reggie Sanders	.15
667	Robin Ventura	.25
668	Joe Girardi	.10
669	Manny Ramirez	3.00
670	Jeff Conine	.15
671	Greg Gohr	.10
672	Andujar Cedeno	.10
673	*Les Norman*	.15
674	*Mike James*	.20
675	*Marshall Boze*	.30
676	B.J. Wallace	.15
677	Kent Hrbek	.12
678	Jack Voight	.10
679	Brien Taylor	.15
680	Curt Schilling	.15
681	Todd Van Poppel	.12
682	Kevin Young	.15
683	Tommy Adams	.10
684	Bernard Gilkey	.12
685	Kevin Brown	.10
686	Fred McGriff	.30
687	Pat Borders	.10
688	Kirt Manwaring	.10
689	Sid Bream	.10
690	John Valentin	.15
691	*Steve Olsen*	.20
692	*Roberto Mejia*	.25
693	Carlos Delgado (Foil)	1.00
694	*Steve Gibralter* (Foil)	.40
695	Gary Mota (Foil)	.25
696	*Jose Malave* (Foil)	.75
697	*Larry Sutton* (Foil)	.75
698	*Dan Frye* (Foil)	.25
699	*Tim Clark* (Foil)	.30
700	*Brian Rupp* (Foil)	.25
701	Felipe Alou, Moises Alou (Foil)	.25
702	Bobby Bonds, Barry Bonds (Foil)	.75
703	Ken Griffey Sr., Ken Griffey Jr. (Foil)	1.50
704	Hal McRae, Brian McRae (Foil)	.25
705	Checklist 1	.10
706	Checklist 2	.10
707	Checklist 3	.10
708	Checklist 4	.10

1994 Bowman Previews

Bowman Preview cards were randomly inserted into Stadium Club 1994 Baseball Series II at a rate of one every 24 packs. This 10-card set featured several proven major league stars, as well as minor league players. Card number 10, James Mouton, is designed as a special MVP foil card.

		MT
Complete Set (10):		35.00
Common Player:		2.00
1	Frank Thomas	10.00
2	Mike Piazza	7.50
3	Albert Belle	5.00
4	Javier Lopez	4.00
5	Cliff Floyd	2.50
6	Alex Gonzalez	2.00
7	Ricky Bottalico	2.00
8	Tony Clark	4.00
9	Mac Suzuki	2.00
10	James Mouton (Foil)	2.50

1994 Bowman

Bowman baseball for 1994 was a 682-card set issued all in one series, including a 52-card foil subset. There were 11 regular cards plus one foil card in each pack, with a suggested retail price of $2. The cards have a full-bleed design, with gold-foil stamping on every card. As in the past, the set includes numerous rookies and prospects, along with the game's biggest stars. The 52-card foil subset features 28 Top Prospects, with the player's team logo in the background; 17 Minor League MVPs, with a stadium in the background; and seven Diamonds in the Rough, with, you guessed it, a diamond as a backdrop.

		MT
Complete Set (682):		125.00
Common Player:		.10
Pack (12):		3.00
Wax Box (24):		65.00
1	Joe Carter	.25
2	Marcus Moore	.10
3	*Doug Creek*	.15
4	Pedro Martinez	1.50
5	Ken Griffey, Jr.	4.00
6	Greg Swindell	.10
7	J.J. Johnson	.10
8	*Homer Bush*	1.50
9	*Arquimedez Pozo*	.30
10	Bryan Harvey	.10
11	J.T. Snow	.20
12	*Alan Benes*	2.00
13	Chad Kreuter	.10
14	Eric Karros	.15
15	Frank Thomas	1.50
16	Bret Saberhagen	.15
17	Terrell Lowery	.10
18	Rod Bolton	.10
19	Harold Baines	.15
20	Matt Walbeck	.10
21	Tom Glavine	.15
22	Todd Jones	.10
23	Alberto Castillo	.10
24	Ruben Sierra	.10
25	Don Mattingly	1.50
26	Mike Morgan	.10
27	*Jim Musselwhite*	.20
28	*Matt Brunson*	.25
29	*Adam Meinershagen*	.20
30	Joe Girardi	.10
31	Shane Halter	.10
32	*Jose Paniagua*	.20
33	Paul Perkins	.10
34	*John Hudek*	.40
35	Frank Viola	.10
36	*David Lamb*	.15
37	Marshall Boze	.10
38	*Jorge Posada*	4.00
39	*Brian Anderson*	1.00
40	Mark Whiten	.10
41	Sean Bergman	.10
42	*Jose Parra*	.20
43	Mike Robertson	.10
44	*Pete Walker*	.15
45	Juan Gonzalez	1.00
46	*Cleveland Ladell*	.20
47	Mark Smith	.10
48	*Kevin Jarvis*	.20
49	*Amaury Telemaco*	.25
50	Andy Van Slyke	.10
51	*Rikkert Faneyte*	.20
52	Curtis Shaw	.10
53	*Matt Drews*	.40
54	Wilson Alvarez	.10
55	Manny Ramirez	2.00
56	Bobby Munoz	.10
57	Ed Sprague	.10
58	*Jamey Wright*	1.50
59	Jeff Montgomery	.10
60	Kirk Rueter	.10
61	Edgar Martinez	.15
62	Luis Gonzalez	.15
63	*Tim Vanegmond*	.15
64	Bip Roberts	.10
65	John Jaha	.10
66	Chuck Carr	.10
67	Chuck Finley	.10
68	Aaron Holbert	.10
69	Cecil Fielder	.25
70	*Tom Engle*	.15
71	Ron Karkovice	.10
72	Joe Orsulak	.10
73	*Duff Brumley*	.25
74	*Craig Clayton*	.15
75	Cal Ripken, Jr.	3.00
76	*Brad Fullmer*	4.00
77	Tony Tarasco	.10
78	*Terry Farrar*	.15
79	Matt Williams	.25
80	Rickey Henderson	.40
81	Terry Mulholland	.10
82	Sammy Sosa	3.00
83	Paul Sorrento	.10
84	Pete Incaviglia	.10
85	*Darren Hall*	.40
86	Scott Klingenbeck	.10
87	*Dario Perez*	.15
88	Ugueth Urbina	.15
89	*Dave Vanhof*	.15
90	Domingo Jean	.10
91	Otis Nixon	.10
92	Andres Berumen	.10
93	Jose Valentin	.10
94	*Edgar Renteria*	2.50
95	Chris Turner	.10
96	Ray Lankford	.15
97	Danny Bautista	.10
98	*Chan Ho Park*	4.00
99	*Glenn DiSarcina*	.15
100	Butch Huskey	.15
101	Ivan Rodriguez	1.50
102	Johnny Ruffin	.10
103	Alex Ochoa	.20
104	*Torii Hunter*	.50
105	Ryan Klesko	.40
106	Jay Bell	.15
107	*Kurt Peltzer*	.15
108	Miguel Jimenez	.10
109	Russ Davis	.15
110	Derek Wallace	.10
111	*Keith Lockhart*	.25
112	Mike Lieberthal	.15
113	Dave Stewart	.10
114	Tom Schmidt	.10
115	Brian McRae	.15
116	Moises Alou	.15
117	Dave Fleming	.10
118	Jeff Bagwell	1.25
119	Luis Ortiz	.10
120	Tony Gwynn	2.00
121	Jaime Navarro	.10
122	Benny Santiago	.10

No.	Player	Price
123	Darrel Whitmore	.10
124	*John Mabry*	.25
125	Mickey Tettleton	.10
126	Tom Candiotti	.10
127	Tim Raines	.15
128	Bobby Bonilla	.15
129	John Dettmer	.10
130	Hector Carrasco	.10
131	Chris Hoiles	.10
132	Rick Aguilera	.10
133	Dave Justice	.40
134	*Esteban Loaiza*	.40
135	Barry Bonds	1.25
136	Bob Welch	.10
137	Mike Stanley	.10
138	Roberto Hernandez	.10
139	Sandy Alomar	.20
140	Darren Daulton	.10
141	*Angel Martinez*	.25
142	Howard Johnson	.10
143	Bob Hamelin	.10
144	*J.J. Thobe*	.20
145	Roger Salkeld	.10
146	Orlando Miller	.10
147	Dmitri Young	.10
148	*Tim Hyers*	.25
149	*Mark Loretta*	.25
150	Chris Hammond	.10
151	*Joel Moore*	.20
152	Todd Zeile	.15
153	Wil Cordero	.10
154	Chris Smith	.10
155	James Baldwin	.15
156	*Edgardo Alfonzo*	12.00
157	*Kym Ashworth*	.50
158	*Paul Bako*	.20
159	*Rick Krivda*	.20
160	Pat Mahomes	.10
161	Damon Hollins	.15
162	*Felix Martinez*	.15
163	*Jason Myers*	.20
164	*Izzy Molina*	.25
165	Brien Taylor	.10
166	*Kevin Orie*	1.50
167	*Casey Whitten*	.20
168	Tony Longmire	.10
169	John Olerud	.35
170	Mark Thompson	.10
171	Jorge Fabregas	.10
172	John Wetteland	.10
173	Dan Wilson	.10
174	Doug Drabek	.10
175	Jeffrey McNeely	.10
176	Melvin Nieves	.10
177	*Doug Glanville*	2.50
178	*Javier De La Hoya*	.20
179	Chad Curtis	.10
180	Brian Barber	.10
181	Mike Henneman	.10
182	Jose Offerman	.10
183	*Robert Ellis*	.20
184	John Franco	.10
185	Benji Gil	.10
186	Hal Morris	.10
187	Chris Sabo	.10
188	*Blaise Ilsley*	.15
189	Steve Avery	.15
190	*Rick White*	.25
191	Rod Beck	.10
(192)	Mark McGwire (no card number)	5.00
193	Jim Abbott	.15
194	Randy Myers	.10
195	Kenny Lofton	.75
196	Mariano Duncan	.10
197	*Lee Daniels*	.15
198	Armando Reynoso	.10
199	Joe Randa	.10
200	Cliff Floyd	.30
201	*Tim Harkrider*	.20
202	*Kevin Gallaher*	.15
203	Scott Cooper	.10
204	*Phil Stidham*	.20
205	*Jeff D'Amico*	3.00
206	Matt Whisenant	.10
207	De Shawn Warren	.10
208	Rene Arocha	.10
209	*Tony Clark*	2.50
210	*Jason Jacome*	.50
211	*Scott Christman*	.20
212	Bill Pulsipher	.15
213	Dean Palmer	.15
214	Chad Mottola	.15
215	Manny Alexander	.10
216	Rich Becker	.15
217	*Andre King*	.30
218	Carlos Garcia	.10
219	*Ron Pezzoni*	.15
220	Steve Karsay	.10
221	*Jose Musset*	.20
222	Karl Rhodes	.10
223	*Frank Cimorelli*	.15
224	*Kevin Jordan*	.25
225	Duane Ward	.10
226	John Burke	.10
227	Mike MacFarlane	.10
228	Mike Lansing	.15
229	Chuck Knoblauch	.35
230	Ken Caminiti	.25
231	*Gar Finnvold*	.15
232	*Derrek Lee*	2.00
233	Brady Anderson	.25
234	*Vic Darensbourg*	.15
235	Mark Langston	.10
236	*T.J. Mathews*	.25
237	Lou Whitaker	.15
238	Roger Cedeno	.15
239	Alex Fernandez	.15
240	Ryan Thompson	.10
241	*Kerry Lacy*	.15
242	Reggie Sanders	.15
243	Brad Pennington	.10
244	*Bryan Eversgerd*	.15
245	Greg Maddux	2.00
246	Jason Kendall	.75
247	J.R. Phillips	.15
248	Bobby Witt	.10
249	Paul O'Neill	.25
250	Ryne Sandberg	.75
251	Charles Nagy	.15
252	Kevin Stocker	.10
253	Shawn Green	.65
254	Charlie Hayes	.10
255	Donnie Elliott	.10
256	*Rob Fitzpatrick*	.15
257	Tim Davis	.10
258	James Mouton	.15
259	Mike Greenwell	.10
260	Ray McDavid	.10
261	Mike Kelly	.10
262	*Andy Larkin*	.25
(263)	Marquis Riley (no card number)	.10
264	Bob Tewksbury	.10
265	Brian Edmondson	.10
266	*Eduardo Lantigua*	.15
267	Brandon Wilson	.10
268	Mike Welch	.10
269	Tom Henke	.10
270	Calvin Reese	.10
271	*Greg Zaun*	.25
272	Todd Ritchie	.10
273	Javier Lopez	.30
274	Kevin Young	.10
275	Kirt Manwaring	.10
276	*Bill Taylor*	.15
277	Robert Eenhoorn	.10
278	Jessie Hollins	.10
279	*Julian Tavarez*	.35
280	Gene Schall	.10
281	Paul Molitor	.90
282	*Neifi Perez*	3.00
283	Greg Gagne	.10
284	Marquis Grissom	.15
285	Randy Johnson	.50
286	Pete Harnisch	.10
287	*Joel Bennett*	.25
288	Derek Bell	.15
289	Darryl Hamilton	.10
290	Gary Sheffield	.25
291	Eduardo Perez	.10
292	Basil Shabazz	.10
293	Eric Davis	.15
294	Pedro Astacio	.10
295	Robin Ventura	.25
296	Jeff Kent	.15
297	Rick Helling	.10
298	Joe Oliver	.10
299	Lee Smith	.15
300	Dave Winfield	.25
301	Deion Sanders	.30
302	*Ravelo Manzanillo*	.15
303	Mark Portugal	.10
304	Brent Gates	.10
305	Wade Boggs	.50
306	Rick Wilkins	.10
307	Carlos Baerga	.15
308	Curt Schilling	.15
309	Shannon Stewart	.50
310	Darren Holmes	.10
311	*Robert Toth*	.20
312	Gabe White	.15
313	*Mac Suzuki*	.40
314	*Alvin Morman*	.15
315	Mo Vaughn	.75
316	*Bryce Florie*	.15
317	*Gabby Martinez*	.25
318	Carl Everett	.15
319	Kerwin Moore	.10
320	Tom Pagnozzi	.10
321	Chris Gomez	.15
322	Todd Williams	.10
323	Pat Hentgen	.10
324	*Kirk Presley*	.50
325	Kevin Brown	.10
326	*Jason Isringhausen*	1.50
327	*Rick Forney*	.25
328	*Carlos Pulido*	.20
329	*Terrell Wade*	.20
330	Al Martin	.10
331	*Dan Carlson*	.20
332	*Mark Acre*	.15
333	Sterling Hitchcock	.10
334	*Jon Ratliff*	.25
335	*Alex Ramirez*	1.00
336	*Phil Geisler*	.20
337	*Eddie Zambrano* (Foil)	.25
338	Jim Thome (Foil)	1.00
339	James Mouton (Foil)	.25
340	Cliff Floyd (Foil)	.40
341	Carlos Delgado (Foil)	.60
342	Roberto Petagine (Foil)	.10
343	Tim Clark (Foil)	.10
344	Bubba Smith (Foil)	.15
345	*Randy Curtis* (Foil)	.20
346	*Joe Biasucci* (Foil)	.20
347	*D.J. Boston* (Foil)	.10
348	*Ruben Rivera* (Foil)	4.00
349	*Bryan Link* (Foil)	.20
350	*Mike Bell* (Foil)	.50
351	*Marty Watson* (Foil)	.20
352	Jason Myers (Foil)	.20
353	Chipper Jones (Foil)	2.50
354	Brooks Kieschnick (Foil)	.65
355	Calvin Reese (Foil)	.10
356	John Burke (Foil)	.10
357	Kurt Miller (Foil)	.10
358	Orlando Miller (Foil)	.10
359	Todd Hollandsworth (Foil)	.75
360	Rondell White (Foil)	.40
361	Bill Pulsipher (Foil)	.25
362	Tyler Green (Foil)	.15
363	Midre Cummings (Foil)	.25
364	Brian Barber (Foil)	.10
365	Melvin Nieves (Foil)	.10
366	Salomon Torres (Foil)	.10
367	Alex Ochoa (Foil)	.20
368	Frank Rodriguez (Foil)	.15
369	Brian Anderson (Foil)	.25
370	James Baldwin (Foil)	.35
371	Manny Ramirez (Foil)	2.00
372	Justin Thompson (Foil)	.15
373	Johnny Damon (Foil)	.85
374	Jeff D'Amico (Foil)	.50
375	Rich Becker (Foil)	.15
376	Derek Jeter (Foil)	4.00
377	Steve Karsay (Foil)	.20
378	Mac Suzuki (Foil)	.30
379	Benji Gil (Foil)	.10
380	Alex Gonzalez (Foil)	.25
381	Jason Bere (Foil)	.25
382	Brett Butler (Foil)	.25
383	Jeff Conine (Foil)	.15
384	Darren Daulton (Foil)	.15
385	Jeff Kent (Foil)	.15
386	Don Mattingly (Foil)	1.00
387	Mike Piazza (Foil)	2.00
388	Ryne Sandberg (Foil)	.75
389	Rich Amaral	.10
390	Craig Biggio	.35
391	*Jeff Suppan*	1.50
392	Andy Benes	.10
393	Cal Eldred	.10
394	Jeff Conine	.15
395	Tim Salmon	.35
396	*Ray Suplee*	.20
397	Tony Phillips	.10
398	Ramon Martinez	.15
399	Julio Franco	.10
400	Dwight Gooden	.15
401	*Kevin Lomon*	.15
402	Jose Rijo	.10
403	Mike Devereaux	.10
404	*Mike Zolecki*	.20
405	Fred McGriff	.25
406	Danny Clyburn	.15
407	Robby Thompson	.10
408	Terry Steinbach	.10
409	Luis Polonia	.10
410	Mark Grace	.35
411	Albert Belle	1.25
412	John Kruk	.10
413	*Scott Spiezio*	1.00
414	Ellis Burks	.15
415	Joe Vitiello	.15
416	Tim Costo	.10
417	Marc Newfield	.10
418	*Oscar Henriquez*	.20
419	*Matt Perisho*	.25
420	Julio Bruno	.10
421	Kenny Felder	.10
422	Tyler Green	.10
423	Jim Edmonds	.35
424	Ozzie Smith	.50
425	Rick Greene	.10
426	Todd Hollandsworth	.25
427	*Eddie Pearson*	.20
428	Quilvio Veras	.10
429	Kenny Rogers	.10
430	Willie Greene	.10
431	Vaughn Eshelman	.20
432	Pat Meares	.10
433	*Jermaine Dye*	10.00
434	Steve Cooke	.10
435	Bill Swift	.10
436	*Fausto Cruz*	.25
437	Mark Hutton	.10
438	*Brooks Kieschnick*	1.50
439	Yorkis Perez	.10
440	Len Dykstra	.10
441	Pat Borders	.10
442	*Doug Walls*	.20
443	Wally Joyner	.15
444	Ken Hill	.10
445	Eric Anthony	.10
446	Mitch Williams	.10
447	*Cory Bailey*	.25
448	Dave Staton	.10
449	Greg Vaughn	.15
450	Dave Magadan	.10
451	Chili Davis	.10
452	*Gerald Santos*	.20
453	Joe Perona	.10
454	Delino DeShields	.10
455	Jack McDowell	.10
456	Todd Hundley	.15
457	Ritchie Moody	.10
458	Bret Boone	.10
459	Ben McDonald	.10
460	Kirby Puckett	.75
461	Gregg Olson	.10
462	*Rich Aude*	.30
463	John Burkett	.10
464	Troy Neel	.10
465	Jimmy Key	.10
466	Ozzie Timmons	.10
467	Eddie Murray	.40
468	*Mark Tranberg*	.15
469	Alex Gonzalez	.25
470	David Nied	.10
471	Barry Larkin	.20
472	*Brian Looney*	.25
473	Shawn Estes	.30
474	*A.J. Sager*	.15
475	Roger Clemens	2.00
476	Vince Moore	.10
477	*Scott Karl*	.15
478	Kurt Miller	.10
479	Garret Anderson	.60
480	Allen Watson	.10
481	*Jose Lima*	2.00
482	Rick Gorecki	.10
483	*Jimmy Hurst*	.50
484	Preston Wilson	.50
485	Will Clark	.35
486	*Mike Ferry*	.15
487	*Curtis Goodwin*	.40
488	Mike Myers	.10
489	Chipper Jones	2.50
490	Jeff King	.10
491	*Bill Van Landingham*	.60
492	*Carlos Reyes*	.20
493	Andy Pettitte	1.50
494	Brant Brown	.15

495 Daron Kirkreit .15
496 *Ricky Bottalico* .40
497 Devon White .15
498 *Jason Johnson* .20
499 Vince Coleman .10
500 Larry Walker .50
501 Bobby Ayala .10
502 Steve Finley .10
503 Scott Fletcher .10
504 Brad Ausmus .10
505 *Scott Talanoa* .20
506 Orestes Destrade .10
507 Gary DiSarcina .10
508 *Willie Smith* .20
509 Alan Trammell .15
510 Mike Piazza 2.50
511 Ozzie Guillen .10
512 Jeromy Burnitz .15
513 Darren Oliver .10
514 Kevin Mitchell .10
515 Rafael Palmeiro .25
516 David McCarty .10
517 Jeff Blauser .10
518 Trey Beamon .15
519 Royce Clayton .10
520 Dennis Eckersley .15
521 Bernie Williams .60
522 Steve Buechele .10
523 Denny Martinez .15
524 Dave Hollins .10
525 Joey Hamilton .30
526 Andres Galarraga .25
527 Jeff Granger .10
528 Joey Eischen .10
529 Desi Relaford .10
530 Roberto Petagine .10
531 Andre Dawson .15
532 Ray Holbert .10
533 Duane Singleton .10
534 *Kurt Abbott* .30
535 Bo Jackson .15
536 Gregg Jefferies .15
537 David Mysel .10
538 Raul Mondesi .75
539 Chris Snopek .15
540 Brook Fordyce .10
541 *Ron Frazier* .25
542 Brian Koelling .10
543 Jimmy Haynes .10
544 Marty Cordova .75
545 *Jason Green* .30
546 Orlando Merced .10
547 *Lou Pote* .20
548 Todd Van Poppel .15
549 Pat Kelly .10
550 Turk Wendell .10
551 *Herb Perry* .15
552 *Ryan Karp* .25
553 Juan Guzman .10
554 *Bryan Rekar* .25
555 Kevin Appier .10
556 *Chris Schwab* .20
557 Jay Buhner .20
558 Andujar Cedeno .10
559 *Ryan McGuire* .60
560 Ricky Gutierrez .10
561 *Keith Kimsey* .20
562 Tim Clark .10
563 Damion Easley .10
564 *Clint Davis* .15
565 Mike Moore .10
566 Orel Hershiser .15
567 Jason Bere .15
568 Kevin McReynolds .10
569 *Leland Macon* .20
570 *John Courtright* .20
571 Sid Fernandez .10
572 Chad Roper .10
573 Terry Pendleton .10
574 Danny Miceli .10
575 Joe Rosselli .10
576 Mike Bordick .10
577 Danny Tartabull .10
578 Jose Guzman .10
579 Omar Vizquel .15
580 Tommy Greene .10
581 Paul Spoljaric .10
582 Walt Weiss .10
583 *Oscar Jimenez* .20
584 Rod Henderson .10
585 Derek Lowe .10
586 *Richard Hidalgo* 12.00
587 *Shayne Bennett* .15
588 *Tim Belk* .20
589 Matt Mieske .10
590 Nigel Wilson .15
591 *Jeff Knox* .15
592 Bernard Gilkey .15
593 David Cone .30
594 *Paul LoDuca* .25
595 Scott Ruffcorn .10
596 Chris Roberts .10
597 *Oscar Munoz* .25
598 *Scott Sullivan* .20
599 *Matt Jarvis* .15
600 Jose Canseco .50
601 *Tony Graffanino* .20
602 Don Slaught .10
603 *Brett King* .20
604 *Jose Herrera* .40
605 Melido Perez .10
606 *Mike Hubbard* .15
607 Chad Ogea .15
608 *Wayne Gomes* .35
609 Roberto Alomar .50
610 *Angel Echevarria* .20
611 Jose Lind .10
612 Darrin Fletcher .10
613 Chris Bosio .10
614 Darryl Kile .10
615 Frank Rodriguez .15
616 Phil Plantier .10
617 Pat Listach .10
618 Charlie Hough .10
619 *Ryan Hancock* .30
620 *Darrel Deak* .20
621 Travis Fryman .15
622 Brett Butler .15
623 Lance Johnson .10
624 Pete Smith .10
625 James Hurst .10
626 Roberto Kelly .10
627 Mike Mussina .50
628 Kevin Tapani .10
629 John Smoltz .15
630 Midre Cummings .15
631 Salomon Torres .10
632 Willie Adams .10
633 Derek Jeter 4.00
634 Steve Trachsel .25
635 Albie Lopez .15
636 Jason Moler .10
637 Carlos Delgado .40
638 Roberto Mejia .10
639 Darren Burton .10
640 B.J. Wallace .10
641 *Brad Clontz* .15
642 *Billy Wagner* 1.00
643 Aaron Sele .25
644 Cameron Cairncross .10
645 Brian Harper .10
(646) Marc Valdes (no card number) .15
647 Mark Ratekin .10
648 *Terry Bradshaw* .35
649 Justin Thompson .15
650 *Mike Busch* .25
651 *Joe Hall* .15
652 Bobby Jones .15
653 *Kelly Stinnett* .25
654 *Rod Steph* .20
655 *Jay Powell* .35
(656) *Keith Garagozzo* (no card number) .15
657 Todd Dunn .15
658 *Charles Peterson* .20
659 Darren Lewis .10
660 *John Wasdin* .50
661 *Tate Seefried* .60
662 *Hector Trinidad* .40
663 *John Carter* .20
664 Larry Mitchell .10
665 *David Catlett* .20
666 Dante Bichette .30
667 Felix Jose .10
668 Rondell White .30
669 Tino Martinez .40
670 Brian Hunter .35
671 Jose Malave .15
672 Archi Cianfrocco .10
673 *Mike Matheny* .15
674 Bret Barberie .10
675 *Andrew Lorraine* .60
676 Brian Jordan .15
677 Tim Belcher .10
678 *Antonio Osuna* .20
679 Checklist I .10
680 Checklist II .10
681 Checklist III .10
682 Checklist IV .10

1994 Bowman Superstar Sampler

As an insert in 1994 Topps retail factory sets, three-card cello packs of "Superstar Sampler" cards were included. The packs contained special versions of the same player's 1994 Bowman, Finest and Stadium Club cards. Forty-five of the game's top stars are represented in the issue. The Bowman cards in this issue are identical to the cards in the regular set except for the appearance of a round "Topps Superstar Sampler" logo on back.

		MT
Complete Set (45):		200.00
Common Player:		2.50
1	Joe Carter	2.50
5	Ken Griffey Jr.	35.00
15	Frank Thomas	25.00
21	Tom Glavine	3.00
25	Don Mattingly	15.00
45	Juan Gonzalez	8.00
50	Andy Van Slyke	2.50
55	Manny Ramirez	5.00
69	Cecil Fielder	3.00
75	Cal Ripken Jr.	30.00
79	Matt Williams	4.00
118	Jeff Bagwell	7.50
120	Tony Gwynn	9.00
128	Bobby Bonilla	2.50
133	Dave Justice	3.00
135	Barry Bonds	12.00
140	Darren Daulton	2.50
169	John Olerud	3.00
200	Cliff Floyd	2.50
245	Greg Maddux	12.00
250	Ryne Sandberg	9.00
281	Paul Molitor	6.00
284	Marquis Grissom	2.50
285	Randy Johnson	4.00
290	Gary Sheffield	3.00
307	Carlos Baerga	2.50
315	Mo Vaughn	6.00
395	Tim Salmon	3.00
405	Fred McGriff	3.00
410	Mark Grace	4.00
411	Albert Belle	6.00
440	Len Dykstra	2.50
455	Jack McDowell	2.50
460	Kirby Puckett	9.00
471	Barry Larkin	2.50
475	Roger Clemens	7.50
485	Will Clark	4.00
500	Larry Walker	4.00
510	Mike Piazza	15.00
515	Rafael Palmeiro	3.00
526	Andres Galarraga	2.50
536	Gregg Jefferies	2.50
538	Raul Mondesi	3.00
600	Jose Canseco	6.00
609	Roberto Alomar	5.00

1994 Bowman's Best

The first ever set of Bowman's Best consisted of 90 Blue cards, 90 Red cards and 20 Mirror Images, featuring a Red veteran and a Blue prospect player matched by position on each card. This 200-card set utilized Topps Finest technology and includes full-color photos front and back with a high-gloss finish. Bowman's Best was available in eight-card wax packs, with each pack containing seven cards and a Mirror Image card. There is also a 200-card parallel set officially titled "Special Effects," which uses Topps' refractor technology. Both the Red and Blue set are numbered 1-90, with the Mirror Image cards numbered 91-110.

		MT
Complete Set (200):		75.00
Common Player:		.25
Red Set		
Pack (7):		4.50
Wax Box (24):		75.00
1	Paul Molitor	1.00
2	Eddie Murray	.75
3	Ozzie Smith	1.50
4	Rickey Henderson	.75
5	Lee Smith	.25
6	Dave Winfield	.50
7	Roberto Alomar	1.00
8	Matt Williams	.75
9	Mark Grace	.50
10	Lance Johnson	.25
11	Darren Daulton	.25
12	Tom Glavine	.50
13	Gary Sheffield	.50
14	Rod Beck	.25
15	Fred McGriff	.50
16	Joe Carter	.25
17	Dante Bichette	.40
18	Danny Tartabull	.25
19	Juan Gonzalez	1.25
20	Steve Avery	.25
21	John Wetteland	.25
22	Ben McDonald	.25
23	Jack McDowell	.25
24	Jose Canseco	1.00
25	Tim Salmon	.50
26	Wilson Alvarez	.25
27	Gregg Jefferies	.25
28	John Burkett	.25
29	Greg Vaughn	.25
30	Robin Ventura	.40
31	Paul O'Neill	.50
32	Cecil Fielder	.35

33 Kevin Mitchell .25
34 Jeff Conine .25
35 Carlos Baerga .25
36 Greg Maddux 2.50
37 Roger Clemens 1.50
38 Deion Sanders .75
39 Delino DeShields .25
40 Ken Griffey, Jr. 5.00
41 Albert Belle 1.00
42 Wade Boggs 1.00
43 Andres Galarraga .60
44 Aaron Sele .25
45 Don Mattingly 1.50
46 David Cone .40
47 Len Dykstra .25
48 Brett Butler .25
49 Bill Swift .25
50 Bobby Bonilla .25
51 Rafael Palmeiro .75
52 Moises Alou .25
53 Jeff Bagwell 1.25
54 Mike Mussina .75
55 Frank Thomas 1.50
56 Jose Rijo .25
57 Ruben Sierra .25
58 Randy Myers .25
59 Barry Bonds 1.50
60 Jimmy Key .25
61 Travis Fryman .25
62 John Olerud .50
63 Dave Justice .75
64 Ray Lankford .25
65 Bob Tewksbury .25
66 Chuck Carr .25
67 Jay Buhner .25
68 Kenny Lofton .75
69 Marquis Grissom .30
70 Sammy Sosa 3.00
71 Cal Ripken, Jr. 4.00
72 Ellis Burks .25
73 Jeff Montgomery .25
74 Julio Franco .25
75 Kirby Puckett 1.50
76 Larry Walker .75
77 Andy Van Slyke .25
78 Tony Gwynn 2.00
79 Will Clark .75
80 Mo Vaughn 1.00
81 Mike Piazza 3.00
82 James Mouton .25
83 Carlos Delgado 1.50
84 Ryan Klesko .40
85 Javier Lopez .50
86 Raul Mondesi .50
87 Cliff Floyd .25
88 Manny Ramirez 1.50
89 Hector Carrasco .25
90 Jeff Granger .25

Blue Set

1 Chipper Jones 4.00
2 Derek Jeter 6.00
3 Bill Pulsipher .50
4 James Baldwin .50
5 *Brooks Kieschnick* .75
6 Justin Thompson .25
7 Midre Cummings .25
8 Joey Hamilton .25
9 Calvin Reese .25
10 Brian Barber .25
11 John Burke .25
12 De Shawn Warren .25
13 *Edgardo Alfonzo* 18.00
14 *Eddie Pearson* .50
15 Jimmy Haynes .25
16 Danny Bautista .25
17 Roger Cedeno .50
18 Jon Lieber .25
19 *Billy Wagner* 1.00
20 *Tate Seefried* .50
21 Chad Mottola .25
22 Jose Malave .25
23 *Terrell Wade* .50
24 Shane Andrews .25
25 *Chan Ho Park* 4.00
26 *Kirk Presley* .50
27 Robbie Beckett .25
28 Orlando Miller .25
29 *Jorge Posada* 6.00
30 Frank Rodriguez .25
31 Brian Hunter .25
32 Billy Ashley .25
33 Rondell White .50
34 John Roper .25
35 Marc Valdes .25
36 Scott Ruffcorn .25
37 Rod Henderson .25
38 Curt Goodwin .25
39 Russ Davis .25
40 Rick Gorecki .25
41 Johnny Damon .25
42 Roberto Petagine .25
43 Chris Snopek .25
44 Mark Acre .25
45 Todd Hollandsworth .25
46 Shawn Green 1.50
47 John Carter .25
48 Jim Pittsley .25
49 *John Wasdin* .50
50 D.J. Boston .25
51 Tim Clark .25
52 Alex Ochoa .25
53 Chad Roper .25
54 Mike Kelly .25
55 *Brad Fullmer* 5.00
56 Carl Everett .50
57 *Tim Belk* .50
58 *Jimmy Hurst* .50
59 *Mac Suzuki* .50
60 Michael Moore .25
61 *Alan Benes* 1.00
62 *Tony Clark* 3.00
63 *Edgar Renteria* 3.00
64 Trey Beamon .25
65 *LaTroy Hawkins* 1.00
66 *Wayne Gomes* 1.00
67 Ray McDavid .25
68 John Dettmer .25
69 Willie Greene .25
70 Dave Stevens .25
71 *Kevin Orie* .50
72 Chad Ogea .25
73 Ben Van Ryn .25
74 Kym Ashworth .25
75 Dmitri Young .25
76 Herb Perry .25
77 Joey Eischen .25
78 *Arquimedez Pozo* .50
79 Ugueth Urbina .25
80 Keith Williams .25
81 *John Frascatore* .50
82 Garey Ingram .25
83 Aaron Small .25
84 *Olmedo Saenz* .50
85 Jesus Tavarez .25
86 *Jose Silva* 1.00
87 *Gerald Witasick, Jr.* .50
88 Jay Maldonado .25
89 Keith Heberling .25
90 *Rusty Greer* 3.00

Mirror Images

91 Frank Thomas, Kevin Young 1.00
92 Fred McGriff, Brooks Kieschnick .50
93 Matt Williams, Shane Andrews .50
94 Cal Ripken, Jr., Kevin Orie 2.50
95 Barry Larkin, Derek Jeter 3.00
96 Ken Griffey, Jr., Johnny Damon 3.00
97 Barry Bonds, Rondell White 1.00
98 Albert Belle, Jimmy Hurst .75
99 Raul Mondesi, *Ruben Rivera* 1.50
100 Roger Clemens, Scott Ruffcorn 1.25
101 Greg Maddux, John Wasdin 1.50
102 Tim Salmon, Chad Mottola .50
103 Carlos Baerga, Arquimedez Pozo .40
104 Mike Piazza, Buddy Hughes 2.00
105 Carlos Delgado, Melvin Nieves 1.00
106 Javier Lopez, Jorge Posada 1.50
107 Manny Ramirez, Jose Malave 1.00
108 Travis Fryman, Chipper Jones 1.50
109 Steve Avery, Bill Pulsipher .50
110 John Olerud, Shawn Green .75

1994 Bowman's Best Refractors

This 200-card parallel set, officially titled "Special Effects," uses Topps' refractor technology. The refractors were packed at the rate of three per wax box of Bowman's Best, but are very difficult to differentiate from the regular high-tech cards.

	MT
Complete Set (200):	750.00
Common Player:	1.00
Superstars:	4-8X
Stars:	3-6X

(See 1994 Bowman's Best for checklist and base card values.)

1995 Bowman

Large numbers of rookie cards and a lengthy run of etched-foil cards distinguishes the 1995 Bowman set. The set's basic cards share a design with a large color photo flanked at left by a severely horizontally compressed mirror image in green, and at bottom by a similar version in brown. Most of the bottom image is covered by the player's last name printed in silver (cards #1-220, rookies) or gold (cards #275-439, veterans) foil. A color team logo is in the lower-left corner of all cards, and the Bowman logo is in red foil at top. In between are the foil-etched subsets of "Minor League MVPs," "1st Impressions," and "Prime Prospects." Each of these cards, seeded one per regular pack and two per jumbo, has the player photo set against a background of textured color foil, with a prismatic silver border. Each of the foil cards can also be found in a gold-toned version, in a ratio of six silver to one gold. Backs of the rookies' cards have a portrait photo at right and a scouting report at left. Veterans' cards have either a scouting report for younger players, or a chart of stats versus each team played in 1994. Backs of all the foil cards have a scouting report.

	MT
Complete Set (439):	250.00
Common Player:	.15
Pack (10):	12.00
Wax Box (24):	290.00

1 Billy Wagner .30
2 Chris Widger .15
3 Brent Bowers .15
4 *Bob Abreu* 15.00
5 *Lou Collier* .30
6 *Juan Acevedo* .40
7 *Jason Kelley* .20
8 Brian Sackinsky .15
9 Scott Christman .15
10 Damon Hollins .15
11 *Willis Otanez* .25
12 *Jason Ryan* .20
13 Jason Giambi .75
14 *Andy Taulbee* .25
15 Mark Thompson .15
16 *Hugo Pivaral* .25
17 Brien Taylor .15
18 Antonio Osuna .15
19 Edgardo Alfonzo .50
20 Carl Everett .15
21 Matt Drews .15
22 *Bartolo Colon* 8.00
23 *Andruw Jones* 50.00
24 *Robert Person* .25
25 Derrek Lee .25
26 *John Ambrose* .20
27 *Eric Knowles* .25
28 Chris Roberts .15
29 Don Wengert .15
30 *Marcus Jensen* .30
31 Brian Barber .15
32 Kevin Brown .15
33 Benji Gil .15
34 Mike Hubbard .15
35 *Bart Evans* .35
36 *Enrique Wilson* 1.00
37 *Brian Buchanan* .20
38 *Ken Ray* .25
39 *Micah Franklin* .40
40 *Ricky Otero* .30
41 Jason Kendall .15
42 Jimmy Hurst .15
43 *Jerry Wolak* .20
44 *Jayson Peterson* .30
45 *Allen Battle* .20
46 Scott Stahoviak .15
47 *Steve Schrenk* .30
48 *Travis Miller* .20
49 *Eddie Rios* .25
50 Mike Hampton .15
51 *Chad Frontera* .25
52 *Tom Evans* .30
53 C.J. Nitkowski .15
54 *Clay Caruthers* .25
55 Shannon Stewart .15
56 Jorge Posada .15
57 Aaron Holbert .15
58 *Harry Berrios* .20
59 Steve Rodriguez .15
60 Shane Andrews .15
61 *Will Cunnane* .25
62 Richard Hidalgo 1.50
63 *Bill Selby* .20
64 *Jay Cranford* .20
65 Jeff Suppan .15
66 Curtis Goodwin .15
67 *John Thomson* .30
68 Justin Thompson .15
69 Troy Percival .15
70 *Matt Wagner* .25
71 Terry Bradshaw .15
72 Greg Hansell .15
73 John Burke .15
74 Jeff D'Amico .15
75 Ernie Young .15
76 Jason Bates .15
77 Chris Stynes .15
78 *Cade Gaspar* .25

79 Melvin Nieves .15
80 Rick Gorecki .15
81 *Felix Rodriguez* .20
82 Ryan Hancock .15
83 *Chris Carpenter* 3.00
84 Ray McDavid .15
85 Chris Wimmer .15
86 Doug Glanville .15
87 DeShawn Warren .15
88 *Damian Moss* .50
89 *Rafael Orellano* .20
90 *Vladimir Guerrero* 90.00
91 *Raul Casanova* .75
92 *Karim Garcia* 1.00
93 Bryce Florie .15
94 Kevin Orie .25
95 *Ryan Nye* .25
96 *Matt Sachse* .25
97 *Ivan Arteaga* .25
98 Glenn Murray .15
99 *Stacy Hollins* .20
100 Jim Pittsley .15
101 *Craig Mattson* .30
102 Neifi Perez .40
103 Keith Williams .15
104 Roger Cedeno .15
105 *Tony Terry* .25
106 Jose Malave .15
107 Joe Rosselli .15
108 Kevin Jordan .15
109 *Sid Roberson* .20
110 Alan Embree .15
111 Terrell Wade .15
112 Bob Wolcott .15
113 *Carlos Perez* .25
114 *Mike Bovee* .30
115 *Tommy Davis* .30
116 *Jeremey Kendall* .25
117 Rich Aude .15
118 Rick Huisman .15
119 Tim Belk .15
120 Edgar Renteria .25
121 *Calvin Maduro* .25
122 *Jerry Martin* .25
123 *Ramon Fermin* .20
124 *Kimera Bartee* .35
125 Mark Farris .25
126 Frank Rodriguez .15
127 *Bobby Higginson* 4.00
128 Bret Wagner .15
129 *Edwin Diaz* .30
130 Jimmy Haynes .15
131 *Chris Weinke* 3.00
132 *Damian Jackson* 1.00
133 Felix Martinez .15
134 *Edwin Hurtado* .40
135 *Matt Raleigh* .30
136 Paul Wilson .25
137 Ron Villone .15
138 *Eric Stuckenschneider* .20
139 Tate Seefried .15
140 *Rey Ordonez* 2.00
141 Eddie Pearson .15
142 Kevin Gallaher .15
143 Torii Hunter .20
144 Daron Kirkreit .15
145 Craig Wilson .15
146 Ugueth Urbina .15
147 Chris Snopek .15
148 Kym Ashworth .15
149 Wayne Gomes .15
150 Mark Loretta .15
151 *Ramon Morel* .25
152 Trot Nixon .25
153 Desi Relaford .15
154 Scott Sullivan .15
155 Marc Barcelo .15
156 Willie Adams .15
157 *Derrick Gibson* .75
158 *Brian Meadows* .20
159 Julian Tavarez .15
160 Bryan Rekar .15
161 Steve Gibralter .15
162 Esteban Loaiza .15
163 John Wasdin .15
164 Kirk Presley .15
165 Mariano Rivera .50
166 Andy Larkin .15
167 *Sean Whiteside* .20
168 *Matt Apana* .25
169 *Shawn Senior* .15
170 Scott Gentile .15
171 Quilvio Veras .15
172 *Elieser Marrero* 2.00
173 *Mendy Lopez* .20
174 Homer Bush .15
175 *Brian Stephenson* .25
176 Jon Nunnally .15
177 Jose Herrera .15
178 *Corey Avrard* .25
179 David Bell .15
180 Jason Isringhausen .50
181 Jamey Wright .15
182 *Lonell Roberts* .15
183 Marty Cordova .15
185 Amaury Telemaco .15
185 John Mabry .15
186 *Andrew Vessel* .20
187 *Jim Cole* .15
188 Marquis Riley .15
189 Todd Dunn .15
190 John Carter .15
191 *Donnie Sadler* 1.00
192 Mike Bell .15
193 *Chris Cumberland* .20
194 Jason Schmidt .15
195 Matt Brunson .15
196 James Baldwin .15
197 *Bill Simas* .20
198 Gus Gandarillas .15
199 Mac Suzuki .15
200 *Rick Holifield* .25
201 *Fernando Lunar* .20
202 Kevin Jarvis .15
203 *Everett Stull* .15
204 Steve Wojciechowski .15
205 Shawn Estes .15
206 Jermaine Dye .20
207 Marc Kroon .15
208 *Peter Munro* .30
209 Pat Watkins .15
210 Matt Smith .15
211 Joe Vitiello .15
212 Gerald Witasick, Jr. .15
213 *Freddy Garcia* .40
214 *Glenn Dishman* .20
215 *Jay Canizaro* .20
216 Angel Martinez .15
217 *Yamil Benitez* .25
218 *Fausto Macey* .20
219 Eric Owens .15
220 Checklist .15
221 *Dwayne Hosey* (Minor League MVPs) .20
222 *Brad Woodall* (Minor League MVPs) .25
223 Billy Ashley (Minor League MVPs) .15
224 *Mark Grudzielanek* (Minor League MVPs) 1.00
225 *Mark Johnson* (Minor League MVPs) .40
226 *Tim Unroe* (Minor League MVPs) .15
227 Todd Greene (Minor League MVPs) .25
228 Larry Sutton (Minor League MVPs) .15
229 Derek Jeter (Minor League MVPs) 4.00
230 *Sal Fasano* (Minor League MVPs) .15
231 Ruben Rivera (Minor League MVPs) 2.00
232 *Chris Truby* (Minor League MVPs) .15
233 John Donati (Minor League MVPs) .15
234 *Decomba Conner* (Minor League MVPs) .25
235 *Sergio Nunez* (Minor League MVPs) .20
236 *Ray Brown* (Minor League MVPs) .50
237 *Juan Melo* (Minor League MVPs) .50
238 *Hideo Nomo* (First Impressions) 4.00
239 *Jaime Bluma* (First Impressions) .20
240 *Jay Payton* (First Impressions) .75
241 Paul Konerko (First Impressions) 3.00
242 *Scott Elarton* (First Impressions) 1.00
243 *Jeff Abbott* (First Impressions) .75
244 *Jim Brower* (First Impressions) .30
245 *Geoff Blum* (First Impressions) .30
246 *Aaron Boone* (First Impressions) .75
247 J.R. Phillips (Top Prospects) .15
248 Alex Ochoa (Top Prospects) .25
249 Nomar Garciaparra (Top Prospects) 15.00
250 Garret Anderson (Top Prospects) .40
251 Ray Durham (Top Prospects) .30
252 Paul Shuey (Top Prospects) .15
253 Tony Clark (Top Prospects) 2.00
254 Johnny Damon (Top Prospects) .50
255 Duane Singleton (Top Prospects) .15
256 LaTroy Hawkins (Top Prospects) .15
257 Andy Pettitte (Top Prospects) .75
258 Ben Grieve (Top Prospects) 5.00
259 Marc Newfield (Top Prospects) .15
260 Terrell Lowery (Top Prospects) .15
261 Shawn Green (Top Prospects) .75
262 Chipper Jones (Top Prospects) 2.00
263 Brooks Kieschnick (Top Prospects) .30
264 Calvin Reese (Top Prospects) .15
265 Doug Million (Top Prospects) .15
266 Marc Valdes (Top Prospects) .15
267 Brian Hunter (Top Prospects) .35
268 Todd Hollandsworth (Top Prospects) .50
269 Rod Henderson (Top Prospects) .20
270 Bill Pulsipher (Top Prospects) .20
271 *Scott Rolen* (Top Prospects) 25.00
272 Trey Beamon (Top Prospects) .15
273 Alan Benes (Top Prospects) .25
274 Dustin Hermanson (Top Prospects) .25
275 Ricky Bottalico .15
276 Albert Belle 1.00
277 Deion Sanders .30
278 Matt Williams .50
279 Jeff Bagwell 1.50
280 Kirby Puckett 1.50
281 Dave Hollins .15
282 Don Mattingly 1.50
283 Joey Hamilton .25
284 Bobby Bonilla .15
285 Moises Alou .25
286 Tom Glavine .40
287 Brett Butler .15
288 Chris Hoiles .15
289 Kenny Rogers .15
290 Larry Walker .50
291 Tim Raines .15
292 Kevin Appier .15
293 Roger Clemens 2.00
294a Chuck Carr .15
294b Cliff Floyd (Should be #394) .20
295 Randy Myers .15
296 Dave Nilsson .15
297 Joe Carter .15
298 Chuck Finley .15
299 Ray Lankford .15
300 Roberto Kelly .15
301 Jon Lieber .15
302 Travis Fryman .25
303 Mark McGwire 5.00
304 Tony Gwynn 2.00
305 Kenny Lofton .75
306 Mark Whiten .15
307 Doug Drabek .15
308 Terry Steinbach .15
309 Ryan Klesko .40
310 Mike Piazza 3.00
311 Ben McDonald .15
312 Reggie Sanders .15
313 Alex Fernandez .15
314 Aaron Sele .15
315 Gregg Jefferies .15
316 Rickey Henderson .50
317 Brian Anderson .15
318 Jose Valentin .15
319 Rod Beck .15
320 Marquis Grissom .15
321 Ken Griffey Jr. 4.00
322 Bret Saberhagen .15
323 Juan Gonzalez 1.00
324 Paul Molitor .50
325 Gary Sheffield .50
326 Darren Daulton .15
327 Bill Swift .15
328 Brian McRae .15
329 Robin Ventura .20
330 Lee Smith .15
331 Fred McGriff .40
332 Delino DeShields .15
333 Edgar Martinez .15
334 Mike Mussina .75
335 Orlando Merced .15
336 Carlos Baerga .15
337 Wil Cordero .15
338 Tom Pagnozzi .15
339 Pat Hentgen .15
340 Chad Curtis .15
341 Darren Lewis .15
342 Jeff Kent .15
343 Bip Roberts .15
344 Ivan Rodriguez 1.50
345 Jeff Montgomery .15
346 Hal Morris .15
347 Danny Tartabull .15
348 Raul Mondesi .40
349 Ken Hill .15
350 Pedro Martinez 1.50
351 Frank Thomas 1.50
352 Manny Ramirez 1.50
353 Tim Salmon .30
354 William Van Landingham .15
355 Andres Galarraga .50
356 Paul O'Neill .40
357 Brady Anderson .15
358 Ramon Martinez .15
359 John Olerud .25
360 Ruben Sierra .15
361 Cal Eldred .15
362 Jay Buhner .15
363 Jay Bell .15
364 Wally Joyner .15
365 Chuck Knoblauch .25
366 Len Dykstra .15
367 John Wetteland .15
368 Roberto Alomar .75
369 Craig Biggio .40
370 Ozzie Smith .75
371 Terry Pendleton .15
372 Sammy Sosa 3.00
373 Carlos Garcia .15
374 Jose Rijo .15
375 Chris Gomez .15
376 Barry Bonds 1.00
377 Steve Avery .15
378 Rick Wilkins .15
379 Pete Harnisch .15
380 Dean Palmer .15
381 Bob Hamelin .15
382 Jason Bere .15
383 Jimmy Key .15
384 Dante Bichette .35
385 Rafael Palmeiro .60
386 David Justice .40
387 Chili Davis .15
388 Mike Greenwell .15
389 Todd Zeile .15
390 Jeff Conine .15
391 Rick Aguilera .15
392 Eddie Murray .40
393 Mike Stanley .15
394 (Not issued - see #294)
395 Randy Johnson .75
396 David Nied .15
397 Devon White .15
398 Royce Clayton .15
399 Andy Benes .15
400 John Hudek .15
401 Bobby Jones .15
402 Eric Karros .25
403 Will Clark .35

404	Mark Langston	.15
405	Kevin Brown	.25
406	Greg Maddux	2.50
407	David Cone	.25
408	Wade Boggs	.35
409	Steve Trachsel	.15
410	Greg Vaughn	.25
411	Mo Vaughn	1.00
412	Wilson Alvarez	.15
413	Cal Ripken Jr.	4.00
414	Rico Brogna	.15
415	Barry Larkin	.30
416	Cecil Fielder	.15
417	Jose Canseco	.40
418	Jack McDowell	.15
419	Mike Lieberthal	.15
420	Andrew Lorraine	.15
421	Rich Becker	.15
422	Tony Phillips	.15
423	Scott Ruffcorn	.15
424	Jeff Granger	.15
425	Greg Pirkl	.15
426	Dennis Eckersley	.15
427	Jose Lima	.15
428	Russ Davis	.15
429	Armando Benitez	.15
430	Alex Gonzalez	.15
431	Carlos Delgado	1.00
432	Chan Ho Park	.15
433	Mickey Tettleton	.15
434	Dave Winfield	.30
435	John Burkett	.15
436	Orlando Miller	.15
437	Rondell White	.25
438	Jose Oliva	.15
439	Checklist	.15

1995 Bowman Gold

The only chase cards in the '95 Bowman set are gold versions of the foil-etched "Minor League MVPs," "1st Impressions" and "Prime Prospects." The gold cards are found in every 6th (regular) or 12th (jumbo) pack, on average, in place of the silver versions.

	MT
Complete Set (54):	100.00
Common Player:	.50
Superstars:	1-1.5X
Stars:	1.5-2X

(See 1995 Bowman #221-274 for checklist and base card values.)

1995 Bowman's Best

Actually made up of three subsets, all cards feature a player photo set against a silver foil background. The 90 veterans' cards have a broad red-foil stripe in the background beneath the team logo; the 90 rookies' cards have a similar stripe in tones of blue. All of those cards are printed in Topps' Finest technology. The 15 Mirror Image cards are in horizontal format, printed more conventionally on metallic foil, and have a rookie and veteran sharing the card. Backs of each card continue the color theme, have '94 and career stats and a highlight or two. Standard packaging was seven-card foil packs with inserts consisting of higher-tech parallel sets of the regular issue.

		MT
Complete Set (195):		325.00
Common Player:		.25
Pack (7):		18.00
Wax Box (24):		375.00
Complete Set Red (90):		50.00
1	Randy Johnson	1.50
2	Joe Carter	.30
3	Chili Davis	.25
4	Moises Alou	.25
5	Gary Sheffield	.50
6	Kevin Appier	.25
7	Denny Neagle	.25
8	Ruben Sierra	.25
9	Darren Daulton	.25
10	Cal Ripken Jr.	5.00
11	Bobby Bonilla	.25
12	Manny Ramirez	1.50
13	Barry Bonds	2.00
14	Eric Karros	.25
15	Greg Maddux	3.00
16	Jeff Bagwell	1.50
17	Paul Molitor	.75
18	Ray Lankford	.25
19	Mark Grace	.50
20	Kenny Lofton	1.00
21	Tony Gwynn	2.00
22	Will Clark	.50
23	Roger Clemens	2.00
24	Dante Bichette	.40
25	Barry Larkin	.40
26	Wade Boggs	.75
27	Kirby Puckett	2.00
28	Cecil Fielder	.30
29	Jose Canseco	.75
30	Juan Gonzalez	1.50
31	David Cone	.40
32	Craig Biggio	.35
33	Tim Salmon	.40
34	David Justice	.50
35	Sammy Sosa	4.00
36	Mike Piazza	4.00
37	Carlos Baerga	.25
38	Jeff Conine	.25
39	Rafael Palmeiro	.75
40	Bret Saberhagen	.25
41	Len Dykstra	.25
42	Mo Vaughn	1.00
43	Wally Joyner	.25
44	Chuck Knoblauch	.30
45	Robin Ventura	.35
46	Don Mattingly	2.00
47	Dave Hollins	.25
48	Andy Benes	.25
49	Ken Griffey Jr.	5.00
50	Albert Belle	1.00
51	Matt Williams	.50
52	Rondell White	.40
53	Raul Mondesi	.40
54	Brian Jordan	.25
55	Greg Vaughn	.35
56	Fred McGriff	.50
57	Roberto Alomar	1.00
58	Dennis Eckersley	.25
59	Lee Smith	.25
60	Eddie Murray	.50
61	Kenny Rogers	.25
62	Ron Gant	.35
63	Larry Walker	.50
64	Chad Curtis	.25
65	Frank Thomas	2.00
66	Paul O'Neill	.40
67	Kevin Seitzer	.25
68	Marquis Grissom	.25
69	Mark McGwire	6.00
70	Travis Fryman	.25
71	Andres Galarraga	.50
72	*Carlos Perez*	.40
73	Tyler Green	.25
74	Marty Cordova	.25
75	Shawn Green	.50
76	Vaughn Eshelman	.25
77	John Mabry	.25
78	Jason Bates	.25
79	Jon Nunnally	.25
80	Ray Durham	.25
81	Edgardo Alfonzo	.75
82	Esteban Loaiza	.25
83	*Hideo Nomo*	5.00
84	Orlando Miller	.25
85	Alex Gonzalez	.25
86	*Mark Grudzielanek*	1.00
87	Julian Tavarez	.25
88	Benji Gil	.25
89	Quilvio Veras	.25
90	Ricky Bottalico	.25
Complete Set Blue (90):		275.00
1	Derek Jeter	5.00
2	*Vladimir Guerrero*	150.00
3	*Bob Abreu*	25.00
4	Chan Ho Park	.50
5	Paul Wilson	.25
6	Chad Ogea	.25
7	*Andruw Jones*	60.00
8	Brian Barber	.25
9	Andy Larkin	.25
10	*Richie Sexson*	15.00
11	*Everett Stull*	.25
12	Brooks Kieschnick	.25
13	Matt Murray	.25
14	John Wasdin	.25
15	Shannon Stewart	.50
16	Luis Ortiz	.25
17	Marc Kroon	.25
18	Todd Greene	.25
19	Juan Acevedo	.25
20	Tony Clark	.50
21	Jermaine Dye	.75
22	Derrek Lee	.25
23	Pat Watkins	.25
24	Calvin Reese	.25
25	Ben Grieve	6.00
26	*Julio Santana*	.25
27	*Felix Rodriguez*	.35
28	Paul Konerko	3.00
29	Nomar Garciaparra	25.00
30	Pat Ahearne	.25
31	Jason Schmidt	.25
32	Billy Wagner	.40
33	*Rey Ordonez*	3.00
34	Curtis Goodwin	.25
35	*Sergio Nunez*	.50
36	Tim Belk	.25
37	*Scott Elarton*	1.00
38	Jason Isringhausen	.40
39	Trot Nixon	.25
40	Sid Roberson	.25
41	Ron Villone	.25
42	Ruben Rivera	.25
43	Rick Huisman	.25
44	Todd Hollandsworth	.40
45	Johnny Damon	.50
46	Garret Anderson	.50
47	Jeff D'Amico	.75
48	Dustin Hermanson	.25
49	*Juan Encarnacion*	15.00
50	Andy Pettitte	.75
51	Chris Stynes	.25
52	Troy Percival	.25
53	LaTroy Hawkins	.25
54	Roger Cedeno	.25
55	Alan Benes	.25
56	*Karim Garcia*	1.50
57	Andrew Lorraine	.25
58	*Gary Rath*	.50
59	Bret Wagner	.25
60	Jeff Suppan	.25
61	Bill Pulsipher	.40
62	*Jay Payton*	5.00
63	Alex Ochoa	.50
64	Ugueth Urbina	.25
65	Armando Benitez	.25
66	George Arias	.25
67	*Raul Casanova*	1.00
68	Matt Drews	.25
69	Jimmy Haynes	.25
70	Jimmy Hurst	.25
71	C.J. Nitkowski	.25
72	*Tommy Davis*	.50
73	*Bartolo Colon*	10.00
74	*Chris Carpenter*	3.00
75	Trey Beamon	.25
76	Bryan Rekar	.25
77	James Baldwin	.25
78	Marc Valdes	.25
79	*Tom Fordham*	.35
80	Marc Newfield	.25
81	Angel Martinez	.25
82	Brian Hunter	.25
83	Jose Herrera	.25
84	*Glenn Dishman*	.35
85	*Jacob Cruz*	1.50
86	Paul Shuey	.25
87	*Scott Rolen*	40.00
88	Doug Million	.25
89	Desi Relaford	.25
90	Michael Tucker	.35
Mirror Image:		.50
1	*Ben Davis*, Ivan Rodriguez	5.00
2	*Mark Redman*, Manny Ramirez	2.00
3	*Reggie Taylor*, Deion Sanders	1.50
4	Ryan Jaroncyk, Shawn Green	1.00
5	Juan LeBron, Juan Gonzalez	1.00
6	Toby McKnight, Craig Biggio	.50
7	*Michael Barrett*, Travis Fryman	10.00
8	Corey Jenkins, Mo Vaughn	1.00
9	Ruben Rivera, Frank Thomas	2.00
10	Curtis Goodwin, Kenny Lofton	1.50
11	Brian Hunter, Tony Gwynn	1.00
12	Todd Greene, Ken Griffey Jr.	5.00
13	Karim Garcia, Matt Williams	1.50
14	Billy Wagner, Randy Johnson	1.00
15	Pat Watkins, Jeff Bagwell	1.50

1995 Bowman's Best Refractors

The large volume of silver foil in the background of the red and blue subsets in '95 Best make the Refractor technology much easier to see than in best issues.

The chase cards, found one per six packs on average, also have a small "REFRACTOR" printed near the lower-left corner on back. The 15-card Mirror Image subset was not paralleled in Refractor technology, but in a process Topps calls "diffraction-foil" which creates a strong vertical-stripe rainbow effect in the background. Cards #72 (Carlos Perez) and 84 (Orlando Miller) can be found both with and without the "REFRACTOR" notice on back; neither version commands a premium.

	MT
Complete Set (195):	1900.
Common Player:	1.00
Superstars:	1.5-3X
Stars:	2-4X

(See 1995 Bowman's Best for checklist and base card values.)

1995 Bowman's Best Refractors - Jumbo

These super-size versions of Bowman's Best Refractors were produced exclusively for inclusion as a one-per-box insert in retail boxes of the product distributed by ANCO to large retail chains. The 4-1/4" x 5-3/4" cards are identical in all ways except size to the regular refractors. The jumbo inserts were not produced in equal quantities, with the most popular players being printed in greater numbers.

		MT
Complete Set (10):		150.00
Common Player:		6.00
10	Cal Ripken Jr.	25.00
15	Greg Maddux	15.00
21	Tony Gwynn	15.00
35	Sammy Sosa	15.00
36	Mike Piazza	20.00
42	Mo Vaughn	7.50
49	Ken Griffey Jr.	30.00
50	Albert Belle	10.00
65	Frank Thomas	15.00
83	Hideo Nomo	6.00

1996 Bowman

In a "Guaranteed Value Program," Topps stated it would pay $100 for this set in 1999, if collectors mail in a request form (one per three packs), a $5 fee and the complete set in numerical order (only one per person). Every set redeemed was destroyed. The 385-card set has 110 veteran stars and 275 prospects. Backs of the prospects' cards provide a detailed scouting report. A "1st Bowman Card" gold-foil stamped logo was included on the card front for 156 players making their first appearance in a Bowman set. Insert sets include Bowman's Best Previews (along with Refractor and Atomic Refractor versions), a 1952 Mickey Mantle Bowman reprint (1 in 48 packs) and Minor League Player of the Year candidates. A 385-card parallel version of the entire base set was also produced on 18-point foilboard; seeded one per pack.

		MT
Complete Set (385):		125.00
Common Player:		.15
Foils:		1x to 2x
Pack (11):		4.00
Wax Box (24):		90.00
1	Cal Ripken Jr.	3.00
2	Ray Durham	.15
3	Ivan Rodriguez	1.50
4	Fred McGriff	.25
5	Hideo Nomo	.75
6	Troy Percival	.15
7	Moises Alou	.15
8	Mike Stanley	.15
9	Jay Buhner	.25
10	Shawn Green	.35
11	Ryan Klesko	.40
12	Andres Galarraga	.25
13	Dean Palmer	.15
14	Jeff Conine	.15
15	Brian Hunter	.15
16	J.T. Snow	.15
17	Larry Walker	.60
18	Barry Larkin	.25
19	Alex Gonzalez	.15
20	Edgar Martinez	.15
21	Mo Vaughn	1.00
22	Mark McGwire	5.00
23	Jose Canseco	.50
24	Jack McDowell	.15
25	Dante Bichette	.25
26	Wade Boggs	.50
27	Mike Piazza	3.00
28	Ray Lankford	.15
29	Craig Biggio	.20
30	Rafael Palmeiro	.35
31	Ron Gant	.25
32	Javy Lopez	.25
33	Brian Jordan	.25
34	Paul O'Neill	.20
35	Mark Grace	.35
36	Matt Williams	.40
37	Pedro Martinez	1.50
38	Rickey Henderson	.25
39	Bobby Bonilla	.20
40	Todd Hollandsworth	.25
41	Jim Thome	.60
42	Gary Sheffield	.75
43	Tim Salmon	.30
44	Gregg Jefferies	.15
45	Roberto Alomar	1.25
45p	Roberto Alomar (unmarked promo card, fielding photo on front)	20.00
46	Carlos Baerga	.15
47	Mark Grudzielanek	.15
48	Randy Johnson	.50
49	Tino Martinez	.20
50	Robin Ventura	.20
51	Ryne Sandberg	1.00
52	Jay Bell	.20
53	Jason Schmidt	.15
54	Frank Thomas	1.50
55	Kenny Lofton	.75
56	Ariel Prieto	.15
57	David Cone	.25
58	Reggie Sanders	.15
59	Michael Tucker	.15
60	Vinny Castilla	.15
61	Lenny Dykstra	.15
62	Todd Hundley	.25
63	Brian McRae	.15
64	Dennis Eckersley	.15
65	Rondell White	.15
66	Eric Karros	.15
67	Greg Maddux	2.50
68	Kevin Appier	.15
69	Eddie Murray	.50
70	John Olerud	.20
71	Tony Gwynn	2.00
72	David Justice	.25
73	Ken Caminiti	.40
74	Terry Steinbach	.15
75	Alan Benes	.15
76	Chipper Jones	2.50
77	Jeff Bagwell	1.25
77p	Jeff Bagwell (unmarked promo card, name in gold)	15.00
78	Barry Bonds	1.00
79	Ken Griffey Jr.	4.00
80	Roger Cedeno	.15
81	Joe Carter	.15
82	Henry Rodriguez	.15
83	Jason Isringhausen	.15
84	Chuck Knoblauch	.25
85	Manny Ramirez	1.50
86	Tom Glavine	.25
87	Jeffrey Hammonds	.15
88	Paul Molitor	.50
89	Roger Clemens	1.50
90	Greg Vaughn	.15
91	Marty Cordova	.20
92	Albert Belle	1.00
93	Mike Mussina	.75
94	Garret Anderson	.15
95	Juan Gonzalez	1.25
96	John Valentin	.15
97	Jason Giambi	.25
98	Kirby Puckett	1.50
99	Jim Edmonds	.25
100	Cecil Fielder	.20
101	Mike Aldrete	.15
102	Marquis Grissom	.15
103	Derek Bell	.15
104	Raul Mondesi	.40
105	Sammy Sosa	2.50
106	Travis Fryman	.15
107	Rico Brogna	.15
108	Will Clark	.30
109	Bernie Williams	.75
110	Brady Anderson	.20
111	Torii Hunter	.15
112	Derek Jeter	2.50
113	*Mike Kusiewicz*	.15
114	Scott Rolen	1.00
115	Ramon Castro	.15
116	*Jose Guillen*	1.00
117	*Wade Walker*	.40
118	Shawn Senior	.15
119	*Onan Masaoka*	.40
120	*Marlon Anderson*	1.00
121	*Katsuhiro Maeda*	.50
122	*Garrett Stephenson*	2.00
123	Butch Huskey	.15
124	*D'Angelo Jimenez*	1.00
125	*Tony Mounce*	.25
126	Jay Canizaro	.15
127	Juan Melo	.20
128	Steve Gibralter	.15
129	Freddy Garcia	.15
130	Julio Santana	.15
131	Richard Hidalgo	.25
132	Jermaine Dye	.20
133	Willie Adams	.15
134	Everett Stull	.15
135	Ramon Morel	.15
136	Chan Ho Park	.20
137	Jamey Wright	.15
138	*Luis Garcia*	.25
139	Dan Serafini	.15
140	*Ryan Dempster*	4.00
141	Tate Seefried	.15
142	Jimmy Hurst	.15
143	Travis Miller	.15
144	Curtis Goodwin	.15
145	*Rocky Coppinger*	.50
146	Enrique Wilson	.40
147	Jaime Bluma	.15
148	Andrew Vessel	.15
149	Damian Moss	.20
150	*Shawn Gallagher*	.50
151	Pat Watkins	.15
152	Jose Paniagua	.15
153	Danny Graves	.15
154	*Bryon Gainey*	.25
155	Steve Soderstrom	.15
156	*Cliff Brumbaugh*	.25
157	*Eugene Kingsale*	.50
158	Lou Collier	.15
159	Todd Walker	.25
160	*Kris Detmers*	.50
161	*Josh Booty*	.35
162	*Greg Whiteman*	.25
163	Damian Jackson	.15
164	Tony Clark	.25
165	Jeff D'Amico	.25
166	Johnny Damon	.25
167	Rafael Orellano	.15
168	Ruben Rivera	.15
169	Alex Ochoa	.20
170	Jay Powell	.15
171	Tom Evans	.15
172	Ron Villone	.15
173	Shawn Estes	.15
174	John Wasdin	.15
175	Bill Simas	.15
176	Kevin Brown	.25
177	Shannon Stewart	.15
178	Todd Greene	.15
179	Bob Wolcott	.15
180	Chris Snopek	.15
181	Nomar Garciaparra	3.00
182	*Cameron Smith*	.25
183	Matt Drews	.15
184	Jimmy Haynes	.15
185	Chris Carpenter	.25
186	Desi Relaford	.15
187	Ben Grieve	.75
188	Mike Bell	.15
189	*Luis Castillo*	2.50
190	Ugueth Urbina	.15
191	Paul Wilson	.15
191p	Paul Wilson (unmarked promo card, name in gold)	3.00
192	Andruw Jones	2.00
193	Wayne Gomes	.15
194	*Craig Counsell*	.40
195	Jim Cole	.15
196	Brooks Kieshnick	.15
197	Trey Beamon	.15
198	*Marino Santana*	.30
199	Bob Abreu	.50
200	Calvin Reese	.15
201	Dante Powell	.20
202	George Arias	.15
202p	George Arias (unmarked promo card, name in gold)	3.00

203 *Jorge Velandia* .25
204 *George Lombard* 2.50
205 *Byron Browne* .30
206 John Frascatore .15
207 Terry Adams .15
208 *Wilson Delgado* .40
209 Billy McMillon .15
210 Jeff Abbott .20
211 Trot Nixon .25
212 Amaury Telemaco .15
213 Scott Sullivan .15
214 Justin Thompson .15
215 Decomba Conner .15
216 Ryan McGuire .15
217 *Matt Luke* .40
218 Doug Million .15
219 *Jason Dickson* .50
220 *Ramon Hernandez* 1.50
221 *Mark Bellhorn* .75
222 *Eric Ludwick* .25
223 *Luke Wilcox* .30
224 *Marty Malloy* .30
225 *Gary Coffee* .30
226 *Wendell Magee* .50
227 *Brett Tomko* .75
228 Derek Lowe .15
229 *Jose Rosado* .75
230 *Steve Bourgeois* .30
231 *Neil Weber* .30
232 Jeff Ware .15
233 Edwin Diaz .20
234 Greg Norton .15
235 Aaron Boone .25
236 Jeff Suppan .15
237 Bret Wagner .15
238 Elieser Marrero .15
239 Will Cunnane .15
240 *Brian Barkley* .40
241 Jay Payton .75
242 Marcus Jensen .15
243 Ryan Nye .15
244 Chad Mottola .15
245 *Scott McClain* .40
246 *Jesse Ibarra* .40
247 *Mike Darr* 1.00
248 *Bobby Estalella* 2.00
249 Michael Barrett .25
250 *Jamie Lopiccolo* .25
251 *Shane Spencer* 3.00
252 *Ben Petrick* 4.00
253 *Jason Bell* .40
254 *Arnold Gooch* .40
255 T.J. Mathews .15
256 Jason Ryan .15
257 *Pat Cline* .40
258 *Rafael Carmona* .40
259 *Carl Pavano* 2.00
260 Ben Davis .25
261 *Matt Lawton* 1.50
262 *Kevin Sefcik* .30
263 *Chris Fussell* .50
264 *Mike Cameron* 2.50
265 *Marty Janzen* .30
266 *Livan Hernandez* 1.50
267 *Raul Ibanez* .50
268 Juan Encarnacion .25
269 *David Yocum* .40
270 *Jonathan Johnson* .40
271 Reggie Taylor .15
272 *Danny Buxbaum* .30
273 Jacob Cruz .20
274 *Bobby Morris* .40
275 *Andy Fox* .40
276 Greg Keagle .15
277 Charles Peterson .15
278 Derrek Lee .35
279 *Bryant Nelson* .40
280 Antone Williamson .15
281 Scott Elarton .15
282 *Shad Williams* .40
283 *Rich Hunter* .40
284 Chris Sheff .15
285 Derrick Gibson .25
286 Felix Rodriguez .15
287 *Brian Banks* .40
288 Jason McDonald .15
289 *Glendon Rusch* 1.50
290 Gary Rath .15
291 Peter Munro .15
292 Tom Fordham .15
293 Jason Kendall .25
294 Russ Johnson .15
295 *Joe Long* .25
296 *Robert Smith* .50
297 *Jarrod Washburn* .75
298 *Dave Coggin* .30
299 *Jeff Yoder* .30
300 *Jed Hansen* .40
301 *Matt Morris* .75
302 *Josh Bishop* .30
303 Dustin Hermanson .15
304 Mike Gulan .15
305 Felipe Crespo .15
306 Quinton McCracken .15
307 *Jim Bonnici* .30
308 Sal Fasano .15
309 *Gabe Alvarez* .40
310 *Heath Murray* .30
311 *Jose Valentin* .50
312 Bartolo Colon .40
313 Olmedo Saenz .15
314 *Norm Hutchins* .50
315 *Chris Holt* .50
316 *David Doster* .40
317 Robert Person .15
318 *Donne Wall* .40
319 *Adam Riggs* .40
320 Homer Bush .15
321 *Brad Rigby* .40
322 *Lou Merloni* .75
323 Neifi Perez .15
324 Chris Cumberland .15
325 *Alvie Shepherd* .40
326 *Jarrod Patterson* .40
327 *Ray Ricken* .40
328 *Danny Klassen* .60
329 *David Miller* .30
330 *Chad Alexander* .60
331 Matt Beaumont .15
332 Damon Hollins .15
333 Todd Dunn .15
334 *Mike Sweeney* 6.00
335 Richie Sexson .50
336 Billy Wagner .25
337 *Ron Wright* .50
338 Paul Konerko .40
339 *Tommy Phelps* .30
340 Karim Garcia .25
341 *Mike Grace* .25
342 *Russell Branyan* 6.00
343 *Randy Winn* .30
344 *A.J. Pierzynski* .40
345 *Mike Busby* .40
346 *Matt Beech* .40
347 *Jose Cepeda* .40
348 Brian Stephenson .15
349 Rey Ordonez .75
350 *Rich Aurilia* .50
351 *Edgard Velazquez* .75
352 Raul Casanova .15
353 *Carlos Guillen* 2.00
354 *Bruce Aven* .40
355 *Ryan Jones* .40
356 *Derek Aucoin* .40
357 *Brian Rose* 1.00
358 *Richard Almanzar* .40
359 *Fletcher Bates* .40
360 *Russ Ortiz* 1.50
361 *Wilton Guerrero* .75
362 *Geoff Jenkins* 6.00
363 Pete Janicki .15
364 Yamil Benitez .15
365 Aaron Holbert .15
366 Tim Belk .15
367 Terrell Wade .15
368 Terrence Long .15
369 Brad Fullmer .25
370 Matt Wagner .15
371 Craig Wilson .15
372 Mark Loretta .15
373 Eric Owens .15
374 Vladimir Guerrero 2.00
375 Tommy Davis .15
376 Donnie Sadler .15
377 Edgar Renteria .60
378 Todd Helton 3.00
379 *Ralph Milliard* .40
380 *Darin Blood* .40
381 Shayne Bennett .15
382 Mark Redman .15
383 Felix Martinez .15
384 *Sean Watkins* .40
385 Oscar Henriquez .15

1996 Bowman Minor League Player of the Year

Fifteen prospects who were candidates for Minor League Player of the Year are featured in this 1996 Bowman baseball insert set. Cards were seeded one per every 12 packs.

		MT
Complete Set (15):		40.00
Common Player:		1.00
1	Andruw Jones	10.00
2	Derrick Gibson	3.00
3	Bob Abreu	1.00
4	Todd Walker	4.00
5	Jamey Wright	1.50
6	Wes Helms	4.00
7	Karim Garcia	4.00
8	Bartolo Colon	1.00
9	Alex Ochoa	1.00
10	Mike Sweeney	1.00
11	Ruben Rivera	1.50
12	Gabe Alvarez	1.50
13	Billy Wagner	3.00
14	Vladimir Guerrero	12.00
15	Edgard Velazquez	5.00

1996 Bowman 1952 Mickey Mantle Reprints

Reprints of Mickey Mantle's 1952 Bowman baseball card were created for insertion in Bowman and Bowman's Best products for 1996. The 2-1/2" x 3-1/2" card can be found in regular (gold seal on front), Finest, Finest Refractor and Atomic Refractor versions.

		MT
Complete Set (4):		60.00
Common Player:		10.00
20	Mickey Mantle (reprint)	10.00
20	Mickey Mantle (Finest)	10.00
20	Mickey Mantle (Refractor)	20.00
20	Mickey Mantle (Atomic Refractor)	30.00

1996 Bowman's Best Preview

These cards use Topps' Finest technology. The cards were seeded one per every 12 packs of 1996 Bowman baseball. Fifteen veterans and 15 prospects are featured in the set.

		MT
Complete Set (30):		100.00
Common Player:		1.50
Refractors:		2-3X
Atomic Refractors:		4-6X
1	Chipper Jones	10.00
2	Alan Benes	1.00
3	Brooks Kieshnick	1.00
4	Barry Bonds	5.00
5	Rey Ordonez	2.00
6	Tim Salmon	1.50
7	Mike Piazza	10.00
8	Billy Wagner	2.00
9	Andruw Jones	6.00
10	Tony Gwynn	8.00
11	Paul Wilson	1.00
12	Calvin Reese	1.00
13	Frank Thomas	6.00
14	Greg Maddux	9.00
15	Derek Jeter	10.00
16	Jeff Bagwell	8.00
17	Barry Larkin	1.50
18	Todd Greene	1.50
19	Ruben Rivera	1.00
20	Richard Hidalgo	1.50
21	Larry Walker	3.00
22	Carlos Baerga	1.00
23	Derrick Gibson	1.50
24	Richie Sexson	1.50
25	Mo Vaughn	4.00
26	Hideo Nomo	2.00
27	Nomar Garciaparra	12.00
28	Cal Ripken Jr.	12.00
29	Karim Garcia	1.50
30	Ken Griffey Jr.	18.00

1996 Bowman's Best

Bowman's Best returns in its traditional format of 180 cards: 90 established stars and 90 up-and-coming prospects and rookies. Three types of insert sets are found in Bowman's Best - Mirror Image, Bowman's Best Cuts and the 1952 Bowman Mickey Mantle reprints. There are also parallel sets of Refractors and Atomic Refractors randomly seeded in packs. Refractors are found on average of one per 12 packs; Atomic Refractors are seeded one per 48 packs. Mirror Image Refractors are found one per 96 packs, while Mirror Image Atomic Refractors are seeded one per 192 packs. in every 48th pack, while Bowman's Best Cuts Atomic Refractors are in every 96th pack. Refractor versions of the Mantle reprint are seeded one per every 96 packs; Atomic Refractor Mantle reprints are seeded in every 192nd pack.

		MT
Complete Set (180):		60.00
Common Player:		.25
1952 Mickey Mantle:		6.00
1952 Mantle Refractor:		15.00
1952 Mantle Atomic Refractor:		30.00
Pack (6):		5.00
Wax Box (24):		100.00
1	Hideo Nomo	.50
2	Edgar Martinez	.25
3	Cal Ripken Jr.	4.00
4	Wade Boggs	.75
5	Cecil Fielder	.25
6	Albert Belle	1.00
7	Chipper Jones	2.50
8	Ryne Sandberg	1.25
9	Tim Salmon	.40
10	Barry Bonds	1.25
11	Ken Caminiti	.25
12	Ron Gant	.25
13	Frank Thomas	1.50
14	Dante Bichette	.40
15	Jason Kendall	.35
16	Mo Vaughn	1.00
17	Rey Ordonez	.25
18	Henry Rodriguez	.25
19	Ryan Klesko	.40
20	Jeff Bagwell	1.25
21	Randy Johnson	1.25
22	Jim Edmonds	.40
23	Kenny Lofton	.75
24	Andy Pettitte	.50
25	Brady Anderson	.35
26	Mike Piazza	3.00
27	Greg Vaughn	.40
28	Joe Carter	.25
29	Jason Giambi	.75
30	Ivan Rodriguez	1.25
31	Jeff Conine	.25
32	Rafael Palmeiro	.75
33	Roger Clemens	2.00
34	Chuck Knoblauch	.40
35	Reggie Sanders	.25
36	Andres Galarraga	.75
37	Paul O'Neill	.50
38	Tony Gwynn	2.00
39	Paul Wilson	.25
40	Garret Anderson	.25
41	David Justice	.50
42	Eddie Murray	.75
43	*Mike Grace*	.40
44	Marty Cordova	.25
45	Kevin Appier	.25
46	Raul Mondesi	.40
47	Jim Thome	.75
48	Sammy Sosa	3.00
49	Craig Biggio	.40
50	Marquis Grissom	.25
51	Alan Benes	.25
52	Manny Ramirez	1.50
53	Gary Sheffield	.75
54	Mike Mussina	1.00
55	Robin Ventura	.40
56	Johnny Damon	.25
57	Jose Canseco	.75
58	Juan Gonzalez	1.25
59	Tino Martinez	.40
60	Brian Hunter	.25
61	Fred McGriff	.50
62	Jay Buhner	.25
63	Carlos Delgado	1.00
64	Moises Alou	.25
65	Roberto Alomar	1.00
66	Barry Larkin	.50
67	Vinny Castilla	.25
68	Ray Durham	.25
69	Travis Fryman	.40
70	Jason Isringhausen	.25
71	Ken Griffey Jr.	5.00
72	John Smoltz	.25
73	Matt Williams	.50
74	Chan Ho Park	.25
75	Mark McGwire	5.00
76	Jeffrey Hammonds	.25
77	Will Clark	.50
78	Kirby Puckett	1.50
79	Derek Jeter	4.00
80	Derek Bell	.25
81	Eric Karros	.25
82	Lenny Dykstra	.25
83	Larry Walker	.75
84	Mark Grudzielanek	.25
85	Greg Maddux	2.50
86	Carlos Baerga	.25
87	Paul Molitor	.50
88	John Valentin	.25
89	Mark Grace	.40
90	Ray Lankford	.25
91	Andruw Jones	3.00
92	Nomar Garciaparra	3.00
93	Alex Ochoa	.25
94	Derrick Gibson	.25
95	Jeff D'Amico	.40
96	Ruben Rivera	.25
97	Vladimir Guerrero	4.00
98	Calvin Reese	.25
99	Richard Hidalgo	.40
100	Bartolo Colon	.40
101	Karim Garcia	.25
102	Ben Davis	.25
103	Jay Powell	.25
104	Chris Snopek	.25
105	*Glendon Rusch*	1.50
106	Enrique Wilson	.25
107	*Antonio Alfonseca*	1.00
108	*Wilton Guerrero*	1.00
109	*Jose Guillen*	2.00
110	*Miguel Mejia*	.40
111	Jay Payton	.40
112	Scott Elarton	.40
113	Brooks Kieschnick	.25
114	Dustin Hermanson	.25
115	Roger Cedeno	.25
116	Matt Wagner	.25
117	Lee Daniels	.25
118	Ben Grieve	.75
119	Ugueth Urbina	.25
120	Danny Graves	.25
121	*Dan Donato*	.40
122	*Matt Ruebel*	.25
123	*Mark Sievert*	.25
124	Chris Stynes	.25
125	Jeff Abbott	.25
126	*Rocky Coppinger*	.50
127	Jermaine Dye	.25
128	Todd Greene	.15
129	Chris Carpenter	.25
130	Edgar Renteria	.40
131	Matt Drews	.25
132	*Edgard Velazquez*	1.50
133	Casey Whitten	.25
134	*Ryan Jones*	.50
135	Todd Walker	.20
136	*Geoff Jenkins*	6.00
137	*Matt Morris*	1.00
138	Richie Sexson	.40
139	*Todd Dunwoody*	1.00
140	*Gabe Alvarez*	1.00
141	J.J. Johnson	.25
142	Shannon Stewart	.25
143	Brad Fullmer	.40
144	Julio Santana	.25
145	Scott Rolen	2.00
146	Amaury Telemaco	.25
147	Trey Beamon	.25
148	Billy Wagner	.20
149	Todd Hollandsworth	.25
150	Doug Million	.25
151	*Jose Valentin*	1.00
152	*Wes Helms*	1.50
153	Jeff Suppan	.25
154	*Luis Castillo*	3.00
155	Bob Abreu	.75
156	Paul Konerko	.40
157	Jamey Wright	.25
158	Eddie Pearson	.25
159	Jimmy Haynes	.25
160	Derrek Lee	.15
161	Damian Moss	.15
162	*Carlos Guillen*	2.00
163	*Chris Fussell*	.75
164	*Mike Sweeney*	8.00
165	Donnie Sadler	.15
166	Desi Relaford	.15
167	Steve Gibralter	.15
168	Neifi Perez	.25
169	Antone Williamson	.15
170	*Marty Janzen*	.25
171	Todd Helton	6.00
172	*Raul Ibanez*	.75
173	Bill Selby	.25
174	*Shane Monahan*	.50
175	*Robin Jennings*	.25
176	*Bobby Chouinard*	.25
177	Einar Diaz	.25
178	Jason Thompson	.15
179	*Rafael Medina*	.50
180	Kevin Orie	.15

1996 Bowman's Best Refractors

Parallel sets of 180 Refractors and Atomic Refractors were randomly seeded in Bowman's Best packs at the average rate of per 12 packs for Refrqctors, with Atomic Refractors seeded one per 48 packs. Mirror Image Refractors are found one per 96 packs, while Mirror Image Atomic Refractors are seeded one per 192 packs.

	MT
Complete Refractor Set (180):	1500.
Common Refractor:	2.00
Refractors:	4-8X
Common Atomic Refractor:	6.00
Atomics:	6-12X

(See 1996 Bowman's Best for checklist and base card values.)

1996 Bowman's Best Cuts

Bowman's Best Cuts gave collectors the first die-cut chromium cards in a 15-card set of top stars. The cards were seeded one per 24 packs. Refractor versions are inserted on average of one per 48 packs; Atomic Refractor versions are found one per 96 packs.

		MT
Complete Set (15):		100.00
Common Player:		2.00
Refractors:		2-3X
Atomic Refractors:		4-6X
1	Ken Griffey Jr.	25.00
2	Jason Isringhausen	2.00
3	Derek Jeter	15.00
4	Andruw Jones	10.00
5	Chipper Jones	12.00
6	Ryan Klesko	2.50
7	Raul Mondesi	3.00
8	Hideo Nomo	4.00
9	Mike Piazza	15.00
10	Manny Ramirez	8.00
11	Cal Ripken Jr.	20.00
12	Ruben Rivera	2.00
13	Tim Salmon	3.00
14	Frank Thomas	10.00
15	Jim Thome	5.00

1996 Bowman's Best Mirror Image

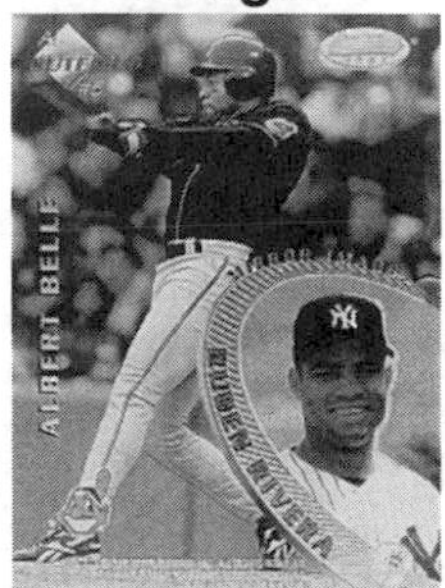

Mirror Image inserts feature four top players at 10 different positions, pairing an American League veteran and a prospect on one side and a National League veteran and prospect on the other. These cards are seeded one per every 48 packs. Mirror Image Refractors (one in every 96 packs) and Mirror Image Atomic Refractors (one in every 192 packs) were also produced.

		MT
Complete Set (10):		90.00
Common Player:		5.00
Refractors:		1.5x to 2x
Atomics:		2x to 4x
1	Jeff Bagwell, Todd Helton, Frank Thomas, Richie Sexson	15.00
2	Craig Biggio, Luis Castillo, Roberto Alomar, Desi Relaford	5.00
3	Chipper Jones, Scott Rolen, Wade Boggs, George Arias	12.50
4	Barry Larkin, Neifi Perez, Cal Ripken Jr., Mark Bellhorn	12.50
5	Larry Walker, Karim Garcia, Albert Belle, Ruben Rivera	5.00
6	Barry Bonds, Andruw Jones, Kenny Lofton, Donnie Sadler	9.00
7	Tony Gwynn, Vladimir Guerrero, Ken Griffey Jr., Ben Grieve	25.00
8	Mike Piazza, Ben Davis, Ivan Rodriguez, Jose Valentin	12.00
9	Greg Maddux, Jamey Wright, Mike Mussina, Bartolo Colon	10.00
10	Tom Glavine, Billy Wagner, Randy Johnson, Jarrod Washburn	5.00

1997 Bowman Pre-production

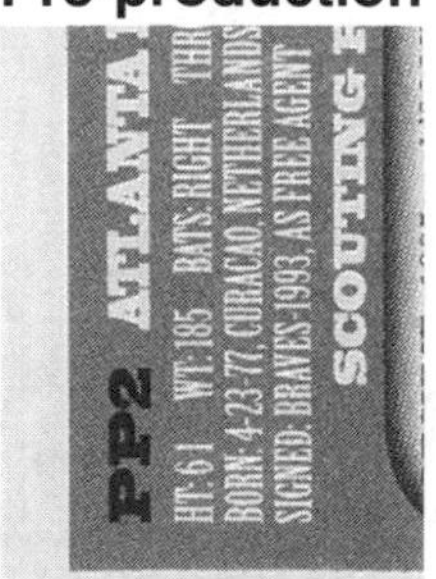

The format for 1997 Bowman's base set was previewed in this sample issue distributed to card dealers and the hobby press. The samples are virtually identical to the issued versions of the same players' cards, except they carry a "PP" prefix to the number on back.

		MT
Complete Set (4):		16.00
Common Player:		3.00
PP1	Jose Cruz, Jr.	3.00
PP2	Andruw Jones	5.00
PP3	Derek Jeter	7.50
PP4	Sammy Sosa	8.00

1997 Bowman

The 1997 Bowman set consists of 440 base cards, an increase of 55 cards from the '96 set. Fronts have a player photo within a red or blue frame with black borders. Backs feature another color photo, along with 1996 statistics broken down by opponent. Players making their first appearance in a Bowman set have a "1st Bowman Card" designation on the card. Prospects' cards have red foil on front; veterans have blue. Inserts include International parallels, Certified Autographs, Scout's Honor Roll and Bowman's Best Previews. Cards were sold in 10-card packs with a suggested retail price of $2.50. Topps offered collectors a $125 guarantee on the value of the set through the year 2000.

		MT
Complete Set (440):		100.00
Complete Series 1 Set (221):		50.00
Complete Series 2 Set (219):		50.00
Common Player:		.15
Series 1 Pack (10):		3.00
Series 1 Wax Box (24):		60.00
Series 2 Pack (10):		3.00
Series 2 Wax Box (24):		55.00
1	Derek Jeter	2.00
2	Edgar Renteria	.15
3	Chipper Jones	1.50
4	Hideo Nomo	.40
5	Tim Salmon	.25
6	Jason Giambi	.40
7	Robin Ventura	.25
8	Tony Clark	.25
9	Barry Larkin	.25
10	Paul Molitor	.50
11	Bernard Gilkey	.15
12	Jack McDowell	.15
13	Andy Benes	.15
14	Ryan Klesko	.25
15	Mark McGwire	3.00
16	Ken Griffey Jr.	3.00
17	Robb Nen	.15
18	Cal Ripken Jr.	2.50
19	John Valentin	.15
20	Ricky Bottalico	.15
21	Mike Lansing	.15
22	Ryne Sandberg	.75
23	Carlos Delgado	.75
24	Craig Biggio	.30
25	Eric Karros	.25
26	Kevin Appier	.15
27	Mariano Rivera	.25
28	Vinny Castilla	.15
29	Juan Gonzalez	1.00
30	Al Martin	.15
31	Jeff Cirillo	.15
32	Eddie Murray	.50
33	Ray Lankford	.15
34	Manny Ramirez	1.00
35	Roberto Alomar	.75
36	Will Clark	.25
37	Chuck Knoblauch	.25
38	Harold Baines	.15
39	Trevor Hoffman	.15
40	Edgar Martinez	.15
41	Geronimo Berroa	.15
42	Rey Ordonez	.25
43	Mike Stanley	.15
44	Mike Mussina	.75
45	Kevin Brown	.25
46	Dennis Eckersley	.15
47	Henry Rodriguez	.15
48	Tino Martinez	.25
49	Eric Young	.15
50	Bret Boone	.15
51	Raul Mondesi	.25
52	Sammy Sosa	2.00
53	John Smoltz	.15
54	Billy Wagner	.15
55	Jeff D'Amico	.25
56	Ken Caminiti	.25
57	Jason Kendall	.25
58	Wade Boggs	.50
59	Andres Galarraga	.40
60	Jeff Brantley	.15
61	Mel Rojas	.15
62	Brian Hunter	.15
63	Bobby Bonilla	.15
64	Roger Clemens	1.50
65	Jeff Kent	.25
66	Matt Williams	.40
67	Albert Belle	.50
68	Jeff King	.15
69	John Wetteland	.15
70	Deion Sanders	.25
71	*Bubba Trammell*	.50
72	*Felix Heredia*	.50
73	*Billy Koch*	1.50
74	*Sidney Ponson*	.75
75	*Ricky Ledee*	1.00
76	Brett Tomko	.15
77	*Braden Looper*	.50
78	Damian Jackson	.15
79	Jason Dickson	.25
80	*Chad Green*	.50
81	*R.A. Dickey*	.40
82	Jeff Liefer	.15
83	Matt Wagner	.15
84	Richard Hidalgo	.40
85	Adam Riggs	.15
86	Robert Smith	.15
87	*Chad Hermansen*	1.00
88	Felix Martinez	.15
89	J.J. Johnson	.15
90	Todd Dunwoody	.25
91	Katsuhiro Maeda	.15
92	Darin Erstad	.75
93	Elieser Marrero	.15
94	Bartolo Colon	.15
95	Chris Fussell	.20
96	Ugueth Urbina	.15
97	*Josh Paul*	.50
98	Jaime Bluma	.15
99	*Seth Greisinger*	.40
100	*Jose Cruz*	2.00
101	Todd Dunn	.15
102	*Joe Young*	.40
103	Jonathan Johnson	.15
104	*Justin Towle*	.50
105	Brian Rose	.20
106	Jose Guillen	.25
107	Andruw Jones	.75
108	*Mark Kotsay*	1.00
109	Wilton Guerrero	.15
110	Jacob Cruz	.15
111	Mike Sweeney	.25
112	Julio Mosquera	.15
113	Matt Morris	.25
114	Wendell Magee	.15
115	John Thomson	.15
116	*Javier Valentin*	.25
117	Tom Fordham	.15
118	Ruben Rivera	.15
119	*Mike Drumright*	.25
120	Chris Holt	.15
121	*Sean Maloney*	.40
122	Michael Barrett	.15
123	*Tony Saunders*	.40
124	Kevin Brown	.25
125	Richard Almanzar	.15
126	Mark Redman	.15
127	*Anthony Sanders*	.50
128	Jeff Abbott	.15
129	Eugene Kingsale	.15
130	Paul Konerko	.40
131	*Randall Simon*	.50
132	Andy Larkin	.15
133	Rafael Medina	.25
134	Mendy Lopez	.15
135	Freddy Garcia	.15
136	Karim Garcia	.25
137	*Larry Rodriguez*	.50
138	Carlos Guillen	.15
139	Aaron Boone	.15
140	Donnie Sadler	.15
141	Brooks Kieschnick	.15
142	Scott Spiezio	.15
143	Everett Stull	.15
144	Enrique Wilson	.15
145	*Milton Bradley*	3.00
146	Kevin Orie	.20
147	Derek Wallace	.15
148	Russ Johnson	.15
149	*Joe Lagarde*	.40
150	Luis Castillo	.40
151	Jay Payton	.25
152	Joe Long	.15
153	Livan Hernandez	.25
154	*Vladimir Nunez*	.50
155	Not issued	.15
156a	George Arias	.15
156b	Calvin Reese (Should be #155)	.15
157	Homer Bush	.15
158	Not issued	.15
159a	*Eric Milton*	1.50
159b	Chris Carpenter (Should be #158)	.15
160	Richie Sexson	.25
161	Carl Pavano	.25
162	*Chris Gissell*	.50
163	Mac Suzuki	.15
164	Pat Cline	.15
165	Ron Wright	.20
166	Dante Powell	.15
167	Mark Bellhorn	.15
168	George Lombard	.25
169	*Pee Wee Lopez*	.40
170	*Paul Wilder*	.50
171	Brad Fullmer	.15
172	*Willie Martinez*	.75
173	*Dario Veras*	.40
174	Dave Coggin	.15
175	*Kris Benson*	3.00
176	Torii Hunter	.15
177	*D.T. Cromer*	.40
178	*Nelson Figueroa*	.50
179	*Hiram Bocachica*	.50
180	Shane Monahan	.15
181	*Jimmy Anderson*	.75
182	Juan Melo	.15
183	*Pablo Ortega*	.50
184	*Calvin Pickering*	.50
185	Reggie Taylor	.15
186	*Jeff Farnsworth*	.40
187	Terrence Long	.15
188	Geoff Jenkins	.40
189	*Steve Rain*	.40
190	*Nerio Rodriguez*	.75
191	Derrick Gibson	.15
192	Darin Blood	.15
193	Ben Davis	.15
194	*Adrian Beltre*	4.00
195	*Damian Sapp*	.50
196	*Kerry Wood*	6.00
197	*Nate Rolison*	.50
198	*Fernando Tatis*	2.50
199	*Brad Penny*	2.50
200	*Jake Westbrook*	.50
201	Edwin Diaz	.15
202	*Joe Fontenot*	.50
203	*Matt Halloran*	.50
204	*Blake Stein*	.40
205	Onan Masaoka	.15
206	Ben Petrick	.15
207	*Matt Clement*	1.00

208 Todd Greene .15
209 Ray Ricken .15
210 *Eric Chavez* 4.00
211 Edgard Velazquez .15
212 *Bruce Chen* 1.00
213 *Danny Patterson* .40
214 Jeff Yoder .15
215 *Luis Ordaz* .40
216 Chris Widger .15
217 Jason Brester .15
218 Carlton Loewer .15
219 *Chris Reitsma* .50
220 Neifi Perez .15
221 *Hideki Irabu* .50
222 Ellis Burks .15
223 Pedro Martinez 1.00
224 Kenny Lofton .50
225 Randy Johnson .75
226 Terry Steinbach .15
227 Bernie Williams .50
228 Dean Palmer .15
229 Alan Benes .15
230 Marquis Grissom .15
231 Gary Sheffield .40
232 Curt Schilling .25
233 Reggie Sanders .15
234 Bobby Higginson .15
235 Moises Alou .25
236 Tom Glavine .30
237 Mark Grace .30
238 Ramon Martinez .15
239 Rafael Palmeiro .30
240 John Olerud .25
241 Dante Bichette .25
242 Greg Vaughn .15
243 Jeff Bagwell .75
244 Barry Bonds 1.00
245 Pat Hentgen .15
246 Jim Thome .50
247 Jermaine Allensworth .15
248 Andy Pettitte .40
249 Jay Bell .15
250 John Jaha .15
251 Jim Edmonds .30
252 Ron Gant .25
253 David Cone .25
254 Jose Canseco .40
255 Jay Buhner .20
256 Greg Maddux 1.50
257 Brian McRae .15
258 Lance Johnson .15
259 Travis Fryman .25
260 Paul O'Neill .30
261 Ivan Rodriguez .75
262 Gregg Jefferies .15
263 Fred McGriff .25
264 Derek Bell .15
265 Jeff Conine .15
266 Mike Piazza 2.00
267 Mark Grudzielanek .15
268 Brady Anderson .25
269 Marty Cordova .15
270 Ray Durham .15
271 Joe Carter .15
272 Brian Jordan .15
273 David Justice .40
274 Tony Gwynn 1.00
275 Larry Walker .40
276 Cecil Fielder .20
277 Mo Vaughn .50
278 Alex Fernandez .15
279 Michael Tucker .15
280 Jose Valentin .15
281 Sandy Alomar .15
282 Todd Hollandsworth .15
283 Rico Brogna .15
284 Rusty Greer .15
285 Roberto Hernandez .15
286 Hal Morris .15
287 Johnny Damon .15
288 Todd Hundley .25
289 Rondell White .25
290 Frank Thomas 1.00
291 *Don Denbow* .25
292 Derrek Lee .15
293 Todd Walker .15
294 Scott Rolen .75
295 Wes Helms .20
296 Bob Abreu .15
297 *John Patterson* .50
298 *Alex Gonzalez* .75
299 *Grant Roberts* .75
300 Jeff Suppan .15
301 Luke Wilcox .15
302 Marlon Anderson .15
303 Ray Brown .15
304 *Mike Caruso* .75
305 *Sam Marsonek* .40
306 *Brady Raggio* .40
307 *Kevin McGlinchy* .50
308 *Roy Halladay* .50
309 *Jeremi Gonzalez* .50
310 *Aramis Ramirez* 2.00
311 *Dermal Brown* 2.00
312 Justin Thompson .15
313 *Jay Tessmer* .20
314 Mike Johnson .15
315 Danny Clyburn .15
316 Bruce Aven .15
317 *Keith Foulke* .40
318 *Jimmy Osting* .40
319 *Valerio DeLosSantos* .40
320 Shannon Stewart .15
321 Willie Adams .15
322 Larry Barnes .15
323 Mark Johnson .15
324 *Chris Stowers* .40
325 Brandon Reed .15
326 Randy Winn .15
327 Steven Chavez .15
328 Nomar Garciaparra 2.00
329 *Jacque Jones* 2.00
330 Chris Clemons .15
331 Todd Helton 1.00
332 *Ryan Brannan* .40
333 *Alex Sanchez* .50
334 Arnold Gooch .15
335 Russell Branyan .40
336 Daryle Ward 1.50
337 *John LeRoy* .40
338 Steve Cox .15
339 Kevin Witt .20
340 Norm Hutchins .15
341 Gabby Martinez .15
342 Kris Detmers .15
343 *Mike Villano* .50
344 Preston Wilson .15
345 *Jim Manias* .40
346 *Deivi Cruz* 1.00
347 *Donzell McDonald* .50
348 *Rod Myers* .40
349 *Shawn Chacon* .40
350 *Elvin Hernandez* .40
351 *Orlando Cabrera* .75
352 Brian Banks .15
353 Robbie Bell .25
354 Brad Rigby .15
355 Scott Elarton .15
356 *Kevin Sweeney* .75
357 Steve Soderstrom .15
358 Ryan Nye .15
359 *Marlon Allen* .40
360 *Donny Leon* .50
361 *Garrett Neubart* .40
362 *Abraham Nunez* .75
363 *Adam Eaton* 1.50
364 *Octavio Dotel* 1.00
365 *Dean Crow* .40
366 *Jason Baker* .40
367 Sean Casey 2.00
368 *Joe Lawrence* 1.00
369 *Adam Johnson* .50
370 *Scott Schoeneweis* .75
371 Gerald Witasick, Jr. .15
372 *Ronnie Belliard* 1.00
373 Russ Ortiz .15
374 *Robert Stratton* 1.00
375 Bobby Estalella .40
376 *Corey Lee* .50
377 Carlos Beltran .40
378 Mike Cameron .25
379 *Scott Randall* .40
380 *Corey Erickson* .75
381 Jay Canizaro .15
382 *Kerry Robinson* .40
383 *Todd Noel* .50
384 *A.J. Zapp* .50
385 Jarrod Washburn .15
386 Ben Grieve .40
387 *Javier Vazquez* 1.00
388 Tony Graffanino .15
389 *Travis Lee* 1.00
390 DaRond Stovall .15
391 *Dennis Reyes* .50
392 Danny Buxbaum .15
393 *Marc Lewis* .50
394 *Kelvim Escobar* .50
395 Danny Klassen .25
396 *Ken Cloude* .50
397 Gabe Alvarez .15
398 *Jaret Wright* 1.00
399 Raul Casanova .15
400 *Clayton Brunner* .50
401 *Jason Marquis* 1.00
402 Marc Kroon .15
403 Jamey Wright .15
404 *Matt Snyder* .40
405 *Josh Garrett* .50
406 Juan Encarnacion .25
407 Heath Murray .15
408 *Brett Herbison* .50
409 *Brent Butler* .75
410 *Danny Peoples* .75
411 *Miguel Tejada* 5.00
412 Damian Moss .15
413 Jim Pittsley .15
414 Dmitri Young .15
415 Glendon Rusch .15
416 Vladimir Guerrero 1.00
417 *Cole Liniak* .75
418 Ramon Hernandez .15
419 *Cliff Politte* .50
420 *Mel Rosario* .50
421 *Jorge Carrion* .50
422 *John Barnes* .40
423 *Chris Stowe* .40
424 *Vernon Wells* 2.00
425 *Brett Caradonna* .75
426 *Scott Hodges* .50
427 *Jon Garland* 2.00
428 *Nathan Haynes* .50
429 *Geoff Goetz* .75
430 *Adam Kennedy* 2.00
431 *T.J. Tucker* .50
432 *Aaron Akin* .75
433 *Jayson Werth* .50
434 *Glenn Davis* .75
435 *Mark Mangum* .50
436 *Troy Cameron* .50
437 *J.J. Davis* 1.00
438 *Lance Berkman* 3.00
439 *Jason Standridge* .50
440 *Jason Dellaero* .50
441 *Hideki Irabu* .50

1997 Bowman Certified Autographs

Ninety players signed autographs for inclusion in Series 1 and 2 packs. Each autograph card features a gold-foil Certified Autograph stamp on front and can be found in one of three versions: Blue, 1:96 packs; black, 1:503 packs and gold, 1:1,509 packs. Derek Jeter's card can also be found in a green-ink autographed version, inserted one per 1,928 packs. Card numbers have a "CA" prefix.

	MT
Complete Set (90):	1000.
Complete Series 1 Set (46):	450.00
Complete Series 2 Set (44):	600.00
Common Blue:	5.00
Black:	1.5-2.5X
Gold:	4-6X
Derek Jeter Green:	1.5X

1 Jeff Abbott 5.00
2 Bob Abreu 20.00
3 Willie Adams 5.00
4 Brian Banks 5.00
5 Kris Benson 25.00
6 Darin Blood 5.00
7 Jaime Bluma 5.00
8 Kevin Brown 5.00
9 Ray Brown 5.00
10 Homer Bush 10.00
11 Mike Cameron 15.00
12 Jay Canizaro 10.00
13 Luis Castillo 10.00
14 Dave Coggin 5.00
15 Bartolo Colon 15.00
16 Rocky Coppinger 10.00
17 Jacob Cruz 15.00
18 Jose Cruz 15.00
19 Jeff D'Amico 15.00
20 Ben Davis 15.00
21 Mike Drumbright 5.00
22 Scott Elarton 15.00
23 Darin Erstad 30.00
24 Bobby Estalella 15.00
25 Joe Fontenot 5.00
26 Tom Fordham 5.00
27 Brad Fullmer 15.00
28 Chris Fussell 5.00
29 Karim Garcia 10.00
30 Kris Detmers 5.00
31 Todd Greene 10.00
32 Ben Grieve 30.00
33 Vladimir Guerrero 60.00
34 Jose Guillen 10.00
35 Roy Halladay 10.00
36 Wes Helms 10.00
37 Chad Hermansen 15.00
38 Richard Hidalgo 25.00
39 Todd Hollandsworth 10.00
40 Damian Jackson 10.00
41 Derek Jeter 90.00
42 Andruw Jones 40.00
43 Brooks Kieschnick 10.00
44 Eugene Kingsale 5.00
45 Paul Konerko 15.00
46 Marc Kroon 5.00
47 Derrek Lee 10.00
48 Travis Lee 15.00
49 Terrence Long 5.00
50 Curt Lyons 5.00
51 Elieser Marrero 10.00
52 Rafael Medina 5.00
53 Juan Melo 10.00
54 Shane Monahan 5.00
55 Julio Mosquera 5.00
56 Heath Murray 5.00
57 Ryan Nye 5.00
58 Kevin Orie 10.00
59 Russ Ortiz 5.00
60 Carl Pavano 10.00
61 Jay Payton 15.00
62 Neifi Perez 15.00
63 Sidney Ponson 10.00
64 Calvin Reese 10.00
65 Ray Ricken 5.00
66 Brad Rigby 10.00
67 Adam Riggs 10.00
68 Ruben Rivera 10.00
69 J.J. Johnson 5.00
70 Scott Rolen 40.00
71 Tony Saunders 10.00
72 Donnie Sadler 10.00
73 Richie Sexson 15.00
74 Scott Spiezio 10.00
75 Everett Stull 5.00
76 Mike Sweeney 10.00
77 Fernando Tatis 40.00
78 Miguel Tejada 40.00
79 Justin Thompson 10.00
80 Justin Towle 10.00
81 Billy Wagner 10.00
82 Todd Walker 10.00
83 Luke Wilcox 5.00
84 Paul Wilder 10.00
85 Enrique Wilson 10.00
86 Kerry Wood 40.00
87 Jamey Wright 10.00
88 Ron Wright 10.00
89 Dmitri Young 10.00
90 Nelson Figueroa 5.00

1997 Bowman International

Inserted at the rate of one per pack, the International parallel set replaces the regular photo background on front and back with the flag of the player's native land. Card #441 from the regular-issue version does not exist as an International parallel.

	MT
Complete Set (440):	125.00
Complete Series 1 (221):	60.00
Complete Series 2 (219):	60.00
Common Player:	.25
Stars and Rookies:	1-2X

(See 1997 Bowman for checklist and base card values.)

1997 Bowman International Best

This Series 2 insert set features a flag design in the background of each card front depicting the player's country of origin. On back is another color photo, player personal data, a record of his best season and colored flags representing 14 nations which have sent players to the major leagues. One International Best card was inserted in every second series pack. Card numbers carry a "BBI" prefix. Refractor versions are a 1:48 parallel with Atomic Refractors found 1:96.

		MT
Complete Set (20):		75.00
Common Player:		1.50
Refractors:		1.5x to 2x
Atomic Refractors:		2x to 3x
1	Frank Thomas	5.00
2	Ken Griffey Jr.	15.00
3	Juan Gonzalez	4.00
4	Bernie Williams	4.00
5	Hideo Nomo	3.00
6	Sammy Sosa	10.00
7	Larry Walker	2.00
8	Vinny Castilla	1.50
9	Mariano Rivera	1.50
10	Rafael Palmeiro	2.00
11	Nomar Garciaparra	10.00
12	Todd Walker	3.00
13	Andruw Jones	6.00
14	Vladimir Guerrero	8.00
15	Ruben Rivera	1.50
16	Bob Abreu	1.50
17	Karim Garcia	2.00
18	Katsuhiro Maeda	1.50
19	Jose Cruz Jr.	2.00
20	Damian Moss	1.50

1997 Bowman Rookie of the Year Candidates

This 15-card insert was inserted in one per 12 packs of Bowman Series 2. Fronts feature a color shot of the player over a textured foil background, with the player's name across the bottom and the words "Rookie of the Year Favorites" across the top with the word "Rookie" in large script letters. Card numbers have a "ROY" prefix.

		MT
Complete Set (15):		30.00
Common Player:		1.50
1	Jeff Abbott	1.50
2	Karim Garcia	1.50
3	Todd Helton	6.00
4	Richard Hidalgo	2.00
5	Geoff Jenkins	3.00
6	Russ Johnson	1.50
7	Paul Konerko	4.00
8	Mark Kotsay	3.00
9	Ricky Ledee	3.00
10	Travis Lee	3.00
11	Derrek Lee	1.50
12	Elieser Marrero	1.50
13	Juan Melo	1.50
14	Brian Rose	1.50
15	Fernando Tatis	4.00

1997 Bowman Scout's Honor Roll

This insert features 15 prospects deemed to have the most potential by Topps' scouts. Each card features a double-etched foil design and is inserted 1:12 packs.

		MT
Complete Set (15):		60.00
Common Player:		1.50
1	Dmitri Young	1.50
2	Bob Abreu	1.50
3	Vladimir Guerrero	6.00
4	Paul Konerko	4.00
5	Kevin Orie	2.00
6	Todd Walker	2.50
7	Ben Grieve	3.00
8	Darin Erstad	6.00
9	Derrek Lee	1.50
10	Jose Cruz	2.00
11	Scott Rolen	6.00
12	Travis Lee	2.00
13	Andruw Jones	5.00
14	Wilton Guerrero	1.50
15	Nomar Garciaparra	8.00

1997 Bowman Chrome

Bowman Chrome was released in one 300-card series following the conclusion of the 1997 season. Four-card foil packs carried an SRP of $3. Each card reprints one of the regular Bowman set, utilizing chromium technology on front. Inserts include: International parallels, Rookie of the Year Favorites and Scout's Honor Roll.

		MT
Complete Set (300):		250.00
Common Player:		.25
Internationals		1.5-2.5X
Pack (3):		10.00
Wax Box (24):		200.00
1	Derek Jeter	4.00
2	Chipper Jones	2.50
3	Hideo Nomo	.50
4	Tim Salmon	.50
5	Robin Ventura	.40
6	Tony Clark	.25
7	Barry Larkin	.75
8	Paul Molitor	1.00
9	Andy Benes	.25
10	Ryan Klesko	.50
11	Mark McGwire	5.00
12	Ken Griffey Jr.	4.00
13	Robb Nen	.25
14	Cal Ripken Jr.	4.00
15	John Valentin	.25
16	Ricky Bottalico	.25
17	Mike Lansing	.25
18	Ryne Sandberg	1.25
19	Carlos Delgado	1.00
20	Craig Biggio	.50
21	Eric Karros	.40
22	Kevin Appier	.25
23	Mariano Rivera	.50
24	Vinny Castilla	.40
25	Juan Gonzalez	1.25
26	Al Martin	.25
27	Jeff Cirillo	.25
28	Ray Lankford	.25
29	Manny Ramirez	1.25
30	Roberto Alomar	1.00
31	Will Clark	.75
32	Chuck Knoblauch	.75
33	Harold Baines	.25
34	Edgar Martinez	.40
35	Mike Mussina	1.00
36	Kevin Brown	.40
37	Dennis Eckersley	.40
38	Tino Martinez	.40
39	Raul Mondesi	.50
40	Sammy Sosa	3.00
41	John Smoltz	.25
42	Billy Wagner	.25
43	Ken Caminiti	.25
44	Wade Boggs	.75
45	Andres Galarraga	.75
46	Roger Clemens	2.00
47	Matt Williams	.50
48	Albert Belle	1.00
49	Jeff King	.25
50	John Wetteland	.25
51	Deion Sanders	.75
52	Ellis Burks	.25
53	Pedro Martinez	1.50
54	Kenny Lofton	.75
55	Randy Johnson	1.25
56	Bernie Williams	1.00
57	Marquis Grissom	.25
58	Gary Sheffield	.75
59	Curt Schilling	.50
60	Reggie Sanders	.25
61	Bobby Higginson	.25
62	Moises Alou	.40
63	Tom Glavine	.75
64	Mark Grace	.50
65	Rafael Palmeiro	.75
66	John Olerud	.50
67	Dante Bichette	.40
68	Jeff Bagwell	1.25
69	Barry Bonds	1.50
70	Pat Hentgen	.25
71	Jim Thome	.75
72	Andy Pettitte	.75
73	Jay Bell	.25
74	Jim Edmonds	.50
75	Ron Gant	.40
76	David Cone	.40
77	Jose Canseco	.75
78	Jay Buhner	.40
79	Greg Maddux	2.50
80	Lance Johnson	.25
81	Travis Fryman	.40
82	Paul O'Neill	.50
83	Ivan Rodriguez	1.25
84	Fred McGriff	.50
85	Mike Piazza	3.00
86	Brady Anderson	.40
87	Marty Cordova	.25
88	Joe Carter	.40
89	Brian Jordan	.25
90	David Justice	.75
91	Tony Gwynn	2.00
92	Larry Walker	.75
93	Mo Vaughn	1.00
94	Sandy Alomar	.40
95	Rusty Greer	.40
96	Roberto Hernandez	.25
97	Hal Morris	.25
98	Todd Hundley	.25
99	Rondell White	.25
100	Frank Thomas	2.00
101	*Bubba Trammell*	1.50
102	*Sidney Ponson*	3.00
103	*Ricky Ledee*	4.00
104	Brett Tomko	.25
105	*Braden Looper*	1.00
106	Jason Dickson	.40

No.	Player	Value
107	*Chad Green*	1.50
108	*R.A. Dickey*	.75
109	Jeff Liefer	.40
110	Richard Hidalgo	.25
111	*Chad Hermansen*	5.00
112	Felix Martinez	.25
113	J.J. Johnson	.25
114	Todd Dunwoody	.50
115	Katsuhiro Maeda	.25
116	Darin Erstad	1.25
117	Elieser Marrero	.25
118	Bartolo Colon	.25
119	Ugueth Urbina	.25
120	Jaime Bluma	.25
121	*Seth Greisinger*	1.50
122	*Jose Cruz Jr.*	4.00
123	Todd Dunn	.25
124	*Justin Towle*	.75
125	Brian Rose	.50
126	Jose Guillen	.25
127	Andruw Jones	1.50
128	*Mark Kotsay*	4.00
129	Wilton Guerrero	.25
130	Jacob Cruz	.25
131	Mike Sweeney	.25
132	Matt Morris	.50
133	John Thomson	.25
134	*Javier Valentin*	.40
135	*Mike Drumright*	.75
136	Michael Barrett	.25
137	*Tony Saunders*	.75
138	Kevin Brown	.40
139	*Anthony Sanders*	.75
140	Jeff Abbott	.25
141	Eugene Kingsale	.25
142	Paul Konerko	.50
143	*Randall Simon*	1.50
144	Freddy Garcia	.25
145	Karim Garcia	.40
146	Carlos Guillen	.25
147	Aaron Boone	.25
148	Donnie Sadler	.25
149	Brooks Kieschnick	.25
150	Scott Spiezio	.25
151	Kevin Orie	.25
152	Russ Johnson	.25
153	Livan Hernandez	.40
154	*Vladimir Nunez*	1.50
155	Calvin Reese	.25
156	Chris Carpenter	.25
157	*Eric Milton*	5.00
158	Richie Sexson	.40
159	Carl Pavano	.50
160	Pat Cline	.25
161	Ron Wright	.25
162	Dante Powell	.25
163	Mark Bellhorn	.25
164	George Lombard	.50
165	*Paul Wilder*	.75
166	Brad Fullmer	.50
167	*Kris Benson*	10.00
168	Torii Hunter	.25
169	D.T. Cromer	.25
170	*Nelson Figueroa*	1.50
171	*Hiram Bocachica*	2.50
172	Shane Monahan	.25
173	Juan Melo	.25
174	*Calvin Pickering*	1.50
175	Reggie Taylor	.25
176	Geoff Jenkins	.75
177	*Steve Rain*	1.50
178	Nerio Rodriguez	.50
179	Derrick Gibson	.50
180	Darin Blood	.25
181	Ben Davis	.25
182	*Adrian Beltre*	15.00
183	*Kerry Wood*	25.00
184	Nate Rolison	3.00
185	*Fernando Tatis*	10.00
186	Jake Westbrook	2.00
187	Edwin Diaz	.25
188	*Joe Fontenot*	1.50
189	*Matt Halloran*	1.50
190	*Matt Clement*	4.00
191	Todd Greene	.25
192	*Eric Chavez*	15.00
193	Edgard Velazquez	.25
194	*Bruce Chen*	4.00
195	Jason Brester	.25
196	*Chris Reitsma*	1.50
197	Neifi Perez	.25
198	*Hideki Irabu*	3.00
199	*Don Denbow*	.50
200	Derrek Lee	.25
201	Todd Walker	.25
202	Scott Rolen	1.25
203	Wes Helms	.50
204	Bob Abreu	.40
205	*John Patterson*	2.50
206	*Alex Gonzalez*	2.00
207	*Grant Roberts*	3.00
208	Jeff Suppan	.25
209	Luke Wilcox	.25
210	Marlon Anderson	.25
211	*Mike Caruso*	1.50
212	*Roy Halladay*	2.00
213	*Jeremi Gonzalez*	.75
214	*Aramis Ramirez*	8.00
215	*Dermal Brown*	8.00
216	Justin Thompson	.25
217	Danny Clyburn	.25
218	Bruce Aven	.25
219	Keith Foulke	.25
220	Shannon Stewart	.25
221	Larry Barnes	.25
222	*Mark Johnson*	1.50
223	Randy Winn	.25
224	Nomar Garciaparra	3.00
225	*Jacque Jones*	8.00
226	Chris Clemons	.25
227	Todd Helton	2.00
228	*Ryan Brannan*	.75
229	*Alex Sanchez*	1.50
230	Russell Branyan	.75
231	Daryle Ward	3.00
232	Kevin Witt	1.00
233	Gabby Martinez	.25
234	Preston Wilson	.25
235	*Donzell McDonald*	1.50
236	*Orlando Cabrera*	2.00
237	Brian Banks	.25
238	Robbie Bell	2.00
239	Brad Rigby	.25
240	Scott Elarton	.25
241	*Donny Leon*	1.50
242	*Abraham Nunez*	1.50
243	*Adam Eaton*	6.00
244	*Octavio Dotel*	4.00
245	Sean Casey	8.00
246	*Joe Lawrence*	2.50
247	*Adam Johnson*	1.50
248	*Ronnie Belliard*	3.00
249	Bobby Estalella	.25
250	*Corey Lee*	.75
251	Mike Cameron	.25
252	*Kerry Robinson*	.75
253	*A.J. Zapp*	2.50
254	Jarrod Washburn	.25
255	Ben Grieve	.75
256	*Javier Vazquez*	4.00
257	*Travis Lee*	4.00
258	*Dennis Reyes*	1.50
259	Danny Buxbaum	.25
260	*Kelvim Escobar*	2.50
261	Danny Klassen	.25
262	*Ken Cloude*	.75
263	Gabe Alvarez	.25
264	*Clayton Brunner*	.75
265	*Jason Marquis*	3.00
266	Jamey Wright	.25
267	*Matt Snyder*	.75
268	*Josh Garrett*	1.50
269	Juan Encarnacion	.50
270	Heath Murray	.25
271	*Brent Butler*	3.00
272	*Danny Peoples*	1.50
273	*Miguel Tejada*	15.00
274	Jim Pittsley	.25
275	Dmitri Young	.25
276	Vladimir Guerrero	1.50
277	*Cole Liniak*	2.00
278	Ramon Hernandez	.40
279	*Cliff Politte*	2.00
280	*Mel Rosario*	.75
281	*Jorge Carrion*	.75
282	*John Barnes*	3.00
283	*Chris Stowe*	.75
284	*Vernon Wells*	8.00
285	*Brett Caradonna*	1.50
286	*Scott Hodges*	2.00
287	*Jon Garland*	6.00
288	*Nathan Haynes*	2.00
289	*Geoff Goetz*	1.50
290	*Adam Kennedy*	6.00
291	*T.J. Tucker*	2.00
292	*Aaron Akin*	1.50
293	*Jayson Werth*	3.00
294	*Glenn Davis*	1.50
295	*Mark Mangum*	1.50
296	*Troy Cameron*	2.00
297	*J.J. Davis*	4.00
298	*Lance Berkman*	10.00
299	*Jason Standridge*	2.00
300	*Jason Dellaero*	1.50

1997 Bowman Chrome Refractors

All 300 cards in Bowman Chrome were reprinted in Refractor versions and inserted one per 12 packs. The cards are very similar to the base cards, but feature a refractive foil finish on front.

	MT
Complete Set (300):	2000.
Common Player:	1.50
Stars:	3-6X
Rookies:	2-4X

(See 1997 Bowman Chrome for checklist and base card values.)

1997 Bowman Chrome ROY Candidates

This 15-card insert set features color action photos of 1998 Rookie of the Year candidates printed on chromium finish cards. Card backs are numbered with a "ROY" prefix and were inserted one per 24 packs of Bowman Chrome. Refractor versions are seeded one per 72 packs.

		MT
Complete Set (15):		50.00
Common Player:		2.00
Refractors:		1.5x to 2.5x
1	Jeff Abbott	2.00
2	Karim Garcia	2.00
3	Todd Helton	10.00
4	Richard Hidalgo	3.00
5	Geoff Jenkins	3.00
6	Russ Johnson	2.00
7	Paul Konerko	5.00
8	Mark Kotsay	4.00
9	Ricky Ledee	4.00
10	Travis Lee	4.00
11	Derrek Lee	2.00
12	Elieser Marrero	2.00
13	Juan Melo	2.00
14	Brian Rose	2.00
15	Fernando Tatis	6.00

1997 Bowman Chrome Scout's Honor Roll

This 15-card set features top prospects and rookies as selected by the Topps' scouts. These chromium cards are numbered with a "SHR" prefix and are inserted one per 12 packs, while Refractor versions are seeded one per 36 packs.

		MT
Complete Set (15):		70.00
Common Player:		1.50
Refractors:		1.5x to 2.5x
1	Dmitri Young	1.50
2	Bob Abreu	1.50
3	Vladimir Guerrero	10.00
4	Paul Konerko	4.00
5	Kevin Orie	1.50
6	Todd Walker	2.00
7	Ben Grieve	5.00
8	Darin Erstad	4.00
9	Derrek Lee	1.50
10	Jose Cruz, Jr.	2.00
11	Scott Rolen	10.00
12	Travis Lee	6.00
13	Andruw Jones	6.00
14	Wilton Guerrero	1.50
15	Nomar Garciaparra	12.00

1997 Bowman's Best Preview

This 20-card set, featuring 10 veterans and 10 prospects, is a preview of the format used in the Bowman's Best product. Three different versions of the Preview cards were available: Regular (1:12

packs), Refractors (1:48) and Atomic Refractors (1:96).

		MT
Complete Set (20):		100.00
Common Player:		1.50
Refractors:		2X
Atomic Refractors:		3-4X
1	Frank Thomas	5.00
2	Ken Griffey Jr.	15.00
3	Barry Bonds	4.00
4	Derek Jeter	10.00
5	Chipper Jones	10.00
6	Mark McGwire	15.00
7	Cal Ripken Jr.	12.00
8	Kenny Lofton	3.00
9	Gary Sheffield	2.00
10	Jeff Bagwell	7.00
11	Wilton Guerrero	1.50
12	Scott Rolen	6.00
13	Todd Walker	2.50
14	Ruben Rivera	1.50
15	Andruw Jones	8.00
16	Nomar Garciaparra	10.00
17	Vladimir Guerrero	8.00
18	Miguel Tejada	4.00
19	Bartolo Colon	1.50
20	Katsuhiro Maeda	1.50

1997 Bowman's Best

The 200-card base set is divided into a 100-card subset featuring current stars on a gold-chromium stock, and 100 cards of top prospects in silver chromium. Packs contain six cards and were issued with a suggested retail price of $5. Autographed cards of 10 different players were randomly inserted into packs, with each player signing regular, Refractor and Atomic Refractor versions of their cards. Bowman's Best Laser Cuts and Mirror Image are the two other inserts, each with Refractor and Atomic Refractor editions.

		MT
Complete Set (200):		50.00
Common Player:		.25
Star Refractors:		6-10X
Young Star & RC Refractors:		2-4X
Star Atomics:		8-15X
Young Star & RC Atomics:		4-8X
Pack (6):		4.00
Wax Box (24):		90.00
1	Ken Griffey Jr.	5.00
2	Cecil Fielder	.25
3	Albert Belle	1.00
4	Todd Hundley	.40
5	Mike Piazza	3.00
6	Matt Williams	.75
7	Mo Vaughn	1.00
8	Ryne Sandberg	1.25
9	Chipper Jones	2.50
10	Edgar Martinez	.25
11	Kenny Lofton	.75
12	Ron Gant	.25
13	Moises Alou	.35
14	Pat Hentgen	.25
15	Steve Finley	.25
16	Mark Grace	.50
17	Jay Buhner	.40
18	Jeff Conine	.25
19	Jim Edmonds	.50
20	Todd Hollandsworth	.25
21	Andy Petitte	.50
22	Jim Thome	.75
23	Eric Young	.25
24	Ray Lankford	.25
25	Marquis Grissom	.25
26	Tony Clark	.35
27	Jermaine Allensworth	.25
28	Ellis Burks	.25
29	Tony Gwynn	2.00
30	Barry Larkin	.50
31	John Olerud	.40
32	Mariano Rivera	.40
33	Paul Molitor	1.00
34	Ken Caminiti	.25
35	Gary Sheffield	.75
36	Al Martin	.25
37	John Valentin	.25
38	Frank Thomas	1.50
39	John Jaha	.25
40	Greg Maddux	2.50
41	Alex Fernandez	.25
42	Dean Palmer	.25
43	Bernie Williams	1.00
44	Deion Sanders	.50
45	Mark McGwire	5.00
46	Brian Jordan	.25
47	Bernard Gilkey	.25
48	Will Clark	.50
49	Kevin Appier	.25
50	Tom Glavine	.50
51	Chuck Knoblauch	.40
52	Rondell White	.25
53	Greg Vaughn	.25
54	Mike Mussina	1.00
55	Brian McRae	.25
56	Chili Davis	.25
57	Wade Boggs	.75
58	Jeff Bagwell	1.25
59	Roberto Alomar	1.00
60	Dennis Eckersley	.25
61	Ryan Klesko	.40
62	Manny Ramirez	1.25
63	John Wetteland	.25
64	Cal Ripken Jr.	4.00
65	Edgar Renteria	.25
66	Tino Martinez	.40
67	Larry Walker	.50
68	Gregg Jefferies	.25
69	Lance Johnson	.25
70	Carlos Delgado	1.00
71	Craig Biggio	.40
72	Jose Canseco	.50
73	Barry Bonds	1.25
74	Juan Gonzalez	1.25
75	Eric Karros	.25
76	Reggie Sanders	.25
77	Robin Ventura	.25
78	Hideo Nomo	.50
79	David Justice	.50
80	Vinny Castilla	.25
81	Travis Fryman	.35
82	Derek Jeter	3.00
83	Sammy Sosa	3.00
84	Ivan Rodriguez	1.25
85	Rafael Palmeiro	.50
86	Roger Clemens	1.50
87	Jason Giambi	.75
88	Andres Galarraga	.75
89	Jermaine Dye	.25
90	Joe Carter	.25
91	Brady Anderson	.35
92	Derek Bell	.25
93	Randy Johnson	1.25
94	Fred McGriff	.40
95	John Smoltz	.25
96	Harold Baines	.25
97	Raul Mondesi	.50
98	Tim Salmon	.50
99	Carlos Baerga	.25
100	Dante Bichette	.40
101	Vladimir Guerrero	1.50
102	Richard Hidalgo	.40
103	Paul Konerko	.50
104	*Alex Gonzalez*	.50
105	Jason Dickson	.25
106	Jose Rosado	.25
107	Todd Walker	.25
108	*Seth Greisinger*	.50
109	Todd Helton	1.50
110	Ben Davis	.25
111	Bartolo Colon	.25
112	Elieser Marrero	.25
113	Jeff D'Amico	.40
114	*Miguel Tejada*	6.00
115	Darin Erstad	1.50
116	*Kris Benson*	4.00
117	*Adrian Beltre*	5.00
118	Neifi Perez	.25
119	Calvin Reese	.25
120	Carl Pavano	.40
121	Juan Melo	.25
122	*Kevin McGlinchy*	.50
123	Pat Cline	.25
124	*Felix Heredia*	.75
125	Aaron Boone	.25
126	Glendon Rusch	.25
127	Mike Cameron	.25
128	Justin Thompson	.25
129	*Chad Hermansen*	1.50
130	*Sidney Ponson*	1.00
131	*Willie Martinez*	.50
132	*Paul Wilder*	.50
133	Geoff Jenkins	.40
134	*Roy Halladay*	.50
135	Carlos Guillen	.25
136	Tony Batista	.25
137	Todd Greene	.25
138	Luis Castillo	.25
139	*Jimmy Anderson*	.50
140	Edgard Velazquez	.40
141	Chris Snopek	.25
142	Ruben Rivera	.25
143	*Javier Valentin*	.40
144	Brian Rose	.25
145	*Fernando Tatis*	3.00
146	*Dean Crow*	.50
147	Karim Garcia	.25
148	Dante Powell	.25
149	*Hideki Irabu*	1.00
150	Matt Morris	.25
151	Wes Helms	.50
152	Russ Johnson	.25
153	Jarrod Washburn	.25
154	*Kerry Wood*	6.00
155	*Joe Fontenot*	.60
156	Eugene Kingsale	.25
157	Terrence Long	.25
158	Calvin Maduro	.25
159	Jeff Suppan	.25
160	DaRond Stovall	.25
161	Mark Redman	.25
162	*Ken Cloude*	.50
163	Bobby Estalella	.25
164	*Abraham Nunez*	.75
165	Derrick Gibson	.25
166	*Mike Drumright*	.50
167	Katsuhiro Maeda	.25
168	Jeff Liefer	.25
169	Ben Grieve	.75
170	Bob Abreu	.40
171	Shannon Stewart	.25
172	*Braden Looper*	.50
173	Brant Brown	.25
174	Marlon Anderson	.25
175	Brad Fullmer	.50
176	Carlos Beltran	.40
177	Nomar Garciaparra	3.00
178	Derrek Lee	.25
179	*Valerio DeLosSantos*	.50
180	Dmitri Young	.25
181	Jamey Wright	.25
182	*Hiram Bocachica*	1.00
183	Wilton Guerrero	.25
184	Chris Carpenter	.25
185	Scott Spiezio	.25
186	Andruw Jones	1.00
187	*Travis Lee*	1.50
188	*Jose Cruz Jr.*	2.00
189	Jose Guillen	.25
190	Jeff Abbott	.25
191	*Ricky Ledee*	1.00
192	Mike Sweeney	.25
193	Donnie Sadler	.25
194	Scott Rolen	1.00
195	Kevin Orie	.25
196	*Jason Conti*	.75
197	*Mark Kotsay*	1.00
198	*Eric Milton*	1.50
199	Russell Branyan	.40
200	*Alex Sanchez*	.50

1997 Bowman's Best Autographs

Ten different players each signed 10 regular versions of their respective Bowman's Best cards (1:170 packs), 10 of their Bowman's Best Refractors (1:2,036 packs) and 10 of their Bowman's Best Atomic Refractors (1:6,107 packs). Each autograph card features a special Certified Autograph stamp on the front.

		MT
Complete Set (10):		600.00
Common Player:		25.00
Refractors:		1.5-2X
Atomics:		4-6X
29	Tony Gwynn	125.00
33	Paul Molitor	40.00
82	Derek Jeter	140.00
91	Brady Anderson	30.00
98	Tim Salmon	35.00
107	Todd Walker	30.00
183	Wilton Guerrero	25.00
185	Scott Spiezio	25.00
188	Jose Cruz Jr.	30.00
194	Scott Rolen	65.00

1997 Bowman's Best Cuts

Each of these 20-card inserts features a laser-cut pattern in the chromium stock. Backs have another color photo and list several of the player's career "Bests". Three different versions of each card are available: Regular (1:24 packs), Refractor (1:48) and Atomic Refractor (1:96). Cards are numbered with a "BC" prefix.

		MT
Complete Set (20):		75.00
Common Player:		1.50
Refractors:		1.5-2X
Atomic Refractors:		2-3X
1	Derek Jeter	6.00
2	Chipper Jones	6.00
3	Frank Thomas	6.00
4	Cal Ripken Jr.	7.50
5	Mark McGwire	12.50
6	Ken Griffey Jr.	12.50
7	Jeff Bagwell	4.00
8	Mike Piazza	6.00
9	Ken Caminiti	1.50
10	Albert Belle	3.00
11	Jose Cruz Jr.	3.00
12	Wilton Guerrero	1.50
13	Darin Erstad	3.50
14	Andruw Jones	5.00
15	Scott Rolen	5.00
16	Jose Guillen	2.50
17	Bob Abreu	1.50
18	Vladimir Guerrero	6.00
19	Todd Walker	2.00
20	Nomar Garciaparra	6.00

1997 Bowman's Best Mirror Image

This 10-card insert features four players on each double-sided card - two veterans and two rookies - utilizing Finest technology. Regular Mirror Image cards are found 1:48 packs, while Refractor versions are seeded 1:96 packs and Atomic Refractors are found 1:192 packs. Cards are numbered with an "MI" prefix.

		MT
Complete Set (10):		90.00
Common Card:		5.00
Refractors:		1.5X
Atomic Refractors:		2-3X
1	Nomar Garciaparra, Derek Jeter, Hiram Bocachica, Barry Larkin	12.00
2	Travis Lee, Frank Thomas, Derrek Lee, Jeff Bagwell	10.00
3	Kerry Wood, Greg Maddux, Kris Benson, John Smoltz	9.00
4	Kevin Brown, Ivan Rodriguez, Elieser Marrero, Mike Piazza	12.00
5	Jose Cruz Jr., Ken Griffey Jr., Andruw Jones, Barry Bonds	15.00
6	Jose Guillen, Juan Gonzalez, Richard Hidalgo, Gary Sheffield	5.00
7	Paul Konerko, Mark McGwire, Todd Helton, Rafael Palmeiro	15.00
8	Wilton Guerrero, Craig Biggio, Donnie Sadler, Chuck Knoblauch	5.00
9	Russell Branyan, Matt Williams, Adrian Beltre, Chipper Jones	10.00
10	Bob Abreu, Kenny Lofton, Vladimir Guerrero, Albert Belle	6.00

1997 Bowman's Best Jumbos

This large-format (4" x 5-5/8") version of 1997 Bowman's Best features 16 of the season's top stars and hottest rookies. Utilizing chromium, Refractor and Atomic Refractor technologies, the cards are identical in every way except size to the regular-issue Bowman's Best. The jumbos were sold only through Topps Stadium Club. Each of the sets consists of 12 chromium cards, plus three randomly packaged Refractors and one Atomic Refractor. About 900 sets were produced according to Topps sales literature, which breaks down to 700 regular cards, 170 Refractors and 60 Atomic Refractors of each player.

		MT
Complete Set (16):		100.00
Common Player:		6.00
Refractor:		3-5X
Atomic Refractor:		6-9X
1	Ken Griffey Jr.	12.00
5	Mike Piazza	8.00
9	Chipper Jones	8.00
11	Kenny Lofton	5.00
29	Tony Gwynn	6.00
33	Paul Molitor	5.00
38	Frank Thomas	6.00
45	Mark McGwire	12.00
64	Cal Ripken Jr.	10.00
73	Barry Bonds	6.00
74	Juan Gonzalez	6.00
82	Derek Jeter	8.00
101	Vladimir Guerrero	6.00
177	Nomar Garciaparra	8.00
186	Andruw Jones	6.00
188	Jose Cruz, Jr.	5.00

1998 Bowman

Bowman was a 441-card set released in a pair of 220-card series in 1998 (Orlando Hernandez, #221, was late Series 1 addition.) Within each series were 150 prospects printed in a silver and blue design and 70 veterans printed in silver and red. Cards feature a Bowman seal, and in cases where it's the player's first Bowman card a "Bowman Rookie Card" stamp is applied. The player's facsimile signature from their first contract runs down the side. The entire set was paralleled twice in Bowman International (one per pack) and Golden Anniversary (serially numbered to 50). Inserts in Series 1 include Autographs, Scout's Choice, and Japanese Rookies. Inserts in Series 2 include Autographs, 1999 Rookie of the Year Favorites, Minor League MVPs and Japanese Rookies.

		MT
Complete Set (441):		120.00
Complete Series 1 set (221):		70.00
Complete Series 2 set (220):		50.00
Common Player:		.20
Unlisted Stars: .		50 to .75
Internationals:		1.5-3X
Inserted 1:1		
Series 1 Pack (10):		3.00
Series 1 Wax Box (24):		70.00
Series 2 Pack (10):		2.50
Series 2 Wax Box (24):		50.00
1	Nomar Garciaparra	2.50
2	Scott Rolen	1.50
3	Andy Pettitte	.75
4	Ivan Rodriguez	1.00
5	Mark McGwire	5.00
6	Jason Dickson	.20
7	Jose Cruz Jr.	.75
8	Jeff Kent	.20
9	Mike Mussina	.75
10	Jason Kendall	.20
11	Brett Tomko	.20
12	Jeff King	.20
13	Brad Radke	.20
14	Robin Ventura	.35
15	Jeff Bagwell	1.50
16	Greg Maddux	2.00
17	John Jaha	.20
18	Mike Piazza	2.50
19	Edgar Martinez	.20
20	David Justice	.40
21	Todd Hundley	.20
22	Tony Gwynn	2.00
23	Larry Walker	.60
24	Bernie Williams	.75
25	Edgar Renteria	.20
26	Rafael Palmeiro	.40
27	Tim Salmon	.50
28	Matt Morris	.40
29	Shawn Estes	.20
30	Vladimir Guerrero	2.00
31	Fernando Tatis	.75
32	Justin Thompson	.20
33	Ken Griffey Jr.	4.00
34	Edgardo Alfonzo	.30
35	Mo Vaughn	1.00
36	Marty Cordova	.20
37	Craig Biggio	.40
38	Roger Clemens	1.50
39	Mark Grace	.50
40	Ken Caminiti	.40
41	Tony Womack	.20
42	Albert Belle	1.00
43	Tino Martinez	.75
44	Sandy Alomar	.40
45	Jeff Cirillo	.20
46	Jason Giambi	.20
47	Darin Erstad	1.00
48	Livan Hernandez	.20
49	Mark Grudzielanek	.20
50	Sammy Sosa	3.00
51	Curt Schilling	.40
52	Brian Hunter	.20
53	Neifi Perez	.20
54	Todd Walker	.40
55	Jose Guillen	.40
56	Jim Thome	.75
57	Tom Glavine	.40
58	Todd Greene	.20
59	Rondell White	.40
60	Roberto Alomar	.75
61	Tony Clark	.60
62	Vinny Castilla	.40
63	Barry Larkin	.40
64	Hideki Irabu	.50
65	Johnny Damon	.20
66	Juan Gonzalez	1.50
67	John Olerud	.40
68	Gary Sheffield	.50
69	Raul Mondesi	.40
70	Chipper Jones	2.50
71	David Ortiz	.75
72	*Warren Morris*	1.00
73	Alex Gonzalez	.35
74	Nick Bierbrodt	.20
75	Roy Halladay	.50
76	Danny Buxbaum	.20
77	Adam Kennedy	.40
78	*Jared Sandberg*	1.50
79	Michael Barrett	.50
80	Gil Meche	.40
81	Jayson Werth	.50
82	Abraham Nunez	.50
83	Ben Petrick	.20
84	Brett Caradonna	.40
85	*Mike Lowell*	1.50
86	*Clay Bruner*	.50
87	*John Curtice*	.50
88	Bobby Estalella	.20
89	Juan Melo	.20
90	Arnold Gooch	.20
91	*Kevin Millwood*	2.00
92	Richie Sexson	.20
93	Orlando Cabrera	.40
94	Pat Cline	.20
95	Anthony Sanders	.50
96	Russ Johnson	.20
97	Ben Grieve	.50
98	Kevin McGlinchy	.20

99 Paul Wilder .20
100 Russ Ortiz .20
101 *Ryan Jackson* .50
102 Heath Murray .20
103 Brian Rose .40
104 *Ryan Radmanovich* .50
105 Ricky Ledee .25
106 *Jeff Wallace* .50
107 *Ryan Minor* .50
108 Dennis Reyes .25
109 *James Manias* .50
110 Chris Carpenter .20
111 Daryle Ward .20
112 Vernon Wells .75
113 Chad Green .40
114 *Mike Stoner* .75
115 Brad Fullmer .20
116 Adam Eaton .20
117 Jeff Liefer .20
118 *Corey Koskie* 1.50
119 Todd Helton .75
120 *Jaime Jones* .50
121 Mel Rosario .20
122 Geoff Goetz .20
123 Adrian Beltre .50
124 Jason Dellaero .50
125 *Gabe Kapler* 4.00
126 Scott Schoeneweis .20
127 Ryan Brannan .20
128 Aaron Akin .20
129 *Ryan Anderson* 5.00
130 Brad Penny .20
131 Bruce Chen .50
132 Eli Marrero .20
133 Eric Chavez .50
134 *Troy Glaus* 8.00
135 Troy Cameron .25
136 *Brian Sikorski* .75
137 *Mike Kinkade* .50
138 Braden Looper .20
139 Mark Mangum .20
140 Danny Peoples .50
141 J.J. Davis .75
142 Ben Davis .20
143 Jacque Jones .50
144 Derrick Gibson .20
145 Bronson Arroyo .50
146 *Cristian Guzman* .50
147 Jeff Abbott .20
148 *Mike Cuddyer* 1.50
149 Jason Romano .75
150 Shane Monahan .20
151 *Ntema Ndungidi* 1.25
152 Alex Sanchez .40
153 *Jack Cust* 3.00
154 Brent Butler .40
155 Ramon Hernandez .20
156 Norm Hutchins .20
157 Jason Marquis .20
158 Jacob Cruz .20
159 *Rob Burger* .50
160 Eric Milton .75
161 Preston Wilson .20
162 *Jason Fitzgerald* .50
163 Dan Serafini .20
164 Peter Munro .20
165 Trot Nixon .20
166 Homer Bush .20
167 Dermal Brown .40
168 Chad Hermansen .40
169 *Julio Moreno* .50
170 *John Roskos* .50
171 Grant Roberts .40
172 Ken Cloude .25
173 Jason Brester .20
174 Jason Conti .20
175 Jon Garland .50
176 Robbie Bell .20
177 Nathan Haynes .20
178 *Ramon Ortiz* 1.50
179 Shannon Stewart .20
180 Pablo Ortega .20
181 *Jimmy Rollins* 1.00
182 Sean Casey .50
183 *Ted Lilly* .50
184 *Chris Enochs* .75
185 *Magglio Ordonez* 8.00
186 Mike Drumright .20
187 Aaron Boone .20
188 Matt Clement .40
189 Todd Dunwoody .40
190 Larry Rodriguez .20
191 Todd Noel .20
192 Geoff Jenkins .20
193 George Lombard .20
194 Lance Berkman .50
195 *Marcus McCain* .50
196 Ryan McGuire .20
197 *Jhensy Sandoval* .50
198 Corey Lee .20
199 Mario Valdez .20
200 *Robert Fick* 1.00
201 Donnie Sadler .20
202 Marc Kroon .20
203 David Miller .20
204 Jarrod Washburn .20
205 Miguel Tejada .50
206 Raul Ibanez .20
207 John Patterson .50
208 Calvin Pickering .75
209 Felix Martinez .20
210 Mark Redman .20
211 Scott Elarton .20
212 *Jose Amado* .50
213 Kerry Wood .50
214 Dante Powell .20
215 Aramis Ramirez .25
216 A.J. Hinch .25
217 *Dustin Carr* .50
218 Mark Kotsay .40
219 Jason Standridge .20
220 Luis Ordaz .20
221 *Orlando Hernandez* 2.00
222 Cal Ripken Jr. 3.00
223 Paul Molitor .75
224 Derek Jeter 2.50
225 Barry Bonds 1.00
226 Jim Edmonds .20
227 John Smoltz .40
228 Eric Karros .30
229 Ray Lankford .20
230 Rey Ordonez .30
231 Kenny Lofton .75
232 Alex Rodriguez 3.00
233 Dante Bichette .35
234 Pedro Martinez .75
235 Carlos Delgado .50
236 Rod Beck .20
237 Matt Williams .50
238 Charles Johnson .20
239 Rico Brogna .20
240 Frank Thomas 1.50
241 Paul O'Neill .50
242 Jaret Wright 1.00
243 Brant Brown .20
244 Ryan Klesko .30
245 Chuck Finley .20
246 Derek Bell .20
247 Delino DeShields .20
248 Chan Ho Park .40
249 Wade Boggs .60
250 Jay Buhner .35
251 Butch Huskey .20
252 Steve Finley .20
253 Will Clark .50
254 John Valentin .20
255 Bobby Higginson .20
256 Darryl Strawberry .40
257 Randy Johnson .75
258 Al Martin .20
259 Travis Fryman .20
260 Fred McGriff .40
261 Jose Valentin .20
262 Andruw Jones 1.00
263 Kenny Rogers .20
264 Moises Alou .40
265 Denny Neagle .20
266 Ugueth Urbina .20
267 Derrek Lee .20
268 Ellis Burks .20
269 Mariano Rivera .40
270 Dean Palmer .20
271 Eddie Taubensee .20
272 Brady Anderson .20
273 Brian Giles .20
274 Quinton McCracken .20
275 Henry Rodriguez .20
276 Andres Galarraga .35
277 Jose Canseco .60
278 David Segui .20
279 Bret Saberhagen .20
280 Kevin Brown .40
281 Chuck Knoblauch .60
282 Jeromy Burnitz .30
283 Jay Bell .20
284 Manny Ramirez 1.50
285 Rick Helling .20
286 Francisco Cordova .20
287 Bob Abreu .20
288 J.T. Snow Jr. .20
289 Hideo Nomo .50
290 Brian Jordan .20
291 Javy Lopez .20
292 Travis Lee 1.00
293 Russell Branyan .20
294 Paul Konerko .40
295 *Masato Yoshii* 1.00
296 Kris Benson .40
297 Juan Encarnacion .20
298 Eric Milton .20
299 Mike Caruso .20
300 *Ricardo Aramboles* 1.00
301 Bobby Smith .20
302 Billy Koch .20
303 Richard Hidalgo .20
304 *Justin Baughman* .50
305 Chris Gissell .20
306 *Donnie Bridges* 1.00
307 *Nelson Lara* .50
308 *Randy Wolf* 1.00
309 *Jason LaRue* .75
310 *Jason Gooding* .50
311 *Edgar Clemente* .50
312 Andrew Vessel .20
313 Chris Reitsma .20
314 *Jesus Sanchez* .50
315 *Buddy Carlyle* .75
316 Randy Winn .20
317 Luis Rivera .50
318 *Marcus Thames* 1.00
319 A.J. Pierzynski .20
320 Scott Randall .20
321 Damian Sapp .20
322 *Eddie Yarnell* 1.00
323 *Luke Allen* .50
324 J.D. Smart .20
325 Willie Martinez .20
326 Alex Ramirez .20
327 *Eric DuBose* .50
328 Kevin Witt .20
329 *Dan McKinley* .75
330 Cliff Politte .20
331 Vladimir Nunez .20
332 *John Halama* .50
333 Nerio Rodriguez .20
334 Desi Relaford .20
335 Robinson Checo .20
336 *John Nicholson* .50
337 *Tom LaRosa* .75
338 *Kevin Nicholson* .75
339 Javier Vazquez .20
340 A.J. Zapp .20
341 Tom Evans .20
342 Kerry Robinson .20
343 *Gabe Gonzalez* .75
344 Ralph Milliard .20
345 Enrique Wilson .20
346 Elvin Hernandez .20
347 *Mike Lincoln* .50
348 *Cesar King* .75
349 *Cristian Guzman* 1.00
350 Donzell McDonald .20
351 *Jim Parque* 1.00
352 *Mike Saipe* .50
353 *Carlos Febles* 1.00
354 *Dernell Stenson* 1.50
355 *Mark Osborne* .50
356 *Odalis Perez* .50
357 *Jason Dewey* .50
358 Joe Fontenot .20
359 *Jason Grilli* .75
360 *Kevin Haverbusch* .75
361 *Jay Yennaco* .50
362 Brian Buchanan .20
363 John Barnes .20
364 Chris Fussell .20
365 *Kevin Gibbs* .75
366 Joe Lawrence .20
367 DaRond Stovall .20
368 *Brian Fuentes* .50
369 Jimmy Anderson .20
370 *Laril Gonzalez* .50
371 *Scott Williamson* .50
372 Milton Bradley .20
373 *Jason Halper* .75
374 *Brent Billingsley* .75
375 *Joe DePastino* .20
376 Jake Westbrook .20
377 Octavio Dotel .20
378 *Jason Williams* .50
379 *Julio Ramirez* 1.00
380 Seth Greisinger .20
381 *Mike Judd* .50
382 *Ben Ford* .50
383 Tom Bennett .20
384 *Adam Butler* .50
385 *Wade Miller* .75
386 *Kyle Peterson* .50
387 *Tommy Peterman* .50
388 Onan Masaoka .20
389 *Jason Rakers* .75
390 Rafael Medina .20
391 Luis Lopez .20
392 Jeff Yoder .20
393 *Vance Wilson* .75
394 *Fernando Seguignol* .75
395 Ron Wright .20
396 *Ruben Mateo* 2.50
397 *Steve Lomasney* .50
398 Damian Jackson .20
399 *Mike Jerzembeck* .75
400 *Luis Rivas* 1.00
401 *Kevin Burford* .75
402 Glenn Davis .20
403 *Robert Luce* .75
404 Cole Liniak .20
405 *Matthew LeCroy* 1.00
406 *Jeremy Giambi* 1.00
407 Shawn Chacon .20
408 *Dewayne Wise* .50
409 *Steve Woodard* .50
410 *Francisco Cordero* .50
411 *Damon Minor* .75
412 Lou Collier .20
413 Justin Towle .20
414 Juan LeBron .20
415 Michael Coleman .20
416 Felix Rodriguez .20
417 *Paul Ah Yat* .50
418 *Kevin Barker* .75
419 Brian Meadows .20
420 *Darnell McDonald* 1.00
421 *Matt Kinney* .75
422 *Mike Vavrek* .75
423 *Courtney Duncan* .75
424 *Kevin Millar* .50
425 Ruben Rivera .20
426 *Steve Shoemaker* .50
427 *Dan Reichert* .75
428 *Carlos Lee* 4.00
429 *Rod Barajas* .75
430 *Pablo Ozuna* 1.50
431 *Todd Belitz* .50
432 Sidney Ponson .20
433 *Steve Carver* .50
434 Esteban Yan .25
435 *Cedrick Bowers* .50
436 Marlon Anderson .20
437 Carl Pavano .20
438 *Jae Weong Seo* .50
439 *Jose Taveras* .50
440 *Matt Anderson* .50
441 *Darron Ingram* .50

1998 Bowman Autographs

Rookies and prospects are featured on the certified autograph cards found as '98 Bowman inserts. Each player signed cards in blue, silver and gold ink. The front of each autographed card bears a certification seal. The base-level blue signatures are found at the rate of one per 149 packs Series 1, and 1:122 in second series. Silver-signed cards are seeded at 1:902 and 1:815, respectively. The rare gold inked versions are found 1:2976 in Series 1 and 1:2445 in Series 2. Relative values in the current market come nowhere near reflecting those scarcities.

		MT
Complete Set, Blue (70):		750.00
Common Player:		7.50
Inserted 1:149		
Silvers:		1.5-2.5X
Inserted 1:992		
Golds:		2-4X
Inserted 1:2,976		
1	Adrian Beltre	20.00
2	Brad Fullmer	15.00
3	Ricky Ledee	15.00
4	David Ortiz	10.00
5	Fernando Tatis	15.00
6	Kerry Wood	30.00
7	Mel Rosario	7.50
8	Cole Liniak	10.00
9	A.J. Hinch	10.00
10	Jhensy Sandoval	7.50
11	Jose Cruz Jr.	10.00
12	Richard Hidalgo	20.00
13	Geoff Jenkins	15.00
14	Carl Pavano	10.00
15	Richie Sexson	15.00
16	Tony Womack	10.00
17	Scott Rolen	30.00
18	Ryan Minor	10.00
19	Elieser Marrero	7.50
20	Jason Marquis	7.50
21	Mike Lowell	10.00
22	Todd Helton	40.00
23	Chad Green	7.50
24	Scott Elarton	7.50
25	Russell Branyan	10.00
26	Mike Drumright	7.50
27	Ben Grieve	25.00
28	Jacque Jones	15.00
29	Jared Sandberg	10.00
30	Grant Roberts	10.00
31	Mike Stoner	10.00
32	Brian Rose	7.50
33	Randy Winn	7.50
34	Justin Towle	10.00
35	Anthony Sanders	7.50
36	Rafael Medina	7.50
37	Corey Lee	7.50
38	Mike Kinkade	7.50
39	Norm Hutchins	7.50
40	Jason Brester	7.50
41	Ben Davis	10.00
42	Nomar Garciaparra	60.00
43	Jeff Liefer	7.50
44	Eric Milton	10.00
45	Preston Wilson	10.00
46	Miguel Tejada	25.00
47	Luis Ordaz	7.50
48	Travis Lee	10.00
49	Kris Benson	10.00
50	Jacob Cruz	10.00
51	Dermal Brown	8.00
52	Marc Kroon	7.50
53	Chad Hermansen	10.00
54	Roy Halladay	8.00
55	Eric Chavez	20.00
56	Jason Conti	7.50
57	Juan Encarnacion	10.00
58	Paul Wilder	8.00
59	Aramis Ramirez	8.00
60	Cliff Politte	7.50
61	Todd Dunwoody	10.00
62	Paul Konerko	15.00
63	Shane Monahan	9.00
64	Alex Sanchez	7.50
65	Jeff Abbott	8.00
66	John Patterson	7.50
67	Peter Munro	7.50
68	Jarrod Washburn	8.00
69	Derrek Lee	10.00
70	Ramon Hernandez	8.00

1998 Bowman Golden Anniversary

This 441-card parallel set celebrates Bowman's 50th anniversary with a gold, rather than black, facsimile autograph on each card. Golden Anniversary cards were inserted in both Series 1 (1:237) and Series 2 (1:194) packs and are sequentially numbered to 50.

	MT
Common Player:	7.50
Veteran Stars:	40-80X
Young Stars:	20-40X
Rookie Cards:	6-12X

(See 1998 Bowman for checklist and base card values.)

1998 Bowman International

All 441 cards in Bowman Series 1 and 2 are paralleled in an International version, with the player's native country highlighted. Background map designs and vital information were translated into the player's native language on these one per pack parallel cards.

	MT
Complete Set (441):	200.00
Common Player:	.25
Stars:	1.5-3X
Inserted 1:1	

(See 1998 Bowman for checklist and base card values.)

1998 Bowman Japanese Rookies

Bowman offered collectors a chance to receive original 1991 BBM-brand Japanese rookie cards of three players. Series 1 had rookie cards of Hideo Nomo and Shigetoshi Hasegawa inserted in one per 2,685 packs, while Series 2 offered Hideki Irabu seeded one per 4,411 packs. Card numbers have a "BBM" prefix.

		MT
Complete Set (3):		40.00
Common Player:		10.00
11	Hideo Nomo	20.00
17	Shigetosi Hasegawa	10.00
	Hideki Irabu	15.00

1998 Bowman Minor League MVP

This 11-card insert set features players who are former Minor League MVPs who had graduated to the majors. Minor League MVPs are seeded one per 12 packs of Series 2 and are numbered with a "MVP" prefix.

		MT
Complete Set (11):		18.00
Common Player:		1.00
1	Jeff Bagwell	3.00
2	Andres Galarraga	1.00
3	Juan Gonzalez	2.00
4	Tony Gwynn	4.00
5	Vladimir Guerrero	3.00
6	Derek Jeter	4.00
7	Andruw Jones	2.00
8	Tino Martinez	1.00
9	Manny Ramirez	2.50
10	Gary Sheffield	1.00
11	Jim Thome	1.00

1998 Bowman Rookie of the Year Favorites

Rookie of the Year Favorites displays 10 players who had a legitimate shot at the 1999 ROY award in the opinion of the Bowman Scouts. The insert was seeded one per 12 packs of Series 2 and numbered with an "ROY" prefix.

		MT
Complete Set (10):		20.00
Common Player:		.75
1	Adrian Beltre	2.50
2	Troy Glaus	7.50
3	Chad Hermansen	1.00
4	Matt Clement	2.00
5	Eric Chavez	6.00
6	Kris Benson	.75
7	Richie Sexson	1.50
8	Randy Wolf	1.50
9	Ryan Minor	4.00
10	Alex Gonzalez	.75

1998 Bowman Scout's Choice

This 21-card insert has players with potential for Major League stardom. Scout's Choice inserts were seeded one per 12 packs of Series 1. Fronts have action photos with gold-foil highlights. Backs have a portrait photo and an assessment of the player's skills in the traditional five areas of raw talent. Cards are numbered with an "SC" prefix.

		MT
Complete Set (21):		35.00
Common Player:		.75
Inserted 1:12		
1	Paul Konerko	2.00
2	Richard Hidalgo	2.00
3	Mark Kotsay	1.50
4	Ben Grieve	2.50
5	Chad Hermansen	1.00
6	Matt Clement	1.00
7	Brad Fullmer	2.00
8	Eli Marrero	.75
9	Kerry Wood	2.50
10	Adrian Beltre	2.50
11	Ricky Ledee	1.50
12	Travis Lee	1.50
13	Abraham Nunez	.75
14	Ryan Anderson	4.00
15	Dermal Brown	1.00
16	Juan Encarnacion	1.00
17	Aramis Ramirez	1.50
18	Todd Helton	6.00
19	Kris Benson	2.00
20	Russell Branyan	1.50
21	Mike Stoner	1.00

1998 Bowman Chrome

All 441 cards in Bowman 1 and 2 were reprinted with a chromium finish for Bowman Chrome. Issued in two Series, Chrome contains International and Golden Anniversary parallels, like Bowman. Internationals are seeded one per four packs, with Refractor versions every 24 packs. Golden Anniversary parallels are exclusive to hobby packs and inserted one per 164 packs and sequentially numbered to 50 sets. Refractor versions are seeded one per 1,279 packs and numbered to just five sets. In addition, 50 Bowman Chrome Reprints were inserted with 25 in each series.

	MT
Complete Set (441):	160.00
Complete Series 1 Set (221):	100.00
Complete Series 2 Set (220):	70.00
Common Player:	.20
Series 1 or Series 2 Pack (4):	4.50
Series 1 or Series 2 Wax Box (24):	95.00

No.	Player	MT
1	Nomar Garciaparra	3.00
2	Scott Rolen	1.00
3	Andy Pettitte	.75
4	Ivan Rodriguez	1.25
5	Mark McGwire	5.00
6	Jason Dickson	.20
7	Jose Cruz Jr.	.25
8	Jeff Kent	.40
9	Mike Mussina	1.00
10	Jason Kendall	.40
11	Brett Tomko	.20
12	Jeff King	.20
13	Brad Radke	.20
14	Robin Ventura	.50
15	Jeff Bagwell	1.25
16	Greg Maddux	2.50
17	John Jaha	.25
18	Mike Piazza	3.00
19	Edgar Martinez	.40
20	David Justice	.75
21	Todd Hundley	.40
22	Tony Gwynn	2.00
23	Larry Walker	.60
24	Bernie Williams	1.00
25	Edgar Renteria	.40
26	Rafael Palmeiro	.75
27	Tim Salmon	.50
28	Matt Morris	.25
29	Shawn Estes	.40
30	Vladimir Guerrero	1.50
31	Fernando Tatis	.40
32	Justin Thompson	.25
33	Ken Griffey Jr.	4.00
34	Edgardo Alfonzo	.40
35	Mo Vaughn	1.00
36	Marty Cordova	.25
37	Craig Biggio	.50
38	Roger Clemens	2.00
39	Mark Grace	.50
40	Ken Caminiti	.40
41	Tony Womack	.40
42	Albert Belle	1.00
43	Tino Martinez	.40
44	Sandy Alomar	.40
45	Jeff Cirillo	.40
46	Jason Giambi	1.00
47	Darin Erstad	1.00
48	Livan Hernandez	.40
49	Mark Grudzielanek	.40
50	Sammy Sosa	3.00
51	Curt Schilling	.50
52	Brian Hunter	.25
53	Neifi Perez	.40
54	Todd Walker	.25
55	Jose Guillen	.25
56	Jim Thome	.75
57	Tom Glavine	.60
58	Todd Greene	.20
59	Rondell White	.40
60	Roberto Alomar	1.00
61	Tony Clark	.50
62	Vinny Castilla	.25
63	Barry Larkin	.75
64	Hideki Irabu	.20
65	Johnny Damon	.40
66	Juan Gonzalez	1.25
67	John Olerud	.50
68	Gary Sheffield	.75
69	Raul Mondesi	.50
70	Chipper Jones	2.50
71	David Ortiz	.40
72	*Warren Morris*	3.00
73	Alex Gonzalez	.50
74	Nick Bierbrodt	.40
75	Roy Halladay	.50
76	Danny Buxbaum	.40
77	Adam Kennedy	.40
78	*Jared Sandberg*	1.00
79	Michael Barrett	.40
80	Gil Meche	1.50
81	Jayson Werth	.75
82	Abraham Nunez	.50
83	Ben Petrick	.25
84	Brett Caradonna	.25
85	*Mike Lowell*	5.00
86	*Clay Bruner*	1.00
87	*John Curtice*	2.00
88	Bobby Estalella	.25
89	Juan Melo	.25
90	Arnold Gooch	.40
91	*Kevin Millwood*	8.00
92	Richie Sexson	.40
93	Orlando Cabrera	.40
94	Pat Cline	.40
95	Anthony Sanders	.50
96	Russ Johnson	.40
97	Ben Grieve	.75
98	Kevin McGlinchy	.40
99	Paul Wilder	.40
100	Russ Ortiz	.40
101	*Ryan Jackson*	1.00
102	Heath Murray	.40
103	Brian Rose	.40
104	*Ryan Radmanovich*	1.00
105	Ricky Ledee	.75
106	*Jeff Wallace*	1.50
107	*Ryan Minor*	2.00
108	Dennis Reyes	.50
109	*James Manias*	1.00
110	Chris Carpenter	.40
111	Daryle Ward	.50
112	Vernon Wells	.50
113	Chad Green	.40
114	*Mike Stoner*	1.00
115	Brad Fullmer	.60
116	Adam Eaton	.40
117	Jeff Liefer	.40
118	*Corey Koskie*	4.00
119	Todd Helton	2.00
120	*Jaime Jones*	2.00
121	Mel Rosario	.40
122	Geoff Goetz	.40
123	Adrian Beltre	.75
124	Jason Dellaero	.25
125	*Gabe Kapler*	12.00
126	Scott Schoeneweis	.40
127	Ryan Brannan	.40
128	Aaron Akin	.40
129	*Ryan Anderson*	15.00
130	Brad Penny	.40
131	Bruce Chen	.50
132	Eli Marrero	.40
133	Eric Chavez	1.00
134	*Troy Glaus*	35.00
135	Troy Cameron	.50
136	*Brian Sikorski*	1.50
137	*Mike Kinkade*	1.50
138	Braden Looper	.40
139	Mark Mangum	.40
140	Danny Peoples	.50
141	J.J. Davis	.75
142	Ben Davis	.40
143	Jacque Jones	.50
144	Derrick Gibson	.40
145	Bronson Arroyo	.50
146	*Luis DeLosSantos*	1.50
147	Jeff Abbott	.40
148	*Mike Cuddyer*	5.00
149	Jason Romano	.75
150	Shane Monahan	.40
151	*Ntema Ndungidi*	4.00
152	Alex Sanchez	.40
153	*Jack Cust*	8.00
154	Brent Butler	.50
155	Ramon Hernandez	.40
156	Norm Hutchins	.40
157	Jason Marquis	.40
158	Jacob Cruz	.40
159	*Rob Burger*	1.50
160	Eric Milton	.60
161	Preston Wilson	.40
162	*Jason Fitzgerald*	1.50
163	Dan Serafini	.40
164	Peter Munro	.40
165	Trot Nixon	.50
166	Homer Bush	.40
167	Dermal Brown	.40
168	Chad Hermansen	.40
169	*Julio Moreno*	1.50
170	*John Roskos*	1.50
171	Grant Roberts	.40
172	Ken Cloude	.50
173	Jason Brester	.40
174	Jason Conti	.40
175	Jon Garland	.50
176	Robbie Bell	.40
177	Nathan Haynes	.40
178	*Ramon Ortiz*	4.00
179	Shannon Stewart	.40
180	Pablo Ortega	.40
181	*Jimmy Rollins*	2.50
182	Sean Casey	.75
183	*Ted Lilly*	1.50
184	*Chris Enochs*	1.50
185	*Magglio Ordonez*	30.00
186	Mike Drumright	.40
187	Aaron Boone	.40
188	Matt Clement	.50
189	Todd Dunwoody	.40
190	Larry Rodriguez	.40
191	Todd Noel	.40
192	Geoff Jenkins	.40
193	George Lombard	.50
194	Lance Berkman	.50
195	*Marcus McCain*	.75
196	Ryan McGuire	.40
197	*Jhensy Sandoval*	.75
198	Corey Lee	.40
199	Mario Valdez	.40
200	*Robert Fick*	3.00
201	Donnie Sadler	.40
202	Marc Kroon	.40
203	David Miller	.40
204	Jarrod Washburn	.40
205	Miguel Tejada	.75
206	Raul Ibanez	.25
207	John Patterson	.40
208	Calvin Pickering	.50
209	Felix Martinez	.25
210	Mark Redman	.40
211	Scott Elarton	.40
212	*Jose Amado*	1.50
213	Kerry Wood	.75
214	Dante Powell	.40
215	Aramis Ramirez	.50
216	A.J. Hinch	.40
217	*Dustin Carr*	1.50
218	Mark Kotsay	.75
219	Jason Standridge	.25
220	Luis Ordaz	.25
221	*Orlando Hernandez*	6.00
222	Cal Ripken Jr.	4.00
223	Paul Molitor	1.00
224	Derek Jeter	3.00
225	Barry Bonds	1.25
226	Jim Edmonds	.40
227	John Smoltz	.25
228	Eric Karros	.40
229	Ray Lankford	.20
230	Rey Ordonez	.20
231	Kenny Lofton	.75
232	Alex Rodriguez	4.00
233	Dante Bichette	.40
234	Pedro Martinez	1.50
235	Carlos Delgado	1.25
236	Rod Beck	.20
237	Matt Williams	.50
238	Charles Johnson	.20
239	Rico Brogna	.20
240	Frank Thomas	1.50
241	Paul O'Neill	.50
242	Jaret Wright	.40
243	Brant Brown	.20
244	Ryan Klesko	.40
245	Chuck Finley	.20
246	Derek Bell	.20
247	Delino DeShields	.20
248	Chan Ho Park	.40
249	Wade Boggs	.75
250	Jay Buhner	.40
251	Butch Huskey	.20
252	Steve Finley	.20
253	Will Clark	.75
254	John Valentin	.20
255	Bobby Higginson	.20
256	Darryl Strawberry	.50
257	Randy Johnson	1.25
258	Al Martin	.20
259	Travis Fryman	.20
260	Fred McGriff	.50
261	Jose Valentin	.20
262	Andruw Jones	1.25
263	Kenny Rogers	.20
264	Moises Alou	.40
265	Denny Neagle	.20
266	Ugueth Urbina	.20
267	Derrek Lee	.20
268	Ellis Burks	.20
269	Mariano Rivera	.50
270	Dean Palmer	.20
271	Eddie Taubensee	.20
272	Brady Anderson	.40
273	Brian Giles	.20
274	Quinton McCracken	.20
275	Henry Rodriguez	.20
276	Andres Galarraga	.75
277	Jose Canseco	.75
278	David Segui	.20
279	Bret Saberhagen	.20
280	Kevin Brown	.40
281	Chuck Knoblauch	.50
282	Jeromy Burnitz	.20
283	Jay Bell	.20
284	Manny Ramirez	1.25
285	Rick Helling	.20
286	Francisco Cordova	.20
287	Bob Abreu	.20
288	J.T. Snow Jr.	.20
289	Hideo Nomo	.75
290	Brian Jordan	.20
291	Javy Lopez	.20
292	*Aaron Akin*	1.00
293	Russell Branyan	.20
294	Paul Konerko	.50
295	*Masato Yoshii*	3.00
296	Kris Benson	.75
297	Juan Encarnacion	.20
298	Eric Milton	.20
299	Mike Caruso	.20
300	*Ricardo Aramboles*	3.00
301	Bobby Smith	.20
302	Billy Koch	.20
303	Richard Hidalgo	.20
304	*Justin Baughman*	.50
305	Chris Gissell	.20
306	*Donnie Bridges*	3.00
307	*Nelson Lara*	1.50
308	*Randy Wolf*	3.00
309	*Jason LaRue*	2.50
310	*Jason Gooding*	.50
311	*Edgar Clemente*	.75
312	Andrew Vessel	.20
313	Chris Reitsma	.20
314	*Jesus Sanchez*	1.50
315	*Buddy Carlyle*	2.00
316	Randy Winn	.20
317	Luis Rivera	2.00
318	*Marcus Thames*	3.00
319	A.J. Pierzynski	.20
320	Scott Randall	.20
321	Damian Sapp	.20
322	*Eddie Yarnell*	2.00
323	*Luke Allen*	2.00
324	J.D. Smart	.20
325	Willie Martinez	.20
326	Alex Ramirez	.20
327	*Eric DuBose*	1.50
328	Kevin Witt	.20
329	*Dan McKinley*	1.50
330	Cliff Politte	.20
331	Vladimir Nunez	.20
332	*John Halama*	2.00
333	Nerio Rodriguez	.20
334	Desi Relaford	.20
335	Robinson Checo	.20
336	*John Nicholson*	.75
337	*Tom LaRosa*	.75
338	*Kevin Nicholson*	1.50
339	Javier Vazquez	.20
340	A.J. Zapp	.20

341	Tom Evans	.20
342	Kerry Robinson	.20
343	*Gabe Gonzalez*	.50
344	Ralph Milliard	.20
345	Enrique Wilson	.20
346	Elvin Hernandez	.20
347	*Mike Lincoln*	1.50
348	*Cesar King*	1.50
349	Cristian Guzman	.40
350	Donzell McDonald	.20
351	*Jim Parque*	4.00
352	*Mike Saipe*	.75
353	*Carlos Febles*	2.50
354	*Dernell Stenson*	4.00
355	*Mark Osborne*	1.50
356	*Odalis Perez*	1.50
357	*Jason Dewey*	1.00
358	Joe Fontenot	.20
359	*Jason Grilli*	1.50
360	*Kevin Haverbusch*	1.00
361	*Jay Yennaco*	1.00
362	Brian Buchanan	.20
363	John Barnes	.20
364	Chris Fussell	.20
365	*Kevin Gibbs*	1.00
366	Joe Lawrence	.20
367	DaRond Stovall	.20
368	*Brian Fuentes*	1.50
369	Jimmy Anderson	.20
370	*Laril Gonzalez*	1.50
371	*Scott Williamson*	1.50
372	Milton Bradley	.20
373	*Jason Halper*	.75
374	*Brent Billingsley*	1.50
375	*Joe DePastino*	.40
376	Jake Westbrook	.20
377	Octavio Dotel	.20
378	*Jason Williams*	.50
379	*Julio Ramirez*	2.50
380	Seth Greisinger	.20
381	*Mike Judd*	1.50
382	*Ben Ford*	.75
383	*Tom Bennett*	.75
384	*Adam Butler*	.75
385	*Wade Miller*	2.00
386	*Kyle Peterson*	2.00
387	*Tommy Peterman*	1.50
388	Onan Masaoka	.20
389	*Jason Rakers*	.75
390	Rafael Medina	.20
391	Luis Lopez	.20
392	Jeff Yoder	.20
393	*Vance Wilson*	.75
394	*Fernando Seguignol*	2.00
395	Ron Wright	.20
396	*Ruben Mateo*	10.00
397	*Steve Lomasney*	2.00
398	Damian Jackson	.20
399	*Mike Jerzembeck*	.75
400	*Luis Rivas*	4.00
401	*Kevin Burford*	2.50
402	Glenn Davis	.20
403	*Robert Luce*	.75
404	Cole Liniak	.20
405	*Matthew LeCroy*	3.00
406	*Jeremy Giambi*	2.50
407	Shawn Chacon	.20
408	*Dewayne Wise*	1.50
409	*Steve Woodard*	.75
410	*Francisco Cordero*	1.50
411	*Damon Minor*	2.00
412	Lou Collier	.20
413	Justin Towle	.20
414	Juan LeBron	.20
415	Michael Coleman	.20
416	Felix Rodriguez	.20
417	*Paul Ah Yat*	.75
418	*Kevin Barker*	1.50
419	Brian Meadows	.20
420	*Darnell McDonald*	2.50
421	*Matt Kinney*	2.00
422	*Mike Vavrek*	.75
423	*Courtney Duncan*	.75
424	*Kevin Millar*	1.50
425	Ruben Rivera	.20
426	*Steve Shoemaker*	.75
427	*Dan Reichert*	2.00
428	*Carlos Lee*	10.00
429	Rod Barajas	.75
430	*Pablo Ozuna*	3.00
431	*Todd Belitz*	1.00
432	Sidney Ponson	.20
433	*Steve Carver*	.75
434	*Esteban Yan*	1.00
435	*Cedrick Bowers*	.75
436	Marlon Anderson	.20
437	Carl Pavano	.20
438	*Jae Weong Seo*	1.00
439	*Jose Taveras*	1.50
440	*Matt Anderson*	1.50
441	*Darron Ingram*	1.00

1998 Bowman Chrome Refractors

Refractor versions for all 441 cards in Bowman Chrome Series I and II were inserted one per 12 packs. The cards contained the word "Refractor" on the back in black letters directly under the card number.

	MT
Complete Set (441):	1500.
Common Player:	2.00
Stars:	5-10X
Young Stars/RCs:	3-6X
Inserted 1:12	
Int'l Refractors:	8-15X
Young Stars/RCs:	4-10X
Inserted 1:24	

(See 1998 Bowman Chrome for checklist and base card values.)

1998 Bowman Chrome Golden Anniversary

Golden Anniversary parallels were printed for all 441 cards in Bowman Chrome. They are exclusive to hobby packs, seeded one per 164 packs and sequentially numbered to 50 sets. Refractor versions were also available, numbered to just five sets and inserted one per 1,279 packs.

	MT
Common Player:	7.50
Veteran Stars:	20-40X
Young Stars:	15-25X

(See 1998 Bowman Chrome for checklist and base card values. Golden Anniversary Refractors cannot be accurately priced due to their rarity (five each).)

1998 Bowman Chrome International

All 441 cards throughout Bowman Chrome Series 1 and 2 were paralleled in International versions. Cards fronts have the regular background replaced by a map denoting the player's birthplace. Backs are written in the player's native language. Regular versions were inserted one per four packs while Refractor versions arrived every 24 packs.

	MT
Complete Set (441):	450.00
Common Player:	.50
Stars and rookies:	1.5-2.5X
Inserted:	1:4

(See 1998 Bowman Chrome for checklist and base card values.)

1998 Bowman Chrome Reprints

Bowman Chrome Reprints showcas 50 of the most popular rookie cards to appear in the brand since 1948. Regular versions were seeded one per 12 packs, while Refractor versions were seeded 1:36. The 25 odd-numbered cards are found in Series 1; the evens in Series 2. The Reprints are numbered with a "BC" prefix.

		MT
Complete Set (50):		65.00
Common Player:		.50
Inserted 1:12		
Refractors:		1.5-2.5X
Inserted 1:36		
1	Yogi Berra	3.00
2	Jackie Robinson	6.00
3	Don Newcombe	.50
4	Satchel Paige	2.50
5	Willie Mays	4.00
6	Gil McDougald	.50
7	Don Larsen	1.00
8	Elston Howard	.50
9	Robin Ventura	.50
10	Brady Anderson	.50
11	Gary Sheffield	.50
12	Tino Martinez	.50
13	Ken Griffey Jr.	7.50
14	John Smoltz	.50
15	Sandy Alomar Jr.	.50
16	Larry Walker	.50
17	Todd Hundley	.50
18	Mo Vaughn	.50
19	Sammy Sosa	5.00
20	Frank Thomas	3.00
21	Chuck Knoblauch	.50
22	Bernie Williams	.50
23	Juan Gonzalez	2.00
24	Mike Mussina	.50
25	Jeff Bagwell	1.00
26	Tim Salmon	.50
27	Ivan Rodriguez	1.00
28	Kenny Lofton	.50
29	Chipper Jones	5.00
30	Javier Lopez	.50
31	Ryan Klesko	.50
32	Raul Mondesi	.50
33	Jim Thome	.50
34	Carlos Delgado	.75
35	Mike Piazza	5.00
36	Manny Ramirez	1.00
37	Andy Pettitte	.50
38	Derek Jeter	5.00
39	Brad Fullmer	.50
40	Richard Hidalgo	.50
41	Tony Clark	.50
42	Andruw Jones	1.50
43	Vladimir Guerrero	3.00
44	Nomar Garciaparra	5.00
45	Paul Konerko	.50
46	Ben Grieve	.50
47	Hideo Nomo	.50
48	Scott Rolen	1.00
49	Jose Guillen	.50
50	Livan Hernandez	.50

1998 Bowman's Best

Bowman's Best was issued in a single 200-card series comprised of 100 prospects and 100 veterans. Prospects are shown on a silver background, while the veterans are showcased on gold. The set was paralleled twice: A Refractor version is seeded one per 20 packs and sequentially numbered to 400, while an Atomic Refractor version is a 1:82 find and numbered to 100 sets. Inserts include regular, Refractor and Atomic Refractor versions of: Autographs, Mirror Image and Performers.

	MT
Complete Set (200):	75.00
Common Player:	.25
Star Refractors:	10-15X
Young Star/RCs Refractors:	2-5X
Production 400 sets	

Star Atomic Refractors: 15-30X
Young Star/RCs Atomics: 5-10X
Production 100 sets
Pack (6): 4.00
Wax Box (24): 80.00
1 Mark McGwire 4.00
2 Hideo Nomo .40
3 Barry Bonds 1.00
4 Dante Bichette .40
5 Chipper Jones 2.00
6 Frank Thomas 1.50
7 Kevin Brown .40
8 Juan Gonzalez 1.00
9 Jay Buhner .40
10 Chuck Knoblauch .40
11 Cal Ripken Jr. 3.00
12 Matt Williams .40
13 Jim Edmonds .40
14 Manny Ramirez 1.00
15 Tony Clark .40
16 Mo Vaughn .75
17 Bernie Williams .75
18 Scott Rolen 1.00
19 Gary Sheffield .50
20 Albert Belle .75
21 Mike Piazza 2.50
22 John Olerud .40
23 Tony Gwynn 1.50
24 Jay Bell .25
25 Jose Cruz Jr. .25
26 Justin Thompson .25
27 Ken Griffey Jr. 4.00
28 Sandy Alomar .40
29 Mark Grudzielanek .25
30 Mark Grace .50
31 Ron Gant .40
32 Javy Lopez .25
33 Jeff Bagwell 1.00
34 Fred McGriff .40
35 Rafael Palmeiro .50
36 Vinny Castilla .40
37 Andy Benes .25
38 Pedro Martinez 1.00
39 Andy Pettitte .50
40 Marty Cordova .25
41 Rusty Greer .25
42 Kevin Orie .25
43 Chan Ho Park .40
44 Ryan Klesko .40
45 Alex Rodriguez 3.00
46 Travis Fryman .25
47 Jeff King .25
48 Roger Clemens 1.50
49 Darin Erstad .75
50 Brady Anderson .40
51 Jason Kendall .25
52 John Valentin .25
53 Ellis Burks .25
54 Brian Hunter .25
55 Paul O'Neill .40
56 Ken Caminiti .25
57 David Justice .60
58 Eric Karros .40
59 Pat Hentgen .25
60 Greg Maddux 2.00
61 Craig Biggio .50
62 Edgar Martinez .25
63 Mike Mussina .75
64 Larry Walker .50
65 Tino Martinez .40
66 Jim Thome .50
67 Tom Glavine .50
68 Raul Mondesi .40
69 Marquis Grissom .25
70 Randy Johnson 1.00
71 Steve Finley .25
72 Jose Guillen .25
73 Nomar Garciaparra 2.50
74 Wade Boggs .75
75 Bobby Higginson .25
76 Robin Ventura .40
77 Derek Jeter 3.00
78 Andruw Jones 1.00
79 Ray Lankford .25
80 Vladimir Guerrero 1.50
81 Kenny Lofton .50
82 Ivan Rodriguez 1.00
83 Neifi Perez .25
84 John Smoltz .25
85 Tim Salmon .40
86 Carlos Delgado 1.00
87 Sammy Sosa 2.50
88 Jaret Wright .25
89 Roberto Alomar .75
90 Paul Molitor .75
91 Dean Palmer .25
92 Barry Larkin .50
93 Jason Giambi .75
94 Curt Schilling .40
95 Eric Young .25
96 Denny Neagle .25
97 Moises Alou .40
98 Livan Hernandez .25
99 Todd Hundley .25
100 Andres Galarraga .50
101 Travis Lee .40
102 Lance Berkman .40
103 Orlando Cabrera .40
104 *Mike Lowell* 1.50
105 Ben Grieve .50
106 *Jae Weong Seo* .75
107 Richie Sexson .40
108 Eli Marrero .25
109 Aramis Ramirez .40
110 Paul Konerko .50
111 Carl Pavano .25
112 Brad Fullmer .50
113 Matt Clement .25
114 Donzell McDonald .25
115 Todd Helton 1.00
116 Mike Caruso .25
117 Donnie Sadler .25
118 Bruce Chen .25
119 Jarrod Washburn .25
120 Adrian Beltre .50
121 *Ryan Jackson* .50
122 *Kevin Millar* .75
123 *Corey Koskie* 1.50
124 Dermal Brown .25
125 Kerry Wood .50
126 Juan Melo .25
127 Ramon Hernandez .25
128 Roy Halladay .40
129 Ron Wright .25
130 *Darnell McDonald* 1.00
131 *Odalis Perez* .75
132 *Alex Cora* 1.00
133 Justin Towle .25
134 Juan Encarnacion .25
135 Brian Rose .40
136 Russell Branyan .25
137 *Cesar King* .50
138 Ruben Rivera .25
139 Ricky Ledee .25
140 Vernon Wells .25
141 *Luis Rivas* 1.50
142 Brent Butler .25
143 Karim Garcia .25
144 George Lombard .40
145 *Masato Yoshii* 1.00
146 Braden Looper .25
147 Alex Sanchez .25
148 Kris Benson .40
149 Mark Kotsay .40
150 Richard Hidalgo .25
151 Scott Elarton .25
152 *Ryan Minor* .75
153 *Troy Glaus* 12.00
154 *Carlos Lee* 6.00
155 Michael Coleman .25
156 *Jason Grilli* .50
157 *Julio Ramirez* 1.00
158 *Randy Wolf* 1.00
159 Ryan Brannan .25
160 *Edgar Clemente* .50
161 Miguel Tejada .40
162 Chad Hermansen .40
163 *Ryan Anderson* 6.00
164 Ben Petrick .25
165 Alex Gonzalez .50
166 Ben Davis .25
167 John Patterson .50
168 Cliff Politte .25
169 Randall Simon .25
170 Javier Vazquez .25
171 Kevin Witt .25
172 Geoff Jenkins .50
173 David Ortiz .50
174 Derrick Gibson .25
175 Abraham Nunez .25
176 A.J. Hinch .25
177 *Ruben Mateo* 4.00
178 *Magglio Ordonez* 10.00
179 Todd Dunwoody .25
180 Daryle Ward .50
181 *Mike Kinkade* .50
182 Willie Martinez .25
183 *Orlando Hernandez* 2.50
184 Eric Milton .40
185 Eric Chavez .40
186 Damian Jackson .25
187 *Jim Parque* 1.00
188 *Dan Reichert* 1.00
189 Mike Drumright .25
190 Todd Walker .25
191 Shane Monahan .25
192 Derrek Lee .25
193 *Jeremy Giambi* .75
194 *Dan McKinley* .50
195 *Tony Armas* 5.00
196 *Matt Anderson* .50
197 *Jim Chamblee* .50
198 *Francisco Cordero* .75
199 Calvin Pickering .25
200 Reggie Taylor .25

1998 Bowman's Best Autographs

This 10-card set offers autographs from five prospects and five veteran stars. Each card has on front the Topps "Certified Autograph Issue" logo for authentication. Regular versions are seeded one per 180 packs, Refractor versions, 1:2158 and Atomic Refractor versions, 1:6437.

MT
Common Player: 10.00
Inserted 1:180
Refractors: 1.5-2.5X
Inserted 1:2,158
Atomics: 2-4X
Inserted 1:6,437
5 Chipper Jones 60.00
10 Chuck Knoblauch 15.00
15 Tony Clark 10.00
20 Albert Belle 20.00
25 Jose Cruz Jr. 10.00
105 Ben Grieve 15.00
110 Paul Konerko 15.00
115 Todd Helton 30.00
120 Adrian Beltre 15.00
125 Kerry Wood 20.00

1998 Bowman's Best Mirror Image Fusion

This 20-card die-cut insert features a veteran star on one side and a young player at the same position on the other. Regular versions are seeded one per 12 packs, while Refractors are found 1:809 packs and numbered within an edition of 100, and Atomic Refractors are a 1:3237 find numbered to 25. All have a "MI" prefix to the card number.

MT
Complete Set (20): 120.00
Common Player (1:12): 1.50
Refractor (1:809): 6-10X
Atomic Refractor (1:3237): 15-25X
1 Frank Thomas, David Ortiz 10.00
2 Chuck Knoblauch, Enrique Wilson 1.50
3 Nomar Garciaparra, Miguel Tejada 10.00
4 Alex Rodriguez, Mike Caruso 10.00
5 Cal Ripken Jr., Ryan Minor 15.00
6 Ken Griffey Jr., Ben Grieve 20.00
7 Juan Gonzalez, Juan Encarnacion 5.00
8 Jose Cruz Jr., Ruben Mateo 4.00
9 Randy Johnson, Ryan Anderson 3.00
10 Ivan Rodriguez, A.J. Hinch 5.00
11 Jeff Bagwell, Paul Konerko 5.00
12 Mark McGwire, Travis Lee 25.00
13 Craig Biggio, Chad Hermanson 1.50
14 Mark Grudzielanek, Alex Gonzalez 2.00
15 Chipper Jones, Adrian Beltre 10.00
16 Larry Walker, Mark Kotsay 2.00
17 Tony Gwynn, Preston Wilson 8.00
18 Barry Bonds, Richard Hidalgo 5.00
19 Greg Maddux, Kerry Wood 10.00
20 Mike Piazza, Ben Petrick 12.00

1998 Bowman's Best Performers

Performers are 10 players who had the best minor league seasons in 1997. Regular versions were inserted one per six packs, while Refractors are seeded 1:809 and serially numbered to 200, and Atomic Refractors are 1:3237 and numbered to 50 sets. All versions have card numbers with a "BP" prefix.

		MT
Complete Set (10):		15.00
Common Player:		1.00
Refractor (1:309):		6-10X
Atomic Refractor (1:3237):		15-25X
1	Ben Grieve	2.00
2	Travis Lee	3.00
3	Ryan Minor	2.00
4	Todd Helton	1.50
5	Brad Fullmer	1.50
6	Paul Konerko	1.00
7	Adrian Beltre	2.00
8	Richie Sexson	1.00
9	Aramis Ramirez	1.00
10	Russell Branyan	1.00

1999 Bowman Pre-Production

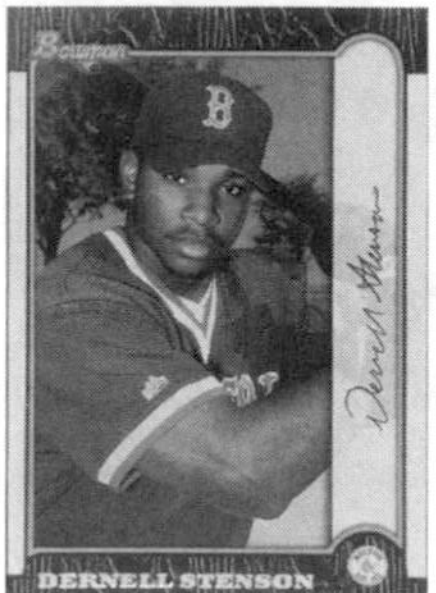

Bowman's 1999 issue was introduced with this group of sample cards. Format is nearly identical to the issued cards, except for the use of a "PP" prefix to the card number on back.

		MT
Complete Set (6):		12.00
Common Player:		2.00
1	Andres Galarraga	2.00
2	Raul Mondesi	2.50
3	Vinny Castilla	2.00
4	Corey Koskie	3.00
5	Octavio Dotel	3.00
6	Dernell Stenson	4.00

1999 Bowman

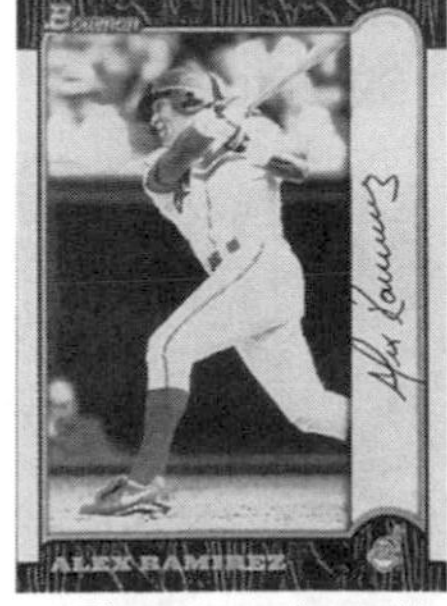

The set was issued in two 220-card series, each comprised of 70 veterans and 150 rookies and prospects. Rookie/prospect cards have blue metallic foil highlights; veteran cards are highlighted with red foil. On each card is the player's facsimile autograph, reproduced from their initial Topps contract.

		MT
Complete Set (440):		130.00
Complete Series 1 (220):		60.00
Complete Series 2 (220):		70.00
Common Player:		.15
Pack (10):		3.00
Series 1 Box (24):		60.00
Series 2 Box (24):		80.00
1	Ben Grieve	.75
2	Kerry Wood	1.00
3	Ruben Rivera	.15
4	Sandy Alomar	.25
5	Cal Ripken Jr.	3.00
6	Mark McGwire	5.00
7	Vladimir Guerrero	2.00
8	Moises Alou	.25
9	Jim Edmonds	.15
10	Greg Maddux	2.50
11	Gary Sheffield	.25
12	John Valentin	.15
13	Chuck Knoblauch	.40
14	Tony Clark	.40
15	Rusty Greer	.15
16	Al Leiter	.15
17	Travis Lee	.75
18	Jose Cruz Jr.	.50
19	Pedro Martinez	.75
20	Paul O'Neill	.40
21	Todd Walker	.25
22	Vinny Castilla	.25
23	Barry Larkin	.40
24	Curt Schilling	.40
25	Jason Kendall	.25
26	Scott Erickson	.15
27	Andres Galarraga	.40
28	Jeff Shaw	.15
29	John Olerud	.25
30	Orlando Hernandez	1.00
31	Larry Walker	.75
32	Andruw Jones	1.00
33	Jeff Cirillo	.15
34	Barry Bonds	1.00
35	Manny Ramirez	2.00
36	Mark Kotsay	.15
37	Ivan Rodriguez	1.00
38	Jeff King	.15
39	Brian Hunter	.15
40	Ray Durham	.15
41	Bernie Williams	.75
42	Darin Erstad	1.00
43	Chipper Jones	2.50
44	Pat Hentgen	.15
45	Eric Young	.15
46	Jaret Wright	.50
47	Juan Guzman	.15
48	Jorge Posada	.25
49	Bobby Higginson	.15
50	Jose Guillen	.15
51	Trevor Hoffman	.15
52	Ken Griffey Jr.	4.00
53	David Justice	.40
54	Matt Williams	.40
55	Eric Karros	.25
56	Derek Bell	.15
57	Ray Lankford	.15
58	Mariano Rivera	.25
59	Brett Tomko	.15
60	Mike Mussina	.60
61	Kenny Lofton	1.00
62	Chuck Finley	.15
63	Alex Gonzalez	.15
64	Mark Grace	.30
65	Raul Mondesi	.30
66	David Cone	.25
67	Brad Fullmer	.25
68	Andy Benes	.15
69	John Smoltz	.25
70	Shane Reynolds	.25
71	Bruce Chen	.40
72	Adam Kennedy	.15
73	Jack Cust	.15
74	Matt Clement	.15
75	Derrick Gibson	.15
76	Darnell McDonald	.15
77	*Adam Everett*	2.00
78	Ricardo Aramboles	.15
79	*Mark Quinn*	2.50
80	Jason Rakers	.15
81	*Seth Etherton*	2.00
82	*Jeff Urban*	1.00
83	Manny Aybar	.15
84	*Mike Nannini*	1.50
85	Onan Masaoka	.15
86	Rod Barajas	.15
87	Mike Frank	.15
88	Scott Randall	.15
89	*Justin Bowles*	.50
90	Chris Haas	.15
91	*Arturo McDowell*	1.00
92	*Matt Belisle*	1.00
93	Scott Elarton	.15
94	Vernon Wells	.15
95	Pat Cline	.15
96	Ryan Anderson	1.00
97	Kevin Barker	.15
98	Ruben Mateo	2.00
99	Robert Fick	.15
100	Corey Koskie	.15
101	Ricky Ledee	.25
102	*Rick Elder*	3.00
103	*Jack Cressend*	.75
104	Joe Lawrence	.15
105	Mike Lincoln	.15
106	*Kit Pellow*	1.00
107	*Matt Burch*	2.00
108	Brent Butler	.15
109	Jason Dewey	.15
110	Cesar King	.15
111	Julio Ramirez	.15
112	Jake Westbrook	.15
113	*Eric Valent*	5.00
114	*Roosevelt Brown*	.75
115	*Choo Freeman*	1.50
116	Juan Melo	.15
117	Jason Grilli	.15
118	Jared Sandberg	.15
119	Glenn Davis	.15
120	*David Riske*	.75
121	Jacque Jones	.15
122	Corey Lee	.15
123	Michael Barrett	.40
124	Lariel Gonzalez	.15
125	Mitch Meluskey	.30
126	Freddy Garcia	.40
127	*Tony Torcato*	1.00
128	Jeff Liefer	.15
129	Ntema Ndungidi	.15
130	*Andy Brown*	1.50
131	*Ryan Mills*	2.00
132	*Andy Abad*	.50
133	Carlos Febles	.15
134	*Jason Tyner*	1.00
135	Mark Osborne	.15
136	*Phil Norton*	1.00
137	Nathan Haynes	.15
138	Roy Halladay	.15
139	Juan Encarnacion	.15
140	Brad Penny	.15
141	Grant Roberts	.15
142	Aramis Ramirez	.15
143	Cristian Guzman	.15
144	*Mamon Tucker*	1.50
145	Ryan Bradley	.15
146	Brian Simmons	.15
147	Dan Reichert	.15
148	Russ Branyon	.15
149	*Victor Valencia*	2.00
150	Scott Schoeneweis	.15
151	*Sean Spencer*	.75
152	Odalis Perez	.15
153	Joe Fontenot	.15
154	Milton Bradley	.15
155	*Josh McKinley*	1.50
156	Terrence Long	.15
157	Danny Klassen	.15
158	*Paul Hoover*	1.00
159	Ron Belliard	.15
160	Armando Rios	.15
161	Ramon Hernandez	.15
162	Jason Conti	.15
163	Chad Hermansen	.15
164	Jason Standridge	.15
165	Jason Dellaero	.15
166	John Curtice	.15
167	*Clayton Andrews*	2.00
168	Jeremy Giambi	.25
169	Alex Ramirez	.15
170	*Gabe Molina*	.15
171	*Mario Encarnacion*	1.50
172	*Mike Zywica*	1.50
173	*Chip Ambres*	1.50
174	Trot Nixon	.15
175	*Pat Burrell*	6.00
176	Jeff Yoder	.15
177	*Chris Jones*	1.00
178	Kevin Witt	.15
179	*Keith Luuloa*	.50
180	Billy Koch	.15
181	*Damaso Marte*	1.00
182	*Ryan Glynn*	1.50
183	Calvin Pickering	.40
184	Michael Cuddyer	.15
185	*Nick Johnson*	2.00
186	*Doug Mientkiewicz*	.50
187	*Nate Cornejo*	.50
188	Octavio Dotel	.15
189	Wes Helms	.15
190	Nelson Lara	.15
191	*Chuck Abbott*	.50
192	Tony Armas, Jr.	.15
193	Gil Meche	.15
194	Ben Petrick	.15
195	*Chris George*	1.00
196	*Scott Hunter*	.75
197	Ryan Brannan	.15
198	*Amaury Garcia*	.75
199	Chris Gissell	.15
200	*Austin Kearns*	3.00
201	Alex Gonzalez	.15
202	Wade Miller	.15
203	Scott Williamson	.15
204	Chris Enochs	.15
205	Fernando Seguignol	.50
206	Marlon Anderson	.15
207	Todd Sears	.75
208	*Nate Bump*	.50
209	*J.M. Gold*	.50
210	*Matt LeCroy*	.15
211	Alex Hernandez	.15
212	Luis Rivera	.15
213	Troy Cameron	.15
214	*Alex Escobar*	2.00
215	Jason LaRue	.15
216	Kyle Peterson	.15
217	Brent Butler	.15
218	Dernell Stenson	.40
219	Adrian Beltre	.75
220	Daryle Ward	.15
----	Series 1 Checklist Folder	.15
221	Jim Thome	.50
222	Cliff Floyd	.15
223	Rickey Henderson	.25
224	Garret Anderson	.15
225	Ken Caminiti	.25
226	Bret Boone	.15
227	Jeromy Burnitz	.15
228	Steve Finley	.15
229	Miguel Tejada	.15
230	Greg Vaughn	.25
231	Jose Offerman	.15
232	Andy Ashby	.15
233	Albert Belle	.50
234	Fernando Tatis	.40
235	Todd Helton	.75
236	Sean Casey	.25
237	Brian Giles	.15
238	Andy Pettitte	.25
239	Fred McGriff	.25
240	Roberto Alomar	.75
241	Edgar Martinez	.15
242	Lee Stevens	.15
243	Shawn Green	.40
244	Ryan Klesko	.25
245	Sammy Sosa	2.50
246	Todd Hundley	.15
247	Shannon Stewart	.15
248	Randy Johnson	.75
249	Rondell White	.25
250	Mike Piazza	2.50
251	Craig Biggio	.50
252	David Wells	.15
253	Brian Jordan	.15
254	Edgar Renteria	.15
255	Bartolo Colon	.15
256	Frank Thomas	1.50
257	Will Clark	.50
258	Dean Palmer	.15
259	Dmitri Young	.15
260	Scott Rolen	1.00
261	Jeff Kent	.15
262	Dante Bichette	.40
263	Nomar Garciaparra	2.50
264	Tony Gwynn	2.00
265	Alex Rodriguez	3.00
266	Jose Canseco	.75
267	Jason Giambi	.15
268	Jeff Bagwell	1.50
269	Carlos Delgado	.50

270 Tom Glavine .25
271 Eric Davis .15
272 Edgardo Alfonzo .25
273 Tim Salmon .25
274 Johnny Damon .15
275 Rafael Palmeiro .75
276 Denny Neagle .15
277 Neifi Perez .15
278 Roger Clemens 1.50
279 Brant Brown .15
280 Kevin Brown .25
281 Jay Bell .15
282 Jay Buhner .25
283 Matt Lawton .15
284 Robin Ventura .25
285 Juan Gonzalez 1.00
286 Mo Vaughn 1.00
287 Kevin Millwood .50
288 Tino Martinez .50
289 Justin Thompson .15
290 Derek Jeter 2.50
291 Ben Davis .15
292 Mike Lowell .15
293 *Joe Crede* .40
294 *Micah Bowie* 1.00
295 Lance Berkman .25
296 Jason Marquis .15
297 Chad Green .15
298 Dee Brown .15
299 Jerry Hairston .15
300 Gabe Kapler .50
301 *Brent Stentz* .50
302 *Scott Mullen* .50
303 Brandon Reed .15
304 *Shea Hillenbrand* .50
305 *J.D. Closser* .50
306 Gary Matthews Jr. .15
307 *Toby Hall* .75
308 *Jason Phillips* .50
309 *Jose Macias* .40
310 *Jung Bong* .50
311 *Ramon Soler* .75
312 *Kelly Dransfeldt* .50
313 *Carlos Hernandez* .50
314 Kevin Haverbusch .15
315 *Aaron Myette* 1.50
316 *Chad Harville* .50
317 *Kyle Farnsworth* .75
318 *Travis Dawkins* 1.00
319 Willie Martinez .15
320 Carlos Lee .15
321 *Carlos Pena* 3.00
322 *Peter Bergeron* 1.00
323 *A.J. Burnett* 1.00
324 *Bucky Jacobsen* .50
325 *Mo Bruce* .50
326 Reggie Taylor .15
327 Jackie Rexrode .15
328 *Alvin Morrow* .50
329 Carlos Beltran .25
330 Eric Chavez .40
331 John Patterson .15
332 Jayson Werth .15
333 Richie Sexson .15
334 Randy Wolf .15
335 Eli Marrero .15
336 Paul LoDuca .15
337 J.D. Smart .15
338 Ryan Minor .15
339 Kris Benson .15
340 George Lombard .15
341 Troy Glaus 1.00
342 Eddie Yarnell .15
343 *Kip Wells* 1.00
344 *C.C. Sabathia* 2.00
345 *Sean Burroughs* 5.00
346 *Felipe Lopez* 1.50
347 *Ryan Rupe* .75
348 *Orber Moreno* .50
349 *Rafael Roque* .75
350 *Alfonso Soriano* 2.00
351 Pablo Ozuna .15
352 *Corey Patterson* 6.00
353 Braden Looper .15
354 Robbie Bell .15
355 *Mark Mulder* 1.00
356 Angel Pena .15
357 Kevin McGlinchy .15
358 *Michael Restovich* 1.00
359 Eric DuBose .15
360 Geoff Jenkins .15
361 *Mark Harriger* 1.00
362 *Junior Herndon* .50
363 *Tim Raines, Jr.* .75
364 *Rafael Furcal* 5.00
365 *Marcus Giles* 2.00
366 Ted Lilly .15
367 *Jorge Toca* .50
368 *David Kelton* .75
369 *Adam Dunn* 3.00
370 *Guillermo Mota* .50
371 *Brett Laxton* .50
372 *Travis Harper* .50
373 *Tom Davey* .50
374 *Darren Blakely* .75
375 *Tim Hudson* 5.00
376 Jason Romano .15
377 Dan Reichert .15
378 *Julio Lugo* .50
379 *Jose Garcia* .50
380 *Erubiel Durazo* 1.00
381 Jose Jimenez .15
382 Chris Fussell .15
383 Steve Lomasney .15
384 *Juan Pena* .50
385 *Allen Levrault* .50
386 *Juan Rivera* 1.00
387 *Steve Colyer* .50
388 *Joe Nathan* 1.50
389 *Ron Walker* .75
390 Nick Bierbrodt .15
391 *Luke Prokopec* 1.00
392 *Dave Roberts* .75
393 Mike Darr .15
394 *Abraham Nunez* 2.00
395 *Giuseppe Chiaramonte* .75
396 *Jermaine Van Buren* .50
397 Mike Kusiewicz .15
398 *Matt Wise* .50
399 *Joe McEwing* 3.00
400 *Matt Holliday* 1.00
401 *Willi Mo Pena* 3.00
402 *Ruben Quevedo* .75
403 *Rob Ryan* .50
404 *Freddy Garcia* 2.00
405 *Kevin Eberwein* .50
406 *Jesus Colome* .75
407 *Chris Singleton* .50
408 *Bubba Crosby* .50
409 *Jesus Cordero* .50
410 Donny Leon .15
411 *Goefrey Tomlinson* .50
412 *Jeff Winchester* 1.00
413 *Adam Piatt* 4.00
414 Robert Stratton .15
415 T.J. Tucker .15
416 *Ryan Langerhans* .50
417 *Anthony Shumaker* .50
418 *Matt Miller* .50
419 *Doug Clark* .50
420 *Kory DeHaan* .40
421 *David Eckstein* .50
422 *Brian Cooper* .50
423 *Brady Clark* .50
424 *Chris Magruder* .50
425 *Bobby Seay* .50
426 *Aubrey Huff* 1.50
427 Mike Jerzembeck .15
428 *Matt Blank* .50
429 *Benny Agbayani* 1.00
430 *Kevin Beirne* .50
431 *Josh Hamilton* 6.00
432 *Josh Girdley* .75
433 *Kyle Snyder* .50
434 *Mike Paradis* .50
435 *Jason Jennings* .75
436 *David Walling* .75
437 *Omar Ortiz* .50
438 *Jay Gehrke* .75
439 *Casey Burns* .50
440 *Carl Crawford* 1.50

1999 Bowman Autographs

Autographs were randomly seeded in Series 1 and 2 packs, with each card bearing a Topps Certified Autograph seal on the front and numbered with a "BA" prefix on back. Levels of scarcity are color coded by the metallic-foil highlights on front: Golds are the most difficult to find at 1:1941 Series 1 packs and 1:1024 Series 2. Silvers are seeded 1:485 in Series 1, 1:256 Series 2. Blues are found at an average rate of 1:162 in first series and 1:85 in second series.

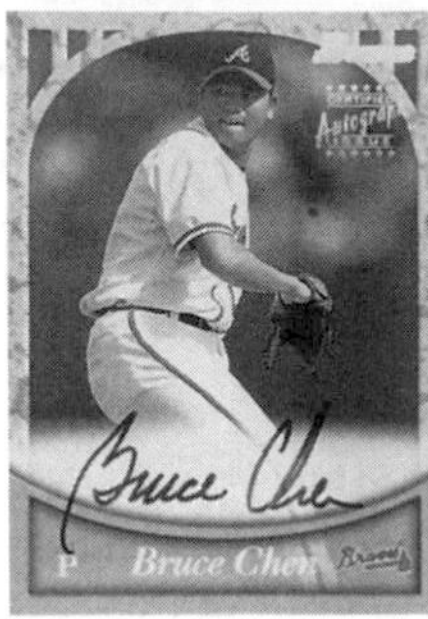

MT
Common Player: 6.00
Blues inserted 1:162 or 1:85
Silvers inserted 1:485 or 1:256
Golds inserted 1:1954 or 1:1024

1 Ruben Mateo B 25.00
2 Troy Glaus G 50.00
3 Ben Davis G 15.00
4 Jayson Werth B 10.00
5 Jerry Hairston Jr. S 15.00
6 Darnell McDonald B 10.00
7 Calvin Pickering S 20.00
8 Ryan Minor S 15.00
9 Alex Escobar B 15.00
10 Grant Roberts B 10.00
11 Carlos Guillen B 10.00
12 Ryan Anderson S 30.00
13 Gil Meche S 15.00
14 Russell Branyan S 15.00
15 Alex Ramirez S 20.00
16 Jason Rakers S 15.00
17 Eddie Yarnall B 10.00
18 Freddy Garcia B 20.00
19 Jason Conti B 6.00
20 Corey Koskie B 8.00
21 Roosevelt Brown B 8.00
22 Willie Martinez B 6.00
23 Mike Jerzembeck B 6.00
24 Lariel Gonzalez B 6.00
25 Fernando Seguignol B 15.00
26 Robert Fick S 15.00
27 J.D. Smart B 6.00
28 Ryan Mills B 6.00
29 Chad Hermansen G 20.00
30 Jason Grilli B 8.00
31 Michael Cuddyer B 10.00
32 Jacque Jones S 20.00
33 Reggie Taylor B 8.00
34 Richie Sexson G 25.00
35 Michael Barrett B 12.00
36 Paul LoDuca B 10.00
37 Adrian Beltre G 25.00
38 Peter Bergeron B 10.00
39 Joe Fontenot B 8.00
40 Randy Wolf B 10.00
41 Nick Johnson B 25.00
42 Ryan Bradley B 15.00
43 Mike Lowell S 15.00
44 Ricky Ledee B 15.00
45 Mike Lincoln S 15.00
46 Jeremy Giambi B 15.00
47 Dermal Brown S 15.00
48 Derrick Gibson B 12.00
49 Scott Randall B 6.00
50 Ben Petrick S 10.00
51 Jason LaRue B 6.00
52 Cole Liniak B 10.00
53 John Curtice B 6.00
54 Jackie Rexrode B 6.00
55 John Patterson B 10.00
56 Brad Penny S 15.00
57 Jared Sandberg B 8.00
58 Kerry Wood G 35.00
59 Eli Marrero B 7.00
60 Jason Marquis B 15.00
61 George Lombard S 15.00
62 Bruce Chen S 15.00
63 Kevin Witt S 8.00
64 Vernon Wells B 15.00
65 Billy Koch B 6.00
66 Roy Halladay B 20.00
67 Nathan Haynes B 6.00
68 Ben Grieve G 50.00
69 Eric Chavez G 25.00
70 Lance Berkman S 20.00

1999 Bowman Early Risers

This insert set features 11 current baseball superstars who have already won a Rookie of the Year award and who continue to excel. The insertion rate is 1:12. Cards have an "ER" prefix to the number on back.

MT
Complete Set (11): 20.00
Common Player: .75
Inserted 1:12

1 Mike Piazza 3.50
2 Cal Ripken Jr. 4.00
3 Jeff Bagwell 2.00
4 Ben Grieve 1.00
5 Kerry Wood .75
6 Mark McGwire 7.00
7 Nomar Garciaparra 3.50
8 Derek Jeter 3.50
9 Scott Rolen 1.25
10 Jose Canseco 1.00
11 Raul Mondesi .75

1999 Bowman Gold

Gold, rather than black, ink for the facsimile autograph, Bowman logo and player name on front, and a serial number on back from within an edition of 99, designate these parallels. Stated odds of finding the Gold cards were one per 111 packs of Series 1, and 1:59 in Series 2.

	MT
Common Player:	5.00
Veteran Stars:	20-40X
Young Stars/RCs:	4-10X

(See 1999 Bowman for checklist and base card values.)

1999 Bowman International

International parallels are a one-per-pack insert. Fronts are printed in metallic silver on which the photo's background has been replaced with a scenic picture supposed to be indicative of the player's native land. That location is spelled out at the lower-left corner of the photo, Backs of the Internationals are printed in the player's native language.

	MT
Complete Set (220):	150.00
Common Player:	.25
Veteran Stars:	1.5-2X
Young Stars/RCs:	1-1.5X

(See 1999 Bowman for checklist and base card values.)

1999 Bowman Late Bloomers

This 10-card set features late-round picks from previous drafts who have emerged as bona fide stars. These inserts are numbered with an "LB" prefix and seeded 1:12 packs.

		MT
Complete Set (10):		12.00
Common Player:		.50
Inserted 1:12		
LB1	Mike Piazza	6.00
LB2	Jim Thome	2.00
LB3	Larry Walker	1.50
LB4	Vinny Castilla	.50
LB5	Andy Pettitte	.75
LB6	Jim Edmonds	.50
LB7	Kenny Lofton	2.50
LB8	John Smoltz	.50
LB9	Mark Grace	.75
LB10	Trevor Hoffman	.50

1999 Bowman Scout's Choice

Scout's Choice inserts were randomly inserted in Series 1 packs and feature a borderless, double-etched design. The 21-card set focuses on prospects who have potential to win a future Rookie of the Year award. These are seeded 1:12 packs.

		MT
Complete Set (21):		45.00
Common Player:		1.00
Inserted 1:12		
SC1	Ruben Mateo	6.00
SC2	Ryan Anderson	4.00
SC3	Pat Burrell	8.00
SC4	Troy Glaus	10.00
SC5	Eric Chavez	5.00
SC6	Adrian Beltre	2.50
SC7	Bruce Chen	1.50
SC8	Carlos Beltran	1.50
SC9	Alex Gonzalez	1.00
SC10	Carlos Lee	2.00
SC11	George Lombard	2.00
SC12	Matt Clement	1.00
SC13	Calvin Pickering	1.00
SC14	Marlon Anderson	1.00
SC15	Chad Hermansen	1.00
SC16	Russell Branyan	1.00
SC17	Jeremy Giambi	2.00
SC18	Ricky Ledee	1.00
SC19	John Patterson	1.00
SC20	Roy Halladay	2.00
SC21	Michael Barrett	1.50

1999 Bowman 2000 Rookie of the Year

Randomly inserted in Series 2 packs at a rate of 1:12, these cards have a borderless, double-etched foil design. The 10-card set focuses on players that have potential to win the 2000 Rookie of the Year award.

		MT
Complete Set (10):		15.00
Common Player:		.75
Inserted 1:12		
1	Ryan Anderson	.75
2	Pat Burrell	3.00
3	A.J. Burnett	1.50
4	Ruben Mateo	1.00
5	Alex Escobar	2.00
6	Pablo Ozuna	.75
7	Mark Mulder	1.00
8	Corey Patterson	2.50
9	George Lombard	.75
10	Nick Johnson	4.00

1999 Bowman Chrome

Bowman Chrome was released in two 220-card series as an upscale chromium parallel version of Bowman Baseball. Like Bowman, each series has 150 prospect cards with blue foil, while 70 veteran cards have red foil. Packs contain four cards with an original SRP of $3.

		MT
Complete Set (440):		350.00
Complete Series 1 (220):		150.00
Complete Series 2 (220):		250.00
Common Player:		.40
International Stars:		1.5-2X
Gold Stars:		3-6X
Refractors:		4X
Int'l Refractor:		8X
Series 1 Pack (4):		4.00
Series 1 Wax Box (24):		80.00
Series 2 Pack (4):		6.00
Series 2 Wax Box (24):		130.00
1	Ben Grieve	1.50
2	Kerry Wood	1.50
3	Ruben Rivera	.40
4	Sandy Alomar	.50
5	Cal Ripken Jr.	6.00
6	Mark McGwire	10.00
7	Vladimir Guerrero	4.00
8	Moises Alou	.75
9	Jim Edmonds	.50
10	Greg Maddux	5.00
11	Gary Sheffield	.75
12	John Valentin	.40
13	Chuck Knoblauch	.75
14	Tony Clark	.75
15	Rusty Greer	.40
16	Al Leiter	.60
17	Travis Lee	1.50
18	Jose Cruz Jr.	1.00
19	Pedro Martinez	2.00
20	Paul O'Neill	.75
21	Todd Walker	.50
22	Vinny Castilla	.50
23	Barry Larkin	.75
24	Curt Schilling	.75
25	Jason Kendall	.50
26	Scott Erickson	.40
27	Andres Galarraga	.75
28	Jeff Shaw	.40
29	John Olerud	.50
30	Orlando Hernandez	2.00
31	Larry Walker	1.50
32	Andruw Jones	2.00
33	Jeff Cirillo	.40
34	Barry Bonds	2.00
35	Manny Ramirez	4.00
36	Mark Kotsay	.40
37	Ivan Rodriguez	2.00
38	Jeff King	.40
39	Brian Hunter	.40
40	Ray Durham	.40
41	Bernie Williams	1.50
42	Darin Erstad	1.50
43	Chipper Jones	5.00
44	Pat Hentgen	.40
45	Eric Young	.40
46	Jaret Wright	.75
47	Juan Guzman	.40
48	Jorge Posada	.50
49	Bobby Higginson	.40
50	Jose Guillen	.40
51	Trevor Hoffman	.40
52	Ken Griffey Jr.	8.00
53	David Justice	.75
54	Matt Williams	.75
55	Eric Karros	.50
56	Derek Bell	.40
57	Ray Lankford	.40
58	Mariano Rivera	.50
59	Brett Tomko	.40
60	Mike Mussina	1.50
61	Kenny Lofton	2.00
62	Chuck Finley	.40
63	Alex Gonzalez	.40
64	Mark Grace	.75
65	Raul Mondesi	.60
66	David Cone	.75
67	Brad Fullmer	.50
68	Andy Benes	.40
69	John Smoltz	.50
70	Shane Reynolds	.50
71	Bruce Chen	.75
72	Adam Kennedy	.40
73	Jack Cust	.40
74	Matt Clement	.40
75	Derrick Gibson	.40
76	Darnell McDonald	.40
77	*Adam Everett*	4.00
78	Ricardo Aramboles	.40
79	*Mark Quinn*	6.00
80	Jason Rakers	.40
81	*Seth Etherton*	4.00
82	*Jeff Urban*	2.50
83	Manny Aybar	.40
84	*Mike Nannini*	3.00
85	Onan Masaoka	.40
86	Rod Barajas	.40
87	Mike Frank	.40
88	Scott Randall	.40
89	*Justin Bowles*	1.00
90	Chris Haas	.40
91	*Arturo McDowell*	2.50
92	*Matt Belisle*	3.00
93	Scott Elarton	.40
94	Vernon Wells	.40
95	Pat Cline	.40
96	Ryan Anderson	2.00
97	Kevin Barker	.40
98	Ruben Mateo	2.00
99	Robert Fick	.40
100	Corey Koskie	.40
101	Ricky Ledee	.50
102	*Rick Elder*	3.00
103	*Jack Cressend*	1.50
104	Joe Lawrence	.40
105	Mike Lincoln	.40
106	*Kit Pellow*	1.50
107	*Matt Burch*	1.50
108	Brent Butler	.40
109	Jason Dewey	.40
110	Cesar King	.40
111	Julio Ramirez	.40
112	Jake Westbrook	.40
113	*Eric Valent*	3.00
114	*Roosevelt Brown*	2.00
115	*Choo Freeman*	2.50
116	Juan Melo	.40

No.	Player	Value
117	Jason Grilli	.40
118	Jared Sandberg	.40
119	Glenn Davis	.40
120	*David Riske*	1.50
121	Jacque Jones	.40
122	Corey Lee	.40
123	Michael Barrett	.40
124	Lariel Gonzalez	.40
125	Mitch Meluskey	.75
126	*Freddy Garcia*	3.00
127	*Tony Torcato*	2.50
128	Jeff Liefer	.40
129	Ntema Ndungidi	.40
130	*Andy Brown*	3.00
131	*Ryan Mills*	1.50
132	*Andy Abad*	.75
133	Carlos Febles	.40
134	*Jason Tyner*	2.50
135	Mark Osborne	.40
136	*Phil Norton*	1.50
137	Nathan Haynes	.40
138	Roy Halladay	.40
139	Juan Encarnacion	.75
140	Brad Penny	.40
141	Grant Roberts	.40
142	Aramis Ramirez	.40
143	Cristian Guzman	.40
144	*Mamon Tucker*	2.00
145	Ryan Bradley	.40
146	Brian Simmons	.40
147	Dan Reichert	.40
148	Russ Branyon	.40
149	*Victor Valencia*	1.50
150	Scott Schoeneweis	.40
151	*Sean Spencer*	1.50
152	Odalis Perez	.75
153	Joe Fontenot	.40
154	Milton Bradley	.40
155	*Josh McKinley*	2.00
156	Terrence Long	.40
157	Danny Klassen	.40
158	*Paul Hoover*	1.50
159	Ron Belliard	.40
160	Armando Rios	.40
161	Ramon Hernandez	.40
162	Jason Conti	.40
163	Chad Hermansen	.40
164	Jason Standridge	.40
165	Jason Dellaero	.40
166	John Curtice	.40
167	*Clayton Andrews*	1.50
168	Jeremy Giambi	.75
169	Alex Ramirez	.40
170	*Gabe Molina*	1.50
171	*Mario Encarnacion*	2.00
172	*Mike Zywica*	.75
173	*Chip Ambres*	2.50
174	Trot Nixon	.40
175	*Pat Burrell*	20.00
176	Jeff Yoder	.40
177	*Chris Jones*	2.00
178	Kevin Witt	.40
179	*Keith Luuloa*	.75
180	Billy Koch	.40
181	*Damaso Marte*	.75
182	*Ryan Glynn*	2.00
183	Calvin Pickering	.40
184	Michael Cuddyer	.40
185	*Nick Johnson*	8.00
186	*Doug Mientkiewicz*	1.50
187	*Nate Cornejo*	1.50
188	Octavio Dotel	.40
189	Wes Helms	.40
190	Nelson Lara	.40
191	*Chuck Abbott*	.75
192	Tony Armas, Jr.	.40
193	Gil Meche	.40
194	Ben Petrick	.40
195	*Chris George*	3.00
196	*Scott Hunter*	1.50
197	Ryan Brannan	.40
198	*Amaury Garcia*	1.50
199	Chris Gissell	.40
200	*Austin Kearns*	8.00
201	Alex Gonzalez	.40
202	Wade Miller	.40
203	Scott Williamson	.40
204	Chris Enochs	.40
205	Fernando Seguignol	.50
206	Marlon Anderson	.40
207	*Todd Sears*	2.00
208	*Nate Bump*	1.50
209	*J.M. Gold*	2.00
210	*Matt LeCroy*	.40
211	Alex Hernandez	.40
212	Luis Rivera	.40
213	Troy Cameron	.40
214	*Alex Escobar*	8.00
215	Jason LaRue	.40
216	Kyle Peterson	.40
217	Brent Butler	.40
218	Dernell Stenson	.40
219	Adrian Beltre	.50
220	Daryle Ward	.40
221	Jim Thome	.75
222	Cliff Floyd	.40
223	Rickey Henderson	.75
224	Garret Anderson	.40
225	Ken Caminiti	.75
226	Bret Boone	.40
227	Jeromy Burnitz	.40
228	Steve Finley	.40
229	Miguel Tejada	.40
230	Greg Vaughn	.75
231	Jose Offerman	.40
232	Andy Ashby	.40
233	Albert Belle	1.50
234	Fernando Tatis	1.00
235	Todd Helton	1.50
236	Sean Casey	1.00
237	Brian Giles	.40
238	Andy Pettitte	.75
239	Fred McGriff	.75
240	Roberto Alomar	1.50
241	Edgar Martinez	.40
242	Lee Stevens	.40
243	Shawn Green	1.50
244	Ryan Klesko	.50
245	Sammy Sosa	5.00
246	Todd Hundley	.40
247	Shannon Stewart	.40
248	Randy Johnson	1.00
249	Rondell White	.75
250	Mike Piazza	5.00
251	Craig Biggio	1.00
252	David Wells	.40
253	Brian Jordan	.40
254	Edgar Renteria	.40
255	Bartolo Colon	.40
256	Frank Thomas	2.50
257	Will Clark	1.00
258	Dean Palmer	.40
259	Dmitri Young	.40
260	Scott Rolen	2.00
261	Jeff Kent	.40
262	Dante Bichette	.75
263	Nomar Garciaparra	5.00
264	Tony Gwynn	4.00
265	Alex Rodriguez	6.00
266	Jose Canseco	2.00
267	Jason Giambi	.40
268	Jeff Bagwell	2.00
269	Carlos Delgado	1.50
270	Tom Glavine	.75
271	Eric Davis	.40
272	Edgardo Alfonzo	.75
273	Tim Salmon	.75
274	Johnny Damon	.40
275	Rafael Palmeiro	1.00
276	Denny Neagle	.40
277	Neifi Perez	.40
278	Roger Clemens	3.00
279	Brant Brown	.40
280	Kevin Brown	.75
281	Jay Bell	.40
282	Jay Buhner	.75
283	Matt Lawton	.40
284	Robin Ventura	.75
285	Juan Gonzalez	2.50
286	Mo Vaughn	1.50
287	Kevin Millwood	1.00
288	Tino Martinez	1.00
289	Justin Thompson	.40
290	Derek Jeter	5.00
291	Ben Davis	.40
292	Mike Lowell	.40
293	*Joe Crede*	.75
294	*Micah Bowie*	2.00
295	Lance Berkman	.40
296	Jason Marquis	.40
297	Chad Green	.40
298	Dee Brown	.40
299	Jerry Hairston	.40
300	Gabe Kapler	.75
301	*Brent Stentz*	1.50
302	*Scott Mullen*	.75
303	Brandon Reed	.40
304	*Shea Hillenbrand*	1.50
305	*J.D. Closser*	2.00
306	Gary Matthews Jr.	.50
307	*Toby Hall*	2.00
308	*Jason Phillips*	2.00
309	*Jose Macias*	.50
310	*Jung Bong*	2.00
311	*Ramon Soler*	1.50
312	*Kelly Dransfeldt*	1.50
313	*Carlos Hernandez*	1.50
314	Kevin Haverbusch	.40
315	*Aaron Myette*	3.00
316	*Chad Harville*	1.50
317	*Kyle Farnsworth*	3.00
318	*Travis Dawkins*	2.50
319	Willie Martinez	.40
320	Carlos Lee	.60
321	*Carlos Pena*	6.00
322	*Peter Bergeron*	3.00
323	*A.J. Burnett*	3.00
324	*Bucky Jacobsen*	1.50
325	*Mo Bruce*	1.50
326	Reggie Taylor	.40
327	Jackie Rexrode	.40
328	*Alvin Morrow*	1.50
329	Carlos Beltran	.40
330	Eric Chavez	.75
331	John Patterson	.40
332	Jayson Werth	.40
333	Richie Sexson	.75
334	Randy Wolf	.40
335	Eli Marrero	.40
336	Paul LoDuca	.40
337	J.D. Smart	.40
338	Ryan Minor	.75
339	Kris Benson	.40
340	George Lombard	.40
341	Troy Glaus	2.00
342	Eddie Yarnell	.40
343	*Kip Wells*	2.50
344	*C.C. Sabathia*	5.00
345	*Sean Burroughs*	12.00
346	*Felipe Lopez*	5.00
347	*Ryan Rupe*	2.00
348	*Orber Moreno*	1.50
349	*Rafael Roque*	.75
350	*Alfonso Soriano*	8.00
351	Pablo Ozuna	.40
352	*Corey Patterson*	18.00
353	Braden Looper	.40
354	Robbie Bell	.40
355	*Mark Mulder*	4.00
356	Angel Pena	.40
357	Kevin McGlinchy	.40
358	*Michael Restovich*	3.00
359	Eric DuBose	.40
360	Geoff Jenkins	.40
361	*Mark Harriger*	1.50
362	*Junior Herndon*	1.50
363	*Tim Raines, Jr.*	3.00
364	*Rafael Furcal*	20.00
365	*Marcus Giles*	6.00
366	Ted Lilly	.40
367	*Jorge Toca*	2.00
368	*David Kelton*	3.00
369	*Adam Dunn*	8.00
370	*Guillermo Mota*	.75
371	*Brett Laxton*	.75
372	*Travis Harper*	1.00
373	*Tom Davey*	1.00
374	*Darren Blakely*	1.50
375	*Tim Hudson*	12.00
376	Jason Romano	.40
377	Dan Reichert	.40
378	*Julio Lugo*	2.00
379	*Jose Garcia*	1.50
380	*Erubiel Durazo*	4.00
381	Jose Jimenez	.40
382	Chris Fussell	.40
383	Steve Lomasney	.40
384	*Juan Pena*	2.00
385	*Allen Levrault*	1.50
386	*Juan Rivera*	3.00
387	*Steve Colyer*	1.50
388	*Joe Nathan*	1.50
389	*Ron Walker*	1.00
390	Nick Bierbrodt	.40
391	*Luke Prokopec*	2.00
392	*Dave Roberts*	.75
393	Mike Darr	.40
394	*Abraham Nunez*	6.00
395	*Giuseppe Chiaramonte*	2.00
396	*Jermaine Van Buren*	1.50
397	Mike Kusiewicz	.40
398	*Matt Wise*	1.50
399	*Joe McEwing*	1.50
400	*Matt Holliday*	3.00
401	*Willi Mo Pena*	8.00
402	*Ruben Quevedo*	2.00
403	*Rob Ryan*	.50
404	*Freddy Garcia*	6.00
405	*Kevin Eberwein*	2.00
406	*Jesus Colome*	2.00
407	*Chris Singleton*	.75
408	*Bubba Crosby*	2.00
409	*Jesus Cordero*	1.00
410	Donny Leon	.40
411	*Goefrey Tomlinson*	1.00
412	*Jeff Winchester*	2.00
413	*Adam Piatt*	10.00
414	Robert Stratton	.40
415	T.J. Tucker	.40
416	*Ryan Langerhans*	1.50
417	*Chris Wakeland*	.50
418	*Matt Miller*	.50
419	*Doug Clark*	1.50
420	*Kory DeHaan*	1.50
421	*David Eckstein*	1.00
422	*Brian Cooper*	1.00
423	*Brady Clark*	1.50
424	*Chris Magruder*	1.00
425	*Bobby Seay*	2.50
426	*Aubrey Huff*	4.00
427	Mike Jerzembeck	.40
428	*Matt Blank*	1.50
429	*Benny Agbayani*	5.00
430	*Kevin Beirne*	.50
431	*Josh Hamilton*	20.00
432	*Josh Girdley*	2.00
433	*Kyle Snyder*	1.50
434	*Mike Paradis*	1.50
435	*Jason Jennings*	2.00
436	*David Walling*	2.00
437	*Omar Ortiz*	1.00
438	*Jay Gehrke*	1.50
439	*Casey Burns*	1.50
440	*Carl Crawford*	5.00

1999 Bowman Chrome Refractors

Refractor versions of all Bowman Chrome base cards and inserts were also created. Base card Refractors are found at the average rate of one per 12 packs. Scout's Choice Refractors are a 1:48 find; International Refractors (serially numbered within an edition of 100 each) are 1:76 and Diamond Aces Refractors are 1:84.

	MT
Common Player:	2.00
Refractor Stars:	4X

(See 1999 Bowman Chrome for checklist and base card values.)

1999 Bowman Chrome Diamond Aces

This 18-card set features nine emerging stars along with nine proven veterans. The cards have a prismatic look with "Diamond Aces" across the top. They are inserted in Series 1 packs at an average rate of 1:21. A parallel Refractor version is also randomly inserted and found 1:84 packs.

	MT
Complete Set (18):	150.00
Common Player:	3.00
Inserted 1:21	
Refractors:	1.5-2X
Inserted 1:84	
DA1 Troy Glaus	10.00
DA2 Eric Chavez	4.00
DA3 Fernando Seguignol	3.00
DA4 Ryan Anderson	3.00
DA5 Ruben Mateo	6.00
DA6 Carlos Beltran	3.00
DA7 Adrian Beltre	4.00
DA8 Bruce Chen	3.00
DA9 Pat Burrell	10.00
DA10Mike Piazza	12.00
DA11Ken Griffey Jr.	20.00
DA12Chipper Jones	10.00
DA13Derek Jeter	12.00
DA14Mark McGwire	25.00
DA15Nomar Garciaparra	12.00
DA16Sammy Sosa	12.00
DA17Juan Gonzalez	5.00
DA18Alex Rodriguez	15.00

1999 Bowman Chrome Impact

The checklist of this Series 2 insert (one per 15 packs, on average) mixes a dozen youngsters - labeled "Early Impact" on front - who are already making a mark in the majors with eight veteran stars, whose cards are labeled "Lasting Impact". A Refractor version - a 1:75 pack insert - is a parallel.

		MT
Complete Set (20):		75.00
Common Player:		1.50
Inserted 1:15		
Refractor:		1.5-3X
Inserted 1:75		
1	Alfonso Soriano	4.00
2	Pat Burrell	6.00
3	Ruben Mateo	2.00
4	A.J. Burnett	2.50
5	Corey Patterson	4.00
6	Daryle Ward	1.50
7	Eric Chavez	1.50
8	Troy Glaus	4.00
9	Sean Casey	2.00
10	Joe McEwing	2.00
11	Gabe Kapler	2.00
12	Michael Barrett	1.50
13	Sammy Sosa	6.00
14	Alex Rodriguez	8.00
15	Mark McGwire	12.00
16	Derek Jeter	6.00
17	Nomar Garciaparra	6.00
18	Mike Piazza	6.00
19	Chipper Jones	6.00
20	Ken Griffey Jr.	10.00

1999 Bowman Chrome Scout's Choice

This is a chromium parallel of the inserts found in Series 1 Bowman. The 21-card set is inserted in Series 1 Chrome packs at a rate of 1:12 and showcases prospects that have potential to win a future Rookie of the Year award. Refractor parallels are also randomly inserted 1:48 packs.

	MT
Complete Set (21):	75.00
Common Player:	2.00
Inserted 1:12	
Refractors:	1.5x to 2x
Inserted 1:48	
SC1 Ruben Mateo	8.00
SC2 Ryan Anderson	6.00
SC3 Pat Burrell	10.00
SC4 Troy Glaus	12.00
SC5 Eric Chavez	8.00
SC6 Adrian Beltre	4.00
SC7 Bruce Chen	3.00
SC8 Carlos Beltran	2.00
SC9 Alex Gonzalez	2.00
SC10Carlos Lee	3.00
SC11George Lombard	3.00
SC12Matt Clement	2.00
SC13Calvin Pickering	2.00
SC14Marlon Anderson	2.00
SC15Chad Hermansen	2.00
SC16Russell Branyan	2.00
SC17Jeremy Giambi	2.00
SC18Ricky Ledee	2.00
SC19John Patterson	2.00
SC20Roy Halladay	2.00
SC21Michael Barrett	3.00

1999 Bowman Chrome 2000 Rookie of the Year

This is a chromium parallel of the inserts found in Series 2 Bowman. The 10-card set is inserted in Series 2 Chrome packs at a rate of 1:20 and showcases prospects that have potential to win the 2000 Rookie of the Year award. Refractor parallels are also randomly inserted 1:100 packs.

		MT
Complete Set (10):		25.00
Common Player:		1.50
Inserted 1:20		
Refractors:		1.5-3X
Inserted 1:100		
1	Ryan Anderson	2.00
2	Pat Burrell	6.00
3	A.J. Burnett	2.50
4	Ruben Mateo	2.00
5	Alex Escobar	3.00
6	Pablo Ozuna	1.50
7	Mark Mulder	2.00
8	Corey Patterson	5.00
9	George Lombard	1.50
10	Nick Johnson	6.00

1999 Bowman's Best Pre-production

These cards were issued to draw interest to the '99 Bowman's Best issue. The promos are virtually identical to the issued version of each player's card except for the card number which is preceeded by a "PP" prefix.

	MT
Complete Set (3):	5.00
Common Player:	2.00
PP1 Javy Lopez	2.00
PP2 Marlon Anderson	2.00
PP3 J.M. Gold	2.00

1999 Bowman's Best

Bowman's Best consists of 200 cards printed on thick 27-point stock. Within the base set are 85 veteran stars printed on gold foil, 15 Best Performers on bronze foil, 50 Prospects on silver foil and 50 rookies on blue foil. The rookies are seeded one per pack. There are also two parallel versions: Refractors and Atomic Refractors. Refractors are inserted 1:15 packs and are sequentially numbered to 400, while Atomic Refractors are found 1:62 packs and are sequentially numbered to 100.

		MT
Complete Set (200):		100.00
Common Player:		.25
Common SP (151-200):		1.50
Inserted 1:1		
Refractors:		8-15X
SP Refractors:		3-5X
Production 400 sets		
Atomic Refractors:		25-40X
SP Atomic Refractors:		6-12X
Production 100 sets		
Pack (6):		5.00
Wax Box (24):		100.00
1	Chipper Jones	2.50
2	Brian Jordan	.25
3	David Justice	.50
4	Jason Kendall	.40
5	Mo Vaughn	1.25
6	Jim Edmonds	.25
7	Wade Boggs	.50
8	Jeromy Burnitz	.25
9	Todd Hundley	.25
10	Rondell White	.40
11	Cliff Floyd	.25
12	Sean Casey	.50
13	Bernie Williams	1.00
14	Dante Bichette	.50
15	Greg Vaughn	.40
16	Andres Galarraga	.75
17	Ray Durham	.25
18	Jim Thome	.75
19	Gary Sheffield	.40
20	Frank Thomas	2.00
21	Orlando Hernandez	1.00
22	Ivan Rodriguez	1.25
23	Jose Cruz Jr.	.50
24	Jason Giambi	.25
25	Craig Biggio	.75
26	Kerry Wood	1.00
27	Manny Ramirez	1.50
28	Curt Schilling	.40
29	Mike Mussina	1.00
30	Tim Salmon	.50
31	Mike Piazza	3.00
32	Roberto Alomar	1.00
33	Larry Walker	1.00
34	Barry Larkin	.75
35	Nomar Garciaparra	3.00
36	Paul O'Neill	.50
37	Todd Walker	.25
38	Eric Karros	.40
39	Brad Fullmer	.25
40	John Olerud	.40
41	Todd Helton	1.00
42	Raul Mondesi	.40
43	Jose Canseco	1.00
44	Matt Williams	.75
45	Ray Lankford	.25
46	Carlos Delgado	.50
47	Darin Erstad	1.00
48	Vladimir Guerrero	2.50
49	Robin Ventura	.40
50	Alex Rodriguez	4.00
51	Vinny Castilla	.25
52	Tony Clark	.50
53	Pedro Martinez	1.25
54	Rafael Palmeiro	.75
55	Scott Rolen	1.50
56	Tino Martinez	.75
57	Tony Gwynn	2.50
58	Barry Bonds	1.25

59	Kenny Lofton	1.25
60	Javy Lopez	.25
61	Mark Grace	.50
62	Travis Lee	1.00
63	Kevin Brown	.50
64	Al Leiter	.25
65	Albert Belle	1.25
66	Sammy Sosa	3.00
67	Greg Maddux	3.00
68	Mark Kotsay	.25
69	Dmitri Young	.25
70	Mark McGwire	6.00
71	Juan Gonzalez	1.50
72	Andruw Jones	1.25
73	Derek Jeter	3.00
74	Randy Johnson	1.00
75	Cal Ripken Jr.	4.00
76	Shawn Green	.50
77	Moises Alou	.40
78	Tom Glavine	.40
79	Sandy Alomar	.25
80	Ken Griffey Jr.	5.00
81	Ryan Klesko	.40
82	Jeff Bagwell	1.25
83	Ben Grieve	1.00
84	John Smoltz	.25
85	Roger Clemens	1.50
86	Ken Griffey Jr.	2.50
87	Roger Clemens	.75
88	Derek Jeter	1.50
89	Nomar Garciaparra	1.50
90	Mark McGwire	3.00
91	Sammy Sosa	1.50
92	Alex Rodriguez	2.00
93	Greg Maddux	1.50
94	Vladimir Guerrero	1.00
95	Chipper Jones	1.25
96	Kerry Wood	.50
97	Ben Grieve	.50
98	Tony Gwynn	1.25
99	Juan Gonzalez	.75
100	Mike Piazza	1.50
101	Eric Chavez	.75
102	Billy Koch	.25
103	Dernell Stenson	.25
104	Marlon Anderson	.25
105	Ron Belliard	.25
106	Bruce Chen	.25
107	Carlos Beltran	.25
108	Chad Hermansen	.25
109	Ryan Anderson	.75
110	Michael Barrett	1.00
111	Matt Clement	.25
112	Ben Davis	.25
113	Calvin Pickering	.25
114	Brad Penny	.25
115	Paul Konerko	.25
116	Alex Gonzalez	.25
117	George Lombard	.25
118	John Patterson	.25
119	Rob Bell	.25
120	Ruben Mateo	1.50
121	*Peter Bergeron*	2.00
122	Ryan Bradley	.25
123	Carlos Lee	.25
124	Gabe Kapler	1.50
125	Ramon Hernandez	.25
126	Carlos Febles	.75
127	Mitch Meluskey	.50
128	Michael Cuddyer	.25
129	Pablo Ozuna	.25
130	Jayson Werth	.25
131	Ricky Ledee	.25
132	Jeremy Giambi	.75
133	Danny Klassen	.25
134	Mark DeRosa	.25
135	Randy Wolf	.25
136	Roy Halladay	.50
137	Derrick Gibson	.25
138	Ben Petrick	.25
139	Warren Morris	.25
140	Lance Berkman	.25
141	Russell Branyan	.25
142	Adrian Beltre	.75
143	Juan Encarnacion	.50
144	Fernando Seguignol	.25
145	Corey Koskie	.25
146	Preston Wilson	.25
147	Homer Bush	.25
148	Daryle Ward	.25
149	*Joe McEwing*	.50
150	*Peter Bergeron*	1.50
151	*Pat Burrell*	10.00
152	*Choo Freeman*	1.00
153	*Matt Belisle*	1.50
154	*Carlos Pena*	3.00
155	*A.J. Burnett*	1.50
156	*Doug Mientkiewicz*	.75
157	*Sean Burroughs*	6.00
158	*Mike Zywica*	.75
159	*Corey Patterson*	10.00
160	*Austin Kearns*	4.00
161	*Chip Ambres*	1.50
162	*Kelly Dransfeldt*	.75
163	*Mike Nannini*	1.50
164	*Mark Mulder*	2.00
165	*Jason Tyner*	1.50
166	*Bobby Seay*	1.50
167	*Alex Escobar*	4.00
168	*Nick Johnson*	4.00
169	*Alfonso Soriano*	4.00
170	*Clayton Andrews*	.75
171	*C.C. Sabathia*	3.00
172	*Matt Holliday*	1.50
173	*Brad Lidge*	.75
174	*Kit Pellow*	.75
175	*J.M. Gold*	1.00
176	*Roosevelt Brown*	.75
177	*Eric Valent*	2.00
178	*Adam Everett*	1.00
179	*Jorge Toca*	1.00
180	*Matt Roney*	1.00
181	*Andy Brown*	1.50
182	*Phil Norton*	.50
183	*Mickey Lopez*	.50
184	*Chris George*	1.00
185	*Arturo McDowell*	1.00
186	*Jose Fernandez*	.50
187	*Seth Etherton*	1.00
188	*Josh McKinley*	1.00
189	*Nate Cornejo*	1.00
190	*Giuseppe Chiaramonte*	1.00
191	*Mamon Tucker*	1.00
192	*Ryan Mills*	.75
193	*Chad Moeller*	.75
194	*Tony Torcato*	1.50
195	*Jeff Winchester*	1.50
196	*Rick Elder*	1.50
197	*Matt Burch*	.75
198	*Jeff Urban*	.75
199	*Chris Jones*	1.00
200	*Masao Kida*	.50

1999 Bowman's Best Franchise Best

Ten league leaders are featured in this insert set on three different technologies: Mach I, Mach II and Mach III. Mach I feature die-cut Serillusion stock and is numbered to 3,000. Mach II features die-cut refractive styrene stock, numbered to 1,000; and, Mach III features die-cut polycarbonate stock and is limited to 500 numbered sets. All cards numbers have an "FB" prefix.

		MT
Complete Set (10):		100.00
Common Player:		5.00
Production 3,000 sets		
Mach II:		1.5-2X
Production 1,000 sets		
Mach III:		2-3X
Production 500 sets		
1	Mark McGwire	25.00
2	Ken Griffey Jr.	20.00
3	Sammy Sosa	12.00
4	Nomar Garciaparra	12.00
5	Alex Rodriguez	15.00
6	Derek Jeter	12.00
7	Mike Piazza	12.00
8	Frank Thomas	8.00
9	Chipper Jones	10.00
10	Juan Gonzalez	5.00

1999 Bowman's Best Franchise Favorites

This six-card set features retired legends and current stars in three versions. Version A features a current star, Version B features a retired player and Version C pairs the current star with the retired player. The insert rate is 1:40 packs. Cards have an "FR" prefix to the number on back.

		MT
Complete Set (6):		40.00
Common Player:		5.00
Inserted 1:75		
1A	Derek Jeter	15.00
1B	Don Mattingly	5.00
1C	Derek Jeter, Don Mattingly	10.00
2A	Scott Rolen	8.00
2B	Mike Schmidt	5.00
2C	Scott Rolen, Mike Schmidt	6.00

1999 Bowman's Best Franchise Favorites Autographs

This is a parallel autographed version of the regular Franchise Favorites inserts. The insert rate is 1:1,548 for Versions A and B, and 1:6,191 packs for Version C.

		MT
Common Player:		100.00
Version A & B 1:1548		
Version C 1:6191		
1A	Derek Jeter	200.00
1B	Don Mattingly	175.00
1C	Derek Jeter, Don Mattingly	400.00
2A	Scott Rolen	100.00
2B	Mike Schmidt	120.00
2C	Scott Rolen, Mike Schmidt	325.00

1999 Bowman's Best Future Foundations

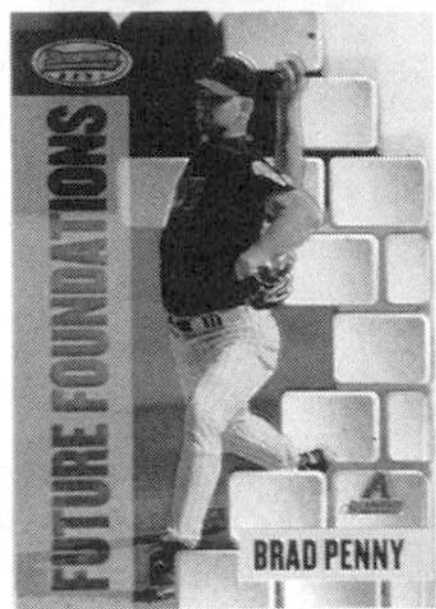

Ten up-and-coming players are featured in this set that has the same technologies as the Franchise Best inserts and broken down the same way. The insert rates are 1:41 packs for Mach I, 1:124 for Mach II and 1:248 for Mach III.

		MT
Complete Set (10):		75.00
Common Player:		3.00
Production 3,000 sets		
Mach II:		1.5-2X
Production 1,000 sets		
Mach III:		2-3X
Production 500 sets		
1	Ruben Mateo	6.00
2	Troy Glaus	8.00
3	Eric Chavez	6.00
4	Pat Burrell	12.00
5	Adrian Beltre	5.00
6	Ryan Anderson	5.00
7	Alfonso Soriano	6.00
8	Brad Penny	3.00
9	Derrick Gibson	3.00
10	Bruce Chen	3.00

1999 Bowman's Best Mirror Image

These inserts feature a veteran player on one side and a prospect on the other side for a total of 10 double-sided cards featuring 20 players. The insert rate is 1:24 packs. There are also parallel Refractor and Atomic Refractor versions. Refractors are inserted 1:96 packs while Atomic Refractors are seeded 1:192 packs.

		MT
Complete Set (10):		100.00
Common Player:		4.00
Inserted 1:24		
Refractors:		1.5-2X
Inserted 1:96		
Atomic Refractors:		2-4X
Inserted 1:192		
1	Alex Rodriguez, Alex Gonzalez	10.00
2	Ken Griffey Jr., Ruben Mateo	18.00
3	Derek Jeter, Alfonso Soriano	15.00
4	Sammy Sosa, Corey Patterson	10.00
5	Greg Maddux, Bruce Chen	10.00
6	Chipper Jones, Eric Chavez	8.00
7	Vladimir Guerrero, Carlos Beltran	6.00
8	Frank Thomas, Nick Johnson	6.00
9	Nomar Garciaparra, Pablo Ozuna	10.00
10	Mark McGwire, Pat Burrell	25.00

1999 Bowman's Best Rookie Locker Room Autographs

This five-card set features autographs of baseball's current hot prospects. Each card is branded with a "Topps Certified Autograph Issue" stamp and the issue is inserted 1:248 packs.

		MT
Complete Set (5):		180.00
Common Player:		25.00
Inserted 1:248		
1	Pat Burrell	60.00
2	Michael Barrett	25.00
3	Troy Glaus	50.00
4	Gabe Kapler	40.00
5	Eric Chavez	30.00

1999 Bowman's Best Rookie Locker Room Game-Worn Jerseys

This four-card set spotlights hot prospects and has a swatch of game-used jersey from the featured player embedded into the card. These are inserted one card per 270 packs.

		MT
Complete Set (4):		200.00
Common Player:		50.00
Inserted 1:270		
1	Richie Sexson	50.00
2	Michael Barrett	50.00
3	Troy Glaus	90.00
4	Eric Chavez	60.00

1999 Bowman's Best Rookie Locker Room Game-Used Lumber

This six-card set features actual pieces of each player's game-used bat embedded into the cards. The insertion rate is about one cards per 258 packs.

		MT
Complete Set (6):		400.00
Common Player:		50.00
Inserted 1:258		
1	Pat Burrell	90.00
2	Michael Barrett	50.00
3	Troy Glaus	90.00
4	Gabe Kapler	75.00
5	Eric Chavez	60.00
6	Richie Sexson	50.00

1999 Bowman's Best Rookie of the Year

This set salutes 1998 AL and NL Rookie of Year award winners Kerry Wood and Ben Grieve. They are inserted 1:95 packs and are numbered with a ROY prefix. Ben Grieve also autographed some of the inserts which feature a "Topps Certified Autograph Issue" stamp. Autographs are seeded 1:1,241 packs.

		MT
Complete Set (2):		12.00
1	Ben Grieve	8.00
2	Kerry Wood	6.00
A1	Ben Grieve (Auto.)	50.00

2000 Bowman

Released in one 440-card series. The card fronts are foil stamped to differentiate Veterans (gold foil) from Rookies and Prospects (silver). All card fronts feature facsimile signatures from the players' original Topps contracts. All bona fide rookie cards also exhibit the "Bowman Rookie Card" stamped under the 2000 Bowman logo.

		MT
Complete Set (440):		125.00
Common Player:		.15
Common Rookie:		.50
Pack (10):		3.00
Wax Box:		65.00
1	Vladimir Guerrero	1.50
2	Chipper Jones	1.50
3	Todd Walker	.15
4	Barry Larkin	.40
5	Bernie Williams	.50
6	Todd Helton	.75
7	Jermaine Dye	.15
8	Brian Giles	.25
9	Freddy Garcia	.15
10	Greg Vaughn	.25
11	Alex Gonzalez	.15
12	Luis Gonzalez	.15
13	Ron Belliard	.15
14	Ben Grieve	.30
15	Carlos Delgado	.50
16	Brian Jordan	.15
17	Fernando Tatis	.25
18	Ryan Rupe	.15
19	Miguel Tejada	.15
20	Mark Grace	.30
21	Kenny Lofton	.50
22	Eric Karros	.25
23	Cliff Floyd	.15
24	John Halama	.15
25	Cristian Guzman	.15
26	Scott Williamson	.15
27	Mike Lieberthal	.15
28	Tim Hudson	.25
29	Warren Morris	.15
30	Pedro Martinez	1.00
31	John Smoltz	.15
32	Ray Durham	.15
33	Chad Allen	.15
34	Tony Clark	.25
35	Tino Martinez	.40
36	J.T. Snow Jr.	.15
37	Kevin Brown	.25
38	Bartolo Colon	.15
39	Rey Ordonez	.15
40	Jeff Bagwell	.75
41	Ivan Rodriguez	.75
42	Eric Chavez	.25
43	Eric Milton	.15
44	Jose Canseco	.75
45	Shawn Green	.50
46	Rich Aurilia	.15
47	Roberto Alomar	.50
48	Brian Daubach	.15
49	Magglio Ordonez	.15
50	Derek Jeter	2.00
51	Kris Benson	.15
52	Albert Belle	.50
53	Rondell White	.25
54	Justin Thompson	.15
55	Nomar Garciaparra	2.00
56	Chuck Finley	.15
57	Omar Vizquel	.25
58	Luis Castillo	.15
59	Richard Hidalgo	.15
60	Barry Bonds	.75
61	Craig Biggio	.40
62	Doug Glanville	.15
63	Gabe Kapler	.30
64	Johnny Damon	.15
65	Pokey Reese	.15
66	Andy Pettitte	.25
67	B.J. Surhoff	.15
68	Richie Sexson	.15
69	Javy Lopez	.25
70	Raul Mondesi	.25
71	Darin Erstad	.30
72	Kevin Millwood	.25
73	Ricky Ledee	.15
74	John Olerud	.25
75	Sean Casey	.40
76	Carlos Febles	.15
77	Paul O'Neill	.40
78	Bob Abreu	.25
79	Neifi Perez	.15
80	Tony Gwynn	1.50
81	Russ Ortiz	.15
82	Matt Williams	.40
83	Chris Carpenter	.15
84	Roger Cedeno	.15
85	Tim Salmon	.30
86	Billy Koch	.15
87	Jeromy Burnitz	.25
88	Edgardo Alfonzo	.25
89	Jay Bell	.15
90	Manny Ramirez	.75
91	Frank Thomas	1.00
92	Mike Mussina	.50
93	J.D. Drew	.40
94	Adrian Beltre	.30
95	Alex Rodriguez	2.50
96	Larry Walker	.50
97	Juan Encarnacion	.15
98	Mike Sweeney	.15
99	Rusty Greer	.15
100	Randy Johnson	.50
101	Jose Vidro	.15
102	Preston Wilson	.15
103	Greg Maddux	1.50
104	Jason Giambi	.25
105	Cal Ripken Jr.	2.50
106	Carlos Beltran	.25
107	Vinny Castilla	.25
108	Mariano Rivera	.25
109	Mo Vaughn	.50
110	Rafael Palmeiro	.50
111	Shannon Stewart	.15
112	Mike Hampton	.15
113	Joe Nathan	.15
114	Ben Davis	.15
115	Andruw Jones	.50
116	Robin Ventura	.25
117	Damion Easley	.15
118	Jeff Cirillo	.25
119	Kerry Wood	.40
120	Scott Rolen	.75
121	Sammy Sosa	2.00
122	Ken Griffey Jr.	3.00
123	Shane Reynolds	.15
124	Troy Glaus	.75
125	Tom Glavine	.30
126	Michael Barrett	.15
127	Al Leiter	.25
128	Jason Kendall	.25
129	Roger Clemens	1.00
130	Juan Gonzalez	.75
131	Corey Koskie	.15
132	Curt Schilling	.25
133	Mike Piazza	2.00
134	Gary Sheffield	.30
135	Jim Thome	.40
136	Orlando Hernandez	.40
137	Ray Lankford	.15
138	Geoff Jenkins	.25
139	Jose Lima	.15
140	Mark McGwire	3.00
141	Adam Piatt	.15
142	*Pat Manning*	1.50
143	*Marcos Castillo*	.50
144	*Lesli Brea*	.50
145	*Humberto Cota*	1.00
146	Ben Petrick	.15
147	Kip Wells	.15
148	Willi Mo Pena	.75
149	*Chris Wakeland*	.50
150	*Brad Baker*	1.50
151	*Robbie Morrison*	.50
152	Reggie Taylor	.15
153	*Brian Cole*	.50
154	Peter Bergeron	.15
155	Roosevelt Brown	.15
156	*Matt Cepicky*	.50
157	Ramon Castro	.15
158	*Brad Baisley*	1.00
159	*Jeff Goldbach*	1.50
160	Mitch Meluskey	.15
161	Chad Harville	.15

No.	Player	Value
162	Brian Cooper	.15
163	Marcus Giles	.15
164	Jim Morris	.15
165	Geoff Goetz	.15
166	*Bobby Bradley*	2.00
167	Rob Bell	.15
168	Joe Crede	.15
169	Michael Restovich	.15
170	*Quincy Foster*	.50
171	*Enrique Cruz*	.75
172	Mark Quinn	.15
173	Nick Johnson	.15
174	Jeff Liefer	.15
175	*Kevin Mench*	1.50
176	Steve Lomasney	.15
177	Jayson Werth	.15
178	Tim Drew	.15
179	Chip Ambres	.15
180	Ryan Anderson	.40
181	Matt Blank	.15
182	Giuseppe Chiaramonte	.15
183	*Corey Myers*	1.50
184	Jeff Yoder	.15
185	*Craig Dingman*	.50
186	*Jon Hamilton*	.50
187	Toby Hall	.15
188	Russell Branyan	.15
189	*Brian Falkenborg*	.50
190	*Aaron Harang*	.50
191	Juan Pena	.15
192	*Travis Thompson*	.50
193	Alfonso Soriano	.75
194	*Alejandro Diaz*	1.00
195	Carlos Pena	.15
196	Kevin Nicholson	.15
197	Mo Bruce	.15
198	C.C. Sabathia	.15
199	Carl Crawford	.15
200	Rafael Furcal	.75
201	*Andrew Beinbrink*	.50
202	Jimmy Osting	.15
203	*Aaron McNeal*	2.00
204	Brett Laxton	.15
205	Chris George	.15
206	Felipe Lopez	.15
207	*Ben Sheets*	4.00
208	*Mike Meyers*	2.00
209	Jason Conti	.15
210	Milton Bradley	.15
211	*Chris Mears*	.50
212	*David Tavarez*	.50
213	Jason Romano	.15
214	Goefrey Tomlinson	.15
215	Jimmy Rollins	.15
216	Pablo Ozuna	.15
217	Steve Cox	.15
218	Terrence Long	.15
219	*Jeff DaVanon*	.50
220	Rick Ankiel	2.00
221	Jason Standridge	.15
222	Tony Armas	.15
223	Jason Tyner	.15
224	Ramon Ortiz	.15
225	Daryle Ward	.15
226	*Enger Veras*	.50
227	*Chris Jones*	.75
228	*Eric Cammack*	.50
229	Ruben Mateo	.15
230	*Ken Harvey*	1.00
231	Jake Westbrook	.15
232	*Rob Purvis*	.50
233	Choo Freeman	.15
234	Aramis Ramirez	.15
235	A.J. Burnett	.15
236	Kevin Barker	.15
237	*Chance Caple*	.75
238	Jarrod Washburn	.15
239	Lance Berkman	.15
240	*Michael Wenner*	.50
241	Alex Sanchez	.15
242	*Jake Esteves*	.50
243	Grant Roberts	.15
244	*Mark Ellis*	1.50
245	Donny Leon	.15
246	David Eckstein	.15
247	*Dicky Gonzalez*	.50
248	John Patterson	.15
249	Chad Green	.15
250	*Scot Shields*	.50
251	Troy Cameron	.15
252	Jose Molina	.15
253	*Rob Pugmire*	.50
254	Rick Elder	.15
255	Sean Burroughs	.75
256	*Josh Kalinowski*	.50
257	Matt LeCroy	.15
258	*Alex Graman*	1.00
259	*Tomokazu Ohka*	1.00
260	Brady Clark	.15
261	*Rico Washington*	.75
262	Gary Matthews Jr.	.15
263	Matt Wise	.15
264	*Keith Reed*	.50
265	*Santiago Ramirez*	.50
266	*Ben Broussard*	5.00
267	Ryan Langerhans	.15
268	Juan Rivera	.15
269	Shawn Gallagher	.15
270	Jorge Toca	.15
271	Brad Lidge	.15
272	*Leo Estrella*	.50
273	Ruben Quevedo	.15
274	Jack Cust	.15
275	T.J. Tucker	.15
276	Mike Colangelo	.15
277	Brian Schneider	.15
278	Calvin Murray	.15
279	Josh Girdley	.15
280	Mike Paradis	.15
281	Chad Hermansen	.15
282	*Ty Howington*	.75
283	Aaron Myette	.15
284	D'Angelo Jimenez	.15
285	Dernell Stenson	.15
286	Jerry Hairston Jr.	.15
287	*Gary Majewski*	.50
288	*Derrin Ebert*	.50
289	*Steve Fish*	.50
290	Carlos Hernandez	.15
291	Allen Levrault	.15
292	*Sean McNally*	.50
293	*Randey Dorame*	.75
294	*Wes Anderson*	1.00
295	B.J. Ryan	.15
296	*Alan Webb*	.50
297	*Brandon Inge*	.75
298	David Walling	.15
299	*Sun-Woo Kim*	1.50
300	Pat Burrell	.50
301	*Rick Guttormson*	.50
302	Gil Meche	.15
303	*Carlos Zambrano*	1.00
304	*Eric Byrnes*	.50
305	*Robb Quinlan*	.50
306	Jackie Rexrode	.15
307	Nate Bump	.15
308	*Sean DePaula*	.50
309	Matt Riley	.15
310	Ryan Minor	.15
311	J.J. Davis	.15
312	Randy Wolf	.15
313	Jason Jennings	.15
314	*Scott Seabol*	.50
315	Doug Davis	.15
316	*Todd Moser*	.50
317	Rob Ryan	.15
318	Bubba Crosby	.15
319	*Ryan Knox*	1.50
320	Mario Encarnacion	.15
321	*Francisco Rodriguez*	.50
322	Michael Cuddyer	.15
323	Eddie Yarnall	.15
324	*Cesar Saba*	.75
325	Travis Dawkins	.15
326	Alex Escobar	.25
327	*Julio Zuleta*	.50
328	Josh Hamilton	1.00
329	*Nick Neugebauer*	.75
330	Matt Belisle	.15
331	*Kurt Ainsworth*	1.50
332	Tim Raines, Jr.	.15
333	Eric Munson	.40
334	Donzell McDonald	.15
335	Larry Bigbie	.15
336	Matt Watson	.15
337	Aubrey Huff	.15
338	Julio Ramirez	.15
339	*Jason Grabowski*	.75
340	Jon Garland	.15
341	Austin Kearns	.15
342	Josh Pressley	.15
343	*Miguel Olivo*	.50
344	Julio Lugo	.15
345	Roberto Vaz	.15
346	Ramon Soler	.15
347	*Brandon Phillips*	.50
348	*Vince Faison*	1.50
349	Mike Venafro	.15
350	*Rick Asadoorian*	4.00
351	*B.J. Garbe*	2.00
352	Dan Reichert	.15
353	*Jason Stumm*	2.00
354	*Ruben Salazar*	.75
355	Francisco Cordero	.15
356	*Juan Guzman*	.50
357	*Mike Bacsik*	.50
358	Jared Sandberg	.15
359	Rod Barajas	.15
360	*Junior Brignac*	.75
361	J.M. Gold	.15
362	Octavio Dotel	.15
363	David Kelton	.15
364	*Scott Morgan*	.50
365	*Wascar Serrano*	1.00
366	Wilton Veras	.15
367	Eugene Kingsale	.15
368	Ted Lilly	.15
369	George Lombard	.15
370	Chris Haas	.15
371	*Wilton Pena*	.75
372	Vernon Wells	.15
373	*Lyle Overbay*	.75
374	*Jeff Heaverlo*	.75
375	Calvin Pickering	.15
376	*Mike Lamb*	1.25
377	Kyle Snyder	.15
378	*Javier Cardona*	.50
379	*Aaron Rowand*	1.00
380	Dee Brown	.15
381	*Brett Myers*	1.50
382	Abraham Nunez	.50
383	Eric Valent	.15
384	*Jody Gerut*	.50
385	Adam Dunn	.40
386	Jay Gehrke	.15
387	Omar Ortiz	.15
388	Darnell McDonald	.15
389	Chad Alexander	.15
390	J.D. Closser	.15
391	*Ben Christensen*	1.00
392	Adam Kennedy	.15
393	*Nick Green*	.50
394	Ramon Hernandez	.15
395	*Roy Oswalt*	1.00
396	*Andy Tracy*	.50
397	Eric Gagne	.15
398	*Michael Tejera*	.50
399	Adam Everett	.15
400	Corey Patterson	.75
401	*Gary Knotts*	.50
402	*Ryan Christianson*	2.00
403	*Eric Ireland*	.50
404	*Andrew Good*	.50
405	Brad Penny	.15
406	Jason LaRue	.15
407	Kit Pellow	.15
408	Kevin Beirne	.15
409	Kelly Dransfeldt	.15
410	Jason Grilli	.15
411	*Scott Downs*	.75
412	Jesus Colome	.15
413	*John Sneed*	.50
414	*Tony McKnight*	.50
415	Luis Rivera	.15
416	Adam Eaton	.15
417	*Mike MacDougal*	.50
418	Mike Nannini	.15
419	*Barry Zito*	4.00
420	Dewayne Wise	.15
421	Jason Dellaero	.15
422	Chad Moeller	.15
423	Jason Marquis	.15
424	*Tim Redding*	.50
425	Mark Mulder	.15
426	Josh Paul	.15
427	Chris Enochs	.15
428	*Wilfredo Rodriguez*	1.00
429	Kevin Witt	.15
430	*Scott Sobkowiak*	.50
431	McKay Christensen	.15
432	Jung Bong	.15
433	*Keith Evans*	.15
434	Garry Maddox Jr.	.15
435	*Ramon Santiago*	1.00
436	Alex Cora	.15
437	Carlos Lee	.15
438	*Jason Repko*	1.50
439	Matt Burch	.15
440	*Shawn Sonnier*	.50

2000 Bowman Retro/Future

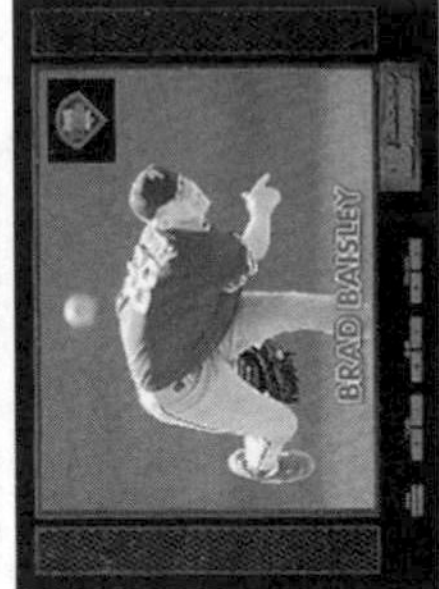

These inserts are a parallel to the 440-card base set. The foiled card fronts have a horizontal format and a design reminiscent of the 1955 Bowman "television set" design. They were seeded one per pack.

	MT
Common Player:	.25
Stars:	2-3X
Rookies:	1-2X
Inserted 1:1	

2000 Bowman Gold

Golds are a 440-card parallel to the base set and are highlighted by gold-stamped facsimile autographs on the card front. Golds are limited to 99 serial numbered sets.

	MT
Stars:	20-40X
Rookies:	5-10X
Production 99 sets	

2000 Bowman Autographs

This set consists of 40 players with card rarity differentiated by either a Blue, Silver or Gold foil Topps "Certified Autograph Issue" stamp. Blues are seeded 1:144, Silver 1:312 and Gold 1:1,604. Card backs are numbered using the player initials and have a Topps serial numbered foil hologram to ensure the authenticity of the autograph.

		MT
Common Player:		10.00
Blue Inserted 1:144		
Silver 1:312		
Gold 1:1,604		
CA	Chip Ambres B	10.00
RA	Rick Ankiel G	100.00
CB	Carlos Beltran G	25.00
LB	Lance Berkman S	15.00
DB	Dee Brown S	15.00
SB	Sean Burroughs S	35.00
JDC	J.D. Closser B	10.00
SC	Steve Cox B	10.00
MC	Michael Cuddyer S	20.00
JC	Jack Cust S	20.00
SD	Scott Downs S	15.00
JDD	J.D. Drew G	40.00
AD	Adam Dunn B	20.00
CF	Choo Freeman B	10.00
RF	Rafael Furcal S	40.00
AH	Aubrey Huff B	10.00
JJ	Jason Jennings B	10.00
NJ	Nick Johnson S	35.00
AK	Austin Kearns B	10.00
DK	David Kelton B	10.00
RM	Ruben Mateo G	30.00
MM	Mike Meyers B	10.00
CP	Corey Patterson S	60.00
BWP	Brad Penny B	10.00
BP	Ben Petrick G	20.00
AP	Adam Piatt S	35.00
MQ	Mark Quinn S	20.00
MR	Mike Restovich B	15.00
MR	Matt Riley S	25.00
JR	Jason Romano B	10.00
BS	Ben Sheets B	25.00
AS	Alfonso Soriano S	25.00
EV	Eric Valent B	10.00
JV	Jose Vidro S	20.00
VW	Vernon Wells G	30.00
SW	Scott Williamson G	20.00
KJW	Kevin Witt S	15.00
KLW	Kerry Wood S	35.00
EY	Eddie Yarnall S	15.00
JZ	Julio Zuleta B	10.00

2000 Bowman Bowman's Best Previews

Inserted 1:18 packs, this 10-card insert set is identical in design to 2000 Bowman's Best. The card fronts have a Refractor like sheen and the card backs are numbered with a "BBP" prefix.

		MT
Complete Set (10):		40.00
Common Player:		1.50
Inserted 1:18		
1	Derek Jeter	5.00
2	Ken Griffey Jr.	8.00
3	Nomar Garciaparra	5.00
4	Mike Piazza	5.00
5	Alex Rodriguez	6.00
6	Sammy Sosa	5.00
7	Mark McGwire	8.00
8	Pat Burrell	2.50
9	Josh Hamilton	3.00
10	Adam Piatt	1.50

2000 Bowman Early Indications

This 10-card set has a blue foiled card front with red foil stamping. Card backs are numbered with an "E" prefix. These were seeded 1:24 packs.

		MT
Complete Set (10):		50.00
Common Player:		2.00
Inserted 1:24		
1	Nomar Garciaparra	6.00
2	Cal Ripken Jr.	8.00
3	Derek Jeter	6.00
4	Mark McGwire	10.00
5	Alex Rodriguez	8.00
6	Chipper Jones	5.00
7	Todd Helton	2.50
8	Vladimir Guerrero	5.00
9	Mike Piazza	6.00
10	Jose Canseco	2.50

2000 Bowman Major Power

This 10-card set spotlights the top home run hitters. Card fronts have a red border on a full foiled card front. These were seeded 1:24 packs and are numbered with an "MP" prefix on the card back.

		MT
Complete Set (10):		50.00
Common Player:		2.00
Inserted 1:24		
1	Mark McGwire	10.00
2	Chipper Jones	5.00
3	Alex Rodriguez	8.00
4	Sammy Sosa	6.00
5	Rafael Palmeiro	2.00
6	Ken Griffey Jr.	10.00
7	Nomar Garciaparra	6.00
8	Barry Bonds	2.50
9	Derek Jeter	6.00
10	Jeff Bagwell	2.50

2000 Bowman Tool Time

This 20-card set focuses on the top minor league Prospects in five different categories: batting, power, speed, arm strength and defense. These are seeded 1:8 packs. Backs are numbered with a "TT" prefix.

		MT
Complete Set (20):		25.00
Common Player:		1.00
Inserted 1:8		
1	Pat Burrell	2.00
2	Aaron Rowand	1.00
3	Chris Wakeland	1.00
4	Ruben Mateo	1.00
5	Pat Burrell	2.00
6	Adam Piatt	1.50
7	Nick Johnson	2.00
8	Jack Cust	1.00
9	Rafael Furcal	3.00
10	Julio Ramirez	1.00
11	Travis Dawkins	1.00
12	Corey Patterson	4.00
13	Ruben Mateo	1.00
14	Jason Dellaero	1.00
15	Sean Burroughs	1.50
16	Ryan Langerhans	1.00
17	D'Angelo Jimenez	1.00
18	Corey Patterson	4.00
19	Troy Cameron	1.00
20	Michael Cuddyer	1.00

2000 Bowman Chrome

Released as a single series 440-card set, Bowman Chrome is identical in design to 2000 Bowman besides the chromium finish on all cards. Foil highlights differentiate rookies and prospects (blue) from veterans (red). Three parallels to the base set are randomly seeded: Refractors, Retro/Future and Retro/Future Refractors.

		MT
Complete Set (440):		325.00
Common Player:		.25
Common Rookie:		1.00
Pack (4):		3.50
Box (24):		80.00
1	Vladimir Guerrero	1.50
2	Chipper Jones	2.00
3	Todd Walker	.25
4	Barry Larkin	.60
5	Bernie Williams	.75
6	Todd Helton	1.00
7	Jermaine Dye	.25
8	Brian Giles	.40
9	Freddy Garcia	.25
10	Greg Vaughn	.40
11	Alex Gonzalez	.25
12	Luis Gonzalez	.25
13	Ron Belliard	.25
14	Ben Grieve	.50
15	Carlos Delgado	1.00
16	Brian Jordan	.25
17	Fernando Tatis	.40
18	Ryan Rupe	.25
19	Miguel Tejada	.25
20	Mark Grace	.40
21	Kenny Lofton	.60
22	Eric Karros	.40
23	Cliff Floyd	.25
24	John Halama	.25
25	Cristian Guzman	.25
26	Scott Williamson	.25
27	Mike Lieberthal	.25
28	Tim Hudson	.40
29	Warren Morris	.25
30	Pedro Martinez	1.50
31	John Smoltz	.25
32	Ray Durham	.25
33	Chad Allen	.25
34	Tony Clark	.30
35	Tino Martinez	.40
36	J.T. Snow Jr.	.25
37	Kevin Brown	.30
38	Bartolo Colon	.25
39	Rey Ordonez	.25
40	Jeff Bagwell	1.00
41	Ivan Rodriguez	1.00
42	Eric Chavez	.40
43	Eric Milton	.25
44	Jose Canseco	.75
45	Shawn Green	.75
46	Rich Aurilia	.25
47	Roberto Alomar	.75
48	Brian Daubach	.25
49	Magglio Ordonez	.25
50	Derek Jeter	2.50
51	Kris Benson	.25
52	Albert Belle	.75
53	Rondell White	.40
54	Justin Thompson	.25
55	Nomar Garciaparra	2.50
56	Chuck Finley	.25
57	Omar Vizquel	.35
58	Luis Castillo	.25
59	Richard Hidalgo	.25
60	Barry Bonds	1.00
61	Craig Biggio	.50
62	Doug Glanville	.25
63	Gabe Kapler	.40
64	Johnny Damon	.25
65	Pokey Reese	.25
66	Andy Pettitte	.40
67	B.J. Surhoff	.25
68	Richie Sexson	.25
69	Javy Lopez	.25
70	Raul Mondesi	.40
71	Darin Erstad	.50
72	Kevin Millwood	.25
73	Ricky Ledee	.25
74	John Olerud	.40
75	Sean Casey	.40
76	Carlos Febles	.25
77	Paul O'Neill	.50
78	Bob Abreu	.40
79	Neifi Perez	.25
80	Tony Gwynn	1.50
81	Russ Ortiz	.25
82	Matt Williams	.50
83	Chris Carpenter	.25
84	Roger Cedeno	.25

85 Tim Salmon .40
86 Billy Koch .25
87 Jeromy Burnitz .25
88 Edgardo Alfonzo .40
89 Jay Bell .15
90 Manny Ramirez 1.00
91 Frank Thomas 1.50
92 Mike Mussina .75
93 J.D. Drew .50
94 Adrian Beltre .40
95 Alex Rodriguez 3.00
96 Larry Walker .50
97 Juan Encarnacion .25
98 Mike Sweeney .25
99 Rusty Greer .25
100 Randy Johnson .75
101 Jose Vidro .25
102 Preston Wilson .25
103 Greg Maddux 2.00
104 Jason Giambi .40
105 Cal Ripken Jr. 3.00
106 Carlos Beltran .25
107 Vinny Castilla .25
108 Mariano Rivera .40
109 Mo Vaughn .75
110 Rafael Palmeiro .50
111 Shannon Stewart .25
112 Mike Hampton .25
113 Joe Nathan .25
114 Ben Davis .25
115 Andruw Jones .75
116 Robin Ventura .40
117 Damion Easley .25
118 Jeff Cirillo .40
119 Kerry Wood .50
120 Scott Rolen .75
121 Sammy Sosa 2.50
122 Ken Griffey Jr. 4.00
123 Shane Reynolds .25
124 Troy Glaus 1.00
125 Tom Glavine .40
126 Michael Barrett .25
127 Al Leiter .25
128 Jason Kendall .25
129 Roger Clemens 1.50
130 Juan Gonzalez 1.00
131 Corey Koskie .25
132 Curt Schilling .35
133 Mike Piazza 2.50
134 Gary Sheffield .40
135 Jim Thome .50
136 Orlando Hernandez .50
137 Ray Lankford .25
138 Geoff Jenkins .40
139 Jose Lima .25
140 Mark McGwire 4.00
141 Adam Piatt .25
142 *Pat Manning* 4.00
143 *Marcos Castillo* 1.00
144 *Lesli Brea* 1.00
145 *Humberto Cota* 3.00
146 Ben Petrick .25
147 Kip Wells .25
148 Willi Mo Pena 1.00
149 *Chris Wakeland* 1.00
150 *Brad Baker* 5.00
151 *Robbie Morrison* 1.00
152 Reggie Taylor .25
153 *Brian Cole* 1.00
154 Peter Bergeron .25
155 Roosevelt Brown .25
156 *Matt Cepicky* 1.00
157 Ramon Castro .25
158 *Brad Baisley* 3.00
159 *Jason Hart* 8.00
160 Mitch Meluskey .25
161 Chad Harville .25
162 Brian Cooper .25
163 Marcus Giles .25
164 Jim Morris .25
165 Geoff Goetz .25
166 *Bobby Bradley* 6.00
167 Rob Bell .25
168 Joe Crede .25
169 Michael Restovich .25
170 *Quincy Foster* 1.00
171 *Enrique Cruz* 2.00
172 Mark Quinn .25
173 Nick Johnson .25
174 Jeff Liefer .25
175 *Kevin Mench* 5.00
176 Steve Lomasney .25
177 Jayson Werth .25
178 Tim Drew .25
179 Chip Ambres .25
180 Ryan Anderson .50
181 Matt Blank .25
182 Giuseppe Chiaramonte .25
183 *Corey Myers* 3.00
184 Jeff Yoder .25
185 *Craig Dingman* 1.00
186 *Jon Hamilton* 1.00
187 Toby Hall .25
188 Russell Branyan .25
189 *Brian Falkenborg* 1.00
190 *Aaron Harang* 1.00
191 Juan Pena .25
192 *Chin-Hui Tsao* 20.00
193 Alfonso Soriano .75
194 *Alejandro Diaz* 3.00
195 Carlos Pena .25
196 Kevin Nicholson .25
197 Mo Bruce .25
198 C.C. Sabathia .25
199 Carl Crawford .25
200 Rafael Furcal 1.25
201 *Andrew Beinbrink* 1.00
202 Jimmy Osting .25
203 *Aaron McNeal* 4.00
204 Brett Laxton .25
205 Chris George .25
206 Felipe Lopez .25
207 *Ben Sheets* 12.00
208 *Mike Meyers* 6.00
209 Jason Conti .25
210 Milton Bradley .25
211 *Chris Mears* 1.00
212 *David Tavarez* 1.00
213 Jason Romano .25
214 Goefrey Tomlinson .25
215 Jimmy Rollins .25
216 Pablo Ozuna .25
217 Steve Cox .25
218 Terrence Long .25
219 *Jeff DaVanon* 1.00
220 Rick Ankiel 3.00
221 Jason Standridge .25
222 Tony Armas .25
223 Jason Tyner .25
224 Ramon Ortiz .25
225 Daryle Ward .25
226 *Enger Veras* 1.00
227 *Chris Jones* 1.50
228 *Eric Cammack* 1.00
229 Ruben Mateo .25
230 *Ken Harvey* 3.00
231 Jake Westbrook .25
232 *Rob Purvis* 1.00
233 Choo Freeman .25
234 Aramis Ramirez .25
235 A.J. Burnett .25
236 Kevin Barker .25
237 *Chance Caple* 2.50
238 Jarrod Washburn .25
239 Lance Berkman .25
240 *Michael Wenner* 1.00
241 Alex Sanchez .25
242 *Jake Esteves* 1.00
243 Grant Roberts .25
244 *Mark Ellis* 4.00
245 Donny Leon .25
246 David Eckstein .25
247 *Dicky Gonzalez* 1.00
248 John Patterson .25
249 Chad Green .25
250 *Scot Shields* 1.00
251 Troy Cameron .25
252 Jose Molina .25
253 *Rob Pugmire* 1.00
254 Rick Elder .25
255 Sean Burroughs .75
256 *Josh Kalinowski* 1.50
257 Matt LeCroy .25
258 *Alex Graman* 3.00
259 *Juan Silvestre* 4.00
260 Brady Clark .25
261 *Rico Washington* 2.00
262 Gary Matthews Jr. .25
263 Matt Wise .25
264 *Keith Reed* 1.00
265 *Santiago Ramirez* 1.00
266 *Ben Broussard* 8.00
267 Ryan Langerhans .25
268 Juan Rivera .25
269 Shawn Gallagher .25
270 Jorge Toca .25
271 Brad Lidge .25
272 *Leo Estrella* 1.00
273 Ruben Quevedo .25
274 Jack Cust .25
275 T.J. Tucker .25
276 Mike Colangelo .25
277 Brian Schneider .25
278 Calvin Murray .25
279 Josh Girdley .25
280 Mike Paradis .25
281 Chad Hermansen .25
282 *Ty Howington* 2.00
283 Aaron Myette .25
284 D'Angelo Jimenez .25
285 Dernell Stenson .25
286 Jerry Hairston Jr. .25
287 *Gary Majewski* 2.00
288 *Derrin Ebert* 1.00
289 *Steve Fish* 1.00
290 Carlos Hernandez .25
291 Allen Levrault .25
292 *Sean McNally* 1.00
293 *Randey Dorame* 2.50
294 *Wes Anderson* 3.00
295 B.J. Ryan .25
296 *Alan Webb* 1.00
297 *Brandon Inge* 3.00
298 David Walling .25
299 *Sun-Woo Kim* 3.00
300 Pat Burrell .75
301 *Rick Guttormson* 1.00
302 Gil Meche .25
303 *Carlos Zambrano* 3.00
304 *Eric Byrnes* 1.00
305 *Robb Quinlan* 1.00
306 Jackie Rexrode .25
307 Nate Bump .25
308 *Sean DePaula* 1.00
309 Matt Riley .25
310 Ryan Minor .25
311 J.J. Davis .25
312 Randy Wolf .25
313 Jason Jennings .25
314 *Scott Seabol* 1.00
315 Doug Davis .25
316 *Todd Moser* 1.00
317 Rob Ryan .25
318 Bubba Crosby .25
319 *Lyle Overbay* 5.00
320 Mario Encarnacion .25
321 *Francisco Rodriguez* 2.00
322 Michael Cuddyer .25
323 Eddie Yarnall .25
324 *Cesar Saba* 3.00
325 Travis Dawkins .25
326 Alex Escobar .25
327 *Julio Zuleta* 1.00
328 Josh Hamilton 1.50
329 *Carlos Urquiola* 3.00
330 Matt Belisle .25
331 *Kurt Ainsworth* 4.00
332 Tim Raines, Jr. .25
333 Eric Munson .60
334 Donzell McDonald .25
335 *Larry Bigbie* 2.00
336 Matt Watson .25
337 Aubrey Huff .25
338 Julio Ramirez .25
339 *Jason Grabowski* 2.50
340 Jon Garland .25
341 Austin Kearns .25
342 Josh Pressley .25
343 *Miguel Olivo* 1.00
344 Julio Lugo .25
345 Roberto Vaz .25
346 Ramon Soler .25
347 *Brandon Phillips* 1.00
348 *Vince Faison* 4.00
349 Mike Venafro .25
350 *Rick Asadoorian* 12.00
351 *B.J. Garbe* 6.00
352 Dan Reichert .25
353 *Jason Stumm* 3.00
354 *Ruben Salazar* 3.00
355 Francisco Cordero .25
356 *Juan Guzman* 1.00
357 *Mike Bacsik* 1.00
358 Jared Sandberg .25
359 Rod Barajas .25
360 *Junior Brignac* 2.50
361 J.M. Gold .25
362 Octavio Dotel .25
363 David Kelton .25
364 *Scott Morgan* 1.00
365 *Wascar Serrano* 3.00
366 Wilton Veras .25
367 Eugene Kingsale .25
368 Ted Lilly .25
369 George Lombard .25
370 Chris Haas .25
371 *Wilton Pena* 2.50
372 Vernon Wells .25
373 *Keith Ginter* 5.00
374 *Jeff Heaverlo* 2.50
375 Calvin Pickering .25
376 *Mike Lamb* 4.00
377 Kyle Snyder .25
378 *Javier Cardona* 1.00
379 *Aaron Rowand* 4.00
380 Dee Brown .25
381 *Brett Myers* 3.00
382 Abraham Nunez .75
383 Eric Valent .25
384 *Jody Gerut* 1.00
385 Adam Dunn .50
386 Jay Gehrke .25
387 Omar Ortiz .25
388 Darnell McDonald .25
389 Chad Alexander .25
390 J.D. Closser .25
391 *Ben Christensen* 3.00
392 Adam Kennedy .25
393 *Nick Green* 1.00
394 Ramon Hernandez .25
395 *Roy Oswalt* 2.50
396 *Andy Tracy* 1.00
397 Eric Gagne .25
398 *Michael Tejera* 1.00
399 Adam Everett .25
400 Corey Patterson 2.00
401 *Gary Knotts* 1.00
402 *Ryan Christianson* 4.00
403 *Eric Ireland* 1.00
404 *Andrew Good* 1.00
405 Brad Penny .25
406 Jason LaRue .25
407 Kit Pellow .25
408 Kevin Beirne .25
409 Kelly Dransfeldt .25
410 Jason Grilli .25
411 *Scott Downs* 1.50
412 Jesus Colome .25
413 *John Sneed* 1.00
414 *Tony McKnight* 1.00
415 Luis Rivera .25
416 Adam Eaton .25
417 *Mike MacDougal* 1.00
418 Mike Nannini .25
419 *Barry Zito* 15.00
420 Dewayne Wise .25
421 Jason Dellaero .25
422 Chad Moeller .25
423 Jason Marquis .25
424 *Tim Redding* 2.00
425 Mark Mulder .25
426 Josh Paul .25
427 Chris Enochs .25
428 *Wilfredo Rodriguez* 3.00
429 Kevin Witt .25
430 *Scott Sobkowiak* 1.50
431 McKay Christensen .25
432 Jung Bong .25
433 *Keith Evans* 1.00
434 Garry Maddox Jr. .25
435 *Ramon Santiago* 3.00
436 Alex Cora .25
437 Carlos Lee .25
438 *Jason Repko* 3.00
439 Matt Burch .25
440 *Shawn Sonnier* 1.00

2000 Bowman Chrome Retro/Future

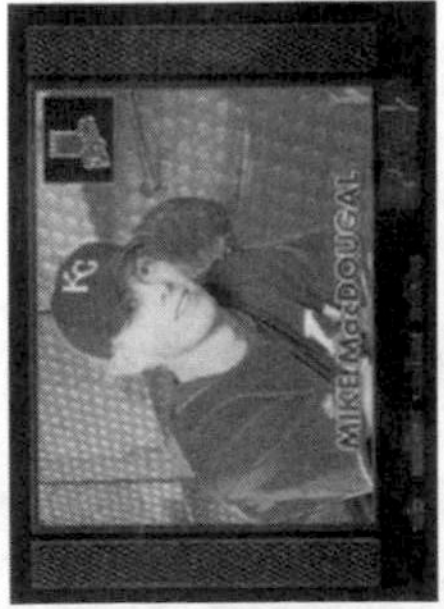

This 440-card parallel to the base set is modeled after the 1955 Bowman "television set" design and are seeded 1:6 packs, with Refractors seeded 1:60 packs.

	MT
Stars:	2-3X
Rookies:	1X
Inserted 1:6	
Refractors:	6-8X
Rookies:	1-3X
Inserted 1:60	

2000 Bowman Chrome Refractors

A parallel to the 440-card base set, these inserts have a mirror like sheen to them on the card front and are listed Refractor underneath the card number on the back. These were seeded 1:12 packs.

	MT
Stars:	15-25X
Rookies:	3-5X

2000 Bowman Chrome Bidding for the Call

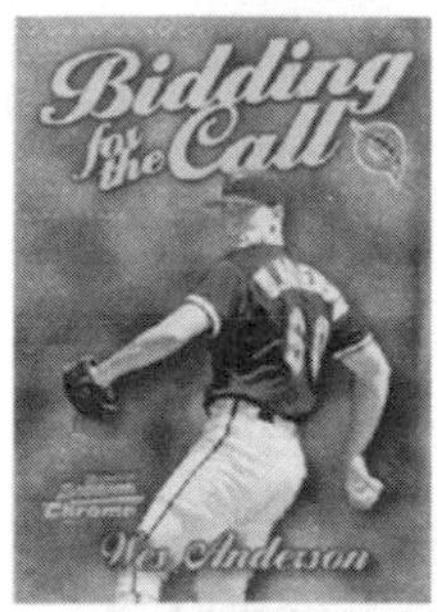

Top minor league prospects are highlighted on a design with gold foil background on an all chromium finish. Card backs are numbered with a "BC" prefix and are seeded 1:16 packs. A Refractor parallel version is seeded 1:160.

		MT
Complete Set (15):		25.00
Common Player:		1.00
Inserted 1:16		
Refractors:		2-4X
Inserted 1:160		
1	Adam Piatt	1.50
2	Pat Burrell	4.00
3	Mark Mulder	1.00
4	Nick Johnson	2.50
5	Alfonso Soriano	2.00
6	Chin-Feng Chen	6.00
7	Scott Sobkowiak	1.00
8	Corey Patterson	5.00
9	Jack Cust	1.00
10	Sean Burroughs	2.00
11	Josh Hamilton	4.00
12	Corey Myers	1.00
13	Eric Munson	2.00
14	Wes Anderson	1.00
15	Lyle Overbay	1.00

2000 Bowman Chrome Meteoric Rise

This 10-card set spotlights players who all made their first All-Star team within their first two years. Card fronts have a futuristic background, with the player in an intergalactic setting. Card backs are numbered with a "MR" prefix. These are seeded 1:24 packs, a Refractor parallel version is seeded 1:240 packs.

		MT
Complete Set (10):		40.00
Common Player:		1.50
Inserted 1:24		
Refractors:		2-4X
Inserted 1:240		
1	Nomar Garciaparra	6.00
2	Mark McGwire	10.00
3	Ken Griffey Jr.	10.00
4	Chipper Jones	5.00
5	Manny Ramirez	2.50
6	Mike Piazza	6.00
7	Cal Ripken Jr.	8.00
8	Ivan Rodriguez	2.50
9	Greg Maddux	5.00
10	Randy Johnson	2.00

2000 Bowman Chrome Oversize

		MT
Complete Set (8):		15.00
Common Player:		1.00
Inserted 1:box		
1	Pat Burrell	4.00
2	Josh Hamilton	4.00
3	Rafael Furcal	3.00
4	Corey Patterson	4.00
5	A.J. Burnett	1.00
6	Eric Munson	1.00
7	Nick Johnson	1.50
8	Alfonso Soriano	1.50

2000 Bowman Chrome Rookie Class 2000

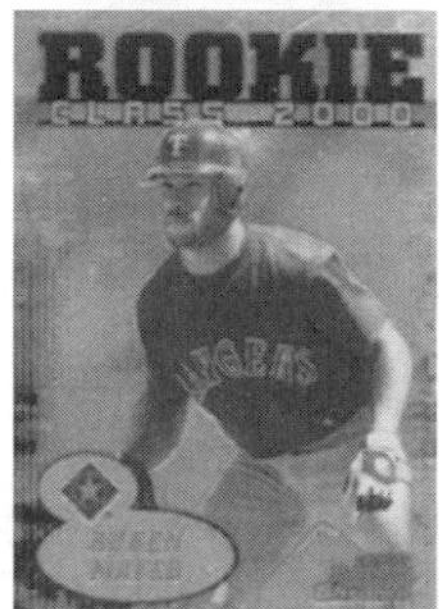

This set highlighted 10 prospects who were thought to contend for the 2000 Rookie of the Year awards. Backs are numbered with a "RC" prefix and are seeded 1:24 packs. A Refractor parallel version is seeded 1:240 packs.

		MT
Complete Set (10):		25.00
Common Player:		1.50
Inserted 1:24		
Refractors:		2-4X
Inserted 1:240		
1	Pat Burrell	4.00
2	Rick Ankiel	8.00
3	Ruben Mateo	1.50
4	Vernon Wells	1.50
5	Mark Mulder	1.50
6	A.J. Burnett	1.50
7	Chad Hermansen	1.50
8	Corey Patterson	5.00
9	Rafael Furcal	4.00
10	Mike Lamb	1.50

2000 Bowman Chrome Teen Idols

This 15-card set highlights top teenagers who are predicted to emerge as major league standouts. These were seeded 1:16 packs with Refractor parallels inserted 1:160 packs.

		MT
Complete Set (15):		40.00
Common Player:		1.50
Inserted 1:16		
Refractors:		2-4X
Inserted 1:160		
1	Alex Rodriguez	8.00
2	Andruw Jones	2.00
3	Juan Gonzalez	2.50
4	Ivan Rodriguez	2.50
5	Ken Griffey Jr.	10.00
6	Bobby Bradley	2.00
7	Brett Myers	1.50
8	C.C. Sabathia	1.50
9	Ty Howington	1.50
10	Brandon Phillips	1.50
11	Rick Asadoorian	6.00
12	Wily Pena	2.50
13	Sean Burroughs	2.00
14	Josh Hamilton	4.00
15	Rafael Furcal	3.00

2000 Bowman's Best

The base set consists of 200-cards on a mirror like sheen, reminiscent of Refractors. Veteran cards have gold highlights while rookies and prospects have blue highlights. There are three subsets: Best Performers (86-100), Prospects (101-150) and Rookies (151-200). Rookies are serially numbered to 2,999 on the card back and are randomly inserted on the average of 1:7 packs.

		MT
Complete Set (200):		650.00
Common Player:		.20
Common Rookie (151-200):		8.00
Production 2,999 sets		
Pack (4):		5.00
Box (24):		100.00
1	Nomar Garciaparra	2.50
2	Chipper Jones	2.00
3	Damion Easley	.20
4	Bernie Williams	.75
5	Barry Bonds	1.00
6	Jermaine Dye	.20
7	John Olerud	.40
8	Mike Hampton	.20
9	Cal Ripken Jr.	3.00
10	Jeff Bagwell	1.00
11	Troy Glaus	1.00
12	J.D. Drew	.40
13	Jeromy Burnitz	.20
14	Carlos Delgado	1.00
15	Shawn Green	.75
16	Kevin Millwood	.20

17	Rondell White	.40
18	Scott Rolen	.75
19	Jeff Cirillo	.20
20	Barry Larkin	.50
21	Brian Giles	.20
22	Roger Clemens	1.50
23	Manny Ramirez	1.00
24	Alex Gonzalez	.20
25	Mark Grace	.40
26	Fernando Tatis	.40
27	Randy Johnson	.75
28	Roger Cedeno	.20
29	Brian Jordan	.20
30	Kevin Brown	.40
31	Greg Vaughn	.20
32	Roberto Alomar	.75
33	Larry Walker	.40
34	Rafael Palmeiro	.50
35	Curt Schilling	.30
36	Orlando Hernandez	.30
37	Todd Walker	.20
38	Juan Gonzalez	1.00
39	Sean Casey	.30
40	Tony Gwynn	1.50
41	Albert Belle	.60
42	Gary Sheffield	.50
43	Michael Barrett	.20
44	Preston Wilson	.20
45	Jim Thome	.50
46	Shannon Stewart	.20
47	Mo Vaughn	.75
48	Ben Grieve	.40
49	Adrian Beltre	.20
50	Sammy Sosa	2.50
51	Bob Abreu	.40
52	Edgardo Alfonzo	.40
53	Carlos Febles	.20
54	Frank Thomas	1.50
55	Alex Rodriguez	3.00
56	Cliff Floyd	.20
57	Jose Canseco	.60
58	Erubiel Durazo	.20
59	Tim Hudson	.40
60	Craig Biggio	.40
61	Eric Karros	.20
62	Mike Mussina	.50
63	Robin Ventura	.30
64	Carlos Beltran	.20
65	Pedro Martinez	1.00
66	Gabe Kapler	.40
67	Jason Kendall	.30
68	Derek Jeter	2.50
69	Magglio Ordonez	.40
70	Mike Piazza	2.50
71	Mike Lieberthal	.20
72	Andres Galarraga	.50
73	Raul Mondesi	.30
74	Eric Chavez	.30
75	Greg Maddux	2.00
76	Matt Williams	.50
77	Kris Benson	.20
78	Ivan Rodriguez	1.00
79	Pokey Reese	.20
80	Vladimir Guerrero	1.50
81	Mark McGwire	4.00
82	Vinny Castilla	.20
83	Todd Helton	1.00
84	Andruw Jones	.50
85	Ken Griffey Jr.	4.00
86	Mark McGwire (Best Performers)	2.00
87	Derek Jeter (Best Performers)	1.25
88	Chipper Jones (Best Performers)	1.00
89	Nomar Garciaparra (Best Performers)	1.25
90	Sammy Sosa (Best Performers)	1.25
91	Cal Ripken Jr. (Best Performers)	1.50
92	Juan Gonzalez (Best Performers)	.50
93	Alex Rodriguez (Best Performers)	1.50
94	Barry Bonds (Best Performers)	.50
95	Sean Casey (Best Performers)	.20
96	Vladimir Guerrero (Best Performers)	.75
97	Mike Piazza (Best Performers)	1.25
98	Shawn Green (Best Performers)	.20
99	Jeff Bagwell (Best Performers)	.50
100	Ken Griffey Jr. (Best Performers)	2.00
101	Rick Ankiel (Prospects)	2.50
102	John Patterson (Prospects)	.20
103	David Walling (Prospects)	.20
104	Michael Restovich (Prospects)	.20
105	A.J. Burnett (Prospects)	.20
106	Matt Riley (Prospects)	.20
107	Chad Hermansen (Prospects)	.20
108	Choo Freeman (Prospects)	.20
109	Mark Quinn (Prospects)	.20
110	Corey Patterson (Prospects)	1.50
111	Ramon Ortiz (Prospects)	.20
112	Vernon Wells (Prospects)	.20
113	Milton Bradley (Prospects)	.20
114	Travis Dawkins (Prospects)	.20
115	Sean Burroughs (Prospects)	.75
116	Willi Mo Pena (Prospects)	1.00
117	Dee Brown (Prospects)	.20
118	C.C. Sabathia (Prospects)	.20
119	Larry Bigbie (Prospects)	.20
120	Octavio Dotel (Prospects)	.20
121	Kip Wells (Prospects)	.20
122	Ben Petrick (Prospects)	.20
123	Mark Mulder (Prospects)	.20
124	Jason Standridge (Prospects)	.20
125	Adam Piatt (Prospects)	.20
126	Steve Lomasney (Prospects)	.20
127	Jayson Werth (Prospects)	.20
128	Alex Escobar (Prospects)	.20
129	Ryan Anderson (Prospects)	.40
130	Adam Dunn (Prospects)	.20
131	Omar Ortiz (Prospects)	.20
132	Brad Penny (Prospects)	.20
133	Daryle Ward (Prospects)	.20
134	Eric Munson (Prospects)	.75
135	Nick Johnson (Prospects)	.75
136	Jason Jennings (Prospects)	.20
137	Tim Raines, Jr. (Prospects)	.20
138	Ruben Mateo (Prospects)	.20
139	Jack Cust (Prospects)	.20
140	Rafael Furcal (Prospects)	1.50
141	Eric Gagne (Prospects)	.20
142	Tony Armas (Prospects)	.20
143	Mike Paradis (Prospects)	.20
144	Chris George (Prospects)	.20
145	Alfonso Soriano (Prospects)	.75
146	Josh Hamilton (Prospects)	1.50
147	Michael Cuddyer (Prospects)	.20
148	Jay Gehrke (Prospects)	.20
149	Josh Girdley (Prospects)	.20
150	Pat Burrell (Prospects)	1.00
151	*Brett Myers*	15.00
152	*Scott Seabol*	8.00
153	*Keith Reed*	8.00
154	*Francisco Rodriguez*	8.00
155	*Barry Zito*	50.00
156	*Pat Manning*	12.00
157	*Ben Christensen*	12.00
158	*Corey Myers*	12.00
159	*Wascar Serrano*	10.00
160	*Wes Anderson*	10.00
161	*Andy Tracy*	8.00
162	*Cesar Saba*	8.00
163	*Mike Lamb*	15.00
164	*Bobby Bradley*	25.00
165	*Vince Faison*	8.00
166	*Ty Howington*	8.00
167	*Ken Harvey*	12.00
168	*Josh Kalinowski*	10.00
169	*Ruben Salazar*	15.00
170	*Aaron Rowand*	12.00
171	*Ramon Santiago*	8.00
172	*Scott Sobkowiak*	10.00
173	*Lyle Overbay*	15.00
174	*Rico Washington*	8.00
175	*Rick Asadoorian*	40.00
176	*Matt Ginter*	8.00
177	*Jason Stumm*	10.00
178	*B.J. Garbe*	20.00
179	*Mike MacDougal*	8.00
180	*Ryan Christianson*	12.00
181	*Kurt Ainsworth*	15.00
182	*Brad Baisley*	8.00
183	*Ben Broussard*	25.00
184	*Aaron McNeal*	12.00
185	*John Sneed*	8.00
186	*Junior Brignac*	8.00
187	*Chance Caple*	10.00
188	*Scott Downs*	8.00
189	*Matt Cepicky*	8.00
190	*Chin-Feng Chen*	75.00
191	*Johan Santana*	10.00
192	*Brad Baker*	10.00
193	*Jason Repko*	8.00
194	*Craig Dingman*	8.00
195	*Chris Wakeland*	10.00
196	*Rogelio Arias*	8.00
197	*Luis Matos*	15.00
198	*Robert Ramsay*	10.00
199	*Willie Bloomquist*	10.00
200	*Tony Pena Jr.*	12.00

2000 Bowman's Best Bets

This 10-card set highlighted prospects who had the best chance of making the big league. The upper left corner and bottom right corner are die-cut. An small action photo is super imposed over a larger background shot of the featured player. Backs are numbered with a "BBB" prefix. These were seeded 1:15 packs.

		MT
Complete Set (10):		25.00
Common Player:		1.50
Inserted 1:15		
1	Pat Burrell	4.00
2	Alfonso Soriano	2.00
3	Corey Patterson	4.00
4	Eric Munson	2.00
5	Sean Burroughs	2.00
6	Rafael Furcal	3.00
7	Rick Ankiel	6.00
8	Nick Johnson	2.00
9	Ruben Mateo	1.50
10	Josh Hamilton	4.00

2000 Bowman's Best Franchise Favorites

Two current players and two retired stars are featured in this six-card set. These were seeded 1:17 packs. Card backs are numbered with a "FR" prefix.

		MT
Complete Set (6):		25.00
Common Player:		1.50
Inserted 1:17		
1A	Sean Casey	1.50
1B	Johnny Bench	4.00
1C	Sean Casey, Johnny Bench	4.00
2A	Cal Ripken Jr.	8.00
2B	Brooks Robinson	3.00
2C	Cal Ripken Jr., Brooks Robinson	8.00

2000 Bowman's Best Franchise 2000

Each of the 25-cards in this set have rounded corners on a holographic silver design. Backs are numbered with a "F" prefix and are seeded 1:18 packs.

		MT
Complete Set (25):		150.00
Common Player:		2.00
Inserted 1:18		
1	Cal Ripken Jr.	15.00
2	Nomar Garciaparra	12.00
3	Frank Thomas	8.00
4	Manny Ramirez	5.00
5	Juan Gonzalez	5.00
6	Carlos Beltran	2.00
7	Derek Jeter	12.00
8	Alex Rodriguez	15.00
9	Ben Grieve	3.00
10	Jose Canseco	3.00
11	Ivan Rodriguez	5.00
12	Mo Vaughn	4.00
13	Randy Johnson	4.00
14	Chipper Jones	10.00
15	Sammy Sosa	12.00
16	Ken Griffey Jr.	20.00
17	Larry Walker	3.00
18	Preston Wilson	2.00
19	Jeff Bagwell	5.00
20	Shawn Green	3.00
21	Vladimir Guerrero	8.00
22	Mike Piazza	12.00
23	Scott Rolen	4.00
24	Tony Gwynn	8.00
25	Barry Bonds	5.00

2000 Bowman's Best Franchise Favorites Autograph

These autographs are seeded 1:1,291 packs, while the two dual autographed versions are inserted 1:5,153 packs.

		MT
Common Player:		30.00
Version A & B 1:1,291		
Version C 1:5,153		
1A	Sean Casey	30.00
1B	Johnny Bench	100.00
1C	Sean Casey, Johnny Bench	125.00
2A	Cal Ripken Jr.	180.00
2B	Brooks Robinson	50.00
2C	Cal Ripken Jr., Brooks Robinson	250.00

2000 Bowman's Best Locker Room Collection Autographs

Part of the Locker Room Collection, these autographs were inserted 1:57 packs and feature 19 players. Backs are numbered with a "LRCA" prefix.

		MT
Complete Set (19):		360.00
Common Player:		15.00
Inserted 1:57		
1	Carlos Beltran	15.00
2	Rick Ankiel	60.00
3	Vernon Wells	15.00
4	Ruben Mateo	15.00
5	Ben Petrick	15.00
6	Adam Piatt	25.00
7	Eric Munson	25.00
8	Alfonso Soriano	25.00
9	Kerry Wood	30.00
10	Jack Cust	20.00
11	Rafael Furcal	30.00
12	Josh Hamilton	40.00
13	Brad Penny	15.00
14	Dee Brown	15.00
15	Milton Bradley	20.00
16	Ryan Anderson	25.00
17	John Patterson	15.00
18	Nick Johnson	20.00
19	Peter Bergeron	15.00

2000 Bowman's Best Locker Room Collection Lumber

These inserts have a piece of game-used bat embedded into them and are seeded 1:376 packs. They are numbered with a "LRCL" prefix on the back.

		MT
Complete Set (11):		
Common Player:		25.00
Inserted 1:376		
1	Carlos Beltran	25.00
2	Rick Ankiel	75.00
3	Vernon Wells	25.00
4	Adam Kennedy	25.00
5	Ben Petrick	25.00
6	Adam Piatt	30.00
7	Eric Munson	30.00
8	Rafael Furcal	40.00
9	J.D. Drew	40.00
10	Pat Burrell	50.00

2000 Bowman's Best Locker Room Collection Jerseys

These inserts have a piece of game-worn jersey embedded into them and are numbered with a "LRCJ" prefix. These are seeded 1:206 packs.

		MT
Complete Set (5):		160.00
Common Player:		25.00
Inserted 1:206		
1	Carlos Beltran	25.00
2	Rick Ankiel	75.00
3	Adam Kennedy	25.00
4	Ben Petrick	25.00
5	Adam Piatt	30.00

2000 Bowman's Best Rookie Signed Baseballs

Redemption inserts, redeemable for Rookie Signed Baseballs are randomly inserted at a rate of 1:688 packs. Each signed baseball displays the Bowman "Rookie Autograph" logo and the Topps "Genuine Issue" sticker.

		MT
Complete Set (5):		250.00
Common Player:		35.00
Inserted 1:688		
1	Josh Hamilton	50.00
2	Rick Ankiel	90.00
3	Alfonso Soriano	35.00
4	Nick Johnson	35.00
5	Corey Patterson	60.00

2000 Bowman's Best Selections

This 15-card set is printed on a luminescent, die-cut design. The set features former Rookies of the Year and former No. 1 overall Draft Picks. These are seeded 1:30 packs. Backs are numbered with a "BBS" prefix.

		MT
Complete Set (15):		120.00
Common Player:		2.50
Inserted 1:30		
1	Alex Rodriguez	15.00
2	Ken Griffey Jr.	20.00
3	Pat Burrell	5.00
4	Mark McGwire	20.00
5	Derek Jeter	12.00
6	Nomar Garciaparra	12.00
7	Mike Piazza	12.00
8	Josh Hamilton	5.00
9	Cal Ripken Jr.	15.00
10	Jeff Bagwell	5.00
11	Chipper Jones	10.00
12	Jose Canseco	3.00
13	Carlos Beltran	2.50
14	Kerry Wood	3.00
15	Ben Grieve	3.00

2000 Bowman's Best Year By Year

This 10-card set highlights 10 duos who began their careers in the same year. They have a horizontal format on a mirror foiled card front. Backs are numbered with a "YY" prefix and are seeded 1:23 packs.

		MT
Complete Set (10):		75.00
Common Player:		4.00
Inserted 1:23		
1	Sammy Sosa, Ken Griffey Jr.	15.00
2	Nomar Garciaparra, Vladimir Guerrero	10.00
3	Alex Rodriguez, Jeff Cirillo	12.00
4	Mike Piazza, Pedro Martinez	10.00
5	Derek Jeter, Edgardo Alfonzo	10.00
6	Alfonso Soriano, Rick Ankiel	5.00
7	Mark McGwire, Barry Bonds	15.00
8	Juan Gonzalez, Larry Walker	4.00
9	Ivan Rodriguez, Jeff Bagwell	4.00
10	Shawn Green, Manny Ramirez	4.00

1996 Circa

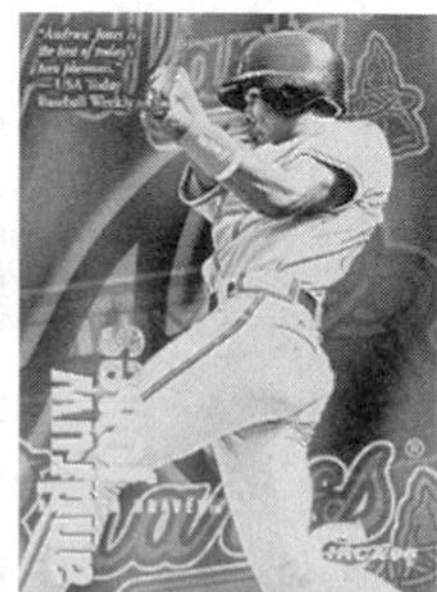

This hobby-exclusive product was limited to

2,000 sequentially numbered cases. The regular-issue set has 196 player cards, including 18 top prospects and four prospects. Circa also has a 200-card parallel set called Rave which is limited to 150 sets. Each Rave card is sequentially numbered from 1-150. Two other insert sets were also produced - Access and Boss.

		MT
Complete Set (200):		25.00
Common Player:		.10
Pack (8):		1.50
Wax Box (24):		35.00
1	Roberto Alomar	.40
2	Brady Anderson	.20
3	*Rocky Coppinger*	.10
4	Eddie Murray	.25
5	Mike Mussina	.30
6	Randy Myers	.10
7	Rafael Palmeiro	.25
8	Cal Ripken Jr.	1.50
9	Jose Canseco	.40
10	Roger Clemens	.75
11	Mike Greenwell	.10
12	Tim Naehring	.10
13	John Valentin	.10
14	Mo Vaughn	.40
15	Tim Wakefield	.10
16	Jim Abbott	.10
17	Garret Anderson	.10
18	Jim Edmonds	.25
19	*Darin Erstad*	2.50
20	Chuck Finley	.10
21	Troy Percival	.10
22	Tim Salmon	.20
23	J.T. Snow	.10
24	Wilson Alvarez	.10
25	Harold Baines	.15
26	Ray Durham	.10
27	Alex Fernandez	.10
28	Tony Phillips	.10
29	Frank Thomas	.75
30	Robin Ventura	.15
31	Sandy Alomar Jr.	.10
32	Albert Belle	.40
33	Kenny Lofton	.25
34	Dennis Martinez	.10
35	Jose Mesa	.10
36	Charles Nagy	.10
37	Manny Ramirez	.50
37p	Manny Ramirez (overprinted "PROMOTIONAL SAMPLE")	3.00
38	Jim Thome	.25
39	Travis Fryman	.15
40	Bob Higginson	.10
41	Melvin Nieves	.10
42	Alan Trammell	.10
43	Kevin Appier	.10
44	Johnny Damon	.10
45	Keith Lockhart	.10
46	Jeff Montgomery	.10
47	Joe Randa	.10
48	Bip Roberts	.10
49	Ricky Bones	.10
50	Jeff Cirillo	.10
51	Marc Newfield	.10
52	Dave Nilsson	.10
53	Kevin Seitzer	.10
54	Ron Coomer	.10
55	Marty Cordova	.10
56	Roberto Kelly	.10
57	Chuck Knoblauch	.20
58	Paul Molitor	.40
59	Kirby Puckett	.50
60	Scott Stahoviak	.10
61	Wade Boggs	.40
62	David Cone	.15
63	Cecil Fielder	.15
64	Dwight Gooden	.15
65	Derek Jeter	1.50
66	Tino Martinez	.20
67	Paul O'Neill	.20
68	Andy Pettitte	.25
69	Ruben Rivera	.10
70	Bernie Williams	.40
71	Geronimo Berroa	.10
72	Jason Giambi	.25
73	Mark McGwire	2.00
74	Terry Steinbach	.10
75	Todd Van Poppel	.10
76	Jay Buhner	.15
77	Norm Charlton	.10
78	Ken Griffey Jr.	2.00
79	Randy Johnson	.50
80	Edgar Martinez	.10
81	Alex Rodriguez	1.50
82	Paul Sorrento	.10
83	Dan Wilson	.10
84	Will Clark	.30
85	Kevin Elster	.10
86	Juan Gonzalez	.50
87	Rusty Greer	.10
88	Ken Hill	.10
89	Mark McLemore	.10
90	Dean Palmer	.10
91	Roger Pavlik	.10
92	Ivan Rodriguez	.50
93	Joe Carter	.15
94	Carlos Delgado	.50
95	Juan Guzman	.10
96	John Olerud	.20
97	Ed Sprague	.10
98	Jermaine Dye	.10
99	Tom Glavine	.20
100	Marquis Grissom	.10
101	Andruw Jones	.75
102	Chipper Jones	1.00
103	David Justice	.25
104	Ryan Klesko	.20
105	Greg Maddux	1.00
106	Fred McGriff	.25
107	John Smoltz	.10
108	Brant Brown	.10
109	Mark Grace	.20
110	Brian McRae	.10
111	Ryne Sandberg	.50
112	Sammy Sosa	1.25
113	Steve Trachsel	.10
114	Bret Boone	.10
115	Eric Davis	.10
116	Steve Gibralter	.10
117	Barry Larkin	.25
118	Reggie Sanders	.10
119	John Smiley	.10
120	Dante Bichette	.15
121	Ellis Burks	.10
122	Vinny Castilla	.10
123	Andres Galarraga	.25
124	Larry Walker	.20
125	Eric Young	.10
126	Kevin Brown	.15
127	Greg Colbrunn	.10
128	Jeff Conine	.10
129	Charles Johnson	.10
130	Al Leiter	.20
131	Gary Sheffield	.30
132	Devon White	.15
133	Jeff Bagwell	.50
134	Derek Bell	.10
135	Craig Biggio	.20
136	Doug Drabek	.10
137	Brian Hunter	.10
138	Darryl Kile	.10
139	Shane Reynolds	.10
140	Brett Butler	.10
141	Eric Karros	.15
142	Ramon Martinez	.10
143	Raul Mondesi	.25
144	Hideo Nomo	.25
145	Chan Ho Park	.15
146	Mike Piazza	1.25
147	Moises Alou	.15
148	Yamil Benitez	.10
149	Mark Grudzielanek	.10
150	Pedro Martinez	.50
151	Henry Rodriguez	.10
152	David Segui	.10
153	Rondell White	.20
154	Carlos Baerga	.10
155	John Franco	.10
156	Bernard Gilkey	.10
157	Todd Hundley	.15
158	Jason Isringhausen	.15
159	Lance Johnson	.10
160	Alex Ochoa	.10
161	Rey Ordonez	.15
162	Paul Wilson	.10
163	Ron Blazier	.10
164	Ricky Bottalico	.10
165	Jim Eisenreich	.10
166	Pete Incaviglia	.10
167	Mickey Morandini	.10
168	Ricky Otero	.10
169	Curt Schilling	.15
170	Jay Bell	.10
171	Charlie Hayes	.10
172	Jason Kendall	.15
173	Jeff King	.10
174	Al Martin	.10
175	Alan Benes	.15
176	Royce Clayton	.10
177	Brian Jordan	.10
178	Ray Lankford	.10
179	John Mabry	.10
180	Willie McGee	.10
181	Ozzie Smith	.40
182	Todd Stottlemyre	.10
183	Andy Ashby	.10
184	Ken Caminiti	.15
185	Steve Finley	.10
186	Tony Gwynn	1.00
187	Rickey Henderson	.25
188	Wally Joyner	.10
189	Fernando Valenzuela	.10
190	Greg Vaughn	.15
191	Rod Beck	.10
192	Barry Bonds	.50
193	Shawon Dunston	.10
194	Chris Singleton	.10
195	Robby Thompson	.10
196	Matt Williams	.20
197	Checklist (Barry Bonds)	.20
198	Checklist (Ken Griffey Jr.)	.50
199	Checklist (Cal Ripken Jr.)	.75
200	Checklist (Frank Thomas)	.25

1996 Circa Rave

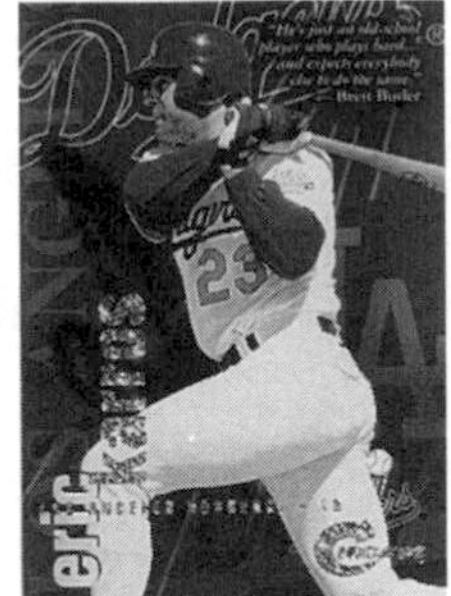

Rainbow metallic foil highlights on front and a serial number on back from within an edition of 150 of each card differentiate this parallel issue from the Circa base cards. Announced insertion rate for Raves was one per 60 packs.

	MT
Complete Set (200):	550.00
Common Player:	4.00
Veteran Stars:	25-50X
Young Stars:	25-50X

(See 1996 Circa for checklist and base card values.)

1996 Circa Access

This 1996 Fleer Circa insert set highlights 30 players on a three-panel foldout design that includes multiple photographs, personal information and statistics. The cards were seeded about one every 12 packs.

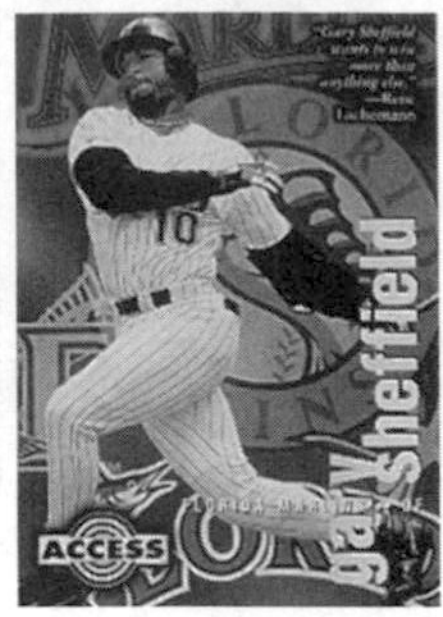

		MT
Complete Set (30):		75.00
Common Player:		1.00
1	Cal Ripken Jr.	7.50
2	Mo Vaughn	2.50
3	Tim Salmon	1.25
4	Frank Thomas	4.00
5	Albert Belle	2.50
6	Kenny Lofton	2.50
7	Manny Ramirez	3.00
8	Paul Molitor	1.50
9	Kirby Puckett	4.00
10	Paul O'Neill	1.00
11	Mark McGwire	12.50
12	Ken Griffey Jr.	10.00
13	Randy Johnson	2.00
14	Greg Maddux	5.00
15	John Smoltz	1.50
16	Sammy Sosa	6.00
17	Barry Larkin	1.50
18	Gary Sheffield	2.00
19	Jeff Bagwell	4.00
20	Hideo Nomo	1.50
21	Mike Piazza	6.00
22	Moises Alou	1.00
23	Henry Rodriguez	1.00
24	Rey Ordonez	1.50
25	Jay Bell	1.00
26	Ozzie Smith	2.00
27	Tony Gwynn	4.00
28	Rickey Henderson	1.50
29	Barry Bonds	2.50
30	Matt Williams	1.50
30p	Matt Williams (overprinted "PROMOTIONAL SAMPLE")	1.50

1996 Circa Boss

This insert set showcases the game's top stars on an embossed design. Cards were seeded one per six packs.

	MT
Complete Set (50):	65.00
Common Player:	.50

#	Player	Price
1	Roberto Alomar	1.50
2	Cal Ripken Jr.	6.00
2p	Cal Ripken Jr. (overprinted "PROMOTIONAL SAMPLE")	4.00
3	Jose Canseco	.80
4	Mo Vaughn	2.00
5	Tim Salmon	.75
6	Frank Thomas	3.00
7	Robin Ventura	.60
8	Albert Belle	2.00
9	Kenny Lofton	2.00
10	Manny Ramirez	2.50
11	Dave Nilsson	.50
12	Chuck Knoblauch	.75
13	Paul Molitor	1.50
14	Kirby Puckett	3.00
15	Wade Boggs	.80
16	Dwight Gooden	.50
17	Paul O'Neill	.50
18	Mark McGwire	10.00
19	Jay Buhner	.75
20	Ken Griffey Jr.	7.50
21	Randy Johnson	1.25
22	Will Clark	.75
23	Juan Gonzalez	2.00
24	Joe Carter	.50
25	Tom Glavine	.50
26	Ryan Klesko	.75
27	Greg Maddux	5.00
28	John Smoltz	.75
29	Ryne Sandberg	2.50
30	Sammy Sosa	4.00
31	Barry Larkin	.80
32	Reggie Sanders	.50
33	Dante Bichette	.75
34	Andres Galarraga	.75
35	Charles Johnson	.50
36	Gary Sheffield	1.00
37	Jeff Bagwell	4.00
38	Hideo Nomo	1.00
39	Mike Piazza	5.00
40	Moises Alou	.50
41	Henry Rodriguez	.50
42	Rey Ordonez	.65
43	Ricky Otero	.50
44	Jay Bell	.50
45	Royce Clayton	.50
46	Ozzie Smith	1.50
47	Tony Gwynn	3.00
48	Rickey Henderson	.80
49	Barry Bonds	2.00
50	Matt Williams	1.00

1997 Circa

Circa baseball returned for the second year in 1997, with a 400-card set, including 393 player cards and seven checklists. Cards feature action photos on a dynamic graphic arts background, and arrived in eight-card packs. The set was paralelled in a Rave insert and was accompanied by five inserts: Boss, Fast Track, Icons, Limited Access and Rave Reviews.

		MT
Complete Set (400):		40.00
Common Player:		.10
Pack (8):		1.50
Retail Wax Box (18):		25.00
Hobby Wax Box (36):		45.00
1	Kenny Lofton	.75
2	Ray Durham	.10
3	Mariano Rivera	.20
4	Jon Lieber	.10
5	Tim Salmon	.20
6	Mark Grudzielanek	.10
7	Neifi Perez	.10
8	Cal Ripken Jr.	2.50
9	John Olerud	.10
10	Edgar Renteria	.10
11	Jose Rosado	.10
12	Mickey Morandini	.10
13	Orlando Miller	.10
14	Ben McDonald	.10
15	Hideo Nomo	.50
16	Fred McGriff	.25
17	Sean Berry	.10
18	Roger Pavlik	.10
19	Aaron Sele	.10
20	Joey Hamilton	.10
21	Roger Clemens	1.00
22	Jose Herrera	.10
23	Ryne Sandberg	.75
24	Ken Griffey Jr.	3.00
25	Barry Bonds	.75
26	Dan Naulty	.10
27	Wade Boggs	.20
28	Ray Lankford	.10
29	Rico Brogna	.10
30	Wally Joyner	.10
31	F.P. Santangelo	.10
32	Vinny Castilla	.10
33	Eddie Murray	.40
34	Kevin Elster	.10
35	Mike Macfarlane	.10
36	Jeff Kent	.10
37	Orlando Merced	.10
38	Jason Isringhausen	.10
39	Chad Ogea	.10
40	Greg Gagne	.10
41	Curt Lyons	.25
42	Mo Vaughn	.75
43	Rusty Greer	.10
44	Shane Reynolds	.10
45	Frank Thomas	1.00
46	Chris Hoiles	.10
47	Scott Sanders	.10
48	Mark Lemke	.10
49	Fernando Vina	.10
50	Mark McGwire	3.00
51	Bernie Williams	.50
52	Bobby Higginson	.10
53	Kevin Tapani	.10
54	Rich Becker	.10
55	*Felix Heredia*	.40
56	Delino DeShields	.10
57	Rick Wilkins	.10
58	Edgardo Alfonzo	.10
59	Brett Butler	.10
60	Ed Sprague	.10
61	Joe Randa	.10
62	Ugueth Urbina	.10
63	Todd Greene	.10
64	Devon White	.10
65	Bruce Ruffin	.10
66	Mark Gardner	.10
67	Omar Vizquel	.10
68	Luis Gonzalez	.10
69	Tom Glavine	.20
70	Cal Eldred	.10
71	William VanLandingham	.10
72	Jay Buhner	.20
73	James Baldwin	.10
74	Robin Jennings	.10
75	Terry Steinbach	.10
76	Billy Taylor	.10
77	Armando Benitez	.10
78	Joe Girardi	.10
79	Jay Bell	.10
80	Damon Buford	.10
81	Deion Sanders	.40
82	Bill Haselman	.10
83	John Flaherty	.10
84	Todd Stottlemyre	.10
85	J.T. Snow	.10
86	Felipe Lira	.10
87	Steve Avery	.10
88	Trey Beamon	.10
89	Alex Gonzalez	.10
90	Mark Clark	.10
91	Shane Andrews	.10
92	Randy Myers	.10
93	Gary Gaetti	.10
94	Jeff Blauser	.10
95	Tony Batista	.10
96	Todd Worrell	.10
97	Jim Edmonds	.10
98	Eric Young	.10
99	Roberto Kelly	.10
100	Alex Rodriguez	3.00
100p	Alex Rodriguez (overprinted "PROMOTIONAL SAMPLE")	5.00
101	Julio Franco	.10
102	Jeff Bagwell	1.25
103	Bobby Witt	.10
104	Tino Martinez	.25
105	Shannon Stewart	.10
106	Brian Banks	.10
107	Eddie Taubensee	.10
108	Terry Mulholland	.10
109	Lyle Mouton	.10
110	Jeff Conine	.10
111	Johnny Damon	.10
112	Quilvio Veras	.10
113	Wilton Guerrero	.20
114	Dmitri Young	.10
115	Garret Anderson	.10
116	Bill Pulsipher	.10
117	Jacob Brumfield	.10
118	Mike Lansing	.10
119	Jose Canseco	.30
120	Mike Bordick	.10
121	Kevin Stocker	.10
122	Frank Rodriguez	.10
123	Mike Cameron	.10
124	*Tony Womack*	.50
125	Bret Boone	.10
126	Moises Alou	.10
127	Tim Naehring	.10
128	Brant Brown	.20
129	Todd Zeile	.10
130	Dave Nilsson	.10
131	Donne Wall	.10
132	Jose Mesa	.10
133	Mark McLemore	.10
134	Mike Stanton	.10
135	Dan Wilson	.10
136	Jose Offerman	.10
137	David Justice	.30
138	Kirt Manwaring	.10
139	Raul Casanova	.10
140	Ron Coomer	.10
141	Dave Hollins	.10
142	Shawn Estes	.10
143	Darren Daulton	.10
144	Turk Wendell	.10
145	Darrin Fletcher	.10
146	Marquis Grissom	.10
147	Andy Benes	.10
148	Nomar Garciaparra	2.00
149	Andy Pettitte	.75
150	Tony Gwynn	1.50
151	Robb Nen	.10
152	Kevin Seitzer	.10
153	Ariel Prieto	.10
154	Scott Karl	.10
155	Carlos Baerga	.10
156	Wilson Alvarez	.10
157	Thomas Howard	.10
158	Kevin Appier	.10
159	Russ Davis	.10
160	Justin Thompson	.10
161	Pete Schourek	.10
162	John Burkett	.10
163	Roberto Alomar	.75
164	Darren Holmes	.10
165	Travis Miller	.10
166	Mark Langston	.10
167	Juan Guzman	.10
168	Pedro Astacio	.10
169	Mark Johnson	.10
170	Mark Leiter	.10
171	Heathcliff Slocumb	.10
172	Dante Bichette	.20
173	*Brian Giles*	1.50
174	Paul Wilson	.10
175	Eric Davis	.10
176	Charles Johnson	.10
177	Willie Greene	.10
178	Geronimo Berroa	.10
179	Mariano Duncan	.10
180	Robert Person	.10
181	David Segui	.10
182	Ozzie Guillen	.10
183	Osvaldo Fernandez	.10
184	Dean Palmer	.10
185	Bob Wickman	.10
186	Eric Karros	.10
187	Travis Fryman	.10
188	Andy Ashby	.10
189	Scott Stahoviak	.10
190	Norm Charlton	.10
191	Craig Paquette	.10
192	John Smoltz	.25
193	Orel Hershiser	.10
194	Glenallen Hill	.10
195	George Arias	.10
196	Brian Jordan	.10
197	Greg Vaughn	.10
198	Rafael Palmeiro	.20
199	Darryl Kile	.10
200	Derek Jeter	2.00
201	Jose Vizcaino	.10
202	Rick Aguilera	.10
203	Jason Schmidt	.10
204	Trot Nixon	.10
205	Tom Pagnozzi	.10
206	Mark Wohlers	.10
207	Lance Johnson	.10
208	Carlos Delgado	.25
209	Cliff Floyd	.10
210	Kent Mercker	.10
211	Matt Mieske	.10
212	Ismael Valdes	.10
213	Shawon Dunston	.10
214	Melvin Nieves	.10
215	Tony Phillips	.10
216	Scott Spiezio	.10
217	Michael Tucker	.10
218	Matt Williams	.25
219	Ricky Otero	.10
220	Kevin Ritz	.10
221	Darryl Strawberry	.10
222	Troy Percival	.10
223	Eugene Kingsale	.10
224	Julian Tavarez	.10
225	Jermaine Dye	.10
226	Jason Kendall	.10
227	Sterling Hitchcock	.10
228	Jeff Cirillo	.10
229	Roberto Hernandez	.10
230	Ricky Bottalico	.10
231	Bobby Bonilla	.10
232	Edgar Martinez	.10
233	John Valentin	.10
234	Ellis Burks	.10
235	Benito Santiago	.10
236	Terrell Wade	.10
237	Armando Reynoso	.10
238	Danny Graves	.10
239	Ken Hill	.10
240	Dennis Eckersley	.10
241	Darin Erstad	1.00
242	Lee Smith	.10
243	Cecil Fielder	.20
244	Tony Clark	.50
245	Scott Erickson	.10
246	Bob Abreu	.10
247	Ruben Sierra	.10
248	Chili Davis	.10
249	Darryl Hamilton	.10
250	Albert Belle	.75
251	Todd Hollandsworth	.10
252	Terry Adams	.10
253	Rey Ordonez	.10
254	Steve Finley	.10
255	Jose Valentin	.10
256	Royce Clayton	.10
257	Sandy Alomar	.10
258	Mike Lieberthal	.10
259	Ivan Rodriguez	.50
260	Rod Beck	.10
261	Ron Karkovice	.10
262	Mark Gubicza	.10
263	Chris Holt	.10
264	Jaime Bluma	.10
265	Francisco Cordova	.15
266	Javy Lopez	.20
267	Reggie Jefferson	.10
268	Kevin Brown	.10
269	Scott Brosius	.10
270	Dwight Gooden	.10
271	Marty Cordova	.10
272	Jeff Brantley	.10
273	Joe Carter	.10
274	Todd Jones	.10
275	Sammy Sosa	1.50
276	Randy Johnson	.50
277	B.J. Surhoff	.10
278	Chan Ho Park	.10
279	Jamey Wright	.10
280	Manny Ramirez	1.00
281	John Franco	.10

#	Player	Value
282	Tim Worrell	.10
283	Scott Rolen	1.25
284	Reggie Sanders	.10
285	Mike Fetters	.10
286	Tim Wakefield	.10
287	Trevor Hoffman	.10
288	Donovan Osborne	.10
289	Phil Nevin	.10
290	Jermaine Allensworth	.10
291	Rocky Coppinger	.10
292	Tim Raines	.10
293	Henry Rodriguez	.10
294	Paul Sorrento	.10
295	Tom Goodwin	.10
296	Raul Mondesi	.25
297	Allen Watson	.10
298	Derek Bell	.10
299	Gary Sheffield	.40
300	Paul Molitor	.40
301	Shawn Green	.10
302	Darren Oliver	.10
303	Jack McDowell	.10
304	Denny Neagle	.10
305	Doug Drabek	.10
306	Mel Rojas	.10
307	Andres Galarraga	.20
308	Alex Ochoa	.10
309	Gary DiSarcina	.10
310	Ron Gant	.10
311	Gregg Jefferies	.10
312	Ruben Rivera	.10
313	Vladimir Guerrero	1.25
314	Willie Adams	.10
315	Bip Roberts	.10
316	Mark Grace	.20
317	Bernard Gilkey	.10
318	Marc Newfield	.10
319	Al Leiter	.10
320	Otis Nixon	.10
321	Tom Candiotti	.10
322	Mike Stanley	.10
323	Jeff Fassero	.10
324	Billy Wagner	.10
325	Todd Walker	.75
326	Chad Curtis	.10
327	Quinton McCracken	.10
328	Will Clark	.25
329	Andruw Jones	1.50
330	Robin Ventura	.10
331	Curtis Pride	.10
332	Barry Larkin	.30
333	Jimmy Key	.10
334	David Wells	.10
335	Mike Holtz	.10
336	Paul Wagner	.10
337	Greg Maddux	2.00
338	Curt Schilling	.10
339	Steve Trachsel	.10
340	John Wetteland	.10
341	Rickey Henderson	.10
342	Ernie Young	.10
343	Harold Baines	.10
344	Bobby Jones	.10
345	Jeff D'Amico	.10
346	John Mabry	.10
347	Pedro Martinez	.10
348	Mark Lewis	.10
349	Dan Miceli	.10
350	Chuck Knoblauch	.10
351	John Smiley	.10
352	Brady Anderson	.10
353	Jim Leyritz	.10
354	Al Martin	.10
355	Pat Hentgen	.10
356	Mike Piazza	2.00
357	Charles Nagy	.10
358	Luis Castillo	.15
359	Paul O'Neill	.10
360	Steve Reed	.10
361	Tom Gordon	.10
362	Craig Biggio	.10
363	Jeff Montgomery	.10
364	Jamie Moyer	.10
365	Ryan Klesko	.25
366	Todd Hundley	.20
367	Bobby Estalella	.10
368	Jason Giambi	.10
369	Brian Hunter	.10
370	Ramon Martinez	.10
371	Carlos Garcia	.10
372	Hal Morris	.10
373	Juan Gonzalez	.75
374	Brian McRae	.10
375	Mike Mussina	.60
376	John Ericks	.10
377	Larry Walker	.35
378	Chris Gomez	.10
379	John Jaha	.10
380	Rondell White	.20
381	Chipper Jones	2.00
382	David Cone	.20
383	Alan Benes	.20
384	Troy O'Leary	.10
385	Ken Caminiti	.30
386	Jeff King	.10
387	Mike Hampton	.10
388	Jaime Navarro	.10
389	Brad Radke	.10
390	Joey Cora	.10
391	Jim Thome	.40
392	Alex Fernandez	.20
393	Chuck Finley	.10
394	Andruw Jones CL	.75
395	Ken Griffey Jr. CL	1.50
396	Frank Thomas CL	.50
397	Alex Rodriguez CL	1.50
398	Cal Ripken Jr. CL	1.25
399	Mike Piazza CL	1.00
400	Greg Maddux CL	1.00

1997 Circa Rave

In its second year, Circa Rave parallel inserts were limited to inclusion only in hobby packs at the stated. rate of one card per "30 to 40" packs. Raves are distinguished from regular-edition Circa cards by the use of purple metallic foil for the brand name and player identification on front. Rave backs carry a silver-foil serial number detailing its position within a production of 150 for each card.

	MT
Complete Set (400):	600.00
Common Player:	5.00
Veteran Stars:	25-40X
Young Stars:	15-30X

(See 1997 Circa for checklist and base card values.)

1997 Circa Boss

Boss was Circa's most common insert series. Twenty embossed cards were seeded one per six packs, displaying some of baseball's best players. A Super Boss parallel insert features metallic-foil background and graphics on front, and is inserted at a rate of one per 36 packs.

		MT
Complete Set (20):		40.00
Common Player:		.50
Super Boss:		2-3X
1	Jeff Bagwell	3.00
2	Albert Belle	2.00
3	Barry Bonds	2.00
4	Ken Caminiti	1.00
5	Juan Gonzalez	2.00
6	Ken Griffey Jr.	8.00
7	Tony Gwynn	3.00
8	Derek Jeter	5.00
9	Andruw Jones	4.00
10	Chipper Jones	5.00
11	Greg Maddux	5.00
12	Mark McGwire	10.00
13	Mike Piazza	5.00
14	Manny Ramirez	2.50
15	Cal Ripken Jr.	6.00
16	Alex Rodriguez	8.00
17	John Smoltz	1.00
18	Frank Thomas	3.00
19	Mo Vaughn	2.00
20	Bernie Williams	1.50

1997 Circa Emerald Autograph Redemption Cards

These box-topper cards were a hobby exclusive redeemable until May 31, 1998, for autographed special cards of six young stars. Fronts have a green-foil enhanced player action photo. Backs provide details of the redemption program.

		MT
Complete Set (6):		20.00
Common Player:		1.50
(1)	Darin Erstad	3.50
(2)	Todd Hollandsworth	1.50
(3)	Alex Ochoa	1.50
(4)	Alex Rodriguez	12.50
(5)	Scott Rolen	5.00
(6)	Todd Walker	2.00

1997 Circa Emerald Autographs

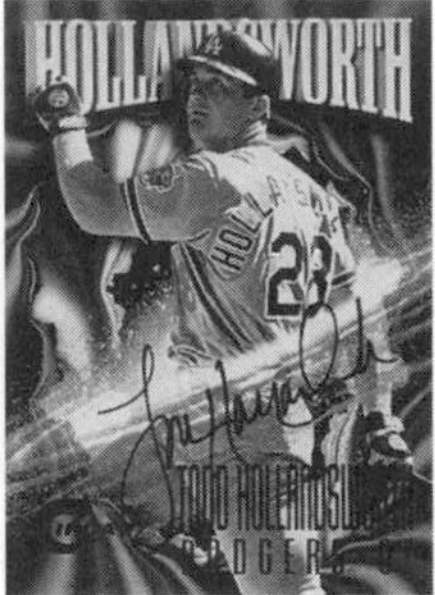

Special green-foil enhanced cards of six top young stars were available via a mail-in redemption. The cards feature authentic player signatures on front and an embossed authentication seal. Backs are identical to the regular card of each featured player.

		MT
Complete Set (6):		200.00
Common Player:		15.00
100	Alex Rodriguez	90.00
241	Darin Erstad	35.00
251	Todd Hollandsworth	15.00
283	Scott Rolen	45.00
308	Alex Ochoa	15.00
325	Todd Walker	20.00

1997 Circa Fast Track

Fast Track highlights 10 top rookies and young stars on a flocked background simulating grass. Cards were inserted every 24 packs.

		MT
Complete Set (10):		30.00
Common Player:		1.00
1	Vladimir Guerrero	4.00
2	Todd Hollandsworth	1.00
3	Derek Jeter	6.00
4	Andruw Jones	3.00
5	Chipper Jones	4.00
6	Andy Pettitte	2.00
7	Mariano Rivera	3.00
8	Alex Rodriguez	8.00
9	Scott Rolen	3.00
10	Todd Walker	2.00

1997 Circa Icons

Twelve of baseball's top sluggers were displayed on 100-percent holofoil cards in Icons. Icons were found at a rate of one per 36 packs.

		MT
Complete Set (12):		55.00
Common Player:		2.00
1	Juan Gonzalez	4.00
2	Ken Griffey Jr.	15.00
3	Tony Gwynn	5.00
4	Derek Jeter	6.00
5	Chipper Jones	6.00
6	Greg Maddux	5.00
7	Mark McGwire	15.00
8	Mike Piazza	6.00
9	Cal Ripken Jr.	7.50
10	Alex Rodriguez	8.00
11	Frank Thomas	4.00
12	Matt Williams	2.00

1997 Circa Limited Access

Limited Access was a retail-only insert found every 18 packs. Cards feature an in-depth, statistical analysis including the player's favorite pitcher to hit and each pitcher's least favorite hitter to face. Limited Access is formatted as a die-cut, bi-fold design resembling a book.

		MT
Complete Set (15):		110.00
Common Player:		2.00
1	Jeff Bagwell	8.00
2	Albert Belle	5.00
3	Barry Bonds	5.00
4	Juan Gonzalez	5.00
5	Ken Griffey Jr.	20.00
6	Tony Gwynn	10.00
7	Derek Jeter	12.00
8	Chipper Jones	12.00
9	Greg Maddux	12.00
10	Mark McGwire	25.00
11	Mike Piazza	12.00
12	Cal Ripken Jr.	15.00
13	Alex Rodriguez	15.00
14	Frank Thomas	8.00
15	Mo Vaughn	5.00

1997 Circa Rave Reviews

Hitters that continually put up great numbers were selected for Rave Reviews. The insert was found every 288 packs and was printed on 100-percent holofoil.

		MT
Complete Set (12):		275.00
Common Player:		10.00
1	Albert Belle	15.00
2	Barry Bonds	15.00
3	Juan Gonzalez	15.00
4	Ken Griffey Jr.	50.00
5	Tony Gwynn	25.00
6	Greg Maddux	25.00
7	Mark McGwire	50.00
8	Eddie Murray	10.00
9	Mike Piazza	30.00
10	Cal Ripken Jr.	40.00
11	Alex Rodriguez	35.00
12	Frank Thomas	20.00

1998 Circa Thunder

Circa Thunder was issued as one series of 300 cards, sold in packs of eight for $1.59. The set marked SkyBox's brand transition from Circa to Thunder so the cards are labeled with both names. Inserts include: Rave and Super Rave parallels, Boss, Fast Track, Quick Strike, Limited Access, Rave Review and Thunder Boomers.

		MT
Complete Set (300):		25.00
Common Player:		.15
Pack (8):		1.75
Wax Box (36):		40.00
1	Ben Grieve	1.25
2	Derek Jeter	2.00
3	Alex Rodriguez	2.50
4	Paul Molitor	.50
5	Nomar Garciaparra	2.00
6	Fred McGriff	.25
7	Kenny Lofton	.75
8a	Cal Ripken Jr.	2.50
8b	Marquis Grissom (should be #280)	.15
8s	Cal Ripken Jr. ("PROMOTIONAL SAMPLE" on back)	3.00
9	Matt Williams	.30
10	Chipper Jones	2.00
11	Barry Larkin	.25
12	Steve Finley	.15
13	Billy Wagner	.15
14	Rico Brogna	.15
15	Tim Salmon	.30
16	Hideo Nomo	.50
17	Tony Clark	.50
18	Jason Kendall	.15
19	Juan Gonzalez	.75
20	Jeromy Burnitz	.15
21	Roger Clemens	1.00
22	Mark Grace	.30
23	Robin Ventura	.25
24	Manny Ramirez	1.00
25	Mark McGwire	4.00
26	Gary Sheffield	.30
27	Vladimir Guerrero	1.00
28	Butch Huskey	.15
29	Cecil Fielder	.25
30	Roderick Myers	.15
31	Greg Maddux	2.00
32	Bill Mueller	.15
33	Larry Walker	.30
34	Henry Rodriguez	.15
35	Mike Mussina	.60
36	Ricky Ledee	.25
37	Bobby Bonilla	.25
38	Curt Schilling	.30
39	Luis Gonzalez	.15
40	Troy Percival	.15
41	Eric Milton	.40
42	Mo Vaughn	.75
43	Raul Mondesi	.30
44	Kenny Rogers	.15
45	Frank Thomas	1.50
46	Jose Canseco	.30
47	Tom Glavine	.25
48	*Rich Butler*	.40
49	Jay Buhner	.25
50	Jose Cruz Jr.	.20
51	Bernie Williams	.50
52	Doug Glanville	.15
53	Travis Fryman	.15
54	Rey Ordonez	.15
55	Jeff Conine	.15
56	Trevor Hoffman	.15
57	Kirk Rueter	.15
58	Ron Gant	.25
59	Carl Everett	.15
60	Joe Carter	.25
61	Livan Hernandez	.25
62	John Jaha	.15
63	Ivan Rodriguez	.75
64	Willie Blair	.15
65	Todd Helton	.75
66	Kevin Young	.15
67	Mike Caruso	.15
68	Steve Trachsel	.15
69	Marty Cordova	.15
70	Alex Fernandez	.15
71	Eric Karros	.25
72	Reggie Sanders	.15
73	Russ Davis	.15
74	Roberto Hernandez	.15
75	Barry Bonds	.75
76	Alex Gonzalez	.15
77	Roberto Alomar	.50
78	Troy O'Leary	.15
79	Bernard Gilkey	.15
80	Ismael Valdes	.15
81	Travis Lee	.75
82	Brant Brown	.15
83	Gary DiSarcina	.15
84	Joe Randa	.15
85	Jaret Wright	1.50
86	Quilvio Veras	.15
87	Rickey Henderson	.15
88	Randall Simon	.25
89	Mariano Rivera	.25
90	Ugueth Urbina	.15
91	Fernando Vina	.15
92	Alan Benes	.25
93	Dante Bichette	.25
94	Karim Garcia	.15
95	A.J. Hinch	.75
96	Shane Reynolds	.15
97	Kevin Stocker	.15
98	John Wetteland	.15
99	Terry Steinbach	.15
100	Ken Griffey Jr.	3.00
101	Mike Cameron	.25
102	Damion Easley	.15
103	Randy Myers	.15
104	Jason Schmidt	.15
105	Jeff King	.15
106	Gregg Jefferies	.15
107	Sean Casey	.40
108	Mark Kotsay	.40
109	Brad Fullmer	.15
110	Wilson Alvarez	.15
111	Sandy Alomar Jr.	.25
112	Walt Weiss	.15
113	Doug Jones	.15
114	Andy Benes	.25
115	Paul O'Neill	.25
116	Dennis Eckersley	.15
117	Todd Greene	.15
118	Bobby Jones	.15
119	Darrin Fletcher	.15
120	Eric Young	.15
121	Jeffrey Hammonds	.15
122	Mickey Morandini	.15
123	Chuck Knoblauch	.40
124	Moises Alou	.25
125	Miguel Tejada	.50
126	Brian Anderson	.15
127	Edgar Renteria	.15
128	Mike Lansing	.15
129	Quinton McCracken	.15
130	Ray Lankford	.15
131	Andy Ashby	.15
132	Kelvim Escobar	.15
133	*Mike Lowell*	.25
134	Randy Johnson	.50
135	Andres Galarraga	.35
136	Armando Benitez	.15
137	Rusty Greer	.15
138	Jose Guillen	.25
139	Paul Konerko	.75
140	Edgardo Alfonzo	.15
141	Jim Leyritz	.15
142	Mark Clark	.15
143	Brian Johnson	.15
144	Scott Rolen	1.00
145	David Cone	.25
146	Jeff Shaw	.15
147	Shannon Stewart	.15
148	Brian Hunter	.15
149	Garret Anderson	.15
150	Jeff Bagwell	1.00
151	James Baldwin	.15
152	Devon White	.15
153	Jim Thome	.40
154	Wally Joyner	.15
155	Mark Wohlers	.15
156	Jeff Cirillo	.15
157	Jason Giambi	.15
158	Royce Clayton	.15
159	Dennis Reyes	.15
160	Raul Casanova	.15
161	Pedro Astacio	.15
162	Todd Dunwoody	.15
163	Sammy Sosa	2.00
164	Todd Hundley	.15
165	Wade Boggs	.25
166	Robb Nen	.15
167	Dan Wilson	.15
168	Hideki Irabu	.50
169	B.J. Surhoff	.15
170	Carlos Delgado	.25
171	Fernando Tatis	.15
172	Bob Abreu	.15
173	David Ortiz	.25
174	Tony Womack	.15
175	*Magglio Ordonez*	1.00
176	Aaron Boone	.15
177	Brian Giles	.15
178	Kevin Appier	.15

179	Chuck Finley	.15
180	Brian Rose	.25
181	Ryan Klesko	.20
182	Mike Stanley	.15
183	Dave Nilsson	.15
184	Carlos Perez	.15
185	Jeff Blauser	.15
186	Richard Hidalgo	.15
187	Charles Johnson	.25
188	Vinny Castilla	.25
189	Joey Hamilton	.15
190	Bubba Trammell	.15
191	Eli Marrero	.15
192	Scott Erickson	.15
193	Pat Hentgen	.15
194	Jorge Fabregas	.15
195	Tino Martinez	.30
196	Bobby Higginson	.15
197	Dave Hollins	.15
198	*Rolando Arrojo*	.40
199	Joey Cora	.15
200	Mike Piazza	2.00
201	Reggie Jefferson	.15
202	John Smoltz	.25
203	Bobby Smith	.15
204	Tom Goodwin	.15
205	Omar Vizquel	.15
206	John Olerud	.25
207	Matt Stairs	.15
208	Bobby Estalella	.15
209	Miguel Cairo	.15
210	Shawn Green	.15
211	Jon Nunnally	.15
212	Al Leiter	.15
213	Matt Lawton	.15
214	Brady Anderson	.15
215	Jeff Kent	.15
216	Ray Durham	.15
217	Al Martin	.15
218	Jeff D'Amico	.15
219	Kevin Tapani	.15
220	Jim Edmonds	.25
221	Jose Vizcaino	.15
222	Jay Bell	.15
223	Ken Caminiti	.25
224	Craig Biggio	.30
225	Bartolo Colon	.25
226	Neifi Perez	.15
227	Delino DeShields	.15
228	Javier Lopez	.15
229	David Wells	.15
230	Brad Rigby	.15
231	John Franco	.15
232	Michael Coleman	.15
233	Edgar Martinez	.25
234	Francisco Cordova	.15
235	Johnny Damon	.15
236	Deivi Cruz	.15
237	J.T. Snow	.15
238	Enrique Wilson	.15
239	Rondell White	.25
240	Aaron Sele	.25
241	Tony Saunders	.15
242	Ricky Bottalico	.15
243	Cliff Floyd	.15
244	Chili Davis	.15
245	Brian McRae	.15
246	Brad Radke	.15
247	Chan Ho Park	.25
248	Lance Johnson	.15
249	Rafael Palmeiro	.25
250	Tony Gwynn	1.50
251	Denny Neagle	.15
252	Dean Palmer	.15
253	Jose Valentin	.15
254	Matt Morris	.15
255	Ellis Burks	.15
256	Jeff Suppan	.15
257	Jimmy Key	.15
258	Justin Thompson	.15
259	Brett Tomko	.15
260	Mark Grudzielanek	.15
261	Mike Hampton	.15
262	Jeff Fassero	.15
263	Charles Nagy	.15
264	Pedro Martinez	.40
265	Todd Zeile	.15
266	Will Clark	.30
267	Abraham Nunez	.15
268	Dave Martinez	.15
269	Jason Dickson	.15
270	Eric Davis	.15
271	Kevin Orie	.15
272	Derrek Lee	.25
273	Andruw Jones	.75
274	Juan Encarnacion	.15
275	Carlos Baerga	.15
276	Andy Pettitte	.50
277	Brent Brede	.15
278	Paul Sorrento	.15
279	Mike Lieberthal	.15
280	(Not issued, see #8)	
281	Darin Erstad	.75
282	Willie Greene	.15
283	Derek Bell	.15
284	Scott Spiezio	.15
285	David Segui	.15
286	Albert Belle	.75
287	Ramon Martinez	.15
288	Jeremi Gonzalez	.15
289	Shawn Estes	.15
290	Ron Coomer	.15
291	John Valentin	.15
292	Kevin Brown	.15
293	Michael Tucker	.15
294	Brian Jordan	.15
295	Darryl Kile	.15
296	David Justice	.30
297	Jose Cruz Jr. CL	.20
298	Alex Rodriguez CL	1.25
299	Ken Griffey Jr. CL	1.50
300	Frank Thomas CL	.75

1998 Circa Thunder Rave

Rave parallels each card in Circa Thunder except for the four checklist cards. A special silver sparkling foil is used on the player's name and the Thunder logo on front. This 296-card set was inserted approximately one per 36 packs and sequentially numbered to 150 sets on the back.

	MT
Complete Set (296):	1650.
Common Player:	5.00
Veteran Stars:	25-50X
Young Stars:	25-50X

(See 1998 Circa Thunder for checklist and base card values.)

1998 Circa Thunder Super Rave

Only 25 Super Rave parallel sets were printed and they were inserted approximately one per 216 packs. The set contains 296 player cards (no checklist cards). Fronts are identified by sparkling gold foil on the player's name and the Thunder logo, with sequential numbering on the back to 25.

	MT
Common Player:	15.00
Veteran Stars:	80-150X
Young Stars:	50-100X

(See 1998 Circa Thunder for checklist and base card values.)

1998 Circa Thunder Boss

This 20-card insert, seeded one per six packs, has cards embossed with the player's last name in large letters across the top.

		MT
Complete Set (20):		25.00
Common Player:		.50
Inserted 1:6		
1B	Jeff Bagwell	1.25
2B	Barry Bonds	.75
3B	Roger Clemens	1.25
4B	Jose Cruz Jr.	.75
5B	Nomar Garciaparra	2.00
6B	Juan Gonzalez	.75
7B	Ken Griffey Jr.	3.00
8B	Tony Gwynn	1.50
9B	Derek Jeter	2.00
10B	Chipper Jones	2.00
11B	Travis Lee	.75
12B	Greg Maddux	1.50
13B	Pedro Martinez	.75
14B	Mark McGwire	4.00
15B	Mike Piazza	2.00
16B	Cal Ripken Jr.	2.50
17B	Alex Rodriguez	2.50
18B	Scott Rolen	1.00
19B	Frank Thomas	1.25
20B	Larry Walker	.50

1998 Circa Thunder Fast Track

This 10-card insert showcases some of the top young stars in baseball and was seeded one per 24 packs. Fronts picture the player over a closeup of a gold foil baseball on the left. The right side has smaller head shots of all 10 players with the featured player's head in gold foil.

		MT
Complete Set (10):		35.00
Common Player:		1.50
Inserted 1:24		
1FT	Jose Cruz Jr.	1.50
2FT	Juan Encarnacion	1.50
3FT	Brad Fullmer	3.00
4FT	Nomar Garciaparra	7.50
5FT	Todd Helton	3.00
6FT	Livan Hernandez	1.50
7FT	Travis Lee	5.00
8FT	Neifi Perez	1.50
9FT	Scott Rolen	5.00
10FT	Jaret Wright	5.00

1998 Circa Thunder Limited Access

This retail exclusive insert was seeded one per 18 packs. Cards are bi-fold and die-cut with foil stamping on front. The theme of the insert was to provide an in-depth statistical scouting analysis of each player.

		MT
Complete Set (15):		90.00
Common Player:		2.00
Inserted 1:18		
1LA	Jeff Bagwell	6.00
2LA	Roger Clemens	6.00
3LA	Jose Cruz Jr.	2.00
4LA	Nomar Garciaparra	10.00
5LA	Juan Gonzalez	4.00
6LA	Ken Griffey Jr.	15.00
7LA	Tony Gwynn	8.00
8LA	Derek Jeter	10.00
9LA	Greg Maddux	10.00
10LA	Pedro Martinez	2.00
11LA	Mark McGwire	20.00
12LA	Mike Piazza	10.00
13LA	Alex Rodriguez	12.00
14LA	Frank Thomas	6.00
15LA	Larry Walker	2.00

1998 Circa Thunder Quick Strike

This insert pictures players over a colorful die-cut foil-board front.

Quick Strikes were seeded one per 36 packs of Circa Thunder.

		MT
Complete Set (12):		90.00
Common Player:		3.00
Inserted 1:36		
1QS	Jeff Bagwell	8.00
2QS	Roger Clemens	8.00
3QS	Jose Cruz Jr.	3.00
4QS	Nomar Garciaparra	12.00
5QS	Ken Griffey Jr.	20.00
6QS	Greg Maddux	12.00
7QS	Pedro Martinez	3.00
8QS	Mark McGwire	25.00
9QS	Mike Piazza	12.00
10QS	Alex Rodriguez	15.00
11QS	Frank Thomas	8.00
12QS	Larry Walker	3.00

1998 Circa Thunder Rave Reviews

Rave Reviews were inserted at one per 288 packs of Circa Thunder. The cards are die-cut in a horizontal design with bronze foil etching and the image of a ballfield in the background.

		MT
Complete Set (15):		500.00
Common Player:		10.00
Inserted 1:288		
1RR	Jeff Bagwell	25.00
2RR	Barry Bonds	20.00
3RR	Roger Clemens	35.00
4RR	Jose Cruz Jr.	10.00
5RR	Nomar Garciaparra	50.00
6RR	Juan Gonzalez	20.00
7RR	Ken Griffey Jr.	80.00
8RR	Tony Gwynn	40.00
9RR	Derek Jeter	50.00
10RR	Greg Maddux	40.00
11RR	Mark McGwire	100.00
12RR	Mike Piazza	50.00
13RR	Alex Rodriguez	60.00
14RR	Frank Thomas	25.00
15RR	Larry Walker	10.00

1998 Circa Thunder Thunder Boomers

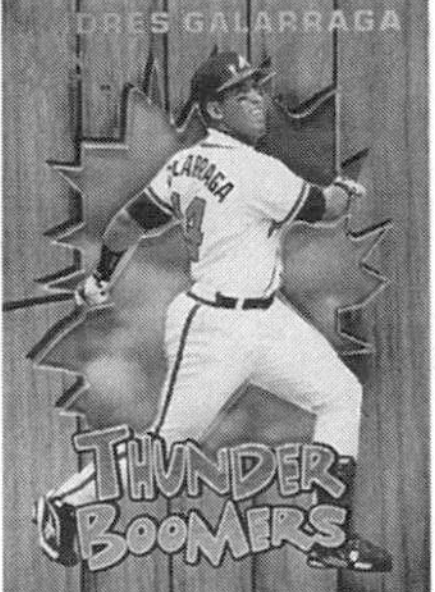

Thunder Boomers feature top power hitters imposed over a see-through cloud-like plastic center with the imagery of a wooden fence with a large hole blasted through the middle of it. This 12-card set was inserted one per 96 packs of Circa Thunder.

		MT
Complete Set (12):		125.00
Common Player:		5.00
Inserted 1:96		
1TB	Jeff Bagwell	15.00
2TB	Barry Bonds	10.00
3TB	Jay Buhner	5.00
4TB	Andres Galarraga	5.00
5TB	Juan Gonzalez	10.00
6TB	Ken Griffey Jr.	40.00
7TB	Tino Martinez	5.00
8TB	Mark McGwire	45.00
9TB	Mike Piazza	25.00
10TB	Frank Thomas	15.00
11TB	Jim Thome	6.00
12TB	Larry Walker	5.00

1987 Classic Major League Baseball Game

The "Classic Major League Baseball Board Game" set consists of 100 full-color cards used to play the game in which participants answer trivia questions found on the card backs. Cards measure 2-1/2" x 3-1/2" and are printed on semi-gloss stock. Backs carry the player's career stats besides the trivia questions. The game was produced by Game Time, Ltd. of Marietta, Ga., and sold for $19.95 in most retail outlets. In 1991-92 the set was selling for $200 or more, with the Bo Jackson card advertised as high as $80.

		MT
Complete Set (100):		35.00
Common Player:		.10
1	Pete Rose	2.50
2	Len Dykstra	.10
3	Darryl Strawberry	.15
4	Keith Hernandez	.10
5	Gary Carter	.25
6	Wally Joyner	.15
7	Andres Thomas	.10
8	Pat Dodson	.10
9	Kirk Gibson	.10
10	Don Mattingly	3.00
11	Dave Winfield	.50
12	Rickey Henderson	.50
13	Dan Pasqua	.10
14	Don Baylor	.10
15	Bo Jackson	4.00
16	Pete Incaviglia	.10
17	Kevin Bass	.10
18	Barry Larkin	.35
19	Dave Magadan	.10
20	Steve Sax	.10
21	Eric Davis	.12
22	Mike Pagliarulo	.10
23	Fred Lynn	.10
24	Reggie Jackson	.50
25	Larry Parrish	.10
26	Tony Gwynn	1.00
27	Steve Garvey	.20
28	Glenn Davis	.10
29	Tim Raines	.12
30	Vince Coleman	.10
31	Willie McGee	.12
32	Ozzie Smith	.75
33	Dave Parker	.10
34	Tony Pena	.10
35	Ryne Sandberg	2.50
36	Brett Butler	.12
37	Dale Murphy	.35
38	Bob Horner	.10
39	Pedro Guerrero	.10
40	Brook Jacoby	.10
41	Carlton Fisk	.25
42	Harold Baines	.12
43	Rob Deer	.10
44	Robin Yount	.75
45	Paul Molitor	.75
46	Jose Canseco	3.00
47	George Brett	3.00
48	Jim Presley	.10
49	Rich Gedman	.10
50	Lance Parrish	.10
51	Eddie Murray	.75
52	Cal Ripken, Jr.	10.00
53	Kent Hrbek	.12
54	Gary Gaetti	.12
55	Kirby Puckett	2.50
56	George Bell	.10
57	Tony Fernandez	.12
58	Jesse Barfield	.10
59	Jim Rice	.12
60	Wade Boggs	.75
61	Marty Barrett	.10
62	Mike Schmidt	1.00
63	Von Hayes	.10
64	Jeff Leonard	.10
65	Chris Brown	.10
66	Dave Smith	.10
67	Mike Krukow	.10
68	Ron Guidry	.12
69	Rob Woodward (photo actually Pat Dodson)	.10
70	Rob Murphy	.10
71	Andres Galarraga	.20
72	Dwight Gooden	.15
73	Bob Ojeda	.10
74	Sid Fernandez	.10
75	Jesse Orosco	.10
76	Roger McDowell	.10
77	John Tutor (Tudor)	.10
78	Tom Browning	.10
79	Rick Aguilera	.10
80	Lance McCullers	.10
81	Mike Scott	.10
82	Nolan Ryan	7.00
83	Bruce Hurst	.10
84	Roger Clemens	1.00
85	Oil Can Boyd	.10
86	Dave Righetti	.10
87	Dennis Rasmussen	.10
88	Bret Saberhagan (Saberhagen)	.15
89	Mark Langston	.10
90	Jack Morris	.10
91	Fernando Valenzuela	.12
92	Orel Hershiser	.12
93	Rick Honeycutt	.10
94	Jeff Reardon	.10
95	John Habyan	.10
96	Goose Gossage	.12
97	Todd Worrell	.10
98	Floyd Youmans	.10
99	Don Aase	.10
100	John Franco	.10

1987 Classic Travel Update (Yellow)

Game Time, Ltd. of Marietta, Ga., issued as an update to its Classic Baseball Board Game a 50-card set entitled "Travel Edition." Cards measure 2-1/2" x 3-1/2" in the same format as the first release, though with yellow, rather than green, borders. Numbered from 101 to 150, the "Travel Edition," besides updating player trades and showcasing rookies, offers several highlights from the 1987 season. All new trivia questions are found on the card backs.

		MT
Complete Set (50):		10.00
Common Player:		.10
101	Mike Schmidt	.75
102	Eric Davis	.12
103	Pete Rose	1.00
104	Don Mattingly	.75
105	Wade Boggs	.50
106	Dale Murphy	.15
107	Glenn Davis	.10
108	Wally Joyner	.12
109	Bo Jackson	.35
110	Cory Snyder	.10
111	Jim Lindeman	.10
112	Kirby Puckett	.75
113	Barry Bonds	1.50
114	Roger Clemens	.75
115	Oddibe McDowell	.10

116	Bret Saberhagen	.12
117	Joe Magrane	.10
118	Scott Fletcher	.10
119	Mark McLemore	.10
120	Who Me? (Joe Niekro)	.25
121	Mark McGwire	2.00
122	Darryl Strawberry	.15
123	Mike Scott	.10
124	Andre Dawson	.12
125	Jose Canseco	.40
126	Kevin McReynolds	.10
127	Joe Carter	.10
128	Casey Candaele	.10
129	Matt Nokes	.10
130	Kal Daniels	.10
131	Pete Incaviglia	.10
132	Benito Santiago	.10
133	Barry Larkin	.20
134	Gary Pettis	.10
135	B.J. Surhoff	.12
136	Juan Nieves	.10
137	Jim Deshaies	.10
138	Pete O'Brien	.10
139	Kevin Seitzer	.10
140	Devon White	.12
141	Rob Deer	.10
142	Kurt Stillwell	.10
143	Edwin Correa	.10
144	Dion James	.10
145	Danny Tartabull	.10
146	Jerry Browne	.10
147	Ted Higuera	.10
148	Jack Clark	.10
149	Ruben Sierra	.10
150	Mark McGwire, Eric Davis	1.50

1988 Classic Travel Update I (Red)

This set was produced for use with the travel edition of Game Time's Classic Baseball Board Game. Special cards in the set include a McGwire/Mattingly, an instruction card with McGwire/Canseco and three different cards featuring Phil Niekro (in different uniforms). Update I card fronts have red borders, a yellow Classic logo in the upper-left corner and a black and beige name banner beneath the photo. Backs are printed in red and pink on white and include the player name, personal info, major league records, a baseball question and space for the player autograph. Classic card series sold via hobby dealers and retail toy stores nationwide. Game Time Ltd., the set's producer, was purchased by Scoreboard of Cherry Hill, N.J. in 1988.

		MT
Complete Set (50):		10.00
Common Player:		.10
151	Don Mattingly, Mark McGwire	2.00
152	Don Mattingly	.80
153	Mark McGwire	3.00
154	Eric Davis	.10
155	Wade Boggs	.50
156	Dale Murphy	.15
157	Andre Dawson	.12
158	Roger Clemens	.75
159	Kevin Seitzer	.10
160	Benito Santiago	.10
161	Kal Daniels	.10
162	John Kruk	.10
163	Bill Ripken	.10
164	Kirby Puckett	.75
165	Jose Canseco	.50
166	Matt Nokes	.10
167	Mike Schmidt	.75
168	Tim Raines	.12
169	Ryne Sandberg	.60
170	Dave Winfield	.25
171	Dwight Gooden	.12
172	Bret Saberhagen	.12
173	Willie McGee	.10
174	Jack Morris	.10
175	Jeff Leonard	.10
176	Cal Ripken, Jr.	3.00
177	Pete Incaviglia	.10
178	Devon White	.10
179	Nolan Ryan	3.00
180	Ruben Sierra	.10
181	Todd Worrell	.10
182	Glenn Davis	.10
183	Frank Viola	.10
184	Cory Snyder	.10
185	Tracy Jones	.10
186	Terry Steinbach	.10
187	Julio Franco	.10
188	Larry Sheets	.10
189	John Marzano	.10
190	Kevin Elster	.10
191	Vincente Palacios	.10
192	Kent Hrbek	.12
193	Eric Bell	.10
194	Kelly Downs	.10
195	Jose Lind	.10
196	Dave Stewart	.10
197	Jose Canseco, Mark McGwire	2.00
198	Phil Niekro	.20
199	Phil Niekro	.20
200	Phil Niekro	.20

1988 Classic Travel Update II (Blue)

This set was produced for use with the travel edition of Game Time's Classic Baseball Board Game. Fronts have blue borders, a yellow Classic logo in the upper-left corner and a black and beige name banner beneath the photo. Backs are printed in blue on white and include the player name, personal info, major league records, a baseball question and space for the player autograph. Classic card series are sold via hobby dealers and retail toy stores nationwide. Game Time Ltd., the set's producer, was purchased by Scoreboard of Cherry Hill, N.J. in 1988.

		MT
Complete Set (50):		9.00
Common Player:		.10
201	Dale Murphy, Eric Davis	.20
202	B.J. Surhoff	.12
203	John Kruk	.10
204	Sam Horn	.10
205	Jack Clark	.10
206	Wally Joyner	.12
207	Matt Nokes	.10
208	Bo Jackson	.30
209	Darryl Strawberry	.15
210	Ozzie Smith	.40
211	Don Mattingly	.75
212	Mark McGwire	2.00
213	Eric Davis	.12
214	Wade Boggs	.50
215	Dale Murphy	.25
216	Andre Dawson	.15
217	Roger Clemens	.65
218	Kevin Seitzer	.10
219	Benito Santiago	.10
220	Tony Gwynn	.75
221	Mike Scott	.10
222	Steve Bedrosian	.10
223	Vince Coleman	.10
224	Rick Sutcliffe	.10
225	Will Clark	.35
226	Pete Rose	1.25
227	Mike Greenwell	.10
228	Ken Caminiti	.15
229	Ellis Burks	.10
230	Dave Magadan	.10
231	Alan Trammell	.12
232	Paul Molitor	.40
233	Gary Gaetti	.10
234	Rickey Henderson	.20
235	Danny Tartabull	.10
236	Bobby Bonilla	.15
237	Mike Dunne	.10
238	Al Leiter	.12
239	John Farrell	.10
240	Joe Magrane	.10
241	Mike Henneman	.10
242	George Bell	.10
243	Gregg Jefferies	.25
244	Jay Buhner	.20
245	Todd Benzinger	.10
246	Matt Williams	.25
(247)	Don Mattingly, Mark McGwire (No card number on back)	2.00
248	George Brett	1.00
249	Jimmy Key	.10
250	Mark Langston	.10

1989 Classic

This 100-card set was released by The Score Board to accompany trivia board games. Fronts have a wide border which graduates from pink at the top to blue at the bottom. Card backs are printed in blue. The flip side includes personal information, and major league record in a boxed area. Another boxed area below the record presents five trivia questions. The lower border on back provides an autograph space. The Classic card series was sold by retail stores and hobby dealers nationwide.

		MT
Complete Set (100):		10.00
Common Player:		.10
1	Orel Hershiser	.12
2	Wade Boggs	.60
3	Jose Canseco	.60
4	Mark McGwire	2.00
5	Don Mattingly	.90
6	Gregg Jefferies	.20
7	Dwight Gooden	.15
8	Darryl Strawberry	.15
9	Eric Davis	.12
10	Joey Meyer	.10
11	Joe Carter	.10
12	Paul Molitor	.50
13	Mark Grace	.35
14	Kurt Stillwell	.10
15	Kirby Puckett	.90
16	Keith Miller	.10
17	Glenn Davis	.10
18	Will Clark	.50
19	Cory Snyder	.10
20	Jose Lind	.10
21	Andres Thomas	.10
22	Dave Smith	.10
23	Mike Scott	.10
24	Kevin McReynolds	.10
25	B.J. Surhoff	.10
26	Mackey Sasser	.10
27	Chad Kreuter	.10
28	Hal Morris	.10
29	Wally Joyner	.12
30	Tony Gwynn	.75
31	Kevin Mitchell	.10
32	Dave Winfield	.25
33	Billy Bean	.10
34	Steve Bedrosian	.10
35	Ron Gant	.10
36	Len Dykstra	.10
37	Andre Dawson	.12
38	Brett Butler	.12
39	Rob Deer	.10
40	Tommy John	.15
41	Gary Gaetti	.10
42	Tim Raines	.12
43	George Bell	.10
44	Dwight Evans	.10
45	Denny Martinez	.12
46	Andres Galarraga	.20
47	George Brett	.90
48	Mike Schmidt	.90
49	Dave Steib	.10
50	Rickey Henderson	.30
51	Craig Biggio	.15
52	Mark Lemke	.10
53	Chris Sabo	.10
54	Jeff Treadway	.10
55	Kent Hrbek	.12
56	Cal Ripken, Jr.	2.00
57	Tim Belcher	.10
58	Ozzie Smith	.50
59	Keith Hernandez	.10
60	Pedro Guerrero	.10
61	Greg Swindell	.10
62	Bret Saberhagen	.12
63	John Tudor	.10

64	Gary Carter	.15
65	Kevin Seitzer	.10
66	Jesse Barfield	.10
67	Luis Medina	.10
68	Walt Weiss	.12
69	Terry Steinbach	.10
70	Barry Larkin	.20
71	Pete Rose	1.50
72	Luis Salazar	.10
73	Benito Santiago	.10
74	Kal Daniels	.10
75	Kevin Elster	.10
76	Rob Dibble	.10
77	Bobby Witt	.10
78	Steve Searcy	.10
79	Sandy Alomar	.15
80	Chili Davis	.12
81	Alvin Davis	.10
82	Charlie Leibrandt	.10
83	Robin Yount	.50
84	Mark Carreon	.10
85	Pascual Perez	.10
86	Dennis Rasmussen	.10
87	Ernie Riles	.10
88	Melido Perez	.10
89	Doug Jones	.10
90	Dennis Eckersley	.12
91	Bob Welch	.10
92	Bob Milacki	.10
93	Jeff Robinson	.10
94	Mike Henneman	.10
95	Randy Johnson	.50
96	Ron Jones	.10
97	Jack Armstrong	.10
98	Willie McGee	.12
99	Ryne Sandberg	.65
100	David Cone, Danny Jackson	.10

1989 Classic Travel Update I (Orange)

Roberto Alomar

Sold only as a 50-card complete set under the official name of "Travel Update I," these cards are identical in format to the 1989 Classic 100-card set with the exception that the borders are orange at the top, graduating to maroon at the bottom. Backs are maroon.

		MT
Complete Set (50):		15.00
Common Player:		.10
101	Gary Sheffield	.35
102	Wade Boggs	.55
103	Jose Canseco	.55
104	Mark McGwire	1.00
105	Orel Hershiser	.12
106	Don Mattingly	.90
107	Dwight Gooden	.15
108	Darryl Strawberry	.15
109	Eric Davis	.15
110	Bam Bam Meulens	.10
111	Andy Van Slyke	.10
112	Al Leiter	.12
113	Matt Nokes	.10
114	Mike Krukow	.10
115	Tony Fernandez	.10
116	Fred McGriff	.15
117	Barry Bonds	.75
118	Gerald Perry	.10
119	Roger Clemens	.50
120	Kirk Gibson	.10
121	Greg Maddux	.55
122	Bo Jackson	.25
123	Danny Jackson	.10
124	Dale Murphy	.15
125	David Cone	.10
126	Tom Browning	.10
127	Roberto Alomar	.50
128	Alan Trammell	.12
129	Ricky Jordan	.10
130	Ramon Martinez	.15
131	Ken Griffey, Jr.	9.00
132	Gregg Olson	.10
133	Carlos Quintana	.10
134	Dave West	.10
135	Cameron Drew	.10
136	Ted Higuera	.10
137	Sil Campusano	.10
138	Mark Gubicza	.10
139	Mike Boddicker	.10
140	Paul Gibson	.10
141	Jose Rijo	.10
142	John Costello	.10
143	Cecil Espy	.10
144	Frank Viola	.10
145	Erik Hanson	.10
146	Juan Samuel	.10
147	Harold Reynolds	.10
148	Joe Magrane	.10
149	Mike Greenwell	.10
150	Darryl Strawberry, Will Clark	.25

1989 Classic Travel Update II (Purple)

Numbered from 151-200, this set features rookies and traded players with their new teams. The cards are purple and gray and were sold as part of a board game with baseball trivia questions.

Complete Set (50):		12.00
Common Player:		.05
151	Jim Abbott	.20
152	Ellis Burks	.10
153	Mike Schmidt	.75
154	Gregg Jefferies	.20
155	Mark Grace	.25
156	Jerome Walton	.05
157	Bo Jackson	.25
158	Jack Clark	.05
159	Tom Glavine	.10
160	Eddie Murray	.25
161	John Dopson	.05
162	Ruben Sierra	.05
163	Rafael Palmeiro	.20
164	Nolan Ryan	1.50
165	Barry Larkin	.12
166	Tommy Herr	.05
167	Roberto Kelly	.05
168	Glenn Davis	.05
169	Glenn Braggs	.05
170	Juan Bell	.05
171	Todd Burns	.05
172	Derek Lilliquist	.05
173	Orel Hershiser	.10
174	John Smoltz	.15
175	Ozzie Guillen, Ellis Burks	.10
176	Kirby Puckett	.75
177	Robin Ventura	.20
178	Allan Anderson	.05
179	Steve Sax	.05
180	Will Clark	.25
181	Mike Devereaux	.05
182	Tom Gordon	.05
183	Rob Murphy	.05
184	Pete O'Brien	.05
185	Cris Carpenter	.05
186	Tom Brunansky	.05
187	Bob Boone	.05
188	Lou Whitaker	.05
189	Dwight Gooden	.10
190	Mark McGwire	1.50
191	John Smiley	.05
192	Tommy Gregg	.05
193	Ken Griffey, Jr.	7.50
194	Bruce Hurst	.05
195	Greg Swindell	.05
196	Nelson Liriano	.05
197	Randy Myers	.05
198	Kevin Mitchell	.05
199	Dante Bichette	.15
200	Deion Sanders	.75

1990 Classic

Classic baseball returned in 1990 with a 150-card set. Cards have a blue border on front, with splashes of pink. The cards were again sold as part of a baseball trivia game.

		MT
Complete Set (150):		5.50
Common Player:		.05
1	Nolan Ryan	.95
2	Bo Jackson	.15
3	Gregg Olson	.05
4	Tom Gordon	.05
5	Robin Ventura	.15
6	Will Clark	.30
7	Ruben Sierra	.05
8	Mark Grace	.25
9	Luis de los Santos	.05
10	Bernie Williams	.30
11	Eric Davis	.10
12	Carney Lansford	.05
13	John Smoltz	.10
14	Gary Sheffield	.25
15	Kent Merker	.05
16	Don Mattingly	.60
17	Tony Gwynn	.45
18	Ozzie Smith	.35
19	Fred McGriff	.15
20	Ken Griffey, Jr.	1.50
21a	Deion Sanders ("Prime Time")	.75
21b	Deion Sanders (Deion "Prime Time" Sanders)	.50
22	Jose Canseco	.35
23	Mitch Williams	.05
24	Cal Ripken, Jr.	.95
25	Bob Geren	.05
26	Wade Boggs	.30
27	Ryne Sandberg	.50
28	Kirby Puckett	.60
29	Mike Scott	.05
30	Dwight Smith	.05
31	Craig Worthington	.05
32	Ricky Jordan	.05
33	Darryl Strawberry	.15
34	Jerome Walton	.05
35	John Olerud	.20
36	Tom Glavine	.10
37	Rickey Henderson	.15
38	Rolando Roomes	.05
39	Mickey Tettleton	.05
40	Jim Abbott	.10
41	Dave Righetti	.05
42	Mike LaValliere	.05
43	Rob Dibble	.05
44	Pete Harnisch	.05
45	Jose Offerman	.05
46	Walt Weiss	.05
47	Mike Greenwell	.05
48	Barry Larkin	.15
49	Dave Gallagher	.05
50	Junior Felix	.05
51	Roger Clemens	.50
52	Lonnie Smith	.05
53	Jerry Browne	.05
54	Greg Briley	.05
55	Delino DeShields	.05
56	Carmelo Martinez	.05
57	Craig Biggio	.10
58	Dwight Gooden	.12
59a	Bo, Ruben, Mark (Bo Jackson, Ruben Sierra, Mark McGwire)	1.00
59b	A.L. Fence Busters (Bo Jackson, Ruben Sierra, Mark McGwire)	1.00
60	Greg Vaughn	.15
61	Roberto Alomar	.15
62	Steve Bedrosian	.05
63	Devon White	.05
64	Kevin Mitchell	.05
65	Marquis Grissom	.08
66	Brian Holman	.05
67	Julio Franco	.05
68	Dave West	.05
69	Harold Baines	.08
70	Eric Anthony	.05
71	Glenn Davis	.05
72	Mark Langston	.05
73	Matt Williams	.20
74	Rafael Palmeiro	.20
75	Pete Rose, Jr.	.25
76	Ramon Martinez	.10
77	Dwight Evans	.05
78	Mackey Sasser	.05
79	Mike Schooler	.05
80	Dennis Cook	.05
81	Orel Hershiser	.10
82	Barry Bonds	.60
83	Geronimo Berroa	.05
84	George Bell	.05
85	Andre Dawson	.12
86	John Franco	.05
87a	Clark/Gwynn (Will Clark, Tony Gwynn)	.50
87b	N.L. Hit Kings (Will Clark, Tony Gwynn)	.40
88	Glenallen Hill	.05
89	Jeff Ballard	.05
90	Todd Zeile	.10
91	Frank Viola	.05
92	Ozzie Guillen	.05
93	Jeff Leonard	.05
94	Dave Smith	.05
95	Dave Parker	.08
96	Jose Gonzalez	.05
97	Dave Steib	.05
98	Charlie Hayes	.05
99	Jesse Barfield	.05
100	Joey Belle	.75
101	Jeff Reardon	.05
102	Bruce Hurst	.05
103	Luis Medina	.05
104	Mike Moore	.05
105	Vince Coleman	.05
106	Alan Trammell	.10
107	Randy Myers	.05
108	Frank Tanana	.05

109	Craig Lefferts	.05
110	John Wetteland	.08
111	Chris Gwynn	.05
112	Mark Carreon	.05
113	Von Hayes	.05
114	Doug Jones	.05
115	Andres Galarraga	.10
116	Carlton Fisk	.15
117	Paul O'Neill	.08
118	Tim Raines	.10
119	Tom Brunansky	.05
120	Andy Benes	.12
121	Mark Portugal	.05
122	Willie Randolph	.05
123	Jeff Blauser	.05
124	Don August	.05
125	Chuck Cary	.05
126	John Smiley	.05
127	Terry Mullholland	.05
128	Harold Reynolds	.05
129	Hubie Brooks	.05
130	Ben McDonald	.05
131	Kevin Ritz	.05
132	Luis Quinones	.05
133a	Bam Bam Muelens (last name incorrect)	.50
133b	Bam Bam Meulens (last name correct)	.05
134	Bill Spiers	.05
135	Andy Hawkins	.05
136	Alvin Davis	.05
137	Lee Smith	.05
138	Joe Carter	.08
139	Bret Saberhagen	.08
140	Sammy Sosa	1.00
141	Matt Nokes	.05
142	Bert Blyleven	.05
143	Bobby Bonilla	.10
144	Howard Johnson	.05
145	Joe Magrane	.05
146	Pedro Guerrero	.05
147	Robin Yount	.45
148	Dan Gladden	.05
149	Steve Sax	.05
150a	Clark/Mitchell (Will Clark, Kevin Mitchell)	.50
150b	Bay Bombers (Will Clark, Kevin Mitchell)	.25

1990 Classic Series II

As in previous years, Classic released a 50-card second series set for use with its trivia board game. Unlike earlier update sets, the 1990 Series II set is numbered 1-50 with a "T" designation accompanying the card number. Cards measure 2-1/2" x 3-1/2" and share the format of the original 1990 Classic cards; Series II cards have pink borders with blue highlights. The cards were issued only in complete set form.

		MT
Complete Set (50):		3.50
Common Player:		.05
1	Gregg Jefferies	.10
2	Steve Adkins	.05
3	Sandy Alomar, Jr.	.10
4	Steve Avery	.05
5	Mike Blowers	.05
6	George Brett	.50
7	Tom Browning	.05
8	Ellis Burks	.05
9	Joe Carter	.05
10	Jerald Clark	.05
11	"Hot Corners" (Matt Williams, Will Clark)	.25
12	Pat Combs	.05
13	Scott Cooper	.05
14	Mark Davis	.05
15	Storm Davis	.05
16	Larry Walker	.10
17	Brian DuBois	.05
18	Len Dykstra	.05
19	John Franco	.05
20	Kirk Gibson	.05
21	Juan Gonzalez	1.50
22	Tommy Greene	.05
23	Kent Hrbek	.08
24	Mike Huff	.05
25	Bo Jackson	.15
26	Nolan Knows Bo (Bo Jackson, Nolan Ryan)	2.00
27	Roberto Kelly	.05
28	Mark Langston	.05
29	Ray Lankford	.10
30	Kevin Maas	.05
31	Julio Machado	.05
32	Greg Maddux	.50
33	Mark McGwire	1.50
34	Paul Molitor	.30
35	Hal Morris	.05
36	Dale Murphy	.15
37	Eddie Murray	.30
38	Jaime Navarro	.05
39	Dean Palmer	.08
40	Derek Parks	.05
41	Bobby Rose	.05
42	Wally Joyner	.08
43	Chris Sabo	.05
44	Benito Santiago	.05
45	Mike Stanton	.05
46	Terry Steinbach	.05
47	Dave Stewart	.05
48	Greg Swindell	.05
49	Jose Vizcaino	.05
---	"Royal Flush" (Bret Saberhagen, Mark Davis)	.08

1990 Classic Series III

Classic's third series of 1990 features the same format as the previous two releases. Series III borders are yellow with blue accents. The cards have trivia questions on back and are numbered 1T-100T. No card 51T or 57T exists. Two cards in the set are unnumbered. Like other Classic issues, the cards are designed for use with the trivia board game and were sold only as complete sets.

		MT
Complete Set (100):		5.50
Common Player:		.05
1	Ken Griffey, Jr.	2.00
2	John Tudor	.05
3	John Kruk	.05
4	Mark Gardner	.05
5	Scott Radinsky	.05
6	John Burkett	.05
7	Will Clark	.15
8	Gary Carter	.08
9	Ted Higuera	.05
10	Dave Parker	.05
11	Dante Bichette	.08
12	Don Mattingly	.65
13	Greg Harris	.05
14	David Hollins	.05
15	Matt Nokes	.05
16	Kevin Tapani	.05
17	Shane Mack	.05
18	Randy Myers	.05
19	Greg Olson	.05
20	Shawn Abner	.05
21	Jim Presley	.05
22	Randy Johnson	.12
23	Edgar Martinez	.05
24	Scott Coolbaugh	.05
25	Jeff Treadway	.05
26	Joe Klink	.05
27	Rickey Henderson	.10
28	Sam Horn	.05
29	Kurt Stillwell	.05
30	Andy Van Slyke	.05
31	Willie Banks	.05
32	Jose Canseco	.30
33	Felix Jose	.05
34	Candy Maldonado	.05
35	Carlos Baerga	.05
36	Keith Hernandez	.05
37	Frank Viola	.05
38	Pete O'Brien	.05
39	Pat Borders	.05
40	Mike Heath	.05
41	Kevin Brown	.05
42	Chris Bosio	.05
43	Shawn Boskie	.05
44	Carlos Quintana	.05
45	Juan Samuel	.05
46	Tim Layana	.05
47	Mike Harkey	.05
48	Gerald Perry	.05
49	Mike Witt	.05
50	Joe Orsulak	.05
51	(Not issued)	
52	Willie Blair	.05
53	Gene Larkin	.05
54	Jody Reed	.05
55	Jeff Reardon	.05
56	Kevin McReynolds	.05
57	(Not issued)	
58	Eric Yelding	.05
59	Fred Lynn	.05
60	Jim Leyritz	.05
61	John Orton	.05
62	Mike Lieberthal	.10
63	Mike Hartley	.05
64	Kal Daniels	.05
65	Terry Shumpert	.05
66	Sil Campusano	.05
67	Tony Pena	.05
68	Barry Bonds	.50
69	Oddibe McDowell	.05
70	Kelly Gruber	.05
71	Willie Randolph	.05
72	Rick Parker	.05
73	Bobby Bonilla	.08
74	Jack Armstrong	.05
75	Hubie Brooks	.05
76	Sandy Alomar, Jr.	.10
77	Ruben Sierra	.05
78	Erik Hanson	.05
79	Tony Phillips	.05
80	Rondell White	.35
81	Bobby Thigpen	.05
82	Ron Walden	.05
83	Don Peters	.05
84	#6 (Nolan Ryan)	.75
85	Lance Dickson	.05
86	Ryne Sandberg	.40
87	Eric Christopherson	.05
88	Shane Andrews	.10
89	Marc Newfield	.05
90	Adam Hyzdu	.05
91	"Texas Heat" (Nolan Ryan, Reid Ryan)	1.00
92	Chipper Jones	2.00
93	Frank Thomas	2.00
94	Cecil Fielder	.05
95	Delino DeShields	.05
96	John Olerud	.15
97	Dave Justice	.50
98	Joe Oliver	.05
99	Alex Fernandez	.08
100	Todd Hundley	.10
---	Mike Marshall (Game instructions on back)	.05
---	4 in 1 (Frank Viola, Nolan/Reid Ryan, Chipper Jones, Don Mattingly)	.50

1991 Classic

Top rookies and draft picks highlight this set from Classic. The cards come with a trivia board game and accessories. Fronts have fading blue borders with a touch of red. A blank-back "4-in-1" micro-player card is included with each game set.

		MT
Complete Set (99):		5.50
Common Player:		.05
1	John Olerud	.10
2	Tino Martinez	.20
3	Ken Griffey, Jr.	1.50
4	Jeromy Burnitz	.08
5	Ron Gant	.05
6	Mike Benjamin	.05
7	Steve Decker	.05
8	Matt Williams	.20
9	Rafael Novoa	.05
10	Kevin Mitchell	.05
11	Dave Justice	.20
12	Leo Gomez	.05
13	Chris Hoiles	.05
14	Ben McDonald	.05
15	David Segui	.05
16	Anthony Telford	.05
17	Mike Mussina	.10
18	Roger Clemens	.50
19	Wade Boggs	.45
20	Tim Naehring	.05
21	Joe Carter	.08
22	Phil Plantier	.05
23	Rob Dibble	.05
24	Mo Vaughn	.60
25	Lee Stevens	.05
26	Chris Sabo	.05
27	Mark Grace	.20
28	Derrick May	.05
29	Ryne Sandberg	.30
30	Matt Stark	.05
31	Bobby Thigpen	.05
32	Frank Thomas	.75

33	Don Mattingly	.75
34	Eric Davis	.08
35	Reggie Jefferson	.05
36	Alex Cole	.05
37	Mark Lewis	.05
38	Tim Costo	.05
39	Sandy Alomar, Jr.	.10
40	Travis Fryman	.08
41	Cecil Fielder	.08
42	Milt Cuyler	.05
43	Andujar Cedeno	.05
44	Danny Darwin	.05
45	Randy Henis	.05
46	George Brett	.65
47	Jeff Conine	.08
48	Bo Jackson	.15
49	Brian McRae	.08
50	Brent Mayne	.05
51	Eddie Murray	.25
52	Ramon Martinez	.05
53	Jim Neidlinger	.05
54	Jim Poole	.05
55	Tim McIntosh	.05
56	Randy Veres	.05
57	Kirby Puckett	.75
58	Todd Ritchie	.05
59	Rich Garces	.05
60	Moises Alou	.15
61	Delino DeShields	.05
62	Oscar Azocar	.05
63	Kevin Maas	.05
64	Alan Mills	.05
65	John Franco	.05
66	Chris Jelic	.05
67	Dave Magadan	.05
68	Darryl Strawberry	.10
69	Hensley Meulens	.05
70	Juan Gonzalez	.75
71	Reggie Harris	.05
72	Rickey Henderson	.15
73	Mark McGwire	.75
74	Willie McGee	.05
75	Todd Van Poppel	.10
76	Bob Welch	.05
77	"Future Aces" "(Todd Van Poppel, Don Peters, David Zancanaro, Kirk Dressendorfer)	.10
78	Lenny Dykstra	.05
79	Mickey Morandini	.05
80	Wes Chamberlain	.05
81	Barry Bonds	.60
82	Doug Drabek	.05
83	Randy Tomlin	.05
84	Scott Chiamparino	.05
85	Rafael Palmeiro	.12
86	Nolan Ryan	1.00
87	Bobby Witt	.05
88	Fred McGriff	.15
89	Dave Steib	.05
90	Ed Sprague	.05
91	Vince Coleman	.05
92	Rod Brewer	.05
93	Bernard Gilkey	.08
94	Roberto Alomar	.15
95	Chuck Finley	.05
96	Dale Murphy	.15
97	Jose Rijo	.05
98	Hal Morris	.05
99	"Friendly Foes" (Dwight Gooden, Darryl Strawberry)	.15
---	John Olerud, Dwight Gooden, Jose Canseco, Darryl Strawberry	.25

1991 Classic Series II

Classic released a 100-card second series in 1991. Cards feature the same format as the first series, with the exception of border color; Series II features maroon borders. The cards are designed for trivia game use. Series II includes several players with new teams and top rookies. Special Four-In-One, 300 Game Winner and Strikout Kings cards are included with each set.

		MT
Complete Set (100):		4.50
Common Player:		.05
1	Ken Griffey, Jr.	1.00
2	Wilfredo Cordero	.08
3	Cal Ripken, Jr.	.90
4	D.J. Dozier	.05
5	Darrin Fletcher	.05
6	Glenn Davis	.05
7	Alex Fernandez	.08
8	Cory Snyder	.05
9	Tim Raines	.08
10	Greg Swindell	.05
11	Mark Lewis	.05
12	Rico Brogna	.05
13	Gary Sheffield	.20
14	Paul Molitor	.45
15	Kent Hrbek	.08
16	Scott Erickson	.08
17	Steve Sax	.05
18	Dennis Eckersley	.08
19	Jose Canseco	.25
20	Kirk Dressendorfer	.05
21	Ken Griffey, Sr.	.05
22	Erik Hanson	.05
23	Dan Peltier	.05
24	John Olerud	.10
25	Eddie Zosky	.05
26	Steve Avery	.05
27	John Smoltz	.10
28	Frank Thomas	.75
29	Jerome Walton	.05
30	George Bell	.05
31	Jose Rijo	.05
32	Randy Myers	.05
33	Barry Larkin	.10
34	Eric Anthony	.05
35	Dave Hansen	.05
36	Eric Karros	.08
37	Jose Offerman	.05
38	Marquis Grissom	.08
39	Dwight Gooden	.10
40	Gregg Jefferies	.10
41	Pat Combs	.05
42	Todd Zeile	.08
43	Benito Santiago	.08
44	Dave Staton	.05
45	Tony Fernandez	.05
46	Fred McGriff	.15
47	Jeff Brantley	.05
48	Junior Felix	.05
49	Jack Morris	.05
50	Chris George	.05
51	Henry Rodriguez	.10
52	Paul Marak	.05
53	Ryan Klesko	.10
54	Darren Lewis	.05
55	Lance Dickson	.05
56	Anthony Young	.05
57	Willie Banks	.05
58	Mike Bordick	.05
59	Roger Salkeld	.05
60	Steve Karsay	.05
61	Bernie Williams	.20
62	Mickey Tettleton	.05
63	Dave Justice	.25
64	Steve Decker	.05
65	Roger Clemens	.45
66	Phil Plantier	.05
67	Ryne Sandberg	.50
68	Sandy Alomar,Jr.	.10
69	Cecil Fielder	.08
70	George Brett	.50
71	Delino DeShields	.05
72	Dave Magadan	.05
73	Darryl Strawberry	.08
74	Juan Gonzalez	.50
75	Rickey Henderson	.15
76	Willie McGee	.05
77	Todd Van Poppel	.08
78	Barry Bonds	.45
79	Doug Drabek	.05
80	Nolan Ryan (300 games)	.75
81	Roberto Alomar	.10
82	Ivan Rodriguez	.25
83	Dan Opperman	.05
84	Jeff Bagwell	.60
85	Braulio Castillo	.05
86	Doug Simons	.05
87	Wade Taylor	.05
88	Gary Scott	.05
89	Dave Stewart	.05
90	Mike Simms	.05
91	Luis Gonzalez	.05
92	Bobby Bonilla	.10
93	Tony Gwynn	.45
94	Will Clark	.20
95	Rich Rowland	.05
96	Alan Trammell	.10
97	"Strikeout Kings" (Nolan Ryan, Roger Clemens)	.75
98	Joe Carter	.05
99	Jack Clark	.05
100	Four-In-One	.25

1991 Classic Series III

Green borders highlight Classic's third series of cards for 1991. The set includes a gameboard and player cards featuring trivia questions on the back. Statistics and biographical information are also found on back.

		MT
Complete Set (100):		5.00
Common Player:		.05
1	Jim Abbott	.10
2	Craig Biggio	.10
3	Wade Boggs	.35
4	Bobby Bonilla	.10
5	Ivan Calderon	.05
6	Jose Canseco	.35
7	Andy Benes	.10
8	Wes Chamberlain	.05
9	Will Clark	.30
10	Royce Clayton	.05
11	Gerald Alexander	.05
12	Chili Davis	.05
13	Eric Davis	.08
14	Andre Dawson	.10
15	Rob Dibble	.05
16	Chris Donnels	.05
17	Scott Erickson	.08
18	Monty Fariss	.05
19	Ruben Amaro, Jr.	.05
20	Chuck Finley	.05
21	Carlton Fisk	.12
22	Carlos Baerga	.10
23	Ron Gant	.10
24	Dave Justice, Ron Gant	.25
25	Mike Gardiner	.05
26	Tom Glavine	.08
27	Joe Grahe	.05
28	Derek Bell	.10
29	Mike Greenwell	.05
30	Ken Griffey, Jr.	1.00
31	Leo Gomez	.05
32	Tom Goodwin	.05
33	Tony Gwynn	.25
34	Mel Hall	.05
35	Brian Harper	.05
36	Dave Henderson	.05
37	Albert Belle	.50
38	Orel Hershiser	.08
39	Brian Hunter	.05
40	Howard Johnson	.05
41	Felix Jose	.05
42	Wally Joyner	.08
43	Jeff Juden	.08
44	Pat Kelly	.05
45	Jimmy Key	.05
46	Chuck Knoblauch	.15
47	John Kruk	.05
48	Ray Lankford	.10
49	Ced Landrum	.05
50	Scott Livingstone	.05
51	Kevin Maas	.05
52	Greg Maddux	.50
53	Dennis Martinez	.10
54	Edgar Martinez	.05
55	Pedro Martinez	.45
56	Don Mattingly	.75
57	Orlando Merced	.05
58	Keith Mitchell	.05
59	Kevin Mitchell	.05
60	Paul Molitor	.25
61	Jack Morris	.05
62	Hal Morris	.05
63	Kevin Morton	.05
64	Pedro Munoz	.05
65	Eddie Murray	.25
66	Jack McDowell	.05
67	Jeff McNeely	.05
68	Brian McRae	.08
69	Kevin McReynolds	.05
70	Gregg Olson	.05
71	Rafael Palmeiro	.15
72	Dean Palmer	.08
73	Tony Phillips	.05
74	Kirby Puckett	.60
75	Carlos Quintana	.05
76	Pat Rice	.05
77	Cal Ripken, Jr.	.90
78	Ivan Rodriguez	.20
79	Nolan Ryan	1.00
80	Bret Saberhagen	.08
81	Tim Salmon	.35
82	Juan Samuel	.05
83	Ruben Sierra	.05
84	Heathcliff Slocumb	.05
85	Joe Slusarski	.05
86	John Smiley	.05
87	Dave Smith	.05
88	Ed Sprague	.05
89	Todd Stottlemyre	.05
90	Mike Timlin	.05
91	Greg Vaughn	.10
92	Frank Viola	.05
93	John Wehner	.05
94	Devon White	.05
95	Matt Williams	.20
96	Rick Wilkins	.05
97	Bernie Williams	.25
98	Starter & Stopper (Goose Gossage, Nolan Ryan)	.20
99	Gerald Williams	.05
----	4-in-1 (Bobby Bonilla, Will Clark, Cal Ripken Jr., Scott Erickson)	.25

1991 Classic Collector's Edition

The Classic Collector's edition made its

debut in 1991. This package includes a board game, trivia baseball player cards, a baseball tips booklet and a certificate of authenticity, all packaged in a collector's edition box. Each box is individually and sequentially numbered on the outside, with a reported 100,000 available.

		MT
Complete Set (200):		15.00
Common Player:		.05
1	Frank Viola	.05
2	Tim Wallach	.05
3	Lou Whitaker	.05
4	Brett Butler	.08
5	Jim Abbott	.08
6	Jack Armstrong	.05
7	Craig Biggio	.10
8	Brian Barnes	.05
9	Dennis "Oil Can" Boyd	.05
10	Tom Browning	.05
11	Tom Brunansky	.05
12	Ellis Burks	.08
13	Harold Baines	.05
14	Kal Daniels	.05
15	Mark Davis	.05
16	Storm Davis	.05
17	Tom Glavine	.10
18	Mike Greenwell	.05
19	Kelly Gruber	.05
20	Mark Gubicza	.05
21	Pedro Guerrero	.05
22	Mike Harkey	.05
23	Orel Hershiser	.08
24	Ted Higuera	.05
25	Von Hayes	.05
26	Andre Dawson	.12
27	Shawon Dunston	.05
28	Roberto Kelly	.05
29	Joe Magrane	.05
30	Dennis Martinez	.08
31	Kevin McReynolds	.05
32	Matt Nokes	.05
33	Dan Plesac	.05
34	Dave Parker	.08
35	Randy Johnson	.20
36	Bret Saberhagen	.08
37	Mackey Sasser	.05
38	Mike Scott	.05
39	Ozzie Smith	.35
40	Kevin Seitzer	.05
41	Ruben Sierra	.05
42	Kevin Tapani	.05
43	Danny Tartabull	.05
44	Robby Thompson	.05
45	Andy Van Slyke	.05
46	Greg Vaughn	.10
47	Harold Reynolds	.05
48	Will Clark	.35
49	Gary Gaetti	.05
50	Joe Grahe	.05
51	Carlton Fisk	.12
52	Robin Ventura	.08
53	Ozzie Guillen	.05
54	Tom Candiotti	.05
55	Doug Jones	.05
56	Eric King	.05
57	Kirk Gibson	.05
58	Tim Costo	.05
59	Robin Yount	.40
60	Sammy Sosa	.75
61	Jesse Barfield	.05
62	Marc Newfield	.05
63	Jimmy Key	.05
64	Felix Jose	.05
65	Mark Whiten	.05
66	Tommy Greene	.05
67	Kent Mercker	.05
68	Greg Maddux	.40
69	Danny Jackson	.05
70	Reggie Sanders	.08
71	Eric Yelding	.05
72	Karl Rhodes	.05
73	Fernando Valenzuela	.08
74	Chris Nabholz	.05
75	Andres Galarraga	.08
76	Howard Johnson	.05
77	Hubie Brooks	.05
78	Terry Mulholland	.05
79	Paul Molitor	.40
80	Roger McDowell	.05
81	Darren Daulton	.05
82	Zane Smith	.05
83	Ray Lankford	.10
84	Bruce Hurst	.05
85	Andy Benes	.10
86	John Burkett	.05
87	Dave Righetti	.05
88	Steve Karsay	.05
89	D.J. Dozier	.05
90	Jeff Bagwell	.60
91	Joe Carter	.05
92	Wes Chamberlain	.05
93	Vince Coleman	.05
94	Pat Combs	.05
95	Jerome Walton	.05
96	Jeff Conine	.05
97	Alan Trammell	.10
98	Don Mattingly	.75
99	Ramon Martinez	.10
100	Dave Magadan	.05
101	Greg Swindell	.05
102	Dave Stewart	.08
103	Gary Sheffield	.25
104	George Bell	.05
105	Mark Grace	.20
106	Steve Sax	.05
107	Ryne Sandberg	.50
108	Chris Sabo	.05
109	Jose Rijo	.05
110	Cal Ripken, Jr.	.90
111	Kirby Puckett	.75
112	Eddie Murray	.30
113	Roberto Alomar	.10
114	Randy Myers	.05
115	Rafael Palmeiro	.15
116	John Olerud	.10
117	Gregg Jefferies	.10
118	Kent Hrbek	.08
119	Marquis Grissom	.08
120	Ken Griffey, Jr.	1.00
121	Dwight Gooden	.08
122	Juan Gonzalez	.75
123	Ron Gant	.08
124	Travis Fryman	.08
125	John Franco	.05
126	Dennis Eckersley	.10
127	Cecil Fielder	.08
128	Phil Plantier	.05
129	Kevin Mitchell	.05
130	Kevin Maas	.05
131	Mark McGwire	1.00
132	Ben McDonald	.05
133	Lenny Dykstra	.05
134	Delino DeShields	.05
135	Jose Canseco	.35
136	Eric Davis	.08
137	George Brett	.50
138	Steve Avery	.05
139	Eric Anthony	.05
140	Bobby Thigpen	.05
141	Ken Griffey, Sr.	.05
142	Barry Larkin	.10
143	Jeff Brantley	.05
144	Bobby Bonilla	.10
145	Jose Offerman	.05
146	Mike Mussina	.10
147	Erik Hanson	.05
148	Dale Murphy	.15
149	Roger Clemens	.50
150	Tino Martinez	.10
151	Todd Van Poppel	.08
152	Mo Vaughn	.50
153	Derrick May	.05
154	Jack Clark	.05
155	Dave Hansen	.05
156	Tony Gwynn	.35
157	Brian McRae	.08
158	Matt Williams	.10
159	Kirk Dressendorfer	.05
160	Scott Erickson	.05
161	Tony Fernandez	.05
162	Willie McGee	.05
163	Fred McGriff	.15
164	Leo Gomez	.05
165	Bernard Gilkey	.08
166	Bobby Witt	.05
167	Doug Drabek	.05
168	Rob Dibble	.05
169	Glenn Davis	.05
170	Danny Darwin	.05
171	Eric Karros	.25
172	Eddie Zosky	.05
173	Todd Zeile	.08
174	Tim Raines	.08
175	Benito Santiago	.05
176	Dan Peltier	.05
177	Darryl Strawberry	.10
178	Hal Morris	.05
179	Hensley Meulens	.05
180	John Smoltz	.10
181	Frank Thomas	.75
182	Dave Staton	.05
183	Scott Chiamparino	.05
184	Alex Fernandez	.08
185	Mark Lewis	.05
186	Bo Jackson	.25
187	Mickey Morandini (photo actually Darren Daulton)	.15
188	Cory Snyder	.05
189	Rickey Henderson	.25
190	Junior Felix	.05
191	Milt Cuyler	.05
192	Wade Boggs	.35
193	"Justice Prevails" (David Justice)	.30
194	Sandy Alomar, Jr.	.10
195	Barry Bonds	.60
196	Nolan Ryan	.90
197	Rico Brogna	.05
198	Steve Decker	.05
199	Bob Welch	.05
200	Andujar Cedeno	.05

1992 Classic Series I

Classic introduced an innovative design with the release of its 1992 set. Fronts feature full-color photos bordered in white, while backs feature statistics, biographical information and trivia questions accented by a fading stadium shot. The cards were released with a gameboard and are numbered on back with a "T" prefix.

		MT
Complete Set (100):		5.00
Common Player:		.05
1	Jim Abbott	.10
2	Kyle Abbott	.05
3	Scott Aldred	.05
4	Roberto Alomar	.15
5	Wilson Alvarez	.08
6	Andy Ashby	.05
7	Steve Avery	.05
8	Jeff Bagwell	.40
9	Bret Barberie	.05
10	Kim Batiste	.05
11	Derek Bell	.10
12	Jay Bell	.05
13	Albert Belle	.35
14	Andy Benes	.10
15	Sean Berry	.05
16	Barry Bonds	.40
17	Ryan Bowen	.05
18	Trifecta (Alejandro Pena, Mark Wohlers, Kent Mercker)	.05
19	Scott Brosius	.05
20	Jay Buhner	.10
21	David Burba	.05
22	Jose Canseco	.25
23	Andujar Cedeno	.05
24	Will Clark	.20
25	Royce Clayton	.05
26	Roger Clemens	.35
27	David Cone	.10
28	Scott Cooper	.05
29	Chris Cron	.05
30	Len Dykstra	.05
31	Cal Eldred	.05
32	Hector Fajardo	.05
33	Cecil Fielder	.10
34	Dave Fleming	.05
35	Steve Foster	.05
36	Julio Franco	.05
37	Carlos Garcia	.05
38	Tom Glavine	.08
39	Tom Goodwin	.05
40	Ken Griffey, Jr.	1.00
41	Chris Haney	.05
42	Bryan Harvey	.05
43	Rickey Henderson	.10
44	Carlos Hernandez	.05
45	Roberto Hernandez	.05
46	Brook Jacoby	.05
47	Howard Johnson	.05
48	Pat Kelly	.05
49	Darryl Kile	.05
50	Chuck Knoblauch	.10
51	Ray Lankford	.08
52	Mark Leiter	.05
53	Darren Lewis	.05
54	Scott Livingstone	.05
55	Shane Mack	.05
56	Chito Martinez	.05
57	Dennis Martinez	.08
58	Don Mattingly	.50
59	Paul McClellan	.05
60	Chuck McElroy	.05
61	Fred McGriff	.15
62	Orlando Merced	.05
63	Luis Mercedes	.05
64	Kevin Mitchell	.05
65	Hal Morris	.05
66	Jack Morris	.05
67	Mike Mussina	.10
68	Denny Neagle	.10
69	Tom Pagnozzi	.05
70	Terry Pendleton	.05
71	Phil Plantier	.05
72	Kirby Puckett	.50
73	Carlos Quintana	.05
74	Willie Randolph	.05
75	Arthur Rhodes	.05
76	Cal Ripken	.75
77	Ivan Rodriguez	.25
78	Nolan Ryan	.75
79	Ryne Sandberg	.25
80	Deion Sanders	.20
81	Reggie Sanders	.10
82	Mo Sanford	.05
83	Terry Shumpert	.05
84	Tim Spehr	.05
85	Lee Stevens	.05
86	Darryl Strawberry	.12
87	Kevin Tapani	.05
88	Danny Tartabull	.05
89	Frank Thomas	.65
90	Jim Thome	.15
91	Todd Van Poppel	.08
92	Andy Van Slyke	.05
93	John Wehner	.05
94	John Wetteland	.05

95	Devon White	.05
96	Brian Williams	.05
97	Mark Wohlers	.08
98	Robin Yount	.25
99	Eddie Zosky	.05
---	4-in-1 (Barry Bonds, Roger Clemens, Steve Avery, Nolan Ryan)	.50

1992 Classic Series II

The 100-cards in Classic's 1992 Series II came packaged with a gameboard and spinner. In a completely different format from Classic's other '92 issues, Series II features player photos bordered at left and right with red or blue color bars which fade toward top and bottom. Backs have biographical data, previous-year and career statistics and five trivia questions, along with a color representation of the team's uniform. Cards, except the 4-In-1, are numbered with a "T" prefix.

		MT
Complete Set (100):		5.00
Common Player:		.05
1	Jim Abbott	.08
2	Jeff Bagwell	.35
3	Jose Canseco	.25
4	Julio Valera	.05
5	Scott Brosius	.05
6	Mark Langston	.05
7	Andy Stankiewicz	.05
8	Gary DiSarcina	.05
9	Pete Harnisch	.05
10	Mark McGwire	.75
11	Ricky Bones	.05
12	Steve Avery	.05
13	Deion Sanders	.20
14	Mike Mussina	.10
15	Dave Justice	.20
16	Pat Hentgen	.05
17	Tom Glavine	.08
18	Juan Guzman	.05
19	Ron Gant	.10
20	Kelly Gruber	.05
21	Eric Karros	.12
22	Derrick May	.05
23	Dave Hansen	.05
24	Andre Dawson	.12
25	Eric Davis	.10
26	Ozzie Smith	.25
27	Sammy Sosa	.50
28	Lee Smith	.10
29	Ryne Sandberg	.25
30	Robin Yount	.20
31	Matt Williams	.15
32	John Vander Wal	.05
33	Bill Swift	.05
34	Delino DeShields	.05
35	Royce Clayton	.05
36	Moises Alou	.08
37	Will Clark	.20
38	Darryl Strawberry	.10
39	Larry Walker	.15
40	Ramon Martinez	.08
41	Howard Johnson	.05
42	Tino Martinez	.10
43	Dwight Gooden	.08
44	Ken Griffey, Jr.	.75
45	David Cone	.05
46	Kenny Lofton	.10
47	Bobby Bonilla	.10
48	Carlos Baerga	.08
49	Don Mattingly	.40
50	Sandy Alomar, Jr.	.08
51	Lenny Dykstra	.05
52	Tony Gwynn	.25
53	Felix Jose	.05
54	Rick Sutcliffe	.05
55	Wes Chamberlain	.05
56	Cal Ripken, Jr.	.50
57	Kyle Abbott	.05
58	Leo Gomez	.05
59	Gary Sheffield	.12
60	Anthony Young	.05
61	Roger Clemens	.25
62	Rafael Palmeiro	.15
63	Wade Boggs	.25
64	Andy Van Slyke	.05
65	Ruben Sierra	.05
66	Denny Neagle	.08
67	Nolan Ryan	.50
68	Doug Drabek	.05
69	Ivan Rodriguez	.15
70	Barry Bonds	.35
71	Chuck Knoblauch	.10
72	Reggie Sanders	.05
73	Cecil Fielder	.10
74	Barry Larkin	.12
75	Scott Aldred	.05
76	Rob Dibble	.05
77	Brian McRae	.08
78	Tim Belcher	.05
79	George Brett	.40
80	Frank Viola	.05
81	Roberto Kelly	.05
82	Jack McDowell	.05
83	Mel Hall	.05
84	Esteban Beltre	.05
85	Robin Ventura	.10
86	George Bell	.05
87	Frank Thomas	.45
88	John Smiley	.05
89	Bobby Thigpen	.05
90	Kirby Puckett	.40
91	Kevin Mitchell	.05
92	Peter Hoy	.05
93	Russ Springer	.08
94	Donovan Osborne	.05
95	Dave Silvestri	.05
96	Chad Curtis	.08
97	Pat Mahomes	.05
98	Danny Tartabull	.05
99	John Doherty	.05
---	4-in-1 (Ryne Sandberg, Mike Mussina, Reggie Sanders, Jose Canseco)	.25

1992 Classic Collector's Edition

The second annual 200-card "Collector's Edition" set was packaged with a gameboard, spinner, generic player pieces, a mechanical scoreboard and a book of tips from star players. The UV-coated card fronts feature color player photos against a deep purple border. Backs have a few biographical details, previous season and career stats, plus five trivia questions in case anyone actually wanted to play the game.

		MT
Complete Set (200):		11.00
Common Player:		.05
1	Chuck Finley	.05
2	Craig Biggio	.10
3	Luis Gonzalez	.05
4	Pete Harnisch	.08
5	Jeff Juden	.08
6	Harold Baines	.08
7	Kirk Dressendorfer	.05
8	Dennis Eckersley	.10
9	Dave Henderson	.05
10	Dave Stewart	.08
11	Joe Carter	.15
12	Juan Guzman	.05
13	Dave Stieb	.05
14	Todd Stottlemyre	.05
15	Ron Gant	.12
16	Brian Hunter	.05
17	Dave Justice	.20
18	John Smoltz	.10
19	Mike Stanton	.05
20	Chris George	.05
21	Paul Molitor	.40
22	Omar Olivares	.05
23	Lee Smith	.08
24	Ozzie Smith	.35
25	Todd Zeile	.08
26	George Bell	.05
27	Andre Dawson	.15
28	Shawon Dunston	.15
29	Mark Grace	.35
30	Greg Maddux	.50
31	Dave Smith	.05
32	Brett Butler	.10
33	Orel Hershiser	.10
34	Eric Karros	.08
35	Ramon Martinez	.08
36	Jose Offerman	.05
37	Juan Samuel	.05
38	Delino DeShields	.05
39	Marquis Grissom	.10
40	Tim Wallach	.05
41	Eric Gunderson	.05
42	Willie McGee	.05
43	Dave Righetti	.05
44	Robby Thompson	.05
45	Matt Williams	.20
46	Sandy Alomar, Jr.	.12
47	Reggie Jefferson	.05
48	Mark Lewis	.05
49	Robin Ventura	.10
50	Tino Martinez	.10
51	Roberto Kelly	.05
52	Vince Coleman	.05
53	Dwight Gooden	.10
54	Todd Hundley	.10
55	Kevin Maas	.05
56	Wade Taylor	.05
57	Bryan Harvey	.05
58	Leo Gomez	.05
59	Ben McDonald	.05
60	Ricky Bones	.05
61	Tony Gwynn	.40
62	Benito Santiago	.10
63	Wes Chamberlain	.05
64	Tommy Greene	.05
65	Dale Murphy	.15
66	Steve Buechele	.05
67	Doug Drabek	.05
68	Joe Grahe	.05
69	Rafael Palmeiro	.15
70	Wade Boggs	.35
71	Ellis Burks	.10
72	Mike Greenwell	.05
73	Mo Vaughn	.40
74	Derek Bell	.08
75	Rob Dibble	.05
76	Barry Larkin	.12
77	Jose Rijo	.05
78	Doug Henry	.05
79	Chris Sabo	.05
80	Pedro Guerrero	.05
81	George Brett	.50
82	Tom Gordon	.05
83	Mark Gubicza	.05
84	Mark Whiten	.05
85	Brian McRae	.08
86	Danny Jackson	.05
87	Milt Cuyler	.05
88	Travis Fryman	.08
89	Mickey Tettleton	.05
90	Alan Trammell	.12
91	Lou Whitaker	.05
92	Chili Davis	.05
93	Scott Erickson	.05
94	Kent Hrbek	.08
95	Alex Fernandez	.08
96	Carlton Fisk	.15
97	Ramon Garcia	.05
98	Ozzie Guillen	.05
99	Tim Raines	.10
100	Bobby Thigpen	.05
101	Kirby Puckett	.65
102	Bernie Williams	.25
103	Dave Hansen	.05
104	Kevin Tapani	.05
105	Don Mattingly	.75
106	Frank Thomas	.75
107	Monty Fariss	.05
108	Bo Jackson	.12
109	Jim Abbott	.12
110	Jose Canseco	.30
111	Phil Plantier	.05
112	Brian Williams	.05
113	Mark Langston	.05
114	Wilson Alvarez	.05
115	Roberto Hernandez	.05
116	Darryl Kile	.05
117	Ryan Bowen	.05
118	Rickey Henderson	.20
119	Mark McGwire	1.50
120	Devon White	.05
121	Roberto Alomar	.20
122	Kelly Gruber	.05
123	Eddie Zosky	.05
124	Tom Glavine	.08
125	Kal Daniels	.05
126	Cal Eldred	.05
127	Deion Sanders	.25
128	Robin Yount	.40
129	Cecil Fielder	.10
130	Ray Lankford	.10
131	Ryne Sandberg	.35
132	Darryl Strawberry	.12
133	Chris Haney	.05
134	Dennis Martinez	.08
135	Bryan Hickerson	.05
136	Will Clark	.25
137	Hal Morris	.05
138	Charles Nagy	.05
139	Jim Thome	.10
140	Albert Belle	.45
141	Reggie Sanders	.12
142	Scott Cooper	.05
143	David Cone	.08
144	Anthony Young	.05
145	Howard Johnson	.05
146	Arthur Rhodes	.05
147	Scott Aldred	.05
148	Mike Mussina	.10
149	Fred McGriff	.15
150	Andy Benes	.10
151	Ruben Sierra	.05
152	Len Dykstra	.05
153	Andy Van Slyke	.05
154	Orlando Merced	.05
155	Barry Bonds	.40
156	John Smiley	.05
157	Julio Franco	.05
158	Juan Gonzalez	.45
159	Ivan Rodriguez	.25
160	Willie Banks	.05
161	Eric Davis	.10
162	Eddie Murray	.25
163	Dave Fleming	.05
164	Wally Joyner	.08
165	Kevin Mitchell	.05

166	Ed Taubensee	.05
167	Danny Tartabull	.05
168	Ken Hill	.05
169	Willie Randolph	.05
170	Kevin McReynolds	.05
171	Gregg Jefferies	.10
172	Patrick Lennon	.05
173	Luis Mercedes	.05
174	Glenn Davis	.05
175	Bret Saberhagen	.10
176	Bobby Bonilla	.10
177	Kenny Lofton	.20
178	Jose Lind	.05
179	Royce Clayton	.05
180	Scott Scudder	.05
181	Chuck Knoblauch	.15
182	Terry Pendleton	.05
183	Nolan Ryan	1.00
184	Rob Maurer	.05
185	Brian Bohanon	.05
186	Ken Griffey, Jr.	1.50
187	Jeff Bagwell	.50
188	Steve Avery	.05
189	Roger Clemens	.40
190	Cal Ripken, Jr.	1.00
191	Kim Batiste	.05
192	Bip Roberts	.05
193	Greg Swindell	.05
194	Dave Winfield	.20
195	Steve Sax	.05
196	Frank Viola	.05
197	Mo Sanford	.05
198	Kyle Abbott	.05
199	Jack Morris	.05
200	Andy Ashby	.05

1993 Classic

A 100-card travel edition of Classic's baseball trivia cards was produced for 1993. Cards feature game-action player photos with dark blue borders. Backs have previous season and career stats along with five trivia questions. Card numbers have a "T" prefix.

		MT
Complete Set (100):		6.00
Common Player:		.05
1	Jim Abbott	.10
2	Roberto Alomar	.15
3	Moises Alou	.08
4	Brady Anderson	.08
5	Eric Anthony	.05
6	Alex Arias	.05
7	Pedro Astacio	.05
8	Steve Avery	.05
9	Carlos Baerga	.08
10	Jeff Bagwell	.35
11	George Bell	.05
12	Albert Belle	.30
13	Craig Biggio	.10
14	Barry Bonds	.30
15	Bobby Bonilla	.10
16	Mike Bordick	.05
17	George Brett	.60
18	Jose Canseco	.30
19	Joe Carter	.08
20	Royce Clayton	.05
21	Roger Clemens	.50
22	Greg Colbrunn	.05
23	David Cone	.08
24	Darren Daulton	.05
25	Delino DeShields	.05
26	Rob Dibble	.05
27	Dennis Eckersley	.08
28	Cal Eldred	.05
29	Scott Erickson	.05
30	Junior Felix	.05
31	Tony Fernandez	.05
32	Cecil Fielder	.08
33	Steve Finley	.05
34	Dave Fleming	.05
35	Travis Fryman	.10
36	Tom Glavine	.08
37	Juan Gonzalez	.50
38	Ken Griffey, Jr.	1.00
39	Marquis Grissom	.10
40	Juan Guzman	.05
41	Tony Gwynn	.40
42	Rickey Henderson	.15
43	Felix Jose	.05
44	Wally Joyner	.08
45	David Justice	.25
46	Eric Karros	.10
47	Roberto Kelly	.05
48	Ryan Klesko	.10
49	Chuck Knoblauch	.15
50	John Kruk	.05
51	Ray Lankford	.10
52	Barry Larkin	.08
53	Pat Listach	.05
54	Kenny Lofton	.15
55	Shane Mack	.05
56	Greg Maddux	.40
57	Dave Magadan	.05
58	Edgar Martinez	.05
59	Don Mattingly	.65
60	Ben McDonald	.05
61	Jack McDowell	.05
62	Fred McGriff	.15
63	Mark McGwire	1.00
64	Kevin McReynolds	.05
65	Sam Militello	.05
66	Paul Molitor	.35
67	Jeff Montgomery	.05
68	Jack Morris	.05
69	Eddie Murray	.25
70	Mike Mussina	.12
71	Otis Nixon	.05
72	Donovan Osborne	.05
73	Terry Pendleton	.05
74	Mike Piazza	.75
75	Kirby Puckett	.50
76	Cal Ripken, Jr.	.80
77	Bip Roberts	.05
78	Ivan Rodriguez	.25
79	Nolan Ryan	.80
80	Ryne Sandberg	.35
81	Deion Sanders	.25
82	Reggie Sanders	.05
83	Frank Seminara	.05
84	Gary Sheffield	.15
85	Ruben Sierra	.05
86	John Smiley	.05
87	Lee Smith	.08
88	Ozzie Smith	.35
89	John Smoltz	.08
90	Danny Tartabull	.05
91	Bob Tewksbury	.05
92	Frank Thomas	.65
93	Andy Van Slyke	.05
94	Mo Vaughn	.35
95	Robin Ventura	.10
96	Tim Wakefield	.05
97	Larry Walker	.15
98	Dave Winfield	.25
99	Robin Yount	.40
---	4-in-1 (Mark McGwire, Sam Militello, Ryan Klesko, Greg Maddux)	.75

1994 Collector's Choice Promos

Upper Deck used a pair of promo cards to preview its new 1994 Collector's Choice brand. Ken Griffey, Jr. was featured on the promos, though the photos differ from those which appear on his regular-issue card, as does the card number. "For Promotional Use Only" is printed diagonally in black on both the front and back of the regular-size card. The 5" x 7-3/8" promo card uses the same front photo as the smaller promo and has advertising on the back describing the Collector's Choice issue.

		MT
Complete Set (2):		10.00
50	Ken Griffey, Jr.	6.00
---	Ken Griffey, Jr. (jumbo)	6.00

1994 Collector's Choice

This base-brand set, released in two series, was more widely available than the regular 1994 Upper Deck issue. Cards feature UD production staples such as UV coating and hologram and have large photos with a narrow pinstripe border. Backs have stats and a color photo. Series 1 has 320 cards and subsets titled Rookie Class, Draft Picks and Top Performers. Series 2 subsets are Up Close and Personal, Future Foundation and Rookie Class. Each of the set's player cards can also be found with either a gold- (1 in 36 packs) or silver-foil replica-autograph card; one silver-signature card appears in every pack.

		MT
Complete Set (670):		30.00
Complete Series 1 (320):		12.00
Complete Series 2 (350):		18.00
Gold Signature:		20-40X
Silver Signature:		1.5-3X
Common Player:		.05
Series 1 or 2 Pack (12):		1.00
Series 1 or 2 Wax Box (36):		25.00
1	*Rich Becker*	.05
2	Greg Blosser	.05
3	Midre Cummings	.05
4	Carlos Delgado	.25
5	*Steve Dreyer*	.05
6	*Carl Everett*	.15
7	Cliff Floyd	.10
8	Alex Gonzalez	.15
9	Shawn Green	.25
10	Butch Huskey	.10
11	Mark Hutton	.05
12	Miguel Jimenez	.05
13	Steve Karsay	.10
14	Marc Newfield	.05
15	Luis Ortiz	.05
16	Manny Ramirez	.75
17	Johnny Ruffin	.05
18	*Scott Stahoviak*	.10
19	Salomon Torres	.05
20	*Gabe White*	.10
21	*Brian Anderson*	.10
22	*Wayne Gomes*	.10
23	Jeff Granger	.10
24	*Steve Soderstrom*	.10
25	*Trot Nixon*	.25
26	*Kirk Presley*	.05
27	*Matt Brunson*	.05
28	*Brooks Kieschnick*	.20
29	*Billy Wagner*	.40
30	*Matt Drews*	.10
31	*Kurt Abbott*	.20
32	Luis Alicea	.05
33	Roberto Alomar	.40
34	Sandy Alomar Jr.	.10
35	Moises Alou	.10
36	Wilson Alvarez	.05
37	Rich Amaral	.05
38	Eric Anthony	.05
39	Luis Aquino	.05
40	Jack Armstrong	.05
41	Rene Arocha	.05
42	*Rich Aude*	.05
43	Brad Ausmus	.05
44	Steve Avery	.05
45	Bob Ayrault	.05
46	Willie Banks	.05
47	Bret Barberie	.05
48	Kim Batiste	.05
49	Rod Beck	.05
50	Jason Bere	.05
51	Sean Berry	.05
52	Dante Bichette	.15
53	Jeff Blauser	.05
54	Mike Blowers	.05
55	Tim Bogar	.05
56	Tom Bolton	.05
57	Ricky Bones	.05
58	Bobby Bonilla	.05
59	Bret Boone	.05
60	Pat Borders	.05
61	Mike Bordick	.05
62	Daryl Boston	.05
63	Ryan Bowen	.05
64	Jeff Branson	.05
65	George Brett	.35
66	Steve Buechele	.05
67	Dave Burba	.05
68	John Burkett	.05
69	Jeromy Burnitz	.10
70	Brett Butler	.05
71	Rob Butler	.05
72	Ken Caminiti	.20
73	Cris Carpenter	.05
74	Vinny Castilla	.10
75	Andujar Cedeno	.05
76	Wes Chamberlain	.05

77 Archi Cianfrocco .05
78 Dave Clark .05
79 Jerald Clark .05
80 Royce Clayton .05
81 David Cone .10
82 Jeff Conine .05
83 Steve Cooke .05
84 Scott Cooper .05
85 Joey Cora .05
86 Tim Costa .05
87 Chad Curtis .05
88 Ron Darling .05
89 Danny Darwin .05
90 Rob Deer .05
91 Jim Deshaies .05
92 Delino DeShields .05
93 Rob Dibble .05
94 Gary DiSarcina .05
95 Doug Drabek .05
96 Scott Erickson .05
97 *Rikkert Faneyte* .05
98 Jeff Fassero .05
99 Alex Fernandez .10
100 Cecil Fielder .05
101 Dave Fleming .05
102 Darrin Fletcher .05
103 Scott Fletcher .05
104 Mike Gallego .05
105 Carlos Garcia .05
106 Jeff Gardner .05
107 Brent Gates .10
108 Benji Gil .05
109 Bernard Gilkey .05
110 Chris Gomez .05
111 Luis Gonzalez .05
112 Tom Gordon .05
113 Jim Gott .05
114 Mark Grace .10
115 Tommy Greene .05
116 Willie Greene .05
117 Ken Griffey, Jr. 1.50
118 Bill Gullickson .05
119 Ricky Gutierrez .05
120 Juan Guzman .05
121 Chris Gwynn .05
122 Tony Gwynn .50
123 Jeffrey Hammonds .10
124 Erik Hanson .05
125 Gene Harris .05
126 Greg Harris .05
127 Bryan Harvey .05
128 Billy Hatcher .05
129 Hilly Hathaway .05
130 Charlie Hayes .05
131 Rickey Henderson .15
132 Mike Henneman .05
133 Pat Hentgen .10
134 Roberto Hernandez .05
135 Orel Hershiser .05
136 Phil Hiatt .10
137 Glenallen Hill .05
138 Ken Hill .05
139 Eric Hillman .05
140 Chris Hoiles .05
141 Dave Hollins .05
142 David Hulse .05
143 Todd Hundley .15
144 Pete Incaviglia .05
145 Danny Jackson .05
146 John Jaha .05
147 Domingo Jean .10
148 Gregg Jefferies .05
149 Reggie Jefferson .05
150 Lance Johnson .05
151 Bobby Jones .10
152 Chipper Jones .75
153 Todd Jones .05
154 Brian Jordan .10
155 Wally Joyner .05
156 Dave Justice .15
157 Ron Karkovice .05
158 Eric Karros .10
159 Jeff Kent .05
160 Jimmy Key .10
161 Mark Kiefer .05
162 Darryl Kile .05
163 Jeff King .05
164 Wayne Kirby .05
165 Ryan Klesko .15
166 Chuck Knoblauch .15
167 Chad Kreuter .05
168 John Kruk .05
169 Mark Langston .05
170 Mike Lansing .05
171 Barry Larkin .15
172 Manuel Lee .05
173 *Phil Leftwich* .05
174 Darren Lewis .05
175 Derek Lilliquist .05
176 Jose Lind .05
177 Albie Lopez .05
178 Javier Lopez .20
179 Torey Lovullo .05
180 Scott Lydy .05
181 Mike Macfarlane .05
182 Shane Mack .05
183 Greg Maddux 1.00
184 Dave Magadan .05
185 Joe Magrane .05
186 Kirt Manwaring .05
187 Al Martin .05
188 *Pedro A. Martinez* .10
189 Pedro J. Martinez .15
190 Ramon Martinez .10
191 Tino Martinez .20
192 Don Mattingly .50
193 Derrick May .05
194 David McCarty .05
195 Ben McDonald .05
196 Roger McDowell .05
197 Fred McGriff .20
198 Mark McLemore .05
199 Greg McMichael .05
200 Jeff McNeely .05
201 Brian McRae .05
202 Pat Meares .05
203 Roberto Mejia .05
204 Orlando Merced .05
205 Jose Mesa .05
206 Blas Minor .05
207 Angel Miranda .05
208 Paul Molitor .35
209 Raul Mondesi .50
210 Jeff Montgomery .05
211 Mickey Morandini .05
212 Mike Morgan .05
213 Jamie Moyer .05
214 Bobby Munoz .05
215 Troy Neel .05
216 Dave Nilsson .05
217 John O'Donoghue .05
218 Paul O'Neill .10
219 Jose Offerman .05
220 Joe Oliver .05
221 Greg Olson .05
222 Donovan Osborne .05
223 Jayhawk Owens .05
224 Mike Pagliarulo .05
225 Craig Paquette .05
226 Roger Pavlik .05
227 Brad Pennington .05
228 Eduardo Perez .05
229 Mike Perez .05
230 Tony Phillips .05
231 Hipolito Pichardo .05
232 Phil Plantier .05
233 *Curtis Pride* .15
234 Tim Pugh .05
235 Scott Radinsky .05
236 Pat Rapp .05
237 Kevin Reimer .05
238 Armando Reynoso .05
239 Jose Rijo .05
240 Cal Ripken, Jr. 1.50
241 Kevin Roberson .05
242 Kenny Rogers .05
243 Kevin Rogers .05
244 Mel Rojas .05
245 John Roper .05
246 Kirk Rueter .05
247 Scott Ruffcorn .05
248 Ken Ryan .05
249 Nolan Ryan .75
250 Bret Saberhagen .10
251 Tim Salmon .25
252 Reggie Sanders .05
253 Curt Schilling .10
254 David Segui .05
255 Aaron Sele .10
256 Scott Servais .05
257 Gary Sheffield .25
258 Ruben Sierra .05
259 Don Slaught .05
260 Lee Smith .05
261 Cory Snyder .05
262 Paul Sorrento .05
263 Sammy Sosa .75
264 Bill Spiers .05
265 Mike Stanley .05
266 Dave Staton .05
267 Terry Steinbach .05
268 Kevin Stocker .05
269 Todd Stottlemyre .10
270 Doug Strange .05
271 Bill Swift .05
272 Kevin Tapani .05
273 Tony Tarasco .05
274 *Julian Tavarez* .05
275 Mickey Tettleton .05
276 Ryan Thompson .05
277 Chris Turner .05
278 John Valentin .05
279 Todd Van Poppel .05
280 Andy Van Slyke .05
281 Mo Vaughn .30
282 Robin Ventura .10
283 Frank Viola .05
284 Jose Vizcaino .05
285 Omar Vizquel .05
286 Larry Walker .20
287 Duane Ware .05
288 Allen Watson .05
289 Bill Wegman .05
290 Turk Wendell .05
291 Lou Whitaker .05
292 Devon White .05
293 Rondell White .15
294 Mark Whiten .05
295 Darrell Whitmore .05
296 Bob Wickman .05
297 Rick Wilkins .05
298 Bernie Williams .25
299 Matt Williams .30
300 Woody Williams .05
301 Nigel Wilson .05
302 Dave Winfield .15
303 Anthony Young .05
304 Eric Young .05
305 Todd Zeile .05
306 Jack McDowell, John Burkett, Tom Glavine (Top Performers) .10
307 Randy Johnson (Top Performers) .15
308 Randy Myers (Top Performers) .05
309 Jack McDowell (Top Performers) .05
310 Mike Piazza (Top Performers) .40
311 Barry Bonds (Top Performers) .25
312 Andres Galarraga (Top Performers) .10
313 Juan Gonzalez, Barry Bonds (Top Performers) .35
314 Albert Belle (Top Performers) .30
315 Kenny Lofton (Top Performers) .10
316 Checklist 1-64 (Barry Bonds) .10
317 Checklist 65-128 (Ken Griffey, Jr.) .30
318 Checklist 129-192 (Mike Piazza) .15
319 Checklist 193-256 (Kirby Puckett) .10
320 Checklist 257-320 (Nolan Ryan) .25
321 Checklist 321-370 (Roberto Alomar) .15
322 Checklist 371-420 (Roger Clemens) .15
323 Checklist 421-470 (Juan Gonzalez) .15
324 Checklist 471-520 (Ken Griffey, Jr.) .30
325 Checklist 521-570 (David Justice) .10
326 Checklist 571-620 (John Kruk) .05
327 Checklist 621-670 (Frank Thomas) .25
328 Angels Checklist (Tim Salmon) .10
329 Astros Checklist (Jeff Bagwell) .15
330 Athletics Checklist (Mark McGwire) .75
331 Blue Jays Checklist (Roberto Alomar) .15
332 Braves Checklist (David Justice) .10
333 Brewers Checklist (Pat Listach) .05
334 Cardinals Checklist (Ozzie Smith) .10
335 Cubs Checklist (Ryne Sandberg) .10
336 Dodgers Checklist (Mike Piazza) .25
337 Expos Checklist (Cliff Floyd) .05
338 Giants Checklist (Barry Bonds) .15
339 Indians Checklist (Albert Belle) .20
340 Mariners Checklist (Ken Griffey, Jr.) .50
341 Marlins Checklist (Gary Sheffield) .20
342 Mets Checklist (Dwight Gooden) .05
343 Orioles Checklist (Cal Ripken, Jr.) .50
344 Padres Checklist (Tony Gwynn) .20
345 Phillies Checklist (Lenny Dykstra) .05
346 Pirates Checklists (Andy Van Slyke) .05
347 Rangers Checklist (Juan Gonzalez) .20
348 Red Sox Checklist (Roger Clemens) .15
349 Reds Checklist (Barry Larkin) .10
350 Rockies Checklist (Andres Galarraga) .10
351 Royals Checklist (Kevin Appier) .05
352 Tigers Checklist (Cecil Fielder) .10
353 Twins Checklist (Kirby Puckett) .20
354 White Sox Checklist (Frank Thomas) .40
355 Yankees Checklist (Don Mattingly) .30
356 Bo Jackson .10
357 Randy Johnson .30
358 Darren Daulton .05
359 Charlie Hough .05
360 Andres Galarraga .10
361 Mike Felder .05
362 Chris Hammond .05
363 Shawon Dunston .05
364 Junior Felix .05
365 Ray Lankford .05
366 Darryl Strawberry .10
367 Dave Magadan .05
368 Gregg Olson .05
369 Len Dykstra .05
370 Darrin Jackson .05
371 Dave Stewart .05
372 Terry Pendleton .05
373 Arthur Rhodes .05
374 Benito Santiago .05
375 Travis Fryman .10
376 Scott Brosius .05
377 Stan Belinda .05
378 Derek Parks .05
379 Kevin Seitzer .05
380 Wade Boggs .20
381 Wally Whitehurst .05
382 Scott Leius .05
383 Danny Tartabull .05
384 Harold Reynolds .05
385 Tim Raines .05
386 Darryl Hamilton .05
387 Felix Fermin .05
388 Jim Eisenreich .05
389 Kurt Abbott .05
390 Kevin Appier .05
391 Chris Bosio .05
392 Randy Tomlin .05
393 Bob Hamelin .05
394 Kevin Gross .05
395 Wil Cordero .05
396 Joe Girardi .05
397 Orestes Destrade .05
398 Chris Haney .05
399 Xavier Hernandez .05
400 Mike Piazza .75
401 Alex Arias .05
402 Tom Candiotti .05
403 Kirk Gibson .05
404 Chuck Carr .05
405 Brady Anderson .10
406 Greg Gagne .05
407 Bruce Ruffin .05

408 Scott Hemond .05
409 Keith Miller .05
410 John Wetteland .05
411 Eric Anthony .05
412 Andre Dawson .05
413 Doug Henry .05
414 John Franco .05
415 Julio Franco .05
416 Dave Hansen .05
417 Mike Harkey .05
418 Jack Armstrong .05
419 Joe Orsulak .05
420 John Smoltz .15
421 Scott Livingstone .05
422 Darren Holmes .05
423 Ed Sprague .05
424 Jay Buhner .10
425 Kirby Puckett .60
426 Phil Clark .05
427 Anthony Young .05
428 Reggie Jefferson .05
429 Mariano Duncan .05
430 Tom Glavine .15
431 Dave Henderson .05
432 Melido Perez .05
433 Paul Wagner .05
434 Tim Worrell .05
435 Ozzie Guillen .05
436 Mike Butcher .05
437 Jim Deshaies .05
438 Kevin Young .05
439 Tom Browning .05
440 Mike Greenwell .05
441 Mike Stanton .05
442 John Doherty .05
443 John Dopson .05
444 Carlos Baerga .05
445 Jack McDowell .05
446 Kent Mercker .05
447 Ricky Jordan .05
448 Jerry Browne .05
449 Fernando Vina .05
450 Jim Abbott .05
451 Teddy Higuera .05
452 Tim Naehring .05
453 Jim Leyritz .05
454 Frank Castillo .05
455 Joe Carter .10
456 Craig Biggio .10
457 Geronimo Pena .05
458 Alejandro Pena .05
459 Mike Moore .05
460 Randy Myers .05
461 Greg Myers .05
462 Greg Hibbard .05
463 Jose Guzman .05
464 Tom Pagnozzi .05
465 Marquis Grissom .05
466 Tim Wallach .05
467 Joe Grahe .05
468 Bob Tewksbury .05
469 B.J. Surhoff .05
470 Kevin Mitchell .05
471 Bobby Witt .05
472 Milt Thompson .05
473 John Smiley .05
474 Alan Trammell .05
475 Mike Mussina .20
476 Rick Aguilera .05
477 Jose Valentin .05
478 Harold Baines .05
479 Bip Roberts .05
480 Edgar Martinez .05
481 Rheal Cormier .05
482 Hal Morris .05
483 Pat Kelly .05
484 Roberto Kelly .05
485 Chris Sabo .05
486 Kent Hrbek .05
487 Scott Kamieniecki .05
488 Walt Weiss .05
489 Karl Rhodes .05
490 Derek Bell .05
491 Chili Davis .05
492 Brian Harper .05
493 Felix Jose .05
494 Trevor Hoffman .05
495 Dennis Eckersley .05
496 Pedro Astacio .05
497 Jay Bell .05
498 Randy Velarde .05
499 David Wells .10
500 Frank Thomas 1.00
501 Mark Lemke .05
502 Mike Devereaux .05
503 Chuck McElroy .05
504 Luis Polonia .05
505 Damion Easley .05
506 Greg A. Harris .05
507 Chris James .05
508 Terry Mulholland .05
509 Pete Smith .05
510 Rickey Henderson .15
511 Sid Fernandez .05
512 Al Leiter .10
513 Doug Jones .05
514 Steve Farr .05
515 Chuck Finley .05
516 Bobby Thigpen .05
517 Jim Edmonds .15
518 Graeme Lloyd .05
519 Dwight Gooden .10
520 Pat Listach .05
521 Kevin Bass .05
522 Willie Banks .05
523 Steve Finley .05
524 Delino DeShields .05
525 Mark McGwire 2.00
526 Greg Swindell .05
527 Chris Nabholz .05
528 Scott Sanders .05
529 David Segui .05
530 Howard Johnson .05
531 Jaime Navarro .05
532 Jose Vizcaino .05
533 Mark Lewis .05
534 Pete Harnisch .05
535 Robby Thompson .05
536 Marcus Moore .05
537 Kevin Brown .10
538 Mark Clark .05
539 Sterling Hitchcock .05
540 Will Clark .20
541 Denis Boucher .05
542 Jack Morris .05
543 Pedro Munoz .05
544 Bret Boone .05
545 Ozzie Smith .25
546 Dennis Martinez .05
547 Dan Wilson .05
548 Rick Sutcliffe .05
549 Kevin McReynolds .05
550 Roger Clemens .35
551 Todd Benzinger .05
552 Bill Haselman .05
553 Bobby Munoz .05
554 Ellis Burks .05
555 Ryne Sandberg .25
556 Lee Smith .05
557 Danny Bautista .05
558 Rey Sanchez .05
559 Norm Charlton .05
560 Jose Canseco .25
561 Tim Belcher .05
562 Denny Neagle .05
563 Eric Davis .05
564 Jody Reed .05
565 Kenny Lofton .15
566 Gary Gaetti .05
567 Todd Worrell .05
568 Mark Portugal .05
569 Dick Schofield .05
570 Andy Benes .10
571 Zane Smith .05
572 Bobby Ayala .05
573 Chip Hale .05
574 Bob Welch .05
575 Deion Sanders .20
576 Dave Nied .05
577 Pat Mahomes .05
578 Charles Nagy .05
579 Otis Nixon .05
580 Dean Palmer .05
581 Roberto Petagine .05
582 Dwight Smith .05
583 Jeff Russell .05
584 Mark Dewey .05
585 Greg Vaughn .10
586 Brian Hunter .05
587 Willie McGee .05
588 Pedro J. Martinez .20
589 Roger Salkeld .05
590 Jeff Bagwell .50
591 Spike Owen .05
592 Jeff Reardon .05
593 Erik Pappas .05
594 Brian Williams .05
595 Eddie Murray .25
596 Henry Rodriguez .05
597 Erik Hanson .05
598 Stan Javier .05
599 Mitch Williams .05
600 John Olerud .10
601 Vince Coleman .05
602 Damon Berryhill .05
603 Tom Brunansky .05
604 Robb Nen .05
605 Rafael Palmeiro .15
606 Cal Eldred .05
607 Jeff Brantley .05
608 Alan Mills .05
609 Jeff Nelson .05
610 Barry Bonds .40
611 *Carlos Pulido* .10
612 *Tim Hyers* .15
613 Steve Howe .05
614 *Brian Turang* .05
615 Leo Gomez .05
616 Jesse Orosco .05
617 Dan Pasqua .05
618 Marvin Freeman .05
619 Tony Fernandez .05
620 Albert Belle .50
621 Eddie Taubensee .05
622 Mike Jackson .05
623 Jose Bautista .05
624 Jim Thome .20
625 Ivan Rodriguez .30
626 Ben Rivera .05
627 Dave Valle .05
628 Tom Henke .05
629 Omar Vizquel .05
630 Juan Gonzalez .40
631 Roberto Alomar (Up Close) .15
632 Barry Bonds (Up Close) .20
633 Juan Gonzalez (Up Close) .25
634 Ken Griffey, Jr. (Up Close) .75
635 Michael Jordan (Up Close) 3.00
636 Dave Justice (Up Close) .10
637 Mike Piazza (Up Close) .40
638 Kirby Puckett (Up Close) .25
639 Tim Salmon (Up Close) .15
640 Frank Thomas (Up Close) .50
641 *Alan Benes* (Future Foundation) .60
642 Johnny Damon (Future Foundation) .10
643 *Brad Fullmer* (Future Foundation) 1.00
644 Derek Jeter (Future Foundation) 2.00
645 *Derrek Lee* (Future Foundation) .50
646 Alex Ochoa (Future Foundation) .10
647 *Alex Rodriguez* (Future Foundation) 5.00
648 *Jose Silva* (Future Foundation) .10
649 *Terrell Wade* (Future Foundation) .05
650 Preston Wilson (Future Foundation) .25
651 Shane Andrews (Rookie Class) .05
652 James Baldwin (Rookie Class) .05
653 *Ricky Bottalico* (Rookie Class) .10
654 Tavo Alvarez (Rookie Class) .05
655 Donnie Elliott (Rookie Class) .10
656 Joey Eischen (Rookie Class) .05
657 Jason Giambi (Rookie Class) .35
658 Todd Hollandsworth (Rookie Class) .20
659 Brian Hunter (Rookie Class) .10
660 Charles Johnson (Rookie Class) .20
661 *Michael Jordan* (Rookie Class) 7.50
662 Jeff Juden (Rookie Class) .05
663 Mike Kelly (Rookie Class) .05
664 James Mouton (Rookie Class) .05
665 Ray Holbert (Rookie Class) .10
666 Pokey Reese (Rookie Class) .05
667 *Ruben Santana* (Rookie Class) .10
668 Paul Spoljaric (Rookie Class) .05
669 Luis Lopez (Rookie Class) .05
670 Matt Walbeck (Rookie Class) .10

1994 Collector's Choice Silver Signature

Each of the cards in the debut edition of Upper Deck's Collector's Choice brand was also issued in a parallel edition bearing a facsimile silver-foil signature on front. The silver-signature cards were inserted at a one-per-pack rate in the set's foil packs, and proportionately in other types of packaging.

	MT
Complete Set (670):	200.00
Complete Series 1 (1-320):	120.00
Complete Series 2 (321-670):	80.00
Common Player:	.25
Stars:	1.5-3X

(See 1994 Collector's Choice for checklist and base card values.)

1994 Collector's Choice Gold Signature

A super-scarce parallel set of the premiere-issue Collector's Choice in 1994 was the gold-signature version found on average of only once per 36 foil packs. In addition to a gold-foil facsimile signature on the card front, this edition features gold-colored borders on the regular player cards.

	MT
Complete Set (670):	2000.
Complete Series 1 (1-320):	1200.
Complete Series 2 (321-670):	1100.
Common Player:	1.50
Stars:	20-40X

(See 1994 Collector's Choice for checklist and base card values.)

1994 Collector's Choice Home Run All-Stars

Among the most attractive of the 1994 chase cards, the perceived high production (over a million sets according to stated odds of winning) of this set keeps it affordable. Sets were available by a mail-in offer to persons who found a winner card in Series 1 foil packs (about one per box). Cards feature a combination of brick-bordered hologram and color player photo on front, along with a gold-foil facsimile autograph. On back the brick border is repeated, as is the photo on the hologram, though this time in full color. There is a stadium photo in the background, over which is printed a description of the player's home run prowess. A numbering error resulted in two cards numbered HA4 and no card with the HA5 number.

	MT
Complete Set (8):	4.00
Common Player:	.25
1HA Juan Gonzalez	1.00
2HA Ken Griffey, Jr.	3.00
3HA Barry Bonds	.75
4HAaBobby Bonilla	.25
4HAbCecil Fielder	.25
6HA Albert Belle	.60
7HA David Justice	.40
8HA Mike Piazza	1.50

1995 Collector's Choice

Issued in a single series, Upper Deck's base-brand baseball series features a number of subsets within the main body of the issue, as well as several insert sets. Basic cards feature large photos on front and back, with the back having full major league stats. The set opens with a 27-card Rookie Class subset featuring front photos on which the background has been rendered in hot pink tones. Backs have a lime-green box with a scouting report on the player and a box featuring 1994 minor and major league stats. The next 18 cards are Future Foundation cards which have the prospects pictured with a posterized background on front, with backs similar to the Rookie Class cards. Career finale cards of five retired superstars follow, then a run of Best of the '90s cards honoring record-setting achievements, followed by cards depicting major award winners of the previous season. Each of the last three named subsets features borderless color photos on front, with backs similar to the regular cards. Immediately preceding the regular cards, which are arranged in team-set order, is a five-card What's the Call? subset featuring cartoon representations of the players. A set of five checklist cards marking career highlights ends the set.

		MT
Complete Set (530):		20.00
Common Player:		.05
Pack (12):		1.00
Wax Box (36):		30.00
1	Charles Johnson (Rookie Class)	.15
2	Scott Ruffcorn (Rookie Class)	.05
3	Ray Durham (Rookie Class)	.15
4	Armando Benitez (Rookie Class)	.05
5	Alex Rodriguez (Rookie Class)	2.00
6	Julian Tavarez (Rookie Class)	.08
7	Chad Ogea (Rookie Class)	.05
8	Quilvio Veras (Rookie Class)	.10
9	Phil Nevin (Rookie Class)	.05
10	Michael Tucker (Rookie Class)	.10
11	Mark Thompson (Rookie Class)	.05
12	Rod Henderson (Rookie Class)	.05
13	Andrew Lorraine (Rookie Class)	.05
14	Joe Randa (Rookie Class)	.05
15	Derek Jeter (Rookie Class)	1.00
16	Tony Clark (Rookie Class)	.60
17	Juan Castillo (Rookie Class)	.05
18	Mark Acre (Rookie Class)	.05
19	Orlando Miller (Rookie Class)	.05
20	Paul Wilson (Rookie Class)	.15
21	John Mabry (Rookie Class)	.05
22	Garey Ingram (Rookie Class)	.05
23	*Garret Anderson* (Rookie Class)	.15
24	Dave Stevens (Rookie Class)	.05
25	Dustin Hermanson (Rookie Class)	.05
26	Paul Shuey (Rookie Class)	.05
27	J.R. Phillips (Rookie Class)	.05
28	Ruben Rivera (Future Foundation)	.40
29	Nomar Garciaparra (Future Foundation)	1.50
30	John Wasdin (Future Foundation)	.05
31	Jim Pittsley (Future Foundation)	.05
32	*Scott Elarton* (Future Foundation)	.20
33	*Raul Casanova* (Future Foundation)	.40
34	Todd Greene (Future Foundation)	.05
35	Bill Pulsipher (Future Foundation)	.15
36	Trey Beamon (Future Foundation)	.10
37	Curtis Goodwin (Future Foundation)	.05
38	Doug Million (Future Foundation)	.05
39	*Karim Garcia* (Future Foundation)	1.00
40	Ben Grieve (Future Foundation)	1.50
41	Mark Farris (Future Foundation)	.10
42	*Juan Acevedo* (Future Foundation)	.15
43	C.J. Nitkowski (Future Foundation)	.05
44	*Travis Miller* (Future Foundation)	.15
45	Reid Ryan (Future Foundation)	.10
46	Nolan Ryan	1.00
47	Robin Yount	.25
48	Ryne Sandberg	.40
49	George Brett	.60
50	Mike Schmidt	.40
51	Cecil Fielder (Best of the 90's)	.10
52	Nolan Ryan (Best of the 90's)	.60
53	Rickey Henderson (Best of the 90's)	.05
54	George Brett, Robin Yount, Dave Winfield (Best of the 90's)	.25
55	Sid Bream (Best of the 90's)	.05
56	Carlos Baerga (Best of the 90's)	.05
57	Lee Smith (Best of the 90's)	.05
58	Mark Whiten (Best of the 90's)	.05
59	Joe Carter (Best of the 90's)	.10
60	Barry Bonds (Best of the 90's)	.25
61	Tony Gwynn (Best of the 90's)	.35
62	Ken Griffey Jr. (Best of the 90's)	1.00
63	Greg Maddux (Best of the 90's)	.75
64	Frank Thomas (Best of the 90's)	.50
65	Dennis Martinez, Kenny Rogers (Best of the 90's)	.05
66	David Cone (Cy Young)	.10
67	Greg Maddux (Cy Young)	1.00
68	Jimmy Key (Most Victories)	.05
69	Fred McGriff (All-Star MVP)	.25
70	Ken Griffey Jr. (HR Champ)	2.00
71	Matt Williams (HR Champ)	.25
72	Paul O'Neill (Batting Title)	.05
73	Tony Gwynn (Batting Title)	.50
74	Randy Johnson (Ks Leader)	.35
75	Frank Thomas (MVP)	1.00
76	Jeff Bagwell (MVP)	.60
77	Kirby Puckett (RBI leader)	.60
78	Bob Hamelin (ROY)	.05
79	Raul Mondesi (ROY)	.25
80	Mike Piazza (All-Star)	.75
81	Kenny Lofton (SB Leader)	.40
82	Barry Bonds (Gold Glove)	.40
83	Albert Belle (All-Star)	.50
84	Juan Gonzalez (HR Champ)	.50
85	Cal Ripken Jr. (2,000 Straight Games)	2.00
86	Barry Bonds (What's the Call?)	.20
87	Mike Piazza (What's the Call?)	.40
88	Ken Griffey Jr. (What's the Call?)	1.00
89	Frank Thomas (What's the Call?)	.50
90	Juan Gonzalez (What's the Call?)	.30
91	Jorge Fabregas	.05
92	J.T. Snow	.10
93	Spike Owen	.05
94	Eduardo Perez	.05
95	Bo Jackson	.10
96	Damion Easley	.05
97	Gary DiSarcina	.05
98	Jim Edmonds	.15

No.	Player	Value
99	Chad Curtis	.05
100	Tim Salmon	.15
101	Chili Davis	.05
102	Chuck Finley	.05
103	Mark Langston	.05
104	Brian Anderson	.05
105	Lee Smith	.05
106	Phil Leftwich	.05
107	Chris Donnels	.05
108	John Hudek	.05
109	Craig Biggio	.10
110	Luis Gonzalez	.05
111	Brian L. Hunter	.10
112	James Mouton	.05
113	Scott Servais	.05
114	Tony Eusebio	.05
115	Derek Bell	.05
116	Doug Drabek	.05
117	Shane Reynolds	.05
118	Darryl Kile	.05
119	Greg Swindell	.05
120	Phil Plantier	.05
121	Todd Jones	.05
122	Steve Ontiveros	.05
123	Bobby Witt	.05
124	Brent Gates	.05
125	Rickey Henderson	.05
126	Scott Brosius	.05
127	Mike Bordick	.05
128	Fausto Cruz	.05
129	Stan Javier	.05
130	Mark McGwire	2.00
131	Geronimo Berroa	.05
132	Terry Steinbach	.05
133	Steve Karsay	.05
134	Dennis Eckersley	.05
135	Ruben Sierra	.05
136	Ron Darling	.05
137	Todd Van Poppel	.05
138	Alex Gonzalez	.10
139	John Olerud	.10
140	Roberto Alomar	.50
141	Darren Hall	.05
142	Ed Sprague	.05
143	Devon White	.05
144	Shawn Green	.10
145	Paul Molitor	.25
146	Pat Borders	.05
147	Carlos Delgado	.25
148	Juan Guzman	.05
149	Pat Hentgen	.05
150	Joe Carter	.10
151	Dave Stewart	.05
152	Todd Stottlemyre	.05
153	Dick Schofield	.05
154	Chipper Jones	1.00
155	Ryan Klesko	.20
156	Dave Justice	.25
157	Mike Kelly	.05
158	Roberto Kelly	.05
159	Tony Tarasco	.05
160	Javier Lopez	.10
161	Steve Avery	.05
162	Greg McMichael	.05
163	Kent Mercker	.05
164	Mark Lemke	.05
165	Tom Glavine	.15
166	Jose Oliva	.05
167	John Smoltz	.15
168	Jeff Blauser	.05
169	Troy O'Leary	.05
170	Greg Vaughn	.05
171	Jody Reed	.05
172	Kevin Seitzer	.05
173	Jeff Cirillo	.05
174	B.J. Surhoff	.05
175	Cal Eldred	.05
176	Jose Valentin	.05
177	Turner Ward	.05
178	Darryl Hamilton	.05
179	Pat Listach	.05
180	Matt Mieske	.05
181	Brian Harper	.05
182	Dave Nilsson	.05
183	Mike Fetters	.05
184	John Jaha	.05
185	Ricky Bones	.05
186	Geronimo Pena	.05
187	Bob Tewksbury	.05
188	Todd Zeile	.05
189	Danny Jackson	.05
190	Ray Lankford	.05
191	Bernard Gilkey	.05
192	Brian Jordan	.05
193	Tom Pagnozzi	.05
194	Rick Sutcliffe	.05
195	Mark Whiten	.05
196	Tom Henke	.05
197	Rene Arocha	.05
198	Allen Watson	.05
199	Mike Perez	.05
200	Ozzie Smith	.25
201	Anthony Young	.05
202	Rey Sanchez	.05
203	Steve Buechele	.05
204	Shawon Dunston	.05
205	Mark Grace	.10
206	Glenallen Hill	.05
207	Eddie Zambrano	.05
208	Rick Wilkins	.05
209	Derrick May	.05
210	Sammy Sosa	.75
211	Kevin Roberson	.05
212	Steve Trachsel	.05
213	Willie Banks	.05
214	Kevin Foster	.05
215	Randy Myers	.05
216	Mike Morgan	.05
217	Rafael Bournigal	.05
218	Delino DeShields	.05
219	Tim Wallach	.05
220	Eric Karros	.10
221	Jose Offerman	.05
222	Tom Candiotti	.05
223	Ismael Valdes	.10
224	Henry Rodriguez	.05
225	Billy Ashley	.10
226	Darren Dreifort	.05
227	Ramon Martinez	.10
228	Pedro Astacio	.05
229	Orel Hershiser	.05
230	Brett Butler	.05
231	Todd Hollandsworth	.10
232	Chan Ho Park	.10
233	Mike Lansing	.05
234	Sean Berry	.05
235	Rondell White	.15
236	Ken Hill	.05
237	Marquis Grissom	.05
238	Larry Walker	.20
239	John Wetteland	.05
240	Cliff Floyd	.10
241	Joey Eischen	.05
242	Lou Frazier	.05
243	Darrin Fletcher	.05
244	Pedro J. Martinez	.15
245	Wil Cordero	.05
246	Jeff Fassero	.05
247	Butch Henry	.05
248	Mel Rojas	.05
249	Kirk Rueter	.05
250	Moises Alou	.10
251	Rod Beck	.05
252	John Patterson	.05
253	Robby Thompson	.05
254	Royce Clayton	.05
255	William Van Landingham	.08
256	Darren Lewis	.05
257	Kirt Manwaring	.05
258	Mark Portugal	.05
259	Bill Swift	.05
260	Rikkert Faneyte	.05
261	Mike Jackson	.05
262	Todd Benzinger	.05
263	Bud Black	.05
264	Salomon Torres	.05
265	Eddie Murray	.25
266	Mark Clark	.05
267	Paul Sorrento	.05
268	Jim Thome	.30
269	Omar Vizquel	.05
270	Carlos Baerga	.05
271	Jeff Russell	.05
272	Herbert Perry	.05
273	Sandy Alomar Jr.	.05
274	Dennis Martinez	.05
275	Manny Ramirez	.50
276	Wayne Kirby	.05
277	Charles Nagy	.05
278	Albie Lopez	.05
279	Jeromy Burnitz	.05
280	Dave Winfield	.08
281	Tim Davis	.05
282	Marc Newfield	.08
283	Tino Martinez	.10
284	Mike Blowers	.05
285	Goose Gossage	.05
286	Luis Sojo	.05
287	Edgar Martinez	.05
288	Rich Amaral	.05
289	Felix Fermin	.05
290	Jay Buhner	.10
291	Dan Wilson	.05
292	Bobby Ayala	.05
293	Dave Fleming	.05
294	Greg Pirkl	.05
295	Reggie Jefferson	.05
296	Greg Hibbard	.05
297	Yorkis Perez	.05
298	Kurt Miller	.05
299	Chuck Carr	.05
300	Gary Sheffield	.20
301	Jerry Browne	.05
302	Dave Magadan	.05
303	Kurt Abbott	.05
304	Pat Rapp	.05
305	Jeff Conine	.05
306	Benito Santiago	.05
307	Dave Weathers	.05
308	Robb Nen	.05
309	Chris Hammond	.05
310	Bryan Harvey	.05
311	Charlie Hough	.05
312	Greg Colbrunn	.05
313	David Segui	.05
314	Rico Brogna	.05
315	Jeff Kent	.05
316	Jose Vizcaino	.05
317	Jim Lindeman	.05
318	Carl Everett	.05
319	Ryan Thompson	.05
320	Bobby Bonilla	.10
321	Joe Orsulak	.05
322	Pete Harnisch	.05
323	Doug Linton	.05
324	Todd Hundley	.15
325	Bret Saberhagen	.05
326	Kelly Stinnett	.05
327	Jason Jacome	.08
328	Bobby Jones	.05
329	John Franco	.05
330	Rafael Palmeiro	.10
331	Chris Hoiles	.05
332	Leo Gomez	.05
333	Chris Sabo	.05
334	Brady Anderson	.10
335	Jeffrey Hammonds	.10
336	Dwight Smith	.05
337	Jack Voigt	.05
338	Harold Baines	.05
339	Ben McDonald	.05
340	Mike Mussina	.30
341	Bret Barberie	.05
342	Jamie Moyer	.05
343	Mike Oquist	.05
344	Sid Fernandez	.05
345	Eddie Williams	.05
346	Joey Hamilton	.05
347	Brian Williams	.05
348	Luis Lopez	.05
349	Steve Finley	.05
350	Andy Benes	.10
351	Andujar Cedeno	.05
352	Bip Roberts	.05
353	Ray McDavid	.05
354	Ken Caminiti	.15
355	Trevor Hoffman	.05
356	Mel Nieves	.05
357	Brad Ausmus	.05
358	Andy Ashby	.05
359	Scott Sanders	.05
360	Gregg Jefferies	.05
361	Mariano Duncan	.05
362	Dave Hollins	.05
363	Kevin Stocker	.05
364	Fernando Valenzuela	.05
365	Lenny Dykstra	.05
366	Jim Eisenreich	.05
367	Ricky Bottalico	.05
368	Doug Jones	.05
369	Ricky Jordan	.05
370	Darren Daulton	.05
371	Mike Lieberthal	.05
372	Bobby Munoz	.05
373	John Kruk	.05
374	Curt Schilling	.05
375	Orlando Merced	.05
376	Carlos Garcia	.05
377	Lance Parrish	.05
378	Steve Cooke	.05
379	Jeff King	.05
380	Jay Bell	.05
381	Al Martin	.05
382	Paul Wagner	.05
383	Rick White	.05
384	Midre Cummings	.05
385	Jon Lieber	.05
386	Dave Clark	.05
387	Don Slaught	.05
388	Denny Neagle	.05
389	Zane Smith	.05
390	Andy Van Slyke	.05
391	Ivan Rodriguez	.40
392	David Hulse	.05
393	John Burkett	.05
394	Kevin Brown	.05
395	Dean Palmer	.05
396	Otis Nixon	.05
397	Rick Helling	.05
398	Kenny Rogers	.05
399	Darren Oliver	.05
400	Will Clark	.25
401	Jeff Frye	.05
402	Kevin Gross	.05
403	John Dettmer	.05
404	Manny Lee	.05
405	Rusty Greer	.05
406	Aaron Sele	.10
407	Carlos Rodriguez	.05
408	Scott Cooper	.05
409	John Valentin	.05
410	Roger Clemens	.50
411	Mike Greenwell	.05
412	Tim Vanegmond	.05
413	Tom Brunansky	.05
414	Steve Farr	.05
415	Jose Canseco	.30
416	Joe Hesketh	.05
417	Ken Ryan	.05
418	Tim Naehring	.05
419	Frank Viola	.05
420	Andre Dawson	.08
421	Mo Vaughn	.40
422	Jeff Brantley	.05
423	Pete Schourek	.05
424	Hal Morris	.05
425	Deion Sanders	.30
426	Brian L. Hunter	.15
427	Bret Boone	.05
428	Willie Greene	.05
429	Ron Gant	.10
430	Barry Larkin	.10
431	Reggie Sanders	.05
432	Eddie Taubensee	.05
433	Jack Morris	.05
434	Jose Rijo	.05
435	Johnny Ruffin	.05
436	John Smiley	.05
437	John Roper	.05
438	David Nied	.05
439	Roberto Mejia	.05
440	Andres Galarraga	.10
441	Mike Kingery	.05
442	Curt Leskanic	.05
443	Walt Weiss	.05
444	Marvin Freeman	.05
445	Charlie Hayes	.05
446	Eric Young	.05
447	Ellis Burks	.05
448	Joe Girardi	.05
449	Lance Painter	.05
450	Dante Bichette	.10
451	Bruce Ruffin	.05
452	Jeff Granger	.05
453	Wally Joyner	.05
454	Jose Lind	.05
455	Jeff Montgomery	.05
456	Gary Gaetti	.05
457	Greg Gagne	.05
458	Vince Coleman	.05
459	Mike Macfarlane	.05
460	Brian McRae	.05
461	Tom Gordon	.05
462	Kevin Appier	.05
463	Billy Brewer	.05
464	Mark Gubicza	.05
465	Travis Fryman	.10
466	Danny Bautista	.05
467	Sean Bergman	.05
468	Mike Henneman	.05
469	Mike Moore	.05
470	Cecil Fielder	.10
471	Alan Trammell	.05
472	Kirk Gibson	.05
473	Tony Phillips	.05
474	Mickey Tettleton	.05
475	Lou Whitaker	.05
476	Chris Gomez	.05
477	John Doherty	.05
478	Greg Gohr	.05
479	Bill Gullickson	.05
480	Rick Aguilera	.05

481	Matt Walbeck	.05
482	Kevin Tapani	.05
483	Scott Erickson	.05
484	Steve Dunn	.05
485	David McCarty	.05
486	Scott Leius	.05
487	Pat Meares	.05
488	Jeff Reboulet	.05
489	Pedro Munoz	.05
490	Chuck Knoblauch	.10
491	Rich Becker	.05
492	Alex Cole	.05
493	Pat Mahomes	.05
494	Ozzie Guillen	.05
495	Tim Raines	.05
496	Kirk McCaskill	.05
497	Olmedo Saenz	.05
498	Scott Sanderson	.05
499	Lance Johnson	.05
500	Michael Jordan	2.50
501	Warren Newson	.05
502	Ron Karkovice	.05
503	Wilson Alvarez	.05
504	Jason Bere	.05
505	Robin Ventura	.05
506	Alex Fernandez	.05
507	Roberto Hernandez	.05
508	Norberto Martin	.05
509	Bob Wickman	.05
510	Don Mattingly	.75
511	Melido Perez	.05
512	Pat Kelly	.05
513	Randy Velarde	.05
514	Tony Fernandez	.05
515	Jack McDowell	.10
516	Luis Polonia	.05
517	Bernie Williams	.35
518	Danny Tartabull	.05
519	Mike Stanley	.05
520	Wade Boggs	.25
521	Jim Leyritz	.05
522	Steve Howe	.05
523	Scott Kamieniecki	.05
524	Russ Davis	.05
525	Jim Abbott	.05
526	Checklist 1-106 (Eddie Murray)	.10
527	Checklist 107-212 (Alex Rodriguez)	.40
528	Checklist 213-318 (Jeff Bagwell)	.15
529	Checklist 319-424 (Joe Carter)	.05
530	Checklist 425-530 (Fred McGriff)	.10
---	National Packtime offer card	.05

1995 Collector's Choice Silver Signature

A silver-foil facsimile autograph added to the card front is the only difference between these chase cards and regular-issue Collector's Choice cards. The silver-signature inserts are found one per pack in regular foil packs, and two per pack in retail jumbo packs.

	MT
Complete Set (530):	50.00
Common Player:	.10
Veteran Stars:	1.5-3X
Young Stars/RCs:	1-2X

(See 1995 Collector's Choice for checklist and base card values.)

1995 Collector's Choice Gold Signature

The top-of-the-line chase card in 1995 Collector's Choice is the Gold Signature parallel set. Each of the 530 cards in the set was created in a special gold version that was found on average only one per box of foil packs. Other than the addition of a gold-foil facsimile autograph on front, the cards are identical to regular-issue Collector's Choice.

	MT
Complete Set (530):	800.00
Common Player:	2.00
Veteran Stars:	8-15X
Young Stars/RCs:	4-8X

(See 1995 Collector's Choice for checklist and base card values.)

1995 Collector's Choice Trade Cards

A series of five mail-in redemption cards was included as inserts into UD Collector's Choice, at the rate of approximately one per 11 packs. The cards could be sent in with $2 to receive 11 Collector's Choice Update cards, as specified on the front of the card. The trade offer expired on Feb. 1, 1996. Cards are numbered with the "TC" prefix.

		MT
Complete Set (5):		2.50
Common Player:		.50
1	Larry Walker (#531-541)	.75
2	David Cone (#542-552)	.75
3	Marquis Grissom (#553-563)	.50
4	Terry Pendleton (#564-574)	.50
5	Fernando Valenzuela (#575-585)	.50

1995 Collector's Choice Redemption Cards

These update cards were available only via a mail-in offer involving trade cards found in foil packs. Each trade card was redeemable for a specific 11-card set of players shown in their new uniforms as a result of rookie call-ups, trades and free agent signings. The cards are are in the same format as the regular 1995 Collector's Choice issue. The update redemption cards are numbered by team nickname from Angels through Yankees, the numbers running contiguously from the body of the CC set.

		MT
Complete Set (55):		6.00
Common Player:		.25
531	Tony Phillips	.25
532	Dave Magadan	.25
533	Mike Gallego	.25
534	Dave Stewart	.25
535	Todd Stottlemyre	.30
536	David Cone	1.00
537	Marquis Grissom	.75
538	Derrick May	.25
539	Joe Oliver	.25
540	Scott Cooper	.25
541	Ken Hill	.25
542	Howard Johnson	.25
543	Brian McRae	.35
544	Jaime Navarro	.25
545	Ozzie Timmons	.25
546	Roberto Kelly	.25
547	Hideo Nomo	2.00
548	Shane Andrews	.60
549	Mark Grudzielanek	.30
550	Carlos Perez	.25
551	Henry Rodriguez	.25
552	Tony Tarasco	.25
553	Glenallen Hill	.25
554	Terry Mulholland	.25
555	Orel Hershiser	.75
556	Darren Bragg	.25
557	John Burkett	.25
558	Bobby Witt	.25
559	Terry Pendleton	.25
560	Andre Dawson	.50
561	Brett Butler	.35
562	Kevin Brown	.75
563	Doug Jones	.25
564	Andy Van Slyke	.25
565	Jody Reed	.25
566	Fernando Valenzuela	.35
567	Charlie Hayes	.25
568	Benji Gil	.25
569	Mark McLemore	.25
570	Mickey Tettleton	.25
571	Bob Tewksbury	.25
572	Rheal Cormier	.25
573	Vaughn Eshelman	.25
574	Mike Macfarlane	.25
575	Mark Whiten	.25
576	Benito Santiago	.25
577	Jason Bates	.25
578	Bill Swift	.25
579	Larry Walker	.60
580	Chad Curtis	.35
581	Bobby Higginson	.35
582	Marty Cordova	.75
583	Mike Devereaux	.25
584	John Kruk	.25
585	John Wetteland	.25

1995 Collector's Choice "You Crash the Game"

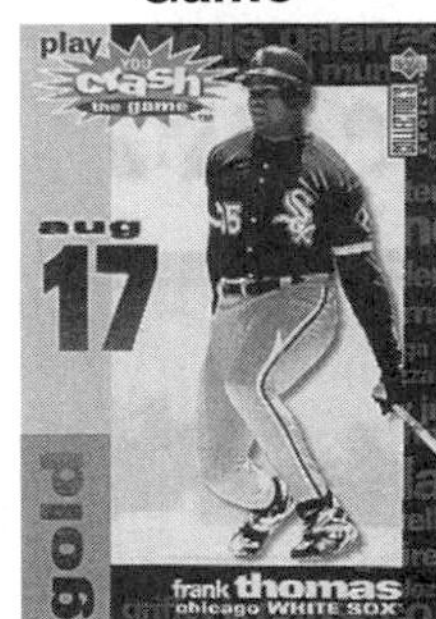

These insert cards gave collectors a reason to follow box scores around the major leagues between June 18-Oct. 1. Each of 20 noted home run hitters can be found with three different dates foil-stamped on the card front. If the player hit a home run on that day, the card could be redeemed for a set of 20 special prize cards. Stated odds of finding a You Crash the Game card were one in five packs. Most of the inserts are silver-foil enhanced, with about one in eight being found with gold foil. Winning cards are much scarcer than the others since they had to be mailed in for redemption.

	MT
Complete Set, Silver (20):	7.00
Common Player, Silver:	.25
Complete Set, Gold (20):	18.00
Common Player, Gold:	.50
Silver Set	7.00
CG1 Jeff Bagwell (July 30)	.25
CG1 Jeff Bagwell (Aug. 13)	.25
CG1 Jeff Bagwell (Sept. 28)	.25
CG2 Albert Belle (June 18)	.40
CG2 Albert Belle (Aug. 26)	.40
CG2 Albert Belle (Sept. 20)	.40
CG3 Barry Bonds (June 28)	.50
CG3 Barry Bonds (July 9)	.50
CG3 Barry Bonds (Sept. 6)	.50
CG4 Jose Canseco (June 30) (winner)	2.00
CG4 Jose Canseco (July 30) (winner)	2.00
CG4 Jose Canseco (Sept. 3)	.50
CG5 Joe Carter (July 14)	.25
CG5 Joe Carter (Aug. 9)	.25
CG5 Joe Carter (Sept. 23)	.25
CG6 Cecil Fielder (July 4)	.25
CG6 Cecil Fielder (Aug. 2)	.25
CG6 Cecil Fielder (Oct. 1)	.25
CG7 Juan Gonzalez (June 29)	.60
CG7 Juan Gonzalez (Aug. 13)	.60
CG7 Juan Gonzalez (Sept. 3) (winner)	2.00
CG8 Ken Griffey Jr. (July 2)	1.00
CG8 Ken Griffey Jr. (Aug. 24) (winner)	5.00
CG8 Ken Griffey Jr. (Sept. 15)	1.00
CG9 Bob Hamelin (July 23)	.25
CG9 Bob Hamelin (Aug. 1)	.25
CG9 Bob Hamelin (Sept. 29)	.25
CG10David Justice (June 24)	.25
CG10David Justice (July 25)	.25
CG10David Justice (Sept. 17)	.25
CG11Ryan Klesko (July 13)	.25
CG11Ryan Klesko (Aug. 20)	.25
CG11Ryan Klesko (Sept. 10)	.25
CG12Fred McGriff (Aug. 25)	.25
CG12Fred McGriff (Sept. 8)	.25
CG12Fred McGriff (Sept. 24)	.25
CG13Mark McGwire (July 23)	1.00
CG13Mark McGwire (Aug. 3) (winner)	3.50
CG13Mark McGwire (Sept. 27)	1.00
CG14Raul Mondesi (July 27) (winner)	2.00
CG14Raul Mondesi (Aug. 13)	.40
CG14Raul Mondesi (Sept. 15) (winner)	2.00
CG15Mike Piazza (July 23) (winner)	3.00
CG15Mike Piazza (Aug. 27) (winner)	3.00
CG15Mike Piazza (Sept. 19)	.65
CG16Manny Ramirez (June 21)	.25
CG16Manny Ramirez (Aug. 13)	.25
CG16Manny Ramirez (Sept. 26)	.25
CG17Alex Rodriguez (Sept. 10)	.50
CG17Alex Rodriguez (Sept. 18)	.50
CG17Alex Rodriguez (Sept. 24)	.50
CG18Gary Sheffield (July 5)	.25
CG18Gary Sheffield (Aug. 13)	.25
CG18Gary Sheffield (Sept. 4) (winner)	2.00
CG19Frank Thomas (July 26)	.75
CG19Frank Thomas (Aug. 17)	.75
CG19Frank Thomas (Sept. 23)	.75
CG20Matt Williams (July 29)	.25
CG20Matt Williams (Aug. 12)	.25
CG20Matt Williams (Sept. 19)	.25
Gold Set	18.00
CG1 Jeff Bagwell (July 30)	1.00
CG1 Jeff Bagwell (Aug. 13)	1.00
CG1 Jeff Bagwell (Sept. 28)	1.00
CG2 Albert Belle (June 18)	1.25
CG2 Albert Belle (Aug. 26)	1.25
CG2 Albert Belle (Sept. 20)	1.25
CG3 Barry Bonds (June 28)	1.50
CG3 Barry Bonds (July 9)	1.50
CG3 Barry Bonds (Sept. 6)	1.50
CG4 Jose Canseco (June 30) (winner)	3.00
CG4 Jose Canseco (July 30) (winner)	3.00
CG4 Jose Canseco (Sept. 3)	1.25
CG5 Joe Carter (July 14)	.75
CG5 Joe Carter (Aug. 9)	.75
CG5 Joe Carter (Sept. 23)	.75
CG6 Cecil Fielder (July 4)	.75
CG6 Cecil Fielder (Aug. 2)	.75
CG6 Cecil Fielder (Oct. 1)	.75
CG7 Juan Gonzalez (June 29)	1.00
CG7 Juan Gonzalez (Aug. 13)	1.00
CG7 Juan Gonzalez (Sept. 3) (winner)	4.00
CG8 Ken Griffey Jr. (July 2)	3.00
CG8 Ken Griffey Jr. (Aug. 24) (winner)	6.00
CG8 Ken Griffey Jr. (Sept. 15)	3.00
CG9 Bob Hamelin (July 23)	.50
CG9 Bob Hamelin (Aug. 1)	.50
CG9 Bob Hamelin (Sept. 29)	.50
CG10David Justice (June 24)	.75
CG10David Justice (July 25)	.75
CG10David Justice (Sept. 17)	.75
CG11Ryan Klesko (July 13)	.75
CG11Ryan Klesko (Aug. 20)	.75
CG11Ryan Klesko (Sept. 10)	.75
CG12Fred McGriff (Aug. 25)	.75
CG12Fred McGriff (Sept. 8)	.75
CG12Fred McGriff (Sept. 24)	.75
CG13Mark McGwire (July 23)	2.00
CG13Mark McGwire (Aug. 3) (winner)	6.00
CG13Mark McGwire (Sept. 27)	2.00
CG14Raul Mondesi (July 27) (winner)	2.50
CG14Raul Mondesi (Aug. 13)	.90
CG14Raul Mondesi (Sept. 15) (winner)	2.50
CG15Mike Piazza (July 23) (winner)	4.00
CG15Mike Piazza (Aug. 27) (winner)	4.00
CG15Mike Piazza (Sept. 19)	1.25
CG16Manny Ramirez (June 21)	.75
CG16Manny Ramirez (Aug. 13)	.75
CG16Manny Ramirez (Sept. 26)	.75
CG17Alex Rodriguez (Sept. 10)	1.25
CG17Alex Rodriguez (Sept. 18)	1.25
CG17Alex Rodriguez (Sept. 24)	1.25
CG18Gary Sheffield (July 5)	.75
CG18Gary Sheffield (Aug. 13)	.75
CG18Gary Sheffield (Sept. 4) (winner)	2.50
CG19Frank Thomas (July 26)	1.50
CG19Frank Thomas (Aug. 17)	1.50
CG19Frank Thomas (Sept. 23)	1.50
CG20Matt Williams (July 29)	1.00
CG20Matt Williams (Aug. 12)	1.00
CG20Matt Williams (Sept. 19)	1.00

1995 Collector's Choice "Crash" Winners

These 20-card sets were awarded to collectors who redeemed "You Crash the Game" winners cards. A silver-foil enhanced set was sent to winners with silver redemption cards, a gold version was sent to gold winners. A $3 redemption fee was required. Fronts are similar to the game cards, except for the foil printing down the left side in the place of the game date. Instead of redemption rules on the back of award cards there are career highlights at left and a panel at right with the names of the players in the set.

	MT
Complete Set, Silver (20):	12.00
Complete Set, Gold (20):	45.00
Common Player, Silver:	.50
Common Player, Gold:	2.00
SILVER SET	
CR1 Jeff Bagwell	1.50
CR2 Albert Belle	1.50
CR3 Barry Bonds	1.50
CR4 Jose Canseco	1.50
CR5 Joe Carter	.75
CR6 Cecil Fielder	.75
CR7 Juan Gonzalez	2.00
CR8 Ken Griffey Jr.	6.00
CR9 Bob Hamelin	.50
CR10Dave Justice	1.00
CR11Ryan Klesko	.75
CR12Fred McGriff	1.00
CR13Mark McGwire	5.00
CR14Raul Mondesi	1.00
CR15Mike Piazza	3.00
CR16Manny Ramirez	1.00
CR17Alex Rodriguez	1.50
CR18Gary Sheffield	.75
CR19Frank Thomas	3.00
CR20Matt Williams	1.00
GOLD SET	
CR1 Jeff Bagwell	5.00
CR2 Albert Belle	5.00
CR3 Barry Bonds	5.00
CR4 Jose Canseco	4.00
CR5 Joe Carter	2.00
CR6 Cecil Fielder	2.00
CR7 Juan Gonzalez	7.50
CR8 Ken Griffey Jr.	15.00
CR9 Bob Hamelin	2.00
CR10Dave Justice	3.50
CR11Ryan Klesko	3.50
CR12Fred McGriff	3.50
CR13Mark McGwire	12.50
CR14Raul Mondesi	3.50
CR15Mike Piazza	7.50
CR16Manny Ramirez	3.50
CR17Alex Rodriguez	5.00
CR18Gary Sheffield	3.00
CR19Frank Thomas	5.00
CR20Matt Williams	4.00

1995 Collector's Choice/SE

The first Upper Deck baseball card issue for 1995 was this 265-card issue which uses blue borders and a blue foil "Special Edition" trapezoidal logo to impart a premium look. The set opens with a Rookie Class subset of 25 cards on which the background has been rendered in orange hues. A series of six Record Pace cards, horizontal with blue and yellow backgrounds, immediately precedes the regular cards. Base cards in the set are arranged in team-alpha order. Front and back have large color photos, while backs offer complete major league stats. Interspersed within the teams are special cards with borderless front designs honoring players who won significant awards in the 1994 season. Another subset, Stat Leaders, pictures various players in a silver dollar-sized circle at the center of the card and lists the 1994 leaders in that category on the back. A dozen-card Fantasy Team subset near the end of the set lists on back the top-rated players at each position, picturing one of them on front, with a giant blue baseball. The set closes with five checklists honoring career highlights from the '94 season.

		MT
Complete Set (265):		20.00
Common Player:		.05
Pack (12):		1.25
Wax Box (36):		35.00
1	Alex Rodriguez	3.00
2	Derek Jeter	1.50
3	Dustin Hermanson	.15
4	Bill Pulsipher	.15
5	Terrell Wade	.05
6	Darren Dreifort	.05
7	LaTroy Hawkins	.15
8	Alex Ochoa	.08
9	Paul Wilson	.15
10	Ernie Young	.08
11	Alan Benes	.15
12	Garret Anderson	.15
13	Armando Benitez	.15
14	Robert Perez	.05
15	Herbert Perry	.05
16	Jose Silva	.05
17	Orlando Miller	.10
18	Russ Davis	.10
19	Jason Isringhausen	.15
20	Ray McDavid	.05
21	Duane Singleton	.05
22	Paul Shuey	.05
23	Steve Dunn	.05
24	Mike Lieberthal	.10
25	Chan Ho Park	.10
26	Ken Griffey Jr. (Record Pace)	1.00
27	Tony Gwynn (Record Pace)	.35
28	Chuck Knoblauch (Record Pace)	.10
29	Frank Thomas (Record Pace)	.75
30	Matt Williams (Record Pace)	.10
31	Chili Davis	.05
32	Chad Curtis	.05
33	Brian Anderson	.05
34	Chuck Finley	.05
35	Tim Salmon	.25
36	Bo Jackson	.10
37	Doug Drabek	.05
38	Craig Biggio	.10
39	Ken Caminiti	.20
40	Jeff Bagwell	1.00
41	Darryl Kile	.05
42	John Hudek	.05
43	Brian L. Hunter	.08
44	Dennis Eckersley	.08
45	Mark McGwire	3.00
46	Brent Gates	.05
47	Steve Karsay	.05
48	Rickey Henderson	.12
49	Terry Steinbach	.05
50	Ruben Sierra	.05
51	Roberto Alomar	.60
52	Carlos Delgado	.25
53	Alex Gonzalez	.10
54	Joe Carter	.08
55	Paul Molitor	.40
56	Juan Guzman	.05
57	John Olerud	.15
58	Shawn Green	.15
59	Tom Glavine	.15
60	Greg Maddux	1.50
61	Roberto Kelly	.05
62	Ryan Klesko	.20
63	Javier Lopez	.15
64	Jose Oliva	.05
65	Fred McGriff	.20
66	Steve Avery	.05
67	Dave Justice	.15
68	Ricky Bones	.05
69	Cal Eldred	.05
70	Greg Vaughn	.10
71	Dave Nilsson	.05
72	Jose Valentin	.05
73	Matt Mieske	.05
74	Todd Zeile	.05
75	Ozzie Smith	.40
76	Bernard Gilkey	.05
77	Ray Lankford	.08
78	Bob Tewksbury	.05
79	Mark Whiten	.05
80	Gregg Jefferies	.05
81	Randy Myers	.05
82	Shawon Dunston	.05
83	Mark Grace	.15
84	Derrick May	.05
85	Sammy Sosa	.75
86	Steve Trachsel	.05
87	Brett Butler	.08
88	Delino DeShields	.05
89	Orel Hershiser	.10
90	Mike Piazza	1.50
91	Todd Hollandsworth	.15
92	Eric Karros	.08
93	Ramon Martinez	.10
94	Tim Wallach	.05
95	Raul Mondesi	.25
96	Larry Walker	.25
97	Wil Cordero	.05
98	Marquis Grissom	.05
99	Ken Hill	.05
100	Cliff Floyd	.10
101	Pedro J. Martinez	.25
102	John Wetteland	.05
103	Rondell White	.15
104	Moises Alou	.10
105	Barry Bonds	.75
106	Darren Lewis	.05
107	Mark Portugal	.05
108	Matt Williams	.25
109	William Van Landingham	.05
110	Bill Swift	.05
111	Robby Thompson	.05
112	Rod Beck	.05
113	Darryl Strawberry	.10
114	Jim Thome	.30
115	Dave Winfield	.10
116	Eddie Murray	.35
117	Manny Ramirez	.75
118	Carlos Baerga	.05
119	Kenny Lofton	.45
120	Albert Belle	.60
121	Mark Clark	.05
122	Dennis Martinez	.05
123	Randy Johnson	.40
124	Jay Buhner	.10
125	Ken Griffey Jr.	3.00
125a	Ken Griffey Jr. (overprinted "For Promotional Use Only")	3.00
126	Rich Gossage	.05
127	Tino Martinez	.10
128	Reggie Jefferson	.05
129	Edgar Martinez	.05
130	Gary Sheffield	.20
131	Pat Rapp	.05
132	Bret Barberie	.05
133	Chuck Carr	.05
134	Jeff Conine	.05
135	Charles Johnson	.15
136	Benito Santiago	.05
137	Matt Williams (Stat Leaders)	.15
138	Jeff Bagwell (Stat Leaders)	.35
139	Kenny Lofton (Stat Leaders)	.15
140	Tony Gwynn (Stat Leaders)	.35
141	Jimmy Key (Stat Leaders)	.05
142	Greg Maddux (Stat Leaders)	.60
143	Randy Johnson (Stat Leaders)	.20
144	Lee Smith (Stat Leaders)	.05
145	Bobby Bonilla	.05
146	Jason Jacome	.05
147	Jeff Kent	.05
148	Ryan Thompson	.05
149	Bobby Jones	.05
150	Bret Saberhagen	.05
151	John Franco	.05
152	Lee Smith	.05
153	Rafael Palmeiro	.15
154	Brady Anderson	.10
155	Cal Ripken Jr.	2.50
156	Jeffrey Hammonds	.10
157	Mike Mussina	.30
158	Chris Hoiles	.05
159	Ben McDonald	.05
160	Tony Gwynn	1.00
161	Joey Hamilton	.10
162	Andy Benes	.05
163	Trevor Hoffman	.08
164	Phil Plantier	.05
165	Derek Bell	.05
166	Bip Roberts	.05
167	Eddie Williams	.05
168	Fernando Valenzuela	.05
169	Mariano Duncan	.05
170	Lenny Dykstra	.05
171	Darren Daulton	.05
172	Danny Jackson	.05
173	Bobby Munoz	.05
174	Doug Jones	.05
175	Jay Bell	.05
176	Zane Smith	.05
177	Jon Lieber	.05
178	Carlos Garcia	.05
179	Orlando Merced	.05
180	Andy Van Slyke	.05
181	Rick Helling	.05
182	Rusty Greer	.05
183	Kenny Rogers	.05
184	Will Clark	.25
185	Jose Canseco	.40
186	Juan Gonzalez	1.00
187	Dean Palmer	.05
188	Ivan Rodriguez	.50
189	John Valentin	.10
190	Roger Clemens	1.00
191	Aaron Sele	.05
192	Scott Cooper	.05
193	Mike Greenwell	.05
194	Mo Vaughn	.60
195	Andre Dawson	.10
196	Ron Gant	.08
197	Jose Rijo	.05
198	Bret Boone	.05
199	Deion Sanders	.15
200	Barry Larkin	.15
201	Hal Morris	.05
202	Reggie Sanders	.05
203	Kevin Mitchell	.05
204	Marvin Freeman	.05
205	Andres Galarraga	.15
206	Walt Weiss	.05
207	Charlie Hayes	.05
208	David Nied	.05
209	Dante Bichette	.15
210	David Cone	.10
211	Jeff Montgomery	.05
212	Felix Jose	.05
213	Mike Macfarlane	.05
214	Wally Joyner	.05
215	Bob Hamelin	.05
216	Brian McRae	.05
217	Kirk Gibson	.05
218	Lou Whitaker	.05
219	Chris Gomez	.05
220	Cecil Fielder	.10
221	Mickey Tettleton	.05
222	Travis Fryman	.08
223	Tony Phillips	.05
224	Rick Aguilera	.05
225	Scott Erickson	.05
226	Chuck Knoblauch	.15
227	Kent Hrbek	.05
228	Shane Mack	.05
229	Kevin Tapani	.05
230	Kirby Puckett	1.00
231	Julio Franco	.05
232	Jack McDowell	.05
233	Jason Bere	.05
234	Alex Fernandez	.08
235	Frank Thomas	1.50
236	Ozzie Guillen	.05
237	Robin Ventura	.08
238	Michael Jordan	3.50
239	Wilson Alvarez	.05
240	Don Mattingly	.75
241	Jim Abbott	.05
242	Jim Leyritz	.05
243	Paul O'Neill	.08
244	Melido Perez	.05
245	Wade Boggs	.35
246	Mike Stanley	.05
247	Danny Tartabull	.05
248	Jimmy Key	.05
249	Greg Maddux (Fantasy Team)	.60
250	Randy Johnson (Fantasy Team)	.20
251	Bret Saberhagen (Fantasy Team)	.05
252	John Wetteland (Fantasy Team)	.05
253	Mike Piazza (Fantasy Team)	.50
254	Jeff Bagwell (Fantasy Team)	.30
255	Craig Biggio (Fantasy Team)	.05
256	Matt Williams (Fantasy Team)	.10
257	Wil Cordero (Fantasy Team)	.05
258	Kenny Lofton (Fantasy Team)	.15
259	Barry Bonds (Fantasy Team)	.30
260	Dante Bichette (Fantasy Team)	.10
261	Checklist 1-53	.05
262	Checklist 54-106	.05
263	Checklist 107-159	.05
264	Checklist 160-212	.05
265	Checklist 213-265	.05

1995 Collector's Choice/SE Silver

The cards in this parallel edition feature the addition of a silver-foil facsimile autograph on the card front. Also, the blue SE logo and card borders have been replaced with silver on the chase cards, which are found on average of one per pack.

	MT
Complete Set (265):	50.00
Common Player:	.15
Stars:	1.5-3X
Young Stars/RCs:	1-2X

(For checklist and base card values, see 1995 Collector's Choice SE.)

1995 Collector's Choice/SE Gold

Each of the cards in the SE issue can be found in a premium chase card version which replaces the blue border and SE logo with gold, and adds a gold-foil facsimile autograph to the front of the card. The gold-version SE inserts are found on average of one per 36 packs.

	MT
Complete Set (265):	1200.
Common Player:	2.00
Stars:	10-20X
Young Stars/RCs:	8-12X

(For checklist and base card values, see 1995 Collector's Choice SE.)

1996 Collector's Choice Promo

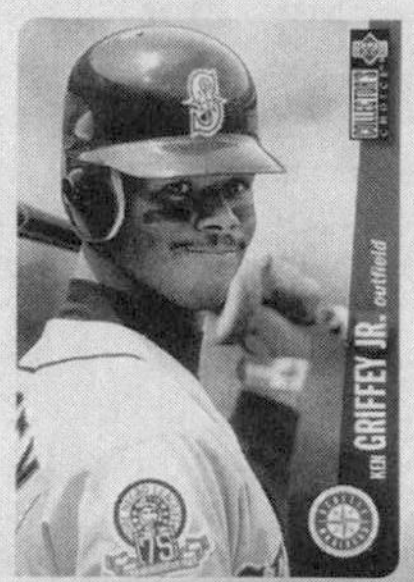

To introduce its base-brand set, Upper Deck issued a promotional sample card of Ken Griffey, Jr. Numbered 100 (he's #310 in the issued set), the back is overprinted "For Promotional Use Only".

		MT
100	Ken Griffey Jr.	6.00

1996 Collector's Choice

The third year for Collector's Choice includes 730 cards in two series with packs formatted in retail and hobby versions. The 280 regular player cards are joined by subsets of Rookie Class, International Flavor, Traditional Threads, Fantasy Team, Stat Leaders, Season Highlights, First Class, Arizona Fall League, Awards and Checklists. Packs feature a number of different insert sets including silver and gold signature parallel sets, interactive "You Make the Play" cards, four cards from the cross-brand Cal Ripken Collection and three postseason trade cards redeemable for 10-card sets recalling the League Championships and World Series. An additional 30 cards (#761-790) featuring traded players in their new uniforms was issued only in factory sets.

		MT
Complete Series 1-2 Set: (760):		20.00
Complete Factory Set (790):		30.00
Complete Series 1 (1-365):		10.00
Complete Series 2 (396-760):		10.00
Traded Set (366T-395T):		6.00
Common Player:		.05
Series 1 Pack (12):		1.00
Series 1 Wax Box (36):		28.00
Series 2 Pack (14):		1.00
Series 2 Wax Box (40):		30.00
1	Cal Ripken Jr.	1.75
2	Edgar Martinez, Tony Gwynn (1995 Stat Leaders)	.35
3	Albert Belle, Dante Bichette (1995 Stat Leaders)	.30
4	Albert Belle, Mo Vaughn, Dante Bichette (1995 Stat Leaders)	.30
5	Kenny Lofton, Quilvio Veras (1995 Stat Leaders)	.30
6	Mike Mussina, Greg Maddux (1995 Stat Leaders)	1.00
7	Randy Johnson, Hideo Nomo (1995 Stat Leaders)	.25
8	Randy Johnson, Greg Maddux (1995 Stat Leaders)	1.00
9	Jose Mesa, Randy Myers (1995 Stat Leaders)	.05
10	Johnny Damon (Rookie Class)	.25
11	Rick Krivda (Rookie Class)	.05
12	Roger Cedeno (Rookie Class)	.05
13	Angel Martinez (Rookie Class)	.05
14	Ariel Prieto (Rookie Class)	.05
15	John Wasdin (Rookie Class)	.05
16	Edwin Hurtado (Rookie Class)	.05
17	Lyle Mouton (Rookie Class)	.05
18	Chris Snopek (Rookie Class)	.10
19	Mariano Rivera (Rookie Class)	.15
20	Ruben Rivera (Rookie Class)	.40
21	*Juan Castro* (Rookie Class)	.15
22	Jimmy Haynes (Rookie Class)	.05
23	Bob Wolcott (Rookie Class)	.05
24	Brian Barber (Rookie Class)	.05
25	Frank Rodriguez (Rookie Class)	.05
26	Jesus Tavarez (Rookie Class)	.05
27	Glenn Dishman (Rookie Class)	.05
28	Jose Herrera (Rookie Class)	.05
29	Chan Ho Park (Rookie Class)	.05
30	Jason Isringhausen (Rookie Class)	.15
31	Doug Johns (Rookie Class)	.05
32	Gene Schall (Rookie Class)	.05
33	Kevin Jordan (Rookie Class)	.05
34	*Matt Lawton* (Rookie Class)	.20
35	Karim Garcia (Rookie Class)	.30
36	George Williams (Rookie Class)	.05
37	Orlando Palmeiro (Rookie Class)	.05
38	Jamie Brewington (Rookie Class)	.05
39	Robert Person (Rookie Class)	.05
40	Greg Maddux	1.00
41	Marquis Grissom	.10
42	Chipper Jones	1.25
43	David Justice	.15
44	Mark Lemke	.05
45	Fred McGriff	.25
46	Javy Lopez	.15
47	Mark Wohlers	.05
48	Jason Schmidt	.10
49	John Smoltz	.15
50	Curtis Goodwin	.05
51	Greg Zaun	.05
52	Armando Benitez	.05
53	Manny Alexander	.05
54	Chris Hoiles	.05
55	Harold Baines	.05
56	Ben McDonald	.05
57	Scott Erickson	.05
58	Jeff Manto	.05
59	Luis Alicea	.05
60	Roger Clemens	.35
61	Rheal Cormier	.05
62	Vaughn Eshelman	.05
63	Zane Smith	.05
64	Mike Macfarlane	.05
65	Erik Hanson	.05
66	Tim Naehring	.05
67	Lee Tinsley	.05
68	Troy O'Leary	.05
69	Garret Anderson	.05
70	Chili Davis	.05
71	Jim Edmonds	.15
72	Troy Percival	.05
73	Mark Langston	.05
74	Spike Owen	.05
75	Tim Salmon	.25
76	Brian Anderson	.05
77	Lee Smith	.05
78	Jim Abbott	.05
79	Jim Bullinger	.05
80	Mark Grace	.10
81	Todd Zeile	.05
82	Kevin Foster	.05
83	Howard Johnson	.05
84	Brian McRae	.05
85	Randy Myers	.05
86	Jaime Navarro	.05
87	Luis Gonzalez	.05
88	Ozzie Timmons	.05
89	Wilson Alvarez	.05
90	Frank Thomas	1.00
91	James Baldwin	.05
92	Ray Durham	.05
93	Alex Fernandez	.05
94	Ozzie Guillen	.05
95	Tim Raines	.05
96	Roberto Hernandez	.05
97	Lance Johnson	.05
98	John Kruk	.05
99	Mark Portugal	.05
100	Don Mattingly (Traditional Threads)	.50
101	Jose Canseco (Traditional Threads)	.20
102	Raul Mondesi (Traditional Threads)	.20
103	Cecil Fielder (Traditional Threads)	.05
104	Ozzie Smith (Traditional Threads)	.15
105	Frank Thomas (Traditional Threads)	.50
106	Sammy Sosa (Traditional Threads)	.50

No.	Card	Value
107	Fred McGriff (Traditional Threads)	.20
108	Barry Bonds (Traditional Threads)	.25
109	Thomas Howard	.05
110	Ron Gant	.05
111	Eddie Taubensee	.05
112	Hal Morris	.05
113	Jose Rijo	.05
114	Pete Schourek	.05
115	Reggie Sanders	.05
116	Benito Santiago	.05
117	Jeff Brantley	.05
118	Julian Tavarez	.05
119	Carlos Baerga	.15
120	Jim Thome	.30
121	Jose Mesa	.05
122	Dennis Martinez	.05
123	Dave Winfield	.05
124	Eddie Murray	.25
125	Manny Ramirez	.75
126	Paul Sorrento	.05
127	Kenny Lofton	.50
128	Eric Young	.05
129	Jason Bates	.05
130	Bret Saberhagen	.05
131	Andres Galarraga	.10
132	Joe Girardi	.05
133	John Vander Wal	.05
134	David Nied	.05
135	Dante Bichette	.20
136	Vinny Castilla	.05
137	Kevin Ritz	.05
138	Felipe Lira	.05
139	Joe Boever	.05
140	Cecil Fielder	.15
141	John Flaherty	.05
142	Kirk Gibson	.05
143	Brian Maxcy	.05
144	Lou Whitaker	.05
145	Alan Trammell	.05
146	Bobby Higginson	.05
147	Chad Curtis	.05
148	Quilvio Veras	.05
149	Jerry Browne	.05
150	Andre Dawson	.05
151	Robb Nen	.05
152	Greg Colbrunn	.05
153	Chris Hammond	.05
154	Kurt Abbott	.05
155	Charles Johnson	.05
156	Terry Pendleton	.05
157	Dave Weathers	.05
158	Mike Hampton	.05
159	Craig Biggio	.05
160	Jeff Bagwell	.75
161	Brian L. Hunter	.10
162	Mike Henneman	.05
163	Dave Magadan	.05
164	Shane Reynolds	.05
165	Derek Bell	.05
166	Orlando Miller	.05
167	James Mouton	.05
168	Melvin Bunch	.05
169	Tom Gordon	.05
170	Kevin Appier	.05
171	Tom Goodwin	.05
172	Greg Gagne	.05
173	Gary Gaetti	.05
174	Jeff Montgomery	.05
175	Jon Nunnally	.05
176	Michael Tucker	.05
177	Joe Vitiello	.05
178	Billy Ashley	.05
179	Tom Candiotti	.05
180	Hideo Nomo	.25
181	Chad Fonville	.05
182	Todd Hollandsworth	.10
183	Eric Karros	.05
184	Roberto Kelly	.05
185	Mike Piazza	1.00
186	Ramon Martinez	.05
187	Tim Wallach	.05
188	Jeff Cirillo	.05
189	Sid Roberson	.05
190	Kevin Seitzer	.05
191	Mike Fetters	.05
192	Steve Sparks	.05
193	Matt Mieske	.05
194	Joe Oliver	.05
195	B.J. Surhoff	.05
196	Alberto Reyes	.05
197	Fernando Vina	.05
198	LaTroy Hawkins	.05
199	Marty Cordova	.10
200	Kirby Puckett	.75
201	Brad Radke	.05
202	(Pedro Munoz)	.05
203	Scott Klingenbeck	.05
204	Pat Meares	.05
205	Chuck Knoblauch	.05
206	Scott Stahoviak	.05
207	Dave Stevens	.05
208	Shane Andrews	.05
209	Moises Alou	.05
210	David Segui	.05
211	Cliff Floyd	.05
212	Carlos Perez	.05
213	Mark Grudzielanek	.05
214	Butch Henry	.05
215	Rondell White	.10
216	Mel Rojas	.05
217	Ugueth Urbina	.05
218	Edgardo Alfonzo	.05
219	Carl Everett	.05
220	John Franco	.05
221	Todd Hundley	.05
222	Bobby Jones	.05
223	Bill Pulsipher	.15
224	Rico Brogna	.05
225	Jeff Kent	.05
226	Chris Jones	.05
227	Butch Huskey	.05
228	Robert Eenhoorn	.05
229	Sterling Hitchcock	.05
230	Wade Boggs	.15
231	Derek Jeter	1.00
232	Tony Fernandez	.05
233	Jack McDowell	.10
234	Andy Pettitte	.50
235	David Cone	.10
236	Mike Stanley	.05
237	Don Mattingly	.75
238	Geronimo Berroa	.05
239	Scott Brosius	.05
240	Rickey Henderson	.10
241	Terry Steinbach	.05
242	Mike Gallego	.05
243	Jason Giambi	.05
244	Steve Ontiveros	.05
245	Dennis Eckersley	.05
246	Dave Stewart	.05
247	Don Wengert	.05
248	Paul Quantrill	.05
249	Ricky Bottalico	.05
250	Kevin Stocker	.05
251	Lenny Dykstra	.05
252	Tony Longmire	.05
253	Tyler Green	.05
254	Mike Mimbs	.05
255	Charlie Hayes	.05
256	Mickey Morandini	.05
257	Heathcliff Slocumb	.05
258	Jeff King	.05
259	Midre Cummings	.05
260	Mark Johnson	.05
261	Freddy Garcia	.05
262	Jon Lieber	.05
263	Esteban Loaiza	.10
264	Danny Miceli	.05
265	Orlando Merced	.05
266	Denny Neagle	.05
267	Steve Parris	.05
268	Fantasy Team '95 (Greg Maddux)	.60
269	Fantasy Team '95 (Randy Johnson)	.10
270	Fantasy Team '95 (Hideo Nomo)	.25
271	Fantasy Team '95 (Jose Mesa)	.05
272	Fantasy Team '95 (Mike Piazza)	.50
273	Fantasy Team '95 (Mo Vaughn)	.30
274	Fantasy Team '95 (Craig Biggio)	.05
275	Fantasy Team '95 (Edgar Martinez)	.05
276	Fantasy Team '95 (Barry Larkin)	.15
277	Fantasy Team '95 (Sammy Sosa)	.50
278	Fantasy Team '95 (Dante Bichette)	.05
279	Fantasy Team '95 (Albert Belle)	.40
280	Ozzie Smith	.30
281	Mark Sweeney	.05
282	Terry Bradshaw	.05
283	Allen Battle	.05
284	Danny Jackson	.05
285	Tom Henke	.05
286	Scott Cooper	.05
287	Tripp Cromer	.05
288	Bernard Gilkey	.05
289	Brian Jordan	.05
290	Tony Gwynn	.75
291	Brad Ausmus	.05
292	Bryce Florie	.05
293	Andres Berumen	.05
294	Ken Caminiti	.10
295	Bip Roberts	.05
296	Trevor Hoffman	.05
297	Roberto Petagine	.05
298	Jody Reed	.05
299	Fernando Valenzuela	.05
300	Barry Bonds	.50
301	Mark Leiter	.05
302	Mark Carreon	.05
303	Royce Clayton	.05
304	Kirt Manwaring	.05
305	Glenallen Hill	.05
306	Deion Sanders	.20
307	Joe Rosselli	.05
308	Robby Thompson	.05
309	William Van Landingham	.05
310	Ken Griffey Jr.	2.00
311	Bobby Ayala	.05
312	Joey Cora	.05
313	Mike Blowers	.05
314	Darren Bragg	.05
315	Randy Johnson	.25
316	Alex Rodriguez	2.00
317	Andy Benes	.05
318	Tino Martinez	.05
319	Dan Wilson	.05
320	Will Clark	.30
321	Jeff Frye	.05
322	Benji Gil	.05
323	Rick Helling	.05
324	Mark McLemore	.05
325	Dave Nilsson (International Flavor)	.05
326	Larry Walker (International Flavor)	.20
327	Jose Canseco (International Flavor)	.20
328	Raul Mondesi (International Flavor)	.25
329	Manny Ramirez (International Flavor)	.40
330	Robert Eenhoorn (International Flavor)	.05
331	Chili Davis (International Flavor)	.05
332	Hideo Nomo (International Flavor)	.25
333	Benji Gil (International Flavor)	.05
334	Fernando Valenzuela (International Flavor)	.05
335	Dennis Martinez (International Flavor)	.05
336	Roberto Kelly (International Flavor)	.05
337	Carlos Baerga (International Flavor)	.10
338	Juan Gonzalez (International Flavor)	.40
339	Roberto Alomar (International Flavor)	.25
340	Chan Ho Park (International Flavor)	.05
341	Andres Galarraga (International Flavor)	.10
342	Midre Cummings (International Flavor)	.05
343	Otis Nixon	.05
344	Jeff Russell	.05
345	Ivan Rodriguez	.25
346	Mickey Tettleton	.05
347	Bob Tewksbury	.05
348	Domingo Cedeno	.05
349	Lance Parrish	.05
350	Joe Carter	.15
351	Devon White	.05
352	Carlos Delgado	.25
353	Alex Gonzalez	.05
354	Darren Hall	.05
355	Paul Molitor	.25
356	Al Leiter	.05
357	Randy Knorr	.05
358	Checklist 1-46 (12-player Astros-Padres trade)	.05
359	Checklist 47-92 (Hideo Nomo)	.10
360	Checklist 93-138 (Ramon Martinez)	.05
361	Checklist 139-184 (Robin Ventura)	.05
362	Checklist 185-230 (Cal Ripken Jr.)	.30
363	Checklist 231-275 (Ken Caminiti)	.05
364	Checklist 276-320 (Eddie Murray)	.10
365	Checklist 321-365 (Randy Johnson)	.10
366	A.L. Divisional Series (Tony Pena)	.10
367	A.L. Divisional Series (Jim Thome)	.10
368	A.L. Divisional Series (Don Mattingly)	.40
369	A.L. Divisional Series (Jim Leyritz)	.10
370	A.L. Divisional Series (Ken Griffey Jr.)	1.25
371	A.L. Divisional Series (Edgar Martinez)	.10
372	N.L. Divisional Series (Pete Schourek)	.10
373	N.L. Divisional Series (Mark Lewis)	.10
374	N.L. Divisonal Series (Chipper Jones)	1.00
375	N.L. Divisonal Series (Fred McGriff)	.25
376	N.L. Championship Series (Javy Lopez)	.15
377	N.L. Championship Series (Fred McGriff)	.25
378	N.L. Championship Series (Charlie O'Brien)	.10
379	N.L. Championship Series (Mike Devereaux)	.10
380	N.L. Championship Series (Mark Wohlers)	.10
381	A.L. Championship Series (Bob Wolcott)	.10
382	A.L. Championship Series (Manny Ramirez)	.25
383	A.L. Championship Series (Jay Buhner)	.15
384	A.L. Championship Series (Orel Hershiser)	.10
385	A.L. Championship Series (Kenny Lofton)	.25
386	World Series (Greg Maddux)	1.00
387	World Series (Javy Lopez)	.15
388	World Series (Kenny Lofton)	.25
389	World Series (Eddie Murray)	.30
390	World Series (Luis Polonia)	.10
391	World Series (Pedro Borbon)	.10
392	World Series (Jim Thome)	.20
393	World Series (Orel Hershiser)	.15
394	World Series (David Justice)	.20
395	World Series (Tom Glavine)	.20
396	Braves Team Checklist (Greg Maddux)	.25
397	Mets Team Checklist (Brett Butler)	.05
398	Phillies Team Checklist (Darren Daulton)	.05

399 Marlins Team Checklist (Gary Sheffield) .10
400 Expos Team Checklist (Moises Alou) .05
401 Reds Team Checklist (Barry Larkin) .10
402 Astros Team Checklist (Jeff Bagwell) .20
403 Cubs Team Checklist (Sammy Sosa) .40
404 Cardinals Team Checklist (Ozzie Smith) .10
405 Pirates Team Checklist (Jeff King) .05
406 Dodgers Team Checklist (Mike Piazza) .25
407 Rockies Team Checklist (Dante Bichette) .10
408 Padres Team Checklist (Tony Gwynn) .15
409 Giants Team Checklist (Barry Bonds) .15
410 Indians Team Checklist (Kenny Lofton) .15
411 Royals Team Checklist (Jon Nunnally) .05
412 White Sox Team Checklist (Frank Thomas) .25
413 Brewers Team Checklist (Greg Vaughn) .05
414 Twins Team Checklist (Paul Molitor) .10
415 Mariners Team Checklist (Ken Griffey Jr.) .50
416 Angels Team Checklist (Jim Edmonds) .05
417 Rangers Team Checklist (Juan Gonzalez) .25
418 Athletics Team Checklist (Mark McGwire) .75
419 Red Sox Team Checklist (Roger Clemens) .15
420 Yankees Team Checklist (Wade Boggs) .05
421 Orioles Team Checklist (Cal Ripken Jr.) .40
422 Tigers Team Checklist (Cecil Fielder) .05
423 Blue Jays Team Checklist (Joe Carter) .05
424 *Osvaldo Fernandez* (Rookie Class) .20
425 Billy Wagner (Rookie Class) .10
426 George Arias (Rookie Class) .05
427 Mendy Lopez (Rookie Class) .05
428 Jeff Suppan (Rookie Class) .05
429 Rey Ordonez (Rookie Class) .25
430 Brooks Kieschnick (Rookie Class) .10
431 *Raul Ibanez* (Rookie Class) .10
432 *Livan Hernandez* (Rookie Class) .75
433 Shannon Stewart (Rookie Class) .05
434 Steve Cox (Rookie Class) .05
435 Trey Beamon (Rookie Class) .05
436 Sergio Nunez (Rookie Class) .05
437 Jermaine Dye (Rookie Class) .15
438 *Mike Sweeney* (Rookie Class) .15
439 Richard Hidalgo (Rookie Class) .05
440 Todd Greene (Rookie Class) .15
441 *Robert Smith* (Rookie Class) .25
442 Rafael Orellano (Rookie Class) .15
443 *Wilton Guerrero* (Rookie Class) .35
444 *David Doster* (Rookie Class) .05
445 Jason Kendall (Rookie Class) .10
446 Edgar Renteria (Rookie Class) .15
447 Scott Spiezio (Rookie Class) .10
448 Jay Canizaro (Rookie Class) .10
449 Enrique Wilson (Rookie Class) .05
450 Bob Abreu (Rookie Class) .05
451 Dwight Smith .05
452 Jeff Blauser .05
453 Steve Avery .05
454 Brad Clontz .05
455 Tom Glavine .10
456 Mike Mordecai .05
457 Rafael Belliard .05
458 Greg McMichael .05
459 Pedro Borbon .05
460 Ryan Klesko .20
461 Terrell Wade .05
462 Brady Anderson .10
463 Roberto Alomar .40
464 Bobby Bonilla .05
465 Mike Mussina .35
466 *Cesar Devarez* .05
467 Jeffrey Hammonds .05
468 Mike Devereaux .05
469 B.J. Surhoff .05
470 Rafael Palmeiro .15
471 John Valentin .05
472 Mike Greenwell .05
473 Dwayne Hosey .05
474 Tim Wakefield .05
475 Jose Canseco .25
476 Aaron Sele .05
477 Stan Belinda .05
478 Mike Stanley .05
479 Jamie Moyer .05
480 Mo Vaughn .50
481 Randy Velarde .05
482 Gary DiSarcina .05
483 Jorge Fabregas .05
484 Rex Hudler .05
485 Chuck Finley .05
486 Tim Wallach .05
487 Eduardo Perez .05
488 Scott Sanderson .05
489 J.T. Snow .05
490 Sammy Sosa .75
491 Terry Adams .05
492 Matt Franco .05
493 Scott Servais .05
494 Frank Castillo .05
495 Ryne Sandberg .35
496 Rey Sanchez .05
497 Steve Trachsel .05
498 Jose Hernandez .05
499 Dave Martinez .05
500 Babe Ruth (First Class) 1.00
501 Ty Cobb (First Class) .50
502 Walter Johnson (First Class) .15
503 Christy Mathewson (First Class) .05
504 Honus Wagner (First Class) .25
505 Robin Ventura .05
506 Jason Bere .05
507 *Mike Cameron* .50
508 Ron Karkovice .05
509 Matt Karchner .05
510 Harold Baines .05
511 Kirk McCaskill .05
512 Larry Thomas .05
513 Danny Tartabull .05
514 Steve Gibralter .05
515 Bret Boone .05
516 Jeff Branson .05
517 Kevin Jarvis .05
518 Xavier Hernandez .05
519 Eric Owens .05
520 Barry Larkin .15
521 Dave Burba .05
522 John Smiley .05
523 Paul Assenmacher .05
524 Chad Ogea .05
525 Orel Hershiser .05
526 Alan Embree .05
527 Tony Pena .05
528 Omar Vizquel .05
529 Mark Clark .05
530 Albert Belle .60
531 Charles Nagy .05
532 Herbert Perry .05
533 Darren Holmes .05
534 Ellis Burks .05
535 Bill Swift .05
536 Armando Reynoso .05
537 Curtis Leskanic .05
538 Quinton McCracken .05
539 Steve Reed .05
540 Larry Walker .15
541 Walt Weiss .05
542 Bryan Rekar .05
543 Tony Clark .50
544 Steve Rodriguez .05
545 C.J. Nitkowski .05
546 Todd Steverson .05
547 Jose Lima .05
548 Phil Nevin .05
549 Chris Gomez .05
550 Travis Fryman .05
551 Mark Lewis .05
552 Alex Arias .05
553 Marc Valdes .05
554 Kevin Brown .05
555 Jeff Conine .05
556 John Burkett .05
557 Devon White .05
558 Pat Rapp .05
559 Jay Powell .05
560 Gary Sheffield .20
561 Jim Dougherty .05
562 Todd Jones .05
563 Tony Eusebio .05
564 Darryl Kile .05
565 Doug Drabek .05
566 Mike Simms .05
567 Derrick May .05
568 *Donne Wall* .05
569 Greg Swindell .05
570 Jim Pittsley .05
571 Bob Hamelin .05
572 Mark Gubicza .05
573 Chris Haney .05
574 Keith Lockhart .05
575 Mike Macfarlane .05
576 Les Norman .05
577 Joe Randa .05
578 Chris Stynes .05
579 Greg Gagne .05
580 Raul Mondesi .25
581 Delino DeShields .05
582 Pedro Astacio .05
583 Antonio Osuna .05
584 Brett Butler .05
585 Todd Worrell .05
586 Mike Blowers .05
587 Felix Rodriguez .05
588 Ismael Valdes .05
589 Ricky Bones .05
590 Greg Vaughn .05
591 Mark Loretta .05
592 Cal Eldred .05
593 Chuck Carr .05
594 Dave Nilsson .05
595 John Jaha .05
596 Scott Karl .05
597 Pat Listach .05
598 *Jose Valentin* .15
599 Mike Trombley .05
600 Paul Molitor .20
601 Dave Hollins .05
602 Ron Coomer .05
603 Matt Walbeck .05
604 Roberto Kelly .05
605 Rick Aguilera .05
606 Pat Mahomes .05
607 Jeff Reboulet .05
608 Rich Becker .05
609 Tim Scott .05
610 Pedro J. Martinez .05
611 Kirk Rueter .05
612 Tavo Alvarez .05
613 Yamil Benitez .05
614 Darrin Fletcher .05
615 Mike Lansing .05
616 Henry Rodriguez .05
617 Tony Tarasco .05
618 Alex Ochoa .05
619 Tim Bogar .05
620 Bernard Gilkey .05
621 Dave Mlicki .05
622 Brent Mayne .05
623 Ryan Thompson .05
624 Pete Harnisch .05
625 Lance Johnson .05
626 Jose Vizcaino .05
627 Doug Henry .05
628 Scott Kamieniecki .05
629 Jim Leyritz .05
630 Ruben Sierra .05
631 Pat Kelly .05
632 Joe Girardi .05
633 John Wetteland .05
634 Melido Perez .05
635 Paul O'Neill .05
636 Jorge Posada .10
637 Bernie Williams .20
638 Mark Acre .25
639 Mike Bordick .05
640 Mark McGwire 2.50
641 Fausto Cruz .05
642 Ernie Young .05
643 Todd Van Poppel .05
644 Craig Paquette .05
645 Brent Gates .05
646 Pedro Munoz .05
647 Andrew Lorraine .05
648 Sid Fernandez .05
649 Jim Eisenreich .05
650 Johnny Damon (Arizona Fall League) .15
651 Dustin Hermanson (Arizona Fall League) .05
652 Joe Randa (Arizona Fall League) .05
653 Michael Tucker (Arizona Fall League) .10
654 Alan Benes (Arizona Fall League) .20
655 Chad Fonville (Arizona Fall League) .05
656 David Bell (Arizona Fall League) .05
657 Jon Nunnally (Arizona Fall League) .05
658 Chan Ho Park (Arizona Fall League) .05
659 LaTroy Hawkins (Arizona Fall League) .05
660 Jamie Brewington (Arizona Fall League) .05
661 Quinton McCracken (Arizona Fall League) .05
662 Tim Unroe (Arizona Fall League) .05
663 Jeff Ware (Arizona Fall League) .05
664 Todd Greene (Arizona Fall League) .15
665 Andrew Lorraine (Arizona Fall League) .05
666 Ernie Young (Arizona Fall League) .05
667 Toby Borland .05
668 Lenny Webster .05
669 Benito Santiago .05
670 Gregg Jefferies .05
671 Darren Daulton .05
672 Curt Schilling .05
673 Mark Whiten .05
674 Todd Zeile .05
675 Jay Bell .05
676 Paul Wagner .05
677 Dave Clark .05
678 Nelson Liriano .05
679 Ramon Morel .10
680 Charlie Hayes .05
681 Angelo Encaracion .05
682 Al Martin .05
683 Jacob Brumfield .05
684 Mike Kingery .05

685	Carlos Garcia	.05
686	Tom Pagnozzi	.05
687	David Bell	.05
688	Todd Stottlemyre	.05
689	Jose Oliva	.05
690	Ray Lankford	.05
691	Mike Morgan	.05
692	John Frascatore	.05
693	John Mabry	.05
694	Mark Petkovsek	.05
695	Alan Benes	.25
696	Steve Finley	.05
697	Marc Newfield	.05
698	Andy Ashby	.05
699	Marc Kroon	.05
700	Wally Joyner	.05
701	Joey Hamilton	.05
702	Dustin Hermanson	.05
703	Scott Sanders	.05
704	Marty Cordova (Award Win.-ROY)	.05
705	Hideo Nomo (Award Win.-ROY)	.20
706	Mo Vaughn (Award Win.-MVP)	.25
707	Barry Larkin (Award Win.-MVP)	.15
708	Randy Johnson (Award Win.-CY)	.15
709	Greg Maddux (Award Win.-CY)	.60
710	Mark McGwire (Award-Comeback)	.75
711	Ron Gant (Award-Comeback)	.05
712	Andujar Cedeno	.05
713	Brian Johnson	.05
714	J.R. Phillips	.05
715	Rod Beck	.05
716	Sergio Valdez	.05
717	*Marvin Benard*	.05
718	Steve Scarsone	.05
719	*Rich Aurilia*	.10
720	Matt Williams	.30
721	John Patterson	.05
722	Shawn Estes	.05
723	Russ Davis	.05
724	Rich Amaral	.05
725	Edgar Martinez	.05
726	Norm Charlton	.05
727	Paul Sorrento	.05
728	Luis Sojo	.05
729	Arquimedez Pozo	.05
730	Jay Buhner	.15
731	Chris Bosio	.05
732	Chris Widger	.05
733	Kevin Gross	.05
734	Darren Oliver	.05
735	Dean Palmer	.05
736	Matt Whiteside	.05
737	Luis Ortiz	.05
738	Roger Pavlik	.05
739	Damon Buford	.05
740	Juan Gonzalez	.75
741	Rusty Greer	.05
742	Lou Frazier	.05
743	Pat Hentgen	.05
744	Tomas Perez	.05
745	Juan Guzman	.05
746	Otis Nixon	.05
747	Robert Perez	.05
748	Ed Sprague	.05
749	Tony Castillo	.05
750	John Olerud	.05
751	Shawn Green	.05
752	Jeff Ware	.05
753	Checklist 396-441/Blake St. Bombers (Dante Bichette, Larry Walker, Andres Galarraga, Vinny Castilla)	.10
754	Checklist 442-487 (Greg Maddux)	.35
755	Checklist 488-533 (Marty Cordova)	.05
756	Checklist 534-579 (Ozzie Smith)	.15
757	Checklist 580-625 (John Vander Wal)	.05
758	Checklist 626-670 (Andres Galarraga)	.10
759	Checklist 671-715 (Frank Thomas)	.25
760	Checklist 716-760 (Tony Gwynn)	.30
761	Randy Myers	.10
762	Kent Mercker	.10
763	David Wells	.10
764	Tom Gordon	.10
765	Wil Cordero	.10
766	Dave Magadan	.10
767	Doug Jones	.10
768	Kevin Tapani	.10
769	Curtis Goodwin	.10
770	Julio Franco	.10
771	Jack McDowell	.15
772	Al Leiter	.10
773	Sean Berry	.10
774	Bip Roberts	.10
775	Jose Offerman	.10
776	Ben McDonald	.15
777	Dan Serafini	.25
778	Ryan McGuire	.25
779	Tim Raines	.10
780	Tino Martinez	.15
781	Kenny Rogers	.10
782	Bob Tewksbury	.10
783	Rickey Henderson	.15
784	Ron Gant	.20
785	Gary Gaetti	.10
786	Andy Benes	.15
787	Royce Clayton	.10
788	Darryl Hamilton	.10
789	Ken Hill	.10
790	Erik Hanson	.10

1996 Collector's Choice Silver Signature

A silver border instead of white, and a facsimile autograph in silver ink on the card front differentiate these parallel insert cards from the regular-issue Collector's Choice. The inserts are seeded at the rate of one per pack.

	MT
Complete Set (730):	75.00
Common Player:	.10
Stars:	1-2.5X

(See 1996 Collector's Choice for checklist and base card values.)

1996 Collector's Choice Gold Signature

This insert set parallels each card in the regular Collector's Choice set. Found on average of one per 35 packs, the cards are nearly identical to the regular version except for the presence of a facsimile autograph in gold ink on the front and gold, instead of white, borders.

	MT
Complete Set (730):	1200.
Common Player:	1.00
Veteran Stars:	10-20X
Young Stars:	8-15X

(See 1996 Collector's Choice for checklist and base card values.)

1996 Collector's Choice Crash the Game

For a second season, UD continued its interactive chase card series, "You Crash the Game." At a ratio of about one per five packs for a silver version and one per 49 packs for a gold version, cards of the game's top sluggers can be found bearing one of three date ranges representing a three- or four-game series in which that player was scheduled to play during the 1996 season. If the player hit a home run during the series shown on the card, the card could be redeemed (for $1.75) by mail for a "Super Premium" wood-and-plastic card of the player. Both silver and gold Crash cards feature silver and red prismatic foil behind the player action photo. Silver versions have the Crash logo, series dates and player ID in silver foil on front; those details are in gold foil on the gold cards. Backs have contest rules printed on a gray (silver) or yellow (gold) background. Card numbers are preceded by a "CG" prefix. Cards were redeemable only until Nov. 25, 1996. Winning cards are indicated with an asterisk; they would be in shorter supply than those which could not be redeemed.

		MT
	Complete Silver Set (90):	40.00
	Common Silver Player:	.50
	Gold Version:	5-6X
1a	Chipper Jones (July 11-14*)	3.00
1b	Chipper Jones (Aug. 27-29*)	3.00
1c	Chipper Jones (Sept. 19-23)	2.00
2a	Fred McGriff (July 1-3)	.50
2b	Fred McGriff (Aug. 30-Sept. 1)	.50
2c	Fred McGriff (Sept. 10-12*)	.90
3a	Rafael Palmeiro (July 4-7*)	.90
3b	Rafael Palmeiro (Aug. 29-Sept. 1)	.50
3c	Rafael Palmeiro (Sept. 26-29)	.50
4a	Cal Ripken Jr. (June 27-30)	3.00
4b	Cal Ripken Jr. (July 25-28*)	6.00
4c	Cal Ripken Jr. (Sept. 2-4)	3.00
5a	Jose Canseco (June 27-30)	.50
5b	Jose Canseco (July 11-14*)	.90
5c	Jose Canseco (Aug. 23-25)	.50
6a	Mo Vaughn (June 21-23*)	.90
6b	Mo Vaughn (July 18-21*)	.90
6c	Mo Vaughn (Sept. 20-22)	.50
7a	Jim Edmonds (July 18-21*)	.90
7b	Jim Edmonds (Aug. 16-18*)	.90
7c	Jim Edmonds (Sept. 20-22)	.50
8a	Tim Salmon (June 20-23)	.50
8b	Tim Salmon (July 30-Aug. 1)	.50
8c	Tim Salmon (Sept. 9-12)	.50
9a	Sammy Sosa (July 4-7*)	3.00
9b	Sammy Sosa (Aug. 1-4*)	3.00
9c	Sammy Sosa (Sept. 2-4)	1.50
10a	Frank Thomas (June 27-30)	1.00
10b	Frank Thomas (July 4-7)	1.00
10c	Frank Thomas (Sept. 2-4*)	2.00
11a	Albert Belle (June 25-26)	.75
11b	Albert Belle (Aug. 2-5*)	1.50
11c	Albert Belle (Sept. 6-8)	.75
12a	Manny Ramirez (July 18-21*)	.90
12b	Manny Ramirez (Aug. 26-28)	.50

12c	Manny Ramirez (Sept. 9-12*)	.90
13a	Jim Thome (June 27-30)	.50
13b	Jim Thome (July 4-7*)	.90
13c	Jim Thome (Sept. 23-25)	.50
14a	Dante Bichette (July 11-14*)	.90
14b	Dante Bichette (Aug. 9-11)	.50
14c	Dante Bichette (Sept. 9-12)	.50
15a	Vinny Castilla (July 1-3)	.50
15b	Vinny Castilla (Aug. 23-25*)	.90
15c	Vinny Castilla (Sept. 13-15*)	.90
16a	Larry Walker (June 24-26)	.65
16b	Larry Walker (July 18-21)	.65
16c	Larry Walker (Sept. 27-29)	.65
17a	Cecil Fielder (June 27-30)	.50
17b	Cecil Fielder (July 30-Aug. 1*)	.90
17c	Cecil Fielder (Sept. 17-19*)	.50
18a	Gary Sheffield (July 4-7)	.50
18b	Gary Sheffield (Aug. 2-4)	.50
18c	Gary Sheffield (Sept. 5-8*)	.90
19a	Jeff Bagwell (July 4-7*)	1.50
19b	Jeff Bagwell (Aug. 16-18)	.90
19c	Jeff Bagwell (Sept. 13-15)	.90
20a	Eric Karros (July 4-7*)	.90
20b	Eric Karros (Aug. 13-15*)	.90
20c	Eric Karros (Sept. 16-18)	.50
21a	Mike Piazza (June 27-30*)	4.00
21b	Mike Piazza (July 26-28)	2.50
21c	Mike Piazza (Sept. 12-15*)	4.00
22a	Ken Caminiti (July 11-14*)	.90
22b	Ken Caminiti (Aug. 16-18*)	.90
22c	Ken Caminiti (Sept. 19-22*)	.90
23a	Barry Bonds (June 27-30*)	3.00
23b	Barry Bonds (July 22-24)	1.50
23c	Barry Bonds (Sept. 24-26)	1.50
24a	Matt Williams (July 11-14*)	1.00
24b	Matt Williams (Aug. 19-21)	.55
24c	Matt Williams (Sept. 27-29)	.55
25a	Jay Buhner (June 20-23)	.50
25b	Jay Buhner (July 25-28)	.50
25c	Jay Buhner (Aug. 29-Sept. 1*)	.90
26a	Ken Griffey Jr. (July 18-21*)	6.00
26b	Ken Griffey Jr. (Aug. 16-18*)	6.00
26c	Ken Griffey Jr. (Sept. 20-22*)	6.00
27a	Ron Gant (June 24-27*)	.90
27b	Ron Gant (July 11-14*)	.90
27c	Ron Gant (Sept. 27-29*)	.90
28a	Juan Gonzalez (June 28-30*)	3.00
28b	Juan Gonzalez (July 15-17*)	3.00
28c	Juan Gonzalez (Aug. 6-8)	1.50
29a	Mickey Tettleton (July 4-7*)	.90
29b	Mickey Tettleton (Aug. 6-8)	.50
29c	Mickey Tettleton (Sept. 6-8*)	.90
30a	Joe Carter (June 25-27)	.50
30b	Joe Carter (Aug. 5-8)	.50
30c	Joe Carter (Sept. 23-25)	.50

1996 Collector's Choice Crash Winners

Collectors who held "You Crash The Game" insert cards with date ranges on which the pictured player hit a home run could redeem them (for $1.75 per card) for a premium card of that player. The redemption cards have a layer of clear plastic bonded to a wood-laminate front. Within a starburst cutout at center is the player photo with a red background. Cards have a Crash/Game logo in the lower-right corner, in either silver or gold, depending on which winning card was submitted for exchange. Backs have 1995 and career stats along with licensing and copyright data. There were no winning cards of Tim Salmon, Larry Walker or Joe Carter.

	MT
Complete Set (27):	140.00
Common Player:	3.00
Gold Version:	4-5X
CR1 Chipper Jones	12.00
CR2 Fred McGriff	3.00
CR3 Rafael Palmeiro	4.00
CR4 Cal Ripken Jr.	12.50
CR5 Jose Canseco	4.00
CR6 Mo Vaughn	5.00
CR7 Jim Edmonds	3.00
CR9 Sammy Sosa	9.00
CR10Frank Thomas	6.00
CR11Albert Belle	6.00
CR12Manny Ramirez	4.00
CR13Jim Thome	3.00
CR14Dante Bichette	3.00
CR15Vinny Castilla	3.00
CR17Cecil Fielder	3.00
CR18Gary Sheffield	3.00
CR19Jeff Bagwell	7.50
CR20Eric Karros	3.00
CR21Mike Piazza	10.00
CR22Ken Caminiti	3.00
CR23Barry Bonds	7.50
CR24Matt Williams	4.00
CR25Jay Buhner	3.00
CR26Ken Griffey Jr.	15.00
CR27Ron Gant	3.00
CR28Juan Gonzalez	7.50
CR29Mickey Tettleton	3.00

1996 Collector's Choice Nomo Scrapbook

The five-card, regular-sized set was randomly inserted in 1996 Collector's Choice baseball. Fronts depict the Dodgers pitcher in action with his name in atypical lower-case type up the right border. Backs feature in-depth text below Nomo's name.

	MT
Complete Set (5):	5.00
Common Player:	1.00
1-5 Hideo Nomo	1.00

1996 Collector's Choice Ripken Collection

The 23-card, regular-sized Cal Ripken Collection was randomly inserted in various Upper Deck baseball releases in 1996. Cards #1-4 were found in Series 1 Collector's Choice; cards 5-8 were found in Upper Deck Series 1; cards 9-12 in Collector's Choice Series 2; cards 13-17 in Upper Deck Series 2; cards 18-22 in SP baseball and the header card in Collector's Choice.

	MT
Complete Set (1-4, 9-12)	40.00
Common Card:	4.00
Header Card:	4.00

(See also Upper Deck Series 1 and 2, and Upper Deck/SP)

1996 Collector's Choice "You Make the Play"

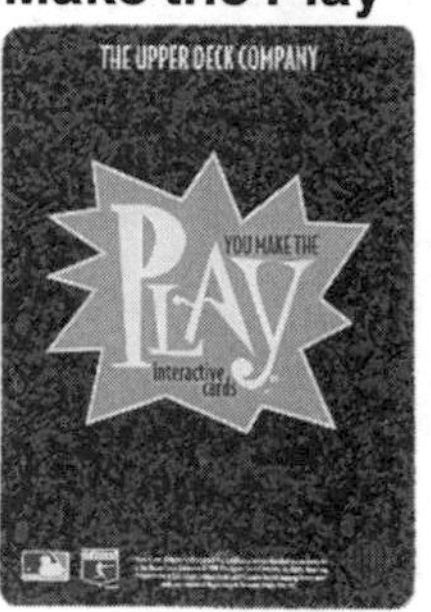

This insert series of interactive game cards was packaged with Series 1 Collector's Choice. Each player's card can be found with one of two play outcomes printed thereon, which are then used to play a baseball card game utilizing a playing field and scorecard found on box bottoms. Regular versions of the cards are seeded one per pack, while gold-signature versions are found one per 36 packs.

		MT
Complete Set (45):		11.00
Common Player:		.25
Gold version:		8-12X
1a	Kevin Appier (Strike out)	.25
1b	Kevin Appier (Pick off)	.25
2a	Carlos Baerga (Home run)	.25
2b	Carlos Baerga (Ground out)	.25
3a	Jeff Bagwell (Walk)	.40
3b	Jeff Bagwell (Strike out)	.40
4a	Jay Bell (Sacrifice)	.25
4b	Jay Bell (Walk)	.25
5a	Albert Belle (Fly out)	.75
5b	Albert Belle (Home run)	.75
6a	Craig Biggio (Single)	.35
6b	Craig Biggio (Strike out)	.35
7a	Wade Boggs (Single)	.45
7b	Wade Boggs (Ground out)	.45

8a	Barry Bonds (Strike out)	.60
8b	Barry Bonds (Reach on error)	.60
9a	Bobby Bonilla (Walk)	.25
9b	Bobby Bonilla (Strike out)	.25
10a	Jose Canseco (Strike out)	.35
10b	Jose Canseco (Double)	.35
11a	Joe Carter (Double)	.25
11b	Joe Carter (Fly out)	.25
12a	Darren Daulton (Ground out)	.25
12b	Darren Daulton (Catcher's interference)	.25
13a	Cecil Fielder (Stolen base)	.25
13b	Cecil Fielder (Home run)	.25
14a	Ron Gant (Home run)	.25
14b	Ron Gant (Fly out)	.25
15a	Juan Gonzalez (Double)	.60
15b	Juan Gonzalez (Fly out)	.60
16a	Ken Griffey Jr. (Home run)	2.00
16b	Ken Griffey Jr. (Hit by pitch)	2.00
17a	Tony Gwynn (Single)	.60
17b	Tony Gwynn (Ground out)	.60
18a	Randy Johnson (Strike out)	.45
18b	Randy Johnson (K - reach on wild pitch)	.45
19a	Chipper Jones (Walk)	.75
19b	Chipper Jones (Strike out)	.75
20a	Barry Larkin (Ground out)	.25
20b	Barry Larkin (Stolen base)	.25
21a	Kenny Lofton (Triple)	.30
21b	Kenny Lofton (Stolen base)	.30
22a	Greg Maddux (Single)	.50
22b	Greg Maddux (Strike out)	.50
23a	Don Mattingly (Fly out)	.50
23b	Don Mattingly (Double)	.50
24a	Fred McGriff (Double)	.30
24b	Fred McGriff (Home run)	.30
25a	Mark McGwire (Strike out)	1.75
25b	Mark McGwire (Home run)	1.75
26a	Paul Molitor (Ground out)	.45
26b	Paul Molitor (Single)	.45
27a	Raul Mondesi (Single)	.35
27b	Raul Mondesi (Fly out)	.35
28a	Eddie Murray (Sacrifice fly)	.45
28b	Eddie Murray (Ground out)	.45
29a	Hideo Nomo (Strike out)	.40
29b	Hideo Nomo (Balk)	.40
30a	Jon Nunnally (Single)	.25
30b	Jon Nunnally (Error)	.25
31a	Mike Piazza (Strike out)	.75
31b	Mike Piazza Single)	.75
32a	Kirby Puckett (Walk)	.45
32b	Kirby Puckett (Ground out)	.45
33a	Cal Ripken Jr. (Home run)	1.75
33b	Cal Ripken Jr. (Double)	1.75
34a	Alex Rodriguez (Strike out)	.75
34b	Alex Rodriguez (Triple)	.75
35a	Tim Salmon (Sacrifice fly)	.35
35b	Tim Salmon (Strike out)	.35
36a	Gary Sheffield (Fly out)	.25
36b	Gary Sheffield (Single)	.25
37a	Lee Smith (Strike out)	.25
37b	Lee Smith (Pick off of lead runner)	.25
38a	Ozzie Smith (Ground out)	.45
38b	Ozzie Smith (Single)	.45
39a	Sammy Sosa (Stolen base)	1.00
39b	Sammy Sosa (Single)	1.00
40a	Frank Thomas (Walk)	1.00
40b	Frank Thomas (Home run)	1.00
41a	Greg Vaughn (Sacrifice fly)	.25
41b	Greg Vaughn (Strike out)	.25
42a	Mo Vaughn (Hit by Pitch)	.35
42b	Mo Vaughn (Stolen base)	.35
43a	Larry Walker (Strike out)	.35
43b	Larry Walker (Walk)	.35
44a	Rondell White (Triple)	.25
44b	Rondell White (Fly out)	.25
45a	Matt Williams (Home run)	.35
45b	Matt Williams (Single)	.35

1997 Collector's Choice

The 246-card, standard-size set contains four subsets: Rookie Class (1-27), Leaders (56-63), Postseason (218-224) and Ken Griffey Jr. Checklists (244-246). Insert sets are: Stick'Ums, Premier Power, Clearly Dominant and The Big Show. Basic card fronts feature a color action shot with the player's name appearing on the bottom edge. The team logo is located in the lower-left corner and each card features a white border. Backs contain another action shot on the upper half with biography, and career/season stats. The cards were issued in 12-card packs retailing for 99 cents.

		MT
	Complete Set (506):	30.00
	Complete Series 1 Set (246):	15.00
	Complete Series 2 Set (260):	18.00
	Common Player:	.05
	Series 1 or 2 Pack (12):	1.00
	Series 1 or 2 Wax Box (36):	30.00
1	Andruw Jones (Rookie Class)	1.00
2	Rocky Coppinger (Rookie Class)	.05
3	Jeff D'Amico (Rookie Class)	.05
4	Dmitri Young (Rookie Class)	.05
5	Darin Erstad (Rookie Class)	.75
6	Jermaine Allensworth (Rookie Class)	.05
7	Damian Jackson (Rookie Class)	.05
8	Bill Mueller (Rookie Class)	.10
9	Jacob Cruz (Rookie Class)	.30
10	Vladimir Guerrero (Rookie Class)	.75
11	Marty Janzen (Rookie Class)	.05
12	Kevin L. Brown (Rookie Class)	.05
13	Willie Adams (Rookie Class)	.05
14	Wendell Magee (Rookie Class)	.05
15	Scott Rolen (Rookie Class)	1.00
16	Matt Beech (Rookie Class)	.05
17	Neifi Perez (Rookie Class)	.05
18	Jamey Wright (Rookie Class)	.05
19	Jose Paniagua (Rookie Class)	.05
20	Todd Walker (Rookie Class)	.40
21	Justin Thompson (Rookie Class)	.05
22	Robin Jennings (Rookie Class)	.05
23	*Dario Veras* (Rookie Class)	.05
24	Brian Lesher (Rookie Class)	.05
25	Nomar Garciaparra (Rookie Class)	1.25
26	Luis Castillo (Rookie Class)	.10
27	*Brian Giles* (Rookie Class)	.75
28	Jermaine Dye	.10
29	Terrell Wade	.05
30	Fred McGriff	.25
31	Marquis Grissom	.05
32	Ryan Klesko	.20
33	Javier Lopez	.10
34	Mark Wohlers	.05
35	Tom Glavine	.15
36	Denny Neagle	.05
37	Scott Erickson	.05
38	Chris Hoiles	.05
39	Roberto Alomar	.50
40	Eddie Murray	.30
41	Cal Ripken Jr.	1.75
42	Randy Myers	.05
43	B.J. Surhoff	.05
44	Rick Krivda	.05
45	Jose Canseco	.25
46	Heathcliff Slocumb	.05
47	Jeff Suppan	.05
48	Tom Gordon	.05
49	Aaron Sele	.05
50	Mo Vaughn	.40
51	Darren Bragg	.05
52	Wil Cordero	.05
53	Scott Bullett	.05
54	Terry Adams	.05
55	Jackie Robinson	.05
56	Tony Gwynn, Alex Rodriguez (Batting Leaders)	.50
57	Andres Galarraga, Mark McGwire (Homer Leaders)	.75
58	Andres Galarraga, Albert Belle (RBI Leaders)	.25
59	Eric Young, Kenny Lofton (SB Leaders)	.10
60	John Smoltz, Andy Pettitte (Victory Leaders)	.25
61	John Smoltz, Roger Clemens (Strikout Leaders)	.30
62	Kevin Brown, Juan Guzman (ERA Leaders)	.05
63	John Wetteland, Todd Worrell, Jeff Brantley (Save Leaders)	.05
64	Scott Servais	.05
65	Sammy Sosa	.85
66	Ryne Sandberg	.60
67	Frank Castillo	.05
68	Rey Sanchez	.05
69	Steve Trachsel	.05
70	Robin Ventura	.05
71	Wilson Alvarez	.05
72	Tony Phillips	.05
73	Lyle Mouton	.05
74	Mike Cameron	.05
75	Harold Baines	.05
76	Albert Belle	.50
77	Chris Snopek	.05
78	Reggie Sanders	.05
79	Jeff Brantley	.05
80	Barry Larkin	.15
81	Kevin Jarvis	.05
82	John Smiley	.05
83	Pete Schourek	.05
84	Thomas Howard	.05
85	Lee Smith	.05
86	Omar Vizquel	.05
87	Julio Franco	.05
88	Orel Hershiser	.05
89	Charles Nagy	.05
90	Matt Williams	.20
91	Dennis Martinez	.05
92	Jose Mesa	.05
93	Sandy Alomar Jr.	.05
94	Jim Thome	.20
95	Vinny Castilla	.05
96	Armando Reynoso	.05
97	Kevin Ritz	.05
98	Larry Walker	.20
99	Eric Young	.05
100	Dante Bichette	.15
101	Quinton McCracken	.05
102	John Vander Wal	.05
103	Phil Nevin	.05
104	Tony Clark	.40
105	Alan Trammell	.05
106	Felipe Lira	.05
107	Curtis Pride	.05
108	Bobby Higginson	.05
109	Mark Lewis	.05
110	Travis Fryman	.05
111	Al Leiter	.05
112	Devon White	.05
113	Jeff Conine	.05
114	Charles Johnson	.05
115	Andre Dawson	.05
116	Edgar Renteria	.20
117	Robb Nen	.05
118	Kevin Brown	.05
119	Derek Bell	.05
120	Bob Abreu	.05

121 Mike Hampton .05
122 Todd Jones .05
123 Billy Wagner .15
124 Shane Reynolds .05
125 Jeff Bagwell 1.00
126 Brian L. Hunter .05
127 Jeff Montgomery .05
128 *Rod Myers* .05
129 Tim Belcher .05
130 Kevin Appier .05
131 Mike Sweeney .05
132 Craig Paquette .05
133 Joe Randa .05
134 Michael Tucker .05
135 Raul Mondesi .20
136 Tim Wallach .05
137 Brett Butler .05
138 Karim Garcia .35
139 Todd Hollandsworth .10
140 Eric Karros .05
141 Hideo Nomo .25
142 Ismael Valdes .05
143 Cal Eldred .05
144 Scott Karl .05
145 Matt Mieske .05
146 Mike Fetters .05
147 Mark Loretta .05
148 Fernando Vina .05
149 Jeff Cirillo .05
150 Dave Nilsson .05
151 Kirby Puckett 1.00
152 Rich Becker .05
153 Chuck Knoblauch .15
154 Marty Cordova .05
155 Paul Molitor .35
156 Rick Aguilera .05
157 Pat Meares .05
158 Frank Rodriguez .05
159 David Segui .05
160 Henry Rodriguez .05
161 Shane Andrews .05
162 Pedro J. Martinez .05
163 Mark Grudzielanek .05
164 Mike Lansing .05
165 Rondell White .05
166 Ugueth Urbina .05
167 Rey Ordonez .20
168 Robert Person .05
169 Carlos Baerga .05
170 Bernard Gilkey .05
171 John Franco .05
172 Pete Harnisch .05
173 Butch Huskey .05
174 Paul Wilson .10
175 Bernie Williams .25
176 Dwight Gooden .05
177 Wade Boggs .25
178 Ruben Rivera .10
179 Jim Leyritz .05
180 Derek Jeter 1.00
181 Tino Martinez .15
182 Tim Raines .05
183 Scott Brosius .05
184 Jason Giambi .15
185 Geronimo Berroa .05
186 Ariel Prieto .05
187 Scott Spiezio .05
188 John Wasdin .05
189 Ernie Young .05
190 Mark McGwire 2.50
191 Jim Eisenreich .05
192 Ricky Bottalico .05
193 Darren Daulton .05
194 David Doster .05
195 Gregg Jefferies .05
196 Lenny Dykstra .05
197 Curt Schilling .05
198 Todd Stottlemyre .05
199 Willie McGee .05
200 Ozzie Smith .35
201 Dennis Eckersley .05
202 Ray Lankford .05
203 John Mabry .05
204 Alan Benes .05
205 Ron Gant .10
206 Archi Cianfrocco .05
207 Fernando Valenzuela .05
208 Greg Vaughn .05
209 Steve Finley .05
210 Tony Gwynn .75
211 Rickey Henderson .05
212 Trevor Hoffman .05
213 Jason Thompson .05
214 Osvaldo Fernandez .05
215 Glenallen Hill .05
216 William VanLandingham .05
217 Marvin Benard .05
218 Juan Gonzalez (Postseason) .40
219 Roberto Alomar (Postseason) .25
220 Brian Jordan (Postseason) .05
221 John Smoltz (Postseason) .15
222 Javy Lopez (Postseason) .05
223 Bernie Williams (Postseason) .15
224 Jim Leyritz, John Wetteland (Postseason) .05
225 Barry Bonds .60
226 Rich Aurilia .05
227 Jay Canizaro .05
228 Dan Wilson .05
229 Bob Wolcott .05
230 Ken Griffey Jr. 2.00
231 Sterling Hitchcock .05
232 Edgar Martinez .05
233 Joey Cora .05
234 Norm Charlton .05
235 Alex Rodriguez 1.50
236 Bobby Witt .05
237 Darren Oliver .05
238 Kevin Elster .05
239 Rusty Greer .05
240 Juan Gonzalez .50
241 Will Clark .20
242 Dean Palmer .05
243 Ivan Rodriguez .30
244 Checklist (Ken Griffey Jr.) .50
245 Checklist (Ken Griffey Jr.) .50
246 Checklist (Ken Griffey Jr.) .50
247 Checklist (Ken Griffey Jr.) .50
248 Checklist (Ken Griffey Jr.) .50
249 Checklist (Ken Griffey Jr.) .50
250 Eddie Murray .25
251 Troy Percival .05
252 Garret Anderson .05
253 Allen Watson .05
254 Jason Dickson .15
255 Jim Edmonds .10
256 Chuck Finley .05
257 Randy Velarde .05
258 Shigetosi Hasegawa .05
259 Todd Greene .05
260 Tim Salmon .20
261 Mark Langston .05
262 Dave Hollins .05
263 Gary DiSarcina .05
264 Kenny Lofton .40
265 John Smoltz .15
266 Greg Maddux 1.00
267 Jeff Blauser .05
268 Alan Embree .05
269 Mark Lemke .05
270 Chipper Jones 1.25
271 Mike Mussina .35
272 Rafael Palmeiro .15
273 Jimmy Key .05
274 Mike Bordick .05
275 Brady Anderson .10
276 Eric Davis .05
277 Jeffrey Hammonds .05
278 Reggie Jefferson .05
279 Tim Naehring .05
280 John Valentin .05
281 Troy O'Leary .05
282 Shane Mack .05
283 Mike Stanley .05
284 Tim Wakefield .05
285 Brian McRae .05
286 Brooks Kieschnick .05
287 Shawon Dunston .05
288 Kevin Foster .05
289 Mel Rojas .05
290 Mark Grace .15
291 Brant Brown .05
292 Amaury Telemaco .05
293 Dave Martinez .05
294 Jaime Navarro .05
295 Ray Durham .05
296 Ozzie Guillen .05
297 Roberto Hernandez .05
298 Ron Karkovice .05
299 James Baldwin .05
300 Frank Thomas 1.00
301 Eddie Taubensee .05
302 Bret Boone .05
303 Willie Greene .05
304 Dave Burba .05
305 Deion Sanders .15
306 Reggie Sanders .05
307 Hal Morris .05
308 Pokey Reese .05
309 Tony Fernandez .05
310 Manny Ramirez .65
311 Chad Ogea .05
312 Jack McDowell .05
313 Kevin Mitchell .05
314 Chad Curtis .05
315 Steve Kline .05
316 Kevin Seitzer .05
317 Kirt Manwaring .05
318 Bill Swift .05
319 Ellis Burks .05
320 Andres Galarraga .10
321 Bruce Ruffin .05
322 Mark Thompson .05
323 Walt Weiss .05
324 Todd Jones .05
325 Andruw Jones (Griffey Hot List) .50
326 Chipper Jones (Griffey Hot List) .60
327 Mo Vaughn (Griffey Hot List) .15
328 Frank Thomas (Griffey Hot List) .50
329 Albert Belle (Griffey Hot List) .30
330 Mark McGwire (Griffey Hot List) 1.00
331 Derek Jeter (Griffey Hot List) .65
332 Alex Rodriguez (Griffey Hot List) 1.00
333 Juan Gonzalez (Griffey Hot List) .25
334 Ken Griffey Jr. (Griffey Hot List) 1.00
335 Brian L. Hunter .05
336 Brian Johnson .05
337 Omar Olivares .05
338 *Deivi Cruz* .05
339 Damion Easley .05
340 Melvin Nieves .05
341 Moises Alou .05
342 Jim Eisenreich .05
343 Mark Hutton .05
344 Alex Fernandez .05
345 Gary Sheffield .15
346 Pat Rapp .05
347 Brad Ausmus .05
348 Sean Berry .05
349 Darryl Kile .05
350 Craig Biggio .10
351 Chris Holt .05
352 Luis Gonzalez .05
353 Pat Listach .05
354 Jose Rosado .05
355 Mike Macfarlane .05
356 Tom Goodwin .05
357 Chris Haney .05
358 Chili Davis .05
359 Jose Offerman .05
360 Johnny Damon .05
361 Bip Roberts .05
362 Ramon Martinez .05
363 Pedro Astacio .05
364 Todd Zeile .05
365 Mike Piazza 1.25
366 Greg Gagne .05
367 Chan Ho Park .05
368 Wilton Guerrero .10
369 Todd Worrell .05
370 John Jaha .05
371 Steve Sparks .05
372 Mike Matheny .05
373 Marc Newfield .05
374 Jeromy Burnitz .05
375 Jose Valentin .05
376 Ben McDonald .05
377 Roberto Kelly .05
378 Bob Tewksbury .05
379 Ron Coomer .05
380 Brad Radke .05
381 Matt Lawton .05
382 Dan Naulty .05
383 Scott Stahoviak .05
384 Matt Wagner .05
385 Jim Bullinger .05
386 Carlos Perez .05
387 Darrin Fletcher .05
388 Chris Widger .05
389 F.P. Santangelo .05
390 Lee Smith .05
391 Bobby Jones .05
392 John Olerud .05
393 Mark Clark .05
394 Jason Isringhausen .05
395 Todd Hundley .15
396 Lance Johnson .05
397 Edgardo Alfonzo .10
398 Alex Ochoa .05
399 Darryl Strawberry .10
400 David Cone .15
401 Paul O'Neill .10
402 Joe Girardi .05
403 Charlie Hayes .05
404 Andy Pettitte .40
405 Mariano Rivera .15
406 Mariano Duncan .05
407 Kenny Rogers .05
408 Cecil Fielder .05
409 George Williams .05
410 Jose Canseco .25
411 Tony Batista .05
412 Steve Karsay .05
413 Dave Telgheder .05
414 Billy Taylor .05
415 Mickey Morandini .05
416 Calvin Maduro .05
417 Mark Leiter .05
418 Kevin Stocker .05
419 Mike Lieberthal .05
420 Rico Brogna .05
421 Mark Portugal .05
422 Rex Hudler .05
423 Mark Johnson .05
424 Esteban Loiaza .05
425 Lou Collier .05
426 Kevin Elster .05
427 Francisco Cordova .05
428 Marc Wilkins .05
429 Joe Randa .05
430 Jason Kendall .05
431 Jon Lieber .05
432 Steve Cooke .05
433 *Emil Brown* .10
434 *Tony Womack* .25
435 Al Martin .05
436 Jason Schmidt .05
437 Andy Benes .05
438 Delino DeShields .05
439 Royce Clayton .05
440 Brian Jordan .05
441 Donovan Osborne .05
442 Gary Gaetti .05
443 Tom Pagnozzi .05
444 Joey Hamilton .05
445 Wally Joyner .05
446 John Flaherty .05
447 Chris Gomez .05
448 Sterling Hitchcock .05
449 Andy Ashby .05
450 Ken Caminiti .15
451 Tim Worrell .05
452 Jose Vizcaino .05
453 Rod Beck .05
454 Wilson Delgado .05
455 Darryl Hamilton .05
456 Mark Lewis .05
457 Mark Gardner .05
458 Rick Wilkins .05
459 Scott Sanders .05
460 Kevin Orie .05
461 Glendon Rusch .05
462 Juan Melo .05
463 Richie Sexson .10
464 Bartolo Colon .05
465 Jose Guillen .50
466 Heath Murray .05
467 Aaron Boone .05
468 *Bubba Trammell* .40
469 Jeff Abbott .05
470 Derrick Gibson .15
471 Matt Morris .15
472 Ryan Jones .05
473 Pat Cline .05
474 Adam Riggs .05
475 Jay Payton .05
476 Derrek Lee .15
477 Elieser Marrero .05
478 Lee Tinsley .05

479	Jamie Moyer	.05
480	Jay Buhner	.10
481	Bob Wells	.05
482	Jeff Fassero	.05
483	Paul Sorrento	.05
484	Russ Davis	.05
485	Randy Johnson	.40
486	Roger Pavlik	.05
487	Damon Buford	.05
488	Julio Santana	.05
489	Mark McLemore	.05
490	Mickey Tettleton	.05
491	Ken Hill	.05
492	Benji Gil	.05
493	Ed Sprague	.05
494	Mike Timlin	.05
495	Pat Hentgen	.05
496	Orlando Merced	.05
497	Carlos Garcia	.05
498	Carlos Delgado	.25
499	Juan Guzman	.05
500	Roger Clemens	.75
501	Erik Hanson	.05
502	Otis Nixon	.05
503	Shawn Green	.05
504	Charlie O'Brien	.05
505	Joe Carter	.10
506	Alex Gonzalez	.05

1997 Collector's Choice All-Star Connection

This 45-card insert from Series 2 highlights All-Star caliber players. Cards feature a large starburst pattern on a metallic-foil background behind the player's photo. They were inserted one per pack.

		MT
Complete Set (45):		9.00
Common Player:		.10
1	Mark McGwire	1.50
2	Chuck Knoblauch	.10
3	Jim Thome	.20
4	Alex Rodriguez	1.25
5	Ken Griffey Jr.	1.50
6	Brady Anderson	.10
7	Albert Belle	.40
8	Ivan Rodriguez	.25
9	Pat Hentgen	.10
10	Frank Thomas	.65
11	Roberto Alomar	.20
12	Robin Ventura	.15
13	Cal Ripken Jr.	1.20
14	Juan Gonzalez	.50
15	Manny Ramirez	.40
16	Bernie Williams	.20
17	Terry Steinbach	.10
18	Andy Pettitte	.25
19	Jeff Bagwell	.50
20	Craig Biggio	.10
21	Ken Caminiti	.10
22	Barry Larkin	.10
23	Tony Gwynn	.45
24	Barry Bonds	.30
25	Kenny Lofton	.25
26	Mike Piazza	.75
27	John Smoltz	.15
28	Andres Galarraga	.10
29	Ryne Sandberg	.25
30	Chipper Jones	.75
31	Mark Grudzielanek	.10
32	Sammy Sosa	.75
.3	Steve Finley	.10
34	Gary Sheffield	.15
35	Todd Hundley	.10
36	Greg Maddux	.65
37	Mo Vaughn	.25
38	Eric Young	.10
39	Vinny Castilla	.10
40	Derek Jeter	.75
41	Lance Johnson	.10
42	Ellis Burks	.10
43	Dante Bichette	.10
44	Javy Lopez	.10
45	Hideo Nomo	.20

1997 Collector's Choice Big Shots

This 20-card insert depicts the game's top stars in unique photos. Cards were inserted 1:12 packs. Gold Signature Editions, featuring a gold foil-stamped facsimile autograph, were inserted 1:144 packs. Fronts are highlighted in silver foil. Backs repeat a portion of the front photo, have a picture of the photographer and his comments about the picture.

		MT
Complete Set (19):		45.00
Common Player:		.50
Gold Signature Edition:		2-3X
1	Ken Griffey Jr.	8.00
2	Nomar Garciaparra	4.50
3	Brian Jordan	.50
4	Scott Rolen	3.00
5	Alex Rodriguez	6.00
6	Larry Walker	.75
7	Mariano Rivera	.50
8	Cal Ripken Jr.	6.00
9	Deion Sanders	.50
10	Frank Thomas	2.50
11	Dean Palmer	.50
12	Ken Caminiti	.50
13	Derek Jeter	4.50
14	Barry Bonds	2.50
15	Chipper Jones	4.50
16	Mo Vaughn	.50
17	Jay Buhner	.50
18	Mike Piazza	6.00
19	Tony Gwynn	3.00

1997 Collector's Choice Big Show

The 45-card, regular-sized set was inserted one per pack of Series 1. Backs feature player comments written by ESPN SportsCenter hosts Keith Olbermann and Dan Patrick, whose portraits appear both front and back. On front, printed on metallic foil, is an action shot of the player, with his name printed along the left border of the horizontal cards. The cards are numbered "X/45." A parallel set to this chase-card series carries a gold-foil "World Headquarters Edition" seal at lower-right and was a 1:35 insert.

		MT
Complete Set (45):		10.00
Common Player:		.25
World Headquarters:		8-15X
1	Greg Maddux	1.00
2	Chipper Jones	1.00
3	Andruw Jones	.50
4	John Smoltz	.35
5	Cal Ripken Jr.	2.00
6	Roberto Alomar	.50
7	Rafael Palmeiro	.35
8	Eddie Murray	.50
9	Jose Canseco	.35
10	Roger Clemens	.60
11	Mo Vaughn	.50
12	Jim Edmonds	.25
13	Tim Salmon	.25
14	Sammy Sosa	1.50
15	Albert Belle	.50
16	Frank Thomas	1.50
17	Barry Larkin	.25
18	Kenny Lofton	.35
19	Manny Ramirez	.50
20	Matt Williams	.40
21	Dante Bichette	.25
22	Gary Sheffield	.25
23	Craig Biggio	.25
24	Jeff Bagwell	1.00
25	Todd Hollandsworth	.25
26	Raul Mondesi	.25
27	Hideo Nomo	.25
28	Mike Piazza	1.00
29	Paul Molitor	.75
30	Kirby Puckett	1.00
31	Rondell White	.25
32	Rey Ordonez	.25
33	Paul Wilson	.25
34	Derek Jeter	2.00
35	Andy Pettitte	.35
36	Mark McGwire	3.00
37	Jason Kendall	.25
38	Ozzie Smith	.75
39	Tony Gwynn	1.00
40	Barry Bonds	.75
41	Alex Rodriguez	2.00
42	Jay Buhner	.25
43	Ken Griffey Jr.	3.00
44	Randy Johnson	.40
45	Juan Gonzalez	.75

1997 Collector's Choice Clearly Dominant

The five-card, regular-sized set features Seattle outfielder Ken Griffey Jr. on each card and was inserted every 144 packs of 1997 Collector's Choice baseball.

	MT
Complete Set (5):	40.00
Common Card:	10.00
CD1 Ken Griffey Jr.	12.00
CD2 Ken Griffey Jr.	12.00
CD3 Ken Griffey Jr.	12.00
CD4 Ken Griffey Jr.	12.00
CD5 Ken Griffey Jr.	12.00

1997 Collector's Choice Clearly Dominant Jumbos

Each of the five Ken Griffey Jr. cards from the Collector's Choice insert set was also produced in a special retail-only 5" x 3-1/2" jumbo version. The supersize Clearly Dominant cards were packaged in a special collectors' kit which also included a Griffey stand-up figure and eight packs of CC cards, retailing for about $15. The cards could also be purchased as a complete set for $10. Cards are numbered with a "CD" prefix.

		MT
Complete Set (5):		10.00
Common Card:		2.00
1	Ken Griffey Jr.	2.00
2	Ken Griffey Jr.	2.00
3	Ken Griffey Jr.	2.00
4	Ken Griffey Jr.	2.00
5	Ken Griffey Jr.	2.00

1997 Collector's Choice Hot List Jumbos

These 5" x 7" versions of the "Ken Griffey Jr.'s Hot List" subset from Series 1 are an exclusive box-topper in certain retail packaging of Series 2 Collector's Choice. Other than size, the jumbos are identical to the regular Hot List cards, including foil background printing on front.

		MT
Complete Set (10):		30.00
Common Player:		2.00
325	Andruw Jones	2.50
326	Chipper Jones	4.00
327	Mo Vaughn	2.00
328	Frank Thomas	2.50
329	Albert Belle	2.00
330	Mark McGwire	6.00
331	Derek Jeter	4.00
332	Alex Rodriguez	5.00
333	Juan Gonzalez	1.50
334	Ken Griffey Jr.	6.00

1997 Collector's Choice New Frontier

This is a 40-card Series 2 insert highlighting anticipated interleague matchups. Cards were designed with each player's action photo superimposed on a metallic-foil background depicting half of a ballfield. Pairs could then be displayed side-by-side. Cards were inserted 1:69 packs. They are numbered and carry a "NF" prefix.

		MT
Complete Set (40):		250.00
Common Player:		2.50
1	Alex Rodriguez	25.00
2	Tony Gwynn	9.00
3	Jose Canseco	5.00
4	Hideo Nomo	2.50
5	Mark McGwire	30.00
6	Barry Bonds	5.00
7	Juan Gonzalez	8.00
8	Ken Caminiti	2.50
9	Tim Salmon	4.00
10	Mike Piazza	12.50
11	Ken Griffey Jr.	30.00
12	Andres Galarraga	2.50
13	Jay Buhner	2.50
14	Dante Bichette	2.50
15	Frank Thomas	10.00
16	Ryne Sandberg	5.00
17	Roger Clemens	7.50
18	Andruw Jones	4.00
19	Jim Thome	2.50
20	Sammy Sosa	10.00
21	David Justice	2.50
22	Deion Sanders	2.50
23	Todd Walker	2.50
24	Kevin Orie	2.50
25	Albert Belle	5.00
26	Jeff Bagwell	7.50
27	Manny Ramirez	6.00
28	Brian Jordan	2.50
29	Derek Jeter	20.00
30	Chipper Jones	15.00
31	Mo Vaughn	5.00
32	Gary Sheffield	2.50
33	Carlos Delgado	2.50
34	Vladimir Guerrero	5.00
35	Cal Ripken Jr.	20.00
36	Greg Maddux	10.00
37	Cecil Fielder	2.50
38	Todd Hundley	2.50
39	Mike Mussina	4.00
40	Scott Rolen	5.00

1997 Collector's Choice Premier Power

The 20-card, regular-sized set was included one per 15 packs of Series 1. Fronts feature an action photo with the "Premier Power" logo in silver foil in the lower half and "spotlights" aiming out toward the sides. The bottom portion of the card is transparent red. Backs are bordered in red with the same card front shot appearing in black-and-white above a brief description and "Power Facts." The cards are numbered with a "PP" prefix. A parallel gold-foil version was available every 69 packs.

		MT
Complete Set (20):		35.00
Common Player:		.50
Gold:		3-4X
1	Mark McGwire	9.00
2	Brady Anderson	.50
3	Ken Griffey Jr.	9.00
4	Albert Belle	2.00
5	Juan Gonzalez	2.50
6	Andres Galarraga	.50
7	Jay Buhner	.50
8	Mo Vaughn	2.00
9	Barry Bonds	2.00
10	Gary Sheffield	.50
11	Todd Hundley	.50
12	Frank Thomas	3.00
13	Sammy Sosa	5.00
14	Ken Caminiti	.50
15	Vinny Castilla	.50
16	Ellis Burks	.50
17	Rafael Palmeiro	.50
18	Alex Rodriguez	6.00
19	Mike Piazza	5.00
20	Eddie Murray	1.00

1997 Collector's Choice Premier Power Jumbo

Each factory set of 1997 Collector's Choice included 10 super-size (3" x 5") versions of the Premier Power inserts. Besides the size, the jumbos differ from the insert version in the addition of a metallic facsimile autograph on front.

		MT
Complete Set (20):		20.00
Common Player:		.50
1	Mark McGwire	5.00
2	Brady Anderson	.50
3	Ken Griffey Jr.	5.00
4	Albert Belle	.50
5	Juan Gonzalez	1.50
6	Andres Galarraga	.50
7	Jay Buhner	.50
8	Mo Vaughn	1.00
9	Barry Bonds	1.00
10	Gary Sheffield	.50
11	Todd Hundley	.50
12	Frank Thomas	1.50
13	Sammy Sosa	2.50
14	Ken Caminiti	.50
15	Vinny Castilla	.50
16	Ellis Burks	.50
17	Rafael Palmeiro	.50
18	Alex Rodriguez	3.00
19	Mike Piazza	2.50
20	Eddie Murray	.50

1997 Collector's Choice Stick'Ums

The 30-piece 2-1/2" x 3-1/2" sticker set was inserted one per three packs of Series 1 Collector's Choice. Fronts feature a bright background color and include five different peel-off stickers: An action shot of the player, a pennant in team colors featuring the player's name, a team logo, an Upper Deck Collector's Choice logo and a "Super Action Stick'Ums" decal. Backs feature the player checklist in black ink over a gray background. An unnumbered version of the stickers (without Smith and Puckett) was sold in a special retail-only package.

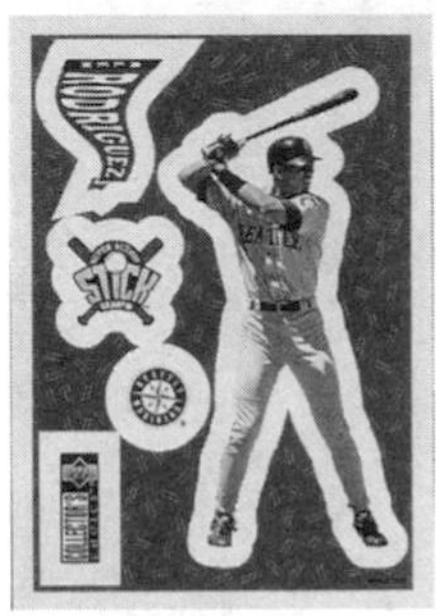

		MT
Complete Set (30):		20.00
Common Player:		.25
1	Ozzie Smith	.75
2	Andruw Jones	1.00
3	Alex Rodriguez	2.50
4	Paul Molitor	.50
5	Jeff Bagwell	1.25
6	Manny Ramirez	1.00
7	Kenny Lofton	.50
8	Albert Belle	.75
9	Jay Buhner	.25
10	Chipper Jones	1.50
11	Barry Larkin	.25
12	Dante Bichette	.25
13	Mike Piazza	1.50
14	Andres Galarraga	.25
15	Barry Bonds	.75
16	Brady Anderson	.25
17	Gary Sheffield	.25
18	Jim Thome	.25
19	Tony Gwynn	1.25
20	Cal Ripken Jr.	2.50
21	Sammy Sosa	1.50
22	Juan Gonzalez	.75
23	Greg Maddux	1.00
24	Ken Griffey Jr.	3.00
25	Mark McGwire	3.00
26	Kirby Puckett	1.00
27	Mo Vaughn	.40
28	Vladimir Guerrero	1.00
29	Ken Caminiti	.25
30	Frank Thomas	1.50

1997 Collector's Choice Toast of the Town

This 30-card Series 2 insert features top stars on foil-enhanced cards. Odds of finding one are 1:35 packs. Cards are numbered with a "T" prefix.

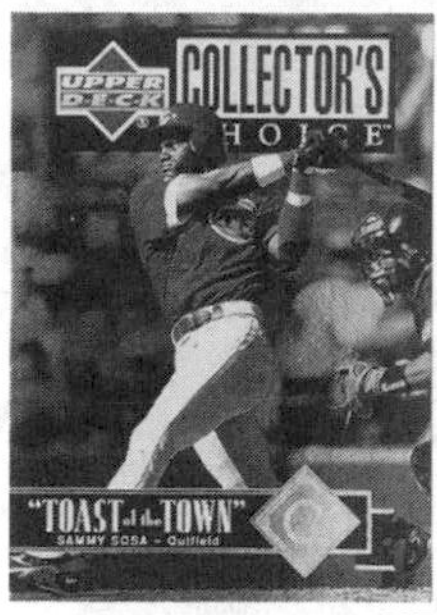

		MT
Complete Set (30):		120.00
Common Player:		1.00
1	Andruw Jones	4.00
2	Chipper Jones	7.50
3	Greg Maddux	6.00
4	John Smoltz	1.00
5	Kenny Lofton	2.00
6	Brady Anderson	1.00
7	Cal Ripken Jr.	12.00
8	Mo Vaughn	2.00
9	Sammy Sosa	7.50
10	Albert Belle	2.00
11	Frank Thomas	4.00
12	Barry Larkin	1.00
13	Manny Ramirez	4.00
14	Jeff Bagwell	5.00
15	Mike Piazza	7.50
16	Paul Molitor	2.00
17	Vladimir Guerrero	6.00
18	Todd Hundley	1.00
19	Derek Jeter	7.50
20	Andy Pettitte	1.00
21	Bernie Williams	1.00
22	Mark McGwire	15.00
23	Scott Rolen	5.00
24	Ken Caminiti	1.00
25	Tony Gwynn	5.00
26	Barry Bonds	3.00
27	Ken Griffey Jr.	15.00
28	Alex Rodriguez	12.50
29	Juan Gonzalez	4.00
30	Roger Clemens	3.00

1997 Collector's Choice Update

This update set was offered via a mail-in redemption offer. Traded players in their new uniforms and 1997 rookies are the focus of the set. Fronts are color photos which are borderless at top and sides. Beneath each photo the player's name and team logo appear in a red (A.L.) or blue (N.L.) baseball design. Backs have another photo, major and minor league career stats and a trivia question. Cards are numbered with a "U" prefix.

		MT
Complete Set (30):		5.00
Common Player:		.15
1	Jim Leyritz	.15
2	Matt Perisho	.15
3	Michael Tucker	.15
4	Mike Johnson	.15
5	Jaime Navarro	.15
6	Doug Drabek	.15
7	Terry Mulholland	.35
8	Brett Tomko	.15
9	Marquis Grissom	.40
10	David Justice	.40
11	Brian Moehler	.15
12	Bobby Bonilla	.30
13	Todd Dunwoody	.40
14	Tony Saunders	.15
15	Jay Bell	.15
16	Jeff King	.15
17	Terry Steinbach	.15
18	Steve Bieser	.15
19	*Takashi Kashiwada*	.40
20	Hideki Irabu	1.00
21	Damon Mashore	.15
22	Quilvio Veras	.15
23	Will Cunnane	.15
24	Jeff Kent	.35
25	J.T. Snow	.40
26	Dante Powell	.15
27	Jose Cruz Jr.	.50
28	John Burkett	.15
29	John Wetteland	.15
30	Benito Santiago	.15

1997 Collector's Choice Team Sets

A special version of Collector's Choice cards for several popular major league teams was produced in two retail packages by Upper Deck. In one version, blister packs containing 13 player cards and a metallic-foil team logo/checklist card was sold for a suggested retail price of $1.99. The second version, exclusive to Wal-Mart, is a hard plastic blister pack containing two cello-wrapped packages. One holds a random assortment of 15 Series 1 Collector's Choice cards. The other has 13 player cards and a foil logo/checklist card for a specific team. The team-set cards are identical to the regular-issue cards, from either Series 1 or Series 2, except each of the team-set cards has a number on back which differs from the regular edition. Packaged with the Wal-Mart version is a 3-1/2" x 5" "Home Team Heroes" card, listed seperately.

		MT
Common Player:		.10
	Atlanta Braves team set:	4.00
AB	Team logo/checklist	.10
AB1	Andruw Jones	1.00
AB2	Kenny Lofton	.30
AB3	Fred McGriff	.20
AB4	Michael Tucker	.10
AB5	Ryan Klesko	.20
AB6	Javy Lopez	.15
AB7	Mark Wohlers	.10
AB8	Tom Glavine	.20
AB9	Denny Neagle	.10
AB10	Chipper Jones	1.25
AB11	Jeff Blauser	.10
AB12	Greg Maddux	1.00
AB13	John Smoltz	.20
	Baltimore Orioles team set:	2.00
BO	Team logo/checklist	.10
BO1	Rocky Coppinger	.10
BO2	Scott Erickson	.10
BO3	Chris Hoiles	.10
BO4	Roberto Alomar	.40
BO5	Cal Ripken Jr.	1.50
BO6	Randy Myers	.10
BO7	B.J. Surhoff	.10
BO8	Mike Mussina	.35
BO9	Rafael Palmeiro	.30
BO10	Jimmy Key	.10
BO11	Mike Bordick	.10
BO12	Brady Anderson	.20
BO13	Eric Davis	.10
	Chicago White Sox team set:	2.50
CW	Team logo/checklist	.10
CW1	Robin Ventura	.10
CW2	Wilson Alvarez	.10
CW3	Tony Phillips	.10
CW4	Lyle Mouton	.10
CW5	James Baldwin	.10
CW6	Harold Baines	.10
CW7	Albert Belle	.75
CW8	Chris Snopek	.10
CW9	Ray Durham	.10
CW10	Frank Thomas	1.00
CW11	Ozzie Guillen	.10
CW12	Roberto Hernandez	.10
CW13	Jaime Navarro	.10
	Cleveland Indians team set:	1.50
CI	Team logo/checklist	.10
CI1	Brian Giles	.10
CI2	Omar Vizquel	.10
CI3	Julio Franco	.10
CI4	Orel Hershiser	.10
CI5	Charles Nagy	.10
CI6	Matt Williams	.20
CI7	Jose Mesa	.10
CI8	Sandy Alomar	.20
CI9	Jim Thome	.35
CI10	David Justice	.25
CI11	Marquis Grissom	.15
CI12	Chad Ogea	.10
CI13	Manny Ramirez	.65
	Colorado Rockies team set:	1.25
CR	Team logo/checklist	.10
CR1	Dante Bichette	.20
CR2	Vinny Castilla	.10
CR3	Kevin Ritz	.10
CR4	Larry Walker	.30
CR5	Eric Young	.10
CR6	Quinton McCracken	.10
CR7	John Vander Wal	.10
CR8	Jamey Wright	.10
CR9	Mark Thompson	.10
CR10	Andres Galarraga	.25
CR11	Ellis Burks	.10
CR12	Kirt Manwaring	.10
CR13	Walt Weiss	.10
	Florida Marlins team set:	2.00
FM	Team logo/checklist	.10
FM1	(Luis Castillo)	.10
FM2	(Al Leiter)	.15
FM3	(Devon White)	.15
FM4	(Jeff Conine)	.10
FM5	(Charles Johnson)	.15
FM6	(Edgar Renteria)	.20
FM7	(Robb Nen)	.10
FM8	(Kevin Brown)	.50
FM9	(Gary Sheffield)	.25
FM10	(Alex Fernandez)	.15
FM11	(Pat Rapp)	.10
FM12	(Moises Alou)	.25
FM13	(Bobby Bonilla)	.10
	L.A. Dodgers team set:	3.00
LA	Team logo/checklist	.10
LA1	(Raul Mondesi)	.35
LA2	(Brett Butler)	.10
LA3	(Todd Hollandsworth)	.10
LA4	(Eric Karros)	.10
LA5	(Hideo Nomo)	.50
LA6	(Ismael Valdes)	.15
LA7	(Wilton Guerrero)	.10
LA8	(Ramon Martinez)	.15
LA9	(Greg Gagne)	.10
LA10	(Mike Piazza)	1.00
LA11	(Chan Ho Park)	.35
LA12	(Todd Worrell)	.10
LA13	(Todd Zeile)	.10

1997 Collector's Choice You Crash the Game

A 30-card interactive set found in Series 2 packs features the game's top home run hitters. Cards were inserted 1:5 packs. Fronts feature a red-foil Crash logo and a range of game dates. Those holding cards of players who homered in that span could (for $2 per card handling fee) redeem them for high-tech versions. Instant winner cards (seeded 1:721) were redeemable for complete 30-card upgrade sets. Winning cards are marked with an asterisk; theoretically they would be scarcer than losing cards because many were redeemed. The contest cards expired on Sept. 8, 1997. Cards are numbered with a "CG" prefix.

		MT
Complete Set (30):		40.00
Common Player:		.50
1	Ryan Klesko July 28-30	.50

No.	Player / Date	MT
	August 8-11	.50
	Sept. 19-21	.50
2	Chipper Jones	
	August 15-17	3.00
	August 29-31	3.00
	Sept. 12-14	3.00
3	Andruw Jones	
	August 22-24*	3.00
	Sept. 1-3	1.50
	Sept. 19-22	1.50
4	Brady Anderson	
	July 31-Aug. 3*	1.00
	Sept. 4-7	.50
	Sept. 19-22	.50
5	Rafael Palmeiro	
	July 29-30	.50
	Aug. 29-31	.50
	Sept. 26-28	.50
6	Cal Ripken Jr.	
	August 8-10*	6.00
	Sept. 1-3*	6.00
	Sept. 11-14	4.00
7	Mo Vaughn	
	August 14-17	.75
	August 29-31*	1.50
	Sept. 23-25*	1.50
8	Sammy Sosa	
	August 1-3*	4.50
	August 29-31	3.00
	Sept. 19-21*	4.50
9	Albert Belle	
	August 7-10	.65
	Sept. 11-14	.65
	Sept. 19-21*	1.25
10	Frank Thomas	
	August 29-31	2.50
	Sept. 1-3	2.50
	Sept. 23-25*	5.00
11	Manny Ramirez	
	August 12-14*	1.00
	August 29-31	.50
	Sept. 11-14*	1.00
12	Jim Thome	
	July 28-30	.50
	August 15-18*	1.00
	Sept. 19-22	.50
13	Matt Williams	
	August 4-5	.50
	Sept. 1-3*	1.00
	Sept. 23-25	.50
14	Dante Bichette	
	July 24-27*	1.00
	August 28-29	.50
	Sept. 26-28*	1.00
15	Vinny Castilla	
	August 12-13	.50
	Sept. 4-7*	1.00
	Sept. 19-21	.50
16	Andres Galarraga	
	August 8-10*	1.00
	August 30-31	.50
	Sept. 12-14	.50
17	Gary Sheffield	
	August 1-3*	1.00
	Sept. 1-3*	1.00
	Sept. 12-14*	1.00
18	Jeff Bagwell	
	Sept. 9-10	.75
	Sept. 19-22*	1.50
	Sept. 23-25*	1.50
19	Eric Karros	
	August 1-3	.50
	August 15-17	.50
	Sept. 25-28*	1.00
20	Mike Piazza	
	August 11-12	2.00
	Sept. 5-8*	4.00
	Sept. 19-21*	4.00
21	Vladimir Guerrero	
	August 22-24	1.00
	August 29-31	1.00
	Sept. 19-22	1.00
22	Cecil Fielder	
	August 29-31	.50
	Sept. 4-7	.50
	Sept. 26-28*	1.00
23	Jose Canseco	
	August 22-24	.65
	Sept. 12-14	.65
	Sept. 26-28	.65
24	Mark McGwire	
	July 31-Aug. 3	2.50
	August 30-31	2.50
	Sept. 19-22*	5.00
25	Ken Caminiti	
	August 8-10	.50
	Sept. 4-7	.50
	Sept. 17-18*	1.00
26	Barry Bonds	
	August 5-7	.90
	Sept. 4-7*	2.00
	Sept. 23-24*	2.00
27	Jay Buhner	
	August 7-10	.50
	August 28-29	.50
	Sept. 1-3	.50
28	Ken Griffey Jr.	
	August 22-24*	5.00
	August 28-29	3.00
	Sept. 19-22*	5.00
29	Alex Rodriguez	
	July 29-31	1.50
	August 30-31	1.50
	Sept. 12-15	1.50
30	Juan Gonzalez	
	August 11-13*	2.00
	August 30-31	1.00
	Sept. 19-21*	2.00

1997 Collector's Choice You Crash the Game Winners

These are the prize cards from CC's interactive "You Crash the Game" cards in Series 2. Persons who redeemed a Crash card with the correct date (s) on which the pictured player homered received (for a $2 handling fee) this high-end version of the Crash card. The redemption cards have the same basic design as the contest cards, but use different player photos with fronts printed on metallic-foil stock, and a team logo in place of the Crash foil logo. Where the contest cards have game rules on back, the redemption cards have another photo of the player and career highlights. Complete redemption sets were available upon redeeming an instant winner card, found on average of one per 721 packs. Because some cards were only available in complete redemption sets (marked with an "SP" here), and others might have been available for more than one date range, some cards will be scarcer than others.

		MT
Complete Set (30):		40.00
Common Player:		1.00
CG1	Ryan Klesko (SP)	1.50
CG2	Chipper Jones (SP)	10.00
CG3	Andruw Jones	1.00
CG4	Brady Anderson	1.00
CG5	Rafael Palmeiro (SP)	4.00
CG6	Cal Ripken Jr.	6.00
CG7	Mo Vaughn	1.00
CG8	Sammy Sosa	3.00
CG9	Albert Belle	1.50
CG10	Frank Thomas	2.00
CG11	Manny Ramirez	1.50
CG12	Jim Thome	1.00
CG13	Matt Williams	1.00
CG14	Dante Bichette	1.00
CG15	Vinny Castilla	1.00
CG16	Andres Galarraga	1.00
CG17	Gary Sheffield	1.00
CG18	Jeff Bagwell	1.50
CG19	Eric Karros	1.00
CG20	Mike Piazza	4.00
CG21	Vladimir Guerrero (SP)	6.00
CG22	Cecil Fielder (SP)	1.50
CG23	Jose Canseco (SP)	4.00
CG24	Mark McGwire	6.00
CG25	Ken Caminiti	1.00
CG26	Barry Bonds	1.50
CG27	Jay Buhner (SP)	1.50
CG28	Ken Griffey Jr.	6.00
CG29	Alex Rodriguez (SP)	15.00
CG30	Juan Gonzalez	1.50

1998 Collector's Choice

The 530-card Collectors Choice set was issued in two 265-card series. Series 1 features 197-regular cards, five checklists and four subsets: Cover Story features 18 of the leagues' top stars, Rookie Class has 27 young players, the nine-card Top of the Charts subset honors 1997's statistical leaders and Masked Marauders is a nine-card subset. Inserts in Series One are Super Action Stick-Ums, Evolution Revolution and StarQuest. Series 2 has 233 regular cards, five checklist cards, an 18-card Rookie Class subset and the nine-card Golden Jubilee subset. Inserts in Series 2 include Mini Bobbing Head Cards, You Crash the Game and StarQuest.

		MT
Complete Set (530):		30.00
Complete Series I Set (265):		15.00
Complete Series II Set (265):		15.00
Common Player:		.05
Pack (14):		1.25
Wax Box (36):		40.00
1	Nomar Garciaparra (Cover Glory)	.60
2	Roger Clemens (Cover Glory)	.30
3	Larry Walker (Cover Glory)	.10
4	Mike Piazza (Cover Glory)	.60
5	Mark McGwire (Cover Glory)	1.00
6	Tony Gwynn (Cover Glory)	.50
7	Jose Cruz Jr. (Cover Glory)	.15
8	Frank Thomas (Cover Glory)	.50
9	Tino Martinez (Cover Glory)	.10
10	Ken Griffey Jr. (Cover Glory)	1.00
11	Barry Bonds (Cover Glory)	.25
12	Scott Rolen (Cover Glory)	.50
13	Randy Johnson (Cover Glory)	.15
14	Ryne Sandberg (Cover Glory)	.25
15	Eddie Murray (Cover Glory)	.10
16	Kevin Brown (Cover Glory)	.05
17	Greg Maddux (Cover Glory)	.60
18	Sandy Alomar Jr. (Cover Glory)	.05
19	Checklist (Ken Griffey Jr., Adam Riggs)	.50
20	Checklist (Nomar Garciaparra, Charlie O'Brien)	.30
21	Checklist (Ben Grieve, Ken Griffey Jr., Larry Walker, Mark McGwire)	1.00
22	Checklist (Mark McGwire, Cal Ripken Jr.)	1.00
23	Checklist (Tino Martinez)	.05
24	Jason Dickson	.05
25	Darin Erstad	.60
26	Todd Greene	.15
27	Chuck Finley	.05
28	Garret Anderson	.05
29	Dave Hollins	.05
30	Rickey Henderson	.05
31	John Smoltz	.15
32	Michael Tucker	.05
33	Jeff Blauser	.05
34	Javier Lopez	.10
35	Andruw Jones	1.00
36	Denny Neagle	.05
37	Randall Simon	.15
38	Mark Wohlers	.05
39	Harold Baines	.05
40	Cal Ripken Jr.	1.50
41	Mike Bordick	.05
42	Jimmy Key	.05
43	Armando Benitez	.05
44	Scott Erickson	.05
45	Eric Davis	.05
46	Bret Saberhagen	.05
47	Darren Bragg	.05
48	Steve Avery	.05
49	Jeff Frye	.05
50	Aaron Sele	.05
51	Scott Hatteberg	.05
52	Tom Gordon	.05

53 Kevin Orie .05
54 Kevin Foster .05
55 Ryne Sandberg .50
56 Doug Glanville .05
57 Tyler Houston .05
58 Steve Trachsel .05
59 Mark Grace .15
60 Frank Thomas 1.00
61 *Scott Eyre* .15
62 Jeff Abbott .05
63 Chris Clemons .05
64 Jorge Fabregas .05
65 Robin Ventura .10
66 Matt Karchner .05
67 Jon Nunnally .05
68 Aaron Boone .05
69 Pokey Reese .05
70 Deion Sanders .15
71 Jeff Shaw .05
72 Eduardo Perez .05
73 Brett Tomko .05
74 Bartolo Colon .05
75 Manny Ramirez .50
76 Jose Mesa .05
77 Brian Giles .05
78 Richie Sexson .05
79 Orel Hershiser .05
80 Matt Williams .20
81 Walt Weiss .05
82 Jerry DiPoto .05
83 Quinton McCracken .05
84 Neifi Perez .05
85 Vinny Castilla .10
86 Ellis Burks .05
87 John Thomson .05
88 Willie Blair .05
89 Bob Hamelin .05
90 Tony Clark .35
91 Todd Jones .05
92 Deivi Cruz .05
93 *Frank Catalanotto* .15
94 Justin Thompson .05
95 Gary Sheffield .25
96 Kevin Brown .15
97 Charles Johnson .10
98 Bobby Bonilla .10
99 Livan Hernandez .05
100 Paul Konerko (Rookie Class) .60
101 Craig Counsell (Rookie Class) .05
102 *Magglio Ordonez* (Rookie Class) .50
103 Garrett Stephenson (Rookie Class) .05
104 Ken Cloude (Rookie Class) .15
105 Miguel Tejada (Rookie Class) .40
106 Juan Encarnacion (Rookie Class) .20
107 Dennis Reyes (Rookie Class) .15
108 Orlando Cabrera (Rookie Class) .05
109 Kelvim Escobar (Rookie Class) .05
110 Ben Grieve (Rookie Class) .75
111 Brian Rose (Rookie Class) .05
112 Fernando Tatis (Rookie Class) .20
113 Tom Evans (Rookie Class) .05
114 Tom Fordham (Rookie Class) .05
115 Mark Kotsay (Rookie Class) .40
116 Mario Valdez (Rookie Class) .05
117 Jeremi Gonzalez (Rookie Class) .05
118 Todd Dunwoody (Rookie Class) .05
119 Javier Valentin (Rookie Class) .05
120 Todd Helton (Rookie Class) .50
121 Jason Varitek (Rookie Class) .05
122 Chris Carpenter (Rookie Class) .05
123 *Kevin Millwood* (Rookie Class) 1.00
124 Brad Fullmer (Rookie Class) .05
125 Jaret Wright (Rookie Class) 1.00
126 Brad Rigby (Rookie Class) .05
127 Edgar Renteria .05
128 Robb Nen .05
129 Tony Pena .05
130 Craig Biggio .15
131 Brad Ausmus .05
132 Shane Reynolds .05
133 Mike Hampton .05
134 Billy Wagner .05
135 Richard Hidalgo .05
136 Jose Rosado .05
137 Yamil Benitez .05
138 Felix Martinez .05
139 Jeff King .05
140 Jose Offerman .05
141 Joe Vitiello .05
142 Tim Belcher .05
143 Brett Butler .05
144 Greg Gagne .05
145 Mike Piazza 1.25
146 Ramon Martinez .10
147 Raul Mondesi .20
148 Adam Riggs .05
149 Eddie Murray .20
150 Jeff Cirillo .05
151 Scott Karl .05
152 Mike Fetters .05
153 Dave Nilsson .05
154 Antone Williamson .05
155 Jeff D'Amico .05
156 Jose Valentin .05
157 Brad Radke .05
158 Torii Hunter .05
159 Chuck Knoblauch .15
160 Paul Molitor .35
161 Travis Miller .05
162 Rich Robertson .05
163 Ron Coomer .05
164 Mark Grudzielanek .05
165 Lee Smith .05
166 Vladimir Guerrero .75
167 Dustin Hermanson .05
168 Ugueth Urbina .05
169 F.P. Santangelo .05
170 Rondell White .15
171 Bobby Jones .05
172 Edgardo Alfonzo .15
173 John Franco .05
174 Carlos Baerga .05
175 Butch Huskey .05
176 Rey Ordonez .10
177 Matt Franco .05
178 Dwight Gooden .15
179 Chad Curtis .05
180 Tino Martinez .15
181 Charlie O'Brien (Masked Marauders) .05
182 Sandy Alomar Jr. (Masked Marauders) .05
183 Raul Casanova (Masked Marauders) .05
184 Jim Leyritz (Masked Marauders) .05
185 Mike Piazza (Masked Marauders) .60
186 Ivan Rodriguez (Masked Marauders) .25
187 Charles Johnson (Masked Marauders) .10
188 Brad Ausmus (Masked Marauders) .05
189 Brian Johnson (Masked Marauders) .05
190 Wade Boggs .20
191 David Wells .05
192 Tim Raines .05
193 Ramiro Mendoza .05
194 Willie Adams .05
195 Matt Stairs .05
196 Jason McDonald .05
197 Dave Magadan .05
198 Mark Bellhorn .05
199 Ariel Prieto .05
200 Jose Canseco .20
201 Bobby Estalella .05
202 *Tony Barron* .05
203 Midre Cummings .05
204 Ricky Bottalico .05
205 Mike Grace .05
206 Rico Brogna .05
207 Mickey Morandini .05
208 Lou Collier .05
209 *Kevin Polcovich* .05
210 Kevin Young .05
211 Jose Guillen .25
212 Esteban Loaiza .05
213 Marc Wilkins .05
214 Jason Schmidt .05
215 Gary Gaetti .05
216 Fernando Valenzuela .05
217 Willie McGee .05
218 Alan Benes .15
219 Eli Marrero .05
220 Mark McGwire 2.50
221 Matt Morris .05
222 Trevor Hoffman .05
223 Will Cunnane .05
224 Joey Hamilton .05
225 Ken Caminiti .15
226 Derrek Lee .15
227 Mark Sweeney .05
228 Carlos Hernandez .05
229 Brian Johnson .05
230 Jeff Kent .05
231 Kirk Rueter .05
232 Bill Mueller .05
233 Dante Powell .05
234 J.T. Snow .15
235 Shawn Estes .05
236 Dennis Martinez .05
237 Jamie Moyer .05
238 Dan Wilson .05
239 Joey Cora .05
240 Ken Griffey Jr. 2.00
241 Paul Sorrento .05
242 Jay Buhner .20
243 *Hanley Frias* .05
244 John Burkett .05
245 Juan Gonzalez .50
246 Rick Helling .05
247 Darren Oliver .05
248 Mickey Tettleton .05
249 Ivan Rodriguez .50
250 Joe Carter .15
251 Pat Hentgen .05
252 Marty Janzen .05
253 Frank Thomas, Tony Gwynn (Top of the Charts) .25
254 Mark McGwire, Ken Griffey Jr., Larry Walker (Top of the Charts) 1.00
255 Ken Griffey Jr., Andres Galarraga (Top of the Charts) .50
256 Brian Hunter, Tony Womack (Top of the Charts) .05
257 Roger Clemens, Denny Neagle (Top of the Charts) .20
258 Roger Clemens, Curt Schilling (Top of the Charts) .20
259 Roger Clemens, Pedro J. Martinez (Top of the Charts) .20
260 Randy Myers, Jeff Shaw (Top of the Charts) .05
261 Nomar Garciaparra, Scott Rolen (Top of the Charts) .30
262 Charlie O'Brien .05
263 Shannon Stewart .05
264 Robert Person .05
265 Carlos Delgado .25
266 Checklist (Matt Williams, Travis Lee) .25
267 Checklist (Nomar Garciaparra, Cal Ripken Jr.) .40
268 Checklist (Mark McGwire, Mike Piazza) .75
269 Checklist (Tony Gwynn, Ken Griffey Jr.) .50
270 Checklist (Fred McGriff, Jose Cruz Jr.) .10
271 Andruw Jones (Golden Jubilee) .25
272 Alex Rodriguez (Golden Jubilee) .60
273 Juan Gonzalez (Golden Jubilee) .25
274 Nomar Garciaparra (Golden Jubilee) .60
275 Ken Griffey Jr (Golden Jubilee) 1.00
276 Tino Martinez (Golden Jubilee) .15
277 Roger Clemens (Golden Jubilee) .40
278 Barry Bonds (Golden Jubilee) .25
279 Mike Piazza (Golden Jubilee) .60
280 Tim Salmon (Golden Jubilee) .15
281 Gary DiSarcina .05
282 Cecil Fielder .15
283 Ken Hill .05
284 Troy Percival .05
285 Jim Edmonds .05
286 Allen Watson .05
287 Brian Anderson .05
288 Jay Bell .05
289 Jorge Fabregas .05
290 Devon White .05
291 Yamil Benitez .05
292 Jeff Suppan .05
293 Tony Batista .05
294 Brent Brede .05
295 Andy Benes .15
296 Felix Rodriguez .05
297 Karim Garcia .05
298 Omar Daal .05
299 Andy Stankiewicz .05
300 Matt Williams .25
301 Willie Blair .05
302 Ryan Klesko .20
303 Tom Glavine .15
304 Walt Weiss .05
305 Greg Maddux 1.25
306 Chipper Jones 1.25
307 Keith Lockhart .05
308 Andres Galarraga .20
309 Chris Hoiles .05
310 Roberto Alomar .40
311 Joe Carter .15
312 Doug Drabek .05
313 Jeffrey Hammonds .05
314 Rafael Palmeiro .20
315 Mike Mussina .40
316 Brady Anderson .05
317 B.J. Surhoff .05
318 Dennis Eckersley .05
319 Jim Leyritz .05
320 Mo Vaughn .50
321 Nomar Garciaparra 1.25
322 Reggie Jefferson .05
323 Tim Naehring .05
324 Troy O'Leary .05
325 Pedro J. Martinez .25
326 John Valentin .05
327 Mark Clark .05
328 Rod Beck .05
329 Mickey Morandini .05
330 Sammy Sosa 1.50
331 Jeff Blauser .05
332 Lance Johnson .05
333 Scott Servais .05
334 Kevin Tapani .05
335 Henry Rodriguez .05
336 Jaime Navarro .05
337 Benji Gil .05
338 James Baldwin .05
339 Mike Cameron .05
340 Ray Durham .05
341 Chris Snopek .05
342 Eddie Taubensee .05
343 Bret Boone .05
344 Willie Greene .05
345 Barry Larkin .15
346 Chris Stynes .05
347 Pete Harnisch .05
348 Dave Burba .05
349 Sandy Alomar Jr. .15
350 Kenny Lofton .50
351 Geronimo Berroa .05
352 Omar Vizquel .05
353 Travis Fryman .05
354 Dwight Gooden .05
355 Jim Thome .40
356 David Justice .25
357 Charles Nagy .05
358 Chad Ogea .05

359	Pedro Astacio	.05
360	Larry Walker	.25
361	Mike Lansing	.05
362	Kirt Manwaring	.05
363	Dante Bichette	.15
364	Jamey Wright	.05
365	Darryl Kile	.05
366	Luis Gonzalez	.05
367	Joe Randa	.05
368	Raul Casanova	.05
369	Damion Easley	.05
370	Brian L. Hunter	.05
371	Bobby Higginson	.05
372	Brian Moehler	.05
373	Scott Sanders	.05
374	Jim Eisenreich	.05
375	Derrek Lee	.05
376	Jay Powell	.05
377	Cliff Floyd	.05
378	Alex Fernandez	.05
379	Felix Heredia	.05
380	Jeff Bagwell	.75
381	Bill Spiers	.05
382	Chris Holt	.05
383	Carl Everett	.05
384	Derek Bell	.05
385	Moises Alou	.15
386	Ramon Garcia	.05
387	Mike Sweeney	.05
388	Glendon Rusch	.05
389	Kevin Appier	.05
390	Dean Palmer	.05
391	Jeff Conine	.05
392	Johnny Damon	.05
393	Jose Vizcaino	.05
394	Todd Hollandsworth	.05
395	Eric Karros	.05
396	Todd Zeile	.05
397	Chan Ho Park	.15
398	Ismael Valdes	.05
399	Eric Young	.05
400	Hideo Nomo	.40
401	Mark Loretta	.05
402	Doug Jones	.05
403	Jeromy Burnitz	.05
404	John Jaha	.05
405	Marquis Grissom	.05
406	Mike Matheny	.05
407	Todd Walker	.05
408	Marty Cordova	.05
409	Matt Lawton	.05
410	Terry Steinbach	.05
411	Pat Meares	.05
412	Rick Aguilera	.05
413	Otis Nixon	.05
414	Derrick May	.05
415	Carl Pavano (Rookie Class)	.05
416	A.J. Hinch (Rookie Class)	.15
417	*David Dellucci* (Rookie Class)	.25
418	Bruce Chen (Rookie Class)	.15
419	*Darron Ingram* (Rookie Class)	.05
420	Sean Casey (Rookie Class)	.05
421	Mark L. Johnson (Rookie Class)	.05
422	Gabe Alvarez (Rookie Class)	.05
423	Alex Gonzalez (Rookie Class)	.05
424	Daryle Ward (Rookie Class)	.15
425	Russell Branyan (Rookie Class)	.05
426	Mike Caruso (Rookie Class)	.05
427	*Mike Kinkade* (Rookie Class)	.25
428	Ramon Hernandez (Rookie Class)	.05
429	Matt Clement (Rookie Class)	.10
430	Travis Lee (Rookie Class)	.60
431	Shane Monahan (Rookie Class)	.05
432	*Rich Butler* (Rookie Class)	.25
433	Chris Widger	.05
434	Jose Vidro	.05
435	Carlos Perez	.05
436	Ryan McGuire	.05
437	Brian McRae	.05
438	Al Leiter	.05
439	Rich Becker	.05
440	Todd Hundley	.05
441	Dave Mlicki	.05
442	Bernard Gilkey	.05
443	John Olerud	.15
444	Paul O'Neill	.15
445	Andy Pettitte	.40
446	David Cone	.15
447	Chili Davis	.05
448	Bernie Williams	.40
449	Joe Girardi	.05
450	Derek Jeter	1.25
451	Mariano Rivera	.15
452	George Williams	.05
453	Kenny Rogers	.05
454	Tom Candiotti	.05
455	Rickey Henderson	.05
456	Jason Giambi	.05
457	Scott Spiezio	.05
458	Doug Glanville	.05
459	Desi Relaford	.05
460	Curt Schilling	.15
461	Bob Abreu	.05
462	Gregg Jefferies	.05
463	Scott Rolen	.75
464	Mike Lieberthal	.05
465	Tony Womack	.05
466	Jermaine Allensworth	.05
467	Francisco Cordova	.05
468	Jon Lieber	.05
469	Al Martin	.05
470	Jason Kendall	.05
471	Todd Stottlemyre	.05
472	Royce Clayton	.05
473	Brian Jordan	.05
474	John Mabry	.05
475	Ray Lankford	.05
476	Delino DeShields	.05
477	Ron Gant	.05
478	Mark Langston	.05
479	Steve Finley	.05
480	Tony Gwynn	1.00
481	Andy Ashby	.05
482	Wally Joyner	.05
483	Greg Vaughn	.05
484	Sterling Hitchcock	.05
485	J. Kevin Brown	.05
486	Orel Hershiser	.05
487	Charlie Hayes	.05
488	Darryl Hamilton	.05
489	Mark Gardner	.05
490	Barry Bonds	.50
491	Robb Nen	.05
492	Kirk Rueter	.05
493	Randy Johnson	.40
494	Jeff Fassero	.05
495	Alex Rodriguez	1.25
496	David Segui	.05
497	Rich Amaral	.05
498	Russ Davis	.05
499	Bubba Trammell	.05
500	Wade Boggs	.20
501	Roberto Hernandez	.05
502	Dave Martinez	.05
503	Dennis Springer	.05
504	Paul Sorrento	.05
505	Wilson Alvarez	.05
506	Mike Kelly	.05
507	Albie Lopez	.05
508	Tony Saunders	.05
509	John Flaherty	.05
510	Fred McGriff	.15
511	Quinton McCracken	.05
512	Terrell Wade	.05
513	Kevin Stocker	.05
514	Kevin Elster	.05
515	Will Clark	.20
516	Bobby Witt	.05
517	Tom Goodwin	.05
518	Aaron Sele	.05
519	Lee Stevens	.05
520	Rusty Greer	.05
521	John Wetteland	.05
522	Darrin Fletcher	.05
523	Jose Canseco	.25
524	Randy Myers	.05
525	Jose Cruz Jr.	.15
526	Shawn Green	.05
527	Tony Fernandez	.05
528	Alex Gonzalez	.05
529	Ed Sprague	.05
530	Roger Clemens	.75

1998 Collector's Choice Evolution Revolution

This 28-card insert features one player from each Major League team. The fronts picture the team jersey and open to reveal the player's top 1997 accomplishment. Evolution Revolution was inserted one per 13 Series 1 packs. Cards are numbered with an "ER" prefix.

		MT
Complete Set (28):		60.00
Common Player:		.75
Inserted 1:13		
1	Tim Salmon	1.25
2	Greg Maddux	5.00
3	Cal Ripken Jr.	8.00
4	Mo Vaughn	2.50
5	Sammy Sosa	6.00
6	Frank Thomas	4.00
7	Barry Larkin	1.00
8	Jim Thome	1.50
9	Larry Walker	1.25
10	Travis Fryman	.75
11	Gary Sheffield	1.50
12	Jeff Bagwell	4.00
13	Johnny Damon	.75
14	Mike Piazza	6.00
15	Jeff Cirillo	.75
16	Paul Molitor	2.00
17	Vladimir Guerrero	4.00
18	Todd Hundley	.75
19	Tino Martinez	.75
20	Jose Canseco	1.00
21	Scott Rolen	5.00
22	Al Martin	.75
23	Mark McGwire	12.00
24	Tony Gwynn	5.00
25	Barry Bonds	2.50
26	Ken Griffey Jr.	10.00
27	Juan Gonzalez	3.00
28	Roger Clemens	4.00

1998 Collector's Choice Mini Bobbing Heads

The cards in this 30-card insert series can be punched out and assembled into a stand-up figure with a removable bobbing head. They were inserted 1:3 in Series 2 packs.

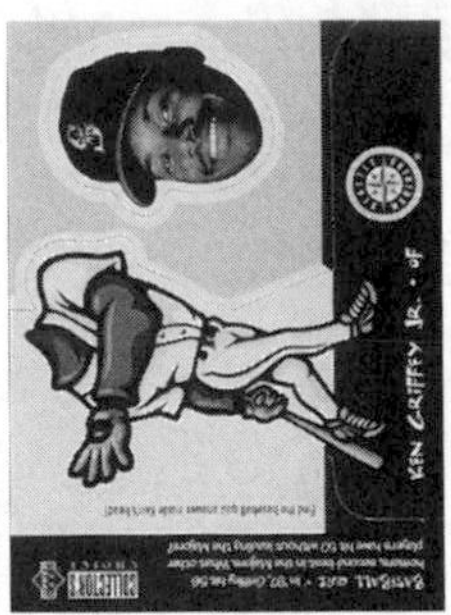

		MT
Complete Set (30):		20.00
Common Player:		.25
Inserted 1:3		
1	Tim Salmon	.40
2	Travis Lee	.75
3	Matt Williams	.25
4	Chipper Jones	1.50
5	Greg Maddux	1.00
6	Cal Ripken Jr.	2.00
7	Nomar Garciaparra	1.50
8	Mo Vaughn	.75
9	Sammy Sosa	1.50
10	Frank Thomas	1.20
11	Kenny Lofton	.75
12	Jaret Wright	.75
13	Larry Walker	.50
14	Tony Clark	.50
15	Edgar Renteria	.25
16	Jeff Bagwell	1.00
17	Mike Piazza	1.50
18	Vladimir Guerrero	1.00
19	Derek Jeter	1.50
20	Ben Grieve	.85
21	Scott Rolen	.80
22	Mark McGwire	3.00
23	Tony Gwynn	1.25
24	Barry Bonds	.90
25	Ken Griffey Jr.	3.00
26	Alex Rodriguez	2.00
27	Fred McGriff	.40
28	Juan Gonzalez	.75
29	Roger Clemens	1.00
30	Jose Cruz Jr.	.25

1998 Collector's Choice Rookie Class: Prime Choice

This 18-card set is a parallel of the Rookie Class subset. Each card is foil-stamped with the words "Prime Choice Reserve." This hobby-only set is sequentially numbered to 500 and was inserted in Series 2 packs.

		MT
Complete Set (18):		100.00
Common Player:		5.00
415	Carl Pavano	7.50
416	A.J. Hinch	7.50
417	David Dellucci	9.00
418	Bruce Chen	10.00
419	Darron Ingram	5.00
420	Sean Casey	15.00
421	Mark L. Johnson	5.00
422	Gabe Alvarez	5.00
423	Alex Gonzalez	7.50
424	Daryle Ward	5.00
425	Russell Branyan	5.00
426	Mike Caruso	7.50
427	Mike Kinkade	5.00
428	Ramon Hernandez	5.00
429	Matt Clement	5.00
430	Travis Lee	15.00
431	Shane Monahan	5.00
432	Rich Butler	10.00

1998 Collector's Choice StarQuest - Series 1

The StarQuest insert in Series 1 consists of 90 cards within four tiers. The tiers are designated by the number of stars found on front, the more the better. Special Delivery (#1-45, one star) was inserted 1:1, Students of the Game (two stars, #46-65) 1:21, Super Powers (three stars, #66-80) 1:71 and Super Star Domain (four stars, #81-90) 1:145. All cards are numbered with a "SQ" prefix.

	MT
Complete Set (90):	500.00
Common Special Delivery (1-45)	.20
Inserted 1:1	
Common Student of the Game (46-65):	1.50
Inserted 1:21	
Common Super Power (66-80):	5.00
Inserted 1:71	
Common Superstar Domain (81-90):	10.00
Inserted 1:145	
1 Nomar Garciaparra	2.00
2 Scott Rolen	1.50
3 Jason Dickson	.20
4 Jaret Wright	1.50
5 Kevin Orie	.20
6 Jose Guillen	.50
7 Matt Morris	.20
8 Mike Cameron	.30
9 Kevin Polcovich	.20
10 Jose Cruz Jr.	.25
11 Miguel Tejada	.50
12 Fernando Tatis	.40
13 Todd Helton	.75
14 Ken Cloude	.20
15 Ben Grieve	1.00
16 Dante Powell	.20
17 Bubba Trammell	.30
18 Juan Encarnacion	.40
19 Derrek Lee	.20
20 Paul Konerko	1.00
21 Richard Hidalgo	.20
22 Denny Neagle	.20
23 David Justice	.40
24 Pedro J. Martinez	.40
25 Greg Maddux	2.00
26 Edgar Martinez	.20
27 Cal Ripken Jr.	2.50
28 Tim Salmon	.40
29 Shawn Estes	.20
30 Ken Griffey Jr.	3.00
31 Brad Radke	.20
32 Andy Pettitte	.50
33 Curt Schilling	.20
34 Raul Mondesi	.40
35 Alex Rodriguez	2.00
36 Jeff Kent	.20
37 Jeff Bagwell	1.25
38 Juan Gonzalez	1.00
39 Barry Bonds	.75
40 Mark McGwire	4.00
41 Frank Thomas	1.50
42 Ray Lankford	.20
43 Tony Gwynn	1.50
44 Mike Piazza	2.00
45 Tino Martinez	.20
46 Nomar Garciaparra	10.00
47 Paul Molitor	3.00
48 Chuck Knoblauch	2.00
49 Rusty Greer	1.50
50 Cal Ripken Jr.	12.00
51 Roberto Alomar	3.00
52 Scott Rolen	7.00
53 Derek Jeter	10.00
54 Mark Grace	2.00
55 Randy Johnson	2.50
56 Craig Biggio	1.50
57 Kenny Lofton	4.00
58 Eddie Murray	2.00
59 Ryne Sandberg	4.00
60 Rickey Henderson	1.50
61 Darin Erstad	4.00
62 Jim Edmonds	1.50
63 Ken Caminiti	2.00
64 Ivan Rodriguez	3.00
65 Tony Gwynn	8.00
66 Tony Clark	8.00
67 Andres Galarraga	6.00
68 Rafael Palmeiro	6.00
69 Manny Ramirez	8.00
70 Albert Belle	10.00
71 Jay Buhner	5.00
72 Mo Vaughn	10.00
73 Barry Bonds	10.00
74 Chipper Jones	25.00
75 Jeff Bagwell	18.00
76 Jim Thome	8.00
77 Sammy Sosa	12.00
78 Todd Hundley	5.00
79 Matt Williams	6.00
80 Vinny Castilla	5.00
81 Jose Cruz Jr.	10.00
82 Frank Thomas	25.00
83 Juan Gonzalez	20.00
84 Mike Piazza	40.00
85 Alex Rodriguez	40.00
86 Larry Walker	12.00
87 Tino Martinez	10.00
88 Greg Maddux	35.00
89 Mark McGwire	70.00
90 Ken Griffey Jr.	65.00

1998 Collector's Choice StarQuest - Series 2

The 30-card StarQuest insert was included in Series 2 packs. The insert has four parallel tiers - Single, Double, Triple and Home Run - designated by the number of baseball diamond icons on the card front. Single cards were inserted 1:1, Doubles 1:21, Triples 1:71 and Home Runs are sequentially numbered to 100. The second series SQ cards feature a front design with the letters "QSUTEASRT" in color block vertically at left.

	MT
Complete Set (30):	18.00
Common Player:	.25
Singles 1:1	
Doubles 1:21	4-8X
Triples 1:71	12-20X
1 Ken Griffey Jr.	2.00
2 Jose Cruz Jr.	.25
3 Cal Ripken Jr.	1.50
4 Roger Clemens	.75
5 Frank Thomas	1.00
6 Derek Jeter	1.00
7 Alex Rodriguez	1.25
8 Andruw Jones	.50
9 Vladimir Guerrero	.50
10 Mark McGwire	3.00
11 Kenny Lofton	.50
12 Pedro J. Martinez	.25
13 Greg Maddux	1.00
14 Larry Walker	.25
15 Barry Bonds	.50
16 Chipper Jones	1.25
17 Jeff Bagwell	.75
18 Juan Gonzalez	1.00
19 Tony Gwynn	1.00
20 Mike Piazza	1.25
21 Tino Martinez	.25
22 Mo Vaughn	.50
23 Ben Grieve	.60
24 Scott Rolen	.60
25 Nomar Garciaparra	1.25
26 Paul Konerko	.25
27 Jaret Wright	.50
28 Gary Sheffield	.25
29 Travis Lee	.60
30 Todd Helton	.50

1998 Collector's Choice StarQuest Home Run

StarQuest Home Run cards are the fourth tier of the insert in Series Two. The cards have four baseball diamond icons to designate their level. Home Run cards are sequentially numbered to 100.

	MT
Common Player:	10.00
Semistars:	25.00
Production 100 sets	
1 Ken Griffey Jr.	150.00
2 Jose Cruz Jr.	20.00
3 Cal Ripken Jr.	120.00
4 Roger Clemens	60.00
5 Frank Thomas	75.00
6 Derek Jeter	80.00
7 Alex Rodriguez	100.00
8 Andruw Jones	40.00
9 Vladimir Guerrero	40.00
10 Mark McGwire	150.00
11 Kenny Lofton	40.00
12 Pedro J. Martinez	20.00
13 Greg Maddux	100.00
14 Larry Walker	25.00
15 Barry Bonds	40.00
16 Chipper Jones	90.00
17 Jeff Bagwell	60.00
18 Juan Gonzalez	50.00
19 Tony Gwynn	75.00
20 Mike Piazza	100.00
21 Tino Martinez	20.00
22 Mo Vaughn	40.00
23 Ben Grieve	50.00
24 Scott Rolen	50.00
25 Nomar Garciaparra	90.00
26 Paul Konerko	10.00
27 Jaret Wright	40.00
28 Gary Sheffield	20.00
29 Travis Lee	30.00
30 Todd Helton	40.00

1998 Collector's Choice Stickums

This 30-card insert was seeded 1:3 Series 1 packs. The stickers can be peeled off the card and reused.

	MT
Complete Set (30):	20.00
Common Player:	.25
Inserted 1:3	
1 Andruw Jones	.60
2 Chipper Jones	1.50
3 Cal Ripken Jr.	2.00
4 Nomar Garciaparra	1.50
5 Mo Vaughn	.60
6 Ryne Sandberg	.60
7 Sammy Sosa	1.25
8 Frank Thomas	1.00
9 Albert Belle	.60
10 Jim Thome	.40
11 Manny Ramirez	.75
12 Larry Walker	.40
13 Gary Sheffield	.40
14 Jeff Bagwell	.75
15 Mike Piazza	1.50
16 Paul Molitor	.50
17 Pedro J. Martinez	.50
18 Todd Hundley	.25
19 Derek Jeter	1.50
20 Tino Martinez	.50
21 Curt Schilling	.25
22 Mark McGwire	3.00
23 Tony Gwynn	1.25
24 Barry Bonds	.60
25 Ken Griffey Jr.	2.50
26 Alex Rodriguez	2.00
27 Juan Gonzalez	.75
28 Ivan Rodriguez	.60
29 Roger Clemens	1.25
30 Jose Cruz Jr.	.25

1998 Collector's Choice You Crash the Game

These 90 game cards were inserted one per five Series 2 packs. Each card features a player and a list of dates. If the pictured player hit a home run on one of those days, collectors with the card could mail it in for a graphically enhanced prize version. Instant Winner cards of each player were also inserted at the rate of 1:721 and could be exchanged for the complete 30-card prize set. Deadline for exchange of all winning cards was Dec. 1, 1998. Winning cards are designated here with an asterisk and can be expected to be somewhat scarcer than non-winning dates.

		MT
Complete Set (90):		90.00
Common Player:		.50
Instant Winner:		25X
Inserted 1:5		
CG1	Ken Griffey Jr. (June 26-28*)	6.00
CG1	Ken Griffey Jr. (July 7)	4.00
CG1	Ken Griffey Jr. (Sept. 21-24*)	6.00
CG2	Travis Lee (July 27-30)	.50
CG2	Travis Lee (Aug. 27-30)	.50
CG2	Travis Lee (Sept. 17-20)	.50
CG3	Larry Walker (July 17-19)	.75
CG3	Larry Walker (Aug. 27-30*)	1.50
CG3	Larry Walker (Sept. 25-27*)	1.50
CG4	Tony Clark (July 9-12*)	.75
CG4	Tony Clark (June 30-July 2)	.50
CG4	Tony Clark (Sept. 4-6)	.50
CG5	Cal Ripken Jr. (June 22-25*)	4.00
CG5	Cal Ripken Jr. (July 7)	3.00
CG5	Cal Ripken Jr. (Sept. 4-6)	4.00
CG6	Tim Salmon (June 22-25)	.50
CG6	Tim Salmon (Aug. 28-30)	.50
CG6	Tim Salmon (Sept. 14-15)	.50
CG7	Vinny Castilla (June 30-July 2*)	.75
CG7	Vinny Castilla (Aug. 27-30*)	.75
CG7	Vinny Castilla (Sept. 7-10*)	.75
CG8	Fred McGriff (June 22-25)	.50
CG8	Fred McGriff (July 3-5)	.50
CG8	Fred McGriff (Sept. 18-20*)	.75
CG9	Matt Williams (July 17-29)	.50
CG9	Matt Williams (Sept. 14-16*)	.75
CG9	Matt Williams (Sept. 18-20)	.50
CG10	Mark McGwire (July 7)	4.00
CG10	Mark McGwire (July 24-26*)	6.00
CG10	Mark McGwire (Aug. 18-19*)	6.00

1998 Collector's Choice You Crash the Game Winners

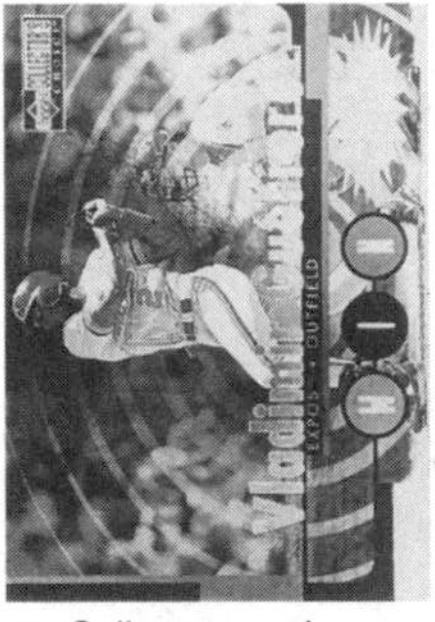

Collectors who redeemed winning "Crash" cards prior to the Dec. 1, 1998, deadline received an upgraded version of that player's card. Similar in format, the winners' cards have an action photo on front (different than the game card), with a metallic foil background. Instead of dates in the three circles at bottom are the letters "W I N". Backs have a career summary and stats, instead of the redemption instructions found on the game cards. The cards are numbered with a "CG" prefix. Cards of players who didn't homer during their designated dates were available only by redeeming a scarce (1:721 packs) Instant Win card. They are indicated here by "SP".

		MT
Complete Set (30):		110.00
Common Player:		1.50
CG1	Ken Griffey Jr.	12.00
CG2	Travis Lee (SP)	15.00
CG3	Larry Walker	2.25
CG4	Tony Clark	2.25
CG5	Cal Ripken Jr.	9.00
CG6	Tim Salmon (SP)	6.00
CG7	Vinny Castilla	1.50
CG8	Fred McGriff	1.50
CG9	Matt Williams	2.25
CG10	Mark McGwire	8.00
CG11	Albert Belle	3.00
CG12	Jay Buhner	1.50
CG13	Vladimir Guerrero	3.00
CG14	Andruw Jones	3.00
CG15	Nomar Garciaparra	7.50
CG16	Ken Caminiti	1.50
CG17	Sammy Sosa	3.00
CG18	Ben Grieve	3.00
CG19	Mo Vaughn	3.00
CG20	Frank Thomas	4.00
CG21	Manny Ramirez	3.00
CG22	Jeff Bagwell	4.50
CG23	Jose Cruz Jr. (SP)	6.00
CG24	Alex Rodriguez	7.50
CG25	Mike Piazza	7.50
CG26	Tino Martinez	2.25
CG27	Chipper Jones (SP)	24.00
CG28	Juan Gonzalez	5.00
CG29	Jim Thome	2.25
CG30	Barry Bonds	3.00

1998 Collector's Choice 5x7

These super-size (5" x 7") cards were one-per-box inserts in Series 2 retail packaging. Besides being four times the size of a normal card, the 5x7s are identical to the regular versions.

		MT
Complete Set (10):		15.00
Common Player:		1.00
306	Chipper Jones	3.00
321	Nomar Garciaparra	3.00
360	Larry Walker	1.00
450	Derek Jeter	3.00
463	Scott Rolen	2.00
480	Tony Gwynn	2.00
490	Barry Bonds	2.00
495	Alex Rodriguez	3.00
525	Jose Cruz Jr.	1.00
530	Roger Clemens	2.50

1998 Collector's Choice Cover Glory 5x7

		MT
Complete Set (10):		10.00
Common Player:		1.00
1	Nomar Garciaparra	2.00
2	Roger Clemens	1.50
3	Larry Walker	1.00
4	Mike Piazza	2.00
5	Mark McGwire	3.00
6	Tony Gwynn	1.50
7	Jose Cruz Jr.	1.00
8	Frank Thomas	1.50
9	Tino Martinez	1.00
10	Ken Griffey Jr.	3.00

D

1981 Donruss

The Donruss Co. of Memphis, Tenn., produced its premiere baseball card issue in 1981 with a set that consisted of 600 numbered cards and five unnumbered checklists. The cards, which measure 2-1/2" x 3-1/2", are printed on thin stock. The card fronts contain the Donruss logo plus the year of issue. The card backs are designed on a vertical format and have black print on red and white. The set, entitled "First Edition Collector Series," contains nearly 40 variations, those being first-printing errors that were corrected in a subsequent print run. The cards were sold in wax packs with bubblegum. The complete set price does not include the higher priced variations.

		MT
Complete Set (605):		45.00
Complete Set, Uncut Sheets (5):		75.00
Common Player:		.08
Eight-card promo sheet:		20.00
Pack (18):		1.75
Wax Box (36):		32.50
1	Ozzie Smith	4.00
2	Rollie Fingers	.75
3	Rick Wise	.08
4	Gene Richards	.08
5	Alan Trammell	.60
6	Tom Brookens	.08
7a	Duffy Dyer (1980 Avg. .185)	.50
7b	Duffy Dyer (1980 Avg. 185)	.10

8	Mark Fidrych	.10
9	Dave Rozema	.08
10	Ricky Peters	.08
11	Mike Schmidt	3.00
12	Willie Stargell	.80
13	Tim Foli	.08
14	Manny Sanguillen	.08
15	Grant Jackson	.08
16	Eddie Solomon	.08
17	Omar Moreno	.08
18	Joe Morgan	.60
19	Rafael Landestoy	.08
20	Bruce Bochy	.08
21	Joe Sambito	.08
22	Manny Trillo	.08
23a	*Dave Smith* (incomplete box around stats)	.50
23b	*Dave Smith* (complete box around stats)	.50
24	Terry Puhl	.08
25	Bump Wills	.08
26a	John Ellis (Danny Walton photo - with bat)	.60
26b	John Ellis (John Ellis photo - with glove)	.10
27	Jim Kern	.08
28	Richie Zisk	.08
29	John Mayberry	.08
30	Bob Davis	.08
31	Jackson Todd	.08
32	Al Woods	.08
33	Steve Carlton	1.50
34	Lee Mazzilli	.08
35	John Stearns	.08
36	Roy Jackson	.08
37	Mike Scott	.15
38	Lamar Johnson	.08
39	Kevin Bell	.08
40	Ed Farmer	.08
41	Ross Baumgarten	.08
42	Leo Sutherland	.08
43	Dan Meyer	.08
44	Ron Reed	.08
45	Mario Mendoza	.08
46	Rick Honeycutt	.08
47	Glenn Abbott	.08
48	Leon Roberts	.08
49	Rod Carew	1.50
50	Bert Campaneris	.10
51a	Tom Donahue (incorrect spelling)	.50
51b	Tom Donohue (Donohue on front)	.10
52	Dave Frost	.08
53	Ed Halicki	.08
54	Dan Ford	.08
55	Garry Maddox	.10
56a	Steve Garvey (Surpassed 25 HR..)	1.25
56b	Steve Garvey (Surpassed 21 HR..)	.60
57	Bill Russell	.10
58	Don Sutton	.65
59	Reggie Smith	.10
60	Rick Monday	.10
61	Ray Knight	.10
62	Johnny Bench	1.25
63	Mario Soto	.08
64	Doug Bair	.08
65	George Foster	.20
66	Jeff Burroughs	.08
67	Keith Hernandez	.20
68	Tom Herr	.08
69	Bob Forsch	.08
70	John Fulgham	.08
71a	Bobby Bonds (lifetime HR 986)	.50
71b	Bobby Bonds (lifetime HR 326)	.15
72a	Rennie Stennett ("...breaking broke leg..." on back)	.50
72b	Rennie Stennett ("...breaking leg..." on back)	.10
73	Joe Strain	.08
74	Ed Whitson	.08
75	Tom Griffin	.08
76	Bill North	.08
77	Gene Garber	.08
78	Mike Hargrove	.08
79	Dave Rosello	.08
80	Ron Hassey	.08
81	Sid Monge	.08
82a	*Joe Charboneau* ("For some reason, Phillies..." on back)	1.00
82b	*Joe Charboneau* ("Phillies..." on back)	.25
83	Cecil Cooper	.15
84	Sal Bando	.08
85	Moose Haas	.08
86	Mike Caldwell	.08
87a	Larry Hisle ("...Twins with 28 RBI." on back)	.50
87b	Larry Hisle ("...Twins with 28 HR" on back)	.10
88	Luis Gomez	.08
89	Larry Parrish	.08
90	Gary Carter	.60
91	*Bill Gullickson*	.15
92	Fred Norman	.08
93	Tommy Hutton	.08
94	Carl Yastrzemski	1.25
95	Glenn Hoffman	.08
96	Dennis Eckersley	1.00
97a	Tom Burgmeier (Throws: Right)	.50
97b	Tom Burgmeier (Throws: Left)	.10
98	Win Remmerswaal	.08
99	Bob Horner	.15
100	George Brett	6.00
101	Dave Chalk	.08
102	Dennis Leonard	.08
103	Renie Martin	.08
104	Amos Otis	.08
105	Graig Nettles	.15
106	Eric Soderholm	.08
107	Tommy John	.20
108	Tom Underwood	.08
109	Lou Piniella	.12
110	Mickey Klutts	.08
111	Bobby Murcer	.10
112	Eddie Murray	4.00
113	Rick Dempsey	.08
114	Scott McGregor	.08
115	Ken Singleton	.10
116	Gary Roenicke	.08
117	Dave Revering	.08
118	Mike Norris	.08
119	Rickey Henderson	4.00
120	Mike Heath	.08
121	Dave Cash	.08
122	Randy Jones	.08
123	Eric Rasmussen	.08
124	Jerry Mumphrey	.08
125	Richie Hebner	.08
126	Mark Wagner	.08
127	Jack Morris	.45
128	Dan Petry	.08
129	Bruce Robbins	.08
130	Champ Summers	.08
131a	Pete Rose ("see card 251" on back)	2.50
131b	Pete Rose ("see card 371" on back)	2.00
132	Willie Stargell	.80
133	Ed Ott	.08
134	Jim Bibby	.08
135	Bert Blyleven	.12
136	Dave Parker	.45
137	Bill Robinson	.08
138	Enos Cabell	.08
139	Dave Bergman	.08
140	J.R. Richard	.10
141	Ken Forsch	.08
142	Larry Bowa	.15
143	Frank LaCorte (photo actually Randy Niemann)	.08
144	Dennis Walling	.08
145	Buddy Bell	.12
146	Fergie Jenkins	.75
147	Danny Darwin	.08
148	John Grubb	.08
149	Alfredo Griffin	.08
150	Jerry Garvin	.08
151	*Paul Mirabella*	.08
152	Rick Bosetti	.08
153	Dick Ruthven	.08
154	Frank Taveras	.08
155	Craig Swan	.08
156	*Jeff Reardon*	1.50
157	Steve Henderson	.08
158	Jim Morrison	.08
159	Glenn Borgmann	.08
160	*Lamarr Hoyt (LaMarr)*	.10
161	Rich Wortham	.08
162	Thad Bosley	.08
163	Julio Cruz	.08
164a	Del Unser (no 3B in stat heads)	.50
164b	Del Unser (3B in stat heads)	.10
165	Jim Anderson	.08
166	Jim Beattie	.08
167	Shane Rawley	.08
168	Joe Simpson	.08
169	Rod Carew	1.50
170	Fred Patek	.08
171	Frank Tanana	.08
172	Alfredo Martinez	.08
173	Chris Knapp	.08
174	Joe Rudi	.10
175	Greg Luzinski	.15
176	Steve Garvey	.65
177	Joe Ferguson	.08
178	Bob Welch	.10
179	Dusty Baker	.10
180	Rudy Law	.08
181	Dave Concepcion	.15
182	Johnny Bench	1.25
183	Mike LaCoss	.08
184	Ken Griffey	.12
185	Dave Collins	.08
186	Brian Asselstine	.08
187	Garry Templeton	.10
188	Mike Phillips	.08
189	Pete Vukovich	.08
190	John Urrea	.08
191	Tony Scott	.08
192	Darrell Evans	.12
193	Milt May	.08
194	Bob Knepper	.08
195	Randy Moffitt	.08
196	Larry Herndon	.08
197	Rick Camp	.08
198	Andre Thornton	.10
199	Tom Veryzer	.08
200	Gary Alexander	.08
201	Rick Waits	.08
202	Rick Manning	.08
203	Paul Molitor	3.00
204	Jim Gantner	.08
205	Paul Mitchell	.08
206	Reggie Cleveland	.08
207	Sixto Lezcano	.08
208	Bruce Benedict	.08
209	Rodney Scott	.08
210	John Tamargo	.08
211	Bill Lee	.08
212	Andre Dawson	1.00
213	Rowland Office	.08
214	Carl Yastrzemski	1.25
215	Jerry Remy	.08
216	Mike Torrez	.08
217	Skip Lockwood	.08
218	Fred Lynn	.20
219	Chris Chambliss	.08
220	Willie Aikens	.08
221	John Wathan	.08
222	Dan Quisenberry	.15
223	Willie Wilson	.15
224	Clint Hurdle	.08
225	Bob Watson	.08
226	Jim Spencer	.08
227	Ron Guidry	.25
228	Reggie Jackson	2.50
229	Oscar Gamble	.08
230	Jeff Cox	.08
231	Luis Tiant	.12
232	Rich Dauer	.08
233	Dan Graham	.08
234	Mike Flanagan	.10
235	John Lowenstein	.08
236	Benny Ayala	.08
237	Wayne Gross	.08
238	Rick Langford	.08
239	Tony Armas	.10
240a	Bob Lacy (incorrect spelling)	.50
240b	Bob Lacey (correct spelling)	.10
241	Gene Tenace	.08
242	Bob Shirley	.08
243	Gary Lucas	.08
244	Jerry Turner	.08
245	John Wockenfuss	.08
246	Stan Papi	.08
247	Milt Wilcox	.08
248	Dan Schatzeder	.08
249	Steve Kemp	.08
250	Jim Lentine	.08
251	Pete Rose	2.50
252	Bill Madlock	.12
253	Dale Berra	.08
254	Kent Tekulve	.08
255	Enrique Romo	.08
256	Mike Easler	.08
257	Chuck Tanner	.08
258	Art Howe	.12
259	Alan Ashby	.08
260	Nolan Ryan	8.00
261a	Vern Ruhle (Ken Forsch photo - head shot)	.50
261b	Vern Ruhle (Vern Ruhle photo - waist to head shot)	.10
262	Bob Boone	.10
263	Cesar Cedeno	.12
264	Jeff Leonard	.08
265	Pat Putnam	.08
266	Jon Matlack	.08
267	Dave Rajsich	.08
268	Billy Sample	.08
269	*Damaso Garcia*	.10
270	Tom Buskey	.08
271	Joey McLaughlin	.08
272	Barry Bonnell	.08
273	Tug McGraw	.10
274	Mike Jorgensen	.08
275	Pat Zachry	.08
276	Neil Allen	.08
277	Joel Youngblood	.08
278	Greg Pryor	.08
279	*Britt Burns*	.10
280	*Rich Dotson*	.25
281	Chet Lemon	.08
282	Rusty Kuntz	.08
283	Ted Cox	.08
284	Sparky Lyle	.10
285	Larry Cox	.08
286	Floyd Bannister	.08
287	Byron McLaughlin	.08
288	Rodney Craig	.08
289	Bobby Grich	.10
290	Dickie Thon	.08
291	Mark Clear	.08
292	Dave Lemanczyk	.08
293	Jason Thompson	.08
294	Rick Miller	.08
295	Lonnie Smith	.08
296	Ron Cey	.12
297	Steve Yeager	.08
298	Bobby Castillo	.08
299	Manny Mota	.08
300	Jay Johnstone	.08
301	Dan Driessen	.08
302	Joe Nolan	.08
303	Paul Householder	.08
304	Harry Spilman	.08
305	Cesar Geronimo	.08
306a	Gary Mathews (Mathews on front)	.65
306b	Gary Matthews (Matthews on front)	.10
307	Ken Reitz	.08
308	Ted Simmons	.10
309	John Littlefield	.08
310	George Frazier	.08
311	Dane Iorg	.08
312	Mike Ivie	.08
313	Dennis Littlejohn	.08
314	Gary LaVelle (Lavelle)	.08
315	Jack Clark	.25
316	Jim Wohlford	.08
317	Rick Matula	.08
318	Toby Harrah	.08
319a	Dwane Kuiper (Dwane on front)	.50
319b	Duane Kuiper (Duane on front)	.10
320	Len Barker	.08
321	Victor Cruz	.08
322	Dell Alston	.08
323	Robin Yount	4.00
324	Charlie Moore	.08
325	Lary Sorensen	.08
326a	Gorman Thomas ("...30-HR mark 4th..." on back)	.65

326b Gorman Thomas ("...30-HR mark 3rd..." on back) .10
327 Bob Rodgers .08
328 Phil Niekro .75
329 Chris Speier .08
330a Steve Rodgers (Rodgers on front) .50
330b Steve Rogers (Rogers on front) .10
331 Woodie Fryman .08
332 Warren Cromartie .08
333 Jerry White .08
334 Tony Perez .25
335 Carlton Fisk 1.50
336 Dick Drago .08
337 Steve Renko .08
338 Jim Rice .30
339 Jerry Royster .08
340 Frank White .10
341 Jamie Quirk .08
342a Paul Spittorff (Spittorff on front) .50
342b Paul Splittorff (Splittorff on front) .10
343 Marty Pattin .08
344 Pete LaCock .08
345 Willie Randolph .10
346 Rick Cerone .08
347 Rich Gossage .20
348 Reggie Jackson 2.50
349 Ruppert Jones .08
350 Dave McKay .08
351 Yogi Berra .45
352 Doug Decinces (DeCinces) .10
353 Jim Palmer 1.00
354 Tippy Martinez .08
355 Al Bumbry .08
356 Earl Weaver .50
357a Bob Picciolo (Bob on front) .50
357b Rob Picciolo (Rob on front) .10
358 Matt Keough .08
359 Dwayne Murphy .08
360 Brian Kingman .08
361 Bill Fahey .08
362 Steve Mura .08
363 Dennis Kinney .08
364 Dave Winfield 2.00
365 Lou Whitaker .45
366 Lance Parrish .20
367 Tim Corcoran .08
368 Pat Underwood .08
369 Al Cowens .08
370 Sparky Anderson .15
371 Pete Rose 2.50
372 Phil Garner .08
373 Steve Nicosia .08
374 John Candelaria .10
375 Don Robinson .08
376 Lee Lacy .08
377 John Milner .08
378 Craig Reynolds .08
379a Luis Pujois (Pujois on front) .50
379b Luis Pujols (Pujols on front) .10
380 Joe Niekro .12
381 Joaquin Andujar .08
382 *Keith Moreland* .20
383 Jose Cruz .12
384 Bill Virdon .08
385 Jim Sundberg .08
386 Doc Medich .08
387 Al Oliver .15
388 Jim Norris .08
389 Bob Bailor .08
390 Ernie Whitt .08
391 Otto Velez .08
392 Roy Howell .08
393 *Bob Walk* .10
394 Doug Flynn .08
395 Pete Falcone .08
396 Tom Hausman .08
397 Elliott Maddox .08
398 Mike Squires .08
399 Marvis Foley .08
400 Steve Trout .08
401 Wayne Nordhagen .08
402 Tony Larussa (LaRussa) .12
403 Bruce Bochte .08
404 Bake McBride .08
405 Jerry Narron .08
406 Rob Dressler .08
407 Dave Heaverlo .08
408 Tom Paciorek .08
409 Carney Lansford .08
410 Brian Downing .10
411 Don Aase .08
412 Jim Barr .08
413 Don Baylor .15
414 Jim Fregosi .08
415 Dallas Green .08
416 Dave Lopes .10
417 Jerry Reuss .10
418 Rick Sutcliffe .20
419 Derrel Thomas .08
420 Tommy LaSorda (Lasorda) .50
421 *Charlie Leibrandt* .50
422 Tom Seaver 2.00
423 Ron Oester .08
424 Junior Kennedy .08
425 Tom Seaver 2.00
426 Bobby Cox .10
427 *Leon Durham* .20
428 Terry Kennedy .08
429 Silvio Martinez .08
430 George Hendrick .08
431 Red Schoendienst .25
432 John LeMaster .08
433 Vida Blue .12
434 John Montefusco .08
435 Terry Whitfield .08
436 Dave Bristol .08
437 Dale Murphy .75
438 Jerry Dybzinski .08
439 Jorge Orta .08
440 Wayne Garland .08
441 Miguel Dilone .08
442 Dave Garcia .08
443 Don Money .08
444a Buck Martinez (photo reversed) .50
444b Buck Martinez (photo correct) .10
445 Jerry Augustine .08
446 Ben Oglivie .08
447 Jim Slaton .08
448 Doyle Alexander .08
449 Tony Bernazard .08
450 Scott Sanderson .08
451 Dave Palmer .08
452 Stan Bahnsen .08
453 Dick Williams .08
454 Rick Burleson .08
455 Gary Allenson .08
456 Bob Stanley .08
457a *John Tudor* (lifetime W/L 9.7) .75
457b *John Tudor* (lifetime W/L 9-7) .50
458 Dwight Evans .15
459 Glenn Hubbard .08
460 U L Washington .08
461 Larry Gura .08
462 Rich Gale .08
463 Hal McRae .10
464 Jim Frey .08
465 Bucky Dent .10
466 Dennis Werth .08
467 Ron Davis .08
468 Reggie Jackson 2.50
469 Bobby Brown .08
470 *Mike Davis* .10
471 Gaylord Perry .75
472 Mark Belanger .08
473 Jim Palmer 1.00
474 Sammy Stewart .08
475 Tim Stoddard .08
476 Steve Stone .10
477 Jeff Newman .08
478 Steve McCatty .08
479 Billy Martin .12
480 Mitchell Page .08
481 Steve Carlton (CY) .40
482 Bill Buckner .12
483a Ivan DeJesus (lifetime hits 702) .50
483b Ivan DeJesus (lifetime hits 642) .10
484 Cliff Johnson .08
485 Lenny Randle .08
486 Larry Milbourne .08
487 Roy Smalley .08
488 John Castino .08
489 Ron Jackson .08
490a Dave Roberts (1980 highlights begins "Showed pop...") .50
490b Dave Roberts (1980 highlights begins "Declared himself...") .10
491 George Brett (MVP) 3.00
492 Mike Cubbage .08
493 Rob Wilfong .08
494 Danny Goodwin .08
495 Jose Morales .08
496 Mickey Rivers .08
497 Mike Edwards .08
498 Mike Sadek .08
499 Lenn Sakata .08
500 Gene Michael .08
501 Dave Roberts .08
502 Steve Dillard .08
503 Jim Essian .08
504 Rance Mulliniks .08
505 Darrell Porter .08
506 Joe Torre .25
507 Terry Crowley .08
508 Bill Travers .08
509 Nelson Norman .08
510 Bob McClure .08
511 *Steve Howe* .15
512 Dave Rader .08
513 Mick Kelleher .08
514 Kiko Garcia .08
515 Larry Biittner .08
516a Willie Norwood (1980 highlights begins "Spent most...") .50
516b Willie Norwood (1980 highlights begins "Traded to...") .10
517 Bo Diaz .08
518 Juan Beniquez .08
519 Scot Thompson .08
520 Jim Tracy .08
521 Carlos Lezcano .08
522 Joe Amalfitano .08
523 Preston Hanna .08
524a Ray Burris (1980 highlights begins "Went on...") .50
524b Ray Burris (1980 highlights begins "Drafted by...") .10
525 Broderick Perkins .08
526 Mickey Hatcher .08
527 John Goryl .08
528 Dick Davis .08
529 Butch Wynegar .08
530 Sal Butera .08
531 Jerry Koosman .10
532a Jeff (Geoff) Zahn (1980 highlights begins "Was 2nd in...") .50
532b Jeff (Geoff) Zahn (1980 highlights begins "Signed a 3 year ...") .10
533 Dennis Martinez .12
534 Gary Thomasson .08
535 Steve Macko .08
536 Jim Kaat .20
537 Best Hitters (George Brett, Rod Carew) 1.50
538 *Tim Raines* 6.00
539 Keith Smith .08
540 Ken Macha .08
541 Burt Hooton .08
542 Butch Hobson .08
543 Bill Stein .08
544 Dave Stapleton .08
545 Bob Pate .08
546 Doug Corbett .08
547 Darrell Jackson .08
548 Pete Redfern .08
549 Roger Erickson .08
550 Al Hrabosky .08
551 Dick Tidrow .08
552 Dave Ford .08
553 Dave Kingman .12
554a Mike Vail (1980 highlights begins "After...") .50
554b Mike Vail (1980 highlights begins "Traded...") .10
555a Jerry Martin (1980 highlights begins "Overcame...") .50
555b Jerry Martin (1980 highlights begins "Traded...") .10
556a Jesus Figueroa (1980 highlights begins "Had...") .50
556b Jesus Figueroa (1980 highlights begins "Traded...") .10
557 Don Stanhouse .08
558 Barry Foote .08
559 Tim Blackwell .08
560 Bruce Sutter .15
561 Rick Reuschel .10
562 Lynn McGlothen .08
563a Bob Owchinko (1980 highlights begins "Traded...") .50
563b Bob Owchinko (1980 highlights begins "Involved...") .10
564 John Verhoeven .08
565 Ken Landreaux .08
566a Glen Adams (Glen on front) .50
566b Glenn Adams (Glenn on front) .10
567 Hosken Powell .08
568 Dick Noles .08
569 *Danny Ainge* 4.00
570 Bobby Mattick .08
571 Joe LeFebvre (Lefebvre) .08
572 Bobby Clark .08
573 Dennis Lamp .08
574 Randy Lerch .08
575 *Mookie Wilson* .30
576 Ron LeFlore .08
577 Jim Dwyer .08
578 Bill Castro .08
579 Greg Minton .08
580 Mark Littell .08
581 Andy Hassler .08
582 Dave Stieb .15
583 Ken Oberkfell .08
584 Larry Bradford .08
585 Fred Stanley .08
586 Bill Caudill .08
587 Doug Capilla .08
588 George Riley .08
589 Willie Hernandez .10
590 Mike Schmidt (MVP) 1.00
591 Steve Stone (Cy Young 1980) .10
592 Rick Sofield .08
593 Bombo Rivera .08
594 Gary Ward .08
595a Dave Edwards (1980 highlights begins "Sidelined...") .50
595b Dave Edwards (1980 highlights begins "Traded...") .10
596 Mike Proly .08
597 Tommy Boggs .08
598 Greg Gross .08
599 Elias Sosa .08
600 Pat Kelly .08
---- Checklist 1-120 (51 Tom Donohue) .50
---- Checklist 1-120 (51 Tom Donahue) .10
---- Checklist 121-240 .10
---- Checklist 241-360 (306 Gary Mathews) .50
---- Checklist 241-360 (306 Gary Matthews) .10
---- Checklist 361-480 (379 Luis Pujois) .50
---- Checklist 361-480 (379 Luis Pujols) .10
---- Checklist 481-600 (566 Glen Adams) .50
---- Checklist 481-600 (566 Glenn Adams) .10

1982 Donruss

Using card stock thicker than the previous year, Donruss issued a 660-card set which includes 653 numbered cards and seven unnumbered checklists. The cards were sold with puzzle pieces rather than gum as a result of a lawsuit by Topps. The puzzle pieces (three pieces on one card per pack) feature Babe Ruth. The first 26 cards of the set, entitled Diamond Kings, showcase the artwork of Dick Perez. Card fronts display the Donruss logo and the year of issue. Backs have black and blue ink on white stock and include the player's career highlights. The complete set price does not include the higher priced variations.

		MT
Complete Set (660):		85.00
Common Player:		.08
Babe Ruth Puzzle:		3.00
Pack (15):		3.50
Wax Box (36):		87.00
1	Pete Rose (Diamond King)	3.00
2	Gary Carter (DK)	.50
3	Steve Garvey (DK)	.30
4	Vida Blue (DK)	.12
5a	Alan Trammel (DK) (last name incorrect)	1.50
5b	Alan Trammell (DK) (corrected)	.40
6	Len Barker (DK)	.08
7	Dwight Evans (DK)	.15
8	Rod Carew (DK)	.60
9	George Hendrick (DK)	.08
10	Phil Niekro (DK)	.60
11	Richie Zisk (DK)	.08
12	Dave Parker (DK)	.30
13	Nolan Ryan (DK)	4.00
14	Ivan DeJesus (DK)	.08
15	George Brett (DK)	1.50
16	Tom Seaver (DK)	.90
17	Dave Kingman (DK)	.15
18	Dave Winfield (DK)	1.00
19	Mike Norris (DK)	.08
20	Carlton Fisk (DK)	.80
21	Ozzie Smith (DK)	1.50
22	Roy Smalley (DK)	.08
23	Buddy Bell (DK)	.12
24	Ken Singleton (DK)	.10
25	John Mayberry (DK)	.08
26	Gorman Thomas (DK)	.10
27	Earl Weaver	.45
28	Rollie Fingers	.60
29	Sparky Anderson	.10
30	Dennis Eckersley	.75
31	Dave Winfield	2.00
32	Burt Hooton	.08
33	Rick Waits	.08
34	George Brett	3.00
35	Steve McCatty	.08
36	Steve Rogers	.08
37	Bill Stein	.08
38	Steve Renko	.08
39	Mike Squires	.08
40	George Hendrick	.08
41	Bob Knepper	.08
42	Steve Carlton	1.00
43	Larry Biittner	.08
44	Chris Welsh	.08
45	Steve Nicosia	.08
46	Jack Clark	.25
47	Chris Chambliss	.08
48	Ivan DeJesus	.08
49	Lee Mazzilli	.08
50	Julio Cruz	.08
51	Pete Redfern	.08
52	Dave Stieb	.12
53	Doug Corbett	.08
54	*George Bell*	1.00
55	Joe Simpson	.08
56	Rusty Staub	.10
57	Hector Cruz	.08
58	Claudell Washington	.10
59	Enrique Romo	.08
60	Gary Lavelle	.08
61	Tim Flannery	.08
62	Joe Nolan	.08
63	Larry Bowa	.15
64	Sixto Lezcano	.08
65	Joe Sambito	.08
66	Bruce Kison	.08
67	Wayne Nordhagen	.08
68	Woodie Fryman	.08
69	Billy Sample	.08
70	Amos Otis	.08
71	Matt Keough	.08
72	Toby Harrah	.08
73	*Dave Righetti*	.30
74	Carl Yastrzemski	1.00
75	Bob Welch	.12
76a	Alan Trammel (last name misspelled)	2.00
76b	Alan Trammell (corrected)	.60
77	Rick Dempsey	.08
78	Paul Molitor	2.50
79	Dennis Martinez	.10
80	Jim Slaton	.08
81	Champ Summers	.08
82	Carney Lansford	.08
83	Barry Foote	.08
84	Steve Garvey	.45
85	Rick Manning	.08
86	John Wathan	.08
87	Brian Kingman	.08
88	Andre Dawson	.75
89	Jim Kern	.08
90	Bobby Grich	.10
91	Bob Forsch	.08
92	Art Howe	.10
93	Marty Bystrom	.08
94	Ozzie Smith	2.50
95	Dave Parker	.30
96	Doyle Alexander	.08
97	Al Hrabosky	.08
98	Frank Taveras	.08
99	Tim Blackwell	.08
100	Floyd Bannister	.08
101	Alfredo Griffin	.08
102	Dave Engle	.08
103	Mario Soto	.08
104	Ross Baumgarten	.08
105	Ken Singleton	.10
106	Ted Simmons	.10
107	Jack Morris	.30
108	Bob Watson	.08
109	Dwight Evans	.15
110	Tom Lasorda	.40
111	Bert Blyleven	.12
112	Dan Quisenberry	.15
113	Rickey Henderson	2.00
114	Gary Carter	.50
115	Brian Downing	.10
116	Al Oliver	.15
117	LaMarr Hoyt	.08
118	Cesar Cedeno	.10
119	Keith Moreland	.10
120	Bob Shirley	.08
121	Terry Kennedy	.08
122	Frank Pastore	.08
123	Gene Garber	.08
124	Tony Pena	.25
125	Allen Ripley	.08
126	Randy Martz	.08
127	Richie Zisk	.08
128	Mike Scott	.15
129	Lloyd Moseby	.10
130	Rob Wilfong	.08
131	Tim Stoddard	.08
132	Gorman Thomas	.08
133	Dan Petry	.08
134	Bob Stanley	.08
135	Lou Piniella	.15
136	Pedro Guerrero	.25
137	Len Barker	.08
138	Richard Gale	.08
139	Wayne Gross	.08
140	*Tim Wallach*	1.00
141	Gene Mauch	.08
142	Doc Medich	.08
143	Tony Bernazard	.08
144	Bill Virdon	.08
145	John Littlefield	.08
146	Dave Bergman	.08
147	Dick Davis	.08
148	Tom Seaver	1.00
149	Matt Sinatro	.08
150	Chuck Tanner	.08
151	Leon Durham	.08
152	Gene Tenace	.08
153	Al Bumbry	.08
154	Mark Brouhard	.08
155	Rick Peters	.08
156	Jerry Remy	.08
157	Rick Reuschel	.10
158	Steve Howe	.08
159	Alan Bannister	.08
160	U L Washington	.08
161	Rick Langford	.08
162	Bill Gullickson	.08
163	Mark Wagner	.08
164	Geoff Zahn	.08
165	Ron LeFlore	.08
166	Dane Iorg	.08
167	Joe Niekro	.12
168	Pete Rose	2.50
169	Dave Collins	.08
170	Rick Wise	.08
171	Jim Bibby	.08
172	Larry Herndon	.08
173	Bob Horner	.12
174	Steve Dillard	.08
175	Mookie Wilson	.12
176	Dan Meyer	.08
177	Fernando Arroyo	.08
178	Jackson Todd	.08
179	Darrell Jackson	.08
180	Al Woods	.08
181	Jim Anderson	.08
182	Dave Kingman	.12
183	Steve Henderson	.08
184	Brian Asselstine	.08
185	Rod Scurry	.08
186	Fred Breining	.08
187	Danny Boone	.08
188	Junior Kennedy	.08
189	Sparky Lyle	.10
190	Whitey Herzog	.08
191	Dave Smith	.08
192	Ed Ott	.08
193	Greg Luzinski	.15
194	Bill Lee	.08
195	Don Zimmer	.08
196	Hal McRae	.15
197	Mike Norris	.08
198	Duane Kuiper	.08
199	Rick Cerone	.08
200	Jim Rice	.30
201	Steve Yeager	.08
202	Tom Brookens	.08
203	Jose Morales	.08
204	Roy Howell	.08
205	Tippy Martinez	.08
206	Moose Haas	.08
207	Al Cowens	.08
208	Dave Stapleton	.08
209	Bucky Dent	.10
210	Ron Cey	.12
211	Jorge Orta	.08
212	Jamie Quirk	.08
213	Jeff Jones	.08
214	Tim Raines	1.00
215	Jon Matlack	.08
216	Rod Carew	1.00
217	Jim Kaat	.20
218	Joe Pittman	.08
219	Larry Christenson	.08
220	Juan Bonilla	.08
221	Mike Easler	.08
222	Vida Blue	.12
223	Rick Camp	.08
224	Mike Jorgensen	.08
225	*Jody Davis*	.15
226	Mike Parrott	.08
227	Jim Clancy	.08
228	Hosken Powell	.08
229	Tom Hume	.08
230	Britt Burns	.08
231	Jim Palmer	1.00
232	Bob Rodgers	.08
233	Milt Wilcox	.08
234	Dave Revering	.08
235	Mike Torrez	.08
236	Robert Castillo	.08
237	*Von Hayes*	.25
238	Renie Martin	.08
239	Dwayne Murphy	.08
240	Rodney Scott	.08
241	Fred Patek	.08
242	Mickey Rivers	.08
243	Steve Trout	.08
244	Jose Cruz	.12
245	Manny Trillo	.08
246	Lary Sorensen	.08
247	Dave Edwards	.08
248	Dan Driessen	.08
249	Tommy Boggs	.08
250	Dale Berra	.08
251	Ed Whitson	.08
252	*Lee Smith*	8.00
253	Tom Paciorek	.08
254	Pat Zachry	.08
255	Luis Leal	.08
256	John Castino	.08
257	Rich Dauer	.08
258	Cecil Cooper	.15
259	Dave Rozema	.08
260	John Tudor	.08
261	Jerry Mumphrey	.08
262	Jay Johnstone	.08
263	Bo Diaz	.08
264	Dennis Leonard	.08
265	Jim Spencer	.08
266	John Milner	.08
267	Don Aase	.08
268	Jim Sundberg	.08
269	Lamar Johnson	.08
270	Frank LaCorte	.08
271	Barry Evans	.08
272	Enos Cabell	.08
273	Del Unser	.08
274	George Foster	.20
275	*Brett Butler*	2.00
276	Lee Lacy	.08
277	Ken Reitz	.08
278	Keith Hernandez	.20
279	Doug DeCinces	.10
280	Charlie Moore	.08
281	Lance Parrish	.20
282	Ralph Houk	.08
283	Rich Gossage	.20
284	Jerry Reuss	.10
285	Mike Stanton	.08
286	Frank White	.10
287	Bob Owchinko	.08
288	Scott Sanderson	.08
289	Bump Wills	.08
290	Dave Frost	.08
291	Chet Lemon	.08
292	Tito Landrum	.08
293	Vern Ruhle	.08
294	Mike Schmidt	2.25
295	Sam Mejias	.08
296	Gary Lucas	.08
297	John Candelaria	.08
298	Jerry Martin	.08
299	Dale Murphy	.75
300	Mike Lum	.08
301	Tom Hausman	.08
302	Glenn Abbott	.08
303	Roger Erickson	.08
304	Otto Velez	.08
305	Danny Goodwin	.08
306	John Mayberry	.08
307	Lenny Randle	.08
308	Bob Bailor	.08
309	Jerry Morales	.08
310	Rufino Linares	.08
311	Kent Tekulve	.08
312	Joe Morgan	.75
313	John Urrea	.08
314	Paul Householder	.08
315	Garry Maddox	.08
316	Mike Ramsey	.08
317	Alan Ashby	.08
318	Bob Clark	.08
319	Tony LaRussa	.15
320	Charlie Lea	.08

No.	Player	Value
321	Danny Darwin	.08
322	Cesar Geronimo	.08
323	Tom Underwood	.08
324	Andre Thornton	.10
325	Rudy May	.08
326	Frank Tanana	.08
327	Davey Lopes	.10
328	Richie Hebner	.08
329	Mike Flanagan	.10
330	Mike Caldwell	.08
331	Scott McGregor	.08
332	Jerry Augustine	.08
333	Stan Papi	.08
334	Rick Miller	.08
335	Graig Nettles	.15
336	Dusty Baker	.10
337	Dave Garcia	.08
338	Larry Gura	.08
339	Cliff Johnson	.08
340	Warren Cromartie	.08
341	Steve Comer	.08
342	Rick Burleson	.08
343	John Martin	.08
344	Craig Reynolds	.08
345	Mike Proly	.08
346	Ruppert Jones	.08
347	Omar Moreno	.08
348	Greg Minton	.08
349	*Rick Mahler*	.10
350	Alex Trevino	.08
351	Mike Krukow	.08
352a	Shane Rawley (Jim Anderson photo - shaking hands)	.75
352b	Shane Rawley (correct photo - kneeling)	.15
353	Garth Iorg	.08
354	Pete Mackanin	.08
355	Paul Moskau	.08
356	Richard Dotson	.10
357	Steve Stone	.10
358	Larry Hisle	.08
359	Aurelio Lopez	.08
360	Oscar Gamble	.08
361	Tom Burgmeier	.08
362	Terry Forster	.08
363	Joe Charboneau	.15
364	Ken Brett	.08
365	Tony Armas	.10
366	Chris Speier	.08
367	Fred Lynn	.20
368	Buddy Bell	.12
369	Jim Essian	.08
370	Terry Puhl	.08
371	Greg Gross	.08
372	Bruce Sutter	.15
373	Joe Lefebvre	.08
374	Ray Knight	.10
375	Bruce Benedict	.08
376	Tim Foli	.08
377	Al Holland	.08
378	Ken Kravec	.08
379	Jeff Burroughs	.08
380	Pete Falcone	.08
381	Ernie Whitt	.08
382	Brad Havens	.08
383	Terry Crowley	.08
384	Don Money	.08
385	Dan Schatzeder	.08
386	Gary Allenson	.08
387	Yogi Berra	.35
388	Ken Landreaux	.08
389	Mike Hargrove	.10
390	Darryl Motley	.08
391	Dave McKay	.08
392	Stan Bahnsen	.08
393	Ken Forsch	.08
394	Mario Mendoza	.08
395	Jim Morrison	.08
396	Mike Ivie	.08
397	Broderick Perkins	.08
398	Darrell Evans	.15
399	Ron Reed	.08
400	Johnny Bench	1.50
401	*Steve Bedrosian*	.20
402	Bill Robinson	.08
403	Bill Buckner	.12
404	Ken Oberkfell	.08
405	*Cal Ripken, Jr.*	50.00
406	Jim Gantner	.08
407	Kirk Gibson	.50
408	Tony Perez	.30
409	Tommy John	.20
410	*Dave Stewart*	2.50
411	Dan Spillner	.08
412	Willie Aikens	.08
413	Mike Heath	.08
414	Ray Burris	.08
415	Leon Roberts	.08
416	*Mike Witt*	.20
417	Bobby Molinaro	.08
418	Steve Braun	.08
419	Nolan Ryan	9.00
420	Tug McGraw	.12
421	Dave Concepcion	.12
422a	Juan Eichelberger (Gary Lucas photo - white player)	.75
422b	Juan Eichelberger (correct photo - black player)	.08
423	Rick Rhoden	.08
424	Frank Robinson	.30
425	Eddie Miller	.08
426	Bill Caudill	.08
427	Doug Flynn	.08
428	Larry Anderson (Andersen)	.08
429	Al Williams	.08
430	Jerry Garvin	.08
431	Glenn Adams	.08
432	Barry Bonnell	.08
433	Jerry Narron	.08
434	John Stearns	.08
435	Mike Tyson	.08
436	Glenn Hubbard	.08
437	Eddie Solomon	.08
438	Jeff Leonard	.08
439	Randy Bass	.08
440	Mike LaCoss	.08
441	Gary Matthews	.08
442	Mark Littell	.08
443	Don Sutton	.45
444	John Harris	.08
445	Vada Pinson	.10
446	Elias Sosa	.08
447	Charlie Hough	.10
448	Willie Wilson	.15
449	Fred Stanley	.08
450	Tom Veryzer	.08
451	Ron Davis	.08
452	Mark Clear	.08
453	Bill Russell	.10
454	Lou Whitaker	.40
455	Dan Graham	.08
456	Reggie Cleveland	.08
457	Sammy Stewart	.08
458	Pete Vuckovich	.08
459	John Wockenfuss	.08
460	Glenn Hoffman	.08
461	Willie Randolph	.10
462	Fernando Valenzuela	.25
463	Ron Hassey	.08
464	Paul Splittorff	.08
465	Rob Picciolo	.08
466	Larry Parrish	.08
467	Johnny Grubb	.08
468	Dan Ford	.08
469	Silvio Martinez	.08
470	Kiko Garcia	.08
471	Bob Boone	.10
472	Luis Salazar	.08
473	Randy Niemann	.08
474	Tom Griffin	.08
475	Phil Niekro	.60
476	Hubie Brooks	.25
477	Dick Tidrow	.08
478	Jim Beattie	.08
479	Damaso Garcia	.08
480	Mickey Hatcher	.08
481	Joe Price	.08
482	Ed Farmer	.08
483	Eddie Murray	2.00
484	Ben Oglivie	.08
485	Kevin Saucier	.08
486	Bobby Murcer	.10
487	Bill Campbell	.08
488	Reggie Smith	.10
489	Wayne Garland	.08
490	Jim Wright	.08
491	Billy Martin	.12
492	Jim Fanning	.08
493	Don Baylor	.12
494	Rick Honeycutt	.08
495	Carlton Fisk	1.00
496	Denny Walling	.08
497	Bake McBride	.08
498	Darrell Porter	.08
499	Gene Richards	.08
500	Ron Oester	.08
501	*Ken Dayley*	.12
502	Jason Thompson	.08
503	Milt May	.08
504	Doug Bird	.08
505	Bruce Bochte	.08
506	Neil Allen	.08
507	Joey McLaughlin	.08
508	Butch Wynegar	.08
509	Gary Roenicke	.08
510	Robin Yount	2.50
511	Dave Tobik	.08
512	*Rich Gedman*	.15
513	*Gene Nelson*	.08
514	Rick Monday	.10
515	Miguel Dilone	.08
516	Clint Hurdle	.08
517	Jeff Newman	.08
518	Grant Jackson	.08
519	Andy Hassler	.08
520	Pat Putnam	.08
521	Greg Pryor	.08
522	Tony Scott	.08
523	Steve Mura	.08
524	Johnnie LeMaster	.08
525	Dick Ruthven	.08
526	John McNamara	.08
527	Larry McWilliams	.08
528	*Johnny Ray*	.10
529	*Pat Tabler*	.10
530	Tom Herr	.10
531a	San Diego Chicken (w/trademark symbol)	.75
531b	San Diego Chicken (no trademark symbol)	.80
532	Sal Butera	.08
533	Mike Griffin	.08
534	Kelvin Moore	.08
535	Reggie Jackson	2.00
536	Ed Romero	.08
537	Derrel Thomas	.08
538	Mike O'Berry	.08
539	Jack O'Connor	.08
540	*Bob Ojeda*	.50
541	Roy Lee Jackson	.08
542	Lynn Jones	.08
543	Gaylord Perry	.60
544a	Phil Garner (photo reversed)	.75
544b	Phil Garner (photo correct)	.10
545	Garry Templeton	.10
546	Rafael Ramirez	.08
547	Jeff Reardon	.40
548	Ron Guidry	.25
549	*Tim Laudner*	.12
550	John Henry Johnson	.08
551	Chris Bando	.08
552	Bobby Brown	.08
553	Larry Bradford	.08
554	*Scott Fletcher*	.40
555	Jerry Royster	.08
556	Shooty Babbitt	.08
557	*Kent Hrbek*	2.00
558	Yankee Winners (Ron Guidry, Tommy John)	.15
559	Mark Bomback	.08
560	Julio Valdez	.08
561	Buck Martinez	.08
562	*Mike Marshall*	.15
563	Rennie Stennett	.08
564	Steve Crawford	.08
565	Bob Babcock	.08
566	Johnny Podres	.10
567	Paul Serna	.08
568	Harold Baines	.65
569	Dave LaRoche	.08
570	Lee May	.08
571	Gary Ward	.10
572	John Denny	.08
573	Roy Smalley	.08
574	*Bob Brenly*	.20
575	Bronx Bombers (Reggie Jackson, Dave Winfield)	2.00
576	Luis Pujols	.08
577	Butch Hobson	.08
578	Harvey Kuenn	.10
579	Cal Ripken, Sr.	.08
580	Juan Berenguer	.08
581	Benny Ayala	.08
582	Vance Law	.08
583	*Rick Leach*	.12
584	George Frazier	.08
585	Phillies Finest (Pete Rose, Mike Schmidt)	1.00
586	Joe Rudi	.10
587	Juan Beniquez	.08
588	*Luis DeLeon*	.08
589	Craig Swan	.08
590	Dave Chalk	.08
591	Billy Gardner	.08
592	Sal Bando	.08
593	Bert Campaneris	.10
594	Steve Kemp	.08
595a	Randy Lerch (Braves)	.75
595b	Randy Lerch (Brewers)	.08
596	Bryan Clark	.08
597	Dave Ford	.08
598	Mike Scioscia	.20
599	John Lowenstein	.08
600	Rene Lachmann (Lachemann)	.08
601	Mick Kelleher	.08
602	Ron Jackson	.08
603	Jerry Koosman	.10
604	Dave Goltz	.08
605	Ellis Valentine	.08
606	Lonnie Smith	.08
607	Joaquin Andujar	.08
608	Garry Hancock	.08
609	Jerry Turner	.08
610	Bob Bonner	.08
611	Jim Dwyer	.08
612	Terry Bulling	.08
613	Joel Youngblood	.08
614	Larry Milbourne	.08
615	Phil Roof (photo actually Gene Roof)	.08
616	Keith Drumright	.08
617	Dave Rosello	.08
618	Rickey Keeton	.08
619	Dennis Lamp	.08
620	Sid Monge	.08
621	Jerry White	.08
622	*Luis Aguayo*	.08
623	Jamie Easterly	.08
624	*Steve Sax*	.75
625	Dave Roberts	.08
626	Rick Bosetti	.08
627	*Terry Francona*	.12
628	Pride of the Reds (Johnny Bench, Tom Seaver)	.80
629	Paul Mirabella	.08
630	Rance Mulliniks	.08
631	Kevin Hickey	.08
632	Reid Nichols	.08
633	Dave Geisel	.08
634	Ken Griffey	.12
635	Bob Lemon	.25
636	Orlando Sanchez	.08
637	Bill Almon	.08
638	Danny Ainge	1.25
639	Willie Stargell	.75
640	Bob Sykes	.08
641	Ed Lynch	.08
642	John Ellis	.08
643	Fergie Jenkins	.50
644	Lenn Sakata	.08
645	Julio Gonzales	.08
646	Jesse Orosco	.10
647	Jerry Dybzinski	.08
648	Tommy Davis	.08
649	Ron Gardenhire	.08
650	Felipe Alou	.12
651	Harvey Haddix	.08
652	Willie Upshaw	.15
653	Bill Madlock	.12
----	Checklist 1-26 DK (5 Trammel)	.50
----	Checklist 1-26 DK (5 Trammell)	.08
----	Checklist 27-130	.08
----	Checklist 131-234	.08
----	Checklist 235-338	.08
----	Checklist 339-442	.08
----	Checklist 443-544	.08
----	Checklist 545-653	.08

1983 Donruss

The 1983 Donruss set consists of 653 numbered

cards plus seven unnumbered checklists. The 2-1/2" x 3-1/2" cards were issued with puzzle pieces (three pieces on one card per pack) that feature Ty Cobb. The first 26 cards in the set were once again the Diamond Kings series. The card fronts display the Donruss logo and the year of issue. The card backs have black print on yellow and white and include statistics, career highlights, and the player's contract status. (DK) in the checklist below indicates cards which belong to the Diamond Kings series.

	MT
Complete Set (660):	90.00
Common Player:	.08
Ty Cobb Puzzle:	3.00
Pack (15 - 2nd print):	4.25
Wax Box (36 - 2nd print):	110.00

No.	Player	MT
1	Fernando Valenzuela (DK)	.25
2	Rollie Fingers (DK)	.50
3	Reggie Jackson (DK)	.75
4	Jim Palmer (DK)	.50
5	Jack Morris (DK)	.25
6	George Foster (DK)	.25
7	Jim Sundberg (DK)	.08
8	Willie Stargell (DK)	.50
9	Dave Stieb (DK)	.12
10	Joe Niekro (DK)	.12
11	Rickey Henderson (DK)	2.00
12	Dale Murphy (DK)	.50
13	Toby Harrah (DK)	.08
14	Bill Buckner (DK)	.15
15	Willie Wilson (DK)	.20
16	Steve Carlton (DK)	.50
17	Ron Guidry (DK)	.20
18	Steve Rogers (DK)	.08
19	Kent Hrbek (DK)	.20
20	Keith Hernandez (DK)	.20
21	Floyd Bannister (DK)	.08
22	Johnny Bench (DK)	.75
23	Britt Burns (DK)	.08
24	Joe Morgan (DK)	.50
25	Carl Yastrzemski (DK)	.80
26	Terry Kennedy (DK)	.08
27	Gary Roenicke	.08
28	Dwight Bernard	.08
29	Pat Underwood	.08
30	Gary Allenson	.08
31	Ron Guidry	.25
32	Burt Hooton	.08
33	Chris Bando	.08
34	Vida Blue	.12
35	Rickey Henderson	2.50
36	Ray Burris	.08
37	John Butcher	.08
38	Don Aase	.08
39	Jerry Koosman	.10
40	Bruce Sutter	.15
41	Jose Cruz	.12
42	Pete Rose	2.50
43	Cesar Cedeno	.12
44	Floyd Chiffer	.08
45	Larry McWilliams	.08
46	Alan Fowlkes	.08
47	Dale Murphy	.75
48	Doug Bird	.08
49	Hubie Brooks	.12
50	Floyd Bannister	.08
51	Jack O'Connor	.08
52	Steve Senteney	.08
53	*Gary Gaetti*	.75
54	Damaso Garcia	.08
55	Gene Nelson	.08
56	Mookie Wilson	.10
57	Allen Ripley	.08
58	Bob Horner	.12
59	Tony Pena	.10
60	Gary Lavelle	.08
61	Tim Lollar	.08
62	Frank Pastore	.08
63	Garry Maddox	.08
64	Bob Forsch	.08
65	Harry Spilman	.08
66	Geoff Zahn	.08
67	Salome Barojas	.08
68	David Palmer	.08
69	Charlie Hough	.08
70	Dan Quisenberry	.15
71	Tony Armas	.10
72	Rick Sutcliffe	.12
73	Steve Balboni	.08
74	Jerry Remy	.08
75	Mike Scioscia	.08
76	John Wockenfuss	.08
77	Jim Palmer	.80
78	Rollie Fingers	.60
79	Joe Nolan	.08
80	Pete Vuckovich	.08
81	Rick Leach	.08
82	Rick Miller	.08
83	Graig Nettles	.15
84	Ron Cey	.12
85	Miguel Dilone	.08
86	John Wathan	.08
87	Kelvin Moore	.08
88a	Byrn Smith (first name incorrect)	.70
88b	Bryn Smith (first name correct)	.08
89	Dave Hostetler	.08
90	Rod Carew	1.00
91	Lonnie Smith	.08
92	Bob Knepper	.08
93	Marty Bystrom	.08
94	Chris Welsh	.08
95	Jason Thompson	.08
96	Tom O'Malley	.08
97	Phil Niekro	.65
98	Neil Allen	.08
99	Bill Buckner	.12
100	*Ed Vande Berg*	.08
101	Jim Clancy	.08
102	Robert Castillo	.08
103	Bruce Berenyi	.08
104	Carlton Fisk	.75
105	Mike Flanagan	.08
106	Cecil Cooper	.10
107	Jack Morris	.45
108	Mike Morgan	.12
109	Luis Aponte	.08
110	Pedro Guerrero	.15
111	Len Barker	.08
112	Willie Wilson	.15
113	Dave Beard	.08
114	Mike Gates	.08
115	Reggie Jackson	1.50
116	George Wright	.08
117	Vance Law	.08
118	Nolan Ryan	8.50
119	Mike Krukow	.08
120	Ozzie Smith	2.00
121	Broderick Perkins	.08
122	Tom Seaver	1.50
123	Chris Chambliss	.08
124	Chuck Tanner	.08
125	Johnnie LeMaster	.08
126	*Mel Hall*	.15
127	Bruce Bochte	.08
128	*Charlie Puleo*	.08
129	Luis Leal	.08
130	John Pacella	.08
131	Glenn Gulliver	.08
132	Don Money	.08
133	Dave Rozema	.08
134	Bruce Hurst	.15
135	Rudy May	.08
136	Tom LaSorda (Lasorda)	.45
137	Dan Spillner (photo actually Ed Whitson)	.08
138	Jerry Martin	.08
139	Mike Norris	.08
140	Al Oliver	.15
141	Daryl Sconiers	.08
142	Lamar Johnson	.08
143	Harold Baines	.20
144	Alan Ashby	.08
145	Garry Templeton	.08
146	Al Holland	.08
147	Bo Diaz	.08
148	Dave Concepcion	.12
149	Rick Camp	.08
150	Jim Morrison	.08
151	Randy Martz	.08
152	Keith Hernandez	.20
153	John Lowenstein	.08
154	Mike Caldwell	.08
155	Milt Wilcox	.08
156	Rich Gedman	.08
157	Rich Gossage	.20
158	Jerry Reuss	.10
159	Ron Hassey	.08
160	Larry Gura	.08
161	Dwayne Murphy	.08
162	Woodie Fryman	.08
163	Steve Comer	.08
164	Ken Forsch	.08
165	Dennis Lamp	.08
166	David Green	.08
167	Terry Puhl	.08
168	Mike Schmidt	2.50
169	*Eddie Milner*	.08
170	John Curtis	.08
171	Don Robinson	.08
172	Richard Gale	.08
173	Steve Bedrosian	.08
174	Willie Hernandez	.08
175	Ron Gardenhire	.08
176	Jim Beattie	.08
177	Tim Laudner	.08
178	Buck Martinez	.08
179	Kent Hrbek	.50
180	Alfredo Griffin	.08
181	Larry Andersen	.08
182	Pete Falcone	.08
183	Jody Davis	.08
184	Glenn Hubbard	.08
185	Dale Berra	.08
186	Greg Minton	.08
187	Gary Lucas	.08
188	Dave Van Gorder	.08
189	Bob Dernier	.08
190	*Willie McGee*	1.50
191	Dickie Thon	.08
192	Bob Boone	.10
193	Britt Burns	.08
194	Jeff Reardon	.50
195	Jon Matlack	.08
196	*Don Slaught*	.20
197	Fred Stanley	.08
198	Rick Manning	.08
199	Dave Righetti	.20
200	Dave Stapleton	.08
201	Steve Yeager	.08
202	Enos Cabell	.08
203	Sammy Stewart	.08
204	Moose Haas	.08
205	Lenn Sakata	.08
206	Charlie Moore	.08
207	Alan Trammell	.40
208	Jim Rice	.25
209	Roy Smalley	.08
210	Bill Russell	.08
211	Andre Thornton	.10
212	Willie Aikens	.08
213	Dave McKay	.08
214	Tim Blackwell	.08
215	Buddy Bell	.12
216	Doug DeCinces	.10
217	Tom Herr	.10
218	Frank LaCorte	.08
219	Steve Carlton	1.00
220	Terry Kennedy	.08
221	Mike Easler	.08
222	Jack Clark	.25
223	Gene Garber	.08
224	Scott Holman	.08
225	Mike Proly	.08
226	Terry Bulling	.08
227	Jerry Garvin	.08
228	Ron Davis	.08
229	Tom Hume	.08
230	Marc Hill	.08
231	Dennis Martinez	.10
232	Jim Gantner	.08
233	Larry Pashnick	.08
234	Dave Collins	.08
235	Tom Burgmeier	.08
236	Ken Landreaux	.08
237	John Denny	.08
238	Hal McRae	.12
239	Matt Keough	.08
240	Doug Flynn	.08
241	Fred Lynn	.15
242	Billy Sample	.08
243	Tom Paciorek	.08
244	Joe Sambito	.08
245	Sid Monge	.08
246	Ken Oberkfell	.08
247	Joe Pittman (photo actually Juan Eichelberger)	.08
248	Mario Soto	.08
249	Claudell Washington	.08
250	Rick Rhoden	.10
251	Darrell Evans	.15
252	Steve Henderson	.08
253	Manny Castillo	.08
254	Craig Swan	.08
255	Joey McLaughlin	.08
256	Pete Redfern	.08
257	Ken Singleton	.10
258	Robin Yount	2.50
259	Elias Sosa	.08
260	Bob Ojeda	.08
261	Bobby Murcer	.10
262	*Candy Maldonado*	.20
263	Rick Waits	.08
264	Greg Pryor	.08
265	Bob Owchinko	.08
266	Chris Speier	.08
267	Bruce Kison	.08
268	Mark Wagner	.08
269	Steve Kemp	.08
270	Phil Garner	.08
271	Gene Richards	.08
272	Renie Martin	.08
273	Dave Roberts	.08
274	Dan Driessen	.08
275	Rufino Linares	.08
276	Lee Lacy	.08
277	*Ryne Sandberg*	14.00
278	Darrell Porter	.08
279	Cal Ripken, Jr.	16.00
280	Jamie Easterly	.08
281	Bill Fahey	.08
282	Glenn Hoffman	.08
283	Willie Randolph	.10
284	Fernando Valenzuela	.25
285	Alan Bannister	.08
286	Paul Splittorff	.08
287	Joe Rudi	.10
288	Bill Gullickson	.08
289	Danny Darwin	.08
290	Andy Hassler	.08
291	Ernesto Escarrega	.08
292	Steve Mura	.08
293	Tony Scott	.08
294	Manny Trillo	.08
295	Greg Harris	.08
296	Luis DeLeon	.08
297	Kent Tekulve	.08
298	Atlee Hammaker	.08
299	Bruce Benedict	.08
300	Fergie Jenkins	.45
301	Dave Kingman	.15
302	Bill Caudill	.08
303	John Castino	.08
304	Ernie Whitt	.08
305	Randy S. Johnson	.08
306	Garth Iorg	.08
307	Gaylord Perry	.60
308	Ed Lynch	.08
309	Keith Moreland	.08
310	Rafael Ramirez	.08
311	Bill Madlock	.12
312	Milt May	.08
313	John Montefusco	.08
314	Wayne Krenchicki	.08
315	George Vukovich	.08
316	Joaquin Andujar	.08
317	Craig Reynolds	.08
318	Rick Burleson	.08
319	Richard Dotson	.08

320 Steve Rogers .08
321 Dave Schmidt .08
322 *Bud Black* .20
323 Jeff Burroughs .08
324 Von Hayes .08
325 Butch Wynegar .08
326 Carl Yastrzemski .80
327 Ron Roenicke .08
328 *Howard Johnson* 1.00
329 Rick Dempsey .08
330a Jim Slaton (one yellow box on back) .70
330b Jim Slaton (two yellow boxes on back) .08
331 Benny Ayala .08
332 Ted Simmons .12
333 Lou Whitaker .25
334 Chuck Rainey .08
335 Lou Piniella .12
336 Steve Sax .15
337 Toby Harrah .08
338 George Brett 3.00
339 Davey Lopes .10
340 Gary Carter .40
341 John Grubb .08
342 Tim Foli .08
343 Jim Kaat .15
344 Mike LaCoss .08
345 Larry Christenson .08
346 Juan Bonilla .08
347 Omar Moreno .08
348 Chili Davis .50
349 Tommy Boggs .08
350 Rusty Staub .10
351 Bump Wills .08
352 Rick Sweet .08
353 *Jim Gott* .20
354 Terry Felton .08
355 Jim Kern .08
356 Bill Almon .08
357 Tippy Martinez .08
358 Roy Howell .08
359 Dan Petry .08
360 Jerry Mumphrey .08
361 Mark Clear .08
362 Mike Marshall .10
363 Lary Sorensen .08
364 Amos Otis .08
365 Rick Langford .08
366 Brad Mills .08
367 Brian Downing .10
368 Mike Richardt .08
369 Aurelio Rodriguez .08
370 Dave Smith .08
371 Tug McGraw .12
372 Doug Bair .08
373 Ruppert Jones .08
374 Alex Trevino .08
375 Ken Dayley .08
376 Rod Scurry .08
377 Bob Brenly .08
378 Scot Thompson .08
379 Julio Cruz .08
380 John Stearns .08
381 Dale Murray .08
382 *Frank Viola* 1.50
383 Al Bumbry .08
384 Ben Oglivie .08
385 Dave Tobik .08
386 Bob Stanley .08
387 Andre Robertson .08
388 Jorge Orta .08
389 Ed Whitson .08
390 Don Hood .08
391 Tom Underwood .08
392 Tim Wallach .20
393 Steve Renko .08
394 Mickey Rivers .08
395 Greg Luzinski .15
396 Art Howe .08
397 Alan Wiggins .08
398 Jim Barr .08
399 Ivan DeJesus .08
400 *Tom Lawless* .08
401 Bob Walk .08
402 Jimmy Smith .08
403 Lee Smith 1.50
404 George Hendrick .08
405 Eddie Murray 2.50
406 Marshall Edwards .08
407 Lance Parrish .35
408 Carney Lansford .08
409 Dave Winfield 1.50
410 Bob Welch .10
411 Larry Milbourne .08
412 Dennis Leonard .08
413 Dan Meyer .08
414 Charlie Lea .08
415 Rick Honeycutt .08
416 Mike Witt .10
417 Steve Trout .08
418 Glenn Brummer .08
419 Denny Walling .08
420 Gary Matthews .10
421 Charlie Liebrandt (Leibrandt) .08
422 Juan Eichelberger .08
423 *Matt Guante (Cecilio)* .08
424 Bill Laskey .08
425 Jerry Royster .08
426 Dickie Noles .08
427 George Foster .15
428 *Mike Moore* .50
429 Gary Ward .08
430 Barry Bonnell .08
431 Ron Washington .08
432 Rance Mulliniks .08
433 Mike Stanton .08
434 Jesse Orosco .10
435 Larry Bowa .10
436 Biff Pocoroba .08
437 Johnny Ray .08
438 Joe Morgan .60
439 *Eric Show* .25
440 Larry Biittner .08
441 Greg Gross .08
442 Gene Tenace .08
443 Danny Heep .08
444 Bobby Clark .08
445 Kevin Hickey .08
446 Scott Sanderson .08
447 Frank Tanana .08
448 Cesar Geronimo .08
449 Jimmy Sexton .08
450 Mike Hargrove .08
451 Doyle Alexander .08
452 Dwight Evans .15
453 Terry Forster .08
454 Tom Brookens .08
455 Rich Dauer .08
456 Rob Picciolo .08
457 Terry Crowley .08
458 Ned Yost .08
459 Kirk Gibson .20
460 Reid Nichols .08
461 Oscar Gamble .08
462 Dusty Baker .12
463 Jack Perconte .08
464 Frank White .10
465 Mickey Klutts .08
466 Warren Cromartie .08
467 Larry Parrish .08
468 Bobby Grich .10
469 Dane Iorg .08
470 Joe Niekro .12
471 Ed Farmer .08
472 Tim Flannery .08
473 Dave Parker .35
474 Jeff Leonard .08
475 Al Hrabosky .08
476 Ron Hodges .08
477 Leon Durham .08
478 Jim Essian .08
479 Roy Lee Jackson .08
480 Brad Havens .08
481 Joe Price .08
482 Tony Bernazard .08
483 Scott McGregor .08
484 Paul Molitor 1.75
485 Mike Ivie .08
486 Ken Griffey .12
487 Dennis Eckersley .65
488 Steve Garvey .45
489 Mike Fischlin .08
490 U.L. Washington .08
491 Steve McCatty .08
492 Roy Johnson .08
493 Don Baylor .12
494 Bobby Johnson .08
495 Mike Squires .08
496 Bert Roberge .08
497 Dick Ruthven .08
498 Tito Landrum .08
499 Sixto Lezcano .08
500 Johnny Bench 1.00
501 Larry Whisenton .08
502 Manny Sarmiento .08
503 Fred Breining .08
504 Bill Campbell .08
505 Todd Cruz .08
506 Bob Bailor .08
507 Dave Stieb .12
508 Al Williams .08
509 Dan Ford .08
510 Gorman Thomas .08
511 Chet Lemon .08
512 Mike Torrez .08
513 Shane Rawley .08
514 Mark Belanger .08
515 Rodney Craig .08
516 Onix Concepcion .08
517 Mike Heath .08
518 Andre Dawson 1.25
519 Luis Sanchez .08
520 Terry Bogener .08
521 Rudy Law .08
522 Ray Knight .10
523 Joe Lefebvre .08
524 Jim Wohlford .08
525 *Julio Franco* 4.00
526 Ron Oester .08
527 Rick Mahler .08
528 Steve Nicosia .08
529 Junior Kennedy .08
530a Whitey Herzog (one yellow box on back) .70
530b Whitey Herzog (two yellow boxes on back) .10
531a Don Sutton (blue frame) .45
531b Don Sutton (green frame) .45
532 Mark Brouhard .08
533a Sparky Anderson (one yellow box on back) .70
533b Sparky Anderson (two yellow boxes on back) .10
534 Roger LaFrancois .08
535 George Frazier .08
536 Tom Niedenfuer .08
537 Ed Glynn .08
538 Lee May .08
539 Bob Kearney .08
540 Tim Raines .35
541 Paul Mirabella .08
542 Luis Tiant .12
543 Ron LeFlore .08
544 *Dave LaPoint* .12
545 Randy Moffitt .08
546 Luis Aguayo .08
547 Brad Lesley .08
548 Luis Salazar .08
549 John Candelaria .08
550 Dave Bergman .08
551 Bob Watson .08
552 Pat Tabler .08
553 Brent Gaff .08
554 Al Cowens .08
555 Tom Brunansky .10
556 Lloyd Moseby .08
557a Pascual Perez (Twins) .90
557b Pascual Perez (Braves) .15
558 Willie Upshaw .08
559 Richie Zisk .08
560 Pat Zachry .08
561 Jay Johnstone .08
562 Carlos Diaz .08
563 John Tudor .10
564 Frank Robinson .25
565 Dave Edwards .08
566 Paul Householder .08
567 Ron Reed .08
568 Mike Ramsey .08
569 Kiko Garcia .08
570 Tommy John .20
571 Tony LaRussa .12
572 Joel Youngblood .08
573 *Wayne Tolleson* .08
574 Keith Creel .08
575 Billy Martin .12
576 Jerry Dybzinski .08
577 Rick Cerone .08
578 Tony Perez .25
579 *Greg Brock* .15
580 Glen Wilson (Glenn) .20
581 Tim Stoddard .08
582 Bob McClure .08
583 Jim Dwyer .08
584 Ed Romero .08
585 Larry Herndon .08
586 *Wade Boggs* 15.00
587 Jay Howell .10
588 Dave Stewart .50
589 Bert Blyleven .12
590 Dick Howser .08
591 Wayne Gross .08
592 Terry Francona .08
593 Don Werner .08
594 Bill Stein .08
595 Jesse Barfield .40
596 Bobby Molinaro .08
597 Mike Vail .08
598 *Tony Gwynn* 30.00
599 Gary Rajsich .08
600 Jerry Ujdur .08
601 Cliff Johnson .08
602 Jerry White .08
603 Bryan Clark .08
604 Joe Ferguson .08
605 Guy Sularz .08
606a Ozzie Virgil (green frame around photo) .90
606b Ozzie Virgil (orange frame around photo) .08
607 Terry Harper .08
608 Harvey Kuenn .08
609 Jim Sundberg .08
610 Willie Stargell .75
611 Reggie Smith .10
612 Rob Wilfong .08
613 Niekro Brothers (Joe Niekro, Phil Niekro) .25
614 Lee Elia .08
615 Mickey Hatcher .08
616 Jerry Hairston .08
617 John Martin .08
618 Wally Backman .08
619 *Storm Davis* .10
620 Alan Knicely .08
621 John Stuper .08
622 Matt Sinatro .08
623 *Gene Petralli* .08
624 Duane Walker .08
625 Dick Williams .08
626 Pat Corrales .08
627 Vern Ruhle .08
628 Joe Torre .08
629 Anthony Johnson .08
630 Steve Howe .08
631 Gary Woods .08
632 Lamarr Hoyt (LaMarr) .08
633 Steve Swisher .08
634 Terry Leach .08
635 Jeff Newman .08
636 Brett Butler .10
637 Gary Gray .08
638 Lee Mazzilli .08
639a Ron Jackson (A's) 6.00
639b Ron Jackson (Angels - green frame around photo) .90
639c Ron Jackson (Angels - red frame around photo) .20
640 Juan Beniquez .08
641 Dave Rucker .08
642 Luis Pujols .08
643 Rick Monday .10
644 Hosken Powell .08
645 San Diego Chicken .20
646 Dave Engle .08
647 Dick Davis .08
648 MVP's (Vida Blue, Joe Morgan, Frank Robinson) .15
649 Al Chambers .08
650 Jesus Vega .08
651 Jeff Jones .08
652 Marvis Foley .08
653 Ty Cobb (puzzle) .08
---- DK checklist (Dick Perez) (no word "Checklist" on back) .70
---- DK Checklist (Dick Perez) (word "Checklist" on back) .08
---- Checklist 27-130 .08
---- Checklist 131-234 .08
---- Checklist 235-338 .08
---- Checklist 339-442 .08
---- Checklist 443-546 .08
---- Checklist 547-653 .08

1983 Donruss Action All-Stars

The cards in this 60-card set are designed on a horizontal format and contain a large close-up photo of the player on the left and a smaller action photo on the right. The 5" x 3-1/2" cards have deep red borders and contain the Donruss logo and the year of issue. Backs are printed in black on red and white and contain statistical and biographical information. The cards were sold with puzzle pieces (three pieces on one card per pack) that feature Mickey Mantle.

		MT
Complete Set (60):		7.00
Common Player:		.05
Mickey Mantle puzzle:		12.50
1	Eddie Murray	.30
2	Dwight Evans	.05
3a	Reggie Jackson (red covers part of statistics on back)	.30
3b	Reggie Jackson (red does not cover any statistics on back)	.30
4	Greg Luzinski	.08
5	Larry Herndon	.05
6	Al Oliver	.05
7	Bill Buckner	.05
8	Jason Thompson	.05
9	Andre Dawson	.15
10	Greg Minton	.05
11	Terry Kennedy	.05
12	Phil Niekro	.20
13	Willie Wilson	.05
14	Johnny Bench	.30
15	Ron Guidry	.05
16	Hal McRae	.05
17	Damaso Garcia	.05
18	Gary Ward	.05
19	Cecil Cooper	.05
20	Keith Hernandez	.05
21	Ron Cey	.05
22	Rickey Henderson	.30
23	Nolan Ryan	2.50
24	Steve Carlton	.30
25	John Stearns	.05
26	Jim Sundberg	.05
27	Joaquin Andujar	.05
28	Gaylord Perry	.20
29	Jack Clark	.05
30	Bill Madlock	.05
31	Pete Rose	1.00
32	Mookie Wilson	.05
33	Rollie Fingers	.20
34	Lonnie Smith	.05
35	Tony Pena	.05
36	Dave Winfield	.30
37	Tim Lollar	.05
38	Rod Carew	.30
39	Toby Harrah	.05
40	Buddy Bell	.05
41	Bruce Sutter	.05
42	George Brett	.75
43	Carlton Fisk	.30
44	Carl Yastrzemski	.50
45	Dale Murphy	.20
46	Bob Horner	.05
47	Dave Concepcion	.05
48	Dave Stieb	.05
49	Kent Hrbek	.08
50	Lance Parrish	.05
51	Joe Niekro	.05
52	Cal Ripken, Jr.	2.50
53	Fernando Valenzuela	.08
54	Rickie Zisk	.05
55	Leon Durham	.05
56	Robin Yount	.30
57	Mike Schmidt	.75
58	Gary Carter	.08
59	Fred Lynn	.05
60	Checklist	.03

1983 Donruss Hall of Fame Heroes

The artwork of Dick Perez is featured in the 44- card Hall of Fame Heroes set issued in 1983. The 2-1/2" x 3-1/2" cards were available in wax packs that contained eight cards plus a Mickey Mantle puzzle piece card (three pieces on one card). Backs display red and blue print on white stock and contain a short biograpical sketch.

		MT
Complete Set (44):		8.00
Common Player:		.10
Mickey Mantle Puzzle:		12.50
1	Ty Cobb	.75
2	Walter Johnson	.15
3	Christy Mathewson	.15
4	Josh Gibson	.15
5	Honus Wagner	.25
6	Jackie Robinson	.75
7	Mickey Mantle	2.00
8	Luke Appling	.10
9	Ted Williams	.75
10	Johnny Mize	.10
11	Satchel Paige	.25
12	Lou Boudreau	.10
13	Jimmie Foxx	.10
14	Duke Snider	.35
15	Monte Irvin	.10
16	Hank Greenberg	.25
17	Roberto Clemente	1.00
18	Al Kaline	.25
19	Frank Robinson	.25
20	Joe Cronin	.10
21	Burleigh Grimes	.10
22	The Waner Brothers (Lloyd Waner, Paul Waner)	.10
23	Grover Alexander	.10
24	Yogi Berra	.35
25	James Bell	.10
26	Bill Dickey	.10
27	Cy Young	.15
28	Charlie Gehringer	.10
29	Dizzy Dean	.15
30	Bob Lemon	.10
31	Red Ruffing	.10
32	Stan Musial	.75
33	Carl Hubbell	.15
34	Hank Aaron	.75
35	John McGraw	.10
36	Bob Feller	.20
37	Casey Stengel	.10
38	Ralph Kiner	.10
39	Roy Campanella	.35
40	Mel Ott	.10
41	Robin Roberts	.10
42	Early Wynn	.10
43	Mickey Mantle Puzzle Card	.10
---	Checklist	.05

1984 Donruss

The 1984 Donruss set consists of 651 numbered cards, seven unnumbered checklists and two "Living Legends" cards (designated A and B). The A and B cards were issued only in wax packs and were not available to hobby dealers purchasing factory sets. The card fronts differ in style from the previous years, however the Donruss logo and year of issue are still included. Backs have black print on green and white and are identical in format to the preceding year. The 2-1/2" x 3-1/2" cards were issued in packs with three pieces of a 63-piece puzzle of Duke Snider. The complete set price in the checklist that follows does not include the higher priced variations. Cards marked with (DK) or (RR) in the checklist refer to the Diamond Kings and Rated Rookies subsets. Each of the Diamond Kings cards and the DK checklist can be found in two varieties. The more common has Frank Steele's name misspelled "Steel" in the credit line at the bottom-right corner on the back. The error was later corrected.

		MT
Complete Set (660):		180.00
Common Player:		.15
Duke Snider Puzzle:		3.50
Pack (15):		9.00
Wax Box (36):		225.00
A	Living Legends (Rollie Fingers, Gaylord Perry)	5.00
B	Living Legends (Johnny Bench, Carl Yastrzemski)	8.00
1a	Robin Yount (DK) (Steel)	3.00
1b	Robin Yount (DK) (Steele)	5.00
2a	Dave Concepcion (DK) (Steel)	.30
2b	Dave Concepcion (DK) (Steele)	.60
3a	Dwayne Murphy (DK) (Steel)	.25
3b	Dwayne Murphy (DK) (Steele)	.60
4a	John Castino (DK) (Steel)	.20
4b	John Castino (DK) (Steele)	.60
5a	Leon Durham (DK) (Steel)	.25
5b	Leon Durham (DK) (Steele)	.60
6a	Rusty Staub (DK) (Steel)	.30
6b	Rusty Staub (DK) (Steele)	.60
7a	Jack Clark (DK) (Steel)	.25
7b	Jack Clark (DK) (Steele)	.60
8a	Dave Dravecky (DK) (Steel)	.25
8b	Dave Dravecky (DK) (Steele)	.60
9a	Al Oliver (DK) (Steel)	.35
9b	Al Oliver (DK) (Steele)	.70
10a	Dave Righetti (DK) (Steel)	.25
10b	Dave Righetti (DK) (Steele)	.60
11a	Hal McRae (DK) (Steel)	.30
11b	Hal McRae (DK) (Steele)	.60
12a	Ray Knight (DK) (Steel)	.25
12b	Ray Knight (DK) (Steele)	.60
13a	Bruce Sutter (DK) (Steel)	.25
13b	Bruce Sutter (DK) (Steele)	.60
14a	Bob Horner (DK) (Steel)	.25
14b	Bob Horner (DK) (Steele)	.60
15a	Lance Parrish (DK) (Steel)	.25
15b	Lance Parrish (DK) (Steele)	.60
16a	Matt Young (DK) (Steel)	.25
16b	Matt Young (DK) (Steele)	.60
17a	Fred Lynn (DK) (Steel)	.35
17b	Fred Lynn (DK) (Steele)	.70
18a	Ron Kittle (DK) (Steel)	.25
18b	Ron Kittle (DK) (Steele)	.60
19a	Jim Clancy (DK) (Steel)	.25
19b	Jim Clancy (DK) (Steele)	.60
20a	Bill Madlock (DK) (Steel)	.30
20b	Bill Madlock (DK) (Steele)	.60
21a	Larry Parrish (DK) (Steel)	.25
21b	Larry Parrish (DK) (Steele)	.60
22a	Eddie Murray (DK) (Steel)	2.00
22b	Eddie Murray (DK) (Steele)	4.00

23a Mike Schmidt (DK) (Steel) 4.00
23b Mike Schmidt (DK) (Steele) 5.00
24a Pedro Guerrero (DK) (Steel) .25
24b Pedro Guerrero (DK) (Steele) .60
25a Andre Thornton (DK) (Steel) .25
25b Andre Thornton (DK) (Steele) .60
26a Wade Boggs (DK) (Steel) 3.00
26b Wade Boggs (DK) (Steele) 4.00
27 *Joel Skinner* (RR) .15
28 Tom Dunbar (RR) .15
29a Mike Stenhouse (RR) (no number on back) .15
29b Mike Stenhouse (RR) (29 on back) 3.00
30a *Ron Darling* (RR) (no number on back) 2.00
30b *Ron Darling* (RR) (30 on back) 3.00
31 *Dion James* (RR) .15
32 *Tony Fernandez* (RR) 3.00
33 Angel Salazar (RR) .15
34 *Kevin McReynolds* (RR) 1.50
35 *Dick Schofield* (RR) .20
36 *Brad Komminsk* (RR) .15
37 *Tim Teufel* (RR) .30
38 Doug Frobel (RR) .15
39 *Greg Gagne* (RR) .80
40 Mike Fuentes (RR) .15
41 *Joe Carter* (RR) 40.00
42 Mike Brown (RR) .15
43 Mike Jeffcoat (RR) .15
44 *Sid Fernandez* (RR) 4.00
45 Brian Dayett (RR) .15
46 Chris Smith (RR) .15
47 Eddie Murray 8.00
48 Robin Yount 6.00
49 Lance Parrish .40
50 Jim Rice .50
51 Dave Winfield 6.00
52 Fernando Valenzuela .40
53 George Brett 12.00
54 Rickey Henderson 5.00
55 Gary Carter .65
56 Buddy Bell .20
57 Reggie Jackson 6.00
58 Harold Baines .30
59 Ozzie Smith 6.00
60 Nolan Ryan 30.00
61 Pete Rose 8.00
62 Ron Oester .15
63 Steve Garvey .75
64 Jason Thompson .15
65 Jack Clark .25
66 Dale Murphy 1.50
67 Leon Durham .15
68 Darryl Strawberry 10.00
69 Richie Zisk .15
70 Kent Hrbek .40
71 Dave Stieb .25
72 Ken Schrom .15
73 George Bell .40
74 John Moses .15
75 Ed Lynch .15
76 Chuck Rainey .15
77 Biff Pocoroba .15
78 Cecilio Guante .15
79 Jim Barr .15
80 Kurt Bevacqua .15
81 Tom Foley .15
82 Joe Lefebvre .15
83 *Andy Van Slyke* 2.00
84 Bob Lillis .15
85 Rick Adams .15
86 Jerry Hairston .15
87 Bob James .15
88 Joe Altobelli .15
89 Ed Romero .15
90 John Grubb .15
91 John Henry Johnson .15
92 Juan Espino .15
93 Candy Maldonado .15
94 Andre Thornton .20
95 Onix Concepcion .15
96 *Don Hill* .15
97 Andre Dawson 2.00
98 Frank Tanana .15
99 *Curt Wilkerson* .15
100 Larry Gura .15
101 Dwayne Murphy .15
102 Tom Brennan .15
103 Dave Righetti .40
104 Steve Sax .30
105 Dan Petry .15
106 Cal Ripken, Jr. 30.00
107 Paul Molitor 8.00
108 Fred Lynn .35
109 Neil Allen .15
110 Joe Niekro .20
111 Steve Carlton 5.00
112 Terry Kennedy .15
113 Bill Madlock .20
114 Chili Davis .20
115 Jim Gantner .15
116 Tom Seaver 5.00
117 Bill Buckner .20
118 Bill Caudill .15
119 Jim Clancy .15
120 John Castino .15
121 Dave Concepcion .20
122 Greg Luzinski .20
123 Mike Boddicker .20
124 Pete Ladd .15
125 Juan Berenguer .15
126 John Montefusco .15
127 Ed Jurak .15
128 Tom Niedenfuer .15
129 Bert Blyleven .30
130 Bud Black .15
131 Gorman Heimueller .15
132 Dan Schatzeder .15
133 Ron Jackson .15
134 *Tom Henke* 1.50
135 Kevin Hickey .15
136 Mike Scott .15
137 Bo Diaz .15
138 Glenn Brummer .15
139 Sid Monge .15
140 Rich Gale .15
141 Brett Butler .20
142 Brian Harper .25
143 John Rabb .15
144 Gary Woods .15
145 Pat Putnam .15
146 *Jim Acker* .15
147 Mickey Hatcher .15
148 Todd Cruz .15
149 Tom Tellmann .15
150 John Wockenfuss .15
151 Wade Boggs 12.00
152 Don Baylor .20
153 Bob Welch .20
154 Alan Bannister .15
155 Willie Aikens .15
156 Jeff Burroughs .15
157 Bryan Little .15
158 Bob Boone .20
159 Dave Hostetler .15
160 Jerry Dybzinski .15
161 Mike Madden .15
162 Luis DeLeon .15
163 Willie Hernandez .15
164 Frank Pastore .15
165 Rick Camp .15
166 Lee Mazzilli .15
167 Scot Thompson .15
168 Bob Forsch .15
169 Mike Flanagan .15
170 Rick Manning .15
171 Chet Lemon .15
172 Jerry Remy .15
173 Ron Guidry .20
174 Pedro Guerrero .25
175 Willie Wilson .25
176 Carney Lansford .15
177 Al Oliver .30
178 Jim Sundberg .15
179 Bobby Grich .20
180 Richard Dotson .15
181 Joaquin Andujar .15
182 Jose Cruz .20
183 Mike Schmidt 12.00
184 *Gary Redus* .25
185 Garry Templeton .15
186 Tony Pena .20
187 Greg Minton .15
188 Phil Niekro 1.00
189 Fergie Jenkins 1.00
190 Mookie Wilson .20
191 Jim Beattie .15
192 Gary Ward .15
193 Jesse Barfield .20
194 Pete Filson .15
195 Roy Lee Jackson .15
196 Rick Sweet .15
197 Jesse Orosco .15
198 *Steve Lake* .15
199 Ken Dayley .15
200 Manny Sarmiento .15
201 Mark Davis .15
202 Tim Flannery .15
203 Bill Scherrer .15
204 Al Holland .15
205 David Von Ohlen .15
206 Mike LaCoss .15
207 Juan Beniquez .15
208 *Juan Agosto* .15
209 Bobby Ramos .15
210 Al Bumbry .15
211 Mark Brouhard .15
212 Howard Bailey .15
213 Bruce Hurst .15
214 Bob Shirley .15
215 Pat Zachry .15
216 Julio Franco 1.00
217 Mike Armstrong .15
218 Dave Beard .15
219 Steve Rogers .15
220 John Butcher .15
221 *Mike Smithson* .15
222 Frank White .20
223 Mike Heath .15
224 Chris Bando .15
225 Roy Smalley .15
226 Dusty Baker .20
227 Lou Whitaker .40
228 John Lowenstein .15
229 Ben Oglivie .15
230 Doug DeCinces .15
231 Lonnie Smith .15
232 Ray Knight .15
233 Gary Matthews .15
234 Juan Bonilla .15
235 Rod Scurry .15
236 Atlee Hammaker .15
237 Mike Caldwell .15
238 Keith Hernandez .25
239 Larry Bowa .20
240 Tony Bernazard .15
241 Damaso Garcia .15
242 Tom Brunansky .15
243 Dan Driessen .15
244 Ron Kittle .15
245 Tim Stoddard .15
246 Bob L. Gibson .15
247 Marty Castillo .15
248 *Don Mattingly* 55.00
249 Jeff Newman .15
250 *Alejandro Pena* .25
251 Toby Harrah .15
252 Cesar Geronimo .15
253 Tom Underwood .15
254 Doug Flynn .15
255 Andy Hassler .15
256 Odell Jones .15
257 Rudy Law .15
258 Harry Spilman .15
259 Marty Bystrom .15
260 Dave Rucker .15
261 Ruppert Jones .15
262 Jeff Jones .15
263 *Gerald Perry* .25
264 Gene Tenace .15
265 Brad Wellman .15
266 Dickie Noles .15
267 Jamie Allen .15
268 Jim Gott .15
269 Ron Davis .15
270 Benny Ayala .15
271 Ned Yost .15
272 Dave Rozema .15
273 Dave Stapleton .15
274 Lou Piniella .20
275 Jose Morales .15
276 Brod Perkins .15
277 Butch Davis .15
278 Tony Phillips 1.00
279 Jeff Reardon .25
280 Ken Forsch .15
281 *Pete O'Brien* .50
282 Tom Paciorek .15
283 Frank LaCorte .15
284 Tim Lollar .15
285 Greg Gross .15
286 Alex Trevino .15
287 Gene Garber .15
288 Dave Parker .50
289 Lee Smith 2.00
290 Dave LaPoint .15
291 *John Shelby* .15
292 Charlie Moore .15
293 Alan Trammell 1.50
294 Tony Armas .20
295 Shane Rawley .15
296 Greg Brock .15
297 Hal McRae .20
298 Mike Davis .15
299 Tim Raines 1.00
300 Bucky Dent .15
301 Tommy John .35
302 Carlton Fisk 4.00
303 Darrell Porter .15
304 Dickie Thon .15
305 Garry Maddox .15
306 Cesar Cedeno .20
307 Gary Lucas .15
308 Johnny Ray .15
309 Andy McGaffigan .15
310 Claudell Washington .15
311 Ryne Sandberg 18.00
312 George Foster .30
313 *Spike Owen* .50
314 Gary Gaetti .35
315 Willie Upshaw .15
316 Al Williams .15
317 Jorge Orta .15
318 Orlando Mercado .15
319 *Junior Ortiz* .15
320 Mike Proly .15
321 Randy S. Johnson .15
322 Jim Morrison .15
323 Max Venable .15
324 Tony Gwynn 20.00
325 Duane Walker .15
326 Ozzie Virgil .15
327 Jeff Lahti .15
328 *Bill Dawley* .15
329 Rob Wilfong .15
330 Marc Hill .15
331 Ray Burris .15
332 Allan Ramirez .15
333 Chuck Porter .15
334 Wayne Krenchicki .15
335 Gary Allenson .15
336 *Bob Meacham* .15
337 Joe Beckwith .15
338 Rick Sutcliffe .25
339 *Mark Huismann* .15
340 *Tim Conroy* .15
341 Scott Sanderson .15
342 Larry Biittner .15
343 Dave Stewart .50
344 Darryl Motley .15
345 *Chris Codiroli* .15
346 Rick Behenna .15
347 Andre Robertson .15
348 Mike Marshall .25
349 Larry Herndon .15
350 Rich Dauer .15
351 Cecil Cooper .15
352 Rod Carew 4.00
353 Willie McGee .40
354 Phil Garner .20
355 Joe Morgan 1.00
356 Luis Salazar .15
357 John Candelaria .15
358 Bill Laskey .15
359 Bob McClure .15
360 Dave Kingman .20
361 Ron Cey .20
362 *Matt Young* .15
363 Lloyd Moseby .20
364 Frank Viola .45
365 Eddie Milner .15
366 Floyd Bannister .15
367 Dan Ford .15
368 Moose Haas .15
369 Doug Bair .15
370 *Ray Fontenot* .15
371 Luis Aponte .15
372 Jack Fimple .15
373 *Neal Heaton* .20
374 Greg Pryor .15
375 Wayne Gross .15
376 Charlie Lea .15
377 Steve Lubratich .15
378 Jon Matlack .15
379 Julio Cruz .15
380 John Mizerock .15
381 *Kevin Gross* .50
382 Mike Ramsey .15
383 Doug Gwosdz .15
384 Kelly Paris .15
385 Pete Falcone .15

#	Player	Price
386	Milt May	.15
387	Fred Breining	.15
388	*Craig Lefferts*	.25
389	Steve Henderson	.15
390	Randy Moffitt	.15
391	Ron Washington	.15
392	Gary Roenicke	.15
393	*Tom Candiotti*	.75
394	Larry Pashnick	.15
395	Dwight Evans	.30
396	Goose Gossage	.25
397	Derrel Thomas	.15
398	Juan Eichelberger	.15
399	Leon Roberts	.15
400	Davey Lopes	.15
401	Bill Gullickson	.15
402	Geoff Zahn	.15
403	Billy Sample	.15
404	Mike Squires	.15
405	Craig Reynolds	.15
406	Eric Show	.15
407	John Denny	.15
408	Dann Bilardello	.15
409	Bruce Benedict	.15
410	Kent Tekulve	.15
411	Mel Hall	.15
412	John Stuper	.15
413	Rick Dempsey	.15
414	Don Sutton	.90
415	Jack Morris	.50
416	John Tudor	.15
417	Willie Randolph	.20
418	Jerry Reuss	.15
419	Don Slaught	.15
420	Steve McCatty	.15
421	Tim Wallach	.25
422	Larry Parrish	.15
423	Brian Downing	.15
424	Britt Burns	.15
425	David Green	.15
426	Jerry Mumphrey	.15
427	Ivan DeJesus	.15
428	Mario Soto	.15
429	Gene Richards	.15
430	Dale Berra	.15
431	Darrell Evans	.25
432	Glenn Hubbard	.15
433	Jody Davis	.15
434	Danny Heep	.15
435	*Ed Nunez*	.15
436	Bobby Castillo	.15
437	Ernie Whitt	.15
438	Scott Ullger	.15
439	Doyle Alexander	.15
440	Domingo Ramos	.15
441	Craig Swan	.15
442	Warren Brusstar	.15
443	Len Barker	.15
444	Mike Easler	.15
445	Renie Martin	.15
446	*Dennis Rasmussen*	.30
447	Ted Power	.15
448	*Charlie Hudson*	.15
449	*Danny Cox*	.50
450	Kevin Bass	.15
451	Daryl Sconiers	.15
452	Scott Fletcher	.15
453	Bryn Smith	.15
454	Jim Dwyer	.15
455	Rob Picciolo	.15
456	Enos Cabell	.15
457	*Dennis Boyd*	.20
458	Butch Wynegar	.15
459	Burt Hooton	.15
460	Ron Hassey	.15
461	*Danny Jackson*	.50
462	Bob Kearney	.15
463	Terry Francona	.15
464	Wayne Tolleson	.15
465	Mickey Rivers	.15
466	John Wathan	.15
467	Bill Almon	.15
468	George Vukovich	.15
469	Steve Kemp	.15
470	Ken Landreaux	.15
471	Milt Wilcox	.15
472	Tippy Martinez	.15
473	Ted Simmons	.15
474	Tim Foli	.15
475	George Hendrick	.15
476	Terry Puhl	.15
477	Von Hayes	.15
478	Bobby Brown	.15
479	Lee Lacy	.15
480	Joel Youngblood	.15
481	Jim Slaton	.15
482	*Mike Fitzgerald*	.15
483	Keith Moreland	.15
484	Ron Roenicke	.15
485	Luis Leal	.15
486	Bryan Oelkers	.15
487	Bruce Berenyi	.15
488	LaMarr Hoyt	.15
489	Joe Nolan	.15
490	Marshall Edwards	.15
491	*Mike Laga*	.15
492	Rick Cerone	.15
493	Mike Miller (Rick)	.15
494	Rick Honeycutt	.15
495	Mike Hargrove	.15
496	Joe Simpson	.15
497	*Keith Atherton*	.15
498	Chris Welsh	.15
499	Bruce Kison	.15
500	Bob Johnson	.15
501	Jerry Koosman	.15
502	Frank DiPino	.15
503	Tony Perez	.75
504	Ken Oberkfell	.15
505	*Mark Thurmond*	.15
506	Joe Price	.15
507	Pascual Perez	.15
508	*Marvell Wynne*	.15
509	Mike Krukow	.15
510	Dick Ruthven	.15
511	Al Cowens	.15
512	Cliff Johnson	.15
513	*Randy Bush*	.15
514	Sammy Stewart	.15
515	*Bill Schroeder*	.15
516	Aurelio Lopez	.15
517	Mike Brown	.15
518	Graig Nettles	.35
519	Dave Sax	.15
520	Gerry Willard	.15
521	Paul Splittorff	.15
522	Tom Burgmeier	.15
523	Chris Speier	.15
524	Bobby Clark	.15
525	George Wright	.15
526	Dennis Lamp	.15
527	Tony Scott	.15
528	Ed Whitson	.15
529	Ron Reed	.15
530	Charlie Puleo	.15
531	Jerry Royster	.15
532	Don Robinson	.15
533	Steve Trout	.15
534	Bruce Sutter	.30
535	Bob Horner	.20
536	Pat Tabler	.15
537	Chris Chambliss	.15
538	Bob Ojeda	.15
539	Alan Ashby	.15
540	Jay Johnstone	.15
541	Bob Dernier	.15
542	*Brook Jacoby*	.25
543	U.L. Washington	.15
544	Danny Darwin	.15
545	Kiko Garcia	.15
546	Vance Law	.15
547	Tug McGraw	.20
548	Dave Smith	.15
549	Len Matuszek	.15
550	Tom Hume	.15
551	Dave Dravecky	.15
552	Rick Rhoden	.15
553	Duane Kuiper	.15
554	Rusty Staub	.20
555	Bill Campbell	.15
556	Mike Torrez	.15
557	Dave Henderson	.15
558	Len Whitehouse	.15
559	Barry Bonnell	.15
560	Rick Lysander	.15
561	Garth Iorg	.15
562	Bryan Clark	.15
563	Brian Giles	.15
564	Vern Ruhle	.15
565	Steve Bedrosian	.20
566	Larry McWilliams	.15
567	Jeff Leonard	.15
568	Alan Wiggins	.15
569	*Jeff Russell*	.50
570	Salome Barojas	.15
571	Dane Iorg	.15
572	Bob Knepper	.15
573	Gary Lavelle	.15
574	Gorman Thomas	.15
575	Manny Trillo	.15
576	Jim Palmer	3.00
577	Dale Murray	.15
578	Tom Brookens	.15
579	Rich Gedman	.15
580	*Bill Doran*	.50
581	Steve Yeager	.15
582	Dan Spillner	.15
583	Dan Quisenberry	.15
584	Rance Mulliniks	.15
585	Storm Davis	.15
586	Dave Schmidt	.15
587	Bill Russell	.15
588	*Pat Sheridan*	.15
589	Rafael Ramirez	.15
590	Bud Anderson	.15
591	George Frazier	.15
592	*Lee Tunnell*	.15
593	Kirk Gibson	.50
594	Scott McGregor	.15
595	Bob Bailor	.15
596	Tom Herr	.15
597	Luis Sanchez	.15
598	Dave Engle	.15
599	*Craig McMurtry*	.15
600	Carlos Diaz	.15
601	Tom O'Malley	.15
602	*Nick Esasky*	.15
603	Ron Hodges	.15
604	Ed Vande Berg	.15
605	Alfredo Griffin	.15
606	Glenn Hoffman	.15
607	Hubie Brooks	.20
608	Richard Barnes (photo actually Neal Heaton)	.15
609	*Greg Walker*	.20
610	Ken Singleton	.20
611	Mark Clear	.15
612	Buck Martinez	.15
613	Ken Griffey	.20
614	Reid Nichols	.15
615	*Doug Sisk*	.15
616	Bob Brenly	.15
617	Joey McLaughlin	.15
618	Glenn Wilson	.15
619	Bob Stoddard	.15
620	Len Sakata (Lenn)	.15
621	*Mike Young*	.15
622	John Stefero	.15
623	*Carmelo Martinez*	.15
624	Dave Bergman	.15
625	Runnin' Reds (David Green, Willie McGee, Lonnie Smith, Ozzie Smith)	.75
626	Rudy May	.15
627	Matt Keough	.15
628	*Jose DeLeon*	.15
629	Jim Essian	.15
630	*Darnell Coles*	.15
631	Mike Warren	.15
632	Del Crandall	.15
633	Dennis Martinez	.20
634	Mike Moore	.15
635	Lary Sorensen	.15
636	Ricky Nelson	.15
637	Omar Moreno	.15
638	Charlie Hough	.15
639	Dennis Eckersley	2.00
640	*Walt Terrell*	.20
641	Denny Walling	.15
642	*Dave Anderson*	.15
643	*Jose Oquendo*	.25
644	Bob Stanley	.15
645	Dave Geisel	.15
646	*Scott Garrelts*	.25
647	*Gary Pettis*	.25
648	Duke Snider Puzzle Card	.15
649	Johnnie LeMaster	.15
650	Dave Collins	.15
651	San Diego Chicken	.25
----	Checklist 1-26 DK (Perez-Steel on back)	.15
----	Checklist 1-26 DK (Perez-Steele on back)	.40
----	Checklist 27-130	.15
----	Checklist 131-234	.15
----	Checklist 235-338	.15
----	Checklist 339-442	.15
----	Checklist 443-546	.15
----	Checklist 547-651	.15

1984 Donruss Action All-Stars

Full-color photos on the card fronts and backs make the 1984 Donruss Action All-Stars set somewhat unusual. Fronts contain a large action photo plus the Donruss logo and year of issue inside a deep red border. The top half of the backs features a close-up photo with the bottom portion containing biographical and statistical information. The 3-1/2" x 5" cards were sold with Ted Williams puzzle pieces.

		MT
Complete Set (60):		7.50
Common Player:		.10
Ted Williams Puzzle:		10.00
1	Gary Lavelle	.10
2	Willie McGee	.10
3	Tony Pena	.10
4	Lou Whitaker	.10
5	Robin Yount	.65
6	Doug DeCinces	.10
7	John Castino	.10
8	Terry Kennedy	.10
9	Rickey Henderson	.65
10	Bob Horner	.10
11	Harold Baines	.10
12	Buddy Bell	.10
13	Fernando Valenzuela	.15
14	Nolan Ryan	2.50
15	Andre Thornton	.10
16	Gary Redus	.10
17	Pedro Guerrero	.10
18	Andre Dawson	.20
19	Dave Stieb	.10
20	Cal Ripken, Jr.	3.00
21	Ken Griffey	.10
22	Wade Boggs	.70
23	Keith Hernandez	.10
24	Steve Carlton	.40
25	Hal McRae	.10
26	John Lowenstein	.10
27	Fred Lynn	.10
28	Bill Buckner	.10
29	Chris Chambliss	.10
30	Richie Zisk	.10
31	Jack Clark	.10
32	George Hendrick	.10
33	Bill Madlock	.10
34	Lance Parrish	.10
35	Paul Molitor	.60
36	Reggie Jackson	.65
37	Kent Hrbek	.10
38	Steve Garvey	.25
39	Carney Lansford	.10
40	Dale Murphy	.25
41	Greg Luzinski	.10
42	Larry Parrish	.10
43	Ryne Sandberg	.65
44	Dickie Thon	.10
45	Bert Blyleven	.10
46	Ron Oester	.10

47	Dusty Baker	.10
48	Steve Rogers	.10
49	Jim Clancy	.10
50	Eddie Murray	.60
51	Ron Guidry	.10
52	Jim Rice	.10
53	Tom Seaver	.50
54	Pete Rose	1.00
55	George Brett	.75
56	Dan Quisenberry	.10
57	Mike Schmidt	.75
58	Ted Simmons	.10
59	Dave Righetti	.10
60	Checklist	.05

1984 Donruss Champions

The 60-card Donruss Champions set includes ten Hall of Famers, forty-nine current players and a numbered checklist. The Hall of Famers' cards (called Grand Champions) feature the artwork of Dick Perez, while cards of the current players (called Champions) are color photos. All cards measure 3-1/2" x 5". The Grand Champions represent hallmarks of excellence in various statistical categories, while the Champions are the leaders among then-active players in each category. The cards were issued with Duke Snider puzzle pieces.

		MT
Complete Set (60):		7.00
Common Player:		.10
Duke Snider Puzzle:		3.50
1	Babe Ruth	1.00
2	George Foster	.10
3	Dave Kingman	.10
4	Jim Rice	.10
5	Gorman Thomas	.10
6	Ben Oglivie	.10
7	Jeff Burroughs	.10
8	Hank Aaron	.75
9	Reggie Jackson	.30
10	Carl Yastrzemski	.35
11	Mike Schmidt	.50
12	Graig Nettles	.10
13	Greg Luzinski	.15
14	Ted Williams	.75
15	George Brett	.60
16	Wade Boggs	.50
17	Hal McRae	.10
18	Bill Buckner	.10
19	Eddie Murray	.40
20	Rogers Hornsby	.15
21	Rod Carew	.25
22	Bill Madlock	.10
23	Lonnie Smith	.10
24	Cecil Cooper	.10
25	Ken Griffey	.10
26	Ty Cobb	.60
27	Pete Rose	.60
28	Rusty Staub	.10
29	Tony Perez	.12
30	Al Oliver	.10
31	Cy Young	.15
32	Gaylord Perry	.15
33	Ferguson Jenkins	.15
34	Phil Niekro	.15
35	Jim Palmer	.20
36	Tommy John	.10
37	Walter Johnson	.20
38	Steve Carlton	.20
39	Nolan Ryan	.75
40	Tom Seaver	.25
41	Don Sutton	.10
42	Bert Blyleven	.10
43	Frank Robinson	.25
44	Joe Morgan	.15
45	Rollie Fingers	.15
46	Keith Hernandez	.10
47	Robin Yount	.35
48	Cal Ripken, Jr.	1.50
49	Dale Murphy	.25
50	Mickey Mantle	2.00
51	Johnny Bench	.40
52	Carlton Fisk	.20
53	Tug McGraw	.10
54	Paul Molitor	.35
55	Carl Hubbell	.10
56	Steve Garvey	.15
57	Dave Parker	.10
58	Gary Carter	.15
59	Fred Lynn	.10
60	Checklist	.05

1985 Donruss

The black-bordered 1985 Donruss set includes 653 numbered cards and seven unnumbered checklists. Displaying the artwork of Dick Perez for the fourth consecutive year, cards #1-26 feature the Diamond Kings series. Donruss, reacting to the hobby craze over rookie cards, included a Rated Rookies subset (cards #27-46). The cards, in standard 2-1/2" x 3-1/2", were issued with a Lou Gehrig puzzle. Backs repeat the format of previous years with black print on yellow and white. The complete set price does not include the higher priced variations. (DK) and (RR) refer to the Diamond Kings and Rated Rookies subsets.

		MT
Complete Set (660):		110.00
Common Player:		.10
Lou Gehrig Puzzle:		3.00
Pack (15):		6.25
Wax Box (36):		155.00
1	Ryne Sandberg (DK)	2.50
2	Doug DeCinces (DK)	.10
3	Rich Dotson (DK)	.10
4	Bert Blyleven (DK)	.15
5	Lou Whitaker (DK)	.15
6	Dan Quisenberry (DK)	.10
7	Don Mattingly (DK)	3.50
8	Carney Lansford (DK)	.10
9	Frank Tanana (DK)	.10
10	Willie Upshaw (DK)	.10
11	Claudell Washington (DK)	.10
12	Mike Marshall (DK)	.10
13	Joaquin Andujar (DK)	.10
14	Cal Ripken, Jr. (DK)	8.00
15	Jim Rice (DK)	.25
16	Don Sutton (DK)	.30
17	Frank Viola (DK)	.15
18	Alvin Davis (DK)	.10
19	Mario Soto (DK)	.10
20	Jose Cruz (DK)	.10
21	Charlie Lea (DK)	.10
22	Jesse Orosco (DK)	.10
23	Juan Samuel (DK)	.10
24	Tony Pena (DK)	.10
25	Tony Gwynn (DK)	3.00
26	Bob Brenly (DK)	.10
27	*Danny Tartabull* (RR)	1.50
28	*Mike Bielecki* (RR)	.15
29	*Steve Lyons* (RR)	.20
30	*Jeff Reed* (RR)	.15
31	Tony Brewer (RR)	.10
32	*John Morris* (RR)	.10
33	*Daryl Boston* (RR)	.15
34	Alfonso Pulido (RR)	.10
35	*Steve Kiefer* (RR)	.10
36	*Larry Sheets* (RR)	.10
37	*Scott Bradley* (RR)	.10
38	*Calvin Schiraldi* (RR)	.10
39	*Shawon Dunston* (RR)	1.50
40	Charlie Mitchell (RR)	.10
41	*Billy Hatcher* (RR)	.50
42	Russ Stephans (RR)	.10
43	Alejandro Sanchez (RR)	.10
44	*Steve Jeltz* (RR)	.10
45	*Jim Traber* (RR)	.10
46	Doug Loman (RR)	.10
47	Eddie Murray	2.50
48	Robin Yount	2.50
49	Lance Parrish	.15
50	Jim Rice	.15
51	Dave Winfield	1.00
52	Fernando Valenzuela	.15
53	George Brett	4.00
54	Dave Kingman	.15
55	Gary Carter	.40
56	Buddy Bell	.12
57	Reggie Jackson	1.50
58	Harold Baines	.25
59	Ozzie Smith	2.50
60	Nolan Ryan	10.00
61	Mike Schmidt	4.00
62	Dave Parker	.35
63	Tony Gwynn	7.50
64	Tony Pena	.12
65	Jack Clark	.15
66	Dale Murphy	.60
67	Ryne Sandberg	6.00
68	Keith Hernandez	.20
69	*Alvin Davis*	.25
70	Kent Hrbek	.20
71	Willie Upshaw	.10
72	Dave Engle	.10
73	Alfredo Griffin	.10
74a	Jack Perconte (last line of highlights begins "Batted .346...")	.10
74b	Jack Perconte (last line of highlights begins "Led the ...")	.75
75	Jesse Orosco	.10
76	Jody Davis	.10
77	Bob Horner	.12
78	Larry McWilliams	.10
79	Joel Youngblood	.10
80	Alan Wiggins	.10
81	Ron Oester	.10
82	Ozzie Virgil	.10
83	*Ricky Horton*	.10
84	Bill Doran	.12
85	Rod Carew	1.00
86	LaMarr Hoyt	.10
87	Tim Wallach	.12
88	Mike Flanagan	.10
89	Jim Sundberg	.10
90	Chet Lemon	.10
91	Bob Stanley	.10
92	Willie Randolph	.12
93	Bill Russell	.10
94	Julio Franco	.50
95	Dan Quisenberry	.12
96	Bill Caudill	.10
97	Bill Gullickson	.10
98	Danny Darwin	.10
99	Curtis Wilkerson	.10
100	Bud Black	.10
101	Tony Phillips	.20
102	Tony Bernazard	.10
103	Jay Howell	.10
104	Burt Hooton	.10
105	Milt Wilcox	.10
106	Rich Dauer	.10
107	Don Sutton	.45
108	Mike Witt	.12
109	Bruce Sutter	.15
110	Enos Cabell	.10
111	John Denny	.10
112	Dave Dravecky	.10
113	Marvell Wynne	.10
114	Johnnie LeMaster	.10
115	Chuck Porter	.10
116	John Gibbons	.10
117	Keith Moreland	.10
118	Darnell Coles	.10
119	Dennis Lamp	.10
120	Ron Davis	.10
121	Nick Esasky	.10
122	Vance Law	.10
123	Gary Roenicke	.10
124	Bill Schroeder	.10
125	Dave Rozema	.10
126	Bobby Meacham	.10
127	Marty Barrett	.15
128	*R.J. Reynolds*	.15
129	Ernie Camacho	.10
130	Jorge Orta	.10
131	Lary Sorensen	.10
132	Terry Francona	.10
133	Fred Lynn	.20
134	Bobby Jones	.10
135	Jerry Hairston	.10
136	Kevin Bass	.10
137	Garry Maddox	.10
138	Dave LaPoint	.10
139	Kevin McReynolds	.20
140	Wayne Krenchicki	.10
141	Rafael Ramirez	.10
142	Rod Scurry	.10
143	Greg Minton	.10
144	Tim Stoddard	.10
145	Steve Henderson	.10
146	George Bell	.20
147	Dave Meier	.10
148	Sammy Stewart	.10
149	Mark Brouhard	.10
150	Larry Herndon	.10
151	Oil Can Boyd	.10
152	Brian Dayett	.10
153	Tom Niedenfuer	.10
154	Brook Jacoby	.10
155	Onix Concepcion	.10
156	Tim Conroy	.10
157	*Joe Hesketh*	.12
158	Brian Downing	.10
159	Tommy Dunbar	.10
160	Marc Hill	.10
161	Phil Garner	.12
162	Jerry Davis	.10
163	Bill Campbell	.10
164	*John Franco*	1.00
165	Len Barker	.10
166	*Benny Distefano*	.10
167	George Frazier	.10
168	Tito Landrum	.10
169	Cal Ripken, Jr.	10.00
170	Cecil Cooper	.10
171	Alan Trammell	.40
172	Wade Boggs	3.00
173	Don Baylor	.15
174	Pedro Guerrero	.12
175	Frank White	.12
176	Rickey Henderson	2.00
177	Charlie Lea	.10
178	Pete O'Brien	.10
179	Doug DeCinces	.12
180	Ron Kittle	.10

No.	Player	Price
181	George Hendrick	.10
182	Joe Niekro	.12
183	Juan Samuel	.10
184	Mario Soto	.10
185	Goose Gossage	.25
186	Johnny Ray	.10
187	Bob Brenly	.10
188	Craig McMurtry	.10
189	Leon Durham	.10
190	Dwight Gooden	1.50
191	Barry Bonnell	.10
192	Tim Teufel	.10
193	Dave Stieb	.15
194	Mickey Hatcher	.10
195	Jesse Barfield	.10
196	Al Cowens	.10
197	Hubie Brooks	.10
198	Steve Trout	.10
199	Glenn Hubbard	.10
200	Bill Madlock	.15
201	*Jeff Robinson*	.10
202	Eric Show	.10
203	Dave Concepcion	.15
204	Ivan DeJesus	.10
205	Neil Allen	.10
206	Jerry Mumphrey	.10
207	Mike Brown	.10
208	Carlton Fisk	.75
209	Bryn Smith	.10
210	Tippy Martinez	.10
211	Dion James	.10
212	Willie Hernandez	.10
213	Mike Easler	.10
214	Ron Guidry	.10
215	Rick Honeycutt	.10
216	Brett Butler	.15
217	Larry Gura	.10
218	Ray Burris	.10
219	Steve Rogers	.10
220	Frank Tanana	.10
221	Ned Yost	.10
222	Bret Saberhagen	1.50
223	Mike Davis	.10
224	Bert Blyleven	.15
225	Steve Kemp	.10
226	Jerry Reuss	.10
227	Darrell Evans	.15
228	Wayne Gross	.10
229	Jim Gantner	.10
230	Bob Boone	.12
231	Lonnie Smith	.10
232	Frank DiPino	.10
233	Jerry Koosman	.10
234	Graig Nettles	.12
235	John Tudor	.10
236	John Rabb	.10
237	Rick Manning	.10
238	Mike Fitzgerald	.10
239	Gary Matthews	.10
240	*Jim Presley*	.10
241	Dave Collins	.10
242	Gary Gaetti	.15
243	Dann Bilardello	.10
244	Rudy Law	.10
245	John Lowenstein	.10
246	Tom Tellmann	.10
247	Howard Johnson	.20
248	Ray Fontenot	.10
249	Tony Armas	.12
250	Candy Maldonado	.10
251	*Mike Jeffcoat*	.10
252	Dane Iorg	.10
253	Bruce Bochte	.10
254	Pete Rose	2.50
255	Don Aase	.10
256	George Wright	.10
257	Britt Burns	.10
258	Mike Scott	.15
259	Len Matuszek	.10
260	Dave Rucker	.10
261	Craig Lefferts	.10
262	*Jay Tibbs*	.10
263	Bruce Benedict	.10
264	Don Robinson	.10
265	Gary Lavelle	.10
266	Scott Sanderson	.10
267	Matt Young	.10
268	Ernie Whitt	.10
269	Houston Jimenez	.10
270	*Ken Dixon*	.10
271	Peter Ladd	.10
272	Juan Berenguer	.10
273	Roger Clemens	50.00
274	Rick Cerone	.10
275	Dave Anderson	.10
276	George Vukovich	.10
277	Greg Pryor	.10
278	Mike Warren	.10
279	Bob James	.10
280	Bobby Grich	.12
281	*Mike Mason*	.10
282	Ron Reed	.10
283	Alan Ashby	.10
284	Mark Thurmond	.10
285	Joe Lefebvre	.10
286	Ted Power	.10
287	Chris Chambliss	.10
288	Lee Tunnell	.10
289	Rich Bordi	.10
290	Glenn Brummer	.10
291	Mike Boddicker	.10
292	Rollie Fingers	.40
293	Lou Whitaker	.20
294	Dwight Evans	.15
295	Don Mattingly	6.00
296	Mike Marshall	.15
297	Willie Wilson	.12
298	Mike Heath	.10
299	Tim Raines	.45
300	Larry Parrish	.10
301	Geoff Zahn	.10
302	Rich Dotson	.10
303	David Green	.10
304	Jose Cruz	.12
305	Steve Carlton	1.25
306	Gary Redus	.10
307	Steve Garvey	.40
308	Jose DeLeon	.10
309	Randy Lerch	.10
310	Claudell Washington	.10
311	Lee Smith	.75
312	Darryl Strawberry	.75
313	Jim Beattie	.10
314	John Butcher	.10
315	Damaso Garcia	.10
316	Mike Smithson	.10
317	Luis Leal	.10
318	Ken Phelps	.10
319	Wally Backman	.10
320	Ron Cey	.12
321	Brad Komminsk	.10
322	Jason Thompson	.10
323	*Frank Williams*	.10
324	Tim Lollar	.10
325	*Eric Davis*	1.50
326	Von Hayes	.10
327	Andy Van Slyke	.30
328	Craig Reynolds	.10
329	Dick Schofield	.10
330	Scott Fletcher	.10
331	Jeff Reardon	.12
332	Rick Dempsey	.10
333	Ben Oglivie	.10
334	Dan Petry	.10
335	Jackie Gutierrez	.10
336	Dave Righetti	.10
337	Alejandro Pena	.10
338	Mel Hall	.10
339	Pat Sheridan	.10
340	Keith Atherton	.10
341	David Palmer	.10
342	Gary Ward	.10
343	Dave Stewart	.15
344	*Mark Gubicza*	.50
345	Carney Lansford	.10
346	Jerry Willard	.10
347	Ken Griffey	.12
348	*Franklin Stubbs*	.10
349	Aurelio Lopez	.10
350	Al Bumbry	.10
351	Charlie Moore	.10
352	Luis Sanchez	.10
353	Darrell Porter	.10
354	Bill Dawley	.10
355	Charlie Hudson	.10
356	Garry Templeton	.10
357	Cecilio Guante	.10
358	Jeff Leonard	.10
359	Paul Molitor	3.00
360	Ron Gardenhire	.10
361	Larry Bowa	.12
362	Bob Kearney	.10
363	Garth Iorg	.10
364	Tom Brunansky	.15
365	Brad Gulden	.10
366	Greg Walker	.10
367	Mike Young	.10
368	Rick Waits	.10
369	Doug Bair	.10
370	Bob Shirley	.10
371	Bob Ojeda	.10
372	Bob Welch	.10
373	Neal Heaton	.10
374	Danny Jackson (photo actually Steve Farr)	.80
375	Donnie Hill	.10
376	Mike Stenhouse	.10
377	Bruce Kison	.10
378	Wayne Tolleson	.10
379	Floyd Bannister	.10
380	Vern Ruhle	.10
381	Tim Corcoran	.10
382	Kurt Kepshire	.10
383	Bobby Brown	.10
384	Dave Van Gorder	.10
385	Rick Mahler	.10
386	Lee Mazzilli	.10
387	Bill Laskey	.10
388	Thad Bosley	.10
389	Al Chambers	.10
390	Tony Fernandez	.50
391	Ron Washington	.10
392	Bill Swaggerty	.10
393	Bob L. Gibson	.10
394	Marty Castillo	.10
395	Steve Crawford	.10
396	Clay Christiansen	.10
397	Bob Bailor	.10
398	Mike Hargrove	.10
399	Charlie Leibrandt	.10
400	Tom Burgmeier	.10
401	Razor Shines	.10
402	Rob Wilfong	.10
403	Tom Henke	.12
404	Al Jones	.10
405	Mike LaCoss	.10
406	Luis DeLeon	.10
407	Greg Gross	.10
408	Tom Hume	.10
409	Rick Camp	.10
410	Milt May	.10
411	*Henry Cotto*	.10
412	Dave Von Ohlen	.10
413	Scott McGregor	.10
414	Ted Simmons	.10
415	Jack Morris	.20
416	Bill Buckner	.15
417	Butch Wynegar	.10
418	Steve Sax	.15
419	Steve Balboni	.10
420	Dwayne Murphy	.10
421	Andre Dawson	.50
422	Charlie Hough	.10
423	Tommy John	.25
424a	Tom Seaver (Floyd Bannister photo, left-hander)	2.00
424b	Tom Seaver (correct photo)	30.00
425	Tom Herr	.10
426	Terry Puhl	.10
427	Al Holland	.10
428	Eddie Milner	.10
429	Terry Kennedy	.10
430	John Candelaria	.10
431	Manny Trillo	.10
432	Ken Oberkfell	.10
433	Rick Sutcliffe	.15
434	Ron Darling	.15
435	Spike Owen	.10
436	Frank Viola	.25
437	Lloyd Moseby	.10
438	Kirby Puckett	30.00
439	Jim Clancy	.10
440	Mike Moore	.10
441	Doug Sisk	.10
442	Dennis Eckersley	.75
443	Gerald Perry	.10
444	Dale Berra	.10
445	Dusty Baker	.12
446	Ed Whitson	.10
447	Cesar Cedeno	.12
448	*Rick Schu*	.10
449	Joaquin Andujar	.10
450	*Mark Bailey*	.10
451	*Ron Romanick*	.10
452	Julio Cruz	.10
453	Miguel Dilone	.10
454	Storm Davis	.10
455	Jaime Cocanower	.10
456	Barbaro Garbey	.10
457	Rich Gedman	.10
458	Phil Niekro	.40
459	Mike Scioscia	.10
460	Pat Tabler	.10
461	Darryl Motley	.10
462	Chris Codoroli (Codiroli)	.10
463	Doug Flynn	.10
464	Billy Sample	.10
465	Mickey Rivers	.10
466	John Wathan	.10
467	Bill Krueger	.10
468	Andre Thornton	.12
469	Rex Hudler	.12
470	*Sid Bream*	.60
471	Kirk Gibson	.20
472	John Shelby	.10
473	Moose Haas	.10
474	Doug Corbett	.10
475	Willie McGee	.15
476	Bob Knepper	.10
477	Kevin Gross	.10
478	Carmelo Martinez	.10
479	Kent Tekulve	.10
480	Chili Davis	.12
481	Bobby Clark	.10
482	Mookie Wilson	.12
483	Dave Owen	.10
484	Ed Nunez	.10
485	Rance Mulliniks	.10
486	Ken Schrom	.10
487	Jeff Russell	.10
488	Tom Paciorek	.10
489	Dan Ford	.10
490	Mike Caldwell	.10
491	Scottie Earl	.10
492	Jose Rijo	.25
493	Bruce Hurst	.10
494	Ken Landreaux	.10
495	Mike Fischlin	.10
496	Don Slaught	.10
497	Steve McCatty	.10
498	Gary Lucas	.10
499	Gary Pettis	.10
500	Marvis Foley	.10
501	Mike Squires	.10
502	*Jim Pankovitz*	.10
503	Luis Aguayo	.10
504	Ralph Citarella	.10
505	Bruce Bochy	.10
506	Bob Owchinko	.10
507	Pascual Perez	.10
508	Lee Lacy	.10
509	Atlee Hammaker	.10
510	Bob Dernier	.10
511	Ed Vande Berg	.10
512	Cliff Johnson	.10
513	Len Whitehouse	.10
514	Dennis Martinez	.12
515	Ed Romero	.10
516	Rusty Kuntz	.10
517	Rick Miller	.10
518	Dennis Rasmussen	.10
519	Steve Yeager	.10
520	Chris Bando	.10
521	U.L. Washington	.10
522	*Curt Young*	.10
523	Angel Salazar	.10
524	Curt Kaufman	.10
525	Odell Jones	.10
526	Juan Agosto	.10
527	Denny Walling	.10
528	Andy Hawkins	.15
529	Sixto Lezcano	.10
530	Skeeter Barnes	.10
531	Randy S. Johnson	.10
532	Jim Morrison	.10
533	Warren Brusstar	.10
534a	*Jeff Pendleton* (error)	3.00
534b	*Terry Pendleton* (correct)	12.00
535	Vic Rodriguez	.10
536	Bob McClure	.10
537	Dave Bergman	.10
538	Mark Clear	.10
539	*Mike Pagliarulo*	.35
540	Terry Whitfield	.10
541	Joe Beckwith	.10
542	Jeff Burroughs	.10
543	Dan Schatzeder	.10
544	Donnie Scott	.10
545	Jim Slaton	.10
546	Greg Luzinski	.12
547	*Mark Salas*	.10
548	Dave Smith	.10
549	John Wockenfuss	.10
550	Frank Pastore	.10
551	Tim Flannery	.10
552	Rick Rhoden	.10
553	Mark Davis	.10
554	*Jeff Dedmon*	.12

555	Gary Woods	.10
556	Danny Heep	.10
557	Mark Langston	1.00
558	Darrell Brown	.10
559	Jimmy Key	1.00
560	Rick Lysander	.10
561	Doyle Alexander	.10
562	Mike Stanton	.10
563	Sid Fernandez	.20
564	Richie Hebner	.10
565	Alex Trevino	.10
566	Brian Harper	.10
567	*Dan Gladden*	.30
568	Luis Salazar	.10
569	Tom Foley	.10
570	Larry Andersen	.10
571	Danny Cox	.10
572	Joe Sambito	.10
573	Juan Beniquez	.10
574	Joel Skinner	.10
575	*Randy St. Claire*	.10
576	Floyd Rayford	.10
577	Roy Howell	.10
578	John Grubb	.10
579	Ed Jurak	.10
580	John Montefusco	.10
581	*Orel Hershiser*	3.50
582	*Tom Waddell*	.10
583	Mark Huismann	.10
584	Joe Morgan	.40
585	Jim Wohlford	.10
586	Dave Schmidt	.10
587	*Jeff Kunkel*	.10
588	Hal McRae	.12
589	Bill Almon	.10
590	Carmen Castillo	.10
591	Omar Moreno	.10
592	*Ken Howell*	.10
593	Tom Brookens	.10
594	Joe Nolan	.10
595	Willie Lozado	.10
596	*Tom Nieto*	.10
597	Walt Terrell	.10
598	Al Oliver	.15
599	Shane Rawley	.10
600	*Denny Gonzalez*	.10
601	*Mark Grant*	.10
602	Mike Armstrong	.10
603	George Foster	.15
604	Davey Lopes	.10
605	Salome Barojas	.10
606	Roy Lee Jackson	.10
607	Pete Filson	.10
608	Duane Walker	.10
609	Glenn Wilson	.10
610	*Rafael Santana*	.10
611	Roy Smith	.10
612	Ruppert Jones	.10
613	Joe Cowley	.10
614	*Al Nipper* (photo actually Mike Brown)	.15
615	Gene Nelson	.10
616	Joe Carter	4.00
617	Ray Knight	.12
618	Chuck Rainey	.10
619	Dan Driessen	.10
620	Daryl Sconiers	.10
621	Bill Stein	.10
622	Roy Smalley	.10
623	Ed Lynch	.10
624	*Jeff Stone*	.10
625	Bruce Berenyi	.10
626	Kelvin Chapman	.10
627	Joe Price	.10
628	Steve Bedrosian	.12
629	Vic Mata	.10
630	Mike Krukow	.10
631	*Phil Bradley*	.15
632	Jim Gott	.10
633	Randy Bush	.10
634	*Tom Browning*	.60
635	Lou Gehrig Puzzle Card	.10
636	Reid Nichols	.10
637	*Dan Pasqua*	.60
638	German Rivera	.10
639	*Don Schulze*	.10
640a	Mike Jones (last line of highlights begins "Was 11- 7...")	.10
640b	Mike Jones (last line of highlights begins "Spent some ...")	.75
641	Pete Rose	2.00
642	*Wade Rowdon*	.10
643	Jerry Narron	.10
644	*Darrell Miller*	.10
645	*Tim Hulett*	.10
646	Andy McGaffigan	.10
647	Kurt Bevacqua	.10
648	*John Russell*	.10
649	*Ron Robinson*	.10
650	Donnie Moore	.10
651a	Two for the Title (Don Mattingly, Dave Winfield) (yellow letters)	4.00
651b	Two for the Title (Don Mattingly, Dave Winfield) (white letters)	6.00
652	Tim Laudner	.10
653	*Steve Farr*	.15
----	Checklist 1-26 DK	.10
----	Checklist 27-130	.10
----	Checklist 131-234	.10
----	Checklist 235-338	.10
----	Checklist 339-442	.10
----	Checklist 443-546	.10
----	Checklist 547-653	.10

1985 Donruss Box Panels

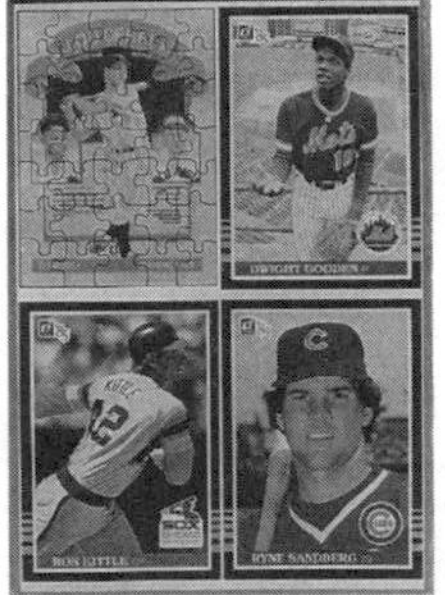

In 1985, Donruss placed on the bottoms of its wax pack boxes a four-card panel which included three player cards and a Lou Gehrig puzzle card. The player cards, numbered PC1 through PC3, have backs identical to the regular 1985 Donruss issue. The card fronts are identical in design to the regular issue, but carry different photos.

		MT
Complete Panel:		5.00
Complete Singles Set (4):		3.50
Common Player:		.10
PC1	Dwight Gooden	1.00
PC2	Ryne Sandberg	3.00
PC3	Ron Kittle	.10
---	Lou Gehrig (puzzle card)	.10
1	Dwight Gooden	1.50
2	Ryne Sandberg	3.00
3	Ron Kittle	.10
----	Lou Gehrig Puzzle Card	.05

1985 Donruss Action All-Stars

In 1985, Donruss issued an Action All-Stars set for the third consecutive year. Card fronts feature an action photo with an inset portrait of the player inside a black border with grey boxes through it. The card backs have black print on blue and white and include statistical and biographical information. The cards were issued with a Lou Gehrig puzzle.

		MT
Complete Set (60):		8.00
Common Player:		.15
Lou Gehrig Puzzle:		3.00
1	Tim Raines	.25
2	Jim Gantner	.15
3	Mario Soto	.15
4	Spike Owen	.15
5	Lloyd Moseby	.15
6	Damaso Garcia	.15
7	Cal Ripken, Jr.	3.50
8	Dan Quisenberry	.15
9	Eddie Murray	.75
10	Tony Pena	.15
11	Buddy Bell	.15
12	Dave Winfield	.50
13	Ron Kittle	.15
14	Rich Gossage	.15
15	Dwight Evans	.15
16	Al Davis	.15
17	Mike Schmidt	.90
18	Pascual Perez	.15
19	Tony Gwynn	1.50
20	Nolan Ryan	3.00
21	Robin Yount	.75
22	Mike Marshall	.15
23	Brett Butler	.20
24	Ryne Sandberg	1.00
25	Dale Murphy	.35
26	George Brett	.90
27	Jim Rice	.20
28	Ozzie Smith	.75
29	Larry Parrish	.15
30	Jack Clark	.15
31	Manny Trillo	.15
32	Dave Kingman	.15
33	Geoff Zahn	.15
34	Pedro Guerrero	.15
35	Dave Parker	.15
36	Rollie Fingers	.25
37	Fernando Valenzuela	.20
38	Wade Boggs	.75
39	Reggie Jackson	.50
40	Kent Hrbek	.20
41	Keith Hernandez	.15
42	Lou Whitaker	.15
43	Tom Herr	.15
44	Alan Trammell	.20
45	Butch Wynegar	.15
46	Leon Durham	.15
47	Dwight Gooden	.30
48	Don Mattingly	1.00
49	Phil Niekro	.25
50	Johnny Ray	.15
51	Doug DeCinces	.15
52	Willie Upshaw	.15
53	Lance Parrish	.15
54	Jody Davis	.15
55	Steve Carlton	.40
56	Juan Samuel	.15
57	Gary Carter	.20
58	Harold Baines	.15
59	Eric Show	.15
60	Checklist	.05

1985 Donruss Diamond Kings Supers

The 1985 Donruss Diamond Kings Supers are enlarged versions of the Diamond Kings cards in the regular 1985 Donruss set. The cards measure 4-15/16" x 6-3/4". The Diamond Kings series features the artwork of Dick Perez. Twenty-eight cards make up the Super set - 26 DK cards, an unnumbered checklist, and an unnumbered Dick Perez card. The back of the Perez card contains a brief history of Dick Perez and the Perez-Steele Galleries. The set could be obtained through a mail-in offer found on wax pack wrappers.

		MT
Complete Set (28):		15.00
Common Player:		.50
1	Ryne Sandberg	4.00
2	Doug DeCinces	.50
3	Richard Dotson	.50
4	Bert Blyleven	.50
5	Lou Whitaker	.50
6	Dan Quisenberry	.50
7	Don Mattingly	5.00
8	Carney Lansford	.50
9	Frank Tanana	.50
10	Willie Upshaw	.50
11	Claudell Washington	.50
12	Mike Marshall	.50
13	Joaquin Andujar	.50
14	Cal Ripken, Jr.	8.00
15	Jim Rice	.75
16	Don Sutton	.75
17	Frank Viola	.50
18	Alvin Davis	.50
19	Mario Soto	.50
20	Jose Cruz	.50
21	Charlie Lea	.50
22	Jesse Orosco	.50
23	Juan Samuel	.50
24	Tony Pena	.50
25	Tony Gwynn	5.00
26	Bob Brenly	.50
---	Checklist	.05
---	Dick Perez (DK artist)	.50

1985 Donruss Highlights

Designed in the style of the regular 1985 Donruss set, this issue features the Player of the Month in the major leagues plus highlight cards of special baseball events and milestones of the 1985 season. Fifty-six cards, including an unnumbered checklist, comprise the set which was available only through hobby dealers. The cards measure 2-1/2" x 3-1/2" and have glossy fronts. The last two cards in the set feature Donruss' picks for the A.L. and N.L. Rookies of the Year. The set was issued in a specially designed box.

MT

Complete Set (56): 7.50
Common Player: .05
1 Sets Opening Day Record (Tom Seaver) .20
2 Establishes A.L. Save Mark (Rollie Fingers) .08
3 A.L. Player of the Month - April (Mike Davis) .05
4 A.L. Pitcher of the Month - April (Charlie Leibrandt) .05
5 N.L. Player of the Month - April (Dale Murphy) .15
6 N.L. Pitcher of the Month - April (Fernando Valenzuela) .08
7 N.L. Shortstop Record (Larry Bowa) .05
8 Joins Reds 2000 Hit Club (Dave Concepcion) .05
9 Eldest Grand Slammer (Tony Perez) .08
10 N.L. Career Run Leader (Pete Rose) .60
11 A.L. Player of the Month - May (George Brett) .45
12 A.L. Pitcher of the Month - May (Dave Stieb) .05
13 N.L. Player of the Month - May (Dave Parker) .05
14 N.L. Pitcher of the Month - May (Andy Hawkins) .05
15 Records 11th Straight Win (Andy Hawkins) .05
16 Two Homers In First Inning (Von Hayes) .05
17 A.L. Player of the Month - June (Rickey Henderson) .30
18 A.L. Pitcher of the Month - June (Jay Howell) .05
19 N.L. Player of the Month - June (Pedro Guerrero) .05
20 N.L. Pitcher of the Month - June (John Tudor) .05
21 Marathon Game Iron Men (Gary Carter, Keith Hernandez) .05
22 Records 4000th K (Nolan Ryan) 1.00
23 All-Star Game MVP (LaMarr Hoyt) .05
24 1st Ranger To Hit For Cycle (Oddibe McDowell) .05
25 A.L. Player of the Month - July (George Brett) .45
26 A.L. Pitcher of the Month - July (Bret Saberhagen) .08
27 N.L. Player of the Month - July (Keith Hernandez) .05
28 N.L. Pitcher of the Month - July (Fernando Valenzuela) .08
29 Record Setting Base Stealers (Vince Coleman, Willie McGee) .10
30 Notches 300th Career Win (Tom Seaver) .20
31 Strokes 3000th Hit (Rod Carew) .20
32 Establishes Met Record (Dwight Gooden) .13
33 Achieves Strikeout Milestone (Dwight Gooden) .13
34 Explodes For 9 RBI (Eddie Murray) .20
35 A.L. Career Hbp Leader (Don Baylor) .05
36 A.L. Player of the Month - August (Don Mattingly) .75
37 A.L. Pitcher of the Month - August (Dave Righetti) .05
38 N.L. Player of the Month (Willie McGee) .05
39 N.L. Pitcher of the Month - August (Shane Rawley) .05
40 Ty-Breaking Hit (Pete Rose) 1.00
41 Hits 3 HRs, Drives In 8 Runs (Andre Dawson) .05
42 Sets Yankee Theft Mark (Rickey Henderson) .30
43 20 Wins In Rookie Season (Tom Browning) .05
44 Yankee Milestone For Hits (Don Mattingly) .75
45 A.L. Player of the Month - September (Don Mattingly) .75
46 A.L. Pitcher of the Month - September (Charlie Leibrandt) .05
47 N.L. Player of the Month - September (Gary Carter) .05
48 N.L. Pitcher of the Month - September (Dwight Gooden) .13
49 Major League Record Setter (Wade Boggs) .60
50 Hurls Shutout For 300th Win (Phil Niekro) .13
51 Venerable HR King (Darrell Evans) .05
52 N.L. Switch-hitting Record (Willie McGee) .05
53 Equals DiMaggio Feat (Dave Winfield) .15
54 Donruss N.L. Rookie of the Year (Vince Coleman) .25
55 Donruss A.L. Rookie of the Year (Ozzie Guillen) .20
---- Checklist .03

1985 Donruss Sluggers of The Hall of Fame

In much the same manner as the 1959-71 Bazooka cards were issued, this eight-player set consists of cards printed on the bottom panel of a box of bubble gum. When cut off the box, cards measure 3-1/2" x 6-1/2", with blank backs. Players are pictured on the cards in paintings done by Dick Perez.

MT

Complete Set (8): 12.00
Common Player: .60
1 Babe Ruth 2.50
2 Ted Williams 1.50
3 Lou Gehrig 2.00
4 Johnny Mize .60
5 Stan Musial 1.50
6 Mickey Mantle 3.00
7 Hank Aaron 1.50
8 Frank Robinson .90

1986 Donruss

In 1986, Donruss issued a 660-card set which included 653 numbered cards and seven unnumbered checklists. The 2-1/2" x 3-1/2" cards have fronts that feature blue borders and backs that have black print on blue and white. For the fifth year in a row, the first 26 cards in the set are Diamond Kings. The Rated Rookies subset (#27-46) appears once again. The cards were distributed with a Hank Aaron puzzle. The complete set price does not include the higher priced variations. In the checklist that follows, (DK) and (RR) refer to the Diamond Kings and Rated Rookies series.

MT

Complete Set (660): 60.00
Complete Factory Set (660): 75.00
Common Player: .08
Hank Aaron Puzzle: 5.00
Pack (15): 3.25
Wax Box (36): 72.00
1 Kirk Gibson (DK) .15
2 Goose Gossage (DK) .15
3 Willie McGee (DK) .15
4 George Bell (DK) .15
5 Tony Armas (DK) .10
6 Chili Davis (DK) .10
7 Cecil Cooper (DK) .12
8 Mike Boddicker (DK) .10
9 Davey Lopes (DK) .10
10 Bill Doran (DK) .10
11 Bret Saberhagen (DK) .25
12 Brett Butler (DK) .15
13 Harold Baines (DK) .25
14 Mike Davis (DK) .10
15 Tony Perez (DK) .25
16 Willie Randolph (DK) .12
17 Bob Boone (DK) .10
18 Orel Hershiser (DK) .20
19 Johnny Ray (DK) .10
20 Gary Ward (DK) .10
21 Rick Mahler (DK) .08
22 Phil Bradley (DK) .10
23 Jerry Koosman (DK) .12
24 Tom Brunansky (DK) .15
25 Andre Dawson (DK) .50
26 Dwight Gooden (DK) .35
27 *Kal Daniels* (RR) .10
28 *Fred McGriff* (RR) 6.00
29 *Cory Snyder* (RR) .20
30 *Jose Guzman* (RR) .10
31 *Ty Gainey* (RR) .08
32 *Johnny Abrego* (RR) .08
33a *Andres Galarraga* (RR) accent mark over e of Andres on back) 10.00
33b *Andres Galarraga* (RR) no accent mark) 10.00
34 *Dave Shipanoff* (RR) .08
35 *Mark McLemore* (RR) .30
36 *Marty Clary* (RR) .08
37 *Paul O'Neill* (RR) 6.00
38 Danny Tartabull (RR) .25
39 *Jose Canseco* (RR) 40.00
40 *Juan Nieves* (RR) .10
41 *Lance McCullers* (RR) .20
42 *Rick Surhoff* (RR) .08
43 *Todd Worrell* (RR) .40
44 Bob Kipper (RR) .08
45 *John Habyan* (RR) .15
46 *Mike Woodard* (RR) .08
47 Mike Boddicker .10
48 Robin Yount 1.75
49 Lou Whitaker .20
50 Dennis Boyd .08

51 Rickey Henderson 1.00
52 Mike Marshall .10
53 George Brett 2.00
54 Dave Kingman .15
55 Hubie Brooks .10
56 *Oddibe McDowell* .10
57 Doug DeCinces .10
58 Britt Burns .08
59 Ozzie Smith 2.00
60 Jose Cruz .10
61 Mike Schmidt 2.00
62 Pete Rose 2.00
63 Steve Garvey .30
64 Tony Pena .10
65 Chili Davis .10
66 Dale Murphy .35
67 Ryne Sandberg 2.00
68 Gary Carter .35
69 Alvin Davis .08
70 Kent Hrbek .20
71 George Bell .15
72 Kirby Puckett 6.00
73 Lloyd Moseby .10
74 Bob Kearney .08
75 Dwight Gooden .50
76 Gary Matthews .08
77 Rick Mahler .08
78 Benny Distefano .08
79 Jeff Leonard .08
80 Kevin McReynolds .20
81 Ron Oester .08
82 John Russell .08
83 Tommy Herr .08
84 Jerry Mumphrey .08
85 Ron Romanick .08
86 Daryl Boston .08
87 Andre Dawson .75
88 Eddie Murray 1.50
89 Dion James .08
90 Chet Lemon .08
91 Bob Stanley .08
92 Willie Randolph .10
93 Mike Scioscia .08
94 Tom Waddell .08
95 Danny Jackson .08
96 Mike Davis .08
97 Mike Fitzgerald .08
98 Gary Ward .08
99 Pete O'Brien .08
100 Bret Saberhagen .45
101 Alfredo Griffin .08
102 Brett Butler .12
103 Ron Guidry .12
104 Jerry Reuss .08
105 Jack Morris .20
106 Rick Dempsey .08
107 Ray Burris .08
108 Brian Downing .08
109 Willie McGee .15
110 Bill Doran .10
111 Kent Tekulve .08
112 Tony Gwynn 3.50
113 Marvell Wynne .08
114 David Green .08
115 Jim Gantner .08
116 George Foster .15
117 Steve Trout .08
118 Mark Langston .30
119 Tony Fernandez .20
120 John Butcher .08
121 Ron Robinson .08
122 Dan Spillner .08
123 Mike Young .08
124 Paul Molitor 2.00
125 Kirk Gibson .20
126 Ken Griffey .12
127 Tony Armas .10
128 *Mariano Duncan* .15
129 Pat Tabler (Mr. Clutch) .08
130 Frank White .10
131 Carney Lansford .08
132 Vance Law .08
133 Dick Schofield .08
134 Wayne Tolleson .08
135 Greg Walker .08
136 Denny Walling .08
137 Ozzie Virgil .08
138 Ricky Horton .08
139 LaMarr Hoyt .08
140 Wayne Krenchicki .08
141 Glenn Hubbard .08
142 Cecilio Guante .08
143 Mike Krukow .08
144 Lee Smith .12
145 Edwin Nunez .08
146 Dave Stieb .12
147 Mike Smithson .08
148 Ken Dixon .08
149 Danny Darwin .08
150 Chris Pittaro .08
151 Bill Buckner .12
152 Mike Pagliarulo .08
153 Bill Russell .08
154 Brook Jacoby .08
155 Pat Sheridan .08
156 *Mike Gallego* .15
157 Jim Wohlford .08
158 Gary Pettis .08
159 Toby Harrah .08
160 Richard Dotson .08
161 Bob Knepper .08
162 Dave Dravecky .08
163 Greg Gross .08
164 Eric Davis .40
165 Gerald Perry .08
166 Rick Rhoden .08
167 Keith Moreland .08
168 Jack Clark .10
169 Storm Davis .08
170 Cecil Cooper .10
171 Alan Trammell .35
172 Roger Clemens 5.00
173 Don Mattingly 4.00
174 Pedro Guerrero .20
175 Willie Wilson .12
176 Dwayne Murphy .08
177 Tim Raines .40
178 Larry Parrish .08
179 Mike Witt .08
180 Harold Baines .20
181 *Vince Coleman* .35
182 *Jeff Heathcock* .08
183 Steve Carlton .75
184 Mario Soto .08
185 Goose Gossage .20
186 Johnny Ray .08
187 Dan Gladden .08
188 Bob Horner .12
189 Rick Sutcliffe .12
190 Keith Hernandez .10
191 Phil Bradley .10
192 Tom Brunansky .10
193 Jesse Barfield .10
194 Frank Viola .10
195 Willie Upshaw .08
196 Jim Beattie .08
197 Darryl Strawberry .35
198 Ron Cey .10
199 Steve Bedrosian .12
200 Steve Kemp .08
201 Manny Trillo .08
202 Garry Templeton .08
203 Dave Parker .15
204 John Denny .08
205 Terry Pendleton .08
206 Terry Puhl .08
207 Bobby Grich .10
208 *Ozzie Guillen* .90
209 Jeff Reardon .12
210 Cal Ripken, Jr. 5.00
211 Bill Schroeder .08
212 Dan Petry .08
213 Jim Rice .20
214 Dave Righetti .08
215 Fernando Valenzuela .20
216 Julio Franco .10
217 Darryl Motley .08
218 Dave Collins .08
219 Tim Wallach .12
220 George Wright .08
221 Tommy Dunbar .08
222 Steve Balboni .08
223 Jay Howell .08
224 Joe Carter .75
225 Ed Whitson .08
226 Orel Hershiser .25
227 Willie Hernandez .08
228 Lee Lacy .08
229 Rollie Fingers .35
230 Bob Boone .10
231 Joaquin Andujar .08
232 Craig Reynolds .08
233 Shane Rawley .08
234 Eric Show .08
235 Jose DeLeon .08
236 *Jose Uribe* .08
237 Moose Haas .08
238 Wally Backman .08
239 Dennis Eckersley .15
240 Mike Moore .08
241 Damaso Garcia .08
242 Tim Teufel .08
243 Dave Concepcion .12
244 Floyd Bannister .08
245 Fred Lynn .20
246 Charlie Moore .08
247 Walt Terrell .08
248 Dave Winfield 1.00
249 Dwight Evans .12
250 *Dennis Powell* .08
251 Andre Thornton .10
252 Onix Concepcion .08
253 Mike Heath .08
254a David Palmer (2B on front) .08
254b David Palmer (P on front) .50
255 Donnie Moore .08
256 Curtis Wilkerson .08
257 Julio Cruz .08
258 Nolan Ryan 6.00
259 Jeff Stone .08
260a John Tudor (1981 Games is .18) .10
260b John Tudor (1981 Games is 18) .50
261 Mark Thurmond .08
262 Jay Tibbs .08
263 Rafael Ramirez .08
264 Larry McWilliams .08
265 Mark Davis .08
266 Bob Dernier .08
267 Matt Young .08
268 Jim Clancy .08
269 Mickey Hatcher .08
270 Sammy Stewart .08
271 Bob L. Gibson .08
272 Nelson Simmons .08
273 Rich Gedman .08
274 Butch Wynegar .08
275 Ken Howell .08
276 Mel Hall .08
277 Jim Sundberg .08
278 Chris Codiroli .08
279 *Herman Winningham* .10
280 Rod Carew 1.00
281 Don Slaught .08
282 Scott Fletcher .08
283 Bill Dawley .08
284 Andy Hawkins .08
285 Glenn Wilson .08
286 Nick Esasky .08
287 Claudell Washington .08
288 Lee Mazzilli .08
289 Jody Davis .08
290 Darrell Porter .08
291 Scott McGregor .08
292 Ted Simmons .08
293 Aurelio Lopez .08
294 Marty Barrett .08
295 Dale Berra .08
296 Greg Brock .08
297 Charlie Leibrandt .08
298 Bill Krueger .08
299 Bryn Smith .08
300 Burt Hooton .08
301 *Stu Cliburn* .08
302 Luis Salazar .08
303 Ken Dayley .08
304 Frank DiPino .08
305 Von Hayes .08
306a Gary Redus (1983 2B is .20) .08
306b Gary Redus (1983 2B is 20) 1.00
307 Craig Lefferts .08
308 Sam Khalifa .08
309 Scott Garrelts .08
310 Rick Cerone .08
311 Shawon Dunston .20
312 Howard Johnson .12
313 Jim Presley .08
314 Gary Gaetti .15
315 Luis Leal .08
316 Mark Salas .08
317 Bill Caudill .08
318 Dave Henderson .08
319 Rafael Santana .08
320 Leon Durham .08
321 Bruce Sutter .12
322 Jason Thompson .08
323 Bob Brenly .08
324 Carmelo Martinez .08
325 Eddie Milner .08
326 Juan Samuel .08
327 Tom Nieto .08
328 Dave Smith .08
329 *Urbano Lugo* .08
330 Joel Skinner .08
331 Bill Gullickson .08
332 Floyd Rayford .08
333 Ben Oglivie .08
334 Lance Parrish .20
335 Jackie Gutierrez .08
336 Dennis Rasmussen .12
337 Terry Whitfield .08
338 Neal Heaton .08
339 Jorge Orta .08
340 Donnie Hill .08
341 Joe Hesketh .08
342 Charlie Hough .10
343 Dave Rozema .08
344 Greg Pryor .08
345 Mickey Tettleton .50
346 George Vukovich .08
347 Don Baylor .15
348 Carlos Diaz .08
349 Barbaro Garbey .08
350 Larry Sheets .08
351 *Ted Higuera* .15
352 Juan Beniquez .08
353 Bob Forsch .08
354 Mark Bailey .08
355 Larry Andersen .08
356 Terry Kennedy .08
357 Don Robinson .08
358 Jim Gott .08
359 *Earnest Riles* .08
360 *John Christensen* .08
361 Ray Fontenot .08
362 Spike Owen .08
363 Jim Acker .08
364a Ron Davis (last line in highlights ends with "...in May.") .08
364b Ron Davis (last line in highlights ends with "...relievers (9).") .50
365 Tom Hume .08
366 Carlton Fisk .60
367 Nate Snell .08
368 Rick Manning .08
369 Darrell Evans .15
370 Ron Hassey .08
371 Wade Boggs 1.50
372 Rick Honeycutt .08
373 Chris Bando .08
374 Bud Black .08
375 Steve Henderson .08
376 Charlie Lea .08
377 Reggie Jackson 1.25
378 Dave Schmidt .08
379 Bob James .08
380 Glenn Davis .15
381 Tim Corcoran .08
382 Danny Cox .08
383 Tim Flannery .08
384 Tom Browning .08
385 Rick Camp .08
386 Jim Morrison .08
387 Dave LaPoint .08
388 Davey Lopes .08
389 Al Cowens .08
390 Doyle Alexander .08
391 Tim Laudner .08
392 Don Aase .08
393 Jaime Cocanower .08
394 Randy O'Neal .08
395 Mike Easler .08
396 Scott Bradley .08
397 Tom Niedenfuer .08
398 Jerry Willard .08
399 Lonnie Smith .08
400 Bruce Bochte .08
401 Terry Francona .08
402 Jim Slaton .08
403 Bill Stein .08
404 Tim Hulett .08
405 Alan Ashby .08
406 Tim Stoddard .08
407 Garry Maddox .08
408 Ted Power .08
409 Len Barker .08
410 Denny Gonzalez .08
411 George Frazier .08
412 Andy Van Slyke .15
413 Jim Dwyer .08
414 Paul Householder .08
415 Alejandro Sanchez .08
416 Steve Crawford .08
417 Dan Pasqua .08

418	Enos Cabell	.08
419	Mike Jones	.08
420	Steve Kiefer	.08
421	*Tim Burke*	.10
422	Mike Mason	.08
423	Ruppert Jones	.08
424	Jerry Hairston	.08
425	Tito Landrum	.08
426	Jeff Calhoun	.08
427	*Don Carman*	.08
428	Tony Perez	.20
429	Jerry Davis	.08
430	Bob Walk	.08
431	Brad Wellman	.08
432	Terry Forster	.08
433	Billy Hatcher	.08
434	Clint Hurdle	.08
435	*Ivan Calderon*	.15
436	Pete Filson	.08
437	Tom Henke	.08
438	Dave Engle	.08
439	Tom Filer	.08
440	Gorman Thomas	.08
441	*Rick Aguilera*	.50
442	Scott Sanderson	.08
443	Jeff Dedmon	.08
444	*Joe Orsulak*	.15
445	Atlee Hammaker	.08
446	Jerry Royster	.08
447	Buddy Bell	.10
448	Dave Rucker	.08
449	Ivan DeJesus	.08
450	Jim Pankovits	.08
451	Jerry Narron	.08
452	Bryan Little	.08
453	Gary Lucas	.08
454	Dennis Martinez	.12
455	Ed Romero	.08
456	*Bob Melvin*	.08
457	Glenn Hoffman	.08
458	Bob Shirley	.08
459	Bob Welch	.10
460	Carmen Castillo	.08
461	Dave Leeper	.08
462	*Tim Birtsas*	.08
463	Randy St. Claire	.08
464	Chris Welsh	.08
465	Greg Harris	.08
466	Lynn Jones	.08
467	Dusty Baker	.12
468	Roy Smith	.08
469	Andre Robertson	.08
470	Ken Landreaux	.08
471	Dave Bergman	.08
472	Gary Roenicke	.08
473	Pete Vuckovich	.08
474	*Kirk McCaskill*	.40
475	Jeff Lahti	.08
476	Mike Scott	.10
477	*Darren Daulton*	1.50
478	Graig Nettles	.15
479	Bill Almon	.08
480	Greg Minton	.08
481	Randy Ready	.08
482	*Len Dykstra*	1.50
483	Thad Bosley	.08
484	*Harold Reynolds*	.40
485	Al Oliver	.12
486	Roy Smalley	.08
487	John Franco	.10
488	Juan Agosto	.08
489	Al Pardo	.08
490	*Bill Wegman*	.15
491	Frank Tanana	.08
492	*Brian Fisher*	.08
493	Mark Clear	.08
494	Len Matuszek	.08
495	Ramon Romero	.08
496	John Wathan	.08
497	Rob Picciolo	.08
498	U.L. Washington	.08
499	John Candelaria	.08
500	Duane Walker	.08
501	Gene Nelson	.08
502	John Mizerock	.08
503	Luis Aguayo	.08
504	Kurt Kepshire	.08
505	Ed Wojna	.08
506	Joe Price	.08
507	*Milt Thompson*	.20
508	Junior Ortiz	.08
509	Vida Blue	.10
510	Steve Engel	.08
511	Karl Best	.08
512	*Cecil Fielder*	3.00
513	Frank Eufemia	.08
514	Tippy Martinez	.08
515	*Billy Robidoux*	.08
516	Bill Scherrer	.08
517	Bruce Hurst	.08
518	Rich Bordi	.08
519	Steve Yeager	.08
520	Tony Bernazard	.08
521	Hal McRae	.10
522	Jose Rijo	.08
523	*Mitch Webster*	.08
524	*Jack Howell*	.08
525	Alan Bannister	.08
526	Ron Kittle	.08
527	Phil Garner	.10
528	Kurt Bevacqua	.08
529	Kevin Gross	.08
530	Bo Diaz	.08
531	Ken Oberkfell	.08
532	Rick Reuschel	.08
533	Ron Meridith	.08
534	Steve Braun	.08
535	Wayne Gross	.08
536	Ray Searage	.08
537	Tom Brookens	.08
538	Al Nipper	.08
539	Billy Sample	.08
540	Steve Sax	.12
541	Dan Quisenberry	.10
542	Tony Phillips	.12
543	*Floyd Youmans*	.08
544	*Steve Buechele*	.35
545	Craig Gerber	.08
546	Joe DeSa	.08
547	Brian Harper	.08
548	Kevin Bass	.08
549	Tom Foley	.08
550	Dave Van Gorder	.08
551	Bruce Bochy	.08
552	R.J. Reynolds	.08
553	*Chris Brown*	.12
554	Bruce Benedict	.08
555	Warren Brusstar	.08
556	Danny Heep	.08
557	Darnell Coles	.08
558	Greg Gagne	.08
559	Ernie Whitt	.08
560	Ron Washington	.08
561	Jimmy Key	.15
562	Billy Swift	.08
563	Ron Darling	.08
564	Dick Ruthven	.08
565	Zane Smith	.10
566	Sid Bream	.10
567a	Joel Youngblood (P on front)	.08
567b	Joel Youngblood (IF on front)	.50
568	Mario Ramirez	.08
569	Tom Runnells	.08
570	Rick Schu	.08
571	Bill Campbell	.08
572	Dickie Thon	.08
573	Al Holland	.08
574	Reid Nichols	.08
575	Bert Roberge	.08
576	Mike Flanagan	.08
577	Tim Leary	.10
578	Mike Laga	.08
579	Steve Lyons	.10
580	Phil Niekro	.45
581	Gilberto Reyes	.08
582	Jamie Easterly	.08
583	Mark Gubicza	.12
584	*Stan Javier*	.10
585	Bill Laskey	.08
586	Jeff Russell	.08
587	Dickie Noles	.08
588	Steve Farr	.08
589	*Steve Ontiveros*	.10
590	Mike Hargrove	.10
591	Marty Bystrom	.08
592	Franklin Stubbs	.08
593	Larry Herndon	.08
594	Bill Swaggerty	.08
595	Carlos Ponce	.08
596	*Pat Perry*	.08
597	Ray Knight	.08
598	*Steve Lombardozzi*	.10
599	Brad Havens	.08
600	*Pat Clements*	.08
601	Joe Niekro	.12
602	Hank Aaron Puzzle Card	.08
603	*Dwayne Henry*	.08
604	Mookie Wilson	.10
605	Buddy Biancalana	.08
606	Rance Mulliniks	.08
607	Alan Wiggins	.08
608	Joe Cowley	.08
609a	Tom Seaver (green stripes around name)	1.00
609b	Tom Seaver (yellow stripes around name)	3.00
610	Neil Allen	.08
611	Don Sutton	.35
612	*Fred Toliver*	.08
613	Jay Baller	.08
614	Marc Sullivan	.08
615	John Grubb	.08
616	Bruce Kison	.08
617	Bill Madlock	.12
618	Chris Chambliss	.08
619	Dave Stewart	.15
620	Tim Lollar	.08
621	Gary Lavelle	.08
622	Charles Hudson	.08
623	*Joel Davis*	.08
624	*Joe Johnson*	.08
625	Sid Fernandez	.12
626	Dennis Lamp	.08
627	Terry Harper	.08
628	Jack Lazorko	.08
629	*Roger McDowell*	.25
630	Mark Funderburk	.08
631	Ed Lynch	.08
632	Rudy Law	.08
633	*Roger Mason*	.08
634	*Mike Felder*	.08
635	Ken Schrom	.08
636	Bob Ojeda	.08
637	Ed Vande Berg	.08
638	Bobby Meacham	.08
639	Cliff Johnson	.08
640	Garth Iorg	.08
641	Dan Driessen	.08
642	Mike Brown	.08
643	John Shelby	.08
644	Pete Rose (RB)	.50
645	Knuckle Brothers (Joe Niekro, Phil Niekro)	.25
646	Jesse Orosco	.08
647	*Billy Beane*	.08
648	Cesar Cedeno	.10
649	Bert Blyleven	.15
650	Max Venable	.08
651	Fleet Feet (Vince Coleman, Willie McGee)	.35
652	Calvin Schiraldi	.08
653	King of Kings (Pete Rose)	2.50
----	Checklist 1-26 DK	.08
----	Checklist 27-130 (45 is Beane)	.08
----	Checklist 27-130 (45 is Habyan)	.30
----	Checklist 131-234	.08
----	Checklist 235-338	.08
----	Checklist 339-442	.08
----	Checklist 443-546	.08
----	Checklist 547-653	.08

1986 Donruss Box Panels

For the second year in a row, Donruss placed baseball cards on the bottom of its wax and cello pack boxes. The cards, printed four to a panel, are standard 2-1/2" x 3-1/2". With numbering that begins where Donruss left off in 1985, cards PC4 through PC6 were found on boxes of regular Donruss issue wax packs. Cards PC7 through PC9 were found on boxes of the 1986 All- Star/Pop-up packs. An unnumbered Hank Aaron puzzle card was included on each box.

		MT
Complete Panel Set (2):		3.00
Complete Singles Set (8):		2.00
Common Single Player:		.15
Panel		1.00
PC4	Kirk Gibson	.25
PC5	Willie Hernandez	.15
PC6	Doug DeCinces	.15
---	Aaron Puzzle Card	.04
Panel		2.00
PC7	Wade Boggs	.75
PC8	Lee Smith	.25
PC9	Cecil Cooper	.15
---	Aaron Puzzle Card	.04

1986 Donruss All-Stars

Issued in conjunction with the 1986 Donruss Pop-Ups set, the All-Stars consist of 60 cards in 3-1/2" x 5" format. Fifty-nine players involved in the 1985 All-Star game plus an unnumbered checklist comprise the set. Card fronts have the same blue border found on the regular 1986 Donruss issue. Retail packs included one Pop-up card, three All-Star cards and one Hank Aaron puzzle-piece card.

		MT
Complete Set (60):		8.00
Common Player:		.10
Hank Aaron puzzle:		5.00
1	Tony Gwynn	1.00
2	Tommy Herr	.10
3	Steve Garvey	.30
4	Dale Murphy	.30
5	Darryl Strawberry	.30
6	Graig Nettles	.10
7	Terry Kennedy	.10
8	Ozzie Smith	.75
9	LaMarr Hoyt	.10
10	Rickey Henderson	.50
11	Lou Whitaker	.10
12	George Brett	.75
13	Eddie Murray	.50

14 Cal Ripken, Jr. 2.50
15 Dave Winfield .50
16 Jim Rice .15
17 Carlton Fisk .35
18 Jack Morris .10
19 Jose Cruz .10
20 Tim Raines .15
21 Nolan Ryan 2.00
22 Tony Pena .10
23 Jack Clark .10
24 Dave Parker .10
25 Tim Wallach .10
26 Ozzie Virgil .10
27 Fernando Valenzuela .15
28 Dwight Gooden .20
29 Glenn Wilson .10
30 Garry Templeton .10
31 Goose Gossage .10
32 Ryne Sandberg .75
33 Jeff Reardon .10
34 Pete Rose 1.50
35 Scott Garrelts .10
36 Willie McGee .10
37 Ron Darling .10
38 Dick Williams .10
39 Paul Molitor .50
40 Damaso Garcia .10
41 Phil Bradley .10
42 Dan Petry .10
43 Willie Hernandez .10
44 Tom Brunansky .10
45 Alan Trammell .20
46 Donnie Moore .10
47 Wade Boggs .60
48 Ernie Whitt .10
49 Harold Baines .10
50 Don Mattingly 1.00
51 Gary Ward .10
52 Bert Blyleven .10
53 Jimmy Key .10
54 Cecil Cooper .10
55 Dave Stieb .10
56 Rich Gedman .10
57 Jay Howell .10
58 Sparky Anderson .10
59 Minneapolis Metrodome .10
--- Checklist .05

1986 Donruss Diamond Kings Supers

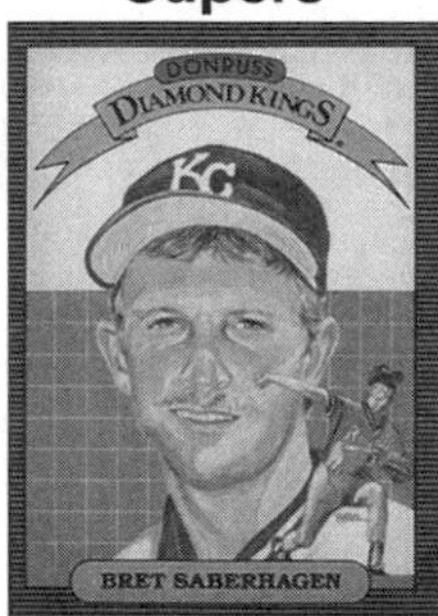

Donruss produced a set of large-format Diamond Kings in 1986 for the second year in a row. The 4-11/16" x 6-3/4" cards are enlarged versions of the 26 Diamond Kings cards found in the regular 1986 Donruss set, plus an unnumbered checklist and an unnumbered Pete Rose "King of Kings" card.

MT
Complete Set (28): 12.00
Common Player: .50
1 Kirk Gibson .75
2 Goose Gossage .60
3 Willie McGee .75
4 George Bell .50
5 Tony Armas .50
6 Chili Davis .60
7 Cecil Cooper .50
8 Mike Boddicker .50
9 Davey Lopes .50
10 Bill Doran .50
11 Bret Saberhagen .75
12 Brett Butler .75
13 Harold Baines .60
14 Mike Davis .50
15 Tony Perez .75
16 Willie Randolph .50
18 Orel Hershiser .75
19 Johnny Ray .50
20 Gary Ward .50
21 Rick Mahler .50
22 Phil Bradley .50
23 Jerry Koosman .50
24 Tom Brunansky .50
25 Andre Dawson .75
26 Dwight Gooden .75
--- Checklist .05
--- King of Kings (Pete Rose) 1.50

1986 Donruss Highlights

Donruss, for the second year in a row, issued a 56-card highlights set featuring cards of each league's Player of the Month plus significant events of the 1986 season. The cards, 2-1/2" x 3-1/2," are similar in design to the regular 1986 Donruss set but have a gold border instead of blue. A "Highlights" logo appears in the lower-left corner of each card front. Backs are designed on a vertical format and feature black print on a yellow background. As in 1985, the set includes Donruss' picks for the Rookies of the Year. A new feature was three cards honoring the 1986 Hall of Fame inductees. The set, available only through hobby dealers, was issued in a specially designed box.

MT
Complete Set (56): 4.50
Common Player: .08
1 Homers In First At-Bat (Will Clark) .75
2 Oakland Milestone For Strikeouts (Jose Rijo) .08
3 Royals' All-Time Hit Man (George Brett) .35
4 Phillies RBI Leader (Mike Schmidt) .35
5 KKKKKKKKKKK KKKKKKKK (Roger Clemens) .75
6 A.L. Pitcher of the Month-April (Roger Clemens) .25
7 A.L. Player of the Month-April (Kirby Puckett) .45
8 N.L. Pitcher of the Month-April (Dwight Gooden) .15
9 N.L. Player of the Month-April (Johnny Ray) .08
10 Eclipses Mantle HR Record (Reggie Jackson) .20
11 First Five Hit Game of Career (Wade Boggs) .20
12 A.L. Pitcher of the Month-May (Don Aase) .08
13 A.L. Player of the Month-May (Wade Boggs) .20
14 N.L. Pitcher of the Month-May (Jeff Reardon) .08
15 N.L. Player of the Month-May (Hubie Brooks) .08
16 Notches 300th Career Win (Don Sutton) .10
17 Starts Season 14-0 (Roger Clemens) .20
18 A.L. Pitcher of the Month-June (Roger Clemens) .20
19 A.L. Player of the Month-June (Kent Hrbek) .08
20 N.L. Pitcher of the Month-June (Rick Rhoden) .08
21 N.L. Player of the Month-June (Kevin Bass) .08
22 Blasts 4 HRS in 1 Game (Bob Horner) .10
23 Starting All Star Rookie (Wally Joyner) .08
24 Starts 3rd Straight All Star Game (Darryl Strawberry) .10
25 Ties All Star Game Record (Fernando Valenzuela) .08
26 All Star Game MVP (Roger Clemens) .20
27 A.L. Pitcher of the Month-July (Jack Morris) .08
28 A.L. Player of the Month-July (Scott Fletcher) .08
29 N.L. Pitcher of the Month-July (Todd Worrell) .08
30 N.L. PLayer of the Month-July (Eric Davis) .08
31 Records 3000th Strikeout (Bert Blyleven) .08
32 1986 Hall of Fame Inductee (Bobby Doerr) .08
33 1986 Hall of Fame Inductee (Ernie Lombardi) .08
34 1986 Hall of Fame Inductee (Willie McCovey) .20
35 Notches 4000th K (Steve Carlton) .20
36 Surpasses DiMaggio Record (Mike Schmidt) .35
37 Records 3rd "Quadruple Double" (Juan Samuel) .08
38 A.L. Pitcher of the Month-August (Mike Witt) .08
39 A.L. Player of the Month-August (Doug DeCinces) .08
40 N.L. Pitcher of the Month-August (Bill Gullickson) .08
41 N.L. Player of the Month-August (Dale Murphy) .10
42 Sets Tribe Offensive Record (Joe Carter) .08
43 Longest HR In Royals Stadium (Bo Jackson) .25
44 Majors 1st No-Hitter In 2 Years (Joe Cowley) .08
45 Sets M.L. Strikeout Record (Jim Deshaies) .08
46 No Hitter Clinches Division (Mike Scott) .08
47 A.L. Pitcher of the Month-September (Bruce Hurst) .08
48 A.L. Player of the Month-September (Don Mattingly) .40
49 N.L. Pitcher of the Month-September (Mike Krukow) .08
50 N.L. Player of the Month-September (Steve Sax) .08
51 A.L. Record For Steals By A Rookie (John Cangelosi) .08
52 Shatters M.L. Save Mark (Dave Righetti) .08
53 Yankee Record For Hits & Doubles (Don Mattingly) .40
54 Donruss N.L. Rookie of the Year (Todd Worrell) .08
55 Donruss A.L. Rookie of the Year (Jose Canseco) 1.00
56 Highlight Checklist .04

1986 Donruss Pop-Ups

Issued in conjunction with the 1986 Donruss All-Stars set, the Pop-Ups (18 unnumbered cards) feature the 1985 All-Star Game starting lineups.

The cards, 2-1/2" x 5", are die-cut and fold out to form a three-dimensional stand-up card. The background for the cards is the Minneapolis Metrodome, site of the 1985 All-Star Game. Retail packs included one Pop-Up card, three All-Star cards and one Hank Aaron puzzle card.

		MT
Complete Set (18):		3.00
Common Player:		.10
Hank Aaron Puzzle:		5.00
(1)	George Brett	.50
(2)	Carlton Fisk	.30
(3)	Steve Garvey	.20
(4)	Tony Gwynn	.75
(5)	Rickey Henderson	.40
(6)	Tommy Herr	.10
(7)	LaMarr Hoyt	.10
(8)	Terry Kennedy	.10
(9)	Jack Morris	.10
(10)	Dale Murphy	.20
(11)	Eddie Murray	.40
(12)	Graig Nettles	.10
(13)	Jim Rice	.10
(14)	Cal Ripken, Jr.	.90
(15)	Ozzie Smith	.40
(16)	Darryl Strawberry	.30
(17)	Lou Whitaker	.10
(18)	Dave Winfield	.30

1986 Donruss Rookies

Entitled "The Rookies," this 56-card set includes the top 55 rookies of 1986 plus an unnumbered checklist. The cards are similar in format to the 1986 Donruss regular issue, except that the borders are green rather than blue. Several of the rookies who had cards in the regular 1986 Donruss set appear again in "The Rookies" set. The sets, which were only available through hobby dealers, came in a specially designed box.

		MT
Comp. Unopened Set (56):		30.00
Complete Opened Set (56):		20.00
Common Player:		.10
1	*Wally Joyner*	.75
2	Tracy Jones	.10
3	Allan Anderson	.10
4	Ed Correa	.10
5	Reggie Williams	.10
6	Charlie Kerfeld	.10
7	Andres Galarraga	3.00
8	Bob Tewksbury	.60
9	Al Newman	.10
10	Andres Thomas	.10
11	*Barry Bonds*	20.00
12	Juan Nieves	.10
13	Mark Eichhorn	.10
14	Dan Plesac	.15
15	Cory Snyder	.10
16	Kelly Gruber	.10
17	*Kevin Mitchell*	.30
18	Steve Lombardozzi	.10
19	Mitch Williams	.15
20	John Cerutti	.10
21	Todd Worrell	.15
22	Jose Canseco	8.00
23	*Pete Incaviglia*	.30
24	Jose Guzman	.10
25	Scott Bailes	.10
26	Greg Mathews	.10
27	Eric King	.10
28	Paul Assenmacher	.10
29	Jeff Sellers	.10
30	*Bobby Bonilla*	1.00
31	*Doug Drabek*	.75
32	*Will Clark*	4.00
33	Bip Roberts	.15
34	Jim Deshaies	.10
35	Mike LaValliere	.10
36	Scott Bankhead	.10
37	Dale Sveum	.10
38	*Bo Jackson*	1.50
39	Rob Thompson	.15
40	Eric Plunk	.10
41	Bill Bathe	.10
42	*John Kruk*	.45
43	Andy Allanson	.10
44	Mark Portugal	.10
45	Danny Tartabull	.25
46	Bob Kipper	.10
47	Gene Walter	.10
48	Rey Quinonez	.10
49	Bobby Witt	.25
50	Bill Mooneyham	.10
51	John Cangelosi	.10
52	*Ruben Sierra*	.35
53	Rob Woodward	.10
54	Ed Hearn	.10
55	Joel McKeon	.10
56	Checklist 1-56	.05

1987 Donruss

The 1987 Donruss set consists of 660 numbered cards, each measuring 2-1/2" x 3-1/2". Color photos are surrounded by a bold black border separated by two narrow bands of yellow which enclose a brown area filled with baseballs. The player's name, team and team logo appear on the card fronts along with the words "Donruss '87". The card backs are designed on a horizontal format and contain black print on a yellow and white background. The backs are very similar to those in previous years' sets. Backs of cards issued in wax and rack packs face to the left when turned over, while those issued in factory sets face to the right. Cards were sold with Roberto Clemente puzzle pieces in each pack. Cards checklisted with a (DK) suffix are Diamond Kings; cards with an (RR) suffix are Rated Rookies.

		MT
Complete Set (660):		60.00
Common Player:		.05
Roberto Clemente Puzzle:		9.00
Wax Box:		55.00
1	Wally Joyner (DK)	.25
2	Roger Clemens (DK)	1.00
3	Dale Murphy (DK)	.15
4	Darryl Strawberry (DK)	.15
5	Ozzie Smith (DK)	.45
6	Jose Canseco (DK)	.65
7	Charlie Hough (DK)	.08
8	Brook Jacoby (DK)	.10
9	Fred Lynn (DK)	.12
10	Rick Rhoden (DK)	.10
11	Chris Brown (DK)	.10
12	Von Hayes (DK)	.10
13	Jack Morris (DK)	.10
14a	Kevin McReynolds (DK) (no yellow stripe on back)	.75
14b	Kevin McReynolds (DK) (yellow stripe on back)	.20
15	George Brett (DK)	.75
16	Ted Higuera (DK)	.05
17	Hubie Brooks (DK)	.10
18	Mike Scott (DK)	.08
19	Kirby Puckett (DK)	.75
20	Dave Winfield (DK)	.45
21	Lloyd Moseby (DK)	.10
22a	Eric Davis (DK) (no yellow stripe on back)	1.00
22b	Eric Davis (DK) (yellow stripe on back)	.15
23	Jim Presley (DK)	.08
24	Keith Moreland (DK)	.08
25a	Greg Walker (DK) (no yellow stripe on back)	.50
25b	Greg Walker (DK) (yellow stripe on back)	.10
26	Steve Sax (DK)	.12
27	Checklist 1-27	.05
28	*B.J. Surhoff* (RR)	.30
29	*Randy Myers* (RR)	.65
30	*Ken Gerhart* (RR)	.08
31	Benito Santiago (RR)	.40
32	*Greg Swindell* (RR)	.15
33	*Mike Birkbeck* (RR)	.10
34	*Terry Steinbach* (RR)	.50
35	Bo Jackson (RR)	2.00
36	*Greg Maddux* (RR)	20.00
37	*Jim Lindeman* (RR)	.05
38	*Devon White* (RR)	.75
39	*Eric Bell* (RR)	.08
40	*Will Fraser* (RR)	.10
41	*Jerry Browne* (RR)	.15
42	*Chris James* (RR)	.10
43	*Rafael Palmeiro* (RR)	8.00
44	*Pat Dodson* (RR)	.05
45	*Duane Ward* (RR)	.25
46	Mark McGwire (RR)	30.00
47	*Bruce Fields* (RR) (Photo actually Darnell Coles)	.10
48	Eddie Murray	.60
49	Ted Higuera	.05
50	Kirk Gibson	.10
51	Oil Can Boyd	.05
52	Don Mattingly	1.00
53	Pedro Guerrero	.10
54	George Brett	1.00
55	Jose Rijo	.05
56	Tim Raines	.30
57	*Ed Correa*	.05
58	Mike Witt	.05
59	Greg Walker	.05
60	Ozzie Smith	.60
61	Glenn Davis	.05
62	Glenn Wilson	.05
63	Tom Browning	.05
64	Tony Gwynn	1.00
65	R.J. Reynolds	.05
66	Will Clark	2.00
67	Ozzie Virgil	.05
68	Rick Sutcliffe	.12
69	Gary Carter	.12
70	Mike Moore	.05
71	Bert Blyleven	.12
72	Tony Fernandez	.15
73	Kent Hrbek	.10
74	Lloyd Moseby	.08
75	Alvin Davis	.05
76	Keith Hernandez	.15
77	Ryne Sandberg	.90
78	Dale Murphy	.30
79	Sid Bream	.05
80	Chris Brown	.05
81	Steve Garvey	.25
82	Mario Soto	.05
83	Shane Rawley	.05
84	Willie McGee	.12
85	Jose Cruz	.08
86	Brian Downing	.08
87	Ozzie Guillen	.05
88	Hubie Brooks	.05
89	Cal Ripken, Jr.	2.50
90	Juan Nieves	.05
91	Lance Parrish	.08
92	Jim Rice	.12
93	Ron Guidry	.15
94	Fernando Valenzuela	.08
95	*Andy Allanson*	.05
96	Willie Wilson	.12
97	Jose Canseco	2.00
98	Jeff Reardon	.10
99	*Bobby Witt*	.20
100	Checklist 28-133	.05
101	Jose Guzman	.05
102	Steve Balboni	.05
103	Tony Phillips	.05
104	Brook Jacoby	.05
105	Dave Winfield	.30
106	Orel Hershiser	.15
107	Lou Whitaker	.10
108	Fred Lynn	.10
109	Bill Wegman	.05
110	Donnie Moore	.05
111	Jack Clark	.10
112	Bob Knepper	.05
113	Von Hayes	.05
114	*Bip Roberts*	.40
115	Tony Pena	.08
116	Scott Garrelts	.05
117	Paul Molitor	.75
118	Darryl Strawberry	.25
119	Shawon Dunston	.05
120	Jim Presley	.05
121	Jesse Barfield	.05
122	Gary Gaetti	.10
123	*Kurt Stillwell*	.10
124	Joel Davis	.05
125	Mike Boddicker	.05
126	Robin Yount	.75
127	Alan Trammell	.25
128	Dave Righetti	.08
129	Dwight Evans	.12
130	Mike Scioscia	.05
131	Julio Franco	.05
132	Bret Saberhagen	.12
133	Mike Davis	.05
134	Joe Hesketh	.05
135	Wally Joyner	.25
136	Don Slaught	.05
137	Daryl Boston	.05
138	Nolan Ryan	2.50
139	Mike Schmidt	1.00
140	Tommy Herr	.10
141	Garry Templeton	.05
142	Kal Daniels	.05
143	Billy Sample	.05
144	Johnny Ray	.05
145	*Rob Thompson*	.25
146	Bob Dernier	.05
147	Danny Tartabull	.05
148	Ernie Whitt	.05

149 Kirby Puckett 1.00
150 Mike Young .05
151 Ernest Riles .05
152 Frank Tanana .05
153 Rich Gedman .05
154 Willie Randolph .10
155a Bill Madlock (name in brown band) .12
155b Bill Madlock (name in red band) .50
156a Joe Carter (name in brown band) .10
156b Joe Carter (name in red band) .40
157 Danny Jackson .05
158 Carney Lansford .05
159 Bryn Smith .05
160 Gary Pettis .05
161 Oddibe McDowell .05
162 *John Cangelosi* .12
163 Mike Scott .10
164 Eric Show .05
165 Juan Samuel .05
166 Nick Esasky .05
167 Zane Smith .05
168 Mike Brown .05
169 Keith Moreland .05
170 John Tudor .05
171 Ken Dixon .05
172 Jim Gantner .05
173 Jack Morris .15
174 Bruce Hurst .05
175 Dennis Rasmussen .05
176 Mike Marshall .05
177 Dan Quisenberry .08
178 Eric Plunk .08
179 Tim Wallach .10
180 Steve Buechele .05
181 Don Sutton .40
182 Dave Schmidt .05
183 Terry Pendleton .08
184 *Jim Deshaies* .15
185 Steve Bedrosian .12
186 Pete Rose 1.25
187 Dave Dravecky .08
188 Rick Reuschel .05
189 Dan Gladden .05
190 Rick Mahler .05
191 Thad Bosley .05
192 Ron Darling .10
193 Matt Young .05
194 Tom Brunansky .10
195 Dave Stieb .12
196 Frank Viola .10
197 Tom Henke .08
198 Karl Best .05
199 Dwight Gooden .25
200 Checklist 134-239 .05
201 Steve Trout .05
202 Rafael Ramirez .05
203 Bob Walk .05
204 Roger Mason .05
205 Terry Kennedy .05
206 Ron Oester .05
207 John Russell .05
208 *Greg Mathews* .05
209 Charlie Kerfeld .05
210 Reggie Jackson .35
211 Floyd Bannister .05
212 Vance Law .05
213 Rich Bordi .05
214 *Dan Plesac* .10
215 Dave Collins .05
216 Bob Stanley .05
217 Joe Niekro .10
218 Tom Niedenfuer .05
219 Brett Butler .12
220 Charlie Leibrandt .05
221 Steve Ontiveros .05
222 Tim Burke .05
223 Curtis Wilkerson .05
224 *Pete Incaviglia* .25
225 Lonnie Smith .05
226 Chris Codiroli .05
227 *Scott Bailes* .05
228 Rickey Henderson .65
229 Ken Howell .05
230 Darnell Coles .05
231 Don Aase .05
232 Tim Leary .05
233 Bob Boone .08
234 Ricky Horton .05
235 Mark Bailey .05
236 Kevin Gross .05
237 Lance McCullers .05
238 Cecilio Guante .05
239 Bob Melvin .05
240 Billy Jo Robidoux .05
241 Roger McDowell .12
242 Leon Durham .05
243 Ed Nunez .05
244 Jimmy Key .12
245 Mike Smithson .05
246 Bo Diaz .05
247 Carlton Fisk .30
248 Larry Sheets .05
249 *Juan Castillo* .05
250 *Eric King* .05
251 Doug Drabek .10
252 Wade Boggs 1.00
253 Mariano Duncan .05
254 Pat Tabler .05
255 Frank White .10
256 Alfredo Griffin .05
257 Floyd Youmans .05
258 Rob Wilfong .05
259 Pete O'Brien .05
260 Tim Hulett .05
261 Dickie Thon .05
262 Darren Daulton .10
263 Vince Coleman .10
264 Andy Hawkins .05
265 Eric Davis .20
266 *Andres Thomas* .05
267 *Mike Diaz* .05
268 Chili Davis .08
269 Jody Davis .05
270 Phil Bradley .05
271 George Bell .08
272 Keith Atherton .05
273 Storm Davis .10
274 Rob Deer .10
275 Walt Terrell .05
276 Roger Clemens 1.00
277 Mike Easler .05
278 Steve Sax .10
279 Andre Thornton .05
280 Jim Sundberg .05
281 Bill Bathe .05
282 Jay Tibbs .05
283 Dick Schofield .05
284 Mike Mason .05
285 Jerry Hairston .05
286 Bill Doran .05
287 Tim Flannery .05
288 Gary Redus .05
289 John Franco .10
290 *Paul Assenmacher* .15
291 Joe Orsulak .05
292 Lee Smith .20
293 Mike Laga .05
294 Rick Dempsey .05
295 Mike Felder .05
296 Tom Brookens .05
297 Al Nipper .05
298 Mike Pagliarulo .10
299 Franklin Stubbs .05
300 Checklist 240-345 .05
301 Steve Farr .05
302 *Bill Mooneyham* .05
303 Andres Galarraga .50
304 Scott Fletcher .05
305 Jack Howell .05
306 *Russ Morman* .10
307 Todd Worrell .10
308 Dave Smith .05
309 Jeff Stone .05
310 Ron Robinson .05
311 Bruce Bochy .05
312 Jim Winn .05
313 Mark Davis .05
314 Jeff Dedmon .05
315 *Jamie Moyer* .08
316 Wally Backman .05
317 Ken Phelps .05
318 Steve Lombardozzi .05
319 Rance Mulliniks .05
320 Tim Laudner .05
321 *Mark Eichhorn* .08
322 *Lee Guetterman* .05
323 Sid Fernandez .05
324 Jerry Mumphrey .05
325 David Palmer .05
326 Bill Almon .05
327 Candy Maldonado .05
328 John Kruk .10
329 John Denny .05
330 Milt Thompson .05
331 *Mike LaValliere* .15
332 Alan Ashby .05
333 Doug Corbett .05
334 *Ron Karkovice* .10
335 Mitch Webster .05
336 Lee Lacy .05
337 *Glenn Braggs* .15
338 Dwight Lowry .05
339 Don Baylor .15
340 Brian Fisher .05
341 *Reggie Williams* .05
342 Tom Candiotti .05
343 Rudy Law .05
344 Curt Young .05
345 Mike Fitzgerald .05
346 Ruben Sierra .10
347 *Mitch Williams* .25
348 Jorge Orta .05
349 Mickey Tettleton .10
350 Ernie Camacho .05
351 Ron Kittle .05
352 Ken Landreaux .05
353 Chet Lemon .05
354 John Shelby .05
355 Mark Clear .05
356 Doug DeCinces .05
357 Ken Dayley .05
358 Phil Garner .08
359 Steve Jeltz .05
360 Ed Whitson .05
361 Barry Bonds 10.00
362 Vida Blue .10
363 Cecil Cooper .05
364 Bob Ojeda .05
365 Dennis Eckersley .25
366 Mike Morgan .05
367 Willie Upshaw .05
368 *Allan Anderson* .05
369 Bill Gullickson .05
370 *Bobby Thigpen* .10
371 Juan Beniquez .05
372 Charlie Moore .05
373 Dan Petry .05
374 Rod Scurry .05
375 Tom Seaver .50
376 Ed Vande Berg .05
377 Tony Bernazard .05
378 Greg Pryor .05
379 Dwayne Murphy .05
380 Andy McGaffigan .05
381 Kirk McCaskill .05
382 Greg Harris .05
383 Rich Dotson .05
384 Craig Reynolds .05
385 Greg Gross .05
386 Tito Landrum .05
387 Craig Lefferts .05
388 Dave Parker .25
389 Bob Horner .10
390 Pat Clements .05
391 Jeff Leonard .05
392 Chris Speier .05
393 John Moses .05
394 Garth Iorg .05
395 Greg Gagne .05
396 Nate Snell .05
397 *Bryan Clutterbuck* .05
398 Darrell Evans .12
399 Steve Crawford .05
400 Checklist 346-451 .05
401 *Phil Lombardi* .05
402 Rick Honeycutt .05
403 Ken Schrom .05
404 Bud Black .05
405 Donnie Hill .05
406 Wayne Krenchicki .05
407 *Chuck Finley* .35
408 Toby Harrah .08
409 Steve Lyons .08
410 Kevin Bass .05
411 Marvell Wynne .05
412 Ron Roenicke .05
413 *Tracy Jones* .08
414 Gene Garber .05
415 Mike Bielecki .05
416 Frank DiPino .05
417 Andy Van Slyke .10
418 Jim Dwyer .05
419 Ben Oglivie .05
420 Dave Bergman .05
421 Joe Sambito .05
422 *Bob Tewksbury* .30
423 Len Matuszek .05
424 *Mike Kingery* .05
425 Dave Kingman .10
426 *Al Newman* .05
427 Gary Ward .05
428 Ruppert Jones .05
429 Harold Baines .15
430 Pat Perry .05
431 Terry Puhl .05
432 Don Carman .05
433 Eddie Milner .05
434 LaMarr Hoyt .05
435 Rick Rhoden .10
436 Jose Uribe .05
437 Ken Oberkfell .05
438 Ron Davis .05
439 Jesse Orosco .08
440 Scott Bradley .05
441 Randy Bush .05
442 *John Cerutti* .10
443 Roy Smalley .05
444 Kelly Gruber .05
445 Bob Kearney .05
446 *Ed Hearn* .05
447 Scott Sanderson .05
448 Bruce Benedict .05
449 Junior Ortiz .05
450 *Mike Aldrete* .05
451 Kevin McReynolds .10
452 *Rob Murphy* .08
453 Kent Tekulve .05
454 Curt Ford .05
455 Davey Lopes .08
456 Bobby Grich .10
457 Jose DeLeon .05
458 Andre Dawson .30
459 Mike Flanagan .05
460 *Joey Meyer* .08
461 *Chuck Cary* .05
462 Bill Buckner .10
463 Bob Shirley .05
464 *Jeff Hamilton* .08
465 Phil Niekro .30
466 Mark Gubicza .12
467 Jerry Willard .05
468 *Bob Sebra* .05
469 Larry Parrish .05
470 Charlie Hough .08
471 Hal McRae .10
472 *Dave Leiper* .05
473 Mel Hall .05
474 Dan Pasqua .10
475 Bob Welch .10
476 Johnny Grubb .05
477 Jim Traber .05
478 *Chris Bosio* .25
479 Mark McLemore .08
480 John Morris .05
481 Billy Hatcher .05
482 Dan Schatzeder .05
483 Rich Gossage .15
484 Jim Morrison .05
485 Bob Brenly .05
486 Bill Schroeder .05
487 Mookie Wilson .10
488 *Dave Martinez* .15
489 Harold Reynolds .10
490 Jeff Hearron .05
491 Mickey Hatcher .05
492 *Barry Larkin* 2.00
493 Bob James .05
494 John Habyan .05
495 *Jim Adduci* .05
496 Mike Heath .05
497 Tim Stoddard .05
498 Tony Armas .08
499 Dennis Powell .05
500 Checklist 452-557 .05
501 Chris Bando .05
502 *David Cone* 2.50
503 Jay Howell .05
504 Tom Foley .05
505 *Ray Chadwick* .05
506 *Mike Loynd* .05
507 Neil Allen .05
508 Danny Darwin .05
509 Rick Schu .05
510 Jose Oquendo .05
511 Gene Walter .05
512 *Terry McGriff* .05
513 Ken Griffey .10
514 Benny Distefano .05
515 *Terry Mulholland* .40
516 Ed Lynch .05
517 Bill Swift .05
518 Manny Lee .05
519 Andre David .05
520 Scott McGregor .05
521 Rick Manning .05
522 Willie Hernandez .05
523 Marty Barrett .05
524 Wayne Tolleson .05

525	*Jose Gonzalez*	.05
526	Cory Snyder	.05
527	Buddy Biancalana	.05
528	Moose Haas	.05
529	*Wilfredo Tejada*	.05
530	Stu Cliburn	.05
531	*Dale Mohorcic*	.05
532	Ron Hassey	.05
533	Ty Gainey	.05
534	Jerry Royster	.05
535	*Mike Maddux*	.05
536	Ted Power	.05
537	Ted Simmons	.05
538	*Rafael Belliard*	.12
539	Chico Walker	.05
540	Bob Forsch	.05
541	John Stefero	.05
542	*Dale Sveum*	.08
543	Mark Thurmond	.05
544	*Jeff Sellers*	.05
545	Joel Skinner	.05
546	Alex Trevino	.05
547	*Randy Kutcher*	.05
548	Joaquin Andujar	.05
549	*Casey Candaele*	.10
550	Jeff Russell	.05
551	John Candelaria	.10
552	Joe Cowley	.05
553	Danny Cox	.05
554	Denny Walling	.05
555	*Bruce Ruffin*	.20
556	Buddy Bell	.10
557	*Jimmy Jones*	.10
558	Bobby Bonilla	.40
559	Jeff Robinson	.05
560	Ed Olwine	.05
561	*Glenallen Hill*	.75
562	Lee Mazzilli	.05
563	Mike Brown	.05
564	George Frazier	.05
565	*Mike Sharperson*	.10
566	*Mark Portugal*	.10
567	Rick Leach	.05
568	Mark Langston	.12
569	Rafael Santana	.05
570	Manny Trillo	.05
571	Cliff Speck	.05
572	Bob Kipper	.05
573	*Kelly Downs*	.10
574	*Randy Asadoor*	.05
575	*Dave Magadan*	.25
576	*Marvin Freeman*	.05
577	Jeff Lahti	.05
578	Jeff Calhoun	.05
579	Gus Polidor	.05
580	Gene Nelson	.05
581	Tim Teufel	.05
582	Odell Jones	.05
583	Mark Ryal	.05
584	Randy O'Neal	.05
585	*Mike Greenwell*	.50
586	Ray Knight	.05
587	*Ralph Bryant*	.05
588	Carmen Castillo	.05
589	Ed Wojna	.05
590	Stan Javier	.05
591	*Jeff Musselman*	.10
592	*Mike Stanley*	.20
593	Darrell Porter	.05
594	*Drew Hall*	.05
595	*Rob Nelson*	.05
596	Bryan Oelkers	.05
597	*Scott Nielsen*	.05
598	*Brian Holton*	.10
599	Kevin Mitchell	.10
600	Checklist 558-660	.05
601	Jackie Gutierrez	.05
602	*Barry Jones*	.10
603	Jerry Narron	.05
604	Steve Lake	.05
605	Jim Pankovits	.05
606	Ed Romero	.05
607	Dave LaPoint	.05
608	Don Robinson	.05
609	Mike Krukow	.05
610	*Dave Valle*	.10
611	Len Dykstra	.10
612	Roberto Clemente Puzzle Card	.25
613	Mike Trujillo	.05
614	Damaso Garcia	.05
615	Neal Heaton	.05
616	Juan Berenguer	.05
617	Steve Carlton	.35
618	Gary Lucas	.05
619	Geno Petralli	.05
620	Rick Aguilera	.05
621	Fred McGriff	.75
622	Dave Henderson	.05
623	*Dave Clark*	.05
624	Angel Salazar	.05
625	Randy Hunt	.05
626	John Gibbons	.05
627	*Kevin Brown*	4.00
628	Bill Dawley	.05
629	Aurelio Lopez	.05
630	Charlie Hudson	.05
631	Ray Soff	.05
632	*Ray Hayward*	.05
633	Spike Owen	.05
634	Glenn Hubbard	.05
635	*Kevin Elster*	.12
636	Mike LaCoss	.05
637	Dwayne Henry	.05
638	*Rey Quinones*	.05
639	Jim Clancy	.05
640	Larry Andersen	.05
641	Calvin Schiraldi	.05
642	*Stan Jefferson*	.05
643	Marc Sullivan	.05
644	Mark Grant	.05
645	Cliff Johnson	.05
646	Howard Johnson	.10
647	Dave Sax	.05
648	Dave Stewart	.10
649	Danny Heep	.05
650	Joe Johnson	.05
651	*Bob Brower*	.05
652	Rob Woodward	.05
653	John Mizerock	.05
654	*Tim Pyznarski*	.05
655	*Luis Aquino*	.05
656	Mickey Brantley	.10
657	Doyle Alexander	.05
658	Sammy Stewart	.05
659	Jim Acker	.05
660	Pete Ladd	.05

1987 Donruss Box Panels

Continuing with an idea they initiated in 1985, Donruss once again placed baseball cards on the bottoms of their retail boxes. The cards, which are 2-1/2" x 3-1/2" in size, come four to a panel with each panel containing an unnumbered Roberto Clemente puzzle card. With numbering that begins where Donruss left off in 1986, cards PC 10 through PC 12 were found on boxes of Donruss regular issue wax packs. Cards PC 13 through PC 15 were located on boxes of the 1987 All-Star/Pop-Up packs.

		MT
Complete Panel Set (2):		3.00
Complete Singles Set (8):		3.00
Common Single Player:		.15
Panel		2.00
10	Dale Murphy	.35
11	Jeff Reardon	.15
12	Jose Canseco	1.50
----	Roberto Clemente Puzzle Card	.15
Panel		2.00
13	Mike Scott	.15
14	Roger Clemens	1.50
15	Mike Krukow	.15
----	Roberto Clemente Puzzle Card	.15

1987 Donruss All-Stars

Issued in conjunction with the Donruss Pop-Ups set for the second consecutive year, the 1987 Donruss All-Stars consist of 59 players (plus a checklist) who were selected to the 1986 All-Star Game. Measuring 3-1/2" x 5" in size, the card fronts feature black borders and American or National League logos. Included on back are the player's career highlights and All-Star Game statistics. Retail packs included one Pop-Up card, three All-Star cards and one Roberto Clemente puzzle card.

		MT
Complete Set (60):		5.00
Common Player:		.10
Roberto Clemente Puzzle:		9.00
1	Wally Joyner	.15
2	Dave Winfield	.40
3	Lou Whitaker	.10
4	Kirby Puckett	.75
5	Cal Ripken, Jr.	2.00
6	Rickey Henderson	.25
7	Wade Boggs	.65
8	Roger Clemens	.75
9	Lance Parrish	.10
10	Dick Howser	.10
11	Keith Hernandez	.10
12	Darryl Strawberry	.15
13	Ryne Sandberg	.75
14	Dale Murphy	.25
15	Ozzie Smith	.45
16	Tony Gwynn	.85
17	Mike Schmidt	.75
18	Dwight Gooden	.15
19	Gary Carter	.15
20	Whitey Herzog	.10
21	Jose Canseco	.60
22	John Franco	.10
23	Jesse Barfield	.10
24	Rick Rhoden	.10
25	Harold Baines	.15
26	Sid Fernandez	.10
27	George Brett	.75
28	Steve Sax	.10
29	Jim Presley	.10
30	Dave Smith	.10
31	Eddie Murray	.40
32	Mike Scott	.10
33	Don Mattingly	.90
34	Dave Parker	.10
35	Tony Fernandez	.10
36	Tim Raines	.12
37	Brook Jacoby	.10
38	Chili Davis	.15
39	Rich Gedman	.10
40	Kevin Bass	.10
41	Frank White	.10
42	Glenn Davis	.10
43	Willie Hernandez	.10
44	Chris Brown	.10
45	Jim Rice	.10
46	Tony Pena	.10
47	Don Aase	.10
48	Hubie Brooks	.10
49	Charlie Hough	.10
50	Jody Davis	.10
51	Mike Witt	.10
52	Jeff Reardon	.10
53	Ken Schrom	.10
54	Fernando Valenzuela	.12
55	Dave Righetti	.10
56	Shane Rawley	.10
57	Ted Higuera	.10
58	Mike Krukow	.10
59	Lloyd Moseby	.10
60	Checklist	.05

1987 Donruss Diamond Kings Supers

For a third season, Donruss produced a set of enlarged Diamond Kings, measuring 4-11/16" x 6-3/4". The 28-cards feature the artwork of Dick Perez, and contain 26 player cards, a checklist and a Roberto Clemente puzzle card. The set was available through a mail-in offer for $9.50 plus three wrappers.

		MT
Complete Set (28):		7.50
Common Player:		.15
1	Wally Joyner	.25
2	Roger Clemens	1.50
3	Dale Murphy	.30
4	Darryl Strawberry	.25
5	Ozzie Smith	.50
6	Jose Canseco	.75
7	Charlie Hough	.15
8	Brook Jacoby	.15
9	Fred Lynn	.15
10	Rick Rhoden	.15
11	Chris Brown	.15
12	Von Hayes	.15
13	Jack Morris	.15
14	Kevin McReynolds	.15
15	George Brett	1.00
16	Ted Higuera	.15
17	Hubie Brooks	.15

18 Mike Scott .15
19 Kirby Puckett .75
20 Dave Winfield .40
21 Lloyd Moseby .15
22 Eric Davis .25
23 Jim Presley .15
24 Keith Moreland .15
25 Greg Walker .15
26 Steve Sax .15
27 Checklist .04
--- Roberto Clemente Puzzle Card .20

1987 Donruss Highlights

For a third consecutive year, Donruss produced a 56-card set which highlighted the special events of the 1987 baseball season. The 2-1/2" x 3-1/2" cards have a front design similar to the regular 1987 Donruss set. A blue border and the "Highlights" logo are the significant differences. The backs feature black print on a white background and include the date the event took place plus the particulars. As in the past, the set includes Donruss' picks for the A.L. and N.L. Rookies of the Year. The set was issued in a specially designed box and was available only through hobby dealers.

MT
Complete Unopended Set (56): 9.00
Complete Set (56): 5.00
Common Player: .10
1 First No-Hitter For Brewers (Juan Nieves) .10
2 Hits 500th Homer (Mike Schmidt) .75
3 N.L. Player of the Month - April (Eric Davis) .15
4 N.L. Pitcher of the Month - April (Sid Fernandez) .10
5 A.L. Player of the Month - April (Brian Downing) .10
6 A.L. Pitcher of the Month - April (Bret Saberhagen) .10
7 Free Agent Holdout Returns (Tim Raines) .10
8 N.L. Player of the Month - May (Eric Davis) .15
9 N.L. Pitcher of the Month - May (Steve Bedrosian) .10
10 A.L. Player of the Month - May (Larry Parrish) .10
11 A.L. Pitcher of the Month - May (Jim Clancy) .10
12 N.L. Player of the Month - June (Tony Gwynn) .35
13 N.L. Pitcher of the Month - June (Orel Hershiser) .10
14 A.L. Player of the Month - June (Wade Boggs) .35
15 A.L. Pitcher of the Month - June (Steve Ontiveros) .10
16 All Star Game Hero (Tim Raines) .10
17 Consecutive Game Homer Streak (Don Mattingly) .75
18 1987 Hall of Fame Inductee (Jim "Catfish" Hunter) .25
19 1987 Hall of Fame Inductee (Ray Dandridge) .25
20 1987 Hall of Fame Inductee (Billy Williams) .25
21 N.L. Player of the Month - July (Bo Diaz) .10
22 N.L. Pitcher of the Month - July (Floyd Youmans) .10
23 A.L. Player of the Month - July (Don Mattingly) .35
24 A.L. Pitcher of the Month - July (Frank Viola) .10
25 Strikes Out 4 Batters In 1 Inning (Bobby Witt) .10
26 Ties A.L. 9-Inning Game Hit Mark (Kevin Seitzer) .10
27 Sets Rookie Home Run Record (Mark McGwire) 1.50
28 Sets Cubs' 1st Year Homer Mark (Andre Dawson) .10
29 Hits In 39 Straight Games (Paul Molitor) .20
30 Record Weekend (Kirby Puckett) .35
31 N.L. Player of the Month - August (Andre Dawson) .10
32 N.L. Pitcher of the Month - August (Doug Drabek) .10
33 A.L. Player of the Month - August (Dwight Evans) .10
34 A.L. Pitcher of the Month - August (Mark Langston) .10
35 100 RBI In 1st 2 Major League Seasons (Wally Joyner) .10
36 100 SB In 1st 3 Major League Seasons (Vince Coleman) .10
37 Orioles' All Time Homer King (Eddie Murray) .25
38 Ends Consecutive Innings Streak (Cal Ripken) 1.50
39 Blue Jays Hit Record 10 Homers In 1 Game (Rob Ducey, Fred McGriff, Ernie Whitt) .10
40 Equal A's RBI Marks (Jose Canseco, Mark McGwire) 1.50
41 Sets All-Time Catching Record (Bob Boone) .10
42 Sets Mets' One-Season HR Mark (Darryl Strawberry) .15
43 N.L.'s All-Time Switch Hit HR King (Howard Johnson) .10
44 Five Straight 200-Hit Seasons (Wade Boggs) .35
45 Eclipses Rookie Game Hitting Streak (Benito Santiago) .10
46 Eclipses Jackson's A's HR Record (Mark McGwire) 2.00
47 13th Rookie To Collect 200 Hits (Kevin Seitzer) .10
48 Sets Slam Record (Don Mattingly) 2.00
49 N.L. Player of the Month - September (Darryl Strawberry) .15
50 N.L. Pitcher of the Month - September (Pascual Perez) .10
51 A.L. Player of the Month - September (Alan Trammell) .10
52 A.L. Pitcher of the Month - September (Doyle Alexander) .10
53 Strikeout King - Again (Nolan Ryan) 1.50
54 Donruss A.L. Rookie of the Year (Mark McGwire) 2.00
55 Donruss N.L. Rookie of the Year (Benito Santiago) .25
56 Highlight Checklist .10

1987 Donruss Opening Day

The Donruss Opening Day set includes all players in major league baseball's starting lineups on the opening day of the 1987 baseball season. Cards in the 272-piece set measure 2-1/2" x 3-1/2" and have a glossy coating. The fronts are identical in design to the regular Donruss set, but new photos were utilized along with maroon borders as opposed to black. The backs carry black printing on white and yellow and offer a brief player biography plus the player's career statistics. The set was packaged in a sturdy 15" by 5" by 2" box with a clear acetate lid.

MT
Complete Set (272): 12.00
Common Player: .10
1 Doug DeCinces .10
2 Mike Witt .10
3 George Hendrick .10
4 Dick Schofield .10
5 Devon White .15
6 Butch Wynegar .10
7 Wally Joyner .25
8 Mark McLemore .10
9 Brian Downing .10
10 Gary Pettis .10
11 Bill Doran .10
12 Phil Garner .10
13 Jose Cruz .10
14 Kevin Bass .10
15 Mike Scott .10
16 Glenn Davis .10
17 Alan Ashby .10
18 Billy Hatcher .10
19 Craig Reynolds .10
20 Carney Lansford .10
21 Mike Davis .10
22 Reggie Jackson .30
23 Mickey Tettleton .15
24 Jose Canseco 1.75
25 Rob Nelson .10
26 Tony Phillips .15
27 Dwayne Murphy .10
28 Alfredo Griffin .10
29 Curt Young .10
30 Willie Upshaw .10
31 Mike Sharperson .10
32 Rance Mulliniks .10
33 Ernie Whitt .10
34 Jesse Barfield .10
35 Tony Fernandez .10
36 Lloyd Moseby .10
37 Jimmy Key .15
38 Fred McGriff .40
39 George Bell .12
40 Dale Murphy .40
41 Rick Mahler .10
42 Ken Griffey .10
43 Andres Thomas .10
44 Dion James .10
45 Ozzie Virgil .10
46 Ken Oberkfell .10
47 Gary Roenicke .10
48 Glenn Hubbard .10
49 Bill Schroeder .10
50 Greg Brock .10
51 Billy Jo Robidoux .10
52 Glenn Braggs .10
53 Jim Gantner .10
54 Paul Molitor .35
55 Dale Sveum .10
56 Ted Higuera .10
57 Rob Deer .10
58 Robin Yount .65
59 Jim Lindeman .10
60 Vince Coleman .10
61 Tommy Herr .10
62 Terry Pendleton .10
63 John Tudor .10
64 Tony Pena .10
65 Ozzie Smith .55
66 Tito Landrum .10
67 Jack Clark .10
68 Bob Dernier .10
69 Rick Sutcliffe .10
70 Andre Dawson .25
71 Keith Moreland .10
72 Jody Davis .10
73 Brian Dayett .10
74 Leon Durham .10
75 Ryne Sandberg .75
76 Shawon Dunston .15
77 Mike Marshall .10
78 Bill Madlock .10
79 Orel Hershiser .15
80 Mike Ramsey .10
81 Ken Landreaux .10
82 Mike Scioscia .10
83 Franklin Stubbs .10
84 Mariano Duncan .10
85 Steve Sax .10
86 Mitch Webster .10
87 Reid Nichols .10
88 Tim Wallach .10
89 Floyd Youmans .10

90	Andres Galarraga	.25
91	Hubie Brooks	.10
92	Jeff Reed	.10
93	Alonzo Powell	.10
94	Vance Law	.10
95	Bob Brenly	.10
96	Will Clark	1.00
97	Chili Davis	.10
98	Mike Krukow	.10
99	Jose Uribe	.10
100	Chris Brown	.10
101	Rob Thompson	.10
102	Candy Maldonado	.10
103	Jeff Leonard	.10
104	Tom Candiotti	.10
105	Chris Bando	.10
106	Cory Snyder	.10
107	Pat Tabler	.10
108	Andre Thornton	.10
109	Joe Carter	.25
110	Tony Bernazard	.10
111	Julio Franco	.12
112	Brook Jacoby	.10
113	Brett Butler	.15
114	Donnell Nixon	.10
115	Alvin Davis	.10
116	Mark Langston	.12
117	Harold Reynolds	.10
118	Ken Phelps	.10
119	Mike Kingery	.10
120	Dave Valle	.10
121	Rey Quinones	.10
122	Phil Bradley	.10
123	Jim Presley	.10
124	Keith Hernandez	.10
125	Kevin McReynolds	.10
126	Rafael Santana	.10
127	Bob Ojeda	.10
128	Darryl Strawberry	.25
129	Mookie Wilson	.10
130	Gary Carter	.15
131	Tim Teufel	.10
132	Howard Johnson	.10
133	Cal Ripken, Jr.	2.50
134	Rick Burleson	.10
135	Fred Lynn	.10
136	Eddie Murray	.40
137	Ray Knight	.10
138	Alan Wiggins	.10
139	John Shelby	.10
140	Mike Boddicker	.10
141	Ken Gerhart	.10
142	Terry Kennedy	.10
143	Steve Garvey	.25
144	Marvell Wynne	.10
145	Kevin Mitchell	.15
146	Tony Gwynn	.75
147	Joey Cora	.10
148	Benito Santiago	.15
149	Eric Show	.10
150	Garry Templeton	.10
151	Carmelo Martinez	.10
152	Von Hayes	.10
153	Lance Parrish	.12
154	Milt Thompson	.10
155	Mike Easler	.10
156	Juan Samuel	.10
157	Steve Jeltz	.10
158	Glenn Wilson	.10
159	Shane Rawley	.10
160	Mike Schmidt	.75
161	Andy Van Slyke	.10
162	Johnny Ray	.10
163a	Barry Bonds (dark jersey, photo actually Johnny Ray)	175.00
163b	Barry Bonds (white jersey, correct photo)	2.50
164	Junior Ortiz	.10
165	Rafael Belliard	.10
166	Bob Patterson	.10
167	Bobby Bonilla	.25
168	Sid Bream	.10
169	Jim Morrison	.10
170	Jerry Browne	.10
171	Scott Fletcher	.10
172	Ruben Sierra	.12
173	Larry Parrish	.10
174	Pete O'Brien	.10
175	Pete Incaviglia	.12
176	Don Slaught	.10
177	Oddibe McDowell	.10
178	Charlie Hough	.10
179	Steve Buechele	.10
180	Bob Stanley	.10
181	Wade Boggs	.75
182	Jim Rice	.10
183	Bill Buckner	.10
184	Dwight Evans	.10
185	Spike Owen	.10
186	Don Baylor	.12
187	Marc Sullivan	.10
188	Marty Barrett	.10
189	Dave Henderson	.10
190	Bo Diaz	.10
191	Barry Larkin	.35
192	Kal Daniels	.10
193	Terry Francona	.10
194	Tom Browning	.10
195	Ron Oester	.10
196	Buddy Bell	.10
197	Eric Davis	.15
198	Dave Parker	.12
199	Steve Balboni	.10
200	Danny Tartabull	.10
201	Ed Hearn	.10
202	Buddy Biancalana	.10
203	Danny Jackson	.10
204	Frank White	.10
205	Bo Jackson	.50
206	George Brett	.75
207	Kevin Seitzer	.10
208	Willie Wilson	.10
209	Orlando Mercado	.10
210	Darrell Evans	.10
211	Larry Herndon	.10
212	Jack Morris	.10
213	Chet Lemon	.10
214	Mike Heath	.10
215	Darnell Coles	.10
216	Alan Trammell	.15
217	Terry Harper	.10
218	Lou Whitaker	.10
219	Gary Gaetti	.15
220	Tom Nieto	.10
221	Kirby Puckett	.75
222	Tom Brunansky	.10
223	Greg Gagne	.10
224	Dan Gladden	.10
225	Mark Davidson	.10
226	Bert Blyleven	.10
227	Steve Lombardozzi	.10
228	Kent Hrbek	.12
229	Gary Redus	.10
230	Ivan Calderon	.10
231	Tim Hulett	.10
232	Carlton Fisk	.15
233	Greg Walker	.10
234	Ron Karkovice	.10
235	Ozzie Guillen	.10
236	Harold Baines	.10
237	Donnie Hill	.10
238	Rich Dotson	.10
239	Mike Pagliarulo	.10
240	Joel Skinner	.10
241	Don Mattingly	1.50
242	Gary Ward	.10
243	Dave Winfield	.40
244	Dan Pasqua	.10
245	Wayne Tolleson	.10
246	Willie Randolph	.10
247	Dennis Rasmussen	.10
248	Rickey Henderson	.40
249	Angels Checklist	.05
250	Astros Checklist	.05
251	Athletics Checklist	.05
252	Blue Jays Checklist	.05
253	Braves Checklist	.05
254	Brewers Checklist	.05
255	Cardinals Checklist	.05
256	Dodgers Checklist	.05
257	Expos Checklist	.05
258	Giants Checklist	.05
259	Indians Checklist	.05
260	Mariners Checklist	.05
261	Orioles Checklist	.05
262	Padres Checklist	.05
263	Phillies Checklist	.05
264	Pirates Checklist	.05
265	Rangers Checklist	.05
266	Red Sox Checklist	.05
267	Reds Checklist	.05
268	Royals Checklist	.05
269	Tigers Checklist	.05
270	Twins Checklist	.05
271	White Sox/Cubs Checklist	.05
272	Yankees/Mets Checklist	.05

1987 Donruss Pop-Ups

For the second straight year, Donruss released in conjunction with its All-Stars issue a set of cards designed to fold out to form a three-dimensional stand-up card. Consisting of 20 cards, as opposed to the previous year's 18, the 1987 Donruss Pop-Ups set contains players selected to the 1986 All-Star Game. Background for the 2-1/2" x 5" cards is the Houston Astrodome, site of the 1986 mid-summer classic. Retail packs included one Pop-Up card, three All-Star cards and one Roberto Clemente puzzle card.

		MT
Complete Set (20):		3.00
Common Player:		.20
Roberto Clemente Puzzle:		9.00
(1)	Wade Boggs	.50
(2)	Gary Carter	.25
(3)	Roger Clemens	.90
(4)	Dwight Gooden	.25
(5)	Tony Gwynn	.80
(6)	Rickey Henderson	.40
(7)	Keith Hernandez	.20
(8)	Whitey Herzog	.20
(9)	Dick Howser	.20
(10)	Wally Joyner	.25
(11)	Dale Murphy	.30
(12)	Lance Parrish	.20
(13)	Kirby Puckett	.75
(14)	Cal Ripken, Jr.	1.50
(15)	Ryne Sandberg	.75
(16)	Mike Schmidt	.75
(17)	Ozzie Smith	.40
(18)	Darryl Strawberry	.25
(19)	Lou Whitaker	.20
(20)	Dave Winfield	.35

1987 Donruss Rookies

As they did in 1986, Donruss issued a 56-card set highlighting the major leagues' most promising rookies. The cards are standard 2-1/2" x 3-1/2" and are identical in design to the regular Donruss issue. The card fronts have green borders as opposed to the black found in the regular issue and carry the words "The Rookies" in the lower-left portion of the card. The set came housed in a specially designed box and was available only through hobby dealers.

		MT
Comp. Unopened Set (56):		35.00
Complete Set (56):		30.00
Common Player:		.05
1	Mark McGwire	20.00
2	Eric Bell	.05
3	Mark Williamson	.05
4	Mike Greenwell	.08
5	Ellis Burks	.10
6	DeWayne Buice	.05
7	Mark Mclemore (McLemore)	.08
8	Devon White	.10
9	Willie Fraser	.05
10	Lester Lancaster	.05
11	Ken Williams	.05
12	Matt Nokes	.05
13	Jeff Robinson	.05
14	Bo Jackson	.50
15	Kevin Seitzer	.05
16	Billy Ripken	.05
17	B.J. Surhoff	.10
18	Chuck Crim	.05
19	Mike Birbeck	.05
20	Chris Bosio	.05
21	Les Straker	.05
22	Mark Davidson	.05
23	Gene Larkin	.05
24	Ken Gerhart	.05
25	Luis Polonia	.05
26	Terry Steinbach	.08
27	Mickey Brantley	.05
28	Mike Stanley	.05
29	Jerry Browne	.05
30	Todd Benzinger	.05
31	Fred McGriff	.75
32	Mike Henneman	.08
33	Casey Candaele	.05
34	Dave Magadan	.05
35	David Cone	1.00
36	Mike Jackson	.05
37	John Mitchell	.05
38	Mike Dunne	.05
39	John Smiley	.05
40	Joe Magrane	.05
41	Jim Lindeman	.05
42	Shane Mack	.05
43	Stan Jefferson	.05
44	Benito Santiago	.08
45	*Matt Williams*	2.00
46	Dave Meads	.05
47	Rafael Palmeiro	5.00
48	Bill Long	.05
49	Bob Brower	.05
50	James Steels	.05
51	Paul Noce	.05
52	Greg Maddux	12.00
53	Jeff Musselman	.05
54	Brian Holton	.05
55	Chuck Jackson	.05
56	Checklist 1-56	.03

1988 Donruss

The 1988 Donruss set consists of 660 cards, each measuring 2-1/2" x 3-1/2". Fronts feature a full-color photo surrounded by a colorful border - alternating stripes of black, red, black, blue, black, blue, black, red and black (in that order) - separated by soft-focus edges and airbrushed fades. The player's name and position appear in a red band at the bottom of the card. The Donruss logo is situated in the upper-left corner, while the team logo is located in the lower-right. For the seventh consecutive season, Donruss included a subset of "Diamond Kings" cards (#1-27) in the issue. And for the fifth straight year, Donruss incorporated the popular "Rated Rookies" (card #28-47) with the set. Twenty-six of the cards between #603-660 were short-printed to accommodate the printing of the 26 MVP insert cards.

		MT
Comp. Factory Set, Sealed (660):		15.00
Complete Set (660):		12.00
Common Player:		.05
Stan Musial Puzzle:		1.00
Pack (15):		.60
Wax Box (36):		11.00
1	Mark McGwire (DK)	.75
2	Tim Raines (DK)	.08
3	Benito Santiago (DK)	.08
4	Alan Trammell (DK)	.08
5	Danny Tartabull (DK)	.05
6	Ron Darling (DK)	.08
7	Paul Molitor (DK)	.15
8	Devon White (DK)	.10
9	Andre Dawson (DK)	.10
10	Julio Franco (DK)	.10
11	Scott Fletcher (DK)	.08
12	Tony Fernandez (DK)	.10
13	Shane Rawley (DK)	.05
14	Kal Daniels (DK)	.05
15	Jack Clark (DK)	.08
16	Dwight Evans (DK)	.08
17	Tommy John (DK)	.08
18	Andy Van Slyke (DK)	.10
19	Gary Gaetti (DK)	.08
20	Mark Langston (DK)	.08
21	Will Clark (DK)	.25
22	Glenn Hubbard (DK)	.05
23	Billy Hatcher (DK)	.05
24	Bob Welch (DK)	.05
25	Ivan Calderon (DK)	.05
26	Cal Ripken, Jr. (DK)	.35
27	Checklist 1-27	.05
28	*Mackey Sasser* (RR)	.10
29	*Jeff Treadway* (RR)	.05
30	*Mike Campbell* (RR)	.05
31	*Lance Johnson* (RR)	.15
32	*Nelson Liriano* (RR)	.08
33	Shawn Abner (RR)	.05
34	*Roberto Alomar* (RR)	1.50
35	*Shawn Hillegas* (RR)	.05
36	Joey Meyer (RR)	.05
37	Kevin Elster (RR)	.10
38	*Jose Lind* (RR)	.12
39	*Kirt Manwaring* (RR)	.15
40	*Mark Grace* (RR)	.50
41	*Jody Reed* (RR)	.15
42	*John Farrell* (RR)	.05
43	*Al Leiter* (RR)	.25
44	*Gary Thurman* (RR)	.08
45	*Vicente Palacios* (RR)	.05
46	*Eddie Williams* (RR)	.10
47	*Jack McDowell* (RR)	.25
48	Ken Dixon	.05
49	Mike Birkbeck	.05
50	Eric King	.05
51	Roger Clemens	.40
52	Pat Clements	.05
53	Fernando Valenzuela	.08
54	Mark Gubicza	.08
55	Jay Howell	.05
56	Floyd Youmans	.05
57	Ed Correa	.05
58	*DeWayne Buice*	.10
59	Jose DeLeon	.05
60	Danny Cox	.05
61	Nolan Ryan	.60
62	Steve Bedrosian	.05
63	Tom Browning	.05
64	Mark Davis	.05
65	R.J. Reynolds	.05
66	Kevin Mitchell	.05
67	Ken Oberkfell	.05
68	Rick Sutcliffe	.08
69	Dwight Gooden	.12
70	Scott Bankhead	.05
71	Bert Blyleven	.10
72	Jimmy Key	.10
73	*Les Straker*	.05
74	Jim Clancy	.05
75	Mike Moore	.05
76	Ron Darling	.08
77	Ed Lynch	.05
78	Dale Murphy	.15
79	Doug Drabek	.08
80	Scott Garrelts	.05
81	Ed Whitson	.05
82	Rob Murphy	.05
83	Shane Rawley	.05
84	Greg Mathews	.05
85	Jim Deshaies	.08
86	Mike Witt	.08
87	Donnie Hill	.05
88	Jeff Reed	.05
89	Mike Boddicker	.05
90	Ted Higuera	.05
91	Walt Terrell	.05
92	Bob Stanley	.05
93	Dave Righetti	.08
94	Orel Hershiser	.10
95	Chris Bando	.05
96	Bret Saberhagen	.10
97	Curt Young	.05
98	Tim Burke	.05
99	Charlie Hough	.08
100a	Checklist 28-137	.05
100b	Checklist 28-133	.10
101	Bobby Witt	.10
102	George Brett	.40
103	Mickey Tettleton	.08
104	Scott Bailes	.05
105	Mike Pagliarulo	.08
106	Mike Scioscia	.05
107	Tom Brookens	.05
108	Ray Knight	.08
109	Dan Plesac	.05
110	Wally Joyner	.12
111	Bob Forsch	.05
112	Mike Scott	.08
113	Kevin Gross	.05
114	Benito Santiago	.10
115	Bob Kipper	.05
116	Mike Krukow	.05
117	Chris Bosio	.05
118	Sid Fernandez	.05
119	Jody Davis	.05
120	Mike Morgan	.05
121	Mark Eichhorn	.05
122	Jeff Reardon	.05
123	John Franco	.08
124	Richard Dotson	.05
125	Eric Bell	.05
126	Juan Nieves	.05
127	Jack Morris	.08
128	Rick Rhoden	.05
129	Rich Gedman	.05
130	Ken Howell	.05
131	Brook Jacoby	.05
132	Danny Jackson	.05
133	Gene Nelson	.05
134	Neal Heaton	.05
135	Willie Fraser	.05
136	Jose Guzman	.05
137	Ozzie Guillen	.08
138	Bob Knepper	.05
139	*Mike Jackson*	.10
140	*Joe Magrane*	.08
141	Jimmy Jones	.05
142	Ted Power	.05
143	Ozzie Virgil	.05
144	*Felix Fermin*	.08
145	Kelly Downs	.05
146	Shawon Dunston	.08
147	Scott Bradley	.05
148	Dave Stieb	.10
149	Frank Viola	.10
150	Terry Kennedy	.05
151	Bill Wegman	.05
152	*Matt Nokes*	.10
153	Wade Boggs	.35
154	Wayne Tolleson	.05
155	Mariano Duncan	.05
156	Julio Franco	.08
157	Charlie Leibrandt	.05
158	Terry Steinbach	.10
159	Mike Fitzgerald	.05
160	Jack Lazorko	.05
161	Mitch Williams	.08
162	Greg Walker	.05
163	Alan Ashby	.05
164	Tony Gwynn	.40
165	Bruce Ruffin	.05
166	Ron Robinson	.05
167	Zane Smith	.05
168	Junior Ortiz	.05
169	Jamie Moyer	.05
170	Tony Pena	.05
171	Cal Ripken, Jr.	.50
172	B.J. Surhoff	.10
173	Lou Whitaker	.10
174	*Ellis Burks*	.25
175	Ron Guidry	.10
176	Steve Sax	.05
177	Danny Tartabull	.05
178	Carney Lansford	.05
179	Casey Candaele	.05
180	Scott Fletcher	.05
181	Mark McLemore	.05
182	Ivan Calderon	.05
183	Jack Clark	.08
184	Glenn Davis	.05
185	Luis Aguayo	.05
186	Bo Diaz	.05
187	Stan Jefferson	.05
188	Sid Bream	.05
189	Bob Brenly	.05
190	Dion James	.05
191	Leon Durham	.05
192	Jesse Orosco	.05
193	Alvin Davis	.05
194	Gary Gaetti	.08
195	Fred McGriff	.25
196	Steve Lombardozzi	.05
197	Rance Mulliniks	.05
198	Rey Quinones	.05
199	Gary Carter	.10
200a	Checklist 138-247	.05
200b	Checklist 134-239	.10
201	Keith Moreland	.05
202	Ken Griffey	.08
203	*Tommy Gregg*	.05
204	Will Clark	.25
205	John Kruk	.08
206	Buddy Bell	.08
207	Von Hayes	.05
208	Tommy Herr	.05
209	Craig Reynolds	.05
210	Gary Pettis	.05
211	Harold Baines	.10
212	Vance Law	.05
213	Ken Gerhart	.05
214	Jim Gantner	.05
215	Chet Lemon	.05
216	Dwight Evans	.10
217	Don Mattingly	.35
218	Franklin Stubbs	.05
219	Pat Tabler	.05
220	Bo Jackson	.25
221	Tony Phillips	.08
222	Tim Wallach	.08
223	Ruben Sierra	.05
224	Steve Buechele	.05
225	Frank White	.05
226	Alfredo Griffin	.05
227	Greg Swindell	.05
228	Willie Randolph	.08
229	Mike Marshall	.05
230	Alan Trammell	.15
231	Eddie Murray	.20
232	Dale Sveum	.05
233	Dick Schofield	.05
234	Jose Oquendo	.05
235	Bill Doran	.05
236	Milt Thompson	.05
237	Marvell Wynne	.05
238	Bobby Bonilla	.15
239	Chris Speier	.05
240	Glenn Braggs	.05
241	Wally Backman	.05
242	Ryne Sandberg	.30
243	Phil Bradley	.05
244	Kelly Gruber	.05
245	Tom Brunansky	.05
246	Ron Oester	.05
247	Bobby Thigpen	.05
248	Fred Lynn	.08
249	Paul Molitor	.30
250	Darrell Evans	.10
251	Gary Ward	.05
252	Bruce Hurst	.05
253	Bob Welch	.08
254	Joe Carter	.10
255	Willie Wilson	.10
256	Mark McGwire	1.50
257	Mitch Webster	.05
258	Brian Downing	.05
259	Mike Stanley	.05
260	Carlton Fisk	.15
261	Billy Hatcher	.05
262	Glenn Wilson	.05
263	Ozzie Smith	.25
264	Randy Ready	.05
265	Kurt Stillwell	.05
266	David Palmer	.05
267	Mike Diaz	.05
268	Rob Thompson	.05
269	Andre Dawson	.15
270	Lee Guetterman	.05
271	Willie Upshaw	.05
272	Randy Bush	.05
273	Larry Sheets	.05
274	Rob Deer	.05
275	Kirk Gibson	.08
276	Marty Barrett	.05
277	Rickey Henderson	.20
278	Pedro Guerrero	.05
279	Brett Butler	.08
280	Kevin Seitzer	.08
281	Mike Davis	.05
282	Andres Galarraga	.20
283	Devon White	.12
284	Pete O'Brien	.05
285	Jerry Hairston	.05
286	Kevin Bass	.05
287	Carmelo Martinez	.05
288	Juan Samuel	.08
289	Kal Daniels	.05
290	Albert Hall	.05
291	Andy Van Slyke	.08
292	Lee Smith	.10
293	Vince Coleman	.08
294	Tom Niedenfuer	.05
295	Robin Yount	.25
296	*Jeff Robinson*	.05
297	*Todd Benzinger*	.10
298	Dave Winfield	.15
299	Mickey Hatcher	.05
300a	Checklist 248-357	.05
300b	Checklist 240-345	.10
301	Bud Black	.05
302	Jose Canseco	.25
303	Tom Foley	.05
304	Pete Incaviglia	.05
305	Bob Boone	.08
306	*Bill Long*	.05
307	Willie McGee	.10
308	*Ken Caminiti*	.50
309	Darren Daulton	.08
310	Tracy Jones	.05

311 Greg Booker .05
312 Mike LaValliere .08
313 Chili Davis .10
314 Glenn Hubbard .05
315 *Paul Noce* .05
316 Keith Hernandez .08
317 Mark Langston .12
318 Keith Atherton .05
319 Tony Fernandez .10
320 Kent Hrbek .08
321 John Cerutti .05
322 Mike Kingery .05
323 Dave Magadan .08
324 Rafael Palmeiro .20
325 Jeff Dedmon .05
326 Barry Bonds .50
327 Jeffrey Leonard .05
328 Tim Flannery .05
329 Dave Concepcion .05
330 Mike Schmidt .30
331 Bill Dawley .05
332 Larry Andersen .05
333 Jack Howell .05
334 *Ken Williams* .05
335 Bryn Smith .05
336 *Billy Ripken* .08
337 Greg Brock .05
338 Mike Heath .05
339 Mike Greenwell .08
340 Claudell Washington .05
341 Jose Gonzalez .05
342 Mel Hall .05
343 Jim Eisenreich .05
344 Tony Bernazard .05
345 Tim Raines .08
346 Bob Brower .05
347 Larry Parrish .05
348 Thad Bosley .05
349 Dennis Eckersley .12
350 Cory Snyder .05
351 Rick Cerone .05
352 John Shelby .05
353 Larry Herndon .05
354 John Habyan .05
355 *Chuck Crim* .05
356 Gus Polidor .05
357 Ken Dayley .05
358 Danny Darwin .05
359 Lance Parrish .10
360 *James Steels* .05
361 *Al Pedrique* .05
362 Mike Aldrete .05
363 Juan Castillo .05
364 Len Dykstra .10
365 Luis Quinones .05
366 Jim Presley .05
367 Lloyd Moseby .05
368 Kirby Puckett .50
369 Eric Davis .12
370 Gary Redus .05
371 Dave Schmidt .05
372 Mark Clear .05
373 Dave Bergman .05
374 Charles Hudson .05
375 Calvin Schiraldi .05
376 Alex Trevino .05
377 Tom Candiotti .05
378 Steve Farr .05
379 Mike Gallego .05
380 Andy McGaffigan .05
381 Kirk McCaskill .08
382 Oddibe McDowell .05
383 Floyd Bannister .05
384 Denny Walling .05
385 Don Carman .05
386 Todd Worrell .08
387 Eric Show .05
388 Dave Parker .08
389 Rick Mahler .05
390 *Mike Dunne* .08
391 Candy Maldonado .05
392 Bob Dernier .05
393 Dave Valle .05
394 Ernie Whitt .05
395 Juan Berenguer .05
396 Mike Young .05
397 Mike Felder .05
398 Willie Hernandez .05
399 Jim Rice .10
400a Checklist 358-467 .05
400b Checklist 346-451 .10
401 Tommy John .15
402 Brian Holton .05
403 Carmen Castillo .05
404 Jamie Quirk .05
405 Dwayne Murphy .05
406 *Jeff Parrett* .05
407 Don Sutton .15
408 Jerry Browne .05
409 Jim Winn .05
410 Dave Smith .05
411 *Shane Mack* .15
412 Greg Gross .05
413 Nick Esasky .05
414 Damaso Garcia .05
415 Brian Fisher .05
416 Brian Dayett .05
417 Curt Ford .05
418 *Mark Williamson* .05
419 Bill Schroeder .05
420 *Mike Henneman* .15
421 *John Marzano* .05
422 Ron Kittle .05
423 Matt Young .05
424 Steve Balboni .05
425 *Luis Polonia* .10
426 Randy St. Claire .05
427 Greg Harris .05
428 Johnny Ray .05
429 Ray Searage .05
430 Ricky Horton .05
431 *Gerald Young* .05
432 Rick Schu .05
433 Paul O'Neill .25
434 Rich Gossage .12
435 John Cangelosi .05
436 Mike LaCoss .05
437 Gerald Perry .05
438 Dave Martinez .05
439 Darryl Strawberry .15
440 John Moses .05
441 Greg Gagne .05
442 Jesse Barfield .05
443 George Frazier .05
444 Garth Iorg .05
445 Ed Nunez .05
446 Rick Aguilera .05
447 Jerry Mumphrey .05
448 Rafael Ramirez .05
449 *John Smiley* .10
450 Atlee Hammaker .05
451 Lance McCullers .05
452 Guy Hoffman .05
453 Chris James .05
454 Terry Pendleton .05
455 *Dave Meads* .05
456 Bill Buckner .08
457 *John Pawlowski* .05
458 Bob Sebra .05
459 Jim Dwyer .05
460 *Jay Aldrich* .05
461 Frank Tanana .05
462 Oil Can Boyd .05
463 Dan Pasqua .08
464 *Tim Crews* .10
465 Andy Allanson .05
466 *Bill Pecota* .05
467 Steve Ontiveros .05
468 Hubie Brooks .05
469 *Paul Kilgus* .05
470 Dale Mohorcic .05
471 Dan Quisenberry .08
472 Dave Stewart .10
473 Dave Clark .05
474 Joel Skinner .05
475 Dave Anderson .05
476 Dan Petry .05
477 *Carl Nichols* .05
478 Ernest Riles .05
479 George Hendrick .05
480 John Morris .05
481 *Manny Hernandez* .05
482 Jeff Stone .05
483 Chris Brown .05
484 Mike Bielecki .05
485 Dave Dravecky .08
486 Rick Manning .05
487 Bill Almon .05
488 Jim Sundberg .05
489 Ken Phelps .05
490 Tom Henke .08
491 Dan Gladden .05
492 Barry Larkin .15
493 *Fred Manrique* .05
494 Mike Griffin .05
495 *Mark Knudson* .05
496 Bill Madlock .10
497 Tim Stoddard .05
498 *Sam Horn* .05
499 *Tracy Woodson* .05
500a Checklist 468-577 .05
500b Checklist 452-557 .10
501 Ken Schrom .05
502 Angel Salazar .05
503 Eric Plunk .05
504 Joe Hesketh .05
505 Greg Minton .05
506 Geno Petralli .05
507 Bob James .05
508 *Robbie Wine* .05
509 Jeff Calhoun .05
510 Steve Lake .05
511 Mark Grant .05
512 Frank Williams .05
513 *Jeff Blauser* .15
514 Bob Walk .05
515 Craig Lefferts .05
516 Manny Trillo .05
517 Jerry Reed .05
518 Rick Leach .05
519 *Mark Davidson* .05
520 *Jeff Ballard* .05
521 *Dave Stapleton* .05
522 Pat Sheridan .05
523 Al Nipper .05
524 Steve Trout .05
525 Jeff Hamilton .05
526 *Tommy Hinzo* .05
527 Lonnie Smith .05
528 *Greg Cadaret* .05
529 Rob McClure (Bob) .05
530 Chuck Finley .10
531 Jeff Russell .05
532 Steve Lyons .05
533 Terry Puhl .05
534 *Eric Nolte* .05
535 Kent Tekulve .05
536 *Pat Pacillo* .05
537 Charlie Puleo .05
538 *Tom Prince* .05
539 Greg Maddux 1.00
540 Jim Lindeman .05
541 *Pete Stanicek* .05
542 Steve Kiefer .05
543 Jim Morrison .05
544 Spike Owen .05
545 *Jay Buhner* .75
546 *Mike Devereaux* .15
547 Jerry Don Gleaton .05
548 Jose Rijo .05
549 Dennis Martinez .10
550 Mike Loynd .05
551 Darrell Miller .05
552 Dave LaPoint .05
553 John Tudor .05
554 *Rocky Childress* .05
555 *Wally Ritchie* .05
556 Terry McGriff .05
557 Dave Leiper .05
558 Jeff Robinson .05
559 Jose Uribe .05
560 Ted Simmons .05
561 *Lester Lancaster* .10
562 *Keith Miller* .05
563 Harold Reynolds .08
564 *Gene Larkin* .05
565 Cecil Fielder .10
566 Roy Smalley .05
567 Duane Ward .08
568 *Bill Wilkinson* .05
569 Howard Johnson .08
570 Frank DiPino .05
571 *Pete Smith* .05
572 Darnell Coles .05
573 Don Robinson .05
574 Rob Nelson .05
575 Dennis Rasmussen .05
576 Steve Jeltz (photo actually Juan Samuel) .05
577 *Tom Pagnozzi* .08
578 Ty Gainey .05
579 Gary Lucas .05
580 Ron Hassey .05
581 Herm Winningham .05
582 *Rene Gonzales* .05
583 Brad Komminsk .05
584 Doyle Alexander .05
585 Jeff Sellers .05
586 Bill Gullickson .05
587 Tim Belcher .08
588 *Doug Jones* .10
589 *Melido Perez* .10
590 Rick Honeycutt .05
591 Pascual Perez .05
592 Curt Wilkerson .05
593 Steve Howe .05
594 *John Davis* .05
595 Storm Davis .05
596 Sammy Stewart .05
597 Neil Allen .05
598 Alejandro Pena .05
599 Mark Thurmond .05
600a Checklist 578-BC26 .05
600b Checklist 558-660 .10
601 *Jose Mesa* .10
602 *Don August* .05
603 Terry Leach (SP) .10
604 *Tom Newell* .05
605 *Randall Byers* (SP) .10
606 Jim Gott .05
607 Harry Spilman .05
608 John Candelaria .05
609 *Mike Brumley* .05
610 Mickey Brantley .05
611 *Jose Nunez* (SP) .10
612 Tom Nieto .05
613 Rick Reuschel .05
614 Lee Mazzilli (SP) .10
615 *Scott Lusader* .05
616 Bobby Meacham .05
617 Kevin McReynolds (SP) .15
618 Gene Garber .05
619 *Barry Lyons* (SP) .10
620 Randy Myers .10
621 Donnie Moore .05
622 Domingo Ramos .05
623 Ed Romero .05
624 *Greg Myers* .08
625 Ripken Baseball Family (Billy Ripken, Cal Ripken, Jr., Cal Ripken, Sr.) .30
626 Pat Perry .05
627 Andres Thomas (SP) .10
628 Matt Williams (SP) .75
629 *Dave Hengel* .05
630 Jeff Musselman (SP) .10
631 Tim Laudner .05
632 Bob Ojeda (SP) .12
633 Rafael Santana .05
634 *Wes Gardner* .05
635 *Roberto Kelly* (SP) .15
636 Mike Flanagan (SP) .10
637 *Jay Bell* .35
638 Bob Melvin .05
639 *Damon Berryhill* .10
640 *David Wells* (SP) .40
641 Stan Musial Puzzle Card .05
642 Doug Sisk .05
643 *Keith Hughes* .05
644 *Tom Glavine* .50
645 Al Newman .05
646 Scott Sanderson .05
647 Scott Terry .05
648 Tim Teufel (SP) .12
649 Garry Templeton (SP) .10
650 Manny Lee (SP) .10
651 Roger McDowell (SP) .15
652 Mookie Wilson (SP) .15
653 David Cone (SP) .25
654 *Ron Gant* (SP) .25
655 Joe Price (SP) .10
656 George Bell (SP) .15
657 *Gregg Jefferies* (SP) .25
658 *Todd Stottlemyre* (SP) .15
659 *Geronimo Berroa* (SP) .30
660 Jerry Royster (SP) .10

1988 Donruss MVP

This 26-card set of standard-size player cards replaced the Donruss box-bottom cards in 1988. The bonus cards (numbered BC1 - BC26) were randomly inserted in Donruss wax or rack packs. Cards feature the company's choice of Most Valuable Player for each major league team and are titled "Donruss MVP." The MVP cards were not included in the factory-collated sets. Fronts carry the same basic red-blue-black border design as the 1988 Donruss basic issue. Backs are the same as the regular issue, except for the numbering system.

		MT
Complete Set (26):		5.00
Common Player:		.15
1	Cal Ripken, Jr.	1.00
2	Eric Davis	.15
3	Paul Molitor	.40
4	Mike Schmidt	.45
5	Ivan Calderon	.15
6	Tony Gwynn	.50
7	Wade Boggs	.40
8	Andy Van Slyke	.15
9	Joe Carter	.15
10	Andre Dawson	.20
11	Alan Trammell	.20
12	Mike Scott	.15
13	Wally Joyner	.20
14	Dale Murphy	.20
15	Kirby Puckett	.60
16	Pedro Guerrero	.15
17	Kevin Seitzer	.15
18	Tim Raines	.20
19	George Bell	.15
20	Darryl Strawberry	.25
21	Don Mattingly	.60
22	Ozzie Smith	.40
23	Mark McGwire	1.00
24	Will Clark	.25
25	Alvin Davis	.15
26	Ruben Sierra	.15

1988 Donruss All-Stars

For the third consecutive year, this set of 64 cards was marketed in conjunction with Donruss Pop-Ups. The 1988 issue included a major change - the cards were reduced in size from 3-1/2" x 5" to a standard 2-1/2" x 3-1/2". The set features players from the 1987 All-Star Game starting lineup. Card fronts feature full-color photos, framed in blue, black and white, with a Donruss logo at upper-left. Player name and position appear in a red banner below the photo, along with the appropriate National or American League logo. Backs include player stats and All-Star Game record. In 1988, All-Stars cards were distributed in individual packages containing three All-Stars, one Pop-Up and three Stan Musial puzzle pieces.

		MT
Complete Set (64):		3.00
Common Player:		.10
Stan Musial Puzzle:		1.00
1	Don Mattingly	.90
2	Dave Winfield	.25
3	Willie Randolph	.10
4	Rickey Henderson	.40
5	Cal Ripken, Jr.	1.25
6	George Bell	.10
7	Wade Boggs	.75
8	Bret Saberhagen	.10
9	Terry Kennedy	.10
10	John McNamara	.10
11	Jay Howell	.10
12	Harold Baines	.10
13	Harold Reynolds	.10
14	Bruce Hurst	.10
15	Kirby Puckett	.75
16	Matt Nokes	.10
17	Pat Tabler	.10
18	Dan Plesac	.10
19	Mark McGwire	1.50
20	Mike Witt	.10
21	Larry Parrish	.10
22	Alan Trammell	.15
23	Dwight Evans	.10
24	Jack Morris	.10
25	Tony Fernandez	.10
26	Mark Langston	.10
27	Kevin Seitzer	.10
28	Tom Henke	.10
29	Dave Righetti	.10
30	Oakland Coliseum	.10
31	Wade Boggs (Top Vote Getter)	.35
32	Checklist 1-32	.05
33	Jack Clark	.10
34	Darryl Strawberry	.15
35	Ryne Sandberg	.75
36	Andre Dawson	.15
37	Ozzie Smith	.40
38	Eric Davis	.15
39	Mike Schmidt	.75
40	Mike Scott	.10
41	Gary Carter	.12
42	Davey Johnson	.10
43	Rick Sutcliffe	.10
44	Willie McGee	.10
45	Hubie Brooks	.10
46	Dale Murphy	.30
47	Bo Diaz	.10
48	Pedro Guerrero	.10
49	Keith Hernandez	.10
50	Ozzie Virgil	.10
51	Tony Gwynn	.60
52	Rick Reuschel	.10
53	John Franco	.10
54	Jeffrey Leonard	.10
55	Juan Samuel	.10
56	Orel Hershiser	.10
57	Tim Raines	.10
58	Sid Fernandez	.10
59	Tim Wallach	.10
60	Lee Smith	.10
61	Steve Bedrosian	.10
62	(Tim Raines) (MVP)	.15
63	(Ozzie Smith) (Top Vote Getter)	.15
64	Checklist 33-64	.05

1988 Donruss Baseball's Best

The design of this 336-card set is similar to the regular 1988 Donruss issue with the exception of the borders which are orange, instead of blue. Player photos on the glossy front are framed by the Donruss logo upper-left, team logo lower-right and a bright red and white player name that spans the bottom margin. Backs are black and white, framed by a yellow border, and include personal information, year-by-year stats and major league totals. This set was packaged in a bright red cardboard box containing six individually shrink-wrapped packs of 56 cards. Donruss marketed the set via retail chain outlets with a suggested retail price of $21.95.

		MT
Complete Set (336):		9.00
Common Player:		.05
1	Don Mattingly	.75
2	Ron Gant	.10
3	Bob Boone	.08
4	Mark Grace	.45
5	Andy Allanson	.05
6	Kal Daniels	.05
7	Floyd Bannister	.05
8	Alan Ashby	.05
9	Marty Barrett	.05
10	Tim Belcher	.05
11	Harold Baines	.08
12	Hubie Brooks	.05
13	Doyle Alexander	.05
14	Gary Carter	.10
15	Glenn Braggs	.05
16	Steve Bedrosian	.05
17	Barry Bonds	.75
18	Bert Blyleven	.08
19	Tom Brunansky	.05
20	John Candelaria	.05
21	Shawn Abner	.05
22	Jose Canseco	.45
23	Brett Butler	.08
24	Scott Bradley	.05
25	Ivan Calderon	.05
26	Rich Gossage	.08
27	Brian Downing	.05
28	Jim Rice	.08
29	Dion James	.05
30	Terry Kennedy	.05
31	George Bell	.05
32	Scott Fletcher	.05
33	Bobby Bonilla	.15
34	Tim Burke	.05
35	Darrell Evans	.08
36	Mike Davis	.05
37	Shawon Dunston	.05
38	Kevin Bass	.05
39	George Brett	.45
40	David Cone	.15
41	Ron Darling	.05
42	Roberto Alomar	.30
43	Dennis Eckersley	.10
44	Vince Coleman	.05
45	Sid Bream	.05
46	Gary Gaetti	.08
47	Phil Bradley	.05
48	Jim Clancy	.05
49	Jack Clark	.05
50	Mike Krukow	.05
51	Henry Cotto	.05
52	Rich Dotson	.05
53	Jim Gantner	.05
54	John Franco	.05
55	Pete Incaviglia	.05
56	Joe Carter	.08
57	Roger Clemens	.75
58	Gerald Perry	.05
59	Jack Howell	.05
60	Vance Law	.05
61	Jay Bell	.08
62	Eric Davis	.10
63	Gene Garber	.05
64	Glenn Davis	.05
65	Wade Boggs	.45
66	Kirk Gibson	.08
67	Carlton Fisk	.10
68	Casey Candaele	.05
69	Mike Heath	.05
70	Kevin Elster	.05
71	Greg Brock	.05
72	Don Carman	.05
73	Doug Drabek	.08
74	Greg Gagne	.05
75	Danny Cox	.05
76	Rickey Henderson	.30
77	Chris Brown	.05
78	Terry Steinbach	.05
79	Will Clark	.35
80	Mickey Brantley	.05
81	Ozzie Guillen	.05
82	Greg Maddux	.75
83	Kirk McCaskill	.05
84	Dwight Evans	.08
85	Ozzie Virgil	.05
86	Mike Morgan	.05
87	Tony Fernandez	.08
88	Jose Guzman	.05
89	Mike Dunne	.05
90	Andres Galarraga	.10
91	Mike Henneman	.05
92	Alfredo Griffin	.05
93	Rafael Palmeiro	.20
94	Jim Deshaies	.05
95	Mark Gubicza	.05
96	Dwight Gooden	.10
97	Howard Johnson	.05
98	Mark Davis	.05
99	Dave Stewart	.08
100	Joe Magrane	.05
101	Brian Fisher	.05
102	Kent Hrbek	.08
103	Kevin Gross	.05
104	Tom Henke	.05
105	Mike Pagliarulo	.05
106	Kelly Downs	.05
107	Alvin Davis	.05
108	Willie Randolph	.05
109	Rob Deer	.05
110	Bo Diaz	.05
111	Paul Kilgus	.05
112	Tom Candiotti	.05
113	Dale Murphy	.15
114	Rick Mahler	.05
115	Wally Joyner	.08
116	Ryne Sandberg	.50
117	John Farrell	.05
118	Nick Esasky	.05
119	Bo Jackson	.25
120	Bill Doran	.05
121	Ellis Burks	.08
122	Pedro Guerrero	.05
123	Dave LaPoint	.05
124	Neal Heaton	.05
125	Willie Hernandez	.05
126	Roger McDowell	.05
127	Ted Higuera	.05
128	Von Hayes	.05
129	Mike LaValliere	.05
130	Dan Gladden	.05
131	Willie McGee	.05
132	Al Lieter	.08
133	Mark Grant	.05

134	Bob Welch	.05
135	Dave Dravecky	.05
136	Mark Langston	.08
137	Dan Pasqua	.05
138	Rick Sutcliffe	.05
139	Dan Petry	.05
140	Rich Gedman	.05
141	Ken Griffey	.05
142	Eddie Murray	.30
143	Jimmy Key	.08
144	Dale Mohorcic	.05
145	Jose Lind	.05
146	Dennis Martinez	.08
147	Chet Lemon	.05
148	Orel Hershiser	.10
149	Dave Martinez	.05
150	Billy Hatcher	.05
151	Charlie Leibrandt	.05
152	Keith Hernandez	.08
153	Kevin McReynolds	.05
154	Tony Gwynn	.75
155	Stan Javier	.05
156	Tony Pena	.05
157	Andy Van Slyke	.05
158	Gene Larkin	.05
159	Chris James	.05
160	Fred McGriff	.10
161	Rick Rhoden	.05
162	Scott Garrelts	.05
163	Mike Campbell	.05
164	Dave Righetti	.05
165	Paul Molitor	.20
166	Danny Jackson	.05
167	Pete O'Brien	.05
168	Julio Franco	.05
169	Mark McGwire	1.00
170	Zane Smith	.05
171	Johnny Ray	.05
172	Lester Lancaster	.05
173	Mel Hall	.05
174	Tracy Jones	.05
175	Kevin Seitzer	.05
176	Bob Knepper	.05
177	Mike Greenwell	.08
178	Mike Marshall	.05
179	Melido Perez	.05
180	Tim Raines	.10
181	Jack Morris	.05
182	Darryl Strawberry	.10
183	Robin Yount	.30
184	Lance Parrish	.05
185	Darnell Coles	.05
186	Kirby Puckett	.45
187	Terry Pendleton	.05
188	Don Slaught	.05
189	Jimmy Jones	.05
190	Dave Parker	.08
191	Mike Aldrete	.05
192	Mike Moore	.05
193	Greg Walker	.05
194	Calvin Schiraldi	.05
195	Dick Schofield	.05
196	Jody Reed	.05
197	Pete Smith	.05
198	Cal Ripken, Jr.	1.00
199	Lloyd Moseby	.05
200	Ruben Sierra	.05
201	R.J. Reynolds	.05
202	Bryn Smith	.05
203	Gary Pettis	.05
204	Steve Sax	.05
205	Frank DiPino	.05
206	Mike Scott	.05
207	Kurt Stillwell	.05
208	Mookie Wilson	.05
209	Lee Mazzilli	.05
210	Lance McCullers	.05
211	Rick Honeycutt	.05
212	John Tudor	.05
213	Jim Gott	.05
214	Frank Viola	.05
215	Juan Samuel	.05
216	Jesse Barfield	.05
217	Claudell Washington	.05
218	Rick Reuschel	.05
219	Jim Presley	.05
220	Tommy John	.05
221	Dan Plesac	.05
222	Barry Larkin	.10
223	Mike Stanley	.05
224	Cory Snyder	.05
225	Andre Dawson	.10
226	Ken Oberkfell	.05
227	Devon White	.08
228	Jamie Moyer	.05
229	Brook Jacoby	.05
230	Rob Murphy	.05
231	Bret Saberhagen	.08
232	Nolan Ryan	.90
233	Bruce Hurst	.05
234	Jesse Orosco	.05
235	Bobby Thigpen	.05
236	Pascual Perez	.05
237	Matt Nokes	.05
238	Bob Ojeda	.05
239	Joey Meyer	.05
240	Shane Rawley	.05
241	Jeff Robinson	.05
242	Jeff Reardon	.05
243	Ozzie Smith	.15
244	Dave Winfield	.30
245	John Kruk	.05
246	Carney Lansford	.05
247	Candy Maldonado	.05
248	Ken Phelps	.05
249	Ken Williams	.05
250	Al Nipper	.05
251	Mark McLemore	.05
252	Lee Smith	.08
253	Albert Hall	.05
254	Billy Ripken	.05
255	Kelly Gruber	.05
256	Charlie Hough	.05
257	John Smiley	.05
258	Tim Wallach	.05
259	Frank Tanana	.05
260	Mike Scioscia	.05
261	Damon Berryhill	.05
262	Dave Smith	.05
263	Willie Wilson	.05
264	Len Dykstra	.05
265	Randy Myers	.05
266	Keith Moreland	.05
267	Eric Plunk	.05
268	Todd Worrell	.05
269	Bob Walk	.05
270	Keith Atherton	.05
271	Mike Schmidt	.50
272	Mike Flanagan	.05
273	Rafael Santana	.05
274	Rob Thompson	.05
275	Rey Quinones	.05
276	Cecilio Guante	.05
277	B.J. Surhoff	.08
278	Chris Sabo	.05
279	Mitch Williams	.05
280	Greg Swindell	.05
281	Alan Trammell	.10
282	Storm Davis	.05
283	Chuck Finley	.05
284	Dave Stieb	.05
285	Scott Bailes	.05
286	Larry Sheets	.05
287	Danny Tartabull	.05
288	Checklist	.05
289	Todd Benzinger	.05
290	John Shelby	.05
291	Steve Lyons	.05
292	Mitch Webster	.05
293	Walt Terrell	.05
294	Pete Stanicek	.05
295	Chris Bosio	.05
296	Milt Thompson	.05
297	Fred Lynn	.08
298	Juan Berenguer	.05
299	Ken Dayley	.05
300	Joel Skinner	.05
301	Benito Santiago	.08
302	Ron Hassey	.05
303	Jose Uribe	.05
304	Harold Reynolds	.05
305	Dale Sveum	.05
306	Glenn Wilson	.05
307	Mike Witt	.05
308	Ron Robinson	.05
309	Denny Walling	.05
310	Joe Orsulak	.05
311	David Wells	.05
312	Steve Buechele	.05
313	Jose Oquendo	.05
314	Floyd Youmans	.05
315	Lou Whitaker	.05
316	Fernando Valenzuela	.08
317	Mike Boddicker	.05
318	Gerald Young	.05
319	Frank White	.05
320	Bill Wegman	.05
321	Tom Niedenfuer	.05
322	Ed Whitson	.05
323	Curt Young	.05
324	Greg Mathews	.05
325	Doug Jones	.05
326	Tommy Herr	.05
327	Kent Tekulve	.05
328	Rance Mulliniks	.05
329	Checklist	.05
330	Craig Lefferts	.05
331	Franklin Stubbs	.05
332	Rick Cerone	.05
333	Dave Schmidt	.05
334	Larry Parrish	.05
335	Tom Browning	.05
336	Checklist	.05

1988 Donruss Diamond Kings Supers

This 28-card set (including the checklist) marks the fourth edition of Donruss' super-size (5" x 7") set. These cards are exact duplicates of the 1988 Diamond Kings that feature player portraits by Dick Perez. A 12-piece Stan Musial puzzle was also included with the purchase of the super-size set which was marketed via a mail-in offer printed on Donruss wrappers.

		MT
Complete Set (28):		10.00
Common Player:		.25
1	Mark McGwire	4.00
2	Tim Raines	.30
3	Benito Santiago	.25
4	Alan Trammell	.30
5	Danny Tartabull	.25
6	Ron Darling	.25
7	Paul Molitor	.50
8	Devon White	.30
9	Andre Dawson	.30
10	Julio Franco	.25
11	Scott Fletcher	.25
12	Tony Fernandez	.25
13	Shane Rawley	.25
14	Kal Daniels	.25
15	Jack Clark	.25
16	Dwight Evans	.25
17	Tommy John	.25
18	Andy Van Slyke	.25
19	Gary Gaetti	.30
20	Mark Langston	.25
21	Will Clark	1.00
22	Glenn Hubbard	.25
23	Billy Hatcher	.25
24	Bob Welch	.25
25	Ivan Calderon	.25
26	Cal Ripken, Jr.	4.00
27	Checklist	.10
641	Stan Musial Puzzle Card	.25

1988 Donruss Pop-Ups

Donruss' 1988 Pop-Up cards were reduced to the standard 2-1/2" x 3-1/2". The set includes 20 cards that fold out so that the upper portion of the player stands upright, giving a three-dimensional effect. Pop-Ups feature players from the All-Star Game starting lineup. Card fronts feature full-color photos, with the player's name, team and position printed in black on a yellow banner near the bottom. As in previous issues, the backs contain only the player's name, league and position. Pop-Ups were distributed in individual packages containing one Pop-Up, three Stan Musial puzzle pieces and three All-Star cards.

		MT
Complete Set (20):		2.00
Common Player:		.10
Stan Musial Puzzle:		1.00
(1)	George Bell	.10
(2)	Wade Boggs	.50
(3)	Gary Carter	.12
(4)	Jack Clark	.10
(5)	Eric Davis	.15
(6)	Andre Dawson	.15
(7)	Rickey Henderson	.35
(8)	Davey Johnson	.10
(9)	Don Mattingly	.75
(10)	Terry Kennedy	.10
(11)	John McNamara	.10
(12)	Willie Randolph	.10
(13)	Cal Ripken, Jr.	1.00
(14)	Bret Saberhagen	.15
(15)	Ryne Sandberg	.65
(16)	Mike Schmidt	.70
(17)	Mike Scott	.10
(18)	Ozzie Smith	.35
(19)	Darryl Strawberry	.15
(20)	Dave Winfield	.30

1988 Donruss Rookies

For the third consecutive year, Donruss issued a 56-card boxed set highlighting current rookies. The complete set includes a checklist and a 15-piece Stan Musial Diamond Kings puzzle. As in previous years, the set is similar to the company's basic issue, with the exception of the logo and border color. Card fronts feature red, green and black-striped borders, with a red-and-white player name printed in the lower-left corner beneath the photo. "The Rookies" logo is printed in red, white and black in the lower-right corner. Backs are printed in black on bright aqua and include personal data, recent performance stats and major league totals, as well as 1984-88 minor league stats. The cards are the standard 2-1/2" x 3-1/2".

		MT
Complete Set (56):		10.00
Common Player:		.10
1	Mark Grace	2.00
2	Mike Campbell	.10
3	Todd Frowirth	.10
4	Dave Stapleton	.10
5	Shawn Abner	.10
6	Jose Cecena	.10
7	Dave Gallagher	.10
8	Mark Parent	.10
9	Cecil Espy	.10
10	Pete Smith	.10
11	Jay Buhner	1.00
12	Pat Borders	.20
13	Doug Jennings	.10
14	*Brady Anderson*	1.00
15	Pete Stanicek	.10
16	Roberto Kelly	.15
17	Jeff Treadway	.10
18	Walt Weiss	.25
19	Paul Gibson	.10
20	Tim Crews	.10
21	Melido Perez	.10
22	Steve Peters	.10
23	Craig Worthington	.10
24	John Trautwein	.10
25	DeWayne Vaughn	.10
26	David Wells	1.50
27	Al Leiter	.15
28	Tim Belcher	.15
29	Johnny Paredes	.10
30	Chris Sabo	.20
31	Damon Berryhill	.10
32	Randy Milligan	.10
33	Gary Thurman	.10
34	Kevin Elster	.15
35	Roberto Alomar	5.00
36	*Edgar Martinez* (photo actually Edwin Nunez)	1.25
37	Todd Stottlemyre	.15
38	Joey Meyer	.10
39	Carl Nichols	.10
40	Jack McDowell	.20
41	Jose Bautista	.10
42	Sil Campusano	.10
43	John Dopson	.10
44	Jody Reed	.15
45	Darrin Jackson	.20
46	Mike Capel	.10
47	Ron Gant	.40
48	John Davis	.10
49	Kevin Coffman	.10
50	Cris Carpenter	.10
51	Mackey Sasser	.10
52	Luis Alicea	.10
53	Bryan Harvey	.10
54	Steve Ellsworth	.10
55	Mike Macfarlane	.10
56	Checklist 1-56	.05

1989 Donruss

This basic annual issue consists of 660 2-1/2" x 3-1/2" cards, including 26 Diamond Kings (DK) portrait cards and 20 Rated Rookies (RR) cards. Top and bottom borders of the cards are printed in a variety of colors that fade from dark to light. A white-lettered player name is printed across the top margin. The team logo appears upper-right and the Donruss logo lower-left. A black outer stripe varnish gives faintly visible film-strip texture to the border. Backs are in orange and black, similar to the 1988 design, with personal info, recent stats and major league totals. Team logo sticker cards (22 total) and Warren Spahn puzzle cards (63 total) are included in individual wax packs of cards. Each regular player card can be found with a back variation in the header line above the stats: i.e., "*Denotes" or "*Denotes*". Neither version carries a premium.

		MT
Factory Set, Unopened (660):		40.00
Complete Set (660):		25.00
Common Player:		.05
Warren Spahn Puzzle:		1.00
Wax Pack (15):		1.25
Wax Box (36):		31.00
1	Mike Greenwell (DK)	.05
2	Bobby Bonilla (DK)	.08
3	Pete Incaviglia (DK)	.05
4	Chris Sabo (DK)	.08
5	Robin Yount (DK)	.15
6	Tony Gwynn (DK)	.25
7	Carlton Fisk (DK)	.12
8	Cory Snyder (DK)	.05
9	David Cone (DK)	.08
10	Kevin Seitzer (DK)	.08
11	Rick Reuschel (DK)	.05
12	Johnny Ray (DK)	.05
13	Dave Schmidt (DK)	.05
14	Andres Galarraga (DK)	.15
15	Kirk Gibson (DK)	.08
16	Fred McGriff (DK)	.15
17	Mark Grace (DK)	.20
18	Jeff Robinson (DK)	.05
19	Vince Coleman (DK)	.05
20	Dave Henderson (DK)	.08
21	Harold Reynolds (DK)	.08
22	Gerald Perry (DK)	.05
23	Frank Viola (DK)	.08
24	Steve Bedrosian (DK)	.08
25	Glenn Davis (DK)	.08
26	Don Mattingly (DK)	.30
27	Checklist 1-27	.05
28	*Sandy Alomar, Jr.* (RR)	.45
29	*Steve Searcy* (RR)	.08
30	*Cameron Drew* (RR)	.05
31	*Gary Sheffield* (RR)	1.00
32	*Erik Hanson* (RR)	.25
33	*Ken Griffey, Jr.* (RR)	15.00
34	*Greg Harris* (RR)	.05
35	Gregg Jefferies (RR)	.35
36	*Luis Medina* (RR)	.05
37	*Carlos Quintana* (RR)	.05
38	*Felix Jose* (RR)	.15
39	*Cris Carpenter* (RR)	.05
40	*Ron Jones* (RR)	.05
41	*Dave West* (RR)	.08
42	*Randy Johnson* (RR)	2.50
43	*Mike Harkey* (RR)	.10
44	*Pete Harnisch* (RR)	.15
45	*Tom Gordon* (RR)	.12
46	*Gregg Olson* (RR)	.10
47	*Alex Sanchez* (RR)	.05
48	Ruben Sierra	.08
49	Rafael Palmeiro	.25
50	Ron Gant	.15
51	Cal Ripken, Jr.	.75
52	Wally Joyner	.10
53	Gary Carter	.10
54	Andy Van Slyke	.08
55	Robin Yount	.25
56	Pete Incaviglia	.08
57	Greg Brock	.05
58	Melido Perez	.05
59	Craig Lefferts	.05
60	Gary Pettis	.05
61	Danny Tartabull	.05
62	Guillermo Hernandez	.05
63	Ozzie Smith	.25
64	Gary Gaetti	.12
65	Mark Davis	.05
66	Lee Smith	.08
67	Dennis Eckersley	.10
68	Wade Boggs	.30
69	Mike Scott	.05
70	Fred McGriff	.30
71	Tom Browning	.08
72	Claudell Washington	.05
73	Mel Hall	.05
74	Don Mattingly	.45
75	Steve Bedrosian	.05
76	Juan Samuel	.05
77	Mike Scioscia	.05
78	Dave Righetti	.05
79	Alfredo Griffin	.05
80	Eric Davis	.10
81	Juan Berenguer	.05
82	Todd Worrell	.08
83	Joe Carter	.25
84	Steve Sax	.05
85	Frank White	.05
86	John Kruk	.08
87	Rance Mulliniks	.05
88	Alan Ashby	.05
89	Charlie Leibrandt	.05
90	Frank Tanana	.05
91	Jose Canseco	.35
92	Barry Bonds	.50
93	Harold Reynolds	.08
94	Mark McLemore	.05
95	Mark McGwire	1.00
96	Eddie Murray	.20
97	Tim Raines	.08
98	Rob Thompson	.05
99	Kevin McReynolds	.08
100	Checklist 28-137	.05
101	Carlton Fisk	.12
102	Dave Martinez	.05
103	Glenn Braggs	.05
104	Dale Murphy	.12
105	Ryne Sandberg	.40
106	Dennis Martinez	.10
107	Pete O'Brien	.05
108	Dick Schofield	.05
109	Henry Cotto	.05
110	Mike Marshall	.05
111	Keith Moreland	.05
112	Tom Brunansky	.05
113	Kelly Gruber	.05
114	Brook Jacoby	.05
115	*Keith Brown*	.05
116	Matt Nokes	.08
117	Keith Hernandez	.05
118	Bob Forsch	.05
119	Bert Blyleven	.10
120	Willie Wilson	.08
121	Tommy Gregg	.05
122	Jim Rice	.08
123	Bob Knepper	.05
124	Danny Jackson	.08
125	Eric Plunk	.05
126	Brian Fisher	.05
127	Mike Pagliarulo	.05
128	Tony Gwynn	.45
129	Lance McCullers	.05
130	Andres Galarraga	.20
131	Jose Uribe	.05
132	Kirk Gibson	.08
133	David Palmer	.05
134	R.J. Reynolds	.05
135	Greg Walker	.05
136	Kirk McCaskill	.05
137	Shawon Dunston	.08
138	Andy Allanson	.05
139	Rob Murphy	.05
140	Mike Aldrete	.05
141	Terry Kennedy	.05
142	Scott Fletcher	.05
143	Steve Balboni	.05
144	Bret Saberhagen	.12
145	Ozzie Virgil	.05
146	Dale Sveum	.05
147	Darryl Strawberry	.12
148	Harold Baines	.10
149	George Bell	.08
150	Dave Parker	.12
151	Bobby Bonilla	.10
152	Mookie Wilson	.05
153	Ted Power	.05
154	Nolan Ryan	.75
155	Jeff Reardon	.05
156	Tim Wallach	.08
157	Jamie Moyer	.05
158	Rich Gossage	.08
159	Dave Winfield	.25
160	Von Hayes	.05
161	Willie McGee	.10
162	Rich Gedman	.05
163	Tony Pena	.05
164	Mike Morgan	.05
165	Charlie Hough	.05
166	Mike Stanley	.05
167	Andre Dawson	.20
168	Joe Boever	.05
169	Pete Stanicek	.05
170	Bob Boone	.08
171	Ron Darling	.08
172	Bob Walk	.05
173	Rob Deer	.05
174	Steve Buechele	.05
175	Ted Higuera	.05
176	Ozzie Guillen	.05
177	Candy Maldonado	.05
178	Doyle Alexander	.05
179	Mark Gubicza	.10
180	Alan Trammell	.15
181	Vince Coleman	.08
182	Kirby Puckett	.45
183	Chris Brown	.05
184	Marty Barrett	.05
185	Stan Javier	.05
186	Mike Greenwell	.08
187	Billy Hatcher	.05
188	Jimmy Key	.08
189	Nick Esasky	.05
190	Don Slaught	.05
191	Cory Snyder	.05
192	John Candelaria	.05
193	Mike Schmidt	.35
194	Kevin Gross	.05
195	John Tudor	.05
196	Neil Allen	.05
197	Orel Hershiser	.08
198	Kal Daniels	.05

No.	Player	Price
199	Kent Hrbek	.15
200	Checklist 138-247	.05
201	Joe Magrane	.05
202	Scott Bailes	.05
203	Tim Belcher	.10
204	George Brett	.40
205	Benito Santiago	.12
206	Tony Fernandez	.10
207	Gerald Young	.05
208	Bo Jackson	.25
209	Chet Lemon	.05
210	Storm Davis	.05
211	Doug Drabek	.05
212	Mickey Brantley (photo actually Nelson Simmons)	.05
213	Devon White	.08
214	Dave Stewart	.08
215	Dave Schmidt	.05
216	Bryn Smith	.05
217	Brett Butler	.08
218	Bob Ojeda	.05
219	*Steve Rosenberg*	.05
220	Hubie Brooks	.05
221	B.J. Surhoff	.05
222	Rick Mahler	.05
223	Rick Sutcliffe	.05
224	Neal Heaton	.05
225	Mitch Williams	.08
226	Chuck Finley	.08
227	Mark Langston	.10
228	Jesse Orosco	.05
229	Ed Whitson	.05
230	Terry Pendleton	.08
231	Lloyd Moseby	.05
232	Greg Swindell	.05
233	John Franco	.05
234	Jack Morris	.10
235	Howard Johnson	.08
236	Glenn Davis	.05
237	Frank Viola	.08
238	Kevin Seitzer	.05
239	Gerald Perry	.05
240	Dwight Evans	.10
241	Jim Deshaies	.05
242	Bo Diaz	.05
243	Carney Lansford	.05
244	Mike LaValliere	.05
245	Rickey Henderson	.20
246	Roberto Alomar	.60
247	Jimmy Jones	.05
248	Pascual Perez	.05
249	Will Clark	.35
250	Fernando Valenzuela	.10
251	Shane Rawley	.05
252	Sid Bream	.05
253	Steve Lyons	.05
254	Brian Downing	.05
255	Mark Grace	.30
256	Tom Candiotti	.05
257	Barry Larkin	.12
258	Mike Krukow	.05
259	Billy Ripken	.05
260	Cecilio Guante	.05
261	Scott Bradley	.05
262	Floyd Bannister	.05
263	Pete Smith	.05
264	Jim Gantner	.05
265	Roger McDowell	.05
266	Bobby Thigpen	.05
267	Jim Clancy	.05
268	Terry Steinbach	.08
269	Mike Dunne	.05
270	Dwight Gooden	.10
271	Mike Heath	.05
272	Dave Smith	.05
273	Keith Atherton	.05
274	Tim Burke	.05
275	Damon Berryhill	.05
276	Vance Law	.05
277	Rich Dotson	.05
278	Lance Parrish	.08
279	Geronimo Berroa	.08
280	Roger Clemens	.40
281	Greg Mathews	.05
282	Tom Niedenfuer	.05
283	Paul Kilgus	.05
284	Jose Guzman	.05
285	Calvin Schiraldi	.05
286	Charlie Puleo	.05
287	Joe Orsulak	.05
288	Jack Howell	.05
289	Kevin Elster	.05
290	Jose Lind	.08
291	Paul Molitor	.25
292	Cecil Espy	.05
293	Bill Wegman	.05
294	Dan Pasqua	.05
295	Scott Garrelts	.05
296	Walt Terrell	.05
297	Ed Hearn	.05
298	Lou Whitaker	.08
299	Ken Dayley	.05
300	Checklist 248-357	.05
301	Tommy Herr	.05
302	Mike Brumley	.05
303	Ellis Burks	.10
304	Curt Young	.05
305	Jody Reed	.10
306	Bill Doran	.05
307	David Wells	.08
308	Ron Robinson	.05
309	Rafael Santana	.05
310	Julio Franco	.10
311	Jack Clark	.05
312	Chris James	.05
313	Milt Thompson	.05
314	John Shelby	.05
315	Al Leiter	.05
316	Mike Davis	.05
317	*Chris Sabo*	.15
318	Greg Gagne	.05
319	Jose Oquendo	.05
320	John Farrell	.05
321	Franklin Stubbs	.05
322	Kurt Stillwell	.05
323	Shawn Abner	.05
324	Mike Flanagan	.05
325	Kevin Bass	.05
326	Pat Tabler	.05
327	Mike Henneman	.08
328	Rick Honeycutt	.05
329	John Smiley	.10
330	Rey Quinones	.05
331	Johnny Ray	.05
332	Bob Welch	.08
333	Larry Sheets	.05
334	Jeff Parrett	.05
335	Rick Reuschel	.05
336	Randy Myers	.10
337	Ken Williams	.05
338	Andy McGaffigan	.05
339	Joey Meyer	.05
340	Dion James	.05
341	Les Lancaster	.05
342	Tom Foley	.05
343	Geno Petralli	.05
344	Dan Petry	.05
345	Alvin Davis	.05
346	Mickey Hatcher	.05
347	Marvell Wynne	.05
348	Danny Cox	.05
349	Dave Stieb	.08
350	Jay Bell	.08
351	Jeff Treadway	.05
352	Luis Salazar	.05
353	Len Dykstra	.15
354	Juan Agosto	.05
355	Gene Larkin	.05
356	Steve Farr	.05
357	Paul Assenmacher	.05
358	Todd Benzinger	.05
359	Larry Andersen	.05
360	Paul O'Neill	.12
361	Ron Hassey	.05
362	Jim Gott	.05
363	Ken Phelps	.05
364	Tim Flannery	.05
365	Randy Ready	.05
366	*Nelson Santovenia*	.05
367	Kelly Downs	.05
368	Danny Heep	.05
369	Phil Bradley	.05
370	Jeff Robinson	.05
371	Ivan Calderon	.05
372	Mike Witt	.05
373	Greg Maddux	.75
374	Carmen Castillo	.05
375	Jose Rijo	.05
376	Joe Price	.05
377	R.C. Gonzalez	.05
378	Oddibe McDowell	.05
379	Jim Presley	.05
380	Brad Wellman	.05
381	Tom Glavine	.25
382	Dan Plesac	.05
383	Wally Backman	.05
384	*Dave Gallagher*	.05
385	Tom Henke	.05
386	Luis Polonia	.05
387	Junior Ortiz	.05
388	David Cone	.12
389	Dave Bergman	.05
390	Danny Darwin	.05
391	Dan Gladden	.05
392	*John Dopson*	.05
393	Frank DiPino	.05
394	Al Nipper	.05
395	Willie Randolph	.05
396	Don Carman	.05
397	Scott Terry	.05
398	Rick Cerone	.05
399	Tom Pagnozzi	.05
400	Checklist 358-467	.05
401	Mickey Tettleton	.08
402	Curtis Wilkerson	.05
403	Jeff Russell	.05
404	Pat Perry	.05
405	*Jose Alvarez*	.05
406	Rick Schu	.05
407	*Sherman Corbett*	.05
408	Dave Magadan	.08
409	Bob Kipper	.05
410	Don August	.05
411	Bob Brower	.05
412	Chris Bosio	.05
413	Jerry Reuss	.05
414	Atlee Hammaker	.05
415	Jim Walewander	.05
416	*Mike Macfarlane*	.08
417	Pat Sheridan	.05
418	Pedro Guerrero	.05
419	Allan Anderson	.05
420	*Mark Parent*	.08
421	Bob Stanley	.05
422	Mike Gallego	.05
423	Bruce Hurst	.05
424	Dave Meads	.05
425	Jesse Barfield	.05
426	*Rob Dibble*	.15
427	Joel Skinner	.05
428	Ron Kittle	.05
429	Rick Rhoden	.05
430	Bob Dernier	.05
431	Steve Jeltz	.05
432	Rick Dempsey	.05
433	Roberto Kelly	.10
434	Dave Anderson	.05
435	Herm Winningham	.05
436	Al Newman	.05
437	Jose DeLeon	.05
438	Doug Jones	.08
439	Brian Holton	.05
440	Jeff Montgomery	.10
441	Dickie Thon	.05
442	Cecil Fielder	.20
443	*John Fishel*	.05
444	Jerry Don Gleaton	.05
445	*Paul Gibson*	.05
446	Walt Weiss	.08
447	Glenn Wilson	.05
448	Mike Moore	.05
449	Chili Davis	.10
450	Dave Henderson	.05
451	*Jose Bautista*	.05
452	Rex Hudler	.05
453	Bob Brenly	.05
454	Mackey Sasser	.05
455	Daryl Boston	.05
456	Mike Fitzgerald	.05
457	Jeffery Leonard	.05
458	Bruce Sutter	.05
459	Mitch Webster	.05
460	Joe Hesketh	.05
461	Bobby Witt	.05
462	Stew Cliburn	.05
463	Scott Bankhead	.05
464	*Ramon Martinez*	.40
465	Dave Leiper	.05
466	*Luis Alicea*	.08
467	John Cerutti	.05
468	Ron Washington	.05
469	Jeff Reed	.05
470	Jeff Robinson	.05
471	Sid Fernandez	.05
472	Terry Puhl	.05
473	Charlie Lea	.05
474	*Israel Sanchez*	.05
475	Bruce Benedict	.05
476	Oil Can Boyd	.05
477	Craig Reynolds	.05
478	Frank Williams	.05
479	Greg Cadaret	.05
480	*Randy Kramer*	.05
481	*Dave Eiland*	.05
482	Eric Show	.05
483	Garry Templeton	.05
484	Wallace Johnson	.05
485	Kevin Mitchell	.08
486	Tim Crews	.05
487	Mike Maddux	.05
488	Dave LaPoint	.05
489	Fred Manrique	.05
490	Greg Minton	.05
491	*Doug Dascenzo*	.08
492	Willie Upshaw	.05
493	*Jack Armstrong*	.10
494	Kirt Manwaring	.10
495	Jeff Ballard	.05
496	Jeff Kunkel	.05
497	Mike Campbell	.05
498	Gary Thurman	.05
499	Zane Smith	.05
500	Checklist 468-577	.05
501	Mike Birkbeck	.05
502	Terry Leach	.05
503	Shawn Hillegas	.05
504	Manny Lee	.05
505	*Doug Jennings*	.08
506	Ken Oberkfell	.05
507	Tim Teufel	.05
508	Tom Brookens	.05
509	Rafael Ramirez	.05
510	Fred Toliver	.05
511	*Brian Holman*	.05
512	Mike Bielecki	.05
513	*Jeff Pico*	.05
514	Charles Hudson	.05
515	Bruce Ruffin	.05
516	Larry McWilliams	.05
517	Jeff Sellers	.05
518	*John Costello*	.05
519	Brady Anderson	.25
520	Craig McMurtry	.05
521	Ray Hayward	.05
522	Drew Hall	.05
523	*Mark Lemke*	.05
524	*Oswald Peraza*	.05
525	*Bryan Harvey*	.10
526	Rick Aguilera	.05
527	Tom Prince	.05
528	Mark Clear	.05
529	Jerry Browne	.05
530	Juan Castillo	.05
531	Jack McDowell	.15
532	Chris Speier	.05
533	Darrell Evans	.08
534	Luis Aquino	.05
535	Eric King	.05
536	*Ken Hill*	.40
537	Randy Bush	.05
538	Shane Mack	.05
539	Tom Bolton	.05
540	Gene Nelson	.05
541	Wes Gardner	.05
542	Ken Caminiti	.10
543	Duane Ward	.05
544	*Norm Charlton*	.12
545	*Hal Morris*	.40
546	Rich Yett	.05
547	*Hensley Meulens*	.10
548	Greg Harris	.05
549	Darren Daulton	.08
550	Jeff Hamilton	.05
551	Luis Aguayo	.05
552	Tim Leary	.05
553	Ron Oester	.05
554	Steve Lombardozzi	.05
555	*Tim Jones*	.05
556	Bud Black	.05
557	Alejandro Pena	.05
558	*Jose DeJesus*	.05
559	Dennis Rasmussen	.05
560	*Pat Borders*	.08
561	*Craig Biggio*	.50
562	*Luis de los Santos*	.05
563	Fred Lynn	.10
564	*Todd Burns*	.05
565	Felix Fermin	.05
566	Darnell Coles	.05
567	Willie Fraser	.05
568	Glenn Hubbard	.05
569	*Craig Worthington*	.05
570	*Johnny Paredes*	.05
571	Don Robinson	.05
572	Barry Lyons	.05
573	Bill Long	.05
574	Tracy Jones	.05
575	Juan Nieves	.05
576	Andres Thomas	.05
577	*Rolando Roomes*	.05
578	Luis Rivera	.05
579	*Chad Kreuter*	.15

580	Tony Armas	.08
581	Jay Buhner	.15
582	Ricky Horton	.05
583	Andy Hawkins	.05
584	*Sil Campusano*	.05
585	Dave Clark	.05
586	*Van Snider*	.05
587	Todd Frohwirth	.05
588	Warren Spahn Puzzle Card	.05
589	*William Brennan*	.05
590	*German Gonzalez*	.05
591	Ernie Whitt	.05
592	Jeff Blauser	.05
593	Spike Owen	.05
594	Matt Williams	.35
595	Lloyd McClendon	.05
596	Steve Ontiveros	.05
597	*Scott Medvin*	.05
598	*Hipolito Pena*	.05
599	*Jerald Clark*	.05
600a	Checklist 578-BC26 (#635 is Kurt Schilling)	.15
600b	Checklist 578-BC26 (#635 is Curt Schilling)	.05
601	Carmelo Martinez	.05
602	Mike LaCoss	.05
603	Mike Devereaux	.05
604	*Alex Madrid*	.05
605	Gary Redus	.05
606	Lance Johnson	.08
607	*Terry Clark*	.05
608	Manny Trillo	.05
609	*Scott Jordan*	.05
610	Jay Howell	.05
611	*Francisco Melendez*	.05
612	Mike Boddicker	.05
613	Kevin Brown	.10
614	Dave Valle	.05
615	Tim Laudner	.05
616	*Andy Nezelek*	.05
617	Chuck Crim	.05
618	Jack Savage	.05
619	Adam Peterson	.05
620	Todd Stottlemyre	.05
621	*Lance Blankenship*	.10
622	*Miguel Garcia*	.05
623	Keith Miller	.05
624	*Ricky Jordan*	.08
625	Ernest Riles	.05
626	John Moses	.05
627	Nelson Liriano	.05
628	Mike Smithson	.05
629	Scott Sanderson	.05
630	Dale Mohorcic	.05
631	Marvin Freeman	.05
632	Mike Young	.05
633	Dennis Lamp	.05
634	*Dante Bichette*	.75
635	*Curt Schilling*	.75
636	*Scott May*	.05
637	*Mike Schooler*	.05
638	Rick Leach	.05
639	*Tom Lampkin*	.05
640	*Brian Meyer*	.05
641	Brian Harper	.05
642	John Smoltz	.75
643	Jose Canseco (40/40)	.20
644	Bill Schroeder	.05
645	Edgar Martinez	.15
646	*Dennis Cook*	.08
647	Barry Jones	.05
648	(Orel Hershiser) (59 and Counting)	.15
649	*Rod Nichols*	.05
650	Jody Davis	.05
651	*Bob Milacki*	.05
652	Mike Jackson	.05
653	*Derek Lilliquist*	.10
654	Paul Mirabella	.05
655	Mike Diaz	.05
656	Jeff Musselman	.05
657	Jerry Reed	.05
658	*Kevin Blankenship*	.08
659	Wayne Tolleson	.05
660	*Eric Hetzel*	.05

1989 Donruss Grand Slammers

One card from this 12-card set was included in each Donruss cello pack. The complete insert set was included in factory sets. The featured players all hit grand slams in 1988. The 2-1/2" x 3-1/2" cards feature full color action photos. Backs tell the story of the player's grand slam. Border color variations on the front of the card have been discovered, but the prices are consistent with all forms of the cards.

		MT
Complete Set (12):		2.50
Common Player:		.25
1	Jose Canseco	.40
2	Mike Marshall	.25
3	Walt Weiss	.25
4	Kevin McReynolds	.25
5	Mike Greenwell	.25
6	Dave Winfield	.30
7	Mark McGwire	1.00
8	Keith Hernandez	.25
9	Franklin Stubbs	.25
10	Danny Tartabull	.25
11	Jesse Barfield	.25
12	Ellis Burks	.25

1989 Donruss MVP

This set, numbered BC1-BC26, was randomly inserted in Donruss wax packs, but not included in factory sets or other card packs. Players highlighted were selected by Donruss, one player per team. MVP cards feature a variation of the design in the basic Donruss issue, with multi-color upper and lower borders and black side borders. The "MVP" designation in large, bright letters serves as a backdrop for the full-color player photo. The cards measure 2-1/2" x 3-1/2".

		MT
Complete Set (26):		3.00
Common Player:		.10
1	Kirby Puckett	.50
2	Mike Scott	.10
3	Joe Carter	.10
4	Orel Hershiser	.10
5	Jose Canseco	.40
6	Darryl Strawberry	.15
7	George Brett	.45
8	Andre Dawson	.20
9	Paul Molitor	.45
10	Andy Van Slyke	.10
11	Dave Winfield	.30
12	Kevin Gross	.10
13	Mike Greenwell	.10
14	Ozzie Smith	.40
15	Cal Ripken	1.00
16	Andres Galarraga	.20
17	Alan Trammell	.15
18	Kal Daniels	.10
19	Fred McGriff	.20
20	Tony Gwynn	.45
21	Wally Joyner	.10
22	Will Clark	.35
23	Ozzie Guillen	.10
24	Gerald Perry	.10
25	Alvin Davis	.10
26	Ruben Sierra	.10

1989 Donruss All-Stars

For the fourth consecutive year Donruss featured a 64-card set with players from the 1988 All-Star Game. The card fronts include a red-to-gold fade or gold-to-red fade border and blue vertical side borders. The top border features the player's name and position along with the "Donruss 89" logo. Each full-color player photo is highlighted by a thin white line and includes a league logo in the lower right corner. Card backs reveal an orange-gold border and black and white printing. The player's ID and personal information is displayed with a gold star on both sides. The star in the left corner includes the card number. 1988 All-Star game statistics and run totals follow along with a career highlights feature surrounded by the team, All-Star Game MLB, MLBPA, and Leaf Inc. logos. The All-Stars were distributed in wax packages containing five All-Stars, one Pop-Up, and one three-piece Warren Spahn puzzle card.

		MT
Complete Set (64):		5.00
Common Player:		.10
Warren Spahn Puzzle:		1.00
1	Mark McGwire	1.00
2	Jose Canseco	.60
3	Paul Molitor	.25
4	Rickey Henderson	.25
5	Cal Ripken, Jr.	1.50
6	Dave Winfield	.25
7	Wade Boggs	.50
8	Frank Viola	.10
9	Terry Steinbach	.10
10	Tom Kelly	.10
11	George Brett	.60
12	Doyle Alexander	.10
13	Gary Gaetti	.10
14	Roger Clemens	.75
15	Mike Greenwell	.10
16	Dennis Eckersley	.15
17	Carney Lansford	.10
18	Mark Gubicza	.10
19	Tim Laudner	.10
20	Doug Jones	.10
21	Don Mattingly	.75
22	Dan Plesac	.10
23	Kirby Puckett	.75
24	Jeff Reardon	.10
25	Johnny Ray	.10
26	Jeff Russell	.10
27	Harold Reynolds	.10
28	Dave Stieb	.10
29	Kurt Stillwell	.10
30	Jose Canseco	.60
31	Terry Steinbach	.10
32	A.L. Checklist	.05
33	Will Clark	.40
34	Darryl Strawberry	.20
35	Ryne Sandberg	.65
36	Andre Dawson	.12
37	Ozzie Smith	.25
38	Vince Coleman	.10
39	Bobby Bonilla	.12
40	Dwight Gooden	.10
41	Gary Carter	.12
42	Whitey Herzog	.10
43	Shawon Dunston	.10
44	David Cone	.12
45	Andres Galarraga	.15
46	Mark Davis	.10
47	Barry Larkin	.15
48	Kevin Gross	.10
49	Vance Law	.10
50	Orel Hershiser	.10
51	Willie McGee	.10
52	Danny Jackson	.10
53	Rafael Palmeiro	.25
54	Bob Knepper	.10
55	Lance Parrish	.10
56	Greg Maddux	.75
57	Gerald Perry	.10
58	Bob Walk	.10
59	Chris Sabo	.10
60	Todd Worrell	.10
61	Andy Van Slyke	.10
62	Ozzie Smith	.25
63	Riverfront Stadium	.10
64	N.L. Checklist	.05

1989 Donruss Baseball's Best

For the second consecutive year, Donruss issued a "Baseball's Best" set in 1989 to highlight the game's top players. The special 336-card set was packaged in a special box and was sold at various retail chains nationwide following the conclusion of the 1989 baseball season. The cards are styled after the regular 1989 Donruss set with green borders and a glossy finish. The set included a Warren Spahn puzzle.

		MT
Complete Unopened Set (336):		200.00
Complete Set (336):		20.00
Common Player:		.05
1	Don Mattingly	.90
2	Tom Glavine	.15
3	Bert Blyleven	.05
4	Andre Dawson	.10
5	Pete O'Brien	.05
6	Eric Davis	.10
7	George Brett	.50
8	Glenn Davis	.05
9	Ellis Burks	.10
10	Kirk Gibson	.08
11	Carlton Fisk	.12
12	Andres Galarraga	.15
13	Alan Trammell	.15
14	Dwight Gooden	.15
15	Paul Molitor	.15
16	Roger McDowell	.05
17	Doug Drabek	.05
18	Kent Hrbek	.08
19	Vince Coleman	.05
20	Steve Sax	.05
21	Roberto Alomar	.35
22	Carney Lansford	.05
23	Will Clark	.50
24	Alvin Davis	.05
25	Bobby Thigpen	.05
26	Ryne Sandberg	.75
27	Devon White	.08
28	Mike Greenwell	.05
29	Dale Murphy	.20
30	Jeff Ballard	.05
31	Kelly Gruber	.05
32	Julio Franco	.08
33	Bobby Bonilla	.10
34	Tim Wallach	.05
35	Lou Whitaker	.08
36	Jay Howell	.05
37	Greg Maddux	.75
38	Bill Doran	.05
39	Danny Tartabull	.05
40	Darryl Strawberry	.10
41	Ron Darling	.05
42	Tony Gwynn	.50
43	Mark McGwire	1.50
44	Ozzie Smith	.25
45	Andy Van Slyke	.05
46	Juan Berenguer	.05
47	Von Hayes	.05
48	Tony Fernandez	.08
49	Eric Plunk	.05
50	Ernest Riles	.05
51	Harold Reynolds	.05
52	Andy Hawkins	.05
53	Robin Yount	.30
54	Danny Jackson	.05
55	Nolan Ryan	1.25
56	Joe Carter	.10
57	Jose Canseco	.75
58	Jody Davis	.05
59	Lance Parrish	.05
60	Mitch Williams	.05
61	Brook Jacoby	.05
62	Tom Browning	.05
63	Kurt Stillwell	.05
64	Rafael Ramirez	.05
65	Roger Clemens	.60
66	Mike Scioscia	.05
67	Dave Gallagher	.05
68	Mark Langston	.08
69	Chet Lemon	.05
70	Kevin McReynolds	.05
71	Rob Deer	.05
72	Tommy Herr	.05
73	Barry Bonds	.75
74	Frank Viola	.05
75	Pedro Guerrero	.05
76	Dave Righetti	.05
77	Bruce Hurst	.05
78	Rickey Henderson	.30
79	Robby Thompson	.05
80	Randy Johnson	.35
81	Harold Baines	.08
82	Calvin Schiraldi	.05
83	Kirk McCaskill	.05
84	Lee Smith	.08
85	John Smoltz	.15
86	Mickey Tettleton	.05
87	Jimmy Key	.08
88	Rafael Palmeiro	.15
89	Sid Bream	.05
90	Dennis Martinez	.08
91	Frank Tanana	.05
92	Eddie Murray	.30
93	Shawon Dunston	.10
94	Mike Scott	.05
95	Bret Saberhagen	.10
96	David Cone	.15
97	Kevin Elster	.05
98	Jack Clark	.05
99	Dave Stewart	.05
100	Jose Oquendo	.05
101	Jose Lind	.05
102	Gary Gaetti	.05
103	Ricky Jordan	.05
104	Fred McGriff	.20
105	Don Slaught	.05
106	Jose Uribe	.05
107	Jeffrey Leonard	.05
108	Lee Guetterman	.05
109	Chris Bosio	.05
110	Barry Larkin	.12
111	Ruben Sierra	.05
112	Greg Swindell	.05
113	Gary Sheffield	.35
114	Lonnie Smith	.05
115	Chili Davis	.05
116	Damon Berryhill	.05
117	Tom Candiotti	.05
118	Kal Daniels	.05
119	Mark Gubicza	.05
120	Jim Deshaies	.05
121	Dwight Evans	.05
122	Mike Morgan	.05
123	Dan Pasqua	.05
124	Bryn Smith	.05
125	Doyle Alexander	.05
126	Howard Johnson	.05
127	Chuck Crim	.05
128	Darren Daulton	.05
129	Jeff Robinson	.05
130	Kirby Puckett	.50
131	Joe Magrane	.05
132	Jesse Barfield	.05
133	Mark Davis (Photo actually Dave Leiper)	.05
134	Dennis Eckersley	.10
135	Mike Krukow	.05
136	Jay Buhner	.10
137	Ozzie Guillen	.05
138	Rick Sutcliffe	.05
139	Wally Joyner	.10
140	Wade Boggs	.50
141	Jeff Treadway	.05
142	Cal Ripken	1.50
143	Dave Steib	.05
144	Pete Incaviglia	.05
145	Bob Walk	.05
146	Nelson Santovenia	.05
147	Mike Heath	.05
148	Willie Randolph	.05
149	Paul Kilgus	.05
150	Billy Hatcher	.05
151	Steve Farr	.05
152	Gregg Jefferies	.10
153	Randy Myers	.05
154	Garry Templeton	.05
155	Walt Weiss	.05
156	Terry Pendleton	.05
157	John Smiley	.05
158	Greg Gagne	.05
159	Lenny Dykstra	.05
160	Nelson Liriano	.05
161	Alvaro Espinoza	.05
162	Rick Reuschel	.05
163	Omar Vizquel	.10
164	Clay Parker	.05
165	Dan Plesac	.05
166	John Franco	.05
167	Scott Fletcher	.05
168	Cory Snyder	.05
169	Bo Jackson	.25
170	Tommy Gregg	.05
171	Jim Abbott	.10
172	Jerome Walton	.05
173	Doug Jones	.05
174	Todd Benzinger	.05
175	Frank White	.05
176	Craig Biggio	.10
177	John Dopson	.05
178	Alfredo Griffin	.05
179	Melido Perez	.05
180	Tim Burke	.05
181	Matt Nokes	.05
182	Gary Carter	.12
183	Ted Higuera	.05
184	Ken Howell	.05
185	Rey Quinones	.05
186	Wally Backman	.05
187	Tom Brunansky	.05
188	Steve Balboni	.05
189	Marvell Wynne	.05
190	Dave Henderson	.05
191	Don Robinson	.05
192	Ken Griffey, Jr.	4.00
193	Ivan Calderon	.05
194	Mike Bielecki	.05
195	Johnny Ray	.05
196	Rob Murphy	.05
197	Andres Thomas	.05
198	Phil Bradley	.05
199	Junior Felix	.05
200	Jeff Russell	.05
201	Mike LaValliere	.05
202	Kevin Gross	.05
203	Keith Moreland	.05
204	Mike Marshall	.05
205	Dwight Smith	.05
206	Jim Clancy	.05
207	Kevin Seitzer	.05
208	Keith Hernandez	.05
209	Bob Ojeda	.05
210	Ed Whitson	.05
211	Tony Phillips	.05
212	Milt Thompson	.05
213	Randy Kramer	.05
214	Randy Bush	.05
215	Randy Ready	.05
216	Duane Ward	.05
217	Jimmy Jones	.05
218	Scott Garrelts	.05
219	Scott Bankhead	.05
220	Lance McCullers	.05
221	B.J. Surhoff	.05
222	Chris Sabo	.05
223	Steve Buechele	.05
224	Joel Skinner	.05
225	Orel Hershiser	.08
226	Derek Lilliquist	.05
227	Claudell Washington	.05
228	Lloyd McClendon	.05
229	Felix Fermin	.05
230	Paul O'Neill	.12
231	Charlie Leibrandt	.05
232	Dave Smith	.05
233	Bob Stanley	.05
234	Tim Belcher	.05
235	Eric King	.05
236	Spike Owen	.05
237	Mike Henneman	.05
238	Juan Samuel	.05
239	Greg Brock	.05
240	John Kruk	.05
241	Glenn Wilson	.05
242	Jeff Reardon	.05
243	Todd Worrell	.05
244	Dave LaPoint	.05
245	Walt Terrell	.05
246	Mike Moore	.05
247	Kelly Downs	.05
248	Dave Valle	.05
249	Ron Kittle	.05
250	Steve Wilson	.05
251	Dick Schofield	.05
252	Marty Barrett	.05
253	Dion James	.05
254	Bob Milacki	.05
255	Ernie Whitt	.05
256	Kevin Brown	.05
257	R.J. Reynolds	.05
258	Tim Raines	.10
259	Frank Williams	.05
260	Jose Gonzalez	.05
261	Mitch Webster	.05
262	Ken Caminiti	.15
263	Bob Boone	.05
264	Dave Magadan	.05
265	Rick Aguilera	.05
266	Chris James	.05
267	Bob Welch	.05
268	Ken Dayley	.05
269	Junior Ortiz	.05
270	Allan Anderson	.05
271	Steve Jeltz	.05
272	George Bell	.05
273	Roberto Kelly	.08
274	Brett Butler	.10
275	Mike Schooler	.05
276	Ken Phelps	.05
277	Glenn Braggs	.05
278	Jose Rijo	.05
279	Bobby Witt	.05
280	Jerry Browne	.05
281	Kevin Mitchell	.10
282	Craig Worthington	.05
283	Greg Minton	.05
284	Nick Esasky	.05
285	John Farrell	.05
286	Rick Mahler	.05
287	Tom Gordon	.05
288	Gerald Young	.05
289	Jody Reed	.05
290	Jeff Hamilton	.05
291	Gerald Perry	.05
292	Hubie Brooks	.05
293	Bo Diaz	.05
294	Terry Puhl	.05
295	Jim Gantner	.05
296	Jeff Parrett	.05
297	Mike Boddicker	.05
298	Dan Gladden	.05
299	Tony Pena	.05
300	Checklist	.05
301	Tom Henke	.05
302	Pascual Perez	.05
303	Steve Bedrosian	.05
304	Ken Hill	.05
305	Jerry Reuss	.05
306	Jim Eisenreich	.05
307	Jack Howell	.05
308	Rick Cerone	.05
309	Tim Leary	.05
310	Joe Orsulak	.05
311	Jim Dwyer	.05
312	Geno Petralli	.05
313	Rick Honeycutt	.05
314	Tom Foley	.05
315	Kenny Rogers	.08
316	Mike Flanagan	.05
317	Bryan Harvey	.05
318	Billy Ripken	.05
319	Jeff Montgomery	.05
320	Erik Hanson	.05
321	Brian Downing	.05
322	Gregg Olson	.05
323	Terry Steinbach	.08
324	Sammy Sosa	10.00
325	Gene Harris	.05
326	Mike Devereaux	.05
327	Dennis Cook	.05
328	David Wells	.08
329	Checklist	.05
330	Kirt Manwaring	.05
331	Jim Presley	.05
332	Checklist	.05
333	Chuck Finley	.05
334	Rob Dibble	.05
335	Cecil Espy	.05
336	Dave Parker	.08

1989 Donruss Diamond King Supers

Once again for 1989, collectors could acquire a 4-3/4" x 6-3/4" version of the Diamond King subset via a wrapper mail-in offer. Other than size, cards are identical to the DKs in the regular issue.

		MT
Complete Set (27):		14.00
Common Player:		.25
1	Mike Greenwell	.25
2	Bobby Bonilla	.50
3	Pete Incaviglia	.25
4	Chris Sabo	.25
5	Robin Yount	1.50
6	Tony Gwynn	2.50
7	Carlton Fisk	1.00
8	Cory Snyder	.25
9	David Cone	.75
10	Kevin Seitzer	.25
11	Rick Reuschel	.25
12	Johnny Ray	.25
13	Dave Schmidt	.25
14	Andres Galarraga	.75
15	Kirk Gibson	.30
16	Fred McGriff	1.00
17	Mark Grace	1.50
18	Jeff Robinson	.25
19	Vince Coleman	.25
20	Dave Henderson	.25
21	Harold Reynolds	.25
22	Gerald Perry	.25
23	Frank Viola	.25
24	Steve Bedrosian	.25
25	Glenn Davis	.25
26	Don Mattingly	4.00
27	Checklist	.05

1989 Donruss Pop-Ups

This set features the eighteen starters from the 1988 Major League All-Star game. The cards are designed with a perforated outline so each player can be popped up to stand upright. The flip side features a red, white, and blue "Cincinnati Reds All-Star Game" logo at the top, a league designation, and the player's name and position. The lower portion displays instructions for creating the base of the Pop-Up. The Pop-Ups were marketed in conjunction with All-Star and Warren Spahn Puzzle Cards.

		MT
Complete Set (20):		3.00
Common Player:		.20
Warren Spahn Puzzle:		1.00
(1)	Mark McGwire	1.00
(2)	Jose Canseco	.60
(3)	Paul Molitor	.35
(4)	Rickey Henderson	.35
(5)	Cal Ripken, Jr.	1.00
(6)	Dave Winfield	.25
(7)	Wade Boggs	.50
(8)	Frank Viola	.20
(9)	Terry Steinbach	.20
(10)	Tom Kelly	.20
(11)	Will Clark	.45
(12)	Darryl Strawberry	.20
(13)	Ryne Sandberg	.50
(14)	Andre Dawson	.20
(15)	Ozzie Smith	.35
(16)	Vince Coleman	.20
(17)	Bobby Bonilla	.20
(18)	Dwight Gooden	.20
(19)	Gary Carter	.20
(20)	Whitey Herzog	.20

1989 Donruss Rookies

For the fourth straight year, Donruss issued a 56-card "Rookies" set in 1989. As in previous years, the set is similar in design to the regular Donruss set, except for a new "The Rookies" logo and a green and black border.

		MT
Complete Unopened Set (56):		30.00
Complete Set (56):		24.00
Common Player:		.10
1	Gary Sheffield	2.00
2	Gregg Jefferies	.25
3	Ken Griffey, Jr.	25.00
4	Tom Gordon	.10
5	Billy Spiers	.10
6	*Deion Sanders*	.75
7	Donn Pall	.10
8	Steve Carter	.10
9	Francisco Oliveras	.10
10	Steve Wilson	.10
11	Bob Geren	.10
12	Tony Castillo	.10
13	*Kenny Rogers*	.20
14	Carlos Martinez	.10
15	Edgar Martinez	.20
16	Jim Abbott	.15
17	Torey Lovullo	.10
18	Mark Carreon	.15
19	Geronimo Berroa	.10
20	Luis Medina	.10
21	Sandy Alomar, Jr.	.30
22	Bob Milacki	.10
23	*Joe Girardi*	.15
24	German Gonzalez	.10
25	Craig Worthington	.10
26	Jerome Walton	.10
27	Gary Wayne	.10
28	Tim Jones	.10
29	*Dante Bichette*	1.50
30	Alexis Infante	.10
31	*Ken Hill*	.15
32	Dwight Smith	.10
33	Luis de los Santos	.10
34	Eric Yelding	.10
35	Gregg Olson	.10
36	Phil Stephenson	.10
37	Ken Patterson	.10
38	Rick Wrona	.10
39	Mike Brumley	.10
40	Cris Carpenter	.10
41	Jeff Brantley	.10
42	Ron Jones	.10
43	Randy Johnson	6.00
44	Kevin Brown	.10
45	*Ramon Martinez*	.40
46	Greg Harris	.10
47	*Steve Finley*	.20
48	Randy Kramer	.10
49	Erik Hanson	.10
50	Matt Merullo	.10
51	Mike Devereaux	.10
52	Clay Parker	.10
53	Omar Vizquel	.25
54	Derek Lilliquist	.10
55	Junior Felix	.10
56	Checklist	.05

1989 Donruss Traded

Donruss issued its first "Traded" set in 1989, releasing a 56-card boxed set designed in the same style as the regular 1989 Donruss set. The set included a Stan Musial puzzle card and a checklist.

		MT
Complete Set (56):		3.00
Common Player:		.10
1	Jeffrey Leonard	.10
2	Jack Clark	.10
3	Kevin Gross	.10
4	Tommy Herr	.10
5	Bob Boone	.10
6	Rafael Palmeiro	.40
7	John Dopson	.10
8	Willie Randolph	.10
9	Chris Brown	.10
10	Wally Backman	.10
11	Steve Ontiveros	.10
12	Eddie Murray	.30
13	Lance McCullers	.10
14	Spike Owen	.10
15	Rob Murphy	.10
16	Pete O'Brien	.10
17	Ken Williams	.10
18	Nick Esasky	.10
19	Nolan Ryan	1.50
20	Brian Holton	.10
21	Mike Moore	.10
22	Joel Skinner	.10
23	Steve Sax	.10
24	Rick Mahler	.10
25	Mike Aldrete	.10
26	Jesse Orosco	.10
27	Dave LaPoint	.10
28	Walt Terrell	.10
29	Eddie Williams	.10
30	Mike Devereaux	.10
31	Julio Franco	.15
32	Jim Clancy	.10
33	Felix Fermin	.10
34	Curtis Wilkerson	.10
35	Bert Blyleven	.10
36	Mel Hall	.10
37	Eric King	.10
38	Mitch Williams	.10
39	Jamie Moyer	.10
40	Rick Rhoden	.10
41	Phil Bradley	.10
42	Paul Kilgus	.10
43	Milt Thompson	.10
44	Jerry Browne	.10
45	Bruce Hurst	.10
46	Claudell Washington	.10
47	Todd Benzinger	.10
48	Steve Balboni	.10
49	Oddibe McDowell	.10
50	Charles Hudson	.10
51	Ron Kittle	.10
52	Andy Hawkins	.10
53	Tom Brookens	.10
54	Tom Niedenfuer	.10
55	Jeff Parrett	.10
56	Checklist	.10

1990 Donruss Previews

To introduce its 1990 baseball issue, Donruss sent two preview cards from a set of 12 to each member of its dealers' network. Though the photos are different than those used on the issued versions, the front format was the same. Backs are printed in black on white and contain career highlights, but no stats. Issued at the dawn of the "promo card" craze, and succeeding the relatively valueless sample sheets used by most companies in earlier years, little value was attached to these preview cards initially.

Today they are among the scarcest of the early-1990s promos.

		MT
Complete Set (12):		225.00
Common Player:		7.50
1	Todd Zeile	7.50
2	Ben McDonald	7.50
3	Bo Jackson	15.00
4	Will Clark	25.00
5	Dave Stewart	7.50
6	Kevin Mitchell	7.50
7	Nolan Ryan	150.00
8	Howard Johnson	7.50
9	Tony Gwynn	50.00
10	Jerome Walton	7.50
11	Wade Boggs	40.00
12	Kirby Puckett	45.00

1990 Donruss

Donruss marked its 10th anniversary in the baseball card hobby with a 715-card set in 1990, up from previous 660-card sets. The standard-size cards feature bright red borders with the player's name in script at the top. The set includes 26 "Diamond Kings" (DK) in the checklist, 20 "Rated Rookies" (RR) and a Carl Yastrzemski puzzle. Each All-Star card back has two variations. The more common has the stats box headed "All-Star Performance". Slightly scarcer versions say "Recent Major League Performance", and are worth about twice the value of the correct version.

		MT
Unopened Factory Set (716):		15.00
Complete Set (716):		10.00
Common Player:		.05
Carl Yastrzemski Puzzle:		1.00
Wax Pack (16 - Final Print):		.85
Wax Box (36- Final Print):		17.50
1	Bo Jackson (Diamond King)	.15
2	Steve Sax (DK)	.08
3a	Ruben Sierra (DK) (no vertical black line at top-right on back)	.25
3b	Ruben Sierra (DK) (vertical line at top-right on back)	.10
4	Ken Griffey, Jr. (DK)	.50
5	Mickey Tettleton (DK)	.08
6	Dave Stewart (DK)	.10
7	Jim Deshaies (DK)	.05
8	John Smoltz (DK)	.10
9	Mike Bielecki (DK)	.05
10a	Brian Downing (DK) (reversed negative)	.50
10b	Brian Downing (DK) (corrected)	.15
11	Kevin Mitchell (DK)	.08
12	Kelly Gruber (DK)	.05
13	Joe Magrane (DK)	.05
14	John Franco (DK)	.05
15	Ozzie Guillen (DK)	.08
16	Lou Whitaker (DK)	.08
17	John Smiley (DK)	.08
18	Howard Johnson (DK)	.08
19	Willie Randolph (DK)	.08
20	Chris Bosio (DK)	.05
21	Tommy Herr (DK)	.05
22	Dan Gladden (DK)	.05
23	Ellis Burks (DK)	.08
24	Pete O'Brien (DK)	.08
25	Bryn Smith (DK)	.05
26	Ed Whitson (DK)	.05
27	Checklist 1-27	.05
28	Robin Ventura (Rated Rookie)	.25
29	*Todd Zeile* (RR)	.15
30	Sandy Alomar, Jr. (RR)	.15
31	*Kent Mercker* (RR)	.20
32	*Ben McDonald* (RR)	.25
33a	*Juan Gonzalez (reversed negative)* (RR)	2.00
33b	*Juan Gonzalez* (RR) (corrected)	2.00
34	*Eric Anthony* (RR)	.15
35	*Mike Fetters* (RR)	.10
36	*Marquis Grissom* (RR)	.50
37	*Greg Vaughn* (RR)	.25
38	*Brian Dubois* (RR)	.08
39	*Steve Avery* (RR)	.20
40	*Mark Gardner* (RR)	.15
41	Andy Benes (RR)	.20
42	*Delino DeShields* (RR)	.15
43	*Scott Coolbaugh* (RR)	.05
44	*Pat Combs* (RR)	.08
45	*Alex Sanchez* (RR)	.05
46	*Kelly Mann* (RR)	.05
47	*Julio Machado* (RR)	.08
48	Pete Incaviglia	.05
49	Shawon Dunston	.08
50	Jeff Treadway	.05
51	Jeff Ballard	.05
52	Claudell Washington	.05
53	Juan Samuel	.05
54	John Smiley	.05
55	Rob Deer	.05
56	Geno Petralli	.05
57	Chris Bosio	.08
58	Carlton Fisk	.12
59	Kirt Manwaring	.05
60	Chet Lemon	.05
61	Bo Jackson	.25
62	Doyle Alexander	.05
63	Pedro Guerrero	.05
64	Allan Anderson	.05
65	Greg Harris	.05
66	Mike Greenwell	.08
67	Walt Weiss	.05
68	Wade Boggs	.25
69	Jim Clancy	.05
70	*Junior Felix*	.08
71	Barry Larkin	.12
72	Dave LaPoint	.05
73	Joel Skinner	.05
74	Jesse Barfield	.05
75	Tommy Herr	.05
76	Ricky Jordan	.05
77	Eddie Murray	.20
78	Steve Sax	.05
79	Tim Belcher	.05
80	Danny Jackson	.05
81	Kent Hrbek	.10
82	Milt Thompson	.05
83	Brook Jacoby	.05
84	Mike Marshall	.05
85	Kevin Seitzer	.05
86	Tony Gwynn	.35
87	Dave Steib	.05
88	Dave Smith	.05
89	Bret Saberhagen	.08
90	Alan Trammell	.10
91	Tony Phillips	.05
92	Doug Drabek	.05
93	Jeffrey Leonard	.05
94	Wally Joyner	.10
95	Carney Lansford	.05
96	Cal Ripken, Jr.	.75
97	Andres Galarraga	.15
98	Kevin Mitchell	.05
99	Howard Johnson	.08
100a	Checklist 28-129	.05
100b	Checklist 28-125	.05
101	Melido Perez	.05
102	Spike Owen	.05
103	Paul Molitor	.25
104	Geronimo Berroa	.05
105	Ryne Sandberg	.25
106	Bryn Smith	.05
107	Steve Buechele	.05
108	Jim Abbott	.10
109	Alvin Davis	.05
110	Lee Smith	.08
111	Roberto Alomar	.25
112	Rick Reuschel	.05
113a	Kelly Gruber (Born 2/22)	.05
113b	Kelly Gruber (Born 2/26)	.25
114	Joe Carter	.10
115	Jose Rijo	.05
116	Greg Minton	.05
117	Bob Ojeda	.05
118	Glenn Davis	.05
119	Jeff Reardon	.05
120	Kurt Stillwell	.05
121	John Smoltz	.15
122	Dwight Evans	.08
123	Eric Yelding	.08
124	John Franco	.05
125	Jose Canseco	.20
126	Barry Bonds	.30
127	Lee Guetterman	.05
128	Jack Clark	.05
129	Dave Valle	.05
130	Hubie Brooks	.05
131	Ernest Riles	.05
132	Mike Morgan	.05
133	Steve Jeltz	.05
134	Jeff Robinson	.05
135	Ozzie Guillen	.05
136	Chili Davis	.08
137	Mitch Webster	.05
138	Jerry Browne	.05
139	Bo Diaz	.05
140	Robby Thompson	.05
141	Craig Worthington	.05
142	Julio Franco	.08
143	Brian Holman	.05
144	George Brett	.25
145	Tom Glavine	.20
146	Robin Yount	.20
147	Gary Carter	.10
148	Ron Kittle	.05
149	Tony Fernandez	.08
150	Dave Stewart	.08
151	Gary Gaetti	.08
152	Kevin Elster	.05
153	Gerald Perry	.05
154	Jesse Orosco	.05
155	Wally Backman	.05
156	Dennis Martinez	.08
157	Rick Sutcliffe	.05
158	Greg Maddux	.60
159	Andy Hawkins	.05
160	John Kruk	.05
161	Jose Oquendo	.05
162	John Dopson	.05
163	Joe Magrane	.05
164	Billy Ripken	.05
165	Fred Manrique	.05
166	Nolan Ryan	.60
167	Damon Berryhill	.05
168	Dale Murphy	.10
169	Mickey Tettleton	.05
170a	Kirk McCaskill (Born 4/19)	.05
170b	Kirk McCaskill (Born 4/9)	.25
171	Dwight Gooden	.10
172	Jose Lind	.05
173	B.J. Surhoff	.05
174	Ruben Sierra	.05
175	Dan Plesac	.05
176	Dan Pasqua	.05
177	Kelly Downs	.05
178	Matt Nokes	.05
179	Luis Aquino	.05
180	Frank Tanana	.05
181	Tony Pena	.05
182	Dan Gladden	.05
183	Bruce Hurst	.05
184	Roger Clemens	.35
185	Mark McGwire	1.00
186	Rob Murphy	.05
187	Jim Deshaies	.05
188	Fred McGriff	.15
189	Rob Dibble	.05
190	Don Mattingly	.35
191	Felix Fermin	.05
192	Roberto Kelly	.05
193	Dennis Cook	.05
194	Darren Daulton	.05
195	Alfredo Griffin	.05
196	Eric Plunk	.05
197	Orel Hershiser	.10
198	Paul O'Neill	.15
199	Randy Bush	.05
200a	Checklist 130-231	.05
200b	Checklist 126-223	.05
201	Ozzie Smith	.20
202	Pete O'Brien	.05
203	Jay Howell	.05
204	Mark Gubicza	.05
205	Ed Whitson	.05
206	George Bell	.05
207	Mike Scott	.05
208	Charlie Leibrandt	.05
209	Mike Heath	.05
210	Dennis Eckersley	.10
211	Mike LaValliere	.05
212	Darnell Coles	.05
213	Lance Parrish	.08
214	Mike Moore	.05
215	*Steve Finley*	.20
216	Tim Raines	.10
217a	Scott Garrelts (Born 10/20)	.05
217b	Scott Garrelts (Born 10/30)	.25
218	Kevin McReynolds	.05
219	Dave Gallagher	.05
220	Tim Wallach	.05
221	Chuck Crim	.05
222	Lonnie Smith	.05
223	Andre Dawson	.12
224	Nelson Santovenia	.05
225	Rafael Palmeiro	.12
226	Devon White	.05
227	Harold Reynolds	.05
228	Ellis Burks	.10
229	Mark Parent	.05
230	Will Clark	.25
231	Jimmy Key	.08
232	John Farrell	.05
233	Eric Davis	.10
234	Johnny Ray	.05
235	Darryl Strawberry	.12
236	Bill Doran	.05
237	Greg Gagne	.05
238	Jim Eisenreich	.05
239	Tommy Gregg	.05
240	Marty Barrett	.05
241	Rafael Ramirez	.05
242	Chris Sabo	.08
243	Dave Henderson	.05
244	Andy Van Slyke	.05
245	Alvaro Espinoza	.05
246	Garry Templeton	.05
247	Gene Harris	.05
248	Kevin Gross	.05
249	Brett Butler	.08
250	Willie Randolph	.05
251	Roger McDowell	.05
252	Rafael Belliard	.05
253	Steve Rosenberg	.05
254	Jack Howell	.05
255	Marvell Wynne	.05
256	Tom Candiotti	.05
257	Todd Benzinger	.05
258	Don Robinson	.05
259	Phil Bradley	.05
260	Cecil Espy	.05
261	Scott Bankhead	.05
262	Frank White	.05
263	Andres Thomas	.05
264	Glenn Braggs	.05
265	David Cone	.10
266	Bobby Thigpen	.05
267	Nelson Liriano	.05
268	Terry Steinbach	.05
269	Kirby Puckett	.35
270	Gregg Jefferies	.15
271	Jeff Blauser	.05
272	Cory Snyder	.05
273	Roy Smith	.05
274	Tom Foley	.05

No.	Player	Price
275	Mitch Williams	.05
276	Paul Kilgus	.05
277	Don Slaught	.05
278	Von Hayes	.05
279	Vince Coleman	.05
280	Mike Boddicker	.05
281	Ken Dayley	.05
282	Mike Devereaux	.05
283	*Kenny Rogers*	.10
284	Jeff Russell	.05
285	*Jerome Walton*	.08
286	Derek Lilliquist	.05
287	Joe Orsulak	.05
288	Dick Schofield	.05
289	Ron Darling	.05
290	Bobby Bonilla	.10
291	Jim Gantner	.05
292	Bobby Witt	.05
293	Greg Brock	.05
294	Ivan Calderon	.05
295	Steve Bedrosian	.05
296	Mike Henneman	.05
297	Tom Gordon	.05
298	Lou Whitaker	.08
299	Terry Pendleton	.05
300a	Checklist 232-333	.05
300b	Checklist 224-321	.05
301	Juan Berenguer	.05
302	Mark Davis	.05
303	Nick Esasky	.05
304	Rickey Henderson	.20
305	Rick Cerone	.05
306	Craig Biggio	.15
307	Duane Ward	.05
308	Tom Browning	.05
309	Walt Terrell	.05
310	Greg Swindell	.05
311	Dave Righetti	.05
312	Mike Maddux	.05
313	Len Dykstra	.08
314	Jose Gonzalez	.05
315	Steve Balboni	.05
316	Mike Scioscia	.05
317	Ron Oester	.05
318	*Gary Wayne*	.05
319	Todd Worrell	.05
320	Doug Jones	.05
321	Jeff Hamilton	.05
322	Danny Tartabull	.05
323	Chris James	.05
324	Mike Flanagan	.05
325	Gerald Young	.05
326	Bob Boone	.08
327	Frank Williams	.05
328	Dave Parker	.08
329	Sid Bream	.05
330	Mike Schooler	.05
331	Bert Blyleven	.08
332	Bob Welch	.05
333	Bob Milacki	.05
334	Tim Burke	.05
335	Jose Uribe	.05
336	Randy Myers	.05
337	Eric King	.05
338	Mark Langston	.10
339	Ted Higuera	.05
340	Oddibe McDowell	.05
341	Lloyd McClendon	.05
342	Pascual Perez	.05
343	Kevin Brown	.05
344	Chuck Finley	.05
345	Erik Hanson	.05
346	Rich Gedman	.05
347	Bip Roberts	.05
348	Matt Williams	.20
349	Tom Henke	.05
350	Brad Komminsk	.05
351	Jeff Reed	.05
352	Brian Downing	.05
353	Frank Viola	.05
354	Terry Puhl	.05
355	Brian Harper	.05
356	Steve Farr	.05
357	Joe Boever	.05
358	Danny Heep	.05
359	Larry Andersen	.05
360	Rolando Roomes	.05
361	Mike Gallego	.05
362	Bob Kipper	.05
363	Clay Parker	.05
364	Mike Pagliarulo	.05
365	Ken Griffey, Jr.	2.00
366	Rex Hudler	.05
367	Pat Sheridan	.05
368	Kirk Gibson	.08
369	Jeff Parrett	.05
370	Bob Walk	.05
371	Ken Patterson	.05
372	Bryan Harvey	.05
373	Mike Bielecki	.05
374	*Tom Magrann*	.05
375	Rick Mahler	.05
376	Craig Lefferts	.05
377	Gregg Olson	.05
378	Jamie Moyer	.05
379	Randy Johnson	.25
380	Jeff Montgomery	.05
381	Marty Clary	.05
382	*Bill Spiers*	.05
383	Dave Magadan	.05
384	*Greg Hibbard*	.05
385	Ernie Whitt	.05
386	Rick Honeycutt	.05
387	Dave West	.05
388	Keith Hernandez	.05
389	Jose Alvarez	.05
390	Albert Belle	.50
391	Rick Aguilera	.05
392	Mike Fitzgerald	.05
393	*Dwight Smith*	.05
394	*Steve Wilson*	.05
395	*Bob Geren*	.05
396	Randy Ready	.05
397	Ken Hill	.05
398	Jody Reed	.05
399	Tom Brunansky	.05
400a	Checklist 334-435	.05
400b	Checklist 322-419	.05
401	Rene Gonzales	.05
402	Harold Baines	.08
403	Cecilio Guante	.05
404	Joe Girardi	.08
405a	*Sergio Valdez* (black line crosses S in Sergio)	.25
405b	Sergio Valdez (corrected)	.05
406	Mark Williamson	.05
407	Glenn Hoffman	.05
408	*Jeff Innis*	.05
409	Randy Kramer	.05
410	Charlie O'Brien	.05
411	Charlie Hough	.05
412	Gus Polidor	.05
413	Ron Karkovice	.05
414	Trevor Wilson	.08
415	*Kevin Ritz*	.10
416	Gary Thurman	.05
417	Jeff Robinson	.05
418	Scott Terry	.05
419	Tim Laudner	.05
420	Dennis Rasmussen	.05
421	Luis Rivera	.05
422	Jim Corsi	.05
423	Dennis Lamp	.05
424	Ken Caminiti	.10
425	David Wells	.08
426	Norm Charlton	.05
427	Deion Sanders	.25
428	Dion James	.05
429	Chuck Cary	.05
430	Ken Howell	.05
431	Steve Lake	.05
432	Kal Daniels	.05
433	Lance McCullers	.05
434	Lenny Harris	.05
435	*Scott Scudder*	.05
436	Gene Larkin	.05
437	Dan Quisenberry	.05
438	*Steve Olin*	.05
439	Mickey Hatcher	.05
440	Willie Wilson	.05
441	Mark Grant	.05
442	Mookie Wilson	.05
443	Alex Trevino	.05
444	Pat Tabler	.05
445	Dave Bergman	.05
446	Todd Burns	.05
447	R.J. Reynolds	.05
448	Jay Buhner	.08
449	*Lee Stevens*	.10
450	Ron Hassey	.05
451	Bob Melvin	.05
452	Dave Martinez	.05
453	*Greg Litton*	.05
454	Mark Carreon	.05
455	Scott Fletcher	.05
456	Otis Nixon	.05
457	*Tony Fossas*	.05
458	John Russell	.05
459	Paul Assenmacher	.05
460	Zane Smith	.05
461	*Jack Daugherty*	.05
462	*Rich Monteleone*	.05
463	Greg Briley	.05
464	Mike Smithson	.05
465	Benito Santiago	.08
466	*Jeff Brantley*	.08
467	Jose Nunez	.05
468	Scott Bailes	.05
469	Ken Griffey	.08
470	Bob McClure	.05
471	Mackey Sasser	.05
472	Glenn Wilson	.05
473	*Kevin Tapani*	.25
474	Bill Buckner	.05
475	Ron Gant	.10
476	Kevin Romine	.05
477	Juan Agosto	.05
478	Herm Winningham	.05
479	Storm Davis	.05
480	Jeff King	.10
481	*Kevin Mmahat*	.05
482	Carmelo Martinez	.05
483	*Omar Vizquel*	.10
484	Jim Dwyer	.05
485	Bob Knepper	.05
486	Dave Anderson	.05
487	Ron Jones	.05
488	Jay Bell	.05
489	*Sammy Sosa*	5.00
490	*Kent Anderson*	.05
491	Domingo Ramos	.05
492	Dave Clark	.05
493	Tim Birtsas	.05
494	Ken Oberkfell	.05
495	Larry Sheets	.05
496	Jeff Kunkel	.05
497	Jim Presley	.05
498	Mike Macfarlane	.05
499	Pete Smith	.05
500a	Checklist 436-537	.05
500b	Checklist 420-517	.05
501	Gary Sheffield	.25
502	*Terry Bross*	.05
503	*Jerry Kutzler*	.05
504	Lloyd Moseby	.05
505	Curt Young	.05
506	Al Newman	.05
507	Keith Miller	.05
508	*Mike Stanton*	.15
509	Rich Yett	.05
510	*Tim Drummond*	.05
511	Joe Hesketh	.05
512	*Rick Wrona*	.10
513	Luis Salazar	.05
514	Hal Morris	.05
515	Terry Mullholland	.08
516	John Morris	.05
517	Carlos Quintana	.05
518	Frank DiPino	.05
519	Randy Milligan	.05
520	Chad Kreuter	.05
521	Mike Jeffcoat	.05
522	Mike Harkey	.05
523a	Andy Nezelek (Born 1985)	.05
523b	Andy Nezelek (Born 1965)	.25
524	Dave Schmidt	.05
525	Tony Armas	.05
526	Barry Lyons	.05
527	*Rick Reed*	.05
528	Jerry Reuss	.05
529	*Dean Palmer*	.15
530	*Jeff Peterek*	.05
531	*Carlos Martinez*	.08
532	Atlee Hammaker	.05
533	Mike Brumley	.05
534	Terry Leach	.05
535	*Doug Strange*	.05
536	Jose DeLeon	.05
537	Shane Rawley	.05
538	Joey Cora	.10
539	Eric Hetzel	.05
540	Gene Nelson	.05
541	Wes Gardner	.05
542	Mark Portugal	.05
543	Al Leiter	.05
544	Jack Armstrong	.05
545	Greg Cadaret	.05
546	Rod Nichols	.05
547	Luis Polonia	.05
548	Charlie Hayes	.05
549	Dickie Thon	.05
550	Tim Crews	.05
551	Dave Winfield	.20
552	Mike Davis	.05
553	Ron Robinson	.05
554	Carmen Castillo	.05
555	John Costello	.05
556	Bud Black	.05
557	Rick Dempsey	.05
558	Jim Acker	.05
559	Eric Show	.05
560	Pat Borders	.05
561	Danny Darwin	.05
562	*Rick Luecken*	.05
563	Edwin Nunez	.05
564	Felix Jose	.05
565	John Cangelosi	.05
566	Billy Swift	.05
567	Bill Schroeder	.05
568	Stan Javier	.05
569	Jim Traber	.05
570	Wallace Johnson	.05
571	Donell Nixon	.05
572	Sid Fernandez	.05
573	Lance Johnson	.08
574	Andy McGaffigan	.05
575	Mark Knudson	.05
576	*Tommy Greene*	.20
577	Mark Grace	.15
578	*Larry Walker*	1.50
579	Mike Stanley	.05
580	Mike Witt	.05
581	Scott Bradley	.05
582	Greg Harris	.05
583a	Kevin Hickey (black stripe over top of "K" vertical stroke)	.05
583b	Kevin Hickey (black stripe under "K")	.05
584	Lee Mazzilli	.05
585	Jeff Pico	.05
586	*Joe Oliver*	.05
587	Willie Fraser	.05
588	Puzzle card (Carl Yastrzemski)	.05
589	Kevin Bass	.05
590	John Moses	.05
591	Tom Pagnozzi	.05
592	*Tony Castillo*	.05
593	Jerald Clark	.05
594	Dan Schatzeder	.05
595	Luis Quinones	.05
596	Pete Harnisch	.08
597	Gary Redus	.05
598	Mel Hall	.05
599	Rick Schu	.05
600a	Checklist 538-639	.05
600b	Checklist 518-617	.05
601	Mike Kingery	.05
602	Terry Kennedy	.05
603	Mike Sharperson	.05
604	Don Carman	.05
605	Jim Gott	.05
606	Donn Pall	.05
607	Rance Mulliniks	.05
608	Curt Wilkerson	.05
609	Mike Felder	.05
610	Guillermo Hernandez	.05
611	Candy Maldonado	.05
612	Mark Thurmond	.05
613	Rick Leach	.05
614	Jerry Reed	.05
615	Franklin Stubbs	.05
616	Billy Hatcher	.05
617	Don August	.05
618	Tim Teufel	.05
619	Shawn Hillegas	.05
620	Manny Lee	.05
621	Gary Ward	.05
622	*Mark Guthrie*	.05
623	Jeff Musselman	.05
624	Mark Lemke	.05
625	Fernando Valenzuela	.08
626	*Paul Sorrento*	.10
627	Glenallen Hill	.05
628	Les Lancaster	.05
629	Vance Law	.05
630	Randy Velarde	.08
631	Todd Frohwirth	.05
632	Willie McGee	.08
633	Oil Can Boyd	.05
634	Cris Carpenter	.05
635	Brian Holton	.05
636	Tracy Jones	.05
637	Terry Steinbach (AS)	.08
638	Brady Anderson	.12

639a Jack Morris (black line crosses J of Jack) .25
639b Jack Morris (corrected) .08
640 *Jaime Navarro* .05
641 Darrin Jackson .05
642 *Mike Dyer* .05
643 Mike Schmidt .25
644 Henry Cotto .05
645 John Cerutti .05
646 *Francisco Cabrera* .05
647 Scott Sanderson .05
648 Brian Meyer .05
649 Ray Searage .05
650 Bo Jackson (AS) .15
651 Steve Lyons .05
652 Mike LaCoss .05
653 Ted Power .05
654 Howard Johnson (AS) .05
655 *Mauro Gozzo* .05
656 *Mike Blowers* .15
657 Paul Gibson .05
658 Neal Heaton .05
659a Nolan Ryan 5,000 K's (King of Kings (#665) back) 2.50
659b Nolan Ryan 5,000 K's (correct back) .50
660a Harold Baines (AS) (black line through star on front, Recent Major League Performance on back) .50
660b Harold Baines (AS) (black line through star on front, All-Star Game Performance on back) 1.50
660c Harold Baines (AS) (black line behind star on front, Recent Major League Performance on back) .75
660d Harold Baines (AS) (black line behind star on front, All-Star Game Performance on back) .10
661 Gary Pettis .05
662 *Clint Zavaras* .05
663 Rick Reuschel (AS) .05
664 Alejandro Pena .05
665a Nolan Ryan (King of Kings) 5,000 K's (#659) back) 2.50
665b Nolan Ryan (King of Kings) (correct back) .50
665c Nolan Ryan (King of Kings) (no number on back) 1.00
666 Ricky Horton .05
667 Curt Schilling .05
668 Bill Landrum .05
669 Todd Stottlemyre .05
670 Tim Leary .05
671 *John Wetteland* .25
672 Calvin Schiraldi .05
673 Ruben Sierra (AS) .05
674 Pedro Guerrero (AS) .05
675 Ken Phelps .05
676 Cal Ripken (AS) .25
677 Denny Walling .05
678 Goose Gossage .05
679 *Gary Mielke* .05
680 Bill Bathe .05
681 Tom Lawless .05
682 *Xavier Hernandez* .15
683 Kirby Puckett (AS) .20
684 Mariano Duncan .05
685 Ramon Martinez .10
686 Tim Jones .05
687 Tom Filer .05
688 Steve Lombardozzi .05
689 *Bernie Williams* 1.00
690 *Chip Hale* .05
691 *Beau Allred* .05
692 Ryne Sandberg (AS) .25
693 *Jeff Huson* .10
694 Curt Ford .05
695 Eric Davis (AS) .05
696 Scott Lusader .05
697 Mark McGwire (AS) .50
698 *Steve Cummings* .05
699 *George Canale* .05
700a Checklist 640-715/ BC1-BC26 .05
700b Checklist 640-716/ BC1-BC26 .05
700c Checklist 618-716 .05
701 Julio Franco (AS) .05
702 *Dave Johnson* .05
703 Dave Stewart (AS) .05
704 *Dave Justice* .50
705 Tony Gwynn (AS) .15
706 Greg Myers .05
707 Will Clark (AS) .10
708 Benito Santiago (AS) .05
709 Larry McWilliams .05
710 Ozzie Smith (AS) .10
711 *John Olerud* .50
712 Wade Boggs (AS) .10
713 *Gary Eave* .05
714 Bob Tewksbury .05
715 Kevin Mitchell (AS) .05
716 A. Bartlett Giamatti .25

1990 Donruss Grand Slammers

For the second consecutive year Donruss produced a set in honor of players who hit grand slams in the previous season. The cards are styled after the 1990 Donruss regular issue. The cards were inserted into 1990 Donruss factory sets, and one card per cello pack. Some, perhaps all, of the cards can be found without the split black stripe near the right end on back.

		MT
Complete Set (12):		2.00
Common Player:		.10
1	Matt Williams	.30
2	Jeffrey Leonard	.10
3	Chris James	.10
4	Mark McGwire	1.00
5	Dwight Evans	.10
6	Will Clark	.25
7	Mike Scioscia	.10
8	Todd Benzinger	.10
9	Fred McGriff	.30
10	Kevin Bass	.10
11	Jack Clark	.10
12	Bo Jackson	.25

1990 Donruss MVP

This special 26-card set includes one player from each Major League team. Numbered BC-1 (the "BC" stands for "Bonus Card") through BC-26, the cards from this set were randomly packed in 1990 Donruss wax packs and were not available in factory sets or other types of packaging. The red-bordered cards are similar in design to the regular 1990 Donruss set, except the player photos are set against a special background made up of the "MVP" logo.

		MT
Complete Set (26):		1.25
Common Player:		.10
1	Bo Jackson	.25
2	Howard Johnson	.10
3	Dave Stewart	.10
4	Tony Gwynn	.35
5	Orel Hershiser	.10
6	Pedro Guerrero	.10
7	Tim Raines	.12
8	Kirby Puckett	.35
9	Alvin Davis	.10
10	Ryne Sandberg	.40
11	Kevin Mitchell	.10
12a	John Smoltz (photo of Tom Glavine)	2.00
12b	John Smoltz (corrected)	.40
13	George Bell	.10
14	Julio Franco	.10
15	Paul Molitor	.25
16	Bobby Bonilla	.15
17	Mike Greenwell	.10
18	Cal Ripken	.60
19	Carlton Fisk	.15
20	Chili Davis	.10
21	Glenn Davis	.10
22	Steve Sax	.10
23	Eric Davis	.15
24	Greg Swindell	.10
25	Von Hayes	.10
26	Alan Trammell	.12

1990 Donruss Best A.L.

This 144-card set features the top players of the American League. The 2-1/2" x 3-1/2" cards feature the same front design as the regular Donruss set, exception with blue borders instead of red. Backs feature a yellow frame with complete statistics and biographical information provided. This marks the first year that Donruss divided its baseball-best issue into two sets designated by league.

		MT
Complete Set (144):		6.00
Common Player:		.05
1	Ken Griffey, Jr.	1.50
2	Bob Milacki	.05
3	Mike Boddicker	.05
4	Bert Blyleven	.05
5	Carlton Fisk	.10
6	Greg Swindell	.05
7	Alan Trammell	.08
8	Mark Davis	.05
9	Chris Bosio	.05
10	Gary Gaetti	.05
11	Matt Nokes	.05
12	Dennis Eckersley	.08
13	Kevin Brown	.05
14	Tom Henke	.05
15	Mickey Tettleton	.05
16	Jody Reed	.05
17	Mark Langston	.08
18	Melido Perez	.05
19	John Farrell	.05
20	Tony Phillips	.05
21	Bret Saberhagen	.08
22	Robin Yount	.10
23	Kirby Puckett	.25
24	Steve Sax	.05
25	Dave Stewart	.05
26	Alvin Davis	.05
27	Geno Petralli	.05
28	Mookie Wilson	.05
29	Jeff Ballard	.05
30	Ellis Burks	.05
31	Wally Joyner	.08
32	Bobby Thigpen	.05
33	Keith Hernandez	.05
34	Jack Morris	.05
35	George Brett	.20
36	Dan Plesac	.05
37	Brian Harper	.05
38	Don Mattingly	.45
39	Dave Henderson	.05
40	Scott Bankhead	.05
41	Rafael Palmeiro	.10
42	Jimmy Key	.05
43	Gregg Olson	.05
44	Tony Pena	.05
45	Jack Howell	.05
46	Eric King	.05
47	Cory Snyder	.05
48	Frank Tanana	.05
49	Nolan Ryan	.60
50	Bob Boone	.05
51	Dave Parker	.08
52	Allan Anderson	.05
53	Tim Leary	.05
54	Mark McGwire	1.50
55	Dave Valle	.05
56	Fred McGriff	.20
57	Cal Ripken	1.50
58	Roger Clemens	.25
59	Lance Parrish	.05
60	Robin Ventura	.10
61	Doug Jones	.05
62	Lloyd Moseby	.05
63	Bo Jackson	.15
64	Paul Molitor	.10
65	Kent Hrbek	.08
66	Mel Hall	.05
67	Bob Welch	.05
68	Erik Hanson	.05
69	Harold Baines	.08
70	Junior Felix	.05
71	Craig Worthington	.05
72	Jeff Reardon	.05

73	Johnny Ray	.05
74	Ozzie Guillen	.05
75	Brook Jacoby	.05
76	Chet Lemon	.05
77	Mark Gubicza	.05
78	B.J. Surhoff	.08
79	Rick Aguilera	.05
80	Pascual Perez	.05
81	Jose Canseco	.35
82	Mike Schooler	.05
83	Jeff Huson	.05
84	Kelly Gruber	.05
85	Randy Milligan	.05
86	Wade Boggs	.35
87	Dave Winfield	.15
88	Scott Fletcher	.05
89	Tom Candiotti	.05
90	Mike Heath	.05
91	Kevin Seitzer	.05
92	Ted Higuera	.05
93	Kevin Tapani	.05
94	Roberto Kelly	.05
95	Walt Weiss	.05
96	Checklist	.05
97	Sandy Alomar	.10
98	Pete O'Brien	.05
99	Jeff Russell	.05
100	John Olerud	.12
101	Pete Harnisch	.05
102	Dwight Evans	.05
103	Chuck Finley	.05
104	Sammy Sosa	1.00
105	Mike Henneman	.05
106	Kurt Stillwell	.05
107	Greg Vaughn	.08
108	Dan Gladden	.05
109	Jesse Barfield	.05
110	Willie Randolph	.05
111	Randy Johnson	.20
112	Julio Franco	.08
113	Tony Fernandez	.05
114	Ben McDonald	.05
115	Mike Greenwell	.05
116	Luis Polonia	.05
117	Carney Lansford	.05
118	Bud Black	.05
119	Lou Whitaker	.05
120	Jim Eisenreich	.05
121	Gary Sheffield	.10
122	Shane Mack	.05
123	Alvaro Espinoza	.05
124	Rickey Henderson	.15
125	Jeffrey Leonard	.05
126	Gary Pettis	.05
127	Dave Steib	.05
128	Danny Tartabull	.05
129	Joe Orsulak	.05
130	Tom Brunansky	.05
131	Dick Schofield	.05
132	Candy Maldonado	.05
133	Cecil Fielder	.05
134	Terry Shumpert	.05
135	Greg Gagne	.05
136	Dave Righetti	.05
137	Terry Steinbach	.05
138	Harold Reynolds	.05
139	George Bell	.05
140	Carlos Quintana	.05
141	Ivan Calderon	.05
142	Greg Brock	.05
143	Ruben Sierra	.05
144	Checklist	.05

1990 Donruss Best N.L.

This 144-card set features the top players in the National League for 1990. The 2-1/2" x 3-1/2" cards feature the same design as the regular 1990 Donruss cards, except they have blue, rather than red borders. Traded players are featured with their new teams. This set, along with the A.L. Best set, was available at select retail stores and within the hobby.

		MT
Complete Set (144):		4.00
Common Player:		.05
1	Eric Davis	.10
2	Tom Glavine	.08
3	Mike Bielecki	.05
4	Jim Deshaies	.05
5	Mike Scioscia	.05
6	Spike Owen	.05
7	Dwight Gooden	.12
8	Ricky Jordan	.05
9	Doug Drabek	.05
10	Bryn Smith	.05
11	Tony Gwynn	.40
12	John Burkett	.05
13	Nick Esasky	.05
14	Greg Maddux	.75
15	Joe Oliver	.05
16	Mike Scott	.05
17	Tim Belcher	.05
18	Kevin Gross	.05
19	Howard Johnson	.05
20	Darren Daulton	.05
21	John Smiley	.05
22	Ken Dayley	.05
23	Craig Lefferts	.05
24	Will Clark	.25
25	Greg Olson	.05
26	Ryne Sandberg	.45
27	Tom Browning	.05
28	Eric Anthony	.08
29	Juan Samuel	.05
30	Dennis Martinez	.08
31	Kevin Elster	.08
32	Tom Herr	.05
33	Sid Bream	.05
34	Terry Pendleton	.05
35	Roberto Alomar	.30
36	Kevin Bass	.05
37	Jim Presley	.05
38	Les Lancaster	.05
39	Paul O'Neill	.10
40	Dave Smith	.05
41	Kirk Gibson	.05
42	Tim Burke	.05
43	David Cone	.08
44	Ken Howell	.05
45	Barry Bonds	.50
46	Joe Magrane	.05
47	Andy Benes	.08
48	Gary Carter	.10
49	Pat Combs	.05
50	John Smoltz	.08
51	Mark Grace	.15
52	Barry Larkin	.15
53	Danny Darwin	.05
54	Orel Hershiser	.08
55	Tim Wallach	.05
56	Dave Magadan	.05
57	Roger McDowell	.05
58	Bill Landrum	.05
59	Jose DeLeon	.05
60	Bip Roberts	.05
61	Matt Williams	.12
62	Dale Murphy	.10
63	Dwight Smith	.05
64	Chris Sabo	.05
65	Glenn Davis	.05
66	Jay Howell	.05
67	Andres Galarraga	.08
68	Frank Viola	.05
69	John Kruk	.05
70	Bobby Bonilla	.08
71	Todd Zeile	.08
72	Joe Carter	.08
73	Robby Thompson	.05
74	Jeff Blauser	.05
75	Mitch Williams	.05
76	Rob Dibble	.05
77	Rafael Ramirez	.05
78	Eddie Murray	.20
79	Dave Martinez	.05
80	Darryl Strawberry	.10
81	Dickie Thon	.05
82	Jose Lind	.05
83	Ozzie Smith	.20
84	Bruce Hurst	.05
85	Kevin Mitchell	.05
86	Lonnie Smith	.05
87	Joe Girardi	.05
88	Randy Myers	.05
89	Craig Biggio	.10
90	Fernando Valenzuela	.08
91	Larry Walker	.15
92	John Franco	.05
93	Dennis Cook	.05
94	Bob Walk	.05
95	Pedro Guerrero	.05
96	Checklist	.05
97	Andre Dawson	.10
98	Ed Whitson	.05
99	Steve Bedrosian	.05
100	Oddibe McDowell	.05
101	Todd Benzinger	.05
102	Bill Doran	.05
103	Alfredo Griffin	.05
104	Tim Raines	.10
105	Sid Fernandez	.05
106	Charlie Hayes	.05
107	Mike LaValliere	.05
108	Jose Oquendo	.05
109	Jack Clark	.05
110	Scott Garrelts	.05
111	Ron Gant	.10
112	Shawon Dunston	.05
113	Mariano Duncan	.05
114	Eric Yelding	.05
115	Hubie Brooks	.05
116	Delino DeShields	.05
117	Gregg Jefferies	.10
118	Len Dykstra	.05
119	Andy Van Slyke	.05
120	Lee Smith	.08
121	Benito Santiago	.05
122	Jose Uribe	.05
123	Jeff Treadway	.05
124	Jerome Walton	.05
125	Billy Hatcher	.05
126	Ken Caminiti	.10
127	Kal Daniels	.05
128	Marquis Grissom	.12
129	Kevin McReynolds	.05
130	Wally Backman	.05
131	Willie McGee	.05
132	Terry Kennedy	.05
133	Garry Templeton	.05
134	Lloyd McClendon	.05
135	Daryl Boston	.05
136	Jay Bell	.05
137	Mike Pagliarulo	.05
138	Vince Coleman	.05
139	Brett Butler	.08
140	Von Hayes	.05
141	Ramon Martinez	.10
142	Jack Armstrong	.05
143	Franklin Stubbs	.05
144	Checklist	.05

1990 Donruss Diamond Kings Supers

Donruss made this set available through a mail-in offer. Three wrappers, $10 and $2 for postage were necessary to obtain this set. The cards are exactly the same design as the regular Donruss Diamond Kings except they measure approximately 5" x 6-3/4" in size. The artwork of Dick Perez is featured.

		MT
Complete Set (26):		6.00
Common Player:		.10
1	Bo Jackson	.50
2	Steve Sax	.10
3	Ruben Sierra	.10
4	Ken Griffey, Jr.	4.00
5	Mickey Tettleton	.10
6	Dave Stewart	.10
7	Jim Deshaies	.10
8	John Smoltz	.35
9	Mike Bielecki	.10
10	Brian Downing	.10
11	Kevin Mitchell	.10
12	Kelly Gruber	.10
13	Joe Magrane	.10
14	John Franco	.10
15	Ozzie Guillen	.10
16	Lou Whitaker	.10
17	John Smiley	.10
18	Howard Johnson	.10
19	Willie Randolph	.10
20	Chris Bosio	.10
21	Tommy Herr	.10
22	Dan Gladden	.10
23	Ellis Burks	.10
24	Pete O'Brien	.10
25	Bryn Smith	.10
26	Ed Whitson	.10

1990 Donruss Learning Series

Cards from this 55-card set were released as part of an educational package available to schools. The cards are styled like the regular-issue 1990 Donruss cards, but feature a special "learning series" logo on the front. The backs feature career highlights, statistics and card numbers. The cards were not released directly to the hobby.

		MT
Complete Set (55):		20.00
Common Player:		.25
1	George Brett (DK)	2.00
2	Kevin Mitchell	.25
3	Andy Van Slyke	.25
4	Benito Santiago	.25
5	Gary Carter	.40
6	Jose Canseco	1.00
7	Rickey Henderson	.85
8	Ken Griffey, Jr.	8.00
9	Ozzie Smith	2.00
10	Dwight Gooden	.35
11	Ryne Sandberg (DK)	2.00
12	Don Mattingly	3.00
13	Ozzie Guillen	.25
14	Dave Righetti	.25

15	Rick Dempsey	.25
16	Tom Herr	.25
17	Julio Franco	.25
18	Von Hayes	.25
19	Cal Ripken	5.00
20	Alan Trammell	.35
21	Wade Boggs	2.00
22	Glenn Davis	.25
23	Will Clark	.75
24	Nolan Ryan	5.00
25	George Bell	.25
26	Cecil Fielder	.25
27	Gregg Olson	.25
28	Tim Wallach	.25
29	Ron Darling	.25
30	Kelly Gruber	.25
31	Shawn Boskie	.25
32	Mike Greenwell	.25
33	Dave Parker	.30
34	Joe Magrane	.25
35	Dave Stewart	.25
36	Kent Hrbek	.25
37	Robin Yount	1.00
38	Bo Jackson	.50
39	Fernando Valenzuela	.25
40	Sandy Alomar, Jr.	.35
41	Lance Parrish	.25
42	Candy Maldonado	.25
43	Mike LaValliere	.25
44	Jim Abbott	.25
45	Edgar Martinez	.25
46	Kirby Puckett	2.50
47	Delino DeShields	.25
48	Tony Gwynn	2.00
49	Carlton Fisk	.40
50	Mike Scott	.25
51	Barry Larkin	.30
52	Andre Dawson	.40
53	Tom Glavine	.35
54	Tom Browning	.25
55	Checklist	.05

1990 Donruss Rookies

For the fifth straight year, Donruss issued a 56-card "Rookies" set in 1990. As in previous years, the set is similar in design to the regular Donruss set, except for a new "The Rookies" logo and green borders instead of red. The set is packaged in a special box and includes a Carl Yastrzemski puzzle card.

		MT
Complete Set (56):		2.00
Common Player:		.10
1	Sandy Alomar	.25
2	John Olerud	.40
3	Pat Combs	.10
4	Brian Dubois	.10
5	Felix Jose	.10
6	Delino DeShields	.10
7	Mike Stanton	.10
8	Mike Munoz	.10
9	Craig Grebeck	.10
10	Joe Kraemer	.10
11	Jeff Huson	.10
12	Bill Sampen	.10
13	Brian Bohanon	.10
14	Dave Justice	.50
15	Robin Ventura	.30
16	Greg Vaughn	.20
17	Wayne Edwards	.10
18	Shawn Boskie	.10
19	*Carlos Baerga*	.20
20	Mark Gardner	.10
21	Kevin Appier	.30
22	Mike Harkey	.10
23	Tim Layana	.10
24	Glenallen Hill	.10
25	Jerry Kutzler	.10
26	Mike Blowers	.10
27	Scott Ruskin	.10
28	Dana Kiecker	.10
29	Willie Blair	.10
30	Ben McDonald	.15
31	Todd Zeile	.15
32	Scott Coolbaugh	.10
33	Xavier Hernandez	.10
34	Mike Hartley	.10
35	Kevin Tapani	.10
36	Kevin Wickander	.10
37	Carlos Hernandez	.10
38	Brian Traxler	.10
39	Marty Brown	.10
40	Scott Radinsky	.10
41	Julio Machado	.10
42	Steve Avery	.10
43	Mark Lemke	.10
44	Alan Mills	.10
45	Marquis Grissom	.50
46	Greg Olson	.10
47	Dave Hollins	.15
48	Jerald Clark	.10
49	Eric Anthony	.10
50	Tim Drummond	.10
51	John Burkett	.15
52	Brent Knackert	.10
53	Jeff Shaw	.10
54	John Orton	.10
55	Terry Shumpert	.10
56	Checklist	.05

1991 Donruss Previews

Once again in late 1990 Donruss distributed individual cards from a 12-card preview issue to its dealer network as an introduction to its 1991 issue. Like the previous year's preview cards, the '91 samples utilized the format which would follow on the regular-issue cards, but the photos were different. This has helped create demand for these cards from superstar collectors. Backs are printed in black-and-white and have little more than a player name, card number and MLB logos.

		MT
Complete Set (12):		750.00
Common Player:		9.00
1	Dave Justice	75.00
2	Doug Drabek	9.00
3	Scott Chiamparino	9.00
4	Ken Griffey, Jr.	250.00
5	Bob Welch	9.00
6	Tino Martinez	45.00
7	Nolan Ryan	250.00
8	Dwight Gooden	15.00
9	Ryne Sandberg	95.00
10	Barry Bonds	100.00
11	Jose Canseco	75.00
12	Eddie Murray	60.00

1991 Donruss

Donruss used a two-series format in 1991. The first series was released in December, 1990, and the second in February, 1991. The 1991 design is somewhat reminiscent of the 1986 set, with blue borders on Series I cards; green on Series II. Limited edition cards including an autographed Ryne Sandberg card (5,000) were randomly inserted in wax packs. Other features of the set include 40 Rated Rookies, (RR) in the checklist, Legends and Elite insert series, and another Diamond King (DK) subset. Cards were distributed in packs with Willie Stargell puzzle pieces.

		MT
Factory Set w/Leaf or Studio Preview:		10.00
Complete Set (792):		8.00
Common Player:		.05
Willie Stargell Puzzle:		1.00
Series 1 or 2 Pack (15):		.35
Series 1 or 2 Wax Box (36):		9.00
1	Dave Steib (Diamond King)	.05
2	Craig Biggio (DK)	.05
3	Cecil Fielder (DK)	.08
4	Barry Bonds (DK)	.20
5	Barry Larkin (DK)	.10
6	Dave Parker (DK)	.05
7	Len Dykstra (DK)	.05
8	Bobby Thigpen (DK)	.05
9	Roger Clemens (DK)	.15
10	Ron Gant (DK)	.08
11	Delino DeShields (DK)	.05
12	Roberto Alomar (DK)	.15
13	Sandy Alomar (DK)	.08
14	Ryne Sandberg (DK)	.15
15	Ramon Martinez (DK)	.05
16	Edgar Martinez (DK)	.05
17	Dave Magadan (DK)	.05
18	Matt Williams (DK)	.12
19	Rafael Palmeiro (DK)	.10
20	Bob Welch (DK)	.05
21	Dave Righetti (DK)	.05
22	Brian Harper (DK)	.05
23	Gregg Olson (DK)	.05
24	Kurt Stillwell (DK)	.05
25	Pedro Guerrero (DK)	.05
26	Chuck Finley (DK)	.05
27	Diamond King checklist	.05
28	Tino Martinez (Rated Rookie)	.15
29	Mark Lewis (RR)	.10
30	*Bernard Gilkey* (RR)	.15
31	Hensley Meulens (RR)	.05
32	*Derek Bell* (RR)	.30
33	Jose Offerman (RR)	.08
34	Terry Bross (RR)	.08
35	*Leo Gomez* (RR)	.08
36	Derrick May (RR)	.08
37	*Kevin Morton* (RR)	.05
38	Moises Alou (RR)	.15
39	*Julio Valera* (RR)	.05
40	Milt Cuyler (RR)	.05
41	*Phil Plantier* (RR)	.10
42	*Scott Chiamparino* (RR)	.05
43	*Ray Lankford* (RR)	.20
44	*Mickey Morandini* (RR)	.10
45	Dave Hansen (RR)	.10
46	*Kevin Belcher* (RR)	.08
47	Darrin Fletcher (RR)	.10
48	Steve Sax (All Star)	.05
49	Ken Griffey, Jr. (AS)	.50
50a	Jose Canseco (AS) (A's in stat line on back)	.12
50b	Jose Canseco (AS) (AL in stat line on back)	.15
51	Sandy Alomar (AS)	.08
52	Cal Ripken, Jr. (AS)	.20
53	Rickey Henderson (AS)	.15
54	Bob Welch (AS)	.05
55	Wade Boggs (AS)	.10
56	Mark McGwire (AS)	.50
57	Jack McDowell	.08
58	Jose Lind	.05
59	Alex Fernandez	.20
60	Pat Combs	.05
61	*Mike Walker*	.05
62	Juan Samuel	.05
63	Mike Blowers	.05
64	Mark Guthrie	.05
65	Mark Salas	.05
66	Tim Jones	.05
67	Tim Leary	.05
68	Andres Galarraga	.10
69	Bob Milacki	.05
70	Tim Belcher	.05
71	Todd Zeile	.08
72	Jerome Walton	.05
73	Kevin Seitzer	.05
74	Jerald Clark	.05
75	John Smoltz	.10
76	Mike Henneman	.05
77	Ken Griffey, Jr.	1.50
78	Jim Abbott	.08
79	Gregg Jefferies	.10
80	Kevin Reimer	.05
81	Roger Clemens	.35
82	Mike Fitzgerald	.05
83	Bruce Hurst	.05
84	Eric Davis	.10
85	Paul Molitor	.25
86	Will Clark	.25
87	Mike Bielecki	.05
88	Bret Saberhagen	.10
89	Nolan Ryan	.50
90	Bobby Thigpen	.05
91	Dickie Thon	.05
92	Duane Ward	.05
93	Luis Polonia	.05
94	Terry Kennedy	.05
95	Kent Hrbek	.08
96	Danny Jackson	.05
97	Sid Fernandez	.05
98	Jimmy Key	.08
99	Franklin Stubbs	.05
100	Checklist 28-103	.05
101	R.J. Reynolds	.05
102	Dave Stewart	.08
103	Dan Pasqua	.05
104	Dan Plesac	.05

105 Mark McGwire 1.00
106 John Farrell .05
107 Don Mattingly .35
108 Carlton Fisk .10
109 Ken Oberkfell .05
110 Darrel Akerfelds .05
111 Gregg Olson .05
112 Mike Scioscia .05
113 Bryn Smith .05
114 Bob Geren .05
115 Tom Candiotti .05
116 Kevin Tapani .08
117 Jeff Treadway .05
118 Alan Trammell .10
119 Pete O'Brien .05
120 Joel Skinner .05
121 Mike LaValliere .05
122 Dwight Evans .08
123 Jody Reed .05
124 Lee Guetterman .05
125 Tim Burke .05
126 Dave Johnson .05
127 Fernando Valenzuela .10
128 Jose DeLeon .05
129 Andre Dawson .10
130 Gerald Perry .05
131 Greg Harris .05
132 Tom Glavine .10
133 Lance McCullers .05
134 Randy Johnson .25
135 Lance Parrish .08
136 Mackey Sasser .05
137 Geno Petralli .05
138 Dennis Lamp .05
139 Dennis Martinez .08
140 Mike Pagliarulo .05
141 Hal Morris .05
142 Dave Parker .08
143 Brett Butler .08
144 Paul Assenmacher .05
145 Mark Gubicza .05
146 Charlie Hough .05
147 Sammy Sosa .75
148 Randy Ready .05
149 Kelly Gruber .05
150 Devon White .10
151 Gary Carter .12
152 Gene Larkin .05
153 Chris Sabo .05
154 David Cone .10
155 Todd Stottlemyre .08
156 Glenn Wilson .05
157 Bob Walk .05
158 Mike Gallego .05
159 Greg Hibbard .05
160 Chris Bosio .05
161 Mike Moore .05
162 Jerry Browne .05
163 Steve Sax .05
164 Melido Perez .05
165 Danny Darwin .05
166 Roger McDowell .05
167 Bill Ripken .05
168 Mike Sharperson .05
169 Lee Smith .08
170 Matt Nokes .05
171 Jesse Orosco .05
172 Rick Aguilera .05
173 Jim Presley .05
174 Lou Whitaker .08
175 Harold Reynolds .08
176 Brook Jacoby .05
177 Wally Backman .05
178 Wade Boggs .25
179 Chuck Cary .05
180 Tom Foley .05
181 Pete Harnisch .05
182 Mike Morgan .05
183 Bob Tewksbury .05
184 Joe Girardi .05
185 Storm Davis .05
186 Ed Whitson .05
187 Steve Avery .05
188 Lloyd Moseby .05
189 Scott Bankhead .05
190 Mark Langston .08
191 Kevin McReynolds .05
192 Julio Franco .08
193 John Dopson .05
194 Oil Can Boyd .05
195 Bip Roberts .05
196 Billy Hatcher .05
197 Edgar Diaz .05
198 Greg Litton .05
199 Mark Grace .20
200 Checklist 104-179 .05
201 George Brett .30
202 Jeff Russell .05
203 Ivan Calderon .05
204 Ken Howell .05
205 Tom Henke .05
206 Bryan Harvey .05
207 Steve Bedrosian .05
208 Al Newman .05
209 Randy Myers .08
210 Daryl Boston .05
211 Manny Lee .05
212 Dave Smith .05
213 Don Slaught .05
214 Walt Weiss .05
215 Donn Pall .05
216 Jamie Navarro .05
217 Willie Randolph .05
218 Rudy Seanez .05
219 *Jim Leyritz* .15
220 Ron Karkovice .05
221 Ken Caminiti .10
222a Von Hayes (Traded players' first names included in How Acquired on back) .05
222b Von Hayes (No first names) .05
223 Cal Ripken, Jr. .75
224 Lenny Harris .05
225 Milt Thompson .05
226 Alvaro Espinoza .05
227 Chris James .05
228 Dan Gladden .05
229 Jeff Blauser .05
230 Mike Heath .05
231 Omar Vizquel .08
232 Doug Jones .05
233 Jeff King .05
234 Luis Rivera .05
235 Ellis Burks .08
236 Greg Cadaret .05
237 Dave Martinez .05
238 Mark Williamson .05
239 Stan Javier .05
240 Ozzie Smith .25
241 *Shawn Boskie* .08
242 Tom Gordon .05
243 Tony Gwynn .35
244 Tommy Gregg .05
245 Jeff Robinson .05
246 Keith Comstock .05
247 Jack Howell .05
248 Keith Miller .05
249 Bobby Witt .05
250 Rob Murphy .05
251 Spike Owen .05
252 Garry Templeton .05
253 Glenn Braggs .05
254 Ron Robinson .05
255 Kevin Mitchell .05
256 Les Lancaster .05
257 *Mel Stottlemyre* .10
258 Kenny Rogers .08
259 Lance Johnson .05
260 John Kruk .08
261 Fred McGriff .15
262 Dick Schofield .05
263 Trevor Wilson .05
264 David West .05
265 Scott Scudder .05
266 Dwight Gooden .10
267 *Willie Blair* .08
268 Mark Portugal .05
269 Doug Drabek .05
270 Dennis Eckersley .10
271 Eric King .05
272 Robin Yount .25
273 Carney Lansford .05
274 Carlos Baerga .08
275 Dave Righetti .05
276 Scott Fletcher .05
277 Eric Yelding .05
278 Charlie Hayes .05
279 Jeff Ballard .05
280 Orel Hershiser .10
281 Jose Oquendo .05
282 Mike Witt .05
283 Mitch Webster .05
284 Greg Gagne .05
285 *Greg Olson* .05
286 Tony Phillips .08
287 Scott Bradley .05
288 Cory Snyder .05
289 Jay Bell .08
290 Kevin Romine .05
291 Jeff Robinson .05
292 Steve Frey .05
293 Craig Worthington .05
294 Tim Crews .05
295 Joe Magrane .05
296 *Hector Villanueva* .05
297 *Terry Shumpert* .05
298 Joe Carter .08
299 Kent Mercker .05
300 Checklist 180-255 .05
301 Chet Lemon .05
302 Mike Schooler .05
303 Dante Bichette .08
304 Kevin Elster .05
305 Jeff Huson .05
306 Greg Harris .05
307 Marquis Grissom .12
308 Calvin Schiraldi .05
309 Mariano Duncan .05
310 Bill Spiers .05
311 Scott Garrelts .05
312 Mitch Williams .05
313 Mike Macfarlane .05
314 Kevin Brown .05
315 Robin Ventura .15
316 Darren Daulton .05
317 Pat Borders .05
318 Mark Eichhorn .05
319 Jeff Brantley .05
320 Shane Mack .05
321 Rob Dibble .05
322 John Franco .05
323 Junior Felix .05
324 Casey Candaele .05
325 Bobby Bonilla .08
326 Dave Henderson .05
327 Wayne Edwards .05
328 Mark Knudson .05
329 Terry Steinbach .08
330 *Colby Ward* .05
331 *Oscar Azocar* .05
332 *Scott Radinsky* .10
333 Eric Anthony .05
334 Steve Lake .05
335 Bob Melvin .05
336 Kal Daniels .05
337 Tom Pagnozzi .05
338 *Alan Mills* .08
339 Steve Olin .05
340 Juan Berenguer .05
341 Francisco Cabrera .05
342 Dave Bergman .05
343 Henry Cotto .05
344 Sergio Valdez .05
345 Bob Patterson .05
346 John Marzano .05
347 *Dana Kiecker* .05
348 Dion James .05
349 Hubie Brooks .05
350 Bill Landrum .05
351 *Bill Sampen* .05
352 Greg Briley .05
353 Paul Gibson .05
354 Dave Eiland .05
355 Steve Finley .05
356 Bob Boone .05
357 Steve Buechele .05
358 Chris Hoiles .08
359 Larry Walker .25
360 Frank DiPino .05
361 Mark Grant .05
362 Dave Magadan .05
363 Robby Thompson .05
364 Lonnie Smith .05
365 Steve Farr .05
366 Dave Valle .05
367 *Tim Naehring* .08
368 Jim Acker .05
369 Jeff Reardon .05
370 Tim Teufel .05
371 Juan Gonzalez .60
372 Luis Salazar .05
373 Rick Honeycutt .05
374 Greg Maddux .75
375 Jose Uribe .05
376 Donnie Hill .05
377 Don Carman .05
378 *Craig Grebeck* .05
379 Willie Fraser .05
380 Glenallen Hill .08
381 Joe Oliver .05
382 Randy Bush .05
383 Alex Cole .05
384 Norm Charlton .05
385 Gene Nelson .05
386a Checklist 256-331 (blue borders) .05
386b Checklist 256-331 (green borders) .05
387 Rickey Henderson (MVP) .15
388 Lance Parrish (MVP) .05
389 Fred McGriff (MVP) .10
390 Dave Parker (MVP) .05
391 Candy Maldonado (MVP) .05
392 Ken Griffey, Jr. (MVP) .40
393 Gregg Olson (MVP) .05
394 Rafael Palmeiro (MVP) .10
395 Roger Clemens (MVP) .20
396 George Brett (MVP) .15
397 Cecil Fielder (MVP) .10
398 Brian Harper (MVP) .05
399 Bobby Thigpen (MVP) .05
400 Roberto Kelly (MVP) .05
401 Danny Darwin (MVP) .05
402 Dave Justice (MVP) .25
403 Lee Smith (MVP) .05
404 Ryne Sandberg (MVP) .15
405 Eddie Murray (MVP) .15
406 Tim Wallach (MVP) .05
407 Kevin Mitchell (MVP) .05
408 Darryl Strawberry (MVP) .08
409 Joe Carter (MVP) .05
410 Len Dykstra (MVP) .05
411 Doug Drabek (MVP) .05
412 Chris Sabo (MVP) .05
413 *Paul Marak* (RR) .05
414 Tim McIntosh (RR) .05
415 *Brian Barnes* (RR) .05
416 *Eric Gunderson* (RR) .05
417 *Mike Gardiner* (RR) .10
418 Steve Carter (RR) .08
419 *Gerald Alexander* (RR) .05
420 *Rich Garces* (RR) .05
421 *Chuck Knoblauch* (RR) .45
422 *Scott Aldred* (RR) .05
423 *Wes Chamberlain* (RR) .10
424 *Lance Dickson* (RR) .08
425 *Greg Colbrunn* (RR) .15
426 *Rich Delucia* (RR) .08
427 *Jeff Conine* (RR) .40
428 *Steve Decker* (RR) .10
429 *Turner Ward* (RR) .10
430 Mo Vaughn (RR) .65
431 *Steve Chitren* (RR) .10
432 Mike Benjamin (RR) .10
433 Ryne Sandberg (AS) .10
434 Len Dykstra (AS) .05
435 Andre Dawson (AS) .10
436 Mike Scioscia (AS) .05
437 Ozzie Smith (AS) .10
438 Kevin Mitchell (AS) .05
439 Jack Armstrong (AS) .05
440 Chris Sabo (AS) .05
441 Will Clark (AS) .10
442 Mel Hall .05
443 Mark Gardner .05
444 Mike Devereaux .05
445 Kirk Gibson .05
446 Terry Pendleton .05
447 Mike Harkey .05
448 Jim Eisenreich .05
449 Benito Santiago .08
450 Oddibe McDowell .05
451 Cecil Fielder .08
452 Ken Griffey, Sr. .08
453 Bert Blyleven .08
454 Howard Johnson .05
455 Monty Farris .05
456 Tony Pena .05
457 Tim Raines .08
458 Dennis Rasmussen .05
459 Luis Quinones .05
460 B.J. Surhoff .08
461 Ernest Riles .05
462 Rick Sutcliffe .05
463 Danny Tartabull .05
464 Pete Incaviglia .05
465 Carlos Martinez .05
466 Ricky Jordan .05
467 John Cerutti .05
468 Dave Winfield .15
469 Francisco Oliveras .05
470 Roy Smith .05

#	Player	Price
471	Barry Larkin	.12
472	Ron Darling	.05
473	David Wells	.08
474	Glenn Davis	.05
475	Neal Heaton	.05
476	Ron Hassey	.05
477	Frank Thomas	.75
478	Greg Vaughn	.08
479	Todd Burns	.05
480	Candy Maldonado	.05
481	Dave LaPoint	.05
482	Alvin Davis	.05
483	Mike Scott	.05
484	Dale Murphy	.12
485	Ben McDonald	.08
486	Jay Howell	.05
487	Vince Coleman	.05
488	Alfredo Griffin	.05
489	Sandy Alomar	.15
490	Kirby Puckett	.35
491	Andres Thomas	.05
492	Jack Morris	.08
493	Matt Young	.05
494	Greg Myers	.05
495	Barry Bonds	.35
496	Scott Cooper	.05
497	Dan Schatzeder	.05
498	Jesse Barfield	.05
499	Jerry Goff	.05
500	Checklist 332-408	.05
501	*Anthony Telford*	.08
502	Eddie Murray	.20
503	*Omar Olivares*	.12
504	Ryne Sandberg	.25
505	Jeff Montgomery	.05
506	Mark Parent	.05
507	Ron Gant	.10
508	Frank Tanana	.05
509	Jay Buhner	.08
510	Max Venable	.05
511	Wally Whitehurst	.05
512	Gary Pettis	.05
513	Tom Brunansky	.05
514	Tim Wallach	.08
515	Craig Lefferts	.05
516	*Tim Layana*	.05
517	Darryl Hamilton	.05
518	Rick Reuschel	.05
519	Steve Wilson	.05
520	Kurt Stillwell	.05
521	Rafael Palmeiro	.20
522	Ken Patterson	.05
523	Len Dykstra	.08
524	Tony Fernandez	.08
525	Kent Anderson	.05
526	*Mark Leonard*	.08
527	Allan Anderson	.05
528	Tom Browning	.05
529	Frank Viola	.05
530	John Olerud	.20
531	Juan Agosto	.05
532	Zane Smith	.05
533	Scott Sanderson	.05
534	Barry Jones	.05
535	Mike Felder	.05
536	Jose Canseco	.25
537	Felix Fermin	.05
538	Roberto Kelly	.05
539	Brian Holman	.05
540	Mark Davidson	.05
541	Terry Mulholland	.08
542	Randy Milligan	.05
543	Jose Gonzalez	.05
544	*Craig Wilson*	.08
545	Mike Hartley	.05
546	Greg Swindell	.05
547	Gary Gaetti	.08
548	Dave Justice	.30
549	Steve Searcy	.05
550	Erik Hanson	.05
551	Dave Stieb	.08
552	Andy Van Slyke	.05
553	Mike Greenwell	.05
554	Kevin Maas	.05
555	Delino Deshields	.08
556	Curt Schilling	.10
557	Ramon Martinez	.08
558	Pedro Guerrero	.05
559	Dwight Smith	.05
560	Mark Davis	.05
561	Shawn Abner	.05
562	Charlie Leibrandt	.05
563	John Shelby	.05
564	Bill Swift	.05
565	Mike Fetters	.05
566	Alejandro Pena	.05
567	Ruben Sierra	.05
568	Carlos Quintana	.05
569	Kevin Gross	.05
570	Derek Lilliquist	.05
571	Jack Armstrong	.05
572	Greg Brock	.05
573	Mike Kingery	.05
574	Greg Smith	.05
575	*Brian McRae*	.25
576	Jack Daugherty	.05
577	Ozzie Guillen	.05
578	Joe Boever	.05
579	Luis Sojo	.05
580	Chili Davis	.08
581	Don Robinson	.05
582	Brian Harper	.05
583	Paul O'Neill	.12
584	Bob Ojeda	.05
585	Mookie Wilson	.05
586	Rafael Ramirez	.05
587	Gary Redus	.05
588	Jamie Quirk	.05
589	Shawn Hilligas	.05
590	*Tom Edens*	.05
591	Joe Klink	.05
592	Charles Nagy	.08
593	Eric Plunk	.05
594	Tracy Jones	.05
595	Craig Biggio	.15
596	Jose DeJesus	.05
597	Mickey Tettleton	.05
598	Chris Gwynn	.05
599	Rex Hudler	.05
600	Checklist 409-506	.05
601	Jim Gott	.05
602	Jeff Manto	.05
603	Nelson Liriano	.05
604	Mark Lemke	.05
605	Clay Parker	.05
606	Edgar Martinez	.08
607	*Mark Whiten*	.20
608	Ted Power	.05
609	Tom Bolton	.05
610	Tom Herr	.05
611	Andy Hawkins	.05
612	Scott Ruskin	.05
613	Ron Kittle	.05
614	John Wetteland	.08
615	*Mike Perez*	.08
616	Dave Clark	.05
617	Brent Mayne	.08
618	Jack Clark	.05
619	Marvin Freeman	.05
620	Edwin Nunez	.05
621	Russ Swan	.05
622	Johnny Ray	.05
623	Charlie O'Brien	.05
624	*Joe Bitker*	.05
625	Mike Marshall	.05
626	Otis Nixon	.05
627	Andy Benes	.10
628	Ron Oester	.05
629	Ted Higuera	.05
630	Kevin Bass	.05
631	Damon Berryhill	.05
632	Bo Jackson	.15
633	Brad Arnsberg	.05
634	Jerry Willard	.05
635	Tommy Greene	.05
636	*Bob MacDonald*	.05
637	Kirk McCaskill	.05
638	John Burkett	.05
639	*Paul Abbott*	.05
640	Todd Benzinger	.05
641	Todd Hundley	.08
642	George Bell	.05
643	*Javier Ortiz*	.05
644	Sid Bream	.05
645	Bob Welch	.05
646	Phil Bradley	.05
647	Bill Krueger	.05
648	Rickey Henderson	.20
649	Kevin Wickander	.05
650	Steve Balboni	.05
651	Gene Harris	.05
652	Jim Deshaies	.05
653	Jason Grimsley	.05
654	Joe Orsulak	.05
655	*Jimmy Poole*	.05
656	Felix Jose	.05
657	Dennis Cook	.05
658	Tom Brookens	.05
659	Junior Ortiz	.05
660	Jeff Parrett	.05
661	Jerry Don Gleaton	.05
662	Brent Knackert	.05
663	Rance Mulliniks	.05
664	John Smiley	.05
665	Larry Andersen	.05
666	Willie McGee	.08
667	*Chris Nabholz*	.05
668	Brady Anderson	.10
669	*Darren Holmes*	.12
670	Ken Hill	.05
671	Gary Varsho	.05
672	Bill Pecota	.05
673	Fred Lynn	.08
674	Kevin D. Brown	.05
675	Dan Petry	.05
676	Mike Jackson	.05
677	Wally Joyner	.08
678	Danny Jackson	.05
679	*Bill Haselman*	.05
680	Mike Boddicker	.05
681	*Mel Rojas*	.12
682	Roberto Alomar	.25
683	Dave Justice (R.O.Y.)	.25
684	Chuck Crim	.05
685a	Matt Williams (Last line of Career Highlights ends, "most DP's in")	.20
685b	Matt Williams (last line ends "8/24-27/87.")	.25
686	Shawon Dunston	.05
687	*Jeff Schulz*	.05
688	*John Barfield*	.05
689	Gerald Young	.05
690	*Luis Gonzalez*	.15
691	Frank Wills	.05
692	Chuck Finley	.05
693	Sandy Alomar (R.O.Y.)	.10
694	Tim Drummond	.05
695	Herm Winningham	.05
696	Darryl Strawberry	.10
697	Al Leiter	.08
698	*Karl Rhodes*	.08
699	Stan Belinda	.05
700	Checklist 507-604	.05
701	Lance Blankenship	.05
702	Willie Stargell (Puzzle Card)	.05
703	Jim Gantner	.05
704	*Reggie Harris*	.05
705	Rob Ducey	.05
706	Tim Hulett	.05
707	Atlee Hammaker	.05
708	Xavier Hernandez	.05
709	Chuck McElroy	.05
710	John Mitchell	.05
711	Carlos Hernandez	.05
712	Geronimo Pena	.05
713	*Jim Neidlinger*	.05
714	John Orton	.05
715	Terry Leach	.05
716	Mike Stanton	.05
717	Walt Terrell	.05
718	Luis Aquino	.05
719	Bud Black	.05
720	Bob Kipper	.05
721	*Jeff Gray*	.05
722	Jose Rijo	.05
723	Curt Young	.05
724	Jose Vizcaino	.08
725	*Randy Tomlin*	.05
726	Junior Noboa	.05
727	Bob Welch (Award Winner)	.05
728	Gary Ward	.05
729	Rob Deer	.05
730	*David Segui*	.08
731	Mark Carreon	.05
732	Vicente Palacios	.05
733	Sam Horn	.05
734	*Howard Farmer*	.08
735	Ken Dayley	.05
736	Kelly Mann	.05
737	*Joe Grahe*	.05
738	Kelly Downs	.05
739	*Jimmy Kremers*	.05
740	Kevin Appier	.12
741	Jeff Reed	.05
742	Jose Rijo (World Series)	.05
743	*Dave Rohde*	.08
744	Dr. Dirt/Mr. Clean (Len Dykstra, Dale Murphy)	.08
745	Paul Sorrento	.05
746	Thomas Howard	.05
747	*Matt Stark*	.05
748	Harold Baines	.08
749	Doug Dascenzo	.05
750	Doug Drabek (Award Winner)	.05
751	Gary Sheffield	.10
752	*Terry Lee*	.05
753	*Jim Vatcher*	.05
754	Lee Stevens	.05
755	Randy Veres	.05
756	Bill Doran	.05
757	Gary Wayne	.05
758	*Pedro Munoz*	.10
759	Chris Hammond	.05
760	Checklist 605-702	.05
761	Rickey Henderson (MVP)	.15
762	Barry Bonds (MVP)	.25
763	Billy Hatcher (World Series)	.05
764	Julio Machado	.05
765	Jose Mesa	.05
766	Willie Randolph (World Series)	.05
767	*Scott Erickson*	.10
768	Travis Fryman	.10
769	*Rich Rodriguez*	.10
770	Checklist 703-770; BC1-BC22	.05

1991 Donruss Elite

Donruss released a series of special inserts in 1991. Ten thousand of each Elite card was released, while 7,500 Legend cards and 5,000 Signature cards were issued. Cards were inserted in wax packs and feature marble borders. The Legend card features a Dick Perez drawing. Each card is designated with a serial number on the back.

		MT
Complete Set (10):		400.00
Common Player:		10.00
1	Barry Bonds	50.00
2	George Brett	90.00
3	Jose Canseco	40.00
4	Andre Dawson	10.00
5	Doug Drabek	10.00
6	Cecil Fielder	10.00
7	Rickey Henderson	25.00
8	Matt Williams	35.00
---	Nolan Ryan (Legend)	200.00
---	Ryne Sandberg (Signature)	275.00

1991 Donruss Grand Slammers

This set features players who hit grand slams in 1990. The cards are styled after the 1991 Donruss regular-issue cards. The featured player is showcased with a star in the background. The set was included in factory sets and randomly in jumbo packs.

		MT
Complete Set (14):		1.50
Common Player:		.10
1	Joe Carter	.10
2	Bobby Bonilla	.15
3	Kal Daniels	.10
4	Jose Canseco	.30
5	Barry Bonds	.35
6	Jay Buhner	.15
7	Cecil Fielder	.10
8	Matt Williams	.25
9	Andres Galarraga	.15
10	Luis Polonia	.10
11	Mark McGwire	.75
12	Ron Karkovice	.10
13	Darryl Strawberry	.15
14	Mike Greenwell	.10

1991 Donruss Highlights

This insert features highlights from the 1990 season. Cards have a "BC" prefix to the number and are styled after the 1991 regular-issue Donruss cards. Cards 1-10 feature blue borders due to their release with Series I cards. Cards 11-22 feature green borders and were released with Series II cards. A highlight logo appears on the front of the card. Each highlight is explained in depth on the card back.

		MT
Complete Set (22):		2.00
Common Player:		.10
1	Mark Langston, Mike Witt (No-Hit Mariners)	.10
2	Randy Johnson (No-Hits Tigers)	.20
3	Nolan Ryan (No-Hits A's)	.40
4	Dave Stewart (No-Hits Blue Jays)	.10
5	Cecil Fielder (50 Homer Club)	.10
6	Carlton Fisk (Record Home Run)	.20
7	Ryne Sandberg (Sets Fielding Records)	.25
8	Gary Carter (Breaks Catching Mark)	.10
9	Mark McGwire (Home Run Milestone)	.50
10	Bo Jackson (4 Consecutive HRs)	.25
11	Fernando Valenzuela (No-Hits Cardinals)	.10
12	Andy Hawkins (No-Hits White Sox)	.10
13	Melido Perez (No-Hits Yankees)	.10
14	Terry Mulholland (No-Hits Giants)	.10
15	Nolan Ryan (300th Win)	.40
16	Delino DeShields (4 Hits In Debut)	.10
17	Cal Ripken (Errorless Games)	.50
18	Eddie Murray (Switch Hit Homers)	.25
19	George Brett (3 Decade Champ)	.25
20	Bobby Thigpen (Shatters Save Mark)	.10
21	Dave Stieb (No-Hits Indians)	.10
22	Willie McGee (NL Batting Champ)	.10

1991 Donruss Rookies

Red borders highlight the 1991 Donruss Rookies cards. This set marks the sixth year that Donruss produced such an issue. As in past years, "The Rookies" logo appears on the card fronts. The set is packaged in a special box and includes a Willie Stargell puzzle card.

		MT
Complete Set (56):		6.00
Common Player:		.10
1	Pat Kelly	.10
2	Rich DeLucia	.10
3	Wes Chamberlain	.10
4	Scott Leius	.10
5	Darryl Kile	.10
6	Milt Cuyler	.10
7	Todd Van Poppel	.10
8	Ray Lankford	.30
9	Brian Hunter	.10
10	Tony Perezchica	.10
11	Ced Landrum	.10
12	Dave Burba	.10
13	Ramon Garcia	.10
14	Ed Sprague	.10
15	Warren Newson	.10
16	Paul Faries	.10
17	Luis Gonzalez	.15
18	Charles Nagy	.15
19	Chris Hammond	.10
20	Frank Castillo	.10
21	Pedro Munoz	.10
22	Orlando Merced	.10
23	Jose Melendez	.10
24	Kirk Dressendorfer	.10
25	Heathcliff Slocumb	.10
26	Doug Simons	.10
27	Mike Timlin	.15
28	Jeff Fassero	.10
29	Mark Leiter	.10
30	*Jeff Bagwell*	4.00
31	Brian McRae	.25
32	Mark Whiten	.10
33	*Ivan Rodriguez*	3.00
34	Wade Taylor	.10
35	Darren Lewis	.15
36	Mo Vaughn	1.00
37	Mike Remlinger	.10
38	Rick Wilkins	.15
39	Chuck Knoblauch	.60
40	Kevin Morton	.10
41	Carlos Rodriguez	.10
42	Mark Lewis	.15
43	Brent Mayne	.10
44	Chris Haney	.10
45	Denis Boucher	.10
46	Mike Gardiner	.10
47	Jeff Johnson	.10
48	Dean Palmer	.15
49	Chuck McElroy	.10
50	Chris Jones	.10
51	Scott Kamieniecki	.10
52	Al Osuna	.10
53	Rusty Meacham	.10
54	Chito Martinez	.10
55	Reggie Jefferson	.10
56	Checklist	.05

1992 Donruss Previews

Four-card cello packs distributed to members of the Donruss dealers' network previewed the forthcoming 1992 baseball card issue. The preview cards have the same format, front and back photos as their counterparts in the regular set. Only the card number, the security underprinting, "Donruss Preview Card", and the stats, complete only through 1990, differ.

		MT
Complete Set (12):		300.00
Common Player:		5.00
1	Wade Boggs	25.00
2	Barry Bonds	35.00
3	Will Clark	20.00
4	Andre Dawson	9.00
5	Dennis Eckersley	9.00
6	Robin Ventura	15.00
7	Ken Griffey, Jr.	90.00
8	Kelly Gruber	5.00
9	Ryan Klesko (Rated Rookie)	25.00
10	Cal Ripken, Jr.	85.00
11	Nolan Ryan (Highlight)	70.00
12	Todd Van Poppel	5.00

1992 Donruss

For the second consecutive year, Donruss released its card set in two series. The 1992 cards feature improved stock, an anti-counterfeit feature and include both front and back photos. Once again Rated Rookies and All-Stars are included in the set. Special highlight cards also can be found in the 1992 Donruss set. Production was reduced in 1992 compared to 1988-1991.

		MT
Complete Factory Set, Retail (788):		15.00
Complete Factory Set, Hobby (784):		12.00
Complete Set (784):		12.00
Common Player:		.05
Series 1 or 2 Pack (15):		.50
Series 1 or 2 Wax Box (36):		15.00
1	*Mark Wohlers* (Rated Rookie)	.30
2	Wil Cordero (Rated Rookie)	.30
3	Kyle Abbott (Rated Rookie)	.08
4	*Dave Nilsson* (Rated Rookie)	.12
5	Kenny Lofton (Rated Rookie)	2.00
6	*Luis Mercedes* (Rated Rookie)	.10
7	*Roger Salkeld* (Rated Rookie)	.15
8	Eddie Zosky (Rated Rookie)	.10
9	*Todd Van Poppel* (Rated Rookie)	.15
10	*Frank Seminara* (Rated Rookie)	.10
11	*Andy Ashby* (Rated Rookie)	.20
12	Reggie Jefferson (Rated Rookie)	.10
13	Ryan Klesko (Rated Rookie)	.75

No.	Player	Price
14	*Carlos Garcia* (Rated Rookie)	.15
15	*John Ramos* (Rated Rookie)	.05
16	Eric Karros (Rated Rookie)	.25
17	*Pat Lennon* (Rated Rookie)	.05
18	*Eddie Taubensee* (Rated Rookie)	.10
19	*Roberto Hernandez* (Rated Rookie)	.10
20	D.J. Dozier (Rated Rookie)	.05
21	Dave Henderson (All-Star)	.05
22	Cal Ripken, Jr. (All-Star)	.30
23	Wade Boggs (All-Star)	.10
24	Ken Griffey, Jr. (All-Star)	.75
25	Jack Morris (All-Star)	.05
26	Danny Tartabull (All-Star)	.05
27	Cecil Fielder (All-Star)	.05
28	Roberto Alomar (All-Star)	.20
29	Sandy Alomar (All-Star)	.08
30	Rickey Henderson (All-Star)	.15
31	Ken Hill	.05
32	John Habyan	.05
33	Otis Nixon (Highlight)	.05
34	Tim Wallach	.08
35	Cal Ripken, Jr.	.75
36	Gary Carter	.10
37	Juan Agosto	.05
38	Doug Dascenzo	.05
39	Kirk Gibson	.05
40	Benito Santiago	.05
41	Otis Nixon	.05
42	Andy Allanson	.05
43	Brian Holman	.05
44	Dick Schofield	.05
45	Dave Magadan	.05
46	Rafael Palmeiro	.20
47	Jody Reed	.05
48	Ivan Calderon	.05
49	Greg Harris	.05
50	Chris Sabo	.05
51	Paul Molitor	.25
52	Robby Thompson	.05
53	Dave Smith	.05
54	Mark Davis	.05
55	Kevin Brown	.05
56	Donn Pall	.05
57	Len Dykstra	.08
58	Roberto Alomar	.30
59	Jeff Robinson	.05
60	Willie McGee	.08
61	Jay Buhner	.10
62	Mike Pagliarulo	.05
63	Paul O'Neill	.15
64	Hubie Brooks	.05
65	Kelly Gruber	.05
66	Ken Caminiti	.12
67	Gary Redus	.05
68	Harold Baines	.08
69	Charlie Hough	.05
70	B.J. Surhoff	.08
71	Walt Weiss	.05
72	Shawn Hillegas	.05
73	Roberto Kelly	.05
74	Jeff Ballard	.05
75	Craig Biggio	.12
76	Pat Combs	.05
77	Jeff Robinson	.05
78	Tim Belcher	.05
79	Cris Carpenter	.05
80	Checklist 1-79	.05
81	Steve Avery	.05
82	Chris James	.05
83	Brian Harper	.05
84	Charlie Leibrandt	.05
85	Mickey Tettleton	.05
86	Pete O'Brien	.05
87	Danny Darwin	.05
88	Bob Walk	.05
89	Jeff Reardon	.05
90	Bobby Rose	.05
91	Danny Jackson	.05
92	John Morris	.05
93	Bud Black	.05
94	Tommy Greene (Highlight)	.05
95	Rick Aguilera	.05
96	Gary Gaetti	.05
97	David Cone	.12
98	John Olerud	.20
99	Joel Skinner	.05
100	Jay Bell	.10
101	Bob Milacki	.05
102	Norm Charlton	.05
103	Chuck Crim	.05
104	Terry Steinbach	.05
105	Juan Samuel	.05
106	Steve Howe	.05
107	Rafael Belliard	.05
108	Joey Cora	.05
109	Tommy Greene	.08
110	Gregg Olson	.05
111	Frank Tanana	.05
112	Lee Smith	.08
113	Greg Harris	.05
114	Dwayne Henry	.05
115	Chili Davis	.08
116	Kent Mercker	.05
117	Brian Barnes	.05
118	Rich DeLucia	.05
119	Andre Dawson	.15
120	Carlos Baerga	.10
121	Mike LaValliere	.05
122	Jeff Gray	.05
123	Bruce Hurst	.05
124	Alvin Davis	.05
125	John Candelaria	.05
126	Matt Nokes	.05
127	George Bell	.05
128	Bret Saberhagen	.10
129	Jeff Russell	.05
130	Jim Abbott	.08
131	Bill Gullickson	.05
132	Todd Zeile	.08
133	Dave Winfield	.15
134	Wally Whitehurst	.05
135	Matt Williams	.20
136	Tom Browning	.05
137	Marquis Grissom	.10
138	Erik Hanson	.05
139	Rob Dibble	.05
140	Don August	.05
141	Tom Henke	.05
142	Dan Pasqua	.05
143	George Brett	.25
144	Jerald Clark	.05
145	Robin Ventura	.15
146	Dale Murphy	.15
147	Dennis Eckersley	.10
148	Eric Yelding	.05
149	Mario Diaz	.05
150	Casey Candaele	.05
151	Steve Olin	.05
152	Luis Salazar	.05
153	Kevin Maas	.05
154	Nolan Ryan (Highlight)	.40
155	Barry Jones	.05
156	Chris Hoiles	.08
157	Bobby Ojeda	.05
158	Pedro Guerrero	.05
159	Paul Assenmacher	.05
160	Checklist 80-157	.05
161	Mike Macfarlane	.05
162	Craig Lefferts	.05
163	*Brian Hunter*	.05
164	Alan Trammell	.12
165	Ken Griffey, Jr.	1.50
166	Lance Parrish	.08
167	Brian Downing	.05
168	John Barfield	.05
169	Jack Clark	.05
170	Chris Nabholz	.05
171	Tim Teufel	.05
172	Chris Hammond	.05
173	Robin Yount	.25
174	Dave Righetti	.05
175	Joe Girardi	.05
176	Mike Boddicker	.05
177	Dean Palmer	.10
178	Greg Hibbard	.05
179	Randy Ready	.05
180	Devon White	.08
181	Mark Eichhorn	.05
182	Mike Felder	.05
183	Joe Klink	.05
184	Steve Bedrosian	.05
185	Barry Larkin	.10
186	John Franco	.05
187	*Ed Sprague*	.15
188	Mark Portugal	.05
189	Jose Lind	.05
190	Bob Welch	.05
191	Alex Fernandez	.15
192	Gary Sheffield	.15
193	Rickey Henderson	.20
194	Rod Nichols	.05
195	*Scott Kamieniecki*	.10
196	Mike Flanagan	.05
197	Steve Finley	.08
198	Darren Daulton	.05
199	Leo Gomez	.05
200	Mike Morgan	.05
201	Bob Tewksbury	.05
202	Sid Bream	.05
203	Sandy Alomar	.12
204	Greg Gagne	.05
205	Juan Berenguer	.05
206	Cecil Fielder	.08
207	Randy Johnson	.25
208	Tony Pena	.05
209	Doug Drabek	.05
210	Wade Boggs	.25
211	Bryan Harvey	.05
212	Jose Vizcaino	.05
213	*Alonzo Powell*	.05
214	Will Clark	.20
215	Rickey Henderson (Highlight)	.10
216	Jack Morris	.08
217	Junior Felix	.05
218	Vince Coleman	.05
219	Jimmy Key	.08
220	Alex Cole	.05
221	Bill Landrum	.05
222	Randy Milligan	.05
223	Jose Rijo	.05
224	Greg Vaughn	.10
225	Dave Stewart	.08
226	Lenny Harris	.05
227	Scott Sanderson	.05
228	Jeff Blauser	.05
229	Ozzie Guillen	.05
230	John Kruk	.05
231	Bob Melvin	.05
232	Milt Cuyler	.05
233	Felix Jose	.05
234	Ellis Burks	.10
235	Pete Harnisch	.05
236	Kevin Tapani	.05
237	Terry Pendleton	.05
238	Mark Gardner	.05
239	Harold Reynolds	.05
240	Checklist 158-237	.05
241	Mike Harkey	.05
242	Felix Fermin	.05
243	Barry Bonds	.35
244	Roger Clemens	.35
245	Dennis Rasmussen	.05
246	Jose DeLeon	.05
247	Orel Hershiser	.10
248	Mel Hall	.05
249	*Rick Wilkins*	.15
250	Tom Gordon	.05
251	Kevin Reimer	.05
252	Luis Polonia	.05
253	Mike Henneman	.05
254	Tom Pagnozzi	.05
255	Chuck Finley	.05
256	Mackey Sasser	.05
257	John Burkett	.05
258	Hal Morris	.05
259	Larry Walker	.20
260	Billy Swift	.05
261	Joe Oliver	.05
262	Julio Machado	.05
263	Todd Stottlemyre	.05
264	Matt Merullo	.05
265	Brent Mayne	.05
266	Thomas Howard	.05
267	Lance Johnson	.05
268	Terry Mulholland	.05
269	Rick Honeycutt	.05
270	Luis Gonzalez	.08
271	Jose Guzman	.05
272	Jimmy Jones	.05
273	Mark Lewis	.05
274	Rene Gonzales	.05
275	*Jeff Johnson*	.05
276	Dennis Martinez (Highlight)	.05
277	Delino DeShields	.05
278	Sam Horn	.05
279	Kevin Gross	.05
280	Jose Oquendo	.05
281	Mark Grace	.20
282	Mark Gubicza	.05
283	Fred McGriff	.15
284	Ron Gant	.10
285	Lou Whitaker	.08
286	Edgar Martinez	.08
287	Ron Tingley	.05
288	Kevin McReynolds	.05
289	Ivan Rodriguez	.25
290	Mike Gardiner	.05
291	*Chris Haney*	.05
292	Darrin Jackson	.05
293	Bill Doran	.05
294	Ted Higuera	.05
295	Jeff Brantley	.05
296	Les Lancaster	.05
297	Jim Eisenreich	.05
298	Ruben Sierra	.05
299	Scott Radinsky	.05
300	Jose DeJesus	.05
301	*Mike Timlin*	.15
302	Luis Sojo	.05
303	Kelly Downs	.05
304	Scott Bankhead	.05
305	Pedro Munoz	.05
306	Scott Scudder	.05
307	Kevin Elster	.05
308	Duane Ward	.05
309	*Darryl Kile*	.15
310	Orlando Merced	.05
311	Dave Henderson	.05
312	Tim Raines	.10
313	Mark Lee	.05
314	Mike Gallego	.05
315	Charles Nagy	.08
316	Jesse Barfield	.05
317	Todd Frohwirth	.05
318	Al Osuna	.05
319	Darrin Fletcher	.05
320	Checklist 238-316	.05
321	David Segui	.05
322	Stan Javier	.05
323	Bryn Smith	.05
324	Jeff Treadway	.05
325	Mark Whiten	.05
326	Kent Hrbek	.08
327	Dave Justice	.25
328	Tony Phillips	.05
329	Rob Murphy	.05
330	Kevin Morton	.05
331	John Smiley	.05
332	Luis Rivera	.05
333	Wally Joyner	.08
334	*Heathcliff Slocumb*	.08
335	Rick Cerone	.05
336	*Mike Remlinger*	.05
337	Mike Moore	.05
338	Lloyd McClendon	.05
339	Al Newman	.05
340	Kirk McCaskill	.05
341	Howard Johnson	.05
342	Greg Myers	.05
343	Kal Daniels	.05
344	Bernie Williams	.25
345	Shane Mack	.05
346	Gary Thurman	.05
347	Dante Bichette	.10
348	Mark McGwire	2.00
349	Travis Fryman	.10
350	Ray Lankford	.08
351	Mike Jeffcoat	.05
352	Jack McDowell	.08
353	Mitch Williams	.05
354	Mike Devereaux	.05
355	Andres Galarraga	.10
356	Henry Cotto	.05
357	Scott Bailes	.05
358	Jeff Bagwell	.75
359	Scott Leius	.05
360	Zane Smith	.05
361	Bill Pecota	.05
362	Tony Fernandez	.08
363	Glenn Braggs	.05
364	Bill Spiers	.05
365	Vicente Palacios	.05
366	Tim Burke	.05
367	Randy Tomlin	.05
368	Kenny Rogers	.08
369	Brett Butler	.08
370	Pat Kelly	.05
371	Bip Roberts	.05
372	Gregg Jefferies	.10
373	Kevin Bass	.05
374	Ron Karkovice	.05
375	Paul Gibson	.05
376	Bernard Gilkey	.08
377	Dave Gallagher	.05

No.	Player	Price
378	Bill Wegman	.05
379	Pat Borders	.05
380	Ed Whitson	.05
381	Gilberto Reyes	.05
382	Russ Swan	.05
383	Andy Van Slyke	.05
384	Wes Chamberlain	.05
385	Steve Chitren	.05
386	Greg Olson	.05
387	Brian McRae	.08
388	Rich Rodriguez	.05
389	Steve Decker	.05
390	Chuck Knoblauch	.12
391	Bobby Witt	.05
392	Eddie Murray	.25
393	Juan Gonzalez	.60
394	Scott Ruskin	.05
395	Jay Howell	.05
396	Checklist 317-396	.05
397	Royce Clayton (Rated Rookie)	.15
398	*John Jaha* (Rated Rookie)	.15
399	Dan Wilson (Rated Rookie)	.10
400	*Archie Corbin* (Rated Rookie)	.08
401	*Barry Manuel* (Rated Rookie)	.05
402	Kim Batiste (Rated Rookie)	.08
403	*Pat Mahomes* (Rated Rookie)	.15
404	Dave Fleming (Rated Rookie)	.05
405	Jeff Juden (Rated Rookie)	.10
406	*Jim Thome* (Rated Rookie)	.45
407	Sam Militello (Rated Rookie)	.10
408	*Jeff Nelson* (Rated Rookie)	.05
409	Anthony Young (Rated Rookie)	.15
410	Tino Martinez (Rated Rookie)	.25
411	*Jeff Mutis* (Rated Rookie)	.08
412	*Rey Sanchez* (Rated Rookie)	.10
413	*Chris Gardner* (Rated Rookie)	.08
414	*John Vander Wal* (Rated Rookie)	.08
415	Reggie Sanders (Rated Rookie)	.15
416	*Brian Williams* (Rated Rookie)	.10
417	Mo Sanford (Rated Rookie)	.15
418	*David Weathers* (Rated Rookie)	.08
419	*Hector Fajardo* (Rated Rookie)	.08
420	*Steve Foster* (Rated Rookie)	.08
421	Lance Dickson (Rated Rookie)	.10
422	Andre Dawson (All-Star)	.08
423	Ozzie Smith (All-Star)	.10
424	Chris Sabo (All-Star)	.05
425	Tony Gwynn (All-Star)	.10
426	Tom Glavine (All-Star)	.05
427	Bobby Bonilla (All-Star)	.08
428	Will Clark (All-Star)	.15
429	Ryne Sandberg (All-Star)	.20
430	Benito Santiago (All-Star)	.08
431	Ivan Calderon (All-Star)	.05
432	Ozzie Smith	.25
433	Tim Leary	.05
434	Bret Saberhagen (Highlight)	.05
435	Mel Rojas	.05
436	Ben McDonald	.08
437	Tim Crews	.05
438	Rex Hudler	.05
439	Chico Walker	.05
440	Kurt Stillwell	.05
441	Tony Gwynn	.35
442	John Smoltz	.10
443	Lloyd Moseby	.05
444	Mike Schooler	.05
445	Joe Grahe	.05
446	Dwight Gooden	.10
447	Oil Can Boyd	.05
448	John Marzano	.05
449	Bret Barberie	.05
450	Mike Maddux	.05
451	Jeff Reed	.05
452	Dale Sveum	.05
453	Jose Uribe	.05
454	Bob Scanlan	.05
455	Kevin Appier	.08
456	Jeff Huson	.05
457	Ken Patterson	.05
458	Ricky Jordan	.05
459	Tom Candiotti	.05
460	Lee Stevens	.05
461	*Rod Beck*	.15
462	Dave Valle	.05
463	Scott Erickson	.10
464	Chris Jones	.05
465	Mark Carreon	.05
466	Rob Ducey	.05
467	Jim Corsi	.05
468	Jeff King	.05
469	Curt Young	.05
470	Bo Jackson	.15
471	Chris Bosio	.05
472	Jamie Quirk	.05
473	Jesse Orosco	.05
474	Alvaro Espinoza	.05
475	Joe Orsulak	.05
476	Checklist 397-477	.05
477	Gerald Young	.05
478	Wally Backman	.05
479	Juan Bell	.05
480	Mike Scioscia	.05
481	Omar Olivares	.05
482	Francisco Cabrera	.05
483	Greg Swindell	.05
484	Terry Leach	.05
485	Tommy Gregg	.05
486	Scott Aldred	.05
487	Greg Briley	.05
488	Phil Plantier	.05
489	Curtis Wilkerson	.05
490	Tom Brunansky	.05
491	Mike Fetters	.05
492	Frank Castillo	.05
493	Joe Boever	.05
494	Kirt Manwaring	.05
495	Wilson Alvarez (Highlight)	.05
496	Gene Larkin	.05
497	Gary DiSarcina	.05
498	Frank Viola	.05
499	Manuel Lee	.05
500	Albert Belle	.35
501	Stan Belinda	.05
502	Dwight Evans	.05
503	Eric Davis	.12
504	Darren Holmes	.05
505	Mike Bordick	.05
506	Dave Hansen	.05
507	Lee Guetterman	.05
508	*Keith Mitchell*	.05
509	Melido Perez	.05
510	Dickie Thon	.05
511	Mark Williamson	.05
512	Mark Salas	.05
513	Milt Thompson	.05
514	Mo Vaughn	.30
515	Jim Deshaies	.05
516	Rich Garces	.05
517	Lonnie Smith	.05
518	Spike Owen	.05
519	Tracy Jones	.05
520	Greg Maddux	.60
521	Carlos Martinez	.05
522	Neal Heaton	.05
523	Mike Greenwell	.05
524	Andy Benes	.08
525	Jeff Schaefer	.05
526	Mike Sharperson	.05
527	Wade Taylor	.05
528	Jerome Walton	.05
529	Storm Davis	.05
530	*Jose Hernandez*	.05
531	Mark Langston	.05
532	Rob Deer	.05
533	Geronimo Pena	.05
534	*Juan Guzman*	.12
535	Pete Schourek	.05
536	Todd Benzinger	.05
537	Billy Hatcher	.05
538	Tom Foley	.05
539	Dave Cochrane	.05
540	Mariano Duncan	.05
541	Edwin Nunez	.05
542	Rance Mulliniks	.05
543	Carlton Fisk	.10
544	Luis Aquino	.05
545	Ricky Bones	.05
546	Craig Grebeck	.05
547	Charlie Hayes	.05
548	Jose Canseco	.25
549	Andujar Cedeno	.05
550	Geno Petralli	.05
551	Javier Ortiz	.05
552	Rudy Seanez	.05
553	Rich Gedman	.05
554	Eric Plunk	.05
555	Nolan Ryan, Rich Gossage (Highlight)	.20
556	Checklist 478-555	.05
557	Greg Colbrunn	.05
558	*Chito Martinez*	.05
559	Darryl Strawberry	.10
560	Luis Alicea	.05
561	Dwight Smith	.05
562	Terry Shumpert	.05
563	Jim Vatcher	.05
564	Deion Sanders	.10
565	Walt Terrell	.05
566	Dave Burba	.05
567	Dave Howard	.05
568	Todd Hundley	.08
569	Jack Daugherty	.05
570	Scott Cooper	.05
571	Bill Sampen	.05
572	Jose Melendez	.05
573	Freddie Benavides	.05
574	Jim Gantner	.05
575	Trevor Wilson	.05
576	Ryne Sandberg	.20
577	Kevin Seitzer	.05
578	Gerald Alexander	.05
579	Mike Huff	.05
580	Von Hayes	.05
581	Derek Bell	.15
582	Mike Stanley	.05
583	Kevin Mitchell	.05
584	Mike Jackson	.05
585	Dan Gladden	.05
586	Ted Power	.05
587	Jeff Innis	.05
588	Bob MacDonald	.05
589	*Jose Tolentino*	.05
590	Bob Patterson	.05
591	*Scott Brosius*	.10
592	Frank Thomas	1.00
593	Darryl Hamilton	.05
594	Kirk Dressendorfer	.05
595	Jeff Shaw	.05
596	Don Mattingly	.35
597	Glenn Davis	.05
598	Andy Mota	.05
599	Jason Grimsley	.05
600	Jimmy Poole	.05
601	Jim Gott	.05
602	Stan Royer	.08
603	Marvin Freeman	.05
604	Denis Boucher	.05
605	Denny Neagle	.05
606	Mark Lemke	.05
607	Jerry Don Gleaton	.05
608	Brent Knackert	.05
609	Carlos Quintana	.05
610	Bobby Bonilla	.12
611	Joe Hesketh	.05
612	Daryl Boston	.05
613	Shawon Dunston	.05
614	Danny Cox	.05
615	Darren Lewis	.10
616	Alejandro Pena, Kent Mercker, Mark Wohlers (Highlight)	.10
617	Kirby Puckett	.35
618	Franklin Stubbs	.05
619	Chris Donnels	.10
620	David Wells	.08
621	Mike Aldrete	.05
622	Bob Kipper	.05
623	Anthony Telford	.05
624	Randy Myers	.05
625	Willie Randolph	.05
626	Joe Slusarski	.05
627	John Wetteland	.05
628	Greg Cadaret	.05
629	Tom Glavine	.10
630	Wilson Alvarez	.10
631	Wally Ritchie	.05
632	Mike Mussina	.30
633	Mark Leiter	.05
634	Gerald Perry	.05
635	Matt Young	.05
636	Checklist 556-635	.05
637	Scott Hemond	.05
638	David West	.05
639	Jim Clancy	.05
640	Doug Piatt	.05
641	Omar Vizquel	.08
642	Rick Sutcliffe	.05
643	Glenallen Hill	.05
644	Gary Varsho	.05
645	Tony Fossas	.05
646	Jack Howell	.05
647	*Jim Campanis*	.10
648	Chris Gwynn	.05
649	Jim Leyritz	.05
650	Chuck McElroy	.05
651	Sean Berry	.08
652	Donald Harris	.05
653	Don Slaught	.05
654	*Rusty Meacham*	.05
655	Scott Terry	.05
656	Ramon Martinez	.10
657	Keith Miller	.05
658	Ramon Garcia	.05
659	*Milt Hill*	.05
660	Steve Frey	.05
661	Bob McClure	.05
662	*Ced Landrum*	.05
663	*Doug Henry*	.05
664	Candy Maldonado	.05
665	Carl Willis	.05
666	Jeff Montgomery	.05
667	*Craig Shipley*	.10
668	*Warren Newson*	.05
669	Mickey Morandini	.05
670	Brook Jacoby	.05
671	*Ryan Bowen*	.10
672	Bill Krueger	.05
673	Rob Mallicoat	.05
674	Doug Jones	.05
675	Scott Livingstone	.05
676	Danny Tartabull	.05
677	Joe Carter (Highlight)	.05
678	Cecil Espy	.05
679	Randy Velarde	.05
680	Bruce Ruffin	.05
681	*Ted Wood*	.05
682	Dan Plesac	.05
683	Eric Bullock	.05
684	Junior Ortiz	.05
685	Dave Hollins	.08
686	Dennis Martinez	.08
687	Larry Andersen	.05
688	Doug Simons	.05
689	*Tim Spehr*	.05
690	*Calvin Jones*	.05
691	Mark Guthrie	.05
692	Alfredo Griffin	.05
693	Joe Carter	.10
694	*Terry Mathews*	.08
695	Pascual Perez	.05
696	Gene Nelson	.05
697	Gerald Williams	.08
698	*Chris Cron*	.08
699	Steve Buechele	.05
700	Paul McClellan	.05
701	Jim Lindeman	.05
702	Francisco Oliveras	.05
703	*Rob Maurer*	.05
704	*Pat Hentgen*	.25
705	Jaime Navarro	.05
706	*Mike Magnante*	.05
707	Nolan Ryan	.75
708	Bobby Thigpen	.05
709	John Cerutti	.05
710	Steve Wilson	.05
711	Hensley Meulens	.05
712	*Rheal Cormier*	.20
713	Scott Bradley	.05
714	Mitch Webster	.05
715	Roger Mason	.05
716	Checklist 636-716	.05
717	*Jeff Fassero*	.10
718	Cal Eldred	.08
719	Sid Fernandez	.05
720	*Bob Zupcic*	.05
721	Jose Offerman	.08
722	*Cliff Brantley*	.10
723	Ron Darling	.05
724	Dave Stieb	.05
725	Hector Villanueva	.05
726	Mike Hartley	.05

727	*Arthur Rhodes*	.15
728	Randy Bush	.05
729	Steve Sax	.05
730	Dave Otto	.05
731	*John Wehner*	.05
732	Dave Martinez	.05
733	*Ruben Amaro*	.05
734	Billy Ripken	.05
735	Steve Farr	.05
736	Shawn Abner	.05
737	*Gil Heredia*	.10
738	Ron Jones	.05
739	Tony Castillo	.05
740	Sammy Sosa	.75
741	Julio Franco	.05
742	Tim Naehring	.05
743	*Steve Wapnick*	.05
744	Craig Wilson	.05
745	*Darrin Chapin*	.08
746	*Chris George*	.08
747	Mike Simms	.05
748	Rosario Rodriguez	.05
749	Skeeter Barnes	.05
750	Roger McDowell	.05
751	Dann Howitt	.05
752	Paul Sorrento	.05
753	*Braulio Castillo*	.08
754	*Yorkis Perez*	.05
755	Willie Fraser	.05
756	*Jeremy Hernandez*	.05
757	Curt Schilling	.10
758	Steve Lyons	.05
759	Dave Anderson	.05
760	Willie Banks	.05
761	Mark Leonard	.05
762	Jack Armstrong	.05
763	Scott Servais	.05
764	Ray Stephens	.05
765	Junior Noboa	.05
766	*Jim Olander*	.05
767	Joe Magrane	.05
768	Lance Blankenship	.05
769	*Mike Humphreys*	.10
770	*Jarvis Brown*	.08
771	Damon Berryhill	.05
772	Alejandro Pena	.05
773	Jose Mesa	.05
774	*Gary Cooper*	.05
775	Carney Lansford	.05
776	Mike Bielecki	.05
777	Charlie O'Brien	.05
778	Carlos Hernandez	.05
779	Howard Farmer	.05
780	Mike Stanton	.05
781	Reggie Harris	.05
782	Xavier Hernandez	.05
783	*Bryan Hickerson*	.05
784	Checklist 717-BC8	.05

1992 Donruss Bonus Cards

The eight bonus cards were randomly inserted in 1992 foil packs and are numbered with a "BC" prefix. Both leagues' MVPs, Cy Young and Rookie of the Year award winners are featured, as are logo cards for the expansion Colorado Rockies and Florida Marlins. Cards are standard size in a format similar to the regular issue.

		MT
Complete Set (8):		3.00
Common Player:		.30
1	Cal Ripken, Jr. (MVP)	1.00
2	Terry Pendleton (MVP)	.30
3	Roger Clemens (Cy Young)	.75
4	Tom Glavine (Cy Young)	.40
5	Chuck Knoblauch (Rookie of the Year)	.60
6	Jeff Bagwell (Rookie of the Year)	1.00
7	Colorado Rockies	.50
8	Florida Marlins	.50

1992 Donruss Diamond Kings

Donruss changed its Diamond Kings style and distribution in 1992. The cards still feature the art of Dick Perez, but quality was improved from past years. The cards were randomly inserted in foil packs. One player from each team is featured. Card numbers have a "DK" prefix.

		MT
Complete Set (27):		25.00
Common Player:		.35
1	Paul Molitor	2.00
2	Will Clark	.50
3	Joe Carter	.35
4	Julio Franco	.25
5	Cal Ripken, Jr.	7.50
6	Dave Justice	.50
7	George Bell	.35
8	Frank Thomas	4.50
9	Wade Boggs	1.50
10	Scott Sanderson	.35
11	Jeff Bagwell	4.00
12	John Kruk	.35
13	Felix Jose	.35
14	Harold Baines	.45
15	Dwight Gooden	.45
16	Brian McRae	.35
17	Jay Bell	.45
18	Brett Butler	.35
19	Hal Morris	.35
20	Mark Langston	.35
21	Scott Erickson	.35
22	Randy Johnson	1.00
23	Greg Swindell	.35
24	Dennis Martinez	.35
25	Tony Phillips	.35
26	Fred McGriff	.75
27	Checklist	.10

1992 Donruss Elite

Donruss continued its Elite series in 1992 by inserting cards in foil packs. Each card was released in the same quantity as the 1991 inserts - 10,000 Elite, 7,500 Legend and 5,000 Signature. The Elite cards, now featuring a prismatic border, are numbered as a continuation of the 1991 issue.

		MT
Complete Set (12):		800.00
Common Player:		10.00
9	Wade Boggs	30.00
10	Joe Carter	10.00
11	Will Clark	25.00
12	Dwight Gooden	15.00
13	Ken Griffey, Jr.	160.00
14	Tony Gwynn	50.00
15	Howard Johnson	10.00
16	Terry Pendleton	10.00
17	Kirby Puckett	65.00
18	Frank Thomas	40.00
---	Rickey Henderson (Legend)	65.00
---	Cal Ripken, Jr. (Signature)	375.00

1992 Donruss Rookie Phenoms

The first 12 cards in this insert set were available in Donruss Rookies foil packs. Cards 13-20 were found randomly packed in jumbo packs. Predominantly black on both front and back, the borders are highlighted with gold. A gold-foil "Phenoms" appears at top front.

		MT
Complete Set (20):		30.00
Common Player:		.40
1	Moises Alou	1.50
2	Bret Boone	1.50
3	Jeff Conine	.75
4	Dave Fleming	.40
5	Tyler Green	.40
6	Eric Karros	1.00
7	Pat Listach	.40
8	Kenny Lofton	5.00
9	Mike Piazza	18.00
10	Tim Salmon	6.00
11	Andy Stankiewicz	.40
12	Dan Walters	.40
13	Ramon Caraballo	.40
14	Brian Jordan	1.50
15	Ryan Klesko	.75
16	Sam Militello	.40
17	Frank Seminara	.40
18	Salomon Torres	.40
19	John Valentin	1.00
20	Wil Cordero	.40

1992 Donruss Update

Each retail factory set of 1992 Donruss cards contained a cello-wrapped four-card selection from this 22-card Update set. The cards feature the same basic format as the regular '92 Donruss, except they carry a "U" prefix to the card number on back. The cards feature rookies, highlights and traded players from the 1992 season.

		MT
Complete Set (22):		40.00
Common Player:		.75
1	Pat Listach (Rated Rookie)	.75
2	Andy Stankiewicz (Rated Rookie)	.75
3	Brian Jordan (Rated Rookie)	2.00
4	Dan Walters (Rated Rookie)	.75
5	Chad Curtis (Rated Rookie)	1.50
6	Kenny Lofton (Rated Rookie)	8.00
7	Mark McGwire (Highlight)	20.00
8	Eddie Murray (Highlight)	2.00
9	Jeff Reardon (Highlight)	.75
10	Frank Viola	.75
11	Gary Sheffield	2.50
12	George Bell	.75
13	Rick Sutcliffe	.75
14	Wally Joyner	.75
15	Kevin Seitzer	.75
16	Bill Krueger	.75
17	Danny Tartabull	.75
18	Dave Winfield	2.50
19	Gary Carter	.75
20	Bobby Bonilla	1.00
21	Cory Snyder	.75
22	Bill Swift	.75

1992 Donruss Rookies

Donruss increased the size of its Rookies set in 1992 to include 132 cards. In the past the cards were released only in boxed set form, but the 1992 cards were available in packs. Special "Phenoms" cards were randomly inserted into Rookies packs. The Phenoms cards feature black borders, while the Rookies cards are styled after the regular 1992 Donruss issue. The cards are numbered alphabetically.

		MT
Complete Set (132):		10.00
Common Player:		.05
Pack (12):		1.00
Wax Box (36):		50.00
1	Kyle Abbott	.05
2	Troy Afenir	.05
3	Rich Amaral	.05
4	Ruben Amaro	.05
5	Billy Ashley	.05
6	Pedro Astacio	.15
7	Jim Austin	.05
8	Robert Ayrault	.05
9	Kevin Baez	.05
10	Estaban Beltre	.05
11	Brian Bohanon	.05
12	Kent Bottenfield	.05
13	Jeff Branson	.05
14	Brad Brink	.05
15	John Briscoe	.05
16	Doug Brocail	.05
17	Rico Brogna	.20
18	J.T. Bruett	.05
19	Jacob Brumfield	.05
20	Jim Bullinger	.05
21	Kevin Campbell	.05
22	Pedro Castellano	.05
23	Mike Christopher	.05
24	Archi Cianfrocco	.05
25	Mark Clark	.05
26	Craig Colbert	.05
27	Victor Cole	.05
28	Steve Cooke	.05
29	Tim Costo	.05
30	Chad Curtis	.30
31	Doug Davis	.05
32	Gary DiSarcina	.05
33	John Doherty	.05
34	Mike Draper	.05
35	Monty Fariss	.05
36	Bien Figueroa	.05
37	John Flaherty	.05
38	Tim Fortugno	.05
39	Eric Fox	.05
40	*Jeff Frye*	.05
41	Ramon Garcia	.05
42	Brent Gates	.20
43	Tom Goodwin	.05
44	Buddy Groom	.05
45	Jeff Grotewold	.05
46	Juan Guerrero	.05
47	Johnny Guzman	.05
48	Shawn Hare	.05
49	Ryan Hawblitzel	.05
50	Bert Heffernan	.05
51	Butch Henry	.05
52	Cesar Hernandez	.05
53	Vince Horsman	.05
54	Steve Hosey	.05
55	Pat Howell	.05
56	Peter Hoy	.05
57	Jon Hurst	.05
58	Mark Hutton	.05
59	Shawn Jeter	.05
60	Joel Johnston	.05
61	Jeff Kent	.40
62	Kurt Knudsen	.05
63	Kevin Koslofski	.05
64	Danny Leon	.05
65	Jesse Levis	.05
66	Tom Marsh	.05
67	Ed Martel	.05
68	Al Martin	.20
69	Pedro Martinez	2.00
70	Derrick May	.05
71	Matt Maysey	.05
72	Russ McGinnis	.05
73	Tim McIntosh	.05
74	Jim McNamara	.05
75	Jeff McNeely	.20
76	Rusty Meacham	.05
77	Tony Melendez	.05
78	Henry Mercedes	.05
79	Paul Miller	.05
80	Joe Millette	.05
81	Blas Minor	.05
82	Dennis Moeller	.05
83	Raul Mondesi	1.00
84	Rob Natal	.05
85	Troy Neel	.15
86	David Nied	.05
87	Jerry Nielsen	.05
88	Donovan Osborne	.05
89	John Patterson	.15
90	Roger Pavlik	.05
91	Dan Peltier	.05
92	Jim Pena	.05
93	William Pennyfeather	.05
94	Mike Perez	.05
95	Hipolito Pichardo	.05
96	Greg Pirkl	.05
97	Harvey Pulliam	.05
98	*Manny Ramirez*	6.00
99	Pat Rapp	.05
100	Jeff Reboulet	.05
101	Darren Reed	.15
102	Shane Reynolds	.05
103	Bill Risley	.05
104	Ben Rivera	.05
105	Henry Rodriguez	.15
106	Rico Rossy	.05
107	Johnny Ruffin	.05
108	Steve Scarsone	.05
109	Tim Scott	.05
110	Steve Shifflett	.05
111	Dave Silvestri	.05
112	Matt Stairs	.10
113	William Suero	.05
114	Jeff Tackett	.05
115	Eddie Taubensee	.25
116	Rick Trlicek	.05
117	Scooter Tucker	.05
118	Shane Turner	.05
119	Julio Valera	.05
120	Paul Wagner	.05
121	Tim Wakefield	.15
122	Mike Walker	.05
123	Bruce Walton	.05
124	Lenny Webster	.05
125	Bob Wickman	.05
126	Mike Williams	.05
127	Kerry Woodson	.05
128	Eric Young	.25
129	Kevin Young	.15
130	Pete Young	.05
131	Checklist	.05
132	Checklist	.05

1993 Donruss Previews

Twenty-two of the game's biggest stars were selected for inclusion in the preview version of Donruss' 1993 baseball card set. The previews follow the same basic format of the regular-issue 1993 except for the addition of the word "PREVIEW" above the card number in the home plate on back. Front photos are different between the preview and issued versions.

		MT
Complete Set (22):		135.00
Common Player:		3.00
1	Tom Glavine	3.00
2	Ryne Sandberg	8.00
3	Barry Larkin	4.00
4	Jeff Bagwell	7.50
5	Eric Karros	3.00
6	Larry Walker	7.00
7	Eddie Murray	7.00
8	Darren Daulton	3.00
9	Andy Van Slyke	3.00
10	Gary Sheffield	5.00
11	Will Clark	7.00
12	Cal Ripken Jr.	15.00
13	Roger Clemens	10.00
14	Frank Thomas	8.00
15	Cecil Fielder	3.00
16	George Brett	8.00
17	Robin Yount	7.50
18	Don Mattingly	12.00
19	Dennis Eckersley	4.00
20	Ken Griffey Jr.	15.00
21	Jose Canseco	7.50
22	Roberto Alomar	5.00

1993 Donruss

Rated Rookies and a randomly inserted Diamond Kings subset once again are featured in the 1993 Donruss set. Series I of the set includes 396 cards. Card fronts feature white borders surrounding a full-color player photo. The flip sides feature an additional photo, biographical information and career statistics. The cards are numbered on the back and the card's series is given with the number. The cards are UV coated. Series II contains a subset of players labeled with an "Expansion Draft" headline over their Marlins or Rockies team logo on front, even though the player photos are in the uniform of their previous team.

		MT
Complete Set (792):		20.00
Common Player:		.05
Series 1 or 2 Pack (14):		.75
Series 1 or 2 Wax Box (36):		24.00
1	Craig Lefferts	.05
2	Kent Mercker	.05
3	Phil Plantier	.05
4	*Alex Arias*	.15
5	Julio Valera	.05
6	Dan Wilson	.12
7	Frank Thomas	1.00
8	Eric Anthony	.05
9	Derek Lilliquist	.05
10	*Rafael Bournigal*	.12
11	*Manny Alexander* (Rated Rookie)	.12
12	Bret Barberie	.05
13	Mickey Tettleton	.05
14	Anthony Young	.08
15	Tim Spehr	.05
16	*Bob Ayrault*	.10
17	Bill Wegman	.05
18	Jay Bell	.08
19	Rick Aguilera	.05
20	Todd Zeile	.08
21	Steve Farr	.05
22	Andy Benes	.08
23	Lance Blankenship	.05
24	Ted Wood	.05
25	Omar Vizquel	.08
26	Steve Avery	.05
27	Brian Bohanon	.05
28	Rick Wilkins	.05
29	Devon White	.08
30	*Bobby Ayala*	.12
31	Leo Gomez	.05
32	Mike Simms	.05
33	Ellis Burks	.08
34	Steve Wilson	.05
35	Jim Abbott	.08
36	Tim Wallach	.05
37	Wilson Alvarez	.05
38	Daryl Boston	.05
39	Sandy Alomar, Jr.	.10
40	Mitch Williams	.05
41	Rico Brogna	.10
42	Gary Varsho	.05
43	Kevin Appier	.08
44	Eric Wedge (Rated Rookie)	.05
45	Dante Bichette	.08
46	Jose Oquendo	.05
47	*Mike Trombley*	.05
48	Dan Walters	.05
49	Gerald Williams	.08
50	Bud Black	.05
51	Bobby Witt	.05
52	Mark Davis	.05
53	*Shawn Barton*	.10
54	Paul Assenmacher	.05
55	Kevin Reimer	.05
56	*Billy Ashley* (Rated Rookie)	.20
57	Eddie Zosky	.05
58	Chris Sabo	.05
59	Billy Ripken	.05
60	*Scooter Tucker*	.10
61	*Tim Wakefield* (Rated Rookie)	.15
62	Mitch Webster	.05
63	Jack Clark	.05
64	Mark Gardner	.05
65	Lee Stevens	.05
66	Todd Hundley	.08
67	Bobby Thigpen	.05
68	Dave Hollins	.10
69	Jack Armstrong	.05
70	Alex Cole	.05
71	Mark Carreon	.05
72	Todd Worrell	.05
73	*Steve Shifflett*	.05
74	Jerald Clark	.05
75	Paul Molitor	.25
76	*Larry Carter*	.05
77	Rich Rowland	.05
78	Damon Berryhill	.05
79	Willie Banks	.05
80	Hector Villanueva	.05
81	Mike Gallego	.05
82	Tim Belcher	.05
83	Mike Bordick	.05
84	Craig Biggio	.10
85	Lance Parrish	.05
86	Brett Butler	.08

No.	Player	Value
87	Mike Timlin	.05
88	Brian Barnes	.05
89	Brady Anderson	.10
90	D.J. Dozier	.05
91	Frank Viola	.05
92	Darren Daulton	.05
93	Chad Curtis	.10
94	Zane Smith	.05
95	George Bell	.05
96	Rex Hudler	.05
97	Mark Whiten	.05
98	Tim Teufel	.05
99	Kevin Ritz	.05
100	Jeff Brantley	.05
101	Jeff Conine	.08
102	Vinny Castilla	.10
103	Greg Vaughn	.08
104	Steve Buechele	.05
105	Darren Reed	.05
106	Bip Roberts	.05
107	John Habyan	.05
108	Scott Servais	.05
109	Walt Weiss	.05
110	*J.T. Snow* (Rated Rookie)	.75
111	Jay Buhner	.08
112	Darryl Strawberry	.08
113	*Roger Pavlik*	.10
114	Chris Nabholz	.05
115	Pat Borders	.05
116	*Pat Howell*	.10
117	Gregg Olson	.05
118	Curt Schilling	.10
119	Roger Clemens	.40
120	*Victor Cole*	.05
121	Gary DiSarcina	.05
122	Checklist 1-80	.05
123	Steve Sax	.05
124	Chuck Carr	.05
125	Mark Lewis	.05
126	Tony Gwynn	.40
127	Travis Fryman	.10
128	Dave Burba	.05
129	Wally Joyner	.08
130	John Smoltz	.08
131	Cal Eldred	.05
132	Checklist 81-159	.05
133	Arthur Rhodes	.05
134	Jeff Blauser	.05
135	Scott Cooper	.05
136	Doug Strange	.05
137	Luis Sojo	.05
138	*Jeff Branson*	.10
139	Alex Fernandez	.08
140	Ken Caminiti	.10
141	Charles Nagy	.08
142	Tom Candiotti	.05
143	Willie Green (Rated Rookie)	.10
144	John Vander Wal	.05
145	*Kurt Knudsen*	.05
146	John Franco	.05
147	*Eddie Pierce*	.05
148	Kim Batiste	.05
149	Darren Holmes	.05
150	*Steve Cooke*	.15
151	Terry Jorgensen	.05
152	*Mark Clark*	.10
153	Randy Velarde	.05
154	Greg Harris	.05
155	*Kevin Campbell*	.10
156	John Burkett	.05
157	Kevin Mitchell	.05
158	Deion Sanders	.20
159	Jose Canseco	.25
160	*Jeff Hartsock*	.05
161	*Tom Quinlan*	.10
162	*Tim Pugh*	.10
163	Glenn Davis	.05
164	*Shane Reynolds*	.12
165	Jody Reed	.05
166	Mike Sharperson	.05
167	Scott Lewis	.05
168	Dennis Martinez	.08
169	Scott Radinsky	.05
170	Dave Gallagher	.05
171	Jim Thome	.25
172	Terry Mulholland	.05
173	Milt Cuyler	.05
174	Bob Patterson	.05
175	Jeff Montgomery	.05
176	Tim Salmon (Rated Rookie)	.50
177	Franklin Stubbs	.05
178	Donovan Osborne	.05
179	*Jeff Reboulet*	.05
180	*Jeremy Hernandez*	.08
181	Charlie Hayes	.05
182	Matt Williams	.20
183	Mike Raczka	.05
184	Francisco Cabrera	.05
185	Rich DeLucia	.05
186	Sammy Sosa	1.00
187	Ivan Rodriguez	.40
188	Bret Boone (Rated Rookie)	.15
189	Juan Guzman	.10
190	Tom Browning	.05
191	Randy Milligan	.05
192	Steve Finley	.08
193	John Patterson (Rated Rookie)	.10
194	Kip Gross	.05
195	Tony Fossas	.05
196	Ivan Calderon	.05
197	Junior Felix	.05
198	Pete Schourek	.05
199	Craig Grebeck	.05
200	Juan Bell	.05
201	Glenallen Hill	.05
202	Danny Jackson	.05
203	John Kiely	.05
204	Bob Tewksbury	.05
205	*Kevin Koslofski*	.10
206	Craig Shipley	.05
207	John Jaha	.10
208	Royce Clayton	.05
209	Mike Piazza (Rated Rookie)	1.50
210	Ron Gant	.08
211	Scott Erickson	.05
212	Doug Dascenzo	.05
213	Andy Stankiewicz	.08
214	Geronimo Berroa	.05
215	Dennis Eckersley	.08
216	Al Osuna	.05
217	Tino Martinez	.10
218	*Henry Rodriguez*	.12
219	Ed Sprague	.05
220	Ken Hill	.05
221	Chito Martinez	.05
222	Bret Saberhagen	.08
223	Mike Greenwell	.05
224	Mickey Morandini	.05
225	Chuck Finley	.05
226	Denny Neagle	.05
227	Kirk McCaskill	.05
228	Rheal Cormier	.05
229	Paul Sorrento	.05
230	Darrin Jackson	.05
231	Rob Deer	.05
232	Bill Swift	.05
233	Kevin McReynolds	.05
234	Terry Pendleton	.05
235	Dave Nilsson	.05
236	Chuck McElroy	.05
237	Derek Parks	.05
238	Norm Charlton	.05
239	Matt Nokes	.05
240	*Juan Guerrero*	.08
241	Jeff Parrett	.05
242	Ryan Thompson (Rated Rookie)	.15
243	Dave Fleming	.05
244	Dave Hansen	.05
245	Monty Fariss	.05
246	*Archi Cianfrocco*	.05
247	*Pat Hentgen*	.15
248	Bill Pecota	.05
249	Ben McDonald	.05
250	Cliff Brantley	.05
251	*John Valentin*	.15
252	Jeff King	.05
253	*Reggie Williams*	.10
254	Checklist 160-238	.05
255	Ozzie Guillen	.05
256	Mike Perez	.05
257	Thomas Howard	.05
258	Kurt Stillwell	.05
259	Mike Henneman	.05
260	Steve Decker	.05
261	Brent Mayne	.05
262	Otis Nixon	.05
263	*Mark Keifer*	.05
264	Checklist 239-317	.05
265	*Richie Lewis*	.05
266	*Pat Gomez*	.10
267	*Scott Taylor*	.10
268	Shawon Dunston	.05
269	Greg Myers	.05
270	Tim Costo	.05
271	Greg Hibbard	.05
272	Pete Harnisch	.05
273	*Dave Mlicki*	.08
274	Orel Hershiser	.08
275	Sean Berry (Rated Rookie)	.08
276	Doug Simons	.05
277	*John Doherty*	.10
278	Eddie Murray	.20
279	Chris Haney	.05
280	Stan Javier	.05
281	Jaime Navarro	.05
282	Orlando Merced	.05
283	Kent Hrbek	.08
284	Bernard Gilkey	.05
285	Russ Springer	.05
286	Mike Maddux	.05
287	*Eric Fox*	.10
288	Mark Leonard	.05
289	Tim Leary	.05
290	Brian Hunter	.05
291	Donald Harris	.05
292	Bob Scanlan	.05
293	Turner Ward	.05
294	Hal Morris	.05
295	Jimmy Poole	.05
296	Doug Jones	.05
297	Tony Pena	.05
298	Ramon Martinez	.08
299	*Tim Fortugno*	.10
300	Marquis Grissom	.10
301	Lance Johnson	.05
302	*Jeff Kent*	.15
303	Reggie Jefferson	.05
304	Wes Chamberlain	.05
305	*Shawn Hare*	.10
306	Mike LaValliere	.05
307	Gregg Jefferies	.08
308	*Troy Neel* (Rated Rookie)	.20
309	Pat Listach	.05
310	Geronimo Pena	.05
311	Pedro Munoz	.05
312	*Guillermo Velasquez*	.10
313	Roberto Kelly	.05
314	Mike Jackson	.05
315	Rickey Henderson	.20
316	Mark Lemke	.05
317	Erik Hanson	.05
318	Derrick May	.05
319	Geno Petralli	.05
320	Melvin Nieves (Rated Rookie)	.10
321	*Doug Linton*	.10
322	Rob Dibble	.05
323	Chris Hoiles	.05
324	Jimmy Jones	.05
325	Dave Staton (Rated Rookie)	.08
326	Pedro Martinez	.05
327	*Paul Quantrill*	.10
328	Greg Colbrunn	.05
329	*Hilly Hathaway*	.10
330	Jeff Innis	.05
331	Ron Karkovice	.05
332	*Keith Shepherd*	.10
333	*Alan Embree*	.12
334	*Paul Wagner*	.10
335	*Dave Haas*	.10
336	Ozzie Canseco	.05
337	Bill Sampen	.05
338	Rich Rodriguez	.05
339	Dean Palmer	.08
340	Greg Litton	.05
341	Jim Tatum (Rated Rookie)	.10
342	*Todd Haney*	.05
343	Larry Casian	.05
344	Ryne Sandberg	.35
345	*Sterling Hitchcock*	.15
346	Chris Hammond	.05
347	*Vince Horsman*	.12
348	*Butch Henry*	.12
349	Dann Howitt	.05
350	Roger McDowell	.05
351	Jack Morris	.05
352	Bill Krueger	.05
353	*Cris Colon*	.08
354	*Joe Vitko*	.10
355	Willie McGee	.08
356	Jay Baller	.05
357	Pat Mahomes	.05
358	Roger Mason	.05
359	*Jerry Nielsen*	.10
360	Tom Pagnozzi	.05
361	*Kevin Baez*	.08
362	*Tim Scott*	.08
363	*Domingo Martinez*	.10
364	Kirt Manwaring	.05
365	Rafael Palmeiro	.20
366	Ray Lankford	.08
367	Tim McIntosh	.05
368	*Jessie Hollins*	.08
369	Scott Leius	.05
370	Bill Doran	.05
371	*Sam Militello*	.10
372	Ryan Bowen	.05
373	Dave Henderson	.05
374	Dan Smith (Rated Rookie)	.10
375	*Steve Reed*	.12
376	Jose Offerman	.05
377	Kevin Brown	.05
378	Darrin Fletcher	.05
379	Duane Ward	.05
380	Wayne Kirby (Rated Rookie)	.12
381	*Steve Scarsone*	.08
382	Mariano Duncan	.05
383	*Ken Ryan*	.15
384	Lloyd McClendon	.05
385	Brian Holman	.05
386	Braulio Castillo	.05
387	*Danny Leon*	.08
388	Omar Olivares	.05
389	Kevin Wickander	.05
390	Fred McGriff	.20
391	Phil Clark	.12
392	Darren Lewis	.08
393	*Phil Hiatt*	.10
394	Mike Morgan	.05
395	Shane Mack	.05
396	Checklist 318-396	.05
397	David Segui	.05
398	Rafael Belliard	.05
399	Tim Naehring	.05
400	Frank Castillo	.05
401	Joe Grahe	.05
402	Reggie Sanders	.08
403	Roberto Hernandez	.05
404	Luis Gonzalez	.08
405	Carlos Baerga	.08
406	Carlos Hernandez	.05
407	Pedro Astacio (Rated Rookie)	.15
408	Mel Rojas	.05
409	Scott Livingstone	.05
410	Chico Walker	.05
411	Brian McRae	.05
412	Ben Rivera	.05
413	Ricky Bones	.05
414	Andy Van Slyke	.05
415	Chuck Knoblauch	.15
416	Luis Alicea	.05
417	Bob Wickman	.05
418	Doug Brocail	.05
419	Scott Brosius	.05
420	Rod Beck	.05
421	Edgar Martinez	.05
422	Ryan Klesko	.25
423	Nolan Ryan	1.00
424	Rey Sanchez	.05
425	Roberto Alomar	.35
426	Barry Larkin	.10
427	Mike Mussina	.25
428	Jeff Bagwell	.75
429	Mo Vaughn	.40
430	Eric Karros	.08
431	John Orton	.05
432	Wil Cordero	.05
433	Jack McDowell	.08
434	Howard Johnson	.05
435	Albert Belle	.50
436	John Kruk	.05
437	Skeeter Barnes	.05
438	Don Slaught	.05
439	Rusty Meacham	.05
440	Tim Laker (Rated Rookie)	.10
441	Robin Yount	.25
442	Brian Jordan	.10
443	Kevin Tapani	.05
444	Gary Sheffield	.15
445	Rich Monteleone	.05
446	Will Clark	.25
447	Jerry Browne	.05
448	Jeff Treadway	.05
449	Mike Schooler	.05
450	Mike Harkey	.05
451	Julio Franco	.05
452	Kevin Young (Rated Rookie)	.20
453	Kelly Gruber	.05

No.	Player	Value
454	Jose Rijo	.05
455	Mike Devereaux	.05
456	Andujar Cedeno	.05
457	Damion Easley (Rated Rookie)	.15
458	Kevin Gross	.05
459	Matt Young	.05
460	Matt Stairs	.05
461	Luis Polonia	.05
462	Dwight Gooden	.08
463	Warren Newson	.05
464	Jose DeLeon	.05
465	Jose Mesa	.05
466	Danny Cox	.05
467	Dan Gladden	.05
468	Gerald Perry	.05
469	Mike Boddicker	.05
470	Jeff Gardner	.05
471	Doug Henry	.05
472	Mike Benajmin	.05
473	Dan Peltier (Rated Rookie)	.05
474	Mike Stanton	.05
475	John Smiley	.05
476	Dwight Smith	.05
477	Jim Leyritz	.05
478	Dwayne Henry	.05
479	Mark McGwire	2.00
480	Pete Incaviglia	.05
481	Dave Cochrane	.05
482	Eric Davis	.08
483	John Olerud	.15
484	Ken Bottenfield	.05
485	Mark McLemore	.05
486	Dave Magadan	.05
487	John Marzano	.05
488	Ruben Amaro	.05
489	Rob Ducey	.05
490	Stan Belinda	.05
491	Dan Pasqua	.05
492	Joe Magrane	.05
493	Brook Jacoby	.05
494	Gene Harris	.05
495	Mark Leiter	.05
496	Bryan Hickerson	.05
497	Tom Gordon	.05
498	Pete Smith	.05
499	Chris Bosio	.05
500	Shawn Boskie	.05
501	Dave West	.05
502	Milt Hill	.05
503	Pat Kelly	.05
504	Joe Boever	.05
505	Terry Steinbach	.05
506	Butch Huskey (Rated Rookie)	.15
507	David Valle	.05
508	Mike Scioscia	.05
509	Kenny Rogers	.08
510	Moises Alou	.10
511	David Wells	.08
512	Mackey Sasser	.05
513	Todd Frohwirth	.05
514	Ricky Jordan	.05
515	Mike Gardiner	.05
516	Gary Redus	.05
517	Gary Gaetti	.05
518	Checklist 397-476	.05
519	Carlton Fisk	.10
520	Ozzie Smith	.25
521	Rod Nichols	.05
522	Benito Santiago	.05
523	Bill Gullickson	.05
524	Robby Thompson	.05
525	Mike Macfarlane	.05
526	Sid Bream	.05
527	Darryl Hamilton	.05
528	Checklist 477-555	.05
529	Jeff Tackett	.05
530	Greg Olson	.05
531	Bob Zupcic	.05
532	Mark Grace	.10
533	Steve Frey	.05
534	Dave Martinez	.05
535	Robin Ventura	.15
536	Casey Candaele	.05
537	Kenny Lofton	.30
538	Jay Howell	.05
539	Fernando Ramsey (Rated Rookie)	.10
540	Larry Walker	.25
541	Cecil Fielder	.08
542	Lee Guetterman	.05
543	Keith Miller	.05
544	Len Dykstra	.05
545	B.J. Surhoff	.08
546	Bob Walk	.05
547	Brian Harper	.05
548	Lee Smith	.05
549	Danny Tartabull	.05
550	Frank Seminara	.05
551	Henry Mercedes	.05
552	Dave Righetti	.05
553	Ken Griffey, Jr.	2.00
554	Tom Glavine	.08
555	Juan Gonzalez	.60
556	Jim Bullinger	.05
557	Derek Bell	.08
558	Cesar Hernandez	.05
559	Cal Ripken, Jr.	2.00
560	Eddie Taubensee	.05
561	John Flaherty	.05
562	Todd Benzinger	.05
563	Hubie Brooks	.05
564	Delino DeShields	.05
565	Tim Raines	.08
566	Sid Fernandez	.05
567	Steve Olin	.05
568	Tommy Greene	.05
569	Buddy Groom	.05
570	Randy Tomlin	.05
571	Hipolito Pichardo	.05
572	Rene Arocha (Rated Rookie)	.08
573	Mike Fetters	.05
574	Felix Jose	.05
575	Gene Larkin	.05
576	Bruce Hurst	.05
577	Bernie Williams	.40
578	Trevor Wilson	.05
579	Bob Welch	.05
580	Dave Justice	.20
581	Randy Johnson	.35
582	Jose Vizcaino	.05
583	Jeff Huson	.05
584	Rob Maurer (Rated Rookie)	.05
585	Todd Stottlemyre	.05
586	Joe Oliver	.05
587	Bob Milacki	.05
588	Rob Murphy	.05
589	Greg Pirkl (Rated Rookie)	.05
590	Lenny Harris	.05
591	Luis Rivera	.05
592	John Wetteland	.05
593	Mark Langston	.05
594	Bobby Bonilla	.08
595	Esteban Beltre	.05
596	Mike Hartley	.05
597	Felix Fermin	.05
598	Carlos Garcia	.05
599	Frank Tanana	.05
600	Pedro Guerrero	.05
601	Terry Shumpert	.05
602	Wally Whitehurst	.05
603	Kevin Seitzer	.05
604	Chris James	.05
605	Greg Gohr (Rated Rookie)	.05
606	Mark Wohlers	.05
607	Kirby Puckett	.40
608	Greg Maddux	1.00
609	Don Mattingly	.60
610	Greg Cadaret	.05
611	Dave Stewart	.08
612	Mark Portugal	.05
613	Pete O'Brien	.05
614	Bobby Ojeda	.05
615	Joe Carter	.08
616	Pete Young	.05
617	Sam Horn	.05
618	Vince Coleman	.05
619	Wade Boggs	.25
620	*Todd Pratt*	.10
621	Ron Tingley	.05
622	Doug Drabek	.05
623	Scott Hemond	.05
624	Tim Jones	.05
625	Dennis Cook	.05
626	Jose Melendez	.05
627	Mike Munoz	.05
628	Jim Pena	.05
629	Gary Thurman	.05
630	Charlie Leibrandt	.05
631	Scott Fletcher	.05
632	Andre Dawson	.10
633	Greg Gagne	.05
634	Greg Swindell	.05
635	Kevin Maas	.05
636	Xavier Hernandez	.05
637	Ruben Sierra	.05
638	Dimitri Young (Rated Rookie)	.12
639	Harold Reynolds	.05
640	Tom Goodwin	.05
641	Todd Burns	.05
642	Jeff Fassero	.05
643	Dave Winfield	.20
644	Willie Randolph	.05
645	Luis Mercedes	.05
646	Dale Murphy	.10
647	Danny Darwin	.05
648	Dennis Moeller	.05
649	Chuck Crim	.05
650	Checklist 556-634	.05
651	Shawn Abner	.05
652	Tracy Woodson	.05
653	Scott Scudder	.05
654	Tom Lampkin	.05
655	Alan Trammell	.10
656	Cory Snyder	.05
657	Chris Gwynn	.05
658	Lonnie Smith	.05
659	Jim Austin	.05
660	Checklist 635-713	.05
661	(Tim Hulett)	.05
662	Marvin Freeman	.05
663	Greg Harris	.05
664	Heathcliff Slocumb	.05
665	Mike Butcher	.05
666	Steve Foster	.05
667	Donn Pall	.05
668	Darryl Kile	.05
669	Jesse Levis	.08
670	Jim Gott	.05
671	*Mark Hutton*	.10
672	Brian Drahman	.05
673	Chad Kreuter	.05
674	Tony Fernandez	.08
675	Jose Lind	.05
676	Kyle Abbott	.05
677	Dan Plesac	.05
678	Barry Bonds	.60
679	Chili Davis	.08
680	Stan Royer	.05
681	Scott Kamieniecki	.05
682	Carlos Martinez	.05
683	Mike Moore	.05
684	Candy Maldanado	.05
685	Jeff Nelson	.05
686	Lou Whitaker	.08
687	Jose Guzman	.05
688	Manuel Lee	.05
689	Bob MacDonald	.05
690	Scott Bankhead	.05
691	Alan Mills	.05
692	Brian Williams	.05
693	Tom Brunansky	.05
694	Lenny Webster	.05
695	Greg Briley	.05
696	Paul O'Neill	.08
697	Joey Cora	.05
698	Charlie O'Brien	.05
699	Junior Ortiz	.05
700	Ron Darling	.05
701	Tony Phillips	.05
702	William Pennyfeather	.05
703	Mark Gubicza	.05
704	Steve Hosey (Rated Rookie)	.12
705	Henry Cotto	.05
706	*David Hulse*	.15
707	Mike Pagliarulo	.05
708	Dave Stieb	.05
709	Melido Perez	.05
710	Jimmy Key	.05
711	Jeff Russell	.05
712	David Cone	.10
713	Russ Swan	.05
714	Mark Guthrie	.05
715	Checklist 714-792	.05
716	Al Martin (Rated Rookie)	.15
717	Randy Knorr	.05
718	Mike Stanley	.05
719	Rick Sutcliffe	.05
720	Terry Leach	.05
721	Chipper Jones (Rated Rookie)	1.50
722	Jim Eisenreich	.05
723	Tom Henke	.05
724	Jeff Frye	.05
725	Harold Baines	.08
726	Scott Sanderson	.05
727	Tom Foley	.05
728	Bryan Harvey (Expansion Draft)	.05
729	Tom Edens	.05
730	Eric Young (Expansion Draft)	.12
731	Dave Weathers (Expansion Draft)	.05
732	Spike Owen	.05
733	Scott Aldred (Expansion Draft)	.05
734	Cris Carpenter (Expansion Draft)	.05
735	Dion James	.05
736	Joe Girardi (Expansion Draft)	.05
737	Nigel Wilson (Expansion Draft)	.08
738	Scott Chiamparino (Expansion Draft)	.05
739	Jeff Reardon	.05
740	Willie Blair (Expansion Draft)	.05
741	Jim Corsi (Expansion Draft)	.05
742	Ken Patterson	.05
743	Andy Ashby (Expansion Draft)	.05
744	Rob Natal (Expansion Draft)	.05
745	Kevin Bass	.05
746	Freddie Benavides (Expansion Draft)	.05
747	Chris Donnels (Expansion Draft)	.05
748	*Kerry Woodson*	.10
749	Calvin Jones (Expansion Draft)	.05
750	Gary Scott	.05
751	Joe Orsulak	.05
752	Armando Reynoso (Expansion Draft)	.05
753	Monty Farriss (Expansion Draft)	.05
754	Billy Hatcher	.05
755	Denis Boucher (Expansion Draft)	.05
756	Walt Weiss	.05
757	Mike Fitzgerald	.05
758	Rudy Seanez	.05
759	Bret Barberie (Expansion Draft)	.05
760	Mo Sanford (Expansion Draft)	.05
761	*Pedro Castellano* (Expansion Draft)	.12
762	Chuck Carr (Expansion Draft)	.05
763	Steve Howe	.05
764	Andres Galarraga	.10
765	Jeff Conine (Expansion Draft)	.08
766	Ted Power	.05
767	Butch Henry (Expansion Draft)	.05
768	Steve Decker (Expansion Draft)	.05
769	Storm Davis	.05
770	Vinny Castilla (Expansion Draft)	.10
771	Junior Felix (Expansion Draft)	.05
772	Walt Terrell	.05
773	Brad Ausmus (Expansion Draft)	.08
774	Jamie McAndrew (Expansion Draft)	.05
775	Milt Thompson	.05
776	Charlie Hayes (Expansion Draft)	.05
777	Jack Armstrong (Expansion Draft)	.05
778	Dennis Rasmussen	.05
779	Darren Holmes (Expansion Draft)	.05
780	*Alex Arias*	.12
781	Randy Bush	.05
782	Javier Lopez (Rated Rookie)	.60
783	Dante Bichette	.10
784	John Johnstone (Expansion Draft)	.05
785	Rene Gonzales	.05
786	Alex Cole (Expansion Draft)	.05
787	Jeromy Burnitz (Rated Rookie)	.15

788	Michael Huff	.05
789	Anthony Telford	.05
790	Jerald Clark (Expansion Draft)	.05
791	Joel Johnston	.05
792	David Nied (Rated Rookie)	.08

1993 Donruss Diamond Kings

The traditional Donruss Diamond Kings cards were again used as an insert in Series I and Series II foil packs in 1993. The first 15 cards were found in Series I packs, while cards 16-31 were available in the second series packs.

		MT
Complete Set (31):		32.50
Common Player:		.75
1	Ken Griffey, Jr.	10.00
2	Ryne Sandberg	4.00
3	Roger Clemens	4.00
4	Kirby Puckett	4.50
5	Bill Swift	.75
6	Larry Walker	1.00
7	Juan Gonzalez	3.00
8	Wally Joyner	.75
9	Andy Van Slyke	.75
10	Robin Ventura	1.00
11	Bip Roberts	.75
12	Roberto Kelly	.75
13	Carlos Baerga	.75
14	Orel Hershiser	.75
15	Cecil Fielder	.75
16	Robin Yount	1.50
17	Darren Daulton	.75
18	Mark McGwire	10.00
19	Tom Glavine	.75
20	Roberto Alomar	2.50
21	Gary Sheffield	.90
22	Bob Tewksbury	.75
23	Brady Anderson	.75
24	Craig Biggio	1.00
25	Eddie Murray	1.50
26	Luis Polonia	.75
27	Nigel Wilson	.75
28	David Nied	.75
29	Pat Listach	.75
30	Eric Karros	.75
31	Checklist	.05

1993 Donruss Elite

Continuing the card numbering from the 1992 Elite set, the Elite '93 inserts utilized a silver-foil prismatic front border with blue back printing. Each card is serial numbered as one of 10,000; this identified production number helping to make the Elites among the more valuable of insert cards.

		MT
Complete Set (20):		500.00
Common Player:		10.00
19	Fred McGriff	10.00
20	Ryne Sandberg	30.00
21	Eddie Murray	30.00
22	Paul Molitor	30.00
23	Barry Larkin	15.00
24	Don Mattingly	45.00
25	Dennis Eckersley	10.00
26	Roberto Alomar	30.00
27	Edgar Martinez	10.00
28	Gary Sheffield	15.00
29	Darren Daulton	10.00
30	Larry Walker	25.00
31	Barry Bonds	30.00
32	Andy Van Slyke	10.00
33	Mark McGwire	60.00
34	Cecil Fielder	10.00
35	Dave Winfield	15.00
36	Juan Gonzalez	30.00
---	Robin Yount (Legend)	25.00
---	Will Clark (Signature)	125.00

1993 Donruss Elite Supers

A Wal-Mart exclusive, Donruss produced 3-1/2" x 5" versions of its 1993 Elite inserts, added Nolan Ryan and Frank Thomas and a new card of Barry Bonds in his Giants uniform and packaged them one per shrink-wrapped box with Series I Donruss left-overs. Each super-size card features a color player photo and silver-foil prismatic borders on front. Backs are printed in blue and include a serial number identifying each of the cards from an edition of 5,000.

		MT
Complete Set (20):		600.00
Common Player:		12.00
1	Fred McGriff	20.00
2	Ryne Sandberg	60.00
3	Eddie Murray	40.00
4	Paul Molitor	40.00
5	Barry Larkin	20.00
6	Don Mattingly	75.00
7	Dennis Eckersley	12.00
8	Roberto Alomar	35.00
9	Edgar Martinez	12.00
10	Gary Sheffield	20.00
11	Darren Daulton	12.00
12	Larry Walker	25.00
13	Barry Bonds	65.00
14	Andy Van Slyke	12.00
15	Mark McGwire	100.00
16	Cecil Fielder	12.00
17	Dave Winfield	35.00
18	Juan Gonzalez	50.00
19	Frank Thomas	75.00
20	Nolan Ryan	150.00

1993 Donruss Long Ball Leaders

Carrying a prefix of "LL" before the card number, these inserts were released in Series I (LL1-9) and Series II (LL10-18) jumbo packs, detailing mammoth home runs of the previous season.

		MT
Complete Set (18):		55.00
Common Player:		.75
1	Rob Deer	.75
2	Fred McGriff	1.50
3	Albert Belle	3.50
4	Mark McGwire	15.00
5	Dave Justice	1.50
6	Jose Canseco	2.50
7	Kent Hrbek	.75
8	Roberto Alomar	2.50
9	Ken Griffey, Jr.	15.00
10	Frank Thomas	6.00
11	Darryl Strawberry	1.25
12	Felix Jose	.75
13	Cecil Fielder	.75
14	Juan Gonzalez	4.00
15	Ryne Sandberg	3.00
16	Gary Sheffield	1.25
17	Jeff Bagwell	5.00
18	Larry Walker	2.00

1993 Donruss MVP's

This set was inserted in jumbo packs of both Series I and Series II. Cards carry a MVP prefix to the card number.

		MT
Complete Set (26):		30.00
Common Player:		.50
1	Luis Polonia	.50
2	Frank Thomas	3.00
3	George Brett	2.50
4	Paul Molitor	1.50
5	Don Mattingly	3.50
6	Roberto Alomar	2.00
7	Terry Pendleton	.50
8	Eric Karros	.75
9	Larry Walker	1.00
10	Eddie Murray	1.25
11	Darren Daulton	.50
12	Ray Lankford	.50
13	Will Clark	1.00
14	Cal Ripken, Jr.	5.00
15	Roger Clemens	2.50
16	Carlos Baerga	.50
17	Cecil Fielder	.50
18	Kirby Puckett	3.50
19	Mark McGwire	6.00
20	Ken Griffey, Jr.	6.00
21	Juan Gonzalez	1.50
22	Ryne Sandberg	2.50
23	Bip Roberts	.50
24	Jeff Bagwell	3.00
25	Barry Bonds	2.00
26	Gary Sheffield	1.00

1993 Donruss Spirit of the Game

Series I and Series II foil and jumbo packs could be found with these cards randomly inserted. Several multi-player cards are included in the set. Card numbers bear an SG prefix.

		MT
Complete Set (20):		25.00
Common Player:		1.00
1	Turning Two (Dave Winfield, Mike Bordick)	1.00
2	Play at the Plate (David Justice)	2.00
3	In There (Roberto Alomar)	2.00

4	Pumped (Dennis Eckersley)	1.00
5	Dynamic Duo (Juan Gonzalez, Jose Canseco)	2.00
6	Gone (Frank Thomas, George Bell)	1.50
7	Safe or Out? (Wade Boggs)	1.50
8	The Thrill (Will Clark)	1.00
9	Safe at Home (Damon Berryhill, Bip Roberts, Glenn Braggs)	1.00
10	Thirty X 31 (Cecil Fielder, Mickey Tettleton, Rob Deer)	1.00
11	Bag Bandit (Kenny Lofton)	2.00
12	Back to Back (Fred McGriff, Gary Sheffield)	1.00
13	Range Rovers (Greg Gagne, Barry Larkin)	1.00
14	The Ball Stops Here (Ryne Sandberg)	2.00
15	Over the Top (Carlos Baerga, Gary Gaetti)	1.00
16	At the Wall (Danny Tartabull)	1.00
17	Head First (Brady Anderson)	1.00
18	Big Hurt (Frank Thomas)	3.00
19	No-Hitter (Kevin Gross)	1.00
20	3,000 (Robin Yount)	1.50

1993 Donruss Elite Dominators

Created as a premium to move left-over boxes of its 1993 product on a home shopping network at $100 apiece, this special edition was produced in standard 2-1/2" x 3-1/2" size in a format similar to the 1991-93 Donruss Elite chase cards. Cards feature green prismatic borders, liberal use of foil stamping, etc. Only 5,000 of each card were produced, and each card is serially numbered on the back. Half of the cards of Nolan Ryan, Juan Gonzalez, Don Mattingly and Paul Molitor were personally autographed by the player.

		MT
Complete Set (20):		750.00
Common Player:		20.00
1	Ryne Sandberg	25.00
2	Fred McGriff	20.00
3	Greg Maddux	50.00
4	Ron Gant	20.00
5	Dave Justice	20.00
6	Don Mattingly	50.00
7	Tim Salmon	20.00
8	Mike Piazza	50.00
9	John Olerud	22.00
10	Nolan Ryan	60.00
11	Juan Gonzalez	25.00
12	Ken Griffey, Jr.	75.00
13	Frank Thomas	30.00
14	Tom Glavine	20.00
15	George Brett	45.00
16	Barry Bonds	35.00
17	Albert Belle	25.00
18	Paul Molitor	25.00
19	Cal Ripken, Jr.	60.00
20	Roberto Alomar	30.00
Autographed Cards:		
6	Don Mattingly	125.00
10	Nolan Ryan	175.00
11	Juan Gonzalez	100.00
18	Paul Molitor	85.00

1993 Donruss Masters of the Game

Donruss issued a series of "Masters of the Game" art cards that were available only at Wal-Mart stores. The oversized cards (3-1/2" x 5") feature the artwork of Dick Perez, creator of the Diamond Kings cards for the same company. The cards came issued one to a pack, along with a foil pack of 1993 Donruss cards for a retail price of about $3.

		MT
Complete Set (16):		45.00
Common Player:		2.50
1	Frank Thomas	4.00
2	Nolan Ryan	6.00
3	Gary Sheffield	2.50
4	Fred McGriff	2.50
5	Ryne Sandberg	3.00
6	Cal Ripken, Jr.	6.00
7	Jose Canseco	3.00
8	Ken Griffey, Jr.	7.50
9	Will Clark	2.50
10	Roberto Alomar	2.50
11	Juan Gonzalez	3.00
12	David Justice	2.50
13	Kirby Puckett	4.00
14	Barry Bonds	4.00
15	Robin Yount	3.50
16	Deion Sanders	2.50

1994 Donruss Promos

To introduce both its regular 1994 issue and the "Special Edition" gold cards, Donruss produced this 12-card promo set for distribution to its dealer network. The promos are virtually identical in format to the regular cards except for the large gray diagonal overprint "Promotional Sample" on both front and back. Card numbers also differ on the promos.

		MT
Complete Set (12):		45.00
Common Player:		1.50
1	Barry Bonds	4.00
2	Darren Daulton	1.50
3	John Olerud	2.50
4	Frank Thomas	4.50
5	Mike Piazza	5.00
6	Tim Salmon	3.00
7	Ken Griffey, Jr.	7.50
8	Fred McGriff	2.50
9	Don Mattingly	5.00
10	Gary Sheffield	3.00
Special Edition Gold:		
1G	Barry Bonds (Special Edition Gold)	5.00
4G	Frank Thomas (Special Edition Gold)	7.50

1994 Donruss

Donruss released its 1994 set in two 330-card series. Each series also includes, 50 Special Edition gold cards and several insert sets. Regular cards have full-bleed photos and are UV coated and foil stamped. Special Edition cards are gold-foil stamped on both sides and are included in each pack. Insert sets titled Spirit of the Game and Decade Dominators were produced in regular and super (3-1/2" x 5") formats. Other inserts were MVPs and Long Ball Leaders in regular size and super-size Award Winners. An Elite series of cards, continuing from previous years with #37-48, was also issued as inserts. A 10th Anniversary insert set features 10 popular 1984 Donruss cards in gold-foil enhanced reprint versions.

		MT
Complete Set (660):		35.00
Common Player:		.05
Series 1 Pack (13):		1.50
Series 1 Wax Box (36):		35.00
Series 2 Pack (13):		1.25
Series 2 Wax Box (36):		30.00
1	Nolan Ryan (Career Salute 27 Years)	2.50
2	Mike Piazza	1.50
3	Moises Alou	.10
4	Ken Griffey, Jr.	3.00
5	Gary Sheffield	.25
6	Roberto Alomar	.75
7	John Kruk	.05
8	Gregg Olson	.05
9	Gregg Jefferies	.08
10	Tony Gwynn	1.25
11	Chad Curtis	.08
12	Craig Biggio	.25
13	John Burkett	.05
14	Carlos Baerga	.08
15	Robin Yount	.40
16	Dennis Eckersley	.08
17	Dwight Gooden	.08
18	Ryne Sandberg	.50
19	Rickey Henderson	.20
20	Jack McDowell	.05
21	Jay Bell	.08
22	Kevin Brown	.08
23	Robin Ventura	.20
24	Paul Molitor	.25
25	Dave Justice	.15
26	Rafael Palmeiro	.30
27	Cecil Fielder	.08
28	Chuck Knoblauch	.15
29	Dave Hollins	.08
30	Jimmy Key	.05
31	Mark Langston	.05
32	Darryl Kile	.05
33	Ruben Sierra	.05
34	Ron Gant	.08
35	Ozzie Smith	.40
36	Wade Boggs	.30
37	Marquis Grissom	.10
38	Will Clark	.25
39	Kenny Lofton	.60
40	Cal Ripken, Jr.	2.50
41	Steve Avery	.05
42	Mo Vaughn	.60
43	Brian McRae	.05
44	Mickey Tettleton	.05
45	Barry Larkin	.25
46	Charlie Hayes	.05
47	Kevin Appier	.05
48	Robby Thompson	.05
49	Juan Gonzalez	.75
50	Paul O'Neill	.15
51	Marcos Armas	.05
52	Mike Butcher	.05
53	Ken Caminiti	.15
54	Pat Borders	.05
55	Pedro Munoz	.05
56	Tim Belcher	.05
57	Paul Assenmacher	.05

No.	Player	Price
58	Damon Berryhill	.05
59	Ricky Bones	.05
60	Rene Arocha	.05
61	Shawn Boskie	.05
62	Pedro Astacio	.05
63	Frank Bolick	.05
64	Bud Black	.05
65	Sandy Alomar, Jr.	.10
66	Rich Amaral	.05
67	Luis Aquino	.05
68	Kevin Baez	.05
69	Mike Devereaux	.05
70	Andy Ashby	.08
71	Larry Andersen	.05
72	Steve Cooke	.05
73	Mario Daiz	.05
74	Rob Deer	.05
75	Bobby Ayala	.05
76	Freddie Benavides	.05
77	Stan Belinda	.05
78	John Doherty	.05
79	Willie Banks	.05
80	Spike Owen	.05
81	Mike Bordick	.05
82	Chili Davis	.08
83	Luis Gonzalez	.08
84	Ed Sprague	.05
85	Jeff Reboulet	.05
86	Jason Bere	.08
87	Mark Hutton	.05
88	Jeff Blauser	.05
89	Cal Eldred	.05
90	Bernard Gilkey	.05
91	Frank Castillo	.05
92	Jim Gott	.05
93	Greg Colbrunn	.05
94	Jeff Brantley	.05
95	Jeremy Hernandez	.05
96	Norm Charlton	.05
97	Alex Arias	.05
98	John Franco	.05
99	Chris Hoiles	.05
100	Brad Ausmus	.05
101	Wes Chamberlain	.05
102	Mark Dewey	.05
103	Benji Gil (Rated Rookie)	.10
104	John Dopson	.05
105	John Smiley	.05
106	David Nied	.05
107	George Brett (Career Salute 21 Years)	1.00
108	Kirk Gibson	.05
109	Larry Casian	.05
110	Checklist (Ryne Sandberg 2,000 Hits)	.15
111	Brent Gates	.08
112	Damion Easley	.08
113	Pete Harnisch	.05
114	Danny Cox	.05
115	Kevin Tapani	.05
116	Roberto Hernandez	.05
117	Domingo Jean	.05
118	Sid Bream	.05
119	Doug Henry	.05
120	Omar Olivares	.05
121	Mike Harkey	.05
122	Carlos Hernandez	.05
123	Jeff Fassero	.08
124	Dave Burba	.05
125	Wayne Kirby	.05
126	John Cummings	.05
127	Bret Barberie	.05
128	Todd Hundley	.10
129	Tim Hulett	.05
130	Phil Clark	.05
131	Danny Jackson	.05
132	Tom Foley	.05
133	Donald Harris	.05
134	Scott Fletcher	.05
135	Johnny Ruffin (Rated Rookie)	.05
136	Jerald Clark	.05
137	Billy Brewer	.05
138	Dan Gladden	.05
139	Eddie Guardado	.05
140	Checklist (Cal Ripken, Jr. 2,000 Hits)	.25
141	Scott Hemond	.05
142	Steve Frey	.05
143	Xavier Hernandez	.05
144	Mark Eichhorn	.05
145	Ellis Burks	.08
146	Jim Leyritz	.05
147	Mark Lemke	.05
148	Pat Listach	.05
149	Donovan Osborne	.05
150	Glenallen Hill	.05
151	Orel Hershiser	.08
152	Darrin Fletcher	.05
153	Royce Clayton	.05
154	Derek Lilliquist	.05
155	Mike Felder	.05
156	Jeff Conine	.08
157	Ryan Thompson	.05
158	Ben McDonald	.05
159	Ricky Gutierrez	.05
160	Terry Mulholland	.05
161	Carlos Garcia	.05
162	Tom Henke	.05
163	Mike Greenwell	.05
164	Thomas Howard	.05
165	Joe Girardi	.05
166	Hubie Brooks	.05
167	Greg Gohr	.05
168	Chip Hale	.05
169	Rick Honeycutt	.05
170	Hilly Hathaway	.05
171	Todd Jones	.05
172	Tony Fernandez	.05
173	Bo Jackson	.15
174	Bobby Munoz	.05
175	Greg McMichael	.05
176	Graeme Lloyd	.05
177	Tom Pagnozzi	.05
178	Derrick May	.05
179	Pedro Martinez	.75
180	Ken Hill	.05
181	Bryan Hickerson	.05
182	Jose Mesa	.05
183	Dave Fleming	.05
184	Henry Cotto	.05
185	Jeff Kent	.05
186	Mark McLemore	.05
187	Trevor Hoffman	.08
188	Todd Pratt	.08
189	Blas Minor	.05
190	Charlie Leibrandt	.05
191	Tony Pena	.05
192	*Larry Luebbers*	.08
193	Greg Harris	.05
194	David Cone	.10
195	Bill Gullickson	.05
196	Brian Harper	.05
197	Steve Karsay (Rated Rookie)	.20
198	Greg Myers	.05
199	Mark Portugal	.05
200	Pat Hentgen	.08
201	Mike La Valliere	.05
202	Mike Stanley	.05
203	Kent Mercker	.05
204	Dave Nilsson	.05
205	Erik Pappas	.05
206	Mike Morgan	.05
207	Roger McDowell	.05
208	Mike Lansing	.08
209	Kirt Manwaring	.05
210	Randy Milligan	.05
211	Erik Hanson	.05
212	Orestes Destrade	.05
213	Mike Maddux	.05
214	Alan Mills	.05
215	Tim Mauser	.05
216	Ben Rivera	.05
217	Don Slaught	.05
218	Bob Patterson	.05
219	Carlos Quintana	.05
220	Checklist (Tim Raines 2,000 Hits)	.05
221	Hal Morris	.05
222	Darren Holmes	.05
223	Chris Gwynn	.05
224	Chad Kreuter	.05
225	Mike Hartley	.05
226	Scott Lydy	.05
227	Eduardo Perez	.05
228	Greg Swindell	.05
229	Al Leiter	.08
230	Scott Radinsky	.05
231	Bob Wickman	.05
232	Otis Nixon	.05
233	Kevin Reimer	.05
234	Geronimo Pena	.05
235	Kevin Roberson (Rated Rookie)	.10
236	Jody Reed	.05
237	Kirk Rueter (Rated Rookie)	.15
238	Willie McGee	.05
239	Charles Nagy	.08
240	Tim Leary	.05
241	Carl Everett	.20
242	Charlie O'Brien	.05
243	Mike Pagliarulo	.05
244	Kerry Taylor	.05
245	Kevin Stocker	.05
246	Joel Johnston	.05
247	Geno Petralli	.05
248	Jeff Russell	.05
249	Joe Oliver	.05
250	Robert Mejia	.05
251	Chris Haney	.05
252	Bill Krueger	.05
253	Shane Mack	.05
254	Terry Steinbach	.05
255	Luis Polonia	.05
256	Eddie Taubensee	.05
257	Dave Stewart	.05
258	Tim Raines	.08
259	Bernie Williams	.50
260	John Smoltz	.10
261	Kevin Seitzer	.05
262	Bob Tewksbury	.05
263	Bob Scanlan	.05
264	Henry Rodriguez	.05
265	Tim Scott	.05
266	Scott Sanderson	.05
267	Eric Plunk	.05
268	Edgar Martinez	.08
269	Charlie Hough	.05
270	Joe Orsulak	.05
271	Harold Reynolds	.05
272	Tim Teufel	.05
273	Bobby Thigpen	.05
274	Randy Tomlin	.05
275	Gary Redus	.05
276	Ken Ryan	.05
277	Tim Pugh	.05
278	Jayhawk Owens	.05
279	Phil Hiatt (Rated Rookie)	.08
280	Alan Trammell	.08
281	Dave McCarty (Rated Rookie)	.08
282	Bob Welch	.05
283	J.T. Snow	.20
284	Brian Williams	.05
285	Devon White	.05
286	Steve Sax	.05
287	Tony Tarasco	.05
288	Bill Spiers	.05
289	Allen Watson	.05
290	Checklist (Rickey Henderson 2,000 Hits)	.05
291	Joe Vizcaino	.05
292	Darryl Strawberry	.08
293	John Wetteland	.05
294	Bill Swift	.05
295	Jeff Treadway	.05
296	Tino Martinez	.20
297	Richie Lewis	.05
298	Bret Saberhagen	.08
299	Arthur Rhodes	.05
300	Guillermo Velasquez	.05
301	Milt Thompson	.05
302	Doug Strange	.05
303	Aaron Sele	.12
304	Bip Roberts	.05
305	Bruce Ruffin	.05
306	Jose Lind	.05
307	David Wells	.08
308	Bobby Witt	.05
309	Mark Wohlers	.05
310	B.J. Surhoff	.08
311	Mark Whiten	.05
312	Turk Wendell	.05
313	Raul Mondesi	.25
314	*Brian Turang*	.08
315	Chris Hammond	.05
316	Tim Bogar	.05
317	Brad Pennington	.05
318	Tim Worrell	.05
319	Mitch Williams	.05
320	Rondell White (Rated Rookie)	.20
321	Frank Viola	.05
322	Manny Ramirez (Rated Rookie)	1.50
323	Gary Wayne	.05
324	Mike Macfarlane	.05
325	Russ Springer	.05
326	Tim Wallach	.05
327	Salomon Torres (Rated Rookie)	.08
328	Omar Vizquel	.08
329	*Andy Tomberlin*	.10
330	Chris Sabo	.05
331	Mike Mussina	.40
332	Andy Benes	.08
333	Darren Daulton	.05
334	Orlando Merced	.05
335	Mark McGwire	3.00
336	Dave Winfield	.25
337	Sammy Sosa	1.50
338	Eric Karros	.10
339	Greg Vaughn	.10
340	Don Mattingly	1.00
341	Frank Thomas	1.00
342	Fred McGriff	.20
343	Kirby Puckett	1.00
344	Roberto Kelly	.05
345	Wally Joyner	.08
346	Andres Galarraga	.40
347	Bobby Bonilla	.08
348	Benito Santiago	.05
349	Barry Bonds	.75
350	Delino DeShields	.08
351	Albert Belle	.60
352	Randy Johnson	.75
353	Tim Salmon	.20
354	John Olerud	.25
355	Dean Palmer	.05
356	Roger Clemens	1.00
357	Jim Abbott	.08
358	Mark Grace	.15
359	Ozzie Guillen	.05
360	Lou Whitaker	.05
361	Jose Rijo	.05
362	Jeff Montgomery	.05
363	Chuck Finley	.05
364	Tom Glavine	.20
365	Jeff Bagwell	1.00
366	Joe Carter	.08
367	Ray Lankford	.05
368	Ramon Martinez	.08
369	Jay Buhner	.10
370	Matt Williams	.25
371	Larry Walker	.25
372	Jose Canseco	.40
373	Len Dykstra	.05
374	Bryan Harvey	.05
375	Andy Van Slyke	.05
376	Ivan Rodriguez	.75
377	Kevin Mitchell	.05
378	Travis Fryman	.15
379	Duane Ward	.05
380	Greg Maddux	1.00
381	Scott Servais	.05
382	Greg Olson	.05
383	Rey Sanchez	.05
384	Tom Kramer	.05
385	David Valle	.05
386	Eddie Murray	.15
387	Kevin Higgins	.05
388	Dan Wilson	.05
389	Todd Frohwirth	.05
390	Gerald Williams	.05
391	Hipolito Pichardo	.05
392	Pat Meares	.05
393	Luis Lopez	.05
394	Ricky Jordan	.05
395	Bob Walk	.05
396	Sid Fernandez	.05
397	Todd Worrell	.05
398	Darryl Hamilton	.05
399	Randy Myers	.05
400	Rod Brewer	.05
401	Lance Blankenship	.05
402	Steve Finley	.05
403	*Phil Leftwich*	.05
404	Juan Guzman	.05
405	Anthony Young	.05
406	Jeff Gardner	.05
407	Ryan Bowen	.05
408	Fernando Valenzuela	.05
409	David West	.05
410	Kenny Rogers	.05
411	Bob Zupcic	.05
412	Eric Young	.08
413	Bret Boone	.08
414	Danny Tartabull	.05
415	Bob MacDonald	.05
416	Ron Karkovice	.05
417	Scott Cooper	.05
418	Dante Bichette	.15
419	Tripp Cromer	.05

420 Billy Ashley .05
421 Roger Smithberg .05
422 Dennis Martinez .08
423 Mike Blowers .05
424 Darren Lewis .05
425 Junior Ortiz .05
426 Butch Huskey .10
427 Jimmy Poole .05
428 Walt Weiss .05
429 Scott Bankhead .05
430 Deion Sanders .15
431 Scott Bullett .05
432 Jeff Huson .05
433 Tyler Green .05
434 Billy Hatcher .05
435 Bob Hamelin .05
436 Reggie Sanders .10
437 Scott Erickson .08
438 Steve Reed .05
439 Randy Velarde .05
440 Checklist (Tony Gwynn 2,000 Hits) .15
441 Terry Leach .05
442 Danny Bautista .05
443 Kent Hrbek .08
444 Rick Wilkins .05
445 Tony Phillips .08
446 Dion James .05
447 Joey Cora .05
448 Andre Dawson .15
449 Pedro Castellano .05
450 Tom Gordon .05
451 Rob Dibble .05
452 Ron Darling .05
453 Chipper Jones 1.00
454 Joe Grahe .05
455 Domingo Cedeno .05
456 Tom Edens .05
457 Mitch Webster .05
458 Jose Bautista .05
459 Troy O'Leary .05
460 Todd Zeile .08
461 Sean Berry .05
462 *Brad Holman* .05
463 Dave Martinez .05
464 Mark Lewis .05
465 Paul Carey .05
466 Jack Armstrong .05
467 David Telgheder .05
468 Gene Harris .05
469 Danny Darwin .05
470 Kim Batiste .05
471 Tim Wakefield .08
472 Craig Lefferts .05
473 Jacob Brumfield .05
474 Lance Painter .05
475 Milt Cuyler .05
476 Melido Perez .05
477 Derek Parks .05
478 Gary DiSarcina .05
479 Steve Bedrosian .05
480 Eric Anthony .05
481 Julio Franco .08
482 Tommy Greene .05
483 Pat Kelly .05
484 Nate Minchey (Rated Rookie) .05
485 William Pennyfeather .05
486 Harold Baines .08
487 Howard Johnson .05
488 Angel Miranda .05
489 Scott Sanders .05
490 Shawon Dunston .05
491 Mel Rojas .05
492 Jeff Nelson .05
493 Archi Cianfrocco .05
494 Al Martin .05
495 Mike Gallego .05
496 Mike Henneman .05
497 Armando Reynoso .05
498 Mickey Morandini .05
499 Rick Renteria .05
500 Rick Sutcliffe .05
501 Bobby Jones (Rated Rookie) .15
502 Gary Gaetti .05
503 Rick Aguilera .05
504 Todd Stottlemyre .05
505 Mike Mohler .05
506 Mike Stanton .05
507 Jose Guzman .05
508 Kevin Rogers .05
509 Chuck Carr .05
510 Chris Jones .05
511 Brent Mayne .05
512 Greg Harris .05
513 Dave Henderson .05
514 Eric Hillman .05
515 Dan Peltier .05
516 Craig Shipley .05
517 John Valentin .08
518 Wilson Alvarez .05
519 Andujar Cedeno .05
520 Troy Neel .05
521 Tom Candiotti .05
522 Matt Mieske .05
523 Jim Thome .30
524 Lou Frazier .05
525 Mike Jackson .05
526 Pedro Martinez .75
527 Roger Pavlik .05
528 Kent Bottenfield .05
529 Felix Jose .05
530 Mark Guthrie .05
531 Steve Farr .05
532 Craig Paquette .05
533 Doug Jones .05
534 Luis Alicea .05
535 Cory Snyder .05
536 Paul Sorrento .05
537 Nigel Wilson .05
538 Jeff King .05
539 Willie Green .05
540 Kirk McCaskill .05
541 Al Osuna .05
542 Greg Hibbard .05
543 Brett Butler .08
544 Jose Valentin .05
545 Wil Cordero .05
546 Chris Bosio .05
547 Jamie Moyer .05
548 Jim Eisenreich .05
549 Vinny Castilla .08
550 Checklist (Dave Winfield 3,000 Hits) .05
551 John Roper .05
552 Lance Johnson .05
553 Scott Kamieniecki .05
554 Mike Moore .05
555 Steve Buechele .05
556 Terry Pendleton .05
557 Todd Van Poppel .05
558 Rob Butler .05
559 Zane Smith .05
560 David Hulse .05
561 Tim Costo .05
562 John Habyan .05
563 Terry Jorgensen .05
564 Matt Nokes .05
565 Kevin McReynolds .05
566 Phil Plantier .05
567 Chris Turner .05
568 Carlos Delgado .50
569 John Jaha .08
570 Dwight Smith .05
571 John Vander Wal .05
572 Trevor Wilson .05
573 Felix Fermin .05
574 Marc Newfield (Rated Rookie) .10
575 Jeromy Burnitz .08
576 Leo Gomez .05
577 Curt Schilling .10
578 Kevin Young .08
579 *Jerry Spradlin* .08
580 Curt Leskanic .05
581 Carl Willis .05
582 Alex Fernandez .08
583 Mark Holzemer .05
584 Domingo Martinez .05
585 Pete Smith .05
586 Brian Jordan .05
587 Kevin Gross .05
588 J.R. Phillips (Rated Rookie) .15
589 Chris Nabholz .05
590 Bill Wertz .05
591 Derek Bell .08
592 Brady Anderson .10
593 Matt Turner .05
594 Pete Incaviglia .05
595 Greg Gagne .05
596 John Flaherty .05
597 Scott Livingstone .05
598 Rod Bolton .05
599 Mike Perez .05
600 Checklist (Roger Clemens 2,000 Strikeouts) .08
601 Tony Castillo .05
602 Henry Mercedes .05
603 Mike Fetters .05
604 Rod Beck .05
605 Damon Buford .05
606 Matt Whiteside .05
607 Shawn Green .40
608 Midre Cummings (Rated Rookie) .10
609 Jeff McNeeley .05
610 Danny Sheaffer .05
611 Paul Wagner .05
612 Torey Lovullo .05
613 Javier Lopez .25
614 Mariano Duncan .05
615 Doug Brocail .05
616 Dave Hansen .05
617 Ryan Klesko .25
618 Eric Davis .10
619 Scott Ruffcorn (Rated Rookie) .10
620 Mike Trombley .05
621 Jaime Navarro .05
622 Rheal Cormier .05
623 Jose Offerman .05
624 David Segui .05
625 Robb Nen (Rated Rookie) .05
626 Dave Gallagher .05
627 *Julian Tavarez* .10
628 Chris Gomez .05
629 Jeffrey Hammonds (Rated Rookie) .15
630 Scott Brosius .05
631 Willie Blair .05
632 Doug Drabek .05
633 Bill Wegman .05
634 Jeff McKnight .05
635 Rich Rodriguez .05
636 Steve Trachsel .10
637 Buddy Groom .05
638 Sterling Hitchcock .08
639 Chuck McElroy .05
640 Rene Gonzales .05
641 Dan Plesac .05
642 Jeff Branson .05
643 Darrell Whitmore .05
644 Paul Quantrill .05
645 Rich Rowland .05
646 *Curtis Pride* .20
647 Erik Plantenberg .05
648 Albie Lopez .05
649 *Rich Batchelor* .05
650 Lee Smith .08
651 Cliff Floyd .10
652 Pete Schourek .05
653 Reggie Jefferson .05
654 Bill Haselman .05
655 Steve Hosey .05
656 Mark Clark .05
657 Mark Davis .05
658 Dave Magadan .05
659 Candy Maldonado .05
660 Checklist (Mark Langston 2,0000 Strikeouts) .05

1994 Donruss Special Edition - Gold

In 1994 Donruss added a Special Edition subset of 100 of the game's top players. Fifty cards each were included one or two per pack in all types of Donruss' Series I and II packaging. The cards use the same photos and format as the regular-issue version, but have special gold-foil stamping on front in the area of the team logo and player name, and on back in a "Special Edition" number box in the upper-left corner.

		MT
Complete Set (100):		30.00
Common Player:		.25
1	Nolan Ryan	3.00
2	Mike Piazza	3.00
3	Moises Alou	.25
4	Ken Griffey, Jr.	5.00
5	Gary Sheffield	.50
6	Roberto Alomar	1.00
7	John Kruk	.25
8	Gregg Olson	.25
9	Gregg Jefferies	.30
10	Tony Gwynn	2.00
11	Chad Curtis	.25
12	Craig Biggio	.50
13	John Burkett	.25
14	Carlos Baerga	.25
15	Robin Yount	.75
16	Dennis Eckersley	.25
17	Dwight Gooden	.35
18	Ryne Sandberg	1.00
19	Rickey Henderson	.40
20	Jack McDowell	.25
21	Jay Bell	.25
22	Kevin Brown	.40
23	Robin Ventura	.40
24	Paul Molitor	.75
25	David Justice	.50
26	Rafael Palmeiro	.75
27	Cecil Fielder	.25
28	Chuck Knoblauch	.40
29	Dave Hollins	.25
30	Jimmy Key	.25
31	Mark Langston	.25
32	Darryl Kile	.25
33	Ruben Sierra	.25
34	Ron Gant	.30
35	Ozzie Smith	1.00
36	Wade Boggs	.60
37	Marquis Grissom	.30
38	Will Clark	.40
39	Kenny Lofton	.75
40	Cal Ripken, Jr.	4.00
41	Steve Avery	.25
42	Mo Vaughn	1.00
43	Brian McRae	.25
44	Mickey Tettleton	.25
45	Barry Larkin	.50
46	Charlie Hayes	.25
47	Kevin Appier	.25
48	Robby Thompson	.25
49	Juan Gonzalez	1.25
50	Paul O'Neill	.30
51	Mike Mussina	.75
52	Andy Benes	.25
53	Darren Daulton	.25
54	Orlando Merced	.25
55	Mark McGwire	5.00
56	Dave Winfield	.35
57	Sammy Sosa	2.50
58	Eric Karros	.25
59	Greg Vaughn	.25
60	Don Mattingly	1.50
61	Frank Thomas	1.50
62	Fred McGriff	.40
63	Kirby Puckett	1.50
64	Roberto Kelly	.25
65	Wally Joyner	.25
66	Andres Galarraga	.75
67	Bobby Bonilla	.25
68	Benito Santiago	.25
69	Barry Bonds	1.50
70	Delino DeShields	.25
71	Albert Belle	1.00
72	Randy Johnson	1.50
73	Tim Salmon	.40
74	John Olerud	.30
75	Dean Palmer	.25

76	Roger Clemens	2.00
77	Jim Abbott	.25
78	Mark Grace	.40
79	Ozzie Guillen	.25
80	Lou Whitaker	.25
81	Jose Rijo	.25
82	Jeff Montgomery	.25
83	Chuck Finley	.25
84	Tom Glavine	.40
85	Jeff Bagwell	1.50
86	Joe Carter	.25
87	Ray Lankford	.25
88	Ramon Martinez	.25
89	Jay Buhner	.25
90	Matt Williams	.50
91	Larry Walker	1.00
92	Jose Canseco	1.00
93	Len Dykstra	.25
94	Bryan Harvey	.25
95	Andy Van Slyke	.25
96	Ivan Rodriguez	1.50
97	Kevin Mitchell	.25
98	Travis Fryman	.40
99	Duane Ward	.25
100	Greg Maddux	2.50

1994 Donruss Anniversary-1984

This set commemorates and features 10 of the most popular cards from Donruss' 1984 set. The cards, inserted in Series I hobby foil packs only, are "holographically enhanced" with foil stamping and UV coating.

		MT
Complete Set (10):		50.00
Common Player:		2.00
1	Joe Carter	2.00
2	Robin Yount	3.50
3	George Brett	5.00
4	Rickey Henderson	2.00
5	Nolan Ryan	15.00
6	Cal Ripken, Jr.	15.00
7	Wade Boggs	2.00
8	Don Mattingly	7.50
9	Ryne Sandberg	4.00
10	Tony Gwynn	6.00

1994 Donruss Award Winners Supers

Major award winners of the 1993 season are honored in in this super-size (3-1/2" x 5") insert set. One card was packaged in each box of U.S. jumbo packs and in each Canadian foil-pack box. On a gold-tone background, the card backs have another player photo, a description of his award winning performance and a white strip with a serial number identifying the card's place in an edition of 10,000.

		MT
Complete Set (10):		45.00
Common Player:		3.00
1	Barry Bonds (N.L. MVP)	5.00
2	Greg Maddux (N.L. Cy Young)	6.00
3	Mike Piazza (N.L. ROY)	7.50
4	Barry Bonds (N.L. HR Champ)	5.00
5	Kirby Puckett (All-Star MVP)	6.00
6	Frank Thomas (A.L. MVP)	6.00
7	Jack McDowell (A.L. Cy Young)	3.00
8	Tim Salmon (A.L. ROY)	4.00
9	Juan Gonzalez (A.L. HR Champ)	6.00
10	Paul Molitor (World Series MVP)	5.00

1994 Donruss Decade Dominators

Donruss selected 10 top home run hitters (Series I) and 10 RBI leaders of the 1990s for this insert set. Cards were issued in all types of Series I and II packs. Full-bleed UV-coated cards were gold-foil enhanced on the front. Backs featured another full-color player photo and charted information on his 1990s home run or RBI output and ranking.

		MT
Complete Set (20):		40.00
Common Player:		.75
Series 1		
1	Cecil Fielder	.75
2	Barry Bonds	2.00
3	Fred McGriff	1.00
4	Matt Williams	.75
5	Joe Carter	.75
6	Juan Gonzalez	2.00
7	Jose Canseco	1.50
8	Ron Gant	.75
9	Ken Griffey, Jr.	8.00
10	Mark McGwire	8.00
Series 2		
1	Tony Gwynn	4.00
2	Frank Thomas	3.00
3	Paul Molitor	2.00
4	Edgar Martinez	.75
5	Kirby Puckett	3.00
6	Ken Griffey, Jr.	8.00
7	Barry Bonds	2.50
8	Willie McGee	.75
9	Len Dykstra	.75
10	John Kruk	.75

1994 Donruss Decade Dominators Supers

Super-size (3-1/2" x 5") versions of the 1994 Donruss Decade Dominators insert cards were produced as a premium, one card being packaged in a paper checklist envelope in each hobby box of Donruss foil packs. The supers are identical in format to the regular-size cards with the exception of a white serial number strip on the back, identifying each card's position in an edition of 10,000.

		MT
Complete Set (20):		60.00
Common Player:		4.00
Series 1		
1	Cecil Fielder	3.00
2	Barry Bonds	6.00
3	Fred McGriff	3.00
4	Matt Williams	3.00
5	Joe Carter	3.00
6	Juan Gonzalez	7.50
7	Jose Canseco	4.00
8	Ron Gant	3.00
9	Ken Griffey, Jr.	9.00
10	Mark McGwire	9.00
Series 2		
1	Tony Gwynn	5.00
2	Frank Thomas	5.00
3	Paul Molitor	4.00
4	Edgar Martinez	3.00
5	Kirby Puckett	5.00
6	Ken Griffey, Jr.	8.00
7	Barry Bonds	7.50
8	Willie McGee	3.00
9	Lenny Dykstra	3.00
10	John Kruk	3.00

1994 Donruss Diamond Kings

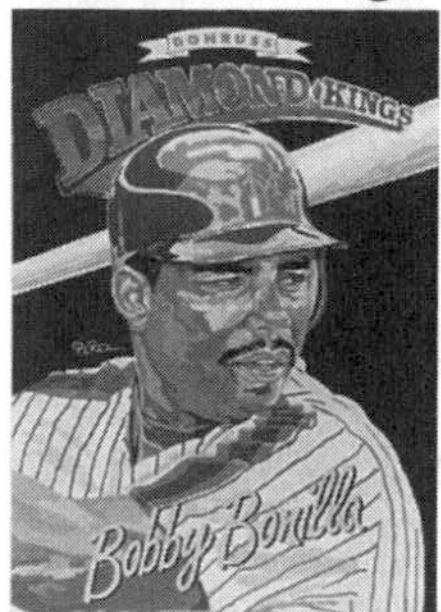

The artwork of Dick Perez is again featured on this insert set included in foil packs. Player art is set against garish color backgrounds with a red-and-silver "Diamond Kings" foil logo above, and the player's name in script at bottom. Backs are printed in red on pale yellow and feature a 1993 season summary. Cards have a DK preface to the number. Cards #1-14 and #29, Dave Winfield, were included in Series I packs; cards #15-28 were found in Series II, along with the checklist card (#30), featuring a Dick Perez self-portrait.

		MT
Complete Set (30):		40.00
Common Player:		.60
1	Barry Bonds	2.50
2	Mo Vaughn	1.50
3	Steve Avery	.60
4	Tim Salmon	1.00
5	Rick Wilkins	.60
6	Brian Harper	.60
7	Andres Galarraga	1.50
8	Albert Belle	2.00
9	John Kruk	.60
10	Ivan Rodriguez	2.50
11	Tony Gwynn	4.00
12	Brian McRae	.60
13	Bobby Bonilla	.60
14	Ken Griffey, Jr.	8.00
15	Mike Piazza	5.00
16	Don Mattingly	3.50
17	Barry Larkin	1.00
18	Ruben Sierra	.60
19	Orlando Merced	.60
20	Greg Vaughn	.60
21	Gregg Jefferies	.60
22	Cecil Fielder	.60
23	Moises Alou	.60
24	John Olerud	.75
25	Gary Sheffield	.75
26	Mike Mussina	1.00
27	Jeff Bagwell	2.50
28	Frank Thomas	3.50
29	Dave Winfield (King of Kings)	1.50
30	Dick Perez (Checklist)	.60

1994 Donruss Diamond Kings Supers

Each retail box of 1994 Donruss foil packs contains one super-size (4-7/8" x 6-13/16") version of the Diamond Kings inserts. Series I boxes offer cards #1-14, while #15-28 are found in Series II boxes. A 29th card, honoring Dave Winfield, was also produced. Super DKs are identical in format to the regular-size inserts, with the exception of a white serial number strip on the back which identifies the card within an edition of 10,000.

		MT
Complete Set (29):		75.00
Common Player:		3.00
1	Barry Bonds	5.00
2	Mo Vaughn	3.00
3	Steve Avery	2.00
4	Tim Salmon	3.00
5	Rick Wilkins	2.00
6	Brian Harper	2.00
7	Andres Galarraga	3.00
8	Albert Belle	4.00
9	John Kruk	2.00
10	Ivan Rodriguez	4.00
11	Tony Gwynn	5.00
12	Brian McRae	3.00
13	Bobby Bonilla	3.00
14	Ken Griffey, Jr.	7.50
15	Mike Piazza	6.00
16	Don Mattingly	5.00
17	Barry Larkin	4.00
18	Ruben Sierra	3.00
19	Orlando Merced	3.00
20	Greg Vaughn	3.00
21	Gregg Jefferies	3.00
22	Cecil Fielder	3.00
23	Moises Alou	3.00
24	John Olerud	3.00
25	Gary Sheffield	3.00
26	Mike Mussina	3.00
27	Jeff Bagwell	5.00
28	Frank Thomas	3.00
29	Dave Winfield	4.00

1994 Donruss Elite

Donruss continued its popular Elite Series with 12 more players in 1994. The cards, numbered #37-48, were inserted in foil packs only. The cards feature the player in a diamond on the front; the back offers an opinion of why the player is considered an elite and is serially numbered to 10,000.

		MT
Complete Set (12):		160.00
Common Player:		6.00
37	Frank Thomas	20.00
38	Tony Gwynn	25.00
39	Tim Salmon	8.00
40	Albert Belle	10.00
41	John Kruk	5.00
42	Juan Gonzalez	12.00
43	John Olerud	8.00
44	Barry Bonds	15.00
45	Ken Griffey, Jr.	45.00
46	Mike Piazza	30.00
47	Jack McDowell	5.00
48	Andres Galarraga	8.00

1994 Donruss Long Ball Leaders

The "Tale of the Tape" for the 1993 season is chronicled in this Series II hobby-only foil-pack insert. Silver prismatic foil highlights the typography on the front of the card which includes the "Long Ball Leaders" logos (complete with embossed baseball), the player's last name and the distance of his blast. Cards backs have another player photo superimposed on the venue in which the home run was hit. The distance is repeated in silver over the ballpark photo. In a wide silver box at bottom are data about the home run.

		MT
Complete Set (10):		18.00
Common Player:		.50
1	Cecil Fielder	.50
2	Dean Palmer	.50
3	Andres Galarraga	1.00
4	Bo Jackson	.75
5	Ken Griffey, Jr.	6.00
6	Dave Justice	1.00
7	Mike Piazza	4.00
8	Frank Thomas	3.00
9	Barry Bonds	2.00
10	Juan Gonzalez	1.50

Player names in *Italic* type indicate a rookie card.

1994 Donruss MVPs

These inserts were included in 1994 jumbo packs only. The fronts have a large metallic blue MVP logo, beneath which is a red stripe with the player's name and position in white. Backs have a portrait photo, stats for 1993 and a summary of why the player was selected as team MVP.

		MT
Complete Set (28):		30.00
Common Player:		.25
1	Dave Justice	.50
2	Mark Grace	.50
3	Jose Rijo	.25
4	Andres Galarraga	1.00
5	Bryan Harvey	.25
6	Jeff Bagwell	2.00
7	Mike Piazza	6.00
8	Moises Alou	.25
9	Bobby Bonilla	.25
10	Len Dykstra	.25
11	Jeff King	.25
12	Gregg Jefferies	.25
13	Tony Gwynn	3.00
14	Barry Bonds	2.00
15	Cal Ripken, Jr.	6.00
16	Mo Vaughn	1.00
17	Tim Salmon	.50
18	Frank Thomas	4.00
19	Albert Belle	1.50
20	Cecil Fielder	.25
21	Wally Joyner	.25
22	Greg Vaughn	.40
23	Kirby Puckett	2.50
24	Don Mattingly	2.00
25	Ruben Sierra	.25
26	Ken Griffey, Jr.	8.00
27	Juan Gonzalez	2.00
28	John Olerud	.40

1994 Donruss Spirit of the Game

Ten players are featured in this insert set, packaged exclusively in retail boxes. Horizontal in format, fronts feature a color player action photo set against a gold-tone background which has the appearance of a multiple-exposure photo. On back a player portrait photo is set against a backdrop of red, white and blue bunting. There is a short previous-season write-up at right. Cards #1-5 were included with Series I, cards 6-10 were in Series II packs.

		MT
Complete Set (10):		25.00
Common Player:		1.50
1	John Olerud	1.50
2	Barry Bonds	2.50
3	Ken Griffey, Jr.	8.00
4	Mike Piazza	6.00
5	Juan Gonzalez	2.00
6	Frank Thomas	3.00
7	Tim Salmon	1.50
8	Dave Justice	1.50
9	Don Mattingly	3.00
10	Len Dykstra	1.00

1994 Donruss Spirit of the Game Supers

Virtually identical in format to the regular-size "Spirit of the Game" cards, these 3-1/2" x 5" versions have gold-foil, rather than holographic printing on the front, and have a serial number on back identifying it from an edition of 10,000. One super card was inserted in each specially designated retail box.

		MT
Complete Set (10):		50.00
Common Player:		3.00
1	John Olerud	5.00
2	Barry Bonds	6.00
3	Ken Griffey, Jr.	9.00
4	Mike Piazza	7.50
5	Juan Gonzalez	6.00
6	Frank Thomas	5.00
7	Tim Salmon	4.00
8	Dave Justice	3.00
9	Don Mattingly	6.00
10	Len Dykstra	3.00

1995 Donruss Samples

The cards in this preview release of Donruss' 1995 baseball issue are virtually identical to the issued versions of the same players' cards except for the overprinted notation of sample status on each side.

		MT
Complete Set (7):		50.00
Common Player:		7.50
5	Mike Piazza	10.00
8	Barry Bonds	7.50
20	Jeff Bagwell	9.00
42	Juan Gonzalez	8.00
55	Don Mattingly	10.00
275	Frank Thomas	8.00
331	Greg Maddux	8.00

1995 Donruss

A pair of player photos on the front of each card and silver-foil highlights are featured on the 1995 Donruss set. Besides the main action photo on front, each card has a second photo in a home plate frame at lower-left. A silver-foil ribbon beneath has the player's team and name embossed. Above the small photo is the player's position, with a half-circle of stars over all; both elements in silver foil. Completing the silver-foil highlights is the Donruss logo at upper-left. Full-bleed backs have yet another action photo at center, with a large team logo at left and five years' worth of stats plus career numbers at bottom. Donruss was issued in retail and hobby 12-card packs, magazine distributor packs of 16 and jumbo packs of 20 cards. New to Donruss in 1995 were Super Packs. These were packs that contained complete insert sets and were seeded every 90 packs.

		MT
Complete Set (550):		35.00
Complete Series 1:		20.00
Complete Series 2:		15.00
Common Player:		.05
Series 1 or 2 Pack (12):		1.00
Series 1 or 2 Wax Box (36):		30.00
1	Dave Justice	.20
2	Rene Arocha	.08
3	Sandy Alomar Jr.	.15
4	Luis Lopez	.08
5	Mike Piazza	1.50
6	Bobby Jones	.08
7	Damion Easley	.08
8	Barry Bonds	.75
9	Mike Mussina	.35
10	Kevin Seitzer	.05
11	John Smiley	.05
12	W. VanLandingham	.05
13	Ron Darling	.05
14	Walt Weiss	.05
15	Mike Lansing	.08
16	Allen Watson	.08
17	Aaron Sele	.10
18	Randy Johnson	.45
19	Dean Palmer	.05
20	Jeff Bagwell	.75
21	Curt Schilling	.15
22	Darrell Whitmore	.08
23	Steve Trachsel	.10
24	Dan Wilson	.10
25	Steve Finley	.05
26	Bret Boone	.10
27	Charles Johnson	.10
28	Mike Stanton	.05
29	Ismael Valdes	.10
30	Salomon Torres	.05
31	Eric Anthony	.05
32	Spike Owen	.05
33	Joey Cora	.05
34	Robert Eenhoorn	.05
35	Rick White	.05
36	Omar Vizquel	.08
37	Carlos Delgado	.40
38	Eddie Williams	.05
39	Shawon Dunston	.05
40	Darrin Fletcher	.05
41	Leo Gomez	.05
42	Juan Gonzalez	1.00
43	Luis Alicea	.05
44	Ken Ryan	.08
45	Lou Whitaker	.05
46	Mike Blowers	.05
47	Willie Blair	.05
48	Todd Van Poppel	.05
49	Roberto Alomar	.60
50	Ozzie Smith	.40
51	Sterling Hitchcock	.08
52	Mo Vaughn	.60
53	Rick Aguilera	.05
54	Kent Mercker	.05
55	Don Mattingly	1.00
56	Bob Scanlan	.05
57	Wilson Alvarez	.08
58	Jose Mesa	.05
59	Scott Kamieniecki	.08
60	Todd Jones	.05
61	John Kruk	.05
62	Mike Stanley	.08
63	Tino Martinez	.10
64	Eddie Zambrano	.08
65	Todd Hundley	.15
66	Jamie Moyer	.05
67	Rich Amaral	.05
68	Jose Valentin	.05
69	Alex Gonzalez	.15
70	Kurt Abbott	.08
71	Delino DeShields	.08
72	Brian Anderson	.10
73	John Vander Wal	.05
74	Turner Ward	.05
75	Tim Raines	.08
76	Mark Acre	.05
77	Jose Offerman	.08
78	Jimmy Key	.08
79	Mark Whiten	.05
80	Mark Gubicza	.05
81	Darren Hall	.05
82	Travis Fryman	.15
83	Cal Ripken, Jr.	2.50
84	Geronimo Berroa	.05
85	Bret Barberie	.08
86	Andy Ashby	.10
87	Steve Avery	.05
88	Rich Becker	.05
89	John Valentin	.10
90	Glenallen Hill	.05
91	Carlos Garcia	.08
92	Dennis Martinez	.10
93	Pat Kelly	.05
94	Orlando Miller	.08
95	Felix Jose	.05
96	Mike Kingery	.05
97	Jeff Kent	.05
98	Pete Incaviglia	.05
99	Chad Curtis	.10
100	Thomas Howard	.05
101	Hector Carrasco	.05
102	Tom Pagnozzi	.05
103	Danny Tartabull	.05
104	Donnie Elliott	.05
105	Danny Jackson	.05
106	Steve Dunn	.05
107	Roger Salkeld	.05
108	Jeff King	.08
109	Cecil Fielder	.08
110	Checklist	.05
111	Denny Neagle	.05
112	Troy Neel	.08
113	Rod Beck	.05
114	Alex Rodriguez	3.00
115	Joey Eischen	.05
116	Tom Candiotti	.05
117	Ray McDavid	.05
118	Vince Coleman	.05
119	Pete Harnisch	.05
120	David Nied	.05
121	Pat Rapp	.08
122	Sammy Sosa	1.50
123	Steve Reed	.05
124	Jose Oliva	.05
125	Rick Bottalico	.08
126	Jose DeLeon	.05
127	Pat Hentgen	.08
128	Will Clark	.35
129	Mark Dewey	.05
130	Greg Vaughn	.08
131	Darren Dreifort	.05
132	Ed Sprague	.08
133	Lee Smith	.08
134	Charles Nagy	.08
135	Phil Plantier	.05
136	Jason Jacome	.05
137	Jose Lima	.10
138	J.R. Phillips	.05
139	J.T. Snow	.08
140	Mike Huff	.05
141	Billy Brewer	.05
142	Jeromy Burnitz	.08
143	Ricky Bones	.05
144	Carlos Rodriguez	.05
145	Luis Gonzalez	.08
146	Mark Lemke	.05
147	Al Martin	.05
148	Mike Bordick	.08
149	Robb Nen	.05
150	Wil Cordero	.05
151	Edgar Martinez	.08
152	Gerald Williams	.08
153	Esteban Beltre	.05
154	Mike Moore	.05
155	Mark Langston	.05
156	Mark Clark	.05
157	Bobby Ayala	.05
158	Rick Wilkins	.05
159	Bobby Munoz	.05
160	Checklist	.05
161	Scott Erickson	.05
162	Paul Molitor	.35
163	Jon Lieber	.05
164	Jason Grimsley	.05
165	Norberto Martin	.05
166	Javier Lopez	.10
167	Brian McRae	.08
168	Gary Sheffield	.30
169	Marcus Moore	.05
170	John Hudek	.05
171	Kelly Stinett	.05
172	Chris Gomez	.05
173	Rey Sanchez	.05
174	Juan Guzman	.05
175	Chan Ho Park	.15
176	Terry Shumpert	.05
177	Steve Ontiveros	.05
178	Brad Ausmus	.05
179	Tim Davis	.05
180	Billy Ashley	.05
181	Vinny Castilla	.10
182	Bill Spiers	.05
183	Randy Knorr	.05
184	Brian Hunter	.05
185	Pat Meares	.05
186	Steve Buechele	.05
187	Kirt Manwaring	.05
188	Tim Naehring	.05
189	Matt Mieske	.05
190	Josias Manzanillo	.05
191	Greg McMichael	.05
192	Chuck Carr	.05
193	Midre Cummings	.08
194	Darryl Strawberry	.10
195	Greg Gagne	.05
196	Steve Cooke	.08
197	Woody Williams	.05
198	Ron Karkovice	.05
199	Phil Leftwich	.05
200	Jim Thome	.30
201	Brady Anderson	.15
202	Pedro Martinez	.15
203	Steve Karsay	.08
204	Reggie Sanders	.08
205	Bill Risley	.05
206	Jay Bell	.08
207	Kevin Brown	.15
208	Tim Scott	.05
209	Len Dykstra	.05
210	Willie Greene	.05
211	Jim Eisenreich	.05
212	Cliff Floyd	.08
213	Otis Nixon	.05
214	Eduardo Perez	.05
215	Manuel Lee	.05
216	*Armando Benitez*	.15
217	Dave McCarty	.05
218	Scott Livingstone	.05
219	Chad Kreuter	.05
220	Checklist	.05
221	Brian Jordan	.10
222	Matt Whiteside	.05
223	Jim Edmonds	.15
224	Tony Gwynn	.75
225	Jose Lind	.05
226	Marvin Freeman	.05
227	Ken Hill	.05
228	David Hulse	.05
229	Joe Hesketh	.05
230	Roberto Petagine	.05
231	Jeffrey Hammonds	.08
232	John Jaha	.05
233	John Burkett	.08
234	Hal Morris	.05
235	Tony Castillo	.05
236	Ryan Bowen	.08
237	Wayne Kirby	.05
238	Brent Mayne	.05
239	Jim Bullinger	.05
240	Mike Lieberthal	.08
241	Barry Larkin	.20
242	David Segui	.05
243	Jose Bautista	.05
244	Hector Fajardo	.05
245	Orel Hershiser	.08
246	James Mouton	.05
247	Scott Leius	.05
248	Tom Glavine	.20
249	Danny Bautista	.05
250	Jose Mercedes	.05
251	Marquis Grissom	.10
252	Charlie Hayes	.05
253	Ryan Klesko	.25
254	Vicente Palacios	.05
255	Matias Carillo	.05
256	Gary DiSarcina	.05
257	Kirk Gibson	.05
258	Garey Ingram	.05
259	Alex Fernandez	.08
260	John Mabry	.05
261	Chris Howard	.05
262	Miguel Jimenez	.05
263	Heath Slocumb	.05
264	Albert Belle	.75
265	Dave Clark	.05
266	Joe Orsulak	.05
267	Joey Hamilton	.08
268	Mark Portugal	.05
269	Kevin Tapani	.05
270	Sid Fernandez	.05
271	Steve Dreyer	.05
272	Denny Hocking	.05
273	Troy O'Leary	.05
274	Milt Cuyler	.05
275	Frank Thomas	1.50
276	Jorge Fabregas	.08
277	Mike Gallego	.05

278 Mickey Morandini .05
279 Roberto Hernandez .08
280 Henry Rodriguez .08
281 Garret Anderson .08
282 Bob Wickman .05
283 Gar Finnvold .05
284 Paul O'Neill .10
285 Royce Clayton .05
286 Chuck Knoblauch .20
287 Johnny Ruffin .05
288 Dave Nilsson .05
289 David Cone .08
290 Chuck McElroy .05
291 Kevin Stocker .05
292 Jose Rijo .05
293 Sean Berry .05
294 Ozzie Guillen .05
295 Chris Hoiles .05
296 Kevin Foster .05
297 Jeff Frye .05
298 Lance Johnson .05
299 Mike Kelly .05
300 Ellis Burks .08
301 Roberto Kelly .05
302 Dante Bichette .15
303 Alvaro Espinoza .05
304 Alex Cole .05
305 Rickey Henderson .10
306 Dave Weathers .05
307 Shane Reynolds .08
308 Bobby Bonilla .08
309 Junior Felix .05
310 Jeff Fassero .08
311 Darren Lewis .05
312 John Doherty .05
313 Scott Servais .05
314 Rick Helling .05
315 Pedro Martinez .15
316 Wes Chamberlain .05
317 Bryan Eversgerd .05
318 Trevor Hoffman .08
319 John Patterson .05
320 Matt Walbeck .05
321 Jeff Montgomery .05
322 Mel Rojas .05
323 Eddie Taubensee .05
324 Ray Lankford .08
325 Jose Vizcaino .05
326 Carlos Baerga .08
327 Jack Voigt .05
328 Julio Franco .05
329 Brent Gates .08
330 Checklist .05
331 Greg Maddux 1.50
332 Jason Bere .08
333 Bill Wegman .05
334 Tuffy Rhodes .05
335 Kevin Young .08
336 Andy Benes .08
337 Pedro Astacio .05
338 Reggie Jefferson .05
339 Tim Belcher .05
340 Ken Griffey Jr. 3.00
341 Mariano Duncan .05
342 Andres Galarraga .10
343 Rondell White .10
344 Cory Bailey .05
345 Bryan Harvey .05
346 John Franco .05
347 Greg Swindell .05
348 David West .05
349 Fred McGriff .30
350 Jose Canseco .30
351 Orlando Merced .05
352 Rheal Cormier .05
353 Carlos Pulido .05
354 Terry Steinbach .05
355 Wade Boggs .25
356 B.J. Surhoff .08
357 Rafael Palmeiro .20
358 Anthony Young .08
359 Tom Brunansky .05
360 Todd Stottlemyre .08
361 Chris Turner .05
362 Joe Boever .05
363 Jeff Blauser .05
364 Derek Bell .08
365 Matt Williams .30
366 Jeremy Hernandez .05
367 Joe Girardi .05
368 Mike Devereaux .05
369 Jim Abbott .08
370 Manny Ramirez 1.00
371 Kenny Lofton .60
372 Mark Smith .05
373 Dave Fleming .05
374 Dave Stewart .08
375 Roger Pavlik .05
376 Hipolito Pichardo .05
377 Bill Taylor .05
378 Robin Ventura .10
379 Bernard Gilkey .10
380 Kirby Puckett 1.00
381 Steve Howe .05
382 Devon White .08
383 Roberto Mejia .05
384 Darrin Jackson .05
385 Mike Morgan .05
386 Rusty Meacham .05
387 Bill Swift .05
388 Lou Frazier .05
389 Andy Van Slyke .05
390 Brett Butler .08
391 Bobby Witt .05
392 Jeff Conine .08
393 Tim Hyers .05
394 Terry Pendleton .05
395 Ricky Jordan .05
396 Eric Plunk .05
397 Melido Perez .05
398 Darryl Kile .08
399 Mark McLemore .05
400 Greg Harris .05
401 Jim Leyritz .05
402 Doug Strange .05
403 Tim Salmon .25
404 Terry Mulholland .05
405 Robby Thompson .05
406 Ruben Sierra .05
407 Tony Phillips .08
408 Moises Alou .10
409 Felix Fermin .05
410 Pat Listach .05
411 Kevin Bass .05
412 Ben McDonald .05
413 Scott Cooper .05
414 Jody Reed .05
415 Deion Sanders .20
416 Ricky Gutierrez .05
417 Gregg Jefferies .08
418 Jack McDowell .08
419 Al Leiter .08
420 Tony Longmire .05
421 Paul Wagner .05
422 Geronimo Pena .05
423 Ivan Rodriguez .60
424 Kevin Gross .05
425 Kirk McCaskill .05
426 Greg Myers .05
427 Roger Clemens 1.00
428 Chris Hammond .05
429 Randy Myers .05
430 Roger Mason .05
431 Bret Saberhagen .08
432 Jeff Reboulet .05
433 John Olerud .20
434 Bill Gullickson .05
435 Eddie Murray .40
436 Pedro Munoz .05
437 Charlie O'Brien .05
438 Jeff Nelson .05
439 Mike Macfarlane .05
440 Checklist .05
441 Derrick May .05
442 John Roper .05
443 Darryl Hamilton .05
444 Dan Miceli .05
445 Tony Eusebio .05
446 Jerry Browne .05
447 Wally Joyner .08
448 Brian Harper .05
449 Scott Fletcher .05
450 Bip Roberts .05
451 Pete Smith .05
452 Chili Davis .08
453 Dave Hollins .08
454 Tony Pena .05
455 Butch Henry .05
456 Craig Biggio .15
457 Zane Smith .05
458 Ryan Thompson .08
459 Mike Jackson .05
460 Mark McGwire 4.00
461 John Smoltz .20
462 Steve Scarsone .05
463 Greg Colbrunn .05
464 Shawn Green .25
465 David Wells .08
466 Jose Hernandez .05
467 Chip Hale .05
468 Tony Tarasco .05
469 Kevin Mitchell .05
470 Billy Hatcher .05
471 Jay Buhner .15
472 Ken Caminiti .20
473 Tom Henke .05
474 Todd Worrell .05
475 Mark Eichhorn .05
476 Bruce Ruffin .05
477 Chuck Finley .05
478 Marc Newfield .05
479 Paul Shuey .05
480 Bob Tewksbury .05
481 Ramon Martinez .08
482 Melvin Nieves .05
483 Todd Zeile .08
484 Benito Santiago .05
485 Stan Javier .05
486 Kirk Rueter .05
487 Andre Dawson .10
488 Eric Karros .08
489 Dave Magadan .05
490 Checklist .05
491 Randy Velarde .05
492 Larry Walker .20
493 Cris Carpenter .05
494 Tom Gordon .05
495 Dave Burba .05
496 Darren Bragg .05
497 Darren Daulton .05
498 Don Slaught .05
499 Pat Borders .05
500 Lenny Harris .05
501 Joe Ausanio .05
502 Alan Trammell .08
503 Mike Fetters .05
504 Scott Ruffcorn .05
505 Rich Rowland .05
506 Juan Samuel .05
507 Bo Jackson .15
508 Jeff Branson .05
509 Bernie Williams .40
510 Paul Sorrento .05
511 Dennis Eckersley .08
512 Pat Mahomes .05
513 Rusty Greer .08
514 Luis Polonia .05
515 Willie Banks .05
516 John Wetteland .05
517 Mike LaVaillere .05
518 Tommy Greene .05
519 Mark Grace .20
520 Bob Hamelin .05
521 Scott Sanderson .05
522 Joe Carter .08
523 Jeff Brantley .05
524 Andrew Lorraine .05
525 Rico Brogna .05
526 Shane Mack .05
527 Mark Wohlers .05
528 Scott Sanders .05
529 Chris Bosio .05
530 Andujar Cedeno .05
531 Kenny Rogers .05
532 Doug Drabek .05
533 Curt Leskanic .05
534 Craig Shipley .05
535 Craig Grebeck .05
536 Cal Eldred .05
537 Mickey Tettleton .05
538 Harold Baines .08
539 Tim Wallach .05
540 Damon Buford .05
541 Lenny Webster .05
542 Kevin Appier .05
543 Raul Mondesi .40
544 Eric Young .08
545 Russ Davis .08
546 Mike Benjamin .05
547 Mike Greenwell .05
548 Scott Brosius .05
549 Brian Dorsett .05
550 Checklist .05

1995 Donruss Press Proofs

Designated as Press Proofs, the first 2,000 cards of each player in the '95 Donruss set were enhanced with gold, rather than silver, foil and inserted into packs at an average rate of one per 20 packs.

	MT
Complete Set (550):	600.00
Complete Series 1 (330):	350.00
Complete Series 2 (220):	250.00
Common Player:	2.00
Stars:	10-20X

(See 1995 Donruss for checklist and base card values.)

1995 Donruss All-Stars

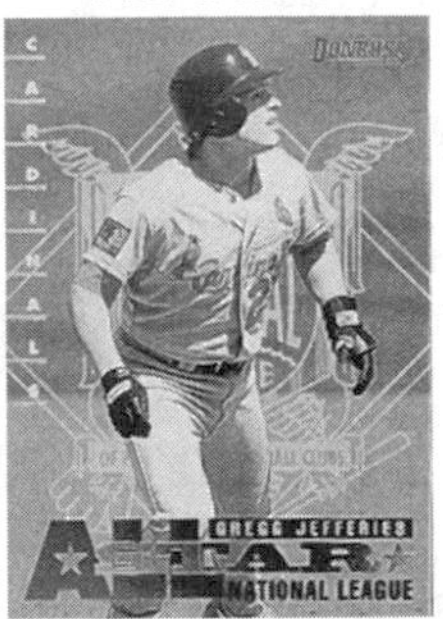

Exclusive to Wal-Mart jumbo packs were Donruss All-Stars. Nine cards featuring American Leaguers were inserted into Series 1, while nine National League All-Stars were inserted into Series 2 jumbos.

	MT
Complete Set (18):	70.00
Common Player:	1.00
AL1 Jimmy Key	1.00
AL2 Ivan Rodriguez	3.50
AL3 Frank Thomas	9.00
AL4 Roberto Alomar	3.00
AL5 Wade Boggs	2.50
AL6 Cal Ripken, Jr.	12.50
AL7 Joe Carter	1.00
AL8 Ken Griffey, Jr.	15.00
AL9 Kirby Puckett	6.00
NL1 Greg Maddux	9.00
NL2 Mike Piazza	10.00

NL3	Gregg Jefferies	1.00
NL4	Mariano Duncan	1.00
NL5	Matt Williams	1.50
NL6	Ozzie Smith	3.00
NL7	Barry Bonds	4.00
NL8	Tony Gwynn	8.00
NL9	Dave Justice	2.00

1995 Donruss Bomb Squad

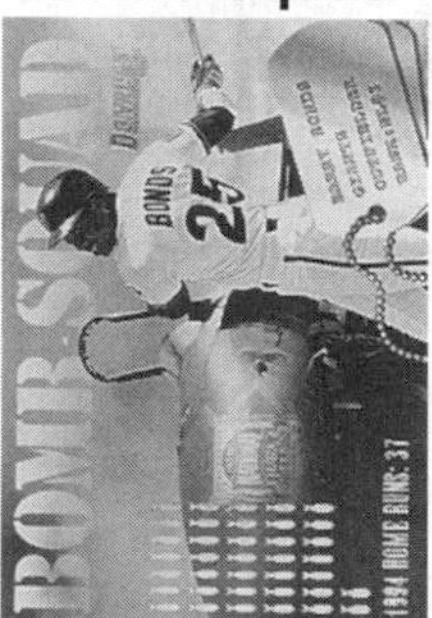

Bomb Squad features the top six home run hitters in each league on double-sided cards. These cards were only inserted into Series I retail and magazine distributor packs at a rate of one per 24 retail packs and one per 16 magazine distributor packs.

		MT
Complete Set (6):		6.00
Common Player:		.50
1	Ken Griffey, Jr., Matt Williams	2.50
2	Frank Thomas, Jeff Bagwell	1.50
3	Albert Belle, Barry Bonds	1.00
4	Jose Canseco, Fred McGriff	.75
5	Cecil Fielder, Andres Galarraga	.50
6	Joe Carter, Kevin Mitchell	.50

1995 Donruss Diamond Kings

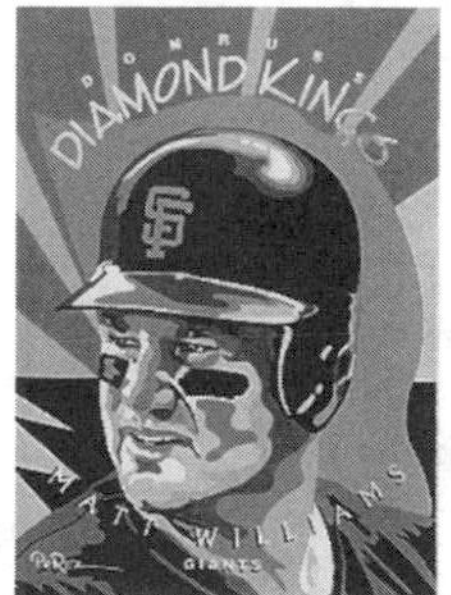

Continuing a tradition begun in 1982, artist Dick Perez painted a series of 28 water colors to produce insert cards of the game's best; 14 in each series. A portrait of the player appears on a party-colored background, with Diamond Kings in gold across the top. DKs were inserted in Series 1 and 2 packs at a rate of one per 10.

		MT
Complete Set (29):		22.00
Common Player:		.50
1	Frank Thomas	3.00
2	Jeff Bagwell	2.50
3	Chili Davis	.50
4	Dante Bichette	.50
5	Ruben Sierra	.50
6	Jeff Conine	.50
7	Paul O'Neill	.50
8	Bobby Bonilla	.50
9	Joe Carter	.50
10	Moises Alou	.50
11	Kenny Lofton	1.00
12	Matt Williams	.50
13	Kevin Seitzer	.50
14	Sammy Sosa	3.00
15	Scott Cooper	.50
16	Raul Mondesi	.50
17	Will Clark	.75
18	Lenny Dykstra	.50
19	Kirby Puckett	2.50
20	Hal Morris	.50
21	Travis Fryman	.50
22	Greg Maddux	3.00
23	Rafael Palmeiro	.60
24	Tony Gwynn	2.50
25	David Cone	.75
26	Al Martin	.50
27	Ken Griffey Jr.	5.00
28	Gregg Jefferies	.50
29	Checklist	.15

1995 Donruss Dominators

Dominators is a nine-card chase set inserted into hobby packs of Series II Donruss baseball at a rate of one per 24 packs. These acetate cards feature three of the top players at each position on a horizontal format.

		MT
Complete Set (9):		15.00
Common Player:		.50
1	David Cone, Mike Mussina, Greg Maddux	1.50
2	Ivan Rodriguez, Mike Piazza, Darren Daulton	2.50
3	Fred McGriff, Frank Thomas, Jeff Bagwell	2.50
4	Roberto Alomar, Carlos Baerga, Craig Biggio	1.00
5	Robin Ventura, Travis Fryman, Matt Williams	1.00
6	Cal Ripken Jr., Barry Larkin, Wil Cordero	4.00
7	Albert Belle, Barry Bonds, Moises Alou	1.50
8	Ken Griffey Jr., Kenny Lofton, Marquis Grissom	4.00
9	Kirby Puckett, Paul O'Neill, Tony Gwynn	2.50

1995 Donruss Elite

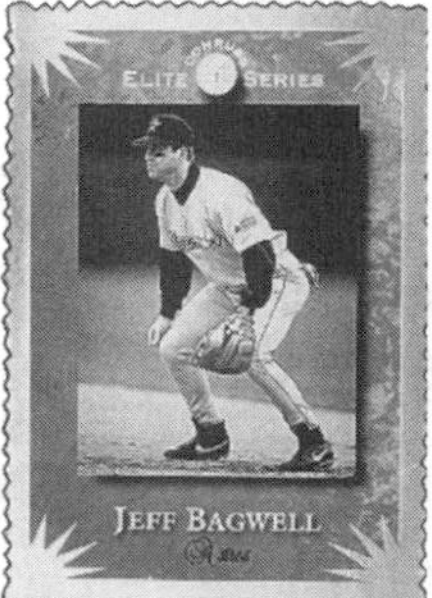

Another Donruss insert tradition continues with the fifth annual presentation of the Elite series. Each of the 12 cards (six each Series 1 and 2) is produced in a numbered edition of 10,000 and inserted into all types of packaging at the rate of one per 210 packs.

		MT
Complete Set (12):		300.00
Common Player:		8.00
49	Jeff Bagwell	30.00
50	Paul O'Neill	8.00
51	Greg Maddux	30.00
52	Mike Piazza	40.00
53	Matt Williams	9.00
54	Ken Griffey, Jr.	75.00
55	Frank Thomas	30.00
56	Barry Bonds	20.00
57	Kirby Puckett	25.00
58	Fred McGriff	9.00
59	Jose Canseco	10.00
60	Albert Belle	15.00

1995 Donruss Long Ball Leaders

Exclusive to Series 1 hobby packs, these cards feature the top long-distance home runs of 1994 in an eye-popping holographic foil presentation. Stated odds of picking one from a hobby pack are one in 24.

		MT
Complete Set (8):		24.00
Common Player:		1.00
1	Frank Thomas	4.00
2	Fred McGriff	1.00
3	Ken Griffey, Jr.	6.00
4	Matt Williams	1.00
5	Mike Piazza	5.00
6	Jose Canseco	1.50
7	Barry Bonds	2.00
8	Jeff Bagwell	3.00

1995 Donruss Mound Marvels

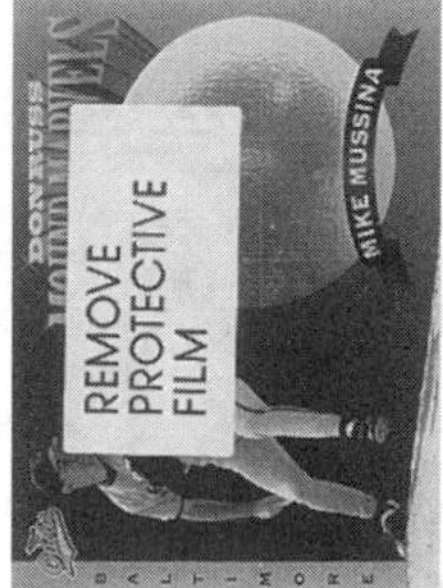

Mound Marvels is an eight-card insert set containing some of the best pitchers in baseball. Cards were inserted into one per 18 retail and magazine packs of Donruss Series II. Each card features a two-way mirror that allows collectors to see the players' face through the mirror.

		MT
Complete Set (8):		15.00
Common Player:		1.00
1	Greg Maddux	6.00
2	David Cone	1.50
3	Mike Mussina	2.00
4	Bret Saberhagen	1.25
5	Jimmy Key	1.00
6	Doug Drabek	1.00
7	Randy Johnson	3.00
8	Jason Bere	1.00

1995 Donruss/ Top of the Order Card Game

In one of the earliest efforts to wed the play factor and collectibility that had made various fantasy card games so successful in 1994-95, Donruss created the interactive Top of the Order baseball card game. Printed on playing card stock with rounded corners and semi-gloss surface, the player cards feature color action photos and all manners of game-action indicators. Backs of each card are printed primarily in green with Donruss logos. Cards were sold in several types of packaging, including 80- and 160-card boxed sets, and 12-card foil "booster" packs. Stars' cards were printed in lesser quantities than those of journeyman players, resulting in values higher than would be the case based on player popularity alone if all cards were printed in equal quantities. The unnumbered cards are checklisted here in alphabetical order within team and league.

	MT
Complete Set (360):	175.00
Common Player:	.10
(1) Brady Anderson	.10
(2) Harold Baines	.10
(3) Bret Barberie	.10
(4) Armando Benitez	.10
(5) Bobby Bonilla	.20
(6) Scott Erickson	.15
(7) Leo Gomez	.10
(8) Curtis Goodwin	.10
(9) Jeffrey Hammonds	.10
(10) Chris Hoiles	.10
(11) Doug Jones	.10
(12) Ben McDonald	.10
(13) Mike Mussina	1.50
(14) Rafael Palmeiro	2.50
(15) Cal Ripken Jr.	25.00
(16) Rick Aguilera	.10
(17) Luis Alicea	.10
(18) Jose Canseco	2.50
(19) Roger Clemens	4.50
(20) Mike Greenwell	.10
(21) Erik Hanson	.10
(22) Mike Macfarlane	.10
(23) Tim Naehring	.10
(24) Troy O'Leary	.10
(25) Ken Ryan	.10
(26) Aaron Sele	.15
(27) Lee Tinsley	.10
(28) John Valentin	.10
(29) Mo Vaughn	3.50
(30) Jim Abbott	.25
(31) Mike Butcher	.10
(32) Chili Davis	.10
(33) Gary DiSarcina	.10
(34) Damion Easley	.10
(35) Jim Edmonds	1.50
(36) Chuck Finley	.10
(37) Mark Langston	.10
(38) Greg Myers	.10
(39) Spike Owen	.10
(40) Troy Percival	.10
(41) Tony Phillips	.10
(42) Tim Salmon	2.00
(43) Lee Smith	.50
(44) J.T. Snow	.15
(45) Jason Bere	.10
(46) Mike Devereaux	.10
(47) Ray Durham	.15
(48) Alex Fernandez	.15
(49) Ozzie Guillen	.10
(50) Roberto Hernandez	.10
(51) Lance Johnson	.10
(52) Ron Karkovice	.10
(53) Tim Raines	.20
(54) Frank Thomas	17.50
(55) Robin Ventura	1.50
(56) Sandy Alomar Jr.	.20
(57) Carlos Baerga	.25
(58) Albert Belle	5.00
(59) Kenny Lofton	5.00
(60) Dennis Martinez	.15
(61) Jose Mesa	.10
(62) Eddie Murray	3.00
(63) Charles Nagy	.10
(64) Tony Pena	.10
(65) Eric Plunk	.10
(66) Manny Ramirez	6.00
(67) Paul Sorrento	.10
(68) Jim Thome	2.00
(69) Omar Vizquel	.10
(70) Danny Bautista	.10
(71) Joe Boever	.10
(72) Chad Curtis	.10
(73) Cecil Fielder	.25
(74) John Flaherty	.10
(75) Travis Fryman	.40
(76) Kirk Gibson	.10
(77) Chris Gomez	.10
(78) Mike Henneman	.10
(79) Bob Higginson	.25
(80) Alan Trammell	.50
(81) Lou Whitaker	.25
(82) Kevin Appier	.10
(83) Billy Brewer	.10
(84) Vince Coleman	.10
(85) Gary Gaetti	.10
(86) Greg Gagne	.10
(87) Tom Goodwin	.10
(88) Tom Gordon	.10
(89) Mark Gubicza	.10
(90) Bob Hamelin	.10
(91) Phil Hiatt	.10
(92) Wally Joyner	.15
(93) Brent Mayne	.10
(94) Jeff Montgomery	.10
(95) Ricky Bones	.10
(96) Mike Fetters	.10
(97) Darryl Hamilton	.10
(98) Pat Listach	.10
(99) Matt Mieske	.10
(100) Dave Nilsson	.10
(101) Joe Oliver	.10
(102) Kevin Seitzer	.10
(103) B.J. Surhoff	.10
(104) Jose Valentin	.10
(105) Greg Vaughn	.15
(106) Bill Wegman	.10
(107) Alex Cole	.10
(108) Marty Cordova	.25
(109) Chuck Knoblauch	1.50
(110) Scott Leius	.10
(111) Pat Meares	.10
(112) Pedro Munoz	.10
(113) Kirby Puckett	17.50
(114) Scott Stahoviak	.10
(115) Mike Trombley	.10
(116) Matt Walbeck	.10
(117) Wade Boggs	12.00
(118) David Cone	.15
(119) Tony Fernandez	.10
(120) Don Mattingly	15.00
(121) Jack McDowell	.10
(122) Paul O'Neill	.15
(123) Melido Perez	.10
(124) Luis Polonia	.10
(125) Ruben Sierra	.10
(126) Mike Stanley	.10
(127) Randy Velarde	.10
(128) John Wetteland	.10
(129) Bob Wickman	.10
(130) Bernie Williams	.35
(131) Gerald Williams	.10
(132) Geronimo Berroa	.10
(133) Mike Bordick	.10
(134) Scott Brosius	.10
(135) Dennis Eckersley	.35
(136) Brent Gates	.10
(137) Rickey Henderson	3.00
(138) Stan Javier	.10
(139) Mark McGwire	25.00
(140) Steve Ontiveros	.10
(141) Terry Steinbach	.10
(142) Todd Stottlemyre	.10
(143) Danny Tartabull	.10
(144) Bobby Ayala	.10
(145) Andy Benes	.15
(146) Mike Blowers	.10
(147) Jay Buhner	.20
(148) Joey Cora	.10
(149) Alex Diaz	.10
(150) Ken Griffey Jr.	25.00
(151) Randy Johnson	4.50
(152) Edgar Martinez	.25
(153) Tino Martinez	.15
(154) Bill Risley	.10
(155) Alex Rodriguez	12.00
(156) Dan Wilson	.10
(157) Will Clark	7.00
(158) Jeff Frye	.10
(159) Benji Gil	.10
(160) Juan Gonzalez	4.00
(161) Rusty Greer	.10
(162) Mark McLemore	.10
(163) Otis Nixon	.10
(164) Dean Palmer	.10
(165) Ivan Rodriguez	3.50
(166) Kenny Rogers	.10
(167) Jeff Russell	.10
(168) Mickey Tettleton	.10
(169) Bob Tewksbury	.10
(170) Bobby Witt	.10
(171) Roberto Alomar	11.00
(172) Joe Carter	1.50
(173) Alex Gonzalez	.25
(174) Candy Maldonado	.10
(175) Paul Molitor	2.50
(176) John Olerud	.25
(177) Lance Parrish	.10
(178) Ed Sprague	.10
(179) Devon White	.10
(180) Woody Williams	.10
(181) Steve Avery	.10
(182) Jeff Blauser	.10
(183) Tom Glavine	1.00
(184) Marquis Grissom	.15
(185) Chipper Jones	12.00
(186) Dave Justice	5.00
(187) Ryan Klesko	.25
(188) Mark Lemke	.10
(189) Javier Lopez	.20
(190) Greg Maddux	17.50
(191) Fred McGriff	2.50
(192) Greg McMichael	.10
(193) John Smoltz	4.00
(194) Mark Wohlers	.10
(195) Jim Bullinger	.10
(196) Shawon Dunston	.10
(197) Kevin Foster	.10
(198) Luis Gonzalez	.10
(199) Mark Grace	3.50
(200) Brian McRae	.10
(201) Randy Myers	.10
(202) Jaime Navarro	.10
(203) Rey Sanchez	.10
(204) Scott Servais	.10
(205) Sammy Sosa	4.00
(206) Steve Trachsel	.10
(207) Todd Zeile	.10
(208) Bret Boone	1.00
(209) Jeff Branson	.10
(210) Jeff Brantley	.10
(211) Hector Carrasco	.10
(212) Ron Gant	.20
(213) Lenny Harris	.10
(214) Barry Larkin	2.50
(215) Darren Lewis	.10
(216) Hal Morris	.10
(217) Mark Portugal	.10
(218) Jose Rijo	.10
(219) Reggie Sanders	.75
(220) Pete Schourek	.10
(221) John Smiley	.10
(222) Eddie Taubensee	.10
(223) Dave Wells	.15
(224) Jason Bates	.10
(225) Dante Bichette	4.00
(226) Vinny Castilla	.20
(227) Andres Galarraga	4.00
(228) Joe Girardi	.10
(229) Mike Kingery	.10
(230) Steve Reed	.10
(231) Bruce Ruffin	.10
(232) Bret Saberhagen	.15
(233) Bill Swift	.10
(234) Larry Walker	3.50
(235) Walt Weiss	.10
(236) Eric Young	.10
(237) Kurt Abbott	.10
(238) John Burkett	.10
(239) Chuck Carr	.10
(240) Greg Colbrunn	.10
(241) Jeff Conine	1.00
(242) Andre Dawson	.25
(243) Chris Hammond	.10
(244) Charles Johnson	.10
(245) Robb Nen	.10
(246) Terry Pendleton	.10
(247) Gary Sheffield	2.50
(248) Quilvio Veras	.10
(249) Jeff Bagwell	4.50
(250) Derek Bell	.20
(251) Craig Biggio	.25
(252) Doug Drabek	.10
(253) Tony Eusebio	.10
(254) John Hudek	.10
(255) Brian Hunter	.10
(256) Todd Jones	.10
(257) Dave Magadan	.10
(258) Orlando Miller	.10
(259) James Mouton	.10
(260) Shane Reynolds	.10
(261) Greg Swindell	.10
(262) Billy Ashley	.10
(263) Tom Candiotti	.10
(264) Delino DeShields	.10
(265) Eric Karros	2.50
(266) Roberto Kelly	.10
(267) Ramon Martinez	.15
(268) Raul Mondesi	2.50
(269) Hideo Nomo	9.00
(270) Jose Offerman	.10
(271) Mike Piazza	20.00
(272) Kevin Tapani	.10
(273) Ismael Valdes	.15
(274) Tim Wallach	.10
(275) Todd Worrell	.10
(276) Moises Alou	1.00
(277) Sean Berry	.10
(278) Wil Cordero	.10
(279) Jeff Fassero	.10
(280) Darrin Fletcher	.10
(281) Mike Lansing	.10
(282) Pedro J. Martinez	.50
(283) Carlos Perez	.15
(284) Mel Rojas	.10
(285) Tim Scott	.10
(286) David Segui	.10
(287) Tony Tarasco	.10
(288) Rondell White	.20
(289) Rico Brogna	.10
(290) Brett Butler	.10
(291) John Franco	.10
(292) Pete Harnisch	.10
(293) Todd Hundley	.15
(294) Bobby Jones	.10
(295) Jeff Kent	.10
(296) Joe Orsulak	.10
(297) Ryan Thompson	.10
(298) Jose Vizcaino	.10
(299) Ricky Bottalico	.10
(300) Darren Daulton	.10
(301) Mariano Duncan	.10
(302) Lenny Dykstra	.10
(303) Jim Eisenreich	.10
(304) Tyler Green	.10
(305) Charlie Hayes	.10
(306) Dave Hollins	.10
(307) Gregg Jefferies	.25
(308) Mickey Morandini	.10
(309) Curt Schilling	.20
(310) Heathcliff Slocumb	.10
(311) Kevin Stocker	.10
(312) Jay Bell	.10
(313) Jacob Brumfield	.10
(314) Dave Clark	.10
(315) Carlos Garcia	.10
(316) Mark Johnson	.10
(317) Jeff King	.10
(318) Nelson Liriano	.10
(319) Al Martin	.10
(320) Orlando Merced	.10
(321) Dan Miceli	.10
(322) Denny Neagle	.10
(323) Mark Parent	.10
(324) Dan Plesac	.10
(325) Scott Cooper	.10
(326) Bernard Gilkey	.10
(327) Tom Henke	.10
(328) Ken Hill	.10
(329) Danny Jackson	.10
(330) Brian Jordan	.15
(331) Ray Lankford	.10
(332) John Mabry	.10
(333) Jose Oquendo	.10
(334) Tom Pagnozzi	.10

No.	Player	Value
(335)	Ozzie Smith	2.50
(336)	Andy Ashby	.15
(337)	Brad Ausmus	.10
(338)	Ken Caminiti	.20
(339)	Andujar Cedeno	.10
(340)	Steve Finley	.10
(341)	Tony Gwynn	15.00
(342)	Joey Hamilton	.10
(343)	Trevor Hoffman	.15
(344)	Jody Reed	.10
(345)	Bip Roberts	.10
(346)	Eddie Williams	.10
(347)	Rod Beck	.10
(348)	Mike Benjamin	.10
(349)	Barry Bonds	12.50
(350)	Royce Clayton	.10
(351)	Glenallen Hill	.10
(352)	Kirt Manwaring	.10
(353)	Terry Mulholland	.10
(354)	John Patterson	.10
(355)	J.R. Phillips	.10
(356)	Deion Sanders	6.00
(357)	Steve Scarsone	.10
(358)	Robby Thompson	.10
(359)	William VanLandingham	.10
(360)	Matt Williams	3.50

1996 Donruss Samples

To introduce its 1996 series to dealers and the hobby press, Donruss issued an eight-card sample set. Identical in format to the issued version, the samples are numbered differently from the same players' cards in the regular issue (except #1, Frank Thomas). The samples also differ in that they lack 1995 stats on back, may have slightly different wording in the career highlights, and have printed on front and back a diagonal gray "PROMOTIONAL SAMPLE".

		MT
Complete Set (8):		30.00
Common Player:		3.50
1	Frank Thomas	4.50
2	Barry Bonds	3.50
3	Hideo Nomo	3.00
4	Ken Griffey Jr.	7.00
5	Cal Ripken Jr.	6.50
6	Manny Ramirez	4.50
7	Mike Piazza	6.00
8	Greg Maddux	4.50

1996 Donruss

A clean, borderless look marks the 1996 Donruss regular-issue cards. Besides the player name in white inside a fading team-color stripe at top-right, the only graphic enhancement on front is a 7/8" square foil box at bottom-center with the company and team name, team logo, player position and uniform number. The foil box is enhanced with team colors, which are carried over to the horizontal backs. Backs also feature a color action photo, a large gray team logo, stats and career highlights. Basic packaging was 12-card foil packs with a suggested retail price of $1.79. Several types of insert cards were offered, each at a virtually unprecedented rate of scarcity. The set was issued in two series; Series 1 with 330 cards, Series 2 with 220 cards.

		MT
Complete Set (550):		45.00
Complete Series 1 (330):		25.00
Complete Series 2 (220):		20.00
Common Player:		.05
Series 1 Pack (12):		1.50
Series 1 Wax Box (36):		40.00
Series 2 Pack (12):		2.00
Series 2 Wax Box (18):		30.00
1	Frank Thomas	1.50
2	Jason Bates	.05
3	Steve Sparks	.05
4	Scott Servais	.05
5	Angelo Encarnacion	.05
6	Scott Sanders	.05
7	Billy Ashley	.05
8	Alex Rodriguez	3.00
9	Sean Bergman	.05
10	Brad Radke	.05
11	Andy Van Slyke	.05
12	Joe Girardi	.05
13	Mark Grudzielanek	.10
14	Rick Aguilera	.05
15	Randy Veres	.05
16	Tim Bogar	.05
17	Dave Veres	.05
18	Kevin Stocker	.05
19	Marquis Grissom	.08
20	Will Clark	.30
21	Jay Bell	.08
22	Allen Battle	.05
23	Frank Rodriguez	.05
24	Terry Steinbach	.05
25	Gerald Williams	.08
26	Sid Roberson	.05
27	Greg Zaun	.05
28	Ozzie Timmons	.05
29	Vaughn Eshelman	.05
30	Ed Sprague	.05
31	Gary DiSarcina	.05
32	Joe Boever	.05
33	Steve Avery	.05
34	Brad Ausmus	.05
35	Kirt Manwaring	.05
36	Gary Sheffield	.40
37	Jason Bere	.05
38	Jeff Manto	.05
39	David Cone	.15
40	Manny Ramirez	1.00
41	Sandy Alomar	.08
42	Curtis Goodwin (Rated Rookie)	.05
43	Tino Martinez	.10
44	Woody Williams	.05
45	Dean Palmer	.08
46	Hipolito Pichardo	.05
47	Jason Giambi	.05
48	Lance Johnson	.05
49	Bernard Gilkey	.08
50	Kirby Puckett	1.00
51	Tony Fernandez	.05
52	Alex Gonzalez	.08
53	Bret Saberhagen	.08
54	Lyle Mouton (Rated Rookie)	.05
55	Brian McRae	.05
56	Mark Gubicza	.05
57	Sergio Valdez	.05
58	Darrin Fletcher	.05
59	Steve Parris	.05
60	Johnny Damon (Rated Rookie)	.20
61	Rickey Henderson	.20
62	Darrell Whitmore	.05
63	Roberto Petagine	.05
64	Trenidad Hubbard	.05
65	Heathcliff Slocumb	.05
66	Steve Finley	.05
67	Mariano Rivera	.35
68	Brian Hunter	.05
69	Jamie Moyer	.05
70	Ellis Burks	.05
71	Pat Kelly	.05
72	Mickey Tettleton	.05
73	Garret Anderson	.15
74	Andy Pettitte (Rated Rookie)	1.00
75	Glenallen Hill	.05
76	Brent Gates	.05
77	Lou Whitaker	.05
78	David Segui	.05
79	Dan Wilson	.05
80	Pat Listach	.05
81	Jeff Bagwell	1.00
82	Ben McDonald	.05
83	John Valentin	.08
84	John Jaha	.05
85	Pete Schourek	.05
86	Bryce Florie	.05
87	Brian Jordan	.10
88	Ron Karkovice	.05
89	Al Leiter	.08
90	Tony Longmire	.05
91	Nelson Liriano	.05
92	David Bell	.05
93	Kevin Gross	.05
94	Tom Candiotti	.05
95	Dave Martinez	.05
96	Greg Myers	.05
97	Rheal Cormier	.05
98	Chris Hammond	.05
99	Randy Myers	.05
100	Bill Pulsipher (Rated Rookie)	.15
101	Jason Isringhausen (Rated Rookie)	.20
102	Dave Stevens	.05
103	Roberto Alomar	.75
104	Bob Higginson (Rated Rookie)	.25
105	Eddie Murray	.35
106	Matt Walbeck	.05
107	Mark Wohlers	.05
108	Jeff Nelson	.05
109	Tom Goodwin	.05
110	Checklist 1-83 (Cal Ripken Jr.) (2,131 Consecutive Games)	1.50
111	Rey Sanchez	.05
112	Hector Carrasco	.05
113	B.J. Surhoff	.08
114	Dan Miceli	.05
115	Dean Hartgraves	.05
116	John Burkett	.05
117	Gary Gaetti	.05
118	Ricky Bones	.05
119	Mike Macfarlane	.05
120	Bip Roberts	.05
121	Dave Mlicki	.05
122	Chili Davis	.08
123	Mark Whiten	.05
124	Herbert Perry	.05
125	Butch Henry	.05
126	Derek Bell	.08
127	Al Martin	.05
128	John Franco	.05
129	William VanLandingham	.05
130	Mike Bordick	.05
131	Mike Mordecai	.05
132	Robby Thompson	.05
133	Greg Colbrunn	.05
134	Domingo Cedeno	.05
135	Chad Curtis	.08
136	Jose Hernandez	.05
137	Scott Klingenbeck	.05
138	Ryan Klesko	.25
139	John Smiley	.05
140	Charlie Hayes	.05
141	Jay Buhner	.15
142	Doug Drabek	.05
143	Roger Pavlik	.05
144	Todd Worrell	.05
145	Cal Ripken Jr.	2.50
146	Steve Reed	.05
147	Chuck Finley	.05
148	Mike Blowers	.05
149	Orel Hershiser	.08
150	Allen Watson	.05
151	Ramon Martinez	.08
152	Melvin Nieves	.05
153	Tripp Cromer	.05
154	Yorkis Perez	.05
155	Stan Javier	.05
156	Mel Rojas	.05
157	Aaron Sele	.05
158	Eric Karros	.10
159	Robb Nen	.05
160	Raul Mondesi	.30
161	John Wetteland	.05
162	Tim Scott	.05
163	Kenny Rogers	.05
164	Melvin Bunch	.05
165	Rod Beck	.05
166	Andy Benes	.05
167	Lenny Dykstra	.05
168	Orlando Merced	.05
169	Tomas Perez	.05
170	Xavier Hernandez	.05
171	Ruben Sierra	.05
172	Alan Trammell	.08
173	Mike Fetters	.05
174	Wilson Alvarez	.05
175	Erik Hanson	.05
176	Travis Fryman	.10
177	Jim Abbott	.05
178	Bret Boone	.08
179	Sterling Hitchcock	.05
180	Pat Mahomes	.05
181	Mark Acre	.05
182	Charles Nagy	.08
183	Rusty Greer	.10
184	Mike Stanley	.05
185	Jim Bullinger	.05
186	Shane Andrews	.05
187	Brian Keyser	.05
188	Tyler Green	.05
189	Mark Grace	.20
190	Bob Hamelin	.05
191	Luis Ortiz	.05
192	Joe Carter	.08
193	Eddie Taubensee	.05
194	Brian Anderson	.08
195	Edgardo Alfonzo	.15
196	Pedro Munoz	.05
197	David Justice	.25
198	Trevor Hoffman	.08
199	Bobby Ayala	.05
200	Tony Eusebio	.05
201	Jeff Russell	.05
202	Mike Hampton	.05
203	Walt Weiss	.05
204	Joey Hamilton	.05
205	Roberto Hernandez	.05
206	Greg Vaughn	.08
207	Felipe Lira	.05
208	Harold Baines	.08
209	Tim Wallach	.05
210	Manny Alexander	.05
211	Tim Laker	.05
212	Chris Haney	.05
213	Brian Maxcy	.05
214	Eric Young	.08
215	Darryl Strawberry	.08

216 Barry Bonds .85
217 Tim Naehring .05
218 Scott Brosius .05
219 Reggie Sanders .05
220 Checklist 84-166 (Eddie Murray) (3,000 Career Hits) .20
221 Luis Alicea .05
222 Albert Belle .75
223 Benji Gil .05
224 Dante Bichette .25
225 Bobby Bonilla .10
226 Todd Stottlemyre .05
227 Jim Edmonds .10
228 Todd Jones .05
229 Shawn Green .15
230 Javy Lopez .15
231 Ariel Prieto .05
232 Tony Phillips .05
233 James Mouton .05
234 Jose Oquendo .05
235 Royce Clayton .05
236 Chuck Carr .05
237 Doug Jones .05
238 Mark Mclemore (McLemore) .05
239 Bill Swift .05
240 Scott Leius .05
241 Russ Davis .05
242 Ray Durham (Rated Rookie) .08
243 Matt Mieske .05
244 Brent Mayne .05
245 Thomas Howard .05
246 Troy O'Leary .05
247 Jacob Brumfield .05
248 Mickey Morandini .05
249 Todd Hundley .20
250 Chris Bosio .05
251 Omar Vizquel .08
252 Mike Lansing .08
253 John Mabry .05
254 Mike Perez .05
255 Delino DeShields .05
256 Wil Cordero .05
257 Mike James .05
258 Todd Van Poppel .05
259 Joey Cora .05
260 Andre Dawson .08
261 Jerry DiPoto .05
262 Rick Krivda .05
263 Glenn Dishman .05
264 Mike Mimbs .05
265 John Ericks .05
266 Jose Canseco .35
267 Jeff Branson .05
268 Curt Leskanic .05
269 Jon Nunnally .05
270 Scott Stahoviak .05
271 Jeff Montgomery .05
272 Hal Morris .05
273 Esteban Loaiza .08
274 Rico Brogna .05
275 Dave Winfield .20
276 J.R. Phillips .05
277 Todd Zeile .08
278 Tom Pagnozzi .05
279 Mark Lemke .05
280 Dave Magadan .05
281 Greg McMichael .05
282 Mike Morgan .05
283 Moises Alou .15
284 Dennis Martinez .08
285 Jeff Kent .05
286 Mark Johnson .05
287 Darren Lewis .05
288 Brad Clontz .05
289 Chad Fonville (Rated Rookie) .15
290 Paul Sorrento .05
291 Lee Smith .08
292 Tom Glavine .20
293 Antonio Osuna .05
294 Kevin Foster .05
295 *Sandy Martinez* .05
296 Mark Leiter .05
297 Julian Tavarez .05
298 Mike Kelly .05
299 Joe Oliver .05
300 John Flaherty .05
301 Don Mattingly .75
302 Pat Meares .05
303 John Doherty .05
304 Joe Vitiello .05
305 Vinny Castilla .08
306 Jeff Brantley .05
307 Mike Greenwell .05
308 Midre Cummings .05
309 Curt Schilling .10
310 Ken Caminiti .25
311 Scott Erickson .05
312 Carl Everett .05
313 Charles Johnson .08
314 Alex Diaz .05
315 Jose Mesa .05
316 Mark Carreon .05
317 Carlos Perez (Rated Rookie) .15
318 Ismael Valdes .08
319 Frank Castillo .05
320 Tom Henke .05
321 Spike Owen .05
322 Joe Orsulak .05
323 Paul Menhart .05
324 Pedro Borbon .05
325 Checklist 167-249 (Paul Molitor) (1,000 Career RBI) .25
326 Jeff Cirillo .05
327 Edwin Hurtado .05
328 Orlando Miller .05
329 Steve Ontiveros .05
330 Checklist 250-330 (Kirby Puckett) (1,000 Career RBI) .50
331 Scott Bullett .05
332 Andres Galarraga .20
333 Cal Eldred .05
334 Sammy Sosa 1.50
335 Don Slaught .05
336 Jody Reed .05
337 Roger Cedeno .05
338 Ken Griffey Jr. 3.00
339 Todd Hollandsworth .08
340 Mike Trombley .05
341 Gregg Jefferies .08
342 Larry Walker .30
343 Pedro Martinez .08
344 Dwayne Hosey .05
345 Terry Pendleton .05
346 Pete Harnisch .05
347 Tony Castillo .05
348 Paul Quantrill .05
349 Fred McGriff .35
350 Ivan Rodriguez .65
351 Butch Huskey .05
352 Ozzie Smith .50
353 Marty Cordova .15
354 John Wasdin .05
355 Wade Boggs .25
356 Dave Nilsson .05
357 Rafael Palmeiro .20
358 Luis Gonzalez .08
359 Reggie Jefferson .05
360 Carlos Delgado .40
361 Orlando Palmeiro .05
362 Chris Gomez .05
363 John Smoltz .20
364 Marc Newfield .05
365 Matt Williams .30
366 Jesus Tavarez .05
367 Bruce Ruffin .05
368 Sean Berry .05
369 Randy Velarde .05
370 Tony Pena .05
371 Jim Thome .50
372 Jeffrey Hammonds .05
373 Bob Wolcott .05
374 Juan Guzman .05
375 Juan Gonzalez 1.00
376 Michael Tucker .05
377 Doug Johns .05
378 *Mike Cameron* 1.00
379 Ray Lankford .08
380 Jose Parra .05
381 Jimmy Key .08
382 John Olerud .15
383 Kevin Ritz .05
384 Tim Raines .08
385 Rich Amaral .05
386 Keith Lockhart .05
387 Steve Scarsone .05
388 Cliff Floyd .08
389 Rich Aude .05
390 Hideo Nomo .60
391 Geronimo Berroa .05
392 Pat Rapp .05
393 Dustin Hermanson .05
394 Greg Maddux 2.00
395 Darren Daulton .05
396 Kenny Lofton .60
397 Ruben Rivera .30
398 Billy Wagner .10
399 Kevin Brown .15
400 Mike Kingery .05
401 Bernie Williams .50
402 Otis Nixon .05
403 Damion Easley .05
404 Paul O'Neill .10
405 Deion Sanders .35
406 Dennis Eckersley .08
407 Tony Clark .50
408 Rondell White .15
409 Luis Sojo .05
410 David Hulse .05
411 Shane Reynolds .05
412 Chris Hoiles .05
413 Lee Tinsley .05
414 Scott Karl .05
415 Ron Gant .15
416 Brian Johnson .05
417 Jose Oliva .05
418 Jack McDowell .08
419 Paul Molitor .35
420 Ricky Bottalico .05
421 Paul Wagner .05
422 Terry Bradshaw .05
423 Bob Tewksbury .05
424 Mike Piazza 2.00
425 *Luis Andujar* .05
426 Mark Langston .05
427 Stan Belinda .05
428 Kurt Abbott .05
429 Shawon Dunston .08
430 Bobby Jones .05
431 Jose Vizcaino .05
432 *Matt Lawton* .05
433 Pat Hentgen .05
434 Cecil Fielder .08
435 Carlos Baerga .08
436 Rich Becker .05
437 Chipper Jones 2.00
438 Bill Risley .05
439 Kevin Appier .05
440 Checklist .05
441 Jaime Navarro .05
442 Barry Larkin .20
443 *Jose Valentin* .10
444 Bryan Rekar .05
445 Rick Wilkins .05
446 Quilvio Veras .05
447 Greg Gagne .05
448 Mark Kiefer .05
449 Bobby Witt .05
450 Andy Ashby .08
451 Alex Ochoa .05
452 Jorge Fabregas .05
453 Gene Schall .05
454 Ken Hill .05
455 Tony Tarasco .05
456 Donnie Wall .05
457 Carlos Garcia .05
458 Ryan Thompson .05
459 *Marvin Benard* .08
460 Jose Herrera .05
461 Jeff Blauser .05
462 Chris Hook .05
463 Jeff Conine .08
464 Devon White .05
465 Danny Bautista .05
466 Steve Trachsel .05
467 C.J. Nitkowski .05
468 Mike Devereaux .05
469 David Wells .08
470 Jim Eisenreich .05
471 Edgar Martinez .08
472 Craig Biggio .10
473 Jeff Frye .05
474 Karim Garcia .50
475 Jimmy Haynes .05
476 Darren Holmes .05
477 Tim Salmon .25
478 Randy Johnson .35
479 Eric Plunk .05
480 Scott Cooper .05
481 Chan Ho Park .08
482 Ray McDavid .05
483 Mark Petkovsek .05
484 Greg Swindell .05
485 George Williams .05
486 Yamil Benitez .08
487 Tim Wakefield .05
488 Kevin Tapani .05
489 Derrick May .05
490 Checklist (Ken Griffey Jr.) 1.50
491 Derek Jeter 2.00
492 Jeff Fassero .08
493 Benito Santiago .05
494 Tom Gordon .05
495 Jamie Brewington .05
496 Vince Coleman .05
497 Kevin Jordan .05
498 Jeff King .05
499 Mike Simms .05
500 Jose Rijo .05
501 Denny Neagle .05
502 Jose Lima .08
503 Kevin Seitzer .05
504 Alex Fernandez .15
505 Mo Vaughn .75
506 Phil Nevin .08
507 J.T. Snow .08
508 Andujar Cedeno .05
509 Ozzie Guillen .05
510 Mark Clark .05
511 Mark McGwire 4.00
512 Jeff Reboulet .05
513 Armando Benitez .05
514 LaTroy Hawkins .05
515 Brett Butler .08
516 Tavo Alvarez .05
517 Chris Snopek .08
518 Mike Mussina .30
519 Darryl Kile .08
520 Wally Joyner .08
521 Willie McGee .08
522 Kent Mercker .05
523 Mike Jackson .05
524 Troy Percival .05
525 Tony Gwynn 1.50
526 Ron Coomer .05
527 Darryl Hamilton .05
528 Phil Plantier .05
529 Norm Charlton .05
530 Craig Paquette .05
531 Dave Burba .05
532 Mike Henneman .05
533 Terrell Wade .05
534 Eddie Williams .05
535 Robin Ventura .10
536 Chuck Knoblauch .20
537 Les Norman .05
538 Brady Anderson .10
539 Roger Clemens 1.50
540 Mark Portugal .05
541 Mike Matheny .05
542 Jeff Parrett .05
543 Roberto Kelly .05
544 Damon Buford .05
545 Chad Ogea .05
546 Jose Offerman .05
547 Brian Barber .05
548 Danny Tartabull .05
549 Duane Singleton .05
550 Checklist (Tony Gwynn) .50

1996 Donruss Press Proofs

The first 2,000 of each regular card issued in the 1996 Donruss set are distinguished by the addition of a gold-foil "PRESS PROOF" stamped along the right side. As opposed to regular-issue cards which have silver-and-black card numbers and personal data strip at bottom, the Press Proof cards have those elements printed in black-on-gold. Stated odds of finding a Press Proof are one per 12 packs in Series 1, one per 10 packs in Series 2, on average.

		MT
Complete Set (550):		1250.
Complete Series 1 (330):		650.00
Complete Series 2 (220):		600.00
Common Player:		1.00

(Star cards valued 8X-15X corresponding regular-issue cards.)

1996 Donruss Diamond Kings

The most "common" of the '96 Donruss inserts are the popular Diamond Kings, featuring the portraits of Dick Perez on a black background within a mottled gold-foil frame. Once again, the DKs feature one player from each team, with 14 issued in each of Series 1 and 2. Like all '96 Donruss inserts, the DKs are numbered on back, within an edition of 10,000. Also on back are color action photos and career highlights. Diamond Kings are inserted at the rate of one per 60 foil packs (Series 1), and one per 30 packs (Series 2), on average.

		MT
Complete Set (31):		190.00
Complete Series 1 (1-14):		110.00
Complete Series 2 (15-31):		80.00
Common Player Series 1:		3.00
Common Player Series 2:		3.00
1	Frank Thomas	12.50
2	Mo Vaughn	6.00
3	Manny Ramirez	8.00
4	Mark McGwire	30.00
5	Juan Gonzalez	8.00
6	Roberto Alomar	6.00
7	Tim Salmon	4.00
8	Barry Bonds	10.00
9	Tony Gwynn	15.00
10	Reggie Sanders	3.00
11	Larry Walker	6.00
12	Pedro Martinez	8.00
13	Jeff King	3.00
14	Mark Grace	5.00
15	Greg Maddux	15.00
16	Don Mattingly	10.00
17	Gregg Jefferies	3.00
18	Chad Curtis	3.00
19	Jason Isringhausen	3.00
20	B.J. Surhoff	3.00
21	Jeff Conine	3.00
22	Kirby Puckett	10.00
23	Derek Bell	3.00
24	Wally Joyner	3.00
25	Brian Jordan	3.00
26	Edgar Martinez	3.00
27	Hideo Nomo	3.00
28	Mike Mussina	5.00
29	Eddie Murray	4.00
30	Cal Ripken Jr.	25.00
31	Checklist	.50

1996 Donruss Elite

The Elite series continued as a Donruss insert in 1996, and they are the elite of the chase cards, being found on average only once per 140 packs (Series 1) or once per 75 packs (Series 2). The '96 Elite cards have a classic look bespeaking value. Player action photos at top center are framed in mottled silver foil and bordered in bright silver. Backs have another action photo, a few words about the player and a serial number from within an edition of 10,000 cards each. As usual, card numbering continues from the previous year.

		MT
Complete Set (12):		110.00
Complete Series 1 (61-66):		50.00
Complete Series 2 (67-72):		65.00
Common Player Series 1:		7.50
Common Player Series 2:		5.00
61	Cal Ripken Jr.	20.00
62	Hideo Nomo	7.50
63	Reggie Sanders	4.00
64	Mo Vaughn	7.50
65	Tim Salmon	5.00
66	Chipper Jones	15.00
67	Manny Ramirez	7.50
68	Greg Maddux	12.50
69	Frank Thomas	12.50
70	Ken Griffey Jr.	25.00
71	Dante Bichette	4.00
72	Tony Gwynn	12.50

1996 Donruss Freeze Frame

One of two insert sets exclusive to Series 2 Donruss is the Freeze Frame issue. Printed on heavy, round-cornered cardboard stock, the inserts feature multiple photos of the player on both front and back. Fronts combine matte and glossy finish plus a gold-foil Donruss logo. Backs are conventionally printed, include 1995 season highlights and a serial number from within the edition of 5,000. Stated odds of pulling a Freeze Frame insert are one per 60 packs.

		MT
Complete Set (8):		85.00
Common Player:		8.00
1	Frank Thomas	12.00
2	Ken Griffey Jr.	17.50
3	Cal Ripken Jr.	15.00
4	Hideo Nomo	4.00
5	Greg Maddux	12.00
6	Albert Belle	6.00
7	Chipper Jones	12.50
8	Mike Piazza	12.50

1996 Donruss Hit List

Printed on metallic foil with gold-foil graphic highlights, players who hit for high average with power or who collected milestone hits are featured in this insert set. Eight inserts were included in each of Series 1 and 2. Backs have a color action photo, a description of the player's batting prowess and a serial number from an edition of 10,000 cards each. Hit List inserts are found at an average rate of once per 106 foil packs in Series 1 and once per 60 packs in Series 2.

		MT
Complete Set (16):		60.00
Complete Set Series 1 (8):		35.00
Complete Set Series 2 (9-16):		25.00
Common Player Series 1:		1.25
Common Player Series 2:		1.75
1	Tony Gwynn	7.50
2	Ken Griffey Jr.	18.00
3	Will Clark	1.75
4	Mike Piazza	10.00
5	Carlos Baerga	1.25
6	Mo Vaughn	2.50
7	Mark Grace	1.50
8	Kirby Puckett	4.00
9	Frank Thomas	7.50
10	Barry Bonds	4.00
11	Jeff Bagwell	4.00
12	Edgar Martinez	1.75
13	Tim Salmon	2.00
14	Wade Boggs	2.50
15	Don Mattingly	3.50
16	Eddie Murray	2.50

1996 Donruss Long Ball Leaders

Once again the previous season's longest home runs are recalled in this retail-only insert set, found at an average rate of once per 96 packs in Series 1 only. Fronts are bordered and trimmed in bright silver foil and feature the player in his home run stroke against a black background. The date, location and distance of his tape-measure shot are in an arc across the card front. Backs feature another batting action photo, further details of the home run and a serial number within an edition of 5,000.

		MT
Complete Set (8):		100.00
Common Player:		4.00
1	Barry Bonds	12.00
2	Ryan Klesko	5.00
3	Mark McGwire	45.00
4	Raul Mondesi	4.00
5	Cecil Fielder	4.00
6	Ken Griffey Jr.	45.00
7	Larry Walker	9.00
8	Frank Thomas	15.00

1996 Donruss Power Alley

Among the most visually dazzling of 1996's inserts is this hobby-only chase set featuring baseball's top sluggers. Action batting photos are found within several layers of prismatic foil in geometric patterns on front. Backs are horizontally formatted, feature portrait photos at left and power stats at right and bottom. In the lower-left corner is an individual serial number from within an edition of 5,000 cards each. The first 500 of each player's cards are specially die-cut at left- and right-center. Found only in Series 1 hobby foil packs, Power Alley inserts are a one per 92 pack pick.

		MT
Complete Set (10):		90.00
Common Player		4.00
Die-cuts		2-3X
1	Frank Thomas	12.00
2	Barry Bonds	10.00
3	Reggie Sanders	4.00
4	Albert Belle	9.00
5	Tim Salmon	6.00
6	Dante Bichette	6.00
7	Mo Vaughn	8.00
8	Jim Edmonds	4.00
9	Manny Ramirez	10.00
10	Ken Griffey Jr.	30.00

1996 Donruss Round Trippers

An embossed white home plate design bearing the player's 1995 dinger output is featured on this Series II insert set. The entire background has been rendered in gold-flecked sepia tones. Typography on front is in bronze foil. Backs repeat the sepia background photo and include a month-by-month bar graph of the player's 1995 and career homers. Within the white home plate frame is the card's unique serial number from within an edition of 5,000. Odds of finding a Round Trippers card are stated at one per 55 packs, in hobby packs only.

		MT
Complete Set (10):		75.00
Common Player:		3.00
1	Albert Belle	5.00
2	Barry Bonds	5.00
3	Jeff Bagwell	7.50
4	Tim Salmon	3.00
5	Mo Vaughn	4.00
6	Ken Griffey Jr.	20.00
7	Mike Piazza	12.50
8	Cal Ripken Jr.	15.00
9	Frank Thomas	7.50
9p	Frank Thomas (Promo)	3.00
10	Dante Bichette	3.00

1996 Donruss Showdown

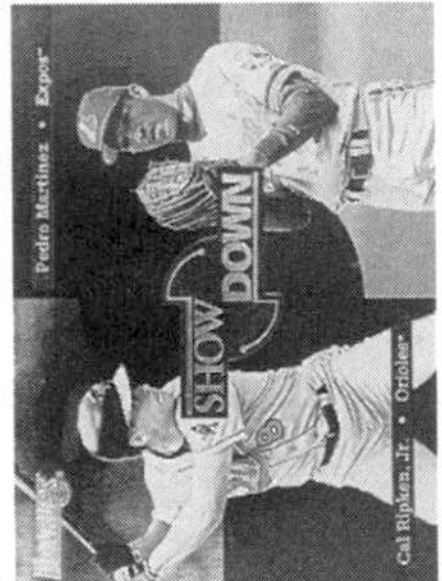

Baseball's top hitters and pitchers are matched on a silver and black foil background in this insert set. Gold-foil graphic highlights complete the horizontal front design. Backs are printed on a black and gold background with color action photos and write-ups about each player. At top is a serial number from within an edition of 10,000 cards each. Showdown inserts are found at an average rate of one per Series 1 foil packs.

		MT
Complete Set (8):		65.00
Common Player:		2.00
1	Frank Thomas, Hideo Nomo	9.00
2	Barry Bonds, Randy Johnson	7.50
3	Greg Maddux, Ken Griffey Jr.	20.00
4	Roger Clemens, Tony Gwynn	12.50
5	Mike Piazza, Mike Mussina	12.50
6	Cal Ripken Jr., Pedro Martinez	15.00
7	Tim Wakefield, Matt Williams	2.00
8	Manny Ramirez, Carlos Perez	4.00

1997 Donruss

Donruss' 1997 Series 1 features 270 base cards with a full-bleed color action photo on the front. Horizontal backs have a photo, career statistics, a brief player profile and biographical tidbits. A Press Proofs parallel was made of the base cards in an edition of 2,000 each. Other Series 1 inserts include the annual Diamond Kings, Elites, Armed and Dangerous cards, Longball Leaders and Rocket Launchers. A 180-card Update set was released later as a follow-up to the regular. '97 Donruss series. The Updates are numbered contiguously, #271-450, from the first series. Press Proofs and Gold Press Proof parallel inserts were available; other Update inserts include Dominators, Franchise Futures, Power Alley, Rookie Diamond Kings and a special Cal Ripken Jr. set.

		MT
Complete Set (450):		30.00
Series 1 Set (270):		15.00
Update Set (180):		15.00
Common Player:		.10
Pack (10):		2.00
Hobby Wax Box (18):		32.00
Retail Wax Box (36):		60.00
Update Pack (10):		2.00
Update Wax Box (24):		45.00
1	Juan Gonzalez	.75
2	Jim Edmonds	.15
3	Tony Gwynn	1.25
4	Andres Galarraga	.15
5	Joe Carter	.15
6	Raul Mondesi	.20
7	Greg Maddux	1.50
8	Travis Fryman	.10
9	Brian Jordan	.10
10	Henry Rodriguez	.10
11	Manny Ramirez	1.00
12	Mark McGwire	3.00
13	Marc Newfield	.10
14	Craig Biggio	.10
15	Sammy Sosa	1.50
16	Brady Anderson	.10
17	Wade Boggs	.25
18	Charles Johnson	.10
19	Matt Williams	.20
20	Denny Neagle	.10
21	Ken Griffey Jr.	2.50
22	Robin Ventura	.15
23	Barry Larkin	.20
24	Todd Zeile	.10
25	Chuck Knoblauch	.15
26	Todd Hundley	.10
27	Roger Clemens	.75
28	Michael Tucker	.10
29	Rondell White	.10
30	Osvaldo Fernandez	.10
31	Ivan Rodriguez	.50
32	Alex Fernandez	.10
33	Jason Isringhausen	.10
34	Chipper Jones	1.50
35	Paul O'Neill	.10
36	Hideo Nomo	.40
37	Roberto Alomar	.75
38	Derek Bell	.10
39	Paul Molitor	.30
40	Andy Benes	.10
41	Steve Trachsel	.10
42	J.T. Snow	.10
43	Jason Kendall	.10
44	Alex Rodriguez	2.50
45	Joey Hamilton	.10
46	Carlos Delgado	.40
47	Jason Giambi	.10
48	Larry Walker	.30
49	Derek Jeter	1.50
50	Kenny Lofton	.75
51	Devon White	.10
52	Matt Mieske	.10
53	Melvin Nieves	.10
54	Jose Canseco	.30
55	Tino Martinez	.30
56	Rafael Palmeiro	.15
57	Edgardo Alfonzo	.15
58	Jay Buhner	.15
59	Shane Reynolds	.10
60	Steve Finley	.10
61	Bobby Higginson	.10
62	Dean Palmer	.10
63	Terry Pendleton	.10
64	Marquis Grissom	.10
65	Mike Stanley	.10
66	Moises Alou	.10
67	Ray Lankford	.10
68	Marty Cordova	.15
69	John Olerud	.10
70	David Cone	.10
71	Benito Santiago	.10
72	Ryne Sandberg	.60
73	Rickey Henderson	.15
74	Roger Cedeno	.10
75	Wilson Alvarez	.10
76	Tim Salmon	.20
77	Orlando Merced	.10
78	Vinny Castilla	.10
79	Ismael Valdes	.10
80	Dante Bichette	.15
81	Kevin Brown	.15
82	Andy Pettitte	.60
83	Scott Stahoviak	.10
84	Mickey Tettleton	.10
85	Jack McDowell	.10
86	Tom Glavine	.10
87	Gregg Jefferies	.10
88	Chili Davis	.10
89	Randy Johnson	.35
90	John Mabry	.10
91	Billy Wagner	.10
92	Jeff Cirillo	.10
93	Trevor Hoffman	.10
94	Juan Guzman	.10
95	Geronimo Berroa	.10
96	Bernard Gilkey	.10
97	Danny Tartabull	.10
98	Johnny Damon	.20
99	Charlie Hayes	.10
100	Reggie Sanders	.10
101	Robby Thompson	.10
102	Bobby Bonilla	.10
103	Reggie Jefferson	.10
104	John Smoltz	.20
105	Jim Thome	.35
106	Ruben Rivera	.25
107	Darren Oliver	.10
108	Mo Vaughn	.80
109	Roger Pavlik	.10
110	Terry Steinbach	.10
111	Jermaine Dye	.10

112 Mark Grudzielanek .10
113 Rick Aguilera .10
114 Jamey Wright .10
115 Eddie Murray .35
116 Brian Hunter .10
117 Hal Morris .10
118 Tom Pagnozzi .10
119 Mike Mussina .35
120 Mark Grace .25
121 Cal Ripken Jr. 2.00
122 Tom Goodwin .10
123 Paul Sorrento .10
124 Jay Bell .10
125 Todd Hollandsworth .10
126 Edgar Martinez .10
127 George Arias .10
128 Greg Vaughn .10
129 Roberto Hernandez .10
130 Delino DeShields .10
131 Bill Pulsipher .10
132 Joey Cora .10
133 Mariano Rivera .25
134 Mike Piazza 1.50
135 Carlos Baerga .10
136 Jose Mesa .10
137 Will Clark .25
138 Frank Thomas 1.50
139 John Wetteland .10
140 Shawn Estes .10
141 Garret Anderson .10
142 Andre Dawson .10
143 Eddie Taubensee .10
144 Ryan Klesko .25
145 Rocky Coppinger .10
146 Jeff Bagwell 1.25
147 Donovan Osborne .10
148 Greg Myers .10
149 Brant Brown .10
150 Kevin Elster .10
151 Bob Wells .10
152 Wally Joyner .10
153 Rico Brogna .10
154 Dwight Gooden .10
155 Jermaine Allensworth .10
156 Ray Durham .10
157 Cecil Fielder .10
158 Ryan Hancock .10
159 Gary Sheffield .20
160 Albert Belle .75
161 Tomas Perez .10
162 David Doster .10
163 John Valentin .10
164 Danny Graves .10
165 Jose Paniagua .10
166 *Brian Giles* 1.00
167 Barry Bonds .75
168 Sterling Hitchcock .10
169 Bernie Williams .50
170 Fred McGriff .25
171 George Williams .10
172 Amaury Telemaco .10
173 Ken Caminiti .10
174 Ron Gant .10
175 David Justice .15
176 James Baldwin .10
177 Pat Hentgen .10
178 Ben McDonald .10
179 Tim Naehring .10
180 Jim Eisenreich .10
181 Ken Hill .10
182 Paul Wilson .10
183 Marvin Benard .10
184 Alan Benes .10
185 Ellis Burks .10
186 Scott Servais .10
187 David Segui .10
188 Scott Brosius .10
189 Jose Offerman .10
190 Eric Davis .10
191 Brett Butler .10
192 Curtis Pride .10
193 Yamil Benitez .10
194 Chan Ho Park .10
195 Bret Boone .10
196 Omar Vizquel .10
197 Orlando Miller .10
198 Ramon Martinez .10
199 Harold Baines .10
200 Eric Young .10
201 Fernando Vina .10
202 Alex Gonzalez .10
203 Fernando Valenzuela .10
204 Steve Avery .10
205 Ernie Young .10
206 Kevin Appier .10
207 Randy Myers .10
208 Jeff Suppan .10
209 James Mouton .10
210 Russ Davis .10
211 Al Martin .10
212 Troy Percival .10
213 Al Leiter .10
214 Dennis Eckersley .10
215 Mark Johnson .10
216 Eric Karros .10
217 Royce Clayton .10
218 Tony Phillips .10
219 Tim Wakefield .10
220 Alan Trammell .10
221 Eduardo Perez .10
222 Butch Huskey .10
223 Tim Belcher .10
224 Jamie Moyer .10
225 F.P. Santangelo .10
226 Rusty Greer .10
227 Jeff Brantley .10
228 Mark Langston .10
229 Ray Montgomery .10
230 Rich Becker .10
231 Ozzie Smith .50
232 Rey Ordonez .20
233 Ricky Otero .10
234 Mike Cameron .10
235 Mike Sweeney .10
236 Mark Lewis .10
237 Luis Gonzalez .10
238 Marcus Jensen .10
239 Ed Sprague .10
240 Jose Valentin .10
241 Jeff Frye .10
242 Charles Nagy .10
243 Carlos Garcia .10
244 Mike Hampton .10
245 B.J. Surhoff .10
246 Wilton Guerrero .10
247 Frank Rodriguez .10
248 Gary Gaetti .10
249 Lance Johnson .10
250 Darren Bragg .10
251 Darryl Hamilton .10
252 John Jaha .10
253 Craig Paquette .10
254 Jaime Navarro .10
255 Shawon Dunston .10
256 Ron Wright .75
257 Tim Belk .10
258 Jeff Darwin .10
259 Ruben Sierra .10
260 Chuck Finley .10
261 Darryl Strawberry .10
262 Shannon Stewart .10
263 Pedro Martinez .10
264 Neifi Perez .10
265 Jeff Conine .10
266 Orel Hershiser .10
267 Checklist 1-90 (Eddie Murray) (500 Career HR) .10
268 Checklist 91-180 (Paul Molitor) (3,000 Career Hits) .10
269 Checklist 181-270 (Barry Bonds) (300 Career HR) .30
270 Checklist - inserts (Mark McGwire) (300 Career HR) .75
271 Matt Williams .30
272 Todd Zeile .10
273 Roger Clemens .75
274 Michael Tucker .10
275 J.T. Snow .10
276 Kenny Lofton .75
277 Jose Canseco .25
278 Marquis Grissom .10
279 Moises Alou .10
280 Benito Santiago .10
281 Willie McGee .10
282 Chili Davis .10
283 Ron Coomer .10
284 Orlando Merced .10
285 Delino DeShields .10
286 John Wetteland .10
287 Darren Daulton .10
288 Lee Stevens .10
289 Albert Belle .75
290 Sterling Hitchcock .10
291 David Justice .20
292 Eric Davis .10
293 Brian Hunter .10
294 Darryl Hamilton .10
295 Steve Avery .10
296 Joe Vitiello .10
297 Jaime Navarro .10
298 Eddie Murray .30
299 Randy Myers .10
300 Francisco Cordova .10
301 Javier Lopez .15
302 Geronimo Berroa .10
303 Jeffrey Hammonds .10
304 Deion Sanders .25
305 Jeff Fassero .10
306 Curt Schilling .10
307 Robb Nen .10
308 Mark McLemore .10
309 Jimmy Key .10
310 Quilvio Veras .10
311 Bip Roberts .10
312 Esteban Loaiza .10
313 Andy Ashby .10
314 Sandy Alomar Jr. .10
315 Shawn Green .10
316 Luis Castillo .10
317 Benji Gil .10
318 Otis Nixon .10
319 Aaron Sele .10
320 Brad Ausmus .10
321 Troy O'Leary .10
322 Terrell Wade .10
323 Jeff King .10
324 Kevin Seitzer .10
325 Mark Wohlers .10
326 Edgar Renteria .10
327 Dan Wilson .10
328 Brian McRae .10
329 Rod Beck .10
330 Julio Franco .10
331 Dave Nilsson .10
332 Glenallen Hill .10
333 Kevin Elster .10
334 Joe Girardi .10
335 David Wells .10
336 Jeff Blauser .10
337 Darryl Kile .10
338 Jeff Kent .10
339 Jim Leyritz .10
340 Todd Stottlemyre .10
341 Tony Clark .25
342 Chris Hoiles .10
343 Mike Lieberthal .10
344 Matt Lawton .10
345 Alex Ochoa .10
346 Chris Snopek .10
347 Rudy Pemberton .10
348 Eric Owens .10
349 Joe Randa .10
350 John Olerud .10
351 Steve Karsay .10
352 Mark Whiten .10
353 Bob Abreu .10
354 Bartolo Colon .10
355 Vladimir Guerrero 1.50
356 Darin Erstad 1.00
357 Scott Rolen 1.25
358 Andruw Jones 1.50
359 Scott Spiezio .10
360 Karim Garcia .10
361 *Hideki Irabu* 1.50
362 Nomar Garciaparra 1.25
363 Dmitri Young .10
364 *Bubba Trammell* 1.00
365 Kevin Orie .10
366 Jose Rosado .10
367 Jose Guillen .75
368 Brooks Kieschnick .10
369 Pokey Reese .10
370 Glendon Rusch .10
371 Jason Dickson .15
372 Todd Walker .60
373 Justin Thompson .10
374 Todd Greene .10
375 Jeff Suppan .10
376 Trey Beamon .10
377 Damon Mashore .10
378 Wendell Magee .10
379 Shigetosi Hasegawa .10
380 Bill Mueller .10
381 Chris Widger .10
382 Tony Grafannino .10
383 Derrek Lee .10
384 Brian Moehler .10
385 Quinton McCracken .10
386 Matt Morris .10
387 Marvin Benard .10
388 *Deivi Cruz* .50
389 *Javier Valentin* .15
390 Todd Dunwoody .40
391 Derrick Gibson .20
392 Raul Casanova .10
393 George Arias .10
394 *Tony Womack* .25
395 Antone Williamson .10
396 *Jose Cruz Jr.* .75
397 Desi Relaford .10
398 Frank Thomas (Hit List) .75
399 Ken Griffey Jr. (Hit List) 1.50
400 Cal Ripken Jr. (Hit List) 1.25
401 Chipper Jones (Hit List) 1.00
402 Mike Piazza (Hit List) 1.00
403 Gary Sheffield (Hit List) .15
404 Alex Rodriguez (Hit List) 1.50
405 Wade Boggs (Hit List) .15
406 Juan Gonzalez (Hit List) .40
407 Tony Gwynn (Hit List) .60
408 Edgar Martinez (Hit List) .10
409 Jeff Bagwell (Hit List) .60
410 Larry Walker (Hit List) .15
411 Kenny Lofton (Hit List) .35
412 Manny Ramirez (Hit List) .50
413 Mark McGwire (Hit List) 1.50
414 Roberto Alomar (Hit List) .25
415 Derek Jeter (Hit List) 1.00
416 Brady Anderson (Hit List) .10
417 Paul Molitor (Hit List) .20
418 Dante Bichette (Hit List) .15
419 Jim Edmonds (Hit List) .10
420 Mo Vaughn (Hit List) .35
421 Barry Bonds (Hit List) .35
422 Rusty Greer (Hit List) .10
423 Greg Maddux (King of the Hill) 1.00
424 Andy Pettitte (King of the Hill) .35
425 John Smoltz (King of the Hill) .10
426 Randy Johnson (King of the Hill) .25
427 Hideo Nomo (King of the Hill) .25
428 Roger Clemens (King of the Hill) .35
429 Tom Glavine (King of the Hill) .15
430 Pat Hentgen (King of the Hill) .10
431 Kevin Brown (King of the Hill) .10
432 Mike Mussina (King of the Hill) .25
433 Alex Fernandez (King of the Hill) .10
434 Kevin Appier (King of the Hill) .10
435 David Cone (King of the Hill) .15
436 Jeff Fassero (King of the Hill) .10
437 John Wetteland (King of the Hill) .10
438 Barry Bonds, Ivan Rodriguez (Interleague Showdown) .25
439 Ken Griffey Jr., Andres Galarraga (Interleague Showdown) 1.00
440 Fred McGriff, Rafael Palmeiro (Interleague Showdown) .15
441 Barry Larkin, Jim Thome (Interleague Showdown) .20

442	Sammy Sosa, Albert Belle (Interleague Showdown)	1.50
443	Bernie Williams, Todd Hundley (Interleague Showdown)	.20
444	Chuck Knoblauch, Brian Jordan (Interleague Showdown)	.15
445	Mo Vaughn, Jeff Conine (Interleague Showdown)	.25
446	Ken Caminiti, Jason Giambi (Interleague Showdown)	.15
447	Raul Mondesi, Tim Salmon (Interleague Showdown)	.15
448	Checklist (Cal Ripken Jr.)	.75
449	Checklist (Greg Maddux)	.60
450	Checklist (Ken Griffey Jr.)	1.00

1997 Donruss Press Proofs

Each of the 450 cards in the Donruss base set was also produced in a Press Proof parallel edition of 2,000 cards. Virtually identical in design to the regular cards, the Press Proofs are printed on a metallic background with silver-foil highlights. Most Press Proof backs carry the notation "1 of 2000". Stated odds of finding a press proof are one per eight packs. A special "gold" press proof chase set features cards with gold-foil highlights, die-cut at top and bottom and the note "1 of 500" on back. Gold press proofs are found on average of once per 32 packs.

	MT
Complete Set (270):	600.00
Common Player:	1.00
Stars/Rookies:	6-10X
Complete Gold Set (270):	1800.
Common Gold Player:	4.00
Gold Stars/Rookies:	15-25X

(See 1997 Donruss for checklist and base card values.)

1997 Donruss Armed and Dangerous

These 15 cards are numbered up to 5,000. They were inserted in 1997 Donruss Series 1 retail packs only.

		MT
Complete Set (15):		70.00
Common Player:		1.50
1	Ken Griffey Jr.	15.00
2	Raul Mondesi	2.50
3	Chipper Jones	10.00
4	Ivan Rodriguez	4.00
5	Randy Johnson	3.00
6	Alex Rodriguez	12.00
7	Larry Walker	2.50
8	Cal Ripken Jr.	12.50
9	Kenny Lofton	3.00
10	Barry Bonds	4.00
11	Derek Jeter	10.00
12	Charles Johnson	1.50
13	Greg Maddux	9.00
14	Roberto Alomar	3.00
15	Barry Larkin	1.50

1997 Donruss Diamond Kings

Diamond Kings for 1997 are sequentially numbered from 1 to 10,000. To celebrate 15 years of this popular insert set, Donruss offered collectors a one-of-a-kind piece of artwork if they find one of the 10 cards with the serial number 1,982 (1982 was the first year of the Diamond Kings). Those who find these cards can redeem them for an original artwork provided by artist Dan Gardiner. In addition, Donruss printed the first 500 of each card on canvas stock.

		MT
Complete Set (10):		60.00
Common Player:		2.50
Canvas (1st 500):		2-4X
1	Ken Griffey Jr.	15.00
2	Cal Ripken Jr.	12.50
3	Mo Vaughn	5.00
4	Chuck Knoblauch	3.50
5	Jeff Bagwell	6.00
6	Henry Rodriguez	2.50
7	Mike Piazza	10.00
8	Ivan Rodriguez	5.00
9	Frank Thomas	7.50
10	Chipper Jones	10.00

1997 Donruss Elite Promos

Each of the 12 cards in Series 1 Donruss Elite inserts can be found in a sample card version. The promos differ from the issued version in the diagonal black overprint "SAMPLE CARD" on front and back, and the "PROMO/2500" at back bottom in place of the issued version's serial number.

		MT
Complete Set (12):		100.00
Common Player:		3.75
1	Frank Thomas	7.50
2	Paul Molitor	6.00
3	Sammy Sosa	7.50
4	Barry Bonds	9.00
5	Chipper Jones	12.50
6	Alex Rodriguez	15.00
7	Ken Griffey Jr.	17.50
8	Jeff Bagwell	7.50
9	Cal Ripken Jr.	15.00
10	Mo Vaughn	3.50
11	Mike Piazza	12.00
12	Juan Gonzalez	6.00

1997 Donruss Elite Inserts

There were 2,500 sets of these insert cards made. The cards were randomly included in 1997 Donruss Series I packs. Fronts have a white marbled border and are graphically enhanced with silver foil, including a large script "E". On back is another photo, a career summary and a serial number from within the edition limit of 2,500.

		MT
Complete Set (12):		260.00
Common Player:		10.00
1	Frank Thomas	20.00
2	Paul Molitor	10.00
3	Sammy Sosa	25.00
4	Barry Bonds	15.00
5	Chipper Jones	25.00
6	Alex Rodriguez	40.00
7	Ken Griffey Jr.	50.00
8	Jeff Bagwell	15.00
9	Cal Ripken Jr.	40.00
10	Mo Vaughn	10.00
11	Mike Piazza	30.00
12	Juan Gonzalez	15.00

1997 Donruss Longball Leaders

These 1997 Donruss Series 1 inserts have an action photo printed on a metallic foil background. Printed on the gold-foil border is a gauge with the player's 1996 home run total indicated. Horizontal backs have a player photo and record of career HRs by season. Each card is serially numbered within an edition of 5,000. The set was seeded in retail packs only.

		MT
Complete Set (15):		45.00
Common Player:		1.00
1	Frank Thomas	5.00
2	Albert Belle	3.00
3	Mo Vaughn	3.00
4	Brady Anderson	1.00
5	Greg Vaughn	1.00
6	Ken Griffey Jr.	12.50
7	Jay Buhner	1.00
8	Juan Gonzalez	3.00
9	Mike Piazza	7.50
10	Jeff Bagwell	5.00
11	Sammy Sosa	7.00
12	Mark McGwire	12.50
13	Cecil Fielder	1.00
14	Ryan Klesko	1.50
15	Jose Canseco	2.00

1997 Donruss Rated Rookies

Although numbered more like an insert set, Rated Rookies qre part of the regular-issue set. Cards are numbered 1-30, with no ratio given on packs. The cards are differentiated by a large silver-foil strip on the top right side with the words Rated Rookie.

		MT
Complete Set (30):		25.00
Common Player:		.75
1	Jason Thompson	.75
2	LaTroy Hawkins	.75
3	Scott Rolen	5.00
4	Trey Beamon	.75
5	Kimera Bartee	.75
6	Nerio Rodriguez	.75
7	Jeff D'Amico	.75
8	Quinton McCracken	.75
9	John Wasdin	.75
10	Robin Jennings	.75
11	Steve Gibralter	.75
12	Tyler Houston	.75
13	Tony Clark	2.00
14	Ugueth Urbina	.90
15	Billy McMillon	.75
16	Raul Casanova	.75
17	Brooks Kieschnick	.75
18	Luis Castillo	.75
19	Edgar Renteria	1.25
20	Andruw Jones	5.00
21	Chad Mottola	.75
22	Makoto Suzuki	.75
23	Justin Thompson	.75
24	Darin Erstad	4.00
25	Todd Walker	2.50
26	Todd Greene	.75
27	Vladimir Guerrero	6.00
28	Darren Dreifort	.75
29	John Burke	.75
30	Damon Mashore	.75

1997 Donruss Rocket Launchers

These 1997 Donruss Series 1 inserts are limited to 5,000 each. They were only included in magazine packs.

		MT
Complete Set (15):		50.00
Common Player:		1.50
1	Frank Thomas	6.00
2	Albert Belle	3.00
3	Chipper Jones	7.50
4	Mike Piazza	7.50
5	Mo Vaughn	3.00
6	Juan Gonzalez	4.00
7	Fred McGriff	2.00
8	Jeff Bagwell	4.00
9	Matt Williams	2.00
10	Gary Sheffield	1.50
11	Barry Bonds	3.00
12	Manny Ramirez	3.00
13	Henry Rodriguez	1.50
14	Jason Giambi	1.50
15	Cal Ripken Jr.	10.00

1997 Donruss Update Press Proofs

This 180-card parallel set is printed on an all-foil stock with bright foil accents. Each card is numbered "1 of 2,000". Special die-cut gold versions are numbered as "1 of 500".

	MT
Complete Set (180):	650.00
Common Player:	2.00
Stars:	
(180):	2500.
Common Player, Gold:	6.00
Gold Stars:	45-60X

(See 1997 Donruss (#271-450) for checklist, base card values.)

Player names in *Italic* type indicate a rookie card.

1997 Donruss Update Dominators

This 20-card insert highlights players known for being able to "take over a game." Each card features silver-foil highlights on front and stats on back.

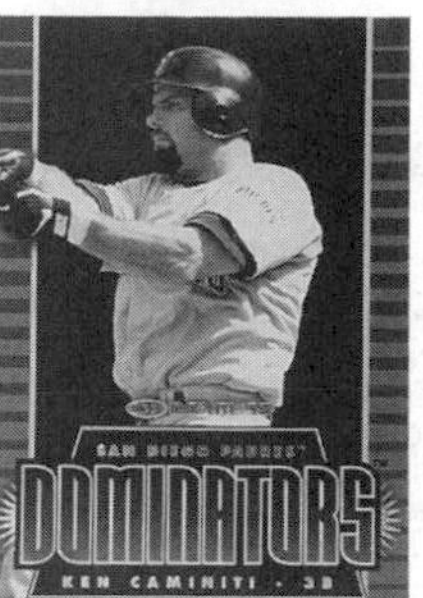

		MT
Complete Set (20):		80.00
Common Player:		2.00
1	Frank Thomas	7.50
2	Ken Griffey Jr.	15.00
3	Greg Maddux	9.00
4	Cal Ripken Jr.	12.00
5	Alex Rodriguez	12.00
6	Albert Belle	4.00
7	Mark McGwire	15.00
8	Juan Gonzalez	4.00
9	Chipper Jones	9.00
10	Hideo Nomo	2.00
11	Roger Clemens	4.00
12	John Smoltz	2.00
13	Mike Piazza	9.00
14	Sammy Sosa	10.00
15	Matt Williams	2.50
16	Kenny Lofton	2.50
17	Barry Larkin	2.00
18	Rafael Palmeiro	2.00
19	Ken Caminiti	2.00
20	Gary Sheffield	2.00

1997 Donruss Update Franchise Features

This hobby-exclusive insert consists of 15 cards designed with a movie poster theme. The double-front design highlights a top veteran player on one side with an up-and-coming rookie on the other. The side featuring the veteran has the designation "Now Playing," while the rookie side carries the banner "Coming Attraction." Each card is printed on an all-foil stock and numbered to 3,000.

		MT
Complete Set (15):		175.00
Common Player:		5.00
1	Ken Griffey Jr., Andruw Jones	25.00
2	Frank Thomas, Darin Erstad	10.00
3	Alex Rodriguez, Nomar Garciaparra	20.00
4	Chuck Knoblauch, Wilton Guerrero	5.00
5	Juan Gonzalez, Bubba Trammell	12.50
6	Chipper Jones, Todd Walker	15.00
7	Barry Bonds, Vladimir Guerrero	8.00
8	Mark McGwire, Dmitri Young	25.00
9	Mike Piazza, Mike Sweeney	15.00
10	Mo Vaughn, Tony Clark	7.50
11	Gary Sheffield, Jose Guillen	2.50
12	Kenny Lofton, Shannon Stewart	7.50
13	Cal Ripken Jr., Scott Rolen	20.00
14	Derek Jeter, Pokey Reese	15.00
15	Tony Gwynn, Bob Abreu	15.00

1997 Donruss Update Power Alley

This 24-card insert is fractured into three different styles: Gold, Blue and Green. Each card is micro-etched and printed on holographic foil board. All cards are sequentially numbered, with the first 250 cards in each level being die-cut. Twelve players' cards feature a green finish and are numbered to 4,000. Eight players are printed on blue cards that are numbered to 2,000. Four players are found on gold cards numbered to 1,000.

		MT
Complete Set (24):		400.00
Common Gold:		20.00
Common Blue:		10.00
Common Green:		5.00
Die-Cuts:		2-4X
1	Frank Thomas (G)	25.00
2	Ken Griffey Jr. (G)	60.00
3	Cal Ripken Jr. (G)	45.00
4	Jeff Bagwell (B)	20.00
5	Mike Piazza (B)	30.00
6	Andruw Jones (GR)	15.00
7	Alex Rodriguez (G)	40.00
8	Albert Belle (GR)	10.00
9	Mo Vaughn (GR)	9.00
10	Chipper Jones (B)	30.00
11	Juan Gonzalez (B)	15.00

12	Ken Caminiti (GR)	10.00
13	Manny Ramirez (GR)	12.00
14	Mark McGwire (GR)	30.00
15	Kenny Lofton (B)	10.00
16	Barry Bonds (GR)	10.00
17	Gary Sheffield (GR)	7.50
18	Tony Gwynn (GR)	15.00
19	Vladimir Guerrero (B)	20.00
20	Ivan Rodriguez (B)	10.00
21	Paul Molitor (B)	10.00
22	Sammy Sosa (GR)	25.00
23	Matt Williams (GR)	5.00
24	Derek Jeter (GR)	20.00

1997 Donruss Update Rookie Diamond Kings

This popular Donruss Update insert set features a new twist - all 10 cards feature promising rookies. Each card is sequentially numbered to 10,000, with the first 500 cards of each player printed on actual canvas.

		MT
Complete Set (10):		80.00
Common Player:		4.00
Canvas:		2-4X
1	Andruw Jones	15.00
2	Vladimir Guerrero	15.00
3	Scott Rolen	15.00
4	Todd Walker	6.00
5	Bartolo Colon	5.00
6	Jose Guillen	7.00
7	Nomar Garciaparra	20.00
8	Darin Erstad	12.00
9	Dmitri Young	4.00
10	Wilton Guerrero	4.00

1997 Donruss Team Sets

A total of 165 cards were part of the Donruss Team Set issue. Packs consisted solely of players from one of 11 different teams. In addition, a full 150-card parallel set called Pennant Edition was available, featuring red and gold foil and a special "Pennant Edition" logo. Cards were sold in five-card packs for $1.99 each. The Angels and Indians set were sold only at their teams' souvenir outlets. Cards #131 Bernie Williams and #144, Russ Davis, were never issued. The Team Set cards utilize team-color foil highlights and the numbers on back differ from the regular-issue version.

		MT
Comp. Angels Set (1-15):		2.50
Comp. Braves Set (16-30):		6.00
Comp. Orioles Set (31-45):		3.50
Comp. Red Sox Set (46-60):		3.00
Comp. White Sox Set (61-75):		4.00
Comp. Indians Set (76-90):		3.00
Comp. Rockies Set (91-105):		2.50
Comp. Dodgers Set (106-120):		3.50
Comp. Yankees Set (121-135):		5.00
Comp. Mariners Set (136-150):		10.00
Common Player:		.10
Pennant Edition Stars:		8-12X
1	Jim Edmonds	.15
2	Tim Salmon	.25
3	Tony Phillips	.10
4	Garret Anderson	.10
5	Troy Percival	.10
6	Mark Langston	.10
7	Chuck Finley	.10
8	Eddie Murray	.50
9	Jim Leyritz	.10
10	Darin Erstad	1.00
11	Jason Dickson	.10
12	Allen Watson	.10
13	Shigetosi Hasegawa	.10
14	Dave Hollins	.10
15	Gary DiSarcina	.10
16	Greg Maddux	2.00
17	Denny Neagle	.15
18	Chipper Jones	2.00
19	Tom Glavine	.20
20	John Smoltz	.20
21	Ryan Klesko	.40
22	Fred McGriff	.30
23	Michael Tucker	.10
24	Kenny Lofton	.75
25	Javier Lopez	.15
26	Mark Wohlers	.10
27	Jeff Blauser	.10
28	Andruw Jones	1.50
29	Tony Graffanino	.10
30	Terrell Wade	.10
31	Brady Anderson	.15
32	Roberto Alomar	.60
33	Rafael Palmeiro	.20
34	Mike Mussina	.60
35	Cal Ripken Jr.	2.50
36	Rocky Coppinger	.10
37	Randy Myers	.10
38	B.J. Surhoff	.10
39	Eric Davis	.10
40	Armando Benitez	.10
41	Jeffrey Hammonds	.10
42	Jimmy Key	.10
43	Chris Hoiles	.10
44	Mike Bordick	.10
45	Pete Incaviglia	.10
46	Mike Stanley	.10
47	Reggie Jefferson	.10
48	Mo Vaughn	.75
49	John Valentin	.10
50	Tim Naehring	.10
51	Jeff Suppan	.10
52	Tim Wakefield	.10
53	Jeff Frye	.10
54	Darren Bragg	.10
55	Steve Avery	.10
56	Shane Mack	.10
57	Aaron Sele	.10
58	Troy O'Leary	.10
59	Rudy Pemberton	.10
60	Nomar Garciaparra	2.00
61	Robin Ventura	.15
62	Wilson Alvarez	.10
63	Roberto Hernandez	.10
64	Frank Thomas	2.00
65	Ray Durham	.10
66	James Baldwin	.10
67	Harold Baines	.10
68	Doug Drabek	.10
69	Mike Cameron	.10
70	Albert Belle	.75
71	Jaime Navarro	.10
72	Chris Snopek	.10
73	Lyle Mouton	.10
74	Dave Martinez	.10
75	Ozzie Guillen	.10
76	Manny Ramirez	1.00
77	Jack McDowell	.10
78	Jim Thome	.50
79	Jose Mesa	.10
80	Brian Giles	.10
81	Omar Vizquel	.10
82	Charles Nagy	.10
83	Orel Hershiser	.10
84	Matt Williams	.25
85	Marquis Grissom	.15
86	David Justice	.20
87	Sandy Alomar	.10
88	Kevin Seitzer	.10
89	Julio Franco	.10
90	Bartolo Colon	.10
91	Andres Galarraga	.20
92	Larry Walker	.30
93	Vinny Castilla	.10
94	Dante Bichette	.15
95	Jamey Wright	.10
96	Ellis Burks	.10
97	Eric Young	.10
98	Neifi Perez	.10
99	Quinton McCracken	.10
100	Bruce Ruffin	.10
101	Walt Weiss	.10
102	Roger Bailey	.10
103	Jeff Reed	.10
104	Bill Swift	.10
105	Kirt Manwaring	.10
106	Raul Mondesi	.20
107	Hideo Nomo	.50
108	Roger Cedeno	.10
109	Ismael Valdes	.10
110	Todd Hollandsworth	.10
111	Mike Piazza	2.00
112	Brett Butler	.10
113	Chan Ho Park	.10
114	Ramon Martinez	.10
115	Eric Karros	.10
116	Wilton Guerrero	.10
117	Todd Zeile	.10
118	Karim Garcia	.20
119	Greg Gagne	.10
120	Darren Dreifort	.10
121	Wade Boggs	.45
122	Paul O'Neill	.20
123	Derek Jeter	2.00
124	Tino Martinez	.25
125	David Cone	.20
126	Andy Pettitte	.60
127	Charlie Hayes	.10
128	Mariano Rivera	.20
129	Dwight Gooden	.15
130	Cecil Fielder	.10
131	Not Issued	
132	Darryl Strawberry	.15
133	Joe Girardi	.10
134	David Wells	.10
135	Hideki Irabu	1.50
136	Ken Griffey Jr.	3.00
137	Alex Rodriguez	2.50
138	Jay Buhner	.10
139	Randy Johnson	.50
140	Paul Sorrento	.10
141	Edgar Martinez	.10
142	Joey Cora	.10
143	Bob Wells	.10
144	Not Issued	
145	Jamie Moyer	.10
146	Jeff Fassero	.10
147	Dan Wilson	.10
148	Jose Cruz, Jr.	.50
149	Scott Sanders	.10
150	Rich Amaral	.10
151	Brian Jordan	.10
152	Andy Benes	.10
153	Ray Lankford	.10
154	John Mabry	.10
155	Tom Pagnozzi	.10
156	Ron Gant	.10
157	Alan Benes	.10
158	Dennis Eckersley	.10
159	Royce Clayton	.10
160	Todd Stottlemyre	.10
161	Gary Gaetti	.10
162	Willie McGee	.10
163	Delino DeShields	.10
164	Dmitri Young	.10
165	Matt Morris	.10

1997 Donruss Team Sets MVP

The top players at each position were available in this 18-card insert set. Each card is sequentially numbered to 1,000. Fronts are printed with a textured foil background and holographic foil highlights. Backs have a portrait photo.

		MT
Complete Set (18):		240.00
Common Player:		2.00
1	Ivan Rodriguez	7.50
2	Mike Piazza	25.00
3	Frank Thomas	25.00
4	Jeff Bagwell	17.50
5	Chuck Knoblauch	3.00
6	Eric Young	2.00
7	Alex Rodriguez	30.00
8	Barry Larkin	2.00
9	Cal Ripken Jr.	30.00
10	Chipper Jones	25.00
11	Albert Belle	7.50
12	Barry Bonds	7.50
13	Ken Griffey Jr.	40.00
14	Kenny Lofton	5.00
15	Juan Gonzalez	10.00
16	Larry Walker	3.00
17	Roger Clemens	12.50
18	Greg Maddux	22.50

1997 Donruss Elite

Donruss Elite Baseball is a 150-card, single-series set distributed as a hobby-only product. The regular-issue cards feature a silver border around the entire card, with a marblized frame around a color player photo at center. Backs feature a color player photo and minimal statistics and personal data. Elite was accompanied by an Elite Stars parallel set and three inserts: Leather and Lumber, Passing the Torch and Turn of the Century.

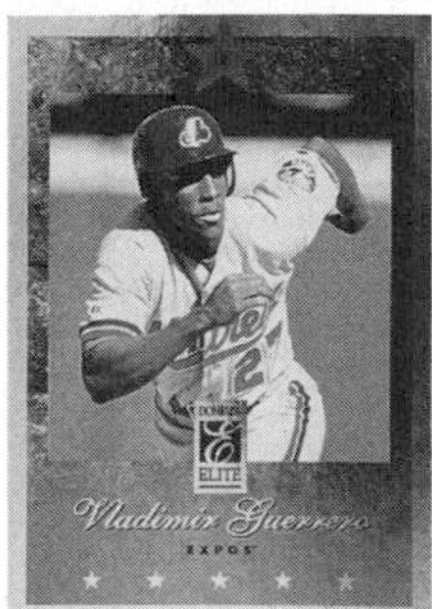

		MT
Complete Set (150):		20.00
Common Player:		.15
Pack (6):		3.50
Wax Box (18):		55.00
1	Juan Gonzalez	1.00
2	Alex Rodriguez	4.00
3	Frank Thomas	2.00
4	Greg Maddux	2.50
5	Ken Griffey Jr.	4.00
6	Cal Ripken Jr.	3.00
7	Mike Piazza	2.50
8	Chipper Jones	2.50
9	Albert Belle	1.00
10	Andruw Jones	2.00
11	Vladimir Guerrero	2.00
12	Mo Vaughn	.75
13	Ivan Rodriguez	1.00
14	Andy Pettitte	.75
15	Tony Gwynn	2.00
16	Barry Bonds	1.00
17	Jeff Bagwell	1.75
18	Manny Ramirez	1.25
19	Kenny Lofton	.60
20	Roberto Alomar	.75
21	Mark McGwire	5.00
22	Ryan Klesko	.30
23	Tim Salmon	.30
24	Derek Jeter	2.50
25	Eddie Murray	.50
26	Jermaine Dye	.15
27	Ruben Rivera	.25
28	Jim Edmonds	.15
29	Mike Mussina	.50
30	Randy Johnson	.50
31	Sammy Sosa	2.00
32	Hideo Nomo	.25
33	Chuck Knoblauch	.35
34	Paul Molitor	.50
35	Rafael Palmeiro	.30
36	Brady Anderson	.20
37	Will Clark	.30
38	Craig Biggio	.30
39	Jason Giambi	.15
40	Roger Clemens	1.50
41	Jay Buhner	.20
42	Edgar Martinez	.15
43	Gary Sheffield	.25
44	Fred McGriff	.20
45	Bobby Bonilla	.15
46	Tom Glavine	.25
47	Wade Boggs	.35
48	Jeff Conine	.15
49	John Smoltz	.25
50	Jim Thome	.30
51	Billy Wagner	.20
52	Jose Canseco	.30
53	Javy Lopez	.15
54	Cecil Fielder	.15
55	Garret Anderson	.15
56	Alex Ochoa	.15
57	Scott Rolen	1.50
58	Darin Erstad	1.25
59	Rey Ordonez	.20
60	Dante Bichette	.20
61	Joe Carter	.20
62	Moises Alou	.25
63	Jason Isringhausen	.15
64	Karim Garcia	.35
65	Brian Jordan	.15
66	Ruben Sierra	.15
67	Todd Hollandsworth	.15
68	Paul Wilson	.15
69	Ernie Young	.15
70	Ryne Sandberg	1.25
71	Raul Mondesi	.30
72	George Arias	.15
73	Ray Durham	.15
74	Dean Palmer	.15
75	Shawn Green	.25
76	Eric Young	.15
77	Jason Kendall	.15
78	Greg Vaughn	.15
79	Terrell Wade	.15
80	Bill Pulsipher	.15
81	Bobby Higginson	.15
82	Mark Grudzielanek	.15
83	Ken Caminiti	.40
84	Todd Greene	.15
85	Carlos Delgado	.50
86	Mark Grace	.25
87	Rondell White	.25
88	Barry Larkin	.25
89	J.T. Snow	.15
90	Alex Gonzalez	.15
91	Raul Casanova	.15
92	Marc Newfield	.15
93	Jermaine Allensworth	.15
94	John Mabry	.15
95	Kirby Puckett	1.50
96	Travis Fryman	.15
97	Kevin Brown	.25
98	Andres Galarraga	.20
99	Marty Cordova	.15
100	Henry Rodriguez	.15
101	Sterling Hitchcock	.15
102	Trey Beamon	.15
103	Brett Butler	.15
104	Rickey Henderson	.25
105	Tino Martinez	.30
106	Kevin Appier	.15
107	Brian Hunter	.15
108	Eric Karros	.15
109	Andre Dawson	.15
110	Darryl Strawberry	.15
111	James Baldwin	.15
112	Chad Mottola	.15
113	Dave Nilsson	.15
114	Carlos Baerga	.15
115	Chan Ho Park	.20
116	John Jaha	.15
117	Alan Benes	.20
118	Mariano Rivera	.25
119	Ellis Burks	.15
120	Tony Clark	.30
121	Todd Walker	.50
122	Dwight Gooden	.15
123	Ugueth Urbina	.15
124	David Cone	.25
125	Ozzie Smith	.60
126	Kimera Bartee	.15
127	Rusty Greer	.15
128	Pat Hentgen	.15
129	Charles Johnson	.15
130	Quinton McCracken	.15
131	Troy Percival	.15
132	Shane Reynolds	.15
133	Charles Nagy	.15
134	Tom Goodwin	.15
135	Ron Gant	.15
136	Dan Wilson	.15
137	Matt Williams	.35
138	LaTroy Hawkins	.15
139	Kevin Seitzer	.15
140	Michael Tucker	.15
141	Todd Hundley	.25
142	Alex Fernandez	.15
143	Marquis Grissom	.15
144	Steve Finley	.15
145	Curtis Pride	.15
146	Derek Bell	.15
147	Butch Huskey	.15
148	Dwight Gooden	.15
149	Al Leiter	.15
150	Hideo Nomo	.25

1997 Donruss Elite Stars

Gold, rather than silver, foil differentiates the parallel set of Elite Stars from the regular-issue versions of each of the base cards in the Elite set. The parallels also have a small "Elite Stars" printed at top, flanking the position. Stated odds of finding a Stars insert are about one per five packs.

	MT
Complete Set (150):	600.00
Common Player:	2.00

(Star players in the Elite Star parallel issue valued at 15-30X regular Elites.)

1997 Donruss Elite Leather & Lumber

Leather and Lumber is a 10-card insert set filled with veterans. Genuine leather is featured on one side of the card, while wood card stock is on the other. There were 500 sequentially numbered sets produced.

		MT
Complete Set (10):		400.00
Common Player:		15.00
1	Ken Griffey Jr.	90.00
2	Alex Rodriguez	60.00
3	Frank Thomas	50.00
4	Chipper Jones	60.00
5	Ivan Rodriguez	25.00
6	Cal Ripken Jr.	75.00
7	Barry Bonds	25.00
8	Chuck Knoblauch	15.00
9	Manny Ramirez	20.00
10	Mark McGwire	90.00

1997 Donruss Elite Passing the Torch

Passing the Torch is a 12-card insert limited to 1,500 individually numbered sets. It features eight different stars, each with their own cards and then featured on a double-sided card with another player from the set.

		MT
Complete Set (12):		300.00
Common Player:		15.00
1	Cal Ripken Jr.	60.00
2	Alex Rodriguez	60.00
3	Cal Ripken Jr., Alex Rodriguez	50.00
4	Kirby Puckett	20.00
5	Andruw Jones	25.00
6	Kirby Puckett, Andruw Jones	25.00
7	Cecil Fielder	15.00
8	Frank Thomas	30.00
9	Cecil Fielder, Frank Thomas	20.00
10	Ozzie Smith	20.00
11	Derek Jeter	40.00
12	Ozzie Smith, Derek Jeter	25.00

1997 Donruss Elite Passing the Torch Autographs

The first 150 individually numbered sets of the Passing the Torch insert were autographed. This means that cards 3, 6, 9 and 12 are dual-autographed on their double-sided format.

		MT
Complete Set (12):		2250.
Common Card:		50.00
1	Cal Ripken Jr.	300.00
2	Alex Rodriguez	250.00
3	Cal Ripken Jr., Alex Rodriguez	1200.
4	Kirby Puckett	150.00
5	Andruw Jones	90.00
6	Kirby Puckett, Andruw Jones	250.00
7	Cecil Fielder	50.00
8	Frank Thomas	150.00
9	Cecil Fielder, Frank Thomas	150.00
10	Ozzie Smith	125.00
11	Derek Jeter	150.00
12	Ozzie Smith, Derek Jeter	225.00

1997 Donruss Elite Turn of the Century

Turn of the Century includes 20 potential year 2000 superstars on an insert set numbered to 3,500. The first 500 of these sets feature an external die-cut design. Cards feature the player over a framed background image on silver foil board, with black strips down each side. Backs have a color photo, a few words about the player and the serial number.

		MT
Complete Set (20):		175.00
Common Player:		4.00
Complete Die-Cut Set (20):		400.00
Die-Cuts:		-4X
1	Alex Rodriguez	30.00
2	Andruw Jones	20.00
3	Chipper Jones	25.00
4	Todd Walker	8.00
5	Scott Rolen	15.00
6	Trey Beamon	4.00
7	Derek Jeter	25.00
7s	Derek Jeter ("SAMPLE" overprint)	10.00
8	Darin Erstad	12.00
9	Tony Clark	8.00
10	Todd Greene	5.00
11	Jason Giambi	4.00
12	Justin Thompson	5.00
13	Ernie Young	4.00
14	Jason Kendall	5.00
15	Alex Ochoa	4.00
15s	Alex Ochoa ("SAMPLE" overprint)	3.00
16	Brooks Kieschnick	4.00
17	Bobby Higginson	5.00
17s	Bobby Higginson ("SAMPLE" overprint)	3.00
18	Ruben Rivera	4.00
18s	Ruben Rivera ("SAMPLE" overprint)	3.00
19	Chan Ho Park	5.00
20	Chad Mottola	4.00

1997 Donruss Limited

Each of the 200 base cards in this set features a double-front design showcasing an action photo on each side. The set is divided into four subsets. Counterparts (100 cards) highlights two different players from the same position; Double Team (40 cards) features some of the majors' top teammate duos; Star Factor (40 cards) consists of two photos of some of the hobby's favorite players; and Unlimited Potential/Talent (20 cards) combines a top veteran with a top prospect. The issue also includes a Limited Exposure parallel set and a multi-tiered insert called Fabric of the Game. Odds of finding any insert card were 1:5 packs. Less than 1,100 base sets were available. Cards were sold in five-card packs for $4.99.

		MT
Complete Set (200):		900.00
Common Counterpart:		.25
Common Double Team:		1.00
Common Star Factor:		2.50
Common Unlimited:		2.00
Pack (5):		4.00
Wax Box (24):		90.00
1	Ken Griffey Jr., Rondell White (Counterparts)	3.00
2	Greg Maddux, David Cone (Counterparts)	1.75
3	Gary Sheffield, Moises Alou (Double Team)	2.00
4	Frank Thomas (Star Factor)	12.50
5	Cal Ripken Jr., Kevin Orie (Counterparts)	2.00
6	Vladimir Guerrero, Barry Bonds (Unlimited Potential/Talent)	15.00
7	Eddie Murray, Reggie Jefferson (Counterparts)	.40
8	Manny Ramirez, Marquis Grissom (Double Team)	4.00
9	Mike Piazza (Star Factor)	25.00
10	Barry Larkin, Rey Ordonez (Counterparts)	.40
11	Jeff Bagwell, Eric Karros (Counterparts)	1.00
12	Chuck Knoblauch, Ray Durham (Counterparts)	.40
13	Alex Rodriguez, Edgar Renteria (Counterparts)	2.00
14	Matt Williams, Vinny Castilla (Counterparts)	.40
15	Todd Hollandsworth, Bob Abreu (Counterparts)	.25
16	John Smoltz, Pedro Martinez (Counterparts)	.40
17	Jose Canseco, Chili Davis (Counterparts)	.40
18	Jose Cruz, Jr., Ken Griffey Jr. (Unlimited Potential/Talent)	30.00
19	Ken Griffey Jr. (Star Factor)	35.00
20	Paul Molitor, John Olerud (Counterparts)	.75
21	Roberto Alomar, Luis Castillo (Counterparts)	.50
22	Derek Jeter, Lou Collier (Counterparts)	2.00
23	Chipper Jones, Robin Ventura (Counterparts)	2.50
24	Gary Sheffield, Ron Gant (Counterparts)	.40
25	Ramon Martinez, Bobby Jones (Counterparts)	.25
26	Mike Piazza, Raul Mondesi (Double Team)	15.00
27	Darin Erstad, Jeff Bagwell (Unlimited Potential/Talent)	7.50
28	Ivan Rodriguez (Star Factor)	10.00
29	J.T. Snow, Kevin Young (Counterparts)	.25
30	Ryne Sandberg, Julio Franco (Counterparts)	.70
31	Travis Fryman, Chris Snopek (Counterparts)	.25
32	Wade Boggs, Russ Davis (Counterparts)	.40
33	Brooks Kieschnick, Marty Cordova (Counterparts)	.25
34	Andy Pettitte, Denny Neagle (Counterparts)	.70
35	Paul Molitor, Matt Lawton (Double Team)	2.00
36	Scott Rolen, Cal Ripken Jr. (Unlimited Potential/Talent)	30.00
37	Cal Ripken Jr. (Star Factor)	30.00
38	Jim Thome, Dave Nilsson (Counterparts)	.50
39	*Tony Womack*, Carlos Baerga (Counterparts)	.25
40	Nomar Garciaparra, Mark Grudzielanek (Counterparts)	1.75
41	Todd Greene, Chris Widger (Counterparts)	.25
42	Deion Sanders, Bernard Gilkey (Counterparts)	.40
43	Hideo Nomo, Charles Nagy (Counterparts)	.40
44	Ivan Rodriguez, Rusty Greer (Double Team)	3.00
45	Todd Walker, Chipper Jones (Unlimited Potential/Talent)	20.00
46	Greg Maddux (Star Factor)	20.00
47	Mo Vaughn, Cecil Fielder (Counterparts)	.75
48	Craig Biggio, Scott Spiezio (Counterparts)	.25
49	Pokey Reese, Jeff Blauser (Counterparts)	.25
50	Ken Caminiti, Joe Randa (Counterparts)	.40
51	Albert Belle, Shawn Green (Counterparts)	.75
52	Randy Johnson, Jason Dickson (Counterparts)	.60
53	Hideo Nomo, Chan Ho Park (Double Team)	2.50
54	Scott Spiezio, Chuck Knoblauch (Unlimited Potential/Talent)	3.00
55	Chipper Jones (Star Factor)	25.00
56	Tino Martinez, Ryan McGuire (Counterparts)	.40
57	Eric Young, Wilton Guerrero (Counterparts)	.25
58	Ron Coomer, Dave Hollins (Counterparts)	.25
59	Sammy Sosa, Angel Echevarria (Counterparts)	1.75
60	*Dennis Reyes*, Jimmy Key (Counterparts)	.25
61	Barry Larkin, Deion Sanders (Double Team)	1.00
62	Wilton Guerrero, Roberto Alomar (Unlimited Potential/Talent)	3.00
63	Albert Belle (Star Factor)	10.00
64	Mark McGwire, Andres Galarraga (Counterparts)	2.00
65	Edgar Martinez, Todd Walker (Counterparts)	.40
66	Steve Finley, Rich Becker (Counterparts)	.25
67	Tom Glavine, Andy Ashby (Counterparts)	.40
68	Sammy Sosa, Ryne Sandberg (Double Team)	15.00
69	Nomar Garciaparra, Alex Rodriguez (Unlimited Potential/Talent)	35.00
70	Jeff Bagwell (Star Factor)	15.00
71	Darin Erstad, Mark Grace (Counterparts)	1.00
72	Scott Rolen, Edgardo Alfonzo (Counterparts)	1.00
73	Kenny Lofton, Lance Johnson (Counterparts)	.60
74	Joey Hamilton, Brett Tomko (Counterparts)	.25
75	Eddie Murray, Tim Salmon (Double Team)	1.50
76	Dmitri Young, Mo Vaughn (Unlimited Potential/Talent)	3.00

77 Juan Gonzalez (Star Factor) 10.00
78 Frank Thomas, Tony Clark (Counterparts) 1.00
79 Shannon Stewart, Bip Roberts (Counterparts) .25
80 Shawn Estes, Alex Fernandez (Counterparts) .25
81 John Smoltz, Javier Lopez (Double Team) 2.00
82 Todd Greene, Mike Piazza (Unlimited Potential/ Talent) 25.00
83 Derek Jeter (Star Factor) 25.00
84 Dmitri Young, Antone Williamson (Counterparts) .25
85 Rickey Henderson, Darryl Hamilton (Counterparts) .35
86 Billy Wagner, Dennis Eckersley (Counterparts) .50
87 Larry Walker, Eric Young (Double Team) 1.50
88 Mark Kotsay, Juan Gonzalez (Unlimited Potential/ Talent) 5.00
89 Barry Bonds (Star Factor) 10.00
90 Will Clark, Jeff Conine (Counterparts) .40
91 Tony Gwynn, Brett Butler (Counterparts) 1.25
92 John Wetteland, Rod Beck (Counterparts) .25
93 Bernie Williams, Tino Martinez (Double Team) 2.00
94 Andruw Jones, Kenny Lofton (Unlimited Potential/ Talent) 8.00
95 Mo Vaughn (Star Factor) 5.00
96 Joe Carter, Derrek Lee (Counterparts) .25
97 John Mabry, F.P. Santangelo (Counterparts) .25
98 Esteban Loaiza, Wilson Alvarez (Counterparts) .25
99 Matt Williams, David Justice (Double Team) 1.25
100 Derrek Lee, Frank Thomas (Unlimited Potential/ Talent) 7.50
101 Mark McGwire (Star Factor) 35.00
102 Fred McGriff, Paul Sorrento (Counterparts) .40
103 Jermaine Allensworth, Bernie Williams (Counterparts) .50
104 Ismael Valdes, Chris Holt (Counterparts) .25
105 Fred McGriff, Ryan Klesko (Double Team) 1.25
106 Tony Clark, Mark McGwire (Unlimited Potential/ Talent) 35.00
107 Tony Gwynn (Star Factor) 20.00
108 Jeffrey Hammonds, Ellis Burks (Counterparts) .25
109 Shane Reynolds, Andy Benes (Counterparts) .25
110 Roger Clemens, Carlos Delgado (Double Team) 4.00
111 Karim Garcia, Albert Belle (Unlimited Potential/ Talent) 4.00
112 Paul Molitor (Star Factor) 7.50
113 Trey Beamon, Eric Owens (Counterparts) .25
114 Curt Schilling, Darryl Kile (Counterparts) .25
115 Tom Glavine, Michael Tucker (Double Team) 1.00
116 Pokey Reese, Derek Jeter (Unlimited Potential/ Talent) 20.00
117 Manny Ramirez (Star Factor) 9.00
118 Juan Gonzalez, Brant Brown (Counterparts) 1.00
119 Juan Guzman, Francisco Cordova (Counterparts) .25
120 Randy Johnson, Edgar Martinez (Double Team) 2.00
121 Hideki Irabu, Greg Maddux (Unlimited Potential/ Talent) 6.50
122 Alex Rodriguez (Star Factor) 30.00
123 Barry Bonds, Quinton McCracken (Counterparts) .75
124 Roger Clemens, Alan Benes (Counterparts) .75
125 Wade Boggs, Paul O'Neill (Double Team) 2.00
126 Mike Cameron, Larry Walker (Unlimited Potential/ Talent) 3.00
127 Gary Sheffield (Star Factor) 2.50
128 Andruw Jones, Raul Mondesi (Counterparts) 1.00
129 Brian Anderson, Terrell Wade (Counterparts) .25
130 Brady Anderson, Rafael Palmeiro (Double Team) 2.50
131 Neifi Perez, Barry Larkin (Unlimited Potential/ Talent) 2.00
132 Ken Caminiti (Star Factor) 4.00
133 Larry Walker, Rusty Greer (Counterparts) .40
134 Mariano Rivera, Mark Wohlers (Counterparts) .30
135 Hideki Irabu, Andy Pettitte (Double Team) 3.00
136 Jose Guillen, Tony Gwynn (Unlimited Potential/ Talent) 6.00
137 Hideo Nomo (Star Factor) 3.50
138 Vladimir Guerrero, Jim Edmonds (Counterparts) .75
139 Justin Thompson, Dwight Gooden (Counterparts) .25
140 Andres Galarraga, Dante Bichette (Double Team) 1.00
141 Kenny Lofton (Star Factor) 5.00
142 Tim Salmon, Manny Ramirez (Counterparts) 1.00
143 Kevin Brown, Matt Morris (Counterparts) .25
144 Craig Biggio, Bob Abreu (Double Team) 1.00
145 Roberto Alomar (Star Factor) 5.00
146 Jose Guillen, Brian Jordan (Counterparts) .50
147 Bartolo Colon, Kevin Appier (Counterparts) .25
148 Ray Lankford, Brian Jordan (Double Team) 1.00
149 Chuck Knoblauch (Star Factor) 5.00
150 Henry Rodriguez, Ray Lankford (Counterparts) .25
151 *Jaret Wright*, Ben McDonald (Counterparts) .65
152 Bobby Bonilla, Kevin Brown (Double Team) 2.50
153 Barry Larkin (Star Factor) 2.50
154 David Justice, Reggie Sanders (Counterparts) .40
155 Mike Mussina, Ken Hill (Counterparts) .50
156 Mark Grace, Brooks Kieschnick (Double Team) 1.25
157 Jim Thome (Star Factor) 2.50
158 Michael Tucker, Curtis Goodwin (Counterparts) .25
159 Jeff Suppan, Jeff Fassero (Counterparts) .25
160 Mike Mussina, Jeffrey Hammonds (Double Team) 2.00
161 John Smoltz (Star Factor) 3.50
162 Moises Alou, Eric Davis (Counterparts) .25
163 Sandy Alomar Jr., Dan Wilson (Counterparts) .25
164 Rondell White, Henry Rodriguez (Double Team) 2.50
165 Roger Clemens (Star Factor) 10.00
166 Brady Anderson, Al Martin (Counterparts) .25
167 Jason Kendall, Charles Johnson (Counterparts) .25
168 Jason Giambi, Jose Canseco (Double Team) 1.25
169 Larry Walker (Star Factor) 4.00
170 Jay Buhner, Geronimo Berroa (Counterparts) .40
171 Ivan Rodriguez, Mike Sweeney (Counterparts) .60
172 Kevin Appier, Jose Rosado (Double Team) 2.50
173 Bernie Williams (Star Factor) 2.50
174 Todd Dunwoody, *Brian Giles* (Counterparts) .75
175 Javier Lopez, Scott Hatteberg (Counterparts) .30
176 John Jaha, Jeff Cirillo (Double Team) 2.50
177 Andy Pettitte Star Factor) 2.50
178 Dante Bichette, Butch Huskey (Counterparts) .40
179 Raul Casanova, Todd Hundley (Counterparts) .40
180 Jim Edmonds, Garret Anderson (Double Team) 2.50
181 Deion Sanders (Star Factor) 2.50
182 Ryan Klesko, Paul O'Neill (Counterparts) .40
183 Joe Carter, Pat Hentgen (Double Team) 2.50
184 Brady Anderson (Star Factor) 2.50
185 Carlos Delgado, Wally Joyner (Counterparts) .50
186 Jermaine Dye, Johnny Damon (Double Team) 2.50
187 Randy Johnson (Star Factor) 5.00
188 Todd Hundley, Carlos Baerga (Double Team) 2.50
189 Tom Glavine (Star Factor) 2.50
190 Damon Mashore, Jason McDonald (Double Team) 2.50
191 Wade Boggs (Star Factor) 5.00
192 Al Martin , Jason Kendall (Double Team) 2.50
193 Matt Williams (Star Factor) 3.00
194 Will Clark, Dean Palmer (Double Team) 1.25
195 Sammy Sosa (Star Factor) 20.00
196 Jose Cruz, Jr., Jay Buhner (Double Team) 1.00
197 Eddie Murray (Star Factor) 5.00
198 Darin Erstad, Jason Dickson (Double Team) 3.00
199 Fred McGriff (Star Factor) 2.50
200 Bubba Trammell, Bobby Higginson (Double Team) 2.00

1997 Donruss Limited Exposure

A complete 200-card parallel set printed with Holographic Poly-Chromium technology on both sides and featuring a special "Limited Exposure" stamp. Less than 40 sets of the Star Factor Limited Exposures are thought to exist.

	MT
Complete Set (200):	6000.
Common Counterparts:	2.00
Counterparts Stars:	4-8X
Common Double Team:	6.00
Double Team Stars:	5-7X
Common Star Factor:	10.00
Star Factor Stars:	3-5X
Common Unlimited:	8.00
Unlimited Stars:	3-5X

(See 1997 Donruss Limited for checklist and base card values.)

1997 Donruss Limited Exposure Non-Glossy

In error, half (100 cards) of the Limited Exposure parallels were produced in regular technology (non-chrome) on regular (non-glossy) cardboard stock. These cards do carry the Limited Exposure identification in the card-number box on back, but do not carry the correct cards' higher values. No checklist of which 100 cards were involved in the error is available.

	MT
Common Non-Glossy:	1.00
Stars:	15-25%

(See 1997 Donruss Limited and Limited Exposure to calculate base card values.)

1997 Donruss Limited Fabric of the Game

This fractured insert set consists of 69 different cards highlighting three different technologies representing three statistical categories: Canvas (stolen bases), Leather (doubles) and Wood (home runs). Each of the 23 cards in each category are found in varying levels of scarcity: Legendary Material (one card per theme; numbered to 100), Hall of Fame Material (four cards numbered to 250), Superstar Material (five cards numbered to 500), Star Material (six cards numbered to 750), and Major League Material (seven cards numbered to 1,000).

	MT
Complete Set: (69):	1650.
Common Player:	5.00
Complete Canvas Set (23):	325.00
Rickey Henderson (100)	45.00
Barry Bonds (250)	30.00
Kenny Lofton (250)	25.00
Roberto Alomar (250)	25.00
Ryne Sandberg (250)	30.00
Tony Gwynn (500)	30.00
Barry Larkin (500)	10.00
Brady Anderson (500)	10.00
Chuck Knoblauch (500)	12.50
Craig Biggio (500)	10.00
Sammy Sosa (750)	30.00
Gary Sheffield (750)	12.50
Eric Young (750)	7.50
Larry Walker (750)	15.00
Ken Griffey Jr. (750)	65.00
Deion Sanders (750)	10.00
Raul Mondesi (1,000)	10.00
Rondell White (1,000)	7.50
Derek Jeter (1,000)	25.00
Nomar Garciaparra (1,000)	20.00
Wilton Guerrero (1,000)	5.00
Pokey Reese (1,000)	5.00
Darin Erstad (1,000)	17.50
Complete Leather Set (23):	350.00
Paul Molitor (100)	60.00
Wade Boggs (250)	25.00
Cal Ripken Jr. (250)	80.00
Tony Gwynn (250)	50.00
Joe Carter (250)	12.50
Rafael Palmeiro (500)	15.00
Mark Grace (500)	15.00
Bobby Bonilla (500)	7.50
Andres Galarraga (500)	7.50
Edgar Martinez (500)	7.50
Ken Caminiti (750)	10.00
Ivan Rodriguez (750)	17.50
Frank Thomas (750)	35.00
Jeff Bagwell (750)	25.00
Albert Belle (750)	15.00
Bernie Williams (750)	15.00
Chipper Jones (1,000)	25.00
Rusty Greer (1,000)	5.00
Todd Walker (1,000)	10.00
Scott Rolen (1,000)	20.00
Bob Abreu (1,000)	5.00
Jose Guillen (1,000)	7.50
Jose Cruz, Jr. (1,000)	5.00
Complete Wood Set (23):	425.00
Eddie Murray (100)	50.00
Cal Ripken Jr. (250)	75.00
Barry Bonds (250)	30.00
Mark McGwire (250)	75.00
Fred McGriff (250)	12.50
Ken Griffey Jr. (500)	70.00
Albert Belle (500)	17.50
Frank Thomas (500)	40.00
Juan Gonzalez (500)	20.00
Matt Williams (500)	12.50
Mike Piazza (750)	30.00
Jeff Bagwell (750)	20.00
Mo Vaughn (750)	15.00
Gary Sheffield (750)	10.00
Tim Salmon (750)	10.00
David Justice (750)	10.00
Manny Ramirez (1,000)	15.00
Jim Thome (1,000)	7.50
Tino Martinez (1,000)	7.50
Andruw Jones (1,000)	10.00
Vladimir Guerrero (1,000)	15.00
Tony Clark (1,000)	7.50
Dmitri Young (1,000)	5.00

1997 Donruss Preferred

Each of the 200 base cards is printed on all-foil microetched stock. Conventional backs have a color player photo and a few stats. The set is fractured into four increasingly scarce levels: 100 Bronze cards, 70 Silver, 20 Gold and 10 Platinum. Instead of traditional packs, cards were sold in five-card collectible tins. Four different inserts were included with the product: Staremaster, X-Ponential Power, Cut To The Chase (a die-cut parallel) and Precious Metals. Odds of finding any insert were 1:4 packs.

		MT
Complete Set (200):		400.00
Common Bronze:		.10
Common Silver:		.75
Common Gold:		2.00
Common Platinum:		5.00
Wax Box (24):		120.00
1	Frank Thomas P	17.50
2	Ken Griffey Jr. P	40.00
3	Cecil Fielder B	.10
4	Chuck Knoblauch G	4.00
5	Garret Anderson B	.10
6	Greg Maddux P	20.00
7	Matt Williams S	1.00
8	Marquis Grissom S	.75
9	Jason Isringhausen B	.10
10	Larry Walker S	1.25
11	Charles Nagy B	.10
12	Dan Wilson B	.10
13	Albert Belle G	6.00
14	Javier Lopez B	.10
15	David Cone B	.15
16	Bernard Gilkey B	.10
17	Andres Galarraga S	.75
18	Bill Pulsipher B	.10
19	Alex Fernandez B	.10
20	Andy Pettitte S	2.00
21	Mark Grudzielanek B	.10
22	Juan Gonzalez P	10.00
23	Reggie Sanders B	.10
24	Kenny Lofton G	4.00
25	Andy Ashby B	.10
26	John Wetteland B	.10
27	Bobby Bonilla B	.10
28	Hideo Nomo G	3.00
29	Joe Carter B	.10
30	Jose Canseco B	.25
31	Ellis Burks B	.10
32	Edgar Martinez S	.75
33	Chan Ho Park B	.10
34	David Justice B	.20
35	Carlos Delgado B	.50
36	Jeff Cirillo S	.75
37	Charles Johnson B	.10
38	Manny Ramirez G	6.00
39	Greg Vaughn B	.10
40	Henry Rodriguez B	.10
41	Darryl Strawberry B	.10
42	Jim Thome G	3.00
43	Ryan Klesko S	1.50
44	Jermaine Allensworth B	.10
45	Brian Jordan G	3.00
46	Tony Gwynn P	20.00
47	Rafael Palmeiro G	5.00
48	Dante Bichette S	.75
49	Ivan Rodriguez G	8.00
50	Mark McGwire G	35.00
51	Tim Salmon S	1.00
52	Roger Clemens B	.50
53	Matt Lawton B	.10
54	Wade Boggs S	1.50
55	Travis Fryman B	.10
56	Bobby Higginson S	.75
57	John Jaha S	.75
58	Rondell White S	.75
59	Tom Glavine S	1.00
60	Eddie Murray S	2.50
61	Vinny Castilla B	.10
62	Todd Hundley B	.20
63	Jay Buhner S	.75
64	Paul O'Neill B	.10
65	Steve Finley B	.10
66	Kevin Appier B	.10
67	Ray Durham B	.10
68	Dave Nilsson B	.10
69	Jeff Bagwell G	10.00
70	Al Martin S	.75
71	Paul Molitor G	5.00
72	Kevin Brown S	1.00
73	Ron Gant B	.10
74	Dwight Gooden B	.10
75	Quinton McCracken B	.10
76	Rusty Greer S	.75
77	Juan Guzman B	.10
78	Fred McGriff S	.75
79	Tino Martinez B	.20
80	Ray Lankford B	.10
81	Ken Caminiti G	3.00
82	James Baldwin B	.10
83	Jermaine Dye G	2.00
84	Mark Grace S	1.00
85	Pat Hentgen S	.75

No.	Player	MT
86	Jason Giambi S	.75
87	Brian Hunter B	.10
88	Andy Benes B	.10
89	Jose Rosado B	.10
90	Shawn Green B	.20
91	Jason Kendall B	.10
92	Alex Rodriguez P	30.00
93	Chipper Jones P	25.00
94	Barry Bonds G	5.00
95	Brady Anderson G	2.00
96	Ryne Sandberg S	2.50
97	Lance Johnson B	.10
98	Cal Ripken Jr. P	30.00
99	Craig Biggio S	.75
100	Dean Palmer B	.10
101	Gary Sheffield G	3.00
102	Johnny Damon B	.10
103	Mo Vaughn G	4.00
104	Randy Johnson S	1.50
105	Raul Mondesi S	.75
106	Roberto Alomar G	4.00
107	Mike Piazza P	25.00
108	Rey Ordonez B	.10
109	Barry Larkin G	2.00
110	Tony Clark S	1.50
111	Bernie Williams S	2.00
112	John Smoltz G	3.00
113	Moises Alou B	.10
114	Will Clark B	.15
115	Sammy Sosa G	15.00
116	Jim Edmonds S	.75
117	Jeff Conine B	.10
118	Joey Hamilton B	.10
119	Todd Hollandsworth B	.10
120	Troy Percival B	.10
121	Paul Wilson B	.10
122	Ken Hill B	.10
123	Mariano Rivera S	.75
124	Eric Karros B	.10
125	Derek Jeter G	20.00
126	Eric Young S	.75
127	John Mabry B	.10
128	Gregg Jefferies B	.10
129	Ismael Valdes S	.75
130	Marty Cordova B	.10
131	Omar Vizquel B	.10
132	Mike Mussina S	2.00
133	Darin Erstad B	.50
134	Edgar Renteria S	.75
135	Billy Wagner B	.10
136	Alex Ochoa B	.10
137	Luis Castillo B	.10
138	Rocky Coppinger B	.10
139	Mike Sweeney B	.10
140	Michael Tucker B	.10
141	Chris Snopek B	.10
142	Dmitri Young S	.75
143	Andruw Jones P	15.00
144	Mike Cameron S	.75
145	Brant Brown B	.10
146	Todd Walker G	2.00
147	Nomar Garciaparra G	20.00
148	Glendon Rusch B	.10
149	Karim Garcia S	.75
150	*Bubba Trammell S*	2.00
151	Todd Greene B	.10
152	Wilton Guerrero G	2.00
153	Scott Spiezio B	.10
154	Brooks Kieschnick B	.10
155	Vladimir Guerrero G	12.00
156	*Brian Giles S*	10.00
157	Pokey Reese B	.10
158	Jason Dickson G	2.00
159	Kevin Orie S	.75
160	Scott Rolen G	9.00
161	Bartolo Colon S	.75
162	Shannon Stewart G	2.00
163	Wendell Magee B	.10
164	Jose Guillen S	2.00
165	Bob Abreu S	.75
166	*Deivi Cruz B*	.25
167	Alex Rodriguez B (National Treasures)	2.00
168	Frank Thomas B (National Treasures)	1.00
169	Cal Ripken Jr. B (National Treasures)	2.50
170	Chipper Jones B (National Treasures)	1.50
171	Mike Piazza B (National Treasures)	1.50
172	Tony Gwynn S (National Treasures)	4.00
173	Juan Gonzalez B (National Treasures)	.50
174	Kenny Lofton S (National Treasures)	2.50
175	Ken Griffey Jr. B (National Treasures)	6.00
176	Mark McGwire B (National Treasures)	4.00
177	Jeff Bagwell B (National Treasures)	.50
178	Paul Molitor S (National Treasures)	1.50
179	Andruw Jones B (National Treasures)	1.00
180	Manny Ramirez S (National Treasures)	2.50
181	Ken Caminiti S (National Treasures)	1.00
182	Barry Bonds B (National Treasures)	.40
183	Mo Vaughn B (National Treasures)	.30
184	Derek Jeter B (National Treasures)	1.00
185	Barry Larkin S (National Treasures)	1.00
186	Ivan Rodriguez B (National Treasures)	.25
187	Albert Belle S (National Treasures)	2.00
188	John Smoltz S (National Treasures)	.75
189	Chuck Knoblauch S (National Treasures)	1.00
190	Brian Jordan S (National Treasures)	.75
191	Gary Sheffield S (National Treasures)	1.00
192	Jim Thome S (National Treasures)	2.00
193	Brady Anderson S (National Treasures)	.75
194	Hideo Nomo S (National Treasures)	1.50
195	Sammy Sosa S (National Treasures)	6.00
196	Greg Maddux B (National Treasures)	.60
197	Checklist (Vladimir Guerrero B)	.50
198	Checklist (Scott Rolen B)	.25
199	Checklist (Todd Walker B)	.10
200	Checklist (Nomar Garciaparra B)	.50

1997 Donruss Preferred Cut To The Chase

Each of the cards in the Donruss Preferred series can also be found in this parallel set with die-cut borders, in the same bronze, silver, gold and platinum finishes. Multiplier values of the die-cuts are inverse to that usually found, with platinum cards the lowest, followed by gold, silver and bronze. Besides die-cutting, the chase cards feature a "CUT TO THE CHASE" designation at bottom.

	MT
Complete Set (200):	4000.
Common Bronze:	.50
Bronze Stars:	3-6X
Common Silver:	1.50
Silver Stars:	1.5-3X
Common Gold:	4.00
Gold Stars:	2X
Common Platinum:	10.00
Platinum Stars:	2X

(See 1997 Donruss Preferred for checklist and base card values.)

1997 Donruss Preferred Precious Metals

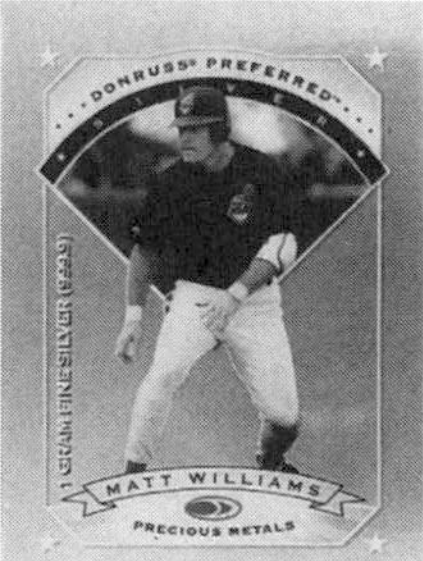

This 25-card partial parallel set features cards printed on actual silver, gold and platinum stock. Only 100 of each card were produced.

		MT
	Complete Set (25):	4000.
	Common Player:	20.00
1	Frank Thomas (P)	125.00
2	Ken Griffey Jr. (P)	250.00
3	Greg Maddux (P)	125.00
4	Albert Belle (G)	60.00
5	Juan Gonzalez (P)	75.00
6	Kenny Lofton (G)	55.00
7	Tony Gwynn (P)	125.00
8	Ivan Rodriguez (G)	60.00
9	Mark McGwire (G)	200.00
10	Matt Williams (S)	25.00
11	Wade Boggs (S)	35.00
12	Eddie Murray (S)	40.00
13	Jeff Bagwell (G)	75.00
14	Ken Caminiti (G)	55.00
15	Alex Rodriguez (P)	150.00
16	Chipper Jones (P)	125.00
17	Barry Bonds (G)	60.00
18	Cal Ripken Jr. (P)	200.00
19	Mo Vaughn (G)	55.00
20	Mike Piazza (P)	150.00
21	Derek Jeter (G)	125.00
22	Bernie Williams (S)	35.00
23	Andruw Jones (P)	90.00
24	Vladimir Guerrero (G)	60.00
25	Jose Guillen (S)	30.00

1997 Donruss Preferred Staremasters

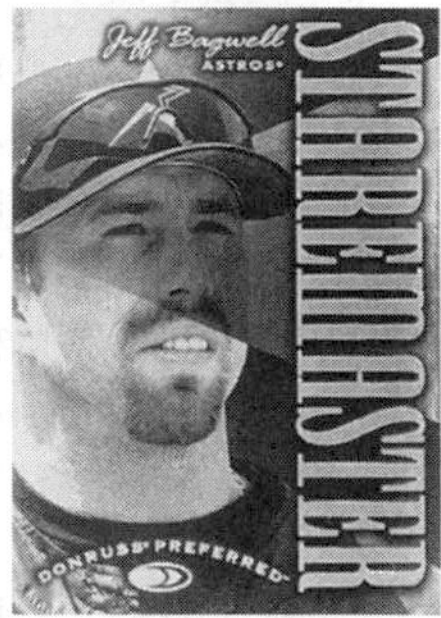

A 20-card insert printed on foil stock and accented with holographic foil, Staremasters is designed to show up-close "game-face" photography. Each card is sequentially numbered to 1,500. Each of the Staremasters inserts can also be found in a version overprinted with a large diagonal black "SAMPLE" on front and back. These were distributed to dealers and the media. The sample cards have a "PROMO/1500" on back in place of a serial number.

		MT
	Complete Set (20):	275.00
	Common Player:	6.00
	Samples:	20%
1	Alex Rodriguez	25.00
2	Frank Thomas	20.00
3	Chipper Jones	25.00
4	Cal Ripken Jr.	30.00
5	Mike Piazza	25.00
6	Juan Gonzalez	10.00
7	Derek Jeter	20.00
8	Jeff Bagwell	15.00
9	Ken Griffey Jr.	40.00
10	Tony Gwynn	17.50
11	Barry Bonds	10.00

12	Albert Belle	7.50
13	Greg Maddux	20.00
14	Mark McGwire	40.00
15	Ken Caminiti	6.00
16	Hideo Nomo	6.00
17	Gary Sheffield	6.00
18	Andruw Jones	15.00
19	Mo Vaughn	7.50
20	Ivan Rodriguez	9.00

1997 Donruss Preferred X-Ponential Power

This 20-card die-cut insert contains two top hitters from 10 different teams. Placing the cards of teammates together forms an "X" shape. Cards are printed on thick plastic stock and gold holographic foil stamping and are sequentially numbered to 3,000.

		MT
Complete Set (20):		200.00
Common Player:		3.50
1A	Manny Ramirez	9.00
1B	Jim Thome	6.00
2A	Paul Molitor	5.50
2B	Chuck Knoblauch	3.50
3A	Ivan Rodriguez	6.50
3B	Juan Gonzalez	10.00
4A	Albert Belle	7.50
4B	Frank Thomas	15.00
5A	Roberto Alomar	6.50
5B	Cal Ripken Jr.	30.00
6A	Tim Salmon	3.50
6B	Jim Edmonds	3.50
7A	Ken Griffey Jr.	35.00
7B	Alex Rodriguez	25.00
8A	Chipper Jones	20.00
8B	Andruw Jones	12.00
9A	Mike Piazza	20.00
9B	Raul Mondesi	3.50
10A	Tony Gwynn	12.00
10B	Ken Caminiti	3.50

1997 Donruss Preferred Tins

Twenty-five different players are featured on the lithographed steel tins which were the "packs" of Donruss Preferred baseball. The 3" x 4-1/2" x 5/8" tins are hinged along the left side and were produced in two versions. Predominantly blue tins are the standard package. A premium parallel version is gold-colored and serially numbered within an edition of 1,200. Gold tins were packed one per 24-pack box of Preferred. Values shown are for opened tins. Shrink-wrapped unopened tins are valued about 1.5-3X the figures shown.

		MT
Complete Set, Blue (25):		15.00
Common Tin:		.50
Gold:		7-10X
1	Frank Thomas	1.00
2	Ken Griffey Jr.	2.00
3	Andruw Jones	1.25
4	Cal Ripken Jr.	1.50
5	Mike Piazza	1.25
6	Chipper Jones	1.25
7	Alex Rodriguez	1.50
8	Derek Jeter	1.00
9	Juan Gonzalez	.75
10	Albert Belle	.60
11	Tony Gwynn	.75
12	Greg Maddux	.75
13	Jeff Bagwell	.60
14	Roger Clemens	.75
15	Mark McGwire	1.50
16	Gary Sheffield	.50
17	Manny Ramirez	.60
18	Hideo Nomo	.50
19	Kenny Lofton	.50
20	Mo Vaughn	.50
21	Ryne Sandberg	.50
22	Barry Bonds	.60
23	Sammy Sosa	1.00
24	John Smoltz	.50
25	Ivan Rodriguez	.60

1997 Donruss Preferred Tin Boxes

Twenty-five different players are featured on the lithographed steel boxes in which the "packs" of Donruss Preferred baseball were sold. Boxes measure about 5-1/4" x 9-1/4" x 5-3/8". Inside the removable lid is a serial number from within an edition of 1,200 (blue) or 299 (gold). The gold versions were a later, hobby-only release.

		MT
Complete Set, Blue (25):		115.00
Common Box:		3.00
Gold:		6-8X
1	Frank Thomas	6.00
2	Ken Griffey Jr.	12.00
3	Andruw Jones	5.00
4	Cal Ripken Jr.	9.00
5	Mike Piazza	7.50
6	Chipper Jones	7.50
7	Alex Rodriguez	7.50
8	Derek Jeter	6.00
9	Juan Gonzalez	4.00
10	Albert Belle	3.50
11	Tony Gwynn	4.50
12	Greg Maddux	4.00
13	Jeff Bagwell	3.50
14	Roger Clemens	4.50
15	Mark McGwire	10.00
16	Gary Sheffield	3.00
17	Manny Ramirez	3.50
18	Hideo Nomo	3.00
19	Kenny Lofton	3.00
20	Mo Vaughn	3.00
21	Ryne Sandberg	3.50
22	Barry Bonds	4.00
23	Sammy Sosa	4.50
24	John Smoltz	3.00
25	Ivan Rodriguez	3.50

1997 Donruss Signature

Donruss ventured in the autograph-per-pack market with this series featuring 100 base cards (unsigned) and various types and versions of authentically autographed cards. The suggested retail price for each five-card pack was $14.99. Base cards have textured silver-foil borders and highlights on front. Backs have a second photo and lengthy stats. A parallel insert edition of each base card was also issued. labeled "Platinum Press Proof", the parallels have blue metallic foil on front and are designated "1 of 150" on the back.

		MT
Complete Set (100):		40.00
Common Player:		.20
Pack (5):		15.00
Wax Box (12):		160.00
1	Mark McGwire	5.00
2	Kenny Lofton	.75
3	Tony Gwynn	2.00
4	Tony Clark	.45
5	Tim Salmon	.40
6	Ken Griffey Jr.	4.00
7	Mike Piazza	2.50
8	Greg Maddux	2.00
9	Roberto Alomar	.75
10	Andres Galarraga	.30
11	Roger Clemens	1.50
12	Bernie Williams	.60
13	Rondell White	.30
14	Kevin Appler	.20
15	Ray Lankford	.20
16	Frank Thomas	2.00
17	Will Clark	.35
18	Chipper Jones	2.50
19	Jeff Bagwell	1.50
20	Manny Ramirez	1.00
21	Ryne Sandberg	1.00
22	Paul Molitor	.65
23	Gary Sheffield	.40
24	Jim Edmonds	.20
25	Barry Larkin	.30
26	Rafael Palmeiro	.30
27	Alan Benes	.20
28	David Justice	.30
29	Randy Johnson	.60
30	Barry Bonds	1.00
31	Mo Vaughn	.75
32	Michael Tucker	.20
33	Larry Walker	.40
34	Tino Martinez	.25
35	Jose Guillen	.60
36	Carlos Delgado	.75
37	Jason Dickson	.20
38	Tom Glavine	.30
39	Raul Mondesi	.30
40	*Jose Cruz Jr.*	.75
41	Johnny Damon	.20
42	Mark Grace	.30
43	Juan Gonzalez	1.00
44	Vladimir Guerrero	2.00
45	Kevin Brown	.25
46	Justin Thompson	.20
47	Eric Young	.20
48	Ron Coomer	.20
49	Mark Kotsay	.40
50	Scott Rolen	1.50
51	Derek Jeter	2.50
52	Jim Thome	.65
53	Fred McGriff	.30
54	Albert Belle	.75
55	Garret Anderson	.20
56	Wilton Guerrero	.20
57	Jose Canseco	.30
58	Cal Ripken Jr.	3.00
59	Sammy Sosa	2.00
60	Dmitri Young	.20
61	Alex Rodriguez	3.00
62	Javier Lopez	.20
63	Sandy Alomar Jr.	.25
64	Joe Carter	.20
65	Dante Bichette	.25
66	Al Martin	.20
67	Darin Erstad	1.25
68	Pokey Reese	.20
69	Brady Anderson	.25
70	Andruw Jones	1.50
71	Ivan Rodriguez	.75
72	Nomar Garciaparra	2.00
73	Moises Alou	.25
74	Andy Pettitte	.60
75	Jay Buhner	.25
76	Craig Biggio	.40
77	Wade Boggs	.50
78	Shawn Estes	.20
79	Neifi Perez	.20
80	Rusty Greer	.20
81	Pedro Martinez	.40
82	Mike Mussina	.60
83	Jason Giambi	.20
84	Hideo Nomo	.45
85	Todd Hundley	.20
86	Deion Sanders	.25
87	Mike Cameron	.20
88	Bobby Bonilla	.25
89	Todd Greene	.20
90	Kevin Orie	.20
91	Ken Caminiti	.30
92	Chuck Knoblauch	.40
93	Matt Morris	.20
94	Matt Williams	.40
95	Pat Hentgen	.20
96	John Smoltz	.30
97	Edgar Martinez	.20
98	Jason Kendall	.20
99	Ken Griffey Jr.	2.00
100	Frank Thomas	.75

1997 Donruss Signature Platinum Press Proofs

This parallel insert set features metallic blue borders and graphics on front and has a "1 of 150" notation on back.

	MT
Complete Set (100):	1500.
Common Player:	4.00
Stars:	15-25X

(See 1997 Donruss Signature for checklist and base card prices.)

1997 Donruss Signature Autographs (Red)

The basic level of authentically autographed cards found one per ($15) pack in Donruss Signature is the unnumbered "red" version. Cards have the background of the front photo printed only in red. For most players, 3,900 cards of the red version were autographed for insertion. Some players, however, signed fewer reds. Exchange cards had to be issued for Raul Mondesi and Edgar Renteria, whose signed cards were not ready when the set was first issued. It has been reported that Mondesi never signed any of the red version autograph cards. Cards are checklisted here in alphabetical order, in concordance with the larger Millenium checklist. The reported number of red cards signed appears in parentheses. This list differs significantly from the original list announced by Donruss in Nov. 1997 due to last minute additions and deletions. Players signed in black and/or blue ink. Some players also added personal touches to some or all of their signatures, such as Bible verse citations, uniform numbers, etc.

		MT
	Complete Set (116):	1300.
	Common Player:	5.00
(1)	Jeff Abbott (3900)	5.00
(2)	Bob Abreu (3900)	6.00
(3)	Edgardo Alfonzo (3900)	15.00
(4)	Roberto Alomar (150)	90.00
(5)	Sandy Alomar Jr. (1400)	15.00
(6)	Moises Alou (900)	20.00
(7)	Garret Anderson (3900)	10.00
(8)	Andy Ashby (3900)	6.00
(10)	Trey Beamon (3900)	5.00
(12)	Alan Benes (3900)	10.00
(13)	Geronimo Berroa (3900)	5.00
(14)	Wade Boggs (150)	100.00
(18)	Kevin L. Brown (3900)	5.00
(20)	Brett Butler (1400)	15.00
(21)	Mike Cameron (3900)	10.00
(22)	Giovanni Carrara (2900)	5.00
(23)	Luis Castillo (3900)	5.00
(24)	Tony Clark (3900)	15.00
(25)	Will Clark (1400)	25.00
(27)	Lou Collier (3900)	5.00
(28)	Bartolo Colon (3900)	9.00
(29)	Ron Coomer (3900)	5.00
(30)	Marty Cordova (3900)	5.00
(31)	Jacob Cruz (3900)	12.00
(32)	Jose Cruz Jr. (900)	35.00
(33)	Russ Davis (3900)	5.00
(34)	Jason Dickson (3900)	6.00
(35)	Todd Dunwoody (3900)	12.00
(36)	Jermaine Dye (3900)	5.00
(37)	Jim Edmonds (3900)	15.00
(38)	Darin Erstad (900)	40.00
(39)	Bobby Estalella (3900)	7.50
(40)	Shawn Estes (3900)	10.00
(41)	Jeff Fassero (3900)	7.50
(42)	Andres Galarraga (900)	20.00
(43)	Karim Garcia (3900)	12.00
(45)	Derrick Gibson (3900)	12.00
(46)	Brian Giles (3900)	7.50
(47)	Tom Glavine (150)	60.00
(49)	Rick Gorecki (900)	5.00
(50)	Shawn Green (1900)	25.00
(51)	Todd Greene (3900)	12.00
(52)	Rusty Greer (3900)	10.00
(53)	Ben Grieve (3900)	20.00
(54)	Mark Grudzielanek (3900)	5.00
(55)	Vladimir Guerrero (1900)	40.00
(56)	Wilton Guerrero (2150)	5.00
(57)	Jose Guillen (2900)	20.00
(59)	Jeffrey Hammonds (2150)	7.50
(60)	Todd Helton (1400)	30.00
(61)	Todd Hollandsworth (2900)	10.00
(62)	Trenidad Hubbard (900)	7.50
(63)	Todd Hundley (1400)	15.00
(66)	Bobby Jones (3900)	5.00
(68)	Brian Jordan (1400)	12.00
(69)	David Justice (900)	35.00
(70)	Eric Karros (650)	20.00
(71)	Jason Kendall (3900)	10.00
(72)	Jimmy Key (3900)	10.00
(73)	Brooks Kieschnick (3900)	5.00
(74)	Ryan Klesko (225)	40.00
(76)	Paul Konerko (3900)	20.00
(77)	Mark Kotsay (2400)	20.00
(78)	Ray Lankford (3900)	7.50
(79)	Barry Larkin (150)	50.00
(80)	Derrek Lee (3900)	12.00
(81)	Esteban Loaiza (3900)	5.00
(82)	Javier Lopez (1400)	20.00
(84)	Edgar Martinez (150)	40.00
(85)	Pedro Martinez (900)	50.00
(87)	Rafael Medina (3900)	5.00
(88)	Raul Mondesi (may not exist)	
(88)	Raul Mondesi (Exchange card)	5.00
(89)	Matt Morris (3900)	5.00
(92)	Paul O'Neill (900)	25.00
(93)	Kevin Orie (3900)	5.00
(94)	David Ortiz (3900)	5.00
(95)	Rafael Palmeiro (900)	25.00
(96)	Jay Payton (3900)	5.00
(97)	Neifi Perez (3900)	6.00
(99)	Manny Ramirez (900)	35.00
(100)	Joe Randa (3900)	5.00
(101)	Calvin Reese (3900)	5.00
(102)	Edgar Renteria (?)	25.00
(102)	Edgar Renteria (Exchange card)	5.00
(103)	Dennis Reyes (3900)	5.00
(106)	Henry Rodriguez (3900)	7.50
(108)	Scott Rolen (1900)	50.00
(109)	Kirk Rueter (2900)	5.00
(110)	Ryne Sandberg (400)	100.00
(112)	Dwight Smith (2900)	5.00
(113)	J.T. Snow (900)	15.00
(114)	Scott Spiezio (3900)	5.00
(115)	Shannon Stewart (2900)	10.00
(116)	Jeff Suppan (1900)	10.00
(117)	Mike Sweeney (3900)	5.00
(118)	Miguel Tejada (3900)	20.00
(121)	Justin Thompson (2400)	10.00
(122)	Brett Tomko (3900)	5.00
(123)	Bubba Trammell (3900)	15.00
(124)	Michael Tucker (3900)	5.00
(125)	Javier Valentin (3900)	5.00
(126)	Mo Vaughn (150)	100.00
(127)	Robin Ventura (1400)	20.00
(128)	Terrell Wade (3900)	5.00
(129)	Billy Wagner (3900)	10.00
(130)	Larry Walker (900)	50.00
(131)	Todd Walker (2400)	12.00
(132)	Rondell White (3900)	15.00
(133)	Kevin Wickander (900)	7.50
(134)	Chris Widger (3900)	5.00
(136)	Matt Williams (150)	50.00
(137)	Antone Williamson (3900)	5.00
(138)	Dan Wilson (3900)	5.00
(139)	Tony Womack (3900)	7.50
(140)	Jaret Wright (3900)	20.00
(141)	Dmitri Young (3900)	5.00
(142)	Eric Young (3900)	6.00
(143)	Kevin Young (3900)	5.00

1997 Donruss Signature Millennium Marks (Green)

One thousand cards of each of the players who signed Signature Autographs are found in an edition marked on front as "Millenium Marks". These cards are also distinguished by the use of green ink in the background of the front photo. On back, the cards have a silver-foil serial number between (generally) 0101-1,000. Some cards as noted in the alphabetical checklist here were produced in lower numbers. The MM autographs were a random insert among the one-per-pack autographed cards found in $15 packs of Donruss Signature. Packs carried exchange cards redeemable for autographed cards of Raul Mondesi, Edgar Renteria and Jim Thome. This checklist differs significantly from that released in Nov., 1997, by Donruss due to the last-minute addition, deletion and substitution of players. It is possible that cards exist of players not shown here.

		MT
Complete Set (143):		1575.
Common Player:		5.00
(1)	Jeff Abbott	5.00
(2)	Bob Abreu	5.00
(3)	Edgardo Alfonzo	12.50
(4)	Roberto Alomar	15.00
(5)	Sandy Alomar Jr.	10.00
(6)	Moises Alou	7.50
(7)	Garret Anderson	5.00
(8)	Andy Ashby	7.50
(9)	Jeff Bagwell (400)	50.00
(10)	Trey Beamon	5.00
(11)	Albert Belle (400)	35.00
(12)	Alan Benes	5.00
(13)	Geronimo Berroa	5.00
(14)	Wade Boggs	30.00
(15)	Barry Bonds (400)	45.00
(16)	Bobby Bonilla (900)	12.50
(17)	Kevin Brown (900)	5.00
(18)	Kevin L. Brown	10.00
(19)	Jay Buhner (900)	6.00
(20)	Brett Butler	7.50
(21)	Mike Cameron	5.00
(22)	Giovanni Carrara	5.00
(23)	Luis Castillo	5.00
(24)	Tony Clark	10.00
(25)	Will Clark	15.00
(26)	Roger Clemens (400)	65.00
(27)	Lou Collier	5.00
(28)	Bartolo Colon	9.00
(29)	Ron Coomer	5.00
(30)	Marty Cordova	5.00
(31)	Jacob Cruz	5.00
(32)	Jose Cruz Jr.	7.50
(33)	Russ Davis	5.00
(34)	Jason Dickson	7.50
(35)	Todd Dunwoody	7.50
(36)	Jermaine Dye	5.00
(37)	Jim Edmonds	7.50
(38)	Darin Erstad	15.00
(39)	Bobby Estalella	5.00
(40)	Shawn Estes	5.00
(41)	Jeff Fassero	5.00
(42)	Andres Galarraga	9.00
(43)	Karim Garcia	7.50
(44)	Nomar Garciaparra (650)	90.00
(45)	Derrick Gibson	10.00
(46)	Brian Giles	7.50
(47)	Tom Glavine	15.00
(48)	Juan Gonzalez (900)	25.00
(49)	Rick Gorecki	5.00
(50)	Shawn Green	25.00
(51)	Todd Greene	7.50
(52)	Rusty Greer	5.00
(53)	Ben Grieve	15.00
(54)	Mark Grudzielanek	5.00
(55)	Vladimir Guerrero	20.00
(56)	Wilton Guerrero	5.00
(57)	Jose Guillen	10.00
(58)	Tony Gwynn (900)	35.00
(59)	Jeffrey Hammonds	5.00
(60)	Todd Helton	25.00
(61)	Todd Hollandsworth	5.00
(62)	Trenidad Hubbard	5.00
(63)	Todd Hundley	6.00
(64)	Derek Jeter (400)	100.00
(65)	Andruw Jones (900)	25.00
(66)	Bobby Jones	5.00
(67)	Chipper Jones	45.00
(68)	Brian Jordan	7.50
(69)	David Justice	9.00
(70)	Eric Karros	7.50
(71)	Jason Kendall	7.50
(72)	Jimmy Key	5.00
(73)	Brooks Kieschnick	5.00
(74)	Ryan Klesko	5.00
(75)	Chuck Knoblauch (900)	15.00
(76)	Paul Konerko	9.00
(77)	Mark Kotsay	12.50
(78)	Ray Lankford	5.00
(79)	Barry Larkin	9.00
(80)	Derrek Lee	6.00
(81)	Esteban Loaiza	5.00
(82)	Javy Lopez	8.00
(83)	Greg Maddux (400)	75.00
(84)	Edgar Martinez	6.00
(85)	Pedro Martinez	25.00
(86)	Tino Martinez (900)	15.00
(87)	Rafael Medina	5.00
(88)	Raul Mondesi	15.00
(88)	Raul Mondesi (Exchange card)	5.00
(89)	Matt Morris	5.00
(90)	Eddie Murray (900)	25.00
(91)	Mike Mussina (900)	12.50
(92)	Paul O'Neill	10.00
(93)	Kevin Orie	5.00
(94)	David Ortiz	5.00
(95)	Rafael Palmeiro	12.50
(96)	Jay Payton	5.00
(97)	Neifi Perez	5.00
(98)	Andy Petitte (900)	9.00
(99)	Manny Ramirez	15.00
(100)	Joe Randa	5.00
(101)	Calvin Reese	5.00
(102)	Edgar Renteria	12.50
(102)	Edgar Renteria (Exchange card)	5.00
(103)	Dennis Reyes	5.00
(104)	Cal Ripken Jr. (400)	150.00
(105)	Alex Rodriguez (400)	100.00
(106)	Henry Rodriguez	6.00
(107)	Ivan Rodriguez (900)	20.00
(108)	Scott Rolen	25.00
(109)	Kirk Rueter	5.00
(110)	Ryne Sandberg	35.00
(111)	Gary Sheffield (400)	25.00
(112)	Dwight Smith	5.00
(113)	J.T. Snow	7.50
(114)	Scott Spiezio	5.00
(115)	Shannon Stewart	5.00
(116)	Jeff Suppan	5.00
(117)	Mike Sweeney	5.00
(118)	Miguel Tejada	7.50
(119)	Frank Thomas (400)	75.00
(120)	Jim Thome (900)	15.00
(120)	Jim Thome (Exchange card)	5.00
(121)	Justin Thompson	5.00
(122)	Brett Tomko	5.00
(123)	Bubba Trammell	9.00
(124)	Michael Tucker	5.00
(125)	Javier Valentin	5.00
(126)	Mo Vaughn	15.00
(127)	Robin Ventura	12.50
(128)	Terrell Wade	5.00
(129)	Billy Wagner	12.50
(130)	Larry Walker	15.00
(131)	Todd Walker	9.00
(132)	Rondell White	7.50
(133)	Kevin Wickander	5.00
(134)	Chris Widger	5.00
(135)	Bernie Williams (400)	25.00
(136)	Matt Williams	15.00
(137)	Antone Williamson	5.00
(138)	Dan Wilson	5.00
(139)	Tony Womack	5.00
(140)	Jaret Wright	9.00
(141)	Dmitri Young	5.00
(142)	Eric Young	6.00
(143)	Kevin Young	5.00

1997 Donruss Signature Century Marks (Blue)

Only the top-name stars and rookies from the Signature series autograph line-up are included in the top level of scarcity. Virtually identical to the more common red and green (Millenium) versions, the Century Marks are identifiable at first glance by the use of blue ink in the background of the front photo and the "Century Marks" designation at top. On back, the cards are numbered from 0001 through 0100 in metallic foil at center. Several players initially had to be represented in the set by exchange cards. The unnumbered cards are checklisted here alphabetically, with the assigned card numbered keyed to the full 143-card issue in green.

		MT
Common Player:		20.00
(4)	Roberto Alomar	50.00
(9)	Jeff Bagwell	75.00
(11)	Albert Belle	60.00
(14)	Wade Boggs	50.00
(15)	Barry Bonds	75.00
(19)	Jay Buhner	20.00
(24)	Tony Clark	25.00
(25)	Will Clark	50.00
(26)	Roger Clemens	150.00
(32)	Jose Cruz Jr.	25.00
(37)	Jim Edmonds	20.00
(38)	Darin Erstad	30.00
(42)	Andres Galarraga	35.00
(44)	Nomar Garciaparra (SP)	200.00
(48)	Juan Gonzalez	80.00
(53)	Ben Grieve	40.00
(55)	Vladimir Guerrero	75.00
(57)	Jose Guillen	25.00
(58)	Tony Gwynn	150.00
(60)	Todd Helton	50.00
(64)	Derek Jeter	150.00
(65)	Andruw Jones	50.00
(67)	Chipper Jones	150.00
(69)	David Justice	30.00
(74)	Ryan Klesko	25.00
(75)	Chuck Knoblauch	30.00
(76)	Paul Konerko	20.00
(77)	Mark Kotsay	20.00
(79)	Barry Larkin	30.00
(83)	Greg Maddux	150.00
(84)	Edgar Martinez	20.00
(85)	Pedro Martinez	60.00
(86)	Tino Martinez	25.00
(88)	Raul Mondesi	35.00
(88)	Raul Mondesi (Exchange card)	5.00
(90)	Eddie Murray	40.00
(90)	Eddie Murray (Exchange card)	5.00
(91)	Mike Mussina	35.00
(95)	Rafael Palmeiro	40.00
(98)	Andy Pettitte	25.00
(99)	Manny Ramirez	60.00
(104)	Cal Ripken Jr.	200.00
(105)	Alex Rodriguez	175.00
(107)	Ivan Rodriguez	75.00
(108)	Scott Rolen	50.00
(110)	Ryne Sandberg	75.00
(111)	Gary Sheffield	35.00
(118)	Miguel Tejada	30.00
(119)	Frank Thomas	75.00
(120)	Jim Thome	35.00
(120)	Jim Thome (Exchange card)	5.00
(126)	Mo Vaughn	40.00
(130)	Larry Walker	40.00
(135)	Bernie Williams	40.00
(136)	Matt Williams	30.00
(140)	Jaret Wright	20.00

1997 Donruss Signature Notable Nicknames

Current and former players whose nicknames are instantly recognized are featured in this Signature Series insert. The autographs are generally enhanced by the appearance of those nicknames, though Roger Clemens omitted "The Rocket" from many of his cards. Backs have a serial number from within an edition of 200 of each card.

		MT
Complete Set (13):		950.00
Common Player:		50.00
(1)	Ernie Banks (Mr. Cub)	100.00
(2)	Tony Clark (The Tiger)	50.00
(3)	Roger Clemens (The Rocket)	150.00
(4)	Reggie Jackson (Mr. October)	125.00
(5)	Randy Johnson (Big Unit)	100.00
(6)	Stan Musial (The Man)	150.00
(7)	Ivan Rodriguez (Pudge)	100.00
(8)	Frank Thomas (The Big Hurt)	125.00
(9)	Mo Vaughn (Hit Dog)	100.00
(10)	Billy Wagner (The Kid)	50.00

1997 Donruss Signature Significant Signatures

Retired superstars from the early 1960s through the mid 1990s are featured in this insert series. Cards are horizontal in format with color photos on front and back.

Generally autographed on front, each card is serially numbered on back from within an edition of 2,000. The unnumbered cards are listed here in alphabetical order.

		MT
Complete Set (22):		850.00
Common Player:		15.00
(1)	Ernie Banks	50.00
(2)	Johnny Bench	60.00
(3)	Yogi Berra	50.00
(4)	George Brett	75.00
(5)	Lou Brock	30.00
(6)	Rod Carew	30.00
(7)	Steve Carlton	30.00
(8)	Larry Doby	30.00
(9)	Carlton Fisk	35.00
(10)	Bob Gibson	30.00
(11)	Reggie Jackson	60.00
(12)	Al Kaline	30.00
(13)	Harmon Killebrew	30.00
(14)	Don Mattingly	75.00
(15)	Stan Musial	75.00
(16)	Jim Palmer	30.00
(17)	Brooks Robinson	40.00
(18)	Frank Robinson	30.00
(19)	Mike Schmidt	75.00
(20)	Tom Seaver	40.00
(21)	Duke Snider	30.00
(22)	Carl Yastrzemski	50.00

1997 Donruss VXP 1.0 CDs

One of the earliest attempts to bring baseball cards into the computer age was Donruss "VXP 1.0 CD ROM" trading cards. Retailed, with 10 special-series player cards for about $10, the 4" x 2-3/4" "card" is a CD with player portrait and action photos on front. The CD was sold in a cardboard folder with the player's picture on front and instructions for use inside. CDs feature player stats, action footage and other interactive elements.

		MT
Complete Set (6):		25.00
Common Player:		4.00
(1)	Ken Griffey Jr.	6.00
(2)	Greg Maddux	4.00
(3)	Mike Piazza	4.00
(4)	Cal Ripken Jr.	5.00
(5)	Alex Rodriguez	5.00
(6)	Frank Thomas	4.00

1997 Donruss VXP 1.0

This set was issued to accompany the hobby's first major effort to bring baseball cards into the computer age. The standard-format cards have motion-variable portrait and action photos on front and another photo on back. Cards were sold in packs of 10 with one of six CD ROMs for about $10.

		MT
Complete Set (50):		35.00
Common Player:		.50
1	Darin Erstad	1.50
2	Jim Thome	.50
3	Alex Rodriguez	2.50
4	Greg Maddux	2.00
5	Scott Rolen	1.50
6	Roberto Alomar	.50
7	Tony Clark	.50
8	Randy Johnson	.75
9	Sammy Sosa	2.00
10	Jose Guillen	.50
11	Cal Ripken Jr.	3.00
12	Paul Molitor	1.50
13	Jose Cruz Jr.	.50
14	Barry Larkin	.50
15	Ken Caminiti	.50
16	Rafael Palmeiro	.75
17	Chuck Knoblauch	.50
18	Juan Gonzalez	1.50
19	Larry Walker	.75
20	Tony Gwynn	1.75
21	Brady Anderson	.50
22	Derek Jeter	2.00
23	Rusty Greer	.50
24	Gary Sheffield	.50
25	Barry Bonds	1.50
26	Mo Vaughn	.75
27	Tino Martinez	.50
28	Ivan Rodriguez	.75
29	Jeff Bagwell	.75
30	Tim Salmon	.50
31	Nomar Garciaparra	1.75
32	Bernie Williams	.50
33	Kenny Lofton	.50
34	Mike Piazza	2.00
35	Jim Edmonds	.50
36	Frank Thomas	2.00
37	Andy Pettitte	.50
38	Andruw Jones	1.50
39	Raul Mondesi	.75
40	John Smoltz	.50
41	Albert Belle	.75
42	Mark McGwire	5.00
43	Chipper Jones	2.50
44	Hideo Nomo	.60
45	David Justice	.50
46	Manny Ramirez	.75
47	Ken Griffey Jr.	5.00
48	Roger Clemens	1.50
49	Vladimir Guerrero	1.50
50	Ryne Sandberg	1.00

1998 Donruss

This 170-card set includes 155 regular player cards, the 10-card Fan Club subset and five checklists. The cards have color photos and the player's name listed at the bottom. The backs have a horizontal layout with stats and a biography on the left and another photo on the right. The base set is paralleled twice. Silver Press Proofs is a silver foil and die-cut parallel numbered "1 of 1,500." Gold Press Proofs is die-cut, has gold foil and is numbered "1 of 500." The inserts are Crusade, Diamond Kings, Longball Leaders, Production Line and Rated Rookies.

		MT
Complete Set (420):		45.00
Complete Series 1 (170):		20.00
Complete Update 2 (250):		25.00
Common Player:		.10
Unlisted Stars:		.30 to .60
Silver Press Proofs:		6-12X
Production 1,500 sets		
Gold Press Proof Stars:		20-40X
Gold Young Stars/RCs:		12-25X
Production 500 sets		
Pack (10):		1.75
Wax Box (24):		35.00
1	Paul Molitor	.50
2	Juan Gonzalez	.75
3	Darryl Kile	.10
4	Randy Johnson	.40
5	Tom Glavine	.20
6	Pat Hentgen	.10
7	David Justice	.25
8	Kevin Brown	.15
9	Mike Mussina	.60
10	Ken Caminiti	.20
11	Todd Hundley	.20
12	Frank Thomas	1.50
13	Ray Lankford	.10
14	Justin Thompson	.10
15	Jason Dickson	.10
16	Kenny Lofton	.75
17	Ivan Rodriguez	.60
18	Pedro Martinez	.40
19	Brady Anderson	.20
20	Barry Larkin	.20
21	Chipper Jones	2.00
22	Tony Gwynn	1.50
23	Roger Clemens	1.00
24	Sandy Alomar Jr.	.15
25	Tino Martinez	.20
26	Jeff Bagwell	1.25
27	Shawn Estes	.10
28	Ken Griffey Jr.	3.00
29	Javier Lopez	.20
30	Denny Neagle	.10
31	Mike Piazza	2.00
32	Andres Galarraga	.20
33	Larry Walker	.25
34	Alex Rodriguez	2.50
35	Greg Maddux	1.50
36	Albert Belle	.75
37	Barry Bonds	.75
38	Mo Vaughn	.75
39	Kevin Appier	.10
40	Wade Boggs	.30
41	Garret Anderson	.10
42	Jeffrey Hammonds	.10
43	Marquis Grissom	.10
44	Jim Edmonds	.10
45	Brian Jordan	.10
46	Raul Mondesi	.20
47	John Valentin	.10
48	Brad Radke	.10
49	Ismael Valdes	.10
50	Matt Stairs	.10
51	Matt Williams	.20
52	Reggie Jefferson	.10
53	Alan Benes	.10
54	Charles Johnson	.10
55	Chuck Knoblauch	.25
56	Edgar Martinez	.10
57	Nomar Garciaparra	1.75
58	Craig Biggio	.20
59	Bernie Williams	.50
60	David Cone	.20
61	Cal Ripken Jr.	2.50
62	Mark McGwire	4.00
63	Roberto Alomar	.50
64	Fred McGriff	.20
65	Eric Karros	.10
66	Robin Ventura	.15
67	Darin Erstad	.75
68	Michael Tucker	.10
69	Jim Thome	.40
70	Mark Grace	.25
71	Lou Collier	.10
72	Karim Garcia	.20
73	Alex Fernandez	.10
74	J.T. Snow	.10
75	Reggie Sanders	.10
76	John Smoltz	.10
77	Tim Salmon	.25
78	Paul O'Neill	.20
79	Vinny Castilla	.10
80	Rafael Palmeiro	.20
81	Jaret Wright	.75
82	Jay Buhner	.20
83	Brett Butler	.10
84	Todd Greene	.10
85	Scott Rolen	1.50
86	Sammy Sosa	2.00
87	Jason Giambi	.10
88	Carlos Delgado	.40
89	Deion Sanders	.15
90	Wilton Guerrero	.10
91	Andy Pettitte	.50
92	Brian Giles	.10
93	Dmitri Young	.10
94	Ron Coomer	.10
95	Mike Cameron	.10
96	Edgardo Alfonzo	.20
97	Jimmy Key	.10
98	Ryan Klesko	.20
99	Andy Benes	.10
100	Derek Jeter	1.75
101	Jeff Fassero	.10
102	Neifi Perez	.10
103	Hideo Nomo	.35
104	Andruw Jones	1.50
105	Todd Helton	.75
106	Livan Hernandez	.15
107	Brett Tomko	.10
108	Shannon Stewart	.10
109	Bartolo Colon	.10
110	Matt Morris	.10
111	Miguel Tejada	.50
112	Pokey Reese	.10
113	Fernando Tatis	.25
114	Todd Dunwoody	.10
115	Jose Cruz Jr.	.25
116	Chan Ho Park	.10
117	Kevin Young	.10
118	Rickey Henderson	.20
119	Hideki Irabu	.75
120	Francisco Cordova	.10
121	Al Martin	.10
122	Tony Clark	.30
123	Curt Schilling	.15
124	Rusty Greer	.10
125	Jose Canseco	.25

No.	Player	Value
126	Edgar Renteria	.10
127	Todd Walker	.20
128	Wally Joyner	.10
129	Bill Mueller	.10
130	Jose Guillen	.40
131	Manny Ramirez	.75
132	Bobby Higginson	.10
133	Kevin Orie	.10
134	Will Clark	.20
135	Dave Nilsson	.10
136	Jason Kendall	.10
137	Ivan Cruz	.10
138	Gary Sheffield	.25
139	Bubba Trammell	.20
140	Vladimir Guerrero	1.50
141	Dennis Reyes	.10
142	Bobby Bonilla	.15
143	Ruben Rivera	.10
144	Ben Grieve	.75
145	Moises Alou	.20
146	Tony Womack	.10
147	Eric Young	.10
148	Paul Konerko	.75
149	Dante Bichette	.20
150	Joe Carter	.15
151	Rondell White	.20
152	Chris Holt	.10
153	Shawn Green	.25
154	Mark Grudzielanek	.10
155	Jermaine Dye	.10
156	Ken Griffey Jr. (Fan Club)	1.50
157	Frank Thomas (Fan Club)	.75
158	Chipper Jones (Fan Club)	1.00
159	Mike Piazza (Fan Club)	1.00
160	Cal Ripken Jr. (Fan Club)	1.25
161	Greg Maddux (Fan Club)	1.00
162	Juan Gonzalez (Fan Club)	.40
163	Alex Rodriguez (Fan Club)	1.25
164	Mark McGwire (Fan Club)	1.50
165	Derek Jeter (Fan Club)	1.00
166	Larry Walker CL	.20
167	Tony Gwynn CL	.75
168	Tino Martinez CL	.15
169	Scott Rolen CL	.75
170	Nomar Garciaparra CL	1.00
171	Mike Sweeney	.10
172	Dustin Hermanson	.10
173	Darren Dreifort	.10
174	Ron Gant	.20
175	Todd Hollandsworth	.10
176	John Jaha	.10
177	Kerry Wood	.50
178	Chris Stynes	.10
179	Kevin Elster	.10
180	Derek Bell	.10
181	Darryl Strawberry	.20
182	Damion Easley	.10
183	Jeff Cirillo	.10
184	John Thomson	.10
185	Dan Wilson	.10
186	Jay Bell	.10
187	Bernard Gilkey	.10
188	Marc Valdes	.10
189	Ramon Martinez	.20
190	Charles Nagy	.10
191	Derek Lowe	.10
192	Andy Benes	.10
193	Delino DeShields	.10
194	*Ryan Jackson*	.40
195	Kenny Lofton	.75
196	Chuck Knoblauch	.25
197	Andres Galarraga	.25
198	Jose Canseco	.25
199	John Olerud	.25
200	Lance Johnson	.10
201	Darryl Kile	.10
202	Luis Castillo	.10
203	Joe Carter	.15
204	Dennis Eckersley	.20
205	Steve Finley	.10
206	Esteban Loaiza	.10
207	*Ryan Christenson*	.25
208	Deivi Cruz	.10
209	Mariano Rivera	.15
210	*Mike Judd*	.25
211	Billy Wagner	.15
212	Scott Spiezio	.10
213	Russ Davis	.10
214	Jeff Suppan	.10
215	Doug Glanville	.10
216	Dmitri Young	.10
217	Rey Ordonez	.10
218	Cecil Fielder	.15
219	*Masato Yoshii*	.50
220	Raul Casanova	.10
221	*Rolando Arrojo*	.40
222	Ellis Burks	.10
223	Butch Huskey	.10
224	Brian Hunter	.10
225	Marquis Grissom	.10
226	Kevin Brown	.15
227	Joe Randa	.10
228	Henry Rodriguez	.10
229	Omar Vizquel	.10
230	Fred McGriff	.25
231	Matt Williams	.25
232	Moises Alou	.20
233	Travis Fryman	.20
234	Wade Boggs	.35
235	Pedro Martinez	.65
236	Rickey Henderson	.25
237	Bubba Trammell	.10
238	Mike Caruso	.20
239	Wilson Alvarez	.10
240	Geronimo Berroa	.10
241	Eric Milton	.10
242	Scott Erickson	.10
243	*Todd Erdos*	.20
244	Bobby Hughes	.10
245	Dave Hollins	.10
246	Dean Palmer	.10
247	Carlos Baerga	.10
248	Jose Silva	.10
249	*Jose Cabrera*	.20
250	Tom Evans	.10
251	Marty Cordova	.10
252	*Hanley Frias*	.20
253	Javier Valentin	.10
254	Mario Valdez	.10
255	Joey Cora	.10
256	Mike Lansing	.10
257	Jeff Kent	.10
258	*David Dellucci*	.50
259	*Curtis King*	.10
260	David Segui	.10
261	Royce Clayton	.10
262	Jeff Blauser	.10
263	*Manny Aybar*	.25
264	*Mike Cather*	.20
265	Todd Zeile	.10
266	Richard Hidalgo	.10
267	Dante Powell	.10
268	*Mike DeJean*	.10
269	Ken Cloude	.10
270	Danny Klassen	.20
271	Sean Casey	.25
272	A.J. Hinch	.50
273	*Rich Butler*	.25
274	*Ben Ford*	.10
275	Billy McMillon	.10
276	Wilson Delgado	.10
277	Orlando Cabrera	.10
278	Geoff Jenkins	.10
279	Enrique Wilson	.10
280	Derrek Lee	.10
281	*Marc Pisciotta*	.10
282	Abraham Nunez	.20
283	Aaron Boone	.10
284	Brad Fullmer	.20
285	*Rob Stanifer*	.25
286	Preston Wilson	.10
287	Greg Norton	.10
288	Bobby Smith	.10
289	Josh Booty	.10
290	Russell Branyan	.10
291	Jeremi Gonzalez	.10
292	Michael Coleman	.10
293	Cliff Politte	.10
294	Eric Ludwick	.10
295	Rafael Medina	.10
296	Jason Varitek	.10
297	Ron Wright	.10
298	Mark Kotsay	.25
299	David Ortiz	.15
300	*Frank Catalanotto*	.20
301	Robinson Checo	.10
302	*Kevin Millwood*	2.50
303	Jacob Cruz	.10
304	Javier Vazquez	.10
305	*Magglio Ordonez*	1.50
306	Kevin Witt	.10
307	Derrick Gibson	.10
308	Shane Monahan	.10
309	Brian Rose	.10
310	Bobby Estalella	.10
311	Felix Heredia	.10
312	Desi Relaford	.10
313	*Esteban Yan*	.20
314	Ricky Ledee	.25
315	*Steve Woodard*	.25
316	Pat Watkins	.10
317	Damian Moss	.10
318	Bob Abreu	.10
319	Jeff Abbott	.10
320	Miguel Cairo	.10
321	*Rigo Beltran*	.10
322	Tony Saunders	.10
323	Randall Simon	.25
324	Hiram Bocachica	.10
325	Richie Sexson	.10
326	Karim Garcia	.10
327	*Mike Lowell*	.40
328	Pat Cline	.10
329	Matt Clement	.10
330	Scott Elarton	.10
331	*Manuel Barrios*	.10
332	Bruce Chen	.40
333	Juan Encarnacion	.10
334	Travis Lee	.75
335	Wes Helms	.10
336	*Chad Fox*	.10
337	Donnie Sadler	.10
338	*Carlos Mendoza*	.35
339	Damian Jackson	.10
340	*Julio Ramirez*	.40
341	*John Halama*	.30
342	Edwin Diaz	.10
343	Felix Martinez	.10
344	Eli Marrero	.10
345	Carl Pavano	.10
346	Vladimir Guerrero (Hit List)	.75
347	Barry Bonds (Hit List)	.40
348	Darin Erstad (Hit List)	.40
349	Albert Belle (Hit List)	.40
350	Kenny Lofton (Hit List)	.40
351	Mo Vaughn (Hit List)	.40
352	Jose Cruz Jr. (Hit List)	.25
353	Tony Clark (Hit List)	.25
354	Roberto Alomar (Hit List)	.25
355	Manny Ramirez (Hit List)	.50
356	Paul Molitor (Hit List)	.25
357	Jim Thome (Hit List)	.25
358	Tino Martinez (Hit List)	.20
359	Tim Salmon (Hit List)	.20
360	David Justice (Hit List)	.20
361	Raul Mondesi (Hit List)	.10
362	Mark Grace (Hit List)	.10
363	Craig Biggio (Hit List)	.10
364	Larry Walker (Hit List)	.10
365	Mark McGwire (Hit List)	1.50
366	Juan Gonzalez (Hit List)	.40
367	Derek Jeter (Hit List)	.75
368	Chipper Jones (Hit List)	1.00
369	Frank Thomas (Hit List)	.50
370	Alex Rodriguez (Hit List)	1.00
371	Mike Piazza (Hit List)	1.00
372	Tony Gwynn (Hit List)	.75
373	Jeff Bagwell (Hit List)	.50
374	Nomar Garciaparra (Hit List)	1.00
375	Ken Griffey Jr. (Hit List)	1.50
376	Livan Hernandez (Untouchables)	.10
377	Chan Ho Park (Untouchables)	.10
378	Mike Mussina (Untouchables)	.25
379	Andy Pettitte (Untouchables)	.25
380	Greg Maddux (Untouchables)	1.00
381	Hideo Nomo (Untouchables)	.25
382	Roger Clemens (Untouchables)	.75
383	Randy Johnson (Untouchables)	.25
384	Pedro Martinez (Untouchables)	.25
385	Jaret Wright (Untouchables)	.40
386	Ken Griffey Jr. (Spirit of the Game)	1.50
387	Todd Helton (Spirit of the Game)	.40
388	Paul Konerko (Spirit of the Game)	.10
389	Cal Ripken Jr. (Spirit of the Game)	1.25
390	Larry Walker (Spirit of the Game)	.10
391	Ken Caminiti (Spirit of the Game)	.10
392	Jose Guillen (Spirit of the Game)	.10
393	Jim Edmonds (Spirit of the Game)	.10
394	Barry Larkin (Spirit of the Game)	.10
395	Bernie Williams (Spirit of the Game)	.25
396	Tony Clark (Spirit of the Game)	.20
397	Jose Cruz Jr. (Spirit of the Game)	.25
398	Ivan Rodriguez (Spirit of the Game)	.40
399	Darin Erstad (Spirit of the Game)	.40
400	Scott Rolen (Spirit of the Game)	.50
401	Mark McGwire (Spirit of the Game)	1.50
402	Andruw Jones (Spirit of the Game)	.40
403	Juan Gonzalez (Spirit of the Game)	.40
404	Derek Jeter (Spirit of the Game)	.75
405	Chipper Jones (Spirit of the Game)	1.00
406	Greg Maddux (Spirit of the Game)	1.00
407	Frank Thomas (Spirit of the Game)	.50
408	Alex Rodriguez (Spirit of the Game)	1.00
409	Mike Piazza (Spirit of the Game)	1.00
410	Tony Gwynn (Spirit of the Game)	.75
411	Jeff Bagwell (Spirit of the Game)	.50
412	Nomar Garciaparra (Spirit of the Game)	1.00
413	Hideo Nomo (Spirit of the Game)	.25
414	Barry Bonds (Spirit of the Game)	.40
415	Ben Grieve (Spirit of the Game)	.50
416	Checklis (Barry Bonds)	.25
417	Checklist (Mark McGwire)	1.00
418	Checklist (Roger Clemens)	.40
419	Checklis t (Livan Hernandez)	.10
420	Checklist (Ken Griffey Jr.)	1.00

1998 Donruss Crusade

This 100-card insert was included in 1998 Donruss (40 cards), Leaf (30) and Donruss Update (30). The cards use refractive technology and the background features heraldic-style lions. The cards are sequentially numbered to 250. Crusade Purple (numbered to 100) and Red (25) parallels were also inserted in the three products.

		MT
Complete Set (40):		600.00
Common Player:		5.00
Production 250 sets		
Purples:		1.5X
Production 100 sets		
Reds:		4-6X
Production 25 sets		
5	Jason Dickson	5.00
6	Todd Greene	10.00
7	Roberto Alomar	15.00
8	Cal Ripken Jr.	75.00
12	Mo Vaughn	20.00
13	Nomar Garciaparra	45.00
16	Mike Cameron	7.50
20	Sandy Alomar Jr.	10.00
21	David Justice	12.50
25	Justin Thompson	5.00
27	Kevin Appier	5.00
33	Tino Martinez	10.00
36	Hideki Irabu	7.50
37	Jose Canseco	12.50
39	Ken Griffey Jr.	100.00
42	Edgar Martinez	5.00
45	Will Clark	12.50
47	Rusty Greer	5.00
50	Shawn Green	17.50
51	Jose Cruz Jr.	7.50
52	Kenny Lofton	15.00
53	Chipper Jones	45.00
62	Kevin Orie	5.00
65	Deion Sanders	7.50
67	Larry Walker	15.00
68	Dante Bichette	7.50
71	Todd Helton	20.00
74	Bobby Bonilla	7.50
75	Kevin Brown	10.00
78	Craig Biggio	10.00
82	Wilton Guerrero	5.00
85	Pedro Martinez	20.00
86	Edgardo Alfonzo	7.50
88	Scott Rolen	35.00
89	Francisco Cordova	5.00
90	Jose Guillen	10.00
92	Ray Lankford	5.00
93	Mark McGwire	125.00
94	Matt Morris	7.50
100	Shawn Estes	5.00

1998 Donruss Diamond Kings

Diamond Kings is a 20-card insert featuring a painted portrait by Dan Gardiner of the player on the card front. The backs have a ghosted image of the portrait with a player biography and the card's number overprinted. A total of 10,000 sets were produced with the first 500 of each card printed on canvas. A Frank Thomas sample card was also created.

		MT
Complete Set (20):		150.00
Common Player:		4.00
Production 9,500 sets		
Canvas (1st 500 sets):		2-4X
1	Cal Ripken Jr.	20.00
2	Greg Maddux	12.50
3	Ivan Rodriguez	7.50
4	Tony Gwynn	10.00
5	Paul Molitor	5.00
6	Kenny Lofton	5.00
7	Andy Pettitte	4.00
8	Darin Erstad	7.50
9	Randy Johnson	5.00
10	Derek Jeter	15.00
11	Hideo Nomo	4.00
12	David Justice	4.00
13	Bernie Williams	4.00
14	Roger Clemens	9.00
15	Barry Larkin	4.00
16	Andruw Jones	7.50
17	Mike Piazza	15.00
18	Frank Thomas	12.50
19	Alex Rodriguez	20.00
20	Ken Griffey Jr.	25.00

1998 Donruss Longball Leaders

Longball Leaders features 24 top home run hitters. The right border features a home run meter with zero at the bottom, 61 at the top and the player's 1997 home run total marked. Each card is sequentially numbered to 5,000.

		MT
Complete Set (24):		125.00
Common Player:		1.00
Production 5,000 sets		
1	Ken Griffey Jr.	20.00
2	Mark McGwire	20.00
3	Tino Martinez	1.00
4	Barry Bonds	3.50
5	Frank Thomas	7.50
6	Albert Belle	2.00
7	Mike Piazza	10.00
8	Chipper Jones	10.00
9	Vladimir Guerrero	5.00
10	Matt Williams	1.50
11	Sammy Sosa	9.00
12	Tim Salmon	1.00
13	Raul Mondesi	1.00
14	Jeff Bagwell	5.00
15	Mo Vaughn	3.00
16	Manny Ramirez	4.00
17	Jim Thome	2.00
18	Jim Edmonds	1.00
19	Tony Clark	2.00
20	Nomar Garciaparra	9.00
21	Juan Gonzalez	5.00
22	Scott Rolen	4.00
23	Larry Walker	4.00
24	Andres Galarraga	1.00

1998 Donruss Production Line-ob

This 20-card insert is printed on holographic foil board. Inserted in magazine packs, this insert features player's with a high on-base percentage in 1997. Each player's card is sequentially numbered to his on-base percentage from that season. The card back has a player photo and a list of the 20 players with their stat.

		MT
Complete Set (20):		500.00
Common Player:		7.50
1	Frank Thomas (456)	40.00
2	Edgar Martinez (456)	7.50
3	Barry Bonds (446)	20.00
4	Barry Larkin (440)	7.50
5	Mike Piazza (431)	70.00
6	Jeff Bagwell (425)	40.00
7	Gary Sheffield (424)	10.00
8	Mo Vaughn (420)	15.00
9	Craig Biggio (415)	10.00
10	Kenny Lofton (409)	15.00
11	Tony Gwynn (409)	50.00
12	Bernie Williams (408)	15.00
13	Rusty Greer (405)	7.50
14	Brady Anderson (393)	7.50
15	Mark McGwire (393)	100.00
16	Chuck Knoblauch (390)	12.50
17	Roberto Alomar (390)	15.00
18	Ken Griffey Jr. (382)	100.00
19	Chipper Jones (371)	70.00
20	Derek Jeter (370)	65.00

1998 Donruss Production Line-pi

This 20-card insert was printed on holographic board. The set features players with a high power index from 1997. Each card is sequentially numbered to that player's power index from that season.

		MT
Complete Set (20):		300.00
Common Player:		5.00
1	Larry Walker (1,172)	9.00
2	Mike Piazza (1,070)	30.00
3	Frank Thomas (1,067)	25.00
4	Mark McGwire (1,039)	50.00
5	Barry Bonds (1,031)	12.50
6	Ken Griffey Jr. (1,028)	50.00
7	Jeff Bagwell (1,017)	20.00
8	David Justice (1,013)	5.00
9	Jim Thome (1,001)	7.50
10	Mo Vaughn (980)	6.00
11	Tony Gwynn (957)	25.00
12	Manny Ramirez (953)	12.50
13	Bernie Williams (952)	7.50
14	Tino Martinez (948)	5.00
15	Brady Anderson (863)	5.00
16	Chipper Jones (850)	30.00
17	Scott Rolen (846)	15.00
18	Alex Rodriguez (846)	40.00
19	Vladimir Guerrero (833)	15.00
20	Albert Belle (823)	12.50

1998 Donruss Production Line-sg

This 20-card insert was printed on holographic board. It featured players with high slugging percentages in 1997. Each card is sequentially numbered to the player's slugging percentage from that season.

		MT
Complete Set (20):		400.00
Common Player:		7.50
1	Larry Walker (720)	10.00
2	Ken Griffey Jr. (646)	75.00
3	Mark McGwire (646)	75.00
4	Mike Piazza (638)	45.00
5	Frank Thomas (611)	35.00
6	Jeff Bagwell (592)	30.00
7	Juan Gonzalez (589)	25.00
8	Andres Galarraga (585)	7.50
9	Barry Bonds (585)	20.00
10	Jim Thome (579)	7.50
11	Tino Martinez (577)	7.50
12	Mo Vaughn (560)	10.00
13	Raul Mondesi (541)	7.50
14	Manny Ramirez (538)	17.50
15	Nomar Garciaparra (534)	40.00
16	Tim Salmon (517)	7.50
17	Tony Clark (500)	7.50
18	Jose Cruz Jr. (499)	7.50
19	Alex Rodriguez (496)	60.00
20	Cal Ripken Jr. (402)	55.00

1998 Donruss Rated Rookies

This 30-card insert features top young players. The fronts have a color player photo in front of a stars and stripes background, with "Rated Rookies" and the player's name printed on the right. The backs have another photo, basic player information and career highlights. A rare (250 each) Medalist version is microetched on gold holographic foil.

		MT
Complete Set (30):		35.00
Common Player:		1.00
Medalists (250 sets):		5-10X
1	Mark Kotsay	2.00
2	Neifi Perez	1.00
3	Paul Konerko	2.00
4	Jose Cruz Jr.	1.50
5	Hideki Irabu	1.25
6	Mike Cameron	1.00
7	Jeff Suppan	1.00
8	Kevin Orie	1.00
9	Pokey Reese	1.00
10	Todd Dunwoody	1.00
11	Miguel Tejada	2.00
12	Jose Guillen	1.50
13	Bartolo Colon	1.00
14	Derrek Lee	1.00
15	Antone Williamson	1.00
16	Wilton Guerrero	1.00
17	Jaret Wright	2.00
18	Todd Helton	2.00
19	Shannon Stewart	1.00
20	Nomar Garciaparra	7.50
21	Brett Tomko	1.00
22	Fernando Tatis	2.00
23	Raul Ibanez	1.00
24	Dennis Reyes	1.00
25	Bobby Estalella	1.00
26	Lou Collier	1.00
27	Bubba Trammell	1.00
28	Ben Grieve	2.50
29	Ivan Cruz	1.00
30	Karim Garcia	1.50

1998 Donruss Update Crusade

This 30-card insert is continued from 1998 Donruss and Leaf baseball sets. Each card features a color action photo in front of a Medieval background. The player's name and background are green and each card is serial numbered to 250. Purple (numbered to 100) and Red (25) parallel versions were also created. Crusade is a 130-card cross-brand insert with 40 cards included in 1998 Donruss and 30 each in 1998 Leaf and Leaf Rookies & Stars.

		MT
Complete Set (30):		400.00
Common Player:		5.00
Production 250 sets		
Purples (100 sets):		1.5X
Reds (25 sets):		4-6X
1	Tim Salmon	8.00
2	Garret Anderson	5.00
9	Rafael Palmeiro	15.00
10	Brady Anderson	5.00
14	Frank Thomas	40.00
17	Robin Ventura	10.00
22	Matt Williams	10.00
23	Tony Clark	8.00
29	Chuck Knoblauch	10.00
31	Bernie Williams	20.00
32	Derek Jeter	75.00
38	Jason Giambi	5.00
43	Jay Buhner	7.50
44	Juan Gonzalez	25.00
49	Carlos Delgado	20.00
55	Greg Maddux	60.00
57	Tom Glavine	9.00
60	Mark Grace	12.50
61	Sammy Sosa	60.00
63	Barry Larkin	12.00
69	Neifi Perez	5.00
72	Gary Sheffield	10.00
77	Jeff Bagwell	30.00
80	Raul Mondesi	7.50
81	Hideo Nomo	7.50
83	Rondell White	7.50
84	Vladimir Guerrero	35.00
87	Todd Hundley	5.00
96	Brian Jordan	5.00
99	Barry Bonds	25.00

1998 Donruss Update Dominators

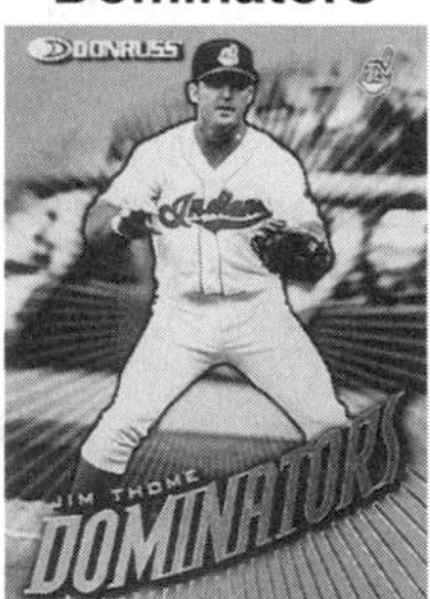

This 30-card insert features color player photos and holographic foil.

		MT
Complete Set (30):		100.00
Common Player:		1.25
Approx: 1:12		
1	Roger Clemens	5.00
2	Tony Clark	1.50
3	Darin Erstad	3.00
4	Jeff Bagwell	5.00
5	Ken Griffey Jr.	12.50
6	Andruw Jones	3.00
7	Juan Gonzalez	3.00
8	Ivan Rodriguez	3.00
9	Randy Johnson	2.00
10	Tino Martinez	1.50
11	Mark McGwire	12.50
12	Chuck Knoblauch	1.50
13	Jim Thome	1.50
14	Alex Rodriguez	10.00
15	Hideo Nomo	1.50
16	Jose Cruz Jr.	1.50
17	Chipper Jones	7.50
18	Tony Gwynn	6.00
19	Barry Bonds	3.00
20	Mo Vaughn	1.50
21	Cal Ripken Jr.	10.00
22	Greg Maddux	6.00
23	Manny Ramirez	2.00
24	Andres Galarraga	1.50
25	Vladimir Guerrero	4.00
26	Albert Belle	2.00
27	Nomar Garciaparra	6.00
28	Kenny Lofton	1.50
29	Mike Piazza	7.50
30	Frank Thomas	5.00

1998 Donruss Update Elite

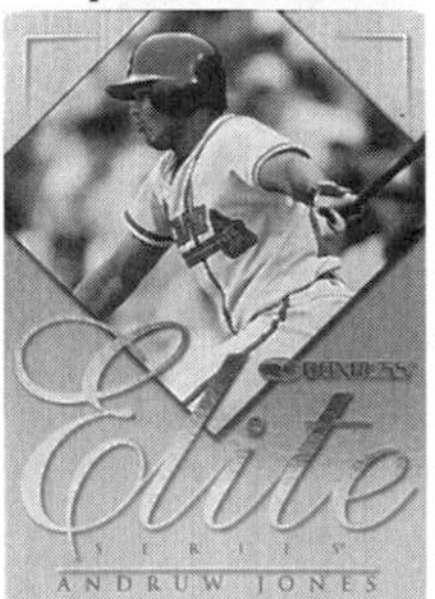

This 20-card insert features color player photos in a diamond-shaped border at the top with the Elite Series logo and player's name at the bottom. The fronts have a cream-colored border. The cards are sequentially numbered to 2,500.

		MT
Complete Set (20):		200.00
Common Player:		2.50
Production 2,500 sets		
1	Jeff Bagwell	10.00
2	Andruw Jones	5.00
3	Ken Griffey Jr.	25.00
4	Derek Jeter	15.00
5	Juan Gonzalez	8.00
6	Mark McGwire	25.00
7	Ivan Rodriguez	7.50
8	Paul Molitor	5.00
9	Hideo Nomo	5.00
10	Mo Vaughn	5.00
11	Chipper Jones	15.00
12	Nomar Garciaparra	12.50
13	Mike Piazza	15.00
14	Frank Thomas	10.00
15	Greg Maddux	12.50
16	Cal Ripken Jr.	20.00
17	Alex Rodriguez	20.00
18	Scott Rolen	7.50
19	Barry Bonds	7.50
20	Tony Gwynn	12.50

1998 Donruss Update FANtasy Team

This 20-card set features the top vote getters from the Donruss online Fan Club ballot box. The top ten make up the 1st Team FANtasy Team and are sequentially numbered to 2,000. The other players are included in the 2nd Team FANtasy Team and are numbered to 4,000. The first 250 cards of each player are die-cut. The front of the cards feature a color photo inside a stars and stripes border.

		MT
Complete Set (20):		250.00
Common Player (1-10) (1,750 sets):		6.00
Common Player (11-20) (3,750 sets):		2.00
Die-Cuts (250 each):		4-6X
1	Frank Thomas	15.00
2	Ken Griffey Jr.	40.00
3	Cal Ripken Jr.	30.00
4	Jose Cruz Jr.	8.00
5	Travis Lee	10.00
6	Greg Maddux	20.00
7	Alex Rodriguez	30.00
8	Mark McGwire	40.00
9	Chipper Jones	25.00
10	Andruw Jones	10.00
11	Mike Piazza	15.00
12	Tony Gwynn	12.00
13	Larry Walker	4.00
14	Nomar Garciaparra	15.00
15	Jaret Wright	6.00
16	Livan Hernandez	4.00
17	Roger Clemens	10.00
18	Derek Jeter	12.50
19	Scott Rolen	8.00
20	Jeff Bagwell	10.00

1998 Donruss Update Rookie Diamond Kings

The Rookie Diamond Kings insert features color portraits by artist Dan Gardiner of young players inside a golden border. Player identification and Rookie Diamond Kings logo are at the bottom. Each card is sequentially numbered to

10,000 with the first 500 printed on canvas.

		MT
Complete Set (12):		60.00
Common Player:		2.00
Production 9,500 sets		
Canvas (500 sets):		3-5X
1	Travis Lee	10.00
2	Fernando Tatis	5.00
3	Livan Hernandez	2.00
4	Todd Helton	10.00
5	Derrek Lee	2.00
6	Jaret Wright	9.00
7	Ben Grieve	10.00
8	Paul Konerko	6.00
9	Jose Cruz Jr.	2.00
10	Mark Kotsay	6.00
11	Todd Greene	2.00
12	Brad Fullmer	6.00

1998 Donruss Update Sony MLB 99

This 20-card set promotes the MLB '99 game for Sony PlayStation systems. The card front has a color player photo with a red border on two sides. The Donruss, PlayStation and MLB '99 logos appear on the front as well. The backs have a MLB '99 Tip and instructions on entering the PlayStation MLB '99 Sweepstakes.

		MT
Complete Set (20):		10.00
Common Player:		.25
1	Cal Ripken Jr.	1.50
2	Nomar Garciaparra	1.20
3	Barry Bonds	.60
4	Mike Mussina	.50
5	Pedro Martinez	.40
6	Derek Jeter	1.25
7	Andruw Jones	.60
8	Kenny Lofton	.50
9	Gary Sheffield	.25
10	Raul Mondesi	.25
11	Jeff Bagwell	.75
12	Tim Salmon	.25
13	Tom Glavine	.25
14	Ben Grieve	.75
15	Matt Williams	.25
16	Juan Gonzalez	.60
17	Mark McGwire	2.00
18	Bernie Williams	.35
19	Andres Galarraga	.25
20	Jose Cruz Jr.	.25

1998 Donruss Elite

Donruss Elite consists of a 150-card base set with two parallels and five inserts. The base cards feature a foil background with player photo on front. Another photo is on the back with stats and basic player information. The Aspirations parallel is numbered to 750 and the Status parallel is numbered to 100. The base set also includes the 30-card Generations subset and three checklists. The inserts are Back to the Future, Back to the Future Autographs, Craftsmen, Prime Numbers and Prime Numbers Die-Cuts.

		MT
Complete Set (150):		25.00
Common Player:		.15
Aspirations (750 sets):		4-8X
Status (100 sets):		30-60X
Pack (5):		5.00
Wax Box (18):		70.00
1	Ken Griffey Jr.	4.00
2	Frank Thomas	2.00
3	Alex Rodriguez	3.00
4	Mike Piazza	2.50
5	Greg Maddux	2.00
6	Cal Ripken Jr.	3.00
7	Chipper Jones	2.50
8	Derek Jeter	2.50
9	Tony Gwynn	2.00
10	Andruw Jones	2.00
11	Juan Gonzalez	1.00
12	Jeff Bagwell	1.50
13	Mark McGwire	4.00
14	Roger Clemens	1.50
15	Albert Belle	.75
16	Barry Bonds	1.00
17	Kenny Lofton	.75
18	Ivan Rodriguez	.75
19	Manny Ramirez	.75
20	Jim Thome	.50
21	Chuck Knoblauch	.40
22	Paul Molitor	.60
23	Barry Larkin	.30
24	Andy Pettitte	.60
25	John Smoltz	.25
26	Randy Johnson	.50
27	Bernie Williams	.75
28	Larry Walker	.30
29	Mo Vaughn	.75
30	Bobby Higginson	.15
31	Edgardo Alfonzo	.20
32	Justin Thompson	.15
33	Jeff Suppan	.15
34	Roberto Alomar	.75
35	Hideo Nomo	.50
36	Rusty Greer	.15
37	Tim Salmon	.30
38	Jim Edmonds	.15
39	Gary Sheffield	.30
40	Ken Caminiti	.25
41	Sammy Sosa	2.50
42	Tony Womack	.15
43	Matt Williams	.30
44	Andres Galarraga	.30
45	Garret Anderson	.15
46	Rafael Palmeiro	.25
47	Mike Mussina	.50
48	Craig Biggio	.25
49	Wade Boggs	.35
50	Tom Glavine	.25
51	Jason Giambi	.15
52	Will Clark	.25
53	David Justice	.25
54	Sandy Alomar Jr.	.20
55	Edgar Martinez	.15
56	Brady Anderson	.20
57	Eric Young	.15
58	Ray Lankford	.15
59	Kevin Brown	.25
60	Raul Mondesi	.30
61	Bobby Bonilla	.20
62	Javier Lopez	.15
63	Fred McGriff	.20
64	Rondell White	.25
65	Todd Hundley	.25
66	Mark Grace	.35
67	Alan Benes	.15
68	Jeff Abbott	.15
69	Bob Abreu	.15
70	Deion Sanders	.20
71	Tino Martinez	.20
72	Shannon Stewart	.15
73	Homer Bush	.15
74	Carlos Delgado	.50
75	Raul Ibanez	.15
76	Hideki Irabu	.75
77	Jose Cruz Jr.	.50
78	Tony Clark	.60
79	Wilton Guerrero	.15
80	Vladimir Guerrero	1.50
81	Scott Rolen	2.00
82	Nomar Garciaparra	2.50
83	Darin Erstad	1.00
84	Chan Ho Park	.25
85	Mike Cameron	.15
86	Todd Walker	.25
87	Todd Dunwoody	.15
88	Neifi Perez	.15
89	Brett Tomko	.15
90	Jose Guillen	.40
91	Matt Morris	.15
92	Bartolo Colon	.15
93	Jaret Wright	1.00
94	Shawn Estes	.15
95	Livan Hernandez	.20
96	Bobby Estalella	.15
97	Ben Grieve	1.50
98	Paul Konerko	1.00
99	David Ortiz	.50
100	Todd Helton	1.00
101	Juan Encarnacion	.30
102	Bubba Trammell	.15
103	Miguel Tejada	.75
104	Jacob Cruz	.15
105	Todd Greene	.15
106	Kevin Orie	.15
107	Mark Kotsay	.60
108	Fernando Tatis	.30
109	Jay Payton	.15
110	Pokey Reese	.15
111	Derrek Lee	.20
112	Richard Hidalgo	.15
113	Ricky Ledee	1.00
114	Lou Collier	.15
115	Ruben Rivera	.15
116	Shawn Green	.25
117	Moises Alou	.25
118	Ken Griffey Jr. (Generations)	2.00
119	Frank Thomas (Generations)	1.00
120	Alex Rodriguez (Generations)	1.50
121	Mike Piazza (Generations)	1.25
122	Greg Maddux (Generations)	1.25
123	Cal Ripken Jr. (Generations)	1.50
124	Chipper Jones (Generations)	1.25
125	Derek Jeter (Generations)	1.25
126	Tony Gwynn (Generations)	1.00
127	Andruw Jones (Generations)	1.00
128	Juan Gonzalez (Generations)	.50
129	Jeff Bagwell (Generations)	.75
130	Mark McGwire (Generations)	2.50
131	Roger Clemens (Generations)	.75
132	Albert Belle (Generations)	.50
133	Barry Bonds (Generations)	.50
134	Kenny Lofton (Generations)	.50
135	Ivan Rodriguez (Generations)	.40
136	Manny Ramirez (Generations)	.40
137	Jim Thome (Generations)	.30
138	Chuck Knoblauch (Generations)	.25
139	Paul Molitor (Generations)	.30
140	Barry Larkin (Generations)	.15
141	Mo Vaughn (Generations)	.50
142	Hideki Irabu (Generations)	.40
143	Jose Cruz Jr. (Generations)	.50
144	Tony Clark (Generations)	.40
145	Vladimir Guerrero (Generations)	.75
146	Scott Rolen (Generations)	1.00
147	Nomar Garciaparra (Generations)	1.25
148	Checklist (Garciaparra) (Hit Streaks)	.75
149	Checklist (Walker) (Long HR-Coors)	.15
150	Checklist (Martinez) (3 HR in game)	.15

1998 Donruss Elite Aspirations

A parallel edition of 750 of each player are found in this die-cut set. Cards have a scalloped treatment cut into the top and sides and red, rather than silver metallic borders. The word "ASPIRATIONS" in printed on front at bottom-right. Backs have the notation "1 of 750".

	MT
Complete Set (150):	550.00
Common Player:	2.00
Stars and rookies:	4-8X

(See 1998 Donruss Elite for checklist and base card values.)

1998 Donruss Elite Status

Just 100 serially numbered cards of each player are found in this die-cut parallel set. Cards have a scalloped treatment cut into the top and sides and red, rather than silver metallic borders.

	MT
Common Player:	6.00
Stars and rookies	30-60X

(See 1998 Donruss Elite for checklist and base card values.)

1998 Donruss Elite Back to the Future

These double-front cards feature a veteran or retired star on one side and a young player on the other. Each player's name, team and "Back to the Future" are printed in the border. The cards are numbered to 1,500, with the first 100 of each card signed by both players. Exceptions are cards #1 and #6. Ripken and Konerko did not sign the same cards and Frank Thomas did not sign his Back to the Future card. Thomas instead signed 100 copies of his Elite base set card which was specially marked.

		MT
Complete Set (8):		175.00
Common Player:		10.00
Production 1,400 sets		
1	Cal Ripken Jr., Paul Konerko	30.00
2	Jeff Bagwell, Todd Helton	20.00
3	Eddie Mathews, Chipper Jones	25.00
4	Juan Gonzalez, Ben Grieve	20.00
5	Hank Aaron, Jose Cruz Jr.	25.00
6	Frank Thomas, David Ortiz	10.00
7	Nolan Ryan, Greg Maddux	35.00
8	Alex Rodriguez, Nomar Garciaparra	35.00

1998 Donruss Elite Back to the Future Autographs

The first 100 of each card in the Back to the Future insert was autographed by both players. Exceptions are cards #1 and #6. Ripken and Konerko did not sign the same cards and Frank Thomas did not sign his Back to the Future card. Thomas instead signed 100 specially marked copies of his Elite base-set card.

		MT
Common Autograph:		125.00
F. Thomas Redemption:		450.00
C. Ripken Redemption:		450.00
Production 100 sets		
1	Paul Konerko	125.00
2	Jeff Bagwell, Todd Helton	350.00
3	Eddie Mathews, Chipper Jones	400.00
4	Juan Gonzalez, Ben Grieve	350.00
5	Hank Aaron, Jose Cruz Jr.	500.00
7	Nolan Ryan, Greg Maddux	1000.
8	Alex Rodriguez, Nomar Garciaparra	600.00

1998 Donruss Elite Craftsmen

This 30-card insert has color player photos on the front and back. The set is sequentially numbered to 3,500. The Master Craftsmen parallel is numbered to 100.

		MT
Complete Set (30):		150.00
Common Player:		2.00
Production 3,500 sets		
Master Craftsman:		3-6X
Production 100 sets		
1	Ken Griffey Jr.	15.00
2	Frank Thomas	7.50
3	Alex Rodriguez	12.00
4	Cal Ripken Jr.	10.00
5	Greg Maddux	8.00
6	Mike Piazza	9.00
7	Chipper Jones	9.00
8	Derek Jeter	9.00
9	Tony Gwynn	7.50
10	Nomar Garciaparra	9.00
11	Scott Rolen	5.00
12	Jose Cruz Jr.	2.00
13	Tony Clark	2.50
14	Vladimir Guerrero	6.00
15	Todd Helton	3.00
16	Ben Grieve	5.00
17	Andruw Jones	5.00
18	Jeff Bagwell	5.00
19	Mark McGwire	15.00
20	Juan Gonzalez	4.00
21	Roger Clemens	7.50
22	Albert Belle	4.00
23	Barry Bonds	4.00
24	Kenny Lofton	3.00
25	Ivan Rodriguez	4.00
26	Paul Molitor	3.00
27	Barry Larkin	2.00
28	Mo Vaughn	3.00
29	Larry Walker	3.00
30	Tino Martinez	2.00

1998 Donruss Elite Prime Numbers Samples

Each of the 36 Elite Prime Numbers inserts was also created in a promo version. They are virtually identical to the much rarer inserts, but have no serial number on back, and display a large black "SAMPLE" overprint.

		MT
Complete Set (36):		175.00
Common Player:		3.00
1A	Ken Griffey Jr. 2 (94)	10.00
1B	Ken Griffey Jr. 9 (204)	10.00
1C	Ken Griffey Jr. 4 (290)	10.00
2A	Frank Thomas 4 (56)	5.00
2B	Frank Thomas 5 (406)	5.00
2C	Frank Thomas 6 (450)	5.00
3A	Mark McGwire 3 (87)	10.00
3B	Mark McGwire 8 (307)	10.00
3C	Mark McGwire 7 (380)	10.00
4A	Cal Ripken Jr. 5 (17)	9.00
4B	Cal Ripken Jr. 1 (507)	9.00
4C	Cal Ripken Jr. 7 (510)	9.00
5A	Mike Piazza 5 (76)	7.50
5B	Mike Piazza 7 (506)	7.50
5C	Mike Piazza 6 (570)	7.50
6A	Chipper Jones 4 (89)	7.50
6B	Chipper Jones 8 (409)	7.50
6C	Chipper Jones 9 (480)	7.50
7A	Tony Gwynn 3 (72)	6.00
7B	Tony Gwynn 7 (302)	6.00
7C	Tony Gwynn 2 (370)	6.00
8A	Barry Bonds 3 (74)	3.00
8B	Barry Bonds 7 (304)	3.00
8C	Barry Bonds 4 (370)	3.00
9A	Jeff Bagwell 4 (25)	3.00
9B	Jeff Bagwell 2 (405)	3.00
9C	Jeff Bagwell 5 (420)	3.00
10A	Juan Gonzalez 5 (89)	3.00
10B	Juan Gonzalez 8 (509)	3.00
10C	Juan Gonzalez 9 (580)	3.00
11A	Alex Rodriguez 5 (34)	7.50
11B	Alex Rodriguez 3 (504)	7.50
11C	Alex Rodriguez 4 (530)	7.50
12A	Kenny Lofton 3 (54)	3.00
12B	Kenny Lofton 5 (304)	3.00
12C	Kenny Lofton 4 (350)	3.00

1998 Donruss Elite Prime Numbers

This 36-card insert includes three cards for each of 12 players. Each card has a single number in the background. The three numbers for each player represent a key statistic for the player (ex. Mark McGwire's cards are 3-8-7; his career home run total at the time was 387). Each card in the set is sequentially numbered. The total is dependent upon the player's statistic.

		MT
Common Player:		10.00
1A	Ken Griffey Jr. 2 (94)	140.00
1B	Ken Griffey Jr. 9 (204)	70.00
1C	Ken Griffey Jr. 4 (290)	60.00
2A	Frank Thomas 4 (56)	80.00

2B Frank Thomas 5 (406) 20.00
2C Frank Thomas 6 (450) 20.00
3A Mark McGwire 3 (87) 140.00
3B Mark McGwire 8 (307) 60.00
3C Mark McGwire 7 (380) 60.00
4A Cal Ripken Jr. 5 (17) 400.00
4B Cal Ripken Jr. 1 (507) 40.00
4C Cal Ripken Jr. 7 (510) 40.00
5A Mike Piazza 5 (76) 90.00
5B Mike Piazza 7 (506) 30.00
5C Mike Piazza 6 (570) 30.00
6A Chipper Jones 4 (89) 75.00
6B Chipper Jones 8 (409) 20.00
6C Chipper Jones 9 (480) 20.00
7A Tony Gwynn 3 (72) 80.00
7B Tony Gwynn 7 (302) 30.00
7C Tony Gwynn 2 (370) 30.00
8A Barry Bonds 3 (74) 40.00
8B Barry Bonds 7 (304) 15.00
8C Barry Bonds 4 (370) 15.00
9A Jeff Bagwell 4 (25) 150.00
9B Jeff Bagwell 2 (405) 20.00
9C Jeff Bagwell 5 (420) 20.00
10A Juan Gonzalez 5 (89) 60.00
10B Juan Gonzalez 8 (509) 15.00
10C Juan Gonzalez 9 (580) 15.00
11A Alex Rodriguez 5 (34) 150.00
11B Alex Rodriguez 3 (504) 30.00
11C Alex Rodriguez 4 (530) 30.00
12A Kenny Lofton 3 (54) 45.00
12B Kenny Lofton 5 (304) 15.00
12C Kenny Lofton 4 (350) 15.00

1998 Donruss Elite Prime Numbers Die-Cuts

This set is a die-cut parallel of the Prime Numbers insert. Each card is sequentially numbered. The production run for each player is the number featured on his first card times 100, his second card times 10 and his third card is sequentially numbered to the number featured on the card.

MT
Common Player: 15.00
1A Ken Griffey Jr. 2 (200) 90.00
1B Ken Griffey Jr. 9 (90) 160.00
1C Ken Griffey Jr. 4 (4) 650.00
2A Frank Thomas 4 (400) 25.00
2B Frank Thomas 5 (50) 80.00
2C Frank Thomas 6 (6) 250.00
3A Mark McGwire 3 (300) 75.00
3B Mark McGwire 8 (80) 200.00
3C Mark McGwire 7 (7) 450.00
4A Cal Ripken Jr. 5 (500) 50.00
4B Cal Ripken Jr. 1 (10) 350.00
4C Cal Ripken Jr. 7 (7) 400.00
5A Mike Piazza 5 (500) 37.00
5B Mike Piazza 7 (70) 100.00
5C Mike Piazza 6 (6) 250.00
6A Chipper Jones 4 (400) 25.00
6B Chipper Jones 8 (80) 100.00
6C Chipper Jones 9 (9) 200.00
7A Tony Gwynn 3 (300) 35.00
7B Tony Gwynn 7 (70) 90.00
7C Tony Gwynn 2 (2) 600.00
8A Barry Bonds 3 (300) 20.00
8B Barry Bonds 7 (70) 50.00
8C Barry Bonds 4 (4) 250.00
9A Jeff Bagwell 4 (400) 15.00
9B Jeff Bagwell 2 (20) 100.00
9C Jeff Bagwell 5 (5) 200.00
10A Juan Gonzalez 5 (500) 15.00
10B Juan Gonzalez 8 (80) 60.00
10C Juan Gonzalez 9 (9) 200.00
11A Alex Rodriguez 5 (500) 30.00
11B Alex Rodriguez 3 (30) 225.00
11C Alex Rodriguez 4 (4) 600.00
12A Kenny Lofton 3 (300) 15.00
12B Kenny Lofton 5 (50) 60.00
12C Kenny Lofton 4 (4) 150.00

1998 Donruss Preferred

The Donruss Preferred 200-card base set is broken down into five subsets: 100 Grand Stand cards (5:1), 40 Mezzanine (1:6), 30 Club Level (1:12), 20 Field Box (1:23) and 10 Executive Suite (1:65). The base set is paralleled in the Preferred Seating set. Each subset has a different die-cut in the parallel. Inserts in this product include Great X-Pectations, Precious Metals and Title Waves.

MT
Complete Set (200): 450.00
Common Grand Stand (5:1): .10
Common Mezzanine (1:6): .75
Common Club Level (1:12): 1.00
Common Field Box: (1:23) 1.50
Common Executive Suite (1:65): 15.00
Pack (5): 5.00
Wax Box (24): 110.00
1 Ken Griffey Jr. EX 45.00
2 Frank Thomas EX 25.00
3 Cal Ripken Jr. EX 30.00
4 Alex Rodriguez EX 30.00
5 Greg Maddux EX 20.00
6 Mike Piazza EX 25.00
7 Chipper Jones EX 25.00
8 Tony Gwynn FB 17.50
9 Derek Jeter FB 15.00
10 Jeff Bagwell EX 17.50
11 Juan Gonzalez EX 10.00
12 Nomar Garciaparra EX 22.50
13 Andruw Jones FB 7.50
14 Hideo Nomo FB 5.00
15 Roger Clemens FB 12.50
16 Mark McGwire FB 30.00
17 Scott Rolen FB 10.00
18 Vladimir Guerrero FB 12.00
19 Barry Bonds FB 7.50
20 Darin Erstad FB 7.50
21 Albert Belle FB 7.50
22 Kenny Lofton FB 7.50
23 Mo Vaughn FB 7.50
24 Tony Clark FB 4.00
25 Ivan Rodriguez FB 7.50
26 Larry Walker CL 2.50
27 Eddie Murray CL 2.00
28 Andy Pettitte CL 4.00
29 Roberto Alomar CL 4.00
30 Randy Johnson CL 4.00
31 Manny Ramirez CL 5.00
32 Paul Molitor FB 6.00
33 Mike Mussina CL 4.00
34 Jim Thome FB 5.00
35 Tino Martinez CL 2.50
36 Gary Sheffield CL 2.50
37 Chuck Knoblauch CL 2.50
38 Bernie Williams CL 4.00
39 Tim Salmon CL 3.00
40 Sammy Sosa CL 10.00
41 Wade Boggs MZ 1.50
42 Will Clark GS .25
43 Andres Galarraga CL 2.50
44 Raul Mondesi CL 2.50
45 Rickey Henderson GS .10
46 Jose Canseco GS .25
47 Pedro Martinez GS .40
48 Jay Buhner GS .25
49 Ryan Klesko GS .25
50 Barry Larkin CL 2.50
51 Charles Johnson GS .10
52 Tom Glavine GS .25
53 Edgar Martinez CL 1.00
54 Fred McGriff GS .25
55 Moises Alou MZ .70
56 Dante Bichette GS .25
57 Jim Edmonds CL 1.00
58 Mark Grace MZ 1.25
59 Chan Ho Park MZ 1.25
60 Justin Thompson MZ .70
61 John Smoltz MZ 1.25
62 Craig Biggio CL 2.00
63 Ken Caminiti MZ 1.25
64 Deion Sanders MZ 1.25
65 Carlos Delgado GS .50
66 David Justice CL 2.00
67 J.T. Snow GS .10
68 Jason Giambi CL 1.00
69 Garret Anderson MZ .10
70 Rondell White MZ .25
71 Matt Williams MZ .30
72 Brady Anderson MZ .20
73 Eric Karros GS .25
74 Javier Lopez GS .20
75 Pat Hentgen GS .20
76 Todd Hundley GS .10
77 Ray Lankford GS .10
78 Denny Neagle GS .10
79 Henry Rodriguez GS .10
80 Sandy Alomar Jr. MZ .70
81 Rafael Palmeiro MZ 1.25
82 Robin Ventura GS .20
83 John Olerud GS .20
84 Omar Vizquel GS .10
85 Joe Randa GS .10
86 Lance Johnson GS .10
87 Kevin Brown GS .20
88 Curt Schilling GS .25
89 Ismael Valdes GS .10
90 Francisco Cordova GS .10
91 David Cone GS .20
92 Paul O'Neill GS .20
93 Jimmy Key GS .10
94 Brad Radke GS .10
95 Kevin Appier GS .10
96 Al Martin GS .10
97 Rusty Greer MZ .70
98 Reggie Jefferson GS .10
99 Ron Coomer GS .10
100 Vinny Castilla GS .20
101 Bobby Bonilla MZ .70
102 Eric Young GS .10
103 Tony Womack GS .10
104 Jason Kendall GS .10
105 Jeff Suppan GS .10
106 Shawn Estes MZ .70
107 Shawn Green GS .10
108 Edgardo Alfonzo MZ .70
109 Alan Benes MZ .70
110 Bobby Higginson GS .10
111 Mark Grudzielanek GS .10
112 Wilton Guerrero GS .10
113 Todd Greene MZ .70
114 Pokey Reese GS .10
115 Jose Guillen CL 1.00
116 Neifi Perez MZ .70
117 Luis Castillo GS .10
118 Edgar Renteria GS .10
119 Karim Garcia GS .10
120 Butch Huskey GS .10
121 Michael Tucker GS .10
122 Jason Dickson GS .10
123 Todd Walker MZ 1.25
124 Brian Jordan GS .10
125 Joe Carter GS .10
126 Matt Morris MZ .70
127 Brett Tomko MZ .70
128 Mike Cameron CL 1.50
129 Russ Davis GS .10
130 Shannon Stewart MZ .70
131 Kevin Orie GS .10
132 Scott Spiezio GS .10
133 Brian Giles GS .10
134 Raul Casanova GS .10
135 Jose Cruz Jr. CL 4.00
136 Hideki Irabu GS .40
137 Bubba Trammell GS .10
138 Richard Hidalgo CL 1.00
139 Paul Konerko CL 3.00
140 Todd Helton FB 7.50
141 Miguel Tejada CL 4.00
142 Fernando Tatis MZ .70
143 Ben Grieve FB 12.50
144 Travis Lee FB 7.50
145 Mark Kotsay CL 4.00
146 Eli Marrero MZ .70
147 David Ortiz CL 2.50

148	Juan Encarnacion MZ	.70
149	Jaret Wright MZ	5.00
150	Livan Hernandez CL	2.00
151	Ruben Rivera GS	.10
152	Brad Fullmer MZ	2.00
153	Dennis Reyes GS	.10
154	Enrique Wilson MZ	.70
155	Todd Dunwoody MZ	.70
156	Derrick Gibson MZ	.70
157	Aaron Boone MZ	.70
158	Ron Wright MZ	.70
159	Preston Wilson MZ	.70
160	Abraham Nunez GS	.10
161	Shane Monahan GS	.10
162	Carl Pavano GS	.25
163	Derrek Lee GS	.25
164	Jeff Abbott GS	.10
165	Wes Helms MZ	.10
166	Brian Rose GS	.15
167	Bobby Estalella GS	.10
168	Ken Griffey Jr. GS	1.50
169	Frank Thomas GS	.70
170	Cal Ripken Jr. GS	1.25
171	Alex Rodriguez GS	1.00
172	Greg Maddux GS	1.00
173	Mike Piazza GS	1.00
174	Chipper Jones GS	1.00
175	Tony Gwynn GS	.70
176	Derek Jeter GS	1.00
177	Jeff Bagwell GS	.50
178	Juan Gonzalez GS	.50
179	Nomar Garciaparra GS	1.00
180	Andruw Jones GS	.40
181	Hideo Nomo GS	.25
182	Roger Clemens GS	.60
183	Mark McGwire GS	2.00
184	Scott Rolen GS	.50
185	Barry Bonds GS	.40
186	Darin Erstad GS	.40
187	Mo Vaughn GS	.40
188	Ivan Rodriguez GS	.50
189	Larry Walker MZ	2.00
190	Andy Pettitte GS	.25
191	Randy Johnson MZ	2.00
192	Paul Molitor GS	.30
193	Jim Thome GS	.20
194	Tino Martinez MZ	2.00
195	Gary Sheffield GS	.20
196	Albert Belle GS	.40
197	Jose Cruz Jr. GS	.25
198	Todd Helton GS	.50
199	Ben Grieve GS	.60
200	Paul Konerko GS	.40

1998 Donruss Preferred Great X-pectations

This 26-card insert features a veteran player on one side and a young player on the other. A large "GX" appears in the background on each side. The cards are sequentially numbered to 2,700, with the first 300 of each die-cut around the "GX".

		MT
Complete Set (26):		225.00
Common Player:		3.00
Die-Cuts:		2-3X
1	Jeff Bagwell, Travis Lee	10.00
2	Jose Cruz Jr., Ken Griffey Jr.	5.00
3	Larry Walker, Ben Grieve	10.00
4	Frank Thomas, Todd Helton	10.00
5	Jim Thome, Paul Konerko	4.00
6	Alex Rodriguez, Miguel Tejada	15.00
7	Greg Maddux, Livan Hernandez	12.50
8	Roger Clemens, Jaret Wright	10.00
9	Albert Belle, Juan Encarnacion	6.00
10	Mo Vaughn, David Ortiz	6.00
11	Manny Ramirez, Mark Kotsay	5.00
12	Tim Salmon, Brad Fullmer	3.00
13	Cal Ripken Jr., Fernando Tatis	20.00
14	Hideo Nomo, Hideki Irabu	3.00
15	Mike Piazza, Todd Greene	15.00
16	Gary Sheffield, Richard Hidalgo	4.00
17	Paul Molitor, Darin Erstad	6.00
18	Ivan Rodriguez, Eli Marrero	6.00
19	Ken Caminiti, Todd Walker	4.00
20	Tony Gwynn, Jose Guillen	12.50
21	Derek Jeter, Nomar Garciaparra	15.00
22	Chipper Jones, Scott Rolen	15.00
23	Juan Gonzalez, Andruw Jones	10.00
24	Barry Bonds, Vladimir Guerrero	8.00
25	Mark McGwire, Tony Clark	25.00
26	Bernie Williams, Mike Cameron	5.00

1998 Donruss Preferred Precious Metals

Precious Metals is a 30-card partial parallel of the Preferred base set. Each card was printed on stock using real silver, gold or platinum. Fifty complete sets were produced.

		MT
Complete Set (30):		3000.
Common Player:		25.00
1	Ken Griffey Jr.	300.00
2	Frank Thomas	100.00
3	Cal Ripken Jr.	250.00
4	Alex Rodriguez	225.00
5	Greg Maddux	175.00
6	Mike Piazza	200.00
7	Chipper Jones	200.00
8	Tony Gwynn	150.00
9	Derek Jeter	200.00
10	Jeff Bagwell	100.00
11	Juan Gonzalez	80.00
12	Nomar Garciaparra	200.00
13	Andruw Jones	75.00
14	Hideo Nomo	30.00
15	Roger Clemens	125.00
16	Mark McGwire	300.00
17	Scott Rolen	75.00
18	Barry Bonds	75.00
19	Darin Erstad	55.00
20	Kenny Lofton	45.00
21	Mo Vaughn	45.00
22	Ivan Rodriguez	50.00
23	Randy Johnson	50.00
24	Paul Molitor	60.00
25	Jose Cruz Jr.	25.00
26	Paul Konerko	25.00
27	Todd Helton	60.00
28	Ben Grieve	60.00
29	Travis Lee	60.00
30	Mark Kotsay	25.00

1998 Donruss Preferred Title Waves

This 30-card set features players who won awards or titles between 1993-1997. Printed on plastic stock, each card is sequentially numbered to the year the player won the award. The card fronts feature the Title Waves logo, a color player photo in front of a background of fans and the name of the award the player won.

		MT
Complete Set (30):		350.00
Common Player:		4.00
1	Nomar Garciaparra	20.00
2	Scott Rolen	10.00
3	Roger Clemens	15.00
4	Gary Sheffield	4.00
5	Jeff Bagwell	15.00
6	Cal Ripken Jr.	25.00
7	Frank Thomas	15.00
8	Ken Griffey Jr.	35.00
9	Larry Walker	5.00
10	Derek Jeter	20.00
11	Juan Gonzalez	10.00
12	Bernie Williams	6.00
13	Andruw Jones	12.50
14	Andy Pettitte	5.00
15	Ivan Rodriguez	10.00
16	Alex Rodriguez	25.00
17	Mark McGwire	35.00
18	Andres Galarraga	4.00
19	Hideo Nomo	5.00
20	Mo Vaughn	7.50
21	Randy Johnson	6.00
22	Chipper Jones	20.00
23	Greg Maddux	17.50
24	Manny Ramirez	7.50
25	Tony Gwynn	17.50
26	Albert Belle	6.00
27	Kenny Lofton	5.00
28	Mike Piazza	20.00
29	Paul Molitor	6.00
30	Barry Bonds	7.50

1998 Donruss Preferred Tins

Donruss Preferred was packaged in collectible tins. Each tin contained five cards and featured one of 24 players on the top. Silver (numbered to 999) and gold (199) parallel tins were also produced and included in hobby-only boxes. The values shown are for empty tins.

		MT
Complete Set (24):		20.00
Common Player:		.25
Gold Tins (199):		15X
Silver Tins (999):		5x
1	Todd Helton	.75
2	Ben Grieve	1.00
3	Cal Ripken Jr.	2.00
4	Alex Rodriguez	1.75
5	Greg Maddux	1.25
6	Mike Piazza	1.50
7	Chipper Jones	1.50
8	Travis Lee	1.00
9	Derek Jeter	1.50
10	Jeff Bagwell	1.00
11	Juan Gonzalez	.75
12	Mark McGwire	2.50
13	Hideo Nomo	.50
14	Roger Clemens	1.00
15	Andruw Jones	.75
16	Paul Molitor	.50
17	Vladimir Guerrero	.75
18	Jose Cruz Jr.	.25
19	Nomar Garciaparra	1.50
20	Scott Rolen	1.00
21	Ken Griffey Jr.	2.50
22	Larry Walker	.25
23	Frank Thomas	1.00
24	Tony Gwynn	1.25

1998 Donruss Signature Series

The 140-card base set has a white border encasing the player photo with the logo stamped with silver foil. Card backs have a small photo and complete year-by-year statistics. Signature Proofs are a parallel to the base set utilizing holo-foil treatment and "Signature Proof" written down the left edge of the card front. Each card is numbered "1 of 150" on the card back.

	MT
Complete Set (140):	75.00
Common Player:	.15
Signature Proofs:	15x to 20x
Pack (5):	15.00
Wax Box (12):	175.00

1 David Justice .30
2 Derek Jeter 2.50
3 Nomar Garciaparra 2.50
4 Ryan Klesko .25
5 Jeff Bagwell 1.00
6 Dante Bichette .25
7 Ivan Rodriguez 1.00
8 Albert Belle .75
9 Cal Ripken Jr. 3.00
10 Craig Biggio .50
11 Barry Larkin .40
12 Jose Guillen .20
13 Will Clark .30
14 J.T. Snow .15
15 Chuck Knoblauch .30
16 Todd Walker .20
17 Scott Rolen .75
18 Rickey Henderson .40
19 Juan Gonzalez .75
20 Justin Thompson .15
21 Roger Clemens 1.25
22 Ray Lankford .15
23 Jose Cruz Jr. .25
24 Ken Griffey Jr. 4.00
25 Andruw Jones .60
26 Darin Erstad .60
27 Jim Thome .30
28 Wade Boggs .40
29 Ken Caminiti .20
30 Todd Hundley .15
31 Mike Piazza 2.50
32 Sammy Sosa 2.50
33 Larry Walker .75
34 Matt Williams .30
35 Frank Thomas 1.00
36 Gary Sheffield .25
37 Alex Rodriguez 2.50
38 Hideo Nomo .25
39 Kenny Lofton .50
40 John Smoltz .20
41 Mo Vaughn .50
42 Edgar Martinez .15
43 Paul Molitor .50
44 Rafael Palmeiro .50
45 Barry Bonds .50
46 Vladimir Guerrero 1.00
47 Carlos Delgado .75
48 Bobby Higginson .15
49 Greg Maddux 2.00
50 Jim Edmonds .15
51 Randy Johnson .75
52 Mark McGwire 4.00
53 Rondell White .20
54 Raul Mondesi .20
55 Manny Ramirez 1.00
56 Pedro Martinez 1.00
57 Tim Salmon .25
58 Moises Alou .20
59 Fred McGriff .20
60 Garret Anderson .15
61 Sandy Alomar Jr. .15
62 Chan Ho Park .20
63 Mark Kotsay .20
64 Mike Mussina .50
65 Tom Glavine .25
66 Tony Clark .40
67 Mark Grace .25
68 Tony Gwynn 2.00
69 Tino Martinez .40
70 Kevin Brown .25
71 Todd Greene .15
72 Andy Pettitte .30
73 Livan Hernandez .15
74 Curt Schilling .25
75 Andres Galarraga .30
76 Rusty Greer .15
77 Jay Buhner .15
78 Bobby Bonilla .20
79 Chipper Jones 2.00
80 Eric Young .15
81 Jason Giambi .15
82 Javy Lopez .20
83 Roberto Alomar .40
84 Bernie Williams .40
85 A.J. Hinch .15
86 Kerry Wood 1.00
87 Juan Encarnacion .25
88 Brad Fullmer .15
89 Ben Grieve .60
90 *Magglio Ordonez* 6.00
91 Todd Helton 1.00
92 Richard Hidalgo .15
93 Paul Konerko .25
94 Aramis Ramirez .25
95 Ricky Ledee .40
96 Derrek Lee .15
97 Travis Lee .50
98 *Matt Anderson* 1.00
99 Jaret Wright .50
100 David Ortiz .20
101 Carl Pavano .20
102 *Orlando Hernandez* 5.00
103 Fernando Tatis .40
104 Miguel Tejada .20
105 *Rolando Arrojo* 2.00
106 *Kevin Millwood* 6.00
107 Ken Griffey Jr. (Checklist) 1.25
108 Frank Thomas (Checklist) .75
109 Cal Ripken Jr. (Checklist) 1.00
110 Greg Maddux (Checklist) .75
111 John Olerud .40
112 David Cone .30
113 Vinny Castilla .20
114 Jason Kendall .20
115 Brian Jordan .15
116 Hideki Irabu .25
117 Bartolo Colon .15
118 Greg Vaughn .25
119 David Segui .15
120 Bruce Chen .25
121 *Julio Ramirez* 1.00
122 *Troy Glaus* 10.00
123 *Jeremy Giambi* 2.00
124 *Ryan Minor* 3.00
125 Richie Sexson .15
126 Dermal Brown .25
127 Adrian Beltre .50
128 Eric Chavez .50
129 *J.D. Drew* 12.00
130 *Gabe Kapler* 6.00
131 *Masato Yoshii* .50
132 *Mike Lowell* 1.00
133 *Jim Parque* 1.00
134 Roy Halladay .40
135 *Carlos Lee* 4.00
136 *Jin Ho Cho* .40
137 Michael Barrett .50
138 *Fernando Seguignol* 2.00
139 *Odalis Perez* 1.50
140 Mark McGwire (Checklist) 1.50

1998 Donruss Signature Series Proofs

This parallel set differs from the regular issue Signature Series base cards in the presence at left-front of a vertical stack of gold refractive foil strips on which SIGNATURE PROOF is spelled out. Also, backs of the proofs have a gold, rather than white, background.

	MT
Complete Set (140):	1200.
Common Player:	2.00
Veteran Stars:	15-20X
Young Stars/Rookies:	8-15X

(See 1998 Donruss Signature Series for checklist and base card values.)

1998 Donruss Signature Series Preview Autographs

This insert was a surprise addition to Donruss Update. The set features autographs from top rookies and stars. The number of cards produced varies for each player. The card fronts have a color player photo in front of a gold checkered border with the signature in a white area near the bottom. Cards of a number of players (Alou, Casey, Jenkins and Wilson) were never officially released, having been returned too late by the players; specimens, have, however made their wau into the hobby market in unknown numbers.

	MT
Common Player:	15.00
Sandy Alomar Jr. (96)	45.00
Moises Alou	75.00
Andy Benes (135)	30.00
Russell Branyan (188)	25.00
Sean Casey	125.00
Tony Clark (188)	40.00
Juan Encarnacion (193)	25.00
Brad Fullmer (396)	25.00
Juan Gonzalez (108)	180.00
Ben Grieve (100)	100.00
Todd Helton (101)	100.00
Richard Hidalgo (380)	25.00
A.J. Hinch (400)	15.00
Damian Jackson (15)	200.00
Geoff Jenkins	275.00
Chipper Jones (112)	300.00
Chuck Knoblauch (98)	80.00
Travis Lee (101)	30.00
Mike Lowell (450)	20.00
Greg Maddux (92)	250.00
Kevin Millwood (395)	60.00
Magglio Ordonez (420)	75.00
David Ortiz (393)	15.00
Rafael Palmeiro (107)	75.00
Cal Ripken Jr. (22)	1200.
Alex Rodriguez (23)	1000.
Curt Schilling (100)	75.00
Randall Simon (380)	15.00
Fernando Tatis (400)	25.00

1998 Donruss Signature Series Autographs (Red)

Autographs were inserted one per pack and feature the player photo over a silver and red foil background. The featured player's autograph appears on the bottom portion on front with the Donruss logo stamped in gold foil. Autographs are un-numbered. The first 100 cards signed by each player are blue, sequentially numbered and designated as "Century Marks". The next 1,000 signed are green, sequentially numbered and designated as "Millennium Marks." Greg Maddux signed only 12 regular Donruss Signature Autographs.

	MT
Common Player:	2.50
Roberto Alomar (150)	50.00
Sandy Alomar Jr. (700)	12.50
Moises Alou (900)	12.50
Gabe Alvarez (2,900)	2.50
Wilson Alvarez (1,600)	4.00
Jay Bell (1,500)	4.00
Adrian Beltre (1,900)	12.50

Andy Benes (2,600) 5.00
Aaron Boone (3,400) 2.50
Russell Branyan (1,650) 4.00
Orlando Cabrera (3,100) 2.50
Mike Cameron (1,150) 7.50
Joe Carter (400) 15.00
Sean Casey (2,275) 15.00
Bruce Chen (150) 25.00
Tony Clark (2,275) 7.50
Will Clark (1,400) 15.00
Matt Clement (1,400) 7.50
Pat Cline (400) 10.00
Ken Cloude (3,400) 4.00
Michael Coleman (2,800) 2.50
David Cone (25) 125.00
Jeff Conine (1,400) 5.00
Jacob Cruz (3,200) 2.50
Russ Davis (3,500) 2.50
Jason Dickson (1,400) 4.00
Todd Dunwoody (3,500) 2.50
Juan Encarnacion (3,400) 7.50
Darin Erstad (700) 25.00
Bobby Estalella (3,400) 2.50
Jeff Fassero (3,400) 2.50
John Franco (1,800) 2.50
Brad Fullmer (3,100) 5.00
Jason Giambi (3,100) 5.00
Derrick Gibson (1,200) 5.00
Todd Greene (1,400) 5.00
Ben Grieve (1,400) 20.00
Mark Grudzielanek (3,200) 4.00
Vladimir Guerrero (2,100) 30.00
Wilton Guerrero (1,900) 4.00
Jose Guillen (2,400) 6.00
Todd Helton (1,300) 20.00
Richard Hidalgo (3,400) 4.00
A.J. Hinch (2,900) 4.00
Butch Huskey (1,900) 4.00
Raul Ibanez (3,300) 2.50
Damian Jackson (900) 2.50
Geoff Jenkins (3,100) 4.00
Eric Karros (650) 9.00
Ryan Klesko (400) 12.00
Mark Kotsay (3,600) 5.00
Ricky Ledee (2,200) 12.50
Derrek Lee (3,400) 4.00
Travis Lee (150) 35.00
Travis Lee (facsimile autograph, "SAMPLE" on back) 3.00
Javier Lopez (650) 10.00
Mike Lowell (3,500) 7.50
Greg Maddux (12) 450.00
Eli Marrero (3,400) 2.50
Al Martin (1,300) 4.00
Rafael Medina (1,400) 2.50
Scott Morgan (900) 7.50
Abraham Nunez (3,500) 2.50
Paul O'Neill (1,000) 12.50
Luis Ordaz (2,700) 4.00
Magglio Ordonez (3,200) 6.00
Kevin Orie (1,350) 5.00
David Ortiz (3,400) 5.00
Rafael Palmeiro (1,000) 15.00
Carl Pavano (2,600) 4.00
Neifi Perez (3,300) 2.50
Dante Powell (3,050) 2.50
Aramis Ramirez (2,800) 7.50
Mariano Rivera (900) 10.00
Felix Rodriguez (1,400) 5.00
Henry Rodriguez (3,400) 4.00
Scott Rolen (1,900) 30.00
Brian Rose (1,400) 5.00
Curt Schilling (900) 12.50
Richie Sexson (3,500) 7.50
Randall Simon (3,500) 5.00
J.T. Snow (400) 10.00
Jeff Suppan (1,400) 5.00
Fernando Tatis (3,900) 5.00
Miguel Tejada (3,800) 5.00
Brett Tomko (3,400) 2.50
Bubba Trammell (3,900) 2.50
Ismael Valdez (1,900) 5.00
Robin Ventura (1,400) 10.00
Billy Wagner (3,900) 4.00
Todd Walker (1,900) 7.50
Daryle Ward (400) 7.50
Rondell White (3,400) 7.50
Antone Williamson (3,350) 2.50
Dan Wilson (2,400) 2.50
Enrique Wilson (3,400) 2.50
Preston Wilson (2,100) 5.00
Tony Womack (3,500) 2.50
Kerry Wood (3,400) 10.00

1998 Donruss Signature Series Millennium Marks (Green)

This is a green-foil parallel version of the Autographs insert set and features 1,000 cards signed by the featured player (unless otherwise shown in the checklist). Cards are not numbered.

	MT
Complete Set (125):	
Common Player:	6.00
Roberto Alomar	25.00
Sandy Alomar Jr.	10.00
Moises Alou	12.50
Gabe Alvarez	6.00
Wilson Alvarez	6.00
Brady Anderson (800)	10.00
Jay Bell	6.00
Albert Belle (400)	50.00
Adrian Beltre	20.00
Andy Benes	7.50
Wade Boggs (900)	30.00
Barry Bonds (400)	65.00
Aaron Boone	6.00
Russell Branyan	7.50
Jay Buhner (400)	17.50
Ellis Burks (900)	7.50
Orlando Cabrera	6.00
Mike Cameron	7.50
Ken Caminiti (900) 15.00	
Joe Carter	10.00
Sean Casey	20.00
Bruce Chen	10.00
Tony Clark	12.50
Will Clark	20.00
Roger Clemens (400)	85.00
Matt Clement (900)	6.00
Pat Cline	6.00
Ken Cloude	6.00
Michael Coleman	6.00
David Cone	17.50
Jeff Conine	6.00
Jacob Cruz	6.00
Jose Cruz Jr. (850)	10.00
Russ Davis (950)	6.00
Jason Dickson (950)	6.00
Todd Dunwoody	6.00
Scott Elarton (900)	6.00
Juan Encarnacion	10.00
Darin Erstad	20.00
Bobby Estalella	6.00
Jeff Fassero	6.00
John Franco (950)	6.00
Brad Fullmer	10.00
Andres Galarraga (900)	12.50
Nomar Garciaparra (400)	100.00
Jason Giambi	7.50
Derrick Gibson	6.00
Tom Glavine (700)	20.00
Juan Gonzalez	50.00
Todd Greene	6.00
Ben Grieve	25.00
Mark Grudzielanek	6.00
Vladimir Guerrero	40.00
Wilton Guerrero	6.00
Jose Guillen	7.50
Tony Gwynn (900)	60.00
Todd Helton	25.00
Richard Hidalgo	7.50
A.J. Hinch	7.50
Butch Huskey	7.50
Raul Ibanez	6.00
Damian Jackson	6.00
Geoff Jenkins	7.50
Derek Jeter (400)	90.00
Randy Johnson (800)	25.00
Chipper Jones (900)	65.00
Eric Karros	7.50
Ryan Klesko	7.50
Chuck Knoblauch (900)	20.00
Mark Kotsay	10.00
Ricky Ledee	15.00
Derrek Lee	7.50
Travis Lee	20.00
Javier Lopez (800)	10.00
Mike Lowell	10.00
Greg Maddux (400)	125.00
Eli Marrero	6.00
Al Martin (950)	6.00
Rafael Medina (850)	6.00
Paul Molitor (900)	30.00
Scott Morgan	7.50
Mike Mussina (900)	15.00
Abraham Nunez	6.00
Paul O'Neill (900)	12.50
Luis Ordaz	6.00
Magglio Ordonez	10.00
Kevin Orie	6.00
David Ortiz	10.00
Rafael Palmeiro (900)	20.00
Carl Pavano	7.50
Neifi Perez	6.00
Andy Pettitte (900)	15.00
Dante Powell (950)	6.00
Aramis Ramirez	12.50
Cal Ripken Jr. (375)	150.00
Mariano Rivera	15.00
Alex Rodriguez (350)	125.00
Felix Rodriguez	7.50
Henry Rodriguez	7.50
Scott Rolen	40.00
Brian Rose	7.50
Curt Schilling	12.50
Richie Sexson	12.50
Randall Simon	10.00
J.T. Snow	6.00
Darryl Strawberry (900)	17.50
Jeff Suppan	7.50
Fernando Tatis	12.50
Miguel Tejada	10.00
Brett Tomko	6.00
Bubba Trammell	6.00
Ismael Valdes	7.50
Robin Ventura	15.00
Billy Wagner (900)	7.50
Todd Walker	12.50
Daryle Ward	6.00
Rondell White	12.50
Matt Williams (820)	20.00
Antone Williamson	6.00
Dan Wilson	6.00
Enrique Wilson	6.00
Preston Wilson (400)	12.50
Tony Womack	6.00
Kerry Wood	25.00

1998 Donruss Signature Series Century Marks (Blue)

This 121-card set is a serially numbered, blue-foil parallel of the Autographs insert set and limited to 100 cards signed by each featured player (unless otherwise shown in the checklist).

	MT
Common Player:	15.00
Roberto Alomar	60.00
Sandy Alomar Jr.	20.00
Moises Alou	20.00
Gabe Alvarez	15.00
Wilson Alvarez	15.00
Brady Anderson	20.00
Jay Bell	15.00
Albert Belle	60.00
Adrian Beltre	50.00
Andy Benes	20.00
Wade Boggs	65.00
Barry Bonds	90.00
Aaron Boone	15.00
Russell Branyan	15.00

Jay Buhner	20.00
Ellis Burks	15.00
Orlando Cabrera	15.00
Mike Cameron	20.00
Ken Caminiti	30.00
Joe Carter	15.00
Sean Casey	20.00
Bruce Chen	20.00
Tony Clark	25.00
Will Clark	35.00
Roger Clemens	125.00
Matt Clement	20.00
Pat Cline	15.00
Ken Cloude	15.00
Michael Coleman	15.00
David Cone	25.00
Jeff Conine	15.00
Jacob Cruz	15.00
Jose Cruz Jr.	20.00
Russ Davis	15.00
Jason Dickson	15.00
Todd Dunwoody	15.00
Scott Elarton	15.00
Darin Erstad	35.00
Bobby Estalella	15.00
Jeff Fassero	15.00
John Franco	15.00
Brad Fullmer	20.00
Andres Galarraga	35.00
Nomar Garciaparra	175.00
Jason Giambi	20.00
Derrick Gibson	20.00
Tom Glavine	25.00
Juan Gonzalez	100.00
Todd Greene	15.00
Ben Grieve	60.00
Mark Grudzielanek	15.00
Vladimir Guerrero	80.00
Wilton Guerrero	15.00
Jose Guillen	20.00
Tony Gwynn	150.00
Todd Helton	50.00
Richard Hidalgo	20.00
A.J. Hinch	20.00
Butch Huskey	20.00
Raul Ibanez	15.00
Damian Jackson	15.00
Geoff Jenkins	20.00
Derek Jeter	150.00
Randy Johnson	50.00
Chipper Jones	150.00
Eric Karros (50)	25.00
Ryan Klesko	25.00
Chuck Knoblauch	45.00
Mark Kotsay	20.00
Ricky Ledee	20.00
Derrek Lee	15.00
Travis Lee	35.00
Javier Lopez	20.00
Mike Lowell	25.00
Greg Maddux	200.00
Eli Marrero	15.00
Al Martin	15.00
Rafael Medina	15.00
Paul Molitor	65.00
Scott Morgan	20.00
Mike Mussina	50.00
Abraham Nunez	15.00
Paul O'Neill	30.00
Luis Ordaz	15.00
Magglio Ordonez	20.00
Kevin Orie	15.00
David Ortiz	20.00
Rafael Palmeiro	40.00
Carl Pavano	20.00
Neifi Perez	15.00
Andy Pettitte	40.00
Aramis Ramirez	20.00
Cal Ripken Jr.	250.00
Mariano Rivera	30.00
Alex Rodriguez	200.00
Felix Rodriguez	15.00
Henry Rodriguez	20.00
Scott Rolen	80.00
Brian Rose	15.00
Curt Schilling	30.00
Richie Sexson	30.00
Randall Simon	20.00
J.T. Snow	15.00
Darryl Strawberry	30.00
Jeff Suppan	20.00
Fernando Tatis	20.00
Brett Tomko	15.00
Bubba Trammell	15.00
Ismael Valdez	20.00
Robin Ventura	30.00
Billy Wagner	20.00
Todd Walker	20.00
Daryle Ward	15.00
Rondell White	25.00
Matt Williams (80)	45.00
Antone Williamson	15.00
Dan Wilson	15.00
Enrique Wilson	15.00
Preston Wilson	20.00
Tony Womack	15.00
Kerry Wood	35.00

1998 Donruss Signature Series Redemption Baseballs

Redemption cards authentically autographed baseballs were randomly inserted in Donruss Signature Series packs. Baseballs are laser burned with a Donruss seal to ensure authenticity. Every ball, except Ben Grieve's, is serial numbered within the edition limit shown. Redemption cards, no longer valid, are valued about 10% of the corresponding ball.

	MT
Common Autographed Ball:	35.00
Signing Bonus Redemption Card:	10%
Roberto Alomar (60)	90.00
Sandy Alomar Jr. (60)	45.00
Ernie Banks (12)	175.00
Ken Caminiti (60)	60.00
Tony Clark (60)	45.00
Jacob Cruz (12)	100.00
Russ Davis (60)	35.00
Juan Encarnacion (60)	60.00
Bobby Estalella (60)	35.00
Jeff Fassero (60)	35.00
Mark Grudzielanek (60)	35.00
Ben Grieve (30)	75.00
Jose Guillen (120)	35.00
Tony Gwynn (60)	200.00
Al Kaline (12)	175.00
Paul Konerko (100)	35.00
Travis Lee (100)	60.00
Mike Lowell (60)	35.00
Eli Marrero (60)	35.00
Eddie Mathews (12)	160.00
Paul Molitor (60)	125.00
Stan Musial (12)	225.00
Abraham Nunez (12)	100.00
Luis Ordaz (12)	75.00
Magglio Ordonez (12)	75.00
Scott Rolen (60)	100.00
Bubba Trammell (24)	60.00
Robin Ventura (60)	75.00
Billy Wagner (60)	50.00
Rondell White (60)	45.00
Antone Williamson (12)	35.00
Tony Womack (60)	35.00

1998 Donruss Signature Series Significant Signatures

This 18-card autographed set features some of baseball's all-time great players. Each card is sequentially numbered to 2,000. The Sandy Koufax autographs weren't received in time prior to release and was redeemable by sending in the Billy Williams autograph, the collector would then receive both the Williams and Koufax back. Exchange cards were also initially released for Nolan Ryan and Ozzie Smith.

	MT
Complete Set (18):	1200.
Common Player:	25.00
Ernie Banks	50.00
Yogi Berra	60.00
George Brett	80.00
Catfish Hunter	25.00
Al Kaline	40.00
Harmon Killebrew	40.00
Ralph Kiner	30.00
Sandy Koufax	150.00
Eddie Mathews	50.00
Don Mattingly	80.00
Willie McCovey	25.00
Stan Musial	75.00
Phil Rizzuto (edition of 1,000)	45.00
Nolan Ryan	150.00
Nolan Ryan (Exchange card)	30.00
Ozzie Smith	60.00
Ozzie Smith (Exchange card)	15.00
Duke Snider	50.00
Don Sutton	25.00
Billy Williams	50.00

1998 Donruss Collections

Collections consists of a 750-card base set made up of cards from the Donruss (200 cards), Leaf (200), Donruss Elite (150) and Donruss Preferred (200) sets. The cards were reproduced with a chromium finish and have the scripted word "Collections" vertically at left-front. The Collections logo is repeated on back and each card has a second number within the 750-piece set. The Donruss and Leaf cards were inserted two per pack, Elite was inserted one per pack and Preferred cards had a production run of less than 1,400, averaging one card per two packs.

	MT
Complete Set (750):	650.00
Complete Donruss Set (200):	75.00
Complete Leaf Set (200):	60.00
Complete Elite Set (150):	150.00
Complete Preferred Set (200):	400.00
Prized Collections Parallel:	4-6X
Pack (5):	4.00
Wax Box (20):	60.00

DONRUSS

1	Paul Molitor	.50
2	Juan Gonzalez	1.00
3	Darryl Kile	.10
4	Randy Johnson	.40
5	Tom Glavine	.20
6	Pat Hentgen	.10
7	David Justice	.25
8	Kevin Brown	.25
9	Mike Mussina	.45
10	Ken Caminiti	.20
11	Todd Hundley	.20
12	Frank Thomas	2.00
13	Ray Lankford	.10
14	Justin Thompson	.10
15	Jason Dickson	.10
16	Kenny Lofton	.60
17	Ivan Rodriguez	.75
18	Pedro Martinez	.40
19	Brady Anderson	.15
20	Barry Larkin	.15
21	Chipper Jones	2.00
22	Tony Gwynn	1.50
23	Roger Clemens	1.00
24	Sandy Alomar Jr.	.15
25	Tino Martinez	.15
26	Jeff Bagwell	1.25
27	Shawn Estes	.10
28	Ken Griffey Jr.	3.00
29	Javier Lopez	.15
30	Denny Neagle	.10
31	Mike Piazza	2.00
32	Andres Galarraga	.15
33	Larry Walker	.25
34	Alex Rodriguez	3.00
35	Greg Maddux	1.50
36	Albert Belle	.75
37	Barry Bonds	.75
38	Mo Vaughn	.60
39	Kevin Appier	.10
40	Wade Boggs	.25
41	Garret Anderson	.10
42	Jeffrey Hammonds	.10
43	Marquis Grissom	.10
44	Jim Edmonds	.10
45	Brian Jordan	.10

46	Raul Mondesi	.20
47	John Valentin	.10
48	Brad Radke	.10
49	Ismael Valdes	.10
50	Matt Stairs	.10
51	Matt Williams	.20
52	Reggie Jefferson	.10
53	Alan Benes	.10
54	Charles Johnson	.10
55	Chuck Knoblauch	.15
56	Edgar Martinez	.10
57	Nomar Garciaparra	2.00
58	Craig Biggio	.20
59	Bernie Williams	.45
60	David Cone	.20
61	Cal Ripken Jr.	2.50
62	Mark McGwire	4.00
63	Roberto Alomar	.50
64	Fred McGriff	.15
65	Eric Karros	.10
66	Robin Ventura	.15
67	Darin Erstad	.50
68	Michael Tucker	.10
69	Jim Thome	.30
70	Mark Grace	.25
71	Lou Collier	.10
72	Karim Garcia	.20
73	Alex Fernandez	.10
74	J.T. Snow	.10
75	Reggie Sanders	.10
76	John Smoltz	.15
77	Tim Salmon	.20
78	Paul O'Neill	.20
79	Vinny Castilla	.10
80	Rafael Palmeiro	.20
81	Jaret Wright	.50
82	Jay Buhner	.15
83	Brett Butler	.10
84	Todd Greene	.10
85	Scott Rolen	1.50
86	Sammy Sosa	1.50
87	Jason Giambi	.10
88	Carlos Delgado	.15
89	Deion Sanders	.20
90	Wilton Guerrero	.10
91	Andy Pettitte	.50
92	Brian Giles	.15
93	Dmitri Young	.10
94	Ron Coomer	.10
95	Mike Cameron	.10
96	Edgardo Alfonzo	.20
97	Jimmy Key	.10
98	Ryan Klesko	.20
99	Andy Benes	.10
100	Derek Jeter	2.00
101	Jeff Fassero	.10
102	Neifi Perez	.10
103	Hideo Nomo	.45
104	Andruw Jones	1.50
105	Todd Helton	.75
106	Livan Hernandez	.20
107	Brett Tomko	.10
108	Shannon Stewart	.10
109	Bartolo Colon	.10
110	Matt Morris	.10
111	Miguel Tejada	.50
112	Pokey Reese	.10
113	Fernando Tatis	.25
114	Todd Dunwoody	.10
115	Jose Cruz Jr.	.50
116	Chan Ho Park	.15
117	Kevin Young	.10
118	Rickey Henderson	.25
119	Hideki Irabu	.50
120	Francisco Cordova	.10
121	Al Martin	.10
122	Tony Clark	.30
123	Curt Schilling	.15
124	Rusty Greer	.10
125	Jose Canseco	.35
126	Edgar Renteria	.10
127	Todd Walker	.20
128	Wally Joyner	.10
129	Bill Mueller	.10
130	Jose Guillen	.40
131	Manny Ramirez	.50
132	Bobby Higginson	.10
133	Kevin Orie	.10
134	Will Clark	.20
135	Dave Nilsson	.10
136	Jason Kendall	.10
137	Ivan Cruz	.10
138	Gary Sheffield	.25
139	Bubba Trammell	.20
140	Vladimir Guerrero	1.00
141	Dennis Reyes	.15
142	Bobby Bonilla	.15
143	Ruben Rivera	.10
144	Ben Grieve	1.00
145	Moises Alou	.20
146	Tony Womack	.10
147	Eric Young	.10
148	Paul Konerko	.50
149	Dante Bichette	.20
150	Joe Carter	.15
151	Rondell White	.20
152	Chris Holt	.10
153	Shawn Green	.25
154	Mark Grudzielanek	.10
155	Jermaine Dye	.10
156	Ken Griffey Jr. (Fan Club)	1.50
157	Frank Thomas (Fan Club)	1.00
158	Chipper Jones (Fan Club)	1.00
159	Mike Piazza (Fan Club)	1.25
160	Cal Ripken Jr. (Fan Club)	1.25
161	Greg Maddux (Fan Club)	.90
162	Juan Gonzalez (Fan Club)	.50
163	Alex Rodriguez (Fan Club)	1.50
164	Mark McGwire (Fan Club)	2.50
165	Derek Jeter (Fan Club)	1.50
166	Larry Walker (Checklist)	.20
167	Tony Gwynn (Checklist)	.75
168	Tino Martinez (Checklist)	.10
169	Scott Rolen (Checklist)	.60
170	Nomar Garciaparra (Checklist)	1.00

DONRUSS RATED ROOKIES

1	Mark Kotsay	2.00
2	Neifi Perez	1.00
3	Paul Konerko	2.00
4	Jose Cruz Jr.	4.00
5	Hideki Irabu	4.00
6	Mike Cameron	1.00
7	Jeff Suppan	1.00
8	Kevin Orie	1.00
9	Pokey Reese	1.00
10	Todd Dunwoody	1.00
11	Miguel Tejada	2.00
12	Jose Guillen	1.50
13	Bartolo Colon	2.00
14	Derrek Lee	1.00
15	Antone Williamson	1.00
16	Wilton Guerrero	1.00
17	Jaret Wright	2.00
18	Todd Helton	2.00
19	Shannon Stewart	1.00
20	Nomar Garciaparra	5.00
21	Brett Tomko	1.00
22	Fernando Tatis	1.50
23	Raul Ibanez	1.00
24	Dennis Reyes	1.00
25	Bobby Estalella	1.00
26	Lou Collier	1.00
27	Bubba Trammell	1.00
28	Ben Grieve	2.50
29	Ivan Cruz	1.00
30	Karim Garcia	1.50

LEAF

1	Rusty Greer	.10
2	Tino Martinez	.20
3	Bobby Bonilla	.15
4	Jason Giambi	.10
5	Matt Morris	.20
6	Craig Counsell	.10
7	Reggie Jefferson	.10
8	Brian Rose	.25
9	Ruben Rivera	.10
10	Shawn Estes	.10
11	Tony Gwynn	1.50
12	Jeff Abbott	.10
13	Jose Cruz Jr.	.75
14	Francisco Cordova	.10
15	Ryan Klesko	.20
16	Tim Salmon	.25
17	Brett Tomko	.10
18	Matt Williams	.25
19	Joe Carter	.15
20	Harold Baines	.15
21	Gary Sheffield	.25
22	Charles Johnson	.15
23	Aaron Boone	.15
24	Eddie Murray	.25
25	Matt Stairs	.10
26	David Cone	.20
27	Jon Nunnally	.10
28	Chris Stynes	.10
29	Enrique Wilson	.10
30	Randy Johnson	.50
31	Garret Anderson	.10
32	Manny Ramirez	.60
33	Jeff Suppan	.10
34	Rickey Henderson	.25
35	Scott Spiezio	.10
36	Rondell White	.20
37	Todd Greene	.20
38	Delino DeShields	.10
39	Kevin Brown	.20
40	Chili Davis	.10
41	Jimmy Key	.10
42	NOT ISSUED	
43	Mike Mussina	.45
44	Joe Randa	.10
45	Chan Ho Park	.20
46	Brad Radke	.10
47	Geronimo Berroa	.10
48	Wade Boggs	.25
49	Kevin Appier	.10
50	Moises Alou	.15
51	David Justice	.25
52	Ivan Rodriguez	.75
53	J.T. Snow	.15
54	Brian Giles	.15
55	Will Clark	.25
56	Justin Thompson	.10
57	Javier Lopez	.15
58	Hideki Irabu	.30
59	Mark Grudzielanek	.10
60	Abraham Nunez	.15
61	Todd Hollandsworth	.10
62	Jay Bell	.10
63	Nomar Garciaparra	2.00
64	Vinny Castilla	.10
65	Lou Collier	.10
66	Kevin Orie	.10
67	John Valentin	.10
68	Robin Ventura	.20
69	Denny Neagle	.10
70	Tony Womack	.10
71	Dennis Reyes	.10
72	Wally Joyner	.10
73	Kevin Brown	.20
74	Ray Durham	.10
75	Mike Cameron	.15
76	Dante Bichette	.20
77	Jose Guillen	.25
78	Carlos Delgado	.20
79	Paul Molitor	.40
80	Jason Kendall	.10
81	Mark Belhorn	.10
82	Damian Jackson	.10
83	Bill Mueller	.10
84	Kevin Young	.10
85	Curt Schilling	.20
86	Jeffrey Hammonds	.10
87	Sandy Alomar Jr.	.15
88	Bartolo Colon	.10
89	Wilton Guerrero	.10
90	Bernie Williams	.50
91	Deion Sanders	.25
92	Mike Piazza	2.00
93	Butch Huskey	.10
94	Edgardo Alfonzo	.25
95	Alan Benes	.10
96	Craig Biggio	.20
97	Mark Grace	.25
98	Shawn Green	.25
99	Derrek Lee	.15
100	Ken Griffey Jr.	3.00
101	Tim Raines	.10
102	Pokey Reese	.10
103	Lee Stevens	.10
104	Shannon Stewart	.10
105	John Smoltz	.15
106	Frank Thomas	1.50
107	Jeff Fassero	.10
108	Jay Buhner	.15
109	Jose Canseco	.25
110	Omar Vizquel	.10
111	Travis Fryman	.10
112	Dave Nilsson	.10
113	John Olerud	.15
114	Larry Walker	.25
115	Jim Edmonds	.15
116	Bobby Higginson	.20
117	Todd Hundley	.10
118	Paul O'Neill	.20
119	Bip Roberts	.10
120	Ismael Valdes	.10
121	Pedro Martinez	.25
122	Jeff Cirillo	.10
123	Andy Benes	.10
124	Bobby Jones	.10
125	Brian Hunter	.10
126	Darryl Kile	.10
127	Pat Hentgen	.10
128	Marquis Grissom	.10
129	Eric Davis	.10
130	Chipper Jones	2.00
131	Edgar Martinez	.10
132	Andy Pettitte	.25
133	Cal Ripken Jr.	2.50
134	Scott Rolen	1.50
135	Ron Coomer	.10
136	Luis Castillo	.10
137	Fred McGriff	.15
138	Neifi Perez	.10
139	Eric Karros	.15
140	Alex Fernandez	.10
141	Jason Dickson	.10
142	Lance Johnson	.10
143	Ray Lankford	.10
144	Sammy Sosa	1.50
145	Eric Young	.10
146	Bubba Trammell	.20
147	Todd Walker	.20
148	Mo Vaughn (Curtain Calls)	1.00
149	Jeff Bagwell (Curtain Calls)	1.00
150	Kenny Lofton (Curtain Calls)	.50
151	Raul Mondesi (Curtain Calls)	.50
152	Mike Piazza (Curtain Calls)	2.00
153	Chipper Jones (Curtain Calls)	2.00
154	Larry Walker (Curtain Calls)	.75
155	Greg Maddux (Curtain Calls)	2.00
156	Ken Griffey Jr. (Curtain Calls)	3.00
157	Frank Thomas (Curtain Calls)	2.00
158	Darin Erstad (Gold Leaf Stars)	1.50
159	Roberto Alomar (Gold Leaf Stars)	1.00
160	Albert Belle (Gold Leaf Stars)	1.50
161	Jim Thome (Gold Leaf Stars)	.75
162	Tony Clark (Gold Leaf Stars)	1.00
163	Chuck Knoblauch (Gold Leaf Stars)	.75
164	Derek Jeter (Gold Leaf Stars)	4.00
165	Alex Rodriguez (Gold Leaf Stars)	5.00
166	Tony Gwynn (Gold Leaf Stars)	4.00
167	Roger Clemens (Gold Leaf Stars)	2.50
168	Barry Larkin (Gold Leaf Stars)	.50
169	Andres Galarraga (Gold Leaf Stars)	.50
170	Vladimir Guerrero (Gold Leaf Stars)	2.00
171	Mark McGwire (Gold Leaf Stars)	5.00
172	Barry Bonds (Gold Leaf Stars)	1.50
173	Juan Gonzalez (Gold Leaf Stars)	2.00
174	Andruw Jones (Gold Leaf Stars)	2.50
175	Paul Molitor (Gold Leaf Stars)	1.50

176 Hideo Nomo (Gold Leaf Stars) 1.50
177 Cal Ripken Jr. (Gold Leaf Stars) 4.00
178 Brad Fullmer (Gold Leaf Rookies) 1.00
179 Jaret Wright (Gold Leaf Rookies) 2.00
180 Bobby Estalella (Gold Leaf Rookies) .75
181 Ben Grieve (Gold Leaf Rookies) 2.00
182 Paul Konerko (Gold Leaf Rookies) 1.50
183 David Ortiz (Gold Leaf Rookies) .75
184 Todd Helton (Gold Leaf Rookies) 1.50
185 Juan Encarnacion (Gold Leaf Rookies) .75
186 Miguel Tejada (Gold Leaf Rookies) 1.50
187 Jacob Cruz (Gold Leaf Rookies) .50
188 Mark Kotsay (Gold Leaf Rookies) .75
189 Fernando Tatis (Gold Leaf Rookies) .50
190 Ricky Ledee (Gold Leaf Rookies) .65
191 Richard Hidalgo (Gold Leaf Rookies) .75
192 Richie Sexson (Gold Leaf Rookies) .75
193 Luis Ordaz (Gold Leaf Rookies) .75
194 Eli Marrero (Gold Leaf Rookies) .50
195 Livan Hernandez (Gold Leaf Rookies) .75
196 Homer Bush (Gold Leaf Rookies) .75
197 Raul Ibanez (Gold Leaf Rookies) .75
198 Checklist (Nomar Garciaparra) .75
199 Checklist (Scott Rolen) .50
200 Checklist (Jose Cruz Jr.) .25
201 (Al Martin) .25

ELITE

1 Ken Griffey Jr. 4.00
2 Frank Thomas 2.00
3 Alex Rodriguez 2.50
4 Mike Piazza 2.50
5 Greg Maddux 2.00
6 Cal Ripken Jr. 3.00
7 Chipper Jones 2.50
8 Derek Jeter 2.50
9 Tony Gwynn 1.50
10 Andruw Jones 1.00
11 Juan Gonzalez 1.00
12 Jeff Bagwell 1.25
13 Mark McGwire 4.00
14 Roger Clemens 1.25
15 Albert Belle .75
16 Barry Bonds .75
17 Kenny Lofton .65
18 Ivan Rodriguez .75
19 Manny Ramirez .75
20 Jim Thome .50
21 Chuck Knoblauch .40
22 Paul Molitor .60
23 Barry Larkin .30
24 Andy Pettitte .50
25 John Smoltz .25
26 Randy Johnson .50
27 Bernie Williams .75
28 Larry Walker .30
29 Mo Vaughn .75
30 Bobby Higginson .25
31 Edgardo Alfonzo .45
32 Justin Thompson .25
33 Jeff Suppan .25
34 Roberto Alomar .75
35 Hideo Nomo .75
36 Rusty Greer .25
37 Tim Salmon .30
38 Jim Edmonds .25
39 Gary Sheffield .30
40 Ken Caminiti .45
41 Sammy Sosa 3.00
42 Tony Womack .25
43 Matt Williams .30
44 Andres Galarraga .25
45 Garret Anderson .25
46 Rafael Palmeiro .35
47 Mike Mussina .75
48 Craig Biggio .35
49 Wade Boggs .40
50 Tom Glavine .30
51 Jason Giambi .25
52 Will Clark .35
53 David Justice .35
54 Sandy Alomar Jr. .25
55 Edgar Martinez .25
56 Brady Anderson .25
57 Eric Young .25
58 Ray Lankford .25
59 Kevin Brown .35
60 Raul Mondesi .30
61 Bobby Bonilla .25
62 Javier Lopez .25
63 Fred McGriff .30
64 Rondell White .25
65 Todd Hundley .25
66 Mark Grace .30
67 Alan Benes .25
68 Jeff Abbott .25
69 Bob Abreu .25
70 Deion Sanders .30
71 Tino Martinez .30
72 Shannon Stewart .25
73 Homer Bush .25
74 Carlos Delgado .30
75 Raul Ibanez .25
76 Hideki Irabu .75
77 Jose Cruz Jr. .75
78 Tony Clark .60
79 Wilton Guerrero .25
80 Vladimir Guerrero 1.00
81 Scott Rolen 1.50
82 Nomar Garciaparra 2.50
83 Darin Erstad .75
84 Chan Ho Park .35
85 Mike Cameron .25
86 Todd Walker .25
87 Todd Dunwoody .25
88 Neifi Perez .25
89 Brett Tomko .25
90 Jose Guillen .40
91 Matt Morris .25
92 Bartolo Colon .45
93 Jaret Wright .75
94 Shawn Estes .25
95 Livan Hernandez .25
96 Bobby Estalella .25
97 Ben Grieve 1.50
98 Paul Konerko .75
99 David Ortiz .55
100 Todd Helton 1.00
101 Juan Encarnacion .30
102 Bubba Trammell .25
103 Miguel Tejada .75
104 Jacob Cruz .25
105 Todd Greene .25
106 Kevin Orie .25
107 Mark Kotsay .60
108 Fernando Tatis .30
109 Jay Payton .25
110 Pokey Reese .25
111 Derrek Lee .25
112 Richard Hidalgo .35
113 Ricky Ledee .75
114 Lou Collier .25
115 Ruben Rivera .25
116 Shawn Green .75
117 Moises Alou .35
118 Ken Griffey Jr. (Generations) 2.00
119 Frank Thomas (Generations) 1.00
120 Alex Rodriguez (Generations) 1.50
121 Mike Piazza (Generations) 1.25
122 Greg Maddux (Generations) 1.00
123 Cal Ripken Jr. (Generations) 1.50
124 Chipper Jones (Generations) 1.25
125 Derek Jeter (Generations) 1.25
126 Tony Gwynn (Generations) 1.00
127 Andruw Jones (Generations) .90
128 Juan Gonzalez (Generations) .50
129 Jeff Bagwell (Generations) .75
130 Mark McGwire (Generations) 3.00
131 Roger Clemens (Generations) .75
132 Albert Belle (Generations) .50
133 Barry Bonds (Generations) .50
134 Kenny Lofton (Generations) .45
135 Ivan Rodriguez (Generations) .40
136 Manny Ramirez (Generations) .50
137 Jim Thome (Generations) .30
138 Chuck Knoblauch (Generations) .25
139 Paul Molitor (Generations) .35
140 Barry Larkin (Generations) .25
141 Mo Vaughn (Generations) .50
142 Hideki Irabu (Generations) .50
143 Jose Cruz Jr. (Generations) .65
144 Tony Clark (Generations) .40
145 Vladimir Guerrero (Generations) 1.00
146 Scott Rolen (Generations) 1.00
147 Nomar Garciaparra (Generations) 1.50
148 Checklist (Garciaparra) .75
149 Checklist (Walker) .25
150 Checklist (Martinez) .25

PREFERRED

1 Ken Griffey Jr. EX 15.00
2 Frank Thomas EX 7.50
3 Cal Ripken Jr. EX 12.50
4 Alex Rodriguez EX 12.50
5 Greg Maddux EX 10.00
6 Mike Piazza EX 15.00
7 Chipper Jones EX 15.00
8 Tony Gwynn FB 10.00
9 Derek Jeter FB 15.00
10 Jeff Bagwell EX 7.50
11 Juan Gonzalez EX 6.00
12 Nomar Garciaparra EX 12.50
13 Andruw Jones FB 7.50
14 Hideo Nomo FB 3.00
15 Roger Clemens FB 6.00
16 Mark McGwire FB 15.00
17 Scott Rolen FB 6.00
18 Vladimir Guerrero FB 6.00
19 Barry Bonds FB 5.00
20 Darin Erstad FB 5.00
21 Albert Belle FB 5.00
22 Kenny Lofton FB 4.00
23 Mo Vaughn FB 4.00
24 Tony Clark FB 3.00
25 Ivan Rodriguez FB 6.00
26 Larry Walker CL 2.00
27 Eddie Murray CL 3.00
28 Andy Pettitte CL 1.50
29 Roberto Alomar CL 3.00
30 Randy Johnson CL 5.00
31 Manny Ramirez CL 7.50
32 Paul Molitor FB 6.00
33 Mike Mussina CL 5.00
34 Jim Thome FB 3.00
35 Tino Martinez CL 3.00
36 Gary Sheffield CL 2.00
37 Chuck Knoblauch CL 2.00
38 Bernie Williams CL 2.00
39 Tim Salmon CL 1.50
40 Sammy Sosa CL 12.50
41 Wade Boggs MZ 4.50
42 Will Clark GS 3.00
43 Andres Galarraga CL 1.50
44 Raul Mondesi CL 1.50
45 Rickey Henderson GS 1.50
46 Jose Canseco GS 1.50
47 Pedro Martinez GS 2.00
48 Jay Buhner GS 1.00
49 Ryan Klesko GS 1.00
50 Barry Larkin CL 1.00
51 Charles Johnson GS 1.00
52 Tom Glavine GS 1.00
53 Edgar Martinez CL 1.00
54 Fred McGriff GS 1.00
55 Moises Alou MZ 1.00
56 Dante Bichette GS 1.00
57 Jim Edmonds CL 1.00
58 Mark Grace MZ 2.00
59 Chan Ho Park MZ 1.50
60 Justin Thompson MZ 1.50
61 John Smoltz MZ 1.00
62 Craig Biggio CL 2.00
63 Ken Caminiti MZ 2.00
64 Deion Sanders MZ 1.50
65 Carlos Delgado GS 1.00
66 David Justice CL 1.50
67 J.T. Snow GS 1.00
68 Jason Giambi CL 1.00
69 Garret Anderson MZ 1.00
70 Rondell White MZ 1.00
71 Matt Williams MZ 1.25
72 Brady Anderson MZ 1.00
73 Eric Karros GS 1.00
74 Javier Lopez GS 1.00
75 Pat Hentgen GS 1.00
76 Todd Hundley GS 1.00
77 Ray Lankford GS 1.00
78 Denny Neagle GS 1.00
79 Henry Rodriguez GS 1.00
80 Sandy Alomar Jr. MZ 1.25
81 Rafael Palmeiro MZ 2.00
82 Robin Ventura GS 2.00
83 John Olerud GS 1.50
84 Omar Vizquel GS 1.00
85 Joe Randa GS 1.00
86 Lance Johnson GS 1.00
87 Kevin Brown GS 1.50
88 Curt Schilling GS 1.25
89 Ismael Valdes GS 1.00
90 Francisco Cordova GS 1.00
91 David Cone GS 1.25
92 Paul O'Neill GS 1.50
93 Jimmy Key GS 1.00
94 Brad Radke GS 1.00
95 Kevin Appier GS 1.00
96 Al Martin GS 1.00
97 Rusty Greer MZ 1.00
98 Reggie Jefferson GS 1.00
99 Ron Coomer GS 1.00
100 Vinny Castilla GS 1.00
101 Bobby Bonilla MZ 1.50
102 Eric Young GS 1.00
103 Tony Womack GS 1.00
104 Jason Kendall GS 1.00
105 Jeff Suppan GS 1.00
106 Shawn Estes MZ 1.00
107 Shawn Green GS 2.00
108 Edgardo Alfonzo MZ 2.00
109 Alan Benes MZ 1.00
110 Bobby Higginson GS 1.50
111 Mark Grudzielanek GS 1.00
112 Wilton Guerrero GS 1.00
113 Todd Greene MZ 1.50
114 Pokey Reese GS 1.00
115 Jose Guillen CL 2.00
116 Neifi Perez MZ 1.00
117 Luis Castillo GS 1.00
118 Edgar Renteria GS 1.50
119 Karim Garcia GS 1.50
120 Butch Huskey GS 1.00
121 Michael Tucker GS 1.00
122 Jason Dickson GS 1.00

123	Todd Walker MZ	2.00
124	Brian Jordan GS	1.00
125	Joe Carter GS	1.00
126	Matt Morris MZ	1.00
127	Brett Tomko MZ	1.00
128	Mike Cameron CL	1.00
129	Russ Davis GS	1.00
130	Shannon Stewart MZ	1.00
131	Kevin Orie GS	1.00
132	Scott Spiezio GS	1.00
133	Brian Giles GS	1.00
134	Raul Casanova GS	1.00
135	Jose Cruz Jr. CL	2.50
136	Hideki Irabu GS	2.50
137	Bubba Trammell GS	1.50
138	Richard Hidalgo CL	2.00
139	Paul Konerko CL	2.00
140	Todd Helton FB	5.00
141	Miguel Tejada CL	2.00
142	Fernando Tatis MZ	1.50
143	Ben Grieve FB	2.00
144	Travis Lee FB	2.00
145	Mark Kotsay CL	1.50
146	Eli Marrero MZ	1.00
147	David Ortiz CL	1.50
148	Juan Encarnacion MZ	1.50
149	Jaret Wright MZ	2.50
150	Livan Hernandez CL	2.00
151	Ruben Rivera GS	1.00
152	Brad Fullmer MZ	2.00
153	Dennis Reyes GS	1.00
154	Enrique Wilson MZ	1.00
155	Todd Dunwoody MZ	1.50
156	Derrick Gibson MZ	1.50
157	Aaron Boone MZ	1.50
158	Ron Wright MZ	1.00
159	Preston Wilson MZ	2.00
160	Abraham Nunez GS	1.25
161	Shane Monahan GS	1.25
162	Carl Pavano GS	1.50
163	Derrek Lee GS	1.50
164	Jeff Abbott GS	1.00
165	Wes Helms MZ	1.00
166	Brian Rose GS	1.00
167	Bobby Estalella GS	1.00
168	Ken Griffey Jr. GS	6.00
169	Frank Thomas GS	4.00
170	Cal Ripken Jr. GS	5.00
171	Alex Rodriguez GS	5.00
172	Greg Maddux GS	4.00
173	Mike Piazza GS	5.00
174	Chipper Jones GS	5.00
175	Tony Gwynn GS	3.00
176	Derek Jeter GS	4.00
177	Jeff Bagwell GS	2.00
178	Juan Gonzalez GS	2.00
179	Nomar Garciaparra GS	4.00
180	Andruw Jones GS	1.50
181	Hideo Nomo GS	1.00
182	Roger Clemens GS	2.50
183	Mark McGwire GS	5.00
184	Scott Rolen GS	2.00
185	Barry Bonds GS	1.50
186	Darin Erstad GS	1.50
187	Mo Vaughn GS	1.50
188	Ivan Rodriguez GS	1.50
189	Larry Walker MZ	2.00
190	Andy Pettitte GS	1.00
191	Randy Johnson MZ	2.50
192	Paul Molitor GS	1.50
193	Jim Thome GS	1.00
194	Tino Martinez MZ	1.00
195	Gary Sheffield GS	1.00
196	Albert Belle GS	1.50
197	Jose Cruz Jr. GS	1.50
198	Todd Helton GS	1.50
199	Ben Grieve GS	2.50
200	Paul Konerko GS	1.50

Player names in *Italic* type indicate a rookie card.

E

2000 E-X

Released as a 90-card set the card fronts have a holo-foil card front, with the E-X logo and player name stamped in silver foil. Card backs have a player image, 1999 stats and the featured player's career totals.

		MT
Complete Set (90):		300.00
Common Player:		.25
Common Prospect (61-90):		5.00
Production 3,499 sets		
Pack:		4.00
Wax Box:		90.00
1	Alex Rodriguez	5.00
2	Jeff Bagwell	1.50
3	Mike Piazza	4.00
4	Tony Gwynn	2.50
5	Ken Griffey Jr.	6.00
6	Juan Gonzalez	1.50
7	Vladimir Guerrero	3.00
8	Cal Ripken Jr.	5.00
9	Mo Vaughn	1.00
10	Chipper Jones	3.00
11	Derek Jeter	4.00
12	Nomar Garciaparra	4.00
13	Mark McGwire	6.00
14	Sammy Sosa	4.00
15	Pedro Martinez	1.50
16	Greg Maddux	3.00
17	Frank Thomas	2.00
18	Shawn Green	1.00
19	Carlos Beltran	.40
20	Roger Clemens	2.00
21	Randy Johnson	1.50
22	Bernie Williams	1.00
23	Carlos Delgado	1.00
24	Manny Ramirez	1.50
25	Freddy Garcia	.25
26	Barry Bonds	1.50
27	Tim Hudson	.50
28	Larry Walker	.75
29	Raul Mondesi	.50
30	Ivan Rodriguez	1.50
31	Magglio Ordonez	.50
32	Scott Rolen	1.50
33	Mike Mussina	.75
34	J.D. Drew	.40
35	Tom Glavine	.40
36	Barry Larkin	.50
37	Jim Thome	.75
38	Erubiel Durazo	.25
39	Curt Schilling	.40
40	Orlando Hernandez	.40
41	Rafael Palmeiro	1.00
42	Gabe Kapler	.25
43	Mark Grace	.50
44	Jeff Cirillo	.25
45	Jeromy Burnitz	.25
46	Sean Casey	.25
47	Kevin Millwood	.25
48	Vinny Castilla	.25
49	Jose Canseco	1.00
50	Roberto Alomar	1.00
51	Craig Biggio	.50
52	Preston Wilson	.25
53	Jeff Weaver	.25
54	Robin Ventura	.40
55	Ben Grieve	.50
56	Troy Glaus	1.50
57	Jacque Jones	.25
58	Brian Giles	.25
59	Kevin Brown	.40
60	Todd Helton	1.50
61	Ben Petrick (Prospects)	5.00
62	Chad Hermansen (Prospects)	5.00
63	Kevin Barker (Prospects)	5.00
64	Matt LeCroy (Prospects)	5.00
65	Brad Penny (Prospects)	5.00
66	D.T. Cromer (Prospects)	5.00
67	Steve Lomasney (Prospects)	5.00
68	Cole Liniak (Prospects)	5.00
69	B.J. Ryan (Prospects)	5.00
70	Wilton Veras (Prospects)	10.00
71	*Aaron McNeal* (Prospects)	12.00
72	Nick Johnson (Prospects)	15.00
73	Adam Piatt (Prospects)	10.00
74	Adam Kennedy (Prospects)	6.00
75	Cesar King (Prospects)	5.00
76	Peter Bergeron (Prospects)	6.00
77	Rob Bell (Prospects)	5.00
78	Wily Pena (Prospects)	20.00
79	Ruben Mateo (Prospects)	5.00
80	Kip Wells (Prospects)	6.00
81	Alex Escobar (Prospects)	5.00
82	*Danys Baez* (Prospects)	10.00
83	Travis Dawkins (Prospects)	5.00
84	Mark Quinn (Prospects)	6.00
85	Jimmy Anderson (Prospects)	5.00
86	Rick Ankiel (Prospects)	30.00
87	Alfonso Soriano (Prospects)	12.00
88	Pat Burrell (Prospects)	15.00
89	Eric Munson (Prospects)	15.00
90	Josh Beckett (Prospects)	18.00

2000 E-X Generation E-X

This 15-card set spotlights the top young players in the game and were seeded 1:8 packs. Card fronts have silver foil stamping over a background resembling a sky. These were seeded 1:8 packs. Card backs are numbered with a "GX" suffix.

		MT
Complete Set (15):		50.00
Common Player:		1.50
Inserted 1:8		
1	Rick Ankiel	10.00
2	Josh Beckett	4.00
3	Carlos Beltran	1.50
4	Pat Burrell	5.00
5	Freddy Garcia	1.50
6	Alex Rodriguez	12.00
7	Derek Jeter	10.00
8	Tim Hudson	2.00
9	Shawn Green	3.00
10	Eric Munson	3.00
11	Adam Piatt	2.50
12	Adam Kennedy	1.50
13	Nick Johnson	3.00
14	Alfonso Soriano	4.00
15	Nomar Garciaparra	10.00

2000 E-X E-Xplosive

These inserts have a traditional format, with a holographic star like image in the background and "explosive" running down the top left side. Card backs are numbered with an "XP" suffix and are serial numbered on the bottom portion in an edition of 2,499 sets.

		MT
Complete Set (20):		150.00
Common Player:		4.00
Production 2,499 sets		
1	Tony Gwynn	8.00
2	Alex Rodriguez	15.00
3	Pedro Martinez	5.00
4	Sammy Sosa	12.00
5	Cal Ripken Jr.	15.00
6	Adam Piatt	4.00
7	Pat Burrell	6.00
8	J.D. Drew	4.00
9	Mike Piazza	12.00
10	Shawn Green	4.00
11	Troy Glaus	5.00
12	Randy Johnson	5.00
13	Juan Gonzalez	5.00
14	Chipper Jones	10.00
15	Ivan Rodriguez	5.00

16	Nomar Garciaparra	12.00
17	Ken Griffey Jr.	20.00
18	Nick Johnson	5.00
19	Mark McGwire	20.00
20	Frank Thomas	8.00

2000 E-X E-Xceptional Red

Die-cut in a shape similar to an oval, these inserts have a cloth like feel with silver foil stamping with a red background. Card backs are numbered consecutively "1 Of 15XC" and so on. These are seeded 1:14 packs. Two parallels are also inserted: Blues are seeded 1:288 packs and Greens are limited to 999 serial numbered sets.

		MT
Complete Set (15):		190.00
Common Player:		6.00
Inserted 1:14		
Blue:		2-3X
Inserted 1:288		
Green:		1-1.5X
Production 999 sets		
1	Ken Griffey Jr.	30.00
2	Derek Jeter	20.00
3	Nomar Garciaparra	20.00
4	Mark McGwire	30.00
5	Sammy Sosa	20.00
6	Mike Piazza	20.00
7	Alex Rodriguez	25.00
8	Cal Ripken Jr.	25.00
9	Chipper Jones	15.00
10	Pedro Martinez	8.00
11	Jeff Bagwell	8.00
12	Greg Maddux	15.00
13	Roger Clemens	10.00
14	Tony Gwynn	12.00
15	Frank Thomas	10.00

2000 E-X E-Xciting

Die-cut in the shape of a jersey, card fronts have a holograpic appearance with silver foil stamping. These were seeded 1:24 packs. Card backs are numbered with an "XT" suffix.

		MT
Complete Set (10):		75.00
Common Player:		4.00
Inserted 1:24		
1	Mark McGwire	20.00
2	Ken Griffey Jr.	20.00
3	Randy Johnson	5.00
4	Sammy Sosa	12.00
5	Manny Ramirez	5.00
6	Jose Canseco	4.00
7	Derek Jeter	12.00
8	Scott Rolen	5.00
9	Juan Gonzalez	5.00
10	Barry Bonds	5.00

2000 E-X Genuine Coverage

		MT
Common Player:		25.00
Inserted 1:144		
1	Alex Rodriguez	180.00
2	Tom Glavine	40.00
3	Cal Ripken Jr.	180.00
4	Edgar Martinez	40.00
5	Raul Mondesi	30.00
6	Carlos Beltran	25.00
7	Chipper Jones	75.00
8	Barry Bonds	75.00
9	Heath Murray	25.00
10	Tim Hudson	40.00
11	Mike Mussina	35.00
12	Derek Jeter	180.00

2000 E-X Essential Credentials Now

Like Future, this is a parallel of the base set, with the production of cards 1-60 limited to that player's card number. Production for cards 61-90 can be determined by subtracting 60 from the card number. Quantity issued is listed in parantheses.

		MT
Common Player:		15.00
1	Alex Rodriguez (1)	NA
2	Jeff Bagwell (2)	NA
3	Mike Piazza (3)	NA
4	Tony Gwynn (4)	NA
5	Ken Griffey Jr. (5)	NA
6	Juan Gonzalez (6)	NA
7	Vladimir Guerrero (7)	NA
8	Cal Ripken Jr. (8)	NA
9	Mo Vaughn (9)	NA
10	Chipper Jones (10)	NA
11	Derek Jeter (11)	NA
12	Nomar Garciaparra (12)	NA
13	Mark McGwire (13)	NA
14	Sammy Sosa (14)	NA
15	Pedro Martinez (15)	NA
16	Greg Maddux (16)	NA
17	Frank Thomas (17)	NA
18	Shawn Green (18)	NA
19	Carlos Beltran (19)	NA
20	Roger Clemens (20)	200.00
21	Randy Johnson (21)	125.00
22	Bernie Williams (22)	125.00
23	Carlos Delgado (23)	90.00
24	Manny Ramirez (24)	100.00
25	Freddy Garcia (25)	30.00
26	Barry Bonds (26)	125.00
27	Tim Hudson (27)	40.00
28	Larry Walker (28)	75.00
29	Raul Mondesi (29)	50.00
30	Ivan Rodriguez (30)	125.00
31	Magglio Ordonez (31)	50.00
32	Scott Rolen (32)	100.00
33	Mike Mussina (33)	75.00
34	J.D. Drew (34)	35.00
35	Tom Glavine (35)	35.00
36	Barry Larkin (36)	40.00
37	Jim Thome (37)	40.00
38	Erubiel Durazo (38)	20.00
39	Curt Schilling (39)	25.00
40	Orlando Hernandez (40)	25.00
41	Rafael Palmeiro (41)	40.00
42	Gabe Kapler (42)	20.00
43	Mark Grace (43)	25.00
44	Jeff Cirillo (44)	20.00
45	Jeromy Burnitz (45)	15.00
46	Sean Casey (46)	15.00
47	Kevin Millwood (47)	15.00
48	Vinny Castilla (48)	15.00
49	Jose Canseco (49)	40.00
50	Roberto Alomar (50)	40.00
51	Craig Biggio (51)	25.00
52	Preston Wilson (52)	10.00
53	Jeff Weaver (53)	10.00
54	Robin Ventura (54)	15.00
55	Ben Grieve (55)	20.00
56	Troy Glaus (56)	20.00
57	Jacque Jones (57)	10.00
58	Brian Giles (58)	10.00
59	Kevin Brown (59)	15.00
60	Todd Helton (60)	40.00
61	Ben Petrick (1) (Prospects)	NA
62	Chad Hermansen (2) (Prospects)	NA
63	Kevin Barker (3) (Prospects)	NA
64	Matt LeCroy (4) (Prospects)	NA
65	Brad Penny (5) (Prospects)	NA
66	D.T. Cromer (6) (Prospects)	NA
67	Steve Lomasney (7) (Prospects)	NA
68	Cole Liniak (8) (Prospects)	NA
69	B.J. Ryan (9) (Prospects)	NA
70	Wilton Veras (10) (Prospects)	NA
71	Aaron McNeal (11) (Prospects)	NA
72	Nick Johnson (12) (Prospects)	NA
73	Adam Piatt (13) (Prospects)	NA
74	Adam Kennedy (14) (Prospects)	NA
75	Cesar King (15) (Prospects)	NA
76	Peter Bergeron (16) (Prospects)	NA
77	Rob Bell (17) (Prospects)	NA
78	Wily Pena (18) (Prospects)	100.00
79	Ruben Mateo (19) (Prospects)	20.00
80	Kip Wells (20) (Prospects)	20.00
81	Alex Escobar (21) (Prospects)	20.00
82	Danys Baez (22) (Prospects)	75.00
83	Travis Dawkins (23) (Prospects)	15.00
84	Mark Quinn (24) (Prospects)	15.00
85	Jimmy Anderson (25) (Prospects)	15.00
86	Rick Ankiel (26) (Prospects)	180.00
87	Alfonso Soriano (27) (Prospects)	65.00
88	Pat Burrell (28) (Prospects)	100.00
89	Eric Munson (29) (Prospects)	75.00
90	Josh Beckett (30) (Prospects)	75.00

2000 E-X Essential Credentials Future

Production varied for these parallel inserts depending on the card number, with the exact production number for cards 1-60 determined by subtracting the card number from 61. Cards 61-90 are determined by subtracting the card number from 91. Quantity issued is listed in parantheses.

		MT
Common Player:		15.00
1	Alex Rodriguez (60)	160.00
2	Jeff Bagwell (59)	60.00
3	Mike Piazza (58)	150.00
4	Tony Gwynn (57)	100.00
5	Ken Griffey Jr. (56)	250.00
6	Juan Gonzalez (55)	60.00
7	Vladimir Guerrero (54)	75.00
8	Cal Ripken Jr. (53)	180.00
9	Mo Vaughn (52)	50.00
10	Chipper Jones (51)	125.00
11	Derek Jeter (50)	160.00
12	Nomar Garciaparra (49)	150.00
13	Mark McGwire (48)	275.00
14	Sammy Sosa (47)	150.00
15	Pedro Martinez (46)	70.00
16	Greg Maddux (45)	125.00
17	Frank Thomas (44)	80.00
18	Shawn Green (43)	50.00
19	Carlos Beltran (42)	25.00
20	Roger Clemens (41)	80.00
21	Randy Johnson (40)	60.00
22	Bernie Williams (39)	50.00

23	Carlos Delgado (38)	50.00
24	Manny Ramirez (37)	60.00
25	Freddy Garcia (36)	25.00
26	Barry Bonds (35)	70.00
27	Tim Hudson (34)	30.00
28	Larry Walker (33)	50.00
29	Raul Mondesi (32)	30.00
30	Ivan Rodriguez (31)	80.00
31	Magglio Ordonez (30)	25.00
32	Scott Rolen (29)	60.00
33	Mike Mussina (28)	40.00
34	J.D. Drew (27)	30.00
35	Tom Glavine (26)	40.00
36	Barry Larkin (25)	40.00
37	Jim Thome (24)	40.00
38	Erubiel Durazo (23)	25.00
39	Curt Schilling (22)	25.00
40	Orlando Hernandez (21)	20.00
41	Rafael Palmeiro (20)	60.00
42	Gabe Kapler (19)	25.00
43	Mark Grace (18)	30.00
44	Jeff Cirillo (17)	20.00
45	Jeromy Burnitz (16)	20.00
46	Sean Casey (15)	20.00
47	Kevin Millwood (14)	20.00
48	Vinny Castilla (13)	25.00
49	Jose Canseco (12)	80.00
50	Roberto Alomar (11)	80.00
51	Craig Biggio (10)	50.00
52	Preston Wilson (9)	NA
53	Jeff Weaver (8)	NA
54	Robin Ventura (7)	NA
55	Ben Grieve (6)	NA
56	Troy Glaus (5)	NA
57	Jacque Jones (4)	NA
58	Brian Giles (3)	NA
59	Kevin Brown (2)	NA
60	Todd Helton (1)	NA
61	Ben Petrick (30) (Prospects)	15.00
62	Chad Hermansen (29) (Prospects)	15.00
63	Kevin Barker (28) (Prospects)	15.00
64	Matt LeCroy (27) (Prospects)	15.00
65	Brad Penny (26) (Prospects)	15.00
66	D.T. Cromer (25) (Prospects)	15.00
67	Steve Lomasney (24) (Prospects)	15.00
68	Cole Liniak (23) (Prospects)	15.00
69	B.J. Ryan (22) (Prospects)	20.00
70	Wilton Veras (21) (Prospects)	75.00
71	Aaron McNeal (20) (Prospects)	90.00
72	Nick Johnson (19) (Prospects)	125.00
73	Adam Piatt (18) (Prospects)	100.00
74	Adam Kennedy (17) (Prospects)	35.00
75	Cesar King (16) (Prospects)	25.00
76	Peter Bergeron (15) (Prospects)	35.00
77	Rob Bell (14) (Prospects)	25.00
78	Wily Pena (13) (Prospects)	150.00
79	Ruben Mateo (12) (Prospects)	25.00
80	Kip Wells (11) (Prospects)	25.00
81	Alex Escobar (10) (Prospects)	35.00
82	Danys Baez (9) (Prospects)	NA
83	Travis Dawkins (8) (Prospects)	NA
84	Mark Quinn (7) (Prospects)	NA
85	Jimmy Anderson (6) (Prospects)	NA
86	Rick Ankiel (5) (Prospects)	NA
87	Alfonso Soriano (4) (Prospects)	NA
88	Pat Burrell (3) (Prospects)	NA
89	Eric Munson (2) (Prospects)	NA
90	Josh Beckett (1) (Prospects)	NA

2000 E-X Autographics

	MT
Common Player:	10.00
Inserted 1:24	
Bob Abreu	20.00
Moises Alou	15.00
Rick Ankiel	75.00
Michael Barrett	10.00
Josh Beckett	25.00
Rob Bell	15.00
Adrian Beltre	20.00
Carlos Beltran	20.00
Wade Boggs	60.00
Barry Bonds	75.00
Kent Bottenfield	10.00
Milton Bradley	15.00
Pat Burrell	40.00
Chris Carpenter	10.00
Sean Casey	20.00
Eric Chavez	15.00
Will Clark	40.00
Johnny Damon	15.00
Mike Darr	10.00
Ben Davis	10.00
Russ Davis	10.00
Carlos Delgado	50.00
Jason Dewey	10.00
Octavio Dotel	10.00
J.D. Drew	40.00
Ray Durham	15.00
Damion Easley	10.00
Kelvim Escobar	10.00
Carlos Febles	10.00
Freddy Garcia	10.00
Jeremy Giambi	10.00
Todd Greene	10.00
Jason Grilli	10.00
Vladimir Guerrero	60.00
Tony Gwynn	75.00
Jerry Hairston	10.00
Mike Hampton	15.00
Todd Helton	40.00
Trevor Hoffman	10.00
Tim Hudson	20.00
John Jaha	10.00
Derek Jeter	200.00
D'Angelo Jimenez	10.00
Randy Johnson	75.00
Jason Kendall	15.00
Adam Kennedy	10.00
Cesar King	10.00
Paul Konerko	15.00
Mark Kotsay	10.00
Ray Lankford	15.00
Jason LaRue	10.00
Matt Lawton	10.00
Carlos Lee	10.00
Mike Lieberthal	10.00
Cole Liniak	10.00
Steve Lomasney	10.00
Jose Macias	10.00
Greg Maddux	150.00
Edgar Martinez	20.00
Pedro Martinez	75.00
Ruben Mateo	15.00
Gary Matthews Jr.	10.00
Aaron McNeal	10.00
Raul Mondesi	20.00
Orber Moreno	10.00
Warren Morris	10.00
Eric Munson	20.00
Heath Murray	10.00
Mike Mussina	30.00
Joe Nathan	15.00
Rafael Palmeiro	40.00
Jim Parque	10.00
Angel Pena	10.00
Wily Pena	25.00
Pokey Reese	15.00
Matt Riley	10.00
Cal Ripken Jr.	200.00
Alex Rodriguez	175.00
Scott Rolen	40.00
Jimmy Rollins	10.00
B.J. Ryan	10.00
Randall Simon	10.00
Chris Singleton	15.00
Alfonso Soriano	20.00
Shannon Stewart	15.00
Mike Sweeney	15.00
Miguel Tejada	15.00
Wilton Veras	25.00
Frank Thomas	75.00
Billy Wagner	15.00
Jeff Weaver	10.00
Rondell White	15.00
Scott Williamson	10.00
Randy Wolf	15.00
Jaret Wright	10.00
Ed Yarnall	15.00
Kevin Young	10.00

1993 Finest Promos

Debuting at the 1993 National Convention in Chicago, this three-card set introduced the hobby to the Topps Finest baseball issue. While the promos are identical in high-tech format to the regular Finest cards issued later, including the same card numbers, there are differences in the promos; some subtle, some glaring. For instance, the Ryan and Alomar cards were issued in promo form in the "gray" style of the basic set. In the regularly issued set, those cards were in the green All-Star format. Each of the promos is overprinted in red on the back, "Promotional Sample 1 of 5000". Of considerably greater rarity are refractor versions of these promo cards, with production numbers unknown.

		MT
	Complete Set (3):	35.00
	Complete Set, Refractors (3):	4500.
88	Roberto Alomar	10.00
88r	Roberto Alomar (refractor)	1500.
98	Don Mattingly	15.00
98r	Don Mattingly (refractor)	1500.
107	Nolan Ryan	20.00
107r	Nolan Ryan (refractor)	2500

1993 Finest

This 199-card set uses a process of multi-color metallization; this chromium technology adds depth and dimension to the card. The set has a 33-card subset of All-Stars; a parallel version of these cards (Refractors) were also created with refracting foil using the metallization enhancement process. There is one refracting foil card in every nine packs. Packs have five cards. Each 18-count box contains a 5" x 7" version of one of the 33 All-Star players in the set.

		MT
	Complete Set (199):	200.00
	Common Player:	1.00
	Pack (6):	32.00
	Wax Box (18):	425.00
1	Dave Justice	2.00
2	Lou Whitaker	1.00
3	Bryan Harvey	1.00
4	Carlos Garcia	1.00
5	Sid Fernandez	1.00
6	Brett Butler	1.00
7	Scott Cooper	1.00
8	B.J. Surhoff	1.00
9	Steve Finley	1.50
10	Curt Schilling	2.00
11	Jeff Bagwell	8.00
12	Alex Cole	1.00
13	John Olerud	1.50
14	John Smiley	1.00
15	Bip Roberts	1.00
16	Albert Belle	5.00
17	Duane Ward	1.00
18	Alan Trammell	1.00
19	Andy Benes	1.50
20	Reggie Sanders	1.00
21	Todd Zeile	1.00
22	Rick Aguilera	1.00
23	Dave Hollins	1.00
24	Jose Rijo	1.00
25	Matt Williams	3.00
26	Sandy Alomar	1.50
27	Alex Fernandez	1.00
28	Ozzie Smith	6.00
29	Ramon Martinez	2.00
30	Bernie Williams	6.00
31	Gary Sheffield	3.00
32	Eric Karros	1.50
33	Frank Viola	1.00
34	Kevin Young	1.00

35 Ken Hill 1.00
36 Tony Fernandez 1.00
37 Tim Wakefield 1.00
38 John Kruk 1.00
39 Chris Sabo 1.00
40 Marquis Grissom 1.50
41 Glenn Davis 1.00
42 Jeff Montgomery 1.00
43 Kenny Lofton 5.00
44 John Burkett 1.00
45 Darryl Hamilton 1.00
46 Jim Abbott 1.00
47 Ivan Rodriguez 7.50
48 Eric Young 1.00
49 Mitch Williams 1.00
50 Harold Reynolds 1.00
51 Brian Harper 1.00
52 Rafael Palmeiro 4.00
53 Bret Saberhagen 1.25
54 Jeff Conine 1.50
55 Ivan Calderon 1.00
56 Juan Guzman 1.00
57 Carlos Baerga 1.00
58 Charles Nagy 1.00
59 Wally Joyner 1.00
60 Charlie Hayes 1.00
61 Shane Mack 1.00
62 Pete Harnisch 1.00
63 George Brett 10.00
64 Lance Johnson 1.00
65 Ben McDonald 1.00
66 Bobby Bonilla 1.50
67 Terry Steinbach 1.00
68 Ron Gant 1.50
69 Doug Jones 1.00
70 Paul Molitor 4.00
71 Brady Anderson 1.50
72 Chuck Finley 1.00
73 Mark Grace 2.00
74 Mike Devereaux 1.00
75 Tony Phillips 1.00
76 Chuck Knoblauch 2.50
77 Tony Gwynn 12.50
78 Kevin Appier 1.00
79 Sammy Sosa 12.50
80 Mickey Tettleton 1.00
81 Felix Jose 1.00
82 Mark Langston 1.00
83 Gregg Jefferies 1.50
84 Andre Dawson (AS) 1.50
85 Greg Maddux (AS) 12.50
86 Rickey Henderson (AS) 2.50
87 Tom Glavine (AS) 2.50
88 Roberto Alomar (AS) 5.00
89 Darryl Strawberry (AS) 1.50
90 Wade Boggs (AS) 3.00
91 Bo Jackson (AS) 2.00
92 Mark McGwire (AS) 25.00
93 Robin Ventura (AS) 1.50
94 Joe Carter (AS) 1.00
95 Lee Smith (AS) 1.00
96 Cal Ripken, Jr. (AS) 17.50
97 Larry Walker (AS) 4.00
98 Don Mattingly (AS) 10.00
99 Jose Canseco (AS) 2.50
100 Dennis Eckersley (AS) 1.00
101 Terry Pendleton (AS) 1.00
102 Frank Thomas (AS) 12.50
103 Barry Bonds (AS) 6.00
104 Roger Clemens 12.00
105 Ryne Sandberg (AS) 6.00
106 Fred McGriff (AS) 2.00
107 Nolan Ryan (AS) 20.00
108 Will Clark (AS) 3.00
109 Pat Listach (AS) 1.00
110 Ken Griffey, Jr. (AS) 25.00
111 Cecil Fielder (AS) 1.00
112 Kirby Puckett (AS) 10.00
113 Dwight Gooden (AS) 1.25
114 Barry Larkin (AS) 3.00
115 David Cone (AS) 1.50
116 Juan Gonzalez (AS) 8.00
117 Kent Hrbek 1.00
118 Tim Wallach 1.00
119 Craig Biggio 2.00
120 Bobby Kelly 1.00
121 Greg Olson 1.00
122 Eddie Murray 4.00
123 Wil Cordero 1.00
124 Jay Buhner 2.00
125 Carlton Fisk 1.50
126 Eric Davis 1.00
127 Doug Drabek 1.00
128 Ozzie Guillen 1.00
129 John Wetteland 1.00
130 Andres Galarraga 2.00
131 Ken Caminiti 1.50
132 Tom Candiotti 1.00
133 Pat Borders 1.00
134 Kevin Brown 1.50
135 Travis Fryman 2.00
136 Kevin Mitchell 1.00
137 Greg Swindell 1.00
138 Benny Santiago 1.00
139 Reggie Jefferson 1.00
140 Chris Bosio 1.00
141 Deion Sanders 2.00
142 Scott Erickson 1.00
143 Howard Johnson 1.00
144 Orestes Destrade 1.00
145 Jose Guzman 1.00
146 Chad Curtis 1.00
147 Cal Eldred 1.00
148 Willie Greene 1.00
149 Tommy Greene 1.00
150 Erik Hanson 1.00
151 Bob Welch 1.00
152 John Jaha 1.00
153 Harold Baines 1.00
154 Randy Johnson 5.00
155 Al Martin 1.00
156 *J.T. Snow* 3.00
157 Mike Mussina 5.00
158 Ruben Sierra 1.00
159 Dean Palmer 1.00
160 Steve Avery 1.00
161 Julio Franco 1.00
162 Dave Winfield 2.00
163 Tim Salmon 4.00
164 Tom Henke 1.00
165 Mo Vaughn 6.00
166 John Smoltz 2.00
167 Danny Tartabull 1.00
168 Delino DeShields 1.00
169 Charlie Hough 1.00
170 Paul O'Neill 1.50
171 Darren Daulton 1.00
172 Jack McDowell 1.00
173 Junior Felix 1.00
174 Jimmy Key 1.00
175 George Bell 1.00
176 Mike Stanton 1.00
177 Len Dykstra 1.00
178 Norm Charlton 1.00
179 Eric Anthony 1.00
180 Bob Dibble 1.00
181 Otis Nixon 1.00
182 Randy Myers 1.00
183 Tim Raines 1.00
184 Orel Hershiser 1.25
185 Andy Van Slyke 1.00
186 *Mike Lansing* 2.00
187 Ray Lankford 1.00
188 Mike Morgan 1.00
189 Moises Alou 2.00
190 Edgar Martinez 1.00
191 John Franco 1.00
192 Robin Yount 4.00
193 Bob Tewksbury 1.00
194 Jay Bell 1.00
195 Luis Gonzalez 1.00
196 Dave Fleming 1.00
197 Mike Greenwell 1.00
198 David Nied 1.00
199 Mike Piazza 30.00

1993 Finest Refractors

This parallel insert set comprises each of the 199 cards from the regular Topps Finest set recreated with refracting foil using the metallization enhancement process. One refracting foil card was inserted in every nine packs, on average. Estimated production is about 250 of each card.

MT

Complete Set (199): 8500.
Common Player: 20.00
1 Dave Justice 65.00
2 Lou Whitaker 25.00
3 Bryan Harvey 25.00
4 Carlos Garcia 20.00
5 Sid Fernandez 20.00
6 Brett Butler 25.00
7 Scott Cooper 20.00
8 B.J. Surhoff 25.00
9 Steve Finley 25.00
10 Curt Schilling 40.00
11 Jeff Bagwell 150.00
12 Alex Cole 20.00
13 John Olerud 45.00
14 John Smiley 20.00
15 Bip Roberts 20.00
16 Albert Belle 100.00
17 Duane Ward 20.00
18 Alan Trammell 25.00
19 Andy Benes 20.00
20 Reggie Sanders 20.00
21 Todd Zeile 20.00
22 Rick Aguilera 20.00
23 Dave Hollins 20.00
24 Jose Rijo 20.00
25 Matt Williams 45.00
26 Sandy Alomar 35.00
27 Alex Fernandez 25.00
28 Ozzie Smith 125.00
29 Ramon Martinez 20.00
30 Bernie Williams 60.00
31 Gary Sheffield 50.00
32 Eric Karros 20.00
33 Frank Viola 20.00
34 Kevin Young 20.00
35 Ken Hill 20.00
36 Tony Fernandez 20.00
37 Tim Wakefield 20.00
38 John Kruk 20.00
39 Chris Sabo 20.00
40 Marquis Grissom 20.00
41 Glenn Davis 20.00
42 Jeff Montgomery 20.00
43 Kenny Lofton 60.00
44 John Burkett 20.00
45 Darryl Hamilton 20.00
46 Jim Abbott 20.00
47 Ivan Rodriguez 200.00
48 Eric Young 20.00
49 Mitch Williams 20.00
50 Harold Reynolds 20.00
51 Brian Harper 20.00
52 Rafael Palmeiro 75.00
53 Bret Saberhagen 25.00
54 Jeff Conine 20.00
55 Ivan Calderon 20.00
56 Juan Guzman 20.00
57 Carlos Baerga 20.00
58 Charles Nagy 30.00
59 Wally Joyner 30.00
60 Charlie Hayes 20.00
61 Shane Mack 20.00
62 Pete Harnisch 20.00
63 George Brett 200.00
64 Lance Johnson 20.00
65 Ben McDonald 20.00
66 Bobby Bonilla 30.00
67 Terry Steinbach 20.00
68 Ron Gant 25.00
69 Doug Jones 20.00
70 Paul Molitor 125.00
71 Brady Anderson 25.00
72 Chuck Finley 20.00
73 Mark Grace 60.00
74 Mike Devereaux 20.00
75 Tony Phillips 20.00
76 Chuck Knoblauch 45.00
77 Tony Gwynn 200.00
78 Kevin Appier 20.00
79 Sammy Sosa 250.00
80 Mickey Tettleton 20.00
81 Felix Jose 20.00
82 Mark Langston 20.00
83 Gregg Jefferies 20.00
84 Andre Dawson (AS) 30.00
85 Greg Maddux (AS) 200.00
86 Rickey Henderson (AS) 50.00
87 Tom Glavine (AS) 45.00
88 Roberto Alomar (AS) 75.00
89 Darryl Strawberry (AS) 30.00
90 Wade Boggs (AS) 45.00
91 Bo Jackson (AS) 35.00
92 Mark McGwire (AS) 750.00
93 Robin Ventura (AS) 40.00
94 Joe Carter (AS) 25.00
95 Lee Smith (AS) 20.00
96 Cal Ripken, Jr. (AS) 700.00
97 Larry Walker (AS) 100.00
98 Don Mattingly (AS) 175.00
99 Jose Canseco (AS) 75.00
100 Dennis Eckersley (AS) 30.00
101 Terry Pendleton (AS) 20.00
102 Frank Thomas (AS) 200.00
103 Barry Bonds (AS) 150.00
104 Roger Clemens 200.00
105 Ryne Sandberg (AS) 150.00
106 Fred McGriff (AS) 50.00
107 Nolan Ryan (AS) 650.00
108 Will Clark (AS) 60.00
109 Pat Listach (AS) 20.00
110 Ken Griffey, Jr. (AS) 800.00
111 Cecil Fielder (AS) 25.00
112 Kirby Puckett (AS) 175.00
113 Dwight Gooden (AS) 30.00
114 Barry Larkin (AS) 35.00
115 David Cone (AS) 25.00
116 Juan Gonzalez (AS) 350.00
117 Kent Hrbek 20.00
118 Tim Wallach 20.00
119 Craig Biggio 45.00
120 Bobby Kelly 20.00
121 Greg Olson 20.00
122 Eddie Murray 90.00
123 Wil Cordero 20.00
124 Jay Buhner 30.00
125 Carlton Fisk 60.00
126 Eric Davis 25.00
127 Doug Drabek 20.00
128 Ozzie Guillen 20.00
129 John Wetteland 20.00
130 Andres Galarraga 40.00
131 Ken Caminiti 40.00
132 Tom Candiotti 20.00
133 Pat Borders 20.00
134 Kevin Brown 45.00
135 Travis Fryman 30.00
136 Kevin Mitchell 20.00
137 Greg Swindell 20.00
138 Benny Santiago 20.00
139 Reggie Jefferson 20.00
140 Chris Bosio 20.00
141 Deion Sanders 30.00
142 Scott Erickson 20.00
143 Howard Johnson 20.00
144 Orestes Destrade 20.00
145 Jose Guzman 20.00
146 Chad Curtis 20.00
147 Cal Eldred 20.00
148 Willie Greene 20.00
149 Tommy Greene 20.00
150 Erik Hanson 20.00
151 Bob Welch 20.00
152 John Jaha 20.00
153 Harold Baines 20.00
154 Randy Johnson 75.00
155 Al Martin 20.00
156 J.T. Snow 25.00
157 Mike Mussina 60.00
158 Ruben Sierra 20.00
159 Dean Palmer 20.00
160 Steve Avery 20.00
161 Julio Franco 20.00
162 Dave Winfield 45.00
163 Tim Salmon 50.00
164 Tom Henke 20.00
165 Mo Vaughn 75.00

#	Player	MT
166	John Smoltz	45.00
167	Danny Tartabull	20.00
168	Delino DeShields	20.00
169	Charlie Hough	20.00
170	Paul O'Neill	60.00
171	Darren Daulton	20.00
172	Jack McDowell	20.00
173	Junior Felix	20.00
174	Jimmy Key	20.00
175	George Bell	20.00
176	Mike Stanton	20.00
177	Len Dykstra	20.00
178	Norm Charlton	20.00
179	Eric Anthony	20.00
180	Bob Dibble	20.00
181	Otis Nixon	20.00
182	Randy Myers	20.00
183	Tim Raines	30.00
184	Orel Hershiser	30.00
185	Andy Van Slyke	20.00
186	*Mike Lansing*	25.00
187	Ray Lankford	20.00
188	Mike Morgan	20.00
189	Moises Alou	30.00
190	Edgar Martinez	25.00
191	John Franco	20.00
192	Robin Yount	90.00
193	Bob Tewksbury	20.00
194	Jay Bell	20.00
195	Luis Gonzalez	20.00
196	Dave Fleming	20.00
197	Mike Greenwell	20.00
198	David Nied	20.00
199	Mike Piazza	300.00

1993 Finest Jumbo All-Stars

These 4-1/2" x 6" cards were produced using the chromium metallization process. Each 18-pack Finest box contains one of the All-Star jumbo cards. Based on '93 Finest production, it is estimated fewer than 1,500 of each were issued.

		MT
Complete Set (33):		225.00
Common Player:		2.00
84	Andre Dawson	2.00
85	Greg Maddux	15.00
86	Rickey Henderson	4.00
87	Tom Glavine	4.00
88	Roberto Alomar	6.00
89	Darryl Strawberry	4.00
90	Wade Boggs	5.00
91	Bo Jackson	2.00
92	Mark McGwire	25.00
93	Robin Ventura	3.00
94	Joe Carter	2.00
95	Lee Smith	2.00
96	Cal Ripken, Jr.	25.00
97	Larry Walker	4.00
98	Don Mattingly	10.00
99	Jose Canseco	4.00
100	Dennis Eckersley	2.00
101	Terry Pendleton	2.00
102	Frank Thomas	15.00
103	Barry Bonds	7.50
104	Roger Clemens	10.00
105	Ryne Sandberg	7.50
106	Fred McGriff	3.00
107	Nolan Ryan	25.00
108	Will Clark	4.00
109	Pat Listach	2.00
110	Ken Griffey, Jr.	30.00
111	Cecil Fielder	2.00
112	Kirby Puckett	10.00
113	Dwight Gooden	2.00
114	Barry Larkin	2.50
115	David Cone	2.50
116	Juan Gonzalez	8.00

1994 Finest Pre-Production

Forty cards premiering the upcoming 1994 Topps Finest set were issued as a random insert in packs of Topps Series 2 regular-issue cards. The promos are in the same format as the regular-issue Finest cards and share the same card numbers. On back there is a red "Pre-Production" notice printed diagonally over the statistics.

		MT
Complete Set (40):		100.00
Common Player:		2.50
22	Deion Sanders	4.00
23	Jose Offerman	2.50
26	Alex Fernandez	2.50
31	Steve Finley	2.50
35	Andres Galarraga	3.00
43	Reggie Sanders	2.50
47	Dave Hollins	2.50
52	David Cone	3.50
59	Dante Bichette	3.00
61	Orlando Merced	2.50
62	Brian McRae	2.50
66	Mike Mussina	4.00
76	Mike Stanley	2.50
78	Mark McGwire	20.00
79	Pat Listach	2.50
82	Dwight Gooden	3.00
84	Phil Plantier	2.50
90	Jeff Russell	2.50
92	Gregg Jefferies	2.50
93	Jose Guzman	2.50
100	John Smoltz	3.00
102	Jim Thome	4.00
121	Moises Alou	3.00
125	Devon White	2.50
126	Ivan Rodriguez	6.00
130	Dave Magadan	2.50
136	Ozzie Smith	9.00
141	Chris Hoiles	2.50
149	Jim Abbott	2.50
151	Bill Swift	2.50
154	Edgar Martinez	2.50
157	J.T. Snow	3.00
159	Alan Trammell	3.00
163	Roberto Kelly	2.50
166	Scott Erickson	2.50
168	Scott Cooper	2.50
169	Rod Beck	2.50
177	Dean Palmer	2.50
182	Todd Van Poppel	2.50
185	Paul Sorrento	2.50

1994 Finest

The 1994 Finest set comprises two series of 220 cards each; subsets of 20 superstars and 20 top rookies are featured in each series. Each card has a metallic look to it, using Topps Finest technology. Backs picture the player on the top half and statistics on the bottom. Baseball's Finest was limited to 4,000 cases and available to dealers through an allocation process, based on their sales the previous year. Along with the regular-issue set, there was a parallel set, called Refractors, of 440 cards and a 4 x 6-inch version of the 80 subset cards.

		MT
Complete Set (440):		150.00
Common Player:		.50
Series 1 or 2 Pack (7):		3.00
Series 1 or 2 Wax Box (24):		65.00
1	Mike Piazza	8.00
2	Kevin Stocker	.50
3	Greg McMichael	.50
4	Jeff Conine	.50
5	Rene Arocha	.50
6	Aaron Sele	.50
7	Brent Gates	.50
8	Chuck Carr	.50
9	Kirk Rueter	.50
10	Mike Lansing	.50
11	Al Martin	.50
12	Jason Bere	.50
13	Troy Neel	.50
14	Armando Reynoso	.50
15	Jeromy Burnitz	.60
16	Rich Amaral	.50
17	David McCarty	.50
18	Tim Salmon	1.00
19	Steve Cooke	.50
20	Wil Cordero	.50
21	Kevin Tapani	.50
22	Deion Sanders	.75
23	Jose Offerman	.50
24	Mark Langston	.50
25	Ken Hill	.50
26	Alex Fernandez	.50
27	Jeff Blauser	.50
28	Royce Clayton	.50
29	Brad Ausmus	.50
30	Ryan Bowen	.50
31	Steve Finley	.50
32	Charlie Hayes	.50
33	Jeff Kent	.50
34	Mike Henneman	.50
35	Andres Galarraga	2.00
36	Wayne Kirby	.50
37	Joe Oliver	.50
38	Terry Steinbach	.50
39	Ryan Thompson	.50
40	Luis Alicea	.50
41	Randy Velarde	.50
42	Bob Tewksbury	.50
43	Reggie Sanders	.50
44	Brian Williams	.50
45	Joe Orsulak	.50
46	Jose Lind	.50
47	Dave Hollins	.50
48	Graeme Lloyd	.50
49	Jim Gott	.50
50	Andre Dawson	.75
51	Steve Buechele	.50
52	David Cone	.75
53	Ricky Gutierrez	.50
54	Lance Johnson	.50
55	Tino Martinez	.75
56	Phil Hiatt	.50
57	Carlos Garcia	.50
58	Danny Darwin	.50
59	Dante Bichette	.75
60	Scott Kamieniecki	.50
61	Orlando Merced	.50
62	Brian McRae	.50
63	Pat Kelly	.50
64	Tom Henke	.50
65	Jeff King	.50
66	Mike Mussina	2.00
67	Tim Pugh	.50
68	Robby Thompson	.50
69	Paul O'Neill	.75
70	Hal Morris	.50
71	Ron Karkovice	.50
72	Joe Girardi	.50
73	Eduardo Perez	.50
74	Raul Mondesi	1.00
75	Mike Gallego	.50
76	Mike Stanley	.50
77	Kevin Roberson	.50
78	Mark McGwire	12.00
79	Pat Listach	.50
80	Eric Davis	.50
81	Mike Bordick	.50
82	Dwight Gooden	.60
83	Mike Moore	.50
84	Phil Plantier	.50
85	Darren Lewis	.50
86	Rick Wilkins	.50
87	Darryl Strawberry	.75
88	Rob Dibble	.50
89	Greg Vaughn	.75
90	Jeff Russell	.50
91	Mark Lewis	.50
92	Gregg Jefferies	.50
93	Jose Guzman	.50
94	Kenny Rogers	.50
95	Mark Lemke	.50
96	Mike Morgan	.50
97	Andujar Cedeno	.50
98	Orel Hershiser	.65
99	Greg Swindell	.50
100	John Smoltz	.50
101	Pedro Martinez	3.00
102	Jim Thome	1.50
103	David Segui	.50
104	Charles Nagy	.50
105	Shane Mack	.50
106	John Jaha	.50
107	Tom Candiotti	.50
108	David Wells	.60
109	Bobby Jones	.50
110	Bob Hamelin	.50
111	Bernard Gilkey	.50
112	Chili Davis	.50
113	Todd Stottlemyre	.50
114	Derek Bell	.50
115	Mark McLemore	.50
116	Mark Whiten	.50
117	Mike Devereaux	.50
118	Terry Pendleton	.50
119	Pat Meares	.50
120	Pete Harnisch	.50
121	Moises Alou	.60
122	Jay Buhner	.75
123	Wes Chamberlain	.50
124	Mike Perez	.50
125	Devon White	.50
126	Ivan Rodriguez	3.00
127	Don Slaught	.50
128	John Valentin	.50
129	Jaime Navarro	.50
130	Dave Magadan	.50
131	Brady Anderson	.75

132	Juan Guzman	.50
133	John Wetteland	.50
134	Dave Stewart	.50
135	Scott Servais	.50
136	Ozzie Smith	2.50
137	Darrin Fletcher	.50
138	Jose Mesa	.50
139	Wilson Alvarez	.50
140	Pete Incaviglia	.50
141	Chris Hoiles	.50
142	Darryl Hamilton	.50
143	Chuck Finley	.50
144	Archi Cianfrocco	.50
145	Bill Wegman	.50
146	Joey Cora	.50
147	Darrell Whitmore	.50
148	David Hulse	.50
149	Jim Abbott	.50
150	Curt Schilling	.75
151	Bill Swift	.50
152	Tommy Greene	.50
153	Roberto Mejia	.50
154	Edgar Martinez	.75
155	Roger Pavlik	.50
156	Randy Tomlin	.50
157	J.T. Snow	.50
158	Bob Welch	.50
159	Alan Trammell	.50
160	Ed Sprague	.50
161	Ben McDonald	.50
162	Derrick May	.50
163	Roberto Kelly	.50
164	Bryan Harvey	.50
165	Ron Gant	.60
166	Scott Erickson	.50
167	Anthony Young	.50
168	Scott Cooper	.50
169	Rod Beck	.50
170	John Franco	.50
171	Gary DiSarcina	.50
172	Dave Fleming	.50
173	Wade Boggs	1.50
174	Kevin Appier	.50
175	Jose Bautista	.50
176	Wally Joyner	.50
177	Dean Palmer	.50
178	Tony Phillips	.50
179	John Smiley	.50
180	Charlie Hough	.50
181	Scott Fletcher	.50
182	Todd Van Poppel	.50
183	Mike Blowers	.50
184	Willie McGee	.50
185	Paul Sorrento	.50
186	Eric Young	.50
187	Bret Barberie	.50
188	Manuel Lee	.50
189	Jeff Branson	.50
190	Jim Deshaies	.50
191	Ken Caminiti	.75
192	Tim Raines	.50
193	Joe Grahe	.50
194	Hipolito Pichardo	.50
195	Denny Neagle	.50
196	Jeff Gardner	.50
197	Mike Benjamin	.50
198	Milt Thompson	.50
199	Bruce Ruffin	.50
200	Chris Hammond	.50
201	Tony Gwynn	5.00
202	Robin Ventura	1.00
203	Frank Thomas	4.00
204	Kirby Puckett	3.00
205	Roberto Alomar	2.50
206	Dennis Eckersley	.50
207	Joe Carter	.75
208	Albert Belle	2.50
209	Greg Maddux	7.50
210	Ryne Sandberg	3.00
211	Juan Gonzalez	3.00
212	Jeff Bagwell	3.00
213	Randy Johnson	3.00
214	Matt Williams	1.00
215	Dave Winfield	.75
216	Larry Walker	1.00
217	Roger Clemens	4.00
218	Kenny Lofton	2.50
219	Cecil Fielder	.75
220	Darren Daulton	.50
221	John Olerud	.75
222	Jose Canseco	2.00
223	Rickey Henderson	1.00
224	Fred McGriff	1.50
225	Gary Sheffield	1.50
226	Jack McDowell	.50
227	Rafael Palmeiro	1.50
228	Travis Fryman	.60
229	Marquis Grissom	.60
230	Barry Bonds	3.00
231	Carlos Baerga	.50
232	Ken Griffey, Jr.	12.00
233	Dave Justice	.75
234	Bobby Bonilla	.60
235	Cal Ripken	10.00
236	Sammy Sosa	6.00
237	Len Dykstra	.50
238	Will Clark	1.00
239	Paul Molitor	2.50
240	Barry Larkin	1.00
241	Bo Jackson	.75
242	Mitch Williams	.50
243	Ron Darling	.50
244	Darryl Kile	.50
245	Geronimo Berroa	.50
246	Gregg Olson	.50
247	Brian Harper	.50
248	Rheal Cormier	.50
249	Rey Sanchez	.50
250	Jeff Fassero	.50
251	Sandy Alomar	.65
252	Chris Bosio	.50
253	Andy Stankiewicz	.50
254	Harold Baines	.50
255	Andy Ashby	.50
256	Tyler Green	.50
257	Kevin Brown	.75
258	Mo Vaughn	2.50
259	Mike Harkey	.50
260	Dave Henderson	.50
261	Kent Hrbek	.50
262	Darrin Jackson	.50
263	Bob Wickman	.50
264	Spike Owen	.50
265	Todd Jones	.50
266	Pat Borders	.50
267	Tom Glavine	1.25
268	Dave Nilsson	.50
269	Rich Batchelor	.50
270	Delino DeShields	.50
271	Felix Fermin	.50
272	Orestes Destrade	.50
273	Mickey Morandini	.50
274	Otis Nixon	.50
275	Ellis Burks	.50
276	Greg Gagne	.50
277	John Doherty	.50
278	Julio Franco	.50
279	Bernie Williams	2.00
280	Rick Aguilera	.50
281	Mickey Tettleton	.50
282	David Nied	.50
283	Johnny Ruffin	.50
284	Dan Wilson	.50
285	Omar Vizquel	.50
286	Willie Banks	.50
287	Erik Pappas	.50
288	Cal Eldred	.50
289	Bobby Witt	.50
290	Luis Gonzalez	.50
291	Greg Pirkl	.50
292	Alex Cole	.50
293	Ricky Bones	.50
294	Denis Boucher	.50
295	John Burkett	.50
296	Steve Trachsel	.50
297	Ricky Jordan	.50
298	Mark Dewey	.50
299	Jimmy Key	.50
300	Mike MacFarlane	.50
301	Tim Belcher	.50
302	Carlos Reyes	.50
303	Greg Harris	.50
304	*Brian Anderson*	1.50
305	Terry Mulholland	.50
306	Felix Jose	.50
307	Darren Holmes	.50
308	Jose Rijo	.50
309	Paul Wagner	.50
310	Bob Scanlan	.50
311	Mike Jackson	.50
312	Jose Vizcaino	.50
313	Rob Butler	.50
314	Kevin Seitzer	.50
315	Geronimo Pena	.50
316	Hector Carrasco	.50
317	Eddie Murray	1.00
318	Roger Salkeld	.50
319	Todd Hundley	.50
320	Danny Jackson	.50
321	Kevin Young	.50
322	Mike Greenwell	.50
323	Kevin Mitchell	.50
324	Chuck Knoblauch	.75
325	Danny Tartabull	.50
326	Vince Coleman	.50
327	Marvin Freeman	.50
328	Andy Benes	.50
329	Mike Kelly	.50
330	Karl Rhodes	.50
331	Allen Watson	.50
332	Damion Easley	.50
333	Reggie Jefferson	.50
334	Kevin McReynolds	.50
335	Arthur Rhodes	.50
336	Brian Hunter	.50
337	Tom Browning	.50
338	Pedro Munoz	.50
339	Billy Ripken	.50
340	Gene Harris	.50
341	Fernando Vina	.50
342	Sean Berry	.50
343	Pedro Astacio	.50
344	B.J. Surhoff	.50
345	Doug Drabek	.50
346	Jody Reed	.50
347	Ray Lankford	.50
348	Steve Farr	.50
349	Eric Anthony	.50
350	Pete Smith	.50
351	Lee Smith	.50
352	Mariano Duncan	.50
353	Doug Strange	.50
354	Tim Bogar	.50
355	Dave Weathers	.50
356	Eric Karros	.50
357	Randy Myers	.50
358	Chad Curtis	.50
359	Steve Avery	.50
360	Brian Jordan	.50
361	Tim Wallach	.50
362	Pedro Martinez	3.00
363	Bip Roberts	.50
364	Lou Whitaker	.50
365	Luis Polonia	.50
366	Benny Santiago	.50
367	Brett Butler	.50
368	Shawon Dunston	.50
369	Kelly Stinnett	.50
370	Chris Turner	.50
371	Ruben Sierra	.50
372	Greg Harris	.50
373	Xavier Hernandez	.50
374	Howard Johnson	.50
375	Duane Ward	.50
376	Roberto Hernandez	.50
377	Scott Leius	.50
378	Dave Valle	.50
379	Sid Fernandez	.50
380	Doug Jones	.50
381	Zane Smith	.50
382	Craig Biggio	1.00
383	Rick White	.50
384	Tom Pagnozzi	.50
385	Chris James	.50
386	Bret Boone	.50
387	Jeff Montgomery	.50
388	Chad Kreuter	.50
389	Greg Hibbard	.50
390	Mark Grace	1.00
391	Phil Leftwich	.50
392	Don Mattingly	4.00
393	Ozzie Guillen	.50
394	Gary Gaetti	.50
395	Erik Hanson	.50
396	Scott Brosius	.50
397	Tom Gordon	.50
398	Bill Gullickson	.50
399	Matt Mieske	.50
400	Pat Hentgen	.50
401	Walt Weiss	.50
402	Greg Blosser	.50
403	Stan Javier	.50
404	Doug Henry	.50
405	Ramon Martinez	.50
406	Frank Viola	.50
407	Mike Hampton	.50
408	Andy Van Slyke	.50
409	Bobby Ayala	.50
410	Todd Zeile	.50
411	Jay Bell	.50
412	Denny Martinez	.50
413	Mark Portugal	.50
414	Bobby Munoz	.50
415	Kirt Manwaring	.50
416	John Kruk	.50
417	Trevor Hoffman	.50
418	Chris Sabo	.50
419	Bret Saberhagen	.50
420	Chris Nabholz	.50
421	James Mouton	.50
422	Tony Tarasco	.50
423	Carlos Delgado	2.50
424	Rondell White	1.50
425	Javier Lopez	.75
426	*Chan Ho Park*	1.50
427	Cliff Floyd	.50
428	Dave Staton	.50
429	J.R. Phillips	.50
430	Manny Ramirez	3.00
431	Kurt Abbott	.50
432	Melvin Nieves	.50
433	Alex Gonzalez	.50
434	Rick Helling	.50
435	Danny Bautista	.50
436	Matt Walbeck	.50
437	Ryan Klesko	.75
438	Steve Karsay	.50
439	Salomon Torres	.50
440	Scott Ruffcorn	.50

1994 Finest Refractors

It takes an experienced eye and good light to detect a Refractor parallel card from a regular-issue Topps Finest. The Refractor utilizes a variation of the Finest metallic printing process to produce rainbow-effect highlights on the card front. The Refractors share the checklist with the regular-issue Finest and were inserted at a rate of about one per 10 packs.

	MT
Complete Set (440):	1750.
Common Player:	1.50
Veteran Stars:	6X
Young Stars:	3X

(See 1994 Finest for checklist and base card prices.).

1994 Finest Superstar Jumbos

Identical in format to the Superstars subset in the Finest issue, these cards measure about 4" x 5-1/2" and were distributed one per box in Finest foil packs. Backs carry a card number under the banner with the player's name and position. Since there were 20 rookies and

20 superstars from both Series 1 and Series 2, this is an 80-card set.

		MT
Complete Set (80):		250.00
Common Player:		1.00
1	Mike Piazza	22.50
2	Kevin Stocker	1.00
3	Greg McMichael	1.00
4	Jeff Conine	1.00
5	Rene Arocha	1.00
6	Aaron Sele	1.00
7	Brent Gates	1.00
8	Chuck Carr	1.00
9	Kirk Rueter	1.00
10	Mike Lansing	1.00
11	Al Martin	1.00
12	Jason Bere	1.00
13	Troy Neel	1.00
14	Armando Reynoso	1.00
15	Jeromy Burnitz	1.50
16	Rich Amaral	1.00
17	David McCarty	1.00
18	Tim Salmon	4.00
19	Steve Cooke	1.00
20	Wil Cordero	1.00
201	Tony Gwynn	9.00
202	Robin Ventura	3.00
203	Frank Thomas	20.00
204	Kirby Puckett	15.00
205	Roberto Alomar	9.00
206	Dennis Eckersley	1.25
207	Joe Carter	1.50
208	Albert Belle	10.00
209	Greg Maddux	20.00
210	Ryne Sandberg	7.50
211	Juan Gonzalez	8.00
212	Jeff Bagwell	12.00
213	Randy Johnson	5.00
214	Matt Williams	4.00
215	Dave Winfield	4.00
216	Larry Walker	3.00
217	Roger Clemens	7.50
218	Kenny Lofton	7.50
219	Cecil Fielder	1.00
220	Darren Daulton	1.00
221	John Olerud	2.00
222	Jose Canseco	6.00
223	Rickey Henderson	4.00
224	Fred McGriff	4.00
225	Gary Sheffield	4.00
226	Jack McDowell	1.00
227	Rafael Palmeiro	3.00
228	Travis Fryman	1.50
229	Marquis Grissom	1.00
230	Barry Bonds	10.00
231	Carlos Baerga	1.00
232	Ken Griffey Jr.	35.00
233	Dave Justice	4.00
234	Bobby Bonilla	1.00
235	Cal Ripken	25.00
236	Sammy Sosa	15.00
237	Len Dykstra	1.00
238	Will Clark	4.50
239	Paul Molitor	4.50
240	Barry Larkin	2.00
421	James Mouton	1.00
422	Tony Tarasco	1.00
423	Carlos Delgado	1.50
424	Rondell White	1.50
425	Javier Lopez	2.00
426	Chan Ho Park	2.00
427	Cliff Floyd	1.50
428	Dave Staton	1.00
429	J.R. Phillips	1.00
430	Manny Ramirez	10.00
431	Kurt Abbott	1.00
432	Melvin Nieves	1.00
433	Alex Gonzalez	1.00
434	Rick Helling	1.00
435	Danny Bautista	1.00
436	Matt Walbeck	1.00
437	Ryan Klesko	2.50
438	Steve Karsay	1.00
439	Salomon Torres	1.00
440	Scott Ruffcorn	1.00

1994 Finest Superstar Sampler

This special version of 45 of the biggest-name stars from the 1994 Topps Finest set was issued in a three-card cello pack with the same player's '94 Bowman and Stadium Club cards. The packs were available only in 1994 Topps retail factory sets. Cards are identical to the regular-issue Finest cards except for a round, red "Topps Superstar Sampler" logo printed at bottom center on back.

		MT
Complete Set (45):		275.00
Common Player:		3.00
1	Mike Piazza	15.00
18	Tim Salmon	4.50
35	Andres Galarraga	4.00
74	Raul Mondesi	4.00
92	Gregg Jefferies	4.00
201	Tony Gwynn	7.50
203	Frank Thomas	20.00
204	Kirby Puckett	10.00
205	Roberto Alomar	6.00
207	Joe Carter	3.00
208	Albert Belle	7.50
209	Greg Maddux	20.00
210	Ryne Sandberg	12.50
211	Juan Gonzalez	10.00
212	Jeff Bagwell	10.00
213	Randy Johnson	5.00
214	Matt Williams	4.50
216	Larry Walker	5.00
217	Roger Clemens	7.50
219	Cecil Fielder	3.00
220	Darren Daulton	3.00
221	John Olerud	4.50
222	Jose Canseco	6.00
224	Fred McGriff	4.00
225	Gary Sheffield	4.50
226	Jack McDowell	3.00
227	Rafael Palmeiro	5.00
229	Marquis Grissom	4.00
230	Barry Bonds	10.00
231	Carlos Baerga	3.00
232	Ken Griffey Jr.	35.00
233	Dave Justice	4.50
234	Bobby Bonilla	3.50
235	Cal Ripken Jr.	30.00
237	Len Dykstra	3.00
238	Will Clark	5.00
239	Paul Molitor	4.50
240	Barry Larkin	4.00
258	Mo Vaughn	6.00
267	Tom Glavine	4.00
390	Mark Grace	5.00
392	Don Mattingly	17.50
408	Andy Van Slyke	3.00
427	Cliff Floyd	3.00
430	Manny Ramirez	7.50

1995 Finest

In its third year Finest baseball was reduced to a 220-card base set. All cards feature the chrome-printing technology associated with the Finest logo and include a peel-off plastic protector on the card front. Backgrounds are green with gold pinstripes. Behind the action photo at center is a large diamond with each corner intersected by a silver semi-circle. On the Finest Rookies subset which makes up the first 30 cards of the issue, the diamond has a graduated pink to orange center, with flecks of red throughout. Veterans cards have a graduated blue to purple center of the diamond. On the rookies cards there is a teal brand name at top, while the vets show a gold "FINEST". Backs repeat the front background motif in shades of green. There is a player photo at right, with biographical data, 1994 and career stats, and a "Finest Moment" career highlight at left. Finest was sold in seven-card packs with a suggested retail price of $4.99.

		MT
Complete Set (220):		80.00
Common Player:		.25
Series 1 Pack (7):		4.00
Series 1 Wax Box (24):		90.00
Series 2 Pack (7):		4.00
Series 2 Wax Box (24):		70.00
1	Raul Mondesi (Rookie Theme)	.75
2	Kurt Abbott (Rookie Theme)	.30
3	Chris Gomez (Rookie Theme)	.25
4	Manny Ramirez (Rookie Theme)	2.50
5	Rondell White (Rookie Theme)	.50
6	William Van Landingham (Rookie Theme)	.25
7	Jon Lieber (Rookie Theme)	.25
8	Ryan Klesko (Rookie Theme)	.75
9	John Hudek (Rookie Theme)	.25
10	Joey Hamilton (Rookie Theme)	.75
11	Bob Hamelin (Rookie Theme)	.25
12	Brian Anderson (Rookie Theme)	.25
13	Mike Lieberthal (Rookie Theme)	.35
14	Rico Brogna (Rookie Theme)	.25
15	Rusty Greer (Rookie Theme)	.30
16	Carlos Delgado (Rookie Theme)	.75
17	Jim Edmonds (Rookie Theme)	.75
18	Steve Trachsel (Rookie Theme)	.25
19	Matt Walbeck (Rookie Theme)	.25
20	Armando Benitez (Rookie Theme)	.30
21	Steve Karsay (Rookie Theme)	.25
22	Jose Oliva (Rookie Theme)	.25
23	Cliff Floyd (Rookie Theme)	.30
24	Kevin Foster (Rookie Theme)	.25
25	Javier Lopez (Rookie Theme)	.75
26	Jose Valentin (Rookie Theme)	.25
27	James Mouton (Rookie Theme)	.25
28	Hector Carrasco (Rookie Theme)	.25
29	Orlando Miller (Rookie Theme)	.25
30	Garret Anderson (Rookie Theme)	.25
31	Marvin Freeman	.25
32	Brett Butler	.25
33	Roberto Kelly	.25
34	Rod Beck	.25
35	Jose Rijo	.25
36	Edgar Martinez	.25
37	Jim Thome	1.50
38	Rick Wilkins	.25
39	Wally Joyner	.30
40	Wil Cordero	.25
41	Tommy Greene	.25
42	Travis Fryman	.30
43	Don Slaught	.25
44	Brady Anderson	.30
45	Matt Williams	.75
46	Rene Arocha	.25
47	Rickey Henderson	.50
48	Mike Mussina	1.00
49	Greg McMichael	.25
50	Jody Reed	.25
51	Tino Martinez	.35
52	Dave Clark	.25
53	John Valentin	.25
54	Bret Boone	.25
55	Walt Weiss	.25
56	Kenny Lofton	2.00
57	Scott Leius	.25
58	Eric Karros	.30
59	John Olerud	.40
60	Chris Hoiles	.25
61	Sandy Alomar	.30
62	Tim Wallach	.25
63	Cal Eldred	.25
64	Tom Glavine	.35
65	Mark Grace	.50
66	Rey Sanchez	.25
67	Bobby Ayala	.25
68	Dante Bichette	.75
69	Andres Galarraga	.35
70	Chuck Carr	.25
71	Bobby Witt	.25
72	Steve Avery	.25
73	Bobby Jones	.25
74	Delino DeShields	.25

No.	Player	MT
75	Kevin Tapani	.25
76	Randy Johnson	1.50
77	David Nied	.25
78	Pat Hentgen	.25
79	Tim Salmon	.75
80	Todd Zeile	.25
81	John Wetteland	.25
82	Albert Belle	2.50
83	Ben McDonald	.25
84	Bobby Munoz	.25
85	Bip Roberts	.25
86	Mo Vaughn	2.00
87	Chuck Finley	.25
88	Chuck Knoblauch	.50
89	Frank Thomas	4.00
90	Danny Tartabull	.25
91	Dean Palmer	.25
92	Len Dykstra	.25
93	J.R. Phillips	.25
94	Tom Candiotti	.25
95	Marquis Grissom	.25
96	Barry Larkin	.50
97	Bryan Harvey	.25
98	Dave Justice	.50
99	David Cone	.40
100	Wade Boggs	.50
101	Jason Bere	.25
102	Hal Morris	.25
103	Fred McGriff	.50
104	Bobby Bonilla	.30
105	Jay Buhner	.30
106	Allen Watson	.25
107	Mickey Tettleton	.25
108	Kevin Appier	.25
109	Ivan Rodriguez	2.50
110	Carlos Garcia	.25
111	Andy Benes	.25
112	Eddie Murray	1.50
113	Mike Piazza	7.00
114	Greg Vaughn	.35
115	Paul Molitor	1.50
116	Terry Steinbach	.25
117	Jeff Bagwell	4.00
118	Ken Griffey Jr.	10.00
119	Gary Sheffield	2.00
120	Cal Ripken Jr.	8.00
121	Jeff Kent	.25
122	Jay Bell	.25
123	Will Clark	.75
124	Cecil Fielder	.25
125	Alex Fernandez	.30
126	Don Mattingly	4.00
127	Reggie Sanders	.25
128	Moises Alou	.30
129	Craig Biggio	.40
130	Eddie Williams	.25
131	John Franco	.25
132	John Kruk	.25
133	Jeff King	.25
134	Royce Clayton	.25
135	Doug Drabek	.25
136	Ray Lankford	.25
137	Roberto Alomar	2.00
138	Todd Hundley	.50
139	Alex Cole	.25
140	Shawon Dunston	.25
141	John Roper	.25
142	Mark Langston	.25
143	Tom Pagnozzi	.25
144	Wilson Alvarez	.25
145	Scott Cooper	.25
146	Kevin Mitchell	.25
147	Mark Whiten	.25
148	Jeff Conine	.25
149	Chili Davis	.25
150	Luis Gonzalez	.25
151	Juan Guzman	.25
152	Mike Greenwell	.25
153	Mike Henneman	.25
154	Rick Aguilera	.25
155	Dennis Eckersley	.30
156	Darrin Fletcher	.25
157	Darren Lewis	.25
158	Juan Gonzalez	2.50
159	Dave Hollins	.25
160	Jimmy Key	.25
161	Roberto Hernandez	.25
162	Randy Myers	.25
163	Joe Carter	.30
164	Darren Daulton	.25
165	Mike MacFarlane	.25
166	Bret Saberhagen	.25
167	Kirby Puckett	4.00
168	Lance Johnson	.25
169	Mark McGwire	10.00
170	Jose Canseco	1.00
171	Mike Stanley	.25
172	Lee Smith	.25
173	Robin Ventura	.45
174	Greg Gagne	.25
175	Brian McRae	.25
176	Mike Bordick	.25
177	Rafael Palmeiro	.50
178	Kenny Rogers	.25
179	Chad Curtis	.25
180	Devon White	.30
181	Paul O'Neill	.35
182	Ken Caminiti	.75
183	Dave Nilsson	.25
184	Tim Naehring	.25
185	Roger Clemens	3.00
186	Otis Nixon	.25
187	Tim Raines	.25
188	Dennis Martinez	.25
189	Pedro Martinez	.40
190	Jim Abbott	.25
191	Ryan Thompson	.25
192	Barry Bonds	2.50
193	Joe Girardi	.25
194	Steve Finley	.25
195	John Jaha	.25
196	Tony Gwynn	4.00
197	Sammy Sosa	5.00
198	John Burkett	.25
199	Carlos Baerga	.25
200	Ramon Martinez	.25
201	Aaron Sele	.25
202	Eduardo Perez	.25
203	Alan Trammell	.25
204	Orlando Merced	.25
205	Deion Sanders	.40
206	Robb Nen	.25
207	Jack McDowell	.25
208	Ruben Sierra	.25
209	Bernie Williams	2.00
210	Kevin Seitzer	.25
211	Charles Nagy	.25
212	Tony Phillips	.25
213	Greg Maddux	6.00
214	Jeff Montgomery	.25
215	Larry Walker	.75
216	Andy Van Slyke	.25
217	Ozzie Smith	1.50
218	Geronimo Pena	.25
219	Gregg Jefferies	.25
220	Lou Whitaker	.25

1995 Finest Refractors

A parallel set with a counterpart to each of the 220 cards in the regular Finest emission, the Refractors are printed in a version of the Finest chrome technology that produces a rainbow effect when viewed at the proper angle. The relatively open spaces of the 1995 Finest design make the Refractors easier to spot than the previous years' versions, but just to assist the identification process, Topps placed a small black "REFRACTOR" in the dark green background on the cards' backs, as well. Advertised rate of insertion for the Refractors was about one per 12 packs.

	MT
Complete Set (220):	2250.
Common Player:	4.00
Stars:	7-12X

(See 1995 Finest for checklist and base card values.)

1995 Finest Flame Throwers

The scarcest of the Finest inserts is the nine-card set of baseball hardest throwing pitchers. Flame Throwers cards are found at an average rate of one per 48 packs. Fronts have a central photo of a pitcher bringing his best heat. Behind the photo is the Flame Throwers typographic logo in tones of red, yellow and orange. Backs have another photo and a bar graph rating the pitcher's skill levels.

No.	Player	MT
	Complete Set (9):	35.00
	Common Player:	2.50
1	Jason Bere	2.50
2	Roger Clemens	15.00
3	Juan Guzman	2.50
4	John Hudek	2.50
5	Randy Johnson	7.50
6	Pedro Martinez	7.50
7	Jose Rijo	2.50
8	Bret Saberhagen	3.00
9	John Wetteland	2.50

1995 Finest Power Kings

The emphasis in on youth in this chase set of baseball's top distance threats. Found at a rate of one per 24 packs, on average, the Power Kings inserts have a central photo of the player in batting action. The background, in shades of blue, features lightning strokes. Backs feature another pair of player photos and a bar graph charting the hitter's power skills.

No.	Player	MT
	Complete Set (18):	90.00
	Common Player:	1.50
1	Bob Hamelin	1.50
2	Raul Mondesi	2.50
3	Ryan Klesko	2.00
4	Carlos Delgado	3.00
5	Manny Ramirez	7.50
6	Mike Piazza	15.00
7	Jeff Bagwell	10.00
8	Mo Vaughn	7.50
9	Frank Thomas	10.00
10	Ken Griffey Jr.	25.00
11	Albert Belle	5.00
12	Sammy Sosa	12.50
13	Dante Bichette	2.00
14	Gary Sheffield	2.00
15	Matt Williams	2.50
16	Fred McGriff	2.00
17	Barry Bonds	7.50
18	Cecil Fielder	1.50

1995 Finest Update

Players who changed teams through trades or free agent signings and more of the season's rookie player crop are included in the Finest Update series of 110 cards. The cards are numbered contiguously with the base Finest set and share the same design. Once again, Refractor cards were found on an average of once per 12 packs. Finest Update was sold in seven-card packs with a suggested retail price of $4.99.

No.	Player	MT
	Complete Set (110):	25.00
	Common Player:	.25
	Refractors:	7-12X
221	Chipper Jones	8.00

222	Benji Gil	.25
223	Tony Phillips	.25
224	Trevor Wilson	.25
225	Tony Tarasco	.25
226	Roberto Petagine	.25
227	Mike MacFarlane	.25
228	*Hideo Nomo*	8.00
229	Mark McLemore	.25
230	Ron Gant	.50
231	Andujar Cedeno	.25
232	*Mike Mimbs*	.40
233	Jim Abbott	.25
234	Ricky Bones	.25
235	Marty Cordova	1.00
236	Mark Johnson	.50
237	Marquis Grissom	.25
238	Tom Henke	.25
239	Terry Pendleton	.25
240	John Wetteland	.25
241	Lee Smith	.25
242	Jaime Navarro	.25
243	Luis Alicea	.25
244	Scott Cooper	.25
245	Gary Gaetti	.25
246	Edgardo Alfonzo	.50
247	Brad Clontz	.25
248	Dave Mlicki	.25
249	Dave Winfield	.75
250	*Mark Grudzielanek*	3.00
251	Alex Gonzalez	.25
252	Kevin Brown	.50
253	Esteban Loaiza	.40
254	Vaughn Eshelman	.25
255	Bill Swift	.25
256	Brian McRae	.25
257	*Bobby Higginson*	5.00
258	Jack McDowell	.25
259	Scott Stahoviak	.25
260	Jon Nunnally	.25
261	Charlie Hayes	.25
262	Jacob Brumfield	.25
263	Chad Curtis	.25
264	Heathcliff Slocumb	.25
265	Mark Whiten	.25
266	Mickey Tettleton	.25
267	Jose Mesa	.25
268	Doug Jones	.25
269	Trevor Hoffman	.50
270	Paul Sorrento	.25
271	Shane Andrews	.25
272	Brett Butler	.25
273	Curtis Goodwin	.25
274	Larry Walker	.75
275	Phil Plantier	.25
276	Ken Hill	.25
277	Vinny Castilla	.35
278	Billy Ashley	.25
279	Derek Jeter	8.00
280	Bob Tewksbury	.25
281	Jose Offerman	.25
282	Glenallen Hill	.25
283	Tony Fernandez	.25
284	Mike Devereaux	.25
285	John Burkett	.25
286	Geronimo Berroa	.25
287	Quilvio Veras	.25
288	Jason Bates	.25
289	Lee Tinsley	.25
290	Derek Bell	.25
291	Jeff Fassero	.25
292	Ray Durham	.50
293	Chad Ogea	.25
294	Bill Pulsipher	.35
295	Phil Nevin	.25
296	*Carlos Perez*	1.00
297	Roberto Kelly	.25
298	Tim Wakefield	.25
299	Jeff Manto	.25
300	Brian Hunter	.25
301	C.J. Nitkowski	.25
302	Dustin Hermanson	.25
303	John Mabry	.25
304	Orel Hershiser	.25
305	Ron Villone	.25
306	Sean Bergman	.25
307	Tom Goodwin	.25
308	Al Reyes	.25
309	Todd Stottlemyre	.25
310	Rich Becker	.25
311	Joey Cora	.25
312	Ed Sprague	.25
313	John Smoltz	.75
314	Frank Castillo	.25
315	Chris Hammond	.25
316	Ismael Valdes	.25
317	Pete Harnisch	.25
318	Bernard Gilkey	.25
319	John Kruk	.25
320	Marc Newfield	.25
321	Brian Johnson	.25
322	Mark Portugal	.25
323	David Hulse	.25
324	Luis Ortiz	.25
325	Mike Benjamin	.25
326	Brian Jordan	.25
327	Shawn Green	1.00
328	Joe Oliver	.25
329	Felipe Lira	.25
330	Andre Dawson	.35

1995 Finest Update Refractors

The special version of Topps' chromium printing process which creates a rainbow effect was applied to a limited number of each card in the Finest Update set to create a parallel Refractor edition. To assist in identification, a small black "REFRACTOR" is printed on the cards' backs, as well. Refractors are found on average once every 12 packs of Finest Update.

	MT
Complete Set (110):	450.00
Common Player:	4.00
Stars:	7-12X

(See 1995 Finest Update for checklist and base card values.)

1996 Finest

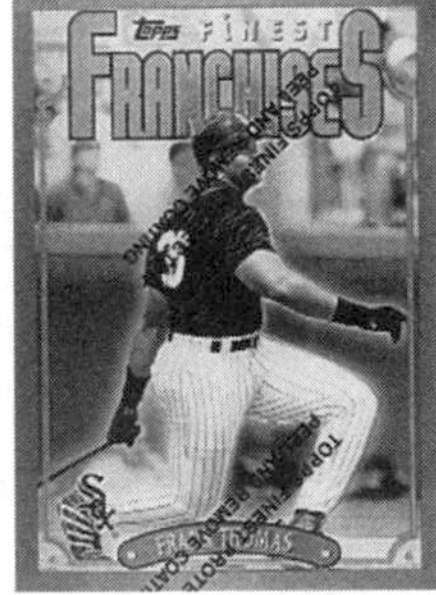

Utilizing three levels of base-card scarcity, the 359-card Finest set comprises 220 Commons (Bronze), 91 Uncommons (Silver) and 49 Rares (Gold). Cards were somewhat randomly assigned a status. Uncommon cards are found one in four packs; Rare cards are seeded one per 24 packs. The set has eight themes. Series 1 themes are Phenoms, Intimidators, Gamers and Sterling, the latter of which consists of star players already included within the first three themes. Series 2 themes are Franchise, Additions, Prodigies and Sterling. Regular-issue cards are not only numbered from 1-359 in the set as a whole, but also numbered within each subset. Finest Refractor parallel cards were also made. Rare Refractor cards are found one every 288 packs (fewer than 150 of each produced), while Uncommon Refractors are found one per 48 packs. Common Refractors are seeded 1:12.

	MT
Complete Set (359):	750.00
Bronze Set (220):	40.00
Common Bronze:	.15
Silver Set (91):	200.00
Typical Silver:	1.00
Gold Set (47):	600.00
Typical Gold:	5.00
Series 1 Pack (6):	5.00
Series 1 Wax Box (24):	90.00
Series 2 Pack (6):	3.50
Series 2 Wax Box (24):	60.00

1	Greg Maddux S (Intimidators)	6.00
2	Bernie Williams S (Gamers)	2.50
3	Ivan Rodriguez S (Intimidators)	4.00
4	Marty Cordova G (Phenoms)	5.00
5	Roberto Hernandez (Intimidators)	.15
6	Tony Gwynn G (Gamers)	15.00
7	Barry Larkin S (Sterling)	1.00
8	Terry Pendleton (Gamers)	.15
9	Albert Belle G (Sterling)	8.00
10	Ray Lankford S (Gamers)	1.00
11	Mike Piazza S (Sterling)	7.50
12	Ken Caminiti (Gamers)	.25
13	Larry Walker S (Intimidators)	2.00
14	Matt Williams S (Intimidators)	1.50
15	Dan Miceli (Phenoms)	.15
16	Chipper Jones (Sterling)	2.50
17	John Wetteland (Intimidators)	.15
18	Kirby Puckett G (Sterling)	12.00
19	Tim Naehring (Gamers)	.15
20	Karim Garcia G (Phenoms)	5.00
21	Eddie Murray (Gamers)	.40
22	Tim Salmon S (Intimidators)	1.50
23	Kevin Appier (Intimidators)	.15
24	Ken Griffey Jr. (Sterling)	5.00
25	Cal Ripken Jr. G (Gamers)	30.00
26	Brian McRae (Gamers)	.15
27	Pedro Martinez (Intimidators)	.40
28	Brian Jordan (Gamers)	.15
29	Mike Fetters (Intimidators)	.15
30	Carlos Delgado (Phenoms)	.50
31	Shane Reynolds (Intimidators)	.15
32	Terry Steinbach (Gamers)	.15
33	Hideo Nomo G (Sterling)	7.50
34	Mark Leiter (Gamers)	.15
35	Edgar Martinez S (Intimidators)	1.00
36	David Segui (Gamers)	.15
37	Gregg Jefferies S (Gamers)	1.00
38	Bill Pulsipher S (Phenoms)	1.00
39	Ryne Sandberg G (Gamers)	10.00
40	Fred McGriff (Intimidators)	.40
41	Shawn Green S (Phenoms)	2.50
42	Jeff Bagwell G (Sterling)	17.50
43	Jim Abbott S (Gamers)	1.00
44	Glenallen Hill (Intimidators)	.15
45	Brady Anderson (Gamers)	.15
46	Roger Clemens S (Intimidators)	3.00
47	Jim Thome (Gamers)	.40
48	Frank Thomas (Sterling)	2.00
49	Chuck Knoblauch (Gamers)	.20
50	Lenny Dykstra (Gamers)	.15
51	Jason Isringhausen G (Phenoms)	5.00
52	Rondell White S (Phenoms)	1.00
53	Tom Pagnozzi (Gamers)	.15
54	Dennis Eckersley S (Intimidators)	1.00
55	Ricky Bones (Gamers)	.15
56	David Justice (Intimidators)	.35
57	Steve Avery (Gamers)	.15
58	Robby Thompson (Gamers)	.15
59	Hideo Nomo S (Phenoms)	2.00
60	Gary Sheffield S (Intimidators)	1.50
61	Tony Gwynn (Sterling)	2.50
62	Will Clark S (Gamers)	1.50
63	Denny Neagle (Gamers)	.15
64	Mo Vaughn G (Intimidators)	10.00
65	Bret Boone S (Gamers)	1.00
66	Dante Bichette G (Sterling)	6.00
67	Robin Ventura (Gamers)	.25
68	Rafael Palmeiro S (Intimidators)	1.50
69	Carlos Baerga S (Gamers)	1.00
70	Kevin Seitzer (Gamers)	.15
71	Ramon Martinez (Intimidators)	.20
72	Tom Glavine S (Gamers)	1.25
73	Garret Anderson S (Phenoms)	1.00
74	Mark McGwire G (Intimidators)	40.00
75	Brian Hunter (Phenoms)	.25
76	Alan Benes (Phenoms)	.25
77	Randy Johnson S (Intimidators)	3.00
78	Jeff King S (Gamers)	1.00
79	Kirby Puckett S (Intimidators)	4.00
80	Ozzie Guillen (Gamers)	.15

81 Kenny Lofton G (Intimidators) 8.00
82 Benji Gil (Phenoms) .15
83 Jim Edmonds G (Gamers) 5.00
84 Cecil Fielder S (Intimidators) 1.00
85 Todd Hundley (Gamers) .35
86 Reggie Sanders S (Intimidators) 1.00
87 Pat Hentgen (Gamers) .15
88 Ryan Klesko S (Intimidators) 1.50
89 Chuck Finley (Gamers) .15
90 Mike Mussina G (Intimidators) 8.00
91 John Valentin S (Intimidators) 1.00
92 Derek Jeter (Phenoms) 4.00
93 Paul O'Neill (Intimidators) .25
94 Darrin Fletcher (Gamers) .15
95 Manny Ramirez S (Phenoms) 5.00
96 Delino DeShields (Gamers) .15
97 Tim Salmon (Sterling) .40
98 John Olerud (Gamers) .25
99 Vinny Castilla S (Intimidators) 1.25
100 Jeff Conine G (Gamers) 5.00
101 Tim Wakefield (Gamers) .15
102 Johnny Damon G (Phenoms) 5.00
103 Dave Stevens (Gamers) .15
104 Orlando Merced (Gamers) .15
105 Barry Bonds G (Sterling) 12.50
106 Jay Bell (Gamers) .15
107 John Burkett (Gamers) .15
108 Chris Hoiles (Gamers) .15
109 Carlos Perez S (Phenoms) 1.00
110 Dave Nilsson (Gamers) .15
111 Rod Beck (Intimidators) .15
112 Craig Biggio S (Gamers) 2.00
113 Mike Piazza (Intimidators) 4.00
114 Mark Langston (Gamers) .15
115 Juan Gonzalez S (Intimidators) 4.00
116 Rico Brogna (Gamers) .15
117 Jose Canseco G (Intimidators) 9.00
118 Tom Goodwin (Gamers) .15
119 Bryan Rekar (Phenoms) .15
120 David Cone (Intimidators) .20
121 Ray Durham S (Phenoms) 1.00
122 Andy Pettitte (Phenoms) .70
123 Chili Davis (Intimidators) .15
124 John Smoltz (Gamers) .25
125 Heathcliff Slocumb (Intimidators) .15
126 Dante Bichette (Intimidators) .25
127 C.J. Nitkowski S (Phenoms) 1.00
128 Alex Gonzalez (Phenoms) .15
129 Jeff Montgomery (Intimidators) .15
130 Raul Mondesi S (Intimidators) 1.25
131 Denny Martinez (Gamers) .15
132 Mel Rojas (Intimidators) .15
133 Derek Bell (Gamers) .15
134 Trevor Hoffman (Intimidators) .20
135 Ken Griffey Jr. G (Intimidators) 45.00
136 Darren Daulton (Gamers) .15
137 Pete Schourek (Gamers) .15
138 Phil Nevin (Phenoms) .15
139 Andres Galarraga (Intimidators) .20
140 Chad Fonville (Phenoms) .15
141 Chipper Jones G (Phenoms) 25.00
142 Lee Smith S (Intimidators) 1.00
143 Joe Carter S (Gamers) 1.00
144 J.T. Snow (Gamers) .15
145 Greg Maddux G (Sterling) 25.00
146 Barry Bonds (Intimidators) .70
147 Orel Hershiser (Gamers) .15
148 Quilvio Veras (Phenoms) .15
149 Will Clark (Sterling) .35
150 Jose Rijo (Gamers) .15
151 Mo Vaughn S (Sterling) 4.00
152 Travis Fryman (Gamers) .20
153 Frank Rodriguez S (Phenoms) 1.00
154 Alex Fernandez (Gamers) .15
155 Wade Boggs (Gamers) .35
156 Troy Percival (Phenoms) .15
157 Moises Alou (Gamers) .25
158 Javy Lopez (Gamers) .25
159 Jason Giambi (Phenoms) .15
160 Steve Finley S (Gamers) 1.00
161 Jeff Bagwell S (Intimidators) 6.00
162 Mark McGwire (Sterling) 5.00
163 Eric Karros (Gamers) .15
164 Jay Buhner G (Intimidators) 6.00
165 Cal Ripken Jr. S (Sterling) 15.00
166 Mickey Tettleton (Intimidators) .15
167 Barry Larkin (Intimidators) .40
168 Lyle Mouton S (Phenoms) 1.00
169 Ruben Sierra (Intimidators) .15
170 Bill Swift (Gamers) .15
171 Sammy Sosa S (Intimidators) 10.00
172 Chad Curtis (Gamers) .15
173 Dean Palmer (Gamers) .15
174 John Franco S (Gamers) 1.00
175 Bobby Bonilla (Intimidators) .15
176 Greg Colbrunn (Gamers) .15
177 Jose Mesa (Intimidators) .15
178 Mike Greenwell (Gamers) .15
179 Greg Vaughn S (Intimidators) 1.25
180 Mark Wohlers S (Intimidators) 1.00
181 Doug Drabek (Gamers) .15
182 Paul O'Neill S (Sterling) 1.50
183 Wilson Alvarez (Gamers) .15
184 Marty Cordova (Sterling) .20
185 Hal Morris (Gamers) .15
186 Frank Thomas G (Intimidators) 15.00
187 Carlos Garcia (Gamers) .15
188 Albert Belle S (Intimidators) 4.00
189 Mark Grace S (Gamers) 2.50
190 Marquis Grissom (Gamers) .15
191 Checklist .15
192 Chipper Jones G 25.00
193 Will Clark .35
194 Paul Molitor .40
195 Kenny Rogers .15
196 Reggie Sanders .15
197 Roberto Alomar G 10.00
198 Dennis Eckersley G 5.00
199 Raul Mondesi .40
200 Lance Johnson .15
201 Alvin Mormon .15
202 George Arias G 5.00
203 Jack McDowell .15
204 Randy Myers .15
205 Harold Baines .15
206 Marty Cordova .20
207 *Rich Hunter* .15
208 Al Leiter .20
209 Greg Gagne .15
210 Ben McDonald .15
211 Ernie Young S 1.00
212 Terry Adams .15
213 Paul Sorrento .15
214 Albert Belle .70
215 Mike Blowers .15
216 Jim Edmonds .40
217 Felipe Crespo .15
218 Fred McGriff S 1.25
219 Shawon Dunston .15
220 Jimmy Haynes .15
221 Jose Canseco .40
222 Eric Davis .15
223 Kimera Bartee S 1.00
224 Tim Raines .15
225 Tony Phillips .15
226 Charlie Hayes .15
227 Eric Owens .15
228 Roberto Alomar .60
229 Rickey Henderson S 2.00
230 Sterling Hitchcock S 1.00
231 Bernard Gilkey S 1.00
232 Hideo Nomo G 7.50
233 Kenny Lofton .70
234 Ryne Sandberg S 3.00
235 Greg Maddux S 7.50
236 Mark McGwire 5.00
237 Jay Buhner .20
238 Craig Biggio .25
239 Todd Stottlemyre S 1.00
240 Barry Bonds .70
241 Jason Kendall S 1.50
242 Paul O'Neill S 1.50
243 Chris Snopek G 5.00
244 Ron Gant .20
245 Paul Wilson .20
246 Todd Hollandsworth .15
247 Todd Zeile .15
248 David Justice .25
249 Tim Salmon G 6.00
250 Moises Alou .20
251 Bob Wolcott .15
252 David Wells .15
253 Juan Gonzalez 1.25
254 Andres Galarraga .25
255 Dave Hollins .15
256 Devon White S 1.00
257 Sammy Sosa 3.00
258 Ivan Rodriguez 1.25
259 Bip Roberts .15
260 Tino Martinez .25
261 Chuck Knoblauch S 1.25
262 Mike Stanley .15
263 Wally Joyner S 1.00
264 Butch Huskey .15
265 Jeff Conine .15
266 Matt Williams G 6.00
267 Mark Grace .25
268 Jason Schmidt .15
269 Otis Nixon .15
270 Randy Johnson G 10.00
271 Kirby Puckett 2.00
272 *Andy Fox S* 1.00
273 Andy Benes .15
274 Sean Berry S 1.00
275 Mike Piazza 4.00
276 Rey Ordonez .40
277 Benito Santiago S 1.00
278 Gary Gaetti .15
279 Paul Molitor G 7.50
280 Robin Ventura .25
281 Cal Ripken Jr. 4.00
282 Carlos Baerga .15
283 Roger Cedeno .25
284 Chad Mottola S 1.00
285 Terrell Wade .15
286 Kevin Brown .25
287 Rafael Palmeiro .25
288 Mo Vaughn .70
289 Dante Bichette S 1.25
290 Cecil Fielder G 5.00
291 Doc Gooden S 1.50
292 Bob Tewksbury .15
293 Kevin Mitchell S 1.00
294 *Livan Hernandez G* 7.00
295 Russ Davis S 1.00
296 Chan Ho Park S 2.00
297 T.J. Mathews .15
298 Manny Ramirez 2.00
299 Jeff Bagwell 1.50
300 *Marty Janzen G* 5.00
301 Wade Boggs .35
302 Larry Walker S 2.00
303 Steve Gibralter .15
304 B.J. Surhoff .15
305 Ken Griffey Jr. S 25.00
306 Royce Clayton .15
307 Sal Fasano .15
308 Ron Gant G 5.00
309 Gary Sheffield .40
310 Ken Hill .15
311 Joe Girardi .15
312 *Matt Lawton* .15
313 Billy Wagner S 2.00
314 Julio Franco .15
315 Joe Carter .20
316 Brooks Kieschnick .15
317 *Mike Grace S* 1.50
318 Heathcliff Slocumb .15
319 Barry Larkin .40
320 Tony Gwynn 2.50
321 Ryan Klesko G 6.00
322 Frank Thomas 1.50
323 Edgar Martinez .15
324 Jermaine Dye G 5.00
325 Henry Rodriguez .15
326 *Marvin Benard* .25
327 Kenny Lofton S 4.00
328 Derek Bell S 1.00
329 Ugueth Urbina .15
330 Jason Giambi G 5.00
331 Roger Salkeld .15
332 Edgar Renteria .25
333 Ryan Klesko .50
334 Ray Lankford .15
335 Edgar Martinez G 5.00
336 Justin Thompson .15
337 Gary Sheffield S 2.00
338 Rey Ordonez G 5.00
339 Mark Clark .15
340 Ruben Rivera .40
341 Mark Grace S 1.50
342 Matt Williams .25
343 *Francisco Cordova* .20
344 Cecil Fielder .20
345 Andres Galarraga S 1.25
346 Brady Anderson S 1.25
347 Sammy Sosa G 20.00
348 Mark Grudzielanek .15
349 Ron Coomer .15
350 Derek Jeter S 9.00
351 Rich Aurilla .15
352 Jose Herrera .15
353 Jay Buhner S 1.50
354 Juan Gonzalez G 12.00
355 Craig Biggio G 7.50
356 Tony Clark .50
357 Tino Martinez S 1.25
358 *Dan Naulty* .15
359 Checklist .15

1996 Finest Refractors

Finest Refractor cards were created as a parallel set to Topps' 1996 Finest set. Rare Refractor cards are found one per every 288 packs (less than 150 of these sets were produced), while uncommon Refractors are found one per every 48 packs. Common Refractors are seeded one per every 12 packs.

	MT
Complete Set (359):	2500.
Bronze Set (220):	600.00
Common Bronze:	2.00
Bronze Stars:	8X
Silver Set (91):	600.00
Typical Silver:	3.50
Silver Stars:	3X
Gold Set (48):	1500.
Typical Gold:	12.50
Gold Stars:	2.5X

(See 1996 Finest for checklist and base card values.)

1997 Finest Samples

Many of the subsets included in the 1997 Finest issue were previewed with a cello-wrapped pack of five cards distributed to hobby dealers. Cards are virtually identical to the issued versions and are designated a Refractor on back. Overprinted on back is a red notice, "PROMOTIONAL SAMPLE / NOT FOR RESALE".

		MT
Complete Set (5):		15.00
Common Player:		2.00
1	Barry Bonds	3.00
15	Derek Jeter	4.00
30	Mark McGwire	4.00
143	Hideo Nomo	2.00
159	Jeff Bagwell	3.00

1997 Finest

Finest returned for 1997 in its three-tiered format from 1996, but added several new twists. Issued in two series of 175 cards each, cards numbered 1-100 and 176-275 are bronze; 101-150 and 276-325 are silver and 151-175 and 326-350 are gold. All cards are designated among one of five different subsets per series. In Series 1 they are: Warriors, Blue Chips, Power, Hurlers and Masters. Series 2 subsets are: Power, Masters, Blue Chips, Competitors and Acquisitions. The bronze cards are the "common" card, while silvers are found every four packs and golds every 24 packs. Each card has a parallel Refractor version: bronze (1:12), silver (1:48) and gold (1:288). In addition, silver and gold cards have an additional parallel set. Silvers are found in an embossed version (1:16) and embossed Refractor version (1:192), while golds are found in a die-cut embossed version (1:96) and a die-cut embossed Refractor (1:1152).

		MT
Complete Set (350):		600.00
Bronze Set (200):		35.00
Common Bronze:		.15
Silver Set (100):		200.00
Typical Silver:		1.00
Complete Gold Set (50):		400.00
Typical Gold:		4.00
Series 1 or 2 Pack (6):		4.00
Series 1 or 2 Wax Box (24):		70.00
1	Barry Bonds B	.75
2	Ryne Sandberg B	.75
3	Brian Jordan B	.15
4	Rocky Coppinger B	.15
5	Dante Bichette B	.25
6	Al Martin B	.15
7	Charles Nagy B	.15
8	Otis Nixon B	.15
9	Mark Johnson B	.15
10	Jeff Bagwell B	1.25
11	Ken Hill B	.15
12	Willie Adams B	.15
13	Raul Mondesi B	.25
14	Reggie Sanders B	.15
15	Derek Jeter B	3.00
16	Jermaine Dye B	.15
17	Edgar Renteria B	.35
18	Travis Fryman B	.15
19	Roberto Hernandez B	.15
20	Sammy Sosa B	3.00
21	Garret Anderson B	.15
22	Rey Ordonez B	.35
23	Glenallen Hill B	.15
24	Dave Nilsson B	.15
25	Kevin Brown B	.25
26	Brian McRae B	.15
27	Joey Hamilton B	.15
28	Jamey Wright B	.15
29	Frank Thomas B	2.00
30	Mark McGwire B	6.00
31	Ramon Martinez B	.15
32	Jaime Bluma B	.15
33	Frank Rodriguez B	.15
34	Andy Benes B	.15
35	Jay Buhner B	.20
36	Justin Thompson B	.15
37	Darin Erstad B	1.25
38	Gregg Jefferies B	.15
39	Jeff D'Amico B	.15
40	Pedro Martinez B	.25
41	Nomar Garciaparra B	1.25
42	Jose Valentin B	.15
43	Pat Hentgen B	.15
44	Will Clark B	.25
45	Bernie Williams B	.50
46	Luis Castillo B	.15
47	B.J. Surhoff B	.15
48	Greg Gagne B	.15
49	Pete Schourek B	.15
50	Mike Piazza B	3.00
51	Dwight Gooden B	.15
52	Javy Lopez B	.20
53	Chuck Finley B	.15
54	James Baldwin B	.15
55	Jack McDowell B	.15
56	Royce Clayton B	.15
57	Carlos Delgado B	.50
58	Neifi Perez B	.15
59	Eddie Taubensee B	.15
60	Rafael Palmeiro B	.25
61	Marty Cordova B	.15
62	Wade Boggs B	.25
63	Rickey Henderson B	.25
64	Mike Hampton B	.15
65	Troy Percival B	.15
66	Barry Larkin B	.20
67	Jermaine Allensworth B	.15
68	Mark Clark B	.15
69	Mike Lansing B	.15
70	Mark Grudzielanek B	.15
71	Todd Stottlemyre B	.15
72	Juan Guzman B	.15
73	John Burkett B	.15
74	Wilson Alvarez B	.15
75	Ellis Burks B	.20
76	Bobby Higginson B	.25
77	Ricky Bottalico B	.15
78	Omar Vizquel B	.15
79	Paul Sorrento B	.15
80	Denny Neagle B	.15
81	Roger Pavlik B	.15
82	Mike Lieberthal B	.15
83	Devon White B	.15
84	John Olerud B	.25
85	Kevin Appier B	.15
86	Joe Girardi B	.15
87	Paul O'Neill B	.20
88	Mike Sweeney B	.15
89	John Smiley B	.15
90	Ivan Rodriguez B	.50
91	Randy Myers B	.15
92	Bip Roberts B	.15
93	Jose Mesa B	.15
94	Paul Wilson B	.20
95	Mike Mussina B	.50
96	Ben McDonald B	.15
97	John Mabry B	.15
98	Tom Goodwin B	.15
99	Edgar Martinez B	.20
100	Andruw Jones B	1.25
101	Jose Canseco S	1.50
102	Billy Wagner S	1.50
103	Dante Bichette S	1.50
104	Curt Schilling S	1.50
105	Dean Palmer S	1.00
106	Larry Walker S	2.50
107	Bernie Williams S	3.00
108	Chipper Jones S	7.50
109	Gary Sheffield S	2.00
110	Randy Johnson S	2.50
111	Roberto Alomar S	3.00
112	Todd Walker S	2.50
113	Sandy Alomar S	1.00
114	John Jaha S	1.00
115	Ken Caminiti S	2.00
116	Ryan Klesko S	2.50
117	Mariano Rivera S	1.50
118	Jason Giambi S	1.00
119	Lance Johnson S	1.00
120	Robin Ventura S	1.50
121	Todd Hollandsworth S	1.00
122	Johnny Damon S	1.00
123	William VanLandingham S	1.00
124	Jason Kendall S	1.25
125	Vinny Castilla S	1.25
126	Harold Baines S	1.00
127	Joe Carter S	1.00
128	Craig Biggio S	1.25
129	Tony Clark S	3.00
130	Ron Gant S	1.00
131	David Segui S	1.00
132	Steve Trachsel S	1.00
133	Scott Rolen S	4.00
134	Mike Stanley S	1.00
135	Cal Ripken Jr. S	10.00
136	John Smoltz S	2.00
137	Bobby Jones S	1.00
138	Manny Ramirez S	4.00
139	Ken Griffey Jr. S	15.00
140	Chuck Knoblauch S	1.50
141	Mark Grace S	1.50
142	Chris Snopek S	1.00
143	Hideo Nomo S	2.00
144	Tim Salmon S	1.50
145	David Cone S	1.50
146	Eric Young S	1.00
147	Jeff Brantley S	1.00
148	Jim Thome S	2.50
149	Trevor Hoffman S	1.25
150	Juan Gonzalez S	4.00
151	Mike Piazza G	20.00
152	Ivan Rodriguez G	7.50
153	Mo Vaughn G	6.00
154	Brady Anderson G	4.00
155	Mark McGwire G	35.00
156	Rafael Palmeiro G	6.00
157	Barry Larkin G	4.00
158	Greg Maddux G	17.50
159	Jeff Bagwell G	12.00
160	Frank Thomas G	15.00
161	Ken Caminiti G	6.00
162	Andruw Jones G	10.00
163	Dennis Eckersley G	4.00
164	Jeff Conine G	4.00
165	Jim Edmonds G	4.00
166	Derek Jeter G	25.00
167	Vladimir Guerrero G	15.00
168	Sammy Sosa G	20.00
169	Tony Gwynn G	15.00
170	Andres Galarraga G	6.00
171	Todd Hundley G	5.00
172	Jay Buhner G	4.00
173	Paul Molitor G	6.00
174	Kenny Lofton G	6.00
175	Barry Bonds G	12.00
176	Gary Sheffield B	.25
177	Dmitri Young B	.15
178	Jay Bell B	.15
179	David Wells B	.15
180	Walt Weiss B	.15
181	Paul Molitor B	.50
182	Jose Guillen B	.75
183	Al Leiter B	.15
184	Mike Fetters B	.15
185	Mark Langston B	.15
186	Fred McGriff B	.20
187	Darrin Fletcher B	.15
188	Brant Brown B	.15
189	Geronimo Berroa B	.15
190	Jim Thome B	.50
191	Jose Vizcaino B	.15
192	Andy Ashby B	.15

193 Rusty Greer B .15
194 Brian Hunter B .15
195 Chris Hoiles B .15
196 Orlando Merced B .15
197 Brett Butler B .15
198 Derek Bell B .15
199 Bobby Bonilla B .15
200 Alex Ochoa B .15
201 Wally Joyner B .15
202 Mo Vaughn B .60
203 Doug Drabek B .15
204 Tino Martinez B .25
205 Roberto Alomar B .50
206 *Brian Giles B* 6.00
207 Todd Worrell B .15
208 Alan Benes B .15
209 Jim Leyritz B .15
210 Darryl Hamilton B .15
211 Jimmy Key B .15
212 Juan Gonzalez B 1.25
213 Vinny Castilla B .15
214 Chuck Knoblauch B .20
215 Tony Phillips B .15
216 Jeff Cirillo B .15
217 Carlos Garcia B .15
218 Brooks Kieschnick B .15
219 Marquis Grissom B .15
220 Dan Wilson B .15
221 Greg Vaughn B .20
222 John Wetteland B .15
223 Andres Galarraga B .20
224 Ozzie Guillen B .15
225 Kevin Elster B .15
226 Bernard Gilkey B .15
227 Mike MacFarlane B .15
228 Heathcliff Slocumb B .15
229 Wendell Magee Jr. B .15
230 Carlos Baerga B .15
231 Kevin Seitzer B .15
232 Henry Rodriguez B .15
233 Roger Clemens B .75
234 Mark Wohlers B .15
235 Eddie Murray B .40
236 Todd Zeile B .15
237 J.T. Snow B .15
238 Ken Griffey Jr. B 5.00
239 Sterling Hitchcock B .15
240 Albert Belle B .60
241 Terry Steinbach B .15
242 Robb Nen B .15
243 Mark McLemore B .15
244 Jeff King B .15
245 Tony Clark B .60
246 Tim Salmon B .20
247 Benito Santiago B .15
248 Robin Ventura B .25
249 *Bubba Trammell B* .75
250 Chili Davis B .15
251 John Valentin B .15
252 Cal Ripken Jr. B 4.00
253 Matt Williams B .25
254 Jeff Kent B .15
255 Eric Karros B .15
256 Ray Lankford B .15
257 Ed Sprague B .15
258 Shane Reynolds B .15
259 Jaime Navarro B .15
260 Eric Davis B .15
261 Orel Hershiser B .15
262 Mark Grace B .25
263 Rod Beck B .15
264 Ismael Valdes B .15
265 Manny Ramirez B .75
266 Ken Caminiti B .20
267 Tim Naehring B .15
268 Jose Rosado B .15
269 Greg Colbrunn B .15
270 Dean Palmer B .15
271 David Justice B .25
272 Scott Spiezio B .15
273 Chipper Jones B 3.00
274 Mel Rojas B .15
275 Bartolo Colon B .15
276 Darin Erstad S 6.00
277 Sammy Sosa S 9.00
278 Rafael Palmeiro S 1.50
279 Frank Thomas S 5.00
280 Ruben Rivera S 1.00
281 Hal Morris S 1.00
282 Jay Buhner S 1.25
283 Kenny Lofton S 4.00
284 Jose Canseco S 1.50
285 Alex Fernandez S 1.00
286 Todd Helton S 4.00
287 Andy Pettitte S 3.00
288 John Franco S 1.00
289 Ivan Rodriguez S 5.00
290 Ellis Burks S 1.00
291 Julio Franco S 1.00
292 Mike Piazza S 9.00
293 Brian Jordan S 1.00
294 Greg Maddux S 7.50
295 Bob Abreu S 1.25
296 Rondell White S 1.25
297 Moises Alou S 1.25
298 Tony Gwynn S 6.00
299 Deion Sanders S 1.25
300 Jeff Montgomery S 1.00
301 Ray Durham S 1.00
302 John Wasdin S 1.00
303 Ryne Sandberg S 5.00
304 Delino DeShields S 1.00
305 Mark McGwire S 15.00
306 Andruw Jones S 4.00
307 Kevin Orie S 1.00
308 Matt Williams S 1.25
309 Karim Garcia S 1.50
310 Derek Jeter S 12.00
311 Mo Vaughn S 4.00
312 Brady Anderson S 1.00
313 Barry Bonds S 5.00
314 Steve Finley S 1.00
315 Vladimir Guerrero S 6.00
316 Matt Morris S 1.00
317 Tom Glavine S 1.50
318 Jeff Bagwell S 6.00
319 Albert Belle S 4.00
320 *Hideki Irabu S* 4.00
321 Andres Galarraga S 2.00
322 Cecil Fielder S 1.00
323 Barry Larkin S 1.00
324 Todd Hundley S 1.50
325 Fred McGriff S 1.50
326 Gary Sheffield G 6.00
327 Craig Biggio G 7.50
328 Raul Mondesi G 6.00
329 Edgar Martinez G 4.00
330 Chipper Jones G 20.00
331 Bernie Williams G 8.00
332 Juan Gonzalez G 10.00
333 Ron Gant G 4.00
334 Cal Ripken Jr. G 25.00
335 Larry Walker G 6.00
336 Matt Williams G 7.50
337 Jose Cruz Jr. G 4.00
338 Joe Carter G 4.00
339 Wilton Guerrero G 4.00
340 Cecil Fielder G 4.00
341 Todd Walker G 4.00
342 Ken Griffey Jr. G 35.00
343 Ryan Klesko G 5.00
344 Roger Clemens G 10.00
345 Hideo Nomo G 5.00
346 Dante Bichette G 4.00
347 Albert Belle G 7.50
348 Randy Johnson G 7.50
349 Manny Ramirez G 10.00
350 John Smoltz G 4.00

1997 Finest Embossed

Each Uncommon (silver) and Rare (gold) card in both Series 1 and 2 Finest was also issued in a parallel Embossed version. The Embossed Silver were a 1:16 find, while the die-cut Embossed Gold were found on average of just one per 96 packs.

	MT
Common Embossed Silver:	1.00
Embossed Silver Stars:	3X
Common Embossed Gold:	5.00
Embossed/Die-Cut Gold Stars:	2X

(See 1997 Finest for checklist and base card values.)

1997 Finest Refractors

Every card in '97 Finest - both regular and embossed parallel - has a Refractor version. The Uncommon parallel set of Refractors features a mosaic pattern in the background while the Rare embossed die-cut parallel set of Refractors are produced with a hyper-plaid foil design. The number of cards and the insertion ratios for each level of Refractors is as follows: Common (200 cards, 1:12 packs), Uncommon (100, 1:48), Rare (50, 1:288), Embossed Uncommon (100, 1:192), Embossed Die-cut Rare (50, 1:1152).

	MT
Common Bronze:	2.00
Bronze Stars:	6X
Typical Silver:	3.00
Silver Stars:	3X
Typical Gold:	8.00
Gold Stars:	2X
Typical Embossed Silver:	7.50
Embossed Silver Stars:	8X
Typical Embossed Gold:	20.00
Embossed Gold Stars:	2X

(See 1997 Finest for cheklist and base card values.)

1998 Finest Pre-Production

Five-card cello packs of '98 Finest were distributed in the hobby market to preview the always-popular issue. The cards are virtually identical to the issued versions except for the card number, which bears a "PP" prefix.

		MT
Complete Set (5):		10.00
Common Player:		1.50
1	Nomar Garciaparra	3.00
2	Mark McGwire	4.00
3	Ivan Rodriguez	3.00
4	Ken Griffey Jr.	4.50
5	Roger Clemens	3.00

1998 Finest

Finest dropped its three-tiered format in 1998 and produced a 275-card set on a thicker 26-point stock, with 150 cards in Series 1 and 125 in Series 2. The catch in 1998 was that each card arrived in Protector, No-Protector, Protector Refractor and No-Protector Refractor versions. Six-card packs sold for a suggested retail price of $5. Finest also included insert sets for the first time since 1995. Included in Series 1 packs were Centurions, Mystery Finest and Power Zone inserts. Series 2 had Mystery Finest, Stadium Stars and The Man. Throughout both series, Finest Protector cards are considered base cards, while No-Protector are inserted one per two packs (HTA odds 1:1), No-Protector Refractors are seeded 1:24 packs (HTA odds 1:10) and Finest Refractors are seeded 1:12 packs (HTA odds 1:5).

		MT
Complete Set (275):		75.00
Complete Series 1 Set (150):		40.00
Complete Series 2 Set (125):		35.00
Common Player:		.15
Refractors:		8X
No-Protector Refractor:		15X
Pack (6):		3.50
Wax Box (24):		75.00
1	Larry Walker	.50
2	Andruw Jones	.75
3	Ramon Martinez	.15
4	Geronimo Berroa	.15
5	David Justice	.50
6	Rusty Greer	.15
7	Chad Ogea	.15
8	Tom Goodwin	.15
9	Tino Martinez	.35
10	Jose Guillen	.25
11	Jeffrey Hammonds	.15
12	Brian McRae	.15
13	Jeremi Gonzalez	.15
14	Craig Counsell	.15
15	Mike Piazza	2.50
16	Greg Maddux	1.75
17	Todd Greene	.15
18	Rondell White	.25
19	Kirk Rueter	.15
20	Tony Clark	.25
21	Brad Radke	.15
22	Jaret Wright	.25
23	Carlos Delgado	1.00

24 Dustin Hermanson .25
25 Gary Sheffield .40
26 Jose Canseco .40
27 Kevin Young .15
28 David Wells .15
29 Mariano Rivera .25
30 Reggie Sanders .15
31 Mike Cameron .15
32 Bobby Witt .15
33 Kevin Orie .15
34 Royce Clayton .15
35 Edgar Martinez .25
36 Neifi Perez .15
37 Kevin Appier .15
38 Darryl Hamilton .15
39 Michael Tucker .15
40 Roger Clemens 1.50
41 Carl Everett .25
42 Mike Sweeney .15
43 Pat Meares .15
44 Brian Giles .30
45 Matt Morris .15
46 Jason Dickson .15
47 Rich Loiselle .15
48 Joe Girardi .15
49 Steve Trachsel .15
50 Ben Grieve .50
51 Jose Vizcaino .15
52 Hideki Irabu .20
53 J.T. Snow .15
54 Mike Hampton .25
55 Dave Nilsson .15
56 Alex Fernandez .15
57 Brett Tomko .15
58 Wally Joyner .15
59 Kelvim Escobar .15
60 Roberto Alomar .60
61 Todd Jones .15
62 Paul O'Neill .40
63 Jamie Moyer .15
64 Mark Wohlers .15
65 Jose Cruz Jr. .25
66 Troy Percival .15
67 Rick Reed .15
68 Will Clark .40
69 Jamey Wright .15
70 Mike Mussina .60
71 David Cone .25
72 Ryan Klesko .30
73 Scott Hatteberg .15
74 James Baldwin .15
75 Tony Womack .15
76 Carlos Perez .15
77 Charles Nagy .15
78 Jeromy Burnitz .15
79 Shane Reynolds .15
80 Cliff Floyd .15
81 Jason Kendall .25
82 Chad Curtis .15
83 Matt Karchner .15
84 Ricky Bottalico .15
85 Sammy Sosa 2.50
86 Javy Lopez .20
87 Jeff Kent .25
88 Shawn Green .40
89 Devon White .15
90 Tony Gwynn 1.50
91 Bob Tewksbury .15
92 Derek Jeter 2.50
93 Eric Davis .25
94 Jeff Fassero .15
95 Denny Neagle .15
96 Ismael Valdes .15
97 Tim Salmon .40
98 Mark Grudzielanek .15
99 Curt Schilling .40
100 Ken Griffey Jr. 3.00
101 Edgardo Alfonzo .40
102 Vinny Castilla .15
103 Jose Rosado .15
104 Scott Erickson .15
105 Alan Benes .15
106 Shannon Stewart .15
107 Delino DeShields .15
108 Mark Loretta .15
109 Todd Hundley .25
110 Chuck Knoblauch .25
111 Quinton McCracken .15
112 F.P. Santangelo .15
113 Gerald Williams .15
114 Omar Vizquel .25
115 John Valentin .15
116 Damion Easley .15
117 Matt Lawton .15
118 Jim Thome .50
119 Sandy Alomar .25
120 Albert Belle .75
121 Chris Stynes .15
122 Butch Huskey .15
123 Shawn Estes .15
124 Terry Adams .15
125 Ivan Rodriguez 1.00
126 Ron Gant .20
127 John Mabry .15
128 Jeff Shaw .15
129 Jeff Montgomery .15
130 Justin Thompson .20
131 Livan Hernandez .20
132 Ugueth Urbina .15
133 Doug Glanville .15
134 Troy O'Leary .15
135 Cal Ripken Jr. 3.00
136 Quilvio Veras .15
137 Pedro Astacio .15
138 Willie Greene .15
139 Lance Johnson .15
140 Nomar Garciaparra 2.50
141 Jose Offerman .15
142 Scott Rolen 1.00
143 Derek Bell .15
144 Johnny Damon .15
145 Mark McGwire 4.00
146 Chan Ho Park .25
147 Edgar Renteria .15
148 Eric Young .15
149 Craig Biggio .35
150 Checklist 1-150 .15
151 Frank Thomas 1.50
152 John Wetteland .15
153 Mike Lansing .15
154 Pedro Martinez 1.00
155 Rico Brogna .15
156 Kevin Brown .30
157 Alex Rodriguez 3.00
158 Wade Boggs .50
159 Richard Hidalgo .25
160 Mark Grace .25
161 Jose Mesa .15
162 John Olerud .25
163 Tim Belcher .15
164 Chuck Finley .15
165 Brian Hunter .15
166 Joe Carter .20
167 Stan Javier .15
168 Jay Bell .15
169 Ray Lankford .15
170 John Smoltz .20
171 Ed Sprague .15
172 Jason Giambi .40
173 Todd Walker .15
174 Paul Konerko .40
175 Rey Ordonez .15
176 Dante Bichette .25
177 Bernie Williams .75
178 Jon Nunnally .15
179 Rafael Palmeiro .60
180 Jay Buhner .20
181 Devon White .15
182 Jeff D'Amico .15
183 Walt Weiss .15
184 Scott Spiezio .15
185 Moises Alou .25
186 Carlos Baerga .15
187 Todd Zeile .15
188 Gregg Jefferies .15
189 Mo Vaughn .75
190 Terry Steinbach .15
191 Ray Durham .15
192 Robin Ventura .30
193 Jeff Reed .15
194 Ken Caminiti .15
195 Eric Karros .25
196 Wilson Alvarez .15
197 Gary Gaetti .15
198 Andres Galarraga .40
199 Alex Gonzalez .15
200 Garret Anderson .15
201 Andy Benes .15
202 Harold Baines .15
203 Ron Coomer .15
204 Dean Palmer .15
205 Reggie Jefferson .15
206 John Burkett .15
207 Jermaine Allensworth .15
208 Bernard Gilkey .15
209 Jeff Bagwell 1.00
210 Kenny Lofton .50
211 Bobby Jones .15
212 Bartolo Colon .25
213 Jim Edmonds .40
214 Pat Hentgen .15
215 Matt Williams .40
216 Bob Abreu .30
217 Jorge Posada .15
218 Marty Cordova .15
219 Ken Hill .15
220 Steve Finley .15
221 Jeff King .15
222 Quinton McCracken .15
223 Matt Stairs .15
224 Darin Erstad .75
225 Fred McGriff .40
226 Marquis Grissom .15
227 Doug Glanville .15
228 Tom Glavine .40
229 John Franco .15
230 Darren Bragg .15
231 Barry Larkin .40
232 Trevor Hoffman .15
233 Brady Anderson .25
234 Al Martin .15
235 B.J. Surhoff .15
236 Ellis Burks .15
237 Randy Johnson 1.00
238 Mark Clark .15
239 Tony Saunders .15
240 Hideo Nomo .25
241 Brad Fullmer .25
242 Chipper Jones 2.00
243 Jose Valentin .15
244 Manny Ramirez 1.00
245 Derrek Lee .15
246 Jimmy Key .15
247 Tim Naehring .15
248 Bobby Higginson .15
249 Charles Johnson .15
250 Chili Davis .15
251 Tom Gordon .15
252 Mike Lieberthal .15
253 Billy Wagner .15
254 Juan Guzman .15
255 Todd Stottlemyre .15
256 Brian Jordan .15
257 Barry Bonds 1.00
258 Dan Wilson .15
259 Paul Molitor .50
260 Juan Gonzalez 1.00
261 Francisco Cordova .15
262 Cecil Fielder .15
263 Travis Lee .15
264 Kevin Tapani .15
265 Raul Mondesi .25
266 Travis Fryman .25
267 Armando Benitez .15
268 Pokey Reese .15
269 Rick Aguilera .15
270 Andy Pettitte .50
271 Jose Vizcaino .15
272 Kerry Wood .50
273 Vladimir Guerrero 1.50
274 John Smiley .15
275 Checklist 151-275 .15

1998 Finest No-Protector

This parallel to the 275-card base set foregoes the peel-off front protector and adds Finest technology to the back of the card. Stated insertion rates were one per two packs or one per pack in Home Team Advantage (HTA) boxes.

	MT
Complete Set (275):	250.00
Common Player:	.50
Stars/Rookies:	2.5X

(See 1998 Finest for checklist and base card values.)

1998 Finest Centurions

Centurions is a 20-card insert found only Series 1 hobby (1:153) and Home Team Advantage packs (1:71). The theme of the insert to top players who will lead the game into the next century. Each card is sequentially numbered on the back to 500, while Refractor versions are numbered to 75.

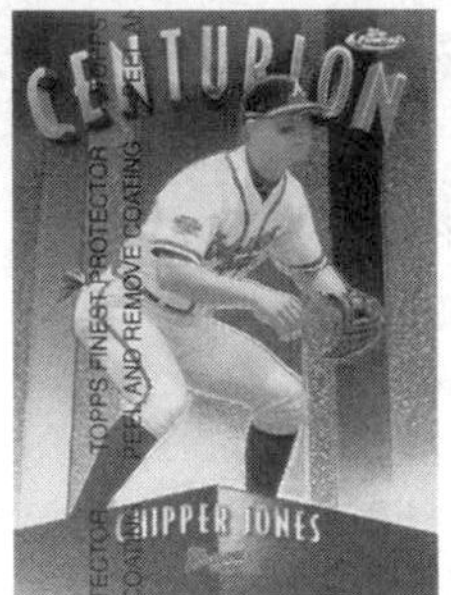

		MT
Complete Set (20):		100.00
Common Player:		2.00
Production 500 sets		
Refractors:		4X
Production 75 sets		
C1	Andruw Jones	4.00
C2	Vladimir Guerrero	8.00
C3	Nomar Garciaparra	12.00
C4	Scott Rolen	5.00
C5	Ken Griffey Jr.	15.00
C6	Jose Cruz Jr.	2.00
C7	Barry Bonds	5.00
C8	Mark McGwire	20.00
C9	Juan Gonzalez	5.00
C10	Jeff Bagwell	5.00
C11	Frank Thomas	6.00
C12	Paul Konerko	2.00
C13	Alex Rodriguez	15.00
C14	Mike Piazza	12.00
C15	Travis Lee	2.00
C16	Chipper Jones	10.00
C17	Larry Walker	3.00
C18	Mo Vaughn	4.00
C19	Livan Hernandez	2.00
C20	Jaret Wright	2.00

1998 Finest Mystery Finest

This 50-card insert was seeded one per 36 Series 1 packs and one per 15 HTA packs. The set includes 20 top players, each matched on a double-sided card with three other players and once with himself. Each side of the card is printed on a chromium finish and arrives with a black opaque protector. Mystery Finest inserts are numbered with an "M" prefix. Refractor versions were seeded one per 64 packs (HTA odds 1:15).

		MT
Complete Set (50):		600.00
Common Player:		5.00
Refractors:		2X
M1	Frank Thomas, Ken Griffey Jr.	25.00
M2	Frank Thomas, Mike Piazza	18.00
M3	Frank Thomas, Mark McGwire	30.00
M4	Frank Thomas, Frank Thomas	12.00
M5	Ken Griffey Jr., Mike Piazza	25.00
M6	Ken Griffey Jr., Mark McGwire	30.00
M7	Ken Griffey Jr., Ken Griffey Jr.	30.00
M8	Mike Piazza, Mark McGwire	30.00
M9	Mike Piazza, Mike Piazza	25.00
M10	Mark McGwire, Mark McGwire	40.00
M11	Nomar Garciaparra, Jose Cruz Jr.	15.00
M12	Nomar Garciaparra, Derek Jeter	20.00
M13	Nomar Garciaparra, Andruw Jones	15.00
M14	Nomar Garciaparra, Nomar Garciaparra	20.00
M15	Jose Cruz Jr., Derek Jeter	18.00
M16	Jose Cruz Jr., Andruw Jones	5.00
M17	Jose Cruz Jr., Jose Cruz Jr.	5.00
M18	Derek Jeter, Andruw Jones	20.00
M19	Derek Jeter, Derek Jeter	25.00
M20	Andruw Jones, Andruw Jones	10.00
M21	Cal Ripken Jr., Tony Gwynn	20.00
M22	Cal Ripken Jr., Barry Bonds	20.00
M23	Cal Ripken Jr., Greg Maddux	20.00
M24	Cal Ripken Jr., Cal Ripken Jr.	25.00
M25	Tony Gwynn, Barry Bonds	12.00
M26	Tony Gwynn, Greg Maddux	15.00
M27	Tony Gwynn, Tony Gwynn	12.00
M28	Barry Bonds, Greg Maddux	12.00
M29	Barry Bonds, Barry Bonds	10.00
M30	Greg Maddux, Greg Maddux	15.00
M31	Juan Gonzalez, Larry Walker	8.00
M32	Juan Gonzalez, Andres Galarraga	8.00
M33	Juan Gonzalez, Chipper Jones	15.00
M34	Juan Gonzalez, Juan Gonzalez	8.00
M35	Larry Walker	6.00
M36	Larry Walker, Chipper Jones	10.00
M37	Larry Walker, Larry Walker	5.00
M38	Andres Galarraga, Chipper Jones	10.00
M39	Andres Galarraga, Andres Galarraga	5.00
M40	Chipper Jones, Chipper Jones	20.00
M41	Gary Sheffield, Sammy Sosa	15.00
M42	Gary Sheffield, Jeff Bagwell	10.00
M43	Gary Sheffield, Tino Martinez	5.00
M44	Gary Sheffield, Gary Sheffield	6.00
M45	Sammy Sosa, Jeff Bagwell	15.00
M46	Sammy Sosa, Tino Martinez	15.00
M47	Sammy Sosa, Sammy Sosa	20.00
M48	Jeff Bagwell, Tino Martinez	8.00
M49	Jeff Bagwell, Jeff Bagwell	12.50
M50	Tino Martinez, Tino Martinez	5.00

1998 Finest Mystery Finest 2

Forty more Mystery Finest inserts were seeded in Series 2 packs at a rate of one per 36 packs (HTA odds 1:15), with Refrators every 1:144 packs (HTA odds 1:64). As with Series 1, 20 players are in the checklist; some players are found with another player on the back or by himself on each side. Each side is printed in Finest technology with an opaque black protector.

		MT
Complete Set (40):		650.00
Common Player:		5.00
Refractors:		2X
M1	Nomar Garciaparra, Frank Thomas	25.00
M2	Nomar Garciaparra, Albert Belle	25.00
M3	Nomar Garciaparra, Scott Rolen	25.00
M4	Frank Thomas, Albert Belle	15.00
M5	Frank Thomas, Scott Rolen	15.00
M6	Albert Belle, Scott Rolen	8.00
M7	Ken Griffey Jr., Jose Cruz	30.00
M8	Ken Griffey Jr., Alex Rodriguez	30.00
M9	Ken Griffey Jr., Roger Clemens	30.00
M10	Jose Cruz, Alex Rodriguez	25.00
M11	Jose Cruz, Roger Clemens	12.00
M12	Alex Rodriguez, Roger Clemens	30.00
M13	Mike Piazza, Barry Bonds	25.00
M14	Mike Piazza, Derek Jeter	25.00
M15	Mike Piazza, Bernie Williams	25.00
M16	Barry Bonds, Derek Jeter	25.00
M17	Barry Bonds, Bernie Williams	10.00
M18	Derek Jeter, Bernie Williams	20.00
M19	Mark McGwire, Jeff Bagwell	40.00
M20	Mark McGwire, Mo Vaughn	35.00
M21	Mark McGwire, Jim Thome	35.00
M22	Jeff Bagwell, Mo Vaughn	10.00
M23	Jeff Bagwell, Jim Thome	10.00
M24	Mo Vaughn, Jim Thome	4.00
M25	Juan Gonzalez, Travis Lee	10.00
M26	Juan Gonzalez, Ben Grieve	10.00
M27	Juan Gonzalez, Fred McGriff	10.00
M28	Travis Lee, Ben Grieve	6.00
M29	Travis Lee, Fred McGriff	6.00
M30	Ben Grieve, Fred McGriff	6.00
M31	Albert Belle, Albert Belle	6.00
M32	Scott Rolen, Scott Rolen	8.00
M33	Alex Rodriguez, Alex Rodriguez	25.00
M34	Roger Clemens, Roger Clemens	12.00
M35	Bernie Williams, Bernie Williams	6.00
M36	Mo Vaughn, Mo Vaughn	5.00
M37	Jim Thome, Jim Thome	5.00
M38	Travis Lee, Travis Lee	5.00
M39	Fred McGriff, Fred McGriff	5.00
M40	Ben Grieve, Ben Grieve	6.00

1998 Finest Mystery Finest Jumbo

Series 2 Home Team Advantage (HTA) boxes were the exclusive venue for these large-format (3" x 5") versions of Mystery Finest. Regular cards were found one per six boxes of HTA, while Refractor versions were a 1:12 seed.

		MT
Complete Set (3):		25.00
Common Card:		5.00
Refractor:		1.5X
1	Ken Griffey Jr., Alex Rodriguez	12.00
2	Derek Jeter, Bernie Williams	5.00
3	Mark McGwire, Jeff Bagwell	10.00

1998 Finest Power Zone

This Series 1 insert features Topps' new "Flop Inks" technology which changes the color of the card depending at what angle it is viewed. They are inserted one per 72 hobby packs (HTA odds 1:32). Cards are numbered with a "P" prefix.

		MT
Complete Set (20):		200.00
Common Player:		3.00
1	Ken Griffey Jr.	40.00
2	Jeff Bagwell	10.00
3	Jose Cruz Jr.	3.00
4	Barry Bonds	10.00
5	Mark McGwire	40.00
6	Jim Thome	5.00
7	Mo Vaughn	6.00
8	Gary Sheffield	4.00
9	Andres Galarraga	6.00
10	Nomar Garciaparra	25.00
11	Rafael Palmeiro	6.00
12	Sammy Sosa	20.00
13	Jay Buhner	3.00
14	Tony Clark	3.00
15	Mike Piazza	25.00
16	Larry Walker	4.00
17	Albert Belle	6.00
18	Tino Martinez	4.00
19	Juan Gonzalez	10.00
20	Frank Thomas	15.00

1998 Finest Stadium Stars

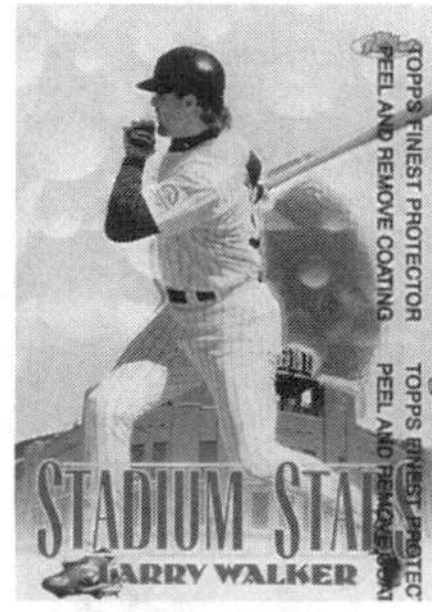

Stadium Stars is a 24-card insert that features Topps' new lenticular holographic chromium technology. These are exclusive to Series 2 packs and carried an insertion rate of one per 72 packs (HTA odds 1:32).

		MT
Complete Set (24):		350.00
Common Player:		4.00
SS1	Ken Griffey Jr.	40.00
SS2	Alex Rodriguez	40.00
SS3	Mo Vaughn	10.00
SS4	Nomar Garciaparra	30.00
SS5	Frank Thomas	20.00
SS6	Albert Belle	10.00
SS7	Derek Jeter	30.00
SS8	Chipper Jones	25.00
SS9	Cal Ripken Jr.	40.00
SS10	Jim Thome	5.00
SS11	Mike Piazza	30.00
SS12	Juan Gonzalez	15.00
SS13	Jeff Bagwell	15.00
SS14	Sammy Sosa	25.00
SS15	Jose Cruz Jr.	5.00
SS16	Gary Sheffield	6.00
SS17	Larry Walker	8.00
SS18	Tony Gwynn	20.00
SS19	Mark McGwire	50.00
SS20	Barry Bonds	15.00
SS21	Tino Martinez	4.00
SS22	Manny Ramirez	15.00
SS23	Ken Caminiti	4.00
SS24	Andres Galarraga	6.00

1998 Finest The Man

This 20-card insert features the top players in baseball and was exlusive found in Series 2 packs. Regular versions are sequentially numbered to 500 and inserted one per 119 packs, while Refractor versions are numbered to 75 and inserted one per 793 packs.

	MT
Complete Set (20):	500.00
Common Player:	7.50
Refractors:	2X
TM1 Ken Griffey Jr.	60.00
TM2 Barry Bonds	20.00
TM3 Frank Thomas	25.00
TM4 Chipper Jones	35.00
TM5 Cal Ripken Jr.	60.00
TM6 Nomar Garciaparra	40.00
TM7 Mark McGwire	75.00
TM8 Mike Piazza	40.00
TM9 Derek Jeter	50.00
TM10Alex Rodriguez	60.00
TM11Jose Cruz Jr.	7.50
TM12Larry Walker	10.00
TM13Jeff Bagwell	20.00
TM14Tony Gwynn	25.00
TM15Travis Lee	7.50
TM16Juan Gonzalez	15.00
TM17Scott Rolen	15.00
TM18Randy Johnson	15.00
TM19Roger Clemens	20.00
TM20Greg Maddux	35.00

1998 Finest Jumbo

Eight oversized cards were inserted into both Series 1 and Series 2 boxes as box toppers. The cards measure 3" x 5" and are inserted one per three boxes, with Refractor versions every six boxes. The oversized cards are similar to the regular-issed cards except for the numbering which designates each "X of 8".

		MT
Complete Set (16):		90.00
Complete Series 1 (8):		60.00
Complete Series 2 (8):		35.00
Common Player:		2.50
Refractors: 1.5X		
	FIRST SERIES	
1	Mark McGwire	15.00
2	Cal Ripken Jr.	12.50
3	Nomar Garciaparra	10.00
4	Mike Piazza	10.00
5	Greg Maddux	8.00
6	Jose Cruz Jr.	2.50
7	Roger Clemens	6.00
8	Ken Griffey Jr.	15.00
	SECOND SERIES	
1	Frank Thomas	10.00
2	Bernie Williams	3.00
3	Randy Johnson	3.00
4	Chipper Jones	10.00
5	Manny Ramirez	4.00
6	Barry Bonds	4.00
7	Juan Gonzalez	7.50
8	Jeff Bagwell	5.00

1999 Finest

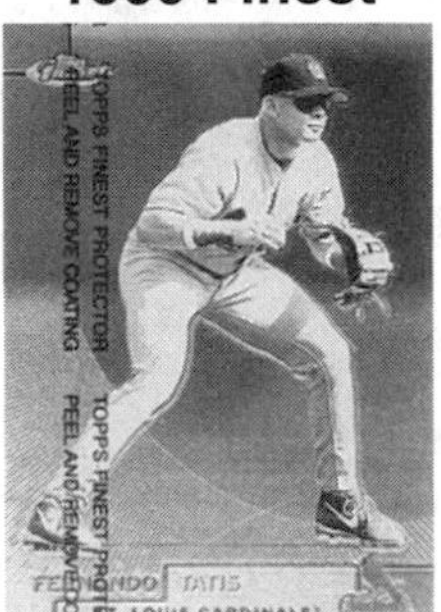

Released in two series, with each consisting of 100 regular and 50 subset cards divided into three categories: Gems, Sensations and Rookies in Series 1, and Sterling, Gamers and Rookies in the second series. The subset cards are shortprinted, seeded one per pack. Cards are printed on 27 pt. stock utilizing chromium technology. There are two parallels: Refractors and die-cut Gold Refractors. Refractors are seeded 1:12 packs, while Gold Refractors are numbered to 100 sets. Six-cards packs carried an SRP of $4.99.

		MT
Complete Set (300):		200.00
Complete Series 1 (150):		100.00
Complete Series 2 (150):		100.00
Common Player:		.15
Common SP (101-150, 251-300):		.50
Pack (6):		4.00
Wax Box (24):		85.00
1	Darin Erstad	.75
2	Javy Lopez	.25
3	Vinny Castilla	.15
4	Jim Thome	.75
5	Tino Martinez	.25
6	Mark Grace	.25
7	Shawn Green	.40
8	Dustin Hermanson	.15
9	Kevin Young	.15
10	Tony Clark	.25
11	Scott Brosius	.15
12	Craig Biggio	.35
13	Brian McRae	.15
14	Chan Ho Park	.25
15	Manny Ramirez	1.00
16	Chipper Jones	2.00
17	Rico Brogna	.15
18	Quinton McCracken	.15
19	J.T. Snow Jr.	.15
20	Tony Gwynn	1.50
21	Juan Guzman	.15
22	John Valentin	.15
23	Rick Helling	.15
24	Sandy Alomar	.15
25	Frank Thomas	1.50
26	Jorge Posada	.15
27	Dmitri Young	.15
28	Rick Reed	.15
29	Kevin Tapani	.15
30	Troy Glaus	1.50
31	Kenny Rogers	.15
32	Jeromy Burnitz	.15
33	Mark Grudzielanek	.15
34	Mike Mussina	.75
35	Scott Rolen	1.00
36	Neifi Perez	.15
37	Brad Radke	.15
38	Darryl Strawberry	.25
39	Robb Nen	.15
40	Moises Alou	.25
41	Eric Young	.15
42	Livan Hernandez	.15
43	John Wetteland	.15
44	Matt Lawton	.15
45	Ben Grieve	.40
46	Fernando Tatis	.25
47	Travis Fryman	.25
48	David Segui	.15
49	Bob Abreu	.25
50	Nomar Garciaparra	2.50
51	Paul O'Neill	.40
52	Jeff King	.15
53	Francisco Cordova	.15
54	John Olerud	.25
55	Vladimir Guerrero	1.50
56	Fernando Vina	.15
57	Shane Reynolds	.15
58	Chuck Finley	.15
59	Rondell White	.25
60	Greg Vaughn	.25
61	Ryan Minor	.25
62	Tom Gordon	.15
63	Damion Easley	.15
64	Ray Durham	.15
65	Orlando Hernandez	.40
66	Bartolo Colon	.15
67	Jaret Wright	.15
68	Royce Clayton	.15
69	Tim Salmon	.40
70	Mark McGwire	4.00
71	Alex Gonzalez	.15
72	Tom Glavine	.40
73	David Justice	.50
74	Omar Vizquel	.15
75	Juan Gonzalez	1.00
76	Bobby Higginson	.15
77	Todd Walker	.15
78	Dante Bichette	.25
79	Kevin Millwood	.25
80	Roger Clemens	1.50
81	Kerry Wood	.40
82	Cal Ripken Jr.	3.00
83	Jay Bell	.15
84	Barry Bonds	1.00
85	Alex Rodriguez	3.00
86	Doug Glanville	.15
87	Jason Kendall	.25
88	Sean Casey	.25
89	Aaron Sele	.15
90	Derek Jeter	3.00
91	Andy Ashby	.15
92	Rusty Greer	.15
93	Rod Beck	.15
94	Matt Williams	.40
95	Mike Piazza	2.50
96	Wally Joyner	.15
97	Barry Larkin	.50
98	Eric Milton	.15
99	Gary Sheffield	.50
100	Greg Maddux	2.00
101	Ken Griffey Jr. (Gem)	5.00
102	Frank Thomas (Gem)	2.00
103	Nomar Garciaparra (Gem)	4.00
104	Mark McGwire (Gem)	6.00
105	Alex Rodriguez (Gem)	5.00
106	Tony Gwynn (Gem)	2.00
107	Juan Gonzalez (Gem)	1.50
108	Jeff Bagwell (Gem)	1.50
109	Sammy Sosa (Gem)	4.00
110	Vladimir Guerrero (Gem)	2.00
111	Roger Clemens (Gem)	2.00
112	Barry Bonds (Gem)	1.50
113	Darin Erstad (Gem)	1.00
114	Mike Piazza (Gem)	4.00
115	Derek Jeter (Gem)	4.00
116	Chipper Jones (Gem)	3.00
117	Larry Walker (Gem)	.75
118	Scott Rolen (Gem)	1.50
119	Cal Ripken Jr. (Gem)	5.00
120	Greg Maddux (Gem)	3.00
121	Troy Glaus (Sensations)	2.50
122	Ben Grieve (Sensations)	.75
123	Ryan Minor (Sensations)	.50
124	Kerry Wood (Sensations)	.75
125	Travis Lee (Sensations)	.50
126	Adrian Beltre (Sensations)	.50
127	Brad Fullmer (Sensations)	.75
128	Aramis Ramirez (Sensations)	.50
129	Eric Chavez (Sensations)	.50
130	Todd Helton (Sensations)	1.50
131	*Pat Burrell* (Finest Rookies)	12.00
132	*Ryan Mills* (Finest Rookies)	1.00
133	*Austin Kearns* (Finest Rookies)	6.00
134	*Josh McKinley* (Finest Rookies)	1.00
135	*Adam Everett* (Finest Rookies)	1.00
136	Marlon Anderson	.50
137	Bruce Chen	.50
138	Matt Clement	.50
139	Alex Gonzalez	.50
140	Roy Halladay	.50
141	Calvin Pickering	.50
142	Randy Wolf	.50
143	Ryan Anderson	.75
144	Ruben Mateo	.75
145	*Alex Escobar*	5.00
146	Jeremy Giambi	.50
147	Lance Berkman	.50
148	Michael Barrett	.50
149	Preston Wilson	.50
150	Gabe Kapler	.75
151	Roger Clemens	1.50
152	Jay Buhner	.20
153	Brad Fullmer	.15
154	Ray Lankford	.15
155	Jim Edmonds	.40
156	Jason Giambi	.40
157	Bret Boone	.15
158	Jeff Cirillo	.15
159	Rickey Henderson	.40
160	Edgar Martinez	.15
161	Ron Gant	.25
162	Mark Kotsay	.15
163	Trevor Hoffman	.15
164	Jason Schmidt	.15
165	Brett Tomko	.15
166	David Ortiz	.15
167	Dean Palmer	.15
168	Hideki Irabu	.20
169	Mike Cameron	.15
170	Pedro Martinez	1.00
171	Tom Goodwin	.15
172	Brian Hunter	.15
173	Al Leiter	.15
174	Charles Johnson	.15
175	Curt Schilling	.25
176	Robin Ventura	.25
177	Travis Lee	.15
178	Jeff Shaw	.15
179	Ugueth Urbina	.15
180	Roberto Alomar	.75
181	Cliff Floyd	.15
182	Adrian Beltre	.40
183	Tony Womack	.15
184	Brian Jordan	.15
185	Randy Johnson	1.00
186	Mickey Morandini	.15
187	Todd Hundley	.15

188	Jose Valentin	.15
189	Eric Davis	.15
190	Ken Caminiti	.20
191	David Wells	.15
192	Ryan Klesko	.25
193	Garret Anderson	.15
194	Eric Karros	.25
195	Ivan Rodriguez	1.00
196	Aramis Ramirez	.15
197	Mike Lieberthal	.15
198	Will Clark	.50
199	Rey Ordonez	.15
200	Ken Griffey Jr.	3.00
201	Jose Guillen	.15
202	Scott Erickson	.15
203	Paul Konerko	.25
204	Johnny Damon	.15
205	Larry Walker	.40
206	Denny Neagle	.15
207	Jose Offerman	.15
208	Andy Pettitte	.25
209	Bobby Jones	.15
210	Kevin Brown	.30
211	John Smoltz	.15
212	Henry Rodriguez	.15
213	Tim Belcher	.15
214	Carlos Delgado	1.00
215	Andruw Jones	1.00
216	Andy Benes	.15
217	Fred McGriff	.40
218	Edgar Renteria	.15
219	Miguel Tejada	.40
220	Bernie Williams	.75
221	Justin Thompson	.15
222	Marty Cordova	.15
223	Delino DeShields	.15
224	Ellis Burks	.15
225	Kenny Lofton	.50
226	Steve Finley	.15
227	Eric Chavez	.25
228	Jose Cruz Jr.	.15
229	Marquis Grissom	.15
230	Jeff Bagwell	1.00
231	Jose Canseco	.50
232	Edgardo Alfonzo	.25
233	Richie Sexson	.25
234	Jeff Kent	.25
235	Rafael Palmeiro	.50
236	David Cone	.25
237	Gregg Jefferies	.15
238	Mike Lansing	.15
239	Mariano Rivera	.25
240	Albert Belle	.50
241	Chuck Knoblauch	.40
242	Derek Bell	.15
243	Pat Hentgen	.15
244	Andres Galarraga	.60
245	Mo Vaughn	.75
246	Wade Boggs	.50
247	Devon White	.15
248	Todd Helton	.75
249	Raul Mondesi	.40
250	Sammy Sosa	2.50
251	Nomar Garciaparra (Sterling)	4.00
252	Mark McGwire (Sterling)	6.00
253	Alex Rodriguez (Sterling)	5.00
254	Juan Gonzalez (Sterling)	1.50
255	Vladimir Guerrero (Sterling)	2.00
256	Ken Griffey Jr. (Sterling)	5.00
257	Mike Piazza (Sterling)	4.00
258	Derek Jeter (Sterling)	4.00
259	Albert Belle (Sterling)	1.00
260	Greg Vaughn (Sterling)	.50
261	Sammy Sosa (Sterling)	4.00
262	Greg Maddux (Sterling)	3.00
263	Frank Thomas (Sterling)	2.00
264	Mark Grace (Sterling)	.50
265	Ivan Rodriguez (Sterling)	1.50
266	Roger Clemens (Gamers)	2.00
267	Mo Vaughn (Gamers)	1.00
268	Jim Thome (Gamers)	1.00
269	Darin Erstad (Gamers)	.75
270	Chipper Jones (Gamers)	3.00
271	Larry Walker (Gamers)	1.00
272	Cal Ripken Jr. (Gamers)	5.00
273	Scott Rolen (Gamers)	1.00
274	Randy Johnson (Gamers)	1.50
275	Tony Gwynn (Gamers)	2.00
276	Barry Bonds (Gamers)	1.50
277	*Sean Burroughs*	8.00
278	*J.M. Gold*	1.00
279	Carlos Lee	.50
280	George Lombard	.50
281	Carlos Beltran	.50
282	Fernando Seguignol	.50
283	Eric Chavez	.50
284	*Carlos Pena*	4.00
285	*Corey Patterson*	10.00
286	*Alfonso Soriano*	5.00
287	*Nick Johnson*	5.00
288	*Jorge Toca*	1.00
289	*A.J. Burnett*	2.00
290	*Andy Brown*	1.50
291	*Doug Mientkiewicz*	1.00
292	*Bobby Seay*	1.00
293	*Chip Ambres*	1.00
294	*C.C. Sabathia*	4.00
295	*Choo Freeman*	1.50
296	*Eric Valent*	2.00
297	*Matt Belisle*	2.00
298	*Jason Tyner*	1.50
299	*Masao Kida*	1.50
300	Hank Aaron, Mark McGwire (Homerun Kings)	4.00

1999 Finest Refractors

Inserted at the rate of one card per 12 packs, Refractors use special technology to impart a more colorful sheen to the card fronts. To eliminate doubt, the backs have the word "REFRACTOR" printed to the right of the card number at top.

	MT
Complete Set (300):	2250.
Common Player:	2.00
Stars:	6-10X
SPs:	3-5X

(See 1999 Finest for checklist and base card values.)

1999 Finest Gold Refractors

At the top of Finest's chase-card line-up for 1999 are the Gold Refractors. Fronts have an overall gold tone in the background. Backs are individually serial numbered in gold foil with an edition of 100 each, and have the words "GOLD REFRACTOR" printed at top, to the right of the card number. The Gold Refractors are die-cut along the edges to create a deckled effect. Stated pack insertion rates were between 1:26 and 1:82 depending on series and type.

	MT
Common Player:	7.50
Stars:	30-50X
SPs:	15-25X

(See 1999 Finest for checklist and base card values.)

1999 Finest Complements

This Series 2 insert set pairs two players on a "split-screen" card front. There are three different versions for each card, Non-Refractor/Refractor (1:56), Refractor/Non-Refractor (1:56) and Refractor/Refractor (1:168). Each card is numbered with a "C" prefix. Values shown are for cards with either the left- or right-side player as Refractor; dual-refractor cards valued at 2X.

		MT
Complete Set (7):		35.00
Common Player:		2.50
Inserted 1:56		
Dual-Refractors:		2X
Inserted 1:168		
1	Mike Piazza, Ivan Rodriguez	6.00
2	Tony Gwynn, Wade Boggs	5.00
3	Kerry Wood, Roger Clemens	3.00
4	Juan Gonzalez, Sammy Sosa	5.00
5	Derek Jeter, Nomar Garciaparra	6.00
6	Mark McGwire, Frank Thomas	7.50
7	Vladimir Guerrero, Andruw Jones	3.00

1999 Finest Double Feature

Similar to Finest Complements, this Series 2 set utilizes split-screen fronts to accomodate two players on a horizontal format. Each card has three versions: Non- Refractor/Refractor (1:56), Refractor/Non-Refractor (1:56) and Refractor/Refractor (1:168). Card numbers have a "DF" prefix. Values shown are for cards with either left- or right-side Refractor; Dual-Refractor cards are valued at 2X.

		MT
Complete Set (7):		30.00
Common Player:		2.00
Dual-Refractors:		2X
1	Ken Griffey Jr., Alex Rodriguez	12.50
2	Chipper Jones, Andruw Jones	5.00
3	Darin Erstad, Mo Vaughn	2.50
4	Craig Biggio, Jeff Bagwell	3.00
5	Ben Grieve, Eric Chavez	2.00
6	Albert Belle, Cal Ripken Jr.	7.50
7	Scott Rolen, Pat Burrell	6.00

1999 Finest Franchise Records

This Series 2 insert set focuses on players who led their teams in various statistical categories. They are randomly seeded in 1:129 packs, while a parallel Refractor version is inserted 1:378. Card numbers have a "FR" prefix.

		MT
Complete Set (10):		165.00
Common Player:		7.50
Refractors:		1.5X
1	Frank Thomas	15.00
2	Ken Griffey Jr.	30.00
3	Mark McGwire	35.00
4	Juan Gonzalez	8.00
5	Nomar Garciaparra	20.00
6	Mike Piazza	20.00
7	Cal Ripken Jr.	25.00
8	Sammy Sosa	20.00
9	Barry Bonds	8.00
10	Tony Gwynn	10.00

1999 Finest Future's Finest

This Series 2 insert focuses on up-and-coming players who are primed to emerge as superstars. These are seeded 1:171 packs and limited to 500 numbered sets. Card numbers have a "FF" prefix.

		MT
Complete Set (10):		75.00
Common Player:		4.00
1	Pat Burrell	25.00
2	Troy Glaus	20.00
3	Eric Chavez	10.00
4	Ryan Anderson	10.00
5	Ruben Mateo	10.00
6	Gabe Kapler	10.00
7	Alex Gonzalez	4.00
8	Michael Barrett	4.00
9	Lance Berkman	4.00
10	Fernando Seguignol	4.00

1999 Finest Hank Aaron Award Contenders

This insert set focuses on nine players who had the best chance to win baseball's newest award. Production varies from card to card, with nine times as many of card #9 as of card #1, and so on. Insertion odds thus vary greatly, from 1:12 to 1:216. Refractor versions are found at odds which vary from 1:96 to 1:1728. Card numbers have an "HA" prefix.

		MT
Complete Set (9):		40.00
Common Player:		3.00
Refractors:		3X
1	Juan Gonzalez	6.00
2	Vladimir Guerrero	6.00
3	Nomar Garciaparra	12.00
4	Albert Belle	4.00
5	Frank Thomas	3.00
6	Sammy Sosa	4.00
7	Alex Rodriguez	5.00
8	Ken Griffey Jr.	6.00
9	Mark McGwire	6.00

1999 Finest Leading Indicators

Utilizing a heat-sensitive, thermal ink technology, these cards highlight the 1998 home run totals of 10 players. Touching the left, right or center field portion of the card behind each player's image reveals his 1998 season home run total in that specific direction. These are seeded 1:24 in Series 1 packs.

		MT
Complete Set (10):		45.00
Common Player:		1.00
Inserted 1:24		
L1	Mark McGwire	12.00
L2	Sammy Sosa	8.00
L3	Ken Griffey Jr.	10.00
L4	Greg Vaughn	1.00
L5	Albert Belle	2.50
L6	Juan Gonzalez	3.00
L7	Andres Galarraga	1.00
L8	Alex Rodriguez	10.00
L9	Barry Bonds	3.00
L10	Jeff Bagwell	3.00

1999 Finest Milestones

This Series 2 insert set is fractured into four subsets, each focusing on a statistical category: Hits, Home Runs, RBIs and Doubles. The Hits category is limited to 3,000 numbered sets. Home Runs are limited to 500 numbered sets. RBIs are limited to 1,400 numbered sets and Doubles is limited to 500 numbered sets. Each card number carries an "M" prefix.

		MT
Complete Set (40):		300.00
Common Hits (1-10):		2.00
Common Homeruns (11-20):		5.00
Common RBI (21-30):		2.00
Common Doubles (31-40):		4.00
1	Tony Gwynn (Hits)	5.00
2	Cal Ripken Jr. (Hits)	7.50
3	Wade Boggs (Hits)	2.00
4	Ken Griffey Jr. (Hits)	10.00
5	Frank Thomas (Hits)	4.00
6	Barry Bonds (Hits)	2.50
7	Travis Lee (Hits)	2.00
8	Alex Rodriguez (Hits)	8.00
9	Derek Jeter (Hits)	6.00
10	Vladimir Guerrero (Hits)	4.00
11	Mark McGwire (Home Runs)	35.00
12	Ken Griffey Jr. (Home Runs)	30.00
13	Vladimir Guerrero (Home Runs)	12.00
14	Alex Rodriguez (Home Runs)	25.00
15	Barry Bonds (Home Runs)	7.50
16	Sammy Sosa (Home Runs)	20.00
17	Albert Belle (Home Runs)	5.00
18	Frank Thomas (Home Runs)	10.00
19	Jose Canseco (Home Runs)	5.00
20	Mike Piazza (Home Runs)	20.00
21	Jeff Bagwell (RBI)	5.00
22	Barry Bonds (RBI)	4.00
23	Ken Griffey Jr. (RBI)	15.00
24	Albert Belle (RBI)	4.00
25	Juan Gonzalez (RBI)	7.50
26	Vinny Castilla (RBI)	2.00
27	Mark McGwire (RBI)	15.00
28	Alex Rodriguez (RBI)	12.00
29	Nomar Garciaparra (RBI)	10.00
30	Frank Thomas (RBI)	6.00
31	Barry Bonds (Doubles)	7.50
32	Albert Belle (Doubles)	7.50
33	Ben Grieve (Doubles)	5.00
34	Craig Biggio (Doubles)	5.00
35	Vladimir Guerrero (Doubles)	12.00
36	Nomar Garciaparra (Doubles)	20.00
37	Alex Rodriguez (Doubles)	25.00
38	Derek Jeter (Doubles)	20.00
39	Ken Griffey Jr. (Doubles)	30.00
40	Brad Fullmer (Doubles)	4.00

1999 Finest Peel & Reveal

This Series 1 insert offers 20 players produced in varying levels of scarcity designated by background design: Sparkle is common, Hyperplaid is uncommon and Stadium Stars is rare. Each card has a peel-off opaque protective coating on both front and back. Stated insertion odds are: Sparkle 1:30; Hyperplaid 1:60, and Stadium Stars 1:120. Home Team Advantage (HTA) boxes have odds which are twice as good.

		MT
Complete Set (20):		80.00
Common Player:		2.00
Hyperplaid:		1.5X
Stadium Stars:		2.5X
1	Kerry Wood	2.50
2	Mark McGwire	15.00
3	Sammy Sosa	8.00
4	Ken Griffey Jr.	12.00
5	Nomar Garciaparra	7.50
6	Greg Maddux	6.00
7	Derek Jeter	7.50
8	Andres Galarraga	2.00
9	Alex Rodriguez	10.00
10	Frank Thomas	4.50
11	Roger Clemens	3.50
12	Juan Gonzalez	3.00
13	Ben Grieve	2.50
14	Jeff Bagwell	2.50
15	Todd Helton	3.00
16	Chipper Jones	4.50
17	Barry Bonds	2.50
18	Travis Lee	2.50
19	Vladimir Guerrero	5.00
20	Pat Burrell	7.50

1999 Finest Prominent Figures

Fifty cards on Refractor technology highlight superstars chasing the all-time records in five different statistical categories: Home Runs, Slugging Percentage, Batting Average, RBIs and Total Bases. Ten players are featured in each category, each sequentially numbered to the all-time single season record statistic for that category. Home Run category is numbered to 70, Slugging Percentage to 847, Batting Average to 424, RBIs to 190 and Total Bases to 457.

	MT
Complete Set (50):	1000.
Common Home Runs (1-10); #d to 70:	12.00
Common Slugging % (11-20); #d to 847:	4.00
Common Batting Ave. (21-30); #d to 424:	6.00
Common RBIs (31-40); #d to 190:	7.50
Common Total Bases (41-50); #d to 457:	7.50
1 Mark McGwire (HR)	150.00
2 Sammy Sosa (HR)	75.00
3 Ken Griffey Jr. (HR)	125.00
4 Mike Piazza (HR)	75.00
5 Juan Gonzalez (HR)	30.00
6 Greg Vaughn (HR)	12.00
7 Alex Rodriguez (HR)	80.00
8 Manny Ramirez (HR)	30.00
9 Jeff Bagwell (HR)	30.00
10 Andres Galarraga (HR)	15.00
11 Mark McGwire (S%)	30.00
12 Sammy Sosa (S%)	20.00
13 Juan Gonzalez (S%)	8.00
14 Ken Griffey Jr. (S%)	25.00
15 Barry Bonds (S%)	8.00
16 Greg Vaughn (S%)	4.00
17 Larry Walker (S%)	5.00
18 Andres Galarraga (S%)	5.00
19 Jeff Bagwell (S%)	8.00
20 Albert Belle (S%)	6.00
21 Tony Gwynn (BA)	20.00
22 Mike Piazza (BA)	25.00
23 Larry Walker (BA)	7.50
24 Alex Rodriguez (BA)	30.00
25 John Olerud (BA)	6.00
26 Frank Thomas (BA)	15.00
27 Bernie Williams (BA)	6.00
28 Chipper Jones (BA)	15.00
29 Jim Thome (BA)	6.00
30 Barry Bonds (BA)	10.00
31 Juan Gonzalez (RBI)	20.00
32 Sammy Sosa (RBI)	45.00
33 Mark McGwire (RBI)	80.00
34 Albert Belle (RBI)	10.00
35 Ken Griffey Jr. (RBI)	75.00
36 Jeff Bagwell (RBI)	18.00
37 Chipper Jones (RBI)	35.00
38 Vinny Castilla (RBI)	7.50
39 Alex Rodriguez (RBI)	50.00
40 Andres Galarraga (RBI)	10.00
41 Sammy Sosa (TB)	25.00
42 Mark McGwire (TB)	45.00
43 Albert Belle (TB)	6.00
44 Ken Griffey Jr. (TB)	40.00
45 Jeff Bagwell (TB)	10.00
46 Juan Gonzalez (TB)	10.00
47 Barry Bonds (TB)	10.00
48 Vladimir Guerrero (TB)	15.00
49 Larry Walker (TB)	7.50
50 Alex Rodriguez (TB)	30.00

1999 Finest Split Screen

Players who share a common bond are highlighted in this Series 1 insert set which includes 14 paired players. Each card is available in three variations: Non-Refractor/Refractor (1:28), Refractor/Non-Refractor (1:28) and Refractor/Refractor (1:84). Values shown are for a card with either left- or right-side Refractor; dual-Refractor cards are worth 2X.

	MT
Complete Set (14):	80.00
Common Card:	3.00
Dual-Refractor:	2X
1 Mark McGwire, Sammy Sosa	15.00
2 Ken Griffey Jr., Alex Rodriguez	12.50
3 Nomar Garciaparra, Derek Jeter	7.50
4 Barry Bonds, Albert Belle	4.00
5 Cal Ripken Jr., Tony Gwynn	10.00
6 Manny Ramirez, Juan Gonzalez	4.00
7 Frank Thomas, Andres Galarraga	6.00
8 Scott Rolen, Chipper Jones	5.00
9 Ivan Rodriguez, Mike Piazza	7.50
10 Kerry Wood, Roger Clemens	6.00
11 Greg Maddux, Tom Glavine	6.00
12 Troy Glaus, Eric Chavez	4.00
13 Ben Grieve, Todd Helton	3.00
14 Travis Lee, Pat Burrell	10.00

1999 Finest Team Finest

The first 10 cards are showcased in Series 1 while the last 10 cards showcased in Series 2. Team Finest are available in three colors: Blue, Red and Gold (Red and Gold are only available in Home Team Advantage packs). All Team Finest are serially numbered as follows: Blue, numbered to 1,500; Blue Refractors to 150; Red to 500; Red Refractors to 50; Gold to 250 and Gold Refractors to 25. Cards have a TF prefix to the card number.

	MT
Complete Set (20):	125.00
Common Blue:	3.00
Production 1,500 sets	
Blue Refractors:	3X
Production 150 sets	
Reds:	1.5X
Production 500 sets	
Red Refractors:	7X
Production 50 sets	
Golds:	2X
Production 250 sets	
Gold Refractors:	10X
Production 25 sets	
1 Greg Maddux	10.00
2 Mark McGwire	20.00
3 Sammy Sosa	10.00
4 Juan Gonzalez	5.00
5 Alex Rodriguez	12.00
6 Travis Lee	2.50
7 Roger Clemens	8.00
8 Darin Erstad	3.00
9 Todd Helton	4.00
10 Mike Piazza	12.00
11 Kerry Wood	4.00
12 Ken Griffey Jr.	15.00
13 Frank Thomas	6.00
14 Jeff Bagwell	5.00
15 Nomar Garciaparra	10.00
16 Derek Jeter	12.00
17 Chipper Jones	8.00
18 Barry Bonds	5.00
19 Tony Gwynn	6.00
20 Ben Grieve	3.00

2000 Finest

The 286-card base set has the traditional chromium finish with the Topps Finest logo in the upper left portion on the front. Also in the upper left portion is a partial image of a baseball with seams in the background of the player photo. Card backs have a small photo with 99 stats and career totals. The Rookies from Series 1 were serial numbered to 2,000 and in Series II to 3,000. Counterpart subset cards are seeded 1:8 packs and Gems are found 1:24 packs.

	MT
Complete Set (286):	1000.
Complete Series 1 (147)	600.00
Complete Series 2 (140): 400.00	
Common Player:	.25
Common Rookie (101-120):	10.00
Production 2,000	
Common Rookie (247-266)	8.00
Production 3,000	
Common Counterpart (267-276)	1.00
Inserted 1:8	
Common Gem (136-145):	
Inserted 1:24	
Pack (6):	5.00
Series 1 & 2 Box:	100.00
1 Nomar Garciaparra	2.50
2 Chipper Jones	2.00
3 Erubiel Durazo	.50
4 Robin Ventura	.50
5 Garret Anderson	.25
6 Dean Palmer	.40
7 Mariano Rivera	.50
8 Rusty Greer	.25
9 Jim Thome	.75
10 Jeff Bagwell	1.00
11 Jason Giambi	.25
12 Jeromy Burnitz	.40
13 Mark Grace	.50
14 Russ Ortiz	.25
15 Kevin Brown	.50
16 Kevin Millwood	.40
17 Scott Williamson	.25
18 Orlando Hernandez	.50
19 Todd Walker	.25
20 Carlos Beltran	.40
21 Ruben Rivera	.25
22 Curt Schilling	.40
23 Brian Giles	.25
24 Eric Karros	.40
25 Preston Wilson	.25
26 Al Leiter	.40
27 Juan Encarnacion	.25
28 Tim Salmon	.40
29 B.J. Surhoff	.25
30 Bernie Williams	.75
31 Lee Stevens	.25
32 Pokey Reese	.25
33 Mike Sweeney	.25
34 Corey Koskie	.25
35 Roberto Alomar	.75
36 Tim Hudson	.25
37 Tom Glavine	.50
38 Jeff Kent	.25

39 Mike Lieberthal .25
40 Barry Larkin .60
41 Paul O'Neill .40
42 Rico Brogna .25
43 Brian Daubach .25
44 Rich Aurilia .25
45 Vladimir Guerrero 1.50
46 Luis Castillo .25
47 Bartolo Colon .25
48 Kevin Appier .25
49 Mo Vaughn .75
50 Alex Rodriguez 3.00
51 Randy Johnson .75
52 Kris Benson .25
53 Tony Clark .50
54 Chad Allen .25
55 Larry Walker .75
56 Freddy Garcia .25
57 Paul Konerko .40
58 Edgardo Alfonzo .40
59 Brady Anderson .40
60 Derek Jeter 2.50
61 Mike Hampton .25
62 Jeff Cirillo .40
63 Shannon Stewart .25
64 Greg Maddux 2.00
65 Mark McGwire 4.00
66 Gary Sheffield .50
67 Kevin Young .25
68 Tony Gwynn 2.00
69 Rey Ordonez .25
70 Cal Ripken Jr. 3.00
71 Todd Helton 1.00
72 Brian Jordan .25
73 Jose Canseco .50
74 Luis Gonzalez .25
75 Barry Bonds 1.00
76 Jermaine Dye .25
77 Jose Offerman .25
78 Magglio Ordonez .25
79 Fred McGriff .50
80 Ivan Rodriguez 1.00
81 Josh Hamilton (Prospects) 2.00
82 Vernon Wells (Prospects) .25
83 Mark Mulder (Prospects) .25
84 John Patterson (Prospects) .25
85 Nick Johnson (Prospects) 1.00
86 Pablo Ozuna (Prospects) .25
87 A.J. Burnett (Prospects) .25
88 Jack Cust (Prospects) .25
89 Adam Piatt (Prospects) 1.00
90 Rob Ryan (Prospects) .25
91 Sean Burroughs (Prospects) 1.50
92 D'Angelo Jimenez (Prospects) .25
93 Chad Hermansen (Prospects) .25
94 Rob Fick (Prospects) .25
95 Ruben Mateo (Prospects) .25
96 Alex Escobar (Prospects) .25
97 Willi Mo Pena (Prospects) 1.00
98 Corey Patterson (Prospects) 1.00
99 Eric Munson (Prospects) .40
100 Pat Burrell (Prospects) 1.50
101 *Michael Tejera* 12.00
102 *Bobby Bradley* 35.00
103 *Larry Bigbie* 20.00
104 *B.J. Garbe* 40.00
105 *Josh Kalinowski* 10.00
106 *Brett Myers* 20.00
107 *Chris Mears* 15.00
108 *Aaron Rowand* 20.00
109 *Corey Myers* 15.00
110 *John Sneed* 10.00
111 *Ryan Christensen* 25.00
112 *Kyle Snyder* 10.00
113 *Mike Paradis* 10.00
114 *Chance Caple* 15.00
115 *Ben Christiansen* 20.00
116 *Brad Baker* 20.00
117 *Rob Purvis* 10.00
118 *Rick Asadoorian* 60.00
119 *Ruben Salazar* 15.00
120 *Julio Zuleta* 10.00
121 Ken Griffey Jr., Alex Rodriguez (Features) 8.00
122 Nomar Garciaparra, Derek Jeter (Features) 5.00
123 Mark McGwire, Sammy Sosa (Features) 8.00
124 Randy Johnson, Pedro Martinez (Features) 2.00
125 Mike Piazza, Ivan Rodriguez (Features) 5.00
126 Manny Ramirez, Roberto Alomar (Features) 2.00
127 Chipper Jones, Andruw Jones (Features) 4.00
128 Cal Ripken Jr., Tony Gwynn (Features) 6.00
129 Jeff Bagwell, Craig Biggio (Features) 2.00
130 Vladimir Guerrero, Barry Bonds (Features) 3.00
131 Alfonso Soriano, Nick Johnson (Features) 3.00
132 Josh Hamilton, Pat Burrell (Features) 3.00
133 Corey Patterson, Ruben Mateo (Features) 3.00
134 Larry Walker, Todd Helton (Features) 1.50
135 Edgardo Alfonzo, Rey Ordonez (Features) 1.00
136 Derek Jete (Gems) 12.00
137 Alex Rodrigue z (Gems) 15.00
138 Chipper Jones (Gems) 10.00
139 Mike Piazza (Gems) 12.00
140 Mark McGwire (Gems) 20.00
141 Ivan Rodriguez (Gems) 5.00
142 Cal Ripken Jr . (Gems) 15.00
143 Vladimir Guerrero (Gems) 8.00
144 Randy Johnson (Gems) 4.00
145 Jeff Bagwell (Gems) 5.00
146 Ken Griffey Jr. field 5.00
146a Ken Griffey Jr. press 5.00
147 Andruw Jones .50
148 Kerry Wood .40
149 Jim Edmonds .40
150 Pedro Martinez 1.00
151 Warren Morris .25
152 Trevor Hoffman .25
153 Eric Young .25
154 Andy Pettitte .25
155 Frank Thomas 1.50
156 Damion Easley .25
157 Cliff Floyd .25
158 Ben Davis .25
159 John Valentin .25
160 Rafael Palmeiro .75
161 Andy Ashby .25
162 J.D. Drew .40
163 Jay Bell .25
164 Adam Kennedy .25
165 Manny Ramirez 1.00
166 John Halama .25
167 Octavio Dotel .25
168 Darin Erstad .50
169 Jose Lima .25
170 Andres Galarraga .75
171 Scott Rolen .75
172 Delino DeShields .25
173 J.T. Snow Jr. .25
174 Tony Womack .25
175 John Olerud .40
176 Jason Kendall .40
177 Carlos Lee .25
178 Eric Milton .25
179 Jeff Cirillo .25
180 Gabe Kapler .50
181 Greg Vaughn .40
182 Denny Neagle .25
183 Tino Martinez .40
184 Doug Mientkiewicz .25
185 Juan Gonzalez 1.00
186 Ellis Burks .25
187 Mike Hampton .25
188 Royce Clayton .25
189 Mike Mussina .50
190 Carlos Delgado .75
191 Ben Grieve .50
192 Fernando Tatis .25
193 Matt Williams .50
194 Rondell White .40
195 Shawn Green .75
196 Justin Thompson .25
197 Troy Glaus 1.00
198 Roger Cedeno .25
199 Ray Lankford .25
200 Sammy Sosa 2.50
201 Kenny Lofton .50
202 Edgar Martinez .40
203 Mark Kotsay .25
204 David Wells .25
205 Craig Biggio .50
206 Ray Durham .25
207 Troy O'Leary .25
208 Rickey Henderson .50
209 Bob Abreu .25
210 Neifi Perez .25
211 Carlos Febles .25
212 Chuck Knoblauch .25
213 Moises Alou .25
214 Omar Vizquel .25
215 Vinny Castilla .25
216 Javy Lopez .25
217 Johnny Damon .40
218 Roger Clemens 1.25
219 Miguel Tejada .25
220 Deion Sanders .40
221 Matt Lawton .25
222 Albert Belle .75
223 Adrian Beltre .40
224 Dante Bichette .40
225 Raul Mondesi .40
226 Mike Piazza 2.50
227 Brad Penny (Prospects) .25
228 Kip Wells (Prospects) .25
229 Adam Everett (Prospects) .25
230 Eddie Yarnall (Prospects) .25
231 Matt LeCroy (Prospects) .25
232 Ryan Anderson (Prospects) .50
233 Rick Ankiel (Prospects) 2.50
234 Daryle Ward (Prospects) .25
235 Rafael Furcal (Prospects) 1.50
236 Dee Brown (Prospects) .25
237 Travis Dawkins (Prospects) .25
238 Eric Valent (Prospects) .25
239 Peter Bergeron (Prospects) .25
240 Alfonso Soriano (Prospects) .75
241 John Patterson (Prospects) .25
242 Jorge Toca (Prospects) .25
243 Ryan Anderson (Prospects) .50
244 Jason Dallaero (Prospects) .25
245 Jason Grilli (Prospects) .25
246 Chad Hermansen (Prospects) .25
247 *Scott Downs* 8.00
248 *Keith Reed* 12.00
249 *Edgar Cruz* 8.00
250 *Wes Anderson* 8.00
251 *Lyle Overbay* 15.00
252 *Mike Lamb* 15.00
253 *Vince Faison* 15.00
254 *Chad Alexander* 8.00
255 *Chris Wakeland* 8.00
256 *Aaron McNeal* 15.00
257 *Tomokazu Ohka* 10.00
258 *Ty Howington* 15.00
259 *Javier Colina* 8.00
260 *Jason Jennings* 8.00
261 *Ramon Santiago* 10.00
262 *Johan Santana* 8.00
263 *Quincey Foster* 8.00
264 *Junior Brignac* 8.00
265 *Rico Washington* 8.00
266 *Scott Sobkowiak* 8.00
267 Pedro Martinez, Rick Ankiel (Counterparts) 5.00
268 Manny Ramirez, Vladimir Guerrero (Counterparts) 3.00
269 A.J. Burnett, Mark Mulder (Counterparts) 1.00
270 Mike Piazza, Eric Munson (Counterparts) 6.00
271 Josh Hamilton, Corey Patterson (Counterparts) 2.50
272 Ken Griffey Jr., Sammy Sosa (Counterparts) 8.00
273 Derek Jeter, Alfonso Soriano (Counterparts) 6.00
274 Mark McGwire, Pat Burrell (Counterparts) 10.00
275 Chipper Jones, Cal Ripken Jr. (Counterparts) 8.00
276 Nomar Garciaparra, Alex Rodriguez (Counterparts) 8.00
277 Pedro Martinez (Gems) 5.00
278 Tony Gwynn (Gems) 8.00
279 Barry Bonds (Gems) 5.00
280 Juan Gonzalez (Gems) 5.00
281 Larry Walker (Gems) 4.00
282 Nomar Garciaparra (Gems) 12.00
283 Ken Griffey Jr. (Gems) 15.00
284 Manny Ramirez (Gems) 5.00
285 Shawn Green (Gems) 4.00
286 Sammy Sosa (Gems) 12.00

2000 Finest Refractor

These are a parallel to the base set and have

a mirror like sheen. Card backs have "refractor" written underneath the card number.

	MT
Stars (1-100):	6-10X
Inserted 1:24	
Rookies (101-120,247-266):	1X
Production 500 sets	
Features (121-135):	2-3X
Inserted 1:96	
Counterparts (267-276):	2-3X
Inserted 1:96	
Gems (136-145,277-286):	2-3X
Inserted 1:288	

2000 Finest Gold Refractor

A parallel to the base set, these have the usual mirror like appearance with a deckle edged border. Regular cards are seeded 1:240 packs, Rookies are limited to 100 serial numbered sets, Features and Counterparts subsets (1:960) and Gems (1:2,880).

	MT
Stars (1-100):	20-40X
Inserted 1:240	
Rookies (101-120, 247-266):	1-2X
Production 100 sets	
Features:	4-8X
Inserted 1:960	
Counterparts:	4-8X
Inserted 1:960	
Gems:	4-8X
Inserted 1:2,880	

2000 Finest Gems Oversized

Each of the 10 Gems subset cards in series 1 and 2 were also done on an oversized format. The oversized cards were added as a box topper to each box. Home Team Advantage stores received Refractor versions of the Gems Oversized cards as a box topper.

		MT
Complete Set (20):		90.00
Complete Series 1 (10):		50.00
Complete Series 2 (10):		40.00
Common Player:		2.00
Inserted 1:box		
1	Derek Jeter	8.00
2	Alex Rodriguez	10.00
3	Chipper Jones	6.00
4	Mike Piazza	8.00
5	Mark McGwire	12.00
6	Ivan Rodriguez	3.00
7	Cal Ripken Jr.	10.00
8	Vladimir Guerrero	5.00
9	Randy Johnson	3.00
10	Jeff Bagwell	3.00
11	Nomar Garciaparra	8.00
12	Ken Griffey Jr.	12.00
13	Manny Ramirez	3.00
14	Shawn Green	2.00
15	Sammy Sosa	8.00
16	Pedro Martinez	3.00
17	Tony Gwynn	5.00
18	Barry Bonds	3.00
19	Juan Gonzalez	3.00
20	Larry Walker	2.00

2000 Finest Ballpark Bounties

Seeded across both series 1 and 2 these 1:24 pack inserts Serigraph Fresnal technology and have a metallic looking image of a baseball in the background of the player photo. Card backs are numbered with a "BB" prefix.

		MT
Complete Set (30):		170.00
Complete Series 1 (15):		80.00
Complete Series 2 (15):		90.00
Common Player:		3.00
Inserted 1:24		
1	Chipper Jones	10.00
2	Mike Piazza	12.00
3	Vladimir Guerrero	8.00
4	Sammy Sosa	12.00
5	Nomar Garciaparra	12.00
6	Manny Ramirez	5.00
7	Jeff Bagwell	5.00
8	Scott Rolen	5.00
9	Carlos Beltran	3.00
10	Pedro Martinez	5.00
11	Greg Maddux	10.00
12	Josh Hamilton	6.00
13	Adam Piatt	3.00
14	Pat Burrell	5.00
15	Alfonso Soriano	4.00
16	Alex Rodriguez	15.00
17	Derek Jeter	12.00
18	Cal Ripken Jr.	15.00
19	Larry Walker	3.00
20	Barry Bonds	5.00
21	Ken Griffey Jr.	20.00
22	Mark McGwire	20.00
23	Ivan Rodriguez	5.00
24	Andruw Jones	4.00
25	Todd Helton	5.00
26	Randy Johnson	5.00
27	Ruben Mateo	3.00
28	Corey Patterson	5.00
29	Sean Burroughs	4.00
30	Eric Munson	3.00

2000 Finest Dream Cast

These inserts are found exclusively in Series 2 packs and utilize Duflex technology. The card fronts try to portray a "dream sequence" with sky and clouds in the background. Found 1:36 packs they are numbered with a "DC" prefix on the card back.

		MT
Complete Set (10):		80.00
Common Player:		4.00
Inserted 1:36		
1	Mark McGwire	20.00
2	Roberto Alomar	4.00
3	Chipper Jones	10.00
4	Derek Jeter	12.00
5	Barry Bonds	5.00
6	Ken Griffey Jr.	20.00
7	Sammy Sosa	12.00
8	Mike Piazza	12.00
9	Pedro Martinez	5.00
10	Randy Johnson	5.00

2000 Finest Finest Moments

This four-card set pays tribute to four milestone achievements accomplished during the 1999 season. Seeded 1:9 packs, these are numbered with a "FM" prefix. A Refractor parallel version is seeded 1:20 packs.

		MT
Complete Set (4):		
Common Player:		1.00
Inserted 1:9		
Refractor:		1-2X
Inserted 1:20		
1	Chipper Jones	3.00
2	Ivan Rodriguez	1.50
3	Tony Gwynn	2.50
4	Wade Boggs	1.00

2000 Finest Moments Autographs

An autographed version of the four-card set, these were seeded 1:425 packs.

		MT
Complete Set (4):		325.00
Common Player:		80.00
Inserted 1:425		
1	Chipper Jones	100.00
2	Ivan Rodriguez	80.00
3	Tony Gwynn	100.00
4	Wade Boggs	80.00

2000 Finest For The Record

Printed on Finest Clear Card technology, each of the 10 players featured has three cards. Each card is sequentially numbered to the distance of the outfield wall in their home ballpark (left, center and right). Combining all three cards forms a panoramic view of the stadium.

		MT
Complete Set (30):		700.00
Common Player:		10.00
1A	Derek Jeter (318)	35.00
1B	Derek Jeter (408)	30.00
1C	Derek Jeter (314)	35.00
2A	Mark McGwire (330)	55.00
2B	Mark McGwire (402)	50.00
2C	Mark McGwire (330)	55.00
3A	Ken Griffey Jr. (331)	55.00
3B	Ken Griffey Jr. (405)	50.00
3C	Ken Griffey Jr. (327)	55.00
4A	Alex Rodriguez (331)	40.00
4B	Alex Rodriguez (405)	35.00
4C	Alex Rodriguez (327)	40.00
5A	Nomar Garciaparra (310)	35.00
5B	Nomar Garciaparra (390)	30.00
5C	Nomar Garciaparra (302)	35.00
6A	Cal Ripken Jr. (333)	40.00
6B	Cal Ripken Jr. (410)	35.00
6C	Cal Ripken Jr. (318)	40.00
7A	Sammy Sosa (355)	30.00
7B	Sammy Sosa (400)	30.00
7C	Sammy Sosa (353)	30.00

8A	Manny Ramirez (325)	15.00
8B	Manny Ramirez (410)	12.00
8C	Manny Ramirez (325)	15.00
9A	Mike Piazza (338)	35.00
9B	Mike Piazza (410)	30.00
9C	Mike Piazza (338)	35.00
10A	Chipper Jones (335)	30.00
10B	Chipper Jones (401)	25.00
10C	Chipper Jones (330)	30.00

2000 Finest Going the Distance

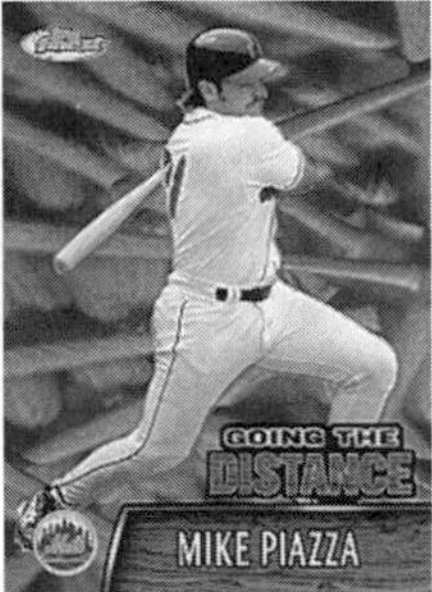

This 12-card set highlights the top hitters in baseball, utilizing Photo-polymer hologram technology. Seeded 1:24 packs, card backs are numbered with a "GTD" prefix.

		MT
Complete Set (12):		90.00
Common Player:		3.00
Inserted 1:24		
1	Tony Gwynn	8.00
2	Alex Rodriguez	12.00
3	Derek Jeter	10.00
4	Chipper Jones	8.00
5	Nomar Garciaparra	10.00
6	Sammy Sosa	10.00
7	Ken Griffey Jr.	15.00
8	Vladimir Guerrero	6.00
9	Mark McGwire	15.00
10	Mike Piazza	10.00
11	Manny Ramirez	4.00
12	Cal Ripken Jr.	12.00

1993 Flair

Designed as Fleer's super-premium card brand, this 300-card set contains extra-thick cards which feature gold-foil highlights and UV coating front and back. Portrait and action photos are combined in a high-tech front picture and there is a muted photo on the back, as well.

		MT
Complete Set (300):		40.00
Common Player:		.25
Pack (10):		2.50
Wax Box (24):		50.00
1	Steve Avery	.25
2	Jeff Blauser	.25
3	Ron Gant	.30
4	Tom Glavine	.40
5	Dave Justice	.50
6	Mark Lemke	.25
7	Greg Maddux	2.50
8	Fred McGriff	.40
9	Terry Pendleton	.25
10	Deion Sanders	.40
11	John Smoltz	.30
12	Mike Stanton	.25
13	Steve Buechele	.25
14	Mark Grace	.40
15	Greg Hibbard	.25
16	Derrick May	.25
17	Chuck McElroy	.25
18	Mike Morgan	.25
19	Randy Myers	.25
20	Ryne Sandberg	1.50
21	Dwight Smith	.25
22	Sammy Sosa	3.00
23	Jose Vizcaino	.25
24	Tim Belcher	.25
25	Rob Dibble	.25
26	Roberto Kelly	.25
27	Barry Larkin	.50
28	Kevin Mitchell	.25
29	Hal Morris	.25
30	Joe Oliver	.25
31	Jose Rijo	.25
32	Bip Roberts	.25
33	Chris Sabo	.25
34	Reggie Sanders	.30
35	Dante Bichette	.50
36	Willie Blair	.25
37	Jerald Clark	.25
38	Alex Cole	.25
39	Andres Galarraga	.75
40	Joe Girardi	.25
41	Charlie Hayes	.25
42	Chris Jones	.25
43	David Nied	.25
44	Eric Young	.25
45	Alex Arias	.25
46	Jack Armstrong	.25
47	Bret Barberie	.25
48	Chuck Carr	.25
49	Jeff Conine	.30
50	Orestes Destrade	.25
51	Chris Hammond	.25
52	Bryan Harvey	.25
53	Benito Santiago	.25
54	Gary Sheffield	.50
55	Walt Weiss	.25
56	Eric Anthony	.25
57	Jeff Bagwell	1.25
58	Craig Biggio	.40
59	Ken Caminiti	.30
60	Andujar Cedeno	.25
61	Doug Drabek	.25
62	Steve Finley	.25
63	Luis Gonzalez	.30
64	Pete Harnisch	.25
65	Doug Jones	.25
66	Darryl Kile	.25
67	Greg Swindell	.25
68	Brett Butler	.25
69	Jim Gott	.25
70	Orel Hershiser	.30
71	Eric Karros	.40
72	Pedro Martinez	1.50
73	Ramon Martinez	.25
74	Roger McDowell	.25
75	Mike Piazza	3.00
76	Jody Reed	.25
77	Tim Wallach	.25
78	Moises Alou	.30
79	Greg Colbrunn	.25
80	Wil Cordero	.25
81	Delino DeShields	.25
82	Jeff Fassero	.25
83	Marquis Grissom	.25
84	Ken Hill	.25
85	*Mike Lansing*	.60
86	Dennis Martinez	.25
87	Larry Walker	.60
88	John Wetteland	.25
89	Bobby Bonilla	.35
90	Vince Coleman	.25
91	Dwight Gooden	.35
92	Todd Hundley	.30
93	Howard Johnson	.25
94	Eddie Murray	.40
95	Joe Orsulak	.25
96	Bret Saberhagen	.25
97	Darren Daulton	.25
98	Mariano Duncan	.25
99	Len Dykstra	.25
100	Jim Eisenreich	.25
101	Tommy Greene	.25
102	Dave Hollins	.25
103	Pete Incaviglia	.25
104	Danny Jackson	.25
105	John Kruk	.25
106	Terry Mulholland	.25
107	Curt Schilling	.35
108	Mitch Williams	.25
109	Stan Belinda	.25
110	Jay Bell	.25
111	Steve Cooke	.25
112	Carlos Garcia	.25
113	Jeff King	.25
114	Al Martin	.30
115	Orlando Merced	.25
116	Don Slaught	.25
117	Andy Van Slyke	.25
118	Tim Wakefield	.25
119	*Rene Arocha*	.40
120	Bernard Gilkey	.30
121	Gregg Jefferies	.25
122	Ray Lankford	.30
123	Donovan Osborne	.25
124	Tom Pagnozzi	.25
125	Erik Pappas	.25
126	Geronimo Pena	.25
127	Lee Smith	.30
128	Ozzie Smith	1.25
129	Bob Tewksbury	.25
130	Mark Whiten	.25
131	Derek Bell	.25
132	Andy Benes	.30
133	Tony Gwynn	2.00
134	Gene Harris	.25
135	Trevor Hoffman	.30
136	Phil Plantier	.25
137	Rod Beck	.25
138	Barry Bonds	1.25
139	John Burkett	.25
140	Will Clark	.50
141	Royce Clayton	.25
142	Mike Jackson	.25
143	Darren Lewis	.25
144	Kirt Manwaring	.25
145	Willie McGee	.30
146	Bill Swift	.25
147	Robby Thompson	.25
148	Matt Williams	.50
149	Brady Anderson	.40
150	Mike Devereaux	.25
151	Chris Hoiles	.25
152	Ben McDonald	.25
153	Mark McLemore	.25
154	Mike Mussina	1.00
155	Gregg Olson	.25
156	Harold Reynolds	.25
157	Cal Ripken, Jr.	4.00
158	Rick Sutcliffe	.25
159	Fernando Valenzuela	.30
160	Roger Clemens	2.00
161	Scott Cooper	.25
162	Andre Dawson	.35
163	Scott Fletcher	.25
164	Mike Greenwell	.25
165	Greg Harris	.25
166	Billy Hatcher	.25
167	Jeff Russell	.25
168	Mo Vaughn	1.00
169	Frank Viola	.25
170	Chad Curtis	.30
171	Chili Davis	.25
172	Gary DiSarcina	.25
173	Damion Easley	.25
174	Chuck Finley	.25
175	Mark Langston	.25
176	Luis Polonia	.25
177	Tim Salmon	.50
178	Scott Sanderson	.25
179	*J.T. Snow*	1.50
180	Wilson Alvarez	.25
181	Ellis Burks	.25
182	Joey Cora	.25
183	Alex Fernandez	.30
184	Ozzie Guillen	.25
185	Roberto Hernandez	.25
186	Bo Jackson	.40
187	Lance Johnson	.25
188	Jack McDowell	.25
189	Frank Thomas	2.00
190	Robin Ventura	.40
191	Carlos Baerga	.30
192	Albert Belle	.75
193	Wayne Kirby	.25
194	Derek Lilliquist	.25
195	Kenny Lofton	.50
196	Carlos Martinez	.25
197	Jose Mesa	.25
198	Eric Plunk	.25
199	Paul Sorrento	.25
200	John Doherty	.25
201	Cecil Fielder	.25
202	Travis Fryman	.40
203	Kirk Gibson	.25
204	Mike Henneman	.25
205	Chad Kreuter	.25
206	Scott Livingstone	.25
207	Tony Phillips	.25
208	Mickey Tettleton	.25
209	Alan Trammell	.40
210	David Wells	.30
211	Lou Whitaker	.25
212	Kevin Appier	.25
213	George Brett	2.00
214	David Cone	.40
215	Tom Gordon	.25
216	Phil Hiatt	.25
217	Felix Jose	.25
218	Wally Joyner	.30
219	Jose Lind	.25
220	Mike Macfarlane	.25
221	Brian McRae	.25
222	Jeff Montgomery	.25
223	Cal Eldred	.25
224	Darryl Hamilton	.25
225	John Jaha	.30
226	Pat Listach	.25
227	*Graeme Lloyd*	.35
228	Kevin Reimer	.25
229	Bill Spiers	.25
230	B.J. Surhoff	.30
231	Greg Vaughn	.40
232	Robin Yount	.75
233	Rick Aguilera	.25
234	Jim Deshaies	.25
235	Brian Harper	.25
236	Kent Hrbek	.30
237	Chuck Knoblauch	.40
238	Shane Mack	.25
239	David McCarty	.25
240	Pedro Munoz	.25
241	Mike Pagliarulo	.25
242	Kirby Puckett	2.00
243	Dave Winfield	.50
244	Jim Abbott	.30
245	Wade Boggs	.75
246	Pat Kelly	.25
247	Jimmy Key	.25
248	Jim Leyritz	.25
249	Don Mattingly	2.00
250	Matt Nokes	.25
251	Paul O'Neill	.40
252	Mike Stanley	.25
253	Danny Tartabull	.25
254	Bob Wickman	.25
255	Bernie Williams	1.00
256	Mike Bordick	.25
257	Dennis Eckersley	.30
258	Brent Gates	.30
259	Goose Gossage	.25
260	Rickey Henderson	.40
261	Mark McGwire	5.00
262	Ruben Sierra	.25
263	Terry Steinbach	.25
264	Bob Welch	.25
265	Bobby Witt	.25
266	Rich Amaral	.25
267	Chris Bosio	.25
268	Jay Buhner	.35
269	Norm Charlton	.25
270	Ken Griffey, Jr.	4.00
271	Erik Hanson	.25

272	Randy Johnson	1.25
273	Edgar Martinez	.40
274	Tino Martinez	.40
275	Dave Valle	.25
276	Omar Vizquel	.30
277	Kevin Brown	.40
278	Jose Canseco	.75
279	Julio Franco	.25
280	Juan Gonzalez	1.25
281	Tom Henke	.25
282	David Hulse	.25
283	Rafael Palmeiro	.75
284	Dean Palmer	.40
285	Ivan Rodriguez	1.25
286	Nolan Ryan	5.00
287	Roberto Alomar	1.00
288	Pat Borders	.25
289	Joe Carter	.30
290	Juan Guzman	.25
291	Pat Hentgen	.35
292	Paul Molitor	1.00
293	John Olerud	.40
294	Ed Sprague	.25
295	Dave Stewart	.30
296	Duane Ward	.25
297	Devon White	.30
298	Checklist	.10
299	Checklist	.10
300	Checklist	.10

1993 Flair Promos

Among the scarcest modern baseball promo cards are those produced to introduce Fleer's new premium product for 1993, Flair. Basically similar to the issued versions, the promo cards have "000" in place of the card number on back. The promos are checklisted here in alphabetical order.

		MT
Complete Set (8):		800.00
Common Player:		50.00
(1)	Will Clark	150.00
(2)	Darren Daulton	50.00
(3)	Andres Galarraga	150.00
(4)	Bryan Harvey	50.00
(5)	David Justice	150.00
(6)	Jody Reed	50.00
(7)	Nolan Ryan	300.00
(8)	Sammy Sosa	250.00

1993 Flair Wave of the Future

The game's top prospects are featured in this insert issue randomly packaged in Flair packs. Cards #19-20, Darrell Whitmore and Nigel Wilson, were printed with each other's back; no corrected version was made.

		MT
Complete Set (20):		35.00
Common Player:		.75
1	Jason Bere	.75
2	Jeremy Burnitz	3.00
3	Russ Davis	.75
4	Jim Edmonds	5.00
5	Cliff Floyd	1.50
6	Jeffrey Hammonds	1.00
7	Trevor Hoffman	2.00
8	Domingo Jean	.75
9	David McCarty	.75
10	Bobby Munoz	.75
11	Brad Pennington	.75
12	Mike Piazza	12.00
13	Manny Ramirez	8.00
14	John Roper	.75
15	Tim Salmon	5.00
16	Aaron Sele	1.50
17	Allen Watson	.75
18	Rondell White	3.00
19	Darell Whitmore	.75
20	Nigel Wilson	.75

1994 Flair

One of the success stories of 1993 returned with the release of Fleer Flair for 1994. At $4 per pack this was pricey stuff, but collectors apparently liked the look that includes an extremely thick card stock, full-bleed photos and gold-foil graphics on both sides with a protective polyester laminate described as "far beyond mere UV coating." In addition to the 250 regular-issue cards, there are three 10-card, insert sets; Wave of the Future, Outfield Power and Hot Numbers in Series 1, the last with players' images printed on 100% etched foil. Series 2 has 200 base cards and Hot Glove, Infield Power and 10 more Wave of the Future insert cards.

		MT
Complete Set (450):		85.00
Common Player:		.15
Series 1 Pack (10):		2.50
Series 1 Wax Box (24):		50.00
Series 2 Pack (10):		7.00
Series 2 Wax Box (24):		150.00
1	Harold Baines	.25
2	Jeffrey Hammonds	.20
3	Chris Hoiles	.15
4	Ben McDonald	.15
5	Mark McLemore	.15
6	Jamie Moyer	.15
7	Jim Poole	.15
8	Cal Ripken, Jr.	4.00
9	Chris Sabo	.15
10	Scott Bankhead	.15
11	Scott Cooper	.15
12	Danny Darwin	.15
13	Andre Dawson	.35
14	Billy Hatcher	.15
15	Aaron Sele	.25
15a	Aaron Sele (overprinted "PROMOTIONAL SAMPLE")	3.00
16	John Valentin	.20
17	Dave Valle	.15
18	Mo Vaughn	1.00
19	*Brian Anderson*	.75
20	Gary DiSarcina	.15
21	Jim Edmonds	.40
22	Chuck Finley	.15
23	Bo Jackson	.35
24	Mark Leiter	.15
25	Greg Myers	.15
26	Eduardo Perez	.15
27	Tim Salmon	.50
28	Wilson Alvarez	.15
29	Jason Bere	.15
30	Alex Fernandez	.20
31	Ozzie Guillen	.15
32	Joe Hall	.15
33	Darrin Jackson	.15
34	Kirk McCaskill	.15
35	Tim Raines	.25
36	Frank Thomas	2.00
37	Carlos Baerga	.15
38	Albert Belle	.75
39	Mark Clark	.15
40	Wayne Kirby	.15
41	Dennis Martinez	.25
42	Charles Nagy	.15
43	Manny Ramirez	1.25
44	Paul Sorrento	.15
45	Jim Thome	.50
46	Eric Davis	.15
47	John Doherty	.15
48	Junior Felix	.15
49	Cecil Fielder	.25
50	Kirk Gibson	.15
51	Mike Moore	.15
52	Tony Phillips	.15
53	Alan Trammell	.30
54	Kevin Appier	.15
55	Stan Belinda	.15
56	Vince Coleman	.15
57	Greg Gagne	.15
58	Bob Hamelin	.15
59	Dave Henderson	.15
60	Wally Joyner	.25
61	Mike Macfarlane	.15
62	Jeff Montgomery	.15
63	Ricky Bones	.15
64	Jeff Bronkey	.15
65	Alex Diaz	.15
66	Cal Eldred	.15
67	Darryl Hamilton	.15
68	John Jaha	.15
69	Mark Kiefer	.15
70	Kevin Seitzer	.15
71	Turner Ward	.15
72	Rich Becker	.15
73	Scott Erickson	.15
74	Keith Garagozzo	.15
75	Kent Hrbek	.25
76	Scott Leius	.15
77	Kirby Puckett	1.50
78	Matt Walkbeck	.15
79	Dave Winfield	.40
80	Mike Gallego	.15
81	Xavier Hernandez	.15
82	Jimmy Key	.15
83	Jim Leyritz	.15
84	Don Mattingly	2.00
85	Matt Nokes	.15
86	Paul O'Neill	.25
87	Melido Perez	.15
88	Danny Tartabull	.15
89	Mike Bordick	.15
90	Ron Darling	.15
91	Dennis Eckersley	.25
92	Stan Javier	.15
93	Steve Karsay	.15
94	Mark McGwire	5.00
95	Troy Neel	.15
96	Terry Steinbach	.15
97	Bill Taylor	.15
98	Eric Anthony	.15
99	Chris Bosio	.15
100	Tim Davis	.15
101	Felix Fermin	.15
102	Dave Fleming	.15
103	Ken Griffey, Jr.	4.00
104	Greg Hibbard	.15
105	Reggie Jefferson	.15
106	Tino Martinez	.30
107	Jack Armstrong	.15
108	Will Clark	.75
109	Juan Gonzalez	1.25
110	Rick Helling	.15
111	Tom Henke	.15
112	David Hulse	.15
113	Manuel Lee	.15
114	Doug Strange	.15
115	Roberto Alomar	1.00
116	Joe Carter	.20
117	Carlos Delgado	1.25
118	Pat Hentgen	.15
119	Paul Molitor	.75
120	John Olerud	.35
121	Dave Stewart	.25
122	Todd Stottlemyre	.15
123	Mike Timlin	.15
124	Jeff Blauser	.15
125	Tom Glavine	.40
126	Dave Justice	.50
127	Mike Kelly	.15
128	Ryan Klesko	.30
129	Javier Lopez	.40
130	Greg Maddux	2.00
131	Fred McGriff	.50
132	Kent Mercker	.15
133	Mark Wohlers	.15
134	Willie Banks	.15
135	Steve Buechele	.15
136	Shawon Dunston	.15
137	Jose Guzman	.15
138	Glenallen Hill	.15
139	Randy Myers	.15
140	Karl Rhodes	.15
141	Ryne Sandberg	1.25
142	Steve Trachsel	.25
143	Bret Boone	.15
144	Tom Browning	.15
145	Hector Carrasco	.15
146	Barry Larkin	.50
147	Hal Morris	.15
148	Jose Rijo	.15
149	Reggie Sanders	.25
150	John Smiley	.15
151	Dante Bichette	.40
152	Ellis Burks	.25
153	Joe Girardi	.15
154	Mike Harkey	.15
155	Roberto Mejia	.15
156	Marcus Moore	.15
157	Armando Reynoso	.15
158	Bruce Ruffin	.15
159	Eric Young	.15
160	*Kurt Abbott*	.40
161	Jeff Conine	.25
162	Orestes Destrade	.15
163	Chris Hammond	.15
164	Bryan Harvey	.15
165	Dave Magadan	.15
166	Gary Sheffield	.50
167	David Weathers	.15
168	Andujar Cedeno	.15
169	Tom Edens	.15
170	Luis Gonzalez	.15
171	Pete Harnisch	.15
172	Todd Jones	.15
173	Darryl Kile	.15
174	James Mouton	.15
175	Scott Servais	.15
176	Mitch Williams	.15

177	Pedro Astacio	.15
178	Orel Hershiser	.25
179	Raul Mondesi	.50
180	Jose Offerman	.15
181	*Chan Ho Park*	1.50
182	Mike Piazza	3.00
183	Cory Snyder	.15
184	Tim Wallach	.15
185	Todd Worrell	.15
186	Sean Berry	.15
187	Wil Cordero	.15
188	Darrin Fletcher	.15
189	Cliff Floyd	.25
190	Marquis Grissom	.25
191	Rod Henderson	.15
192	Ken Hill	.15
193	Pedro Martinez	1.50
194	Kirk Rueter	.15
195	Jeromy Burnitz	.20
196	John Franco	.15
197	Dwight Gooden	.25
198	Todd Hundley	.25
199	Bobby Jones	.15
200	Jeff Kent	.25
201	Mike Maddux	.15
202	Ryan Thompson	.15
203	Jose Vizcaino	.15
204	Darren Daulton	.15
205	Len Dykstra	.15
206	Jim Eisenreich	.15
207	Dave Hollins	.15
208	Danny Jackson	.15
209	Doug Jones	.15
210	Jeff Juden	.15
211	Ben Rivera	.15
212	Kevin Stocker	.15
213	Milt Thompson	.15
214	Jay Bell	.15
215	Steve Cooke	.15
216	Mark Dewey	.15
217	Al Martin	.15
218	Orlando Merced	.15
219	Don Slaught	.15
220	Zane Smith	.15
221	Rick White	.15
222	Kevin Young	.15
223	Rene Arocha	.15
224	Rheal Cormier	.15
225	Brian Jordan	.25
226	Ray Lankford	.25
227	Mike Perez	.15
228	Ozzie Smith	1.00
229	Mark Whiten	.15
230	Todd Zeile	.25
231	Derek Bell	.25
232	Archi Cianfrocco	.15
233	Ricky Gutierrez	.15
234	Trevor Hoffman	.20
235	Phil Plantier	.15
236	Dave Staton	.15
237	Wally Whitehurst	.15
238	Todd Benzinger	.15
239	Barry Bonds	1.50
240	John Burkett	.15
241	Royce Clayton	.15
242	Bryan Hickerson	.15
243	Mike Jackson	.15
244	Darren Lewis	.15
245	Kirt Manwaring	.15
246	Mark Portugal	.15
247	Salomon Torres	.15
248	Checklist	.15
249	Checklist	.15
250	Checklist	.15
251	Brady Anderson	.30
252	Mike Devereaux	.15
253	Sid Fernandez	.15
254	Leo Gomez	.15
255	Mike Mussina	1.00
256	Mike Oquist	.15
257	Rafael Palmeiro	.75
258	Lee Smith	.25
259	Damon Berryhill	.15
260	Wes Chamberlain	.15
261	Roger Clemens	2.00
262	Gar Finnvold	.15
263	Mike Greenwell	.15
264	Tim Naehring	.15
265	Otis Nixon	.15
266	Ken Ryan	.15
267	Chad Curtis	.15
268	Chili Davis	.25
269	Damion Easley	.15
270	Jorge Fabregas	.15
271	Mark Langston	.15
272	Phil Leftwich	.15
273	Harold Reynolds	.15
274	J.T. Snow	.25
275	Joey Cora	.15
276	Julio Franco	.15
277	Roberto Hernandez	.15
278	Lance Johnson	.15
279	Ron Karkovice	.15
280	Jack McDowell	.15
281	Robin Ventura	.30
282	Sandy Alomar Jr.	.25
283	Kenny Lofton	.50
284	Jose Mesa	.15
285	Jack Morris	.15
286	Eddie Murray	.35
287	Chad Ogea	.15
288	Eric Plunk	.15
289	Paul Shuey	.15
290	Omar Vizquel	.20
291	Danny Bautista	.15
292	Travis Fryman	.30
293	Greg Gohr	.15
294	Chris Gomez	.15
295	Mickey Tettleton	.15
296	Lou Whitaker	.15
297	David Cone	.20
298	Gary Gaetti	.15
299	Tom Gordon	.15
300	Felix Jose	.15
301	Jose Lind	.15
302	Brian McRae	.15
303	Mike Fetters	.15
304	Brian Harper	.15
305	Pat Listach	.15
306	Matt Mieske	.20
307	Dave Nilsson	.15
308	Jody Reed	.15
309	Greg Vaughn	.25
310	Bill Wegman	.15
311	Rick Aguilera	.15
312	Alex Cole	.15
313	Denny Hocking	.15
314	Chuck Knoblauch	.30
315	Shane Mack	.15
316	Pat Meares	.25
317	Kevin Tapani	.15
318	Jim Abbott	.25
319	Wade Boggs	.50
320	Sterling Hitchcock	.15
321	Pat Kelly	.15
322	Terry Mulholland	.15
323	Luis Polonia	.15
324	Mike Stanley	.15
325	Bob Wickman	.15
326	Bernie Williams	1.00
327	Mark Acre	.15
328	Geronimo Berroa	.15
329	Scott Brosius	.15
330	Brent Gates	.15
331	Rickey Henderson	.40
332	Carlos Reyes	.15
333	Ruben Sierra	.15
334	Bobby Witt	.15
335	Bobby Ayala	.15
336	Jay Buhner	.25
337	Randy Johnson	1.25
338	Edgar Martinez	.25
339	Bill Risley	.15
340	*Alex Rodriguez*	50.00
341	Roger Salkeld	.25
342	Dan Wilson	.15
343	Kevin Brown	.25
344	Jose Canseco	.75
345	Dean Palmer	.15
346	Ivan Rodriguez	1.25
347	Kenny Rogers	.15
348	Pat Borders	.15
349	Juan Guzman	.15
350	Ed Sprague	.15
351	Devon White	.15
352	Steve Avery	.15
353	Roberto Kelly	.15
354	Mark Lemke	.15
355	Greg McMichael	.15
356	Terry Pendleton	.15
357	John Smoltz	.30
358	Mike Stanton	.15
359	Tony Tarasco	.15
360	Mark Grace	.30
361	Derrick May	.15
362	Rey Sanchez	.15
363	Sammy Sosa	3.00
364	Rick Wilkins	.15
365	Jeff Brantley	.15
366	Tony Fernandez	.15
367	Chuck McElroy	.15
368	Kevin Mitchell	.15
369	John Roper	.15
370	Johnny Ruffin	.15
371	Deion Sanders	.40
372	Marvin Freeman	.15
373	Andres Galarraga	.75
374	Charlie Hayes	.15
375	Nelson Liriano	.15
376	David Nied	.15
377	Walt Weiss	.15
378	Bret Barberie	.15
379	Jerry Browne	.15
380	Chuck Carr	.15
381	Greg Colbrunn	.15
382	Charlie Hough	.15
383	Kurt Miller	.25
384	Benito Santiago	.20
385	Jeff Bagwell	1.25
386	Craig Biggio	.40
387	Ken Caminiti	.25
388	Doug Drabek	.15
389	Steve Finley	.15
390	John Hudek	.15
391	Orlando Miller	.15
392	Shane Reynolds	.15
393	Brett Butler	.20
394	Tom Candiotti	.15
395	Delino DeShields	.15
396	Kevin Gross	.15
397	Eric Karros	.30
398	Ramon Martinez	.25
399	Henry Rodriguez	.25
400	Moises Alou	.25
401	Jeff Fassero	.15
402	Mike Lansing	.15
403	Mel Rojas	.15
404	Larry Walker	.60
405	John Wetteland	.15
406	Gabe White	.30
407	Bobby Bonilla	.30
408	Josias Manzanillo	.15
409	Bret Saberhagen	.15
410	David Segui	.15
411	Mariano Duncan	.15
412	Tommy Greene	.15
413	Billy Hatcher	.15
414	Ricky Jordan	.15
415	John Kruk	.15
416	Bobby Munoz	.15
417	Curt Schilling	.25
418	Fernando Valenzuela	.25
419	David West	.15
420	Carlos Garcia	.15
421	Brian Hunter	.15
422	Jeff King	.15
423	Jon Lieber	.15
424	Ravelo Manzanillo	.15
425	Denny Neagle	.15
426	Andy Van Slyke	.15
427	Bryan Eversgerd	.15
428	Bernard Gilkey	.25
429	Gregg Jefferies	.25
430	Tom Pagnozzi	.15
431	Bob Tewksbury	.15
432	Allen Watson	.15
433	Andy Ashby	.15
434	Andy Benes	.25
435	Donnie Elliott	.15
436	Tony Gwynn	1.50
437	Joey Hamilton	.25
438	Tim Hyers	.15
439	Luis Lopez	.15
440	Bip Roberts	.15
441	Scott Sanders	.15
442	Rod Beck	.15
443	Dave Burba	.15
444	Darryl Strawberry	.25
445	Bill Swift	.15
446	Robby Thompson	.15
447	*William VanLandingham*	.50
448	Matt Williams	.50
449	Checklist	.15
450	Checklist	.15

1994 Flair Hot Gloves

Hot Glove is a 10-card Series 2 insert set. It focuses on players with outstanding defensive ability. Cards feature a die-cut design, with the player photo in front of a baseball glove. Player identification and a "Hot Glove" logo are in gold foil in the lower-left corner.

		MT
Complete Set (10):		110.00
Common Player:		5.00
1	Barry Bonds	10.00
2	Will Clark	5.00
3	Ken Griffey, Jr.	40.00
4	Kenny Lofton	6.00
5	Greg Maddux	20.00
6	Don Mattingly	12.00
7	Kirby Puckett	10.00
8	Cal Ripken, Jr.	30.00
9	Tim Salmon	5.00
10	Matt Williams	5.00

1994 Flair Hot Numbers

Hot Numbers is an insert set found in Series 1 packs at an average rate of 1:24. Each card is printed on 100% etched foil and displays the player in the forefront with a background made up of floating numbers. The player's name is in gold foil across the bottom-right side and a large foil "Hot Numbers" and that player's uniform number are in a square at bottom-left.

		MT
Complete Set (10):		50.00
Common Player:		1.00
1	Roberto Alomar	5.00
2	Carlos Baerga	1.00
3	Will Clark	3.00
4	Fred McGriff	1.50
5	Paul Molitor	4.00
6	John Olerud	1.50
7	Mike Piazza	15.00
8	Cal Ripken, Jr.	20.00
9	Ryne Sandberg	6.00
10	Frank Thomas	8.00

1994 Flair Infield Power

Infield Power is a horizontally formatted insert set. Cards show the player batting on one half and in the field on the other half of the card, divided by a black, diagonal strip that reads "Infield Power" and the player's name. The set spotlights infielders that often hit the longball. Infield Power was inserted into Series 2 packs at an average rate of 1:5.

		MT
Complete Set (10):		12.00
Common Player:		.50
1	Jeff Bagwell	1.50
2	Will Clark	.60
3	Darren Daulton	.50
4	Don Mattingly	1.50
5	Fred McGriff	.50
6	Rafael Palmeiro	.60
7	Mike Piazza	4.00
8	Cal Ripken, Jr.	5.00
9	Frank Thomas	2.50
10	Matt Williams	.60

1994 Flair Outfield Power

Flair's Outfield Power was randomly inserted in Series 1 packs at a 1:5 rate. This vertically formatted card shows the player in the field on top, while the bottom half shows the player at the plate. The photos divided by a black strip with "Outfield Power" and the player's name on it.

		MT
Complete Set (10):		15.00
Common Player:		.75
1	Albert Belle	1.50
2	Barry Bonds	2.00
3	Joe Carter	.75
4	Len Dykstra	.75
5	Juan Gonzalez	2.00
6	Ken Griffey, Jr.	8.00
7	Dave Justice	1.25
8	Kirby Puckett	2.50
9	Tim Salmon	1.25
10	Dave Winfield	.75

1994 Flair Wave of the Future

Series 1 Wave of the Future is horizontally formatted and depicts 10 outstanding 1994 rookies who have the potential to become superstars. Each player is featured on a colorful wavelike background. A Wave of the Future gold-foil stamp is placed in the bottom-right corner with the player name in gold foil starting in the opposite bottom corner and running across the bottom. Advertised insertion rate was 1:5.

		MT
Complete Set (10):		15.00
Common Player:		.50
1	Kurt Abbott	.50
2	Carlos Delgado	8.00
3	Steve Karsay	.50
4	Ryan Klesko	3.00
5	Javier Lopez	3.00
6	Raul Mondesi	4.00
7	James Mouton	.50
8	Chan Ho Park	2.00
9	Dave Staton	.50
10	Rick White	.50

1994 Flair Wave of the Future 2

Series 2 Flair also has a Wave of the Future insert set. Unlike the earlier series, this 10-card set is vertically formated. The Wave of the Future logo appears in the bottom-left with the player's name stretching across the rest of the bottom. The background has a swirling water effect, on which the player is superimposed. Insertion rate is one per five packs.

		MT
Complete Set (10):		45.00
Common Player:		.75
1	Mark Acre	.75
2	Chris Gomez	.75
3	Joey Hamilton	1.00
4	John Hudek	.75
5	Jon Lieber	.75
6	Matt Mieske	1.00
7	Orlando Miller	1.00
8	Alex Rodriguez	50.00
9	Tony Tarasco	.75
10	Bill VanLandingham	.75

1995 Flair

There's no mistaking that 1995 Flair is Fleer's super-premium brand. Cards are printed on double-thick cardboard with a background of etched metallic foil: Gold for National Leaguers, silver for American. A portrait and an action photo are featured on the horizontal front design. Backs are vertically formatted with a borderless action photo, several years worth of stats and foil trim. The basic set was issued in two series of 216 basic cards each, along with several insert sets exclusive to each series. Cards were sold in a hard pack of nine with a suggested retail price of $5.

		MT
Complete Set (432):		55.00
Common Player:		.20
Series 1 or 2 Pack (9):		3.00
Series 1 or 2 Wax Box (24):		65.00
1	Brady Anderson	.30
2	Harold Baines	.25
3	Leo Gomez	.20
4	Alan Mills	.20
5	Jamie Moyer	.20
6	Mike Mussina	.75
7	Mike Oquist	.20
8	Arthur Rhodes	.20
9	Cal Ripken Jr.	4.00
10	Roger Clemens	1.50
11	Scott Cooper	.20
12	Mike Greenwell	.20
13	Aaron Sele	.20
14	John Valentin	.25
15	Mo Vaughn	1.00
16	Chad Curtis	.20
17	Gary DiSarcina	.20
18	Chuck Finley	.20
19	Andrew Lorraine	.20
20	Spike Owen	.20
21	Tim Salmon	.40
22	J.T. Snow	.25
23	Wilson Alvarez	.20
24	Jason Bere	.20
25	Ozzie Guillen	.20
26	Mike LaValliere	.20
27	Frank Thomas	1.50
28	Robin Ventura	.30
29	Carlos Baerga	.20
30	Albert Belle	.75
31	Jason Grimsley	.20
32	Dennis Martinez	.25
33	Eddie Murray	.50
34	Charles Nagy	.25
35	Manny Ramirez	1.25
36	Paul Sorrento	.20
37	John Doherty	.20
38	Cecil Fielder	.20
39	Travis Fryman	.25
40	Chris Gomez	.20
41	Tony Phillips	.20
42	Lou Whitaker	.20
43	David Cone	.25
44	Gary Gaetti	.20
45	Mark Gubicza	.20
46	Bob Hamelin	.20
47	Wally Joyner	.25
48	Rusty Meacham	.20
49	Jeff Montgomery	.20
50	Ricky Bones	.20
51	Cal Eldred	.20
52	Pat Listach	.20
53	Matt Mieske	.20
54	Dave Nilsson	.20
55	Greg Vaughn	.25
56	Bill Wegman	.20
57	Chuck Knoblauch	.35
58	Scott Leius	.20
59	Pat Mahomes	.20
60	Pat Meares	.20
61	Pedro Munoz	.20
62	Kirby Puckett	2.00
63	Wade Boggs	.50
64	Jimmy Key	.20
65	Jim Leyritz	.20
66	Don Mattingly	2.00
67	Paul O'Neill	.40
68	Melido Perez	.20
69	Danny Tartabull	.20
70	John Briscoe	.20
71	Scott Brosius	.20
72	Ron Darling	.20
73	Brent Gates	.20
74	Rickey Henderson	.40
75	Stan Javier	.20
76	Mark McGwire	5.00
77	Todd Van Poppel	.20
78	Bobby Ayala	.20
79	Mike Blowers	.20
80	Jay Buhner	.25
81	Ken Griffey Jr.	4.00
82	Randy Johnson	1.25
83	Tino Martinez	.30
84	Jeff Nelson	.20
85	Alex Rodriguez	4.00
86	Will Clark	.50
87	Jeff Frye	.20
88	Juan Gonzalez	1.25
89	Rusty Greer	.25
90	Darren Oliver	.20
91	Dean Palmer	.20
92	Ivan Rodriguez	1.25
93	Matt Whiteside	.20
94	Roberto Alomar	1.00
95	Joe Carter	.20
96	Tony Castillo	.20
97	Juan Guzman	.20
98	Pat Hentgen	.20

No.	Player	Value
99	Mike Huff	.20
100	John Olerud	.30
101	Woody Williams	.20
102	Roberto Kelly	.20
103	Ryan Klesko	.40
104	Javier Lopez	.35
105	Greg Maddux	2.50
106	Fred McGriff	.40
107	Jose Oliva	.20
108	John Smoltz	.25
109	Tony Tarasco	.20
110	Mark Wohlers	.20
111	Jim Bullinger	.20
112	Shawon Dunston	.20
113	Derrick May	.20
114	Randy Myers	.20
115	Karl Rhodes	.20
116	Rey Sanchez	.20
117	Steve Trachsel	.20
118	Eddie Zambrano	.20
119	Bret Boone	.20
120	Brian Dorsett	.20
121	Hal Morris	.20
122	Jose Rijo	.20
123	John Roper	.20
124	Reggie Sanders	.25
125	Pete Schourek	.20
126	John Smiley	.20
127	Ellis Burks	.25
128	Vinny Castilla	.25
129	Marvin Freeman	.20
130	Andres Galarraga	.50
131	Mike Munoz	.20
132	David Nied	.20
133	Bruce Ruffin	.20
134	Walt Weiss	.20
135	Eric Young	.20
136	Greg Colbrunn	.20
137	Jeff Conine	.25
138	Jeremy Hernandez	.20
139	Charles Johnson	.25
140	Robb Nen	.20
141	Gary Sheffield	.60
142	Dave Weathers	.20
143	Jeff Bagwell	1.25
144	Craig Biggio	.30
145	Tony Eusebio	.20
146	Luis Gonzalez	.20
147	John Hudek	.20
148	Darryl Kile	.20
149	Dave Veres	.20
150	Billy Ashley	.20
151	Pedro Astacio	.20
152	Rafael Bournigal	.20
153	Delino DeShields	.20
154	Raul Mondesi	.50
155	Mike Piazza	3.00
156	Rudy Seanez	.20
157	Ismael Valdes	.20
158	Tim Wallach	.20
159	Todd Worrell	.20
160	Moises Alou	.25
161	Cliff Floyd	.20
162	Gil Heredia	.20
163	Mike Lansing	.20
164	Pedro Martinez	1.25
165	Kirk Rueter	.20
166	Tim Scott	.20
167	Jeff Shaw	.20
168	Rondell White	.30
169	Bobby Bonilla	.25
170	Rico Brogna	.20
171	Todd Hundley	.30
172	Jeff Kent	.20
173	Jim Lindeman	.20
174	Joe Orsulak	.20
175	Bret Saberhagen	.20
176	Toby Borland	.20
177	Darren Daulton	.20
178	Lenny Dykstra	.20
179	Jim Eisenreich	.20
180	Tommy Greene	.20
181	Tony Longmire	.20
182	Bobby Munoz	.20
183	Kevin Stocker	.20
184	Jay Bell	.20
185	Steve Cooke	.20
186	Ravelo Manzanillo	.20
187	Al Martin	.20
188	Denny Neagle	.20
189	Don Slaught	.20
190	Paul Wagner	.20
191	Rene Arocha	.20
192	Bernard Gilkey	.20
193	Jose Oquendo	.20
194	Tom Pagnozzi	.20
195	Ozzie Smith	1.00
196	Allen Watson	.20
197	Mark Whiten	.20
198	Andy Ashby	.25
199	Donnie Elliott	.20
200	Bryce Florie	.20
201	Tony Gwynn	1.50
202	Trevor Hoffman	.25
203	Brian Johnson	.20
204	Tim Mauser	.20
205	Bip Roberts	.20
206	Rod Beck	.20
207	Barry Bonds	1.25
208	Royce Clayton	.20
209	Darren Lewis	.20
210	Mark Portugal	.20
211	Kevin Rogers	.20
212	William Van Landingham	.20
213	Matt Williams	.50
214	Checklist	.20
215	Checklist	.20
216	Checklist	.20
217	Bret Barberie	.20
218	Armando Benitez	.20
219	Kevin Brown	.25
220	Sid Fernandez	.20
221	Chris Hoiles	.20
222	Doug Jones	.20
223	Ben McDonald	.20
224	Rafael Palmeiro	.60
225	Andy Van Slyke	.20
226	Jose Canseco	.50
227	Vaughn Eshelman	.20
228	Mike Macfarlane	.20
229	Tim Naehring	.20
230	Frank Rodriguez	.20
231	Lee Tinsley	.20
232	Mark Whiten	.20
233	Garret Anderson	.20
234	Chili Davis	.25
235	Jim Edmonds	.40
236	Mark Langston	.20
237	Troy Percival	.20
238	Tony Phillips	.20
239	Lee Smith	.20
240	Jim Abbott	.25
241	James Baldwin	.20
242	Mike Devereaux	.20
243	Ray Durham	.25
244	Alex Fernandez	.25
245	Roberto Hernandez	.20
246	Lance Johnson	.20
247	Ron Karkovice	.20
248	Tim Raines	.25
249	Sandy Alomar Jr.	.25
250	Orel Hershiser	.25
251	Julian Tavarez	.20
252	Jim Thome	.60
253	Omar Vizquel	.25
254	Dave Winfield	.40
255	Chad Curtis	.20
256	Kirk Gibson	.20
257	Mike Henneman	.20
258	*Bob Higginson*	1.50
259	Felipe Lira	.20
260	Rudy Pemberton	.20
261	Alan Trammell	.25
262	Kevin Appier	.20
263	Pat Borders	.20
264	Tom Gordon	.20
265	Jose Lind	.20
266	Jon Nunnally	.20
267	Dilson Torres	.20
268	Michael Tucker	.20
269	Jeff Cirillo	.20
270	Darryl Hamilton	.20
271	David Hulse	.20
272	Mark Kiefer	.20
273	Graeme Lloyd	.20
274	Joe Oliver	.20
275	Al Reyes	.20
276	Kevin Seitzer	.20
277	Rick Aguilera	.20
278	Marty Cordova	.20
279	Scott Erickson	.20
280	LaTroy Hawkins	.20
281	Brad Radke	.20
282	Kevin Tapani	.20
283	Tony Fernandez	.20
284	Sterling Hitchcock	.20
285	Pat Kelly	.20
286	Jack McDowell	.20
287	Andy Pettitte	.60
288	Mike Stanley	.20
289	John Wetteland	.25
290	Bernie Williams	1.00
291	Mark Acre	.20
292	Geronimo Berroa	.20
293	Dennis Eckersley	.25
294	Steve Ontiveros	.20
295	Ruben Sierra	.20
296	Terry Steinbach	.20
297	Dave Stewart	.25
298	Todd Stottlemyre	.20
299	Darren Bragg	.20
300	Joey Cora	.20
301	Edgar Martinez	.25
302	Bill Risley	.20
303	Ron Villone	.20
304	Dan Wilson	.20
305	Benji Gil	.20
306	Wilson Heredia	.20
307	Mark McLemore	.20
308	Otis Nixon	.20
309	Kenny Rogers	.20
310	Jeff Russell	.20
311	Mickey Tettleton	.20
312	Bob Tewksbury	.20
313	David Cone	.25
314	Carlos Delgado	1.00
315	Alex Gonzalez	.20
316	Shawn Green	.50
317	Paul Molitor	.40
318	Ed Sprague	.20
319	Devon White	.25
320	Steve Avery	.20
321	Jeff Blauser	.20
322	Brad Clontz	.20
323	Tom Glavine	.50
324	Marquis Grissom	.25
325	Chipper Jones	2.50
326	Dave Justice	.50
327	Mark Lemke	.20
328	Kent Mercker	.20
329	Jason Schmidt	.20
330	Steve Buechele	.20
331	Kevin Foster	.20
332	Mark Grace	.35
333	Brian McRae	.20
334	Sammy Sosa	3.00
335	Ozzie Timmons	.20
336	Rick Wilkins	.20
337	Hector Carrasco	.20
338	Ron Gant	.25
339	Barry Larkin	.50
340	Deion Sanders	.30
341	Benito Santiago	.20
342	Roger Bailey	.20
343	Jason Bates	.20
344	Dante Bichette	.30
345	Joe Girardi	.20
346	Bill Swift	.20
347	Mark Thompson	.20
348	Larry Walker	.50
349	Kurt Abbott	.20
350	John Burkett	.20
351	Chuck Carr	.20
352	Andre Dawson	.25
353	Chris Hammond	.20
354	Charles Johnson	.25
355	Terry Pendleton	.20
356	Quilvio Veras	.20
357	Derek Bell	.25
358	Jim Dougherty	.20
359	Doug Drabek	.20
360	Todd Jones	.20
361	Orlando Miller	.20
362	James Mouton	.20
363	Phil Plantier	.20
364	Shane Reynolds	.20
365	Todd Hollandsworth	.25
366	Eric Karros	.25
367	Ramon Martinez	.20
368	*Hideo Nomo*	3.00
369	Jose Offerman	.20
370	Antonio Osuna	.20
371	Todd Williams	.20
372	Shane Andrews	.20
373	Wil Cordero	.20
374	Jeff Fassero	.20
375	Darrin Fletcher	.20
376	*Mark Grudzielanek*	.60
377	*Carlos Perez*	.25
378	Mel Rojas	.20
379	Tony Tarasco	.20
380	Edgardo Alfonzo	.40
381	Brett Butler	.20
382	Carl Everett	.25
383	John Franco	.20
384	Pete Harnisch	.20
385	Bobby Jones	.20
386	Dave Mlicki	.20
387	Jose Vizcaino	.20
388	Ricky Bottalico	.20
389	Tyler Green	.20
390	Charlie Hayes	.20
391	Dave Hollins	.20
392	Gregg Jefferies	.25
393	*Michael Mimbs*	.20
394	Mickey Morandini	.20
395	Curt Schilling	.30
396	Heathcliff Slocumb	.20
397	Jason Christiansen	.20
398	Midre Cummings	.20
399	Carlos Garcia	.20
400	Mark Johnson	.25
401	Jeff King	.20
402	Jon Lieber	.20
403	Esteban Loaiza	.30
404	Orlando Merced	.20
405	*Gary Wilson*	.20
406	Scott Cooper	.20
407	Tom Henke	.20
408	Ken Hill	.20
409	Danny Jackson	.20
410	Brian Jordan	.30
411	Ray Lankford	.25
412	John Mabry	.20
413	Todd Zeile	.25
414	Andy Benes	.25
415	Andres Berumen	.20
416	Ken Caminiti	.30
417	Andujar Cedeno	.20
418	Steve Finley	.20
419	Joey Hamilton	.30
420	Dustin Hermanson	.25
421	Melvin Nieves	.20
422	Roberto Petagine	.20
423	Eddie Williams	.20
424	Glenallen Hill	.20
425	Kirt Manwaring	.20
426	Terry Mulholland	.20
427	J.R. Phillips	.20
428	Joe Rosselli	.20
429	Robby Thompson	.20
430	Checklist	.20
431	Checklist	.20
432	Checklist	.20

1995 Flair Cal Ripken, Jr. Enduring Flair

The career of Cal Ripken, Jr., is traced in this insert set found in Series 2 Flair at the average rate of once per dozen packs. Each card has a vintage photo on front, with a large silver-foil "ENDURING" logo toward bottom. Backs have another color photo, a quote and other information about the milestone. The series was extended by a special mail-in offer for five additional cards which chronicled Ripken's record-breaking 1995 season.

		MT
Complete Set (15):		50.00
Common Card:		3.50
1	Rookie Of The Year	3.50
2	1st MVP Season	3.50
3	World Series Highlight	3.50
4	Family Tradition	3.50
5	8,243 Consecutive Innings	3.50
6	95 Consecutive Errorless Games	3.50
7	All-Star MVP	3.50
8	1,000th RBI	3.50
9	287th Home Run	3.50
10	2,000th Consecutive Game	3.50
11	Record-tying Game	4.00
12	Record-breaking Game	4.00
13	Defensive Prowess	4.00
14	Literacy Work	4.00
15	2,153 and Counting	4.00

1995 Flair Hot Gloves

The cream of the crop among Series 2 Flair inserts is this set featuring fine fielders. Cards have a background of an embossed gold-foil glove, with a color player photo centered in front. Silver foil comprises the card title and player name at bottom and the Flair logo at top. Backs have a white background, a photo of a glove with a career summary overprinted and a player portrait photo in a lower corner. These inserts are found at the average rate of once per 25 packs.

		MT
Complete Set (12):		100.00
Common Player:		4.00
1	Roberto Alomar	8.00
2	Barry Bonds	10.00
3	Ken Griffey Jr.	30.00
4	Marquis Grissom	4.00
5	Barry Larkin	5.00
6	Darren Lewis	4.00
7	Kenny Lofton	6.00
8	Don Mattingly	12.50
9	Cal Ripken Jr.	25.00
10	Ivan Rodriguez	8.00
11	Devon White	4.00
12	Matt Williams	5.00

1995 Flair Hot Numbers

These Series 1 inserts are a 1:9 find. Gold metallic-foil background with 1994 seasonal stat numbers are the background for a color action photo on front. Horizontal backs have a ghosted portrait photo at right and career highlights at left.

		MT
Complete Set (10):		45.00
Common Player:		2.50
1	Jeff Bagwell	4.00
2	Albert Belle	3.00
3	Barry Bonds	4.00
4	Ken Griffey Jr.	12.00
5	Kenny Lofton	2.50
6	Greg Maddux	6.00
7	Mike Piazza	8.00
8	Cal Ripken Jr.	9.00
9	Frank Thomas	5.00
10	Matt Williams	2.50

1995 Flair Infield Power

Power rays and waves eminating from the player's bat in an action photo are the front design of this Series 2 chase set. The card title, name and team at bottom, and the Flair logo at top are in silver foil. Backs repeat the wave theme with a player photo on one end and a career summary at the other. These inserts are seeded at the average rate of one per five packs.

		MT
Complete Set (10):		8.00
Common Player:		.50
1	Jeff Bagwell	1.50
2	Darren Daulton	.50
3	Cecil Fielder	.50
4	Andres Galarraga	.50
5	Fred McGriff	.75
6	Rafael Palmeiro	.75
7	Mike Piazza	2.00
8	Frank Thomas	2.00
9	Mo Vaughn	1.00
10	Matt Williams	.50

1995 Flair Outfield Power

Laser-like colored rays are the background to the action photo on front and portrait on back of this series. The card title, player identification and Flair logo on front are in silver foil. Backs are horizontal, silver-foil enhanced and include a career summary. This chase set is seeded at the average rate of one card per six packs of Series 1 Flair.

		MT
Complete Set (10):		12.00
Common Player:		.50
1	Albert Belle	1.25
2	Dante Bichette	.75
3	Barry Bonds	1.25
4	Jose Canseco	1.25
5	Joe Carter	.50
6	Juan Gonzalez	1.50
7	Ken Griffey Jr.	6.00
8	Kirby Puckett	1.50
9	Gary Sheffield	.75
10	Ruben Sierra	.50

1995 Flair Today's Spotlight

The premier insert set in Flair Series I, found once every 30 packs or so, this die-cut issue has the player action photo spotlighted in a 2-3/8" bright spot, with the rest of the photo muted in gray and dark gray. The card title, Flair logo, player name and team are in silver foil. The horizontal backs have a portrait photo in the spotlight and career summary on the side.

		MT
Complete Set (12):		60.00
Common Player:		3.00
1	Jeff Bagwell	12.00
2	Jason Bere	3.00
3	Cliff Floyd	3.00
4	Chuck Knoblauch	6.00
5	Kenny Lofton	6.00
6	Javier Lopez	4.00
7	Raul Mondesi	5.00
8	Mike Mussina	6.00
9	Mike Piazza	20.00
10	Manny Ramirez	10.00
11	Tim Salmon	4.00
12	Frank Thomas	15.00

1995 Flair Wave Of The Future

The cream of baseball's rookie crop is featured in this Series 2 insert set, found once per eight packs on average. Fronts have a graduated color background with a baseball/wave morph, which is repeated at the bottom in silver foil, along with the player name. A color action photo is at center. The player's name, team and "Wave of the Future" are repeated in horizontal rows behind the photo. Horizontal backs repeat the wave logo, have another player photo and a career summary.

		MT
Complete Set (10):		20.00
Common Player:		.50
1	Jason Bates	.50
2	Armando Benitez	.75
3	Marty Cordova	.50
4	Ray Durham	1.50
5	Vaughn Eshelman	.50
6	Carl Everett	2.00
7	Shawn Green	5.00
8	Dustin Hermanson	1.50
9	Chipper Jones	12.00
10	Hideo Nomo	5.00

1996 Flair Promotional Sheet

Three samples of Flair's 1996 issue and an information card are included on this 5" x 7" promotional sheet.

	MT
Complete Sheet: Manny Ramirez, Cal Ripken Jr., Matt Williams, Information card	7.50

1996 Flair

Fleer's 1996 Flair baseball set has 400 cards, a parallel set and four insert types. Regular card fronts have two photos of the featured player; backs have a photo and career statistics. All cards have a silver-foil version and a gold-foil version, with each version appearing in equal numbers. Seven-card packs carried an issue price of $4.99.

		MT
Complete Set (400):		125.00
Common Player:		.25
Unlisted Stars:		.50 to .75
Pack (9):		5.00
Wax Box (18):		75.00
1	Roberto Alomar	2.00
2	Brady Anderson	.35
3	Bobby Bonilla	.30
4	Scott Erickson	.25
5	Jeffrey Hammonds	.25
6	Jimmy Haynes	.25
7	Chris Hoiles	.25
8	Kent Mercker	.25
9	Mike Mussina	1.50
10	Randy Myers	.25
11	Rafael Palmeiro	1.00
12	Cal Ripken Jr.	8.00
(12p)	Cal Ripken Jr. (no card #, overprinted "PROMOTIONAL SAMPLE")	5.00
13	B.J. Surhoff	.30
14	David Wells	.30
15	Jose Canseco	.75
16	Roger Clemens	3.00
17	Wil Cordero	.25
18	Tom Gordon	.25
19	Mike Greenwell	.25
20	Dwayne Hosey	.25
21	Jose Malave	.25
22	Tim Naehring	.25
23	Troy O'Leary	.25
24	Aaron Sele	.25
25	Heathcliff Slocumb	.25
26	Mike Stanley	.25
27	Jeff Suppan	.25
28	John Valentin	.25
29	Mo Vaughn	2.00
30	Tim Wakefield	.25
31	Jim Abbott	.25
32	Garret Anderson	.25
33	George Arias	.25
34	Chili Davis	.25
35	Gary DiSarcina	.25
36	Jim Edmonds	.50
37	Chuck Finley	.25
38	Todd Greene	.25
39	Mark Langston	.25
40	Troy Percival	.25
41	Tim Salmon	.50
42	Lee Smith	.25
43	J.T. Snow	.30
44	Randy Velarde	.25
45	Tim Wallach	.25
46	Wilson Alvarez	.25
47	Harold Baines	.30
48	Jason Bere	.25
49	Ray Durham	.25
50	Alex Fernandez	.25
51	Ozzie Guillen	.25
52	Roberto Hernandez	.25
53	Ron Karkovice	.25
54	Darren Lewis	.25
55	Lyle Mouton	.25
56	Tony Phillips	.25
57	Chris Snopek	.25
58	Kevin Tapani	.25
59	Danny Tartabull	.25
30	Frank Thomas	5.00
61	Robin Ventura	.35
62	Sandy Alomar	.30
63	Carlos Baerga	.25
64	Albert Belle	2.00
65	Julio Franco	.25
66	Orel Hershiser	.25
67	Kenny Lofton	1.50
68	Dennis Martinez	.25
69	Jack McDowell	.25
70	Jose Mesa	.25
71	Eddie Murray	1.00
72	Charles Nagy	.25
73	Tony Pena	.25
74	Manny Ramirez	2.50
75	Julian Tavarez	.25
76	Jim Thome	1.00
77	Omar Vizquel	.25
78	Chad Curtis	.25
79	Cecil Fielder	.25
80	Travis Fryman	.40
81	Chris Gomez	.25
82	Bob Higginson	.25
83	Mark Lewis	.25
84	Felipe Lira	.25
85	Alan Trammell	.25
86	Kevin Appier	.25
87	Johnny Damon	.40
88	Tom Goodwin	.25
89	Mark Gubicza	.25
90	Bob Hamelin	.25
91	Keith Lockhart	.25
92	Jeff Montgomery	.25
93	Jon Nunnally	.25
94	Bip Roberts	.25
95	Michael Tucker	.25
96	Joe Vitiello	.25
97	Ricky Bones	.25
98	Chuck Carr	.25
99	Jeff Cirillo	.25
100	Mike Fetters	.25
101	John Jaha	.25
102	Mike Matheny	.25
103	Ben McDonald	.25
104	Matt Mieske	.25
105	Dave Nilsson	.25
106	Kevin Seitzer	.25
107	Steve Sparks	.25
108	Jose Valentin	.25
109	Greg Vaughn	.30
110	Rick Aguilera	.25
111	Rich Becker	.25
112	Marty Cordova	.25
113	LaTroy Hawkins	.25
114	Dave Hollins	.25
115	Roberto Kelly	.25
116	Chuck Knoblauch	.50
117	*Matt Lawton*	2.50
118	Pat Meares	.25
119	Paul Molitor	1.50
120	Kirby Puckett	4.00
121	Brad Radke	.25
122	Frank Rodriguez	.25
123	Scott Stahoviak	.25
124	Matt Walbeck	.25
125	Wade Boggs	.60
126	David Cone	.40
127	Joe Girardi	.25
128	Dwight Gooden	.35
129	Derek Jeter	6.00
130	Jimmy Key	.25
131	Jim Leyritz	.25
132	Tino Martinez	.40
133	Paul O'Neill	.50
134	Andy Pettitte	1.00
135	Tim Raines	.25
136	Ruben Rivera	.25
137	Kenny Rogers	.25
138	Ruben Sierra	.25
139	John Wetteland	.25
140	Bernie Williams	2.00
141	*Tony Batista*	10.00
142	Allen Battle	.25
143	Geronimo Berroa	.25
144	Mike Bordick	.25
145	Scott Brosius	.25
146	Steve Cox	.25
147	Brent Gates	.25
148	Jason Giambi	.75
149	Doug Johns	.25
150	Mark McGwire	10.00
151	Pedro Munoz	.25
152	Ariel Prieto	.25
153	Terry Steinbach	.25
154	Todd Van Poppel	.25
155	Bobby Ayala	.25
156	Chris Bosio	.25
157	Jay Buhner	.30
158	Joey Cora	.25
159	Russ Davis	.25
160	Ken Griffey Jr.	10.00
161	Sterling Hitchcock	.25
162	Randy Johnson	2.50
163	Edgar Martinez	.25
164	Alex Rodriguez	8.00
165	Paul Sorrento	.25
166	Dan Wilson	.25
167	Will Clark	.50
168	Benji Gil	.25
169	Juan Gonzalez	2.50
170	Rusty Greer	.25
171	Kevin Gross	.25
172	Darryl Hamilton	.25
173	Mike Henneman	.25
174	Ken Hill	.25
175	Mark McLemore	.25
176	Dean Palmer	.25
177	Roger Pavlik	.25
178	Ivan Rodriguez	2.50
179	Mickey Tettleton	.25
180	Bobby Witt	.25
181	Joe Carter	.30
182	Felipe Crespo	.25
183	Alex Gonzalez	.25
184	Shawn Green	.75
185	Juan Guzman	.25
186	Erik Hanson	.25
187	Pat Hentgen	.25
188	*Sandy Martinez*	.25
189	Otis Nixon	.25
190	John Olerud	.40
191	Paul Quantrill	.25
192	Bill Risley	.25
193	Ed Sprague	.25
194	Steve Avery	.25
195	Jeff Blauser	.25
196	Brad Clontz	.25
197	Jermaine Dye	.25
198	Tom Glavine	.60
199	Marquis Grissom	.25
200	Chipper Jones	6.00
201	David Justice	.75
202	Ryan Klesko	.50
203	Mark Lemke	.25
204	Javier Lopez	.40
205	Greg Maddux	6.00
206	Fred McGriff	1.00
207	Greg McMichael	.25
208	Wonderful Monds	.25
209	Jason Schmidt	.25
210	John Smoltz	.25
211	Mark Wohlers	.25
212	Jim Bullinger	.25
213	Frank Castillo	.25
214	Kevin Foster	.25
215	Luis Gonzalez	.25
216	Mark Grace	.40
217	*Robin Jennings*	.25
218	Doug Jones	.25
219	Dave Magadan	.25
220	Brian McRae	.25
221	Jaime Navarro	.25
222	Rey Sanchez	.25
223	Ryne Sandberg	2.00
224	Scott Servais	.25
225	Sammy Sosa	6.00
226	Ozzie Timmons	.25
227	Bret Boone	.25
228	Jeff Branson	.25
229	Jeff Brantley	.25
230	Dave Burba	.25
231	Vince Coleman	.25
232	Steve Gibralter	.25
233	Mike Kelly	.25
234	Barry Larkin	1.00
235	Hal Morris	.25
236	Mark Portugal	.25
237	Jose Rijo	.25
238	Reggie Sanders	.25
239	Pete Schourek	.25
240	John Smiley	.25
241	Eddie Taubensee	.25
242	Jason Bates	.25
243	Dante Bichette	1.00
244	Ellis Burks	.25
245	Vinny Castilla	.25
246	Andres Galarraga	.75
247	Darren Holmes	.25
248	Curt Leskanic	.25
249	Steve Reed	.25
250	Kevin Ritz	.25
251	Bret Saberhagen	.25
252	Bill Swift	.25
253	Larry Walker	.50
254	Walt Weiss	.25
255	Eric Young	.25
256	Kurt Abbott	.25
257	Kevin Brown	.25
258	John Burkett	.25
259	Greg Colbrunn	.25
260	Jeff Conine	.25
261	Andre Dawson	.40
262	Chris Hammond	.25
263	Charles Johnson	.25
264	Al Leiter	.25
265	Robb Nen	.25
266	Terry Pendleton	.25
267	Pat Rapp	.25
268	Gary Sheffield	1.00
269	Quilvio Veras	.25
270	Devon White	.25
271	Bob Abreu	.50
272	Jeff Bagwell	4.00
273	Derek Bell	.25
274	Sean Berry	.25
275	Craig Biggio	.50
276	Doug Drabek	.25
277	Tony Eusebio	.25
278	Richard Hidalgo	.50
279	Brian Hunter	.25
280	Todd Jones	.25
281	Derrick May	.25
282	Orlando Miller	.25
283	James Mouton	.25
284	Shane Reynolds	.25
285	Greg Swindell	.25
286	Mike Blowers	.25
287	Brett Butler	.25
288	Tom Candiotti	.25
289	Roger Cedeno	.25
290	Delino DeShields	.25
291	Greg Gagne	.25
292	Karim Garcia	1.00
293	Todd Hollandsworth	.25
294	Eric Karros	.25
295	Ramon Martinez	.25
296	Raul Mondesi	.50

297 Hideo Nomo 1.00
298 Mike Piazza 6.00
299 Ismael Valdes .25
300 Todd Worrell .25
301 Moises Alou .25
302 Shane Andrews .25
303 Yamil Benitez .25
304 Jeff Fassero .25
305 Darrin Fletcher .25
306 Cliff Floyd .25
307 Mark Grudzielanek .25
308 Mike Lansing .25
309 Pedro Martinez 2.50
310 Ryan McGuire .25
311 Carlos Perez .25
312 Mel Rojas .25
313 David Segui .25
314 Rondell White .25
315 Edgardo Alfonzo .40
316 Rico Brogna .25
317 Carl Everett .25
318 John Franco .25
319 Bernard Gilkey .25
320 Todd Hundley .40
321 Jason Isringhausen .25
322 Lance Johnson .25
323 Bobby Jones .25
324 Jeff Kent .25
325 Rey Ordonez .25
326 Bill Pulsipher .25
327 Jose Vizcaino .25
328 Paul Wilson .25
329 Ricky Bottalico .25
330 Darren Daulton .25
331 *David Doster* .25
332 Lenny Dykstra .25
333 Jim Eisenreich .25
334 Sid Fernandez .25
335 Gregg Jefferies .25
336 Mickey Morandini .25
337 Benito Santiago .25
338 Curt Schilling .30
339 Kevin Stocker .25
340 David West .25
341 Mark Whiten .25
342 Todd Zeile .25
343 Jay Bell .25
344 John Ericks .25
345 Carlos Garcia .25
346 Charlie Hayes .25
347 Jason Kendall .25
348 Jeff King .25
349 Mike Kingery .25
350 Al Martin .25
351 Orlando Merced .25
352 Dan Miceli .25
353 Denny Neagle .25
354 Alan Benes .25
355 Andy Benes .25
356 Royce Clayton .25
357 Dennis Eckersley .25
358 Gary Gaetti .25
359 Ron Gant .30
360 Brian Jordan .30
361 Ray Lankford .25
362 John Mabry .25
363 T.J. Mathews .25
364 Mike Morgan .25
365 Donovan Osborne .25
366 Tom Pagnozzi .25
367 Ozzie Smith 1.50
368 Todd Stottlemyre .25
369 Andy Ashby .25
370 Brad Ausmus .25
371 Ken Caminiti .25
372 Andujar Cedeno .25
373 Steve Finley .25
374 Tony Gwynn 4.00
375 Joey Hamilton .25
376 Rickey Henderson .50
377 Trevor Hoffman .25
378 Wally Joyner .25
379 Marc Newfield .25
380 Jody Reed .25
381 Bob Tewksbury .25
382 Fernando Valenzuela .25
383 Rod Beck .25
384 Barry Bonds 2.50
385 Mark Carreon .25
386 Shawon Dunston .25
387 *Osvaldo Fernandez* .40
388 Glenallen Hill .25
389 Stan Javier .25
390 Mark Leiter .25
391 Kirt Manwaring .25
392 Robby Thompson .25
393 William VanLandingham .25
394 Allen Watson .25
395 Matt Williams .50
396 Checklist .25
397 Checklist .25
398 Checklist .25
399 Checklist .25
400 Checklist .25

1996 Flair Diamond Cuts

Ten of the game's top stars are showcased on these 1996 Flair inserts. They are seeded one per 20 packs. Fronts have a textured background rainbow metallic foil and silver glitter.

		MT
Complete Set (12):		90.00
Common Player:		2.50
1	Jeff Bagwell	7.50
2	Albert Belle	4.50
3	Barry Bonds	5.00
4	Juan Gonzalez	5.00
5	Ken Griffey Jr.	20.00
6	Greg Maddux	10.00
7	Eddie Murray	4.00
8	Mike Piazza	12.50
9	Cal Ripken Jr.	15.00
10	Frank Thomas	10.00
11	Mo Vaughn	4.00
12	Matt Williams	2.50

1996 Flair Hot Gloves

Ten top defensive players are highlighted on these die-cut insert cards, a design first made popular in 1994. Hot Gloves can only be found in hobby packs, at a rate of one per every 90 packs.

		MT
Complete Set (10):		225.00
Common Player:		10.00
1	Roberto Alomar	17.50
2	Barry Bonds	30.00
3	Will Clark	10.00
4	Ken Griffey Jr.	60.00
5	Kenny Lofton	20.00
6	Greg Maddux	40.00
7	Mike Piazza	45.00
8	Cal Ripken Jr.	50.00
9	Ivan Rodriguez	25.00
10	Matt Williams	10.00

1996 Flair Powerline

Ten of baseball's top sluggers are featured on these Flair inserts. They are the easiest of the Flair inserts to obtain; seeded one per six packs. Fronts combine yellow-green artwork with the player photo. Backs have a vertical color photo and career information.

		MT
Complete Set (10):		20.00
Common Player:		1.00
1	Albert Belle	1.50
2	Barry Bonds	1.75
3	Juan Gonzalez	2.00
4	Ken Griffey Jr.	7.50
5	Mark McGwire	7.50
6	Mike Piazza	4.00
7	Manny Ramirez	2.00
8	Sammy Sosa	3.50
9	Frank Thomas	3.50
10	Matt Williams	1.00

1996 Flair Wave of the Future

These inserts feature up-and-coming young talent in baseball. Twenty 1996 rookies and prospects are printed on lenticular cards. They are seeded one per every 72 packs.

		MT
Complete Set (20):		125.00
Common Player:		6.00
1	Bob Abreu	15.00
2	George Arias	6.00
3	Tony Batista	30.00
4	Alan Benes	6.00
5	Yamil Benitez	6.00
6	Steve Cox	6.00
7	David Doster	6.00
8	Jermaine Dye	15.00
9	Osvaldo Fernandez	6.00
10	Karim Garcia	6.00
11	Steve Gibralter	6.00
12	Todd Greene	6.00
13	Richard Hidalgo	20.00
14	Robin Jennings	6.00
15	Jason Kendall	18.00
16	Jose Malave	6.00
17	Wonderful Monds	6.00
18	Rey Ordonez	6.00
19	Ruben Rivera	6.00
20	Paul Wilson	6.00

1997 Flair Showcase Promo Strip

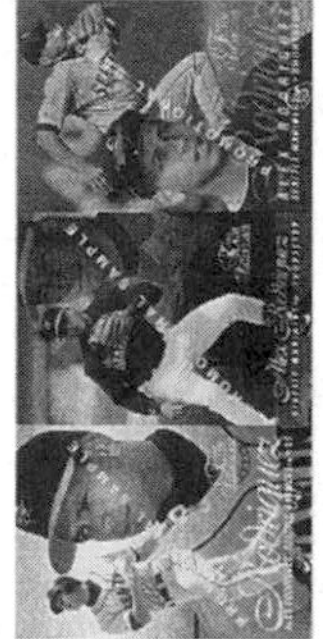

The concept of Flair Showcase's Style-Grace-Showcase set composition is debuted on this 7-1/2" x 3-1/2" strip featuring three cards of Alex Rodriguez. The cards are overprinted in gold on front and black on back with "PROMOTIONAL SAMPLE".

	MT
Complete Strip (3):	10.00
ROW0 Alex Rodriguez (Showcase)	
ROW1 Alex Rodriguez (Grace)	
ROW2 Alex Rodriguez (Style)	

1997 Flair Showcase Row 2 (Style)

The 540-card 1997 Flair issue is actually a 180-player set printed in three different versions, all on a super-glossy thick stock. The most common version, Style, is designated Row 2 on back. Fronts have a color action photo with a black-and-white portrait image in the background, all printed on silver foil. Cards #1-60 are designated "Showtime" on back; #61-120 are "Showpiece" and #121-180 are labeled "Showstopper" and were inserted in varying ratios: Showtime - 1.5:1; Showpiece 1:1.5 and Showstopper 1:1. Cards were sold exclusively at hobby shops in five-card packs for $4.99.

		MT
Complete Set (180):		40.00
Common Style/Showtime (1-60):		.20
Common Style/Showpiece (61-120):		.35
Common Style/Showstopper (121-180):		.25
A-Rod Glove Exchange:		250.00
Pack (5):		4.00
Wax Box (24):		90.00
1	Andruw Jones	1.50
2	Derek Jeter	3.00
3	Alex Rodriguez	4.00
4	Paul Molitor	1.00
5	Jeff Bagwell	1.50
6	Scott Rolen	1.50
7	Kenny Lofton	1.00
8	Cal Ripken Jr.	4.00
9	Brady Anderson	.20
10	Chipper Jones	3.00
11	Todd Greene	.20
12	Todd Walker	.50
13	Billy Wagner	.30
14	Craig Biggio	.75
15	Kevin Orie	.20
16	Hideo Nomo	.50
17	Kevin Appier	.20
18	*Bubba Trammell*	1.00
19	Juan Gonzalez	1.50
20	Randy Johnson	1.00
21	Roger Clemens	1.50
22	Johnny Damon	.25
23	Ryne Sandberg	1.00
24	Ken Griffey Jr.	5.00
25	Barry Bonds	1.50
26	Nomar Garciaparra	3.00
27	Vladimir Guerrero	2.00
28	Ron Gant	.20
29	Joe Carter	.20
30	Tim Salmon	.75
31	Mike Piazza	3.00
32	Barry Larkin	.75
33	Manny Ramirez	1.50
34	Sammy Sosa	3.00
35	Frank Thomas	1.50
36	Melvin Nieves	.20
37	Tony Gwynn	2.50
38	Gary Sheffield	.50
39	Darin Erstad	1.50
40	Ken Caminiti	.50
41	Jermaine Dye	.20
42	Mo Vaughn	1.25
43	Raul Mondesi	.50
44	Greg Maddux	3.00
45	Chuck Knoblauch	.75
46	Andy Pettitte	.75
47	Deion Sanders	.50
48	Albert Belle	1.00
49	Jamey Wright	.20
50	Rey Ordonez	.35
51	Bernie Williams	1.00
52	Mark McGwire	6.00
53	Mike Mussina	1.00
54	Bob Abreu	.25
55	Reggie Sanders	.20
56	Brian Jordan	.20
57	Ivan Rodriguez	1.50
58	Roberto Alomar	1.00
59	Tim Naehring	.20
60	Edgar Renteria	.25
61	Dean Palmer	.35
62	Benito Santiago	.35
63	David Cone	.50
64	Carlos Delgado	1.00
65	*Brian Giles*	3.00
66	Alex Ochoa	.35
67	Rondell White	.35
68	Robin Ventura	.50
69	Eric Karros	.35
70	Jose Valentin	.35
71	Rafael Palmeiro	.75
72	Chris Snopek	.35
73	David Justice	.75
74	Tom Glavine	.50
75	Rudy Pemberton	.35
76	Larry Walker	1.00
77	Jim Thome	1.00
78	Charles Johnson	.35
79	Dante Powell	.35
80	Derrek Lee	.35
81	Jason Kendall	.35
82	Todd Hollandsworth	.35
83	Bernard Gilkey	.35
84	Mel Rojas	.35
85	Dmitri Young	.35
86	Bret Boone	.35
87	Pat Hentgen	.35
88	Bobby Bonilla	.35
89	John Wetteland	.35
90	Todd Hundley	.25
91	Wilton Guerrero	.25
92	Geronimo Berroa	.35
93	Al Martin	.35
94	Danny Tartabull	.35
95	Brian McRae	.35
96	Steve Finley	.35
97	Todd Stottlemyre	.35
98	John Smoltz	.40
99	Matt Williams	1.00
100	Eddie Murray	1.00
101	Henry Rodriguez	.35
102	Marty Cordova	.35
103	Juan Guzman	.35
104	Chili Davis	.35
105	Eric Young	.35
106	Jeff Abbott	.35
107	Shannon Stewart	.35
108	Rocky Coppinger	.35
109	Jose Canseco	1.00
110	Dante Bichette	.75
111	Dwight Gooden	.35
112	Scott Brosius	.35
113	Steve Avery	.35
114	Andres Galarraga	.75
115	Sandy Alomar Jr.	.40
116	Ray Lankford	.35
117	Jorge Posada	.35
118	Ryan Klesko	.40
119	Jay Buhner	.50
120	Jose Guillen	.40
121	Paul O'Neill	.50
122	Jimmy Key	.25
123	Hal Morris	.25
124	Travis Fryman	.25
125	Jim Edmonds	.25
126	Jeff Cirillo	.25
127	Fred McGriff	.50
128	Alan Benes	.35
129	Derek Bell	.25
130	Tony Graffanino	.25
131	Shawn Green	.75
132	Denny Neagle	.25
133	Alex Fernandez	.25
134	Mickey Morandini	.25
135	Royce Clayton	.25
136	Jose Mesa	.25
137	Edgar Martinez	.25
138	Curt Schilling	.50
139	Lance Johnson	.25
140	Andy Benes	.25
141	Charles Nagy	.25
142	Mariano Rivera	.50
143	Mark Wohlers	.25
144	Ken Hill	.25
145	Jay Bell	.25
146	Bob Higginson	.40
147	Mark Grudzielanek	.25
148	Ray Durham	.25
149	John Olerud	.50
150	Joey Hamilton	.25
151	Trevor Hoffman	.30
152	Dan Wilson	.25
153	J.T. Snow	.25
154	Marquis Grissom	.40
155	Yamil Benitez	.25
156	Rusty Greer	.25
157	Darryl Kile	.25
158	Ismael Valdes	.25
159	Jeff Conine	.25
160	Darren Daulton	.25
161	Chan Ho Park	.25
162	Troy Percival	.25
163	Wade Boggs	.75
164	Dave Nilsson	.25
165	Vinny Castilla	.25
166	Kevin Brown	.40
167	Dennis Eckersley	.25
168	Wendell Magee Jr.	.25
169	John Jaha	.25
170	Garret Anderson	.25
171	Jason Giambi	.25
172	Mark Grace	.50
173	Tony Clark	.75
174	Moises Alou	.40
175	Brett Butler	.25
176	Cecil Fielder	.25
177	Chris Widger	.25
178	Doug Drabek	.25
179	Ellis Burks	.25
180	Shigetosi Hasegawa	.25

1997 Flair Showcase Row 1 (Grace)

The second level of '97 Flair scarcity is represented by the Row 1/Grace cards (so designated on back). These are visually differentiated on front by the use of a full background to the action photo, and the addition of a color portrait. Row 1/Grace cards are further broken down by their designation on back as: "Showstopper" (#1-60; seeded 1:2.5 packs), "Showtime" (#61-120; 1:2) and "Showpiece" (#121-180; 1:3) with varying insertion rates as shown.

	MT
Complete Set (180):	150.00
Common Showstopper (1-60):	.50
Stars:	2X
Common Showtime (#61-120):	.35
Stars:	1X
Common Showpiece (#121-180):	.75
Stars:	2X

(See 1997 Flair Showcase Row 2 for checklist and base card values.)

1997 Flair Showcase Row 0 (Showcase)

The scarcest level of '97 Flair is the Row 0/Showcase cards (so designated on front and back). These are identifiable on front by the use of a color portrait in the foreground, with a large action photo behind, printed on a gold-flecked metallic background. Row 0/Showcase cards are further broken down by their designation on back as: "Showpiece" (#1-60; seeded 1:24 packs), "Showstopper" (#61-120; 1:12) and "Showtime" (#121-180; 1:5) with varying insertion rates as shown.

	MT
Complete Set (180):	950.00
Common Showpiece (1-60):	3.00
Stars:	10X
Common Showstopper (61-120):	1.50
Stars:	4X
Common Showtime (121-180):	.50
Stars:	3X

(See 1997 Flair Showcase Row 2 for checklist and base card values.)

1997 Flair Showcase Legacy Collection

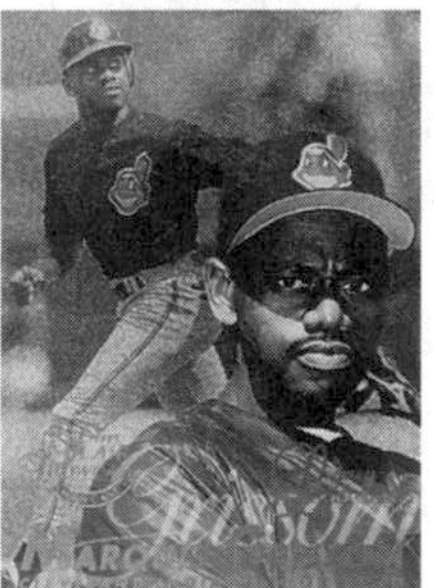

This 540-card parallel set is printed on matte-finish stock rather than the high-gloss of the regular cards. Front graphic highlights are in blue foil, as is the serial number on back from within each card's edition of just 100. Stated odds of insertion are one per 30 packs. Because all Legacies are printed in identical numbers, there is no premium for cards of different rows.

	MT
Common Player:	10.00
Stars:	25-50X

(See 1997 Flair Showcase Row 2 for checkist and base card values.)

1997 Flair Showcase Legacy Masterpiece

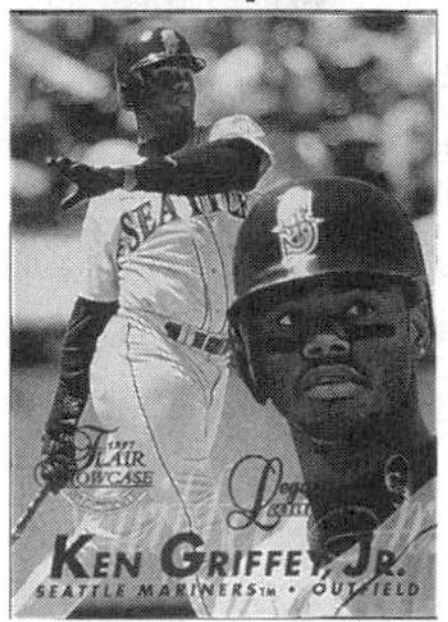

The insert card chase reached its inevitable zenith with the creation of this series of one-of-a-kind inserts. Each of the 180 players' three cards (Row 2/Style, Row 1/Grace, Row 0/Showcase) in the '97 Flair Legacy Collection was also produced in an edition of one card and inserted at a rate of about one per 3,000 packs. Instead of the blue metallic foil on front and highlights on back of the regular Legacy cards, the one-of-a-kind cards are highlighted in purple and carry a notation on back that they are "The Only 1 of 1 Masterpiece". Because of the unique nature of each card, value depends solely on demand, thus presentation of meaningful "catalog" values is not possible.

	MT
Common Player:	100.00
Stars:	15x to 25x

(Values undertermined)

1997 Flair Showcase Diamond Cuts

This 20-card insert, found 1:20 packs, features a die-cut design with an action photo of the player appearing above a baseball diamond in the lower background.

		MT
Complete Set (20):		130.00
Common Player:		2.50
1	Jeff Bagwell	7.50
2	Albert Belle	5.00
3	Ken Caminiti	2.50
4	Juan Gonzalez	5.00
5	Ken Griffey Jr.	15.00
6	Tony Gwynn	9.00
7	Todd Hundley	2.50
8	Andruw Jones	5.00
9	Chipper Jones	12.00
10	Greg Maddux	10.00
11	Mark McGwire	15.00
12	Mike Piazza	12.00
13	Derek Jeter	12.00
14	Manny Ramirez	5.00
15	Cal Ripken Jr.	12.50
16	Alex Rodriguez	12.00
17	Frank Thomas	7.50
18	Mo Vaughn	4.00
19	Bernie Williams	4.00
20	Matt Williams	2.50

1997 Flair Showcase Hot Gloves

Inserted 1:90 packs, Hot Gloves features 15 cards with a die-cut "flaming glove" design printed in thermally active inks and saluting some of baseball's best defensive players.

		MT
Complete Set (15):		275.00
Common Player:		5.00
1	Roberto Alomar	10.00
2	Barry Bonds	12.50
3	Juan Gonzalez	15.00
4	Ken Griffey Jr.	50.00
5	Marquis Grissom	5.00
6	Derek Jeter	30.00
7	Chipper Jones	30.00
8	Barry Larkin	5.00
9	Kenny Lofton	10.00
10	Greg Maddux	25.00
11	Mike Piazza	30.00
12	Cal Ripken Jr.	40.00
13	Alex Rodriguez	40.00
14	Ivan Rodriguez	12.50
15	Frank Thomas	25.00

1997 Flair Showcase Wave of the Future

This insert focuses on some of the up-and-coming young stars in the game. Cards were seeded 1:4 packs. A large ocean wave makes up the background of each card front.

		MT
Complete Set (27):		45.00
Common Player:		1.00
1	Todd Greene	1.25
2	Andruw Jones	5.00
3	Randall Simon	1.00
4	Wady Almonte	1.00
5	Pat Cline	1.50
6	Jeff Abbott	1.00
7	Justin Towle	1.00
8	Richie Sexson	1.50
9	Bubba Trammell	2.50
10	Bob Abreu	1.50
11	David Arias (last name actually Ortiz)	2.00
12	Todd Walker	3.00
13	Orlando Cabrera	1.00
14	Vladimir Guerrero	6.00
15	Ricky Ledee	3.00
16	Jorge Posada	2.00
17	Ruben Rivera	1.25
18	Scott Spiezio	1.00
19	Scott Rolen	5.00
20	Emil Brown	1.00
21	Jose Guillen	2.50
22	T.J. Staton	1.00
23	Elieser Marrero	1.00
24	Fernando Tatis	2.50
25	Ryan Jones	1.00
WF1	Hideki Irabu	3.00
WF2	Jose Cruz Jr.	2.50

1998 Flair Showcase Promo Strip

Each of the Row 0, 1, 2 and 3 variations of Cal Ripken's cards are featured on this 10" x 3-1/2" promo strip. The front of each card has "PROMOTIONAL SAMPLE" printed diagonally in gold; on the back the notice is printed in black-and-white.

	MT
Complete Promo Strip: Cal Ripken Jr.	10.00

1998 Flair Showcase Row 3

Row 3, or Flair, cards are considered the base cards of '98 Showcase. They feature a close-up black-and-white portrait photo in the background and an action shot in front, overprinted on a silver-foil background. Flair/Showtime (#1-30) cards are inserted 1:.9 packs, Flair/Showstopper (#31-60) are found 1:1.1 packs, Flair/Showdown (#61-90) cards are inserted 1:1.5 packs and Flair/Showdown (#91-120) cards are inserted 1:2 packs.

		MT
Complete Set (120):		30.00
Common Player (1-30):		.25
Common Player (31-60):		.25
Common Player (61-90):		.35
Common Player (91-120):		.45
1	Ken Griffey Jr.	6.00
2	Travis Lee	1.25
3	Frank Thomas	3.00
4	Ben Grieve	2.00
5	Nomar Garciaparra	4.00
6	Jose Cruz Jr.	.40
7	Alex Rodriguez	4.00
8	Cal Ripken Jr.	5.00
9	Mark McGwire	8.00
10	Chipper Jones	3.00
11	Paul Konerko	1.00
12	Todd Helton	1.50
13	Greg Maddux	4.00
14	Derek Jeter	4.00
15	Jaret Wright	1.00
16	Livan Hernandez	.25
17	Mike Piazza	4.00
18	Juan Encarnacion	.25
19	Tony Gwynn	3.00
20	Scott Rolen	2.00
21	Roger Clemens	3.00
22	Tony Clark	1.00
23	Albert Belle	1.50
24	Mo Vaughn	1.50
25	Andruw Jones	1.50
26	Jason Dickson	.25
27	Fernando Tatis	.50
28	Ivan Rodriguez	1.50
29	Ricky Ledee	.50
30	Darin Erstad	1.50
31	Brian Rose	.25
32	*Magglio Ordonez*	5.00
33	Larry Walker	1.00
34	Bobby Higginson	.25
35	Chili Davis	.25
36	Barry Bonds	1.50
37	Vladimir Guerrero	2.50
38	Jeff Bagwell	1.50
39	Kenny Lofton	1.50
40	Ryan Klesko	.50
41	Mike Cameron	.25
42	Charles Johnson	.25
43	Andy Pettitte	1.00
44	Juan Gonzalez	1.50
45	Tim Salmon	1.00
46	Hideki Irabu	.75
47	Paul Molitor	1.00
48	Edgar Renteria	.25
49	Manny Ramirez	2.00
50	Jim Edmonds	.50
51	Bernie Williams	1.00
52	Roberto Alomar	1.00

53	David Justice	.50
54	Rey Ordonez	.25
55	Ken Caminiti	.50
56	Jose Guillen	.50
57	Randy Johnson	1.00
58	Brady Anderson	.25
59	Hideo Nomo	.50
60	Tino Martinez	1.00
61	John Smoltz	.50
62	Joe Carter	.50
63	Matt Williams	.50
64	Robin Ventura	.50
65	Barry Larkin	.50
66	Dante Bichette	.75
67	Travis Fryman	.35
68	Gary Sheffield	.75
69	Eric Karros	.40
70	Matt Stairs	.35
71	Al Martin	.35
72	Jay Buhner	.60
73	Ray Lankford	.35
74	Carlos Delgado	.50
75	Edgardo Alfonzo	.50
76	Rondell White	.50
77	Chuck Knoblauch	.75
78	Raul Mondesi	.50
79	Johnny Damon	.35
80	Matt Morris	.35
81	Tom Glavine	.50
82	Kevin Brown	.50
83	Garret Anderson	.35
84	Mike Mussina	1.00
85	Pedro Martinez	1.00
86	Craig Biggio	.50
87	Darryl Kile	.35
88	Rafael Palmeiro	.75
89	Jim Thome	1.00
90	Andres Galarraga	1.00
91	Sammy Sosa	4.00
92	Willie Greene	.45
93	Vinny Castilla	.60
94	Justin Thompson	.45
95	Jeff King	.45
96	Jeff Cirillo	.45
97	Mark Grudzielanek	.45
98	Brad Radke	.45
99	John Olerud	.75
100	Curt Schilling	.60
101	Steve Finley	.45
102	J.T. Snow	.45
103	Edgar Martinez	.45
104	Wilson Alvarez	.45
105	Rusty Greer	.45
106	Pat Hentgen	.45
107	David Cone	.50
108	Fred McGriff	.50
109	Jason Giambi	.45
110	Tony Womack	.45
111	Bernard Gilkey	.45
112	Alan Benes	.45
113	Mark Grace	.50
114	Reggie Sanders	.45
115	Moises Alou	.50
116	John Jaha	.45
117	Henry Rodriguez	.45
118	Dean Palmer	.45
119	Mike Lieberthal	.50
120	Shawn Estes	.45

1998 Flair Showcase Row 2

Row 2, or Style (as they are designated on front) cards in Flair Showcase are the second easiest type of card to pull from packs. Fronts are similar to Row 3 base cards, but include the entire background of the action photo and have a color portrait photo. Cards #1-30 are inserted one per three packs, #31-60 are found 1:2.5 packs, #61-90 cards are 1:4 and #91-120 are inserted one per three packs.

	MT
Complete Set (120):	75.00
Common Player (1-30):	.50
Stars:	2X
Common Player (31-60):	.50
Stars:	1.5X
Common Player (61-90):	.75
Stars:	2X
Common Player (91-120):	.75
Stars:	1.5X

(See 1998 Flair Showcase Row 3 for checklist and base card values.)

1998 Flair Showcase Row 1

Row 1, also referred to as Grace, was the second most difficult type of card to pull from Flair Showcase. The front design has an action photo overprinted on a large portrait which is printed on a rainbow metallic-foil background. Cards #1-30 are seeded one per 16 packs, #31-60 are 1:24, #61-90 are 1:6 and #91-120 are 1:10.

	MT
Complete Set (1-120):	400.00
Commons (1-30):	2.00
Stars:	4X
Commons (31-60):	2.50
Stars:	6X
Commons (61-90):	.75
Stars:	2X
Commons (91-120):	1.50
Stars:	3X

(See 1998 Flair Showcase Row 3 for checklist and base cards values.)

1998 Flair Showcase Row 0

Row 0 is the most difficult of the four tiers to obtain from packs. Two action photos are combined on a horizontal format with one in a prismatic foil background. The first 30 cards are serially numbered to 250, cards #30-60 are numbered to 500, #61-90 are numbered to 1,000 and #91-120 are numbered within an edition of 2,000.

	MT
Complete Set (120):	1500.
Common Player (1-30):	5.00
Stars:	20X
Common Player (31-60):	3.00
Stars:	15X
Common Player (61-90):	2.00
Stars:	9X
Common Player (91-120):	1.00
Stars:	5X

(See 1998 Flair Showcase Row 3 for checklist and base card values.)

1998 Flair Showcase Legacy Collection

Legacy Collection parallels all 480 cards in the Flair Showcase set. Each Legacy Collection card displays the player's name in black plate laminated on the back, with the card's sequential numbering to 100 in gold foil.

	MT
Common Player:	6.00
Stars:	15-25X

(See 1998 Flair Showcase Row 3 for checklist and base card values.)

1998 Flair Showcase Legacy Masterpiece

Each of the 120 players' four cards (Rows 3, 2, 1 and 0) in the '98 Flair Legacy Collection was also produced in an edition of one card and inserted at a rate of about one per 3,000 packs. The one-of-a-kind cards carry a notation on back: "The Only 1 of 1 Masterpiece". With supply a fixed quantity, value depends on demand at any particular time, thus it is not possible to present meaningful "catalog" values.

	MT
Common Player:	100.00

(Values undetermined)

1998 Flair Showcase Perfect 10

Perfect 10 features the game's most popular players on a silk-screen technology design. The cards were serial numbered to 10 on the back and were inserted into packs of Flair Showcase.

		MT
Complete Set (10):		6000.
Common Player:		150.00
1	Ken Griffey Jr.	1250.
2	Cal Ripken Jr.	1000.
3	Frank Thomas	450.00
4	Mike Piazza	750.00
5	Greg Maddux	600.00
6	Nomar Garciaparra	750.00
7	Mark McGwire	1200.
8	Scott Rolen	150.00
9	Alex Rodriguez	1000.
10	Roger Clemens	300.00

1998 Flair Showcase Wave of the Future

Twelve up-and-coming players with hot minor league stats and Major League potential are displayed in Wave of the Future. The cards contain a clear acetate card inside a plastic covering that is filled with vegetable oil and glitter. These were inserted one per 20 packs and are numbered with a "WF" prefix.

	MT
Complete Set (12):	25.00
Common Player:	1.00
WF1 Travis Lee	10.00
WF2 Todd Helton	6.00
WF3 Ben Grieve	7.50
WF4 Juan Encarnacion	1.00
WF5 Brad Fullmer	3.00
WF6 Ruben Rivera	1.00
WF7 Paul Konerko	2.50
WF8 Derrek Lee	1.00
WF9 Mike Lowell	1.00
WF10Magglio Ordonez	2.00
WF11Rich Butler	2.00
WF12Eli Marrero	1.00

1999 Flair Showcase Row 3 (Power)

Power is one of three tiers in 1999 in Showcase. The card front on this base-level version is rainbow holofoil including the large portrait photo in the background. In the foreground is a color action photo. Matte textured silver spot embossing is printed over the player's name and team at lower-right. All three Rows of Showcase can be found with three different back designs. Showtime presents traditional annual and carere stats; horizontally formatted Showpiece cards have a black-and-white player photo as a "Classic Matchup" of the player's stats to those of a past star. Showdown card backs have a color action photo on a brightly-colored wave-pattern background. A stat box at center offers career numbers broken-down into four unique categories like day-night, grass-turf, etc. Each of these three back-design levels of scarcity has a different advertised insertion rate. Within Row 3/Power, these vary only between one card in .9 packs, and one card in 1.2 packs, thus there is no practical value differential. Five-card packs of Flair Showcase had a $4.99 SRP.

		MT
Complete Set (144):		35.00
Common Player:		.25
Pack (5):		5.00
Wax Box (24):		105.00
1	Mark McGwire	6.00
2	Sammy Sosa	3.00
3	Ken Griffey Jr.	5.00
4	Chipper Jones	2.50
5	Ben Grieve	1.00
6	J.D. Drew	.50
7	Jeff Bagwell	1.25
8	Cal Ripken Jr.	4.00
9	Tony Gwynn	2.50
10	Nomar Garciaparra	3.00
11	Travis Lee	1.00
12	Troy Glaus	2.00
13	Mike Piazza	3.00
14	Alex Rodriguez	4.00
15	Kevin Brown	.50
16	Darin Erstad	1.00
17	Scott Rolen	1.50
18	*Micah Bowie*	.75
19	Juan Gonzalez	1.50
20	Kerry Wood	1.00
21	Roger Clemens	2.00
22	Derek Jeter	3.00
23	*Pat Burrell*	10.00
24	Tim Salmon	.75
25	Barry Bonds	1.25
26	*Roosevelt Brown*	1.00
27	Vladimir Guerrero	2.00
28	Randy Johnson	1.00
29	Mo Vaughn	1.00
30	Fernando Seguignol	.25
31	Greg Maddux	3.00
32	Tony Clark	.75
33	Eric Chavez	.50
34	Kris Benson	.25
35	Frank Thomas	2.00
36	Mario Encarnacion	.25
37	Gabe Kapler	1.25
38	Jeremy Giambi	.40
39	*Peter Tucci*	.75
40	Manny Ramirez	2.00
41	Albert Belle	1.25
42	Warren Morris	.25
43	Michael Barrett	1.00
44	Andruw Jones	1.25
45	Carlos Delgado	.75
46	Jaret Wright	.50
47	Juan Encarnacion	.40
48	Scott Hunter	.75
49	Tino Martinez	.75
50	Craig Biggio	.75
51	Jim Thome	.75
52	Vinny Castilla	.40
53	Tom Glavine	.40
54	Bob Higginson	.25
55	Moises Alou	.40
56	Robin Ventura	.25
57	Bernie Williams	1.00
58	Pedro J. Martinez	1.25
59	Greg Vaughn	.40
60	Ray Lankford	.25
61	Jose Canseco	1.00
62	Ivan Rodriguez	1.25
63	Shawn Green	.75
64	Rafael Palmeiro	.75
65	Ellis Burks	.25
66	Jason Kendall	.50
67	David Wells	.25
68	Rondell White	.40
69	Gary Sheffield	.40
70	Ken Caminiti	.25
71	Cliff Floyd	.25
72	Larry Walker	1.00
73	Bartolo Colon	.25
74	Barry Larkin	.75
75	Calvin Pickering	.25
76	Jim Edmonds	.25
77	Henry Rodriguez	.25
78	Roberto Alomar	1.00
79	Andres Galarraga	.75
80	Richie Sexson	.50
81	Todd Helton	1.50
82	Damion Easley	.25
83	Livan Hernandez	.25
84	Carlos Beltran	.40
85	Todd Hundley	.25
86	Todd Walker	.25
87	Scott Brosius	.25
88	Bob Abreu	.25
89	Corey Koskie	.25
90	Ruben Rivera	.25
91	Edgar Renteria	.25
92	Quinton McCracken	.25
93	Bernard Gilkey	.25
94	Shannon Stewart	.25
95	Dustin Hermanson	.25
96	Mike Caruso	.25
97	Alex Gonzalez	.25
98	Raul Mondesi	.40
99	David Cone	.50
100	Curt Schilling	.40
101	Brian Giles	.25
102	Edgar Martinez	.25
103	Rolando Arrojo	.25
104	Derek Bell	.25
105	Denny Neagle	.25
106	Marquis Grissom	.25
107	Bret Boone	.25
108	Mike Mussina	1.00
109	John Smoltz	.25
110	Brett Tomko	.25
111	David Justice	.50
112	Andy Pettitte	.40
113	Eric Karros	.25
114	Dante Bichette	.75
115	Jeromy Burnitz	.25
116	Paul Konerko	.25
117	Steve Finley	.25
118	Ricky Ledee	.50
119	Edgardo Alfonzo	.25
120	Dean Palmer	.25
121	Rusty Greer	.25
122	Luis Gonzalez	.25
123	Randy Winn	.25
124	Jeff Kent	.25
125	Doug Glanville	.25
126	Justin Thompson	.25
127	Bret Saberhagen	.25
128	Wade Boggs	.75
129	Al Leiter	.25
130	Paul O'Neill	.75
131	Chan Ho Park	.50
132	Johnny Damon	.25
133	Darryl Kile	.25
134	Reggie Sanders	.25
135	Kevin Millwood	.75
136	Charles Johnson	.25
137	Ray Durham	.25
138	Rico Brogna	.25
139	Matt Williams	.75
140	Sandy Alomar	.25
141	Jeff Cirillo	.25
142	Devon White	.25
143	Andy Benes	.25
144	Mike Stanley	.25

1999 Flair Showcase Row 2 (Passion)

The metallic-foil background in the second level of Flair Showcase - Row 2/Passion - has an action photo printed in front of large textured numerals representing the player's uniform number. In the foreground is another action shot. Backs have the same three designs as Row 3, but only vary in insertion rate from one card per 1.3 packs to one card per three packs.

	MT
Complete Set:	100.00
Common Player:	.25
Showdown (1-48):	2X
Showpiece (49-96):	1X
Showtime (97-144):	1X

(See 1999 Flair Showcase Row 3 for checklist and base card values.)

1999 Flair Showcase Row 1 (Showcase)

Showcase level - Row 1 - presents two portraits and an action photo and the player's uniform number on a platic laminate in a horizontal format. A gold-foil serial number is stamped into the upper-left corner in one of three levels of scarcity: Showpiece (#1-48) is limited to 1,500 numbered sets, Showtime (#49-96) is limited to 3,000 sets and Showdown (#97-144) is numbered to 6,000 sets.

	MT
Complete Set (144):	800.00
Common Showpiece (1-48):	2.00
Showpiece Stars:	7X
Common Showtime (49-96):	1.00
Showtime Stars:	5X
Common Showdown (97-144):	.75
Showdown Stars:	2X

(See 1999 Flair Showcase Row 1 for checklist and base card values.)

1999 Flair Showcase Legacy / Masterpiece

Each of the 432 total cards in Flair Showcase was also produced in a pair of extremely limited parallels. The blue-foil enhanced Legacy Collection cards are serially numbered within an edition of just 99. The presence of purple foil on front signifies a Legacy Masterpiece card, which is identified on back by the notation, "The Only 1 of 1 Masterpiece". Because of their unique nature, determination of a "book value" for Masterpiece cards is not possible.

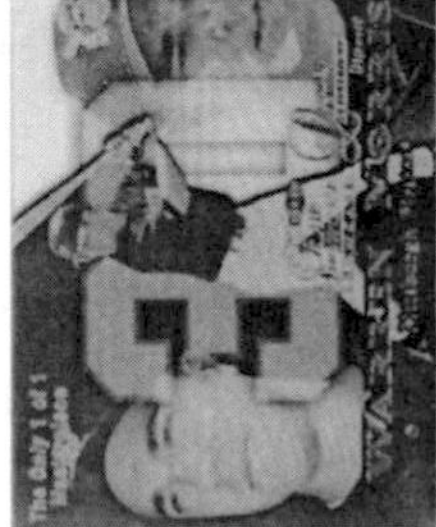

	MT
Common Legacy:	4.00
Legacy Stars:	15x to 20x
Common Masterpiece:	75.00

(See 1999 Flair Showcase for checklist.)

1999 Flair Showcase Measure of Greatness

This 15-card set captures baseball's top superstars who were closing in on milestones during the 1999 season. Each card is sequentially numbered to 500.

		MT
Complete Set (15):		350.00
Common Player:		10.00
Production 500 sets		
1	Roger Clemens	15.00
2	Nomar Garciaparra	20.00
3	Juan Gonzalez	15.00
4	Ken Griffey Jr.	50.00
5	Vladimir Guerrero	15.00
6	Tony Gwynn	15.00
7	Derek Jeter	25.00
8	Chipper Jones	25.00
9	Mark McGwire	50.00
10	Mike Piazza	25.00
11	Manny Ramirez	10.00
12	Cal Ripken Jr.	35.00
13	Alex Rodriguez	35.00
14	Sammy Sosa	25.00
15	Frank Thomas	10.00

1999 Flair Showcase Wave of the Future

This insert set spotlights young stars on the rise and is limited to 1,000 serial numbered sets.

		MT
Complete Set (15):		80.00
Common Player:		3.00
Production 1,000 sets		
1	Kerry Wood	5.00
2	Ben Grieve	5.00
3	J.D. Drew	6.00
4	Juan Encarnacion	4.00
5	Travis Lee	4.00
6	Todd Helton	10.00
7	Troy Glaus	12.00
8	Ricky Ledee	4.00
9	Eric Chavez	8.00
10	Ben Davis	3.00
11	George Lombard	3.00
12	Jeremy Giambi	3.00
13	Roosevelt Brown	4.00
14	Pat Burrell	25.00
15	Preston Wilson	3.00

1981 Fleer

For the first time in 18 years, Fleer issued a baseball card set featuring current players. The 660-card effort included numerous errors in the first print run which were subsequently corrected. The 2-1/2" x 3-1/2" cards are numbered by team in order of the previous season's finish. Card fronts feature a full-color photo inside a border which is color-coded by team. Backs are printed in black, grey and yellow on white stock and carry full player statistical information. The player's batting average or earned run average is located in a circle in the upper-right corner of the back. The complete set price in the checklist that follows does not include the higher priced variations.

		MT
Complete Set (660):		50.00
Common Player:		.08
Pack (17 - 2nd print):		1.75
Wax Box (38 - 2nd print)_:		33.00
1	Pete Rose	2.50
2	Larry Bowa	.10
3	Manny Trillo	.08
4	Bob Boone	.10
5a	Mike Schmidt (portrait)	2.00
5b	Mike Schmidt (batting)	2.00
6a	Steve Carlton ("Lefty" on front)	1.00
6b	Steve Carlton (Pitcher of the Year on front, date 1066 on back)	2.00
6c	Steve Carlton (Pitcher of the Year on front, date 1966 on back)	3.00
7a	Tug McGraw (Game Saver on front)	.50
7b	Tug McGraw (Pitcher on front)	.12
8	Larry Christenson	.08
9	Bake McBride	.08
10	Greg Luzinski	.15
11	Ron Reed	.08
12	Dickie Noles	.08
13	*Keith Moreland*	.08
14	*Bob Walk*	.10
15	Lonnie Smith	.08
16	Dick Ruthven	.08
17	Sparky Lyle	.10
18	Greg Gross	.08
19	Garry Maddox	.10
20	Nino Espinosa	.08
21	George Vukovich	.08
22	John Vukovich	.08
23	Ramon Aviles	.08
24a	Kevin Saucier (Ken Saucier on back)	.15
24b	Kevin Saucier (Kevin Saucier on back)	.50
25	Randy Lerch	.08
26	Del Unser	.08
27	Tim McCarver	.15
28a	George Brett (batting)	4.00
28b	George Brett (portrait)	1.00
29a	Willie Wilson (portrait)	.50
29b	Willie Wilson (batting)	.15
30	Paul Splittorff	.08
31	Dan Quisenberry	.15
32a	Amos Otis (batting)	.50
32b	Amos Otis (portrait)	.10
33	Steve Busby	.08
34	U.L. Washington	.08
35	Dave Chalk	.08
36	Darrell Porter	.08
37	Marty Pattin	.08
38	Larry Gura	.08
39	Renie Martin	.08
40	Rich Gale	.08
41a	Hal McRae (dark blue "Royals" on front)	.40
41b	Hal McRae (light blue "Royals" on front)	.10
42	Dennis Leonard	.08
43	Willie Aikens	.08
44	Frank White	.08
45	Clint Hurdle	.08
46	John Wathan	.08
47	Pete LaCock	.08
48	Rance Mulliniks	.08
49	Jeff Twitty	.08
50	Jamie Quirk	.08
51	Art Howe	.08
52	Ken Forsch	.08
53	Vern Ruhle	.08
54	Joe Niekro	.12
55	Frank LaCorte	.08
56	J.R. Richard	.10
57	Nolan Ryan	8.00
58	Enos Cabell	.08
59	Cesar Cedeno	.12
60	Jose Cruz	.12
61	Bill Virdon	.08
62	Terry Puhl	.08
63	Joaquin Andujar	.08
64	Alan Ashby	.08
65	Joe Sambito	.08
66	Denny Walling	.08
67	Jeff Leonard	.08
68	Luis Pujols	.08
69	Bruce Bochy	.08
70	Rafael Landestoy	.08
71	*Dave Smith*	.08
72	*Danny Heep*	.08
73	Julio Gonzalez	.08
74	Craig Reynolds	.08
75	Gary Woods	.08
76	Dave Bergman	.08
77	Randy Niemann	.08
78	Joe Morgan	.75
79a	Reggie Jackson (portrait)	4.00
79b	Reggie Jackson (batting)	2.00
80	Bucky Dent	.10
81	Tommy John	.20
82	Luis Tiant	.12
83	Rick Cerone	.08
84	Dick Howser	.08
85	Lou Piniella	.12
86	Ron Davis	.08
87a	Graig Nettles (Craig on back)	10.00
87b	Graig Nettles (Graig on back)	.15
88	Ron Guidry	.15
89	Rich Gossage	.10
90	Rudy May	.08
91	Gaylord Perry	.75
92	Eric Soderholm	.08
93	Bob Watson	.08
94	Bobby Murcer	.10
95	Bobby Brown	.08
96	Jim Spencer	.08
97	Tom Underwood	.08
98	Oscar Gamble	.08
99	Johnny Oates	.08
100	Fred Stanley	.08
101	Ruppert Jones	.08
102	Dennis Werth	.08
103	Joe Lefebvre	.08
104	Brian Doyle	.08
105	Aurelio Rodriguez	.08
106	Doug Bird	.08
107	Mike Griffin	.08
108	Tim Lollar	.08
109	Willie Randolph	.08
110	Steve Garvey	.40
111	Reggie Smith	.10
112	Don Sutton	.45
113	Burt Hooton	.08
114a	Davy Lopes (Davey) (no finger on back)	.08
114b	Davy Lopes (Davey) (small finger on back)	1.00
115	Dusty Baker	.10
116	Tom Lasorda	.45
117	Bill Russell	.12
118	Jerry Reuss	.08
119	Terry Forster	.08
120a	Bob Welch (Bob on back)	.10
120b	Bob Welch (Robert)	.50
121	Don Stanhouse	.08
122	Rick Monday	.08
123	Derrel Thomas	.08
124	Joe Ferguson	.08
125	Rick Sutcliffe	.10
126a	Ron Cey (no finger on back)	.10
126b	Ron Cey (small finger on back)	1.00
127	Dave Goltz	.08
128	Jay Johnstone	.08
129	Steve Yeager	.08
130	Gary Weiss	.08
131	*Mike Scioscia*	.25
132	Vic Davalillo	.08
133	Doug Rau	.08
134	Pepe Frias	.08
135	Mickey Hatcher	.08
136	*Steve Howe*	.10
137	Robert Castillo	.08
138	Gary Thomasson	.08
139	Rudy Law	.08
140	*Fernando Valenzuela*	1.50
141	Manny Mota	.08
142	Gary Carter	.65
143	Steve Rogers	.08
144	Warren Cromartie	.08
145	Andre Dawson	1.00
146	Larry Parrish	.08
147	Rowland Office	.08
148	Ellis Valentine	.08
149	Dick Williams	.08
150	*Bill Gullickson*	.15
151	Elias Sosa	.08
152	John Tamargo	.08
153	Chris Speier	.08
154	Ron LeFlore	.08
155	Rodney Scott	.08
156	Stan Bahnsen	.08
157	Bill Lee	.08
158	Fred Norman	.08
159	Woodie Fryman	.08
160	Dave Palmer	.08
161	Jerry White	.08
162	Roberto Ramos	.08
163	John D'Acquisto	.08
164	Tommy Hutton	.08
165	*Charlie Lea*	.12
166	Scott Sanderson	.08

167 Ken Macha .08
168 Tony Bernazard .08
169 Jim Palmer 1.00
170 Steve Stone .08
171 Mike Flanagan .08
172 Al Bumbry .08
173 Doug DeCinces .08
174 Scott McGregor .08
175 Mark Belanger .08
176 Tim Stoddard .08
177a Rick Dempsey (no finger on front) .08
177b Rick Dempsey (small finger on front) 1.00
178 Earl Weaver .40
179 Tippy Martinez .08
180 Dennis Martinez .10
181 Sammy Stewart .08
182 Rich Dauer .08
183 Lee May .08
184 Eddie Murray 3.00
185 Benny Ayala .08
186 John Lowenstein .08
187 Gary Roenicke .08
188 Ken Singleton .10
189 Dan Graham .08
190 Terry Crowley .08
191 Kiko Garcia .08
192 Dave Ford .08
193 Mark Corey .08
194 Lenn Sakata .08
195 Doug DeCinces .08
196 Johnny Bench 1.50
197 Dave Concepcion .15
198 Ray Knight .10
199 Ken Griffey .12
200 Tom Seaver 1.50
201 Dave Collins .08
202 George Foster .12
203 Junior Kennedy .08
204 Frank Pastore .08
205 Dan Driessen .08
206 Hector Cruz .08
207 Paul Moskau .08
208 *Charlie Leibrandt* .25
209 Harry Spilman .08
210 *Joe Price* .08
211 Tom Hume .08
212 Joe Nolan .08
213 Doug Bair .08
214 Mario Soto .08
215a Bill Bonham (no finger on back) .08
215b Bill Bonham (small finger on back) 1.00
216a George Foster (Slugger on front) .25
216b George Foster (Outfield on front) .20
217 Paul Householder .08
218 Ron Oester .08
219 Sam Mejias .08
220 Sheldon Burnside .08
221 Carl Yastrzemski 1.50
222 Jim Rice .15
223 Fred Lynn .15
224 Carlton Fisk 1.00
225 Rick Burleson .08
226 Dennis Eckersley .75
227 Butch Hobson .08
228 Tom Burgmeier .08
229 Garry Hancock .08
230 Don Zimmer .08
231 Steve Renko .08
232 Dwight Evans .15
233 Mike Torrez .08
234 Bob Stanley .08
235 Jim Dwyer .08
236 Dave Stapleton .08
237 Glenn Hoffman .08
238 Jerry Remy .08
239 Dick Drago .08
240 Bill Campbell .08
241 Tony Perez .20
242 Phil Niekro .75
243 Dale Murphy .75
244 Bob Horner .12
245 Jeff Burroughs .08
246 Rick Camp .08
247 Bob Cox .10
248 Bruce Benedict .08
249 Gene Garber .08
250 Jerry Royster .08
251a Gary Matthews (no finger on back) .08
251b Gary Matthews (small finger on back) 1.00
252 Chris Chambliss .08
253 Luis Gomez .08
254 Bill Nahorodny .08
255 Doyle Alexander .08
256 Brian Asselstine .08
257 Biff Pocoroba .08
258 Mike Lum .08
259 Charlie Spikes .08
260 Glenn Hubbard .08
261 Tommy Boggs .08
262 Al Hrabosky .08
263 Rick Matula .08
264 Preston Hanna .08
265 Larry Bradford .08
266 *Rafael Ramirez* .08
267 Larry McWilliams .08
268 Rod Carew 1.50
269 Bobby Grich .10
270 Carney Lansford .08
271 Don Baylor .15
272 Joe Rudi .08
273 Dan Ford .08
274 Jim Fregosi .08
275 Dave Frost .08
276 Frank Tanana .08
277 Dickie Thon .08
278 Jason Thompson .08
279 Rick Miller .08
280 Bert Campaneris .08
281 Tom Donohue .08
282 Brian Downing .08
283 Fred Patek .08
284 Bruce Kison .08
285 Dave LaRoche .08
286 Don Aase .08
287 Jim Barr .08
288 Alfredo Martinez .08
289 Larry Harlow .08
290 Andy Hassler .08
291 Dave Kingman .12
292 Bill Buckner .12
293 Rick Reuschel .08
294 Bruce Sutter .08
295 Jerry Martin .08
296 Scot Thompson .08
297 Ivan DeJesus .08
298 Steve Dillard .08
299 Dick Tidrow .08
300 Randy Martz .08
301 Lenny Randle .08
302 Lynn McGlothen .08
303 Cliff Johnson .08
304 Tim Blackwell .08
305 Dennis Lamp .08
306 Bill Caudill .08
307 Carlos Lezcano .08
308 Jim Tracy .08
309 Doug Capilla .08
310 Willie Hernandez .08
311 Mike Vail .08
312 Mike Krukow .08
313 Barry Foote .08
314 Larry Biittner .08
315 Mike Tyson .08
316 Lee Mazzilli .08
317 John Stearns .08
318 Alex Trevino .08
319 Craig Swan .08
320 Frank Taveras .08
321 Steve Henderson .08
322 Neil Allen .08
323 Mark Bomback .08
324 Mike Jorgensen .08
325 Joe Torre .15
326 Elliott Maddox .08
327 Pete Falcone .08
328 Ray Burris .08
329 Claudell Washington .08
330 Doug Flynn .08
331 Joel Youngblood .08
332 Bill Almon .08
333 Tom Hausman .08
334 Pat Zachry .08
335 *Jeff Reardon* 2.00
336 *Wally Backman* .15
337 Dan Norman .08
338 Jerry Morales .08
339 Ed Farmer .08
340 Bob Molinaro .08
341 Todd Cruz .08
342a *Britt Burns* (no finger on front) .10
342b *Britt Burns* (small finger on front) 1.00
343 Kevin Bell .08
344 Tony LaRussa .12
345 Steve Trout .08
346 *Harold Baines* 4.00
347 Richard Wortham .08
348 Wayne Nordhagen .08
349 Mike Squires .08
350 Lamar Johnson .08
351 Rickey Henderson 6.00
352 Francisco Barrios .08
353 Thad Bosley .08
354 Chet Lemon .08
355 Bruce Kimm .08
356 *Richard Dotson* .08
357 Jim Morrison .08
358 Mike Proly .08
359 Greg Pryor .08
360 Dave Parker .15
361 Omar Moreno .08
362a Kent Tekulve (1071 Waterbury on back) .15
362b Kent Tekulve (1971 Waterbury on back) .50
363 Willie Stargell .75
364 Phil Garner .08
365 Ed Ott .08
366 Don Robinson .08
367 Chuck Tanner .08
368 Jim Rooker .08
369 Dale Berra .08
370 Jim Bibby .08
371 Steve Nicosia .08
372 Mike Easler .08
373 Bill Robinson .08
374 Lee Lacy .08
375 John Candelaria .08
376 Manny Sanguillen .08
377 Rick Rhoden .08
378 Grant Jackson .08
379 Tim Foli .08
380 *Rod Scurry* .08
381 Bill Madlock .10
382a Kurt Bevacqua (photo reversed, backwards "P" on cap) .15
382b Kurt Bevacqua (correct photo) .50
383 Bert Blyleven .08
384 Eddie Solomon .08
385 Enrique Romo .08
386 John Milner .08
387 Mike Hargrove .08
388 Jorge Orta .08
389 Toby Harrah .08
390 Tom Veryzer .08
391 Miguel Dilone .08
392 Dan Spillner .08
393 Jack Brohamer .08
394 Wayne Garland .08
395 Sid Monge .08
396 Rick Waits .08
397 *Joe Charboneau* .25
398 Gary Alexander .08
399 Jerry Dybzinski .08
400 Mike Stanton .08
401 Mike Paxton .08
402 Gary Gray .08
403 Rick Manning .08
404 Bo Diaz .08
405 Ron Hassey .08
406 Ross Grimsley .08
407 Victor Cruz .08
408 Len Barker .08
409 Bob Bailor .08
410 Otto Velez .08
411 Ernie Whitt .08
412 Jim Clancy .08
413 Barry Bonnell .08
414 Dave Stieb .25
415 *Damaso Garcia* .10
416 John Mayberry .08
417 Roy Howell .08
418 *Dan Ainge* 5.00
419a Jesse Jefferson (Pirates on back) .10
419b Jesse Jefferson (Blue Jays on back) .50
420 Joey McLaughlin .08
421 *Lloyd Moseby* .10
422 Al Woods .08
423 Garth Iorg .08
424 Doug Ault .08
425 *Ken Schrom* .08
426 Mike Willis .08
427 Steve Braun .08
428 Bob Davis .08
429 Jerry Garvin .08
430 Alfredo Griffin .08
431 Bob Mattick .08
432 Vida Blue .12
433 Jack Clark .12
434 Willie McCovey 1.00
435 Mike Ivie .08
436a Darrel Evans (Darrel on front) .15
436b Darrell Evans (Darrell on front) .50
437 Terry Whitfield .08
438 Rennie Stennett .08
439 John Montefusco .08
440 Jim Wohlford .08
441 Bill North .08
442 Milt May .08
443 Max Venable .08
444 Ed Whitson .08
445 *Al Holland* .08
446 Randy Moffitt .08
447 Bob Knepper .08
448 Gary Lavelle .08
449 Greg Minton .08
450 Johnnie LeMaster .08
451 Larry Herndon .08
452 Rich Murray .08
453 Joe Pettini .08
454 Allen Ripley .08
455 Dennis Littlejohn .08
456 Tom Griffin .08
457 Alan Hargesheimer .08
458 Joe Strain .08
459 Steve Kemp .08
460 Sparky Anderson .12
461 Alan Trammell 1.00
462 Mark Fidrych .12
463 Lou Whitaker .45
464 Dave Rozema .08
465 Milt Wilcox .08
466 Champ Summers .08
467 Lance Parrish .20
468 Dan Petry .08
469 Pat Underwood .08
470 Rick Peters .08
471 Al Cowens .08
472 John Wockenfuss .08
473 Tom Brookens .08
474 Richie Hebner .08
475 Jack Morris .15
476 Jim Lentine .08
477 Bruce Robbins .08
478 Mark Wagner .08
479 Tim Corcoran .08
480a Stan Papi (Pitcher on front) .15
480b Stan Papi (Shortstop on front) .50
481 *Kirk Gibson* 3.00
482 Dan Schatzeder .08
483 Amos Otis .15
484 Dave Winfield 2.50
485 Rollie Fingers 1.00
486 Gene Richards .08
487 Randy Jones .08
488 Ozzie Smith 3.00
489 Gene Tenace .08
490 Bill Fahey .08
491 John Curtis .08
492 Dave Cash .08
493a Tim Flannery (photo reversed, batting righty) .15
493b Tim Flannery (photo correct, batting lefty) .50
494 Jerry Mumphrey .08
495 Bob Shirley .08
496 Steve Mura .08
497 Eric Rasmussen .08
498 Broderick Perkins .08
499 Barry Evans .08
500 Chuck Baker .08
501 *Luis Salazar* .08
502 Gary Lucas .08
503 Mike Armstrong .08
504 Jerry Turner .08
505 Dennis Kinney .08
506 Willy Montanez (Willie) .08
507 Gorman Thomas .08
508 Ben Oglivie .08
509 Larry Hisle .08

510 Sal Bando .08
511 Robin Yount 3.00
512 Mike Caldwell .08
513 Sixto Lezcano .08
514a Jerry Augustine (Billy Travers photo) .15
514b Billy Travers (correct name with photo) .50
515 Paul Molitor 3.00
516 Moose Haas .08
517 Bill Castro .08
518 Jim Slaton .08
519 Lary Sorensen .08
520 Bob McClure .08
521 Charlie Moore .08
522 Jim Gantner .08
523 Reggie Cleveland .08
524 Don Money .08
525 Billy Travers .08
526 Buck Martinez .08
527 Dick Davis .08
528 Ted Simmons .08
529 Garry Templeton .08
530 Ken Reitz .08
531 Tony Scott .08
532 Ken Oberkfell .08
533 Bob Sykes .08
534 Keith Smith .08
535 John Littlefield .08
536 Jim Kaat .20
537 Bob Forsch .08
538 Mike Phillips .08
539 *Terry Landrum* .08
540 *Leon Durham* .10
541 Terry Kennedy .08
542 George Hendrick .08
543 Dane Iorg .08
544 Mark Littell (photo actually Jeff Little) .08
545 Keith Hernandez .12
546 Silvio Martinez .08
547a Pete Vuckovich (photo actually Don Hood) .15
547b Don Hood (correct name with photo) .50
548 Bobby Bonds .10
549 Mike Ramsey .08
550 Tom Herr .08
551 Roy Smalley .08
552 Jerry Koosman .08
553 Ken Landreaux .08
554 John Castino .08
555 Doug Corbett .08
556 Bombo Rivera .08
557 Ron Jackson .08
558 Butch Wynegar .08
559 Hosken Powell .08
560 Pete Redfern .08
561 Roger Erickson .08
562 Glenn Adams .08
563 Rick Sofield .08
564 Geoff Zahn .08
565 Pete Mackanin .08
566 Mike Cubbage .08
567 Darrell Jackson .08
568 Dave Edwards .08
569 Rob Wilfong .08
570 Sal Butera .08
571 Jose Morales .08
572 Rick Langford .08
573 Mike Norris .08
574 Rickey Henderson 7.00
575 Tony Armas .08
576 Dave Revering .08
577 Jeff Newman .08
578 Bob Lacey .08
579 Brian Kingman (photo actually Alan Wirth) .08
580 Mitchell Page .08
581 Billy Martin .12
582 Rob Picciolo .08
583 Mike Heath .08
584 Mickey Klutts .08
585 Orlando Gonzalez .08
586 *Mike Davis* .08
587 Wayne Gross .08
588 Matt Keough .08
589 Steve McCatty .08
590 Dwayne Murphy .08
591 Mario Guerrero .08
592 Dave McKay .08
593 Jim Essian .08
594 Dave Heaverlo .08
595 Maury Wills .10
596 Juan Beniquez .08
597 Rodney Craig .08
598 Jim Anderson .08
599 Floyd Bannister .08
600 Bruce Bochte .08
601 Julio Cruz .08
602 Ted Cox .08
603 Dan Meyer .08
604 Larry Cox .08
605 Bill Stein .08
606 Steve Garvey .45
607 Dave Roberts .08
608 Leon Roberts .08
609 Reggie Walton .08
610 Dave Edler .08
611 Larry Milbourne .08
612 Kim Allen .08
613 Mario Mendoza .08
614 Tom Paciorek .08
615 Glenn Abbott .08
616 Joe Simpson .08
617 Mickey Rivers .08
618 Jim Kern .08
619 Jim Sundberg .08
620 Richie Zisk .08
621 Jon Matlack .08
622 Fergie Jenkins .75
623 Pat Corrales .08
624 Ed Figueroa .08
625 Buddy Bell .12
626 Al Oliver .15
627 Doc Medich .08
628 Bump Wills .08
629 Rusty Staub .10
630 Pat Putnam .08
631 John Grubb .08
632 Danny Darwin .08
633 Ken Clay .08
634 Jim Norris .08
635 John Butcher .08
636 Dave Roberts .08
637 Billy Sample .08
638 Carl Yastrzemski 1.25
639 Cecil Cooper .08
640 Mike Schmidt 2.00
641a Checklist 1-50 (41 Hal McRae) .10
641b Checklist 1-50 (41 Hal McRae Double Threat) .25
642 Checklist 51-109 .08
643 Checklist 110-168 .08
644a Checklist 169-220 (202 George Foster) .10
644b Checklist 169-220 (202 George Foster "Slugger") .25
(645a) Triple Threat (Larry Bowa, Pete Rose, Mike Schmidt) (no number on back) 2.00
645b Triple Threat (Pete Rose, Larry Bowa, Mike Schmidt) (number on back) 2.00
646 Checklist 221-267 .08
647 Checklist 268-315 .08
648 Checklist 316-359 .08
649 Checklist 360-408 .08
650 Reggie Jackson 2.50
651 Checklist 409-458 .08
652a Checklist 459-509 (483 Aurelio Lopez) .10
652b Checklist 459-506 (no 483) .25
653 Willie Wilson .25
654a Checklist 507-550 (514 Jerry Augustine) .10
654b Checklist 507-550 (514 Billy Travers) .25
655 George Brett 4.00
656 Checklist 551-593 .08
657 Tug McGraw .15
658 Checklist 594-637 .08
659a Checklist 640-660 (last number on front is 551) .10
659b Checklist 640-660 (last number on front is 483) .25
660a Steve Carlton (date 1066 on back) 1.00
660b Steve Carlton (date 1966 on back) 2.00

1981 Fleer Star Stickers

The 128-card 1981 Fleer Star Sticker set was designed to allow the card fronts to be peeled away from the cardboard backs. Fronts feature color photos with blue and yellow trim. Backs are identical in design to the regular 1981 Fleer set except for color and numbering. The set contains three unnumbered checklist cards whose fronts depict Reggie Jackson, George Brett and Mike Schmidt. The sticker-cards, which are the standard 2-1/2" x 3-1/2", were issued in gum wax packs.

	MT
Complete Set (128):	40.00
Common Player:	.15
Wax Box:	35.00

1 Steve Garvey .50
2 Ron LeFlore .13
3 Ron Cey .13
4 Dave Revering .13
5 Tony Armas .13
6 Mike Norris .13
7 Steve Kemp .13
8 Bruce Bochte .13
9 Mike Schmidt 5.00
10 Scott McGregor .13
11 Buddy Bell .13
12 Carney Lansford .13
13 Carl Yastrzemski 4.50
14 Ben Oglivie .13
15 Willie Stargell 3.75
16 Cecil Cooper .13
17 Gene Richards .13
18 Jim Kern .13
19 Jerry Koosman .13
20 Larry Bowa .13
21 Kent Tekulve .13
22 Dan Driessen .13
23 Phil Niekro 2.00
24 Dan Quisenberry .13
25 Dave Winfield 3.75
26 Dave Parker .40
27 Rick Langford .13
28 Amos Otis .13
29 Bill Buckner .15
30 Al Bumbry .13
31 Bake McBride .13
32 Mickey Rivers .13
33 Rick Burleson .13
34 Dennis Eckersley 1.00
35 Cesar Cedeno .13
36 Enos Cabell .13
37 Johnny Bench 4.50
38 Robin Yount 3.75
39 Mark Belanger .13
40 Rod Carew 3.75
41 George Foster .13
42 Lee Mazzilli .13
43 Triple Threat (Larry Bowa, Pete Rose, Mike Schmidt) 3.00
44 J.R. Richard .15
45 Lou Piniella .15
46 Ken Landreaux .13
47 Rollie Fingers 2.00
48 Joaquin Andujar .13
49 Tom Seaver 4.50
50 Bobby Grich .13
51 Jon Matlack .13
52 Jack Clark .13
53 Jim Rice .15
54 Rickey Henderson 4.00
55 Roy Smalley .13
56 Mike Flanagan .13
57 Steve Rogers .13
58 Carlton Fisk .60
59 Don Sutton .75
60 Ken Griffey .20
61 Burt Hooton .13
62 Dusty Baker .20
63 Vida Blue .13
64 Al Oliver .13
65 Jim Bibby .13
66 Tony Perez .25
67 Davy Lopes (Davey) .13
68 Bill Russell .15
69 Larry Parrish .13
70 Garry Maddox .13
71 Phil Garner .13
72 Graig Nettles .13
73 Gary Carter .60
74 Pete Rose 6.00
75 Greg Luzinski .20
76 Ron Guidry .15
77 Gorman Thomas .13
78 Jose Cruz .13
79 Bob Boone .20
80 Bruce Sutter .13
81 Chris Chambliss .13
82 Paul Molitor 3.75
83 Tug McGraw .13
84 Ferguson Jenkins 1.50
85 Steve Carlton 3.75
86 Miguel Dilone .13
87 Reggie Smith .13
88 Rick Cerone .13
89 Alan Trammell .75
90 Doug DeCinces .13
91 Sparky Lyle .13
92 Warren Cromartie .13
93 Rick Reuschel .13
94 Larry Hisle .13
95 Paul Splittorff .13
96 Manny Trillo .13
97 Frank White .13
98 Fred Lynn .20
99 Bob Horner .13
100 Omar Moreno .13
101 Dave Concepcion .13
102 Larry Gura .13
103 Ken Singleton .13
104 Steve Stone .13
105 Richie Zisk .13
106 Willie Wilson .13
107 Willie Randolph .13
108 Nolan Ryan 9.00
109 Joe Morgan 2.00
110 Bucky Dent .13
111 Dave Kingman .20
112 John Castino .13
113 Joe Rudi .13
114 Ed Farmer .13
115 Reggie Jackson 5.00
116 George Brett 5.00
117 Eddie Murray 2.00
118 Rich Gossage .20
119 Dale Murphy 1.00
120 Ted Simmons .13
121 Tommy John .25
122 Don Baylor .25
123 Andre Dawson 1.00
124 Jim Palmer 3.75
125 Garry Templeton .13
---- Checklist 1-42 (Reggie Jackson) 1.00
---- Checklist 43-83 (George Brett) 1.00
---- Checklist 84-125 (Mike Schmidt) 1.00

1982 Fleer

Fleer's 1982 set did not match the quality of the previous year's effort. Many of the card photos are blurred and have muddied backgrounds. The 2-1/2" x 3-1/2" cards feature color photos bordered by a frame which is color-coded by team. Backs are blue, white, and yellow and contain the player's team logo plus the logos of Major League Baseball and the Major League Baseball Players Association. Due to a lawsuit by Topps, Fleer was forced to issue the set with team logo stickers rather than gum. The complete set price does not include the higher priced variations.

	MT
Complete Set (660):	60.00
Common Player:	.08
Pack (15 - 2nd print):	3.25
Wax Box (36 - 2nd print):	82.00

No.	Player	MT
1	Dusty Baker	.10
2	Robert Castillo	.08
3	Ron Cey	.08
4	Terry Forster	.08
5	Steve Garvey	.20
6	Dave Goltz	.08
7	Pedro Guerrero	.08
8	Burt Hooton	.08
9	Steve Howe	.08
10	Jay Johnstone	.08
11	Ken Landreaux	.08
12	Davey Lopes	.08
13	*Mike Marshall*	.12
14	Bobby Mitchell	.08
15	Rick Monday	.08
16	*Tom Niedenfuer*	.08
17	*Ted Power*	.08
18	Jerry Reuss	.08
19	Ron Roenicke	.08
20	Bill Russell	.08
21	*Steve Sax*	.45
22	Mike Scioscia	.08
23	Reggie Smith	.08
24	*Dave Stewart*	2.00
25	Rick Sutcliffe	.08
26	Derrel Thomas	.08
27	Fernando Valenzuela	.15
28	Bob Welch	.08
29	Steve Yeager	.08
30	Bobby Brown	.08
31	Rick Cerone	.08
32	Ron Davis	.08
33	Bucky Dent	.10
34	Barry Foote	.08
35	George Frazier	.08
36	Oscar Gamble	.08
37	Rich Gossage	.10
38	Ron Guidry	.15
39	Reggie Jackson	1.50
40	Tommy John	.15
41	Rudy May	.08
42	Larry Milbourne	.08
43	Jerry Mumphrey	.08
44	Bobby Murcer	.10
45	*Gene Nelson*	.08
46	Graig Nettles	.10
47	Johnny Oates	.08
48	Lou Piniella	.12
49	Willie Randolph	.08
50	Rick Reuschel	.08
51	Dave Revering	.08
52	*Dave Righetti*	.45
53	Aurelio Rodriguez	.08
54	Bob Watson	.08
55	Dennis Werth	.08
56	Dave Winfield	2.00
57	Johnny Bench	1.00
58	Bruce Berenyi	.08
59	Larry Biittner	.08
60	Scott Brown	.08
61	Dave Collins	.08
62	Geoff Combe	.08
63	Dave Concepcion	.08
64	Dan Driessen	.08
65	Joe Edelen	.08
66	George Foster	.10
67	Ken Griffey	.12
68	Paul Householder	.08
69	Tom Hume	.08
70	Junior Kennedy	.08
71	Ray Knight	.10
72	Mike LaCoss	.08
73	Rafael Landestoy	.08
74	Charlie Leibrandt	.08
75	Sam Mejias	.08
76	Paul Moskau	.08
77	Joe Nolan	.08
78	Mike O'Berry	.08
79	Ron Oester	.08
80	Frank Pastore	.08
81	Joe Price	.08
82	Tom Seaver	1.00
83	Mario Soto	.08
84	Mike Vail	.08
85	Tony Armas	.08
86	Shooty Babitt	.08
87	Dave Beard	.08
88	Rick Bosetti	.08
89	Keith Drumright	.08
90	Wayne Gross	.08
91	Mike Heath	.08
92	Rickey Henderson	2.50
93	Cliff Johnson	.08
94	Jeff Jones	.08
95	Matt Keough	.08
96	Brian Kingman	.08
97	Mickey Klutts	.08
98	Rick Langford	.08
99	Steve McCatty	.08
100	Dave McKay	.08
101	Dwayne Murphy	.08
102	Jeff Newman	.08
103	Mike Norris	.08
104	Bob Owchinko	.08
105	Mitchell Page	.08
106	Rob Picciolo	.08
107	Jim Spencer	.08
108	Fred Stanley	.08
109	Tom Underwood	.08
110	Joaquin Andujar	.08
111	Steve Braun	.08
112	Bob Forsch	.08
113	George Hendrick	.08
114	Keith Hernandez	.08
115	Tom Herr	.08
116	Dane Iorg	.08
117	Jim Kaat	.10
118	Tito Landrum	.08
119	Sixto Lezcano	.08
120	Mark Littell	.08
121	John Martin	.08
122	Silvio Martinez	.08
123	Ken Oberkfell	.08
124	Darrell Porter	.08
125	Mike Ramsey	.08
126	Orlando Sanchez	.08
127	Bob Shirley	.08
128	Lary Sorensen	.08
129	Bruce Sutter	.08
130	Bob Sykes	.08
131	Garry Templeton	.08
132	Gene Tenace	.08
133	Jerry Augustine	.08
134	Sal Bando	.08
135	Mark Brouhard	.08
136	Mike Caldwell	.08
137	Reggie Cleveland	.08
138	Cecil Cooper	.08
139	Jamie Easterly	.08
140	Marshall Edwards	.08
141	Rollie Fingers	.65
142	Jim Gantner	.08
143	Moose Haas	.08
144	Larry Hisle	.08
145	Roy Howell	.08
146	Rickey Keeton	.08
147	Randy Lerch	.08
148	Paul Molitor	3.00
149	Don Money	.08
150	Charlie Moore	.08
151	Ben Oglivie	.08
152	Ted Simmons	.08
153	Jim Slaton	.08
154	Gorman Thomas	.08
155	Robin Yount	3.00
156	Pete Vukovich	.08
157	Benny Ayala	.08
158	Mark Belanger	.08
159	Al Bumbry	.08
160	Terry Crowley	.08
161	Rich Dauer	.08
162	Doug DeCinces	.08
163	Rick Dempsey	.08
164	Jim Dwyer	.08
165	Mike Flanagan	.08
166	Dave Ford	.08
167	Dan Graham	.08
168	Wayne Krenchicki	.08
169	John Lowenstein	.08
170	Dennis Martinez	.10
171	Tippy Martinez	.08
172	Scott McGregor	.08
173	Jose Morales	.08
174	Eddie Murray	3.00
175	Jim Palmer	.75
176	*Cal Ripken, Jr.*	50.00
177	Gary Roenicke	.08
178	Lenn Sakata	.08
179	Ken Singleton	.08
180	Sammy Stewart	.08
181	Tim Stoddard	.08
182	Steve Stone	.08
183	Stan Bahnsen	.08
184	Ray Burris	.08
185	Gary Carter	.25
186	Warren Cromartie	.08
187	Andre Dawson	.75
188	*Terry Francona*	.08
189	Woodie Fryman	.08
190	Bill Gullickson	.08
191	Grant Jackson	.08
192	Wallace Johnson	.08
193	Charlie Lea	.08
194	Bill Lee	.08
195	Jerry Manuel	.08
196	Brad Mills	.08
197	John Milner	.08
198	Rowland Office	.08
199	David Palmer	.08
200	Larry Parrish	.08
201	Mike Phillips	.08
202	Tim Raines	.75
203	Bobby Ramos	.08
204	Jeff Reardon	.12
205	Steve Rogers	.08
206	Scott Sanderson	.08
207	Rodney Scott (photo actually Tim Raines)	.10
208	Elias Sosa	.08
209	Chris Speier	.08
210	*Tim Wallach*	1.00
211	Jerry White	.08
212	Alan Ashby	.08
213	Cesar Cedeno	.12
214	Jose Cruz	.12
215	Kiko Garcia	.08
216	Phil Garner	.08
217	Danny Heep	.08
218	Art Howe	.08
219	Bob Knepper	.08
220	Frank LaCorte	.08
221	Joe Niekro	.12
222	Joe Pittman	.08
223	Terry Puhl	.08
224	Luis Pujols	.08
225	Craig Reynolds	.08
226	J.R. Richard	.10
227	Dave Roberts	.08
228	Vern Ruhle	.08
229	Nolan Ryan	9.00
230	Joe Sambito	.08
231	Tony Scott	.08
232	Dave Smith	.08
233	Harry Spilman	.08
234	Don Sutton	.50
235	Dickie Thon	.08
236	Denny Walling	.08
237	Gary Woods	.08
238	*Luis Aguayo*	.08
239	Ramon Aviles	.08
240	Bob Boone	.10
241	Larry Bowa	.08
242	Warren Brusstar	.08
243	Steve Carlton	1.00
244	Larry Christenson	.08
245	Dick Davis	.08
246	Greg Gross	.08
247	Sparky Lyle	.08
248	Garry Maddox	.08
249	Gary Matthews	.08
250	Bake McBride	.08
251	Tug McGraw	.10
252	Keith Moreland	.08
253	Dickie Noles	.08
254	Mike Proly	.08
255	Ron Reed	.08
256	Pete Rose	2.50
257	Dick Ruthven	.08
258	Mike Schmidt	3.00
259	Lonnie Smith	.08
260	Manny Trillo	.08
261	Del Unser	.08
262	George Vukovich	.08
263	Tom Brookens	.08
264	George Cappuzzello	.08
265	Marty Castillo	.08
266	Al Cowens	.08
267	Kirk Gibson	.12
268	Richie Hebner	.08
269	Ron Jackson	.08
270	Lynn Jones	.08
271	Steve Kemp	.08
272	*Rick Leach*	.12
273	Aurelio Lopez	.08
274	Jack Morris	.10
275	Kevin Saucier	.08
276	Lance Parrish	.10
277	Rick Peters	.08
278	Dan Petry	.08
279	David Rozema	.08
280	Stan Papi	.08
281	Dan Schatzeder	.08
282	Champ Summers	.08
283	Alan Trammell	.60
284	Lou Whitaker	.15
285	Milt Wilcox	.08
286	John Wockenfuss	.08
287	Gary Allenson	.08
288	Tom Burgmeier	.08
289	Bill Campbell	.08
290	Mark Clear	.08
291	Steve Crawford	.08
292	Dennis Eckersley	.75
293	Dwight Evans	.15
294	*Rich Gedman*	.20
295	Garry Hancock	.08
296	Glenn Hoffman	.08
297	Bruce Hurst	.08
298	Carney Lansford	.08
299	Rick Miller	.08
300	Reid Nichols	.08
301	*Bob Ojeda*	.25
302	Tony Perez	.20
303	Chuck Rainey	.08
304	Jerry Remy	.08
305	Jim Rice	.15
306	Joe Rudi	.08
307	Bob Stanley	.08
308	Dave Stapleton	.08
309	Frank Tanana	.08
310	Mike Torrez	.08
311	John Tudor	.08
312	Carl Yastrzemski	1.00
313	Buddy Bell	.10
314	Steve Comer	.08
315	Danny Darwin	.08
316	John Ellis	.08
317	John Grubb	.08
318	Rick Honeycutt	.08
319	Charlie Hough	.08
320	Fergie Jenkins	.65
321	John Henry Johnson	.08
322	Jim Kern	.08
323	Jon Matlack	.08
324	Doc Medich	.08
325	Mario Mendoza	.08

No.	Player	Price
326	Al Oliver	.10
327	Pat Putnam	.08
328	Mickey Rivers	.08
329	Leon Roberts	.08
330	Billy Sample	.08
331	Bill Stein	.08
332	Jim Sundberg	.08
333	Mark Wagner	.08
334	Bump Wills	.08
335	Bill Almon	.08
336	Harold Baines	.25
337	Ross Baumgarten	.08
338	Tony Bernazard	.08
339	Britt Burns	.08
340	Richard Dotson	.08
341	Jim Essian	.08
342	Ed Farmer	.08
343	Carlton Fisk	.90
344	Kevin Hickey	.08
345	Lamarr Hoyt (LaMarr)	.08
346	Lamar Johnson	.08
347	Jerry Koosman	.08
348	Rusty Kuntz	.08
349	Dennis Lamp	.08
350	Ron LeFlore	.08
351	Chet Lemon	.08
352	Greg Luzinski	.10
353	Bob Molinaro	.08
354	Jim Morrison	.08
355	Wayne Nordhagen	.08
356	Greg Pryor	.08
357	Mike Squires	.08
358	Steve Trout	.08
359	Alan Bannister	.08
360	Len Barker	.08
361	Bert Blyleven	.08
362	Joe Charboneau	.10
363	John Denny	.08
364	Bo Diaz	.08
365	Miguel Dilone	.08
366	Jerry Dybzinski	.08
367	Wayne Garland	.08
368	Mike Hargrove	.08
369	Toby Harrah	.08
370	Ron Hassey	.08
371	*Von Hayes*	.25
372	Pat Kelly	.08
373	Duane Kuiper	.08
374	Rick Manning	.08
375	Sid Monge	.08
376	Jorge Orta	.08
377	Dave Rosello	.08
378	Dan Spillner	.08
379	Mike Stanton	.08
380	Andre Thornton	.08
381	Tom Veryzer	.08
382	Rick Waits	.08
383	Doyle Alexander	.08
384	Vida Blue	.10
385	Fred Breining	.08
386	Enos Cabell	.08
387	Jack Clark	.08
388	Darrell Evans	.10
389	Tom Griffin	.08
390	Larry Herndon	.08
391	Al Holland	.08
392	Gary Lavelle	.08
393	Johnnie LeMaster	.08
394	Jerry Martin	.08
395	Milt May	.08
396	Greg Minton	.08
397	Joe Morgan	.75
398	Joe Pettini	.08
399	Alan Ripley	.08
400	Billy Smith	.08
401	Rennie Stennett	.08
402	Ed Whitson	.08
403	Jim Wohlford	.08
404	Willie Aikens	.08
405	George Brett	4.00
406	Ken Brett	.08
407	Dave Chalk	.08
408	Rich Gale	.08
409	Cesar Geronimo	.08
410	Larry Gura	.08
411	Clint Hurdle	.08
412	Mike Jones	.08
413	Dennis Leonard	.08
414	Renie Martin	.08
415	Lee May	.08
416	Hal McRae	.12
417	Darryl Motley	.08
418	Rance Mulliniks	.08
419	Amos Otis	.08
420	*Ken Phelps*	.10
421	Jamie Quirk	.08
422	Dan Quisenberry	.10
423	Paul Splittorff	.08
424	U.L. Washington	.08
425	John Wathan	.08
426	Frank White	.08
427	Willie Wilson	.10
428	Brian Asselstine	.08
429	Bruce Benedict	.08
430	Tom Boggs	.08
431	Larry Bradford	.08
432	Rick Camp	.08
433	Chris Chambliss	.08
434	Gene Garber	.08
435	Preston Hanna	.08
436	Bob Horner	.08
437	Glenn Hubbard	.08
438a	Al Hrabosky (All Hrabosky, 5'1" on back)	16.00
438b	Al Hrabosky (Al Hrabosky, 5'1" on back)	1.25
438c	Al Hrabosky (Al Hrabosky, 5'10" on back)	.35
439	Rufino Linares	.08
440	*Rick Mahler*	.12
441	Ed Miller	.08
442	John Montefusco	.08
443	Dale Murphy	.60
444	Phil Niekro	.90
445	Gaylord Perry	.65
446	Biff Pocoroba	.08
447	Rafael Ramirez	.08
448	Jerry Royster	.08
449	Claudell Washington	.08
450	Don Aase	.08
451	Don Baylor	.15
452	Juan Beniquez	.08
453	Rick Burleson	.08
454	Bert Campaneris	.08
455	Rod Carew	1.00
456	Bob Clark	.08
457	Brian Downing	.08
458	Dan Ford	.08
459	Ken Forsch	.08
460	Dave Frost	.08
461	Bobby Grich	.08
462	Larry Harlow	.08
463	John Harris	.08
464	Andy Hassler	.08
465	Butch Hobson	.08
466	Jesse Jefferson	.08
467	Bruce Kison	.08
468	Fred Lynn	.12
469	Angel Moreno	.08
470	Ed Ott	.08
471	Fred Patek	.08
472	Steve Renko	.08
473	*Mike Witt*	.25
474	Geoff Zahn	.08
475	Gary Alexander	.08
476	Dale Berra	.08
477	Kurt Bevacqua	.08
478	Jim Bibby	.08
479	John Candelaria	.08
480	Victor Cruz	.08
481	Mike Easler	.08
482	Tim Foli	.08
483	Lee Lacy	.08
484	Vance Law	.08
485	Bill Madlock	.08
486	Willie Montanez	.08
487	Omar Moreno	.08
488	Steve Nicosia	.08
489	Dave Parker	.20
490	Tony Pena	.10
491	Pascual Perez	.10
492	*Johnny Ray*	.08
493	Rick Rhoden	.08
494	Bill Robinson	.08
495	Don Robinson	.08
496	Enrique Romo	.08
497	Rod Scurry	.08
498	Eddie Solomon	.08
499	Willie Stargell	.75
500	Kent Tekulve	.08
501	Jason Thompson	.08
502	Glenn Abbott	.08
503	Jim Anderson	.08
504	Floyd Bannister	.08
505	Bruce Bochte	.08
506	Jeff Burroughs	.08
507	Bryan Clark	.08
508	Ken Clay	.08
509	Julio Cruz	.08
510	Dick Drago	.08
511	Gary Gray	.08
512	Dan Meyer	.08
513	Jerry Narron	.08
514	Tom Paciorek	.08
515	Casey Parsons	.08
516	Lenny Randle	.08
517	Shane Rawley	.08
518	Joe Simpson	.08
519	Richie Zisk	.08
520	Neil Allen	.08
521	Bob Bailor	.08
522	Hubie Brooks	.10
523	Mike Cubbage	.08
524	Pete Falcone	.08
525	Doug Flynn	.08
526	Tom Hausman	.08
527	Ron Hodges	.08
528	Randy Jones	.08
529	Mike Jorgensen	.08
530	Dave Kingman	.12
531	Ed Lynch	.08
532	Mike Marshall	.08
533	Lee Mazzilli	.08
534	Dyar Miller	.08
535	Mike Scott	.10
536	Rusty Staub	.10
537	John Stearns	.08
538	Craig Swan	.08
539	Frank Taveras	.08
540	Alex Trevino	.08
541	Ellis Valentine	.08
542	Mookie Wilson	.15
543	Joel Youngblood	.08
544	Pat Zachry	.08
545	Glenn Adams	.08
546	Fernando Arroyo	.08
547	John Verhoeven	.08
548	Sal Butera	.08
549	John Castino	.08
550	Don Cooper	.08
551	Doug Corbett	.08
552	Dave Engle	.08
553	Roger Erickson	.08
554	Danny Goodwin	.08
555a	Darrell Jackson (black cap)	1.00
555b	Darrell Jackson (red cap with emblem)	.10
555c	Darrell Jackson (red cap, no emblem)	.25
556	Pete Mackanin	.08
557	Jack O'Connor	.08
558	Hosken Powell	.08
559	Pete Redfern	.08
560	Roy Smalley	.08
561	Chuck Baker	.08
562	Gary Ward	.08
563	Rob Wilfong	.08
564	Al Williams	.08
565	Butch Wynegar	.08
566	Randy Bass	.08
567	Juan Bonilla	.08
568	Danny Boone	.08
569	John Curtis	.08
570	Juan Eichelberger	.08
571	Barry Evans	.08
572	Tim Flannery	.08
573	Ruppert Jones	.08
574	Terry Kennedy	.08
575	Joe Lefebvre	.08
576a	John Littlefield (pitching lefty)	200.00
576b	John Littlefield (pitching righty)	.08
577	Gary Lucas	.08
578	Steve Mura	.08
579	Broderick Perkins	.08
580	Gene Richards	.08
581	Luis Salazar	.08
582	Ozzie Smith	3.00
583	John Urrea	.08
584	Chris Welsh	.08
585	Rick Wise	.08
586	Doug Bird	.08
587	Tim Blackwell	.08
588	Bobby Bonds	.10
589	Bill Buckner	.08
590	Bill Caudill	.08
591	Hector Cruz	.08
592	*Jody Davis*	.10
593	Ivan DeJesus	.08
594	Steve Dillard	.08
595	Leon Durham	.08
596	Rawly Eastwick	.08
597	Steve Henderson	.08
598	Mike Krukow	.08
599	Mike Lum	.08
600	Randy Martz	.08
601	Jerry Morales	.08
602	Ken Reitz	.08
603a	*Lee Smith* (Cubs logo reversed on back)	8.00
603b	*Lee Smith* (corrected)	8.00
604	Dick Tidrow	.08
605	Jim Tracy	.08
606	Mike Tyson	.08
607	Ty Waller	.08
608	Danny Ainge	1.25
609	*Jorge Bell*	1.00
610	Mark Bomback	.08
611	Barry Bonnell	.08
612	Jim Clancy	.08
613	Damaso Garcia	.08
614	Jerry Garvin	.08
615	Alfredo Griffin	.08
616	Garth Iorg	.08
617	Luis Leal	.08
618	Ken Macha	.08
619	John Mayberry	.08
620	Joey McLaughlin	.08
621	Lloyd Moseby	.08
622	Dave Stieb	.08
623	Jackson Todd	.08
624	Willie Upshaw	.08
625	Otto Velez	.08
626	Ernie Whitt	.08
627	Al Woods	.08
628	1981 All-Star Game	.08
629	All-Star Infielders (Bucky Dent, Frank White)	.08
630	Big Red Machine (Dave Concepcion, Dan Driessen, George Foster)	.10
631	Top N.L. Relief Pitcher (Bruce Sutter)	.08
632	Steve & Carlton (Steve Carlton, Carlton Fisk)	.25
633	3000th Game, May 25, 1981 (Carl Yastrzemski)	.35
634	Dynamic Duo (Johnny Bench, Tom Seaver)	.30
635	West Meets East (Gary Carter, Fernando Valenzuela)	.20
636a	N.L. Strikeout King (Fernando Valenzuela) ("...led the National League...")	1.00
636b	N.L. Strikeout King (Fernando Valenzuela) ("... led the National League)	.35
637	Home Run King (Mike Schmidt)	.50
638	N.L. All-Stars (Gary Carter, Dave Parker)	.20
639	Perfect Game! (Len Barker, Bo Diaz)	.08
640	Pete Rose, Pete Rose, Jr. (Re-Pete)	2.00
641	Phillies' Finest (Steve Carlton, Mike Schmidt, Lonnie Smith)	.50
642	Red Sox Reunion (Dwight Evans, Fred Lynn)	.15
643	Most Hits and Runs (Rickey Henderson)	1.50
644	Most Saves 1981 A.L. (Rollie Fingers)	.15
645	Most 1981 Wins (Tom Seaver)	.25
646a	Yankee Powerhouse (Reggie Jackson, Dave Winfield)	

(comma after "outfielder" on back) 2.00
646b Yankee Powerhouse (Reggie Jackson, Dave Winfield) (no comma) 2.00
647 Checklist 1-56 .08
648 Checklist 57-109 .08
649 Checklist 110-156 .08
650 Checklist 157-211 .08
651 Checklist 212-262 .08
652 Checklist 263-312 .08
653 Checklist 313-358 .08
654 Checklist 359-403 .08
655 Checklist 404-449 .08
656 Checklist 450-501 .08
657 Checklist 502-544 .08
658 Checklist 545-585 .08
659 Checklist 586-627 .08
660 Checklist 628-646 .08

1982 Fleer Stamps

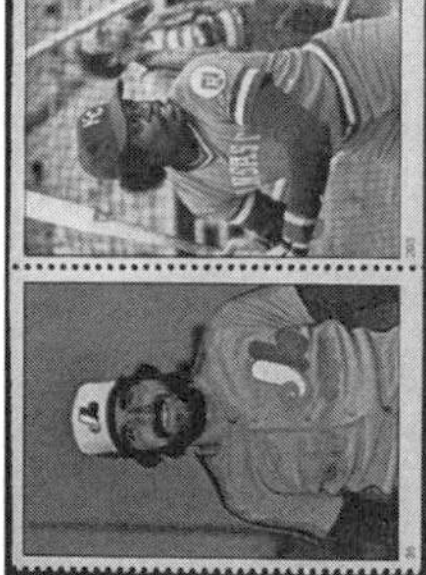

Issued by Fleer in 1982, this set consists of 242 player stamps, each measuring 1-13/16" x 2-1/2". Originally issued in perforated strips of 10, the full-color stamps are numbered in the lower-left corner and were designed to be placed in an album. Six stamps feature two players each.

MT
Complete Set (242): 12.00
Common Player: .05
Stamp Album: 1.50
1 Fernando Valenzuela .10
2 Rick Monday .05
3 Ron Cey .05
4 Dusty Baker .08
5 Burt Hooton .05
6 Pedro Guerrero .05
7 Jerry Reuss .05
8 Bill Russell .05
9 Steve Garvey .20
10 Davey Lopes .05
11 Tom Seaver .25
12 George Foster .05
13 Frank Pastore .05
14 Dave Collins .05
15 Dave Concepcion .05
16 Ken Griffey .08
17 Johnny Bench .25
18 Ray Knight .05
19 Mario Soto .05
20 Ron Oester .05
21 Ken Oberkfell .05
22 Bob Forsch .05
23 Keith Hernandez .05
24 Dane Iorg .05
25 George Hendrick .05
26 Gene Tenace .05
27 Garry Templeton .05
28 Bruce Sutter .05
29 Darrell Porter .05
30 Tom Herr .05
31 Tim Raines .10
32 Chris Speier .05
33 Warren Cromartie .05
34 Larry Parrish .05
35 Andre Dawson .15
36 Steve Rogers .05
37 Jeff Reardon .05
38 Rodney Scott .05
39 Gary Carter .15
40 Scott Sanderson .05
41 Cesar Cedeno .05
42 Nolan Ryan 1.00
43 Don Sutton .20
44 Terry Puhl .05
45 Joe Niekro .05
46 Tony Scott .05
47 Joe Sambito .05
48 Art Howe .05
49 Bob Knepper .05
50 Jose Cruz .05
51 Pete Rose .35
52 Dick Ruthven .05
53 Mike Schmidt .30
54 Steve Carlton .25
55 Tug McGraw .05
56 Larry Bowa .05
57 Garry Maddox .05
58 Gary Matthews .05
59 Manny Trillo .05
60 Lonnie Smith .05
61 Vida Blue .05
62 Milt May .05
63 Joe Morgan .25
64 Enos Cabell .05
65 Jack Clark .05
66 Claudell Washington .05
67 Gaylord Perry .20
68 Phil Niekro .20
69 Bob Horner .05
70 Chris Chambliss .05
71 Dave Parker .10
72 Tony Pena .05
73 Kent Tekulve .05
74 Mike Easler .05
75 Tim Foli .05
76 Willie Stargell .25
77 Bill Madlock .05
78 Jim Bibby .05
79 Omar Moreno .05
80 Lee Lacy .05
81 Hubie Brooks .05
82 Rusty Staub .08
83 Ellis Valentine .05
84 Neil Allen .05
85 Dave Kingman .08
86 Mookie Wilson .05
87 Doug Flynn .05
88 Pat Zachry .05
89 John Stearns .05
90 Lee Mazzilli .05
91 Ken Reitz .05
92 Mike Krukow .05
93 Jerry Morales .05
94 Leon Durham .05
95 Ivan DeJesus .05
96 Bill Buckner .05
97 Jim Tracy .05
98 Steve Henderson .05
99 Dick Tidrow .05
100 Mike Tyson .05
101 Ozzie Smith .25
102 Ruppert Jones .05
103 Broderick Perkins .05
104 Gene Richrds .05
105 Terry Kennedy .05
106 Jim Bibby, Willie Stargell .08
107 Larry Bowa, Pete Rose .10
108 Warren Spahn, Fernando Valenzuela .15
109 Dave Concepcion, Pete Rose .15
110 Reggie Jackson, Dave Winfield .20
111 Tom Lasorda, Fernando Valenzuela .20
112 Reggie Jackson .25
113 Dave Winfield .20
114 Lou Piniella .08
115 Tommy John .08
116 Rich Gossage .08
117 Ron Davis .05
118 Rick Cerone .05
119 Graig Nettles .05
120 Ron Guidry .05
121 Willie Randolph .05
122 Dwayne Murphy .05
123 Rickey Henderson .25
124 Wayne Gross .05
125 Mike Norris .05
126 Rick Langford .05
127 Jim Spencer .05
128 Tony Armas .05
129 Matt Keough .05
130 Jeff Jones .05
131 Steve McCatty .05
132 Rollie Fingers .20
133 Jim Gantner .05
134 Gorman Thomas .05
135 Robin Yount .35
136 Paul Molitor .30
137 Ted Simmons .05
138 Ben Oglivie .05
139 Moose Haas .05
140 Cecil Cooper .05
141 Pete Vuckovich .05
142 Doug DeCinces .05
143 Jim Palmer .25
144 Steve Stone .05
145 Mike Flanagan .05
146 Rick Dempsey .05
147 Al Bumbry .05
148 Mark Belanger .05
149 Scott McGregor .05
150 Ken Singleton .05
151 Eddie Murray .25
152 Lance Parrish .08
153 David Rozema .05
154 Champ Summers .05
155 Alan Trammell .10
156 Lou Whitaker .08
157 Milt Wilcox .05
158 Kevin Saucier .05
159 Jack Morris .05
160 Steve Kemp .05
161 Kirk Gibson .05
162 Carl Yastrzemski .25
163 Jim Rice .08
164 Carney Lansford .05
165 Dennis Eckersley .08
166 Mike Torrez .05
167 Dwight Evans .05
168 Glenn Hoffman .05
169 Bob Stanley .05
170 Tony Perez .08
171 Jerry Remy .05
172 Buddy Bell .05
173 Ferguson Jenkins .20
174 Mickey Rivers .05
175 Bump Wills .05
176 Jon Matlack .05
177 Steve Comer .05
178 Al Oliver .05
179 Bill Stein .05
180 Pat Putnam .05
181 Jim Sundberg .05
182 Ron LeFlore .05
183 Carlton Fisk .15
184 Harold Baines .08
185 Bill Almon .05
186 Richard Dotson .05
187 Greg Luzinski .05
188 Mike Squires .05
189 Britt Burns .05
190 Lamarr Hoyt .05
191 Chet Lemon .05
192 Joe Charboneau .05
193 Toby Harrah .05
194 John Denny .05
195 Rick Manning .05
196 Miguel Dilone .05
197 Bo Diaz .05
198 Mike Hargrove .05
199 Bert Blyleven .05
200 Len Barker .05
201 Andre Thornton .05
202 George Brett .25
203 U.L. Washington .05
204 Dan Quisenberry .05
205 Larry Gura .05
206 Willie Aikens .05
207 Willie Wilson .05
208 Dennis Leonard .05
209 Frank White .05
210 Hal McRae .05
211 Amos Otis .05
212 Don Aase .05
213 Butch Hobson .05
214 Fred Lynn .08
215 Brian Downing .05
216 Dan Ford .05
217 Rod Carew .25
218 Bobby Grich .05
219 Rick Burleson .05
220 Don Baylor .08
221 Ken Forsch .05
222 Bruce Bochte .05
223 Richie Zisk .05
224 Tom Paciorek .05
225 Julio Cruz .05
226 Jeff Burroughs .05
227 Doug Corbett .05
228 Roy Smalley .05
229 Gary Ward .05
230 John Castino .05
231 Rob Wilfong .05
232 Dave Stieb .05
233 Otto Velez .05
234 Damaso Garcia .05
235 John Mayberry .05
236 Alfredo Griffin .05
237 Ted Williams, Carl Yastrzemski .35
238 Rick Cerone, Graig Nettles .05
239 Buddy Bell, George Brett .15
240 Steve Carlton, Jim Kaat .10
241 Steve Carlton, Dave Parker .10
242 Ron Davis, Nolan Ryan .40

1983 Fleer Star Stamps

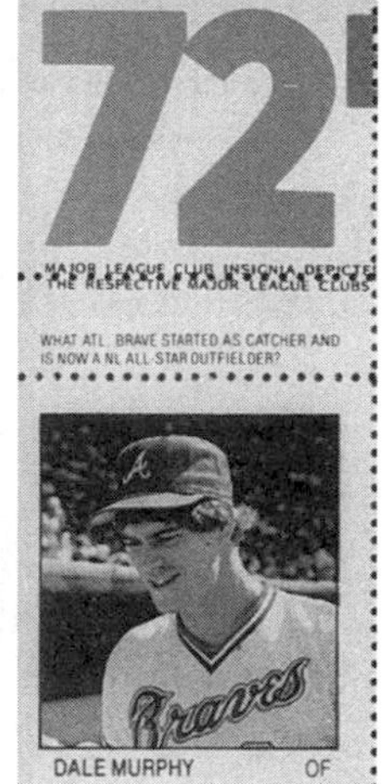

The 1983 Fleer Stamp set consists of 288 stamps, including 224 player stamps and 64 team logo stamps. They were originally issued on four different sheets of 72 stamps each (checklisted below) and in "Vend-A-Stamp" dispensers of 18 stamps each. Sixteen different dispenser strips were needed to complete the set (strips 1-4 comprise Sheet 1; strips 5-8 comprise Sheet 2; strips 9-12 comprise Sheet 3; and strips 13-16 comprise Sheet 4.) Stamps measure 1-1/4" x 1-13/16".

MT
Complete Sheet Set (4): 9.00
Complete Vend-A-Stamp Set (288): 9.00

Common Sheet: 3.50
Common Stamp Dispenser: .50
Common Single Stamp: .02

1 Sheet 1 (A's Logo, Angels Logo, Astros Logo, Cardinals Logo, Cubs Logo, Dodgers Logo, Expos Logo, Giants Logo, Indians Logo, Mets Logo, Orioles Logo, Phillies Logo, Pirates Logo, Red Sox Logo, Twins Logo, White Sox Logo

2 Sheet 2 (Angels Logo, Astros Logo, Braves Logo, Cardinals Logo, Dodgers Logo, Expos Logo, Indians Logo, Mariners Logo, Mets Logo, Phillies Logo, Pirates Logo, Rangers Logo, Reds Logo, Royals Logo, Tigers Logo, Yankees Logo

3 Sheet 3 (A's Logo, Angels Logo, Blue Jays Logo, Braves Logo, Brewers Logo, Dodgers Logo, Giants Logo, Indians Logo, Mariners Logo, Orioles Logo, Padres Logo, Reds Logo, Royals Logo, Tigers Logo, Twins Logo, White Sox Logo

4 Sheet 4 (Blue Jays Logo, Braves logo, Brewers Logo, Cubs Logo, Expos Logo, Giants Logo, Padres Logo, Phillies Logo, Pirates Logo, Rangers Logo, Red Sox Logo, Reds Logo, Royals Logo, Twins Logo, White Sox Logo, Yankees Logo

1983 Fleer

The 1983 Fleer set features color photos set inside a light brown border. The cards are standard 2-1/2" x 3-1/2". A team logo is located at the card bottom and the word "Fleer" is found at the top. The card backs are designed on a vertical format and include a small black and white photo of the player along with biographical and statistical information. The reverses are done in two shades of brown on white stock. The set was issued with team logo stickers.

		MT
Complete Set (660):		100.00
Common Player:		.08
Pack (15):		4.25
Wax Box (38):		115.00
1	Joaquin Andujar	.08
2	Doug Bair	.08
3	Steve Braun	.08
4	Glenn Brummer	.08
5	Bob Forsch	.08
6	David Green	.08
7	George Hendrick	.08
8	Keith Hernandez	.10
9	Tom Herr	.08
10	Dane Iorg	.08
11	Jim Kaat	.12
12	Jeff Lahti	.08
13	Tito Landrum	.08
14	*Dave LaPoint*	.08
15	*Willie McGee*	1.50
16	Steve Mura	.08
17	Ken Oberkfell	.08
18	Darrell Porter	.08
19	Mike Ramsey	.08
20	Gene Roof	.08
21	Lonnie Smith	.08
22	Ozzie Smith	2.50
23	John Stuper	.08
24	Bruce Sutter	.08
25	Gene Tenace	.08
26	Jerry Augustine	.08
27	Dwight Bernard	.08
28	Mark Brouhard	.08
29	Mike Caldwell	.08
30	Cecil Cooper	.08
31	Jamie Easterly	.08
32	Marshall Edwards	.08
33	Rollie Fingers	.60
34	Jim Gantner	.08
35	Moose Haas	.08
36	Roy Howell	.08
37	Peter Ladd	.08
38	Bob McClure	.08
39	Doc Medich	.08
40	Paul Molitor	2.50
41	Don Money	.08
42	Charlie Moore	.08
43	Ben Oglivie	.08
44	Ed Romero	.08
45	Ted Simmons	.08
46	Jim Slaton	.08
47	Don Sutton	.40
48	Gorman Thomas	.08
49	Pete Vuckovich	.08
50	Ned Yost	.08
51	Robin Yount	2.50
52	Benny Ayala	.08
53	Bob Bonner	.08
54	Al Bumbry	.08
55	Terry Crowley	.08
56	*Storm Davis*	.10
57	Rich Dauer	.08
58	Rick Dempsey	.08
59	Jim Dwyer	.08
60	Mike Flanagan	.08
61	Dan Ford	.08
62	Glenn Gulliver	.08
63	John Lowenstein	.08
64	Dennis Martinez	.10
65	Tippy Martinez	.08
66	Scott McGregor	.08
67	Eddie Murray	2.50
68	Joe Nolan	.08
69	Jim Palmer	.90
70	Cal Ripken, Jr.	15.00
71	Gary Roenicke	.08
72	Lenn Sakata	.08
73	Ken Singleton	.08
74	Sammy Stewart	.08
75	Tim Stoddard	.08
76	Don Aase	.08
77	Don Baylor	.10
78	Juan Beniquez	.08
79	Bob Boone	.08
80	Rick Burleson	.08
81	Rod Carew	1.00
82	Bobby Clark	.08
83	Doug Corbett	.08
84	John Curtis	.08
85	Doug DeCinces	.08
86	Brian Downing	.08
87	Joe Ferguson	.08
88	Tim Foli	.08
89	Ken Forsch	.08
90	Dave Goltz	.08
91	Bobby Grich	.08
92	Andy Hassler	.08
93	Reggie Jackson	1.00
94	Ron Jackson	.08
95	Tommy John	.10
96	Bruce Kison	.08
97	Fred Lynn	.10
98	Ed Ott	.08
99	Steve Renko	.08
100	Luis Sanchez	.08
101	Rob Wilfong	.08
102	Mike Witt	.08
103	Geoff Zahn	.08
104	Willie Aikens	.08
105	Mike Armstrong	.08
106	Vida Blue	.08
107	*Bud Black*	.50
108	George Brett	3.50
109	Bill Castro	.08
110	Onix Concepcion	.08
111	Dave Frost	.08
112	Cesar Geronimo	.08
113	Larry Gura	.08
114	Steve Hammond	.08
115	Don Hood	.08
116	Dennis Leonard	.08
117	Jerry Martin	.08
118	Lee May	.08
119	Hal McRae	.08
120	Amos Otis	.08
121	Greg Pryor	.08
122	Dan Quisenberry	.08
123	*Don Slaught*	.20
124	Paul Splittorff	.08
125	U.L. Washington	.08
126	John Wathan	.08
127	Frank White	.08
128	Willie Wilson	.08
129	Steve Bedrosian	.08
130	Bruce Benedict	.08
131	Tommy Boggs	.08
132	Brett Butler	.15
133	Rick Camp	.08
134	Chris Chambliss	.08
135	Ken Dayley	.08
136	Gene Garber	.08
137	Terry Harper	.08
138	Bob Horner	.08
139	Glenn Hubbard	.08
140	Rufino Linares	.08
141	Rick Mahler	.08
142	Dale Murphy	.45
143	Phil Niekro	.60
144	Pascual Perez	.08
145	Biff Pocoroba	.08
146	Rafael Ramirez	.08
147	Jerry Royster	.08
148	Ken Smith	.08
149	Bob Walk	.08
150	Claudell Washington	.08
151	Bob Watson	.08
152	Larry Whisenton	.08
153	Porfirio Altamirano	.08
154	Marty Bystrom	.08
155	Steve Carlton	1.00
156	Larry Christenson	.08
157	Ivan DeJesus	.08
158	John Denny	.08
159	Bob Dernier	.08
160	Bo Diaz	.08
161	Ed Farmer	.08
162	Greg Gross	.08
163	Mike Krukow	.08
164	Garry Maddox	.08
165	Gary Matthews	.08
166	Tug McGraw	.08
167	Bob Molinaro	.08
168	Sid Monge	.08
169	Ron Reed	.08
170	Bill Robinson	.08
171	Pete Rose	3.00
172	Dick Ruthven	.08
173	Mike Schmidt	2.50
174	Manny Trillo	.08
175	Ozzie Virgil	.08
176	George Vukovich	.08
177	Gary Allenson	.08
178	Luis Aponte	.08
179	*Wade Boggs*	17.50
180	Tom Burgmeier	.08
181	Mark Clear	.08
182	Dennis Eckersley	.30
183	Dwight Evans	.10
184	Rich Gedman	.08
185	Glenn Hoffman	.08
186	Bruce Hurst	.08
187	Carney Lansford	.08
188	Rick Miller	.08
189	Reid Nichols	.08
190	Bob Ojeda	.08
191	Tony Perez	.10
192	Chuck Rainey	.08
193	Jerry Remy	.08
194	Jim Rice	.12
195	Bob Stanley	.08
196	Dave Stapleton	.08
197	Mike Torrez	.08
198	John Tudor	.08
199	Julio Valdez	.08
200	Carl Yastrzemski	1.00
201	Dusty Baker	.08
202	Joe Beckwith	.08
203	*Greg Brock*	.08
204	Ron Cey	.08
205	Terry Forster	.08
206	Steve Garvey	.30
207	Pedro Guerrero	.08
208	Burt Hooton	.08
209	Steve Howe	.08
210	Ken Landreaux	.08
211	Mike Marshall	.08
212	*Candy Maldonado*	.10
213	Rick Monday	.08
214	Tom Niedenfuer	.08
215	Jorge Orta	.08
216	Jerry Reuss	.08
217	Ron Roenicke	.08
218	Vicente Romo	.08
219	Bill Russell	.10
220	Steve Sax	.08
221	Mike Scioscia	.08
222	Dave Stewart	.25
223	Derrel Thomas	.08
224	Fernando Valenzuela	.10
225	Bob Welch	.08
226	Ricky Wright	.08
227	Steve Yeager	.08
228	Bill Almon	.08
229	Harold Baines	.15
230	Salome Barojas	.08
231	Tony Bernazard	.08
232	Britt Burns	.08
233	Richard Dotson	.08
234	Ernesto Escarrega	.08
235	Carlton Fisk	.45
236	Jerry Hairston	.08
237	Kevin Hickey	.08
238	LaMarr Hoyt	.08
239	Steve Kemp	.08
240	Jim Kern	.08
241	*Ron Kittle*	.15
242	Jerry Koosman	.08
243	Dennis Lamp	.08
244	Rudy Law	.08
245	Vance Law	.08
246	Ron LeFlore	.08
247	Greg Luzinski	.10
248	Tom Paciorek	.08
249	Aurelio Rodriguez	.08
250	Mike Squires	.08
251	Steve Trout	.08
252	Jim Barr	.08
253	Dave Bergman	.08
254	Fred Breining	.08
255	Bob Brenly	.08
256	Jack Clark	.08
257	Chili Davis	.20
258	Darrell Evans	.10
259	Alan Fowlkes	.08
260	Rich Gale	.08
261	Atlee Hammaker	.08
262	Al Holland	.08
263	Duane Kuiper	.08
264	Bill Laskey	.08
265	Gary Lavelle	.08
266	Johnnie LeMaster	.08
267	Renie Martin	.08
268	Milt May	.08
269	Greg Minton	.08
270	Joe Morgan	.60
271	Tom O'Malley	.08
272	Reggie Smith	.08
273	Guy Sularz	.08
274	Champ Summers	.08
275	Max Venable	.08
276	Jim Wohlford	.08
277	Ray Burris	.08
278	Gary Carter	.20
279	Warren Cromartie	.08
280	Andre Dawson	.50
281	Terry Francona	.08
282	Doug Flynn	.08

283 Woody Fryman .08
284 Bill Gullickson .08
285 Wallace Johnson .08
286 Charlie Lea .08
287 Randy Lerch .08
288 Brad Mills .08
289 Dan Norman .08
290 Al Oliver .08
291 David Palmer .08
292 Tim Raines .25
293 Jeff Reardon .10
294 Steve Rogers .08
295 Scott Sanderson .08
296 Dan Schatzeder .08
297 Bryn Smith .08
298 Chris Speier .08
299 Tim Wallach .10
300 Jerry White .08
301 Joel Youngblood .08
302 Ross Baumgarten .08
303 Dale Berra .08
304 John Candelaria .08
305 Dick Davis .08
306 Mike Easler .08
307 Richie Hebner .08
308 Lee Lacy .08
309 Bill Madlock .08
310 Larry McWilliams .08
311 John Milner .08
312 Omar Moreno .08
313 Jim Morrison .08
314 Steve Nicosia .08
315 Dave Parker .12
316 Tony Pena .08
317 Johnny Ray .08
318 Rick Rhoden .08
319 Don Robinson .08
320 Enrique Romo .08
321 Manny Sarmiento .08
322 Rod Scurry .08
323 Jim Smith .08
324 Willie Stargell .60
325 Jason Thompson .08
326 Kent Tekulve .08
327a Tom Brookens (narrow (1/4") brown box at bottom on back) .45
327b Tom Brookens (wide (1-1/4") brown box at bottom on back) .08
328 Enos Cabell .08
329 Kirk Gibson .08
330 Larry Herndon .08
331 Mike Ivie .08
332 *Howard Johnson* 1.00
333 Lynn Jones .08
334 Rick Leach .08
335 Chet Lemon .08
336 Jack Morris .10
337 Lance Parrish .10
338 Larry Pashnick .08
339 Dan Petry .08
340 Dave Rozema .08
341 Dave Rucker .08
342 Elias Sosa .08
343 Dave Tobik .08
344 Alan Trammell .45
345 Jerry Turner .08
346 Jerry Ujdur .08
347 Pat Underwood .08
348 Lou Whitaker .10
349 Milt Wilcox .08
350 *Glenn Wilson* .08
351 John Wockenfuss .08
352 Kurt Bevacqua .08
353 Juan Bonilla .08
354 Floyd Chiffer .08
355 Luis DeLeon .08
356 *Dave Dravecky* .30
357 Dave Edwards .08
358 Juan Eichelberger .08
359 Tim Flannery .08
360 *Tony Gwynn* 25.00
361 Ruppert Jones .08
362 Terry Kennedy .08
363 Joe Lefebvre .08
364 Sixto Lezcano .08
365 Tim Lollar .08
366 Gary Lucas .08
367 John Montefusco .08
368 Broderick Perkins .08
369 Joe Pittman .08
370 Gene Richards .08
371 Luis Salazar .08
372 *Eric Show* .08
373 Garry Templeton .08
374 Chris Welsh .08
375 Alan Wiggins .08
376 Rick Cerone .08
377 Dave Collins .08
378 Roger Erickson .08
379 George Frazier .08
380 Oscar Gamble .08
381 Goose Gossage .08
382 Ken Griffey .10
383 Ron Guidry .10
384 Dave LaRoche .08
385 Rudy May .08
386 John Mayberry .08
387 Lee Mazzilli .08
388 Mike Morgan .08
389 Jerry Mumphrey .08
390 Bobby Murcer .08
391 Graig Nettles .08
392 Lou Piniella .10
393 Willie Randolph .08
394 Shane Rawley .08
395 Dave Righetti .08
396 Andre Robertson .08
397 Roy Smalley .08
398 Dave Winfield 2.00
399 Butch Wynegar .08
400 Chris Bando .08
401 Alan Bannister .08
402 Len Barker .08
403 Tom Brennan .08
404 *Carmelo Castillo* .08
405 Miguel Dilone .08
406 Jerry Dybzinski .08
407 Mike Fischlin .08
408 Ed Glynn (photo actually Bud Anderson) .08
409 Mike Hargrove .08
410 Toby Harrah .08
411 Ron Hassey .08
412 Von Hayes .08
413 Rick Manning .08
414 Bake McBride .08
415 Larry Milbourne .08
416 Bill Nahorodny .08
417 Jack Perconte .08
418 Larry Sorensen .08
419 Dan Spillner .08
420 Rick Sutcliffe .08
421 Andre Thornton .08
422 Rick Waits .08
423 Eddie Whitson .08
424 Jesse Barfield .08
425 Barry Bonnell .08
426 Jim Clancy .08
427 Damaso Garcia .08
428 Jerry Garvin .08
429 Alfredo Griffin .08
430 Garth Iorg .08
431 Roy Lee Jackson .08
432 Luis Leal .08
433 Buck Martinez .08
434 Joey McLaughlin .08
435 Lloyd Moseby .08
436 Rance Mulliniks .08
437 Dale Murray .08
438 Wayne Nordhagen .08
439 *Gene Petralli* .08
440 Hosken Powell .08
441 Dave Stieb .08
442 Willie Upshaw .08
443 Ernie Whitt .08
444 Al Woods .08
445 Alan Ashby .08
446 Jose Cruz .08
447 Kiko Garcia .08
448 Phil Garner .08
449 Danny Heep .08
450 Art Howe .08
451 Bob Knepper .08
452 Alan Knicely .08
453 Ray Knight .08
454 Frank LaCorte .08
455 Mike LaCoss .08
456 Randy Moffitt .08
457 Joe Niekro .08
458 Terry Puhl .08
459 Luis Pujols .08
460 Craig Reynolds .08
461 Bert Roberge .08
462 Vern Ruhle .08
463 Nolan Ryan 8.00
464 Joe Sambito .08
465 Tony Scott .08
466 Dave Smith .08
467 Harry Spilman .08
468 Dickie Thon .08
469 Denny Walling .08
470 Larry Andersen .08
471 Floyd Bannister .08
472 Jim Beattie .08
473 Bruce Bochte .08
474 Manny Castillo .08
475 Bill Caudill .08
476 Bryan Clark .08
477 Al Cowens .08
478 Julio Cruz .08
479 Todd Cruz .08
480 Gary Gray .08
481 Dave Henderson .10
482 *Mike Moore* .25
483 Gaylord Perry .50
484 Dave Revering .08
485 Joe Simpson .08
486 Mike Stanton .08
487 Rick Sweet .08
488 *Ed Vande Berg* .08
489 Richie Zisk .08
490 Doug Bird .08
491 Larry Bowa .08
492 Bill Buckner .10
493 Bill Campbell .08
494 Jody Davis .08
495 Leon Durham .08
496 Steve Henderson .08
497 Willie Hernandez .08
498 Fergie Jenkins .50
499 Jay Johnstone .08
500 Junior Kennedy .08
501 Randy Martz .08
502 Jerry Morales .08
503 Keith Moreland .08
504 Dickie Noles .08
505 Mike Proly .08
506 Allen Ripley .08
507 *Ryne Sandberg* 15.00
508 Lee Smith 1.25
509 Pat Tabler .08
510 Dick Tidrow .08
511 Bump Wills .08
512 Gary Woods .08
513 Tony Armas .08
514 Dave Beard .08
515 Jeff Burroughs .08
516 John D'Acquisto .08
517 Wayne Gross .08
518 Mike Heath .08
519 Rickey Henderson 2.50
520 Cliff Johnson .08
521 Matt Keough .08
522 Brian Kingman .08
523 Rick Langford .08
524 Davey Lopes .08
525 Steve McCatty .08
526 Dave McKay .08
527 Dan Meyer .08
528 Dwayne Murphy .08
529 Jeff Newman .08
530 Mike Norris .08
531 Bob Owchinko .08
532 Joe Rudi .08
533 Jimmy Sexton .08
534 Fred Stanley .08
535 Tom Underwood .08
536 Neil Allen .08
537 Wally Backman .08
538 Bob Bailor .08
539 Hubie Brooks .08
540 Carlos Diaz .08
541 Pete Falcone .08
542 George Foster .08
543 Ron Gardenhire .08
544 Brian Giles .08
545 Ron Hodges .08
546 Randy Jones .08
547 Mike Jorgensen .08
548 Dave Kingman .10
549 Ed Lynch .08
550 Jesse Orosco .08
551 Rick Ownbey .08
552 *Charlie Puleo* .08
553 Gary Rajsich .08
554 Mike Scott .08
555 Rusty Staub .10
556 John Stearns .08
557 Craig Swan .08
558 Ellis Valentine .08
559 Tom Veryzer .08
560 Mookie Wilson .08
561 Pat Zachry .08
562 Buddy Bell .08
563 John Butcher .08
564 Steve Comer .08
565 Danny Darwin .08
566 Bucky Dent .08
567 John Grubb .08
568 Rick Honeycutt .08
569 Dave Hostetler .08
570 Charlie Hough .08
571 Lamar Johnson .08
572 Jon Matlack .08
573 Paul Mirabella .08
574 Larry Parrish .08
575 Mike Richardt .08
576 Mickey Rivers .08
577 Billy Sample .08
578 *Dave Schmidt* .08
579 Bill Stein .08
580 Jim Sundberg .08
581 Frank Tanana .08
582 Mark Wagner .08
583 George Wright .08
584 Johnny Bench 1.00
585 Bruce Berenyi .08
586 Larry Biittner .08
587 Cesar Cedeno .08
588 Dave Concepcion .08
589 Dan Driessen .08
590 Greg Harris .08
591 Ben Hayes .08
592 Paul Householder .08
593 Tom Hume .08
594 Wayne Krenchicki .08
595 Rafael Landestoy .08
596 Charlie Leibrandt .08
597 *Eddie Milner* .08
598 Ron Oester .08
599 Frank Pastore .08
600 Joe Price .08
601 Tom Seaver 1.00
602 Bob Shirley .08
603 Mario Soto .08
604 Alex Trevino .08
605 Mike Vail .08
606 Duane Walker .08
607 Tom Brunansky .08
608 Bobby Castillo .08
609 John Castino .08
610 Ron Davis .08
611 Lenny Faedo .08
612 Terry Felton .08
613 *Gary Gaetti* .35
614 Mickey Hatcher .08
615 Brad Havens .08
616 Kent Hrbek .25
617 Randy S. Johnson .08
618 Tim Laudner .08
619 Jeff Little .08
620 Bob Mitchell .08
621 Jack O'Connor .08
622 John Pacella .08
623 Pete Redfern .08
624 Jesus Vega .08
625 *Frank Viola* .90
626 Ron Washington .08
627 Gary Ward .08
628 Al Williams .08
629 Red Sox All-Stars (Mark Clear, Dennis Eckersley, Carl Yastrzemski) .25
630 300 Career Wins (Terry Bulling, Gaylord Perry) .15
631 Pride of Venezuela (Dave Concepcion, Manny Trillo) .10
632 All-Star Infielders (Buddy Bell, Robin Yount) .20
633 Mr. Vet & Mr. Rookie (Kent Hrbek, Dave Winfield) .25
634 Fountain of Youth (Pete Rose, Willie Stargell) .40
635 Big Chiefs (Toby Harrah, Andre Thornton) .08
636 "Smith Bros." (Lonnie Smith, Ozzie Smith) .10
637 Base Stealers' Threat (Gary Carter, Bo Diaz) .10
638 All-Star Catchers (Gary Carter, Carlton Fisk) .20

639	Rickey Henderson (In Action)	.50
640	Home Run Threats (Reggie Jackson, Ben Oglivie)	.25
641	Two Teams - Same Day (Joel Youngblood)	.08
642	Last Perfect Game (Len Barker, Ron Hassey)	.08
643	Blue (Vida Blue)	.08
644	Black & (Bud Black)	.08
645	Power (Reggie Jackson)	.30
646	Speed & (Rickey Henderson)	.30
647	Checklist 1-51	.08
648	Checklist 52-103	.08
649	Checklist 104-152	.08
650	Checklist 153-200	.08
651	Checklist 201-251	.08
652	Checklist 252-301	.08
653	Checklist 302-351	.08
654	Checklist 352-399	.08
655	Checklist 400-444	.08
656	Checklist 445-489	.08
657	Checklist 490-535	.08
658	Checklist 536-583	.08
659	Checklist 584-628	.08
660	Checklist 629-646	.08

1983 Fleer Stickers

This 270-sticker set consists of both player stickers and team logo stickers, all measuring 1-13/16" x 2-1/2". The player stickers are numbered on the back. The front features a full-color photo surrounded by a blue border with two stars at the top. The stickers were issued in strips of ten player stickers plus two team logo stickers. The 26 logo stickers have been assigned numbers 271 through 296.

		MT
Complete Set (296):		13.00
Common Player:		.05
1	Bruce Sutter	.05
2	Willie McGee	.08
3	Darrell Porter	.05
4	Lonnie Smith	.05
5	Dane Iorg	.05
6	Keith Hernandez	.05
7	Joaquin Andujar	.05
8	Ken Oberkfell	.05
9	John Stuper	.05
10	Ozzie Smith	.20
11	Bob Forsch	.05
12	Jim Gantner	.05
13	Rollie Fingers	.15
14	Pete Vuckovich	.05
15	Ben Oglivie	.05
16	Don Sutton	.12
17	Bob McClure	.05
18	Robin Yount	.20
19	Paul Molitor	.20
20	Gorman Thomas	.05
21	Mike Caldwell	.05
22	Ted Simmons	.05
23	Cecil Cooper	.05
24	Steve Renko	.05
25	Tommy John	.08
26	Rod Carew	.25
27	Bruce Kison	.05
28	Ken Forsch	.05
29	Geoff Zahn	.05
30	Doug DiCinces	.05
31	Fred Lynn	.08
32	Reggie Jackson	.25
33	Don Baylor	.08
34	Bob Boone	.05
35	Brian Downing	.05
36	Goose Gossage	.05
37	Roy Smalley	.05
38	Graig Nettles	.05
39	Dave Winfield	.20
40	Lee Mazzilli	.05
41	Jerry Mumphrey	.05
42	Dave Collins	.05
43	Rick Cerone	.05
44	Willie Randolph	.05
45	Lou Piniella	.08
46	Ken Griffey	.08
47	Ron Guidry	.05
48	Jack Clark	.05
49	Reggie Smith	.05
50	Atlee Hammaker	.05
51	Fred Breining	.05
52	Gary Lavelle	.05
53	Chili Davis	.08
54	Greg Minton	.05
55	Joe Morgan	.15
56	Al Holland	.05
57	Bill Laskey	.05
58	Duane Kuiper	.05
59	Tom Burgmeier	.05
60	Carl Yastrzemski	.25
61	Mark Clear	.05
62	Mike Torrez	.05
63	Dennis Eckersley	.08
64	Wade Boggs	.40
65	Bob Stanley	.05
66	Jim Rice	.10
67	Carney Lansford	.05
68	Jerry Remy	.05
69	Dwight Evans	.08
70	John Candelaria	.05
71	Bill Madlock	.05
72	Dave Parker	.08
73	Kent Tekulve	.05
74	Tony Pena	.05
75	Manny Sarmiento	.05
76	Johnny Ray	.05
77	Dale Berra	.05
78	Lee Lacy	.05
79	Jason Thompson	.05
80	Mike Easler	.05
81	Willie Stargell	.20
82	Rick Camp	.05
83	Bob Watson	.05
84	Bob Horner	.05
85	Rafael Ramirez	.05
86	Chris Chambliss	.05
87	Gene Garber	.05
88	Claudell Washington	.05
89	Steve Bedrosian	.05
90	Dale Murphy	.15
91	Phil Niekro	.15
92	Jerry Royster	.05
93	Bob Walk	.05
94	Frank White	.05
95	Dennis Leonard	.05
96	Vida Blue	.05
97	U.L. Washington	.05
98	George Brett	.45
99	Amos Otis	.05
100	Dan Quisenberry	.05
101	Willie Aikens	.05
102	Hal McRae	.05
103	Larry Gura	.05
104	Willie Wilson	.05
105	Damaso Garcia	.05
106	Hosken Powell	.05
107	Joey McLaughlin	.05
108	Jim Clancy	.05
109	Barry Bonnell	.05
110	Garth Lorg	.05
111	Dave Stieb	.05
112	Fernando Valenzuela	.08
113	Steve Garvey	.12
114	Rick Monday	.05
115	Burt Hooton	.05
116	Bill Russell	.08
117	Pedro Guerrero	.05
118	Steve Sax	.05
119	Steve Howe	.05
120	Ken Landreaux	.05
121	Dusty Baker	.08
122	Ron Cey	.05
123	Jerry Reuss	.05
124	Bump Wills	.05
125	Keith Moreland	.05
126	Dick Tidrow	.05
127	Bill Campbell	.05
128	Larry Bowa	.05
129	Randy Martz	.05
130	Ferguson Jenkins	.15
131	Leon Durham	.05
132	Bill Buckner	.05
133	Ron Davis	.05
134	Jack O'Connor	.05
135	Kent Hrbek	.08
136	Gary Ward	.05
137	Al Williams	.05
138	Tom Brunansky	.05
139	Bobby Castillo	.05
140	Dusty Baker, Dale Murphy	.08
141	Nolan Ryan	.50
142	Lee Lacey (Lacy), Omar Moreno	.05
143	Al Oliver, Pete Rose	.25
144	Rickey Henderson	.25
145	Ray Knight, Pete Rose, Mike Schmidt	.30
146	Hal McRae, Ben Oglivie	.05
147	Tom Hume, Ray Knight	.05
148	Buddy Bell, Carlton Fisk	.05
149	Steve Kemp	.05
150	Rudy Law	.05
151	Ron LeFlore	.05
152	Jerry Koosman	.05
153	Carlton Fisk	.10
154	Salome Barojas	.05
155	Harold Baines	.08
156	Britt Burns	.05
157	Tom Paciorek	.05
158	Greg Luzinski	.05
159	LaMarr Hoyt	.05
160	George Wright	.05
161	Danny Darwin	.05
162	Lamar Johnson	.05
163	Charlie Hough	.05
164	Buddy Bell	.05
165	John Matlack (Jon)	.05
166	Billy Sample	.05
167	John Grubb	.05
168	Larry Parrish	.05
169	Ivan DeJesus	.05
170	Mike Schmidt	.40
171	Tug McGraw	.05
172	Ron Reed	.05
173	Garry Maddox	.05
174	Pete Rose	.45
175	Manny Trillo	.05
176	Steve Carlton	.20
177	Bo Diaz	.05
178	Gary Matthews	.05
179	Bill Caudill	.05
180	Ed Vande Berg	.05
181	Gaylord Perry	.15
182	Floyd Bannister	.05
183	Richie Zisk	.05
184	Al Cowens	.05
185	Bruce Bochte	.05
186	Jeff Burroughs	.05
187	Dave Beard	.05
188	Davey Lopes	.05
189	Dwayne Murphy	.05
190	Rick Langford	.05
191	Tom Underwood	.05
192	Rickey Henderson	.25
193	Mike Flanagan	.05
194	Scott McGregor	.05
195	Ken Singleton	.05
196	Rich Dauer	.05
197	John Lowenstein	.05
198	Cal Ripken, Jr.	1.00
199	Dennis Martinez	.08
200	Jim Palmer	.20
201	Tippy Martinez	.05
202	Eddie Murray	.20
203	Al Bumbry	.05
204	Dickie Thon	.05
205	Phil Garner	.05
206	Jose Cruz	.05
207	Nolan Ryan	.50
208	Ray Knight	.05
209	Terry Puhl	.05
210	Joe Niekro	.05
211	Art Howe	.05
212	Alan Ashby	.05
213	Tom Hume	.05
214	Johnny Bench	.25
215	Larry Biittner	.05
216	Mario Soto	.05
217	Dan Driessen	.05
218	Tom Seaver	.25
219	Dave Concepcion	.05
220	Wayne Krenchicki	.05
221	Cesar Cedeno	.05
222	Ruppert Jones	.05
223	Terry Kennedy	.05
224	Luis DeLeon	.05
225	Eric Show	.05
226	Tim Flannery	.05
227	Garry Templeton	.05
228	Tim Lollar	.05
229	Sixto Lezcano	.05
230	Bob Bailor	.05
231	Craig Swan	.05
232	Dave Kingman	.08
233	Mookie Wilson	.05
234	John Stearns	.05
235	Ellis Valentine	.05
236	Neil Allen	.05
237	Pat Zachry	.05
238	Rusty Staub	.08
239	George Foster	.08
240	Rick Sutcliffe	.05
241	Andre Thornton	.05
242	Mike Hargrove	.05
243	Dan Spillner	.05
244	Lary Sorensen	.05
245	Len Barker	.05
246	Rick Manning	.05
247	Toby Harrah	.05
248	Milt Wilcox	.05
249	Lou Whitaker	.05
250	Tom Brookens	.05
251	Chet Lemon	.05
252	Jack Morris	.05
253	Alan Trammell	.10
254	John Wockenfuss	.05
255	Lance Parrish	.05
256	Larry Herndon	.05
257	Chris Speier	.05
258	Woody Fryman	.05
259	Scott Sanderson	.05
260	Steve Rogers	.05
261	Warren Cromartie	.05
262	Gary Carter	.12
263	Bill Gullickson	.05
264	Andre Dawson	.12
265	Tim Raines	.08
266	Charlie Lea	.05
267	Jeff Reardon	.05
268	Al Oliver	.05
269	George Hendrick	.05
270	John Montefusco	.05
(271)	A's Logo	.05
(272)	Angels Logo	.05
(273)	Astros Logo	.05
(274)	Blue Jays Logo	.05
(275)	Braves Logo	.05
(276)	Brewers Logo	.05
(277)	Cardinals Logo	.05
(278)	Cubs Logo	.05
(279)	Dodgers Logo	.05
(280)	Expos Logo	.05
(281)	Giants Logo	.05
(282)	Indians Logo	.05
(283)	Mariners Logo	.05
(284)	Mets Logo	.05
(285)	Orioles Logo	.05
(286)	Padres Logo	.05
(287)	Phillies Logo	.05
(288)	Pirates Logo	.05
(289)	Rangers Logo	.05
(290)	Red Sox Logo	.05
(291)	Reds Logo	.05
(292)	Royals Logo	.05
(293)	Tigers Logo	.05
(294)	Twins Logo	.05
(295)	Yankees Logo	.05
(296)	White Sox Logo	.05

1984 Fleer

The 1984 Fleer set contained 660 cards for the fourth consecutive year. The 2-1/2" x 3-1/2" cards feature a color photo surrounded by white borders and horizontal dark blue stripes. The top stripe contains the word "Fleer" with the lower carrying the player's name. Backs have a small black-and-white player photo and are done in blue ink on white stock. The set was issued with team logo stickers.

		MT
Complete Set (660):		75.00
Common Player:		.08
Pack (15):		4.00
Wax Box (36):		100.00
1	Mike Boddicker	.08
2	Al Bumbry	.08
3	Todd Cruz	.08
4	Rich Dauer	.08
5	Storm Davis	.08
6	Rick Dempsey	.08
7	Jim Dwyer	.08
8	Mike Flanagan	.08
9	Dan Ford	.08
10	John Lowenstein	.08
11	Dennis Martinez	.12
12	Tippy Martinez	.08
13	Scott McGregor	.08
14	Eddie Murray	4.00
15	Joe Nolan	.08
16	Jim Palmer	1.00
17	Cal Ripken, Jr.	12.50
18	Gary Roenicke	.08
19	Lenn Sakata	.08
20	*John Shelby*	.08
21	Ken Singleton	.08
22	Sammy Stewart	.08
23	Tim Stoddard	.08
24	Marty Bystrom	.08
25	Steve Carlton	3.50
26	Ivan DeJesus	.08
27	John Denny	.08
28	Bob Dernier	.08
29	Bo Diaz	.08
30	Kiko Garcia	.08
31	Greg Gross	.08
32	*Kevin Gross*	.08
33	Von Hayes	.08
34	Willie Hernandez	.08
35	Al Holland	.08
36	*Charles Hudson*	.08
37	Joe Lefebvre	.08
38	Sixto Lezcano	.08
39	Garry Maddox	.08
40	Gary Matthews	.08
41	Len Matuszek	.08
42	Tug McGraw	.08
43	Joe Morgan	.75
44	Tony Perez	.15
45	Ron Reed	.08
46	Pete Rose	7.50
47	*Juan Samuel*	.75
48	Mike Schmidt	8.00
49	Ozzie Virgil	.08
50	*Juan Agosto*	.08
51	Harold Baines	.12
52	Floyd Bannister	.08
53	Salome Barojas	.08
54	Britt Burns	.08
55	Julio Cruz	.08
56	Richard Dotson	.08
57	Jerry Dybzinski	.08
58	Carlton Fisk	1.00
59	Scott Fletcher	.08
60	Jerry Hairston	.08
61	Kevin Hickey	.08
62	Marc Hill	.08
63	LaMarr Hoyt	.08
64	Ron Kittle	.08
65	Jerry Koosman	.08
66	Dennis Lamp	.08
67	Rudy Law	.08
68	Vance Law	.08
69	Greg Luzinski	.12
70	Tom Paciorek	.08
71	Mike Squires	.08
72	Dick Tidrow	.08
73	*Greg Walker*	.08
74	Glenn Abbott	.08
75	Howard Bailey	.08
76	Doug Bair	.08
77	Juan Berenguer	.08
78	Tom Brookens	.08
79	Enos Cabell	.08
80	Kirk Gibson	.08
81	John Grubb	.08
82	Larry Herndon	.08
83	Wayne Krenchicki	.08
84	Rick Leach	.08
85	Chet Lemon	.08
86	Aurelio Lopez	.08
87	Jack Morris	.08
88	Lance Parrish	.12
89	Dan Petry	.08
90	Dave Rozema	.08
91	Alan Trammell	.30
92	Lou Whitaker	.12
93	Milt Wilcox	.08
94	Glenn Wilson	.08
95	John Wockenfuss	.08
96	Dusty Baker	.12
97	Joe Beckwith	.08
98	Greg Brock	.08
99	Jack Fimple	.08
100	Pedro Guerrero	.08
101	Rick Honeycutt	.08
102	Burt Hooton	.08
103	Steve Howe	.08
104	Ken Landreaux	.08
105	Mike Marshall	.08
106	Rick Monday	.08
107	Jose Morales	.08
108	Tom Niedenfuer	.08
109	*Alejandro Pena*	.08
110	Jerry Reuss	.08
111	Bill Russell	.12
112	Steve Sax	.08
113	Mike Scioscia	.08
114	Derrel Thomas	.08
115	Fernando Valenzuela	.12
116	Bob Welch	.08
117	Steve Yeager	.08
118	Pat Zachry	.08
119	Don Baylor	.15
120	Bert Campaneris	.08
121	Rick Cerone	.08
122	*Ray Fontenot*	.08
123	George Frazier	.08
124	Oscar Gamble	.08
125	Goose Gossage	.10
126	Ken Griffey	.12
127	Ron Guidry	.10
128	Jay Howell	.08
129	Steve Kemp	.08
130	Matt Keough	.08
131	*Don Mattingly*	30.00
132	John Montefusco	.08
133	Omar Moreno	.08
134	Dale Murray	.08
135	Graig Nettles	.10
136	Lou Piniella	.10
137	Willie Randolph	.08
138	Shane Rawley	.08
139	Dave Righetti	.08
140	Andre Robertson	.08
141	Bob Shirley	.08
142	Roy Smalley	.08
143	Dave Winfield	3.00
144	Butch Wynegar	.08
145	*Jim Acker*	.08
146	Doyle Alexander	.08
147	Jesse Barfield	.08
148	George Bell	.08
149	Barry Bonnell	.08
150	Jim Clancy	.08
151	Dave Collins	.08
152	*Tony Fernandez*	1.00
153	Damaso Garcia	.08
154	Dave Geisel	.08
155	Jim Gott	.08
156	Alfredo Griffin	.08
157	Garth Iorg	.08
158	Roy Lee Jackson	.08
159	Cliff Johnson	.08
160	Luis Leal	.08
161	Buck Martinez	.08
162	Joey McLaughlin	.08
163	Randy Moffitt	.08
164	Lloyd Moseby	.08
165	Rance Mulliniks	.08
166	Jorge Orta	.08
167	Dave Stieb	.10
168	Willie Upshaw	.08
169	Ernie Whitt	.08
170	Len Barker	.08
171	Steve Bedrosian	.08
172	Bruce Benedict	.08
173	Brett Butler	.10
174	Rick Camp	.08
175	Chris Chambliss	.08
176	Ken Dayley	.08
177	Pete Falcone	.08
178	Terry Forster	.08
179	Gene Garber	.08
180	Terry Harper	.08
181	Bob Horner	.08
182	Glenn Hubbard	.08
183	Randy S. Johnson	.08
184	*Craig McMurtry*	.08
185	Donnie Moore	.08
186	Dale Murphy	.75
187	Phil Niekro	.75
188	Pascual Perez	.08
189	Biff Pocoroba	.08
190	Rafael Ramirez	.08
191	Jerry Royster	.08
192	Claudell Washington	.08
193	Bob Watson	.08
194	Jerry Augustine	.08
195	Mark Brouhard	.08
196	Mike Caldwell	.08
197	*Tom Candiotti*	.60
198	Cecil Cooper	.08
199	Rollie Fingers	.50
200	Jim Gantner	.08
201	Bob L. Gibson	.08
202	Moose Haas	.08
203	Roy Howell	.08
204	Pete Ladd	.08
205	Rick Manning	.08
206	Bob McClure	.08
207	Paul Molitor	4.00
208	Don Money	.08
209	Charlie Moore	.08
210	Ben Oglivie	.08
211	Chuck Porter	.08
212	Ed Romero	.08
213	Ted Simmons	.08
214	Jim Slaton	.08
215	Don Sutton	.45
216	Tom Tellmann	.08
217	Pete Vuckovich	.08
218	Ned Yost	.08
219	Robin Yount	4.00
220	Alan Ashby	.08
221	Kevin Bass	.08
222	Jose Cruz	.08
223	*Bill Dawley*	.08
224	Frank DiPino	.08
225	*Bill Doran*	.08
226	Phil Garner	.08
227	Art Howe	.08
228	Bob Knepper	.08
229	Ray Knight	.08
230	Frank LaCorte	.08
231	Mike LaCoss	.08
232	Mike Madden	.08
233	Jerry Mumphrey	.08
235	Terry Puhl	.08
236	Luis Pujols	.08
237	Craig Reynolds	.08
238	Vern Ruhle	.08
239	Nolan Ryan	17.50
240	Mike Scott	.08
241	Tony Scott	.08
242	Dave Smith	.08
243	Dickie Thon	.08
244	Denny Walling	.08
245	Dale Berra	.08
246	Jim Bibby	.08
247	John Candelaria	.08
248	*Jose DeLeon*	.08
249	Mike Easler	.08
250	Cecilio Guante	.08
251	Richie Hebner	.08
252	Lee Lacy	.08
253	Bill Madlock	.08
254	Milt May	.08
255	Lee Mazzilli	.08
256	Larry McWilliams	.08
257	Jim Morrison	.08
258	Dave Parker	.12
259	Tony Pena	.08
260	Johnny Ray	.08
261	Rick Rhoden	.08
262	Don Robinson	.08
263	Manny Sarmiento	.08
264	Rod Scurry	.08
265	Kent Tekulve	.08
266	Gene Tenace	.08
267	Jason Thompson	.08
268	*Lee Tunnell*	.08
269	*Marvell Wynne*	.08
270	Ray Burris	.08
271	Gary Carter	.45
272	Warren Cromartie	.08
273	Andre Dawson	1.00
274	Doug Flynn	.08
275	Terry Francona	.08
276	Bill Gullickson	.08
277	Bob James	.08
278	Charlie Lea	.08
279	Bryan Little	.08
280	Al Oliver	.10
281	Tim Raines	.45
282	Bobby Ramos	.08
283	Jeff Reardon	.08
284	Steve Rogers	.08
285	Scott Sanderson	.08
286	Dan Schatzeder	.08
287	Bryn Smith	.08
288	Chris Speier	.08
289	Manny Trillo	.08
290	Mike Vail	.08
291	Tim Wallach	.12
292	Chris Welsh	.08
293	Jim Wohlford	.08
294	Kurt Bevacqua	.08
295	Juan Bonilla	.08
296	Bobby Brown	.08
297	Luis DeLeon	.08
298	Dave Dravecky	.08
299	Tim Flannery	.08
300	Steve Garvey	.45
301	Tony Gwynn	12.00
302	*Andy Hawkins*	.20
303	Ruppert Jones	.08
304	Terry Kennedy	.08
305	Tim Lollar	.08
306	Gary Lucas	.08
307	*Kevin McReynolds*	.60
308	Sid Monge	.08
309	Mario Ramirez	.08
310	Gene Richards	.08
311	Luis Salazar	.08
312	Eric Show	.08
313	Elias Sosa	.08
314	Garry Templeton	.08
315	*Mark Thurmond*	.08
316	Ed Whitson	.08
317	Alan Wiggins	.08
318	Neil Allen	.08
319	Joaquin Andujar	.08
320	Steve Braun	.08
321	Glenn Brummer	.08
322	Bob Forsch	.08
323	David Green	.08
324	George Hendrick	.08
325	Tom Herr	.08
326	Dane Iorg	.08
327	Jeff Lahti	.08
328	Dave LaPoint	.08
329	Willie McGee	.12
330	Ken Oberkfell	.08
331	Darrell Porter	.08
332	Jamie Quirk	.08
333	Mike Ramsey	.08
334	Floyd Rayford	.08
335	Lonnie Smith	.08
336	Ozzie Smith	4.00
337	John Stuper	.08

No.	Player	Price
338	Bruce Sutter	.08
339	*Andy Van Slyke*	2.00
340	Dave Von Ohlen	.08
341	Willie Aikens	.08
342	Mike Armstrong	.08
343	Bud Black	.08
344	George Brett	7.50
345	Onix Concepcion	.08
346	Keith Creel	.08
347	Larry Gura	.08
348	Don Hood	.08
349	Dennis Leonard	.08
350	Hal McRae	.12
351	Amos Otis	.08
352	Gaylord Perry	.60
353	Greg Pryor	.08
354	Dan Quisenberry	.08
355	Steve Renko	.08
356	Leon Roberts	.08
357	*Pat Sheridan*	.08
358	Joe Simpson	.08
359	Don Slaught	.08
360	Paul Splittorff	.08
361	U.L. Washington	.08
362	John Wathan	.08
363	Frank White	.08
364	Willie Wilson	.12
365	Jim Barr	.08
366	Dave Bergman	.08
367	Fred Breining	.08
368	Bob Brenly	.08
369	Jack Clark	.08
370	Chili Davis	.12
371	Mark Davis	.08
372	Darrell Evans	.08
373	Atlee Hammaker	.08
374	Mike Krukow	.08
375	Duane Kuiper	.08
376	Bill Laskey	.08
377	Gary Lavelle	.08
378	Johnnie LeMaster	.08
379	Jeff Leonard	.08
380	Randy Lerch	.08
381	Renie Martin	.08
382	Andy McGaffigan	.08
383	Greg Minton	.08
384	Tom O'Malley	.08
385	Max Venable	.08
386	Brad Wellman	.08
387	Joel Youngblood	.08
388	Gary Allenson	.08
389	Luis Aponte	.08
390	Tony Armas	.08
391	Doug Bird	.08
392	Wade Boggs	4.00
393	*Dennis Boyd*	.08
394	Mike Brown	.08
395	Mark Clear	.08
396	Dennis Eckersley	.15
397	Dwight Evans	.10
398	Rich Gedman	.08
399	Glenn Hoffman	.08
400	Bruce Hurst	.08
401	John Henry Johnson	.08
402	Ed Jurak	.08
403	Rick Miller	.08
404	Jeff Newman	.08
405	Reid Nichols	.08
406	Bob Ojeda	.08
407	Jerry Remy	.08
408	Jim Rice	.15
409	Bob Stanley	.08
410	Dave Stapleton	.08
411	John Tudor	.08
412	Carl Yastrzemski	1.00
413	Buddy Bell	.08
414	Larry Biittner	.08
415	John Butcher	.08
416	Danny Darwin	.08
417	Bucky Dent	.08
418	Dave Hostetler	.08
419	Charlie Hough	.08
420	Bobby Johnson	.08
421	Odell Jones	.08
422	Jon Matlack	.08
423	*Pete O'Brien*	.30
424	Larry Parrish	.08
425	Mickey Rivers	.08
426	Billy Sample	.08
427	Dave Schmidt	.08
428	*Mike Smithson*	.08
429	Bill Stein	.08
430	Dave Stewart	.15
431	Jim Sundberg	.08
432	Frank Tanana	.08
433	Dave Tobik	.08
434	Wayne Tolleson	.08
435	George Wright	.08
436	Bill Almon	.08
437	*Keith Atherton*	.08
438	Dave Beard	.08
439	Tom Burgmeier	.08
440	Jeff Burroughs	.08
441	*Chris Codiroli*	.08
442	*Tim Conroy*	.08
443	Mike Davis	.08
444	Wayne Gross	.08
445	Garry Hancock	.08
446	Mike Heath	.08
447	Rickey Henderson	3.00
448	*Don Hill*	.08
449	Bob Kearney	.08
450	Bill Krueger	.08
451	Rick Langford	.08
452	Carney Lansford	.08
453	Davey Lopes	.08
454	Steve McCatty	.08
455	Dan Meyer	.08
456	Dwayne Murphy	.08
457	Mike Norris	.08
458	Ricky Peters	.08
459	Tony Phillips	.25
460	Tom Underwood	.08
461	Mike Warren	.08
462	Johnny Bench	1.00
463	Bruce Berenyi	.08
464	Dann Bilardello	.08
465	Cesar Cedeno	.08
466	Dave Concepcion	.08
467	Dan Driessen	.08
468	*Nick Esasky*	.08
469	Rich Gale	.08
470	Ben Hayes	.08
471	Paul Householder	.08
472	Tom Hume	.08
473	Alan Knicely	.08
474	Eddie Milner	.08
475	Ron Oester	.08
476	Kelly Paris	.08
477	Frank Pastore	.08
478	Ted Power	.08
479	Joe Price	.08
480	Charlie Puleo	.08
481	*Gary Redus*	.25
482	Bill Scherrer	.08
483	Mario Soto	.08
484	Alex Trevino	.08
485	Duane Walker	.08
486	Larry Bowa	.08
487	Warren Brusstar	.08
488	Bill Buckner	.08
489	Bill Campbell	.08
490	Ron Cey	.08
491	Jody Davis	.08
492	Leon Durham	.08
493	Mel Hall	.08
494	Fergie Jenkins	.60
495	Jay Johnstone	.08
496	*Craig Lefferts*	.20
497	*Carmelo Martinez*	.08
498	Jerry Morales	.08
499	Keith Moreland	.08
500	Dickie Noles	.08
501	Mike Proly	.08
502	Chuck Rainey	.08
503	Dick Ruthven	.08
504	Ryne Sandberg	8.00
505	Lee Smith	.15
506	Steve Trout	.08
507	Gary Woods	.08
508	Juan Beniquez	.08
509	Bob Boone	.08
510	Rick Burleson	.08
511	Rod Carew	1.00
512	Bobby Clark	.08
513	John Curtis	.08
514	Doug DeCinces	.08
515	Brian Downing	.08
516	Tim Foli	.08
517	Ken Forsch	.08
518	Bobby Grich	.08
519	Andy Hassler	.08
520	Reggie Jackson	1.50
521	Ron Jackson	.08
522	Tommy John	.12
523	Bruce Kison	.08
524	Steve Lubratich	.08
525	Fred Lynn	.12
526	*Gary Pettis*	.08
527	Luis Sanchez	.08
528	Daryl Sconiers	.08
529	Ellis Valentine	.08
530	Rob Wilfong	.08
531	Mike Witt	.08
532	Geoff Zahn	.08
533	Bud Anderson	.08
534	Chris Bando	.08
535	Alan Bannister	.08
536	Bert Blyleven	.08
537	Tom Brennan	.08
538	Jamie Easterly	.08
539	Juan Eichelberger	.08
540	Jim Essian	.08
541	Mike Fischlin	.08
542	Julio Franco	.25
543	Mike Hargrove	.08
544	Toby Harrah	.08
545	Ron Hassey	.08
546	*Neal Heaton*	.08
547	Bake McBride	.08
548	Broderick Perkins	.08
549	Lary Sorensen	.08
550	Dan Spillner	.08
551	Rick Sutcliffe	.08
552	Pat Tabler	.08
553	Gorman Thomas	.08
554	Andre Thornton	.08
555	George Vukovich	.08
556	Darrell Brown	.08
557	Tom Brunansky	.08
558	*Randy Bush*	.08
559	Bobby Castillo	.08
560	John Castino	.08
561	Ron Davis	.08
562	Dave Engle	.08
563	Lenny Faedo	.08
564	Pete Filson	.08
565	Gary Gaetti	.12
566	Mickey Hatcher	.08
567	Kent Hrbek	.20
568	Rusty Kuntz	.08
569	Tim Laudner	.08
570	Rick Lysander	.08
571	Bobby Mitchell	.08
572	Ken Schrom	.08
573	Ray Smith	.08
574	*Tim Teufel*	.30
575	Frank Viola	.08
576	Gary Ward	.08
577	Ron Washington	.08
578	Len Whitehouse	.08
579	Al Williams	.08
580	Bob Bailor	.08
581	Mark Bradley	.08
582	Hubie Brooks	.08
583	Carlos Diaz	.08
584	George Foster	.08
585	Brian Giles	.08
586	Danny Heep	.08
587	Keith Hernandez	.08
588	Ron Hodges	.08
589	Scott Holman	.08
590	Dave Kingman	.15
591	Ed Lynch	.08
592	*Jose Oquendo*	.15
593	Jesse Orosco	.08
594	*Junior Ortiz*	.08
595	Tom Seaver	1.50
596	*Doug Sisk*	.08
597	Rusty Staub	.12
598	John Stearns	.08
599	Darryl Strawberry	7.50
600	Craig Swan	.08
601	*Walt Terrell*	.12
602	Mike Torrez	.08
603	Mookie Wilson	.08
604	Jamie Allen	.08
605	Jim Beattie	.08
606	Tony Bernazard	.08
607	Manny Castillo	.08
608	Bill Caudill	.08
609	Bryan Clark	.08
610	Al Cowens	.08
611	Dave Henderson	.08
612	Steve Henderson	.08
613	Orlando Mercado	.08
614	Mike Moore	.08
615	Ricky Nelson	.08
616	*Spike Owen*	.20
617	Pat Putnam	.08
618	Ron Roenicke	.08
619	Mike Stanton	.08
620	Bob Stoddard	.08
621	Rick Sweet	.08
622	Roy Thomas	.08
623	Ed Vande Berg	.08
624	*Matt Young*	.08
625	Richie Zisk	.08
626	'83 All-Star Game Record Breaker (Fred Lynn)	.08
627	'83 All-Star Game Record Breaker (Manny Trillo)	.08
628	N.L. Iron Man (Steve Garvey)	.20
629	A.L. Batting Runner-Up (Rod Carew)	.25
630	A.L. Batting Champion (Wade Boggs)	1.00
631	Letting Go Of The Raines (Tim Raines)	.20
632	Double Trouble (Al Oliver)	.08
633	All-Star Second Base (Steve Sax)	.08
634	All-Star Shortstop (Dickie Thon)	.08
635	Ace Firemen (Tippy Martinez, Dan Quisenberry)	.08
636	Reds Reunited (Joe Morgan, Tony Perez, Pete Rose)	.75
637	Backstop Stars (Bob Boone, Lance Parrish)	.12
638	The Pine Tar Incident, 7/24/83 (George Brett, Gaylord Perry)	.45
639	1983 No-Hitters (Bob Forsch, Dave Righetti, Mike Warren)	.08
640	Retiring Superstars (Johnny Bench, Carl Yastrzemski)	1.00
641	Going Out In Style (Gaylord Perry)	.15
642	300 Club & Strikeout Record (Steve Carlton)	.20
643	The Managers (Joe Altobelli, Paul Owens)	.08
644	The MVP (Rick Dempsey)	.08
645	The Rookie Winner (Mike Boddicker)	.08
646	The Clincher (Scott McGregor)	.08
647	Checklist: Orioles/Royals (Joe Altobelli)	.08
648	Checklist: Phillies/Giants (Paul Owens)	.08
649	Checklist: White Sox/Red Sox (Tony LaRussa)	.08
650	Checklist: Tigers/Rangers (Sparky Anderson)	.08
651	Checklist: Dodgers/A's (Tommy Lasorda)	.10
652	Checklist: Yankees/Reds (Billy Martin)	.08
653	Checklist: Blue Jays/Cubs (Bobby Cox)	.08
654	Checklist: Braves/Angels (Joe Torre)	.08
655	Checklist: Brewers/Indians (Rene Lacheman)	.08
656	Checklist: Astros/Twins (Bob Lillis)	.08
657	Checklist: Pirates/Mets (Chuck Tanner)	.08
658	Checklist: Expos/Mariners (Bill Virdon)	.08
659	Checklist: Padres/Specials (Dick Williams)	.08
660	Checklist: Cardinals/Specials (Whitey Herzog)	.08

1984 Fleer Update

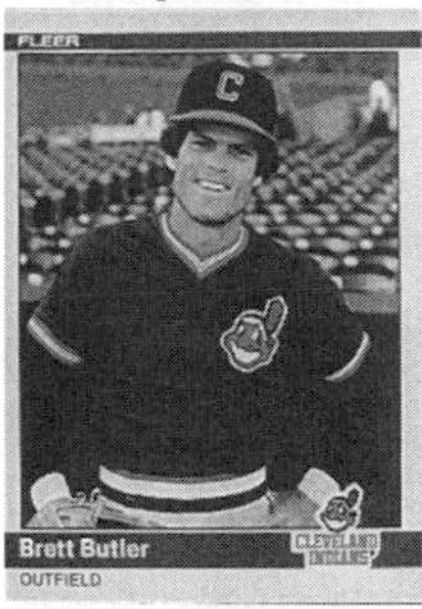

Following the lead of Topps, Fleer issued near the end of the baseball season a 132-card set to update player trades and include rookies not depicted in the regular issue. The cards are identical in design to the regular issue but are numbered U-1 through U-132. Available only as a boxed set through hobby dealers, the set was printed in limited quantities.

		MT
Complete Set (132):		400.00
Common Player:		.25
1	Willie Aikens	.25
2	Luis Aponte	.25
3	Mark Bailey	.25
4	Bob Bailor	.25
5	Dusty Baker	.35
6	Steve Balboni	.25
7	Alan Bannister	.25
8	Marty Barrett	.25
9	Dave Beard	.25
10	Joe Beckwith	.25
11	Dave Bergman	.25
12	Tony Bernazard	.25
13	Bruce Bochte	.25
14	Barry Bonnell	.25
15	Phil Bradley	.25
16	Fred Breining	.25
17	Mike Brown	.25
18	Bill Buckner	.35
19	Ray Burris	.25
20	John Butcher	.25
21	Brett Butler	.50
22	Enos Cabell	.25
23	Bill Campbell	.25
24	Bill Caudill	.25
25	Bobby Clark	.25
26	Bryan Clark	.25
27	*Roger Clemens*	240.00
28	Jaime Cocanower	.25
29	*Ron Darling*	2.50
30	Alvin Davis	.25
31	Bob Dernier	.25
32	Carlos Diaz	.25
33	Mike Easler	.25
34	Dennis Eckersley	10.00
35	Jim Essian	.25
36	Darrell Evans	.35
37	Mike Fitzgerald	.25
38	Tim Foli	.25
39	John Franco	6.00
40	George Frazier	.25
41	Rich Gale	.25
42	Barbaro Garbey	.25
43	*Dwight Gooden*	10.00
44	Goose Gossage	.40
45	Wayne Gross	.25
46	Mark Gubicza	2.00
47	Jackie Gutierrez	.25
48	Toby Harrah	.25
49	Ron Hassey	.25
50	Richie Hebner	.25
51	Willie Hernandez	.25
52	Ed Hodge	.25
53	Ricky Horton	.25
54	Art Howe	.25
55	Dane Iorg	.25
56	Brook Jacoby	.40
57	Dion James	.25
58	Mike Jeffcoat	.25
59	Ruppert Jones	.25
60	Bob Kearney	.25
61	*Jimmy Key*	8.00
62	Dave Kingman	.50
63	Brad Komminsk	.25
64	Jerry Koosman	.25
65	Wayne Krenchicki	.25
66	Rusty Kuntz	.25
67	Frank LaCorte	.25
68	Dennis Lamp	.25
69	Tito Landrum	.25
70	*Mark Langston*	8.00
71	Rick Leach	.25
72	Craig Lefferts	.25
73	Gary Lucas	.25
74	Jerry Martin	.25
75	Carmelo Martinez	.25
76	Mike Mason	.25
77	Gary Matthews	.25
78	Andy McGaffigan	.25
79	Joey McLaughlin	.25
80	Joe Morgan	6.00
81	Darryl Motley	.25
82	Graig Nettles	.50
83	Phil Niekro	4.00
84	Ken Oberkfell	.25
85	Al Oliver	.35
86	Jorge Orta	.25
87	Amos Otis	.25
88	Bob Owchinko	.25
89	Dave Parker	2.00
90	Jack Perconte	.25
91	Tony Perez	4.00
92	Gerald Perry	.25
93	*Kirby Puckett*	150.00
94	Shane Rawley	.25
95	Floyd Rayford	.25
96	Ron Reed	.25
97	R.J. Reynolds	.25
98	Gene Richards	.25
99	*Jose Rijo*	10.00
100	Jeff Robinson	.25
101	Ron Romanick	.25
102	Pete Rose	15.00
103	*Bret Saberhagen*	15.00
104	Scott Sanderson	.25
105	Dick Schofield	.25
106	Tom Seaver	15.00
107	Jim Slaton	.25
108	Mike Smithson	.25
109	Lary Sorensen	.25
110	Tim Stoddard	.25
111	Jeff Stone	.25
112	Champ Summers	.25
113	Jim Sundberg	.25
114	Rick Sutcliffe	.35
115	Craig Swan	.25
116	Derrel Thomas	.25
117	Gorman Thomas	.25
118	Alex Trevino	.25
119	Manny Trillo	.25
120	John Tudor	.25
121	Tom Underwood	.25
122	Mike Vail	.25
123	Tom Waddell	.25
124	Gary Ward	.25
125	Terry Whitfield	.25
126	Curtis Wilkerson	.25
127	Frank Williams	.25
128	Glenn Wilson	.25
129	John Wockenfuss	.25
130	Ned Yost	.25
131	Mike Young	.25
132	Checklist 1-132	.10

1984 Fleer Stickers

This set was designed to be housed in a special collector's album that was organized according to various league leader categories, resulting in some players being pictured on more than one sticker. Each full-color sticker measures 1-15/16" x 2-1/2" and is framed with a beige border. The stickers, which were sold in packs of six, are numbered on the back.

		MT
Complete Set (126):		10.00
Common Player:		.05
Sticker Album:		1.00
1	Dickie Thon	.05
2	Ken Landreaux	.05
3	Darrell Evans	.05
4	Harold Baines	.08
5	Dave Winfield	.20
6	Bill Madlock	.05
7	Lonnie Smith	.05
8	Jose Cruz	.05
9	George Hendrick	.05
10	Ray Knight	.05
11	Wade Boggs	.40
12	Rod Carew	.25
13	Lou Whitaker	.10
14	Alan Trammell	.10
15	Cal Ripken, Jr.	.50
16	Mike Schmidt	.40
17	Dale Murphy	.20
18	Andre Dawson	.15
19	Pedro Guerrero	.05
20	Jim Rice	.08
21	Tony Armas	.05
22	Ron Kittle	.05
23	Eddie Murray	.25
24	Jose Cruz	.05
25	Andre Dawson	.15
26	Rafael Ramirez	.05
27	Al Oliver	.05
28	Wade Boggs	.40
29	Cal Ripken, Jr.	.50
30	Lou Whitaker	.10
31	Cecil Cooper	.05
32	Dale Murphy	.20
33	Andre Dawson	.15
34	Pedro Guerrero	.05
35	Mike Schmidt	.40
36	George Brett	.40
37	Jim Rice	.08
38	Eddie Murray	.25
39	Carlton Fisk	.10
40	Rusty Staub	.05
41	Duane Walker	.05
42	Steve Braun	.05
43	Kurt Bevacqua	.05
44	Hal McRae	.05
45	Don Baylor	.08
46	Ken Singleton	.05
47	Greg Luzinski	.08
48	Mike Schmidt	.40
49	Keith Hernandez	.05
50	Dale Murphy	.20
51	Tim Raines	.10
52	Wade Boggs	.40
53	Rickey Henderson	.25
54	Rod Carew	.25
55	Ken Singleton	.05
56	John Denny	.05
57	John Candelaria	.05
58	Larry McWilliams	.05
59	Pascual Perez	.05
60	Jesse Orosco	.05
61	Moose Haas	.05
62	Richard Dotson	.05
63	Mike Flanagan	.05
64	Scott McGregor	.05
65	Atlee Hammaker	.05
66	Rick Honeycutt	.05
67	Lee Smith	.08
68	Al Holland	.05
69	Greg Minton	.05
70	Bruce Sutter	.05
71	Jeff Reardon	.05
72	Frank DiPino	.05
73	Dan Quisenberry	.05
74	Bob Stanley	.05
75	Ron Davis	.05
76	Bill Caudill	.05
77	Peter Ladd	.05
78	Steve Carlton	.20
79	Mario Soto	.05
80	Larry McWilliams	.05
81	Fernando Valenzuela	.08
82	Nolan Ryan	.75
83	Jack Morris	.05
84	Floyd Bannister	.05
85	Dave Stieb	.05
86	Dave Righetti	.05
87	Rick Sutcliffe	.05
88	Tim Raines	.10
89	Alan Wiggins	.05
90	Steve Sax	.05
91	Mookie Wilson	.05
92	Rickey Henderson	.25
93	Rudy Law	.05
94	Willie Wilson	.05
95	Julio Cruz	.05
96	Johnny Bench	.30
97	Carl Yastrzemski	.25
98	Gaylord Perry	.15
99	Pete Rose	.45
100	Joe Morgan	.20
101	Steve Carlton	.20
102	Jim Palmer	.20
103	Rod Carew	.25
104	Darryl Strawberry	.20
105	Craig McMurtry	.05
106	Mel Hall	.05
107	Lee Tunnell	.05
108	Bill Dawley	.05
109	Ron Kittle	.05
110	Mike Boddicker	.05
111	Julio Franco	.05
112	Daryl Sconiers	.05
113	Neal Heaton	.05
114	John Shelby	.05
115	Rick Dempsey	.05
116	John Lowenstein	.05
117	Jim Dwyer	.05
118	Bo Diaz	.05
119	Pete Rose	.45
120	Joe Morgan	.20
121	Gary Matthews	.05
122	Garry Maddox	.05
123	Paul Owens	.05
124	Tom Lasorda	.10
125	Joe Altobelli	.05
126	Tony LaRussa	.05

1985 Fleer

The 1985 Fleer set consists of 660 cards, each measuring 2-1/2" x 3-1/2". Card fronts feature a color photo plus the player's team logo and the word "Fleer." The photos have a color-coded frame which corresponds to the player's team. A grey border surrounds the frame. Backs are similar in design to previous years, but have two shades of red and black ink on white stock. For the fourth consecutive year, Fleer included special cards and team checklists in the set. Also incorporated in a set for the first time were ten "Major League Prospect" cards, each featuring two rookie hopefuls. The set was issued with team logo stickers.

		MT
Complete Set (660):		110.00
Common Player:		.06
Pack (15):		6.00
Wax Box (36):		150.00
1	Doug Bair	.06
2	Juan Berenguer	.06
3	Dave Bergman	.06
4	Tom Brookens	.06
5	Marty Castillo	.06
6	Darrell Evans	.10
7	Barbaro Garbey	.06
8	Kirk Gibson	.06
9	John Grubb	.06
10	Willie Hernandez	.06
11	Larry Herndon	.06
12	Howard Johnson	.06
13	Ruppert Jones	.06
14	Rusty Kuntz	.06
15	Chet Lemon	.06
16	Aurelio Lopez	.06
17	Sid Monge	.06
18	Jack Morris	.10
19	Lance Parrish	.10
20	Dan Petry	.06
21	Dave Rozema	.06
22	Bill Scherrer	.06
23	Alan Trammell	.25
24	Lou Whitaker	.10
25	Milt Wilcox	.06
26	Kurt Bevacqua	.06
27	*Greg Booker*	.06
28	Bobby Brown	.06
29	Luis DeLeon	.06
30	Dave Dravecky	.06
31	Tim Flannery	.06
32	Steve Garvey	.35
33	Goose Gossage	.12
34	Tony Gwynn	6.00
35	Greg Harris	.06
36	Andy Hawkins	.06
37	Terry Kennedy	.06
38	Craig Lefferts	.06
39	Tim Lollar	.06
40	Carmelo Martinez	.06
41	Kevin McReynolds	.06
42	Graig Nettles	.10
43	Luis Salazar	.06
44	Eric Show	.06
45	Garry Templeton	.06
46	Mark Thurmond	.06
47	Ed Whitson	.06
48	Alan Wiggins	.06
49	Rich Bordi	.06
50	Larry Bowa	.06
51	Warren Brusstar	.06
52	Ron Cey	.06
53	*Henry Cotto*	.06
54	Jody Davis	.06
55	Bob Dernier	.06
56	Leon Durham	.06
57	Dennis Eckersley	.30
58	George Frazier	.06
59	Richie Hebner	.06
60	Dave Lopes	.06
61	Gary Matthews	.06
62	Keith Moreland	.06
63	Rick Reuschel	.06
64	Dick Ruthven	.06
65	Ryne Sandberg	5.00
66	Scott Sanderson	.06
67	Lee Smith	.10
68	Tim Stoddard	.06
69	Rick Sutcliffe	.06
70	Steve Trout	.06
71	Gary Woods	.06
72	Wally Backman	.06
73	Bruce Berenyi	.06
74	Hubie Brooks	.06
75	Kelvin Chapman	.06
76	Ron Darling	.06
77	Sid Fernandez	.06
78	Mike Fitzgerald	.06
79	George Foster	.06
80	Brent Gaff	.06
81	Ron Gardenhire	.06
82	Dwight Gooden	1.00
83	Tom Gorman	.06
84	Danny Heep	.06
85	Keith Hernandez	.06
86	Ray Knight	.06
87	Ed Lynch	.06
88	Jose Oquendo	.06
89	Jesse Orosco	.06
90	*Rafael Santana*	.06
91	Doug Sisk	.06
92	Rusty Staub	.10
93	Darryl Strawberry	1.00
94	Walt Terrell	.06
95	Mookie Wilson	.06
96	Jim Acker	.06
97	Willie Aikens	.06
98	Doyle Alexander	.06
99	Jesse Barfield	.06
100	George Bell	.06
101	Jim Clancy	.06
102	Dave Collins	.06
103	Tony Fernandez	.06
104	Damaso Garcia	.06
105	Jim Gott	.06
106	Alfredo Griffin	.06
107	Garth Iorg	.06
108	Roy Lee Jackson	.06
109	Cliff Johnson	.06
110	Jimmy Key	2.00
111	Dennis Lamp	.06
112	Rick Leach	.06
113	Luis Leal	.06
114	Buck Martinez	.06
115	Lloyd Moseby	.06
116	Rance Mulliniks	.06
117	Dave Stieb	.06
118	Willie Upshaw	.06
119	Ernie Whitt	.06
120	Mike Armstrong	.06
121	Don Baylor	.12
122	Marty Bystrom	.06
123	Rick Cerone	.06
124	Joe Cowley	.06
125	Brian Dayett	.06
126	Tim Foli	.06
127	Ray Fontenot	.06
128	Ken Griffey	.10
129	Ron Guidry	.10
130	Toby Harrah	.06
131	Jay Howell	.06
132	Steve Kemp	.06
133	Don Mattingly	9.00
134	Bobby Meacham	.06
135	John Montefusco	.06
136	Omar Moreno	.06
137	Dale Murray	.06
138	Phil Niekro	.50
139	*Mike Pagliarulo*	.20
140	Willie Randolph	.06
141	Dennis Rasmussen	.06
142	Dave Righetti	.06
143	Jose Rijo	.10
144	Andre Robertson	.06
145	Bob Shirley	.06
146	Dave Winfield	3.00
147	Butch Wynegar	.06
148	Gary Allenson	.06
149	Tony Armas	.06
150	Marty Barrett	.06
151	Wade Boggs	4.50
152	Dennis Boyd	.06
153	Bill Buckner	.06
154	Mark Clear	.06
155	Roger Clemens	50.00
156	Steve Crawford	.06
157	Mike Easler	.06
158	Dwight Evans	.06
159	Rich Gedman	.06
160	Jackie Gutierrez	.06
161	Bruce Hurst	.06
162	John Henry Johnson	.06
163	Rick Miller	.06
164	Reid Nichols	.06
165	*Al Nipper*	.06
166	Bob Ojeda	.06
167	Jerry Remy	.06
168	Jim Rice	.06
169	Bob Stanley	.06
170	Mike Boddicker	.06
171	Al Bumbry	.06
172	Todd Cruz	.06
173	Rich Dauer	.06
174	Storm Davis	.06
175	Rick Dempsey	.06
176	Jim Dwyer	.06
177	Mike Flanagan	.06
178	Dan Ford	.06
179	Wayne Gross	.06
180	John Lowenstein	.06
181	Dennis Martinez	.10
182	Tippy Martinez	.06
183	Scott McGregor	.06
184	Eddie Murray	2.50
185	Joe Nolan	.06
186	Floyd Rayford	.06
187	Cal Ripken, Jr.	10.00
188	Gary Roenicke	.06
189	Lenn Sakata	.06
190	John Shelby	.06
191	Ken Singleton	.06
192	Sammy Stewart	.06
193	Bill Swaggerty	.06
194	Tom Underwood	.06
195	Mike Young	.06
196	Steve Balboni	.06
197	Joe Beckwith	.06
198	Bud Black	.06
199	George Brett	4.50
200	Onix Concepcion	.06
201	*Mark Gubicza*	.80
202	Larry Gura	.06
203	Mark Huismann	.06
204	Dane Iorg	.06
205	Danny Jackson	.06
206	Charlie Leibrandt	.06
207	Hal McRae	.10
208	Darryl Motley	.06
209	Jorge Orta	.06
210	Greg Pryor	.06
211	Dan Quisenberry	.06
212	Bret Saberhagen	2.00
213	Pat Sheridan	.06
214	Don Slaught	.06
215	U.L. Washington	.06
216	John Wathan	.06
217	Frank White	.06
218	Willie Wilson	.06
219	Neil Allen	.06
220	Joaquin Andujar	.06
221	Steve Braun	.06
222	Danny Cox	.06
223	Bob Forsch	.06
224	David Green	.06
225	George Hendrick	.06
226	Tom Herr	.06
227	*Ricky Horton*	.06
228	Art Howe	.06
229	Mike Jorgensen	.06
230	Kurt Kepshire	.06
231	Jeff Lahti	.06
232	Tito Landrum	.06
233	Dave LaPoint	.06
234	Willie McGee	.15
235	*Tom Nieto*	.06
236	*Terry Pendleton*	2.00
237	Darrell Porter	.06
238	Dave Rucker	.06
239	Lonnie Smith	.06
240	Ozzie Smith	3.00
241	Bruce Sutter	.06
242	Andy Van Slyke	.06
243	Dave Von Ohlen	.06
244	Larry Andersen	.06
245	Bill Campbell	.06
246	Steve Carlton	1.50
247	Tim Corcoran	.06
248	Ivan DeJesus	.06
249	John Denny	.06
250	Bo Diaz	.06
251	Greg Gross	.06
252	Kevin Gross	.06
253	Von Hayes	.06
254	Al Holland	.06
255	Charles Hudson	.06
256	Jerry Koosman	.06
257	Joe Lefebvre	.06
258	Sixto Lezcano	.06
259	Garry Maddox	.06
260	Len Matuszek	.06
261	Tug McGraw	.06
262	Al Oliver	.06
263	Shane Rawley	.06
264	Juan Samuel	.06
265	Mike Schmidt	5.00
266	*Jeff Stone*	.06
267	Ozzie Virgil	.06
268	Glenn Wilson	.06
269	John Wockenfuss	.06
270	Darrell Brown	.06
271	Tom Brunansky	.06
272	Randy Bush	.06
273	John Butcher	.06
274	Bobby Castillo	.06
275	Ron Davis	.06
276	Dave Engle	.06
277	Pete Filson	.06
278	Gary Gaetti	.10
279	Mickey Hatcher	.06
280	Ed Hodge	.06
281	Kent Hrbek	.20
282	Houston Jimenez	.06
283	Tim Laudner	.06
284	Rick Lysander	.06
285	Dave Meier	.06
286	Kirby Puckett	30.00
287	Pat Putnam	.06
288	Ken Schrom	.06
289	Mike Smithson	.06
290	Tim Teufel	.06
291	Frank Viola	.06
292	Ron Washington	.06
293	Don Aase	.06
294	Juan Beniquez	.06
295	Bob Boone	.06
296	Mike Brown	.06
297	Rod Carew	1.50
298	Doug Corbett	.06
299	Doug DeCinces	.06
300	Brian Downing	.06
301	Ken Forsch	.06
302	Bobby Grich	.06
303	Reggie Jackson	2.00
304	Tommy John	.10
305	Curt Kaufman	.06
306	Bruce Kison	.06
307	Fred Lynn	.10
308	Gary Pettis	.06
309	*Ron Romanick*	.06
310	Luis Sanchez	.06
311	Dick Schofield	.06
312	Daryl Sconiers	.06
313	Jim Slaton	.06
314	Derrel Thomas	.06
315	Rob Wilfong	.06
316	Mike Witt	.06
317	Geoff Zahn	.06
318	Len Barker	.06
319	Steve Bedrosian	.06
320	Bruce Benedict	.06
321	Rick Camp	.06
322	Chris Chambliss	.06
323	*Jeff Dedmon*	.06
324	Terry Forster	.06
325	Gene Garber	.06
326	*Albert Hall*	.06
327	Terry Harper	.06
328	Bob Horner	.06
329	Glenn Hubbard	.06
330	Randy S. Johnson	.06
331	Brad Komminsk	.06
332	Rick Mahler	.06
333	Craig McMurtry	.06
334	Donnie Moore	.06
335	Dale Murphy	.50
336	Ken Oberkfell	.06
337	Pascual Perez	.06
338	Gerald Perry	.06
339	Rafael Ramirez	.06
340	Jerry Royster	.06
341	Alex Trevino	.06
342	Claudell Washington	.06
343	Alan Ashby	.06
344	*Mark Bailey*	.06
345	Kevin Bass	.06
346	Enos Cabell	.06
347	Jose Cruz	.06
348	Bill Dawley	.06
349	Frank DiPino	.06
350	Bill Doran	.06
351	Phil Garner	.06
352	Bob Knepper	.06
353	Mike LaCoss	.06
354	Jerry Mumphrey	.06
355	Joe Niekro	.06
356	Terry Puhl	.06

357 Craig Reynolds .06
358 Vern Ruhle .06
359 Nolan Ryan 10.00
360 Joe Sambito .06
361 Mike Scott .06
362 Dave Smith .06
363 *Julio Solano* .06
364 Dickie Thon .06
365 Denny Walling .06
366 Dave Anderson .06
367 Bob Bailor .06
368 Greg Brock .06
369 Carlos Diaz .06
370 Pedro Guerrero .06
371 *Orel Hershiser* 3.50
372 Rick Honeycutt .06
373 Burt Hooton .06
374 *Ken Howell* .15
375 Ken Landreaux .06
376 Candy Maldonado .06
377 Mike Marshall .06
378 Tom Niedenfuer .06
379 Alejandro Pena .06
380 Jerry Reuss .06
381 *R.J. Reynolds* .06
382 German Rivera .06
383 Bill Russell .06
384 Steve Sax .06
385 Mike Scioscia .06
386 *Franklin Stubbs* .06
387 Fernando Valenzuela .10
388 Bob Welch .06
389 Terry Whitfield .06
390 Steve Yeager .06
391 Pat Zachry .06
392 Fred Breining .06
393 Gary Carter .40
394 Andre Dawson .90
395 Miguel Dilone .06
396 Dan Driessen .06
397 Doug Flynn .06
398 Terry Francona .06
399 Bill Gullickson .06
400 Bob James .06
401 Charlie Lea .06
402 Bryan Little .06
403 Gary Lucas .06
404 David Palmer .06
405 Tim Raines .20
406 Mike Ramsey .06
407 Jeff Reardon .06
408 Steve Rogers .06
409 Dan Schatzeder .06
410 Bryn Smith .06
411 Mike Stenhouse .06
412 Tim Wallach .10
413 Jim Wohlford .06
414 Bill Almon .06
415 Keith Atherton .06
416 Bruce Bochte .06
417 Tom Burgmeier .06
418 Ray Burris .06
419 Bill Caudill .06
420 Chris Codiroli .06
421 Tim Conroy .06
422 Mike Davis .06
423 Jim Essian .06
424 Mike Heath .06
425 Rickey Henderson 3.00
426 Donnie Hill .06
427 Dave Kingman .10
428 Bill Krueger .06
429 Carney Lansford .06
430 Steve McCatty .06
431 Joe Morgan .40
432 Dwayne Murphy .06
433 Tony Phillips .10
434 Lary Sorensen .06
435 Mike Warren .06
436 *Curt Young* .06
437 Luis Aponte .06
438 Chris Bando .06
439 Tony Bernazard .06
440 Bert Blyleven .06
441 Brett Butler .10
442 Ernie Camacho .06
443 Joe Carter 4.00
444 Carmelo Castillo .06
445 Jamie Easterly .06
446 *Steve Farr* .10
447 Mike Fischlin .06
448 Julio Franco .06
449 Mel Hall .06
450 Mike Hargrove .06
451 Neal Heaton .06
452 Brook Jacoby .06
453 *Mike Jeffcoat* .06
454 *Don Schulze* .06
455 Roy Smith .06
456 Pat Tabler .06
457 Andre Thornton .06
458 George Vukovich .06
459 Tom Waddell .06
460 Jerry Willard .06
461 Dale Berra .06
462 John Candelaria .06
463 Jose DeLeon .06
464 Doug Frobel .06
465 Cecilio Guante .06
466 Brian Harper .06
467 Lee Lacy .06
468 Bill Madlock .06
469 Lee Mazzilli .06
470 Larry McWilliams .06
471 Jim Morrison .06
472 Tony Pena .06
473 Johnny Ray .06
474 Rick Rhoden .06
475 Don Robinson .06
476 Rod Scurry .06
477 Kent Tekulve .06
478 Jason Thompson .06
479 John Tudor .06
480 Lee Tunnell .06
481 Marvell Wynne .06
482 Salome Barojas .06
483 Dave Beard .06
484 Jim Beattie .06
485 Barry Bonnell .06
486 *Phil Bradley* .06
487 Al Cowens .06
488 *Alvin Davis* .06
489 Dave Henderson .06
490 Steve Henderson .06
491 Bob Kearney .06
492 Mark Langston 1.50
493 Larry Milbourne .06
494 Paul Mirabella .06
495 Mike Moore .06
496 Edwin Nunez .06
497 Spike Owen .06
498 Jack Perconte .06
499 Ken Phelps .06
500 *Jim Presley* .06
501 Mike Stanton .06
502 Bob Stoddard .06
503 Gorman Thomas .06
504 Ed Vande Berg .06
505 Matt Young .06
506 Juan Agosto .06
507 Harold Baines .15
508 Floyd Bannister .06
509 Britt Burns .06
510 Julio Cruz .06
511 Richard Dotson .06
512 Jerry Dybzinski .06
513 Carlton Fisk .75
514 Scott Fletcher .06
515 Jerry Hairston .06
516 Marc Hill .06
517 LaMarr Hoyt .06
518 Ron Kittle .06
519 Rudy Law .06
520 Vance Law .06
521 Greg Luzinski .10
522 Gene Nelson .06
523 Tom Paciorek .06
524 Ron Reed .06
525 Bert Roberge .06
526 Tom Seaver 1.25
527 Roy Smalley .06
528 Dan Spillner .06
529 Mike Squires .06
530 Greg Walker .06
531 Cesar Cedeno .06
532 Dave Concepcion .06
533 *Eric Davis* 2.50
534 Nick Esasky .06
535 Tom Foley .06
536 *John Franco* .75
537 Brad Gulden .06
538 Tom Hume .06
539 Wayne Krenchicki .06
540 Andy McGaffigan .06
541 Eddie Milner .06
542 Ron Oester .06
543 Bob Owchinko .06
544 Dave Parker .25
545 Frank Pastore .06
546 Tony Perez .15
547 Ted Power .06
548 Joe Price .06
549 Gary Redus .06
550 Pete Rose 3.00
551 Jeff Russell .06
552 Mario Soto .06
553 *Jay Tibbs* .06
554 Duane Walker .06
555 Alan Bannister .06
556 Buddy Bell .06
557 Danny Darwin .06
558 Charlie Hough .06
559 Bobby Jones .06
560 Odell Jones .06
561 *Jeff Kunkel* .06
562 *Mike Mason* .06
563 Pete O'Brien .06
564 Larry Parrish .06
565 Mickey Rivers .06
566 Billy Sample .06
567 Dave Schmidt .06
568 Donnie Scott .06
569 Dave Stewart .12
570 Frank Tanana .06
571 Wayne Tolleson .06
572 Gary Ward .06
573 Curtis Wilkerson .06
574 George Wright .06
575 Ned Yost .06
576 Mark Brouhard .06
577 Mike Caldwell .06
578 Bobby Clark .06
579 Jaime Cocanower .06
580 Cecil Cooper .06
581 Rollie Fingers .40
582 Jim Gantner .06
583 Moose Haas .06
584 Dion James .06
585 Pete Ladd .06
586 Rick Manning .06
587 Bob McClure .06
588 Paul Molitor 3.00
589 Charlie Moore .06
590 Ben Oglivie .06
591 Chuck Porter .06
592 *Randy Ready* .06
593 Ed Romero .06
594 Bill Schroeder .06
595 Ray Searage .06
596 Ted Simmons .06
597 Jim Sundberg .06
598 Don Sutton .35
599 Tom Tellmann .06
600 Rick Waits .06
601 Robin Yount 3.00
602 Dusty Baker .10
603 Bob Brenly .06
604 Jack Clark .06
605 Chili Davis .15
606 Mark Davis .06
607 *Dan Gladden* .45
608 Atlee Hammaker .06
609 Mike Krukow .06
610 Duane Kuiper .06
611 Bob Lacey .06
612 Bill Laskey .06
613 Gary Lavelle .06
614 Johnnie LeMaster .06
615 Jeff Leonard .06
616 Randy Lerch .06
617 Greg Minton .06
618 Steve Nicosia .06
619 Gene Richards .06
620 *Jeff Robinson* .06
621 Scot Thompson .06
622 Manny Trillo .06
623 Brad Wellman .06
624 *Frank Williams* .06
625 Joel Youngblood .06
626 Cal Ripken, Jr. (In Action) 4.00
627 Mike Schmidt (In Action) 1.50
628 Giving the Signs (Sparky Anderson) .10
629 A.L. Pitcher's Nightmare (Rickey Henderson, Dave Winfield) 1.00
630 N.L. Pitcher's Nightmare (Ryne Sandberg Mike Schmidt) 2.00
631 N.L. All-Stars (Gary Carter, Steve Garvey, Ozzie Smith, Darryl Strawberry) .25
632 All-Star Game Winning Battery (Gary Carter, Charlie Lea) .10
633 N.L. Pennant Clinchers (Steve Garvey, Goose Gossage) .20
634 N.L. Rookie Phenoms (Dwight Gooden, Juan Samuel) .25
635 Toronto's Big Guns (Willie Upshaw) .06
636 Toronto's Big Guns (Lloyd Moseby) .06
637 Holland (Al Holland) .06
638 Tunnell (Lee Tunnell) .06
639 Reggie Jackson (In Action) .50
640 Pete Rose (In Action) .75
641 Father & Son (Cal Ripken, Jr., Cal Ripken, Sr.) 4.00
642 Cubs team .10
643 1984's Two Perfect Games & One No-Hitter (Jack Morris, David Palmer, Mike Witt) .06
644 Major League Prospect (Willie Lozado, Vic Mata) .06
645 Major League Prospect (*Kelly Gruber*), (*Randy O'Neal*) .15
646 Major League Prospect (*Jose Roman*), (*Joel Skinner*) .06
647 Major League Prospect (*Steve Kiefer*), (*Danny Tartabull*) 1.00
648 Major League Prospect (*Rob Deer*), (*Alejandro Sanchez*) .15
649 Major League Prospect (*Shawon Dunston*), (*Bill Hatcher*) 2.00
650 Major League Prospect (*Mike Bielecki*), (*Ron Robinson*) .10
651 Major League Prospect (*Zane Smith*), (*Paul Zuvella*) .15
652 Major League Prospect (*Glenn Davis*), (*Joe Hesketh*) .20
653 Major League Prospect (*Steve Jeltz*), (*John Russell*) .10
654 Checklist 1-95 .06
655 Checklist 96-195 .06
656 Checklist 196-292 .06
657 Checklist 293-391 .06
658 Checklist 392-481 .06
659 Checklist 482-575 .06
660 Checklist 576-660 .06

1985 Fleer Update

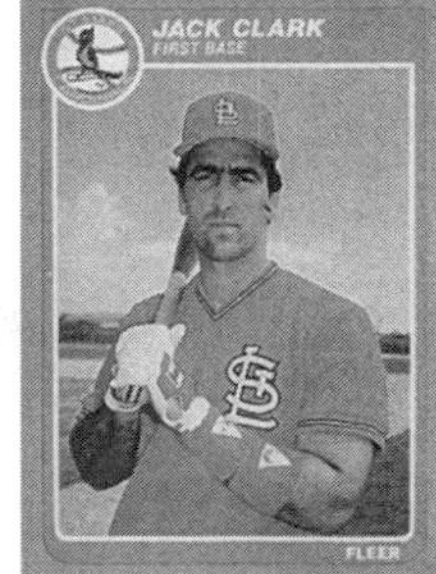

For the second straight year, Fleer issued a 132-card update set. Cards portray traded players on their new teams and also include rookies not depicted in the regular issue. The cards are identical in design to the 1985 Fleer set but are numbered U-1 through U-132. The set was issued with team logo stickers in a specially designed box and was available only through hobby dealers.

		MT
Complete Set (132):		12.00
Common Player:		.10
1	Don Aase	.10
2	Bill Almon	.10
3	Dusty Baker	.20
4	Dale Berra	.10
5	Karl Best	.10
6	Tim Birtsas	.10
7	Vida Blue	.10
8	Rich Bordi	.10
9	Daryl Boston	.15
10	Hubie Brooks	.10
11	Chris Brown	.10
12	Tom Browning	.35
13	Al Bumbry	.10
14	Tim Burke	.10
15	Ray Burris	.10
16	Jeff Burroughs	.10
17	Ivan Calderon	.10
18	Jeff Calhoun	.10
19	Bill Campbell	.10
20	Don Carman	.10
21	Gary Carter	.75
22	Bobby Castillo	.10
23	Bill Caudill	.10
24	Rick Cerone	.10
25	Jack Clark	.15
26	Pat Clements	.10
27	Stewart Cliburn	.10
28	Vince Coleman	.60
29	Dave Collins	.10
30	Fritz Connally	.10
31	Henry Cotto	.10
32	Danny Darwin	.10
33	*Darren Daulton*	3.00
34	Jerry Davis	.10
35	Brian Dayett	.10
36	Ken Dixon	.10
37	Tommy Dunbar	.10
38	Mariano Duncan	.40
39	Bob Fallon	.10
40	Brian Fisher	.10
41	Mike Fitzgerald	.10
42	Ray Fontenot	.10
43	Greg Gagne	.50
44	Oscar Gamble	.10
45	Jim Gott	.10
46	David Green	.10
47	Alfredo Griffin	.10
48	*Ozzie Guillen*	1.50
49	Toby Harrah	.10
50	Ron Hassey	.10
51	Rickey Henderson	3.00
52	Steve Henderson	.10
53	George Hendrick	.10
54	Teddy Higuera	.10
55	Al Holland	.10
56	Burt Hooton	.10
57	Jay Howell	.10
58	LaMarr Hoyt	.10
59	Tim Hulett	.10
60	Bob James	.10
61	Cliff Johnson	.10
62	Howard Johnson	.15
63	Ruppert Jones	.10
64	Steve Kemp	.10
65	Bruce Kison	.10
66	Mike LaCoss	.10
67	Lee Lacy	.10
68	Dave LaPoint	.10
69	Gary Lavelle	.10
70	Vance Law	.10
71	Manny Lee	.10
72	Sixto Lezcano	.10
73	Tim Lollar	.10
74	Urbano Lugo	.10
75	Fred Lynn	.25
76	Steve Lyons	.15
77	Mickey Mahler	.10
78	Ron Mathis	.10
79	Len Matuszek	.10
80	Oddibe McDowell	.10
81	Roger McDowell	.40
82	Donnie Moore	.10
83	Ron Musselman	.10
84	Al Oliver	.15
85	Joe Orsulak	.15
86	Dan Pasqua	.40
87	Chris Pittaro	.10
88	Rick Reuschel	.10
89	Earnie Riles	.10
90	Jerry Royster	.10
91	Dave Rozema	.10
92	Dave Rucker	.10
93	Vern Ruhle	.10
94	Mark Salas	.10
95	Luis Salazar	.10
96	Joe Sambito	.10
97	Billy Sample	.10
98	Alex Sanchez	.10
99	Calvin Schiraldi	.10
100	Rick Schu	.10
101	Larry Sheets	.10
102	Ron Shepherd	.10
103	Nelson Simmons	.10
104	Don Slaught	.10
105	Roy Smalley	.10
106	Lonnie Smith	.10
107	Nate Snell	.10
108	Lary Sorensen	.10
109	Chris Speier	.10
110	Mike Stenhouse	.10
111	Tim Stoddard	.10
112	John Stuper	.10
113	Jim Sundberg	.10
114	Bruce Sutter	.10
115	Don Sutton	.75
116	Bruce Tanner	.10
117	Kent Tekulve	.10
118	Walt Terrell	.10
119	*Mickey Tettleton*	2.00
120	Rich Thompson	.10
121	Louis Thornton	.10
122	Alex Trevino	.10
123	John Tudor	.10
124	Jose Uribe	.10
125	Dave Valle	.15
126	Dave Von Ohlen	.10
127	Curt Wardle	.10
128	U.L. Washington	.10
129	Ed Whitson	.10
130	Herm Winningham	.10
131	Rich Yett	.10
132	Checklist	.10

1985 Fleer Star Stickers

The 1985 Fleer sticker set consists of 126 player stickers, each measuring 1-15/16" x 2-1/2". Numbered on the back, the stickers were designed to be put in a special album. Distributed in packs of six, the 1985 stickers are the scarcest of all Fleer baseball sticker issues.

		MT
Complete Set (126):		50.00
Common Player:		.15
Sticker Album:		2.50
1	Pete Rose	1.00
2	Pete Rose	1.00
3	Pete Rose	1.00
4	Don Mattingly	3.00
5	Dave Winfield	.75
6	Wade Boggs	2.25
7	Buddy Bell	.15
8	Tony Gwynn	2.50
9	Lee Lacy	.15
10	Chili Davis	.15
11	Ryne Sandberg	3.00
12	Tony Armas	.15
13	Jim Rice	.25
14	Dave Kingman	.15
15	Alvin Davis	.15
16	Gary Carter	.25
17	Mike Schmidt	2.00
18	Dale Murphy	.40
19	Ron Cey	.15
20	Eddie Murray	.75
21	Harold Baines	.20
22	Kirk Gibson	.15
23	Jim Rice	.25
24	Gary Matthews	.15
25	Keith Hernandez	.15
26	Gary Carter	.25
27	George Hendrick	.15
28	Tony Armas	.15
29	Dave Kingman	.20
30	Dwayne Murphy	.15
31	Lance Parrish	.15
32	Andre Thornton	.15
33	Dale Murphy	.40
34	Mike Schmidt	2.00
35	Gary Carter	.25
36	Darryl Strawberry	.40
37	Don Mattingly	3.00
38	Larry Parrish	.15
39	George Bell	.15
40	Dwight Evans	.15
41	Cal Ripken, Jr.	5.00
42	Tim Raines	.25
43	Johnny Ray	.15
44	Juan Samuel	.15
45	Ryne Sandberg	3.00
46	Mike Easler	.15
47	Andre Thornton	.15
48	Dave Kingman	.20
49	Don Baylor	.20
50	Rusty Staub	.15
51	Steve Braun	.15
52	Kevin Bass	.15
53	Greg Gross	.15
54	Rickey Henderson	.75
55	Dave Collins	.15
56	Brett Butler	.20
57	Gary Pettis	.15
58	Tim Raines	.25
59	Juan Samuel	.15
60	Alan Wiggins	.15
61	Lonnie Smith	.15
62	Eddie Murray	.25
63	Eddie Murray	.25
64	Eddie Murray	.25
65	Eddie Murray	.25
66	Eddie Murray	.25
67	Eddie Murray	.25
68	Tom Seaver	.25
69	Tom Seaver	.25
70	Tom Seaver	.25
71	Tom Seaver	.25
72	Tom Seaver	.25
73	Tom Seaver	.25
74	Mike Schmidt	.50
75	Mike Schmidt	.50
76	Mike Schmidt	.50
77	Mike Schmidt	.50
78	Mike Schmidt	.50
79	Mike Schmidt	.50
80	Mike Boddicker	.15
81	Bert Blyleven	.15
82	Jack Morris	.15
83	Dan Petry	.15
84	Frank Viola	.15
85	Joaquin Andujar	.15
86	Mario Soto	.15
87	Dwight Gooden	.25
88	Joe Niekro	.15
89	Rick Sutcliffe	.15
90	Mike Boddicker	.15
91	Dave Stieb	.15
92	Bert Blyleven	.15
93	Phil Niekro	.50
94	Alejandro Pena	.15
95	Dwight Gooden	.25
96	Orel Hershiser	.25
97	Rick Rhoden	.15
98	John Candelaria	.15
99	Dan Quisenberry	.15
100	Bill Caudill	.15
101	Willie Hernandez	.15
102	Dave Righetti	.15
103	Ron Davis	.15
104	Bruce Sutter	.15
105	Lee Smith	.25
106	Jesse Orosco	.15
107	Al Holland	.15
108	Goose Gossage	.15
109	Mark Langston	.20
110	Dave Stieb	.15
111	Mike Witt	.15
112	Bert Blyleven	.15
113	Dwight Gooden	.25
114	Fernando Valenzuela	.20
115	Nolan Ryan	4.50
116	Mario Soto	.15
117	Ron Darling	.15
118	Dan Gladden	.15
119	Jeff Stone	.15
120	John Franco	.15
121	Barbaro Garbey	.15
122	Kirby Puckett	5.00
123	Roger Clemens	5.00
124	Bret Saberhagen	.15
125	Sparky Anderson	.20
126	Dick Williams	.15

1986 Fleer

The 1986 Fleer set contains 660 color cards measuring 2-1/2" x 3-1/2". The card fronts feature a player photo enclosed by a dark blue border. The card backs are minus the black-and-white photo that was included in past Fleer efforts. Player biographical and statistical information appear in black and yellow on white stock. As in 1985, Fleer devoted ten cards, entitled "Major League Prospects," to twenty promising rookie players. The 1986 set, as in the previous four years was issued with team logo stickers.

		MT
Complete Set (660):		40.00
Factory Set (660):		50.00
Common Player:		.08
Wax Box:		100.00
1	Steve Balboni	.08
2	Joe Beckwith	.08
3	Buddy Biancalana	.08
4	Bud Black	.08
5	George Brett	2.25
6	Onix Concepcion	.08
7	Steve Farr	.08
8	Mark Gubicza	.08
9	Dane Iorg	.08
10	Danny Jackson	.08

No.	Player	Price
11	Lynn Jones	.08
12	Mike Jones	.08
13	Charlie Leibrandt	.08
14	Hal McRae	.10
15	Omar Moreno	.08
16	Darryl Motley	.08
17	Jorge Orta	.08
18	Dan Quisenberry	.08
19	Bret Saberhagen	.15
20	Pat Sheridan	.08
21	Lonnie Smith	.08
22	Jim Sundberg	.08
23	John Wathan	.08
24	Frank White	.08
25	Willie Wilson	.08
26	Joaquin Andujar	.08
27	Steve Braun	.08
28	Bill Campbell	.08
29	Cesar Cedeno	.08
30	Jack Clark	.08
31	*Vince Coleman*	.40
32	Danny Cox	.08
33	Ken Dayley	.08
34	Ivan DeJesus	.08
35	Bob Forsch	.08
36	Brian Harper	.08
37	Tom Herr	.08
38	Ricky Horton	.08
39	Kurt Kepshire	.08
40	Jeff Lahti	.08
41	Tito Landrum	.08
42	Willie McGee	.10
43	Tom Nieto	.08
44	Terry Pendleton	.08
45	Darrell Porter	.08
46	Ozzie Smith	2.00
47	John Tudor	.08
48	Andy Van Slyke	.08
49	*Todd Worrell*	.40
50	Jim Acker	.08
51	Doyle Alexander	.08
52	Jesse Barfield	.08
53	George Bell	.08
54	Jeff Burroughs	.08
55	Bill Caudill	.08
56	Jim Clancy	.08
57	Tony Fernandez	.10
58	Tom Filer	.08
59	Damaso Garcia	.08
60	Tom Henke	.08
61	Garth Iorg	.08
62	Cliff Johnson	.08
63	Jimmy Key	.10
64	Dennis Lamp	.08
65	Gary Lavelle	.08
66	Buck Martinez	.08
67	Lloyd Moseby	.08
68	Rance Mulliniks	.08
69	Al Oliver	.08
70	Dave Stieb	.08
71	Louis Thornton	.08
72	Willie Upshaw	.08
73	Ernie Whitt	.08
74	*Rick Aguilera*	1.00
75	Wally Backman	.08
76	Gary Carter	.35
77	Ron Darling	.08
78	*Len Dykstra*	2.00
79	Sid Fernandez	.08
80	George Foster	.08
81	Dwight Gooden	.45
82	Tom Gorman	.08
83	Danny Heep	.08
84	Keith Hernandez	.08
85	Howard Johnson	.08
86	Ray Knight	.08
87	Terry Leach	.08
88	Ed Lynch	.08
89	*Roger McDowell*	.40
90	Jesse Orosco	.08
91	Tom Paciorek	.08
92	Ronn Reynolds	.08
93	Rafael Santana	.08
94	Doug Sisk	.08
95	Rusty Staub	.10
96	Darryl Strawberry	.75
97	Mookie Wilson	.08
98	Neil Allen	.08
99	Don Baylor	.12
100	Dale Berra	.08
101	Rich Bordi	.08
102	Marty Bystrom	.08
103	Joe Cowley	.08
104	*Brian Fisher*	.08
105	Ken Griffey	.10
106	Ron Guidry	.12
107	Ron Hassey	.08
108	Rickey Henderson	1.00
109	Don Mattingly	3.00
110	Bobby Meacham	.08
111	John Montefusco	.08
112	Phil Niekro	.50
113	Mike Pagliarulo	.08
114	Dan Pasqua	.08
115	Willie Randolph	.08
116	Dave Righetti	.08
117	Andre Robertson	.08
118	Billy Sample	.08
119	Bob Shirley	.08
120	Ed Whitson	.08
121	Dave Winfield	1.25
122	Butch Wynegar	.08
123	Dave Anderson	.08
124	Bob Bailor	.08
125	Greg Brock	.08
126	Enos Cabell	.08
127	Bobby Castillo	.08
128	Carlos Diaz	.08
129	*Mariano Duncan*	.15
130	Pedro Guerrero	.08
131	Orel Hershiser	.15
132	Rick Honeycutt	.08
133	Ken Howell	.08
134	Ken Landreaux	.08
135	Bill Madlock	.08
136	Candy Maldonado	.08
137	Mike Marshall	.08
138	Len Matuszek	.08
139	Tom Niedenfuer	.08
140	Alejandro Pena	.08
141	Jerry Reuss	.08
142	Bill Russell	.08
143	Steve Sax	.08
144	Mike Scioscia	.08
145	Fernando Valenzuela	.10
146	Bob Welch	.08
147	Terry Whitfield	.08
148	Juan Beniquez	.08
149	Bob Boone	.08
150	John Candelaria	.08
151	Rod Carew	.75
152	*Stewart Cliburn*	.08
153	Doug DeCinces	.08
154	Brian Downing	.08
155	Ken Forsch	.08
156	Craig Gerber	.08
157	Bobby Grich	.08
158	George Hendrick	.08
159	Al Holland	.08
160	Reggie Jackson	1.00
161	Ruppert Jones	.08
162	*Urbano Lugo*	.08
163	*Kirk McCaskill*	.25
164	Donnie Moore	.08
165	Gary Pettis	.08
166	Ron Romanick	.08
167	Dick Schofield	.08
168	Daryl Sconiers	.08
169	Jim Slaton	.08
170	Don Sutton	.35
171	Mike Witt	.08
172	Buddy Bell	.08
173	Tom Browning	.08
174	Dave Concepcion	.08
175	Eric Davis	.45
176	Bo Diaz	.08
177	Nick Esasky	.08
178	John Franco	.08
179	Tom Hume	.08
180	Wayne Krenchicki	.08
181	Andy McGaffigan	.08
182	Eddie Milner	.08
183	Ron Oester	.08
184	Dave Parker	.10
185	Frank Pastore	.08
186	Tony Perez	.15
187	Ted Power	.08
188	Joe Price	.08
189	Gary Redus	.08
190	Ron Robinson	.08
191	Pete Rose	1.00
192	Mario Soto	.08
193	John Stuper	.08
194	Jay Tibbs	.08
195	Dave Van Gorder	.08
196	Max Venable	.08
197	Juan Agosto	.08
198	Harold Baines	.10
199	Floyd Bannister	.08
200	Britt Burns	.08
201	Julio Cruz	.08
202	*Joel Davis*	.08
203	Richard Dotson	.08
204	Carlton Fisk	.50
205	Scott Fletcher	.08
206	*Ozzie Guillen*	.80
207	Jerry Hairston	.08
208	Tim Hulett	.08
209	Bob James	.08
210	Ron Kittle	.08
211	Rudy Law	.08
212	Bryan Little	.08
213	Gene Nelson	.08
214	Reid Nichols	.08
215	Luis Salazar	.08
216	Tom Seaver	1.00
217	Dan Spillner	.08
218	Bruce Tanner	.08
219	Greg Walker	.08
220	Dave Wehrmeister	.08
221	Juan Berenguer	.08
222	Dave Bergman	.08
223	Tom Brookens	.08
224	Darrell Evans	.10
225	Barbaro Garbey	.08
226	Kirk Gibson	.08
227	John Grubb	.08
228	Willie Hernandez	.08
229	Larry Herndon	.08
230	Chet Lemon	.08
231	Aurelio Lopez	.08
232	Jack Morris	.08
233	Randy O'Neal	.08
234	Lance Parrish	.08
235	Dan Petry	.08
236	Alex Sanchez	.08
237	Bill Scherrer	.08
238	Nelson Simmons	.08
239	Frank Tanana	.08
240	Walt Terrell	.08
241	Alan Trammell	.25
242	Lou Whitaker	.10
243	Milt Wilcox	.08
244	Hubie Brooks	.08
245	*Tim Burke*	.10
246	Andre Dawson	.30
247	Mike Fitzgerald	.08
248	Terry Francona	.08
249	Bill Gullickson	.08
250	Joe Hesketh	.08
251	Bill Laskey	.08
252	Vance Law	.08
253	Charlie Lea	.08
254	Gary Lucas	.08
255	David Palmer	.08
256	Tim Raines	.30
257	Jeff Reardon	.08
258	Bert Roberge	.08
259	Dan Schatzeder	.08
260	Bryn Smith	.08
261	Randy St. Claire	.08
262	Scot Thompson	.08
263	Tim Wallach	.08
264	U.L. Washington	.08
265	*Mitch Webster*	.08
266	*Herm Winningham*	.08
267	*Floyd Youmans*	.08
268	Don Aase	.08
269	Mike Boddicker	.08
270	Rich Dauer	.08
271	Storm Davis	.08
272	Rick Dempsey	.08
273	Ken Dixon	.08
274	Jim Dwyer	.08
275	Mike Flanagan	.08
276	Wayne Gross	.08
277	Lee Lacy	.08
278	Fred Lynn	.10
279	Tippy Martinez	.08
280	Dennis Martinez	.10
281	Scott McGregor	.08
282	Eddie Murray	1.50
283	Floyd Rayford	.08
284	Cal Ripken, Jr.	8.00
285	Gary Roenicke	.08
286	Larry Sheets	.08
287	John Shelby	.08
288	Nate Snell	.08
289	Sammy Stewart	.08
290	Alan Wiggins	.08
291	Mike Young	.08
292	Alan Ashby	.08
293	Mark Bailey	.08
294	Kevin Bass	.08
295	Jeff Calhoun	.08
296	Jose Cruz	.08
297	Glenn Davis	.08
298	Bill Dawley	.08
299	Frank DiPino	.08
300	Bill Doran	.08
301	Phil Garner	.08
302	*Jeff Heathcock*	.08
303	*Charlie Kerfeld*	.08
304	Bob Knepper	.08
305	Ron Mathis	.08
306	Jerry Mumphrey	.08
307	Jim Pankovits	.08
308	Terry Puhl	.08
309	Craig Reynolds	.08
310	Nolan Ryan	8.00
311	Mike Scott	.08
312	Dave Smith	.08
313	Dickie Thon	.08
314	Denny Walling	.08
315	Kurt Bevacqua	.08
316	Al Bumbry	.08
317	Jerry Davis	.08
318	Luis DeLeon	.08
319	Dave Dravecky	.08
320	Tim Flannery	.08
321	Steve Garvey	.30
322	Goose Gossage	.08
323	Tony Gwynn	4.00
324	Andy Hawkins	.08
325	LaMarr Hoyt	.08
326	Roy Lee Jackson	.08
327	Terry Kennedy	.08
328	Craig Lefferts	.08
329	Carmelo Martinez	.08
330	*Lance McCullers*	.08
331	Kevin McReynolds	.08
332	Graig Nettles	.08
333	Jerry Royster	.08
334	Eric Show	.08
335	Tim Stoddard	.08
336	Garry Templeton	.08
337	Mark Thurmond	.08
338	Ed Wojna	.08
339	Tony Armas	.08
340	Marty Barrett	.08
341	Wade Boggs	2.00
342	Dennis Boyd	.08
343	Bill Buckner	.10
344	Mark Clear	.08
345	Roger Clemens	7.00
346	Steve Crawford	.08
347	Mike Easler	.08
348	Dwight Evans	.08
349	Rich Gedman	.08
350	Jackie Gutierrez	.08
351	Glenn Hoffman	.08
352	Bruce Hurst	.08
353	Bruce Kison	.08
354	Tim Lollar	.08
355	Steve Lyons	.08
356	Al Nipper	.08
357	Bob Ojeda	.08
358	Jim Rice	.12
359	Bob Stanley	.08
360	Mike Trujillo	.08
361	Thad Bosley	.08
362	Warren Brusstar	.08
363	Ron Cey	.08
364	Jody Davis	.08
365	Bob Dernier	.08
366	Shawon Dunston	.10
367	Leon Durham	.08
368	Dennis Eckersley	.12
369	Ray Fontenot	.08
370	George Frazier	.08
371	Bill Hatcher	.08
372	Dave Lopes	.08
373	Gary Matthews	.08
374	Ron Meredith	.08
375	Keith Moreland	.08
376	Reggie Patterson	.08
377	Dick Ruthven	.08
378	Ryne Sandberg	3.00
379	Scott Sanderson	.08
380	Lee Smith	.12
381	Lary Sorensen	.08
382	Chris Speier	.08
383	Rick Sutcliffe	.08
384	Steve Trout	.08
385	Gary Woods	.08
386	Bert Blyleven	.08
387	Tom Brunansky	.08
388	Randy Bush	.08
389	John Butcher	.08
390	Ron Davis	.08
391	Dave Engle	.08
392	Frank Eufemia	.08
393	Pete Filson	.08

394	Gary Gaetti	.10
395	Greg Gagne	.08
396	Mickey Hatcher	.08
397	Kent Hrbek	.20
398	Tim Laudner	.08
399	Rick Lysander	.08
400	Dave Meier	.08
401	Kirby Puckett	6.00
402	Mark Salas	.08
403	Ken Schrom	.08
404	Roy Smalley	.08
405	Mike Smithson	.08
406	Mike Stenhouse	.08
407	Tim Teufel	.08
408	Frank Viola	.08
409	Ron Washington	.08
410	Keith Atherton	.08
411	Dusty Baker	.10
412	*Tim Birtsas*	.08
413	Bruce Bochte	.08
414	Chris Codiroli	.08
415	Dave Collins	.08
416	Mike Davis	.08
417	Alfredo Griffin	.08
418	Mike Heath	.08
419	Steve Henderson	.08
420	Donnie Hill	.08
421	Jay Howell	.08
422	Tommy John	.10
423	Dave Kingman	.10
424	Bill Krueger	.08
425	Rick Langford	.08
426	Carney Lansford	.08
427	Steve McCatty	.08
428	Dwayne Murphy	.08
429	*Steve Ontiveros*	.08
430	Tony Phillips	.10
431	Jose Rijo	.08
432	Mickey Tettleton	.25
433	Luis Aguayo	.08
434	Larry Andersen	.08
435	Steve Carlton	.60
436	*Don Carman*	.08
437	Tim Corcoran	.08
438	*Darren Daulton*	2.50
439	John Denny	.08
440	Tom Foley	.08
441	Greg Gross	.08
442	Kevin Gross	.08
443	Von Hayes	.08
444	Charles Hudson	.08
445	Garry Maddox	.08
446	Shane Rawley	.08
447	Dave Rucker	.08
448	John Russell	.08
449	Juan Samuel	.08
450	Mike Schmidt	1.50
451	Rick Schu	.08
452	Dave Shipanoff	.08
453	Dave Stewart	.10
454	Jeff Stone	.08
455	Kent Tekulve	.08
456	Ozzie Virgil	.08
457	Glenn Wilson	.08
458	Jim Beattie	.08
459	Karl Best	.08
460	Barry Bonnell	.08
461	Phil Bradley	.08
462	*Ivan Calderon*	.08
463	Al Cowens	.08
464	Alvin Davis	.08
465	Dave Henderson	.08
466	Bob Kearney	.08
467	Mark Langston	.10
468	Bob Long	.08
469	Mike Moore	.08
470	Edwin Nunez	.08
471	Spike Owen	.08
472	Jack Perconte	.08
473	Jim Presley	.08
474	Donnie Scott	.08
475	Bill Swift	.08
476	Danny Tartabull	.10
477	Gorman Thomas	.08
478	Roy Thomas	.08
479	Ed Vande Berg	.08
480	Frank Wills	.08
481	Matt Young	.08
482	Ray Burris	.08
483	Jaime Cocanower	.08
484	Cecil Cooper	.08
485	Danny Darwin	.08
486	Rollie Fingers	.25
487	Jim Gantner	.08
488	Bob Gibson	.08
489	Moose Haas	.08
490	*Teddy Higuera*	.08
491	Paul Householder	.08
492	Pete Ladd	.08
493	Rick Manning	.08
494	Bob McClure	.08
495	Paul Molitor	2.00
496	Charlie Moore	.08
497	Ben Oglivie	.08
498	Randy Ready	.08
499	*Earnie Riles*	.08
500	Ed Romero	.08
501	Bill Schroeder	.08
502	Ray Searage	.08
503	Ted Simmons	.08
504	Pete Vuckovich	.08
505	Rick Waits	.08
506	Robin Yount	2.00
507	Len Barker	.08
508	Steve Bedrosian	.08
509	Bruce Benedict	.08
510	Rick Camp	.08
511	Rick Cerone	.08
512	Chris Chambliss	.08
513	Jeff Dedmon	.08
514	Terry Forster	.08
515	Gene Garber	.08
516	Terry Harper	.08
517	Bob Horner	.08
518	Glenn Hubbard	.08
519	*Joe Johnson*	.08
520	Brad Komminsk	.08
521	Rick Mahler	.08
522	Dale Murphy	.35
523	Ken Oberkfell	.08
524	Pascual Perez	.08
525	Gerald Perry	.08
526	Rafael Ramirez	.08
527	*Steve Shields*	.08
528	Zane Smith	.08
529	Bruce Sutter	.08
530	*Milt Thompson*	.10
531	Claudell Washington	.08
532	Paul Zuvella	.08
533	Vida Blue	.08
534	Bob Brenly	.08
535	*Chris Brown*	.08
536	Chili Davis	.10
537	Mark Davis	.08
538	Rob Deer	.08
539	Dan Driessen	.08
540	Scott Garrelts	.08
541	Dan Gladden	.08
542	Jim Gott	.08
543	David Green	.08
544	Atlee Hammaker	.08
545	Mike Jeffcoat	.08
546	Mike Krukow	.08
547	Dave LaPoint	.08
548	Jeff Leonard	.08
549	Greg Minton	.08
550	Alex Trevino	.08
551	Manny Trillo	.08
552	*Jose Uribe*	.08
553	Brad Wellman	.08
554	Frank Williams	.08
555	Joel Youngblood	.08
556	Alan Bannister	.08
557	Glenn Brummer	.08
558	*Steve Buechele*	.10
559	*Jose Guzman*	.08
560	Toby Harrah	.08
561	Greg Harris	.08
562	*Dwayne Henry*	.08
563	Burt Hooton	.08
564	Charlie Hough	.08
565	Mike Mason	.08
566	*Oddibe McDowell*	.08
567	Dickie Noles	.08
568	Pete O'Brien	.08
569	Larry Parrish	.08
570	Dave Rozema	.08
571	Dave Schmidt	.08
572	Don Slaught	.08
573	Wayne Tolleson	.08
574	Duane Walker	.08
575	Gary Ward	.08
576	Chris Welsh	.08
577	Curtis Wilkerson	.08
578	George Wright	.08
579	Chris Bando	.08
580	Tony Bernazard	.08
581	Brett Butler	.10
582	Ernie Camacho	.08
583	Joe Carter	.50
584	Carmello Castillo (Carmelo)	.08
585	Jamie Easterly	.08
586	Julio Franco	.10
587	Mel Hall	.08
588	Mike Hargrove	.08
589	Neal Heaton	.08
590	Brook Jacoby	.08
591	*Otis Nixon*	.30
592	Jerry Reed	.08
593	Vern Ruhle	.08
594	Pat Tabler	.08
595	Rich Thompson	.08
596	Andre Thornton	.08
597	Dave Von Ohlen	.08
598	George Vukovich	.08
599	Tom Waddell	.08
600	Curt Wardle	.08
601	Jerry Willard	.08
602	Bill Almon	.08
603	Mike Bielecki	.08
604	Sid Bream	.08
605	Mike Brown	.08
606	*Pat Clements*	.08
607	Jose DeLeon	.08
608	Denny Gonzalez	.08
609	Cecilio Guante	.08
610	Steve Kemp	.08
611	Sam Khalifa	.08
612	Lee Mazzilli	.08
613	Larry McWilliams	.08
614	Jim Morrison	.08
615	*Joe Orsulak*	.25
616	Tony Pena	.08
617	Johnny Ray	.08
618	Rick Reuschel	.08
619	R.J. Reynolds	.08
620	Rick Rhoden	.08
621	Don Robinson	.08
622	Jason Thompson	.08
623	Lee Tunnell	.08
624	Jim Winn	.08
625	Marvell Wynne	.08
626	Dwight Gooden (In Action)	.25
627	Don Mattingly (In Action)	1.25
628	Pete Rose (4,192 hits)	.75
629	Rod Carew (3,000 Hits)	.50
630	Phil Niekro, Tom Seaver (300 Wins)	.25
631	Ouch! (Don Baylor)	.10
632	Instant Offense (Tim Raines, Darryl Strawberry)	.25
633	Shortstops Supreme (Cal Ripken, Jr., Alan Trammell)	1.00
634	Boggs & "Hero" (Wade Boggs, George Brett)	1.00
635	Braves Dynamic Duo (Bob Horner, Dale Murphy)	.30
636	Cardinal Ignitors (Vince Coleman, Willie McGee)	.25
637	Terror on the Basepaths (Vince Coleman)	.10
638	Charlie Hustle & Dr. K (Dwight Gooden, Pete Rose)	.50
639	1984 and 1985 A.L. Batting Champs (Wade Boggs, Don Mattingly)	1.00
640	N.L. West Sluggers (Steve Garvey, Dale Murphy, Dave Parker)	.30
641	Staff Aces (Dwight Gooden, Fernando Valenzuela)	.20
642	Blue Jay Stoppers (Jimmy Key, Dave Stieb)	.10
643	A.L. All-Star Backstops (Carlton Fisk, Rich Gedman)	.10
644	Major League Prospect (*Benito Santiago*), (*Gene Walter*)	.90
645	Major League Prospect (*Colin Ward*), (*Mike Woodard*)	.10
646	Major League Prospect (*Kal Daniels*), (*Paul O'Neill*)	5.00
647	Major League Prospect (*Andres Galarraga*), (*Fred Toliver*)	6.00
648	Major League Prospect (*Curt Ford*), (*Bob Kipper*)	.10
649	Major League Prospect (*Jose Canseco*), (*Eric Plunk*)	20.00
650	Major League Prospect (*Mark McLemore*), (*Gus Polidor*)	.45
651	Major League Prospect (*Mickey Brantley*), (*Rob Woodward*)	.10
652	Major League Prospect (*Mark Funderburk*), (*Billy Joe Robidoux*)	.10
653	Major League Prospect (*Cecil Fielder*), (*Cory Snyder*)	1.50
654	Checklist 1-97	.08
655	Checklist 98-196	.08
656	Checklist 197-291	.08
657	Checklist 292-385	.08
658	Checklist 386-482	.08
659	Checklist 483-578	.08
660	Checklist 579-660	.08

1986 Fleer All Stars

Fleer's choices for a major league All-Star team make up this 12-card set. The cards were randomly inserted in 35¢ wax packs and 59¢ cello packs. The card fronts have a color photo set against a bright red background for A.L. players or a bright blue background for N.L. players. Backs feature the player's career highlights on a red and blue background.

		MT
Complete Set (12):		19.00
Common Player:		.25
1	Don Mattingly	5.00
2	Tom Herr	.25
3	George Brett	5.00
4	Gary Carter	.75
5	Cal Ripken, Jr.	12.00
6	Dave Parker	.35
7	Rickey Henderson	2.00
8	Pedro Guerrero	.25
9	Dan Quisenberry	.25
10	Dwight Gooden	.50
11	Gorman Thomas	.25
12	John Tudor	.25

1986 Fleer Future Hall Of Famers

The 1986 Future Hall of Famers set is comprised of six players Fleer felt would gain eventual entrance into the Baseball Hall of Fame. The cards are the standard 2-1/2" x 3-1/2" and were randomly inserted in three-pack rack packs. Card fronts feature a player photo set against a blue background with horizontal light blue stripes. Backs are printed in black on blue and feature career highlights in narrative form.

		MT
Complete Set (6):		15.00
Common Player:		1.75
1	Pete Rose	2.50
2	Steve Carlton	2.00
3	Tom Seaver	2.00
4	Rod Carew	2.00
5	Nolan Ryan	9.00
6	Reggie Jackson	2.00

1986 Fleer Box Panels

Picking up on a Donruss idea, Fleer issued eight cards in panels of four on the bottoms of the wax and cello pack boxes. The cards are numbered C-1 through C-8 and are 2-1/2" x 3-1/2", with a complete panel measuring 5" x 7-1/8". Included in the eight cards are six players and two team logo/checklist cards.

		MT
Complete Panel Set (2):		3.50
Complete Singles Set (8):		1.75
Common Single Player:		.20
Panel		2.50
1	Royals logo/checklist	.05
2	George Brett	.90
3	Ozzie Guillen	.20
4	Dale Murphy	.40
Panel		1.50
5	Cardinals Logo/ Checklist	.05
6	Tom Browning	.20
7	Gary Carter	.35
8	Carlton Fisk	.35

1986 Fleer Update

Issued near the end of the baseball season, the 1986 Fleer Update set consists of cards numbered U-1 through U-132. The 2-1/2" x 3-1/2" cards are identical in design to the regular 1986 Fleer set. The purpose of the set is to update player trades and include rookies not depicted in the regular issue. The set was issued with team logo stickers in a specially designed box and was available only through hobby dealers.

		MT
Complete Set (132):		25.00
Common Player:		.08
1	Mike Aldrete	.08
2	Andy Allanson	.08
3	Neil Allen	.08
4	Joaquin Andujar	.08
5	Paul Assenmacher	.08
6	Scott Bailes	.08
7	Jay Baller	.08
8	Scott Bankhead	.08
9	Bill Bathe	.08
10	Don Baylor	.25
11	Billy Beane	.08
12	Steve Bedrosian	.08
13	Juan Beniquez	.08
14	*Barry Bonds*	20.00
15	*Bobby Bonilla*	1.50
16	Rich Bordi	.08
17	Bill Campbell	.08
18	Tom Candiotti	.08
19	John Cangelosi	.08
20	*Jose Canseco*	6.00
21	Chuck Cary	.08
22	Juan Castillo	.08
23	Rick Cerone	.08
24	John Cerutti	.10
25	*Will Clark*	3.00
26	Mark Clear	.08
27	Darnell Coles	.08
28	Dave Collins	.08
29	Tim Conroy	.08
30	Ed Correa	.08
31	Joe Cowley	.08
32	Bill Dawley	.08
33	Rob Deer	.08
34	John Denny	.08
35	Jim DeShaies	.10
36	*Doug Drabek*	1.00
37	Mike Easler	.08
38	Mark Eichhorn	.12
39	Dave Engle	.08
40	Mike Fischlin	.08
41	Scott Fletcher	.08
42	Terry Forster	.08
43	Terry Francona	.08
44	Andres Galarraga	5.00
45	Lee Guetterman	.08
46	Bill Gullickson	.08
47	Jackie Gutierrez	.08
48	Moose Haas	.08
49	Billy Hatcher	.08
50	Mike Heath	.08
51	Guy Hoffman	.08
52	Tom Hume	.08
53	*Pete Incaviglia*	.40
54	Dane Iorg	.08
55	Chris James	.08
56	Stan Javier	.10
57	Tommy John	.15
58	Tracy Jones	.08
59	*Wally Joyner*	1.50
60	Wayne Krenchicki	.08
61	*John Kruk*	.50
62	Mike LaCoss	.08
63	Pete Ladd	.08
64	Dave LaPoint	.08
65	Mike LaValliere	.20
66	Rudy Law	.08
67	Dennis Leonard	.08
68	Steve Lombardozzi	.08
69	Aurelio Lopez	.08
70	Mickey Mahler	.08
71	Candy Maldonado	.08
72	Roger Mason	.08
73	Greg Mathews	.08
74	Andy McGaffigan	.08
75	Joel McKeon	.08
76	*Kevin Mitchell*	.50
77	Bill Mooneyham	.08
78	Omar Moreno	.08
79	Jerry Mumphrey	.08
80	Al Newman	.08
81	Phil Niekro	.50
82	Randy Niemann	.08
83	Juan Nieves	.08
84	Bob Ojeda	.08
85	Rick Ownbey	.08
86	Tom Paciorek	.08
87	David Palmer	.08
88	Jeff Parrett	.08
89	Pat Perry	.08
90	Dan Plesac	.08
91	Darrell Porter	.08
92	Luis Quinones	.08
93	Rey Quinonez	.08
94	Gary Redus	.08
95	Jeff Reed	.08
96	Bip Roberts	.60
97	Billy Joe Robidoux	.08
98	Gary Roenicke	.08
99	Ron Roenicke	.08
100	Angel Salazar	.08
101	Joe Sambito	.08
102	Billy Sample	.08
103	Dave Schmidt	.08
104	Ken Schrom	.08
105	*Ruben Sierra*	.75
106	Ted Simmons	.08
107	Sammy Stewart	.08
108	Kurt Stillwell	.08
109	Dale Sveum	.08
110	Tim Teufel	.08
111	Bob Tewksbury	.75
112	Andres Thomas	.08
113	Jason Thompson	.08
114	Milt Thompson	.08
115	Rob Thompson	.20
116	Jay Tibbs	.08
117	Fred Toliver	.08
118	Wayne Tolleson	.08
119	Alex Trevino	.08
120	Manny Trillo	.08
121	Ed Vande Berg	.08
122	Ozzie Virgil	.08
123	Tony Walker	.08
124	Gene Walter	.08
125	Duane Ward	.25
126	Jerry Willard	.08
127	Mitch Williams	.30
128	Reggie Williams	.08
129	Bobby Witt	.30
130	Marvell Wynne	.08
131	Steve Yeager	.08
132	Checklist	.05

1986 Fleer Mini

Fleer's 1986 "Classic Miniatures" set contains 120 cards that measure 1-13/16" x 2-9/16". The design of the high-gloss cards is identical to the regular 1986 Fleer set but the player photos are entirely different. The set, which was issued in a specially designed box along with 18 team logo stickers, was available only through hobby dealers.

		MT
Complete Set (120):		6.00
Common Player:		.05
1	George Brett	.80
2	Dan Quisenberry	.05
3	Bret Saberhagen	.08
4	Lonnie Smith	.05
5	Willie Wilson	.05
6	Jack Clark	.05
7	Vince Coleman	.05
8	Tom Herr	.05
9	Willie McGee	.08
10	Ozzie Smith	.50
11	John Tudor	.05
12	Jesse Barfield	.05
13	George Bell	.05
14	Tony Fernandez	.08
15	Damaso Garcia	.05
16	Dave Stieb	.05
17	Gary Carter	.12
18	Ron Darling	.05
19	Dwight Gooden	.15
20	Keith Hernandez	.05
21	Darryl Strawberry	.10
22	Ron Guidry	.10
23	Rickey Henderson	.45
24	Don Mattingly	1.00
25	Dave Righetti	.05
26	Dave Winfield	.45
27	Mariano Duncan	.05
28	Pedro Guerrero	.05
29	Bill Madlock	.05
30	Mike Marshall	.05
31	Fernando Valenzuela	.10
32	Reggie Jackson	.30
33	Gary Pettis	.05
34	Ron Romanick	.05
35	Don Sutton	.15
36	Mike Witt	.05
37	Buddy Bell	.05
38	Tom Browning	.05
39	Dave Parker	.08
40	Pete Rose	.85
41	Mario Soto	.05
42	Harold Baines	.08
43	Carlton Fisk	.12
44	Ozzie Guillen	.05
45	Ron Kittle	.05

46	Tom Seaver	.20
47	Kirk Gibson	.05
48	Jack Morris	.05
49	Lance Parrish	.05
50	Alan Trammell	.15
51	Lou Whitaker	.08
52	Hubie Brooks	.05
53	Andre Dawson	.12
54	Tim Raines	.10
55	Bryn Smith	.05
56	Tim Wallach	.05
57	Mike Boddicker	.05
58	Eddie Murray	.40
59	Cal Ripken, Jr.	2.50
60	John Shelby	.05
61	Mike Young	.05
62	Jose Cruz	.05
63	Glenn Davis	.05
64	Phil Garner	.05
65	Nolan Ryan	2.00
66	Mike Scott	.05
67	Steve Garvey	.12
68	Goose Gossage	.05
69	Tony Gwynn	.60
70	Andy Hawkins	.05
71	Garry Templeton	.05
72	Wade Boggs	.80
73	Roger Clemens	.90
74	Dwight Evans	.05
75	Rich Gedman	.05
76	Jim Rice	.10
77	Shawon Dunston	.15
78	Leon Durham	.05
79	Keith Moreland	.05
80	Ryne Sandberg	.75
81	Rick Sutcliffe	.05
82	Bert Blyleven	.05
83	Tom Brunansky	.05
84	Kent Hrbek	.08
85	Kirby Puckett	.95
86	Bruce Bochte	.05
87	Jose Canseco	1.00
88	Mike Davis	.05
89	Jay Howell	.05
90	Dwayne Murphy	.05
91	Steve Carlton	.20
92	Von Hayes	.05
93	Juan Samuel	.05
94	Mike Schmidt	.50
95	Glenn Wilson	.05
96	Phil Bradley	.05
97	Alvin Davis	.05
98	Jim Presley	.05
99	Danny Tartabull	.05
100	Cecil Cooper	.05
101	Paul Molitor	.50
102	Earnie Riles	.05
103	Robin Yount	.50
104	Bob Horner	.05
105	Dale Murphy	.20
106	Bruce Sutter	.05
107	Claudell Washington	.05
108	Chris Brown	.05
109	Chili Davis	.08
110	Scott Garrelts	.05
111	Oddibe McDowell	.05
112	Pete O'Brien	.05
113	Gary Ward	.05
114	Brett Butler	.10
115	Julio Franco	.08
116	Brook Jacoby	.05
117	Mike Brown	.05
118	Joe Orsulak	.05
119	Tony Pena	.05
120	R.J. Reynolds	.05

1986 Fleer Star Stickers

Fleer's 1986 sticker-card set again measures 2-1/2" x 3-1/2" and features color photos inside dark maroon borders. Backs are identical to the 1986 baseball card issue except for the 1-132 numbering system and blue ink instead of yellow. Card #132 is a multi-player card featuring Dwight Gooden and Dale Murphy on the front and a complete checklist for the set on the reverse. The cards were sold in wax packs with team logo stickers.

		MT
Complete Set (132):		22.00
Common Player:		.10
1	Harold Baines	.15
2	Jesse Barfield	.10
3	Don Baylor	.15
4	Juan Beniquez	.10
5	Tim Birtsas	.10
6	Bert Blyleven	.10
7	Bruce Bochte	.10
8	Wade Boggs	1.75
9	Dennis Boyd	.10
10	Phil Bradley	.10
11	George Brett	2.00
12	Hubie Brooks	.10
13	Chris Brown	.10
14	Tom Browning	.10
15	Tom Brunansky	.10
16	Bill Buckner	.12
17	Britt Burns	.10
18	Brett Butler	.12
19	Jose Canseco	2.00
20	Rod Carew	.80
21	Steve Carlton	.80
22	Don Carman	.10
23	Gary Carter	.30
24	Jack Clark	.10
25	Vince Coleman	.10
26	Cecil Cooper	.10
27	Jose Cruz	.10
28	Ron Darling	.10
29	Alvin Davis	.10
30	Jody Davis	.10
31	Mike Davis	.10
32	Andre Dawson	.30
33	Mariano Duncan	.10
34	Shawon Dunston	.10
35	Leon Durham	.10
36	Darrell Evans	.10
37	Tony Fernandez	.10
38	Carlton Fisk	.25
39	John Franco	.10
40	Julio Franco	.10
41	Damaso Garcia	.10
42	Scott Garrelts	.10
43	Steve Garvey	.30
44	Rich Gedman	.10
45	Kirk Gibson	.10
46	Dwight Gooden	.25
47	Pedro Guerrero	.10
48	Ron Guidry	.10
49	Ozzie Guillen	.10
50	Tony Gwynn	1.00
51	Andy Hawkins	.10
52	Von Hayes	.10
53	Rickey Henderson	.80
54	Tom Henke	.10
55	Keith Hernandez	.10
56	Willie Hernandez	.10
57	Tom Herr	.10
58	Orel Hershiser	.15
59	Teddy Higuera	.10
60	Bob Horner	.10
61	Charlie Hough	.10
62	Jay Howell	.10
63	LaMarr Hoyt	.10
64	Kent Hrbek	.15
65	Reggie Jackson	1.00
66	Bob James	.10
67	Dave Kingman	.12
68	Ron Kittle	.10
69	Charlie Leibrandt	.10
70	Fred Lynn	.12
71	Mike Marshall	.10
72	Don Mattingly	2.00
73	Oddibe McDowell	.10
74	Willie McGee	.12
75	Scott McGregor	.10
76	Paul Molitor	.75
77	Donnie Moore	.10
78	Keith Moreland	.10
79	Jack Morris	.10
80	Dale Murphy	.30
81	Eddie Murray	.75
82	Phil Niekro	.75
83	Joe Orsulak	.10
84	Dave Parker	.25
85	Lance Parrish	.12
86	Larry Parrish	.10
87	Tony Pena	.10
88	Gary Pettis	.10
89	Jim Presley	.10
90	Kirby Puckett	2.00
91	Dan Quisenberry	.10
92	Tim Raines	.15
93	Johnny Ray	.10
94	Jeff Reardon	.10
95	Rick Reuschel	.10
96	Jim Rice	.15
97	Dave Righetti	.10
98	Earnie Riles	.10
99	Cal Ripken, Jr.	3.00
100	Ron Romanick	.10
101	Pete Rose	1.50
102	Nolan Ryan	3.00
103	Bret Saberhagen	.12
104	Mark Salas	.10
105	Juan Samuel	.10
106	Ryne Sandberg	1.00
107	Mike Schmidt	1.75
108	Mike Scott	.10
109	Tom Seaver	.60
110	Bryn Smith	.10
111	Dave Smith	.10
112	Lee Smith	.15
113	Ozzie Smith	.75
114	Mario Soto	.10
115	Dave Stieb	.10
116	Darryl Strawberry	.40
117	Bruce Sutter	.10
118	Garry Templeton	.10
119	Gorman Thomas	.10
120	Andre Thornton	.10
121	Alan Trammell	.15
122	John Tudor	.10
123	Fernando Valenzuela	.15
124	Frank Viola	.10
125	Gary Ward	.10
126	Lou Whitaker	.12
127	Frank White	.10
128	Glenn Wilson	.10
129	Willie Wilson	.10
130	Dave Winfield	.80
131	Robin Yount	.75
132	Dwight Gooden, Dale Murphy	.50

1986 Fleer Star Stickers Box Panels

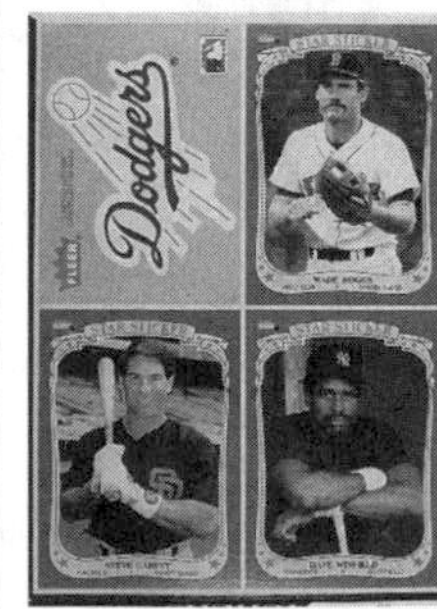

Four cards, numbered S-1 through S-4, were placed on the bottoms of 1986 Fleer Star Stickers wax pack boxes. The cards are nearly identical in format to the regular issue sticker cards. Individual cards measure 2-1/2" x 3-1/2" in size, while a complete panel of four measures 5" x 7-1/8".

		MT
Complete Panel Set:		2.00
Complete Singles Set (4):		1.00
Common Single Player:		.30
1	Dodgers logo	.05
2	Wade Boggs	1.00
3	Steve Garvey	.30
4	Dave Winfield	.50

1987 Fleer

The 1987 Fleer set consists of 660 cards. Fronts feature a graduated blue-to-white border design. The player's name and position appear in the upper-left corner of the card; his team logo is located in the lower-right. Backs are done in blue, red and white and contain an innovative "Pro Scouts Report" feature which rates the player's batting or pitching skills. For the third year in a row, Fleer included its "Major League Prospects" subset. Fleer produced a glossy-finish Collectors Edition set which came housed in a specially-designed tin box. After experiencing a dramatic hike in price during 1987, the glossy set now sells for only a few dollars more than the regular issue.

		MT
Complete Set (660):		50.00
Factory Set (672):		60.00
Common Player:		.06
Wax Pack (15 - Red Test):		4.00
Wax Box (36 - Red Test):		80.00
Wax Pack (17 - Blue Wr.)		4.25
Wax Box (36 - Blue Wr.)		85.00
1	Rick Aguilera	.06
2	Richard Anderson	.06
3	Wally Backman	.06
4	Gary Carter	.20
5	Ron Darling	.06

No.	Player	Price
6	Len Dykstra	.15
7	*Kevin Elster*	.15
8	Sid Fernandez	.06
9	Dwight Gooden	.25
10	*Ed Hearn*	.06
11	Danny Heep	.06
12	Keith Hernandez	.08
13	Howard Johnson	.08
14	Ray Knight	.06
15	Lee Mazzilli	.06
16	Roger McDowell	.06
17	Kevin Mitchell	.10
18	Randy Niemann	.06
19	Bob Ojeda	.06
20	Jesse Orosco	.06
21	Rafael Santana	.06
22	Doug Sisk	.06
23	Darryl Strawberry	.20
24	Tim Teufel	.06
25	Mookie Wilson	.06
26	Tony Armas	.06
27	Marty Barrett	.06
28	Don Baylor	.12
29	Wade Boggs	1.50
30	Oil Can Boyd	.06
31	Bill Buckner	.08
32	Roger Clemens	3.50
33	Steve Crawford	.06
34	Dwight Evans	.08
35	Rich Gedman	.06
36	Dave Henderson	.06
37	Bruce Hurst	.06
38	Tim Lollar	.06
39	Al Nipper	.06
40	Spike Owen	.06
41	Jim Rice	.08
42	Ed Romero	.06
43	Joe Sambito	.06
44	Calvin Schiraldi	.06
45	Tom Seaver	.75
46	*Jeff Sellers*	.06
47	Bob Stanley	.06
48	Sammy Stewart	.06
49	Larry Andersen	.06
50	Alan Ashby	.06
51	Kevin Bass	.06
52	Jeff Calhoun	.06
53	Jose Cruz	.06
54	Danny Darwin	.06
55	Glenn Davis	.06
56	*Jim Deshaies*	.15
57	Bill Doran	.06
58	Phil Garner	.06
59	Billy Hatcher	.06
60	Charlie Kerfeld	.06
61	Bob Knepper	.06
62	Dave Lopes	.06
63	Aurelio Lopez	.06
64	Jim Pankovits	.06
65	Terry Puhl	.06
66	Craig Reynolds	.06
67	Nolan Ryan	4.00
68	Mike Scott	.06
69	Dave Smith	.06
70	Dickie Thon	.06
71	Tony Walker	.06
72	Denny Walling	.06
73	Bob Boone	.06
74	Rick Burleson	.06
75	John Candelaria	.06
76	Doug Corbett	.06
77	Doug DeCinces	.06
78	Brian Downing	.06
79	*Chuck Finley*	1.00
80	Terry Forster	.06
81	Bobby Grich	.06
82	George Hendrick	.06
83	Jack Howell	.06
84	Reggie Jackson	1.00
85	Ruppert Jones	.06
86	Wally Joyner	.75
87	Gary Lucas	.06
88	Kirk McCaskill	.06
89	Donnie Moore	.06
90	Gary Pettis	.06
91	Vern Ruhle	.06
92	Dick Schofield	.06
93	Don Sutton	.30
94	Rob Wilfong	.06
95	Mike Witt	.06
96	Doug Drabek	.10
97	Mike Easler	.06
98	Mike Fischlin	.06
99	Brian Fisher	.06
100	Ron Guidry	.10
101	Rickey Henderson	.45
102	Tommy John	.10
103	Ron Kittle	.06
104	Don Mattingly	2.25
105	Bobby Meacham	.06
106	Joe Niekro	.06
107	Mike Pagliarulo	.06
108	Dan Pasqua	.06
109	Willie Randolph	.06
110	Dennis Rasmussen	.06
111	Dave Righetti	.06
112	Gary Roenicke	.06
113	Rod Scurry	.06
114	Bob Shirley	.06
115	Joel Skinner	.06
116	Tim Stoddard	.06
117	*Bob Tewksbury*	.50
118	Wayne Tolleson	.06
119	Claudell Washington	.06
120	Dave Winfield	.35
121	Steve Buechele	.06
122	*Ed Correa*	.06
123	Scott Fletcher	.06
124	Jose Guzman	.06
125	Toby Harrah	.06
126	Greg Harris	.06
127	Charlie Hough	.06
128	Pete Incaviglia	.08
129	Mike Mason	.06
130	Oddibe McDowell	.06
131	*Dale Mohorcic*	.06
132	Pete O'Brien	.06
133	Tom Paciorek	.06
134	Larry Parrish	.06
135	Geno Petralli	.06
136	Darrell Porter	.06
137	Jeff Russell	.06
138	Ruben Sierra	.10
139	Don Slaught	.06
140	Gary Ward	.06
141	Curtis Wilkerson	.06
142	*Mitch Williams*	.40
143	*Bobby Witt*	.40
144	Dave Bergman	.06
145	Tom Brookens	.06
146	Bill Campbell	.06
147	*Chuck Cary*	.06
148	Darnell Coles	.06
149	Dave Collins	.06
150	Darrell Evans	.06
151	Kirk Gibson	.06
152	John Grubb	.06
153	Willie Hernandez	.06
154	Larry Herndon	.06
155	*Eric King*	.06
156	Chet Lemon	.06
157	Dwight Lowry	.06
158	Jack Morris	.06
159	Randy O'Neal	.06
160	Lance Parrish	.10
161	Dan Petry	.06
162	Pat Sheridan	.06
163	Jim Slaton	.06
164	Frank Tanana	.06
165	Walt Terrell	.06
166	Mark Thurmond	.06
167	Alan Trammell	.25
168	Lou Whitaker	.12
169	Luis Aguayo	.06
170	Steve Bedrosian	.06
171	Don Carman	.06
172	Darren Daulton	.15
173	Greg Gross	.06
174	Kevin Gross	.06
175	Von Hayes	.06
176	Charles Hudson	.06
177	Tom Hume	.06
178	Steve Jeltz	.06
179	*Mike Maddux*	.06
180	Shane Rawley	.06
181	Gary Redus	.06
182	Ron Roenicke	.06
183	*Bruce Ruffin*	.10
184	John Russell	.06
185	Juan Samuel	.06
186	Dan Schatzeder	.06
187	Mike Schmidt	1.00
188	Rick Schu	.06
189	Jeff Stone	.06
190	Kent Tekulve	.06
191	Milt Thompson	.06
192	Glenn Wilson	.06
193	Buddy Bell	.06
194	Tom Browning	.06
195	Sal Butera	.06
196	Dave Concepcion	.06
197	Kal Daniels	.06
198	Eric Davis	.15
199	John Denny	.06
200	Bo Diaz	.06
201	Nick Esasky	.06
202	John Franco	.06
203	Bill Gullickson	.06
204	*Barry Larkin*	5.00
205	Eddie Milner	.06
206	*Rob Murphy*	.06
207	Ron Oester	.06
208	Dave Parker	.12
209	Tony Perez	.15
210	Ted Power	.06
211	Joe Price	.06
212	Ron Robinson	.06
213	Pete Rose	1.00
214	Mario Soto	.06
215	*Kurt Stillwell*	.06
216	Max Venable	.06
217	Chris Welsh	.06
218	*Carl Willis*	.06
219	Jesse Barfield	.06
220	George Bell	.06
221	Bill Caudill	.06
222	*John Cerutti*	.06
223	Jim Clancy	.06
224	*Mark Eichhorn*	.10
225	Tony Fernandez	.08
226	Damaso Garcia	.06
227	Kelly Gruber	.06
228	Tom Henke	.06
229	Garth Iorg	.06
230	Cliff Johnson	.06
231	Joe Johnson	.06
232	Jimmy Key	.10
233	Dennis Lamp	.06
234	Rick Leach	.06
235	Buck Martinez	.06
236	Lloyd Moseby	.06
237	Rance Mulliniks	.06
238	Dave Stieb	.06
239	Willie Upshaw	.06
240	Ernie Whitt	.06
241	*Andy Allanson*	.06
242	*Scott Bailes*	.06
243	Chris Bando	.06
244	Tony Bernazard	.06
245	John Butcher	.06
246	Brett Butler	.10
247	Ernie Camacho	.06
248	Tom Candiotti	.06
249	Joe Carter	.50
250	Carmen Castillo	.06
251	Julio Franco	.08
252	Mel Hall	.06
253	Brook Jacoby	.06
254	Phil Niekro	.25
255	Otis Nixon	.06
256	Dickie Noles	.06
257	Bryan Oelkers	.06
258	Ken Schrom	.06
259	Don Schulze	.06
260	Cory Snyder	.06
261	Pat Tabler	.06
262	Andre Thornton	.06
263	*Rich Yett*	.06
264	*Mike Aldrete*	.06
265	Juan Berenguer	.06
266	Vida Blue	.06
267	Bob Brenly	.06
268	Chris Brown	.06
269	Will Clark	3.00
270	Chili Davis	.08
271	Mark Davis	.06
272	*Kelly Downs*	.06
273	Scott Garrelts	.06
274	Dan Gladden	.06
275	Mike Krukow	.06
276	*Randy Kutcher*	.06
277	Mike LaCoss	.06
278	Jeff Leonard	.06
279	Candy Maldonado	.06
280	Roger Mason	.06
281	Bob Melvin	.06
282	Greg Minton	.06
283	Jeff Robinson	.06
284	Harry Spilman	.06
285	*Rob Thompson*	.25
286	Jose Uribe	.06
287	Frank Williams	.06
288	Joel Youngblood	.06
289	Jack Clark	.06
290	Vince Coleman	.08
291	Tim Conroy	.06
292	Danny Cox	.06
293	Ken Dayley	.06
294	Curt Ford	.06
295	Bob Forsch	.06
296	Tom Herr	.06
297	Ricky Horton	.06
298	Clint Hurdle	.06
299	Jeff Lahti	.06
300	Steve Lake	.06
301	Tito Landrum	.06
302	*Mike LaValliere*	.20
303	*Greg Mathews*	.06
304	Willie McGee	.08
305	Jose Oquendo	.06
306	Terry Pendleton	.06
307	Pat Perry	.06
308	Ozzie Smith	1.00
309	Ray Soff	.06
310	John Tudor	.06
311	Andy Van Slyke	.06
312	Todd Worrell	.06
313	Dann Bilardello	.06
314	Hubie Brooks	.06
315	Tim Burke	.06
316	Andre Dawson	.25
317	Mike Fitzgerald	.06
318	Tom Foley	.06
319	Andres Galarraga	.60
320	Joe Hesketh	.06
321	Wallace Johnson	.06
322	Wayne Krenchicki	.06
323	Vance Law	.06
324	Dennis Martinez	.10
325	Bob McClure	.06
326	Andy McGaffigan	.06
327	*Al Newman*	.06
328	Tim Raines	.25
329	Jeff Reardon	.06
330	*Luis Rivera*	.06
331	*Bob Sebra*	.06
332	Bryn Smith	.06
333	Jay Tibbs	.06
334	Tim Wallach	.06
335	Mitch Webster	.06
336	Jim Wohlford	.06
337	Floyd Youmans	.06
338	*Chris Bosio*	.25
339	*Glenn Braggs*	.06
340	Rick Cerone	.06
341	Mark Clear	.06
342	*Bryan Clutterbuck*	.06
343	Cecil Cooper	.06
344	Rob Deer	.06
345	Jim Gantner	.06
346	Ted Higuera	.06
347	John Henry Johnson	.06
348	Tim Leary	.06
349	Rick Manning	.06
350	Paul Molitor	1.00
351	Charlie Moore	.06
352	Juan Nieves	.06
353	Ben Oglivie	.06
354	*Dan Plesac*	.12
355	Ernest Riles	.06
356	Billy Joe Robidoux	.06
357	Bill Schroeder	.06
358	*Dale Sveum*	.06
359	Gorman Thomas	.06
360	Bill Wegman	.10
361	Robin Yount	1.00
362	Steve Balboni	.06
363	*Scott Bankhead*	.06
364	Buddy Biancalana	.06
365	Bud Black	.06
366	George Brett	2.00
367	Steve Farr	.06
368	Mark Gubicza	.06
369	Bo Jackson	3.00
370	Danny Jackson	.06
371	*Mike Kingery*	.06
372	Rudy Law	.06
373	Charlie Leibrandt	.06
374	Dennis Leonard	.06
375	Hal McRae	.08
376	Jorge Orta	.06
377	Jamie Quirk	.06
378	Dan Quisenberry	.06
379	Bret Saberhagen	.08
380	Angel Salazar	.06
381	Lonnie Smith	.06
382	Jim Sundberg	.06
383	Frank White	.06
384	Willie Wilson	.08
385	Joaquin Andujar	.06
386	Doug Bair	.06
387	Dusty Baker	.10
388	Bruce Bochte	.06
389	Jose Canseco	3.00

390 Chris Codiroli .06
391 Mike Davis .06
392 Alfredo Griffin .06
393 Moose Haas .06
394 Donnie Hill .06
395 Jay Howell .06
396 Dave Kingman .10
397 Carney Lansford .06
398 *David Leiper* .06
399 *Bill Mooneyham* .06
400 Dwayne Murphy .06
401 Steve Ontiveros .06
402 Tony Phillips .12
403 Eric Plunk .06
404 Jose Rijo .06
405 *Terry Steinbach* .60
406 Dave Stewart .10
407 Mickey Tettleton .08
408 Dave Von Ohlen .06
409 Jerry Willard .06
410 Curt Young .06
411 Bruce Bochy .06
412 Dave Dravecky .06
413 Tim Flannery .06
414 Steve Garvey .25
415 Goose Gossage .12
416 Tony Gwynn 2.50
417 Andy Hawkins .06
418 LaMarr Hoyt .06
419 Terry Kennedy .06
420 John Kruk .10
421 Dave LaPoint .06
422 Craig Lefferts .06
423 Carmelo Martinez .06
424 Lance McCullers .06
425 Kevin McReynolds .06
426 Graig Nettles .06
427 *Bip Roberts* .75
428 Jerry Royster .06
429 Benito Santiago .15
430 Eric Show .06
431 Bob Stoddard .06
432 Garry Templeton .06
433 Gene Walter .06
434 Ed Whitson .06
435 Marvell Wynne .06
436 Dave Anderson .06
437 Greg Brock .06
438 Enos Cabell .06
439 Mariano Duncan .06
440 Pedro Guerrero .06
441 Orel Hershiser .10
442 Rick Honeycutt .06
443 Ken Howell .06
444 Ken Landreaux .06
445 Bill Madlock .06
446 Mike Marshall .06
447 Len Matuszek .06
448 Tom Niedenfuer .06
449 Alejandro Pena .06
450 Dennis Powell .06
451 Jerry Reuss .06
452 Bill Russell .08
453 Steve Sax .06
454 Mike Scioscia .06
455 Franklin Stubbs .06
456 Alex Trevino .06
457 Fernando Valenzuela .10
458 Ed Vande Berg .06
459 Bob Welch .06
460 *Reggie Williams* .06
461 Don Aase .06
462 Juan Beniquez .06
463 Mike Boddicker .06
464 Juan Bonilla .06
465 Rich Bordi .06
466 Storm Davis .06
467 Rick Dempsey .06
468 Ken Dixon .06
469 Jim Dwyer .06
470 Mike Flanagan .06
471 Jackie Gutierrez .06
472 Brad Havens .06
473 Lee Lacy .06
474 Fred Lynn .12
475 Scott McGregor .06
476 Eddie Murray 1.00
477 Tom O'Malley .06
478 Cal Ripken, Jr. 4.00
479 Larry Sheets .06
480 John Shelby .06
481 Nate Snell .06
482 Jim Traber .06
483 Mike Young .06
484 Neil Allen .06
485 Harold Baines .10
486 Floyd Bannister .06
487 Daryl Boston .06
488 Ivan Calderon .06
489 *John Cangelosi* .06
490 Steve Carlton .50
491 Joe Cowley .06
492 Julio Cruz .06
493 Bill Dawley .06
494 Jose DeLeon .06
495 Richard Dotson .06
496 Carlton Fisk .75
497 Ozzie Guillen .06
498 Jerry Hairston .06
499 Ron Hassey .06
500 Tim Hulett .06
501 Bob James .06
502 Steve Lyons .06
503 *Joel McKeon* .06
504 Gene Nelson .06
505 Dave Schmidt .06
506 Ray Searage .06
507 *Bobby Thigpen* .15
508 Greg Walker .06
509 Jim Acker .06
510 Doyle Alexander .06
511 *Paul Assenmacher* .06
512 Bruce Benedict .06
513 Chris Chambliss .06
514 Jeff Dedmon .06
515 Gene Garber .06
516 Ken Griffey .10
517 Terry Harper .06
518 Bob Horner .06
519 Glenn Hubbard .06
520 Rick Mahler .06
521 Omar Moreno .06
522 Dale Murphy .25
523 Ken Oberkfell .06
524 Ed Olwine .06
525 David Palmer .06
526 Rafael Ramirez .06
527 Billy Sample .06
528 Ted Simmons .06
529 Zane Smith .06
530 Bruce Sutter .06
531 *Andres Thomas* .06
532 Ozzie Virgil .06
533 *Allan Anderson* .06
534 Keith Atherton .06
535 Billy Beane .06
536 Bert Blyleven .06
537 Tom Brunansky .06
538 Randy Bush .06
539 George Frazier .06
540 Gary Gaetti .10
541 Greg Gagne .06
542 Mickey Hatcher .06
543 Neal Heaton .06
544 Kent Hrbek .15
545 Roy Lee Jackson .06
546 Tim Laudner .06
547 Steve Lombardozzi .06
548 *Mark Portugal* .35
549 Kirby Puckett 2.50
550 Jeff Reed .06
551 Mark Salas .06
552 Roy Smalley .06
553 Mike Smithson .06
554 Frank Viola .06
555 Thad Bosley .06
556 Ron Cey .06
557 Jody Davis .06
558 Ron Davis .06
559 Bob Dernier .06
560 Frank DiPino .06
561 Shawon Dunston .10
562 Leon Durham .06
563 Dennis Eckersley .20
564 Terry Francona .06
565 Dave Gumpert .06
566 Guy Hoffman .06
567 Ed Lynch .06
568 Gary Matthews .06
569 Keith Moreland .06
570 *Jamie Moyer* .06
571 Jerry Mumphrey .06
572 Ryne Sandberg 1.00
573 Scott Sanderson .06
574 Lee Smith .10
575 Chris Speier .06
576 Rick Sutcliffe .06
577 Manny Trillo .06
578 Steve Trout .06
579 Karl Best .06
580 Scott Bradley .06
581 Phil Bradley .06
582 Mickey Brantley .06
583 Mike Brown .06
584 Alvin Davis .06
585 *Lee Guetterman* .06
586 Mark Huismann .06
587 Bob Kearney .06
588 Pete Ladd .06
589 Mark Langston .06
590 Mike Moore .06
591 Mike Morgan .06
592 John Moses .06
593 Ken Phelps .06
594 Jim Presley .06
595 *Rey Quinonez (Quinones)* .06
596 Harold Reynolds .06
597 Billy Swift .06
598 Danny Tartabull .05
599 Steve Yeager .06
600 Matt Young .06
601 Bill Almon .06
602 *Rafael Belliard* .06
603 Mike Bielecki .06
604 Barry Bonds 35.00
605 Bobby Bonilla 1.00
606 Sid Bream .06
607 Mike Brown .06
608 Pat Clements .06
609 *Mike Diaz* .06
610 Cecillo Guante .06
611 *Barry Jones* .06
612 Bob Kipper .06
613 Larry McWilliams .06
614 Jim Morrison .06
615 Joe Orsulak .06
616 Junior Ortiz .06
617 Tony Pena .06
618 Johnny Ray .06
619 Rick Reuschel .06
620 R.J. Reynolds .06
621 Rick Rhoden .06
622 Don Robinson .06
623 Bob Walk .06
624 Jim Winn .06
625 Youthful Power (Jose Canseco, Pete Incaviglia) .40
626 300 Game Winners (Phil Niekro, Don Sutton) .25
627 A.L. Firemen (Don Aase, Dave Righetti) .06
628 Rookie All-Stars (Jose Canseco, Wally Joyner) .40
629 Magic Mets (Gary Carter, Dwight Gooden, Keith Hernandez, Darryl Strawberry) .15
630 N.L. Best Righties (Mike Krukow, Mike Scott) .06
631 Sensational Southpaws (John Franco, Fernando Valenzuela) .06
632 Count 'Em (Bob Horner) .08
633 A.L. Pitcher's Nightmare (Jose Canseco, Kirby Puckett, Jim Rice) .40
634 All Star Battery (Gary Carter, Roger Clemens) .25
635 4,000 Strikeouts (Steve Carlton) .12
636 Big Bats At First Sack (Glenn Davis, Eddie Murray) .25
637 On Base (Wade Boggs, Keith Hernandez) .20
638 Sluggers From Left Side (Don Mattingly, Darryl Strawberry) .40
639 Former MVP's (Dave Parker, Ryne Sandberg) .12
640 Dr. K. & Super K (Roger Clemens, Dwight Gooden) .50
641 A.L. West Stoppers (Charlie Hough, Mike Witt) .06
642 Doubles & Triples (Tim Raines, Juan Samuel) .06
643 Outfielders With Punch (Harold Baines, Jesse Barfield) .06
644 Major League Prospects (*Dave Clark*), (*Greg Swindell*) .30
645 Major League Prospects (*Ron Karkovice*), (*Russ Morman*) .25
646 Major League Prospects (*Willie Fraser*), (*Devon White*) 1.00
647 Major League Prospects (*Jerry Browne*), (*Mike Stanley*) .25
648 Major League Prospects (*Phil Lombardi*), (*Dave Magadan*) .20
649 Major League Prospects (*Ralph Bryant*), (*Jose Gonzalez*) .10
650 Major League Prospects (*Randy Asadoor*), (*Jimmy Jones*) .10
651 Major League Prospects (*Marvin Freeman*), (*Tracy Jones*) .10
652 Major League Prospects (*Kevin Seitzer*, John Stefero) .25
653 Major League Prospects (*Steve Fireovid*), (*Rob Nelson*) .10
654 Checklist 1-95 .06
655 Checklist 96-192 .06
656 Checklist 193-288 .06
657 Checklist 289-384 .06
658 Checklist 385-483 .06
659 Checklist 484-578 .06
660 Checklist 579-660 .06

1987 Fleer Glossy Tin

The three-year run of limited edition, glossy collectors' issues by Fleer from 1987-89 has become known to the hobby as "tins" for the colorful lithographed metal boxes in which complete sets were sold. In their debut year a reported 100,000 sets were made, each serial numbered on a sticker attached to the shrink-wrapped tin box. While the glossy version of the 1987 Fleer set once enjoyed a significant premium over regular cards, today that premium has evaporated and, indeed, it can be harder to find a buyer for the glossy version.

	MT
Complete Set (672):	60.00
Common Player:	.10

(Single star cards valued at .75-1X regular-issue 1987 Fleer.)

1987 Fleer All Stars

As in 1986, Fleer All Star Team cards were randomly inserted in wax and cello packs. Twelve cards, measuring the standard 2-1/2" x 3-1/2", comprise the set. Fronts feature a full-color player photo set against a gray background for American League players and a black background for National Leaguers. Backs are printed in black, red and white and feature a lengthy player biography. Fleer's choices for a major league All-Star team is once again the theme for the set.

		MT
Complete Set (12):		15.00
Common Player:		.30
1	Don Mattingly	4.00
2	Gary Carter	.50
3	Tony Fernandez	.30
4	Steve Sax	.30
5	Kirby Puckett	5.00
6	Mike Schmidt	3.50
7	Mike Easler	.30
8	Todd Worrell	.30
9	George Bell	.30
10	Fernando Valenzuela	.45
11	Roger Clemens	5.00
12	Tim Raines	.50

1987 Fleer Headliners

A continuation of the 1986 Future Hall of Famers idea, Fleer encountered legal problems with using the Hall of Fame name and abated them by entitling the set "Headliners." The cards were randomly inserted in three-pack rack packs. Fronts feature a player photo set against a beige background with bright red stripes. Backs are printed in black, red and gray and offer a brief biography with an emphasis on the player's performance during the 1986 season.

		MT
Complete Set (6):		6.00
Common Player:		.45
1	Wade Boggs	2.25
2	Jose Canseco	2.00
3	Dwight Gooden	.60
4	Rickey Henderson	1.50
5	Keith Hernandez	.45
6	Jim Rice	.65

1987 Fleer '86 World Series

Fleer issued a set of 12 cards highlighting the 1986 World Series between the Boston Red Sox and New York Mets. The sets were available only with Fleer factory sets, both regular and glossy. The cards, 2-1/2" x 3-1/2", have either horizontal or vertical formats. The fronts are bordered in red, white and blue stars and stripes with a thin gold frame around the photo. Backs are printed in red and blue on white stock and include information regarding the photo on the card fronts.

		MT
Complete Set, Regular (12):		2.00
Complete Set, Glossy (12):		3.00
Common Card:		.25
1	Left-Hand Finesse Beats Mets (Bruce Hurst)	.25
2	Wade Boggs, Keith Hernandez	.50
3	Roger Clemens	.75
4	Gary Carter	.35
5	Ron Darling	.25
6	.433 Series Batting Average (Marty Barrett)	.25
7	Dwight Gooden	.35
8	Strategy At Work	.25
9	Dewey! (Dwight Evans)	.25
10	One Strike From Boston Victory (Dave Henderson, Spike Owen)	.25
11	Ray Knight, D arryl Strawberry	.25
12	Series M.V.P. (Ray Knight)	.25

1987 Fleer Box Panels

For the second straight year, Fleer produced a special set of cards designed to stimulate sales of their wax and cello pack boxes. In 1987, Fleer issued 16 cards in panels of four on the bottoms of retail boxes. The cards are numbered C-1 through C-16 and are 2-1/2" x 3-1/2" in size. The cards have the same design as the regular issue set with the player photos and card numbers being different.

		MT
Complete Panel Set (4):		8.00
Complete Singles Set (16):		3.50
Common Panel:		2.25
Common Single Player:		.15
Panel		2.50
1	Mets Logo	.05
6	Keith Hernandez	.15
8	Dale Murphy	.30
14	Ryne Sandberg	.80
Panel		2.25
2	Jesse Barfield	.15
3	George Brett	.80
5	Red Sox Logo	.05
11	Kirby Puckett	.90
Panel		2.75
4	Dwight Gooden	.30
9	Astros Logo	.05
10	Dave Parker	.15
15	Mike Schmidt	.80
Panel		2.50
7	Wally Joyner	.25
12	Dave Righetti	.15
13	Angels Logo	.05
16	Robin Yount	.50

1987 Fleer Update

The 1987 update edition brings the regular Fleer set up to date by including traded players and hot rookies. The cards measure 2-1/2" x 3-1/2" and are housed in a specially designed box with 25 team logo stickers. A glossy-coated Fleer Collectors Edition set was also produced.

		MT
Complete Set (132):		30.00
Common Player:		.08
1	Scott Bankhead	.08
2	Eric Bell	.08
3	Juan Beniquez	.08
4	Juan Berenguer	.08
5	Mike Birkbeck	.08
6	Randy Bockus	.08
7	Rod Booker	.08
8	Thad Bosley	.08
9	Greg Brock	.08
10	Bob Brower	.08
11	Chris Brown	.08
12	Jerry Browne	.08
13	Ralph Bryant	.08
14	DeWayne Buice	.08
15	Ellis Burks	.75
16	Casey Candaele	.08
17	Steve Carlton	.40
18	Juan Castillo	.08
19	Chuck Crim	.08
20	Mark Davidson	.08
21	Mark Davis	.08
22	Storm Davis	.08
23	Bill Dawley	.08
24	Andre Dawson	.35
25	Brian Dayett	.08
26	Rick Dempsey	.08
27	Ken Dowell	.08
28	Dave Dravecky	.08
29	Mike Dunne	.08
30	Dennis Eckersley	.25
31	Cecil Fielder	.50
32	Brian Fisher	.08
33	Willie Fraser	.08
34	Ken Gerhart	.08
35	Jim Gott	.08
36	Dan Gladden	.08
37	Mike Greenwell	.15
38	Cecilio Guante	.08
39	Albert Hall	.08
40	Atlee Hammaker	.08
41	Mickey Hatcher	.08
42	Mike Heath	.08
43	Neal Heaton	.08
44	Mike Henneman	.20
45	Guy Hoffman	.08
46	Charles Hudson	.08
47	Chuck Jackson	.08
48	Mike Jackson	.08
49	Reggie Jackson	.60
50	Chris James	.08
51	Dion James	.08
52	Stan Javier	.08
53	Stan Jefferson	.08
54	Jimmy Jones	.08
55	Tracy Jones	.08
56	Terry Kennedy	.08
57	Mike Kingery	.08
58	Ray Knight	.10
59	Gene Larkin	.08
60	Mike LaValliere	.08
61	Jack Lazorko	.08
62	Terry Leach	.08
63	Rick Leach	.08
64	Craig Lefferts	.08
65	Jim Lindeman	.08
66	Bill Long	.08
67	Mike Loynd	.08
68	*Greg Maddux*	10.00
69	Bill Madlock	.08
70	Dave Magadan	.10
71	Joe Magrane	.10
72	Fred Manrique	.08
73	Mike Mason	.08
74	Lloyd McClendon	.08
75	Fred McGriff	2.00
76	Mark McGwire	20.00
77	Mark McLemore	.08
78	Kevin McReynolds	.08

79	Dave Meads	.08
80	Greg Minton	.08
81	John Mitchell	.08
82	Kevin Mitchell	.10
83	John Morris	.08
84	Jeff Musselman	.10
85	Randy Myers	.35
86	Gene Nelson	.08
87	Joe Niekro	.08
88	Tom Nieto	.08
89	Reid Nichols	.08
90	Matt Nokes	.08
91	Dickie Noles	.08
92	Edwin Nunez	.08
93	Jose Nunez	.08
94	Paul O'Neill	.75
95	Jim Paciorek	.08
96	Lance Parrish	.08
97	Bill Pecota	.08
98	Tony Pena	.08
99	Luis Polonia	.10
100	Randy Ready	.08
101	Jeff Reardon	.08
102	Gary Redus	.08
103	Rick Rhoden	.08
104	Wally Ritchie	.08
105	Jeff Robinson	.08
106	Mark Salas	.08
107	Dave Schmidt	.08
108	Kevin Seitzer	.08
109	John Shelby	.08
110	John Smiley	.10
111	Lary Sorenson	.08
112	Chris Speier	.08
113	Randy St. Claire	.08
114	Jim Sundberg	.08
115	B.J. Surhoff	.25
116	Greg Swindell	.10
117	Danny Tartabull	.08
118	Dorn Taylor	.08
119	Lee Tunnell	.08
120	Ed Vande Berg	.08
121	Andy Van Slyke	.08
122	Gary Ward	.08
123	Devon White	.35
124	Alan Wiggins	.08
125	Bill Wilkinson	.08
126	Jim Winn	.08
127	Frank Williams	.08
128	Ken Williams	.08
129	*Matt Williams*	3.00
130	Herm Winningham	.08
131	Matt Young	.08
132	Checklist 1-132	.08

1987 Fleer Update Glossy Tin

The 1987 Fleer glossy tin update set is identical to the regular-issue updates, except for the high-gloss coating on the cards' fronts and the lithographed metal box in which the sets were sold. Production was estimated at 100,000. Because of perceived overproduction, the glossy tin update set and singles currently carry little, if any, premium over the regular-issue updates.

	MT
Complete Set (132):	35.00
Common Player:	.10

(Star cards valued at .75-1X regular version 1987 Fleer updates.)

1987 Fleer Mini

Continuing with an idea originated the previous year, the Fleer "Classic Miniatures" set consists of 120 cards that measure 1-13/16" x 2-9/16". The cards are identical in design to the regular-issue set, but use completely different photos. The set was issued in a specially prepared collectors box along with 18 team logo stickers. The mini set was available only through hobby dealers.

		MT
Complete Set (120):		4.00
Common Player:		.05
1	Don Aase	.05
2	Joaquin Andujar	.05
3	Harold Baines	.08
4	Jesse Barfield	.05
5	Kevin Bass	.05
6	Don Baylor	.08
7	George Bell	.05
8	Tony Bernazard	.05
9	Bert Blyleven	.05
10	Wade Boggs	.75
11	Phil Bradley	.05
12	Sid Bream	.05
13	George Brett	.60
14	Hubie Brooks	.05
15	Chris Brown	.05
16	Tom Candiotti	.05
17	Jose Canseco	.90
18	Gary Carter	.15
19	Joe Carter	.08
20	Roger Clemens	.85
21	Vince Coleman	.05
22	Cecil Cooper	.05
23	Ron Darling	.05
24	Alvin Davis	.05
25	Chili Davis	.08
26	Eric Davis	.15
27	Glenn Davis	.05
28	Mike Davis	.05
29	Doug DeCinces	.05
30	Rob Deer	.05
31	Jim Deshaies	.05
32	Bo Diaz	.05
33	Richard Dotson	.05
34	Brian Downing	.05
35	Shawon Dunston	.05
36	Mark Eichhorn	.05
37	Dwight Evans	.05
38	Tony Fernandez	.05
39	Julio Franco	.05
40	Gary Gaetti	.05
41	Andres Galarraga	.15
42	Scott Garrelts	.05
43	Steve Garvey	.15
44	Kirk Gibson	.05
45	Dwight Gooden	.10
46	Ken Griffey	.08
47	Mark Gubicza	.05
48	Ozzie Guillen	.05
49	Bill Gullickson	.05
50	Tony Gwynn	.75
51	Von Hayes	.05
52	Rickey Henderson	.50
53	Keith Hernandez	.05
54	Willie Hernandez	.05
55	Ted Higuera	.05
56	Charlie Hough	.05
57	Kent Hrbek	.08
58	Pete Incaviglia	.05
59	Wally Joyner	.08
60	Bob Knepper	.05
61	Mike Krukow	.05
62	Mark Langston	.05
63	Carney Lansford	.05
64	Jim Lindeman	.05
65	Bill Madlock	.05
66	Don Mattingly	1.00
67	Kirk McCaskill	.05
68	Lance McCullers	.05
69	Keith Moreland	.05
70	Jack Morris	.05
71	Jim Morrison	.05
72	Lloyd Moseby	.05
73	Jerry Mumphrey	.05
74	Dale Murphy	.15
75	Eddie Murray	.40
76	Pete O'Brien	.05
77	Bob Ojeda	.05
78	Jesse Orosco	.05
79	Dan Pasqua	.05
80	Dave Parker	.05
81	Larry Parrish	.05
82	Jim Presley	.05
83	Kirby Puckett	.90
84	Dan Quisenberry	.05
85	Tim Raines	.10
86	Dennis Rasmussen	.05
87	Johnny Ray	.05
88	Jeff Reardon	.05
89	Jim Rice	.10
90	Dave Righetti	.05
91	Earnest Riles	.05
92	Cal Ripken, Jr.	2.00
93	Ron Robinson	.05
94	Juan Samuel	.05
95	Ryne Sandberg	.75
96	Steve Sax	.05
97	Mike Schmidt	.50
98	Ken Schrom	.05
99	Mike Scott	.05
100	Ruben Sierra	.05
101	Lee Smith	.08
102	Ozzie Smith	.30
103	Cory Snyder	.05
104	Kent Tekulve	.05
105	Andres Thomas	.05
106	Rob Thompson	.05
107	Alan Trammell	.10
108	John Tudor	.05
109	Fernando Valenzuela	.10
110	Greg Walker	.05
111	Mitch Webster	.05
112	Lou Whitaker	.08
113	Frank White	.05
114	Reggie Williams	.05
115	Glenn Wilson	.05
116	Willie Wilson	.05
117	Dave Winfield	.30
118	Mike Witt	.05
119	Todd Worrell	.05
120	Floyd Youmans	.05

1987 Fleer Star Stickers

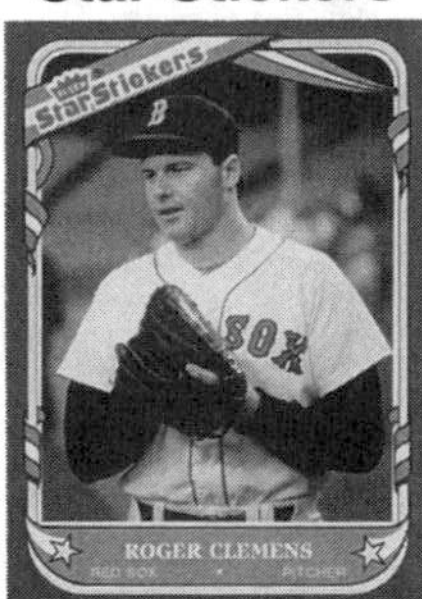

The 1987 Fleer Star Stickers set contains 132 cards which become stickers if the back is bent and peeled off. As in the previous year, the card backs are identical, save the numbering system, to the regular-issue cards. The cards measure 2-1/2" x 3-1/2" and were sold in wax packs with team logo stickers. The fronts have a green border with a red and white banner wrapped across the upper left corner and the sides. The backs are printed in green and yellow.

		MT
Complete Set (132):		15.00
Common Player:		.05
1	Don Aase	.05
2	Harold Baines	.08
3	Floyd Bannister	.05
4	Jesse Barfield	.05
5	Marty Barrett	.05
6	Kevin Bass	.05
7	Don Baylor	.08
8	Steve Bedrosian	.05
9	George Bell	.05
10	Bert Blyleven	.05
11	Mike Boddicker	.05
12	Wade Boggs	.75
13	Phil Bradley	.05
14	Sid Bream	.05
15	George Brett	.75
16	Hubie Brooks	.05
17	Tom Brunansky	.05
18	Tom Candiotti	.05
19	Jose Canseco	.90
20	Gary Carter	.20
21	Joe Carter	.08
22	Will Clark	.50
23	Mark Clear	.05
24	Roger Clemens	.90
25	Vince Coleman	.05
26	Jose Cruz	.05
27	Ron Darling	.05
28	Alvin Davis	.05
29	Chili Davis	.08
30	Eric Davis	.12
31	Glenn Davis	.05
32	Mike Davis	.05
33	Andre Dawson	.20
34	Doug DeCinces	.05
35	Brian Downing	.05
36	Shawon Dunston	.05
37	Mark Eichhorn	.05
38	Dwight Evans	.05
39	Tony Fernandez	.05
40	Bob Forsch	.05
41	John Franco	.05
42	Julio Franco	.05
43	Gary Gaetti	.05
44	Gene Garber	.05
45	Scott Garrelts	.05
46	Steve Garvey	.20
47	Kirk Gibson	.05
48	Dwight Gooden	.15
49	Ken Griffey	.08
50	Ozzie Guillen	.05
51	Bill Gullickson	.05
52	Tony Gwynn	.75
53	Mel Hall	.05
54	Greg Harris	.05
55	Von Hayes	.05
56	Rickey Henderson	.50
57	Tom Henke	.05
58	Keith Hernandez	.05
59	Willie Hernandez	.05
60	Ted Higuera	.05
61	Bob Horner	.05
62	Charlie Hough	.05
63	Jay Howell	.05
64	Kent Hrbek	.05
65	Bruce Hurst	.05
66	Pete Incaviglia	.05
67	Bob James	.05
68	Wally Joyner	.10
69	Mike Krukow	.05
70	Mark Langston	.05
71	Carney Lansford	.05
72	Fred Lynn	.05
73	Bill Madlock	.05
74	Don Mattingly	1.00
75	Kirk McCaskill	.05
76	Lance McCullers	.05
77	Oddibe McDowell	.05

78	Paul Molitor	.50
79	Keith Moreland	.05
80	Jack Morris	.05
81	Jim Morrison	.05
82	Jerry Mumphrey	.05
83	Dale Murphy	.20
84	Eddie Murray	.50
85	Ben Oglivie	.05
86	Bob Ojeda	.05
87	Jesse Orosco	.05
88	Dave Parker	.05
89	Larry Parrish	.05
90	Tony Pena	.05
91	Jim Presley	.05
92	Kirby Puckett	.75
93	Dan Quisenberry	.05
94	Tim Raines	.10
95	Dennis Rasmussen	.05
96	Shane Rawley	.05
97	Johnny Ray	.05
98	Jeff Reardon	.05
99	Jim Rice	.10
100	Dave Righetti	.05
101	Cal Ripken, Jr.	2.50
102	Pete Rose	.75
103	Nolan Ryan	2.00
104	Juan Samuel	.05
105	Ryne Sandberg	.75
106	Steve Sax	.05
107	Mike Schmidt	.80
108	Mike Scott	.05
109	Dave Smith	.05
110	Lee Smith	.05
111	Lonnie Smith	.05
112	Ozzie Smith	.50
113	Cory Snyder	.05
114	Darryl Strawberry	.15
115	Don Sutton	.20
116	Kent Tekulve	.05
117	Gorman Thomas	.05
118	Alan Trammell	.10
119	John Tudor	.05
120	Fernando Valenzuela	.08
121	Bob Welch	.05
122	Lou Whitaker	.05
123	Frank White	.05
124	Reggie Williams	.05
125	Willie Wilson	.05
126	Dave Winfield	.40
127	Mike Witt	.05
128	Todd Worrell	.05
129	Curt Young	.05
130	Robin Yount	.50
131	Checklist (Jose Canseco, Don Mattingly)	.50
132	Checklist (Bo Jackson, Eric Davis)	.20

1987 Fleer Star Stickers Box Panels

Fleer issued on the bottoms of its Fleer Star Stickers wax pack boxes six player cards plus two team logo/checklist cards. The cards, which measure 2-1/2" x 3-1/2", are numbered S-1 through S-8, and are identical in design to the Star Stickers.

		MT
Complete Panel Set (2):		4.00
Complete Singles Set (8):		2.50
Common Single Player:		.10
Panel		3.50
2	Wade Boggs	1.00
3	Bert Blyleven	.10
6	Phillies Logo	.05
8	Don Mattingly	1.00
Panel		1.00
1	Tigers Logo	.05
4	Jose Cruz	.10
5	Glenn Davis	.10
7	Bob Horner	.10

1988 Fleer

A clean, uncluttered look was the trademark of the 660-card 1988 Fleer set. The cards, which are the standard 2-1/2" x 3-1/2" format, feature blue and red diagonal lines set inside a white border. The player name and position are located on a slant in the upper left corner of the card. The player's team logo appears in the upper right corner. Below the player photo, a blue and red band with the word "Fleer" appears. Card backs include the card number, player personal information and career statistics, plus a new feature called "At Their Best." This feature graphically shows a player's pitching or hitting statistics for home and road games and how he fared during day games as opposed to night contests. The set includes 19 special cards (#622-640) and 12 "Major League Prospects" cards.

		MT
Complete Set (660):		15.00
Common Player:		.06
Pack (15):		1.00
Wax Box (36):		19.50
1	Keith Atherton	.06
2	Don Baylor	.10
3	Juan Berenguer	.06
4	Bert Blyleven	.06
5	Tom Brunansky	.06
6	Randy Bush	.06
7	Steve Carlton	.25
8	*Mark Davidson*	.06
9	George Frazier	.06
10	Gary Gaetti	.08
11	Greg Gagne	.06
12	Dan Gladden	.06
13	Kent Hrbek	.15
14	*Gene Larkin*	.06
15	Tim Laudner	.06
16	Steve Lombardozzi	.06
17	Al Newman	.06
18	Joe Niekro	.06
19	Kirby Puckett	.75
20	Jeff Reardon	.06
21a	Dan Schatzader (incorrect spelling)	.20
21b	Dan Schatzeder (correct spelling)	.06
22	Roy Smalley	.06
23	Mike Smithson	.06
24	*Les Straker*	.06
25	Frank Viola	.06
26	Jack Clark	.06
27	Vince Coleman	.06
28	Danny Cox	.06
29	Bill Dawley	.06
30	Ken Dayley	.06
31	Doug DeCinces	.06
32	Curt Ford	.06
33	Bob Forsch	.06
34	David Green	.06
35	Tom Herr	.06
36	Ricky Horton	.06
37	*Lance Johnson*	.50
38	Steve Lake	.06
39	Jim Lindeman	.06
40	*Joe Magrane*	.10
41	Greg Mathews	.06
42	Willie McGee	.08
43	John Morris	.06
44	Jose Oquendo	.06
45	Tony Pena	.06
46	Terry Pendleton	.06
47	Ozzie Smith	.65
48	John Tudor	.06
49	Lee Tunnell	.06
50	Todd Worrell	.06
51	Doyle Alexander	.06
52	Dave Bergman	.06
53	Tom Brookens	.06
54	Darrell Evans	.08
55	Kirk Gibson	.06
56	Mike Heath	.06
57	*Mike Henneman*	.20
58	Willie Hernandez	.06
59	Larry Herndon	.06
60	Eric King	.06
61	Chet Lemon	.06
62	*Scott Lusader*	.06
63	Bill Madlock	.06
64	Jack Morris	.06
65	Jim Morrison	.06
66	*Matt Nokes*	.15
67	Dan Petry	.06
68a	*Jeff Robinson* (Born 12-13-60 on back)	.25
68b	*Jeff Robinson* (Born 12/14/61 on back)	.10
69	Pat Sheridan	.06
70	Nate Snell	.06
71	Frank Tanana	.06
72	Walt Terrell	.06
73	Mark Thurmond	.06
74	Alan Trammell	.10
75	Lou Whitaker	.06
76	Mike Aldrete	.06
77	Bob Brenly	.06
78	Will Clark	.50
79	Chili Davis	.10
80	Kelly Downs	.06
81	Dave Dravecky	.06
82	Scott Garrelts	.06
83	Atlee Hammaker	.06
84	Dave Henderson	.06
85	Mike Krukow	.06
86	Mike LaCoss	.06
87	Craig Lefferts	.06
88	Jeff Leonard	.06
89	Candy Maldonado	.06
90	Ed Milner	.06
91	Bob Melvin	.06
92	Kevin Mitchell	.06
93	*Jon Perlman*	.06
94	Rick Reuschel	.06
95	Don Robinson	.06
96	Chris Speier	.06
97	Harry Spilman	.06
98	Robbie Thompson	.06
99	Jose Uribe	.06
100	*Mark Wasinger*	.06
101	Matt Williams	1.50
102	Jesse Barfield	.06
103	George Bell	.06
104	Juan Beniquez	.06
105	John Cerutti	.06
106	Jim Clancy	.06
107	*Rob Ducey*	.06
108	Mark Eichhorn	.06
109	Tony Fernandez	.06
110	Cecil Fielder	.15
111	Kelly Gruber	.06
112	Tom Henke	.06
113	Garth Iorq (Iorg)	.06
114	Jimmy Key	.08
115	Rick Leach	.06
116	Manny Lee	.06
117	*Nelson Liriano*	.06
118	Fred McGriff	.50
119	Lloyd Moseby	.06
120	Rance Mulliniks	.06
121	Jeff Musselman	.06
122	*Jose Nunez*	.06
123	Dave Stieb	.06
124	Willie Upshaw	.06
125	Duane Ward	.06
126	Ernie Whitt	.06
127	Rick Aguilera	.06
128	Wally Backman	.06
129	*Mark Carreon*	.12
130	Gary Carter	.10
131	David Cone	.50
132	Ron Darling	.06
133	Len Dykstra	.08
134	Sid Fernandez	.06
135	Dwight Gooden	.10
136	Keith Hernandez	.06
137	*Gregg Jefferies*	.75
138	Howard Johnson	.06
139	Terry Leach	.06
140	*Barry Lyons*	.06
141	Dave Magadan	.06
142	Roger McDowell	.06
143	Kevin McReynolds	.06
144	*Keith Miller*	.06
145	*John Mitchell*	.06
146	Randy Myers	.06
147	Bob Ojeda	.06
148	Jesse Orosco	.06
149	Rafael Santana	.06
150	Doug Sisk	.06
151	Darryl Strawberry	.15
152	Tim Teufel	.06
153	Gene Walter	.06
154	Mookie Wilson	.06
155	*Jay Aldrich*	.06
156	Chris Bosio	.06
157	Glenn Braggs	.06
158	Greg Brock	.06
159	Juan Castillo	.06
160	Mark Clear	.06
161	Cecil Cooper	.06
162	*Chuck Crim*	.06
163	Rob Deer	.06
164	Mike Felder	.06
165	Jim Gantner	.06
166	Ted Higuera	.06
167	Steve Kiefer	.06
168	Rick Manning	.06
169	Paul Molitor	.65
170	Juan Nieves	.06
171	Dan Plesac	.06
172	Earnest Riles	.06
173	Bill Schroeder	.06
174	*Steve Stanicek*	.06
175	B.J. Surhoff	.08
176	Dale Sveum	.06
177	Bill Wegman	.06
178	Robin Yount	.75
179	Hubie Brooks	.06
180	Tim Burke	.06
181	Casey Candaele	.06
182	Mike Fitzgerald	.06
183	Tom Foley	.06
184	Andres Galarraga	.25
185	Neal Heaton	.06
186	Wallace Johnson	.06
187	Vance Law	.06
188	Dennis Martinez	.08
189	Bob McClure	.06
190	Andy McGaffigan	.06
191	Reid Nichols	.06
192	Pascual Perez	.06
193	Tim Raines	.10
194	Jeff Reed	.06
195	Bob Sebra	.06
196	Bryn Smith	.06
197	Randy St. Claire	.06
198	Tim Wallach	.06
199	Mitch Webster	.06
200	Herm Winningham	.06
201	Floyd Youmans	.06
202	*Brad Arnsberg*	.06
203	Rick Cerone	.06
204	Pat Clements	.06
205	Henry Cotto	.06
206	Mike Easler	.06
207	Ron Guidry	.10
208	Bill Gullickson	.06
209	Rickey Henderson	.40
210	Charles Hudson	.06
211	Tommy John	.10
212	*Roberto Kelly*	.40
213	Ron Kittle	.06
214	Don Mattingly	.75
215	Bobby Meacham	.06

216 Mike Pagliarulo .06
217 Dan Pasqua .06
218 Willie Randolph .06
219 Rick Rhoden .06
220 Dave Righetti .06
221 Jerry Royster .06
222 Tim Stoddard .06
223 Wayne Tolleson .06
224 Gary Ward .06
225 Claudell Washington .06
226 Dave Winfield .50
227 Buddy Bell .06
228 Tom Browning .06
229 Dave Concepcion .06
230 Kal Daniels .06
231 Eric Davis .10
232 Bo Diaz .06
233 Nick Esasky .06
234 John Franco .06
235 Guy Hoffman .06
236 Tom Hume .06
237 Tracy Jones .06
238 *Bill Landrum* .06
239 Barry Larkin .20
240 Terry McGriff .06
241 Rob Murphy .06
242 Ron Oester .06
243 Dave Parker .10
244 Pat Perry .06
245 Ted Power .06
246 Dennis Rasmussen .06
247 Ron Robinson .06
248 Kurt Stillwell .06
249 *Jeff Treadway* .06
250 Frank Williams .06
251 Steve Balboni .06
252 Bud Black .06
253 Thad Bosley .06
254 George Brett .75
255 *John Davis* .06
256 Steve Farr .06
257 Gene Garber .06
258 Jerry Gleaton .06
259 Mark Gubicza .06
260 Bo Jackson .25
261 Danny Jackson .06
262 *Ross Jones* .06
263 Charlie Leibrandt .06
264 *Bill Pecota* .06
265 *Melido Perez* .15
266 Jamie Quirk .06
267 Dan Quisenberry .06
268 Bret Saberhagen .10
269 Angel Salazar .06
270 Kevin Seitzer .06
271 Danny Tartabull .06
272 *Gary Thurman* .06
273 Frank White .06
274 Willie Wilson .06
275 Tony Bernazard .06
276 Jose Canseco .65
277 Mike Davis .06
278 Storm Davis .06
279 Dennis Eckersley .10
280 Alfredo Griffin .06
281 Rick Honeycutt .06
282 Jay Howell .06
283 Reggie Jackson .30
284 Dennis Lamp .06
285 Carney Lansford .06
286 Mark McGwire 4.00
287 Dwayne Murphy .06
288 Gene Nelson .06
289 Steve Ontiveros .06
290 Tony Phillips .12
291 Eric Plunk .06
292 *Luis Polonia* .15
293 *Rick Rodriguez* .06
294 Terry Steinbach .06
295 Dave Stewart .10
296 Curt Young .06
297 Luis Aguayo .06
298 Steve Bedrosian .06
299 Jeff Calhoun .06
300 Don Carman .06
301 *Todd Frohwirth* .06
302 Greg Gross .06
303 Kevin Gross .06
304 Von Hayes .06
305 *Keith Hughes* .06
306 *Mike Jackson* .06
307 Chris James .06
308 Steve Jeltz .06
309 Mike Maddux .06
310 Lance Parrish .08
311 Shane Rawley .06
312 *Wally Ritchie* .06
313 Bruce Ruffin .06
314 Juan Samuel .06
315 Mike Schmidt .75
316 Rick Schu .06
317 Jeff Stone .06
318 Kent Tekulve .06
319 Milt Thompson .06
320 Glenn Wilson .06
321 Rafael Belliard .06
322 Barry Bonds 1.00
323 Bobby Bonilla .15
324 Sid Bream .06
325 John Cangelosi .06
326 Mike Diaz .06
327 Doug Drabek .06
328 *Mike Dunne* .06
329 Brian Fisher .06
330 *Brett Gideon* .06
331 Terry Harper .06
332 Bob Kipper .06
333 Mike LaValliere .06
334 *Jose Lind* .15
335 Junior Ortiz .06
336 *Vicente Palacios* .06
337 *Bob Patterson* .12
338 *Al Pedrique* .06
339 R.J. Reynolds .06
340 *John Smiley* .20
341 Andy Van Slyke .06
342 Bob Walk .06
343 Marty Barrett .06
344 *Todd Benzinger* .06
345 Wade Boggs .65
346 *Tom Bolton* .06
347 Oil Can Boyd .06
348 Ellis Burks .50
349 Roger Clemens 1.00
350 Steve Crawford .06
351 Dwight Evans .06
352 *Wes Gardner* .06
353 Rich Gedman .06
354 Mike Greenwell .15
355 *Sam Horn* .06
356 Bruce Hurst .06
357 *John Marzano* .06
358 Al Nipper .06
359 Spike Owen .06
360 *Jody Reed* .30
361 Jim Rice .08
362 Ed Romero .06
363 Kevin Romine .06
364 Joe Sambito .06
365 Calvin Schiraldi .06
366 Jeff Sellers .06
367 Bob Stanley .06
368 Scott Bankhead .06
369 Phil Bradley .06
370 Scott Bradley .06
371 Mickey Brantley .06
372 *Mike Campbell* .06
373 Alvin Davis .06
374 Lee Guetterman .06
375 *Dave Hengel* .06
376 Mike Kingery .06
377 Mark Langston .06
378 *Edgar Martinez* 1.50
379 Mike Moore .06
380 Mike Morgan .06
381 John Moses .06
382 *Donnell Nixon* .06
383 Edwin Nunez .06
384 Ken Phelps .06
385 Jim Presley .06
386 Rey Quinones .06
387 Jerry Reed .06
388 Harold Reynolds .06
389 Dave Valle .06
390 *Bill Wilkinson* .06
391 Harold Baines .08
392 Floyd Bannister .06
393 Daryl Boston .06
394 Ivan Calderon .06
395 Jose DeLeon .06
396 Richard Dotson .06
397 Carlton Fisk .20
398 Ozzie Guillen .06
399 Ron Hassey .06
400 Donnie Hill .06
401 Bob James .06
402 Dave LaPoint .06
403 *Bill Lindsey* .06
404 *Bill Long* .06
405 Steve Lyons .06
406 *Fred Manrique* .06
407 *Jack McDowell* .75
408 Gary Redus .06
409 Ray Searage .06
410 Bobby Thigpen .06
411 Greg Walker .06
412 *Kenny Williams* .06
413 Jim Winn .06
414 Jody Davis .06
415 Andre Dawson .20
416 Brian Dayett .06
417 Bob Dernier .06
418 Frank DiPino .06
419 Shawon Dunston .06
420 Leon Durham .06
421 *Les Lancaster* .10
422 Ed Lynch .06
423 Greg Maddux 2.00
424 Dave Martinez .06
425a Keith Moreland (bunting, photo actually Jody Davis) 3.00
425b Keith Moreland (standing upright, scorrect photo) .06
426 Jamie Moyer .06
427 Jerry Mumphrey .06
428 *Paul Noce* .06
429 Rafael Palmeiro .75
430 Wade Rowdon .06
431 Ryne Sandberg .75
432 Scott Sanderson .06
433 Lee Smith .10
434 Jim Sundberg .06
435 Rick Sutcliffe .06
436 Manny Trillo .06
437 Juan Agosto .06
438 Larry Andersen .06
439 Alan Ashby .06
440 Kevin Bass .06
441 *Ken Caminiti* 1.50
442 *Rocky Childress* .06
443 Jose Cruz .06
444 Danny Darwin .06
445 Glenn Davis .06
446 Jim Deshaies .06
447 Bill Doran .06
448 Ty Gainey .06
449 Billy Hatcher .06
450 Jeff Heathcock .06
451 Bob Knepper .06
452 *Rob Mallicoat* .06
453 *Dave Meads* .06
454 Craig Reynolds .06
455 Nolan Ryan 1.50
456 Mike Scott .06
457 Dave Smith .06
458 Denny Walling .06
459 *Robbie Wine* .06
460 *Gerald Young* .06
461 Bob Brower .06
462a Jerry Browne (white player, photo actually Bob Brower) 2.50
462b Jerry Browne (black player, correct photo) .06
463 Steve Buechele .06
464 Edwin Correa .06
465 *Cecil Espy* .06
466 Scott Fletcher .06
467 Jose Guzman .06
468 Greg Harris .06
469 Charlie Hough .06
470 Pete Incaviglia .06
471 *Paul Kilgus* .06
472 Mike Loynd .06
473 Oddibe McDowell .06
474 Dale Mohorcic .06
475 Pete O'Brien .06
476 Larry Parrish .06
477 Geno Petralli .06
478 Jeff Russell .06
479 Ruben Sierra .06
480 Mike Stanley .06
481 Curtis Wilkerson .06
482 Mitch Williams .06
483 Bobby Witt .06
484 Tony Armas .06
485 Bob Boone .06
486 Bill Buckner .06
487 *DeWayne Buice* .06
488 Brian Downing .06
489 Chuck Finley .06
490 Willie Fraser .06
491 Jack Howell .06
492 Ruppert Jones .06
493 Wally Joyner .10
494 Jack Lazorko .06
495 Gary Lucas .06
496 Kirk McCaskill .06
497 Mark McLemore .06
498 Darrell Miller .06
499 Greg Minton .06
500 Donnie Moore .06
501 Gus Polidor .06
502 Johnny Ray .06
503 Mark Ryal .06
504 Dick Schofield .06
505 Don Sutton .20
506 Devon White .10
507 Mike Witt .06
508 Dave Anderson .06
509 Tim Belcher .06
510 Ralph Bryant .06
511 *Tim Crews* .15
512 *Mike Devereaux* .10
513 Mariano Duncan .06
514 Pedro Guerrero .06
515 Jeff Hamilton .06
516 Mickey Hatcher .06
517 Brad Havens .06
518 Orel Hershiser .10
519 *Shawn Hillegas* .06
520 Ken Howell .06
521 Tim Leary .06
522 Mike Marshall .06
523 Steve Sax .06
524 Mike Scioscia .06
525 Mike Sharperson .06
526 John Shelby .06
527 Franklin Stubbs .06
528 Fernando Valenzuela .08
529 Bob Welch .06
530 Matt Young .06
531 Jim Acker .06
532 Paul Assenmacher .06
533 *Jeff Blauser* .40
534 *Joe Boever* .06
535 Martin Clary .06
536 *Kevin Coffman* .06
537 Jeff Dedmon .06
538 *Ron Gant* 2.50
539 *Tom Glavine* 3.00
540 Ken Griffey .08
541 Al Hall .06
542 Glenn Hubbard .06
543 Dion James .06
544 Dale Murphy .20
545 Ken Oberkfell .06
546 David Palmer .06
547 Gerald Perry .06
548 Charlie Puleo .06
549 Ted Simmons .06
550 Zane Smith .06
551 Andres Thomas .06
552 Ozzie Virgil .06
553 Don Aase .06
554 *Jeff Ballard* .06
555 Eric Bell .06
556 Mike Boddicker .06
557 Ken Dixon .06
558 Jim Dwyer .06
559 Ken Gerhart .06
560 *Rene Gonzales* .06
561 Mike Griffin .06
562 John Hayban (Habyan) .06
563 Terry Kennedy .06
564 Ray Knight .06
565 Lee Lacy .06
566 Fred Lynn .08
567 Eddie Murray .55
568 Tom Niedenfuer .06
569 *Bill Ripken* .06
570 Cal Ripken, Jr. 1.50
571 Dave Schmidt .06
572 Larry Sheets .06
573 *Pete Stanicek* .06
574 *Mark Williamson* .06
575 Mike Young .06
576 Shawn Abner .06
577 Greg Booker .06
578 Chris Brown .06
579 *Keith Comstock* .06
580 *Joey Cora* .06
581 Mark Davis .06
582 Tim Flannery .06
583 Goose Gossage .08
584 Mark Grant .06
585 Tony Gwynn .75
586 Andy Hawkins .06

587 Stan Jefferson .06
588 Jimmy Jones .06
589 John Kruk .06
590 *Shane Mack* .25
591 Carmelo Martinez .06
592 Lance McCullers .06
593 *Eric Nolte* .06
594 Randy Ready .06
595 Luis Salazar .06
596 Benito Santiago .08
597 Eric Show .06
598 Garry Templeton .06
599 Ed Whitson .06
600 Scott Bailes .06
601 Chris Bando .06
602 *Jay Bell* .75
603 Brett Butler .08
604 Tom Candiotti .06
605 Joe Carter .10
606 Carmen Castillo .06
607 *Brian Dorsett* .06
608 *John Farrell* .06
609 Julio Franco .06
610 Mel Hall .06
611 *Tommy Hinzo* .06
612 Brook Jacoby .06
613 *Doug Jones* .30
614 Ken Schrom .06
615 Cory Snyder .06
616 Sammy Stewart .06
617 Greg Swindell .06
618 Pat Tabler .06
619 Ed Vande Berg .06
620 *Eddie Williams* .06
621 Rich Yett .06
622 Slugging Sophomores (Wally Joyner, Cory Snyder) .25
623 Dominican Dynamite (George Bell, Pedro Guerrero) .06
624 Oakland's Power Team (Jose Canseco, Mark McGwire) 2.00
625 Classic Relief (Dan Plesac, Dave Righetti) .06
626 All Star Righties (Jack Morris, Bret Saberhagen, Mike Witt) .06
627 Game Closers (Steve Bedrosian, John Franco) Double Play (Ryne Sandberg, Ozzie Smith) .35
629 Rookie Record Setter (Mark McGwire) 2.00
630 Changing the Guard in Boston (Todd Benzinger, Ellis Burks, Mike Greenwell) .25
631 N.L. Batting Champs (Tony Gwynn, Tim Raines) .20
632 Pitching Magic (Orel Hershiser, Mike Scott) .06
633 Big Bats At First (Mark McGwire, Pat Tabler) 1.00
634 Hitting King and the Thief (Tony Gwynn, Vince Coleman) .12
635 A.L. Slugging Shortstops (Tony Fernandez, Cal Ripken, Jr., Alan Trammell) .30
636 Tried and True Sluggers (Gary Carter, Mike Schmidt) .25
637 Crunch Time (Eric Davis) .10
638 A.L. All Stars (Matt Nokes, Kirby Puckett) .25
639 N.L. All Stars (Keith Hernandez, Dale Murphy) .10
640 The "O's" Brothers (Bill Ripken, Cal Ripken, Jr.) .50
641 Major League Prospects (*Mark Grace*), (*Darrin Jackson*) 3.00
642 Major League Prospects (*Damon Berryhill*), (*Jeff Montgomery*) .20
643 Major League Prospects (*Felix Fermin*), (*Jessie Reid*) .10
644 Major League Prospects (*Greg Myers*), (*Greg Tabor*) .10
645 Major League Prospects (*Jim Eppard*, Joey Meyer) .06
646 Major League Prospects (*Adam Peterson*), (*Randy Velarde*) .15
647 Major League Prospects (*Chris Gwynn*), (*Peter Smith*) .15
648 Major League Prospects (*Greg Jelks*), (*Tom Newell*) .06
649 Major League Prospects (*Mario Diaz*), (*Clay Parker*) .06
650 Major League Prospects (*Jack Savage*), (*Todd Simmons*) .06
651 Major League Prospects (*John Burkett*), (*Kirt Manwaring*) .25
652 Major League Prospects (*Dave Otto*), (*Walt Weiss*) .40
653 Major League Prospects (*Randell Byers*) (*Randall*), (*Jeff King*) .75
654a Checklist 1-101 (21 is Schatzader) .08
654b Checklist 1-101 (21 is Schatzeder) .06
655 Checklist 102-201 .06
656 Checklist 202-296 .06
657 Checklist 297-390 .06
658 Checklist 391-483 .06
659 Checklist 484-575 .06
660 Checklist 576-660 .06

1988 Fleer Glossy Tin

In its second year of production, Fleer radically reduced production numbers on its glossy version of the 1988 baseball card set. With production estimates in the 60,000 set range, values of the '88 tin glossies are about double those of the regular issue cards. Once again the issue was sold only as complete sets in colorful lithographed metal boxes.

	MT
Complete Set (672):	50.00
Common Player:	.15

(Star cards valued at 3-5X regular-issue 1988 Fleer version.)

1988 Fleer All Stars

For the third consecutive year, Fleer randomly inserted All Star Team cards in its wax and cello packs. Twelve cards make up the set, with players chosen for the set being Fleer's idea of a major league All-Star team.

		MT
Complete Set (12):		6.00
Common Player:		.25
1	Matt Nokes	.25
2	Tom Henke	.25
3	Ted Higuera	.25
4	Roger Clemens	3.00
5	George Bell	.25
6	Andre Dawson	.45
7	Eric Davis	.35
8	Wade Boggs	1.00
9	Alan Trammell	.35
10	Juan Samuel	.25
11	Jack Clark	.25
12	Paul Molitor	2.00

1988 Fleer Headliners

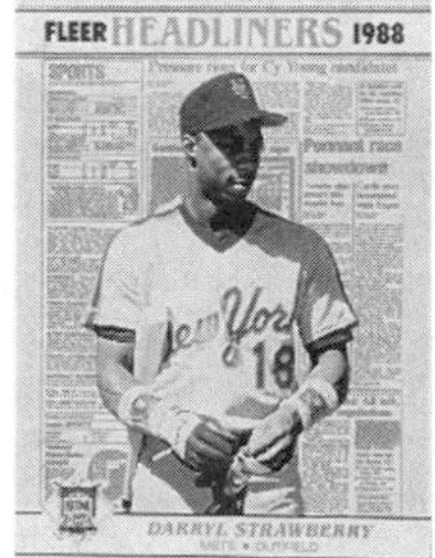

This six-card set was inserted in Fleer three-packs, sold by retail outlets and hobby dealers nationwide. The card fronts feature crisp full-color player cut-outs printed on a grey and white facsimile sports page. "Fleer Headliners 1988" is printed in black and red on a white banner across the top of the card, both front and back. A similar white banner across the card bottom bears the black and white National or American League logo and a red player/team name. Card backs are black on grey with red accents and include the card number and a narrative career summary.

		MT
Complete Set (6):		6.00
Common Player:		.50
1	Don Mattingly	2.00
2	Mark McGwire	4.00
3	Jack Morris	.50
4	Darryl Strawberry	.50
5	Dwight Gooden	.75
6	Tim Raines	.50

1988 Fleer '87 World Series

Highlights of the 1987 Series are captured in this full-color insert set found only in Fleer's regular 660-card factory sets. This second World Series edition by Fleer features cards framed in red, with a blue and white starred bunting draped over the upper edges of the photo and a brief photo caption printed on a yellow band across the lower border. Numbered card backs are red, white and blue and include a description of the action pictured on the front, with stats for the Series.

		MT
Complete Set (12):		2.50
Common Player:		.20
1	"Grand" Hero In Game 1 (Dan Gladden)	.20
2	The Cardinals "Bush" Whacked (Randy Bush, Tony Pena)	.20
3	Masterful Performance Turns Momentum (John Tudor)	.20
4	Ozzie Smith	.75
5	Throw Smoke! (Tony Pena, Todd Worrell)	.20
6	Cardinal Attack - Disruptive Speed (Vince Coleman)	.20
7	Herr's Wallop (Dan Driessen, Tom Herr)	.20
8	Kirby Puckett	1.00
9	Kent Hrbek	.30
10	Rich Hacker (coach), Tom Herr, Lee Weyer (umpire)	.20
11	Game 7's Play At The Plate (Don Baylor, Dave Phillips (umpire)	.20
12	Frank Viola	.20

1988 Fleer Box Panels

Fleer's third annual box-bottom issue once

again included 16 full-color trading cards printed on the bottoms of four different wax and cello pack retail display boxes. Each box contains three player cards and one team logo card. Player cards follow the same design as the basic 1988 Fleer issue. Standard size, the cards are numbered C-1 through C-16.

		MT
Complete Panel Set (4):		8.00
Complete Singles Set (16):		3.00
Common Panel:		2.00
Common Single Player:		.15
Panel		2.00
1	Cardinals Logo	.05
11	Mike Schmidt	.75
14	Dave Stewart	.20
15	Tim Wallach	.15
Panel		2.75
2	Dwight Evans	.15
8	Shane Rawley	.15
10	Ryne Sandberg	.75
13	Tigers Logo	.05
Panel		2.00
3	Andres Galarraga	.30
6	Dale Murphy	.30
9	Giants Logo	.05
12	Kevin Seitzer	.15
Panel		2.75
4	Wally Joyner	.20
5	Twins Logo	.05
7	Kirby Puckett	1.00
16	Todd Worrell	.15

1988 Fleer Update

This update set (numbered U-1 through U-132 are 2-1/2" x 3-1/2") features traded veterans and rookies in a mixture of full-color action shots and close-ups, framed by white borders with red and blue stripes. The backs are red, white and blue-grey and include personal info, along with yearly and "At Their Best" (day, night, home, road) stats charts. The set was packaged in white cardboard boxes with red and blue stripes. A glossy-coated edition of the update set was issued in its own box and is valued at two times the regular issue.

		MT
Complete Set (132):		10.00
Common Player:		.06
1	Jose Bautista	.06
2	Joe Orsulak	.06
3	Doug Sisk	.06
4	Craig Worthington	.06
5	Mike Boddicker	.06
6	Rick Cerone	.06
7	Larry Parrish	.06
8	Lee Smith	.10
9	Mike Smithson	.06
10	John Trautwein	.06
11	Sherman Corbett	.06
12	Chili Davis	.10
13	Jim Eppard	.06
14	Bryan Harvey	.25
15	John Davis	.06
16	Dave Gallagher	.06
17	Ricky Horton	.06
18	Dan Pasqua	.06
19	Melido Perez	.06
20	Jose Segura	.06
21	Andy Allanson	.06
22	Jon Perlman	.06
23	Domingo Ramos	.06
24	Rick Rodriguez	.06
25	Willie Upshaw	.06
26	Paul Gibson	.06
27	Don Heinkel	.06
28	Ray Knight	.06
29	Gary Pettis	.06
30	Luis Salazar	.06
31	Mike MacFarlane	.06
32	Jeff Montgomery	.25
33	Ted Power	.06
34	Israel Sanchez	.06
35	Kurt Stillwell	.06
36	Pat Tabler	.06
37	Don August	.06
38	Darryl Hamilton	.30
39	Jeff Leonard	.06
40	Joey Meyer	.06
41	Allan Anderson	.06
42	Brian Harper	.06
43	Tom Herr	.06
44	Charlie Lea	.06
45	John Moses	.06
46	John Candelaria	.06
47	Jack Clark	.06
48	Richard Dotson	.06
49	Al Leiter	.10
50	Rafael Santana	.06
51	Don Slaught	.06
52	Todd Burns	.06
53	Dave Henderson	.06
54	Doug Jennings	.06
55	Dave Parker	.08
56	Walt Weiss	.10
57	Bob Welch	.06
58	Henry Cotto	.06
59	Marion Diaz (Mario)	.06
60	Mike Jackson	.06
61	Bill Swift	.06
62	Jose Cecena	.06
63	Ray Hayward	.06
64	Jim Steels	.06
65	Pat Borders	.10
66	Sil Campusano	.06
67	Mike Flanagan	.06
68	Todd Stottlemyre	.15
69	David Wells	1.50
70	Jose Alvarez	.06
71	Paul Runge	.06
72	Cesar Jimenez (German)	.06
73	Pete Smith	.08
74	*John Smoltz*	2.00
75	Damon Berryhill	.06
76	Goose Gossage	.08
77	Mark Grace	1.50
78	Darrin Jackson	.10
79	Vance Law	.06
80	Jeff Pico	.06
81	Gary Varsho	.06
82	Tim Birtsas	.06
83	Rob Dibble	.10
84	Danny Jackson	.06
85	Paul O'Neill	.35
86	Jose Rijo	.06
87	*Chris Sabo*	.20
88	John Fishel	.06
89	*Craig Biggio*	2.50
90	Terry Puhl	.06
91	Rafael Ramirez	.06
92	Louie Meadows	.06
93	Kirk Gibson	.06
94	Alfredo Griffin	.06
95	Jay Howell	.06
96	Jesse Orosco	.06
97	Alejandro Pena	.06
98	Tracy Woodson	.06
99	John Dopson	.06
100	Brian Holman	.06
101	Rex Hudler	.06
102	Jeff Parrett	.06
103	Nelson Santovenia	.06
104	Kevin Elster	.08
105	Jeff Innis	.06
106	Mackey Sasser	.06
107	Phil Bradley	.06
108	Danny Clay	.06
109	Greg Harris	.06
110	Ricky Jordan	.06
111	David Palmer	.06
112	Jim Gott	.06
113	Tommy Gregg (photo actually Randy Milligan)	.06
114	Barry Jones	.06
115	Randy Milligan	.10
116	Luis Alicea	.10
117	Tom Brunansky	.06
118	John Costello	.06
119	Jose DeLeon	.06
120	Bob Horner	.06
121	Scott Terry	.06
122	*Roberto Alomar*	5.00
123	Dave Leiper	.06
124	Keith Moreland	.06
125	Mark Parent	.06
126	Dennis Rasmussen	.06
127	Randy Bockus	.06
128	Brett Butler	.08
129	Donell Nixon	.06
130	Earnest Riles	.06
131	Roger Samuels	.06
132	Checklist	.06

1988 Fleer Update Glossy Tin

The glossy version of the 1988 Fleer Update set differs from the regular-issue Update set only in the high-gloss finish applied to the cards' fronts and the lithographed metal box in which sets were sold.

	MT
Complete Set (132):	25.00
Common Player:	.15

(Star cards valued about 2X regular-issue 1988 Fleer Updates)

1988 Fleer Mini

This third annual issue of miniatures (1-7/8" x 2-5/8") includes 120 high-gloss cards featuring new photos, not copies from the regular issue, although the card designs are identical. Card backs are red, white and blue and include personal data, yearly career stats and a stats breakdown of batting average, slugging percentage and on-base average, listed for day, night, home and road games. Card backs are numbered in alphabetical order by teams which are also listed alphabetically. The set includes 18 team logo stickers with black-and-white aerial stadium photos on the flip sides.

		MT
Complete Set (120):		8.00
Common Player:		.05
1	Eddie Murray	.40
2	Dave Schmidt	.05
3	Larry Sheets	.05
4	Wade Boggs	.65
5	Roger Clemens	.75
6	Dwight Evans	.05
7	Mike Greenwell	.05
8	Sam Horn	.05
9	Lee Smith	.08
10	Brian Downing	.05
11	Wally Joyner	.08
12	Devon White	.08
13	Mike Witt	.05
14	Ivan Calderon	.05
15	Ozzie Guillen	.05
16	Jack McDowell	.05
17	Kenny Williams	.05
18	Joe Carter	.08
19	Julio Franco	.05
20	Pat Tabler	.05
21	Doyle Alexander	.05
22	Jack Morris	.05
23	Matt Nokes	.05
24	Walt Terrell	.05
25	Alan Trammell	.10
26	Bret Saberhagen	.05
27	Kevin Seitzer	.05
28	Danny Tartabull	.05
29	Gary Thurman	.05
30	Ted Higuera	.05
31	Paul Molitor	.50
32	Dan Plesac	.05
33	Robin Yount	.50
34	Gary Gaetti	.05
35	Kent Hrbek	.05
36	Kirby Puckett	.75
37	Jeff Reardon	.05
38	Frank Viola	.05
39	Jack Clark	.05
40	Rickey Henderson	.50
41	Don Mattingly	1.00
42	Willie Randolph	.05
43	Dave Righetti	.05
44	Dave Winfield	.50
45	Jose Canseco	.65
46	Mark McGwire	2.00
47	Dave Parker	.05
48	Dave Stewart	.05
49	Walt Weiss	.05
50	Bob Welch	.05
51	Mickey Brantley	.05
52	Mark Langston	.05
53	Harold Reynolds	.05
54	Scott Fletcher	.05
55	Charlie Hough	.05
56	Pete Incaviglia	.05
57	Larry Parrish	.05
58	Ruben Sierra	.05
59	George Bell	.05
60	Mark Eichhorn	.05
61	Tony Fernandez	.05
62	Tom Henke	.05
63	Jimmy Key	.05
64	Dion James	.05
65	Dale Murphy	.15
66	Zane Smith	.05
67	Andre Dawson	.15
68	Mark Grace	.75

69	Jerry Mumphrey	.05
70	Ryne Sandberg	.65
71	Rick Sutcliffe	.05
72	Kal Daniels	.05
73	Eric Davis	.10
74	John Franco	.05
75	Ron Robinson	.05
76	Jeff Treadway	.05
77	Kevin Bass	.05
78	Glenn Davis	.05
79	Nolan Ryan	1.00
80	Mike Scott	.05
81	Dave Smith	.05
82	Kirk Gibson	.05
83	Pedro Guerrero	.05
84	Orel Hershiser	.08
85	Steve Sax	.05
86	Fernando Valenzuela	.08
87	Tim Burke	.05
88	Andres Galarraga	.15
89	Neal Heaton	.05
90	Tim Raines	.10
91	Tim Wallach	.05
92	Dwight Gooden	.10
93	Keith Hernandez	.05
94	Gregg Jefferies	.25
95	Howard Johnson	.05
96	Roger McDowell	.05
97	Darryl Strawberry	.15
98	Steve Bedrosian	.05
99	Von Hayes	.05
100	Shane Rawley	.05
101	Juan Samuel	.05
102	Mike Schmidt	.60
103	Bobby Bonilla	.08
104	Mike Dunne	.05
105	Andy Van Slyke	.05
106	Vince Coleman	.05
107	Bob Horner	.05
108	Willie McGee	.08
109	Ozzie Smith	.50
110	John Tudor	.05
111	Todd Worrell	.05
112	Tony Gwynn	.75
113	John Kruk	.05
114	Lance McCullers	.05
115	Benito Santiago	.08
116	Will Clark	.40
117	Jeff Leonard	.05
118	Candy Maldonado	.05
119	Kirt Manwaring	.05
120	Don Robinson	.05

1988 Fleer Star Stickers

This set of 132 standard-size sticker cards (including a checklist card) features exclusive player photos, different from those in the Fleer regular issue. Card fronts have light gray borders sprinkled with multi-colored stars. Card backs are printed in red, gray and black on white and include personal data and a breakdown of pitching and batting stats into day, night, home and road categories. Cards were marketed in two different display boxes that feature six players and two team logos on the bottoms.

		MT
Complete Set (132):		20.00
Common Player:		.05
1	Mike Boddicker	.05
2	Eddie Murray	.60
3	Cal Ripken, Jr.	2.50
4	Larry Sheets	.05
5	Wade Boggs	.60
6	Ellis Burks	.05
7	Roger Clemens	.75
8	Dwight Evans	.05
9	Mike Greenwell	.05
10	Bruce Hurst	.05
11	Brian Downing	.05
12	Wally Joyner	.10
13	Mike Witt	.05
14	Ivan Calderon	.05
15	Jose DeLeon	.05
16	Ozzie Guillen	.05
17	Bobby Thigpen	.05
18	Joe Carter	.08
19	Julio Franco	.05
20	Brook Jacoby	.05
21	Cory Snyder	.05
22	Pat Tabler	.05
23	Doyle Alexander	.05
24	Kirk Gibson	.05
25	Mike Henneman	.05
26	Jack Morris	.05
27	Matt Nokes	.05
28	Walt Terrell	.05
29	Alan Trammell	.08
30	George Brett	.75
31	Charlie Leibrandt	.05
32	Bret Saberhagen	.08
33	Kevin Seitzer	.05
34	Danny Tartabull	.05
35	Frank White	.05
36	Rob Deer	.05
37	Ted Higuera	.05
38	Paul Molitor	.75
39	Dan Plesac	.05
40	Robin Yount	.60
41	Bert Blyleven	.05
42	Tom Brunansky	.05
43	Gary Gaetti	.05
44	Kent Hrbek	.05
45	Kirby Puckett	.90
46	Jeff Reardon	.05
47	Frank Viola	.05
48	Don Mattingly	1.00
49	Mike Pagliarulo	.05
50	Willie Randolph	.05
51	Rick Rhoden	.05
52	Dave Righetti	.05
53	Dave Winfield	.50
54	Jose Canseco	.60
55	Carney Lansford	.05
56	Mark McGwire	3.00
57	Dave Stewart	.05
58	Curt Young	.05
59	Alvin Davis	.05
60	Mark Langston	.05
61	Ken Phelps	.05
62	Harold Reynolds	.05
63	Scott Fletcher	.05
64	Charlie Hough	.05
65	Pete Incaviglia	.05
66	Oddibe McDowell	.05
67	Pete O'Brien	.05
68	Larry Parrish	.05
69	Ruben Sierra	.05
70	Jesse Barfield	.05
71	George Bell	.05
72	Tony Fernandez	.05
73	Tom Henke	.05
74	Jimmy Key	.05
75	Lloyd Moseby	.05
76	Dion James	.05
77	Dale Murphy	.15
78	Zane Smith	.05
79	Andre Dawson	.15
80	Ryne Sandberg	.65
81	Rick Sutcliffe	.05
82	Kal Daniels	.05
83	Eric Davis	.10
84	John Franco	.05
85	Kevin Bass	.05
86	Glenn Davis	.05
87	Bill Doran	.05
88	Nolan Ryan	2.50
89	Mike Scott	.05
90	Dave Smith	.05
91	Pedro Guerrero	.05
92	Orel Hershiser	.08
93	Steve Sax	.05
94	Fernando Valenzuela	.10
95	Tim Burke	.05
96	Andres Galarraga	.12
97	Tim Raines	.10
98	Tim Wallach	.05
99	Mitch Webster	.05
100	Ron Darling	.05
101	Sid Fernandez	.05
102	Dwight Gooden	.10
103	Keith Hernandez	.05
104	Howard Johnson	.05
105	Roger McDowell	.05
106	Darryl Strawberry	.10
107	Steve Bedrosian	.05
108	Von Hayes	.05
109	Shane Rawley	.05
110	Juan Samuel	.05
111	Mike Schmidt	.75
112	Milt Thompson	.05
113	Sid Bream	.05
114	Bobby Bonilla	.08
115	Mike Dunne	.05
116	Andy Van Slyke	.05
117	Vince Coleman	.05
118	Willie McGee	.05
119	Terry Pendleton	.05
120	Ozzie Smith	.60
121	John Tudor	.05
122	Todd Worrell	.05
123	Tony Gwynn	.75
124	John Kruk	.05
125	Benito Santiago	.08
126	Will Clark	.60
127	Dave Dravecky	.05
128	Jeff Leonard	.05
129	Candy Maldonado	.05
130	Rick Rueschel	.05
131	Don Robinson	.05
132	Checklist	.05

1988 Fleer Star Stickers Box Panels

This set of eight box-bottom cards was printed on two different retail display boxes. Six players and two team logo sticker cards are included in the set, three player photos and one team photo per box. The full-color player photos are exclusive to the Fleer Star Sticker set. The cards, which measure 2-1/2" x 3-1/2", have a light gray border sprinkled with multi-color stars. The backs are printed in navy blue and red.

		MT
Complete Panel Set (2):		2.00
Complete Singles Set (8):		1.00
Common Singles Player:		.15
Panel		1.00
1	Eric Davis	.25
3	Kevin Mitchell	.10
5	Rickey Henderson	.50
7	Tigers Logo	.05
Panel		1.00
2	Gary Carter	.15
4	Ron Guidry	.10
6	Don Baylor	.10
8	Giants Logo	.05

1989 Fleer

This set includes 660 standard-size cards and was issued with 45 team logo stickers. Individual card fronts feature a grey and white striped background with full-color player photos framed by a bright line of color that slants upward to the right. The set also includes two subsets: 15 Major League Prospects and 12 SuperStar Specials. A special bonus set of 12 All-Star Team cards was randomly inserted in individual wax packs of 15 cards. The last seven cards in the set are checklists, with players listed alphabetically by teams.

		MT
Fact. Set, Unopened (660):		35.00
Complete Set (660):		30.00
Common Player:		.05
Wax Pack (15 - final print):		1.50
Wax Box (36- final print):		36.00
1	Don Baylor	.12
2	*Lance Blankenship*	.10
3	*Todd Burns*	.08
4	Greg Cadaret	.05
5	Jose Canseco	.35
6	Storm Davis	.05
7	Dennis Eckersley	.08
8	Mike Gallego	.05
9	Ron Hassey	.05
10	Dave Henderson	.05
11	Rick Honeycutt	.05
12	Glenn Hubbard	.05
13	Stan Javier	.05
14	*Doug Jennings*	.05
15	*Felix Jose*	.08
16	Carney Lansford	.05
17	Mark McGwire	1.00
18	Gene Nelson	.05
19	Dave Parker	.10
20	Eric Plunk	.05
21	Luis Polonia	.05
22	Terry Steinbach	.05
23	Dave Stewart	.08
24	Walt Weiss	.05
25	Bob Welch	.05
26	Curt Young	.05
27	Rick Aguilera	.05
28	Wally Backman	.05
29	Mark Carreon	.05
30	Gary Carter	.15
31	David Cone	.12
32	Ron Darling	.05
33	Len Dykstra	.10
34	Kevin Elster	.05
35	Sid Fernandez	.05
36	Dwight Gooden	.10
37	Keith Hernandez	.05
38	Gregg Jefferies	.20
39	Howard Johnson	.05
40	Terry Leach	.05

No.	Player	Price
41	Dave Magadan	.05
42	Bob McClure	.05
43	Roger McDowell	.05
44	Kevin McReynolds	.05
45	Keith Miller	.05
46	Randy Myers	.05
47	Bob Ojeda	.05
48	Mackey Sasser	.05
49	Darryl Strawberry	.15
50	Tim Teufel	.05
51	*Dave West*	.12
52	Mookie Wilson	.05
53	Dave Anderson	.05
54	Tim Belcher	.05
55	Mike Davis	.05
56	Mike Devereaux	.05
57	Kirk Gibson	.05
58	Alfredo Griffin	.05
59	Chris Gwynn	.05
60	Jeff Hamilton	.05
61a	Danny Heep (Home: San Antonio, TX)	.50
61b	Danny Heep (Home: Lake Hills, TX)	.05
62	Orel Hershiser	.08
63	Brian Holton	.05
64	Jay Howell	.05
65	Tim Leary	.05
66	Mike Marshall	.05
67	*Ramon Martinez*	.40
68	Jesse Orosco	.05
69	Alejandro Pena	.05
70	Steve Sax	.05
71	Mike Scioscia	.05
72	Mike Sharperson	.05
73	John Shelby	.05
74	Franklin Stubbs	.05
75	John Tudor	.05
76	Fernando Valenzuela	.08
77	Tracy Woodson	.05
78	Marty Barrett	.05
79	Todd Benzinger	.05
80	Mike Boddicker	.05
81	Wade Boggs	.25
82	"Oil Can" Boyd	.05
83	Ellis Burks	.08
84	Rick Cerone	.05
85	Roger Clemens	.50
86	*Steve Curry*	.05
87	Dwight Evans	.05
88	Wes Gardner	.05
89	Rich Gedman	.05
90	Mike Greenwell	.08
91	Bruce Hurst	.05
92	Dennis Lamp	.05
93	Spike Owen	.05
94	Larry Parrish	.05
95	*Carlos Quintana*	.08
96	Jody Reed	.05
97	Jim Rice	.10
98a	Kevin Romine (batting follow-thru, photo actually Randy Kutcher)	.40
98b	Kevin Romine (arms crossed on chest, correct photo)	.40
99	Lee Smith	.10
100	Mike Smithson	.05
101	Bob Stanley	.05
102	Allan Anderson	.05
103	Keith Atherton	.05
104	Juan Berenguer	.05
105	Bert Blyleven	.05
106	*Eric Bullock*	.05
107	Randy Bush	.05
108	John Christensen	.05
109	Mark Davidson	.05
110	Gary Gaetti	.08
111	Greg Gagne	.05
112	Dan Gladden	.05
113	*German Gonzalez*	.05
114	Brian Harper	.05
115	Tom Herr	.05
116	Kent Hrbek	.08
117	Gene Larkin	.05
118	Tim Laudner	.05
119	Charlie Lea	.05
120	Steve Lombardozzi	.05
121a	John Moses (Home: Phoenix, AZ)	.25
121b	John Moses (Home: Tempe, AZ)	.05
122	Al Newman	.05
123	Mark Portugal	.05
124	Kirby Puckett	.40
125	Jeff Reardon	.05
126	Fred Toliver	.05
127	Frank Viola	.05
128	Doyle Alexander	.05
129	Dave Bergman	.05
130a	Tom Brookens (Mike Heath stats on back)	2.00
130b	Tom Brookens (correct stats on back)	.20
131	*Paul Gibson*	.05
132a	Mike Heath (Tom Brookens stats on back)	2.00
132b	Mike Heath (correct stats on back)	.20
133	*Don Heinkel*	.05
134	Mike Henneman	.05
135	Guillermo Hernandez	.05
136	Eric King	.05
137	Chet Lemon	.05
138	Fred Lynn	.08
139	Jack Morris	.05
140	Matt Nokes	.05
141	Gary Pettis	.05
142	Ted Power	.05
143	Jeff Robinson	.05
144	Luis Salazar	.05
145	*Steve Searcy*	.10
146	Pat Sheridan	.05
147	Frank Tanana	.05
148	Alan Trammell	.10
149	Walt Terrell	.05
150	Jim Walewander	.05
151	Lou Whitaker	.05
152	Tim Birtsas	.05
153	Tom Browning	.05
154	*Keith Brown*	.05
155	*Norm Charlton*	.15
156	Dave Concepcion	.05
157	Kal Daniels	.05
158	Eric Davis	.10
159	Bo Diaz	.05
160	*Rob Dibble*	.20
161	Nick Esasky	.05
162	John Franco	.05
163	Danny Jackson	.05
164	Barry Larkin	.15
165	Rob Murphy	.05
166	Paul O'Neill	.15
167	Jeff Reed	.05
168	Jose Rijo	.05
169	Ron Robinson	.05
170	*Chris Sabo*	.15
171	*Candy Sierra*	.05
172	*Van Snider*	.05
173a	Jeff Treadway (blue "target" above head)	15.00
173b	Jeff Treadway (no "target")	.05
174	Frank Williams	.05
175	Herm Winningham	.05
176	Jim Adduci	.05
177	Don August	.05
178	Mike Birkbeck	.05
179	Chris Bosio	.05
180	Glenn Braggs	.05
181	Greg Brock	.05
182	Mark Clear	.05
183	Chuck Crim	.05
184	Rob Deer	.05
185	Tom Filer	.05
186	Jim Gantner	.05
187	*Darryl Hamilton*	.25
188	Ted Higuera	.05
189	Odell Jones	.05
190	Jeffrey Leonard	.05
191	Joey Meyer	.05
192	Paul Mirabella	.05
193	Paul Molitor	.30
194	Charlie O'Brien	.05
195	Dan Plesac	.05
196	*Gary Sheffield*	1.50
197	B.J. Surhoff	.08
198	Dale Sveum	.05
199	Bill Wegman	.05
200	Robin Yount	.30
201	Rafael Belliard	.05
202	Barry Bonds	.50
203	Bobby Bonilla	.10
204	Sid Bream	.05
205	Benny Distefano	.05
206	Doug Drabek	.05
207	Mike Dunne	.05
208	Felix Fermin	.05
209	Brian Fisher	.05
210	Jim Gott	.05
211	Bob Kipper	.05
212	Dave LaPoint	.05
213	Mike LaValliere	.05
214	Jose Lind	.05
215	Junior Ortiz	.05
216	Vicente Palacios	.05
217	Tom Prince	.05
218	Gary Redus	.05
219	R.J. Reynolds	.05
220	Jeff Robinson	.05
221	John Smiley	.05
222	Andy Van Slyke	.05
223	Bob Walk	.05
224	Glenn Wilson	.05
225	Jesse Barfield	.05
226	George Bell	.05
227	*Pat Borders*	.15
228	John Cerutti	.05
229	Jim Clancy	.05
230	Mark Eichhorn	.05
231	Tony Fernandez	.05
232	Cecil Fielder	.15
233	Mike Flanagan	.05
234	Kelly Gruber	.05
235	Tom Henke	.05
236	Jimmy Key	.05
237	Rick Leach	.05
238	Manny Lee	.05
239	Nelson Liriano	.05
240	Fred McGriff	.20
241	Lloyd Moseby	.05
242	Rance Mulliniks	.05
243	Jeff Musselman	.05
244	Dave Stieb	.05
245	Todd Stottlemyre	.05
246	Duane Ward	.05
247	David Wells	.08
248	Ernie Whitt	.05
249	Luis Aguayo	.05
250a	Neil Allen (Home: Sarasota, FL)	.25
250b	Neil Allen (Home: Syosset, NY)	.05
251	John Candelaria	.05
252	Jack Clark	.05
253	Richard Dotson	.05
254	Rickey Henderson	.30
255	Tommy John	.10
256	Roberto Kelly	.05
257	Al Leiter	.08
258	Don Mattingly	.50
259	Dale Mohorcic	.05
260	*Hal Morris*	.25
261	Scott Nielsen	.05
262	Mike Pagliarulo	.05
263	*Hipolito Pena*	.05
264	Ken Phelps	.05
265	Willie Randolph	.05
266	Rick Rhoden	.05
267	Dave Righetti	.05
268	Rafael Santana	.05
269	Steve Shields	.05
270	Joel Skinner	.05
271	Don Slaught	.05
272	Claudell Washington	.05
273	Gary Ward	.05
274	Dave Winfield	.25
275	Luis Aquino	.05
276	Floyd Bannister	.05
277	George Brett	.35
278	Bill Buckner	.05
279	*Nick Capra*	.05
280	*Jose DeJesus*	.05
281	Steve Farr	.05
282	Jerry Gleaton	.05
283	Mark Gubicza	.05
284	*Tom Gordon*	.20
285	Bo Jackson	.20
286	Charlie Leibrandt	.05
287	*Mike Macfarlane*	.15
288	Jeff Montgomery	.08
289	Bill Pecota	.05
290	Jamie Quirk	.05
291	Bret Saberhagen	.08
292	Kevin Seitzer	.05
293	Kurt Stillwell	.05
294	Pat Tabler	.05
295	Danny Tartabull	.05
296	Gary Thurman	.05
297	Frank White	.05
298	Willie Wilson	.05
299	Roberto Alomar	.40
300	*Sandy Alomar, Jr.*	.40
301	Chris Brown	.05
302	Mike Brumley	.05
303	Mark Davis	.05
304	Mark Grant	.05
305	Tony Gwynn	.40
306	*Greg Harris*	.05
307	Andy Hawkins	.05
308	Jimmy Jones	.05
309	John Kruk	.05
310	Dave Leiper	.05
311	Carmelo Martinez	.05
312	Lance McCullers	.05
313	Keith Moreland	.05
314	Dennis Rasmussen	.05
315	Randy Ready	.05
316	Benito Santiago	.05
317	Eric Show	.05
318	Todd Simmons	.05
319	Garry Templeton	.05
320	Dickie Thon	.05
321	Ed Whitson	.05
322	Marvell Wynne	.05
323	Mike Aldrete	.05
324	Brett Butler	.08
325	Will Clark	.25
326	Kelly Downs	.05
327	Dave Dravecky	.05
328	Scott Garrelts	.05
329	Atlee Hammaker	.05
330	*Charlie Hayes*	.25
331	Mike Krukow	.05
332	Craig Lefferts	.05
333	Candy Maldonado	.05
334	Kirt Manwaring	.05
335	Bob Melvin	.05
336	Kevin Mitchell	.05
337	Donell Nixon	.05
338	*Tony Perezchica*	.05
339	Joe Price	.05
340	Rick Reuschel	.05
341	Earnest Riles	.05
342	Don Robinson	.05
343	Chris Speier	.05
344	Robby Thompson	.05
345	Jose Uribe	.05
346	Matt Williams	.25
347	*Trevor Wilson*	.15
348	Juan Agosto	.05
349	Larry Andersen	.05
350a	Alan Ashby ("Throws Rig")	.50
350b	Alan Ashby ("Throws Right")	.05
351	Kevin Bass	.05
352	Buddy Bell	.05
353	Craig Biggio	.50
354	Danny Darwin	.05
355	Glenn Davis	.05
356	Jim Deshaies	.05
357	Bill Doran	.05
358	*John Fishel*	.05
359	Billy Hatcher	.05
360	Bob Knepper	.05
361	*Louie Meadows*	.05
362	Dave Meads	.05
363	Jim Pankovits	.05
364	Terry Puhl	.05
365	Rafael Ramirez	.05
366	Craig Reynolds	.05
367	Mike Scott	.05
368	Nolan Ryan	.75
369	Dave Smith	.05
370	Gerald Young	.05
371	Hubie Brooks	.05
372	Tim Burke	.05
373	*John Dopson*	.10
374	Mike Fitzgerald	.05
375	Tom Foley	.05
376	Andres Galarraga	.15
377	Neal Heaton	.05
378	Joe Hesketh	.05
379	*Brian Holman*	.10
380	Rex Hudler	.05
381	*Randy Johnson*	2.50
382	Wallace Johnson	.05
383	Tracy Jones	.05
384	Dave Martinez	.05
385	Dennis Martinez	.08
386	Andy McGaffigan	.05
387	Otis Nixon	.05
388	*Johnny Paredes*	.05
389	Jeff Parrett	.05
390	Pascual Perez	.05

391 Tim Raines .08
392 Luis Rivera .05
393 *Nelson Santovenia* .05
394 Bryn Smith .05
395 Tim Wallach .05
396 Andy Allanson .05
397 *Rod Allen* .05
398 Scott Bailes .05
399 Tom Candiotti .05
400 Joe Carter .10
401 Carmen Castillo .05
402 Dave Clark .05
403 John Farrell .05
404 Julio Franco .08
405 Don Gordon .05
406 Mel Hall .05
407 Brad Havens .05
408 Brook Jacoby .05
409 Doug Jones .05
410 *Jeff Kaiser* .05
411 *Luis Medina* .05
412 Cory Snyder .05
413 Greg Swindell .05
414 *Ron Tingley* .05
415 Willie Upshaw .05
416 Ron Washington .05
417 Rich Yett .05
418 Damon Berryhill .05
419 Mike Bielecki .05
420 *Doug Dascenzo* .05
421 Jody Davis .05
422 Andre Dawson .15
423 Frank DiPino .05
424 Shawon Dunston .15
425 "Goose" Gossage .08
426 Mark Grace .30
427 *Mike Harkey* .05
428 Darrin Jackson .05
429 Les Lancaster .05
430 Vance Law .05
431 Greg Maddux .65
432 Jamie Moyer .05
433 Al Nipper .05
434 Rafael Palmeiro .25
435 Pat Perry .05
436 *Jeff Pico* .05
437 Ryne Sandberg .40
438 Calvin Schiraldi .05
439 Rick Sutcliffe .05
440a Manny Trillo ("Throws Rig") 1.50
440b Manny Trillo ("Throws Right") .05
441 *Gary Varsho* .05
442 Mitch Webster .05
443 *Luis Alicea* .15
444 Tom Brunansky .05
445 Vince Coleman .05
446 *John Costello* .05
447 Danny Cox .05
448 Ken Dayley .05
449 Jose DeLeon .05
450 Curt Ford .05
451 Pedro Guerrero .05
452 Bob Horner .05
453 *Tim Jones* .05
454 Steve Lake .05
455 Joe Magrane .05
456 Greg Mathews .05
457 Willie McGee .08
458 Larry McWilliams .05
459 Jose Oquendo .05
460 Tony Pena .05
461 Terry Pendleton .05
462 *Steve Peters* .05
463 Ozzie Smith .35
464 Scott Terry .05
465 Denny Walling .05
466 Todd Worrell .05
467 Tony Armas .05
468 *Dante Bichette* .50
469 Bob Boone .05
470 *Terry Clark* .05
471 Stew Cliburn .05
472 *Mike Cook* .05
473 *Sherman Corbett* .05
474 Chili Davis .08
475 Brian Downing .05
476 Jim Eppard .05
477 Chuck Finley .05
478 Willie Fraser .05
479 *Bryan Harvey* .25
480 Jack Howell .05
481 Wally Joyner .08
482 Jack Lazorko .05
483 Kirk McCaskill .05
484 Mark McLemore .05
485 Greg Minton .05
486 Dan Petry .05
487 Johnny Ray .05
488 Dick Schofield .05
489 Devon White .08
490 Mike Witt .05
491 Harold Baines .08
492 Daryl Boston .05
493 Ivan Calderon .05
494 Mike Diaz .05
495 Carlton Fisk .15
496 *Dave Gallagher* .05
497 Ozzie Guillen .05
498 Shawn Hillegas .05
499 Lance Johnson .05
500 Barry Jones .05
501 Bill Long .05
502 Steve Lyons .05
503 Fred Manrique .05
504 Jack McDowell .05
505 *Donn Pall* .12
506 Kelly Paris .05
507 Dan Pasqua .05
508 *Ken Patterson* .10
509 Melido Perez .05
510 Jerry Reuss .05
511 Mark Salas .05
512 Bobby Thigpen .05
513 Mike Woodard .05
514 Bob Brower .05
515 Steve Buechele .05
516 *Jose Cecena* .05
517 Cecil Espy .05
518 Scott Fletcher .05
519 Cecilio Guante .05
520 Jose Guzman .05
521 Ray Hayward .05
522 Charlie Hough .05
523 Pete Incaviglia .05
524 Mike Jeffcoat .05
525 Paul Kilgus .05
526 *Chad Kreuter* .15
527 Jeff Kunkel .05
528 Oddibe McDowell .05
529 Pete O'Brien .05
530 Geno Petralli .05
531 Jeff Russell .05
532 Ruben Sierra .05
533 Mike Stanley .05
534 Ed Vande Berg .05
535 Curtis Wilkerson .05
536 Mitch Williams .05
537 Bobby Witt .05
538 Steve Balboni .05
539 Scott Bankhead .05
540 Scott Bradley .05
541 Mickey Brantley .05
542 Jay Buhner .15
543 Mike Campbell .05
544 Darnell Coles .05
545 Henry Cotto .05
546 Alvin Davis .05
547 Mario Diaz .05
548 *Ken Griffey, Jr.* 20.00
549 *Erik Hanson* .15
550 Mike Jackson .05
551 Mark Langston .05
552 Edgar Martinez .10
553 *Bill McGuire* .05
554 Mike Moore .05
555 Jim Presley .05
556 Rey Quinones .05
557 Jerry Reed .05
558 Harold Reynolds .05
559 *Mike Schooler* .05
560 Bill Swift .05
561 Dave Valle .05
562 Steve Bedrosian .05
563 Phil Bradley .05
564 Don Carman .05
565 Bob Dernier .05
566 Marvin Freeman .05
567 Todd Frohwirth .05
568 Greg Gross .05
569 Kevin Gross .05
570 Greg Harris .05
571 Von Hayes .05
572 Chris James .05
573 Steve Jeltz .05
574 *Ron Jones* .05
575 *Ricky Jordan* .05
576 Mike Maddux .05
577 David Palmer .05
578 Lance Parrish .08
579 Shane Rawley .05
580 Bruce Ruffin .05
581 Juan Samuel .05
582 Mike Schmidt .30
583 Kent Tekulve .05
584 Milt Thompson .05
585 *Jose Alvarez* .05
586 Paul Assenmacher .05
587 Bruce Benedict .05
588 Jeff Blauser .05
589 *Terry Blocker* .05
590 Ron Gant .15
591 Tom Glavine .20
592 Tommy Gregg .05
593 Albert Hall .05
594 Dion James .05
595 Rick Mahler .05
596 Dale Murphy .15
597 Gerald Perry .05
598 Charlie Puleo .05
599 Ted Simmons .05
600 Pete Smith .05
601 Zane Smith .05
602 John Smoltz .20
603 Bruce Sutter .05
604 Andres Thomas .05
605 Ozzie Virgil .05
606 Brady Anderson .30
607 Jeff Ballard .05
608 *Jose Bautista* .05
609 Ken Gerhart .05
610 Terry Kennedy .05
611 Eddie Murray .30
612 Carl Nichols .05
613 Tom Niedenfuer .05
614 Joe Orsulak .05
615 *Oswaldo Peraza* (Oswald) .05
616a Bill Ripken (vulgarity on bat knob) 8.00
616b Bill Ripken (scribble over vulgarity) 8.00
616c Bill Ripken (black box over vulgarity) .10
616d Bill Ripken (vulgarity whited out) 30.00
616e Billy Ripken (strip cut out of bottom of card) .10
617 Cal Ripken, Jr. .75
618 Dave Schmidt .05
619 Rick Schu .05
620 Larry Sheets .05
621 Doug Sisk .05
622 Pete Stanicek .05
623 Mickey Tettleton .05
624 Jay Tibbs .05
625 Jim Traber .05
626 Mark Williamson .05
627 *Craig Worthington* .10
628 Speed and Power (Jose Canseco) .25
629 Pitcher Perfect (Tom Browning) .05
630 Like Father Like Sons (Roberto Alomar, Sandy Alomar, Jr.) .25
631 N.L. All-Stars (Will Clark, Rafael Palmeiro) .20
632 Homeruns Coast to Coast (Will Clark, Darryl Strawberry) .25
633 Hot Corner's Hot Hitters (Wade Boggs, Carney Lansford) .10
634 Triple A's (Jose Canseco, Mark McGwire, Terry Steinbach) .75
635 Dual Heat (Mark Davis, Dwight Gooden) .10
636 N.L. Pitching Power (David Cone, Danny Jackson) .05
637 Cannon Arms (Bobby Bonilla, Chris Sabo) .10
638 Double Trouble (Andres Galarraga, Gerald Perry) .10
639 Power Center (Eric Davis) .10
640 Major League Prospects (*Cameron Drew*), (*Steve Wilson*) .05
641 Major League Prospects (Kevin Brown), (*Kevin Reimer*) .30
642 Major League Prospects (*Jerald Clark*), (*Brad Pounders*) .08
643 Major League Prospects (*Mike Capel*), (*Drew Hall*) .05
644 Major League Prospects (*Joe Girardi*), (*Rolando Roomes*) .20
645 Major League Prospects (*Marty Brown*), (*Lenny Harris*) .12
646 Major League Prospects (*Luis de los Santos*), (*Jim Campbell*) .05
647 Major League Prospects (*Miguel Garcia*), (*Randy Kramer*) .05
648 Major League Prospects (*Torey Lovullo*), (*Robert Palacios*) .08
649 Major League Prospects (*Jim Corsi*), (*Bob Milacki*) .12
650 Major League Prospects (*Grady Hall*), (*Mike Rochford*) .05
651 Major League Prospects (*Vance Lovelace*), (*Terry Taylor*) .05
652 Major League Prospects (*Dennis Cook*), (*Ken Hill*) .25
653 Major League Prospects (*Scott Service*), (*Shane Turner*) .08
654 Checklist 1-101 .05
655 Checklist 102-200 .05
656 Checklist 201-298 .05
657 Checklist 299-395 .05
658 Checklist 396-490 .05
659 Checklist 491-584 .05

1989 Fleer Glossy Tin

The last of the limited-edition, collector-version glossy tin sets is estimated to have been produced in an edition of 30,000-60,000, creating a significant premium over their counterparts in the regualr Fleer set. The issue was sold only in complete-set form in a lithographed metal box. The 1989 glossies differ from the regular cards on back in the use of blue, rather than yellow ink, and the appearance at center of a large baseball logo with 1989 / Collector's Edition / Fleer at center. No glossy version of the '89 Update set was made. Fleer glossy sets were originally wholesaled at $40 each.

	MT
Complete Set, Unopened (672):	250.00
Complete Set (672):	80.00
Common Player:	.25

(Star cards valued at 3X-5X regular 1989 Fleer cards.)

1989 Fleer All-Stars

This special 12-card set represents Fleer's choices for its 1989 Major League All-Star Team. For the fourth consecutive year, Fleer inserted the special cards randomly inside its regular 1989 wax and cello packs. The cards feature two player photos set against a green background with the "1989 Fleer All Star Team" logo bannered across the top, and the player's name, position and team in the lower left corner. The backs contain a narrative player profile.

		MT
Complete Set (12):		8.00
Common Player:		.50
1	Bobby Bonilla	.60
2	Jose Canseco	1.50
3	Will Clark	1.00
4	Dennis Eckersley	.50
5	Julio Franco	.50
6	Mike Greenwell	.50
7	Orel Hershiser	.50
8	Paul Molitor	2.00
9	Mike Scioscia	.50
10	Darryl Strawberry	.60
11	Alan Trammell	.50
12	Frank Viola	.50

1989 Fleer For The Record

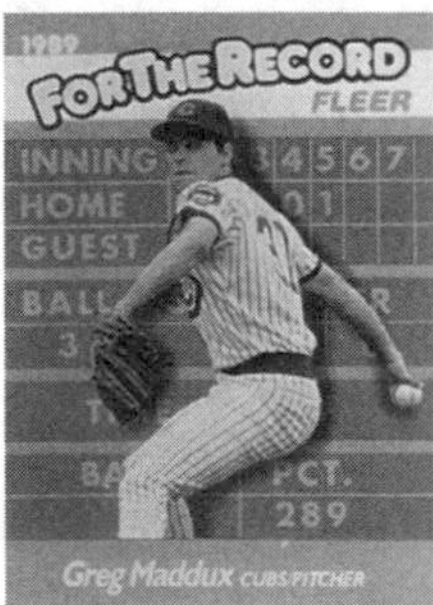

Fleer's "For the Record" set features six players and their achievements from 1988. Fronts of the standard 2-1/2" x 3-1/2" cards feature a photo of the player set against a red scoreboard background. Card backs are grey and describe individual accomplishments. The cards were distributed randomly in rack packs.

		MT
Complete Set (6):		5.00
Common Player:		.50
1	Wade Boggs	1.00
2	Roger Clemens	1.50
3	Andres Galarraga	.75
4	Kirk Gibson	.50
5	Greg Maddux	2.00
6	Don Mattingly	1.50

1989 Fleer World Series

This 12-card set, which depicts highlights of the 1988 World Series, was included as a special sub-set with the regular and glossy factory-collated Fleer set. It was not available as individual cards in wax packs, cello packs or any other form.

		MT
Complete Set, Regular (12):		1.50
Complete Set, Glossy (12):		1.00
Common Card:		.15
1	Dodgers Secret Weapon (Mickey Hatcher)	.15
2	Rookie Starts Series (Tim Belcher)	.15
3	Jose Canseco	.40
4	Dramatic Comeback (Mike Scioscia)	.15
5	Kirk Gibson	.30
6	Orel Hershiser	.30
7	One Swings, Three RBIs (Mike Marshall)	.15
8	Mark McGwire	.75
9	Sax's Speed Wins Game 4 (Steve Sax)	.15
10	Series Caps Award Winning Year (Walt Weiss)	.15
11	Orel Hershiser	.25
12	Dodger Blue, World Champs	.25

1989 Fleer Box Panels

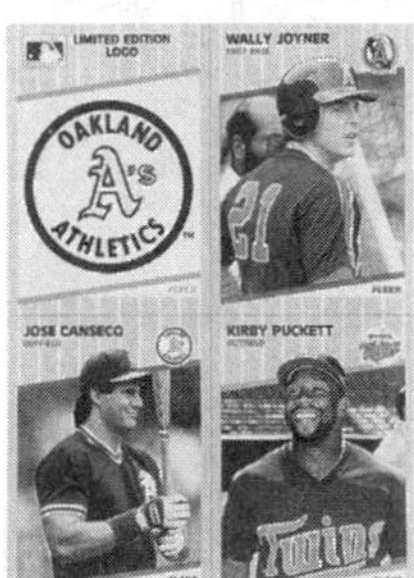

For the fourth consecutive year, Fleer issued a series of cards on the bottom panels of its regular 1989 wax pack boxes. The 28-card set includes 20 players and eight team logo cards, all designed in the identical style of the regular 1989 Fleer set. The box-bottom cards were randomly printed, four cards (three player cards and one team logo) on each bottom panel. The cards are numbered from C-1 to C-28.

		MT
Complete Panel Set (7):		6.00
Complete Singles Set (28):		3.00
Common Single Player:		.15
1	Mets Logo	.05
2	Wade Boggs	.45
3	George Brett	.50
4	Jose Canseco	.50
5	A's Logo	.05
6	Will Clark	.35
7	David Cone	.15
8	Andres Galarraga	.20
9	Dodgers Logo	.05
10	Kirk Gibson	.15
11	Mike Greenwell	.10
12	Tony Gwynn	.75
13	Tigers Logo	.05
14	Orel Hershiser	.15
15	Danny Jackson	.10
16	Wally Joyner	.15
17	Red Sox Logo	.05
18	Yankees Logo	.05
19	Fred McGriff	.25
20	Kirby Puckett	.50
21	Chris Sabo	.15
22	Kevin Seitzer	.10
23	Pirates logo	.05
24	Astros logo	.05
25	Darryl Strawberry	.20
26	Alan Trammell	.20
27	Andy Van Slyke	.10
28	Frank Viola	.10

1989 Fleer Update

Fleer produced its sixth consecutive "Update" set in 1989 to supplement the company's regular set. As in the past, the set consisted of 132 cards (numbered U-1 through U-132) that were sold by hobby dealers in special collector's boxes.

		MT
Complete Set (132):		8.00
Common Player:		.06
1	Phil Bradley	.06
2	Mike Devereaux	.06
3	Steve Finley	.30
4	Kevin Hickey	.06
5	Brian Holton	.06
6	Bob Milacki	.06
7	Randy Milligan	.06
8	John Dopson	.06
9	Nick Esasky	.06
10	Rob Murphy	.06
11	Jim Abbott	.20
12	Bert Blyleven	.06
13	Jeff Manto	.06
14	Bob McClure	.06
15	Lance Parrish	.08
16	Lee Stevens	.06
17	Claudell Washington	.06
18	Mark Davis	.06
19	Eric King	.06
20	Ron Kittle	.06
21	Matt Merullo	.06
22	Steve Rosenberg	.06
23	Robin Ventura	.40
24	Keith Atherton	.06
25	*Joey (Albert) Belle*	3.00
26	Jerry Browne	.06
27	Felix Fermin	.06
28	Brad Komminsk	.06
29	Pete O'Brien	.06
30	Mike Brumley	.06
31	Tracy Jones	.06
32	Mike Schwabe	.06
33	Gary Ward	.06
34	Frank Williams	.06
35	*Kevin Appier*	.40
36	Bob Boone	.06
37	Luis de los Santos	.06
38	Jim Eisenreich	.06
39	*Jaime Navarro*	.20
40	Bill Spiers	.06
41	*Greg Vaughn*	1.50
42	Randy Veres	.06
43	Wally Backman	.06
44	Shane Rawley	.06
45	Steve Balboni	.06
46	Jesse Barfield	.06
47	Alvaro Espinoza	.06
48	Bob Geren	.06
49	Mel Hall	.06
50	Andy Hawkins	.06
51	Hensley Meulens	.06
52	Steve Sax	.06
53	*Deion Sanders*	.75
54	Rickey Henderson	.25
55	Mike Moore	.06
56	Tony Phillips	.10
57	Greg Briley	.06
58	Gene Harris	.06
59	Randy Johnson	3.00
60	Jeffrey Leonard	.06
61	Dennis Powell	.06
62	Omar Vizquel	.30
63	Kevin Brown	.10
64	Julio Franco	.08
65	Jamie Moyer	.06
66	Rafael Palmeiro	.25
67	Nolan Ryan	1.00
68	Francisco Cabrera	.06
69	Junior Felix	.06
70	Al Leiter	.08
71	Alex Sanchez	.06
72	Geronimo Berroa	.10
73	Derek Lilliquist	.06
74	Lonnie Smith	.06
75	Jeff Treadway	.06
76	Paul Kilgus	.06
77	Lloyd McClendon	.06
78	Scott Sanderson	.06
79	Dwight Smith	.06
80	Jerome Walton	.06
81	Mitch Williams	.06
82	Steve Wilson	.06
83	Todd Benzinger	.06
84	Ken Griffey	.08
85	Rick Mahler	.06
86	Rolando Roomes	.06
87	Scott Scudder	.06
88	Jim Clancy	.06
89	Rick Rhoden	.06
90	Dan Schatzeder	.06
91	Mike Morgan	.06
92	Eddie Murray	.25
93	Willie Randolph	.06
94	Ray Searage	.06
95	Mike Aldrete	.06
96	Kevin Gross	.06
97	Mark Langston	.06
98	Spike Owen	.06
99	Zane Smith	.06
100	Don Aase	.06
101	Barry Lyons	.06
102	Juan Samuel	.06
103	Wally Whitehurst	.06
104	Dennis Cook	.06
105	Len Dykstra	.08
106	Charlie Hayes	.15
107	Tommy Herr	.06

108 Ken Howell .06
109 John Kruk .06
110 Roger McDowell .06
111 Terry Mulholland .10
112 Jeff Parrett .06
113 Neal Heaton .06
114 Jeff King .10
115 Randy Kramer .06
116 Bill Landrum .06
117 Cris Carpenter .06
118 Frank DiPino .06
119 Ken Hill .15
120 Dan Quisenberry .06
121 Milt Thompson .06
122 *Todd Zeile* .25
123 Jack Clark .06
124 Bruce Hurst .06
125 Mark Parent .06
126 Bip Roberts .06
127 Jeff Brantley .15
128 Terry Kennedy .06
129 Mike LaCoss .06
130 Greg Litton .06
131 Mike Schmidt .50
132 Checklist .06

1990 Fleer

Fleer's 1990 set, its 10th annual baseball card offering, again consisted of 660 cards numbered by team. The front of the cards feature mostly action photos surrounded by one of several different color bands and a white border. The set includes various special cards, including a series of "Major League Prospects," Players of the Decade, team checklist cards and a series of multi-player cards. The backs include complete career stats, player data, and a special "Vital Signs" section showing on-base percentage, slugging percentage, etc. for batters; and strikeout and walk ratios, opposing batting averages, etc. for pitchers.

	MT
Complete Set (660):	10.00
Common Player:	.05
Wax Pack (15 - Final Print):	1.10
Wax Box (36- Final Print):	21.50

1 Lance Blankenship .05
2 Todd Burns .05
3 Jose Canseco .25
4 Jim Corsi .05
5 Storm Davis .05
6 Dennis Eckersley .10
7 Mike Gallego .05
8 Ron Hassey .05
9 Dave Henderson .05
10 Rickey Henderson .25
11 Rick Honeycutt .05
12 Stan Javier .05
13 Felix Jose .05
14 Carney Lansford .05
15 Mark McGwire 1.00
16 Mike Moore .05
17 Gene Nelson .05
18 Dave Parker .08
19 Tony Phillips .05
20 Terry Steinbach .05
21 Dave Stewart .08
22 Walt Weiss .08
23 Bob Welch .05
24 Curt Young .05
25 Paul Assenmacher .05
26 Damon Berryhill .05
27 Mike Bielecki .05
28 Kevin Blankenship .05
29 Andre Dawson .12
30 Shawon Dunston .08
31 Joe Girardi .08
32 Mark Grace .25
33 Mike Harkey .05
34 Paul Kilgus .05
35 Les Lancaster .05
36 Vance Law .05
37 Greg Maddux .60
38 Lloyd McClendon .05
39 Jeff Pico .05
40 Ryne Sandberg .30
41 Scott Sanderson .05
42 Dwight Smith .05
43 Rick Sutcliffe .05
44 *Jerome Walton* .05
45 Mitch Webster .05
46 Curt Wilkerson .05
47 *Dean Wilkins* .05
48 Mitch Williams .05
49 Steve Wilson .05
50 Steve Bedrosian .05
51 *Mike Benjamin* .08
52 *Jeff Brantley* .10
53 Brett Butler .08
54 Will Clark .25
55 Kelly Downs .05
56 Scott Garrelts .05
57 Atlee Hammaker .05
58 Terry Kennedy .05
59 Mike LaCoss .05
60 Craig Lefferts .05
61 *Greg Litton* .05
62 Candy Maldonado .05
63 Kirt Manwaring .05
64 *Randy McCament* .05
65 Kevin Mitchell .05
66 Donell Nixon .05
67 Ken Oberkfell .05
68 Rick Reuschel .05
69 Ernest Riles .05
70 Don Robinson .05
71 Pat Sheridan .05
72 Chris Speier .05
73 Robby Thompson .05
74 Jose Uribe .05
75 Matt Williams .25
76 George Bell .05
77 Pat Borders .05
78 John Cerutti .05
79 *Junior Felix* .05
80 Tony Fernandez .05
81 Mike Flanagan .05
82 *Mauro Gozzo* .05
83 Kelly Gruber .05
84 Tom Henke .05
85 Jimmy Key .08
86 Manny Lee .05
87 Nelson Liriano .05
88 Lee Mazzilli .05
89 Fred McGriff .20
90 Lloyd Moseby .05
91 Rance Mulliniks .05
92 Alex Sanchez .05
93 Dave Steib .05
94 Todd Stottlemyre .05
95 Duane Ward .05
96 David Wells .08
97 Ernie Whitt .05
98 Frank Wills .05
99 Mookie Wilson .05
100 *Kevin Appier* .25
101 Luis Aquino .05
102 Bob Boone .05
103 George Brett .30
104 Jose DeJesus .05
105 Luis de los Santos .05
106 Jim Eisenreich .05
107 Steve Farr .05
108 Tom Gordon .05
109 Mark Gubicza .05
110 Bo Jackson .20
111 Terry Leach .05
112 Charlie Leibrandt .05
113 *Rick Luecken* .05
114 Mike Macfarlane .05
115 Jeff Montgomery .05
116 Bret Saberhagen .08
117 Kevin Seitzer .05
118 Kurt Stillwell .05
119 Pat Tabler .05
120 Danny Tartabull .05
121 Gary Thurman .05
122 Frank White .05
123 Willie Wilson .05
124 *Matt Winters* .05
125 Jim Abbott .08
126 Tony Armas .05
127 Dante Bichette .20
128 Bert Blyleven .05
129 Chili Davis .08
130 Brian Downing .05
131 *Mike Fetters* .08
132 Chuck Finley .05
133 Willie Fraser .05
134 Bryan Harvey .05
135 Jack Howell .05
136 Wally Joyner .10
137 *Jeff Manto* .08
138 Kirk McCaskill .05
139 Bob McClure .05
140 Greg Minton .05
141 Lance Parrish .05
142 Dan Petry .05
143 Johnny Ray .05
144 Dick Schofield .05
145 *Lee Stevens* .08
146 Claudell Washington .05
147 Devon White .08
148 Mike Witt .05
149 Roberto Alomar .25
150 Sandy Alomar, Jr. .12
151 Andy Benes .20
152 Jack Clark .05
153 Pat Clements .05
154 Joey Cora .05
155 Mark Davis .05
156 Mark Grant .05
157 Tony Gwynn .40
158 Greg Harris .05
159 Bruce Hurst .05
160 Darrin Jackson .05
161 Chris James .05
162 Carmelo Martinez .05
163 Mike Pagliarulo .05
164 Mark Parent .05
165 Dennis Rasmussen .05
166 Bip Roberts .05
167 Benito Santiago .05
168 Calvin Schiraldi .05
169 Eric Show .05
170 Garry Templeton .05
171 Ed Whitson .05
172 Brady Anderson .12
173 Jeff Ballard .05
174 Phil Bradley .05
175 Mike Devereaux .05
176 *Steve Finley* .10
177 Pete Harnisch .10
178 Kevin Hickey .05
179 Brian Holton .05
180 *Ben McDonald* .25
181 Bob Melvin .05
182 Bob Milacki .05
183 Randy Milligan .05
184 Gregg Olson .05
185 Joe Orsulak .05
186 Bill Ripken .05
187 Cal Ripken, Jr. .60
188 Dave Schmidt .05
189 Larry Sheets .05
190 Mickey Tettleton .05
191 Mark Thurmond .05
192 Jay Tibbs .05
193 Jim Traber .05
194 Mark Williamson .05
195 Craig Worthington .05
196 Don Aase .05
197 *Blaine Beatty* .05
198 Mark Carreon .05
199 Gary Carter .10
200 David Cone .08
201 Ron Darling .05
202 Kevin Elster .05
203 Sid Fernandez .05
204 Dwight Gooden .10
205 Keith Hernandez .05
206 *Jeff Innis* .05
207 Gregg Jefferies .12
208 Howard Johnson .05
209 Barry Lyons .05
210 Dave Magadan .05
211 Kevin McReynolds .05
212 Jeff Musselman .05
213 Randy Myers .05
214 Bob Ojeda .05
215 Juan Samuel .05
216 Mackey Sasser .05
217 Darryl Strawberry .08
218 Tim Teufel .05
219 Frank Viola .05
220 Juan Agosto .05
221 Larry Anderson .05
222 *Eric Anthony* .15
223 Kevin Bass .05
224 Craig Biggio .15
225 Ken Caminiti .15
226 Jim Clancy .05
227 Danny Darwin .05
228 Glenn Davis .05
229 Jim Deshaies .05
230 Bill Doran .05
231 Bob Forsch .05
232 Brian Meyer .05
233 Terry Puhl .05
234 Rafael Ramirez .05
235 Rick Rhoden .05
236 Dan Schatzeder .05
237 Mike Scott .05
238 Dave Smith .05
239 Alex Trevino .05
240 Glenn Wilson .05
241 Gerald Young .05
242 Tom Brunansky .05
243 Cris Carpenter .05
244 *Alex Cole* .05
245 Vince Coleman .05
246 John Costello .05
247 Ken Dayley .05
248 Jose DeLeon .05
249 Frank DiPino .05
250 Pedro Guerrero .05
251 Ken Hill .05
252 Joe Magrane .05
253 Willie McGee .08
254 John Morris .05
255 Jose Oquendo .05
256 Tony Pena .05
257 Terry Pendleton .05
258 Ted Power .05
259 Dan Quisenberry .05
260 Ozzie Smith .25
261 Scott Terry .05
262 Milt Thompson .05
263 Denny Walling .05
264 Todd Worrell .05
265 *Todd Zeile* .15
266 Marty Barrett .05
267 Mike Boddicker .05
268 Wade Boggs .35
269 Ellis Burks .05
270 Rick Cerone .05
271 Roger Clemens .50
272 John Dopson .05
273 Nick Esasky .05
274 Dwight Evans .05
275 Wes Gardner .05
276 Rich Gedman .05
277 Mike Greenwell .05
278 Danny Heep .05
279 Eric Hetzel .05
280 Dennis Lamp .05
281 Rob Murphy .05
282 Joe Price .05
283 Carlos Quintana .05
284 Jody Reed .05
285 Luis Rivera .05
286 Kevin Romine .05
287 Lee Smith .08
288 Mike Smithson .05
289 Bob Stanley .05
290 Harold Baines .08
291 Kevin Brown .10
292 Steve Buechele .05
293 *Scott Coolbaugh* .05
294 *Jack Daugherty* .05
295 Cecil Espy .05
296 Julio Franco .05
297 *Juan Gonzalez* 3.00

No.	Player	Value
298	Cecilio Guante	.05
299	Drew Hall	.05
300	Charlie Hough	.05
301	Pete Incaviglia	.05
302	Mike Jeffcoat	.05
303	Chad Kreuter	.05
304	Jeff Kunkel	.05
305	Rick Leach	.05
306	Fred Manrique	.05
307	Jamie Moyer	.05
308	Rafael Palmeiro	.15
309	Geno Petralli	.05
310	Kevin Reimer	.05
311	*Kenny Rogers*	.15
312	Jeff Russell	.05
313	Nolan Ryan	.60
314	Ruben Sierra	.05
315	Bobby Witt	.05
316	Chris Bosio	.05
317	Glenn Braggs	.05
318	Greg Brock	.05
319	Chuck Crim	.05
320	Rob Deer	.05
321	Mike Felder	.05
322	Tom Filer	.05
323	*Tony Fossas*	.05
324	Jim Gantner	.05
325	Darryl Hamilton	.05
326	Ted Higuera	.05
327	Mark Knudson	.05
328	Bill Krueger	.05
329	*Tim McIntosh*	.05
330	Paul Molitor	.30
331	*Jaime Navarro*	.15
332	Charlie O'Brien	.05
333	*Jeff Peterek*	.05
334	Dan Plesac	.05
335	Jerry Reuss	.05
336	Gary Sheffield	.25
337	*Bill Spiers*	.05
338	B.J. Surhoff	.08
339	Greg Vaughn	.20
340	Robin Yount	.30
341	Hubie Brooks	.05
342	Tim Burke	.05
343	Mike Fitzgerald	.05
344	Tom Foley	.05
345	Andres Galarraga	.15
346	Damaso Garcia	.05
347	*Marquis Grissom*	.50
348	Kevin Gross	.05
349	Joe Hesketh	.05
350	*Jeff Huson*	.10
351	Wallace Johnson	.05
352	Mark Langston	.05
353	Dave Martinez	.05
354	Dennis Martinez	.08
355	Andy McGaffigan	.05
356	Otis Nixon	.05
357	Spike Owen	.05
358	Pascual Perez	.05
359	Tim Raines	.10
360	Nelson Santovenia	.05
361	Bryn Smith	.05
362	Zane Smith	.05
363	*Larry Walker*	1.25
364	Tim Wallach	.05
365	Rick Aguilera	.05
366	Allan Anderson	.05
367	Wally Backman	.05
368	Doug Baker	.05
369	Juan Berenguer	.05
370	Randy Bush	.05
371	Carmen Castillo	.05
372	*Mike Dyer*	.05
373	Gary Gaetti	.05
374	Greg Gagne	.05
375	Dan Gladden	.05
376	German Gonzalez	.05
377	Brian Harper	.05
378	Kent Hrbek	.08
379	Gene Larkin	.05
380	Tim Laudner	.05
381	John Moses	.05
382	Al Newman	.05
383	Kirby Puckett	.35
384	Shane Rawley	.05
385	Jeff Reardon	.05
386	Roy Smith	.05
387	*Gary Wayne*	.05
388	Dave West	.05
389	Tim Belcher	.05
390	Tim Crews	.05
391	Mike Davis	.05
392	Rick Dempsey	.05
393	Kirk Gibson	.05
394	Jose Gonzalez	.05
395	Alfredo Griffin	.05
396	Jeff Hamilton	.05
397	Lenny Harris	.05
398	Mickey Hatcher	.05
399	Orel Hershiser	.08
400	Jay Howell	.05
401	Mike Marshall	.05
402	Ramon Martinez	.08
403	Mike Morgan	.05
404	Eddie Murray	.25
405	Alejandro Pena	.05
406	Willie Randolph	.05
407	Mike Scioscia	.05
408	Ray Searage	.05
409	Fernando Valenzuela	.08
410	*Jose Vizcaino*	.25
411	*John Wetteland*	.25
412	Jack Armstrong	.05
413	Todd Benzinger	.05
414	Tim Birtsas	.05
415	Tom Browning	.05
416	Norm Charlton	.05
417	Eric Davis	.08
418	Rob Dibble	.05
419	John Franco	.05
420	Ken Griffey, Sr.	.08
421	*Chris Hammond*	.15
422	Danny Jackson	.05
423	Barry Larkin	.15
424	Tim Leary	.05
425	Rick Mahler	.05
426	*Joe Oliver*	.05
427	Paul O'Neill	.15
428	Luis Quinones	.05
429	Jeff Reed	.05
430	Jose Rijo	.05
431	Ron Robinson	.05
432	Rolando Roomes	.05
433	Chris Sabo	.05
434	*Scott Scudder*	.10
435	Herm Winningham	.05
436	Steve Balboni	.05
437	Jesse Barfield	.05
438	*Mike Blowers*	.15
439	Tom Brookens	.05
440	Greg Cadaret	.05
441	Alvaro Espinoza	.05
442	*Bob Geren*	.05
443	Lee Guetterman	.05
444	Mel Hall	.05
445	Andy Hawkins	.05
446	Roberto Kelly	.05
447	Don Mattingly	.40
448	Lance McCullers	.05
449	Hensley Meulens	.05
450	Dale Mohorcic	.05
451	Clay Parker	.05
452	Eric Plunk	.05
453	Dave Righetti	.05
454	Deion Sanders	.25
455	Steve Sax	.05
456	Don Slaught	.05
457	Walt Terrell	.05
458	Dave Winfield	.25
459	Jay Bell	.08
460	Rafael Belliard	.05
461	Barry Bonds	.40
462	Bobby Bonilla	.08
463	Sid Bream	.05
464	Benny Distefano	.05
465	Doug Drabek	.05
466	Jim Gott	.05
467	Billy Hatcher	.05
468	Neal Heaton	.05
469	Jeff King	.08
470	Bob Kipper	.05
471	Randy Kramer	.05
472	Bill Landrum	.05
473	Mike LaValliere	.05
474	Jose Lind	.05
475	Junior Ortiz	.05
476	Gary Redus	.05
477	*Rick Reed*	.05
478	R.J. Reynolds	.05
479	Jeff Robinson	.05
480	John Smiley	.05
481	Andy Van Slyke	.05
482	Bob Walk	.05
483	Andy Allanson	.05
484	Scott Bailes	.05
485	Albert Belle	.50
486	Bud Black	.05
487	Jerry Browne	.05
488	Tom Candiotti	.05
489	Joe Carter	.08
490	David Clark	.05
491	John Farrell	.05
492	Felix Fermin	.05
493	Brook Jacoby	.05
494	Dion James	.05
495	Doug Jones	.05
496	Brad Komminsk	.05
497	Rod Nichols	.05
498	Pete O'Brien	.05
499	*Steve Olin*	.10
500	Jesse Orosco	.05
501	Joel Skinner	.05
502	Cory Snyder	.05
503	Greg Swindell	.05
504	Rich Yett	.05
505	Scott Bankhead	.05
506	Scott Bradley	.05
507	Greg Briley	.05
508	Jay Buhner	.08
509	Darnell Coles	.05
510	Keith Comstock	.05
511	Henry Cotto	.05
512	Alvin Davis	.05
513	Ken Griffey, Jr.	2.00
514	Erik Hanson	.05
515	Gene Harris	.05
516	Brian Holman	.05
517	Mike Jackson	.05
518	Randy Johnson	.35
519	Jeffrey Leonard	.05
520	Edgar Martinez	.08
521	Dennis Powell	.05
522	Jim Presley	.05
523	Jerry Reed	.05
524	Harold Reynolds	.05
525	Mike Schooler	.05
526	Bill Swift	.05
527	David Valle	.05
528	*Omar Vizquel*	.25
529	Ivan Calderon	.05
530	Carlton Fisk	.10
531	Scott Fletcher	.05
532	Dave Gallagher	.05
533	Ozzie Guillen	.05
534	*Greg Hibbard*	.05
535	Shawn Hillegas	.05
536	Lance Johnson	.05
537	Eric King	.05
538	Ron Kittle	.05
539	Steve Lyons	.05
540	Carlos Martinez	.05
541	*Tom McCarthy*	.05
542	*Matt Merullo*	.05
543	Donn Pall	.05
544	Dan Pasqua	.05
545	Ken Patterson	.05
546	Melido Perez	.05
547	Steve Rosenberg	.05
548	*Sammy Sosa*	5.00
549	Bobby Thigpen	.05
550	Robin Ventura	.15
551	Greg Walker	.05
552	Don Carman	.05
553	*Pat Combs*	.10
554	Dennis Cook	.05
555	Darren Daulton	.05
556	Len Dykstra	.08
557	Curt Ford	.05
558	Charlie Hayes	.05
559	Von Hayes	.05
560	Tom Herr	.05
561	Ken Howell	.05
562	Steve Jeltz	.05
563	Ron Jones	.05
564	Ricky Jordan	.05
565	John Kruk	.05
566	Steve Lake	.05
567	Roger McDowell	.05
568	Terry Mulholland	.05
569	Dwayne Murphy	.05
570	Jeff Parrett	.05
571	Randy Ready	.05
572	Bruce Ruffin	.05
573	Dickie Thon	.05
574	Jose Alvarez	.05
575	Geronimo Berroa	.05
576	Jeff Blauser	.05
577	Joe Boever	.05
578	Marty Clary	.05
579	Jody Davis	.05
580	Mark Eichhorn	.05
581	Darrell Evans	.08
582	Ron Gant	.10
583	Tom Glavine	.10
584	*Tommy Greene*	.15
585	Tommy Gregg	.05
586	*Dave Justice*	.40
587	Mark Lemke	.05
588	Derek Lilliquist	.05
589	Oddibe McDowell	.05
590	*Kent Mercker*	.20
591	Dale Murphy	.10
592	Gerald Perry	.05
593	Lonnie Smith	.05
594	Pete Smith	.05
595	John Smoltz	.15
596	*Mike Stanton*	.15
597	Andres Thomas	.05
598	Jeff Treadway	.05
599	Doyle Alexander	.05
600	Dave Bergman	.05
601	*Brian Dubois*	.08
602	Paul Gibson	.05
603	Mike Heath	.05
604	Mike Henneman	.05
605	Guillermo Hernandez	.05
606	*Shawn Holman*	.05
607	Tracy Jones	.05
608	Chet Lemon	.05
609	Fred Lynn	.05
610	Jack Morris	.05
611	Matt Nokes	.05
612	Gary Pettis	.05
613	*Kevin Ritz*	.08
614	Jeff Robinson	.05
615	Steve Searcy	.05
616	Frank Tanana	.05
617	Alan Trammell	.10
618	Gary Ward	.05
619	Lou Whitaker	.05
620	Frank Williams	.05
621a	Players of the Decade - 1980 (George Brett) (... 10 .390 hitting ...)	2.00
621b	Players of the Decade - 1980 (George Brett)	.20
622	Players of the Decade - 1981 (Fernando Valenzuela)	.05
623	Players of the Decade - 1982 (Dale Murphy)	.05
624a	Players of the Decade - 1983 (Cal Ripkin, Jr.) (Ripkin)	3.00
624b	Players of the Decade - 1983 (Cal Ripken, Jr.)	.25
625	Players of the Decade - 1984 (Ryne Sandberg)	.25
626	Players of the Decade - 1985 (Don Mattingly)	.25
627	Players of the Decade - 1986 (Roger Clemens)	.25
628	Players of the Decade - 1987 (George Bell)	.05
629	Players of the Decade - 1988 (Jose Canseco)	.20
630a	Players of the Decade - 1989 (Will Clark) (total bases 32)	.85
630b	Players of the Decade - 1989 (Will Clark) (total bases 321)	.20
631	Game Savers (Mark Davis, Mitch Williams)	.05
632	Boston Igniters (Wade Boggs, Mike Greenwell)	.10
633	Starter & Stopper (Mark Gubicza, Jeff Russell)	.05
634	League's Best Shortstops (Tony Fernandez, Cal Ripken Jr.)	.15

635	Human Dynamos (Kirby Puckett, Bo Jackson)	.20
636	300 Strikeout Club (Mike Scott, Nolan Ryan)	.20
637	The Dymanic Duo (Will Clark, Kevin Mitchell)	.10
638	A.L. All-Stars (Don Mattingly, Mark McGwire)	.50
639	N.L. East Rivals (Howard Johnson, Ryne Sandberg)	.10
640	Major League Prospects *(Rudy Seanez)*, *(Colin Charland)*	.15
641	Major League Prospects *(George Canale)*, *(Kevin Maas)*	.15
642	Major League Prospects *(Kelly Mann)*, *(Dave Hansen)*	.15
643	Major League Prospects *(Greg Smith)*, *(Stu Tate)*	.10
644	Major League Prospects *(Tom Drees)*, *(Dan Howitt)*	.08
645	Major League Prospects *(Mike Roesler)*, *(Derrick May)*	.15
646	Major League Prospects *(Scott Hemond)*, *(Mark Gardner)*	.15
647	Major League Prospects *(John Orton)*, *(Scott Leius)*	.15
648	Major League Prospects *(Rich Monteleone)*, *(Dana Williams)*	.08
649	Major League Prospects *(Mike Huff)*, *(Steve Frey)*	.10
650	Major League Prospects *(Chuck McElroy)*, *(Moises Alou)*	.50
651	Major League Prospects *(Bobby Rose)*, *(Mike Hartley)*	.10
652	Major League Prospects *(Matt Kinzer)*, *(Wayne Edwards)*	.08
653	Major League Prospects *(Delino DeShields)*, *(Jason Grimsley)*	.20
654	Athletics, Cubs, Giants & Blue Jays (Checklist)	.05
655	Royals, Angels, Padres & Orioles (Checklist)	.05
656	Mets, Astros, Cardinals & Red Sox (Checklist)	.05
657	Rangers, Brewers, Expos & Twins (Checklist)	.05
658	Dodgers, Reds, Yankees & Pirates (Checklist)	.05
659	Indians, Mariners, White Sox & Phillies (Checklist)	.05
660	Braves, Tigers & Special Cards (Checklist)	.05

1990 Fleer All-Stars

The top players at each position, as selected by Fleer, are featured in this 12-card set inserted in cello packs and some wax packs. The cards measure 2-1/2" x 3-1/2" and feature a unique two-photo format on the card fronts.

		MT
Complete Set (12):		5.00
Common Player:		.20
1	Harold Baines	.25
2	Will Clark	.50
3	Mark Davis	.20
4	Howard Johnson	.20
5	Joe Magrane	.20
6	Kevin Mitchell	.20
7	Kirby Puckett	1.50
8	Cal Ripken	3.00
9	Ryne Sandberg	1.50
10	Mike Scott	.20
11	Ruben Sierra	.20
12	Mickey Tettleton	.20

1990 Fleer League Standouts

Fleer's "League Standouts" are six of baseball's top players distributed randomly in Fleer rack packs. Fronts feature full color photos with a six-dimensional effect. A black and gold frame borders the photo. Backs are yellow and describe the player's accomplishments. The cards measure 2-1/2" x 3-1/2".

		MT
Complete Set (6):		4.00
Common Player:		.50
1	Barry Larkin	.50
2	Don Mattingly	1.00
3	Darryl Strawberry	.50
4	Jose Canseco	.75
5	Wade Boggs	.75
6	Mark Grace	.60

1990 Fleer Soaring Stars

Cards from this 12-card set could be found in 1990 Fleer jumbo cello packs. The cards are styled with a cartoon flavor, featuring astronomical graphics surrounding the player. Backs feature information about the promising young player.

		MT
Complete Set (12):		15.00
Common Player:		.25
1	Todd Zeile	.50
2	Mike Stanton	.25
3	Larry Walker	3.00
4	Robin Ventura	2.00
5	Scott Coolbaugh	.25
6	Ken Griffey, Jr.	12.00
7	Tom Gordon	.35
8	Jerome Walton	.25
9	Junior Felix	.25
10	Jim Abbott	.50
11	Ricky Jordan	.25
12	Dwight Smith	.25

1990 Fleer World Series

This 12-card set depicts highlights of the 1989 World Series and was included in the factory-collated Fleer set. Single World Series cards were discovered in cello and rack packs, but this was not intended to happen. Fronts of the 2-1/2" x 3-1/2" cards feature action photos set against a white background with a red and blue "89 World Series" banner. Backs are pink and white and describe the events of the 1989 Fall Classic.

		MT
Complete Set (12):		1.50
Common Player:		.10
1	The Final Piece To The Puzzle (Mike Moore)	.10
2	Kevin Mitchell	.15
3	Game Two's Crushing Blow	.20
4	Will Clark	.60
5	Jose Canseco	.75
6	Great Leather in the Field	.10
7	Game One And A's Break Out On Top	.10
8	Dave Stewart	.25
9	Parker's Bat Produces Power (Dave Parker)	.25
10	World Series Record Book Game 3	.10
11	Rickey Henderson	.45
12	Oakland A's - Baseball's Best In '89	.25

1990 Fleer Box Panels

For the fifth consecutive year, Fleer issued a series of cards on the bottom panels of its wax pack boxes. This 28-card set features both players and team logo cards. The cards were numbered C-1 to C-28.

		MT
Complete Set, Panels (7):		4.00
Complete Set, Singles (28):		
Common Player:		.05
1	Giants Logo	.05
2	Tim Belcher	.05
3	Roger Clemens	.50
4	Eric Davis	.10
5	Glenn Davis	.05
6	Cubs Logo	.05
7	John Franco	.05
8	Mike Greenwell	.08
9	Athletics logo	.05
10	Ken Griffey, Jr.	2.50
11	Pedro Guerrero	.05
12	Tony Gwynn	.60
13	Blue Jays Logo	.05
14	Orel Hershiser	.10
15	Bo Jackson	.25
16	Howard Johnson	.05
17	Mets Logo	.05
18	Cardinals Logo	.05
19	Don Mattingly	1.00
20	Mark McGwire	1.00
21	Kevin Mitchell	.08
22	Kirby Puckett	.75
23	Royals Logo	.05
24	Orioles Logo	.05
25	Ruben Sierra	.10
26	Dave Stewart	.08
27	Jerome Walton	.05
28	Robin Yount	.25

1990 Fleer Update

Fleer produced its seventh consecutive "Update" set in 1990. As in the past, the set consists of 132 cards (numbered U-1 through U-132) that were sold by hobby dealers in special collectors boxes. The cards are designed in the same style as the regular issue. A special Nolan Ryan commemorative card is included in the set.

		MT
Complete Set (132):		5.00
Common Player:		.06
1	Steve Avery	.15
2	Francisco Cabrera	.06
3	Nick Esasky	.06
4	Jim Kremers	.06
5	Greg Olson	.06
6	Jim Presley	.06
7	Shawn Boskie	.06
8	Joe Kraemer	.06
9	Luis Salazar	.06
10	Hector Villanueva	.06
11	Glenn Braggs	.06
12	Mariano Duncan	.06
13	Billy Hatcher	.06
14	Tim Layana	.06
15	Hal Morris	.20
16	Javier Ortiz	.06
17	Dave Rohde	.06
18	Eric Yelding	.10
19	Hubie Brooks	.06
20	Kal Daniels	.06
21	Dave Hansen	.06
22	Mike Hartley	.06
23	Stan Javier	.06
24	Jose Offerman	.15
25	Juan Samuel	.06
26	Dennis Boyd	.06
27	Delino DeShields	.10
28	Steve Frey	.06
29	Mark Gardner	.06
30	Chris Nabholz	.06
31	Bill Sampen	.06
32	Dave Schmidt	.06
33	Daryl Boston	.06
34	Chuck Carr	.20
35	John Franco	.06
36	*Todd Hundley*	.75
37	Julio Machado	.06
38	Alejandro Pena	.06
39	Darren Reed	.06
40	Kelvin Torve	.06
41	Darrel Akerfelds	.06
42	Jose DeJesus	.06
43	Dave Hollins	.20
44	Carmelo Martinez	.06
45	Brad Moore	.06
46	Dale Murphy	.15
47	Wally Backman	.06
48	Stan Belinda	.10
49	Bob Patterson	.06
50	Ted Power	.06
51	Don Slaught	.06
52	Geronimo Pena	.15
53	Lee Smith	.08
54	John Tudor	.06
55	Joe Carter	.15
56	Tom Howard	.06
57	Craig Lefferts	.06
58	Rafael Valdez	.06
59	Dave Anderson	.06
60	Kevin Bass	.06
61	John Burkett	.08
62	Gary Carter	.10
63	Rick Parker	.06
64	Trevor Wilson	.10
65	Chris Hoiles	.20
66	Tim Hulett	.06
67	Dave Johnson	.06
68	Curt Schilling	.30
69	David Segui	.15
70	Tom Brunansky	.06
71	Greg Harris	.06
72	Dana Kiecker	.06
73	Tim Naehring	.15
74	Tony Pena	.06
75	Jeff Reardon	.06
76	Jerry Reed	.06
77	Mark Eichhorn	.06
78	Mark Langston	.06
79	John Orton	.06
80	Luis Polonia	.06
81	Dave Winfield	.15
82	Cliff Young	.06
83	Wayne Edwards	.06
84	Alex Fernandez	.20
85	Craig Grebeck	.06
86	Scott Radinsky	.10
87	Frank Thomas	3.00
88	Beau Allred	.06
89	Sandy Alomar, Jr.	.15
90	*Carlos Baerga*	.25
91	Kevin Bearse	.06
92	Chris James	.06
93	Candy Maldonado	.06
94	Jeff Manto	.06
95	Cecil Fielder	.20
96	*Travis Fryman*	.35
97	Lloyd Moseby	.06
98	Edwin Nunez	.06
99	Tony Phillips	.10
100	Larry Sheets	.06
101	Mark Davis	.06
102	Storm Davis	.06
103	Gerald Perry	.06
104	Terry Shumpert	.06
105	Edgar Diaz	.06
106	Dave Parker	.12
107	Tim Drummond	.06
108	Junior Ortiz	.06
109	Park Pittman	.06
110	Kevin Tapani	.25
111	Oscar Azocar	.06
112	Jim Leyritz	.15
113	Kevin Maas	.06
114	Alan Mills	.12
115	Matt Nokes	.06
116	Pascual Perez	.06
117	Ozzie Canseco	.08
118	Scott Sanderson	.06
119	Tino Martinez	.40
120	Jeff Schaefer	.06
121	Matt Young	.06
122	Brian Bohanon	.10
123	Jeff Huson	.06
124	Ramon Manon	.06
125	Gary Mielke	.06
126	Willie Blair	.06
127	Glenallen Hill	.10
128	*John Olerud*	.35
129	Luis Sojo	.06
130	Mark Whiten	.15
131	Three Decades of No Hitters (Nolan Ryan)	.70
132	Checklist	.06

1990 Fleer "Printed in Canada"

Whether these cards were printed for distribution in Canada or simply the work of a Canadian printer engaged by Fleer to meet U.S. demand is unknown. Each of the 660 cards in the 1990 Fleer issue can be found with a "1990 FLEER LTD./LTEE PTD. IN CANADA" copyright notice on back in the bottom border. Except for various superstar cards, little demand attaches to this variation.

	MT
Complete Set (660):	50.00
Common Player:	.25

(See 1990 Fleer for checklist and base values; stars bring 5X-10X base price.)

1991 Fleer Promo Strip

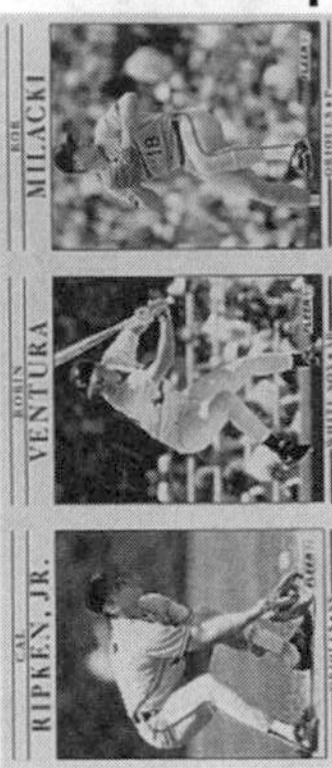

This three-card strip was issued to introduce Fleer's 1991 baseball card set. The cards on the 7-1/2" x 3-1/2" strip are identical to the players' regular issue cards.

	MT
Three-card Strip: Cal Ripken Jr., Robin Ventura, Bob Milacki	30.00

1991 Fleer

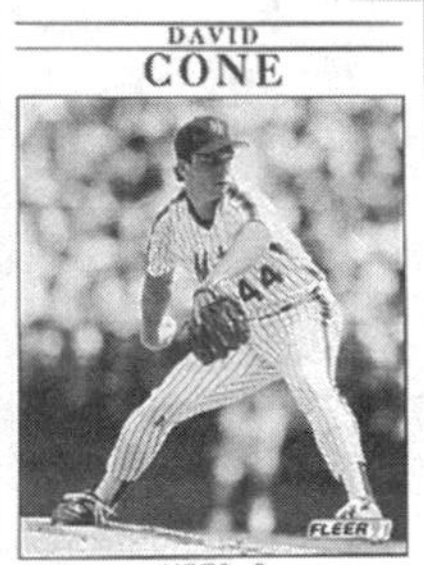

Fleer expanded its 1991 set to include 720 cards. The cards feature yellow borders surrounding full-color action photos. Backs feature a circular portrait photo, biographical information, complete statistics, and career highlights. Once again the cards are numbered alphabetically within team. Because Fleer used more than one printer, many minor variations in photo cropping and typography can be found. The most notable are included in the checklist here.

		MT
Unopened Factory Set (732):		10.00
Complete Set (720):		8.00
Common Player:		.05
Pack (15):		.35
Wax Box (36):		8.00
1	*Troy Afenir*	.05
2	Harold Baines	.08
3	Lance Blankenship	.05
4	Todd Burns	.05
5	Jose Canseco	.35
6	Dennis Eckersley	.08
7	Mike Gallego	.05
8	Ron Hassey	.05
9	Dave Henderson	.05
10	Rickey Henderson	.25
11	Rick Honeycutt	.05
12	Doug Jennings	.05
13	*Joe Klink*	.05
14	Carney Lansford	.05
15	*Darren Lewis*	.15
16	Willie McGee	.08
17a	Mark McGwire (six-line career summary)	1.50
17b	Mark McGwire (seven-line career summary)	1.50
18	Mike Moore	.05
19	Gene Nelson	.05
20	Dave Otto	.05
21	Jamie Quirk	.05
22	Willie Randolph	.05
23	Scott Sanderson	.05
24	Terry Steinbach	.05
25	Dave Stewart	.08
26	Walt Weiss	.05
27	Bob Welch	.05
28	Curt Young	.05
29	Wally Backman	.05
30	*Stan Belinda*	.05
31	Jay Bell	.05
32	Rafael Belliard	.05
33	Barry Bonds	.35
34	Bobby Bonilla	.08
35	Sid Bream	.05
36	Doug Drabek	.05
37	*Carlos Garcia*	.15
38	Neal Heaton	.05
39	Jeff King	.05
40	Bob Kipper	.05
41	Bill Landrum	.05
42	Mike LaValliere	.05
43	Jose Lind	.05
44	Carmelo Martinez	.05
45	Bob Patterson	.05
46	Ted Power	.05
47	Gary Redus	.05
48	R.J. Reynolds	.05
49	Don Slaught	.05
50	John Smiley	.05
51	Zane Smith	.05
52	*Randy Tomlin*	.10
53	Andy Van Slyke	.05
54	Bob Walk	.05
55	Jack Armstrong	.05
56	Todd Benzinger	.05
57	Glenn Braggs	.05
58	Keith Brown	.05
59	Tom Browning	.05
60	Norm Charlton	.05
61	Eric Davis	.08
62	Rob Dibble	.05
63	Bill Doran	.05
64	Mariano Duncan	.05
65	Chris Hammond	.05
66	Billy Hatcher	.05
67	Danny Jackson	.05
68	Barry Larkin	.10
69	*Tim Layana*	.05
70	*Terry Lee*	.05
71	Rick Mahler	.05
72	Hal Morris	.05
73	Randy Myers	.05
74	Ron Oester	.05
75	Joe Oliver	.05
76	Paul O'Neill	.10
77	Luis Quinones	.05
78	Jeff Reed	.05
79	Jose Rijo	.05
80	Chris Sabo	.05
81	Scott Scudder	.05
82	Herm Winningham	.05
83	Larry Andersen	.05
84	Marty Barrett	.05
85	Mike Boddicker	.05
86	Wade Boggs	.35
87	Tom Bolton	.05
88	Tom Brunansky	.05
89	Ellis Burks	.05
90	Roger Clemens	.50
91	Scott Cooper	.10

No.	Player	Price
92	John Dopson	.05
93	Dwight Evans	.05
94	Wes Gardner	.05
95	*Jeff Gray*	.05
96	Mike Greenwell	.05
97	Greg Harris	.05
98	*Daryl Irvine*	.05
99	*Dana Kiecker*	.05
100	Randy Kutcher	.05
101	Dennis Lamp	.05
102	Mike Marshall	.05
103	John Marzano	.05
104	Rob Murphy	.05
105a	*Tim Naehring* (seven-line career summary)	.08
105b	*Tim Naehring* (nine-line career summary)	.08
106	Tony Pena	.05
107	*Phil Plantier*	.10
108	Carlos Quintana	.05
109	Jeff Reardon	.05
110	Jerry Reed	.05
111	Jody Reed	.05
112	Luis Rivera	.05
113a	Kevin Romine (one-line career summary)	.05
113b	Kevin Romine (two-line career summary)	.05
114	Phil Bradley	.05
115	Ivan Calderon	.05
116	Wayne Edwards	.05
117	Alex Fernandez	.10
118	Carlton Fisk	.10
119	Scott Fletcher	.05
120	*Craig Grebeck*	.08
121	Ozzie Guillen	.05
122	Greg Hibbard	.05
123	Lance Johnson	.05
124	Barry Jones	.05
125a	Ron Karkovice (two-line career summary)	.05
125b	Ron Karkovice (one-line career summary)	.05
126	Eric King	.05
127	Steve Lyons	.05
128	Carlos Martinez	.05
129	Jack McDowell	.05
130	Donn Pall	.05
131	Dan Pasqua	.05
132	Ken Patterson	.05
133	Melido Perez	.05
134	Adam Peterson	.05
135	*Scott Radinsky*	.08
136	Sammy Sosa	.75
137	Bobby Thigpen	.05
138	Frank Thomas	1.00
139	Robin Ventura	.15
140	Daryl Boston	.05
141	*Chuck Carr*	.15
142	Mark Carreon	.05
143	David Cone	.08
144	Ron Darling	.05
145	Kevin Elster	.05
146	Sid Fernandez	.05
147	John Franco	.05
148	Dwight Gooden	.10
149	Tom Herr	.05
150	Todd Hundley	.10
151	Gregg Jefferies	.10
152	Howard Johnson	.05
153	Dave Magadan	.05
154	Kevin McReynolds	.05
155	Keith Miller	.05
156	Bob Ojeda	.05
157	Tom O'Malley	.05
158	Alejandro Pena	.05
159	*Darren Reed*	.08
160	Mackey Sasser	.05
161	Darryl Strawberry	.10
162	Tim Teufel	.05
163	Kelvin Torve	.05
164	Julio Valera	.05
165	Frank Viola	.05
166	Wally Whitehurst	.05
167	Jim Acker	.05
168	*Derek Bell*	.15
169	George Bell	.05
170	*Willie Blair*	.05
171	Pat Borders	.05
172	John Cerutti	.05
173	Junior Felix	.05
174	Tony Fernandez	.05
175	Kelly Gruber	.05
176	Tom Henke	.05
177	Glenallen Hill	.05
178	Jimmy Key	.08
179	Manny Lee	.05
180	Fred McGriff	.20
181	Rance Mulliniks	.05
182	Greg Myers	.05
183	John Olerud	.15
184	Luis Sojo	.05
185	Dave Steib	.05
186	Todd Stottlemyre	.05
187	Duane Ward	.05
188	David Wells	.08
189	*Mark Whiten*	.15
190	Ken Williams	.05
191	Frank Wills	.05
192	Mookie Wilson	.05
193	Don Aase	.05
194	Tim Belcher	.05
195	Hubie Brooks	.05
196	Dennis Cook	.05
197	Tim Crews	.05
198	Kal Daniels	.05
199	Kirk Gibson	.05
200	Jim Gott	.05
201	Alfredo Griffin	.05
202	Chris Gwynn	.05
203	Dave Hansen	.05
204	Lenny Harris	.05
205	Mike Hartley	.05
206	Mickey Hatcher	.05
207	*Carlos Hernandez*	.10
208	Orel Hershiser	.08
209	Jay Howell	.05
210	Mike Huff	.05
211	Stan Javier	.05
212	Ramon Martinez	.08
213	Mike Morgan	.05
214	Eddie Murray	.20
215	*Jim Neidlinger*	.05
216	Jose Offerman	.05
217	*Jim Poole*	.05
218	Juan Samuel	.05
219	Mike Scioscia	.05
220	Ray Searage	.05
221	Mike Sharperson	.05
222	Fernando Valenzuela	.08
223	Jose Vizcaino	.05
224	Mike Aldrete	.05
225	*Scott Anderson*	.05
226	Dennis Boyd	.05
227	Tim Burke	.05
228	Delino DeShields	.08
229	Mike Fitzgerald	.05
230	Tom Foley	.05
231	Steve Frey	.05
232	Andres Galarraga	.10
233	Mark Gardner	.05
234	Marquis Grissom	.10
235	Kevin Gross	.05
236	Drew Hall	.05
237	Dave Martinez	.05
238	Dennis Martinez	.08
239	Dale Mohorcic	.05
240	*Chris Nabholz*	.05
241	Otis Nixon	.05
242	Junior Noboa	.05
243	Spike Owen	.05
244	Tim Raines	.08
245	*Mel Rojas*	.12
246	*Scott Ruskin*	.05
247	*Bill Sampen*	.05
248	Nelson Santovenia	.05
249	Dave Schmidt	.05
250	Larry Walker	.25
251	Tim Wallach	.05
252	Dave Anderson	.05
253	Kevin Bass	.05
254	Steve Bedrosian	.05
255	Jeff Brantley	.05
256	John Burkett	.08
257	Brett Butler	.08
258	Gary Carter	.08
259	Will Clark	.20
260	*Steve Decker*	.05
261	Kelly Downs	.05
262	Scott Garrelts	.05
263	Terry Kennedy	.05
264	Mike LaCoss (photo on back actually Ken Oberkfell)	.05
265	*Mark Leonard*	.05
266	Greg Litton	.05
267	Kevin Mitchell	.05
268	Randy O'Neal	.05
269	*Rick Parker*	.05
270	Rick Reuschel	.05
271	Ernest Riles	.05
272	Don Robinson	.05
273	Robby Thompson	.05
274	Mark Thurmond	.05
275	Jose Uribe	.05
276	Matt Williams	.20
277	Trevor Wilson	.05
278	*Gerald Alexander*	.05
279	Brad Arnsberg	.05
280	*Kevin Belcher*	.05
281	*Joe Bitker*	.05
282	Kevin Brown	.10
283	Steve Buechele	.05
284	Jack Daugherty	.05
285	Julio Franco	.05
286	Juan Gonzalez	.50
287	*Bill Haselman*	.15
288	Charlie Hough	.05
289	Jeff Huson	.05
290	Pete Incaviglia	.05
291	Mike Jeffcoat	.05
292	Jeff Kunkel	.05
293	Gary Mielke	.05
294	Jamie Moyer	.05
295	Rafael Palmeiro	.12
296	Geno Petralli	.05
297	Gary Pettis	.05
298	Kevin Reimer	.05
299	Kenny Rogers	.05
300	Jeff Russell	.05
301	John Russell	.05
302	Nolan Ryan	.65
303	Ruben Sierra	.05
304	Bobby Witt	.05
305	Jim Abbott	.08
306	Kent Anderson	.05
307	Dante Bichette	.08
308	Bert Blyleven	.05
309	Chili Davis	.08
310	Brian Downing	.05
311	Mark Eichhorn	.05
312	Mike Fetters	.05
313	Chuck Finley	.05
314	Willie Fraser	.05
315	Bryan Harvey	.05
316	Donnie Hill	.05
317	Wally Joyner	.10
318	Mark Langston	.05
319	Kirk McCaskill	.05
320	John Orton	.05
321	Lance Parrish	.08
322	Luis Polonia	.05
323	Johnny Ray	.05
324	Bobby Rose	.05
325	Dick Schofield	.05
326	Rick Schu	.05
327a	Lee Stevens (six-line career summary)	.10
327b	Lee Stevens (seven-line career summary)	.10
328	Devon White	.08
329	Dave Winfield	.20
330	*Cliff Young*	.05
331	Dave Bergman	.05
332	*Phil Clark*	.08
333	Darnell Coles	.05
334	Milt Cuyler	.05
335	Cecil Fielder	.08
336	Travis Fryman	.08
337	Paul Gibson	.05
338	Jerry Don Gleaton	.05
339	Mike Heath	.05
340	Mike Henneman	.05
341	Chet Lemon	.05
342	Lance McCullers	.05
343	Jack Morris	.05
344	Lloyd Moseby	.05
345	Edwin Nunez	.05
346	Clay Parker	.05
347	Dan Petry	.05
348	Tony Phillips	.05
349	Jeff Robinson	.05
350	Mark Salas	.05
351	*Mike Schwabe*	.05
352	Larry Sheets	.05
353	John Shelby	.05
354	Frank Tanana	.05
355	Alan Trammell	.10
356	Gary Ward	.05
357	Lou Whitaker	.08
358	Beau Allred	.05
359	Sandy Alomar,Jr.	.10
360	Carlos Baerga	.05
361	*Kevin Bearse*	.05
362	Tom Brookens	.05
363	Jerry Browne	.05
364	Tom Candiotti	.05
365	Alex Cole	.05
366	John Farrell	.05
367	Felix Fermin	.05
368	Keith Hernandez	.05
369	Brook Jacoby	.05
370	Chris James	.05
371	Dion James	.05
372	Doug Jones	.05
373	Candy Maldonado	.05
374	Steve Olin	.05
375	Jesse Orosco	.05
376	Rudy Seanez	.05
377	Joel Skinner	.05
378	Cory Snyder	.05
379	Greg Swindell	.05
380	Sergio Valdez	.05
381	*Mike Walker*	.05
382	*Colby Ward*	.05
383	*Turner Ward*	.10
384	Mitch Webster	.05
385	Kevin Wickander	.05
386	Darrel Akerfelds	.05
387	Joe Boever	.05
388a	Rod Booker (no 1981 stats)	.05
388b	Rod Booker (1981 stats included)	.10
389	Sil Campusano	.05
390	Don Carman	.05
391	*Wes Chamberlain*	.10
392	Pat Combs	.05
393	Darren Daulton	.05
394	Jose DeJesus	.05
395	Len Dykstra	.08
396	Jason Grimsley	.05
397	Charlie Hayes	.05
398	Von Hayes	.05
399	*Dave Hollins*	.25
400	Ken Howell	.05
401	Ricky Jordan	.05
402	John Kruk	.05
403	Steve Lake	.05
404	*Chuck Malone*	.05
405	Roger McDowell	.05
406	Chuck McElroy	.05
407	*Mickey Morandini*	.10
408	Terry Mulholland	.05
409	Dale Murphy	.10
410	Randy Ready	.05
411	Bruce Ruffin	.05
412	Dickie Thon	.05
413	Paul Assenmacher	.05
414	Damon Berryhill	.05
415	Mike Bielecki	.05
416	*Shawn Boskie*	.08
417	Dave Clark	.05
418	Doug Dascenzo	.05
419a	Andre Dawson (no 1976 stats)	.10
419b	Andre Dawson (1976 stats included)	.10
420	Shawon Dunston	.05
421	Joe Girardi	.05
422	Mark Grace	.20
423	Mike Harkey	.05
424	Les Lancaster	.05
425	Bill Long	.05
426	Greg Maddux	.60
427	Derrick May	.05
428	Jeff Pico	.05
429	Domingo Ramos	.05
430	Luis Salazar	.05
431	Ryne Sandberg	.25
432	Dwight Smith	.05
433	Greg Smith	.05
434	Rick Sutcliffe	.05
435	Gary Varsho	.05
436	*Hector Villanueva*	.05
437	Jerome Walton	.05
438	Curtis Wilkerson	.05
439	Mitch Williams	.05
440	Steve Wilson	.05
441	Marvell Wynne	.05
442	Scott Bankhead	.05
443	Scott Bradley	.05
444	Greg Briley	.05
445	Mike Brumley	.05
446	Jay Buhner	.08

447 *Dave Burba* .10
448 Henry Cotto .05
449 Alvin Davis .05
450 Ken Griffey, Jr. 1.50
451 Erik Hanson .05
452 Gene Harris .05
453 Brian Holman .05
454 Mike Jackson .05
455 Randy Johnson .25
456 Jeffrey Leonard .05
457 Edgar Martinez .08
458 Tino Martinez .20
459 Pete O'Brien .05
460 Harold Reynolds .05
461 Mike Schooler .05
462 Bill Swift .05
463 David Valle .05
464 Omar Vizquel .08
465 Matt Young .05
466 Brady Anderson .20
467 Jeff Ballard .05
468 Juan Bell .05
469a Mike Devereaux ("six" last word in career summary top line) .08
469b Mike Devereaux ("runs" last word in career summary top line) .08
470 Steve Finley .05
471 Dave Gallagher .05
472 *Leo Gomez* .10
473 Rene Gonzales .05
474 Pete Harnisch .05
475 Kevin Hickey .05
476 *Chris Hoiles* .10
477 Sam Horn .05
478 Tim Hulett .05
479 Dave Johnson .05
480 Ron Kittle .05
481 Ben McDonald .05
482 Bob Melvin .05
483 Bob Milacki .05
484 Randy Milligan .05
485 *John Mitchell* .05
486 Gregg Olson .05
487 Joe Orsulak .05
488 Joe Price .05
489 Bill Ripken .05
490 Cal Ripken, Jr. .75
491 Curt Schilling .08
492 *David Segui* .05
493 *Anthony Telford* .05
494 Mickey Tettleton .05
495 Mark Williamson .05
496 Craig Worthington .05
497 Juan Agosto .05
498 Eric Anthony .05
499 Craig Biggio .12
500 Ken Caminiti .12
501 Casey Candaele .05
502 *Andujar Cedeno* .05
503 Danny Darwin .05
504 Mark Davidson .05
505 Glenn Davis .05
506 Jim Deshaies .05
507 *Luis Gonzalez* .25
508 Bill Gullickson .05
509 Xavier Hernandez .05
510 Brian Meyer .05
511 Ken Oberkfell .05
512 Mark Portugal .05
513 Rafael Ramirez .05
514 *Karl Rhodes* .08
515 Mike Scott .05
516 *Mike Simms* .05
517 Dave Smith .05
518 Franklin Stubbs .05
519 Glenn Wilson .05
520 Eric Yelding .05
521 Gerald Young .05
522 Shawn Abner .05
523 Roberto Alomar .25
524 Andy Benes .10
525 Joe Carter .08
526 Jack Clark .05
527 Joey Cora .05
528 *Paul Faries* .05
529 Tony Gwynn .40
530 Atlee Hammaker .05
531 Greg Harris .05
532 *Thomas Howard* .08
533 Bruce Hurst .05
534 Craig Lefferts .05
535 Derek Lilliquist .05
536 Fred Lynn .05
537 Mike Pagliarulo .05
538 Mark Parent .05
539 Dennis Rasmussen .05
540 Bip Roberts .05
541 *Richard Rodriguez* .05
542 Benito Santiago .05
543 Calvin Schiraldi .05
544 Eric Show .05
545 Phil Stephenson .05
546 Garry Templeton .05
547 Ed Whitson .05
548 Eddie Williams .05
549 Kevin Appier .05
550 Luis Aquino .05
551 Bob Boone .05
552 George Brett .25
553 *Jeff Conine* .30
554 Steve Crawford .05
555 Mark Davis .05
556 Storm Davis .05
557 Jim Eisenreich .05
558 Steve Farr .05
559 Tom Gordon .05
560 Mark Gubicza .05
561 Bo Jackson .15
562 Mike Macfarlane .05
563 *Brian McRae* .25
564 Jeff Montgomery .05
565 Bill Pecota .05
566 Gerald Perry .05
567 Bret Saberhagen .08
568 *Jeff Schulz* .05
569 Kevin Seitzer .05
570 *Terry Shumpert* .05
571 Kurt Stillwell .05
572 Danny Tartabull .05
573 Gary Thurman .05
574 Frank White .05
575 Willie Wilson .05
576 Chris Bosio .05
577 Greg Brock .05
578 George Canale .05
579 Chuck Crim .05
580 Rob Deer .05
581 *Edgar Diaz* .05
582 *Tom Edens* .05
583 Mike Felder .05
584 Jim Gantner .05
585 Darryl Hamilton .05
586 Ted Higuera .05
587 Mark Knudson .05
588 Bill Krueger .05
589 Tim McIntosh .05
590 Paul Mirabella .05
591 Paul Molitor .30
592 Jaime Navarro .05
593 Dave Parker .05
594 Dan Plesac .05
595 Ron Robinson .05
596 Gary Sheffield .20
597 Bill Spiers .05
598 B.J. Surhoff .08
599 Greg Vaughn .08
600 Randy Veres .05
601 Robin Yount .25
602a Rick Aguilera (five-line career summary) .08
602b Rick Aguilera (four-line career summary) .08
603 Allan Anderson .05
604 Juan Berenguer .05
605 Randy Bush .05
606 Carmen Castillo .05
607 Tim Drummond .05
608 *Scott Erickson* .10
609 Gary Gaetti .05
610 Greg Gagne .05
611 Dan Gladden .05
612 Mark Guthrie .05
613 Brian Harper .05
614 Kent Hrbek .08
615 Gene Larkin .05
616 Terry Leach .05
617 Nelson Liriano .05
618 Shane Mack .05
619 John Moses .05
620 *Pedro Munoz* .10
621 Al Newman .05
622 Junior Ortiz .05
623 Kirby Puckett .40
624 Roy Smith .05
625 Kevin Tapani .05
626 Gary Wayne .05
627 David West .05
628 Cris Carpenter .05
629 Vince Coleman .05
630 Ken Dayley .05
631 Jose DeLeon .05
632 Frank DiPino .05
633 *Bernard Gilkey* .25
634 Pedro Guerrero .05
635 Ken Hill .05
636 Felix Jose .05
637 *Ray Lankford* .25
638 Joe Magrane .05
639 Tom Niedenfuer .05
640 Jose Oquendo .05
641 Tom Pagnozzi .05
642 Terry Pendleton .05
643 *Mike Perez* .10
644 Bryn Smith .05
645 Lee Smith .08
646 Ozzie Smith .30
647 Scott Terry .05
648 Bob Tewksbury .05
649 Milt Thompson .05
650 John Tudor .05
651 Denny Walling .05
652 *Craig Wilson* .05
653 Todd Worrell .05
654 Todd Zeile .08
655 *Oscar Azocar* .05
656 Steve Balboni .05
657 Jesse Barfield .05
658 Greg Cadaret .05
659 Chuck Cary .05
660 Rick Cerone .05
661 Dave Eiland .05
662a Alvaro Espinoza (no 1979-80 stats) .08
662b Alvaro Espinoza (1979-80 stats included) .08
663 Bob Geren .05
664 Lee Guetterman .05
665 Mel Hall .05
666a Andy Hawkins (no 1978 stats) .08
666b Andy Hawkins (1978 stats included) .08
667 Jimmy Jones .05
668 Roberto Kelly .05
669 Dave LaPoint .05
670 Tim Leary .05
671 *Jim Leyritz* .20
672 Kevin Maas .05
673 Don Mattingly .40
674 Matt Nokes .05
675 Pascual Perez .05
676 Eric Plunk .05
677 Dave Righetti .05
678 Jeff Robinson .05
679 Steve Sax .05
680 Mike Witt .05
681 Steve Avery .05
682 Mike Bell .05
683 Jeff Blauser .05
684 Francisco Cabrera .05
685 Tony Castillo .05
686 Marty Clary .05
687 Nick Esasky .05
688 Ron Gant .10
689 Tom Glavine .10
690 Mark Grant .05
691 Tommy Gregg .05
692 Dwayne Henry .05
693 Dave Justice .25
694 *Jimmy Kremers* .05
695 Charlie Leibrandt .05
696 Mark Lemke .05
697 Oddibe McDowell .05
698 *Greg Olson* .05
699 Jeff Parrett .05
700 Jim Presley .05
701 *Victor Rosario* .05
702 Lonnie Smith .05
703 Pete Smith .05
704 John Smoltz .10
705 Mike Stanton .05
706 Andres Thomas .05
707 Jeff Treadway .05
708 *Jim Vatcher* .05
709 Home Run Kings (Ryne Sandberg, Cecil Fielder) .15
710 Second Generation Superstars (Barry Bonds, Ken Griffey, Jr.) .50
711 NLCS Team Leaders (Bobby Bonilla, Barry Larkin) .15
712 Top Game Savers (Bobby Thigpen, John Franco) .05
713 Chicago's 100 Club (Andre Dawson, Ryne Sandberg) .15
714 Checklists (Athletics, Pirates, Reds, Red Sox) .05
715 Checklists - White Sox, Mets, Blue Jays, Dodgers .05
716 Checklists (Expos, Giants, Rangers, Angels) .05
717 Checklists (Tigers, Indians, Phillies, Cubs) .05
718 Checklists (Mariners, Orioles, Astros, Padres) .05
719 Checklists (Royals, Brewers, Twins, Cardinals) .05
720 Checklists (Yankees, Braves, Super Stars) .05

1991 Fleer All Stars

Three player photos are featured on each card in this special insert set. An action shot and portrait close-up are featured on the front, while a full-figure pose is showcased on the back. The cards were inserted into 1991 Fleer cello packs.

		MT
Complete Set (10):		9.00
Common Player:		.50
1	Ryne Sandberg	1.50
2	Barry Larkin	.50
3	Matt Williams	.60
4	Cecil Fielder	.50
5	Barry Bonds	2.00
6	Rickey Henderson	.60
7	Ken Griffey, Jr.	6.00
8	Jose Canseco	.75
9	Benito Santiago	.50
10	Roger Clemens	1.75

1991 Fleer ProVisions

The illustrations of artist Terry Smith are showcased in this special set. Twelve fantasy portraits were produced for cards inserted into rack packs. Four other ProVision cards were inserted into factory sets. The rack pack cards feature black borders, while the factory set cards have white borders. Information on the card backs explains the manner in which Smith painted each player. Factory insert ProVisions are indicated by an "F" suffix in the checklist here.

		MT
Complete Set (12):		3.00
Common Player:		.15
Complete Factory Set (4):		3.00
Common Player:		.40
1	Kirby Puckett	.80
2	Will Clark	.40
3	Ruben Sierra	.15
4	Mark McGwire	1.50
5	Bo Jackson	.25
6	Jose Canseco	.50
7	Dwight Gooden	.25
8	Mike Greenwell	.15
9	Roger Clemens	.75
10	Eric Davis	.20
11	Don Mattingly	1.00
12	Darryl Strawberry	.25
1F	Barry Bonds	1.25
2F	Rickey Henderson	.50
3F	Ryne Sandberg	1.00
4F	Dave Stewart	.40

1991 Fleer World Series

Once again Fleer released a set in honor of the World Series from the previous season. The 1991 issue features only eight cards compared to twelve in 1990. The cards feature white borders surrounding full-color action shots from the 1990 Fall Classic. The card backs feature an overview of the World Series action.

		MT
Complete Set (8):		1.50
Common Player:		.20
1	Eric Davis	.25
2	Billy Hatcher	.20
3	Jose Canseco	.35
4	Rickey Henderson	.25
5	Chris Sabo, Carney Lansford	.20
6	Dave Stewart	.25
7	Jose Rijo	.20
8	Reds Celebrate	.20

1991 Fleer Box Panels

Unlike past box panel sets, the 1991 Fleer box panels feature a theme; 1990 no-hitters are celebrated on the three different boxes. The cards feature blank backs and are numbered in order of no-hitter on the front. A team logo was included on each box. The card fronts are styled after the 1991 Fleer cards. A special no-hitter logo appears in the lower left corner.

		MT
Complete Set (10):		3.00
Common Player:		.10
1	Mark Langston, Mike Witt	.10
2	Randy Johnson	.50
3	Nolan Ryan	2.50
4	Dave Stewart	.20
5	Fernando Valenzuela	.15
6	Andy Hawkins	.10
7	Melido Perez	.10
8	Terry Mulholland	.10
9	Dave Steib	.10
----	Team Logos	.05

1991 Fleer Update

Fleer produced its eighth consecutive "Update" set in 1991 to supplement the company's regular set. As in the past, the set consists of 132 cards that were sold by hobby dealers in special collectors boxes. The cards are designed in the same style as the regular Fleer issue.

		MT
Complete Set (132):		6.00
Common Player:		.06
1	Glenn Davis	.06
2	Dwight Evans	.06
3	Jose Mesa	.12
4	Jack Clark	.06
5	Danny Darwin	.06
6	Steve Lyons	.06
7	Mo Vaughn	.65
8	Floyd Bannister	.06
9	Gary Gaetti	.08
10	Dave Parker	.10
11	Joey Cora	.06
12	Charlie Hough	.06
13	Matt Merullo	.06
14	Warren Newson	.08
15	Tim Raines	.10
16	Albert Belle	.30
17	Glenallen Hill	.08
18	Shawn Hillegas	.06
19	Mark Lewis	.06
20	Charles Nagy	.25
21	Mark Whiten	.06
22	John Cerutti	.06
23	Rob Deer	.06
24	Mickey Tettleton	.06
25	Warren Cromartie	.06
26	Kirk Gibson	.06
27	David Howard	.08
28	Brent Mayne	.10
29	Dante Bichette	.10
30	Mark Lee	.06
31	Julio Machado	.06
32	Edwin Nunez	.06
33	Willie Randolph	.06
34	Franklin Stubbs	.06
35	Bill Wegman	.06
36	Chili Davis	.08
37	Chuck Knoblauch	.50
38	Scott Leius	.06
39	Jack Morris	.06
40	Mike Pagliarulo	.06
41	Lenny Webster	.06
42	John Habyan	.06
43	Steve Howe	.06
44	Jeff Johnson	.06
45	Scott Kamieniecki	.10
46	Pat Kelly	.10
47	Hensley Meulens	.06
48	Wade Taylor	.10
49	Bernie Williams	.30
50	Kirk Dressendorfer	.15
51	Ernest Riles	.06
52	Rich DeLucia	.06
53	Tracy Jones	.06
54	Bill Krueger	.06
55	Alonzo Powell	.06
56	Jeff Schaefer	.06
57	Russ Swan	.06
58	John Barfield	.06
59	Rich Gossage	.08
60	Jose Guzman	.06
61	Dean Palmer	.20
62	*Ivan Rodriguez*	3.00
63	Roberto Alomar	.30
64	Tom Candiotti	.06
65	Joe Carter	.10
66	Ed Sprague	.10
67	Pat Tabler	.06
68	Mike Timlin	.15
69	Devon White	.08
70	Rafael Belliard	.06
71	Juan Berenguer	.06
72	Sid Bream	.06
73	Marvin Freeman	.06
74	Kent Mercker	.06
75	Otis Nixon	.06
76	Terry Pendleton	.06
77	George Bell	.06
78	Danny Jackson	.06
79	Chuck McElroy	.06
80	Gary Scott	.06
81	Heathcliff Slocumb	.06
82	Dave Smith	.06
83	Rick Wilkins	.10
84	Freddie Benavides	.06
85	Ted Power	.06
86	Mo Sanford	.15
87	*Jeff Bagwell*	3.00
88	Steve Finley	.06
89	Pete Harnisch	.06
90	Darryl Kile	.10
91	Brett Butler	.10
92	John Candelaria	.06
93	Gary Carter	.12
94	Kevin Gross	.06
95	Bob Ojeda	.06
96	Darryl Strawberry	.15
97	Ivan Calderon	.06
98	Ron Hassey	.06
99	Gilberto Reyes	.06
100	Hubie Brooks	.06
101	Rick Cerone	.06
102	Vince Coleman	.06
103	Jeff Innis	.06
104	Pete Schourek	.15
105	Andy Ashby	.15
106	Wally Backman	.06
107	Darrin Fletcher	.10
108	Tommy Greene	.08
109	John Morris	.06
110	Mitch Williams	.06
111	Lloyd McClendon	.06
112	Orlando Merced	.25
113	Vicente Palacios	.06
114	Gary Varsho	.06
115	John Wehner	.06
116	Rex Hudler	.06
117	Tim Jones	.06
118	Geronimo Pena	.10
119	Gerald Perry	.06
120	Larry Andersen	.06
121	Jerald Clark	.06
122	Scott Coolbaugh	.06
123	Tony Fernandez	.06
124	Darrin Jackson	.06
125	Fred McGriff	.20
126	Jose Mota	.06
127	Tim Teufel	.06
128	Bud Black	.06
129	Mike Felder	.06
130	Willie McGee	.08
131	Dave Righetti	.06
132	Checklist	.06

1992 Fleer

For the second consecutive year, Fleer produced a 720-card set. The standard card fronts feature full-color action photos bordered in green with the player's name, position and team logo on the right border. The backs feature another full-color action photo, biographical information and statistics. A special 12-card Roger Clemens subset is also included in the 1992 Fleer set. Three more Clemens cards were available through a mail-in offer, and 2,000 Roger Clemens autographed cards were inserted in 1992 packs. Once again the cards are numbered according to team. Subsets in the issue included Major League Propects (#652-680), Record Setters (#681-687), League Leaders (#688-697), Superstar Specials (#698-707) and ProVisions (#708-713), which for the first time were part of the regular numbered set rather than limited edition insert cards.

		MT
Complete Set (720):		15.00
Common Player:		.05
Pack (15):		.75
Wax Box (36):		20.00
1	Brady Anderson	.10
2	Jose Bautista	.05
3	Juan Bell	.05
4	Glenn Davis	.05
5	Mike Devereaux	.05
6	Dwight Evans	.05
7	Mike Flanagan	.05
8	Leo Gomez	.05
9	Chris Hoiles	.05
10	Sam Horn	.05
11	Tim Hulett	.05
12	Dave Johnson	.05
13	*Chito Martinez*	.08
14	Ben McDonald	.05
15	Bob Melvin	.05
16	*Luis Mercedes*	.10
17	Jose Mesa	.05
18	Bob Milacki	.05
19	Randy Milligan	.05
20	Mike Mussina	.25
21	Gregg Olson	.05
22	Joe Orsulak	.05
23	Jim Poole	.05
24	*Arthur Rhodes*	.10
25	Billy Ripken	.05
26	Cal Ripken, Jr.	1.00
27	David Segui	.05
28	Roy Smith	.05
29	Anthony Telford	.05
30	Mark Williamson	.05
31	Craig Worthington	.05
32	Wade Boggs	.20
33	Tom Bolton	.05
34	Tom Brunansky	.05
35	Ellis Burks	.05
36	Jack Clark	.05
37	Roger Clemens	.40
38	Danny Darwin	.05
39	Mike Greenwell	.05
40	Joe Hesketh	.05
41	Daryl Irvine	.05
42	Dennis Lamp	.05
43	Tony Pena	.05
44	Phil Plantier	.05
45	Carlos Quintana	.05
46	Jeff Reardon	.05
47	Jody Reed	.05
48	Luis Rivera	.05
49	Mo Vaughn	.30
50	Jim Abbott	.08
51	Kyle Abbott	.05
52	*Ruben Amaro, Jr.*	.05
53	Scott Bailes	.05
54	*Chris Beasley*	.05
55	Mark Eichhorn	.05
56	Mike Fetters	.05
57	Chuck Finley	.05
58	Gary Gaetti	.05
59	Dave Gallagher	.05
60	Donnie Hill	.05
61	Bryan Harvey	.05
62	Wally Joyner	.08
63	Mark Langston	.05
64	Kirk McCaskill	.05
65	John Orton	.05
66	Lance Parrish	.05
67	Luis Polonia	.05
68	Bobby Rose	.05
69	Dick Schofield	.05
70	Luis Sojo	.05
71	Lee Stevens	.05
72	Dave Winfield	.15
73	Cliff Young	.05
74	Wilson Alvarez	.08
75	*Esteban Beltre*	.08
76	Joey Cora	.05
77	*Brian Drahman*	.08
78	Alex Fernandez	.10
79	Carlton Fisk	.12
80	Scott Fletcher	.05
81	Craig Grebeck	.05
82	Ozzie Guillen	.05
83	Greg Hibbard	.05
84	Charlie Hough	.05
85	Mike Huff	.05
86	Bo Jackson	.15
87	Lance Johnson	.05
88	Ron Karkovice	.05
89	Jack McDowell	.05
90	Matt Merullo	.05
91	*Warren Newson*	.10
92	Donn Pall	.05
93	Dan Pasqua	.05
94	Ken Patterson	.05
95	Melido Perez	.05
96	Scott Radinsky	.05
97	Tim Raines	.08
98	Sammy Sosa	.50
99	Bobby Thigpen	.05
100	Frank Thomas	1.00
101	Robin Ventura	.15
102	Mike Aldrete	.05
103	Sandy Alomar, Jr.	.08
104	Carlos Baerga	.05
105	Albert Belle	.35
106	Willie Blair	.05
107	Jerry Browne	.05
108	Alex Cole	.05
109	Felix Fermin	.05
110	Glenallen Hill	.05
111	Shawn Hillegas	.05
112	Chris James	.05
113	Reggie Jefferson	.10
114	Doug Jones	.05
115	Eric King	.05
116	Mark Lewis	.05
117	Carlos Martinez	.05
118	Charles Nagy	.08
119	Rod Nichols	.05
120	Steve Olin	.05
121	Jesse Orosco	.05
122	Rudy Seanez	.05
123	Joel Skinner	.05
124	Greg Swindell	.05
125	Jim Thome	.40
126	Mark Whiten	.05
127	Scott Aldred	.05
128	Andy Allanson	.05
129	John Cerutti	.05
130	Milt Cuyler	.05
131	*Mike Dalton*	.05
132	Rob Deer	.05
133	Cecil Fielder	.08
134	Travis Fryman	.08
135	*Dan Gakeler*	.05
136	Paul Gibson	.05
137	Bill Gullickson	.05
138	Mike Henneman	.05
139	Pete Incaviglia	.05
140	*Mark Leiter*	.05
141	*Scott Livingstone*	.15
142	Lloyd Moseby	.05
143	Tony Phillips	.05
144	Mark Salas	.05
145	Frank Tanana	.05
146	Walt Terrell	.05
147	Mickey Tettleton	.05
148	Alan Trammell	.10
149	Lou Whitaker	.08
150	Kevin Appier	.05
151	Luis Aquino	.05
152	Todd Benzinger	.05
153	Mike Boddicker	.05
154	George Brett	.35
155	Storm Davis	.05
156	Jim Eisenreich	.05
157	Kirk Gibson	.05
158	Tom Gordon	.05
159	Mark Gubicza	.05
160	*David Howard*	.08
161	Mike Macfarlane	.05
162	Brent Mayne	.05
163	Brian McRae	.05
164	Jeff Montgomery	.05
165	Bill Pecota	.05
166	*Harvey Pulliam*	.05
167	Bret Saberhagen	.08
168	Kevin Seitzer	.05
169	Terry Shumpert	.05
170	Kurt Stillwell	.05
171	Danny Tartabull	.05
172	Gary Thurman	.05
173	Dante Bichette	.12
174	Kevin Brown	.05
175	Chuck Crim	.05
176	Jim Gantner	.05
177	Darryl Hamilton	.05
178	Ted Higuera	.05
179	Darren Holmes	.05
180	Mark Lee	.05
181	Julio Machado	.05
182	Paul Molitor	.25
183	Jaime Navarro	.05
184	Edwin Nunez	.05
185	Dan Plesac	.05
186	Willie Randolph	.05
187	Ron Robinson	.05
188	Gary Sheffield	.25
189	Bill Spiers	.05
190	B.J. Surhoff	.08
191	Dale Sveum	.05
192	Greg Vaughn	.08
193	Bill Wegman	.05
194	Robin Yount	.25
195	Rick Aguilera	.05
196	Allan Anderson	.05
197	Steve Bedrosian	.05
198	Randy Bush	.05
199	Larry Casian	.05
200	Chili Davis	.08
201	Scott Erickson	.05
202	Greg Gagne	.05
203	Dan Gladden	.05
204	Brian Harper	.05
205	Kent Hrbek	.08
206	Chuck Knoblauch	.15
207	Gene Larkin	.05
208	Terry Leach	.05
209	Scott Leius	.05
210	Shane Mack	.05
211	Jack Morris	.05
212	Pedro Munoz	.08
213	*Denny Neagle*	.12
214	Al Newman	.05
215	Junior Ortiz	.05
216	Mike Pagliarulo	.05
217	Kirby Puckett	.60
218	Paul Sorrento	.05
219	Kevin Tapani	.05
220	Lenny Webster	.05
221	Jesse Barfield	.05
222	Greg Cadaret	.05
223	Dave Eiland	.05
224	Alvaro Espinoza	.05
225	Steve Farr	.05
226	Bob Geren	.05
227	Lee Guetterman	.05
228	John Habyan	.05
229	Mel Hall	.05
230	Steve Howe	.05
231	*Mike Humphreys*	.05
232	*Scott Kamieniecki*	.10
233	Pat Kelly	.05
234	Roberto Kelly	.05
235	Tim Leary	.05
236	Kevin Maas	.05
237	Don Mattingly	.75
238	Hensley Meulens	.05
239	Matt Nokes	.05
240	Pascual Perez	.05
241	Eric Plunk	.05
242	*John Ramos*	.05
243	Scott Sanderson	.05
244	Steve Sax	.05
245	*Wade Taylor*	.15
246	Randy Velarde	.05
247	Bernie Williams	.20
248	Troy Afenir	.05
249	Harold Baines	.08
250	Lance Blankenship	.05
251	*Mike Bordick*	.10
252	Jose Canseco	.20
253	Steve Chitren	.05
254	Ron Darling	.05
255	Dennis Eckersley	.08
256	Mike Gallego	.05
257	Dave Henderson	.05
258	Rickey Henderson	.20
259	Rick Honeycutt	.05
260	Brook Jacoby	.05
261	Carney Lansford	.05
262	Mark McGwire	1.00
263	Mike Moore	.05
264	Gene Nelson	.05
265	Jamie Quirk	.05
266	*Joe Slusarski*	.15
267	Terry Steinbach	.05
268	Dave Stewart	.08
269	Todd Van Poppel	.08
270	Walt Weiss	.05
271	Bob Welch	.05
272	Curt Young	.05
273	Scott Bradley	.05
274	Greg Briley	.05
275	Jay Buhner	.08
276	Henry Cotto	.05
277	Alvin Davis	.05
278	Rich DeLucia	.05
279	Ken Griffey, Jr.	1.50
280	Erik Hanson	.05
281	Brian Holman	.05
282	Mike Jackson	.05
283	Randy Johnson	.20
284	Tracy Jones	.05
285	Bill Krueger	.05
286	Edgar Martinez	.08
287	Tino Martinez	.12
288	Rob Murphy	.05
289	Pete O'Brien	.05
290	Alonzo Powell	.05
291	Harold Reynolds	.05
292	Mike Schooler	.05
293	Russ Swan	.05
294	Bill Swift	.05
295	Dave Valle	.05
296	Omar Vizquel	.08
297	Gerald Alexander	.05
298	Brad Arnsberg	.05
299	Kevin Brown	.08
300	Jack Daugherty	.05
301	Mario Diaz	.05
302	Brian Downing	.05
303	Julio Franco	.05
304	Juan Gonzalez	.60
305	Rich Gossage	.08
306	Jose Guzman	.05
307	*Jose Hernandez*	.05
308	Jeff Huson	.05
309	Mike Jeffcoat	.05
310	*Terry Mathews*	.05
311	Rafael Palmeiro	.12
312	Dean Palmer	.05
313	Geno Petralli	.05
314	Gary Pettis	.05
315	Kevin Reimer	.05
316	Ivan Rodriguez	.20
317	Kenny Rogers	.05
318	*Wayne Rosenthal*	.05
319	Jeff Russell	.05
320	Nolan Ryan	.45
321	Ruben Sierra	.05
322	Jim Acker	.05
323	Roberto Alomar	.25
324	Derek Bell	.05
325	Pat Borders	.05
326	Tom Candiotti	.05
327	Joe Carter	.08
328	Rob Ducey	.05
329	Kelly Gruber	.05
330	*Juan Guzman*	.25
331	Tom Henke	.05
332	Jimmy Key	.05
333	Manny Lee	.05
334	Al Leiter	.08
335	*Bob MacDonald*	.05
336	Candy Maldonado	.05
337	Rance Mulliniks	.05
338	Greg Myers	.05
339	John Olerud	.20
340	*Ed Sprague*	.10
341	Dave Stieb	.05
342	Todd Stottlemyre	.05
343	*Mike Timlin*	.15
344	Duane Ward	.05
345	David Wells	.08
346	Devon White	.08
347	Mookie Wilson	.05
348	Eddie Zosky	.05
349	Steve Avery	.05
350	Mike Bell	.05
351	Rafael Belliard	.05
352	Juan Berenguer	.05
353	Jeff Blauser	.05
354	Sid Bream	.05

No.	Player	Price
355	Francisco Cabrera	.05
356	Marvin Freeman	.05
357	Ron Gant	.05
358	Tom Glavine	.10
359	*Brian Hunter*	.05
360	Dave Justice	.15
361	Charlie Leibrandt	.05
362	Mark Lemke	.05
363	Kent Mercker	.05
364	*Keith Mitchell*	.05
365	Greg Olson	.05
366	Terry Pendleton	.05
367	*Armando Reynoso*	.05
368	Deion Sanders	.15
369	Lonnie Smith	.05
370	Pete Smith	.05
371	John Smoltz	.10
372	Mike Stanton	.05
373	Jeff Treadway	.05
374	*Mark Wohlers*	.15
375	Paul Assenmacher	.05
376	George Bell	.05
377	Shawn Boskie	.05
378	*Frank Castillo*	.05
379	Andre Dawson	.12
380	Shawon Dunston	.05
381	Mark Grace	.20
382	Mike Harkey	.05
383	Danny Jackson	.05
384	Les Lancaster	.05
385	*Cedric Landrum*	.05
386	Greg Maddux	.60
387	Derrick May	.05
388	Chuck McElroy	.05
389	Ryne Sandberg	.35
390	*Heathcliff Slocumb*	.08
391	Dave Smith	.05
392	Dwight Smith	.05
393	Rick Sutcliffe	.05
394	Hector Villanueva	.05
395	*Chico Walker*	.05
396	Jerome Walton	.05
397	*Rick Wilkins*	.15
398	Jack Armstrong	.05
399	*Freddie Benavides*	.10
400	Glenn Braggs	.05
401	Tom Browning	.05
402	Norm Charlton	.05
403	Eric Davis	.08
404	Rob Dibble	.05
405	Bill Doran	.05
406	Mariano Duncan	.05
407	*Kip Gross*	.05
408	Chris Hammond	.05
409	Billy Hatcher	.05
410	*Chris Jones*	.10
411	Barry Larkin	.10
412	Hal Morris	.05
413	Randy Myers	.05
414	Joe Oliver	.05
415	Paul O'Neill	.08
416	Ted Power	.05
417	Luis Quinones	.05
418	Jeff Reed	.05
419	Jose Rijo	.05
420	Chris Sabo	.05
421	Reggie Sanders	.15
422	Scott Scudder	.05
423	Glenn Sutko	.05
424	Eric Anthony	.05
425	Jeff Bagwell	.75
426	Craig Biggio	.15
427	Ken Caminiti	.15
428	Casey Candaele	.05
429	Mike Capel	.05
430	Andujar Cedeno	.05
431	Jim Corsi	.05
432	Mark Davidson	.05
433	Steve Finley	.05
434	Luis Gonzalez	.08
435	Pete Harnisch	.05
436	Dwayne Henry	.05
437	Xavier Hernandez	.05
438	Jimmy Jones	.05
439	*Darryl Kile*	.10
440	*Rob Mallicoat*	.05
441	*Andy Mota*	.08
442	Al Osuna	.05
443	Mark Portugal	.05
444	*Scott Servais*	.10
445	Mike Simms	.05
446	Gerald Young	.05
447	Tim Belcher	.05
448	Brett Butler	.08
449	John Candelaria	.05
450	Gary Carter	.08
451	Dennis Cook	.05
452	Tim Crews	.05
453	Kal Daniels	.05
454	Jim Gott	.05
455	Alfredo Griffin	.05
456	Kevin Gross	.05
457	Chris Gwynn	.05
458	Lenny Harris	.05
459	Orel Hershiser	.08
460	Jay Howell	.05
461	Stan Javier	.05
462	Eric Karros	.15
463	Ramon Martinez	.08
464	Roger McDowell	.05
465	Mike Morgan	.05
466	Eddie Murray	.25
467	Jose Offerman	.05
468	Bob Ojeda	.05
469	Juan Samuel	.05
470	Mike Scioscia	.05
471	Darryl Strawberry	.10
472	*Bret Barberie*	.10
473	Brian Barnes	.05
474	Eric Bullock	.05
475	Ivan Calderon	.05
476	Delino DeShields	.08
477	*Jeff Fassero*	.10
478	Mike Fitzgerald	.05
479	Steve Frey	.05
480	Andres Galarraga	.12
481	Mark Gardner	.05
482	Marquis Grissom	.10
483	*Chris Haney*	.05
484	Barry Jones	.05
485	Dave Martinez	.05
486	Dennis Martinez	.08
487	Chris Nabholz	.05
488	Spike Owen	.05
489	Gilberto Reyes	.05
490	Mel Rojas	.05
491	Scott Ruskin	.05
492	Bill Sampen	.05
493	Larry Walker	.20
494	Tim Wallach	.05
495	Daryl Boston	.05
496	Hubie Brooks	.05
497	Tim Burke	.05
498	Mark Carreon	.05
499	Tony Castillo	.05
500	Vince Coleman	.05
501	David Cone	.08
502	Kevin Elster	.05
503	Sid Fernandez	.05
504	John Franco	.05
505	Dwight Gooden	.12
506	Todd Hundley	.08
507	Jeff Innis	.05
508	Gregg Jefferies	.12
509	Howard Johnson	.05
510	Dave Magadan	.05
511	*Terry McDaniel*	.05
512	Kevin McReynolds	.05
513	Keith Miller	.05
514	Charlie O'Brien	.05
515	Mackey Sasser	.05
516	*Pete Schourek*	.10
517	Julio Valera	.05
518	Frank Viola	.05
519	Wally Whitehurst	.05
520	*Anthony Young*	.10
521	*Andy Ashby*	.20
522	*Kim Batiste*	.05
523	Joe Boever	.05
524	Wes Chamberlain	.05
525	Pat Combs	.05
526	Danny Cox	.05
527	Darren Daulton	.05
528	Jose DeJesus	.05
529	Len Dykstra	.08
530	Darrin Fletcher	.05
531	Tommy Greene	.05
532	Jason Grimsley	.05
533	Charlie Hayes	.05
534	Von Hayes	.05
535	Dave Hollins	.08
536	Ricky Jordan	.05
537	John Kruk	.05
538	Jim Lindeman	.05
539	Mickey Morandini	.05
540	Terry Mulholland	.05
541	Dale Murphy	.12
542	Randy Ready	.05
543	Wally Ritchie	.05
544	Bruce Ruffin	.05
545	Steve Searcy	.05
546	Dickie Thon	.05
547	Mitch Williams	.05
548	Stan Belinda	.05
549	Jay Bell	.05
550	Barry Bonds	.35
551	Bobby Bonilla	.08
552	Steve Buechele	.05
553	Doug Drabek	.05
554	Neal Heaton	.05
555	Jeff King	.05
556	Bob Kipper	.05
557	Bill Landrum	.05
558	Mike LaValliere	.05
559	Jose Lind	.05
560	Lloyd McClendon	.05
561	Orlando Merced	.05
562	Bob Patterson	.05
563	*Joe Redfield*	.05
564	Gary Redus	.05
565	Rosario Rodriguez	.05
566	Don Slaught	.05
567	John Smiley	.05
568	Zane Smith	.05
569	Randy Tomlin	.05
570	Andy Van Slyke	.05
571	Gary Varsho	.05
572	Bob Walk	.05
573	*John Wehner*	.15
574	Juan Agosto	.05
575	Cris Carpenter	.05
576	Jose DeLeon	.05
577	Rich Gedman	.05
578	Bernard Gilkey	.05
579	Pedro Guerrero	.05
580	Ken Hill	.05
581	Rex Hudler	.05
582	Felix Jose	.05
583	Ray Lankford	.05
584	Omar Olivares	.05
585	Jose Oquendo	.05
586	Tom Pagnozzi	.05
587	Geronimo Pena	.05
588	Mike Perez	.05
589	Gerald Perry	.05
590	Bryn Smith	.05
591	Lee Smith	.08
592	Ozzie Smith	.25
593	Scott Terry	.05
594	Bob Tewksbury	.05
595	Milt Thompson	.05
596	Todd Zeile	.08
597	Larry Andersen	.05
598	Oscar Azocar	.05
599	Andy Benes	.08
600	*Ricky Bones*	.08
601	Jerald Clark	.05
602	Pat Clements	.05
603	Paul Faries	.05
604	Tony Fernandez	.05
605	Tony Gwynn	.35
606	Greg Harris	.05
607	Thomas Howard	.05
608	Bruce Hurst	.05
609	Darrin Jackson	.05
610	Tom Lampkin	.05
611	Craig Lefferts	.05
612	*Jim Lewis*	.05
613	Mike Maddux	.05
614	Fred McGriff	.15
615	*Jose Melendez*	.08
616	*Jose Mota*	.08
617	Dennis Rasmussen	.05
618	Bip Roberts	.05
619	Rich Rodriguez	.05
620	Benito Santiago	.05
621	*Craig Shipley*	.05
622	Tim Teufel	.05
623	*Kevin Ward*	.05
624	Ed Whitson	.05
625	Dave Anderson	.05
626	Kevin Bass	.05
627	*Rod Beck*	.10
628	Bud Black	.05
629	Jeff Brantley	.05
630	John Burkett	.05
631	Will Clark	.20
632	Royce Clayton	.05
633	Steve Decker	.05
634	Kelly Downs	.05
635	Mike Felder	.05
636	Scott Garrelts	.05
637	Eric Gunderson	.05
638	*Bryan Hickerson*	.10
639	Darren Lewis	.05
640	Greg Litton	.05
641	Kirt Manwaring	.05
642	*Paul McClellan*	.05
643	Willie McGee	.08
644	Kevin Mitchell	.05
645	Francisco Olivares	.05
646	*Mike Remlinger*	.08
647	Dave Righetti	.05
648	Robby Thompson	.05
649	Jose Uribe	.05
650	Matt Williams	.15
651	Trevor Wilson	.05
652	Tom Goodwin (Prospects)	.25
653	Terry Bross (Prospects)	.05
654	*Mike Christopher* (Prospects)	.10
655	Kenny Lofton (Prospects)	2.50
656	*Chris Cron* (Prospects)	.10
657	Willie Banks (Prospects)	.10
658	*Pat Rice* (Prospects)	.05
659a	*Rob Mauer* (Prospects) (last name misspelled)	1.00
659b	*Rob Maurer* (Prospects) (corrected)	.12
660	Don Harris (Prospects)	.12
661	Henry Rodriguez (Prospects)	.25
662	*Cliff Brantley* (Prospects)	.08
663	*Mike Linskey* (Prospects)	.05
664	Gary Disarcina (Prospects)	.10
665	*Gil Heredia* (Prospects)	.12
666	*Vinny Castilla* (Prospects)	1.00
667	Paul Abbott (Prospects)	.08
668	Monty Fariss (Prospects)	.08
669	*Jarvis Brown* (Prospects)	.08
670	*Wayne Kirby* (Prospects)	.15
671	*Scott Brosius* (Prospects)	.15
672	Bob Hamelin (Prospects)	.10
673	*Joel Johnston* (Prospects)	.08
674	*Tim Spehr* (Prospects)	.15
675	*Jeff Gardner* (Prospects)	.10
676	*Rico Rossy* (Prospects)	.10
677	*Roberto Hernandez* (Prospects)	.20
678	*Ted Wood* (Prospects)	.08
679	Cal Eldred (Prospects)	.15
680	Sean Berry (Prospects)	.10
681	Rickey Henderson (Stolen Base Record)	.15
682	Nolan Ryan (Record 7th No-hitter)	.25
683	Dennis Martinez (Perfect Game)	.05
684	Wilson Alvarez (Rookie No-hitter)	.05
685	Joe Carter (3 100 RBI Seasons)	.05
686	Dave Winfield (400 Home Runs)	.10
687	David Cone (Ties NL Record Strikeouts)	.05
688	Jose Canseco (League Leaders)	.15
689	Howard Johnson (League Leaders)	.05
690	Julio Franco (League Leaders)	.05
691	Terry Pendleton (League Leaders)	.05
692	Cecil Fielder (League Leaders)	.10

693	Scott Erickson (League Leaders)	.05
694	Tom Glavine (League Leaders)	.05
695	Dennis Martinez (League Leaders)	.05
696	Bryan Harvey (League Leaders)	.05
697	Lee Smith (League Leaders)	.05
698	Super Siblings (Roberto & Sandy Alomar, Roberto & Sandy Alomar)	.15
699	The Indispensables (Bobby Bonilla, Will Clark)	.10
700	Teamwork (Mark Wohlers, Kent Mercker, Alejandro Pena)	.08
701	Tiger Tandems (Chris Jones, Bo Jackson, Gregg Olson, Frank Thomas)	.40
702	The Ignitors (Brett Butler, Paul Molitor)	.20
703	The Indispensables II (Cal Ripken Jr., Joe Carter)	.15
704	Power Packs (Barry Larkin, Kirby Puckett)	.15
705	Today and Tomorrow (Mo Vaughn, Cecil Fielder)	.10
706	Teenage Sensations (Ramon Martinez, Ozzie Guillen)	.08
707	Designated Hitters (Harold Baines, Wade Boggs)	.10
708	Robin Yount (ProVision)	.20
709	Ken Griffey, Jr. (ProVision)	1.00
710	Nolan Ryan (ProVision)	.85
711	Cal Ripken, Jr. (ProVision)	.50
712	Frank Thomas (ProVision)	1.00
713	Dave Justice (ProVision)	.20
714	Checklist 1-101	.05
715	Checklist 102-194	.05
716	Checklist 195-296	.05
717	Checklist 297-397	.05
718	Checklist 398-494	.05
719	Checklist 495-596	.05
720a	Checklist 597-720 (659 Rob Mauer)	.05
720b	Checklist 597-720 (659 Rob Maurer)	.05

1992 Fleer All-Stars

Black borders with gold highlights are featured on these special wax pack insert cards. The fronts feature glossy action photos with a portrait photo inset. Backs feature career highlights.

		MT
Complete Set (24):		20.00
Common Player:		.20
1	Felix Jose	.20
2	Tony Gwynn	2.00
3	Barry Bonds	1.50
4	Bobby Bonilla	.30
5	Mike LaValliere	.20
6	Tom Glavine	.30
7	Ramon Martinez	.25
8	Lee Smith	.20
9	Mickey Tettleton	.20
10	Scott Erickson	.20
11	Frank Thomas	2.50
12	Danny Tartabull	.20
13	Will Clark	.50
14	Ryne Sandberg	.75
15	Terry Pendleton	.20
16	Barry Larkin	.30
17	Rafael Palmeiro	.50
18	Julio Franco	.20
19	Robin Ventura	.40
20	Cal Ripken, Jr.	3.00
21	Joe Carter	.20
22	Kirby Puckett	2.00
23	Ken Griffey, Jr.	4.50
24	Jose Canseco	.75

1992 Fleer Lumber Co.

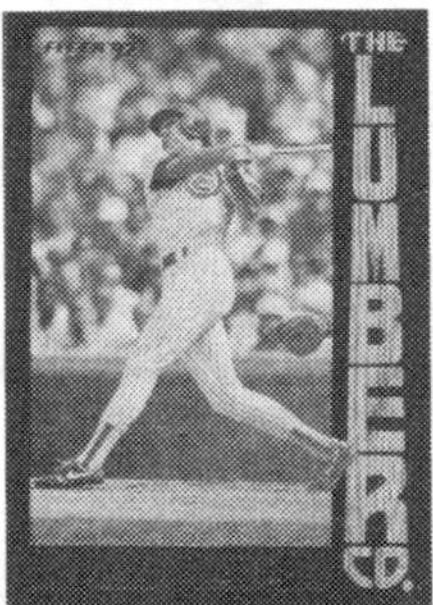

Baseball's top power hitters at each position are featured in this nine-card set. Fronts feature full-color action photos bordered in black. Backs feature posed player photos and career highlights. The set was included only in factory sets released to the hobby trade.

		MT
Complete Set (9):		7.50
Common Player:		.50
1	Cecil Fielder	.50
2	Mickey Tettleton	.50
3	Darryl Strawberry	.75
4	Ryne Sandberg	1.00
5	Jose Canseco	1.00
6	Matt Williams	.75
7	Cal Ripken, Jr.	2.50
8	Barry Bonds	1.25
9	Ron Gant	.50

1992 Fleer Roger Clemens

This set chronicles the career highlights of Roger Clemens. The initial 12 cards from the set were inserted in 1992 Fleer wax packs. A limited number of autographed cards were inserted as well. The additional three cards from the set were available through a mail-in offer. The card fronts feature black borders with metallic gold type. The flip side is yellow with black borders.

		MT
Complete Set (15):		7.00
Common Card:		.50
Autographed Card:		50.00
1	Quiet Storm	.50
2	Courted by the Mets and Twins	.50
3	The Show	.50
4	A Rocket Launched	.50
5	Time of Trial	.50
6	Break Through	.50
7	Play it Again Roger	.50
8	Business as Usual	.50
9	Heee's Back	.50
10	Blood, Sweat and Tears	.50
11	Prime of Life	.50
12	Man for Every Season	.50
13	Cooperstown Bound	1.00
14	The Heat of the Moment	1.00
15	Final Words	1.00

1992 Fleer Rookie Sensations

This 20-card set features the top rookies of 1991 and rookie prospects from 1992. The card fronts feature blue borders with "Rookie Sensations" in gold along the top border. The flip sides feature background information on the player. The cards were randomly inserted in 1992 Fleer cello packs. This issue saw very high prices when initially released then suffered long-term declines as the hobby became inundated with more and more insert sets.

		MT
Complete Set (20):		25.00
Common Player:		.50
1	Frank Thomas	7.50
2	Todd Van Poppel	.50
3	Orlando Merced	.50
4	Jeff Bagwell	6.50
5	Jeff Fassero	.50
6	Darren Lewis	1.00
7	Milt Cuyler	.50
8	Mike Timlin	.50
9	Brian McRae	1.00
10	Chuck Knoblauch	2.50
11	Rich DeLucia	.50
12	Ivan Rodriguez	5.00
13	Juan Guzman	.75
14	Steve Chitren	.50
15	Mark Wohlers	.50
16	Wes Chamberlain	.50
17	Ray Lankford	1.00
18	Chito Martinez	.50
19	Phil Plantier	.50
20	Scott Leius	.50

1992 Fleer Smoke 'N Heat

This 12-card set of top pitchers was included in factory sets designated for sale within the general retail trade. Card numbers have an "S" prefix.

		MT
Complete Set (12):		7.50
Common Player:		.25
1	Lee Smith	.25
2	Jack McDowell	.30
3	David Cone	.50
4	Roger Clemens	1.50
5	Nolan Ryan	3.00
6	Scott Erickson	.25
7	Tom Glavine	.40
8	Dwight Gooden	.40
9	Andy Benes	.30
10	Steve Avery	.25
11	Randy Johnson	.75
12	Jim Abbott	.30

1992 Fleer Team Leaders

White and green borders highlight this insert set from Fleer. The card fronts also feature a special gold-foil "team leaders" logo beneath the full-color player photo. The card backs feature player information. The cards were randomly inserted in 1992 Fleer rack packs.

		MT
Complete Set (20):		40.00
Common Player:		.40
1	Don Mattingly	8.00
2	Howard Johnson	.40
3	Chris Sabo	.40
4	Carlton Fisk	.75
5	Kirby Puckett	6.00
6	Cecil Fielder	.50
7	Tony Gwynn	6.00
8	Will Clark	2.50
9	Bobby Bonilla	.50
10	Len Dykstra	.40
11	Tom Glavine	1.25
12	Rafael Palmeiro	1.50
13	Wade Boggs	1.50
14	Joe Carter	.50
15	Ken Griffey, Jr.	12.50
16	Darryl Strawberry	.50
17	Cal Ripken, Jr.	11.00
18	Danny Tartabull	.40
19	Jose Canseco	1.50
20	Andre Dawson	.50

1992 Fleer Update

This 132-card set was released in boxed set form and features traded players, free agents and top rookies from 1992. The cards are styled after the regular 1992 Fleer and are numbered alphabetically according to team. This set marks the ninth year that Fleer has released an update set. The set includes four black-bordered "Headliner" cards.

		MT
Complete Set (136):		140.00
Common Player:		.20
H1	1992 All-Star Game MVP (Ken Griffey, Jr.)	20.00
H2	3000 Career Hits (Robin Yount)	3.00
H3	Major League Career Saves Record (Jeff Reardon)	.25
H4	Record RBI Performance (Cecil Fielder)	1.00
1	Todd Frohwirth	.20
2	Alan Mills	.20
3	Rick Sutcliffe	.20
4	*John Valentin*	2.00
5	Frank Viola	.20
6	Bob Zupcic	.20
7	Mike Butcher	.20
8	*Chad Curtis*	1.00
9	*Damion Easley*	1.50
10	Tim Salmon	15.00
11	Julio Valera	.20
12	George Bell	.20
13	Roberto Hernandez	.35
14	Shawn Jeter	.20
15	Thomas Howard	.20
16	Jesse Levis	.40
17	Kenny Lofton	10.00
18	Paul Sorrento	.20
19	Rico Brogna	.35
20	John Doherty	.20
21	Dan Gladden	.20
22	Buddy Groom	.20
23	Shawn Hare	.20
24	John Kiely	.20
25	Kurt Knudsen	.20
26	Gregg Jefferies	.30
27	Wally Joyner	.30
28	Kevin Koslofski	.20
29	Kevin McReynolds	.20
30	Rusty Meacham	.20
31	Keith Miller	.20
32	Hipolito Pichardo	.20
33	James Austin	.20
34	Scott Fletcher	.20
35	*John Jaha*	3.00
36	Pat Listach	.50
37	Dave Nilsson	2.00
38	Kevin Seitzer	.20
39	Tom Edens	.20
40	Pat Mahomes	.65
41	John Smiley	.20
42	Charlie Hayes	.20
43	Sam Militello	.20
44	Andy Stankiewicz	.35
45	Danny Tartabull	.20
46	Bob Wickman	.20
47	Jerry Browne	.20
48	Kevin Campbell	.20
49	Vince Horsman	.20
50	Troy Neel	.50
51	Ruben Sierra	.20
52	Bruce Walton	.20
53	Willie Wilson	.20
54	Bret Boone	3.00
55	Dave Fleming	.65
56	Kevin Mitchell	.20
57	*Jeff Nelson*	.20
58	Shane Turner	.20
59	Jose Canseco	4.00
60	*Jeff Frye*	.30
61	Danilo Leon	.20
62	Roger Pavlik	.30
63	David Cone	.35
64	Pat Hentgen	2.00
65	Randy Knorr	.20
66	Jack Morris	.20
67	Dave Winfield	1.00
68	*David Nied*	.20
69	Otis Nixon	.20
70	Alejandro Pena	.20
71	Jeff Reardon	.20
72	Alex Arias	.25
73	Jim Bullinger	.20
74	Mike Morgan	.20
75	Rey Sanchez	.20
76	Bob Scanlan	.20
77	Sammy Sosa	15.00
78	Scott Bankhead	.20
79	Tim Belcher	.20
80	Steve Foster	.20
81	Willie Greene	.50
82	Bip Roberts	.20
83	Scott Ruskin	.20
84	Greg Swindell	.20
85	Juan Guerrero	.20
86	Butch Henry	.20
87	Doug Jones	.20
88	Brian Williams	.30
89	Tom Candiotti	.20
90	Eric Davis	.25
91	Carlos Hernandez	.20
92	*Mike Piazza*	90.00
93	Mike Sharperson	.20
94	Eric Young	1.50
95	Moises Alou	2.50
96	Greg Colbrunn	.20
97	Wil Cordero	1.50
98	Ken Hill	.25
99	John Vander Wal	.25
100	John Wetteland	.20
101	Bobby Bonilla	.35
102	Eric Hilman	.20
103	Pat Howell	.20
104	*Jeff Kent*	6.00
105	Dick Schofield	.20
106	*Ryan Thompson*	.25
107	Chico Walker	.20
108	Juan Bell	.20
109	Mariano Duncan	.20
110	Jeff Grotewold	.25
111	Ben Rivera	.20
112	Curt Schilling	1.50
113	Victor Cole	.20
114	Al Martin	1.00
115	Roger Mason	.20
116	Blas Minor	.35
117	Tim Wakefield	.50
118	*Mark Clark*	.50
119	Rheal Cormier	.35
120	Donovan Osborne	.20
121	Todd Worrell	.20
122	Jeremy Hernandez	.25
123	Randy Myers	.20
124	Frank Seminara	.20
125	Gary Sheffield	2.50
126	Dan Walters	.20
127	Steve Hosey	.40
128	Mike Jackson	.20
129	Jim Pena	.20
130	Cory Snyder	.20
131	Bill Swift	.20
132	Checklist	.05

1993 Fleer

The card fronts feature silver borders with the player's name, team and position in a banner along the left side of the card. The backs feature an action photo of the player with his name in bold behind him. A box featuring biographical information, statistics and player information is located to the right of the action photo. The cards are numbered alphabetically by team. The basic Fleer issue for 1993 was issued in two series of 360 cards each. The 720-card set included a number of subsets and could be found in many different types of packaging with an unprecedented number of inserts sets to spice up each offering.

		MT
Complete Set (720):		35.00
Common Player:		.05
Series 1 or 2 Pack (15):		1.00
Series 1 or 2 Wax Box (36):		26.00
1	Steve Avery	.05
2	Sid Bream	.05
3	Ron Gant	.10
4	Tom Glavine	.10
5	Brian Hunter	.05
6	Ryan Klesko	.25
7	Charlie Leibrandt	.05
8	Kent Mercker	.05
9	David Nied	.05
10	Otis Nixon	.05
11	Greg Olson	.05
12	Terry Pendleton	.05
13	Deion Sanders	.15
14	John Smoltz	.12
15	Mike Stanton	.05
16	Mark Wohlers	.05
17	Paul Assenmacher	.05
18	Steve Buechele	.05
19	Shawon Dunston	.05
20	Mark Grace	.15
21	Derrick May	.05
22	Chuck McElroy	.05
23	Mike Morgan	.05
24	Rey Sanchez	.05
25	Ryne Sandberg	.30
26	Bob Scanlan	.05
27	Sammy Sosa	.75
28	Rick Wilkins	.05
29	*Bobby Ayala*	.05
30	Tim Belcher	.05
31	*Jeff Branson*	.12
32	Norm Charlton	.05
33	*Steve Foster*	.05
34	Willie Greene	.08
35	Chris Hammond	.05
36	Milt Hill	.05
37	Hal Morris	.05
38	Joe Oliver	.05
39	Paul O'Neill	.15
40	*Tim Pugh*	.12
41	Jose Rijo	.05
42	Bip Roberts	.05
43	Chris Sabo	.05
44	Reggie Sanders	.08
45	Eric Anthony	.05
46	Jeff Bagwell	.75
47	Craig Biggio	.15
48	Joe Boever	.05
49	Casey Candaele	.05
50	Steve Finley	.05
51	Luis Gonzalez	.08
52	Pete Harnisch	.05
53	Xavier Hernandez	.05
54	Doug Jones	.05
55	Eddie Taubensee	.05
56	Brian Williams	.05
57	*Pedro Astacio*	.12
58	Todd Benzinger	.05
59	Brett Butler	.08
60	Tom Candiotti	.05
61	Lenny Harris	.05
62	Carlos Hernandez	.05
63	Orel Hershiser	.08
64	Eric Karros	.12
65	Ramon Martinez	.08
66	Jose Offerman	.05
67	Mike Scioscia	.05
68	Mike Sharperson	.05
69	*Eric Young*	.08
70	Moises Alou	.10
71	Ivan Calderon	.05
72	*Archi Cianfrocco*	.05
73	Wil Cordero	.08
74	Delino DeShields	.08
75	Mark Gardner	.05
76	Ken Hill	.05
77	*Tim Laker*	.08
78	Chris Nabholz	.05
79	Mel Rojas	.05
80	*John Vander Wal*	.12
81	Larry Walker	.20
82	Tim Wallach	.05
83	John Wetteland	.05
84	Bobby Bonilla	.08
85	Daryl Boston	.05
86	Sid Fernandez	.05

87 *Eric Hillman* .08
88 Todd Hundley .12
89 Howard Johnson .05
90 Jeff Kent .12
91 Eddie Murray .30
92 Bill Pecota .05
93 Bret Saberhagen .08
94 Dick Schofield .05
95 Pete Schourek .05
96 Anthony Young .05
97 Ruben Amaro Jr. .05
98 Juan Bell .05
99 Wes Chamberlain .05
100 Darren Daulton .05
101 Mariano Duncan .05
102 Mike Hartley .05
103 Ricky Jordan .05
104 John Kruk .05
105 Mickey Morandini .05
106 Terry Mulholland .05
107 *Ben Rivera* .05
108 Curt Schilling .08
109 *Keith Shepherd* .05
110 Stan Belinda .05
111 Jay Bell .05
112 Barry Bonds .40
113 Jeff King .05
114 Mike LaValliere .05
115 Jose Lind .05
116 Roger Mason .05
117 Orlando Merced .05
118 Bob Patterson .05
119 Don Slaught .05
120 Zane Smith .05
121 Randy Tomlin .05
122 Andy Van Slyke .05
123 *Tim Wakefield* .08
124 Rheal Cormier .05
125 Bernard Gilkey .05
126 Felix Jose .05
127 Ray Lankford .05
128 Bob McClure .05
129 Donovan Osborne .05
130 Tom Pagnozzi .05
131 Geronimo Pena .05
132 Mike Perez .05
133 Lee Smith .08
134 Bob Tewksbury .05
135 Todd Worrell .05
136 Todd Zeile .08
137 Jerald Clark .05
138 Tony Gwynn .40
139 Greg Harris .05
140 Jeremy Hernandez .05
141 Darrin Jackson .05
142 Mike Maddux .05
143 Fred McGriff .20
144 Jose Melendez .05
145 Rich Rodriguez .05
146 Frank Seminara .05
147 Gary Sheffield .20
148 Kurt Stillwell .05
149 *Dan Walters* .10
150 Rod Beck .05
151 Bud Black .05
152 Jeff Brantley .05
153 John Burkett .05
154 Will Clark .20
155 Royce Clayton .05
156 Mike Jackson .05
157 Darren Lewis .05
158 Kirt Manwaring .05
159 Willie McGee .08
160 Cory Snyder .05
161 Bill Swift .05
162 Trevor Wilson .05
163 Brady Anderson .10
164 Glenn Davis .05
165 Mike Devereaux .05
166 Todd Frohwirth .05
167 Leo Gomez .05
168 Chris Hoiles .05
169 Ben McDonald .05
170 Randy Milligan .05
171 Alan Mills .05
172 Mike Mussina .30
173 Gregg Olson .05
174 Arthur Rhodes .05
175 David Segui .05
176 Ellis Burks .08
177 Roger Clemens .75
178 Scott Cooper .05
179 Danny Darwin .05
180 Tony Fossas .05
181 *Paul Quantrill* .08
182 Jody Reed .05
183 *John Valentin* .15
184 Mo Vaughn .35
185 Frank Viola .05
186 Bob Zupcic .05
187 Jim Abbott .08
188 Gary DiSarcina .05
189 *Damion Easley* .10
190 Junior Felix .05
191 Chuck Finley .05
192 Joe Grahe .05
193 Bryan Harvey .05
194 Mark Langston .05
195 John Orton .05
196 Luis Polonia .05
197 Tim Salmon .40
198 Luis Sojo .05
199 Wilson Alvarez .05
200 George Bell .05
201 Alex Fernandez .08
202 Craig Grebeck .05
203 Ozzie Guillen .05
204 Lance Johnson .05
205 Ron Karkovice .05
206 Kirk McCaskill .05
207 Jack McDowell .05
208 Scott Radinsky .05
209 Tim Raines .08
210 Frank Thomas 1.00
211 Robin Ventura .12
212 Sandy Alomar Jr. .08
213 Carlos Baerga .08
214 Dennis Cook .05
215 Thomas Howard .05
216 Mark Lewis .05
217 Derek Lilliquist .05
218 Kenny Lofton .50
219 Charles Nagy .08
220 Steve Olin .05
221 Paul Sorrento .05
222 Jim Thome .25
223 Mark Whiten .05
224 Milt Cuyler .05
225 Rob Deer .05
226 *John Doherty* .12
227 Cecil Fielder .08
228 Travis Fryman .10
229 Mike Henneman .05
230 *John Kiely* .05
231 *Kurt Knudsen* .08
232 Scott Livingstone .05
233 Tony Phillips .05
234 Mickey Tettleton .05
235 Kevin Appier .05
236 George Brett .40
237 Tom Gordon .05
238 Gregg Jefferies .10
239 Wally Joyner .08
240 *Kevin Koslofski* .12
241 Mike Macfarlane .05
242 Brian McRae .05
243 Rusty Meacham .05
244 Keith Miller .05
245 Jeff Montgomery .05
246 *Hipolito Pichardo* .05
247 Ricky Bones .05
248 Cal Eldred .05
249 Mike Fetters .05
250 Darryl Hamilton .05
251 Doug Henry .05
252 John Jaha .05
253 Pat Listach .05
254 Paul Molitor .30
255 Jaime Navarro .05
256 Kevin Seitzer .05
257 B.J. Surhoff .08
258 Greg Vaughn .08
259 Bill Wegman .05
260 Robin Yount .30
261 Rick Aguilera .05
262 Chili Davis .08
263 Scott Erickson .05
264 Greg Gagne .05
265 Mark Guthrie .05
266 Brian Harper .05
267 Kent Hrbek .08
268 Terry Jorgensen .05
269 Gene Larkin .05
270 Scott Leius .05
271 Pat Mahomes .05
272 Pedro Munoz .05
273 Kirby Puckett .50
274 Kevin Tapani .05
275 Carl Willis .05
276 Steve Farr .05
277 John Habyan .05
278 Mel Hall .05
279 Charlie Hayes .05
280 Pat Kelly .05
281 Don Mattingly .50
282 Sam Militello .05
283 Matt Nokes .05
284 Melido Perez .05
285 Andy Stankiewicz .05
286 Danny Tartabull .05
287 Randy Velarde .05
288 Bob Wickman .05
289 Bernie Williams .40
290 Lance Blankenship .05
291 Mike Bordick .05
292 Jerry Browne .05
293 Dennis Eckersley .08
294 Rickey Henderson .20
295 *Vince Horsman* .12
296 Mark McGwire 2.00
297 Jeff Parrett .05
298 Ruben Sierra .05
299 Terry Steinbach .05
300 Walt Weiss .05
301 Bob Welch .05
302 Willie Wilson .05
303 Bobby Witt .05
304 Bret Boone .05
305 Jay Buhner .08
306 Dave Fleming .05
307 Ken Griffey, Jr. 2.00
308 Erik Hanson .05
309 Edgar Martinez .08
310 Tino Martinez .15
311 Jeff Nelson .05
312 Dennis Powell .05
313 Mike Schooler .05
314 Russ Swan .05
315 Dave Valle .05
316 Omar Vizquel .08
317 Kevin Brown .05
318 Todd Burns .05
319 Jose Canseco .30
320 Julio Franco .05
321 Jeff Frye .08
322 Juan Gonzalez .50
323 Jose Guzman .05
324 Jeff Huson .05
325 Dean Palmer .08
326 Kevin Reimer .05
327 Ivan Rodriguez .40
328 Kenny Rogers .05
329 Dan Smith .05
330 Roberto Alomar .35
331 Derek Bell .08
332 Pat Borders .05
333 Joe Carter .08
334 Kelly Gruber .05
335 Tom Henke .05
336 Jimmy Key .05
337 Manuel Lee .05
338 Candy Maldonado .05
339 John Olerud .15
340 Todd Stottlemyre .05
341 Duane Ward .05
342 Devon White .08
343 Dave Winfield .15
344 Edgar Martinez (League Leaders) .05
345 Cecil Fielder (League Leaders) .05
346 Kenny Lofton (League Leaders) .15
347 Jack Morris (League Leaders) .05
348 Roger Clemens (League Leaders) .25
349 Fred McGriff (Round Trippers) .10
350 Barry Bonds (Round Trippers) .15
351 Gary Sheffield (Round Trippers) .10
352 Darren Daulton (Round Trippers) .05
353 Dave Hollins (Round Trippers) .05
354 Brothers In Blue (Pedro Martinez, Ramon Martinez) .50
355 Power Packs (Ivan Rodriguez, Kirby Puckett) .35
356 Triple Threats (Ryne Sandberg, Gary Sheffield) .15
357 Infield Trifecta (Roberto Alomar, Chuck Knoblauch, Carlos Baerga) .15
358 Checklist .05
359 Checklist .05
360 Checklist .05
361 Rafael Belliard .05
362 Damon Berryhill .05
363 Mike Bielecki .05
364 Jeff Blauser .05
365 Francisco Cabrera .05
366 Marvin Freeman .05
367 Dave Justice .20
368 Mark Lemke .05
369 Alejandro Pena .05
370 Jeff Reardon .05
371 Lonnie Smith .05
372 Pete Smith .05
373 Shawn Boskie .05
374 Jim Bullinger .05
375 Frank Castillo .05
376 Doug Dascenzo .05
377 Andre Dawson .12
378 Mike Harkey .05
379 Greg Hibbard .05
380 Greg Maddux 1.00
381 Ken Patterson .05
382 Jeff Robinson .05
383 Luis Salazar .05
384 Dwight Smith .05
385 Jose Vizcaino .05
386 Scott Bankhead .05
387 Tom Browning .05
388 Darnell Coles .05
389 Rob Dibble .05
390 Bill Doran .05
391 Dwayne Henry .05
392 Cesar Hernandez .05
393 Roberto Kelly .05
394 Barry Larkin .10
395 Dave Martinez .05
396 Kevin Mitchell .05
397 Jeff Reed .05
398 Scott Ruskin .05
399 Greg Swindell .05
400 Dan Wilson .08
401 Andy Ashby .08
402 Freddie Benavides .05
403 Dante Bichette .10
404 Willie Blair .05
405 Denis Boucher .05
406 Vinny Castilla .10
407 Braulio Castillo .05
408 Alex Cole .05
409 Andres Galarraga .15
410 Joe Girardi .05
411 Butch Henry .05
412 Darren Holmes .05
413 Calvin Jones .05
414 *Steve Reed* .10
415 Kevin Ritz .05
416 *Jim Tatum* .05
417 Jack Armstrong .05
418 Bret Barberie .05
419 Ryan Bowen .05
420 Cris Carpenter .05
421 Chuck Carr .05
422 Scott Chiamparino .05
423 Jeff Conine .08
424 Jim Corsi .05
425 Steve Decker .05
426 Chris Donnels .05
427 Monty Fariss .05
428 Bob Natal .05
429 *Pat Rapp* .08
430 Dave Weathers .05
431 *Nigel Wilson* .10
432 Ken Caminiti .15
433 Andujar Cedeno .05
434 Tom Edens .05
435 Juan Guerrero .05
436 Pete Incaviglia .05
437 Jimmy Jones .05
438 Darryl Kile .05
439 Rob Murphy .05
440 Al Osuna .05
441 Mark Portugal .05
442 Scott Servais .05
443 John Candelaria .05
444 Tim Crews .05
445 Eric Davis .08
446 Tom Goodwin .05
447 Jim Gott .05
448 Kevin Gross .05
449 Dave Hansen .05
450 Jay Howell .05
451 Roger McDowell .05

452 Bob Ojeda .05
453 Henry Rodriguez .08
454 Darryl Strawberry .10
455 Mitch Webster .05
456 Steve Wilson .05
457 Brian Barnes .05
458 Sean Berry .05
459 Jeff Fassero .05
460 Darrin Fletcher .05
461 Marquis Grissom .08
462 Dennis Martinez .08
463 Spike Owen .05
464 Matt Stairs .05
465 Sergio Valdez .05
466 Kevin Bass .05
467 Vince Coleman .05
468 Mark Dewey .05
469 Kevin Elster .05
470 Tony Fernandez .05
471 John Franco .05
472 Dave Gallagher .05
473 Paul Gibson .05
474 Dwight Gooden .12
475 Lee Guetterman .05
476 Jeff Innis .05
477 Dave Magadan .05
478 Charlie O'Brien .05
479 Willie Randolph .05
480 Mackey Sasser .05
481 Ryan Thompson .05
482 Chico Walker .05
483 Kyle Abbott .05
484 Bob Ayrault .05
485 Kim Batiste .05
486 Cliff Brantley .05
487 Jose DeLeon .05
488 Len Dykstra .05
489 Tommy Greene .05
490 Jeff Grotewold .05
491 Dave Hollins .08
492 Danny Jackson .05
493 Stan Javier .05
494 Tom Marsh .05
495 Greg Matthews .05
496 Dale Murphy .12
497 *Todd Pratt* .10
498 Mitch Williams .05
499 Danny Cox .05
500 Doug Drabek .05
501 Carlos Garcia .05
502 Lloyd McClendon .05
503 Denny Neagle .05
504 Gary Redus .05
505 Bob Walk .05
506 John Wehner .05
507 Luis Alicea .05
508 Mark Clark .05
509 Pedro Guerrero .05
510 Rex Hudler .05
511 Brian Jordan .10
512 Omar Olivares .05
513 Jose Oquendo .05
514 Gerald Perry .05
515 Bryn Smith .05
516 Craig Wilson .05
517 Tracy Woodson .05
518 Larry Anderson .05
519 Andy Benes .05
520 Jim Deshaies .05
521 Bruce Hurst .05
522 Randy Myers .05
523 Benito Santiago .05
524 Tim Scott .05
525 Tim Teufel .05
526 Mike Benjamin .05
527 Dave Burba .05
528 Craig Colbert .05
529 Mike Felder .05
530 Bryan Hickerson .05
531 Chris James .05
532 Mark Leonard .05
533 Greg Litton .05
534 Francisco Oliveras .05
535 John Patterson .05
536 Jim Pena .05
537 Dave Righetti .05
538 Robby Thompson .05
539 Jose Uribe .05
540 Matt Williams .30
541 Storm Davis .05
542 Sam Horn .05
543 Tim Hulett .05
544 Craig Lefferts .05
545 Chito Martinez .05
546 Mark McLemore .05
547 Luis Mercedes .05
548 Bob Milacki .05
549 Joe Orsulak .05
550 Billy Ripken .05
551 Cal Ripken, Jr. 1.25
552 Rick Sutcliffe .05
553 Jeff Tackett .05
554 Wade Boggs .35
555 Tom Brunansky .05
556 Jack Clark .05
557 John Dopson .05
558 Mike Gardiner .05
559 Mike Greenwell .05
560 Greg Harris .05
561 Billy Hatcher .05
562 Joe Hesketh .05
563 Tony Pena .05
564 Phil Plantier .05
565 Luis Rivera .05
566 Herm Winningham .05
567 Matt Young .05
568 Bert Blyleven .05
569 Mike Butcher .05
570 Chuck Crim .05
571 *Chad Curtis* .15
572 Tim Fortugno .05
573 Steve Frey .05
574 Gary Gaetti .05
575 Scott Lewis .05
576 Lee Stevens .05
577 Ron Tingley .05
578 Julio Valera .05
579 Shawn Abner .05
580 Joey Cora .05
581 Chris Cron .05
582 Carlton Fisk .10
583 Roberto Hernandez .05
584 Charlie Hough .05
585 Terry Leach .05
586 Donn Pall .05
587 Dan Pasqua .05
588 Steve Sax .05
589 Bobby Thigpen .05
590 Albert Belle .40
591 Felix Fermin .05
592 Glenallen Hill .05
593 Brook Jacoby .05
594 Reggie Jefferson .05
595 Carlos Martinez .05
596 Jose Mesa .05
597 Rod Nichols .05
598 Junior Ortiz .05
599 Eric Plunk .05
600 Ted Power .05
601 Scott Scudder .05
602 Kevin Wickander .05
603 Skeeter Barnes .05
604 Mark Carreon .05
605 Dan Gladden .05
606 Bill Gullickson .05
607 Chad Kreuter .05
608 Mark Leiter .05
609 Mike Munoz .05
610 Rich Rowland .05
611 Frank Tanana .05
612 Walt Terrell .05
613 Alan Trammell .10
614 Lou Whitaker .08
615 Luis Aquino .05
616 Mike Boddicker .05
617 Jim Eisenreich .05
618 Mark Gubicza .05
619 David Howard .05
620 Mike Magnante .05
621 Brent Mayne .05
622 Kevin McReynolds .05
623 *Eddie Pierce* .05
624 Bill Sampen .05
625 Steve Shifflett .05
626 Gary Thurman .05
627 Curtis Wikerson .05
628 Chris Bosio .05
629 Scott Fletcher .05
630 Jim Gantner .05
631 Dave Nilsson .05
632 Jesse Orosco .05
633 Dan Plesac .05
634 Ron Robinson .05
635 Bill Spiers .05
636 Franklin Stubbs .05
637 Willie Banks .05
638 Randy Bush .05
639 Chuck Knoblauch .20
640 Shane Mack .05
641 Mike Pagliarulo .05
642 Jeff Reboulet .05
643 John Smiley .05
644 *Mike Trombley* .08
645 Gary Wayne .05
646 Lenny Webster .05
647 Tim Burke .05
648 Mike Gallego .05
649 Dion James .05
650 Jeff Johnson .05
651 Scott Kamieniecki .05
652 Kevin Maas .05
653 Rich Monteleone .05
654 Jerry Nielsen .05
655 Scott Sanderson .05
656 Mike Stanley .05
657 Gerald Williams .05
658 Curt Young .05
659 Harold Baines .08
660 Kevin Campbell .05
661 Ron Darling .05
662 Kelly Downs .05
663 Eric Fox .05
664 Dave Henderson .05
665 Rick Honeycutt .05
666 Mike Moore .05
667 Jamie Quirk .05
668 Jeff Russell .05
669 Dave Stewart .08
670 Greg Briley .05
671 Dave Cochrane .05
672 Henry Cotto .05
673 Rich DeLucia .05
674 Brian Fisher .05
675 Mark Grant .05
676 Randy Johnson .35
677 Tim Leary .05
678 Pete O'Brien .05
679 Lance Parrish .08
680 Harold Reynolds .05
681 Shane Turner .05
682 Jack Daugherty .05
683 *David Hulse* .10
684 Terry Mathews .05
685 Al Newman .05
686 Edwin Nunez .05
687 Rafael Palmeiro .15
688 Roger Pavlik .05
689 Geno Petralli .05
690 Nolan Ryan .75
691 David Cone .10
692 Alfredo Griffin .05
693 Juan Guzman .08
694 Pat Hentgen .05
695 Randy Knorr .05
696 Bob MacDonald .05
697 Jack Morris .05
698 Ed Sprague .05
699 Dave Stieb .05
700 Pat Tabler .05
701 Mike Timlin .05
702 David Wells .08
703 Eddie Zosky .05
704 Gary Sheffield (League Leaders) .10
705 Darren Daulton (League Leaders) .05
706 Marquis Grissom (League Leaders) .10
707 Greg Maddux (League Leaders) .20
708 Bill Swift (League Leaders) .05
709 Juan Gonzalez (Round Trippers) .25
710 Mark McGwire (Round Trippers) 1.00
711 Cecil Fielder (Round Trippers) .10
712 Albert Belle (Round Trippers) .25
713 Joe Carter (Round Trippers) .10
714 Power Brokers (Frank Thomas, Cecil Fielder) .40
715 Unsung Heroes (Larry Walker, Darren Daulton) .10
716 Hot Corner Hammers (Edgar Martinez, Robin Ventura) .10
717 Start to Finish (Roger Clemens, Dennis Eckersley) .25
718 Checklist .05
719 Checklist .05
720 Checklist .05

1993 Fleer All-Stars

Horizontal-format All-Star cards comprised one of the many 1993 Fleer insert issues. Twelve cards of National League All-Stars were included in Series I wax packs, while a dozen American League All-Stars were found in Series II packs. They are among the more popular and valuable of the '93 Fleer inserts.

		MT
Complete Set A.L. (12):		20.00
Complete Set N.L. (12):		12.00
Common Player:		.50
AMERICAN LEAGUE		
1	Frank Thomas	3.50
2	Roberto Alomar	1.50
3	Edgar Martinez	.60
4	Pat Listach	.50
5	Cecil Fielder	.75
6	Juan Gonzalez	2.00
7	Ken Griffey, Jr.	8.00
8	Joe Carter	.60
9	Kirby Puckett	3.00
10	Brian Harper	.50
11	Dave Fleming	.50
12	Jack McDowell	.60
NATIONAL LEAGUE		
1	Fred McGriff	.60
2	Delino DeShields	.50
3	Gary Sheffield	1.00
4	Barry Larkin	.60
5	Felix Jose	.50
6	Larry Walker	1.50
7	Barry Bonds	2.50
8	Andy Van Slyke	.50
9	Darren Daulton	.50
10	Greg Maddux	5.00
11	Tom Glavine	.75
12	Lee Smith	.60

1993 Fleer Golden Moments

Three cards of this insert set were available in both series of wax packs. Fronts feature black borders with gold-foil baseballs in the corners. The player's name appears in a "Golden Moments" banner at the bottom of the photo. Backs have a portrait photo of the player at top-center and a information on the highlight. The cards are unnumbered and are checklisted here alphabetically within series.

		MT
Complete Set (6):		11.00
Common Player:		.75
	SERIES 1	4.00
(1)	George Brett	3.00
(2)	Mickey Morandini	.75
(3)	Dave Winfield	1.25
	SERIES 2	7.00
(1)	Dennis Eckersley	.75
(2)	Bip Roberts	.75
(3)	Frank Thomas, Juan Gonzalez	4.00

1993 Fleer Major League Prospects

Yet another way to package currently hot rookies and future prospects to increase sales of the base product, there were 18 insert cards found in each series' wax packs. Fronts are bordered in black and have gold-foil highlights. Most of the depicted players were a few seasons away from everyday play in the major leagues.

		MT
Complete Set (36):		25.00
Common Player:		.60
	SERIES 1	18.00
1	Melvin Nieves	.50
2	Sterling Hitchcock	.50
3	Tim Costo	.50
4	Manny Alexander	.50
5	Alan Embree	.50
6	Kevin Young	1.00
7	J.T. Snow	1.50
8	Russ Springer	.50
9	Billy Ashley	.50
10	Kevin Rogers	.50
11	Steve Hosey	.50
12	Eric Wedge	.50
13	Mike Piazza	11.00
14	Jesse Levis	.50
15	Rico Brogna	.50
16	Alex Arias	.50
17	Rod Brewer	.50
18	Troy Neel	.50
	SERIES 2	9.00
1	Scooter Tucker	.50
2	Kerry Woodson	.50
3	Greg Colbrunn	.50
4	Pedro Martinez	3.50
5	Dave Silvestri	.50
6	Kent Bottenfield	.75
7	Rafael Bournigal	.50
8	J.T. Bruett	.50
9	Dave Mlicki	.50
10	Paul Wagner	.50
11	Mike Williams	.50
12	Henry Mercedes	.50
13	Scott Taylor	.50
14	Dennis Moeller	.50
15	Javier Lopez	3.50
16	Steve Cooke	.50
17	Pete Young	.50
18	Ken Ryan	.50

1993 Fleer ProVisions

This three-card insert set in Series I wax packs features the baseball art of Wayne Still. Black-bordered fronts feature a player-fantasy painting at center, with the player's name gold-foil stamped beneath. Backs are also bordered in black and have a white box with a career summary.

		MT
Complete Set (6):		8.00
Common Player:		.75
	SERIES 1	4.00
1	Roberto Alomar	2.00
2	Dennis Eckersley	.75
3	Gary Sheffield	2.00
	SERIES 2	3.00
1	Andy Van Slyke	.75
2	Tom Glavine	1.50
3	Cecil Fielder	1.00

1993 Fleer Rookie Sensations

Ten rookie sensations - some of whom had not been true rookies for several seasons - were featured in this insert issue packaged exclusively in Series 1 and Series 2 cello packs. Card fronts have a player photo set against a silver background and surrounded by a blue border. The player's name and other front printing are in gold foil. Backs are also printed in silver with a blue border. There is a player portrait photo and career summary.

		MT
Complete Set (20):		18.50
Common Player:		.75
	SERIES 1	15.00
1	Kenny Lofton	11.00
2	Cal Eldred	.75
3	Pat Listach	.75
4	Roberto Hernandez	.75
5	Dave Fleming	.75
6	Eric Karros	2.00
7	Reggie Sanders	1.50
8	Derrick May	.75
9	Mike Perez	.75
10	Donovan Osborne	.75
	SERIES 2	7.50
1	Moises Alou	2.75
2	Pedro Astacio	1.25
3	Jim Austin	.75
4	Chad Curtis	.75
5	Gary DiSarcina	.75
6	Scott Livingstone	.75
7	Sam Militello	.75
8	Arthur Rhodes	.75
9	Tim Wakefield	.75
10	Bob Zupcic	.75

1993 Fleer Team Leaders

This 20-card insert issue was exclusive to Series 1 and 2 rack packs. Fronts have a portrait photo, with a small action photo superimposed. At the side is a colored bar with the player's name and "Team Leaders" printed vertically. On back is a career summary. Card borders are a light metallic green and both sides of the card are UV coated.

		MT
Complete Set (20):		45.00
Common Player:		.50
	SERIES 1	35.00
1	Kirby Puckett	5.00
2	Mark McGwire	12.50
3	Pat Listach	.50
4	Roger Clemens	3.00
5	Frank Thomas	4.00
6	Carlos Baerga	.50
7	Brady Anderson	.50
8	Juan Gonzalez	3.00
9	Roberto Alomar	1.25
10	Ken Griffey, Jr.	12.50
	SERIES 2	12.00
1	Will Clark	1.00
2	Terry Pendleton	.50
3	Ray Lankford	.50
4	Eric Karros	.75
5	Gary Sheffield	1.25
6	Ryne Sandberg	2.50
7	Marquis Grissom	.75
8	John Kruk	.50
9	Jeff Bagwell	5.00
10	Andy Van Slyke	.50

1993 Fleer Tom Glavine Career Highlights

This 15-card insert set spotlighted career highlights of Fleer's 1993 spokesman, Tom Glavine. Twelve cards were available in Series 1 and Series 2 packs; cards #13-15 could be obtained only via a special mail offer. A limited number of certified autograph cards were also inserted into packs. Cards #1-4 and 7-10 can each be found with two variations of the writeups on the back. The versions found in Series 2 packaging are the "correct" backs. Neither version carries a premium value.

		MT
Complete Set (15):		5.00
Common Card:		.50
Autographed Card:		75.00
1	Tom Glavine	.50
2	Tom Glavine	.50
3	Tom Glavine	.50
4	Tom Glavine	.50
5	Tom Glavine	.50
6	Tom Glavine	.50
7	Tom Glavine	.50
8	Tom Glavine	.50
9	Tom Glavine	.50
10	Tom Glavine	.50
11	Tom Glavine	.50
12	Tom Glavine	.50
13	Tom Glavine	.50
14	Tom Glavine	.50
15	Tom Glavine	.50

1993 Fleer Final Edition

This 310-card set was sold as a complete set in its own box. Card numbers have the prefix "F". The set also includes 10 Diamond Tribute cards, which are numbered DT1-DT10.

		MT
Complete Set (310):		10.00
Common Player:		.05
1	Steve Bedrosian	.05
2	Jay Howell	.05
3	Greg Maddux	1.50
4	*Greg McMichael*	.05
5	*Tony Tarasco*	.05
6	Jose Bautista	.05
7	Jose Guzman	.05
8	Greg Hibbard	.05
9	Candy Maldonado	.05
10	Randy Myers	.05
11	*Matt Walbeck*	.10
12	Turk Wendell	.05
13	Willie Nelson	.05
14	Greg Cadaret	.05
15	Roberto Kelly	.05
16	Randy Milligan	.05
17	Kevin Mitchell	.05
18	Jeff Reardon	.05
19	John Roper	.05
20	John Smiley	.05
21	Andy Ashby	.08
22	Dante Bichette	.30
23	Willie Blair	.05
24	Pedro Castellano	.05
25	Vinny Castilla	.20
26	Jerald Clark	.05
27	Alex Cole	.05
28	*Scott Fredrickson*	.05
29	*Jay Gainer*	.05
30	Andres Galarraga	.25
31	Joe Girardi	.05
32	Ryan Hawblitzel	.05
33	Charlie Hayes	.05
34	Darren Holmes	.05
35	Chris Jones	.05
36	David Nied	.05
37	*J. Owens*	.10
38	*Lance Painter*	.05
39	Jeff Parrett	.05
40	*Steve Reed*	.05
41	Armando Reynoso	.05
42	Bruce Ruffin	.05
43	*Danny Sheaffer*	.08
44	Keith Shepherd	.05
45	Jim Tatum	.05
46	Gary Wayne	.05
47	Eric Young	.10
48	Luis Aquino	.05
49	Alex Arias	.05
50	Jack Armstrong	.05
51	Bret Barberie	.05
52	Geronimo Berroa	.05
53	Ryan Bowen	.05
54	Greg Briley	.05
55	Chris Carpenter	.05
56	Chuck Carr	.05
57	Jeff Conine	.10
58	Jim Corsi	.05
59	Orestes Destrade	.05
60	Junior Felix	.05
61	Chris Hammond	.05
62	Bryan Harvey	.05
63	Charlie Hough	.05
64	Joe Klink	.05
65	*Richie Lewis*	.10
66	*Mitch Lyden*	.05
67	Bob Natal	.05
68	*Scott Pose*	.05
69	Rich Renteria	.05
70	Benito Santiago	.05
71	Gary Sheffield	.40
72	*Matt Turner*	.10
73	Walt Weiss	.05
74	*Darrell Whitmore*	.10
75	Nigel Wilson	.05
76	Kevin Bass	.05
77	Doug Drabek	.05
78	Tom Edens	.05
79	Chris James	.05
80	Greg Swindell	.05
81	*Omar Daal*	.10
82	Raul Mondesi	1.00
83	Jody Reed	.05
84	Cory Snyder	.05
85	Rick Trlicek	.05
86	Tim Wallach	.05
87	Todd Worrell	.05
88	Tavo Alvarez	.05
89	Frank Bolick	.05
90	Kent Bottenfield	.05
91	Greg Colbrunn	.05
92	Cliff Floyd	.15
93	*Lou Frazier*	.08
94	Mike Gardiner	.05
95	*Mike Lansing*	.30
96	Bill Risley	.05
97	Jeff Shaw	.05
98	Kevin Baez	.05
99	*Tim Bogar*	.10
100	Jeromy Burnitz	.15
101	Mike Draper	.05
102	Darrin Jackson	.05
103	Mike Maddux	.05
104	Joe Orsulak	.05
105	Doug Saunders	.05
106	Frank Tanana	.05
107	Dave Telgheder	.05
108	Larry Anderson	.05
109	Jim Eisenreich	.05
110	Pete Incaviglia	.05
111	Danny Jackson	.05
112	David West	.05
113	Al Martin	.10
114	Blas Minor	.05
115	Dennis Moeller	.05
116	Will Pennyfeather	.05
117	Rich Robertson	.05
118	Ben Shelton	.05
119	Lonnie Smith	.05
120	Freddie Toliver	.05
121	Paul Wagner	.05
122	Kevin Young	.08
123	*Rene Arocha*	.10
124	Gregg Jefferies	.10
125	Paul Kilgus	.05
126	Les Lancaster	.05
127	Joe Magrane	.05
128	Rob Murphy	.05
129	Erik Pappas	.05
130	Stan Royer	.10
131	Ozzie Smith	.75
132	Tom Urbani	.05
133	Mark Whiten	.05
134	Derek Bell	.10
135	Doug Brocail	.05
136	Phil Clark	.05
137	*Mark Ettles*	.05
138	Jeff Gardner	.05
139	*Pat Gomez*	.08
140	Ricky Gutierrez	.05
141	Gene Harris	.05
142	*Kevin Higgins*	.05
143	Trevor Hoffman	.05
144	Phil Plantier	.05
145	*Kerry Taylor*	.05
146	Guillermo Velasquez	.05
147	Wally Whitehurst	.05
148	*Tim Worrell*	.05
149	Todd Benzinger	.05
150	Barry Bonds	.90
151	Greg Brummett	.05
152	Mark Carreon	.05
153	Dave Martinez	.05
154	Jeff Reed	.05
155	Kevin Rogers	.05
156	Harold Baines	.08
157	Damon Buford	.05
158	*Paul Carey*	.05
159	Jeffrey Hammonds	.10
160	Jaime Moyer	.05
161	*Sherman Obando*	.10
162	*John O'Donoghue*	.10
163	Brad Pennington	.05
164	Jim Poole	.05
165	Harold Reynolds	.05
166	Fernando Valenzuela	.08
167	*Jack Voight*	.05
168	Mark Williamson	.05
169	Scott Bankhead	.05
170	Greg Blosser	.05
171	*Jim Byrd*	.05
172	Ivan Calderon	.05
173	Andre Dawson	.12
174	Scott Fletcher	.05
175	Jose Melendez	.05
176	Carlos Quintana	.05
177	Jeff Russell	.05
178	Aaron Sele	.10
179	*Rod Correia*	.05
180	Chili Davis	.08
181	*Jim Edmonds*	1.50
182	Rene Gonzales	.05
183	*Hilly Hathaway*	.05
184	Torey Lovullo	.05
185	Greg Myers	.05
186	Gene Nelson	.05
187	Troy Percival	.05
188	Scott Sanderson	.05
189	*Darryl Scott*	.05
190	*J.T. Snow*	.50
191	Russ Springer	.05
192	Jason Bere	.10
193	Rodney Bolton	.05
194	Ellis Burks	.08
195	Bo Jackson	.12
196	Mike LaValliere	.05
197	Scott Ruffcorn	.05
198	*Jeff Schwartz*	.05
199	Jerry DiPoto	.05
200	Alvaro Espinoza	.05
201	Wayne Kirby	.05
202	*Tom Kramer*	.05
203	Jesse Levis	.05
204	Manny Ramirez	1.50
205	Jeff Treadway	.05
206	*Bill Wertz*	.05
207	Cliff Young	.05
208	Matt Young	.05
209	Kirk Gibson	.05
210	Greg Gohr	.05
211	Bill Krueger	.05
212	Bob MacDonald	.05
213	Mike Moore	.05
214	David Wells	.08
215	*Billy Brewer*	.05
216	David Cone	.15
217	Greg Gagne	.05
218	Mark Gardner	.05
219	Chis Haney	.05
220	Phil Hiatt	.05
221	Jose Lind	.05
222	Juan Bell	.05
223	Tom Brunansky	.05
224	Mike Ignasiak	.05
225	Joe Kmak	.05
226	Tom Lampkin	.05
227	*Graeme Lloyd*	.10
228	Carlos Maldonado	.05
229	Matt Mieske	.08
230	Angel Miranda	.05
231	*Troy O'Leary*	.10
232	Kevin Reimer	.05
233	Larry Casian	.05
234	Jim Deshaies	.05
235	*Eddie Guardado*	.10
236	Chip Hale	.05
237	*Mike Maksudian*	.05
238	David McCarty	.05
239	*Pat Meares*	.10
240	*George Tsamis*	.05
241	Dave Winfield	.15
242	Jim Abbott	.10
243	Wade Boggs	.50
244	*Andy Cook*	.05
245	*Russ Davis*	.15
246	Mike Humphreys	.05
247	Jimmy Key	.05
248	Jim Leyritz	.08
249	Bobby Munoz	.05
250	Paul O'Neill	.10
251	Spike Owen	.05
252	Dave Silvestri	.05
253	*Marcos Armas*	.05
254	Brent Gates	.10
255	Goose Gossage	.05
256	*Scott Lydy*	.05
257	Henry Mercedes	.05
258	*Mike Mohler*	.05
259	Troy Neel	.05
260	Edwin Nunez	.05
261	Craig Paquette	.10
262	Kevin Seitzer	.05
263	Rich Amaral	.05
264	Mike Blowers	.05
265	Chris Bosio	.05
266	Norm Charlton	.05
267	*Jim Converse*	.05
268	*John Cummings*	.10
269	Mike Felder	.05
270	Mike Hampton	.05
271	Bill Haselman	.05
272	Dwayne Henry	.05
273	Greg Litton	.05
274	Mackey Sasser	.05
275	Lee Tinsley	.05
276	David Wainhouse	.05
277	*Jeff Bronkey*	.05
278	Benji Gil	.05
279	Tom Henke	.05
280	Charlie Leibrandt	.05
281	Robb Nen	.10
282	Bill Ripken	.05
283	*Jon Shave*	.05
284	Doug Strange	.05
285	*Matt Whiteside*	.10
286	*Scott Brow*	.05
287	*Willie Canate*	.05
288	Tony Castillo	.05
289	*Domingo Cedeno*	.10
290	Darnell Coles	.05
291	Danny Cox	.05
292	Mark Eichhorn	.05
293	Tony Fernandez	.05
294	Al Leiter	.08
295	Paul Molitor	.75
296	Dave Stewart	.08
297	*Woody Williams*	.05
298	Checklist	.05
299	Checklist	.05
300	Checklist	.05
	DIAMOND TRIBUTE	
1DT	Wade Boggs	.75
2DT	George Brett	1.50
3DT	Andre Dawson	.25
4DT	Carlton Fisk	.25
5DT	Paul Molitor	.90
6DT	Nolan Ryan	4.50
7DT	Lee Smith	.10
8DT	Ozzie Smith	.90
9DT	Dave Winfield	.90
10DT	Robin Yount	.90

1DT	Wade Boggs	.50
2DT	George Brett	1.50
3DT	Andre Dawson	.20
4DT	Carlton Fisk	.20
5DT	Paul Molitor	.60
6DT	Nolan Ryan	4.50
7DT	Lee Smith	.20
8DT	Ozzie Smith	.50
9DT	Dave Winfield	.30
10DT	Robin Yount	1.00

1994 Fleer "Highlights" Promo Sheet

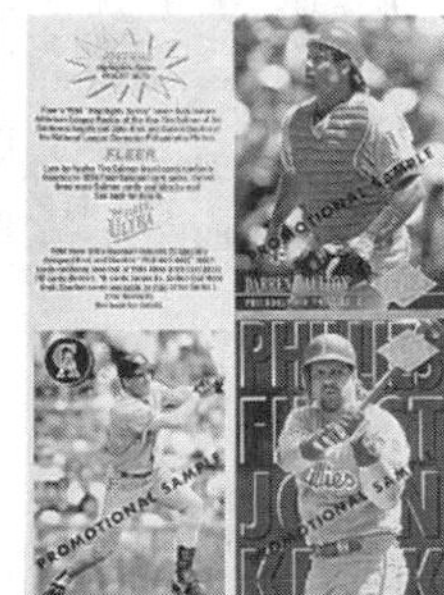

To introduce its special insert card series honoring 1993 A.L. Rookie of the Year Tim Salmon and Phillies stars John Kruk and Darren Daulton, Fleer issued this 5" x 7" promo sheet. The three player cards on the sheet are similar to the issued versions except they have black overprinting on front and back which reads, "PROMOTIONAL SAMPLE". The non-player segment of the sheet has details about the inserts and special mail-in offers for additional cards.

		MT
Complete Set, Sheet:		8.00
Common Card:		3.00
9	John Kruk (Fleer Ultra Phillies Finest)	3.00
69	Tim Salmon (Fleer)	4.00
243	Darren Daulton (Fleer Ultra)	3.00

1994 Fleer

Fleer's 720-card 1994 set, released in one series, includes another 204 insert cards to be pursued by collectors. Every pack includes one of the cards, randomly inserted from among the 12 insert sets. Regular cards have action photos on front, with a team logo in one of the lower corners. The player's name and position is stamped in gold foil around the logo. On back, another color player photo is overprinted with color boxes, data and stats, leaving a clear image of the player's face, 1-1/2" x 1-3/4" in size. Cards are UV coated on both sides.

		MT
Complete Set (720):		45.00
Common Player:		.05
Pack (15):		1.00
Wax Box (36):		30.00
1	Brady Anderson	.15
2	Harold Baines	.08
3	Mike Devereaux	.05
4	Todd Frohwirth	.05
5	Jeffrey Hammonds	.08
6	Chris Hoiles	.05
7	Tim Hulett	.05
8	Ben McDonald	.05
9	Mark McLemore	.05
10	Alan Mills	.05
11	Jamie Moyer	.05
12	Mike Mussina	.50
13	Gregg Olson	.05
14	Mike Pagliarulo	.05
15	Brad Pennington	.05
16	Jim Poole	.05
17	Harold Reynolds	.05
18	Arthur Rhodes	.05
19	Cal Ripken, Jr.	2.50
20	David Segui	.05
21	Rick Sutcliffe	.05
22	Fernando Valenzuela	.08
23	Jack Voigt	.05
24	Mark Williamson	.05
25	Scott Bankhead	.05
26	Roger Clemens	1.50
27	Scott Cooper	.05
28	Danny Darwin	.05
29	Andre Dawson	.10
30	Rob Deer	.05
31	John Dopson	.05
32	Scott Fletcher	.05
33	Mike Greenwell	.05
34	Greg Harris	.05
35	Billy Hatcher	.05
36	Bob Melvin	.05
37	Tony Pena	.05
38	Paul Quantrill	.05
39	Carlos Quintana	.05
40	Ernest Riles	.05
41	Jeff Russell	.05
42	Ken Ryan	.05
43	Aaron Sele	.08
44	John Valentin	.10
45	Mo Vaughn	.50
46	Frank Viola	.05
47	Bob Zupcic	.05
48	Mike Butcher	.05
49	Rod Correia	.05
50	Chad Curtis	.10
51	Chili Davis	.08
52	Gary DiSarcina	.05
53	Damion Easley	.10
54	Jim Edmonds	.25
55	Chuck Finley	.05
56	Steve Frey	.05
57	Rene Gonzales	.05
58	Joe Grahe	.05
59	Hilly Hathaway	.05
60	Stan Javier	.05
61	Mark Langston	.05
62	Phil Leftwich	.05
63	Torey Lovullo	.05
64	Joe Magrane	.05
65	Greg Myers	.05
66	Ken Patterson	.05
67	Eduardo Perez	.05
68	Luis Polonia	.05
69	Tim Salmon	.25
69a	Tim Salmon (overprinted PROMOTIONAL SAMPLE)	3.00
70	J.T. Snow	.15
71	Ron Tingley	.05
72	Julio Valera	.05
73	Wilson Alvarez	.05
74	Tim Belcher	.05
75	George Bell	.05
76	Jason Bere	.05
77	Rod Bolton	.05
78	Ellis Burks	.05
79	Joey Cora	.05
80	Alex Fernandez	.08
81	Craig Grebeck	.05
82	Ozzie Guillen	.05
83	Roberto Hernandez	.05
84	Bo Jackson	.15
85	Lance Johnson	.05
86	Ron Karkovice	.05
87	Mike LaValliere	.05
88	Kirk McCaskill	.05
89	Jack McDowell	.05
90	Warren Newson	.05
91	Dan Pasqua	.05
92	Scott Radinsky	.05
93	Tim Raines	.08
94	Steve Sax	.05
95	Jeff Schwarz	.05
96	Frank Thomas	1.50
97	Robin Ventura	.15
98	Sandy Alomar, Jr.	.08
99	Carlos Baerga	.05
100	Albert Belle	.75
101	Mark Clark	.05
102	Jerry DiPoto	.05
103	Alvaro Espinoza	.05
104	Felix Fermin	.05
105	Jeremy Hernandez	.05
106	Reggie Jefferson	.05
107	Wayne Kirby	.05
108	Tom Kramer	.05
109	Mark Lewis	.05
110	Derek Lilliquist	.05
111	Kenny Lofton	.50
112	Candy Maldonado	.05
113	Jose Mesa	.05
114	Jeff Mutis	.05
115	Charles Nagy	.08
116	Bob Ojeda	.05
117	Junior Ortiz	.05
118	Eric Plunk	.05
119	Manny Ramirez	1.00
120	Paul Sorrento	.05
121	Jim Thome	.40
122	Jeff Treadway	.05
123	Bill Wertz	.05
124	Skeeter Barnes	.05
125	Milt Cuyler	.05
126	Eric Davis	.08
127	John Doherty	.05
128	Cecil Fielder	.08
129	Travis Fryman	.10
130	Kirk Gibson	.05
131	Dan Gladden	.05
132	Greg Gohr	.05
133	Chris Gomez	.05
134	Bill Gullickson	.05
135	Mike Henneman	.05
136	Kurt Knudsen	.05
137	Chad Kreuter	.05
138	Bill Krueger	.05
139	Scott Livingstone	.05
140	Bob MacDonald	.05
141	Mike Moore	.05
142	Tony Phillips	.05
143	Mickey Tettleton	.05
144	Alan Trammell	.08
145	David Wells	.08
146	Lou Whitaker	.05
147	Kevin Appier	.05
148	Stan Belinda	.05
149	George Brett	.50
150	Billy Brewer	.05
151	Hubie Brooks	.05
152	David Cone	.15
153	Gary Gaetti	.05
154	Greg Gagne	.05
155	Tom Gordon	.05
156	Mark Gubicza	.05
157	Chris Gwynn	.05
158	John Habyan	.05
159	Chris Haney	.05
160	Phil Hiatt	.05
161	Felix Jose	.05
162	Wally Joyner	.08
163	Jose Lind	.05
164	Mike Macfarlane	.05
165	Mike Magnante	.05
166	Brent Mayne	.05
167	Brian McRae	.05
168	Kevin McReynolds	.05
169	Keith Miller	.05
170	Jeff Montgomery	.05
171	Hipolito Pichardo	.05
172	Rico Rossy	.05
173	Juan Bell	.05
174	Ricky Bones	.05
175	Cal Eldred	.05
176	Mike Fetters	.05
177	Darryl Hamilton	.05
178	Doug Henry	.05
179	Mike Ignasiak	.05
180	John Jaha	.08
181	Pat Listach	.05
182	Graeme Lloyd	.05
183	Matt Mieske	.05
184	Angel Miranda	.05
185	Jaime Navarro	.05
186	Dave Nilsson	.05
187	Troy O'Leary	.05
188	Jesse Orosco	.05
189	Kevin Reimer	.05
190	Kevin Seitzer	.05
191	Bill Spiers	.05
192	B.J. Surhoff	.08
193	Dickie Thon	.05
194	Jose Valentin	.05
195	Greg Vaughn	.10
196	Bill Wegman	.05
197	Robin Yount	.25
198	Rick Aguilera	.05
199	Willie Banks	.05
200	Bernardo Brito	.05
201	Larry Casian	.05
202	Scott Erickson	.05
203	Eddie Guardado	.05
204	Mark Guthrie	.05
205	Chip Hale	.05
206	Brian Harper	.05
207	Mike Hartley	.05
208	Kent Hrbek	.08
209	Terry Jorgensen	.05
210	Chuck Knoblauch	.20
211	Gene Larkin	.05
212	Shane Mack	.05
213	David McCarty	.05
214	Pat Meares	.05
215	Pedro Munoz	.05
216	Derek Parks	.05
217	Kirby Puckett	1.25
218	Jeff Reboulet	.05
219	Kevin Tapani	.05
220	Mike Trombley	.05
221	George Tsamis	.05
222	Carl Willis	.05
223	Dave Winfield	.25
224	Jim Abbott	.08
225	Paul Assenmacher	.05
226	Wade Boggs	.40
227	Russ Davis	.05
228	Steve Farr	.05
229	Mike Gallego	.05
230	Paul Gibson	.05
231	Steve Howe	.05
232	Dion James	.05
233	Domingo Jean	.05
234	Scott Kamieniecki	.05
235	Pat Kelly	.05
236	Jimmy Key	.05
237	Jim Leyritz	.08
238	Kevin Maas	.05
239	Don Mattingly	1.50
240	Rich Monteleone	.05
241	Bobby Munoz	.05
242	Matt Nokes	.05
243	Paul O'Neill	.20
244	Spike Owen	.05
245	Melido Perez	.05
246	Lee Smith	.08
247	Mike Stanley	.05
248	Danny Tartabull	.05
249	Randy Velarde	.05
250	Bob Wickman	.05
251	Bernie Williams	.50
252	Mike Aldrete	.05
253	Marcos Armas	.05
254	Lance Blankenship	.05
255	Mike Bordick	.05
256	Scott Brosius	.05
257	Jerry Browne	.05
258	Ron Darling	.05
259	Kelly Downs	.05
260	Dennis Eckersley	.08
261	Brent Gates	.05
262	Goose Gossage	.05
263	Scott Hemond	.05
264	Dave Henderson	.05
265	Rick Honeycutt	.05
266	Vince Horsman	.05
267	Scott Lydy	.05
268	Mark McGwire	3.00
269	Mike Mohler	.05
270	Troy Neel	.05
271	Edwin Nunez	.05
272	Craig Paquette	.05
273	Ruben Sierra	.05
274	Terry Steinbach	.05
275	Todd Van Poppel	.05
276	Bob Welch	.05
277	Bobby Witt	.05
278	Rich Amaral	.05
279	Mike Blowers	.05
280	Bret Boone	.08
281	Chris Bosio	.05
282	Jay Buhner	.08
283	Norm Charlton	.05
284	Mike Felder	.05
285	Dave Fleming	.05
286	Ken Griffey, Jr.	3.00
287	Erik Hanson	.05
288	Bill Haselman	.05
289	*Brad Holman*	.10
290	Randy Johnson	.75
291	Tim Leary	.05
292	Greg Litton	.05
293	Dave Magadan	.05
294	Edgar Martinez	.08
295	Tino Martinez	.12
296	Jeff Nelson	.05
297	*Erik Plantenberg*	.08
298	Mackey Sasser	.05
299	*Brian Turang*	.08
300	Dave Valle	.05
301	Omar Vizquel	.08
302	Brian Bohanon	.05
303	Kevin Brown	.05
304	Jose Canseco	.50
305	Mario Diaz	.05
306	Julio Franco	.05
307	Juan Gonzalez	.75
308	Tom Henke	.05
309	David Hulse	.05
310	Manuel Lee	.05
311	Craig Lefferts	.05

No.	Player	Price
312	Charlie Leibrandt	.05
313	Rafael Palmeiro	.40
314	Dean Palmer	.05
315	Roger Pavlik	.05
316	Dan Peltier	.05
317	Geno Petralli	.05
318	Gary Redus	.05
319	Ivan Rodriguez	.75
320	Kenny Rogers	.05
321	Nolan Ryan	2.50
322	Doug Strange	.05
323	Matt Whiteside	.05
324	Roberto Alomar	.75
325	Pat Borders	.05
326	Joe Carter	.08
327	Tony Castillo	.05
328	Darnell Coles	.05
329	Danny Cox	.05
330	Mark Eichhorn	.05
331	Tony Fernandez	.05
332	Alfredo Griffin	.05
333	Juan Guzman	.05
334	Rickey Henderson	.25
335	Pat Hentgen	.05
336	Randy Knorr	.05
337	Al Leiter	.08
338	Paul Molitor	.40
339	Jack Morris	.05
340	John Olerud	.25
341	Dick Schofield	.05
342	Ed Sprague	.05
343	Dave Stewart	.08
344	Todd Stottlemyre	.05
345	Mike Timlin	.05
346	Duane Ward	.05
347	Turner Ward	.05
348	Devon White	.08
349	Woody Williams	.05
350	Steve Avery	.05
351	Steve Bedrosian	.05
352	Rafael Belliard	.05
353	Damon Berryhill	.05
354	Jeff Blauser	.05
355	Sid Bream	.05
356	Francisco Cabrera	.05
357	Marvin Freeman	.05
358	Ron Gant	.08
359	Tom Glavine	.25
360	Jay Howell	.05
361	Dave Justice	.20
362	Ryan Klesko	.20
363	Mark Lemke	.05
364	Javier Lopez	.15
365	Greg Maddux	2.00
366	Fred McGriff	.20
367	Greg McMichael	.05
368	Kent Mercker	.05
369	Otis Nixon	.05
370	Greg Olson	.05
371	Bill Pecota	.05
372	Terry Pendleton	.05
373	Deion Sanders	.25
374	Pete Smith	.05
375	John Smoltz	.12
376	Mike Stanton	.05
377	Tony Tarasco	.05
378	Mark Wohlers	.05
379	Jose Bautista	.05
380	Shawn Boskie	.05
381	Steve Buechele	.05
382	Frank Castillo	.05
383	Mark Grace	.15
384	Jose Guzman	.05
385	Mike Harkey	.05
386	Greg Hibbard	.05
387	Glenallen Hill	.05
388	Steve Lake	.05
389	Derrick May	.05
390	Chuck McElroy	.05
391	Mike Morgan	.05
392	Randy Myers	.05
393	Dan Plesac	.05
394	Kevin Roberson	.05
395	Rey Sanchez	.05
396	Ryne Sandberg	.50
397	Bob Scanlan	.05
398	Dwight Smith	.05
399	Sammy Sosa	1.50
400	Jose Vizcaino	.05
401	Rick Wilkins	.05
402	Willie Wilson	.05
403	Eric Yelding	.05
404	Bobby Ayala	.05
405	Jeff Branson	.05
406	Tom Browning	.05
407	Jacob Brumfield	.05
408	Tim Costo	.05
409	Rob Dibble	.05
410	Willie Greene	.05
411	Thomas Howard	.05
412	Roberto Kelly	.05
413	Bill Landrum	.05
414	Barry Larkin	.25
415	*Larry Luebbers*	.05
416	Kevin Mitchell	.05
417	Hal Morris	.05
418	Joe Oliver	.05
419	Tim Pugh	.05
420	Jeff Reardon	.05
421	Jose Rijo	.05
422	Bip Roberts	.05
423	John Roper	.05
424	Johnny Ruffin	.05
425	Chris Sabo	.05
426	Juan Samuel	.05
427	Reggie Sanders	.05
428	Scott Service	.05
429	John Smiley	.05
430	*Jerry Spradlin*	.05
431	Kevin Wickander	.05
432	Freddie Benavides	.05
433	Dante Bichette	.25
434	Willie Blair	.05
435	Daryl Boston	.05
436	Kent Bottenfield	.05
437	Vinny Castilla	.15
438	Jerald Clark	.05
439	Alex Cole	.05
440	Andres Galarraga	.40
441	Joe Girardi	.05
442	Greg Harris	.05
443	Charlie Hayes	.05
444	Darren Holmes	.05
445	Chris Jones	.05
446	Roberto Mejia	.05
447	David Nied	.05
448	J. Owens	.05
449	Jeff Parrett	.05
450	Steve Reed	.05
451	Armando Reynoso	.05
452	Bruce Ruffin	.05
453	Mo Sanford	.05
454	Danny Sheaffer	.05
455	Jim Tatum	.05
456	Gary Wayne	.05
457	Eric Young	.08
458	Luis Aquino	.05
459	Alex Arias	.05
460	Jack Armstrong	.05
461	Bret Barberie	.05
462	Ryan Bowen	.05
463	Chuck Carr	.05
464	Jeff Conine	.08
465	Henry Cotto	.05
466	Orestes Destrade	.05
467	Chris Hammond	.05
468	Bryan Harvey	.05
469	Charlie Hough	.05
470	Joe Klink	.05
471	Richie Lewis	.05
472	*Bob Natal*	.10
473	*Pat Rapp*	.15
474	*Rich Renteria*	.08
475	Rich Rodriguez	.05
476	Benito Santiago	.05
477	Gary Sheffield	.20
478	Matt Turner	.05
479	David Weathers	.05
480	Walt Weiss	.05
481	Darrell Whitmore	.05
482	Eric Anthony	.05
483	Jeff Bagwell	1.00
484	Kevin Bass	.05
485	Craig Biggio	.25
486	Ken Caminiti	.15
487	Andujar Cedeno	.05
488	Chris Donnels	.05
489	Doug Drabek	.05
490	Steve Finley	.05
491	Luis Gonzalez	.08
492	Pete Harnisch	.05
493	Xavier Hernandez	.05
494	Doug Jones	.05
495	Todd Jones	.05
496	Darryl Kile	.05
497	Al Osuna	.05
498	Mark Portugal	.05
499	Scott Servais	.05
500	Greg Swindell	.05
501	Eddie Taubensee	.05
502	Jose Uribe	.05
503	Brian Williams	.05
504	Billy Ashley	.05
505	Pedro Astacio	.10
506	Brett Butler	.05
507	Tom Candiotti	.05
508	Omar Daal	.05
509	Jim Gott	.05
510	Kevin Gross	.05
511	Dave Hansen	.05
512	Carlos Hernandez	.05
513	Orel Hershiser	.08
514	Eric Karros	.12
515	Pedro Martinez	.75
516	Ramon Martinez	.08
517	Roger McDowell	.05
518	Raul Mondesi	.50
519	Jose Offerman	.05
520	Mike Piazza	2.00
521	Jody Reed	.05
522	Henry Rodriguez	.08
523	Mike Sharperson	.05
524	Cory Snyder	.05
525	Darryl Strawberry	.10
526	Rick Trlicek	.05
527	Tim Wallach	.05
528	Mitch Webster	.05
529	Steve Wilson	.05
530	Todd Worrell	.05
531	Moises Alou	.10
532	Brian Barnes	.05
533	Sean Berry	.05
534	Greg Colbrunn	.05
535	Delino DeShields	.05
536	Jeff Fassero	.05
537	Darrin Fletcher	.05
538	Cliff Floyd	.10
539	Lou Frazier	.05
540	Marquis Grissom	.10
541	Butch Henry	.05
542	Ken Hill	.05
543	Mike Lansing	.10
544	*Brian Looney*	.10
545	Dennis Martinez	.08
546	Chris Nabholz	.05
547	Randy Ready	.05
548	Mel Rojas	.05
549	Kirk Rueter	.05
550	Tim Scott	.05
551	Jeff Shaw	.05
552	Tim Spehr	.05
553	John VanderWal	.05
554	Larry Walker	.40
555	John Wetteland	.05
556	Rondell White	.25
557	Tim Bogar	.08
558	Bobby Bonilla	.08
559	Jeremy Burnitz	.08
560	Sid Fernandez	.05
561	John Franco	.05
562	Dave Gallagher	.05
563	Dwight Gooden	.10
564	Eric Hillman	.05
565	Todd Hundley	.12
566	Jeff Innis	.05
567	Darrin Jackson	.05
568	Howard Johnson	.05
569	Bobby Jones	.05
570	Jeff Kent	.05
571	Mike Maddux	.05
572	Jeff McKnight	.05
573	Eddie Murray	.20
574	Charlie O'Brien	.05
575	Joe Orsulak	.05
576	Bret Saberhagen	.08
577	Pete Schourek	.05
578	Dave Telgheder	.05
579	Ryan Thompson	.05
580	Anthony Young	.05
581	Ruben Amaro	.05
582	Larry Andersen	.05
583	Kim Batiste	.05
584	Wes Chamberlain	.05
585	Darren Daulton	.05
586	Mariano Duncan	.05
587	Len Dykstra	.05
588	Jim Eisenreich	.05
589	Tommy Greene	.05
590	Dave Hollins	.08
591	Pete Incaviglia	.05
592	Danny Jackson	.05
593	Ricky Jordan	.05
594	John Kruk	.05
595	Roger Mason	.05
596	Mickey Morandini	.05
597	Terry Mulholland	.05
598	Todd Pratt	.05
599	Ben Rivera	.05
600	Curt Schilling	.08
601	Kevin Stocker	.05
602	Milt Thompson	.05
603	David West	.05
604	Mitch Williams	.05
605	Jay Bell	.05
606	Dave Clark	.05
607	Steve Cooke	.05
608	Tom Foley	.05
609	Carlos Garcia	.05
610	Joel Johnston	.05
611	Jeff King	.05
612	Al Martin	.08
613	Lloyd McClendon	.05
614	Orlando Merced	.05
615	Blas Minor	.05
616	Denny Neagle	.05
617	*Mark Petkovsek*	.10
618	Tom Prince	.05
619	Don Slaught	.05
620	Zane Smith	.05
621	Randy Tomlin	.05
622	Andy Van Slyke	.05
623	Paul Wagner	.05
624	Tim Wakefield	.05
625	Bob Walk	.05
626	Kevin Young	.10
627	Luis Alicea	.05
628	Rene Arocha	.05
629	Rod Brewer	.05
630	Rheal Cormier	.05
631	Bernard Gilkey	.08
632	Lee Guetterman	.05
633	Gregg Jefferies	.08
634	Brian Jordan	.10
635	Les Lancaster	.05
636	Ray Lankford	.08
637	Rob Murphy	.05
638	Omar Olivares	.05
639	Jose Oquendo	.05
640	Donovan Osborne	.05
641	Tom Pagnozzi	.05
642	Erik Pappas	.05
643	Geronimo Pena	.05
644	Mike Perez	.05
645	Gerald Perry	.05
646	Ozzie Smith	.40
647	Bob Tewksbury	.05
648	Allen Watson	.05
649	Mark Whiten	.05
650	Tracy Woodson	.05
651	Todd Zeile	.08
652	Andy Ashby	.08
653	Brad Ausmus	.05
654	Billy Bean	.05
655	Derek Bell	.08
656	Andy Benes	.08
657	Doug Brocail	.05
658	Jarvis Brown	.05
659	Archi Cianfrocco	.05
660	Phil Clark	.05
661	Mark Davis	.05
662	Jeff Gardner	.05
663	Pat Gomez	.05
664	Ricky Gutierrez	.05
665	Tony Gwynn	1.25
666	Gene Harris	.05
667	Kevin Higgins	.05
668	Trevor Hoffman	.10
669	*Pedro A. Martinez*	.05
670	Tim Mauser	.05
671	Melvin Nieves	.05
672	Phil Plantier	.05
673	Frank Seminara	.05
674	Craig Shipley	.05
675	Kerry Taylor	.05
676	Tim Teufel	.05
677	Guillermo Velasquez	.05
678	Wally Whitehurst	.05
679	Tim Worrell	.05
680	Rod Beck	.05
681	Mike Benjamin	.05
682	Todd Benzinger	.05
683	Bud Black	.05
684	Barry Bonds	.75
685	Jeff Brantley	.05
686	Dave Burba	.05
687	John Burkett	.05
688	Mark Carreon	.05
689	Will Clark	.25
690	Royce Clayton	.05
691	Bryan Hickerson	.05
692	Mike Jackson	.05
693	Darren Lewis	.05
694	Kirt Manwaring	.05
695	Dave Martinez	.05

696	Willie McGee	.08
697	John Patterson	.05
698	Jeff Reed	.05
699	Kevin Rogers	.05
700	Scott Sanderson	.05
701	Steve Scarsone	.05
702	Billy Swift	.05
703	Robby Thompson	.05
704	Matt Williams	.25
705	Trevor Wilson	.05
706	"Brave New World" (Fred McGriff, Ron Gant, Dave Justice)	.10
707	"1-2 Punch" (Paul Molitor, John Olerud)	.15
708	"American Heat" (Mike Mussina, Jack McDowell)	.10
709	"Together Again" (Lou Whitaker, Alan Trammell)	.10
710	"Lone Star Lumber" (Rafael Palmeiro, Juan Gonzalez)	.25
711	"Batmen" (Brett Butler, Tony Gwynn)	.10
712	"Twin Peaks" (Kirby Puckett, Chuck Knoblauch)	.25
713	"Back to Back" (Mike Piazza, Eric Karros)	.50
714	Checklist	.05
715	Checklist	.05
716	Checklist	.05
717	Checklist	.05
718	Checklist	.05
719	Checklist	.05
720	Checklist	.05

1994 Fleer All-Stars

Each league's 25 representatives for the 1993 All-Star Game are featured in this insert set. Fronts have a player action photo with a rippling American flag in the top half of the background. The '93 All-Star logo is featured at the bottom, along with a gold-foil impression of the player's name. The flag motif is repeated at top of the card back, along with a player portrait photo set against a red (American League) or blue (National League) background. Odds of finding one of the 50 All-Star inserts are one in every two 15-card foil packs.

		MT
Complete Set (50):		20.00
Common Player:		.25
1	Roberto Alomar	1.00
2	Carlos Baerga	.25
3	Albert Belle	.75
4	Wade Boggs	.75
5	Joe Carter	.25
6	Scott Cooper	.25
7	Cecil Fielder	.25
8	Travis Fryman	.25
9	Juan Gonzalez	1.00
10	Ken Griffey, Jr.	4.00
11	Pat Hentgen	.25
12	Randy Johnson	1.00
13	Jimmy Key	.25
14	Mark Langston	.25
15	Jack McDowell	.25
16	Paul Molitor	.75
17	Jeff Montgomery	.25
18	Mike Mussina	.75
19	John Olerud	.35
20	Kirby Puckett	1.00
21	Cal Ripken, Jr.	4.00
22	Ivan Rodriguez	1.00
23	Frank Thomas	2.00
24	Greg Vaughn	.25
25	Duane Ward	.25
26	Steve Avery	.25
27	Rod Beck	.25
28	Jay Bell	.25
29	Andy Benes	.25
30	Jeff Blauser	.25
31	Barry Bonds	1.00
32	Bobby Bonilla	.25
33	John Burkett	.25
34	Darren Daulton	.25
35	Andres Galarraga	.50
36	Tom Glavine	.35
37	Mark Grace	.50
38	Marquis Grissom	.25
39	Tony Gwynn	1.50
40	Bryan Harvey	.25
41	Dave Hollins	.25
42	Dave Justice	.35
43	Darryl Kile	.25
44	John Kruk	.25
45	Barry Larkin	.40
46	Terry Mulholland	.25
47	Mike Piazza	2.50
48	Ryne Sandberg	1.00
49	Gary Sheffield	.50
50	John Smoltz	.50

1994 Fleer Award Winners

The 1993 MVP, Cy Young and Rookie of the Year award winners from each league are featured in this insert set. Cards are UV coated on both sides. Three different croppings of the same player action photo are featured on the front, with the player's name and other printing in gold foil. Backs have a player portrait and short summary of his previous season's performance. According to the company, odds of finding one of these horizontal-format inserts were one in 37 packs.

		MT
Complete Set (6):		9.00
Common Player:		.75
1	Frank Thomas	3.00
2	Barry Bonds	1.50
3	Jack McDowell	.75
4	Greg Maddux	3.00
5	Tim Salmon	1.00
6	Mike Piazza	3.00

1994 Fleer Golden Moments

Ten highlights from the 1993 Major League baseball season are commemorated in this insert set. Each of the cards has a title which summarizes the historical moment. These inserts were available exclusively in Fleer cards packaged for large retail outlets.

		MT
Complete Set (10):		20.00
Common Player:		.50
1	"Four in One" (Mark Whiten)	.50
2	"Left and Right" (Carlos Baerga)	.50
3	"3,000 Hit Club" (Dave Winfield)	1.50
4	"Eight Straight" (Ken Griffey, Jr.)	10.00
5	"Triumphant Return" (Bo Jackson)	1.50
6	"Farewell to Baseball" (George Brett)	3.00
7	"Farewell to Baseball" (Nolan Ryan)	8.00
8	"Thirty Times Six" (Fred McGriff)	.75
9	"Enters 5th Dimension" (Frank Thomas)	4.00
10	"The No-Hit Parade" (Chris Bosio, Jim Abbott, Darryl Kile)	.50

1994 Fleer Golden Moments Super

Super-size (3-1/2" x 5") versions of the Golden Moments insert set were included in hobby cases at the rate of one set, in a specially-printed folder, per 20-box case. Each card carries a serial number designating its position in an edition of 10,000.

		MT
Complete Set (10):		37.00
Common Player:		2.50
1	"Four in One" (Mark Whiten)	2.50
2	"Left and Right" (Carlos Baerga)	2.50
3	"3,000 Hit Club" (Dave Winfield)	3.75
4	"Eight Straight" (Ken Griffey, Jr.)	12.00
5	"Triumphant Return" (Bo Jackson)	3.75
6	"Farewell to Baseball" (George Brett)	5.00
7	"Farewell to Baseball" (Nolan Ryan)	7.50
8	"Thirty Times Six" (Fred McGriff)	3.00
9	"Enters 5th Dimension" (Frank Thomas)	5.00
10	"The No-Hit Parade" (Chris Bosio, Jim Abbott, Darryl Kile)	2.50

1994 Fleer League Leaders

Twelve players who led the major leagues in various statistical categories in 1993 are featured in this insert set. Cards are UV coated and have gold-foil stamping on both sides. Within a light metallic green border, card fronts feature a color action photo superimposed over a similar photo in black-and-white. The category in which the player led his league is printed down the right border.

Other printing is gold-foil. On back is a color photo and details of the league-leading performance. Stated odds of finding a League Leaders card were one per 17 packs.

		MT
Complete Set (12):		3.00
Common Player:		.10
1	John Olerud	.15
2	Albert Belle	.50
3	Rafael Palmeiro	.25
4	Kenny Lofton	.50
5	Jack McDowell	.10
6	Kevin Appier	.10
7	Andres Galarraga	.25
8	Barry Bonds	.50
9	Len Dykstra	.10
10	Chuck Carr	.10
11	Tom Glavine	.20
12	Greg Maddux	1.25

1994 Fleer Lumber Co.

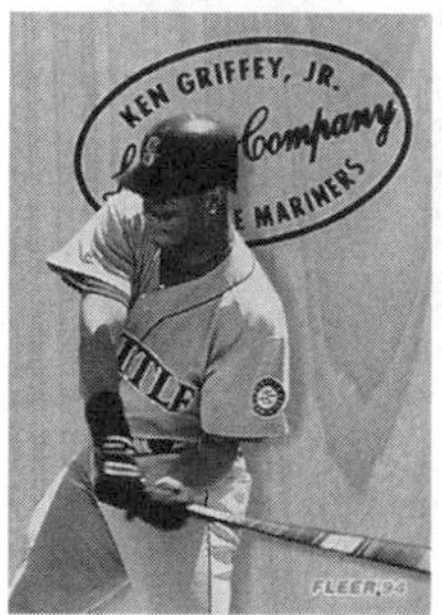

This insert set features the major leagues' top home run hitters. Inserted only in 21-card jumbo packs, odds of finding one were given as one per five packs. Card fronts feature player action photos against a background resembling the label area of a baseball bat. On back is a background photo of a row of bats on the dirt. A player write-up and close-up photo complete the design.

		MT
Complete Set (10):		11.00
Common Player:		.60
1	Albert Belle	1.25
2	Barry Bonds	1.25
3	Ron Gant	.60
4	Juan Gonzalez	2.00
5	Ken Griffey, Jr.	5.00
6	Dave Justice	.75
7	Fred McGriff	.60
8	Rafael Palmeiro	1.00
9	Frank Thomas	1.50
10	Matt Williams	.75

1994 Fleer Major League Prospects

Thirty-five of the game's promising young stars are featured in this insert set. A light green metallic border frames a player photo, with his team logo lightly printed over the background. Most of the printing is gold-foil stamped. Backs have a player photo against a pinstriped background. A light blue box contains career details. Given odds of finding a "Major League Prospects" card are one in six packs.

		MT
Complete Set (35):		9.00
Common Player:		.20
1	Kurt Abbott	.30
2	Brian Anderson	.20
3	Rich Aude	.20
4	Cory Bailey	.20
5	Danny Bautista	.20
6	Marty Cordova	.50
7	Tripp Cromer	.20
8	Midre Cummings	.20
9	Carlos Delgado	2.00
10	Steve Dreyer	.20
11	Steve Dunn	.20
12	Jeff Granger	.20
13	Tyrone Hill	.20
14	Denny Hocking	.20
15	John Hope	.20
16	Butch Huskey	.40
17	Miguel Jimenez	.20
18	Chipper Jones	6.00
19	Steve Karsay	.20
20	Mike Kelly	.20
21	Mike Lieberthal	.50
22	Albie Lopez	.20
23	Jeff McNeely	.20
24	Dan Miceli	.30
25	Nate Minchey	.20
26	Marc Newfield	.20
27	Darren Oliver	.20
28	Luis Ortiz	.20
29	Curtis Pride	.40
30	Roger Salkeld	.25
31	Scott Sanders	.30
32	Dave Staton	.20
33	Salomon Torres	.20
34	Steve Trachsel	.30
35	Chris Turner	.25

1994 Fleer ProVisions

Nine players are featured in this insert set. Cards feature the fantasy artwork of Wayne Still in a format that produces one large image when all nine cards are properly arranged. Besides the art, card fronts feature the player's name in gold-foil. Backs have a background in several shades of red, with the player's name and team at the top in white. A short career summary is printed in black. Odds of finding this particular insert in a pack are one in 12.

		MT
Complete Set (9):		3.00
Common Player:		.20
1	Darren Daulton	.20
2	John Olerud	.25
3	Matt Williams	.50
4	Carlos Baerga	.20
5	Ozzie Smith	.75
6	Juan Gonzalez	1.00
7	Jack McDowell	.20
8	Mike Piazza	2.00
9	Tony Gwynn	1.50

1994 Fleer Rookie Sensations

This insert set features the top rookies from 1993. These inserts were available only in 21-card jumbo packs, with stated odds of one in four packs. Full-bleed fronts have a pair of player photos - one highlighted by a neon outline - superimposed on a graduated background approximating the team colors. Team uniform logo details appear vertically at the right or left side. The player's name is gold-foil stamped in a banner at bottom. The Rookie Sensations and Fleer logos are also gold-imprinted. On back, the team uniform logo is repeated on a white background, along with another player photo and a short write-up.

		MT
Complete Set (20):		15.00
Common Player:		.40
1	Rene Arocha	.40
2	Jason Bere	.40
3	Jeromy Burnitz	.75
4	Chuck Carr	.40
5	Jeff Conine	.50
6	Steve Cooke	.40
7	Cliff Floyd	.60
8	Jeffrey Hammonds	.40
9	Wayne Kirby	.40
10	Mike Lansing	.50
11	Al Martin	.45
12	Greg McMichael	.40
13	Troy Neel	.40
14	Mike Piazza	6.00
15	Armando Reynoso	.40
16	Kirk Rueter	.40
17	Tim Salmon	2.00
18	Aaron Sele	.60
19	J.T. Snow	.75
20	Kevin Stocker	.40

1994 Fleer Smoke N' Heat

Among the scarcest of the '94 Fleer inserts, available at a stated rate of one per 30 packs, these feature 10 of the top strikeout pitchers in the major leagues. "Metallized" card fronts have a player photo set against an infernal background with large letters, "Smoke 'N Heat". The player's name is in gold foil at bottom. Backs have a similar chaotic hot-red background, a player photo and career summary.

		MT
Complete Set (12):		40.00
Common Player:		.50
1	Roger Clemens	10.00
2	David Cone	1.50
3	Juan Guzman	.50
4	Pete Harnisch	.50
5	Randy Johnson	5.00
6	Mark Langston	.50
7	Greg Maddux	12.50
8	Mike Mussina	3.00
9	Jose Rijo	.50
10	Nolan Ryan	17.50
11	Curt Schilling	1.50
12	John Smoltz	2.50

1994 Fleer Team Leaders

A player from each major league team has been chosen for this 28-card insert set. Fronts feature a team logo against a backgound of graduated team colors. Player portrait and action photos are superimposed. At bottom is the player name, team and position, all in gold foil. Backs have a team logo and player photo set against a white background, with a short write-up justifying the player's selection as a "Team Leader." Odds of finding one of these inserts were given as one in eight packs.

		MT
Complete Set (28):		30.00
Common Player:		.25
1	Cal Ripken, Jr.	5.00
2	Mo Vaughn	1.00
3	Tim Salmon	.75
4	Frank Thomas	2.00
5	Carlos Baerga	.25
6	Cecil Fielder	.25
7	Brian McRae	.25
8	Greg Vaughn	.25
9	Kirby Puckett	2.00
10	Don Mattingly	2.00
11	Mark McGwire	6.00
12	Ken Griffey, Jr.	6.00
13	Juan Gonzalez	1.50
14	Paul Molitor	.75
15	Dave Justice	.35
16	Ryne Sandberg	1.00
17	Barry Larkin	.50
18	Andres Galarraga	.75
19	Gary Sheffield	.75
20	Jeff Bagwell	1.50
21	Mike Piazza	4.00
22	Marquis Grissom	.25
23	Bobby Bonilla	.25
24	Len Dykstra	.25
25	Jay Bell	.25
26	Gregg Jefferies	.25
27	Tony Gwynn	2.50
28	Will Clark	.50

1994 Fleer Tim Salmon A.L. Rookie of the Year

The popular Angels Rookie of the Year is featured in a 15-card set produced in what Fleer terms "metallized" format. The first 12 cards in the set were inserted into foil packs at the rate of about one card per box. Three additional cards could be obtained by sending $1.50 and 10 '94 Fleer wrappers to a mail-in offer. On both front and back, the cards have a color player photo set against a metallic-image background.

		MT
Complete Set (15):		25.00
Common Card:		2.00
Autograph/2,000:		35.00
1	Tim Salmon	2.00
2	Tim Salmon	2.00
3	Tim Salmon	2.00
4	Tim Salmon	2.00
5	Tim Salmon	2.00
6	Tim Salmon	2.00
7	Tim Salmon	2.00
8	Tim Salmon	2.00
9	Tim Salmon	2.00
10	Tim Salmon	2.00
11	Tim Salmon	2.00
12	Tim Salmon	2.00
13	Tim Salmon	3.00
14	Tim Salmon	3.00
15	Tim Salmon	3.00
--	Tim Salmon (autographed edition of 2,000)	75.00

1994 Fleer All-Rookie Team

Sharing the format of the basic 1994 Fleer issue, this nine-card set of rookies was available only by redemption of a trade card randomly inserted into foil packs. The exchange card expired Sept. 30, 1994. The cards are numbered with a "M" prefix.

		MT
Complete Set (9):		5.00
Common Player:		.50
Exchange Card:		.50
1	Kurt Abbott	.75
2	Rich Becker	.75
3	Carlos Delgado	3.00
4	Jorge Fabregas	1.00
5	Bob Hamelin	.50
6	John Hudek	.75
7	Tim Hyers	.50
8	Luis Lopez	.50
9	James Mouton	.50

1994 Fleer Update

Rookies, traded players and free agents who changed teams are included in the annual update issue. Cards are in the same format as the regular-issue '94 Fleer set. Cards are numbered alphabetically within team.

		MT
Complete Set (200):		65.00
Common Player:		.10
1	Mark Eichhorn	.10
2	Sid Fernandez	.10
3	Leo Gomez	.10
4	Mike Oquist	.10
5	Rafael Palmeiro	.50
6	Chris Sabo	.10
7	Dwight Smith	.10
8	Lee Smith	.12
9	Damon Berryhill	.10
10	Wes Chamberlain	.10
11	Gar Finnvold	.10
12	Chris Howard	.10
13	Tim Naehring	.10
14	Otis Nixon	.10
15	Brian Anderson	.10
16	Jorge Fabregas	.10
17	Rex Hudler	.10
18	Bo Jackson	.20
19	Mark Leiter	.10
20	Spike Owen	.10
21	Harold Reynolds	.10
22	Chris Turner	.10
23	Dennis Cook	.10
24	Jose DeLeon	.10
25	Julio Franco	.10
26	Joe Hall	.10
27	Darrin Jackson	.10
28	Dane Johnson	.10
29	Norberto Martin	.10
30	Scott Sanderson	.10
31	Jason Grimsley	.10
32	Dennis Martinez	.12
33	Jack Morris	.10
34	Eddie Murray	.25
35	Chad Ogea	.10
36	Tony Pena	.10
37	Paul Shuey	.10
38	Omar Vizquel	.12
39	Danny Bautista	.10
40	Tim Belcher	.10
41	Joe Boever	.10
42	Storm Davis	.10
43	Junior Felix	.10
44	Mike Gardiner	.10
45	Buddy Groom	.10
46	Juan Samuel	.10
47	Vince Coleman	.10
48	Bob Hamelin	.10
49	Dave Henderson	.10
50	Rusty Meacham	.10
51	Terry Shumpert	.10
52	Jeff Bronkey	.10
53	Alex Diaz	.10
54	Brian Harper	.10
55	Jose Mercedes	.10
56	Jody Reed	.10
57	Bob Scanlan	.10
58	Turner Ward	.10
59	Rich Becker	.10
60	Alex Cole	.10
61	Denny Hocking	.10
63	Pat Mahomes	.15
64	Carlos Pulido	.10
65	Dave Stevens	.10
66	Matt Walbeck	.10
67	Xavier Hernandez	.10
68	Sterling Hitchcock	.10
69	Terry Mulholland	.10
70	Luis Polonia	.10
71	Gerald Williams	.10
72	Mark Acre	.10
73	Geronimo Berroa	.10
74	Rickey Henderson	.40
75	Stan Javier	.10
76	Steve Karsay	.10
77	Carlos Reyes	.10
78	Bill Taylor	.10
79	Eric Anthony	.10
80	Bobby Ayala	.10
81	Tim Davis	.10
82	Felix Fermin	.10
83	Reggie Jefferson	.10
84	Keith Mitchell	.10
85	Bill Risley	.10
86	*Alex Rodriguez*	60.00
87	Roger Salkeld	.12
88	Dan Wilson	.12
89	Cris Carpenter	.10
90	Will Clark	.40
91	Jeff Frye	.10
92	Rick Helling	.10
93	Chris James	.10
94	Oddibe McDowell	.10
95	Billy Ripken	.10
96	Carlos Delgado	1.50
97	Alex Gonzalez	.25
98	Shawn Green	1.00
100	Mike Huff	.10
101	Mike Kelly	.10
102	Roberto Kelly	.10
103	Charlie O'Brien	.10
104	Jose Oliva	.10
105	Gregg Olson	.10
106	Willie Banks	.10
107	Jim Bullinger	.10
108	Chuck Crim	.10
109	Shawon Dunston	.10
110	Karl Rhodes	.10
111	Steve Trachsel	.20
112	Anthony Young	.10
113	Eddie Zambrano	.10
114	Bret Boone	.10
115	Jeff Brantley	.10
116	Hector Carrasco	.10
117	Tony Fernandez	.10
118	Tim Fortugno	.10
119	Erik Hanson	.10
120	Chuck McElroy	.10
121	Deion Sanders	.25
122	Ellis Burks	.10
123	Marvin Freeman	.10
124	Mike Harkey	.10
125	Howard Johnson	.10
126	Mike Kingery	.10
127	Nelson Liriano	.10
128	Marcus Moore	.10
129	Mike Munoz	.10
130	Kevin Ritz	.10
131	Walt Weiss	.10
132	Kurt Abbott	.15
133	Jerry Browne	.10
134	Greg Colbrunn	.10
135	Jeremy Hernandez	.10
136	Dave Magadan	.10
137	Kurt Miller	.10
138	Robb Nen	.15
139	Jesus Taverez	.10
140	Sid Bream	.10
141	Tom Edens	.10
142	Tony Eusebio	.10
143	John Hudek	.10
144	Brian Hunter	.25
145	Orlando Miller	.15
146	James Mouton	.10
147	Shane Reynolds	.10

148	Rafael Bournigal	.10
149	Delino DeShields	.10
150	Garey Ingram	.10
151	Chan Ho Park	.20
152	Wil Cordero	.15
153	Pedro Martinez	1.50
154	Randy Milligan	.10
155	Lenny Webster	.10
156	Rico Brogna	.10
157	Josias Manzanillo	.10
158	Kevin McReynolds	.10
159	Mike Remlinger	.10
160	David Segui	.10
161	Pete Smith	.10
162	Kelly Stinnett	.10
163	Jose Vizcaino	.10
164	Billy Hatcher	.10
165	Doug Jones	.10
166	Mike Lieberthal	.20
167	Tony Longmire	.10
168	Bobby Munoz	.10
169	Paul Quantrill	.10
170	Heathcliff Slocumb	.10
171	Fernando Valenzuela	.12
172	Mark Dewey	.10
173	Brian Hunter	.10
174	Jon Lieber	.10
175	Ravelo Manzanillo	.10
176	Dan Miceli	.10
177	Rick White	.10
178	Bryan Eversgerd	.10
179	John Habyan	.10
180	Terry McGriff	.10
181	Vicente Palacios	.10
182	Rich Rodriguez	.10
183	Rick Sutcliffe	.10
184	Donnie Elliott	.10
185	Joey Hamilton	.25
186	Tim Hyers	.10
187	Luis Lopez	.10
188	Ray McDavid	.10
189	Bip Roberts	.10
190	Scott Sanders	.10
191	Eddie Williams	.10
192	Steve Frey	.10
193	Pat Gomez	.10
194	Rich Monteleone	.10
195	Mark Portugal	.10
196	Darryl Strawberry	.15
197	Salomon Torres	.10
198	W. Van Landingham	.15
199	Checklist	.10
200	Checklist	.10

1994 Fleer Update Diamond Tribute

These special cards included in the 1994 Fleer Update set feature 10 of baseball's proven superstars. The card front has a color action shot of the player, against a skyline with a baseball pattern among the clouds. The card back is numbered 1 of 8, etc., and includes another photo against a background similar to that used for the card front. A "Diamond Tribute" logo and career summary are also included on the back.

		MT
Complete Set (10):		7.50
Common Player:		.50
1	Barry Bonds	1.00
2	Joe Carter	.50
3	Will Clark	.60
4	Roger Clemens	1.00
5	Tony Gwynn	1.00
6	Don Mattingly	1.00
7	Fred McGriff	.60
8	Eddie Murray	.60
9	Kirby Puckett	1.00
10	Cal Ripken Jr.	3.00

1994 Fleer/Extra Bases

Extra Bases was a 400-card, oversized set, plus 80 insert cards in four different subsets. The cards, 4-11/16" by 2-1/2", have a full-bleed photo on the front and back, as well as UV coating and color coding by team. As was the case in other Fleer products, Extra Bases contained an insert card in every pack. All 80 insert cards feature gold or silver foil stamping.

		MT
Complete Set (400):		30.00
Common Player:		.10
Wax Box:		30.00
1	Brady Anderson	.15
2	Harold Baines	.12
3	Mike Devereaux	.10
4	Sid Fernandez	.10
5	Jeffrey Hammonds	.15
6	Chris Hoiles	.10
7	Ben McDonald	.10
8	Mark McLemore	.10
9	Mike Mussina	.50
10	Mike Oquist	.10
11	Rafael Palmeiro	.25
12	Cal Ripken, Jr.	2.50
13	Chris Sabo	.10
14	Lee Smith	.12
15	Wes Chamberlain	.10
16	Roger Clemens	.90
17	Scott Cooper	.10
18	Danny Darwin	.10
19	Andre Dawson	.15
20	Mike Greenwell	.10
21	Tim Naehring	.10
22	Otis Nixon	.10
23	Jeff Russell	.10
24	Ken Ryan	.10
25	Aaron Sele	.15
26	John Valentin	.15
27	Mo Vaughn	.50
28	Frank Viola	.10
29	*Brian Anderson*	.15
30	Chad Curtis	.10
31	Chili Davis	.12
32	Gary DiSarcina	.10
33	Damion Easley	.10
34	Jim Edmonds	.30
35	Chuck Finley	.10
36	Bo Jackson	.15
37	Mark Langston	.10
38	Harold Reynolds	.10
39	Tim Salmon	.40
40	Wilson Alvarez	.10
41	James Baldwin	.10
42	Jason Bere	.10
43	Joey Cora	.10
44	*Ray Durham*	.60
45	Alex Fernandez	.15
46	Julio Franco	.10
47	Ozzie Guillen	.10
48	Darrin Jackson	.10
49	Lance Johnson	.10
50	Ron Karkovice	.10
51	Jack McDowell	.12
52	Tim Raines	.12
53	Frank Thomas	1.50
54	Robin Ventura	.15
55	Sandy Alomar Jr.	.12
56	Carlos Baerga	.10
57	Albert Belle	.75
58	Mark Clark	.10
59	Wayne Kirby	.10
60	Kenny Lofton	.60
61	Dennis Martinez	.12
62	Jose Mesa	.10
63	Jack Morris	.10
64	Eddie Murray	.20
65	Charles Nagy	.12
66	Manny Ramirez	1.00
67	Paul Shuey	.10
68	Paul Sorrento	.10
69	Jim Thome	.35
70	Omar Vizquel	.12
71	Eric Davis	.12
72	John Doherty	.10
73	Cecil Fielder	.10
74	Travis Fryman	.10
75	Kirk Gibson	.10
76	Gene Harris	.10
77	Mike Henneman	.10
78	Mike Moore	.10
79	Tony Phillips	.10
80	Mickey Tettleton	.10
81	Alan Trammell	.15
82	Lou Whitaker	.10
83	Kevin Appier	.10
84	Vince Coleman	.10
85	David Cone	.15
86	Gary Gaetti	.10
87	Greg Gagne	.10
88	Tom Gordon	.10
89	Jeff Granger	.10
90	Bob Hamelin	.10
91	Dave Henderson	.10
92	Felix Jose	.10
93	Wally Joyner	.12
94	Jose Lind	.10
95	Mike Macfarlane	.10
96	Brian McRae	.10
97	Jeff Montgomery	.10
98	Ricky Bones	.10
99	Jeff Bronkey	.10
100	Alex Diaz	.10
101	Cal Eldred	.10
102	Darryl Hamilton	.10
103	Brian Harper	.10
104	John Jaha	.10
105	Pat Listach	.10
106	Dave Nilsson	.10
107	Jody Reed	.10
108	Kevin Seitzer	.10
109	Greg Vaughn	.15
110	Turner Ward	.10
111	Wes Weger	.12
112	Bill Wegman	.10
113	Rick Aguilera	.10
114	Rich Becker	.10
115	Alex Cole	.10
116	Scott Erickson	.10
117	Kent Hrbek	.10
118	Chuck Knoblauch	.20
119	Scott Leius	.10
120	Shane Mack	.10
121	Pat Mahomes	.10
122	Pat Meares	.10
123	Kirby Puckett	1.00
124	Kevin Tapani	.10
125	Matt Walbeck	.10
126	Dave Winfield	.35
127	Jim Abbott	.15
128	Wade Boggs	.50
129	Mike Gallego	.10
130	Xavier Hernandez	.10
131	Pat Kelly	.10
132	Jimmy Key	.10
133	Don Mattingly	1.00
134	Terry Mulholland	.10
135	Matt Nokes	.10
136	Paul O'Neill	.15
137	Melido Perez	.10
138	Luis Polonia	.10
139	Mike Stanley	.10
140	Danny Tartabull	.10
141	Randy Velarde	.10
142	Bernie Williams	.40
143	Mark Acre	.10
144	Geronimo Berroa	.10
145	Mike Bordick	.10
146	Scott Brosius	.10
147	Ron Darling	.10
148	Dennis Eckersley	.12
149	Brent Gates	.10
150	Rickey Henderson	.40
151	Stan Javier	.10
152	Steve Karsay	.10
153	Mark McGwire	3.00
154	Troy Neel	.10
155	Ruben Sierra	.10
156	Terry Steinbach	.10
157	Bill Taylor	.10
158	Rich Amaral	.10
159	Eric Anthony	.10
160	Bobby Ayala	.10
161	Chris Bosio	.10
162	Jay Buhner	.10
163	Tim Davis	.10
164	Felix Fermin	.10
165	Dave Fleming	.10
166	Ken Griffey, Jr.	3.00
167	Reggie Jefferson	.10
168	Randy Johnson	.60
169	Edgar Martinez	.12
170	Tino Martinez	.15
171	Bill Risley	.10
172	Roger Salkeld	.10
173	*Mac Suzuki*	.20
174	Dan Wilson	.10
175	Kevin Brown	.20
176	Jose Canseco	.40
177	Will Clark	.35
178	Juan Gonzalez	.75
179	Rick Helling	.10
180	Tom Henke	.10
181	Chris James	.10
182	Manuel Lee	.10
183	Dean Palmer	.10
184	Ivan Rodriguez	.40
185	Kenny Rogers	.10
186	Roberto Alomar	.60
187	Pat Borders	.10
188	Joe Carter	.10
189	Carlos Delgado	.25
190	Juan Guzman	.10
191	Pat Hentgen	.10
192	Paul Molitor	.50
192a	Paul Molitor (promotional sample)	6.00
193	John Olerud	.15
194	Ed Sprague	.10
195	Dave Stewart	.12
196	Todd Stottlemyre	.10
197	Duane Ward	.10
198	Devon White	.12
199	Steve Avery	.10
200	Jeff Blauser	.10
201	Tom Glavine	.20
202	Dave Justice	.40
203	Mike Kelly	.10
204	Roberto Kelly	.10
205	Ryan Klesko	.25
206	Mark Lemke	.10
207	Javier Lopez	.25

208	Greg Maddux	1.50
209	Fred McGriff	.35
210	Greg McMichael	.10
211	Kent Mercker	.10
212	Terry Pendleton	.10
213	John Smoltz	.15
214	Tony Tarasco	.10
215	Willie Banks	.10
216	Steve Buechele	.10
217	Shawon Dunston	.10
218	Mark Grace	.20
219	*Brooks Kieschnick*	.35
220	Derrick May	.10
221	Randy Myers	.10
222	Karl Rhodes	.10
223	Rey Sanchez	.10
224	Sammy Sosa	1.50
225	Steve Traschel	.20
226	Rick Wilkins	.10
227	Bret Boone	.10
228	Jeff Brantley	.10
229	Tom Browning	.10
230	Hector Carrasco	.10
231	Rob Dibble	.10
232	Erik Hanson	.10
233	Barry Larkin	.15
234	Kevin Mitchell	.10
235	Hal Morris	.10
236	Joe Oliver	.10
237	Jose Rijo	.10
238	Johnny Ruffin	.10
239	Deion Sanders	.40
240	Reggie Sanders	.15
241	John Smiley	.10
242	Dante Bichette	.30
243	Ellis Burks	.10
244	Andres Galarraga	.20
245	Joe Girardi	.10
246	Greg Harris	.10
247	Charlie Hayes	.10
248	Howard Johnson	.10
249	Roberto Mejia	.10
250	Marcus Moore	.10
251	David Nied	.10
252	Armando Reynoso	.10
253	Bruce Ruffin	.10
254	Mark Thompson	.10
255	Walt Weiss	.10
256	*Kurt Abbott*	.20
257	Bret Barberie	.10
258	Chuck Carr	.10
259	Jeff Conine	.15
260	Chris Hammond	.10
261	Bryan Harvey	.10
262	Jeremy Hernandez	.10
263	Charlie Hough	.10
264	Dave Magadan	.10
265	Benito Santiago	.10
266	Gary Sheffield	.20
267	David Weathers	.10
268	Jeff Bagwell	1.00
269	Craig Biggio	.15
270	Ken Caminiti	.15
271	Andujar Cedeno	.10
272	Doug Drabek	.10
273	Steve Finley	.10
274	Luis Gonzalez	.10
275	Pete Harnisch	.10
276	John Hudek	.10
277	Darryl Kile	.10
278	Orlando Miller	.10
279	James Mouton	.10
280	Shane Reynolds	.10
281	Scott Servais	.10
282	Greg Swindell	.10
283	Pedro Astacio	.10
284	Brett Butler	.10
285	Tom Candiotti	.10
286	Delino DeShields	.10
287	Kevin Gross	.10
288	Orel Hershiser	.12
289	Eric Karros	.15
290	Ramon Martinez	.12
291	Raul Mondesi	.50
292	Jose Offerman	.10
293	*Chan Ho Park*	.50
294	Mike Piazza	2.00
295	Henry Rodriguez	.12
296	Cory Snyder	.10
297	Tim Wallach	.10
298	Todd Worrell	.10
299	Moises Alou	.15
300	Sean Berry	.10
301	Wil Cordero	.10
302	Joey Eischen	.10
303	Jeff Fassero	.10
304	Darrin Fletcher	.10
305	Cliff Floyd	.20
306	Marquis Grissom	.15
307	Ken Hill	.10
308	Mike Lansing	.10
309	Pedro Martinez	.50
310	Mel Rojas	.10
311	Kirk Rueter	.10
312	Larry Walker	.35
313	John Wetteland	.10
314	Rondell White	.30
315	Bobby Bonilla	.15
316	John Franco	.10
317	Dwight Gooden	.15
318	Todd Hundley	.15
319	Bobby Jones	.10
320	Jeff Kent	.10
321	Kevin McReynolds	.10
322	Bill Pulsipher	.10
323	Bret Saberhagen	.10
324	David Segui	.10
325	Pete Smith	.10
326	Kelly Stinnett	.15
327	Ryan Thompson	.10
328	Jose Vizcaino	.10
329	Ricky Bottalico	.10
330	Darren Daulton	.10
331	Mariano Duncan	.10
332	Len Dykstra	.10
333	Tommy Greene	.10
334	Billy Hatcher	.10
335	Dave Hollins	.10
336	Pete Incaviglia	.10
337	Danny Jackson	.10
338	Doug Jones	.10
339	Ricky Jordan	.10
340	John Kruk	.10
341	Curt Schilling	.15
342	Kevin Stocker	.10
343	Jay Bell	.10
344	Steve Cooke	.10
345	Carlos Garcia	.10
346	Brian Hunter	.10
347	Jeff King	.10
348	Al Martin	.10
349	Orlando Merced	.10
350	Denny Neagle	.10
351	Don Slaught	.10
352	Andy Van Slyke	.10
353	Paul Wagner	.10
354	Rick White	.10
355	Luis Alicea	.10
356	Rene Arocha	.10
357	Rheal Cormier	.10
358	Bernard Gilkey	.10
359	Gregg Jefferies	.15
360	Ray Lankford	.10
361	Tom Pagnozzi	.10
362	Mike Perez	.10
363	Ozzie Smith	.50
364	Bob Tewksbury	.10
365	Mark Whiten	.10
366	Todd Zeile	.10
367	Andy Ashby	.12
368	Brad Ausmus	.10
369	Derek Bell	.10
370	Andy Benes	.12
371	Archi Cianfrocco	.10
372	Tony Gwynn	1.00
373	Trevor Hoffman	.12
374	Tim Hyers	.10
375	Pedro Martinez	.20
376	Phil Plantier	.10
377	Bip Roberts	.10
378	Scott Sanders	.10
379	Dave Staton	.10
380	Wally Whitehurst	.10
381	Rod Beck	.10
382	Todd Benzinger	.10
383	Barry Bonds	.75
384	John Burkett	.10
385	Royce Clayton	.10
386	Bryan Hickerson	.10
387	Mike Jackson	.10
388	Darren Lewis	.10
389	Kirt Manwaring	.10
390	Willie McGee	.12
391	Mark Portugal	.10
392	Bill Swift	.10
393	Robby Thompson	.10
394	Salomon Torres	.10
395	Matt Williams	.35
396	Checklist	.10
397	Checklist	.10
398	Checklist	.10
399	Checklist	.10
400	Checklist	.10

1994 Fleer/Extra Bases Game Breakers

Game Breakers featured 30 big-name stars from both leagues who have exhibited offensive firepower. This insert set was done in a horizontal format picturing the player in two different shots, one close-up and one slightly further away. The words "Game Breakers" is written across the bottom, with the player name and team in much smaller letters, printed under it.

		MT
Complete Set (30):		15.00
Common Player:		.25
1	Jeff Bagwell	1.50
2	Rod Beck	.25
3	Albert Belle	1.00
4	Barry Bonds	1.50
5	Jose Canseco	.75
6	Joe Carter	.35
7	Roger Clemens	1.00
8	Darren Daulton	.25
9	Len Dykstra	.25
10	Cecil Fielder	.30
11	Tom Glavine	.30
12	Juan Gonzalez	1.00
13	Mark Grace	.35
14	Ken Griffey, Jr.	4.00
15	Dave Justice	.55
16	Greg Maddux	2.00
17	Don Mattingly	1.75
18	Ben McDonald	.25
19	Fred McGriff	.50
20	Paul Molitor	.65
21	John Olerud	.40
22	Mike Piazza	2.50
23	Kirby Puckett	1.50
24	Cal Ripken, Jr.	3.00
25	Tim Salmon	.75
26	Gary Sheffield	.45
27	Frank Thomas	2.00
28	Mo Vaughn	.75
29	Matt Williams	.50
30	Dave Winfield	.50

1994 Fleer/Extra Bases Major League Hopefuls

Minor league standouts with impressive credentials were showcased in Major League Hopefuls. Each card in this insert set shows the player over a computer enhanced background, with three smaller photos running down the top half, on the left side of the card. The insert set title runs across the bottom and the player's name is just under it on a black strip.

		MT
Complete Set (10):		4.00
Common Player:		.25
1	James Baldwin	.50
2	Ricky Bottalico	.50
3	Ray Durham	1.00
4	Joey Eischen	.35
5	Brooks Kieschnick	.50
6	Orlando Miller	.35
7	Bill Pulsipher	.25
8	Mac Suzuki	.35
9	Mark Thompson	.25
10	Wes Weger	.35

1994 Fleer/Extra Bases Pitcher's Duel

Pitcher's Duel was available to collectors who mailed in 10 Extra Bases wrappers. The set features 20 of the top pitchers is baseball. Contained in the set were five American League and five National League cards, with two pitchers from the same league on each card. The front background pictures a wide-angle photo of a major league stadium, viewed from above the diamond, behind home plate. Backs have two more action photos set against a sepia-toned background photo of an Old West street to enhance the shootout theme of the set. Cards are numbered with an "M" prefix.

		MT
Complete Set (10):		12.00
Common Player:		.75
1	Roger Clemens, Jack McDowell	3.00
2	Ben McDonald, Randy Johnson	2.00
3	Jimmy Key, David Cone	1.00
4	Mike Mussina, Aaron Sele	1.50
5	Chuck Finley, Wilson Alvarez	.75
6	Steve Avery, Curt Schilling	.75
7	Greg Maddux, Jose Rijo	5.00
8	Bret Saberhagen, Bob Tewksbury	.75
9	Tom Glavine, Bill Swift	1.00
10	Doug Drabek, Orel Hershiser	.75

1994 Fleer/Extra Bases Rookie Standouts

Rookie Standouts highlights 20 of the best and brightest first-year players of the 1994 season. Cards picture the player on a baseball background, with a black, jagged-edged "aura" around the player. Names and teams were placed in the bottom-left corner, running up the side. The Rookie Standouts logo, which is a gold glove with a baseball in it and "Rookie Standouts" printed under it, was placed in the bottom-right corner and the Extra Bases logo appears in the upper-left.

		MT
Complete Set (20):		10.00
Common Player:		.25
1	Kurt Abbott	.50
2	Brian Anderson	.35
3	Hector Carrasco	.35
4	Tim Davis	.25
5	Carlos Delgado	.75
6	Cliff Floyd	.60
7	Bob Hamelin	.30
8	Jeffrey Hammonds	.35
9	Rick Helling	.40
10	Steve Karsay	.30
11	Ryan Klesko	1.00
12	Javier Lopez	1.00
13	Raul Mondesi	2.00
14	James Mouton	.35
15	Chan Ho Park	.75
16	Manny Ramirez	2.00
17	Tony Tarasco	.25
18	Steve Trachsel	.25
19	Rick White	.25
20	Rondell White	1.00

1994 Fleer/Extra Bases Second Year Stars

Second-Year Stars contains 1993 rookies who were expected to have an even bigger impact in the 1994 season. Each card features five photos of the player. Four are in a filmstrip down the left side; the remaining two-thirds of the card contain a larger photo. "Second-Year Stars" is printed across the bottom, along with the player name and team. Backs repeat the film-strip motif.

		MT
Complete Set (20):		9.00
Common Player:		.25
1	Bobby Ayala	.25
2	Jason Bere	.25
3	Chuck Carr	.25
4	Jeff Conine	.40
5	Steve Cooke	.25
6	Wil Cordero	.30
7	Carlos Garcia	.25
8	Brent Gates	.30
9	Trevor Hoffman	.50
10	Wayne Kirby	.25
11	Al Martin	.25
12	Pedro Martinez	1.50
13	Greg McMichael	.25
14	Troy Neel	.25
15	David Nied	.25
16	Mike Piazza	3.50
17	Kirk Rueter	.25
18	Tim Salmon	1.00
19	Aaron Sele	.35
20	Kevin Stocker	.25

1995 Fleer Promos

This eight-player (plus a header card), cello-wrapped promo set was included in a special "Fleer" national newsstand magazine in early 1995. At first glance the cards seem identical to the regularly issued cards of the same players, but there are subtle differences on the back of each card.

		MT
Complete Set (9):		12.50
Common Player:		1.25
26	Roger Clemens (1988 291 SO and 1992 2.41 ERA boxed)	2.50
78	Paul O'Neill (1991 boxed)	1.25
155	David Cone (1990 233 SO boxed, white shadow on team names)	1.25
235	Tim Salmon (No box on 1992 101 R)	2.00
285	Juan Gonzalez (Black stats, 1993 boxed)	2.50
351	Marquis Grissom (No box on 1988 291 AB)	1.25
509	Ozzie Smith (Black stats, no box on 1986 Cardinals)	2.00
514	Dante Bichette (Black stats)	1.25
--	Header card "Different by Design"	.10

1995 Fleer

Fleer baseball arrived in 1995 with six different designs, one for each division. The basic set contains 600 cards and was sold in 12-card and 18-card packs. National League West cards feature many smaller pictures in the background that are identical to the picture in the forefront, while AL West cards contain an action photo over top of a close-up on the right side and a water colored look on the left side. AL Central cards exhibit numbers pertinant to each player througout the front design, with the player in the middle. NL East players appear in action on the left half of the card with a colorful, encripted look on the rest. National League Central and American League East feature more standard designs with the player in the forefront, with vital numbers and a color background.

		MT
Complete Set (600):		50.00
Common Player:		.05
Pack (12):		1.25
Wax Box (36):		35.00
1	Brady Anderson	.15
2	Harold Baines	.08
3	Damon Buford	.05
4	Mike Devereaux	.05
5	Mark Eichhorn	.05
6	Sid Fernandez	.05
7	Leo Gomez	.05
8	Jeffrey Hammonds	.08
9	Chris Hoiles	.05
10	Rick Krivda	.05
11	Ben McDonald	.05
12	Mark McLemore	.05
13	Alan Mills	.05
14	Jamie Moyer	.05
15	Mike Mussina	.40
16	Mike Oquist	.05
17	Rafael Palmeiro	.30
18	Arthur Rhodes	.05
19	Cal Ripken, Jr.	2.50
20	Chris Sabo	.05
21	Lee Smith	.08
22	Jack Voight	.05
23	Damon Berryhill	.05
24	Tom Brunansky	.05
25	Wes Chamberlain	.05
26	Roger Clemens	1.00
27	Scott Cooper	.05
28	Andre Dawson	.15
29	Gar Finnvold	.05
30	Tony Fossas	.05
31	Mike Greenwell	.05
32	Joe Hesketh	.05
33	Chris Howard	.05
34	Chris Nabholz	.05
35	Tim Naehring	.05
36	Otis Nixon	.05
37	Carlos Rodriguez	.05
38	Rich Rowland	.05
39	Ken Ryan	.05
40	Aaron Sele	.08
41	John Valentin	.08
42	Mo Vaughn	.50

No.	Player	Price
43	Frank Viola	.05
44	Danny Bautista	.05
45	Joe Boeven	.05
46	Milt Cuyler	.05
47	Storm Davis	.05
48	John Doherty	.05
49	Junior Felix	.05
50	Cecil Fielder	.08
51	Travis Fryman	.08
52	Mike Gardiner	.05
53	Kirk Gibson	.05
54	Chris Gomez	.05
55	Buddy Groom	.05
56	Mike Henneman	.05
57	Chad Kreuter	.05
58	Mike Moore	.05
59	Tony Phillips	.05
60	Juan Samuel	.05
61	Mickey Tettleton	.05
62	Alan Trammell	.10
63	David Wells	.08
64	Lou Whitaker	.05
65	Jim Abbott	.10
66	Joe Ausanio	.05
67	Wade Boggs	.30
68	Mike Gallego	.05
69	Xavier Hernandez	.05
70	Sterling Hitchcock	.05
71	Steve Howe	.05
72	Scott Kamieniecki	.05
73	Pat Kelly	.05
74	Jimmy Key	.05
75	Jim Leyritz	.05
76	Don Mattingly	1.00
77	Terry Mulholland	.05
78	Paul O'Neill	.15
79	Melido Perez	.05
80	Luis Polonia	.05
81	Mike Stanley	.05
82	Danny Tartabull	.05
83	Randy Velarde	.05
84	Bob Wickman	.05
85	Bernie Williams	.50
86	Gerald Williams	.05
87	Roberto Alomar	.50
88	Pat Borders	.05
89	Joe Carter	.08
90	Tony Castillo	.05
91	Brad Cornett	.05
92	Carlos Delgado	.50
93	Alex Gonzalez	.10
94	Shawn Green	.50
95	Juan Guzman	.05
96	Darren Hall	.05
97	Pat Hentgen	.05
98	Mike Huff	.05
99	Randy Knorr	.05
100	Al Leiter	.08
101	Paul Molitor	.35
102	John Olerud	.20
103	Dick Schofield	.05
104	Ed Sprague	.05
105	Dave Stewart	.08
106	Todd Stottlemyre	.05
107	Devon White	.05
108	Woody Williams	.05
109	Wilson Alvarez	.05
110	Paul Assenmacher	.05
111	Jason Bere	.05
112	Dennis Cook	.05
113	Joey Cora	.05
114	Jose DeLeon	.05
115	Alex Fernandez	.10
116	Julio Franco	.05
117	Craig Graboeck	.05
118	Ozzie Guillen	.05
119	Roberto Hernandez	.05
120	Darrin Jackson	.05
121	Lance Johnson	.05
122	Ron Karkovice	.05
123	Mike LaValliere	.05
124	Norberto Martin	.05
125	Kirk McCaskill	.05
126	Jack McDowell	.05
127	Tim Raines	.08
128	Frank Thomas	1.00
129	Robin Ventura	.10
130	Sandy Alomar Jr.	.10
131	Carlos Baerga	.05
132	Albert Belle	.60
133	Mark Clark	.05
134	Alvaro Espinoza	.05
135	Jason Grimsley	.05
136	Wayne Kirby	.05
137	Kenny Lofton	.60
138	Albie Lopez	.05
139	Dennis Martinez	.08
140	Jose Mesa	.05
141	Eddie Murray	.25
142	Charles Nagy	.05
143	Tony Pena	.05
144	Eric Plunk	.05
145	Manny Ramirez	1.00
146	Jeff Russell	.05
147	Paul Shuey	.05
148	Paul Sorrento	.05
149	Jim Thome	.40
150	Omar Vizquel	.08
151	Dave Winfield	.25
152	Kevin Appier	.05
153	Billy Brewer	.05
154	Vince Coleman	.05
155	David Cone	.08
156	Gary Gaetti	.05
157	Greg Gagne	.05
158	Tom Gordon	.05
159	Mark Gubicza	.05
160	Bob Hamelin	.05
161	Dave Henderson	.05
162	Felix Jose	.05
163	Wally Joyner	.08
164	Jose Lind	.05
165	Mike Macfarlane	.05
166	Mike Magnante	.05
167	Brent Mayne	.05
168	Brian McRae	.05
169	Rusty Meacham	.05
170	Jeff Montgomery	.05
171	Hipolito Pichardo	.05
172	Terry Shumpert	.05
173	Michael Tucker	.08
174	Ricky Bones	.05
175	*Jeff Cirillo*	.40
176	Alex Diaz	.05
177	Cal Eldred	.05
178	Mike Fetters	.05
179	Darryl Hamilton	.05
180	Brian Harper	.05
181	John Jaha	.05
182	Pat Listach	.05
183	Graeme Lloyd	.05
184	Jose Mercedes	.05
185	Matt Mieske	.05
186	Dave Nilsson	.05
187	Jody Reed	.05
188	Bob Scanlan	.05
189	Kevin Seitzer	.05
190	Bill Spiers	.05
191	B.J. Surhoff	.08
192	Jose Valentin	.05
193	Greg Vaughn	.15
194	Turner Ward	.05
195	Bill Wegman	.05
196	Rick Aguilera	.05
197	Rich Becker	.05
198	Alex Cole	.05
199	Marty Cordova	.08
200	Steve Dunn	.05
201	Scott Erickson	.05
202	Mark Guthrie	.05
203	Chip Hale	.05
204	LaTroy Hawkins	.10
205	Denny Hocking	.05
206	Chuck Knoblauch	.20
207	Scott Leius	.05
208	Shane Mack	.05
209	Pat Mahomes	.05
210	Pat Meares	.05
211	Pedro Munoz	.05
212	Kirby Puckett	.75
213	Jeff Reboulet	.08
214	Dave Stevens	.05
215	Kevin Tapani	.05
216	Matt Walbeck	.05
217	Carl Willis	.05
218	Brian Anderson	.08
219	Chad Curtis	.05
220	Chili Davis	.08
221	Gary DiSarcina	.05
222	Damion Easley	.05
223	Jim Edmonds	.25
224	Chuck Finley	.05
225	Joe Grahe	.05
226	Rex Hudler	.05
227	Bo Jackson	.10
228	Mark Langston	.05
229	Phil Leftwich	.05
230	Mark Leiter	.05
231	Spike Owen	.05
232	Bob Patterson	.05
233	Troy Percival	.05
234	Eduardo Perez	.05
235	Tim Salmon	.25
236	J.T. Snow	.12
237	Chris Turner	.05
238	Mark Acre	.05
239	Geronimo Berroa	.05
240	Mike Bordick	.05
241	John Briscoe	.05
242	Scott Brosius	.05
243	Ron Darling	.05
244	Dennis Eckersley	.08
245	Brent Gates	.05
246	Rickey Henderson	.30
247	Stan Javier	.05
248	Steve Karsay	.10
249	Mark McGwire	3.00
250	Troy Neel	.05
251	Steve Ontiveros	.05
252	Carlos Reyes	.05
253	Ruben Sierra	.05
254	Terry Steinbach	.05
255	Bill Taylor	.05
256	Todd Van Poppel	.05
257	Bobby Witt	.05
258	Rich Amaral	.05
259	Eric Anthony	.05
260	Bobby Ayala	.05
261	Mike Blowers	.05
262	Chris Bosio	.05
263	Jay Buhner	.08
264	John Cummings	.05
265	Tim Davis	.05
266	Felix Fermin	.05
267	Dave Fleming	.05
268	Goose Gossage	.05
269	Ken Griffey, Jr.	3.00
270	Reggie Jefferson	.05
271	Randy Johnson	.75
272	Edgar Martinez	.08
273	Tino Martinez	.20
274	Greg Pirkl	.05
275	Bill Risley	.05
276	Roger Salkeld	.05
277	Luis Sojo	.05
278	Mac Suzuki	.08
279	Dan Wilson	.05
280	Kevin Brown	.12
281	Jose Canseco	.50
282	Cris Carpenter	.05
283	Will Clark	.30
284	Jeff Frye	.05
285	Juan Gonzalez	.75
286	Rick Helling	.05
287	Tom Henke	.05
288	David Hulse	.05
289	Chris James	.05
290	Manuel Lee	.05
291	Oddibe McDowell	.05
292	Dean Palmer	.05
293	Roger Pavlik	.05
294	Bill Ripken	.05
295	Ivan Rodriguez	.75
296	Kenny Rogers	.05
297	Doug Strange	.05
298	Matt Whiteside	.05
299	Steve Avery	.05
300	Steve Bedrosian	.05
301	Rafael Belliard	.05
302	Jeff Blauser	.05
303	Dave Gallagher	.05
304	Tom Glavine	.25
305	Dave Justice	.20
306	Mike Kelly	.05
307	Roberto Kelly	.05
308	Ryan Klesko	.15
309	Mark Lemke	.05
310	Javier Lopez	.15
311	Greg Maddux	1.00
312	Fred McGriff	.25
313	Greg McMichael	.05
314	Kent Mercker	.05
315	Charlie O'Brien	.05
316	Jose Oliva	.05
317	Terry Pendleton	.05
318	John Smoltz	.20
319	Mike Stanton	.05
320	Tony Tarasco	.05
321	Terrell Wade	.05
322	Mark Wohlers	.05
323	Kurt Abbott	.05
324	Luis Aquino	.05
325	Bret Barberie	.05
326	Ryan Bowen	.05
327	Jerry Browne	.05
328	Chuck Carr	.05
329	Matias Carrillo	.05
330	Greg Colbrunn	.05
331	Jeff Conine	.12
332	Mark Gardner	.05
333	Chris Hammond	.05
334	Bryan Harvey	.05
335	Richie Lewis	.05
336	Dave Magadan	.05
337	Terry Mathews	.05
338	Robb Nen	.05
339	Yorkis Perez	.05
340	Pat Rapp	.05
341	Benito Santiago	.08
342	Gary Sheffield	.35
343	Dave Weathers	.05
344	Moises Alou	.10
345	Sean Berry	.05
346	Wil Cordero	.05
347	Joe Eischen	.05
348	Jeff Fassero	.05
349	Darrin Fletcher	.05
350	Cliff Floyd	.08
351	Marquis Grissom	.10
352	Butch Henry	.05
353	Gil Heredia	.05
354	Ken Hill	.05
355	Mike Lansing	.05
356	Pedro Martinez	.75
357	Mel Rojas	.05
358	Kirk Rueter	.05
359	Tim Scott	.05
360	Jeff Shaw	.05
361	Larry Walker	.30
362	Lenny Webster	.05
363	John Wetteland	.05
364	Rondell White	.12
365	Bobby Bonilla	.08
366	Rico Brogna	.05
367	Jeromy Burnitz	.08
368	John Franco	.05
369	Dwight Gooden	.10
370	Todd Hundley	.15
371	Jason Jacome	.05
372	Bobby Jones	.05
373	Jeff Kent	.05
374	Jim Lindeman	.05
375	Josias Manzanillo	.05
376	Roger Mason	.05
377	Kevin McReynolds	.05
378	Joe Orsulak	.05
379	Bill Pulsipher	.05
380	Bret Saberhagen	.08
381	David Segui	.05
382	Pete Smith	.05
383	Kelly Stinnett	.05
384	Ryan Thompson	.05
385	Jose Vizcaino	.05
386	Toby Borland	.05
387	Ricky Bettalico	.05
388	Darren Daulton	.05
389	Mariano Duncan	.05
390	Len Dykstra	.05
391	Jim Eisenreich	.05
392	Tommy Greene	.05
393	Dave Hollins	.05
394	Pete Incaviglia	.05
395	Danny Jackson	.05
396	Doug Jones	.05
397	Ricky Jordan	.05
398	John Kruk	.05
399	Mike Lieberthal	.08
400	Tony Longmire	.05
401	Mickey Morandini	.05
402	Bobby Munoz	.05
403	Curt Schilling	.15
404	Heathcliff Slocumb	.05
405	Kevin Stocker	.05
406	Fernando Valenzuela	.05
407	David West	.05
408	Willie Banks	.05
409	Jose Bautista	.05
410	Steve Buechele	.05
411	Jim Bullinger	.05
412	Chuck Crim	.05
413	Shawon Dunston	.05
414	Kevin Foster	.05
415	Mark Grace	.20
416	Jose Hernandez	.05
417	Glenallen Hill	.05

418	Brooks Kieschnick	.08
419	Derrick May	.05
420	Randy Myers	.05
421	Dan Plesac	.05
422	Karl Rhodes	.05
423	Rey Sanchez	.05
424	Sammy Sosa	1.50
425	Steve Trachsel	.05
426	Rick Wilkins	.05
427	Anthony Young	.05
428	Eddie Zambrano	.05
429	Bret Boone	.05
430	Jeff Branson	.05
431	Jeff Brantley	.05
432	Hector Carrasco	.05
433	Brian Dorsett	.05
434	Tony Fernandez	.05
435	Tim Fortugno	.05
436	Erik Hanson	.05
437	Thomas Howard	.05
438	Kevin Jarvis	.05
439	Barry Larkin	.30
440	Chuck McElroy	.05
441	Kevin Mitchell	.05
442	Hal Morris	.05
443	Jose Rijo	.05
444	John Roper	.05
445	Johnny Ruffin	.05
446	Deion Sanders	.20
447	Reggie Sanders	.10
448	Pete Schourek	.05
449	John Smiley	.05
450	Eddie Taubensee	.05
451	Jeff Bagwell	.75
452	Kevin Bass	.05
453	Craig Biggio	.25
454	Ken Caminiti	.15
455	Andujar Cedeno	.05
456	Doug Drabek	.05
457	Tony Eusebio	.05
458	Mike Felder	.05
459	Steve Finley	.05
460	Luis Gonzalez	.08
461	Mike Hampton	.05
462	Pete Harnisch	.05
463	John Hudek	.05
464	Todd Jones	.05
465	Darryl Kile	.05
466	James Mouton	.05
467	Shane Reynolds	.05
468	Scott Servais	.05
469	Greg Swindell	.05
470	Dave Veres	.05
471	Brian Williams	.05
472	Jay Bell	.05
473	Jacob Brumfield	.05
474	Dave Clark	.05
475	Steve Cooke	.05
476	Midre Cummings	.05
477	Mark Dewey	.05
478	Tom Foley	.05
479	Carlos Garcia	.05
480	Jeff King	.05
481	Jon Lieber	.05
482	Ravelo Manzanillo	.05
483	Al Martin	.05
484	Orlando Merced	.05
485	Danny Miceli	.05
486	Denny Neagle	.05
487	Lance Parrish	.05
488	Don Slaught	.05
489	Zane Smith	.05
490	Andy Van Slyke	.05
491	Paul Wagner	.05
492	Rick White	.05
493	Luis Alicea	.05
494	Rene Arocha	.05
495	Rheal Cormier	.05
496	Bryan Eversgerd	.05
497	Bernard Gilkey	.08
498	John Habyan	.05
499	Gregg Jefferies	.10
500	Brian Jordan	.10
501	Ray Lankford	.08
502	John Mabry	.05
503	Terry McGriff	.05
504	Tom Pagnozzi	.05
505	Vicente Palacios	.05
506	Geronimo Pena	.05
507	Gerald Perry	.05
508	Rich Rodriguez	.05
509	Ozzie Smith	.40
510	Bob Tewksbury	.05
511	Allen Watson	.08
512	Mark Whiten	.05
513	Todd Zeile	.05
514	Dante Bichette	.25
515	Willie Blair	.05
516	Ellis Burks	.05
517	Marvin Freeman	.05
518	Andres Galarraga	.40
519	Joe Girardi	.05
520	Greg Harris	.05
521	Charlie Hayes	.05
522	Mike Kingery	.05
523	Nelson Liriano	.05
524	Mike Munoz	.05
525	David Nied	.05
526	Steve Reed	.05
527	Kevin Ritz	.05
528	Bruce Ruffin	.05
529	John Vander Wal	.05
530	Walt Weiss	.05
531	Eric Young	.05
532	Billy Ashley	.05
533	Pedro Astacio	.05
534	Rafael Bournigal	.05
535	Brett Butler	.08
536	Tom Candiotti	.05
537	Omar Daal	.05
538	Delino DeShields	.05
539	Darren Dreifort	.05
540	Kevin Gross	.05
541	Orel Hershiser	.08
542	Garey Ingram	.05
543	Eric Karros	.10
544	Ramon Martinez	.08
545	Raul Mondesi	.40
546	Chan Ho Park	.15
547	Mike Piazza	2.00
548	Henry Rodriguez	.08
549	Rudy Seanez	.05
550	Ismael Valdes	.08
551	Tim Wallach	.05
552	Todd Worrell	.05
553	Andy Ashby	.08
554	Brad Ausmus	.05
555	Derek Bell	.10
556	Andy Benes	.08
557	Phil Clark	.05
558	Donnie Elliott	.05
559	Ricky Gutierrez	.05
560	Tony Gwynn	1.00
561	Joey Hamilton	.12
562	Trevor Hoffman	.08
563	Luis Lopez	.05
564	Pedro Martinez	.05
565	Tim Mauser	.05
566	Phil Plantier	.05
567	Bip Roberts	.05
568	Scott Sanders	.05
569	Craig Shipley	.05
570	Jeff Tabaka	.05
571	Eddie Williams	.05
572	Rod Beck	.05
573	Mike Benjamin	.05
574	Barry Bonds	.75
575	Dave Burba	.05
576	John Burkett	.05
577	Mark Carreon	.05
578	Royce Clayton	.05
579	Steve Frey	.05
580	Bryan Hickerson	.05
581	Mike Jackson	.05
582	Darren Lewis	.05
583	Kirt Manwaring	.05
584	Rich Monteleone	.05
585	John Patterson	.05
586	J.R. Phillips	.05
587	Mark Portugal	.05
588	Joe Rosselli	.05
589	Darryl Strawberry	.10
590	Bill Swift	.05
591	Robby Thompson	.05
592	William Van Landingham	.05
593	Matt Williams	.20
594	Checklist	.05
595	Checklist	.05
596	Checklist	.05
597	Checklist	.05
598	Checklist	.05
599	Checklist	.05
600	Checklist	.05

1995 Fleer All-Fleer 9

Available only by mailing in 10 Fleer wrappers and $3, this set presents an all-star lineup in a unique design. Colored scribbles down one side of the card front offer a background for gold-foil printing of the card title, player name, position and team. Backs repeat the colored scribbles across virtually the entire surface, making it extremely difficult to read the career summary printed in white over it.

		MT
Complete Set (9):		9.00
Common Player:		.50
1	Mike Piazza	1.50
2	Frank Thomas	1.50
3	Roberto Alomar	.75
4	Cal Ripken Jr.	2.00
5	Matt Williams	.50
6	Barry Bonds	1.00
7	Ken Griffey Jr.	2.50
8	Tony Gwynn	1.00
9	Greg Maddux	1.25

1995 Fleer All-Rookies

This mail-in set was available by redeeming a randomly inserted trade card found in packs. The cards feature action player photos on a muted background, with the player ID in gold-foil beneath a huge rookie banner. Horizontal backs have a player photo at left and professional highlights at right. Cards have an "M" prefix to the card number.

		MT
Complete Set (9):		5.00
Common Player:		.50
Trade card (expired Sept. 30, 1995):		.50
1	Edgardo Alfonzo	2.00
2	Jason Bates	.75
3	Brian Boehringer	.50
4	Darren Bragg	.75
5	Brad Clontz	.50
6	Jim Dougherty	.50
7	Todd Hollandsworth	.75
8	Rudy Pemberton	.50
9	Frank Rodriguez	.75

1995 Fleer All-Stars

All-Stars are a horizontal, two-sided insert set consisting of 25 cards. A National League All-Star is on one side, while an American League All-Star is on the other, by position. All-Stars are the most common insert in Fleer 1995 baseball, with an insertion ratio of one per three packs.

		MT
Complete Set (25):		8.00
Common Player:		.15
1	Ivan Rodriguez, Mike Piazza	1.50
2	Frank Thomas, Gregg Jefferies	1.00
3	Roberto Alomar, Mariano Duncan	.50
4	Wade Boggs, Matt Williams	.50
5	Cal Ripken, Jr., Ozzie Smith	1.75
6	Joe Carter, Barry Bonds	.40
7	Ken Griffey, Jr., Tony Gwynn	2.00
8	Kirby Puckett, Dave Justice	1.00
9	Jimmy Key, Greg Maddux	1.25
10	Chuck Knoblauch, Wil Cordero	.20
11	Scott Cooper, Ken Caminiti	.15
12	Will Clark, Carlos Garcia	.25
13	Paul Molitor, Jeff Bagwell	.40
14	Travis Fryman, Craig Biggio	.20
15	Mickey Tettleton, Fred McGriff	.15
16	Kenny Lofton, Moises Alou	.20
17	Albert Belle, Marquis Grissom	.50
18	Paul O'Neill, Dante Bichette	.15
19	David Cone, Ken Hill	.15
20	Mike Mussina, Doug Drabek	.20
21	Randy Johnson, John Hudek	.40
22	Pat Hentgen, Danny Jackson	.15
23	Wilson Alvarez, Rod Beck	.15
24	Lee Smith, Randy Myers	.15
25	Jason Bere, Doug Jones	.15

1995 Fleer Award Winners

Fleer Award Winners contain Fleer's choices of baseball's most outstanding players. This six-card set was only inserted at a rate of one per 24 packs. Each card has an embossed gold foil design, with the gold strip running up the left side and containing the words "Fleer Award Winner" and the player name.

		MT
Complete Set (6):		7.00
Common Player:		.40
1	Frank Thomas	3.00
2	Jeff Bagwell	2.00
3	David Cone	.50
4	Greg Maddux	3.00
5	Bob Hamelin	.40
6	Raul Mondesi	.50

1995 Fleer League Leaders

League Leaders feature players on a horizontal format from 10 statistical categories from both leagues. "League Leader" is placed in a blue strip down the left-side of the card, with their respective league and their name in it. These were inserted at a rate of one per 12 packs.

		MT
Complete Set (10):		7.50
Common Player:		.40
1	Paul O'Neill	.45
2	Ken Griffey, Jr.	4.00
3	Kirby Puckett	1.25
4	Jimmy Key	.40
5	Randy Johnson	1.00
6	Tony Gwynn	1.50
7	Matt Williams	.50
8	Jeff Bagwell	1.25
9	Greg Maddux, Ken Hill	1.50
10	Andy Benes	.40

1995 Fleer Lumber Company

Ten of the top longball hitters were featured in Lumber Company, which were inserted into every 24 12-card retailer packs. They show the power hitter in action, with a woodgrain Lumber Co. logo across the bottom, contain the player's name and team.

		MT
Complete Set (10):		25.00
Common Player:		.75
1	Jeff Bagwell	3.50
2	Albert Belle	2.50
3	Barry Bonds	3.00
4	Jose Canseco	2.00
5	Joe Carter	.75
6	Ken Griffey, Jr.	12.00
7	Fred McGriff	1.50
8	Kevin Mitchell	.75
9	Frank Thomas	4.00
10	Matt Williams	1.00

1995 Fleer Major League Prospects

Major League Prospects showcases 10 of 1995's most promising young players. The set title is repeatedly printed across the background, with the player's name and team in a grey strip across the bottom. These cards were inserted into one every six packs.

		MT
Complete Set (10):		7.00
Common Player:		.25
1	Garret Anderson	.75
2	James Baldwin	.25
3	Alan Benes	.75
4	Armando Benitez	.25
5	Ray Durham	.75
6	Brian Hunter	.35
7a	Derek Jeter (no licensor logos on back)	5.00
7b	Derek Jeter (licensor logos on back)	5.00
8	Charles Johnson	.40
9	Orlando Miller	.25
10	Alex Rodriguez	6.00

1995 Fleer Pro-Visions

Pro-Visions contain six interlocking cards that form one giant picture. These original art cards exhibit the player in a fantasy art background and are inserted into every nine packs.

		MT
Complete Set (6):		2.00
Common Player:		.25
1	Mike Mussina	.25
2	Raul Mondesi	.25
3	Jeff Bagwell	.75
4	Greg Maddux	1.00
5	Tim Salmon	.25
6	Manny Ramirez	.75

1995 Fleer Rookie Sensations

A perenial favorite within Fleer products, Rookie Sensations cards were inserted in 18-card packs only, at a rate of one per 16 packs. This 20-card set featured the top rookies from the 1994 season. The player's name and team run up the right side of the card, while the words "Rookie Sensations" appear in the bottom-left corner, separated by a colorful, zig-zagged image of a player.

		MT
Complete Set (20):		25.00
Common Player:		1.00
1	Kurt Abbott	1.00
2	Rico Brogna	1.00
3	Hector Carrasco	1.00
4	Kevin Foster	1.00
5	Chris Gomez	1.00
6	Darren Hall	1.00
7	Bob Hamelin	1.00
8	Joey Hamilton	1.00
9	John Hudek	1.00
10	Ryan Klesko	1.50
11	Javier Lopez	2.50
12	Matt Mieske	1.00
13	Raul Mondesi	3.00
14	Manny Ramirez	10.00
15	Shane Reynolds	1.00
16	Bill Risley	1.00
17	Johnny Ruffin	1.00
18	Steve Trachsel	1.00
19	William Van Landingham	1.00
20	Rondell White	3.00

1995 Fleer Team Leaders

Team Leaders are two-player cards featuring the leading hitter and pitcher from each major league team, one on each side. Inserted at a rate of one per 24 packs, these are only found in 12-card hobby packs. Team Leaders consisted of 28 cards and included a Team Leader logo in the bottom-left corner.

		MT
Complete Set (28):		140.00
Common Player:		1.25
1	Cal Ripken, Jr., Mike Mussina	20.00
2	Mo Vaughn, Roger Clemens	12.00
3	Tim Salmon, Chuck Finley	2.00
4	Frank Thomas, Jack McDowell	10.00
5	Albert Belle, Dennis Martinez	6.00
6	Cecil Fielder, Mike Moore	1.25

7	Bob Hamelin, David Cone	1.25
8	Greg Vaughn, Ricky Bones	1.25
9	Kirby Puckett, Rick Aguilera	8.00
10	Don Mattingly, Jimmy Key	10.00
11	Ruben Sierra, Dennis Eckersley	1.50
12	Ken Griffey, Jr., Randy Johnson	25.00
13	Jose Canseco, Kenny Rogers	5.00
14	Joe Carter, Pat Hentgen	1.25
15	Dave Justice, Greg Maddux	15.00
16	Sammy Sosa, Steve Trachsel	15.00
17	Kevin Mitchell, Jose Rijo	1.25
18	Dante Bichette, Bruce Ruffin	2.00
19	Jeff Conine, Robb Nen	1.50
20	Jeff Bagwell, Doug Drabek	8.00
21	Mike Piazza, Ramon Martinez	15.00
22	Moises Alou, Ken Hill	1.50
23	Bobby Bonilla, Bret Saberhagen	1.25
24	Darren Daulton, Danny Jackson	1.25
25	Jay Bell, Zane Smith	1.25
26	Gregg Jefferies, Bob Tewksbury	1.25
27	Tony Gwynn, Andy Benes	10.00
28	Matt Williams, Rod Beck	1.50

1995 Fleer Update

Fleer carried its "different by design" concept of six formats (one for each division in each league) from the regular set into its 1995 Update issue. The issue consists of 200 cards of 1995's traded, rookie and free agent players, plus five different insert sets. One insert card was found in each regular (12-card, $1.49) and jumbo (18-card, $2.29) pack. Cards are numbered with a "U" prefix.

		MT
Complete Set (200):		14.00
Common Player:		.10
Pack (12):		1.25
Wax Box (36):		35.00
1	Manny Alexander	.10
2	Bret Barberie	.10
3	Armando Benitez	.10
4	Kevin Brown	.10
5	Doug Jones	.10
6	Sherman Obando	.10
7	Andy Van Slyke	.10
8	Stan Belinda	.10
9	Jose Canseco	.30
10	Vaughn Eshelman	.10
11	Mike Macfarlane	.10
12	Troy O'Leary	.10
13	Steve Rodriguez	.10
14	Lee Tinsley	.10
15	Tim Vanegmond	.10
16	Mark Whiten	.10
17	Sean Bergman	.10
18	Chad Curtis	.10
19	John Flaherty	.10
20	*Bob Higginson*	.25
21	Felipe Lira	.10
22	Shannon Penn	.10
23	Todd Steverson	.10
24	Sean Whiteside	.10
25	Tony Fernandez	.10
26	Jack McDowell	.10
27	Andy Petitte	.12
28	John Wetteland	.10
29	David Cone	.15
30	Mike Timlin	.10
31	Duane Ward	.10
32	Jim Abbott	.15
33	James Baldwin	.10
34	Mike Devereaux	.10
35	Ray Durham	.25
36	Tim Fortugno	.10
37	Scott Ruffcorn	.10
38	Chris Sabo	.10
39	Paul Assenmacher	.10
40	Bud Black	.10
41	Orel Hershiser	.12
42	Julian Tavarez	.10
43	Dave Winfield	.15
44	Pat Borders	.10
45	*Melvin Bunch*	.15
46	Tom Goodwin	.10
47	Jon Nunnally	.10
48	Joe Randa	.10
49	*Dilson Torres*	.10
50	Joe Vitiello	.10
51	David Hulse	.10
52	Scott Karl	.10
53	Mark Kiefer	.10
54	Derrick May	.10
55	Joe Oliver	.10
56	Al Reyes	.10
57	*Steve Sparks*	.15
58	Jerald Clark	.10
59	Eddie Guardado	.10
60	Kevin Maas	.10
61	David McCarty	.10
62	*Brad Radke*	.15
63	Scott Stahoviak	.10
64	Garret Anderson	.15
65	Shawn Boskie	.10
66	Mike James	.10
67	Tony Phillips	.10
68	Lee Smith	.12
69	Mitch Williams	.10
70	Jim Corsi	.10
71	Mark Harkey	.10
72	Dave Stewart	.12
73	Todd Stottlemyre	.10
74	Joey Cora	.10
75	Chad Kreuter	.10
76	Jeff Nelson	.10
77	Alex Rodriguez	2.00
78	Ron Villone	.10
79	*Bob Wells*	.15
80	*Jose Alberro*	.15
81	Terry Burrows	.10
82	Kevin Gross	.10
83	Wilson Heredia	.10
84	Mark McLemore	.10
85	Otis Nixon	.10
86	Jeff Russell	.10
87	Mickey Tettleton	.10
88	Bob Tewksbury	.10
89	Pedro Borbon	.10
90	Marquis Grissom	.12
91	Chipper Jones	.75
92	Mike Mordecai	.10
93	*Jason Schmidt*	.25
94	John Burkett	.10
95	Andre Dawson	.15
96	*Matt Dunbar*	.15
97	Charles Johnson	.15
98	Terry Pendleton	.10
99	Rich Scheid	.10
100	Quilvio Veras	.10
101	Bobby Witt	.10
102	Eddie Zosky	.10
103	Shane Andrews	.10
104	Reid Cornelius	.10
105	*Chad Fonville*	.20
106	*Mark Grudzielanek*	.30
107	Roberto Kelly	.10
108	*Carlos Perez*	.15
109	Tony Tarasco	.10
110	Brett Butler	.15
111	Carl Everett	.10
112	Pete Harnisch	.10
113	Doug Henry	.10
114	Kevin Lomon	.10
115	Blas Minor	.10
116	Dave Mlicki	.10
117	*Ricky Otero*	.15
118	Norm Charlton	.10
119	Tyler Green	.10
120	Gene Harris	.10
121	Charlie Hayes	.10
122	Gregg Jefferies	.15
123	*Michael Mimbs*	.20
124	Paul Quantrill	.10
125	Frank Castillo	.10
126	Brian McRae	.10
127	Jaime Navarro	.10
128	Mike Perez	.10
129	Tanyon Sturtze	.10
130	Ozzie Timmons	.10
131	John Courtright	.10
132	Ron Gant	.15
133	Xavier Hernandez	.10
134	Brian Hunter	.10
135	Benito Santiago	.10
136	Pete Smith	.10
137	Scott Sullivan	.10
138	Derek Bell	.15
139	Doug Brocail	.10
140	Ricky Gutierrez	.10
141	Pedro Martinez	.25
142	Orlando Miller	.10
143	Phil Plantier	.10
144	Craig Shipley	.10
145	Rich Aude	.10
146	*Jason Christiansen*	.15
147	*Freddy Garcia*	.15
148	Jim Gott	.10
149	*Mark Johnson*	.20
150	Esteban Loaiza	.15
151	Dan Plesac	.10
152	*Gary Wilson*	.10
153	Allen Battle	.10
154	Terry Bradshaw	.10
155	Scott Cooper	.10
156	Tripp Cromer	.10
157	John Frascatore	.10
158	John Habyan	.10
159	Tom Henke	.10
160	Ken Hill	.10
161	Danny Jackson	.10
162	Donovan Osborne	.10
163	Tom Urbani	.10
164	Roger Bailey	.10
165	*Jorge Brito*	.15
166	Vinny Castilla	.15
167	Darren Holmes	.10
168	Roberto Mejia	.10
169	Bill Swift	.10
170	Mark Thompson	.10
171	Larry Walker	.40
172	Greg Hansell	.10
173	Dave Hansen	.10
174	Carlos Hernandez	.10
175	*Hideo Nomo*	2.00
176	Jose Offerman	.10
177	Antonio Osuna	.10
178	Reggie Williams	.10
179	Todd Williams	.10
180	Andres Berumen	.10
181	Ken Caminiti	.15
182	Andujar Cedeno	.10
183	Steve Finley	.10
184	Bryce Florie	.10
185	Dustin Hermanson	.15
186	Ray Holbert	.10
187	Melvin Nieves	.10
188	Roberto Petagine	.10
189	Jody Reed	.10
190	Fernando Valenzuela	.10
191	Brian Williams	.10
192	Mark Dewey	.10
193	Glenallen Hill	.10
194	*Chris Hook*	.15
195	Terry Mulholland	.10
196	Steve Scarsone	.10
197	Trevor Wilson	.10
198	Checklist	.10
199	Checklist	.10
200	Checklist	.10

1995 Fleer Update Diamond Tribute

Borderless action photos and gold-foil graphics are front features of this chase set honoring perhaps the 10 top names among baseball's veteran players. Backs have another photo and a few sentences describing what makes the player worthy of inclusion in such a set. The Diamond Tribute cards are found on the average of one per five packs.

		MT
Complete Set (10):		7.00
Common Player:		.25
1	Jeff Bagwell	.75
2	Albert Belle	.75
3	Barry Bonds	.60
4	David Cone	.25
5	Dennis Eckersley	.25
6	Ken Griffey Jr.	2.50
7	Rickey Henderson	.50
8	Greg Maddux	2.00
9	Frank Thomas	2.00
10	Matt Williams	.40

1995 Fleer Update Headliners

The most common of the Fleer Update inserts are the Headliners cards found on average of one per three packs. Fronts have an action photo set against a collage of newspaper clippings. The graphics are gold-foil. Backs have another color photo and a "Fleer Times" newspaper background with career summary and/or quotes about the featured player.

		MT
Complete Set (20):		10.00
Common Player:		.25
1	Jeff Bagwell	.75
2	Albert Belle	.75
3	Barry Bonds	.75
4	Jose Canseco	.50
5	Joe Carter	.25
6	Will Clark	.35
7	Roger Clemens	.75
8	Lenny Dykstra	.25
9	Cecil Fielder	.25
10	Juan Gonzalez	1.00
11	Ken Griffey Jr.	3.00
12	Kenny Lofton	1.00
13	Greg Maddux	2.00
14	Fred McGriff	.40
15	Mike Piazza	2.00
16	Kirby Puckett	1.00
17	Tim Salmon	.40
18	Frank Thomas	2.00
19	Mo Vaughn	.60
20	Matt Williams	.40

1995 Fleer Update Rookie Update

Ten of 1995's top rookies are featured in this horizontally formatted insert set. Fronts have an action photo with a large gold-foil "ROOKIE UPDATE" headline at top. Backs have another photo and career summary. Rookie Update chase cards are found on the average of one per four packs.

		MT
Complete Set (10):		9.00
Common Player:		.15
1	Shane Andrews	.25
2	Ray Durham	.75
3	Shawn Green	2.00
4	Charles Johnson	.75
5	Chipper Jones	3.25
6	Esteban Loaiza	.25
7	Hideo Nomo	1.50
8	Jon Nunnally	.20
9	Alex Rodriguez	4.00
10	Julian Tavarez	.15

1995 Fleer Update Smooth Leather

These inserts featuring top fielders were found only in pre-priced (magazine) foil packs, at an average rate of one card per 12 packs. Fronts are highlighted with gold-foil graphics. Backs have a glove in the background and explain the player's defensive abilities.

		MT
Complete Set (10):		20.00
Common Player:		.50
1	Roberto Alomar	1.25
2	Barry Bonds	1.50
3	Ken Griffey Jr.	7.50
4	Marquis Grissom	.50
5	Darren Lewis	.50
6	Kenny Lofton	1.25
7	Don Mattingly	2.50
8	Cal Ripken Jr.	9.00
9	Ivan Rodriguez	1.00
10	Matt Williams	.90

1995 Fleer Update Soaring Stars

A metallic foil-etched background behind the color player action photo identifies this chase set as the toughest among those in the 1995 Fleer Update issue. The Soaring Star cards are found at the average rate of one per box. Backs are conventionally printed and featured a colorful posterized version of the front background, along with another color photo and a career summary.

		MT
Complete Set (9):		30.00
Common Player:		1.25
1	Moises Alou	1.50
2	Jason Bere	1.25
3	Jeff Conine	1.25
4	Cliff Floyd	1.25
5	Pat Hentgen	1.25
6	Kenny Lofton	7.00
7	Raul Mondesi	4.00
8	Mike Piazza	9.00
9	Tim Salmon	2.00

1995 Fleer-Panini Stickers

Following Fleer's purchase of the well-known Italian sticker company, Panini, it was no surprise to see the companies produce a 1995 baseball issue. Titled "Major League Baseball All-Stars," the set consists of 156 player and team logo stickers. A 36-page color album to house the stickers was sold for $1.19. Sold in six-sticker packs for about .50, the individual stickers measure 1-15/16" x 3". Borders are team color-coded and have the player name and team logo at bottom, with the position abbreviation in a diamond at top-right. Backs are printed in black-and-white and include a sticker number, copyright notice and large logos of the licensors and Fleer/Panini. Each sticker can be found with backs that do, or do not, include a promotional message beginning, "Collect all 156 . . ."

		MT
Complete Set (156):		18.00
Common Player:		.10
Album:		1.25
1	Tom Glavine	.12
2	Doug Drabek	.10
3	Rod Beck	.10
4	Pedro J. Martinez	.15
5	Danny Jackson	.10
6	Greg Maddux	.30
7	Bret Saberhagen	.10
8	Ken Hill	.10
9	Marvin Freeman	.10
10	Andy Benes	.10
11	Wilson Alvarez	.10
12	Jimmy Key	.10
13	Mike Mussina	.12
14	Roger Clemens	.25
15	Pat Hentgen	.10
16	Randy Johnson	.20
17	Lee Smith	.12
18	David Cone	.12
19	Jason Bere	.10
20	Dennis Martinez	.12
21	Darren Daulton	.10
22	Darrin Fletcher	.10
23	Tom Pagnozzi	.10
24	Mike Piazza	.30
25	Benito Santiago	.10
26	Sandy Alomar Jr.	.15
27	Chris Hoiles	.10
28	Ivan Rodriguez	.20
29	Mike Stanley	.10
30	Dave Nilsson	.10
31	Jeff Bagwell	.25
32	Mark Grace	.20
33	Gregg Jefferies	.10
34	Andres Galarraga	.12
35	Fred McGriff	.15
36	Will Clark	.15
37	Mo Vaughn	.20
38	Don Mattingly	.40
39	Frank Thomas	.25
40	Cecil Fielder	.15
41	Robby Thompson	.10
42	Delino DeShields	.10
43	Carlos Garcia	.10
44	Bret Boone	.10
45	Craig Biggio	.15
46	Roberto Alomar	.20
47	Chuck Knoblauch	.15
48	Jose Lind	.10
49	Carlos Baerga	.10
50	Lou Whitaker	.10
51	Bobby Bonilla	.12
52	Tim Wallach	.10
53	Todd Zeile	.10
54	Matt Williams	.12
55	Ken Caminiti	.12
56	Robin Ventura	.12
57	Wade Boggs	.20
58	Scott Cooper	.10
59	Travis Fryman	.10
60	Dean Palmer	.10
61	Jay Bell	.10
62	Barry Larkin	.12
63	Ozzie Smith	.20
64	Wil Cordero	.10
65	Royce Clayton	.10
66	Chris Gomez	.10
67	Ozzie Guillen	.10
68	Cal Ripken Jr.	.50
69	Omar Vizquel	.10
70	Gary DiSarcina	.10
71	Dante Bichette	.15
72	Lenny Dykstra	.10
73	Barry Bonds	.25
74	Gary Sheffield	.15
75	Larry Walker	.20
76	Raul Mondesi	.15
77	Dave Justice	.15
78	Moises Alou	.12
79	Tony Gwynn	.30
80	Deion Sanders	.15
81	Kenny Lofton	.20
82	Kirby Puckett	.40
83	Juan Gonzalez	.30
84	Jay Buhner	.10
85	Joe Carter	.10
86	Ken Griffey Jr.	.50
87	Ruben Sierra	.10
88	Tim Salmon	.15
89	Paul O'Neill	.12
90	Albert Belle	.20
91	Danny Tartabull	.10
92	Jose Canseco	.20
93	Harold Baines	.10
94	Kirk Gibson	.10
95	Chili Davis	.10
96	Eddie Murray	.20
97	Bob Hamelin	.10
98	Paul Molitor	.20
99	Raul Mondesi	.15
100	Ryan Klesko	.15
101	Cliff Floyd	.10
102	William VanLandingham	.10
103	Joey Hamilton	.10
104	John Hudek	.10
105	Manny Ramirez	.20

106	Bob Hamelin	.10
107	Rusty Greer	.10
108	Chris Gomez	.10
	Award Winners	
109	Greg Maddux	.15
110	Jeff Bagwell	.12
111	Raul Mondesi	.15
112	David Cone	.10
113	Frank Thomas	.35
114	Bob Hamelin	.10
	League Leaders	
115	Tony Gwynn	.15
116	Matt Williams	.10
117	Jeff Bagwell	.15
118	Craig Biggio	.10
119	Andy Benes	.10
120	Greg Maddux	.20
121	John Franco	.10
122	Paul O'Neill	.10
123	Ken Griffey Jr.	.35
124	Kirby Puckett	.20
125	Kenny Lofton	.25
126	Randy Johnson	.10
127	Jimmy Key	.10
128	Lee Smith	.10
129	San Francisco Giants logo	.10
130	Montreal Expos logo	.10
131	Cincinnati Reds logo	.10
132	Los Angeles Dodgers logo	.10
133	New York Mets logo	.10
134	San Diego Padres logo	.10
135	Colorado Rockies logo	.10
136	Pittsburgh Pirates logo	.10
137	Florida Marlins logo	.10
138	Philadelphia Phillies logo	.10
139	Atlanta Braves logo	.10
140	Houston Astros logo	.10
141	St. Louis Cardinals logo	.10
142	Chicago Cubs logo	.10
143	Cleveland Indians logo	.10
144	New York Yankees logo	.10
145	Kansas City Royals logo	.10
146	Chicago White Sox logo	.10
147	Baltimore Orioles logo	.10
148	Seattle Mariners logo	.10
149	Boston Red Sox logo	.10
150	California Angels logo	.10
151	Toronto Blue Jays logo	.10
152	Detroit Tigers logo	.10
153	Texas Rangers logo	.10
154	Oakland A's logo	.10
155	Milwaukee Brewers logo	.10
156	Minnesota Twins logo	.10

1996 Fleer

In a radical departure from the UV-coated standard for even base-brand baseball cards, Fleer's 1996 issue is printed on a matte surface. Fronts feature borderless game-action photos with minimal (player ID, Fleer logo) graphic enhancement in gold foil. Backs have a white background, a portrait photo, full pro stats and a few career highlights. The single-series set was sold in basic 11-card packs with one of nearly a dozen insert-set cards in each $1.49 pack. The set is arranged alphabetically by player within team and league. A glossy-surface Tiffany Collection parallel was included in each pack.

	MT
Complete Set (600):	60.00
Common Player:	.05
Complete Tiffany Set (600):	150.00
Tiffanies:	3X
Pack (11):	1.50
Wax Box (36):	45.00

1	Manny Alexander	.05
2	Brady Anderson	.10
3	Harold Baines	.08
4	Armando Benitez	.05
5	Bobby Bonilla	.10
6	Kevin Brown	.05
7	Scott Erickson	.05
8	Curtis Goodwin	.05
9	Jeffrey Hammonds	.05
10	Jimmy Haynes	.05
11	Chris Hoiles	.05
12	Doug Jones	.05
13	Rick Krivda	.05
14	Jeff Manto	.05
15	Ben McDonald	.05
16	Jamie Moyer	.05
17	Mike Mussina	.30
18	Jesse Orosco	.05
19	Rafael Palmeiro	.20
20	Cal Ripken Jr.	2.50
20 (p)	Cal Ripken Jr. (overprinted "PROMOTIONAL SAMPLE")	8.00
21	Rick Aguilera	.05
22	Luis Alicea	.05
23	Stan Belinda	.05
24	Jose Canseco	.30
25	Roger Clemens	.75
26	Vaughn Eshelman	.05
27	Mike Greenwell	.05
28	Erik Hanson	.05
29	Dwayne Hosey	.05
30	Mike Macfarlane	.05
31	Tim Naehring	.05
32	Troy O'Leary	.05
33	Aaron Sele	.05
34	Zane Smith	.05
35	Jeff Suppan	.05
36	Lee Tinsley	.05
37	John Valentin	.10
38	Mo Vaughn	.75
39	Tim Wakefield	.05
40	Jim Abbott	.10
41	Brian Anderson	.05
42	Garret Anderson	.10
43	Chili Davis	.08
44	Gary DiSarcina	.05
45	Damion Easley	.05
46	Jim Edmonds	.10
47	Chuck Finley	.05
48	Todd Greene	.05
49	Mike Harkey	.05
50	Mike James	.05
51	Mark Langston	.05
52	Greg Myers	.05
53	Orlando Palmeiro	.05
54	Bob Patterson	.05
55	Troy Percival	.05
56	Tony Phillips	.05
57	Tim Salmon	.20
58	Lee Smith	.08
59	J.T. Snow	.10
60	Randy Velarde	.05
61	Wilson Alvarez	.05
62	*Luis Andujar*	.05
63	Jason Bere	.05
64	Ray Durham	.05
65	Alex Fernandez	.05
66	Ozzie Guillen	.05
67	Roberto Hernandez	.05
68	Lance Johnson	.05
69	Matt Karchner	.05
70	Ron Karkovice	.05
71	Norberto Martin	.05
72	Dave Martinez	.05
73	Kirk McCaskill	.05
74	Lyle Mouton	.05
75	Tim Raines	.10
76	*Mike Sirotka*	.75
77	Frank Thomas	1.00
78	Larry Thomas	.05
79	Robin Ventura	.15
80	Sandy Alomar Jr.	.10
81	Paul Assenmacher	.05
82	Carlos Baerga	.08
83	Albert Belle	.75
84	Mark Clark	.05
85	Alan Embree	.05
86	Alvaro Espinoza	.05
87	Orel Hershiser	.08
88	Ken Hill	.05
89	Kenny Lofton	.75
90	Dennis Martinez	.08
91	Jose Mesa	.05
92	Eddie Murray	.35
93	Charles Nagy	.08
94	Chad Ogea	.05
95	Tony Pena	.05
96	Herb Perry	.05
97	Eric Plunk	.05
98	Jim Poole	.05
99	Manny Ramirez	1.00
100	Paul Sorrento	.05
101	Julian Travarez	.05
102	Jim Thome	.40
103	Omar Vizquel	8.00
104	Dave Winfield	.20
105	Danny Bautista	.05
106	Joe Boever	.05
107	Chad Curtis	.05
108	John Doherty	.05
109	Cecil Fielder	.08
110	John Flaherty	.05
111	Travis Fryman	.08
112	Chris Gomez	.05
113	Bob Higginson	.10
114	Mark Lewis	.05
115	Jose Lima	.08
116	Felipe Lira	.05
117	Brian Maxcy	.05
118	C.J. Nitkowski	.05
119	Phil Plantier	.05
120	Clint Sodowsky	.05
121	Alan Trammell	.10
122	Lou Whitaker	.05
123	Kevin Appier	.05
124	Johnny Damon	.20
125	Gary Gaetti	.05
126	Tom Goodwin	.05
127	Tom Gordon	.05
128	Mark Gubicza	.05
129	Bob Hamelin	.05
130	David Howard	.05
131	Jason Jacome	.05
132	Wally Joyner	.08
133	Keith Lockhart	.05
134	Brent Mayne	.05
135	Jeff Montgomery	.05
136	Jon Nunnally	.05
137	Juan Samuel	.05
138	*Mike Sweeney*	2.00
139	Michael Tucker	.08
140	Joe Vitiello	.05
141	Ricky Bones	.05
142	Chuck Carr	.05
143	Jeff Cirillo	.05
144	Mike Fetters	.05
145	Darryl Hamilton	.05
146	David Hulse	.05
147	John Jaha	.05
148	Scott Karl	.05
149	Mark Kiefer	.05
150	Pat Listach	.05
151	Mark Loretta	.05
152	Mike Matheny	.05
153	Matt Mieske	.05
154	Dave Nilsson	.05
155	Joe Oliver	.05
156	Al Reyes	.05
157	Kevin Seitzer	.05
158	Steve Sparks	.05
159	B.J. Surhoff	.08
160	Jose Valentin	.05
161	Greg Vaughn	.10
162	Fernando Vina	.05
163	Rich Becker	.05
164	Ron Coomer	.05
165	Marty Cordova	.10
166	Chuck Knoblauch	.20
167	*Matt Lawton*	.50
168	Pat Meares	.05
169	Paul Molitor	.40
170	Pedro Munoz	.05
171	Jose Parra	.05
172	Kirby Puckett	1.00
173	Brad Radke	.05
174	Jeff Reboulet	.05
175	Rich Robertson	.05
176	Frank Rodriguez	.05
177	Scott Stahoviak	.05
178	Dave Stevens	.05
179	Matt Walbeck	.05
180	Wade Boggs	.30
181	David Cone	.08
182	Tony Fernandez	.05
183	Joe Girardi	.05
184	Derek Jeter	1.50
185	Scott Kamieniecki	.05
186	Pat Kelly	.05
187	Jim Leyritz	.05
188	Tino Martinez	.15
189	Don Mattingly	1.00
190	Jack McDowell	.05
191	Jeff Nelson	.05
192	Paul O'Neill	.10
193	Melido Perez	.05
194	Andy Pettitte	1.00
195	Mariano Rivera	.15
196	Ruben Sierra	.05
197	Mike Stanley	.05
198	Darryl Strawberry	.10
199	John Wetteland	.05
200	Bob Wickman	.05
201	Bernie Williams	.40
202	Mark Acre	.05
203	Geronimo Berroa	.05
204	Mike Bordick	.05
205	Scott Brosius	.05
206	Dennis Eckersley	.08
207	Brent Gates	.05
208	Jason Giambi	.10
209	Rickey Henderson	.30
210	Jose Herrera	.05
211	Stan Javier	.05
212	Doug Johns	.05
213	Mark McGwire	4.00
214	Steve Ontiveros	.05
215	Craig Paquette	.05
216	Ariel Prieto	.05
217	Carlos Reyes	.05
218	Terry Steinbach	.05
219	Todd Stottlemyre	.05
220	Danny Tartabull	.05
221	Todd Van Poppel	.05
222	John Wasdin	.05
223	George Williams	.05
224	Steve Wojciechowski	.05
225	Rich Amaral	.05
226	Bobby Ayala	.05
227	Tim Belcher	.05
228	Andy Benes	.08
229	Chris Bosio	.05
230	Darren Bragg	.05
231	Jay Buhner	.10
232	Norm Charlton	.05
233	Vince Coleman	.05
234	Joey Cora	.05
235	Russ Davis	.05
236	Alex Diaz	.05
237	Felix Fermin	.05
238	Ken Griffey Jr.	3.00
239	Sterling Hitchcock	.05
240	Randy Johnson	.25
241	Edgar Martinez	.08
242	Bill Risley	.05
243	Alex Rodriquez	2.50
244	Luis Sojo	.05
245	Dan Wilson	.05
246	Bob Wolcott	.05
247	Will Clark	.30
248	Jeff Frye	.05

No.	Player	Value
249	Benji Gil	.05
250	Juan Gonzalez	.75
251	Rusty Greer	.05
252	Kevin Gross	.05
253	Roger McDowell	.05
254	Mark McLemore	.05
255	Otis Nixon	.05
256	Luis Ortiz	.05
257	Mike Pagliarulo	.05
258	Dean Palmer	.05
259	Roger Pavlik	.05
260	Ivan Rodriguez	.65
261	Kenny Rogers	.05
262	Jeff Russell	.05
263	Mickey Tettleton	.05
264	Bob Tewksbury	.05
265	Dave Valle	.05
266	Matt Whiteside	.05
267	Roberto Alomar	.75
268	Joe Carter	.08
269	Tony Castillo	.05
270	Domingo Cedeno	.05
271	Timothy Crabtree	.05
272	Carlos Delgado	.40
273	Alex Gonzalez	.05
274	Shawn Green	.15
275	Juan Guzman	.05
276	Pat Hentgen	.05
277	Al Leiter	.08
278	*Sandy Martinez*	.05
279	Paul Menhart	.05
280	John Olerud	.12
281	Paul Quantrill	.05
282	Ken Robinson	.05
283	Ed Sprague	.05
284	Mike Timlin	.05
285	Steve Avery	.05
286	Rafael Belliard	.05
287	Jeff Blauser	.05
288	Pedro Borbon	.05
289	Brad Clontz	.05
290	Mike Devereaux	.05
291	Tom Glavine	.15
292	Marquis Grissom	.08
293	Chipper Jones	1.75
294	David Justice	.20
295	Mike Kelly	.05
296	Ryan Klesko	.25
297	Mark Lemke	.05
298	Javier Lopez	.15
299	Greg Maddux	1.50
300	Fred McGriff	.35
301	Greg McMichael	.05
302	Kent Mercker	.05
303	Mike Mordecai	.05
304	Charlie O'Brien	.05
305	Eduardo Perez	.05
306	Luis Polonia	.05
307	Jason Schmidt	.05
308	John Smoltz	.20
309	Terrell Wade	.05
310	Mark Wohlers	.05
311	Scott Bullett	.05
312	Jim Bullinger	.05
313	Larry Casian	.05
314	Frank Castillo	.05
315	Shawon Dunston	.05
316	Kevin Foster	.05
317	Matt Franco	.05
318	Luis Gonzalez	.08
319	Mark Grace	.25
320	Jose Hernandez	.05
321	Mike Hubbard	.05
322	Brian McRae	.05
323	Randy Myers	.05
324	Jaime Navarro	.05
325	Mark Parent	.05
326	Mike Perez	.05
327	Rey Sanchez	.05
328	Ryne Sandberg	.75
329	Scott Servais	.05
330	Sammy Sosa	1.50
331	Ozzie Timmons	.05
332	Steve Trachsel	.05
333	Todd Zeile	.08
334	Bret Boone	.05
335	Jeff Branson	.05
336	Jeff Brantley	.05
337	Dave Burba	.05
338	Hector Carrasco	.05
339	Mariano Duncan	.05
340	Ron Gant	.10
341	Lenny Harris	.05
342	Xavier Hernandez	.05
343	Thomas Howard	.05
344	Mike Jackson	.05
345	Barry Larkin	.10
346	Darren Lewis	.05
347	Hal Morris	.05
348	Eric Owens	.05
349	Mark Portugal	.05
350	Jose Rijo	.05
351	Reggie Sanders	.08
352	Benito Santiago	.05
353	Pete Schourek	.05
354	John Smiley	.05
355	Eddie Taubensee	.05
356	Jerome Walton	.05
357	David Wells	.08
358	Roger Bailey	.05
359	Jason Bates	.05
360	Dante Bichette	.15
361	Ellis Burks	.08
362	Vinny Castilla	.12
363	Andres Galarraga	.15
364	Darren Holmes	.05
365	Mike Kingery	.05
366	Curt Leskanic	.05
367	Quinton McCracken	.05
368	Mike Munoz	.05
369	David Nied	.05
370	Steve Reed	.05
371	Bryan Rekar	.05
372	Kevin Ritz	.05
373	Bruce Ruffin	.05
374	Bret Saberhagen	.08
375	Bill Swift	.05
376	John Vander Wal	.05
377	Larry Walker	.30
378	Walt Weiss	.05
379	Eric Young	.05
380	Kurt Abbott	.05
381	Alex Arias	.05
382	Jerry Browne	.05
383	John Burkett	.05
384	Greg Colbrunn	.05
385	Jeff Conine	.10
386	Andre Dawson	.20
387	Chris Hammond	.05
388	Charles Johnson	.10
389	Terry Mathews	.05
390	Robb Nen	.05
391	Joe Orsulak	.05
392	Terry Pendleton	.05
393	Pat Rapp	.05
394	Gary Sheffield	.40
395	Jesus Tavarez	.05
396	Marc Valdes	.05
397	Quilvio Veras	.05
398	Randy Veres	.05
399	Devon White	.05
400	Jeff Bagwell	1.00
401	Derek Bell	.10
402	Craig Biggio	.10
403	John Cangelosi	.05
404	Jim Dougherty	.05
405	Doug Drabek	.05
406	Tony Eusebio	.05
407	Ricky Gutierrez	.05
408	Mike Hampton	.05
409	Dean Hartgraves	.05
410	John Hudek	.05
411	Brian Hunter	.08
412	Todd Jones	.05
413	Darryl Kile	.05
414	Dave Magadan	.05
415	Derrick May	.05
416	Orlando Miller	.05
417	James Mouton	.05
418	Shane Reynolds	.05
419	Greg Swindell	.05
420	Jeff Tabaka	.05
421	Dave Veres	.05
422	Billy Wagner	.10
423	*Donne Wall*	.05
424	Rick Wilkins	.05
425	Billy Ashley	.05
426	Mike Blowers	.05
427	Brett Butler	.08
428	Tom Candiotti	.05
429	Juan Castro	.05
430	John Cummings	.05
431	Delino DeShields	.05
432	Joey Eischen	.05
433	Chad Fonville	.10
434	Greg Gagne	.05
435	Dave Hansen	.05
436	Carlos Hernandez	.05
437	Todd Hollandsworth	.08
438	Eric Karros	.10
439	Roberto Kelly	.05
440	Ramon Martinez	.08
441	Raul Mondesi	.30
442	Hideo Nomo	.45
443	Antonio Osuna	.05
444	Chan Ho Park	.08
445	Mike Piazza	1.75
446	Felix Rodriguez	.05
447	Kevin Tapani	.05
448	Ismael Valdes	.05
449	Todd Worrell	.05
450	Moises Alou	.10
451	Shane Andrews	.05
452	Yamil Benitez	.05
453	Sean Berry	.05
454	Wil Cordero	.05
455	Jeff Fassero	.05
456	Darrin Fletcher	.05
457	Cliff Floyd	.05
458	Mark Grudzielanek	.08
459	Gil Heredia	.05
460	Tim Laker	.05
461	Mike Lansing	.05
462	Pedro Martinez	.25
463	Carlos Perez	.05
464	Curtis Pride	.05
465	Mel Rojas	.05
466	Kirk Rueter	.05
467	*F.P. Santangelo*	.10
468	Tim Scott	.05
469	David Segui	.05
470	Tony Tarasco	.05
471	Rondell White	.10
472	Edgardo Alfonzo	.12
473	Tim Bogar	.05
474	Rico Brogna	.05
475	Damon Buford	.05
476	Paul Byrd	.05
477	Carl Everett	.05
478	John Franco	.05
479	Todd Hundley	.15
480	Butch Huskey	.10
481	Jason Isringhausen	.08
482	Bobby Jones	.05
483	Chris Jones	.05
484	Jeff Kent	.05
485	Dave Mlicki	.05
486	Robert Person	.05
487	Bill Pulsipher	.05
488	Kelly Stinnett	.05
489	Ryan Thompson	.05
490	Jose Vizcaino	.05
491	Howard Battle	.05
492	Toby Borland	.05
493	Ricky Bottalico	.05
494	Darren Daulton	.05
495	Lenny Dykstra	.05
496	Jim Eisenreich	.05
497	Sid Fernandez	.05
498	Tyler Green	.05
499	Charlie Hayes	.05
500	Gregg Jefferies	.10
501	Kevin Jordan	.05
502	Tony Longmire	.05
503	Tom Marsh	.05
504	Michael Mimbs	.05
505	Mickey Morandini	.05
506	Gene Schall	.05
507	Curt Schilling	.08
508	Heathcliff Slocumb	.05
509	Kevin Stocker	.05
510	Andy Van Slyke	.05
511	Lenny Webster	.05
512	Mark Whiten	.05
513	Mike Williams	.05
514	Jay Bell	.05
515	Jacob Brumfield	.05
516	Jason Christiansen	.05
517	Dave Clark	.05
518	Midre Cummings	.05
519	Angelo Encarnacion	.05
520	John Ericks	.05
521	Carlos Garcia	.05
522	Mark Johnson	.08
523	Jeff King	.05
524	Nelson Liriano	.05
525	Esteban Loaiza	.08
526	Al Martin	.05
527	Orlando Merced	.05
528	Dan Miceli	.05
529	Ramon Morel	.05
530	Denny Neagle	.05
531	Steve Parris	.05
532	Dan Plesac	.05
533	Don Slaught	.05
534	Paul Wagner	.05
535	John Wehner	.05
536	Kevin Young	.05
537	Allen Battle	.05
538	David Bell	.05
539	Alan Benes	.10
540	Scott Cooper	.05
541	Tripp Cromer	.05
542	Tony Fossas	.05
543	Bernard Gilkey	.10
544	Tom Henke	.05
545	Brian Jordan	.15
546	Ray Lankford	.10
547	John Mabry	.05
548	T.J. Mathews	.05
549	Mike Morgan	.05
550	Jose Oliva	.05
551	Jose Oquendo	.05
552	Donovan Osborne	.05
553	Tom Pagnozzi	.05
554	Mark Petkovsek	.05
555	Danny Sheaffer	.05
556	Ozzie Smith	.40
557	Mark Sweeney	.05
558	Allen Watson	.05
559	Andy Ashby	.08
560	Brad Ausmus	.05
561	Willie Blair	.05
562	Ken Caminiti	.15
563	Andujar Cedeno	.05
564	Glenn Dishman	.05
565	Steve Finley	.05
566	Bryce Florie	.05
567	Tony Gwynn	.75
568	Joey Hamilton	.10
569	Dustin Hermanson	.10
570	Trevor Hoffman	.08
571	Brian Johnson	.05
572	Marc Kroon	.05
573	Scott Livingstone	.05
574	Marc Newfield	.05
575	Melvin Nieves	.05
576	Jody Reed	.05
577	Bip Roberts	.05
578	Scott Sanders	.05
579	Fernando Valenzuela	.08
580	Eddie Williams	.05
581	Rod Beck	.05
582	*Marvin Benard*	.10
583	Barry Bonds	.75
584	Jamie Brewington	.05
585	Mark Carreon	.05
586	Royce Clayton	.05
587	Shawn Estes	.05
588	Glenallen Hill	.05
589	Mark Leiter	.05
590	Kirt Manwaring	.05
591	David McCarty	.05
592	Terry Mulholland	.05
593	John Patterson	.05
594	J.R. Phillips	.05
595	Deion Sanders	.15
596	Steve Scarsone	.05
597	Robby Thompson	.05
598	Sergio Valdez	.05
599	William VanLandingham	.05
600	Matt Williams	.25

1996 Fleer Checklists

Checklist cards are treated as an insert set in 1996 Fleer, appearing on average once every six packs. Like all other Fleer hobby inserts in the baseball set, the checklists are UV-coated front and back, in contrast to the matte-finish regular issue cards. Checklists have borderless game-action photos on front, with gold-foil typography. Backs have a large Fleer logo and checklist data on a white background.

		MT
Complete Set (10):		3.00
Common Player:		.25
1	Barry Bonds	.40
2	Ken Griffey Jr.	1.50
3	Chipper Jones	.75
4	Greg Maddux	.65
5	Mike Piazza	.75
6	Manny Ramirez	.50
7	Cal Ripken Jr.	1.00
8	Frank Thomas	.50
9	Mo Vaughn	.35
10	Matt Williams	.25

1996 Fleer Tiffany

While Fleer's basic card set for 1996 feature matte-surface cards, a glossy version of each regular card was also issued as a parallel insert set. Other than the UV coating on front and back and the use of silver- rather than gold-foil typography on front, the cards are identical to the regular '96 Fleer player cards. One glossy version card is found in each pack.

	MT
Complete Set (600):	150.00
Common Player:	.15
Stars:	3X

(See 1996 Fleer for checklist and base card values.)

1996 Fleer Golden Memories

Some of the 1995 season's greatest moments are captured in this insert set, a one per 10 pack pick. Fronts have two photos of the player, one in full color in the foreground and one in monochrome as a backdrop. Typography is in prismatic foil vertically down one side. Backs have another color player photo, along with details of the milestone. Two of the cards feature multiple players.

		MT
Complete Set (10):		6.00
Common Player:		.15
1	Albert Belle	.40
2	Barry Bonds, Sammy Sosa	1.00
3	Greg Maddux	1.00
4	Edgar Martinez	.15
5	Ramon Martinez	.15
6	Mark McGwire	2.50
7	Eddie Murray	.25
8	Cal Ripken Jr.	1.50
9	Frank Thomas	.75
10	Alan Trammell, Lou Whitaker	.15

1996 Fleer Lumber Company

Once again for 1996, a Fleer "Lumber Company" chase set honors the game's top sluggers. The '96 version has a horizontal format with a rather small player action photo on a background resembling the trademark area of a bat. The "trademark" is actually the player and team name along with the "Lumber Company" ID, printed in textured glossy black ink. Backs repeat the trademark motif and also include a close-up player photo and a few words about his power-hitting numbers. Lumber Company cards are a one per nine pack pick, on average, found only in retail packs.

		MT
Complete Set (12):		18.00
Common Player:		.50
1	Albert Belle	1.00
2	Dante Bichette	.75
3	Barry Bonds	1.25
4	Ken Griffey Jr.	5.00
5	Mark McGwire	6.00
6	Mike Piazza	3.00
7	Manny Ramirez	1.50
8	Tim Salmon	.75
9	Sammy Sosa	2.50
10	Frank Thomas	2.00
11	Mo Vaughn	1.00
12	Matt Williams	.75

1996 Fleer Post-Season Glory

Highlights of the 1995 postseason are featured in this small chase card set. Against a stadium background are multiple photos of the featured player, arranged horizontally. The vertical backs have another player photo down one side, and a description of his play-off performance on the other. Stated odds of picking one of these cards are one per five packs.

		MT
Complete Set (5):		2.50
Common Player:		.15
1	Tom Glavine	.20
2	Ken Griffey Jr.	2.00
3	Orel Hershiser	.15
4	Randy Johnson	.30
5	Jim Thome	.20

1996 Fleer Prospects

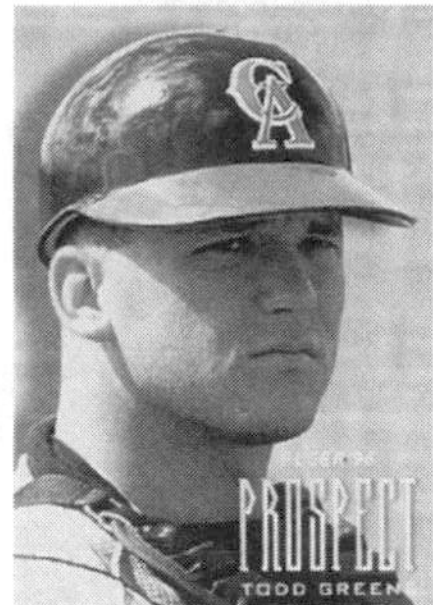

Minor leaguers who are expected to make it big in the big time are featured in this insert issue. Fronts feature large portrait photos against pastel backgrounds with player and set ID in prismatic foil. Backs have an action photo and repeat the front background color in a box which details the player's potential and career to date. Average odds of finding a Prospects card are one per six packs.

		MT
Complete Set (10):		3.00
Common Player:		.25
1	Yamil Benitez	.25
2	Roger Cedeno	.50
3	Tony Clark	1.00
4	Micah Franklin	.25
5	Karim Garcia	.75
6	Todd Greene	.25
7	Alex Ochoa	.25
8	Ruben Rivera	.75
9	Chris Snopek	.25
10	Shannon Stewart	.25

1996 Fleer Road Warriors

A black-and-white country highway photo is the background for the color player action photo on this insert set. Front typography is in silver foil. The players featured are those whose performance on the road is considered outstanding. Backs have a white background, portrait photo and stats bearing out the away-game superiority. These inserts are found at an average pace of one per 13 packs.

		MT
Complete Set (10):		9.00
Common Player:		.35
1	Derek Bell	.40
2	Tony Gwynn	1.25
3	Greg Maddux	1.50
4	Mark McGwire	4.00
5	Mike Piazza	2.00
6	Manny Ramirez	1.00
7	Tim Salmon	.50
8	Frank Thomas	1.25
9	Mo Vaughn	.90
10	Matt Williams	.40

1996 Fleer Rookie Sensations

Top rookies of the 1995 season are featured on this chase card set. Horizontally formatted, the cards have an action photo on one side and a large prismatic-foil end strip which displays the player name, team logo and card company identifiers. Backs have a portrait photo on as white background with a few sentences about the player's rookie season. Stated odds of finding one of these inserts is one per 11 packs, on average.

		MT
Complete Set (15):		12.00
Common Player:		.50
1	Garret Anderson	.75
2	Marty Cordova	.75
3	Johnny Damon	.75
4	Ray Durham	.50
5	Carl Everett	.75
6	Shawn Green	1.50
7	Brian Hunter	.50
8	Jason Isringhausen	.50
9	Charles Johnson	.75
10	Chipper Jones	6.00
11	John Mabry	.50
12	Hideo Nomo	1.50
13	Troy Percival	.50
14	Andy Pettitte	3.00
15	Quilvio Veras	.50

1996 Fleer Smoke 'N Heat

Once more using the "Smoke 'N Heat" identifier for a chase set of the game's hardest throwers, Fleer presents these select pitchers in action photos against a black-and-flame background. Front typography is in gold foil. Backs have a large portrait photo, repeat the flame motif as background and have a description of the pitcher's prowess in a black box. The cards are found, on average, once per nine packs.

		MT
Complete Set (10):		5.00
Common Player:		.25
1	Kevin Appier	.25
2	Roger Clemens	2.00
3	David Cone	.25
4	Chuck Finley	.25
5	Randy Johnson	.50
6	Greg Maddux	2.50
7	Pedro Martinez	.50
8	Hideo Nomo	.50
9	John Smoltz	.50
10	Todd Stottlemyre	.25

1996 Fleer Team Leaders

One player from each club has been selected for inclusion in the "Team Leaders" chase set. Fronts have action player photos on a background of metallic foil littered with multiple representations of the team logo. Gold-foil lettering identifies the player, team and chase set. Backs have a white background, portrait photo and description of the player's leadership role. Stated rate of insertion for this set is one card per nine packs, on average, found only in hobby packs.

		MT
Complete Set (28):		50.00
Common Player:		.60
1	Cal Ripken Jr.	10.00
2	Mo Vaughn	2.00
3	Jim Edmonds	.75
4	Frank Thomas	4.00
5	Kenny Lofton	2.00
6	Travis Fryman	.60
7	Gary Gaetti	.60
8	B.J. Surhoff	.60
9	Kirby Puckett	5.00
10	Don Mattingly	5.00
11	Mark McGwire	15.00
12	Ken Griffey Jr.	15.00
13	Juan Gonzalez	4.00
14	Joe Carter	.60
15	Greg Maddux	6.00
16	Sammy Sosa	6.00
17	Barry Larkin	1.00
18	Dante Bichette	1.50
19	Jeff Conine	.75
20	Jeff Bagwell	4.00
21	Mike Piazza	7.50
22	Rondell White	.75
23	Rico Brogna	.60
24	Darren Daulton	.60
25	Jeff King	.60
26	Ray Lankford	.60
27	Tony Gwynn	5.00
28	Barry Bonds	2.50

1996 Fleer Tomorrow's Legends

In this insert set the projected stars of tomorrow are featured in action poses on a busy multi-colored, quartered background of baseball symbols and the globe. Typography is in silver foil. Backs have a portrait photo and large team logo along with an early-career summary. Odds of finding a "Tomorrow's Legends" card are posted at one per 13 packs, on average.

		MT
Complete Set (10):		10.00
Common Player:		.40
1	Garret Anderson	.40
2	Jim Edmonds	.50
3	Brian Hunter	.40
4	Jason Isringhausen	.40
5	Charles Johnson	.40
6	Chipper Jones	5.00
7	Ryan Klesko	.75
8	Hideo Nomo	1.00
9	Manny Ramirez	2.50
10	Rondell White	.40

1996 Fleer Zone

The toughest pull (one in 90 packs, average) among the '96 Fleer chase cards is this set evoking the "zone" that the game's great players seek in which their performance is at its peak. The cards have action photos with a background of prismatic foil. Backs are conventionally printed but simulate the foil background and include a player portrait photo plus quotes about the player.

		MT
Complete Set (12):		75.00
Common Player:		3.00
1	Albert Belle	5.00
2	Barry Bonds	5.00
3	Ken Griffey Jr.	20.00
4	Tony Gwynn	10.00
5	Randy Johnson	5.00
6	Kenny Lofton	5.00
7	Greg Maddux	12.50
8	Edgar Martinez	3.00
9	Mike Piazza	15.00
10	Frank Thomas	7.50
11	Mo Vaughn	4.00
12	Matt Williams	4.00

1996 Fleer Update

Fleer Update Baseball has 250 cards, including more than 55 rookies, plus traded players and free agents in their new uniforms, 35 Encore subset cards and five checklists. Each card in the regular-issue set also has a parallel "Tiffany Collection" version, which has UV coating and holographic foil stamping in contrast to the matte finish and gold foil of the regular cards. Insert cards include Diamond Tribute, New Horizons, Smooth Leather and Soaring Stars. Each pack also contains a Fleer "Thanks a Million" scratch-off game card, redeemable for prizes. Cards are numbered with a "U" prefix.

		MT
Complete Set (250):		20.00
Common Player:		.05
Complete Glossy Set (250):		100.00
Glossy Stars:		3X
Pack (11):		1.50
Wax Box (24):		35.00
1	Roberto Alomar	.75
2	Mike Devereaux	.05
3	*Scott McClain*	.05
4	Roger McDowell	.05
5	Kent Mercker	.05
6	Jimmy Myers	.05
7	Randy Myers	.05
8	B.J. Surhoff	.08
9	Tony Tarasco	.05
10	David Wells	.08
11	Wil Cordero	.05
12	Tom Gordon	.05
13	Reggie Jefferson	.05
14	Jose Malave	.05
15	Kevin Mitchell	.05
16	Jamie Moyer	.05
17	Heathcliff Slocumb	.05
18	Mike Stanley	.05
19	George Arias	.05
20	Jorge Fabregas	.05
21	Don Slaught	.05
22	Randy Velarde	.05
23	Harold Baines	.05
24	*Mike Cameron*	1.00

25	Darren Lewis	.05
26	Tony Phillips	.05
27	Bill Simas	.05
28	Chris Snopek	.05
29	Kevin Tapani	.05
30	Danny Tartabull	.05
31	Julio Franco	.05
32	Jack McDowell	.08
33	Kimera Bartee	.05
34	Mark Lewis	.05
35	Melvin Nieves	.05
36	Mark Parent	.05
37	Eddie Williams	.05
38	Tim Belcher	.05
39	Sal Fasano	.05
40	Chris Haney	.05
41	Mike Macfarlane	.05
42	Jose Offerman	.05
43	Joe Randa	.05
44	Bip Roberts	.05
45	Chuck Carr	.05
46	Bobby Hughes	.05
47	Graeme Lloyd	.05
48	Ben McDonald	.05
49	Kevin Wickander	.05
50	Rick Aguilera	.05
51	Mike Durant	.05
52	Chip Hale	.05
53	LaTroy Hawkins	.05
54	Dave Hollins	.05
55	Roberto Kelly	.05
56	Paul Molitor	.25
57	*Dan Naulty*	.10
58	Mariano Duncan	.05
59	*Andy Fox*	.05
60	Joe Girardi	.05
61	Dwight Gooden	.10
62	Jimmy Key	.05
63	*Matt Luke*	.08
64	Tino Martinez	.08
65	Jeff Nelson	.05
66	Tim Raines	.08
67	Ruben Rivera	.25
68	Kenny Rogers	.05
69	Gerald Williams	.05
70	*Tony Batista*	8.00
71	Allen Battle	.05
72	Jim Corsi	.05
73	Steve Cox	.05
74	Pedro Munoz	.05
75	Phil Plantier	.05
76	Scott Spiezio	.05
77	Ernie Young	.05
78	Russ Davis	.05
79	Sterling Hitchcock	.05
80	Edwin Hurtado	.05
81	*Raul Ibanez*	.05
82	Mike Jackson	.05
83	Ricky Jordan	.05
84	Paul Sorrento	.05
85	Doug Strange	.05
86	Mark Brandenburg	.05
87	Damon Buford	.05
88	Kevin Elster	.05
89	Darryl Hamilton	.05
90	Ken Hill	.05
91	Ed Vosberg	.05
92	Craig Worthington	.05
93	Tilson Brito	.05
94	Giovanni Carrara	.05
95	Felipe Crespo	.05
96	Erik Hanson	.05
97	*Marty Janzen*	.05
98	Otis Nixon	.05
99	Charlie O'Brien	.05
100	Robert Perez	.05
101	Paul Quantrill	.05
102	Bill Risley	.05
103	Juan Samuel	.05
104	Jermaine Dye	.25
105	Wonderful Monds	.05
106	Dwight Smith	.05
107	Jerome Walton	.05
108	Terry Adams	.05
109	Leo Gomez	.05
110	*Robin Jennings*	.05
111	Doug Jones	.05
112	Brooks Kieschnick	.08
113	Dave Magadan	.05
114	*Jason Maxwell*	.05
115	Rodney Myers	.05
116	Eric Anthony	.05
117	Vince Coleman	.05
118	Eric Davis	.08
119	Steve Gibralter	.05
120	Curtis Goodwin	.05
121	Willie Greene	.05
122	Mike Kelly	.05
123	Marcus Moore	.05
124	Chad Mottola	.05
125	Chris Sabo	.05
126	Roger Salkeld	.05
127	Pedro Castellano	.05
128	Trenidad Hubbard	.05
129	Jayhawk Owens	.05
130	Jeff Reed	.05
131	Kevin Brown	.10
132	Al Leiter	.08
133	*Matt Mantei*	.75
134	Dave Weathers	.05
135	Devon White	.05
136	Bob Abreu	.15
137	Sean Berry	.05
138	Doug Brocail	.05
139	Richard Hidalgo	.08
140	Alvin Morman	.05
141	Mike Blowers	.05
142	Roger Cedeno	.08
143	Greg Gagne	.05
144	Karim Garcia	.75
145	*Wilton Guerrero*	.50
146	Israel Alcantara	.05
147	Omar Daal	.05
148	Ryan McGuire	.08
149	Sherman Obando	.05
150	Jose Paniagua	.05
151	Henry Rodriguez	.05
152	Andy Stankiewicz	.05
153	Dave Veres	.05
154	Juan Acevedo	.05
155	Mark Clark	.05
156	Bernard Gilkey	.05
157	Pete Harnisch	.05
158	Lance Johnson	.05
159	Brent Mayne	.05
160	Rey Ordonez	.30
161	Kevin Roberson	.05
162	Paul Wilson	.10
163	*David Doster*	.05
164	*Mike Grace*	.40
165	*Rich Hunter*	.05
166	Pete Incaviglia	.05
167	Mike Lieberthal	.08
168	Terry Mulholland	.05
169	Ken Ryan	.05
170	Benito Santiago	.05
171	*Kevin Sefcik*	.05
172	Lee Tinsley	.05
173	Todd Zeile	.05
174	*Francisco Cordova*	.10
175	Danny Darwin	.05
176	Charlie Hayes	.05
177	Jason Kendall	.08
178	Mike Kingery	.05
179	Jon Lieber	.05
180	Zane Smith	.05
181	Luis Alicea	.05
182	Cory Bailey	.05
183	Andy Benes	.05
184	Pat Borders	.05
185	*Mike Busby*	.05
186	Royce Clayton	.05
187	Dennis Eckersley	.08
188	Gary Gaetti	.05
189	Ron Gant	.10
190	Aaron Holbert	.05
191	Willie McGee	.05
192	*Miguel Mejia*	.05
193	Jeff Parrett	.05
194	Todd Stottlemyre	.05
195	Sean Bergman	.05
196	Archi Cianfrocco	.05
197	Rickey Henderson	.20
198	Wally Joyner	.08
199	Craig Shipley	.05
200	Bob Tewksbury	.05
201	Tim Worrell	.05
202	*Rich Aurilia*	.05
203	Doug Creek	.05
204	Shawon Dunston	.05
205	*Osvaldo Fernandez*	.10
206	Mark Gardner	.05
207	Stan Javier	.05
208	Marcus Jensen	.05
209	*Chris Singleton*	4.00
210	Allen Watson	.05
211	Jeff Bagwell (Encore)	.60
212	Derek Bell (Encore)	.05
213	Albert Belle (Encore)	.40
214	Wade Boggs (Encore)	.15
215	Barry Bonds (Encore)	.40
216	Jose Canseco (Encore)	.15
217	Marty Cordova (Encore)	.08
218	Jim Edmonds (Encore)	.10
219	Cecil Fielder (Encore)	.08
220	Andres Galarraga (Encore)	.15
221	Juan Gonzalez (Encore)	.50
222	Mark Grace (Encore)	.10
223	Ken Griffey Jr. (Encore)	1.50
224	Tony Gwynn (Encore)	.60
225	Jason Isringhausen (Encore)	.08
226	Derek Jeter (Encore)	.75
227	Randy Johnson (Encore)	.35
228	Chipper Jones (Encore)	1.00
229	Ryan Klesko (Encore)	.25
230	Barry Larkin (Encore)	.15
231	Kenny Lofton (Encore)	.50
232	Greg Maddux (Encore)	1.00
233	Raul Mondesi (Encore)	.20
234	Hideo Nomo (Encore)	.40
235	Mike Piazza (Encore)	1.00
236	Manny Ramirez (Encore)	.75
237	Cal Ripken Jr. (Encore)	1.25
238	Tim Salmon (Encore)	.15
239	Ryne Sandberg (Encore)	.40
240	Reggie Sanders (Encore)	.05
241	Gary Sheffield (Encore)	.20
242	Sammy Sosa (Encore)	1.00
243	Frank Thomas (Encore)	1.00
244	Mo Vaughn (Encore)	.50
245	Matt Williams (Encore)	.15
246	Checklist	.05
247	Checklist	.05
248	Checklist	.05
249	Checklist	.05
250	Checklist	.05

1996 Fleer Update Tiffany

	MT
Complete Set (250):	100.00
Common Player:	.15
Glossy Stars:	3X

(See 1996 Fleer Update for checklist and base card values.)

1996 Fleer Update Diamond Tribute

These insert cards are the most difficult to pull from 1996 Fleer Update packs; they are seeded one per every 100 packs. The 10-card set features cards of future Hall of Famers on stock utilizing two different holographic foils and a diamond design, similar to the "Zone" insert cards in Fleer Baseball.

		MT
Complete Set (10):		140.00
Common Player:		6.00
1	Wade Boggs	7.50
2	Barry Bonds	10.00
3	Ken Griffey Jr.	40.00
4	Tony Gwynn	20.00
5	Rickey Henderson	6.00
6	Greg Maddux	25.00
7	Eddie Murray	6.00
8	Cal Ripken Jr.	30.00
9	Ozzie Smith	7.50
10	Frank Thomas	15.00

1996 Fleer Update New Horizons

These 1996 Fleer Update inserts feature 20 promising youngsters with bright futures in the majors. The cards were seeded one per every five hobby packs.

		MT
Complete Set (20):		8.00
Common Player:		.30
1	Bob Abreu	1.50
2	George Arias	.30
3	Tony Batista	.30
4	Steve Cox	.30
5	David Doster	.30
6	Jermaine Dye	1.00
7	Andy Fox	.60
8	Mike Grace	.60
9	Todd Greene	.60
10	Wilton Guerrero	.75
11	Richard Hidalgo	.65
12	Raul Ibanez	.45
13	Robin Jennings	.30
14	Marcus Jensen	.30
15	Jason Kendall	1.00
16	Brooks Kieschnick	.60
17	Ryan McGuire	.45
18	Miguel Mejia	.30
19	Rey Ordonez	2.00
20	Paul Wilson	.60

1996 Fleer Update Headliners

These 20 cards feature newsmakers from 1996. The cards were random inserts in 1996 Fleer Update packs, one per every five retail packs.

		MT
Complete Set (20):		35.00
Common Player:		.35
1	Roberto Alomar	1.00
2	Jeff Bagwell	1.75
3	Albert Belle	1.25
4	Barry Bonds	1.25
5	Cecil Fielder	.35
6	Juan Gonzalez	1.50
7	Ken Griffey Jr.	6.00
8	Tony Gwynn	2.00
9	Randy Johnson	1.00
10	Chipper Jones	4.00
11	Ryan Klesko	.50
12	Kenny Lofton	1.25
13	Greg Maddux	3.50
14	Hideo Nomo	.75
15	Mike Piazza	4.00
16	Manny Ramirez	1.50
17	Cal Ripken Jr.	5.00
18	Tim Salmon	.50
19	Frank Thomas	2.00
20	Matt Williams	.50

1996 Fleer Update Smooth Leather

Ten of the game's top fielders are showcased on these 1996 Fleer Update insert cards. The cards were seeded one per every five packs.

		MT
Complete Set (10):		7.50
Common Player:		.40
1	Roberto Alomar	.60
2	Barry Bonds	.60
3	Will Clark	.40
4	Ken Griffey Jr.	3.00
5	Kenny Lofton	.60
6	Greg Maddux	1.50
7	Raul Mondesi	.50
8	Rey Ordonez	.60
9	Cal Ripken Jr.	2.50
10	Matt Williams	.40

1996 Fleer Update Soaring Stars

Ten of the game's top players are spotlighted on these 1996 Fleer Update inserts. The cards were seeded one per every 11 packs.

		MT
Complete Set (10):		20.00
Common Player:		.50
1	Jeff Bagwell	1.50
2	Barry Bonds	1.25
3	Juan Gonzalez	1.50
4	Ken Griffey Jr.	5.00
5	Chipper Jones	3.00
6	Greg Maddux	2.50
7	Mike Piazza	3.00
8	Manny Ramirez	1.50
9	Frank Thomas	2.00
10	Matt Williams	.50

1996 Fleer-Panini Stickers

For the second year of distribution by Fleer/SkyBox, the annual baseball sticker set once again used Panini as the dominant brand identification. Printed in Italy, the stickers were sold in packs of six for 49 cents in the U.S., 69 cents in Canada. At 2-1/8" x 3", the basic player stickers have a green border around the color action photo; a second, ghosted, version of the photo appear in the background. Team logo and player ID are in a bat at bottom. Backs are printed in blue with the sticker number, Panini and licensor logos, along with copyright information. Team logo and special rookie stickers were printed on silver foil. A 60-page album was issued to house the set.

		MT
Complete Set (246):		15.00
Common Player:		.20
Album:		2.00
1	David Justice	.30
2	Tom Glavine	.25
3	Javier Lopez	.25
4	Greg Maddux	.75
5	Marquis Grissom	.25
6	Braves logo	.20
7	Ryan Klesko	.25
8	Chipper Jones	.75
9	Quilvio Veras	.20
10	Chris Hammond	.20
11	Charles Johnson	.30
12	John Burkett	.20
13	Marlins logo	.20
14	Jeff Conine	.25
15	Gary Sheffield	.50
16	Greg Colbrunn	.20
17	Moises Alou	.25
18	Pedro J. Martinez	.30
19	Rondell White	.20
20	Tony Tarasco	.20
21	Expos logo	.20
22	Carlos Perez	.20
23	David Segui	.20
24	Wil Cordero	.20
25	Jason Isringhausen	.20
26	Rico Brogna	.20
27	Edgardo Alfonzo	.25
28	Todd Hundley	.25
29	Mets logo	.20
30	Bill Pulsipher	.20
31	Carl Everett	.20
32	Jose Vizcaino	.20
33	Lenny Dykstra	.20
34	Charlie Hayes	.20
35	Heathcliff Slocumb	.20
36	Darren Daulton	.20
37	Phillies logo	.20
38	Mickey Morandini	.20
39	Gregg Jefferies	.25
40	Jim Eisenreich	.20
41	Brian McRae	.20
42	Luis Gonzalez	.20
43	Randy Myers	.20
44	Shawon Dunston	.20
45	Cubs logo	.20
46	Jaime Navarro	.20
47	Mark Grace	.50
48	Sammy Sosa	.75
49	Barry Larkin	.25
50	Pete Schourek	.20
51	John Smiley	.20
52	Reggie Sanders	.20
53	Reds logo	.20
54	Hal Morris	.20
55	Ron Gant	.20
56	Bret Boone	.25
57	Craig Biggio	.30
58	Brian L. Hunter	.20
59	Jeff Bagwell	.50
60	Shane Reynolds	.20
61	Astros logo	.20
62	Derek Bell	.20
63	Doug Drabek	.20
64	Orlando Miller	.20
65	Jay Bell	.20
66	Dan Miceli	.20
67	Orlando Merced	.20
68	Jeff King	.20
69	Carlos Garcia	.20
70	Pirates logo	.20
71	Al Martin	.20
72	Denny Neagle	.20
73	Ray Lankford	.20
74	Ozzie Smith	.50
75	Bernard Gilkey	.20
76	John Mabry	.20
77	Cardinals logo	.20
78	Brian Jordan	.30
79	Scott Cooper	.20
80	Allen Watson	.20
81	Dante Bichette	.30
82	Bret Saberhagen	.20
83	Walt Weiss	.20
84	Andres Galarraga	.30
85	Rockies logo	.20
86	Larry Walker	.50
87	Bill Swift	.20
88	Vinny Castilla	.25
89	Raul Mondesi	.40
90	Roger Cedeno	.20
91	Chad Fonville	.20
92	Hideo Nomo	.50
93	Dodgers logo	.20
94	Ramon Martinez	.25
95	Mike Piazza	.75
96	Eric Karros	.25
97	Tony Gwynn	.50
98	Brad Ausmus	.20
99	Trevor Hoffman	.20
100	Ken Caminiti	.30
101	Padres logo	.20
102	Andy Ashby	.20
103	Steve Finley	.20
104	Joey Hamilton	.25
105	Matt Williams	.30
106	Rod Beck	.20
107	Barry Bonds	.50
108	William VanLandingham	.20
109	Giants logo	.20
110	Deion Sanders	.20
111	Royce Clayton	.20
112	Glenallen Hill	.20
113	Tony Gwynn (League Leader - BA)	.20
114	Dante Bichette (League Leader - HR)	.20
115	Dante Bichette (League Leader - RBI)	.20
116	Quilvio Veras (League Leader - SB)	.20
117	Hideo Nomo (League Leader - K)	.40
118	Greg Maddux League Leader - W)	.40
119	Randy Myers (League Leader - Saves)	.20
120	Edgar Martinez (League Leader - BA)	.20
121	Albert Belle (League Leader - HR)	.40
122	Mo Vaughn (League Leader - RBI)	.20
123	Kenny Lofton (League Leader - SB)	.20
124	Randy Johnson (League Leader - K)	.20
125	Mike Mussina (League Leader - W)	.20
126	Jose Mesa (League Leader - Saves)	.20
127	Mike Mussina	.25
128	Cal Ripken Jr.	1.50
129	Rafael Palmeiro	.25
130	Ben McDonald	.20
131	Orioles logo	.20
132	Chris Hoiles	.20
133	Bobby Bonilla	.25
134	Brady Anderson	.20
135	Jose Canseco	.35
136	Roger Clemens	.50
137	Mo Vaughn	.35
138	Mike Greenwell	.20
139	Red Sox logo	.20
140	Tim Wakefield	.20
141	John Valentin	.20
142	Tim Naehring	.20
143	Travis Fryman	.20
144	Chad Curtis	.20
145	Felipe Lira	.20
146	Cecil Fielder	.20

147	Tigers logo	.20
148	John Flaherty	.20
149	Chris Gomez	.20
150	Sean Bergman	.20
151	Don Mattingly	1.00
152	Andy Pettitte	.25
153	Wade Boggs	.35
154	Paul O'Neill	.20
155	Yankees logo	.20
156	Bernie Williams	.30
157	Jack McDowell	.20
158	David Cone	.25
159	Roberto Alomar	.35
160	Paul Molitor	.50
161	Shawn Green	.25
162	Joe Carter	.20
163	Blue Jays logo	.20
164	Alex Gonzalez	.20
165	Al Leiter	.20
166	John Olerud	.25
167	Alex Fernandez	.20
168	Ray Durham	.20
169	Lance Johnson	.20
170	Ozzie Guillen	.20
171	White Sox logo	.20
172	Robin Ventura	.30
173	Frank Thomas	1.00
174	Tim Raines	.25
175	Albert Belle	.75
176	Manny Ramirez	.50
177	Eddie Murray	.40
178	Orel Hershiser	.25
179	Indians logo	.20
180	Kenny Lofton	.50
181	Carlos Baerga	.20
182	Jose Mesa	.20
183	Gary Gaetti	.20
184	Tom Goodwin	.20
185	Kevin Appier	.20
186	Jon Nunnally	.05
187	Royals logo	.20
188	Wally Joyner	.25
189	Jeff Montgomery	.20
190	Johnny Damon	.30
191	B.J. Surhoff	.20
192	Ricky Bones	.20
193	John Jaha	.20
194	Dave Nilsson	.20
195	Brewers logo	.20
196	Greg Vaughn	.25
197	Kevin Seitzer	.20
198	Joe Oliver	.20
199	Chuck Knoblauch	.30
200	Kirby Puckett	1.00
201	Marty Cordova	.20
202	Pat Meares	.20
203	Twins logo	.20
204	Scott Stahoviak	.20
205	Matt Walbeck	.20
206	Pedro Munoz	.20
207	Garret Anderson	.25
208	Chili Davis	.25
209	Tim Salmon	.25
210	J.T. Snow	.25
211	Angels logo	.20
212	Jim Edmonds	.25
213	Chuck Finley	.20
214	Mark Langston	.20
215	Dennis Eckersley	.25
216	Todd Stottlemyre	.20
217	Geronimo Berroa	.20
218	Mark McGwire	1.50
219	A's logo	.20
220	Brent Gates	.20
221	Terry Steinbach	.20
222	Rickey Henderson	.40
223	Ken Griffey Jr.	2.00
224	Alex Rodriguez	1.50
225	Tino Martinez	.20
226	Randy Johnson	.25
227	Mariners logo	.20
228	Jay Buhner	.25
229	Vince Coleman	.20
230	Edgar Martinez	.20
231	Will Clark	.30
232	Juan Gonzalez	.60
233	Kenny Rogers	.20
234	Ivan Rodriguez	.30
235	Rangers logo	.20
236	Mickey Tettleton	.20
237	Dean Palmer	.20
238	Otis Nixon	.20
239	Hideo Nomo (Rookie)	.65
240	Quilvio Veras (Rookie)	.25
241	Jason Isringhausen (Rookie)	.25
242	Andy Pettitte (Rookie)	.20
243	Chipper Jones (Rookie)	1.50
244	Garret Anderson (Rookie)	.25
245	Charles Johnson (Rookie)	.30
246	Marty Cordova (Rookie)	.25

1997 Fleer

Fleer maintained its matte-finish coating for 1997 after it debuted in the 1996 product. The regular-issue Series 1 has 500 cards equipped with icons designating All-Stars, League Leaders and World Series cards. There were also 10 checklist cards in the regular-issue set, featuring stars on the front. Fleer arrived in 10-card packs and had a Tiffany Collection parallel set and six different insert sets, including Rookie Sensations, Golden Memories, Team Leaders, Night and Day, Zone and Lumber Company. Series 2 comprises 261 cards plus inserts Decade of Excellence, Bleacher Bashers, Diamond Tributes, Goudey Greats, Headliners, New Horizons and Soaring Stars.

		MT
Complete Set (761):		80.00
Complete Series 1 Set (500):		45.00
Complete Series 2 Set (261):		35.00
Common Player:		.05
A. Jones Circa AU/200:		60.00
Series 1 or 2 Pack (10):		1.50
Series 1 or 2 Wax Box (36):		50.00
1	Roberto Alomar	.60
2	Brady Anderson	.10
3	Bobby Bonilla	.08
4	Rocky Coppinger	.05
5	Cesar Devarez	.05
6	Scott Erickson	.05
7	Jeffrey Hammonds	.05
8	Chris Hoiles	.05
9	Eddie Murray	.40
10	Mike Mussina	.60
11	Randy Myers	.05
12	Rafael Palmeiro	.20
13	Cal Ripken Jr.	2.50
14	B.J. Surhoff	.08
15	David Wells	.08
16	Todd Zeile	.05
17	Darren Bragg	.05
18	Jose Canseco	.25
19	Roger Clemens	.75
20	Wil Cordero	.05
21	Jeff Frye	.05
22	Nomar Garciaparra	2.00
23	Tom Gordon	.05
24	Mike Greenwell	.05
25	Reggie Jefferson	.05
26	Jose Malave	.05
27	Tim Naehring	.05
28	Troy O'Leary	.05
29	Heathcliff Slocumb	.05
30	Mike Stanley	.05
31	John Valentin	.05
32	Mo Vaughn	1.00
33	Tim Wakefield	.05
34	Garret Anderson	.05
35	George Arias	.05
36	Shawn Boskie	.05
37	Chili Davis	.05
38	Jason Dickson	.25
39	Gary DiSarcina	.05
40	Jim Edmonds	.05
41	Darin Erstad	1.25
42	Jorge Fabregas	.05
43	Chuck Finley	.05
44	Todd Greene	.05
45	*Mike Holtz*	.10
46	Rex Hudler	.05
47	Mike James	.05
48	Mark Langston	.05
49	Troy Percival	.05
50	Tim Salmon	.20
51	Jeff Schmidt	.05
52	J.T. Snow	.08
53	Randy Velarde	.05
54	Wilson Alvarez	.05
55	Harold Baines	.05
56	James Baldwin	.05
57	Jason Bere	.05
58	Mike Cameron	.05
59	Ray Durham	.05
60	Alex Fernandez	.05
61	Ozzie Guillen	.05
62	Roberto Hernandez	.05
63	Ron Karkovice	.05
64	Darren Lewis	.05
65	Dave Martinez	.05
66	Lyle Mouton	.05
67	Greg Norton	.05
68	Tony Phillips	.05
69	Chris Snopek	.05
70	Kevin Tapani	.05
71	Danny Tartabull	.05
72	Frank Thomas	1.50
73	Robin Ventura	.10
74	Sandy Alomar Jr.	.08
75	Albert Belle	.75
76	Mark Carreon	.05
77	Julio Franco	.05
78	*Brian Giles*	1.50
79	Orel Hershiser	.05
80	Kenny Lofton	.75
81	Dennis Martinez	.05
82	Jack McDowell	.05
83	Jose Mesa	.05
84	Charles Nagy	.08
85	Chad Ogea	.05
86	Eric Plunk	.05
87	Manny Ramirez	1.00
88	Kevin Seitzer	.05
89	Julian Tavarez	.05
90	Jim Thome	.25
91	Jose Vizcaino	.05
92	Omar Vizquel	.08
93	Brad Ausmus	.05
94	Kimera Bartee	.05
95	Raul Casanova	.05
96	Tony Clark	.60
97	John Cummings	.05
98	Travis Fryman	.08
99	Bob Higginson	.12
100	Mark Lewis	.05
101	Felipe Lira	.05
102	Phil Nevin	.05
103	Melvin Nieves	.05
104	Curtis Pride	.05
105	A.J. Sager	.05
106	Ruben Sierra	.05
107	Justin Thompson	.05
108	Alan Trammell	.05
109	Kevin Appier	.05
110	Tim Belcher	.05
111	Jaime Bluma	.05
112	Johnny Damon	.15
113	Tom Goodwin	.05
114	Chris Haney	.05
115	Keith Lockhart	.05
116	Mike Macfarlane	.05
117	Jeff Montgomery	.05
118	Jose Offerman	.05
119	Craig Paquette	.05
120	Joe Randa	.05
121	Bip Roberts	.05
122	Jose Rosado	.05
123	Mike Sweeney	.05
124	Michael Tucker	.05
125	Jeromy Burnitz	.08
126	Jeff Cirillo	.05
127	Jeff D'Amico	.05
128	Mike Fetters	.05
129	John Jaha	.05
130	Scott Karl	.05
131	Jesse Levis	.05
132	Mark Loretta	.05
133	Mike Matheny	.05
134	Ben McDonald	.05
135	Matt Mieske	.05
136	Marc Newfield	.05
137	Dave Nilsson	.05
138	Jose Valentin	.05
139	Fernando Vina	.05
140	Bob Wickman	.05
141	Gerald Williams	.05
142	Rick Aguilera	.05
143	Rich Becker	.05
144	Ron Coomer	.05
145	Marty Cordova	.10
146	Roberto Kelly	.05
147	Chuck Knoblauch	.10
148	Matt Lawton	.05
149	Pat Meares	.05
150	Travis Miller	.05
151	Paul Molitor	.40
152	Greg Myers	.05
153	Dan Naulty	.05
154	Kirby Puckett	1.00
155	Brad Radke	.05
156	Frank Rodriguez	.05
157	Scott Stahoviak	.05
158	Dave Stevens	.05
159	Matt Walbeck	.05
160	Todd Walker	.50
161	Wade Boggs	.25
162	David Cone	.10
163	Mariano Duncan	.05
164	Cecil Fielder	.08
165	Joe Girardi	.05
166	Dwight Gooden	.08
167	Charlie Hayes	.05
168	Derek Jeter	2.00
169	Jimmy Key	.05
170	Jim Leyritz	.05
171	Tino Martinez	.30
172	*Ramiro Mendoza*	.50
173	Jeff Nelson	.05
174	Paul O'Neill	.10
175	Andy Pettitte	.75
176	Mariano Rivera	.10
177	Ruben Rivera	.25
178	Kenny Rogers	.05
179	Darryl Strawberry	.08
180	John Wetteland	.05
181	Bernie Williams	.40
182	Willie Adams	.05
183	Tony Batista	.05
184	Geronimo Berroa	.05
185	Mike Bordick	.05
186	Scott Brosius	.05
187	Bobby Chouinard	.05
188	Jim Corsi	.05
189	Brent Gates	.05
190	Jason Giambi	.05
191	Jose Herrera	.05
192	*Damon Mashore*	.05
193	Mark McGwire	4.00
194	Mike Mohler	.05
195	Scott Spiezio	.05
196	Terry Steinbach	.05
197	Bill Taylor	.05
198	John Wasdin	.05
199	Steve Wojciechowski	.05
200	Ernie Young	.05
201	Rich Amaral	.05
202	Jay Buhner	.10
203	Norm Charlton	.05
204	Joey Cora	.05
205	Russ Davis	.05
206	Ken Griffey Jr.	3.00
207	Sterling Hitchcock	.05

208 Brian Hunter .05
209 Raul Ibanez .05
210 Randy Johnson .30
211 Edgar Martinez .05
212 Jamie Moyer .05
213 Alex Rodriguez 3.00
214 Paul Sorrento .05
215 Matt Wagner .05
216 Bob Wells .05
217 Dan Wilson .05
218 Damon Buford .05
219 Will Clark .25
220 Kevin Elster .05
221 Juan Gonzalez .75
222 Rusty Greer .05
223 Kevin Gross .05
224 Darryl Hamilton .05
225 Mike Henneman .05
226 Ken Hill .05
227 Mark McLemore .05
228 Darren Oliver .05
229 Dean Palmer .05
230 Roger Pavlik .05
231 Ivan Rodriguez .60
232 Mickey Tettleton .05
233 Bobby Witt .05
234 Jacob Brumfield .05
235 Joe Carter .08
236 Tim Crabtree .05
237 Carlos Delgado .40
238 Huck Flener .05
239 Alex Gonzalez .05
240 Shawn Green .10
241 Juan Guzman .05
242 Pat Hentgen .05
243 Marty Janzen .05
244 Sandy Martinez .05
245 Otis Nixon .05
246 Charlie O'Brien .05
247 John Olerud .10
248 Robert Perez .05
249 Ed Sprague .05
250 Mike Timlin .05
251 Steve Avery .05
252 Jeff Blauser .05
253 Brad Clontz .05
254 Jermaine Dye .10
255 Tom Glavine .10
256 Marquis Grissom .05
257 Andruw Jones 1.50
258 Chipper Jones 2.00
259 David Justice .15
260 Ryan Klesko .25
261 Mark Lemke .05
262 Javier Lopez .10
263 Greg Maddux 2.00
264 Fred McGriff .35
265 Greg McMichael .05
266 Denny Neagle .05
267 Terry Pendleton .05
268 Eddie Perez .05
269 John Smoltz .15
270 Terrell Wade .05
271 Mark Wohlers .05
272 Terry Adams .05
273 Brant Brown .05
274 Leo Gomez .05
275 Luis Gonzalez .08
276 Mark Grace .15
277 Tyler Houston .05
278 Robin Jennings .05
279 Brooks Kieschnick .05
280 Brian McRae .05
281 Jaime Navarro .05
282 Ryne Sandberg .75
283 Scott Servais .05
284 Sammy Sosa 1.50
285 *Dave Swartzbaugh* .05
286 Amaury Telemaco .05
287 Steve Trachsel .05
288 *Pedro Valdes* .05
289 Turk Wendell .05
290 Bret Boone .05
291 Jeff Branson .05
292 Jeff Brantley .05
293 Eric Davis .08
294 Willie Greene .05
295 Thomas Howard .05
296 Barry Larkin .15
297 Kevin Mitchell .05
298 Hal Morris .05
299 Chad Mottola .05
300 Joe Oliver .05
301 Mark Portugal .05
302 Roger Salkeld .05
303 Reggie Sanders .05
304 Pete Schourek .05
305 John Smiley .05
306 Eddie Taubensee .05
307 Dante Bichette .10
308 Ellis Burks .05
309 Vinny Castilla .08
310 Andres Galarraga .15
311 Curt Leskanic .05
312 Quinton McCracken .05
313 Neifi Perez .05
314 Jeff Reed .05
315 Steve Reed .05
316 Armando Reynoso .05
317 Kevin Ritz .05
318 Bruce Ruffin .05
319 Larry Walker .30
320 Walt Weiss .05
321 Jamey Wright .05
322 Eric Young .05
323 Kurt Abbott .05
324 Alex Arias .05
325 Kevin Brown .10
326 Luis Castillo .15
327 Greg Colbrunn .05
328 Jeff Conine .05
329 Andre Dawson .08
330 Charles Johnson .08
331 Al Leiter .08
332 Ralph Milliard .05
333 Robb Nen .05
334 Pat Rapp .05
335 Edgar Renteria .25
336 Gary Sheffield .25
337 Devon White .08
338 Bob Abreu .08
339 Jeff Bagwell 1.25
340 Derek Bell .08
341 Sean Berry .05
342 Craig Biggio .10
343 Doug Drabek .05
344 Tony Eusebio .05
345 Ricky Gutierrez .05
346 Mike Hampton .05
347 Brian Hunter .05
348 Todd Jones .05
349 Darryl Kile .05
350 Derrick May .05
351 Orlando Miller .05
352 James Mouton .05
353 Shane Reynolds .05
354 Billy Wagner .08
355 Donne Wall .05
356 Mike Blowers .05
357 Brett Butler .05
358 Roger Cedeno .08
259 Chad Curtis .05
360 Delino DeShields .05
361 Greg Gagne .05
362 Karim Garcia .50
363 Wilton Guerrero .08
364 Todd Hollandsworth .08
365 Eric Karros .08
366 Ramon Martinez .08
367 Raul Mondesi .25
368 Hideo Nomo .50
369 Antonio Osuna .05
370 Chan Ho Park .08
371 Mike Piazza 2.00
372 Ismael Valdes .05
373 Todd Worrell .05
374 Moises Alou .08
375 Shane Andrews .05
376 Yamil Benitez .05
377 Jeff Fassero .05
378 Darrin Fletcher .05
379 Cliff Floyd .05
380 Mark Grudzielanek .05
381 Mike Lansing .05
382 Barry Manuel .05
383 Pedro Martinez .10
384 Henry Rodriguez .05
385 Mel Rojas .05
386 F.P. Santangelo .05
387 David Segui .05
388 Ugueth Urbina .05
389 Rondell White .08
390 Edgardo Alfonzo .10
391 Carlos Baerga .08
392 Mark Clark .05
393 Alvaro Espinoza .05
394 John Franco .05
395 Bernard Gilkey .05
396 Pete Harnisch .05
397 Todd Hundley .08
398 Butch Huskey .05
399 Jason Isringhausen .08
400 Lance Johnson .05
401 Bobby Jones .05
402 Alex Ochoa .05
403 Rey Ordonez .20
404 Robert Person .05
405 Paul Wilson .08
406 Matt Beech .05
407 Ron Blazier .05
408 Ricky Bottalico .05
409 Lenny Dykstra .05
410 Jim Eisenreich .05
411 Bobby Estalella .05
412 Mike Grace .05
413 Gregg Jefferies .05
414 Mike Lieberthal .08
415 Wendell Magee Jr. .05
416 Mickey Morandini .05
417 Ricky Otero .05
418 Scott Rolen 1.50
419 Ken Ryan .05
420 Benito Santiago .05
421 Curt Schilling .10
422 Kevin Sefcik .05
423 Jermaine Allensworth .05
424 Trey Beamon .05
425 Jay Bell .05
426 Francisco Cordova .10
427 Carlos Garcia .05
428 Mark Johnson .05
429 Jason Kendall .08
430 Jeff King .05
431 Jon Lieber .05
432 Al Martin .05
433 Orlando Merced .05
434 Ramon Morel .05
435 Matt Ruebel .05
436 Jason Schmidt .05
437 *Marc Wilkins* .05
438 Alan Benes .10
439 Andy Benes .05
440 Royce Clayton .05
441 Dennis Eckersley .05
442 Gary Gaetti .05
443 Ron Gant .10
444 Aaron Holbert .05
445 Brian Jordan .05
446 Ray Lankford .05
447 John Mabry .05
448 T.J. Mathews .05
449 Willie McGee .05
450 Donovan Osborne .05
451 Tom Pagnozzi .05
452 Ozzie Smith .40
453 Todd Stottlemyre .05
454 Mark Sweeney .05
455 Dmitri Young .05
456 Andy Ashby .05
457 Ken Caminiti .15
458 Archi Cianfrocco .05
459 Steve Finley .05
460 John Flaherty .05
461 Chris Gomez .05
462 Tony Gwynn 1.25
463 Joey Hamilton .05
464 Rickey Henderson .15
465 Trevor Hoffman .08
466 Brian Johnson .05
467 Wally Joyner .05
468 Jody Reed .05
469 Scott Sanders .05
470 Bob Tewksbury .05
471 Fernando Valenzuela .05
472 Greg Vaughn .08
473 Tim Worrell .05
474 Rich Aurilla .05
475 Rod Beck .05
476 Marvin Benard .05
477 Barry Bonds .75
478 Jay Canizaro .05
479 Shawon Dunston .05
480 Shawn Estes .05
481 Mark Gardner .05
482 Glenallen Hill .05
483 Stan Javier .05
484 Marcus Jensen .05
485 *Bill Mueller* .25
486 William VanLandingham .05
487 Allen Watson .05
488 Rick Wilkins .05
489 Matt Williams .25
489p Matt Williams ("PROMOTIONAL SAMPLE") 3.00
490 Desi Wilson .05
491 Checklist (Albert Belle) .35
492 Checklist (Ken Griffey Jr.) 1.00
493 Checklist (Andruw Jones) .50
494 Checklist (Chipper Jones) .60
495 Checklist (Mark McGwire) 1.50
496 Checklist (Paul Molitor) .15
497 Checklist (Mike Piazza) .60
498 Checklist (Cal Ripken Jr.) .75
499 Checklist (Alex Rodriguez) 1.00
500 Checklist (Frank Thomas) .75
501 Kenny Lofton .75
502 Carlos Perez .05
503 Tim Raines .05
504 *Danny Patterson* .10
505 Derrick May .05
506 Dave Hollins .05
507 Felipe Crespo .05
508 Brian Banks .05
509 Jeff Kent .05
510 *Bubba Trammell* .75
511 Robert Person .05
512 *David Arias* (last name actually Ortiz) 1.00
513 Ryan Jones .05
514 David Justice .15
515 Will Cunnane .05
516 Russ Johnson .05
517 John Burkett .05
518 *Robinson Checo* .25
519 *Ricardo Rincon* .15
520 Woody Williams .05
521 Rick Helling .05
522 Jorge Posada .05
523 Kevin Orie .05
524 *Fernando Tatis* 3.00
525 Jermaine Dye .05
526 Brian Hunter .05
527 Greg McMichael .05
528 Matt Wagner .05
529 Richie Sexson .05
530 Scott Ruffcorn .05
531 Luis Gonzalez .05
532 Mike Johnson .05
533 Mark Petkovsek .05
534 Doug Drabek .05
535 Jose Canseco .25
536 Bobby Bonilla .05
537 J.T. Snow .08
538 Shawon Dunston .05
539 John Ericks .05
540 Terry Steinbach .05
541 Jay Bell .05
542 Joe Borowski .05
543 David Wells .08
544 *Justin Towle* .25
545 Mike Blowers .05
546 Shannon Stewart .05
547 Rudy Pemberton .05
548 Bill Swift .05
549 Osvaldo Fernandez .05
550 Eddie Murray .35
551 Don Wengert .05
552 Brad Ausmus .05
553 Carlos Garcia .05
554 Jose Guillen .60
555 Rheal Cormier .05
556 Doug Brocail .05
557 Rex Hudler .05
558 Armando Benitez .05
559 Elieser Marrero .05
560 *Ricky Ledee* 1.00
561 Bartolo Colon .05
562 Quilvio Veras .05
563 Alex Fernandez .05
564 Darren Dreifort .05
565 Benji Gil .05
566 Kent Mercker .05
567 Glendon Rusch .05
568 *Ramon Tatis* .05
569 Roger Clemens 1.25
570 Mark Lewis .05
571 *Emil Brown* .15
572 Jaime Navarro .05
573 Sherman Obando .05

No.	Player	Value
574	John Wasdin	.05
575	Calvin Maduro	.05
576	Todd Jones	.05
577	Orlando Merced	.05
578	Cal Eldred	.05
579	Mark Gubicza	.05
580	Michael Tucker	.05
581	*Tony Saunders*	.50
582	Garvin Alston	.05
583	Joe Roa	.05
584	*Brady Raggio*	.05
585	Jimmy Key	.05
586	*Marc Sagmoen*	.05
587	Jim Bullinger	.05
588	Yorkis Perez	.05
589	*Jose Cruz Jr.*	.75
590	Mike Stanton	.05
591	*Deivi Cruz*	.50
592	Steve Karsay	.05
593	Mike Trombley	.05
594	Doug Glanville	.05
595	Scott Sanders	.05
596	Thomas Howard	.05
597	T.J. Staton	.05
598	Garrett Stephenson	.05
599	Rico Brogna	.05
600	Albert Belle	.75
601	Jose Vizcaino	.05
602	Chili Davis	.05
603	Shane Mack	.05
604	Jim Eisenreich	.05
605	Todd Zeile	.05
606	Brian Boehringer	.05
607	Paul Shuey	.05
608	Kevin Tapani	.05
609	John Wetteland	.05
610	Jim Leyritz	.05
611	Ray Montgomery	.05
612	Doug Bochtler	.05
613	Wady Almonte	.05
614	Danny Tartabull	.05
615	Orlando Miller	.05
616	Bobby Ayala	.05
617	Tony Graffanino	.05
618	Marc Valdes	.05
619	Ron Villone	.05
620	Derrek Lee	.05
621	Greg Colbrunn	.05
622	*Felix Heredia*	.25
623	Carl Everett	.05
624	Mark Thompson	.05
625	Jeff Granger	.05
626	Damian Jackson	.05
627	Mark Leiter	.05
628	Chris Holt	.05
629	*Dario Veras*	.15
630	Dave Burba	.05
631	Darryl Hamilton	.05
632	Mark Acre	.05
633	Fernando Hernandez	.05
634	Terry Mulholland	.05
635	Dustin Hermanson	.05
636	Delino DeShields	.05
637	Steve Avery	.05
638	*Tony Womack*	.25
639	Mark Whiten	.05
640	Marquis Grissom	.05
641	Xavier Hernandez	.05
642	Eric Davis	.08
643	Bob Tewksbury	.05
644	Dante Powell	.05
645	Carlos Castillo	.05
646	Chris Widger	.05
647	Moises Alou	.08
648	Pat Listach	.05
649	Edgar Ramos	.05
650	Deion Sanders	.20
651	John Olerud	.10
652	Todd Dunwoody	.30
653	*Randall Simon*	1.50
654	Dan Carlson	.05
655	Matt Williams	.25
656	Jeff King	.05
657	Luis Alicea	.05
658	Brian Moehler	.05
659	Ariel Prieto	.05
660	Kevin Elster	.05
661	Mark Hutton	.05
662	Aaron Sele	.05
663	Graeme Lloyd	.05
664	John Burke	.05
665	Mel Rojas	.05
666	Sid Fernandez	.05
667	Pedro Astacio	.05
668	Jeff Abbott	.05
669	Darren Daulton	.05
670	Mike Bordick	.05
671	Sterling Hitchcock	.05
672	Damion Easley	.05
673	Armando Reynoso	.05
674	Pat Cline	.05
675	*Orlando Cabrera*	.30
676	Alan Embree	.05
677	Brian Bevil	.05
678	David Weathers	.05
679	Cliff Floyd	.05
680	Joe Randa	.05
681	Bill Haselman	.05
682	Jeff Fassero	.05
683	Matt Morris	.05
684	Mark Portugal	.05
685	Lee Smith	.05
686	Pokey Reese	.05
687	Benito Santiago	.05
688	Brian Johnson	.05
689	*Brent Brede*	.05
690	Shigetosi Hasegawa	.05
691	Julio Santana	.05
692	Steve Kline	.05
693	Julian Tavarez	.05
694	John Hudek	.05
695	Manny Alexander	.05
696	Roberto Alomar (Encore)	.30
697	Jeff Bagwell (Encore)	.60
698	Barry Bonds (Encore)	.40
699	Ken Caminiti (Encore)	.10
700	Juan Gonzalez (Encore)	.40
701	Ken Griffey Jr. (Encore)	1.50
702	Tony Gwynn (Encore)	.60
703	Derek Jeter (Encore)	1.00
704	Andruw Jones (Encore)	.75
705	Chipper Jones (Encore)	1.00
706	Barry Larkin (Encore)	.05
707	Greg Maddux (Encore)	1.00
708	Mark McGwire (Encore)	2.00
709	Paul Molitor (Encore)	.15
710	Hideo Nomo (Encore)	.25
711	Andy Pettitte (Encore)	.40
712	Mike Piazza (Encore)	1.00
713	Manny Ramirez (Encore)	.50
714	Cal Ripken Jr. (Encore)	1.25
715	Alex Rodriguez (Encore)	1.50
716	Ryne Sandberg (Encore)	.40
717	John Smoltz (Encore)	.05
718	Frank Thomas (Encore)	.75
719	Mo Vaughn (Encore)	.40
720	Bernie Williams (Encore)	.30
721	Checklist (Tim Salmon)	.05
722	Checklist (Greg Maddux)	.50
723	Checklist (Cal Ripken Jr.)	.75
724	Checklist (Mo Vaughn)	.25
725	Checklist (Ryne Sandberg)	.25
726	Checklist (Frank Thomas)	.50
727	Checklist (Barry Larkin)	.05
728	Checklist (Manny Ramirez)	.30
729	Checklist (Andres Galarraga)	.05
730	Checklist (Tony Clark)	.25
731	Checklist (Gary Sheffield)	.15
732	Checklist (Jeff Bagwell)	.35
733	Checklist (Kevin Appier)	.05
734	Checklist (Mike Piazza)	.50
735	Checklist (Jeff Cirillo)	.05
736	Checklist (Paul Molitor)	.15
737	Checklist (Henry Rodriguez)	.05
738	Checklist (Todd Hundley)	.10
739	Checklist (Derek Jeter)	.50
740	Checklist (Mark McGwire)	.75
741	Checklist (Curt Schilling)	.05
742	Checklist (Jason Kendall)	.05
743	Checklist (Tony Gwynn)	.40
744	Checklist (Barry Bonds)	.25
745	Checklist (Ken Griffey Jr.)	1.00
746	Checklist (Brian Jordan)	.05
747	Checklist (Juan Gonzalez)	.40
748	Checklist (Joe Carter)	.05
749	Arizona Diamondbacks	.05
750	Tampa Bay Devil Rays	.05
751	*Hideki Irabu*	1.00
752	*Jeremi Gonzalez*	.60
753	*Mario Valdez*	.50
754	Aaron Boone	.05
755	Brett Tomko	.05
756	*Jaret Wright*	2.00
757	Ryan McGuire	.05
758	Jason McDonald	.05
759	*Adrian Brown*	.20
760	*Keith Foulke*	.25
761	Checklist	.05

1997 Fleer Tiffany

Insertion odds were considerably lengthened for the UV-coated Tiffany Collection parallels in 1997 Fleer - to one card per 20 packs.

	MT
Complete Set (761):	3500.
Common Player:	2.00
Veteran Stars:	15-25X
Young Stars/RCs:	10-20X

(See 1997 Fleer for checklist and base card values.)

1997 Fleer Bleacher Blasters

This 10-card insert features some of the game's top power hitters and was found in retail packs only. Cards featured a die-cut "burst" pattern on an etched foil background. Backs have a portrait photo and career highlights. Cards were inserted 1:36 packs.

		MT
Complete Set (10):		60.00
Common Player:		2.00
1	Albert Belle	4.00
2	Barry Bonds	5.00
3	Juan Gonzalez	4.00
4	Ken Griffey Jr.	15.00
5	Mark McGwire	15.00
6	Mike Piazza	9.00
7	Alex Rodriguez	15.00
8	Frank Thomas	5.00
9	Mo Vaughn	4.00
10	Matt Williams	2.00

1997 Fleer Decade of Excellence

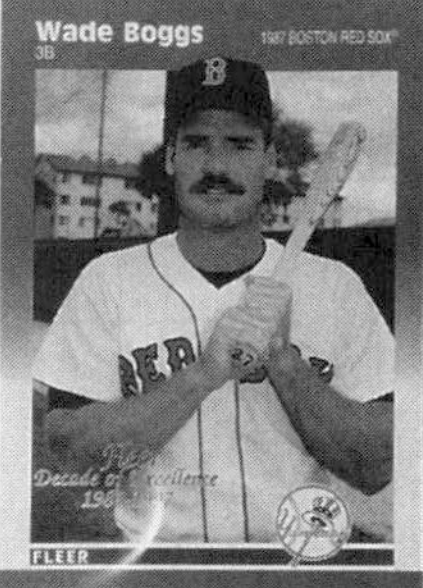

A 12-card insert found 1:36 in hobby shop packs, cards are in a format similar to the 1987 Fleer set and feature vintage photos of players who started their careers no later than the '87 season. Ten percent of the press run (1:360 packs) received a special foil treatment and designation as "Rare Traditions."

		MT
Complete Set (12):		70.00
Common Player:		3.00
Rare Tradition:		15X
1	Wade Boggs	5.00
2	Barry Bonds	6.00
3	Roger Clemens	10.00
4	Tony Gwynn	10.00
5	Rickey Henderson	4.00
6	Greg Maddux	12.50
7	Mark McGwire	20.00
8	Paul Molitor	5.00
9	Eddie Murray	4.00
10	Cal Ripken Jr.	15.00
11	Ryne Sandberg	6.00
12	Matt Williams	3.00

1997 Fleer Diamond Tribute

Twelve of the game's top stars are highlighted in this set. Fronts feature an embossed rainbow prismatic foil background and gold lettering. Backs have an action photo and a few sentences about the player. They were inserted 1:288 packs.

		MT
Complete Set (12):		400.00
Common Player:		8.00
1	Albert Belle	15.00
2	Barry Bonds	16.00
3	Juan Gonzalez	15.00
4	Ken Griffey Jr.	75.00
5	Tony Gwynn	35.00
6	Greg Maddux	40.00
7	Mark McGwire	75.00
8	Eddie Murray	8.00
9	Mike Piazza	45.00
10	Cal Ripken Jr.	50.00
11	Alex Rodriguez	50.00
12	Frank Thomas	20.00

1997 Fleer Golden Memories

Golden Memories captures 10 different highlights from the 1996 season, and is inserted one per 16 packs. Moments like Dwight Gooden's no hitter, Paul Molitor's 3000th hit and Eddie Murray's 500th home run are highlighted on a horizontal format.

		MT
Complete Set (10):		10.00
Common Player:		.35
1	Barry Bonds	1.00
2	Dwight Gooden	.40
3	Todd Hundley	.50
4	Mark McGwire	3.00
5	Paul Molitor	1.00
6	Eddie Murray	.75
7	Hideo Nomo	.50
8	Mike Piazza	2.00
9	Cal Ripken Jr.	2.50
10	Ozzie Smith	1.00

1997 Fleer Goudey Greats

Using a 2-3/8" x 2-7/8" format reminiscent of 1933 Goudey cards, this 15-card insert offers today's top players in classic old-time design. Cards were inserted 1:8 packs. A limited number (1% of press run) of cards received a special gold-foil treatment and were found only in hobby packs.

		MT
Complete Set (15):		30.00
Common Player:		.50
Foils:		20-30X
1	Barry Bonds	1.00
2	Ken Griffey Jr.	5.00
3	Tony Gwynn	2.00
4	Derek Jeter	3.00
5	Chipper Jones	3.00
6	Kenny Lofton	.75
7	Greg Maddux	2.50
8	Mark McGwire	5.00
9	Eddie Murray	.75
10	Mike Piazza	3.00
11	Cal Ripken Jr.	4.00
12	Alex Rodriguez	4.00
13	Ryne Sandberg	1.00
14	Frank Thomas	2.00
15	Mo Vaughn	.75

1997 Fleer Headliners

This 20-card insert highlights the personal achievements of each of the players depicted. Cards were inserted 1:2 packs and feature multi-color foil stamping on the fronts and a newspaper-style account of the player's achievement on the back.

		MT
Complete Set (20):		12.00
Common Player:		.20
1	Jeff Bagwell	.75
2	Albert Belle	.50
3	Barry Bonds	.50
4	Ken Caminiti	.25
5	Juan Gonzalez	.75
6	Ken Griffey Jr.	2.50
7	Tony Gwynn	.75
8	Derek Jeter	1.25
9	Andruw Jones	.75
10	Chipper Jones	1.25
11	Greg Maddux	1.00
12	Mark McGwire	2.50
13	Paul Molitor	.40
14	Eddie Murray	.30
15	Mike Piazza	1.25
16	Cal Ripken Jr.	2.00
17	Alex Rodriguez	2.00
18	Ryne Sandberg	.45
19	John Smoltz	.20
20	Frank Thomas	1.00

1997 Fleer Lumber Company

Lumber Company inserts were found every 48 retail packs. The cards were printed on a die-cut, spherical wood-like pattern, with the player imposed on the left side. Eighteen of the top power hitters in baseball are highlighted.

		MT
Complete Set (18):		150.00
Common Player:		3.00
1	Brady Anderson	3.00
2	Jeff Bagwell	10.00
3	Albert Belle	8.00
4	Barry Bonds	8.00
5	Jay Buhner	4.00
6	Ellis Burks	3.00
7	Andres Galarraga	4.00
8	Juan Gonzalez	8.00
9	Ken Griffey Jr.	30.00
10	Todd Hundley	3.00
11	Ryan Klesko	3.00
12	Mark McGwire	30.00
13	Mike Piazza	20.00
14	Alex Rodriguez	25.00
15	Gary Sheffield	4.00
16	Sammy Sosa	20.00
17	Frank Thomas	10.00
18	Mo Vaughn	6.00

1997-98 Fleer Million Dollar Moments

By assembling a complete set of 50 baseball "Million Dollar Moments" cards prior to July 31, 1998, a collector could win $50,000 a year through 2018. The catch, of course, is that cards #46-50 were printed in very limited quantities, with only one card #50. (Stated odds of winning the million were one in nearly 46,000,000.) The Moments cards have player action photos on front vignetted into a black border. The Fleer Million Dollar Moments logo is at top, with the player name and the date and details of his highlight at bottom in orange and white. Backs have the contest rules in fine print. Instant Win versions of some cards were also issued.

		MT
Complete Set (45):		4.00
Common Player:		.05
1	Checklist	.05
2	Derek Jeter	.10
3	Babe Ruth	.25
4	Barry Bonds	.05
5	Brooks Robinson	.05
6	Todd Hundley	.05
7	Johnny Vander Meer	.05
8	Cal Ripken Jr.	.25
9	Bill Mazeroski	.10
10	Chipper Jones	.15
11	Frank Robinson	.05
12	Roger Clemens	.10
13	Bob Feller	.05
14	Mike Piazza	.10
15	Joe Nuxhall	.05
16	Hideo Nomo	.08
17	Jackie Robinson	.25
18	Orel Hershiser	.05
19	Bobby Thomson	.05
20	Joe Carter	.05
21	Al Kaline	.05
22	Bernie Williams	.05
23	Don Larsen	.05
24	Rickey Henderson	.05
25	Maury Wills	.05
26	Andruw Jones	.10
27	Bobby Richardson	.05
28	Alex Rodriguez	.45
29	Jim Bunning	.05
30	Ken Caminiti	.05
31	Bob Gibson	.05
32	Frank Thomas	.40
33	Mickey Lolich	.05
34	John Smoltz	.05
35	Ron Swoboda	.05
36	Albert Belle	.10
37	Chris Chambliss	.05
38	Juan Gonzalez	.10
39	Ron Blomberg	.05
40	John Wetteland	.05
41	Carlton Fisk	.05
42	Mo Vaughn	.08
43	Bucky Dent	.05
44	Greg Maddux	.10
45	Willie Stargell	.05
46	Tony Gwynn	
47	Joel Youngblood	

48	Andy Pettitte ($500 winner)	
49	Mookie Wilson	
50	Jeff Bagwell ($1 million winner)	

1997 Fleer New Horizons

Rookies and prospects expected to make an impact during the 1996 season were featured in this 15-card insert set. Card fronts feature a rainbow foil background with the words "New Horizon" featured prominently on the bottom under the player's name. Cards were inserted 1:4 packs.

		MT
Complete Set (15):		5.00
Common Player:		.10
1	Bob Abreu	.15
2	Jose Cruz Jr.	.30
3	Darin Erstad	.60
4	Nomar Garciaparra	1.00
5	Vladimir Guerrero	1.00
6	Wilton Guerrero	.10
7	Jose Guillen	.35
8	Hideki Irabu	.50
9	Andruw Jones	1.00
10	Kevin Orie	.10
11	Scott Rolen	.75
12	Scott Spiezio	.10
13	Bubba Trammell	.25
14	Todd Walker	.15
15	Dmitri Young	.10

1997 Fleer Night & Day

Night and Day spotlighted 10 stars with unusual prowess during night or day games. These lenticular cards carried the toughest insert ratios in Fleer Baseball at one per 288 packs.

		MT
Complete Set (10):		200.00
Common Player:		5.00
1	Barry Bonds	9.00
2	Ellis Burks	5.00
3	Juan Gonzalez	10.00
4	Ken Griffey Jr.	40.00
5	Mark McGwire	40.00
6	Mike Piazza	25.00
7	Manny Ramirez	10.00
8	Alex Rodriguez	30.00
9	John Smoltz	5.00
10	Frank Thomas	15.00

1997 Fleer Rookie Sensations

Rookies Sensations showcased 20 of the top up-and-coming stars in baseball. Appearing every six packs, these inserts have the feaured player in the foreground, with the background look of painted brush strokes.

		MT
Complete Set (20):		18.00
Common Player:		.40
1	Jermaine Allensworth	.40
2	James Baldwin	.40
3	Alan Benes	.60
4	Jermaine Dye	.50
5	Darin Erstad	2.00
6	Todd Hollandsworth	.75
7	Derek Jeter	4.00
8	Jason Kendall	.60
9	Alex Ochoa	.50
10	Rey Ordonez	1.00
11	Edgar Renteria	.60
12	Bob Abreu	1.50
13	Nomar Garciaparra	3.50
14	Wilton Guerrero	.50
15	Andruw Jones	3.50
16	Wendell Magee	.75
17	Neifi Perez	.50
18	Scott Rolen	2.50
19	Scott Spiezio	.40
20	Todd Walker	1.00

1997 Fleer Soaring Stars

A 12-card insert found 1:12 packs designed to profile players with outstanding statistical performances early in their careers. Fronts have player action photos set against a background of rainbow holographic stars which appear, disappear and twinkle as the viewing angle is changed. Conventionally printed backs have another player photo and a few sentences about his career. A parallel version on which the background stars glow was issued at a greatly reduced rate.

		MT
Complete Set (12):		35.00
Common Player:		.75
Glowing:		15X
1	Albert Belle	1.50
2	Barry Bonds	1.50
3	Juan Gonzalez	2.00
4	Ken Griffey Jr.	7.50
5	Derek Jeter	4.00
6	Andruw Jones	3.00
7	Chipper Jones	4.00
8	Greg Maddux	3.00
9	Mark McGwire	7.50
10	Mike Piazza	4.00
11	Alex Rodriguez	5.00
12	Frank Thomas	3.00

1997 Fleer Team Leaders

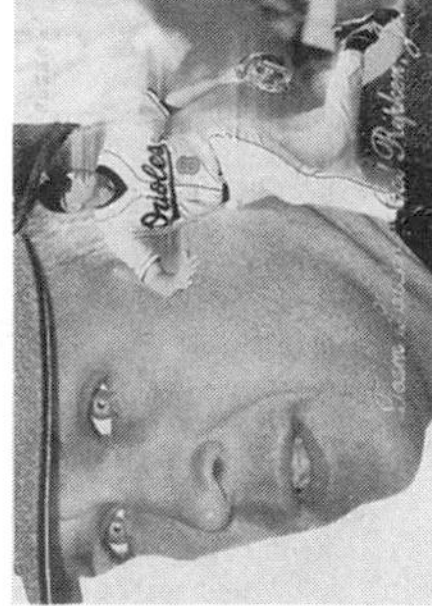

Team Leaders captured the statistical and/or inspirational leaders from all 28 teams. Inserted every 20 packs, these inserts were printed on a horizontal format, with the player's face die-cut in the perimeter of the card.

		MT
Complete Set (28):		90.00
Common Player:		1.50
1	Cal Ripken Jr.	12.50
2	Mo Vaughn	4.00
3	Jim Edmonds	1.50
4	Frank Thomas	5.00
5	Albert Belle	4.00
6	Bob Higginson	1.50
7	Kevin Appier	1.50
8	John Jaha	1.50
9	Paul Molitor	2.50
10	Andy Pettitte	2.00
11	Mark McGwire	17.50
12	Ken Griffey Jr.	17.50
13	Juan Gonzalez	4.00
14	Pat Hentgen	1.50
15	Chipper Jones	9.00
16	Mark Grace	2.50
17	Barry Larkin	1.50
18	Ellis Burks	1.50
19	Gary Sheffield	2.25
20	Jeff Bagwell	7.50
21	Mike Piazza	9.00
22	Henry Rodriguez	1.50
23	Todd Hundley	1.50
24	Curt Schilling	1.50
25	Jeff King	1.50
26	Brian Jordan	1.50
27	Tony Gwynn	7.50
28	Barry Bonds	3.75

1997 Fleer Zone

Twenty of the top hitters in baseball are featured on these holographic cards with the words Zone printed across the front. Zone inserts were found only in hobby packs at a rate of one per 80.

		MT
Complete Set (20):		175.00
Common Player:		3.00
1	Jeff Bagwell	9.00
2	Albert Belle	6.00
3	Barry Bonds	6.00
4	Ken Caminiti	3.50
5	Andres Galarraga	3.00
6	Juan Gonzalez	8.00
7	Ken Griffey Jr.	30.00
8	Tony Gwynn	10.00
9	Chipper Jones	15.00
10	Greg Maddux	12.50
11	Mark McGwire	30.00
12	Dean Palmer	3.00
13	Andy Petitte	4.00
14	Mike Piazza	15.00
15	Alex Rodriguez	25.00
16	Gary Sheffield	4.00
17	John Smoltz	3.00
18	Frank Thomas	9.00
19	Jim Thome	4.00
20	Matt Williams	3.50

1998 Fleer

Fleer was issued in two series in 1998, with 350 cards in Series 1 and 250 in Series 2. Each card features a borderless color action shot, with backs containing player information. Subsets in Series 1 included Smoke

'N Heat (301-310), Golden Memories (311-320) and Tale of the Tape (321-340). Golden Memories (1:6 packs) and Tale of the Tape (1:4) were short-printed. Series 2 subsets included 25 Unforgetable Moments (571-595). Inserts in Series 1 were Vintage '63, Vintage '63 Classic, Decade of Excellence, Decade of Excellence Rare Traditions, Diamond Ink, Diamond Standouts, Lumber Company, Power Game, Rookie Sensations and Zone. Series 2 inserts include: Vintage '63, Vintage '63 Classic, Promising Forecast, In the Clutch, Mickey Mantle: Monumental Moments, Mickey Mantle: Monumental Moments Gold Edition, Diamond Tribute and Diamond Ink. Card No. 7 in the regular set pictures Mickey Mantle.

	MT
Complete Set (600):	100.00
Complete Series 1 (350):	60.00
Complete Series 2 (250):	40.00
Common Player:	.10
Series 1 or 2 Pack (10):	1.75
Series 1 or 2 Wax Box (36):	55.00

No.	Player	MT
1	Ken Griffey Jr.	3.00
2	Derek Jeter	2.00
3	Gerald Williams	.10
4	Carlos Delgado	.40
5	Nomar Garciaparra	2.00
6	Gary Sheffield	.30
7	Jeff King	.10
8	Cal Ripken Jr.	2.50
9	Matt Williams	.25
10	Chipper Jones	2.00
11	Chuck Knoblauch	.25
12	Mark Grudzielanek	.10
13	Edgardo Alfonzo	.15
14	Andres Galarraga	.20
15	Tim Salmon	.25
16	Reggie Sanders	.10
17	Tony Clark	.40
18	Jason Kendall	.12
19	Juan Gonzalez	.75
20	Ben Grieve	1.00
21	Roger Clemens	1.00
22	Raul Mondesi	.20
23	Robin Ventura	.15
24	Derrek Lee	.10
25	Mark McGwire	4.00
26	Luis Gonzalez	.10
27	Kevin Brown	.20
28	Kirk Rueter	.10
29	Bobby Estalella	.10
30	Shawn Green	.15
31	Greg Maddux	2.00
32	Jorge Velandia	.10
33	Larry Walker	.25
34	Joey Cora	.10
35	Frank Thomas	1.50
36	*Curtis King*	.10
37	Aaron Boone	.10
38	Curt Schilling	.12
39	Bruce Aven	.10
40	Ben McDonald	.10
41	Andy Ashby	.12
42	Jason McDonald	.10
43	Eric Davis	.12
44	Mark Grace	.25
45	Pedro Martinez	.25
46	Lou Collier	.10
47	Chan Ho Park	.12
48	Shane Halter	.10
49	Brian Hunter	.10
50	Jeff Bagwell	1.25
51	Bernie Williams	.50
52	J.T. Snow	.12
53	Todd Greene	.10
54	Shannon Stewart	.10
55	Darren Bragg	.10
56	Fernando Tatis	.20
57	Darryl Kile	.10
58	Chris Stynes	.10
59	Javier Valentin	.10
60	Brian McRae	.10
61	Tom Evans	.10
62	Randall Simon	.20
63	Darrin Fletcher	.10
64	Jaret Wright	1.50
65	Luis Ordaz	.10
66	Jose Canseco	.20
67	Edgar Renteria	.10
68	Jay Buhner	.20
69	Paul Konerko	1.00
70	Adrian Brown	.10
71	Chris Carpenter	.10
72	Mike Lieberthal	.12
73	Dean Palmer	.10
74	Jorge Fabregas	.10
75	Stan Javier	.10
76	Damion Easley	.10
77	David Cone	.20
78	Aaron Sele	.10
79	Antonio Alfonseca	.10
80	Bobby Jones	.10
81	David Justice	.25
82	Jeffrey Hammonds	.10
83	Doug Glanville	.10
84	Jason Dickson	.10
85	Brad Radke	.10
86	David Segui	.10
87	Greg Vaughn	.12
88	*Mike Cather*	.20
89	Alex Fernandez	.10
90	Billy Taylor	.10
91	Jason Schmidt	.10
92	*Mike DeJean*	.10
93	Domingo Cedeno	.10
94	Jeff Cirillo	.10
95	*Manny Aybar*	.25
96	Jaime Navarro	.10
97	Dennis Reyes	.10
98	Barry Larkin	.15
99	Troy O'Leary	.10
100	Alex Rodriguez	2.50
100p	Alex Rodriguez (pverprinted PROMOTIONAL SAMPLE)	3.00
101	Pat Hentgen	.10
102	Bubba Trammell	.20
103	Glendon Rusch	.10
104	Kenny Lofton	.75
105	Craig Biggio	.20
106	Kelvim Escobar	.10
107	Mark Kotsay	.40
108	Rondell White	.20
109	Darren Oliver	.10
110	Jim Thome	.40
111	Rich Becker	.10
112	Chad Curtis	.10
113	Dave Hollins	.10
114	Bill Mueller	.10
115	Antone Williamson	.10
116	Tony Womack	.10
117	Randy Myers	.10
118	Rico Brogna	.10
119	Pat Watkins	.10
120	Eli Marrero	.10
121	Jay Bell	.10
122	Kevin Tapani	.10
123	*Todd Erdos*	.20
124	Neifi Perez	.10
125	Todd Hundley	.12
126	Jeff Abbott	.10
127	Todd Zeile	.10
128	Travis Fryman	.12
129	Sandy Alomar	.12
130	Fred McGriff	.20
131	Richard Hidalgo	.10
132	Scott Spiezio	.10
133	John Valentin	.10
134	Quilvio Veras	.10
135	Mike Lansing	.10
136	Paul Molitor	.50
137	Randy Johnson	.40
138	Harold Baines	.10
139	Doug Jones	.10
140	Abraham Nunez	.25
141	Alan Benes	.20
142	Matt Perisho	.10
143	Chris Clemons	.10
144	Andy Pettitte	.50
145	Jason Giambi	.10
146	Moises Alou	.20
147	*Chad Fox*	.25
148	Felix Martinez	.10
149	*Carlos Mendoza*	.25
150	Scott Rolen	1.50
151	*Jose Cabrera*	.20
152	Justin Thompson	.10
153	Ellis Burks	.10
154	Pokey Reese	.10
155	Bartolo Colon	.10
156	Ray Durham	.10
157	Ugueth Urbina	.10
158	Tom Goodwin	.10
159	*David Dellucci*	.50
160	Rod Beck	.10
161	Ramon Martinez	.10
162	Joe Carter	.12
163	Kevin Orie	.10
164	Trevor Hoffman	.10
165	Emil Brown	.10
166	Robb Nen	.10
167	Paul O'Neill	.20
168	Ryan Long	.10
169	Ray Lankford	.10
170	Ivan Rodriguez	.60
171	Rick Aguilera	.10
172	Deivi Cruz	.10
173	Ricky Bottalico	.10
174	Garret Anderson	.10
175	Jose Vizcaino	.10
176	Omar Vizquel	.10
177	Jeff Blauser	.10
178	Orlando Cabrera	.10
179	Russ Johnson	.10
180	Matt Stairs	.10
181	Will Cunnane	.10
182	Adam Riggs	.10
183	Matt Morris	.10
184	Mario Valdez	.10
185	Larry Sutton	.10
186	*Marc Pisciotta*	.10
187	Dan Wilson	.10
188	John Franco	.10
189	Darren Daulton	.10
190	Todd Helton	.75
191	Brady Anderson	.15
192	Ricardo Rincon	.10
193	Kevin Stocker	.10
194	Jose Valentin	.10
195	Ed Sprague	.10
196	Ryan McGuire	.10
197	*Scott Eyre*	.25
198	Steve Finley	.10
199	T.J. Mathews	.10
200	Mike Piazza	2.00
201	Mark Wohlers	.10
202	Brian Giles	.10
203	Eduardo Perez	.10
204	Shigetosi Hasegawa	.10
205	Mariano Rivera	.15
206	Jose Rosado	.10
207	Michael Coleman	.10
208	James Baldwin	.10
209	Russ Davis	.10
210	Billy Wagner	.12
211	Sammy Sosa	1.50
212	*Frank Catalanotto*	.25
213	Delino DeShields	.10
214	John Olerud	.15
215	Heath Murray	.10
216	Jose Vidro	.10
217	Jim Edmonds	.20
218	Shawon Dunston	.10
219	Homer Bush	.10
220	Midre Cummings	.10
221	Tony Saunders	.20
222	Jeromy Burnitz	.10
223	Enrique Wilson	.10
224	Chili Davis	.10
225	Jerry DiPoto	.10
226	Dante Powell	.10
227	Javier Lopez	.20
228	*Kevin Polcovich*	.20
229	Deion Sanders	.15
230	Jimmy Key	.10
231	Rusty Greer	.10
232	Reggie Jefferson	.10
233	Ron Coomer	.10
234	Bobby Higginson	.20
235	*Magglio Ordonez*	2.00
236	Miguel Tejada	.50
237	Rick Gorecki	.10
238	Charles Johnson	.10
239	Lance Johnson	.10
240	Derek Bell	.10
241	Will Clark	.20
242	Brady Raggio	.10
243	Orel Hershiser	.10
244	Vladimir Guerrero	1.50
245	John LeRoy	.10
246	Shawn Estes	.10
247	Brett Tomko	.10
248	Dave Nilsson	.10
249	Edgar Martinez	.10
250	Tony Gwynn	1.50
251	Mark Bellhorn	.10
252	Jed Hansen	.10
253	Butch Huskey	.10
254	Eric Young	.10
255	Vinny Castilla	.10
256	Hideki Irabu	.75
257	Mike Cameron	.10
258	Juan Encarnacion	.25
259	Brian Rose	.25
260	Brad Ausmus	.10
261	Dan Serafini	.10
262	Willie Greene	.10
263	Troy Percival	.10
264	*Jeff Wallace*	.20
265	Richie Sexson	.10
266	Rafael Palmeiro	.20
267	Brad Fullmer	.10
268	Jeremi Gonzalez	.10
269	*Rob Stanifer*	.25
270	Mickey Morandini	.10
271	Andruw Jones	1.50
272	Royce Clayton	.10
273	Takashi Kashiwada	.40
274	*Steve Woodard*	.25
275	Jose Cruz Jr.	.50
276	Keith Foulke	.10
277	Brad Rigby	.10
278	Tino Martinez	.20
279	Todd Jones	.10
280	John Wetteland	.10
281	Alex Gonzalez	.10
282	Ken Cloude	.25
283	Jose Guillen	.40
284	Danny Clyburn	.10
285	David Ortiz	.40
286	John Thomson	.10
287	Kevin Appier	.10
288	Ismael Valdes	.10
289	Gary DiSarcina	.10
290	Todd Dunwoody	.12
291	Wally Joyner	.10
292	Charles Nagy	.10
293	Jeff Shaw	.10
294	*Kevin Millwood*	2.50
295	*Rigo Beltran*	.20
296	Jeff Frye	.10
297	Oscar Henriquez	.10
298	Mike Thurman	.10
299	Garrett Stephenson	.10
300	Barry Bonds	.75
301	Roger Clemens (Smoke 'N Heat)	.50
302	David Cone (Smoke 'N Heat)	.15
303	Hideki Irabu (Smoke 'N Heat)	.40
304	Randy Johnson (Smoke 'N Heat)	.20
305	Greg Maddux (Smoke 'N Heat)	1.00
306	Pedro Martinez (Smoke 'N Heat)	.15
307	Mike Mussina (Smoke 'N Heat)	.30

No.	Player	Price
308	Andy Pettitte (Smoke 'N Heat)	.25
309	Curt Schilling (Smoke 'N Heat)	.15
310	John Smoltz (Smoke 'N Heat)	.15
311	Roger Clemens (Golden Memories)	.50
312	Jose Cruz Jr. (Golden Memories)	.25
313	Nomar Garciaparra (Golden Memories)	1.00
314	Ken Griffey Jr. (Golden Memories)	1.50
315	Tony Gwynn (Golden Memories)	.75
316	Hideki Irabu (Golden Memories)	.40
317	Randy Johnson (Golden Memories)	.20
318	Mark McGwire (Golden Memories)	2.00
319	Curt Schilling (Golden Memories)	.15
320	Larry Walker (Golden Memories)	.15
321	Jeff Bagwell (Tale of the Tape)	.60
322	Albert Belle (Tale of the Tape)	.40
323	Barry Bonds (Tale of the Tape)	.40
324	Jay Buhner (Tale of the Tape)	.15
325	Tony Clark (Tale of the Tape)	.20
326	Jose Cruz Jr. (Tale of the Tape)	.25
327	Andres Galarraga (Tale of the Tape)	.15
328	Juan Gonzalez (Tale of the Tape)	.40
329	Ken Griffey Jr. (Tale of the Tape)	1.50
330	Andruw Jones (Tale of the Tape)	.75
331	Tino Martinez (Tale of the Tape)	.15
332	Mark McGwire (Tale of the Tape)	2.00
333	Rafael Palmeiro (Tale of the Tape)	.15
334	Mike Piazza (Tale of the Tape)	1.00
335	Manny Ramirez (Tale of the Tape)	.50
336	Alex Rodriguez (Tale of the Tape)	1.25
337	Frank Thomas (Tale of the Tape)	.75
338	Jim Thome (Tale of the Tape)	.20
339	Mo Vaughn (Tale of the Tape)	.40
340	Larry Walker (Tale of the Tape)	.15
341	Checklist (Jose Cruz Jr.)	.25
342	Checklist (Ken Griffey Jr.)	1.00
343	Checklist (Derek Jeter)	.60
344	Checklist (Andruw Jones)	.50
345	Checklist (Chipper Jones)	.60
346	Checklist (Greg Maddux)	.60
347	Checklist (Mike Piazza)	.60
348	Checklist (Cal Ripken Jr.)	.75
349	Checklist (Alex Rodriguez)	.75
350	Checklist (Frank Thomas)	.50
351	Mo Vaughn	.75
352	Andres Galarraga	.25
353	Roberto Alomar	.50
354	Darin Erstad	.75
355	Albert Belle	.75
356	Matt Williams	.25
357	Darryl Kile	.10
358	Kenny Lofton	.75
359	Orel Hershiser	.10
360	Bob Abreu	.10
361	Chris Widger	.10
362	Glenallen Hill	.10
363	Chili Davis	.10
364	Kevin Brown	.15
365	Marquis Grissom	.12
366	Livan Hernandez	.10
367	Moises Alou	.20
368	Matt Lawton	.10
369	Rey Ordonez	.10
370	Kenny Rogers	.10
371	Lee Stevens	.10
372	Wade Boggs	.20
373	Luis Gonzalez	.10
374	Jeff Conine	.10
375	Esteban Loaiza	.10
376	Jose Canseco	.25
377	Henry Rodriguez	.10
378	Dave Burba	.10
379	Todd Hollandsworth	.10
380	Ron Gant	.20
381	Pedro Martinez	.40
382	Ryan Klesko	.25
383	Derrek Lee	.10
384	Doug Glanville	.10
385	David Wells	.10
386	Ken Caminiti	.20
387	Damon Hollins	.10
388	Manny Ramirez	1.00
389	Mike Mussina	.60
390	Jay Bell	.10
391	Mike Piazza	.40
392	Mike Lansing	.10
393	Mike Hampton	.10
394	Geoff Jenkins	.10
395	Jimmy Haynes	.10
396	Scott Servais	.10
397	Kent Mercker	.10
398	Jeff Kent	.10
399	Kevin Elster	.10
400	*Masato Yoshii*	.40
401	Jose Vizcaino	.10
402	Javier Martinez	.10
403	David Segui	.10
404	Tony Saunders	.10
405	Karim Garcia	.10
406	Armando Benitez	.10
407	Joe Randa	.10
408	Vic Darensbourg	.10
409	Sean Casey	.20
410	Eric Milton	.20
411	Trey Moore	.10
412	Mike Stanley	.10
413	Tom Gordon	.10
414	Hal Morris	.10
415	Braden Looper	.10
416	Mike Kelly	.10
417	John Smoltz	.12
418	Roger Cedeno	.10
419	Al Leiter	.20
420	Chuck Knoblauch	.30
421	Felix Rodriguez	.10
422	Bip Roberts	.10
423	Ken Hill	.10
424	Jermaine Allensworth	.10
425	Esteban Yan	.10
426	Scott Karl	.10
427	Sean Berry	.10
428	Rafael Medina	.10
429	Javier Vazquez	.10
430	Rickey Henderson	.20
431	*Adam Butler*	.10
432	Todd Stottlemyre	.10
433	Yamil Benitez	.10
434	Sterling Hitchcock	.10
435	Paul Sorrento	.10
436	Bobby Ayala	.10
437	Tim Raines	.10
438	Chris Hoiles	.10
439	Rod Beck	.10
440	Donnie Sadler	.10
441	Charles Johnson	.10
442	Russ Ortiz	.10
443	Pedro Astacio	.10
444	Wilson Alvarez	.10
445	Mike Blowers	.10
446	Todd Zeile	.10
447	Mel Rojas	.10
448	F.P. Santangelo	.10
449	Dmitri Young	.10
450	Brian Anderson	.10
451	Cecil Fielder	.12
452	Roberto Hernandez	.10
453	Todd Walker	.20
454	Tyler Green	.10
455	Jorge Posada	.10
456	Geronimo Berroa	.10
457	Jose Silva	.10
458	Bobby Bonilla	.15
459	Walt Weiss	.10
460	Darren Dreifort	.10
461	B.J. Surhoff	.10
462	Quinton McCracken	.10
463	Derek Lowe	.10
464	Jorge Fabregas	.10
465	Joey Hamilton	.10
466	Brian Jordan	.10
467	Allen Watson	.10
468	John Jaha	.10
469	Heathcliff Slocumb	.10
470	Gregg Jefferies	.10
471	Scott Brosius	.10
472	Chad Ogea	.10
473	A.J. Hinch	.20
474	Bobby Smith	.10
475	Brian Moehler	.10
476	DaRond Stovall	.10
477	Kevin Young	.10
478	Jeff Suppan	.10
479	Marty Cordova	.10
480	*John Halama*	.25
481	Bubba Trammell	.10
482	Mike Caruso	.10
483	Eric Karros	.20
484	Jamey Wright	.10
485	Mike Sweeney	.10
486	Aaron Sele	.10
487	Cliff Floyd	.10
488	Jeff Brantley	.10
489	Jim Leyritz	.10
490	Denny Neagle	.10
491	Travis Fryman	.10
492	Carlos Baerga	.10
493	Eddie Taubensee	.10
494	Darryl Strawberry	.15
495	Brian Johnson	.10
496	Randy Myers	.10
497	Jeff Blauser	.10
498	Jason Wood	.10
499	*Rolando Arrojo*	.40
500	Johnny Damon	.10
501	Jose Mercedes	.10
502	Tony Batista	.10
503	Mike Piazza	2.00
504	Hideo Nomo	.25
505	Chris Gomez	.10
506	*Jesus Sanchez*	.25
507	Al Martin	.10
508	Brian Edmondson	.10
509	Joe Girardi	.10
510	Shayne Bennett	.10
511	Joe Carter	.12
512	Dave Mlicki	.10
513	*Rich Butler*	.50
514	Dennis Eckersley	.10
515	Travis Lee	.75
516	John Mabry	.10
517	Jose Mesa	.10
518	Phil Nevin	.10
519	Raul Casanova	.10
520	Mike Fetters	.10
521	Gary Sheffield	.25
522	Terry Steinbach	.10
523	Steve Trachsel	.10
524	Josh Booty	.10
525	Darryl Hamilton	.10
526	Mark McLemore	.10
527	Kevin Stocker	.10
528	Bret Boone	.10
529	Shane Andrews	.10
530	Robb Nen	.10
531	Carl Everett	.10
532	LaTroy Hawkins	.10
533	Fernando Vina	.10
534	Michael Tucker	.10
535	Mark Langston	.10
536	Mickey Mantle	5.00
537	Bernard Gilkey	.10
538	Francisco Cordova	.10
539	Mike Bordick	.10
540	Fred McGriff	.20
541	Cliff Politte	.10
542	Jason Varitek	.10
543	Shawon Dunston	.10
544	Brian Meadows	.10
545	Pat Meares	.10
546	Carlos Perez	.10
547	Desi Relaford	.10
548	Antonio Osuna	.10
549	Devon White	.10
550	Sean Runyan	.10
551	Mickey Morandini	.10
552	Dave Martinez	.10
553	Jeff Fassero	.10
554	*Ryan Jackson*	.25
555	Stan Javier	.10
556	Jaime Navarro	.10
557	Jose Offerman	.10
558	*Mike Lowell*	.40
559	Darrin Fletcher	.10
560	Mark Lewis	.10
561	Dante Bichette	.25
562	Chuck Finley	.10
563	Kerry Wood	1.00
564	Andy Benes	.10
565	Freddy Garcia	.10
566	Tom Glavine	.20
567	Jon Nunnally	.05
568	Miguel Cairo	.10
569	Shane Reynolds	.10
570	Roberto Kelly	.10
571	Checklist (Jose Cruz Jr.)	.25
572	Checklist (Ken Griffey Jr.)	1.50
573	Checklist (Mark McGwire)	1.50
574	Checklist (Cal Ripken Jr.)	1.00
575	Checklist (Frank Thomas)	.50
576	Jeff Bagwell (Unforgettable Moments)	1.50
577	Barry Bonds (Unforgettable Moments)	1.00
578	Tony Clark (Unforgettable Moments)	.75
579	Roger Clemens (Unforgettable Moments)	1.50
580	Jose Cruz Jr. (Unforgettable Moments)	.50
581	Nomar Garciaparra (Unforgettable Moments)	2.50
582	Juan Gonzalez (Unforgettable Moments)	1.50
583	Ben Grieve (Unforgettable Moments)	1.50
584	Ken Griffey Jr. (Unforgettable Moments)	4.00
585	Tony Gwynn (Unforgettable Moments)	2.00
586	Derek Jeter (Unforgettable Moments)	2.50
587	Randy Johnson (Unforgettable Moments)	.75
588	Chipper Jones (Unforgettable Moments)	2.50
589	Greg Maddux (Unforgettable Moments)	2.50
590	Mark McGwire (Unforgettable Moments)	5.00
591	Andy Pettitte (Unforgettable Moments)	.60
592	Paul Molitor (Unforgettable Moments)	.50
593	Cal Ripken Jr. (Unforgettable Moments)	3.00
594	Alex Rodriguez (Unforgettable Moments)	2.50
595	Scott Rolen (Unforgettable Moments)	1.25
596	Curt Schilling (Unforgettable Moments)	.40
597	Frank Thomas (Unforgettable Moments)	1.50

598	Jim Thome (Unforgettable Moments)	.75
599	Larry Walker (Unforgettable Moments)	.50
600	Bernie Williams (Unforgettable Moments)	.75

1998 Fleer Decade of Excellence

Decade of Excellence inserts were found in one per 72 Series 1 hobby packs of Fleer Tradition. The 12-card set features 1988 season photos in Fleer's 1988 card design. The set includes only those current players who have been in baseball for ten years or more. The use of blue and red metallic foil stripes in the background differentiates a scarcer (1:720 hobby packs) "Rare Traditions" parallel to the insert.

		MT
Complete Set (12):		100.00
Common Player:		4.00
Inserted 1:72		
Rare Traditions:		5X
Inserted 1:720		
1	Roberto Alomar	6.00
2	Barry Bonds	10.00
3	Roger Clemens	12.00
4	David Cone	4.00
5	Andres Galarraga	4.00
6	Mark Grace	5.00
7	Tony Gwynn	15.00
8	Randy Johnson	6.00
9	Greg Maddux	24.00
10	Mark McGwire	40.00
11	Paul O'Neill	4.00
12	Cal Ripken Jr.	30.00

1998 Fleer Diamond Ink

These one-per-pack inserts offer collectors a chance to acquire genuine autographed baseballs. Issued in denominations of 1, 5 and 10 points, the cards had to be accumulated to a total of 500 points of the same player to be redeemed for an autographed ball of that player. Cards are the standard 3-1/2" x 2-1/2" and are printed in black and purple on front and black and yellow on back. The point value of each card is embossed at center to prevent counterfeiting. The rules of the exchange program are printed on back. The deadline for redemption was Dec. 31, 1998. Values shown are for 1-pt. cards, and the unnumbered players in the series are listed alphabetically.

		MT
Complete Set, 1 pt. (11):		1.25
Common Player, 1 pt.:		.05
5-pt. cards:		5X
10-pt. cards:		12X
(1)	Jay Buhner	.05
(2)	Roger Clemens	.10
(3)	Jose Cruz Jr.	.15
(4)	Nomar Garciaparra	.10
(5)	Tony Gwynn	.10
(6)	Roberto Hernandez	.05
(7)	Greg Maddux	.10
(8)	Cal Ripken Jr.	.20
(9)	Alex Rodriguez	.20
(10)	Scott Rolen	.10
(11)	Tony Womack	.05

1998 Fleer Diamond Standouts

Diamond Standouts were inserted into Series I packs at a rate of one per 12. The 20-card insert set features players over a diamond design silver foil background.

		MT
Complete Set (20):		50.00
Common Player:		1.50
1	Jeff Bagwell	5.00
2	Barry Bonds	2.50
3	Roger Clemens	5.00
4	Jose Cruz Jr.	1.50
5	Andres Galarraga	1.50
6	Nomar Garciaparra	8.00
7	Juan Gonzalez	4.00
8	Ken Griffey Jr.	15.00
9	Derek Jeter	7.50
10	Randy Johnson	2.00
11	Chipper Jones	8.00
12	Kenny Lofton	2.00
13	Greg Maddux	6.00
14	Pedro Martinez	1.50
15	Mark McGwire	15.00
16	Mike Piazza	8.00
17	Alex Rodriguez	12.00
18	Curt Schilling	1.50
19	Frank Thomas	5.00
20	Larry Walker	2.00

1998 Fleer Diamond Tribute

This 10-card insert was exclusive to Series II packs and seeded one per 300 packs. Cards were printed on a leather- like laminated stock and had silver holofoil stamping.

		MT
Complete Set (10):		325.00
Common Player:		30.00
DT1	Jeff Bagwell	15.00
DT2	Roger Clemens	20.00
DT3	Nomar Garciaparra	40.00
DT4	Juan Gonzalez	15.00
DT5	Ken Griffey Jr.	60.00
DT6	Mark McGwire	60.00
DT7	Mike Piazza	40.00
DT8	Cal Ripken Jr.	50.00
DT9	Alex Rodriguez	50.00
DT10	Frank Thomas	20.00

1998 Fleer In the Clutch

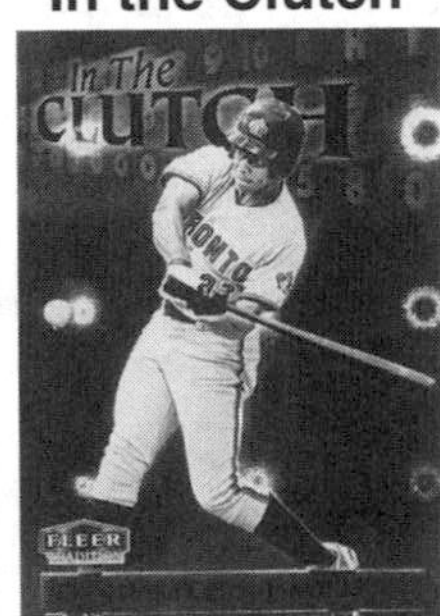

This Series 2 insert features stars who can stand up to pressure of big league ball. Fronts have embossed action photos on a prismatic metallic foil background. Backs have a portrait photo and a few words about the player. Stated insertion rate for the inserts was one per 20 packs on average.

		MT
Complete Set (15):		75.00
Common Player:		1.50
IC1	Jeff Bagwell	5.00
IC2	Barry Bonds	3.00
IC3	Roger Clemens	5.00
IC4	Jose Cruz Jr.	1.50
IC5	Nomar Garciaparra	8.00
IC6	Juan Gonzalez	4.00
IC7	Ken Griffey Jr.	15.00
IC8	Tony Gwynn	6.00
IC9	Derek Jeter	6.00
IC10	Chipper Jones	8.00
IC11	Greg Maddux	6.00
IC12	Mark McGwire	15.00
IC13	Mike Piazza	8.00
IC14	Frank Thomas	5.00
IC15	Larry Walker	1.50

1998 Fleer Lumber Company

This 15-card set was exclusive to Series I retail packs and inserted one per 36 packs. It included power hitters and featured the insert name in large letters across the top.

		MT
Complete Set (15):		100.00
Common Player:		1.50
Inserted 1:36 R		
1	Jeff Bagwell	5.00
2	Barry Bonds	5.00
3	Jose Cruz Jr.	1.50
4	Nomar Garciaparra	10.00
5	Juan Gonzalez	4.00
6	Ken Griffey Jr.	18.00
7	Tony Gwynn	6.00
8	Chipper Jones	8.00
9	Tino Martinez	1.50
10	Mark McGwire	18.00
11	Mike Piazza	10.00
12	Cal Ripken Jr.	15.00
13	Alex Rodriguez	15.00
14	Frank Thomas	6.00
15	Larry Walker	2.00

1998 Fleer Mickey Mantle Monumental Moments

This 10-card insert honors Hall of Famer Mickey Mantle's legendary career and was seeded one per 68 packs of Series 2. Fleer/SkyBox worked closely with Mantle's family with each photo in the set personally selected by them. A gold-enhanced version was issued with each card serially numbered to 51.

		MT
Complete Set (10):		150.00
Common Card:		20.00
Inserted 1:68		
Golds (51 sets):		10X
1	Armed and Dangerous	20.00
2	Getting Ready in Spring Training	20.00
3	Mantle and Rizzuto Celebrate	20.00
4	Posed for Action	20.00
5	Signed, Sealed and Ready to Deliver	20.00
6	Triple Crown 1956 Season	20.00
7	Number 7 . . .	20.00
8	Mantle's Powerful Swing . . .	20.00
9	Old-Timers Day Introduction	20.00
10	Portrait of Determination	20.00

1998 Fleer The Power Game

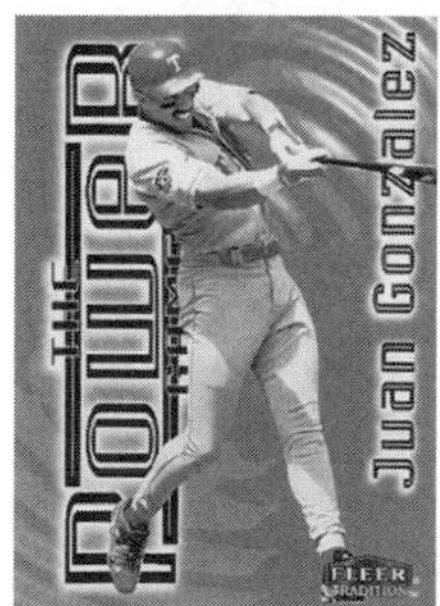

Pitchers and hitters are pictured over a purple metallic background with UV coating in this 20-card insert. Power Game inserts were exclusive to Series I and seeded one per 36 packs.

		MT
Complete Set (20):		100.00
Common Player:		1.50
Inserted 1:36		
1	Jeff Bagwell	5.00
2	Albert Belle	4.00
3	Barry Bonds	5.00
4	Tony Clark	2.00
5	Roger Clemens	7.50
6	Jose Cruz Jr.	1.50
7	Andres Galarraga	3.00
8	Nomar Garciaparra	12.00
9	Juan Gonzalez	5.00
10	Ken Griffey Jr.	20.00
11	Randy Johnson	5.00
12	Greg Maddux	10.00
13	Pedro Martinez	5.00
14	Tino Martinez	2.00
15	Mark McGwire	20.00
16	Mike Piazza	12.00
17	Curt Schilling	2.00
18	Frank Thomas	7.50
19	Jim Thome	3.00
20	Larry Walker	3.00

1998 Fleer Promising Forecast

Potential future stars are showcased in this Series 2 insert. Both front and back have a background of a colorful weather map. Fronts have a glossy player action photo on a matte-finish background. Backs are all-glossy and have a second photo and a few words about the player's potential. Average odds of pulling a Promising Forecast card were stated as one per 12 packs.

		MT
Complete Set (20):		10.00
Common Player:		.25
Inserted 1:12		
PF1	Rolando Arrojo	.60
PF2	Sean Casey	1.00
PF3	Brad Fullmer	1.00
PF4	Karim Garcia	.25
PF5	Ben Grieve	2.00
PF6	Todd Helton	1.50
PF7	Richard Hidalgo	.25
PF8	A.J. Hinch	.25
PF9	Paul Konerko	.75
PF10	Mark Kotsay	.50
PF11	Derrek Lee	.25
PF12	Travis Lee	1.50
PF13	Eric Milton	.25
PF14	Magglio Ordonez	.75
PF15	David Ortiz	.75
PF16	Brian Rose	.25
PF17	Miguel Tejada	.75
PF18	Jason Varitek	.25
PF19	Enrique Wilson	.25
PF20	Kerry Wood	1.25

1998 Fleer Rookie Sensations

Rookie Sensations included 20 gray-bordered cards of the 1997 most promising players who were eligible for the Rookie of the Year award. Each card contained a multi-colored background and was inserted one per 18 packs.

		MT
Complete Set (20):		45.00
Common Player:		2.00
Inserted 1:18		
1	Mike Cameron	2.00
2	Jose Cruz Jr.	2.00
3	Jason Dickson	2.00
4	Kelvim Escobar	2.00
5	Nomar Garciaparra	12.00
6	Ben Grieve	5.00
7	Vladimir Guerrero	8.00
8	Wilton Guerrero	2.00
9	Jose Guillen	3.00
10	Todd Helton	4.00
11	Livan Hernandez	2.00
12	Hideki Irabu	4.00
13	Andruw Jones	6.00
14	Matt Morris	2.00
15	Magglio Ordonez	2.50
16	Neifi Perez	2.00
17	Scott Rolen	8.00
18	Fernando Tatis	4.00
19	Brett Tomko	2.00
20	Jaret Wright	4.00

1998 Fleer Vintage '63

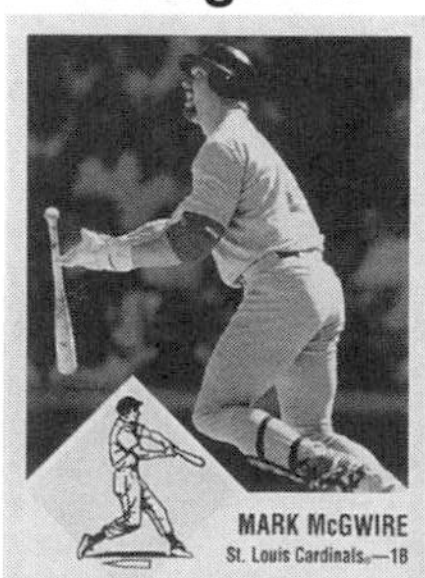

Vintage featured 126 different players, with 63 in Series I and 63 in Series II, on the design of 1963 Fleer cards. The insert commemorated the 35th anniversary of Fleer and was seeded one per hobby pack. In addition, Series II featured Mickey Mantle on card No. 67, which completed the original 1963 Fleer set that ended at card No. 66 and wasn't able to include Mantle for licensing reasons. The Mantle card was printed in vintage looking stock and was purposely made to look and feel like the originals. Fleer also printed a Classic parallel version to this insert that contained gold foil on the front and was sequentially numbered to 63 with a "C" prefix on the back.

		MT
Complete Set (126):		35.00
Complete Series 1 (63):		20.00
Complete Series 2 (63):		15.00
Common Player:		.25
1	Jason Dickson	.25
2	Tim Salmon	.40
3	Andruw Jones	1.00
4	Chipper Jones	1.50
5	Kenny Lofton	.75
6	Greg Maddux	1.50
7	Rafael Palmeiro	.30
8	Cal Ripken Jr.	2.00
9	Nomar Garciaparra	1.50
10	Mark Grace	.40
11	Sammy Sosa	1.50
12	Frank Thomas	1.50
13	Deion Sanders	.30
14	Sandy Alomar	.25
15	David Justice	.40
16	Jim Thome	.50
17	Matt Williams	.30
18	Jaret Wright	1.00
19	Vinny Castilla	.25
20	Andres Galarraga	.40
21	Todd Helton	.75
22	Larry Walker	.40
23	Tony Clark	.40
24	Moises Alou	.25
25	Kevin Brown	.25
26	Charles Johnson	.25
27	Edgar Renteria	.25
28	Gary Sheffield	.40
29	Jeff Bagwell	1.00
30	Craig Biggio	.25
31	Raul Mondesi	.25
32	Mike Piazza	1.50
33	Chuck Knoblauch	.40
34	Paul Molitor	.50
35	Vladimir Guerrero	2.00
36	Pedro Martinez	.40
37	Todd Hundley	.25
38	Derek Jeter	1.50
39	Tino Martinez	.35
40	Paul O'Neill	.25
41	Andy Pettitte	.35
42	Mariano Rivera	.25
43	Bernie Williams	.35
44	Ben Grieve	1.00
45	Scott Rolen	1.00
46	Curt Schilling	.25
47	Jason Kendall	.25
48	Tony Womack	.25
49	Ray Lankford	.25
50	Mark McGwire	4.00
51	Matt Morris	.25
52	Tony Gwynn	1.25
53	Barry Bonds	.75
54	Jay Buhner	.25
55	Ken Griffey Jr.	4.00
56	Randy Johnson	.40
57	Edgar Martinez	.25
58	Alex Rodriguez	2.00
59	Juan Gonzalez	1.00
60	Rusty Greer	.25
61	Ivan Rodriguez	.75
62	Roger Clemens	1.25
63	Jose Cruz Jr.	.35
	Checklist (Vintage '63)	.25
64	Darin Erstad	.75

65	Jay Bell	.25
66	Andy Benes	.25
67	Mickey Mantle	5.00
68	Travis Lee	1.00
69	Matt Williams	.40
70	Andres Galarraga	.35
71	Tom Glavine	.40
72	Ryan Klesko	.40
73	Denny Neagle	.25
74	John Smoltz	.25
75	Roberto Alomar	.50
76	Joe Carter	.25
77	Mike Mussina	.50
78	B.J. Surhoff	.25
79	Dennis Eckersley	.25
80	Pedro Martinez	.40
81	Mo Vaughn	.60
82	Jeff Blauser	.25
83	Henry Rodriguez	.25
84	Albert Belle	.60
85	Sean Casey	.50
86	Travis Fryman	.25
87	Kenny Lofton	.60
88	Darryl Kile	.25
89	Mike Lansing	.25
90	Bobby Bonilla	.25
91	Cliff Floyd	.25
92	Livan Hernandez	.25
93	Derrek Lee	.25
94	Moises Alou	.25
95	Shane Reynolds	.25
96	Jeff Conine	.25
97	Johnny Damon	.25
98	Eric Karros	.25
99	Hideo Nomo	.25
100	Marquis Grissom	.25
101	Matt Lawton	.25
102	Todd Walker	.25
103	Carlos Baerga	.25
104	Bernard Gilkey	.25
105	Rey Ordonez	.25
106	Chili Davis	.25
107	Jason Giambi	.40
108	Chuck Knoblauch	.40
109	Tim Raines	.25
110	Rickey Henderson	.30
111	Bob Abreu	.25
112	Doug Glanville	.25
113	Gregg Jefferies	.25
114	Al Martin	.25
115	Kevin Young	.25
116	Ron Gant	.25
117	Kevin Brown	.25
118	Ken Caminiti	.25
119	Joey Hamilton	.25
120	Jeff Kent	.25
121	Wade Boggs	.50
122	Quinton McCracken	.25
123	Fred McGriff	.40
124	Paul Sorrento	.25
125	Jose Canseco	.40
126	Randy Myers	.25

1998 Fleer Vintage '63 Classic

Vintage '63 Classic paralleled all 126 Vintage '63 inserts throughout Series 1 and 2, plus the checklist. These cards feature gold-foil stamping on front, specifically around the diamond in the lower-left corner, and are sequentailly numbered to 63 sets. Cards have a "C" suffix to the card number.

	MT
Complete Set (127):	3500.
Common Player:	10.00
Stars:	40x to 70x
Young Stars/RCs:	30x to 60x

(See 1998 Fleer Vintage '63 for checklist and base card values.)

1998 Fleer Zone

Inserted in one per 288 packs of Series I Fleer Tradition, Zone featured 15 top players printed on rainbow foil and etching.

		MT
Complete Set (15):		350.00
Common Player:		8.00
Inserted 1:288		
1	Jeff Bagwell	15.00
2	Barry Bonds	15.00
3	Roger Clemens	20.00
4	Jose Cruz Jr.	8.00
5	Nomar Garciaparra	35.00
6	Juan Gonzalez	15.00
7	Ken Griffey Jr.	60.00
8	Tony Gwynn	25.00
9	Chipper Jones	30.00
10	Greg Maddux	30.00
11	Mark McGwire	60.00
12	Mike Piazza	35.00
13	Alex Rodriguez	50.00
14	Frank Thomas	20.00
15	Larry Walker	10.00

1998 Fleer Update

Fleer produced its first Update set since 1994 with this 100-card boxed set. It arrived soon after the conclusion of the 1998 World Series and focused on rookies like J.D. Drew, Rich Croushore, Ryan Bradley, John Rocker, Mike Frank and Benj Sampson, who made their major league debut in September and have not yet had a rookie card yet. The set had 70 rookies, including 15 making their major league debut, 20 traded players and free agents. There was one subset called Season's Highlights that focused on feats like Mark McGwire's 70th home run, Sammy Sosa's single-month home run record and Kerry Wood's 20 strikeout performance.

		MT
Complete Set (100):		30.00
Common Player:		.10
U1	Mark McGwire (Season Highlights)	2.50
U2	Sammy Sosa (Season Highlights)	1.50
U3	Roger Clemens (Season Highlights)	.75
U4	Barry Bonds (Season Highlights)	.50
U5	Kerry Wood (Season Highlights)	.75
U6	Paul Molitor (Season Highlights)	.25
U7	Ken Griffey Jr. (Season Highlights)	2.50
U8	Cal Ripken Jr. (Season Highlights)	1.50
U9	David Wells (Season Highlights)	.10
U10	Alex Rodriguez (Season Highlights)	2.00
U11	*Angel Pena*	1.00
U12	Bruce Chen	.10
U13	Craig Wilson	.10
U14	*Orlando Hernandez*	4.00
U15	Aramis Ramirez	.25
U16	Aaron Boone	.10
U17	Bob Henley	.10
U18	Juan Guzman	.10
U19	Darryl Hamilton	.10
U20	Jay Payton	.10
U21	*Jeremy Powell*	.25
U22	Ben Davis	.10
U23	Preston Wilson	.10
U24	*Jim Parque*	1.50
U25	*Odalis Perez*	2.00
U26	Ron Belliard	.10
U27	Royce Clayton	.10
U28	George Lombard	.25
U29	Tony Phillips	.10
U30	*Fernando Seguignol*	4.00
U31	*Armando Rios*	.50
U32	*Jerry Hairston*	1.00
U33	*Justin Baughman*	.75
U34	Seth Greisinger	.10
U35	Alex Gonzalez	.10
U36	Michael Barrett	.50
U37	Carlos Beltran	.40
U38	Ellis Burks	.10
U39	Jose Jimenez	.40
U40	Carlos Guillen	.10
U41	Marlon Anderson	.10
U42	Scott Elarton	.10
U43	Glenallen Hill	.10
U44	Shane Monahan	.10
U45	Dennis Martinez	.10
U46	*Carlos Febles*	.20
U47	Carlos Perez	.10
U48	Wilton Guerrero	.10
U49	Randy Johnson	.10
U50	*Brian Simmons*	1.00
U51	Carlton Loewer	.10
U52	*Mark DeRosa*	.25
U53	*Tim Young*	.25
U54	Gary Gaetti	.10
U55	Eric Chavez	1.00
U56	Carl Pavano	.10
U57	Mike Stanley	.10
U58	Todd Stottlemyre	.10
U59	*Gabe Kapler*	5.00
U60	*Mike Jerzembeck*	.25
U61	*Mitch Meluskey*	2.00
U62	Bill Pulsipher	.10
U63	Derrick Gibson	.10
U64	*John Rocker*	1.50
U65	Calvin Pickering	.10
U66	Blake Stein	.10
U67	Fernando Tatis	.15
U68	Gabe Alvarez	.10
U69	Jeffrey Hammonds	.10
U70	Adrian Beltre	.50
U71	*Ryan Bradley*	2.00
U72	*Edgar Clemente*	.20
U73	*Rick Croushore*	.20
U74	Matt Clement	.25
U75	Dermal Brown	.10
U76	Paul Bako	.10
U77	*Placido Polanco*	.75
U78	Jay Tessmer	.10
U79	Jarrod Washburn	.10
U80	Kevin Witt	.10
U81	Mike Metcalfe	.10
U82	Daryle Ward	.10
U83	*Benj Sampson*	.20
U84	*Mike Kinkade*	.50
U85	Randy Winn	.10
U86	Jeff Shaw	.10
U87	*Troy Glaus*	6.00
U88	Hideo Nomo	.15
U89	Mark Grudzielanek	.10
U90	*Mike Frank*	1.50
U91	*Bobby Howry*	.50
U92	*Ryan Minor*	3.00
U93	*Corey Koskie*	1.00
U94	*Matt Anderson*	2.00
U95	Joe Carter	.10
U96	Paul Konerko	.15
U97	Sidney Ponson	.10
U98	*Jeremy Giambi*	3.00
U99	*Jeff Kubenka*	.20
U100	*J.D. Drew*	8.00

1999 Fleer

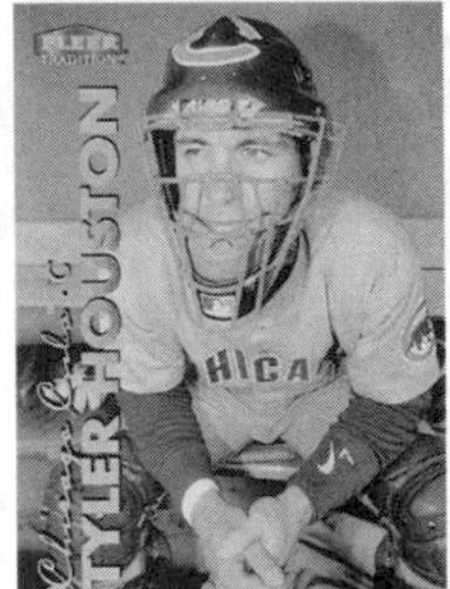

Released as a single series in 10-card packs with a suggested retail price of $1.59, the base set consists of 600 cards, including 10 checklists and a 15-card Franchise Futures subset. Cards are UV coated, with borderless photos and gold-foil graphics. Backs have personal bio-information along with year-by-year career stats and a small photo. There are two parallels, Starting Nine, which are hobby-exclusive, numbered to nine sets with blue foil stamping and Warning Track. Found exclusively in retail packs, Warning Tracks can be identified by red foil stamping and a Warning Track logo.

		MT
Complete Set (600):		60.00
Common Player:		.10
Warning Track:		2x to 4x
Common Warning Track:		.25
Inserted 1:1 R		
Pack (10):		1.75
Wax Box (36):		55.00
1	Mark McGwire	4.00
2	Sammy Sosa	2.50
3	Ken Griffey Jr.	3.00
4	Kerry Wood	.75
5	Derek Jeter	2.00
6	Stan Musial	4.00
7	J.D. Drew	.75
7p	J.D. Drew (overprinted PROMOTIONAL SAMPLE)	1.50
8	Cal Ripken Jr.	2.50
9	Alex Rodriguez	2.50
10	Travis Lee	.75
11	Andres Galarraga	.50
12	Nomar Garciaparra	2.00
13	Albert Belle	.75
14	Barry Larkin	.15
15	Dante Bichette	.20
16	Tony Clark	.40
17	Moises Alou	.20
18	Rafael Palmeiro	.25
19	Raul Mondesi	.25
20	Vladimir Guerrero	1.50
21	John Olerud	.20

No.	Player	Value
22	Bernie Williams	.50
23	Ben Grieve	.75
24	Scott Rolen	.75
25	Jeromy Burnitz	.10
26	Ken Caminiti	.20
27	Barry Bonds	.75
28	Todd Helton	.75
29	Juan Gonzalez	1.00
30	Roger Clemens	1.25
31	Andruw Jones	.75
32	Mo Vaughn	.75
33	Larry Walker	.40
34	Frank Thomas	1.00
35	Manny Ramirez	1.00
36	Randy Johnson	.50
37	Vinny Castilla	.10
38	Juan Encarnacion	.10
39	Jeff Bagwell	.75
40	Gary Sheffield	.25
41	Mike Piazza	2.00
42	Richie Sexson	.10
43	Tony Gwynn	1.50
44	Chipper Jones	1.50
45	Jim Thome	.50
46	Craig Biggio	.30
47	Carlos Delgado	.40
48	Greg Vaughn	.20
49	Greg Maddux	2.00
50	Troy Glaus	.75
51	Roberto Alomar	.50
52	Dennis Eckersley	.10
53	Mike Caruso	.10
54	Bruce Chen	.10
55	Aaron Boone	.10
56	Bartolo Colon	.10
57	Derrick Gibson	.10
58	Brian Anderson	.10
59	Gabe Alvarez	.10
60	Todd Dunwoody	.10
61	Rod Beck	.10
62	Derek Bell	.10
63	Francisco Cordova	.10
64	Johnny Damon	.10
65	Adrian Beltre	.10
66	Garret Anderson	.10
67	Armando Benitez	.10
68	Edgardo Alfonzo	.10
69	Ryan Bradley	.10
70	Eric Chavez	1.00
71	Bobby Abreu	.10
72	Andy Ashby	.10
73	Ellis Burks	.10
74	Jeff Cirillo	.10
75	Jay Buhner	.15
76	Ron Gant	.20
77	Rolando Arrojo	.25
78	Will Clark	.40
79	Chris Carpenter	.10
80	Jim Edmonds	.10
81	Tony Batista	.10
82	Shane Andrews	.10
83	Mark DeRosa	.10
84	Brady Anderson	.10
85	Tony Gordon	.10
86	Brant Brown	.10
87	Ray Durham	.10
88	Ron Coomer	.10
89	Bret Boone	.10
90	Travis Fryman	.10
91	Darryl Kile	.10
92	Paul Bako	.10
93	Cliff Floyd	.10
94	Scott Elarton	.10
95	Jeremy Giambi	.10
96	Darren Dreifort	.10
97	Marquis Grissom	.10
98	Marty Cordova	.10
99	Fernando Seguignol	.25
100	Orlando Hernandez	1.00
101	Jose Cruz Jr.	.50
102	Jason Giambi	.10
103	Damion Easley	.10
104	Freddy Garcia	.10
105	Marlon Anderson	.10
106	Kevin Brown	.20
107	Joe Carter	.20
108	Russ Davis	.10
109	Brian Jordan	.10
110	Wade Boggs	.40
111	Tom Goodwin	.10
112	Scott Brosius	.10
113	Darin Erstad	.75
114	Jay Bell	.10
115	Tom Glavine	.25
116	Pedro Martinez	.50
117	Mark Grace	.25
118	Russ Ortiz	.10
119	Magglio Ordonez	.20
120	Sean Casey	.25
121	*Rafael Roque*	.25
122	Brian Giles	.10
123	Mike Lansing	.10
124	David Cone	.25
125	Alex Gonzalez	.10
126	Carl Everett	.10
127	Jeff King	.10
128	Charles Johnson	.10
129	Geoff Jenkins	.10
130	Corey Koskie	.10
131	Brad Fullmer	.25
132	Al Leiter	.20
133	Rickey Henderson	.25
134	Rico Brogna	.10
135	Jose Guillen	.25
136	Matt Clement	.20
137	Carlos Guillen	.10
138	Orel Hershiser	.10
139	Ray Lankford	.10
140	Miguel Cairo	.10
141	Chuck Finley	.10
142	Rusty Greer	.10
143	Kelvim Escobar	.10
144	Ryan Klesko	.25
145	Andy Benes	.20
146	Eric Davis	.10
147	David Wells	.10
148	Trot Nixon	.25
149	Jose Hernandez	.10
150	Mark Johnson	.10
151	Mike Frank	.10
152	Joey Hamilton	.10
153	David Justice	.30
154	Mike Mussina	.50
155	Neifi Perez	.10
156	Luis Gonzalez	.10
157	Livan Hernandez	.10
158	Dermal Brown	.10
159	Jose Lima	.10
160	Eric Karros	.20
161	Ronnie Belliard	.10
162	Matt Lawton	.10
163	Dustin Hermanson	.10
164	Brian McRae	.10
165	Mike Kinkade	.10
166	A.J. Hinch	.10
167	Doug Glanville	.10
168	Hideo Nomo	.20
169	Jason Kendall	.10
170	Steve Finley	.10
171	Jeff Kent	.10
172	Ben Davis	.10
173	Edgar Martinez	.10
174	Eli Marrero	.10
175	Quinton McCracken	.10
176	Rick Helling	.10
177	Tom Evans	.10
178	Carl Pavano	.10
179	Todd Greene	.10
180	Omar Daal	.10
181	George Lombard	.25
182	Ryan Minor	.40
183	Troy O'Leary	.10
184	Robb Nen	.10
185	Mickey Morandini	.10
186	Robin Ventura	.20
187	Pete Harnisch	.10
188	Kenny Lofton	.60
189	Eric Milton	.10
190	Bobby Higginson	.10
191	Jamie Moyer	.10
192	Mark Kotsay	.25
193	Shane Reynolds	.10
194	Carlos Febles	.10
195	Jeff Kubenka	.10
196	Chuck Knoblauch	.40
197	Kenny Rogers	.10
198	Bill Mueller	.10
199	Shane Monahan	.10
200	Matt Morris	.10
201	Fred McGriff	.30
202	Ivan Rodriguez	.75
203	Kevin Witt	.10
204	Troy Percival	.10
205	David Dellucci	.10
206	Kevin Millwood	.50
207	Jerry Hairston	.50
208	Mike Stanley	.10
209	Henry Rodriguez	.10
210	Trevor Hoffman	.10
211	Craig Wilson	.10
212	Reggie Sanders	.10
213	Carlton Loewer	.10
214	Omar Vizquel	.10
215	Gabe Kapler	1.00
216	Derrek Lee	.10
217	Billy Wagner	.10
218	Dean Palmer	.10
219	Chan Ho Park	.40
220	Fernando Vina	.10
221	Roy Halladay	.50
222	Paul Molitor	.50
223	Ugueth Urbina	.10
224	Rey Ordonez	.10
225	Ricky Ledee	.25
226	Scott Spiezio	.10
227	Wendell Magee Jr.	.10
228	Aramis Ramirez	.10
229	Brian Simmons	.10
230	Fernando Tatis	.10
231	Bobby Smith	.10
232	Aaron Sele	.10
233	Shawn Green	.10
234	Mariano Rivera	.25
235	Tim Salmon	.40
236	Andy Fox	.10
237	Denny Neagle	.10
238	John Valentin	.10
239	Kevin Tapani	.10
240	Paul Konerko	.25
241	Robert Fick	.10
242	Edgar Renteria	.10
243	Brett Tomko	.10
244	Daryle Ward	.10
245	Carlos Beltran	.10
246	Angel Pena	.10
247	Steve Woodard	.10
248	David Ortiz	.10
249	Justin Thompson	.10
250	Rondell White	.25
251	Jaret Wright	.50
252	Ed Sprague	.10
253	Jay Payton	.10
254	Mike Lowell	.25
255	Orlando Cabrera	.10
256	Jason Schmidt	.10
257	David Segui	.10
258	Paul Sorrento	.10
259	John Wetteland	.10
260	Devon White	.10
261	Odalis Perez	.40
262	Calvin Pickering	.10
263	Alex Ramirez	.10
264	Preston Wilson	.10
265	Brad Radke	.10
266	Walt Weiss	.10
267	Tim Young	.10
268	Tino Martinez	.40
269	Matt Stairs	.10
270	Curt Schilling	.20
271	Tony Womack	.10
272	Ismael Valdes	.10
273	Wally Joyner	.10
274	Armando Rios	.10
275	Andy Pettitte	.50
276	Bubba Trammell	.10
277	Todd Zeile	.10
278	Shannon Stewart	.10
279	Matt Williams	.40
280	John Rocker	.10
281	B.J. Surhoff	.10
282	Eric Young	.10
283	Dmitri Young	.10
284	John Smoltz	.25
285	Todd Walker	.25
286	Paul O'Neill	.25
287	Blake Stein	.10
288	Kevin Young	.10
289	Quilvio Veras	.10
290	Kirk Rueter	.10
291	Randy Winn	.10
292	Miguel Tejada	.10
293	J.T. Snow	.10
294	Michael Tucker	.10
295	Jay Tessmer	.10
296	Scott Erickson	.10
297	Tim Wakefield	.10
298	Jeff Abbott	.10
299	Eddie Taubensee	.10
300	Darryl Hamilton	.10
301	Kevin Orie	.10
302	Jose Offerman	.10
303	Scott Karl	.10
304	Chris Widger	.10
305	Todd Hundley	.10
306	Desi Relaford	.10
307	Sterling Hitchcock	.10
308	Delino DeShields	.10
309	Alex Gonzalez	.10
310	Justin Baughman	.10
311	Jamey Wright	.10
312	Wes Helms	.10
313	Dante Powell	.10
314	Jim Abbott	.10
315	Manny Alexander	.10
316	Harold Baines	.10
317	Danny Graves	.10
318	Sandy Alomar	.10
319	Pedro Astacio	.10
320	Jermaine Allensworth	.10
321	Matt Anderson	.10
322	Chad Curtis	.10
323	Antonio Osuna	.10
324	Brad Ausmus	.10
325	Steve Trachsel	.10
326	Mike Blowers	.10
327	Brian Bohanon	.10
328	Chris Gomez	.10
329	Valerio de los Santos	.10
330	Rich Aurilia	.10
331	Michael Barrett	.50
332	Rick Aguilera	.10
333	Adrian Brown	.10
334	Bill Spiers	.10
335	Matt Beech	.10
336	David Bell	.10
337	Juan Acevedo	.10
338	Jose Canseco	.40
339	Wilson Alvarez	.10
340	Luis Alicea	.10
341	Jason Dickson	.10
342	Mike Bordick	.10
343	Ben Ford	.10
344	Keith Lockhart	.10
345	Jason Christiansen	.10
346	Darren Bragg	.10
347	Doug Brocail	.10
348	Jeff Blauser	.10
349	James Baldwin	.10
350	Jeffrey Hammonds	.10
351	Ricky Bottalico	.10
352	Russ Branyon	.10
353	Mark Brownson	.75
354	Dave Berg	.10
355	Sean Bergman	.10
356	Jeff Conine	.10
357	Shayne Bennett	.10
358	Bobby Bonilla	.20
359	Bob Wickman	.10
360	Carlos Baerga	.10
361	Chris Fussell	.10
362	Chili Davis	.10
363	Jerry Spradlin	.10
364	Carlos Hernandez	.10
365	Roberto Hernandez	.10
366	Marvin Benard	.10
367	Ken Cloude	.10
368	Tony Fernandez	.10
369	John Burkett	.10
370	Gary DiSarcina	.10
371	Alan Benes	.10
372	Karim Garcia	.10
373	Carlos Perez	.10
374	Damon Buford	.10
375	Mark Clark	.10
376	*Edgard Clemente*	.10
377	Chad Bradford	.50
378	Frank Catalanotto	.10
379	Vic Darensbourg	.10
380	Sean Berry	.10
381	Dave Burba	.10
382	Sal Fasano	.10
383	Steve Parris	.10
384	Roger Cedeno	.10
385	Chad Fox	.10
386	Wilton Guerrero	.10
387	Dennis Cook	.10
388	Joe Girardi	.10
389	LaTroy Hawkins	.10
390	Ryan Christenson	.10
391	Paul Byrd	.10
392	Lou Collier	.10
393	Jeff Fassero	.10
394	Jim Leyritz	.10
395	Shawn Estes	.10
396	Mike Kelly	.10
397	Rich Croushore	.10
398	Royce Clayton	.10
399	Rudy Seanez	.10
400	Darrin Fletcher	.10
401	Shigetosi Hasegawa	.10
402	Bernard Gilkey	.10
403	Juan Guzman	.10

#	Player	MT
404	Jeff Frye	.10
405	Marino Santana	.10
406	Alex Fernandez	.10
407	Gary Gaetti	.10
408	Dan Miceli	.10
409	Mike Cameron	.10
410	Mike Remlinger	.10
411	Joey Cora	.10
412	Mark Gardner	.10
413	Aaron Ledesma	.10
414	Jerry Dipoto	.10
415	Ricky Gutierrez	.10
416	John Franco	.10
417	Mendy Lopez	.10
418	Hideki Irabu	.25
419	Mark Grudzielanek	.10
420	Bobby Hughes	.10
421	Pat Meares	.10
422	Jimmy Haynes	.10
423	Bob Henley	.10
424	Bobby Estalella	.10
425	Jon Lieber	.10
426	*Giomar Guevara*	.50
427	Jose Jimenez	.10
428	Deivi Cruz	.10
429	Jonathan Johnson	.10
430	Ken Hill	.10
431	Craig Grebeck	.10
432	Jose Rosado	.10
433	Danny Klassen	.10
434	Bobby Howry	.10
435	Gerald Williams	.10
436	Omar Olivares	.10
437	Chris Hoiles	.10
438	Seth Greisinger	.10
439	Scott Hatteberg	.10
440	Jeremi Gonzalez	.10
441	Wil Cordero	.10
442	Jeff Montgomery	.10
443	Chris Stynes	.10
444	Tony Saunders	.10
445	Einar Diaz	.10
446	Laril Gonzalez	.10
447	Ryan Jackson	.10
448	Mike Hampton	.10
449	Todd Hollandsworth	.10
450	Gabe White	.10
451	John Jaha	.10
452	Bret Saberhagen	.10
453	Otis Nixon	.10
454	Steve Kline	.10
455	Butch Huskey	.10
456	Mike Jerzembeck	.10
457	Wayne Gomes	.10
458	Mike Macfarlane	.10
459	Jesus Sanchez	.10
460	Al Martin	.10
461	Dwight Gooden	.20
462	Ruben Rivera	.10
463	Pat Hentgen	.10
464	Jose Valentin	.10
465	Vladimir Nunez	.10
466	Charlie Hayes	.10
467	Jay Powell	.10
468	Raul Ibanez	.10
469	Kent Mercker	.10
470	John Mabry	.10
471	Woody Williams	.10
472	Roberto Kelly	.10
473	Jim Mecir	.10
474	Dave Hollins	.10
475	Rafael Medina	.10
476	Darren Lewis	.10
477	Felix Heredia	.10
478	Brian Hunter	.10
479	Matt Mantei	.10
480	Richard Hidalgo	.10
481	Bobby Jones	.10
482	Hal Morris	.10
483	Ramiro Mendoza	.10
484	Matt Luke	.10
485	Esteban Loaiza	.10
486	Mark Loretta	.10
487	A.J. Pierzynski	.10
488	Charles Nagy	.10
489	Kevin Sefcik	.10
490	Jason McDonald	.10
491	Jeremy Powell	.10
492	Scott Servais	.10
493	Abraham Nunez	.10
494	Stan Spencer	.10
495	Stan Javier	.10
496	Jose Paniagua	.10
497	Gregg Jefferies	.10
498	Gregg Olson	.10
499	Derek Lowe	.10
500	Willis Otanez	.10
501	Brian Moehler	.10
502	Glenallen Hill	.10
503	Bobby Jones	.10
504	Greg Norton	.10
505	Mike Jackson	.10
506	Kirt Manwaring	.10
507	Eric Weaver	.75
508	Mitch Meluskey	.15
509	Todd Jones	.10
510	Mike Matheny	.10
511	Benj Sampson	.10
512	Tony Phillips	.10
513	Mike Thurman	.10
514	Jorge Posada	.10
515	Bill Taylor	.10
516	Mike Sweeney	.10
517	Jose Silva	.10
518	Mark Lewis	.10
519	Chris Peters	.10
520	Brian Johnson	.10
521	Mike Timlin	.10
522	Mark McLemore	.10
523	Dan Plesac	.10
524	Kelly Stinnett	.10
525	Sidney Ponson	.10
526	Jim Parque	.10
527	Tyler Houston	.10
528	John Thomson	.10
529	Mike Metcalfe	.10
530	Robert Person	.10
531	Marc Newfield	.10
532	Javier Vazquez	.10
533	Terry Steinbach	.10
534	Turk Wendell	.10
535	Tim Raines	.10
536	Brian Meadows	.10
537	Mike Lieberthal	.10
538	Ricardo Rincon	.10
539	Dan Wilson	.10
540	John Johnstone	.10
541	Todd Stottlemyre	.10
542	Kevin Stocker	.10
543	Ramon Martinez	.10
544	Mike Simms	.10
545	Paul Quantrill	.10
546	Matt Walbeck	.10
547	Turner Ward	.10
548	Bill Pulsipher	.10
549	Donnie Sadler	.10
550	Lance Johnson	.10
551	Bill Simas	.10
552	Jeff Reed	.10
553	Jeff Shaw	.10
554	Joe Randa	.10
555	Paul Shuey	.10
556	Mike Redmond	.50
557	Sean Runyan	.10
558	Enrique Wilson	.10
559	Scott Radinsky	.10
560	Larry Sutton	.10
561	Masato Yoshii	.10
562	David Nilsson	.10
563	Mike Trombley	.10
564	Darryl Strawberry	.25
565	Dave Mlicki	.10
566	Placido Polanco	.10
567	Yorkis Perez	.10
568	Esteban Yan	.10
569	Lee Stevens	.10
570	Steve Sinclair	.10
571	Jarrod Washburn	.10
572	Lenny Webster	.10
573	Mike Sirotka	.10
574	Jason Varitek	.10
575	Terry Mulholland	.10
576	Adrian Beltre (Franchise Futures)	.25
577	Eric Chavez (Franchise Futures)	.50
578	J.D. Drew (Franchise Futures)	.50
579	Juan Encarnacion (Franchise Futures)	.10
580	Nomar Garciaparra (Franchise Futures)	1.00
581	Troy Glaus (Franchise Futures)	.40
582	Ben Grieve (Franchise Futures)	.40
583	Vladimir Guerrero (Franchise Futures)	.75
584	Todd Helton (Franchise Futures)	.40
585	Derek Jeter (Franchise Futures)	1.00
586	Travis Lee (Franchise Futures)	.40
587	Alex Rodriguez (Franchise Futures)	1.25
588	Scott Rolen (Franchise Futures)	.40
589	Richie Sexson (Franchise Futures)	.10
590	Kerry Wood (Franchise Futures)	.40
591	Ken Griffey Jr.	1.50
592	Chipper Jones	.75
593	Alex Rodriguez	1.25
594	Sammy Sosa	1.00
595	Mark McGwire	2.00
596	Cal Ripken Jr.	1.25
597	Nomar Garciaparra	1.00
598	Derek Jeter	1.00
599	Kerry Wood	.40
600	J.D. Drew	.40

1999 Fleer Starting Nine

This ultra-scarce, hobby-only parallel insert, found at the rate of about two cards per case, includes just nine cards of each player. Sharing the basic design of the Fleer Traditional set, the cards have blue metallic foil printing on front, including a "STARTING 9 NINE" logo at lower-right. At bottom right, the card's individual serial number from within the edition of nine is printed. Backs have an "S" suffix to the card number.

	MT
Common Player:	20.00

(Star and rookie cards valued at 200-250X base versions.)

1999 Fleer Warning Track Collection

Each of the cards in '99 Fleer Tradition was paralleled in this retail-only issue found one per pack. Warning Track cards are distinguished by the use of red metallic foil on front for the player's name, team, position that are in gold-foil on the regular version. There is also a special "Warning Track Collection" logo in red foil at bottom-right. On back, WTC cards have a "W" suffix to the card number.

	MT
Complete Set (600):	250.00
Common Player:	.20
Stars:	3X

(See 1999 Fleer for checklist and base card values.)

1999 Fleer Date With Destiny

This 10-card set takes a look at what Hall of Fame plaques might look like for some of today's great players. These are serially numbered to 100 sets.

		MT
Complete Set (10):		500.00
Common Player:		25.00
Production 100 sets		
1	Barry Bonds	25.00
2	Roger Clemens	30.00
3	Ken Griffey Jr.	80.00
4	Tony Gwynn	30.00
5	Greg Maddux	50.00
6	Mark McGwire	100.00
7	Mike Piazza	60.00
8	Cal Ripken Jr.	80.00
9	Alex Rodriguez	80.00
10	Frank Thomas	30.00

1999 Fleer Diamond Magic

A multi-layer card, where collectors turn a "wheel" for a kaleidoscope effect behind the player image. These are seeded 1:96 packs.

	MT
Complete Set (15):	250.00
Common Player:	6.00

Inserted 1:96
1 Barry Bonds 10.00
2 Roger Clemens 15.00
3 Nomar Garciaparra 25.00
4 Ken Griffey Jr. 30.00
5 Tony Gwynn 15.00
6 Orlando Hernandez 6.00
7 Derek Jeter 25.00
8 Randy Johnson 10.00
9 Chipper Jones 20.00
10 Greg Maddux 20.00
11 Mark McGwire 40.00
12 Alex Rodriguez 30.00
13 Sammy Sosa 25.00
14 Bernie Williams 8.00
15 Kerry Wood 6.00

1999 Fleer Going Yard

This 15-card set features the top home run hitters from the '98 season. These 1:18 pack inserts unfold to be twice as wide as regular cards and takes an unorthodox look at how far the longest home runs went.

	MT
Complete Set (15):	45.00
Common Player:	.75
Inserted 1:18	
1 Moises Alou	.75
2 Albert Belle	2.50
3 Jose Canseco	1.50
4 Vinny Castilla	.75
5 Andres Galarraga	1.50
6 Juan Gonzalez	2.50
7 Ken Griffey Jr.	10.00
8 Chipper Jones	5.00
9 Mark McGwire	12.00
10 Rafael Palmeiro	1.00
11 Mike Piazza	6.00
12 Alex Rodriguez	8.00
13 Sammy Sosa	6.00
14 Greg Vaughn	.75
15 Mo Vaughn	2.50

1999 Fleer Golden Memories

This 15-card set pays tribute to the great moments from the 1998 season including David Wells perfect game and McGwire's record breaking season. These are seeded 1:54 packs on an embossed frame design.

	MT
Complete Set (15):	150.00
Common Player:	3.00
Inserted 1:54	
1 Albert Belle	5.00
2 Barry Bonds	6.00
3 Roger Clemens	10.00
4 Nomar Garciaparra	15.00
5 Juan Gonzalez	6.00
6 Ken Griffey Jr.	20.00
7 Randy Johnson	6.00
8 Greg Maddux	12.00
9 Mark McGwire	25.00
10 Mike Piazza	15.00
11 Cal Ripken Jr.	20.00
12 Alex Rodriguez	20.00
13 Sammy Sosa	15.00
14 David Wells	3.00
15 Kerry Wood	4.00

1999 Fleer Rookie Flashback

This 15-card set features the impact rookies from the 1998 season. These are seeded 1:6 packs and feature sculpture embossing.

	MT
Complete Set (15):	18.00
Common Player:	.25
Inserted 1:6	
1 Matt Anderson	.25
2 Rolando Arrojo	.40
3 Adrian Beltre	.75
4 Mike Caruso	.25
5 Eric Chavez	1.50
6 J.D. Drew	2.00
7 Juan Encarnacion	.75
8 Brad Fullmer	.40
9 Troy Glaus	1.50
10 Ben Grieve	1.50
11 Todd Helton	1.00
12 Orlando Hernandez	1.50
13 Travis Lee	1.50
14 Richie Sexson	.50
15 Kerry Wood	1.00

1999 Fleer Stan Musial Monumental Moments

Great moments and insight from and about the St. Louis Cardinals great. This 10-card tribute set chronicles Musial's legendary career. These are seeded 1:36 packs with 500 autographed cards randomly seeded.

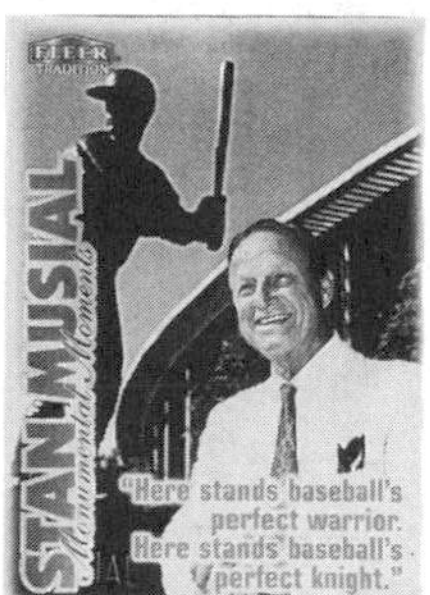

	MT
Complete Set (10):	40.00
Common Musial:	5.00
Autographed Card:	95.00
1 Life in Donora	6.00
2 Values	6.00
3 In the Beginning	6.00
4 In the Navy	6.00
5 The 1948 Season (w/Red Schoendienst)	6.00
6 Success Stories (w/Pres. Kennedy)	6.00
7 Mr. Cardinal	6.00
8 Most Valuable Player	6.00
9 ... baseball's perfect knight	6.00
10 Hall of Fame	6.00

1999 Fleer Vintage '61

This 50-card set takes the first 50 cards from the base set and showcases them in the 1961 Fleer "Baseball Greats" card design. These are seeded one per hobby pack.

	MT
Complete Set (50):	25.00
Common Player:	.20
Inserted 1:1	
1 Mark McGwire	4.00
2 Sammy Sosa	2.50
3 Ken Griffey Jr.	3.00
4 Kerry Wood	.75
5 Derek Jeter	2.00
6 Stan Musial	4.00
7 J.D. Drew	.50
8 Cal Ripken Jr.	2.50
9 Alex Rodriguez	2.50
10 Travis Lee	.75
11 Andres Galarraga	.50
12 Nomar Garciaparra	2.00
13 Albert Belle	.75
14 Barry Larkin	.40
15 Dante Bichette	.40
16 Tony Clark	.40
17 Moises Alou	.30
18 Rafael Palmeiro	.30
19 Raul Mondesi	.20
20 Vladimir Guerrero	1.50
21 John Olerud	.20
22 Bernie Williams	.40
23 Ben Grieve	.75
24 Scott Rolen	.75
25 Jeromy Burnitz	.20
26 Ken Caminiti	.20
27 Barry Bonds	.75
28 Todd Helton	.75
29 Juan Gonzalez	1.00
30 Roger Clemens	1.25
31 Andruw Jones	.75
32 Mo Vaughn	.75
33 Larry Walker	.50
34 Frank Thomas	1.00
35 Manny Ramirez	1.00
36 Randy Johnson	.50
37 Vinny Castilla	.20
38 Juan Encarnacion	.50
39 Jeff Bagwell	.75
40 Gary Sheffield	.30
41 Mike Piazza	2.00
42 Richie Sexson	.20
43 Tony Gwynn	1.50
44 Chipper Jones	1.50
45 Jim Thome	.50
46 Craig Biggio	.40
47 Carlos Delgado	.50
48 Greg Vaughn	.30
49 Greg Maddux	2.00
50 Troy Glaus	.75

1999 Fleer Update

Distributed as a 150-card boxed set, the main focus for this release is the inclusion of rookie cards of players called up late in the '99 season, including Rick Ankiel. Besides rookies, the set also features 10 traded players/ free agents and a 10-card Season Highlights subset.

	MT
Complete Set (150):	40.00
Common Player:	.10
1 *Rick Ankiel*	15.00
2 *Peter Bergeron*	1.00
3 *Pat Burrell*	4.00
4 *Eric Munson*	3.00
5 *Alfonso Soriano*	2.00
6 *Tim Hudson*	3.00
7 *Erubiel Durazo*	3.00
8 Chad Hermansen	.10
9 Jeff Zimmerman	1.00
10 *Jesus Pena*	.25
11 Ramon Hernandez	.10
12 *Trent Durrington*	.25
13 Tony Armas, Jr.	.15
14 *Mike Fyhrie*	.25
15 *Danny Kolb*	.50
16 *Mike Porzio*	.40
17 *Will Brunson*	.40
18 *Mike Duvall*	.25
19 Doug Mientkiewicz	.10
20 *Gabe Molina*	.50
21 *Luis Vizcaino*	.25
22 *Robinson Cancel*	.50
23 *Brett Laxton*	.50
24 *Joe McEwing*	1.50
25 *Justin Speier*	.40
26 *Kip Wells*	1.00
27 *Armando Almanza*	.25
28 *Joe Davenport*	.50
29 *Yamid Haad*	.25
30 John Halama	.10
31 Adam Kennedy	.10
32 Vicente Padilla	.10
33 *Travis Dawkins*	.75
34 *Ryan Rupe*	.50
35 *B.J. Ryan*	.40
36 *Chance Sanford*	.25
37 *Anthony Shumaker*	.25
38 *Ryan Glynn*	.40
39 Matt Herges	.10
40 Ben Molina	.40
41 Scott Williamson	.10
42 *Eric Gagne*	1.00

43 *John McDonald* .25
44 *Scott Sauerbeck* .40
45 *Mike Venafro* .25
46 *Edwards Guzman* .50
47 *Richard Barker* .40
48 Braden Looper .10
49 *Chad Meyers* .25
50 *Scott Strickland* .50
51 Billy Koch .10
52 *Dave Newhan* .40
53 *David Riske* .40
54 Jose Santiago .10
55 *Miguel Del Toro* .25
56 *Orber Moreno* .40
57 Dave Roberts .10
58 *Tim Byrdak* .25
59 *David Lee* .25
60 *Guillermo Mota* .50
61 *Wilton Veras* 1.50
62 *Mike Colangelo* .25
63 *Jose Fernandez* .50
64 *Ray King* .25
65 *Chris Petersen* .40
66 Vernon Wells .40
67 Ruben Mateo .50
68 Ben Petrick .10
69 *Chris Tremie* .25
70 Lance Berkman .10
71 Dan Smith .10
72 *Carlos Hernandez* .10
73 *Chad Harville* .25
74 Damaso Marte .10
75 *Aaron Myette* 1.00
76 *Willis Roberts* .25
77 *Erik Sabel* .50
78 *Hector Almonte* .50
79 Kris Benson .10
80 *Pat Daneker* .25
81 *Freddy Garcia* 4.00
82 *Byung-Hyun Kim* 1.00
83 *Wily Pena* 2.50
84 *Dan Wheeler* .25
85 *Tim Harikkala* .25
86 *Derrin Ebert* .25
87 *Horacio Estrada* .50
88 *Liu Rodriguez* .25
89 *Jordan Zimmerman* .25
90 *A.J. Burnett* 1.00
91 *Doug Davis* .25
92 *Robert Ramsey* .25
93 Ryan Franklin .10
94 *Charlie Greene* .25
95 *Bo Porter* .25
96 *Jorge Toca* 1.00
97 *Casey Blake* .25
98 *Amaury Garcia* .50
99 *Jose Molina* .25
100 *Melvin Mora* 1.50
101 *Joe Nathan* .10
102 *Juan Pena* .10
103 *Dave Borkowski* .10
104 *Eddie Gaillard* .10
105 Rob Radlosky .10
106 *Brett Hinchliffe* .10
107 Carlos Lee .10
108 *Rob Ryan* .10
109 *Jeff Weaver* 1.00
110 Ed Yarnall .10
111 *Nelson Cruz* .10
112 *Cleatus Davidson* .25
113 *Tim Kubinski* .10
114 *Sean Spencer* .10
115 *Joe Winkelsas* .10
116 Chris Clapinski .10
117 *Tom Davey* .10
118 Warren Morris .10
119 *Dan Murray* .10
120 *Jose Nieves* .10
121 *Mark Quinn* 1.50
122 *Josh Beckett* 4.00
123 *Chad Allen* .10
124 Mike Figga .10
125 *Beiker Graterol* .10
126 *Aaron Scheffer* .10
127 *Wiki Gonzalez* .50
128 Ramon E. Martinez .10
129 *Matt Riley* 1.50
130 *Chris Woodward* .25
131 Albert Belle .10
132 Roger Cedeno .10
133 Roger Clemens .10
134 Brian Giles .10
135 Rickey Henderson .10
136 Randy Johnson .10
137 Brian Jordan .10
138 Paul Konerko .10
139 Hideo Nomo .10
140 Kenny Rogers .10
141 Wade Boggs .25
142 Jose Canseco .50
143 Roger Clemens .75
144 David Cone .10
145 Tony Gwynn 1.00
146 Mark McGwire 2.50
147 Cal Ripken Jr. 1.50
148 Alex Rodriguez 1.00
149 Fernando Tatis .10
150 Robin Ventura .10

1999 Fleer Brilliants

This 175-card set features an action photo on a complete silver-foiled background swirl pattern. The featured player's name, team and postion are stamped in gold foil. Card backs have a small photo, vital information, 1998 statistics and a brief overview of the player's '98 season. Cards numbered 126-175 are part of a short-printed Rookies subset and are seeded 1:2 packs.

	MT
Complete Set (175):	100.00
Common Player:	.40
Common SP (126-175):	.75
Pack (5):	5.00
Wax Box (24):	105.00

1 Mark McGwire 5.00
2 Derek Jeter 4.00
3 Nomar Garciaparra 3.00
4 Travis Lee .40
5 Jeff Bagwell 1.25
6 Andres Galarraga .75
7 Pedro Martinez 1.25
8 Cal Ripken Jr. 4.00
9 Vladimir Guerrero 1.50
10 Chipper Jones 2.50
11 Rusty Greer .40
12 Omar Vizquel .40
13 Quinton McCracken .40
14 Jaret Wright .60
15 Mike Mussina .75
16 Jason Giambi .40
17 Tony Clark .40
18 Troy O'Leary .40
19 Troy Percival .40
20 Kerry Wood .75
21 Vinny Castilla .40
22 Chris Carpenter .40
23 Richie Sexson .40
24 Ken Griffey Jr. 4.00
25 Barry Bonds 1.25
26 Carlos Delgado 1.25
27 Frank Thomas 1.50
28 Manny Ramirez 1.25
29 Shawn Green .75
30 Mike Piazza 3.00
31 Tino Martinez .40
32 Dante Bichette .40
33 Scott Rolen 1.25
34 Gabe Alvarez .40
35 Raul Mondesi .60
36 Damion Easley .40
37 Jeff Kent .40
38 Al Leiter .40
39 Alex Rodriguez 4.00
40 Jeff King .40
41 Mark Grace .50
42 Larry Walker .60
43 Moises Alou .60
44 Juan Gonzalez 1.25
45 Rolando Arrojo .40
46 Tom Glavine .60
47 Johnny Damon .40
48 Livan Hernandez .40
49 Craig Biggio .50
50 Dmitri Young .40
51 Chan Ho Park .60
52 Todd Walker .40
53 Derrek Lee .40
54 Todd Helton 1.00
55 Ray Lankford .40
56 Jim Thome .75
57 Matt Lawton .40
58 Matt Anderson .40
59 Jose Offerman .40
60 Eric Karros .40
61 Orlando Hernandez .60
62 Ben Grieve .60
63 Bobby Abreu .40
64 Kevin Young .40
65 John Olerud .50
66 Sammy Sosa 3.00
67 Andy Ashby .40
68 Juan Encarnacion .40
69 Shane Reynolds .40
70 Bernie Williams 1.00
71 Mike Cameron .40
72 Troy Glaus 2.50
73 Gary Sheffield .60
74 Jeromy Burnitz .40
75 Mike Caruso .40
76 Chuck Knoblauch .50
77 Kenny Rogers .40
78 David Cone .60
79 Tony Gwynn 1.50
80 Aramis Ramirez .40
81 Paul O'Neill .75
82 Charles Nagy .40
83 Javy Lopez .60
84 Scott Erickson .40
85 Trevor Hoffman .40
86 Andruw Jones 1.00
87 Ray Durham .40
88 Jorge Posada .40
89 Edgar Martinez .40
90 Tim Salmon .75
91 Bobby Higginson .40
92 Adrian Beltre .75
93 Jason Kendall .60
94 Henry Rodriguez .40
95 Greg Maddux 2.50
96 David Justice .75
97 Ivan Rodriguez 1.25
98 Curt Schilling .60
99 Matt Williams .75
100 Darin Erstad 1.00
101 Rafael Palmeiro .75
102 David Wells .40
103 Barry Larkin .75
104 Robin Ventura .60
105 Edgar Renteria .40
106 Andy Pettitte .60
107 Albert Belle .75
108 Steve Finley .40
109 Fernando Vina .40
110 Rondell White .60
111 Kevin Brown .60
112 Jose Canseco .75
113 Roger Clemens 1.50
114 Todd Hundley .40
115 Will Clark .75
116 Jim Edmonds .40
117 Randy Johnson 1.25
118 Denny Neagle .40
119 Brian Jordan .40
120 Dean Palmer .40
121 Roberto Alomar 1.00
122 Ken Caminiti .60
123 Brian Giles .40
124 Todd Stottlemyre .40
125 Mo Vaughn 1.00
126 J.D. Drew .75
127 Ryan Minor .75
128 Gabe Kapler 1.00
129 Jeremy Giambi .75
130 Eric Chavez .75
131 Ben Davis .75
132 Rob Fick .75
133 George Lombard .75
134 Calvin Pickering .75
135 Preston Wilson .75
136 Corey Koskie .75
137 Russell Branyan .75
138 Bruce Chen .75
139 Matt Clement .75
140 *Pat Burrell* 10.00
141 *Freddy Garcia* 3.00
142 Brian Simmons .75
143 Carlos Febles .75
144 Carlos Guillen .75
145 Fernando Seguignol 1.00
146 Carlos Beltran .75
147 Edgard Clemente .75
148 Mitch Meluskey .75
149 Ryan Bradley .75
150 Marlon Anderson .75
151 *A.J. Burnett* 1.50
152 *Scott Hunter* .75
153 Mark Johnson .75
154 Angel Pena .75
155 Roy Halladay .75
156 *Chad Allen* 1.00
157 Trot Nixon .75
158 Ricky Ledee .75
159 *Gary Bennett* 1.00
160 *Micah Bowie* 1.00
161 Doug Mientkiewicz .75
162 Danny Klassen .75
163 Willis Otanez .75
164 Jin Ho Cho .75
165 Mike Lowell 1.00
166 Armando Rios .75
167 Tom Evans .75
168 Michael Barrett .75
169 Alex Gonzalez .75
170 *Masao Kida* 1.00
171 *Peter Tucci* 1.00
172 Luis Saturria .75
173 Kris Benson 1.00
174 *Mario Encarnacion* 1.50
175 *Roosevelt Brown* 1.00

1999 Fleer Brilliants Blue/Golds

The 175 Fleer Brilliants base cards are paralleled in three insert sets of differing degrees of scarcity. Brilliant Blue parallels have a mirrored blue foil background on front and a "B" suffix to the card number on back. They are seeded one per three packs (125 veterans) and one per six packs (50 rookies). Gold parallels are printed with gold foil background and a "G" suffix. Each card is serially numbered on back within an edition of 99. The 24-karat Gold parallels have

gold rainbow holographic foil backgrounds, a 24-karat gold logo and are serially numbered to just 24 of each card; numbers have a TG sugffix.

	MT
Brilliants Blue Common:	1.00
Brilliants Blue Stars:	2X
Brilliants Blue Rookies:	1.5X
Brilliants Gold Common:	5.00
Brilliants Gold Stars:	15X
Brilliants Gold Rookies:	5X
Brilliants 24K Gold Common:	15.00
Brilliants 24K Gold Stars:	50X
Brilliants 24K Gold Rookies:	15X

(See 1999 Fleer Brilliants for checklist and base card values.)

1999 Fleer Brilliants Illuminators

This 15-card set highlights baseball's top young prospects on a team color-coded fully foiled front. Card backs are numbered with an "I" suffix and are inserted 1:10 packs.

		MT
Complete Set (15):		35.00
Common Player:		1.50
Inserted 1:10		
1	Kerry Wood	2.50
2	Ben Grieve	2.50
3	J.D. Drew	2.00
4	Juan Encarnacion	2.00
5	Travis Lee	1.50
6	Todd Helton	4.00
7	Troy Glaus	6.00
8	Ricky Ledee	1.50
9	Eric Chavez	3.00
10	Ben Davis	1.50
11	George Lombard	1.50
12	Jeremy Giambi	1.50
13	Richie Sexson	2.00
14	Corey Koskie	1.50

1999 Fleer Brilliants Shining Stars

Shining Stars is a 15-card set printed on styrene with two-sided mirrored foil. Card backs are numbered with a "S" suffix and are seeded 1:20 packs. Pulsars are a parallel set that are printed on two-sided rainbow holographic foil and styrene with an embossed star pattern in the background. Pulsars are seeded 1:400 packs.

		MT
Complete Set (15):		125.00
Common Player:		4.00
Inserted 1:20		
Pulsars:		4x to 8x
Inserted 1:400		
1	Ken Griffey Jr.	15.00
2	Mark McGwire	20.00
3	Sammy Sosa	12.00
4	Derek Jeter	12.00
5	Nomar Garciaparra	12.00
6	Alex Rodriguez	15.00
7	Mike Piazza	12.00
8	Juan Gonzalez	5.00
9	Chipper Jones	10.00
10	Cal Ripken Jr.	15.00
11	Frank Thomas	6.00
12	Greg Maddux	10.00
13	Roger Clemens	6.00
14	Vladimir Guerrero	6.00
15	Manny Ramirez	5.00

1999 Fleer Mystique

		MT
Complete Set (160):		325.00
Common Player:		.20
Common SP (1-100):		.75
Common (101-150):		2.50
Production 2,999 sets		
Common (151-160):		10.00
Production 2,500 sets		
Pack (4):		5.00
Wax Box (24):		100.00
1	Ken Griffey Jr.	6.00
2	Livan Hernandez	.20
3	Jeff Kent	.20
4	Brian Jordan	.20
5	Kevin Young	.20
6	Vinny Castilla	.20
7	Orlando Hernandez	.75
8	Bobby Abreu	.20
9	Vladimir Guerrero	3.00
10	Chuck Knoblauch	.50
11	Nomar Garciaparra	4.00
12	Jeff Bagwell	1.00
13	Todd Walker	.20
14	Johnny Damon	.20
15	Mike Caruso	.20
16	Cliff Floyd	.20
17	Andy Pettitte	.40
18	Cal Ripken Jr.	5.00
19	Brian Giles	.20
20	Robin Ventura	.40
21	Alex Gonzalez	.20
22	Randy Johnson	.75
23	Raul Mondesi	.40
24	Ken Caminiti	.40
25	Tom Glavine	.40
26	Derek Jeter	4.00
27	Carlos Delgado	.75
28	Adrian Beltre	.50
29	Tino Martinez	.50
30	Todd Helton	1.50
31	Juan Gonzalez	1.50
32	Henry Rodriguez	.20
33	Jim Thome	.50
34	Paul O'Neill	.40
35	Scott Rolen	1.50
36	Rafael Palmeiro	.75
37	Will Clark	.40
38	Todd Hundley	.20
39	Andruw Jones	1.00
40	Luis Rolando Arrojo	.20
41	Barry Larkin	.50
42	Tim Salmon	.40
43	Rondell White	.40
44	Curt Schilling	.40
45	Chipper Jones	4.00
46	Jeromy Burnitz	.20
47	Mo Vaughn	1.00
48	Tony Clark	.50
49	Fernando Tatis	.40
50	Dmitri Young	.20
51	Wade Boggs	.50
52	Rickey Henderson	.40
53	Manny Ramirez	2.00
54	Edgar Martinez	.20
55	Jason Giambi	.20
56	Jason Kendall	.20
57	Eric Karros	.20
58	Jose Canseco	1.00
59	Shawn Green	.50
60	Ellis Burks	.20
61	Derek Bell	.20
62	Shannon Stewart	.20
63	Roger Clemens	2.00
64	Sean Casey	1.00
65	Jose Offerman	.20
66	Sammy Sosa	4.00
67	Frank Thomas	1.50
68	Tony Gwynn	3.00
69	Roberto Alomar	.75
70	Mark McGwire	8.00
71	Troy Glaus	1.50
72	Ray Durham	.20
73	Jeff Cirillo	.20
74	Alex Rodriguez	5.00
75	Jose Cruz Jr.	.20
76	Juan Encarnacion	.20
77	Mark Grace	.40
78	Barry Bonds	1.50
79	Ivan Rodriguez	1.50
80	Greg Vaughn	.40
81	Greg Maddux	4.00
82	Albert Belle	1.00
83	John Olerud	.50
84	Kenny Lofton	.75
85	Bernie Williams	.75
86	Matt Williams	.50
87	Ray Lankford	.20
88	Darin Erstad	.50
89	Ben Grieve	.50
90	Craig Biggio	.50
91	Dean Palmer	.20
92	Reggie Sanders	.20
93	Dante Bichette	.40
94	Pedro J. Martinez	1.50
95	Larry Walker	.50
96	David Wells	.20
97	Travis Lee	.75
98	Mike Piazza	2.50
99	Mike Mussina	.75
100	Kevin Brown	.40
101	Ruben Mateo (Rookie)	4.00
102	Roberto Ramirez (Rookie)	2.50
103	*Glen Barker* (Rookie)	2.50
104	*Clay Bellinger* (Rookie)	2.50
105	Carlos Guillen (Rookie)	2.50
106	Scott Schoeneweis (Rookie)	2.50
107	Creighton Gubanich (Rookie)	2.50
108	Scott Williamson (Rookie)	3.00
109	*Edwards Guzman* (Rookie)	4.00
110	*A.J. Burnett* (Rookie)	6.00
111	Jeremy Giambi (Rookie)	3.00
112	Trot Nixon (Rookie)	2.50
113	J.D. Drew (Rookie)	10.00
114	Roy Halladay (Rookie)	3.00
115	*Jose Macias* (Rookie)	3.00
116	Corey Koskie (Rookie)	2.50
117	*Ryan Rupe* (Rookie)	5.00
118	Scott Hunter (Rookie)	4.00
119	Rob Fick (Rookie)	2.50
120	McKay Christensen (Rookie)	2.50
121	Carlos Febles (Rookie)	3.00
122	Gabe Kapler (Rookie)	4.00
123	Jeff Liefer (Rookie)	2.50
124	Warren Morris (Rookie)	3.00
125	Chris Pritchett (Rookie)	2.50
126	Torii Hunter (Rookie)	2.50
127	Armando Rios (Rookie)	3.00
128	Ricky Ledee (Rookie)	2.50
129	*Kelly Dransfeldt* (Rookie)	5.00
130	Jeff Zimmerman (Rookie)	6.00
131	Eric Chavez (Rookie)	4.00
132	Freddy Garcia (Rookie)	15.00
133	Jose Jimenez (Rookie)	2.50
134	*Pat Burrell* (Rookie)	80.00
135	*Joe McEwing* (Rookie)	5.00
136	Kris Benson (Rookie)	2.50
137	*Joe Mays* (Rookie)	5.00
138	Rafael Roque (Rookie)	2.50
139	Cristian Guzman (Rookie)	2.50
140	Michael Barrett (Rookie)	2.50
141	Doug Mientkiewicz (Rookie)	4.00
142	*Jeff Weaver* (Rookie)	10.00
143	Mike Lowell (Rookie)	2.50
144	*Jason Phillips* (Rookie)	3.00
145	Marlon Anderson (Rookie)	2.50
146	*Brett Hinchliffe* (Rookie)	2.50
147	Matt Clement (Rookie)	2.50
148	Terrence Long (Rookie)	2.50
149	Carlos Beltran (Rookie)	3.00
150	Preston Wilson (Rookie)	2.50
151	Ken Griffey Jr. (Stars)	15.00
152	Mark McGwire (Stars)	20.00
153	Sammy Sosa (Stars)	12.00
154	Mike Piazza (Stars)	12.00
155	Alex Rodriguez (Stars)	12.00
156	Nomar Garciaparra (Stars)	12.00
157	Cal Ripken Jr. (Stars)	15.00
158	Greg Maddux (Stars)	10.00
159	Derek Jeter (Stars)	15.00
160	Juan Gonzalez (Stars)	5.00

1999 Fleer Mystique Destiny

		MT
Complete Set (10):		90.00
Common Player:		8.00
Production 999 sets		
1	Tony Gwynn	15.00
2	Juan Gonzalez	10.00
3	Scott Rolen	8.00
4	Nomar Garciaparra	30.00
5	Orlando Hernandez	6.00
6	Andruw Jones	10.00
7	Vladimir Guerrero	12.00
8	Darin Erstad	8.00
9	Manny Ramirez	10.00
10	Roger Clemens	15.00

1999 Fleer Mystique Established

		MT
Complete Set (10):		750.00
Common Player:		40.00
Production 100 sets		
1	Ken Griffey Jr.	100.00
2	Derek Jeter	100.00
3	Chipper Jones	60.00
4	Greg Maddux	60.00
5	Mark McGwire	125.00
6	Mike Piazza	75.00
7	Cal Ripken Jr.	100.00
8	Alex Rodriguez	100.00
9	Sammy Sosa	75.00
10	Frank Thomas	40.00

1999 Fleer Mystique Feel the Game

	MT
Complete Set (7):	650.00
Common Player:	50.00
Adrian Beltre (shoe, 430)	40.00
J.D. Drew (jersey, 450)	60.00
Juan Gonzalez (bat glove, 415)	80.00
Tony Gwynn (jersey, 435)	125.00
Kevin Millwood (jersey, 435)	60.00
Alex Rodriguez (bat glove, 345)	225.00
Frank Thomas (jersey, 450)	100.00

Player names in *Italic* type indicate a rookie card.

1999 Fleer Mystique Fresh Ink

	MT
Complete Set (26):	1000.
Common Player:	10.00
Inserted 1:48	
Roberto Alomar (500)	40.00
Michael Barrett (1,000)	15.00
Kris Benson (500)	10.00
Micah Bowie (1,000)	10.00
A.J. Burnett (500)	20.00
Pat Burrell (250)	60.00
Ken Caminiti (250)	30.00
Jose Canseco (250)	120.00
Sean Casey (1,000)	30.00
Edgard Clemente (1,000)	10.00
Bartolo Colon (500)	15.00
J.D. Drew (400)	40.00
Juan Encarnacion (1,000)	10.00
Troy Glaus (400)	40.00
Juan Gonzalez (250)	80.00
Shawn Green (250)	60.00
Tony Gwynn (250)	120.00
Chipper Jones (500)	100.00
Gabe Kapler (750)	30.00
Barry Larkin (250)	40.00
Doug Mientkiewicz (500)	10.00
Alex Rodriguez (200)	250.00
Scott Rolen (140)	80.00
Fernando Tatis (750)	20.00
Robin Ventura (500)	20.00
Todd Walker (1,000)	10.00

1999 Fleer Mystique Masterpiece

Each of the cards in Fleer Mystique was also produced in a unique Masterpiece version. The super-rarities are labeled on front "The Only 1 of 1 / Masterpiece".

	MT
Common Player:	100.00

(Because of their unique nature Masterpiece values cannot be determined.)

1999 Fleer Mystique Prophetic

		MT
Complete Set (10):		60.00
Common Player:		4.00
Production 1,999 sets		
1	Eric Chavez	4.00
2	J.D. Drew	4.00
3	A.J. Burnett	4.00
4	Ben Grieve	5.00
5	Gabe Kapler	4.00
6	Todd Helton	8.00
7	Troy Glaus	12.00
8	Travis Lee	4.00
9	Pat Burrell	25.00
10	Kerry Wood	4.00

2000 Fleer Focus

The 250-card base set has two versions for the Prospects subset card numbers 226-250. The portrait versions are serial numbered from 1-999, while the remaining serial numbered from 1,000 to 3,999 capture an action shot. The base set design has a white border with gold foil stamping. Card backs have complete year-by-year statistics along with a career note and small photo.

		MT
Complete Set (250):		200.00
Common Player:		.15
Common Prospect (226-250):		4.00
Production 2,999 sets		
Common Portrait (226-250):		8.00
Portraits:		2X
Production 999 sets		
Pack:		3.00
Wax Box (24):		60.00
1	Nomar Garciaparra	2.00
2	Adrian Beltre	.25
3	Miguel Tejada	.15
4	Joe Randa	.15
5	Larry Walker	.50
6	Jeff Weaver	.15
7	Jay Bell	.15
8	Ivan Rodriguez	.75
9	Edgar Martinez	.15
10	Desi Relaford	.15
11	Derek Jeter	2.00
12	Delino DeShields	.15
13	Craig Biggio	.50
14	Chuck Knoblauch	.25
15	Chuck Finley	.15
16	Brett Tomko	.15
17	Bobby Higginson	.15
18	Pedro Martinez	.75
19	Troy O'Leary	.15
20	Rickey Henderson	.30
21	Robb Nen	.15
22	Rolando Arrojo	.15
23	Rondell White	.25
24	Royce Clayton	.15
25	Rusty Greer	.15
26	Stan Spencer	.15
27	Steve Finley	.25
28	Tom Goodwin	.15
29	Troy Percival	.15
30	Wilton Guerrero	.15
31	Roberto Alomar	.50
32	Mike Hampton	.15
33	Michael Barrett	.15
34	Curt Schilling	.25
35	Bill Mueller	.15
36	Bernie Williams	.50
37	John Smoltz	.15
38	B.J. Surhoff	.25
39	Pete Harnisch	.15
40	Juan Encarnacion	.25
41	Derrek Lee	.15
42	Jeff Shaw	.15
43	David Cone	.25
44	Jason Christiansen	.15
45	Jeff Kent	.25
46	Randy Johnson	.60
47	Todd Walker	.15
48	Jose Lima	.15
49	Jason Giambi	.25
50	Ken Griffey Jr.	3.00
51	Bartolo Colon	.15
52	Mike Lieberthal	.15
53	Shane Reynolds	.25
54	Travis Lee	.25
55	Travis Fryman	.25
56	John Valentin	.15
57	Joey Hamilton	.15
58	Jay Buhner	.25
59	Brad Radke	.15
60	A.J. Burnett	.15
61	Roy Halladay	.15
62	Raul Mondesi	.25
63	Matt Mantei	.15
64	Mark Grace	.30
65	David Justice	.30
66	Billy Wagner	.15
67	Eric Milton	.15
68	Eric Chavez	.25
69	Doug Glanville	.15

70	Ray Durham	.15
71	Mike Sirotka	.15
72	Greg Vaughn	.25
73	Brian Jordan	.25
74	Alex Gonzalez	.15
75	Alex Rodriguez	2.50
76	David Nilsson	.15
77	Robin Ventura	.25
78	Kevin Young	.25
79	Wilson Alvarez	.15
80	Matt Williams	.40
81	Ismael Valdes	.15
82	Kenny Lofton	.50
83	Carlos Beltran	.20
84	Doug Mientkiewicz	.15
85	Wally Joyner	.15
86	J.D. Drew	.25
87	Carlos Delgado	.50
88	Tony Womack	.15
89	Eric Young	.15
90	Manny Ramirez	.75
91	Johnny Damon	.15
92	Torii Hunter	.15
93	Kenny Rogers	.15
94	Trevor Hoffman	.15
95	John Wetteland	.15
96	Ray Lankford	.15
97	Tom Glavine	.25
98	Carlos Lee	.15
99	Richie Sexson	.25
100	Carlos Febles	.15
101	Chad Allen	.15
102	Sterling Hitchcock	.15
103	Joe McEwing	.15
104	Justin Thompson	.15
105	Jim Edmonds	.25
106	Kerry Wood	.40
107	Jim Thome	.40
108	Jeremy Giambi	.15
109	Mike Piazza	2.00
110	Darryl Kile	.15
111	Darin Erstad	.25
112	Kyle Farnsworth	.15
113	Omar Vizquel	.25
114	Orber Moreno	.15
115	Al Leiter	.25
116	John Olerud	.30
117	Aaron Sele	.15
118	Chipper Jones	1.50
119	Paul Konerko	.25
120	Chris Singleton	.15
121	Fernando Vina	.15
122	Andy Ashby	.15
123	Eli Marrero	.15
124	Edgar Renteria	.15
125	Roberto Hernandez	.15
126	Andruw Jones	.50
127	Magglio Ordonez	.30
128	Bob Wickman	.15
129	Tony Gwynn	1.50
130	Mark McGwire	3.00
131	Albert Belle	.50
132	Pokey Reese	.15
133	Tony Clark	.25
134	Jeff Bagwell	.75
135	Mark Grudzielanek	.15
136	Dustin Hermanson	.15
137	Reggie Sanders	.15
138	Ryan Rupe	.15
139	Kevin Millwood	.30
140	Bret Saberhagen	.15
141	Juan Guzman	.15
142	Alex Gonzalez	.15
143	Gary Sheffield	.30
144	Roger Clemens	1.00
145	Ben Grieve	.30
146	Bobby Abreu	.30
147	Brian Giles	.15
148	Quinton McCracken	.15
149	Freddy Garcia	.25
150	Erubiel Durazo	.25
151	Sidney Ponson	.15
152	Scott Williamson	.15
153	Ken Caminiti	.25
154	Vladimir Guerrero	1.50
155	Andy Pettitte	.30
156	Edwards Guzman	.15
157	Shannon Stewart	.15
158	Greg Maddux	1.50
159	Mike Stanley	.15
160	Sean Casey	.30
161	Cliff Floyd	.15
162	Devon White	.15
163	Scott Brosius	.15
164	Marlon Anderson	.15
165	Jason Kendall	.25
166	Ryan Klesko	.15
167	Sammy Sosa	2.00
168	Frank Thomas	1.00
169	Geoff Jenkins	.25
170	Jason Schmidt	.15
171	Dan Wilson	.15
172	Jose Canseco	.75
173	Troy Glaus	.50
174	Mariano Rivera	.25
175	Scott Rolen	.75
176	J.T. Snow	.15
177	Rafael Palmeiro	.40
178	A.J. Hinch	.15
179	Jose Offerman	.15
180	Jeff Cirillo	.15
181	Dean Palmer	.25
182	Jose Rosado	.15
183	Armando Benitez	.15
184	Brady Anderson	.25
185	Cal Ripken Jr.	2.50
186	Barry Larkin	.40
187	Damion Easley	.15
188	Moises Alou	.25
189	Todd Hundley	.25
190	Tim Hudson	.25
191	Livan Hernandez	.15
192	Fred McGriff	.30
193	Orlando Hernandez	.30
194	Tim Salmon	.25
195	Mike Mussina	.50
196	Todd Helton	.75
197	Juan Gonzalez	.75
198	Kevin Brown	.25
199	Ugueth Urbina	.15
200	Matt Stairs	.15
201	Shawn Estes	.15
202	Gabe Kapler	.25
203	Javy Lopez	.25
204	Henry Rodriguez	.15
205	Dante Bichette	.25
206	Jeromy Burnitz	.25
207	Todd Zeile	.15
208	Rico Brogna	.15
209	Warren Morris	.15
210	David Segui	.15
211	Vinny Castilla	.25
212	Mo Vaughn	.50
213	Charles Johnson	.15
214	Neifi Perez	.15
215	Shawn Green	.50
216	Carl Pavano	.15
217	Tino Martinez	.30
218	Barry Bonds	.75
219	David Wells	.15
220	Paul O'Neill	.30
221	Masato Yoshii	.15
222	Kris Benson	.15
223	Fernando Tatis	.30
224	Lee Stevens	.15
225	Jose Cruz Jr.	.15
226	Rick Ankiel (Prospect)	25.00
227	Matt Riley (Prospect)	6.00
228	Norm Hutchins (Prospect)	4.00
229	Ruben Mateo (Prospect)	4.00
229		8.00
230	Ben Petrick (Prospect)	4.00
231	Mario Encarnacion (Prospect)	4.00
232	Nick Johnson (Prospect)	10.00
233	Adam Piatt (Prospect)	10.00
234	Mike Darr (Prospect)	4.00
235	Chad Hermansen (Prospect)	4.00
236	Wily Pena (Prospect)	12.00
237	Octavio Dotel (Prospect)	4.00
238	Vernon Wells (Prospect)	6.00
239	Daryle Ward (Prospect)	5.00
240	Adam Kennedy (Prospect)	6.00
241	Angel Pena Prospect)	4.00
242	Lance Berkman (Prospect)	5.00
243	Gabe Molina (Prospect)	4.00
244	Steve Lomasney (Prospect)	4.00
245	Jacob Cruz (Prospect)	4.00
246	Mark Quinn (Prospect)	5.00
247	Eric Munson (Prospect)	12.00
248	Alfonso Soriano (Prospect)	6.00
249	Kip Wells (Prospect)	4.00
250	Josh Beckett (Prospect)	12.00
	Checklist #171	.05
	Checklist #172-25, inserts	.05
	Checklist inserts	.05

2000 Fleer Focus Masterpiece

Each of the cards in Fleer Focus was issued in a parallel edition of just one piece each. Fronts of Masterpiece 1/1s have purple metallic ink, instead of gold, for the player identification. On back, there is a notation "The Only 1 of 1 Masterpiece" along with an "M" suffix to the card number. An error version has all the attributes of the true Masterpiece, but lacks the "Only 1 . . . " notation on back (see 2000 Fleer Focus Masterpiece Errors).

	MT
Common Player:	100.00

(Values undetermined due to rarity and fluctuating demand. See 2000 Fleer Focus for checklist.)

2000 Fleer Focus Masterpiece Mania

Green, rather than gold, ink is used on front for the player name, team and position to distinguish this parallel insert set. On back, each card is numbered from within an edition of 300 each.

	MT
Common Player:	3.00
Stars:	8-15X
Yng Stars & RCs (226-250):	1-2X
Production 300 sets	

(See 2000 Fleer Focus for checklist and base card values.)

2000 Fleer Focus Masterpiece Errors

Thousands of collectors' hopes were crushed when it was determined that an unknown number of uncompleted Masterpiece 1-of-1 cards were erroneously inserted in Focus foil packs. Like the true Masterpiece cards, the fronts of the error cards have the player name, team and position at bottom front in purple, rather than gold foil. On back, the cards even have the "M" suffix to the card number at lower-right. Unfortunately, these do not have the foil-stamped "The Only 1 of 1 Masterpiece" notation on back; greatly reducing the value. Because of uncertain supply and variability of demand these error cards cannot be priced.

	MT
Complete Set (25):	250.00
Common Player:	4.00
50M Ken Griffey Jr.	100.00
202MGabe Kapler	8.00
203MJavy Lopez	6.00
204MHenry Rodriguez	4.00
205MDante Bichette	5.00
206MJeromy Burnitz	5.00
207MTodd Zeile	4.00
208MRico Brogna	4.00
209MWarren Morris	4.00
210MDavid Segui	4.00
211MVinny Castilla	5.00
212MMo Vaughn	6.00
213MCharles Johnson	5.00
214MNeifi Perez	5.00
215MShawn Green	20.00
216MCarl Pavano	4.00
217MTino Martinez	5.00
218MBarry Bonds	30.00
219MDavid Wells	8.00
220MPaul O'Neill	6.00
221MMasato Yoshii	5.00
222MKris Benson	8.00
223MFernando Tatis	6.00
224MLee Stevens	4.00
225MJose Cruz Jr.	6.00

2000 Fleer Focus Club 3000

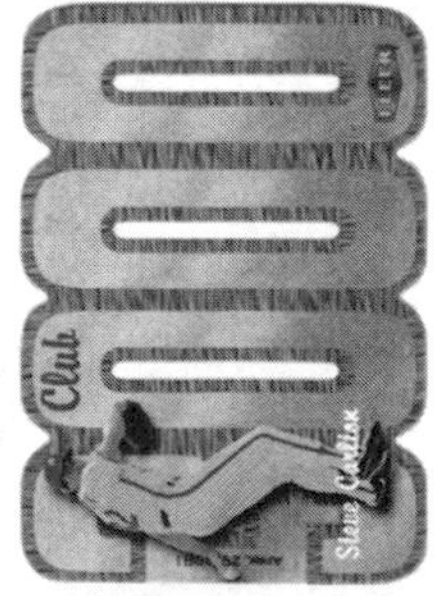

These inserts are die-cut around the number 3,000 and features three players who either have 3,000 hits or strikeouts. This set spotlights Stan Musial, Steve Carlton and Paul Molitor. These are seeded 1:36 packs.

		MT
Complete Set (3):		4.00
Common Player:		1.50
(1)	Steve Carlton	1.50
(2)	Paul Molitor	1.50
(3)	Stan Musial	1.50

2000 Fleer Focus Club 3000 Memorabilia

Five tiers featuring memorabilia from game-used bats, caps etc... make up this hand numbered set. Besides a bat and cap insert others include jersey, bat and jersey combo and a bat, jersey and cap combo.

	MT
Steve Carlton - bat/325	75.00
Steve Carlton - hat/65	215.00
Steve Carlton - jersey/750	50.00
Steve Carlton - bat-hat-jersey/25	450.00
Paul Molitor - bat/355	85.00
Paul Molitor - hat/65	175.00
Paul Molitor - jersey/975	50.00
Stan Musial - bat/325	150.00
Stan Musial - jersey/975	100.00
Stan Musial - bat-jersey/100	300.00

2000 Fleer Focus Feel the Game

This 10-card set offers pieces of player-worn jerseys from some of baseball's biggest stars embedded into the card front. These were seeded 1:288 packs.

	MT
Common Player:	25.00
Inserted 1:288	
Adrian Beltre	30.00
Tom Glavine	30.00
Vladimir Guerrero	75.00
Randy Johnson	75.00
Javy Lopez	30.00
Alex Rodriguez	150.00
Scott Rolen	50.00
Cal Ripken Jr.	150.00
Tim Salmon	30.00
Miguel Tejada	25.00

2000 Fleer Focus Focal Points

This 15-card set has silver foil etching around the border and silver foil stamping. These were seeded 1:6 packs and are numbered with an "F" suffix on the card back.

		MT
Complete Set (15):		35.00
Common Player:		1.00
Inserted 1:6		
1	Mark McGwire	5.00
2	Tony Gwynn	2.50
3	Nomar Garciaparra	3.00
4	Juan Gonzalez	1.25
5	Jeff Bagwell	1.25
6	Chipper Jones	2.50
7	Cal Ripken Jr.	4.00
8	Alex Rodriguez	4.00
9	Scott Rolen	1.00
10	Vladimir Guerrero	2.50
11	Mike Piazza	3.00
12	Frank Thomas	2.00
13	Ken Griffey Jr.	5.00
14	Sammy Sosa	3.00
15	Derek Jeter	3.00

2000 Fleer Focus Focus Pocus

This 10-card set has a silver prismatic, holofoil background with silver foil stamping. These were seeded 1:14 packs and are numbered with an "FP" suffix.

		MT
Complete Set (10):		40.00
Common Player:		1.50
Inserted 1:14		
1	Cal Ripken Jr.	6.00
2	Tony Gwynn	4.00
3	Nomar Garciaparra	5.00
4	Juan Gonzalez	2.00
5	Mike Piazza	5.00
6	Mark McGwire	8.00
7	Chipper Jones	4.00
8	Ken Griffey Jr.	8.00
9	Derek Jeter	5.00
10	Alex Rodriguez	6.00

Player names in *Italic* type indicate a rookie card.

2000 Fleer Focus Fresh Ink

These autographed inserts are seeded 1:96 packs.

	MT
Common Player:	10.00
Inserted 1:96	
Chad Allen	10.00
Michael Barrett	10.00
Josh Beckett	35.00
Rob Bell	15.00
Adrian Beltre	20.00
Milton Bradley	10.00
Rico Brogna	15.00
Mike Cameron	10.00
Eric Chavez	15.00
Bruce Chen	10.00
Johnny Damon	15.00
Ben Davis	10.00
J.D. Drew	30.00
Erubiel Durazo	20.00
Jeremy Giambi	10.00
Jason Giambi	20.00
Doug Glanville	10.00
Troy Glaus	40.00
Shawn Green	50.00
Mike Hampton	15.00
Tim Hudson	15.00
John Jaha	15.00
Derek Jeter	220.00
D'Angelo Jimenez	10.00
Nick Johnson	20.00
Andruw Jones	20.00
Jason Kendall	20.00
Adam Kennedy	15.00
Mike Lieberthal	15.00
Edgar Martinez	15.00
Aaron McNeal	10.00
Kevin Millwood	20.00
Mike Mussina	40.00
Magglio Ordonez	20.00
Eric Owens	10.00
Rafael Palmeiro	50.00
Wily Pena	30.00
Adam Piatt	25.00
Cal Ripken Jr.	200.00
Alex Rodriguez	200.00
Scott Rolen	60.00
Tim Salmon	20.00
Chris Singleton	15.00
Mike Sweeney	15.00
Jose Vidro	15.00
Rondell White	15.00
Jaret Wright	15.00

2000 Fleer Focus Future Vision

This 15-card set highlights the top prospects over a holofoiled background with red foil etching and stamping. These were seeded 1:9 packs and are numbered with an "FV" suffix.

		MT
Complete Set (15):		25.00
Common Player:		1.00
Inserted 1:9		
1	Rick Ankiel	8.00
2	Matt Riley	1.50
3	Ruben Mateo	1.50
4	Ben Petrick	1.00
5	Mario Encarnacion	1.00
6	Octavio Dotel	1.00
7	Vernon Wells	1.50
8	Adam Kennedy	2.00
9	Lance Berkman	1.00
10	Chad Hermansen	1.00
11	Mark Quinn	1.00
12	Eric Munson	2.50
13	Alfonso Soriano	2.00
14	Kip Wells	1.00
15	Josh Beckett	3.00

2000 Fleer Gamers

The 120-card base set has silver foil etching down the left portion of the card with vertical stripes running down the right portion of the card front. The card back has career statistical totals as well as a small photo. Two short-printed subsets also make up the 120-card set. Next Gamers (91-110) are seeded 1:3 packs and Fame Game (111-120) are seeded 1:8 packs.

	MT
Complete Set (120):	125.00
Common Player (1-90):	.15
Common (91-110):	1.00
Inserted 1:3	
Common (111-120):	4.00
Inserted 1:8	
Pack:	4.00
Wax Box:	90.00

1	Cal Ripken Jr.	2.50
2	Derek Jeter	2.00
3	Alex Rodriguez	2.50
4	Alex Gonzalez	.15
5	Nomar Garciaparra	2.00
6	Brian Giles	.25
7	Chris Singleton	.15
8	Kevin Brown	.25
9	J.D. Drew	.40
10	Raul Mondesi	.40
11	Sammy Sosa	2.00
12	Carlos Beltran	.20
13	Eric Chavez	.15
14	Gabe Kapler	.25
15	Tim Salmon	.25
16	Manny Ramirez	.75
17	Orlando Hernandez	.40
18	Jeff Kent	.15
19	Juan Gonzalez	.75
20	Moises Alou	.25
21	Jason Giambi	.25
22	Ivan Rodriguez	.75
23	Geoff Jenkins	.25
24	Ken Griffey Jr.	3.00
25	Mark McGwire	3.00
26	Jose Canseco	.75
27	Roberto Alomar	.50
28	Craig Biggio	.40
29	Scott Rolen	.75
30	Vinny Castilla	.25
31	Greg Maddux	1.50
32	Pedro J. Martinez	.75
33	Mike Piazza	2.00
34	Albert Belle	.50
35	Frank Thomas	1.00
36	Bobby Abreu	.25
37	Edgar Martinez	.25
38	Pokey Reese	.15
39	Preston Wilson	.15
40	Mike Lieberthal	.15
41	Andruw Jones	.50
42	Damion Easley	.15
43	Mike Cameron	.15
44	Todd Walker	.15
45	Jason Kendall	.25
46	Sean Casey	.30
47	Corey Koskie	.15
48	Warren Morris	.15
49	Andres Galarraga	.50
50	Dean Palmer	.15
51	Jose Vidro	.15
52	Brian Jordan	.15
53	Tony Clark	.25
54	Vladimir Guerrero	1.50
55	Mo Vaughn	.50
56	Richie Sexson	.15
57	Tino Martinez	.40
58	Eric Owens	.15
59	Matt Williams	.40
60	Omar Vizquel	.25
61	Rickey Henderson	.40
62	J.T. Snow	.15
63	Mark Grace	.30
64	Carlos Febles	.15
65	Paul O'Neill	.40
66	Randy Johnson	.75
67	Kenny Lofton	.50
68	Roger Cedeno	.15
69	Shawn Green	.50
70	Chipper Jones	1.50
71	Jeff Cirillo	.25
72	Robin Ventura	.25
73	Paul Konerko	.25
74	Jeromy Burnitz	.25
75	Ben Grieve	.40
76	Troy Glaus	.50
77	Jim Thome	.40
78	Bernie Williams	.50
79	Barry Bonds	.75
80	Ray Durham	.15
81	Adrian Beltre	.25
82	Ray Lankford	.15
83	Carlos Delgado	.50
84	Erubiel Durazo	.15
85	Larry Walker	.50
86	Edgardo Alfonzo	.25
87	Rafael Palmeiro	.50
88	Magglio Ordonez	.25
89	Jeff Bagwell	.75
90	Tony Gwynn	1.50
91	Norm Hutchins (Next Gamers)	1.00
92	*Derrick Turnbow* (Next Gamers)	3.00
93	Matt Riley (Next Gamers)	2.50
94	David Eckstein (Next Gamers)	1.00
95	Dernell Stenson (Next Gamers)	2.00
96	Joe Crede (Next Gamers)	1.00
97	Ben Petrick (Next Gamers)	1.00
98	Eric Munson (Next Gamers)	4.00
99	Pablo Ozuna (Next Gamers)	1.50
100	Josh Beckett (Next Gamers)	5.00
101	*Aaron McNeal* (Next Gamers)	4.00
102	Milton Bradley (Next Gamers)	2.00
103	Alex Escobar (Next Gamers)	2.00
104	Alfonso Soriano (Next Gamers)	2.50
105	Wily Pena (Next Gamers)	5.00
106	Nick Johnson (Next Gamers)	4.00
107	Adam Piatt (Next Gamers)	3.00
108	Pat Burrell (Next Gamers)	5.00
109	Rick Ankiel (Next Gamers)	8.00
110	(Vernon Wells) (Next Gamers)	2.00
111	Alex Rodriguez (Fame Game)	6.00
112	Cal Ripken Jr. (Fame Game)	6.00
113	Mark McGwire (Fame Game)	8.00
114	Ken Griffey Jr. (Fame Game)	8.00
115	Mike Piazza (Fame Game)	5.00
116	Nomar Garciaparra (Fame Game)	5.00
117	Derek Jeter (Fame Game)	5.00
118	Chipper Jones (Fame Game)	4.00
119	Sammy Sosa (Fame Game)	5.00
120	Tony Gwynn (Fame Game)	4.00

2000 Fleer Gamers Extra

A parallel to the 120-card base set, the gold foiled card front and "Extra" written down the right portion of the card can be used to differentiate these from regular cards. "Extra" is also written underneath the card number on the back as well. Extras 1-90 are seeded 1:24 packs and numbers 91-120 are seeded 1:36 packs.

	MT
Stars (1-90):	6-12X
Inserted 1:24	
Next Gamers (91-110):	2X
Inserted 1:36	
Fame Game (110-120):	2X
Inserted 1:36	

2000 Fleer Gamers Change the Game

This 15-card set has a holofoiled front with Change the Game printed behind the player image. Seeded 1:24 packs, card backs are numbered with a "CG" suffix.

		MT
Complete Set (15):		125.00
Common Player:		3.00
Inserted 1:24		
1	Alex Rodriguez	15.00
2	Cal Ripken Jr.	15.00
3	Chipper Jones	10.00
4	Derek Jeter	12.00
5	Ken Griffey Jr.	20.00
6	Mark McGwire	20.00
7	Mike Piazza	12.00
8	Nomar Garciaparra	12.00
9	Sammy Sosa	12.00
10	Tony Gwynn	10.00
11	Ivan Rodriguez	6.00
12	Pedro Martinez	6.00
13	Juan Gonzalez	6.00
14	Vladimir Guerrero	10.00
15	Manny Ramirez	6.00

2000 Fleer Gamers Cal to Greatness

This 15-card tribute insert set to baseball's "Iron Man" is broken into three tiers. Cards 1-5 are seeded 1:9 packs, cards 6-10 are found 1:25 packs and cards 11-15 are inserted 1:144 packs. Card backs are numbered with a "C" suffix.

		MT
Complete Set (15):		
Common Ripken (1-5):		5.00
Inserted 1:9		
Common Ripken (6-10):		10.00
Inserted 1:25		
Common Ripken (11-15):		40.00
Inserted 1:144		
1	Cal Ripken Jr.	5.00
2	Cal Ripken Jr.	5.00
3	Cal Ripken Jr.	5.00
4	Cal Ripken Jr.	5.00
5	Cal Ripken Jr.	5.00
6	Cal Ripken Jr.	10.00
7	Cal Ripken Jr.	10.00
8	Cal Ripken Jr.	10.00
9	Cal Ripken Jr.	10.00
10	Cal Ripken Jr.	10.00
11	Cal Ripken Jr.	40.00
12	Cal Ripken Jr.	40.00
13	Cal Ripken Jr.	40.00
14	Cal Ripken Jr.	40.00
15	Cal Ripken Jr.	40.00

2000 Fleer Gamers Determined

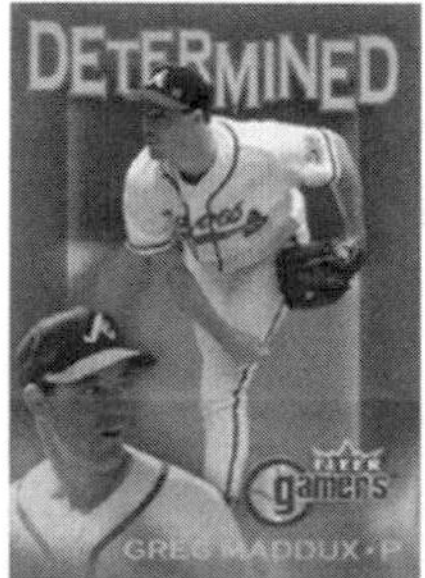

This 15-card set has a holofoiled front with two player images on the card front. The second player photo is smaller than the primary image and is a close-up shot. Card backs are numbered with a "D" suffix and are seeded 1:12 packs.

		MT
Complete Set (15):		70.00
Common Player:		1.50
Inserted 1:12		
1	Nomar Garciaparra	6.00
2	Chipper Jones	5.00
3	Derek Jeter	6.00
4	Mike Piazza	6.00
5	Jeff Bagwell	2.50
6	Mark McGwire	10.00
7	Greg Maddux	5.00
8	Sammy Sosa	6.00
9	Ken Griffey Jr.	10.00
10	Alex Rodriguez	8.00
11	Tony Gwynn	5.00
12	Cal Ripken Jr.	8.00
13	Barry Bonds	2.50
14	Juan Gonzalez	2.50
15	Sean Casey	1.50

2000 Fleer Gamers Lumber

Seeded 1:36 packs, these inserts have a piece of game-used bat embedded into the card front and are numbered with a "GL" suffix

		MT
Common Player:		15.00
Inserted 1:36		
1	Alex Rodriguez	150.00
2	Carlos Delgado	40.00
3	Jose Vidro	20.00
4	Carlos Febles	15.00
5	J.D. Drew	40.00
6	Mike Cameron	15.00
7	Derek Jeter	150.00
8	Eric Chavez	20.00
9	Cal Ripken Jr.	150.00
10	Gabe Kapler	25.00
11	Damion Easley	15.00
12	Frank Thomas	70.00
13	Chris Singleton	15.00
14	Norm Hutchins	15.00
15	Pokey Reese	20.00
16	Rafael Palmeiro	40.00
17	Ray Durham	20.00
18	Ray Lankford	20.00
19	Roger Cedeno	20.00
20	Shawn Green	50.00
21	Wade Boggs	50.00
22	Roberto Alomar	60.00
23	Moises Alou	20.00
24	Adrian Beltre	25.00
25	Barry Bonds	75.00
26	Jason Giambi	25.00
27	Jason Kendall	25.00
28	Paul Konerko	25.00
29	Mike Lieberthal	20.00
30	Edgar Martinez	20.00
31	Raul Mondesi	30.00
32	Scott Rolen	40.00
33	Alfonso Soriano	30.00
34	Ivan Rodriguez	75.00
35	Magglio Ordonez	25.00
36	Chipper Jones	90.00
37	Sean Casey	25.00
38	Edgardo Alfonzo	25.00
39	Robin Ventura	25.00
40	Bernie Williams	50.00
41	Vladimir Guerrero	75.00
42	Tony Clark	25.00
43	Carlos Beltran	15.00
44	Warren Morris	15.00
45	Jim Thome	40.00
46	Jeromy Burnitz	30.00
47	Matt Williams	40.00
48	Erubiel Durazo	25.00

2000 Fleer Gamers Lumber Autograph

Twelve players also signed a limited number of their Lumber inserts. The number signed by each player is listed after the player name. These were seeded 1:287 packs.

		MT
Common Player:		60.00
Inserted 1:287		
1	Derek Jeter	375.00
2	Eric Chavez	60.00
3	Rafael Palmeiro	100.00
4	Shawn Green	125.00
5	Roberto Alomar	175.00
6	Paul Konerko	75.00
7	Sean Casey	75.00
8	Alex Rodriguez	350.00
9	Robin Ventura	80.00
10	Erubiel Durazo	90.00
11	Tony Clark	60.00
12	Alfonso Soriano	75.00

2000 Fleer Greats of the Game

The base set consists of 107-cards of retired stars. Card fronts have a brown border with "Fleer Greats of the Game" stamped in silver foil. Backs have a small photo along with complete career statistics and a brief career highlight.

		MT
Complete Set (108):		90.00
Common Player:		.50
Pack (6):		15.00
Wax Box:		300.00
1	Mickey Mantle	15.00
2	Gil Hodges	1.50
3	Monte Irvin	.50
4	Satchel Paige	2.50
5	Roy Campanella	2.00
6	Richie Ashburn	1.00
7	Roger Maris	2.00
8	Ozzie Smith	2.00
9	Reggie Jackson	2.50
10	Eddie Mathews	2.50
11	Dave Righetti	.50
12	Dave Winfield	1.00
13	Lou Whitaker	.50
14	Phil Garner	.50
15	Ron Cey	.50
16	Brooks Robinson	2.50
17	Bruce Sutter	.50
18	Dave Parker	.50
19	Johnny Bench	2.50
20	Fernando Valenzuela	.50
21	George Brett	3.00
22	Paul Molitor	2.00
23	Hoyt Wilhelm	.50
24	Luis Aparicio	.50
25	Frank White	.50
26	Herb Score	.50
27	Kirk Gibson	.50
28	Mike Schmidt	3.00
29	Don Baylor	.50
30	Joe Pepitone	.50
31	Hal McRae	.50
32	Lee Smith	.50
33	Nolan Ryan	7.00
34	Bill Mazeroski	.50
35	Bobby Doerr	.50
36	Duke Snider	1.00
37	Dick Groat	.50
38	Larry Doby	.50
39	Kirby Puckett	2.00
40	Steve Carlton	1.00
41	Dennis Eckersley	.50
42	Jim Bunning	.50
43	Ron Guidry	.50
44	Alan Trammell	1.00
45	Bob Feller	1.50
46	Dave Concepcion	.50
47	Dwight Evans	.50
48	Enos Slaughter	.50
49	Tom Seaver	2.50
50	Tony Oliva	1.00
51	Mel Stottlemyre	.50
52	Tommy John	.50
53	Willie McCovey	1.00
54	Red Schoendienst	.50
55	Gorman Thomas	.50
56	Ralph Kiner	1.00
57	Robin Yount	2.00
58	Andre Dawson	1.00
59	Al Kaline	2.00
60	Dom DiMaggio	.50
61	Juan Marichal	1.00
62	Jack Morris	.50
63	Warren Spahn	2.00
64	Preacher Roe	.50
65	Darrell Evans	.50
66	Jim Bouton	.50
67	Rocky Colavito	1.00
68	Bob Gibson	2.00
69	Whitey Ford	1.50
70	Moose Skowron	.50
71	Boog Powell	1.00
72	Al Lopez	.50
73	Lou Brock	1.50
74	Mickey Lolich	.50
75	Rod Carew	2.50
76	Bob Lemon	.50
77	Frank Howard	.50
78	Phil Rizzuto	1.50
79	Carl Yastrzemski	2.00
80	Rico Carty	.50
81	Jim Kaat	.50
82	Bert Blyleven	.50
83	George Kell	.50
84	Jim Palmer	2.00
85	Maury Wills	1.00
86	Jim Rice	.50
87	Joe Carter	.50
88	Clete Boyer	.50
89	Yogi Berra	3.00
90	Cecil Cooper	.50
91	Davey Johnson	.50
92	Lou Boudreau	.50
93	Orlando Cepeda	1.00
94	Tommy Henrich	.50
95	Hank Bauer	.50
96	Don Larsen	1.50
97	Vida Blue	1.00
98	Ben Oglivie	.50
99	Don Mattingly	3.00
100	Dale Murphy	1.00
101	Ferguson Jenkins	1.00
102	Bobby Bonds	1.00
103	Dick Allen	.50
104	Stan Musial	3.00
105	Gaylord Perry	.50
106	Willie Randolph	.50
107	Willie Stargell	1.50
108	Checklist	.50

2000 Fleer Greats of the Game Autographs

Seeded in every six packs, Autographs feature the signature on the bottom half of the card front in black Sharpie. The autographed set features 89 retired players. Some cards were issued in considierably lower quantities than others, as noted in the checklist.

	MT
Common Player:	10.00
Inserted 1:6	
Luis Aparicio	20.00
Hank Bauer	10.00
Don Baylor	20.00
Johnny Bench	200.00
Yogi Berra	125.00
Vida Blue	20.00
Bert Blyleven	10.00
Bobby Bonds	30.00
Lou Boudreau	40.00
Jim Bouton	20.00
Clete Boyer	25.00
George Brett (275 or less)	200.00
Lou Brock	35.00
Jim Bunning	30.00
Rod Carew	40.00
Steve Carlton	35.00
Joe Carter	75.00
Orlando Cepeda	25.00
Ron Cey	15.00
Rocky Colavito	30.00
Dave Concepcion (black autograph)	20.00
Dave Concepcion (red autograph)	20.00
Cecil Cooper	10.00
Andre Dawson	30.00
Dom DiMaggio	75.00
Bobby Doerr	20.00
Darrell Evans	20.00
Bob Feller	20.00
Whitey Ford (300 or less)	180.00
Phil Garner	10.00
Bob Gibson	35.00
Kirk Gibson	30.00
Dick Groat	10.00
Ron Guidry	25.00
Tommy Henrich (300 or less)	200.00
Frank Howard	20.00
Reggie Jackson (250 or less)	180.00
Ferguson Jenkins	25.00
Tommy John	10.00

Davey Johnson	10.00
Jim Kaat	15.00
Al Kaline	50.00
George Kell	20.00
Ralph Kiner	35.00
Don Larsen	40.00
Mickey Lolich	10.00
Juan Marichal	50.00
Eddie Mathews	80.00
Don Mattingly (300 or less)	200.00
Bill Mazeroski	25.00
Willie McCovey	50.00
Hal McRae	10.00
Paul Molitor	60.00
Jack Morris	10.00
Dale Murphy	50.00
Stan Musial	125.00
Ben Oglivie	10.00
Tony Oliva	30.00
Jim Palmer	80.00
Dave Parker	20.00
Joe Pepitone	20.00
Gaylord Perry	25.00
Boog Powell	20.00
Kirby Puckett (200 or less)	200.00
Willie Randolph	20.00
Jim Rice	20.00
Dave Righetti	15.00
Phil Rizzuto (200 or less)	200.00
Brooks Robinson	50.00
Preacher Roe	30.00
Nolan Ryan	250.00
Mike Schmidt (175 or less)	300.00
Red Schoendienst	20.00
Herb Score	25.00
Tom Seaver	75.00
Moose Skowron	20.00
Enos Slaughter	25.00
Lee Smith	10.00
Ozzie Smith	250.00
Duke Snider	80.00
Warren Spahn	200.00
Bruce Sutter	10.00
Gorman Thomas	10.00
Alan Trammell	20.00
Frank White	10.00
Hoyt Wilhelm	20.00
Maury Wills	20.00
Dave Winfield	150.00
Carl Yastrzemski	80.00
Robin Yount	80.00

2000 Fleer Greats of the Game Memorable Moments Auto.

		MT
Common Player:		150.00
1	Ron Guidry /78	250.00
2	Nolan Ryan /99	500.00
3	Herb Score /55	150.00
4	Tom Seaver /69	300.00

2000 Fleer Greats of the Game Retrospection

The 15-card Retrospection insert set highlights some of the all-time greats with a design borrowed from 1960 Fleer. Former greats including Stan Musial and Al Kaline are featured. They were seeded 1:6 packs.

		MT
Complete Set (15):		120.00
Common Player:		4.00
Inserted 1:6		
1	Rod Carew	8.00
2	Stan Musial	12.00
3	Nolan Ryan	20.00
4	Tom Seaver	12.00
5	Brooks Robinson	8.00
6	Al Kaline	6.00
7	Mike Schmidt	10.00
8	Thurman Munson	8.00
9	Steve Carlton	6.00
10	Roger Maris	10.00
11	Duke Snider	8.00
12	Yogi Berra	12.00
13	Carl Yastrzemski	8.00
14	Reggie Jackson	12.00
15	Johnny Bench	12.00

2000 Fleer Greats of the Game Yankees Clippings

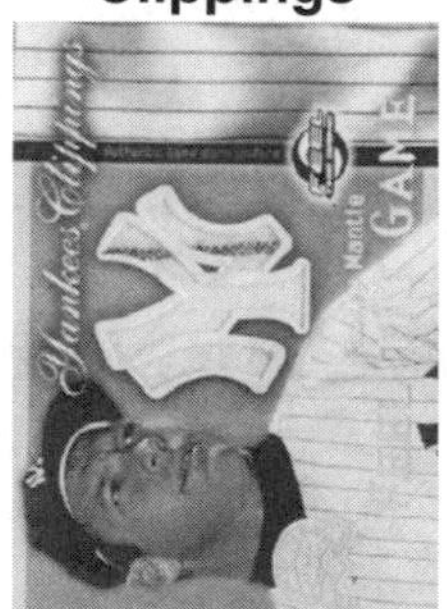

This 15-card memorabilia insert features an actual piece of New York Yankee uniform worn by former Yankee greats. The jersey swatch is formed in the shape of the interlocking "NY" logo and are seeded 1:48 packs. Players featured include Mickey Mantle and Don Mattingly.

		MT
Common Player:		80.00
Inserted 1:48		
1	Mickey Mantle	750.00
2	Ron Guidry	80.00
3	Don Larsen	125.00
4	Elston Howard	80.00
5	Mel Stottlemyre	80.00
6	Don Mattingly	300.00
7	Reggie Jackson	250.00
8	Tommy John	80.00
9	Dave Winfield	150.00
10	Willie Randolph	80.00
11	Tommy Henrich	80.00
12	Billy Martin	200.00
13	Dave Righetti	80.00
14	Joe Pepitone	80.00
15	Thurman Munson	250.00

2000 Fleer Impact

The base set consists of 200 cards with 25 of those being Prospect subset cards. The featured player's team logo appears beside the player name on the bottom portion with the Impact logo on the top left portion. Card backs have a maximum of 10 years of statistics along with a small photo and vital information. Impact was sold in 10-card packs with an SRP of $.99 per pack.

		MT
Complete Set (200):		15.00
Common Player:		.10
Pack (10):		1.00
Box (36):		32.00
1	Cal Ripken Jr.	1.50
2	Jose Canseco	.30
3	Manny Ramirez	.50
4	Bernie Williams	.40
5	Troy Glaus	.25
6	Jeff Bagwell	.50
7	Corey Koskie	.10
8	Barry Larkin	.25
9	Mark Quinn	.10
10	Russ Ortiz	.10
11	Tim Salmon	.15
12	Preston Wilson	.10
13	Mo Vaughn	.30
14	Ray Lankford	.10
15	Sterling Hitchcock	.10
16	Al Leiter	.10
17	Jim Morris	.10
18	Freddy Garcia	.10
19	Adrian Beltre	.10
20	Eric Chavez	.20
21	Robinson Cancel	.10
22	Edgar Renteria	.10
23	John Jaha	.10
24	Chuck Finley	.10
25	Andres Galarraga	.25
26	Paul Byrd	.10
27	John Halama	.10
28	Eric Karros	.15
29	Mike Piazza	1.25
30	Ryan Rupe	.10
31	Frank Thomas	.75
32	Randy Velarde	.10
33	Bobby Abreu	.10
34	Randy Johnson	.50
35	Matt Williams	.20
36	Tony Gwynn	.75
37	Dean Palmer	.10
38	Aaron Sele	.10
39	Rondell White	.15
40	Erubiel Durazo	.10
41	Curt Schilling	.10
42	Kip Wells	.10
43	Craig Biggio	.20
44	Tom Glavine	.20
45	Trevor Hoffman	.10
46	Greg Vaughn	.10
47	Edgar Martinez	.10
48	Magglio Ordonez	.10
49	Mark Mulder	.10
50	John Rocker	.10
51	Kenny Rogers	.10
52	Gary Sheffield	.20
53	Brian Simmons	.10
54	Tony Womack	.10
55	Ken Caminiti	.10
56	Jeff Cirillo	.10
57	Ray Durham	.10
58	Mike Lieberthal	.10
59	Ruben Mateo	.10
60	Mike Cameron	.10
61	Rusty Greer	.10
62	Alex Rodriguez	1.50
63	Robin Ventura	.10
64	Pokey Reese	.10
65	Jose Lima	.10
66	Neifi Perez	.10
67	Rafael Palmeiro	.25
68	Scott Rolen	.40
69	Mike Hampton	.10
70	Sammy Sosa	1.25
71	Mike Stanley	.10
72	Dan Wilson	.10
73	Kerry Wood	.25
74	Mike Mussina	.30
75	Masato Yoshii	.10
76	Peter Bergeron	.10
77	Carlos Delgado	.50
78	Juan Encarnacion	.10
79	Nomar Garciaparra	1.25
80	Jason Kendall	.10
81	Pedro Martinez	.50
82	Darin Erstad	.20
83	Larry Walker	.20
84	Rick Ankiel	1.00
85	Scott Erickson	.10
86	Roger Clemens	.75
87	Matt Lawton	.10
88	Jon Lieber	.10
89	Shane Reynolds	.10
90	Ivan Rodriguez	.50
91	Pat Burrell	.30
92	Kent Bottenfield	.10
93	David Cone	.15
94	Mark Grace	.15
95	Paul Konerko	.10
96	Eric Milton	.10
97	Lee Stevens	.10
98	B.J. Surhoff	.10
99	Billy Wagner	.10
100	Ken Griffey Jr.	2.00
101	Randy Wolf	.10
102	Henry Rodriguez	.10
103	Carlos Beltran	.10
104	Rich Aurilia	.10
105	Chipper Jones	1.00
106	Homer Bush	.10
107	Johnny Damon	.10
108	J.D. Drew	.20
109	Orlando Hernandez	.10
110	Brad Radke	.10
111	Wilton Veras	.10
112	Dmitri Young	.10
113	Jermaine Dye	.10
114	Kris Benson	.10
115	Derek Jeter	1.25
116	Cole Liniak	.10
117	Jim Thome	.25
118	Pedro Astacio	.10
119	Carlos Febles	.10
120	Darryl Kile	.10
121	Alfonso Soriano	.20
122	Michael Barrett	.10
123	Ellis Burks	.10
124	Chad Hermansen	.10
125	Trot Nixon	.10
126	Bobby Higginson	.10
127	Rick Helling	.10
128	Chris Carpenter	.10
129	Vinny Castilla	.10
130	Brian Giles	.10
131	Todd Helton	.50
132	Jason Varitek	.10
133	Rob Ducey	.10
134	Octavio Dotel	.10
135	Adam Kennedy	.10

136	Jeff Kent	.10
137	Aaron Boone	.10
138	Todd Walker	.10
139	Jeromy Burnitz	.10
140	Roberto Hernandez	.10
141	Matt LeCroy	.10
142	Ugueth Urbina	.10
143	David Wells	.10
144	Luis Gonzalez	.10
145	Andruw Jones	.25
146	Juan Gonzalez	.50
147	Moises Alou	.10
148	Michael Tejera	.10
149	Brian Jordan	.10
150	Mark McGwire	2.00
151	Shawn Green	.30
152	Jay Bell	.10
153	Fred McGriff	.20
154	Rey Ordonez	.10
155	Matt Stairs	.10
156	A.J. Burnett	.10
157	Omar Vizquel	.10
158	Damion Easley	.10
159	Dante Bichette	.10
160	Javy Lopez	.10
161	Fernando Seguignol	.10
162	Richie Sexson	.10
163	Vladimir Guerrero	.75
164	Kevin Young	.10
165	Josh Beckett	.10
166	Albert Belle	.30
167	Cliff Floyd	.10
168	Gabe Kapler	.20
169	Nick Johnson	.10
170	Raul Mondesi	.15
171	Warren Morris	.10
172	Kenny Lofton	.20
173	Reggie Sanders	.10
174	Mike Sweeney	.10
175	Robert Fick	.10
176	Barry Bonds	.50
177	Luis Castillo	.10
178	Roger Cedeno	.10
179	Jim Edmonds	.15
180	Geoff Jenkins	.15
181	Adam Piatt	.10
182	Phil Nevin	.10
183	Roberto Alomar	.40
184	Kevin Brown	.15
185	D.T. Cromer	.10
186	Jason Giambi	.20
187	Fernando Tatis	.20
188	Brady Anderson	.15
189	Tony Clark	.10
190	Alex Fernandez	.10
191	Matt Blank	.10
192	Greg Maddux	1.00
193	Kevin Millwood	.10
194	Jason Schmidt	.10
195	Shannon Stewart	.10
196	Rolando Arrojo	.10
197	Darren Dreifort	.10
198	Ben Grieve	.20
199	Bartolo Colon	.10
200	Sean Casey	.20

2000 Fleer Impact Mighty Fine in '99

This 40-card set honors the 1999 World Series Champion New York Yankees as well as other various award winners from the '99 season. These were seeded one per pack.

		MT
Complete Set (40):		15.00
Common Player:		.15
Inserted 1:1		
1	Clay Bellinger	.15
2	Scott Brosius	.15
3	Roger Clemens	1.00
4	David Cone	.25
5	Chad Curtis	.15
6	Chili Davis	.15
7	Joe Girardi	.15
8	Jason Grimsley	.15
9	Orlando Hernandez	.25
10	Hideki Irabu	.15
11	Derek Jeter	1.50
12	Chuck Knoblauch	.25
13	Ricky Ledee	.15
14	Jim Leyritz	.15
15	Tino Martinez	.25
16	Ramiro Mendoza	.15
17	Jeff Nelson	.15
18	Paul O'Neill	.25
19	Andy Pettitte	.25
20	Jorge Posada	.25
21	Mariano Rivera	.25
22	Luis Sojo	.15
23	Mike Stanton	.15
24	Allen Watson	.15
25	Bernie Williams	.50
26	Chipper Jones	1.25
27	Ivan Rodriguez	.60
28	Randy Johnson	.60
29	Pedro Martinez	.60
30	Scott Williamson	.15
31	Carlos Beltran	.15
32	Mark McGwire	2.50
33	Ken Griffey Jr.	2.50
34	Robin Ventura	.15
35	Tony Gwynn	1.00
36	Wade Boggs	.40
37	Cal Ripken Jr.	2.00
38	Jose Canseco	.40
39	Alex Rodriguez	2.00
40	Fernando Tatis	.15

2000 Fleer Impact Genuine Coverage

This memorabilia insert set has pieces of game-used batting gloves embedded into the card front. They were seeded 1:720 packs.

		MT
Common Player:		25.00
Inserted 1:720		
1	Alex Rodriguez	150.00
2	Cole Liniak	25.00
3	Barry Bonds	75.00
4	Ben Davis	25.00
5	Bobby Abreu	50.00
6	Mike Sweeney	40.00
7	Rafael Palmeiro	50.00
8	Carlos Lee	30.00
9	Glen Barker	25.00
10	Jason Giambi	50.00
11	Jacque Jones	25.00
12	Joe Nathan	25.00
13	Jason LaRue	25.00
14	Magglio Ordonez	40.00
15	Shannon Stewart	40.00
16	Matt Lawton	25.00
18	Trevor Hoffman	30.00

2000 Fleer Impact Autographics

This autographed set has the player signature on the bottom portion of the card. These were seeded 1:216 packs.

		MT
Common Player:		10.00
Inserted 1:216		
1	Bobby Abreu	20.00
2	Marlon Anderson	10.00
3	Rick Ankiel	75.00
4	Rob Bell	10.00
5	Carlos Beltran	10.00
6	Wade Boggs	60.00
7	Barry Bonds	75.00
8	Milton Bradley	15.00
9	Pat Burrell	40.00
10	Orlando Cabrera	10.00
11	Chris Carpenter	10.00
12	Sean Casey	20.00
13	Carlos Delgado	50.00
14	J.D. Drew	40.00
15	Ray Durham	15.00
16	Kelvim Escobar	10.00
17	Vladimir Guerrero	60.00
18	Tony Gwynn	75.00
19	Jerry Hairston Jr.	10.00
20	Todd Helton	40.00
21	Nick Johnson	20.00
22	Jason Kendall	15.00
23	Mark Kotsay	10.00
24	Cole Liniak	10.00
25	Jose Macias	10.00
26	Greg Maddux	150.00
27	Ruben Mateo	15.00
28	Ober Moreno	10.00
29	Eric Munson	20.00
30	Joe Nathan	10.00
31	Angel Pena	10.00
32	Adam Piatt	15.00
33	Matt Riley	10.00
34	Cal Ripken Jr.	200.00
35	Alex Rodriguez	175.00
36	Scott Rolen	40.00
37	Jimmy Rollins	10.00
38	B.J. Ryan	10.00
39	Alfonso Soriano	20.00
40	Frank Thomas	75.00
41	Wilton Veras	10.00
42	Billy Wagner	10.00
43	Jeff Weaver	10.00
44	Scott Williamson	10.00

2000 Fleer Impact Point of Impact

Point of Impact honors some of the game's top sluggers on a die-cut design. Card fronts have silver foil stamping and cross hairs where the featured player finds his sweet spot. These were seeded 1:30 packs and are numbered with a "PI" suffix on the card back.

		MT
Complete Set (10):		50.00
Common Player:		2.00
Inserted 1:30		
1	Ken Griffey Jr.	10.00
2	Mark McGwire	10.00
3	Sammy Sosa	6.00
4	Jeff Bagwell	2.50
5	Derek Jeter	6.00
6	Chipper Jones	5.00
7	Nomar Garciaparra	6.00
8	Cal Ripken Jr.	8.00
9	Barry Bonds	2.50
10	Alex Rodriguez	8.00

2000 Fleer Mystique

The base set consists of 175-cards including a 50-card Prospects subset that each card is serially numbered to 2,000 and covered. The card fronts have a full bleed design with gold foil stamping. Card backs have complete year-by-year statistics and a small photo.

		MT
Complete Set (175):		500.00
Common Player:		.20
Common 126-175		8.00
Production 2,000 sets		
Pack (5):		5.00
Box (20):		90.00
1	Derek Jeter	2.50
2	David Justice	.40
3	Kevin Brown	.40
4	Jason Giambi	.40
5	Jose Canseco	.60
6	Mark Grace	.40
7	Hideo Nomo	.20
8	Edgardo Alfonzo	.40
9	Barry Bonds	1.00
10	Pedro Martinez	1.00
11	Juan Gonzalez	1.00
12	Vladimir Guerrero	1.50
13	Chuck Finley	.20
14	Brian Jordan	.20
15	Richie Sexson	.20
16	Chan Ho Park	.20
17	Tim Hudson	.40
18	Fred McGriff	.40
19	Darin Erstad	.40
20	Chris Singleton	.20
21	Jeff Bagwell	1.00
22	David Cone	.40
23	Edgar Martinez	.20
24	Greg Maddux	2.00
25	Jim Thome	.50
26	Eric Karros	.30
27	Bobby Abreu	.30
28	Greg Vaughn	.30
29	Kevin Millwood	.30
30	Omar Vizquel	.20
31	Marquis Grissom	.20
32	Mike Lieberthal	.20
33	Gabe Kapler	.40
34	Brady Anderson	.30
35	Jeff Cirillo	.20
36	Geoff Jenkins	.40
37	Scott Rolen	.75
38	Rafael Palmeiro	.60
39	Randy Johnson	1.00
40	Barry Larkin	.50

41	Johnny Damon	.20
42	Andy Pettitte	.40
43	Mark McGwire	4.00
44	Albert Belle	.60
45	Derrick Gibson	.20
46	Corey Koskie	.20
47	Curt Schilling	.30
48	Ivan Rodriguez	1.00
49	Mike Mussina	.60
50	Todd Helton	1.00
51	Matt Lawton	.20
52	Jason Kendall	.20
53	Kenny Rogers	.20
54	Cal Ripken Jr.	3.00
55	Larry Walker	.50
56	Eric Milton	.20
57	Warren Morris	.20
58	Carlos Delgado	1.00
59	Kerry Wood	.40
60	Cliff Floyd	.20
61	Mike Piazza	2.50
62	Jeff Kent	.20
63	Sammy Sosa	2.50
64	Alex Fernandez	.20
65	Mike Hampton	.20
66	Livan Hernandez	.20
67	Matt Williams	.40
68	Roberto Alomar	.75
69	Jermaine Dye	.20
70	Bernie Williams	.75
71	Edgar Renteria	.20
72	Tom Glavine	.40
73	Bartolo Colon	.20
74	Jason Varitek	.20
75	Eric Chavez	.40
76	Fernando Tatis	.20
77	Adrian Beltre	.40
78	Paul Konerko	.20
79	Mike Lowell	.20
80	Robin Ventura	.20
81	Russ Ortiz	.20
82	Troy Glaus	.75
83	Frank Thomas	1.50
84	Craig Biggio	.40
85	Orlando Hernandez	.20
86	John Olerud	.40
87	Chipper Jones	2.00
88	Manny Ramirez	1.00
89	Shawn Green	.40
90	Ben Grieve	.40
91	Vinny Castilla	.20
92	Tim Salmon	.40
93	Dante Bichette	.30
94	Ken Caminiti	.20
95	Andruw Jones	.50
96	Alex Rodriguez	3.00
97	Erubiel Durazo	.20
98	Sean Casey	.30
99	Carlos Beltran	.20
100	Paul O'Neill	.30
101	Ray Lankford	.20
102	Troy O'Leary	.20
103	Bobby Higginson	.20
104	Rondell White	.20
105	Tony Gwynn	1.50
106	Jim Edmonds	.30
107	Magglio Ordonez	.40
108	Preston Wilson	.20
109	Roger Clemens	1.50
110	Ken Griffey Jr.	4.00
111	Nomar Garciaparra	2.50
112	Juan Encarnacion	.20
113	Michael Barrett	.20
114	Matt Clement	.20
115	David Wells	.20
116	Mo Vaughn	.50
117	Mike Cameron	.20
118	Jose Lima	.20
119	Tino Martinez	.40
120	J.D. Drew	.40
121	Carl Everett	.20
122	Tony Clark	.20
123	Brad Radke	.20
124	Kevin Young	.20
125	Raul Mondesi	.40
126	Cole Liniak (Prospects)	8.00
127	Alfonso Soriano (Prospects)	10.00
128	Lance Berkman (Prospects)	10.00
129	Danny Young (Prospects)	8.00
130	Francisco Cordero (Prospects)	8.00
131	Rob Fick (Prospects)	10.00
132	Matt LeCroy (Prospects)	8.00
133	Adam Piatt (Prospects)	15.00
134	Derrick Turnbow (Prospects)	8.00
135	Mark Quinn (Prospects)	12.00
136	Kip Wells (Prospects)	10.00
137	Rob Bell (Prospects)	8.00
138	Brad Penny (Prospects)	8.00
139	Pat Burrell (Prospects)	25.00
140	*Danys Baez* (Prospects)	12.00
141	Chad Hermansen (Prospects)	8.00
142	Steve Lomasney (Prospects)	8.00
143	Peter Bergeron (Prospects)	12.00
144	Jimmy Anderson (Prospects)	8.00
145	Mike Darr (Prospects)	8.00
146	Jacob Cruz (Prospects)	8.00
147	*Kazuhiro Sasaki* (Prospects)	40.00
148	Ben Petrick (Prospects)	10.00
149	Rick Ankiel (Prospects)	30.00
150	*Aaron McNeal* (Prospects)	15.00
152	Octavio Dotel (Prospects)	8.00
152	Juan Pena (Prospects)	8.00
153	Nick Johnson (Prospects)	15.00
154	Wilton Veras (Prospects)	8.00
155	Wily Pena (Prospects)	15.00
156	Mark Mulder (Prospects)	8.00
157	Daryle Ward (Prospects)	10.00
158	Chad Durbin (Prospects)	8.00
159	Angel Pena (Prospects)	10.00
160	Dewayne Wise (Prospects)	8.00
161	Tarrik Brock (Prospects)	8.00
162	Marcus Jensen (Prospects)	8.00
163	Kevin Barker (Prospects)	10.00
164	B.J. Ryan (Prospects)	8.00
165	Cesar King (Prospects)	8.00
166	Geoff Blum (Prospects)	8.00
167	Ruben Mateo (Prospects)	10.00
168	Ramon Ortiz (Prospects)	8.00
169	Eric Munson (Prospects)	15.00
170	Josh Beckett (Prospects)	15.00
171	Rafael Furcal (Prospects)	35.00
172	Matt Riley (Prospects)	12.00
173	Johan Santana (Prospects)	8.00
174	Mark Johnson (Prospects)	8.00
175	Adam Kennedy (Prospects)	12.00

2000 Fleer Mystique Club 3000

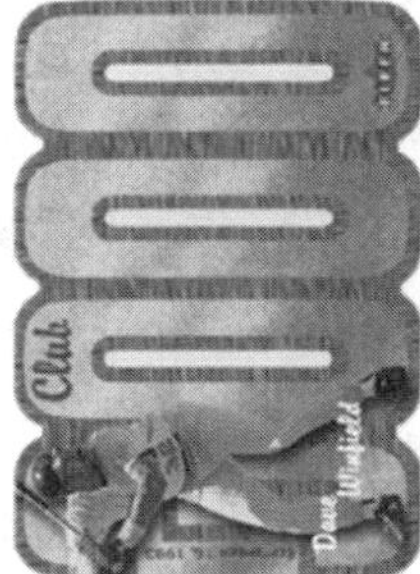

This three-card set is die-cut around the 3,000 numerals with a date on the left side when the featured player reached the 3,000 milestone. The player name is stamped in silver holofoil. Card backs are not numbered and have a brief career note. These were seeded 1:20 packs.

		MT
Complete Set (3):		8.00
Common Player:		2.00
Inserted 1:20		
1	Cal Ripken Jr.	6.00
2	Bob Gibson	2.00
3	Dave Winfield	2.00

2000 Fleer Mystique Club 3000 Memorabilia

Five different memorabilia versions of each player exist, using pieces of game-used bat, jersey and cap which are embedded into each card. The amount of each card produced is listed after the player name.

	MT
Common Card:	2.00
Cal Ripken Jr. jersey/825	150.00
Cal Ripken Jr. bat/265	200.00
Cal Ripken Jr. cap/55	400.00
Cal Ripken Jr. bat/jersey/100	350.00
Cal Ripken bat/cap/jersey/25	
Bob Gibson jersey/825	50.00
Bob Gibson bat/265	60.00
Bob Gibson cap/jersey/100	100.00
Bob Gibson cap/55	125.00
Bob Gibson bat/cap/jersey/25	
Dave Winfield jersey/825	50.00
Dave Winfield bat/270	60.00
Dave Winfield bat/jersey/100	100.00
Dave Winfield cap/55	175.00
Dave Winfield bat/cap/jersey/25	

2000 Fleer Mystique Diamond Dominators

This 10-card set spotlights baseball's most dominating performers. Card fronts have a holofoil appearance. These were seeded 1:5 packs and are numbered with an "DD" suffix.

		MT
Complete Set (10):		15.00
Common Player:		.75
Inserted 1:5		
1	Manny Ramirez	1.00
2	Pedro Martinez	1.00
3	Sean Casey	.75
4	Vladimir Guerrero	1.50
5	Sammy Sosa	2.50
6	Nomar Garciaparra	2.50
7	Mark McGwire	4.00
8	Ken Griffey Jr.	4.00
9	Derek Jeter	2.50
10	Alex Rodriguez	3.00

2000 Fleer Mystique Feel the Game

This game-used memorabilia set features either game-used jerseys or bats from today's top stars. These were seeded 1:120 packs.

		MT
Common Player:		20.00
Inserted 1:120		
1	Tony Gwynn jersey	90.00
2	Alex Rodriguez jersey	140.00

3	Chipper Jones jersey	100.00
4	Cal Ripken Jr. jersey	160.00
5	Derek Jeter pants	140.00
7	Frank Thomas bat	75.00
8	Barry Bonds bat	60.00
9	Carlos Beltran bat	25.00
10	Shawn Green bat	40.00
11	Michael Barrett bat	20.00
12	Rafael Palmeiro bat	40.00
13	Vladimir Guerrero bat	60.00
14	Pat Burrell bat	60.00

2000 Fleer Mystique Fresh Ink

This autographed set features signatures from many of the game's top players and are seeded 1:40 packs.

		MT
Common Player:		10.00
Inserted 1:40		
1	Chad Allen	10.00
2	Glen Barker	10.00
3	Michael Barrett	10.00
4	Josh Beckett	30.00
5	Rob Bell	15.00
6	Lance Berkman	10.00
7	Kent Bottenfield	10.00
8	Milton Bradley	15.00
9	Orlando Cabrera	10.00
10	Sean Casey	20.00
11	Roger Cedeno	15.00
12	Will Clark	25.00
13	Russ Davis	10.00
14	Carlos Delgado	50.00
15	Einar Diaz	10.00
16	J.D. Drew	30.00
17	Erubiel Durazo	20.00
18	Damion Easley	10.00
19	Carlos Febles	15.00
20	Doug Glanville	10.00
21	Alex Gonzalez	10.00
22	Tony Gwynn	100.00
23	Mike Hampton	15.00
24	Bobby Howry	10.00
25	John Jaha	10.00
26	Nick Johnson	20.00
27	Andruw Jones	30.00
28	Adam Kennedy	15.00
29	Mike Lieberthal	15.00
30	Jose Macias	10.00
31	Ruben Mateo	15.00
32	Raul Mondesi	20.00
33	Heath Murray	10.00
34	Mike Mussina	25.00
35	Hideo Nomo	400.00
36	Magglio Ordonez	20.00
37	Eric Owens	10.00
38	Adam Piatt	20.00
39	Cal Ripken Jr.	200.00
40	Tim Salmon	20.00
41	Chris Singleton	10.00
42	J.T. Snow	10.00
43	Mike Sweeney	15.00
44	Wilton Veras	10.00
45	Jose Vidro	15.00
46	Rondell White	15.00
47	Jaret Wright	10.00

2000 Fleer Mystique High Praise

This 10-card set has a holofoiled card front with a "sky" background. These were inserted 1:20 packs and are numbered on the card back with an "HP" suffix.

		MT
Complete Set (10):		55.00
Common Player:		2.00
Inserted 1:20		
1	Mark McGwire	10.00
2	Ken Griffey Jr.	10.00
3	Alex Rodriguez	8.00
4	Derek Jeter	6.00
5	Sammy Sosa	6.00
6	Mike Piazza	6.00
7	Nomar Garciaparra	6.00
8	Cal Ripken Jr.	8.00
9	Tony Gwynn	4.00
10	Shawn Green	2.00

2000 Fleer Mystique Rookie I.P.O.

This 10-card set highlights the top young rookies on a holofoil design. Card backs are numbered with an "RI" suffix and are seeded 1:10 packs.

		MT
Complete Set (10):		15.00
Common Player:		1.00
Inserted 1:10		
1	Josh Beckett	2.00
2	Eric Munson	2.00
3	Pat Burrell	4.00
4	Alfonso Soriano	2.00
5	Rick Ankiel	5.00
6	Ruben Mateo	1.50
7	Mark Quinn	1.00
8	Kip Wells	1.00
9	Ben Petrick	1.00
10	Nick Johnson	2.00

2000 Fleer Mystique Seismic Activity

This 10-card set spotlights the top power hitters in the game. The player image is in the foreground of a warp like setting with golden highlights. Card backs are numbered with an "SA" suffix and are seeded 1:40 packs. A serial numbered parallel called Richter 100 is randomly seeded and is limited to 100 serial numbered sets.

		MT
Complete Set (10):		80.00
Common Player:		3.00
Inserted 1:40		
Richter parallel:		3-5X
Production 100 sets		
1	Ken Griffey Jr.	18.00
2	Sammy Sosa	10.00
3	Derek Jeter	10.00
4	Mark McGwire	18.00
5	Manny Ramirez	5.00
6	Mike Piazza	10.00
7	Vladimir Guerrero	6.00
8	Chipper Jones	8.00
9	Alex Rodriguez	12.00
10	Jeff Bagwell	5.00

2000 Fleer Mystique Dave Winfield Auto. Memorabilia

This two-card set consists of 40 game-used helmet Winfield cards and 20 game-used ball cards.

		MT
Complete Set (2):		
1	Dave Winfield helmet/40	125.00

2000 Fleer Mystique Supernaturals

This 10-card set has a warp like image of the player on the front with silver holofoil highlights around the player image and gold foil stamping. Card backs are numbered with an "S" suffix. These were seeded 1:10 packs.

		MT
Complete Set (10):		30.00
Common Player:		1.50
Inserted 1:10		
1	Alex Rodriguez	5.00
2	Chipper Jones	3.00
3	Derek Jeter	4.00
4	Ivan Rodriguez	1.50
5	Ken Griffey Jr.	6.00
6	Mark McGwire	6.00
7	Mike Piazza	4.00
8	Nomar Garciaparra	4.00
9	Sammy Sosa	4.00
10	Vladimir Guerrero	2.00

2000 Fleer Showcase

The base set consists of 140 cards, including 40 Prospect Showcase subset cards. Cards 101-115 are serially numbered to 1,000 and cards 116-140 are serially numbered to 2,000. The card fronts are holofoiled, with the player name and team stamped in gold foil. Card backs have year-by-year statistics and a small close-up photo. Five-card packs carried an SRP of $4.99.

		MT
Complete Set (140):		450.00
Common Player (1-100):		.25
Common (101-115):		8.00
Production 1,000 sets		
Common (116-140):		6.00
Production 2,000 sets		
Pack (5):		5.00
Box (24):		110.00
1	Alex Rodriguez	3.00
2	Derek Jeter	2.50
3	Jeromy Burnitz	.25
4	John Olerud	.25
5	Paul Konerko	.25
6	Johnny Damon	.25
7	Curt Schilling	.25
8	Barry Larkin	.50
9	Adrian Beltre	.25
10	Scott Rolen	1.00
11	Carlos Delgado	1.00
12	Pedro J. Martinez	1.00
13	Todd Helton	1.00
14	Jacque Jones	.25
15	Jeff Kent	.40
16	Darin Erstad	.50
17	Juan Encarnacion	.25
18	Roger Clemens	1.50
19	Tony Gwynn	1.50

20	Nomar Garciaparra	2.50
21	Roberto Alomar	.75
22	Matt Lawton	.25
23	Rich Aurilia	.25
24	Charles Johnson	.25
25	Jim Thome	.40
26	Eric Milton	.25
27	Barry Bonds	1.00
28	Albert Belle	.50
29	Travis Fryman	.25
30	Ken Griffey Jr.	3.00
31	Phil Nevin	.25
32	Chipper Jones	2.00
33	Craig Biggio	.40
34	Mike Hampton	.25
35	Fred McGriff	.40
36	Cal Ripken Jr.	3.00
37	Manny Ramirez	1.00
38	Jose Vidro	.25
39	Trevor Hoffman	.25
40	Tom Glavine	.50
41	Frank Thomas	1.50
42	Chris Widger	.25
43	J.D. Drew	.25
44	Andres Galarraga	.40
45	Pokey Reese	.25
46	Mike Piazza	2.50
47	Kevin Young	.25
48	Sean Casey	.25
49	Carlos Beltran	.25
50	Jason Kendall	.25
51	Vladimir Guerrero	1.50
52	Jermaine Dye	.25
53	Brian Giles	.25
54	Andruw Jones	.75
55	Richard Hidalgo	.40
56	Robin Ventura	.25
57	Ivan Rodriguez	1.00
58	Greg Maddux	2.00
59	Billy Wagner	.25
60	Ruben Mateo	.25
61	Troy Glaus	1.00
62	Dean Palmer	.25
63	Eric Chavez	.25
64	Edgar Martinez	.25
65	Randy Johnson	1.00
66	Preston Wilson	.25
67	Orlando Hernandez	.40
68	Jim Edmonds	.40
69	Carl Everett	.25
70	Larry Walker	.40
71	Ron Belliard	.25
72	Sammy Sosa	2.50
73	Matt Williams	.40
74	Cliff Floyd	.25
75	Bernie Williams	.75
76	Fernando Tatis	.25
77	Steve Finley	.25
78	Jeff Bagwell	1.00
79	Edgardo Alfonzo	.40
80	Jose Canseco	.50
81	Magglio Ordonez	.25
82	Shawn Green	.40
83	Bobby Abreu	.25
84	Tony Batista	.25
85	Mo Vaughn	.50
86	Juan Gonzalez	1.00
87	Paul O'Neill	.40
88	Mark McGwire	4.00
89	Mark Grace	.40
90	Kevin Brown	.40
91	Ben Grieve	.40
92	Shannon Stewart	.25
93	Erubiel Durazo	.25
94	Antonio Alfonseca	.25
95	Jeff Cirillo	.25
96	Greg Vaughn	.25
97	Kerry Wood	.40
98	Geoff Jenkins	.25
99	Jason Giambi	.40
100	Rafael Palmeiro	.50
101	Rafael Furcal	35.00
102	Pablo Ozuna	8.00
103	Brad Penny	8.00
104	Mark Mulder	10.00
105	Adam Piatt	15.00
106	*Mike Lamb*	15.00
107	*Kazuhiro Sasaki*	75.00
108	*Aaron McNeal*	20.00
109	Pat Burrell	25.00
110	Rick Ankiel	25.00
111	Eric Munson	15.00
112	Josh Beckett	20.00
113	Adam Kennedy	10.00
114	Alex Escobar	10.00
115	Chad Hermansen	8.00
116	Kip Wells	6.00
117	Matt LeCroy	6.00
118	Julio Ramirez	6.00
119	Ben Petrick	6.00
120	Nick Johnson	10.00
121	Gookie Dawkins	8.00
122	*Julio Zuleta*	6.00
123	Alfonso Soriano	8.00
124	*Keith McDonald*	8.00
125	Kory DeHaan	10.00
126	Vernon Wells	6.00
127	Dernell Stenson	8.00
128	David Eckstein	10.00
129	Robert Fick	8.00
130	Cole Liniak	8.00
131	Mark Quinn	10.00
132	Eric Gagne	8.00
133	Wily Pena	10.00
134	*Andy Thompson*	10.00
135	*Steve Sisco*	10.00
136	*Paul Rigdon*	15.00
137	Rob Bell	8.00
138	Carlos Guillen	6.00
139	Jimmy Rollins	6.00
140	Jason Conti	8.00

2000 Fleer Showcase Legacy

A parallel to the 140-card base set, these feature a matte and holofoil design and are serially numbered to 20.

	MT
Stars (1-100):	50-75X
Prospects (101-140):	4-8X
Production 20 sets	

2000 Fleer Showcase Prospect Showcase First

A parallel of the 40-card Prospects subset. These differ from the base cards in that they have a horizontal format and are serially numbered to 500.

	MT
Prospects (101-140):	1-2X
Production 500 sets	

2000 Fleer Showcase Club 3000

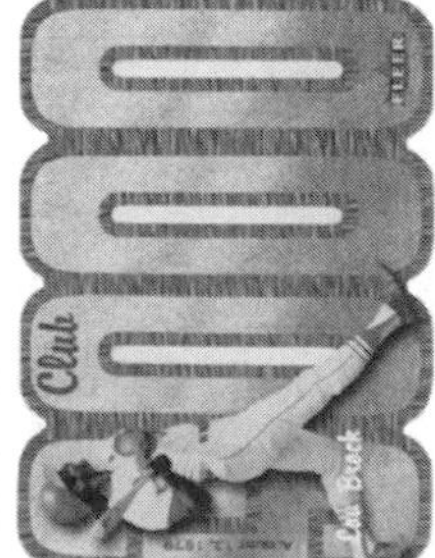

This two-card set pays tribute to Lou Brock and Nolan Ryan. Each card is die-cut around the numerals 3,000 with a date displaying the day Brock or Ryan reached their 3,000 milestone. The player name is stamped in silver holofoil. These were inserted 1:24 packs.

		MT
Complete Set (2):		10.00
Common Player:		3.00
Inserted 1:24		
1	Lou Brock	3.00
2	Nolan Ryan	10.00

2000 Fleer Showcase Club 3000 Memorabilia

These inserts feature actual game-used pieces of memorabilia from Nolan Ryan and Lou Brock and are serial numbered. The number produced is listed after the player name.

	MT
Common Card:	50.00
Lou Brock jersey/680	50.00
Lou Brock bat/270	60.00
Nolan Ryan Jersey/780	175.00
Nolan Ryan bat/265	250.00

2000 Fleer Showcase Consummate Prose

This 15-card set has an image of a worn scroll of paper with "Consummate Prose" written on it in the background of the player image. The Showcase logo, player name and Consummate Prose are stamped in gold foil. Card backs are numbered with an "CP" suffix and are inserted 1:6 packs.

		MT
Complete Set (15):		40.00
Common Player:		1.00
Inserted 1:6		
1	Jeff Bagwell	1.50
2	Alex Rodriguez	5.00
3	Chipper Jones	3.00
4	Derek Jeter	4.00
5	Manny Ramirez	1.50
6	Tony Gwynn	2.00
7	Sammy Sosa	4.00
8	Ivan Rodriguez	1.50
9	Greg Maddux	3.00
10	Ken Griffey Jr.	5.00
11	Rick Ankiel	1.00
12	Cal Ripken Jr.	5.00
13	Pedro Martinez	1.50
14	Mike Piazza	4.00
15	Mark McGwire	6.00

2000 Fleer Showcase Final Answer

These foiled inserts have a green border with the player inside a frame with question marks in the background. The card backs have trivia questions about the featured player. Card backs are numbered with an "FA" suffix. These were seeded 1:10 packs.

		MT
Complete Set (10):		30.00
Common Player:		1.50
Inserted 1:10		
1	Alex Rodriguez	5.00
2	Vladimir Guerrero	2.00
3	Cal Ripken Jr.	5.00
4	Sammy Sosa	4.00
5	Barry Bonds	1.50
6	Derek Jeter	4.00
7	Ken Griffey Jr.	5.00
8	Mike Piazza	4.00
9	Nomar Garciaparra	4.00
10	Mark McGwire	6.00

2000 Fleer Showcase Feel the Game

This 20-card set has swatches of game worn jersey embedded into the card front. These were seeded 1:72 packs.

		MT
Common Player:		20.00
Inserted 1:72		
1	Barry Bonds	60.00
2	Gookie Dawkins	20.00
3	Darin Erstad	50.00
4	Troy Glaus	50.00
5	Scott Rolen	50.00
6	Alex Rodriguez	100.00
7	Andruw Jones	50.00
8	Robin Ventura	30.00
9	Sean Casey	40.00
10	Cal Ripken Jr.	125.00

2000 Fleer Showcase Fresh Ink

These autographed inserts are inserted 1:24 packs.

		MT
Common Player:		10.00
Inserted 1:24		
1	Rick Ankiel	40.00
2	Josh Beckett	25.00
3	Barry Bonds	75.00
4	A.J. Burnett	10.00
5	Pat Burrell	40.00
6	Ken Caminiti	15.00
7	Sean Casey	20.00
8	Jose Cruz Jr.	15.00
9	Gookie Dawkins	15.00
10	Erubiel Durazo	20.00
11	Juan Encarnacion	10.00
12	Darin Erstad	30.00
13	Rafael Furcal	40.00
14	Nomar Garciaparra	125.00
15	Jason Giambi	30.00
16	Jeremy Giambi	10.00
17	Brian Giles	20.00
18	Troy Glaus	40.00
19	Mark Grace	
20	Vladimir Guerrero	50.00
21	Chad Hermansen	10.00
22	Orlando Hernandez	
23	Trevor Hoffman	10.00
24	Randy Johnson	60.00
25	Andruw Jones	30.00
26	Jason Kendall	15.00
27	Paul Konerko	20.00
28	Mike Lowell	10.00
29	Aaron McNeal	15.00
30	Warren Morris	10.00
31	Paul O'Neill	25.00
32	Magglio Ordonez	25.00
33	Pablo Ozuna	10.00
34	Brad Penny	10.00
35	Ben Petrick	10.00
36	Pokey Reese	15.00
37	Cal Ripken Jr.	150.00
38	Alex Rodriguez	150.00
39	Scott Rolen	40.00
40	Jose Vidro	15.00
41	Kip Wells	10.00

2000 Fleer Showcase License to Skill

License to Skill have a rounded, die-cut top with a background similar to that of a bullseye on a target. Silver and gold foil etching and foil stamping are used as well. Card backs are numbered with an "LS" suffix and are inserted 1:20 packs.

		MT
Complete Set (10):		40.00
Common Player:		2.50
Inserted 1:20		
1	Vladimir Guerrero	3.00
2	Pedro J. Martinez	2.50
3	Nomar Garciaparra	6.00
4	Ivan Rodriguez	2.50
5	Mark McGwire	10.00
6	Derek Jeter	6.00
7	Ken Griffey Jr.	8.00
8	Randy Johnson	2.50
9	Sammy Sosa	6.00
10	Alex Rodriguez	8.00

2000 Fleer Showcase Long Gone

These inserts are die-cut around the card top to mimic the outfield dimensions of the featured players' stadium. Gold foil stamping is also used. Card backs are numbered with an "LG" suffix and have an insertion ratio of 1:20 packs.

		MT
Complete Set (10):		45.00
Common Player:		2.50
Inserted 1:20		
1	Sammy Sosa	6.00
2	Derek Jeter	6.00
3	Nomar Garciaparra	6.00
4	Juan Gonzalez	2.50
5	Vladimir Guerrero	3.00
6	Barry Bonds	2.50
7	Jeff Bagwell	2.50
8	Alex Rodriguez	8.00
9	Ken Griffey Jr.	8.00
10	Mark McGwire	10.00

2000 Fleer Showcase Noise of Summer

This 10-card set has a kaleidoscope background with the insert name stamped in red foil and the logo, player name and team name stamped in gold foil. Card backs are numbered with an "NS" suffix. These were seeded 1:10 packs.

		MT
Complete Set (10):		25.00
Common Player:		1.50
Inserted 1:10		
1	Chipper Jones	3.00
2	Jeff Bagwell	1.50
3	Manny Ramirez	1.50
4	Mark McGwire	6.00
5	Ken Griffey Jr.	5.00
6	Mike Piazza	4.00
7	Pedro J. Martinez	1.50
8	Alex Rodriguez	5.00
9	Derek Jeter	4.00
10	Randy Johnson	1.50

2000 Fleer Showcase Sweet Sigs

These autographed inserts have the featured players' autograph on an actual "sweet spot" from an authentic Major League baseball. These have an insertion ratio of 1:250 packs.

		MT
Common Player:		25.00
Inserted 1:250		
1	Nomar Garciaparra	200.00
2	Alex Rodriguez	200.00
3	Tony Gwynn	80.00
4	Roger Clemens	125.00
5	Scott Rolen	50.00
6	Greg Maddux	125.00
7	Jose Cruz Jr.	25.00
8	Tony Womack	25.00
9	Jay Buhner	40.00
10	Nolan Ryan	250.00

2000 Fleer Tradition

The Fleer Tradition base set consists of 450 cards including a 30-card Rookies/Prospects subset, 30 team cards, 10 league leaders, 6 award winners, 10 postseason recaps and 6 checklists. The card fronts have a close-up photo of the featured player as well as a small action photo surrounded by a white border. Like the fronts, the card backs have a "throwback" look, which includes complete year-by-year statistics, a brief career note and vital information. 10-card packs had a SRP of $1.49.

		MT
Complete Set (450):		75.00
Common Player:		.10
Pack (10):		2.00
Wax Box:		70.00
1	AL HRs	.75
2	NL HRs	.75
3	AL RBIs	.75
4	NL RBIs	.75
5	AL Avg.	.50
6	NL Avg.	.15
7	AL Wins	.20
8	NL Wins	.40
9	AL ERA	.20
10	NL ERA	.25
11	Matt Mantei	.10
12	John Rocker	.10
13	Kyle Farnsworth	.10
14	Juan Guzman	.10
15	Manny Ramirez	1.00
16	Matt Riley-P, Calvin Pickering-1B	.10
17	Tony Clark	.40
18	Brian Meadows	.10
19	Orber Moreno	.10
20	Eric Karros	.20
21	Steve Woodard	.10
22	Scott Brosius	.10
23	Gary Bennett	.10
24	Jason Wood-3B, Dave Borkowski-P	.10
25	Joe McEwing	.10
26	Juan Gonzalez	1.00
27	Roy Halladay	.10
28	Trevor Hoffman	.10
29	Arizona Diamondbacks	.10
30	*Domingo Guzman-P*, Wiki Gonzalez-C	.50
31	Bret Boone	.10
32	Nomar Garciaparra	2.50
33	Bo Porter	.10
34	Eddie Taubensee	.10
35	Pedro Astacio	.10
36	Derek Bell	.10
37	Jacque Jones	.10
38	Ricky Ledee	.20
39	Jeff Kent	.10
40	Matt Williams	.50
41	Alfonso Soriano-SS, D'Angelo Jimenez-3B	.50
42	B.J. Surhoff	.10
43	Denny Neagle	.10
44	Omar Vizquel	.10
45	Jeff Bagwell	1.00
46	Mark Grudzielanek	.10
47	LaTroy Hawkins	.10
48	Orlando Hernandez	.40
49	Ken Griffey Jr.	4.00
50	Fernando Tatis	.20
51	Quilvio Veras	.10
52	Wayne Gomes	.10
53	Rick Helling	.10
54	Shannon Stewart	.10
55	Dermal Brown-OF, Mark Quinn-OF	.25
56	Randy Johnson	.75
57	Greg Maddux	2.00
58	Mike Cameron	.10
59	Matt Anderson	.10
60	Milwaukee Brewers	.10
61	Derrek Lee	.10
62	Mike Sweeney	.10
63	Fernando Vina	.10
64	Orlando Cabrera	.10
65	Doug Glanville	.10
66	Stan Spencer	.10
67	Ray Lankford	.10
68	Kelly Dransfeldt	.10
69	Alex Gonzalez	.10
70	Russell Branyan-3B, Danny Peoples-OF	.10
71	Jim Edmonds	.10
72	Brady Anderson	.20
73	Mike Stanley	.10
74	Travis Fryman	.20

75 Carlos Febles .10
76 Bobby Higginson .10
77 Carlos Perez .10
78 Steve Cox-1B, Alex Sanchez-OF .10
79 Dustin Hermanson .10
80 Kenny Rogers .10
81 Miguel Tejada .10
82 Ben Davis .10
83 Reggie Sanders .10
84 Eric Davis .20
85 J.D. Drew .40
86 Ryan Rupe .10
87 Bobby Smith .10
88 Jose Cruz Jr. .10
89 Carlos Delgado .75
90 Toronto Blue Jays .10
91 *Denny Stark-P*, Gil Meche-P .25
92 Randy Velarde .10
93 Aaron Boone .10
94 Javy Lopez .10
95 Johnny Damon .10
96 Jon Lieber .10
97 Montreal Expos .10
98 Mark Kotsay .10
99 Luis Gonzalez .10
100 Larry Walker .75
101 Adrian Beltre .25
102 Alex Ochoa .10
103 Michael Barrett .10
104 Tampa Bay Devil Rays .10
105 Rey Ordonez .10
106 Derek Jeter 2.50
107 Mike Lieberthal .10
108 Ellis Burks .10
109 Steve Finley .10
110 Ryan Klesko .20
111 Steve Avery .10
112 Dave Veres .10
113 Cliff Floyd .10
114 Shane Reynolds .10
115 Kevin Brown .20
116 David Nilsson .10
117 Mike Trombley .10
118 Todd Walker .10
119 John Olerud .25
120 Chuck Knoblauch .40
121 Nomar Garciaparra 2.00
122 Trot Nixon .10
123 Erubiel Durazo .25
124 Edwards Guzman .10
125 Curt Schilling .20
126 Brian Jordan .10
127 Cleveland Indians .10
128 Benito Santiago .10
129 Frank Thomas 1.00
130 Neifi Perez .10
131 Alex Fernandez .10
132 Jose Lima .10
133 Jorge Toca-1B, Melvin Mora-OF .10
134 Scott Karl .10
135 Brad Radke .10
136 Paul O'Neill .25
137 Kris Benson .10
138 Colorado Rockies .10
139 Jason Phillips .10
140 Robb Nen .10
141 Ken Hill .10
142 Charles Johnson .10
143 Paul Konerko .10
144 Dmitri Young .10
145 Justin Thompson .10
146 Mark Loretta .10
147 Edgardo Alfonzo .25
148 Armando Benitez .10
149 Octavio Dotel .10
150 Wade Boggs .50
151 Ramon Hernandez .10
152 Freddy Garcia .25
153 Edgar Martinez .20
154 Ivan Rodriguez 1.00
155 Kansas City Royals .10
156 Cleatus Davidson-2B, Cristian Guzman-SS .10
157 Andy Benes .10
158 Todd Dunwoody .10
159 Pedro Martinez 1.00
160 Mike Caruso .10
161 Mike Sirotka .10
162 Houston Astros .10
163 Darryl Kile .10
164 Chipper Jones 2.00
165 Carl Everett .10
166 Geoff Jenkins .10
167 Dan Perkins .10
168 Andy Pettitte .25
169 Francisco Cordova .10
170 Jay Buhner .20
171 Jay Bell .10
172 Andruw Jones .75
173 Bobby Howry .10
174 Chris Singleton .10
175 Todd Helton .75
176 A.J. Burnett .25
177 Marquis Grissom .10
178 Eric Milton .10
179 Los Angeles Dodgers .10
180 Kevin Appier .10
181 Brian Giles .10
182 Tom Davey .10
183 Mo Vaughn .75
184 Jose Hernandez .10
185 Jim Parque .10
186 Derrick Gibson .10
187 Bruce Aven .10
188 Jeff Cirillo .10
189 Doug Mientkiewicz .10
190 Eric Chavez .10
191 Al Martin .10
192 Tom Glavine .25
193 Butch Huskey .10
194 Ray Durham .10
195 Greg Vaughn .25
196 Vinny Castilla .10
197 Ken Caminiti .20
198 Joe Mays .10
199 Chicago White Sox .10
200 Mariano Rivera .25
201 Mark McGwire 4.00
202 Pat Meares .10
203 Andres Galarraga .50
204 Tom Gordon .10
205 Henry Rodriguez .10
206 Brett Tomko .10
207 Dante Bichette .25
208 Craig Biggio .50
209 Matt Lawton .10
210 Tino Martinez .40
211 Aaron Myette-P, Josh Paul-C .10
212 Warren Morris .10
213 San Diego Padres .10
214 Ramon E. Martinez .10
215 Troy Percival .10
216 Jason Johnson .10
217 Carlos Lee .10
218 Scott Williamson .10
219 Jeff Weaver .10
220 Ronnie Belliard .10
221 Jason Giambi .10
222 Ken Griffey Jr. 4.00
223 John Halama .10
224 Brett Hinchliffe .10
225 Wilson Alvarez .10
226 Rolando Arrojo .10
227 Ruben Mateo .40
228 Rafael Palmeiro .75
229 David Wells .10
230 Eric Gagne-P, Jeff Williams-P .10
231 Tim Salmon .40
232 Mike Mussina .75
233 Magglio Ordonez .25
234 Ron Villone .10
235 Antonio Alfonseca .10
236 Jeromy Burnitz .10
237 Ben Grieve .40
238 Giomar Guevara .10
239 Garret Anderson .10
240 John Smoltz .20
241 Mark Grace .25
242 Cole Liniak-3B, Jose Molina-C .10
243 Damion Easley .10
244 Jeff Montgomery .10
245 Kenny Lofton .60
246 Masato Yoshii .10
247 Philadelphia Phillies .10
248 Raul Mondesi .25
249 Marlon Anderson .10
250 Shawn Green .75
251 Sterling Hitchcock .10
252 Randy Wolf-P, Anthony Shumaker-P .10
253 Jeff Fassero .10
254 Eli Marrero .10
255 Cincinnati Reds .10
256 Rick Ankiel-P, Adam Kennedy-2B 6.00
257 Darin Erstad .25
258 Albert Belle .75
259 Bartolo Colon .10
260 Bret Saberhagen .10
261 Carlos Beltran .25
262 Glenallen Hill .10
263 Gregg Jefferies .10
264 Matt Clement .10
265 Miguel Del Toro .10
266 Robinson Cancel-C, Kevin Barker-1B .10
267 San Francisco Giants .10
268 Kent Bottenfield .10
269 Fred McGriff .25
270 Chris Carpenter .10
271 Atlanta Braves .10
272 Wilton Veras-3B,*Tomokazu Ohka-P* .50
273 Will Clark .50
274 Troy O'Leary .10
275 Sammy Sosa 2.50
276 Travis Lee .25
277 Sean Casey .50
278 Ron Gant .25
279 Roger Clemens 1.50
280 Phil Nevin .10
281 Mike Piazza 2.50
282 Mike Lowell .10
283 Kevin Millwood .25
284 Joe Randa .10
285 Jeff Shaw .10
286 Jason Varitek .10
287 Harold Baines .10
288 Gabe Kapler .25
289 Chuck Finley .10
290 Carl Pavano .10
291 Brad Ausmus .10
292 Brad Fullmer .10
293 Boston Red Sox .10
294 Bob Wickman .10
295 Billy Wagner .10
296 Shawn Estes .10
297 Gary Sheffield .25
298 Fernando Seguignol .10
299 Omar Olivares .10
300 Baltimore Orioles .10
301 Matt Stairs .10
302 Andy Ashby .10
303 Todd Greene .10
304 Jesse Garcia .10
305 Kerry Wood .40
306 Roberto Alomar .75
307 New York Mets .10
308 Dean Palmer .10
309 Mike Hampton .10
310 Devon White .10
311 Chad Hermansen-OF, Mike Garcia-P .10
312 Tim Hudson .40
313 John Franco .10
314 Jason Schmidt .10
315 J.T. Snow .10
316 Ed Sprague .10
317 Chris Widger .10
318 Ben Petrick-C, *Luther Hackman-P* .50
319 Jose Mesa .10
320 Jose Canseco 1.00
321 John Wetteland .10
322 Minnesota Twins .10
323 *Jeff DaVanon-OF*, Brian Cooper-P .50
324 Tony Womack .10
325 Rod Beck .10
326 Mickey Morandini .10
327 Pokey Reese .10
328 Jaret Wright .10
329 Glen Barker .10
330 Darren Dreifort .10
331 Torii Hunter .10
332 Tony Armas, Jr.-P, PeterBergeron-OF .10
333 Hideki Irabu .20
334 Desi Relaford .10
335 Barry Bonds 1.00
336 Gary DiSarcina .10
337 Gerald Williams .10
338 John Valentin .10
339 David Justice .25
340 Juan Encarnacion .10
341 Jeremy Giambi .10
342 Chan Ho Park .10
343 Vladimir Guerrero 2.00
344 Robin Ventura .25
345 Bobby Abreu .10
346 Tony Gwynn 2.00
347 Jose Jimenez .10
348 Royce Clayton .10
349 Kelvim Escobar .10
350 Chicago Cubs .10
351 Travis Dawkins-SS, Jason LaRue-C .10
352 Barry Larkin .50
353 Cal Ripken Jr. 2.50
354 Alex Rodriguez 3.00
355 Todd Stottlemyre .20
356 Terry Adams .10
357 Pittsburgh Pirates .10
358 Jim Thome .50
359 Corey Lee-P, Doug Davis-P .10
360 Moises Alou .20
361 Todd Hollandsworth .10
362 Marty Cordova .10
363 David Cone .20
364 Joe Nathan-P, Wilson Delgado-SS .10
365 Paul Byrd .10
366 Edgar Renteria .10
367 Rusty Greer .10
368 David Segui .10
369 New York Yankees .50
370 Daryle Ward-OF/1B, Carlos Hernandez-2B .10
371 Troy Glaus .50
372 Delino DeShields .10
373 Jose Offerman .10
374 Sammy Sosa 2.50
375 Sandy Alomar Jr. .20
376 Masao Kida .10
377 Richard Hidalgo .10
378 Ismael Valdes .10
379 Ugueth Urbina .10
380 Darryl Hamilton .10
381 John Jaha .10
382 St. Louis Cardinals .10
383 Scott Sauerbeck .10
384 Russ Ortiz .10
385 Jamie Moyer .10
386 Dave Martinez .10
387 Todd Zeile .10
388 Anaheim Angels .10
389 Rob Ryan-OF, Nick Bierbrodt-P .10
390 Rickey Henderson .40
391 Alex Rodriguez 3.00
392 Texas Rangers .10
393 Roberto Hernandez .10
394 Tony Batista .10
395 Oakland Athletics .10
396 Randall Simon-1B, *David Cortes-P* .40
397 Gregg Olson .10
398 Sidney Ponson .10
399 Micah Bowie .10
400 Mark McGwire 4.00
401 Florida Marlins .10
402 Chad Allen .10
403 Casey Blake-3B, Vernon Wells-OF .10
404 Pete Harnisch .10
405 Preston Wilson .10
406 Richie Sexson .10
407 Rico Brogna .10
408 Todd Hundley .10
409 Wally Joyner .10
410 Tom Goodwin .10
411 Joey Hamilton .10
412 Detroit Tigers .10
413 *Michael Tejera-P*, Ramon Castro-C .25
414 Alex Gonzalez .10
415 Jermaine Dye .10
416 Jose Rosado .10
417 Wilton Guerrero .10
418 Rondell White .20
419 Al Leiter .20
420 Bernie Williams .75
421 A.J. Hinch .10
422 Pat Burrell 2.50
423 Scott Rolen 1.00
424 Jason Kendall .25
425 Kevin Young .10
426 Eric Owens .10
427 Derek Jeter 2.50

428	Livan Hernandez	.10
429	Russ Davis	.10
430	Dan Wilson	.10
431	Quinton McCracken	.10
432	Homer Bush	.10
433	Seattle Mariners	.10
434	Chad Harville-P, Luis Vizcaino-P	.10
435	Carlos Beltran	.15
436	Scott Williamson	.10
437	Pedro Martinez	.50
438	Randy Johnson	.40
439	Ivan Rodriguez	.50
440	Chipper Jones	1.00
441	AL Division (Bernie Williams)	.40
442	AL Division (Pedro Martinez)	.50
443	AL Champ (Derek Jeter)	1.25
444	NL Division (Brian Jordan)	.10
445	NL Division (Todd Pratt)	.10
446	NL Champ (Kevin Millwood)	.10
447	World Series (Orlando Hernandez)	.20
448	World Series (Derek Jeter)	1.25
449	World Series (Chad Curtis)	.10
450	World Series (Roger Clemens)	.75

2000 Fleer Tradition Dividends

This insert set consists of 15 cards and spotlights the top players on a horizontal format. Card fronts have silver foil stamping, a red border and are seeded 1:6 packs. They are numbered on the back with a "D" suffix.

		MT
Complete Set (15):		30.00
Common Player:		.75
Inserted 1:6		
1	Alex Rodriguez	5.00
2	Ben Grieve	1.00
3	Cal Ripken Jr.	4.00
4	Chipper Jones	3.00
5	Derek Jeter	4.00
6	Frank Thomas	1.50
7	Jeff Bagwell	1.50
8	Sammy Sosa	4.00
9	Tony Gwynn	3.00
10	Scott Rolen	1.50
11	Nomar Garciaparra	4.00
12	Mike Piazza	4.00
13	Mark McGwire	6.00
14	Ken Griffey Jr.	6.00
15	Juan Gonzalez	1.50

2000 Fleer Tradition Grasskickers

This 15-card set has a close-up photo of the featured player with holographic silver foil stamping. These are seeded 1:30 packs and are numbered on the back with a "GK" suffix.

		MT
Complete Set (15):		125.00
Common Player:		3.00
Inserted 1:30		
1	Tony Gwynn	10.00
2	Scott Rolen	5.00
3	Nomar Garciaparra	12.00
4	Mike Piazza	12.00
5	Mark McGwire	20.00
6	Frank Thomas	5.00
7	Cal Ripken Jr.	12.00
8	Chipper Jones	10.00
9	Greg Maddux	10.00
10	Ken Griffey Jr.	20.00
11	Juan Gonzalez	5.00
12	Derek Jeter	12.00
13	Sammy Sosa	12.00
14	Roger Clemens	8.00
15	Alex Rodriguez	15.00

2000 Fleer Tradition Club 3000

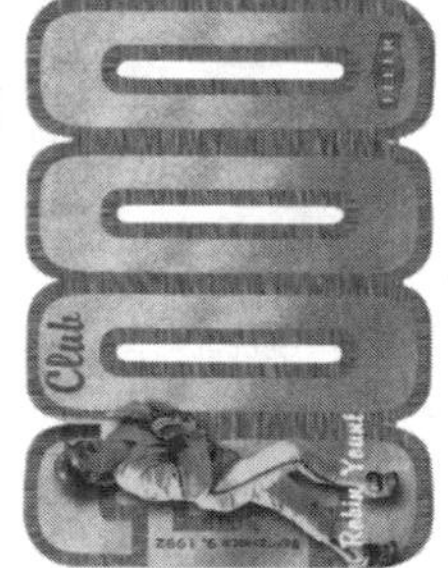

The Club 3000 inserts are die-cut around the number 3,000, commemorating their reaching the 3,000 hit achievement. These are seeded 1:36 packs and feature George Brett, Rod Carew and Robin Yount.

		MT
Complete Set (3):		10.00
Common Player:		3.00
Inserted 1:36		
(1)	George Brett	5.00
(2)	Rod Carew	3.00
(3)	Robin Yount	3.00

2000 Fleer Tradition Club 3000 Memorabilia

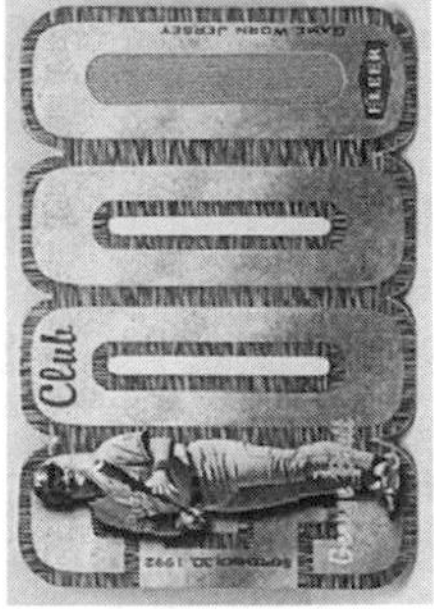

These are a parallel to the base version and has five different memorabilia based tiers. Level 2 (cap), Level 3 (bat), Level 4 (jersey), Level 5 (bat and jersey) and Level 6 (bat, jersey and cap). Each card is hand-numbered.

	MT
Common Card:	75.00
George Brett bat/250	125.00
George Brett hat/100	180.00
George Brett jersey/440	100.00
George Brett bat-jersey/100	200.00
George Brett bat-hat-jersey/25	
Rod Carew bat/250	75.00
Rod Carew hat/100	100.00
Rod Carew jersey/440	75.00
Rod Carew bat-jersey/100	125.00
Rod Carew bat-hat-jersey/25	
Robin Yount bat/250	75.00
Robin Yount hat/100	100.00
Robin Yount jersey/440	75.00
Robin Yount bat-jersey/100	125.00
Robin Yount bat-hat-jersey/25	

2000 Fleer Tradition Diamond Skills Commemorative Sheet

Utilizing the same format and card reproductions as the souvenir sheet issued in conjunction with the season-opener Cubs-Mets series in Japan, Fleer issued this commemorative sheet for distribution to participants in the 2000 Diamond Skills competition. The 10" x 9" sheets depict star cards from Fleer's 2000 Tradition set.

	MT
Derek Jeter, Chipper Jones, Pedro Martinez, Mike Piazza, Cal Ripken Jr., Ivan Rodriguez, Sammy Sosa, Mo Vaughn	10.00

2000 Fleer Tradition Fresh Ink

This autographed insert set consists of 38 cards on a vertical format with the autograph on the bottom third of the card below the player image. These were inserted 1:144 packs.

	MT
Common Player:	10.00
Inserted 1:144	
Rick Ankiel	75.00
Carlos Beltran	25.00
Pat Burrell	30.00
Miguel Cairo	10.00
Sean Casey	20.00
Will Clark	25.00
Mike Darr	10.00
J.D. Drew	40.00
Erubiel Durazo	15.00
Carlos Febles	15.00
Freddy Garcia	25.00
Greg Maddux	175.00
Jason Grilli	10.00
Vladimir Guerrero	75.00
Tony Gwynn	120.00
Jerry Hairston Jr.	10.00
Tim Hudson	25.00
John Jaha	10.00
D'Angelo Jimenez	10.00
Andruw Jones	25.00
Gabe Kapler	25.00
Cesar King	10.00
Jason LaRue	10.00
Mike Lieberthal	10.00
Pedro Martinez	75.00
Gary Matthews Jr.	10.00
Orber Moreno	10.00
Eric Munson	25.00
Rafael Palmeiro	35.00
Jim Parque	10.00
Willi Mo Pena	25.00
Cal Ripken Jr.	200.00
Alex Rodriguez	200.00
Tim Salmon	25.00
Chris Singleton	10.00
Alfonso Soriano	20.00
Ed Yarnall	20.00

2000 Fleer Tradition Hall's Well

This 15-card set spotlights superstars destined for Cooperstown, featured on a transparent plastic stock with overlays of silver foil stamping. These were seeded 1:30 packs and are numbered with a "HW" suffix.

		MT
Complete Set (15):		125.00
Common Player:		3.00
Inserted 1:30		
1	Mark McGwire	20.00
2	Alex Rodriguez	15.00
3	Cal Ripken Jr.	12.00
4	Chipper Jones	10.00
5	Derek Jeter	12.00
6	Frank Thomas	5.00
7	Greg Maddux	10.00
8	Juan Gonzalez	5.00
9	Ken Griffey Jr.	20.00
10	Mike Piazza	12.00
11	Nomar Garciaparra	12.00
12	Sammy Sosa	12.00
13	Roger Clemens	8.00
14	Ivan Rodriguez	5.00
15	Tony Gwynn	10.00

2000 Fleer Tradition Ripken Collection

This 10-card set is devoted to Cal Ripken Jr. and features 10 different Fleer retro designs. These were seeded 1:30 packs.

	MT
Complete Set (10):	70.00
Common Card:	8.00
Inserted 1:30	

(Inserted at the rate of 1:30 packs.)

2000 Fleer Tradition Ten-4

This 10-card insert set focuses on baseball's home run kings on a die-cut design enhanced with silver foil stamping. These were seeded 1:18 packs and are numbered on the card back with a "TF" suffix.

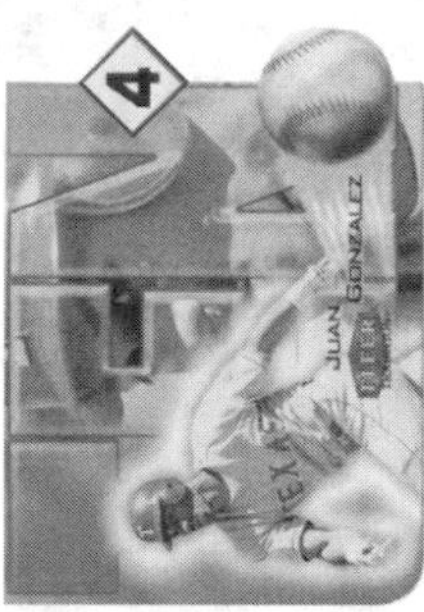

		MT
Complete Set (10):		60.00
Common Player:		2.00
Inserted 1:18		
1	Sammy Sosa	6.00
2	Nomar Garciaparra	6.00
3	Mike Piazza	6.00
4	Mark McGwire	10.00
5	Ken Griffey Jr.	10.00
6	Juan Gonzalez	3.00
7	Derek Jeter	6.00
8	Chipper Jones	5.00
9	Cal Ripken Jr.	6.00
10	Alex Rodriguez	8.00

2000 Fleer Tradition Who To Watch

Top prospects for the 2000 season are highlighted in this 15-card set, including Rick Ankiel. They have a die-cut design with gold foil stamping. These were inserted 1:3 packs and numbered on the back with a "WW" suffix.

		MT
Complete Set (15):		12.00
Common Player:		.50
Inserted 1:3		
1	Rick Ankiel	6.00
2	Matt Riley	.50
3	Wilton Veras	.50
4	Ben Petrick	.50
5	Chad Hermansen	.50
6	Peter Bergeron	1.00
7	Mark Quinn	1.00
8	Russell Branyan	.50
9	Alfonso Soriano	1.00
10	Randy Wolf	.50
11	Ben Davis	.50
12	Jeff DaVanon	.50
13	D'Angelo Jimenez	.50
14	Vernon Wells	1.00
15	Adam Kennedy	.50

2000 Fleer Tradition Update

		MT
Complete Set (150):		30.00
Common Player:		.15
1	Ken Griffey Jr. (Season Highlights)	1.00
2	Cal Ripken Jr. (Season Highlights)	1.00
3	Randy Velarde (Season Highlights)	.15
4	Fred McGriff (Season Highlights)	.15
5	Derek Jeter (Season Highlights)	1.00
6	Tom Glavine (Season Highlights)	.25
7	Brent Mayne (Season Highlights)	.15
8	Alex Ochoa (Season Highlights)	.15
9	Scott Sheldon (Season Highlights)	.15
10	Randy Johnson (Season Highlights)	.25
11	*Daniel Garibay*	.25
12	Brad Fullmer	.15
13	*Kazuhiro Sasaki*	2.50
14	Andy Tracy	.15
15	Bret Boone	.15
16	Chad Durbin	.25
17	Mark Buehrle	.15
18	Julio Zuleta	.15
19	Jeremy Giambi	.15
20	Gene Stechschulte	.15
21	Lou Pote	.15
22	Darrell Einertson	.15
23	Ken Griffey Jr.	2.50
24	Jeff Sparks	.15
25	Aaron Fultz	.15
26	Derek Bell	.15
27	Rob Bell	.15
28	Rob Fick	.15
29	Darryl Kile	.15
30	Clayton Andrews	.15
31	Dave Veres	.15
32	Hector Mercado	.15
33	Willie Morales	.15
34	Kelly Wunsch	.15
35	Hideki Irabu	.15
36	Sean DePaula	.15
37	Dewayne Wise	.15
38	Curt Schilling	.15
39	Mark Johnson	.15
40	Mike Cameron	.15
41	Scott Sheldon	.15
42	Brett Tomko	.15
43	Johan Santana	.15
44	Andy Benes	.15
45	Matt LeCroy	.15
46	Ryan Klesko	.15
47	Andy Ashby	.15
48	Octavio Dotel	.15
49	Eric Byrnes	.15
50	C.C. Sabathia	.15
51	Kenny Rogers	.15
52	Ben Weber	.15
53	Matt Blank	.15
54	Tom Goodwin	.15
55	Jim Edmonds	.50
56	Derrick Turnbow	.15
57	Mark Mulder	.15
58	Tarrik Brock	.15
59	Danny Young	.15
60	Fernando Vina	.15
61	Justin Brunette	.15
62	Jimmy Anderson	.15
63	Reggie Sanders	.15
64	Adam Kennedy	.15
65	Jesse Garcia	.15
66	Al Martin	.15
67	Kevin Walker	.15
68	Brad Penny	.15
69	B.J. Surhoff	.15
70	Geoff Blum	.15
71	Jose Jimenez	.15
72	Chuck Finley	.15
73	Valerio DeLosSantos	.15
74	Terry Adams	.15
75	Rafael Furcal	1.50
76	Mike Darr	.15
77	Quilvio Veras	.15
78	Armando Almanza	.15
79	Greg Vaughn	.15
80	Keith McDonald	.15
81	Eric Cammack	.15
82	Horacio Estrada	.15
83	Kory DeHaan	.15
84	Kevin Hodges	.15
85	Mike Lamb	.50
86	Shawn Green	.40
87	Dan Reichert	.15
88	Adam Piatt	.25
89	Mike Garcia	.15
90	Rodrigo Lopez	.15
91	John Olerud	.25
92	Barry Zito	3.00
93	Jimmy Rollins	.15
94	Denny Neagle	.15
95	Rickey Henderson	.40
96	Adam Eaton	.15
97	Brian O'Connor	.15
98	Andy Thompson	.15
99	Jason Boyd	.15
100	Carlos Guillen	.15
101	Raul Gonzalez	.15
102	Brandon Kolb	.15
103	Jason Maxwell	.15
104	Luis Matos	.50
105	Morgan Burkhart	.15
106	Ismael Villegas	.15
107	David Justice	.50
108	Pablo Ozuna	.15
109	Jose Canseco	.50
110	Alex Cora	.15
111	Will Clark	.50
112	Keith Luuloa	.15
113	Bruce Chen	.15
114	Adam Hyzdu	.15
115	Scott Forster	.15
116	Allen McDill	.15
117	Kevin Nicholson	.15
118	Israel Alcantara	.15
119	Juan Alvarez	.15
120	Julio Lugo	.15
121	B.J. Waszgis	.15
122	Jeff D'Amico	.15
123	Ricky Ledee	.15
124	Mark DeRosa	.15
125	Alex Cabrera	.50
126	Gary Matthews	.15
127	Richie Sexson	.15
128	Santiago Perez	.15
129	Rondell White	.15
130	Craig House	.15
131	Kevin Beirne	.15
132	Wayne Franklin	.15
133	Henry Rodriguez	.15
134	Jay Payton	.15
135	Ron Gant	.15
136	Paxton Crawford	.15
137	Kent Bottenfield	.15
138	Rocky Biddle	.15
139	Travis Lee	.15
140	Ryan Vogelsong	.15
141	Jason Conti	.15
142	Tim Drew	.15
143	John Parrish	.15
144	Javier Cardona	.15
145	Tike Redman	.15
146	Brian Schneider	.15
147	Pasqual Coco	.15
148	Lorenzo Barcelo	.15
149	Jace Brewer	.15
150	Milton Bradley	.15

2000 Fleer Tradition Update Mantle Pieces

		MT
Inserted 1:80 sets		
1	Mickey Mantle	400.00

L

1990 Leaf Previews

This 12-card set was produced for dealer distribution to introduce Leaf as Donruss' premium-quality brand in mid-1990. Cards have the same format as the regular-issue versions with metallic silver ink highlights on front and back. The preview cards have a white undertype on back over the stats and career highlights. It reads "Special Preview Card".

		MT
Complete Set (12):		800.00
Common Player:		20.00
1	Steve Sax	20.00
2	Joe Carter	35.00
3	Dennis Eckersley	65.00
4	Ken Griffey, Jr.	450.00
5	Barry Larkin	50.00
6	Mark Langston	25.00
7	Eric Anthony	20.00
8	Robin Ventura	60.00
9	Greg Vaughn	35.00
10	Bobby Bonilla	25.00
11	Gary Gaetti	20.00
12	Ozzie Smith	150.00

1990 Leaf

This 528-card set was issued in two 264-card series. The cards were printed on heavy quality stock and both the card fronts and backs have full color player photos. Cards also have an ultra-glossy finish on both the fronts and the backs. A high-tech foil Hall of Fame puzzle features former Yankee great Yogi Berra.

		MT
Complete Set (528):		240.00
Complete Series 1 (264):		140.00
Complete Series 2 (264):		100.00
Common Player:		.25
Series 1 Foil Pack (15):		10.00
Series 1 Foil Wax Box (36):		325.00
Series 2 Foil Pack (15):		7.50
Series 2 Foil Wax Box (36):		195.00
1	Introductory card	.25
2	Mike Henneman	.25
3	Steve Bedrosian	.25
4	Mike Scott	.25
5	Allan Anderson	.25
6	Rick Sutcliffe	.25
7	Gregg Olson	.25
8	Kevin Elster	.25
9	Pete O'Brien	.25
10	Carlton Fisk	.50
11	Joe Magrane	.25
12	Roger Clemens	3.00
13	Tom Glavine	2.00
14	Tom Gordon	.25
15	Todd Benzinger	.25
16	Hubie Brooks	.25
17	Roberto Kelly	.25
18	Barry Larkin	.75
19	Mike Boddicker	.25
20	Roger McDowell	.25
21	Nolan Ryan	8.00
22	John Farrell	.25
23	Bruce Hurst	.25
24	Wally Joyner	.40
25	Greg Maddux	8.00
26	Chris Bosio	.25
27	John Cerutti	.25
28	Tim Burke	.25
29	Dennis Eckersley	.40
30	Glenn Davis	.25
31	Jim Abbott	.50
32	Mike LaValliere	.25
33	Andres Thomas	.25
34	Lou Whitaker	.35
35	Alvin Davis	.25
36	Melido Perez	.25
37	Craig Biggio	.75
38	Rick Aguilera	.25
39	Pete Harnisch	.25
40	David Cone	.50
41	Scott Garrelts	.25
42	Jay Howell	.25
43	Eric King	.25
44	Pedro Guerrero	.25
45	Mike Bielecki	.25
46	Bob Boone	.25
47	Kevin Brown	1.50
48	Jerry Browne	.25
49	Mike Scioscia	.25
50	Chuck Cary	.25
51	Wade Boggs	1.00
52	Von Hayes	.25
53	Tony Fernandez	.25
54	Dennis Martinez	.35
55	Tom Candiotti	.25
56	Andy Benes	.50
57	Rob Dibble	.25
58	Chuck Crim	.25
59	John Smoltz	.50
60	Mike Heath	.25
61	Kevin Gross	.25
62	Mark McGwire	8.00
63	Bert Blyleven	.25
64	Bob Walk	.25
65	Mickey Tettleton	.25
66	Sid Fernandez	.25
67	Terry Kennedy	.25
68	Fernando Valenzuela	.30
69	Don Mattingly	3.00
70	Paul O'Neill	.50
71	Robin Yount	1.00
72	Bret Saberhagen	.30
73	Geno Petralli	.25
74	Brook Jacoby	.25
75	Roberto Alomar	2.50
76	Devon White	.35
77	Jose Lind	.25
78	Pat Combs	.25
79	Dave Steib	.25
80	Tim Wallach	.25
81	Dave Stewart	.30
82	*Eric Anthony*	.25
83	Randy Bush	.25
84	Checklist	.25
85	Jaime Navarro	.25
86	Tommy Gregg	.25
87	Frank Tanana	.25
88	Omar Vizquel	1.50
89	Ivan Calderon	.25
90	Vince Coleman	.25
91	Barry Bonds	3.00
92	Randy Milligan	.25
93	Frank Viola	.25
94	Matt Williams	1.50
95	Alfredo Griffin	.25
96	Steve Sax	.25
97	Gary Gaetti	.30
98	Ryne Sandberg	2.00
99	Danny Tartabull	.25
100	Rafael Palmeiro	1.50
101	Jesse Orosco	.25
102	Garry Templeton	.25
103	Frank DiPino	.25
104	Tony Pena	.25
105	Dickie Thon	.25
106	Kelly Gruber	.25
107	*Marquis Grissom*	2.00
108	Jose Canseco	1.50
109	Mike Blowers	.25
110	Tom Browning	.25
111	Greg Vaughn	3.00
112	Oddibe McDowell	.25
113	Gary Ward	.25
114	Jay Buhner	.50
115	Eric Show	.25
116	Bryan Harvey	.25
117	Andy Van Slyke	.25
118	Jeff Ballard	.25
119	Barry Lyons	.25
120	Kevin Mitchell	.25
121	Mike Gallego	.25
122	Dave Smith	.25
123	Kirby Puckett	2.00
124	Jerome Walton	.25
125	Bo Jackson	.75
126	Harold Baines	.35
127	Scott Bankhead	.25
128	Ozzie Guillen	.25
129	Jose Oquendo	.25
130	John Dopson	.25
131	Charlie Hayes	.25
132	Fred McGriff	.75
133	Chet Lemon	.25
134	Gary Carter	.40
135	Rafael Ramirez	.25
136	Shane Mack	.25
137	Mark Grace	.75
138	Phil Bradley	.25
139	Dwight Gooden	.40
140	Harold Reynolds	.25
141	Scott Fletcher	.25
142	Ozzie Smith	1.50
143	Mike Greenwell	.30
144	Pete Smith	.25
145	Mark Gubicza	.30
146	Chris Sabo	.25
147	Ramon Martinez	.35
148	Tim Leary	.25
149	Randy Myers	.25
150	Jody Reed	.25
151	Bruce Ruffin	.25
152	Jeff Russell	.25
153	Doug Jones	.25
154	Tony Gwynn	3.00
155	Mark Langston	.30
156	Mitch Williams	.25
157	Gary Sheffield	3.00
158	Tom Henke	.25
159	Oil Can Boyd	.25
160	Rickey Henderson	.75
161	Bill Doran	.25
162	Chuck Finley	.25
163	Jeff King	.35
164	Nick Esasky	.25
165	Cecil Fielder	.40
166	Dave Valle	.25
167	Robin Ventura	2.00
168	Jim Deshaies	.25
169	Juan Berenguer	.25
170	Craig Worthington	.25
171	Gregg Jefferies	.40
172	Will Clark	.75
173	Kirk Gibson	.25
174	Checklist	.25
175	Bobby Thigpen	.25
176	John Tudor	.25
177	Andre Dawson	.50
178	George Brett	3.00
179	Steve Buechele	.25
180	Albert Belle	8.00
181	Eddie Murray	.75
182	Bob Geren	.25
183	Rob Murphy	.25
184	Tom Herr	.25
185	George Bell	.25
186	Spike Owen	.25
187	Cory Snyder	.25
188	Fred Lynn	.30
189	Eric Davis	.40
190	Dave Parker	.35
191	Jeff Blauser	.25
192	Matt Nokes	.25
193	*Delino DeShields*	.50
194	Scott Sanderson	.25
195	Lance Parrish	.25
196	Bobby Bonilla	.40
197	Cal Ripken, Jr.	6.00
198	Kevin McReynolds	.25
199	Robby Thompson	.25
200	Tim Belcher	.25
201	Jesse Barfield	.25
202	Mariano Duncan	.25
203	Bill Spiers	.25
204	Frank White	.25
205	Julio Franco	.25
206	Greg Swindell	.25
207	Benito Santiago	.25
208	Johnny Ray	.25
209	Gary Redus	.25
210	Jeff Parrett	.25
211	Jimmy Key	.35
212	Tim Raines	.35
213	Carney Lansford	.25
214	Gerald Young	.25
215	Gene Larkin	.25
216	Dan Plesac	.25
217	Lonnie Smith	.25
218	Alan Trammell	.40
219	Jeffrey Leonard	.25
220	*Sammy Sosa*	80.00
221	Todd Zeile	.30
222	Bill Landrum	.25
223	Mike Devereaux	.25
224	Mike Marshall	.25
225	Jose Uribe	.25
226	Juan Samuel	.25
227	Mel Hall	.25
228	Kent Hrbek	.35
229	Shawon Dunston	.25
230	Kevin Seitzer	.25
231	Pete Incaviglia	.25
232	Sandy Alomar	.35
233	Bip Roberts	.25
234	Scott Terry	.25
235	Dwight Evans	.25
236	Ricky Jordan	.25
237	*John Olerud*	6.00
238	Zane Smith	.25
239	Walt Weiss	.25
240	Alvaro Espinoza	.25
241	Billy Hatcher	.25
242	Paul Molitor	2.00
243	Dale Murphy	.30
244	Dave Bergman	.25
245	Ken Griffey, Jr.	20.00
246	Ed Whitson	.25
247	Kirk McCaskill	.25
248	Jay Bell	.25
249	*Ben McDonald*	.50
250	Darryl Strawberry	.50
251	Brett Butler	.30
252	Terry Steinbach	.25
253	Ken Caminiti	.50
254	Dan Gladden	.25

No.	Player	MT
255	Dwight Smith	.25
256	Kurt Stillwell	.25
257	Ruben Sierra	.25
258	Mike Schooler	.25
259	Lance Johnson	.25
260	Terry Pendleton	.25
261	Ellis Burks	.35
262	Len Dykstra	.25
263	Mookie Wilson	.25
264	Checklist (Nolan Ryan)	.25
265	Nolan Ryan (No-Hit King)	4.00
266	Brian DuBois	.25
267	Don Robinson	.25
268	Glenn Wilson	.25
269	*Kevin Tapani*	.75
270	Marvell Wynne	.25
271	Billy Ripken	.25
272	Howard Johnson	.25
273	Brian Holman	.25
274	Dan Pasqua	.25
275	Ken Dayley	.25
276	Jeff Reardon	.25
277	Jim Presley	.25
278	Jim Eisenreich	.25
279	Danny Jackson	.25
280	Orel Hershiser	.35
281	Andy Hawkins	.25
282	Jose Rijo	.25
283	Luis Rivera	.25
284	John Kruk	.25
285	Jeff Huson	.25
286	Joel Skinner	.25
287	Jack Clark	.25
288	Chili Davis	.35
289	Joe Girardi	.30
290	B.J. Surhoff	.30
291	Luis Sojo	.25
292	Tom Foley	.25
293	Mike Moore	.25
294	Ken Oberkfell	.25
295	Luis Polonia	.25
296	Doug Drabek	.25
297	*Dave Justice*	10.00
298	Paul Gibson	.25
299	Edgar Martinez	.75
300	*Frank Thomas*	50.00
301	Eric Yelding	.25
302	Greg Gagne	.25
303	Brad Komminsk	.25
304	Ron Darling	.25
305	Kevin Bass	.25
306	Jeff Hamilton	.25
307	Ron Karkovice	.25
308	Milt Thompson	.25
309	Mike Harkey	.25
310	Mel Stottlemyre	.25
311	Kenny Rogers	.35
312	Mitch Webster	.25
313	Kal Daniels	.25
314	Matt Nokes	.25
315	Dennis Lamp	.25
316	Ken Howell	.25
317	Glenallen Hill	.25
318	Dave Martinez	.25
319	Chris James	.25
320	Mike Pagliarulo	.25
321	Hal Morris	.25
322	Rob Deer	.25
323	Greg Olson	.25
324	Tony Phillips	.30
325	*Larry Walker*	8.00
326	Ron Hassey	.25
327	Jack Howell	.25
328	John Smiley	.25
329	Steve Finley	.50
330	Dave Magadan	.25
331	Greg Litton	.25
332	Mickey Hatcher	.25
333	Lee Guetterman	.25
334	Norm Charlton	.25
335	Edgar Diaz	.25
336	Willie Wilson	.25
337	Bobby Witt	.25
338	Candy Maldonado	.25
339	Craig Lefferts	.25
340	Dante Bichette	1.00
341	Wally Backman	.25
342	Dennis Cook	.25
343	Pat Borders	.25
344	Wallace Johnson	.25
345	Willie Randolph	.25
346	Danny Darwin	.25
347	Al Newman	.25
348	Mark Knudson	.25
349	Joe Boever	.25
350	Larry Sheets	.25
351	Mike Jackson	.25
352	Wayne Edwards	.25
353	*Bernard Gilkey*	2.00
354	Don Slaught	.25
355	Joe Orsulak	.25
356	John Franco	.25
357	Jeff Brantley	.25
358	Mike Morgan	.25
359	Deion Sanders	.75
360	Terry Leach	.25
361	Les Lancaster	.25
362	Storm Davis	.25
363	Scott Coolbaugh	.25
364	Checklist	.25
365	Cecilio Guante	.25
366	Joey Cora	.25
367	Willie McGee	.35
368	Jerry Reed	.25
369	Darren Daulton	.25
370	Manny Lee	.25
371	Mark Gardner	.25
372	Rick Honeycutt	.25
373	Steve Balboni	.25
374	Jack Armstrong	.25
375	Charlie O'Brien	.25
376	Ron Gant	.50
377	Lloyd Moseby	.25
378	Gene Harris	.25
379	Joe Carter	.30
380	Scott Bailes	.25
381	R.J. Reynolds	.25
382	Bob Melvin	.25
383	Tim Teufel	.25
384	John Burkett	.30
385	Felix Jose	.25
386	Larry Andersen	.25
387	David West	.25
388	Luis Salazar	.25
389	Mike Macfarlane	.25
390	Charlie Hough	.25
391	Greg Briley	.25
392	Donn Pall	.25
393	Bryn Smith	.25
394	Carlos Quintana	.25
395	Steve Lake	.25
396	*Mark Whiten*	.50
397	Edwin Nunez	.25
398	Rick Parker	.25
399	Mark Portugal	.25
400	Roy Smith	.25
401	Hector Villanueva	.25
402	Bob Milacki	.25
403	Alejandro Pena	.25
404	Scott Bradley	.25
405	Ron Kittle	.25
406	Bob Tewksbury	.25
407	Wes Gardner	.25
408	Ernie Whitt	.25
409	Terry Shumpert	.25
410	Tim Layana	.25
411	Chris Gwynn	.25
412	Jeff Robinson	.25
413	Scott Scudder	.25
414	Kevin Romine	.25
415	Jose DeJesus	.25
416	Mike Jeffcoat	.25
417	Rudy Seanez	.25
418	Mike Dunne	.25
419	Dick Schofield	.25
420	Steve Wilson	.25
421	Bill Krueger	.25
422	Junior Felix	.25
423	Drew Hall	.25
424	Curt Young	.25
425	Franklin Stubbs	.25
426	Dave Winfield	.50
427	Rick Reed	.25
428	Charlie Leibrandt	.25
429	Jeff Robinson	.25
430	Erik Hanson	.25
431	Barry Jones	.25
432	Alex Trevino	.25
433	John Moses	.25
434	Dave Johnson	.25
435	Mackey Sasser	.25
436	Rick Leach	.25
437	Lenny Harris	.25
438	Carlos Martinez	.25
439	Rex Hudler	.25
440	Domingo Ramos	.25
441	Gerald Perry	.25
442	John Russell	.25
443	*Carlos Baerga*	.75
444	Checklist	.25
445	Stan Javier	.25
446	*Kevin Maas*	.25
447	Tom Brunansky	.25
448	Carmelo Martinez	.25
449	*Willie Blair*	.25
450	Andres Galarraga	1.50
451	Bud Black	.25
452	Greg Harris	.25
453	Joe Oliver	.25
454	Greg Brock	.25
455	Jeff Treadway	.25
456	Lance McCullers	.25
457	Dave Schmidt	.25
458	Todd Burns	.25
459	Max Venable	.25
460	Neal Heaton	.25
461	Mark Williamson	.25
462	Keith Miller	.25
463	Mike LaCoss	.25
464	*Jose Offerman*	.50
465	*Jim Leyritz*	.50
466	Glenn Braggs	.25
467	Ron Robinson	.25
468	Mark Davis	.25
469	Gary Pettis	.25
470	Keith Hernandez	.25
471	Dennis Rasmussen	.25
472	Mark Eichhorn	.25
473	Ted Power	.25
474	Terry Mulholland	.30
475	Todd Stottlemyre	.30
476	Jerry Goff	.25
477	Gene Nelson	.25
478	Rich Gedman	.25
479	Brian Harper	.25
480	Mike Felder	.25
481	Steve Avery	.25
482	Jack Morris	.25
483	Randy Johnson	6.00
484	Scott Radinsky	.25
485	Jose DeLeon	.25
486	*Stan Belinda*	.25
487	Brian Holton	.25
488	Mark Carreon	.25
489	Trevor Wilson	.25
490	Mike Sharperson	.25
491	*Alan Mills*	.25
492	John Candelaria	.25
493	Paul Assenmacher	.25
494	Steve Crawford	.25
495	Brad Arnsberg	.25
496	Sergio Valdez	.25
497	Mark Parent	.25
498	Tom Pagnozzi	.25
499	Greg Harris	.25
500	Randy Ready	.25
501	Duane Ward	.25
502	Nelson Santovenia	.25
503	Joe Klink	.25
504	Eric Plunk	.25
505	Jeff Reed	.25
506	Ted Higuera	.25
507	Joe Hesketh	.25
508	Dan Petry	.25
509	Matt Young	.25
510	Jerald Clark	.25
511	*John Orton*	.25
512	Scott Ruskin	.25
513	*Chris Hoiles*	.75
514	Daryl Boston	.25
515	Francisco Oliveras	.25
516	Ozzie Canseco	.30
517	*Xavier Hernandez*	.40
518	Fred Manrique	.25
519	Shawn Boskie	.30
520	Jeff Montgomery	.30
521	Jack Daugherty	.25
522	Keith Comstock	.25
523	*Greg Hibbard*	.30
524	Lee Smith	.30
525	Dana Kiecker	.25
526	Darrel Akerfelds	.25
527	Greg Myers	.25
528	Checklist	.25

1991 Leaf Previews

Cello packs of four cards previewing the 1991 Leaf set were included in each 1991 Donruss hobby factory set. The cards are identical in format to the regular 1991 Leafs, except there is a notation, "1991 PREVIEW CARD" in white print beneath the statistics and career information on the back.

		MT
Complete Set (26):		55.00
Common Player:		1.00
1	Dave Justice	3.00
2	Ryne Sandberg	5.00
3	Barry Larkin	1.50
4	Craig Biggio	1.50
5	Ramon Martinez	1.50
6	Tim Wallach	1.00
7	Dwight Gooden	1.50
8	Len Dykstra	1.00
9	Barry Bonds	6.00
10	Ray Lankford	1.00
11	Tony Gwynn	6.00
12	Will Clark	2.50
13	Leo Gomez	1.00
14	Wade Boggs	3.50
15	Chuck Finley	1.00
16	Carlton Fisk	1.50
17	Sandy Alomar, Jr.	1.50
18	Cecil Fielder	1.50
19	Bo Jackson	2.00
20	Paul Molitor	3.50
21	Kirby Puckett	6.00
22	Don Mattingly	6.00
23	Rickey Henderson	2.00
24	Tino Martinez	2.00
25	Nolan Ryan	9.00
26	Dave Steib	1.00

1991 Leaf

Silver borders and black insets surround the color action photos on the 1991 Leaf cards. The set was once again released in two series. Series I consists of cards 1-264. Card backs feature an additional player photo, biographical information, statistics and career highlights. The 1991 issue is not considered as scarce as the 1990 release.

		MT
Complete Set (528):		25.00
Common Player:		.05
Series 1 or 2 Pack (15):		1.00
Series 1 or 2 Wax Box (36):		25.00
1	The Leaf Card	.05
2	Kurt Stillwell	.05
3	Bobby Witt	.05
4	Tony Phillips	.05
5	Scott Garrelts	.05
6	Greg Swindell	.05
7	Billy Ripken	.05
8	Dave Martinez	.05
9	Kelly Gruber	.05
10	Juan Samuel	.05
11	Brian Holman	.05
12	Craig Biggio	.25
13	Lonnie Smith	.05
14	Ron Robinson	.05
15	Mike LaValliere	.05
16	Mark Davis	.05
17	Jack Daugherty	.05
18	Mike Henneman	.05
19	Mike Greenwell	.05
20	Dave Magadan	.05
21	Mark Williamson	.05
22	Marquis Grissom	.15
23	Pat Borders	.05
24	Mike Scioscia	.05
25	Shawon Dunston	.05
26	Randy Bush	.05
27	John Smoltz	.20
28	Chuck Crim	.05
29	Don Slaught	.05
30	Mike Macfarlane	.05
31	Wally Joyner	.05
32	Pat Combs	.05
33	Tony Pena	.05
34	Howard Johnson	.05
35	Leo Gomez	.05
36	Spike Owen	.05
37	Eric Davis	.10
38	Roberto Kelly	.05
39	Jerome Walton	.05
40	Shane Mack	.05
41	Kent Mercker	.05
42	B.J. Surhoff	.10
43	Jerry Browne	.05
44	Lee Smith	.05
45	Chuck Finley	.05
46	Terry Mulholland	.05
47	Tom Bolton	.05
48	Tom Herr	.05
49	Jim Deshaies	.05
50	Walt Weiss	.05
51	Hal Morris	.05
52	Lee Guetterman	.05
53	Paul Assenmacher	.05
54	Brian Harper	.05
55	Paul Gibson	.05
56	John Burkett	.05
57	Doug Jones	.05
58	Jose Oquendo	.05
59	Dick Schofield	.05
60	Dickie Thon	.05
61	Ramon Martinez	.10
62	Jay Buhner	.10
63	Mark Portugal	.05
64	Bob Welch	.05
65	Chris Sabo	.05
66	Chuck Cary	.05
67	Mark Langston	.10
68	Joe Boever	.05
69	Jody Reed	.05
70	Alejandro Pena	.05
71	Jeff King	.05
72	Tom Pagnozzi	.05
73	Joe Oliver	.05
74	Mike Witt	.05
75	Hector Villanueva	.05
76	Dan Gladden	.05
77	Dave Justice	.25
78	Mike Gallego	.05
79	Tom Candiotti	.05
80	Ozzie Smith	.50
81	Luis Polonia	.05
82	Randy Ready	.05
83	Greg Harris	.05
84	Checklist (Dave Justice)	.15
85	Kevin Mitchell	.05
86	Mark McLemore	.05
87	Terry Steinbach	.05
88	Tom Browning	.05
89	Matt Nokes	.05
90	Mike Harkey	.05
91	Omar Vizquel	.10
92	Dave Bergman	.05
93	Matt Williams	.40
94	Steve Olin	.05
95	Craig Wilson	.05
96	Dave Stieb	.05
97	Ruben Sierra	.05
98	Jay Howell	.05
99	Scott Bradley	.05
100	Eric Yelding	.05
101	Rickey Henderson	.25
102	Jeff Reed	.05
103	Jimmy Key	.10
104	Terry Shumpert	.05
105	Kenny Rogers	.05
106	Cecil Fielder	.10
107	Robby Thompson	.05
108	Alex Cole	.05
109	Randy Milligan	.05
110	Andres Galarraga	.15
111	Bill Spiers	.05
112	Kal Daniels	.05
113	Henry Cotto	.05
114	Casy Candaele	.05
115	Jeff Blauser	.05
116	Robin Yount	.40
117	Ben McDonald	.05
118	Bret Saberhagen	.10
119	Juan Gonzalez	1.00
120	Lou Whitaker	.05
121	Ellis Burks	.10
122	Charlie O'Brien	.05
123	John Smiley	.05
124	Tim Burke	.05
125	John Olerud	.20
126	Eddie Murray	.30
127	Greg Maddux	1.50
128	Kevin Tapani	.05
129	Ron Gant	.15
130	Jay Bell	.05
131	Chris Hoiles	.05
132	Tom Gordon	.05
133	Kevin Seitzer	.05
134	Jeff Huson	.05
135	Jerry Don Gleaton	.05
136	Jeff Brantley	.05
137	Felix Fermin	.05
138	Mike Devereaux	.05
139	Delino DeShields	.05
140	David Wells	.10
141	Tim Crews	.05
142	Erik Hanson	.05
143	Mark Davidson	.05
144	Tommy Gregg	.05
145	Jim Gantner	.05
146	Jose Lind	.05
147	Danny Tartabull	.05
148	Geno Petralli	.05
149	Travis Fryman	.15
150	Tim Naehring	.05
151	Kevin McReynolds	.05
152	Joe Orsulak	.05
153	Steve Frey	.05
154	Duane Ward	.05
155	Stan Javier	.05
156	Damon Berryhill	.05
157	Gene Larkin	.05
158	Greg Olson	.05
159	Mark Knudson	.05
160	Carmelo Martinez	.05
161	Storm Davis	.05
162	Jim Abbott	.10
163	Len Dykstra	.05
164	Tom Brunansky	.05
165	Dwight Gooden	.15
166	Jose Mesa	.05
167	Oil Can Boyd	.05
168	Barry Larkin	.15
169	Scott Sanderson	.05
170	Mark Grace	.15
171	Mark Guthrie	.05
172	Tom Glavine	.40
173	Gary Sheffield	.25
174	Checklist (Roger Clemens)	.15
175	Chris James	.05
176	Milt Thompson	.05
177	Donnie Hill	.05
178	Wes Chamberlain	.05
179	John Marzano	.05
180	Frank Viola	.05
181	Eric Anthony	.05
182	Jose Canseco	.50
183	Scott Scudder	.05
184	Dave Eiland	.05
185	Luis Salazar	.05
186	Pedro Munoz	.05
187	Steve Searcy	.05
188	Don Robinson	.05
189	Sandy Alomar	.10
190	Jose DeLeon	.05
191	John Orton	.05
192	Darren Daulton	.05
193	Mike Morgan	.05
194	Greg Briley	.05
195	Karl Rhodes	.05
196	Harold Baines	.10
197	Bill Doran	.05
198	Alvaro Espinoza	.05
199	Kirk McCaskill	.05
200	Jose DeJesus	.05
201	Jack Clark	.05
202	Daryl Boston	.05
203	Randy Tomlin	.05
204	Pedro Guerrero	.05
205	Billy Hatcher	.05
206	Tim Leary	.05
207	Ryne Sandberg	.60
208	Kirby Puckett	.75
209	Charlie Leibrandt	.05
210	Rick Honeycutt	.05
211	Joel Skinner	.05
212	Rex Hudler	.05
213	Bryan Harvey	.05
214	Charlie Hayes	.05
215	Matt Young	.05
216	Terry Kennedy	.05
217	Carl Nichols	.05
218	Mike Moore	.05
219	Paul O'Neill	.10
220	Steve Sax	.05
221	Shawn Boskie	.05
222	Rich DeLucia	.05
223	Lloyd Moseby	.05
224	Mike Kingery	.05
225	Carlos Baerga	.10
226	Bryn Smith	.05
227	Todd Stottlemyre	.05
228	Julio Franco	.10
229	Jim Gott	.05
230	Mike Schooler	.05
231	Steve Finley	.05
232	Dave Henderson	.05
233	Luis Quinones	.05
234	Mark Whiten	.05
235	Brian McRae	.10
236	Rich Gossage	.05
237	Rob Deer	.05
238	Will Clark	.25
239	Albert Belle	.50
240	Bob Melvin	.05
241	Larry Walker	.30
242	Dante Bichette	.20
243	Orel Hershiser	.15
244	Pete O'Brien	.05
245	Pete Harnisch	.10
246	Jeff Treadway	.05
247	Julio Machado	.05
248	Dave Johnson	.05
249	Kirk Gibson	.05
250	Kevin Brown	.05
251	Milt Cuyler	.05
252	Jeff Reardon	.05
253	David Cone	.10
254	Gary Redus	.05
255	Junior Noboa	.05
256	Greg Myers	.05
257	Dennis Cook	.05
258	Joe Girardi	.05
259	Allan Anderson	.05
260	Paul Marak	.05
261	Barry Bonds	.75
262	Juan Bell	.05
263	Russ Morman	.05
264	Checklist (George Brett)	.20
265	Jerald Clark	.05
266	Dwight Evans	.05
267	Roberto Alomar	.50
268	Danny Jackson	.05
269	Brian Downing	.05
270	John Cerutti	.05
271	Robin Ventura	.20
273	Wade Boggs	.40
274	Dennis Martinez	.15
275	Andy Benes	.10
276	Tony Fossas	.05
277	Franklin Stubbs	.05
278	John Kruk	.05
279	Kevin Gross	.05
280	Von Hayes	.05
281	Frank Thomas	1.50
282	Rob Dibble	.05
283	Mel Hall	.05
284	Rick Mahler	.05
285	Dennis Eckersley	.15
286	Bernard Gilkey	.10
287	Dan Plesac	.05
288	Jason Grimsley	.05
289	Mark Lewis	.10
290	Tony Gwynn	.75
291	Jeff Russell	.05
292	Curt Schilling	.10
293	Pascual Perez	.05
294	Jack Morris	.05
295	Hubie Brooks	.05
296	Alex Fernandez	.40
297	Harold Reynolds	.05
298	Craig Worthington	.05
299	Willie Wilson	.05
300	Mike Maddux	.05
301	Dave Righetti	.05
302	Paul Molitor	.40
303	Gary Gaetti	.10
304	Terry Pendleton	.05
305	Kevin Elster	.05
306	Scott Fletcher	.05
307	Jeff Robinson	.05
308	Jesse Barfield	.05
309	Mike LaCoss	.05
310	Andy Van Slyke	.05
311	Glenallen Hill	.05
312	Bud Black	.05
313	Kent Hrbek	.10
314	Tim Teufel	.05
315	Tony Fernandez	.05
316	Beau Allred	.05
317	Curtis Wilkerson	.05
318	Bill Sampen	.05
319	Randy Johnson	.40
320	Mike Heath	.05
321	Sammy Sosa	2.00
322	Mickey Tettleton	.05
323	Jose Vizcaino	.05
324	John Candelaria	.05
325	David Howard	.05
326	Jose Rijo	.05
327	Todd Zeile	.10
328	Gene Nelson	.05
329	Dwayne Henry	.05
330	Mike Boddicker	.05
331	Ozzie Guillen	.05
332	Sam Horn	.05
333	Wally Whitehurst	.05
334	Dave Parker	.10
335	George Brett	.40
336	Bobby Thigpen	.05
337	Ed Whitson	.05
338	Ivan Calderon	.05
339	Mike Pagliarulo	.05
340	Jack McDowell	.05
341	Dana Kiecker	.05
342	Fred McGriff	.40
343	Mark Lee	.05
344	Alfredo Griffin	.05
345	Scott Bankhead	.05
346	Darrin Jackson	.05
347	Rafael Palmeiro	.25
348	Steve Farr	.05
349	Hensley Meulens	.05
350	Danny Cox	.05
351	Alan Trammell	.15
352	Edwin Nunez	.05
353	Joe Carter	.10
354	Eric Show	.05
355	Vance Law	.05
356	Jeff Gray	.05
357	Bobby Bonilla	.15
358	Ernest Riles	.05
359	Ron Hassey	.05
360	Willie McGee	.12
361	Mackey Sasser	.05
362	Glenn Braggs	.05
363	Mario Diaz	.05
364	Checklist (Barry Bonds)	.15
365	Kevin Bass	.05
366	Pete Incaviglia	.05
367	Luis Sojo	.05
368	Lance Parrish	.10
369	Mark Leonard	.05
370	Heathcliff Slocumb	.05
371	Jimmy Jones	.05
372	Ken Griffey, Jr.	3.50
373	Chris Hammond	.05
374	Chili Davis	.10
375	Joey Cora	.05

376	Ken Hill	.10
377	Darryl Strawberry	.15
378	Ron Darling	.05
379	Sid Bream	.05
380	Bill Swift	.05
381	Shawn Abner	.05
382	Eric King	.05
383	Mickey Morandini	.05
384	Carlton Fisk	.15
385	Steve Lake	.05
386	Mike Jeffcoat	.05
387	Darren Holmes	.05
388	Tim Wallach	.05
389	George Bell	.05
390	Craig Lefferts	.05
391	Ernie Whitt	.05
392	Felix Jose	.05
393	Kevin Maas	.05
394	Devon White	.12
395	Otis Nixon	.05
396	Chuck Knoblauch	.40
397	Scott Coolbaugh	.05
398	Glenn Davis	.05
399	Manny Lee	.05
400	Andre Dawson	.15
401	Scott Chiamparino	.05
402	Bill Gullickson	.05
403	Lance Johnson	.05
404	Juan Agosto	.05
405	Danny Darwin	.05
406	Barry Jones	.05
407	Larry Andersen	.05
408	Luis Rivera	.05
409	Jaime Navarro	.05
410	Roger McDowell	.05
411	Brett Butler	.10
412	Dale Murphy	.15
413	Tim Raines	.15
414	Norm Charlton	.05
415	Greg Cadaret	.05
416	Chris Nabholz	.05
417	Dave Stewart	.05
418	Rich Gedman	.05
419	Willie Randolph	.05
420	Mitch Williams	.05
421	Brook Jacoby	.05
422	Greg Harris	.05
423	Nolan Ryan	2.00
424	Dave Rohde	.05
425	Don Mattingly	.75
426	Greg Gagne	.05
427	Vince Coleman	.05
428	Dan Pasqua	.05
429	Alvin Davis	.05
430	Cal Ripken, Jr.	2.00
431	Jamie Quirk	.05
432	Benito Santiago	.05
433	Jose Uribe	.05
434	Candy Maldonado	.05
435	Junior Felix	.05
436	Deion Sanders	.45
437	John Franco	.05
438	Greg Hibbard	.05
439	Floyd Bannister	.05
440	Steve Howe	.05
441	Steve Decker	.05
442	Vicente Palacios	.05
443	Pat Tabler	.05
444	Checklist (Darryl Strawberry)	.10
445	Mike Felder	.05
446	Al Newman	.05
447	Chris Donnels	.05
448	Rich Rodriguez	.05
449	Turner Ward	.05
450	Bob Walk	.05
451	Gilberto Reyes	.05
452	Mike Jackson	.05
453	Rafael Belliard	.05
454	Wayne Edwards	.05
455	Andy Allanson	.05
456	Dave Smith	.05
457	Gary Carter	.15
458	Warren Cromartie	.05
459	Jack Armstrong	.05
460	Bob Tewksbury	.10
461	Joe Klink	.05
462	Xavier Hernandez	.05
463	Scott Radinsky	.05
464	Jeff Robinson	.05
465	Gregg Jefferies	.15
466	Denny Neagle	.05
467	Carmelo Martinez	.05
468	Donn Pall	.05
469	Bruce Hurst	.05
470	Eric Bullock	.05
471	Rick Aguilera	.05
472	Charlie Hough	.05
473	Carlos Quintana	.05
474	Marty Barrett	.05
475	Kevin Brown	.10
476	Bobby Ojeda	.05
477	Edgar Martinez	.10
478	Bip Roberts	.05
479	Mike Flanagan	.05
480	John Habyan	.05
481	Larry Casian	.05
482	Wally Backman	.05
483	Doug Dascenzo	.05
484	Rick Dempsey	.05
485	Ed Sprague	.10
486	Steve Chitren	.05
487	Mark McGwire	3.00
488	Roger Clemens	.65
489	Orlando Merced	.05
490	Rene Gonzales	.05
491	Mike Stanton	.05
492	Al Osuna	.05
493	Rick Cerone	.05
494	Mariano Duncan	.05
495	Zane Smith	.05
496	John Morris	.05
497	Frank Tanana	.05
498	Junior Ortiz	.05
499	Dave Winfield	.35
500	Gary Varsho	.05
501	Chico Walker	.05
502	Ken Caminiti	.25
503	Ken Griffey, Sr.	.10
504	Randy Myers	.05
505	Steve Bedrosian	.05
506	Cory Snyder	.05
507	Cris Carpenter	.05
508	Tim Belcher	.05
509	Jeff Hamilton	.05
510	Steve Avery	.05
511	Dave Valle	.05
512	Tom Lampkin	.05
513	Shawn Hillegas	.05
514	Reggie Jefferson	.10
515	Ron Karkovice	.05
516	Doug Drabek	.05
517	Tom Henke	.05
518	Chris Bosio	.05
519	Gregg Olson	.05
520	Bob Scanlan	.05
521	Alonzo Powell	.05
522	Jeff Ballard	.05
523	Ray Lankford	.10
524	Tommy Greene	.05
525	Mike Timlin	.10
526	Juan Berenguer	.05
527	Scott Erickson	.10
528	Checklist (Sandy Alomar Jr.)	.05

1991 Leaf Gold Rookies

Special gold rookie and gold bonus cards were randomly inserted in 1991 Leaf packs. Backs have a design similar to the regular-issue cards, but have gold, rather than silver background. Fronts have gold-foil highlights. Card numbers of the issued version have a "BC" prefix, but there is a much rarer second version of the Series 1 cards, which carry card numbers between 265-276.

		MT
Complete Set (26):		30.00
Common Player:		.50
1	Scott Leius	.50
2	Luis Gonzalez	.75
3	Wil Cordero	.75
4	Gary Scott	.50
5	Willie Banks	.50
6	Arthur Rhodes	.50
7	Mo Vaughn	8.00
8	Henry Rodriguez	.75
9	Todd Van Poppel	.50
10	Reggie Sanders	.75
11	Rico Brogna	.50
12	Mike Mussina	7.50
13	Kirk Dressendorfer	.50
14	Jeff Bagwell	12.00
15	Pete Schourek	.50
16	Wade Taylor	.50
17	Pat Kelly	.50
18	Tim Costo	.50
19	Roger Salkeld	.50
20	Andujar Cedeno	.50
21	Ryan Klesko	1.50
22	Mike Huff	.50
23	Anthony Young	.75
24	Eddie Zosky	.50
25	Nolan Ryan (7th no-hitter)	10.00
26	Rickey Henderson (record steal)	2.00
265	Scott Leius	9.00
266	Luis Gonzalez	12.00
267	Wil Cordero	12.00
268	Gary Scott	9.00
269	Willie Banks	9.00
270	Arthur Rhodes	9.00
271	Mo Vaughn	65.00
272	Henry Rodriguez	9.00
273	Todd Van Poppel	9.00
274	Reggie Sanders	12.00
275	Rico Brogna	9.00
276	Mike Mussina	60.00

1992 Leaf Previews

In a format identical to the regular-issue 1992 Leaf cards, this 26-card preview set was issued as a bonus in packs of four cards in each 1992 Donruss hobby factory set.

		MT
Complete Set (26):		150.00
Common Player:		1.00
1	Steve Avery	1.00
2	Ryne Sandberg	9.00
3	Chris Sabo	1.00
4	Jeff Bagwell	15.00
5	Darryl Strawberry	2.50
6	Bret Barberie	1.00
7	Howard Johnson	1.00
8	John Kruk	1.00
9	Andy Van Slyke	1.00
10	Felix Jose	1.00
11	Fred McGriff	6.00
12	Will Clark	7.50
13	Cal Ripken, Jr.	20.00
14	Phil Plantier	1.00
15	Lee Stevens	1.00
16	Frank Thomas	15.00
17	Mark Whiten	1.00
18	Cecil Fielder	2.00
19	George Brett	10.00
20	Robin Yount	7.50
21	Scott Erickson	1.00
22	Don Mattingly	10.00
23	Jose Canseco	7.50
24	Ken Griffey, Jr.	25.00
25	Nolan Ryan	20.00
26	Joe Carter	2.00

1992 Leaf

Two 264-card series comprise this 528-card set. The cards feature action photos on both the front and the back. Silver borders surround the photo on the card front. Each leaf card was also produced in a gold foil version. One gold card was issued per pack and a complete Leaf Gold Edition set can be assembled. Traded players and free agents are shown in uniform with their new teams.

		MT
Complete Set (528):		20.00
Common Player:		.05
Series 1 or 2 Wax Box:		20.00
Gold Stars:		4X
Young Stars/RCs:		2X
Series 1 or 2 Pack (15):		.75
Series 1 or 2 Wax Box (36):		20.00
1	Jim Abbott	.10
2	Cal Eldred	.05
3	Bud Black	.05
4	Dave Howard	.05
5	Luis Sojo	.05
6	Gary Scott	.05
7	Joe Oliver	.05
8	Chris Gardner	.05
9	Sandy Alomar	.12
10	Greg Harris	.05
11	Doug Drabek	.05
12	Darryl Hamilton	.10
13	Mike Mussina	.60
14	Kevin Tapani	.10
15	Ron Gant	.10
16	Mark McGwire	2.50
17	Robin Ventura	.25
18	Pedro Guerrero	.05
19	Roger Clemens	.65
20	Steve Farr	.05
21	Frank Tanana	.05
22	Joe Hesketh	.05
23	Erik Hanson	.05
24	Greg Cadaret	.05
25	Rex Hudler	.05
26	Mark Grace	.15
27	Kelly Gruber	.05
28	Jeff Bagwell	1.00
29	Darryl Strawberry	.10
30	Dave Smith	.05
31	Kevin Appier	.10
32	Steve Chitren	.05
33	Kevin Gross	.05
34	Rick Aguilera	.05
35	Juan Guzman	.10
36	Joe Orsulak	.05
37	Tim Raines	.15
38	Harold Reynolds	.05
39	Charlie Hough	.05
40	Tony Phillips	.05
41	Nolan Ryan	1.50
42	Vince Coleman	.05
43	Andy Van Slyke	.05
44	Tim Burke	.05
45	Luis Polonia	.05
46	Tom Browning	.05

No.	Player	Value
47	Willie McGee	.10
48	Gary DiSarcina	.05
49	Mark Lewis	.10
50	Phil Plantier	.05
51	Doug Dascenzo	.05
52	Cal Ripken, Jr.	2.00
53	Pedro Munoz	.05
54	Carlos Hernandez	.05
55	Jerald Clark	.05
56	Jeff Brantley	.05
57	Don Mattingly	.60
58	Roger McDowell	.05
59	Steve Avery	.05
60	John Olerud	.20
61	Bill Gullickson	.05
62	Juan Gonzalez	.75
63	Felix Jose	.05
64	Robin Yount	.25
65	Greg Briley	.05
66	Steve Finley	.05
67	Checklist	.05
68	Tom Gordon	.05
69	Rob Dibble	.05
70	Glenallen Hill	.05
71	Calvin Jones	.05
72	Joe Girardi	.05
73	Barry Larkin	.15
74	Andy Benes	.05
75	Milt Cyler	.05
76	Kevin Bass	.05
77	Pete Harnisch	.05
78	Wilson Alvarez	.05
79	Mike Devereaux	.05
80	Doug Henry	.05
81	Orel Hershiser	.15
82	Shane Mack	.05
83	Mike Macfarlane	.05
84	Thomas Howard	.05
85	Alex Fernandez	.05
86	Reggie Jefferson	.10
87	Leo Gomez	.05
88	Mel Hall	.05
89	Mike Greenwell	.05
90	Jeff Russell	.05
91	Steve Buechele	.05
92	David Cone	.12
93	Kevin Reimer	.05
94	Mark Lemke	.05
95	Bob Tewksbury	.05
96	Zane Smith	.05
97	Mark Eichhorn	.05
98	Kirby Puckett	.75
99	Paul O'Neill	.12
100	Dennis Eckersley	.10
101	Duane Ward	.05
102	Matt Nokes	.05
103	Mo Vaughn	.50
104	Pat Kelly	.05
105	Ron Karkovice	.05
106	Bill Spiers	.05
107	Gary Gaetti	.10
108	Mackey Sasser	.05
109	Robby Thompson	.05
110	Marvin Freeman	.05
111	Jimmy Key	.05
112	Dwight Gooden	.12
113	Charlie Leibrandt	.05
114	Devon White	.10
115	Charles Nagy	.10
116	Rickey Henderson	.25
117	Paul Assenmacher	.05
118	Junior Felix	.05
119	Julio Franco	.05
120	Norm Charlton	.05
121	Scott Servais	.05
122	Gerald Perry	.05
123	Brian McRae	.10
124	Don Slaught	.05
125	Juan Samuel	.05
126	Harold Baines	.12
127	Scott Livingstone	.05
128	Jay Buhner	.10
129	Darrin Jackson	.05
130	Luis Mercedes	.05
131	Brian Harper	.05
132	Howard Johnson	.05
133	Checklist	.05
134	Dante Bichette	.10
135	Dave Righetti	.05
136	Jeff Montgomery	.05
137	Joe Grahe	.05
138	Delino DeShields	.10
139	Jose Rijo	.05
140	Ken Caminiti	.15
141	Steve Olin	.05
142	Kurt Stillwell	.05
143	Jay Bell	.05
144	Jaime Navarro	.05
145	Ben McDonald	.05
146	Greg Gagne	.05
147	Jeff Blauser	.05
148	Carney Lansford	.05
149	Ozzie Guillen	.05
150	Milt Thompson	.05
151	Jeff Reardon	.05
152	Scott Sanderson	.05
153	Cecil Fielder	.10
154	Greg Harris	.05
155	Rich DeLucia	.05
156	Roberto Kelly	.05
157	Bryn Smith	.05
158	Chuck McElroy	.05
159	Tom Henke	.05
160	Luis Gonzalez	.10
161	Steve Wilson	.05
162	Shawn Boskie	.05
163	Mark Davis	.05
164	Mike Moore	.05
165	Mike Scioscia	.05
166	Scott Erickson	.10
167	Todd Stottlemyre	.10
168	Alvin Davis	.05
169	Greg Hibbard	.05
170	David Valle	.05
171	Dave Winfield	.25
172	Alan Trammell	.12
173	Kenny Rogers	.05
174	John Franco	.05
175	Jose Lind	.05
176	Pete Schourek	.05
177	Von Hayes	.05
178	Chris Hammond	.05
179	John Burkett	.05
180	Dickie Thon	.05
181	Joel Skinner	.05
182	Scott Cooper	.05
183	Andre Dawson	.15
184	Billy Ripken	.05
185	Kevin Mitchell	.05
186	Brett Butler	.10
187	Tony Fernandez	.05
188	Cory Snyder	.05
189	John Habyan	.05
190	Dennis Martinez	.12
191	John Smoltz	.15
192	Greg Myers	.05
193	Rob Deer	.05
194	Ivan Rodriguez	.50
195	Ray Lankford	.10
196	Bill Wegman	.05
197	Edgar Martinez	.10
198	Darryl Kile	.10
199	Checklist	.05
200	Brent Mayne	.05
201	Larry Walker	.25
202	Carlos Baerga	.10
203	Russ Swan	.05
204	Mike Morgan	.05
205	Hal Morris	.10
206	Tony Gwynn	.75
207	Mark Leiter	.05
208	Kirt Manwaring	.05
209	Al Osuna	.05
210	Bobby Thigpen	.05
211	Chris Hoiles	.05
212	B.J. Surhoff	.10
213	Lenny Harris	.05
214	Scott Leius	.05
215	Gregg Jefferies	.10
216	Bruce Hurst	.05
217	Steve Sax	.05
218	Dave Otto	.05
219	Sam Horn	.05
220	Charlie Hayes	.05
221	Frank Viola	.05
222	Jose Guzman	.05
223	Gary Redus	.05
224	Dave Gallagher	.05
225	Dean Palmer	.05
226	Greg Olson	.05
227	Jose DeLeon	.05
228	Mike LaValliere	.05
229	Mark Langston	.05
230	Chuck Knoblauch	.20
231	Bill Doran	.05
232	Dave Henderson	.05
233	Roberto Alomar	.50
234	Scott Fletcher	.05
235	Tim Naehring	.05
236	Mike Gallego	.05
237	Lance Johnson	.05
238	Paul Molitor	.25
239	Dan Gladden	.05
240	Willie Randolph	.05
241	Will Clark	.30
242	Sid Bream	.05
243	Derek Bell	.10
244	Bill Pecota	.05
245	Terry Pendleton	.05
246	Randy Ready	.05
247	Jack Armstrong	.05
248	Todd Van Poppel	.10
249	Shawon Dunston	.05
250	Bobby Rose	.05
251	Jeff Huson	.05
252	Bip Roberts	.05
253	Doug Jones	.05
254	Lee Smith	.10
255	George Brett	.40
256	Randy Tomlin	.05
257	Todd Benzinger	.05
258	Dave Stewart	.05
259	Mark Carreon	.05
260	Pete O'Brien	.05
261	Tim Teufel	.05
262	Bob Milacki	.05
263	Mark Guthrie	.05
264	Darrin Fletcher	.05
265	Omar Vizquel	.10
266	Chris Bosio	.05
267	Jose Canseco	.25
268	Mike Boddicker	.05
269	Lance Parrish	.10
270	Jose Vizcaino	.05
271	Chris Sabo	.05
272	Royce Clayton	.05
273	Marquis Grissom	.10
274	Fred McGriff	.25
275	Barry Bonds	.60
276	Greg Vaughn	.15
277	Gregg Olson	.05
278	Dave Hollins	.10
279	Tom Glavine	.15
280	Bryan Hickerson	.05
281	Scott Radinsky	.05
282	Omar Olivares	.05
283	Ivan Calderon	.05
284	Kevin Maas	.05
285	Mickey Tettleton	.05
286	Wade Boggs	.25
287	Stan Belinda	.05
288	Bret Barberie	.05
289	Jose Oquendo	.05
290	Frank Castillo	.05
291	Dave Stieb	.05
292	Tommy Greene	.05
293	Eric Karros	.10
294	Greg Maddux	1.50
295	Jim Eisenreich	.05
296	Rafael Palmeiro	.15
297	Ramon Martinez	.10
298	Tim Wallach	.05
299	Jim Thome	.50
300	Chito Martinez	.05
301	Mitch Williams	.05
302	Randy Johnson	.30
303	Carlton Fisk	.10
304	Travis Fryman	.10
305	Bobby Witt	.05
306	Dave Magadan	.05
307	Alex Cole	.05
308	Bobby Bonilla	.12
309	Bryan Harvey	.05
310	Rafael Belliard	.05
311	Mariano Duncan	.05
312	Chuck Crim	.05
313	John Kruk	.05
314	Ellis Burks	.10
315	Craig Biggio	.15
316	Glenn Davis	.05
317	Ryne Sandberg	.35
318	Mike Sharperson	.05
319	Rich Rodriguez	.05
320	Lee Guetterman	.05
321	Benito Santiago	.05
322	Jose Offerman	.05
323	Tony Pena	.05
324	Pat Borders	.05
325	Mike Henneman	.05
326	Kevin Brown	.15
327	Chris Nabholz	.05
328	Franklin Stubbs	.05
329	Tino Martinez	.15
330	Mickey Morandini	.05
331	Checklist	.05
332	Mark Gubicza	.05
333	Bill Landrum	.05
334	Mark Whiten	.05
335	Darren Daulton	.05
336	Rick Wilkins	.05
337	*Brian Jordan*	1.50
338	Kevin Ward	.05
339	Ruben Amaro	.05
340	Trevor Wilson	.05
341	Andujar Cedeno	.05
342	Michael Huff	.05
343	Brady Anderson	.10
344	Craig Grebeck	.05
345	Bobby Ojeda	.05
346	Mike Pagliarulo	.05
347	Terry Shumpert	.05
348	Dann Bilardello	.05
349	Frank Thomas	2.00
350	Albert Belle	.40
351	Jose Mesa	.05
352	Rich Monteleone	.05
353	Bob Walk	.05
354	Monty Fariss	.05
355	Luis Rivera	.05
356	Anthony Young	.05
357	Geno Petralli	.05
358	Otis Nixon	.05
359	Tom Pagnozzi	.05
360	Reggie Sanders	.10
361	Lee Stevens	.05
362	Kent Hrbek	.10
363	Orlando Merced	.05
364	Mike Bordick	.05
365	Dion James	.05
366	Jack Clark	.05
367	Mike Stanley	.05
368	Randy Velarde	.05
369	Dan Pasqua	.05
370	Pat Listach	.05
371	Mike Fitzgerald	.05
372	Tom Foley	.05
373	Matt Williams	.20
374	Brian Hunter	.05
375	Joe Carter	.10
376	Bret Saberhagen	.10
377	Mike Stanton	.05
378	Hubie Brooks	.05
379	Eric Bell	.05
380	Walt Weiss	.05
381	Danny Jackson	.05
382	Manuel Lee	.05
383	Ruben Sierra	.05
384	Greg Swindell	.05
385	Ryan Bowen	.05
386	Kevin Ritz	.05
387	Curtis Wilkerson	.05
388	Gary Varsho	.05
389	Dave Hansen	.05
390	Bob Welch	.05
391	Lou Whitaker	.05
392	Ken Griffey, Jr.	3.00
393	Mike Maddux	.05
394	Arthur Rhodes	.05
395	Chili Davis	.10
396	Eddie Murray	.20
397	Checklist	.05
398	Dave Cochrane	.05
399	Kevin Seitzer	.05
400	Ozzie Smith	.25
401	Paul Sorrento	.05
402	Les Lancaster	.05
403	Junior Noboa	.05
404	Dave Justice	.25
405	Andy Ashby	.10
406	Danny Tartabull	.05
407	Bill Swift	.05
408	Craig Lefferts	.05
409	Tom Candiotti	.05
410	Lance Blankenship	.05
411	Jeff Tackett	.05
412	Sammy Sosa	2.00
413	Jody Reed	.05
414	Bruce Ruffin	.05
415	Gene Larkin	.05
416	John Vanderwal	.05
417	Tim Belcher	.05
418	Steve Frey	.05
419	Dick Schofield	.05
420	Jeff King	.05
421	Kim Batiste	.05
422	Jack McDowell	.05
423	Damon Berryhill	.05
424	Gary Wayne	.05
425	Jack Morris	.05
426	Moises Alou	.10
427	Mark McLemore	.05
428	Juan Guerrero	.05
429	Scott Scudder	.05
430	Eric Davis	.10
431	Joe Slusarski	.05
432	Todd Zeile	.15
433	Dwayne Henry	.05

434 Cliff Brantley .05
435 Butch Henry .05
436 Todd Worrell .05
437 Bob Scanlan .05
438 Wally Joyner .10
439 John Flaherty .05
440 Brian Downing .05
441 Darren Lewis .05
442 Gary Carter .10
443 Wally Ritchie .05
444 Chris Jones .05
445 Jeff Kent .10
446 Gary Sheffield .25
447 Ron Darling .05
448 Deion Sanders .15
449 Andres Galarraga .20
450 Chuck Finley .05
451 Derek Lilliquist .05
452 Carl Willis .05
453 Wes Chamberlain .05
454 Roger Mason .05
455 Spike Owen .05
456 Thomas Howard .05
457 Dave Martinez .05
458 Pete Incaviglia .05
459 Keith Miller .05
460 Mike Fetters .05
461 Paul Gibson .05
462 George Bell .05
463 Checklist .05
464 Terry Mulholland .05
465 Storm Davis .05
466 Gary Pettis .05
467 Randy Bush .05
468 Ken Hill .05
469 Rheal Cormier .05
470 Andy Stankiewicz .05
471 Dave Burba .05
472 Henry Cotto .05
473 Dale Sveum .05
474 Rich Gossage .05
475 William Suero .05
476 Doug Strange .05
477 Bill Krueger .05
478 John Wetteland .10
479 Melido Perez .05
480 Lonnie Smith .05
481 Mike Jackson .05
482 Mike Gardiner .05
483 David Wells .10
484 Barry Jones .05
485 Scott Bankhead .05
486 Terry Leach .05
487 Vince Horsman .05
488 Dave Eiland .05
489 Alejandro Pena .05
490 Julio Valera .05
491 Joe Boever .05
492 Paul Miller .05
493 *Arci Cianfrocco* .10
494 Dave Fleming .05
495 Kyle Abbott .10
496 Chad Kreuter .05
497 Chris James .05
498 Donnie Hill .05
499 Jacob Brumfield .05
500 Ricky Bones .05
501 Terry Steinbach .05
502 Bernard Gilkey .10
503 Dennis Cook .05
504 Len Dykstra .05
505 Mike Bielecki .05
506 Bob Kipper .05
507 Jose Melendez .05
508 Rick Sutcliffe .05
509 Ken Patterson .05
510 Andy Allanson .05
511 Al Newman .05
512 Mark Gardner .05
513 Jeff Schaefer .05
514 Jim McNamara .05
515 Peter Hoy .05
516 Curt Schilling .12
517 Kirk McCaskill .05
518 Chris Gwynn .05
519 Sid Fernandez .05
520 Jeff Parrett .05
521 Scott Ruskin .05
522 Kevin McReynolds .05
523 Rick Cerone .05
524 Jesse Orosco .05
525 Troy Afenir .05
526 John Smiley .05
527 Dale Murphy .12
528 Leaf Set Card .05

1992 Leaf Gold Previews

In the same format as the chase cards which would be included in the regular 1992 Leaf packs, this preview set was produced for distribution to the Donruss dealer network. Cards feature the same black borders and gold highlights as the regular-issue Leaf Gold cards, but are numbered "X of 33" on the back.

		MT
Complete Set (33):		100.00
Common Player:		1.50
1	Steve Avery	1.50
2	Ryne Sandberg	4.50
3	Chris Sabo	1.50
4	Jeff Bagwell	4.50
5	Darryl Strawberry	2.50
6	Bret Barbarie	1.50
7	Howard Johnson	1.50
8	John Kruk	1.50
9	Andy Van Slyke	1.50
10	Felix Jose	1.50
11	Fred McGriff	2.00
12	Will Clark	3.00
13	Cal Ripken, Jr.	8.00
14	Phil Plantier	1.50
15	Lee Stevens	1.50
16	Frank Thomas	5.00
17	Mark Whiten	1.50
18	Cecil Fielder	2.00
19	George Brett	6.00
20	Robin Yount	3.50
21	Scott Erickson	1.50
22	Don Mattingly	5.00
23	Jose Canseco	3.75
24	Ken Griffey, Jr.	9.00
25	Nolan Ryan	8.00
26	Joe Carter	2.00
27	Deion Sanders	3.00
28	Dean Palmer	1.50
29	Andy Benes	1.50
30	Gary DiSarcina	1.50
31	Chris Hoiles	1.50
32	Mark McGwire	9.00
33	Reggie Sanders	1.50

1992 Leaf Gold Edition

This set is a parallel version of Leaf's regular 1992 set. Card fronts do not have silver borders like the regular cards do; black borders and gold foil highlights are seen instead. A Gold Edition card was inserted in each 15-card 1992 Leaf foil pack.

	MT
Complete Set (528):	100.00
Common Player:	.10
Veteran Stars:	4X
Young Stars:	2X

(See 1992 Leaf for checklist and base card values)

1992 Leaf Gold Rookies

Two dozen of the major leagues' most promising players are featured in this insert set. Cards 1-12 were randomly included in Series I foil packs, while cards 13-24 were in Series II packs. Cards, numbered with a BC prefix, are standard size and enhanced with gold foil.

		MT
Complete Set (24):		10.00
Common Player:		.25
1	Chad Curtis	.25
2	Brent Gates	.40
3	Pedro Martinez	2.50
4	Kenny Lofton	4.00
5	Turk Wendell	.25
6	Mark Hutton	.25
7	Todd Hundley	.75
8	Matt Stairs	.25
9	Ed Taubensee	.25
10	David Nied	.25
11	Salomon Torres	.25
12	Bret Boone	.40
13	John Ruffin	.25
14	Ed Martel	.25
15	Rick Trlicek	.25
16	Raul Mondesi	2.00
17	Pat Mahomes	.35
18	Dan Wilson	.25
19	Donovan Osborne	.25
20	Dave Silvestri	.25
21	Gary DiSarcina	.25
22	Denny Neagle	.25
23	Steve Hosey	.25
24	John Doherty	.25

1993 Leaf

Leaf issued this set in three series: two 220-card series and a 110-card update set. Card fronts have full-bleed action photos and players' names stamped in gold foil. Color-coded slate corners are used to differentiate teams. Backs have player photos against cityscapes or landmarks from the team's home city, a holographic embossed team logo and 1992 and career statistics. Players from the National League's expansion teams, the Colorado Rockies and Florida Marlins, along with the Cincinnati Reds, California Angels and Seattle Mariners were featured in Series II packs so they could be pictured in their new uniforms. The Update series included a specially numbered "DW" insert card honoring Dave Winfield's 3,000-hit landmark, plus 3,500 special Frank Thomas autographed cards.

		MT
Complete Set (550):		35.00
Common Player:		.10
Series 1 or 2 Pack (14):		1.00
Series 1 or 2 Wax Box (36):		30.00
Update Pack (14):		1.50
Update Wax Box (36):		40.00
1	Ben McDonald	.10
2	Sid Fernandez	.10
3	Juan Guzman	.10
4	Curt Schilling	.15
5	Ivan Rodriguez	.65
6	Don Slaught	.10
7	Terry Steinbach	.10
8	Todd Zeile	.15
9	Andy Stankiewicz	.10
10	Tim Teufel	.10
11	Marvin Freeman	.10
12	Jim Austin	.10
13	Bob Scanlan	.10
14	Rusty Meacham	.10
15	Casey Candaele	.10
16	Travis Fryman	.20
17	Jose Offerman	.10
18	Albert Belle	.75
19	John Vander Wahl (Vander Wal)	.10
20	Dan Pasqua	.10
21	Frank Viola	.10
22	Terry Mulholland	.10
23	Gregg Olson	.10
24	Randy Tomlin	.10
25	Todd Stottlemyre	.10
26	Jose Oquendo	.10
27	Julio Franco	.10

No.	Player	Value
28	Tony Gwynn	1.25
29	Ruben Sierra	.10
30	Bobby Thigpen	.10
31	Jim Bullinger	.10
32	Rick Aguilera	.10
33	Scott Servais	.10
34	Cal Eldred	.10
35	Mike Piazza	2.00
36	Brent Mayne	.10
37	Wil Cordero	.10
38	Milt Cuyler	.10
39	Howard Johnson	.10
40	Kenny Lofton	.75
41	Alex Fernandez	.15
42	Denny Neagle	.10
43	Tony Pena	.10
44	Bob Tewksbury	.10
45	Glenn Davis	.10
46	Fred McGriff	.25
47	John Olerud	.20
48	Steve Hosey	.10
49	Rafael Palmeiro	.20
50	Dave Justice	.20
51	Pete Harnisch	.10
52	Sam Militello	.10
53	Orel Hershiser	.15
54	Pat Mahomes	.10
55	Greg Colbrunn	.10
56	Greg Vaughn	.15
57	Vince Coleman	.10
58	Brian McRae	.10
59	Len Dykstra	.10
60	Dan Gladden	.10
61	Ted Power	.10
62	Donovan Osborne	.10
63	Ron Karkovice	.10
64	Frank Seminara	.10
65	Bob Zupcic	.10
66	Kirt Manwaring	.10
67	Mike Devereaux	.10
68	Mark Lemke	.10
69	Devon White	.10
70	Sammy Sosa	1.50
71	Pedro Astacio	.10
72	Dennis Eckersley	.15
73	Chris Nabholz	.10
74	Melido Perez	.10
75	Todd Hundley	.20
76	Kent Hrbek	.10
77	Mickey Morandini	.10
78	Tim McIntosh	.10
79	Andy Van Slyke	.10
80	Kevin McReynolds	.10
81	Mike Henneman	.10
82	Greg Harris	.10
83	Sandy Alomar Jr.	.15
84	Mike Jackson	.10
85	Ozzie Guillen	.10
86	Jeff Blauser	.10
87	John Valentin	.20
88	Rey Sanchez	.10
89	Rick Sutcliffe	.10
90	Luis Gonzalez	.10
91	Jeff Fassero	.10
92	Kenny Rogers	.10
93	Bret Saberhagen	.10
94	Bob Welch	.10
95	Darren Daulton	.10
96	Mike Gallego	.10
97	Orlando Merced	.10
98	Chuck Knoblauch	.25
99	Bernard Gilkey	.10
100	Billy Ashley	.10
101	Kevin Appier	.10
102	Jeff Brantley	.10
103	Bill Gullickson	.10
104	John Smoltz	.20
105	Paul Sorrento	.10
106	Steve Buechele	.10
107	Steve Sax	.10
108	Andujar Cedeno	.10
109	Billy Hatcher	.10
110	Checklist	.10
111	Alan Mills	.10
112	John Franco	.10
113	Jack Morris	.10
114	Mitch Williams	.10
115	Nolan Ryan	2.00
116	Jay Bell	.10
117	Mike Bordick	.10
118	Geronimo Pena	.10
119	Danny Tartabull	.10
120	Checklist	.10
121	Steve Avery	.10
122	Ricky Bones	.10
123	Mike Morgan	.10
124	Jeff Montgomery	.10
125	Jeff Bagwell	1.00
126	Tony Phillips	.10
127	Lenny Harris	.10
128	Glenallen Hill	.10
129	Marquis Grissom	.15
130	Bernie Williams (name on front is Gerald Williams)	.60
131	Greg Harris	.10
132	Tommy Greene	.10
133	Chris Hoiles	.10
134	Bob Walk	.10
135	Duane Ward	.10
136	Tom Pagnozzi	.10
137	Jeff Huson	.10
138	Kurt Stillwell	.10
139	Dave Henderson	.10
140	Darrin Jackson	.10
141	Frank Castillo	.10
142	Scott Erickson	.10
143	Darryl Kile	.10
144	Bill Wegman	.10
145	Steve Wilson	.10
146	George Brett	.75
147	Moises Alou	.15
148	Lou Whitaker	.10
149	Chico Walker	.10
150	Jerry Browne	.10
151	Kirk McCaskill	.10
152	Zane Smith	.10
153	Matt Young	.10
154	Lee Smith	.15
155	Leo Gomez	.10
156	Dan Walters	.10
157	Pat Borders	.10
158	Matt Williams	.25
159	Dean Palmer	.15
160	John Patterson	.10
161	Doug Jones	.10
162	John Habyan	.10
163	Pedro Martinez	.35
164	Carl Willis	.10
165	Darrin Fletcher	.10
166	B.J. Surhoff	.10
167	Eddie Murray	.40
168	Keith Miller	.10
169	Ricky Jordan	.10
170	Juan Gonzalez	.75
171	Charles Nagy	.10
172	Mark Clark	.10
173	Bobby Thigpen	.10
174	Tim Scott	.10
175	Scott Cooper	.10
176	Royce Clayton	.10
177	Brady Anderson	.15
178	Sid Bream	.10
179	Derek Bell	.15
180	Otis Nixon	.10
181	Kevin Gross	.10
182	Ron Darling	.10
183	John Wetteland	.10
184	Mike Stanley	.10
185	Jeff Kent	.10
186	Brian Harper	.10
187	Mariano Duncan	.10
188	Robin Yount	.50
189	Al Martin	.10
190	Eddie Zosky	.10
191	Mike Munoz	.10
192	Andy Benes	.10
193	Dennis Cook	.10
194	Bill Swift	.10
195	Frank Thomas	1.50
196	Damon Berryhill	.10
197	Mike Greenwell	.10
198	Mark Grace	.20
199	Darryl Hamilton	.10
200	Derrick May	.10
201	Ken Hill	.10
202	Kevin Brown	.15
203	Dwight Gooden	.15
204	Bobby Witt	.10
205	Juan Bell	.10
206	Kevin Maas	.10
207	Jeff King	.10
208	Scott Leius	.10
209	Rheal Cormier	.10
210	Darryl Strawberry	.15
211	Tom Gordon	.10
212	Bud Black	.10
213	Mickey Tettleton	.10
214	Pete Smith	.10
215	Felix Fermin	.10
216	Rick Wilkins	.10
217	George Bell	.10
218	Eric Anthony	.10
219	Pedro Munoz	.10
220	Checklist	.10
221	Lance Blankenship	.10
222	Deion Sanders	.40
223	Craig Biggio	.20
224	Ryne Sandberg	.60
225	Ron Gant	.15
226	Tom Brunansky	.10
227	Chad Curtis	.10
228	Joe Carter	.15
229	Brian Jordan	.15
230	Brett Butler	.10
231	Frank Bolick	.10
232	Rod Beck	.10
233	Carlos Baerga	.10
234	Eric Karros	.15
235	Jack Armstrong	.10
236	Bobby Bonilla	.15
237	Don Mattingly	1.00
238	Jeff Gardner	.10
239	Dave Hollins	.10
240	Steve Cooke	.10
241	Jose Canseco	.25
242	Ivan Calderon	.10
243	Tim Belcher	.10
244	Freddie Benavides	.10
245	Roberto Alomar	.50
246	Rob Deer	.10
247	Will Clark	.25
248	Mike Felder	.10
249	Harold Baines	.15
250	David Cone	.15
251	Mark Guthrie	.10
252	Ellis Burks	.10
253	Jim Abbott	.15
254	Chili Davis	.10
255	Chris Bosio	.10
256	Bret Barberie	.10
257	Hal Morris	.10
258	Dante Bichette	.25
259	Storm Davis	.10
260	Gary DiSarcina	.10
261	Ken Caminiti	.25
262	Paul Molitor	.50
263	Joe Oliver	.10
264	Pat Listach	.10
265	Gregg Jefferies	.15
266	Jose Guzman	.10
267	Eric Davis	.15
268	Delino DeShields	.10
269	Barry Bonds	.75
270	Mike Bielecki	.10
271	Jay Buhner	.15
272	*Scott Pose*	.15
273	Tony Fernandez	.10
274	Chito Martinez	.10
275	Phil Plantier	.10
276	Pete Incaviglia	.10
277	Carlos Garcia	.10
278	Tom Henke	.10
279	Roger Clemens	1.00
280	Rob Dibble	.10
281	Daryl Boston	.10
282	Greg Gagne	.10
283	Cecil Fielder	.10
284	Carlton Fisk	.15
285	Wade Boggs	.25
286	Damion Easley	.10
287	Norm Charlton	.10
288	Jeff Conine	.15
289	Roberto Kelly	.10
290	Jerald Clark	.10
291	Rickey Henderson	.25
292	Chuck Finley	.10
293	Doug Drabek	.10
294	Dave Stewart	.10
295	Tom Glavine	.20
296	Jaime Navarro	.10
297	Ray Lankford	.15
298	Greg Hibbard	.10
299	Jody Reed	.10
300	Dennis Martinez	.10
301	Dave Martinez	.10
302	Reggie Jefferson	.10
303	*John Cummings*	.25
304	Orestes Destrade	.10
305	Mike Maddux	.10
306	David Segui	.10
307	Gary Sheffield	.30
308	Danny Jackson	.10
309	Criag Lefferts	.10
310	Andre Dawson	.15
311	Barry Larkin	.15
312	Alex Cole	.10
313	Mark Gardner	.10
314	Kirk Gibson	.10
315	Shane Mack	.10
316	Bo Jackson	.15
317	Jimmy Key	.10
318	Greg Myers	.10
319	Ken Griffey, Jr.	3.00
320	Monty Fariss	.10
321	Kevin Mitchell	.10
322	Andres Galarraga	.20
323	Mark McGwire	3.00
324	Mark Langston	.10
325	Steve Finley	.10
326	Greg Maddux	1.50
327	Dave Nilsson	.10
328	Ozzie Smith	.50
329	Candy Maldonado	.10
330	Checklist	.10
331	*Tim Pugh*	.10
332	Joe Girardi	.10
333	Junior Feliz	.10
334	Greg Swindell	.10
335	Ramon Martinez	.15
336	Sean Berry	.10
337	Joe Orsulak	.10
338	Wes Chamberlain	.10
339	Stan Belinda	.10
340	Checklist	.10
341	Bruce Hurst	.10
342	John Burkett	.10
343	Mike Mussina	.60
344	Scott Fletcher	.10
345	Rene Gonzales	.10
346	Roberto Hernandez	.10
347	Carlos Martinez	.10
348	Bill Krueger	.10
349	Felix Jose	.10
350	John Jaha	.15
351	Willie Banks	.10
352	Matt Nokes	.10
353	Kevin Seitzer	.10
354	Erik Hanson	.10
355	*David Hulse*	.10
356	*Domingo Martinez*	.10
357	Greg Olson	.10
358	Randy Myers	.10
359	Tom Browning	.10
360	Charlie Hayes	.10
361	Bryan Harvey	.10
362	Eddie Taubensee	.10
363	Tim Wallach	.10
364	Mel Rojas	.10
365	Frank Tanana	.10
366	John Kruk	.10
367	*Tim Laker*	.10
368	Rich Rodriguez	.10
369	Darren Lewis	.10
370	Harold Reynolds	.10
371	Jose Melendez	.10
372	Joe Grahe	.10
373	Lance Johnson	.10
374	Jose Mesa	.10
375	Scott Livingstone	.10
376	Wally Joyner	.10
377	Kevin Reimer	.10
378	Kirby Puckett	1.00
379	Paul O'Neill	.20
380	Randy Johnson	.40
381	Manuel Lee	.10
382	Dick Schofield	.10
383	Darren Holmes	.10
384	Charlie Hough	.10
385	John Orton	.10
386	Edgar Martinez	.10
387	Terry Pendleton	.10
388	Dan Plesac	.10
389	Jeff Reardon	.10
390	David Nied	.10
391	Dave Magadan	.10
392	Larry Walker	.25
393	Ben Rivera	.10
394	Lonnie Smith	.10
395	Craig Shipley	.10
396	Willie McGee	.10
397	Arthur Rhodes	.10
398	Mike Stanton	.10
399	Luis Polonia	.10
400	Jack McDowell	.10
401	Mike Moore	.10
402	Jose Lind	.10
403	Bill Spiers	.10
404	Kevin Tapani	.10
405	Spike Owen	.10
406	Tino Martinez	.25
407	Charlie Leibrandt	.10
408	Ed Sprague	.10
409	Bryn Smith	.10

410 Benito Santiago .10
411 Jose Rijo .10
412 Pete O'Brien .10
413 Willie Wilson .10
414 Bip Roberts .10
415 Eric Young .15
416 Walt Weiss .10
417 Milt Thompson .10
418 Chris Sabo .10
419 Scott Sanderson .10
420 Tim Raines .15
421 Alan Trammell .15
422 Mike Macfarlane .10
423 Dave Winfield .30
424 Bob Wickman .10
425 David Valie .10
426 Gary Redus .10
427 Turner Ward .10
428 Reggie Sanders .10
429 Todd Worrell .10
430 Julio Valera .10
431 Cal Ripken, Jr. 2.50
432 Mo Vaughn .65
433 John Smiley .10
434 Omar Vizquel .10
435 Billy Ripken .10
436 Cory Snyder .10
437 Carlos Quintana .10
438 Omar Olivares .10
439 Robin Ventura .15
440 Checklist .10
441 Kevin Higgins .10
442 Carlos Hernandez .10
443 Dan Peltier .10
444 Derek Lilliquist .10
445 Tim Salmon .50
446 *Sherman Obando* .10
447 Pat Kelly .10
448 Todd Van Poppel .10
449 Mark Whiten .10
450 Checklist .10
451 Pat Meares .10
452 *Tony Tarasco* .10
453 Chris Gwynn .10
454 Armando Reynoso .10
455 Danny Darwin .10
456 Willie Greene .10
457 Mike Blowers .10
458 *Kevin Roberson* .15
459 *Graeme Lloyd* .10
460 David West .10
461 Joey Cora .10
462 Alex Arias .10
463 Chad Kreuter .10
464 Mike Lansing .15
465 Mike Timlin .10
466 Paul Wagner .10
467 Mark Portugal .10
468 Jim Leyritz .10
469 Ryan Klesko .25
470 Mario Diaz .10
471 Guillermo Velasquez .10
472 Fernando Valenzuela .10
473 Raul Mondesi 1.50
474 Mike Pagliarulo .10
475 Chris Hammond .10
476 Torey Lovullo .10
477 Trevor Wilson .10
478 *Marcos Armas* .10
479 Dave Gallagher .10
480 Jeff Treadway .10
481 Jeff Branson .10
482 Dickie Thon .10
483 Eduardo Perez .10
484 David Wells .15
485 Brian Williams .10
486 Domingo Cedeno .10
487 Tom Candiotti .10
488 Steve Frey .10
489 Greg McMichael .10
490 Marc Newfield .10
491 Larry Andersen .10
492 Damon Buford .15
493 Ricky Gutierrez .10
494 Jeff Russell .10
495 Vinny Castilla .20
496 Wilson Alvarez .10
497 Scott Bullett .10
498 Larry Casian .10
499 Jose Vizcaino .10
500 *J.T. Snow* .75
501 Bryan Hickerson .10
502 Jeremy Hernandez .10
503 Jeromy Burnitz .15
504 Steve Farr .10
505 J. Owens .10
506 Craig Paquette .10
507 Jim Eisenreich .10
508 Matt Whiteside .10
509 Luis Aquino .10
510 Mike LaValliere .10
511 Jim Gott .10
512 Mark McLemore .10
513 Randy Milligan .10
514 Gary Gaetti .10
515 Lou Frazier .10
516 Rich Amaral .10
517 Gene Harris .10
518 Aaron Sele .15
519 Mark Wohlers .10
520 Scott Kamieniecki .10
521 Kent Mercker .10
522 Jim Deshaies .10
523 Kevin Stocker .10
524 Jason Bere .10
525 Tim Bogar .10
526 Brad Pennington .15
527 *Curt Leskanic* .15
528 Wayne Kirby .10
529 Tim Costo .10
530 Doug Henry .10
531 Trevor Hoffman .20
532 Kelly Gruber .10
533 Mike Harkey .10
534 John Doherty .10
535 Erik Pappas .10
536 Brent Gates .15
537 Roger McDowell .10
538 Chris Haney .10
539 Blas Minor .10
540 Pat Hentgen .10
541 Chuck Carr .10
542 Doug Strange .10
543 Xavier Hernandez .10
544 Paul Quantrill .10
545 Anthony Young .10
546 Bret Boone .15
547 Dwight Smith .10
548 Bobby Munoz .10
549 Russ Springer .10
550 Roger Pavlik .10
---- Dave Winfield (3000 Hits) 4.00
---- Frank Thomas (Autograph) 200.00

1993 Leaf Fasttrack

This 20-card insert set was released in two series; cards 1-10 were randomly included in Leaf Series I retail packs, while 11-20 were in Series II packs. Card fronts and backs are similar with a player photo and a diagonal white strip with "on the Fasttrack" printed in black and red. Fronts have the gold embossed Leaf logo, backs have the silver holographic team logo.

		MT
Complete Set (20):		60.00
Common Player:		1.50
1	Frank Thomas	12.00
2	Tim Wakefield	1.50
3	Kenny Lofton	6.00
4	Mike Mussina	4.00
5	Juan Gonzalez	8.00
6	Chuck Knoblauch	3.00
7	Eric Karros	2.00
8	Ray Lankford	1.50
9	Juan Guzman	1.50
10	Pat Listach	1.50
11	Carlos Baerga	1.50
12	Felix Jose	1.50
13	Steve Avery	1.50
14	Robin Ventura	2.50
15	Ivan Rodriguez	6.00
16	Cal Eldred	1.50
17	Jeff Bagwell	10.00
18	Dave Justice	3.00
19	Travis Fryman	1.50
20	Marquis Grissom	1.50

1993 Leaf Frank Thomas

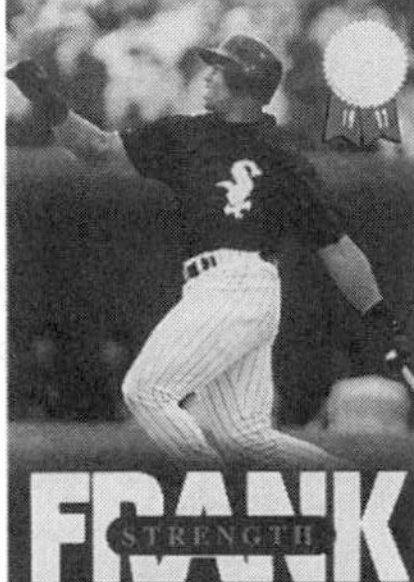

Leaf signed Frank Thomas as its spokesman for 1993, and honored him with a 10-card insert set. Cards 1-5 were randomly included in Series I packs; cards 6-10 were in Series II packs. A custom designed "Frank" logo in a holographic foil stamp is featured on each card front which includes a one-word character trait. On back is a color portrait photo of Thomas superimposed on a Chicago skyline. A paragraph on back describes how the character trait on front applies to Thomas.

		MT
Complete Set:		25.00
Common Card:		3.00
Autographed Card:		200.00
1	Aggressive (Frank Thomas)	3.00
2	Serious (Frank Thomas)	3.00
3	Intense (Frank Thomas)	3.00
4	Confident (Frank Thomas)	3.00
5	Assertive (Frank Thomas)	3.00
6	Power (Frank Thomas)	3.00
7	Control (Frank Thomas)	3.00
8	Strength (Frank Thomas)	3.00
9	Concentration (Frank Thomas)	3.00
10	Preparation (Frank Thomas)	3.00

1993 Leaf Gold All-Stars

Cards 1-10 in this insert set were randomly inserted one per Leaf Series I jumbo packs, while cards 11-20 were in Series II jumbo packs. Cards feature two players per card, one on each side. Only one side is numbered, but both sides have gold foil.

		MT
Complete Set (20):		35.00
Common Player:		.50
1	Ivan Rodriguez, Darren Daulton	1.50
2	Don Mattingly, Fred McGriff	2.50
3	Cecil Fielder, Jeff Bagwell	3.00
4	Carlos Baerga, Ryne Sandberg	2.00
5	Chuck Knoblauch, Delino DeShields	.50
6	Robin Ventura, Terry Pendleton	.75
7	Ken Griffey, Jr., Andy Van Slyke	7.50
8	Joe Carter, Dave Justice	1.00
9	Jose Canseco, Tony Gwynn	2.50
10	Dennis Eckersley, Rob Dibble	.50
11	Mark McGwire, Will Clark	7.50
12	Frank Thomas, Mark Grace	4.00
13	Roberto Alomar, Craig Biggio	2.00
14	Barry Larkin, Cal Ripken, Jr.	6.00
15	Gary Sheffield, Edgar Martinez	1.50
16	Juan Gonzalez, Barry Bonds	3.00
17	Kirby Puckett, Marquis Grissom	2.50
18	Jim Abbott, Tom Glavine	1.00
19	Nolan Ryan, Greg Maddux	7.50
20	Roger Clemens, Doug Drabek	2.00

1993 Leaf Gold Rookies

These cards, numbered 1 of 20 etc., feature 1993 rookies and were randomly inserted into hobby foil packs, 10 players per series. Card fronts feature action photos, while the backs show a player photo against a landmark from his team's city.

		MT
Complete Set (20):		40.00
Common Player:		.50
1	Kevin Young	.50
2	Wil Cordero	1.00
3	Mark Kiefer	.50
4	Gerald Williams	1.00
5	Brandon Wilson	.50
6	Greg Gohr	.50
7	Ryan Thompson	1.50
8	Tim Wakefield	.50
9	Troy Neel	1.00
10	Tim Salmon	8.00
11	Kevin Rogers	.50
12	Rod Bolton	.50
13	Ken Ryan	.50
14	Phil Hiatt	.50
15	Rene Arocha	1.00
16	Nigel Wilson	.50
17	J.T. Snow	3.00
18	Benji Gil	.50
19	Chipper Jones	18.00
20	Darrell Sherman	.50

1993 Leaf Heading for the Hall

Ten players on the way to the Baseball Hall of Fame are featured in this insert set. Series I Leaf packs had cards 1-5 randomly included; Series II packs had cards 6-10.

		MT
Complete Set (10):		30.00
Common Player:		2.00
1	Nolan Ryan	9.00
2	Tony Gwynn	5.00
3	Robin Yount	2.50
4	Eddie Murray	2.00
5	Cal Ripken, Jr.	12.00
6	Roger Clemens	4.00
7	George Brett	4.00
8	Ryne Sandberg	3.00
9	Kirby Puckett	6.00
10	Ozzie Smith	3.00

1993 Leaf Update Gold All-Stars

These 10 cards, featuring 20 all-stars, were randomly inserted in Leaf Update packs. Each card features two players, one on each side. Cards are distinguished from the regular Gold All-Stars by indicating on the front the card is number X of 10, with a tiny white "Update" in the red stripe above the card number.

		MT
Complete Set (10):		15.00
Common Player:		.50
1	Mark Langston, Terry Mulholland	.50
2	Ivan Rodriguez, Darren Daulton	1.00
3	John Olerud, John Kruk	.50
4	Roberto Alomar, Ryne Sandberg	2.00
5	Wade Boggs, Gary Sheffield	1.00
6	Cal Ripken, Jr., Barry Larkin	6.00
7	Kirby Puckett, Barry Bonds	4.00
8	Marquis Grissom, Ken Griffey Jr.	7.50
9	Joe Carter, Dave Justice	1.00
10	Mark Grace, Paul Molitor	1.50

1993 Leaf Update Gold Rookies

These five cards were randomly inserted in Leaf Update packs. Cards are similiar in design to the regular Gold Rookies cards, except the logo on the back indicates they are from the Update series.

		MT
Complete Set (5):		22.00
Common Player:		2.00
1	Allen Watson	2.00
2	Jeffrey Hammonds	2.00
3	David McCarty	2.00
4	Mike Piazza	20.00
5	Roberto Meija	2.00

1993 Leaf Update Frank Thomas Super

This 10-card insert set features Leaf's 1993 spokesman, Frank Thomas. Cards, which measure 5" x 7", were included one per every Leaf Update foil box and are identical to the inserts found in Series I and II except in size. Cards are individually numbered. Thomas autographed 3,500 cards.

		MT
Complete Set (10):		45.00
Common Thomas:		5.00
1	Aggressive (Frank Thomas)	5.00
2	Serious (Frank Thomas)	5.00
3	Intense (Frank Thomas)	5.00
4	Confident (Frank Thomas)	5.00
5	Assertive (Frank Thomas)	5.00
6	Power (Frank Thomas)	5.00
7	Control (Frank Thomas)	5.00
8	Strength (Frank Thomas)	5.00
9	Concentration (Frank Thomas)	5.00
10	Preparation (Frank Thomas)	5.00

1993 Leaf Update Frank Thomas Autograph

This card was a random insert in '93 Leaf Update packs and features a genuine Frank Thomas autograph on front. Unlike the other cards in the set, this has a silver-gray border on front and back. Front has a gold-foil seal in upper-left. Back has a photo of Thomas in his batting follow-through. At bottom on back is a white strip bearing the card's individual serial number from within an edition of 3,500.

		MT
FT	Frank Thomas	125.00

1994 Leaf Promos

Identical in format to the regular issue, this nine-card set was produced as a preview for the 1994 Leaf cards. The only differences on the promo cards are a large, black "Promotional Sample" notice overprinted diagonally on both the front and back of the cards. Instead of the regular card numbers, the promos are numbered "X of 9" at top to the left of the team logo hologram.

		MT
Complete Set (9):		20.00
Common Player:		1.00
1	Roberto Alomar	2.00
2	Darren Daulton	1.00
3	Ken Griffey, Jr.	6.00
4	David Justice	2.00
5	Don Mattingly	4.00
6	Mike Piazza	4.00
7	Cal Ripken, Jr.	5.00
8	Ryne Sandberg	3.00
9	Frank Thomas	3.00

1994 Leaf

Donruss returned its premium-brand Leaf set in

1994 with an announced 25% production cut from the previous season - fewer than 20,000 20-box cases of each 220-card series. Game-action photos dominate the fronts of the cards, borderless at the top and sides. At bottom are team color-coded faux-marble borders with the player's name (last name in gold foil) and team. Backs have a background of the player's home stadium with another action photo superimposed. In a ticket-stub device at upper-left is a portrait photo and a few personal numbers. Previous season and career stats are in white stripes at bottom. The team logo is presented in holographic foil at upper-right. To feature 1994's new stadiums and uniforms, cards of the Indians, Rangers, Brewers and Astros were included only in the second series. Seven different types of insert cards were produced and distributed among the various types of Leaf packaging.

		MT
Complete Set (440):		30.00
Complete Series 1 (220):		15.00
Complete Series 2 (220):		15.00
Common Player:		.10
Series 1 or 2 Pack (12):		1.25
Series 1 or 2 Wax Box (36):		40.00
1	Cal Ripken, Jr.	2.50
2	Tony Tarasco	.10
3	Joe Girardi	.10
4	Bernie Williams	.60
5	Chad Kreuter	.10
6	Troy Neel	.15
7	Tom Pagnozzi	.10
8	Kirk Rueter	.10
9	Chris Bosio	.10
10	Dwight Gooden	.15
11	Mariano Duncan	.10
12	Jay Bell	.10
13	Lance Johnson	.10
14	Richie Lewis	.10
15	Dave Martinez	.10
16	Orel Hershiser	.15
17	Rob Butler	.10
18	Glenallen Hill	.10
19	Chad Curtis	.10
20	Mike Stanton	.10
21	Tim Wallach	.10
22	Milt Thompson	.10
23	Kevin Young	.10
24	John Smiley	.10
25	Jeff Montgomery	.10
26	Robin Ventura	.20
27	Scott Lydy	.10
28	Todd Stottlemyre	.10
29	Mark Whiten	.10
30	Robby Thompson	.10
31	Bobby Bonilla	.15
32	Andy Ashby	.10
33	Greg Myers	.10
34	Billy Hatcher	.10
35	Brad Holman	.10
36	Mark McLemore	.10
37	Scott Sanders	.10
38	Jim Abbott	.10
39	David Wells	.15
40	Roberto Kelly	.10
41	Jeff Conine	.10
42	Sean Berry	.10
43	Mark Grace	.20
44	Eric Young	.10
45	Rick Aguilera	.10
46	Chipper Jones	1.50
47	Mel Rojas	.10
48	Ryan Thompson	.10
49	Al Martin	.10
50	Cecil Fielder	.15
51	Pat Kelly	.10
52	Kevin Tapani	.10
53	Tim Costo	.10
54	Dave Hollins	.10
55	Kirt Manwaring	.10
56	Gregg Jefferies	.15
57	Ron Darling	.10
58	Bill Haselman	.10
59	Phil Plantier	.10
60	Frank Viola	.10
61	Todd Zeile	.10
62	Bret Barberie	.10
63	Roberto Mejia	.10
64	Chuck Knoblauch	.15
65	Jose Lind	.10
66	Brady Anderson	.15
67	Ruben Sierra	.10
68	Jose Vizcaino	.10
69	Joe Grahe	.10
70	Kevin Appier	.10
71	Wilson Alvarez	.10
72	Tom Candiotti	.10
73	John Burkett	.10
74	Anthony Young	.10
75	Scott Cooper	.10
76	Nigel Wilson	.10
77	John Valentin	.10
78	Dave McCarty	.10
79	Archi Cianfrocco	.10
80	Lou Whitaker	.10
81	Dante Bichette	.15
82	Mark Dewey	.10
83	Danny Jackson	.10
84	Harold Baines	.10
85	Todd Benzinger	.10
86	Damion Easley	.10
87	Danny Cox	.10
88	Jose Bautista	.10
89	Mike Lansing	.10
90	Phil Hiatt	.10
91	Tim Pugh	.10
92	Tino Martinez	.20
93	Raul Mondesi	.40
94	Greg Maddux	1.50
95	Al Leiter	.15
96	Benito Santiago	.10
97	Len Dykstra	.10
98	Sammy Sosa	1.50
99	Tim Bogar	.10
100	Checklist	.10
101	Deion Sanders	.20
102	Bobby Witt	.10
103	Wil Cordero	.10
104	Rich Amaral	.10
105	Mike Mussina	.40
106	Reggie Sanders	.10
107	Ozzie Guillen	.10
108	Paul O'Neill	.15
109	Tim Salmon	.35
110	Rheal Cormier	.10
111	Billy Ashley	.10
112	Jeff Kent	.10
113	Derek Bell	.15
114	Danny Darwin	.10
115	Chip Hale	.10
116	Tim Raines	.10
117	Ed Sprague	.10
118	Darrin Fletcher	.10
119	Darren Holmes	.10
120	Alan Trammell	.15
121	Don Mattingly	1.00
122	Greg Gagne	.10
123	Jose Offerman	.10
124	Joe Orsulak	.10
125	Jack McDowell	.10
126	Barry Larkin	.25
127	Ben McDonald	.10
128	Mike Bordick	.10
129	Devon White	.10
130	Mike Perez	.10
131	Jay Buhner	.10
132	Phil Leftwich	.10
133	Tommy Greene	.10
134	Charlie Hayes	.10
135	Don Slaught	.10
136	Mike Gallego	.10
137	Dave Winfield	.25
138	Steve Avery	.10
139	Derrick May	.10
140	Bryan Harvey	.10
141	Wally Joyner	.10
142	Andre Dawson	.15
143	Andy Benes	.10
144	John Franco	.10
145	Jeff King	.10
146	Joe Oliver	.10
147	Bill Gullickson	.10
148	Armando Reynoso	.10
149	Dave Fleming	.10
150	Checklist	.10
151	Todd Van Poppel	.10
152	Bernard Gilkey	.10
153	Kevin Gross	.10
154	Mike Devereaux	.10
155	Tim Wakefield	.10
156	Andres Galarraga	.40
157	Pat Meares	.10
158	Jim Leyritz	.10
159	Mike Macfarlane	.10
160	Tony Phillips	.10
161	Brent Gates	.10
162	Mark Langston	.10
163	Allen Watson	.10
164	Randy Johnson	.75
165	Doug Brocail	.10
166	Rob Dibble	.10
167	Roberto Hernandez	.10
168	Felix Jose	.10
169	Steve Cooke	.10
170	Darren Daulton	.10
171	Eric Karros	.10
172	Geronimo Pena	.10
173	Gary DiSarcina	.10
174	Marquis Grissom	.10
175	Joey Cora	.10
176	Jim Eisenreich	.10
177	Brad Pennington	.10
178	Terry Steinbach	.10
179	Pat Borders	.10
180	Steve Buechele	.10
181	Jeff Fassero	.10
182	Mike Greenwell	.10
183	Mike Henneman	.10
184	Ron Karkovice	.10
185	Pat Hentgen	.10
186	Jose Guzman	.10
187	Brett Butler	.10
188	Charlie Hough	.10
189	Terry Pendleton	.10
190	Melido Perez	.10
191	Orestes Destrade	.10
192	Mike Morgan	.10
193	Joe Carter	.10
194	Jeff Blauser	.10
195	Chris Hoiles	.10
196	Ricky Gutierrez	.10
197	Mike Moore	.10
198	Carl Willis	.10
199	Aaron Sele	.10
200	Checklist	.10
201	Tim Naehring	.10
202	Scott Livingstone	.10
203	Luis Alicea	.10
204	*Torey Lovullo*	.10
205	Jim Gott	.10
206	Bob Wickman	.10
207	Greg McMichael	.10
208	Scott Brosius	.10
209	Chris Gwynn	.10
210	Steve Sax	.10
211	Dick Schofield	.10
212	Robb Nen	.10
213	Ben Rivera	.10
214	Vinny Castilla	.15
215	Jamie Moyer	.10
216	Wally Whitehurst	.10
217	Frank Castillo	.10
218	Mike Blowers	.10
219	Tim Scott	.10
220	Paul Wagner	.10
221	Jeff Bagwell	.75
222	Ricky Bones	.10
223	Sandy Alomar Jr.	.15
224	Rod Beck	.10
225	Roberto Alomar	.60
226	Jack Armstrong	.10
227	Scott Erickson	.10
228	Rene Arocha	.10
229	Eric Anthony	.10
230	Jeromy Burnitz	.15
231	Kevin Brown	.15
232	Tim Belcher	.10
233	Bret Boone	.10
234	Dennis Eckersley	.10
235	Tom Glavine	.20
236	Craig Biggio	.20
237	Pedro Astacio	.10
238	Ryan Bowen	.10
239	Brad Ausmus	.10
240	Vince Coleman	.10
241	Jason Bere	.10
242	Ellis Burks	.10
243	Wes Chamberlain	.10
244	Ken Caminiti	.15
245	Willie Banks	.10
246	Sid Fernandez	.10
247	Carlos Baerga	.10
248	Carlos Garcia	.10
249	Jose Canseco	.40
250	Alex Diaz	.10
251	Albert Belle	.60
252	Moises Alou	.15
253	Bobby Ayala	.10
254	Tony Gwynn	1.25
255	Roger Clemens	1.00
256	Eric Davis	.15
257	Wade Boggs	.30
258	Chili Davis	.10
259	Rickey Henderson	.35
260	Andujar Cedeno	.10
261	Cris Carpenter	.10
262	Juan Guzman	.10
263	Dave Justice	.20
264	Barry Bonds	.75
265	Pete Incaviglia	.10
266	Tony Fernandez	.10
267	Cal Eldred	.10
268	Alex Fernandez	.10
269	Kent Hrbek	.10
270	Steve Farr	.10
271	Doug Drabek	.10
272	Brian Jordan	.15
273	Xavier Hernandez	.10
274	David Cone	.15
275	Brian Hunter	.10
276	Mike Harkey	.10
277	Delino DeShields	.10
278	David Hulse	.10
279	Mickey Tettleton	.10
280	Kevin McReynolds	.10
281	Darryl Hamilton	.10
282	Ken Hill	.10
283	Wayne Kirby	.10
284	Chris Hammond	.10
285	Mo Vaughn	.60
286	Ryan Klesko	.25
287	Rick Wilkins	.10
288	Bill Swift	.10
289	Rafael Palmeiro	.40
290	Brian Harper	.10
291	Chris Turner	.10
292	Luis Gonzalez	.10
293	Kenny Rogers	.10
294	Kirby Puckett	1.00
295	Mike Stanley	.10
296	Carlos Reyes	.10
297	Charles Nagy	.10
298	Reggie Jefferson	.10
299	Bip Roberts	.10
300	Darrin Jackson	.10
301	Mike Jackson	.10
302	Dave Nilsson	.10
303	Ramon Martinez	.15
304	Bobby Jones	.10
305	Johnny Ruffin	.10
306	Brian McRae	.10
307	Bo Jackson	.15
308	Dave Stewart	.10
309	John Smoltz	.15
310	Dennis Martinez	.10
311	Dean Palmer	.10
312	David Nied	.10
313	Eddie Murray	.25
314	Darryl Kile	.10
315	Rick Sutcliffe	.10
316	Shawon Dunston	.10
317	John Jaha	.10
318	Salomon Torres	.10
319	Gary Sheffield	.15
320	Curt Schilling	.15
321	Greg Vaughn	.10
322	Jay Howell	.10
323	Todd Hundley	.15
324	Chris Sabo	.10
325	Stan Javier	.10
326	Willie Greene	.10
327	Hipolito Pichardo	.10
328	Doug Strange	.10
329	Dan Wilson	.10
330	Checklist	.10
331	Omar Vizquel	.10

332	Scott Servais	.10
333	Bob Tewksbury	.10
334	Matt Williams	.30
335	Tom Foley	.10
336	Jeff Russell	.10
337	Scott Leius	.10
338	Ivan Rodriguez	.75
339	Kevin Seitzer	.10
340	Jose Rijo	.10
341	Eduardo Perez	.10
342	Kirk Gibson	.10
343	Randy Milligan	.10
344	Edgar Martinez	.10
345	Fred McGriff	.25
346	Kurt Abbott	.10
347	John Kruk	.10
348	Mike Felder	.10
349	Dave Staton	.10
350	Kenny Lofton	.60
351	Graeme Lloyd	.10
352	David Segui	.10
353	Danny Tartabull	.10
354	Bob Welch	.10
355	Duane Ward	.10
356	Tuffy Rhodes	.10
357	Lee Smith	.10
358	Chris James	.10
359	Walt Weiss	.10
360	Pedro Munoz	.10
361	Paul Sorrento	.10
362	Todd Worrell	.10
363	Bob Hamelin	.10
364	Julio Franco	.10
365	Roberto Petagine	.10
366	Willie McGee	.10
367	Pedro Martinez	.75
368	Ken Griffey, Jr.	3.00
369	B.J. Surhoff	.10
370	Kevin Mitchell	.10
371	John Doherty	.10
372	Manuel Lee	.10
373	Terry Mulholland	.10
374	Zane Smith	.10
375	Otis Nixon	.10
376	Jody Reed	.10
377	Doug Jones	.10
378	John Olerud	.20
379	Greg Swindell	.10
380	Checklist	.10
381	Royce Clayton	.10
382	Jim Thome	.40
383	Steve Finley	.10
384	Ray Lankford	.10
385	Henry Rodriguez	.10
386	Dave Magadan	.10
387	Gary Redus	.10
388	Orlando Merced	.10
389	Tom Gordon	.10
390	Luis Polonia	.10
391	Mark McGwire	3.00
392	Mark Lemke	.10
393	Doug Henry	.10
394	Chuck Finley	.10
395	Paul Molitor	.40
396	Randy Myers	.10
397	Larry Walker	.20
398	Pete Harnisch	.10
399	Darren Lewis	.10
400	Frank Thomas	1.00
401	Jack Morris	.10
402	Greg Hibbard	.10
403	Jeffrey Hammonds	.10
404	Will Clark	.25
405	Travis Fryman	.15
406	Scott Sanderson	.10
407	Gene Harris	.10
408	Chuck Carr	.10
409	Ozzie Smith	.50
410	Kent Mercker	.10
411	Andy Van Slyke	.10
412	Jimmy Key	.10
413	Pat Mahomes	.10
414	John Wetteland	.10
415	Todd Jones	.10
416	Greg Harris	.10
417	Kevin Stocker	.10
418	Juan Gonzalez	.75
419	Pete Smith	.10
420	Pat Listach	.10
421	Trevor Hoffman	.15
422	Scott Fletcher	.10
423	Mark Lewis	.10
424	Mickey Morandini	.10
425	Ryne Sandberg	.75
426	Erik Hanson	.10
427	Gary Gaetti	.10
428	Harold Reynolds	.10
429	Mark Portugal	.10
430	David Valle	.10
431	Mitch Williams	.10
432	Howard Johnson	.10
433	Hal Morris	.10
434	Tom Henke	.10
435	Shane Mack	.10
436	Mike Piazza	2.00
437	Bret Saberhagen	.10
438	Jose Mesa	.10
439	Jaime Navarro	.10
440	Checklist	.10

1994 Leaf Clean-Up Crew

The number four spot in the line-up is featured on this 12-card insert set (six per series) found only in magazine distributor packaging. Fronts are gold-foil enhanced; backs feature an action photo set against a background of a lineup card on which the player is pencilled into the #4 spot. His 1993 stats when batting clean-up are presented.

		MT
Complete Set (12):		20.00
Common Player:		1.00
1	Larry Walker	2.50
2	Andres Galarraga	2.50
3	Dave Hollins	1.00
4	Bobby Bonilla	1.00
5	Cecil Fielder	1.00
6	Danny Tartabull	1.00
7	Juan Gonzalez	5.00
8	Joe Carter	1.00
9	Fred McGriff	2.00
10	Matt Williams	2.00
11	Albert Belle	5.00
12	Harold Baines	1.00

1994 Leaf 5th Anniversary

The card which insured the success of the Leaf brand name when it was re-introduced in 1990, the Frank Thomas rookie card, was re-issued in a 5th anniversary commemorative form as an insert in the 1994 set. On the chase card, silver foil rays emanate from the White Sox logo at lower-left, while a silver-foil 5th anniversary logo at upper-right replaces the Leaf script on the 1990 version. The card back carries a 1994 copyright. The Thomas anniversary card is found on average of once every 36 Series I hobby packs.

		MT
300	Frank Thomas	2.50

1994 Leaf Frank Thomas Super

An edition of 20,000 super-size versions of Frank Thomas' 1994 Leaf card was produced for inclusion in Series II hobby boxes as a bonus. Except for its 5" x 7" format and a white strip on back bearing a serial number, the card is identical to the normal-size issue.

		MT
400	Frank Thomas	8.00

1994 Leaf Gamers

Leaf jumbo packs are the exclusive venue for the six cards of this insert set which were issued in each series.

		MT
Complete Set (12):		65.00
Common Player:		1.50
1	Ken Griffey, Jr.	20.00
2	Len Dykstra	1.00
3	Juan Gonzalez	5.00
4	Don Mattingly	6.00
5	Dave Justice	2.00
6	Mark Grace	2.00
7	Frank Thomas	8.00
8	Barry Bonds	5.00
9	Kirby Puckett	5.00
10	Will Clark	2.00
11	John Kruk	1.00
12	Mike Piazza	15.00

1994 Leaf Gold Rookies

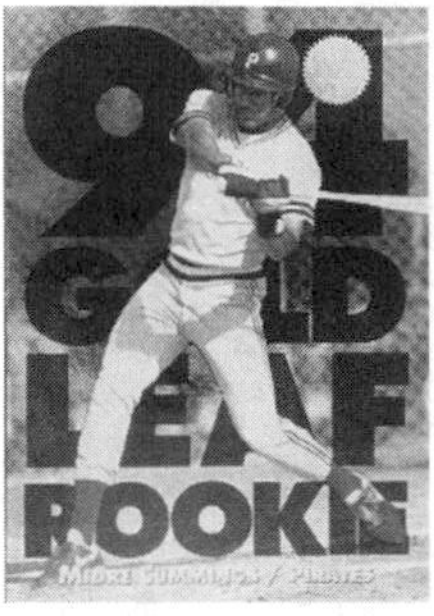

A gold-foil rendered stadium background and huge black "94 Gold Leaf Rookie" serve as a backdrop for a player photo on these insert cards found at the rate of about one per 18 foil packs. The player's name and team are in silver at bottom. Horizontal backs have a ghosted action photo of the player in the background. A portrait photo is in the upper-right corner, above some personal data and stats. Cards are numbered "X of 20".

		MT
Complete Set (20):		15.00
Common Player:		.50
1	Javier Lopez	2.00
2	Rondell White	2.50
3	Butch Huskey	.75
4	Midre Cummings	.50
5	Scott Ruffcorn	.50
6	Manny Ramirez	6.00
7	Danny Bautista	.50
8	Russ Davis	.50
9	Steve Karsay	.50
10	Carlos Delgado	4.00
11	Bob Hamelin	.50
12	Marcus Moore	.50
13	Miguel Jimenez	.50
14	Matt Walbeck	.50
15	James Mouton	.50
16	Rich Becker	.50
17	Brian Anderson	.50
18	Cliff Floyd	.75
19	Steve Trachsel	.75
20	Hector Carrasco	.50

1994 Leaf Gold Stars

The "Cadillac" of 1994 Leaf inserts, this 15-card series (#1-8 in Series I; 9-15 in Series II) is found on average only one card per 90 packs. The edition of 10,000 of each player's card is serially numbered. Fronts feature a rather small photo in a diamond-shaped frame against a green marble-look background. The border, facsimile autograph and several other graphic elements are presented in prismatic foil. The back repeats the basic front design with a few sentences about the player and a serial number strip at bottom.

		MT
Complete Set (15):		140.00
Common Player:		5.00
1	Roberto Alomar	8.00
2	Barry Bonds	10.00
3	Dave Justice	6.00
4	Ken Griffey, Jr.	40.00
5	Len Dykstra	5.00
6	Don Mattingly	15.00
7	Andres Galarraga	6.00
8	Greg Maddux	25.00
9	Carlos Baerga	5.00
10	Paul Molitor	7.50
11	Frank Thomas	15.00
12	John Olerud	6.00
13	Juan Gonzalez	10.00
14	Fred McGriff	6.00
15	Jack McDowell	5.00

1994 Leaf MVP Contenders

Found on an average of about once per 36-pack foil box, these inserts were produced in an edition of 10,000 each. Cards found in packs were marked "Silver Collection" on the horizontal fronts, and featured a silver-foil Leaf seal and other enhancements. Persons holding cards of the players selected as N.L. and A.L. MVPs could trade in their Contender card for an individually numbered 5" x 7" card of Leaf spokesman Frank Thomas and be entered in a drawing for one of 5,000 Gold Collection MVP Contender 28-card sets. Winning cards were punch-cancelled and returned to the winner along with his prize.

		MT
Complete Set, Silver:		150.00
Complete Set, Gold:		200.00
Common Player, Silver:		1.00
Common Player, Gold:		2.00
AMERICAN LEAGUE		8.00
1a	Albert Belle (silver)	4.00
1b	Albert Belle (gold)	8.00
2a	Jose Canseco (silver)	3.00
2b	Jose Canseco (gold)	6.00
3a	Joe Carter (silver)	2.00
3b	Joe Carter (gold)	4.00
4a	Will Clark (silver)	2.00
4b	Will Clark (gold)	4.00
5a	Cecil Fielder (silver)	1.00
5b	Cecil Fielder (gold)	2.00
6a	Juan Gonzalez (silver)	8.00
6b	Juan Gonzalez (gold)	15.00
7a	Ken Griffey, Jr. (silver)	35.00
7b	Ken Griffey, Jr. (gold)	60.00
8a	Paul Molitor (silver)	4.00
8b	Paul Molitor (gold)	8.00
9a	Rafael Palmeiro (silver)	2.00
9b	Rafael Palmeiro (gold)	4.00
10a	Kirby Puckett (silver)	8.00
10b	Kirby Puckett (gold)	15.00
11a	Cal Ripken, Jr. (silver)	25.00
11b	Cal Ripken, Jr. (gold)	50.00
12a	Frank Thomas (silver)	12.50
12b	Frank Thomas (gold)	25.00
13a	Mo Vaughn (silver)	2.00
13b	Mo Vaughn (gold)	4.00
14a	Carlos Baerga (silver)	1.00
14b	Carlos Baerga (gold)	2.00
15	AL Bonus Card (silver)	2.00
NATIONAL LEAGUE		2.50
1a	Gary Sheffield (silver)	2.50
1b	Gary Sheffield (gold)	5.00
2a	Jeff Bagwell (silver)	12.00
2b	Jeff Bagwell (gold)	24.00
3a	Dante Bichette (silver)	1.00
3b	Dante Bichette (gold)	2.00
4a	Barry Bonds (silver)	5.00
4b	Barry Bonds (gold)	10.00
5a	Darren Daulton (silver)	1.00
5b	Darren Daulton (gold)	2.00
6a	Andres Galarraga (silver)	1.50
6b	Andres Galarraga (gold)	3.00
7a	Gregg Jefferies (silver)	1.00
7b	Gregg Jefferies (gold)	2.00
8a	Dave Justice (silver)	2.00
8b	Dave Justice (gold)	4.00
9a	Ray Lankford (silver)	1.00
9b	Ray Lankford (gold)	2.00
10a	Fred McGriff (silver)	2.00
10b	Fred McGriff (gold)	4.00
11a	Barry Larkin (silver)	1.00
11b	Barry Larkin (gold)	2.00
12a	Mike Piazza (silver)	12.00
12b	Mike Piazza (gold)	24.00
13a	Deion Sanders (silver)	2.50
13b	Deion Sanders (gold)	5.00
14a	Matt Williams (silver)	2.00
14b	Matt Williams (gold)	4.00
15	NL Bonus Card (silver)	2.50

1994 Leaf Power Brokers

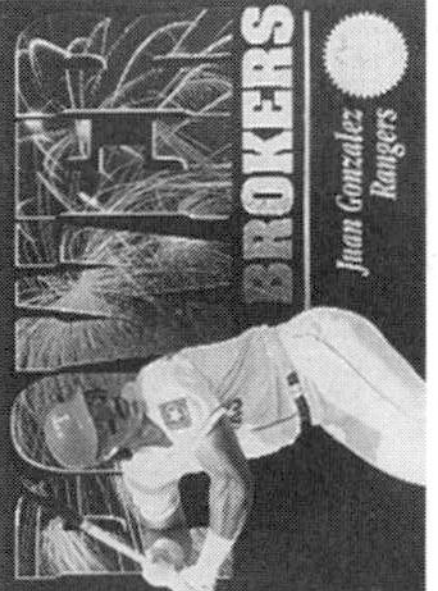

This insert set was unique to Leaf Series II packs and features the game's top sluggers. Horizontal-format fronts have a player photo at left, depicting his power stroke. A fireworks display is featured in the large letters of "POWER" at top. Other gold and silver foil highlights are featured on the black background. Backs have pie charts showing home run facts along with another player photo and a few stats. Stated odds of finding a Power Brokers insert card were one per dozen packs, on average.

		MT
Complete Set (10):		25.00
Common Player:		1.00
1	Frank Thomas	4.00
2	Dave Justice	1.00
3	Barry Bonds	2.50
4	Juan Gonzalez	2.50
5	Ken Griffey, Jr.	10.00
6	Mike Piazza	6.00
7	Cecil Fielder	1.00
8	Fred McGriff	1.00
9	Joe Carter	1.00
10	Albert Belle	2.00

1994 Leaf Slide Show

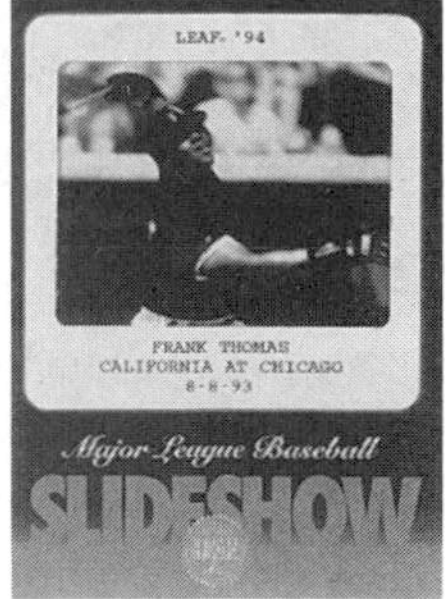

A new level of high-tech insert card production values was reached with the creation of Leaf's "Slide Show" chase cards. The cards feature a printed acetate center sandwiched between cardboard front and back. The see-through acetate portion of the card is bordered in white to give it the appearance of a slide. The player's name, location and date of the photo are printed on the front of the "slide," with the card number on back. The pseudo-slide is bordered in black (Series I) or white (Series II), with a blue "Slide Show" logo at bottom and a silver-foil Leaf logo. Backs of the Slide Show inserts have a few sentences about the featured player from Frank Thomas, Leaf's official spokesman again in 1994. The first five cards were released in Series I; cards 6-10 in Series II. Stated odds of finding a Slide Show insert are one per 54 packs.

		MT
Complete Set (10):		50.00
Common Player:		1.00
1	Frank Thomas	8.00
2	Mike Piazza	10.00
3	Darren Daulton	1.00
4	Ryne Sandberg	5.00
5	Roberto Alomar	4.00
6	Barry Bonds	5.00
7	Juan Gonzalez	5.00
8	Tim Salmon	2.50
9	Ken Griffey, Jr.	20.00
10	Dave Justice	1.00

1994 Leaf Statistical Standouts

Significant statistical acheivements from the 1993 season are marked in this insert set found in both retail and hobby packs at a rate of about once every 12 packs. Fronts feature player action photos set against a foil background of silver at right and a team color at left. A gold embossed Leaf seal is at upper-left. Backs are bordered in the complementary team color at right, silver at left and have a vertical player photo along with the statistical achievement. Cards are numbered "x-10".

		MT
Complete Set (10):		25.00
Common Player:		1.00
1	Frank Thomas	3.00
2	Barry Bonds	2.50
3	Juan Gonzalez	2.00
4	Mike Piazza	5.00
5	Greg Maddux	5.00
6	Ken Griffey, Jr.	7.50
7	Joe Carter	1.00
8	Dave Winfield	1.50
9	Tony Gwynn	4.00
10	Cal Ripken, Jr.	6.00

1994 Leaf/Limited

Leaf Limited was a 160-card high-end, super premium set printed on the highest quality board stock ever used by Donruss. Production was limited to 3,000 20-box case equivalents, making this the most limited product up to that point in 1994 by Donruss. Card fronts feature silver holographic Spectra Tech foiling and a silhouetted layer action photo over full silver foil. Cards have the team name and logo in silver and player name written in black at the bottom of the card. Leaf Limited appears in silver at the top and the player is bordered in silver on the front. The backs are dull grey or silver with a quote from a baseball personality and a player picture in the top-right corner. Leaf Limited and the card number are printed above the player photo. This card set was highly sought after and very limited. The cards look very unique and truly can't be described in words.

		MT
Complete Set (160):		75.00
Common Player:		.25
Pack (5):		4.50
Wax Box (20):		65.00
1	Jeffrey Hammonds	.25
2	Ben McDonald	.25
3	Mike Mussina	2.00
4	Rafael Palmeiro	1.50
5	Cal Ripken, Jr.	8.00
6	Lee Smith	.45
7	Roger Clemens	4.00
8	Scott Cooper	.25
9	Andre Dawson	.75
10	Mike Greenwell	.25
11	Aaron Sele	.25
12	Mo Vaughn	2.00
13	*Brian Anderson*	1.50
14	Chad Curtis	.25
15	Chili Davis	.25
16	Gary DiSarcina	.25
17	Mark Langston	.25
18	Tim Salmon	1.00
19	Wilson Alvarez	.25
20	Jason Bere	.25
21	Julio Franco	.25
22	Jack McDowell	.25
23	Tim Raines	.25
24	Frank Thomas	4.00
25	Robin Ventura	.75
26	Carlos Baerga	.25
27	Albert Belle	2.00
28	Kenny Lofton	2.00
29	Eddie Murray	1.00
30	Manny Ramirez	3.00
31	Cecil Fielder	.25
32	Travis Fryman	.35
33	Mickey Tettleton	.25
34	Alan Trammell	.50
35	Lou Whitaker	.25
36	David Cone	.40
37	Gary Gaetti	.25
38	Greg Gagne	.25
39	Bob Hamelin	.25
40	Wally Joyner	.40
41	Brian McRae	.25
42	Ricky Bones	.25
43	Brian Harper	.25
44	John Jaha	.25
45	Pat Listach	.25
46	Dave Nilsson	.25
47	Greg Vaughn	.40
48	Kent Hrbek	.25
49	Chuck Knoblauch	.75
50	Shane Mack	.25
51	Kirby Puckett	2.50
52	Dave Winfield	1.00
53	Jim Abbott	.50
54	Wade Boggs	1.50
55	Jimmy Key	.25
56	Don Mattingly	2.50
57	Paul O'Neill	.40
58	Danny Tartabull	.25
59	Dennis Eckersley	.60
60	Rickey Henderson	1.00
61	Mark McGwire	10.00
62	Troy Neel	.25
63	Ruben Sierra	.25
64	Eric Anthony	.25
65	Jay Buhner	.50
66	Ken Griffey, Jr.	10.00
67	Randy Johnson	2.50
68	Edgar Martinez	.35
69	Tino Martinez	.50
70	Jose Canseco	1.50
71	Will Clark	1.00
72	Juan Gonzalez	2.50
73	Dean Palmer	.25
74	Ivan Rodriguez	2.50
75	Roberto Alomar	1.50
76	Joe Carter	.50
77	Carlos Delgado	2.00
78	Paul Molitor	1.50
79	John Olerud	.50
80	Devon White	.25
81	Steve Avery	.25
82	Tom Glavine	.75
83	Dave Justice	.75
84	Roberto Kelly	.25
85	Ryan Klesko	.75
86	Javier Lopez	.75
87	Greg Maddux	5.00
88	Fred McGriff	.75
89	Shawon Dunston	.25
90	Mark Grace	.75
91	Derrick May	.25
92	Sammy Sosa	6.00
93	Rick Wilkins	.25
94	Bret Boone	.25
95	Barry Larkin	.75
96	Kevin Mitchell	.25
97	Hal Morris	.25
98	Deion Sanders	.75
99	Reggie Sanders	.25
100	Dante Bichette	.50
101	Ellis Burks	.25
102	Andres Galarraga	1.00
103	Joe Girardi	.25
104	Charlie Hayes	.25
105	Chuck Carr	.25
106	Jeff Conine	.25
107	Bryan Harvey	.25
108	Benito Santiago	.25
109	Gary Sheffield	.75
110	Jeff Bagwell	3.00
111	Craig Biggio	.75
112	Ken Caminiti	.75
113	Andujar Cedeno	.25
114	Doug Drabek	.25
115	Luis Gonzalez	.25
116	Brett Butler	.25
117	Delino DeShields	.25
118	Eric Karros	.25
119	Raul Mondesi	1.00
120	Mike Piazza	6.00
121	Henry Rodriguez	.25
122	Tim Wallach	.25
123	Moises Alou	.50
124	Cliff Floyd	.25
125	Marquis Grissom	.25
126	Ken Hill	.25
127	Larry Walker	1.00
128	John Wetteland	.25
129	Bobby Bonilla	.25
130	John Franco	.25
131	Jeff Kent	.25
132	Bret Saberhagen	.25
133	Ryan Thompson	.25
134	Darren Daulton	.25
135	Mariano Duncan	.25
136	Len Dykstra	.25
137	Danny Jackson	.25
138	John Kruk	.25
139	Jay Bell	.25
140	Jeff King	.25
141	Al Martin	.25
142	Orlando Merced	.25
143	Andy Van Slyke	.25
144	Bernard Gilkey	.25
145	Gregg Jefferies	.35
146	Ray Lankford	.25
147	Ozzie Smith	1.50
148	Mark Whiten	.25
149	Todd Zeile	.25
150	Derek Bell	.25
151	Andy Benes	.25
152	Tony Gwynn	5.00
153	Phil Plantier	.25
154	Bip Roberts	.25
155	Rod Beck	.25
156	Barry Bonds	2.50
157	John Burkett	.25
158	Royce Clayton	.25
159	Bill Swift	.25
160	Matt Williams	1.00

1994 Leaf/Limited Gold

Leaf Limited Gold was an 18-card insert set randomly packed into Leaf Limited. All cards are individually numbered and feature the starting lineups at each position in both the National League and American League for the 1994 All-Star Game. There were only 10,000 cards of each player produced in this insert set.

		MT
Complete Set (18):		125.00
Common Player:		1.00
1	Frank Thomas	12.00
2	Gregg Jefferies	1.00
3	Roberto Alomar	6.00
4	Mariano Duncan	1.00
5	Wade Boggs	4.00
6	Matt Williams	4.00
7	Cal Ripken, Jr.	25.00
8	Ozzie Smith	6.00
9	Kirby Puckett	8.00
10	Barry Bonds	8.00
11	Ken Griffey, Jr.	30.00
12	Tony Gwynn	15.00
13	Joe Carter	1.00
14	Dave Justice	3.00
15	Ivan Rodriguez	8.00
16	Mike Piazza	20.00
17	Jimmy Key	1.00
18	Greg Maddux	20.00

1994 Leaf/Limited Rookies

Similar in format to the super-premium Leaf Limited issue, this separate issue features 80 of baseball's brightest young talents.

		MT
Complete Set (80):		25.00
Common Player:		.35
Pack (5):		4.00
Wax Box (20):		60.00
1	Charles Johnson	2.00
2	Rico Brogna	.50
3	Melvin Nieves	.35
4	Rich Becker	.35
5	Russ Davis	.50
6	Matt Mieske	.50
7	Paul Shuey	.35
8	Hector Carrasco	.50
9	J.R. Phillips	1.00
10	Scott Ruffcorn	.35
11	Kurt Abbott	.35
12	Danny Bautista	.35
13	Rick White	.35
14	Steve Dunn	.35
15	Joe Ausanio	.35
16	Salomon Torres	.35
17	Rick Bottalico	.50
18	Johnny Ruffin	.35
19	Kevin Foster	.35
20	*W. Van Landingham*	.50
21	Troy O'Leary	.40
22	Mark Acre	.35
23	Norberto Martin	.35
24	*Jason Jacome*	.40
25	Steve Trachsel	.75
26	Denny Hocking	.35
27	Mike Lieberthal	.50
28	Gerald Williams	.50
29	John Mabry	.50
30	Greg Blosser	.35
31	Carl Everett	.50
32	Steve Karsay	.40
33	Jose Valentin	.35
34	Jon Lieber	.35
35	Chris Gomez	.50
36	Jesus Tavarez	.35
37	Tony Longmire	.50
38	Luis Lopez	.35
39	Matt Walbeck	.35
40	Rikkert Faneyte	.35
41	Shane Reynolds	.45
42	Joey Hamilton	1.50
43	Ismael Valdes	1.00
44	Danny Miceli	.40
45	Darren Bragg	.35
46	Alex Gonzalez	1.00
47	Rick Helling	.35
48	Jose Oliva	.35
49	Jim Edmonds	2.50
50	Miguel Jimenez	.35
51	Tony Eusebio	.45
52	Shawn Green	5.00
53	Billy Ashley	.35
54	Rondell White	3.00
55	Cory Bailey	.45
56	Tim Davis	.35
57	John Hudek	.35
58	Darren Hall	.35
59	Darren Dreifort	.35
60	Mike Kelly	.35
61	Marcus Moore	.35
62	Garret Anderson	1.00
63	Brian Hunter	1.00
64	Mark Smith	.45
65	Garey Ingram	.35
66	*Rusty Greer*	1.50
67	Marc Newfield	.35
68	Gar Finnvold	.35
69	Paul Spoljaric	.35
70	Ray McDavid	.35
71	Orlando Miller	.75
72	Jorge Fabregas	.45
73	Ray Holbert	.35
74	Armando Benitez	.50
75	Ernie Young	.35
76	James Mouton	.35
77	*Robert Perez*	.45
78	*Chan Ho Park*	2.00
79	Roger Salkeld	.35
80	Tony Tarasco	.35

1994 Leaf/Limited Rookies Rookie Phenoms

Similar in format to the other Leaf Limited cards for 1994, these Phenom inserts feature gold-foil background and graphics, rather than silver. Each card is numbered from within an edition of 5,000 of each player.

		MT
Complete Set (10):		200.00
Common Player:		3.00
1	Raul Mondesi	10.00
2	Bob Hamelin	3.00
3	Midre Cummings	3.00
4	Carlos Delgado	25.00
5	Cliff Floyd	4.00
6	Jeffrey Hammonds	3.00
7	Ryan Klesko	6.00
8	Javier Lopez	10.00
9	Manny Ramirez	25.00
10	Alex Rodriguez	150.00

1995 Leaf

Two series of 200 basic cards each, plus numerous insert sets, are featured in 1995 Leaf. The basic card design has a borderless action photo on front, with a small portrait photo printed at upper-left on holographic silver foil. The team name is printed in the same foil in large letters down the left side. A script rendition of the player's name is at bottom-right, with the Leaf logo under the portrait photo; both elements are in gold foil. Backs have a couple more player photos. The card number is in white in a silver-foil seal at upper-right. Previous season and career stats are at lower-left. Several of the inserts sets are unique to various package configurations, while others are found in all types of packs.

		MT
Complete Set (400):		40.00
Complete Series 1 (200):		15.00
Complete Series 2 (200):		25.00
Common Player:		.10
Series 1 or 2 Pack (12):		1.50
Series 1 or 2 Wax Box (36):		45.00
1	Frank Thomas	1.00
2	Carlos Garcia	.10
3	Todd Hundley	.15
4	Damion Easley	.10
5	Roberto Mejia	.10
6	John Mabry	.10
7	Aaron Sele	.10
8	Kenny Lofton	.75
9	John Doherty	.10
10	Joe Carter	.15
11	Mike Lansing	.10
12	John Valentin	.15
13	Ismael Valdes	.15
14	Dave McCarty	.10
15	Melvin Nieves	.10
16	Bobby Jones	.10
17	Trevor Hoffman	.15
18	John Smoltz	.25
19	Leo Gomez	.10
20	Roger Pavlik	.10
21	Dean Palmer	.10
22	Rickey Henderson	.25
23	Eddie Taubensee	.10
24	Damon Buford	.10
25	Mark Wohlers	.10
26	Jim Edmonds	.15
27	Wilson Alvarez	.10
28	Matt Williams	.35
29	Jeff Montgomery	.10
30	Shawon Dunston	.10
31	Tom Pagnozzi	.10
32	Jose Lind	.10
33	Royce Clayton	.10
34	Cal Eldred	.10
35	Chris Gomez	.10
36	Henry Rodriguez	.10
37	Dave Fleming	.10
38	Jon Lieber	.10
39	Scott Servais	.10
40	Wade Boggs	.30
41	John Olerud	.15
42	Eddie Williams	.10
43	Paul Sorrento	.10
44	Ron Karkovice	.10
45	Kevin Foster	.10
46	Miguel Jimenez	.10
47	Reggie Sanders	.10
48	Rondell White	.15
49	Scott Leius	.10
50	Jose Valentin	.10
51	William Van Landingham	.10
52	Denny Hocking	.10
53	Jeff Fassero	.10
54	Chris Hoiles	.10
55	Walt Weiss	.10
56	Geronimo Berroa	.10
57	Rich Rowland	.10
58	Dave Weathers	.10
59	Sterling Hitchcock	.10
60	Raul Mondesi	.50
61	Rusty Greer	.10
62	Dave Justice	.25
63	Cecil Fielder	.10
64	Brian Jordan	.15
65	Mike Lieberthal	.10
66	Rick Aguilera	.10
67	Chuck Finley	.10
68	Andy Ashby	.10
69	Alex Fernandez	.15
70	Ed Sprague	.10
71	Steve Buechele	.10
72	Willie Greene	.10
73	Dave Nilsson	.10
74	Bret Saberhagen	.10
75	Jimmy Key	.10
76	Darren Lewis	.10
77	Steve Cooke	.10
78	Kirk Gibson	.10
79	Ray Lankford	.10
80	Paul O'Neill	.15
81	Mike Bordick	.10
82	Wes Chamberlain	.10
83	Rico Brogna	.10
84	Kevin Appier	.10
85	Juan Guzman	.10
86	Kevin Seitzer	.10
87	Mickey Morandini	.10
88	Pedro Martinez	.20
89	Matt Mieske	.10
90	Tino Martinez	.15
91	Paul Shuey	.10
92	Bip Roberts	.10
93	Chili Davis	.10
94	Deion Sanders	.25
95	Darrell Whitmore	.10
96	Joe Orsulak	.10
97	Bret Boone	.10
98	Kent Mercker	.10
99	Scott Livingstone	.10
100	Brady Anderson	.15
101	James Mouton	.10
102	Jose Rijo	.10
103	Bobby Munoz	.10
104	Ramon Martinez	.15
105	Bernie Williams	.60
106	Troy Neel	.10
107	Ivan Rodriguez	.50
108	Salomon Torres	.10
109	Johnny Ruffin	.10
110	Darryl Kile	.10
111	Bobby Ayala	.10
112	Ron Darling	.10
113	Jose Lima	.10
114	Joey Hamilton	.15
115	Greg Maddux	1.50
116	Greg Colbrunn	.10
117	Ozzie Guillen	.10
118	Brian Anderson	.10
119	Jeff Bagwell	1.00
120	Pat Listach	.10
121	Sandy Alomar	.15
122	Jose Vizcaino	.10
123	Rick Helling	.10
124	Allen Watson	.10
125	Pedro Munoz	.10
126	Craig Biggio	.15
127	Kevin Stocker	.10
128	Wil Cordero	.10
129	Rafael Palmeiro	.25
130	Gar Finnvold	.10
131	Darren Hall	.10
132	Heath Slocumb	.10
133	Darrin Fletcher	.10
134	Cal Ripken Jr.	2.50
135	Dante Bichette	.15
136	Don Slaught	.10
137	Pedro Astacio	.10
138	Ryan Thompson	.10
139	Greg Gohr	.10
140	Javier Lopez	.20
141	Lenny Dykstra	.10
142	Pat Rapp	.10
143	Mark Kiefer	.10
144	Greg Gagne	.10
145	Eduardo Perez	.10
146	Felix Fermin	.10
147	Jeff Frye	.10
148	Terry Steinbach	.10
149	Jim Eisenreich	.10
150	Brad Ausmus	.10
151	Randy Myers	.10
152	Rick White	.10
153	Mark Portugal	.10
154	Delino DeShields	.10
155	Scott Cooper	.10
156	Pat Hentgen	.10
157	Mark Gubicza	.10
158	Carlos Baerga	.10
159	Joe Girardi	.10
160	Rey Sanchez	.10
161	Todd Jones	.10
162	Luis Polonia	.10
163	Steve Trachsel	.10
164	Roberto Hernandez	.10
165	John Patterson	.10
166	Rene Arocha	.10
167	Will Clark	.30

168	Jim Leyritz	.10
169	Todd Van Poppel	.10
170	Robb Nen	.10
171	Midre Cummings	.10
172	Jay Buhner	.15
173	Kevin Tapani	.10
174	Mark Lemke	.10
175	Marcus Moore	.10
176	Wayne Kirby	.10
177	Rich Amaral	.10
178	Lou Whitaker	.10
179	Jay Bell	.10
180	Rick Wilkins	.10
181	Paul Molitor	.40
182	Gary Sheffield	.40
183	Kirby Puckett	1.00
184	Cliff Floyd	.10
185	Darren Oliver	.10
186	Tim Naehring	.10
187	John Hudek	.10
188	Eric Young	.10
189	Roger Salkeld	.10
190	Kirt Manwaring	.10
191	Kurt Abbott	.10
192	David Nied	.10
193	Todd Zeile	.10
194	Wally Joyner	.10
195	Dennis Martinez	.10
196	Billy Ashley	.10
197	Ben McDonald	.10
198	Bob Hamelin	.10
199	Chris Turner	.10
200	Lance Johnson	.10
201	Willie Banks	.10
202	Juan Gonzalez	.75
203	Scott Sanders	.10
204	Scott Brosius	.10
205	Curt Schilling	.15
206	Alex Gonzalez	.10
207	Travis Fryman	.15
208	Tim Raines	.15
209	Steve Avery	.10
210	Hal Morris	.10
211	Ken Griffey Jr.	3.00
212	Ozzie Smith	.40
213	Chuck Carr	.10
214	Ryan Klesko	.25
215	Robin Ventura	.20
216	Luis Gonzalez	.10
217	Ken Ryan	.10
218	Mike Piazza	1.50
219	Matt Walbeck	.10
220	Jeff Kent	.10
221	Orlando Miller	.10
222	Kenny Rogers	.10
223	J.T. Snow	.15
224	Alan Trammell	.15
225	John Franco	.10
226	Gerald Williams	.10
227	Andy Benes	.10
228	Dan Wilson	.10
229	Dave Hollins	.10
230	Vinny Castilla	.10
231	Devon White	.10
232	Fred McGriff	.35
233	Quilvio Veras	.10
234	Tom Candiotti	.10
235	Jason Bere	.10
236	Mark Langston	.10
237	Mel Rojas	.10
238	Chuck Knoblauch	.20
239	Bernard Gilkey	.10
240	Mark McGwire	3.00
241	Kirk Rueter	.10
242	Pat Kelly	.10
243	Ruben Sierra	.10
244	Randy Johnson	.40
245	Shane Reynolds	.10
246	Danny Tartabull	.10
247	Darryl Hamilton	.10
248	Danny Bautista	.10
249	Tom Gordon	.10
250	Tom Glavine	.20
251	Orlando Merced	.10
252	Eric Karros	.15
253	Benji Gil	.10
254	Sean Bergman	.10
255	Roger Clemens	1.00
256	Roberto Alomar	.60
257	Benito Santiago	.10
258	Robby Thompson	.10
259	Marvin Freeman	.10
260	Jose Offerman	.10
261	Greg Vaughn	.15
262	David Segui	.10
263	Geronimo Pena	.10
264	Tim Salmon	.25
265	Eddie Murray	.40
266	Mariano Duncan	.10
267	*Hideo Nomo*	2.00
268	Derek Bell	.10
269	Mo Vaughn	.75
270	Jeff King	.10
271	Edgar Martinez	.10
272	Sammy Sosa	1.50
273	Scott Ruffcorn	.10
274	Darren Daulton	.10
275	John Jaha	.10
276	Andres Galarraga	.20
277	Mark Grace	.20
278	Mike Moore	.10
279	Barry Bonds	.75
280	Manny Ramirez	1.00
281	Ellis Burks	.10
282	Greg Swindell	.10
283	Barry Larkin	.20
284	Albert Belle	.75
285	Shawn Green	.20
286	John Roper	.10
287	Scott Erickson	.10
288	Moises Alou	.15
289	Mike Blowers	.10
290	Brent Gates	.10
291	Sean Berry	.10
292	Mike Stanley	.10
293	Jeff Conine	.10
294	Tim Wallach	.10
295	Bobby Bonilla	.15
296	Bruce Ruffin	.10
297	Chad Curtis	.10
298	Mike Greenwell	.10
299	Tony Gwynn	1.00
300	Russ Davis	.10
301	Danny Jackson	.10
302	Pete Harnisch	.10
303	Don Mattingly	1.00
304	Rheal Cormier	.10
305	Larry Walker	.30
306	Hector Carrasco	.10
307	Jason Jacome	.10
308	Phil Plantier	.10
309	Harold Baines	.10
310	Mitch Williams	.10
311	Charles Nagy	.10
312	Ken Caminiti	.20
313	Alex Rodriguez	3.00
314	Chris Sabo	.10
315	Gary Gaetti	.10
316	Andre Dawson	.15
317	Mark Clark	.10
318	Vince Coleman	.10
319	Brad Clontz	.10
320	Steve Finley	.10
321	Doug Drabek	.10
322	Mark McLemore	.10
323	Stan Javier	.10
324	Ron Gant	.15
325	Charlie Hayes	.10
326	Carlos Delgado	.50
327	Ricky Bottalico	.10
328	Rod Beck	.10
329	Mark Acre	.10
330	Chris Bosio	.10
331	Tony Phillips	.10
332	Garret Anderson	.15
333	Pat Meares	.10
334	Todd Worrell	.10
335	Marquis Grissom	.10
336	Brent Mayne	.10
337	Lee Tinsley	.10
338	Terry Pendleton	.10
339	David Cone	.15
340	Tony Fernandez	.10
341	Jim Bullinger	.10
342	Armando Benitez	.10
343	John Smiley	.10
344	Dan Miceli	.10
345	Charles Johnson	.15
346	Lee Smith	.15
347	Brian McRae	.10
348	Jim Thome	.35
349	Jose Oliva	.10
350	Terry Mulholland	.10
351	Tom Henke	.10
352	Dennis Eckersley	.15
353	Sid Fernandez	.10
354	Paul Wagner	.10
355	John Dettmer	.10
356	John Wetteland	.10
357	John Burkett	.10
358	Marty Cordova	.15
359	Norm Charlton	.10
360	Mike Devereaux	.10
361	Alex Cole	.10
362	Brett Butler	.10
363	Mickey Tettleton	.10
364	Al Martin	.10
365	Tony Tarasco	.10
366	Pat Mahomes	.10
367	Gary DiSarcina	.10
368	Bill Swift	.10
369	Chipper Jones	1.50
370	Orel Hershiser	.15
371	Kevin Gross	.10
372	Dave Winfield	.25
373	Andujar Cedeno	.10
374	Jim Abbott	.10
375	Glenallen Hill	.10
376	Otis Nixon	.10
377	Roberto Kelly	.10
378	Chris Hammond	.10
379	Mike Macfarlane	.10
380	J.R. Phillips	.10
381	Luis Alicea	.10
382	Bret Barberie	.10
383	Tom Goodwin	.10
384	Mark Whiten	.10
385	Jeffrey Hammonds	.10
386	Omar Vizquel	.10
387	Mike Mussina	.35
388	Rickey Bones	.10
389	Steve Ontiveros	.10
390	Jeff Blauser	.10
391	Jose Canseco	.30
392	Bob Tewksbury	.10
393	Jacob Brumfield	.10
394	Doug Jones	.10
395	Ken Hill	.10
396	Pat Borders	.10
397	Carl Everett	.10
398	Gregg Jefferies	.15
399	Jack McDowell	.10
400	Denny Neagle	.10

1995 Leaf Checklists

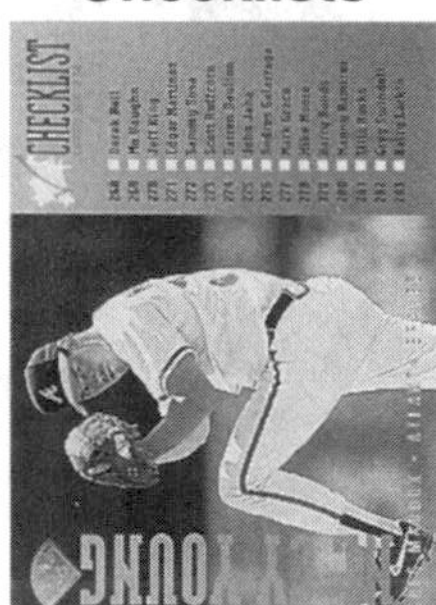

Honoring the major 1994 award winners in the American (Series I) and National (Series II) Leagues, checklists for the 1995 Leaf set are not numbered among the regular issue. Horizontal cards have a player action photo at left with his name and team in gold foil at bottom. The award is printed vertically at left with the checklist beginning on the right. Backs continue the checklist on a graduated purple background with the checklist number in a silver-foil seal at top-right.

		MT
Complete Set (8):		3.00
Common Player:		.25
1	Checklist 1-67 (Bob Hamelin) (Rookie of the Year)	.25
2	Checklist 68-134 (David Cone) (Cy Young)	.25
3	Checklist 135-200 (Frank Thomas) (MVP)	.75
4	Series II inserts checklist (Paul O'Neill) (Batting title)	.25
5	Checklist 201-267 (Raul Mondesi) (Rookie of the Year)	.50
6	Checklist 268-334 (Greg Maddux) (Cy Young)	.60
7	Checklist 335-400 (Jeff Bagwell) (MVP)	.50
8	Series 2 inserts checklist (Tony Gwynn) (Batting title)	.75

1995 Leaf Cornerstones

Cornerstones, six of the best first baseman-third baseman combos in baseball, are a six-card insert series found, on average, once every 18 packs in Series I Leaf. Card fronts are horizontally oriented and have a silver prismatic border and player names. Player defensive action photos are set against a background resembling their team logo chiseled into a stone block. Backs have player batting photos at each end with offensive and defensive stats from 1994, and a few words about the duo.

		MT
Complete Set (6):		7.50
Common Player:		.50
1	Frank Thomas, Robin Ventura	2.00
2	Cecil Fielder, Travis Fryman	.50
3	Don Mattingly, Wade Boggs	2.00
4	Jeff Bagwell, Ken Caminiti	2.00
5	Will Clark, Dean Palmer	.75
6	J.R. Phillips, Matt Williams	.50

1995 Leaf Frank Thomas

The Big Hurt's six seasons in the major leagues are chronicled in this flashy insert set. Silver and gold foil squares are the background for a photo of Thomas on front. Backs repeat the motif with standard print technology and another photo, along with a few words about Thomas' season. The Frank Thomas inserts are found in all types of Series II packs, with odds varying from one in 42 packs to one in 14 packs, depending on card count per pack.

		MT
Complete Set (6):		25.00
Common Thomas:		5.00
1	The Rookie	5.00
2	Sophomore Stardom	5.00
3	Super Star	5.00
4	AL MVP	5.00
5	Back-To-Back	5.00
6	The Big Hurt	5.00

1995 Leaf Gold Rookies

Every other pack of Series I Leaf Series I is seeded with a Gold Leaf Rookie card. Fronts have a largely white background with a large player photo at left-center and a smaller picture in a rectangle at upper-right. A team-color stripe is at left, while a smaller gray stripe is at top-right. The team name is printed in large gray letters across the center of the card, with the player name in a team color beneath that and above the gold-foil Leaf logo at lower-left. "Gold Leaf Rookies" is printed in gold foil down the right side. Backs repeat the team-color motif with a large action photo of the player in a single color and a smaller color portrait. Full career stats are at bottom.

		MT
Complete Set (16):		5.00
Common Player:		.25
1	Alex Rodriguez	4.00
2	Garret Anderson	.50
3	Shawn Green	1.00
4	Armando Benitez	.35
5	Darren Dreifort	.25
6	Orlando Miller	.25
7	Jose Oliva	.25
8	Ricky Bottalico	.25
9	Charles Johnson	.50
10	Brian Hunter	.35
11	Ray McDavid	.25
12	Chan Ho Park	.75
13	Mike Kelly	.25
14	Cory Bailey	.25
15	Alex Gonzalez	.75
16	Andrew Lorraine	.25

1995 Leaf Gold Stars

Once again the toughest pull among the Leaf inserts are the Gold Leaf Stars found in both series. Found on average of one card per 90-270 packs, depending on pack card count, each of these chase cards is numbered on back within an edition of 10,000. Cards have fronts printed on metallic foil with the player name at top, the series title at bottom and a vertical stars and stripe device at right all printed in gold foil. A die-cut star appears at bottom-left. Backs are coventionally printed with another player photo and a few sentences about the star. The serial number is in gold foil in a white strip at top.

		MT
Complete Set (14):		150.00
Common Player:		5.00
1	Jeff Bagwell	15.00
2	Albert Belle	10.00
3	Tony Gwynn	20.00
4	Ken Griffey Jr.	30.00
5	Barry Bonds	10.00
6	Don Mattingly	15.00
7	Raul Mondesi	8.00
8	Joe Carter	5.00
9	Greg Maddux	20.00
10	Frank Thomas	15.00
11	Mike Piazza	25.00
12	Jose Canseco	8.00
13	Kirby Puckett	15.00
14	Matt Williams	5.00

1995 Leaf Great Gloves

While the stated emphasis is on fielding prowess in this Series II chase set, players who don't also swing a big stick are ignored. Found as frequently as one per two packs, cards have a detail photo of a glove at left, with an action photo at right. The player name in the Great Gloves logo at bottom-right is in gold foil, as are the Leaf logo at top-left and the team name vertically at right. Backs repeat the glove photo and series logo as background for another player photo and a few words and stats about the player's defense.

		MT
Complete Set (16):		7.50
Common Player:		.25
1	Jeff Bagwell	.65
2	Roberto Alomar	.40
3	Barry Bonds	.40
4	Wade Boggs	.50
5	Andres Galarraga	.25
6	Ken Griffey Jr.	3.00
7	Marquis Grissom	.25
8	Kenny Lofton	.40
9	Barry Larkin	.25
10	Don Mattingly	.75
11	Greg Maddux	1.50
12	Kirby Puckett	.75
13	Ozzie Smith	.50
14	Cal Ripken Jr.	2.50
15	Matt Williams	.25
16	Ivan Rodriguez	.50

1995 Leaf Heading For The Hall

Series II hobby packs were the home of this scarce (one per 75 packs, average) chase set. Eight players deemed to be sure shots for Cooperstown are pictured in a semblance of the famed tombstone-shaped plaque they will someday adorn at the Hall of Fame; in fact the cards are die-cut to that shape. Backs have a sepia-toned photo, career stats and a serial number placing the card within an edition of 5,000.

		MT
Complete Set (8):		125.00
Common Player:		10.00
1	Frank Thomas	15.00
2	Ken Griffey Jr.	40.00
3	Jeff Bagwell	15.00
4	Barry Bonds	10.00
5	Kirby Puckett	15.00
6	Cal Ripken Jr.	30.00
7	Tony Gwynn	20.00
8	Paul Molitor	10.00

1995 Leaf Slideshow

The hold-to-light technology which Leaf debuted with its 1994 Slideshow inserts continued in 1995 with a cross-series concept. The same eight players are featured on these cards in both Series I and II. Each has three clear photos at center, between the spokes of a silver-foil wheel. When both the player's cards are placed side-by-side, the six-picture see-through photo device is complete. Silver-foil and black borders surround the photo wheel on each side of the card. The Slideshow inserts are found on average of just over one per box among all types of pack configurations. Cards were issued with a peelable plastic protector on the front.

		MT
Complete Set (16):		80.00
Complete Series 1 (1a-8a):		40.00
Complete Series 2 (1b-8b):		40.00
Same CL and prices for both series		
Common Player:		4.00
1a	Raul Mondesi	5.00
1b	Raul Mondesi	5.00
2a	Frank Thomas	6.00
2b	Frank Thomas	6.00
3a	Fred McGriff	4.00
3b	Fred McGriff	4.00
4a	Cal Ripken Jr.	12.00
4b	Cal Ripken Jr.	12.00
5a	Jeff Bagwell	7.50
5b	Jeff Bagwell	7.50
6a	Will Clark	4.00
6b	Will Clark	4.00
7a	Matt Williams	4.00
7b	Matt Williams	4.00
8a	Ken Griffey Jr.	15.00
8b	Ken Griffey Jr.	15.00

1995 Leaf Statistical Standouts

Embossed red stitches on the large baseball background make the Statistical Standouts chase cards stand out among the inserts in Series I hobby packs (one per 70, average). The leather surface of the ball is also lightly textured, as is the player action photo at center. Printed in gold foil on front are the series name at top, the player's facsimile autograph at lower-center and the Leaf logo and team name at bottom. Backs have a graduated black background with a large team logo at bottom, and a circular player portrait at center. A few words explain why the player's stats stand out among his peers.

		MT
Complete Set (9):		350.00
Common Player:		10.00
1	Joe Carter	10.00
2	Ken Griffey Jr.	125.00
3	Don Mattingly	40.00
4	Fred McGriff	10.00
5	Paul Molitor	25.00
6	Kirby Puckett	40.00
7	Cal Ripken Jr.	100.00
8	Frank Thomas	40.00
9	Matt Williams	12.50

1995 Leaf 300 Club

Issued in both Series I and II Leaf, but only in the retail and magazine packs, at a rate of one per 12-30 packs, depending on pack configuration, 300 Club inserts feature the 18 active players with lifetime .300+ batting averages in a minimum of 1,000 AB. Fronts have color player photos with a large white "300" in the background and "club" in gold foil near the bottom. The player name is in gold foil in an arc above the silver Leaf logo at bottom-center. Large embossed silver triangles in each bottom corner have the team name and player position (left) and career BA (right). Backs have another player photo and highlight his place on the list of .300+ batters.

		MT
Complete Set (18):		80.00
Common Player:		1.00
1	Frank Thomas	12.50
2	Paul Molitor	4.00
3	Mike Piazza	15.00
4	Moises Alou	1.50
5	Mike Greenwell	1.00
6	Will Clark	2.50
7	Hal Morris	1.00
8	Edgar Martinez	1.00
9	Carlos Baerga	1.00
10	Ken Griffey Jr.	25.00
11	Wade Boggs	3.50
12	Jeff Bagwell	8.00
13	Tony Gwynn	12.50
14	John Kruk	1.00
15	Don Mattingly	6.00
16	Mark Grace	3.00
17	Kirby Puckett	7.50
18	Kenny Lofton	4.00

1995 Leaf/Limited

Issued in two series of 96 basic cards each, plus inserts, Leaf Limited was a hobby-only product limited to 90,000 numbered 20-pack boxes. Five-card packs had a suggested retail price of $4.99. Fronts of the basic cards have a player action photo on a background of silver holographic foil highlighted with team colors and a gold-foil Leaf Limited logo. Horizontal-format backs have two more player photos, career stats and holographic foil team logos and card numbers.

		MT
Complete Set (192):		50.00
Complete Series 1 (96):		30.00
Complete Series 2 (96):		30.00
Common Player:		.25
Series 1 or 2 Pack (5):		4.00
Series 1 or 2 Wax Box (20):		65.00
1	Frank Thomas	2.50
2	Geronimo Berroa	.25
3	Tony Phillips	.25
4	Roberto Alomar	1.25
5	Steve Avery	.25
6	Darryl Hamilton	.25
7	Scott Cooper	.25
8	Mark Grace	.60
9	Billy Ashley	.25
10	Wil Cordero	.25
11	Barry Bonds	1.50
12	Kenny Lofton	1.25
13	Jay Buhner	.35
14	Alex Rodriguez	5.00
15	Bobby Bonilla	.40
16	Brady Anderson	.45
17	Ken Caminiti	.50
18	Charlie Hayes	.25
19	Jay Bell	.25
20	Will Clark	.50
21	Jose Canseco	.50
22	Bret Boone	.25
23	Dante Bichette	.40
24	Kevin Appier	.25
25	Chad Curtis	.25
26	Marty Cordova	.25
27	Jason Bere	.25
28	Jimmy Key	.25
29	Rickey Henderson	.40
30	Tim Salmon	.60
31	Joe Carter	.25
32	Tom Glavine	.40
33	Pat Listach	.25
34	Brian Jordan	.35
35	Brian McRae	.25
36	Eric Karros	.35
37	Pedro Martinez	.65
38	Royce Clayton	.25
39	Eddie Murray	.75
40	Randy Johnson	1.00
41	Jeff Conine	.25
42	Brett Butler	.25
43	Jeffrey Hammonds	.25
44	Andujar Cedeno	.25
45	Dave Hollins	.25
46	Jeff King	.25
47	Benji Gil	.25
48	Roger Clemens	2.00
49	Barry Larkin	.40
50	Joe Girardi	.25
51	Bob Hamelin	.25
52	Travis Fryman	.25
53	Chuck Knoblauch	.50
54	Ray Durham	.35
55	Don Mattingly	2.00
56	Ruben Sierra	.25
57	J.T. Snow	.40
58	Derek Bell	.25
59	David Cone	.35
60	Marquis Grissom	.35
61	Kevin Seitzer	.25
62	Ozzie Smith	1.00
63	Rick Wilkins	.25
64	*Hideo Nomo*	2.50
65	Tony Tarasco	.25
66	Manny Ramirez	2.00
67	Charles Johnson	.35
68	Craig Biggio	.50
69	Bobby Jones	.25
70	Mike Mussina	.75
71	Alex Gonzalez	.25
72	Gregg Jefferies	.25
73	Rusty Greer	.25
74	Mike Greenwell	.25
75	Hal Morris	.25
76	Paul O'Neill	.40
77	Luis Gonzalez	.25
78	Chipper Jones	4.00
79	Mike Piazza	4.00
80	Rondell White	.50
81	Glenallen Hill	.25
82	Shawn Green	.60
83	Bernie Williams	1.25
84	Jim Thome	.75
85	Terry Pendleton	.25
86	Rafael Palmeiro	.50
87	Tony Gwynn	3.00
88	Mickey Tettleton	.25
89	John Valentin	.25
90	Deion Sanders	.50
91	Larry Walker	.75
92	Michael Tucker	.25
93	Alan Trammell	.25
94	Tim Raines	.25
95	Dave Justice	.50
96	Tino Martinez	.40
97	Cal Ripken Jr.	5.00
98	Deion Sanders	.75
99	Darren Daulton	.25
100	Paul Molitor	1.00
101	Randy Myers	.25
102	Wally Joyner	.25
103	Carlos Perez	.25
104	Brian Hunter	.25
105	Wade Boggs	.75
106	*Bobby Higginson*	3.00
107	Jeff Kent	.25
108	Jose Offerman	.25
109	Dennis Eckersley	.35
110	Dave Nilsson	.25
111	Chuck Finley	.25
112	Devon White	.25
113	Bip Roberts	.25
114	Ramon Martinez	.25
115	Greg Maddux	4.00
116	Curtis Goodwin	.25
117	John Jaha	.25
118	Ken Griffey Jr.	6.00
119	Geronimo Pena	.25
120	Shawon Dunston	.25
121	Ariel Prieto	.25
122	Kirby Puckett	2.00
123	Carlos Baerga	.25
124	Todd Hundley	.50
125	Tim Naehring	.25
126	Gary Sheffield	.60
127	Dean Palmer	.25
128	Rondell White	.50
129	Greg Gagne	.25
130	Jose Rijo	.25
131	Ivan Rodriguez	1.00
132	Jeff Bagwell	2.00
133	Greg Vaughn	.35
134	Chili Davis	.25
135	Al Martin	.25
136	Kenny Rogers	.25
137	Aaron Sele	.25
138	Raul Mondesi	.50
139	Cecil Fielder	.25
140	Tim Wallach	.25
141	Andres Galarraga	.50
142	Lou Whitaker	.25
143	Jack McDowell	.25
144	Matt Williams	.50
145	Ryan Klesko	.40
146	Carlos Garcia	.25
147	Albert Belle	1.50
148	Ryan Thompson	.25

149	Roberto Kelly	.25
150	Edgar Martinez	.25
151	Robby Thompson	.25
152	Mo Vaughn	1.25
153	Todd Zeile	.25
154	Harold Baines	.25
155	Phil Plantier	.25
156	Mike Stanley	.25
157	Ed Sprague	.25
158	Moises Alou	.35
159	Quilvio Veras	.25
160	Reggie Sanders	.25
161	Delino DeShields	.25
162	Rico Brogna	.25
163	Greg Colbrunn	.25
164	Steve Finley	.25
165	Orlando Merced	.25
166	Mark McGwire	6.00
167	Garret Anderson	.25
168	Paul Sorrento	.25
169	Mark Langston	.25
170	Danny Tartabull	.25
171	Vinny Castilla	.25
172	Javier Lopez	.40
173	Bret Saberhagen	.25
174	Eddie Williams	.25
175	Scott Leius	.25
176	Juan Gonzalez	1.50
177	Gary Gaetti	.25
178	Jim Edmonds	.40
179	John Olerud	.35
180	Lenny Dykstra	.25
181	Ray Lankford	.25
182	Ron Gant	.25
183	Doug Drabek	.25
184	Fred McGriff	.50
185	Andy Benes	.25
186	Kurt Abbott	.25
187	Bernard Gilkey	.25
188	Sammy Sosa	3.00
189	Lee Smith	.25
190	Dennis Martinez	.25
191	Ozzie Guillen	.25
192	Robin Ventura	.35

1995 Leaf/Limited Gold

Seeded one per pack in Series I only, this insert set follows the format of the basic Leaf Limited cards, but is distinguished by the presence of gold, rather than silver, holographic foil.

		MT
Complete Set (24):		30.00
Common Player:		.50
1	Frank Thomas	2.50
2	Jeff Bagwell	2.00
3	Raul Mondesi	.75
4	Barry Bonds	1.25
5	Albert Belle	1.25
6	Ken Griffey Jr.	5.00
7	Cal Ripken Jr.	4.00
8	Will Clark	.75
9	Jose Canseco	.75
10	Larry Walker	.75
11	Kirby Puckett	1.50
12	Don Mattingly	1.50
13	Tim Salmon	.50
14	Roberto Alomar	1.00
15	Greg Maddux	2.50
16	Mike Piazza	3.00
17	Matt Williams	.50
18	Kenny Lofton	1.00
19	Alex Rodriquez (Rodriguez)	4.00
20	Tony Gwynn	2.50
21	Mo Vaughn	1.00
22	Chipper Jones	3.00
23	Manny Ramirez	1.50
24	Deion Sanders	.50

1995 Leaf/Limited Bat Patrol

Yet another insert of the game's top veteran hitters was featured as chase cards in Series 2 Leaf Limited. The cards have player action photos on front with large silver-foil "BAT / PATROL" lettering at lower-left. Backs are printed on a silver background and include career stats plus another color player photo. The cards were seeded at the rate of one per pack.

		MT
Complete Set (24):		20.00
Common Player:		.25
1	Frank Thomas	2.00
2	Tony Gwynn	2.50
3	Wade Boggs	.75
4	Larry Walker	.60
5	Ken Griffey Jr.	5.00
6	Jeff Bagwell	2.00
7	Manny Ramirez	1.50
8	Mark Grace	.60
9	Kenny Lofton	1.00
10	Mike Piazza	3.00
11	Will Clark	.50
12	Mo Vaughn	1.00
13	Carlos Baerga	.25
14	Rafael Palmeiro	.50
15	Barry Bonds	1.25
16	Kirby Puckett	2.00
17	Roberto Alomar	1.00
18	Barry Larkin	.35
19	Eddie Murray	.75
20	Tim Salmon	.45
21	Don Mattingly	1.50
22	Fred McGriff	.45
23	Albert Belle	1.00
24	Dante Bichette	.40

1995 Leaf/Limited Lumberjacks

Among the scarcest of 1995 chase cards are the Lumberjacks inserts found in both Series 1 and 2 Leaf Limited at a rate of one per 23 packs on average (less than one per box). Fronts are printed on woodgrain veneer with a large team logo behind a batting action photo of the game's top sluggers. Backs have another photo against a background of tree trunks. A white stripe at bottom carries each card's unique serial number within an edition of 5,000. An even more limited version with black background is limited to 500 numbered cards of each player. Each player can also be found in a promo version.

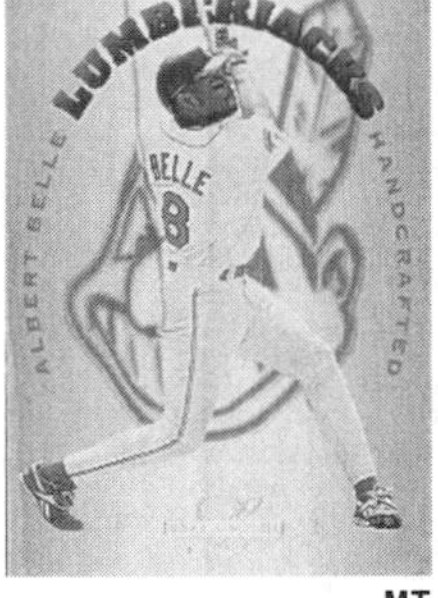

		MT
Complete Set (16):		250.00
Common Player:		8.00
Black:		5X
Promo:		25-50%
1	Albert Belle	12.00
2	Barry Bonds	12.00
3	Juan Gonzalez	15.00
4	Ken Griffey Jr.	50.00
5	Fred McGriff	8.00
6	Mike Piazza	30.00
7	Kirby Puckett	15.00
8	Mo Vaughn	10.00
9	Frank Thomas	20.00
10	Jeff Bagwell	20.00
11	Matt Williams	8.00
12	Jose Canseco	10.00
13	Raul Mondesi	8.00
14	Manny Ramirez	15.00
15	Cecil Fielder	8.00
16	Cal Ripken Jr.	40.00

1995 Leaf/ Opening Day

Issued in celebration of the 1995's season's delayed debut, this set was only available via a mail-in offer for $2 and eight wrappers. Cards were advertised as featuring front and back photos shot on opening day. Fronts have a player photo bordered on the left with a vertical "1995 Opening Day" stripe featuring exploding fireworks at the bottom. The player's name and position appear in a silver-foil strip at bottom; a silver-foil Leaf logo is at upper-right. Backs have a player action photo set against a background of exploding fireworks and a re-cap of the player's 1995 Opening Day performance.

		MT
Complete Set (8):		8.00
Common Player:		.50
1	Frank Thomas	1.50
2	Jeff Bagwell	1.50
3	Barry Bonds	1.00
5	Ken Griffey Jr.	3.00
5	Mike Piazza	2.00
6	Cal Ripken Jr.	2.50
7	Jose Canseco	.50
8	Larry Walker	.50

1996 Leaf

Reverting to a single-series issue of 220 basic cards, plus numerous insert set bells and whistles, this was the final Leaf set under Donruss' ownership. Regular cards offer large action photos on front and back with a side and bottom border subdued through darkening (front) or lightening (back). Fronts feature silver prismatic-foil graphic highlights while the back includes a circular portrait photo with vital data around. Leaf was sold in both hobby and retail versions, each with some unique inserts. Basic unit was the 12-card foil pack, with suggested retail of $2.49.

		MT
Complete Set (220):		20.00
Common Player:		.10
Pack (12):		2.50
Wax Box (30):		55.00
1	John Smoltz	.25
2	Dennis Eckersley	.15
3	Delino DeShields	.10

4	Cliff Floyd	.10
5	Chuck Finley	.10
6	Cecil Fielder	.10
7	Tim Naehring	.10
8	Carlos Perez	.10
9	Brad Ausmus	.10
10	*Matt Lawton*	.75
11	Alan Trammell	.15
12	Steve Finley	.10
13	Paul O'Neill	.15
14	Gary Sheffield	.40
15	Mark McGwire	3.00
16	Bernie Williams	.50
17	Jeff Montgomery	.10
18	Chan Ho Park	.15
19	Greg Vaughn	.15
20	Jeff Kent	.10
21	Cal Ripken Jr.	2.50
22	Charles Johnson	.10
23	Eric Karros	.10
24	Alex Rodriguez	2.50
25	Chris Snopek	.10
26	Jason Isringhausen	.10
27	Chili Davis	.10
28	Chipper Jones	2.00
29	Bret Saberhagen	.10
30	Tony Clark	.35
31	Marty Cordova	.10
32	Dwayne Hosey	.10
33	Fred McGriff	.35
34	Deion Sanders	.25
35	Orlando Merced	.10
36	Brady Anderson	.15
37	Ray Lankford	.15
38	Manny Ramirez	1.00
39	Alex Fernandez	.15
40	Greg Colbrunn	.10
41	Ken Griffey Jr.	3.00
42	Mickey Morandini	.10
43	Chuck Knoblauch	.20
44	Quinton McCracken	.10
45	Tim Salmon	.25
46	Jose Mesa	.10
47	Marquis Grissom	.10
48	Checklist	.10
49	Raul Mondesi	.25
50	Mark Grudzielanek	.10
51	Ray Durham	.10
52	Matt Williams	.25
53	Bob Hamelin	.10
54	Lenny Dykstra	.10
55	Jeff King	.10
56	LaTroy Hawkins	.10
57	Terry Pendleton	.10
58	Kevin Stocker	.10
59	Ozzie Timmons	.10
60	David Justice	.20
61	Ricky Bottalico	.10
62	Andy Ashby	.10
63	Larry Walker	.35
64	Jose Canseco	.25
65	Bret Boone	.10
66	Shawn Green	.15
67	Chad Curtis	.10
68	Travis Fryman	.10
69	Roger Clemens	.75
70	David Bell	.10
71	Rusty Greer	.10
72	Bob Higginson	.10
73	Joey Hamilton	.10
74	Kevin Seitzer	.10
75	Julian Tavarez	.10
76	Troy Percival	.10
77	Kirby Puckett	1.00
78	Barry Bonds	.75
79	Michael Tucker	.10
80	Paul Molitor	.35
81	Carlos Garcia	.10
82	Johnny Damon	.15
83	Mike Hampton	.10
84	Ariel Prieto	.10
85	Tony Tarasco	.10
86	Pete Schourek	.10
87	Tom Glavine	.20
88	Rondell White	.15
89	Jim Edmonds	.10
90	Robby Thompson	.10
91	Wade Boggs	.35
92	Pedro Martinez	.15
93	Gregg Jefferies	.15
94	Albert Belle	.75
95	Benji Gil	.10
96	Denny Neagle	.10
97	Mark Langston	.10
98	Sandy Alomar	.15
99	Tony Gwynn	1.25
100	Todd Hundley	.20
101	Dante Bichette	.15
102	Eddie Murray	.40
103	Lyle Mouton	.10
104	John Jaha	.10
105	Checklist	.10
106	Jon Nunnally	.10
107	Juan Gonzalez	.75
108	Kevin Appier	.10
109	Brian McRae	.10
110	Lee Smith	.10
111	Tim Wakefield	.10
112	Sammy Sosa	1.50
113	Jay Buhner	.15
114	Garret Anderson	.10
115	Edgar Martinez	.10
116	Edgardo Alfonzo	.15
117	Billy Ashley	.10
118	Joe Carter	.10
119	Javy Lopez	.15
120	Bobby Bonilla	.15
121	Ken Caminiti	.25
122	Barry Larkin	.15
123	Shannon Stewart	.10
124	Orel Hershiser	.10
125	Jeff Conine	.10
126	Mark Grace	.20
127	Kenny Lofton	.60
128	Luis Gonzalez	.10
129	Rico Brogna	.10
130	Mo Vaughn	.60
131	Brad Radke	.10
132	Jose Herrera	.10
133	Rick Aguilera	.10
134	Gary DiSarcina	.10
135	Andres Galarraga	.15
136	Carl Everett	.10
137	Steve Avery	.10
138	Vinny Castilla	.10
139	Dennis Martinez	.10
140	John Wetteland	.10
141	Alex Gonzalez	.10
142	Brian Jordan	.15
143	Todd Hollandsworth	.15
144	Terrell Wade	.10
145	Wilson Alvarez	.10
146	Reggie Sanders	.10
147	Will Clark	.25
148	Hideo Nomo	.50
149	J.T. Snow	.10
150	Frank Thomas	1.50
151	Ivan Rodriguez	.60
152	Jay Bell	.10
153	Checklist	.10
154	David Cone	.15
155	Roberto Alomar	.75
156	Carlos Delgado	.50
157	Carlos Baerga	.10
158	Geronimo Berroa	.10
159	Joe Vitiello	.10
160	Terry Steinbach	.10
161	Doug Drabek	.10
162	David Segui	.10
163	Ozzie Smith	.40
164	Kurt Abbott	.10
165	Randy Johnson	.40
166	John Valentin	.10
167	Mickey Tettleton	.10
168	Ruben Sierra	.10
169	Jim Thome	.35
170	Mike Greenwell	.10
171	Quilvio Veras	.10
172	Robin Ventura	.15
173	Bill Pulsipher	.10
174	Rafael Palmeiro	.20
175	Hal Morris	.10
176	Ryan Klesko	.25
177	Eric Young	.10
178	Shane Andrews	.10
179	Brian Hunter	.10
180	Brett Butler	.10
181	John Olerud	.15
182	Moises Alou	.10
183	Glenallen Hill	.10
184	Ismael Valdes	.10
185	Andy Pettitte	.75
186	Yamil Benitez	.10
187	Jason Bere	.10
188	Dean Palmer	.10
189	Jimmy Haynes	.10
190	Trevor Hoffman	.10
191	Mike Mussina	.30
192	Greg Maddux	1.50
193	Ozzie Guillen	.10
194	Pat Listach	.10
195	Derek Bell	.10
196	Darren Daulton	.10
197	John Mabry	.10
198	Ramon Martinez	.10
199	Jeff Bagwell	1.25
200	Mike Piazza	2.00
201	Al Martin	.10
202	Aaron Sele	.10
203	Ed Sprague	.10
204	Rod Beck	.10
205	Checklist	.10
206	Mike Lansing	.10
207	Craig Biggio	.15
208	Jeffrey Hammonds	.10
209	Dave Nilsson	.10
210	Checklist, Inserts (Dante Bichette, Albert Belle)	.10
211	Derek Jeter	2.00
212	Alan Benes	.10
213	Jason Schmidt	.10
214	Alex Ochoa	.10
215	Ruben Rivera	.15
216	Roger Cedeno	.20
217	Jeff Suppan	.10
218	Billy Wagner	.10
219	Mark Loretta	.10
220	Karim Garcia	.50

1996 Leaf Press Proofs

Carrying the parallel edition concept to its inevitable next level, '96 Leaf offered the Press Proof insert cards in three degrees of scarcity, each highlighted with appropriate holographic foil. Like the other '96 Leaf inserts, these are individually serially numbered within its edition limit. At the top of the line are Gold Press Proofs in an edition of only 500 of each card. Silver and Bronze versions were produced in editions of 1,000 and 2,000, respectively. Press Proofs are inserted into both hobby and retail packs at an average rate of one card per 10 packs.

	MT
Complete Set, Gold (220):	2000.
Complete Set, Silver (220):	1000.
Complete Set, Bronze(220):	500.00
Common Player, Gold:	4.00
Common Player, Silver:	2.50
Common Player, Bronze:	1.00

(Press Proof stars valued as follows in comparison to regular-issue '96 Leaf - Gold: 20-30X; Silver: 10-15X; Bronze: 7-10X.)

1996 Leaf All-Star MVP Contenders

A surprise insert in Leaf boxes was this interactive redemption issue. Twenty leading candidates for MVP honors at the 1996 All-Star Game in Philadelphia were presented in a silver-foil highlighted horizontal format. The player's league logo serves as a background to the color action photo on front; the All-Star logo is in the lower-left corner. Backs have details of the redemption offer. Persons who sent in the Mike Piazza card for redemption received a gold version of the set and had their Piazza card punch-cancelled and returned.

		MT
Complete Set (20):		30.00
Common Card:		1.00
Expired:		8-15-96
1	Frank Thomas	3.00
2	Mike Piazza	4.00
2c	Mike Piazza (redeemed and punch-cancelled)	3.00
3	Sammy Sosa	3.00
4	Cal Ripken Jr.	5.00
5	Jeff Bagwell	2.00
6	Reggie Sanders	.75
7	Mo Vaughn	1.00
8	Tony Gwynn	3.00
9	Dante Bichette	1.00
10	Tim Salmon	1.00
11	Chipper Jones	4.00
12	Kenny Lofton	1.00
13	Manny Ramirez	2.00
14	Barry Bonds	1.50
15	Raul Mondesi	1.00
16	Kirby Puckett	1.50
17	Albert Belle	1.50
18	Ken Griffey Jr.	6.00
19	Greg Maddux	3.00
20	Bonus card	.75

1996 Leaf All-Star MVP Contenders Gold

A surprise insert in Leaf boxes was an interactive redemption issue of 20 leading candidates for MVP honors at the 1996 All-Star Game in Philadelphia. The first 5,000 persons who sent in the Mike Piazza card for redemption received a gold version of the set and had their Piazza card punch-cancelled and returned.

		MT
Complete Set (19):		45.00
Common Card:		1.00
1	Frank Thomas	5.00
2	Mike Piazza	6.00
3	Sammy Sosa	5.00
4	Cal Ripken Jr.	7.50
5	Jeff Bagwell	7.50
6	Reggie Sanders	1.00
7	Mo Vaughn	2.00
8	Tony Gwynn	7.50
9	Dante Bichette	1.00
10	Tim Salmon	1.00
11	Chipper Jones	6.00
12	Kenny Lofton	2.00
13	Manny Ramirez	10.00
14	Barry Bonds	3.00
15	Raul Mondesi	2.00
16	Kirby Puckett	3.00
17	Albert Belle	2.00
18	Ken Griffey Jr.	10.00
19	Greg Maddux	5.00

1996 Leaf Frank Thomas' Greatest Hits

Die-cut plastic with a background of prismatic foil to simulate a segment of a compact disc is the format for this insert issue chronicling the career-to-date of Frank Thomas. Backs include a few stats and a portrait photo, plus a gold-foil serial number from within an edition of 5,000. Cards #1-4 are found only in hobby packs; cards #5-7 are exclusive to retail packs (average insertion rate one per 210 packs) and card #8 could be had only through a wrapper redemption.

		MT
Complete Set (8):		145.00
Common Card:		20.00
1	1990	20.00
2	1991	20.00
3	1992	20.00
4	1993	20.00
5	1994	20.00
6	1995	20.00
7	Career	20.00
8	MVP	20.00

1996 Leaf Gold Leaf Stars

A vignetted background of embossed gold metallic cardboard and a Gold Leaf Stars logo in 22-karat gold foil are featured on this limited (2,500 of each) edition insert. Backs include a second color photo of the player and a serial number from within the edition. Gold Leaf Stars were included in both hobby and retail packaging, with an average insertion rate of one per 210 packs.

		MT
Complete Set (15):		300.00
Common Player:		7.50
1	Frank Thomas	25.00
2	Dante Bichette	7.50
3	Sammy Sosa	40.00
4	Ken Griffey Jr.	60.00
5	Mike Piazza	40.00
6	Tim Salmon	7.50
7	Hideo Nomo	7.50
8	Cal Ripken Jr.	50.00
9	Chipper Jones	40.00
10	Albert Belle	12.00
11	Tony Gwynn	30.00
12	Mo Vaughn	10.00
13	Barry Larkin	7.50
14	Manny Ramirez	15.00
15	Greg Maddux	30.00

1996 Leaf Hats Off

The most technically innovative inserts of 1996 have to be the Hats Off series exclusive to Leaf retail packs. Front player photos are on a background that is both flocked to simulate the cloth of a baseball cap, plus enhanced with a stiched team logo. The graphics are all in raised textured gold foil. Backs are conventionally printed and include a gold-foil serial number placing each card within an edition of 5,000 per player.

		MT
Complete Set (8):		120.00
Common Player:		5.00
1	Cal Ripken Jr.	30.00
2	Barry Larkin	5.00
3	Frank Thomas	20.00
4	Mo Vaughn	8.00
5	Ken Griffey Jr.	40.00
6	Hideo Nomo	6.00
7	Albert Belle	10.00
8	Greg Maddux	20.00

1996 Leaf Picture Perfect

Leaf calls the glossy central area of these inserts "pearlized foil," which allows the player action photo to stand out in contrast to the actual wood veneer background. Gold foil graphic highlights complete the design. Backs are conventionally printed and include a gold-foil serial number from within the edition of 5,000 of each player's card. Cards #1-6 are hobby-only inserts, while #7-12 are found in retail packs. Average insertion rate is one per 140 packs.

		MT
Complete Set (12):		220.00
Common Player:		5.00
1	Frank Thomas	15.00
2	Cal Ripken Jr.	30.00
3	Greg Maddux	20.00
4	Manny Ramirez	12.00
5	Chipper Jones	25.00
6	Tony Gwynn	20.00
7	Ken Griffey Jr.	40.00
8	Albert Belle	10.00
9	Jeff Bagwell	15.00
10	Mike Piazza	25.00
11	Mo Vaughn	10.00
12	Barry Bonds	12.00

1996 Leaf Statistical Standouts

The feel of leather complements the game-used baseball background on these hobby-only inserts featuring the game's top names. Backs offer statistical data and a gold-foil serial number placing the card within an edition of 2,500 for each player. Average insertion rate is one per 210 packs.

		MT
Complete Set (8):		150.00
Common Player:		10.00
1	Cal Ripken Jr.	35.00
2	Tony Gwynn	20.00
3	Frank Thomas	20.00
4	Ken Griffey Jr.	45.00
5	Hideo Nomo	10.00
6	Greg Maddux	20.00
7	Albert Belle	10.00
8	Chipper Jones	25.00

1996 Leaf Total Bases

Total-base leaders from 1991-95 are featured in this hobby-only insert set. Card fronts are printed on textured canvas to simulate a base. Fronts are highlighted with gold foil. Backs have stats ranking the player in this category plus a gold-foil serial number from an edition of 5,000 of each player. Total Bases inserts are seeded at an average rate of one per 72 packs.

		MT
Complete Set (12):		110.00
Common Player:		3.00
1	Frank Thomas	15.00
2	Albert Belle	8.00
3	Rafael Palmeiro	5.00
4	Barry Bonds	8.00
5	Kirby Puckett	12.50
6	Joe Carter	3.00
7	Paul Molitor	5.00
8	Fred McGriff	5.00
9	Ken Griffey Jr.	30.00
10	Carlos Baerga	3.00
11	Juan Gonzalez	8.00
12	Cal Ripken Jr.	25.00

1996 Leaf/Limited

Leaf's 1996 Limited set contains 90 of the top rookies and veterans in baseball. There is also a 100-card Limited Gold parallel set which includes the 90 main cards, plus 10 cards from a Limited Rookies insert set. The gold parallel cards are seeded one per every 11 packs. Regular Limited Rookies inserts were seeded one per every seven packs. Two other insert sets were also made - two versions of Lumberjacks and Pennant Craze.

		MT
Complete Set (90):		50.00
Common Player:		.25
Limited Gold Set (90):		250.00
Limited Golds:		5X
Pack (5):		4.00
Wax Box (14):		50.00
1	Ivan Rodriguez	1.50
2	Roger Clemens	3.00
3	Gary Sheffield	1.00
4	Tino Martinez	.35
5	Sammy Sosa	5.00
6	Reggie Sanders	.25
7	Ray Lankford	.25
8	Manny Ramirez	2.50
9	Jeff Bagwell	3.00
10	Greg Maddux	4.50
11	Ken Griffey Jr.	8.00
12	Rondell White	.25
13	Mike Piazza	5.00
14	Marc Newfield	.25
15	Cal Ripken Jr.	6.00
16	Carlos Delgado	.50
17	Tim Salmon	.50
18	Andres Galarraga	.50
19	Chuck Knoblauch	.50
20	Matt Williams	.50
21	Mark McGwire	8.00
22	Ben McDonald	.25
23	Frank Thomas	3.00
24	Johnny Damon	.25
25	Gregg Jefferies	.25
26	Travis Fryman	.25
27	Chipper Jones	5.00
28	David Cone	.35
29	Kenny Lofton	2.00
30	Mike Mussina	1.00
31	Alex Rodriguez	7.50
32	Carlos Baerga	.25
33	Brian Hunter	.25
34	Juan Gonzalez	2.00
35	Bernie Williams	1.50
36	Wally Joyner	.25
37	Fred McGriff	.75
38	Randy Johnson	1.00
39	Marty Cordova	.25
40	Garret Anderson	.25
41	Albert Belle	2.00
42	Edgar Martinez	.25
43	Barry Larkin	.40
44	Paul O'Neill	.40
45	Cecil Fielder	.25
46	Rusty Greer	.25
47	Mo Vaughn	2.00
48	Dante Bichette	.75
49	Ryan Klesko	.50
50	Roberto Alomar	2.00
51	Raul Mondesi	.75
52	Robin Ventura	.40
53	Tony Gwynn	3.00
54	Mark Grace	.50
55	Jim Thome	1.00
56	Jason Giambi	.25
57	Tom Glavine	.50
58	Jim Edmonds	.40
59	Pedro Martinez	.40
60	Charles Johnson	.25
61	Wade Boggs	.50
62	Orlando Merced	.25
63	Craig Biggio	.40
64	Brady Anderson	.25
65	Hideo Nomo	.75
66	Ozzie Smith	1.00
67	Eddie Murray	.75
68	Will Clark	.75
69	Jay Buhner	.25
70	Kirby Puckett	3.00
71	Barry Bonds	2.50
72	Ray Durham	.25
73	Sterling Hitchcock	.25
74	John Smoltz	.75
75	Andre Dawson	.35
76	Joe Carter	.25
77	Ryne Sandberg	1.50
78	Rickey Henderson	.40
79	Brian Jordan	.25
80	Greg Vaughn	.35
81	Andy Pettitte	1.50
82	Dean Palmer	.25
83	Paul Molitor	1.00
84	Rafael Palmeiro	.50
85	Henry Rodriguez	.25
86	Larry Walker	.75
87	Ismael Valdes	.25
88	Derek Bell	.25
89	J.T. Snow	.25
90	Jack McDowell	.25

1996 Leaf/Limited Lumberjacks

Lumberjacks inserts return to Leaf Limited, but the 1996 versions feature an improved maple stock that puts wood grains on both sides of the card. Ten different Lumberjacks are available in two different versions. Regular versions are serial numbered to 5,000, while a special black-bordered Limited Edition version is numbered to 500.

		MT
Complete Set (10):		180.00
Common Player:		6.00
Lumberjack Blacks (500):		3X
1	Ken Griffey Jr.	35.00
2	Sammy Sosa	20.00
3	Cal Ripken Jr.	30.00
4	Frank Thomas	20.00
5	Alex Rodriguez	30.00
6	Mo Vaughn	10.00
7	Chipper Jones	25.00
8	Mike Piazza	25.00
9	Jeff Bagwell	15.00
10	Mark McGwire	35.00

1996 Leaf/Limited Pennant Craze

Each card in this insert set is sequentially numbered to 2,500 in silver foil on the back. The top-front of the cards have a die-cut pennant shape and is felt-textured.

		MT
Complete Set (10):		150.00
Common Player:		7.50
1	Juan Gonzalez	10.00
2	Cal Ripken Jr.	30.00
3	Frank Thomas	15.00
4	Ken Griffey Jr.	35.00
5	Albert Belle	7.50
6	Greg Maddux	20.00
7	Paul Molitor	7.50
8	Alex Rodriguez	30.00
9	Barry Bonds	10.00
10	Chipper Jones	25.00

1996 Leaf/Limited Rookies

There are two versions of this 1996 Limited insert set. The cards are reprinted as part of a Limited Gold parallel set, which also includes the regular issue's 90 cards. The gold cards are seeded one per every 11 packs. The top young players are also featured on regular Limited Rookies inserts; these versions are seeded one per every seven packs.

		MT
Complete Set (10):		40.00
Common Player:		2.00
Limited Gold:		5X
1	Alex Ochoa	2.00
2	Darin Erstad	10.00
3	Ruben Rivera	2.00
4	Derek Jeter	15.00
5	Jermaine Dye	2.00
6	Jason Kendall	2.50
7	Mike Grace	2.00
8	Andruw Jones	10.00
9	Rey Ordonez	5.00
10	George Arias	2.00

1996 Leaf/Preferred Leaf Gold Promos

Each of the 77 gold cards in the Preferred Steel set can also be found in a promo card version. The samples differ from the issued versions only in an overprint diagonally on the back which reads "PROMOTIONAL CARD". This parallel promo edition represents one of the largest promo card issues of the mid-1990s.

		MT
Complete Set (77):		750.00
Common Player:		5.00
1	Frank Thomas	15.00
2	Paul Molitor	15.00
3	Kenny Lofton	15.00
4	Travis Fryman	5.00
5	Jeff Conine	5.00
6	Barry Bonds	30.00
7	Gregg Jefferies	5.00
8	Alex Rodriguez	40.00
9	Wade Boggs	12.50
10	David Justice	7.50
11	Hideo Nomo	12.50
12	Roberto Alomar	2.00
13	Todd Hollandsworth	7.50
14	Mark McGwire	45.00
15	Rafael Palmeiro	7.50
16	Will Clark	7.50
17	Cal Ripken Jr.	40.00
18	Derek Bell	5.00
19	Gary Sheffield	12.50
20	Juan Gonzalez	20.00
21	Garret Anderson	5.00
22	Mo Vaughn	15.00
23	Robin Ventura	5.00
24	Carlos Baerga	5.00
25	Tim Salmon	10.00
26	Matt Williams	7.50
27	Fred McGriff	10.00
28	Rondell White	5.00
29	Ray Lankford	5.00
30	Lenny Dykstra	5.00
31	J.T. Snow	5.00
32	Sammy Sosa	15.00
33	Chipper Jones	35.00
34	Bobby Bonilla	5.00
35	Paul Wilson	5.00
36	Darren Daulton	5.00
37	Larry Walker	7.50
38	Raul Mondesi	7.50
39	Jeff Bagwell	25.00
40	Derek Jeter	25.00
41	Kirby Puckett	25.00
42	Jason Isringhausen	5.00
43	Vinny Castilla	5.00
44	Jim Edmonds	7.50
45	Ron Gant	5.00
46	Carlos Delgado	5.00
47	Jose Canseco	10.00
48	Tony Gwynn	25.00

49	Mike Mussina	7.50
50	Charles Johnson	5.00
51	Mike Piazza	35.00
52	Ken Griffey Jr.	50.00
53	Greg Maddux	32.00
54	Mark Grace	10.00
55	Ryan Klesko	7.50
56	Dennis Eckersley	5.00
57	Rickey Henderson	7.50
58	Michael Tucker	5.00
59	Joe Carter	7.50
60	Randy Johnson	12.50
61	Brian Jordan	5.00
62	Shawn Green	5.00
63	Roger Clemens	20.00
64	Andres Galarraga	7.50
65	Johnny Damon	7.50
66	Ryne Sandberg	15.00
67	Alan Benes	5.00
68	Albert Belle	20.00
69	Barry Larkin	7.50
70	Marty Cordova	6.25
71	Dante Bichette	7.50
72	Craig Biggio	5.00
73	Reggie Sanders	5.00
74	Moises Alou	5.00
75	Chuck Knoblauch	7.50
76	Cecil Fielder	7.50
77	Manny Ramirez	7.50

1996 Leaf/Preferred

Leaf Preferred consists of 150 cards, a Press Proof parallel set and three insert sets, one of which has its own parallel set, too. While no individual odds are given for insert sets, the overall odds of getting an insert card are one per 10 packs. The Press Proof inserts replace the silver foil name and strip down the left side of the card with gold foil. Press Proof parallels were limited to 250 sets. Another insert set, Silver Leaf Steel, has a card seeded one per pack. This insert set is paralleled by a Gold Leaf Steel set, which appears in much more limited numbers. The two other insert sets are Steel Power and Staremaster.

		MT
Complete Set (150):		40.00
Common Player:		.15
Pack (6):		3.00
Wax Box (24):		50.00
1	Ken Griffey Jr.	4.00
2	Rico Brogna	.15
3	Gregg Jefferies	.15
4	Reggie Sanders	.15
5	Manny Ramirez	1.50
6	Shawn Green	.15
7	Tino Martinez	.15
8	Jeff Bagwell	2.00
9	Marc Newfield	.15
10	Ray Lankford	.15
11	Jay Bell	.15
12	Greg Maddux	2.50
13	Frank Thomas	1.50
14	Travis Fryman	.15
15	Mark McGwire	4.00
16	Chuck Knoblauch	.25
17	Sammy Sosa	2.00
18	Matt Williams	.35
19	Roger Clemens	1.00
20	Rondell White	.15
21	Ivan Rodriguez	.75
22	Cal Ripken Jr.	3.00
23	Ben McDonald	.15
24	Kenny Lofton	1.00
25	Mike Piazza	2.50
26	David Cone	.25
27	Gary Sheffield	.75
28	Tim Salmon	.40
29	Andres Galarraga	.30
30	Johnny Damon	.20
31	Ozzie Smith	1.00
32	Carlos Baerga	.20
33	Raul Mondesi	.35
34	Moises Alou	.15
35	Alex Rodriguez	5.00
36	Mike Mussina	1.00
37	Jason Isringhausen	.40
38	Barry Larkin	.40
39	Bernie Williams	.75
40	Chipper Jones	2.50
41	Joey Hamilton	.15
42	Charles Johnson	.15
43	Juan Gonzalez	1.00
44	Greg Vaughn	.15
45	Robin Ventura	.15
46	Albert Belle	1.00
47	Rafael Palmeiro	.25
48	Brian Hunter	.15
49	Mo Vaughn	1.50
50	Paul O'Neill	.15
51	Mark Grace	.25
52	Randy Johnson	.60
53	Pedro Martinez	.15
54	Marty Cordova	.20
55	Garret Anderson	.20
56	Joe Carter	.40
57	Jim Thome	.75
58	Edgardo Alfonzo	.15
59	Dante Bichette	.40
60	Darryl Hamilton	.15
61	Roberto Alomar	1.25
62	Fred McGriff	.60
63	Kirby Puckett	2.00
64	Hideo Nomo	.75
65	Alex Fernandez	.15
66	Ryan Klesko	.40
67	Wade Boggs	.25
68	Eddie Murray	.50
69	Eric Karros	.15
70	Jim Edmonds	.25
71	Edgar Martinez	.15
72	Andy Pettitte	1.00
73	Mark Grudzielanek	.15
74	Tom Glavine	.25
75	Ken Caminiti	.50
76	Will Clark	.30
77	Craig Biggio	.15
78	Brady Anderson	.20
79	Tony Gwynn	2.00
80	Larry Walker	.40
81	Brian Jordan	.25
82	Lenny Dykstra	.15
83	Butch Huskey	.15
84	Jack McDowell	.15
85	Cecil Fielder	.25
86	Jose Canseco	.30
87	Jason Giambi	.20
88	Rickey Henderson	.15
89	Kevin Seitzer	.15
90	Carlos Delgado	.75
91	Ryne Sandberg	1.25
92	Dwight Gooden	.15
93	Michael Tucker	.15
94	Barry Bonds	1.25
95	Eric Young	.15
96	Dean Palmer	.15
97	Henry Rodriguez	.15
98	John Mabry	.15
99	J.T. Snow	.15
100	Andre Dawson	.15
101	Ismael Valdes	.15
102	Charles Nagy	.15
103	Jay Buhner	.40
104	Derek Bell	.15
105	Paul Molitor	.75
106	Hal Morris	.15
107	Ray Durham	.15
108	Bernard Gilkey	.15
109	John Valentin	.15
110	Melvin Nieves	.15
111	John Smoltz	.40
112	Terrell Wade	.15
113	Chad Mottola	.15
114	Tony Clark	.75
115	John Wasdin	.15
116	Derek Jeter	2.00
117	Rey Ordonez	.50
118	Jason Thompson	.15
119	*Robin Jennings*	.15
120	*Rocky Coppinger*	.40
121	Billy Wagner	.30
122	Steve Gibralter	.15
123	Jermaine Dye	.40
124	Jason Kendall	.15
125	*Mike Grace*	.50
126	Jason Schmidt	.15
127	Paul Wilson	.25
128	Alan Benes	.25
129	Justin Thompson	.15
130	Brooks Kieschnick	.15
131	George Arias	.15
132	*Osvaldo Fernandez*	.40
133	Todd Hollandsworth	.20
134	Eric Owens	.15
135	Chan Ho Park	.15
136	Mark Loretta	.15
137	Ruben Rivera	.75
138	Jeff Suppan	.15
139	Ugueth Urbina	.15
140	LaTroy Hawkins	.15
141	Chris Snopek	.15
142	Edgar Renteria	.40
143	Raul Casanova	.15
144	Jose Herrera	.15
145	*Matt Lawton*	.75
146	*Ralph Milliard*	.15
147	Checklist	.15
148	Checklist	.15
149	Checklist	.15
150	Checklist	.15

1996 Leaf/Preferred Press Proofs

Inserted at a rate of about one per 48 packs, Press Proof parallels of the 150 cards in Leaf Preferred are identifiable only by the use of gold foil, rather than silver, on the card fronts, and gold ink on back. The cards are not otherwise marked or numbered. It is believed the issue was limited to 250-500 of each card.

	MT
Complete Set (150):	1500.
Common Player:	2.00
Stars:	25X

(See 1996 Leaf Preferred for checklist and base card values.)

1996 Leaf/Preferred Leaf Steel

This 77-card insert set has two versions - a silver one and a much more limited gold one. A Silver Leaf Steel card is included in every pack; the parallel versions appear about one per 24 packs.

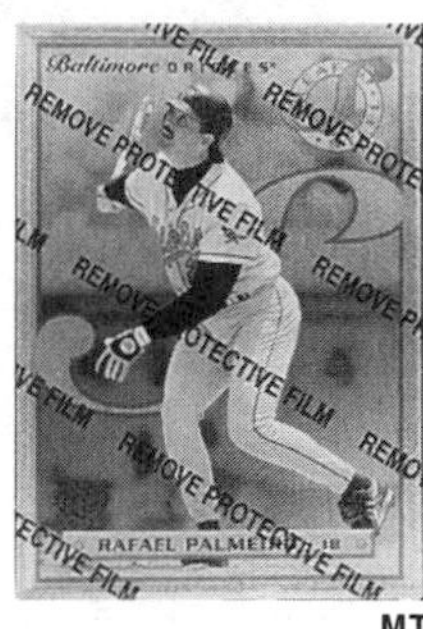

		MT
Complete Set (77):		100.00
Common Player:		.25
Golds:		6X
1	Frank Thomas	5.00
2	Paul Molitor	2.00
3	Kenny Lofton	1.50
4	Travis Fryman	.25
5	Jeff Conine	.25
6	Barry Bonds	2.50
7	Gregg Jefferies	.25
8	Alex Rodriguez	7.50
9	Wade Boggs	.50
10	David Justice	1.00
11	Hideo Nomo	1.00
12	Roberto Alomar	2.00
13	Todd Hollandsworth	.25
14	Mark McGwire	10.00
15	Rafael Palmeiro	1.00
16	Will Clark	1.00
17	Cal Ripken Jr.	8.00
18	Derek Bell	.25
19	Gary Sheffield	1.50
20	Juan Gonzalez	2.50
21	Garret Anderson	.25
22	Mo Vaughn	1.50
23	Robin Ventura	.50
24	Carlos Baerga	.25
25	Tim Salmon	1.00
26	Matt Williams	1.00
27	Fred McGriff	.75
28	Rondell White	.75
29	Ray Lankford	.25
30	Lenny Dykstra	.25
31	J.T. Snow	.25
32	Sammy Sosa	6.00
33	Chipper Jones	6.00
34	Bobby Bonilla	.25
35	Paul Wilson	.25
36	Darren Daulton	.25
37	Larry Walker	1.50
38	Raul Mondesi	1.00
39	Jeff Bagwell	3.00
40	Derek Jeter	5.00
41	Kirby Puckett	2.50
42	Jason Isringhausen	.25
43	Vinny Castilla	.25
44	Jim Edmonds	.50
45	Ron Gant	.25
46	Carlos Delgado	.75
47	Jose Canseco	1.00
48	Tony Gwynn	5.00
49	Mike Mussina	2.00
50	Charles Johnson	.25
51	Mike Piazza	6.00
52	Ken Griffey Jr.	10.00
53	Greg Maddux	5.00
54	Mark Grace	1.00
55	Ryan Klesko	.75
56	Dennis Eckersley	.25
57	Rickey Henderson	.50
58	Michael Tucker	.25
59	Joe Carter	.50
60	Randy Johnson	1.50
61	Brian Jordan	.25
62	Shawn Green	.50
63	Roger Clemens	3.00
64	Andres Galarraga	.50
65	Johnny Damon	.25
66	Ryne Sandberg	2.50
67	Alan Benes	.25
68	Albert Belle	2.00
69	Barry Larkin	.50
70	Marty Cordova	.25
71	Dante Bichette	.50
72	Craig Biggio	.75
73	Reggie Sanders	.25

74	Moises Alou	.50
75	Chuck Knoblauch	1.00
76	Cecil Fielder	.25
77	Manny Ramirez	3.00

1996 Leaf/Preferred Staremaster

These 1996 Leaf Preferred inserts provide a photographic tribute to the stares of 12 top players. Each card is printed on silver holographic card stock and is numbered up to 2,500.

		MT
Complete Set (12):		300.00
Common Player:		10.00
1	Chipper Jones	30.00
2	Alex Rodriguez	40.00
3	Derek Jeter	25.00
4	Tony Gwynn	25.00
5	Frank Thomas	20.00
6	Ken Griffey Jr.	50.00
7	Cal Ripken Jr.	40.00
8	Greg Maddux	30.00
9	Albert Belle	12.00
10	Barry Bonds	12.00
11	Jeff Bagwell	15.00
12	Mike Piazza	35.00

1996 Leaf/Preferred Steel Power

This eight-card Leaf Steel insert set combines micro-etched foil with interior die-cutting to honor the game's top power hitters. Each insert card carries a serial number up to 5,000.

		MT
Complete Set (8):		125.00
Common Player:		6.00
1	Albert Belle	10.00
2	Mo Vaughn	6.00
3	Ken Griffey Jr.	40.00
4	Cal Ripken Jr.	30.00
5	Mike Piazza	25.00
6	Barry Bonds	7.50
7	Jeff Bagwell	15.00
8	Frank Thomas	20.00

1996 Leaf/Signature Series

There were 245 Major League players who autographed cards for Leaf's Signature Series. At least one authentic signature is guaranteed in every pack. There were 235 players who signed cards in these quantities: Gold (500 autographs), Silver (1,000) and Bronze (3,500). The other 10 players signed fewer autographs - 100 Gold, 200 Silver and 700 Bronze. Each major leaguer signed his cards, including an affidavit that was notarized to guarantee each signature was authentic. In addition, Pinnacle used team clubhouse officials to witness autographs. One out of every 48 packs is a super pack containing nothing but autographed cards. In addition, the regular-issue base set is paralleled in Gold and Platinum Press Proof insert sets. The gold version is seeded one per 12 packs in Series 1 and one per eight in the Extended Series. Platinums are found only in the Extended Series packs at the rate of one per 24 packs. Four-card packs of Leaf Signature Series carried a suggested retail price at issue of $9.99.

		MT
Complete Set (150):		75.00
Complete 1st Series (100):		50.00
Complete Extended Series (50):		25.00
Common Player:		.20
Gold Press Proofs Set (150):		900.00
Gold PP Stars:		10X
Complete Platinum Set (150):		3000.
Platinum PP Ser. 1 Stars:		30X
Platinum PP Ser. 2 Stars:		15X
Platinum PP Ser. 1Yng Stars:		20X
Platinum PP Ser. 2Yng Stars:		12X
Pack (4):		10.00
Wax Box (12):		100.00
1	Mike Piazza	3.00
2	Juan Gonzalez	1.50
3	Greg Maddux	3.00
4	Marc Newfield	.20
5	Wade Boggs	.50
6	Ray Lankford	.20
7	Frank Thomas	2.00
8	Rico Brogna	.20
9	Tim Salmon	.40
10	Ken Griffey Jr.	5.00
11	Manny Ramirez	1.50
12	Cecil Fielder	.25
13	Gregg Jefferies	.20
14	Rondell White	.40
15	Cal Ripken Jr.	4.00
16	Alex Rodriguez	4.00
17	Bernie Williams	1.00
18	Andres Galarraga	.40
19	Mike Mussina	1.00
20	Chuck Knoblauch	.30
21	Joe Carter	.25
22	Jeff Bagwell	2.50
23	Mark McGwire	5.00
24	Sammy Sosa	2.00
25	Reggie Sanders	.20
26	Chipper Jones	3.00
27	Jeff Cirillo	.20
28	Roger Clemens	1.25
29	Craig Biggio	.35
30	Gary Sheffield	.50
31	Paul O'Neill	.35
32	Johnny Damon	.50
33	Jason Isringhausen	.20
34	Jay Bell	.20
35	Henry Rodriguez	.20
36	Matt Williams	.40
37	Randy Johnson	.75
38	Fred McGriff	.50
39	Jason Giambi	.20
40	Ivan Rodriguez	.75
41	Raul Mondesi	.50
42	Barry Larkin	.50
43	Ryan Klesko	.40
44	Joey Hamilton	.20
45	Todd Hundley	.25
46	Jim Edmonds	.50
47	Dante Bichette	.35
48	Roberto Alomar	1.25
49	Mark Grace	.40
50	Brady Anderson	.30
51	Hideo Nomo	1.00
52	Ozzie Smith	1.00
53	Robin Ventura	.35
54	Andy Pettitte	1.00
55	Kenny Lofton	1.00
56	John Mabry	.20
57	Paul Molitor	.75
58	Rey Ordonez	.75
59	Albert Belle	1.00
60	Charles Johnson	.20
61	Edgar Martinez	.20
62	Derek Bell	.20
63	Carlos Delgado	.75
64	Raul Casanova	.20
65	Ismael Valdes	.20
66	J.T. Snow	.20
67	Derek Jeter	3.00
68	Jason Kendall	.20
69	John Smoltz	.50
70	Chad Mottola	.20
71	Jim Thome	.30
72	Will Clark	.50
73	Mo Vaughn	1.00
74	John Wasdin	.20
75	Rafael Palmeiro	.50
76	Mark Grudzielanek	.20
77	Larry Walker	.40
78	Alan Benes	.25
79	Michael Tucker	.20
80	Billy Wagner	.25
81	Paul Wilson	.25
82	Greg Vaughn	.25
83	Dean Palmer	.20
84	Ryne Sandberg	1.25
85	Eric Young	.20
86	Jay Buhner	.25
87	Tony Clark	.35
88	Jermaine Dye	.20
89	Barry Bonds	1.25
90	Ugueth Urbina	.20
91	Charles Nagy	.20
92	Ruben Rivera	.25
93	Todd Hollandsworth	.20
94	*Darin Erstad*	8.00
95	Brooks Kieschnick	.20
96	Edgar Renteria	.35
97	Lenny Dykstra	.20
98	Tony Gwynn	2.00
99	Kirby Puckett	1.50
100	Checklist	.20
101	Andruw Jones	2.50
102	Alex Ochoa	.20
103	David Cone	.20
104	Rusty Greer	.20
105	Jose Canseco	.40
106	Ken Caminiti	.40
107	Mariano Rivera	.50
108	Ron Gant	.20
109	Darryl Strawberry	.20
110	Vladimir Guerrero	2.00
111	George Arias	.20
112	Jeff Conine	.20
113	Bobby Higginson	.20
114	Eric Karros	.20
115	Brian Hunter	.20
116	Eddie Murray	.50
117	Todd Walker	.75
118	Chan Ho Park	.20
119	John Jaha	.20
120	David Justice	.40
121	Makoto Suzuki	.20
122	Scott Rolen	1.50
123	Tino Martinez	.20
124	Kimera Bartee	.20
125	Garret Anderson	.20
126	Brian Jordan	.20
127	Andre Dawson	.20
128	Javier Lopez	.30
129	Bill Pulsipher	.20
130	Dwight Gooden	.20
131	Al Martin	.20
132	Terrell Wade	.20
133	Steve Gibralter	.20
134	Tom Glavine	.30
135	Kevin Appier	.20
136	Tim Raines	.20
137	Curtis Pride	.20
138	Todd Greene	.20
139	Bobby Bonilla	.20
140	Trey Beamon	.20
141	Marty Cordova	.20
142	Rickey Henderson	.35
143	Ellis Burks	.20
144	Dennis Eckersley	.20
145	Kevin Brown	.25
146	Carlos Baerga	.20
147	Brett Butler	.20
148	Marquis Grissom	.20
149	Karim Garcia	.75
150	Checklist	.20

1996 Leaf/Signature Series Autograph Promos

To introduce its Autograph Series, Leaf sent dealers one of two promo card versions of the Frank Thomas card. Most received a card with a preprinted facsimile autograph, duly noted in small type beneath the signature. Others (500) received a genuine Frank Thomas autograph on their promo. All of the cards are marked "PROMOTIONAL CARD" diagonally on both front and back.

	MT
Frank Thomas (facsimile signature)	5.00
Frank Thomas (genuine autograph)	150.00

1996 Leaf/Signature Series Autographs

Every pack of 1996 Leaf Signature Series includes at least one authentically signed card from one of 245 players. There were 235 players who signed three versions in these quantities - 500 Gold, 1,000 Silver and 3,500 Bronze. There are also short-printed autographs for 10 players in quantities of 100 Gold, 200 Silver and 700 Bronze. The short-printed players are designated with an "SP" in the checklist. Cards are numbered alphabetically in the checklist since the autographed cards are unnumbered. Each major leaguer signed a notarized affidavit to guarantee each signature was authentic. Series 1 cards of Carlos Delgado, Brian Hunter, Phil Plantier, Jim Thome, Terrell Wade and Ernie Young were signed too late for inclusion in Series 1 packs, and were inserted with Extended. No Bronze cards of Thome were signed.

		MT
	Complete Bronze Set (251):	2000.
	Common Bronze Player:	2.00
	Silver:	2X
	Gold:	3X-4X
	SP Signatures: 200 Silver, 700 Bronze	100 Gold,
(1)	Kurt Abbott	3.00
(2)	Juan Acevedo	2.00
(3)	Terry Adams	2.00
(4)	Manny Alexander	2.00
(5)	Roberto Alomar (SP)	60.00
(6)	Moises Alou	12.00
(7)	Wilson Alvarez	4.00
(8)	Garret Anderson	3.00
(9)	Shane Andrews	4.00
(10)	Andy Ashby	4.00
(11)	Pedro Astacio	3.00
(12)	Brad Ausmus	3.00
(13)	Bobby Ayala	2.00
(14)	Carlos Baerga	2.00
(15)	Harold Baines	5.00
(16)	Jason Bates	2.00
(17)	Allen Battle	2.00
(18)	Rich Becker	2.00
(19)	David Bell	2.00
(20)	Rafael Belliard	2.00
(21)	Andy Benes	4.00
(22)	Armando Benitez	2.00
(23)	Jason Bere	2.00
(24)	Geronimo Berroa	2.00
(25)	Willie Blair	2.00
(26)	Mike Blowers	2.00
(27)	Wade Boggs (SP)	120.00
(28)	Ricky Bones	2.00
(29)	Mike Bordick	2.00
(30)	Toby Borland	2.00
(31)	Ricky Bottalico	2.00
(32)	Darren Bragg	2.00
(33)	Jeff Branson	2.00
(34)	Tilson Brito	2.00
(35)	Rico Brogna	3.00
(36)	Scott Brosius	4.00
(37)	Damon Buford	4.00
(38)	Mike Busby	2.00
(39)	Tom Candiotti	2.00
(40)	Frank Castillo	2.00
(41)	Andujar Cedeno	2.00
(42)	Domingo Cedeno	2.00
(43)	Roger Cedeno	5.00
(44)	Norm Charlton	2.00
(45)	Jeff Cirillo	3.00
(46)	Will Clark	20.00
(47)	Jeff Conine	3.00
(48)	Steve Cooke	4.00
(49)	Joey Cora	3.00
(50)	Marty Cordova	3.00
(51)	Rheal Cormier	2.00
(52)	Felipe Crespo	2.00
(53)	Chad Curtis	4.00
(54)	Johnny Damon	12.00
(55)	Russ Davis	3.00
(56)	Andre Dawson	20.00
(57a)	Carlos Delgado (black autograph)	25.00
(57b)	Carlos Delgado (blue autograph)	25.00
(58)	Doug Drabek	4.00
(59)	Darren Dreifort	4.00
(60)	Shawon Dunston	3.00
(61)	Ray Durham	4.00
(62)	Jim Edmonds	5.00
(63)	Joey Eischen	2.00
(64)	Jim Eisenreich	4.00
(65)	Sal Fasano	2.00
(66)	Jeff Fassero	2.00
(67)	Alex Fernandez	7.50
(68)	Darrin Fletcher	4.00
(69)	Chad Fonville	4.00
(70)	Kevin Foster	4.00
(71)	John Franco	4.00
(72)	Julio Franco	3.00
(73)	Marvin Freeman	2.00
(74)	Travis Fryman	3.00
(75)	Gary Gaetti	3.00
(76)	Carlos Garcia	4.00
(77)	Jason Giambi	3.00
(78)	Benji Gil	2.00
(79)	Greg Gohr	2.00
(80)	Chris Gomez	2.00
(81)	Leo Gomez	2.00
(82)	Tom Goodwin	3.00
(83)	Mike Grace	2.00
(84)	Mike Greenwell	4.00
(85)	Rusty Greer	3.00
(86)	Mark Grudzielanek	2.00
(87)	Mark Gubicza	4.00
(88)	Juan Guzman	4.00
(89)	Darryl Hamilton	4.00
(90)	Joey Hamilton	3.00
(91)	Chris Hammond	4.00
(92)	Mike Hampton	2.00
(93)	Chris Haney	2.00
(94)	Todd Haney	2.00
(95)	Erik Hanson	2.00
(96)	Pete Harnisch	3.00
(97)	LaTroy Hawkins	2.00
(98)	Charlie Hayes	2.00
(99)	Jimmy Haynes	2.00
(100)	Roberto Hernandez	4.00
(101)	Bobby Higginson	9.00
(102)	Glenallen Hill	3.00
(103)	Ken Hill	4.00
(104)	Sterling Hitchcock	4.00
(105)	Trevor Hoffman	6.00
(106)	Dave Hollins	4.00
(107)	Dwayne Hosey	3.00
(108)	Thomas Howard	2.00
(109)	Steve Howe	6.00
(110)	John Hudek	2.00
(111)	Rex Hudler	2.00
(112)	Brian Hunter	2.00
(113)	Butch Huskey	5.00
(114)	Mark Hutton	2.00
(115)	Jason Jacome	2.00
(116)	John Jaha	4.00
(117)	Reggie Jefferson	4.00
(118)	Derek Jeter (SP)	150.00
(119)	Bobby Jones	4.00
(120)	Todd Jones	3.00
(121)	Brian Jordan	4.00
(122)	Kevin Jordan	2.00
(123)	Jeff Juden	3.00
(124)	Ron Karkovice	3.00
(125)	Roberto Kelly	3.00
(126)	Mark Kiefer	2.00
(127)	Brooks Kieschnick	2.00
(128)	Jeff King	4.00
(129)	Mike Lansing	4.00
(130)	Matt Lawton	4.00
(131)	Al Leiter	4.00
(132)	Mark Leiter	2.00
(133)	Curtis Leskanic	4.00
(134)	Darren Lewis	3.00
(135)	Mark Lewis	4.00
(136)	Felipe Lira	2.00
(137)	Pat Listach	3.00
(138)	Keith Lockhart	3.00
(139)	Kenny Lofton (SP)	25.00
(140)	John Mabry	4.00
(141)	Mike Macfarlane	3.00
(142)	Kirt Manwaring	3.00
(143)	Al Martin	4.00
(144)	Norberto Martin	3.00
(145)	Dennis Martinez	5.00
(146)	Pedro Martinez	50.00
(147)	Sandy Martinez	4.00
(148)	Mike Matheny	4.00
(149)	T.J. Mathews	2.00
(150)	David McCarty	3.00
(151)	Ben McDonald	4.00
(152)	Pat Meares	4.00
(153)	Orlando Merced	4.00
(154)	Jose Mesa	3.00
(155)	Matt Mieske	4.00
(156)	Orlando Miller	4.00
(157)	Mike Mimbs	2.00
(158)	Paul Molitor (SP)	50.00
(159)	Raul Mondesi (SP)	25.00
(160)	Jeff Montgomery	4.00
(161)	Mickey Morandini	3.00
(162)	Lyle Mouton	2.00
(163)	James Mouton	2.00
(164)	Jamie Moyer	4.00
(165)	Rodney Myers	2.00
(166)	Denny Neagle	2.00
(167)	Robb Nen	3.00
(168)	Marc Newfield	2.00
(169)	Dave Nilsson	4.00
(170)	Jon Nunnally	4.00
(171)	Chad Ogea	4.00
(172)	Troy O'Leary	4.00
(173)	Rey Ordonez	7.50
(174)	Jayhawk Owens	2.00
(175)	Tom Pagnozzi	3.00
(176)	Dean Palmer	4.00
(177)	Roger Pavlik	3.00
(178)	Troy Percival	4.00
(179)	Carlos Perez	4.00
(180)	Robert Perez	2.00
(181)	Andy Pettitte	20.00
(182)	Phil Plantier	4.00
(183)	Mike Potts	2.00
(184)	Curtis Pride	4.00
(185)	Ariel Prieto	2.00
(186)	Bill Pulsipher	3.00
(187)	Brad Radke	4.00
(188)	Manny Ramirez(SP)	50.00
(189)	Joe Randa	4.00
(190)	Pat Rapp	4.00
(191)	Bryan Rekar	2.00
(192)	Shane Reynolds	4.00
(193)	Arthur Rhodes	4.00
(194)	Mariano Rivera	6.00
(195a)	Alex Rodriguez (SP, black autograph)	200.00
(195b)	Alex Rodriguez(SP, blue autograph)	200.00
(196)	Frank Rodriguez	3.00
(197)	Mel Rojas	2.00
(198)	Ken Ryan	3.00
(199)	Bret Saberhagen	6.00
(200)	Tim Salmon	6.00
(201)	Rey Sanchez	3.00
(202)	Scott Sanders	2.00
(203)	Steve Scarsone	2.00
(204)	Curt Schilling	6.00
(205)	Jason Schmidt	2.00
(206)	David Segui	4.00
(207)	Kevin Seitzer	4.00
(208)	Scott Servais	2.00
(209)	Don Slaught	3.00
(210)	Zane Smith	3.00
(211)	Paul Sorrento	2.00
(212)	Scott Stahoviak	2.00
(213)	Mike Stanley	2.00
(214)	Terry Steinbach	4.00
(215)	Kevin Stocker	2.00
(216)	Jeff Suppan	3.00
(217)	Bill Swift	2.00
(218)	Greg Swindell	3.00
(219)	Kevin Tapani	4.00
(220)	Danny Tartabull	3.00
(221)	Julian Tavarez	2.00
(222a)	Frank Thomas (SP) (blue autograph)	100.00
(222b)	Frank Thomas (SP) (black autograph)	100.00
(223)	Ozzie Timmons	2.00
(224a)	Michael Tucker (black autograph)	4.00
(224b)	Michael Tucker (blue autograph)	4.00
(225)	Ismael Valdez	3.00
(226)	Jose Valentin	2.00
(227)	Todd Van Poppel	4.00
(228)	Mo Vaughn (SP)	40.00
(229)	Quilvio Veras	5.00
(230)	Fernando Vina	5.00
(231)	Joe Vitiello	3.00
(232)	Jose Vizcaino	2.00
(233)	Omar Vizquel	5.00
(234)	Terrell Wade	2.00
(235)	Paul Wagner	2.00
(236)	Matt Walbeck	3.00
(237)	Jerome Walton	2.00
(238)	Turner Ward	2.00
(239)	Allen Watson	2.00
(240)	David Weathers	2.00
(241)	Walt Weiss	4.00
(242)	Turk Wendell	4.00
(243)	Rondell White	5.00
(244)	Brian Williams	2.00
(245)	George Williams	2.00
(246)	Paul Wilson	2.00
(247)	Bobby Witt	3.00
(248)	Bob Wolcott	2.00
(249)	Eric Young	4.00
(250)	Ernie Young	2.00
(251)	Greg Zaun	4.00

1996 Leaf/Signature Series Extended Autographs

Leaf Signature Series Exended Autograph cards consist of 31 stars and rising prospects, six autographs from Series 1 that were late inclusions and 186 other major leaguers. The 186 regular players signed 5,000 each, while other signees' totals are listed in parentheses. Signature cards for Alex Rodriguez, Juan Gonzalez and Andruw Jones were only available through redemption cards. Autographed versions are different designs from the regular-issue cards, with two available in each pack. The unnumbered cards are checklisted here in alphabetical order.

		MT
Complete Set (217):		2000.
Common Player:		2.00
Extended Box:		150.00
(1)	Scott Aldred	2.00
(2)	Mike Aldrete	2.00
(3)	Rich Amaral	2.00
(4)	Alex Arias	2.00
(5)	Paul Assenmacher	2.00
(6)	Roger Bailey	2.00
(7)	Erik Bennett	2.00
(8)	Sean Bergman	2.00
(9)	Doug Bochtler	2.00
(10)	Tim Bogar	2.00
(11)	Pat Borders	2.00
(12)	Pedro Borbon	2.00
(13)	Shawn Boskie	2.00
(14)	Rafael Bournigal	2.00
(15)	Mark Brandenburg	2.00
(16)	John Briscoe	2.00
(17)	Jorge Brito	2.00
(18)	Doug Brocail	2.00
(19)	Jay Buhner (SP, 1000)	20.00
(20)	Scott Bullett	2.00
(21)	Dave Burba	2.00
(22)	Ken Caminiti (SP, 1000)	25.00
(23)	John Cangelosi	2.00
(24)	Cris Carpenter	2.00
(25)	Chuck Carr	2.00
(26)	Larry Casian	2.00
(27)	Tony Castillo	2.00
(28)	Jason Christiansen	2.00
(29)	Archi Cianfrocco	2.00
(30)	Mark Clark	2.00
(31)	Terry Clark	2.00
(32)	Roger Clemens (SP, 1000)	80.00
(33)	Jim Converse	2.00
(34)	Dennis Cook	2.00
(35)	Francisco Cordova	3.00
(36)	Jim Corsi	2.00
(37)	Tim Crabtree	2.00
(38)	Doug Creek (SP, 1950)	3.00
(39)	John Cummings	2.00
(40)	Omar Daal	2.00
(41)	Rich DeLucia	2.00
(42)	Mark Dewey	2.00
(43)	Alex Diaz	2.00
(44)	Jermaine Dye (SP, 2500)	8.00
(45)	Ken Edenfield	2.00
(46)	Mark Eichhorn	2.00
(47)	John Ericks	2.00
(48)	Darin Erstad	30.00
(49)	Alvaro Espinoza	2.00
(50)	Jorge Fabregas	2.00
(51)	Mike Fetters	2.00
(52)	John Flaherty	2.00
(53)	Bryce Florie	2.00
(54)	Tony Fossas	2.00
(55)	Lou Frazier	2.00
(56)	Mike Gallego	2.00
(57)	Karim Garcia (SP, 2500)	20.00
(58)	Jason Giambi	2.00
(59)	Ed Giovanola	2.00
(60)	Tom Glavine (SP, 1250)	25.00
(61)	Juan Gonzalez (SP, 1000)	60.00
(62)	Craig Grebeck	2.00
(63)	Buddy Groom	2.00
(64)	Kevin Gross	2.00
(65)	Eddie Guardado	2.00
(66)	Mark Guthrie	2.00
(67)	Tony Gwynn (SP, 1000)	70.00
(68)	Chip Hale	2.00
(69)	Darren Hall	2.00
(70)	Lee Hancock	2.00
(71)	Dave Hansen	2.00
(72)	Bryan Harvey	2.00
(73)	Bill Haselman	2.00
(74)	Mike Henneman	2.00
(75)	Doug Henry	2.00
(76)	Gil Heredia	2.00
(77)	Carlos Hernandez	2.00
(78)	Jose Hernandez	2.00
(79)	Darren Holmes	2.00
(80)	Mark Holzemer	2.00
(81)	Rick Honeycutt	2.00
(82)	Chris Hook	2.00
(83)	Chris Howard	2.00
(84)	Jack Howell	2.00
(85)	David Hulse	2.00
(86)	Edwin Hurtado	2.00
(87)	Jeff Huson	2.00
(88)	Mike James	2.00
(89)	Derek Jeter (SP, 1000)	100.00
(90)	Brian Johnson	2.00
(91)	Randy Johnson (SP, 1000)	30.00
(92)	Mark Johnson	2.00
(93)	Andruw Jones (SP, 2000)	30.00
(94)	Chris Jones	2.00
(95)	Ricky Jordan	2.00
(96)	Matt Karchner	2.00
(97)	Scott Karl	2.00
(98)	Jason Kendall (SP, 2500)	7.50
(99)	Brian Keyser	2.00
(100)	Mike Kingery	2.00
(101)	Wayne Kirby	2.00
(102)	Ryan Klesko (SP, 1000)	10.00
(103)	Chuck Knoblauch (SP, 1000)	30.00
(104)	Chad Kreuter	2.00
(105)	Tom Lampkin	2.00
(106)	Scott Leius	2.00
(107)	Jon Lieber	2.00
(108)	Nelson Liriano	2.00
(109)	Scott Livingstone	2.00
(110)	Graeme Lloyd	2.00
(111)	Kenny Lofton (SP, 1000)	25.00
(112)	Luis Lopez	2.00
(113)	Torey Lovullo	2.00
(114)	Greg Maddux (SP, 500)	175.00
(115)	Mike Maddux	2.00
(116)	Dave Magadan	2.00
(117)	Mike Magnante	2.00
(118)	Joe Magrane	2.00
(119)	Pat Mahomes	2.00
(120)	Matt Mantei	2.00
(121)	John Marzano	2.00
(122)	Terry Matthews	2.00
(123)	Chuck McElroy	2.00
(124)	Fred McGriff (SP, 1000)	15.00
(125)	Mark McLemore	2.00
(126)	Greg McMichael	2.00
(127)	Blas Minor	2.00
(128)	Dave Mlicki	2.00
(129)	Mike Mohler	2.00
(130)	Paul Molitor (SP, 1000)	40.00
(131)	Steve Montgomery	2.00
(132)	Mike Mordecai	2.00
(133)	Mike Morgan	2.00
(134)	Mike Munoz	2.00
(135)	Greg Myers	2.00
(136)	Jimmy Myers	2.00
(137)	Mike Myers	2.00
(138)	Bob Natal	2.00
(139)	Dan Naulty	2.00
(140)	Jeff Nelson	2.00
(141)	Warren Newson	2.00
(142)	Chris Nichting	2.00
(143)	Melvin Nieves	2.00
(144)	Charlie O'Brien	2.00
(145)	Alex Ochoa	2.00
(146)	Omar Olivares	2.00
(147)	Joe Oliver	2.00
(148)	Lance Painter	2.00
(149)	Rafael Palmeiro (SP, 2000)	25.00
(150)	Mark Parent	2.00
(151)	Steve Parris (SP, 1800)	6.00
(152)	Bob Patterson	2.00
(153)	Tony Pena	2.00
(154)	Eddie Perez	2.00
(155)	Yorkis Perez	2.00
(156)	Robert Person	2.00
(157)	Mark Petkovsek	2.00
(158)	Andy Pettitte (SP, 1000)	25.00
(159)	J.R. Phillips	2.00
(160)	Hipolito Pichardo	2.00
(161)	Eric Plunk	2.00
(162)	Jimmy Poole	2.00
(163)	Kirby Puckett (SP, 1000)	75.00
(164)	Paul Quantrill	2.00
(165)	Tom Quinlan	2.00
(166)	Jeff Reboulet	2.00
(167)	Jeff Reed	2.00
(168)	Steve Reed	2.00
(169)	Carlos Reyes	2.00
(170)	Bill Risley	2.00
(171)	Kevin Ritz	2.00
(172)	Kevin Roberson	2.00
(173)	Rich Robertson	2.00
(174)	Alex Rodriguez (SP, 500)	200.00
(175)	Ivan Rodriguez (SP, 1250)	50.00
(176)	Bruce Ruffin	2.00
(177)	Juan Samuel	2.00
(178)	Tim Scott	2.00
(179)	Kevin Sefcik	2.00
(180)	Jeff Shaw	2.00
(181)	Danny Sheaffer	2.00
(182)	Craig Shipley	2.00
(183)	Dave Silvestri	2.00
(184)	Aaron Small	2.00
(185)	John Smoltz (SP, 1000)	20.00
(186)	Luis Sojo	2.00
(187)	Sammy Sosa (SP, 1000)	250.00
(188)	Steve Sparks	2.00
(189)	Tim Spehr	2.00
(190)	Russ Springer	2.00
(191)	Matt Stairs	2.00
(192)	Andy Stankiewicz	2.00
(193)	Mike Stanton	2.00
(194)	Kelly Stinnett	2.00
(195)	Doug Strange	2.00
(196)	Mark Sweeney	2.00
(197)	Jeff Tabaka	2.00
(198)	Jesus Tavarez	2.00
(199)	Frank Thomas (SP, 1000)	75.00
(200)	Larry Thomas	2.00
(201)	Mark Thompson	2.00
(202)	Mike Timlin	2.00
(203)	Steve Trachsel	4.00
(204)	Tom Urbani	2.00
(205)	Julio Valera	2.00
(206)	Dave Valle	2.00
(207)	William VanLandingham	2.00
(208)	Mo Vaughn (SP, 1000)	25.00
(209)	Dave Veres	2.00
(210)	Ed Vosberg	2.00
(211)	Don Wengert	2.00
(212)	Matt Whiteside	2.00
(213)	Bob Wickman	2.00
(214)	Matt Williams (SP, 1250)	25.00
(215)	Mike Williams	2.00
(216)	Woody Williams	2.00
(217)	Craig Worthington	2.00
---	Frank Thomas (Autographed jumbo)	75.00

1996 Leaf/Signature Extended Autographs - Century Marks

Century Marks represent the first 100 autographs by the 31 stars and top prospects, and are designated with a "Century Marks" blue holographic foil logo. Several players' autographed cards were available only by mail-in redemption cards.

		MT
Common Player:		20.00
(1)	Jay Buhner	25.00
(2)	Ken Caminiti	25.00
(3)	Roger Clemens	150.00
(4)	Jermaine Dye	20.00
(5)	Darin Erstad	60.00
(6)	Karim Garcia	20.00
(7)	Jason Giambi	20.00
(8)	Tom Glavine	25.00
(9)	Juan Gonzalez	75.00
(9)	Juan Gonzalez (redemption card)	25.00
(10)	Tony Gwynn	135.00
(11)	Derek Jeter	200.00
(11)	Derek Jeter (redemption card)	30.00
(12)	Randy Johnson	50.00
(13)	Andruw Jones	100.00
(13)	Andruw Jones (redemption card)	15.00
(14)	Jason Kendall	20.00
(15)	Ryan Klesko	20.00
(16)	Chuck Knoblauch	35.00
(17)	Kenny Lofton	50.00
(18)	Greg Maddux	200.00
(19)	Fred McGriff	30.00
(20)	Paul Molitor	50.00
(21)	Alex Ochoa	20.00
(22)	Rafael Palmeiro	20.00
(22)	Rafael Palmeiro (redemption card)	5.00
(23)	Andy Pettitte	25.00
(24)	Kirby Puckett	100.00
(25)	Alex Rodriguez	275.00
(25)	Alex Rodriguez (redemption card)	40.00
(26)	Ivan Rodriguez	75.00
(27)	John Smoltz	25.00
(28)	Sammy Sosa	400.00
(29)	Frank Thomas	50.00
(30)	Mo Vaughn	40.00
(31)	Matt Williams	30.00

1997 Leaf

Leaf produced a 400-card set in two series in 1997. The cards feature a grey border with the player photo vignetted at center. The player's name, team and a Leaf logo are displayed at bottom in silver foil. A team logo is in the upper-right corner. Besides the base cards, 10-card packs retailing for $2.99 could contain one of the following inserts: Banner Season, Dress for Success, Get-A-Grip, Knot-hole Gang, Statistical Standouts, Fractal Matrix or Fractal Matrix Die-cut.

	MT
Complete Set (400):	40.00
Common Player:	.10
Jackie Robinson 1948 Leaf Reprint:	60.00
Series 1 Pack (12):	3.00
Series 1 Wax Box (18):	50.00
Series 2 Pack (12):	3.00
Series 2 Wax Box (24):	60.00

1	Wade Boggs	.30
2	Brian McRae	.10
3	Jeff D'Amico	.10
4	George Arias	.10
5	Billy Wagner	.15
6	Ray Lankford	.10
7	Will Clark	.25
8	Edgar Renteria	.10
9	Alex Ochoa	.10
10	Roberto Hernandez	.10
11	Joe Carter	.15
12	Gregg Jefferies	.10
13	Mark Grace	.25
14	Roberto Alomar	.75
15	Joe Randa	.10
16	Alex Rodriguez	3.00
17	Tony Gwynn	1.25
18	Steve Gibralter	.10
19	Scott Stahoviak	.10
20	Matt Williams	.25
21	Quinton McCracken	.10
22	Ugueth Urbina	.10
23	Jermaine Allensworth	.10
24	Paul Molitor	.40
25	Carlos Delgado	.40
26	Bob Abreu	.10
27	John Jaha	.10
28	Rusty Greer	.10
29	Kimera Bartee	.10
30	Ruben Rivera	.15
31	Jason Kendall	.10
32	Lance Johnson	.10
33	Robin Ventura	.15
34	Kevin Appier	.10
35	John Mabry	.10
36	Ricky Otero	.10
37	Mike Lansing	.10
38	Mark McGwire	4.00
39	Tim Naehring	.10
40	Tom Glavine	.20
41	Rey Ordonez	.25
42	Tony Clark	.50
43	Rafael Palmeiro	.25
44	Pedro Martinez	.30
45	Keith Lockhart	.10
46	Dan Wilson	.10
47	John Wetteland	.10
48	Chan Ho Park	.15
49	Gary Sheffield	.40
50	Shawn Estes	.10
51	Royce Clayton	.10
52	Jaime Navarro	.10
53	Raul Casanova	.10
54	Jeff Bagwell	1.25
55	Barry Larkin	.20
56	Charles Nagy	.10
57	Ken Caminiti	.30
58	Todd Hollandsworth	.10
59	Pat Hentgen	.10
60	Jose Valentin	.10
61	Frank Rodriguez	.10
62	Mickey Tettleton	.10
63	Marty Cordova	.10
64	Cecil Fielder	.15
65	Barry Bonds	.75
66	Scott Servais	.10
67	Ernie Young	.10
68	Wilson Alvarez	.10
69	Mike Grace	.10
70	Shane Reynolds	.10
71	Henry Rodriguez	.10
72	Eric Karros	.10
73	Mark Langston	.10
74	Scott Karl	.10
75	Trevor Hoffman	.15
76	Orel Hershiser	.10
77	John Smoltz	.20
78	Raul Mondesi	.25
79	Jeff Brantley	.10
80	Donne Wall	.10
81	Joey Cora	.10
82	Mel Rojas	.10
83	Chad Mottola	.10
84	Omar Vizquel	.10
85	Greg Maddux	2.00
86	Jamey Wright	.10
87	Chuck Finley	.10
88	Brady Anderson	.10
89	Alex Gonzalez	.10
90	Andy Benes	.10
91	Reggie Jefferson	.10
92	Paul O'Neill	.15
93	Javier Lopez	.20
94	Mark Grudzielanek	.10
95	Marc Newfield	.10
96	Kevin Ritz	.10
97	Fred McGriff	.25
98	Dwight Gooden	.10
99	Hideo Nomo	.50
100	Steve Finley	.10
101	Juan Gonzalez	.75
102	Jay Buhner	.15
103	Paul Wilson	.10
104	Alan Benes	.10
105	Manny Ramirez	1.00
106	Kevin Elster	.10
107	Frank Thomas	1.50
108	Orlando Miller	.10
109	Ramon Martinez	.10
110	Kenny Lofton	.75
111	Bernie Williams	.50
112	Robby Thompson	.10
113	Bernard Gilkey	.10
114	Ray Durham	.10
115	Jeff Cirillo	.10
116	Brian Jordan	.10
117	Rich Becker	.10
118	Al Leiter	.10
119	Mark Johnson	.10
120	Ellis Burks	.10
121	Sammy Sosa	1.50
122	Willie Greene	.10
123	Michael Tucker	.10
124	Eddie Murray	.40
125	Joey Hamilton	.10
126	Antonio Osuna	.10
127	Bobby Higginson	.10
128	Tomas Perez	.10
129	Tim Salmon	.25
130	Mark Wohlers	.10
131	Charles Johnson	.10
132	Randy Johnson	.50
133	Brooks Kieschnick	.10
134	Al Martin	.10
135	Dante Bichette	.20
136	Andy Pettitte	.75
137	Jason Giambi	.10
138	James Baldwin	.10
139	Ben McDonald	.10
140	Shawn Green	.15
141	Geronimo Berroa	.10
142	Jose Offerman	.10
143	Curtis Pride	.10
144	Terrell Wade	.10
145	Ismael Valdes	.10
146	Mike Mussina	.60
147	Mariano Rivera	.20
148	Ken Hill	.10
149	Darin Erstad	1.25
150	Jay Bell	.10
151	Mo Vaughn	.75
152	Ozzie Smith	.50
153	Jose Mesa	.10
154	Osvaldo Fernandez	.10
155	Vinny Castilla	.10
156	Jason Isringhausen	.10
157	B.J. Surhoff	.10
158	Robert Perez	.10
159	Ron Coomer	.10
160	Darren Oliver	.10
161	Mike Mohler	.10
162	Russ Davis	.10
163	Bret Boone	.10
164	Ricky Bottalico	.10
165	Derek Jeter	2.00
166	Orlando Merced	.10
167	John Valentin	.10
168	Andruw Jones	1.50
169	Angel Echevarria	.10
170	Todd Walker	.75
171	Desi Relaford	.10
172	Trey Beamon	.10
173	*Brian Giles*	1.50
174	Scott Rolen	1.25
175	Shannon Stewart	.10
176	Dmitri Young	.10
177	Justin Thompson	.10
178	Trot Nixon	.10
179	Josh Booty	.10
180	Robin Jennings	.10
181	Marvin Benard	.10
182	Luis Castillo	.15
183	Wendell Magee	.10
184	Vladimir Guerrero	2.00
185	Nomar Garciaparra	2.00
186	Ryan Hancock	.10
187	Mike Cameron	.10
188	Cal Ripken Jr. (Legacy)	1.25
189	Chipper Jones (Legacy)	1.00
190	Albert Belle (Legacy)	.50
191	Mike Piazza (Legacy)	1.00
192	Chuck Knoblauch (Legacy)	.10
193	Ken Griffey Jr. (Legacy)	1.50
194	Ivan Rodriguez (Legacy)	.25
195	Jose Canseco (Legacy)	.20
196	Ryne Sandberg (Legacy)	.35
197	Jim Thome (Legacy)	.20
198	Andy Pettitte (Checklist)	.35
199	Andruw Jones (Checklist)	.75
200	Derek Jeter (Checklist)	.60
201	Chipper Jones	2.00
202	Albert Belle	.75
203	Mike Piazza	2.00
204	Ken Griffey Jr.	4.00
205	Ryne Sandberg	.75
206	Jose Canseco	.25
207	Chili Davis	.10
208	Roger Clemens	1.00
209	Deion Sanders	.15
210	Darryl Hamilton	.10
211	Jermaine Dye	.10
212	Matt Williams	.25
213	Kevin Elster	.10
214	John Wetteland	.10
215	Garret Anderson	.10
216	Kevin Brown	.10
217	Matt Lawton	.10
218	Cal Ripken Jr.	2.50
219	Moises Alou	.10
220	Chuck Knoblauch	.20
221	Ivan Rodriguez	.60
222	Travis Fryman	.10
223	Jim Thome	.40
224	Eddie Murray	.35
225	Eric Young	.10
226	Ron Gant	.10
227	Tony Phillips	.10
228	Reggie Sanders	.10
229	Johnny Damon	.10
230	Bill Pulsipher	.10
231	Jim Edmonds	.10
232	Melvin Nieves	.10
233	Ryan Klesko	.25
234	David Cone	.20
235	Derek Bell	.10
236	Julio Franco	.10
237	Juan Guzman	.10
238	Larry Walker	.25
239	Delino DeShields	.10
240	Troy Percival	.10
241	Andres Galarraga	.15
242	Rondell White	.15
243	John Burkett	.10
244	J.T. Snow	.10
245	Alex Fernandez	.10
246	Edgar Martinez	.10
247	Craig Biggio	.15
248	Todd Hundley	.15
249	Jimmy Key	.10
250	Cliff Floyd	.10
251	Jeff Conine	.10
252	Curt Schilling	.10
253	Jeff King	.10
254	Tino Martinez	.15
255	Carlos Baerga	.10
256	Jeff Fassero	.10
257	Dean Palmer	.10
258	Robb Nen	.10
259	Sandy Alomar Jr.	.15
260	Carlos Perez	.10
261	Rickey Henderson	.20
262	Bobby Bonilla	.10
263	Darren Daulton	.10
264	Jim Leyritz	.10
265	Dennis Martinez	.10
266	Butch Huskey	.10
267	Joe Vitiello	.10
268	Steve Trachsel	.10
269	Glenallen Hill	.10
270	Terry Steinbach	.10
271	Mark McLemore	.10
272	Devon White	.10
273	Jeff Kent	.10
274	Tim Raines	.10
275	Carlos Garcia	.10
276	Hal Morris	.10
277	Gary Gaetti	.10
278	John Olerud	.15
279	Wally Joyner	.10
280	Brian Hunter	.10
281	Steve Karsay	.10
282	Denny Neagle	.10
283	Jose Herrera	.10
284	Todd Stottlemyre	.10
285	Bip Roberts	.10
286	Kevin Seitzer	.10
287	Benji Gil	.10
288	Dennis Eckersley	.10
289	Brad Ausmus	.10
290	Otis Nixon	.10
291	Darryl Strawberry	.10
292	Marquis Grissom	.10
293	Darryl Kile	.10
294	Quilvio Veras	.10
295	Tom Goodwin	.10
296	Benito Santiago	.10
297	Mike Bordick	.10
298	Roberto Kelly	.10
299	David Justice	.20
300	Carl Everett	.10
301	Mark Whiten	.10
302	Aaron Sele	.10
303	Darren Dreifort	.10
304	Bobby Jones	.10
305	Fernando Vina	.10
306	Ed Sprague	.10
307	Andy Ashby	.10
308	Tony Fernandez	.10
309	Roger Pavlik	.10
310	Mark Clark	.10
311	Mariano Duncan	.10
312	Tyler Houston	.10
313	Eric Davis	.10
314	Greg Vaughn	.15
315	David Segul	.10
316	Dave Nilsson	.10
317	F.P. Santangelo	.10
318	Wilton Guerrero	.10
319	Jose Guillen	1.00
320	Kevin Orie	.10
321	Derrek Lee	.10
322	*Bubba Trammell*	.75
323	Pokey Reese	.10
324	*Hideki Irabu*	.75
325	Scott Spiezio	.10
326	Bartolo Colon	.10
327	Damon Mashore	.10
328	Ryan McGuire	.10
329	Chris Carpenter	.10
330	*Jose Cruz Jr.*	.75
331	Todd Greene	.10
332	Brian Moehler	.10
333	Mike Sweeney	.10
334	Neifi Perez	.10

335 Matt Morris .10
336 Marvin Benard .10
337 Karim Garcia .10
338 Jason Dickson .10
339 Brant Brown .10
340 Jeff Suppan .10
341 *Deivi Cruz* .50
342 Antone Williamson .10
343 Curtis Goodwin .10
344 Brooks Kieschnick .10
345 *Tony Womack* .50
346 Rudy Pemberton .10
347 Todd Dunwoody .30
348 Frank Thomas (Legacy) .75
349 Andruw Jones (Legacy) .75
350 Alex Rodriguez (Legacy) 1.25
351 Greg Maddux (Legacy) 1.00
352 Jeff Bagwell (Legacy) .75
353 Juan Gonzalez (Legacy) .40
354 Barry Bonds (Legacy) .40
355 Mark McGwire (Legacy) 2.00
356 Tony Gwynn (Legacy) .75
357 Gary Sheffield (Legacy) .20
358 Derek Jeter (Legacy) 1.00
359 Manny Ramirez (Legacy) .50
360 Hideo Nomo (Legacy) .25
361 Sammy Sosa (Legacy) .75
362 Paul Molitor (Legacy) .20
363 Kenny Lofton (Legacy) .40
364 Eddie Murray (Legacy) .20
365 Barry Larkin (Legacy) .10
366 Roger Clemens (Legacy) .50
367 John Smoltz (Legacy) .10
368 Alex Rodriguez (Gamers) 1.25
369 Frank Thomas (Gamers) .75
370 Cal Ripken Jr. (Gamers) 1.25
371 Ken Griffey Jr. (Gamers) 1.50
372 Greg Maddux (Gamers) 1.00
373 Mike Piazza (Gamers) 1.00
374 Chipper Jones (Gamers) 1.00
375 Albert Belle (Gamers) .40
376 Chuck Knoblauch (Gamers) .15
377 Brady Anderson (Gamers) .10
378 David Justice (Gamers) .10
379 Randy Johnson (Gamers) .20
380 Wade Boggs (Gamers) .15
381 Kevin Brown (Gamers) .10
382 Tom Glavine (Gamers) .10
383 Raul Mondesi (Gamers) .10
384 Ivan Rodriguez (Gamers) .30
385 Larry Walker (Gamers) .10
386 Bernie Williams (Gamers) .30
387 Rusty Greer (Gamers) .10
388 Rafael Palmeiro (Gamers) .10
389 Matt Williams (Gamers) .15
390 Eric Young (Gamers) .10
391 Fred McGriff (Gamers) .10
392 Ken Caminiti (Gamers) .10
393 Roberto Alomar (Gamers) .30
394 Brian Jordan (Gamers) .10
395 Mark Grace (Gamers) .10
396 Jim Edmonds (Gamers) .10
397 Deion Sanders (Gamers) .10
398 Checklist (Vladimir Guerrero) .75
399 Checklist (Darin Erstad) .60
400 Checklist (Nomar Garciaparra) .75

1997 Leaf Fractal Matrix

Leaf introduced Fractal Matrix inserts, a 400-card parallel set broken down into three colors and three unique die-cuts. Two fractures break the insert set down by foil background color only (80 Golds, 120 Silvers and 200 Bronze). A second fracture breaks those cards down into color and die-cutting variations. No production numbers or insert ratios were released for either fracture. Each player is available in only one color.

	MT
Common Bronze:	1.00
Common Silver:	2.00
Common Gold:	4.00
Common Gold Z-Axis:	5.00
Common Gold Y-Axis:	10.00
Common Gold X-Axis:	20.00

1 Wade Boggs G/Y 17.50
2 Brian McRae B/Y 1.00
3 Jeff D'Amico B/Y 1.00
4 George Arias S/Y 2.00
5 Billy Wagner S/Y 2.00
6 Ray Lankford B/Z 1.00
7 Will Clark S/Y 5.00
8 Edgar Renteria S/Y 2.00
9 Alex Ochoa S/Y 2.00
10 Roberto Hernandez 2.00
11 Joe Carter S/Y 3.00
12 Gregg Jefferies B/Y 1.00
13 Mark Grace S/Y 4.00
14 Roberto Alomar G/Y 25.00
15 Joe Randa B/X 1.00
16 Alex Rodriguez G/Z 65.00
17 Tony Gwynn G/Z 35.00
18 Steve Gibralter B/Y 1.00
19 Scott Stahoviak B/X 1.00
20 Matt Williams S/Z 7.50
21 Quinton McCracken B/Y 1.00
22 Ugueth Urbina B/X 1.00
23 Jermaine Allensworth S/X 3.00
24 Paul Molitor G/X 30.00
25 Carlos Delgado S/Y 4.00
26 Bob Abreu S/Y 3.00
27 John Jaha S/Y 3.00
28 Rusty Greer S/Z 2.00
29 Kimera Bartee B/X 1.00
30 Ruben Rivera S/Y 3.00
31 Jason Kendall S/Y 3.00
32 Lance Johnson B/X 1.00
33 Robin Ventura B/Y 1.00
34 Kevin Appier S/X 2.00
35 John Mabry S/Y 2.00
36 Ricky Otero B/X 1.00
37 Mike Lansing B/X 1.00
38 Mark McGwire G/Z 75.00
39 Tim Naehring B/X 1.00
40 Tom Glavine S/Z 3.00
41 Rey Ordonez S/Y 3.00
42 Tony Clark S/Y 10.00
43 Rafael Palmeiro S/Z 5.00
44 Pedro Martinez B/X 2.00
45 Keith Lockhart B/X 1.00
46 Dan Wilson B/Y 1.00
47 John Wetteland B/Y 1.00
48 Chan Ho Park B/X 1.00
49 Gary Sheffield G/Z 12.50
50 Shawn Estes B/X 1.00
51 Royce Clayton B/X 1.00
52 Jaime Navarro B/X 1.00
53 Raul Casanova B/X 1.00
54 Jeff Bagwell G/Z 30.00
55 Barry Larkin G/X 15.00
56 Charles Nagy B/Y 1.00
57 Ken Caminiti G/Y 20.00
58 Todd Hollandsworth S/Z 2.00
59 Pat Hentgen S/X 2.00
60 Jose Valentin B/X 1.00
61 Frank Rodriguez B/X 1.00
62 Mickey Tettleton B/X 1.00
63 Marty Cordova G/X 15.00
64 Cecil Fielder S/X 4.00
65 Barry Bonds G/Z 20.00
66 Scott Servais B/X 1.00
67 Ernie Young B/X 1.00
68 Wilson Alvarez B/X 1.00
69 Mike Grace B/X 1.00
70 Shane Reynolds S/X 3.00
71 Henry Rodriguez S/Y 2.00
72 Eric Karros B/X 1.00
73 Mark Langston B/X 1.00
74 Scott Karl B/X 1.00
75 Trevor HoffmanB/X 1.00
76 Orel Hershiser S/X 2.00
77 John Smoltz G/Y 15.00
78 Raul Mondesi G/Z 12.50
79 Jeff Brantley B/X 1.00
80 Donne Wall B/X 1.00
81 Joey Cora B/X 1.00
82 Mel Rojas B/X 1.00
83 Chad Mottola B/X 1.00
84 Omar Vizquel B/X 1.00
85 Greg Maddux G/Z 60.00
86 Jamey Wright S/Y 3.00
87 Chuck Finley B/X 1.00
88 Brady AndersonG/Y 10.00
89 Alex Gonzalez S/X 3.00
90 Andy Benes B/X 1.00
91 Reggie JeffersonB/X 1.00
92 Paul O'Neill B/Y 2.00
93 Javier Lopez S/X 4.00
94 Mark GrudzielanekS/X 3.00
95 Marc Newfield B/X 1.00
96 Kevin Ritz B/X 1.00
97 Fred McGriff G/Y 12.50
98 Dwight Gooden S/X 3.00
99 Hideo Nomo S/Y 12.50
100 Steve Finley B/X 1.00
101 Juan Gonzalez G/Z 30.00
102 Jay Buhner S/Z 4.00
103 Paul Wilson S/Y 2.00
104 Alan Benes B/Y 2.00
105 Manny Ramirez G/Z 15.00
106 Kevin Elster B/X 1.00
107 Frank Thomas G/Z 30.00
108 Orlando Miller B/X 1.00
109 Ramon Martinez B/X 2.00
110 Kenny Lofton G/Z 20.00
111 Bernie Williams G/Y 25.00
112 Robby Thompson B/X 1.00
113 Bernard Gilkey B/Z 1.00
114 Ray Durham B/X 1.00
115 Jeff Cirillo S/Z 2.00
116 Brian Jordan G/Z 5.00
117 Rich Becker S/Y 2.00
118 Al Leiter B/X 1.00
119 Mark Johnson B/X 1.00
120 Ellis Burks B/Y 2.00
121 Sammy Sosa G/Z 40.00
122 Willie Greene B/X 1.00
123 Michael Tucker B/X 1.00
124 Eddie Murray G/Y 20.00
125 Joey Hamilton S/Y 2.00
126 Antonio Osuna B/X 1.00
127 Bobby Higginson S/Y 3.00
128 Tomas Perez B/X 1.00
129 Tim Salmon G/Z 10.00
130 Mark Wohlers B/X 1.00
131 Charles Johnson S/X 2.00
132 Randy Johnson S/Y 10.00
133 Brooks Kieschnick S/X 3.00
134 Al Martin S/Y 2.00
135 Dante Bichette B/X 2.00
136 Andy Pettitte G/Z 20.00
137 Jason Giambi G/Y 10.00
138 James Baldwin S/X 2.00
139 Ben McDonald B/X 1.00
140 Shawn Green S/X 2.00
141 Geronimo Berroa B/Y 1.00
142 Jose Offerman B/X 1.00
143 Curtis Pride B/X 1.00
144 Terrell Wade B/X 1.00
145 Ismael Valdes S/X 2.00
146 Mike Mussina S/Y 12.50
147 Mariano Rivera S/X 5.00
148 Ken Hill B/Y 1.00
149 Darin Erstad G/Z 35.00
150 Jay Bell B/X 1.00
151 Mo Vaughn G/Z 20.00
152 Ozzie Smith G/Y 30.00
153 Jose Mesa B/X 1.00
154 Osvaldo Fernandez B/X 1.00
155 Vinny Castilla B/Y 1.00

156 Jason Isringhausen S/Y 2.00
157 B.J. Surhoff B/X 1.00
158 Robert Perez B/X 1.00
159 Ron Coomer B/X 1.00
160 Darren Oliver B/X 1.00
161 Mike Mohler B/X 1.00
162 Russ Davis B/X 1.00
163 Bret Boone B/X 1.00
164 Ricky Bottalico B/X 1.00
165 Derek Jeter G/Z 50.00
166 Orlando Merced B/X 1.00
167 John Valentin B/X 1.00
168 Andruw JonesG/Z 40.00
169 Angel EchevarriaB/X 1.00
170 Todd Walker G/Z 15.00
171 Desi Relaford B/Y 1.00
172 Trey Beamon S/X 2.00
173 Brian Giles S/Y 2.00
174 Scott Rolen G/Z 35.00
175 Shannon StewartS/Z 2.00
176 Dmitri Young G/Z 5.00
177 Justin Thompson B/X 1.00
178 Trot Nixon S/Y 2.00
179 Josh Booty S/Y 2.00
180 Robin Jennings B/X 1.00
181 Marvin Benard B/X 1.00
182 Luis Castillo B/Y 1.00
183 Wendell Magee B/X 1.00
184 Vladimir Guerrero G/X 50.00
185 Nomar Garciaparra G/X 60.00
186 Ryan Hancock B/X 1.00
187 Mike Cameron S/X 6.00
188 Cal Ripken Jr. B/Z (Legacy) 15.00
189 Chipper Jones S/Z (Legacy) 25.00
190 Albert Belle S/Z (Legacy) 10.00
191 Mike Piazza B/Z (Legacy) 12.50
192 Chuck Knoblauch S/Y (Legacy) 6.00
193 Ken Griffey Jr. B/Z (Legacy) 20.00
194 Ivan Rodriguez G/Z (Legacy) 15.00
195 Jose Canseco S/X (Legacy) 10.00
196 Ryne Sandberg S/X (Legacy) 20.00
197 Jim Thome G/Y (Legacy) 20.00
198 Checklist (Andy Pettitte B/Y) 6.00
199 Checklist (Andruw Jones B/Y) 10.00
200 Checklist (Derek Jeter S/Y) 30.00
201 Chipper Jones G/X 60.00
202 Albert Belle G/Y 25.00
203 Mike Piazza G/Y 50.00
204 Ken Griffey Jr. G/X 175.00
205 Ryne Sandberg G/Z 12.50
206 Jose Canseco S/Y 4.00
207 Chili Davis B/X 1.00
208 Roger Clemens G/Z 15.00
209 Deion Sanders G/Z 7.50
210 Darryl Hamilton B/X 1.00
211 Jermaine Dye S/X 2.00
212 Matt Williams G/Y 12.50
213 Kevin Elster B/X 1.00
214 John Wetteland S/X 2.00
215 Garret Anderson G/Z 5.00
216 Kevin Brown G/Y 10.00
217 Matt Lawton S/Y 2.00
218 Cal Ripken Jr. G/X 125.00
219 Moises Alou G/Y 10.00
220 Chuck KnoblauchG/Z 7.50
221 Ivan Rodriguez G/Y 20.00
222 Travis Fryman B/Y 1.00
223 Jim Thome G/Z 10.00
224 Eddie Murray S/Z 7.50
225 Eric Young G/Z 5.00
226 Ron Gant S/X 2.00
227 Tony Phillips B/X 1.00
228 Reggie Sanders B/Y 1.00
229 Johnny Damon S/Z 2.00
230 Bill Pulsipher B/X 1.00
231 Jim Edmonds G/Z 5.00
232 Melvin Nieves B/X 1.00
233 Ryan Klesko G/Z 7.50
234 David Cone S/X 2.00
235 Derek Bell B/Y 1.00
236 Julio Franco S/X 2.00
237 Juan Guzman B/X 1.00
238 Larry Walker G/Z 7.50
239 Delino DeShields B/X 1.00
240 Troy Percival B/Y 1.00
241 Andres Galarraga G/Z 6.00
242 Rondell White G/Z 5.00
243 John Burkett B/X 1.00
244 J.T. Snow B/Y 1.00
245 Alex Fernandez S/Y 2.00
246 Edgar Martinez G/Z 5.00
247 Craig Biggio G/Z 5.00
248 Todd Hundley G/Y 10.00
249 Jimmy Key S/X 2.00
250 Cliff Floyd B/Y 1.00
251 Jeff Conine B/Y 1.00
252 Curt Schilling B/X 1.00
253 Jeff King B/X 1.00
254 Tino Martinez G/Z 7.50
255 Carlos Baerga S/Y 2.00
256 Jeff Fassero B/Y 1.00
257 Dean Palmer S/Y 2.00
258 Robb Nen B/X 1.00
259 Sandy Alomar Jr. S/Y 2.00
260 Carlos Perez B/X 1.00
261 Rickey Henderson S/Y 2.00
262 Bobby Bonilla S/Y 2.00
263 Darren Daulton B/X 1.00
264 Jim Leyritz B/X 1.00
265 Dennis Martinez B/X 1.00
266 Butch Huskey B/X 1.00
267 Joe Vitiello S/Y 2.00
268 Steve Trachsel B/X 1.00
269 Glenallen Hill B/X 1.00
270 Terry Steinbach B/X 1.00
271 Mark McLemore B/X 1.00
272 Devon White B/X 1.00
273 Jeff Kent B/X 1.00
274 Tim Raines B/X 1.00
275 Carlos Garcia B/X 1.00
276 Hal Morris B/X 1.00
277 Gary Gaetti B/X 1.00
278 John Olerud S/Y 2.00
279 Wally Joyner B/X 1.00
280 Brian Hunter S/X 2.00
281 Steve Karsay B/X 1.00
282 Denny Neagle S/X 2.00
283 Jose Herrera B/X 1.00
284 Todd Stottlemyre B/X 1.00
285 Bip Roberts S/X 2.00
286 Kevin Seitzer B/X 1.00
287 Benji Gil B/X 1.00
288 Dennis Eckersley S/X 2.00
289 Brad Ausmus B/X 1.00
290 Otis Nixon B/X 1.00
291 Darryl Strawberry B/X 1.00
292 Marquis Grissom S/Y 2.00
293 Darryl Kile B/X 1.00
294 Quilvio Veras B/X 1.00
295 Tom Goodwin B/X 1.00
296 Benito Santiago B/X 1.00
297 Mike Bordick B/X 1.00
298 Roberto Kelly B/X 1.00
299 David Justice G/Z 7.50
300 Carl Everett B/X 1.00
301 Mark Whiten B/X 1.00
302 Aaron Sele B/X 1.00
303 Darren Dreifort B/X 1.00
304 Bobby Jones B/X 1.00
305 Fernando Vina B/X 1.00
306 Ed Sprague B/X 1.00
307 Andy Ashby S/X 2.00
308 Tony Fernandez B/X 1.00
309 Roger Pavlik B/X 1.00
310 Mark Clark B/X 1.00
311 Mariano Duncan B/X 1.00
312 Tyler Houston B/X 1.00
313 Eric Davis S/Y 2.00
314 Greg Vaughn B/Y 1.00
315 David Segui S/Y 2.00
316 Dave Nilsson S/X 2.00
317 F.P. Santangelo S/X 2.00
318 Wilton Guerrero G/Z 5.00
319 Jose Guillen G/Z 12.50
320 Kevin Orie S/Y 2.00
321 Derrek Lee G/Z 5.00
322 Bubba Trammell S/Y 7.50
323 Pokey Reese G/Z 5.00
324 Hideki Irabu G/X 30.00
325 Scott Spiezio S/Z 2.00
326 Bartolo Colon G/Z 5.00
327 Damon Mashore S/Y 2.00
328 Ryan McGuire S/Y 2.00
329 Chris Carpenter B/X 1.00
330 Jose Cruz, Jr. G/X 20.00
331 Todd Greene S/Z 3.00
332 Brian Moehler B/X 1.00
333 Mike Sweeney B/Y 1.00
334 Neifi Perez G/Z 5.00
335 Matt Morris S/Y 2.00
336 Marvin Benard B/Y 1.00
337 Karim Garcia S/Z 2.00
338 Jason Dickson S/Y 2.00
339 Brant Brown S/Y 2.00
340 Jeff Suppan S/Z 2.00
341 Deivi Cruz B/X 2.00
342 Antone Williamson G/Z 5.00
343 Curtis Goodwin B/X 1.00
344 Brooks Kieschnick S/Y 2.00
345 Tony Womack B/X 1.00
346 Rudy Pemberton B/X 1.00
347 Todd Dunwoody B/X 1.00
348 Frank Thomas S/Y (Legacy) 12.50
349 Andruw Jones S/X (Legacy) 12.50
350 Alex Rodriguez B/Y (Legacy) 15.00
351 Greg Maddux S/Y (Legacy) 20.00
352 Jeff Bagwell B/Y (Legacy) 10.00
353 Juan Gonzalez S/Y (Legacy) 10.00
354 Barry Bonds B/Y (Legacy) 5.00
355 Mark McGwire B/Y (Legacy) 15.00
356 Tony Gwynn B/Y (Legacy) 10.00
357 Gary Sheffield B/X (Legacy) 2.00
358 Derek Jeter S/X (Legacy) 15.00
359 Manny Ramirez S/Y (Legacy) 7.50
360 Hideo Nomo G/Z (Legacy) 7.50
361 Sammy Sosa B/X (Legacy) 10.00
362 Paul Molitor S/Z (Legacy) 4.00
363 Kenny Lofton B/Y (Legacy) 5.00
364 Eddie Murray B/X (Legacy) 3.00
365 Barry Larkin S/Z (Legacy) 3.00
366 Roger Clemens S/Y (Legacy) 10.00
367 John Smoltz B/Z (Legacy) 1.00
368 Alex Rodriguez S/X (Gamers) 20.00
369 Frank Thomas B/X (Gamers) 7.50
370 Cal Ripken Jr. S/Y (Gamers) 25.00
371 Ken Griffey Jr. S/Y (Gamers) 35.00
372 Greg Maddux B/X (Gamers) 10.00
373 Mike Piazza S/X (Gamers) 15.00
374 Chipper Jones B/Y (Gamers) 10.00
375 Albert Belle B/X (Gamers) 5.00
376 Chuck Knoblauch B/X (Gamers) 2.00
377 Brady Anderson B/Z (Gamers) 1.00
378 David Justice S/X (Gamers) 4.00
379 Randy Johnson B/Z (Gamers) 4.00
380 Wade Boggs B/X (Gamers) 2.00
381 Kevin Brown B/X (Gamers) 1.00
382 Tom Glavine G/Y (Gamers) 10.00
383 Raul Mondesi S/X (Gamers) 3.00
384 Ivan Rodriguez S/X (Gamers) 5.00
385 Larry Walker B/Y (Gamers) 2.00
386 Bernie Williams B/Z (Gamers) 3.00
387 Rusty Greer G/Y (Gamers) 10.00
388 Rafael Palmeiro G/Y (Gamers) 10.00
389 Matt Williams B/X (Gamers) 2.00
390 Eric Young B/X (Gamers) 1.00
391 Fred McGriff B/X (Gamers) 2.00
392 Ken Caminiti B/X (Gamers) 1.50
393 Roberto Alomar B/Z (Gamers) 4.00
394 Brian Jordan B/X (Gamers) 1.00
395 Mark Grace G/Z (Gamers) 7.50
396 Jim Edmonds B/Y (Gamers) 1.00
397 Deion Sanders S/Y (Gamers) 3.00
398 Checklist (Vladimir Guerrero S/Z) 7.50
399 Checklist (Darin Erstad S/Y) 10.00
400 Checklist (Nomar Garciaparra S/Z) 12.50

1997 Leaf Fractal Matrix Die-Cut

A second parallel set to the Leaf product, the Fractal Matrix Die-Cuts offer three different die-cut designs with three different styles for each. The Axis-X die-cuts consist of 200 cards (150 bronze, 40 silver and 10 gold), the Axis-Y die-cuts consist of 120 cards (60 silver, 40 bronze, 20 gold), and the Axis-Z die-cuts consist of 80 cards (50 gold, 20 silver, 10 bronze). Odds of finding any of these inserts are 1:6 packs. Each player was issued in only one color/cut combination.

		MT
	Complete Set (400):	
	Common X-Axis:	4.00
	Common Y-Axis:	6.00
	Y-Axis Unlisted Stars:	10.00
	Common Z-Axis:	10.00
	Z-Axis Unlisted Stars:	15.00
1	Wade Boggs G/Y	17.50
2	Brian McRae B/Y	6.00
3	Jeff D'Amico B/Y	6.00
4	George Arias S/Y	6.00
5	Billy Wagner S/Y	6.00
6	Ray Lankford B/Z	10.00
7	Will Clark S/Y	10.00
8	Edgar Renteria S/Y	6.00
9	Alex Ochoa S/Y	6.00
11	Joe Carter S/Y	6.00
12	Gregg Jefferies B/Y	6.00
13	Mark Grace S/Y	9.00
14	Roberto Alomar G/Y	25.00
15	Joe Randa B/X	4.00
16	Alex Rodriguez G/Z	125.00
17	Tony Gwynn G/Z	75.00
18	Steve Gibralter B/Y	6.00
19	Scott Stahoviak B/X	4.00
20	Matt Williams S/Z	25.00
21	Quinton McCracken B/Y	6.00
22	Ugueth Urbina B/X	4.00
23	Jermaine Allensworth S/X	4.00
24	Paul Molitor G/X	12.50
25	Carlos Delgado S/Y	6.00
26	Bob Abreu S/Y	6.00
27	John Jaha S/Y	6.00
28	Rusty Greer S/Z	10.00
29	Kimera Bartee B/X	4.00
30	Ruben Rivera S/Y	6.00
31	Jason Kendall S/Y	6.00
32	Lance Johnson B/X	4.00
33	Robin Ventura B/Y	6.00
34	Kevin Appier S/X	4.00
35	John Mabry S/Y	6.00
36	Ricky Otero B/X	4.00
37	Mike Lansing B/X	4.00
38	Mark McGwireG/Z	150.00
39	Tim Naehring B/X	4.00
40	Tom Glavine S/Z	12.50
41	Rey Ordonez S/Y	6.00
42	Tony Clark S/Y	20.00
43	Rafael Palmeiro S/Z	12.50
44	Pedro Martinez B/X	5.00
45	Keith Lockhart B/X	4.00
46	Dan Wilson B/Y	6.00
47	John Wetteland B/Y	6.00
48	Chan Ho Park B/X	4.00
49	Gary Sheffield G/Z	30.00
50	Shawn Estes B/X	4.00
51	Royce Clayton B/X	4.00
52	Jaime Navarro B/X	4.00
53	Raul Casanova B/X	4.00
54	Jeff Bagwell G/Z	75.00
55	Barry Larkin G/X	6.00
56	Charles Nagy B/Y	6.00
57	Ken Caminiti G/Y	20.00
58	Todd Hollandsworth S/Z	10.00
59	Pat Hentgen S/X	4.00
60	Jose Valentin B/X	4.00
61	Frank Rodriguez B/X	4.00
62	Mickey Tettleton B/X	4.00
63	Marty Cordova G/X	5.00
64	Cecil Fielder S/X	6.00
65	Barry Bonds G/Z	40.00
66	Scott Servais B/X	4.00
67	Ernie Young B/X	4.00
68	Wilson Alvarez B/X	4.00
69	Mike Grace B/X	6.00
70	Shane Reynolds S/X	4.00
71	Henry Rodriguez S/Y	6.00
72	Eric Karros B/X	4.00
73	Mark Langston B/X	4.00
74	Scott Karl B/X	4.00
75	Trevor HoffmanB/X	4.00
76	Orel Hershiser S/X	4.00
77	John Smoltz G/Y	20.00
78	Raul Mondesi G/Z	15.00
79	Jeff Brantley B/X	4.00
80	Donne Wall B/X	4.00
81	Joey Cora B/X	4.00
82	Mel Rojas B/X	4.00
83	Chad Mottola B/X	4.00
84	Omar Vizquel B/X	4.00
85	Greg Maddux G/Z	100.00
86	Jamey Wright S/Y	6.00
87	Chuck Finley B/X	4.00
88	Brady AndersonG/Y	7.50
89	Alex Gonzalez S/X	4.00
90	Andy Benes B/X	4.00
91	Reggie JeffersonB/X	4.00
92	Paul O'Neill B/Y	7.50
93	Javier Lopez S/X	6.00
94	Mark Grudzielanek S/X	4.00
95	Marc Newfield B/X	4.00
96	Kevin Ritz B/X	4.00
97	Fred McGriff G/Y	10.00
98	Dwight Gooden S/X	5.00
99	Hideo Nomo S/Y	25.00
100	Steve Finley B/X	4.00
101	Juan GonzalezG/Z	60.00
102	Jay Buhner S/Z	12.50
103	Paul Wilson S/Y	6.00
104	Alan Benes B/Y	6.00
105	Manny RamirezG/Z	30.00
106	Kevin Elster B/X	4.00
107	Frank Thomas G/Z	60.00
108	Orlando Miller B/X	4.00
109	Ramon Martinez B/X	4.00
110	Kenny Lofton G/Z	40.00
111	Bernie Williams G/Y	25.00
112	Robby Thompson B/X	4.00
113	Bernard Gilkey B/Z	10.00
114	Ray Durham B/X	4.00
115	Jeff Cirillo S/Z	10.00
116	Brian Jordan G/Z	10.00
117	Rich Becker S/Y	6.00
118	Al Leiter B/X	4.00
119	Mark Johnson B/X	4.00
120	Ellis Burks B/Y	6.00
121	Sammy Sosa G/Z	65.00
122	Willie Greene B/X	4.00
123	Michael Tucker B/X	4.00
124	Eddie Murray G/Y	20.00
125	Joey Hamilton S/Y	6.00
126	Antonio Osuna B/X	4.00
127	Bobby Higginson S/Y	7.50
128	Tomas Perez B/X	4.00
129	Tim Salmon G/Z	15.00
130	Mark Wohlers B/X	4.00
131	Charles Johnson S/X	4.00
132	Randy JohnsonS/Y	20.00
133	Brooks Kieschnick S/X	4.00
134	Al Martin S/Y	4.00
135	Dante Bichette B/X	6.00
136	Andy Pettitte G/Z	30.00
137	Jason Giambi G/Y	10.00
138	James Baldwin S/X	4.00
139	Ben McDonald B/X	4.00
140	Shawn Green S/X	4.00
141	Geronimo Berroa B/Y	6.00
142	Jose Offerman B/X	4.00
143	Curtis Pride B/X	4.00
144	Terrell Wade B/X	4.00
145	Ismael Valdes S/X	4.00
146	Mike Mussina S/Y	20.00
147	Mariano Rivera S/X	7.50
148	Ken Hill B/Y	6.00
149	Darin Erstad G/Z	50.00
150	Jay Bell B/X	4.00
151	Mo Vaughn G/Z	40.00
152	Ozzie Smith G/Y	30.00
153	Jose Mesa B/X	4.00
154	Osvaldo FernandezB/X	4.00
155	Vinny Castilla B/Y	6.00
156	Jason Isringhausen S/Y	6.00
157	B.J. Surhoff B/X	4.00
158	Robert Perez B/X	4.00
159	Ron Coomer B/X	4.00
160	Darren Oliver B/X	4.00
161	Mike Mohler B/X	4.00
162	Russ Davis B/X	4.00
163	Bret Boone B/X	4.00
164	Ricky Bottalico B/X	4.00
165	Derek Jeter G/Z	100.00
166	Orlando Merced B/X	4.00
167	John Valentin B/X	4.00
168	Andruw Jones G/Z	80.00
169	Angel Echevarria B/X	4.00
170	Todd Walker G/Z	25.00
171	Desi Relaford B/Y	6.00
172	Trey Beamon S/X	4.00
173	Brian Giles S/Y	6.00
174	Scott Rolen G/Z	50.00
175	Shannon Stewart S/Z	10.00
176	Dmitri Young G/Z	10.00
177	Justin ThompsonB/X	4.00
178	Trot Nixon S/Y	6.00
179	Josh Booty S/Y	5.00
180	Robin Jennings B/X	4.00
181	Marvin Benard B/X	4.00
182	Luis Castillo B/Y	6.00
183	Wendell MageeB/X	4.00
184	Vladimir GuerreroG/X	25.00
185	Nomar GarciaparraG/X	30.00
186	Ryan Hancock B/X	4.00
187	Mike Cameron S/X	7.50
188	Cal Ripken Jr. B/Z (Legacy)	125.00
189	Chipper Jones S/Z (Legacy)	100.00
190	Albert Belle S/Z (Legacy)	40.00
191	Mike Piazza B/Z (Legacy)	100.00
192	Chuck Knoblauch S/Y (Legacy)	10.00
193	Ken Griffey Jr. B/Z (Legacy)	150.00
194	Ivan Rodriguez G/Z (Legacy)	30.00
195	Jose Canseco S/X (Legacy)	10.00
196	Ryne Sandberg S/X (Legacy)	20.00
197	Jim Thome G/Y (Legacy)	25.00
198	Checklist (Andy Pettitte B/Y)	20.00
199	Checklist (Andruw Jones B/Y)	50.00
200	Checklist (Derek Jeter S/Y)	60.00
201	Chipper Jones G/X	30.00
202	Albert Belle G/Y	35.00
203	Mike Piazza G/Y	60.00
204	Ken Griffey Jr. G/X	50.00
205	Ryne SandbergG/Z	35.00
206	Jose Canseco S/Y	10.00
207	Chili Davis B/X	4.00
208	Roger Clemens G/Z	50.00
209	Deion Sanders G/Z	15.00
210	Darryl Hamilton B/X	4.00
211	Jermaine Dye S/X	4.00
212	Matt Williams G/Y	17.50
213	Kevin Elster B/X	4.00
214	John Wetteland S/X	4.00
215	Garret Anderson G/Z	10.00
216	Kevin Brown G/Y	6.00
217	Matt Lawton S/Y	6.00
218	Cal Ripken Jr.G/X	35.00
219	Moises Alou G/Y	7.50
220	Chuck Knoblauch G/Z	20.00
221	Ivan Rodriguez G/Y	25.00
222	Travis Fryman B/Y	6.00
223	Jim Thome G/Z	25.00

No.	Player	Price
224	Eddie Murray S/Z	25.00
225	Eric Young G/Z	10.00
226	Ron Gant S/X	4.00
227	Tony Phillips B/X	4.00
228	Reggie Sanders B/Y	6.00
229	Johnny Damon S/Z	10.00
230	Bill Pulsipher B/X	4.00
231	Jim Edmonds G/Z	12.50
232	Melvin Nieves B/X	4.00
233	Ryan Klesko G/Z	25.00
234	David Cone S/X	4.00
235	Derek Bell B/Y	6.00
236	Julio Franco S/X	4.00
237	Juan Guzman B/X	4.00
238	Larry Walker G/Z	20.00
239	Delino DeShields B/X	4.00
240	Troy Percival B/Y	6.00
241	Andres Galarraga G/Z	15.00
242	Rondell White G/Z	10.00
243	John Burkett B/X	4.00
244	J.T. Snow B/Y	6.00
245	Alex Fernandez S/Y	6.00
246	Edgar Martinez G/Z	10.00
247	Craig Biggio G/Z	10.00
248	Todd Hundley G/Y	7.50
249	Jimmy Key S/X	4.00
250	Cliff Floyd B/Y	6.00
251	Jeff Conine B/Y	6.00
252	Curt Schilling B/X	4.00
253	Jeff King B/X	4.00
254	Tino Martinez G/Z	17.50
255	Carlos Baerga S/Y	6.00
256	Jeff Fassero B/Y	6.00
257	Dean Palmer S/Y	6.00
258	Robb Nen B/X	4.00
259	Sandy Alomar Jr.S/Y	6.00
260	Carlos Perez B/X	4.00
261	Rickey Henderson S/Y	6.00
262	Bobby Bonilla S/Y	6.00
263	Darren Daulton B/X	4.00
264	Jim Leyritz B/X	4.00
265	Dennis Martinez B/X	4.00
266	Butch Huskey B/X	4.00
267	Joe Vitiello S/Y	6.00
268	Steve Trachsel B/X	4.00
269	Glenallen Hill B/X	4.00
270	Terry Steinbach B/X	4.00
271	Mark McLemore B/X	4.00
272	Devon White B/X	4.00
273	Jeff Kent B/X	4.00
274	Tim Raines B/X	4.00
275	Carlos Garcia B/X	4.00
276	Hal Morris B/X	4.00
277	Gary Gaetti B/X	4.00
278	John Olerud S/Y	6.00
279	Wally Joyner B/X	4.00
280	Brian Hunter S/X	4.00
281	Steve Karsay B/X	4.00
282	Denny Neagle S/X	4.00
283	Jose Herrera B/X	4.00
284	Todd Stottlemyre B/X	4.00
285	Bip Roberts S/X	4.00
286	Kevin Seitzer B/X	4.00
287	Benji Gil B/X	4.00
288	Dennis Eckersley S/X	4.00
289	Brad Ausmus B/X	4.00
290	Otis Nixon B/X	4.00
291	Darryl Strawberry B/X	4.00
292	Marquis Grissom S/Y	6.00
293	Darryl Kile B/X	4.00
294	Quilvio Veras B/X	4.00
295	Tom Goodwin B/X	4.00
296	Benito Santiago B/X	4.00
297	Mike Bordick B/X	4.00
298	Roberto Kelly B/X	4.00
299	David Justice G/Z	15.00
300	Carl Everett B/X	4.00
301	Mark Whiten B/X	4.00
302	Aaron Sele B/X	4.00
303	Darren Dreifort B/X	4.00
304	Bobby Jones B/X	4.00
305	Fernando Vina B/X	4.00
306	Ed Sprague B/X	4.00
307	Andy Ashby S/X	4.00
308	Tony Fernandez B/X	4.00
309	Roger Pavlik B/X	4.00
310	Mark Clark B/X	4.00
311	Mariano Duncan B/X	4.00
312	Tyler Houston B/X	4.00
313	Eric Davis S/Y	6.00
314	Greg Vaughn B/Y	6.00
315	David Segui S/Y	6.00
316	Dave Nilsson S/X	4.00
317	F.P. Santangelo S/X	4.00
318	Wilton GuerreroG/Z	10.00
319	Jose Guillen G/Z	35.00
320	Kevin Orie S/Y	6.00
321	Derrek Lee G/Z	10.00
322	Bubba Trammell S/Y	25.00
323	Pokey Reese G/Z	10.00
324	Hideki Irabu G/X	20.00
325	Scott Spiezio S/Z	10.00
326	Bartolo Colon G/Z	10.00
327	Damon MashoreS/Y	6.00
328	Ryan McGuire S/Y	6.00
329	Chris Carpenter B/X	4.00
330	Jose Cruz, Jr. G/X	12.50
331	Todd Greene S/Z	15.00
332	Brian Moehler B/X	4.00
333	Mike Sweeney B/Y	6.00
334	Neifi Perez G/Z	10.00
335	Matt Morris S/Y	6.00
336	Marvin Benard B/Y	6.00
337	Karim Garcia S/Z	12.50
338	Jason Dickson S/Y	6.00
339	Brant Brown S/Y	6.00
340	Jeff Suppan S/Z	10.00
341	Deivi Cruz B/X	5.00
342	Antone WilliamsonG/Z	10.00
343	Curtis Goodwin B/X	4.00
344	Brooks Kieschnick S/Y	6.00
345	Tony Womack B/X	4.00
346	Rudy Pemberton B/X	4.00
347	Todd Dunwoody B/X	4.00
348	Frank Thomas S/Y (Legacy)	35.00
349	Andruw Jones S/X (Legacy)	20.00
350	Alex Rodriguez B/Y (Legacy)	60.00
351	Greg Maddux S/Y (Legacy)	50.00
352	Jeff Bagwell B/Y (Legacy)	35.00
353	Juan Gonzalez S/Y (Legacy)	25.00
354	Barry Bonds B/Y (Legacy)	25.00
355	Mark McGwire B/Y (Legacy)	75.00
356	Tony Gwynn B/Y (Legacy)	35.00
357	Gary Sheffield B/X (Legacy)	6.00
358	Derek Jeter S/X (Legacy)	20.00
359	Manny Ramirez S/Y (Legacy)	17.50
360	Hideo Nomo G/Z (Legacy)	15.00
361	Sammy Sosa B/X (Legacy)	15.00
362	Paul Molitor S/Z (Legacy)	15.00
363	Kenny Lofton B/Y (Legacy)	25.00
364	Eddie Murray B/X (Legacy)	7.50
365	Barry Larkin S/Z (Legacy)	12.50
366	Roger Clemens S/Y (Legacy)	25.00
367	John Smoltz B/Z (Legacy)	10.00
368	Alex Rodriguez S/X (Gamers)	35.00
369	Frank Thomas B/X (Gamers)	20.00
370	Cal Ripken Jr. S/Y (Gamers)	60.00
371	Ken Griffey Jr. S/Y (Gamers)	85.00
372	Greg Maddux B/X (Gamers)	20.00
373	Mike Piazza S/X (Gamers)	20.00
374	Chipper Jones B/Y (Gamers)	45.00
375	Albert Belle B/X (Gamers)	7.50
376	Chuck Knoblauch B/X (Gamers)	7.50
377	Brady Anderson B/Z (Gamers)	10.00
378	David Justice S/X (Gamers)	6.00
379	Randy Johnson B/Z (Gamers)	20.00
380	Wade Boggs B/X (Gamers)	6.00
381	Kevin Brown B/X (Gamers)	4.00
382	Tom Glavine G/Y (Gamers)	6.00
383	Raul Mondesi S/X (Gamers)	6.00
384	Ivan Rodriguez S/X (Gamers)	7.50
385	Larry Walker B/Y (Gamers)	10.00
386	Bernie Williams B/Z (Gamers)	20.00
387	Rusty Greer G/Y (Gamers)	6.00
388	Rafael Palmeiro G/Y (Gamers)	7.50
389	Matt Williams B/X (Gamers)	6.00
390	Eric Young B/X (Gamers)	4.00
391	Fred McGriff B/X (Gamers)	6.00
392	Ken Caminiti B/X (Gamers)	5.00
393	Roberto Alomar B/Z (Gamers)	20.00
394	Brian Jordan B/X (Gamers)	4.00
395	Mark Grace G/Z (Gamers)	15.00
396	Jim Edmonds B/Y (Gamers)	6.00
397	Deion Sanders S/Y (Gamers)	9.00
398	Checklist (Vladimir Guerrero S/Z)	25.00
399	Checklist (Darin Erstad S/Y)	25.00
400	Checklist (Nomar GarciaparraS/Z)	35.00

1997 Leaf Banner Season

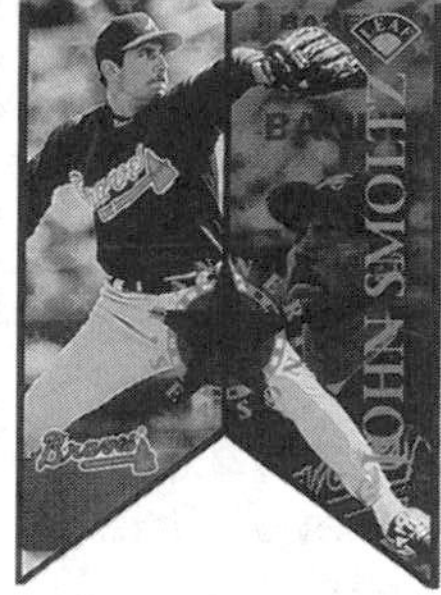

Banner Season was a 15-card insert set that was die-cut and printed on a canvas card stock. Only 2,500 individually numbered sets were produced, with cards only found in pre-priced packs.

		MT
Complete Set (15):		200.00
Common Player:		2.50
1	Jeff Bagwell	20.00
2	Ken Griffey Jr.	50.00
3	Juan Gonzalez	15.00
4	Frank Thomas	20.00
5	Alex Rodriguez	40.00
6	Kenny Lofton	12.00
7	Chuck Knoblauch	5.00
8	Mo Vaughn	12.00
9	Chipper Jones	30.00
10	Ken Caminiti	5.00
11	Craig Biggio	5.00
12	John Smoltz	2.50
13	Pat Hentgen	2.50
14	Derek Jeter	25.00
15	Todd Hollandsworth	2.50

1997 Leaf Dress for Success

Exclusive to retail packs was an insert called Dress for Success. It included 18 players printed on nylon and flocking card stock. Dress for Success was limited to 3,500 individually numbered sets.

		MT
Complete Set (18):		150.00
Common Player:		2.50
1	Greg Maddux	10.00
2	Cal Ripken Jr.	15.00
3	Albert Belle	5.00
4	Frank Thomas	10.00

5	Dante Bichette	2.50
6	Gary Sheffield	4.00
7	Jeff Bagwell	9.00
8	Mike Piazza	12.50
9	Mark McGwire	25.00
10	Ken Caminiti	4.00
11	Alex Rodriguez	20.00
12	Ken Griffey Jr.	25.00
13	Juan Gonzalez	8.00
14	Brian Jordan	2.50
15	Mo Vaughn	5.00
16	Ivan Rodriguez	4.00
17	Andruw Jones	10.00
18	Chipper Jones	12.50

1997 Leaf Get-A-Grip

Get a Grip included 16 double-sided cards, with a star hitter on one side and a star pitcher on the other. The card slated the two stars against each other and explained how the hitter would hit against the pitcher, while featuring the pitcher's top pitch. This insert was printed on silver foilboard with the right side die-cut, and limited to 3,500 numbered sets found only in hobby packs.

		MT
Complete Set (16):		250.00
Common Player:		6.00
1	Ken Griffey Jr., Greg Maddux	40.00
2	John Smoltz, Frank Thomas	15.00
3	Mike Piazza, Andy Pettitte	25.00
4	Randy Johnson, Chipper Jones	25.00
5	Tom Glavine, Alex Rodriguez	35.00
6	Pat Hentgen, Jeff Bagwell	15.00
7	Kevin Brown, Juan Gonzalez	10.00
8	Barry Bonds, Mike Mussina	12.00
9	Hideo Nomo, Albert Belle	9.00
10	Troy Percival, Andruw Jones	15.00
11	Roger Clemens, Brian Jordan	15.00
12	Paul Wilson, Ivan Rodriguez	10.00
13	Andy Benes, Mo Vaughn	6.00
14	Al Leiter, Derek Jeter	25.00
15	Bill Pulsipher, Cal Ripken Jr.	30.00
16	Mariano Rivera, Ken Caminiti	6.00

1997 Leaf Knot-Hole Gang

Knot-Hole Gang pictured 12 hitters against a wood picket fence in the background. Cards were die-cut along the top of the fence and printed on a wood card stock. Set production was limited to 5,000 and these inserts were found in all types of packs.

		MT
Complete Set (12):		90.00
Common Player:		2.50
1	Chuck Knoblauch	3.00
2	Ken Griffey Jr.	20.00
3	Frank Thomas	10.00
4	Tony Gwynn	10.00
5	Mike Piazza	15.00
6	Jeff Bagwell	10.00
7	Rusty Greer	2.50
8	Cal Ripken Jr.	17.50
9	Chipper Jones	15.00
10	Ryan Klesko	2.50
11	Barry Larkin	2.50
12	Paul Molitor	5.00

1997 Leaf Leagues of the Nation

A 15-card insert set featuring a double-sided die-cut design. The players on each card represent matchups from the initial rounds of interleague play. Cards were numbered to 2,500 and feature a flocked texture.

		MT
Complete Set (15):		300.00
Common Player:		10.00
1	Juan Gonzalez, Barry Bonds	10.00
2	Cal Ripken Jr., Chipper Jones	35.00
3	Mark McGwire, Ken Caminiti	40.00
4	Derek Jeter, Kenny Lofton	25.00
5	Ivan Rodriguez, Mike Piazza	25.00
6	Ken Griffey Jr., Larry Walker	45.00
7	Frank Thomas, Sammy Sosa	30.00
8	Paul Molitor, Barry Larkin	10.00
9	Albert Belle, Deion Sanders	10.00
10	Matt Williams, Jeff Bagwell	15.00
11	Mo Vaughn, Gary Sheffield	10.00
12	Alex Rodriguez, Tony Gwynn	35.00
13	Tino Martinez, Scott Rolen	15.00
14	Darin Erstad, Wilton Guerrero	15.00
15	Tony Clark, Vladimir Guerrero	15.00

1997 Leaf Statistical Standouts

Statistical Standouts were limited to only 1,000 individually numbered sets. Inserts were printed on leather and die-cut. The set included 15 top stars who excelled beyond their competition in many statistical categories.

		MT
Complete Set (15):		450.00
Common Player:		10.00
1	Albert Belle	15.00
2	Juan Gonzalez	15.00
3	Ken Griffey Jr.	65.00
4	Alex Rodriguez	50.00
5	Frank Thomas	30.00
6	Chipper Jones	40.00
7	Greg Maddux	35.00
8	Mike Piazza	40.00
9	Cal Ripken Jr.	50.00
10	Mark McGwire	65.00
11	Barry Bonds	15.00
12	Derek Jeter	40.00
13	Ken Caminiti	10.00
14	John Smoltz	10.00
15	Paul Molitor	10.00

1997 Leaf Thomas Collection

This six-card insert from Series II features pieces of various game-used Frank Thomas items built into the texture of each card. Jerseys, bats, hats, batting gloves and sweatbands are all featured on the various cards, which are numbered to 100 each.

		MT
Complete Set (6):		2000.
Common Thomas:		350.00
1	Frank Thomas Hat	300.00
2	Frank Thomas Home Jersey	400.00
3	Frank Thomas Batting Glove	300.00
4	Frank Thomas Bat	300.00
5	Frank Thomas Sweatband	300.00
6	Frank Thomas Away Jersey	400.00

1997 Leaf 22kt Gold Stars

A 36-card insert from Series II Leaf, each card features a special 22kt. gold foil embossed stamp on front which is printed on gold foil cardboard. Horizontal backs have a portrait photo on a dark background and are serially numbered to a limit of 2,500 each.

		MT
Complete Set (36):		300.00
Common Player:		2.50
1	Frank Thomas	15.00
2	Alex Rodriguez	25.00
3	Ken Griffey Jr.	30.00
4	Andruw Jones	12.50
5	Chipper Jones	20.00
6	Jeff Bagwell	10.00
7	Derek Jeter	17.50
8	Deion Sanders	2.50
9	Ivan Rodriguez	7.50
10	Juan Gonzalez	8.00
11	Greg Maddux	17.50
12	Andy Pettitte	6.00
13	Roger Clemens	12.50
14	Hideo Nomo	5.00
15	Tony Gwynn	15.00
16	Barry Bonds	7.50
17	Kenny Lofton	6.00
18	Paul Molitor	6.00
19	Jim Thome	4.00
20	Albert Belle	7.50
21	Cal Ripken Jr.	25.00
22	Mark McGwire	30.00
23	Barry Larkin	3.00
24	Mike Piazza	20.00
25	Darin Erstad	10.00
26	Chuck Knoblauch	3.00
27	Vladimir Guerrero	12.00
28	Tony Clark	4.00
29	Scott Rolen	15.00

30	Nomar Garciaparra	20.00
31	Eric Young	2.50
32	Ryne Sandberg	7.50
33	Roberto Alomar	6.00
34	Eddie Murray	3.00
35	Rafael Palmeiro	3.00
36	Jose Guillen	4.00

1997 Leaf Warning Track

A 12-card insert printed on embossed canvas depicting players who are known for making tough catches. Cards were numbered to 3,500.

		MT
Complete Set (18):		100.00
Common Player:		2.00
1	Ken Griffey Jr.	30.00
2	Albert Belle	8.00
3	Barry Bonds	8.00
4	Andruw Jones	8.00
5	Kenny Lofton	6.00
6	Tony Gwynn	15.00
7	Manny Ramirez	10.00
8	Rusty Greer	2.00
9	Bernie Williams	6.00
10	Gary Sheffield	5.00
11	Juan Gonzalez	8.00
12	Raul Mondesi	5.00
13	Brady Anderson	2.00
14	Rondell White	2.00
15	Sammy Sosa	20.00
16	Deion Sanders	3.00
17	David Justice	3.00
18	Jim Edmonds	2.00

1998 Leaf

The 50th Anniversary edition of Leaf Baseball consists of a 200-card base set with three subsets, three parallels and four inserts. The base set has 147 regular cards, a 10-card Curtain Calls subset, Gold Leaf Stars subset (20 cards), Gold Leaf Rookies subset (20 cards) and three checklists. Card #42 does not exist because Leaf retired the number in honor of Jackie Robinson. The base set was paralleled in Fractal Matrix, Fractal Matrix Die-Cuts and Fractal Diamond Axis. Inserts include Crusade, Heading for the Hall, State Representatives and Statistical Standouts.

		MT
Complete Set (200):		200.00
Common Player:		.10
Diamond Axis Stars:		50X
SP Diamond Axis (148-177):		12X
Pack (10):		3.50
Wax Box (24):		75.00
1	Rusty Greer	.10
2	Tino Martinez	.25
3	Bobby Bonilla	.15
4	Jason Giambi	.10
5	Matt Morris	.20
6	Craig Counsell	.10
7	Reggie Jefferson	.10
8	Brian Rose	.20
9	Ruben Rivera	.10
10	Shawn Estes	.10
11	Tony Gwynn	1.50
12	Jeff Abbott	.10
13	Jose Cruz Jr.	.20
14	Francisco Cordova	.10
15	Ryan Klesko	.25
16	Tim Salmon	.30
17	Brett Tomko	.10
18	Matt Williams	.25
19	Joe Carter	.15
20	Harold Baines	.10
21	Gary Sheffield	.25
22	Charles Johnson	.15
23	Aaron Boone	.20
24	Eddie Murray	.20
25	Matt Stairs	.10
26	David Cone	.20
27	Jon Nunnally	.10
28	Chris Stynes	.10
29	Enrique Wilson	.10
30	Randy Johnson	.50
31	Garret Anderson	.10
32	Manny Ramirez	1.00
33	Jeff Suppan	.10
34	Rickey Henderson	.20
35	Scott Spiezio	.10
36	Rondell White	.20
37	Todd Greene	.20
38	Delino DeShields	.10
39	Kevin Brown	.20
40	Chili Davis	.10
41	Jimmy Key	.10
42	NOT ISSUED	
43	Mike Mussina	.60
44	Joe Randa	.10
45	Chan Ho Park	.20
46	Brad Radke	.10
47	Geronimo Berroa	.10
48	Wade Boggs	.25
49	Kevin Appier	.10
50	Moises Alou	.20
51	David Justice	.25
52	Ivan Rodriguez	.75
53	J.T. Snow	.20
54	Brian Giles	.10
55	Will Clark	.25
56	Justin Thompson	.10
57	Javier Lopez	.20
58	Hideki Irabu	.30
59	Mark Grudzielanek	.10
60	Abraham Nunez	.10
61	Todd Hollandsworth	.10
62	Jay Bell	.10
63	Nomar Garciaparra	2.00
64	Vinny Castilla	.10
65	Lou Collier	.10
66	Kevin Orie	.10
67	John Valentin	.10
68	Robin Ventura	.20
69	Denny Neagle	.10
70	Tony Womack	.10
71	Dennis Reyes	.10
72	Wally Joyner	.10
73	Kevin Brown	.20
74	Ray Durham	.10
75	Mike Cameron	.15
76	Dante Bichette	.15
77	Jose Guillen	.25
78	Carlos Delgado	.50
79	Paul Molitor	.40
80	Jason Kendall	.10
81	Mark Belhorn	.10
82	Damian Jackson	.10
83	Bill Mueller	.10
84	Kevin Young	.10
85	Curt Schilling	.20
86	Jeffrey Hammonds	.10
87	Sandy Alomar Jr.	.20
88	Bartolo Colon	.10
89	Wilton Guerrero	.10
90	Bernie Williams	.50
91	Deion Sanders	.20
92	Mike Piazza	2.00
93	Butch Huskey	.10
94	Edgardo Alfonzo	.10
95	Alan Benes	.20
96	Craig Biggio	.20
97	Mark Grace	.25
98	Shawn Green	.20
99	Derrek Lee	.20
100	Ken Griffey Jr.	3.00
101	Tim Raines	.10
102	Pokey Reese	.10
103	Lee Stevens	.10
104	Shannon Stewart	.10
105	John Smoltz	.20
106	Frank Thomas	1.00
107	Jeff Fassero	.10
108	Jay Buhner	.15
109	Jose Canseco	.25
110	Omar Vizquel	.10
111	Travis Fryman	.10
112	Dave Nilsson	.10
113	John Olerud	.15
114	Larry Walker	.25
115	Jim Edmonds	.15
116	Bobby Higginson	.20
117	Todd Hundley	.10
118	Paul O'Neill	.20
119	Bip Roberts	.10
120	Ismael Valdes	.10
121	Pedro Martinez	.25
122	Jeff Cirillo	.10
123	Andy Benes	.15
124	Bobby Jones	.10
125	Brian Hunter	.10
126	Darryl Kile	.10
127	Pat Hentgen	.10
128	Marquis Grissom	.10
129	Eric Davis	.10
130	Chipper Jones	2.00
131	Edgar Martinez	.10
132	Andy Pettitte	.40
133	Cal Ripken Jr.	2.50
134	Scott Rolen	1.50
135	Ron Coomer	.10
136	Luis Castillo	.10
137	Fred McGriff	.20
138	Neifi Perez	.10
139	Eric Karros	.20
140	Alex Fernandez	.10
141	Jason Dickson	.10
142	Lance Johnson	.10
143	Ray Lankford	.10
144	Sammy Sosa	3.00
145	Eric Young	.10
146	Bubba Trammell	.20
147	Todd Walker	.20
148	Mo Vaughn (Curtain Calls)	3.00
149	Jeff Bagwell (Curtain Calls)	5.00
150	Kenny Lofton (Curtain Calls)	3.00
151	Raul Mondesi (Curtain Calls)	1.50
152	Mike Piazza (Curtain Calls)	10.00
153	Chipper Jones (Curtain Calls)	8.00
154	Larry Walker (Curtain Calls)	1.50
155	Greg Maddux (Curtain Calls)	10.00
156	Ken Griffey Jr. (Curtain Calls)	15.00
157	Frank Thomas (Curtain Calls)	6.00
158	Darin Erstad (Gold Leaf Stars)	3.00
159	Roberto Alomar (Gold Leaf Stars)	2.00
160	Albert Belle (Gold Leaf Stars)	3.00
161	Jim Thome (Gold Leaf Stars)	1.50
162	Tony Clark (Gold Leaf Stars)	2.00
163	Chuck Knoblauch (Gold Leaf Stars)	1.50
164	Derek Jeter (Gold Leaf Stars)	8.00
165	Alex Rodriguez (Gold Leaf Stars)	10.00
166	Tony Gwynn (Gold Leaf Stars)	6.00
167	Roger Clemens (Gold Leaf Stars)	5.00
168	Barry Larkin (Gold Leaf Stars)	1.00
169	Andres Galarraga (Gold Leaf Stars)	1.00
170	Vladimir Guerrero (Gold Leaf Stars)	5.00
171	Mark McGwire (Gold Leaf Stars)	20.00
172	Barry Bonds (Gold Leaf Stars)	3.00
173	Juan Gonzalez (Gold Leaf Stars)	5.00
174	Andruw Jones (Gold Leaf Stars)	6.00
175	Paul Molitor (Gold Leaf Stars)	2.00
176	Hideo Nomo (Gold Leaf Stars)	1.50
177	Cal Ripken Jr. (Gold Leaf Stars)	12.00
178	Brad Fullmer (Gold Leaf Rookies)	1.50
179	Jaret Wright (Gold Leaf Rookies)	8.00
180	Bobby Estalella (Gold Leaf Rookies)	.75
181	Ben Grieve (Gold Leaf Rookies)	5.00
182	Paul Konerko (Gold Leaf Rookies)	4.00
183	David Ortiz (Gold Leaf Rookies)	1.00
184	Todd Helton (Gold Leaf Rookies)	3.00
185	Juan Encarnacion (Gold Leaf Rookies)	.75
186	Miguel Tejada (Gold Leaf Rookies)	3.00
187	Jacob Cruz (Gold Leaf Rookies)	1.00
188	Mark Kotsay (Gold Leaf Rookies)	1.50
189	Fernando Tatis (Gold Leaf Rookies)	1.00
190	Ricky Ledee (Gold Leaf Rookies)	1.50
191	Richard Hidalgo (Gold Leaf Rookies)	.75
192	Richie Sexson (Gold leaf Rookies)	.75
193	Luis Ordaz (Gold Leaf Rookies)	.75
194	Eli Marrero (Gold Leaf Rookies)	.75
195	Livan Hernandez Gold Leaf Rookies)	1.50
196	Homer Bush (Gold Leaf Rookies)	.75
197	Raul Ibanez (Gold Leaf Rookies)	.75
198	Checklist (Nomar Garciaparra)	1.50
199	Checklist (Scott Rolen)	1.00
200	Checklist (Jose Cruz Jr.)	.10
201	Al Martin	

1998 Leaf Fractal Matrix

Fractal Matrix parallels the 1998 Leaf set. The

cards have a metallic-colored finish, with 100 done in bronze, 60 in silver and 40 in gold, and each color having some cards in X, Y and Z axis. Stated print runs are: Bronze: X - 1,600; Y - 1,800; Z - 1,900. Silver: X - 600; Y - 800; Z - 900. Gold: X - 100; Y - 300; Z - 400. Each player is found only in a single color/axis combination.

		MT
Complete Set (200):		750.00
Common Bronze:		.75
Common Silver:		2.50
Common Gold:		5.00
1	Rusty Greer G/Z	5.00
2	Tino Martinez G/Z	5.00
3	Bobby Bonilla S/Y	2.50
4	Jason Giambi S/Y	2.50
5	Matt Morris S/Y	2.50
6	Craig Counsell B/X	.75
7	Reggie Jefferson B/X	.75
8	Brian Rose S/Y	3.50
9	Ruben Rivera B/X	.75
10	Shawn Estes S/Y	2.50
11	Tony Gwynn G/Z	20.00
12	Jeff Abbott B/Y	.75
13	Jose Cruz Jr. G/Z	6.50
14	Francisco Cordova B/X	.75
15	Ryan Klesko B/X	1.00
16	Tim Salmon G/Y	7.50
17	Brett Tomko B/X	.75
18	Matt Williams S/Y	3.00
19	Joe Carter B/X	.75
20	Harold Baines B/X	.75
21	Gary Sheffield S/Z	5.00
22	Charles Johnson S/X	2.50
23	Aaron Boone B/X	1.00
24	Eddie Murray G/Y	5.00
25	Matt Stairs B/X	.75
26	David Cone B/X	1.00
27	Jon Nunnally B/X	.75
28	Chris Stynes B/X	.75
29	Enrique Wilson B/Y	.75
30	Randy Johnson S/Z	7.50
31	Garret Anderson S/Y	2.50
32	Manny Ramirez G/Z	9.00
33	Jeff Suppan S/X	2.50
34	Rickey Henderson B/X	1.00
35	Scott Spiezio B/X	.75
36	Rondell White S/Y	2.50
37	Todd Greene S/Z	2.50
38	Delino DeShields B/X	.75
39	Kevin Brown S/X	3.00
40	Chili Davis B/X	.75
41	Jimmy Key B/X	.75
42	NOT ISSUED	
43	Mike Mussina G/Y	10.00
44	Joe Randa B/X	.75
45	Chan Ho Park S/Z	3.00
46	Brad Radke B/X	.75
47	Geronimo Berroa B/X	.75
48	Wade Boggs S/Y	5.00
49	Kevin Appier B/X	.75
50	Moises Alou S/Y	2.50
51	David Justice G/Y	5.00
52	Ivan Rodriguez G/Z	10.00
53	J.T. Snow B/X	.75
54	Brian Giles B/X	.75
55	Will Clark B/Y	1.25
56	Justin Thompson S/Y	2.50
57	Javier Lopez S/X	3.50
58	Hideki Irabu B/Z	2.00
59	Mark Grudzielanek B/X	.75
60	Abraham Nunez S/X	2.50
61	Todd Hollandsworth B/X	.75
62	Jay Bell B/X	.75
63	Nomar Garciaparra G/Z	25.00
64	Vinny Castilla B/Y	.75
65	Lou Collier B/Y	.75
66	Kevin Orie S/X	2.50
67	John Valentin B/X	.75
68	Robin Ventura B/X	1.00
69	Denny Neagle B/X	.75
70	Tony Womack S/Y	2.50
71	Dennis Reyes S/Y	2.50
72	Wally Joyner B/X	.75
73	Kevin Brown B/Y	1.00
74	Ray Durham B/X	.75
75	Mike Cameron S/Z	2.50
76	Dante Bichette B/X	1.00
77	Jose Guillen G/Y	5.00
78	Carlos Delgado B/Y	.75
79	Paul Molitor G/Z	7.50
80	Jason Kendall B/X	.75
81	Mark Belhorn B/X	.75
82	Damian Jackson B/X	.75
83	Bill Mueller B/X	.75
84	Kevin Young B/X	.75
85	Curt Schilling B/X	1.00
86	Jeffrey Hammonds B/X	.75
87	Sandy Alomar Jr. S/Y	3.50
88	Bartolo Colon B/Y	.75
89	Wilton Guerrero B/Y	.75
90	Bernie Williams G/Y	10.00
91	Deion Sanders S/Y	3.00
92	Mike Piazza G/X	75.00
93	Butch Huskey B/X	.75
94	Edgardo Alfonzo S/X	3.00
95	Alan Benes S/Y	2.50
96	Craig Biggio S/Y	3.50
97	Mark Grace S/Y	3.00
98	Shawn Green S/Y	3.00
99	Derrek Lee S/Y	2.50
100	Ken Griffey Jr. G/Z	40.00
101	Tim Raines B/X	.75
102	Pokey Reese S/X	2.50
103	Lee Stevens B/X	.75
104	Shannon Stewart S/Y	2.50
105	John Smoltz S/Y	3.50
106	Frank Thomas G/X	45.00
107	Jeff Fassero B/X	.75
108	Jay Buhner B/Y	1.00
109	Jose Canseco B/X	1.00
110	Omar Vizquel B/X	.75
111	Travis Fryman B/X	.75
112	Dave Nilsson B/X	.75
113	John Olerud B/X	1.00
114	Larry Walker G/Z	6.50
115	Jim Edmonds S/Y	2.50
116	Bobby Higginson S/X	2.50
117	Todd Hundley S/X	3.50
118	Paul O'Neill B/X	1.00
119	Bip Roberts B/X	.75
120	Ismael Valdes B/X	.75
121	Pedro Martinez S/Y	5.00
122	Jeff Cirillo B/X	.75
123	Andy Benes B/X	.75
124	Bobby Jones B/X	.75
125	Brian Hunter B/X	.75
126	Darryl Kile B/X	.75
127	Pat Hentgen B/X	.75
128	Marquis Grissom B/X	.75
129	Eric Davis B/X	.75
130	Chipper Jones G/Z	25.00
131	Edgar Martinez S/Z	2.50
132	Andy Pettitte G/Z	7.50
133	Cal Ripken Jr. G/X	100.00
134	Scott Rolen G/Z	18.50
135	Ron Coomer B/X	.75
136	Luis Castillo B/Y	.75
137	Fred McGriff B/Y	1.00
138	Neifi Perez S/Y	2.50
139	Eric Karros B/X	.75
140	Alex Fernandez B/X	.75
141	Jason Dickson B/X	.75
142	Lance Johnson B/X	.75
143	Ray Lankford B/Y	.75
144	Sammy Sosa G/Y	18.50
145	Eric Young B/Y	.75
146	Bubba Trammell S/Y	2.50
147	Todd Walker S/Y	2.50
148	Mo Vaughn S/X (Curtain Calls)	5.00
149	Jeff Bagwell S/X (Curtain Calls)	7.50
150	Kenny Lofton S/X (Curtain Calls)	5.00
151	Raul Mondesi S/X (Curtain Calls)	2.50
152	Mike Piazza S/X (Curtain Calls)	12.50
153	Chipper Jones S/X (Curtain Calls)	12.50
154	Larry Walker S/X (Curtain Calls)	2.50
155	Greg Maddux S/X (Curtain Calls)	12.50
156	Ken Griffey Jr. S/X (Curtain Calls)	20.00
157	Frank Thomas S/X (Curtain Calls)	7.50
158	Darin Erstad B/Z (Gold Leaf Stars)	2.00
159	Roberto Alomar B/Y (Gold Leaf Stars)	1.50
160	Albert Belle G/Y (Gold Leaf Stars)	6.50
161	Jim Thome G/Y (Gold Leaf Stars)	5.00
162	Tony Clark G/Y (Gold Leaf Stars)	5.00
163	Chuck Knoblauch B/Y (Gold Leaf Stars)	1.00
164	Derek Jeter G/Z (Gold Leaf Stars)	12.50
165	Alex Rodriguez G/Z (Gold Leaf Stars)	12.50
166	Tony Gwynn B/X (Gold Leaf Stars)	6.50
167	Roger Clemens G/Z (Gold Leaf Stars)	7.50
168	Barry Larkin B/Y (Gold Leaf Stars)	1.00
169	Andres Galarraga B/Y (Gold Leaf Stars)	1.00
170	Vladimir Guerrero G/Z (Gold Leaf Stars)	6.00
171	Mark McGwire B/Z (Gold Leaf Stars)	7.50
172	Barry Bonds B/Z (Gold Leaf Stars)	3.00
173	Juan Gonzalez G/Z (Gold Leaf Stars)	5.00
174	Andruw Jones G/Z (Gold Leaf Stars)	10.00
175	Paul Molitor B/X (Gold Leaf Stars)	1.50
176	Hideo Nomo B/Z (Gold Leaf Stars)	2.50
177	Cal Ripken Jr. B/X (Gold Leaf Stars)	5.00
178	Brad Fullmer S/Z (Gold Leaf Rookies)	3.00
179	Jaret Wright G/Z (Gold Leaf Rookies)	12.50
180	Bobby Estalella B/Y (Gold Leaf Rookies)	.75
181	Ben Grieve G/X (Gold Leaf Rookies)	30.00
182	Paul Konerko G/Z (Gold Leaf Rookies)	7.50
183	David Ortiz G/Z (Gold Leaf Rookies)	5.00
184	Todd Helton G/X (Gold Leaf Rookies)	20.00
185	Juan Encarnacion G/Z (Gold Leaf Rookies)	5.00
186	Miguel Tejada G/Z (Gold Leaf Rookies)	6.50
187	Jacob Cruz B/Y (Gold Leaf Rookies)	.75
188	Mark Kotsay G/Z (Gold Leaf Rookies)	5.00
189	Fernando Tatis S/Z (Gold Leaf Rookies)	2.50
190	Ricky Ledee S/Y (Gold Leaf Rookies)	3.00
191	Richard Hidalgo S/Y (Gold Leaf Rookies)	2.50
192	Richie Sexson S/Y (Gold Leaf Rookies)	2.50
193	Luis Ordaz B/X (Gold Leaf Rookies)	.75
194	Eli Marrero S/Z (Gold Leaf Rookies)	2.50
195	Livan Hernandez S/Z (Gold Leaf Rookies)	2.50
196	Homer Bush B/X (Gold Leaf Rookies)	.75
197	Raul Ibanez B/X (Gold Leaf Rookies)	.75
198	Checklist (Nomar Garciaparra B/X)	4.00
199	Checklist (Scott Rolen B/X)	2.50
200	Checklist (Jose Cruz Jr. B/X)	2.50

1998 Leaf Fractal Matrix Die-Cut

This parallel set adds a die-cut to the Fractal Matrix set. Three different die-cut versions were created: X-axis, Y-axis and Z-axis. An X-axis die-cut was added to 75 bronze, 20 silver and 5 gold cards. A Y-axis die-cut was added to 20 bronze, 30 silver and 10 gold cards. Of the 40 Z-axis cards, 5 are bronze, 10 silver and 25 gold. Stated print runs were 400 of each X-axis card; 200 Y and 100 Z.

	MT
Complete Set (200):	1875.
Common X-Axis:	3.00

Common Y-Axis: 5.00
Common Z-Axis: 10.00
1 Rusty Greer G/Z 10.00
2 Tino Martinez G/Z 15.00
3 Bobby Bonilla S/Y 7.50
4 Jason Giambi S/Y 6.00
5 Matt Morris S/Y 7.50
6 Craig Counsell B/X 3.00
7 Reggie Jefferson B/X 3.00
8 Brian Rose S/Y 7.50
9 Ruben Rivera B/X 5.00
10 Shawn Estes S/Y 5.00
11 Tony Gwynn G/Z 75.00
12 Jeff Abbott B/Y 5.00
13 Jose Cruz Jr. G/Z 20.00
14 Francisco Cordova B/X 3.00
15 Ryan Klesko B/X 4.00
16 Tim Salmon G/Y 12.50
17 Brett Tomko B/X 3.00
18 Matt Williams S/Y 10.00
19 Joe Carter B/X 5.00
20 Harold Baines B/X 3.00
21 Gary Sheffield S/Z 20.00
22 Charles Johnson S/X 4.00
23 Aaron Boone B/X 4.00
24 Eddie Murray G/Y 10.00
25 Matt Stairs B/X 3.00
26 David Cone B/X 5.00
27 Jon Nunnally B/X 3.00
28 Chris Stynes B/X 3.00
29 Enrique Wilson B/Y 5.00
30 Randy Johnson S/Z 25.00
31 Garret Anderson S/Y 5.00
32 Manny Ramirez G/Z 30.00
33 Jeff Suppan S/X 3.00
34 Rickey Henderson B/X 3.00
35 Scott Spiezio B/X 3.00
36 Rondell White S/Y 10.00
37 Todd Greene S/Z 15.00
38 Delino DeShields B/X 3.00
39 Kevin Brown S/X 4.00
40 Chili Davis B/X 3.00
41 Jimmy Key B/X 3.00
42 NOT ISSUED
43 Mike Mussina G/Y 20.00
44 Joe Randa B/X 3.00
45 Chan Ho Park S/Z 15.00
46 Brad Radke B/X 3.00
47 Geronimo Berroa B/X 3.00
48 Wade Boggs S/Y 12.50
49 Kevin Appier B/X 3.00
50 Moises Alou S/Y 7.50
51 David Justice G/Y 12.50
52 Ivan Rodriguez G/Z 40.00
53 J.T. Snow B/X 4.00
54 Brian Giles B/X 3.00
55 Will Clark B/Y 10.00
56 Justin Thompson S/Y 5.00
57 Javier Lopez S/X 4.00
58 Hideki Irabu B/Z 20.00
59 Mark Grudzielanek B/X 3.00
60 Abraham Nunez S/X 5.00
61 Todd Hollandsworth B/X 3.00
62 Jay Bell B/X 3.00
63 Nomar Garciaparra G/Z 100.00
64 Vinny Castilla B/Y 5.00
65 Lou Collier B/Y 5.00
66 Kevin Orie S/X 3.00
67 John Valentin B/X 3.00
68 Robin Ventura B/X 4.00
69 Denny Neagle B/X 4.00
70 Tony Womack S/Y 5.00
71 Dennis Reyes S/Y 5.00
72 Wally Joyner B/X 3.00
73 Kevin Brown B/Y 7.50
74 Ray Durham B/X 3.00
75 Mike Cameron S/Z 15.00
76 Dante Bichette B/X 5.00
77 Jose Guillen G/Y 10.00
78 Carlos Delgado B/Y 7.50
79 Paul Molitor G/Z 30.00
80 Jason Kendall B/X 3.00
81 Mark Belhorn B/X 3.00
82 Damian Jackson B/X 3.00
83 Bill Mueller B/X 3.00
84 Kevin Young B/X 3.00
85 Curt Schilling B/X 5.00
86 Jeffrey Hammonds B/X 3.00
87 Sandy Alomar Jr. S/Y 10.00
88 Bartolo Colon B/Y 5.00
89 Wilton Guerrero B/Y 5.00
90 Bernie Williams G/Y 20.00
91 Deion Sanders S/Y 10.00
92 Mike Piazza G/X 40.00
93 Butch Huskey B/X 3.00
94 Edgardo Alfonzo S/X 3.00
95 Alan Benes S/Y 7.50
96 Craig Biggio S/Y 10.00
97 Mark Grace S/Y 12.50
98 Shawn Green S/Y 7.50
99 Derrek Lee S/Y 10.00
100 Ken Griffey Jr. G/Z 150.00
101 Tim Raines B/X 3.00
102 Pokey Reese S/X 3.00
103 Lee Stevens B/X 3.00
104 Shannon Stewart S/Y 5.00
105 John Smoltz S/Y 10.00
106 Frank Thomas G/X 25.00
107 Jeff Fassero B/X 3.00
108 Jay Buhner B/Y 10.00
109 Jose Canseco B/X 5.00
110 Omar Vizquel B/X 3.00
111 Travis Fryman B/X 4.00
112 Dave Nilsson B/X 3.00
113 John Olerud B/X 5.00
114 Larry Walker G/Z 20.00
115 Jim Edmonds S/Y 10.00
116 Bobby Higginson S/X 5.00
117 Todd Hundley S/X 4.00
118 Paul O'Neill B/X 5.00
119 Bip Roberts B/X 3.00
120 Ismael Valdes B/X 3.00
121 Pedro Martinez S/Y 12.50
122 Jeff Cirillo B/X 3.00
123 Andy Benes B/X 3.00
124 Bobby Jones B/X 3.00
125 Brian Hunter B/X 3.00
126 Darryl Kile B/X 3.00
127 Pat Hentgen B/X 3.00
128 Marquis Grissom B/X 3.00
129 Eric Davis B/X 3.00
130 Chipper Jones G/Z 100.00
131 Edgar Martinez S/Z 10.00
132 Andy Pettitte G/Z 30.00
133 Cal Ripken Jr. G/X 50.00
134 Scott Rolen G/Z 75.00
135 Ron Coomer B/X 3.00
136 Luis Castillo B/Y 5.00
137 Fred McGriff B/Y 10.00
138 Neifi Perez S/Y 5.00
139 Eric Karros B/X 4.00
140 Alex Fernandez B/X 3.00
141 Jason Dickson B/X 3.00
142 Lance Johnson B/X 3.00
143 Ray Lankford B/Y 5.00
144 Sammy Sosa G/Y 40.00
145 Eric Young B/Y 5.00
146 Bubba Trammell S/Y 7.50
147 Todd Walker S/Y 10.00
148 Mo Vaughn S/X (Curtain Calls) 7.50
149 Jeff Bagwell S/X (Curtain Calls) 12.50
150 Kenny Lofton S/X (Curtain Calls) 7.50
151 Raul Mondesi S/X (Curtain Calls) 5.00
152 Mike Piazza S/X (Curtain Calls) 20.00
153 Chipper Jones S/X (Curtain Calls) 20.00
154 Larry Walker S/X (Curtain Calls) 5.00
155 Greg Maddux S/X (Curtain Calls) 20.00
156 Ken Griffey Jr. S/X (Curtain Calls) 40.00
157 Frank Thomas S/X (Curtain Calls) 15.00
158 Darin Erstad B/Z (Gold Leaf Stars) 20.00
159 Roberto Alomar B/Y (Gold Leaf Stars) 10.00
160 Albert Belle G/Y (Gold Leaf Stars) 12.50
161 Jim Thome G/Y (Gold Leaf Stars) 9.00
162 Tony Clark G/Y (Gold Leaf Stars) 9.00
163 Chuck Knoblauch B/Y (Gold Leaf Stars) 10.00
164 Derek Jeter G/Z (Gold Leaf Stars) 50.00
165 Alex Rodriguez G/Z (Gold Leaf Stars) 50.00
166 Tony Gwynn B/X (Gold Leaf Stars) 17.50
167 Roger Clemens G/Z (Gold Leaf Stars) 30.00
168 Barry Larkin B/Y (Gold Leaf Stars) 10.00
169 Andres Galarraga B/Y (Gold Leaf Stars) 10.00
170 Vladimir Guerrero G/Z (Gold Leaf Stars) 25.00
171 Mark McGwire B/Z (Gold Leaf Stars) 50.00
172 Barry Bonds B/Z (Gold Leaf Stars) 20.00
173 Juan Gonzalez G/Z(Gold Leaf Stars) 25.00
174 Andruw Jones G/Z (Gold Leaf Stars) 35.00
175 Paul Molitor B/X (Gold Leaf Stars) 7.50
176 Hideo Nomo B/Z (Gold Leaf Stars) 30.00
177 Cal Ripken Jr. B/X (Gold Leaf Stars) 25.00
178 Brad Fullmer S/Z (Gold Leaf Rookies) 17.50
179 Jaret Wright G/Z (Gold Leaf Rookies) 35.00
180 Bobby Estalella B/Y (Gold Leaf Rookies) 5.00
181 Ben Grieve G/X (Gold Leaf Rookies) 15.00
182 Paul Konerko G/Z (Gold Leaf Rookies) 25.00
183 David Ortiz G/Z (Gold Leaf Rookies) 15.00
184 Todd Helton G/X (Gold Leaf Rookies) 7.50
185 Juan Encarnacion G/Z (Gold Leaf Rookies) 15.00
186 Miguel Tejada G/Z (Gold Leaf Rookies) 20.00
187 Jacob Cruz B/Y (Gold Leaf Rookies) 7.50
188 Mark Kotsay G/Z (Gold Leaf Rookies) 17.50
189 Fernando Tatis S/Z (Gold Leaf Rookies) 12.50
190 Ricky Ledee S/Y (Gold Leaf Rookies) 10.00
191 Richard Hidalgo S/Y (Gold Leaf Rookies) 5.00
192 Richie Sexson S/Y (Gold Leaf Rookies) 5.00
193 Luis Ordaz B/X (Gold Leaf Rookies) 3.00
194 Eli Marrero S/Z (Gold Leaf Rookies) 10.00
195 Livan Hernandez S/Z (Gold Leaf Rookies) 15.00
196 Homer Bush B/X (Gold Leaf Rookies) 3.00
197 Raul Ibanez B/X (Gold Leaf Rookies) 3.00
198 Checklist (Nomar Garciaparra B/X) 20.00
199 Checklist (Scott Rolen B/X) 15.00
200 Checklist (Jose Cruz Jr. B/X) 5.00

1998 Leaf Crusade

Thirty cards from the cross-brand Crusade insert appear in 1998 Leaf. The cards had Green (250 sets), Purple (100 sets) and Red (25 sets) versions. Forty Crusade cards were in 1998 Donruss and 30 each in 1998 Donruss Update and Leaf Rookies & Stars.

MT
Complete Set (30): 475.00
Common Player: 5.00
Purples: 1.5X
Reds: 5X
3 Jim Edmonds 5.00
4 Darin Erstad 25.00
11 Mike Mussina 20.00
15 Albert Belle 30.00
18 Manny Ramirez 25.00
19 Jim Thome 20.00
24 Bubba Trammell 7.50
26 Bobby Higginson 5.00
28 Paul Molitor 20.00
30 Todd Walker 10.00
34 Andy Pettitte 20.00
35 Wade Boggs 25.00
40 Alex Rodriguez 75.00
41 Randy Johnson 20.00
46 Ivan Rodriguez 30.00
48 Roger Clemens 50.00
54 John Smoltz 10.00
56 Andruw Jones 60.00
58 Javier Lopez 7.50
59 Fred McGriff 10.00
64 Pokey Reese 5.00
66 Andres Galarraga 12.50
70 Eric Young 5.00
73 Moises Alou 5.00
76 Ben Grieve 30.00
79 Mike Piazza 75.00
91 Jason Kendall 5.00
95 Alan Benes 5.00
97 Tony Gwynn 60.00
98 Ken Caminiti 15.00

Player names in *Italic* type indicate a rookie card.

1998 Leaf Heading for the Hall

This 20-card insert features players destined for the Hall of Fame. The set is sequentially numbered to 3,500.

		MT
Complete Set (20):		185.00
Common Player:		4.50
1	Roberto Alomar	6.00
2	Jeff Bagwell	12.50
3	Albert Belle	7.50
4	Wade Boggs	6.00
5	Barry Bonds	7.50
6	Roger Clemens	12.50
7	Juan Gonzalez	8.00
8	Ken Griffey Jr.	30.00
9	Tony Gwynn	15.00
10	Barry Larkin	4.50
11	Kenny Lofton	6.00
12	Greg Maddux	17.50
13	Mark McGwire	30.00
14	Paul Molitor	6.00
15	Eddie Murray	4.50
16	Mike Piazza	20.00
16s	Mike Piazza (SAMPLE overprint on back)	4.00
17	Cal Ripken Jr.	25.00
18	Ivan Rodriguez	7.50
19	Ryne Sandberg	7.50
20	Frank Thomas	12.50

1998 Leaf State Representatives

This 30-card insert features top players. The background has a picture of the state in which he plays. "State Representatives" is printed at the top with the player's name at the bottom. This set is sequentially numbered to 5,000.

		MT
Complete Set (30):		200.00
Common Player:		2.00
1	Ken Griffey Jr.	20.00
2	Frank Thomas	8.00
3	Alex Rodriguez	20.00
4	Cal Ripken Jr.	20.00
5	Chipper Jones	12.00
6	Andruw Jones	5.00
7	Scott Rolen	5.00
8	Nomar Garciaparra	15.00
9	Tim Salmon	4.00
10	Manny Ramirez	6.00
11	Jose Cruz Jr.	2.00
12	Vladimir Guerrero	8.00
13	Tino Martinez	3.00
14	Larry Walker	4.00
15	Mo Vaughn	4.00
16	Jim Thome	4.00
17	Tony Clark	3.00
18	Derek Jeter	20.00
19	Juan Gonzalez	6.00
20	Jeff Bagwell	6.00
21	Ivan Rodriguez	6.00
22	Mark McGwire	25.00
23	David Justice	4.00
24	Chuck Knoblauch	3.00
25	Andy Pettitte	3.00
26	Raul Mondesi	3.00
27	Randy Johnson	6.00
28	Greg Maddux	12.00
29	Bernie Williams	5.00
30	Rusty Greer	2.00

1998 Leaf Statistical Standouts

This 24-card insert features players with impressive statistics. The cards have a horizontal layout and the feel of leather. The background has a ball and glove with the player's facsimile signature on the ball. Statistical Standouts is numbered to 2,500. A parallel die-cut version of each card was produced to the number of 250.

		MT
Complete Set (24):		260.00
Common Player:		4.00
Die-Cuts:		2X
1	Frank Thomas	10.00
2	Ken Griffey Jr.	25.00
3	Alex Rodriguez	25.00
4	Mike Piazza	20.00
5	Greg Maddux	15.00
6	Cal Ripken Jr.	25.00
7	Chipper Jones	15.00
8	Juan Gonzalez	8.00
9	Jeff Bagwell	8.00
10	Mark McGwire	30.00
11	Tony Gwynn	10.00
12	Mo Vaughn	5.00
13	Nomar Garciaparra	20.00
14	Jose Cruz Jr.	4.00
15	Vladimir Guerrero	10.00
16	Scott Rolen	6.00
17	Andy Pettitte	4.00
18	Randy Johnson	8.00
19	Larry Walker	4.00
20	Kenny Lofton	4.00
21	Tony Clark	4.00
22	David Justice	5.00
23	Derek Jeter	20.00
24	Barry Bonds	8.00

1998 Leaf Fractal Foundation

Fractal Foundations is a stand-alone product but it parallels the 1998 Leaf set. It contains the Curtain Calls, Gold Leaf Stars and Gold Leaf Rookies subsets and is missing card #42 which Leaf retired in honor of Jackie Robinson. The set was printed on foil board and each card is numbered to 3,999. The set is paralleled in Fractal Materials, Fractal Materials Die-Cuts and Fractal Materials Z2 Axis.

		MT
Complete Set (200):		250.00
Common Player:		.50
Pack (3):		6.00
Wax Box (18):		90.00
1	Rusty Greer	.50
2	Tino Martinez	1.50
3	Bobby Bonilla	1.00
4	Jason Giambi	.50
5	Matt Morris	1.00
6	Craig Counsell	.50
7	Reggie Jefferson	.50
8	Brian Rose	1.50
9	Ruben Rivera	.50
10	Shawn Estes	.50
11	Tony Gwynn	5.00
12	Jeff Abbott	.50
13	Jose Cruz Jr.	1.00
14	Francisco Cordova	.50
15	Ryan Klesko	1.50
16	Tim Salmon	1.50
17	Brett Tomko	.50
18	Matt Williams	1.50
19	Joe Carter	1.00
20	Harold Baines	.50
21	Gary Sheffield	1.50
22	Charles Johnson	1.00
23	Aaron Boone	.50
24	Eddie Murray	1.50
25	Matt Stairs	.50
26	David Cone	1.00
27	Jon Nunnally	.50
28	Chris Stynes	.50
29	Enrique Wilson	.50
30	Randy Johnson	2.00
31	Garret Anderson	.50
32	Manny Ramirez	2.50
33	Jeff Suppan	.50
34	Rickey Henderson	.50
35	Scott Spiezio	.50
36	Rondell White	1.00
37	Todd Greene	.50
38	Delino DeShields	.50
39	Kevin Brown	1.00
40	Chili Davis	.50
41	Jimmy Key	.50
42	NOT ISSUED	
42		.50
43	Mike Mussina	2.50
44	Joe Randa	.50
45	Chan Ho Park	1.00
46	Brad Radke	.50
47	Geronimo Berroa	.50
48	Wade Boggs	1.50
49	Kevin Appier	.50
50	Moises Alou	1.00
51	David Justice	1.50
52	Ivan Rodriguez	2.50
53	J.T. Snow	.50
54	Brian Giles	.50
55	Will Clark	1.50
56	Justin Thompson	.50
57	Javier Lopez	1.00
58	Hideki Irabu	1.00
59	Mark Grudzielanek	.50
60	Abraham Nunez	.50
61	Todd Hollandsworth	.50
62	Jay Bell	.50
63	Nomar Garciaparra	6.00
64	Vinny Castilla	1.00
65	Lou Collier	.50
66	Kevin Orie	.50
67	John Valentin	.50
68	Robin Ventura	1.00
69	Denny Neagle	1.00
70	Tony Womack	.50
71	Dennis Reyes	.50
72	Wally Joyner	.50
73	Kevin Brown	1.00
74	Ray Durham	.50
75	Mike Cameron	1.00
76	Dante Bichette	1.50
77	Jose Guillen	1.50
78	Carlos Delgado	1.50
79	Paul Molitor	2.00
80	Jason Kendall	.50
81	Mark Belhorn	.50
82	Damian Jackson	.50
83	Bill Mueller	.50
84	Kevin Young	.50
85	Curt Schilling	1.00
86	Jeffrey Hammonds	.50
87	Sandy Alomar Jr.	1.00
88	Bartolo Colon	.50
89	Wilton Guerrero	.50
90	Bernie Williams	2.00
91	Deion Sanders	1.50
92	Mike Piazza	6.00
93	Butch Huskey	.50
94	Edgardo Alfonzo	.50
95	Alan Benes	1.00
96	Craig Biggio	1.00
97	Mark Grace	1.25
98	Shawn Green	.50
99	Derrek Lee	1.50
100	Ken Griffey Jr.	10.00
101	Tim Raines	.50
102	Pokey Reese	.50
103	Lee Stevens	.50
104	Shannon Stewart	.50
105	John Smoltz	1.00
106	Frank Thomas	4.00
107	Jeff Fassero	.50
108	Jay Buhner	1.50
109	Jose Canseco	1.50
110	Omar Vizquel	.50
111	Travis Fryman	.50
112	Dave Nilsson	.50
113	John Olerud	.50
114	Larry Walker	1.50
115	Jim Edmonds	1.00
116	Bobby Higginson	1.00
117	Todd Hundley	.50
118	Paul O'Neill	1.00
119	Bip Roberts	.50
120	Ismael Valdes	.50
121	Pedro Martinez	2.00
122	Jeff Cirillo	.50
123	Andy Benes	1.00
124	Bobby Jones	.50
125	Brian Hunter	.50
126	Darryl Kile	.50
127	Pat Hentgen	.50
128	Marquis Grissom	.50
129	Eric Davis	.50
130	Chipper Jones	6.00
131	Edgar Martinez	.50
132	Andy Pettitte	1.50

133 Cal Ripken Jr. 7.50
134 Scott Rolen 4.00
135 Ron Coomer .50
136 Luis Castillo .50
137 Fred McGriff 1.00
138 Neifi Perez .50
139 Eric Karros 1.00
140 Alex Fernandez .50
141 Jason Dickson .50
142 Lance Johnson .50
143 Ray Lankford .50
144 Sammy Sosa 5.00
145 Eric Young .50
146 Bubba Trammell 1.00
147 Todd Walker 1.00
148 Mo Vaughn (Curtain Calls) 3.00
149 Jeff Bagwell (Curtain Calls) 4.00
150 Kenny Lofton (Curtain Calls) 2.50
151 Raul Mondesi (Curtain Calls) 1.00
152 Mike Piazza (Curtain Calls) 6.00
153 Chipper Jones (Curtain Calls) 6.00
154 Larry Walker (Curtain Calls) 1.50
155 Greg Maddux (Curtain Calls) 6.00
156 Ken Griffey Jr. (Curtain Calls) 10.00
157 Frank Thomas (Curtain Calls) 4.00
158 Darin Erstad (Gold Leaf Stars) 2.50
159 Roberto Alomar (Gold Leaf Stars) 2.00
160 Albert Belle (Gold Leaf Stars) 2.50
161 Jim Thome (Gold Leaf Stars) 1.50
162 Tony Clark (Gold Leaf Stars) 1.50
163 Chuck Knoblauch (Gold Leaf Stars) 1.25
164 Derek Jeter (Gold Leaf Stars) 8.00
165 Alex Rodriguez (Gold Leaf Stars) 8.00
166 Tony Gwynn (Gold Leaf Stars) 5.00
167 Roger Clemens (Gold Leaf Stars) 4.00
168 Barry Larkin (Gold Leaf Stars) 1.50
169 Andres Galarraga (Gold Leaf Stars) 1.50
170 Vladimir Guerrero (Gold Leaf Stars) 3.00
171 Mark McGwire (Gold Leaf Stars) 15.00
172 Barry Bonds (Gold Leaf Stars) 2.50
173 Juan Gonzalez (Gold Leaf Stars) 4.00
174 Andruw Jones (Gold Leaf Stars) 3.00
175 Paul Molitor (Gold Leaf Stars) 2.00
176 Hideo Nomo (Gold Leaf Stars) 2.00
177 Cal Ripken Jr. (Gold Leaf Stars) 7.50
178 Brad Fullmer (Gold Leaf Rookies) 1.50
179 Jaret Wright (Gold Leaf Rookies) 4.00
180 Bobby Estalella (Gold Leaf Rookies) .50
181 Ben Grieve (Gold Leaf Rookies) 4.00
182 Paul Konerko (Gold Leaf Rookies) 2.00
183 David Ortiz (Gold Leaf Rookies) 1.00
184 Todd Helton (Gold Leaf Rookies) 2.50
185 Juan Encarnacion (Gold Leaf Rookies) .50
186 Miguel Tejada (Gold Leaf Rookies) 2.00
187 Jacob Cruz (Gold Leaf Rookies) .50
188 Mark Kotsay (Gold Leaf Rookies) 1.00
189 Fernando Tatis (Gold Leaf Rookies) .50
190 Ricky Ledee (Gold Leaf Rookies) 1.00
191 Richard Hidalgo (Gold Leaf Rookies) .50
192 Richie Sexson (Gold Leaf Rookies) .50
193 Luis Ordaz (Gold Leaf Rookies) .50
194 Eli Marrero (Gold Leaf Rookies) .50
195 Livan Hernandez (Gold Leaf Rookies) 1.00
196 Homer Bush (Gold Leaf Rookies) .50
197 Raul Ibanez (Gold Leaf Rookies) .50
198 Checklist (Nomar Garciaparra) 3.00
199 Checklist (Scott Rolen) 2.00
200 Checklist (Jose Cruz Jr.) .50

1998 Leaf Fractal Foundation Z2 Axis

This 200-card set parallels Leaf Fractal Materials and was numbered to 20 sets.

	MT
Common Player:	15.00
Z2 Stars:	15-20X
Production 20 sets	

(See 1998 Leaf Fractal Foundation for checklist and base card prices.)

1998 Leaf Diamond Axis

	MT
Common Player:	10.00
Diamond Axis Stars:	50X
Young Stars/RCs:	30X
SP (148-177):	12X

(See 1998 Leaf for checklist and base card values.)

1998 Leaf Fractal Materials

The Fractal Materials set parallels 1998 Leaf Fractal Foundations. Every card in the set is sequentially numbered. The 200 card set was printed on four different materials: 100 plastic cards (numbered to 3,250), 50 leather (numbered to 1,000), 30 nylon (500) and 20 wood (250). This set was inserted one per pack.

	MT
Common Plastic (3,250):	.50
Common Leather (1,000):	2.00
Common Nylon (500):	5.00
Common Wood (250):	20.00
Wax Box:	120.00

1 Rusty Greer N 5.00
2 Tino Martinez W 15.00
3 Bobby Bonilla N 7.50
4 Jason Giambi N 5.00
5 Matt Morris L 4.00
6 Craig Counsell P .50
7 Reggie Jefferson P .50
8 Brian Rose P .50
9 Ruben Rivera L 2.00
10 Shawn Estes L 4.00
11 Tony Gwynn W 50.00
12 Jeff Abbott P .50
13 Jose Cruz Jr. W 15.00
14 Francisco Cordova P .50
15 Ryan Klesko L 7.50
16 Tim Salmon W 15.00
17 Brett Tomko L 2.00
18 Matt Williams N 10.00
19 Joe Carter P .50
20 Harold Baines P .50
21 Gary Sheffield N 12.50
22 Charles Johnson L 4.00
23 Aaron Boone P .50
24 Eddie Murray N 12.50
25 Matt Stairs P .50
26 David Cone P 1.00
27 Jon Nunnally P .50
28 Chris Stynes P .50
29 Enrique Wilson P .50
30 Randy Johnson W 20.00
31 Garret Anderson N 5.00
32 Manny Ramirez W 25.00
33 Jeff Suppan L 2.00
34 Rickey Henderson N 10.00
35 Scott Spiezio P .50
36 Rondell White L 4.00
37 Todd Greene N 5.00
38 Delino DeShields P .50
39 Kevin Brown L 4.00
40 Chili Davis P .50
41 Jimmy Key P .50
42 NOT ISSUED
43 Mike Mussina N 15.00
44 Joe Randa P .50
45 Chan Ho Park N 7.50
46 Brad Radke P .50
47 Geronimo Berroa P .50
48 Wade Boggs N 12.50
49 Kevin Appier P .50
50 Moises Alou N 7.50
51 David Justice N 10.00
52 Ivan Rodriguez W 25.00
53 J.T. Snow L 3.00
54 Brian Giles P .50
55 Will Clark L 7.50
56 Justin Thompson N 5.00
57 Javier Lopez P 1.00
58 Hideki Irabu L 7.50
59 Mark Grudzielanek P .50
60 Abraham Nunez P .50
61 Todd Hollandsworth P .50
62 Jay Bell P .50
63 Nomar Garciaparra W 60.00
64 Vinny Castilla P 1.00
65 Lou Collier P .50
66 Kevin Orie L 2.00
67 John Valentin P .50
68 Robin Ventura P 1.00
69 Denny Neagle P .50
70 Tony Womack L 2.00
71 Dennis Reyes L 2.00
72 Wally Joyner P .50
73 Kevin Brown P 1.00
74 Ray Durham P .50
75 Mike Cameron N 7.50
76 Dante Bichette L 6.00
77 Jose Guillen N 7.50
78 Carlos Delgado L 4.00
79 Paul Molitor W 20.00
80 Jason Kendall P .50
81 Mark Belhorn L 2.00
82 Damian Jackson P .50
83 Bill Mueller P .50
84 Kevin Young P .50
85 Curt Schilling P 1.00
86 Jeffrey Hammonds P .50
87 Sandy Alomar Jr. L 4.00
88 Bartolo Colon P 1.00
89 Wilton Guerrero L 2.00
90 Bernie Williams N 15.00
91 Deion Sanders N 10.00
92 Mike Piazza W 65.00
93 Butch Huskey L 2.00
94 Edgardo Alfonzo L 2.00
95 Alan Benes L 4.00
96 Craig Biggio N 10.00
97 Mark Grace L 6.00
98 Shawn Green L 2.00
99 Derrek Lee L 5.00
100 Ken Griffey Jr. W 100.00
101 Tim Raines P .50
102 Pokey Reese P .50
103 Lee Stevens P .50
104 Shannon Stewart N 5.00
105 John Smoltz L 5.00
106 Frank Thomas W 40.00
107 Jeff Fassero P .50
108 Jay Buhner L 6.00
109 Jose Canseco L 7.50
110 Omar Vizquel P .50
111 Travis Fryman P .50
112 Dave Nilsson P .50
113 John Olerud P .75
114 Larry Walker W 15.00
115 Jim Edmonds N 7.50
116 Bobby Higginson L 2.00
117 Todd Hundley L 4.00
118 Paul O'Neill P 1.00
119 Bip Roberts P .50
120 Ismael Valdes P .50
121 Pedro Martinez N 12.50
122 Jeff Cirillo P .50
123 Andy Benes P .50
124 Bobby Jones P .50
125 Brian Hunter P .50
126 Darryl Kile P .50
127 Pat Hentgen P .50
128 Marquis Grissom P .50
129 Eric Davis P .50
130 Chipper Jones W 65.00
131 Edgar Martinez N 7.50
132 Andy Pettitte W 20.00
133 Cal Ripken Jr. W 75.00
134 Scott Rolen W 40.00
135 Ron Coomer P .50
136 Luis Castillo L 2.00
136 Luis Castillo ("SAMPLE" overprint on back) 1.50
137 Fred McGriff L 6.00
138 Neifi Perez L 2.00
139 Eric Karros P 1.00
140 Alex Fernandez P .50
141 Jason Dickson P .50
142 Lance Johnson P .50
143 Ray Lankford P .50
144 Sammy Sosa N 25.00
145 Eric Young P .50
146 Bubba Trammell L 4.00
147 Todd Walker L 4.00
148 Mo Vaughn P (Curtain Calls) 3.00
149 Jeff Bagwell P (Curtain Calls) 4.00
150 Kenny Lofton P (Curtain Calls) 3.00
151 Raul Mondesi P (Curtain Calls) 1.00

152 Mike Piazza P (Curtain Calls) 7.50
153 Chipper Jones P (Curtain Calls) 7.50
154 Larry Walker P (Curtain Calls) 2.00
155 Greg Maddux P (Curtain Calls) 7.50
156 Ken Griffey Jr. P (Curtain Calls) 12.50
157 Frank Thomas P (Curtain Calls) 6.00
158 Darin Erstad L (Gold Leaf Stars) 10.00
159 Roberto Alomar P (Gold Leaf Stars) 2.50
160 Albert Belle L (Gold Leaf Stars) 3.00
161 Jim Thome L (Gold Leaf Stars) 2.00
162 Tony Clark L (Gold Leaf Stars) 2.50
163 Chuck Knoblauch L (Gold Leaf Stars) 2.00
164 Derek Jeter P (Gold Leaf Stars) 6.00
165 Alex Rodriguez P (Gold Leaf Stars) 7.50
166 Tony Gwynn P (Gold Leaf Stars) 6.00
167 Roger Clemens L (Gold Leaf Stars) 17.50
168 Barry Larkin P (Gold Leaf Stars) 1.50
169 Andres Galarraga P (Gold Leaf Stars) 1.50
170 Vladimir Guerrero L (Gold Leaf Stars) 10.00
171 Mark McGwire L (Gold Leaf Stars) 40.00
172 Barry Bonds L (Gold Leaf Stars) 12.50
173 Juan Gonzalez P (Gold Leaf Stars) 5.00
174 Andruw Jones P (Gold Leaf Stars) 4.00
175 Paul Molitor P (Gold Leaf Stars) 2.50
176 Hideo Nomo L (Gold Leaf Stars) 10.00
177 Cal Ripken Jr. P (Gold Leaf Stars) 10.00
178 Brad Fullmer P (Gold Leaf Rookies) 1.50
179 Jaret Wright N (Gold Leaf Rookies) 30.00
180 Bobby Estalella P (Gold Leaf Rookies) .50
181 Ben Grieve W (Gold Leaf Rookies) 30.00
182 Paul Konerko W (Gold Leaf Rookies) 12.50
183 David Ortiz N (Gold Leaf Rookies) 6.00
184 Todd Helton W (Gold Leaf Rookies) 20.00
185 Juan Encarnacion N (Gold Leaf Rookies) 5.00
186 Miguel Tejada N (Gold Leaf Rookies) 12.50
187 Jacob Cruz P (Gold Leaf Rookies) .50
188 Mark Kotsay N (Gold Leaf Rookies) 12.50
189 Fernando Tatis L (Gold Leaf Rookies) 5.00
190 Ricky Ledee P (Gold Leaf Rookies) 1.00
191 Richard Hidalgo P (Gold Leaf Rookies) .50
192 Richie Sexson P (Gold Leaf Rookies) .50
193 Luis Ordaz P (Gold Leaf Rookies) .50
194 Eli Marrero L (Gold Leaf Rookies) 4.00
195 Livan Hernandez L (Gold Leaf Rookies) 4.00
196 Homer Bush P (Gold Leaf Rookies) .50
197 Raul Ibanez P (Gold Leaf Rookies) .50
198 Checklist (Nomar Garciaparra P) 5.00
199 Checklist (Scott Rolen P) 2.50
200 Checklist (Jose Cruz Jr. P) 2.50

1998 Leaf Fractal Materials Die-Cut

This parallel set adds a die-cut to the Fractal Materials set. The first 200 of 75 plastic, 15 Leather, 5 nylon and 5 wood cards have an x-axis die-cut. The first 100 of 20 plastic, 25 leather, 10 nylon and 5 wood cards have a y-axis die-cut. The first 50 of 5 plastic, 10 leather, 15 nylon and 10 wood cards have a z-axis die-cut.

MT
Common X (200 of each): 4.00
Common Y (100): 10.00
Common Z (50): 20.00
1 Rusty Greer Z 20.00
2 Tino Martinez Y 20.00
3 Bobby Bonilla Y 15.00
4 Jason Giambi Z 20.00
5 Matt Morris Y 15.00
6 Craig Counsell X 4.00
7 Reggie Jefferson X 4.00
8 Brian Rose X 12.50
9 Ruben Rivera Y 10.00
10 Shawn Estes Y 10.00
11 Tony Gwynn X 50.00
12 Jeff Abbott Y 10.00
13 Jose Cruz Jr. Z 20.00
14 Francisco Cordova Y 10.00
15 Ryan Klesko X 12.50
16 Tim Salmon Y 20.00
17 Brett Tomko Y 10.00
18 Matt Williams Y 20.00
19 Joe Carter X 10.00
20 Harold Baines X 4.00
21 Gary Sheffield Z 40.00
22 Charles Johnson Y 15.00
23 Aaron Boone Y 10.00
24 Eddie Murray Y 20.00
25 Matt Stairs X 4.00
26 David Cone X 10.00
27 Jon Nunnally X 4.00
28 Chris Stynes X 4.00
29 Enrique Wilson Y 10.00
30 Randy Johnson Y 20.00
31 Garret Anderson Y 10.00
32 Manny Ramirez Y 35.00
33 Jeff Suppan Y 10.00
34 Rickey Henderson X 7.50
35 Scott Spiezio Y 10.00
36 Rondell White Y 15.00
37 Todd Greene Z 30.00
38 Delino DeShields Y 10.00
39 Kevin Brown X 7.50
40 Chili Davis X 4.00
41 Jimmy Key X 4.00
42 NOT ISSUED
43 Mike Mussina Z 60.00
44 Joe Randa X 4.00
45 Chan Ho Park Y 12.50
46 Brad Radke X 4.00
47 Geronimo Berroa X 4.00
48 Wade Boggs Y 15.00
49 Kevin Appier X 4.00
50 Moises Alou X 7.50
51 David Justice Z 35.00
52 Ivan Rodriguez X 20.00
53 J.T. Snow X 7.50
54 Brian Giles Y 10.00
55 Will Clark X 10.00
56 Justin Thompson Y 12.50
57 Javier Lopez Y 12.50
58 Hideki Irabu X 10.00
59 Mark Grudzielanek X 4.00
60 Abraham Nunez Z 20.00
61 Todd Hollandsworth X 4.00
62 Jay Bell X 4.00
63 Nomar Garciaparra Z 175.00
64 Vinny Castilla Y 12.50
65 Lou Collier Y 10.00
66 Kevin Orie X 4.00
67 John Valentin X 4.00
68 Robin Ventura X 7.50
69 Denny Neagle X 7.50
70 Tony Womack X 4.00
71 Dennis Reyes Y 10.00
72 Wally Joyner X 4.00
73 Kevin Brown X 4.00
74 Ray Durham X 4.00
75 Mike Cameron Y 15.00
76 Dante Bichette X 12.50
77 Jose Guillen Z 30.00
78 Carlos Delgado Y 15.00
79 Paul Molitor X 20.00
80 Jason Kendall X 4.00
81 Mark Belhorn X 4.00
82 Damian Jackson Y 10.00
83 Bill Mueller X 4.00
84 Kevin Young X 4.00
85 Curt Schilling X 10.00
86 Jeffrey Hammonds X 4.00
87 Sandy Alomar Jr. Y 15.00
88 Bartolo Colon Y 10.00
89 Wilton Guerrero Y 10.00
90 Bernie Williams Z 60.00
91 Deion Sanders Y 15.00
92 Mike Piazza Z 200.00
93 Butch Huskey X 4.00
94 Edgardo Alfonzo Y 10.00
95 Alan Benes Z 20.00
96 Craig Biggio X 10.00
97 Mark Grace Y 20.00
98 Shawn Green Y 10.00
99 Derrek Lee Y 15.00
100 Ken Griffey Jr. Z 300.00
101 Tim Raines X 4.00
102 Pokey Reese Y 10.00
103 Lee Stevens X 4.00
104 Shannon Stewart X 4.00
105 John Smoltz Y 15.00
106 Frank Thomas Z 125.00
107 Jeff Fassero X 4.00
108 Jay Buhner Y 20.00
109 Jose Canseco X 12.50
110 Omar Vizquel X 4.00
111 Travis Fryman X 4.00
112 Dave Nilsson X 4.00
113 John Olerud X 7.50
114 Larry Walker X 15.00
115 Jim Edmonds Z 20.00
116 Bobby Higginson Y 10.00
117 Todd Hundley Z 20.00
118 Paul O'Neill X 10.00
119 Bip Roberts X 4.00
120 Ismael Valdes X 7.50
121 Pedro Martinez X 12.50
122 Jeff Cirillo X 4.00
123 Andy Benes X 10.00
124 Bobby Jones X 4.00
125 Brian Hunter X 4.00
126 Darryl Kile X 4.00
127 Pat Hentgen X 4.00
128 Marquis Grissom X 4.00
129 Eric Davis X 4.00
130 Chipper Jones Z 200.00
131 Edgar Martinez Z 30.00
132 Andy Pettitte Y 30.00
133 Cal Ripken Jr. Z 225.00
134 Scott Rolen X 40.00
135 Ron Coomer X 4.00
136 Luis Castillo X 4.00
137 Fred McGriff X 12.50
138 Neifi Perez Y 10.00
139 Eric Karros X 10.00
140 Alex Fernandez X 4.00
141 Jason Dickson X 4.00
142 Lance Johnson X 4.00
143 Ray Lankford Y 10.00
144 Sammy Sosa Y 40.00
145 Eric Young Y 10.00
146 Bubba Trammell Z 20.00
147 Todd Walker Z 30.00
148 Mo Vaughn X (Curtain Calls) 20.00
149 Jeff Bagwell X (Curtain Calls) 40.00
150 Kenny Lofton X (Curtain Calls) 20.00
151 Raul Mondesi X (Curtain Calls) 10.00
152 Mike Piazza X (Curtain Calls) 60.00
153 Chipper Jones X (Curtain Calls) 60.00
154 Larry Walker X (Curtain Calls) 15.00
155 Greg Maddux X (Curtain Calls) 60.00
156 Ken Griffey Jr. X (Curtain Calls) 100.00
157 Frank Thomas X (Curtain Calls) 40.00
158 Darin Erstad Y (Gold Leaf Stars) 35.00
159 Roberto Alomar X (Gold Leaf Stars) 20.00
160 Albert Belle X (Gold Leaf Stars) 20.00
161 Jim Thome X (Gold Leaf Stars) 15.00
162 Tony Clark Z (Gold Leaf Stars) 50.00
163 Chuck Knoblauch Z (Gold Leaf Stars) 35.00
164 Derek Jeter X (Gold Leaf Stars) 50.00
165 Alex Rodriguez Y (Gold Leaf Stars) 90.00
166 Tony Gwynn X (Gold Leaf Stars) 50.00
167 Roger Clemens Y (Gold Leaf Stars) 60.00
168 Barry Larkin Y (Gold Leaf Stars) 20.00
169 Andres Galarraga Y (Gold Leaf Stars) 20.00
170 Vladimir Guerrero Y (Gold Leaf Stars) 30.00
171 Mark McGwire Z (Gold Leaf Stars) 200.00
172 Barry Bonds Y (Gold Leaf Stars) 35.00

173 Juan Gonzalez Y (Gold Leaf Stars) 40.00
174 Andruw Jones X (Gold Leaf Stars) 20.00
175 Paul Molitor X (Gold Leaf Stars) 17.50
176 Hideo Nomo Z (Gold Leaf Stars) 50.00
177 Cal Ripken Jr. X (Gold Leaf Stars) 75.00
178 Brad Fullmer Z (Gold Leaf Rookies) 30.00
179 Jaret Wright Z (Gold Leaf Rookies) 120.00
180 Bobby Estalella Y (Gold Leaf Rookies) 10.00
181 Ben Grieve Z (Gold Leaf Rookies) 90.00
182 Paul Konerko Z (Gold Leaf Rookies) 50.00
183 David Ortiz Z (Gold Leaf Rookies) 30.00
184 Todd Helton Z (Gold Leaf Rookies) 60.00
185 Juan Encarnacion Z (Gold Leaf Rookies) 20.00
186 Miguel Tejada Z (Gold Leaf Rookies) 40.00
187 Jacob Cruz X (Gold Leaf Rookies) 4.00
188 Mark Kotsay Z (Gold Leaf Rookies) 40.00
189 Fernando Tatis Y (Gold Leaf Rookies) 20.00
190 Ricky Ledee X (Gold Leaf Rookies) 12.50
191 Richard Hidalgo Z (Gold Leaf Rookies) 20.00
192 Richie Sexson Z (Gold Leaf Rookies) 20.00
193 Luis Ordaz X (Gold Leaf Rookies) 4.00
194 Eli Marrero Z (Gold Leaf Rookies) 20.00
195 Livan Hernandez Z (Gold Leaf Rookies) 30.00
196 Homer Bush X (Gold Leaf Rookies) 4.00
197 Raul Ibanez X (Gold Leaf Rookies) 4.00
198 Checklist (Nomar Garciaparra X) 30.00
199 Checklist (Scott Rolen Z) 60.00
200 Checklist (Jose Cruz Jr. X) 7.50

1998 Leaf Rookies & Stars

This 339-card set consists of three subsets: Power Tools, Lineup Card and Rookies. Fronts feature full-bleed photos and silver-foil graphics.Backs have complete year-by-year statistics and a small photo. The base set has short-printed base cards, numbers 131-230, 301-339, which are seeded 1:2 packs. Rookies and Stars has two parallels to the base set: True Blue and Longevity. True Blue's feature blue foil stamping and are each numbered "1 Of 500" on the card back. Longevity's are printed on a full-foiled card front with gold foil stamping and limited to 50 serially numbered sets.

	MT
Complete Set (339):	600.00
Common Player:	.10
Common SP (131-230):	.40
Common SP (301-339):	1.00
Inserted 1:2	
Pack (9):	6.00
Wax Box (24):	150.00

1 Andy Pettitte .30
2 Roberto Alomar .30
3 Randy Johnson .30
4 Manny Ramirez .60
5 Paul Molitor .30
6 Mike Mussina .30
7 Jim Thome .25
8 Tino Martinez .20
9 Gary Sheffield .15
10 Chuck Knoblauch .20
11 Bernie Williams .30
12 Tim Salmon .15
13 Sammy Sosa 1.25
14 Wade Boggs .15
15 Andres Galarraga .30
16 Pedro Martinez .30
17 David Justice .20
18 Chan Ho Park .20
19 Jay Buhner .15
20 Ryan Klesko .15
21 Barry Larkin .15
22 Will Clark .20
23 Raul Mondesi .15
24 Rickey Henderson .12
25 Jim Edmonds .10
26 Ken Griffey Jr. 2.00
27 Frank Thomas 1.00
28 Cal Ripken Jr. 1.50
29 Alex Rodriguez 1.50
30 Mike Piazza 1.25
31 Greg Maddux 1.25
32 Chipper Jones 1.00
33 Tony Gwynn 1.00
34 Derek Jeter 1.00
35 Jeff Bagwell .45
36 Juan Gonzalez .75
37 Nomar Garciaparra 1.25
38 Andruw Jones .45
39 Hideo Nomo .15
40 Roger Clemens .75
41 Mark McGwire 2.50
42 Scott Rolen .45
43 Vladimir Guerrero 1.00
44 Barry Bonds .45
45 Darin Erstad .45
46 Albert Belle .45
47 Kenny Lofton .45
48 Mo Vaughn .45
49 Ivan Rodriguez .45
50 Jose Cruz Jr. .30
51 Tony Clark .30
52 Larry Walker .25
53 Mark Grace .15
54 Edgar Martinez .10
55 Fred McGriff .15
56 Rafael Palmeiro .15
57 Matt Williams .15
58 Craig Biggio .15
59 Ken Caminiti .12
60 Jose Canseco .20
61 Brady Anderson .10
62 Moises Alou .15
63 Justin Thompson .10
64 John Smoltz .12
65 Carlos Delgado .75
66 J.T. Snow .10
67 Jason Giambi .10
68 Garret Anderson .10
69 Rondell White .15
70 Eric Karros .10
71 Javier Lopez .15
72 Pat Hentgen .10
73 Dante Bichette .15
74 Charles Johnson .10
75 Tom Glavine .15
76 Rusty Greer .10
77 Travis Fryman .10
78 Todd Hundley .10
79 Ray Lankford .10
80 Denny Neagle .10
81 Henry Rodriguez .10
82 Sandy Alomar Jr. .10
83 Robin Ventura .10
84 John Olerud .15
85 Omar Vizquel .10
86 Darren Dreifort .10
87 Kevin Brown .15
88 Curt Schilling .15
89 Francisco Cordova .10
90 Brad Radke .10
91 David Cone .15
92 Paul O'Neill .15
93 Vinny Castilla .10
94 Marquis Grissom .10
95 Brian Hunter .10
96 Kevin Appier .10
97 Bobby Bonilla .10
98 Eric Young .10
99 Jason Kendall .15
100 Shawn Green .10
101 Edgardo Alfonzo .10
102 Alan Benes .10
103 Bobby Higginson .10
104 Todd Greene .10
105 Jose Guillen .15
106 Neifi Perez .10
107 Edgar Renteria .10
108 Chris Stynes .10
109 Todd Walker .15
110 Brian Jordan .10
111 Joe Carter .15
112 Ellis Burks .10
113 Brett Tomko .10
114 Mike Cameron .10
115 Shannon Stewart .10
116 Kevin Orie .10
117 Brian Giles .10
118 Hideki Irabu .20
119 Delino DeShields .10
120 David Segui .10
121 Dustin Hermanson .10
122 Kevin Young .10
123 Jay Bell .10
124 Doug Glanville .10
125 *John Roskos* .10
126 *Damon Hollins* .10
127 Matt Stairs .10
128 Cliff Floyd .10
129 Derek Bell .10
130 Darryl Strawberry .10
131 Ken Griffey Jr. (Power Tools) 9.00
132 Tim Salmon (Power Tools) .75
133 Manny Ramirez (Power Tools) 3.00
134 Paul Konerko (Power Tools) .60
135 Frank Thomas (Power Tools) 3.50
136 Todd Helton (Power Tools) 3.00
137 Larry Walker (Power Tools) 1.25
138 Mo Vaughn (Power Tools) 2.50
139 Travis Lee (Power Tools) 2.00
140 Ivan Rodriguez (Power Tools) 2.50
141 Ben Grieve (Power Tools) 2.50
142 Brad Fullmer (Power Tools) .60
143 Alex Rodriguez (Power Tools) 8.00
144 Mike Piazza (Power Tools) 6.00
145 Greg Maddux (Power Tools) 6.00
146 Chipper Jones (Power Tools) 5.00
147 Kenny Lofton (Power Tools) 2.50
148 Albert Belle (Power Tools) 2.50
149 Barry Bonds (Power Tools) 2.50
150 Vladimir Guerrero (Power Tools) 4.00
151 Tony Gwynn (Power Tools) 5.00
152 Derek Jeter (Power Tools) 6.00
153 Jeff Bagwell (Power Tools) 3.00
154 Juan Gonzalez (Power Tools) 2.50
155 Nomar Garciaparra (Power Tools) 6.00
156 Andruw Jones (Power Tools) 2.00
157 Hideo Nomo (Power Tools) .75
158 Roger Clemens (Power Tools) 3.50
159 Mark McGwire (Power Tools) 12.00
160 Scott Rolen (Power Tools) 2.50
161 Travis Lee (Team Line-Up) 1.50
162 Ben Grieve (Team Line-Up) 2.50
163 Jose Guillen (Team Line-Up) .40
164 John Olerud (Team Line-Up) .50
165 Kevin Appier (Team Line-Up) .40
166 Marquis Grissom (Team Line-Up) .40
167 Rusty Greer (Team Line-Up) .40
168 Ken Caminiti (Team Line-Up) .50
169 Craig Biggio (Team Line-Up) .60
170 Ken Griffey Jr. (Team Line-Up) 9.00
171 Larry Walker (Team Line-Up) 1.25
172 Barry Larkin (Team Line-Up) .60
173 Andres Galarraga (Team Line-Up) 1.50
174 Wade Boggs (Team Line-Up) .60
175 Sammy Sosa (Team Line-Up) 7.50
176 Mike Piazza (Team Line-Up) 6.00
177 Jim Thome (Team Line-Up) 1.50
178 Paul Molitor (Team Line-Up) 2.00
179 Tony Clark (Team Line-Up) 1.00
180 Jose Cruz Jr. (Team Line-Up) 1.00
181 Darin Erstad (Team Line-Up) 2.50
182 Barry Bonds (Team Line-Up) 2.50
183 Vladimir Guerrero (Team Line-Up) 4.00
184 Scott Rolen (Team Line-Up) 2.50
185 Mark McGwire (Team Line-Up) 12.00
186 Nomar Garciaparra (Team Line-Up) 6.00
187 Gary Sheffield (Team Line-Up) .60

188	Cal Ripken Jr. (Team Line-Up)	7.50
189	Frank Thomas (Team Line-Up)	3.50
190	Andy Petitte (Team Line-Up)	1.00
191	Paul Konerko	.60
192	Todd Helton	3.00
193	Mark Kotsay	.45
194	Brad Fullmer	.45
195	*Kevin Millwood*	20.00
196	David Ortiz	.45
197	Kerry Wood	1.50
198	Miguel Tejada	.60
199	Fernando Tatis	.45
200	Jaret Wright	2.00
201	Ben Grieve	2.50
202	Travis Lee	2.00
203	Wes Helms	.40
204	Geoff Jenkins	6.00
205	Russell Branyan	.40
206	*Esteban Yan*	3.00
207	*Ben Ford*	2.00
208	*Rich Butler*	2.50
209	*Ryan Jackson*	1.50
210	A.J. Hinch	.40
211	*Magglio Ordonez*	50.00
212	*David Dellucci*	2.50
213	Billy McMillon	.40
214	*Mike Lowell*	5.00
215	*Todd Erdos*	1.50
216	*Carlos Mendoza*	1.00
217	*Frank Catalanotto*	1.50
218	*Julio Ramirez*	6.00
219	*John Halama*	1.50
220	Wilson Delgado	.40
221	*Mike Judd*	2.50
222	*Rolando Arrojo*	4.00
223	*Jason LaRue*	2.50
224	*Manny Aybar*	1.00
225	Jorge Velandia	.40
226	*Mike Kinkade*	1.50
227	*Carlos Lee*	15.00
228	Bobby Hughes	.40
229	*Ryan Christenson*	1.50
230	*Masato Yoshii*	2.00
231	Richard Hidalgo	.10
232	Rafael Medina	.10
233	Damian Jackson	.10
234	Derek Lowe	.10
235	Mario Valdez	.10
236	Eli Marrero	.10
237	Juan Encarnacion	.10
238	Livan Hernandez	.10
239	Bruce Chen	.40
240	Eric Milton	.10
241	Jason Varitek	.10
242	Scott Elarton	.10
243	*Manuel Barrios*	.40
244	Mike Caruso	.10
245	Tom Evans	.10
246	Pat Cline	.10
247	Matt Clement	.10
248	Karim Garcia	.10
249	Richie Sexson	.15
250	Sidney Ponson	.10
251	Randall Simon	.15
252	Tony Saunders	.10
253	Javier Valentin	.10
254	Danny Clyburn	.10
255	Michael Coleman	.10
256	*Hanley Frias*	.15
257	Miguel Cairo	.10
258	*Rob Stanifer*	.10
259	Lou Collier	.10
260	Abraham Nunez	.10
261	Ricky Ledee	.40
262	Carl Pavano	.10
263	Derrek Lee	.10
264	Jeff Abbott	.10
265	Bob Abreu	.10
266	Bartolo Colon	.10
267	Mike Drumright	.10
268	Daryle Ward	.10
269	Gabe Alvarez	.10
270	Josh Booty	.10
271	Damian Moss	.10
272	Brian Rose	.10
273	Jarrod Washburn	.10
274	Bobby Estalella	.10
275	Enrique Wilson	.10
276	Derrick Gibson	.10
277	Ken Cloude	.10
278	Kevin Witt	.10
279	Donnie Sadler	.10
280	Sean Casey	.15
281	Jacob Cruz	.10
282	Ron Wright	.10
283	Jeremi Gonzalez	.10
284	Desi Relaford	.10
285	Bobby Smith	.10
286	Javier Vazquez	.10
287	*Steve Woodard*	.20
288	Greg Norton	.10
289	Cliff Politte	.10
290	Felix Heredia	.10
291	Braden Looper	.10
292	Felix Martinez	.10
293	Brian Meadows	.10
294	Edwin Diaz	.10
295	Pat Watkins	.10
296	*Marc Pisciotta*	.10
297	Rick Gorecki	.10
298	DaRond Stovall	.10
299	Andy Larkin	.10
300	Felix Rodriguez	.10
301	Blake Stein	1.00
302	*John Rocker*	10.00
303	*Justin Baughman*	1.50
304	*Jesus Sanchez*	2.50
305	Randy Winn	1.00
306	Lou Merloni	1.00
307	*Jim Parque*	4.00
308	Dennis Reyes	1.00
309	*Orlando Hernandez*	20.00
310	Jason Johnson	1.00
311	Torii Hunter	1.00
312	Mike Piazza	9.00
313	*Mike Frank*	2.50
314	*Troy Glaus*	180.00
315	*Jin Cho*	1.50
316	*Ruben Mateo*	30.00
317	*Ryan Minor*	20.00
318	Aramis Ramirez	1.50
319	Adrian Beltre	3.00
320	*Matt Anderson*	6.00
321	*Gabe Kapler*	40.00
322	*Jeremy Giambi*	6.00
323	Carlos Beltran	3.00
324	Dermal Brown	.60
325	Ben Davis	1.50
326	Eric Chavez	3.00
327	*Bob Howry*	5.00
328	Roy Halladay	.45
329	George Lombard	1.50
330	Michael Barrett	.75
331	*Fernando Seguignol*	8.00
332	*J.D. Drew*	40.00
333	*Odalis Perez*	5.00
334	*Alex Cora*	3.00
335	*Placido Polanco*	2.50
336	*Armando Rios*	1.00
337	Sammy Sosa (HR commemorative)	15.00
338	Mark McGwire (HR commemorative)	25.00
339	Sammy Sosa Mark McGwire (Checklist)	20.00

1998 Leaf Rookies & Stars True Blue

This parallel edition of the Rookies & Stars base set is labeled at top-back "1 of 500". The parallels feature blue foil graphic highlights on front with TRUE BLUE at top.

	MT
Complete Set (339):	2000.
Common Player:	2.00
Stars:	8-12X
SP Stars (131-230):	2X
SP Stars (301-339):	1.5X

(See 1998 Leaf Rookies & Stars for checklist and base card values.)

1998 Leaf Rookies & Stars Longevity

Only 50 sets of this parallel edition were issued. Each card is serially numbered on back. Fronts are printed with gold foil background and have LONGEVITY printed at top. Special Longevity holographic 1 of 1 cards exist, but cannot be priced due to rarity.

	MT
Common Player:	7.50
Stars:	40-60X
SP Stars (131-230):	10-15X
SP Stars (301-339):	5-7X

(See 1998 Leaf Rookies & Stars for checklist and base card values.)

1998 Leaf Rookies & Stars Cross Training

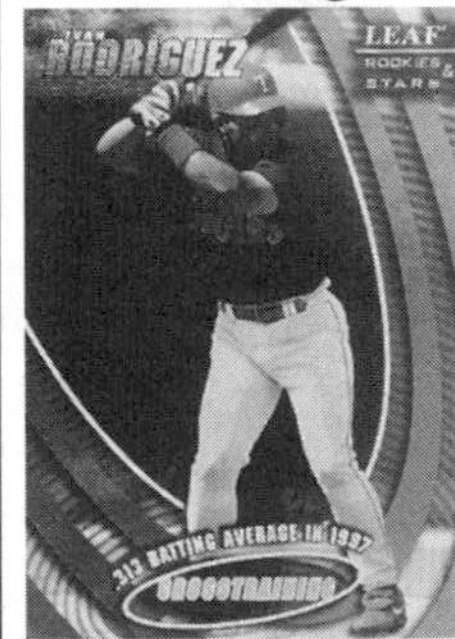

This 10-card insert set highlights players who excel at multiple aspects of the game. Card fronts are full-foiled and sequentially numbered on the card back to 1,000.

		MT
	Complete Set (10):	150.00
	Common Player:	6.00
	Production 1,000 sets	
1	Kenny Lofton	6.00
2	Ken Griffey Jr.	30.00
3	Alex Rodriguez	30.00
4	Greg Maddux	20.00
5	Barry Bonds	10.00
6	Ivan Rodriguez	10.00
7	Chipper Jones	20.00
8	Jeff Bagwell	10.00
9	Nomar Garciaparra	25.00
10	Derek Jeter	30.00

1998 Leaf Rookies & Stars Crusade

This 30-card set is a continuation of this cross-brand insert. Cards are printed on a holographic green foil front and limited to 250 serial numbered sets. Two parallels are also randomly seeded: Purple and Red. Purples have purple holographic foil fronts and limited to 100 serial numbered sets. Reds are printed on red holographic foil fronts and limited to 25 serial numbered sets.

		MT
	Complete Green Set (30):	400.00
	Common Player:	4.00
	Production 250 sets	
	Purples:	2X
	Production 100 sets	
	Reds:	4X
	Production 25 sets	
101	Richard Hidalgo	4.00
102	Paul Konerko	10.00
103	Miguel Tejada	12.50
104	Fernando Tatis	4.00
105	Travis Lee	20.00
106	Wes Helms	4.00
107	Rich Butler	10.00
108	Mark Kotsay	7.50
109	Eli Marrero	4.00
110	David Ortiz	4.00
111	Juan Encarnacion	4.00
112	Jaret Wright	20.00
113	Livan Hernandez	4.00
114	Ron Wright	7.50
115	Ryan Christenson	4.00
116	Eric Milton	4.00
117	Brad Fullmer	7.50
118	Karim Garcia	4.00

119	Abraham Nunez	4.00
120	Ricky Ledee	12.50
121	Carl Pavano	4.00
122	Derrek Lee	4.00
123	A.J. Hinch	4.00
124	Brian Rose	4.00
125	Bobby Estalella	4.00
126	Kevin Millwood	30.00
127	Kerry Wood	25.00
128	Sean Casey	12.50
129	Russell Branyan	4.00
130	Magglio Ordonez	20.00

1998 Leaf Rookies & Stars Donruss MVPs

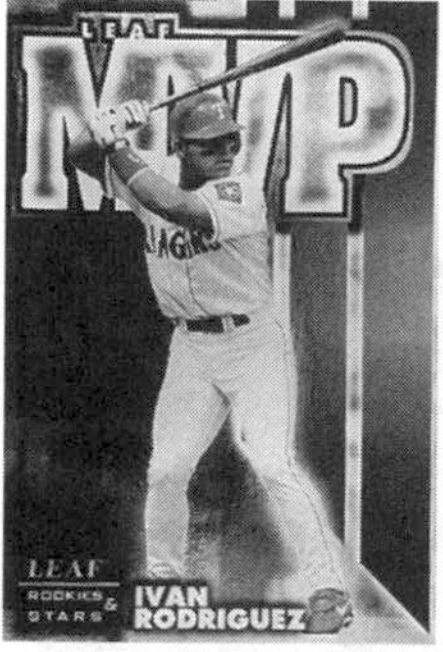

This 20-card set is printed on a full silver-foil card stock and sequentially numbered to 5,000. The first 500 of each card is treated with a "Pennant Edition" logo and unique color coating.

		MT
Complete Set (20):		60.00
Common Player:		1.00
Production 4,500 sets		
Pennant Editions:		5X
Production 500 sets		
1	Frank Thomas	4.00
2	Chuck Knoblauch	1.00
3	Cal Ripken Jr.	7.50
4	Alex Rodriguez	8.00
5	Ivan Rodriguez	2.50
6	Albert Belle	1.50
7	Ken Griffey Jr.	10.00
8	Juan Gonzalez	2.50
9	Roger Clemens	4.00
10	Mo Vaughn	1.00
11	Jeff Bagwell	2.50
12	Craig Biggio	1.00
13	Chipper Jones	5.00
14	Barry Larkin	1.00
15	Mike Piazza	6.00
16	Barry Bonds	2.50
17	Andruw Jones	2.00
18	Tony Gwynn	3.00
19	Greg Maddux	5.00
20	Mark McGwire	10.00

1998 Leaf Rookies & Stars Extreme Measures

These inserts are each printed on a full-foiled card front. Each card highlights an outstanding statistic for the featured player. Each card is sequentially numbered to 1,000.

		MT
Complete Set (10):		150.00
Common Player:		10.00
1	Ken Griffey Jr. (944)	30.00
2	Frank Thomas (653)	20.00
3	Tony Gwynn (628)	15.00
4	Mark McGwire (942)	30.00
5	Larry Walker (280)	10.00
6	Mike Piazza (960)	25.00
7	Roger Clemens (708)	15.00
8	Greg Maddux (980)	20.00
9	Jeff Bagwell (873)	10.00
10	Nomar Garciaparra (989)	20.00

1998 Leaf Rookies & Stars Extreme Measures Die-Cut

Each card highlights an outstanding statistic for each featured player, is die-cut and limited to the featured statistic.

		MT
Complete Set (10):		950.00
Common Player:		5.00
Die-Cut to featured stat		
1	Ken Griffey Jr. (56)	200.00
2	Frank Thomas (347)	25.00
3	Tony Gwynn (372)	30.00
4	Mark McGwire (58)	250.00
5	Larry Walker (720)	5.00
6	Mike Piazza (40)	135.00
7	Roger Clemens (292)	25.00
8	Greg Maddux (20) 250.00	
9	Jeff Bagwell (127)	45.00
10	Nomar Garciaparra (11)	325.00

1998 Leaf Rookies & Stars Freshman Orientation

Card fronts are printed on holographic foil with silver foil stamping and features top young prospects. Card backs highlight the date of the featured player's Major League debut, have a small photo and are serially numbered to 5,000 sets.

		MT
Complete Set (20):		20.00
Common Player:		.70
Production 5,000 sets		
1	Todd Helton	4.00
2	Ben Grieve	2.00
3	Travis Lee	.75
4	Paul Konerko	1.00
5	Jaret Wright	1.00
6	Livan Hernandez	.75
7	Brad Fullmer	1.00
8	Carl Pavano	.75
9	Richard Hidalgo	1.00
10	Miguel Tejada	1.50
11	Mark Kotsay	1.00
12	David Ortiz	.75
13	Juan Encarnacion	.75
14	Fernando Tatis	1.00
15	Kevin Millwood	2.00
15s	Kevin Millwood ("SAMPLE" overprint on back)	1.50
16	Kerry Wood	2.00
16s	Kerry Wood ("SAMPLE" overprint on back)	2.50
17	Magglio Ordonez	5.00
18	Derrek Lee	.75
19	Jose Cruz Jr.	.75
20	A.J. Hinch	.75

1998 Leaf Rookies & Stars Great American Heroes

Card fronts are stamped with a holographic silver foil and done on a horizontal format. Card backs have a photo and are serially numbered to 2,500.

		MT
Complete Set (20):		90.00
Common Player:		2.00
Production 2,500 sets		
1	Frank Thomas	5.00
2	Cal Ripken Jr.	12.00
3	Ken Griffey Jr.	12.00
4	Alex Rodriguez	12.00
5	Greg Maddux	8.00
6	Mike Piazza	10.00
7	Chipper Jones	8.00
8	Tony Gwynn	5.00
9	Jeff Bagwell	4.00
10	Juan Gonzalez	4.00
11	Hideo Nomo	2.00
12	Roger Clemens	5.00
13	Mark McGwire	15.00
14	Barry Bonds	4.00
15	Kenny Lofton	2.00
16	Larry Walker	1.50
17	Paul Molitor	3.00
18	Wade Boggs	2.00
19	Barry Larkin	2.00
20	Andres Galarraga	2.00

1998 Leaf Rookies & Stars Greatest Hits

These inserts feature holographic silver foil stamping on the card front done on a horizontal format. Card backs have a photo and serially numbered to 2,500.

		MT
Complete Set (20):		100.00
Common Player:		2.00
Production 2,500 sets		
1	Ken Griffey Jr.	12.00
2	Frank Thomas	5.00
3	Cal Ripken Jr.	12.00
4	Alex Rodriguez	12.00
5	Ben Grieve	2.00
6	Mike Piazza	10.00
7	Chipper Jones	8.00
8	Tony Gwynn	5.00
9	Derek Jeter	12.00
10	Jeff Bagwell	4.00
11	Tino Martinez	2.00
12	Juan Gonzalez	4.00
13	Nomar Garciaparra	10.00
14	Mark McGwire	15.00
15	Scott Rolen	3.00
16	David Justice	2.00
17	Darin Erstad	4.00
18	Mo Vaughn	2.00
19	Ivan Rodriguez	4.00
20	Travis Lee	2.00

1998 Leaf Rookies & Stars Home Run Derby

This 20-card set spotlights the top home run hitters on a bronze full-foiled card front. Card backs have a portrait photo and are serially numbered to 2,500.

		MT
Complete Set (20):		80.00
Common Player:		2.00
Production 2,500 sets		
1	Tino Martinez	2.00
2	Jim Thome	2.50
3	Larry Walker	2.50
4	Tony Clark	2.00
5	Jose Cruz Jr.	2.00
6	Barry Bonds	4.00
7	Scott Rolen	3.00
8	Paul Konerko	2.00
9	Travis Lee	2.00
10	Todd Helton	4.00
11	Mark McGwire	15.00
12	Andruw Jones	3.00
13	Nomar Garciaparra	10.00
14	Juan Gonzalez	4.00
15	Jeff Bagwell	4.00
16	Chipper Jones	8.00
17	Mike Piazza	10.00
18	Frank Thomas	5.00
19	Ken Griffey Jr.	12.00
20	Albert Belle	2.50

1998 Leaf Rookies & Stars ML Hard Drives

Card fronts are stamped with silver holographic foil. Card backs detail which field (left, center and right) the featured player hit each of his singles, doubles, triples and homeruns. Each card is serially numbered to 2,500.

		MT
Complete Set (20):		100.00
Common Player:		2.00
Production 2,500 sets		
1	Jeff Bagwell	4.00
2	Juan Gonzalez	4.00
3	Nomar Garciaparra	10.00
4	Ken Griffey Jr.	12.00
5	Frank Thomas	5.00
6	Cal Ripken Jr.	12.00
7	Alex Rodriguez	12.00
8	Mike Piazza	10.00
9	Chipper Jones	8.00
10	Tony Gwynn	5.00
11	Derek Jeter	12.00
12	Mo Vaughn	2.00
13	Ben Grieve	2.00
14	Manny Ramirez	4.00
15	Vladimir Guerrero	5.00
16	Scott Rolen	3.00
17	Darin Erstad	4.00
18	Kenny Lofton	2.00
19	Brad Fullmer	2.00
20	David Justice	2.00

1998 Leaf Rookies & Stars Standing Ovation

Card fronts are stamped with silver holographic foil and card backs have a small photo of the featured player and serially numbered to 5,000.

		MT
Complete Set (10):		45.00
Common Player:		2.00
Production 5,000 sets		
1	Barry Bonds	2.50
2	Mark McGwire	12.50
3	Ken Griffey Jr.	12.50
4	Frank Thomas	5.00
5	Tony Gwynn	5.00
6	Cal Ripken Jr.	7.50
7	Greg Maddux	6.00
8	Roger Clemens	4.00
9	Paul Molitor	2.00
10	Ivan Rodriguez	2.50

1998 Leaf Rookies & Stars Ticket Masters

Card fronts are printed on a full-foiled card stock with silver foil stamping and have a photo of one of the two players featured from the same team. Card backs have a photo of the other featured player and are serially numbered to 2,500. The first 250 of each card are die-cut.

		MT
Complete Set (20):		110.00
Common Player:		2.00
Production 2,250 sets		
Die-Cuts:		2X
Production 250 sets		
1	Ken Griffey Jr., Alex Rodriguez	20.00
2	Frank Thomas, Albert Belle	7.50
3	Cal Ripken Jr., Roberto Alomar	12.50
4	Greg Maddux, Chipper Jones	10.00
5	Tony Gwynn, Ken Caminiti	7.50
6	Derek Jeter, Andy Pettitte	12.00
7	Jeff Bagwell, Craig Biggio	4.00
8	Juan Gonzalez, Ivan Rodriguez	5.00
9	Nomar Garciaparra, Mo Vaughn	10.00
10	Vladimir Guerrero, Brad Fullmer	5.00
11	Andruw Jones, Andres Galarraga	4.00
12	Tino Martinez, Chuck Knoblauch	3.00
13	Raul Mondesi, Paul Konerko	2.00
14	Roger Clemens, Jose Cruz Jr.	6.00
15	Mark McGwire, Brian Jordan	20.00
16	Kenny Lofton, Manny Ramirez	5.00
17	Larry Walker, Todd Helton	4.00
18	Darin Erstad, Tim Salmon	4.00
19	Travis Lee, Matt Williams	2.00

M

1996 Metal Universe Sample Sheet

To introduce its premiere edition of Metal Universe baseball cards, Fleer sent a nine-card sample sheet to dealers. The 8" x 11" sheet has a black border on each side of each card. The cards are identical in format to the issued version, printed on etched foil and overprinted "PROMOTIONAL SAMPLE" in gold diagonally on front and back.

		MT
Complete Sheet:		24.00
28	Todd Greene	
67	Jon Nunnally	
81	Brad Radke	
90	Don Mattingly	
110	Alex Rodriguez	
116	Ivan Rodriguez	
129	Chipper Jones	
183	Eric Karros	
216	Jeff King	

1996 Metal Universe

Certainly one of the most unusual baseball card issues of its era, Fleer's Metal Universe set is distinguished by its colored, textured metallic-foil backgrounds created by comic book illustrators. The effects range from gaudy to grotesque. Glossy player action photos are featured on front, with a steel-colored metallic strip at bottom carrying set and player ID. Conventionally printed backs have a heavy-metal theme with a color player portrait photo at top and a few stats and person data around. The issue was sold in hobby and retail packaging with the basic hobby pack containing eight cards at a suggested retail price of $2.49. Several insert sets were included, along with a platinum parallel edition of the player cards.

		MT
Complete Set (250):		30.00
Common Player:		.10
Pack (8):		2.00
Wax Box (24):		40.00
1	Roberto Alomar	.50
2	Brady Anderson	.20
3	Bobby Bonilla	.15
4	Chris Holles	.10
5	Ben McDonald	.10
6	Mike Mussina	.40
7	Randy Myers	.10

8	Rafael Palmeiro	.30
9	Cal Ripken Jr.	2.50
10	B.J. Surhoff	.15
11	Luis Alicea	.10
12	Jose Canseco	.40
13	Roger Clemens	1.00
14	Wil Cordero	.10
15	Tom Gordon	.10
16	Mike Greenwell	.10
17	Tim Naehring	.10
18	Troy O'Leary	.10
19	Mike Stanley	.10
20	John Valentin	.10
21	Mo Vaughn	.40
22	Tim Wakefield	.10
23	Garret Anderson	.15
24	Chili Davis	.15
25	Gary DiSarcina	.10
26	Jim Edmonds	.20
27	Chuck Finley	.10
28	Todd Greene	.10
29	Mark Langston	.10
30	Troy Percival	.10
31	Tony Phillips	.10
32	Tim Salmon	.25
33	Lee Smith	.15
34	J.T. Snow	.10
35	Ray Durham	.10
36	Alex Fernandez	.10
37	Ozzie Guillen	.10
38	Roberto Hernandez	.10
39	Lyle Mouton	.10
40	Frank Thomas	1.00
41	Robin Ventura	.20
42	Sandy Alomar	.20
43	Carlos Baerga	.10
44	Albert Belle	.40
45	Orel Hershiser	.15
46	Kenny Lofton	.40
47	Dennis Martinez	.10
48	Jack McDowell	.10
49	Jose Mesa	.10
50	Eddie Murray	.25
51	Charles Nagy	.10
52	Manny Ramirez	.75
53	Julian Tavarez	.10
54	Jim Thome	.50
55	Omar Vizquel	.15
56	Chad Curtis	.10
57	Cecil Fielder	.15
58	John Flaherty	.10
59	Travis Fryman	.20
60	Chris Gomez	.10
61	Felipe Lira	.10
62	Kevin Appier	.10
63	Johnny Damon	.15
64	Tom Goodwin	.10
65	Mark Gubicza	.10
66	Jeff Montgomery	.10
67	Jon Nunnally	.10
68	Ricky Bones	.10
69	Jeff Cirillo	.10
70	John Jaha	.10
71	Dave Nilsson	.10
72	Joe Oliver	.10
73	Kevin Seitzer	.10
74	Greg Vaughn	.15
75	Marty Cordova	.15
76	Chuck Knoblauch	.20
77	Pat Meares	.10
78	Paul Molitor	.40
79	Pedro Munoz	.10
80	Kirby Puckett	1.00
81	Brad Radke	.10
82	Scott Stahoviak	.10
83	Matt Walbeck	.10
84	Wade Boggs	.40
85	David Cone	.15
86	Joe Girardi	.10
87	Derek Jeter	2.50
88	Jim Leyritz	.10
89	Tino Martinez	.15
90	Don Mattingly	1.00
91	Paul O'Neill	.20
92	Andy Pettitte	.30
93	Tim Raines	.15
94	Kenny Rogers	.10
95	Ruben Sierra	.10
96	John Wetteland	.10
97	Bernie Williams	.60
98	Geronimo Berroa	.10
99	Dennis Eckersley	.15
100	Brent Gates	.10
101	Mark McGwire	3.00
102	Steve Ontiveros	.10
103	Terry Steinbach	.10
104	Jay Buhner	.15
105	Vince Coleman	.10
106	Joey Cora	.10
107	Ken Griffey Jr.	2.50
108	Randy Johnson	.75
109	Edgar Martinez	.15
110	Alex Rodriguez	2.50
111	Paul Sorrento	.10
112	Will Clark	.40
113	Juan Gonzalez	.75
114	Rusty Greer	.10
115	Dean Palmer	.10
116	Ivan Rodriguez	.75
117	Mickey Tettleton	.10
118	Joe Carter	.15
119	Alex Gonzalez	.15
120	Shawn Green	.20
121	Erik Hanson	.10
122	Pat Hentgen	.10
123	*Sandy Martinez*	.10
124	Otis Nixon	.10
125	John Olerud	.20
126	Steve Avery	.10
127	Tom Glavine	.25
128	Marquis Grissom	.15
129	Chipper Jones	1.50
130	David Justice	.30
131	Ryan Klesko	.20
132	Mark Lemke	.10
133	Javier Lopez	.20
134	Greg Maddux	2.00
135	Fred McGriff	.30
136	John Smoltz	.15
137	Mark Wohlers	.10
138	Frank Castillo	.10
139	Shawon Dunston	.10
140	Luis Gonzalez	.10
141	Mark Grace	.25
142	Brian McRae	.10
143	Jaime Navarro	.10
144	Rey Sanchez	.10
145	Ryne Sandberg	.75
146	Sammy Sosa	2.00
147	Bret Boone	.10
148	Curtis Goodwin	.10
149	Barry Larkin	.30
150	Hal Morris	.10
151	Reggie Sanders	.10
152	Pete Schourek	.10
153	John Smiley	.10
154	Dante Bichette	.15
155	Vinny Castilla	.15
156	Andres Galarraga	.30
157	Bret Saberhagen	.10
158	Bill Swift	.10
159	Larry Walker	.30
160	Walt Weiss	.10
161	Kurt Abbott	.10
162	John Burkett	.10
163	Greg Colbrunn	.10
164	Jeff Conine	.15
165	Chris Hammond	.10
166	Charles Johnson	.15
167	Al Leiter	.15
168	Pat Rapp	.10
169	Gary Sheffield	.30
170	Quilvio Veras	.10
171	Devon White	.10
172	Jeff Bagwell	.75
173	Derek Bell	.15
174	Sean Berry	.10
175	Craig Biggio	.15
176	Doug Drabek	.10
177	Tony Eusebio	.10
178	Brian Hunter	.10
179	Orlando Miller	.10
180	Shane Reynolds	.10
181	Mike Blowers	.10
182	Roger Cedeno	.10
183	Eric Karros	.15
184	Ramon Martinez	.15
185	Raul Mondesi	.25
186	Hideo Nomo	.50
187	Mike Piazza	2.00
188	Moises Alou	.15
189	Yamil Benitez	.10
190	Darrin Fletcher	.10
191	Cliff Floyd	.10
192	Pedro Martinez	.75
193	Carlos Perez	.10
194	David Segul	.10
195	Tony Tarasco	.10
196	Rondell White	.15
197	Edgardo Alfonzo	.20
198	Rico Brogna	.10
199	Carl Everett	.10
200	Todd Hundley	.10
201	Jason Isringhausen	.10
202	Lance Johnson	.10
203	Bobby Jones	.10
204	Jeff Kent	.10
205	Bill Pulsipher	.10
206	Jose Vizcaino	.10
207	Ricky Bottalico	.10
208	Darren Daulton	.10
209	Lenny Dykstra	.10
210	Jim Eisenreich	.10
211	Gregg Jefferies	.15
212	Mickey Morandini	.10
213	Heathcliff Slocumb	.10
214	Jay Bell	.10
215	Carlos Garcia	.10
216	Jeff King	.10
217	Al Martin	.10
218	Orlando Merced	.10
219	Dan Miceli	.10
220	Denny Neagle	.10
221	Andy Benes	.15
222	Royce Clayton	.10
223	Gary Gaetti	.10
224	Ron Gant	.15
225	Bernard Gilkey	.10
226	Brian Jordan	.15
227	Ray Lankford	.10
228	John Mabry	.10
229	Ozzie Smith	.40
230	Todd Stottlemyre	.10
231	Andy Ashby	.15
232	Brad Ausmus	.10
233	Ken Caminiti	.20
234	Steve Finley	.10
235	Tony Gwynn	1.00
236	Joey Hamilton	.10
237	Rickey Henderson	.30
238	Trevor Hoffman	.10
239	Wally Joyner	.15
240	Rod Beck	.10
241	Barry Bonds	.75
242	Glenallen Hill	.10
243	Stan Javier	.10
244	Mark Leiter	.10
245	Deion Sanders	.20
246	William VanLandingham	.10
247	Matt Williams	.25
248	Checklist	.10
249	Checklist	.10
250	Checklist	.10

1996 Metal Universe Platinum Edition

One of the eight cards in each pack of Fleer Metal baseball is a Platinum Edition parallel insert. Each of the 247 player cards (no checklists) in this special version has the textured foil background rendered only in silver. The second line of the logo/ID strip at bottom also identifies the card as part of the Platinum Edition.

	MT
Complete Set (247):	100.00
Common Player:	.25
Stars:	3X

(See 1996 Metal Universe for checklist and base card values.)

1996 Metal Universe Heavy Metal

Some of the game's biggest hitters are included in this insert set. Action photos of players at bat are set on a silver-foil background on front. Backs have a close-up photo down one side, with praise for the player's power potential down the other. The Heavy Metal inserts can be expected to turn up at an average rate of one per eight packs.

		MT
Complete Set (10):		20.00
Common Player:		1.00
1	Albert Belle	1.00
2	Barry Bonds	1.50
3	Juan Gonzalez	1.50
4	Ken Griffey Jr.	6.00
5	Mark McGwire	6.00
6	Mike Piazza	4.00
7	Sammy Sosa	3.00
8	Frank Thomas	2.50
9	Mo Vaughn	1.00
10	Matt Williams	1.00

1996 Metal Universe Mining for Gold

Available only in retail packs, at an average rate of one per dozen packs, the Mining for Gold insert series focuses on 1995's top rookies. Fronts have player action photos frame and backgrounded with several different gold tones in etched metal foil. Backs are conventionally printed, carrying on the same format with a portrait photo and a few words about the player.

		MT
Complete Set (12):		32.50
Common Player:		1.00
1	Yamil Benitez	1.00
2	Marty Cordova	2.00
3	Shawn Green	3.00
4	Todd Greene	1.50
5	Brian Hunter	1.00
6	Derek Jeter	10.00
7	Charles Johnson	1.00
8	Chipper Jones	10.00
9	Hideo Nomo	4.00
10	Alex Ochoa	1.00
11	Andy Pettitte	4.50
12	Quilvio Veras	1.00

Player names in *Italic* type indicate a rookie card.

1996 Metal Universe Mother Lode

Medieval designs rendered in textured silver-foil on a plain white background are the setting for the color player photos in this hobby-only insert. Backs also have a silver and white background along with another player photo and some kind words about his skills. The cards are found at an average rate of one per 12 packs.

		MT
Complete Set (12):		40.00
Common Player:		1.50
1	Barry Bonds	4.00
2	Jim Edmonds	1.50
3	Ken Griffey Jr.	15.00
4	Kenny Lofton	3.00
5	Raul Mondesi	2.00
6	Rafael Palmeiro	2.50
7	Manny Ramirez	5.00
8	Cal Ripken Jr.	12.00
9	Tim Salmon	1.50
10	Ryne Sandberg	4.00
11	Frank Thomas	6.00
12	Matt Williams	2.00

1996 Metal Universe Platinum Portraits

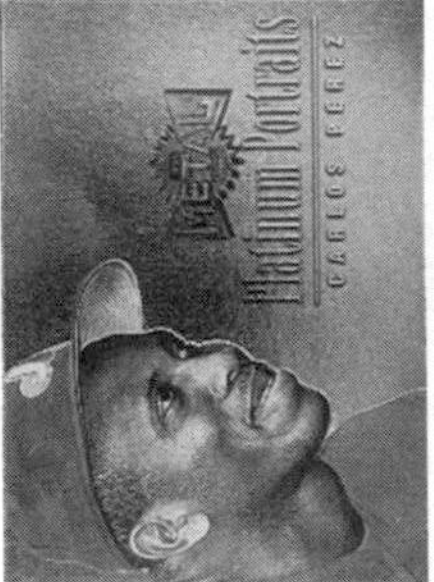

Close-up color photos on a plain metallic-foil background are featured in this insert set. The checklist is heavy in rookie and sophomore players, who are featured in an action photo on back, with a few career details. Platinum Portraits inserts are found in every fourth pack, on average.

		MT
Complete Set (10):		10.00
Common Player:		.50
1	Garret Anderson	.50
2	Marty Cordova	.50
3	Jim Edmonds	.75
4	Jason Isringhausen	.50
5	Chipper Jones	6.00
6	Ryan Klesko	.75
7	Hideo Nomo	2.00
8	Carlos Perez	.50
9	Manny Ramirez	4.00
10	Rondell White	.75

1996 Metal Universe Titanium

A huge purple-highlighted silver baseball in a star-studded night sky is the background for the action photos of the game's biggest names in this insert series. Backs have a second, more up-close, photo and a few words about the player. Titanium inserts are found in Metal Universe packs at an average rate of one per 24 packs.

		MT
Complete Set (10):		90.00
Common Player:		4.00
1	Albert Belle	4.00
2	Barry Bonds	6.00
3	Ken Griffey Jr.	25.00
4	Tony Gwynn	8.00
5	Greg Maddux	12.00
6	Mike Piazza	15.00
7	Cal Ripken Jr.	20.00
8	Frank Thomas	8.00
9	Mo Vaughn	4.00
10	Matt Williams	4.00

1997 Metal Universe

Metal Universe Baseball arrived in a 250-card set, including three checklists. Each card is printed on 100-percent etched foil with "comic book" art full-bleed backgrounds, with the player's name, team, position and the Metal Universe logo near the bottom of the card. Backs contain another player photo and key statistics. Metal Universe sold in eight-card packs and contained six different insert sets. They included: Blast Furnace, Magnetic Field, Mining for Gold, Mother Lode, Platinum Portraits and Titanium.

		MT
Complete Set (250):		35.00
Common Player:		.10
Pack (8):		2.50
Wax Box (24):		50.00
1	Roberto Alomar	.60
2	Brady Anderson	.15
3	Rocky Coppinger	.10
4	Chris Hoiles	.10
5	Eddie Murray	.25
6	Mike Mussina	.50
7	Rafael Palmeiro	.40
8	Cal Ripken Jr.	2.50
9	B.J. Surhoff	.15
10	Brant Brown	.10
11	Mark Grace	.25
12	Brian McRae	.10
13	Jaime Navarro	.10
14	Ryne Sandberg	.75
15	Sammy Sosa	1.50
16	Amaury Telemaco	.10
17	Steve Trachsel	.10
18	Darren Bragg	.10
19	Jose Canseco	.40
20	Roger Clemens	1.00
21	Nomar Garciaparra	2.00
22	Tom Gordon	.10
23	Tim Naehring	.10
24	Mike Stanley	.10
25	John Valentin	.10
26	Mo Vaughn	.40
27	Jermaine Dye	.10
28	Tom Glavine	.25
29	Marquis Grissom	.10
30	Andruw Jones	.75
31	Chipper Jones	1.50
32	Ryan Klesko	.20
33	Greg Maddux	1.50
34	Fred McGriff	.25
35	John Smoltz	.15
36	Garret Anderson	.10
37	George Arias	.10
38	Gary DiSarcina	.10
39	Jim Edmonds	.25
40	Darin Erstad	.75
41	Chuck Finley	.10
42	Troy Percival	.10
43	Tim Salmon	.25
44	Bret Boone	.10
45	Jeff Brantley	.10
46	Eric Davis	.15
47	Barry Larkin	.30
48	Hal Morris	.10
49	Mark Portugal	.10
50	Reggie Sanders	.10
51	John Smiley	.10
52	Wilson Alvarez	.10
53	Harold Baines	.10
54	James Baldwin	.10
55	Albert Belle	.40
56	Mike Cameron	.10
57	Ray Durham	.10
58	Alex Fernandez	.10
59	Roberto Hernandez	.10
60	Tony Phillips	.10
61	Frank Thomas	1.00
62	Robin Ventura	.15
63	Jeff Cirillo	.10
64	Jeff D'Amico	.10
65	John Jaha	.10
66	Scott Karl	.10
67	Ben McDonald	.10
68	Marc Newfield	.10
69	Dave Nilsson	.10
70	Jose Valentin	.10
71	Dante Bichette	.15
72	Ellis Burks	.10
73	Vinny Castilla	.10
74	Andres Galarraga	.25
75	Kevin Ritz	.10
76	Larry Walker	.30
77	Walt Weiss	.10
78	Jamey Wright	.10
79	Eric Young	.10
80	Julio Franco	.10
81	Orel Hershiser	.10
82	Kenny Lofton	.40
83	Jack McDowell	.10
84	Jose Mesa	.10
85	Charles Nagy	.10
86	Manny Ramirez	.75
87	Jim Thome	.40
88	Omar Vizquel	.10
89	Matt Williams	.25
90	Kevin Appier	.10
91	Johnny Damon	.10
92	Chili Davis	.10
93	Tom Goodwin	.10
94	Keith Lockhart	.10
95	Jeff Montgomery	.10
96	Craig Paquette	.10
97	Jose Rosado	.10
98	Michael Tucker	.10
99	Wilton Guerrero	.10
100	Todd Hollandsworth	.10
101	Eric Karros	.10
102	Ramon Martinez	.10
103	Raul Mondesi	.25
104	Hideo Nomo	.50
105	Mike Piazza	2.00
106	Ismael Valdes	.10
107	Todd Worrell	.10
108	Tony Clark	.20
109	Travis Fryman	.20
110	Bob Higginson	.10
111	Mark Lewis	.10
112	Melvin Nieves	.10
113	Justin Thompson	.10
114	Wade Boggs	.40
115	David Cone	.15
116	Cecil Fielder	.15
117	Dwight Gooden	.10
118	Derek Jeter	2.50
119	Tino Martinez	.20
120	Paul O'Neill	.20

121	Andy Pettitte	.30
122	Mariano Rivera	.15
123	Darryl Strawberry	.20
124	John Wetteland	.10
125	Bernie Williams	.50
126	Tony Batista	.25
127	Geronimo Berroa	.10
128	Scott Brosius	.10
129	Jason Giambi	.30
130	Jose Herrera	.10
131	Mark McGwire	3.00
132	John Wasdin	.10
133	Bob Abreu	.20
134	Jeff Bagwell	.75
135	Derek Bell	.10
136	Craig Biggio	.20
137	Brian Hunter	.10
138	Darryl Kile	.10
139	Orlando Miller	.10
140	Shane Reynolds	.10
141	Billy Wagner	.10
142	Donne Wall	.10
143	Jay Buhner	.15
144	Jeff Fassero	.10
145	Ken Griffey Jr.	2.50
146	Sterling Hitchcock	.10
147	Randy Johnson	.75
148	Edgar Martinez	.15
149	Alex Rodriguez	2.50
149p	Alex Rodriguez ("PROMOTIONAL SAMPLE")	3.00
150	Paul Sorrento	.10
151	Dan Wilson	.10
152	Moises Alou	.10
153	Darrin Fletcher	.10
154	Cliff Floyd	.10
155	Mark Grudzielanek	.10
156	Vladimir Guerrero	1.00
157	Mike Lansing	.10
158	Pedro Martinez	.75
159	Henry Rodriguez	.10
160	Rondell White	.15
161	Will Clark	.40
162	Juan Gonzalez	.75
163	Rusty Greer	.10
164	Ken Hill	.10
165	Mark McLemore	.10
166	Dean Palmer	.10
167	Roger Pavlik	.10
168	Ivan Rodriguez	.75
169	Mickey Tettleton	.10
170	Bobby Bonilla	.10
171	Kevin Brown	.15
172	Greg Colbrunn	.10
173	Jeff Conine	.10
174	Jim Eisenreich	.10
175	Charles Johnson	.10
176	Al Leiter	.15
177	Robb Nen	.10
178	Edgar Renteria	.20
179	Gary Sheffield	.40
180	Devon White	.10
181	Joe Carter	.15
182	Carlos Delgado	.75
183	Alex Gonzalez	.10
184	Shawn Green	.25
185	Juan Guzman	.10
186	Pat Hentgen	.10
187	Orlando Merced	.10
188	John Olerud	.20
189	Robert Perez	.10
190	Ed Sprague	.10
191	Mark Clark	.10
192	John Franco	.10
193	Bernard Gilkey	.10
194	Todd Hundley	.10
195	Lance Johnson	.10
196	Bobby Jones	.10
197	Alex Ochoa	.10
198	Rey Ordonez	.15
199	Paul Wilson	.10
200	Ricky Bottalico	.10
201	Gregg Jefferies	.10
202	Wendell Magee Jr.	.10
203	Mickey Morandini	.10
204	Ricky Otero	.10
205	Scott Rolen	.50
206	Benito Santiago	.10
207	Curt Schilling	.20
208	Rich Becker	.10
209	Marty Cordova	.10
210	Chuck Knoblauch	.20
211	Pat Meares	.10
212	Paul Molitor	.40
213	Frank Rodriguez	.10
214	Terry Steinbach	.10
215	Todd Walker	.10
216	Andy Ashby	.10
217	Ken Caminiti	.20
218	Steve Finley	.10
219	Tony Gwynn	1.00
220	Joey Hamilton	.10
221	Rickey Henderson	.25
222	Trevor Hoffman	.10
223	Wally Joyner	.10
224	Scott Sanders	.10
225	Fernando Valenzuela	.10
226	Greg Vaughn	.15
227	Alan Benes	.10
228	Andy Benes	.10
229	Dennis Eckersley	.15
230	Ron Gant	.15
231	Brian Jordan	.15
232	Ray Lankford	.10
233	John Mabry	.10
234	Tom Pagnozzi	.10
235	Todd Stottlemyre	.10
236	Jermaine Allensworth	.10
237	Francisco Cordova	.10
238	Jason Kendall	.20
239	Jeff King	.10
240	Al Martin	.10
241	Rod Beck	.10
242	Barry Bonds	.75
243	Shawn Estes	.10
244	Mark Gardner	.10
245	Glenallen Hill	.10
246	Bill Mueller	.10
247	J.T. Snow	.10
248	Checklist	.10
249	Checklist	.10
250	Checklist	.10

1997 Metal Universe Blast Furnace

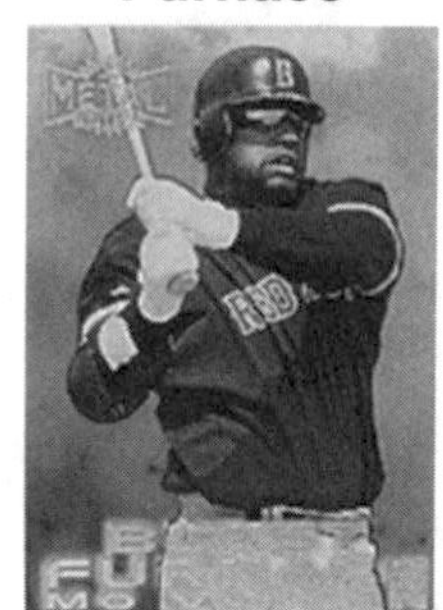

Blast Furnace inserts were found only in hobby packs, at a rate of one per 48 packs. The 12-card set was printed on a red-tinted plastic, with the words "Blast Furnace" near the bottom in gold foil with a fire-like border.

		MT
Complete Set (12):		125.00
Common Player:		3.00
1	Jeff Bagwell	12.00
2	Albert Belle	6.00
3	Barry Bonds	7.50
4	Andres Galarraga	3.00
5	Juan Gonzalez	8.00
6	Ken Griffey Jr.	30.00
7	Todd Hundley	3.00
8	Mark McGwire	30.00
9	Mike Piazza	20.00
10	Alex Rodriguez	25.00
11	Frank Thomas	10.00
12	Mo Vaughn	6.00

1997 Metal Universe Emerald Autograph Redemption

Six different young stars were featured in this insert, which was found every 480 hobby packs of Metal Universe. The cards are similar to regular-issue cards, but have green foil highlights. Redemption cards are numbered AU1-AU6. The redemption period expired Jan. 15, 1998.

		MT
Complete Set (6):		50.00
Common Player:		3.00
1	Darin Erstad	7.50
2	Todd Hollandsworth	3.00
3	Alex Ochoa	3.00
4	Alex Rodriguez	25.00
5	Scott Rolen	7.50
6	Todd Walker	5.00

1997 Metal Universe Emerald Autographs

Six different young stars were featured in this insert, which was found every 480 hobby packs of Metal Universe. The cards are similar to regular-issue cards, but have a green foil finish and autograph on the front. Redemption cards are numbered AU1-AU6, the autographed cards have a notation on back, "Certified Emerald Autograph Card".

		MT
Complete Set (6):		175.00
Common Autograph:		12.50
1	Darin Erstad	30.00
2	Todd Hollandsworth	12.50
3	Alex Ochoa	12.50
4	Alex Rodriguez	100.00
5	Scott Rolen	35.00
6	Todd Walker	15.00

1997 Metal Universe Magnetic Field

Magnetic Field inserts are printed in a horizontal format with prismatic foil backgrounds. This 10-card insert was found every 12 packs of Metal Universe.

		MT
Complete Set (10):		20.00
Common Player:		1.00
1	Roberto Alomar	1.25
2	Jeff Bagwell	2.00
3	Barry Bonds	1.25
4	Ken Griffey Jr.	7.50
5	Derek Jeter	3.00
6	Kenny Lofton	1.00
7	Edgar Renteria	1.00
8	Cal Ripken Jr.	5.00
9	Alex Rodriguez	6.00
10	Matt Williams	1.00

1997 Metal Universe Mining for Gold

Mining for Gold was a 10-card insert that featured some of baseball's brightest stars on a die-cut "ingot" design with pearlized gold coating. This insert was found every nine packs.

	MT
Complete Set (10):	20.00
Common Player:	.75

1	Bob Abreu	1.00
2	Kevin Brown	.75
3	Nomar Garciaparra	5.00
4	Vladimir Guerrero	3.00
5	Wilton Guerrero	.75
6	Andruw Jones	4.00
7	Curt Lyons	.75
8	Neifi Perez	.75
9	Scott Rolen	3.00
10	Todd Walker	2.00

1997 Metal Universe Mother Lode

Mother lode was the most difficult insert out of Metal Universe with a one per 288 pack insertion ratio. Each card in this 10-card inert was printed on etched foil with a plant-type monument in back of the player.

		MT
Complete Set (12):		240.00
Common Player:		6.00
1	Roberto Alomar	10.00
2	Jeff Bagwell	15.00
3	Barry Bonds	15.00
4	Ken Griffey Jr.	45.00
5	Andruw Jones	12.00
6	Chipper Jones	30.00
7	Kenny Lofton	8.00
8	Mike Piazza	30.00
9	Cal Ripken Jr.	40.00
10	Alex Rodriguez	40.00
11	Frank Thomas	15.00
12	Matt Williams	6.00

1997 Metal Universe Platinum Portraits

Each card in the Platinum Portraits insert is printed on a background of platinum-colored etched foil. The 10-card set includes some of the top prospects and rising stars in baseball, and is included every 36 packs.

		MT
Complete Set (10):		30.00
Common Player:		1.25
1	James Baldwin	1.00
2	Jermaine Dye	1.00
3	Todd Hollandsworth	1.00
4	Derek Jeter	10.00
5	Chipper Jones	10.00
6	Jason Kendall	1.00
7	Rey Ordonez	2.00
8	Andy Pettitte	3.00
9	Edgar Renteria	2.00
10	Alex Rodriguez	12.50

1997 Metal Universe Titanium

These retail exclusive inserts include 10 cards and were found every 24 packs. Each card is die-cut on the top-left and bottom-right corner with a silver foil background. Titanium includes some of the most popular players in baseball on cards that are also embossed.

		MT
Complete Set (10):		90.00
Common Player:		4.00
1	Jeff Bagwell	7.00
2	Albert Belle	4.00
3	Ken Griffey Jr.	20.00
4	Chipper Jones	10.00
5	Greg Maddux	10.00
6	Mark McGwire	20.00
7	Mike Piazza	10.00
8	Cal Ripken Jr.	15.00
9	Alex Rodriguez	15.00
10	Frank Thomas	8.00

1998 Metal Universe

This 220-card single series release captured players over a foil etched, art background that related in some way to them or the city they played in. Metal Universe included a 15-card Hardball Galaxy subset and dealers and media were given an Alex Rodriguez promo card that was identical the base card except for the words "Promotional Sample" written across the back. The set arrived with a parallel called Precious Metal Gems, and included the following insert sets: All-Galactic Team, Diamond Heroes, Platinum Portraits, Titanium and Universal Language.

		MT
Complete Set (220):		30.00
Common Player:		.10
Pack (8):		2.75
Wax Box (24):		60.00
1	Jose Cruz Jr.	.15
2	Jeff Abbott	.10
3	Rafael Palmeiro	.40
4	Ivan Rodriguez	.75
5	Jaret Wright	.20
6	Derek Bell	.10
7	Chuck Finley	.10
8	Travis Fryman	.20
9	Randy Johnson	.75
10	Derrek Lee	.10
11	Bernie Williams	.50
12	Carlos Baerga	.10
13	Ricky Bottalico	.10
14	Ellis Burks	.10
15	Russ Davis	.10
16	Nomar Garciaparra	2.00
17	Joey Hamilton	.10
18	Jason Kendall	.20
19	Darryl Kile	.10
20	Edgardo Alfonzo	.20
21	Moises Alou	.20
22	Bobby Bonilla	.20
23	Jim Edmonds	.20
24	Jose Guillen	.15
25	Chuck Knoblauch	.20
26	Javy Lopez	.20
27	Billy Wagner	.10
28	Kevin Appier	.10
29	Joe Carter	.15
30	Todd Dunwoody	.10
31	Gary Gaetti	.10
32	Juan Gonzalez	.75
33	Jeffrey Hammonds	.10
34	Roberto Hernandez	.10
35	Dave Nilsson	.10
36	Manny Ramirez	.75
37	Robin Ventura	.20
38	Rondell White	.20
39	Vinny Castilla	.20
40	Will Clark	.40
41	Scott Hatteberg	.10
42	Russ Johnson	.10
43	Ricky Ledee	.15
44	Kenny Lofton	.40
45	Paul Molitor	.50
46	Justin Thompson	.10
47	Craig Biggio	.20
48	Damion Easley	.10
49	Brad Radke	.10
50	Ben Grieve	.40
51	Mark Bellhorn	.10
52	*Henry Blanco*	.10
53	Mariano Rivera	.20
54	Reggie Sanders	.10
55	Paul Sorrento	.10
56	Terry Steinbach	.10
57	Mo Vaughn	.40
58	Brady Anderson	.20
59	Tom Glavine	.25
60	Sammy Sosa	2.00
61	Larry Walker	.30
62	Rod Beck	.10
63	Jose Canseco	.40
64	Steve Finley	.10
65	Pedro Martinez	.75
66	John Olerud	.25
67	Scott Rolen	.50
68	Ismael Valdes	.10
69	Andrew Vessel	.10
70	Mark Grudzielanek	.10
71	Eric Karros	.15
72	Jeff Shaw	.10
73	Lou Collier	.10
74	Edgar Martinez	.15
75	Vladimir Guerrero	1.00
76	Paul Konerko	.20
77	Kevin Orie	.10
78	Kevin Polcovich	.10
79	Brett Tomko	.10
80	Jeff Bagwell	.75
81	Barry Bonds	.75
82	David Justice	.30
83	Hideo Nomo	.50
84	Ryne Sandberg	.75
85	Shannon Stewart	.10
86	Derek Wallace	.10
87	Tony Womack	.10
88	Jason Giambi	.40
89	Mark Grace	.25
90	Pat Hentgen	.10
91	Raul Mondesi	.25
92	Matt Morris	.10
93	Matt Perisho	.10
94	Tim Salmon	.25
95	Jeremi Gonzalez	.10
96	Shawn Green	.25
97	Todd Greene	.10
98	Ruben Rivera	.10
99	Deion Sanders	.20
100	Alex Rodriguez	2.50
101	Will Cunnane	.10
102	Ray Lankford	.10
103	Ryan McGuire	.10
104	Charles Nagy	.10
105	Rey Ordonez	.10
106	Mike Piazza	2.00
107	Tony Saunders	.10
108	Curt Schilling	.20
109	Fernando Tatis	.10
110	Mark McGwire	3.00
111	*David Dellucci*	.40
112	Garret Anderson	.15
113	Shane Bowers	.10
114	David Cone	.20
115	Jeff King	.10
116	Matt Williams	.25
117	Aaron Boone	.10
118	Dennis Eckersley	.20
119	Livan Hernandez	.15
120	Richard Hidalgo	.15
121	Bobby Higginson	.10
122	Tino Martinez	.20
123	Tim Naehring	.10
124	Jose Vidro	.10
125	John Wetteland	.10
126	Jay Bell	.10
127	Albert Belle	.40
128	Marty Cordova	.10
129	Chili Davis	.10
130	Jason Dickson	.10
131	Rusty Greer	.15
132	Hideki Irabu	.20
133	Greg Maddux	1.50
134	Billy Taylor	.10
135	Jim Thome	.40
136	Gerald Williams	.10
137	Jeff Cirillo	.10
138	Delino DeShields	.10
139	Andres Galarraga	.30
140	Willie Greene	.10
141	John Jaha	.10
142	Charles Johnson	.15
143	Ryan Klesko	.15
144	Paul O'Neill	.25
145	Robinson Checo	.10
146	Roberto Alomar	.50
147	Wilson Alvarez	.10
148	Bobby Jones	.10
149	Raul Casanova	.10
150	Andruw Jones	.75
151	Mike Lansing	.10
152	Mickey Morandini	.10
153	Neifi Perez	.10
154	Pokey Reese	.10
155	Edgar Renteria	.10
156	Eric Young	.10
157	Darin Erstad	.75
158	Kelvim Escobar	.10
159	Carl Everett	.10

160	Tom Gordon	.10
161	Ken Griffey Jr.	2.50
162	Al Martin	.10
163	Bubba Trammell	.20
164	Carlos Delgado	.75
165	Kevin Brown	.20
166	Ken Caminiti	.20
167	Roger Clemens	1.00
168	Ron Gant	.20
169	Jeff Kent	.15
170	Mike Mussina	.50
171	Dean Palmer	.10
172	Henry Rodriguez	.10
173	Matt Stairs	.10
174	Jay Buhner	.20
175	Frank Thomas	1.00
176	Mike Cameron	.10
177	Johnny Damon	.10
178	Tony Gwynn	1.00
179	John Smoltz	.20
180	B.J. Surhoff	.10
181	Antone Williamson	.10
182	Alan Benes	.20
183	Jeromy Burnitz	.10
184	Tony Clark	.20
185	Shawn Estes	.10
186	Todd Helton	.75
187	Todd Hundley	.10
188	Chipper Jones	1.50
189	Mark Kotsay	.15
190	Barry Larkin	.40
191	Mike Lieberthal	.10
192	Andy Pettitte	.25
193	Gary Sheffield	.30
194	Jeff Suppan	.10
195	Mark Wohlers	.10
196	Dante Bichette	.15
197	Trevor Hoffman	.10
198	J.T. Snow	.20
199	Derek Jeter	2.50
200	Cal Ripken Jr.	2.50
201	*Steve Woodard*	.25
202	Ray Durham	.10
203	Barry Bonds (Hardball Galaxy)	.40
204	Tony Clark (Hardball Galaxy)	.10
205	Roger Clemens (Hardball Galaxy)	.50
206	Ken Griffey Jr. (Hardball Galaxy)	1.25
207	Tony Gwynn (Hardball Galaxy)	.50
208	Derek Jeter (Hardball Galaxy)	1.00
209	Randy Johnson (Hardball Galaxy)	.40
210	Mark McGwire (Hardball Galaxy)	1.50
211	Hideo Nomo (Hardball Galaxy)	.25
212	Mike Piazza (Hardball Galaxy)	1.00
213	Cal Ripken Jr. (Hardball Galaxy)	1.25
214	Alex Rodriguez (Hardball Galaxy)	1.25
215	Frank Thomas (Hardball Galaxy)	.50
216	Mo Vaughn (Hardball Galaxy)	.20
217	Larry Walker (Hardball Galaxy)	.15
218	Checklist (Ken Griffey Jr.)	1.00
219	Checklist (Alex Rodriguez)	.75
220	Checklist (Frank Thomas)	.50

1998 Metal Universe Precious Metal Gems

Precious Metal Gems includes 217 (no checklists) player cards from Metal Universe and are serial numbered to 50 sets. Because there were five Ultimate Metal Gems redemption cards (good for a complete set of Metal Gems) available, only serial numberes 1-45 were found in packs (46-50 were held back for the exchage program).

	MT
Common Player:	10.00
Stars:	25-40X
Production 50 sets	

(See 1998 Metal Universe for checklist and base card values.)

1998 Metal Universe All-Galactic Team

This 18-card insert captures players over a planet holofoil background. Cards were inserted one per 192 packs.

		MT
Complete Set (18):		400.00
Common Player:		8.00
Inserted 1:192		
1	Ken Griffey Jr.	60.00
2	Frank Thomas	20.00
3	Chipper Jones	30.00
4	Albert Belle	10.00
5	Juan Gonzalez	15.00
6	Jeff Bagwell	15.00
7	Andruw Jones	12.00
8	Cal Ripken Jr.	40.00
9	Derek Jeter	30.00
10	Nomar Garciaparra	30.00
11	Darin Erstad	15.00
12	Greg Maddux	25.00
13	Alex Rodriguez	50.00
14	Mike Piazza	30.00
15	Vladimir Guerrero	20.00
16	Jose Cruz Jr.	8.00
17	Mark McGwire	60.00
18	Scott Rolen	10.00

1998 Metal Universe Diamond Heroes

Diamond Heroes displayed six players in a comic book setting. This insert was seeded one per 18 packs and contained a foil etched image of a Marvel comic in the background.

		MT
Complete Set (6):		20.00
Common Player:		1.50
Inserted 1:18		
1	Ken Griffey Jr.	7.50
2	Frank Thomas	4.00
3	Andruw Jones	4.00
4	Alex Rodriguez	6.00
5	Jose Cruz Jr.	1.50
6	Cal Ripken Jr.	6.00

1998 Metal Universe Platinum Portraits

This 12-card insert set featured color portraits of top players highlighted with a platinum-colored etched foil frame over it. Platinum Portraits are seeded one per 360 packs of Metal Universe.

		MT
Complete Set (12):		350.00
Common Player:		12.50
Inserted 1:360		
1	Ken Griffey Jr.	60.00
2	Frank Thomas	20.00
3	Chipper Jones	40.00
4	Jose Cruz Jr.	12.50
5	Andruw Jones	15.00
6	Cal Ripken Jr.	45.00
7	Derek Jeter	35.00
8	Darin Erstad	15.00
9	Greg Maddux	35.00
10	Alex Rodriguez	50.00
11	Mike Piazza	40.00
12	Vladimir Guerrero	25.00

1998 Metal Universe Titanium

This die-cut 15-card insert contained color photos printed on embossed, sculpted cards on etched foil. Titanium inserts were seeded one per 96 packs.

		MT
Complete Set (15):		175.00
Common Player:		5.00
Inserted 1:96		
1	Ken Griffey Jr.	30.00
2	Frank Thomas	12.50
3	Chipper Jones	20.00
4	Jose Cruz Jr.	5.00
5	Juan Gonzalez	8.00
6	Scott Rolen	10.00
7	Andruw Jones	10.00
8	Cal Ripken Jr.	25.00
9	Derek Jeter	20.00
10	Nomar Garciaparra	15.00
11	Darin Erstad	7.50
12	Greg Maddux	15.00
13	Alex Rodriguez	25.00
14	Mike Piazza	20.00
15	Vladimir Guerrero	10.00

1998 Metal Universe Universal Language

This 20-card insert features illustration and copy done in the player's native language. Cards were die-cut and inserted one per six packs.

		MT
Complete Set (20):		40.00
Common Player:		1.00
Inserted 1:6		
1	Ken Griffey Jr.	7.50
2	Frank Thomas	2.50
3	Chipper Jones	3.50
4	Albert Belle	1.50
5	Juan Gonzalez	2.00
6	Jeff Bagwell	2.50
7	Andruw Jones	2.50
8	Cal Ripken Jr.	5.00
9	Derek Jeter	3.50
10	Nomar Garciaparra	3.50
11	Darin Erstad	1.75
12	Greg Maddux	3.00
13	Alex Rodriguez	4.00
14	Mike Piazza	3.50
15	Vladimir Guerrero	3.00
16	Jose Cruz Jr.	1.00
17	Hideo Nomo	1.00
18	Kenny Lofton	1.00
19	Tony Gwynn	3.00
20	Scott Rolen	3.00

1999 Metal Universe Sample Sheet

To introduce its annual issue of embossed cards this six-card sheet of Metal Universe samples was issued. The 5" x 10-1/2" sheet has five regular cards and an example of the Building Blocks insert set. Cards on the sheet are virtually identical to the issued versions except they have the word "SAMPLE" on back in place of card numbers.

	MT
Complete Sheet:	15.00
Albert Belle	
Derek Jeter	
Mark McGwire (Building Blocks)	
Mike Piazza	
Alex Rodriguez	
Sammy Sosa	

1999 Metal Universe

The 300-card base set offers 232 player cards and three subsets: Building Blocks, M.L.P.D. and Caught on the Fly. Base cards feature an action photo framed in an ethed-foil and metallic, embossed name plate. Packs consist of eight cards with a S.R.P. of $2.69. There are two parallels, Precious Metal Gems and Gem Masters. Metal Gems are numbered to 50 with gold-foil etching. Gem Masters are limited to only one set, with silver foil etching and serial numbered "one of one".

		MT
Complete Set (300):		40.00
Common Player:		.15
Pack (8):		2.75
Wax Box (24):		55.00
1	Mark McGwire	3.00
2	Jim Edmonds	.25
3	Travis Fryman	.25
4	Tom Gordon	.15
5	Jeff Bagwell	.75
6	Rico Brogna	.15
7	Tom Evans	.15
8	John Franco	.15
9	Juan Gonzalez	.75
10	Paul Molitor	.50
11	Roberto Alomar	.50
12	Mike Hampton	.15
13	Orel Hershiser	.15
14	Todd Stottlemyre	.15
15	Robin Ventura	.20
16	Todd Walker	.15
17	Bernie Williams	.50
18	Shawn Estes	.15
19	Richie Sexson	.25
20	Kevin Millwood	.25
21	David Ortiz	.15
22	Mariano Rivera	.25
23	Ivan Rodriguez	.75
24	Mike Sirotka	.15
25	David Justice	.30
26	Carl Pavano	.15
27	Albert Belle	.40
28	Will Clark	.40
29	Jose Cruz Jr.	.15
30	Trevor Hoffman	.15
31	Dean Palmer	.15
32	Edgar Renteria	.15
33	David Segui	.15
34	B.J. Surhoff	.15
35	Miguel Tejada	.25
36	Bob Wickman	.15
37	Charles Johnson	.15
38	Andruw Jones	.50
39	Mike Lieberthal	.15
40	Eli Marrero	.15
41	Neifi Perez	.15
42	Jim Thome	.40
43	Barry Bonds	.75
44	Carlos Delgado	.75
45	Chuck Finley	.15
46	Brian Meadows	.15
47	Tony Gwynn	1.00
48	Jose Offerman	.15
49	Cal Ripken Jr.	2.50
50	Alex Rodriguez	2.50
51	Esteban Yan	.15
52	Matt Stairs	.15
53	Fernando Vina	.15
54	Rondell White	.25
55	Kerry Wood	.40
56	Dmitri Young	.15
57	Ken Caminiti	.25
58	Alex Gonzalez	.15
59	Matt Mantei	.15
60	Tino Martinez	.20
61	Hal Morris	.15
62	Rafael Palmeiro	.40
63	Troy Percival	.15
64	Bobby Smith	.15
65	Ed Sprague	.15
66	Brett Tomko	.15
67	Steve Trachsel	.15
68	Ugueth Urbina	.15
69	Jose Valentin	.15
70	Kevin Brown	.25
71	Shawn Green	.25
72	Dustin Hermanson	.15
73	Livan Hernandez	.15
74	Geoff Jenkins	.25
75	Jeff King	.15
76	Chuck Knoblauch	.25
77	Edgar Martinez	.20
78	Fred McGriff	.25
79	Mike Mussina	.50
80	Dave Nilsson	.15
81	Kenny Rogers	.15
82	Tim Salmon	.25
83	Reggie Sanders	.15
84	Wilson Alvarez	.15
85	Rod Beck	.15
86	Jose Guillen	.15
87	Bob Higginson	.15
88	Gregg Olson	.15
89	Jeff Shaw	.15
90	Masato Yoshii	.15
91	Todd Helton	.75
92	David Dellucci	.15
93	Johnny Damon	.15
94	Cliff Floyd	.15
95	Ken Griffey Jr.	2.50
96	Juan Guzman	.15
97	Derek Jeter	2.50
98	Barry Larkin	.30
99	Quinton McCracken	.15
100	Sammy Sosa	2.00
101	Kevin Young	.15
102	Jay Bell	.15
103	Jay Buhner	.20
104	Jeff Conine	.15
105	Ryan Jackson	.15
106	Sidney Ponson	.15
107	Jeromy Burnitz	.15
108	Roberto Hernandez	.15
109	A.J. Hinch	.15
110	Hideki Irabu	.15
111	Paul Konerko	.25
112	Henry Rodriguez	.15
113	Shannon Stewart	.15
114	Tony Womack	.15
115	Wilton Guerrero	.15
116	Andy Benes	.15
117	Jeff Cirillo	.15
118	Chili Davis	.15
119	Eric Davis	.15
120	Vladimir Guerrero	1.00
121	Dennis Reyes	.15
122	Rickey Henderson	.30
123	Mickey Morandini	.15
124	Jason Schmidt	.15
125	J.T. Snow	.15
126	Justin Thompson	.15
127	Billy Wagner	.15
128	Armando Benitez	.15
129	Sean Casey	.25
130	Brad Fullmer	.25
131	Ben Grieve	.40
132	Robb Nen	.15
133	Shane Reynolds	.15
134	Todd Zeile	.15
135	Brady Anderson	.15
136	Aaron Boone	.15
137	Orlando Cabrera	.15
138	Jason Giambi	.40
139	Randy Johnson	.75
140	Jeff Kent	.15
141	John Wetteland	.15
142	Rolando Arrojo	.15
143	Scott Brosius	.15
144	Mark Grace	.30
145	Jason Kendall	.25
146	Travis Lee	.15
147	Gary Sheffield	.30
148	David Cone	.25
149	Jose Hernandez	.15
150	Todd Jones	.15
151	Al Martin	.15
152	Ismael Valdes	.15
153	Wade Boggs	.30
154	Garret Anderson	.15
155	Bobby Bonilla	.20
156	Darryl Kile	.15
157	Ryan Klesko	.25
158	Tim Wakefield	.15
159	Kenny Lofton	.40
160	Jose Canseco	.40
161	Doug Glanville	.15
162	Todd Hundley	.15
163	Brian Jordan	.15
164	Steve Finley	.15
165	Tom Glavine	.25
166	Al Leiter	.25
167	Raul Mondesi	.25
168	Desi Relaford	.15
169	Bret Saberhagen	.15
170	Omar Vizquel	.20
171	Larry Walker	.30
172	Bobby Abreu	.25
173	Moises Alou	.25
174	Mike Caruso	.15
175	Royce Clayton	.15
176	Bartolo Colon	.25
177	Marty Cordova	.15
178	Darin Erstad	.75
179	Nomar Garciaparra	2.00
180	Andy Ashby	.15
181	Dan Wilson	.15
182	Larry Sutton	.15
183	Tony Clark	.20
184	Andres Galarraga	.30
185	Ray Durham	.15
186	Hideo Nomo	.25
187	Steve Woodard	.15
188	Scott Rolen	.50
189	Mike Stanley	.15
190	Jaret Wright	.15
191	Vinny Castilla	.15
192	Jason Christiansen	.15
193	Paul Bako	.15
194	Carlos Perez	.15
195	Mike Piazza	2.00
196	Fernando Tatis	.15
197	Mo Vaughn	.40
198	Devon White	.15
199	Ricky Gutierrez	.15
200	Charlie Hayes	.15
201	Brad Radke	.15
202	Rick Helling	.15
203	John Smoltz	.20
204	Frank Thomas	1.00
205	David Wells	.15
206	Roger Clemens	1.00
207	Mark Grudzielanek	.15
208	Chipper Jones	1.50
209	Ray Lankford	.15
210	Pedro Martinez	.75
211	Manny Ramirez	.75
212	Greg Vaughn	.25
213	Craig Biggio	.30
214	Rusty Greer	.15
215	Greg Maddux	1.50
216	Rick Aguilera	.15
217	Andy Pettitte	.30

218 Dante Bichette .20
219 Damion Easley .15
220 Matt Morris .15
221 John Olerud .25
222 Chan Ho Park .20
223 Curt Schilling .25
224 John Valentin .15
225 Matt Williams .40
226 Ellis Burks .15
227 Tom Goodwin .15
228 Javy Lopez .25
229 Eric Milton .15
230 Paul O'Neill .30
231 Magglio Ordonez .25
232 Derrek Lee .15
233 Ken Griffey Jr. (Caught on the Fly) 1.25
234 Randy Johnson (Caught on the Fly) .30
235 Alex Rodriguez (Caught on the Fly) 1.25
236 Darin Erstad (Caught on the Fly) .40
237 Juan Gonzalez (Caught on the Fly) .40
238 Derek Jeter (Caught on the Fly) 1.00
239 Tony Gwynn (Caught on the Fly) .50
240 Kerry Wood (Caught on the Fly) .20
241 Cal Ripken Jr. (Caught on the Fly) 1.25
242 Sammy Sosa (Caught on the Fly) 1.00
243 Greg Maddux (Caught on the Fly) .50
244 Mark McGwire (Caught on the Fly) 1.50
245 Chipper Jones (Caught on the Fly) .75
246 Barry Bonds (Caught on the Fly) .40
247 Ben Grieve (Caught on the Fly) .20
248 Ben Davis (Building Blocks) .15
249 Robert Fick (Building Blocks) .15
250 Carlos Guillen (Building Blocks) .15
251 Mike Frank (Building Blocks) .15
252 Ryan Minor (Building Blocks) .15
253 Troy Glaus (Building Blocks) 1.00
254 Matt Anderson (Building Blocks) .15
255 Josh Booty (Building Blocks) .15
256 Gabe Alvarez (Building Blocks) .15
257 Gabe Kapler (Building Blocks) .25
258 Enrique Wilson (Building Blocks) .15
259 Alex Gonzalez (Building Blocks) .15
260 Preston Wilson (Building Blocks) .15
261 Eric Chavez (Building Blocks) .20
262 Adrian Beltre (Building Blocks) .30
263 Corey Koskie (Building Blocks) .15
264 *Robert Machado* (Building Blocks) .25
265 Orlando Hernandez (Building Blocks) .40
266 Matt Clement (Building Blocks) .15
267 Luis Ordaz (Building Blocks) .15
268 Jeremy Giambi (Building Blocks) .25
269 J.D. Drew (Building Blocks) .25
270 Cliff Politte (Building Blocks) .15
271 Carlton Loewer (Building Blocks) .15
272 Aramis Ramirez (Building Blocks) .15
273 Ken Griffey Jr. (M.I.P.D.) 1.25
274 Randy Johnson (M.I.P.D.) .40
275 Alex Rodriguez (M.I.P.D.) 1.00
276 Darin Erstad (M.I.P.D.) .40
277 Scott Rolen (M.I.P.D.) .25
278 Juan Gonzalez (M.I.P.D.) .40
279 Jeff Bagwell (M.I.P.D.) .40
280 Mike Piazza (M.I.P.D.) 1.00
281 Derek Jeter (M.I.P.D.) 1.00
282 Travis Lee (M.I.P.D.) .15
283 Tony Gwynn (M.I.P.D.) .50
284 Kerry Wood (M.I.P.D.) .20
285 Albert Belle (M.I.P.D.) .20
286 Sammy Sosa (M.I.P.D.) 1.00
287 Mo Vaughn (M.I.P.D.) .20
288 Nomar Garciaparra (M.I.P.D.) 1.00
289 Frank Thomas (M.I.P.D.) .50
290 Cal Ripken Jr. (M.I.P.D.) 1.25
291 Greg Maddux (M.I.P.D.) .75
292 Chipper Jones (M.I.P.D.) .75
293 Ben Grieve (M.I.P.D.) .20
294 Andruw Jones (M.I.P.D.) .40
295 Mark McGwire (M.I.P.D.) 1.50
296 Roger Clemens (M.I.P.D.) .50
297 Barry Bonds (M.I.P.D.) .40
298 Ken Griffey Jr. -Checklist (M.I.P.D.) 1.00
299 Kerry Wood -Checklist (M.I.P.D.) .25
300 Alex Rodriguez -Checklist (M.I.P.D.) .75

1999 Metal Universe Precious Metal Gems

A 300-card parallel of the base set, these cards feature gold-foil etching and are inserted exclusively in hobby packs. Each card is serially numbered to 50. A Gem Master 1 of 1 parallel was also issued, but is too rare to value.

	MT
Common Player:	10.00
Stars:	25-40X
Gem Master 1 of 1:	(Value undetermined)

(See 1999 Metal Universe for checklist and base card values.)

1999 Metal Universe Boyz With The Wood

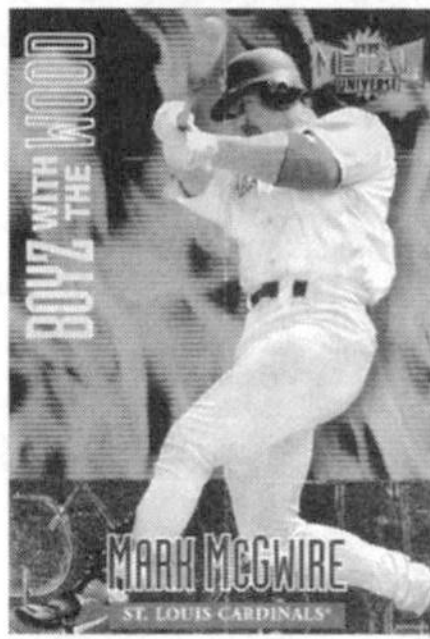

The top hitters in the game are featured on these folded cards with four sides. These are inserted 1:18.

		MT
Complete Set (15):		75.00
Common Player:		2.00
Inserted 1:18		
1	Ken Griffey Jr.	15.00
2	Frank Thomas	5.00
3	Jeff Bagwell	4.00
4	Juan Gonzalez	4.00
5	Mark McGwire	15.00
6	Scott Rolen	3.00
7	Travis Lee	2.00
8	Tony Gwynn	6.00
9	Mike Piazza	7.50
10	Chipper Jones	7.50
11	Nomar Garciaparra	7.50
12	Derek Jeter	7.50
13	Cal Ripken Jr.	10.00
14	Andruw Jones	3.00
15	Alex Rodriguez	12.00

1999 Metal Universe Diamond Soul

Utilizing lenticular technology these inserts showcase a soulful "galactic" design. The set consists of 15 cards which are seeded at 1:72 packs.

		MT
Complete Set (15):		140.00
Common Player:		3.00
Inserted 1:72		
1	Cal Ripken Jr.	20.00
2	Alex Rodriguez	20.00
3	Chipper Jones	12.00
4	Derek Jeter	20.00
5	Frank Thomas	8.00
6	Greg Maddux	12.00
7	Juan Gonzalez	6.00
8	Ken Griffey Jr.	25.00
9	Kerry Wood	3.00
10	Mark McGwire	25.00
11	Mike Piazza	15.00
12	Nomar Garciaparra	15.00
13	Scott Rolen	5.00
14	Tony Gwynn	8.00
15	Travis Lee	3.00

1999 Metal Universe Linchpins

This 10-card set features a laser die-cut background and highlights key players who hold their teams together on the field and in the clubhouse. These are seeded 1:360 packs.

		MT
Complete Set (10):		250.00
Common Player:		8.00
Inserted 1:360		
1	Mike Piazza	30.00
2	Mark McGwire	50.00
3	Kerry Wood	8.00
4	Ken Griffey Jr.	40.00
5	Greg Maddux	25.00
6	Frank Thomas	15.00
7	Derek Jeter	40.00
8	Chipper Jones	25.00
9	Cal Ripken Jr.	40.00
10	Alex Rodriguez	40.00

1999 Metal Universe Neophytes

This 15-card insert set showcases young stars like J.D. Drew and Troy Glaus. The cards feature silver foil stamping on a horizontal format, found on an average of 1:6 packs.

		MT
Complete Set (15):		20.00
Common Player:		.50
Inserted 1:6		
1	Troy Glaus	4.00
2	Travis Lee	1.50
3	Scott Elarton	.50
4	Ricky Ledee	.50
5	Richard Hidalgo	.50
6	J.D. Drew	1.00
7	Paul Konerko	1.00
8	Orlando Hernandez	5.00
9	Mike Caruso	.50
10	Mike Frank	.50
11	Miguel Tejada	1.00
12	Matt Anderson	.75
13	Kerry Wood	1.50
14	Gabe Alvarez	.50
15	Adrian Beltre	1.50

1999 Metal Universe Planet Metal

These die-cut cards feature a metallic view of the planet behind pop-out action photography. The 15-card set features the top players in the game and are seeded 1:36 packs.

		MT
Complete Set (15):		150.00
Common Player:		5.00
Inserted 1:36		
1	Alex Rodriguez	20.00
2	Andruw Jones	6.00
3	Cal Ripken Jr.	20.00
4	Chipper Jones	15.00
5	Darin Erstad	6.00
6	Derek Jeter	15.00
7	Frank Thomas	10.00
8	Travis Lee	5.00
9	Scott Rolen	6.00
10	Nomar Garciaparra	15.00
11	Mike Piazza	15.00
12	Mark McGwire	30.00
13	Ken Griffey Jr.	30.00
14	Juan Gonzalez	8.00
15	Jeff Bagwell	8.00

2000 Metal

		MT
Complete Set (250):		50.00
Common Player:		.15
Common Prospect (201-250):		.75
Inserted 1:2		
Pack (10):		2.00
Wax Box:		45.00
1	Tony Gwynn	1.00
2	Derek Jeter	2.50
3	Johnny Damon	.15
4	Javy Lopez	.25
5	Preston Wilson	.15
6	Derek Bell	.15
7	Richie Sexson	.25
8	Vinny Castilla	.15
9	Billy Wagner	.15
10	Carlos Beltran	.15
11	Chris Singleton	.15
12	Nomar Garciaparra	2.00
13	Carlos Febles	.15
14	Jason Varitek	.15
15	Luis Gonzalez	.15
16	Jon Lieber	.15
17	Mo Vaughn	.40
18	Dave Burba	.15
19	Brady Anderson	.25
20	Carlos Lee	.25
21	Chuck Finley	.15
22	Alex Gonzalez	.15
23	Matt Williams	.30
24	Chipper Jones	1.50
25	Pokey Reese	.15
26	Todd Helton	.75
27	Mike Mussina	.50
28	Butch Huskey	.15
29	Jeff Bagwell	.75
30	Juan Encarnacion	.15
31	A.J. Burnett	.15
32	Micah Bowie	.15
33	Brian Jordan	.15
34	Scott Erickson	.15
35	Sean Casey	.25
36	John Smoltz	.15
37	Edgard Clemente	.15
38	Mike Hampton	.15
39	Tom Glavine	.25
40	Albert Belle	.40
41	Jim Thome	.30
42	Jermaine Dye	.15
43	Sammy Sosa	2.00
44	Pedro Martinez	.75
45	Paul Konerko	.15
46	Damion Easley	.15
47	Cal Ripken Jr.	2.50
48	Jose Lima	.15
49	Mike Lowell	.15
50	Randy Johnson	.75
51	Dean Palmer	.20
52	Tim Salmon	.25
53	Kevin Millwood	.25
54	Mark Grace	.25
55	Aaron Boone	.15
56	Omar Vizquel	.15
57	Moises Alou	.25
58	Travis Fryman	.25
59	Erubiel Durazo	.15
60	Carl Everett	.15
61	Charles Johnson	.15
62	Trot Nixon	.15
63	Andres Galarraga	.30
64	Magglio Ordonez	.25
65	Pedro Astacio	.15
66	Roberto Alomar	.50
67	Pete Harnisch	.15
68	Scott Williamson	.15
69	Alex Fernandez	.15
70	Robin Ventura	.25
71	Chad Allen	.15
72	Darin Erstad	.30
73	Ron Coomer	.15
74	Ellis Burks	.25
75	Kent Bottenfield	.15
76	Ken Griffey Jr.	2.50
77	Mike Piazza	2.00
78	Jorge Posada	.25
79	Dante Bichette	.25
80	Adrian Beltre	.25
81	Andruw Jones	.50
82	Wilson Alvarez	.15
83	Edgardo Alfonzo	.25
84	Brian Giles	.25
85	Gary Sheffield	.30
86	Matt Stairs	.15
87	Bret Boone	.15
88	Kenny Rogers	.15
89	Barry Bonds	.75
90	Scott Rolen	.50
91	Edgar Renteria	.15
92	Larry Walker	.30
93	Roger Cedeno	.15
94	Kevin Brown	.25
95	Lee Stevens	.15
96	Brad Radke	.15
97	Andy Pettitte	.25
98	Bobby Higginson	.15
99	Eric Chavez	.25
100	Alex Rodriguez	2.50
101	Shannon Stewart	.15
102	Ryan Rupe	.15
103	Freddy Garcia	.15
104	John Jaha	.15
105	Greg Maddux	1.50
106	Hideki Irabu	.15
107	Rey Ordonez	.15
108	Troy O'Leary	.15
109	Frank Thomas	1.00
110	Corey Koskie	.15
111	Bernie Williams	.50
112	Barry Larkin	.40
113	Kevin Appier	.15
114	Curt Schilling	.25
115	Bartolo Colon	.15
116	Edgar Martinez	.15
117	Ray Lankford	.15
118	Todd Walker	.15
119	John Wetteland	.15
120	David Nilsson	.15
121	Tino Martinez	.25
122	Phil Nevin	.15
123	Ben Grieve	.25
124	Ron Gant	.25
125	Jeff Kent	.15
126	Rick Helling	.15
127	Russ Ortiz	.15
128	Troy Glaus	.75
129	Chan Ho Park	.25
130	Jeromy Burnitz	.15
131	Aaron Sele	.15
132	Mike Sirotka	.15
133	Brad Ausmus	.15
134	Jose Rosado	.15
135	Mariano Rivera	.25
136	Jason Giambi	.40
137	Mike Lieberthal	.15
138	Chris Carpenter	.15
139	Henry Rodriguez	.15
140	Mike Sweeney	.15
141	Vladimir Guerrero	1.00
142	Charles Nagy	.15
143	Jason Kendall	.25
144	Matt Lawton	.15
145	Michael Barrett	.15
146	David Cone	.25
147	Bobby Abreu	.15
148	Fernando Tatis	.25
149	Jose Canseco	.50
150	Craig Biggio	.25
151	Matt Mantei	.15
152	Jacque Jones	.15
153	John Halama	.15
154	Trevor Hoffman	.15
155	Rondell White	.25
156	Reggie Sanders	.15
157	Steve Finley	.15
158	Roberto Hernandez	.15
159	Geoff Jenkins	.25
160	Chris Widger	.15
161	Orel Hershiser	.15
162	Tim Hudson	.25
163	Kris Benson	.15
164	Kevin Young	.15
165	Rafael Palmeiro	.40
166	David Wells	.15
167	Ben Davis	.15
168	Jamie Moyer	.15
169	Randy Wolf	.15
170	Jeff Cirillo	.15
171	Warren Morris	.15
172	Billy Koch	.15
173	Marquis Grissom	.15
174	Geoff Blum	.15
175	Octavio Dotel	.15
176	Orlando Hernandez	.30
177	J.D. Drew	.25
178	Carlos Delgado	.75
179	Sterling Hitchcock	.15
180	Shawn Green	.30
181	Tony Clark	.20
182	Joe McEwing	.15
183	Fred McGriff	.25
184	Tony Batista	.20
185	Al Leiter	.25
186	Roger Clemens	1.00
187	Al Martin	.15
188	Eric Milton	.15
189	Bobby Smith	.15
190	Rusty Greer	.15
191	Shawn Estes	.15
192	Ken Caminiti	.20
193	Eric Karros	.25
194	Manny Ramirez	.75
195	Jim Edmonds	.25
196	Paul O'Neill	.25
197	Rico Brogna	.15
198	Ivan Rodriguez	.75
199	Doug Glanville	.15
200	Mark McGwire	3.00
201	Mark Quinn (Prospect)	.75
202	Norm Hutchins (Prospect)	.75
203	Ramon Ortiz (Prospect)	.75
204	Brett Laxton (Prospect)	.75
205	Jimmy Anderson (Prospect)	.75
206	Calvin Murray (Prospect)	.75
207	Wilton Veras (Prospect)	.75
208	Chad Hermansen (Prospect)	.75
209	Nick Johnson (Prospect)	.75
210	Kevin Barker (Prospect)	.75
211	Casey Blake (Prospect)	.75
212	Chad Meyers (Prospect)	.75
213	Kip Wells (Prospect)	.75
214	Eric Munson (Prospect)	1.00
215	Lance Berkman (Prospect)	.75
216	Wily Pena (Prospect)	1.00
217	Gary Matthews Jr. (Prospect)	.75
218	Travis Dawkins (Prospect)	.75
219	Josh Beckett (Prospect)	1.00
220	Tony Armas, Jr. (Prospect)	.75
221	Alfonso Soriano (Prospect)	.75
222	Pat Burrell (Prospect)	2.50
223	*Danys Baez* (Prospect)	1.50
224	Adam Kennedy (Prospect)	.75
225	Ruben Mateo (Prospect)	.75
226	Vernon Wells (Prospect)	.75
227	Brian Cooper (Prospect)	.75
228	*Jeff DaVanon* (Prospect)	.75
229	Glen Barker (Prospect)	.75
230	Robinson Cancel (Prospect)	.75
231	D'Angelo Jimenez (Prospect)	.75
232	Adam Piatt (Prospect)	1.00
233	Buddy Carlyle (Prospect)	.75
234	Chad Hutchinson (Prospect)	.75
235	Matt Riley (Prospect)	.75
236	Cole Liniak (Prospect)	.75
237	Ben Petrick (Prospect)	.75
238	Peter Bergeron Prospect)	.75
239	Cesar King (Prospect)	.75
240	Aaron Myette (Prospect)	.75
241	Eric Gagne (Prospect)	.75
242	Joe Nathan (Prospect)	.75
243	Bruce Chen (Prospect)	.75
244	Rob Bell (Prospect)	.75
245	*Juan Sosa* (Prospect)	1.00
246	Julio Ramirez (Prospect)	.75
247	Wade Miller (Prospect)	.75
248	*Trace Coquillette* (Prospect)	1.00
249	Robert Ramsay (Prospect)	.75
250	Rick Ankiel (Prospect)	3.00

2000 Metal Emerald

	MT
Common Player:	
Stars:	5X-10X
Inserted 1:4	
Prospects (201-250):	2X
Inserted 1:8	

2000 Metal Autographics

	MT
Common Player:	10.00
Bobby Abreu	25.00
Chad Allen	10.00
Marlon Anderson	10.00
Rick Ankiel	75.00
Glen Barker	10.00
Rob Bell	15.00
Mark Bellhorn	10.00
Peter Bergeron	20.00
Lance Berkman	10.00
Wade Boggs	60.00
Barry Bonds	75.00
Kent Bottenfield	10.00
Pat Burrell	50.00
Miguel Cairo	10.00
Mike Cameron	15.00
Chris Carpenter	10.00
Roger Cedeno	15.00
Mike Darr	10.00
Einar Diaz	10.00
J.D. Drew	40.00
Erubiel Durazo	30.00
Ray Durham	15.00
Damion Easley	15.00
Scott Elarton	10.00
Jeremy Giambi	15.00
Doug Glanville	10.00
Shawn Green	50.00
Jerry Hairston	10.00
Bob Howry	10.00
Norm Hutchins	10.00
Randy Johnson	60.00
Jacque Jones	15.00
Gabe Kapler	20.00
Cesar King	10.00
Mark Kotsay	15.00
Cole Liniak	10.00
Greg Maddux	150.00
Pedro Martinez	75.00
Ruben Mateo	20.00
Warren Morris	10.00
Heath Murray	10.00
Joe Nathan	15.00
Jim Parque	10.00
Angel Pena	15.00
Cal Ripken Jr.	200.00
Alex Rodriguez	160.00
Ryan Rupe	15.00
Randall Simon	10.00
Chris Singleton	15.00
Mike Sweeney	20.00
Wilton Veras	25.00
Scott Williamson	10.00
Randy Wolf	10.00
Tony Womack	10.00

2000 Metal Base Shredders

	MT
Complete Set (18):	500.00
Common Player:	20.00
Inserted 1:288	
Roberto Alomar	50.00
Michael Barrett	20.00
Tony Clark	20.00
Ben Davis	20.00
Erubiel Durazo	20.00
Troy Glaus	30.00
Ben Grieve	30.00
Vladimir Guerrero	60.00
Tony Gwynn	60.00
Todd Helton	30.00
Eric Munson	25.00
Rafael Palmeiro	30.00
Manny Ramirez	60.00
Ivan Rodriguez	60.00
Miguel Tejada	25.00
Mo Vaughn	30.00
Larry Walker	30.00
Matt Williams	25.00

2000 Metal Fusion

		MT
Complete Set (15):		25.00
Common Player:		.50
Inserted 1:4		
1	Ken Griffey Jr., Alex Rodriguez	4.00
2	Mark McGwire, Rick Ankiel	5.00
3	Scott Rolen, Curt Schilling	1.00
4	Pedro Martinez, Nomar Garciaparra	2.50
5	Carlos Beltran, Carlos Febles	.50
6	Sammy Sosa, Mark Grace	2.50
7	Vladimir Guerrero, Ugueth Urbina	1.50
8	Roger Clemens, Derek Jeter	2.50
9	Jeff Bagwell, Craig Biggio	1.00
10	Chipper Jones, Andruw Jones	2.00
11	Cal Ripken Jr., Mike Mussina	3.00
12	Manny Ramirez, Roberto Alomar	1.00
13	Sean Casey, Barry Larkin	.50
14	Ivan Rodriguez, Rafael Palmeiro	1.00
15	Mike Piazza, Robin Ventura	2.50

2000 Metal Heavy Metal

		MT
Complete Set (10):		50.00
Common Player:		2.00
Inserted 1:20		
1	Sammy Sosa	6.00
2	Mark McGwire	10.00
3	Ken Griffey Jr.	8.00
4	Mike Piazza	6.00
5	Nomar Garciaparra	6.00
6	Alex Rodriguez	8.00
7	Manny Ramirez	2.50
8	Jeff Bagwell	2.50
9	Chipper Jones	5.00
10	Vladimir Guerrero	4.00

2000 Metal Hit Machines

		MT
Complete Set (10):		40.00
Common Player:		2.00
Inserted 1:20		
1	Ken Griffey Jr.	8.00
2	Mark McGwire	10.00
3	Frank Thomas	3.00
4	Tony Gwynn	3.00
5	Rafael Palmeiro	2.00
6	Bernie Williams	2.00
7	Derek Jeter	8.00
8	Sammy Sosa	6.00
9	Mike Piazza	6.00
10	Chipper Jones	5.00

2000 Metal Platinum Portraits

		MT
Complete Set (10):		15.00
Common Player:		.50
Inserted 1:8		
1	Carlos Beltran	.50
2	Vladimir Guerrero	2.50
3	Manny Ramirez	1.50
4	Ivan Rodriguez	1.50
5	Sean Casey	.75
6	Alex Rodriguez	5.00
7	Derek Jeter	4.00
8	Nomar Garciaparra	4.00
9	Vernon Wells	.50
10	Shawn Green	1.00

2000 Metal Talent Show

		MT
Complete Set (15):		8.00
Common Player:		.25
Inserted 1:4		
1	Rick Ankiel	2.00
2	Matt Riley	.25
3	Chad Hermansen	.25
4	Ruben Mateo	.50
5	Eric Munson	.75
6	Alfonso Soriano	.75
7	Wilton Veras	.25
8	Vernon Wells	.50
9	Erubiel Durazo	.25
10	Pat Burrell	1.50
11	Ben Davis	.25
12	A.J. Burnett	.50
13	Peter Bergeron	.50
14	Mark Quinn	.50
15	Ben Petrick	.25

P

1993 Pacific

This set marks the first time a major league set was designed entirely for the Spanish-speaking market. Distribution areas included retail markets in the United States, Mexico, South America and the Caribbean. The cards are glossy and are written in Spanish on both sides. Cards are numbered in alphabetical order by team, beginning with Atlanta. Insert sets are titled Prism

(20 cards featuring Spanish players and their accomplishments), Beisbol De Estralla (Stars of Baseball), Hot Players and Amigos (a 30-card set which features two players per card).

	MT
Complete Set (660):	20.00
Common Player:	.05

1 Rafael Belliard .05
2 Sid Bream .05
3 Francisco Cabrera .05
4 Marvin Freeman .05
5 Ron Gant .10
6 Tom Glavine .25
7 Brian Hunter .05
8 Dave Justice .25
9 Ryan Klesko .20
10 Melvin Nieves .05
11 Deion Sanders .15
12 John Smoltz .15
13 Mark Wohlers .05
14 Brady Anderson .15
15 Glenn Davis .05
16 Mike Devereaux .05
17 Leo Gomez .05
18 Chris Hoiles .05
19 Chito Martinez .05
20 Ben McDonald .05
21 Mike Mussina .30
22 Gregg Olson .05
23 Joe Orsulak .05
24 Cal Ripken, Jr. 1.50
25 David Segui .05
26 Rick Sutcliffe .05
27 Wade Boggs .40
28 Tom Brunansky .05
29 Ellis Burks .10
30 Roger Clemens .50
31 John Dopson .05
32 John Flaherty .05
33 Mike Greenwell .05
34 Tony Pena .05
35 Carlos Quintana .05
36 Luis Rivera .05
37 Mo Vaughn .40
38 Frank Viola .05
39 Matt Young .05
40 Scott Bailes .05
41 Bert Blyleven .05
42 Chad Curtis .10
43 Gary DiSarcina .05
44 Chuck Finley .05
45 Mike Fitzgerald .05
46 Gary Gaetti .05
47 Rene Gonzales .05
48 Mark Langston .05
49 Scott Lewis .05
50 Luis Polonia .05
51 Tim Salmon .25
52 Lee Stevens .05
53 Steve Buechele .05
54 Frank Castillo .05
55 Doug Dascenzo .05
56 Andre Dawson .15
57 Shawon Dunston .05
58 Mark Grace .15
59 Mike Morgan .05
60 Luis Salazar .05
61 Rey Sanchez .05
62 Ryne Sandberg .50
63 Dwight Smith .05
64 Jerome Walton .05
65 Rick Wilkins .05
66 Wilson Alvarez .05
67 George Bell .05
68 Joey Cora .05
69 Alex Fernandez .10
70 Carlton Fisk .10
71 Craig Grebeck .05
72 Ozzie Guillen .05
73 Jack McDowell .05
74 Scott Radinsky .05
75 Tim Raines .10
76 Bobby Thigpen .05
77 Frank Thomas .75
78 Robin Ventura .20
79 Tom Browning .05
80 Jacob Brumfield .05
81 Rob Dibble .05
82 Bill Doran .05
83 Billy Hatcher .05
84 Barry Larkin .25
85 Hal Morris .05
86 Joe Oliver .05
87 Jeff Reed .05
88 Jose Rijo .05
89 Bip Roberts .05
90 Chris Sabo .05
91 Sandy Alomar, Jr. .10
92 Brad Arnsberg .05
93 Carlos Baerga .10
94 Albert Belle .30
95 Felix Fermin .05
96 Mark Lewis .05
97 Kenny Lofton .25
98 Carlos Martinez .05
99 Rod Nicholos .05
100 Dave Rohde .05
101 Scott Scudder .05
102 Paul Sorrento .05
103 Mark Whiten .05
104 Mark Carreon .05
105 Milt Cuyler .05
106 Rob Deer .05
107 Cecil Fielder .10
108 Travis Fryman .15
109 Dan Gladden .05
110 Bill Gullickson .05
111 Les Lancaster .05
112 Mark Leiter .05
113 Tony Phillips .05
114 Mickey Tettleton .05
115 Alan Trammell .10
116 Lou Whitaker .05
117 Jeff Bagwell .50
118 Craig Biggio .20
119 Joe Boever .05
120 Casey Candaele .05
121 Andujar Cedeno .05
122 Steve Finley .05
123 Luis Gonzalez .05
124 Pete Harnisch .05
125 Jimmy Jones .05
126 Mark Portugal .05
127 Rafael Ramirez .05
128 Mike Simms .05
129 Eric Yelding .05
130 Luis Aquino .05
131 Kevin Appier .05
132 Mike Boddicker .05
133 George Brett .50
134 Tom Gordon .05
135 Mark Gubicza .05
136 David Howard .05
137 Gregg Jefferies .10
138 Wally Joyner .10
139 Brian McRae .05
140 Jeff Montgomery .05
141 Terry Shumpert .05
142 Curtis Wilkerson .05
143 Brett Butler .10
144 Eric Davis .10
145 Kevin Gross .05
146 Dave Hansen .05
147 Lenny Harris .05
148 Carlos Hernandez .05
149 Orel Hershiser .10
150 Jay Howell .05
151 Eric Karros .10
152 Ramon Martinez .10
153 Jose Offerman .05
154 Mike Sharperson .05
155 Darryl Strawberry .10
156 Jim Gantner .05
157 Darryl Hamilton .05
158 Doug Henry .05
159 John Jaha .05
160 Pat Listach .05
161 Jaime Navarro .05
162 Dave Nilsson .05
163 Jesse Orosco .05
164 Kevin Seitzer .05
165 B.J. Surhoff .10
166 Greg Vaughn .15
167 Robin Yount .30
168 Rick Aguilera .05
169 Scott Erickson .05
170 Mark Guthrie .05
171 Kent Hrbek .10
172 Chuck Knoblauch .15
173 Gene Larkin .05
174 Shane Mack .05
175 Pedro Munoz .05
176 Mike Pagliarulo .05
177 Kirby Puckett .60
178 Kevin Tapani .05
179 Gary Wayne .05
180 Moises Alou .10
181 Brian Barnes .05
182 Archie Cianfrocco .05
183 Delino DeShields .10
184 Darrin Fletcher .05
185 Marquis Grissom .10
186 Ken Hill .05
187 Dennis Martinez .10
188 Bill Sampen .05
189 John VanderWal .05
190 Larry Walker .15
191 Tim Wallach .05
192 Bobby Bonilla .10
193 Daryl Boston .05
194 Vince Coleman .05
195 Kevin Elster .05
196 Sid Fernandez .05
197 John Franco .05
198 Dwight Gooden .10
199 Howard Johnson .05
200 Willie Randolph .05
201 Bret Saberhagen .05
202 Dick Schofield .05
203 Pete Schourek .05
204 Greg Cadaret .05
205 John Habyan .05
206 Pat Kelly .05
207 Kevin Maas .05
208 Don Mattingly .50
209 Matt Nokes .05
210 Melido Perez .05
211 Scott Sanderson .05
212 Andy Stankiewicz .05
213 Danny Tartabull .05
214 Randy Velarde .05
215 Bernie Williams .40
216 Harold Baines .10
217 Mike Bordick .05
218 Scott Brosius .05
219 Jerry Browne .05
220 Ron Darling .05
221 Dennis Eckersley .10
222 Rickey Henderson .30
223 Rick Honeycutt .05
224 Mark McGwire 2.00
225 Ruben Sierra .05
226 Terry Steinbach .05
227 Bob Welch .05
228 Willie Wilson .05
229 Ruben Amaro .05
230 Kim Batiste .05
231 Juan Bell .05
232 Wes Chamberlain .05
233 Darren Daulton .05
234 Mariano Duncan .05
235 Len Dykstra .05
236 Dave Hollins .05
237 Stan Javier .05
238 John Kruk .05
239 Mickey Morandini .05
240 Terry Mulholland .05
241 Mitch Williams .05
242 Stan Belinda .05
243 Jay Bell .05
244 Carlos Garcia .05
245 Jeff King .05
246 Mike LaValliere .05
247 Lloyd McClendon .05
248 Orlando Merced .05
249 Paul Miller .05
250 Gary Redus .05
251 Don Slaught .05
252 Zane Smith .05
253 Andy Van Slyke .05
254 Tim Wakefield .05
255 Andy Benes .05
256 Dann Bilardello .05
257 Tony Gwynn .50
258 Greg Harris .05
259 Darrin Jackson .05
260 Mike Maddux .05
261 Fred McGriff .25
262 Rich Rodriguez .05
263 Benito Santiago .05
264 Gary Sheffield .25
265 Kurt Stillwell .05
266 Tim Teufel .05
267 Bud Black .05
268 John Burkett .05
269 Will Clark .30
270 Royce Calyton .05
271 Bryan Hickerson .05
272 Chris James .05
273 Darren Lewis .05
274 Willie McGee .05
275 Jim McNamara .05
276 Francisco Oliveras .05
277 Robby Thompson .05
278 Matt Williams .25
279 Trevor Wilson .05
280 Bret Boone .10
281 Greg Briley .05
282 Jay Buhner .10
283 Henry Cotto .05
284 Rich DeLucia .05
285 Dave Fleming .05
286 Ken Griffey, Jr. 2.00
287 Erik Hanson .05
288 Randy Johnson .50
289 Tino Martinez .15
290 Edgar Martinez .10
291 Dave Valle .05
292 Omar Vizquel .10
293 Luis Alicea .05
294 Bernard Gilkey .10
295 Felix Jose .05
296 Ray Lankford .10
297 Omar Olivares .05
298 Jose Oquendo .05
299 Tom Pagnozzi .05
300 Geronimo Pena .05
301 Gerald Perry .05
302 Ozzie Smith .40
303 Lee Smith .10
304 Bob Tewksbury .05
305 Todd Zeile .10
306 Kevin Brown .10
307 Todd Burns .05
308 Jose Canseco .40
309 Hector Fajardo .05
310 Julio Franco .05
311 Juan Gonzalez .50
312 Jeff Huson .05
313 Rob Maurer .05
314 Rafael Palmeiro .25
315 Dean Palmer .10
316 Ivan Rodriguez .40
317 Nolan Ryan 1.00
318 Dickie Thon .05
319 Roberto Alomar .50
320 Derek Bell .10
321 Pat Borders .05
322 Joe Carter .10
323 Kelly Gruber .05
324 Juan Guzman .05
325 Manny Lee .05
326 Jack Morris .05
327 John Olerud .15
328 Ed Sprague .05
329 Todd Stottlemyre .05
330 Duane Ward .05
331 Steve Avery .05
332 Damon Berryhill .05
333 Jeff Blauser .05
334 Mark Lemke .05
335 Greg Maddux 1.00
336 Kent Mercker .05
337 Otis Nixon .05
338 Greg Olson .05
339 Bill Pecota .05
340 Terry Pendleton .05
341 Mike Stanton .05
342 Todd Frohwirth .05
343 Tim Hulett .05
344 Mark McLemore .05
345 Luis Mercedes .05
346 Alan Mills .05
347 Sherman Obando .05
348 Jim Poole .05
349 Harold Reynolds .05
350 Arthur Rhodes .05
351 Jeff Tackett .05
352 Fernando Valenzuela .05
353 Scott Bankhead .05
354 Ivan Calderon .05
355 Scott Cooper .05
356 Danny Darwin .05
357 Scott Fletcher .05
358 Tony Fossas .05
359 Greg Harris .05
360 Joe Hesketh .05
361 Jose Melendez .05
362 Paul Quantrill .05
363 John Valentin .10
364 Mike Butcher .05
365 Chuck Crim .05
366 Chili Davis .05
367 Damion Easley .05
368 Steve Frey .05
369 Joe Grahe .05
370 Greg Myers .05

371	John Orton	.05
372	J.T. Snow	.15
373	Ron Tingley	.05
374	Julio Valera	.05
375	Paul Assenmacher	.05
376	Jose Bautista	.05
377	Jose Guzman	.05
378	Greg Hibbard	.05
379	Candy Maldonado	.05
380	Derrick May	.05
381	Dan Plesac	.05
382	Tommy Shields	.05
383	Sammy Sosa	1.00
384	Jose Vizcaino	.05
385	Greg Walbeck	.05
386	Ellis Burks	.10
387	Roberto Hernandez	.05
388	Mike Huff	.05
389	Bo Jackson	.15
390	Lance Johnson	.05
391	Ron Karkovice	.05
392	Kirk McCaskill	.05
393	Donn Pall	.05
394	Dan Pasqua	.05
395	Steve Sax	.05
396	Dave Stieb	.05
397	Bobby Ayala	.05
398	Tim Belcher	.05
399	Jeff Branson	.05
400	Cesar Hernandez	.05
401	Roberto Kelly	.05
402	Randy Milligan	.05
403	Kevin Mitchell	.05
404	Juan Samuel	.05
405	Reggie Sanders	.10
406	John Smiley	.05
407	Dan Wilson	.05
408	Mike Christopher	.05
409	Dennis Cook	.05
410	Alvaro Espinoza	.05
411	Glenallen Hill	.05
412	Reggie Jefferson	.05
413	Derek Lilliquist	.05
414	Jose Mesa	.05
415	Charles Nagy	.05
416	Junior Ortiz	.05
417	Eric Plunk	.05
418	Ted Power	.05
419	Scott Aldred	.05
420	Andy Ashby	.05
421	Freddie Benavides	.05
422	Dante Bichette	.15
423	Willie Blair	.05
424	Vinny Castilla	.10
425	Jerald Clark	.05
426	Alex Cole	.05
427	Andres Galarraga	.20
428	Joe Girardi	.05
429	Charlie Hayes	.05
430	Butch Henry	.05
431	Darren Holmes	.05
432	Dale Murphy	.15
433	David Nied	.05
434	Jeff Parrett	.05
435	*Steve Reed*	.05
436	Armando Reynoso	.05
437	Bruce Ruffin	.05
438	Bryn Smith	.05
439	Jim Tatum	.05
440	Eric Young	.10
441	Skeeter Barnes	.05
442	Tom Bolton	.05
443	Kirk Gibson	.05
444	Chad Krueter	.05
445	Bill Krueger	.05
446	Scott Livingstone	.05
447	Bob MacDonald	.05
448	Mike Moore	.05
449	Mike Munoz	.05
450	Gary Thurman	.05
451	David Wells	.10
452	Alex Arias	.05
453	Jack Armstrong	.05
454	Bret Barberie	.05
455	Ryan Bowen	.05
456	Cris Carpenter	.05
457	Chuck Carr	.05
458	Jeff Conine	.10
459	Steve Decker	.05
460	Orestes Destrade	.05
461	Monty Fariss	.05
462	Junior Felix	.05
463	Bryan Harvey	.05
464	Trevor Hoffman	.10
465	Charlie Hough	.05
466	Dave Magadan	.05
467	Bob McClure	.05
468	Rob Natal	.05
469	Scott Pose	.05
470	Rich Renteria	.05
471	Benito Santiago	.05
472	Matt Turner	.05
473	Walt Weiss	.05
474	Eric Anthony	.05
475	Chris Donnels	.05
476	Doug Drabek	.05
477	Xavier Hernandez	.05
478	Doug Jones	.05
479	Darryl Kile	.05
480	Scott Servais	.05
481	Greg Swindell	.05
482	Eddie Taubensee	.05
483	Jose Uribe	.05
484	Brian Williams	.05
485	Billy Brewer	.05
486	David Cone	.15
487	Greg Gagne	.05
488	Phil Hiatt	.05
489	Jose Lind	.05
490	Brent Mayne	.05
491	Kevin McReynolds	.05
492	Keith Miller	.05
493	Hipolito Pichardo	.05
494	Harvey Pulliam	.05
495	Rico Rossay	.05
496	Pedro Astacio	.05
497	Tom Candiotti	.05
498	Tom Goodwin	.05
499	Jim Gott	.05
500	Pedro Martinez	.50
501	Roger McDowell	.05
502	Mike Piazza	1.00
503	Jody Reed	.05
504	Rick Trlicek	.05
505	Mitch Weber	.05
506	Steve Wilson	.05
507	James Austin	.05
508	Ricky Bones	.05
509	Alex Diaz	.05
510	Mike Fetters	.05
511	Teddy Higuera	.05
512	Graeme Lloyd	.05
513	Carlos Maldonado	.05
514	Josias Manzanillo	.05
515	Kevin Reimer	.05
516	Bill Spiers	.05
517	Bill Wegman	.05
518	Willie Banks	.05
519	J.T. Bruett	.05
520	Brian Harper	.05
521	Terry Jorgensen	.05
522	Scott Leius	.05
523	Pat Mahomes	.05
524	Dave McCarty	.05
525	Jeff Reboulet	.10
526	Mike Trombley	.05
527	Carl Willis	.05
528	Dave Winfield	.25
529	Sean Berry	.05
530	Frank Bolick	.05
531	Kent Bottenfield	.05
532	Wil Cordero	.05
533	Jeff Fassero	.05
534	Tim Laker	.05
535	Mike Lansing	.10
536	Chris Nabholz	.05
537	Mel Rojas	.05
538	John Wetteland	.05
539	Ted Wood (Front photo actually Frank Bollick)	.05
540	Mike Draper	.05
541	Tony Fernandez	.05
542	Todd Hundley	.10
543	Jeff Innis	.05
544	Jeff McKnight	.05
545	Eddie Murray	.30
546	Charlie O'Brien	.05
547	Frank Tanana	.05
548	Ryan Thompson	.10
549	Chico Walker	.05
550	Anthony Young	.05
551	Jim Abbott	.10
552	Wade Boggs	.40
553	Steve Farr	.05
554	Neal Heaton	.05
555	Steve Howe	.05
556	Dion James	.05
557	Scott Kamieniecki	.05
558	Jimmy Key	.05
559	Jim Leyritz	.05
560	Paul O'Neill	.20
561	Spike Owen	.05
562	Lance Blankenship	.05
563	Joe Boever	.05
564	Storm Davis	.05
565	Kelly Downs	.05
566	Eric Fox	.05
567	Rich Gossage	.05
568	Dave Henderson	.05
569	Shawn Hillegas	.05
570	*Mike Mohler*	.05
571	Troy Neel	.10
572	Dale Sveum	.05
573	Larry Anderson	.05
574	Bob Ayrault	.05
575	Jose DeLeon	.05
576	Jim Eisenreich	.05
577	Pete Incaviglia	.05
578	Danny Jackson	.05
579	Ricky Jordan	.05
580	Ben Rivera	.05
581	Curt Schilling	.10
582	Milt Thompson	.05
583	David West	.05
584	John Candelaria	.05
585	Steve Cooke	.05
586	Tom Foley	.05
587	Al Martin	.05
588	Blas Minor	.05
589	Dennis Moeller	.05
590	Denny Neagle	.05
591	Tom Prince	.05
592	Randy Tomlin	.05
593	Bob Walk	.05
594	Kevin Young	.05
595	Pat Gomez	.05
596	Ricky Gutierrez	.05
597	Gene Harris	.05
598	Jeremy Hernandez	.05
599	Phil Plantier	.05
600	Tim Scott	.05
601	Frank Seminara	.05
602	Darrell Sherman	.05
603	Craig Shipley	.05
604	Guillermo Velasquez	.05
605	Dan Walters	.05
606	Mike Benjamin	.05
607	Barry Bonds	.50
608	Jeff Brantley	.05
609	Dave Burba	.05
610	Craig Colbert	.05
611	Mike Jackson	.05
612	Kirt Manwaring	.05
613	Dave Martinez	.05
614	Dave Righetti	.05
615	Kevin Rogers	.05
616	Bill Swift	.05
617	Rich Amaral	.05
618	Mike Blowers	.05
619	Chris Bosio	.05
620	Norm Charlton	.05
621	John Cummings	.05
622	Mike Felder	.05
623	Bill Haselman	.05
624	Tim Leary	.05
625	Pete O'Brien	.05
626	Russ Swan	.05
627	Fernando Vina	.05
628	Rene Arocha	.05
629	Rod Brewer	.05
630	Ozzie Canseco	.05
631	Rheal Cormier	.05
632	Brian Jordan	.10
633	Joe Magrane	.05
634	Donovan Osborne	.05
635	Mike Perez	.05
636	Stan Royer	.05
637	Hector Villanueva	.05
638	Tracy Woodson	.05
639	Benji Gil	.05
640	Tom Henke	.05
641	David Hulse	.05
642	Charlie Leibrandt	.05
643	Robb Nen	.05
644	Dan Peltier	.05
645	Billy Ripken	.05
646	Kenny Rogers	.05
647	John Russell	.05
648	Dan Smith	.05
649	Matt Whiteside	.05
650	William Canate	.05
651	Darnell Coles	.05
652	Al Leiter	.20
653	Dominigo Martinez	.05
654	Paul Molitor	.30
655	Luis Sojo	.05
656	Dave Stewart	.05
657	Mike Timlin	.05
658	Turner Ward	.05
659	Devon White	.10
660	Eddie Zosky	.05

1993 Pacific Beisbol Amigos

In groups of two, three or more, and generally from the same team, Latin players are paired in this second series insert set. The cards feature player photos (sometimes posed, sometimes superimposed) on a background of red, white and black baseballs. The players' last names and a card title are printed in Spanish on front and repeated on back. Also on back a few career highlights and stats are printed in red on a marbled background - again all in Spanish.

		MT
Complete Set (30):		12.00
Common Player:		.50
1	Edgar Martinez	.70
2	Luis Polonia, Stan Javier	.50
3	George Bell, Julio Franco	.50
4	Ozzie Guillen, Ivan Rodriguez	.75
5	Carlos Baerga, Sandy Alomar Jr.	.50
6	Sandy Alomar Jr., Alvaro Espinoza, Paul Sorrento, Carlos Baerga, Felix Fermin, Junior Ortiz, Jose Mesa, Carlos Martinez	.50
7	Sandy Alomar Jr., Roberto Alomar	1.00
8	Jose Lind, Felix Jose	.50
9	Ricky Bones, Jaime Navarro	.50
10	Jaime Navarro, Jesse Orosco	.50
11	Tino Martinez, Edgar Martinez	.50
12	Juan Gonzalez, Ivan Rodriguez	1.50
13	Juan Gonzalez, Julio Franco	.75
14	Julio Franco, Jose Canseco, Rafael Palmeiro	.60
15	Juan Gonzalez, Jose Canseco	1.00
16	Ivan Rodriguez, Benji Gil	.60
17	Jose Guzman, Frank Castillo	.50

18	Rey Sanchez, Jose Vizcaino	.50
19	Derrick May, Sammy Sosa	1.50
20	Sammy Sosa, Candy Maldonado	1.50
21	Jose Rijo, Juan Samuel	.50
22	Freddie Benavides, Andres Galarraga	.50
23	Guillermo Velasquez, Benito Santiago	.50
24	Luis Gonzalez, Andujar Cedeno	.50
25	Wil Cordero, Dennis Martinez	.50
26	Moises Alou, Wil Cordero	.50
27	Ozzie Canseco, Jose Canseco	.75
28	Jose Oquendo, Luis Alicea	.50
29	Luis Alicea, Rene Arocha	.50
30	Geronimo Pena, Luis Alicea	.50

1993 Pacific Estrellas de Beisbol

Pacific produced a gold-foil "Stars of Baseball" set of 20 that was randomly inserted as part of the company's first series Spanish language Major League set in 1993. Each card features a color action photo on the front surrounded by a gold-foil border. Production was limited to 10,000 of each card.

		MT
Complete Set (20):		37.00
Common Player:		1.50
1	Moises Alou	2.00
2	Bobby Bonilla	2.00
3	Tony Fernandez	1.50
4	Felix Jose	1.50
5	Dennis Martinez	2.00
6	Orlando Merced	1.50
7	Jose Oquendo	1.50
8	Geronimo Pena	1.50
9	Jose Rijo	1.50
10	Benito Santiago	1.50
11	Sandy Alomar Jr.	3.00
12	Carlos Baerga	1.50
13	Jose Canseco	4.00
14	Juan "Igor" Gonzalez	6.00
15	Juan Guzman	1.50
16	Edgar Martinez	1.50
17	Rafael Palmeiro	3.00
18	Ruben Sierra	1.50
19	Danny Tartabull	1.50
20	Omar Vizquel	1.50

1993 Pacific Jugadores Calientes

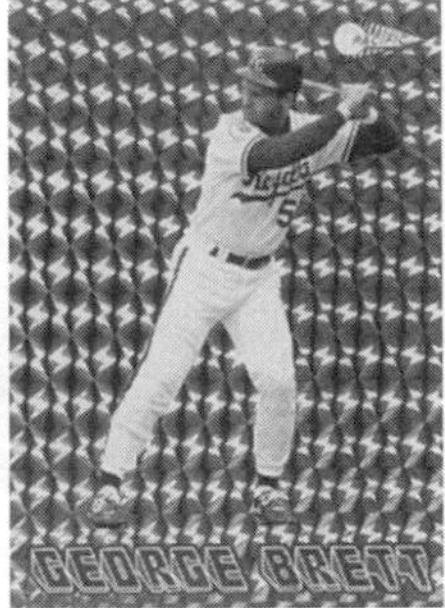

Three dozen "hot players" with a decidedly Hispanic predominance are featured in this glittery Series II insert set. Player action photos appear in front of a silver prismatic foil background. Names appear at bottom in boldly styled but hard to read letters in bright colors. Horizontal backs have a pair of player photos and a large team logo, along with a few stats, all printed in Spanish.

		MT
Complete Set (36):		25.00
Common Player:		.50
1	Rich Amaral	.50
2	George Brett	2.00
3	Jay Buhner	.50
4	Roger Clemens	1.20
5	Kirk Gibson	.50
6	Juan Gonzalez	1.50
7	Ken Griffey Jr.	3.00
8	Bo Jackson	.50
9	Kenny Lofton	.75
10	Mark McGwire	3.00
11	Sherman Obando	.50
12	John Olerud	.60
13	Carlos Quintana	.50
14	Ivan Rodriguez	.75
15	Nolan Ryan	2.50
16	J.T. Snow	.75
17	Fernando Valenzuela	.50
18	Dave Winfield	.75
19	Moises Alou	.60
20	Jeff Bagwell	1.25
21	Barry Bonds	1.25
22	Bobby Bonilla	.50
23	Vinny Castilla	.50
24	Andujar Cedeno	.50
25	Orestes Destrade	.50
26	Andres Galarraga	.60
27	Mark Grace	.75
28	Tony Gwynn	1.20
29	Roberto Kelly	.50
30	John Kruk	.50
31	Dave Magadan	.50
32	Derrick May	.50
33	Orlando Merced	.50
34	Mike Piazza	2.00
35	Armadno Reynoso	.50
36	Jose Vizcaino	.50

1993 Pacific Prism Insert

Pacific produced a prism card that was randomly inserted in its Series I Spanish-language set in 1993. Each of the 20 cards has a color photo of a star Latino player on the front superimposed over a prismatic silver-foil background. Card backs contain an action photo and a brief player biography on a marbled background. Production was limited to 10,000 of each card.

		MT
Complete Set (20):		125.00
Common Player:		6.00
1	Francisco Cabrera	6.00
2	Jose Lind	6.00
3	Dennis Martinez	6.00
4	Ramon Martinez	7.00
5	Jose Rijo	6.00
6	Benito Santiago	6.00
7	Roberto Alomar	12.50
8	Sandy Alomar Jr.	7.00
9	Carlos Baerga	6.00
10	George Bell	6.00
11	Jose Canseco	10.00
12	Alex Fernandez	6.00
13	Julio Franco	6.00
14	Igor (Juan) Gonzalez	20.00
15	Ozzie Guillen	6.00
16	Teddy Higuera	6.00
17	Edgar Martinez	6.00
18	Hipolito Pichardo	6.00
19	Luis Polonia	6.00
20	Ivan Rodriguez	8.00

1994 Pacific Crown Promos

Virtually identical in format to the regular 1994 Pacific Crown issue, the eight cards in the promo set have a "P-" prefix to the card number. Each side has a large "For Promotional Use Only" printed diagonally in black. The cards were sent to dealers as a preview to Pacific's 1994 bilingual issue.

		MT
Complete Set (8):		20.00
Common Player:		1.50
1	Carlos Baerga	1.50
2	Joe Carter	1.50
3	Juan Gonzalez	3.00
4	Ken Griffey, Jr.	4.00
5	Greg Maddux	3.00
6	Mike Piazza	3.00
7	Tim Salmon	2.00
8	Frank Thomas	3.00

1994 Pacific Crown

Following its 1993 Spanish-language set, Pacific's 1994 "Crown Collection" offering is bilingual, featuring both English and Spanish for most of the back printing. Fronts have an action photo which is borderless at the top and sides. A gold-foil line separates the bottom of the photo from a marbled strip that is color-coded by team. The player's name appears in two lines at the left of the strip, a gold-foil crown logo is at left. A Pacific logo appears in one of the upper corners of the photo. Backs have a photo, again borderless at top and sides, with a Pacific logo in one upper corner and the card number and MLB logos in the lower corners. At bottom is a gray marble strip with a few biographical details, 1993 and career stats and a ghost-image color team logo. The 660 cards in the set were issued in a single series.

		MT
Complete Set (660):		35.00
Common Player:		.05
Pack (12):		1.00
Wax Box (36):		25.00
1	Steve Avery	.05
2	Steve Bedrosian	.05
3	Damon Beryhill	.05
4	Jeff Blauser	.05
5	Sid Bream	.05
6	Francisco Cabrera	.05
7	Ramon Caraballo	.05
8	Ron Gant	.10
9	Tom Glavine	.15
10	Chipper Jones	1.50

No.	Player	Price
11	Dave Justice	.25
12	Ryan Klesko	.20
13	Mark Lemke	.05
14	Javier Lopez	.20
15	Greg Maddux	1.25
16	Fred McGriff	.25
17	Greg McMichael	.05
18	Kent Mercker	.05
19	Otis Nixon	.05
20	Terry Pendleton	.05
21	Deion Sanders	.15
22	John Smoltz	.15
23	Tony Tarasco	.05
24	Manny Alexander	.05
25	Brady Anderson	.15
26	Harold Baines	.05
27	Damion Buford (Damon)	.10
28	Paul Carey	.05
29	Mike Devereaux	.05
30	Todd Frohwirth	.05
31	Leo Gomez	.05
32	Jeffrey Hammonds	.05
33	Chris Hoiles	.05
34	Tim Hullett	.05
35	Ben McDonald	.05
36	Mark McLemore	.05
37	Alan Mills	.05
38	Mike Mussina	.20
39	Sherman Obando	.05
40	Gregg Olson	.05
41	Mike Pagliarulo	.05
42	Jim Poole	.05
43	Harold Reynolds	.05
44	Cal Ripken, Jr.	2.00
45	David Segui	.05
46	Fernando Valenzuela	.05
47	Jack Voight	.05
48	Scott Bankhead	.05
49	Roger Clemens	.75
50	Scott Cooper	.05
51	Danny Darwin	.05
52	Andre Dawson	.10
53	John Dopson	.05
54	Scott Fletcher	.05
55	Tony Fossas	.05
56	Mike Greenwell	.05
57	Billy Hatcher	.05
58	Jeff McNeely	.05
59	Jose Melendez	.05
60	Tim Naehring	.05
61	Tony Pena	.05
62	Carlos Quintana	.05
63	Paul Quantrill	.05
64	Luis Rivera	.05
65	Jeff Russell	.05
66	Aaron Sele	.05
67	John Valentin	.05
68	Mo Vaughn	.40
69	Frank Viola	.05
70	Bob Zupcic	.05
71	Mike Butcher	.05
72	Ron Correia	.05
73	Chad Curtis	.05
74	Chili Davis	.05
75	Gary DiSarcia	.05
76	Damion Easley	.05
77	John Farrell	.05
78	Chuck Finley	.05
79	Joe Grahe	.05
80	Stan Javier	.05
81	Mark Langston	.05
82	Phil Leftwich	.05
83	Torey Lovullo	.05
84	Joe Magrane	.05
85	Greg Myers	.05
86	Eduardo Perez	.05
87	Luis Polonia	.05
88	Tim Salmon	.25
89	J.T. Snow	.15
90	Kurt Stillwell	.05
91	Ron Tingley	.05
92	Chris Turner	.05
93	Julio Valera	.05
94	Jose Bautista	.05
95	Shawn Boskie	.05
96	Steve Buechele	.05
97	Frank Castillo	.05
98	Mark Grace	.15
99	Jose Guzman	.05
100	Mike Harkey	.05
101	Greg Hibbard	.05
102	Doug Jennings	.05
103	Derrick May	.05
104	Mike Morgan	.05
105	Randy Myers	.05
106	Karl Rhodes	.05
107	Kevin Robinson	.05
108	Rey Sanchez	.05
109	Ryne Sandberg	.50
110	Tommy Shields	.05
111	Dwight Smith	.05
112	Sammy Sosa	1.00
113	Jose Vizcaino	.05
114	Turk Wendell	.05
115	Rick Wilkins	.05
116	Willie Wilson	.05
117	Eddie Zambrano	.05
118	Wilson Alvarez	.05
119	Tim Belcher	.05
120	Jason Bere	.05
121	Rodney Bolton	.05
122	Ellis Burks	.10
123	Joey Cora	.05
124	Alex Fernandez	.10
125	Ozzie Guillen	.05
126	Craig Grebeck	.05
127	Roberto Hernandez	.05
128	Bo Jackson	.15
129	Lance Johnson	.05
130	Ron Karkovice	.05
131	Mike Lavalliere	.05
132	Norberto Martin	.05
133	Kirk McCaskill	.05
134	Jack McDowell	.05
135	Scott Radinsky	.05
136	Tim Raines	.10
137	Steve Sax	.05
138	Frank Thomas	1.00
139	Dan Pasqua	.05
140	Robin Ventura	.15
141	Jeff Branson	.05
142	Tom Browning	.05
143	Jacob Brumfield	.05
144	Tim Costo	.05
145	Rob Dibble	.05
146	Brian Dorsett	.05
147	Steve Foster	.05
148	Cesar Hernandez	.05
149	Roberto Kelly	.05
150	Barry Larkin	.15
151	Larry Luebbers	.05
152	Kevin Mitchell	.05
153	Joe Oliver	.05
154	Tim Pugh	.05
155	Jeff Reardon	.05
156	Jose Rijo	.05
157	Bip Roberts	.05
158	Chris Sabo	.05
159	Juan Samuel	.05
160	Reggie Sanders	.05
161	John Smiley	.05
162	Jerry Spradlin	.05
163	Gary Varsho	.05
164	Sandy Alomar Jr.	.10
165	Carlos Baerga	.05
166	Albert Belle	.60
167	Mark Clark	.05
168	Alvaro Espinoza	.05
169	Felix Fermin	.05
170	Reggie Jefferson	.05
171	Wayne Kirby	.05
172	Tom Kramer	.05
173	Jesse Levis	.05
174	Kenny Lofton	.50
175	Candy Maldonado	.05
176	Carlos Martinez	.05
177	Jose Mesa	.05
178	Jeff Mutis	.05
179	Charles Nagy	.05
180	Bob Ojeda	.05
181	Junior Ortiz	.05
182	Eric Plunk	.05
183	Manny Ramirez	.75
184	Paul Sorrento	.05
185	Jeff Treadway	.05
186	Bill Wertz	.05
187	Freddie Benavides	.05
188	Dante Bichette	.25
189	Willie Blair	.05
190	Daryl Boston	.05
191	Pedro Castellano	.05
192	Vinny Castilla	.10
193	Jerald Clark	.05
194	Alex Cole	.05
195	Andres Galarraga	.10
196	Joe Girardi	.05
197	Charlie Hayes	.05
198	Darren Holmes	.05
199	Chris Jones	.05
200	Curt Leskanic	.05
201	Roberto Mejia	.05
202	David Nied	.05
203	J. Owens	.05
204	Steve Reed	.05
205	Armando Reynoso	.05
206	Bruce Ruffin	.05
207	Keith Shepherd	.05
208	Jim Tatum	.05
209	Eric Young	.05
210	Skeeter Barnes	.05
211	Danny Bautista	.05
212	Tom Bolton	.05
213	Eric Davis	.10
214	Storm Davis	.05
215	Cecil Fielder	.10
216	Travis Fryman	.10
217	Kirk Gibson	.05
218	Dan Gladden	.05
219	John Doherty	.05
220	Chris Gomez	.05
221	David Haas	.05
222	Bill Krueger	.05
223	Chad Kreuter	.05
224	Mark Leiter	.05
225	Bob MacDonald	.05
226	Mike Moore	.05
227	Tony Phillips	.05
228	Rich Rowland	.05
229	Mickey Tettleton	.05
230	Alan Trammell	.10
231	David Wells	.10
232	Lou Whitaker	.05
233	Luis Aquino	.05
234	Alex Arias	.05
235	Jack Armstrong	.05
236	Ryan Bowen	.05
237	Chuck Carr	.05
238	Matias Carrillo	.05
239	Jeff Conine	.10
240	Henry Cotto	.05
241	Orestes Destrade	.05
242	Chris Hammond	.05
243	Bryan Harvey	.05
244	Charlie Hough	.05
245	Richie Lewis	.05
246	Mitch Lyden	.05
247	Dave Magadan	.05
248	Bob Natal	.05
249	Benito Santiago	.05
250	Gary Sheffield	.20
251	Matt Turner	.05
252	David Weathers	.05
253	Walt Weiss	.05
254	Darrell Whitmore	.05
255	Nigel Wilson	.05
256	Eric Anthony	.05
257	Jeff Bagwell	.75
258	Kevin Bass	.05
259	Craig Biggio	.15
260	Ken Caminiti	.15
261	Andujar Cedeno	.05
262	Chris Donnels	.05
263	Doug Drabek	.05
264	Tom Edens	.05
265	Steve Finley	.05
266	Luis Gonzalez	.05
267	Pete Harnisch	.05
268	Xavier Hernandez	.05
269	Todd Jones	.05
270	Darryl Kile	.05
271	Al Osuna	.05
272	Rick Parker	.05
273	Mark Portugal	.05
274	Scott Servais	.05
275	Greg Swindell	.05
276	Eddie Taubensee	.05
277	Jose Uribe	.05
278	Brian Williams	.05
279	Kevin Appier	.05
280	Billy Brewer	.05
281	David Cone	.10
282	Greg Gagne	.05
283	Tom Gordon	.05
284	Chris Gwynn	.05
285	John Habyan	.05
286	Chris Haney	.05
287	Phil Hiatt	.05
288	David Howard	.05
289	Felix Jose	.05
290	Wally Joyner	.05
291	Kevin Koslofski	.05
292	Jose Lind	.05
293	Brent Mayne	.05
294	Mike Mcfarlane	.05
295	Brian McRae	.05
296	Kevin McReynolds	.05
297	Keith Miller	.05
298	Jeff Montgomery	.05
299	Hipolito Pichardo	.05
300	Rico Rossy	.05
301	Curtis Wilkerson	.05
302	Pedro Astacio	.05
303	Rafael Bournigal	.05
304	Brett Butler	.10
305	Tom Candiotti	.05
306	Omar Daal	.05
307	Jim Gott	.05
308	Kevin Gross	.05
309	Dave Hansen	.05
310	Carlos Hernandez	.05
311	Orel Hershiser	.10
312	Eric Karros	.10
313	Pedro Martinez	.15
314	Ramon Martinez	.10
315	Roger McDowell	.05
316	Raul Mondesi	.40
317	Jose Offerman	.05
318	Mike Piazza	1.50
319	Jody Reed	.05
320	Henry Rodriguez	.05
321	Cory Snyder	.05
322	Darryl Strawberry	.10
323	Tim Wallach	.05
324	Steve Wilson	.05
325	Juan Bell	.05
326	Ricky Bones	.05
327	Alex Diaz	.05
328	Cal Eldred	.05
329	Darryl Hamilton	.05
330	Doug Henry	.05
331	John Jaha	.05
332	Pat Listach	.05
333	Graeme Lloyd	.05
334	Carlos Maldonado	.05
335	Angel Miranda	.05
336	Jaime Navarro	.05
337	Dave Nilsson	.05
338	Rafael Novoa	.05
339	Troy O'Leary	.05
340	Jesse Orosco	.05
341	Kevin Seitzer	.05
342	Bill Spiers	.05
343	William Suero	.05
344	B.J. Surhoff	.10
345	Dickie Thon	.05
346	Jose Valentin	.05
347	Greg Vaughn	.10
348	Robin Yount	.30
349	Willie Banks	.05
350	Bernardo Brito	.05
351	Scott Erickson	.05
352	Mark Guthrie	.05
353	Chip Hale	.05
354	Brian Harper	.05
355	Kent Hrbek	.10
356	Terry Jorgenson	.05
357	Chuck Knoblauch	.15
358	Gene Larkin	.05
359	Scott Leius	.05
360	Shane Mack	.05
361	David McCarty	.05
362	Pat Meares	.05
363	Pedro Munoz	.05
364	Derek Parks	.05
365	Kirby Puckett	.75
366	Jeff Reboulet	.10
367	Kevin Tapani	.05
368	Mike Trombley	.05
369	George Tsamis	.05
370	Carl Willis	.05
371	Dave Winfield	.20
372	Moises Alou	.10
373	Brian Barnes	.05
374	Sean Berry	.05
375	Frank Bolick	.05
376	Wil Cordero	.05
377	Delino DeShields	.05
378	Jeff Fassero	.05
379	Darren Fletcher	.05
380	Cliff Floyd	.05
381	Lou Frazier	.05
382	Marquis Grissom	.10
383	Gil Heredia	.05
384	Mike Lansing	.05
385	Oreste Marrero	.05
386	Dennis Martinez	.10
387	Curtis Pride	.10
388	Mel Rojas	.05
389	Kirk Rueter	.05
390	Joe Siddall	.05
391	John Vander Wal	.05
392	Larry Walker	.20

393	John Wetteland	.05
394	Rondell White	.10
395	Tom Bogar	.05
396	Bobby Bonilla	.10
397	Jeromy Burnitz	.05
398	Mike Draper	.05
399	Sid Fernandez	.05
400	John Franco	.05
401	Dave Gallagher	.05
402	Dwight Gooden	.10
403	Eric Hillman	.05
404	Todd Hundley	.10
405	Butch Huskey	.10
406	Jeff Innis	.05
407	Howard Johnson	.05
408	Jeff Kent	.05
409	Ced Landrum	.05
410	Mike Maddux	.05
411	Josias Manzanillo	.05
412	Jeff McKnight	.05
413	Eddie Murray	.25
414	Tito Navarro	.05
415	Joe Orsulak	.05
416	Bret Saberhagen	.05
417	Dave Telgheder	.05
418	Ryan Thompson	.05
419	Chico Walker	.05
420	Jim Abbott	.10
421	Wade Boggs	.30
422	Mike Gallego	.05
423	Mark Hutton	.05
424	Dion James	.05
425	Domingo Jean	.05
426	Pat Kelly	.05
427	Jimmy Key	.05
428	Jim Leyritz	.05
429	Kevin Maas	.05
430	Don Mattingly	1.00
431	Bobby Munoz	.05
432	Matt Nokes	.05
433	Paul O'Neill	.10
434	Spike Owen	.05
435	Melido Perez	.05
436	Lee Smith	.10
437	Andy Stankiewicz	.05
438	Mike Stanley	.05
439	Danny Tartabull	.05
440	Randy Velarde	.05
441	Bernie Williams	.35
442	Gerald Williams	.10
443	Mike Witt	.05
444	Marcos Armas	.05
445	Lance Blankenship	.05
446	Mike Bordick	.05
447	Ron Darling	.05
448	Dennis Eckersley	.10
449	Brent Gates	.05
450	Goose Gossage	.05
451	Scott Hemond	.05
452	Dave Henderson	.05
453	Shawn Hillegas	.05
454	Rick Honeycutt	.05
455	Scott Lydy	.05
456	Mark McGwire	3.00
457	Henry Mercedes	.05
458	Mike Mohler	.05
459	Troy Neel	.10
460	Edwin Nunez	.05
461	Craig Paquette	.05
462	Ruben Sierra	.05
463	Terry Steinbach	.05
464	Todd Van Poppel	.05
465	Bob Welch	.05
466	Bobby Witt	.05
467	Ruben Amaro	.05
468	Larry Anderson	.05
469	Kim Batiste	.05
470	Wes Chamberlain	.05
471	Darren Daulton	.05
472	Mariano Duncan	.05
473	Len Dykstra	.05
474	Jim Eisenreich	.05
475	Tommy Greene	.05
476	Dave Hollins	.05
477	Pete Incaviglia	.05
478	Danny Jackson	.05
479	John Kruk	.05
480	Tony Longmire	.05
481	Jeff Manto	.05
482	Mike Morandini	.05
483	Terry Mulholland	.05
484	Todd Pratt	.05
485	Ben Rivera	.05
486	Curt Schilling	.10
487	Kevin Stocker	.05
488	Milt Thompson	.05
489	David West	.05
490	Mitch Williams	.05
491	Jeff Ballard	.05
492	Jay Bell	.05
493	Scott Bullett	.05
494	Dave Clark	.05
495	Steve Cooke	.05
496	Midre Cummings	.05
497	Mark Dewey	.05
498	Carlos Garcia	.05
499	Jeff King	.05
500	Al Martin	.05
501	Lloyd McClendon	.05
502	Orlando Merced	.05
503	Blas Minor	.05
504	Denny Neagle	.05
505	Tom Prince	.05
506	Don Slaught	.05
507	Zane Smith	.05
508	Randy Tomlin	.05
509	Andy Van Slyke	.05
510	Paul Wagner	.05
511	Tim Wakefield	.05
512	Bob Walk	.05
513	John Wehner	.05
514	Kevin Young	.10
515	Billy Bean	.05
516	Andy Benes	.10
517	Derek Bell	.10
518	Doug Brocail	.05
519	Jarvis Brown	.05
520	Phil Clark	.05
521	Mark Davis	.05
522	Jeff Gardner	.05
523	Pat Gomez	.05
524	Ricky Gutierrez	.05
525	Tony Gwynn	.40
526	Gene Harris	.05
527	Kevin Higgins	.05
528	Trevor Hoffman	.10
529	Luis Lopez	.05
530	Pedro A. Martinez	.05
531	Melvin Nieves	.05
532	Phil Plantier	.05
533	Frank Seminara	.05
534	Craig Shipley	.05
535	Tim Tuefel	.05
536	Guillermo Velasquez	.05
537	Wally Whitehurst	.05
538	Rod Beck	.05
539	Todd Benzinger	.05
540	Barry Bonds	.50
541	Jeff Brantley	.05
542	Dave Burba	.05
543	John Burkett	.05
544	Will Clark	.25
545	Royce Clayton	.05
546	Brian Hickerson (Bryan)	.05
547	Mike Jackson	.05
548	Darren Lewis	.05
549	Kirt Manwaring	.05
550	Dave Martinez	.05
551	Willie McGee	.05
552	Jeff Reed	.05
553	Dave Righetti	.05
554	Kevin Rogers	.05
555	Steve Scarsone	.05
556	Bill Swift	.05
557	Robby Thompson	.05
558	Salomon Torres	.05
559	Matt Williams	.20
560	Trevor Wilson	.05
561	Rich Amaral	.05
562	Mike Blowers	.05
563	Chris Bosio	.05
564	Jay Buhner	.10
565	Norm Charlton	.05
566	Jim Converse	.05
567	Rich DeLucia	.05
568	Mike Felder	.05
569	Dave Fleming	.05
570	Ken Griffey, Jr.	3.00
571	Bill Haselman	.05
572	Dwayne Henry	.05
573	Brad Holman	.05
574	Randy Johnson	.25
575	Greg Litton	.05
576	Edgar Martinez	.10
577	Tino Martinez	.10
578	Jeff Nelson	.05
579	Mark Newfield	.05
580	Roger Salkeld	.05
581	Mackey Sasser	.05
582	Brian Turang	.05
583	Omar Vizquel	.05
584	Dave Valle	.05
585	Luis Alicea	.05
586	Rene Arocha	.05
587	Rheal Cormier	.05
588	Tripp Cromer	.05
589	Bernard Gilkey	.05
590	Lee Guetterman	.05
591	Gregg Jefferies	.10
592	Tim Jones	.05
593	Paul Kilgus	.05
594	Les Lancaster	.05
595	Omar Olivares	.05
596	Jose Oquendo	.05
597	Donovan Osborne	.05
598	Tom Pagnozzi	.05
599	Erik Pappas	.05
600	Geronimo Pena	.05
601	Mike Perez	.05
602	Gerald Perry	.05
603	Stan Royer	.05
604	Ozzie Smith	.25
605	Bob Tewksbury	.05
606	Allen Watson	.05
607	Mark Whiten	.05
608	Todd Zeile	.05
609	Jeff Bronkey	.05
610	Kevin Brown	.10
611	Jose Canseco	.25
612	Doug Dascenzo	.05
613	Butch Davis	.05
614	Mario Diaz	.05
615	Julio Franco	.05
616	Benji Gil	.05
617	Juan Gonzalez	.75
618	Tom Henke	.05
619	Jeff Huson	.05
620	David Hulse	.05
621	Craig Lefferts	.05
622	Rafael Palmeiro	.15
623	Dean Palmer	.05
624	Bob Patterson	.05
625	Roger Pavlik	.05
626	Gary Redus	.05
627	Ivan Rodriguez	.40
628	Kenny Rogers	.05
629	Jon Shave	.05
630	Doug Strange	.05
631	Matt Whiteside	.05
632	Roberto Alomar	.50
633	Pat Borders	.05
634	Scott Brow	.05
635	Rob Butler	.05
636	Joe Carter	.10
637	Tony Castillo	.05
638	Mark Eichhorn	.05
639	Tony Fernandez	.05
640	*Huck Flener*	.05
641	Alfredo Griffin	.05
642	Juan Guzman	.05
643	Rickey Henderson	.25
644	Pat Hentgen	.05
645	Randy Knorr	.05
646	Al Leiter	.10
647	Dominigo Martinez	.05
648	Paul Molitor	.40
649	Jack Morris	.05
650	John Olerud	.15
651	Ed Sprague	.05
652	Dave Stewart	.05
653	Devon White	.10
654	Woody Williams	.05
655	Barry Bonds (MVP)	.40
656	Greg Maddux (CY)	.75
657	Jack McDowell (CY)	.05
658	Mike Piazza (ROY)	.75
659	Tim Salmon (ROY)	.25
660	Frank Thomas (MVP)	1.00

1994 Pacific Crown All Latino All-Star Team

Latino All-Stars is the theme of the third insert set found randomly packed in Pacific Spanish for 1994. Cards feature a player action photo on front, with a gold foil pinstripe around the sides and top. The player's name appears in gold script at bottom and there is a baseball logo in the corner. On backs a portrait photo of the player is set against a background of his native flag. Season highlights of 1993 are presented in English and Spanish. Eight thousand sets were produced.

		MT
Complete Set (20):		13.00
Common Player:		.50
1	Benito Santiago	.50
2	Dave Magadan	.50
3	Andres Galarraga	.75
4	Luis Gonzalez	.50
5	Jose Offerman	.50
6	Bobby Bonilla	.60
7	Dennis Martinez	.50
8	Mariano Duncan	.50
9	Orlando Merced	.50
10	Jose Rijo	.50
11	Danny Tartabull	.50
12	Ruben Sierra	.50
13	Ivan Rodriguez	2.00
14	Juan Gonzalez	4.00
15	Jose Canseco	1.50
16	Rafael Palmeiro	1.00
17	Roberto Alomar	2.00
18	Eduardo Perez	.50
19	Alex Fernandez	.50
20	Omar Vizquel	.60

1994 Pacific Crown Homerun Leaders

A gold prismatic background behind a color action player photo is the featured design on this Pacific insert set. Backs have another player photo against a ballfield backdrop. A huge baseball is overprinted with the player's name and number of 1993 homers. A league designation is among the logos featured on back. A total of 8,000 of these inserts sets was the announced production.

		MT
Complete Set (20):		30.00
Common Player:		1.00
1	Juan Gonzalez	2.50
2	Ken Griffey, Jr.	7.50
3	Frank Thomas	3.00
4	Albert Belle	2.50
5	Rafael Palmeiro	1.50
6	Joe Carter	1.50
7	Dean Palmer	1.00
8	Mickey Tettleton	1.00
9	Tim Salmon	1.50
10	Danny Tartabull	1.00
11	Barry Bonds	2.50
12	Dave Justice	2.00
13	Matt Williams	1.50
14	Fred McGriff	1.50
15	Ron Gant	1.00
16	Mike Piazza	4.50
17	Bobby Bonilla	1.00
18	Phil Plantier	1.00
19	Sammy Sosa	5.00
20	Rick Wilkins	1.00

1994 Pacific Crown Jewels of the Crown

One of three inserts into 1994 Pacific Spanish foil packs. The design features a player action photo set against a silver prismatic background. On back is another color player photo against a background of colored silk and a large jewel. Season highlight stats and awards won are presented in both English and Spanish. The announced production run of these inserts was 8,000 sets.

		MT
Complete Set (36):		60.00
Common Player:		1.00
1	Robin Yount	2.00
2	Juan Gonzalez	4.00
3	Rafael Palmeiro	1.50
4	Paul Molitor	2.50
5	Roberto Alomar	2.50
6	John Olerud	1.50
7	Randy Johnson	2.50
8	Ken Griffey, Jr.	9.00
9	Wade Boggs	2.50
10	Don Mattingly	4.00
11	Kirby Puckett	4.00
12	Tim Salmon	2.00
13	Frank Thomas	4.00
14	Fernando Valenzuela (Comeback Player)	1.00
15	Cal Ripken, Jr.	7.50
16	Carlos Baerga	1.00
17	Kenny Lofton	3.00
18	Cecil Fielder	1.00
19	John Burkett	1.00
20	Andres Galarraga (Comeback Player)	1.00
21	Charlie Hayes	1.00
22	Orestes Destrade	1.00
23	Jeff Conine	1.00
24	Jeff Bagwell	3.00
25	Mark Grace	1.50
26	Ryne Sandberg	2.50
27	Gregg Jefferies	1.00
28	Barry Bonds	2.50
29	Mike Piazza	6.00
30	Greg Maddux	5.00
31	Darren Daulton	1.00
32	John Kruk	1.00
33	Len Dykstra	1.00
34	Orlando Merced	1.00
35	Tony Gwynn	4.50
36	Robby Thompson	1.00

1994 Pacific Crown Jewels of the Crown - Retail

Using the same design, photos, graphics and card numbers, the retail version of the Jewels of the Crown insert set varies only in the silver prismatic foil background on front. While the scarcer hobby version has a diamond-shaped pattern to the foil, the retail version has numerous circles as a background pattern. The retail cards were inserted one per pack of retail product and are thus much more common than the hobby version.

		MT
Complete Set (36):		60.00
Common Player:		1.00
1	Robin Yount	2.00
2	Juan Gonzalez	3.00
3	Rafael Palmeiro	2.00
4	Paul Molitor	2.00
5	Roberto Alomar	2.50
6	John Olerud	1.50
7	Randy Johnson	2.00
8	Ken Griffey, Jr.	9.00
9	Wade Boggs	2.00
10	Don Mattingly	4.00
11	Kirby Puckett	4.00
12	Tim Salmon	1.50
13	Frank Thomas	5.00
14	Fernando Valenzuela (Comeback Player)	1.00
15	Cal Ripken, Jr.	7.50
16	Carlos Baerga	1.00
17	Kenny Lofton	1.50
18	Cecil Fielder	1.00
19	John Burkett	1.00
20	Andres Galarraga (Comeback Player)	1.00
21	Charlie Hayes	1.00
22	Orestes Destrade	1.00
23	Jeff Conine	1.00
24	Jeff Bagwell	3.00
25	Mark Grace	1.50
26	Ryne Sandberg	2.50
27	Gregg Jefferies	1.00
28	Barry Bonds	2.50
29	Mike Piazza	6.00
30	Greg Maddux	5.00
31	Darren Daulton	1.00
32	John Kruk	1.00
33	Len Dykstra	1.00
34	Orlando Merced	1.00
35	Tony Gwynn	4.50
36	Robby Thompson	1.00

1995 Pacific

The base cards in Pacific's Crown Collection baseball issue for 1995 feature borderless color action photos on front, graphically highlighted by the player name at bottom in gold foil and a color team logo in a baseball at lower-left. Backs have a playing field design in the background with a portrait photo at left. At right are 1994 stats, career highlights and a ghosted image of the team logo. Most back printing is in both English and Spanish. The 450 cards in the series are arranged alphabetically within team, with the teams arranged in city-alpha order. Several chase cards series are found in the 12-card foil packs.

		MT
Complete Set (450):		22.00
Common Player:		.05
Pack (12):		2.00
Wax Box (36):		60.00
1	Steve Avery	.05
2	Rafael Belliard	.05
3	Jeff Blauser	.05
4	Tom Glavine	.10
5	Dave Justice	.35
6	Mike Kelly	.05
7	Roberto Kelly	.05
8	Ryan Klesko	.20
9	Mark Lemke	.05
10	Javier Lopez	.15
11	Greg Maddux	1.50
12	Fred McGriff	.25
13	Greg McMichael	.05
14	Jose Oliva	.05
15	John Smoltz	.10
16	Tony Tarasco	.05
17	Brady Anderson	.10
18	Harold Baines	.05
19	Armando Benitez	.05
20	Mike Devereaux	.05
21	Leo Gomez	.05
22	Jeffrey Hammonds	.05
23	Chris Hoiles	.05
24	Ben McDonald	.05
25	Mark McLemore	.05
26	Jamie Moyer	.05
27	Mike Mussina	.20
28	Rafael Palmeiro	.15
29	Jim Poole	.05
30	Cal Ripken Jr.	2.50
31	Lee Smith	.05
32	Mark Smith	.05
33	Jose Canseco	.30
34	Roger Clemens	.60
35	Scott Cooper	.05
36	Andre Dawson	.10
37	Tony Fossas	.05
38	Mike Greenwell	.05
39	Chris Howard	.05
40	Jose Melendez	.05
41	Nate Minchey	.05
42	Tim Naehring	.05
43	Otis Nixon	.05
44	Carlos Rodriguez	.05
45	Aaron Sele	.05
46	Lee Tinsley	.05
47	Sergio Valdez	.05
48	John Valentin	.05
49	Mo Vaughn	.50
50	Brian Anderson	.05
51	Garret Anderson	.05
52	Rod Correia	.05
53	Chad Curtis	.05
54	Mark Dalesandro	.05
55	Chili Davis	.05
56	Gary DiSarcina	.05
57	Damion Easley	.05
58	Jim Edmonds	.10
59	Jorge Fabregas	.05
60	Chuck Finley	.05
61	Bo Jackson	.10
62	Mark Langston	.05
63	Eduardo Perez	.05
64	Tim Salmon	.15
65	J.T. Snow	.10
66	Willie Banks	.05
67	Jose Bautista	.05
68	Shawon Dunston	.05
69	Kevin Foster	.05
70	Mark Grace	.20
71	Jose Guzman	.05
72	Jose Hernandez	.05
73	Blaise Ilsley	.05
74	Derrick May	.05
75	Randy Myers	.05
76	Karl Rhodes	.05
77	Kevin Roberson	.05
78	Rey Sanchez	.05
79	Sammy Sosa	1.00
80	Steve Trachsel	.05
81	Eddie Zambrano	.05
82	Wilson Alvarez	.05
83	Jason Bere	.05
84	Joey Cora	.05
85	Jose DeLeon	.05
86	Alex Fernandez	.05
87	Julio Franco	.05
88	Ozzie Guillen	.05
89	Joe Hall	.05
90	Roberto Hernandez	.05
91	Darrin Jackson	.05
92	Lance Johnson	.05
93	Norberto Martin	.05
94	Jack McDowell	.05
95	Tim Raines	.10
96	Olmedo Saenz	.05
97	Frank Thomas	1.00
98	Robin Ventura	.10
99	Bret Boone	.05
100	Jeff Brantley	.05
101	Jacob Brumfield	.05
102	Hector Carrasco	.05
103	Brian Dorsett	.05
104	Tony Fernandez	.05
105	Willie Greene	.05
106	Erik Hanson	.05
107	Kevin Jarvis	.05
108	Barry Larkin	.15
109	Kevin Mitchell	.05
110	Hal Morris	.05
111	Jose Rijo	.05
112	Johnny Ruffin	.05
113	Deion Sanders	.15
114	Reggie Sanders	.05
115	Sandy Alomar Jr.	.10
116	Ruben Amaro	.05
117	Carlos Baerga	.05
118	Albert Belle	.60
119	Alvaro Espinoza	.05
120	Rene Gonzales	.05
121	Wayne Kirby	.05
122	Kenny Lofton	.45
123	Candy Maldonado	.05
124	Dennis Martinez	.05

125	Eddie Murray	.25
126	Charles Nagy	.05
127	Tony Pena	.05
128	Manny Ramirez	.50
129	Paul Sorrento	.05
130	Jim Thome	.20
131	Omar Vizquel	.05
132	Dante Bichette	.25
133	Ellis Burks	.10
134	Vinny Castilla	.10
135	Marvin Freeman	.05
136	Andres Galarraga	.10
137	Joe Girardi	.05
138	Charlie Hayes	.05
139	Mike Kingery	.05
140	Nelson Liriano	.05
141	Roberto Mejia	.05
142	David Nied	.05
143	Steve Reed	.05
144	Armando Reynoso	.05
145	Bruce Ruffin	.05
146	John Vander Wal	.05
147	Walt Weiss	.05
148	Skeeter Barnes	.05
149	Tim Belcher	.05
150	Junior Felix	.05
151	Cecil Fielder	.10
152	Travis Fryman	.10
153	Kirk Gibson	.05
154	Chris Gomez	.05
155	Buddy Groom	.05
156	Chad Kreuter	.05
157	Mike Moore	.05
158	Tony Phillips	.05
159	Juan Samuel	.05
160	Mickey Tettleton	.05
161	Alan Trammell	.10
162	David Wells	.10
163	Lou Whitaker	.05
164	Kurt Abbott	.05
165	Luis Aquino	.05
166	Alex Arias	.05
167	Bret Barberie	.05
168	Jerry Browne	.05
169	Chuck Carr	.05
170	Matias Carrillo	.05
171	Greg Colbrunn	.05
172	Jeff Conine	.05
173	Carl Everett	.05
174	Robb Nen	.05
175	Yorkis Perez	.05
176	Pat Rapp	.05
177	Benito Santiago	.05
178	Gary Sheffield	.15
179	Darrell Whitmore	.05
180	Jeff Bagwell	.75
181	Kevin Bass	.05
182	Craig Biggio	.10
183	Andujar Cedeno	.05
184	Doug Drabek	.05
185	Tony Eusebio	.05
186	Steve Finley	.05
187	Luis Gonzalez	.05
188	Pete Harnisch	.05
189	John Hudek	.05
190	Orlando Miller	.05
191	James Mouton	.05
192	Roberto Petagine	.05
193	Shane Reynolds	.05
194	Greg Swindell	.05
195	Dave Veres	.05
196	Kevin Appier	.05
197	Stan Belinda	.05
198	Vince Coleman	.05
199	David Cone	.10
200	Gary Gaetti	.05
201	Greg Gagne	.05
202	Mark Gubicza	.05
203	Bob Hamelin	.05
204	Dave Henderson	.05
205	Felix Jose	.05
206	Wally Joyner	.05
207	Jose Lind	.05
208	Mike Macfarlane	.05
209	Brian McRae	.05
210	Jeff Montgomery	.05
211	Hipolito Pichardo	.05
212	Pedro Astacio	.05
213	Brett Butler	.10
214	Omar Daal	.05
215	Delino DeShields	.05
216	Darren Dreifort	.05
217	Carlos Hernandez	.05
218	Orel Hershiser	.05
219	Garey Ingram	.05
220	Eric Karros	.10
221	Ramon Martinez	.10
222	Raul Mondesi	.50
223	Jose Offerman	.05
224	Mike Piazza	1.50
225	Henry Rodriguez	.05
226	Ismael Valdes	.10
227	Tim Wallach	.05
228	Jeff Cirillo	.05
229	Alex Diaz	.05
230	Cal Eldred	.05
231	Mike Fetters	.05
232	Brian Harper	.05
233	Ted Higuera	.05
234	John Jaha	.05
235	Graeme Lloyd	.05
236	Jose Mercedes	.05
237	Jaime Navarro	.05
238	Dave Nilsson	.05
239	Jesse Orosco	.05
240	Jody Reed	.05
241	Jose Valentin	.05
242	Greg Vaughn	.10
243	Turner Ward	.05
244	Rick Aguilera	.05
245	Rich Becker	.05
246	Jim Deshaies	.05
247	Steve Dunn	.05
248	Scott Erickson	.05
249	Kent Hrbek	.05
250	Chuck Knoblauch	.15
251	Scott Leius	.05
252	David McCarty	.05
253	Pat Meares	.05
254	Pedro Munoz	.05
255	Kirby Puckett	.75
256	Carlos Pulido	.05
257	Kevin Tapani	.05
258	Matt Walbeck	.05
259	Dave Winfield	.15
260	Moises Alou	.10
261	Juan Bell	.05
262	Freddie Benavides	.05
263	Sean Berry	.05
264	Wil Cordero	.05
265	Jeff Fassero	.05
266	Darrin Fletcher	.05
267	Cliff Floyd	.05
268	Marquis Grissom	.05
269	Gil Heredia	.05
270	Ken Hill	.05
271	Pedro Martinez	.15
272	Mel Rojas	.05
273	Larry Walker	.25
274	John Wetteland	.05
275	Rondell White	.15
276	Tim Bogar	.05
277	Bobby Bonilla	.10
278	Rico Brogna	.05
279	Jeromy Burnitz	.05
280	John Franco	.05
281	Eric Hillman	.05
282	Todd Hundley	.10
283	Jeff Kent	.05
284	Mike Maddux	.05
285	Joe Orsulak	.05
286	Luis Rivera	.05
287	Bret Saberhagen	.05
288	David Segui	.05
289	Ryan Thompson	.05
290	Fernando Vina	.05
291	Jose Vizcaino	.05
292	Jim Abbott	.05
293	Wade Boggs	.25
294	Russ Davis	.05
295	Mike Gallego	.05
296	Xavier Hernandez	.05
297	Steve Howe	.05
298	Jimmy Key	.05
299	Don Mattingly	.75
300	Terry Mulholland	.05
301	Paul O'Neill	.10
302	Luis Polonia	.05
303	Mike Stanley	.05
304	Danny Tartabull	.05
305	Randy Velarde	.05
306	Bob Wickman	.05
307	Bernie Williams	.35
308	Mark Acre	.05
309	Geronimo Berroa	.05
310	Mike Bordick	.05
311	Dennis Eckersley	.05
312	Rickey Henderson	.20
313	Stan Javier	.05
314	Miguel Jimenez	.05
315	Francisco Matos	.05
316	Mark McGwire	3.00
317	Troy Neel	.05
318	Steve Ontiveros	.05
319	Carlos Reyes	.05
320	Ruben Sierra	.05
321	Terry Steinbach	.05
322	Bob Welch	.05
323	Bobby Witt	.05
324	Larry Andersen	.05
325	Kim Batiste	.05
326	Darren Daulton	.05
327	Mariano Duncan	.05
328	Lenny Dykstra	.05
329	Jim Eisenreich	.05
330	Danny Jackson	.05
331	John Kruk	.05
332	Tony Longmire	.05
333	Tom Marsh	.05
334	Mickey Morandini	.05
335	Bobby Munoz	.05
336	Todd Pratt	.05
337	Tom Quinlan	.05
338	Kevin Stocker	.05
339	Fernando Valenzuela	.05
340	Jay Bell	.05
341	Dave Clark	.05
342	Steve Cooke	.05
343	Carlos Garcia	.05
344	Jeff King	.05
345	Jon Lieber	.05
346	Ravelo Manzanillo	.05
347	Al Martin	.05
348	Orlando Merced	.05
349	Denny Neagle	.05
350	Alejandro Pena	.05
351	Don Slaught	.05
352	Zane Smith	.05
353	Andy Van Slyke	.05
354	Rick White	.05
355	Kevin Young	.05
356	Andy Ashby	.05
357	Derek Bell	.10
358	Andy Benes	.10
359	Phil Clark	.05
360	Donnie Elliott	.05
361	Ricky Gutierrez	.05
362	Tony Gwynn	.50
363	Trevor Hoffman	.10
364	Tim Hyers	.05
365	Luis Lopez	.05
366	Jose Martinez	.05
367	Pedro A. Martinez	.05
368	Phil Plantier	.05
369	Bip Roberts	.05
370	A.J. Sager	.05
371	Jeff Tabaka	.05
372	Todd Benzinger	.05
373	Barry Bonds	.50
374	John Burkett	.05
375	Mark Carreon	.05
376	Royce Clayton	.05
377	Pat Gomez	.05
378	Erik Johnson	.05
379	Darren Lewis	.05
380	Kirt Manwaring	.05
381	Dave Martinez	.05
382	John Patterson	.05
383	Mark Portugal	.05
384	Darryl Strawberry	.10
385	Salomon Torres	.05
386	Bill Van Landingham	.05
387	Matt Williams	.20
388	Rich Amaral	.05
389	Bobby Ayala	.05
390	Mike Blowers	.05
391	Chris Bosio	.05
392	Jay Buhner	.10
393	Jim Converse	.05
394	Tim Davis	.05
395	Felix Fermin	.05
396	Dave Fleming	.05
397	Goose Gossage	.05
398	Ken Griffey Jr.	3.00
399	Randy Johnson	.25
400	Edgar Martinez	.05
401	Tino Martinez	.10
402	Alex Rodriguez	3.00
403	Dan Wilson	.05
404	Luis Alicea	.05
405	Rene Arocha	.05
406	Bernard Gilkey	.05
407	Gregg Jefferies	.05
408	Ray Lankford	.10
409	Terry McGriff	.05
410	Omar Olivares	.05
411	Jose Oquendo	.05
412	Vicente Palacios	.05
413	Geronimo Pena	.05
414	Mike Perez	.05
415	Gerald Perry	.05
416	Ozzie Smith	.35
417	Bob Tewksbury	.05
418	Mark Whiten	.05
419	Todd Zeile	.05
420	Esteban Beltre	.05
421	Kevin Brown	.10
422	Cris Carpenter	.05
423	Will Clark	.25
424	Hector Fajardo	.05
425	Jeff Frye	.05
426	Juan Gonzalez	.50
427	Rusty Greer	.05
428	Rick Honeycutt	.05
429	David Hulse	.05
430	Manny Lee	.05
431	Junior Ortiz	.05
432	Dean Palmer	.05
433	Ivan Rodriguez	.45
434	Dan Smith	.05
435	Roberto Alomar	.50
436	Pat Borders	.05
437	Scott Brow	.05
438	Rob Butler	.05
439	Joe Carter	.10
440	Tony Castillo	.05
441	Domingo Cedeno	.05
442	Brad Cornett	.05
443	Carlos Delgado	.20
444	Alex Gonzalez	.10
445	Juan Guzman	.05
446	Darren Hall	.05
447	Paul Molitor	.25
448	John Olerud	.10
449	Robert Perez	.05
450	Devon White	.05

1995 Pacific Gold Crown Die-cut

A die-cut gold holographic foil crown in the background is featured in this chase set. The player's name at bottom is rendered in the same foil. Backs have a dark blue background, a portrait photo and a 1994 season recap.

		MT
Complete Set (20):		125.00
Common Player:		1.50
1	Greg Maddux	12.50
2	Fred McGriff	2.50
3	Rafael Palmeiro	2.50
4	Cal Ripken Jr.	16.00
5	Jose Canseco	2.50
6	Frank Thomas	6.00
7	Albert Belle	5.00
8	Manny Ramirez	5.00
9	Andres Galarraga	1.50
10	Jeff Bagwell	7.50
11	Chan Ho Park	1.50
12	Raul Mondesi	2.00
13	Mike Piazza	12.50
14	Kirby Puckett	7.50
15	Barry Bonds	5.00
16	Ken Griffey Jr.	20.00
17	Alex Rodriguez	18.00

18	Juan Gonzalez	5.00
19	Roberto Alomar	4.00
20	Carlos Delgado	1.50

1995 Pacific Hot Hispanics

Acknowledging its bilingual card license and market niche, this insert set of Latinos Destacados (Hot Hispanics) features top Latin players in the majors. The series logo and a gold-foil holographic player name rise from a row of flames at bottom-front. On the reverse is another player photo, on an inferno background, along with 1994 season highlights and a large team logo.

		MT
Complete Set (36):		45.00
Common Player:		1.25
1	Roberto Alomar	5.00
2	Moises Alou	1.50
3	Wilson Alvarez	1.25
4	Carlos Baerga	1.25
5	Geronimo Berroa	1.25
6	Jose Canseco	3.00
7	Hector Carrasco	1.25
8	Wil Cordero	1.25
9	Carlos Delgado	1.50
10	Damion Easley	1.25
11	Tony Eusebio	1.25
12	Hector Fajardo	1.25
13	Andres Galarraga	2.00
14	Carlos Garcia	1.25
15	Chris Gomez	1.25
16	Alex Gonzalez	1.25
17	Juan Gonzalez	5.00
18	Luis Gonzalez	1.25
19	Felix Jose	1.25
20	Javier Lopez	2.00
21	Luis Lopez	1.25
22	Dennis Martinez	1.25
23	Orlando Miller	1.25
24	Raul Mondesi	2.00
25	Jose Oliva	1.25
26	Rafael Palmeiro	2.00
27	Yorkis Perez	1.25
28	Manny Ramirez	8.00
29	Jose Rijo	1.25
30	Alex Rodriguez	15.00
31	Ivan Rodriguez	5.00
32	Carlos Rodriguez	1.25
33	Sammy Sosa	10.00
34	Tony Tarasco	1.25
35	Ismael Valdes	1.25
36	Bernie Williams	4.00

1995 Pacific Marquee Prism

Etched gold holographic foil is the background to the action photos in this insert set. Player names at bottom-front are shadowed in team colors. Backs repeat the front photo in miniature version in a box at one side that offers career stats and a highlight. On the other end is a portrait photo on a background of baseballs.

		MT
Complete Set (36):		125.00
Common Player:		1.50
1	Jose Canseco	2.50
2	Gregg Jefferies	1.50
3	Fred McGriff	2.00
4	Joe Carter	2.00
5	Tim Salmon	2.50
6	Wade Boggs	4.00
7	Dave Winfield	2.50
8	Bob Hamelin	1.50
9	Cal Ripken Jr.	15.00
10	Don Mattingly	8.00
11	Juan Gonzalez	5.00
12	Carlos Delgado	1.75
13	Barry Bonds	7.50
14	Albert Belle	6.00
15	Raul Mondesi	3.00
16	Jeff Bagwell	8.00
17	Mike Piazza	10.00
18	Rafael Palmeiro	2.50
19	Frank Thomas	8.00
20	Matt Williams	2.50
21	Ken Griffey Jr.	20.00
22	Will Clark	3.00
23	Bobby Bonilla	1.50
24	Kenny Lofton	5.00
25	Paul Molitor	6.00
26	Kirby Puckett	8.00
27	Dave Justice	2.00
28	Jeff Conine	1.50
29	Bret Boone	1.50
30	Larry Walker	2.50
31	Cecil Fielder	1.50
32	Manny Ramirez	7.50
33	Javier Lopez	2.00
34	Jimmy Key	1.50
35	Andres Galarraga	2.00
36	Tony Gwynn	8.00

1995 Pacific Prism

The rainbow prismatic foil which is the background ot the action photos on the card fronts provides the visual punch to Pacific's premium brand cards. In a throwback to the 1950s, the cards were sold in single-card packs for $1.75. Production was limited to 2,999 cases of 36-pack boxes. Backs have a large portrait photo on a conventionally printed rainbow background. In keeping with the company's license, the 1994 season summary printed at bottom on back is in both English and Spanish. One checklist, team or Pacific logo was inserted into each pack to protect the Prism card.

		MT
Complete Set (144):		150.00
Common Player:		.50
Pack (2):		1.50
Wax Box (36):		48.00
1	Dave Justice	1.00
2	Ryan Klesko	1.00
3	Javier Lopez	.75
4	Greg Maddux	10.00
5	Fred McGriff	1.00
6	Tony Tarasco	.50
7	Jeffrey Hammonds	.50
8	Mike Mussina	1.50
9	Rafael Palmeiro	.75
10	Cal Ripken Jr.	12.00
11	Lee Smith	.50
12	Roger Clemens	2.50
13	Scott Cooper	.50
14	Mike Greenwell	.50
15	Carlos Rodriguez	.50
16	Mo Vaughn	4.00
17	Chili Davis	.50
18	Jim Edmonds	.50
19	Jorge Fabregas	.50
20	Bo Jackson	.60
21	Tim Salmon	.60
22	Mark Grace	.75
23	Jose Guzman	.50
24	Randy Myers	.50
25	Rey Sanchez	.50
26	Sammy Sosa	8.00
27	Wilson Alvarez	.50
28	Julio Franco	.50
29	Ozzie Guillen	.50
30	Jack McDowell	.50
31	Frank Thomas	6.00
32	Bret Boone	.50
33	Barry Larkin	1.00
34	Hal Morris	.50
35	Jose Rijo	.50
36	Deion Sanders	1.50
37	Carlos Baerga	.50
38	Albert Belle	4.00
39	Kenny Lofton	2.00
40	Dennis Martinez	.50
41	Manny Ramirez	4.00
42	Omar Vizquel	.50
43	Dante Bichette	1.00
44	Marvin Freeman	.50
45	Andres Galarraga	.60
46	Mike Kingery	.50
47	Danny Bautista	.50
48	Cecil Fielder	.50
49	Travis Fryman	.50
50	Tony Phillips	.50
51	Alan Trammell	.50
52	Lou Whitaker	.50
53	Alex Arias	.50
54	Bret Barberie	.50
55	Jeff Conine	.50
56	Charles Johnson	.50
57	Gary Sheffield	3.00
58	Jeff Bagwell	6.00
59	Craig Biggio	.50
60	Doug Drabek	.50
61	Tony Eusebio	.50
62	Luis Gonzalez	.50
63	David Cone	.60
64	Bob Hamelin	.50
65	Felix Jose	.50
66	Wally Joyner	.50
67	Brian McRae	.50
68	Brett Butler	.50
69	Garey Ingram	.50
70	Ramon Martinez	.50
71	Raul Mondesi	1.00
72	Mike Piazza	10.00
73	Henry Rodriguez	.50
74	Ricky Bones	.50
75	Pat Listach	.50
76	Dave Nilsson	.50
77	Jose Valentin	.50
78	Rick Aguilera	.50
79	Denny Hocking	.50
80	Shane Mack	.50
81	Pedro Munoz	.50
82	Kirby Puckett	6.00
83	Dave Winfield	.75
84	Moises Alou	.60
85	Wil Cordero	.50
86	Cliff Floyd	.50
87	Marquis Grissom	.50
88	Pedro Martinez	.75
89	Larry Walker	.75
90	Bobby Bonilla	.50
91	Jeremy Burnitz	.50
92	John Franco	.50
93	Jeff Kent	.50
94	Jose Vizcaino	.50
95	Wade Boggs	1.50
96	Jimmy Key	.50
97	Don Mattingly	7.00
98	Paul O'Neill	.60
99	Luis Polonia	.50
100	Danny Tartabull	.50
101	Geronimo Berroa	.50
102	Rickey Henderson	.75
103	Ruben Sierra	.50
104	Terry Steinbach	.50
105	Darren Daulton	.50
106	Mariano Duncan	.50
107	Lenny Dykstra	.50
108	Mike Lieberthal	.50
109	Tony Longmire	.50
110	Tom Marsh	.50
111	Jay Bell	.50
112	Carlos Garcia	.50
113	Orlando Merced	.50
114	Andy Van Slyke	.50
115	Derek Bell	.50
116	Tony Gwynn	6.00
117	Luis Lopez	.50
118	Bip Roberts	.50
119	Rod Beck	.50
120	Barry Bonds	5.00
121	Darryl Strawberry	.60
122	Bill Van Landingham	.50
123	Matt Williams	1.00
124	Jay Buhner	.50
125	Felix Fermin	.50
126	Ken Griffey Jr.	15.00
127	Randy Johnson	1.00
128	Edgar Martinez	.50
129	Alex Rodriguez	15.00
130	Rene Arocha	.50
131	Gregg Jefferies	.50
132	Mike Perez	.50
133	Ozzie Smith	3.00
134	Jose Canseco	.75
135	Will Clark	.75
136	Juan Gonzalez	4.00
137	Ivan Rodriguez	3.00
138	Roberto Alomar	3.00
139	Joe Carter	.50
140	Carlos Delgado	.50
141	Alex Gonzalez	.50
142	Juan Guzman	.50
143	Paul Molitor	2.00
144	John Olerud	.65

1995 Pacific Prism Team Logos

Inserted one card per pack to provide some protection to the Prism card was a checklist, team or Pacific logo card. The large color logos are on a background of a playing field. Backs have a short English/Spanish history of the team.

		MT
Complete Set (31):		2.00
Common Player:		.10
1	Baltimore Orioles	.10
2	Boston Red Sox	.10
3	California Angels	.10
4	Chicago White Sox	.10
5	Cleveland Indians	.10
6	Detroit Tigers	.10
7	Kansas City Royals	.10
8	Milwaukee Brewers	.10
9	Minnesota Twins	.10
10	New York Yankees	.10
11	Oakland Athletics	.10
12	Seattle Mariners	.10
13	Texas Rangers	.10
14	Toronto Blue Jays	.10
15	Atlanta Braves	.10
16	Chicago Cubs	.10
17	Cincinnati Reds	.10
18	Colorado Rockies	.10
19	Florida Marlins	.10
20	Houston Astros	.10
21	Los Angeles Dodgers	.10
22	Montreal Expos	.10
23	New York Mets	.10
24	Philadelphia Phillies	.10
25	Pittsburgh Pirates	.10
26	St. Louis Cardinals	.10
27	San Diego Padres	.10
28	San Francisco Giants	.10
1	Checklist 1-72	.05
2	Checklist 73-144	.05
---	Pacific logo card	.05

1996 Pacific Crown Collection

Pacific's base set for 1996 features 450 gold-foil enhanced cards. Fronts have borderless game-action photos with the issuer's logo in an upper corner and the player's name at bottom center in gold. Horizontal backs have a portrait photo at right, career highlights in both English and Spanish at left, and 1995 stats at top. Cards were sold in 12-card foil packs which could include one of six types of insert cards.

		MT
Complete Set (450):		30.00
Common Player:		.05
Pack (12):		2.00
Wax Box (36):		45.00
1	Steve Avery	.05
2	Ryan Klesko	.20
3	Pedro Borbon	.05
4	Chipper Jones	2.00
5	Kent Mercker	.05
6	Greg Maddux	2.00
7	Greg McMichael	.05
8	Mark Wohlers	.05
9	Fred McGriff	.20
10	John Smoltz	.20
11	Rafael Belliard	.05
12	Mark Lemke	.05
13	Tom Glavine	.15
14	Javier Lopez	.15
15	Jeff Blauser	.05
16	Dave Justice	.25
17	Marquis Grissom	.05
18	Greg Maddux (NL Cy Young)	1.00
19	Randy Myers	.05
20	Scott Servais	.05
21	Sammy Sosa	1.50
22	Kevin Foster	.05
23	Jose Hernandez	.05
24	Jim Bullinger	.05
25	Mike Perez	.05
26	Shawon Dunston	.05
27	Rey Sanchez	.05
28	Frank Castillo	.05
29	Jaime Navarro	.05
30	Brian McRae	.05
31	Mark Grace	.15
32	Roberto Rivera	.05
33	Luis Gonzalez	.05
34	Hector Carrasco	.05
35	Bret Boone	.05
36	Thomas Howard	.05
37	Hal Morris	.05
38	John Smiley	.05
39	Jeff Brantley	.05
40	Barry Larkin	.15
41	Mariano Duncan	.05
42	Xavier Hernandez	.05
43	Pete Schourek	.05
44	Reggie Sanders	.05
45	Dave Burba	.05
46	Jeff Branson	.05
47	Mark Portugal	.05
48	Ron Gant	.10
49	Benito Santiago	.05
50	Barry Larkin (NL MVP)	.05
51	Steve Reed	.05
52	Kevin Ritz	.05
53	Dante Bichette	.20
54	Darren Holmes	.05
55	Ellis Burks	.05
56	Walt Weiss	.05
57	Armando Reynoso	.05
58	Vinny Castilla	.05
59	Jason Bates	.05
60	Mike Kingery	.05
61	Bryan Rekar	.05
62	Curtis Leskanic	.05
63	Bret Saberhagen	.05
64	Andres Galarraga	.10
65	Larry Walker	.25
66	Joe Girardi	.05
67	Quilvio Veras	.05
68	Robb Nen	.05
69	Mario Diaz	.05
70	Chuck Carr	.05
71	Alex Arias	.05
72	Pat Rapp	.05
73	Rich Garces	.05
74	Kurt Abbott	.05
75	Andre Dawson	.10
76	Greg Colbrunn	.05
77	John Burkett	.05
78	Terry Pendleton	.05
79	Jesus Tavarez	.05
80	Charles Johnson	.10
81	Yorkis Perez	.05
82	Jeff Conine	.05
83	Gary Sheffield	.35
84	Brian Hunter	.05
85	Derrick May	.05
86	Greg Swindell	.05
87	Derek Bell	.05
88	Dave Veres	.05
89	Jeff Bagwell	.75
90	Todd Jones	.05
91	Orlando Miller	.05
92	Pedro A. Martinez	.05
93	Tony Eusebio	.05
94	Craig Biggio	.15
95	Shane Reynolds	.05
96	James Mouton	.05
97	Doug Drabek	.05
98	Dave Magadan	.05
99	Ricky Gutierrez	.05
100	Hideo Nomo	.50
101	Delino DeShields	.05
102	Tom Candiotti	.05
103	Mike Piazza	2.00
104	Ramon Martinez	.10
105	Pedro Astacio	.05
106	Chad Fonville	.05
107	Raul Mondesi	.20
108	Ismael Valdes	.05
109	Jose Offerman	.05
110	Todd Worrell	.05
111	Eric Karros	.10
112	Brett Butler	.05
113	Juan Castro	.05
114	Roberto Kelly	.05
115	Omar Daal	.05
116	Antonio Osuna	.05
117	Hideo Nomo (NL Rookie of Year)	.25
118	Mike Lansing	.05
119	Mel Rojas	.05
120	Sean Berry	.05
121	David Segui	.05
122	Tavo Alvarez	.05
123	Pedro Martinez	.15
124	*F.P. Santangelo*	.10
125	Rondell White	.10
126	Cliff Floyd	.05
127	Henry Rodriguez	.05
128	Tony Tarasco	.05
129	Yamil Benitez	.05
130	Carlos Perez	.05
131	Wil Cordero	.05
132	Jeff Fassero	.05
133	Moises Alou	.10
134	John Franco	.05
135	Rico Brogna	.05
136	Dave Mlicki	.05
137	Bill Pulsipher	.05
138	Jose Vizcaino	.05
139	Carl Everett	.05
140	Edgardo Alfonzo	.10
141	Bobby Jones	.05
142	Alberto Castillo	.05
143	Joe Orsulak	.05
144	Jeff Kent	.05
145	Ryan Thompson	.05
146	Jason Isringhausen	.05
147	Todd Hundley	.15
148	Alex Ochoa	.05
149	Charlie Hayes	.05
150	Michael Mimbs	.05
151	Darren Daulton	.05
152	Toby Borland	.05
153	Andy Van Slyke	.05
154	Mickey Morandini	.05
155	Sid Fernandez	.05
156	Tom Marsh	.05
157	Kevin Stocker	.05
158	Paul Quantrill	.05
159	Gregg Jefferies	.05
160	Ricky Bottalico	.05
161	Lenny Dykstra	.05
162	Mark Whiten	.05
163	Tyler Green	.05
164	Jim Eisenreich	.05
165	Heathcliff Slocumb	.05
166	Esteban Loaiza	.10
167	Rich Aude	.05
168	Jason Christiansen	.05
169	Ramon Morel	.05
170	Orlando Merced	.05
171	Paul Wagner	.05
172	Jeff King	.05
173	Jay Bell	.05
174	Jacob Brumfield	.05
175	Nelson Liriano	.05
176	Dan Miceli	.05
177	Carlos Garcia	.05
178	Denny Neagle	.05
179	Angelo Encarnacion	.05
180	Al Martin	.05
181	Midre Cummings	.05
182	Eddie Williams	.05
183	Roberto Petagine	.05
184	Tony Gwynn	.75
185	Andy Ashby	.05
186	Melvin Nieves	.05
187	Phil Clark	.05
188	Brad Ausmus	.05
189	Bip Roberts	.05
190	Fernando Valenzuela	.05
191	Marc Newfield	.05
192	Steve Finley	.05
193	Trevor Hoffman	.05
194	Andujar Cedeno	.05
195	Jody Reed	.05
196	Ken Caminiti	.25
197	Joey Hamilton	.05
198	Tony Gwynn (NL Batting Champ)	.30
199	Shawn Barton	.05
200	Deion Sanders	.15
201	Rikkert Faneyte	.05
202	Barry Bonds	.75
203	Matt Williams	.25
204	Jose Bautista	.05
205	Mark Leiter	.05
206	Mark Carreon	.05
207	Robby Thompson	.05
208	Terry Mulholland	.05
209	Rod Beck	.05
210	Royce Clayton	.05
211	J.R. Phillips	.05
212	Kirt Manwaring	.05
213	Glenallen Hill	.05
214	William Van Landingham	.05
215	Scott Cooper	.05
216	Bernard Gilkey	.05
217	Allen Watson	.05
218	Donovan Osborne	.05
219	Ray Lankford	.05
220	Tony Fossas	.05
221	Tom Pagnozzi	.05
222	John Mabry	.05
223	Tripp Cromer	.05
224	Mark Petkovsek	.05
225	Mike Morgan	.05
226	Ozzie Smith	.40
227	Tom Henke	.05
228	Jose Oquendo	.05
229	Brian Jordan	.05
230	Cal Ripken Jr.	2.50
231	Scott Erickson	.05
232	Harold Baines	.05
233	Jeff Manto	.05
234	Jesse Orosco	.05
235	Jeffrey Hammonds	.05
236	Brady Anderson	.10
237	Manny Alexander	.05
238	Chris Hoiles	.05
239	Rafael Palmeiro	.15
240	Ben McDonald	.05
241	Curtis Goodwin	.05
242	Bobby Bonilla	.05
243	Mike Mussina	.40
244	Kevin Brown	.10
245	Armando Benitez	.05
246	Jose Canseco	.35
247	Erik Hanson	.05
248	Mo Vaughn	.50
249	Tim Naehring	.05
250	Vaughn Eshelman	.05
251	Mike Greenwell	.05
252	Troy O'Leary	.05
253	Tim Wakefield	.05
254	Dwayne Hosey	.05
255	John Valentin	.05
256	Rick Aguilera	.05
257	Mike MacFarlane	.05
258	Roger Clemens	.75
259	Luis Alicea	.05
260	Mo Vaughn (AL MVP)	.25

261	Mark Langston	.05
262	Jim Edmonds	.10
263	Rod Correia	.05
264	Tim Salmon	.25
265	J.T. Snow	.10
266	Orlando Palmeiro	.05
267	Jorge Fabregas	.05
268	Jim Abbott	.05
269	Eduardo Perez	.05
270	Lee Smith	.05
271	Gary DiSarcina	.05
272	Damion Easley	.05
273	Tony Phillips	.05
274	Garret Anderson	.05
275	Chuck Finley	.05
276	Chili Davis	.05
277	Lance Johnson	.05
278	Alex Fernandez	.10
279	Robin Ventura	.15
280	Chris Snopek	.05
281	Brian Keyser	.05
282	Lyle Mouton	.05
283	*Luis Andujar*	.05
284	Tim Raines	.10
285	Larry Thomas	.05
286	Ozzie Guillen	.05
287	Frank Thomas	1.50
288	Roberto Hernandez	.05
289	Dave Martinez	.05
290	Ray Durham	.05
291	Ron Karkovice	.05
292	Wilson Alvarez	.05
293	Omar Vizquel	.05
294	Eddie Murray	.40
295	Sandy Alomar	.10
296	Orel Hershiser	.05
297	Jose Mesa	.05
298	Julian Tavarez	.05
299	Dennis Martinez	.05
300	Carlos Baerga	.05
301	Manny Ramirez	1.00
302	Jim Thome	.25
303	Kenny Lofton	.50
304	Tony Pena	.05
305	Alvaro Espinoza	.05
306	Paul Sorrento	.05
307	Albert Belle	.75
308	Danny Bautista	.05
309	Chris Gomez	.05
310	Jose Lima	.10
311	Phil Nevin	.05
312	Alan Trammell	.10
313	Chad Curtis	.05
314	John Flaherty	.05
315	Travis Fryman	.05
316	Todd Steverson	.05
317	Brian Bohanon	.05
318	Lou Whitaker	.05
319	Bobby Higginson	.15
320	Steve Rodriguez	.05
321	Cecil Fielder	.10
322	Felipe Lira	.05
323	Juan Samuel	.05
324	Bob Hamelin	.05
325	Tom Goodwin	.05
326	Johnny Damon	.15
327	Hipolito Pichardo	.05
328	Dilson Torres	.05
329	Kevin Appier	.05
330	Mark Gubicza	.05
331	Jon Nunnally	.05
332	Gary Gaetti	.05
333	Brent Mayne	.05
334	Brent Cookson	.05
335	Tom Gordon	.05
336	Wally Joyner	.05
337	Greg Gagne	.05
338	Fernando Vina	.05
339	Joe Oliver	.05
340	John Jaha	.05
341	Jeff Cirillo	.05
342	Pat Listach	.05
343	Dave Nilsson	.05
344	Steve Sparks	.05
345	Ricky Bones	.05
346	David Hulse	.05
347	Scott Karl	.05
348	Darryl Hamilton	.05
349	B.J. Surhoff	.10
350	Angel Miranda	.05
351	Sid Roberson	.05
352	Matt Mieske	.05
353	*Jose Valentin*	.05
354	*Matt Lawton*	.50
355	Eddie Guardado	.05
356	Brad Radke	.05
357	Pedro Munoz	.05
358	Scott Stahoviak	.05
359	Erik Schullstrom	.05
360	Pat Meares	.05
361	Marty Cordova	.10
362	Scott Leius	.05
363	Matt Walbeck	.05
364	Rich Becker	.05
365	Kirby Puckett	.75
366	Oscar Munoz	.05
367	Chuck Knoblauch	.20
368	Marty Cordova (AL Rookie of Year)	.10
369	Bernie Williams	.40
370	Mike Stanley	.05
371	Andy Pettitte	.60
372	Jack McDowell	.05
373	Sterling Hitchcock	.05
374	David Cone	.10
375	Randy Velarde	.05
376	Don Mattingly	1.00
377	Melido Perez	.05
378	Wade Boggs	.25
379	Ruben Sierra	.05
380	Tony Fernandez	.05
381	John Wetteland	.05
382	Mariano Rivera	.15
383	Derek Jeter	2.00
384	Paul O'Neill	.10
385	Mark McGwire	3.00
386	Scott Brosius	.05
387	Don Wengert	.05
388	Terry Steinbach	.05
389	Brent Gates	.05
390	Craig Paquette	.05
391	Mike Bordick	.05
392	Ariel Prieto	.05
393	Dennis Eckersley	.05
394	Carlos Reyes	.05
395	Todd Stottlemyre	.05
396	Rickey Henderson	.25
397	Geronimo Berroa	.05
398	Steve Ontiveros	.05
399	Mike Gallego	.05
400	Stan Javier	.05
401	Randy Johnson	.30
402	Norm Charlton	.05
403	Mike Blowers	.05
404	Tino Martinez	.10
405	Dan Wilson	.05
406	Andy Benes	.05
407	Alex Diaz	.05
408	Edgar Martinez	.05
409	Chris Bosio	.05
410	Ken Griffey Jr.	2.50
411	Luis Sojo	.05
412	Bob Wolcott	.05
413	Vince Coleman	.05
414	Rich Amaral	.05
415	Jay Buhner	.10
416	Alex Rodriguez	2.50
417	Joey Cora	.05
418	Randy Johnson (AL Cy Young)	.20
419	Edgar Martinez (AL Batting Champ)	.05
420	Ivan Rodriguez	.40
421	Mark McLemore	.05
422	Mickey Tettleton	.05
423	Juan Gonzalez	.75
424	Will Clark	.25
425	Kevin Gross	.05
426	Dean Palmer	.05
427	Kenny Rogers	.05
428	Bob Tewksbury	.05
429	Benji Gil	.05
430	Jeff Russell	.05
431	Rusty Greer	.05
432	Roger Pavlik	.05
433	Esteban Beltre	.05
434	Otis Nixon	.05
435	Paul Molitor	.40
436	Carlos Delgado	.25
437	Ed Sprague	.05
438	Juan Guzman	.05
439	Domingo Cedeno	.05
440	Pat Hentgen	.05
441	Tomas Perez	.05
442	John Olerud	.10
443	Shawn Green	.20
444	Al Leiter	.10
445	Joe Carter	.10
446	Robert Perez	.05
447	Devon White	.05
448	Tony Castillo	.05
449	Alex Gonzalez	.05
450	Roberto Alomar	.60
450p	Roberto Alomar (unmarked promo card, "Games: 128" on back)	7.50

1996 Pacific Crown Cramer's Choice

One of the most unusually shaped baseball cards of all time is the Cramer's Choice insert set from the 1996 Pacific Crown Collection. The set features the 10 best players as chosen by Pacific founder and president Mike Cramer. Cards are in a die-cut pyramidal design 3-1/2" tall and 2-1/2" at the base. The player picture on front is set against a silver-foil background, while the player name and other information is in gold foil on a faux marble base at bottom; the effect is a simulation of a trophy. Backs repeat the marbled background and have a bi-lingual justification from Cramer concerning his choice of the player as one of the 10 best. Average insertion rate is one card per case (720 packs). Cards are numbered with a "CC" prefix.

		MT
Complete Set (10):		575.00
Common Player:		40.00
1	Roberto Alomar	30.00
2	Wade Boggs	30.00
3	Cal Ripken Jr.	125.00
4	Greg Maddux	75.00
5	Frank Thomas	50.00
6	Tony Gwynn	50.00
7	Mike Piazza	90.00
8	Ken Griffey Jr.	125.00
9	Manny Ramirez	40.00
10	Edgar Martinez	40.00

1996 Pacific Crown Estrellas Latinas

Three dozen of the best contemporary Latino ballplayers are honored in this chase set. Cards feature action photos silhouetted on a black background shot through with gold-foil streaks and stars. The player name, set and insert set logos are in gold at left. Backs have a player portrait photo and English/Spanish career summary. The Latino Stars insert cards are inserted at an average rate of one per nine packs; about four per foil box. Cards are numbered with an "EL" prefix.

		MT
Complete Set (36):		35.00
Common Player:		.75
1	Roberto Alomar	4.50
2	Moises Alou	.90
3	Carlos Baerga	.75
4	Geronimo Berroa	.75
5	Ricky Bones	.75
6	Bobby Bonilla	.75
7	Jose Canseco	1.50
8	Vinny Castilla	.90
9	Pedro Martinez	1.50
10	John Valentin	.75
11	Andres Galarraga	1.25
12	Juan Gonzalez	5.00
13	Ozzie Guillen	.75
14	Esteban Loaiza	.90
15	Javier Lopez	1.50
16	Dennis Martinez	.75
17	Edgar Martinez	.75
18	Tino Martinez	.90
19	Orlando Merced	.75
20	Jose Mesa	.75
21	Raul Mondesi	1.50
22	Jaime Navarro	.75
23	Rafael Palmeiro	1.50
24	Carlos Perez	.75
25	Manny Ramirez	4.00
26	Alex Rodriguez	10.00
27	Ivan Rodriguez	3.00
28	David Segui	.75
29	Ruben Sierra	.75
30	Sammy Sosa	7.50
31	Julian Tavarez	.75
32	Ismael Valdes	.75
33	Fernando Valenzuela	.75
34	Quilvio Veras	.75
35	Omar Vizquel	.75
36	Bernie Williams	2.00

1996 Pacific Crown Gold Crown Die-Cuts

One of Pacific's most popular inserts of the previous year returns in 1996. The Gold Crown die-cuts have the top of the card cut away to form a gold-foil crown design with an action photo below. The player's name is also in gold foil. Backs repeat the gold crown design at top, have a portrait photo at lower-right and a few words about the player, in both English and Spanish. Insertion rate was advertised as one per 37 packs, on average. Cards are numbered with a "DC" prefix.

		MT
Complete Set (36):		180.00
Common Player:		2.50
1	Roberto Alomar	5.00
2	Will Clark	4.00
3	Johnny Damon	2.50
4	Don Mattingly	8.00
5	Edgar Martinez	2.50
6	Manny Ramirez	6.00
7	Mike Piazza	15.00
8	Quilvio Veras	2.50
9	Rickey Henderson	3.50
10	Jeff Bagwell	6.00
11	Andres Galarraga	2.50
12	Tim Salmon	3.00
13	Ken Griffey Jr.	25.00
14	Sammy Sosa	15.00
15	Cal Ripken Jr.	20.00
16	Raul Mondesi	3.00
17	Jose Canseco	4.00
18	Frank Thomas	8.00
19	Hideo Nomo	4.00
20	Wade Boggs	3.50
21	Reggie Sanders	2.50
22	Carlos Baerga	2.50
23	Mo Vaughn	4.00
24	Ivan Rodriguez	6.00
25	Kirby Puckett	6.00
26	Albert Belle	4.00
27	Vinny Castilla	2.50
28	Greg Maddux	12.00
29	Dante Bichette	3.00
30	Deion Sanders	3.00
31	Chipper Jones	12.00
32	Cecil Fielder	2.50
33	Randy Johnson	6.00
34	Mark McGwire	25.00
35	Tony Gwynn	8.00
36	Barry Bonds	6.00

1996 Pacific Crown Hometown of the Players

The hometown roots of 20 top players are examined in this chase set. Fronts have action photos with large areas of the background replaced with textured gold foil, including solid and outline versions of the player's name. Backs have a portrait photo, a representation of the player's native flag and a few words about his hometown. Card numbers have an "HP" prefix and are inserted at an average rate of one per 18 packs; about two per box.

		MT
Complete Set (20):		50.00
Common Player:		1.50
1	Mike Piazza	6.00
2	Greg Maddux	5.00
3	Tony Gwynn	3.00
4	Carlos Baerga	1.50
5	Don Mattingly	4.00
6	Cal Ripken Jr.	7.50
7	Chipper Jones	5.00
8	Andres Galarraga	1.50
9	Manny Ramirez	2.50
10	Roberto Alomar	2.50
11	Ken Griffey Jr.	8.00
12	Jose Canseco	2.50
13	Frank Thomas	3.00
14	Vinny Castilla	1.50
15	Roberto Kelly	1.50
16	Dennis Martinez	1.50
17	Kirby Puckett	3.00
18	Raul Mondesi	2.00
19	Hideo Nomo	2.50
20	Edgar Martinez	1.50

1996 Pacific Crown Milestones

A textured metallic blue-foil background is featured in this insert set. Behind the player action photo is a spider's web design with flying baseballs, team logo and a number representing the milestone. The player's name is in purple foil, outlined in white, vertically at right. Backs have a portrait photo and bi-lingual description of the milestone. Average insertion rate for this insert series is one per 37 packs. Cards are numbered with a "M" prefix.

		MT
Complete Set (10):		35.00
Common Player:		1.50
1	Albert Belle	3.00
2	Don Mattingly	5.00
3	Tony Gwynn	5.00
4	Jose Canseco	2.50
5	Marty Cordova	1.50
6	Wade Boggs	2.00
7	Greg Maddux	6.00
8	Eddie Murray	2.50
9	Ken Griffey Jr.	10.00
10	Cal Ripken Jr.	7.50

1996 Pacific Crown October Moments

Post-season baseball has never been better represented on a card than in Pacific's "October Moments" chase set. Color action photos are set again a background of a stadium decked in the traditional Fall Classic bunting, all rendered in metallic copper foil. At bottom is a textured silver strip with the player name in copper and a swirl of fallen leaves. Backs have a repeat of the leaves and bunting themes with a player portrait at center and English/Spanish description of his October heroics. These cards are found at an average rate of once per 37 packs. Cards are numbered with an "OM" prefix.

		MT
Complete Set (20):		75.00
Common Player:		1.50
1	Carlos Baerga	1.50
2	Albert Belle	4.00
3	Dante Bichette	2.00
4	Jose Canseco	2.50
5	Tom Glavine	2.00
6	Ken Griffey Jr.	15.00
7	Randy Johnson	5.00
8	Chipper Jones	10.00
9	Dave Justice	2.50
10	Ryan Klesko	1.50
11	Kenny Lofton	3.00
12	Javier Lopez	1.50
13	Greg Maddux	10.00
14	Edgar Martinez	1.50
15	Don Mattingly	7.50
16	Hideo Nomo	4.00
17	Mike Piazza	10.00
18	Manny Ramirez	6.00
19	Reggie Sanders	1.50
20	Jim Thome	1.50

1996 Pacific Prism

Only the best in baseball make the cut for the Prism checklist. Sold in one-card foil packs the cards feature action photos set against an etched silver-foil background highlighted by slashes approximating team colors. Backs are conventionally printed in a horizontal format with a player portrait photo at left center on a purple background. A short 1995 season recap is feature in both English and Spanish. Card numbers are prefixed with a "P".

		MT
Complete Set (144):		150.00
Common Player:		1.00
Pack (2):		1.50
Wax Box (36):		48.00
1	Tom Glavine	1.50
2	Chipper Jones	8.00
3	David Justice	1.50
4	Ryan Klesko	1.50
5	Javier Lopez	1.50
6	Greg Maddux	8.00
7	Fred McGriff	1.50
8	Frank Castillo	1.00
9	Luis Gonzalez	1.00
10	Mark Grace	1.50
11	Brian McRae	1.00
12	Jaime Navarro	1.00
13	Sammy Sosa	9.00
14	Bret Boone	1.00
15	Ron Gant	1.50
16	Barry Larkin	1.50
17	Reggie Sanders	1.00
18	Benito Santiago	1.00
19	Dante Bichette	1.50
20	Vinny Castilla	1.00
21	Andres Galarraga	1.50
22	Bryan Rekar	1.00
23	Roberto Alomar	3.00
23p	Roberto Alomar ("Azulejos" rather than "Los Azulajos" on back, unmarked promo card)	7.50
24	Jeff Conine	1.00
25	Andre Dawson	1.00

26 Charles Johnson 1.00
27 Gary Sheffield 2.00
28 Quilvio Veras 1.00
29 Jeff Bagwell 4.00
30 Derek Bell 1.00
31 Craig Biggio 1.50
32 Tony Eusebio 1.00
33 Karim Garcia 1.00
34 Eric Karros 1.00
35 Ramon Martinez 1.00
36 Raul Mondesi 1.50
37 Hideo Nomo 2.00
38 Mike Piazza 10.00
39 Ismael Valdes 1.00
40 Moises Alou 1.00
41 Wil Cordero 1.00
42 Pedro Martinez 4.00
43 Mel Rojas 1.00
44 David Segui 1.00
45 Edgardo Alfonzo 1.00
46 Rico Brogna 1.00
47 John Franco 1.00
48 Jason Isringhausen 1.00
49 Jose Vizcaino 1.00
50 Ricky Bottalico 1.00
51 Darren Daulton 1.00
52 Lenny Dykstra 1.00
53 Tyler Green 1.00
54 Gregg Jefferies 1.00
55 Jay Bell 1.00
56 Jason Christiansen 1.00
57 Carlos Garcia 1.00
58 Esteban Loaiza 1.00
59 Orlando Merced 1.00
60 Andujar Cedeno 1.00
61 Tony Gwynn 5.00
62 Melvin Nieves 1.00
63 Phil Plantier 1.00
64 Fernando Valenzuela 1.00
65 Barry Bonds 5.00
66 J.R. Phillips 1.00
67 Deion Sanders 1.50
68 Matt Williams 1.50
69 Bernard Gilkey 1.00
70 Tom Henke 1.00
71 Brian Jordan 1.00
72 Ozzie Smith 3.00
73 Manny Alexander 1.00
74 Bobby Bonilla 1.00
75 Mike Mussina 2.00
76 Rafael Palmeiro 2.00
77 Cal Ripken Jr. 12.00
78 Jose Canseco 2.50
79 Roger Clemens 5.00
80 John Valentin 1.00
81 Mo Vaughn 2.50
82 Tim Wakefield 1.00
83 Garret Anderson 1.00
84 Damion Easley 1.00
85 Jim Edmonds 1.50
86 Tim Salmon 1.50
87 Wilson Alvarez 1.00
88 Alex Fernandez 1.00
89 Ozzie Guillen 1.00
90 Roberto Hernandez 1.00
91 Frank Thomas 5.00
92 Robin Ventura 1.00
93 Carlos Baerga 1.00
94 Albert Belle 2.50
95 Kenny Lofton 2.50
96 Dennis Martinez 1.00
97 Eddie Murray 2.00
98 Manny Ramirez 4.00
99 Omar Vizquel 1.00
100 Chad Curtis 1.00
101 Cecil Fielder 1.00
102 Felipe Lira 1.00
103 Alan Trammell 1.00
104 Kevin Appier 1.00
105 Johnny Damon 1.00
106 Gary Gaetti 1.00
107 Wally Joyner 1.00
108 Ricky Bones 1.00
109 John Jaha 1.00
110 B.J. Surhoff 1.00
111 Jose Valentin 1.00
112 Fernando Vina 1.00
113 Marty Cordova 1.00
114 Chuck Knoblauch 1.00
115 Scott Leius 1.00
116 Pedro Munoz 1.00
117 Kirby Puckett 6.00
118 Wade Boggs 2.00
119 Don Mattingly 6.00
120 Jack McDowell 1.00
121 Paul O'Neill 1.50
122 Ruben Rivera 1.00
123 Bernie Williams 3.00
124 Geronimo Berroa 1.00
125 Rickey Henderson 2.00
126 Mark McGwire 15.00
127 Terry Steinbach 1.00
128 Danny Tartabull 1.00
129 Jay Buhner 1.00
130 Joey Cora 1.00
131 Ken Griffey Jr. 12.00
132 Randy Johnson 4.00
133 Edgar Martinez 1.00
134 Tino Martinez 1.00
135 Will Clark 2.00
136 Juan Gonzalez 4.00
137 Dean Palmer 1.00
138 Ivan Rodriguez 4.00
139 Mickey Tettleton 1.00
140 Larry Walker 1.50
141 Joe Carter 1.00
142 Carlos Delgado 3.00
143 Alex Gonzalez 1.00
144 Paul Molitor 2.00

1996 Pacific Prism Gold

Exactly paralleling the cards in the regular Prism set, this chase card insert replaces the silver foil on front with gold foil. All else remains the same. Stated odds of picking a Gold Prism parallel card are about one per 18 packs, on average (two per box).

	MT
Complete Set (144):	500.00
Common Player:	2.50
Stars:	2.5X

(See 1996 Pacific Prism for checklist and base card values.)

1996 Pacific Prism Fence Busters

Home run heroes are featured in this insert set. The player's big swing is photographed in the foreground while a baseball flies out of the etched metallic foil stadium background. The player's name is in blue foil. Backs have another player photo and details of his 1995 season home run output, in both English and Spanish. Cards are numbered with an FB prefix. Stated odds of finding a Fence Busters insert are one per 37 packs, on average.

		MT
Complete Set (19):		130.00
Common Player:		4.50
1	Albert Belle	7.50
2	Dante Bichette	5.00
3	Barry Bonds	7.50
4	Jay Buhner	4.50
5	Jose Canseco	6.00
6	Ken Griffey Jr.	30.00
7	Chipper Jones	20.00
8	David Justice	5.00
9	Eric Karros	4.50
10	Edgar Martinez	4.50
11	Mark McGwire	30.00
12	Eddie Murray	6.00
13	Mike Piazza	20.00
14	Kirby Puckett	10.00
15	Cal Ripken Jr.	25.00
16	Tim Salmon	6.00
17	Sammy Sosa	15.00
18	Frank Thomas	10.00
19	Mo Vaughn	6.00

Player names in *Italic* type indicate a rookie card.

1996 Pacific Prism Flame Throwers

Burning baseballs are the background for the game's best pitchers in this die-cut insert set. The gold-foil highlighted flames have their tails die-cut at the card's left end. The featured pitcher is shown in action in the foreground. The name at bottom and company logo are in gold foil. Backs are conventionally printed with another action photo and 1995 highlight printed in both English and Spanish. Card numbers carry an FT prefix. Stated odds of finding a Flame Throwers card are one in 73 boxes, about every two boxes.

		MT
Complete Set (10):		95.00
Common Player:		6.00
1	Roger Clemens	25.00
2	David Cone	8.00
3	Tom Glavine	8.00
4	Randy Johnson	15.00
5	Greg Maddux	30.00
6	Ramon Martinez	6.00
7	Jose Mesa	6.00
8	Mike Mussina	12.00
9	Hideo Nomo	15.00
10	Jose Rijo	6.00

1996 Pacific Prism Red Hot Stars

Bright red metallic foil provides the background for these inserts. Color action photos are in the foreground, while player name and multiple team logos are worked into the background. Backs are conventionally printed with another player photo and a few words - in both English and Spanish - about the player's 1995 season. Card numbers have an RH prefix. Stated odds of finding a Red Hot Stars insert are one per 37 packs.

		MT
Complete Set (19):		175.00
Common Player:		3.00
1	Roberto Alomar	5.00
2	Jeff Bagwell	10.00
3	Albert Belle	7.50
4	Wade Boggs	3.50
5	Barry Bonds	7.50
6	Jose Canseco	3.50
7	Ken Griffey Jr.	27.50
8	Tony Gwynn	10.00
9	Randy Johnson	4.50
10	Chipper Jones	15.00
11	Greg Maddux	12.50
12	Edgar Martinez	3.00
13	Don Mattingly	12.50
14	Mike Piazza	15.00
15	Kirby Puckett	9.00
16	Manny Ramirez	6.00
17	Cal Ripken Jr.	20.00
18	Tim Salmon	3.00
19	Frank Thomas	10.00

1997 Pacific Crown

The 450-card, regular-sized set was available in

12-card packs. The card fronts feature the player's name in gold foil along the left border with the team logo in the bottom right corner. The card backs feature a head shot of the player in the lower left quadrant with a short highlight in both Spanish and English. Inserted in packs were: Card-Supials, Cramer's Choice, Latinos Of The Major Leagues, Fireworks Die-Cuts, Gold Crown Die-Cuts and Triple Crown Die-Cuts. A parallel silver version (67 sets) was available.

		MT
Complete Set (450):		35.00
Common Player:		.05
Pack (12):		2.00
Wax Box (36):		60.00
1	Garret Anderson	.05
2	George Arias	.05
3	Chili Davis	.05
4	Gary DiSarcina	.05
5	Jim Edmonds	.15
6	Darin Erstad	.75
7	Jorge Fabregas	.05
8	Chuck Finley	.05
9	Rex Hudler	.05
10	Mark Langston	.05
11	Orlando Palmeiro	.05
12	Troy Percival	.05
13	Tim Salmon	.25
14	J.T. Snow	.05
15	Randy Velarde	.05
16	Manny Alexander	.05
17	Roberto Alomar	.60
18	Brady Anderson	.10
19	Armando Benitez	.05
20	Bobby Bonilla	.10
21	Rocky Coppinger	.05
22	Scott Erickson	.05
23	Jeffrey Hammonds	.05
24	Chris Hoiles	.05
25	Eddie Murray	.30
26	Mike Mussina	.60
27	Randy Myers	.05
28	Rafael Palmeiro	.20
29	Cal Ripken Jr.	2.50
30	B.J. Surhoff	.05
31	Tony Tarasco	.05
32	Esteban Beltre	.05
33	Darren Bragg	.05
34	Jose Canseco	.40
35	Roger Clemens	1.00
36	Wil Cordero	.05
37	Alex Delgado	.05
38	Jeff Frye	.05
39	Nomar Garciaparra	1.50
40	Tom Gordon	.05
41	Mike Greenwell	.05
42	Reggie Jefferson	.05
43	Tim Naehring	.05
44	Troy O'Leary	.05
45	Heathcliff Slocumb	.05
46	Lee Tinsley	.05
47	John Valentin	.05
48	Mo Vaughn	.40
49	Wilson Alvarez	.05
50	Harold Baines	.05
51	Ray Durham	.05
52	Alex Fernandez	.05
53	Ozzie Guillen	.05
54	Roberto Hernandez	.05
55	Ron Karkovice	.05
56	Darren Lewis	.05
57	Norberto Martin	.05
58	Dave Martinez	.05
59	Lyle Mouton	.05
60	Jose Munoz	.05
61	Tony Phillips	.05
62	Rich Sauveur	.05
63	Danny Tartabull	.05
64	Frank Thomas	1.00
65	Robin Ventura	.15
66	Sandy Alomar Jr.	.10
67	Albert Belle	.40
68	Julio Franco	.05
69	*Brian Giles*	1.50
70	Danny Graves	.05
71	Orel Hershiser	.05
72	Jeff Kent	.05
73	Kenny Lofton	.30
74	Dennis Martinez	.05
75	Jack McDowell	.05
76	Jose Mesa	.05
77	Charles Nagy	.05
78	Manny Ramirez	.75
79	Julian Tavarez	.05
80	Jim Thome	.25
81	Jose Vizcaino	.05
82	Omar Vizquel	.05
83	Brad Ausmus	.05
84	Kimera Bartee	.05
85	Raul Casanova	.05
86	Tony Clark	.20
87	Travis Fryman	.15
88	Bobby Higginson	.10
89	Mark Lewis	.05
90	Jose Lima	.05
91	Felipe Lira	.05
92	Phil Nevin	.05
93	Melvin Nieves	.05
94	Curtis Pride	.05
95	Ruben Sierra	.05
96	Alan Trammell	.05
97	Kevin Appier	.05
98	Tim Belcher	.05
99	Johnny Damon	.20
100	Tom Goodwin	.05
101	Bob Hamelin	.05
102	David Howard	.05
103	Jason Jacome	.05
104	Keith Lockhart	.05
105	Mike Macfarlane	.05
106	Jeff Montgomery	.05
107	Jose Offerman	.05
108	Hipolito Pichardo	.05
109	Joe Randa	.05
110	Bip Roberts	.05
111	Chris Stynes	.05
112	Mike Sweeney	.05
113	Joe Vitiello	.05
114	Jeromy Burnitz	.05
115	Chuck Carr	.05
116	Jeff Cirillo	.05
117	Mike Fetters	.05
118	David Hulse	.05
119	John Jaha	.05
120	Scott Karl	.05
121	Jesse Levis	.05
122	Mark Loretta	.05
123	Mike Matheny	.05
124	Ben McDonald	.05
125	Matt Mieske	.05
126	Angel Miranda	.05
127	Dave Nilsson	.05
128	Jose Valentin	.05
129	Fernando Vina	.05
130	Ron Villone	.05
131	Gerald Williams	.05
132	Rick Aguilera	.05
133	Rich Becker	.05
134	Ron Coomer	.05
135	Marty Cordova	.05
136	Eddie Guardado	.05
137	Denny Hocking	.05
138	Roberto Kelly	.05
139	Chuck Knoblauch	.10
140	Matt Lawton	.05
141	Pat Meares	.05
142	Paul Molitor	.35
143	Greg Myers	.05
144	Jeff Reboulet	.05
145	Scott Stahoviak	.05
146	Todd Walker	.10
147	Wade Boggs	.25
148	David Cone	.10
149	Mariano Duncan	.05
150	Cecil Fielder	.10
151	Dwight Gooden	.05
152	Derek Jeter	2.50
153	Jim Leyritz	.05
154	Tino Martinez	.15
155	Paul O'Neill	.15
156	Andy Pettitte	.30
157	Tim Raines	.05
158	Mariano Rivera	.15
159	Ruben Rivera	.10
160	Kenny Rogers	.05
161	Darryl Strawberry	.15
162	John Wetteland	.05
163	Bernie Williams	.50
164	Tony Batista	.05
165	Geronimo Berroa	.05
166	Mike Bordick	.05
167	Scott Brosius	.05
168	Brent Gates	.05
169	Jason Giambi	.30
170	Jose Herrera	.05
171	Brian Lesher	.05
172	*Damon Mashore*	.05
173	Mark McGwire	3.00
174	Ariel Prieto	.05
175	Carlos Reyes	.05
176	Matt Stairs	.05
177	Terry Steinbach	.05
178	John Wasdin	.05
179	Ernie Young	.05
180	Rich Amaral	.05
181	Bobby Ayala	.05
182	Jay Buhner	.10
183	Rafael Carmona	.05
184	Norm Charlton	.05
185	Joey Cora	.05
186	Ken Griffey Jr.	2.50
187	Sterling Hitchcock	.05
188	Dave Hollins	.05
189	Randy Johnson	.75
190	Edgar Martinez	.05
191	Jamie Moyer	.05
192	Alex Rodriguez	2.50
193	Paul Sorrento	.05
194	Salomon Torres	.05
195	Bob Wells	.05
196	Dan Wilson	.05
197	Will Clark	.30
198	Kevin Elster	.05
199	Rene Gonzales	.05
200	Juan Gonzalez	.75
201	Rusty Greer	.05
202	Darryl Hamilton	.05
203	Mike Henneman	.05
204	Ken Hill	.05
205	Mark McLemore	.05
206	Darren Oliver	.05
207	Dean Palmer	.05
208	Roger Pavlik	.05
209	Ivan Rodriguez	.75
210	Kurt Stillwell	.05
211	Mickey Tettleton	.05
212	Bobby Witt	.05
213	Tilson Brito	.05
214	Jacob Brumfield	.05
215	Miguel Cairo	.10
216	Joe Carter	.10
217	Felipe Crespo	.05
218	Carlos Delgado	.50
219	Alex Gonzalez	.05
220	Shawn Green	.20
221	Juan Guzman	.05
222	Pat Hentgen	.05
223	Charlie O'Brien	.05
224	John Olerud	.15
225	Robert Perez	.05
226	Tomas Perez	.05
227	Juan Samuel	.05
228	Ed Sprague	.05
229	Mike Timlin	.05
230	Rafael Belliard	.05
231	Jermaine Dye	.10
232	Tom Glavine	.20
233	Marquis Grissom	.05
234	Andruw Jones	.75
235	Chipper Jones	1.50
236	David Justice	.25
237	Ryan Klesko	.15
238	Mark Lemke	.05
239	Javier Lopez	.15
240	Greg Maddux	1.50
241	Fred McGriff	.35
242	Denny Neagle	.05
243	Eddie Perez	.05
244	John Smoltz	.10
245	Mark Wohlers	.05
246	Brant Brown	.05
247	Scott Bullett	.05
248	Leo Gomez	.05
249	Luis Gonzalez	.05
250	Mark Grace	.15
251	Jose Hernandez	.05
252	Brooks Kieschnick	.05
253	Brian McRae	.05
254	Jaime Navarro	.05
255	Mike Perez	.05
256	Rey Sanchez	.05
257	Ryne Sandberg	.75
258	Scott Servais	.05
259	Sammy Sosa	1.50
260	*Pedro Valdes*	.05
261	Turk Wendell	.05
262	Bret Boone	.05
263	Jeff Branson	.05
264	Jeff Brantley	.05
265	Dave Burba	.05
266	Hector Carrasco	.05
267	Eric Davis	.05
268	Willie Greene	.05
269	Lenny Harris	.05
270	Thomas Howard	.05
271	Barry Larkin	.20
272	Hal Morris	.05
273	Joe Oliver	.05
274	Eric Owens	.05
275	Jose Rijo	.05
276	Reggie Sanders	.05
277	Eddie Taubensee	.05
278	Jason Bates	.05
279	Dante Bichette	.15
280	Ellis Burks	.05
281	Vinny Castilla	.05
282	Andres Galarraga	.20
283	Quinton McCracken	.05
284	Jayhawk Owens	.05
285	Jeff Reed	.05
286	Bryan Rekar	.05
287	Armando Reynoso	.05
288	Kevin Ritz	.05
289	Bruce Ruffin	.05
290	John Vander Wal	.05
291	Larry Walker	.25
292	Walt Weiss	.05
293	Eric Young	.05
294	Kurt Abbott	.05
295	Alex Arias	.05
296	Miguel Batista	.05
297	Kevin Brown	.10
298	Luis Castillo	.05
299	Greg Colbrunn	.05
300	Jeff Conine	.05
301	Charles Johnson	.05
302	Al Leiter	.05
303	Robb Nen	.05
304	Joe Orsulak	.05
305	Yorkis Perez	.05
306	Edgar Renteria	.15
307	Gary Sheffield	.25
308	Jesus Tavarez	.05
309	Quilvio Veras	.05
310	Devon White	.05
311	Jeff Bagwell	.75
312	Derek Bell	.05
313	Sean Berry	.05
314	Craig Biggio	.15
315	Doug Drabek	.05
316	Tony Eusebio	.05
317	Ricky Gutierrez	.05
318	Xavier Hernandez	.05
319	Brian L. Hunter	.05
320	Darryl Kile	.05
321	Derrick May	.05
322	Orlando Miller	.05
323	James Mouton	.05
324	Bill Spiers	.05
325	Pedro Astacio	.05
326	Brett Butler	.05
327	Juan Castro	.05
328	Roger Cedeno	.05
329	Delino DeShields	.05
330	Karim Garcia	.10
331	Todd Hollandsworth	.05
332	Eric Karros	.05
333	Oreste Marrero	.05
334	Ramon Martinez	.05
335	Raul Mondesi	.20
336	Hideo Nomo	.50
337	Antonio Osuna	.05
338	Chan Ho Park	.05
339	Mike Piazza	2.00
340	Ismael Valdes	.05
341	Moises Alou	.05
342	Omar Daal	.05
343	Jeff Fassero	.05
344	Cliff Floyd	.05
345	Mark Grudzielanek	.05
346	Mike Lansing	.05
347	Pedro Martinez	.75
348	Sherman Obando	.05
349	Jose Paniagua	.05
350	Henry Rodriguez	.05
351	Mel Rojas	.05
352	F.P. Santangelo	.05
353	Dave Segui	.05
354	Dave Silvestri	.05
355	Ugueth Urbina	.05
356	Rondell White	.10

357 Edgardo Alfonzo .10
358 Carlos Baerga .05
359 Tim Bogar .05
360 Rico Brogna .05
361 Alvaro Espinoza .05
362 Carl Everett .10
363 John Franco .05
364 Bernard Gilkey .05
365 Todd Hundley .05
366 Butch Huskey .05
367 Jason Isringhausen .05
368 Bobby Jones .05
369 Lance Johnson .05
370 Brent Mayne .05
371 Alex Ochoa .05
372 Rey Ordonez .10
373 Ron Blazier .05
374 Ricky Bottalico .05
375 David Doster .05
376 Lenny Dykstra .05
377 Jim Eisenreich .05
378 Bobby Estalella .05
379 Gregg Jefferies .05
380 Kevin Jordan .05
381 Ricardo Jordan .05
382 Mickey Morandini .05
383 Ricky Otero .05
384 Benito Santiago .05
385 Gene Schall .05
386 Curt Schilling .15
387 Kevin Sefcik .05
388 Kevin Stocker .05
389 Jermaine Allensworth .05
390 Jay Bell .05
391 Jason Christiansen .05
392 Francisco Cordova .05
393 Mark Johnson .05
394 Jason Kendall .05
395 Jeff King .05
396 Jon Lieber .05
397 Nelson Liriano .05
398 Esteban Loaiza .10
399 Al Martin .05
400 Orlando Merced .05
401 Ramon Morel .05
402 Luis Alicea .05
403 Alan Benes .10
404 Andy Benes .05
405 Terry Bradshaw .05
406 Royce Clayton .05
407 Dennis Eckersley .05
408 Gary Gaetti .05
409 Mike Gallego .05
410 Ron Gant .10
411 Brian Jordan .05
412 Ray Lankford .05
413 John Mabry .05
414 Willie McGee .05
415 Tom Pagnozzi .05
416 Ozzie Smith .40
417 Todd Stottlemyre .05
418 Mark Sweeney .05
419 Andy Ashby .05
420 Ken Caminiti .10
421 Archi Cianfrocco .05
422 Steve Finley .05
423 Chris Gomez .05
424 Tony Gwynn 1.00
425 Joey Hamilton .05
426 Rickey Henderson .20
427 Trevor Hoffman .05
428 Brian Johnson .05
429 Wally Joyner .05
430 Scott Livingstone .05
431 Jody Reed .05
432 Craig Shipley .05
433 Fernando Valenzuela .05
434 Greg Vaughn .10
435 Rich Aurilia .05
436 Kim Batiste .05
437 Jose Bautista .05
438 Rod Beck .05
439 Marvin Benard .05
440 Barry Bonds .75
441 Shawon Dunston .05
442 Shawn Estes .05
443 Osvaldo Fernandez .05
444 Stan Javier .05
445 David McCarty .05
446 *Bill Mueller* .05
447 Steve Scarsone .05
448 Robby Thompson .05
449 Rick Wilkins .05
450 Matt Williams .25

1997 Pacific Crown Light Blue

This parallel insert was produced exclusively for insertion in Wal-Mart/Sam's jumbo packs at the rate of one per pack. Following the format of the regular-issue, they use light blue foil, rather than the standard gold. Light blue inserts should not be confused with the much scarcer silver inserts which are visually similar.

	MT
Complete Set (450):	250.00
Common Player:	.25
Stars:	2X

(See 1997 Pacific Crown for checklist and base card values.)

1997 Pacific Crown Silver

This parallel insert was produced in an edition of only 67 cards per player. Following the format of the regular-issue, they use silver foil, rather than the standard gold. Silver parallels were inserted at an advertised rate of one per 73 packs. Silver inserts should not be confused with the much more common light blue inserts which are visually similar.

	MT
Common Player:	5.00
Stars:	35-50X
Rookies:	25-40X

(See 1997 Pacific Crown for checklist and base card values.)

1997 Pacific Crown Card-Supials

The 36-card, regular-sized set was inserted every 37 packs of 1997 Pacific Crown baseball. The card fronts feature a gold-foil spiral with the player's name printed along a curve on the bottom edge. The team logo appears in the lower right corner. The card backs feature an action shot and are numbered "x of 36." The cards come with a mini (1-1/4" x 1-3/4") card that slides into a pocket on the back. The mini cards are of a different player, but depict the same action shot as the larger card backs.

		MT
Complete Set (72):		250.00
Complete Large Set (36):		175.00
Complete Small Set (36):		90.00
Common Large:		2.00
Small Cards:		50%
1	Roberto Alomar	3.00
2	Brady Anderson	2.00
3	Eddie Murray	3.00
4	Cal Ripken Jr.	12.50
5	Jose Canseco	2.50
6	Mo Vaughn	3.50
7	Frank Thomas	7.50
8	Albert Belle	4.00
9	Omar Vizquel	2.00
10	Chuck Knoblauch	2.00
11	Paul Molitor	3.00
12	Wade Boggs	2.50
13	Derek Jeter	10.00
14	Andy Pettitte	3.50
15	Mark McGwire	15.00
16	Jay Buhner	2.00
17	Ken Griffey Jr.	15.00
18	Alex Rodriguez	12.50
19	Juan Gonzalez	4.00
20	Ivan Rodriguez	3.00
21	Andruw Jones	7.50
22	Chipper Jones	10.00
23	Ryan Klesko	2.00
24	Greg Maddux	10.00
25	Ryne Sandberg	4.00
26	Andres Galarraga	2.00
27	Gary Sheffield	2.50
28	Jeff Bagwell	7.50
29	Todd Hollandsworth	2.00
30	Hideo Nomo	2.50
31	Mike Piazza	10.00
32	Todd Hundley	2.00
33	Dennis Eckersley	2.00
34	Ken Caminiti	2.00
35	Tony Gwynn	7.50
36	Barry Bonds	4.00

1997 Pacific Crown Cramer's Choice Awards

The 10-card, regular-sized set was inserted every 721 packs and features a die-cut pyramid design. A color player photo is imaged over silver foil with the player's name and position in gold foil over a green marble background along the bottom. The card backs feature a headshot with a brief career highlight in both Spanish and English. The cards are numbered with a "CC" prefix.

		MT
Complete Set (10):		450.00
Common Player:		20.00
1	Roberto Alomar	20.00
2	Frank Thomas	45.00
3	Albert Belle	25.00
4	Andy Pettitte	20.00
5	Ken Griffey Jr.	100.00
6	Alex Rodriguez	75.00
7	Chipper Jones	60.00
8	John Smoltz	20.00
9	Mike Piazza	60.00
10	Tony Gwynn	50.00

1997 Pacific Crown Fireworks Die-Cuts

The 20-card, regular-sized, die-cut set was inserted every 73 packs of 1997 Crown. The card fronts feature a color action shot with generic fireworks over a stadium on the upper half. The horizontal card backs contain close-up shots with highlights in Spanish and English. The cards are numbered with the "FW" prefix.

		MT
Complete Set (20):		240.00
Common Player:		3.50
1	Roberto Alomar	7.50
2	Brady Anderson	3.50
3	Eddie Murray	4.50
4	Cal Ripken Jr.	25.00
5	Frank Thomas	15.00
6	Albert Belle	7.50
7	Derek Jeter	20.00
8	Andy Pettitte	6.00
9	Bernie Williams	6.00
10	Mark McGwire	30.00
11	Ken Griffey Jr.	30.00
12	Alex Rodriguez	25.00
13	Juan Gonzalez	8.00
14	Andruw Jones	15.00
15	Chipper Jones	20.00
16	Hideo Nomo	4.50
17	Mike Piazza	20.00
18	Henry Rodriguez	3.50
19	Tony Gwynn	15.00
20	Barry Bonds	7.50

1997 Pacific Crown Gold Crown Die-Cuts

The 36-card, regular-sized, die-cut set was inserted every 37 packs. The card fronts feature a die-cut, gold-foil crown on the top border and the player's name appears in gold along the bottom edge. The card backs contain a headshot and a Spanish/English highlight and are numbered with the "GC" prefix.

		MT
Complete Set (36):		240.00
Common Player:		2.50
1	Roberto Alomar	6.00
2	Brady Anderson	2.50
3	Mike Mussina	4.00
4	Eddie Murray	4.50
5	Cal Ripken Jr.	20.00
6	Jose Canseco	3.50
7	Frank Thomas	12.50
8	Albert Belle	6.00
9	Omar Vizquel	2.50
10	Wade Boggs	3.50
11	Derek Jeter	12.50
12	Andy Pettitte	5.00
13	Mariano Rivera	2.50
14	Bernie Williams	4.00
15	Mark McGwire	25.00
16	Ken Griffey Jr.	25.00
17	Edgar Martinez	2.50
18	Alex Rodriquez	20.00
19	Juan Gonzalez	8.00
20	Ivan Rodriguez	7.50
21	Andruw Jones	12.00
22	Chipper Jones	15.00
23	Ryan Klesko	2.50
24	John Smoltz	3.00
25	Ryne Sandberg	6.00
26	Andres Galarraga	2.50
27	Edgar Renteria	3.50
28	Jeff Bagwell	10.00
29	Todd Hollandsworth	2.50
30	Hideo Nomo	3.50
31	Mike Piazza	15.00
32	Todd Hundley	2.50
33	Brian Jordan	2.50
34	Ken Caminiti	3.00
35	Tony Gwynn	10.00
36	Barry Bonds	6.00

1997 Pacific Crown Latinos of the Major Leagues

The 36-card, regular-sized set was inserted twice every 37 packs. The card fronts feature a color action shot over the player's name in gold foil. The card backs have another action shot and a Spanish/English highlight.

		MT
Complete Set (36):		60.00
Common Player:		1.50
1	George Arias	1.50
2	Roberto Alomar	4.00
3	Rafael Palmeiro	3.00
4	Bobby Bonilla	2.00
5	Jose Canseco	2.50
6	Wilson Alvarez	1.50
7	Dave Martinez	1.50
8	Julio Franco	1.50
9	Manny Ramirez	6.00
10	Omar Vizquel	1.50
11	Marty Cordova	1.50
12	Roberto Kelly	1.50
13	Tino Martinez	2.00
14	Mariano Rivera	2.50
15	Ruben Rivera	1.50
16	Bernie Williams	4.00
17	Geronimo Berroa	1.50
18	Joey Cora	1.50
19	Edgar Martinez	1.50
20	Alex Rodriguez	12.50
21	Juan Gonzalez	5.00
22	Ivan Rodriguez	7.50
23	Andruw Jones	10.00
24	Javier Lopez	2.00
25	Sammy Sosa	10.00
26	Vinny Castilla	2.00
27	Andres Galarraga	2.00
28	Ramon Martinez	2.00
29	Raul Mondesi	3.00
30	Ismael Valdes	1.50
31	Pedro Martinez	6.00
32	Henry Rodriguez	1.50
33	Carlos Baerga	1.50
34	Rey Ordonez	2.00
35	Fernando Valenzuela	1.50
36	Osvaldo Fernandez	1.50

1997 Pacific Crown Triple Crown Die-Cuts

The 20-card, regular-sized, die-cut set was inserted every 145 packs of Crown baseball. The horizontal card fronts feature the same gold-foil, die-cut crown as on the Gold Crown Die-Cut inserts. The card backs feature a headshot, Spanish/English text and are numbered with the "TC" prefix.

		MT
Complete Set (20):		250.00
Common Player:		10.00
1	Brady Anderson	5.00
2	Rafael Palmeiro	8.00
3	Mo Vaughn	8.00
4	Frank Thomas	15.00
5	Albert Belle	8.00
6	Jim Thome	8.00
7	Cecil Fielder	5.00
8	Mark McGwire	50.00
9	Ken Griffey Jr.	40.00
10	Alex Rodriguez	40.00
11	Juan Gonzalez	12.00
12	Andruw Jones	12.00
13	Chipper Jones	25.00
14	Dante Bichette	5.00
15	Ellis Burks	5.00
16	Andres Galarraga	6.00
17	Jeff Bagwell	12.00
18	Mike Piazza	30.00
19	Ken Caminiti	5.00
20	Barry Bonds	12.00

1997 Pacific Invincible

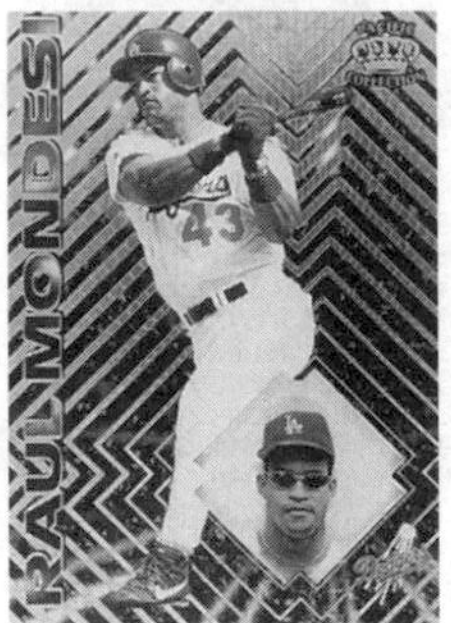

The 1997 Pacific Invincible 150-card set was sold in three-card packs. The card fronts feature gold foil parallel lines with a color action shot. The bottom right quadrant contains a transparent cel headshot. The card backs have Spanish/English text and another color action shot. The reverse cel has the player's hat team logo air-brushed off to prevent reverse print. Insert sets are: Sluggers & Hurlers, Sizzling Lumber, Gate Attractions, Gems of the Diamond (2:1), and Light Blue (retail only) and Platinum (hobby) parallel sets of the 150 baseb cards.

		MT
Complete Set (150):		100.00
Common Player:		.75
Light Blues:		2X
Platinums:		2X
Pack (3):		1.50
Wax Box (36):		48.00
1	Chili Davis	.75
2	Jim Edmonds	1.50
3	Darin Erstad	1.50
4	Orlando Palmeiro	.75
5	Tim Salmon	1.00
6	J.T. Snow	.75
7	Roberto Alomar	2.00
8	Brady Anderson	1.00
9	Eddie Murray	1.00
10	Mike Mussina	1.50
11	Rafael Palmeiro	1.00
12	Cal Ripken Jr.	8.00
13	Jose Canseco	1.50
14	Roger Clemens	3.00
15	Nomar Garciaparra	6.00
16	Reggie Jefferson	.75
17	Mo Vaughn	1.50
18	Wilson Alvarez	.75
19	Harold Baines	.75
20	Alex Fernandez	.75
21	Danny Tartabull	.75
22	Frank Thomas	3.00
23	Robin Ventura	1.00
24	Sandy Alomar Jr.	.75
25	Albert Belle	1.50
26	Kenny Lofton	1.50
27	Jim Thome	1.50
28	Omar Vizquel	.75
29	Raul Casanova	.75
30	Tony Clark	1.00
31	Travis Fryman	1.00
32	Bobby Higginson	.75
33	Melvin Nieves	.75
34	Justin Thompson	.75
35	Johnny Damon	.75
36	Tom Goodwin	.75
37	Jeff Montgomery	.75
38	Jose Offerman	.75
39	John Jaha	.75

40	Jeff Cirillo	.75
41	Dave Nilsson	.75
42	Jose Valentin	.75
43	Fernando Vina	.75
44	Marty Cordova	.75
45	Roberto Kelly	.75
46	Chuck Knoblauch	1.00
47	Paul Molitor	1.50
48	Todd Walker	.75
49	Wade Boggs	2.00
50	Cecil Fielder	.75
51	Derek Jeter	8.00
52	Tino Martinez	1.00
53	Andy Pettitte	1.00
54	Mariano Rivera	1.00
55	Bernie Williams	2.00
56	Tony Batista	.75
57	Geronimo Berroa	.75
58	Jason Giambi	1.50
59	Mark McGwire	10.00
60	Terry Steinbach	.75
61	Jay Buhner	.75
62	Joey Cora	.75
63	Ken Griffey Jr.	8.00
64	Edgar Martinez	1.00
65	Alex Rodriguez	8.00
66	Paul Sorrento	.75
67	Will Clark	1.50
68	Juan Gonzalez	2.50
69	Rusty Greer	.75
70	Dean Palmer	.75
71	Ivan Rodriguez	2.50
72	Joe Carter	.75
73	Carlos Delgado	2.00
74	Juan Guzman	.75
75	Pat Hentgen	.75
76	Ed Sprague	.75
77	Jermaine Dye	.75
78	Andruw Jones	2.50
79	Chipper Jones	5.00
80	Ryan Klesko	1.00
81	Javier Lopez	1.00
82	Greg Maddux	5.00
83	John Smoltz	1.00
84	Mark Grace	1.00
85	Luis Gonzalez	.75
86	Brooks Kieschnick	.75
87	Jaime Navarro	.75
88	Ryne Sandberg	2.50
89	Sammy Sosa	6.00
90	Bret Boone	.75
91	Jeff Brantley	.75
92	Eric Davis	.75
93	Barry Larkin	1.50
94	Reggie Sanders	.75
95	Ellis Burks	.75
96	Dante Bichette	1.00
97	Vinny Castilla	.75
98	Andres Galarraga	1.50
99	Eric Young	.75
100	Kevin Brown	1.00
101	Jeff Conine	.75
102	Charles Johnson	.75
103	Edgar Renteria	1.00
104	Gary Sheffield	1.50
105	Jeff Bagwell	2.50
106	Derek Bell	.75
107	Sean Berry	.75
108	Craig Biggio	1.00
109	Shane Reynolds	.75
110	Karim Garcia	.75
111	Todd Hollandsworth	.75
112	Ramon Martinez	.75
113	Raul Mondesi	1.00
114	Hideo Nomo	1.50
115	Mike Piazza	6.00
116	Ismael Valdes	.75
117	Moises Alou	.75
118	Mark Grudzielanek	.75
119	Pedro Martinez	2.50
120	Henry Rodriguez	.75
121	F.P. Santangelo	.75
122	Carlos Baerga	.75
123	Bernard Gilkey	.75
124	Todd Hundley	.75
125	Lance Johnson	.75
126	Alex Ochoa	.75
127	Rey Ordonez	.75
128	Lenny Dykstra	.75
129	Gregg Jefferies	.75
130	Ricky Otero	.75
131	Benito Santiago	.75
132	Jermaine Allensworth	.75
133	Francisco Cordova	.75
134	Carlos Garcia	.75
135	Jason Kendall	.75
136	Al Martin	.75
137	Dennis Eckersley	.75
138	Ron Gant	.75
139	Brian Jordan	.75
140	John Mabry	.75
141	Ozzie Smith	2.50
142	Ken Caminiti	1.00
143	Steve Finley	.75
144	Tony Gwynn	3.00
145	Wally Joyner	.75
146	Fernando Valenzuela	.75
147	Barry Bonds	2.50
148	Jacob Cruz	.75
149	Osvaldo Fernandez	.75
150	Matt Williams	1.00

1997 Pacific Invincible Gate Attractions

The 32-card, regular-sized set was inserted every 73 packs of Pacific Invincible baseball. The card fronts feature a generic baseball glove background with the player's name and position in a gold-foil circle. The center of the card is a cel action shot within a common baseball image. The player's team logo appears in the upper right corner. The card backs contain a headshot in the upper left corner with highlights in Spanish and English. The player's image in the cel is etched in gray in reverse. The cards are numbered with the "GA" prefix.

		MT
Complete Set (32):		350.00
Common Player:		4.00
1	Roberto Alomar	7.50
2	Brady Anderson	4.00
3	Cal Ripken Jr.	30.00
4	Frank Thomas	18.00
5	Kenny Lofton	5.00
6	Omar Vizquel	4.00
7	Paul Molitor	7.50
8	Wade Boggs	7.50
9	Derek Jeter	25.00
10	Andy Pettitte	5.00
11	Bernie Williams	5.00
12	Geronimo Berroa	4.00
13	Mark McGwire	35.00
14	Ken Griffey Jr.	35.00
15	Alex Rodriguez	30.00
16	Juan Gonzalez	10.00
17	Andruw Jones	18.00
18	Chipper Jones	25.00
19	Greg Maddux	24.00
20	Ryne Sandberg	9.00
21	Sammy Sosa	18.00
22	Andres Galarraga	4.00
23	Jeff Bagwell	15.00
24	Todd Hollandsworth	4.00
25	Hideo Nomo	4.00
26	Mike Piazza	25.00
27	Todd Hundley	4.00
28	Lance Johnson	4.00
29	Ozzie Smith	9.00
30	Ken Caminiti	6.00
31	Tony Gwynn	20.00
32	Barry Bonds	9.00

1997 Pacific Invincible Gems of the Diamond

Essentially the base set for 1997 Pacific Prism Invincible, these cards are found two per three-card pack. Fronts of the 2-1/2" x 3-1/2" cards have action photos with earth-tone borders and a color team logo at bottom. Backs have a large player portrait photos in a diamond at right-center and are numbered with a "GD-" prefix.

		MT
Complete Set (220):		20.00
Common Player:		.15
1	Jim Abbott	.15
2	Shawn Boskie	.15
3	Gary DiSarcina	.15
4	Jim Edmonds	.25
5	Todd Greene	.15
6	Jack Howell	.15
7	Jeff Schmidt	.15
8	Shad Williams	.15
9	Roberto Alomar	.50
10	Cesar Devarez	.15
11	Alan Mills	.15
12	Eddie Murray	.25
13	Jesse Orosco	.15
14	Arthur Rhodes	.15
15	Bill Ripken	.15
16	Cal Ripken Jr.	2.50
17	Mark Smith	.15
18	Roger Clemens	1.00
19	Vaughn Eshelman	.15
20	Rich Garces	.15
21	Bill Haselman	.15
22	Dwayne Hosey	.15
23	Mike Maddux	.15
24	Jose Malave	.15
25	Aaron Sele	.15
26	James Baldwin	.15
27	Pat Borders	.15
28	Mike Cameron	.15
29	Tony Castillo	.15
30	Domingo Cedeno	.15
31	Greg Norton	.15
32	Frank Thomas	1.00
33	Albert Belle	.40
34	Einar Diaz	.15
35	Alan Embree	.15
36	Albie Lopez	.15
37	Chad Ogea	.15
38	Tony Pena	.15
39	Joe Roa	.15
40	Fausto Cruz	.15
41	Joey Eischen	.15
42	Travis Fryman	.30
43	Mike Myers	.15
44	A.J. Sager	.15
45	Duane Singleton	.15
46	Justin Thompson	.15
47	Jeff Granger	.15
48	Les Norman	.15
49	Jon Nunnally	.15
50	Craig Paquette	.15
51	Michael Tucker	.15
52	Julio Valera	.15
53	Kevin Young	.15
54	Cal Eldred	.15
55	Ramon Garcia	.15
56	Marc Newfield	.15
57	Al Reyes	.15
58	Tim Unroe	.15
59	Tim Vanegmond	.15
60	Turner Ward	.15
61	Bob Wickman	.15
62	Chuck Knoblauch	.25
63	Paul Molitor	.50
64	Kirby Puckett	.75
65	Tom Quinlan	.15
66	Rich Robertson	.15
67	Dave Stevens	.15
68	Matt Walbeck	.15
69	Wade Boggs	.50
70	Tony Fernandez	.15
71	Andy Fox	.15
72	Joe Girardi	.15
73	Charlie Hayes	.15
74	Pat Kelly	.15
75	Jeff Nelson	.15
76	Melido Perez	.15
77	Mark Acre	.15
78	Allen Battle	.15
79	Rafael Bournigal	.15
80	Mark McGwire	3.00
81	Pedro Munoz	.15
82	Scott Spiezio	.15
83	Don Wengert	.15
84	Steve Wojciechowski	.15
85	Alex Diaz	.15
86	Ken Griffey Jr.	2.50
87	Raul Ibanez	.15
88	Mike Jackson	.15
89	John Marzano	.15
90	Greg McCarthy	.15
91	Alex Rodriguez	2.50
92	Andy Sheets	.15
93	Makoto Suzuki	.15
94	Benji Gil	.15
95	Juan Gonzalez	.75
96	Kevin Gross	.15
97	Gil Heredia	.15
98	Luis Ortiz	.15
99	Jeff Russell	.15
100	Dave Valle	.15
101	Marty Janzen	.15
102	Sandy Martinez	.15
103	Julio Mosquera	.15
104	Otis Nixon	.15
105	Paul Spoljaric	.15
106	Shannon Stewart	.15
107	Woody Williams	.15
108	Steve Avery	.15
109	Mike Bielecki	.15
110	Pedro Borbon	.15
111	Ed Giovanola	.15
112	Chipper Jones	1.50
113	Greg Maddux	1.50
114	Mike Mordecai	.15
115	Terrell Wade	.15
116	Terry Adams	.15
117	Brian Dorsett	.15
118	Doug Glanville	.15
119	Tyler Houston	.15
120	Robin Jennings	.15
121	Ryne Sandberg	.75
122	Terry Shumpert	.15
123	Amaury Telemaco	.15
124	Steve Trachsel	.15
125	Curtis Goodwin	.15
126	Mike Kelly	.15
127	Chad Mottola	.15
128	Mark Portugal	.15
129	Roger Salkeld	.15
130	John Smiley	.15

131	Lee Smith	.15
132	Roger Bailey	.15
133	Andres Galarraga	.25
134	Darren Holmes	.15
135	Curtis Leskanic	.15
136	Mike Munoz	.15
137	Jeff Reed	.15
138	Mark Thompson	.15
139	Jamey Wright	.15
140	Andre Dawson	.20
141	Craig Grebeck	.15
142	Matt Mantei	.15
143	Billy McMillon	.15
144	Kurt Miller	.15
145	Ralph Milliard	.15
146	Bob Natal	.15
147	Joe Siddall	.15
148	Bob Abreu	.25
149	Doug Brocail	.15
150	Danny Darwin	.15
151	Mike Hampton	.15
152	Todd Jones	.15
153	Kirt Manwaring	.15
154	Alvin Morman	.15
155	Billy Ashley	.15
156	Tom Candiotti	.15
157	Darren Dreifort	.15
158	Greg Gagne	.15
159	Wilton Guerrero	.15
160	Hideo Nomo	.50
161	Mike Piazza	2.00
162	Tom Prince	.15
163	Todd Worrell	.15
164	Moises Alou	.20
165	Shane Andrews	.15
166	Derek Aucoin	.15
167	Raul Chavez	.15
168	Darrin Fletcher	.15
169	Mark Leiter	.15
170	Henry Rodriguez	.15
171	Dave Veres	.15
172	Paul Byrd	.15
173	Alberto Castillo	.15
174	Mark Clark	.15
175	Rey Ordonez	.20
176	Roberto Petagine	.15
177	Andy Tomberlin	.15
178	Derek Wallace	.15
179	Paul Wilson	.15
180	Ruben Amaro, Jr.	.15
181	Toby Borland	.15
182	Rich Hunter	.15
183	Tony Longmire	.15
184	Wendell Magee Jr.	.15
185	Bobby Munoz	.15
186	Scott Rolen	.50
187	Mike Williams	.15
188	Trey Beamon	.15
189	Jason Christiansen	.15
190	Elmer Dessens	.15
191	Angelo Encarnacion	.15
192	Carlos Garcia	.15
193	Mike Kingery	.15
194	Chris Peters	.15
195	Tony Womack	.20
196	Brian Barber	.15
197	David Bell	.15
198	Tony Fossas	.15
199	Rick Honeycutt	.15
200	T.J. Mathews	.15
201	Miguel Mejia	.15
202	Donovan Osborne	.15
203	Ozzie Smith	.50
204	Andres Berumen	.15
205	Ken Caminiti	.20
206	Chris Gwynn	.15
207	Tony Gwynn	1.00
208	Rickey Henderson	.30
209	Scott Sanders	.15
210	Jason Thompson	.15
211	Fernando Valenzuela	.15
212	Tim Worrell	.15
213	Barry Bonds	.75
214	Jay Canizaro	.15
215	Doug Creek	.15
216	Jacob Cruz	.15
217	Glenallen Hill	.15
218	Tom Lampkin	.15
219	Jim Poole	.15
220	Desi Wilson	.15

1997 Pacific Invincible Sizzling Lumber

The 36-card, regular-sized, die-cut set was inserted every 37 packs of Ivincible. The cards have die-cut flames along the right border with a bat running parallel. The player's name appears in gold foil along the top border with his position in English and Spanish in gold foil along the bottom. The card backs feature a headshot in the upper half and contain Spanish and English text. The cards are numbered with the "SL" prefix.

		MT
Complete Set (36):		200.00
Common Player:		2.50
1A	Cal Ripken Jr.	20.00
1B	Rafael Palmeiro	3.00
1C	Roberto Alomar	4.00
2A	Frank Thomas	10.00
2B	Robin Ventura	2.50
2C	Harold Baines	2.50
3A	Albert Belle	6.00
3B	Manny Ramirez	6.00
3C	Kenny Lofton	4.50
4A	Derek Jeter	15.00
4B	Bernie Williams	3.50
4C	Wade Boggs	3.00
5A	Mark McGwire	25.00
5B	Jason Giambi	2.50
5C	Geronimo Berroa	2.50
6A	Ken Griffey Jr.	25.00
6B	Alex Rodriguez	20.00
6C	Jay Buhner	2.50
7A	Juan Gonzalez	8.00
7B	Dean Palmer	2.50
7C	Ivan Rodriguez	6.00
8A	Ryan Klesko	2.50
8B	Chipper Jones	15.00
8C	Andruw Jones	12.50
9A	Dante Bichette	2.50
9B	Andres Galarraga	2.50
9C	Vinny Castilla	2.50
10A	Jeff Bagwell	12.50
10B	Craig Biggio	2.50
10C	Derek Bell	2.50
11A	Mike Piazza	15.00
11B	Raul Mondesi	3.50
11C	Karim Garcia	3.50
12A	Tony Gwynn	12.50
12B	Ken Caminiti	3.50
12C	Greg Vaughn	2.50

Player names in *Italic* type indicate a rookie card.

1997 Pacific Invincible Sluggers & Hurlers

The 24-card, regular-sized set was inserted every 145 packs of Pacific Invincible baseball. The cards are numbered with an "SH-xA" or "SH-xaB." Each "A" card is the left half of a two-card set with the two players from the same team having their logo in the fit-together center. Each card has the player's name printed in gold foil along the bottom border with gold-foil swirls around the team logo. The card backs have a circular headshot with text in English and Spanish.

		MT
Complete Set (24):		500.00
Common Player:		7.50
SH-1a	Cal Ripken Jr.	40.00
SH-1b	Mike Mussina	10.00
SH-2a	Jose Canseco	10.00
SH-2b	Roger Clemens	15.00
SH-3a	Frank Thomas	20.00
SH-3b	Wilson Alvarez	7.50
SH-4a	Kenny Lofton	10.00
SH-4b	Orel Hershiser	7.50
SH-5a	Derek Jeter	30.00
SH-5b	Andy Pettitte	10.00
SH-6a	Ken Griffey Jr.	50.00
SH-6b	Randy Johnson	10.00
SH-7a	Alex Rodriguez	40.00
SH-7b	Jamie Moyer	7.50
SH-8a	Andruw Jones	25.00
SH-8b	Greg Maddux	30.00
SH-9a	Chipper Jones	30.00
SH-9b	John Smoltz	9.00
SH-10a	Jeff Bagwell	20.00
SH-10b	Shane Reynolds	7.50
SH-11a	Mike Piazza	30.00
SH-11b	Hideo Nomo	10.00
SH-12a	Tony Gwynn	20.00
SH-12b	Fernando Valenzuela	7.50

1998 Pacific

1998 Pacific Baseball is a 450-card, bilingual set. The base set features full-bleed photos with the Pacific Crown Collection logo in the upper left and the player's name, position and team at the bottom. Inserts include Cramer's Choice Awards, In The Cage Laser-Cuts, Home Run Hitters, Team Checklist Laser-Cuts, Gold Crown Die-Cuts and Latinos of the Major Leagues.

		MT
Complete Set (450):		40.00
Common Player:		.10
Platinum Blues:		30-45X
Inserted 1:73		
Pack (12):		2.50
Wax Box (36):		75.00
1	Luis Alicea	.10
2	Garret Anderson	.10
3	Jason Dickson	.10
4	Gary DiSarcina	.10
5	Jim Edmonds	.25
6	Darin Erstad	.50
7	Chuck Finley	.10
8	Shigetosi Hasegawa	.10
9	Rickey Henderson	.25
10	Dave Hollins	.10
11	Mark Langston	.10
12	Orlando Palmeiro	.10
13	Troy Percival	.10
14	Tony Phillips	.10
15	Tim Salmon	.25
16	Allen Watson	.10
17	Roberto Alomar	.60
18	Brady Anderson	.10
19	Harold Baines	.10
20	Armando Benitez	.10
21	Geronimo Berroa	.10
22	Mike Bordick	.10
23	Eric Davis	.10
24	Scott Erickson	.10
25	Chris Hoiles	.10
26	Jimmy Key	.10
27	Aaron Ledesma	.10
28	Mike Mussina	.50
29	Randy Myers	.10
30	Jesse Orosco	.10
31	Rafael Palmeiro	.25
32	Jeff Reboulet	.10
33	Cal Ripken Jr.	2.50
34	B.J. Surhoff	.10
35	Steve Avery	.10
36	Darren Bragg	.10
37	Wil Cordero	.10
38	Jeff Frye	.10
39	Nomar Garciaparra	2.00
40	Tom Gordon	.10
41	Bill Haselman	.10
42	Scott Hatteberg	.10
43	Butch Henry	.10
44	Reggie Jefferson	.10
45	Tim Naehring	.10
46	Troy O'Leary	.10
47	Jeff Suppan	.10
48	John Valentin	.10

49 Mo Vaughn .40
50 Tim Wakefield .10
51 James Baldwin .10
52 Albert Belle .40
53 Tony Castillo .10
54 Doug Drabek .10
55 Ray Durham .10
56 Jorge Fabregas .10
57 Ozzie Guillen .10
58 Matt Karchner .10
59 Norberto Martin .10
60 Dave Martinez .10
61 Lyle Mouton .10
62 Jaime Navarro .10
63 Frank Thomas 1.00
64 Mario Valdez .10
65 Robin Ventura .20
66 Sandy Alomar Jr. .20
67 Paul Assenmacher .10
68 Tony Fernandez .10
69 Brian Giles .20
70 Marquis Grissom .10
71 Orel Hershiser .10
72 Mike Jackson .10
73 David Justice .30
74 Albie Lopez .10
75 Jose Mesa .10
76 Charles Nagy .10
77 Chad Ogea .10
78 Manny Ramirez .75
79 Jim Thome .25
80 Omar Vizquel .10
81 Matt Williams .25
82 Jaret Wright .15
83 Willie Blair .10
84 Raul Casanova .10
85 Tony Clark .15
86 Deivi Cruz .10
87 Damion Easley .10
88 Travis Fryman .20
89 Bobby Higginson .15
90 Brian Hunter .10
91 Todd Jones .10
92 Dan Miceli .10
93 Brian Moehler .10
94 Melvin Nieves .10
95 Jody Reed .10
96 Justin Thompson .10
97 Bubba Trammell .10
98 Kevin Appier .10
99 Jay Bell .10
100 Yamil Benitez .10
101 Johnny Damon .10
102 Chili Davis .10
103 Jermaine Dye .10
104 Jed Hansen .10
105 Jeff King .10
106 Mike Macfarlane .10
107 Felix Martinez .10
108 Jeff Montgomery .10
109 Jose Offerman .10
110 Dean Palmer .10
111 Hipolito Pichardo .10
112 Jose Rosado .10
113 Jeromy Burnitz .10
114 Jeff Cirillo .10
115 Cal Eldred .10
116 John Jaha .10
117 Doug Jones .10
118 Scott Karl .10
119 Jesse Levis .10
120 Mark Loretta .10
121 Ben McDonald .10
122 Jose Mercedes .10
123 Matt Mieske .10
124 Dave Nilsson .10
125 Jose Valentin .10
126 Fernando Vina .10
127 Gerald Williams .10
128 Rick Aguilera .10
129 Rich Becker .10
130 Ron Coomer .10
131 Marty Cordova .10
132 Eddie Guardado .10
133 LaTroy Hawkins .10
134 Denny Hocking .10
135 Chuck Knoblauch .20
136 Matt Lawton .10
137 Pat Meares .10
138 Paul Molitor .50
139 David Ortiz .10
140 Brad Radke .10
141 Terry Steinbach .10
142 Bob Tewksbury .10
143 Javier Valentin .10
144 Wade Boggs .25
145 David Cone .15
146 Chad Curtis .10
147 Cecil Fielder .10
148 Joe Girardi .10
149 Dwight Gooden .10
150 Hideki Irabu .20
151 Derek Jeter 2.50
152 Tino Martinez .15
153 Ramiro Mendoza .10
154 Paul O'Neill .25
155 Andy Pettitte .25
156 Jorge Posada .15
157 Mariano Rivera .25
158 Rey Sanchez .10
159 Luis Sojo .10
160 David Wells .10
161 Bernie Williams .50
162 Rafael Bournigal .10
163 Scott Brosius .10
164 Jose Canseco .40
165 Jason Giambi .40
166 Ben Grieve .30
167 Dave Magadan .10
168 Brent Mayne .10
169 Jason McDonald .10
170 Izzy Molina .10
171 Ariel Prieto .10
172 Carlos Reyes .10
173 Scott Spiezio .10
174 Matt Stairs .10
175 Bill Taylor .10
176 Dave Telgheder .10
177 Steve Wojciechowski .10
178 Rich Amaral .10
179 Bobby Ayala .10
180 Jay Buhner .15
181 Rafael Carmona .10
182 Ken Cloude .10
183 Joey Cora .10
184 Russ Davis .10
185 Jeff Fassero .10
186 Ken Griffey Jr. 2.50
187 Raul Ibanez .10
188 Randy Johnson .75
189 Roberto Kelly .10
190 Edgar Martinez .10
191 Jamie Moyer .10
192 Omar Olivares .10
193 Alex Rodriguez 2.50
194 Heathcliff Slocumb .10
195 Paul Sorrento .10
196 Dan Wilson .10
197 Scott Bailes .10
198 John Burkett .10
199 Domingo Cedeno .10
200 Will Clark .40
201 *Hanley Frias* .10
202 Juan Gonzalez .75
203 Tom Goodwin .10
204 Rusty Greer .10
205 Wilson Heredia .10
206 Darren Oliver .10
207 Billy Ripken .10
208 Ivan Rodriguez .75
209 Lee Stevens .10
210 Fernando Tatis .15
211 John Wetteland .10
212 Bobby Witt .10
213 Jacob Brumfield .10
214 Joe Carter .10
215 Roger Clemens 1.00
216 Felipe Crespo .10
217 Jose Cruz Jr. .30
218 Carlos Delgado .60
219 Mariano Duncan .10
220 Carlos Garcia .10
221 Alex Gonzalez .10
222 Juan Guzman .10
223 Pat Hentgen .10
224 Orlando Merced .10
225 Tomas Perez .10
226 Paul Quantrill .10
227 Benito Santiago .10
228 Woody Williams .10
229 Rafael Belliard .10
230 Jeff Blauser .10
231 Pedro Borbon .10
232 Tom Glavine .25
233 Tony Graffanino .10
234 Andruw Jones .75
235 Chipper Jones 1.50
236 Ryan Klesko .20
237 Mark Lemke .10
238 Kenny Lofton .30
239 Javier Lopez .20
240 Fred McGriff .25
241 Greg Maddux 1.50
242 Denny Neagle .10
243 John Smoltz .15
244 Michael Tucker .10
245 Mark Wohlers .10
246 Manny Alexander .10
247 Miguel Batista .10
248 Mark Clark .10
249 Doug Glanville .10
250 Jeremi Gonzalez .10
251 Mark Grace .25
252 Jose Hernandez .10
253 Lance Johnson .10
254 Brooks Kieschnick .10
255 Kevin Orie .10
256 Ryne Sandberg .75
257 Scott Servais .10
258 Sammy Sosa 2.00
259 Kevin Tapani .10
260 Ramon Tatis .10
261 Bret Boone .10
262 Dave Burba .10
263 Brook Fordyce .10
264 Willie Greene .10
265 Barry Larkin .25
266 Pedro A. Martinez .15
267 Hal Morris .10
268 Joe Oliver .10
269 Eduardo Perez .10
270 Pokey Reese .10
271 Felix Rodriguez .10
272 Deion Sanders .15
273 Reggie Sanders .10
274 Jeff Shaw .10
275 Scott Sullivan .10
276 Brett Tomko .10
277 Roger Bailey .10
278 Dante Bichette .20
279 Ellis Burks .10
280 Vinny Castilla .15
281 Frank Castillo .10
282 *Mike DeJean* .10
283 Andres Galarraga .25
284 Darren Holmes .10
285 Kirt Manwaring .10
286 Quinton McCracken .10
287 Neifi Perez .10
288 Steve Reed .10
289 John Thomson .10
290 Larry Walker .30
291 Walt Weiss .10
292 Kurt Abbott .10
293 Antonio Alfonseca .10
294 Moises Alou .20
295 Alex Arias .10
296 Bobby Bonilla .10
297 Kevin Brown .20
298 Craig Counsell .10
299 Darren Daulton .10
300 Jim Eisenreich .10
301 Alex Fernandez .10
302 Felix Heredia .10
303 Livan Hernandez .15
304 Charles Johnson .10
305 Al Leiter .10
306 Robb Nen .10
307 Edgar Renteria .15
308 Gary Sheffield .30
309 Devon White .10
310 Bob Abreu .10
311 Brad Ausmus .10
312 Jeff Bagwell .75
313 Derek Bell .10
314 Sean Berry .10
315 Craig Biggio .20
316 Ramon Garcia .10
317 Luis Gonzalez .10
318 Ricky Gutierrez .10
319 Mike Hampton .10
320 Richard Hidalgo .10
321 Thomas Howard .10
322 Darryl Kile .10
323 Jose Lima .10
324 Shane Reynolds .10
325 Bill Spiers .10
326 Tom Candiotti .10
327 Roger Cedeno .15
328 Greg Gagne .10
329 Karim Garcia .10
330 Wilton Guerrero .10
331 Todd Hollandsworth .10
332 Eric Karros .15
333 Ramon Martinez .10
334 Raul Mondesi .25
335 Otis Nixon .10
336 Hideo Nomo .50
337 Antonio Osuna .10
338 Chan Ho Park .15
339 Mike Piazza 2.00
340 Dennis Reyes .10
341 Ismael Valdes .10
342 Todd Worrell .10
343 Todd Zeile .10
344 Darrin Fletcher .10
345 Mark Grudzielanek .10
346 Vladimir Guerrero 1.00
347 Dustin Hermanson .10
348 Mike Lansing .10
349 Pedro Martinez .75
350 Ryan McGuire .10
351 Jose Paniagua .10
352 Carlos Perez .10
353 Henry Rodriguez .10
354 F.P. Santangelo .10
355 David Segui .10
356 Ugueth Urbina .10
357 Marc Valdes .10
358 Jose Vidro .10
359 Rondell White .15
360 Juan Acevedo .10
361 Edgardo Alfonzo .15
362 Carlos Baerga .10
363 Carl Everett .10
364 John Franco .10
365 Bernard Gilkey .10
366 Todd Hundley .15
367 Butch Huskey .10
368 Bobby Jones .10
369 Takashi Kashiwada .10
370 Greg McMichael .10
371 Brian McRae .10
372 Alex Ochoa .10
373 John Olerud .15
374 Rey Ordonez .15
375 Turk Wendell .10
376 Ricky Bottalico .10
377 Rico Brogna .10
378 Lenny Dykstra .10
379 Bobby Estalella .10
380 Wayne Gomes .10
381 Tyler Green .10
382 Gregg Jefferies .10
383 Mark Leiter .10
384 Mike Lieberthal .10
385 Mickey Morandini .10
386 Scott Rolen .50
387 Curt Schilling .20
388 Kevin Stocker .10
389 Danny Tartabull .10
390 Jermaine Allensworth .10
391 Adrian Brown .10
392 Jason Christiansen .10
393 Steve Cooke .10
394 Francisco Cordova .10
395 Jose Guillen .15
396 Jason Kendall .10
397 Jon Lieber .10
398 Esteban Loaiza .10
399 Al Martin .10
400 *Kevin Polcovich* .15
401 Joe Randa .10
402 Ricardo Rincon .10
403 Tony Womack .10
404 Kevin Young .10
405 Andy Benes .10
406 Royce Clayton .10
407 Delino DeShields .10
408 Mike Difelice .10
409 Dennis Eckersley .10
410 John Frascatore .10
411 Gary Gaetti .10
412 Ron Gant .10
413 Brian Jordan .10
414 Ray Lankford .10
415 Willie McGee .10
416 Mark McGwire 3.00
417 Matt Morris .10
418 Luis Ordaz .10
419 Todd Stottlemyre .10
420 Andy Ashby .10
421 Jim Bruske .10
422 Ken Caminiti .25
423 Will Cunnane .10
424 Steve Finley .10
425 John Flaherty .10
426 Chris Gomez .10
427 Tony Gwynn 1.00
428 Joey Hamilton .10
429 Carlos Hernandez .10
430 Sterling Hitchcock .10

431	Trevor Hoffman	.10
432	Wally Joyner	.10
433	Greg Vaughn	.15
434	Quilvio Veras	.10
435	Wilson Alvarez	.10
436	Rod Beck	.10
437	Barry Bonds	.75
438	Jacob Cruz	.10
439	Shawn Estes	.10
440	Darryl Hamilton	.10
441	Roberto Hernandez	.10
442	Glenallen Hill	.10
443	Stan Javier	.10
444	Brian Johnson	.10
445	Jeff Kent	.10
446	Bill Mueller	.10
447	Kirk Rueter	.10
448	J.T. Snow	.10
449	Julian Tavarez	.10
450	Jose Vizcaino	.10

1998 Pacific Red/Silver

Red and Silver parallels reprinted all 450 cards in Pacific, with the gold foil used on base cards replaced by red or silver foil. Red foil versions were inserted one per Wal-Mart pack (retail), while Silver versions were inserted one per hobby pack.

	MT
Reds:	2x to 4x
Inserted 1:1 Retail	
Silvers:	2x to 4x
Inserted 1:1 Hobby	

(See 1998 Pacific for checklist and base card values.)

1998 Pacific Cramer's Choice

Cramer's Choice Awards is a 10-card die-cut insert. The cards feature the top player at each position as selected by Pacific CEO Mike Cramer. Each card is shaped like a trophy. Cramer's Choice Awards were inserted one per 721 packs of 1998 Pacific Baseball.

		MT
Complete Set (10):		700.00
Common Player:		30.00
Inserted 1:721		
1	Greg Maddux	75.00
2	Roberto Alomar	30.00
3	Cal Ripken Jr.	125.00
4	Nomar Garciaparra	100.00
5	Larry Walker	30.00
6	Mike Piazza	100.00
7	Mark McGwire	150.00
8	Tony Gwynn	50.00
9	Ken Griffey Jr.	125.00
10	Roger Clemens	50.00

1998 Pacific Gold Crown Die-Cuts

Gold Crown Die-Cuts is a 36-card insert seeded one per 37 packs. Each card has a holographic silver foil background and gold etching. The cards are die-cut around a crown design at the top.

		MT
Complete Set (36):		300.00
Common Player:		4.00
1	Chipper Jones	15.00
2	Greg Maddux	15.00
3	Denny Neagle	4.00
4	Roberto Alomar	6.00
5	Rafael Palmeiro	5.00
6	Cal Ripken Jr.	25.00
7	Nomar Garciaparra	20.00
8	Mo Vaughn	5.00
9	Frank Thomas	10.00
10	Sandy Alomar Jr.	4.00
11	David Justice	5.00
12	Manny Ramirez	8.00
13	Andres Galarraga	5.00
14	Larry Walker	5.00
15	Moises Alou	4.00
16	Livan Hernandez	4.00
17	Gary Sheffield	5.00
18	Jeff Bagwell	8.00
19	Raul Mondesi	5.00
20	Hideo Nomo	5.00
21	Mike Piazza	20.00
22	Derek Jeter	25.00
23	Tino Martinez	4.00
24	Bernie Williams	6.00
25	Ben Grieve	5.00
26	Mark McGwire	30.00
27	Tony Gwynn	10.00
28	Barry Bonds	8.00
29	Ken Griffey Jr.	25.00
30	Randy Johnson	8.00
31	Edgar Martinez	4.00
32	Alex Rodriguez	25.00
33	Juan Gonzalez	8.00
34	Ivan Rodriguez	8.00
35	Roger Clemens	10.00
36	Jose Cruz Jr.	4.00

1998 Pacific Home Run Hitters

This 20-card set was inserted one per 73 packs. The full-foil cards feature a color player photo with their home run total from 1997 embossed in the background.

		MT
Complete Set (20):		220.00
Common Player:		6.00
1	Rafael Palmeiro	6.00
2	Mo Vaughn	10.00
3	Sammy Sosa	25.00
4	Albert Belle	10.00
5	Frank Thomas	20.00
6	David Justice	6.00
7	Jim Thome	8.00
8	Matt Williams	6.00
9	Vinny Castilla	6.00
10	Andres Galarraga	6.00
11	Larry Walker	8.00
12	Jeff Bagwell	15.00
13	Mike Piazza	25.00
14	Tino Martinez	6.00
15	Mark McGwire	40.00
16	Barry Bonds	10.00
17	Jay Buhner	6.00
18	Ken Griffey Jr.	40.00
19	Alex Rodriguez	30.00
20	Juan Gonzalez	10.00

1998 Pacific In the Cage

This 20-card insert features top players in a die-cut batting cage. The netting on the cage is laser-cut. In The Cage Laser-Cuts were inserted one per 145 packs.

		MT
Complete Set (20):		450.00
Common Player:		8.00
1	Chipper Jones	40.00
2	Roberto Alomar	12.00
3	Cal Ripken Jr.	50.00
4	Nomar Garciaparra	40.00
5	Frank Thomas	35.00
6	Sandy Alomar Jr.	8.00
7	David Justice	8.00
8	Larry Walker	10.00
9	Bobby Bonilla	8.00
10	Mike Piazza	40.00
11	Tino Martinez	8.00
12	Bernie Williams	8.00
13	Mark McGwire	60.00
14	Tony Gwynn	35.00
15	Barry Bonds	16.00
16	Ken Griffey Jr.	60.00
17	Edgar Martinez	8.00
18	Alex Rodriguez	50.00
19	Juan Gonzalez	15.00
20	Ivan Rodriguez	12.00

The values of some parallel-card issues will have to be calculated based on figures presented in the heading for the regular-issue card set.

1998 Pacific Latinos of the Major Leagues

This 36-card set (2:37) features Major League players of Hispanic descent. The background has a world map on the left, the player's team logo in the center and an American flag on the right.

		MT
Complete Set (36):		75.00
Common Player:		1.50
Inserted 2:37		
1	Andruw Jones	8.00
2	Javier Lopez	1.50
3	Roberto Alomar	4.00
4	Geronimo Berroa	1.50
5	Rafael Palmeiro	2.00
6	Nomar Garciaparra	9.00
7	Sammy Sosa	10.00
8	Ozzie Guillen	1.50
9	Sandy Alomar Jr.	1.50
10	Manny Ramirez	7.50
11	Omar Vizquel	1.50
12	Vinny Castilla	1.50
13	Andres Galarraga	2.50
14	Moises Alou	1.50
15	Bobby Bonilla	1.50
16	Livan Hernandez	1.50
17	Edgar Renteria	1.50
18	Wilton Guerrero	1.50
19	Raul Mondesi	2.50
20	Ismael Valdes	1.50
21	Fernando Vina	1.50
22	Pedro Martinez	2.00
23	Edgardo Alfonzo	1.50
24	Carlos Baerga	1.50
25	Rey Ordonez	1.50
26	Tino Martinez	1.50
27	Mariano Rivera	1.50
28	Bernie Williams	4.00
29	Jose Canseco	3.00
30	Joey Cora	1.50
31	Roberto Kelly	1.50
32	Edgar Martinez	1.50
33	Alex Rodriguez	10.00
34	Juan Gonzalez	5.00
35	Ivan Rodriguez	5.00
36	Jose Cruz Jr.	1.50

1998 Pacific Team Checklists

Team Checklists is a 30-card insert in the bilingual Pacific Baseball set. One card was created for each team. A player photo is featured on the right with the team logo laser-cut into a bat barrel design on the left.

		MT
Complete Set (30):		240.00
Common Player:		3.00
1	Tim Salmon, Jim Edmonds	4.00
2	Cal Ripken Jr., Roberto Alomar	25.00
3	Nomar Garciaparra, Mo Vaughn	20.00
4	Frank Thomas, Albert Belle	20.00
5	Sandy Alomar Jr., Manny Ramirez	8.00
6	Justin Thompson, Tony Clark	5.00
7	Johnny Damon, Jermaine Dye	3.00
8	Dave Nilsson, Jeff Cirillo	3.00
9	Paul Molitor, Chuck Knoblauch	5.00
10	Tino Martinez, Derek Jeter	10.00
11	Ben Grieve, Jose Canseco	12.00
12	Ken Griffey Jr., Alex Rodriguez	30.00
13	Juan Gonzalez, Ivan Rodriguez	8.00
14	Jose Cruz Jr., Roger Clemens	3.00
15	Greg Maddux, Chipper Jones	20.00
16	Sammy Sosa, Mark Grace	15.00
17	Barry Larkin, Deion Sanders	4.00
18	Larry Walker, Andres Galarraga	4.00
19	Moises Alou, Bobby Bonilla	3.00
20	Jeff Bagwell, Craig Biggio	15.00
21	Mike Piazza, Hideo Nomo	20.00
22	Pedro Martinez, Henry Rodriguez	4.00
23	Rey Ordonez, Carlos Baerga	3.00
24	Curt Schilling, Scott Rolen	10.00
25	Al Martin, Tony Womack	3.00
26	Mark McGwire, Dennis Eckersley	30.00
27	Tony Gwynn, Wally Joyner	15.00
28	Barry Bonds, J.T. Snow	8.00
29	Matt Williams, Jay Bell	5.00
30	Fred McGriff, Roberto Hernandez	4.00

1998 Pacific Aurora

The Aurora base set consists of 200 cards printed on 24-point board. The cards have a color photo bordered on two sides by a thick green (National League) or red (A.L.) border. A portrait photo appears in the upper-right corner. Back has another portrait photo, 1997 and career stats, career highlights and personal data. Aurora was sold in six-card foil packs. Inserts include Pennant Fever (with three parallels), Hardball Cel-Fusions, Kings of the Major Leagues, On Deck Laser-Cuts and Pacific Cubes.

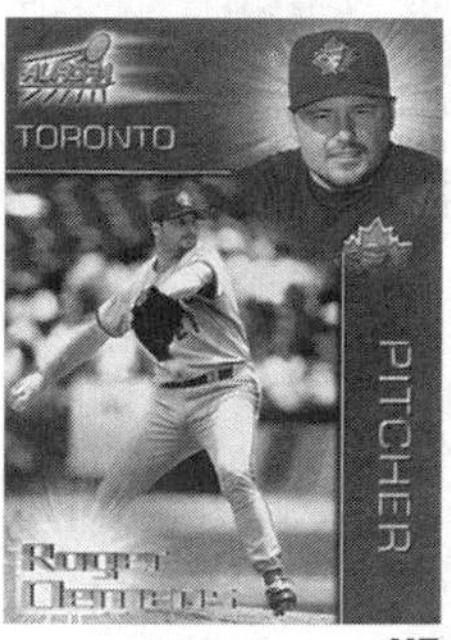

		MT
Complete Set (200):		40.00
Common Player:		.15
Pack (6):		3.00
Wax Box (36):		70.00
1	Garret Anderson	.15
2	Jim Edmonds	.25
3	Darin Erstad	.75
4	Cecil Fielder	.15
5	Chuck Finley	.15
6	Todd Greene	.15
7	Ken Hill	.15
8	Tim Salmon	.25
9	Roberto Alomar	.60
10	Brady Anderson	.20
11	Joe Carter	.15
12	Mike Mussina	.50
13	Rafael Palmeiro	.25
14	Cal Ripken Jr.	2.50
15	B.J. Surhoff	.15
16	Steve Avery	.15
17	Nomar Garciaparra	2.00
18	Pedro Martinez	.75
19	John Valentin	.15
20	Jason Varitek	.15
21	Mo Vaughn	.40
22	Albert Belle	.40
23	Ray Durham	.15
24	*Magglio Ordonez*	1.00
25	Frank Thomas	1.00
26	Robin Ventura	.20
27	Sandy Alomar Jr.	.20
28	Travis Fryman	.25
29	Dwight Gooden	.25
30	David Justice	.40
31	Kenny Lofton	.30
32	Manny Ramirez	.75
33	Jim Thome	.30
34	Omar Vizquel	.15
35	Enrique Wilson	.15
36	Jaret Wright	.15
37	Tony Clark	.20
38	Bobby Higginson	.15
39	Brian Hunter	.15
40	Bip Roberts	.15
41	Justin Thompson	.15
42	Jeff Conine	.15
43	Johnny Damon	.15
44	Jermaine Dye	.15
45	Jeff King	.15
46	Jeff Montgomery	.15
47	Hal Morris	.15
48	Dean Palmer	.15
49	Terry Pendleton	.15
50	Rick Aguilera	.15
51	Marty Cordova	.15
52	Paul Molitor	.50
53	Otis Nixon	.15
54	Brad Radke	.15
55	Terry Steinbach	.15
56	Todd Walker	.15
57	Chili Davis	.15
58	Derek Jeter	2.50
59	Chuck Knoblauch	.25
60	Tino Martinez	.25
61	Paul O'Neill	.25
62	Andy Pettitte	.30
63	Mariano Rivera	.25
64	Bernie Williams	.60
65	Jason Giambi	.40
66	Ben Grieve	.40
67	Rickey Henderson	.25
68	A.J. Hinch	.15
69	Kenny Rogers	.15
70	Jay Buhner	.20
71	Joey Cora	.15
72	Ken Griffey Jr.	2.50
73	Randy Johnson	.75
74	Edgar Martinez	.20
75	Jamie Moyer	.15
76	Alex Rodriguez	2.50
77	David Segui	.15
78	*Rolando Arrojo*	.40
79	Wade Boggs	.40
80	Roberto Hernandez	.15
81	Dave Martinez	.15
82	Fred McGriff	.40
83	Paul Sorrento	.15
84	Kevin Stocker	.15
85	Will Clark	.40
86	Juan Gonzalez	.75
87	Tom Goodwin	.15
88	Rusty Greer	.20
89	Ivan Rodriguez	.75
90	John Wetteland	.15
91	Jose Canseco	.50
92	Roger Clemens	1.00
93	Jose Cruz Jr.	.25
94	Carlos Delgado	.75
95	Pat Hentgen	.15
96	Jay Bell	.15
97	Andy Benes	.25
98	Karim Garcia	.20
99	Travis Lee	.20
100	Devon White	.15
101	Matt Williams	.30
102	Andres Galarraga	.40
103	Tom Glavine	.25
104	Andruw Jones	.75
105	Chipper Jones	1.50
106	Ryan Klesko	.25
107	Javy Lopez	.25
108	Greg Maddux	1.50
109	Walt Weiss	.15
110	Rod Beck	.15
111	Jeff Blauser	.15
112	Mark Grace	.40
113	Lance Johnson	.15
114	Mickey Morandini	.15
115	Henry Rodriguez	.15
116	Sammy Sosa	1.50
117	Kerry Wood	.40
118	Lenny Harris	.15
119	Damian Jackson	.15
120	Barry Larkin	.40
121	Reggie Sanders	.15
122	Brett Tomko	.15
123	Dante Bichette	.25
124	Ellis Burks	.15
125	Vinny Castilla	.15
126	Todd Helton	.75
127	Darryl Kile	.15
128	Larry Walker	.40
129	Bobby Bonilla	.20
130	Livan Hernandez	.20
131	Charles Johnson	.15
132	Derrek Lee	.15
133	Edgar Renteria	.20
134	Gary Sheffield	.40
135	Moises Alou	.25
136	Jeff Bagwell	.75
137	Derek Bell	.15
138	Craig Biggio	.25
139	*John Halama*	.40
140	Mike Hampton	.15
141	Richard Hidalgo	.15
142	Wilton Guerrero	.15
143	Todd Hollandsworth	.15
144	Eric Karros	.20
145	Paul Konerko	.20
146	Raul Mondesi	.25
147	Hideo Nomo	.50
148	Chan Ho Park	.25
149	Mike Piazza	2.00
150	Jeromy Burnitz	.15
151	Todd Dunn	.15
152	Marquis Grissom	.15
153	John Jaha	.15
154	Dave Nilsson	.15
155	Fernando Vina	.15
156	Mark Grudzielanek	.15
157	Vladimir Guerrero	1.00
158	F.P. Santangelo	.15
159	Jose Vidro	.15
160	Rondell White	.25
161	Edgardo Alfonzo	.20
162	Carlos Baerga	.15
163	John Franco	.15
164	Todd Hundley	.15
165	Brian McRae	.15
166	John Olerud	.25
167	Rey Ordonez	.15
168	*Masato Yoshii*	.50
169	Ricky Bottalico	.15
170	Doug Glanville	.15
171	Gregg Jefferies	.15
172	Desi Relaford	.15
173	Scott Rolen	.50
174	Curt Schilling	.25
175	Jose Guillen	.15
176	Jason Kendall	.15
177	Al Martin	.15
178	Abraham Nunez	.15
179	Kevin Young	.15
180	Royce Clayton	.15
181	Delino DeShields	.15
182	Gary Gaetti	.15
183	Ron Gant	.15
184	Brian Jordan	.15
185	Ray Lankford	.15
186	Willie McGee	.15
187	Mark McGwire	3.00
188	Kevin Brown	.25
189	Ken Caminiti	.25
190	Steve Finley	.15
191	Tony Gwynn	1.00
192	Wally Joyner	.15
193	Ruben Rivera	.15
194	Quilvio Veras	.15
195	Barry Bonds	.75
196	Shawn Estes	.15
197	Orel Hershiser	.15
198	Jeff Kent	.15
199	Robb Nen	.15
200	J.T. Snow	.15

1998 Pacific Aurora Cubes

A cardboard cube presenting player photos on top and three sides, plus a side of stats was created as a hobby-only insert for Pacific Aurora. The assembled, shrink-wrapped cubes were packed one per box.

		MT
Complete Set (20):		100.00
Common Player:		2.00
Inserted 1:box		
1	Travis Lee	2.00
2	Chipper Jones	8.00

3	Greg Maddux	8.00
4	Cal Ripken Jr.	12.00
5	Nomar Garciaparra	10.00
6	Frank Thomas	5.00
7	Manny Ramirez	4.00
8	Larry Walker	2.50
9	Hideo Nomo	3.00
10	Mike Piazza	10.00
11	Derek Jeter	10.00
12	Ben Grieve	2.50
13	Mark McGwire	15.00
14	Tony Gwynn	5.00
15	Barry Bonds	4.00
16	Ken Griffey Jr.	12.00
17	Alex Rodriguez	12.00
18	Wade Boggs	3.00
19	Juan Gonzalez	4.00
20	Jose Cruz Jr.	2.00

1998 Pacific Aurora Hardball Cel-Fusion

Hardball Cel-Fusions is a 20-card insert seeded one per 73 packs. The cards feature a die-cut cel baseball fused to a foiled and etched card.

		MT
Complete Set (20):		500.00
Common Player:		10.00
Inserted 1:73		
1	Travis Lee	12.00
2	Chipper Jones	40.00
3	Greg Maddux	40.00
4	Cal Ripken Jr.	50.00
5	Nomar Garciaparra	40.00
6	Frank Thomas	25.00
7	David Justice	10.00
8	Jeff Bagwell	20.00
9	Hideo Nomo	10.00
10	Mike Piazza	40.00
11	Derek Jeter	40.00
12	Ben Grieve	20.00
13	Scott Rolen	20.00
14	Mark McGwire	60.00
15	Tony Gwynn	30.00
16	Ken Griffey Jr.	60.00
17	Alex Rodriguez	50.00
18	Ivan Rodriguez	15.00
19	Roger Clemens	20.00
20	Jose Cruz Jr.	10.00

1998 Pacific Aurora Kings of the Major Leagues

This 10-card insert features star players on fully-foiled cards. Kings of the Major Leagues was seeded one per 361 packs.

		MT
Complete Set (10):		425.00
Common Player:		35.00
Inserted 1:361		
1	Chipper Jones	45.00
2	Greg Maddux	45.00
3	Cal Ripken Jr.	55.00
4	Nomar Garciaparra	45.00
5	Frank Thomas	35.00
6	Mike Piazza	45.00
7	Mark McGwire	75.00
8	Tony Gwynn	35.00
9	Ken Griffey Jr.	75.00
10	Alex Rodriguez	60.00

1998 Pacific Aurora On Deck Laser-Cut

On Deck Laser-Cuts is a 20-card insert seeded four per 37 packs of 1998 Pacific Aurora Baseball. Fronts have an action pphoto at top, with an intricately die-cut pattern in gold foil below. Backs feature a portrait photo.

		MT
Complete Set (20):		70.00
Common Player:		1.00
Inserted 1:9		
1	Travis Lee	2.00
2	Chipper Jones	6.00
3	Greg Maddux	6.00
4	Cal Ripken Jr.	8.00
5	Nomar Garciaparra	6.00
6	Frank Thomas	5.00
7	Manny Ramirez	4.00
8	Larry Walker	1.00
9	Hideo Nomo	1.50
10	Mike Piazza	6.00
11	Derek Jeter	6.00
12	Ben Grieve	4.00
13	Mark McGwire	12.50
14	Tony Gwynn	5.00
15	Barry Bonds	2.50
16	Ken Griffey Jr.	12.50
17	Alex Rodriguez	8.00
18	Wade Boggs	1.50
19	Juan Gonzalez	4.00
20	Jose Cruz Jr.	1.00

1998 Pacific Aurora Pennant Fever

Pennant Fever is a 50-card insert seeded one per pack. Each card is fully foiled and etched. The color player image is duplicated in the upper-left corner with an image stamped in gold foil. Pennant Fever has four parallels. Red cards are a 1:4 retail insert. The Silver retail parallel is numbered to 250, Platinum Blue is numbered to 100 and the Copper hobby parallel is numbered to 20. Tony Gwynn signed his card serially numbered one in each insert.

		MT
Complete Set (50):		20.00
Common Player:		.25
Inserted 1:1		
Reds:		2.5X
Inserted 1:4 Retail		
Silvers:		15-25X
Production 250 sets		
Platinum Blues:		35-50X
Production 100 sets		
Coppers:		75-125X
Production 20 sets		
1	Tony Gwynn	1.00
2	Derek Jeter	1.50
3	Alex Rodriguez	2.00
4	Paul Molitor	.40
5	Nomar Garciaparra	1.25
6	Jeff Bagwell	.75
7	Ivan Rodriguez	.50
8	Cal Ripken Jr.	2.00
9	Matt Williams	.25
10	Chipper Jones	1.25
11	Edgar Martinez	.25
12	Wade Boggs	.35
13	Paul Konerko	.25
14	Ben Grieve	.75
15	Sandy Alomar Jr.	.25
16	Travis Lee	.50
17	Scott Rolen	.75
18	Ryan Klesko	.25
19	Juan Gonzalez	.75
20	Albert Belle	.50
21	Roger Clemens	1.00
22	Javy Lopez	.25
23	Jose Cruz Jr.	.25
24	Ken Griffey Jr.	2.50
25	Mark McGwire	2.50
26	Brady Anderson	.25
27	Jaret Wright	.50
28	Roberto Alomar	.40
29	Joe Carter	.25
30	Hideo Nomo	.40
31	Mike Piazza	1.50
32	Andres Galarraga	.25
33	Larry Walker	.35
34	Tim Salmon	.25
35	Frank Thomas	1.00
36	Moises Alou	.25
37	David Justice	.40
38	Manny Ramirez	.75
39	Jim Edmonds	.25
40	Barry Bonds	.50
41	Jim Thome	.40
42	Mo Vaughn	.50
43	Rafael Palmeiro	.35
44	Darin Erstad	.50
45	Pedro Martinez	.50
46	Greg Maddux	1.25
47	Jose Canseco	.35
48	Vladimir Guerrero	1.00
49	Bernie Williams	.40
50	Randy Johnson	.40

1998 Pacific Crown Royale

The Crown Royale base set consists of 144 die-cut cards. The cards have a horizontal layout and are die-cut around a crown design at the top. The cards are double-foiled and etched. Inserts include Diamond Knights, Pillars of the Game, Race to the Record, All-Star Die-Cuts, Firestone on Baseball and Cramer's Choice Awards.

		MT
Complete Set (144):		125.00
Common Player:		.50
Pack (6):		5.00
Wax Box (24):		90.00
1	Garret Anderson	.50
2	Jim Edmonds	.75
3	Darin Erstad	2.00
4	Tim Salmon	1.00
5	Jarrod Washburn	.50
6	David Dellucci	.50
7	Travis Lee	.50
8	Devon White	.50
9	Matt Williams	1.00
10	Andres Galarraga	1.00
11	Tom Glavine	1.00
12	Andruw Jones	2.00
13	Chipper Jones	5.00
14	Ryan Klesko	.75
15	Javy Lopez	.75
16	Greg Maddux	5.00
17	Walt Weiss	.50
18	Roberto Alomar	1.50
19	Harold Baines	.50
20	Eric Davis	.50
21	Mike Mussina	2.00
22	Rafael Palmeiro	1.00
23	Cal Ripken Jr.	8.00
24	Nomar Garciaparra	6.00
25	Pedro Martinez	2.50
26	Troy O'Leary	.50
27	Mo Vaughn	1.50
28	Tim Wakefield	.50
29	Mark Grace	1.00
30	Mickey Morandini	.50
31	Sammy Sosa	6.00
32	Kerry Wood	1.50
33	Albert Belle	1.50
34	Mike Caruso	.50
35	Ray Durham	.50
36	Frank Thomas	3.00
37	Robin Ventura	.75
38	Bret Boone	.50
39	Sean Casey	.75
40	Barry Larkin	1.00
41	Reggie Sanders	.50
42	Sandy Alomar Jr.	.50
43	David Justice	1.00
44	Kenny Lofton	1.00
45	Manny Ramirez	2.50
46	Jim Thome	1.00
47	Omar Vizquel	.50
48	Jaret Wright	.75
49	Dante Bichette	.75
50	Ellis Burks	.50
51	Vinny Castilla	.75
52	Todd Helton	2.50
53	Larry Walker	1.00
54	Tony Clark	.75
55	Damion Easley	.50
56	Bobby Higginson	.50
57	Cliff Floyd	.50
58	Livan Hernandez	.50
59	Derrek Lee	.50
60	Edgar Renteria	.50
61	Moises Alou	.75
62	Jeff Bagwell	2.50
63	Derek Bell	.50
64	Craig Biggio	.75
65	Johnny Damon	.50
66	Jeff King	.50
67	Hal Morris	.50
68	Dean Palmer	.50
69	Bobby Bonilla	.50
70	Eric Karros	.75
71	Raul Mondesi	.75
72	Gary Sheffield	1.00
73	Jeromy Burnitz	.50
74	Jeff Cirillo	.50
75	Marquis Grissom	.50
76	Fernando Vina	.50
77	Marty Cordova	.50
78	Pat Meares	.50
79	Paul Molitor	1.50
80	Terry Steinbach	.50
81	Todd Walker	.50
82	Brad Fullmer	1.00
83	Vladimir Guerrero	3.00
84	Carl Pavano	.50
85	Rondell White	.75
86	Carlos Baerga	.50
87	Hideo Nomo	1.00
88	John Olerud	.75

89	Rey Ordonez	.50
90	Mike Piazza	6.00
91	*Masato Yoshii*	1.50
92	*Orlando Hernandez*	4.00
93	Hideki Irabu	.50
94	Derek Jeter	8.00
95	Chuck Knoblauch	1.00
96	Ricky Ledee	.50
97	Tino Martinez	.50
98	Paul O'Neill	.75
99	Bernie Williams	2.00
100	Jason Giambi	1.00
101	Ben Grieve	1.00
102	Rickey Henderson	1.00
103	Matt Stairs	.50
104	Bob Abreu	.50
105	Doug Glanville	.50
106	Scott Rolen	1.50
107	Curt Schilling	.75
108	Jose Guillen	.50
109	Jason Kendall	.75
110	Jason Schmidt	.50
111	Kevin Young	.50
112	Delino DeShields	.50
113	Brian Jordan	.50
114	Ray Lankford	.50
115	Mark McGwire	10.00
116	Tony Gwynn	3.00
117	Wally Joyner	.50
118	Ruben Rivera	.50
119	Greg Vaughn	.75
120	Rich Aurilia	.50
121	Barry Bonds	2.50
122	Bill Mueller	.50
123	Robb Nen	.50
124	Jay Buhner	.50
125	Ken Griffey Jr.	8.00
126	Edgar Martinez	.50
127	Shane Monahan	.50
128	Alex Rodriguez	8.00
129	David Segui	.50
130	*Rolando Arrojo*	1.50
131	Wade Boggs	.75
132	Quinton McCracken	.50
133	Fred McGriff	.75
134	Bobby Smith	.50
135	Will Clark	1.00
136	Juan Gonzalez	2.50
137	Rusty Greer	.50
138	Ivan Rodriguez	2.50
139	Aaron Sele	.50
140	John Wetteland	.50
141	Jose Canseco	1.50
142	Roger Clemens	4.00
143	Carlos Delgado	2.00
144	Shawn Green	1.00

1998 Pacific Crown Royale All-Star

This 20-card insert was seeded one per 25 packs. The featured players all participated in the 1998 All-Star Game. The background features the sun rising over a mountain with a die-cut at the top of the card.

		MT
Complete Set (20):		350.00
Common Player:		5.00
Inserted 1:25		
1	Roberto Alomar	10.00
2	Cal Ripken Jr.	40.00
3	Kenny Lofton	10.00
4	Jim Thome	8.00
5	Derek Jeter	30.00
6	David Wells	5.00
7	Ken Griffey Jr.	50.00
8	Alex Rodriguez	40.00
9	Juan Gonzalez	15.00
10	Ivan Rodriguez	15.00
11	Gary Sheffield	5.00
12	Chipper Jones	30.00
13	Greg Maddux	30.00
14	Walt Weiss	5.00
15	Larry Walker	8.00
16	Craig Biggio	5.00
17	Mike Piazza	30.00
18	Mark McGwire	50.00
19	Tony Gwynn	25.00
20	Barry Bonds	15.00

1998 Pacific Crown Royale Cramer's Choice Awards

Premium-sized Cramer's Choice Awards were inserted one per box. The ten players in the set are featured on a die-cut card designed to resemble a trophy. Pacific CEO Mike Cramer signed and hand-numbered ten sets of Cramer's Choice Awards.

		MT
Complete Set (10):		100.00
Common Player:		5.00
Inserted 1:box		
1	Cal Ripken Jr.	15.00
2	Ken Griffey Jr.	20.00
3	Alex Rodriguez	15.00
4	Juan Gonzalez	5.00
5	Travis Lee	5.00
6	Chipper Jones	12.00
7	Greg Maddux	12.00
8	Kerry Wood	5.00
9	Mark McGwire	20.00
10	Tony Gwynn	10.00

1998 Pacific Crown Royale Diamond Knights

Diamond Knights is a 25-card, one per pack insert. Each card features a color action photo and the player's name, team and position listed in a Medieval-type border at the bottom.

		MT
Complete Set (25):		40.00
Common Player:		.75
Inserted 1:1		
1	Andres Galarraga	1.00
2	Chipper Jones	3.00
3	Greg Maddux	3.00
4	Cal Ripken Jr.	4.00
5	Nomar Garciaparra	3.00
6	Mo Vaughn	1.00
7	Kerry Wood	1.50
8	Frank Thomas	2.50
9	Vinny Castilla	.75
10	Jeff Bagwell	1.50
11	Craig Biggio	1.00
12	Paul Molitor	1.00
13	Mike Piazza	3.00
14	Orlando Hernandez	3.00
15	Derek Jeter	3.00
16	Ricky Ledee	.75
17	Mark McGwire	6.00
18	Tony Gwynn	2.50
19	Barry Bonds	1.25
20	Ken Griffey Jr.	6.00
21	Alex Rodriguez	4.00
22	Wade Boggs	1.00
23	Juan Gonzalez	1.50
24	Ivan Rodriguez	1.25
25	Jose Canseco	1.00

1998 Pacific Crown Royale Firestone on Baseball

This 26-card insert features star players with commentary by sports personality Roy Firestone. The fronts have a color photo of the player and a portrait of Firestone in the lower right corner. The card backs have text by Firestone on what makes the featured player great. Firestone signed a total of 300 cards in this insert.

		MT
Complete Set (26):		200.00
Common Player:		2.00
Inserted 1:12		
1	Travis Lee	4.00
2	Chipper Jones	15.00
3	Greg Maddux	15.00
4	Cal Ripken Jr.	20.00
5	Nomar Garciaparra	15.00
6	Mo Vaughn	5.00
7	Kerry Wood	5.00
8	Frank Thomas	10.00
9	Manny Ramirez	6.50
10	Larry Walker	3.00
11	Gary Sheffield	2.00
12	Paul Molitor	4.00
13	Hideo Nomo	2.50
14	Mike Piazza	15.00
15	Ben Grieve	7.50
16	Mark McGwire	25.00
17	Tony Gwynn	12.50
18	Barry Bonds	5.00
19	Ken Griffey Jr.	25.00
20	Randy Johnson	4.00
21	Alex Rodriquez	20.00
22	Wade Boggs	2.50
23	Juan Gonzalez	6.00
24	Ivan Rodriguez	5.00
25	Roger Clemens	10.00
26	Roy Firestone	2.00

1998 Pacific Crown Royale Home Run Fever

Home Run Fever (10 cards, 1:73) features players who had a shot at breaking Roger Maris' home run record in 1998. The card fronts have a player photo on the left and a blackboard with numbers from 1 to 60 on the right. Ten circles featuring disappearing ink contained numbers 61 through 70. Collectors could rub the circles to reveal the player's potential record home run total.

		MT
Complete Set (10):		225.00
Common Player:		7.50
Inserted 1:73		
1	Andres Galarraga	7.50
2	Sammy Sosa	35.00
3	Albert Belle	15.00
4	Jim Thome	7.50
5	Mark McGwire	60.00
6	Greg Vaughn	7.50
7	Ken Griffey Jr.	60.00
8	Alex Rodriguez	55.00
9	Juan Gonzalez	15.00
10	Jose Canseco	10.00

1998 Pacific Crown Royale Pillars of the Game

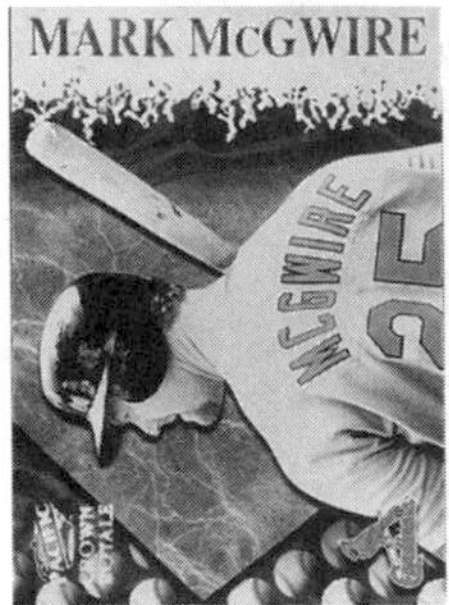

This 25-card insert was seeded one per pack. Each card features a star player with a background of holographic silver foil.

		MT
Complete Set (25):		40.00
Common Player:		.75
Inserted 1:1		
1	Jim Edmonds	.75
2	Travis Lee	1.00
3	Chipper Jones	3.00
4	Tom Glavine, John Smoltz, Greg Maddux	2.00
5	Cal Ripken Jr.	4.00
6	Nomar Garciaparra	3.00
7	Mo Vaughn	1.25
8	Sammy Sosa	4.00
9	Kerry Wood	1.50
10	Frank Thomas	2.50
11	Jim Thome	1.00
12	Larry Walker	1.00
13	Moises Alou	.75
14	Raul Mondesi	1.00
15	Mike Piazza	3.00
16	Hideki Irabu	1.00
17	Bernie Williams	1.00
18	Ben Grieve	1.50
19	Scott Rolen	1.50
20	Mark McGwire	6.00
21	Tony Gwynn	2.50
22	Ken Griffey Jr.	6.00
23	Alex Rodriguez	4.00
24	Juan Gonzalez	1.50
25	Roger Clemens	2.00

1998 Pacific Invincible

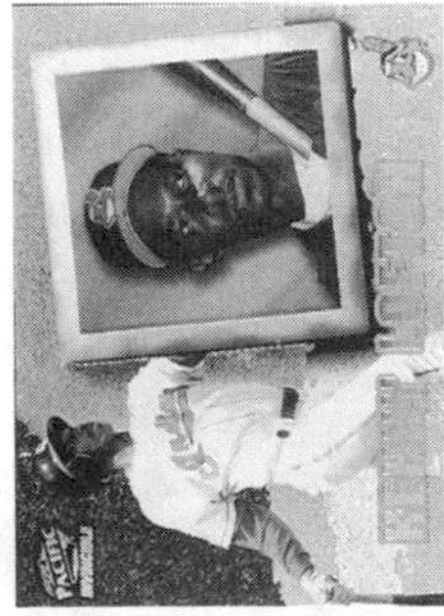

Invincible Baseball consists of a 150-card base set. The base cards have a horizontal layout and feature a player photo on the left and a headshot in a cel window on the right. The regular cards were inserted one per five-card pack. Silver (2:37) and Platinum Blue (1:73) parallels were also created. Inserts include Moments in Time, Team Checklists, Photoengravings, Interleague Players, Gems of the Diamond and Cramer's Choice Awards.

		MT
Complete Set (150):		175.00
Common Player:		1.00
Silvers:		3X
Inserted 2:37		
Platinum Blues:		8X
Inserted 1:73		
Pack (5):		4.00
Wax Box (36):		100.00
1	Garret Anderson	1.00
2	Jim Edmonds	1.50
3	Darin Erstad	4.00
4	Chuck Finley	1.00
5	Tim Salmon	2.00
6	Roberto Alomar	3.00
7	Brady Anderson	1.50
8	Geronimo Berroa	1.00
9	Eric Davis	1.00
10	Mike Mussina	3.00
11	Rafael Palmeiro	2.50
12	Cal Ripken Jr.	12.00
13	Steve Avery	1.00
14	Nomar Garciaparra	9.00
15	John Valentin	1.00
16	Mo Vaughn	3.00
17	Albert Belle	4.00
18	Ozzie Guillen	1.00
19	Norberto Martin	1.00
20	Frank Thomas	7.00
21	Robin Ventura	1.50
22	Sandy Alomar Jr.	1.00
23	David Justice	1.50
24	Kenny Lofton	3.00
25	Manny Ramirez	5.00
26	Jim Thome	1.50
27	Omar Vizquel	1.00
28	Matt Williams	2.00
29	Jaret Wright	6.00
30	Raul Casanova	1.00
31	Tony Clark	1.50
32	Deivi Cruz	1.00
33	Bobby Higginson	1.00
34	Justin Thompson	1.00
35	Yamil Benitez	1.00
36	Johnny Damon	1.00
37	Jermaine Dye	1.00
38	Jed Hansen	1.00
39	Larry Sutton	1.00
40	Jeromy Burnitz	1.00
41	Jeff Cirillo	1.00
42	Dave Nilsson	1.00
43	Jose Valentin	1.00
44	Fernando Vina	1.00
45	Marty Cordova	1.00
46	Chuck Knoblauch	2.00
47	Paul Molitor	3.00
48	Brad Radke	1.00
49	Terry Steinbach	1.00
50	Wade Boggs	2.00
51	Hideki Irabu	1.00
52	Derek Jeter	10.00
53	Tino Martinez	1.50
54	Andy Pettitte	3.00
55	Mariano Rivera	1.50
56	Bernie Williams	3.00
57	Jose Canseco	1.50
58	Jason Giambi	1.00
59	Ben Grieve	6.00
60	Aaron Small	1.00
61	Jay Buhner	1.00
62	Ken Cloude	1.00
63	Joey Cora	1.00
64	Ken Griffey Jr.	15.00
65	Randy Johnson	3.00
66	Edgar Martinez	1.00
67	Alex Rodriguez	12.00
68	Will Clark	1.50
69	Juan Gonzalez	4.00
70	Rusty Greer	1.00
71	Ivan Rodriguez	4.00
72	Joe Carter	1.00
73	Roger Clemens	5.00
74	Jose Cruz Jr.	1.00
75	Carlos Delgado	1.50
76	Andruw Jones	7.00
77	Chipper Jones	9.00
78	Ryan Klesko	1.00
79	Javier Lopez	1.50
80	Greg Maddux	9.00
81	Miguel Batista	1.00
82	Jeremi Gonzalez	1.00
83	Mark Grace	2.50
84	Kevin Orie	1.00
85	Sammy Sosa	10.00
86	Barry Larkin	1.50
87	Deion Sanders	1.50
88	Reggie Sanders	1.00
89	Chris Stynes	1.00
90	Dante Bichette	1.50
91	Vinny Castilla	1.00
92	Andres Galarraga	2.00
93	Neifi Perez	1.00
94	Larry Walker	2.50
95	Moises Alou	1.00
96	Bobby Bonilla	1.00
97	Kevin Brown	1.50
98	Craig Counsell	1.00
99	Livan Hernandez	1.50
100	Edgar Renteria	1.00
101	Gary Sheffield	2.00
102	Jeff Bagwell	7.00
103	Craig Biggio	1.50
104	Luis Gonzalez	1.00
105	Darryl Kile	1.00
106	Wilton Guerrero	1.00
107	Eric Karros	1.50
108	Ramon Martinez	1.50
109	Raul Mondesi	2.00
110	Hideo Nomo	3.00
111	Chan Ho Park	1.50
112	Mike Piazza	9.00
113	Mark Grudzielanek	1.00
114	Vladimir Guerrero	5.00
115	Pedro Martinez	3.00
116	Henry Rodriguez	1.00
117	David Segui	1.00
118	Edgardo Alfonzo	1.00
119	Carlos Baerga	1.00
120	John Franco	1.00
121	John Olerud	1.50
122	Rey Ordonez	1.00
123	Ricky Bottalico	1.00
124	Gregg Jefferies	1.00
125	Mickey Morandini	1.00
126	Scott Rolen	6.00
127	Curt Schilling	1.50
128	Jose Guillen	2.00
129	Esteban Loaiza	1.00
130	Al Martin	1.00
131	Tony Womack	1.00
132	Dennis Eckersley	1.00
133	Gary Gaetti	1.00
134	Curtis King	1.00
135	Ray Lankford	1.00
136	Mark McGwire	15.00
137	Ken Caminiti	1.50
138	Steve Finley	1.00
139	Tony Gwynn	7.00
140	Carlos Hernandez	1.00
141	Wally Joyner	1.00
142	Barry Bonds	4.00
143	Jacob Cruz	1.00
144	Shawn Estes	1.00
145	Stan Javier	1.00
146	J.T. Snow	1.50
147	Nomar Garciaparra	7.00
148	Scott Rolen	4.00
149	Ken Griffey Jr.	10.00
150	Larry Walker	1.50

1998 Pacific Invincible Cramer's Choice

The 10-card Cramer's Choice Awards insert features top players on cards with a die-cut trophy design. This set has six different foil variations, each with a different production number. Green (99 hand-numbered sets), Dark Blue (80), Light Blue (50), Red (25), Gold (15) and Purple (10) versions were included in Invincible.

		MT
Complete Green Set (10):		1100.
Common Green (99 sets):		50.00
Dark Blues (80 sets):		1X
Light Blues (50 sets):		1.5X
Reds (25 sets):		2X
Golds (15 sets):		3X
Purples (10 sets):		5X
1	Greg Maddux	125.00
2	Roberto Alomar	50.00
3	Cal Ripken Jr.	200.00
4	Nomar Garciaparra	125.00
5	Larry Walker	50.00
6	Mike Piazza	150.00
7	Mark McGwire	250.00
8	Tony Gwynn	125.00
9	Ken Griffey Jr.	250.00
10	Roger Clemens	100.00

1998 Pacific Invincible Gems of the Diamond

Gems of the Diamond is a 220-card insert seeded four per pack. The cards feature a color photo inside a white border.

		MT
Complete Set (220):		30.00
Common Player:		.10
1	Jim Edmonds	.20
2	Todd Greene	.20
3	Ken Hill	.10
4	Mike Holtz	.10
5	Mike James	.10
6	Chad Kreuter	.10
7	Tim Salmon	.30
8	Roberto Alomar	.60
9	Brady Anderson	.15
10	David Dellucci	.10
11	Jeffrey Hammonds	.10
12	Mike Mussina	.60
13	Rafael Palmeiro	.25
14	Arthur Rhodes	.10
15	Cal Ripken Jr.	2.50
16	Nerio Rodriguez	.10
17	Tony Tarasco	.10
18	Lenny Webster	.10
19	Mike Benjamin	.10
20	Rich Garces	.10
21	Nomar Garciaparra	2.00
22	Shane Mack	.10
23	Jose Malave	.10
24	Jesus Tavarez	.10
25	Mo Vaughn	.60
26	John Wasdin	.10

27	Jeff Abbott	.10
28	Albert Belle	.50
29	Mike Cameron	.25
30	Al Levine	.10
31	Robert Machado	.10
32	Greg Norton	.10
33	Maggilo Ordonez	.35
34	Mike Sirotka	.10
35	Frank Thomas	1.00
36	Mario Valdez	.10
37	Sandy Alomar Jr.	.20
38	David Justice	.25
39	Jack McDowell	.10
40	Eric Plunk	.10
41	Manny Ramirez	.75
42	Kevin Seitzer	.10
43	Paul Shuey	.10
44	Omar Vizquel	.10
45	Kimera Bartee	.10
46	Glenn Dishman	.10
47	Orlando Miller	.10
48	Mike Myers	.10
49	Phil Nevin	.10
50	A.J. Sager	.10
51	Ricky Bones	.10
52	Scott Cooper	.10
53	Shane Halter	.10
54	David Howard	.10
55	Glendon Rusch	.10
56	Joe Vitiello	.10
57	Jeff D'Amico	.10
58	Mike Fetters	.10
59	Mike Matheny	.10
60	Jose Mercedes	.10
61	Ron Villone	.10
62	Jack Voigt	.10
63	Brent Brede	.10
64	Chuck Knoblauch	.25
65	Paul Molitor	.50
66	Todd Ritchie	.10
67	Frankie Rodriguez	.10
68	Scott Stahoviak	.10
69	Greg Swindell	.10
70	Todd Walker	.20
71	Wade Boggs	.25
72	Hideki Irabu	.30
73	Derek Jeter	2.00
74	Pat Kelly	.10
75	Graeme Lloyd	.10
76	Tino Martinez	.25
77	Jeff Nelson	.10
78	Scott Pose	.10
79	Mike Stanton	.10
80	Darryl Strawberry	.10
81	Bernie Williams	.50
82	Tony Batista	.10
83	Mark Bellhorn	.10
84	Ben Grieve	.50
85	Pat Lennon	.10
86	Brian Lesher	.10
87	Miguel Tejada	.25
88	George Williams	.10
89	Joey Cora	.10
90	Rob Ducey	.10
91	Ken Griffey Jr.	2.50
92	Randy Johnson	.50
93	Edgar Martinez	.10
94	John Marzano	.10
95	Greg McCarthy	.10
96	Alex Rodriguez	2.50
97	Andy Sheets	.10
98	Mike Timlin	.10
99	Lee Tinsley	.10
100	Damon Buford	.10
101	Alex Diaz	.10
102	Benji Gil	.10
103	Juan Gonzalez	.75
104	Eric Gunderson	.10
105	Danny Patterson	.10
106	Ivan Rodriguez	.75
107	Mike Simms	.10
108	Luis Andujar	.10
109	Joe Carter	.15
110	Roger Clemens	1.00
111	Jose Cruz Jr.	.40
112	Shawn Green	.15
113	Robert Perez	.10
114	Juan Samuel	.10
115	Ed Sprague	.10
116	Shannon Stewart	.10
117	Danny Bautista	.10
118	Chipper Jones	2.00
119	Ryan Klesko	.20
120	Keith Lockhart	.10
121	Javier Lopez	.15
122	Greg Maddux	2.00
123	Kevin Millwood	.75
124	Mike Mordecai	.10
125	Eddie Perez	.10
126	Randall Simon	.25
127	Miguel Cairo	.10
128	Dave Clark	.10
129	Kevin Foster	.10
130	Mark Grace	.25
131	Tyler Houston	.10
132	Mike Hubbard	.10
133	Kevin Orie	.10
134	Ryne Sandberg	.75
135	Sammy Sosa	1.50
136	Lenny Harris	.10
137	Kent Mercker	.10
138	Mike Morgan	.10
139	Deion Sanders	.15
140	Chris Stynes	.10
141	Gabe White	.10
142	Jason Bates	.10
143	Vinny Castilla	.10
144	Andres Galarraga	.25
145	Curtis Leskanic	.10
146	Jeff McCurry	.10
147	Mike Munoz	.10
148	Larry Walker	.30
149	Jamey Wright	.10
150	Moises Alou	.20
151	Bobby Bonilla	.10
152	Kevin Brown	.15
153	John Cangelosi	.10
154	Jeff Conine	.10
155	Cliff Floyd	.10
156	Jay Powell	.10
157	Edgar Renteria	.10
158	Tony Saunders	.10
159	Gary Sheffield	.25
160	Jeff Bagwell	.75
161	Tim Bogar	.10
162	Tony Eusebio	.10
163	Chris Holt	.10
164	Ray Montgomery	.10
165	Luis Rivera	.10
166	Eric Anthony	.10
167	Brett Butler	.10
168	Juan Castro	.10
169	Tripp Cromer	.10
170	Raul Mondesi	.25
171	Hideo Nomo	.50
172	Mike Piazza	2.00
173	Tom Prince	.10
174	Adam Riggs	.10
175	Shane Andrews	.10
176	Shayne Bennett	.10
177	Raul Chavez	.10
178	Pedro Martinez	.30
179	Sherman Obando	.10
180	Andy Stankiewicz	.10
181	Alberto Castillo	.10
182	Shawn Gilbert	.10
183	Luis Lopez	.10
184	Roberto Petagine	.10
185	Armando Reynoso	.10
186	Midre Cummings	.10
187	Kevin Jordan	.10
188	Desi Relaford	.10
189	Scott Rolen	.50
190	Ken Ryan	.10
191	Kevin Sefcik	.10
192	Emil Brown	.10
193	Lou Collier	.10
194	Francisco Cordova	.10
195	Kevin Elster	.10
196	Mark Smith	.10
197	Marc Wilkins	.10
198	Manny Aybar	.25
199	Jose Bautista	.10
200	David Bell	.10
201	Rigo Beltran	.10
202	Delino DeShields	.10
203	Dennis Eckersley	.10
204	John Mabry	.10
205	Eli Marrero	.10
206	Willie McGee	.10
207	Mark McGwire	3.00
208	Ken Caminiti	.20
209	Tony Gwynn	1.00
210	Chris Jones	.10
211	Craig Shipley	.10
212	Pete Smith	.10
213	Jorge Velandia	.10
214	Dario Veras	.10
215	Rich Aurilia	.10
216	Damon Berryhill	.10
217	Barry Bonds	.75
218	Osvaldo Fernandez	.10
219	Dante Powell	.10
220	Rich Rodriguez	.10

1998 Pacific Invincible Interleague Players

Interleague Players is a 30-card insert featuring 15 sets of players - one National League and one American League player. The dark blue backgrounds have red lightning bolts and the white borders are made of a leather-like material. When a set of players is placed next to each other, they form the MLB Interleague logo in the center. Interleague Players cards were inserted one per 73 packs.

		MT
Complete Set (30):		475.00
Common Player:		4.00
Inserted 1:73		
1A	Roberto Alomar	10.00
1N	Craig Biggio	6.00
2A	Cal Ripken Jr.	40.00
2N	Chipper Jones	30.00
3A	Nomar Garciaparra	30.00
3N	Scott Rolen	20.00
4A	Mo Vaughn	10.00
4N	Andres Galarraga	6.00
5A	Frank Thomas	20.00
5N	Tony Gwynn	25.00
6A	Albert Belle	12.50
6N	Barry Bonds	12.50
7A	Hideki Irabu	5.00
7N	Hideo Nomo	7.50
8A	Derek Jeter	30.00
8N	Rey Ordonez	5.00
9A	Tino Martinez	7.50
9N	Mark McGwire	50.00
10A	Alex Rodriguez	40.00
10N	Edgar Renteria	5.00
11A	Ken Griffey Jr.	50.00
11N	Larry Walker	7.50
12A	Randy Johnson	10.00
12N	Greg Maddux	30.00
13A	Ivan Rodriguez	12.50
13N	Mike Piazza	30.00
14A	Roger Clemens	20.00
14N	Pedro Martinez	7.50
15A	Jose Cruz Jr.	4.00
15N	Wilton Guerrero	4.00

1998 Pacific Invincible Moments in Time

Moments in Time (20 cards, 1:145) is designed as a baseball scoreboard. The cards have a horizontal layout with the date of an important game in the player's career at the top. The player's stats from the game are featured and a picture is located on the scoreboard screen.

		MT
Complete Set (20):		500.00
Common Player:		9.00
Inserted 1:145		
1	Chipper Jones	45.00
2	Cal Ripken Jr.	60.00
3	Frank Thomas	30.00
4	David Justice	9.00
5	Andres Galarraga	9.00
6	Larry Walker	15.00
7	Livan Hernandez	9.00
8	Wilton Guerrero	9.00
9	Hideo Nomo	18.00
10	Mike Piazza	45.00
11	Pedro Martinez	15.00
12	Bernie Williams	9.00
13	Ben Grieve	25.00
14	Scott Rolen	25.00
15	Mark McGwire	75.00
16	Tony Gwynn	35.00
17	Ken Griffey Jr.	75.00
18	Alex Rodriguez	60.00
19	Juan Gonzalez	20.00
20	Jose Cruz Jr.	9.00

1998 Pacific Invincible Photoen gravings

Photoengravings is an 18-card insert seeded one per 37 packs. Each card has a unique "old-style" design with a player photo in a frame in the center.

		MT
Complete Set (18):		150.00
Common Player:		2.00
Inserted 1:37		
1	Greg Maddux	12.50
2	Cal Ripken Jr.	15.00

3	Nomar Garciaparra	12.50
4	Frank Thomas	9.00
5	Larry Walker	4.00
6	Mike Piazza	12.50
7	Hideo Nomo	3.00
8	Pedro Martinez	4.00
9	Derek Jeter	12.50
10	Tino Martinez	2.00
11	Mark McGwire	20.00
12	Tony Gwynn	10.00
13	Barry Bonds	5.00
14	Ken Griffey Jr.	20.00
15	Alex Rodriguez	15.00
16	Ivan Rodriguez	5.00
17	Roger Clemens	7.50
18	Jose Cruz Jr.	2.00

1998 Pacific Invincible Team Checklists

Team Checklists is a 30-card insert seeded 2:37. The fronts feature a player collage with the team logo in the background. The back has a complete checklist for that team in Invincible.

		MT
Complete Set (30):		200.00
Common Player:		3.00
Inserted 2:37		
1	Anaheim Angels	6.00
2	Atlanta Braves	15.00
3	Baltimore Orioles	20.00
4	Boston Red Sox	15.00
5	Chicago Cubs	10.00
6	Chicago White Sox	20.00
7	Cincinnati Reds	3.00
8	Cleveland Indians	5.00
9	Colorado Rockies	4.00
10	Detroit Tigers	5.00
11	Florida Marlins	4.00
12	Houston Astros	10.00
13	Kansas City Royals	3.00
14	Los Angeles Dodgers	15.00
15	Milwaukee Brewers	3.00
16	Minnesota Twins	5.00
17	Montreal Expos	6.00
18	New York Mets	3.00
19	New York Yankees	15.00
20	Oakland Athletics	10.00
21	Philadelphia Phillies	10.00
22	Pittsburgh Pirates	3.00
23	St. Louis Cardinals	10.00
24	San Diego Padres	12.00
25	San Francisco Giants	6.00
26	Seattle Mariners	25.00
27	Texas Rangers	12.00
28	Toronto Blue Jays	15.00
29	Arizona Diamondbacks	5.00
30	Tampa Bay Devil Rays	5.00

1998 Pacific Omega

The Omega base set consists of 250 three-image cards. The horizontal cards feature a color player photo in the center with the image duplicated in foil on the right. Another color photo is on the left. The photos are divided by a baseball seam design. Inserts in the set include Prisms, Face to Face, EO Portraits, Online and Rising Stars.

		MT
Complete Set (250):		35.00
Common Player:		.10
Reds: 6-8X		
Pack (6):		2.00
Wax Box (36):		55.00
1	Garret Anderson	.10
2	Gary DiSarcina	.10
3	Jim Edmonds	.20
4	Darin Erstad	.75
5	Cecil Fielder	.15
6	Chuck Finley	.10
7	Shigetosi Hasegawa	.10
8	Tim Salmon	.25
9	Brian Anderson	.10
10	Jay Bell	.10
11	Andy Benes	.10
12	Yamil Benitez	.10
13	Jorge Fabregas	.10
14	Travis Lee	.75
15	Devon White	.10
16	Matt Williams	.30
17	Andres Galarraga	.25
18	Tom Glavine	.20
19	Andruw Jones	.75
20	Chipper Jones	2.00
21	Ryan Klesko	.25
22	Javy Lopez	.15
23	Greg Maddux	2.00
24	*Kevin Millwood*	2.50
25	Denny Neagle	.10
26	John Smoltz	.20
27	Roberto Alomar	.60
28	Brady Anderson	.10
29	Joe Carter	.15
30	Eric Davis	.10
31	Jimmy Key	.10
32	Mike Mussina	.60
33	Rafael Palmeiro	.25
34	Cal Ripken Jr.	2.50
35	B.J. Surhoff	.10
36	Dennis Eckersley	.10
37	Nomar Garciaparra	2.00
38	Reggie Jefferson	.10
39	Derek Lowe	.10
40	Pedro Martinez	.50
41	Brian Rose	.10
42	John Valentin	.10
43	Jason Varitek	.15
44	Mo Vaughn	.60
45	Jeff Blauser	.10
46	Jeremi Gonzalez	.10
47	Mark Grace	.25
48	Lance Johnson	.10
49	Kevin Orie	.10
50	Henry Rodriguez	.10
51	Sammy Sosa	1.50
52	Kerry Wood	.75
53	Albert Belle	.75
54	Mike Cameron	.10
55	Mike Caruso	.10
56	Ray Durham	.10
57	Jaime Navarro	.10
58	Greg Norton	.10
59	*Magglio Ordonez*	1.00
60	Frank Thomas	1.50
61	Robin Ventura	.20
62	Bret Boone	.10
63	Willie Greene	.10
64	Barry Larkin	.20
65	Jon Nunnally	.10
66	Eduardo Perez	.10
67	Reggie Sanders	.10
68	Brett Tomko	.10
69	Sandy Alomar Jr.	.20
70	Travis Fryman	.10
71	David Justice	.25
72	Kenny Lofton	.60
73	Charles Nagy	.10
74	Manny Ramirez	.75
75	Jim Thome	.40
76	Omar Vizquel	.10
77	Enrique Wilson	.10
78	Jaret Wright	.60
79	Dante Bichette	.25
80	Ellis Burks	.10
81	Vinny Castilla	.20
82	Todd Helton	.75
83	Darryl Kile	.10
84	Mike Lansing	.10
85	Neifi Perez	.10
86	Larry Walker	.40
87	Raul Casanova	.10
88	Tony Clark	.30
89	Luis Gonzalez	.10
90	Bobby Higginson	.10
91	Brian Hunter	.10
92	Bip Roberts	.10
93	Justin Thompson	.10
94	Josh Booty	.10
95	Craig Counsell	.10
96	Livan Hernandez	.10
97	*Ryan Jackson*	.50
98	Mark Kotsay	.25
99	Derrek Lee	.10
100	Mike Piazza	2.00
101	Edgar Renteria	.10
102	Cliff Floyd	.10
103	Moises Alou	.20
104	Jeff Bagwell	1.00
105	Derrick Bell	.10
106	Sean Berry	.10
107	Craig Biggio	.20
108	*John Halama*	.25
109	Richard Hidalgo	.10
110	Shane Reynolds	.10
111	Tim Belcher	.10
112	Brian Bevil	.10
113	Jeff Conine	.10
114	Johnny Damon	.10
115	Jeff King	.10
116	Jeff Montgomery	.10
117	Dean Palmer	.10
118	Terry Pendleton	.10
119	Bobby Bonilla	.15
120	Wilton Guerrero	.10
121	Todd Hollandsworth	.10
122	Charles Johnson	.10
123	Eric Karros	.15
124	Paul Konerko	.25
125	Ramon Martinez	.10
126	Raul Mondesi	.25
127	Hideo Nomo	.40
128	Gary Sheffield	.30
129	Ismael Valdes	.10
130	Jeromy Burnitz	.10
131	Jeff Cirillo	.10
132	Todd Dunn	.10
133	Marquis Grissom	.10
134	John Jaha	.10
135	Scott Karl	.10
136	Dave Nilsson	.10
137	Jose Valentin	.10
138	Fernando Vina	.10
139	Rick Aguilera	.10
140	Marty Cordova	.10
141	Pat Meares	.10
142	Paul Molitor	.50
143	David Ortiz	.20
144	Brad Radke	.10
145	Terry Steinbach	.10
146	Todd Walker	.20
147	Shane Andrews	.10
148	Brad Fullmer	.25
149	Mark Grudzielanek	.10
150	Vladimir Guerrero	1.25
151	F.P. Santangelo	.10
152	Jose Vidro	.10
153	Rondell White	.20
154	Carlos Baerga	.10
155	Bernard Gilkey	.10
156	Todd Hundley	.10
157	Butch Huskey	.10
158	Bobby Jones	.10
159	Brian McRae	.10
160	John Olerud	.20
161	Rey Ordonez	.10
162	*Masato Yoshii*	.50
163	David Cone	.20
164	Hideki Irabu	.25
165	Derek Jeter	2.00
166	Chuck Knoblauch	.30
167	Tino Martinez	.25
168	Paul O'Neill	.20
169	Andy Pettitte	.35
170	Mariano Rivera	.20
171	Darryl Strawberry	.20
172	David Wells	.10
173	Bernie Williams	.25
174	*Ryan Christenson*	.20
175	Jason Giambi	.10
176	Ben Grieve	1.00
177	Rickey Henderson	.20
178	A.J. Hinch	.30
179	Kenny Rogers	.10
180	Ricky Bottalico	.10
181	Rico Brogna	.10
182	Doug Glanville	.10
183	Gregg Jefferies	.10
184	Mike Lieberthal	.10
185	Scott Rolen	1.00
186	Curt Schilling	.20
187	Jermaine Allensworth	.10
188	Lou Collier	.10
189	Jose Guillen	.25
190	Jason Kendall	.10
191	Al Martin	.10
192	Tony Womack	.10
193	Kevin Young	.10
194	Royce Clayton	.10
195	Delino DeShields	.10
196	Gary Gaetti	.10
197	Ron Gant	.15
198	Brian Jordan	.10
199	Ray Lankford	.10
200	Mark McGwire	3.50
201	Todd Stottlemyre	.10
202	Kevin Brown	.20
203	Ken Caminiti	.20
204	Steve Finley	.10
205	Tony Gwynn	1.50
206	Carlos Hernandez	.10
207	Wally Joyner	.10
208	Greg Vaughn	.25
209	Barry Bonds	.75
210	Shawn Estes	.10
211	Orel Hershiser	.10
212	Stan Javier	.10
213	Jeff Kent	.10
214	Bill Mueller	.10
215	Robb Nen	.10
216	J.T. Snow	.10
217	Jay Buhner	.15
218	Ken Cloude	.25
219	Joey Cora	.10
220	Ken Griffey Jr.	3.50
221	Glenallen Hill	.10
222	Randy Johnson	.50
223	Edgar Martinez	.10
224	Jamie Moyer	.10
225	Alex Rodriguez	2.50
226	David Segui	.10
227	Dan Wilson	.10
228	*Rolando Arrojo*	.40
229	Wade Boggs	.25
230	Miguel Cairo	.10
231	Roberto Hernandez	.10
232	Quinton McCracken	.10

233 Fred McGriff .20
234 Paul Sorrento .10
235 Kevin Stocker .10
236 Will Clark .20
237 Juan Gonzalez .75
238 Rusty Greer .10
239 Rick Helling .10
240 Roberto Kelly .10
241 Ivan Rodriguez .75
242 Aaron Sele .10
243 John Wetteland .10
244 Jose Canseco .25
245 Roger Clemens 1.00
246 Jose Cruz Jr. .15
247 Carlos Delgado .25
248 Alex Gonzalez .10
249 Ed Sprague .10
250 Shannon Stewart .10

1998 Pacific Omega EO Portraits

EO Portraits is a 20-card insert seeded 1:73. Each card has a color action photo with a player portrait laser-cut into the card. A "1-of-1" parallel features a laser-cut number on the card as well. The "EO" stands for "Electro Optical" technology.

MT
Complete Set (20): 350.00
Common Player: 5.00
Inserted 1:73
1 Cal Ripken Jr. 30.00
2 Nomar Garciaparra 25.00
3 Mo Vaughn 10.00
4 Frank Thomas 15.00
5 Manny Ramirez 12.50
6 Ben Grieve 15.00
7 Ken Griffey Jr. 40.00
8 Alex Rodriguez 30.00
9 Juan Gonzalez 10.00
10 Ivan Rodriguez 10.00
11 Travis Lee 8.00
12 Greg Maddux 25.00
13 Chipper Jones 25.00
14 Kerry Wood 10.00
15 Larry Walker 5.00
16 Jeff Bagwell 15.00
17 Mike Piazza 25.00
18 Mark McGwire 40.00
19 Tony Gwynn 20.00
20 Barry Bonds 10.00

1998 Pacific Omega Face to Face

Face to Face features two star players on each card. It is a 10-card insert seeded one per 145 packs.

MT
Complete Set (10): 200.00
Common Player: 8.00
Inserted 1:145
1 Alex Rodriguez, Nomar Garciaparra 35.00
2 Mark McGwire, Ken Griffey Jr. 60.00
3 Mike Piazza, Sandy Alomar Jr. 25.00
4 Kerry Wood, Roger Clemens 20.00
5 Cal Ripken Jr., Paul Molitor 30.00
6 Tony Gwynn, Wade Boggs 20.00
7 Frank Thomas, Chipper Jones 20.00
8 Travis Lee, Ben Grieve 15.00
9 Hideo Nomo, Hideki Irabu 5.00
10 Juan Gonzalez, Manny Ramirez 15.00

1998 Pacific Omega Online

Online is a 36-card insert seeded about one per nine packs. The foiled and etched cards feature a color player photo in front of a hi-tech designed background. The card fronts also include the internet address for the player's web site on bigleaguers.com.

MT
Complete Set (36): 140.00
Common Player: 1.00
Inserted 1:9
1 Cal Ripken Jr. 10.00
2 Nomar Garciaparra 8.00
3 Pedro Martinez 2.00
4 Mo Vaughn 2.00
5 Frank Thomas 6.00
6 Sandy Alomar Jr. 1.00
7 Manny Ramirez 5.00
8 Jaret Wright 1.50
9 Paul Molitor 2.50
10 Derek Jeter 6.00
11 Bernie Williams 1.50
12 Ben Grieve 4.00
13 Ken Griffey Jr. 15.00
14 Edgar Martinez 1.00
15 Alex Rodriguez 12.00
16 Wade Boggs 2.00
17 Juan Gonzalez 4.00
18 Ivan Rodriguez 3.00
19 Roger Clemens 5.00
20 Travis Lee 2.50
21 Matt Williams 1.50
22 Andres Galarraga 1.50
23 Chipper Jones 8.00
24 Greg Maddux 7.50
25 Sammy Sosa 6.00
26 Kerry Wood 3.00
27 Barry Larkin 1.50
28 Larry Walker 2.00
29 Derrek Lee 1.00
30 Jeff Bagwell 4.00
31 Hideo Nomo 1.00
32 Mike Piazza 8.00
33 Scott Rolen 4.00
34 Mark McGwire 15.00
35 Tony Gwynn 6.00
36 Barry Bonds 3.00

1998 Pacific Omega Prism

This 20-card insert was seeded one per 37 packs. Horizontal card fronts feature prismatic foil technology.

MT
Complete Set (20): 145.00
Common Player: 2.00
Inserted 1:37
1 Cal Ripken Jr. 12.00
2 Nomar Garciaparra 10.00
3 Pedro Martinez 2.50
4 Frank Thomas 8.00
5 Manny Ramirez 5.00
6 Brian Giles 2.00
7 Derek Jeter 9.00
8 Ben Grieve 5.00
9 Ken Griffey Jr. 16.00
10 Alex Rodriguez 12.00
11 Juan Gonzalez 4.00
12 Travis Lee 3.00
13 Chipper Jones 10.00
14 Greg Maddux 9.00
15 Kerry Wood 4.00
16 Larry Walker 2.50
17 Hideo Nomo 2.00
18 Mike Piazza 10.00
19 Mark McGwire 16.00
20 Tony Gwynn 8.00

1998 Pacific Omega Rising Stars

Rising Stars is a four-tiered hobby-only insert. The 20 cards were seeded four per 37 packs. Each card featured three rookies and each tier has a different foil color. A parallel of the insert is sequentially numbered. Tier One cards are numbered to 100, Tier Two to 50, Tier Three to 25 and Tier 4 to one.

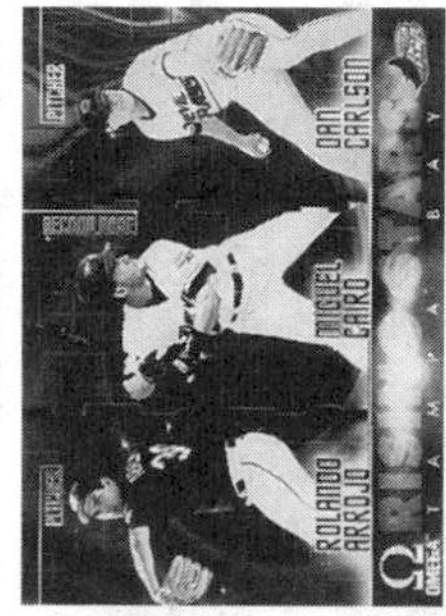

MT
Complete Set (30): 55.00
Common Player: 1.00
Inserted 1:9
1 Nerio Rodriguez, Sidney Ponson 1.00
2 Frank Catalanotto, Roberto Duran, Sean Runyan 1.00
3 Kevin L. Brown, Carlos Almanzar 1.00
4 Aaron Boone, Pat Watkins, Scott Winchester 1.00
5 Brian Meadows, Andy Larkin, Antonio Alfonseca 1.00
6 DaRond Stovall, Trey Moore, Shayne Bennett 1.00
7 Felix Martinez, Larry Sutton, Brian Bevil 1.00
8 Homer Bush, Mike Buddie 1.00
9 Rich Butler, Esteban Yan 2.50
10 Damon Hollins, Brian Edmondson 1.00
11 Lou Collier, Jose Silva, Javier Martinez 1.00
12 Steve Sinclair, Mark Dalesandro 1.00
13 Jason Varitek, Brian Rose, Brian Shouse 2.00
14 Mike Caruso, Jeff Abbott, Tom Fordham 2.00
15 Jason Johnson, Bobby Smith 1.00
16 Dave Berg, Mark Kotsay, Jesus Sanchez 3.00
17 Richard Hidalgo, John Halama, Trever Miller 2.00
18 Geoff Jenkins, Bobby Hughes, Steve Woodard 2.00
19 Eli Marrero, Cliff Politte, Mike Busby 1.00
20 Desi Relaford, Darrin Winston 1.00
21 Todd Helton, Bobby Jones 5.00
22 Rolando Arrojo, Miguel Cairo, Dan Carlson 3.00
23 David Ortiz, Javier Valentin, Eric Milton 2.00

24 Maggio Ordonez, Greg Norton 3.00
25 Brad Fullmer, Javier Vazquez, Rick DeHart 2.00
26 Paul Konerko, Matt Luke 3.00
27 Derrek Lee, Ryan Jackson, John Roskos 2.00
28 Ben Grieve, A.J. Hinch, Ryan Christenson 5.00
29 Travis Lee, Karim Garcia, David Dellucci 6.00
30 Kerry Wood, Marc Pisciotta 4.00

1998 Pacific Online

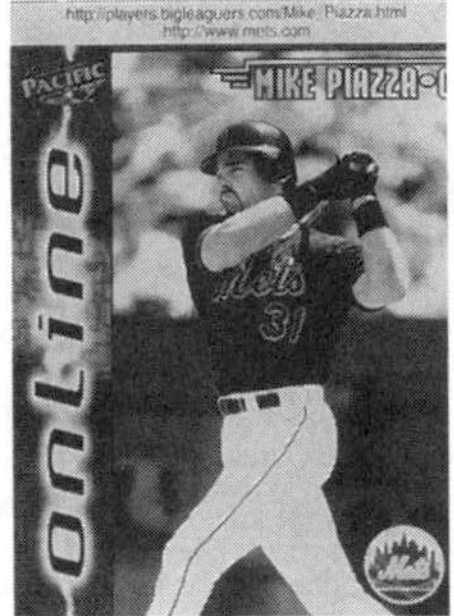

Online Baseball consists of an 800-card base set featuring 750 players on cards that list the internet address of the player's home page on the bigleaguers.com web site. Twenty players have two cards, each with different front and back photos but sharing a card number. Each of the 30 teams has a checklist that lists the team's web site. The Web Cards set parallels the 750 player cards. It has a serial number that can be entered at the bigleaguers.com web site to determine if a prize has been won. Red-foil versions of each card were produced for retail-only jumbo packs; they may carry a modest premium.

	MT
Complete Set (800):	100.00
Common Player:	.15
Web Star Cards:	3X
Young Stars/RCs:	2X
Inserted 1:1	
Pack (9):	1.50
Wax Box (36):	50.00

1 Garret Anderson .15
2 *Rich DeLucia* .40
3 Jason Dickson .15
4 Gary DiSarcina .15
5 Jim Edmonds .15
6 Darin Erstad 1.50
7 Cecil Fielder .15
8 Chuck Finley .15
9 Carlos Carcia .15
10 Shigetosi Hasegawa .15
11 Ken Hill .15
12 Dave Hollins .15
13 Mike Holtz .15
14 Mike James .15
15 Norberto Martin .15
16 Damon Mashore .15
17 Jack McDowell .15
18 Phil Nevin .15
19 Omar Olivares .15
20 Troy Percival .15
21 Rich Robertson .15
22 Tim Salmon .30
23 Craig Shipley .15
24 Matt Walbeck .15
25 Allen Watson .15
26 Jim Edmonds (Angels checklist) .15
27 Brian Anderson .15
28 Tony Batista .15
29 Jay Bell .15
30 Andy Benes .15
31 Yamil Benitez .15
32 Willie Blair .15
33 Brent Brede .15
34 Scott Brow .15
35 Omar Daal .15
36 David Dellucci .15
37 Edwin Diaz .15
38 Jorge Fabregas .15
39 Andy Fox .15
40 Karim Garcia .20
41a Travis Lee (batting) .75
41b Travis Lee (fielding) .75
42 Barry Manuel .15
43 Gregg Olson .15
44 Felix Rodriguez .15
45 Clint Sodowsky .15
46 Russ Springer .15
47 Andy Stankiewicz .15
48 Kelly Stinnett .15
49 Jeff Suppan .15
50 Devon White .15
51 Matt Williams .20
52 Travis Lee (Diamondbacks checklist) .75
53 Danny Bautista .15
54 Rafael Belliard .15
55 *Adam Butler* .30
56 Mike Cather .15
57 Brian Edmondson .15
58 Alan Embree .15
59 Andres Galarraga .40
60 Tom Glavine .30
61 Tony Graffanino .15
62 Andruw Jones 1.00
63a Chipper Jones (batting) 2.50
63b Chipper Jones (fielding) 2.50
64 Ryan Klesko .25
65 Keith Lockhart .15
66 Javy Lopez .20
67a Greg Maddux (batting) 2.50
67b Greg Maddux (pitching) 2.50
68 Dennis Martinez .15
69 *Kevin Millwood* 3.00
70 Denny Neagle .15
71 Eddie Perez .15
72 Curtis Pride .15
73 John Smoltz .25
74 Michael Tucker .15
75 Walt Weiss .15
76 Gerald Williams .15
77 Mark Wohlers .15
78 Chipper Jones (Braves checklist) 2.50
79 Roberto Alomar .40
80 Brady Anderson .15
81 Harold Baines .15
82 Armando Benitez .15
83 Mike Bordick .15
84 Joe Carter .15
85 Norm Charlton .15
86 Eric Davis .15
87 Doug Drabek .15
88 Scott Erickson .15
89 Jeffrey Hammonds .15
90 Chris Hoiles .15
91 Scott Kamieniecki .15
92 Jimmy Key .15
93 Terry Mathews .15
94 Alan Mills .15
95 Mike Mussina .75
96 Jesse Orosco .15
97 Rafael Palmeiro .25
98 Sidney Ponson .15
99 Jeff Reboulet .15
100 Arthur Rhodes .15
101a Cal Ripken Jr. (batting) 3.00
101b Cal Ripken Jr. (batting, close-up) 3.00
102 Nerio Rodriguez .15
103 B.J. Surhoff .15
104 Lenny Webster .15
105 Cal Ripken Jr. (Orioles checklist) 3.00
106 Steve Avery .15
107 Mike Benjamin .15
108 Darren Bragg .15
109 Damon Buford .15
110 Jim Corsi .15
111 Dennis Eckersley .15
112 Rich Garces .15
113a Nomar Garciaparra (batting) 2.50
113b Nomar Garciaparra (fielding) 2.50
114 Tom Gordon .15
115 Scott Hatteberg .15
116 Butch Henry .15
117 Reggie Jefferson .15
118 Mark Lemke .15
119 Darren Lewis .15
120 Jim Leyritz .15
121 Derek Lowe .15
122 Pedro Martinez .75
123 Troy O'Leary .15
124 Brian Rose .15
125 Bret Saberhagen .15
126 Donnie Sadler .15
127 Brian Shouse .15
128 John Valentin .15
129 Jason Varitek .15
130 Mo Vaughn 1.00
131 Tim Wakefield .15
132 John Wasdin .15
133 Nomar Garciaparra (Red Sox checklist) 2.50
134 Terry Adams .15
135 Manny Alexander .15
136 Rod Beck .15
137 Jeff Blauser .15
138 Brant Brown .15
139 Mark Clark .15
140 Jeremi Gonzalez .15
141 Mark Grace .25
142 Jose Hernandez .15
143 Tyler Houston .15
144 Lance Johnson .15
145 Sandy Martinez .15
146 Matt Mieske .15
147 Mickey Morandini .15
148 Terry Mulholland .15
149 Kevin Orie .15
150 Bob Patterson .15
151 Marc Pisciotta .15
152 Henry Rodriguez .15
153 Scott Servais .15
154 Sammy Sosa 2.50
155 Kevin Tapani .15
156 Steve Trachsel .15
157a Kerry Wood (pitching) 1.00
157b Kerry Wood (pitching, close-up) 1.00
158 Kerry Wood (Cubs checklist) .50
159 Jeff Abbott .15
160 James Baldwin .15
161 Albert Belle 1.00
162 Jason Bere .15
163 Mike Cameron .15
164 Mike Caruso .15
165 Carlos Castillo .15
166 Tony Castillo .15
167 Ray Durham .15
168 Scott Eyre .15
169 Tom Fordham .15
170 Keith Foulke .15
171 Lou Frazier .15
172 Matt Karchner .15
173 Chad Kreuter .15
174 Jaime Navarro .15
175 Greg Norton .15
176 Charlie O'Brien .15
177 Magglio Ordonez .50
178 Ruben Sierra .15
179 Bill Simas .15
180 Mike Sirotka .15
181 Chris Snopek .15
182a Frank Thomas (in batter's box) 1.50
182b Frank Thomas (swinging) 1.50
183 Robin Ventura .25
184 Frank Thomas (White Sox checklist) .75
185 Stan Belinda .15
186 Aaron Boone .15
187 Bret Boone .15
188 Brook Fordyce .15
189 Willie Greene .15
190 Pete Harnisch .15
191 Lenny Harris .15
192 Mark Hutton .15
193 Damian Jackson .15
194 Ricardo Jordan .15
195 Barry Larkin .30
196 Eduardo Perez .15
197 Pokey Reese .15
198 Mike Remlinger .15
199 Reggie Sanders .15
200 Jeff Shaw .15
201 Chris Stynes .15
202 Scott Sullivan .15
203 Eddie Taubensee .15
204 Brett Tomko .15
205 Pat Watkins .15
206 David Weathers .15
207 Gabe White .15
208 Scott Winchester .15
209 Barry Larkin (Reds checklist) .25
210 Sandy Alomar Jr. .20
211 Paul Assenmacher .15
212 Geronimo Berroa .15
213 Pat Borders .15
214 Jeff Branson .15
215 Dave Burba .15
216 Bartolo Colon .30
217 Shawon Dunston .15
218 Travis Fryman .15
219 Brian Giles .15
220 Dwight Gooden .15
221 Mike Jackson .15
222 David Justice .40
223 Kenny Lofton 1.00
224 Jose Mesa .15
225 Alvin Morman .15
226 Charles Nagy .15
227 Chad Ogea .15
228 Eric Plunk .15
229 Manny Ramirez 1.50
230 Paul Shuey .15
231 Jim Thome .60
232 Ron Villone .15
233 Omar Vizquel .15
234 Enrique Wilson .15
235 Jaret Wright 1.00
236 Manny Ramirez (Indians checklist) .75
237 Pedro Astacio .15
238 Jason Bates .15
239 Dante Bichette .30
240 Ellis Burks .15
241 Vinny Castilla .25
242 Greg Colbrunn .15
243 Mike DeJean .15
244 Jerry Dipoto .15
245 Curtis Goodwin .15
246 Todd Helton 1.00
247 Bobby Jones .15
248 Darryl Kile .15
249 Mike Lansing .15
250 Curtis Leskanic .15
251 Nelson Liriano .15
252 Kirt Manwaring .15
253 Chuck McElroy .15
254 Mike Munoz .15
255 Neifi Perez .15
256 Jeff Reed .15
257 Mark Thompson .15
258 John Vander Wal .15
259 Dave Veres .15
260a Larry Walker (batting) .40
260b Larry Walker (batting, close-up) .40
261 Jamey Wright .15
262 Larry Walker (Rockies checklist) .25
263 Kimera Bartee .15
264 Doug Brocail .15
265 Raul Casanova .15
266 Frank Castillo .15
267 Frank Catalanotto .15

268 Tony Clark .40
269 Deivi Cruz .15
270 Roberto Duran .15
271 Damion Easley .15
272 Bryce Florie .15
273 Luis Gonzalez .15
274 Bob Higginson .15
275 Brian Hunter .15
276 Todd Jones .15
277 Greg Keagle .15
278 Jeff Manto .15
279 Brian Moehler .15
280 Joe Oliver .15
281 Joe Randa .15
282 Billy Ripken .15
283 Bip Roberts .15
284 Sean Runyan .15
285 A.J. Sager .15
286 Justin Thompson .15
287 Tony Clark (Tigers checklist) .40
288 Antonio Alfonseca .15
289 Dave Berg .15
290 Josh Booty .15
291 John Cangelosi .15
292 Craig Counsell .15
293 Vic Darensbourg .15
294 Cliff Floyd .15
295 Oscar Henriquez .15
296 Felix Heredia .15
297 *Ryan Jackson* .15
298 Mark Kotsay .40
299 Andy Larkin .15
300 Derrek Lee .15
301 Brian Meadows .15
302 Rafael Medina .15
303 Jay Powell .15
304 Edgar Renteria .15
305 *Jesus Sanchez* .30
306 Rob Stanifer .15
307 Greg Zaun .15
308 Derrek Lee (Marlins checklist) .15
309 Moises Alou .25
310 Brad Ausmus .15
311a Jeff Bagwell (batting) 1.50
311b Jeff Bagwell (fielding) 1.50
312 Derek Bell .15
313 Sean Bergman .15
314 Sean Berry .15
315 Craig Biggio .25
316 Tim Bogar .15
317 Jose Cabrera .15
318 Dave Clark .15
319 Tony Eusebio .15
320 Carl Everett .15
321 Ricky Gutierrez .15
322 John Halama .15
323 Mike Hampton .15
324 Doug Henry .15
325 Richard Hidalgo .15
326 Jack Howell .15
327 Jose Lima .15
328 Mike Magnante .15
329 Trever Miller .15
330 C.J. Nitkowski .15
331 Shane Reynolds .15
332 Bill Spiers .15
333 Billy Wagner .20
334 Jeff Bagwell (Astros checklist) .75
335 Tim Belcher .15
336 Brian Bevil .15
337 Johnny Damon .15
338 Jermaine Dye .15
339 Sal Fasano .15
340 Shane Halter .15
341 Chris Haney .15
342 Jed Hansen .15
343 Jeff King .15
344 Jeff Montgomery .15
345 Hal Morris .15
346 Jose Offerman .15
347 Dean Palmer .15
348 Terry Pendleton .15
349 Hipolito Pichardo .15
350 Jim Pittsley .15
351 Pat Rapp .15
352 Jose Rosado .15
353 Glendon Rusch .15
354 Scott Service .15
355 Larry Sutton .15
356 Mike Sweeney .15
357 Joe Vitiello .15
358 Matt Whisenant .15
359 Ernie Young .15
360 Jeff King (Royals checklist) .15
361 Bobby Bonilla .15
362 Jim Bruske .15
363 Juan Castro .15
364 Roger Cedeno .15
365 Mike Devereaux .15
366 Darren Dreifort .15
367 Jim Eisenreich .15
368 Wilton Guerrero .15
369 Mark Guthrie .15
370 Darren Hall .15
371 Todd Hollandsworth .15
372 Thomas Howard .15
373 Trenidad Hubbard .15
374 Charles Johnson .15
375 Eric Karros .15
376 Paul Konerko .40
377 Matt Luke .15
378 Ramon Martinez .15
379 Raul Mondesi .30
380 Hideo Nomo .50
381 Antonio Osuna .15
382 Chan Ho Park .30
383 Tom Prince .15
384 Scott Radinsky .15
385 Gary Sheffield .40
386 Ismael Valdes .15
387 Jose Vizcaino .15
388 Eric Young .15
389 Gary Sheffield (Dodgers checklist) .30
390 Jeromy Burnitz .15
391 Jeff Cirillo .15
392 Cal Eldred .15
393 Chad Fox .15
394 Marquis Grissom .15
395 Bob Hamelin .15
396 Bobby Hughes .15
397 Darrin Jackson .15
398 John Jaha .15
399 Geoff Jenkins .15
400 Doug Jones .15
401 Jeff Juden .15
402 Scott Karl .15
403 Jesse Levis .15
404 Mark Loretta .15
405 Mike Matheny .15
406 Jose Mercedes .15
407 Mike Myers .15
408 Marc Newfield .15
409 Dave Nilsson .15
410 Al Reyes .15
411 Jose Valentin .15
412 Fernando Vina .15
413 Paul Wagner .15
414 Bob Wickman .15
415 Steve Woodard .15
416 Marquis Grissom (Brewers checklist) .15
417 Rick Aguilera .15
418 Ron Coomer .15
419 Marty Cordova .15
420 Brent Gates .15
421 Eddie Guardado .15
422 Denny Hocking .15
423 Matt Lawton .15
424 Pat Meares .15
425 Orlando Merced .15
426 Eric Milton .15
427 Paul Molitor .75
428 Mike Morgan .15
429 Dan Naulty .15
430 Otis Nixon .15
431 Alex Ochoa .15
432 David Ortiz .15
433 Brad Radke .15
434 Todd Ritchie .15
435 Frank Rodriguez .15
436 Terry Steinbach .15
437 Greg Swindell .15
438 Bob Tewksbury .15
439 Mike Trombley .15
440 Javier Valentin .15
441 Todd Walker .40
442 Paul Molitor (Twins checklist) .60
443 Shane Andrews .15
444 Miguel Batista .15
445 Shayne Bennett .15
446 Rick DeHart .15
447 Brad Fullmer .40
448 Mark Grudzielanek .15
449 Vladimir Guerrero 1.50
450 Dustin Hermanson .15
451 Steve Kline .15
452 Scott Livingstone .15
453 Mike Maddux .15
454 Derrick May .15
455 Ryan McGuire .15
456 Trey Moore .15
457 Mike Mordecai .15
458 Carl Pavano .15
459 Carlos Perez .15
460 F.P. Santangelo .15
461 DaRond Stovall .15
462 Anthony Telford .15
463 Ugueth Urbina .15
464 Marc Valdes .15
465 Jose Vidro .15
466 Rondell White .25
467 Chris Widger .15
468 Vladimir Guerrero (Expos checklist) .75
469 Edgardo Alfonzo .20
470 Carlos Baerga .15
471 Rich Becker .15
472 Brian Bohanon .15
473 Alberto Castillo .15
474 Dennis Cook .15
475 John Franco .15
476 Matt Franco .15
477 Bernard Gilkey .15
478 John Hudek .15
479 Butch Huskey .15
480 Bobby Jones .15
481 Al Leiter .25
482 Luis Lopez .15
483 Brian McRae .15
484 Dave Mlicki .15
485 John Olerud .25
486 Rey Ordonez .20
487 Craig Paquette .15
488a Mike Piazza (batting) 2.50
488b Mike Piazza (batting, close-up) 2.50
489 Todd Pratt .15
490 Mel Rojas .15
491 Tim Spehr .15
492 Turk Wendell .15
493 *Masato Yoshii* .40
494 Mike Piazza (Mets checklist) .75
495 Willie Banks .15
496 Scott Brosius .15
497 Mike Buddie .15
498 Homer Bush .15
499 David Cone .20
500 Chad Curtis .15
501 Chili Davis .15
502 Joe Girardi .15
503 Darren Holmes .15
504 Hideki Irabu .40
505a Derek Jeter (batting) 2.50
505b Derek Jeter (fielding) 2.50
506 Chuck Knoblauch .50
507 Graeme Lloyd .15
508 Tino Martinez .40
509 Ramiro Mendoza .15
510 Jeff Nelson .15
511 Paul O'Neill .40
512 Andy Pettitte .60
513 Jorge Posada .25
514 Tim Raines .15
515 Mariano Rivera .25
516 Luis Sojo .15
517 Mike Stanton .15
518 Darryl Strawberry .25
519 Dale Sveum .15
520 David Wells .20
521 Bernie Williams .75
522 Bernie Williams (Yankees checklist) .40
523 Kurt Abbott .15
524 Mike Blowers .15
525 Rafael Bournigal .15
526 Tom Candiotti .15
527 Ryan Christenson .15
528 Mike Fetters .15
529 Jason Giambi .15
530a Ben Grieve (batting) 1.25
530b Ben Grieve (running) 1.25
531 Buddy Groom .15
532 Jimmy Haynes .15
533 Rickey Henderson .25
534 A.J. Hinch .15
535 Mike Macfarlane .15
536 Dave Magadan .15
537 T.J. Mathews .15
538 Jason McDonald .15
539 Kevin Mitchell .15
540 Mike Mohler .15
541 Mike Oquist .15
542 Ariel Prieto .15
543 Kenny Rogers .15
544 Aaron Small .15
545 Scott Spiezio .15
546 Matt Stairs .15
547 Bill Taylor .15
548 Dave Telgheder .15
549 Jack Voigt .15
550 Ben Grieve (A's checklist) .75
551 Bob Abreu .15
552 Ruben Amaro .15
553 Alex Arias .15
554 Matt Beech .15
555 Ricky Bottalico .15
556 Billy Brewer .15
557 Rico Brogna .15
558 Doug Glanville .15
559 Wayne Gomes .15
560 Mike Grace .15
561 Tyler Green .15
562 Rex Hudler .15
563 Gregg Jefferies .15
564 Kevin Jordan .15
565 Mark Leiter .15
566 Mark Lewis .15
567 Mike Lieberthal .15
568 Mark Parent .15
569 Yorkis Perez .15
570 Desi Relaford .15
571 Scott Rolen 1.25
572 Curt Schilling .25
573 Kevin Sefcik .15
574 Jerry Spradlin .15
575 Garrett Stephenson .15
576 Darrin Winston .15
577 Scott Rolen (Phillies checklist) .75
578 Jermaine Allensworth .15
579 Jason Christiansen .15
580 Lou Collier .15
581 Francisco Cordova .15
582 Elmer Dessens .15
583 Freddy Garcia .15
584 Jose Guillen .25
585 Jason Kendall .15
586 Jon Lieber .15
587 Esteban Loaiza .15
588 Al Martin .15
589 Javier Martinez .15
590 *Chris Peters* .15
591 Kevin Polcovich .15
592 Ricardo Rincon .15
593 Jason Schmidt .15
594 Jose Silva .15
595 Mark Smith .15
596 Doug Strange .15
597 Turner Ward .15
598 Marc Wilkins .15
599 Mike Williams .15
600 Tony Womack .15
601 Kevin Young .15
602 Tony Womack (Pirates checklist) .15
603 Manny Aybar .25
604 Kent Bottenfield .15
605 Jeff Brantley .15
606 Mike Busby .15
607 Royce Clayton .15
608 Delino DeShields .15
609 John Frascatore .15
610 Gary Gaetti .15
611 Ron Gant .15
612 David Howard .15
613 Brian Hunter .15
614 Brian Jordan .15
615 Tom Lampkin .15
616 Ray Lankford .15
617 Braden Looper .15
618 John Mabry .15
619 Eli Marrero .15
620 Willie McGee .15
621a Mark McGwire (batting) 4.00
621b Mark McGwire (fielding) 4.00
622 Kent Mercker .15
623 Matt Morris .15

624	Donovan Osborne	.15
625	Tom Pagnozzi	.15
626	Lance Painter	.15
627	Mark Petkovsek	.15
628	Todd Stottlemyre	.15
629	Mark McGwire (Cardinals checklist)	2.00
630	Andy Ashby	.15
631	Brian Boehringer	.15
632	Kevin Brown	.25
633	Ken Caminiti	.25
634	Steve Finley	.15
635	Ed Giovanola	.15
636	Chris Gomez	.15
637a	Tony Gwynn (blue jersey)	2.00
637b	Tony Gwynn (white jersey)	2.00
SAMPLE	Tony Gwynn (SAMPLE overprint on back)	3.00
638	Joey Hamilton	.15
639	Carlos Hernandez	.15
640	Sterling Hitchcock	.15
641	Trevor Hoffman	.15
642	Wally Joyner	.15
643	Dan Miceli	.15
644	James Mouton	.15
645	Greg Myers	.15
646	Carlos Reyes	.15
647	Andy Sheets	.15
648	Pete Smith	.15
649	Mark Sweeney	.15
650	Greg Vaughn	.20
651	Quilvio Veras	.15
652	Tony Gwynn (Padres checklist)	1.00
653	Rich Aurilla	.15
654	Marvin Benard	.15
655a	Barry Bonds (batting)	1.00
655b	Barry Bonds (batting, close-up)	1.00
656	Danny Darwin	.15
657	Shawn Estes	.15
658	Mark Gardner	.15
659	Darryl Hamilton	.15
660	Charlie Hayes	.15
661	Orel Hershiser	.15
662	Stan Javier	.15
663	Brian Johnson	.15
664	John Johnstone	.15
665	Jeff Kent	.15
666	Brent Mayne	.15
667	Bill Mueller	.15
668	Robb Nen	.15
669	Jim Poole	.15
670	Steve Reed	.15
671	Rich Rodriguez	.15
672	Kirk Rueter	.15
673	Rey Sanchez	.15
674	J.T. Snow	.15
675	Julian Tavarez	.15
676	Barry Bonds (Giants checklist)	.50
677	Rich Amaral	.15
678	Bobby Ayala	.15
679	Jay Buhner	.30
680	Ken Cloude	.15
681	Joey Cora	.15
682	Russ Davis	.15
683	Rob Ducey	.15
684	Jeff Fassero	.15
685	Tony Fossas	.15
686a	Ken Griffey Jr. (batting)	4.00
686b	Ken Griffey Jr. (fielding)	4.00
687	Glenallen Hill	.15
688	Jeff Huson	.15
689	Randy Johnson	.75
690	Edgar Martinez	.15
691	John Marzano	.15
692	Jamie Moyer	.15
693a	Alex Rodriguez (batting)	3.00
693b	Alex Rodriguez (fielding)	3.00
694	David Segui	.15
695	Heathcliff Slocumb	.15
696	Paul Spoljaric	.15
697	Bill Swift	.15
698	Mike Timlin	.15
699	Bob Wells	.15
700	Dan Wilson	.15
701	Ken Griffey Jr. (Mariners checklist)	2.00
702	Wilson Alvarez	.15
703	*Rolando Arrojo*	.75
704a	Wade Boggs (batting)	.50
704b	Wade Boggs (fielding)	.50
705	Rich Butler	.15
706	Miguel Cairo	.15
707	Mike Difelice	.15
708	John Flaherty	.15
709	Roberto Hernandez	.15
710	Mike Kelly	.15
711	Aaron Ledesma	.15
712	Albie Lopez	.15
713	Dave Martinez	.15
714	Quinton McCracken	.15
715	Fred McGriff	.25
716	Jim Mecir	.15
717	Tony Saunders	.15
718	Bobby Smith	.15
719	Paul Sorrento	.15
720	Dennis Springer	.15
721	Kevin Stocker	.15
722	Ramon Tatis	.15
723	Bubba Trammell	.15
724	Esteban Yan	.15
725	Wade Boggs (Devil Rays checklist)	.30
726	Luis Alicea	.15
727	Scott Bailes	.15
728	John Burkett	.15
729	Domingo Cedeno	.15
730	Will Clark	.40
731	Kevin Elster	.15
732a	Juan Gonzalez (bat)	1.00
732b	Juan Gonzalez (no bat)	1.00
733	Tom Goodwin	.15
734	Rusty Greer	.15
735	Eric Gunderson	.15
736	Bill Haselman	.15
737	Rick Helling	.15
738	Roberto Kelly	.15
739	Mark McLemore	.15
740	Darren Oliver	.15
741	Danny Patterson	.15
742	Roger Pavlik	.15
743a	Ivan Rodriguez (batting)	1.00
743b	Ivan Rodriguez (fielding)	1.00
744	Aaron Sele	.15
745	Mike Simms	.15
746	Lee Stevens	.15
747	Fernando Tatis	.25
748	John Wetteland	.15
749	Bobby Witt	.15
750	Juan Gonzalez (Rangers checklist)	.50
751	Carlos Almanzar	.15
752	Kevin Brown	.25
753	Jose Canseco	.40
754	Chris Carpenter	.15
755	Roger Clemens	1.50
756	Felipe Crespo	.15
757	Jose Cruz Jr.	.15
758	Mark Dalesandro	.15
759	Carlos Delgado	.40
760	Kelvim Escobar	.15

1998 Pacific Online Web Cards

This 800-card parallel set allowed collectors to use Pacific's web site to find out the prize they had won. The cards used gold foil on the front instead of the silver foil used on base cards, and contained an eight-digit code on the back that was the claim number. These were inserted one per pack in Online Baseball.

	MT
Web Stars:	3X
Young Stars/RCs:	2X
Inserted 1:1	

(See 1998 Pacific Online for checklist and base card values.)

1998 Pacific Paramount

Paramount was Pacific's first fully-licensed baseball card product. The 250 base cards feature full-bleed photos with the player's name and team listed at the bottom. The base set is paralleled three times. Gold retail (1:1), Copper hobby (1:1) and Platinum Blue (1:73) versions were included. Inserts in the product are Special Delivery Die-Cuts, Team Checklist Die-Cuts, Cooperstown Bound, Fielder's Choice Laser-Cuts and Inaugural Issue.

		MT
Complete Set (250):		20.00
Common Player:		.10
Pack (6):		1.50
Wax Box (36):		50.00
1	Garret Anderson	.10
2	Gary DiSarcina	.10
3	Jim Edmonds	.15
4	Darin Erstad	.50
5	Cecil Fielder	.10
6	Chuck Finley	.10
7	Todd Greene	.15
8	Shigetosi Hasegawa	.10
9	Tim Salmon	.30
10	Roberto Alomar	.50
11	Brady Anderson	.15
12	Joe Carter	.15
13	Eric Davis	.10
14	Ozzie Guillen	.10
15	Mike Mussina	.50
16	Rafael Palmeiro	.30
17	Cal Ripken Jr.	2.00
18	B.J. Surhoff	.10
19	Steve Avery	.10
20	Nomar Garciaparra	1.50
21	Reggie Jefferson	.10
22	Pedro Martinez	.25
23	Tim Naehring	.10
24	John Valentin	.10
25	Mo Vaughn	.60
26	James Baldwin	.10
27	Albert Belle	.60
28	Ray Durham	.10
29	Benji Gil	.10
30	Jaime Navarro	.10
31	*Magglio Ordonez*	1.00
32	Frank Thomas	1.25
33	Robin Ventura	.20
34	Sandy Alomar Jr.	.20
35	Geronimo Berroa	.10
36	Travis Fryman	.10
37	David Justice	.25
38	Kenny Lofton	.60
39	Charles Nagy	.10
40	Manny Ramirez	.75
41	Jim Thome	.25
42	Omar Vizquel	.10
43	Jaret Wright	.75
44	Raul Casanova	.10
45	*Frank Catalanotto*	.20
46	Tony Clark	.25
47	Bobby Higginson	.10
48	Brian Hunter	.10
49	Todd Jones	.10
50	Bip Roberts	.10
51	Justin Thompson	.10
52	Kevin Appier	.10
53	Johnny Damon	.10
54	Jermaine Dye	.10
55	Jeff King	.10
56	Jeff Montgomery	.10
57	Dean Palmer	.10
58	Jose Rosado	.10
59	Larry Sutton	.10
60	Rick Aguilera	.10
61	Marty Cordova	.10
62	Pat Meares	.10
63	Paul Molitor	.40
64	Otis Nixon	.10
65	Brad Radke	.10
66	Terry Steinbach	.10
67	Todd Walker	.25
68	Hideki Irabu	.25
69	Derek Jeter	1.50
70	Chuck Knoblauch	.30
71	Tino Martinez	.25
72	Paul O'Neill	.20
73	Andy Pettitte	.25
74	Mariano Rivera	.25
75	Bernie Williams	.35
76	Mark Bellhorn	.10
77	Tom Candiotti	.10
78	Jason Giambi	.10
79	Ben Grieve	1.00
80	Rickey Henderson	.20
81	Jason McDonald	.10
82	Aaron Small	.10
83	Miguel Tejada	.10
84	Jay Buhner	.15
85	Joey Cora	.10
86	Jeff Fassero	.10
87	Ken Griffey Jr.	3.00
88	Randy Johnson	.40
89	Edgar Martinez	.10
90	Alex Rodriguez	2.50
91	David Segui	.10
92	Dan Wilson	.10
93	Wilson Alvarez	.10
94	Wade Boggs	.25
95	Miguel Cairo	.10
96	John Flaherty	.10
97	Dave Martinez	.10
98	Quinton McCracken	.10
99	Fred McGriff	.25
100	Paul Sorrento	.10
101	Kevin Stocker	.10
102	John Burkett	.10
103	Will Clark	.25
104	Juan Gonzalez	.75
105	Rusty Greer	.10
106	Roberto Kelly	.10
107	Ivan Rodriguez	.60
108	Fernando Tatis	.15
109	John Wetteland	.10
110	Jose Canseco	.25
111	Roger Clemens	1.00

112	Jose Cruz Jr.	.20
113	Carlos Delgado	.20
114	Alex Gonzalez	.10
115	Pat Hentgen	.10
116	Ed Sprague	.10
117	Shannon Stewart	.10
118	Brian Anderson	.10
119	Jay Bell	.10
120	Andy Benes	.15
121	Yamil Benitez	.10
122	Jorge Fabregas	.10
123	Travis Lee	.75
124	Devon White	.10
125	Matt Williams	.25
126	Bob Wolcott	.10
127	Andres Galarraga	.25
128	Tom Glavine	.20
129	Andruw Jones	.60
130	Chipper Jones	1.50
131	Ryan Klesko	.25
132	Javy Lopez	.15
133	Greg Maddux	1.50
134	Denny Neagle	.10
135	John Smoltz	.20
136	Rod Beck	.10
137	Jeff Blauser	.10
138	Mark Grace	.25
139	Lance Johnson	.10
140	Mickey Morandini	.10
141	Kevin Orie	.10
142	Sammy Sosa	1.50
143	Aaron Boone	.10
144	Bret Boone	.10
145	Dave Burba	.10
146	Lenny Harris	.10
147	Barry Larkin	.15
148	Reggie Sanders	.10
149	Brett Tomko	.10
150	Pedro Astacio	.10
151	Dante Bichette	.20
152	Ellis Burks	.10
153	Vinny Castilla	.20
154	Todd Helton	.75
155	Darryl Kile	.10
156	Jeff Reed	.10
157	Larry Walker	.30
158	Bobby Bonilla	.10
159	Todd Dunwoody	.15
160	Livan Hernandez	.15
161	Charles Johnson	.15
162	Mark Kotsay	.35
163	Derrek Lee	.10
164	Edgar Renteria	.15
165	Gary Sheffield	.30
166	Moises Alou	.20
167	Jeff Bagwell	1.00
168	Derek Bell	.10
169	Craig Biggio	.20
170	Mike Hampton	.10
171	Richard Hidalgo	.10
172	Chris Holt	.10
173	Shane Reynolds	.10
174	Wilton Guerrero	.10
175	Eric Karros	.15
176	Paul Konerko	.25
177	Ramon Martinez	.20
178	Raul Mondesi	.25
179	Hideo Nomo	.40
180	Chan Ho Park	.20
181	Mike Piazza	1.50
182	Ismael Valdes	.10
183	Jeromy Burnitz	.10
184	Jeff Cirillo	.10
185	Todd Dunn	.10
186	Marquis Grissom	.10
187	John Jaha	.10
188	Doug Jones	.10
189	Dave Nilsson	.10
190	Jose Valentin	.10
191	Fernando Vina	.10
192	Orlando Cabrera	.10
193	Steve Falteisek	.10
194	Mark Grudzielanek	.10
195	Vladimir Guerrero	1.25
196	Carlos Perez	.10
197	F.P. Santangelo	.10
198	Jose Vidro	.10
199	Rondell White	.20
200	Edgardo Alfonzo	.15
201	Carlos Baerga	.10
202	John Franco	.10
203	Bernard Gilkey	.10
204	Todd Hundley	.20
205	Butch Huskey	.10
206	Bobby Jones	.10
207	Brian McRae	.10
208	John Olerud	.20
209	Rey Ordonez	.15
210	Ricky Bottalico	.10
211	Bobby Estalella	.10
212	Doug Glanville	.10
213	Gregg Jefferies	.10
214	Mike Lieberthal	.10
215	Desi Relaford	.10
216	Scott Rolen	.75
217	Curt Schilling	.25
218	Adrian Brown	.10
219	Emil Brown	.10
220	Francisco Cordova	.10
221	Jose Guillen	.40
222	Al Martin	.10
223	Abraham Nunez	.10
224	Tony Womack	.10
225	Kevin Young	.10
226	Alan Benes	.15
227	Royce Clayton	.10
228	Gary Gaetti	.10
229	Ron Gant	.10
230	Brian Jordan	.10
231	Ray Lankford	.10
232	Mark McGwire	3.00
233	Todd Stottlemyre	.10
234	Kevin Brown	.20
235	Ken Caminiti	.20
236	Steve Finley	.10
237	Tony Gwynn	1.25
238	Wally Joyner	.10
239	Ruben Rivera	.10
240	Greg Vaughn	.15
241	Quilvio Veras	.10
242	Barry Bonds	.60
243	Jacob Cruz	.10
244	Shawn Estes	.10
245	Orel Hershiser	.10
246	Stan Javier	.10
247	Brian Johnson	.10
248	Jeff Kent	.10
249	Robb Nen	.10
250	J.T. Snow	.10

1998 Pacific Paramount Gold/Copper/Red

Gold, Copper and Red foil versions of all 250 cards in Paramount were reprinted and inserted at a rate of one per pack. Gold versions were retail exclusive, Copper versions were hobby exclusive and Red versions were ANCO pack exclusive. The only difference is these parallels use a different color foil than the base cards.

	MT
Common Gold/Copper Player:	.25
Gold/Copper Stars:	2X
Inserted 1:1	
Common Red Player:	.30
Red Stars:	3X
Inserted 1:ANCO pack	

(See 1998 Pacific Paramount for checklist and base card values.)

1998 Pacific Paramount Platinum Blue

This paralled set reprinted all 250 cards in Paramount using blue foil stamping on the card front. These were inserted one per 73 packs.

	MT
Common Platinum Blue Player:	3.00
Platinum Blue Stars:	15-30X
Inserted 1:73	

(See 1998 Pacific Paramount for checklist and base card values.)

1998 Pacific Paramount Holographic Silver

Holographics Silver parallel cards were issued for all 250 cards in the Paramount set. These were inserted into hobby packs, while only 99 sets were produced.

	MT
Common Player:	5.00
Holographic Silver Stars:	40-60X
Production 99 sets	

(See 1998 Pacific Paramount for checklist and base card values.)

1998 Pacific Paramount Inaugural Issue

A special edition of Pacific's premiere Paramount issue was created to mark the new brand's introduction on May 27 at the debut SportsFest '98 show in Philadelphia. Each of the cards from the Paramount issue was printed with a gold-foil "INAUGURAL ISSUE May 27, 1998" logo, was embossed with Pacific and SportsFest logos at center and hand-numbered at bottom from within an edition of just 20 cards each.

	MT
Common Player:	6.00

(Stars and rookies valued at 50-75X regular Paramount version.)

1998 Pacific Paramount Cooperstown Bound

Cooperstown Bound is a 10-card insert seeded one per 361 packs. Each card features a color player photo with a silver foil column on the left. The cards are fully foiled and etched.

		MT
Complete Set (10):		450.00
Common Player:		15.00
Inserted 1:361		
Pacific Proofs:		6X
Production 20 sets		
1	Greg Maddux	60.00
2	Cal Ripken Jr.	80.00
3	Frank Thomas	40.00
4	Mike Piazza	60.00
5	Paul Molitor	20.00
6	Mark McGwire	100.00
7	Tony Gwynn	50.00
8	Barry Bonds	25.00
9	Ken Griffey Jr.	100.00
10	Wade Boggs	15.00

1998 Pacific Paramount Fielder's Choice

Fielder's Choice Laser-Cuts is a 20-card insert seeded one per 73 packs. Each card is die-cut around a baseball glove that appears in the background. The webbing of the glove is laser-cut.

		MT
Complete Set (20):		400.00
Common Player:		5.00
Inserted 1:73		
1	Chipper Jones	30.00
2	Greg Maddux	25.00
3	Cal Ripken Jr.	40.00
4	Nomar Garciaparra	30.00
5	Frank Thomas	20.00
6	David Justice	5.00
7	Larry Walker	7.50
8	Jeff Bagwell	15.00
9	Hideo Nomo	5.00
10	Mike Piazza	30.00
11	Derek Jeter	30.00
12	Ben Grieve	10.00
13	Mark McGwire	50.00
14	Tony Gwynn	25.00
15	Barry Bonds	15.00
16	Ken Griffey Jr.	50.00
17	Alex Rodriguez	40.00
18	Wade Boggs	6.00
19	Ivan Rodriguez	15.00
20	Jose Cruz Jr.	5.00

1998 Pacific Paramount Special Delivery

Special Delivery cards are die-cut to resemble a postage stamp. Each card front is foiled and etched and features three photos of the player. Special Delivery is a 20-card insert seeded one per 37 packs.

		MT
Complete Set (20):		150.00
Common Player:		1.50
Inserted 1:37		
1	Chipper Jones	10.00
2	Greg Maddux	10.00
3	Cal Ripken Jr.	12.50
4	Nomar Garciaparra	10.00
5	Pedro Martinez	3.00
6	Frank Thomas	7.50
7	David Justice	2.00
8	Larry Walker	2.50
9	Jeff Bagwell	6.00
10	Hideo Nomo	2.00
11	Mike Piazza	10.00
12	Vladimir Guerrero	6.00
13	Derek Jeter	10.00
14	Ben Grieve	5.00
15	Mark McGwire	15.00
16	Tony Gwynn	7.50
17	Barry Bonds	4.00
18	Ken Griffey Jr.	15.00
19	Alex Rodriguez	12.50
20	Jose Cruz Jr.	1.50

1998 Pacific Paramount Team Checklist

Team Checklists (30 cards, 2:37) feature a player photo surrounded by two bats. The card is die-cut around the photo and the bats at the top. The bottom has the player's name, position and team.

		MT
Complete Set (30):		150.00
Common Player:		1.50
Inserted 1:18		
1	Tim Salmon	3.00
2	Cal Ripken Jr.	15.00
3	Nomar Garciaparra	12.00
4	Frank Thomas	10.00
5	Manny Ramirez	7.50
6	Tony Clark	4.00
7	Dean Palmer	1.50
8	Paul Molitor	4.00
9	Derek Jeter	12.00
10	Ben Grieve	8.00
11	Ken Griffey Jr.	25.00
12	Wade Boggs	2.50
13	Ivan Rodriguez	6.00
14	Roger Clemens	8.00
15	Matt Williams	2.50
16	Chipper Jones	12.00
17	Sammy Sosa	10.00
18	Barry Larkin	2.00
19	Larry Walker	3.00
20	Livan Hernandez	1.50
21	Jeff Bagwell	8.00
22	Mike Piazza	12.00
23	John Jaha	1.50
24	Vladimir Guerrero	10.00
25	Todd Hundley	1.50
26	Scott Rolen	8.00
27	Kevin Young	1.50
28	Mark McGwire	25.00
29	Tony Gwynn	10.00
30	Barry Bonds	5.00

1998 Pacific Revolution

Pacific Revolution Baseball consists of a 150-card base set. The base cards are dual-foiled, etched and embossed. Inserts include Showstoppers, Prime Time Performers Laser-Cuts, Foul Pole Laser-Cuts, Major League Icons and Shadow Series.

		MT
Complete Set (150):		90.00
Common Player:		.40
Pack (3):		4.00
Wax Box (24):		80.00
1	Garret Anderson	.40
2	Jim Edmonds	.40
3	Darin Erstad	1.50
4	Chuck Finley	.40
5	Tim Salmon	1.00
6	Jay Bell	.40
7	Travis Lee	2.00
8	Devon White	.40
9	Matt Williams	1.00
10	Andres Galarraga	1.00
11	Tom Glavine	.60
12	Andruw Jones	2.50
13	Chipper Jones	6.00
14	Ryan Klesko	.50
15	Javy Lopez	.60
16	Greg Maddux	6.00
17	Walt Weiss	.40
18	Roberto Alomar	2.00
19	Joe Carter	.60
20	Mike Mussina	2.00
21	Rafael Palmeiro	1.00
22	Cal Ripken Jr.	8.00
23	B.J. Surhoff	.40
24	Nomar Garciaparra	6.00
25	Reggie Jefferson	.40
26	Pedro Martinez	2.00
27	Troy O'Leary	.40
28	Mo Vaughn	1.50
29	Mark Grace	1.00
30	Mickey Morandini	.40
31	Henry Rodriguez	.40
32	Sammy Sosa	5.00
33	Kerry Wood	2.50
34	Albert Belle	2.50
35	Ray Durham	.40
36	*Magglio Ordonez*	4.00
37	Frank Thomas	5.00
38	Robin Ventura	.60
39	Bret Boone	.40
40	Barry Larkin	.60
41	Reggie Sanders	.40
42	Brett Tomko	.40
43	Sandy Alomar	.60
44	David Justice	.75
45	Kenny Lofton	1.50
46	Manny Ramirez	4.00
47	Jim Thome	1.50
48	Omar Vizquel	.40
49	Jaret Wright	1.50
50	Dante Bichette	.75
51	Ellis Burks	.40
52	Vinny Castilla	.40
53	Todd Helton	3.00
54	Larry Walker	1.50
55	Tony Clark	1.00
56	Deivi Cruz	.40
57	Damion Easley	.40
58	Bobby Higginson	.40
59	Brian Hunter	.40
60	Cliff Floyd	.40
61	Livan Hernandez	.40
62	Derrek Lee	.40
63	Edgar Renteria	.50
64	Moises Alou	.75
65	Jeff Bagwell	3.00
66	Derek Bell	.40
67	Craig Biggio	.75
68	Richard Hidalgo	.40
69	Johnny Damon	.40
70	Jeff King	.40
71	Hal Morris	.40
72	Dean Palmer	.40
73	Bobby Bonilla	.40
74	Charles Johnson	.40
75	Paul Konerko	.75
76	Raul Mondesi	.75
77	Gary Sheffield	1.00
78	Jeromy Burnitz	.40
79	Marquis Grissom	.40
80	Dave Nilsson	.40
81	Fernando Vina	.40
82	Marty Cordova	.40
83	Pat Meares	.40
84	Paul Molitor	2.00
85	Brad Radke	.40
86	Terry Steinbach	.40
87	Todd Walker	.75
88	Brad Fullmer	.75
89	Vladimir Guerrero	5.00
90	Carl Pavano	.40
91	Rondell White	.75
92	Bernard Gilkey	.40
93	Hideo Nomo	1.00
94	John Olerud	.75
95	Rey Ordonez	.50
96	Mike Piazza	6.00
97	*Masato Yoshii*	1.50
98	Hideki Irabu	1.00
99	Derek Jeter	6.00
100	Chuck Knoblauch	1.00
101	Tino Martinez	.75
102	Paul O'Neill	.75
103	Darryl Strawberry	.60
104	Bernie Williams	1.50
105	Jason Giambi	.40
106	Ben Grieve	3.00
107	Rickey Henderson	.75
108	Matt Stairs	.40
109	Doug Glanville	.40
110	Desi Relaford	.40
111	Scott Rolen	3.00
112	Curt Schilling	.75
113	Jason Kendall	.75
114	Al Martin	.40
115	Jason Schmidt	.40
116	Kevin Young	.40
117	Delino DeShields	.40
118	Gary Gaetti	.40
119	Brian Jordan	.40
120	Ray Lankford	.40
121	Mark McGwire	12.00
122	Kevin Brown	.60
123	Steve Finley	.40
124	Tony Gwynn	5.00
125	Wally Joyner	.40
126	Greg Vaughn	.50
127	Barry Bonds	2.50
128	Orel Hershiser	.40
129	Jeff Kent	.40
130	Bill Mueller	.40
131	Jay Buhner	.75
132	Ken Griffey Jr.	12.00
133	Randy Johnson	2.00
134	Edgar Martinez	.40
135	Alex Rodriguez	8.00
136	David Segui	.40
137	*Rolando Arrojo*	3.00
138	Wade Boggs	.75
139	Quinton McCracken	.40
140	Fred McGriff	.60
141	Will Clark	.75
142	Juan Gonzalez	3.00
143	Tom Goodwin	.40
144	Ivan Rodriguez	2.50
145	Aaron Sele	.40
146	John Wetteland	.40
147	Jose Canseco	1.00
148	Roger Clemens	3.00
149	Jose Cruz Jr.	.50
150	Carlos Delgado	.75

1998 Pacific Revolution Shadows

Shadows is a full parallel of the Revolution base set. Limited to 99 sequentially numbered sets, each card is embossed with a special "Shadow Series" stamp.

	MT
Common Player:	5.00
Veteran Stars:	12X
Young Stars:	8X

(See 1998 Pacific Revolution for checklist and base card values.)

1998 Pacific Revolution Foul Pole

Foul Pole Laser-Cuts is a 20-card insert seeded one per 49 packs. Each card features a color player photo on the left and a foul pole on the right. The foul pole design includes netting that is laser cut.

		MT
Complete Set (20):		350.00
Common Player:		6.00
Inserted 1:49		
1	Cal Ripken Jr.	35.00
2	Nomar Garciaparra	30.00
3	Mo Vaughn	12.00
4	Frank Thomas	20.00
5	Manny Ramirez	15.00
6	Bernie Williams	8.00
7	Ben Grieve	15.00
8	Ken Griffey Jr.	50.00
9	Alex Rodriguez	35.00
10	Juan Gonzalez	15.00
11	Ivan Rodriguez	12.00
12	Travis Lee	10.00
13	Chipper Jones	30.00
14	Sammy Sosa	25.00
15	Vinny Castilla	6.00
16	Moises Alou	6.00
17	Gary Sheffield	6.00
18	Mike Piazza	30.00
19	Mark McGwire	50.00
20	Barry Bonds	12.00

1998 Pacific Revolution Major League Icons

Major League Icons is a 10-card insert seeded one per 121 packs. Each card features a player photo on a die-cut shield, with the shield on a flaming stand.

		MT
Complete Set (10):		400.00
Common Player:		20.00
Inserted 1:121		
1	Cal Ripken Jr.	50.00
2	Nomar Garciaparra	40.00
3	Frank Thomas	25.00
4	Ken Griffey Jr.	75.00
5	Alex Rodriguez	50.00
6	Chipper Jones	40.00
7	Kerry Wood	20.00
8	Mike Piazza	40.00
9	Mark McGwire	75.00
10	Tony Gwynn	30.00

1998 Pacific Revolution Prime Time Performers

Prime Time Performers is a 20-card insert seeded one per 25 packs. The cards are designed like a TV program guide with the team logo laser-cut on the TV screen. The color player photo is located on the left.

		MT
Complete Set (20):		250.00
Common Player:		4.00
Inserted 1:25		
1	Cal Ripken Jr.	20.00
2	Nomar Garciaparra	17.50
3	Frank Thomas	12.50
4	Jim Thome	4.00
5	Hideki Irabu	4.00
6	Derek Jeter	17.50
7	Ben Grieve	7.50
8	Ken Griffey Jr.	25.00
9	Alex Rodriguez	20.00
10	Juan Gonzalez	6.00
11	Ivan Rodriguez	7.50
12	Travis Lee	5.00
13	Chipper Jones	17.50
14	Greg Maddux	17.50
15	Kerry Wood	5.00
16	Larry Walker	4.00
17	Jeff Bagwell	10.00
18	Mike Piazza	17.50
19	Mark McGwire	25.00
20	Tony Gwynn	15.00

1998 Pacific Revolution Rookies and Hardball Heroes

This hobby-only insert combines 20 hot prospects with 10 veteran stars. Horizontal cards have action photos on a flashy metallic-foil background. A portrait photo is on back. The first 20 cards in the set, the youngsters, are paralleled in a gold edition which was limited to just 50 cards of each.

		MT
Complete Set (30):		100.00
Common Player:		.50
Inserted 1:6		
Gold (1-20):		15X
Production 50 sets		
1	Justin Baughman	.50
2	Jarrod Washburn	.50
3	Travis Lee	4.00
4	Kerry Wood	8.00
5	Magglio Ordonez	2.00
6	Todd Helton	2.50
7	Derrek Lee	1.50
8	Richard Hidalgo	1.00
9	Mike Caruso	1.00
10	David Ortiz	1.00
11	Brad Fullmer	2.00
12	Masato Yoshii	1.00
13	Orlando Hernandez	8.00
14	Ricky Ledee	1.00
15	Ben Grieve	5.00
16	Carlton Loewer	.50
17	Desi Relaford	.50
18	Ruben Rivera	.50
19	Rolando Arrojo	3.00
20	Matt Perisho	.50
21	Chipper Jones	8.00
22	Greg Maddux	8.00
23	Cal Ripken Jr.	10.00
24	Nomar Garciaparra	8.00
25	Frank Thomas	6.00
26	Mark McGwire	15.00
27	Tony Gwynn	6.00
28	Ken Griffey Jr.	15.00
29	Alex Rodriguez	10.00
30	Juan Gonzalez	4.00

1998 Pacific Revolution Showstoppers

This 36-card insert was seeded two per 25 packs. The cards feature holographic foil. The color photo is centered above the team logo and the Showstoppers logo.

		MT
Complete Set (36):		275.00
Common Player:		2.00
Inserted 1:12		
1	Cal Ripken Jr.	20.00
2	Nomar Garciaparra	15.00
3	Pedro Martinez	5.00
4	Mo Vaughn	4.00
5	Frank Thomas	10.00
6	Manny Ramirez	9.00
7	Jim Thome	4.00
8	Jaret Wright	4.00
9	Paul Molitor	6.00
10	Orlando Hernandez	12.00
11	Derek Jeter	15.00
12	Bernie Williams	3.00
13	Ben Grieve	7.50
14	Ken Griffey Jr.	25.00
15	Alex Rodriguez	20.00
16	Wade Boggs	3.00
17	Juan Gonzalez	8.00
18	Ivan Rodriguez	6.00
19	Jose Canseco	4.00
20	Roger Clemens	10.00
21	Travis Lee	5.00
22	Andres Galarraga	3.00
23	Chipper Jones	15.00
24	Greg Maddux	15.00
25	Sammy Sosa	12.00
26	Kerry Wood	6.00
27	Vinny Castilla	2.00
28	Larry Walker	4.00
29	Moises Alou	2.00
30	Raul Mondesi	3.00
31	Gary Sheffield	3.00
32	Hideo Nomo	3.00
33	Mike Piazza	15.00
34	Mark McGwire	25.00
35	Tony Gwynn	12.00
36	Barry Bonds	6.00

1999 Pacific

The 450-card base set features full bleed fronts enhanced with silver foil stamping. Card backs have year-by-year statistics, a small photo and a brief career highlight caption. There are two parallels, Platinum Blues and Reds. Platinum Blues have blue foil stamping and are seeded 1:73 packs. Reds are retail exclusive with red foil stamping and are seeded one per retail pack.

	MT
Complete Set (500):	40.00
Common Player:	.10
Inserted 1:73	
Reds:	4X
Inserted 1:1 R	
Pack (10):	2.50
Wax Box (36):	60.00

1 Garret Anderson .10
2 Jason Dickson .10
3 Gary DiSarcina .10
4 Jim Edmonds .20
5 Darin Erstad .75
6 Chuck Finley .10
7 Shigetosi Hasegawa .10
8 Ken Hill .10
9 Dave Hollins .10
10 Phil Nevin .10
11 Troy Percival .10
12a Tim Salmon (action) .25
12b Tim Salmon (portrait) .25
13 Brian Anderson .10
14 Tony Batista .10
15 Jay Bell .10
16 Andy Benes .10
17 Yamil Benitez .10
18 Omar Daal .10
19 David Dellucci .10
20 Karim Garcia .15
21 Bernard Gilkey .10
22a Travis Lee (action) .60
22b Travis Lee (portrait) .60
23 Aaron Small .10
24 Kelly Stinnett .10
25 Devon White .10
26 Matt Williams .25
27a Bruce Chen (action) .15
27b Bruce Chen (portrait) .15
28a Andres Galarraga (action) .35
28b Andres Galarraga (portrait) .35
29 Tom Glavine .20
30 Ozzie Guillen .10
31 Andruw Jones .75
32a Chipper Jones (action) 2.00
32b Chipper Jones (portrait) 2.00
33 Ryan Klesko .20
34 George Lombard .10
35 Javy Lopez .15
36a Greg Maddux (action) 2.00
36b Greg Maddux (portrait) 2.00
37a Marty Malloy (action) .10
37b Marty Malloy (portrait) .10
38 Dennis Martinez .10
39 Kevin Millwood .25
40a Alex Rodriguez (action) 2.50
40b Alex Rodriguez (portrait) 2.50
41 Denny Neagle .10
42 John Smoltz .20
43 Michael Tucker .10
44 Walt Weiss .10
45a Roberto Alomar (action) .50
45b Roberto Alomar (portrait) .50
46 Brady Anderson .10
47 Harold Baines .10
48 Mike Bordick .10
49a Danny Clyburn (action) .10
49b Danny Clyburn (portrait) .10
50 Eric Davis .10
51 Scott Erickson .10
52 Chris Hoiles .10
53 Jimmy Key .10
54a Ryan Minor (action) .40
54b Ryan Minor (portrait) .40
55 Mike Mussina .50
56 Jesse Orosco .10
57a Rafael Palmeiro (action) .25
57b Rafael Palmeiro (portrait) .25
58 Sidney Ponson .10
59 Arthur Rhodes .10
60a Cal Ripken Jr. (action) 2.50
60b Cal Ripken Jr. (portrait) 2.50
61 B.J. Surhoff .10
62 Steve Avery .10
63 Darren Bragg .10
64 Dennis Eckersley .10
65a Nomar Garciaparra (action) 2.00
65b Nomar Garciaparra (portrait) 2.00
66a Sammy Sosa (action) 2.50
66b Sammy Sosa (portrait) 2.50
67 Tom Gordon .10
68 Reggie Jefferson .10
69 Darren Lewis .10
70a Mark McGwire (action) 3.50
70b Mark McGwire (portrait) 3.50
71 Pedro Martinez .50
72 Troy O'Leary .10
73 Bret Saberhagen .10
74 Mike Stanley .10
75 John Valentin .10
76 Jason Varitek .10
77 Mo Vaughn .60
78 Tim Wakefield .10
79 Manny Alexander .10
80 Rod Beck .10
81 Brant Brown .10
82 Mark Clark .10
83 Gary Gaetti .10
84 Mark Grace .25
85 Jose Hernandez .10
86 Lance Johnson .10
87a Jason Maxwell (action) .10
87b Jason Maxwell (portrait) .10
88 Mickey Morandini .10
89 Terry Mulholland .10
90 Henry Rodriguez .10
91 Scott Servais .10
92 Kevin Tapani .10
93 Pedro Valdes .10
94 Kerry Wood .75
95 Jeff Abbott .10
96 James Baldwin .10
97 Albert Belle .75
98 Mike Cameron .10
99 Mike Caruso .10
100 Wil Cordero .10
101 Ray Durham .10
102 Jaime Navarro .10
103 Greg Norton .10
104 Magglio Ordonez .20
105 Mike Sirotka .10
106a Frank Thomas (action) 1.00
106b Frank Thomas (portrait) 1.00
107 Robin Ventura .15
108 Craig Wilson .10
109 Aaron Boone .10
110 Bret Boone .10
111 Sean Casey .20
112 Pete Harnisch .10
113 John Hudek .10
114 Barry Larkin .15
115 Eduardo Perez .10
116 Mike Remlinger .10
117 Reggie Sanders .10
118 Chris Stynes .10
119 Eddie Taubensee .10
120 Brett Tomko .10
121 Pat Watkins .10
122 Dmitri Young .10
123 Sandy Alomar Jr. .15
124 Dave Burba .10
125 Bartolo Colon .15
126 Joey Cora .10
127 Brian Giles .10
128 Dwight Gooden .10
129 Mike Jackson .10
130 David Justice .25
131 Kenny Lofton .60
132 Charles Nagy .10
133 Chad Ogea .10
134a Manny Ramirez (action) 1.00
134b Manny Ramirez (portrait) 1.00
135 Richie Sexson .20
136a Jim Thome (action) .40
136b Jim Thome (portrait) .40
137 Omar Vizquel .10
138 Jaret Wright .40
139 Pedro Astacio .10
140 Jason Bates .10
141a Dante Bichette (action) .25
141b Dante Bichette (portrait) .25
142a Vinny Castilla (action) .10
142b Vinny Castilla (portrait) .10
143a Edgar Clemente (action) .10
143b Edgar Clemente (portrait) .10
144a Derrick Gibson (action) .10
144b Derrick Gibson (portrait) .10
145 Curtis Goodwin .10
146a Todd Helton (action) .75
146b Todd Helton (portrait) .75
147 Bobby Jones .10
148 Darryl Kile .10
149 Mike Lansing .10
150 Chuck McElroy .10
151 Neifi Perez .10
152 Jeff Reed .10
153 John Thomson .10
154a Larry Walker (action) .30
154b Larry Walker (portrait) .30
155 Jamey Wright .10
156 Kimera Bartee .10
157 Geronimo Berroa .10
158 Raul Casanova .10
159 Frank Catalanotto .10
160 Tony Clark .40
161 Deivi Cruz .10
162 Damion Easley .10
163 Juan Encarnacion .10
164 Luis Gonzalez .10
165 Seth Greisinger .10
166 Bob Higginson .10
167 Brian Hunter .10
168 Todd Jones .10
169 Justin Thompson .10
170 Antonio Alfonseca .10
171 Dave Berg .10
172 John Cangelosi .10
173 Craig Counsell .10
174 Todd Dunwoody .10
175 Cliff Floyd .10
176 Alex Gonzalez .10
177 Livan Hernandez .10
178 Ryan Jackson .10
179 Mark Kotsay .20
180 Derrek Lee .10
181 Matt Mantei .10
182 Brian Meadows .10
183 Edgar Renteria .10
184a Moises Alou (action) .25
184b Moises Alou (portrait) .25
185 Brad Ausmus .10
186a Jeff Bagwell (action) 1.00
186b Jeff Bagwell (portrait) 1.00
187 Derek Bell .10
188 Sean Berry .10
189 Craig Biggio .25
190 Carl Everett .10
191 Ricky Gutierrez .10
192 Mike Hampton .10
193 Doug Henry .10
194 Richard Hidalgo .10
195 Randy Johnson .50
196a Russ Johnson (action) .10
196b Russ Johnson (portrait) .10
197 Shane Reynolds .10
198 Bill Spiers .10
199 Kevin Appier .10
200 Tim Belcher .10
201 Jeff Conine .10
202 Johnny Damon .10
203 Jermaine Dye .10
204a Jeremy Giambi (batting stance) .20
204b Jeremy Giambi (follow-through) .20
205 Jeff King .10
206 Shane Mack .10
207 Jeff Montgomery .10
208 Hal Morris .10
209 Jose Offerman .10
210 Dean Palmer .10
211 Jose Rosado .10
212 Glendon Rusch .10
213 Larry Sutton .10
214 Mike Sweeney .10
215 Bobby Bonilla .15
216 Alex Cora .10
217 Darren Dreifort .10
218 Mark Grudzielanek .10
219 Todd Hollandsworth .10
220 Trenidad Hubbard .10
221 Charles Johnson .10
222 Eric Karros .15
223 Matt Luke .10
224 Ramon Martinez .20
225 Raul Mondesi .25
226 Chan Ho Park .20
227 Jeff Shaw .10
228 Gary Sheffield .25
229 Eric Young .10
230 Jeromy Burnitz .10
231 Jeff Cirillo .10
232 Marquis Grissom .10
233 Bobby Hughes .10
234 John Jaha .10
235 Geoff Jenkins .10
236 Scott Karl .10
237 Mark Loretta .10
238 Mike Matheny .10
239 Mike Myers .10
240 Dave Nilsson .10
241 Bob Wickman .10
242 Jose Valentin .10
243 Fernando Vina .10
244 Rick Aguilera .10
245 Ron Coomer .10
246 Marty Cordova .10
247 Denny Hocking .10
248 Matt Lawton .10
249 Pat Meares .10
250a Paul Molitor (action) .50
250b Paul Molitor (portrait) .50
251 Otis Nixon .10
252 Alex Ochoa .10
253 David Ortiz .20
254 A.J. Pierzynski .10
255 Brad Radke .10
256 Terry Steinbach .10
257 Bob Tewksbury .10
258 Todd Walker .25
259 Shane Andrews .10
260 Shayne Bennett .10
261 Orlando Cabrera .10
262 Brad Fullmer .25
263 Vladimir Guerrero 1.50
264 Wilton Guerrero .10
265 Dustin Hermanson .10
266 Terry Jones .10
267 Steve Kline .10
268 Carl Pavano .10
269 F.P. Santangelo .10
270a Fernando Seguignol (action) .15
270b Fernando Seguignol (portrait) .15
271 Ugueth Urbina .10
272 Jose Vidro .10
273 Chris Widger .10
274 Edgardo Alfonzo .15
275 Carlos Baerga .10
276 John Franco .10
277 Todd Hundley .10
278 Butch Huskey .10
279 Bobby Jones .10
280 Al Leiter .20
281 Greg McMichael .10
282 Brian McRae .10
283 Hideo Nomo .25

284 John Olerud .20
285 Rey Ordonez .15
286a Mike Piazza (action) 2.00
286b Mike Piazza (portrait) 2.00
287 Turk Wendell .10
288 Masato Yoshii .10
289 David Cone .20
290 Chad Curtis .10
291 Joe Girardi .10
292 Orlando Hernandez 1.50
293a Hideki Irabu (action) .20
293b Hideki Irabu (portrait) .20
294a Derek Jeter (action) 2.00
294b Derek Jeter (portrait) 2.00
295 Chuck Knoblauch .25
296a Mike Lowell (action) .20
296b Mike Lowell (portrait) .20
297 Tino Martinez .25
298 Ramiro Mendoza .20
299 Paul O'Neill .25
300 Andy Pettitte .40
301 Jorge Posada .15
302 Tim Raines .10
303 Mariano Rivera .20
304 David Wells .20
305a Bernie Williams (action) .50
305b Bernie Williams (portrait) .50
306 Mike Blowers .10
307 Tom Candiotti .10
308a Eric Chavez (action) .40
308b Eric Chavez (portrait) .40
309 Ryan Christenson .10
310 Jason Giambi .10
311a Ben Grieve (action) .75
311b Ben Grieve (portrait) .75
312 Rickey Henderson .20
313 A.J. Hinch .10
314 Jason McDonald .10
315 Bip Roberts .10
316 Kenny Rogers .10
317 Scott Spiezio .10
318 Matt Stairs .10
319 Miguel Tejada .25
320 Bob Abreu .10
321 Alex Arias .10
322a *Gary Bennett* (action) .25
322b *Gary Bennett* (portrait) .25
323 Ricky Bottalico .10
324 Rico Brogna .10
325 Bobby Estalella .10
326 Doug Glanville .10
327 Kevin Jordan .10
328 Mark Leiter .10
329 Wendell Magee .10
330 Mark Portugal .10
331 Desi Relaford .10
332 Scott Rolen .75
333 Curt Schilling .20
334 Kevin Sefcik .10
335 Adrian Brown .10
336 Emil Brown .10
337 Lou Collier .10
338 Francisco Cordova .10
339 Freddy Garcia .10
340 Jose Guillen .20
341 Jason Kendall .20
342 Al Martin .10
343 Abraham Nunez .10
344 Aramis Ramirez .20
345 Ricardo Rincon .10
346 Jason Schmidt .10
347 Turner Ward .10
348 Tony Womack .10
349 Kevin Young .10
350 Juan Acevedo .10
351 Delino DeShields .10
352a J.D. Drew (action) .25
352b J.D. Drew (portrait) .25
353 Ron Gant .15
354 Brian Jordan .10
355 Ray Lankford .15
356 Eli Marrero .10
357 Kent Mercker .10
358 Matt Morris .10
359 Luis Ordaz .10
360 Donovan Osborne .10
361 Placido Polanco .10
362 Fernando Tatis .15
363 Andy Ashby .10
364 Kevin Brown .20
365 Ken Caminiti .20
366 Steve Finley .10
367 Chris Gomez .10
368a Tony Gwynn (action) 1.50
368b Tony Gwynn (portrait) 1.50
369 Joey Hamilton .10
370 Carlos Hernandez .10
371 Trevor Hoffman .10
372 Wally Joyner .10
373 Jim Leyritz .10
374 Ruben Rivera .10
375 Greg Vaughn .20
376 Quilvio Veras .10
377 Rich Aurilla .10
378a Barry Bonds (action) .75
378b Barry Bonds (portrait) .75
379 Ellis Burks .10
380 Joe Carter .15
381 Stan Javier .10
382 Brian Johnson .10
383 Jeff Kent .10
384 Jose Mesa .10
385 Bill Mueller .10
386 Robb Nen .10
387a Armando Rios (action) .10
387b Armando Rios (portrait) .10
388 Kirk Rueter .10
389 Rey Sanchez .10
390 J.T. Snow .10
391 David Bell .10
392 Jay Buhner .15
393 Ken Cloude .10
394 Russ Davis .10
395 Jeff Fassero .10
396a Ken Griffey Jr. (action) 3.50
396b Ken Griffey Jr. (portrait) 3.50
397 *Giomar Guevara* .25
398 Carlos Guillen .10
399 Edgar Martinez .10
400 Shane Monahan .10
401 Jamie Moyer .10
402 David Segui .10
403 Makoto Suzuki .10
404 Mike Timlin .10
405 Dan Wilson .10
406 Wilson Alvarez .10
407 Rolando Arrojo .25
408 Wade Boggs .25
409 Miguel Cairo .10
410 Roberto Hernandez .10
411 Mike Kelly .10
412 Aaron Ledesma .10
413 Albie Lopez .10
414 Dave Martinez .10
415 Quinton McCracken .10
416 Fred McGriff .25
417 Bryan Rekar .10
418 Paul Sorrento .10
419 Randy Winn .10
420 John Burkett .10
421 Will Clark .25
422 Royce Clayton .10
423a Juan Gonzalez (action) .75
423b Juan Gonzalez (portrait) .75
424 Tom Goodwin .10
425 Rusty Greer .10
426 Rick Helling .10
427 Roberto Kelly .10
428 Mark McLemore .10
429a Ivan Rodriguez (action) .75
429b Ivan Rodriguez (portrait) .75
430 Aaron Sele .10
431 Lee Stevens .10
432 Todd Stottlemyre .10
433 John Wetteland .10
434 Todd Zeile .10
435 Jose Canseco .40
436a Roger Clemens (action) 1.50
436b Roger Clemens (portrait) 1.50
437 Felipe Crespo .10
438a Jose Cruz Jr. (action) .15
438b Jose Cruz Jr. (portrait) .15
439 Carlos Delgado .40
440a Tom Evans (action) .10
440b Tom Evans (portrait) .10
441 Tony Fernandez .10
442 Darrin Fletcher .10
443 Alex Gonzalez .10
444 Shawn Green .15
445 Roy Halladay .25
446 Pat Hentgen .10
447 Juan Samuel .10
448 Benito Santiago .10
449 Shannon Stewart .10
450 Woody Williams .10

1999 Pacific Platinum Blue

This 450-card parallel set reprinted each card in Pacific, but used a platinum blue foil on the front instead of the gold foil used on base cards. These were inserted one per 73 packs.

	MT
Platinum Blue Stars:	15x-25x
Yng Stars & RCs:	8x-15x
Inserted 1:73	

(See 1999 Pacific for checklist and base card values.)

1999 Pacific Cramer's Choice

Pacific CEO/President Michael Cramer personally chose this 10-card set. Die-cut into a trophy shape, the cards are enhanced with silver holographic etching and gold foil stamping across the card bottom. These are seeded 1:721 packs.

		MT
Complete Set (10):		600.00
Common Player:		25.00
Inserted 1:721		
1	Cal Ripken Jr.	75.00
2	Nomar Garciaparra	60.00
3	Frank Thomas	50.00
4	Ken Griffey Jr.	100.00
5	Alex Rodriguez	80.00
6	Greg Maddux	60.00
7	Sammy Sosa	75.00
8	Kerry Wood	25.00
9	Mark McGwire	125.00
10	Tony Gwynn	50.00

Player names in *Italic* type indicate a rookie card.

1999 Pacific Dynagon Diamond

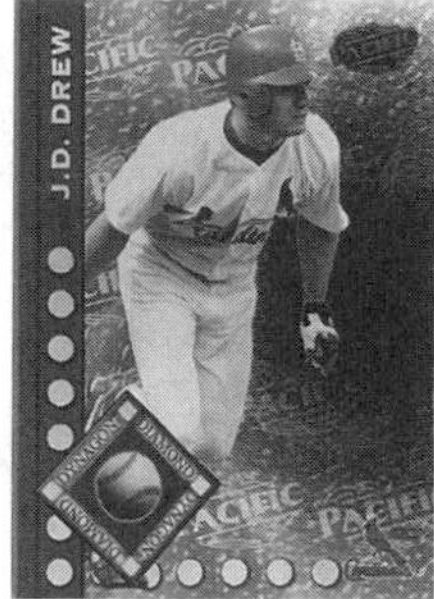

Dynagon Diamond captures 20 of baseball's biggest stars in action against a mirror-patterned full-foil background. These are seeded 4:37.

		MT
Complete Set (20):		75.00
Common Player:		1.00
Inserted 1:9		
1	Cal Ripken Jr.	7.50
2	Nomar Garciaparra	6.00
3	Frank Thomas	4.00
4	Derek Jeter	6.00
5	Ben Grieve	2.00
6	Ken Griffey Jr.	10.00
7	Alex Rodriguez	8.00
8	Juan Gonzalez	2.50
9	Travis Lee	1.50
10	Chipper Jones	6.00
11	Greg Maddux	5.00
12	Sammy Sosa	7.50
13	Kerry Wood	2.00
14	Jeff Bagwell	3.00
15	Hideo Nomo	1.00
16	Mike Piazza	6.00
17	J.D. Drew	2.00
18	Mark McGwire	10.00
19	Tony Gwynn	4.00
20	Barry Bonds	2.00

1999 Pacific Dynagon Diamond Titanium

A parallel to Dynagon Diamond, these are serially numbered to 99 sets and exclusive to hobby packs.

	MT
Common Player:	7.50
Titanium Stars:	8X
Production 99 sets	

(See 1999 Pacific Dynagon Diamond for checklist and base card values.)

1999 Pacific Gold Crown Die-Cuts

This 36-card die-cut set is shaped like a crown at the top and features dual foiling, 24-pt. stock and gold foil stamping. These are seeded 1:37 packs.

		MT
Complete Set (36):		400.00
Common Player:		4.00
Inserted 1:37		
1	Darin Erstad	10.00
2	Cal Ripken Jr.	30.00
3	Nomar Garciaparra	25.00
4	Pedro Martinez	8.00
5	Mo Vaughn	6.00
6	Frank Thomas	20.00
7	Kenny Lofton	6.00
8	Manny Ramirez	12.50
9	Jaret Wright	6.00
10	Paul Molitor	8.00
11	Derek Jeter	25.00
12	Bernie Williams	6.00
13	Ben Grieve	10.00
14	Ken Griffey Jr.	45.00
15	Alex Rodriguez	30.00
16	Rolando Arrojo	4.00
17	Wade Boggs	5.00
18	Juan Gonzalez	10.00
19	Ivan Rodriguez	10.00
20	Roger Clemens	20.00
21	Travis Lee	8.00
22	Chipper Jones	25.00
23	Greg Maddux	20.00
24	Sammy Sosa	30.00
25	Kerry Wood	10.00
26	Todd Helton	8.00
27	Jeff Bagwell	10.00
28	Craig Biggio	5.00
29	Vladimir Guerrero	10.00
30	Hideo Nomo	5.00
31	Mike Piazza	25.00
32	Scott Rolen	10.00
33	J.D. Drew	5.00
34	Mark McGwire	45.00
35	Tony Gwynn	20.00
36	Barry Bonds	10.00

1999 Pacific Hot Cards

This dealer-only 10-card set was awarded to any dealer that had sold any packs/boxes that produced a card for the Pacific Hot Cards Registry Program. Sets are limited to 500 serial numbered sets.

		MT
Complete Set (10):		200.00
Common Player:		8.00
1	Alex Rodriguez	30.00
2	Tony Gwynn	20.00
3	Ken Griffey Jr.	45.00
4	Sammy Sosa	25.00
5	Ivan Rodriguez	10.00
6	Derek Jeter	25.00
7	Cal Ripken Jr.	30.00
8	Mark McGwire	45.00
9	J.D. Drew	15.00
10	Bernie Williams	8.00

1999 Pacific Team Checklists

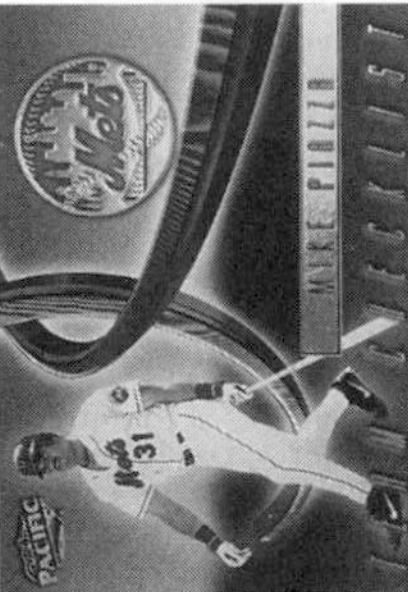

This 30-card horizontal insert set features a star player from each team on the card front, with each team's complete checklist on the card back. Fronts feature a holographic silver-foiled and embossed logo of the player's respective team. These are seeded 2:37 packs.

		MT
Complete Set (30):		100.00
Common Player:		1.50
Inserted 1:18		
1	Darin Erstad	3.00
2	Cal Ripken Jr.	9.00
3	Nomar Garciaparra	8.00
4	Frank Thomas	5.00
5	Manny Ramirez	3.00
6	Damion Easley	1.50
7	Jeff King	1.50
8	Paul Molitor	2.50
9	Derek Jeter	8.00
10	Ben Grieve	3.00
11	Ken Griffey Jr.	15.00
12	Wade Boggs	2.00
13	Juan Gonzalez	4.00
14	Roger Clemens	6.00
15	Travis Lee	2.00
16	Chipper Jones	6.00
17	Sammy Sosa	10.00
18	Barry Larkin	2.00
19	Todd Helton	2.50
20	Mark Kotsay	1.50
21	Jeff Bagwell	3.00
22	Raul Mondesi	2.00
23	Jeff Cirillo	1.50
24	Vladimir Guerrero	6.00
25	Mike Piazza	8.00
26	Scott Rolen	3.00
27	Jason Kendall	1.50
28	Mark McGwire	15.00
29	Tony Gwynn	5.00
30	Barry Bonds	3.00

1999 Pacific Timelines

Timelines features 20 superstars, giving a chronological history of each player complete with photos from early in their careers. Three photos of the player are on the card front. Inserted exclusively in hobby packs these are limited to 199 serially numbered sets.

		MT
Complete Set (20):		900.00
Common Player:		15.00
Inserted 1:181 H		
1	Cal Ripken Jr.	90.00
2	Frank Thomas	50.00
3	Jim Thome	15.00
4	Paul Molitor	20.00
5	Bernie Williams	15.00
6	Derek Jeter	75.00
7	Ken Griffey Jr.	125.00
8	Alex Rodriguez	90.00
9	Wade Boggs	15.00
10	Jose Canseco	15.00
11	Roger Clemens	60.00
12	Andres Galarraga	15.00
13	Chipper Jones	75.00
14	Greg Maddux	75.00
15	Sammy Sosa	90.00
16	Larry Walker	15.00
17	Randy Johnson	15.00
18	Mike Piazza	75.00
19	Mark McGwire	125.00
20	Tony Gwynn	60.00

1999 Pacific Aurora

The 200-card set features two photos on the card front and one on the back. Card backs also have '98 and career stats along with personal information. The player's name and Aurora logo are stamped with gold foil.

		MT
Complete Set (200):		50.00
Common Player:		.20
Pack (6):		3.00
Wax Box (36):		70.00
1	Garret Anderson	.20
2	Jim Edmonds	.40
3	Darin Erstad	.75
4	Matt Luke	.20
5	Tim Salmon	.30
6	Mo Vaughn	.50
7	Jay Bell	.20
8	David Dellucci	.20
9	Steve Finley	.20
10	Bernard Gilkey	.20
11	Randy Johnson	1.00
12	Travis Lee	.20
13	Matt Williams	.40
14	Andres Galarraga	.40
15	Tom Glavine	.40
16	Andruw Jones	1.00
17	Chipper Jones	2.00
18	Brian Jordan	.20
19	Javy Lopez	.30
20	Greg Maddux	2.00
21	Albert Belle	.50
22	Will Clark	.50
23	Scott Erickson	.20
24	Mike Mussina	.75
25	Cal Ripken Jr.	3.00
26	B.J. Surhoff	.20
27	Nomar Garciaparra	2.50
28	Reggie Jefferson	.20
29	Darren Lewis	.20
30	Pedro Martinez	1.00
31	John Valentin	.20
32	Rod Beck	.20
33	Mark Grace	.40
34	Lance Johnson	.20
35	Mickey Morandini	.20
36	Sammy Sosa	2.50
37	Kerry Wood	.40
38	James Baldwin	.20
39	Mike Caruso	.20
40	Ray Durham	.20
41	Magglio Ordonez	.35
42	Frank Thomas	1.50
43	Aaron Boone	.20
44	Sean Casey	.30
45	Barry Larkin	.40
46	Hal Morris	.20
47	Denny Neagle	.20
48	Greg Vaughn	.30
49	Pat Watkins	.20
50	Roberto Alomar	.75
51	Sandy Alomar Jr.	.30
52	David Justice	.40
53	Kenny Lofton	.40
54	Manny Ramirez	1.00
55	Richie Sexson	.25
56	Jim Thome	.50
57	Omar Vizquel	.20
58	Dante Bichette	.25
59	Vinny Castilla	.25
60	*Edgard Clemente*	.50
61	Derrick Gibson	.20
62	Todd Helton	1.00
63	Darryl Kile	.20
64	Larry Walker	.40
65	Tony Clark	.25
66	Damion Easley	.20
67	Bob Higginson	.20
68	Brian Hunter	.20
69	Dean Palmer	.20
70	Justin Thompson	.20
71	Craig Counsell	.20
72	Todd Dunwoody	.25
73	Cliff Floyd	.20
74	Alex Gonzalez	.20
75	Livan Hernandez	.20
76	Mark Kotsay	.25
77	Derrek Lee	.20
78	Moises Alou	.30
79	Jeff Bagwell	1.00
80	Derek Bell	.20
81	Craig Biggio	.30
82	Ken Caminiti	.30
83	Richard Hidalgo	.20
84	Shane Reynolds	.20
85	Jeff Conine	.20
86	Johnny Damon	.20
87	Jermaine Dye	.20
88	Jeff King	.20
89	Jeff Montgomery	.20
90	Mike Sweeney	.20
91	Kevin Brown	.40
92	Mark Grudzielanek	.20
93	Eric Karros	.20
94	Raul Mondesi	.40
95	Chan Ho Park	.30
96	Gary Sheffield	.40
97	Jeromy Burnitz	.20
98	Jeff Cirillo	.20
99	Marquis Grissom	.20
100	Geoff Jenkins	.20
101	Dave Nilsson	.20
102	Jose Valentin	.20
103	Fernando Vina	.20
104	Marty Cordova	.20
105	Matt Lawton	.20
106	David Ortiz	.20
107	Brad Radke	.20
108	Todd Walker	.20
109	Shane Andrews	.20
110	Orlando Cabrera	.20
111	Brad Fullmer	.30
112	Vladimir Guerrero	1.50
113	Wilton Guerrero	.20
114	Carl Pavano	.20
115	Fernando Seguignol	.20
116	Ugueth Urbina	.20
117	Edgardo Alfonzo	.25
118	Bobby Bonilla	.20
119	Rickey Henderson	.40
120	Hideo Nomo	.35
121	John Olerud	.40
122	Rey Ordonez	.25
123	Mike Piazza	2.50
124	Masato Yoshii	.20
125	Scott Brosius	.20
126	Orlando Hernandez	.30
127	Hideki Irabu	.30
128	Derek Jeter	3.00
129	Chuck Knoblauch	.30
130	Tino Martinez	.30
131	Jorge Posada	.30

132	Bernie Williams	.75
133	Eric Chavez	.25
134	Ryan Christenson	.20
135	Jason Giambi	.50
136	Ben Grieve	.40
137	A.J. Hinch	.20
138	Matt Stairs	.20
139	Miguel Tejada	.30
140	Bob Abreu	.20
141	*Gary Bennett*	.30
142	Desi Relaford	.20
143	Scott Rolen	.75
144	Curt Schilling	.30
145	Kevin Sefcik	.20
146	Brian Giles	.30
147	Jose Guillen	.20
148	Jason Kendall	.30
149	Aramis Ramirez	.20
150	Tony Womack	.20
151	Kevin Young	.20
152	Eric Davis	.30
153	J.D. Drew	.25
154	Ray Lankford	.20
155	Eli Marrero	.20
156	Mark McGwire	4.00
157	Luis Ordaz	.20
158	Edgar Renteria	.20
159	Andy Ashby	.20
160	Tony Gwynn	1.50
161	Trevor Hoffman	.20
162	Wally Joyner	.20
163	Jim Leyritz	.20
164	Ruben Rivera	.20
165	Reggie Sanders	.20
166	Quilvio Veras	.20
167	Rich Aurilia	.20
168	Marvin Benard	.20
169	Barry Bonds	1.00
170	Ellis Burks	.20
171	Jeff Kent	.30
172	Bill Mueller	.20
173	J.T. Snow	.20
174	Jay Buhner	.30
175	Jeff Fassero	.20
176	Ken Griffey Jr.	4.00
177	Carlos Guillen	.20
178	Edgar Martinez	.25
179	Alex Rodriguez	3.00
180	David Segui	.20
181	Dan Wilson	.20
182	Rolando Arrojo	.20
183	Wade Boggs	.50
184	Jose Canseco	.75
185	Aaron Ledesma	.20
186	Dave Martinez	.20
187	Quinton McCracken	.20
188	Fred McGriff	.40
189	Juan Gonzalez	1.00
190	Tom Goodwin	.20
191	Rusty Greer	.20
192	Roberto Kelly	.20
193	Rafael Palmeiro	.50
194	Ivan Rodriguez	1.00
195	Roger Clemens	1.50
196	Jose Cruz Jr.	.25
197	Carlos Delgado	.75
198	Alex Gonzalez	.20
199	Roy Halladay	.20
200	Pat Hentgen	.20

1999 Pacific Aurora Complete Players

The 10 players featured in this serial numbered 20-card set each have two cards, designed to fit together. Card fronts feature a red border on the top and bottom with the rest of the card done in gold foil etching. Each card is serially numbered to 299.

		MT
Complete Set (10):		200.00
Common Player:		15.00
Production 299 sets		
1	Cal Ripken Jr.	30.00
2	Nomar Garciaparra	25.00
3	Sammy Sosa	25.00
4	Kerry Wood	8.00
5	Frank Thomas	15.00
6	Mike Piazza	25.00
7	Mark McGwire	40.00
8	Tony Gwynn	15.00
9	Ken Griffey Jr.	30.00
10	Alex Rodriguez	30.00

1999 Pacific Aurora Kings of the Major Leagues

The full foiled card fronts also utilize gold foil stamping. Pacific's crown as well as the featured player's team are shadow boxed in the background with the player's image in the foreground. These are seeded 1:361.

		MT
Complete Set (10):		750.00
Common Player:		30.00
Inserted 1:361		
1	Cal Ripken Jr.	90.00
2	Nomar Garciaparra	75.00
3	Sammy Sosa	75.00
4	Kerry Wood	30.00
5	Frank Thomas	60.00
6	Mike Piazza	75.00
7	Mark McGwire	125.00
8	Tony Gwynn	60.00
9	Ken Griffey Jr.	125.00
10	Alex Rodriguez	90.00

1999 Pacific Aurora On Deck

Twenty of the game's hottest players are featured in this laser-cut and silver foil stamped set. The player's team logo is laser cut into the bottom half of the card beneath the player photo. These are seeded 4:37 packs.

		MT
Complete Set (20):		100.00
Common Player:		2.00
Inserted 1:9		
1	Chipper Jones	8.00
2	Cal Ripken Jr.	10.00
3	Nomar Garciaparra	8.00
4	Sammy Sosa	8.00
5	Frank Thomas	6.00
6	Manny Ramirez	4.00
7	Todd Helton	4.00
8	Larry Walker	2.00
9	Jeff Bagwell	3.00
10	Vladimir Guerrero	6.00
11	Mike Piazza	8.00
12	Derek Jeter	8.00
13	Bernie Williams	2.00
14	J.D. Drew	2.00
15	Mark McGwire	15.00
16	Tony Gwynn	6.00
17	Ken Griffey Jr.	15.00
18	Alex Rodriguez	12.00
19	Juan Gonzalez	4.00
20	Ivan Rodriguez	3.00

1999 Pacific Aurora Pennant Fever

Regular Pennant Fever inserts feature gold foil stamping of 20 of the hottest players in the hobby. These are seeded 4:37 packs. There are also three parallel versions which consist of: Platinum Blue, Silver and Copper. Platinum Blues are limited to 100 serial numbered sets, Silvers are retail exclusive and limited to 250 numbered sets and Coppers are hobby exclusive and limited to 20 numbered sets. Pacific spokesman Tony Gwynn autographed 97 regular Pennent Fever cards and one each of the Silver, Blue and Copper.

		MT
Complete Set (20):		90.00
Common Player:		1.00
Silver (250 each):		2X
Platinum Blue (100 each):		6X
Copper (20 each):		20X
Tony Gwynn Autograph:		200.00
1	Chipper Jones	6.00
2	Greg Maddux	6.00
3	Cal Ripken Jr.	8.00
4	Nomar Garciaparra	6.00
5	Sammy Sosa	6.00
6	Kerry Wood	2.50
7	Frank Thomas	5.00
8	Manny Ramirez	3.00
9	Todd Helton	2.00
10	Jeff Bagwell	3.00
11	Mike Piazza	6.00
12	Derek Jeter	6.00
13	Bernie Williams	2.00
14	J.D. Drew	2.00
15	Mark McGwire	12.00
16	Tony Gwynn	5.00
17	Ken Griffey Jr.	12.00
18	Alex Rodriguez	10.00
19	Juan Gonzalez	3.00
20	Ivan Rodriguez	2.50

1999 Pacific Aurora Styrotechs

This 20-card set features styrene stock, make the cards more resilient. Fronts have a black border and stamped with gold foil. Backs have a photo and a brief career highlight caption. These are seeded 1:37 packs.

		MT
Complete Set (20):		150.00
Common Player:		3.00
Inserted 1:37		
1	Chipper Jones	10.00
2	Greg Maddux	10.00
3	Cal Ripken Jr.	15.00
4	Nomar Garciaparra	12.00
5	Sammy Sosa	12.00
6	Kerry Wood	3.00
7	Frank Thomas	6.00
8	Manny Ramirez	5.00
9	Larry Walker	3.00
10	Jeff Bagwell	5.00
11	Mike Piazza	12.00
12	Derek Jeter	15.00
13	Bernie Williams	4.00
14	J.D. Drew	4.00
15	Mark McGwire	20.00
16	Tony Gwynn	6.00
17	Ken Griffey Jr.	15.00
18	Alex Rodriguez	15.00
19	Juan Gonzalez	5.00
20	Ivan Rodriguez	5.00

1999 Pacific Crown Collection

Released in one series the 300-card set has white borders and gold foil stamping on the card fronts. Backs have a small photo along with english and spanish translation. There is one parallel to the base set Platinum Blues, which are stamped with a platinum blue holographic tint and are seeded 1:73. Packs consist of 12 cards with a S.R.P. of $2.49.

		MT
Complete Set (300):		30.00
Common Player:		.10
Platinum Blue Stars:		30X
Inserted 1:73		
Pack (12):		2.50
Wax Box (36):		75.00
1	Garret Anderson	.10
2	Gary DiSarcina	.10
3	Jim Edmonds	.25
4	Darin Erstad	.40
5	Shigetosi Hasegawa	.10
6	Norberto Martin	.10
7	Omar Olivares	.10
8	Orlando Palmeiro	.10
9	Tim Salmon	.25
10	Randy Velarde	.10
11	Tony Batista	.10
12	Jay Bell	.10
13	Yamil Benitez	.10
14	Omar Daal	.10
15	David Dellucci	.10
16	Karim Garcia	.10
17	Travis Lee	.15
18	Felix Rodriguez	.10
19	Devon White	.10
20	Matt Williams	.25
21	Andres Galarraga	.30
22	Tom Glavine	.25
23	Ozzie Guillen	.10
24	Andruw Jones	.50
25	Chipper Jones	1.50
26	Ryan Klesko	.25
27	Javy Lopez	.20
28	Greg Maddux	1.50
29	Dennis Martinez	.10
30	Odaliz Perez	.10
31	Rudy Seanez	.10
32	John Smoltz	.10
33	Roberto Alomar	.50
34	Armando Benitez	.10
35	Scott Erickson	.10
36	Juan Guzman	.10
37	Mike Mussina	.50
38	Jesse Orosco	.10
39	Rafael Palmeiro	.40
40	Sidney Ponson	.10
41	Cal Ripken Jr.	2.50
42	B.J. Surhoff	.10
43	Lenny Webster	.10
44	Dennis Eckersley	.10
45	Nomar Garciaparra	2.00
46	Darren Lewis	.10
47	Pedro Martinez	.75
48	Troy O'Leary	.10
49	Bret Saberhagen	.10
50	John Valentin	.10
51	Mo Vaughn	.40
52	Tim Wakefield	.10
53	Manny Alexander	.10
54	Rod Beck	.10
55	Gary Gaetti	.10
56	Mark Grace	.25
57	Felix Heredia	.10
58	Jose Hernandez	.10
59	Henry Rodriguez	.10
60	Sammy Sosa	2.00
61	Kevin Tapani	.10
62	Kerry Wood	.40
63	James Baldwin	.10
64	Albert Belle	.40
65	Mike Caruso	.10
66	Carlos Castillo	.10
67	Wil Cordero	.10
68	Jaime Navarro	.10
69	Magglio Ordonez	.20
70	Frank Thomas	1.00
71	Robin Ventura	.20
72	Bret Boone	.10
73	Sean Casey	.25
74	*Guillermo Garcia*	.10
75	Barry Larkin	.30
76	Melvin Nieves	.10
77	Eduardo Perez	.10
78	Roberto Petagine	.10
79	Reggie Sanders	.10
80	Eddie Taubensee	.10
81	Brett Tomko	.10
82	Sandy Alomar Jr.	.15
83	Bartolo Colon	.10
84	Joey Cora	.10
85	Einar Diaz	.10
86	David Justice	.30
87	Kenny Lofton	.30
88	Manny Ramirez	.75
89	Jim Thome	.30
90	Omar Vizquel	.10
91	Enrique Wilson	.10
92	Pedro Astacio	.10
93	Dante Bichette	.30
94	Vinny Castilla	.15
95	*Edgard Clemente*	.15
96	Todd Helton	.75
97	Darryl Kile	.10
98	Mike Munoz	.10
99	Neifi Perez	.10
100	Jeff Reed	.10
101	Larry Walker	.30
102	Gabe Alvarez	.10
103	Kimera Bartee	.10
104	Frank Castillo	.10
105	Tony Clark	.20
106	Deivi Cruz	.10
107	Damion Easley	.10
108	Luis Gonzalez	.10
109	Marino Santana	.10
110	Justin Thompson	.10
111	Antonio Alfonseca	.10
112	Alex Fernandez	.10
113	Cliff Floyd	.10
114	Alex Gonzalez	.10
115	Livan Hernandez	.10
116	Mark Kotsay	.10
117	Derrek Lee	.10
118	Edgar Renteria	.15
119	Jesus Sanchez	.10
120	Moises Alou	.20
121	Jeff Bagwell	.75
122	Derek Bell	.10
123	Craig Biggio	.25
124	Tony Eusebio	.10
125	Ricky Gutierrez	.10
126	Richard Hidalgo	.10
127	Randy Johnson	.75
128	Jose Lima	.10
129	Shane Reynolds	.10
130	Johnny Damon	.10
131	Carlos Febles	.10
132	Jeff King	.10
133	Mendy Lopez	.10
134	Hal Morris	.10
135	Jose Offerman	.10
136	Jose Rosado	.10
137	Jose Santiago	.10
138	Bobby Bonilla	.10
139	Roger Cedeno	.10
140	Alex Cora	.10
141	Eric Karros	.15
142	Raul Mondesi	.25
143	Antonio Osuna	.10
144	Chan Ho Park	.20
145	Gary Sheffield	.25
146	Ismael Valdes	.10
147	Jeromy Burnitz	.10
148	Jeff Cirillo	.10
149	Valerio de los Santos	.10
150	Marquis Grissom	.10
151	Scott Karl	.10
152	Dave Nilsson	.10
153	Al Reyes	.10
154	Rafael Roque	.10
155	Jose Valentin	.10
156	Fernando Vina	.10
157	Rick Aguilera	.10
158	Hector Carrasco	.10
159	Marty Cordova	.10
160	Eddie Guardado	.10
161	Paul Molitor	.50
162	Otis Nixon	.10
163	Alex Ochoa	.10
164	David Ortiz	.10
165	Frank Rodriguez	.10
166	Todd Walker	.10
167	Miguel Batista	.10
168	Orlando Cabrera	.10
169	Vladimir Guerrero	1.00
170	Wilton Guerrero	.10
171	Carl Pavano	.10
172	Robert Perez	.10
173	F.P. Santangelo	.10
174	Fernando Seguignol	.10
175	Ugueth Urbina	.10
176	Javier Vazquez	.10
177	Edgardo Alfonzo	.15
178	Carlos Baerga	.10
179	John Franco	.10
180	Luis Lopez	.10
181	Hideo Nomo	.25
182	John Olerud	.20
183	Rey Ordonez	.15
184	Mike Piazza	2.00
185	Armando Reynoso	.10
186	Masato Yoshii	.10
187	David Cone	.20
188	Orlando Hernandez	.30
189	Hideki Irabu	.10
190	Derek Jeter	2.50
191	Ricky Ledee	.10
192	Tino Martinez	.20
193	Ramiro Mendoza	.10
194	Paul O'Neill	.25
195	Jorge Posada	.20
196	Mariano Rivera	.20
197	Luis Sojo	.10
198	Bernie Williams	.50
199	Rafael Bournigal	.10
200	Eric Chavez	.25
201	Ryan Christenson	.10
202	Jason Giambi	.40
203	Ben Grieve	.30
204	Rickey Henderson	.25
205	A.J. Hinch	.10
206	Kenny Rogers	.10
207	Miguel Tejada	.20
208	Jorge Velandia	.10
209	Bobby Abreu	.10
210	Marlon Anderson	.10
211	Alex Arias	.10
212	Bobby Estalella	.10
213	Doug Glanville	.10
214	Scott Rolen	.50
215	Curt Schilling	.20
216	Kevin Sefcik	.10
217	Adrian Brown	.10
218	Francisco Cordova	.10
219	Freddy Garcia	.10
220	Jose Guillen	.10
221	Jason Kendall	.10
222	Al Martin	.10
223	Abraham Nunez	.10
224	Aramis Ramirez	.10
225	Ricardo Rincon	.10
226	Kevin Young	.10
227	J.D. Drew	.25
228	Ron Gant	.10
229	Jose Jimenez	.10
230	Brian Jordan	.10
231	Ray Lankford	.10
232	Eli Marrero	.10
233	Mark McGwire	3.00
234	Luis Ordaz	.10
235	Placido Polanco	.10
236	Fernando Tatis	.15
237	Andy Ashby	.10
238	Kevin Brown	.15
239	Ken Caminiti	.20
240	Steve Finley	.10
241	Chris Gomez	.10
242	Tony Gwynn	1.00
243	Carlos Hernandez	.10
244	Trevor Hoffman	.10
245	Wally Joyner	.10
246	Ruben Rivera	.10
247	Greg Vaughn	.20
248	Quilvio Veras	.10
249	Rich Aurilia	.10
250	Barry Bonds	.75
251	Stan Javier	.10
252	Jeff Kent	.10
253	Ramon Martinez	.10
254	Jose Mesa	.10
255	Armando Rios	.10
256	Rich Rodriguez	.10
257	Rey Sanchez	.10
258	J.T. Snow	.10
259	Julian Tavarez	.10
260	Jeff Fassero	.10
261	Ken Griffey Jr.	2.50
262	*Giomar Guevara*	.10
263	Carlos Guillen	.10
264	Raul Ibanez	.10
265	Edgar Martinez	.10
266	Jamie Moyer	.10
267	Alex Rodriguez	2.50
268	David Segui	.10
269	Makoto Suzuki	.10
270	Wilson Alvarez	.10
271	Rolando Arrojo	.10
272	Wade Boggs	.40
273	Miguel Cairo	.10
274	Roberto Hernandez	.10
275	Aaron Ledesma	.10
276	Albie Lopez	.10
277	Quinton McCracken	.10
278	Fred McGriff	.40
279	Esteban Yan	.10
280	Luis Alicea	.10
281	Will Clark	.40
282	Juan Gonzalez	.75
283	Rusty Greer	.10
284	Rick Helling	.10
285	Xavier Hernandez	.10
286	Roberto Kelly	.10
287	Esteban Loaiza	.10
288	Ivan Rodriguez	.75
289	Aaron Sele	.10
290	John Wetteland	.10
291	Jose Canseco	.50
292	Roger Clemens	1.00
293	Felipe Crespo	.10
294	Jose Cruz Jr.	.20
295	Carlos Delgado	.75
296	Kelvim Escobar	.10
297	Tony Fernandez	.10
298	Alex Gonzalez	.10
299	Tomas Perez	.10
300	Juan Samuel	.10

1999 Pacific Crown Collection In The Cage

These die-cut inserts have a netting like background with laser cutting, giving the look that the player is hitting in a batting cage. These are seeded 1:145 packs.

		MT
Complete Set (20):		600.00
Common Player:		10.00
Inserted 1:145		
1	Chipper Jones	40.00
2	Cal Ripken Jr.	50.00
3	Nomar Garciaparra	40.00
4	Sammy Sosa	50.00
5	Frank Thomas	30.00
6	Manny Ramirez	20.00
7	Todd Helton	15.00
8	Moises Alou	10.00
9	Vladimir Guerrero	30.00
10	Mike Piazza	40.00
11	Derek Jeter	40.00
12	Ben Grieve	15.00
13	J.D. Drew	10.00
14	Mark McGwire	75.00
15	Tony Gwynn	30.00
16	Ken Griffey Jr.	75.00
17	Edgar Martinez	10.00
18	Alex Rodriguez	50.00
19	Juan Gonzalez	20.00
20	Ivan Rodriguez	15.00

1999 Pacific Crown Collection Latinos/Major Leagues

This 36-card set salutes the many latino players in the major league including Roberto Alomar, Manny Ramirez and Juan Gonzalez. These are seeded 2:37 packs.

		MT
Complete Set (36):		80.00
Common Player:		1.25
Inserted 1:18		
1	Roberto Alomar	3.00
2	Rafael Palmeiro	2.50
3	Nomar Garciaparra	10.00
4	Pedro Martinez	4.00
5	Magglio Ordonez	2.00
6	Sandy Alomar Jr.	2.00
7	Bartolo Colon	1.50
8	Manny Ramirez	6.00
9	Omar Vizquel	1.50
10	Enrique Wilson	1.50
11	David Ortiz	1.50
12	Orlando Hernandez	10.00
13	Tino Martinez	1.50
14	Mariano Rivera	2.00
15	Bernie Williams	2.50
16	Edgar Martinez	1.50
17	Alex Rodriguez	15.00
18	David Segui	1.50
19	Rolando Arrojo	2.00
20	Juan Gonzalez	5.00
21	Ivan Rodriguez	4.00
22	Jose Canseco	3.00
23	Jose Cruz Jr.	1.50
24	Andres Galarraga	3.00
25	Andruw Jones	4.00
26	Javy Lopez	2.00
27	Sammy Sosa	12.50
28	Vinny Castilla	1.50
29	Alex Gonzalez	1.50
30	Moises Alou	2.00
31	Bobby Bonilla	1.50
32	Raul Mondesi	2.00
33	Fernando Vina	1.50
34	Vladimir Guerrero	6.00
35	Carlos Baerga	1.50
36	Rey Ordonez	1.50

1999 Pacific Crown Collection Pacific Cup

These die-cut inserts are shaped like a trophy with the featured player's photo in the foreground. These are seeded 1:721 packs.

		MT
Complete Set (10):		700.00
Common Player:		30.00
Inserted 1:721		
1	Cal Ripken Jr.	90.00
2	Nomar Garciaparra	75.00
3	Frank Thomas	50.00
4	Ken Griffey Jr.	125.00
5	Alex Rodriguez	100.00
6	Greg Maddux	75.00
7	Sammy Sosa	90.00
8	Kerry Wood	30.00
9	Mark McGwire	125.00
10	Tony Gwynn	60.00

1999 Pacific Crown Collection Tape Measure

This 20-card insert set is fully foiled in platinum blue with rainbow highlights in the background of the player photo. Saluting the top power hitters in the game today, these are seeded 1:73 packs.

		MT
Complete Set (20):		325.00
Common Player:		6.00
Inserted 1:73		
1	Andres Galarraga	6.00
2	Chipper Jones	25.00
3	Nomar Garciaparra	25.00
4	Sammy Sosa	35.00
5	Frank Thomas	15.00
6	Manny Ramirez	15.00
7	Vinny Castilla	6.00
8	Moises Alou	6.00
9	Jeff Bagwell	12.50
10	Raul Mondesi	6.00
11	Vladimir Guerrero	20.00
12	Mike Piazza	25.00
13	J.D. Drew	6.00
14	Mark McGwire	45.00
15	Greg Vaughn	6.00
16	Ken Griffey Jr.	45.00
17	Alex Rodriguez	35.00
18	Juan Gonzalez	15.00
19	Ivan Rodriguez	10.00
20	Jose Canseco	6.00

1999 Pacific Crown Collection Team Checklists

This 30-card set features is highlighted with holographic silver foil stamping and done in a horizontal format. The backs have a complete team checklist for the featured player's team. These have an insertion rate of 1:37 packs.

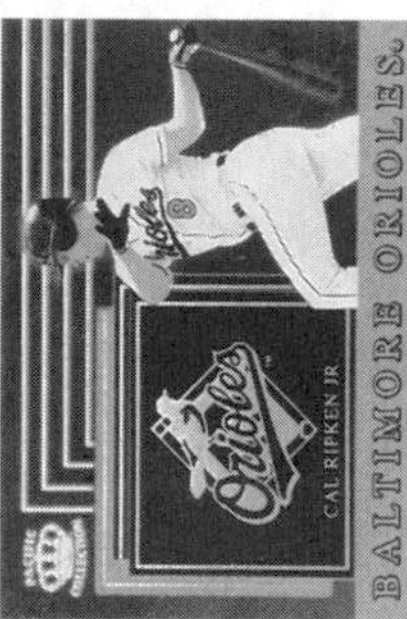

		MT
Complete Set (30):		275.00
Common Player:		4.00
Inserted 1:37		
1	Darin Erstad	8.00
2	Travis Lee	6.00
3	Chipper Jones	20.00
4	Cal Ripken Jr.	25.00
5	Nomar Garciaparra	20.00
6	Sammy Sosa	25.00
7	Frank Thomas	15.00
8	Barry Larkin	5.00
9	Manny Ramirez	12.50
10	Larry Walker	6.00
11	Bob Higginson	4.00
12	Livan Hernandez	4.00
13	Moises Alou	5.00
14	Jeff King	4.00
15	Raul Mondesi	5.00
16	Marquis Grissom	4.00
17	David Ortiz	4.00
18	Vladimir Guerrero	15.00
19	Mike Piazza	20.00
20	Derek Jeter	20.00
21	Ben Grieve	8.00
22	Scott Rolen	8.00
23	Jason Kendall	4.00
24	Mark McGwire	40.00
25	Tony Gwynn	15.00
26	Barry Bonds	8.00
27	Ken Griffey Jr.	40.00
28	Wade Boggs	6.00
29	Juan Gonzalez	10.00
30	Jose Canseco	6.00

1999 Pacific Crown Royale

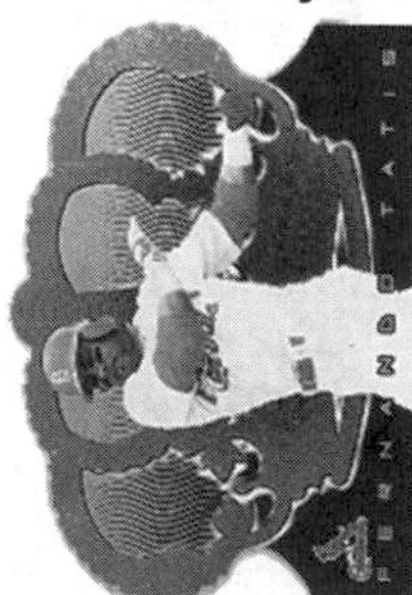

The Crown Royale 144-card base set has a horizontal format die-cut around a crown design at the top. The cards are double foiled and etched. There are two parallels: Limited Series and Opening Day. Limited Series is produced on 24-point stock with silver foil and limited to 99 numbered sets. Opening Day is limited to 72 numbered sets.

		MT
Complete Set (144):		200.00
Common Player:		.50
Common SP:		4.00
Limited Series:		8X
SPs:		2X
Production 99 sets		
Opening Day:		15X
SPs:		3X
Production 72 sets		
Pack (6):		5.00
Wax Box (24):		90.00
1	Jim Edmonds	.50
2	Darin Erstad	1.50
3	Troy Glaus	2.00
4	Tim Salmon	1.00
5	Mo Vaughn	1.00
6	Jay Bell	.50
7	Steve Finley	.50
8	Randy Johnson	2.00
9	Travis Lee	.50
10	Matt Williams	1.00
11	Andruw Jones	1.50
12	Chipper Jones	4.00
13	Brian Jordan	.50
14	Ryan Klesko	.50
15	Javy Lopez	.75
16	Greg Maddux	4.00
17	Randall Simon	.50
18	Albert Belle	1.00
19	Will Clark	1.00
20	Delino DeShields	.50
21	Mike Mussina	1.25
22	Cal Ripken Jr.	6.00
23	Nomar Garciaparra	5.00
24	Pedro Martinez	2.00
25	Jose Offerman	.50
26	John Valentin	.50
27	Mark Grace	1.00
28	Lance Johnson	.50
29	Henry Rodriguez	.50
30	Sammy Sosa	5.00
31	Kerry Wood	1.00
32	Mike Caruso	.50
33	Ray Durham	.50
34	Magglio Ordonez	1.00
35	Brian Simmons	.50
36	Frank Thomas	3.00
37	Mike Cameron	.50
38	Barry Larkin	1.00
39	Greg Vaughn	.50
40	Dmitri Young	.50
41	Roberto Alomar	1.50
42	Sandy Alomar Jr.	.50
43	David Justice	1.00
44	Kenny Lofton	1.00
45	Manny Ramirez	2.00
46	Jim Thome	1.00
47	Dante Bichette	.75
48	Vinny Castilla	.50
49	Todd Helton	2.00
50	Larry Walker	1.00
51	Tony Clark	.75
52	Damion Easley	.50
53	Bob Higginson	.50
54	Brian Hunter	.50
55	Gabe Kapler	5.00
56	*Jeff Weaver*	10.00
57	Cliff Floyd	.50
58	Alex Gonzalez	.50
59	Mark Kotsay	.50
60	Derrek Lee	.50
61	Preston Wilson	4.00
62	Moises Alou	.75
63	Jeff Bagwell	2.00
64	Derek Bell	.50
65	Craig Biggio	.75
66	Ken Caminiti	.75
67	Carlos Beltran	4.00
68	Johnny Damon	.50
69	Carlos Febles	4.00
70	Jeff King	.50
71	Kevin Brown	.75
72	Todd Hundley	.50
73	Eric Karros	.50
74	Raul Mondesi	.75
75	Gary Sheffield	.75
76	Jeromy Burnitz	.50
77	Jeff Cirillo	.50
78	Marquis Grissom	.50
79	Fernando Vina	.50

80	*Chad Allen*	4.00
81	Matt Lawton	.50
82	Doug Mientkiewicz	4.00
83	Brad Radke	.50
84	Todd Walker	.50
85	Michael Barrett	4.00
86	Brad Fullmer	.50
87	Vladimir Guerrero	3.00
88	Wilton Guerrero	.50
89	Ugueth Urbina	.50
90	Bobby Bonilla	.50
91	Rickey Henderson	1.00
92	Rey Ordonez	.50
93	Mike Piazza	5.00
94	Robin Ventura	.50
95	Roger Clemens	3.00
96	Orlando Hernandez	1.00
97	Derek Jeter	6.00
98	Chuck Knoblauch	.75
99	Tino Martinez	.50
100	Bernie Williams	1.50
101	Eric Chavez	5.00
102	Jason Giambi	.50
103	Ben Grieve	1.00
104	Tim Raines	.50
105	Marlon Anderson	4.00
106	Doug Glanville	.50
107	Scott Rolen	1.50
108	Curt Schilling	.75
109	Brian Giles	.50
110	Jose Guillen	.50
111	Jason Kendall	.75
112	Kevin Young	.50
113	J.D. Drew	5.00
114	Jose Jimenez	4.00
115	Ray Lankford	.50
116	Mark McGwire	8.00
117	Fernando Tatis	.50
118	Matt Clement	4.00
119	Tony Gwynn	3.00
120	Trevor Hoffman	.50
121	Wally Joyner	.50
122	Reggie Sanders	.50
123	Barry Bonds	2.00
124	Ellis Burks	.50
125	Jeff Kent	.50
126	J.T. Snow	.50
127	Freddy Garcia	15.00
128	Ken Griffey Jr.	6.00
129	Edgar Martinez	.50
130	Alex Rodriguez	6.00
131	David Segui	.50
132	Rolando Arrojo	.50
133	Wade Boggs	1.00
134	Jose Canseco	1.00
135	Quinton McCracken	.50
136	Fred McGriff	.75
137	Juan Gonzalez	2.00
138	Rusty Greer	.50
139	Rafael Palmeiro	1.00
140	Ivan Rodriguez	2.00
141	Jose Cruz Jr.	.50
142	Carlos Delgado	.75
143	Shawn Green	.75
144	Roy Halladay	4.00

1999 Pacific Crown Royale Century 21

This 10-card set features some of baseball's most dominating players, on a full silver foil front. These are seeded 1:25 packs.

		MT
Complete Set (10):		100.00
Common Player:		10.00
Inserted 1:25		
1	Cal Ripken Jr.	25.00
2	Nomar Garciaparra	20.00
3	Sammy Sosa	20.00
4	Frank Thomas	15.00
5	Mike Piazza	20.00
6	J.D. Drew	5.00
7	Mark McGwire	30.00
8	Tony Gwynn	15.00
9	Ken Griffey Jr.	30.00
10	Alex Rodriguez	25.00

1999 Pacific Crown Royale Cramer's Choice Premiums

This enlarged 10-card set is die-cut into a trophy shape. Cards are enhanced with silver holographic fronts with silver holographic etching and gold foil stamping across the card bottom. They are seeded one per box. Six serially numbered parallels are also randomly seeded: Dark Blue (35 each), Green (30), Red (25), Light Blue (20), Gold (10) and Purple (1).

		MT
Complete Set (10):		120.00
Common Player:		10.00
Inserted 1:box		
Dark Blue (35 each):		5X
Green (30 each):		6X
Red (25 each):		8X
Light Blue (20 each):		10X
Gold (10 each):		15X
Purple (one set produced)		
1	Cal Ripken Jr.	15.00
2	Nomar Garciaparra	12.00
3	Sammy Sosa	12.00
4	Frank Thomas	10.00
5	Mike Piazza	12.00
6	Derek Jeter	12.00
7	J.D. Drew	5.00
8	Mark McGwire	25.00
9	Tony Gwynn	10.00
10	Ken Griffey Jr.	25.00

1999 Pacific Crown Royale Gold Crown Die-Cut Premiums

This enlarged six-card set is identical to Crown Die-cuts besides their larger size. These were limited to 1,036 numbered sets.

		MT
Complete Set (6):		65.00
Common Player:		8.00
Inserted 6:10 boxes		
1	Cal Ripken Jr.	15.00
2	Mike Piazza	10.00
3	Ken Griffey Jr.	20.00
4	Tony Gwynn	8.00
5	Mark McGwire	20.00
6	J.D. Drew	8.00

1999 Pacific Crown Royale Living Legends

This 10-card set spotlights baseball's top stars on an full foiled card front. These are serial numbered to 375 sets.

		MT
Complete Set (10):		225.00
Common Player:		20.00
Production 375 sets		
1	Greg Maddux	25.00
2	Cal Ripken Jr.	30.00
3	Nomar Garciaparra	25.00
4	Sammy Sosa	25.00
5	Frank Thomas	20.00
6	Mike Piazza	25.00
7	Mark McGwire	40.00
8	Tony Gwynn	20.00
9	Ken Griffey Jr.	40.00
10	Alex Rodriguez	30.00

1999 Pacific Crown Royale Master Performers

This 20-card set features a full foiled front with the player photo in a frame like border. Master Performers are seeded 2:25 packs.

		MT
Complete Set (20):		150.00
Common Player:		2.50
Inserted 2:25		
1	Chipper Jones	12.00
2	Greg Maddux	12.00
3	Cal Ripken Jr.	15.00
4	Nomar Garciaparra	12.00
5	Sammy Sosa	12.00
6	Frank Thomas	9.00
7	Raul Mondesi	2.50
8	Vladimir Guerrero	8.00
9	Mike Piazza	12.00
10	Roger Clemens	8.00
11	Derek Jeter	12.00
12	Scott Rolen	4.00
13	J.D. Drew	2.50
14	Mark McGwire	20.00
15	Tony Gwynn	9.00
16	Barry Bonds	4.00
17	Ken Griffey Jr.	20.00
18	Alex Rodriguez	15.00
19	Juan Gonzalez	5.00
20	Ivan Rodriguez	4.00

1999 Pacific Crown Royale Pillars of the Game

This 25-card set features holographic silver foil fronts on a horizontal format. These are seeded one per pack.

		MT
Complete Set (25):		30.00
Common Player:		.60
Inserted 1:1		
1	Mo Vaughn	.75
2	Chipper Jones	2.00
3	Greg Maddux	2.00
4	Albert Belle	.75
5	Cal Ripken Jr.	2.50
6	Nomar Garciaparra	2.00
7	Sammy Sosa	2.00
8	Frank Thomas	1.50
9	Manny Ramirez	1.00
10	Jeff Bagwell	.75
11	Raul Mondesi	.60
12	Vladimir Guerrero	1.50
13	Mike Piazza	2.00
14	Roger Clemens	1.25
15	Derek Jeter	2.00
16	Bernie Williams	.60
17	Ben Grieve	.60
18	J.D. Drew	.75
19	Mark McGwire	3.50
20	Tony Gwynn	1.50
21	Barry Bonds	.75
22	Ken Griffey Jr.	3.50
23	Alex Rodriguez	2.50
24	Juan Gonzalez	1.00
25	Ivan Rodriguez	.75

1999 Pacific Crown Royale Pivotal Players

This 25-card set features holographic silver foil fronts with a flame in the background of the player photo. These are seeded one per pack.

		MT
Complete Set (25):		30.00
Common Player:		.60
Inserted 1:1		
1	Mo Vaughn	.75
2	Chipper Jones	2.00
3	Greg Maddux	2.00
4	Albert Belle	.75
5	Cal Ripken Jr.	2.50
6	Nomar Garciaparra	2.00
7	Sammy Sosa	2.00
8	Frank Thomas	1.50
9	Manny Ramirez	1.00
10	Craig Biggio	.60
11	Raul Mondesi	.60
12	Vladimir Guerrero	1.50
13	Mike Piazza	2.00
14	Roger Clemens	1.25
15	Derek Jeter	2.00
16	Bernie Williams	.60
17	Ben Grieve	.60
18	Scott Rolen	.75
19	J.D. Drew	.75
20	Mark McGwire	3.50
21	Tony Gwynn	1.50
22	Ken Griffey Jr.	3.50
23	Alex Rodriguez	2.50
24	Juan Gonzalez	1.00
25	Ivan Rodriguez	.75

1999 Pacific Invincible

The base set consists of 150 base cards and feature a player photo and a headshot in a cel window on the bottom right portion of the card. There are also two parallels to the base set: Opening Day and Platinum Blue. Both parallels are limited to 67 serial numbered sets.

		MT
Complete Set (150):		175.00
Common Player:		.75
Opening Day:		9X
Production 67 sets		
Platinum Blues:		9X
Production 67 sets		
Pack (3):		4.00
Wax Box (24):		85.00
1	Jim Edmonds	.75
2	Darin Erstad	3.00
3	Troy Glaus	4.00
4	Tim Salmon	1.50
5	Mo Vaughn	2.00
6	Steve Finley	.75
7	Randy Johnson	2.00
8	Travis Lee	2.50
9	Dante Powell	.75
10	Matt Williams	1.50
11	Bret Boone	.75
12	Andruw Jones	2.00
13	Chipper Jones	8.00
14	Brian Jordan	.75
15	Ryan Klesko	.75
16	Javy Lopez	.75
17	Greg Maddux	7.50
18	Brady Anderson	.75
19	Albert Belle	3.00
20	Will Clark	1.50
21	Mike Mussina	2.00
22	Cal Ripken Jr.	10.00
23	Nomar Garciaparra	8.00
24	Pedro Martinez	2.50
25	Trot Nixon	.75
26	Jose Offerman	.75
27	Donnie Sadler	.75
28	John Valentin	.75
29	Mark Grace	1.00
30	Lance Johnson	.75
31	Henry Rodriguez	.75
32	Sammy Sosa	8.00
33	Kerry Wood	3.00
34	McKay Christensen	.75
35	Ray Durham	.75
36	Jeff Liefer	.75
37	Frank Thomas	6.00
38	Mike Cameron	.75
39	Barry Larkin	1.00
40	Greg Vaughn	1.00
41	Dmitri Young	.75
42	Roberto Alomar	2.50
43	Sandy Alomar Jr.	.75
44	David Justice	1.00
45	Kenny Lofton	2.00
46	Manny Ramirez	5.00
47	Jim Thome	1.00
48	Dante Bichette	1.00
49	Vinny Castilla	1.00
50	Darryl Hamilton	.75
51	Todd Helton	3.00
52	Neifi Perez	.75
53	Larry Walker	2.00
54	Tony Clark	1.50
55	Damion Easley	.75
56	Bob Higginson	.75
57	Brian Hunter	.75
58	Gabe Kapler	4.00
59	Cliff Floyd	.75
60	Alex Gonzalez	.75
61	Mark Kotsay	.75
62	Derrek Lee	.75
63	Braden Looper	.75
64	Moises Alou	1.00
65	Jeff Bagwell	3.00
66	Craig Biggio	1.50
67	Ken Caminiti	1.00
68	Scott Elarton	.75
69	Mitch Meluskey	.75
70	Carlos Beltran	.75
71	Johnny Damon	.75
72	Carlos Febles	1.00
73	Jeremy Giambi	.75
74	Kevin Brown	1.00
75	Todd Hundley	.75
76	Paul Loduca	.75
77	Raul Mondesi	1.00
78	Gary Sheffield	1.00
79	Geoff Jenkins	.75
80	Jeromy Burnitz	.75
81	Marquis Grissom	.75
82	Jose Valentin	.75
83	Fernando Vina	.75
84	Corey Koskie	.75
85	Matt Lawton	.75
86	Christian Guzman	.75
87	Torii Hunter	.75
88	Doug Mientkiewicz	.75
89	Michael Barrett	.75
90	Brad Fullmer	.75
91	Vladimir Guerrero	5.00
92	Fernando Seguignol	1.00
93	Ugueth Urbina	.75
94	Bobby Bonilla	.75
95	Rickey Henderson	1.50
96	Rey Ordonez	.75
97	Mike Piazza	8.00
98	Robin Ventura	.75
99	Roger Clemens	4.00
100	Derek Jeter	8.00
101	Chuck Knoblauch	1.00
102	Tino Martinez	1.00
103	Paul O'Neill	1.00
104	Bernie Williams	1.50
105	Eric Chavez	3.00
106	Ryan Christenson	.75
107	Jason Giambi	.75
108	Ben Grieve	3.00
109	Miguel Tejada	.75
110	Marlon Anderson	.75
111	Doug Glanville	.75
112	Scott Rolen	3.00
113	Curt Schilling	1.00
114	Brian Giles	.75
115	Warren Morris	.75
116	Jason Kendall	1.00
117	Kris Benson	.75
118	J.D. Drew	1.00
119	Ray Lankford	.75
120	Mark McGwire	12.50
121	Matt Clement	.75
122	Tony Gwynn	6.00
123	Trevor Hoffman	.75
124	Wally Joyner	.75
125	Reggie Sanders	.75
126	Barry Bonds	3.00
127	Ellis Burks	.75
128	Jeff Kent	.75
129	Stan Javier	.75
130	J.T. Snow	.75
131	Jay Buhner	.75
132	Freddy Garcia	.75
133	Ken Griffey Jr.	12.50
134	Russ Davis	.75
135	Edgar Martinez	.75
136	Alex Rodriguez	10.00
137	David Segui	.75
138	Rolando Arrojo	.75
139	Wade Boggs	1.50
140	Jose Canseco	2.50
141	Quinton McCracken	.75
142	Fred McGriff	1.00
143	Juan Gonzalez	3.00
144	Tom Goodwin	.75
145	Rusty Greer	.75
146	Ivan Rodriguez	3.00
147	Jose Cruz Jr.	.75
148	Carlos Delgado	1.50
149	Shawn Green	1.00
150	Roy Halladay	1.00

1999 Pacific Invincible Diamond Magic

This 10-card set features a horizontal format with silver foil stamping on the front. Diamond Magic's are seeded 1:49 packs.

		MT
Complete Set (10):		80.00
Common Player:		7.50
Inserted 1:49		
1	Cal Ripken Jr.	12.50
2	Nomar Garciaparra	10.00
3	Sammy Sosa	10.00
4	Frank Thomas	7.50
5	Mike Piazza	10.00
6	J.D. Drew	6.00
7	Mark McGwire	15.00
8	Tony Gwynn	7.50
9	Ken Griffey Jr.	15.00
10	Alex Rodriguez	12.00

1999 Pacific Invincible Flash Point

This 20-card set features gold etching and gold foil stamping on the card front. These were seeded 1:25 packs.

		MT
Complete Set (20):		200.00
Common Player:		4.00
Inserted 1:25		
1	Mo Vaughn	4.00
2	Chipper Jones	15.00
3	Greg Maddux	15.00
4	Cal Ripken Jr.	20.00
5	Nomar Garciaparra	15.00
6	Sammy Sosa	15.00
7	Frank Thomas	12.50
8	Manny Ramirez	9.00
9	Vladimir Guerrero	10.00
10	Mike Piazza	15.00
11	Roger Clemens	8.00
12	Derek Jeter	15.00
13	Ben Grieve	4.00
14	Scott Rolen	4.00
15	J.D. Drew	4.00
16	Mark McGwire	25.00
17	Tony Gwynn	12.50
18	Ken Griffey Jr.	25.00
19	Alex Rodriguez	20.00
20	Juan Gonzalez	8.00

1999 Pacific Invincible Giants of the Game

This insert set features 10 of baseball's top stars and are limited to 10 serially numbered sets. Due to their scarcity no pricing is available.

		MT
Complete Set (10):		
Common Player:		
Production 10 sets		
1	Cal Ripken Jr.	
2	Nomar Garciaparra	
3	Sammy Sosa	
4	Frank Thomas	
5	Mike Piazza	
6	J.D. Drew	
7	Mark McGwire	
8	Tony Gwynn	
9	Ken Griffey Jr.	
10	Alex Rodriguez	

1999 Pacific Invincible Sandlot Heroes

Sandlot Heroes salutes baseball's top players on a horizontal format with holographic silver foil stamping on the card front. These were inserted one per pack.

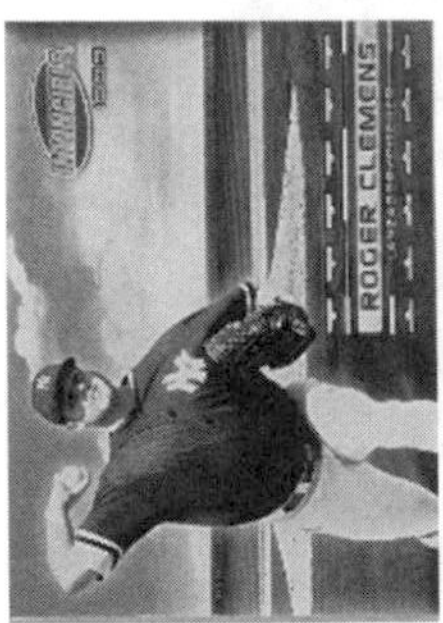

		MT
Complete Set (20):		25.00
Common Player:		.75
Inserted 1:1		
1	Mo Vaughn	.75
2	Chipper Jones	2.00
3	Greg Maddux	2.00
4	Cal Ripken Jr.	2.50
5	Nomar Garciaparra	2.00
6	Sammy Sosa	2.00
7	Frank Thomas	1.50
8	Manny Ramirez	1.00
9	Vladimir Guerrero	1.50
10	Mike Piazza	2.00
11	Roger Clemens	1.00
12	Derek Jeter	2.00
13	Eric Chavez	.75
14	Ben Grieve	.75
15	J.D. Drew	.75
16	Mark McGwire	4.00
17	Tony Gwynn	1.50
18	Ken Griffey Jr.	4.00
19	Alex Rodriguez	2.50
20	Juan Gonzalez	1.00

1999 Pacific Invincible Seismic Force

This 20-card set has a dot pattern behind the featured player with the left side and bottom of the card in a gold border. These were seeded one per pack.

		MT
Complete Set (20):		25.00
Common Player:		.50
Inserted 1:1		
1	Mo Vaughn	.50
2	Chipper Jones	2.00
3	Greg Maddux	2.00
4	Cal Ripken Jr.	2.50
5	Nomar Garciaparra	2.00
6	Sammy Sosa	2.00
7	Frank Thomas	1.50
8	Manny Ramirez	1.00
9	Vladimir Guerrero	1.50
10	Mike Piazza	2.00
11	Bernie Williams	.50
12	Derek Jeter	2.00
13	Ben Grieve	.50
14	J.D. Drew	.75
15	Mark McGwire	3.50
16	Tony Gwynn	1.50
17	Ken Griffey Jr.	3.50
18	Alex Rodriguez	2.50
19	Juan Gonzalez	1.00
20	Ivan Rodriguez	.75

1999 Pacific Invincible Thunder Alley

Thunder Alley focuses on baseball's top power hitters. These were inserted 1:121 packs.

		MT
Complete Set (20):		500.00
Common Player:		10.00
Inserted 1:121		
1	Mo Vaughn	10.00
2	Chipper Jones	40.00
3	Cal Ripken Jr.	50.00
4	Nomar Garciaparra	40.00
5	Sammy Sosa	40.00
6	Frank Thomas	25.00
7	Manny Ramirez	20.00
8	Todd Helton	15.00
9	Vladimir Guerrero	20.00
10	Mike Piazza	40.00
11	Derek Jeter	40.00
12	Ben Grieve	12.50
13	Scott Rolen	15.00
14	J.D. Drew	10.00
15	Mark McGwire	60.00
16	Tony Gwynn	30.00
17	Ken Griffey Jr.	60.00
18	Alex Rodriguez	50.00
19	Juan Gonzalez	15.00
20	Ivan Rodriguez	15.00

1999 Pacific Omega

		MT
Complete Set (250):		35.00
Common Player:		.10
Copper Stars:		20X
Young Stars/RCs:		8X
Production 99 sets H		
Platinum Blue Stars:		30X
Young Stars/RCs:		10X
Production 75 sets		
Wax Box:		65.00
1	Garret Anderson	.10
2	Jim Edmonds	.10
3	Darin Erstad	.40
4	Chuck Finley	.10
5	Troy Glaus	.75
6	Troy Percival	.10
7	Chris Pritchett	.10
8	Tim Salmon	.25
9	Mo Vaughn	.50
10	Jay Bell	.10
11	Steve Finley	.10
12	Luis Gonzalez	.10
13	Randy Johnson	.50
14	*Byung-Hyun Kim*	2.00
15	Travis Lee	.40
16	Matt Williams	.40
17	Tony Womack	.10
18	Bret Boone	.10
19	Mark DeRosa	.10
20	Tom Glavine	.25
21	Andruw Jones	.50
22	Chipper Jones	2.00
23	Brian Jordan	.10
24	Ryan Klesko	.20
25	Javy Lopez	.20
26	Greg Maddux	1.50
27	John Smoltz	.15
28	Bruce Chen, Odalis Perez	.10
29	Brady Anderson	.10
30	Harold Baines	.10
31	Albert Belle	.75
32	Will Clark	.40
33	Delino DeShields	.10
34	Jerry Hairston Jr.	.25
35	Charles Johnson	.10
36	Mike Mussina	.50
37	Cal Ripken Jr.	2.50
38	B.J. Surhoff	.10
39	Jin Ho Cho	.10
40	Nomar Garciaparra	2.00
41	Pedro Martinez	1.00
42	Jose Offerman	.10
43	Troy O'Leary	.10
44	John Valentin	.10
45	Jason Varitek	.10
46	*Juan Pena*, Brian Rose	.10
47	Mark Grace	.25
48	Glenallen Hill	.10
49	Tyler Houston	.10
50	Mickey Morandini	.10
51	Henry Rodriguez	.10
52	Sammy Sosa	2.00
53	Kevin Tapani	.10
54	Mike Caruso	.10
55	Ray Durham	.10
56	Paul Konerko	.10
57	Carlos Lee	.10
58	Magglio Ordonez	.20
59	Mike Sirotka	.10
60	Frank Thomas	1.50
61	Mark L. Johnson, Chris Singleton	.10
62	Mike Cameron	.10
63	Sean Casey	.25
64	Pete Harnisch	.10
65	Barry Larkin	.20
66	Pokey Reese	.10
67	Greg Vaughn	.25
68	Scott Williamson	.10
69	Dmitri Young	.10
70	Roberto Alomar	.50
71	Sandy Alomar Jr.	.20
72	Travis Fryman	.20
73	David Justice	.20
74	Kenny Lofton	.50
75	Manny Ramirez	1.00
76	Richie Sexson	.10
77	Jim Thome	.30
78	Omar Vizquel	.10
79	Jaret Wright	.10
80	Dante Bichette	.25
81	Vinny Castilla	.10
82	Todd Helton	.75
83	Darryl Hamilton	.10
84	Darryl Kile	.10
85	Neifi Perez	.10
86	Larry Walker	.50
87	Tony Clark	.30
88	Damion Easley	.10
89	Juan Encarnacion	.10
90	Bobby Higginson	.10
91	Gabe Kapler	.75
92	Dean Palmer	.10
93	Justin Thompson	.10
94	*Masao Kida*, *Jeff Weaver*	.30
95	Bruce Aven	.10
96	Luis Castillo	.10
97	Alex Fernandez	.10
98	Cliff Floyd	.10
99	Alex Gonzalez	.10
100	Mark Kotsay	.10
101	Preston Wilson	.10
102	Moises Alou	.15
103	Jeff Bagwell	.75
104	Derek Bell	.10
105	Craig Biggio	.40
106	Mike Hampton	.10
107	Richard Hidalgo	.10
108	Jose Lima	.10
109	Billy Wagner	.10
110	Russ Johnson, Daryle Ward	.10
111	Carlos Beltran	.20
112	Johnny Damon	.10
113	Jermaine Dye	.10
114	Carlos Febles	.40
115	Jeremy Giambi	.10
116	Joe Randa	.10
117	Mike Sweeney	.10
118	*Orber Moreno*, Jose Santiago	.10
119	Kevin Brown	.20
120	Todd Hundley	.10
121	Eric Karros	.20
122	Raul Mondesi	.20
123	Chan Ho Park	.20
124	Angel Pena	.10
125	Gary Sheffield	.25
126	Devon White	.10
127	Eric Young	.10
128	Ron Belliard	.25
129	Jeromy Burnitz	.20
130	Jeff Cirillo	.10
131	Marquis Grissom	.10
132	Geoff Jenkins	.10
133	David Nilsson	.10
134	Hideo Nomo	.15
135	Fernando Vina	.10
136	Ron Coomer	.10
137	Marty Cordova	.10
138	Corey Koskie	.10
139	Brad Radke	.10
140	Todd Walker	.20
141	*Chad Allen*, Torii Hunter	.10
142	Cristian Guzman, Jacque Jones	.10
143	Michael Barrett	.40
144	Orlando Cabrera	.10
145	Vladimir Guerrero	1.25
146	Wilton Guerrero	.10
147	Ugueth Urbina	.10
148	Rondell White	.20
149	Chris Widger	.10
150	Edgardo Alfonzo	.25
151	Roger Cedeno	.10
152	Octavio Dotel	.10
153	Rickey Henderson	.25
154	John Olerud	.25
155	Rey Ordonez	.10
156	Mike Piazza	2.00
157	Robin Ventura	.25
158	Scott Brosius	.10
159	Roger Clemens	1.00
160	David Cone	.25
161	Chili Davis	.10
162	Orlando Hernandez	.50
163	Derek Jeter	2.00
164	Chuck Knoblauch	.25
165	Tino Martinez	.20
166	Paul O'Neill	.25
167	Bernie Williams	.60
168	Jason Giambi	.10
169	Ben Grieve	.50
170	*Chad Harville*	.10
171	*Tim Hudson*	2.00
172	Tony Phillips	.10
173	Kenny Rogers	.10
174	Matt Stairs	.10
175	Miguel Tejada	.20
176	Eric Chavez	.25
177	Bobby Abreu	.10
178	Ron Gant	.15
179	Doug Glanville	.10
180	Mike Lieberthal	.10
181	Desi Relaford	.10
182	Scott Rolen	.75
183	Curt Schilling	.25
184	Marlon Anderson, Randy Wolf	.10
185	Brant Brown	.10

186	Brian Giles	.10
187	Jason Kendall	.20
188	Al Martin	.10
189	Ed Sprague	.10
190	Kevin Young	.10
191	Kris Benson, Warren Morris	.10
192	Kent Bottenfield	.10
193	Eric Davis	.10
194	J.D. Drew	.25
195	Ray Lankford	.10
196	*Joe McEwing*	.75
197	Mark McGwire	3.50
198	Edgar Renteria	.10
199	Fernando Tatis	.25
200	Andy Ashby	.10
201	Ben Davis	.20
202	Tony Gwynn	1.50
203	Trevor Hoffman	.10
204	Wally Joyner	.10
205	Gary Matthews Jr.	.10
206	Ruben Rivera	.10
207	Reggie Sanders	.10
208	Rich Aurilia	.10
209	Marvin Benard	.10
210	Barry Bonds	.75
211	Ellis Burks	.10
212	Stan Javier	.10
213	Jeff Kent	.10
214	Robb Nen	.10
215	J.T. Snow	.10
216	David Bell	.10
217	Jay Buhner	.15
218	Freddy Garcia	.40
219	Ken Griffey Jr.	3.50
220	Brian Hunter	.10
221	Butch Huskey	.10
222	Edgar Martinez	.10
223	Jamie Moyer	.10
224	Alex Rodriguez	2.50
225	David Segui	.10
226	Rolando Arrojo	.10
227	Wade Boggs	.40
228	Miguel Cairo	.10
229	Jose Canseco	.75
230	Dave Martinez	.10
231	Fred McGriff	.25
232	Kevin Stocker	.10
233	*Mike Duvall*, David Lamb	.10
234	Royce Clayton	.10
235	Juan Gonzalez	.75
236	Rusty Greer	.10
237	Ruben Mateo	.25
238	Rafael Palmeiro	.50
239	Ivan Rodriguez	.75
240	John Wetteland	.10
241	Todd Zeile	.10
242	Jeff Zimmerman	.10
243	Homer Bush	.10
244	Jose Cruz Jr.	.10
245	Carlos Delgado	.30
246	Tony Fernandez	.10
247	Shawn Green	.25
248	Shannon Stewart	.10
249	David Wells	.15
250	Roy Halladay, Billy Koch	.15

1999 Pacific Omega Debut Duos

		MT
Complete Set (10):		275.00
Common Player:		10.00
Inserted 1:145		
1	Nomar Garciaparra, Vladimir Guerrero	30.00
2	Derek Jeter, Andy Pettitte	35.00
3	Garret Anderson, Alex Rodriguez	30.00
4	Chipper Jones, Raul Mondesi	30.00
5	Pedro Martinez, Mike Piazza	35.00
6	Mo Vaughn, Bernie Williams	10.00
7	Juan Gonzalez, Ken Griffey Jr.	50.00
8	Sammy Sosa, Larry Walker	30.00
9	Barry Bonds, Mark McGwire	50.00
10	Wade Boggs, Tony Gwynn	25.00

Modern cards in Near Mint condition are valued at about 75% of the Mint value shown here. Excellent-condition cards are worth 50%. Cards in lower grades are not generally collectible.

1999 Pacific Omega Diamond Masters

		MT
Complete Set (24):		75.00
Common Player:		1.00
Inserted 4:37		
1	Darin Erstad	1.50
2	Mo Vaughn	1.00
3	Matt Williams	1.00
4	Andruw Jones	2.50
5	Chipper Jones	8.00
6	Greg Maddux	7.50
7	Cal Ripken Jr.	10.00
8	Nomar Garciaparra	8.00
9	Pedro Martinez	4.00
10	Sammy Sosa	8.00
11	Frank Thomas	6.00
12	Kenny Lofton	2.50
13	Manny Ramirez	5.00
14	Larry Walker	2.50
15	Gabe Kapler	2.50
16	Jeff Bagwell	3.00
17	Craig Biggio	2.00
18	Raul Mondesi	1.00
19	Vladimir Guerrero	5.00
20	Mike Piazza	8.00
21	Roger Clemens	4.00
22	Derek Jeter	8.00
23	Bernie Williams	2.00
24	Scott Rolen	3.00

1999 Pacific Omega EO Portraits

		MT
Complete Set (20):		350.00
Common Player:		5.00
Inserted 1:73		
1	Mo Vaughn	5.00
2	Chipper Jones	25.00
3	Greg Maddux	20.00
4	Cal Ripken Jr.	30.00
5	Nomar Garciaparra	25.00
6	Sammy Sosa	25.00
7	Frank Thomas	20.00
8	Manny Ramirez	12.50
9	Jeff Bagwell	10.00
10	Mike Piazza	25.00
11	Roger Clemens	15.00
12	Derek Jeter	25.00
13	Scott Rolen	10.00
14	Mark McGwire	40.00
15	Tony Gwynn	20.00
16	Barry Bonds	10.00
17	Ken Griffey Jr.	40.00
18	Alex Rodriguez	30.00
19	Jose Canseco	7.50
20	Juan Gonzalez	10.00

1999 Pacific Omega 5-Tool Talents

		MT
Complete Set (30):		100.00
Common Player:		1.00
Inserted 4:37		
1	Randy Johnson	2.00
2	Carlos Lee	1.00
3	Chipper Jones	8.00
4	Nomar Garciaparra	8.00
5	Barry Bonds	3.00
6	Jeff Bagwell	3.00
7	Greg Maddux	6.00
8	Gabe Kapler	2.50
9	Manny Ramirez	4.00
10	Frank Thomas	5.00
11	Ivan Rodriguez	3.00
12	Ken Griffey Jr.	15.00
13	Pedro Martinez	4.00
14	Carlos Beltran	1.00
15	Mark McGwire	15.00
16	Larry Walker	2.50
17	Cal Ripken Jr.	10.00
18	Derek Jeter	8.00
19	Kevin Brown	1.00
20	J.D. Drew	1.00
21	Sammy Sosa	8.00
22	Tony Gwynn	6.00
23	Alex Rodriguez	10.00
24	Jose Canseco	3.00
25	Roger Clemens	4.00
26	Ruben Mateo	1.50
27	Vladimir Guerrero	6.00
28	Mike Piazza	8.00
29	Scott Rolen	2.50
30	Juan Gonzalez	3.00

1999 Pacific Omega 5-Tool Talents Tiered

A parallel of the 5-Tool Talents inserts is fractured into five tiers of increasing scarcity, differentiated by the color of foil highlights and the serially numbered limited edition. The breakdown is: Tier 1, blue, 100 sets; Tier 2, red, 75 sets; Tier 3, green, 50 sets; Tier 4, purple, 25 sets; Tier 5, gold, 1 set. The unique gold cards are not priced due to their rarity.

		MT
	TIER 1 (BLUE, 100 SETS)	
1	Randy Johnson	6.00
6	Carlos Lee	3.00
11	Chipper Jones	15.00
18	Nomar Garciaparra	15.00
21	Jeff Bagwell	9.00
28	Barry Bonds	9.00
	TIER 2 (RED, 75 SETS)	
2	Greg Maddux	25.00
7	Gabe Kapler	5.00
13	Manny Ramirez	15.00
16	Ken Griffey Jr.	50.00
19	Frank Thomas	15.00
30	Ivan Rodriguez	12.50
	TIER 3 (GREEN, 50 SETS)	
3	Pedro Martinez	25.00
8	Carlos Beltran	10.00
15	Mark McGwire	100.00
20	Larry Walker	15.00
25	Cal Ripken Jr.	80.00
26	Derek Jeter	60.00
	TIER 4 (PURPLE, 25 SETS)	
4	Kevin Brown	15.00
9	J.D. Drew	25.00
12	Sammy Sosa	60.00
17	Jose Canseco	40.00
23	Tony Gwynn	50.00
29	Alex Rodriguez	75.00
	TIER 5 (GOLD 1 SET)	
5	Roger Clemens	
10	Ruben Mateo	
14	Vladimir Guerrero	
22	Mike Piazza	
24	Juan Gonzalez	
27	Scott Rolen	

1999 Pacific Omega Hit Machine 3000

Within days of Tony Gwynn's 3,000 hit on Aug. 6, Pacific had rushed into production a special insert set honoring the achievement of its long-time spokesman. A total of 3,000 serially numbered sets of 20 cards were issued as random packs inserts in Omega. Fronts feature various game-action and studio photos of Gwynn, and are highlighted in silver foil. Backs have two more color photos of Gwynn and a few sentences about the player. A serial number in printed on front.

		MT
Complete Set (20):		150.00
Common Card:		15.00
1	The Hitting Machine	15.00
2	The Eyes Have It	15.00
3	The Art of Hitting	15.00
4	Solid as a Rock	15.00
5	Seeing Doubles	15.00
6	Pithcer's Worst Nightmare	15.00
7	Portrait of an All-Star	15.00
8	An American Hero	15.00
9	Fan Favorite	15.00
10	Mr. Batting Title	15.00
11	4-for-5!	15.00
12	Mission Accomplished	15.00
13	One Hit Away	15.00
14	A Tip of the Hat	15.00
15	It's a Base Hit!	15.00
16	2997th - Grand Slam!	15.00
17	2998th Hit	15.00
18	2999th Hit - 2-Run Double	15.00
19	3000th Hit!	15.00
20	3000 Hits, 8874 At-Bats, 18 Years	15.00

1999 Pacific Omega HR '99

		MT
Complete Set (20):		125.00
Common Player:		2.50
Inserted 1:37		
1	Mo Vaughn	2.50
2	Matt Williams	2.50
3	Chipper Jones	12.50
4	Albert Belle	4.00
5	Nomar Garciaparra	12.50
6	Sammy Sosa	12.50
7	Frank Thomas	6.00
8	Manny Ramirez	5.00
9	Jeff Bagwell	4.00
10	Raul Mondesi	2.50
11	Vladimir Guerrero	8.00
12	Mike Piazza	12.50
13	Derek Jeter	12.50
14	Mark McGwire	20.00
15	Fernando Tatis	2.50
16	Barry Bonds	4.00
17	Ken Griffey Jr.	20.00
18	Alex Rodriguez	15.00
19	Jose Canseco	4.00
20	Juan Gonzalez	5.00

1999 Pacific Paramount

The 250-card base set is highlighted by silver foil stamping and a white border. Card backs have a small photo along with 1998 statistics and career totals and a a brief career note. There are six parallels to the base set: Copper, Platinum Blue, Holographic Silver, Opening Day Issue, Gold and Holographic Gold. Each parallel is enhanced with the appropriate foil color. Coppers are found exclusively in hobby packs at a rate of one per pack. Platinum Blues are seeded one per 73 packs, Holographic Silvers are hobby only and limited to 99 serial numbered sets. Opening Day Issue is limited to 74 numbered sets. Golds are found one per retail pack. Holographic Golds are limited to 199 numbered sets.

		MT
Complete Set (250):		35.00
Common Player:		.10
Common Copper:		.25
Copper Stars:		3X
Common Platinum Blue:		3.00
Platinum Blue Stars:		20X
Common Holographic Silver:		4.00
Holographic Silver Stars:		30X
Common Opening Day:		5.00
Opening Day Stars:		40X
Common Gold:		.35
Gold Stars:		4X
Common Holographic Gold:		2.50
Holographic Gold Stars:		20X
Pack (6):		1.50
Wax Box (36):		50.00
1	Garret Anderson	.10
2	Gary DiSarcina	.10
3	Jim Edmonds	.20
4	Darin Erstad	.60
5	Chuck Finley	.10
6	Troy Glaus	.75
7	Troy Percival	.10
8	Tim Salmon	.25
9	Mo Vaughn	.40
10	Tony Batista	.10
11	Jay Bell	.10
12	Andy Benes	.10
13	Steve Finley	.10
14	Luis Gonzalez	.10
15	Randy Johnson	.50
16	Travis Lee	.60
17	Todd Stottlemyre	.10
18	Matt Williams	.25
19	David Dellucci	.10
20	Bret Boone	.10
21	Andres Galarraga	.40
22	Tom Glavine	.25
23	Andruw Jones	.50
24	Chipper Jones	1.50
25	Brian Jordan	.10
26	Ryan Klesko	.15
27	Javy Lopez	.20
28	Greg Maddux	1.50
29	John Smoltz	.20
30	Brady Anderson	.10
31	Albert Belle	.60
32	Will Clark	.30
33	Delino DeShields	.10
34	Charles Johnson	.10
35	Mike Mussina	.50
36	Cal Ripken Jr.	2.00
37	B.J. Surhoff	.10
38	Nomar Garciaparra	1.50
39	Reggie Jefferson	.10
40	Darren Lewis	.10
41	Pedro Martinez	.50
42	Troy O'Leary	.10
43	Jose Offerman	.10
44	Donnie Sadler	.10
45	John Valentin	.10
46	Rod Beck	.10
47	Gary Gaetti	.10
48	Mark Grace	.25
49	Lance Johnson	.10
50	Mickey Morandini	.10
51	Henry Rodriguez	.10
52	Sammy Sosa	1.50
53	Kerry Wood	.60
54	Mike Caruso	.10
55	Ray Durham	.10
56	Paul Konerko	.20
57	Jaime Navarro	.10
58	Greg Norton	.10
59	Magglio Ordonez	.10
60	Frank Thomas	1.00
61	Aaron Boone	.10
62	Mike Cameron	.10
63	Barry Larkin	.15
64	Hal Morris	.10
65	Pokey Reese	.10
66	Brett Tomko	.10
67	Greg Vaughn	.20
68	Dmitri Young	.10
69	Roberto Alomar	.50
70	Sandy Alomar Jr.	.20
71	Bartolo Colon	.10
72	Travis Fryman	.10
73	David Justice	.25
74	Kenny Lofton	.40
75	Manny Ramirez	1.00
76	Richie Sexson	.10
77	Jim Thome	.25
78	Omar Vizquel	.10
79	Dante Bichette	.30
80	Vinny Castilla	.20
81	Darryl Hamilton	.10
82	Todd Helton	.75
83	Darryl Kile	.10
84	Mike Lansing	.10
85	Neifi Perez	.10
86	Larry Walker	.50
87	Tony Clark	.30
88	Damion Easley	.10
89	Bob Higginson	.10
90	Brian Hunter	.10
91	Dean Palmer	.10
92	Justin Thompson	.10
93	Todd Dunwoody	.10
94	Cliff Floyd	.10
95	Alex Gonzalez	.10
96	Livan Hernandez	.10
97	Mark Kotsay	.10
98	Derrek Lee	.10
99	Kevin Orie	.10
100	Moises Alou	.20
101	Jeff Bagwell	.75
102	Derek Bell	.10
103	Craig Biggio	.40
104	Ken Caminiti	.20
105	Ricky Gutierrez	.10
106	Richard Hidalgo	.10
107	Billy Wagner	.15
108	Jeff Conine	.10
109	Johnny Damon	.10
110	Carlos Febles	.20
111	Jeremy Giambi	.10
112	Jeff King	.10
113	Jeff Montgomery	.10
114	Joe Randa	.10
115	Kevin Brown	.25
116	Mark Grudzielanek	.10
117	Todd Hundley	.10
118	Eric Karros	.10
119	Raul Mondesi	.25
120	Chan Ho Park	.25
121	Gary Sheffield	.25
122	Devon White	.10
123	Eric Young	.10
124	Jeromy Burnitz	.10
125	Jeff Cirillo	.10
126	Marquis Grissom	.10
127	Geoff Jenkins	.10
128	Dave Nilsson	.10
129	Jose Valentin	.10
130	Fernando Vina	.10
131	Rick Aguilera	.10
132	Ron Coomer	.10
133	Marty Cordova	.10
134	Matt Lawton	.10
135	David Ortiz	.10
136	Brad Radke	.10
137	Terry Steinbach	.10
138	Javier Valentin	.10
139	Todd Walker	.10
140	Orlando Cabrera	.10
141	Brad Fullmer	.10
142	Vladimir Guerrero	1.25
143	Wilton Guerrero	.10
144	Carl Pavano	.10
145	Ugueth Urbina	.10
146	Rondell White	.15
147	Chris Widger	.10
148	Edgardo Alfonzo	.15
149	Bobby Bonilla	.10
150	Rickey Henderson	.25
151	Brian McRae	.10
152	Hideo Nomo	.25
153	John Olerud	.25
154	Rey Ordonez	.15
155	Mike Piazza	1.50
156	Robin Ventura	.20
157	Masato Yoshii	.10
158	Roger Clemens	1.00
159	David Cone	.20
160	Orlando Hernandez	.75
161	Hideki Irabu	.15
162	Derek Jeter	1.50
163	Chuck Knoblauch	.25
164	Tino Martinez	.20
165	Paul O'Neill	.25
166	Darryl Strawberry	.20
167	Bernie Williams	.40
168	Eric Chavez	.60
169	Ryan Christenson	.10
170	Jason Giambi	.10
171	Ben Grieve	.60
172	Tony Phillips	.10
173	Tim Raines	.10
174	Scott Spiezio	.10
175	Miguel Tejada	.25
176	Bobby Abreu	.10
177	Rico Brogna	.10
178	Ron Gant	.15
179	Doug Glanville	.10
180	Desi Relaford	.10
181	Scott Rolen	.75
182	Curt Schilling	.25
183	Brant Brown	.10
184	Brian Giles	.15
185	Jose Guillen	.10
186	Jason Kendall	.20
187	Al Martin	.10

188	Ed Sprague	.10
189	Kevin Young	.10
190	Eric Davis	.10
191	J.D. Drew	.25
192	Ray Lankford	.10
193	Eli Marrero	.10
194	Mark McGwire	3.00
195	Edgar Renteria	.10
196	Fernando Tatis	.15
197	Andy Ashby	.10
198	Tony Gwynn	1.25
199	Carlos Hernandez	.10
200	Trevor Hoffman	.10
201	Wally Joyner	.10
202	Jim Leyritz	.10
203	Ruben Rivera	.10
204	Matt Clement	.10
205	Quilvio Veras	.10
206	Rich Aurilia	.10
207	Marvin Benard	.10
208	Barry Bonds	.60
209	Ellis Burks	.10
210	Jeff Kent	.10
211	Bill Mueller	.10
212	Robb Nen	.10
213	J.T. Snow	.10
214	Jay Buhner	.20
215	Jeff Fassero	.10
216	Ken Griffey Jr.	3.00
217	Carlos Guillen	.10
218	Butch Huskey	.10
219	Edgar Martinez	.10
220	Alex Rodriguez	2.50
221	David Segui	.10
222	Dan Wilson	.10
223	Rolando Arrojo	.10
224	Wade Boggs	.25
225	Jose Canseco	.50
226	Roberto Hernandez	.10
227	Dave Martinez	.10
228	Quinton McCracken	.10
229	Fred McGriff	.20
230	Kevin Stocker	.10
231	Randy Winn	.10
232	Royce Clayton	.10
233	Juan Gonzalez	.75
234	Tom Goodwin	.10
235	Rusty Greer	.10
236	Rick Helling	.10
237	Rafael Palmeiro	.25
238	Ivan Rodriguez	.60
239	Aaron Sele	.10
240	John Wetteland	.10
241	Todd Zeile	.10
242	Jose Cruz Jr.	.15
243	Carlos Delgado	.40
244	Tony Fernandez	.10
245	Cecil Fielder	.10
246	Alex Gonzalez	.10
247	Shawn Green	.20
248	Roy Halladay	.15
249	Shannon Stewart	.10
250	David Wells	.15

1999 Pacific Paramount Cooperstown Bound

This 10-card set focuses on players who seem destined for the Hall of Fame. These inserts feature silver foil stamping and are seeded 1:361 packs.

		MT
Complete Set (10):		500.00
Common Player:		40.00
Inserted 1:361		
1	Greg Maddux	60.00
2	Cal Ripken Jr.	75.00
3	Nomar Garciaparra	60.00
4	Sammy Sosa	60.00
5	Frank Thomas	40.00
6	Mike Piazza	60.00
7	Mark McGwire	90.00
8	Tony Gwynn	50.00
9	Ken Griffey Jr.	90.00
10	Alex Rodriguez	75.00

1999 Pacific Paramount Fielder's Choice

This 20-card set is die-cut into a glove shape and enhanced with gold foil stamping. These are seeded 1:73 packs.

		MT
Complete Set (20):		400.00
Common Player:		7.50
Inserted 1:73		
1	Chipper Jones	30.00
2	Greg Maddux	30.00
3	Cal Ripken Jr.	40.00
4	Nomar Garciaparra	30.00
5	Sammy Sosa	30.00
6	Kerry Wood	10.00
7	Frank Thomas	20.00
8	Manny Ramirez	15.00
9	Todd Helton	7.50
10	Jeff Bagwell	12.50
11	Mike Piazza	30.00
12	Derek Jeter	30.00
13	Bernie Williams	7.50
14	J.D. Drew	8.00
15	Mark McGwire	50.00
16	Tony Gwynn	25.00
17	Ken Griffey Jr.	50.00
18	Alex Rodriguez	40.00
19	Juan Gonzalez	15.00
20	Ivan Rodriguez	10.00

1999 Pacific Paramount Personal Bests

This 36-card set features holographic silver foil stamping on the card front. Card backs include a close-up photo of the featured player and a career note. These are seeded 1:37 packs.

		MT
Complete Set (36):		475.00
Common Player:		3.00
Inserted 1:37		
1	Darin Erstad	10.00
2	Mo Vaughn	6.00
3	Travis Lee	8.00
4	Chipper Jones	25.00
5	Greg Maddux	25.00
6	Albert Belle	10.00
7	Cal Ripken Jr.	30.00
8	Nomar Garciaparra	25.00
9	Sammy Sosa	25.00
10	Kerry Wood	10.00
11	Frank Thomas	20.00
12	Greg Vaughn	3.00
13	Manny Ramirez	12.00
14	Todd Helton	8.00
15	Larry Walker	8.00
16	Jeff Bagwell	12.00
17	Craig Biggio	5.00
18	Raul Mondesi	3.00
19	Vladimir Guerrero	15.00
20	Hideo Nomo	3.00
21	Mike Piazza	25.00
22	Roger Clemens	15.00
23	Derek Jeter	25.00
24	Bernie Williams	4.50
25	Eric Chavez	10.00
26	Ben Grieve	8.00
27	Scott Rolen	10.00
28	J.D. Drew	4.00
29	Mark McGwire	40.00
30	Tony Gwynn	20.00
31	Barry Bonds	10.00
32	Ken Griffey Jr.	40.00
33	Alex Rodriguez	30.00
34	Jose Canseco	7.50
35	Juan Gonzalez	10.00
36	Ivan Rodriguez	10.00

1999 Pacific Paramount Team Checklists

This 30-card set features gold foil etching and stamping on the card front. Card backs feature the featured player's team checklist for the main set. These were seeded 2:37 packs.

		MT
Complete Set (30):		150.00
Common Player:		1.50
Inserted 2:37		
1	Mo Vaughn	5.00
2	Travis Lee	4.00
3	Chipper Jones	12.00
4	Cal Ripken Jr.	15.00
5	Nomar Garciaparra	12.00
6	Sammy Sosa	12.00
7	Frank Thomas	8.00
8	Greg Vaughn	1.50
9	Manny Ramirez	5.00
10	Larry Walker	4.00
11	Damion Easley	1.50
12	Mark Kotsay	1.50
13	Jeff Bagwell	6.00
14	Jeremy Giambi	1.50
15	Raul Mondesi	2.50
16	Marquis Grissom	1.50
17	Brad Radke	1.50
18	Vladimir Guerrero	8.00
19	Mike Piazza	12.00
20	Roger Clemens	8.00
21	Ben Grieve	5.00
22	Scott Rolen	5.00
23	Brian Giles	2.00
24	Mark McGwire	20.00
25	Tony Gwynn	10.00
26	Barry Bonds	5.00
27	Ken Griffey Jr.	20.00
28	Jose Canseco	4.00
29	Juan Gonzalez	5.00
30	Jose Cruz Jr.	1.50

1999 Pacific Prism

This 150-card base set has a full, holographic silver card front. Card backs feature two more player photos along with 1998 and career statistics. Hobby packs consist of five cards. There are also five parallels including Holographic Gold, Holographic Mirror, Holographic Blue, Holographic Purple and Red. Golds are limited to 480 serial numbered sets, Mirrors 160 sets, Blues 80 numbered sets, and, Purples 320 sets. Red parallels are a retail-only insert and are seeded at a rate of one per 12.5 packs.

		MT
Complete Set (150):		80.00
Common Player:		.50
Reds:		3X
Holographic Gold:		5X
Production 480 sets		
Holographic Purple:		6X
Production 320 sets		
Holographic Mirror:		10X
Production 160 sets		
Holographic Blue:		20X
Production 80 sets		
Pack (5):		7.00
Wax Box (24):		100.00
1	Garret Anderson	.50
2	Jim Edmonds	.50
3	Darin Erstad	1.50
4	Chuck Finley	.50
5	Tim Salmon	1.00
6	Jay Bell	.50
7	David Dellucci	.50
8	Travis Lee	1.00
9	Matt Williams	1.00
10	Andres Galarraga	1.00
11	Tom Glavine	.75
12	Andruw Jones	1.50
13	Chipper Jones	4.00
14	Ryan Klesko	.75
15	Javy Lopez	.75
16	Greg Maddux	4.00
17	Roberto Alomar	1.00
18	Ryan Minor	.50
19	Mike Mussina	.75
20	Rafael Palmeiro	1.00
21	Cal Ripken Jr.	5.00
22	Nomar Garciaparra	4.00
23	Pedro Martinez	1.00
24	John Valentin	.50
25	Mo Vaughn	.75
26	Tim Wakefield	.50
27	Rod Beck	.50
28	Mark Grace	.75
29	Lance Johnson	.50
30	Sammy Sosa	4.00
31	Kerry Wood	1.50
32	Albert Belle	1.50
33	Mike Caruso	.50
34	Magglio Ordonez	.75

35	Frank Thomas	3.00
36	Robin Ventura	.75
37	Aaron Boone	.50
38	Barry Larkin	.60
39	Reggie Sanders	.50
40	Brett Tomko	.50
41	Sandy Alomar Jr.	.65
42	Bartolo Colon	.50
43	David Justice	.75
44	Kenny Lofton	.75
45	Manny Ramirez	2.50
46	Richie Sexson	.50
47	Jim Thome	1.00
48	Omar Vizquel	.50
49	Dante Bichette	.75
50	Vinny Castilla	.50
51	*Edgard Clemente*	.50
52	Todd Helton	1.50
53	Quinton McCracken	.50
54	Larry Walker	1.00
55	Tony Clark	1.00
56	Damion Easley	.50
57	Luis Gonzalez	.50
58	Bob Higginson	.50
59	Brian Hunter	.50
60	Cliff Floyd	.50
61	Alex Gonzalez	.50
62	Livan Hernandez	.50
63	Derrek Lee	.50
64	Edgar Renteria	.50
65	Moises Alou	.75
66	Jeff Bagwell	1.50
67	Derek Bell	.50
68	Craig Biggio	1.00
69	Randy Johnson	1.00
70	Johnny Damon	.50
71	Jeff King	.50
72	Hal Morris	.50
73	Dean Palmer	.50
74	Eric Karros	.50
75	Raul Mondesi	.75
76	Chan Ho Park	1.00
77	Gary Sheffield	.75
78	Jeromy Burnitz	.50
79	Jeff Cirillo	.50
80	Marquis Grissom	.50
81	Jose Valentin	.50
82	Fernando Vina	.50
83	Paul Molitor	1.00
84	Otis Nixon	.50
85	David Ortiz	.50
86	Todd Walker	.75
87	Vladimir Guerrero	2.50
88	Carl Pavano	.50
89	Fernando Seguignol	.50
90	Ugueth Urbina	.50
91	Carlos Baerga	.50
92	Bobby Bonilla	.50
93	Hideo Nomo	.60
94	John Olerud	.75
95	Rey Ordonez	.65
96	Mike Piazza	4.00
97	David Cone	.75
98	Orlando Hernandez	1.50
99	Hideki Irabu	.75
100	Derek Jeter	4.00
101	Tino Martinez	.60
102	Bernie Williams	1.00
103	Eric Chavez	.50
104	Jason Giambi	.50
105	Ben Grieve	.75
106	Rickey Henderson	.75
107	Bob Abreu	.50
108	Doug Glanville	.50
109	Scott Rolen	1.00
110	Curt Schilling	.75
111	Emil Brown	.50
112	Jose Guillen	.50
113	Jason Kendall	.50
114	Al Martin	.50
115	Aramis Ramirez	.50
116	Kevin Young	.50
117	J.D. Drew	.75
118	Ron Gant	.50
119	Brian Jordan	.50
120	Eli Marrero	.50
121	Mark McGwire	7.50
122	Kevin Brown	.75
123	Tony Gwynn	3.00
124	Trevor Hoffman	.50
125	Wally Joyner	.50
126	Greg Vaughn	.60
127	Barry Bonds	1.50
128	Ellis Burks	.50
129	Jeff Kent	.50
130	Robb Nen	.50
131	J.T. Snow	.50
132	Jay Buhner	.50
133	Ken Griffey Jr.	7.50
134	Edgar Martinez	.50
135	Alex Rodriguez	5.00
136	David Segui	.50
137	Rolando Arrojo	.75
138	Wade Boggs	.75
139	Aaron Ledesma	.50
140	Fred McGriff	.75
141	Will Clark	1.00
142	Juan Gonzalez	2.00
143	Rusty Greer	.50
144	Ivan Rodriguez	1.50
145	Aaron Sele	.50
146	Jose Canseco	1.00
147	Roger Clemens	2.00
148	Jose Cruz Jr.	.50
149	Carlos Delgado	1.00
150	Alex Gonzalez	.50

1999 Pacific Prism Ahead of the Game

Each card features full gold foil and etching with a close- up photo of baseball's top 20 stars. These are seeded 1:49 packs.

		MT
Complete Set (20):		200.00
Common Player:		4.00
Inserted 1:49		
1	Darin Erstad	6.00
2	Travis Lee	5.00
3	Chipper Jones	12.50
4	Cal Ripken Jr.	15.00
5	Nomar Garciaparra	12.50
6	Sammy Sosa	12.50
7	Kerry Wood	5.00
8	Frank Thomas	10.00
9	Manny Ramirez	8.00
10	Todd Helton	5.00
11	Jeff Bagwell	6.00
12	Mike Piazza	12.50
13	Derek Jeter	12.50
14	Bernie Williams	4.00
15	J.D. Drew	4.00
16	Mark McGwire	25.00
17	Tony Gwynn	10.00
18	Ken Griffey Jr.	25.00
19	Alex Rodriguez	20.00
20	Ivan Rodriguez	6.00

1999 Pacific Prism Ballpark Legends

This 10 card set salutes baseball's biggest stars. These inserts feature silver foil stamping and etching with an image of a ballpark in the background of the player photo. These are seeded 1:193 packs.

		MT
Complete Set (10):		200.00
Common Player:		10.00
Inserted 1:193		
1	Cal Ripken Jr.	30.00
2	Nomar Garciaparra	25.00
3	Frank Thomas	17.50
4	Ken Griffey Jr.	40.00
5	Alex Rodriguez	30.00
6	Greg Maddux	25.00
7	Sammy Sosa	25.00
8	Kerry Wood	10.00
9	Mark McGwire	40.00
10	Tony Gwynn	17.50

1999 Pacific Prism Diamond Glory

Card fronts feature full copper foil stamping with a star in the background of the player's photo. The 20-card set features 20 of baseball's most exciting players including several top 1999 rookies. These are seeded 2:25 packs.

		MT
Complete Set (20):		125.00
Common Player:		2.50
Inserted 2:25		
1	Darin Erstad	4.00
2	Travis Lee	3.00
3	Chipper Jones	10.00
4	Greg Maddux	10.00
5	Cal Ripken Jr.	12.00
6	Nomar Garciaparra	10.00
7	Sammy Sosa	10.00
8	Kerry Wood	4.00
9	Frank Thomas	8.00
10	Todd Helton	4.00
11	Jeff Bagwell	4.00
12	Mike Piazza	10.00
13	Derek Jeter	10.00
14	Bernie Williams	2.50
15	J.D. Drew	3.00
16	Mark McGwire	15.00
17	Tony Gwynn	8.00
18	Ken Griffey Jr.	15.00
19	Alex Rodriguez	12.00
20	Juan Gonzalez	4.00

1999 Pacific Prism Epic Performers

This hobby-only set features the 10 of the top hobby favorites and seeded at 1:97 packs.

		MT
Complete Set (10):		185.00
Common Player:		10.00
Inserted 1:97 H		
1	Cal Ripken Jr.	25.00
2	Nomar Garciaparra	20.00
3	Frank Thomas	20.00
4	Ken Griffey Jr.	35.00
5	Alex Rodriguez	25.00
6	Greg Maddux	20.00
7	Sammy Sosa	20.00
8	Kerry Wood	10.00
9	Mark McGwire	35.00
10	Tony Gwynn	15.00

1999 Pacific Private Stock

The premiere issue of Private Stock base cards features holographic silver foil on 30-pt. cardboard. Card backs have selected box scores from the '98 season, with a brief commentary on the player. Packs consist of six cards.

		MT
Complete Set (150):		60.00
Common Player:		.25
Pack (6):		4.00
Wax Box (24):		75.00
1	Jeff Bagwell	1.50

2	Roger Clemens	2.00
3	J.D. Drew	.25
4	Nomar Garciaparra	3.00
5	Juan Gonzalez	1.50
6	Ken Griffey Jr.	5.00
7	Tony Gwynn	2.50
8	Derek Jeter	3.00
9	Chipper Jones	3.00
10	Travis Lee	1.00
11	Greg Maddux	3.00
12	Mark McGwire	5.00
13	Mike Piazza	3.00
14	Manny Ramirez	1.50
15	Cal Ripken Jr.	4.00
16	Alex Rodriguez	4.00
17	Ivan Rodriguez	1.25
18	Sammy Sosa	3.00
19	Frank Thomas	2.50
20	Kerry Wood	1.50
21	Roberto Alomar	.75
22	Moises Alou	.40
23	Albert Belle	1.25
24	Craig Biggio	.30
25	Wade Boggs	.50
26	Barry Bonds	1.25
27	Jose Canseco	.75
28	Jim Edmonds	.25
29	Darin Erstad	1.25
30	Andres Galarraga	.75
31	Tom Glavine	.40
32	Ben Grieve	1.25
33	Vladimir Guerrero	2.00
34	Wilton Guerrero	.25
35	Todd Helton	1.25
36	Andruw Jones	1.25
37	Ryan Klesko	.30
38	Kenny Lofton	.75
39	Javy Lopez	.40
40	Pedro Martinez	1.00
41	Paul Molitor	1.00
42	Raul Mondesi	.40
43	Rafael Palmeiro	.50
44	Tim Salmon	.40
45	Jim Thome	.75
46	Mo Vaughn	.75
47	Larry Walker	.75
48	David Wells	.25
49	Bernie Williams	.75
50	Jaret Wright	.75
51	Bobby Abreu	.25
52	Garret Anderson	.25
53	Rolando Arrojo	.25
54	Tony Batista	.25
55	Rod Beck	.25
56	Derek Bell	.25
57	Marvin Benard	.25
58	Dave Berg	.25
59	Dante Bichette	.50
60	Aaron Boone	.25
61	Bret Boone	.25
62	Scott Brosius	.25
63	Brant Brown	.25
64	Kevin Brown	.40
65	Jeromy Burnitz	.25
66	Ken Caminiti	.40
67	Mike Caruso	.25
68	Sean Casey	.40
69	Vinny Castilla	.25
70	Eric Chavez	.75
71	Ryan Christenson	.25
72	Jeff Cirillo	.25
73	Tony Clark	.75
74	Will Clark	.50
75	*Edgard Clemente*	.25
76	David Cone	.40
77	Marty Cordova	.25
78	Jose Cruz Jr.	.25
79	Eric Davis	.25
80	Carlos Delgado	.50
81	David Dellucci	.25
82	Delino DeShields	.25
83	Gary DiSarcina	.25
84	Damion Easley	.25
85	Dennis Eckersley	.25
86	Cliff Floyd	.25
87	Jason Giambi	.25
88	Doug Glanville	.25
89	Alex Gonzalez	.25
90	Mark Grace	.50
91	Rusty Greer	.25
92	Jose Guillen	.40
93	Carlos Guillen	.25
94	Jeffrey Hammonds	.25
95	Rick Helling	.25
96	Bob Henley	.25
97	Livan Hernandez	.25
98	Orlando Hernandez	2.00
99	Bob Higginson	.25
100	Trevor Hoffman	.25
101	Randy Johnson	.75
102	Brian Jordan	.25
103	Wally Joyner	.25
104	Eric Karros	.25
105	Jason Kendall	.40
106	Jeff Kent	.25
107	Jeff King	.25
108	Mark Kotsay	.40
109	Ray Lankford	.25
110	Barry Larkin	.30
111	Mark Loretta	.25
112	Edgar Martinez	.25
113	Tino Martinez	.50
114	Quinton McCracken	.25
115	Fred McGriff	.40
116	Ryan Minor	.75
117	Hal Morris	.25
118	Bill Mueller	.25
119	Mike Mussina	.75
120	Dave Nilsson	.25
121	Otis Nixon	.25
122	Hideo Nomo	.50
123	Paul O'Neill	.50
124	Jose Offerman	.25
125	John Olerud	.40
126	Rey Ordonez	.25
127	David Ortiz	.25
128	Dean Palmer	.25
129	Chan Ho Park	.50
130	Aramis Ramirez	.50
131	Edgar Renteria	.25
132	Armando Rios	.25
133	Henry Rodriguez	.25
134	Scott Rolen	1.25
135	Curt Schilling	.40
136	David Segui	.25
137	Richie Sexson	.25
138	Gary Sheffield	.50
139	John Smoltz	.40
140	Matt Stairs	.25
141	Justin Thompson	.25
142	Greg Vaughn	.40
143	Omar Vizquel	.25
144	Tim Wakefield	.25
145	Todd Walker	.40
146	Devon White	.25
147	Rondell White	.40
148	Matt Williams	.50
149	*Enrique Wilson*	.25
150	Kevin Young	.25

1999 Pacific Private Stock Exclusive Series

This 20-card set is a partial parallel to the base set. Taking the first 20 cards from the set and serially numbering them to 299 sets. These are inserted exclusively in hobby packs.

		MT
Complete Set (20):		350.00
Common Player:		7.50
Production 299 sets H		
1	Jeff Bagwell	10.00
2	Roger Clemens	15.00
3	J.D. Drew	5.00
4	Nomar Garciaparra	25.00
5	Juan Gonzalez	10.00
6	Ken Griffey Jr.	40.00
7	Tony Gwynn	20.00
8	Derek Jeter	25.00
9	Chipper Jones	25.00
10	Travis Lee	7.50
11	Greg Maddux	25.00
12	Mark McGwire	40.00
13	Mike Piazza	25.00
14	Manny Ramirez	10.00
15	Cal Ripken Jr.	30.00
16	Alex Rodriguez	30.00
17	Ivan Rodriguez	10.00
18	Sammy Sosa	25.00
19	Frank Thomas	15.00
20	Kerry Wood	10.00

1999 Pacific Private Stock Homerun History

This holographic silver foiled commemorative set honors Mark McGwire and Sammy Sosa's historic '98 seasons. Two cards were added to the end of the set, which are Silver Crown Die-Cuts honoring Ripken Jr.'s consecutive games streak and McGwire's 70 home runs. These are inserted 2:25 packs.

		MT
Complete Set (22):		200.00
Common McGwire:		12.00
Common Sosa:		8.00
Inserted 1:12		
1	Home Run #61 (Mark McGwire)	15.00
2	Home Run #59 (Sammy Sosa)	10.00
3	Home Run #62 (Mark McGwire)	15.00
4	Home Run #60 (Sammy Sosa)	10.00
5	Home Run #63 (Mark McGwire)	15.00
6	Home Run #61 (Sammy Sosa)	10.00
7	Home Run #64 (Mark McGwire)	15.00
8	Home Run #62 (Sammy Sosa)	10.00
9	Home Run #65 (Mark McGwire)	15.00
10	Home Run #63 (Sammy Sosa)	10.00
11	Home Run #67 (Mark McGwire)	15.00
12	Home Run #64 (Sammy Sosa)	10.00
13	Home Run #68 (Mark McGwire)	15.00
14	Home Run #65 (Sammy Sosa)	10.00
15	Home Run #70 (Mark McGwire)	15.00
16	Home Run #66 (Sammy Sosa)	10.00
17	A Season of Celebration (Mark McGwire)	15.00
18	A Season of Celebration (Sammy Sosa)	10.00
19	Awesome Power (Sammy Sosa, Mark McGwire)	15.00
20	Transcending Sports (Mark McGwire, Sammy Sosa)	15.00
21	Crown Die-Cut (Mark McGwire)	15.00
22	Crown Die-Cut (Cal Ripken Jr.)	10.00

1999 Pacific Private Stock Preferred Series

Another partial parallel of the first 20 base cards. Each card is stamped with a holographic Preferred logo and are numbered to 399 sets.

		MT
Complete Set (20):		400.00
Common Player:		5.00
Production 399 sets		
1	Jeff Bagwell	7.50
2	Roger Clemens	15.00
3	J.D. Drew	5.00
4	Nomar Garciaparra	30.00
5	Juan Gonzalez	10.00
6	Ken Griffey Jr.	50.00
7	Tony Gwynn	20.00
8	Derek Jeter	30.00
9	Chipper Jones	30.00
10	Travis Lee	5.00
11	Greg Maddux	30.00
12	Mark McGwire	50.00
13	Mike Piazza	30.00
14	Manny Ramirez	10.00
15	Cal Ripken Jr.	40.00
16	Alex Rodriguez	40.00
17	Ivan Rodriguez	7.50
18	Sammy Sosa	30.00
19	Frank Thomas	15.00
20	Kerry Wood	5.00

1999 Pacific Private Stock Platinum Series

Another partial parallel of the first 50 cards in the base set. Cards have a platinum holographic sheen to them with a Platinum stamp on the front. These are limited to 199 numbered sets.

		MT
Complete Set (50):		700.00
Common Player:		4.00
Production 199 sets		
1	Jeff Bagwell	25.00
2	Roger Clemens	25.00
3	J.D. Drew	5.00
4	Nomar Garciaparra	40.00
5	Juan Gonzalez	20.00
6	Ken Griffey Jr.	65.00
7	Tony Gwynn	30.00
8	Derek Jeter	40.00
9	Chipper Jones	40.00
10	Travis Lee	12.50
11	Greg Maddux	35.00
12	Mark McGwire	65.00
13	Mike Piazza	40.00
14	Manny Ramirez	20.00
15	Cal Ripken Jr.	50.00
16	Alex Rodriguez	50.00
17	Ivan Rodriguez	15.00
18	Sammy Sosa	40.00
19	Frank Thomas	25.00
20	Kerry Wood	15.00
21	Roberto Alomar	12.50
22	Moises Alou	5.00
23	Albert Belle	15.00
24	Craig Biggio	10.00
25	Wade Boggs	10.00
26	Barry Bonds	15.00
27	Jose Canseco	10.00
28	Jim Edmonds	5.00
29	Darin Erstad	15.00
30	Andres Galarraga	10.00
31	Tom Glavine	5.00
32	Ben Grieve	10.00
33	Vladimir Guerrero	25.00
34	Wilton Guerrero	4.00
35	Todd Helton	12.50
36	Andruw Jones	15.00
37	Ryan Klesko	5.00
38	Kenny Lofton	10.00
39	Javy Lopez	5.00
40	Pedro Martinez	12.50
41	Paul Molitor	12.50
42	Raul Mondesi	7.50
43	Rafael Palmeiro	7.50
44	Tim Salmon	5.00
45	Jim Thome	10.00
46	Mo Vaughn	10.00
47	Larry Walker	10.00
48	David Wells	4.00
49	Bernie Williams	10.00
50	Jaret Wright	10.00

1999 Pacific Private Stock PS-206

This 150-card set takes reverent reach back into collecting history with its smaller format (1.5" x 2.5"). Card fronts have a white border with silver foil stamping and a blue back, these are found one per pack. A parallel also exists with a red back, which are seeded 1:25 packs.

		MT
Complete Set (150):		25.00
Common Player:		.25
Inserted 1:1		
Red Parallels:		4X
Inserted 1:25		
1	Jeff Bagwell	.75
2	Roger Clemens	1.00
3	J.D. Drew	.40
4	Nomar Garciaparra	2.00
5	Juan Gonzalez	1.00
6	Ken Griffey Jr.	3.50
7	Tony Gwynn	1.50
8	Derek Jeter	2.00
9	Chipper Jones	2.00
10	Travis Lee	.75
11	Greg Maddux	2.00
12	Mark McGwire	3.50
13	Mike Piazza	2.00
14	Manny Ramirez	1.00
15	Cal Ripken Jr.	2.50
16	Alex Rodriguez	2.50
17	Ivan Rodriguez	.75
18	Sammy Sosa	2.00
19	Frank Thomas	1.50
20	Kerry Wood	.75
21	Roberto Alomar	.50
22	Moises Alou	.25
23	Albert Belle	.75
24	Craig Biggio	.35
25	Wade Boggs	.40
26	Barry Bonds	.75
27	Jose Canseco	.40
28	Jim Edmonds	.25
29	Darin Erstad	.75
30	Andres Galarraga	.50
31	Tom Glavine	.40
32	Ben Grieve	.75
33	Vladimir Guerrero	1.50
34	Wilton Guerrero	.25
35	Todd Helton	.75
36	Andruw Jones	.75
37	Ryan Klesko	.30
38	Kenny Lofton	.60
39	Javy Lopez	.30
40	Pedro Martinez	.60
41	Paul Molitor	.50
42	Raul Mondesi	.35
43	Rafael Palmeiro	.35
44	Tim Salmon	.40
45	Jim Thome	.50
46	Mo Vaughn	.60
47	Larry Walker	.40
48	David Wells	.25
49	Bernie Williams	.60
50	Jaret Wright	.50
51	Bobby Abreu	.25
52	Garret Anderson	.25
53	Rolando Arrojo	.25
54	Tony Batista	.25
55	Rod Beck	.25
56	Derek Bell	.25
57	Marvin Benard	.25
58	Dave Berg	.25
59	Dante Bichette	.40
60	Aaron Boone	.25
61	Bret Boone	.25
62	Scott Brosius	.25
63	Brant Brown	.25
64	Kevin Brown	.35
65	Jeromy Burnitz	.25
66	Ken Caminiti	.35
67	Mike Caruso	.25
68	Sean Casey	.35
69	Vinny Castilla	.25
70	Eric Chavez	.50
71	Ryan Christenson	.25
72	Jeff Cirillo	.25
73	Tony Clark	.50
74	Will Clark	.40
75	Edgard Clemente	.25
76	David Cone	.25
77	Marty Cordova	.25
78	Jose Cruz Jr.	.25
79	Eric Davis	.25
80	Carlos Delgado	.50
81	David Dellucci	.25
82	Delino DeShields	.25
83	Gary DiSarcina	.25
84	Damion Easley	.25
85	Dennis Eckersley	.25
86	Cliff Floyd	.25
87	Jason Giambi	.25
88	Doug Glanville	.25
89	Alex Gonzalez	.25
90	Mark Grace	.40
91	Rusty Greer	.25
92	Jose Guillen	.25
93	Carlos Guillen	.25
94	Jeffrey Hammonds	.25
95	Rick Helling	.25
96	Bob Henley	.25
97	Livan Hernandez	.25
98	Orlando Hernandez	1.50
99	Bob Higginson	.25
100	Trevor Hoffman	.25
101	Randy Johnson	.50
102	Brian Jordan	.25
103	Wally Joyner	.25
104	Eric Karros	.25
105	Jason Kendall	.40
106	Jeff Kent	.25
107	Jeff King	.25
108	Mark Kotsay	.40
109	Ray Lankford	.25
110	Barry Larkin	.30
111	Mark Loretta	.25
112	Edgar Martinez	.25
113	Tino Martinez	.30
114	Quinton McCracken	.25
115	Fred McGriff	.40
116	Ryan Minor	.75
117	Hal Morris	.25
118	Bill Mueller	.25
119	Mike Mussina	.50
120	Dave Nilsson	.25
121	Otis Nixon	.25
122	Hideo Nomo	.40
123	Paul O'Neill	.40
124	Jose Offerman	.25
125	John Olerud	.40
126	Rey Ordonez	.25
127	David Ortiz	.25
128	Dean Palmer	.25
129	Chan Ho Park	.40
130	Aramis Ramirez	.40
131	Edgar Renteria	.25
132	Armando Rios	.25
133	Henry Rodriguez	.25
134	Scott Rolen	.75
135	Curt Schilling	.35
136	David Segui	.25
137	Richie Sexson	.25
138	Gary Sheffield	.40
139	John Smoltz	.25
140	Matt Stairs	.25
141	Justin Thompson	.25
142	Greg Vaughn	.40
143	Omar Vizquel	.25
144	Tim Wakefield	.25
145	Todd Walker	.40
146	Devon White	.25
147	Rondell White	.35
148	Matt Williams	.40
149	Enrique Wilson	.25
150	Kevin Young	.25

1999 Pacific Private Stock Vintage Series

This insert set is a partial parallel of the first 50 cards in the base set and have a Vintage holograpic stamp on the card fronts. These are limited to 99 numbered sets.

		MT
Complete Set (50):		900.00
Common Player:		5.00
Production 99 sets		
1	Jeff Bagwell	20.00
2	Roger Clemens	30.00
3	J.D. Drew	10.00
4	Nomar Garciaparra	50.00
5	Juan Gonzalez	25.00
6	Ken Griffey Jr.	80.00
7	Tony Gwynn	35.00
8	Derek Jeter	50.00
9	Chipper Jones	50.00
10	Travis Lee	10.00
11	Greg Maddux	45.00
12	Mark McGwire	80.00
13	Mike Piazza	50.00
14	Manny Ramirez	20.00
15	Cal Ripken Jr.	65.00
16	Alex Rodriguez	65.00
17	Ivan Rodriguez	20.00
18	Sammy Sosa	50.00
19	Frank Thomas	30.00
20	Kerry Wood	10.00
21	Roberto Alomar	15.00
22	Moises Alou	5.00
23	Albert Belle	15.00
24	Craig Biggio	12.50
25	Wade Boggs	12.50
26	Barry Bonds	15.00
27	Jose Canseco	12.50
28	Jim Edmonds	5.00
29	Darin Erstad	12.50
30	Andres Galarraga	5.00
31	Tom Glavine	12.50
32	Ben Grieve	7.50
33	Vladimir Guerrero	30.00
34	Wilton Guerrero	5.00
35	Todd Helton	12.50
36	Andruw Jones	15.00
37	Ryan Klesko	5.00
38	Kenny Lofton	5.00
39	Javy Lopez	5.00
40	Pedro Martinez	12.50
41	Paul Molitor	12.50
42	Raul Mondesi	7.50
43	Rafael Palmeiro	12.50
44	Tim Salmon	5.00
45	Jim Thome	5.00
46	Mo Vaughn	5.00
47	Larry Walker	5.00
48	David Wells	5.00
49	Bernie Williams	5.00
50	Jaret Wright	5.00

1999 Pacific Revolution

The 150-card set features dual foiled etching and embossing enhanced by gold-foil stamping. Card backs have year-by- year statistics along with a close-up photo. There are three parallels to the base set: Opening Day, Red and Shadow. Reds are retail exclusive and are limited to 299 numbered sets. Shadows have light blue foil stamping and are limited to 99 numbered sets. Opening Day are seeded exclusively in hobby packs at a rate of 1:25 packs.

		MT
Complete Set (150):		125.00
Common Player:		.50
1	Jim Edmonds	.50
2	Darin Erstad	2.00
3	Troy Glaus	3.00
4	Tim Salmon	1.00
5	Mo Vaughn	1.50
6	Steve Finley	.50
7	Luis Gonzalez	.50
8	Randy Johnson	2.00
9	Travis Lee	2.00
10	Matt Williams	1.00
11	Andruw Jones	2.50
12	Chipper Jones	6.00
13	Brian Jordan	.50
14	Javy Lopez	.75
15	Greg Maddux	6.00
16	*Kevin McGlinchy*	.50
17	John Smoltz	.50
18	Brady Anderson	.50
19	Albert Belle	2.50
20	Will Clark	1.00
21	*Willis Otanez*	.50
23	*Calvin Pickering*	.50
23	Cal Ripken Jr.	8.00
24	Nomar Garciaparra	6.00
25	Pedro Martinez	2.50
26	Troy O'Leary	.50
27	Jose Offerman	.50
28	Mark Grace	.75
29	Mickey Morandini	.50
30	Henry Rodriguez	.50
31	Sammy Sosa	6.00
32	Ray Durham	.50
33	Carlos Lee	.50
34	*Jeff Liefer*	.50
35	Magglio Ordonez	.75
36	Frank Thomas	4.00
37	Mike Cameron	.50
38	Sean Casey	.75
39	Barry Larkin	.75
40	Greg Vaughn	.75
41	Roberto Alomar	2.00
42	Sandy Alomar Jr.	.50
43	David Justice	.75
44	Kenny Lofton	1.50
45	Manny Ramirez	3.00
46	Richie Sexson	.50
47	Jim Thome	1.50
48	Dante Bichette	1.00
49	Vinny Castilla	.50
50	Darryl Hamilton	.50
51	Todd Helton	3.00
52	Larry Walker	2.00
53	Tony Clark	1.00
54	Damion Easley	.50
55	Bob Higginson	.50
56	*Gabe Kapler*	5.00
57	*Alex Gonzalez*	.50
58	Mark Kotsay	.50
59	Kevin Orie	.50
60	Preston Wilson	.50
61	Jeff Bagwell	3.00
62	Derek Bell	.50
63	Craig Biggio	1.00
64	Ken Caminiti	.75
65	Carlos Beltran	.50

66	Johnny Damon	.50
67	Jermaine Dye	.50
68	Carlos Febles	.50
69	Kevin Brown	.75
70	Todd Hundley	.50
71	Eric Karros	.50
72	Raul Mondesi	.75
73	Gary Sheffield	.75
74	Jeromy Burnitz	.50
75	Jeff Cirillo	.50
76	Marquis Grissom	.50
77	Fernando Vina	.50
78	*Chad Allen*	.50
79	*Corey Koskie*	.50
80	*Doug Mientkiewicz*	.50
81	Brad Radke	.50
82	Todd Walker	.50
83	*Michael Barrett*	.75
84	Vladimir Guerrero	5.00
85	Wilton Guerrero	.50
86	*Guillermo Mota*	.50
87	Rondell White	.75
88	Edgardo Alfonzo	.50
89	Rickey Henderson	.75
90	John Olerud	.75
91	Mike Piazza	6.00
92	Robin Ventura	.75
93	Roger Clemens	3.00
94	Chili Davis	.50
95	Derek Jeter	6.00
96	Chuck Knoblauch	1.00
97	Tino Martinez	.75
98	Paul O'Neill	.75
99	Bernie Williams	1.50
100	Eric Chavez	1.50
101	Jason Giambi	.50
102	Ben Grieve	2.00
103	John Jaha	.50
104	*Olmedo Saenz*	.50
105	Bobby Abreu	.50
106	Doug Glanville	.50
107	Desi Relaford	.50
108	Scott Rolen	2.50
109	Curt Schilling	.75
110	Brian Giles	.50
111	Jason Kendall	.75
112	Pat Meares	.50
113	Kevin Young	.50
114	J.D. Drew	.75
115	Ray Lankford	.50
116	Eli Marrero	.50
117	*Joe McEwing*	.50
118	Mark McGwire	12.00
119	Fernando Tatis	.50
120	Tony Gwynn	5.00
121	Trevor Hoffman	.50
122	Wally Joyner	.50
123	Reggie Sanders	.50
124	Barry Bonds	2.50
125	Ellis Burks	.50
126	Jeff Kent	.50
127	*Ramon Martinez*	.50
128	*Joe Nathan*	.50
129	*Freddy Garcia*	15.00
130	Ken Griffey Jr.	12.00
131	Brian Hunter	.50
132	Edgar Martinez	.50
133	Alex Rodriguez	8.00
134	David Segui	.50
135	Wade Boggs	1.00
136	Jose Canseco	1.50
137	Quinton McCracken	.50
138	Fred McGriff	.75
139	*Kelly Dransfeldt*	.50
140	Juan Gonzalez	3.00
141	Rusty Greer	.50
142	Rafael Palmeiro	1.00
143	Ivan Rodriguez	2.50
144	Lee Stevens	.50
145	Jose Cruz Jr.	.50
146	Carlos Delgado	1.00
147	Shawn Green	.75
148	*Roy Halladay*	1.00
149	Shannon Stewart	.50
150	*Kevin Witt*	.50

1999 Pacific Revolution Premiere Date

A Premiere Date seal and a serial number from within an edition of 49 sets differentiates these inserts from the base cards they parallel. This version is a 1:25 pack hobby-only insert.

	MT
Common Player:	6.00
Stars:	15X
SPs:	6X

(See 1999 Pacific Revolution for checklist and base card values.)

1999 Pacific Revolution Red

Serially numbered within an edition of 299 each, the Red parallels are a retail-only insert. They feature red metallic-foil background and highlights on front, but otherwise are identical to the base cards, except for the serial number printed on back.

	MT
Common Player:	1.50
Stars:	3X
SPs:	1.5X

(See 1999 Pacific Revolution for checklist and base card values.)

1999 Pacific Revolution Shadow

This hobby-only parallel insert features blue metallic-foil background and graphics on front. Backs are identical to the base version except they include a dot-matrix applied serial number at left within an edition of 99.

	MT
Common Player:	4.00
Stars:	6X
SPs:	3X

(See 1999 Pacific Revolution for checklist and base card values.)

1999 Pacific Revolution Diamond Legacy

This 36-card set features a holographic patterned foil card front. Card backs have a small close-up photo along with a career note. These were seeded 2:25 packs.

		MT
Complete Set (36):		250.00
Common Player:		2.00
Inserted 2:25		
1	Troy Glaus	8.00
2	Mo Vaughn	4.00
3	Matt Williams	3.00
4	Chipper Jones	15.00
5	Andruw Jones	6.00
6	Greg Maddux	15.00
7	Albert Belle	6.00
8	Cal Ripken Jr.	20.00
9	Nomar Garciaparra	15.00
10	Sammy Sosa	15.00
11	Frank Thomas	12.00
12	Manny Ramirez	10.00
13	Todd Helton	8.00
14	Larry Walker	4.00
15	Gabe Kapler	8.00
16	Jeff Bagwell	8.00
17	Craig Biggio	4.00
18	Raul Mondesi	2.00
19	Vladimir Guerrero	12.00
20	Mike Piazza	15.00
21	Roger Clemens	10.00
22	Derek Jeter	15.00
23	Bernie Williams	3.00
24	Ben Grieve	4.00
25	Scott Rolen	6.00
26	J.D. Drew	2.00
27	Mark McGwire	30.00
28	Fernando Tatis	2.00
29	Tony Gwynn	12.00
30	Barry Bonds	6.00
31	Ken Griffey Jr.	30.00
32	Alex Rodriguez	20.00
33	Jose Canseco	4.00
34	Juan Gonzalez	8.00
35	Ivan Rodriguez	6.00
36	Shawn Green	6.00

1999 Pacific Revolution Foul Pole

This 20-card set features netting down the right side of each card, with the player photo on the left side. The player name, position and logo are stamped with gold foil. These were seeded 1:49 packs.

		MT
Complete Set (20):		450.00
Common Player:		5.00
Inserted 1:49		
1	Chipper Jones	30.00
2	Andruw Jones	15.00
3	Cal Ripken Jr.	40.00
4	Nomar Garciaparra	30.00
5	Sammy Sosa	30.00
6	Frank Thomas	25.00
7	Manny Ramirez	20.00
8	Jeff Bagwell	15.00
9	Raul Mondesi	5.00
10	Vladimir Guerrero	20.00
11	Mike Piazza	30.00
12	Derek Jeter	30.00
13	Bernie Williams	5.00
14	Scott Rolen	15.00
15	J.D. Drew	5.00
16	Mark McGwire	50.00
17	Tony Gwynn	25.00
18	Ken Griffey Jr.	50.00
19	Alex Rodriguez	40.00
20	Juan Gonzalez	15.00

1999 Pacific Revolution Icons

This 10-card set spotlights the top players, each card is die-cut in the shape of a shield with silver foil etching and stamping. These were seeded 1:121 packs.

		MT
Complete Set (10):		450.00
Common Player:		40.00
Inserted 1:121		
1	Cal Ripken Jr.	60.00
2	Nomar Garciaparra	50.00
3	Sammy Sosa	50.00
4	Frank Thomas	40.00
5	Mike Piazza	50.00
6	Derek Jeter	50.00
7	Mark McGwire	80.00
8	Tony Gwynn	40.00
9	Ken Griffey Jr.	80.00
10	Alex Rodriguez	60.00

1999 Pacific Revolution Thorn in the Side

This 20-card set features full holographic silver foil and is die-cut in the upper right portion. Card backs analyzes the featured player's success against a certain opponent over the years. These were seeded 1:25 packs.

		MT
Complete Set (20):		250.00
Common Player:		5.00
Inserted 1:25		
1	Mo Vaughn	5.00
2	Chipper Jones	20.00
3	Greg Maddux	20.00
4	Cal Ripken Jr.	25.00
5	Nomar Garciaparra	20.00
6	Sammy Sosa	20.00
7	Frank Thomas	15.00
8	Manny Ramirez	10.00
9	Jeff Bagwell	8.00
10	Mike Piazza	20.00
11	Derek Jeter	20.00
12	Bernie Williams	5.00
13	J.D. Drew	5.00
14	Mark McGwire	35.00
15	Tony Gwynn	15.00
16	Barry Bonds	8.00
17	Ken Griffey Jr.	35.00
18	Alex Rodriguez	25.00
19	Juan Gonzalez	10.00
20	Ivan Rodriguez	8.00

1999 Pacific Revolution Tripleheader

This 30-card set features spotted gold foil blotching around the player image with the name, postion, team and logo stamped in gold foil. These were seeded 4:25 hobby packs. The set is also broken down into three separate tiers of 10 cards. Tier 1 (cards 1-10) are limited to 99 numbered sets. Tier 2 (11-20) 199 numbered sets and Tier 3 (21-30) 299 numbered sets.

		MT
Complete Set (30):		120.00
Common Player:		1.00
Inserted 4:25 H		
Tier 1 (1-10):		6X
Production 99 sets H		
Tier 2 (11-20):		3X
Production 199 sets H		
Tier 3 (21-30):		1.5X
Production 299 sets H		
1	Greg Maddux	8.00
2	Cal Ripken Jr.	10.00
3	Nomar Garciaparra	8.00
4	Sammy Sosa	8.00
5	Frank Thomas	6.00
6	Mike Piazza	8.00
7	Mark McGwire	15.00
8	Tony Gwynn	6.00
9	Ken Griffey Jr.	15.00
10	Alex Rodriguez	10.00
11	Mo Vaughn	2.00
12	Chipper Jones	6.00
13	Manny Ramirez	4.00
14	Larry Walker	1.00
15	Jeff Bagwell	3.00
16	Vladimir Guerrero	6.00
17	Derek Jeter	8.00
18	J.D. Drew	1.50
19	Barry Bonds	3.00
20	Juan Gonzalez	4.00
21	Troy Glaus	4.00
22	Andruw Jones	3.00
23	Matt Williams	1.00
24	Craig Biggio	1.00
25	Raul Mondesi	1.00
26	Roger Clemens	4.00
27	Bernie Williams	1.00
28	Scott Rolen	3.00
29	Jose Canseco	1.50
30	Ivan Rodriguez	3.00

2000 Pacific

The base set consists of 500-cards with the Pacific logo and player name stamped in silver foil on the card front. Card backs have a small photo along with complete career statistics and a brief career highlight. 50 players in the base set also have another version and are priced equally.

		MT
Complete Set (500):		60.00
Common Player:		.10
Pack (12):		2.50
Wax Box (24):		55.00
1	Garret Anderson	.10
2	Tim Belcher	.10
3	Gary DiSarcina	.10
4	Trent Durrington	.10
5	Jim Edmonds	.10
6	Darin Erstad	.25
6b	Darin Erstad	.25
7	Chuck Finley	.10
8	Troy Glaus	.75
9	Todd Greene	.10
10	Bret Hemphill	.10
11	Ken Hill	.10
12	Ramon Ortiz	.10
13	Troy Percival	.10
14	Mark Petkovsek	.10
15	Tim Salmon	.20
16	Mo Vaughn	.50
16b	Mo Vaughn	.50
17	Jay Bell	.10
18	Omar Daal	.10
19	Erubiel Durazo	.10
20	Steve Finley	.10
21	Bernard Gilkey	.10
22	Luis Gonzalez	.20
23	Randy Johnson	.50
24	Byung-Hyun Kim	.10
25	Travis Lee	.25
26	Matt Mantei	.10
27	Armando Reynoso	.10
28	Rob Ryan	.10
29	Kelly Stinnett	.10
30	Todd Stottlemyre	.10
31	Matt Williams	.30
31b	Matt Williams	.30
32	Tony Womack	.10
33	Bret Boone	.10
34	Andres Galarraga	.40
35	Tom Glavine	.25
36	Ozzie Guillen	.10
37	Andruw Jones	.40
37b	Andruw Jones	.40
38	Chipper Jones	1.50
38b	Chipper Jones	1.50
39	Brian Jordan	.10
40	Ryan Klesko	.20
41	Javy Lopez	.20
42	Greg Maddux	1.50
42b	Greg Maddux	1.50
43	Kevin Millwood	.10
44	John Rocker	.10
45	Randall Simon	.10
46	John Smoltz	.20
47	Gerald Williams	.10
48	Brady Anderson	.20
49	Albert Belle	.60
49b	Albert Belle	.60
50	Mike Bordick	.10
51	Will Clark	.25
52	Jeff Conine	.10
53	Delino DeShields	.10
54	Jerry Hairston Jr.	.10
55	Charles Johnson	.10
56	Eugene Kingsale	.10
57	Ryan Minor	.20
58	Mike Mussina	.50
59	Sidney Ponson	.10
60	Cal Ripken Jr.	2.00
60b	Cal Ripken Jr.	2.00
61	B.J. Surhoff	.10
62	Mike Timlin	.10
63	Rod Beck	.10
64	Nomar Garciaparra	2.00
64b	Nomar Garciaparra	2.00
65	Tom Gordon	.10
66	Butch Huskey	.10
67	Derek Lowe	.10
68	Pedro Martinez	.75
68b	Pedro Martinez	.75
69	Trot Nixon	.10
70	Jose Offerman	.10
71	Troy O'Leary	.10
72	Pat Rapp	.10
73	Donnie Sadler	.10
74	Mike Stanley	.10
75	John Valentin	.10
76	Jason Varitek	.10
77	Wilton Veras	.25
78	Tim Wakefield	.10
79	Rick Aguilera	.10
80	Mann Alexander	.10
81	Roosevelt Brown	.10
82	Mark Grace	.20
83	Glenallen Hill	.10
84	Lance Johnson	.10
85	Jon Lieber	.10
86	Cole Liniak	.10
87	Chad Meyers	.10
88	Mickey Morandini	.10
89	Jose Nieves	.10
90	Henry Rodriguez	.10
91	Sammy Sosa	2.00
91b	Sammy Sosa	2.00
92	Kevin Tapani	.10
93	Kerry Wood	.40
94	Mike Caruso	.10
95	Ray Durham	.10
96	Brook Fordyce	.10
97	Bobby Howry	.10
98	Paul Konerko	.10
99	Carlos Lee	.10
100	Aaron Myette	.10
101	Greg Norton	.10
102	Magglio Ordonez	.25
103	Jim Parque	.10
104	Liu Rodriguez	.10
105	Chris Singleton	.10
106	Mike Sirotka	.10
107	Frank Thomas	.75
107b	Frank Thomas	.75
108	Kip Wells	.10
109	Aaron Boone	.10
110	Mike Cameron	.10
111	Sean Casey	.40
111b	Sean Casey	.40
112	Jeffrey Hammonds	.10
113	Pete Harnisch	.10
114	Barry Larkin	.40
114b	Barry Larkin	.40
115	Jason LaRue	.10
116	Denny Neagle	.10
117	Pokey Reese	.10
118	Scott Sullivan	.10
119	Eddie Taubensee	.10
120	Greg Vaughn	.20
121	Scott Williamson	.10
122	Dmitri Young	.10
123	Roberto Alomar	.50
123b	Roberto Alomar	.50
124	Sandy Alomar Jr.	.10
125	Harold Baines	.10
126	Russell Branyan	.10
127	Dave Burba	.10
128	Bartolo Colon	.10
129	Travis Fryman	.20
130	Mike Jackson	.10
131	David Justice	.25
132	Kenny Lofton	.50
132b	Kenny Lofton	.50
133	Charles Nagy	.10
134	Manny Ramirez	.75
134b	Manny Ramirez	.75
135	Dave Roberts	.10
136	Richie Sexson	.10
137	Jim Thome	.40
138	Omar Vizquel	.10
139	Jaret Wright	.10
140	Pedro Astacio	.10
141	Dante Bichette	.25
142	Brian Bohanon	.10
143	Vinny Castilla	.10
143b	Vinny Castilla	.10
144	Edgard Clemente	.10
145	Derrick Gibson	.10
146	Todd Helton	.75
147	Darryl Kile	.10
148	Mike Lansing	.10
149	Kirt Manwaring	.10
150	Neifi Perez	.10
151	Ben Petrick	.10
152	*Juan Sosa*	.40
153	Dave Veres	.10
154	Larry Walker	.50
154b	Larry Walker	.50
155	Brad Ausmus	.10
156	Dave Borkowski	.10
157	Tony Clark	.25
158	Francisco Cordero	.10
159	Deivi Cruz	.10
160	Damion Easley	.10
161	Juan Encarnacion	.10
162	Robert Fick	.10
163	Bobby Higginson	.10
164	Gabe Kapler	.25
165	Brian Moehler	.10
166	Dean Palmer	.10
167	Luis Polonia	.10
168	Justin Thompson	.10
169	Jeff Weaver	.10
170	Antonio Alfonseca	.10
171	Bruce Aven	.10
172	A.J. Burnett	.25
173	Luis Castillo	.10
174	Ramon Castro	.10
175	Ryan Dempster	.10
176	Alex Fernandez	.10
177	Cliff Floyd	.10
178	Amaury Garcia	.10
179	Alex Gonzalez	.10
180	Mark Kotsay	.10
181	Mike Lowell	.10
182	Brian Meadows	.10
183	Kevin Orie	.10
184	Julio Ramirez	.10
185	Preston Wilson	.10
186	Moises Alou	.20
187	Jeff Bagwell	.75
187b	Jeff Bagwell	.75
188	Glen Barker	.10
189	Derek Bell	.10
190	Craig Biggio	.40
190b	Craig Biggio	.40
191	Ken Caminiti	.20
192	Scott Elarton	.10
193	Carl Everett	.10
194	Mike Hampton	.10
195	Carlos Hernandez	.10
196	Richard Hidalgo	.10
197	Jose Lima	.10
198	Shane Reynolds	.20
199	Bill Spiers	.10
200	Billy Wagner	.10
201	Carlos Beltran	.20
201b	Carlos Beltran	.20
202	Dermal Brown	.10
203	Johnny Damon	.10
204	Jermaine Dye	.10
205	Carlos Febles	.10
206	Jeremy Giambi	.10
207	Mark Quinn	.10
208	Joe Randa	.10
209	Dan Reichert	.10
210	Jose Rosado	.10
211	Rey Sanchez	.10
212	Jeff Suppan	.10
213	Mike Sweeney	.10
214	Kevin Brown	.20
214b	Kevin Brown	.20
215	Darren Dreifort	.10
216	Eric Gagne	.10
217	Mark Grudzielanek	.10
218	Todd Hollandsworth	.10
219	Todd Hundley	.10
220	Eric Karros	.20
221	Raul Mondesi	.20
222	Chan Ho Park	.20
223	Jeff Shaw	.10
224	Gary Sheffield	.25
224b	Gary Sheffield	.25
225	Ismael Valdes	.10
226	Devon White	.10
227	Eric Young	.10
228	Kevin Barker	.10
229	Ron Belliard	.10
230	Jeromy Burnitz	.10
230b	Jeromy Burnitz	.10

231	Jeff Cirillo	.10
232	Marquis Grissom	.10
233	Geoff Jenkins	.10
234	Mark Loretta	.10
235	David Nilsson	.10
236	Hideo Nomo	.10
237	Alex Ochoa	.10
238	Kyle Peterson	.10
239	Fernando Vina	.10
240	Bob Wickman	.10
241	Steve Woodard	.10
242	Chad Allen	.10
243	Ron Coomer	.10
244	Marty Cordova	.10
245	Cristian Guzman	.10
246	Denny Hocking	.10
247	Jacque Jones	.10
248	Corey Koskie	.10
249	Matt Lawton	.10
250	Joe Mays	.10
251	Eric Milton	.10
252	Brad Radke	.10
253	Mark Redman	.10
254	Terry Steinbach	.10
255	Todd Walker	.10
256	Tony Armas, Jr.	.10
257	Michael Barrett	.10
258	Peter Bergeron	.10
259	Geoff Blum	.10
260	Orlando Cabrera	.10
261	*Trace Coquillette*	.25
262	Brad Fullmer	.10
263	Vladimir Guerrero	1.25
263b	Vladimir Guerrero	1.25
264	Wilton Guerrero	.10
265	Dustin Hermanson	.10
266	Manny Martinez	.10
267	Ryan McGuire	.10
268	Ugueth Urbina	.10
269	Jose Vidro	.10
270	Rondell White	.20
271	Chris Widger	.10
272	Edgardo Alfonzo	.25
273	Armando Benitez	.10
274	Roger Cedeno	.10
275	Dennis Cook	.10
276	Octavio Dotel	.10
277	John Franco	.10
278	Darryl Hamilton	.10
279	Rickey Henderson	.25
280	Orel Hershiser	.10
281	Al Leiter	.20
282	John Olerud	.25
282b	John Olerud	.25
283	Rey Ordonez	.10
284	Mike Piazza	2.00
284b	Mike Piazza	2.00
285	Kenny Rogers	.10
286	Jorge Toca	.10
287	Robin Ventura	.20
288	Scott Brosius	.10
289	Roger Clemens	1.00
289b	Roger Clemens	1.00
290	David Cone	.20
291	Chili Davis	.10
292	Orlando Hernandez	.25
293	Hideki Irabu	.10
294	Derek Jeter	2.00
294b	Derek Jeter	2.00
295	Chuck Knoblauch	.25
296	Ricky Ledee	.10
297	Jim Leyritz	.10
298	Tino Martinez	.40
299	Paul O'Neill	.25
300	Andy Pettitte	.25
301	Jorge Posada	.10
302	Mariano Rivera	.25
303	Alfonso Soriano	.50
304	Bernie Williams	.50
304b	Bernie Williams	.50
305	Ed Yarnall	.10
306	Kevin Appier	.10
307	Rich Becker	.10
308	Eric Chavez	.10
309	Jason Giambi	.10
310	Ben Grieve	.25
311	Ramon Hernandez	.10
312	Tim Hudson	.40
313	John Jaha	.10
314	Doug Jones	.10
315	Omar Olivares	.10
316	Mike Oquist	.10
317	Matt Stairs	.10
318	Miguel Tejada	.10
319	Randy Velarde	.10
320	Bobby Abreu	.10
321	Marlon Anderson	.10
322	Alex Arias	.10
323	Rico Brogna	.10
324	Paul Byrd	.10
325	Ron Gant	.10
326	Doug Glanville	.10
327	Wayne Gomes	.10
328	Mike Lieberthal	.10
329	Robert Person	.10
330	Desi Relaford	.10
331	Scott Rolen	.75
331b	Scott Rolen	.75
332	Curt Schilling	.20
332b	Curt Schilling	.20
333	Kris Benson	.10
334	Adrian Brown	.10
335	Brant Brown	.10
336	Brian Giles	.10
337	Chad Hermansen	.10
338	Jason Kendall	.20
339	Al Martin	.10
340	Pat Meares	.10
341	Warren Morris	.10
341b	Warren Morris	.10
342	Todd Ritchie	.10
343	Jason Schmidt	.10
344	Ed Sprague	.10
345	Mike Williams	.10
346	Kevin Young	.10
347	Rick Ankiel	2.50
348	Ricky Bottalico	.10
349	Kent Bottenfield	.10
350	Darren Bragg	.10
351	Eric Davis	.20
352	J.D. Drew	.25
352b	J.D. Drew	.25
353	Adam Kennedy	.10
354	Ray Lankford	.10
355	Joe McEwing	.10
356	Mark McGwire	3.00
356b	Mark McGwire	3.00
357	Matt Morris	.10
358	Darren Oliver	.10
359	Edgar Renteria	.10
360	Fernando Tatis	.25
361	Andy Ashby	.10
362	Ben Davis	.10
363	Tony Gwynn	1.50
363b	Tony Gwynn	1.50
364	Sterling Hitchcock	.10
365	Trevor Hoffman	.10
366	Damian Jackson	.10
367	Wally Joyner	.10
368	Dave Magadan	.10
369	Gary Matthews Jr.	.10
370	Phil Nevin	.10
371	Eric Owens	.10
372	Ruben Rivera	.10
373	Reggie Sanders	.10
373b	Reggie Sanders	.10
374	Quilvio Veras	.10
375	Rich Aurilia	.10
376	Marvin Benard	.10
377	Barry Bonds	.75
377b	Barry Bonds	.75
378	Ellis Burks	.10
379	Shawn Estes	.10
380	Livan Hernandez	.10
381	Jeff Kent	.10
381b	Jeff Kent	.10
382	Brent Mayne	.10
383	Bill Mueller	.10
384	Calvin Murray	.10
385	Robb Nen	.10
386	Russ Ortiz	.10
387	Kirk Rueter	.10
388	J.T. Snow	.10
389	David Bell	.10
390	Jay Buhner	.20
391	Russ Davis	.10
392	Freddy Garcia	.25
392b	Freddy Garcia	.25
393	Ken Griffey Jr.	3.00
393b	Ken Griffey Jr.	3.00
394	Carlos Guillen	.10
395	John Halama	.10
396	Brian Hunter	.10
397	Ryan Jackson	.10
398	Edgar Martinez	.10
399	Gil Meche	.10
400	Jose Mesa	.10
401	Jamie Moyer	.10
402	Alex Rodriguez	2.50
402b	Alex Rodriguez	2.50
403	Dan Wilson	.10
404	Wilson Alvarez	.10
405	Rolando Arrojo	.10
406	Wade Boggs	.25
406b	Wade Boggs	.25
407	Miguel Cairo	.10
408	Jose Canseco	.75
408b	Jose Canseco	.75
409	John Flaherty	.10
410	Jose Guillen	.10
411	Roberto Hernandez	.10
412	Terrell Lowery	.10
413	Dave Martinez	.10
414	Quinton McCracken	.10
415	Fred McGriff	.25
415b	Fred McGriff	.25
416	Ryan Rupe	.10
417	Kevin Stocker	.10
418	Bubba Trammell	.10
419	Royce Clayton	.10
420	Juan Gonzalez	.75
420b	Juan Gonzalez	.75
421	Tom Goodwin	.10
422	Rusty Greer	.10
423	Rick Helling	.10
424	Roberto Kelly	.10
425	Ruben Mateo	.10
426	Mark McLemore	.10
427	Mike Morgan	.10
428	Rafael Palmeiro	.40
429	Ivan Rodriguez	.75
429b	Ivan Rodriguez	.75
430	Aaron Sele	.10
431	Lee Stevens	.10
432	John Wetteland	.10
433	Todd Zeile	.10
434	Jeff Zimmerman	.10
435	Tony Batista	.10
436	Casey Blake	.10
437	Homer Bush	.10
438	Chris Carpenter	.10
439	Jose Cruz Jr.	.10
440	Carlos Delgado	.50
440b	Carlos Delgado	.50
441	Tony Fernandez	.10
442	Darrin Fletcher	.10
443	Alex Gonzalez	.10
444	Shawn Green	.50
444b	Shawn Green	.50
445	Roy Halladay	.10
446	Billy Koch	.10
447	David Segui	.10
448	Shannon Stewart	.10
449	David Wells	.10
450	Vernon Wells	.10

2000 Pacific Copper

Coppers are a parallel set to the 500-card base set and are identical to the base cards besides the copper foil stamping. Inserted exclusively in hobby packs Coppers are limited to 99 serial numbered sets.

	MT
Common Copper:	5.00
Stars:	15x to 25x
Yng. Stars & RCs:	8x to 15x
Production 99 sets	

2000 Pacific Platinum Blue

A parallel to the 500-card base set these have identical photos as the regular cards besides platinum blue foil stamping. A total of 75 serial numbered sets were produced.

	MT
Common Player:	8.00
Stars:	20x to 30x
Yng Stars & RCs:	10x to 20x
Production 75 sets	

2000 Pacific Premiere Date

A parallel to the 500-card base set these are sequentially numbered to 37 sets.

	MT
Common Player:	15.00
Stars:	25x to 50x
Yng Stars & RCs:	20x to 40x
Production 37 sets	

2000 Pacific Cramer's Choice Awards

This die-cut set is shaped in a trophy-like design on a holographic silver foil design. Cramer's Choice are seeded 1:721 packs.

		MT
Complete Set (10):		575.00
Common Player:		25.00
Inserted 1:721		
1	Chipper Jones	50.00
2	Cal Ripken Jr.	60.00
3	Nomar Garciaparra	60.00
4	Sammy Sosa	60.00
5	Mike Piazza	60.00
6	Derek Jeter	60.00
7	Mark McGwire	100.00
8	Tony Gwynn	50.00
9	Ken Griffey Jr.	100.00
10	Alex Rodriguez	75.00

2000 Pacific Diamond Leaders

Designed on a horizontal format each card features three statistical leaders from the 1999 season for each respective team. Card fronts have gold holofoil stamping while card backs give statistical leaders for eight categories for the featured team. These were seeded 2:25 packs.

		MT
Complete Set (30):		60.00
Common Player:		1.00
Inserted 2:25		
1	Anaheim Angels (Garret Anderson, Chuck Finley, Troy Percival, Mo Vaughn)	2.00
2	Baltimore Orioles (Albert Belle, Mike Mussina, B.J. Surhoff)	2.00
3	Boston Red Sox (Nomar Garciaparra, Pedro J. Martinez, Troy O'Leary)	6.00
4	Chicago White Sox (Ray Durham, Magglio Ordonez, Frank Thomas)	2.50
5	Cleveland Indians (Bartolo Colon, Manny Ramirez, Omar Vizquel)	2.50
6	Detroit Tigers (Deivi Cruz, Dave Mlicki, David Palmer)	1.00
7	Kansas City Royals (Johnny Damon, Jermaine Dye, Jose Rosado, Mike Sweeney)	1.00
8	Minnesota Twins (Corey Koskie, Eric Milton, Brad Radke)	1.00
9	New York Yankees (Orlando Hernandez, Derek Jeter, Mariano Rivera, Bernie Williams)	6.00
10	Oakland Athletics (Jeremy Giambi, Tim Hudson, Matt Stairs)	1.00
11	Seattle Mariners (Freddy Garcia, Ken Griffey Jr., Edgar Martinez)	10.00
12	Tampa Bay Devil Rays (Jose Canseco, Roberto Hernandez, Fred McGriff)	2.00
13	Texas Rangers (Rafael Palmeiro, Ivan Rodriguez, John Wetteland)	2.50
14	Toronto Blue Jays (Carlos Delgado, Shannon Stewart, David Wells)	1.50
15	Arizona Diamondbacks (Luis Gonzalez, Randy Johnson, Matt Williams)	2.00
16	Atlanta Braves (Chipper Jones, Brian Jordan, Greg Maddux)	5.00
17	Chicago Cubs (Mark Grace, Jon Lieber, Sammy Sosa)	6.00
18	Cincinnati Reds (Sean Casey, Pete Harnisch, Greg Vaughn)	1.00
19	Colorado Rockies (Pedro Astacio, Dante Bichette, Larry Walker)	2.00
20	Florida Marlins (Luis Castillo, Alex Fernandez, Preston Wilson)	1.00
21	Houston Astros (Jeff Bagwell, Mike Hampton, Billy Wagner)	2.50
22	Los Angeles Dodgers (Kevin Brown, Mark Grudzielanek, Eric Karros)	1.00
23	Milwaukee Brewers (Jeromy Burnitz, Jeff Cirillo, Marquis Grissom, Hideo Nomo)	1.00
24	Montreal Expos (Vladimir Guerrero, Dustin Hermanson, Ugueth Urbina)	3.00
25	New York Mets (Roger Cedeno, Rickey Henderson, Mike Piazza)	6.00
26	Philadelphia Phillies (Bobby Abreu, Mike Lieberthal, Curt Schilling)	1.00
27	Pittsburgh Pirates (Brian Giles, Jason Kendall, Kevin Young)	1.00
28	St. Louis Cardinals (Kent Bottenfield, Ray Lankford, Mark McGwire)	10.00
29	San Diego Padres (Tony Gwynn, Trevor Hoffman, Reggie Sanders)	5.00
30	San Francisco Giants (Barry Bonds, Jeff Kent, Russ Ortiz)	2.50

2000 Pacific Gold Crown Die-Cuts

Printed on a 24-point stock this set features Pacific's classic crown shaped design on a dual foiled holographic gold and silver stock. These were seeded 1:25 packs.

		MT
Complete Set (36):		250.00
Common Player:		3.00
Inserted 1:25		
1	Mo Vaughn	5.00
2	Matt Williams	4.00
3	Andruw Jones	4.00
4	Chipper Jones	15.00
5	Greg Maddux	12.00
6	Cal Ripken Jr.	15.00
7	Nomar Garciaparra	15.00
8	Pedro Martinez	6.00
9	Sammy Sosa	15.00
10	Magglio Ordonez	4.00
11	Frank Thomas	6.00
12	Sean Casey	4.00
13	Roberto Alomar	5.00
14	Manny Ramirez	6.00
15	Larry Walker	5.00
16	Jeff Bagwell	6.00
17	Craig Biggio	4.00
18	Carlos Beltran	3.00
19	Vladimir Guerrero	10.00
20	Mike Piazza	15.00
21	Roger Clemens	10.00
22	Derek Jeter	15.00
23	Bernie Williams	5.00
24	Scott Rolen	6.00
25	Warren Morris	3.00
26	J.D. Drew	3.00
27	Mark McGwire	25.00
28	Tony Gwynn	12.00
29	Barry Bonds	6.00
30	Ken Griffey Jr.	25.00
31	Alex Rodriguez	20.00
32	Jose Canseco	6.00
33	Juan Gonzalez	6.00
34	Rafael Palmeiro	5.00
35	Ivan Rodriguez	6.00
36	Shawn Green	4.00

2000 Pacific Reflections

This 20-card die-cut set features a unique sunglasses-on- cap design utilizing cel technology for added effect on the sunglasses portion of the insert. The backs have a small photo of the featured player. These were seeded 1:97 packs.

		MT
Complete Set (20):		350.00
Common Player:		8.00
Inserted 1:97		
1	Andruw Jones	8.00
2	Chipper Jones	30.00
3	Cal Ripken Jr.	30.00
4	Nomar Garciaparra	30.00
5	Sammy Sosa	30.00
6	Frank Thomas	12.00
7	Manny Ramirez	12.00
8	Jeff Bagwell	12.00
9	Vladimir Guerrero	20.00
10	Mike Piazza	30.00
11	Derek Jeter	30.00
12	Bernie Williams	10.00
13	Scott Rolen	12.00
14	J.D. Drew	8.00
15	Mark McGwire	50.00
16	Tony Gwynn	25.00
17	Ken Griffey Jr.	50.00
18	Alex Rodriguez	40.00
19	Juan Gonzalez	12.00
20	Ivan Rodriguez	12.00

2000 Pacific Past & Present

Inserted exclusively in hobby packs at a rate of 1:49, these inserts have a silver prism front and a cardboard textured back. The fronts have a current photo of the player while the backs have a photo taken years before.

		MT
Complete Set (20):		240.00
Common Player:		4.00
Inserted 1:49 H		
1	Chipper Jones	20.00
2	Greg Maddux	15.00
3	Cal Ripken Jr.	20.00
4	Nomar Garciaparra	20.00
5	Pedro Martinez	8.00
6	Sammy Sosa	20.00
7	Frank Thomas	8.00
8	Manny Ramirez	8.00
9	Larry Walker	6.00
10	Jeff Bagwell	8.00
11	Mike Piazza	20.00
12	Roger Clemens	10.00
13	Derek Jeter	20.00
14	Mark McGwire	30.00
15	Tony Gwynn	15.00
16	Barry Bonds	8.00
17	Ken Griffey Jr.	30.00
18	Alex Rodriguez	25.00
19	Wade Boggs	6.00
20	Ivan Rodriguez	8.00

2000 Pacific Ornaments

This 20-card set features a number of different Christmas patterned die-cut shapes, including ornaments, wreaths and Christmas trees. Each card comes with a string intended to hang from a tree on a holographic foil design. These were seeded 2:25 packs.

		MT
Complete Set (20):		140.00
Common Player:		3.00
Inserted 2:25		
1	Mo Vaughn	4.00
2	Chipper Jones	12.00
3	Greg Maddux	10.00
4	Cal Ripken Jr.	12.00
5	Nomar Garciaparra	12.00
6	Sammy Sosa	12.00
7	Frank Thomas	5.00
8	Manny Ramirez	5.00
9	Larry Walker	4.00
10	Jeff Bagwell	5.00
11	Mike Piazza	12.00
12	Roger Clemens	8.00
13	Derek Jeter	12.00
14	Scott Rolen	5.00
15	J.D. Drew	3.00
16	Mark McGwire	20.00
17	Tony Gwynn	10.00
18	Ken Griffey Jr.	20.00
19	Alex Rodriguez	15.00
20	Ivan Rodriguez	5.00

2000 Pacific Aurora

		MT
Complete Set (151):		50.00
Common Player:		.15
Pack (10):		3.00
Wax Box (24):		65.00
1	Darin Erstad	.25
2	Troy Glaus	1.00
3	Tim Salmon	.40
4	Mo Vaughn	.75
5	Jay Bell	.15
6	Erubiel Durazo	.50
7	Luis Gonzalez	.15
8	Randy Johnson	.75
9	Matt Williams	.50
10	Tom Glavine	.40
11	Andruw Jones	.75
12	Chipper Jones	2.00
13	Brian Jordan	.15
14	Greg Maddux	2.00
15	Kevin Millwood	.25
16	Albert Belle	.75
17	Will Clark	.50
18	Mike Mussina	.75
19	Cal Ripken Jr.	3.00
20	B.J. Surhoff	.15
21	Nomar Garciaparra	2.50
22	Pedro Martinez	1.00
23	Troy O'Leary	.15
24	Wilton Veras	.40
25	Mark Grace	.40
26	Henry Rodriguez	.15
27	Sammy Sosa	2.50
28	Kerry Wood	.40
29	Ray Durham	.15
30	Paul Konerko	.25
31	Carlos Lee	.15
32	Magglio Ordonez	.40
33	Chris Singleton	.15
34	Frank Thomas	1.25
35	Mike Cameron	.15
36	Sean Casey	.40
37	Barry Larkin	.50
38	Pokey Reese	.15
39	Eddie Taubensee	.15
40	Roberto Alomar	.75
41	David Justice	.40
42	Kenny Lofton	.50
43	Manny Ramirez	1.00
44	Richie Sexson	.15
45	Jim Thome	.50
46	Omar Vizquel	.15
47	Todd Helton	.75
48	Mike Lansing	.15
49	Neifi Perez	.15
50	Ben Petrick	.15
51	Larry Walker	.75
52	Tony Clark	.40
53	Damion Easley	.15
54	Juan Encarnacion	.15
55	Juan Gonzalez	1.25
56	Dean Palmer	.15
57	Luis Castillo	.15
58	Cliff Floyd	.15
59	Alex Gonzalez	.15
60	Mike Lowell	.15
61	Preston Wilson	.15
62	Jeff Bagwell	1.00
63	Craig Biggio	.50
64	Ken Caminiti	.25
65	Jose Lima	.15
66	Billy Wagner	.15
67	Carlos Beltran	.20
68	Johnny Damon	.15
69	Jermaine Dye	.15
70	Mark Quinn	.15
71	Mike Sweeney	.15
72	Kevin Brown	.25
73	Shawn Green	.75
74	Eric Karros	.25
75	Chan Ho Park	.15
76	Gary Sheffield	.40
77	Ron Belliard	.15
78	Jeromy Burnitz	.15
79	Marquis Grissom	.15
80	Geoff Jenkins	.15
81	David Nilsson	.15
82	Ron Coomer	.15
83	Jacque Jones	.15
84	Brad Radke	.15
85	Todd Walker	.15
86	Michael Barrett	.15
87	Peter Bergeron	.15
88	Vladimir Guerrero	1.50
89	Jose Vidro	.15
90	Rondell White	.25
91	Edgardo Alfonzo	.25
92	Darryl Hamilton	.15
93	Rey Ordonez	.15
94	Mike Piazza	2.50
95	Robin Ventura	.25
96	Roger Clemens	1.50
97	Orlando Hernandez	.50
98	Derek Jeter	2.50
99	Tino Martinez	.40
100	Mariano Rivera	.25
101	Bernie Williams	.75
102	Eric Chavez	.40
103	Jason Giambi	.15
104	Ben Grieve	.40
105	Tim Hudson	.50
106	John Jaha	.15
107	Matt Stairs	.15
108	Bobby Abreu	.15
109	Doug Glanville	.15
110	Mike Lieberthal	.15
111	Scott Rolen	1.00
112	Curt Schilling	.25
113	Brian Giles	.15
114	Chad Hermansen	.15
115	Jason Kendall	.25
116	Warren Morris	.15
117	Kevin Young	.15
118	Rick Ankiel	4.00
119	J.D. Drew	.25
120	Ray Lankford	.15
121	Mark McGwire	4.00
122	Edgar Renteria	.15
123	Fernando Tatis	.25
124	Ben Davis	.15
125	Tony Gwynn	2.00
126	Trevor Hoffman	.15
127	Phil Nevin	.15
128	Barry Bonds	1.00
129	Ellis Burks	.15
130	Jeff Kent	.15
131	J.T. Snow	.15
132	Freddy Garcia	.40
133	Ken Griffey Jr.	4.00
133a	Ken Griffey Jr. Reds	10.00
134	Edgar Martinez	.15
135	Alex Rodriguez	3.00
136	Dan Wilson	.15
137	Jose Canseco	1.00
138	Roberto Hernandez	.15
139	Dave Martinez	.15
140	Fred McGriff	.40
141	Rusty Greer	.15
142	Ruben Mateo	.40
143	Rafael Palmeiro	.75
144	Ivan Rodriguez	1.00
145	Jeff Zimmerman	.15
146	Homer Bush	.15
147	Carlos Delgado	.75
148	Raul Mondesi	.40
149	Shannon Stewart	.15
150	Vernon Wells	.25

2000 Pacific Aurora Copper

	MT
Stars:	4x-8x
Yng. Stars & Rookies:	2x-4x
Production 399 sets	

2000 Pacific Aurora Silver

	MT
Stars:	6x-12x
Yng. Stars & RCs:	3x-6x
Production 199 sets	

2000 Pacific Aurora Platinum Blue

	MT
Stars:	20x-35x
Yng. Stars & RCs:	10x-20x
Production 67 sets	

2000 Pacific Aurora Pinstripes

		MT
Complete Set (50):		200.00
Common Player:		1.00
Premiere Date:		4x-8x
Production 51 sets		
4	Mo Vaughn	2.00
8	Randy Johnson	2.50
9	Matt Williams	2.50
11	Andruw Jones	2.50
12	Chipper Jones	6.00
14	Greg Maddux	6.00
19	Cal Ripken Jr.	10.00
21	Nomar Garciaparra	8.00
22	Pedro Martinez	4.00
27	Sammy Sosa	8.00
32	Magglio Ordonez	1.00
34	Frank Thomas	4.00
36	Sean Casey	1.50
37	Barry Larkin	2.00
42	Kenny Lofton	1.50
43	Manny Ramirez	3.00
45	Jim Thome	2.50
47	Todd Helton	2.00
51	Larry Walker	2.00
55	Juan Gonzalez	4.00
62	Jeff Bagwell	3.00
63	Craig Biggio	2.00
67	Carlos Beltran	2.00
73	Shawn Green	3.00
76	Gary Sheffield	1.50
78	Jeromy Burnitz	1.00
88	Vladimir Guerrero	4.00
91	Edgardo Alfonzo	2.00
94	Mike Piazza	8.00
96	Roger Clemens	5.00
97	Orlando Hernandez	1.50
98	Derek Jeter	8.00
101	Bernie Williams	2.00
102	Eric Chavez	1.00
105	Tim Hudson	1.50
111	Scott Rolen	3.00
112	Curt Schilling	1.50
113	Brian Giles	1.00
114	Rick Ankiel	10.00
121	Mark McGwire	12.00
125	Tony Gwynn	6.00
128	Barry Bonds	3.00
130	Jeff Kent	1.00
133	Ken Griffey Jr.	2.00
135	Alex Rodriguez	8.00
137	Jose Canseco	3.00
140	Fred McGriff	2.00
143	Rafael Palmeiro	2.00
144	Ivan Rodriguez	3.00
147	Carlos Delgado	2.50

2000 Pacific Aurora Pennant Fever

		MT
Complete Set (20):		60.00
Common Player:		1.00
T. Gwynn Auto./147		100.00
Inserted 4:37		
1	Andruw Jones	1.50
2	Chipper Jones	4.00
3	Greg Maddux	4.00
4	Cal Ripken Jr.	6.00
5	Nomar Garciaparra	5.00
6	Pedro Martinez	2.00
7	Sammy Sosa	5.00
8	Manny Ramirez	2.00
9	Jim Thome	1.00
10	Jeff Bagwell	2.00
11	Mike Piazza	5.00
12	Roger Clemens	3.00
13	Derek Jeter	5.00
14	Bernie Williams	1.50
15	Mark McGwire	8.00
16	Tony Gwynn	4.00
17	Ken Griffey Jr.	8.00
18	Alex Rodriguez	6.00
19	Rafael Palmeiro	1.00
20	Ivan Rodriguez	2.00

2000 Pacific Aurora Dugout View Net-Fusions

		MT
Complete Set (20):		160.00
Common Player:		4.00
Inserted 1:37		
1	Mo Vaughn	5.00
2	Chipper Jones	12.00
3	Cal Ripken Jr.	20.00
4	Nomar Garciaparra	15.00
5	Sammy Sosa	15.00
6	Manny Ramirez	6.00
7	Larry Walker	5.00
8	Juan Gonzalez	8.00
9	Jeff Bagwell	6.00
10	Craig Biggio	5.00
11	Shawn Green	4.00
12	Vladimir Guerrero	10.00
13	Mike Piazza	15.00
14	Derek Jeter	15.00
15	Scott Rolen	6.00
16	Mark McGwire	8.00
17	Tony Gwynn	12.00
18	Ken Griffey Jr.	25.00
19	Alex Rodriguez	20.00
20	Rafael Palmeiro	4.00

2000 Pacific Aurora Star Factor

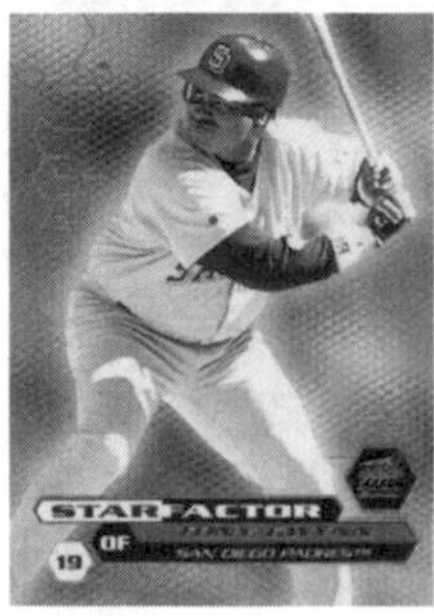

		MT
Complete Set (10):		675.00
Common Player:		25.00
Inserted 1:361		
1	Chipper Jones	60.00
2	Cal Ripken Jr.	100.00
3	Nomar Garciaparra	75.00
4	Sammy Sosa	75.00
5	Mike Piazza	75.00
6	Derek Jeter	75.00
7	Mark McGwire	120.00
8	Tony Gwynn	60.00
9	Ken Griffey Jr.	120.00
10	Alex Rodriguez	90.00

2000 Pacific Aurora At-Bat Styrotechs

		MT
Complete Set (20):		375.00
Common Player:		8.00
Production 299 sets		
1	Chipper Jones	25.00
2	Cal Ripken Jr.	40.00
3	Nomar Garciaparra	30.00
4	Sammy Sosa	30.00
5	Frank Thomas	15.00
6	Manny Ramirez	12.00
7	Larry Walker	10.00
8	Jeff Bagwell	12.00
9	Carlos Beltran	8.00
10	Vladimir Guerrero	20.00
11	Mike Piazza	30.00
12	Derek Jeter	30.00
13	Bernie Williams	10.00
14	Mark McGwire	50.00
15	Tony Gwynn	25.00
16	Barry Bonds	12.00
17	Ken Griffey Jr.	50.00
18	Alex Rodriguez	40.00
19	Jose Canseco	12.00
20	Ivan Rodriguez	12.00

2000 Pacific Crown Collection

This 300-card base set has a white bordered design with the logo, player name and team stamped in gold foil. Card backs have a small close-up photo, a brief career highlight and 1999 statistics along with career totals.

		MT
Complete Set (300):		35.00
Common Player:		.10
Pack (10):		2.50
Wax Box (36):		70.00
1	Garret Anderson	.10
2	Darin Erstad	.25
3	Ben Molina	.10
4	(Ramon Ortiz)	.10
5	Orlando Palmeiro	.10
6	Troy Percival	.10
7	Tim Salmon	.20
8	Mo Vaughn	.50
9	Checklist (Mo Vaughn)	.25
10	Jay Bell	.10
11	Omar Daal	.10
12	Erubiel Durazo	.25
13	Steve Finley	.10
14	Hanley Frias	.10
15	Luis Gonzalez	.10
16	Randy Johnson	.50
17	Matt Williams	.40
18	Checklist (Matt Williams)	.20
19	Andres Galarraga	.40
20	Tom Glavine	.20
21	Andruw Jones	.40
22	Chipper Jones	1.50
23	Brian Jordan	.10
24	Javy Lopez	.10
25	Greg Maddux	1.50
26	Kevin Millwood	.20
27	Eddie Perez	.10
28	John Smoltz	.20
29	Checklist (Chipper Jones)	.75
30	Albert Belle	.50
31	Jesse Garcia	.10
32	Jerry Hairston Jr.	.10
33	Charles Johnson	.10
34	Mike Mussina	.50
35	Sidney Ponson	.10
36	Cal Ripken Jr.	2.00
37	B.J. Surhoff	.10
38	Checklist (Cal Ripken Jr.)	1.00
39	Nomar Garciaparra	2.00
40	Pedro Martinez	.75
41	Ramon Martinez	.10
42	Trot Nixon	.10
43	Jose Offerman	.10
44	Troy O'Leary	.10
45	John Valentin	.10
46	Wilton Veras	.10
47	Checklist (Nomar Garciaparra)	1.00
48	Mark Grace	.20
49	Felix Heredia	.10
50	Jose Molina	.10
51	Jose Nieves	.10
52	Henry Rodriguez	.10
53	Sammy Sosa	2.00
54	Kerry Wood	.40
55	Checklist (Sammy Sosa)	1.00
56	Mike Caruso	.10
57	Carlos Castillo	.10
58	Jason Dellaero	.10
59	Carlos Lee	.10
60	Magglio Ordonez	.25
61	Jesus Pena	.10
62	Liu Rodriguez	.10
63	Frank Thomas	1.00
64	Checklist (Magglio Ordonez)	.15
65	Aaron Boone	.10
66	Mike Cameron	.10
67	Sean Casey	.40
68	Juan Guzman	.10
69	Barry Larkin	.40
70	Pokey Reese	.10
71	Eddie Taubensee	.10
72	Greg Vaughn	.25
73	Checklist (Sean Casey)	.20
74	Roberto Alomar	.25
75	Sandy Alomar Jr.	.15
76	Bartolo Colon	.10
77	Jacob Cruz	.10
78	Einar Diaz	.10
79	David Justice	.20
80	Kenny Lofton	.50
81	Manny Ramirez	.75
82	Richie Sexson	.10
83	Jim Thome	.40
84	Omar Vizquel	.10
85	Enrique Wilson	.10
86	Checklist (Manny Ramirez)	.40
87	Pedro Astacio	.10
88	Henry Blanco	.10
89	Vinny Castilla	.20
90	Edgard Clemente	.10
91	Todd Helton	.75
92	Neifi Perez	.10
93	Terry Shumpert	.10
94	*Juan Sosa*	.40
95	Larry Walker	.50
96	Checklist (Vinny Castilla)	.10
97	Tony Clark	.25
98	Deivi Cruz	.10
99	Damion Easley	.10
100	Juan Encarnacion	.10
101	Karim Garcia	.10
102	Luis Garcia	.10
103	Juan Gonzalez	1.00
104	Jose Macias	.10
105	Dean Palmer	.10
106	Checklist (Juan Encarnacion)	.10
107	Antonio Alfonseca	.10
108	Armando Almanza	.10
109	Bruce Aven	.10
110	Luis Castillo	.10
111	Ramon Castro	.10
112	Alex Fernandez	.10
113	Cliff Floyd	.10
114	Alex Gonzalez	.10
115	*Michael Tejera*	.10
116	Preston Wilson	.10
117	Checklist (Luis Castillo)	.10
118	Jeff Bagwell	.75
119	Craig Biggio	.50
120	Jose Cabrera	.10
121	Tony Eusebio	.10
122	Carl Everett	.10
123	Ricky Gutierrez	.10
124	Mike Hampton	.10
125	Richard Hidalgo	.10
126	Jose Lima	.10
127	Billy Wagner	.10
128	Checklist (Jeff Bagwell)	.40
129	Carlos Beltran	.20
130	Johnny Damon	.10
131	Jermaine Dye	.10
132	Carlos Febles	.10
133	Jeremy Giambi	.10
134	Jose Rosado	.10
135	Rey Sanchez	.10
136	Jose Santiago	.10
137	Checklist (Carlos Beltran)	.10
138	Kevin Brown	.20
139	Craig Counsell	.10
140	Shawn Green	.40
141	Eric Karros	.20
142	Angel Pena	.10
143	Gary Sheffield	.25
144	Ismael Valdes	.10
145	Jose Vizcaino	.10
146	Devon White	.10
147	Checklist (Eric Karros)	.10
148	Ron Belliard	.10
149	Jeromy Burnitz	.10
150	Jeff Cirillo	.10
151	Marquis Grissom	.10
152	Geoff Jenkins	.10
153	Dave Nilsson	.10
154	Rafael Roque	.10
155	Jose Valentin	.10
156	Fernando Vina	.10
157	Jeromy Burnitz	.10
158	Chad Allen	.10
159	Ron Coomer	.10
160	Eddie Guardado	.10
161	Cristian Guzman	.10
162	Jacque Jones	.10
163	Javier Valentin	.10
164	Todd Walker	.10
165	Checklist (Ron Coomer)	.10
166	Michael Barrett	.10
167	Miguel Batista	.10
168	Vladimir Guerrero	1.25
169	Wilton Guerrero	.10
170	Fernando Seguignol	.10
171	Ugueth Urbina	.10
172	Javier Vazquez	.10
173	Jose Vidro	.10
174	Rondell White	.20
175	Checklist (Vladimir Guerrero)	.60
176	Edgardo Alfonzo	.25
177	Armando Benitez	.10

178	Roger Cedeno	.10
179	Octavio Dotel	.10
180	Melvin Mora	.10
181	Rey Ordonez	.10
182	Mike Piazza	2.00
183	Jorge Toca	.10
184	Robin Ventura	.25
185	Checklist (Edgardo Alfonzo)	.15
186	Roger Clemens	1.00
187	David Cone	.20
188	Orlando Hernandez	.25
189	Derek Jeter	2.00
190	Ricky Ledee	.10
191	Tino Martinez	.25
192	Ramiro Mendoza	.10
193	Jorge Posada	.20
194	Mariano Rivera	.25
195	Alfonso Soriano	.75
196	Bernie Williams	.50
197	Checklist (Derek Jeter)	1.00
198	Eric Chavez	.10
199	Jason Giambi	.10
200	Ben Grieve	.25
201	Ramon Hernandez	.10
202	Tim Hudson	.40
203	John Jaha	.10
204	Omar Olivares	.10
205	Olmedo Saenz	.10
206	Matt Stairs	.10
207	Miguel Tejada	.10
208	Checklist (Tim Hudson)	.25
209	Rico Brogna	.10
210	Bobby Abreu	.10
211	Marlon Anderson	.10
212	Alex Arias	.10
213	Doug Glanville	.10
214	Robert Person	.10
215	Scott Rolen	.75
216	Curt Schilling	.20
217	Checklist (Scott Rolen)	.40
218	Francisco Cordova	.10
219	Brian Giles	.10
220	Jason Kendall	.20
221	Warren Morris	.10
222	Abraham Nunez	.10
223	Aramis Ramirez	.10
224	Jose Silva	.10
225	Kevin Young	.10
226	Checklist (Brian Giles)	.10
227	Rick Ankiel	5.00
228	Ricky Bottalico	.10
229	J.D. Drew	.25
230	Ray Lankford	.10
231	Mark McGwire	3.00
232	Eduardo Perez	.10
233	Placido Polanco	.10
234	Edgar Renteria	.10
235	Fernando Tatis	.10
236	Checklist (Mark McGwire)	1.50
237	Carlos Almanzar	.10
238	Wiki Gonzalez	.10
239	Tony Gwynn	1.50
240	Trevor Hoffman	.10
241	Damian Jackson	.10
242	Wally Joyner	.10
243	Ruben Rivera	.10
244	Reggie Sanders	.10
245	Quilvio Veras	.10
246	Checklist (Tony Gwynn)	.75
247	Rich Aurilia	.10
248	Marvin Benard	.10
249	Barry Bonds	.75
250	Ellis Burks	.10
251	Miguel Del Toro	.10
252	Edwards Guzman	.10
253	Livan Hernandez	.10
254	Jeff Kent	.10
255	Russ Ortiz	.10
256	Armando Rios	.10
257	Checklist (Barry Bonds)	.40
258	Rafael Bournigal	.10
259	Freddy Garcia	.50
260	Ken Griffey Jr.	3.00
261	Carlos Guillen	.10
262	Raul Ibanez	.10
263	Edgar Martinez	.20
264	Jose Mesa	.10
265	Jamie Moyer	.10
266	John Olerud	.25
267	Jose Paniagua	.10
268	Alex Rodriguez	2.50
269	Checklist (Alex Rodriguez)	1.25
270	Wilson Alvarez	.10
271	Rolando Arrojo	.10
272	Wade Boggs	.40
273	Miguel Cairo	.10
274	Jose Canseco	.75
275	Jose Guillen	.10
276	Roberto Hernandez	.10
277	Albie Lopez	.10
278	Fred McGriff	.25
279	Esteban Yan	.10
280	Checklist (Jose Canseco)	.40
281	Rusty Greer	.10
282	Roberto Kelly	.10
283	Esteban Loaiza	.10
284	Ruben Mateo	.25
285	Rafael Palmeiro	.50
286	Ivan Rodriguez	.75
287	Aaron Sele	.10
288	John Wetteland	.10
289	Checklist (Ivan Rodriguez)	.40
290	Tony Batista	.10
291	Jose Cruz Jr.	.10
292	Carlos Delgado	.50
293	Kelvim Escobar	.10
294	Tony Fernandez	.10
295	Billy Koch	.10
296	Raul Mondesi	.20
297	Willis Otanez	.10
298	David Segui	.10
299	David Wells	.10
300	Checklist (Carlos Delgado)	.25

2000 Pacific Crown Collection Holographic Purple

A parallel to the 300-card base set, holographic purple stamping replaces the gold foil to differentiate these from the base cards. These are limited to 199 numbered sets.

	MT
Stars:	10x-15x
Yng Stars:	5x-10x
Production 199 sets	

2000 Pacific Crown Collection Platinum Blue

A parallel to the 300-card base set, these have blue foil stamping in place of gold foil and are limited to 67 serial numbered sets.

	MT
Stars:	20x-40x
Yng Stars & RCs:	15x-25x
Production 67 sets	

2000 Pacific Crown Coll. Latinos of the Major Leagues

This set salutes major leagues who have a latino heritage. These were seeded 2:37 packs and have a horizontal format with two images of the featured player on the card front.

		MT
Complete Set (36):		80.00
Common Player:		1.50
Inserted 2:37		
Parallel:		2-3X
Production 99 sets		
1	Erubiel Durazo	1.50
2	Luis Gonzalez	1.50
3	Andruw Jones	3.00
4	Nomar Garciaparra	10.00
5	Pedro Martinez	4.00
6	Sammy Sosa	10.00
7	Carlos Lee	1.50
8	Magglio Ordonez	2.50
9	Roberto Alomar	3.00
10	Manny Ramirez	4.00
11	Omar Vizquel	1.50
12	Vinny Castilla	1.50
13	Juan Gonzalez	4.00
14	Luis Castillo	1.50
15	Jose Lima	1.50
16	Carlos Beltran	1.50
17	Vladimir Guerrero	5.00
18	Edgardo Alfonzo	1.50
19	Roger Cedeno	1.50
20	Rey Ordonez	1.50
21	Orlando Hernandez	1.50
22	Tino Martinez	1.50
23	Mariano Rivera	1.50
24	Bernie Williams	3.00
25	Miguel Tejada	1.50
26	Bobby Abreu	1.50
27	Fernando Tatis	1.50
28	Freddy Garcia	1.50
29	Edgar Martinez	1.50
30	Alex Rodriguez	12.00
31	Jose Canseco	2.50
32	Ruben Mateo	1.50
33	Rafael Palmeiro	2.50
34	Ivan Rodriguez	4.00
35	Carlos Delgado	4.00
36	Raul Mondesi	2.00

Player names in *Italic* type indicate a rookie card.

2000 Pacific Crown Collection Moment of Truth

These inserts feature gold foil stamping and a shadow image of the player in the background of the player photo. These were inserted 1:37 packs.

		MT
Complete Set (30):		300.00
Common Player:		3.00
Inserted 1:37		
1	Mo Vaughn	6.00
2	Chipper Jones	18.00
3	Greg Maddux	18.00
4	Albert Belle	6.00
5	Cal Ripken Jr.	20.00
6	Nomar Garciaparra	20.00
7	Pedro Martinez	8.00
8	Sammy Sosa	20.00
9	Frank Thomas	8.00
10	Barry Larkin	5.00
11	Kenny Lofton	5.00
12	Manny Ramirez	8.00
13	Larry Walker	6.00
14	Juan Gonzalez	8.00
15	Jeff Bagwell	8.00
16	Craig Biggio	5.00
17	Carlos Beltran	3.00
18	Vladimir Guerrero	15.00
19	Mike Piazza	20.00
20	Roger Clemens	12.00
21	Derek Jeter	20.00
22	Bernie Williams	6.00
23	Mark McGwire	35.00
24	Tony Gwynn	18.00
25	Barry Bonds	8.00
26	Ken Griffey Jr.	35.00
27	Alex Rodriguez	25.00
28	Rafael Palmeiro	6.00
29	Ivan Rodriguez	8.00
30	Carlos Delgado	6.00

2000 Pacific Crown Collection Timber 2000

These 1:73 pack inserts have a horizontal format highlighted by gold foil stamping. A black bat is in the background of the player image with 2000 written in the bat head.

		MT
Complete Set (20):		275.00
Common Player:		5.00
Inserted 1:73		
1	Chipper Jones	25.00

2	Nomar Garciaparra	30.00
3	Sammy Sosa	30.00
4	Magglio Ordonez	5.00
5	Manny Ramirez	12.00
6	Vinny Castilla	5.00
7	Juan Gonzalez	12.00
8	Jeff Bagwell	12.00
9	Shawn Green	8.00
10	Vladimir Guerrero	20.00
11	Mike Piazza	25.00
12	Derek Jeter	30.00
13	Bernie Williams	10.00
14	Mark McGwire	50.00
15	Ken Griffey Jr.	50.00
16	Alex Rodriguez	40.00
17	Jose Canseco	12.00
18	Rafael Palmeiro	8.00
19	Ivan Rodriguez	12.00
20	Carlos Delgado	8.00

2000 Pacific Crown Collection In The Cage

These inserts have a die-cut design around an image of a batting cage, with net-fusion technology used to mimic the netting in a batting cage. These were inserted 1:145 packs.

		MT
Complete Set (20):		600.00
Common Player:		10.00
Inserted 1:145		
1	Mo Vaughn	15.00
2	Chipper Jones	40.00
3	Cal Ripken Jr.	50.00
4	Nomar Garciaparra	50.00
5	Sammy Sosa	50.00
6	Frank Thomas	20.00
7	Roberto Alomar	15.00
8	Manny Ramirez	20.00
9	Larry Walker	15.00
10	Jeff Bagwell	20.00
11	Vladimir Guerrero	30.00
12	Mike Piazza	50.00
13	Derek Jeter	50.00
14	Bernie Williams	15.00
15	Mark McGwire	80.00
16	Tony Gwynn	40.00
17	Ken Griffey Jr.	80.00
18	Alex Rodriguez	50.00
19	Rafael Palmeiro	15.00
20	Ivan Rodriguez	20.00

2000 Pacific Crown Collection Pacific Cup

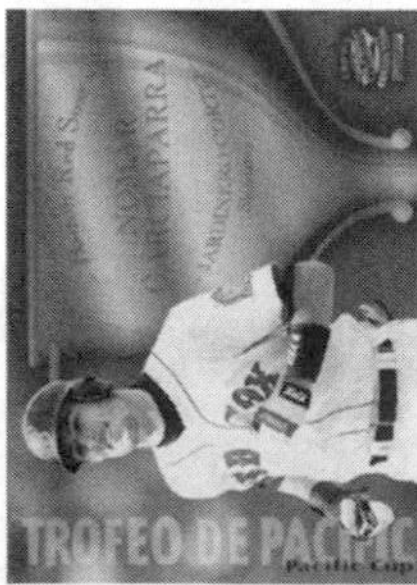

Pacific Cup's have a horizontal format with gold foil stamping and an image of a trophy cup beside the player photo. These were inserted 1:721 packs.

		MT
Complete Set (10):		650.00
Common Player:		25.00
Inserted 1:721		
1	Cal Ripken Jr.	80.00
2	Nomar Garciaparra	80.00
3	Pedro Martinez	30.00
4	Sammy Sosa	80.00
5	Vladimir Guerrero	50.00
6	Derek Jeter	80.00
7	Mark McGwire	120.00
8	Tony Gwynn	60.00
9	Ken Griffey Jr.	120.00
10	Alex Rodriguez	90.00

2000 Pacific Crown Royale

The Crown Royale 144-card base set has a horizontal format die-cut around a crown design at the top. The cards are double foiled with gold and silver foil etching.

		MT
Complete Set (144):		150.00
Common Player:		.25
Common SP:		1.50
Pack (6):		5.00
Box (24):		110.00
1	Darin Erstad	.50
2	Troy Glaus	2.00
3	Adam Kennedy SP	2.00
4	*Derrick Turnbow SP*	1.50
5	Mo Vaughn	1.50
6	Erubiel Durazo	.50
7	Steve Finley	.25
8	Randy Johnson	2.00
9	Travis Lee	.25
10	Matt Williams	.75
11	Rafael Furcal SP	3.00
12	Andres Galarraga	1.00
13	Andruw Jones	.75
14	Chipper Jones	4.00
15	Javy Lopez	.25
16	Greg Maddux	4.00
17	Albert Belle	1.50
18	Will Clark	1.00
19	Mike Mussina	1.00
20	Cal Ripken Jr.	6.00
21	Carl Everett	.25
22	Nomar Garciaparra	5.00
23	Pedro Martinez	2.00
24	Jason Varitek	.25
25	*Scott Downs SP*	2.00
26	Mark Grace	.50
27	Sammy Sosa	5.00
28	Kerry Wood	.75
29	Ray Durham	.25
30	Paul Konerko	.25
31	Carlos Lee	.25
32	Magglio Ordonez	.50
33	Frank Thomas	3.00
34	Rob Bell SP	1.50
35	Sean Casey	.25
36	Ken Griffey Jr.	8.00
37	Barry Larkin	1.00
38	Pokey Reese	.25
39	Roberto Alomar	1.50
40	David Justice	.50
41	Kenny Lofton	1.00
42	Manny Ramirez	2.00
43	Richie Sexson	.25
44	Jim Thome	1.00
45	Rolando Arrojo	.25
46	Jeff Cirillo	.25
47	Tom Goodwin	.25
48	Todd Helton	2.00
49	Larry Walker	1.00
50	Tony Clark	.25
51	Juan Encarnacion	.50
52	Juan Gonzalez	2.00
53	Hideo Nomo	.25
54	Dean Palmer	.25
55	Cliff Floyd	.25
56	Alex Gonzalez	.25
57	Mike Lowell	.25
58	Brad Penny SP	1.50
59	Preston Wilson	.25
60	Moises Alou	.25
61	Jeff Bagwell	2.00
62	Craig Biggio	.75
63	Roger Cedeno	.25
64	Julio Lugo SP	1.50
65	Carlos Beltran	.25
66	Johnny Damon	.25
67	Jermaine Dye	.25
68	Carlos Febles	.25
69	Mark Quinn SP	1.50
70	Kevin Brown	.50
71	Shawn Green	1.50
72	Eric Karros	.50
73	Gary Sheffield	.75
74	Kevin Barker SP	2.00
75	Ron Belliard	.25
76	Jeromy Burnitz	.25
77	Geoff Jenkins	.50
78	Jacque Jones	.25
79	Corey Koskie	.25
80	Matt LeCroy SP	1.50
81	Brad Radke	.25
82	Peter Bergeron SP	2.00
83	Matt Blank SP	1.50
84	Vladimir Guerrero	4.00
85	Hideki Irabu	.25
86	Rondell White	.50
87	Edgardo Alfonzo	.50
88	Mike Hampton	.25
89	Rickey Henderson	.50
90	Rey Ordonez	.25
91	Jay Payton SP	1.50
92	Mike Piazza	5.00
93	Roger Clemens	2.50
94	Orlando Hernandez	.75
95	Derek Jeter	5.00
96	Tino Martinez	.50
97	Alfonso Soriano SP	2.50
98	Bernie Williams	1.50
99	Eric Chavez	.50
100	Jason Giambi	.50
101	Ben Grieve	.50
102	Tim Hudson	.50
103	Terrence Long SP	1.50
104	Mark Mulder SP	1.50
105	Adam Piatt SP	1.50
106	Bobby Abreu	.25
107	Doug Glanville	.25
108	Mike Lieberthal	.25
109	Scott Rolen	1.50
110	Brian Giles	.25
111	Chad Hermansen SP	1.50
112	Jason Kendall	.50
113	Warren Morris	.25
114	Rick Ankiel SP	6.00
115	*Justin Brunette SP*	1.50
116	J.D. Drew	.40
117	Mark McGwire	8.00
118	Fernando Tatis	.50
119	Wiki Gonzalez SP	1.50
120	Tony Gwynn	3.00
121	Trevor Hoffman	.25
122	Ryan Klesko	.25
123	Barry Bonds	2.50
124	Ellis Burks	.25
125	Jeff Kent	.25
126	Calvin Murray SP	1.50
127	J.T. Snow	.25
128	Freddy Garcia	.25
129	John Olerud	.50
130	Alex Rodriguez	6.00
131	*Kazuhiro Sasaki SP*	8.00
132	Jose Canseco	1.00
133	Vinny Castilla	.25
134	Fred McGriff	.50
135	Greg Vaughn	.25
136	Gabe Kapler	.50
137	*Mike Lamb SP*	2.00
138	Ruben Mateo SP	1.50
139	Rafael Palmeiro	1.00
140	Ivan Rodriguez	2.00
141	Tony Batista	.25
142	Carlos Delgado	1.50
143	Raul Mondesi	.50
144	Shannon Stewart	.25

2000 Pacific Crown Royale Platinum Blue

A parallel to the 144-card base set these have blue foil in place of gold foil to differentiate them from regular cards. They are limited to 75 serial numbered sets.

	MT
Stars:	6-10X
Production 75 sets	

2000 Pacific Crown Royale Limited Series

A parallel to the 144-card base set, silver foil replaces gold foil to differentiate these from regular cards. They are also limited to 144 serial numbered sets.

	MT
Stars:	4-6X
Production 144 sets	

2000 Pacific Crown Royale Premiere Date

A parallel to the 144-card base set these are found exclusively in hobby packs and are limited to 144 serial numbered sets.

	MT
Stars:	3-6X
Production 121 sets	

2000 Pacific Crown Royale Red

Identical in design to the base set, these have red foil instead of gold and are the base cards in retail packaging.

	MT
All singles:	1X
base cards in retail packs	

2000 Pacific Crown Royale Feature Attractions

This 25-card set has a horizontal format with the

featured players achievements on a billboard in the background. These were seeded 1 per hobby pack and one per two retail packs. An Exclusive Showing parallel is also randomly inserted and is limited to 20 serial numbered sets.

		MT
Complete Set (25):		25.00
Common Player:		.25
Inserted 1:1		
Exclusive Showing:		30-50X
Production 20 sets		
1	Erubiel Durazo	.25
2	Chipper Jones	1.50
3	Greg Maddux	1.50
4	Cal Ripken Jr.	2.50
5	Nomar Garciaparra	2.00
6	Pedro Martinez	.75
7	Sammy Sosa	2.00
8	Frank Thomas	1.00
9	Ken Griffey Jr.	3.00
10	Manny Ramirez	1.00
11	Larry Walker	.40
12	Juan Gonzalez	.75
13	Jeff Bagwell	.75
14	Carlos Beltran	.25
15	Shawn Green	.50
16	Vladimir Guerrero	1.50
17	Mike Piazza	2.00
18	Roger Clemens	1.00
19	Derek Jeter	2.00
20	Ben Grieve	.25
21	Rick Ankiel	2.00
22	Mark McGwire	3.00
23	Tony Gwynn	1.50
24	Alex Rodriguez	2.00
25	Ivan Rodriguez	.75

2000 Pacific Crown Royale Final Numbers

These inserts are found one per hobby pack and one per two retail packs. The logo, player name and team are stamped in silver foil and has "Final Numbers" written down the right hand portion of the front. A Holographic parallel limited to 10 serial numbered sets is also randomly inserted.

		MT
Complete Set (25):		25.00
Common Player:		.25
Inserted 1:1		
1	Randy Johnson	.75
2	Andruw Jones	.50
3	Chipper Jones	1.50
4	Cal Ripken Jr.	2.50
5	Nomar Garciaparra	2.00
6	Pedro Martinez	.75
7	Sammy Sosa	2.00
8	Ken Griffey Jr.	3.00
9	Sean Casey	.25
10	Manny Ramirez	1.00
11	Larry Walker	.50
12	Jeff Bagwell	.75
13	Craig Biggio	.40
14	Shawn Green	.50
15	Vladimir Guerrero	1.50
16	Mike Piazza	2.00
17	Derek Jeter	2.00
18	Bernie Williams	.50
19	Scott Rolen	.50
20	Mark McGwire	3.00
21	Tony Gwynn	1.00
22	Barry Bonds	1.00
23	Alex Rodriguez	2.50
24	Jose Canseco	.50
25	Ivan Rodriguez	.75

2000 Pacific Crown Royale Team Card-Supials

These inserts feature a superstar's regular sized card paired with a top prospect teammate's smaller card. The standard sized card has a horizontal format with gold foil stamping, the small prospect card has gold foil stamping on a vertical format. These were seeded 2:25 packs.

		MT
Complete Set (20):		120.00
Common Player:		2.50
Inserted 2:25		
1	Randy Johnson, Erubiel Durazo	4.00
2	Chipper Jones, Andruw Jones	8.00
3	Cal Ripken Jr., Matt Riley	12.00
4	Nomar Garciaparra, Jason Varitek	10.00
5	Sammy Sosa, Kerry Wood	10.00
6	Frank Thomas, Magglio Ordonez	5.00
7	Ken Griffey Jr., Sean Casey	15.00
8	Manny Ramirez, Richie Sexson	5.00
9	Larry Walker, Ben Petrick	2.50
10	Juan Gonzalez, Juan Encarnacion	4.00
11	Jeff Bagwell, Lance Berkman	4.00
12	Shawn Green, Eric Gagne	3.00
13	Vladimir Guerrero, Peter Bergeron	8.00
14	Mike Piazza, Edgardo Alfonzo	10.00
15	Derek Jeter, Alfonso Soriano	10.00
16	Scott Rolen, Bobby Abreu	3.00
17	Mark McGwire, Rick Ankiel	20.00
18	Tony Gwynn, Ben Davis	6.00
19	Alex Rodriguez, Freddy Garcia	12.00
20	Ivan Rodriguez, Ruben Mateo	4.00

2000 Pacific Crown Royale Proofs

Proofs are the actual printer's proofs used to produce this set. The inserts are transparent and have a coal black tint. These were inserted 1:25 packs. A parallel is also randomly inserted and is limited to 50 serial numbered sets.

		MT
Complete Set (36):		325.00
Common Player:		4.00
Inserted 1:25		
Proofs:		2-3X
1	Erubiel Durazo	4.00
2	Randy Johnson	8.00
3	Chipper Jones	15.00
4	Greg Maddux	15.00
5	Cal Ripken Jr.	25.00
6	Nomar Garciaparra	20.00
7	Pedro Martinez	8.00
8	Sammy Sosa	20.00
9	Frank Thomas	10.00
10	Sean Casey	4.00
11	Ken Griffey Jr.	30.00
12	Manny Ramirez	10.00
13	Jim Thome	5.00
14	Larry Walker	5.00
15	Juan Gonzalez	8.00
16	Jeff Bagwell	8.00
17	Craig Biggio	5.00
18	Carlos Beltran	4.00
19	Shawn Green	6.00
20	Vladimir Guerrero	12.00
21	Edgardo Alfonzo	4.00
22	Mike Piazza	20.00
23	Roger Clemens	10.00
24	Derek Jeter	20.00
25	Alfonso Soriano	6.00
26	Bernie Williams	6.00
27	Ben Grieve	5.00
28	Rick Ankiel	15.00
29	Mark McGwire	30.00
30	Tony Gwynn	10.00
31	Barry Bonds	10.00
32	Alex Rodriguez	25.00
33	Jose Canseco	6.00
34	Vinny Castilla	4.00
35	Ivan Rodriguez	8.00
36	Rafael Palmeiro	6.00

2000 Pacific Crown Royale Sweet Spot Signatures

These die-cut autographed cards are done on a horizontal format with an image of a baseball beside the player photo. The signature is on the "sweet spot" of the baseball image. Red foil stamping is used on the seams of the baseball and the player name. No insertion ratio was announced.

		MT
Common Player:		15.00
1	Adam Kennedy	15.00
2	Trot Nixon	15.00
3	Magglio Ordonez	25.00
4	Sean Casey	25.00
5	Travis Dawkins	15.00
6	Todd Helton	35.00
7	Ben Petrick	15.00
8	Jeff Weaver	15.00
9	Preston Wilson	20.00
10	Lance Berkman	20.00
11	Roger Cedeno	20.00
12	Eric Gagne	15.00
13	Kevin Barker	15.00
14	Kyle Peterson	15.00
15	Tony Armas, Jr.	20.00
16	Peter Bergeron	20.00
17	Alfonso Soriano	25.00
18	Ben Grieve	25.00
19	Ramon Hernandez	15.00
20	Brian Giles	20.00
21	Chad Hermansen	15.00
22	Warren Morris	15.00
23	Ben Davis	15.00
24	Rick Ankiel	75.00
25	Chad Hutchinson	15.00
26	Freddy Garcia	20.00
27	Gabe Kapler	25.00
28	Ruben Mateo	20.00
29	Billy Koch	15.00
30	Vernon Wells	15.00

2000 Pacific Crown Royale Cramer's Choice Jumbo

This enlarged 10-card set is die-cut into a trophy shape. The jumbo cards are enhanced with a silver holofoiled front with gold foil stamping and etching across the bottom portion. These were found one per box exclusively in hobby boxes. Six parallels also were randomly inserted with each individual color replacing the gold foil stamping. Aqua's are limited to 20 numbered sets, Blue's 35 sets, Gold's 10 sets, Green's 30 sets, Purple's one set and Red's 25 sets.

		MT
Complete Set (10):		100.00
Common Player:		5.00
Inserted 1:box H		
Aqua:		5-10X
Production 20 sets		
Blue:		2-5X
Production 35 sets		
Gold:		10-20X
Production 10 sets		
Green:		3-6X
Production 30 sets		
Red:		4-8X
Production 25 sets		
1	Cal Ripken Jr.	15.00
2	Nomar Garciaparra	12.00
3	Ken Griffey Jr.	20.00
4	Sammy Sosa	12.00
5	Mike Piazza	12.00
6	Derek Jeter	12.00
7	Rick Ankiel	10.00
8	Mark McGwire	20.00
9	Tony Gwynn	8.00
10	Alex Rodriguez	15.00

2000 Pacific Crown Royale Jumbo

These jumbo cards are identical in design to the base cards besides their enlarged size. These were found exclusively in hobby boxes and were found as a box topper in 6:10 boxes.

		MT
Complete Set (6):		75.00
Common Player:		5.00
Inserted 6:10 boxes H		
1	Cal Ripken Jr.	15.00
2	Nomar Garciaparra	12.00

3	Ken Griffey Jr.	20.00
4	Derek Jeter	12.00
5	Mark McGwire	20.00
6	Alex Rodriguez	15.00

2000 Pacific Invincible

The base set consists of 150 cards. The player image is on an acetate stock with a blue sky background. The rest of the card is on standard UV coated stock and has the player name stamped in gold foil.

		MT
Complete Set (150):		120.00
Common Player:		.50
Pack (3):		3.00
Box (36):		85.00
1	Darin Erstad	1.00
2	Troy Glaus	2.00
3	Ramon Ortiz	.50
4	Tim Salmon	.75
5	Mo Vaughn	1.00
6	Erubiel Durazo	.50
7	Luis Gonzalez	.50
8	Randy Johnson	2.00
9	Matt Williams	.75
10	Rafael Furcal	.75
11	Andres Galarraga	1.50
12	Tom Glavine	.75
13	Andruw Jones	.75
14	Chipper Jones	4.00
15	Greg Maddux	4.00
16	Kevin Millwood	.50
17	Albert Belle	1.00
18	Will Clark	.75
19	Mike Mussina	1.00
20	Matt Riley	.50
21	Cal Ripken Jr.	6.00
22	Carl Everett	.50
23	Nomar Garciaparra	5.00
24	Steve Lomasney	.50
25	Pedro Martinez	2.00
26	*Tomo Ohka*	.50
27	Wilton Veras	.50
28	Mark Grace	.75
29	Sammy Sosa	5.00
30	Kerry Wood	.75
31	Eric Young	.50
32	*Julio Zuleta*	.50
33	Paul Konerko	.50
34	Carlos Lee	.50
35	Magglio Ordonez	.75
36	Josh Paul	.50
37	Frank Thomas	3.00
38	Rob Bell	.50
39	Dante Bichette	.75
40	Sean Casey	.50
41	Ken Griffey Jr.	8.00
42	Barry Larkin	1.00
43	Pokey Reese	.50
44	Roberto Alomar	1.50
45	Manny Ramirez	2.00
46	Richie Sexson	.50
47	Jim Thome	1.00
48	Omar Vizquel	.50
49	Jeff Cirillo	.75
50	Todd Helton	2.00
51	Neifi Perez	.50
52	Larry Walker	1.00
53	Tony Clark	.50
54	Juan Encarnacion	.50
55	Juan Gonzalez	2.00
56	Hideo Nomo	.50
57	Luis Castillo	.50
58	Alex Gonzalez	.50
59	Brad Penny	.50
60	Preston Wilson	.50
61	Moises Alou	.50
62	Jeff Bagwell	2.00
63	Lance Berkman	.50
64	Craig Biggio	.75
65	Roger Cedeno	.50
66	Jose Lima	.50
67	Carlos Beltran	.50
68	Johnny Damon	.50
69	*Chad Durbin*	.50
70	Jermaine Dye	.50
71	Carlos Febles	.50
72	Mark Quinn	.50
73	Kevin Brown	.75
74	Eric Gagne	.50
75	Shawn Green	1.50
76	Eric Karros	.75
77	Gary Sheffield	1.00
78	Kevin Barker	.50
79	Ron Belliard	.50
80	Jeromy Burnitz	.50
81	Geoff Jenkins	.75
82	Jacque Jones	.50
83	Corey Koskie	.50
84	Matt LeCroy	.50
85	David Ortiz	.50
86	*Johan Santana*	.50
87	Todd Walker	.50
88	Peter Bergeron	.50
89	Vladimir Guerrero	3.00
90	Jose Vidro	.50
91	Rondell White	.50
92	Edgardo Alfonzo	.75
93	Derek Bell	.50
94	Mike Hampton	.50
95	Rey Ordonez	.50
96	Mike Piazza	5.00
97	Robin Ventura	.75
98	Roger Clemens	3.00
99	Orlando Hernandez	.75
100	Derek Jeter	5.00
101	Alfonso Soriano	1.00
102	Bernie Williams	1.50
103	Eric Chavez	.50
104	Jason Giambi	.75
105	Ben Grieve	.75
106	Tim Hudson	.75
107	Miguel Tejada	.50
108	Bobby Abreu	.50
109	Doug Glanville	.50
110	Mike Lieberthal	.50
111	Scott Rolen	1.50
112	Brian Giles	.50
113	Chad Hermansen	.50
114	Jason Kendall	.50
115	Warren Morris	.50
116	Aramis Ramirez	.50
117	Rick Ankiel	3.00
118	J.D. Drew	.50
119	Mark McGwire	8.00
120	Fernando Tatis	.75
121	Fernando Vina	.50
122	Bret Boone	.50
123	Ben Davis	.50
124	Tony Gwynn	3.00
125	Trevor Hoffman	.50
126	Ryan Klesko	.50
127	Rich Aurilia	.50
128	Barry Bonds	2.50
129	Ellis Burks	.50
130	Jeff Kent	.75
131	Freddy Garcia	.50
132	Carlos Guillen	.50
133	Edgar Martinez	.50
134	John Olerud	.75
135	Robert Ramsay	.50
136	Alex Rodriguez	6.00
137	*Kazuhiro Sasaki*	4.00
138	Jose Canseco	1.50
139	Vinny Castilla	.50
140	Fred McGriff	.75
141	Greg Vaughn	.75
142	Dan Wheeler	.50
143	Gabe Kapler	.75
144	Ruben Mateo	.50
145	Rafael Palmeiro	1.00
146	Ivan Rodriguez	2.00
147	Tony Batista	.75
148	Carlos Delgado	1.50
149	Raul Mondesi	.75
150	Vernon Wells	.50

2000 Pacific Invincible Holographic Purple

A parallel to the 150-card set, holographic purple stamping replaces the gold foil from the base cards. These are limited to 299 serial numbered sets.

	MT
Stars:	2-3X
Production 299 sets	

2000 Pacific Invincible Platinum Blue

A parallel to the 150-card base set these differ only from the regular cards in that blue foil stamping replaces gold. Each card is also serially numbered on the card front in an edition of 67 sets.

	MT
Stars:	6-10X
Production 67 sets	

2000 Pacific Invincible Game Gear

		MT
Complete Set (32):		
Common Player:		
1	Jeff Bagwell Jsy/1000	
2	Tom Glavine Jsy/1000	
3	Mark Grace Jsy/1000	
4	Eric Karros Jsy/1000	
5	Edgar Martinez Jsy/800	
6	Manny Ramirez Jsy/975	
7	Cal Ripken Jr. Jsy/1000	
8	Alex Rodriguez Jsy/900	
9	Ivan Rodriguez Jsy/675	
10	Mo Vaughn Jsy/1000	
11	Edgar Martinez Bat-Jsy/200	
12	Manny Ramirez Jsy/145	
13	Alex Rodriguez Bat-Jsy/200	
14	Ivan Rodriguez Bat-Jsy/200	
15	Edgar Martinez Bat/200	
16	Manny Ramirez Bat/200	
17	Ivan Rodriguez Bat/200	
18	Alex Rodriguez Bat/200	
19	Jeff Bagwell Patch/125	
20	Tom Glavine Patch/110	
21	Mark Grace Patch/125	
22	Tony Gwynn Patch/65	
23	Chipper Jones Patch/80	
24	Eric Karros Patch/125	
25	Greg Maddux Patch/80	
26	Edgar Martinez Patch/125	
27	Manny Ramirez Patch/125	
28	Cal Ripken Jr. Patch/125	
29	Alex Rodriguez Patch/125	
30	Ivan Rodriguez Patch/125	
31	Frank Thomas Patch/125	
32	Mo Vaughn Patch/125	

2000 Pacific Invincible Eyes of the World

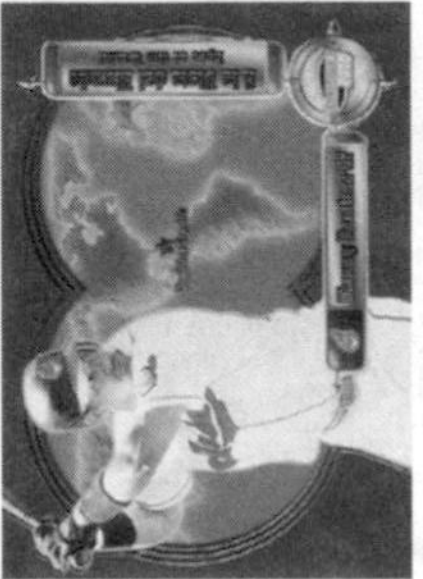

This 20-card set has a horizontal format with gold foil stamping. The background of the player photo has a partial globe with a star and the country the featured player is from stamped in gold foil. These were inserted 1:25 packs.

		MT
Complete Set (20):		125.00
Common Player:		3.00
Inserted 1:25		
1	Erubiel Durazo	3.00
2	Andruw Jones	4.00
3	Cal Ripken Jr.	15.00
4	Nomar Garciaparra	12.00
5	Pedro Martinez	5.00
6	Sammy Sosa	12.00
7	Ken Griffey Jr.	20.00
8	Manny Ramirez	5.00
9	Larry Walker	4.00
10	Juan Gonzalez	5.00
11	Carlos Beltran	3.00
12	Vladimir Guerrero	8.00
13	Orlando Hernandez	3.00
14	Derek Jeter	12.00
15	Mark McGwire	20.00
16	Tony Gwynn	8.00
17	Freddy Garcia	3.00
18	Alex Rodriguez	15.00
19	Jose Canseco	4.00
20	Ivan Rodriguez	5.00

2000 Pacific Invincible Ticket To Stardom

These unique cards have a design intended to replicate a ticket stub. Two images of the featured player are on the front, the bigger primary photo is vertical, while the smaller photo is horizontal. Silver foil stamping is used throughout. These are found 1:121 packs.

		MT
Complete Set (20):		475.00
Common Player:		10.00
Inserted 1:121		
1	Andruw Jones	10.00
2	Chipper Jones	30.00
3	Cal Ripken Jr.	50.00
4	Nomar Garciaparra	40.00
5	Pedro Martinez	15.00
6	Ken Griffey Jr.	60.00
7	Sammy Sosa	40.00
8	Manny Ramirez	15.00
9	Jeff Bagwell	15.00
10	Shawn Green	12.00
11	Vladimir Guerrero	25.00
12	Mike Piazza	40.00
13	Derek Jeter	40.00
14	Alfonso Soriano	10.00
15	Scott Rolen	10.00
16	Rick Ankiel	20.00
17	Mark McGwire	60.00
18	Tony Gwynn	25.00
19	Alex Rodriguez	50.00
20	Ivan Rodriguez	15.00

2000 Pacific Invincible Lighting he Fire

These full foiled inserts are die-cut in the shape of a flame, with an image of a baseball at the core of the fiery image. These were inserted 1:49 packs.

		MT
Complete Set (20):		250.00
Common Player:		5.00
Inserted 1:49		
1	Chipper Jones	15.00
2	Greg Maddux	15.00
3	Cal Ripken Jr.	25.00
4	Nomar Garciaparra	20.00
5	Pedro Martinez	8.00
6	Ken Griffey Jr.	30.00
7	Sammy Sosa	20.00
8	Manny Ramirez	8.00
9	Juan Gonzalez	8.00
10	Jeff Bagwell	8.00
11	Shawn Green	6.00
12	Vladimir Guerrero	12.00
13	Mike Piazza	20.00
14	Roger Clemens	10.00
15	Derek Jeter	20.00
16	Mark McGwire	30.00
17	Tony Gwynn	12.00
18	Alex Rodriguez	25.00
19	Jose Canseco	6.00
20	Ivan Rodriguez	8.00

2000 Pacific Invincible Diamond Aces

This 20-card set highlights the top pitchers in the game. Silver foil stamping is used on the card fronts and are designed to duplicate the look of an Ace in a playing deck of cards. These were seeded 1 per pack. A parallel version limited to 299 serial numbered sets is also randomly seeded.

		MT
Complete Set (20):		8.00
Common Player:		.40
Inserted 1:1		
1	Randy Johnson	.75
2	Greg Maddux	1.50
3	Tom Glavine	.40
4	John Smoltz	.40
5	Mike Mussina	.50
6	Pedro Martinez	.75
7	Kerry Wood	.40
8	Bartolo Colon	.40
9	Brad Penny	.40
10	Billy Wagner	.40
11	Kevin Brown	.40
12	Mike Hampton	.40
13	Roger Clemens	1.00
14	David Cone	.40
15	Orlando Hernandez	.40
16	Mariano Rivera	.40
17	Tim Hudson	.40
18	Trevor Hoffman	.40
19	Rick Ankiel	2.00
20	Freddy Garcia	.40

2000 Pacific Invincible Kings of the Diamond

Twenty of the top hitters in the game are featured on a design intended to duplicate the look of a King card in a playing deck of cards. These were seeded 1 per pack. A parallel version limited to 299 serial numbered sets is also randomly seeded.

		MT
Complete Set (30):		25.00
Common Player:		.40
Inserted 1:1		
1	Mo Vaughn	.50
2	Erubiel Durazo	.40
3	Andruw Jones	.50
4	Chipper Jones	1.50
5	Cal Ripken Jr.	2.50
6	Nomar Garciaparra	2.00
7	Sammy Sosa	2.00
8	Frank Thomas	1.00
9	Sean Casey	.40
10	Ken Griffey Jr.	3.00
11	Manny Ramirez	.75
12	Larry Walker	.50
13	Juan Gonzalez	.75
14	Jeff Bagwell	.75
15	Craig Biggio	.50
16	Carlos Beltran	.40
17	Shawn Green	.50
18	Vladimir Guerrero	1.25
19	Mike Piazza	2.00
20	Derek Jeter	2.00
21	Bernie Williams	.50
22	Ben Grieve	.40
23	Scott Rolen	.50
24	Mark McGwire	3.00
25	Tony Gwynn	1.50
26	Barry Bonds	.75
27	Alex Rodriguez	2.50
28	Jose Canseco	.50
29	Rafael Palmeiro	.50
30	Ivan Rodriguez	.75

The values of some parallel-card issues will have to be calculated based on figures presented in the heading for the regular-issue card set.

2000 Pacific Invincible Wild Vinyl

This scarce 10-card insert set is serial numbered on the card front, limited to only 10 sets.

		MT
Complete Set (10):		N/A
Common Player:		M/A
Production 10 sets		N/A
1	Chipper Jones	
2	Cal Ripken Jr.	
3	Nomar Garciaparra	
4	Ken Griffey Jr.	
5	Sammy Sosa	
6	Mike Piazza	
7	Derek Jeter	
8	Mark McGwire	
9	Tony Gwynn	
10	Alex Rodriguez	

2000 Pacific Paramount

		MT
Complete Set (250):		35.00
Common Player:		.10
Pack (6):		1.75
Wax Box (36):		50.00
1	Garret Anderson	.10
2	Jim Edmonds	.10
3	Darin Erstad	.20
4	Chuck Finley	.10
5	Troy Glaus	.75
6	Troy Percival	.10
7	Tim Salmon	.20
8	Mo Vaughn	.40
9	Jay Bell	.10
10	Erubiel Durazo	.20
11	Steve Finley	.10
12	Luis Gonzalez	.10
13	Randy Johnson	.40
14	Travis Lee	.20
15	Matt Mantei	.10
16	Matt Williams	.25
17	Tony Womack	.10
18	Bret Boone	.10
19	Tom Glavine	.20
20	Andruw Jones	.40
21	Chipper Jones	1.00
22	Brian Jordan	.10
23	Javy Lopez	.15
24	Greg Maddux	1.00
25	Kevin Millwood	.20
26	John Rocker	.10
27	John Smoltz	.15
28	Brady Anderson	.15
29	Albert Belle	.40
30	Will Clark	.25
31	Charles Johnson	.10
32	Mike Mussina	.40
33	Cal Ripken Jr.	1.25
34	B.J. Surhoff	.10
35	Nomar Garciaparra	1.25
36	Derek Lowe	.10
37	Pedro Martinez	.50
38	Trot Nixon	.10
39	Troy O'Leary	.10
40	Jose Offerman	.10
41	John Valentin	.10
42	Jason Varitek	.10
43	Mark Grace	.20
44	Glenallen Hill	.10
45	Jon Lieber	.10
46	Cole Liniak	.10
47	Jose Nieves	.10
48	Henry Rodriguez	.10
49	Sammy Sosa	1.25
50	Kerry Wood	.40
51	Jason Dellaero	.10
52	Ray Durham	.10
53	Paul Konerko	.10
54	Carlos Lee	.10
55	Greg Norton	.10
56	Magglio Ordonez	.25
57	Chris Singleton	.10
58	Frank Thomas	.60
59	Aaron Boone	.10
60	Mike Cameron	.10
61	Sean Casey	.40
62	Pete Harnisch	.10
63	Barry Larkin	.25
64	Pokey Reese	.10
65	Greg Vaughn	.25
66	Scott Williamson	.10
67	Roberto Alomar	.40
68	*Sean DePaula*	.25
69	Travis Fryman	.20

70	David Justice	.20
71	Kenny Lofton	.40
72	Manny Ramirez	.50
73	Richie Sexson	.10
74	Jim Thome	.25
75	Omar Vizquel	.10
76	Pedro Astacio	.10
77	Vinny Castilla	.15
78	Derrick Gibson	.10
79	Todd Helton	.75
80	Neifi Perez	.10
81	Ben Petrick	.10
82	Larry Walker	.40
83	Brad Ausmus	.10
84	Tony Clark	.20
85	Deivi Cruz	.10
86	Damion Easley	.10
87	Juan Encarnacion	.10
88	Juan Gonzalez	.50
89	Bobby Higginson	.10
90	Dave Mlicki	.10
91	Dean Palmer	.15
92	Bruce Aven	.10
93	Luis Castillo	.10
94	Ramon Castro	.10
95	Cliff Floyd	.10
96	Alex Gonzalez	.10
97	Mike Lowell	.10
98	Preston Wilson	.10
99	Jeff Bagwell	.50
100	Derek Bell	.10
101	Craig Biggio	.30
102	Ken Caminiti	.15
103	Carl Everett	.15
104	Mike Hampton	.10
105	Jose Lima	.10
106	Billy Wagner	.10
107	Daryle Ward	.10
108	Carlos Beltran	.15
109	Johnny Damon	.10
110	Jermaine Dye	.10
111	Carlos Febles	.10
112	Mark Quinn	.10
113	Joe Randa	.10
114	Jose Rosado	.10
115	Mike Sweeney	.10
116	Kevin Brown	.15
117	Shawn Green	.40
118	Mark Grudzielanek	.10
119	Todd Hollandsworth	.10
120	Eric Karros	.15
121	Chan Ho Park	.15
122	Gary Sheffield	.25
123	Devon White	.10
124	Eric Young	.10
125	Kevin Barker	.10
126	Ron Belliard	.10
127	Jeromy Burnitz	.10
128	Jeff Cirillo	.10
129	Marquis Grissom	.10
130	Geoff Jenkins	.10
131	David Nilsson	.10
132	Chad Allen	.10
133	Ron Coomer	.10
134	Jacque Jones	.10
135	Corey Koskie	.10
136	Matt Lawton	.10
137	Brad Radke	.10
138	Todd Walker	.10
139	Michael Barrett	.10
140	Peter Bergeron	.10
141	Brad Fullmer	.10
142	Vladimir Guerrero	.75
143	Ugueth Urbina	.10
144	Jose Vidro	.10
145	Rondell White	.15
146	Edgardo Alfonzo	.20
147	Armando Benitez	.10
148	Roger Cedeno	.10
149	Rickey Henderson	.30
150	Melvin Mora	.10
151	John Olerud	.25
152	Rey Ordonez	.10
153	Mike Piazza	1.25
154	Jorge Toca	.10
155	Robin Ventura	.20
156	Roger Clemens	.75
157	David Cone	.20
158	Orlando Hernandez	.20
159	Derek Jeter	1.25
160	Chuck Knoblauch	.25
161	Ricky Ledee	.10
162	Tino Martinez	.25
163	Paul O'Neill	.20
164	Mariano Rivera	.20
165	Alfonso Soriano	.40
166	Bernie Williams	.40
167	Eric Chavez	.10
168	Jason Giambi	.10
169	Ben Grieve	.20
170	Tim Hudson	.20
171	John Jaha	.10
172	Matt Stairs	.10
173	Miguel Tejada	.10
174	Randy Velarde	.10
175	Bobby Abreu	.10
176	Marlon Anderson	.10
177	Rico Brogna	.10
178	Ron Gant	.20
179	Doug Glanville	.10
180	Mike Lieberthal	.10
181	Scott Rolen	.50
182	Curt Schilling	.15
183	Brian Giles	.10
184	Chad Hermansen	.10
185	Jason Kendall	.10
186	Al Martin	.10
187	Pat Meares	.10
188	Warren Morris	.10
189	Ed Sprague	.10
190	Kevin Young	.10
191	Rick Ankiel	5.00
192	Kent Bottenfield	.10
193	Eric Davis	.20
194	J.D. Drew	.25
195	Adam Kennedy	.10
196	Ray Lankford	.10
197	Joe McEwing	.10
198	Mark McGwire	2.00
199	Edgar Renteria	.10
200	Fernando Tatis	.20
201	Mike Darr	.10
202	Ben Davis	.10
203	Tony Gwynn	1.00
204	Trevor Hoffman	.10
205	Damian Jackson	.10
206	Phil Nevin	.10
207	Reggie Sanders	.10
208	Quilvio Veras	.10
209	Rich Aurilia	.10
210	Marvin Benard	.10
211	Barry Bonds	.50
212	Ellis Burks	.10
213	Livan Hernandez	.10
214	Jeff Kent	.10
215	Russ Ortiz	.10
216	J.T. Snow	.10
217	Paul Abbott	.10
218	David Bell	.10
219	Freddy Garcia	.25
220	Ken Griffey Jr.	2.00
221	Carlos Guillen	.10
222	Brian Hunter	.10
223	Edgar Martinez	.15
224	Jamie Moyer	.10
225	Alex Rodriguez	1.50
226	Wade Boggs	.25
227	Miguel Cairo	.10
228	Jose Canseco	.50
229	Roberto Hernandez	.10
230	Dave Martinez	.10
231	Quinton McCracken	.10
232	Fred McGriff	.20
233	Kevin Stocker	.10
234	Royce Clayton	.10
235	Rusty Greer	.10
236	Ruben Mateo	.10
237	Rafael Palmeiro	.30
238	Ivan Rodriguez	.50
239	Aaron Sele	.10
240	John Wetteland	.10
241	Todd Zeile	.10
242	Tony Batista	.10
243	Homer Bush	.10
244	Carlos Delgado	.40
245	Tony Fernandez	.10
246	Billy Koch	.10
247	Raul Mondesi	.20
248	Shannon Stewart	.10
249	David Wells	.10
250	Vernon Wells	.10

2000 Pacific Paramount Copper

	MT
Stars:	2x to 4x
Yng Stars & RCs:	1x to 2x
Inserted 1:1 H	

2000 Pacific Paramount Premiere Date

	MT
Stars:	30x to 60x
Yng Stars & RCs:	15x to 40x
Production 50 sets	

2000 Pacific Paramount Holographic Silver

	MT
Stars:	20x to 40x
Yng Stars & RCs:	10x to 20x
Production 99 sets	

2000 Pacific Paramount Platinum Blue

	MT
Stars:	25x to 50x
Yng Stars & RCs:	20x to 40x
Production 67 sets	

2000 Pacific Paramount Ruby Red

	MT
Stars:	1-2X
RCs:	1X
Inserted 9 per 7-11 pack	

2000 Pacific Paramount Cooperstown Bound

		MT
Complete Set (10):		550.00
Common Player:		30.00
Inserted 1:361		
1	Greg Maddux	50.00
2	Cal Ripken Jr.	70.00
3	Nomar Garciaparra	60.00
4	Sammy Sosa	60.00
5	Roger Clemens	40.00
6	Derek Jeter	60.00
7	Mark McGwire	100.00
8	Tony Gwynn	50.00
9	Ken Griffey Jr.	100.00
10	Alex Rodriguez	70.00

2000 Pacific Paramount Fielder's Choice

		MT
Complete Set (20):		400.00
Common Player:		8.00
Inserted 1:73		
1	Andruw Jones	10.00
2	Chipper Jones	25.00
3	Greg Maddux	25.00
4	Cal Ripken Jr.	30.00
5	Nomar Garciaparra	30.00
6	Sammy Sosa	30.00
7	Sean Casey	8.00
8	Manny Ramirez	15.00
9	Larry Walker	12.00
10	Jeff Bagwell	15.00
11	Mike Piazza	30.00
12	Derek Jeter	30.00
13	Bernie Williams	12.00
14	Scott Rolen	15.00
15	Mark McGwire	50.00
16	Tony Gwynn	25.00
17	Barry Bonds	15.00
18	Ken Griffey Jr.	50.00
19	Alex Rodriguez	35.00
20	Ivan Rodriguez	15.00

2000 Pacific Paramount Double Vision

		MT
Complete Set (36):		350.00
Common Player:		3.00
Inserted 1:37		
1	Chipper Jones	15.00
2	Cal Ripken Jr.	15.00
3	Nomar Garciaparra	15.00
4	Pedro Martinez	6.00
5	Sammy Sosa	15.00
6	Manny Ramirez	6.00
7	Jeff Bagwell	6.00
8	Craig Biggio	3.00
9	Vladimir Guerrero	10.00
10	Mike Piazza	15.00
11	Roger Clemens	10.00

12	Derek Jeter	15.00
13	Mark McGwire	25.00
14	Tony Gwynn	12.00
15	Ken Griffey Jr.	25.00
16	Alex Rodriguez	20.00
17	Rafael Palmeiro	4.00
18	Ivan Rodriguez	6.00
19	Chipper Jones	12.00
20	Cal Ripken Jr.	15.00
21	Nomar Garciaparra	15.00
22	Pedro Martinez	6.00
23	Sammy Sosa	15.00
24	Manny Ramirez	6.00
25	Jeff Bagwell	6.00
26	Craig Biggio	3.00
27	Vladimir Guerrero	10.00
28	Mike Piazza	15.00
29	Roger Clemens	10.00
30	Derek Jeter	15.00
31	Mark McGwire	25.00
32	Tony Gwynn	12.00
33	Ken Griffey Jr.	25.00
34	Alex Rodriguez	20.00
35	Rafael Palmeiro	4.00
36	Ivan Rodriguez	6.00

2000 Pacific Paramount Season in Review

		MT
Complete Set (30):		125.00
Common Player:		2.00
Inserted 2:37		
1	Randy Johnson	3.00
2	Matt Williams	2.00
3	Chipper Jones	8.00
4	Greg Maddux	8.00
5	Cal Ripken Jr.	10.00
6	Nomar Garciaparra	10.00
7	Pedro Martinez	4.00
8	Sammy Sosa	10.00
9	Manny Ramirez	4.00
10	Larry Walker	3.00
11	Jeff Bagwell	4.00
12	Craig Biggio	2.00
13	Carlos Beltran	2.00
14	Mark Quinn	2.00
15	Vladimir Guerrero	6.00
16	Mike Piazza	10.00
17	Robin Ventura	2.00
18	Roger Clemens	5.00
19	David Cone	2.00
20	Derek Jeter	10.00
21	Mark McGwire	15.00
22	Fernando Tatis	2.00
23	Tony Gwynn	8.00
24	Barry Bonds	4.00
25	Ken Griffey Jr.	15.00
26	Alex Rodriguez	12.00
27	Wade Boggs	2.50
28	Jose Canseco	4.00
29	Rafael Palmeiro	3.00
30	Ivan Rodriguez	4.00

2000 Pacific Prism

		MT
Complete Set (150):		70.00
Common Player:		.40
Pack (5):		4.00
Wax Box (24):		80.00
1	*Jeff DaVanon*	.50
2	Troy Glaus	1.50
3	Tim Salmon	.75
4	Mo Vaughn	1.00
5	Jay Bell	.40
6	Erubiel Durazo	1.00
7	Luis Gonzalez	.50
8	Randy Johnson	1.25
9	Matt Williams	1.00
10	Andres Galarraga	1.00
11	Andruw Jones	1.00
12	Chipper Jones	3.00
13	Brian Jordan	.40
14	Greg Maddux	3.00
15	Kevin Millwood	.75
16	John Smoltz	.50
17	Albert Belle	1.00
18	Mike Mussina	1.25
19	Calvin Pickering	.40
20	Cal Ripken Jr.	5.00
21	B.J. Surhoff	.50
22	Nomar Garciaparra	4.00
23	Pedro Martinez	1.50
24	Troy O'Leary	.50
25	John Valentin	.40
26	Jason Varitek	.40
27	Mark Grace	.75
28	Henry Rodriguez	.50
29	Sammy Sosa	4.00
30	Kerry Wood	1.00
31	Ray Durham	.40
32	Carlos Lee	.40
33	Magglio Ordonez	.75
34	Chris Singleton	.40
35	Frank Thomas	2.00
36	Sean Casey	.75
37	Travis Dawkins	.40
38	Barry Larkin	1.00
39	Pokey Reese	.40
40	Scott Williamson	.40
41	Roberto Alomar	1.25
42	Bartolo Colon	.50
43	David Justice	.75
44	Manny Ramirez	1.50
45	Richie Sexson	.40
46	Jim Thome	1.00
47	Omar Vizquel	.60
48	Pedro Astacio	.40
49	Todd Helton	1.50
50	Neifi Perez	.40
51	Ben Petrick	.40
52	Larry Walker	1.00
53	Tony Clark	.75
54	Damion Easley	.40
55	Juan Gonzalez	1.50
56	Dean Palmer	.40
57	A.J. Burnett	.40
58	Luis Castillo	.40
59	Cliff Floyd	.40
60	Alex Gonzalez	.40
61	Preston Wilson	.40
62	Jeff Bagwell	1.50
63	Craig Biggio	1.00
64	Ken Caminiti	.60
65	Jose Lima	.40
66	Billy Wagner	.40
67	Carlos Beltran	.40
68	Johnny Damon	.40
69	Jermaine Dye	.50
70	Carlos Febles	.40
71	Mike Sweeney	.40
72	Kevin Brown	.75
73	Shawn Green	1.00
74	Eric Karros	.75
75	Chan Ho Park	.75
76	Gary Sheffield	.75
77	Ron Belliard	.40
78	Jeromy Burnitz	.50
79	Marquis Grissom	.40
80	Geoff Jenkins	.50
81	Mark Loretta	.40
82	Ron Coomer	.40
83	Jacque Jones	.40
84	Corey Koskie	.40
85	Brad Radke	.40
86	Todd Walker	.40
87	Michael Barrett	.40
88	Peter Bergeron	.40
89	Vladimir Guerrero	3.00
90	Jose Vidro	.40
91	Rondell White	.60
92	Edgardo Alfonzo	.60
93	Rickey Henderson	.75
94	Rey Ordonez	.40
95	Mike Piazza	4.00
96	Robin Ventura	.75
97	Roger Clemens	2.50
98	Orlando Hernandez	1.00
99	Derek Jeter	4.00
100	Tino Martinez	.75
101	Mariano Rivera	.75
102	Alfonso Soriano	1.50
103	Bernie Williams	1.00
104	Eric Chavez	.50
105	Jason Giambi	.50
106	Ben Grieve	.75
107	Tim Hudson	.75
108	John Jaha	.40
109	Bobby Abreu	.75
110	Doug Glanville	.40
111	Mike Lieberthal	.40
112	Scott Rolen	1.50
113	Curt Schilling	.75
114	Brian Giles	.50
115	Jason Kendall	.75
116	Warren Morris	.40
117	Kevin Young	.40
118	Rick Ankiel	5.00
119	J.D. Drew	.50
120	Chad Hutchinson	.40
121	Ray Lankford	.40
122	Mark McGwire	6.00
123	Fernando Tatis	.50
124	Bret Boone	.40
125	Ben Davis	.40
126	Tony Gwynn	3.00
127	Trevor Hoffman	.40
128	Barry Bonds	1.50
129	Ellis Burks	.40
130	Jeff Kent	.40
131	J.T. Snow	.40
132	Freddy Garcia	.75
133	Ken Griffey Jr.	8.00
134	Edgar Martinez	.40
135	John Olerud	.75
136	Alex Rodriguez	5.00
137	Jose Canseco	1.50
138	Vinny Castilla	.50
139	Roberto Hernandez	.50
140	Fred McGriff	.75
141	Rusty Greer	.50
142	Ruben Mateo	.75
143	Rafael Palmeiro	1.00
144	Ivan Rodriguez	1.50
145	Lee Stevens	.40
146	Tony Batista	.50
147	Carlos Delgado	1.00
148	Shannon Stewart	.40
149	David Wells	.40
150	Vernon Wells	.50

2000 Pacific Prism Holographic Blue

	MT
Stars:	15x-25x
Yng. Stars & RCs:	8x-15x
Production 80 sets	

2000 Pacific Prism Holographic Mirror

	MT
Stars:	5x-12x
Yng. Stars & RCs:	3x-6x
Production 160 sets	

2000 Pacific Prism Holographic Gold

	MT
Stars:	2x-5x
Yng. Stars & RCs:	1x-2x
Production 480 sets	

2000 Pacific Prism Silver Drops

	MT
Stars:	1X-2X
Yng. Stars & RCs:	1X

2000 Pacific Prism Holographic Purple

	MT
Stars:	8X-15X
Yng. Stars & RCs:	5X-10X
Production 99 sets	

2000 Pacific Prism Premiere Date

	MT
Stars:	15X-25X
Yng. Stars & RCs:	8X-15X
Production 61 sets	

2000 Pacific Prism Rapture Silver

	MT
Stars:	1X-2X
Yng. Stars & RCs:	1X

The values of some parallel-card issues will have to be calculated based on figures presented in the heading for the regular-issue card set.

2000 Pacific Prism Diamond Dial-A-Stats

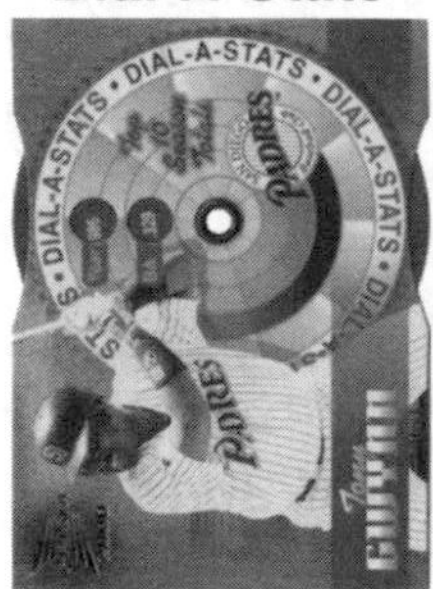

		MT
Complete Set (10):		400.00
Common Player:		10.00
Inserted 1:193		
1	Chipper Jones	40.00
2	Greg Maddux	40.00
3	Cal Ripken Jr.	60.00
4	Sammy Sosa	50.00
5	Mike Piazza	50.00
6	Roger Clemens	30.00
7	Mark McGwire	75.00
8	Tony Gwynn	35.00
9	Ken Griffey Jr.	75.00
10	Alex Rodriguez	60.00

2000 Pacific Prism Center Stage

		MT
Complete Set (20):		180.00
Common Player:		4.00
Inserted 1:25		
1	Chipper Jones	12.00
2	Cal Ripken Jr.	20.00
3	Nomar Garciaparra	15.00
4	Pedro Martinez	6.00
5	Sammy Sosa	15.00
6	Sean Casey	4.00
7	Manny Ramirez	6.00
8	Jim Thome	5.00
9	Jeff Bagwell	6.00
10	Carlos Beltran	4.00
11	Vladimir Guerrero	10.00
12	Mike Piazza	15.00
13	Derek Jeter	15.00
14	Bernie Williams	5.00
15	Scott Rolen	6.00
16	Mark McGwire	25.00
17	Tony Gwynn	12.00
18	Ken Griffey Jr.	25.00
19	Alex Rodriguez	20.00
20	Ivan Rodriguez	6.00

2000 Pacific Prism A.L. Legends

		MT
Complete Set (10):		60.00
Common Player:		2.00
Inserted 1:25		
1	Mo Vaughn	3.00
2	Cal Ripken Jr.	12.00
3	Nomar Garciaparra	10.00
4	Manny Ramirez	4.00
5	Roger Clemens	5.00
6	Derek Jeter	10.00
7	Ken Griffey Jr.	15.00
8	Alex Rodriguez	12.00
9	Jose Canseco	4.00
10	Rafael Palmeiro	3.00

2000 Pacific Prism N.L. Legends

		MT
Complete Set (10):		60.00
Common Player:		2.00
Inserted 1:25		
1	Chipper Jones	8.00
2	Greg Maddux	8.00
3	Sammy Sosa	10.00
4	Larry Walker	3.00
5	Jeff Bagwell	4.00
6	Vladimir Guerrero	6.00
7	Mike Piazza	10.00
8	Mark McGwire	15.00
9	Tony Gwynn	8.00
10	Barry Bonds	4.00

Modern cards in Near Mint condition are valued at about 75% of the Mint value shown here. Excellent-condition cards are worth 50%. Cards in lower grades are not generally collectible.

2000 Pacific Prism Prospects

		MT
Complete Set (10):		70.00
Common Player:		4.00
Inserted 1:97		
1	Erubiel Durazo	6.00
2	Wilton Veras	5.00
3	Ben Petrick	4.00
4	Mark Quinn	6.00
5	Peter Bergeron	4.00
6	Alfonso Soriano	15.00
7	Tim Hudson	8.00
8	Chad Hermansen	4.00
9	Rick Ankiel	30.00
10	Ruben Mateo	6.00

2000 Pacific Private Stock

This base set consists of 150-cards, each card image uses an artist's computer generated brush strokes. Short-printed prospects are seeded 1:4 packs. The logo, player name and team are stamped in gold foil.

		MT
Complete Set (150):		125.00
Common Player:		.25
Common SP Prospect:		2.00
Inserted 1:4		
Pack (7):		4.00
Wax Box (24):		85.00
1	Darin Erstad	.50
2	Troy Glaus	1.50
3	Tim Salmon	.40
4	Mo Vaughn	1.00
5	Jay Bell	.25
6	Luis Gonzalez	.25
7	Randy Johnson	1.00
8	Matt Williams	.75
9	Andruw Jones	1.00
10	Chipper Jones	2.50
11	Brian Jordan	.25
12	Greg Maddux	2.50
13	Kevin Millwood	.50
14	Albert Belle	1.00
15	Mike Mussina	1.00
16	Cal Ripken Jr.	3.00
17	B.J. Surhoff	.25
18	Nomar Garciaparra	3.00
19	Butch Huskey	.25
20	Pedro Martinez	1.50
21	Troy O'Leary	.25
22	Mark Grace	.50
23	Bo Porter (SP)	2.00
24	Henry Rodriguez	.25
25	Sammy Sosa	3.00
26	Kerry Wood	.75
27	Jason Dellaero (SP)	3.00
28	Ray Durham	.25
29	Paul Konerko	.25
30	Carlos Lee	.25
31	Magglio Ordonez	.50
32	Frank Thomas	1.50
33	Mike Cameron	.25
34	Sean Casey	.75
35	Barry Larkin	.75
36	Greg Vaughn	.50
37	Roberto Alomar	1.00
38	Russell Branyan (SP)	3.00
39	Kenny Lofton	1.00
40	Manny Ramirez	1.50
41	Richie Sexson	.25
42	Jim Thome	.75
43	Omar Vizquel	.25
44	Dante Bichette	.50
45	Vinny Castilla	.40
46	Todd Helton	1.00
47	Ben Petrick (SP)	3.00
48	Juan Sosa (SP)	3.00
49	Larry Walker	1.00
50	Tony Clark	.50
51	Damion Easley	.25
52	Juan Encarnacion	.25
53	Robert Fick (SP)	2.00
54	Dean Palmer	.25
55	A.J. Burnett (SP)	4.00
56	Luis Castillo	.25
57	Alex Gonzalez	.25
58	Julio Ramirez (SP)	3.00
59	Preston Wilson	.25
60	Jeff Bagwell	1.50
61	Craig Biggio	.75
62	Ken Caminiti	.40
63	Carl Everett	.25
64	Mike Hampton	.25
65	Billy Wagner	.25
66	Carlos Beltran	.25
67	Dermal Brown (SP)	2.00
68	Jermaine Dye	.25
69	Carlos Febles	.25
70	Mark Quinn (SP)	4.00
71	Mike Sweeney	.25
72	Kevin Brown	.40
73	Eric Gagne (SP)	2.00
74	Eric Karros	.40
75	Raul Mondesi	.40
76	Gary Sheffield	.50
77	Jeromy Burnitz	.25
78	Jeff Cirillo	.25
79	Geoff Jenkins	.25
80	David Nilsson	.25
81	Ron Coomer	.25
82	Jacque Jones	.25
83	Corey Koskie	.25
84	Brad Radke	.25
85	Tony Armas, Jr. (SP)	3.00
86	Peter Bergeron (SP)	3.00
87	Vladimir Guerrero	2.00
88	Jose Vidro	.25
89	Rondell White	.40
90	Edgardo Alfonzo	.50
91	Roger Cedeno	.25
92	Rickey Henderson	.75
93	Jay Payton (SP)	2.00
94	Mike Piazza	3.00
95	Jorge Toca (SP)	4.00
96	Robin Ventura	.50
97	Roger Clemens	2.00
98	David Cone	.40
99	Derek Jeter	3.00
100	D'Angelo Jimenez (SP)	2.00
101	Tino Martinez	.50
102	Alfonso Soriano (SP)	6.00
103	Bernie Williams	1.00
104	Jason Giambi	.25
105	Ben Grieve	.50
106	Tim Hudson	.50

107	Matt Stairs	.25
108	Bobby Abreu	.25
109	Doug Glanville	.25
110	Scott Rolen	1.50
111	Curt Schilling	.40
112	Brian Giles	.25
113	Chad Hermansen (SP)	3.00
114	Jason Kendall	.25
115	Warren Morris	.25
116	Rick Ankiel (SP)	20.00
117	J.D. Drew	.25
118	Adam Kennedy (SP)	2.00
119	Ray Lankford	.25
120	Mark McGwire	5.00
121	Fernando Tatis	.50
122	Mike Darr (SP)	2.00
123	Ben Davis	.25
124	Tony Gwynn	2.50
125	Trevor Hoffman	.25
126	Reggie Sanders	.25
127	Barry Bonds	1.50
128	Ellis Burks	.25
129	Jeff Kent	.25
130	J.T. Snow	.25
131	Freddy Garcia	.75
132	Ken Griffey Jr.	5.00
133	Carlos Guillen (SP)	2.00
134	Edgar Martinez	.25
135	Alex Rodriguez	4.00
136	Miguel Cairo	.25
137	Jose Canseco	1.00
138	Steve Cox (SP)	2.00
139	Roberto Hernandez	.25
140	Fred McGriff	.50
141	Juan Gonzalez	1.50
142	Rusty Greer	.25
143	Ruben Mateo (SP)	4.00
144	Rafael Palmeiro	.75
145	Ivan Rodriguez	1.50
146	Carlos Delgado	.75
147	Tony Fernandez	.25
148	Shawn Green	1.00
149	Shannon Stewart	.25
150	Vernon Wells (SP)	3.00

2000 Pacific Private Stock Gold Portraits

A parallel to the 150-card base set these have a gold foiled border. These are found exclusively in hobby packs and are limited to 99 serial numbered sets.

	MT
Stars:	10x to 20x
Prospects:	1.5x to 3x
Production 99 sets	

2000 Pacific Private Stock Premiere Date

A parallel to the 150-card base set these are limited to 34 serial numbered sets.

	MT
Stars:	20x to 40x
Prospects:	3x to 5x
Inserted 1:24	

2000 Pacific Private Stock Silver Portraits

A parallel to the 150-card base set. These have a silver foiled border. Found exclusively in retail packs, these are limited to 199 serial numbered sets.

	MT
Stars:	5x to 10x
Prospects:	1x to 2x
Production 199 sets	

2000 Pacific Private Stock Extreme Action

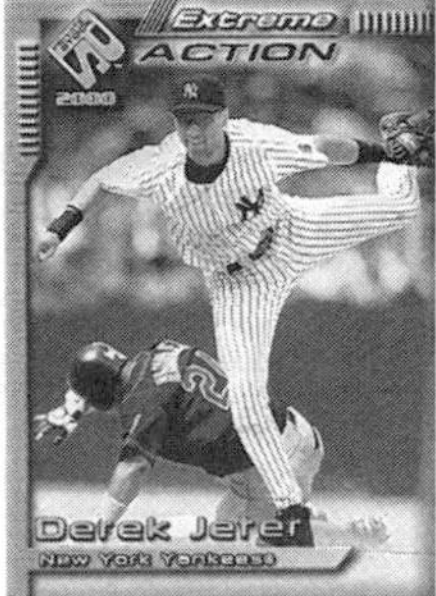

The focus of this 20-card set is the action photography, hence the name Extreme Action. They are seeded 2:25 packs.

		MT
Complete Set (20):		100.00
Common Player:		2.50
Inserted 2:25		
1	Andruw Jones	3.00
2	Chipper Jones	8.00
3	Cal Ripken Jr.	10.00
4	Nomar Garciaparra	10.00
5	Sammy Sosa	10.00
6	Frank Thomas	4.00
7	Roberto Alomar	3.00
8	Manny Ramirez	4.00
9	Larry Walker	3.00
10	Jeff Bagwell	4.00
11	Vladimir Guerrero	6.00
12	Mike Piazza	10.00
13	Derek Jeter	10.00
14	Bernie Williams	3.00
15	Scott Rolen	4.00
16	Mark McGwire	15.00
17	Tony Gwynn	8.00
18	Ken Griffey Jr.	15.00
19	Alex Rodriguez	10.00
20	Ivan Rodriguez	4.00

2000 Pacific Private Stock Private Stock Canvas

This 20-card set is printed on real artist's canvas and have the look of a miniature piece of art. They are seeded 1:49 packs.

		MT
Complete Set (20):		400.00
Common Player:		10.00
Inserted 1:49		
1	Chipper Jones	25.00
2	Greg Maddux	25.00
3	Cal Ripken Jr.	30.00
4	Nomar Garciaparra	30.00
5	Sammy Sosa	30.00
6	Frank Thomas	15.00
7	Manny Ramirez	15.00
8	Larry Walker	10.00
9	Jeff Bagwell	15.00
10	Vladimir Guerrero	18.00
11	Mike Piazza	30.00
12	Roger Clemens	20.00
13	Derek Jeter	30.00
14	Mark McGwire	50.00
15	Tony Gwynn	25.00
16	Barry Bonds	15.00
17	Ken Griffey Jr.	50.00
18	Alex Rodriguez	40.00
19	Juan Gonzalez	15.00
20	Ivan Rodriguez	15.00

2000 Pacific Private Stock Private Stock Reserve

Found exclusively in hobby packs these have a paper thin stock, enhanced with gold foil stamping. These are seeded 1:25 packs.

		MT
Complete Set (20):		175.00
Common Player:		4.00
Inserted 1:25		
1	Chipper Jones	12.00
2	Greg Maddux	12.00
3	Cal Ripken Jr.	15.00
4	Nomar Garciaparra	15.00
5	Sammy Sosa	15.00
6	Frank Thomas	6.00
7	Manny Ramirez	6.00
8	Larry Walker	5.00
9	Jeff Bagwell	6.00
10	Vladimir Guerrero	10.00
11	Mike Piazza	15.00
12	Roger Clemens	10.00
13	Derek Jeter	15.00
14	Mark McGwire	25.00
15	Tony Gwynn	12.00
16	Barry Bonds	6.00
17	Ken Griffey Jr.	25.00
18	Alex Rodriguez	20.00
19	Ivan Rodriguez	6.00
20	Shawn Green	4.00

2000 Pacific Private Stock PS-2000

This miniature 60-card set has a white border with gold foil stamping and are seeded 2 per pack.

		MT
Complete Set (60):		40.00
Common Player:		.25
Inserted 2:pack		
1	Mo Vaughn	.75
2	Greg Maddux	2.00
3	Andruw Jones	.75
4	Chipper Jones	2.00
5	Cal Ripken Jr.	2.50
6	Nomar Garciaparra	2.50
7	Pedro Martinez	1.00
8	Sammy Sosa	2.50
9	Jason Dellaero	.25
10	Magglio Ordonez	.25
11	Frank Thomas	1.00
12	Sean Casey	.50
13	Russell Branyan	.25
14	Manny Ramirez	1.00
15	Richie Sexson	.25
16	Ben Petrick	.25
17	Juan Sosa	.25
18	Larry Walker	.75
19	Robert Fick	.25
20	Craig Biggio	.50
21	Jeff Bagwell	1.00
22	Carlos Beltran	.25
23	Dermal Brown	.25
24	Mark Quinn	.25
25	Eric Gagne	.25
26	Jeromy Burnitz	.25
27	Tony Armas, Jr.	.25
28	Peter Bergeron	.25
29	Vladimir Guerrero	1.50
30	Edgardo Alfonzo	.50
31	Mike Piazza	2.50
32	Jorge Toca	.25
33	Roger Clemens	1.50
34	Alfonso Soriano	1.00
35	Bernie Williams	.75
36	Derek Jeter	2.50
37	Tim Hudson	.50
38	Bobby Abreu	.25
39	Scott Rolen	1.00
40	Brian Giles	.25
41	Chad Hermansen	.25
42	Warren Morris	.25
43	Rick Ankiel	5.00
44	J.D. Drew	.50
45	Adam Kennedy	.25
46	Mark McGwire	4.00
47	Mike Darr	.25
48	Tony Gwynn	2.00
49	Barry Bonds	1.00
50	Ken Griffey Jr.	4.00
51	Carlos Guillen	.25
52	Alex Rodriguez	3.00
53	Juan Gonzalez	1.00
54	Ruben Mateo	.50
55	Ivan Rodriguez	1.00
56	Rafael Palmeiro	.50
57	Jose Canseco	1.00
58	Steve Cox	.25
59	Shawn Green	.75
60	Vernon Wells	.25

2000 Pacific Private Stock PS-2000 Stars

This miniature 20-card set is limited to 299 serial numbered sets.

		MT
Complete Set (20):		260.00
Common Player:		6.00
Production 299 sets		
1	Mo Vaughn	8.00
2	Greg Maddux	20.00
3	Cal Ripken Jr.	25.00
4	Pedro Martinez	10.00
5	Sammy Sosa	25.00
6	Frank Thomas	10.00

7	Larry Walker	8.00
8	Craig Biggio	6.00
9	Jeff Bagwell	10.00
10	Mike Piazza	25.00
11	Roger Clemens	15.00
12	Bernie Williams	8.00
13	Mark McGwire	40.00
14	Tony Gwynn	20.00
15	Barry Bonds	10.00
16	Ken Griffey Jr.	40.00
17	Juan Gonzalez	10.00
18	Ivan Rodriguez	10.00
19	Rafael Palmeiro	6.00
20	Jose Canseco	10.00

2000 Pacific Private Stock PS-2000 New Wave

This miniature 20-card set has copper foil stamping and is limited to 199 serial numbered sets.

		MT
Complete Set (20):		160.00
Common Player:		3.00
Production 199 sets		
1	Andruw Jones	8.00
2	Chipper Jones	20.00
3	Nomar Garciaparra	30.00
4	Magglio Ordonez	5.00
5	Sean Casey	8.00
6	Manny Ramirez	12.00
7	Richie Sexson	3.00
8	Carlos Beltran	3.00
9	Jeromy Burnitz	3.00
10	Vladimir Guerrero	15.00
11	Edgardo Alfonzo	5.00
12	Derek Jeter	30.00
13	Tim Hudson	3.00
14	Bobby Abreu	3.00
15	Scott Rolen	12.00
16	Brian Giles	3.00
17	Warren Morris	3.00
18	J.D. Drew	4.00
19	Alex Rodriguez	35.00
20	Shawn Green	8.00

2000 Pacific Private Stock PS-2000 Rookies

This miniature 20-card set has holographic silver foil stamping and is limited to 99 serial numbered sets.

		MT
Complete Set (20):		160.00
Common Player:		8.00
Inserted 99 sets		
1	Jason Dellaero	8.00
2	Russell Branyan	8.00
3	Ben Petrick	8.00
4	Juan Sosa	8.00
5	Robert Fick	8.00
6	Dermal Brown	8.00
7	Mark Quinn	12.00
8	Eric Gagne	8.00
9	Tony Armas, Jr.	8.00
10	Peter Bergeron	8.00
11	Jorge Toca	8.00
12	Alfonso Soriano	20.00
13	Chad Hermansen	8.00
14	Rick Ankiel	50.00
15	Adam Kennedy	8.00
16	Mike Darr	8.00
17	Carlos Guillen	8.00
18	Steve Cox	8.00
19	Ruben Mateo	12.00
20	Vernon Wells	10.00

2000 Pacific Revolution

The base set consists of 150 cards with silver holofoil throughout the card front. "Revolution" is embossed on the left portion and the logo is stamped in gold foil. Twenty- five short-printed prospects are seeded 1:4 packs.

		MT
Complete Set (150):		150.00
Common Player:		.50
Common SP:		2.00
Pack (3):		4.00
Box:		80.00
1	Darin Erstad	.75
2	Troy Glaus	2.00
3	Adam Kennedy SP	2.00
4	Mo Vaughn	1.00
5	Erubiel Durazo	.50
6	Steve Finley	.50
7	Luis Gonzalez	.75
8	Randy Johnson	2.00
9	Travis Lee	.50
10	Vicente Padilla SP	2.00
11	Matt Williams	.75
12	Rafael Furcal SP	4.00
13	Andres Galarraga	1.00
14	Andruw Jones	1.00
15	Chipper Jones	4.00
16	Greg Maddux	4.00
17	Luis Rivera SP	2.00
18	Albert Belle	1.00
19	Mike Bordick	.50
20	Will Clark	.75
21	Mike Mussina	1.00
22	Cal Ripken Jr.	6.00
23	B.J. Surhoff	.50
24	Carl Everett	.50
25	Nomar Garciaparra	5.00
26	Pedro Martinez	2.00
27	Jason Varitek	.50
28	Wilton Veras SP	3.00
29	Shane Andrews	.50
30	*Scott Downs SP*	2.00
31	Mark Grace	.75
32	Sammy Sosa	5.00
33	Kerry Wood	.75
34	Ray Durham	.50
35	Paul Konerko	.50
36	Carlos Lee	.50
37	Magglio Ordonez	.75
38	Frank Thomas	3.00
39	Rob Bell SP	2.00
40	Sean Casey	.50
41	Ken Griffey Jr.	8.00
42	Barry Larkin	1.00
43	Pokey Reese	.50
44	Roberto Alomar	1.50
45	David Justice	.75
46	Kenny Lofton	.75
47	Manny Ramirez	2.00
48	Richie Sexson	.50
49	Jim Thome	1.00
50	Jeff Cirillo	.75
51	Jeffrey Hammonds	.50
52	Todd Helton	2.00
53	Larry Walker	1.00
54	Tony Clark	.50
55	Juan Gonzalez	2.00
56	Hideo Nomo	.50
57	Dean Palmer	.50
58	Alex Gonzalez	.50
59	Mike Lowell	.50
60	Pablo Ozuna SP	2.00
61	Brad Penny SP	2.00
62	Preston Wilson	.50
63	Moises Alou	.50
64	Jeff Bagwell	2.00
65	Craig Biggio	.75
66	Ken Caminiti	.50
67	Julio Lugo SP	2.00
68	Carlos Beltran	.50
69	Johnny Damon	.50
70	Jermaine Dye	.50
71	Carlos Febles	.50
72	Mark Quinn SP	3.00
73	Kevin Brown	.75
74	Shawn Green	1.00
75	Chan Ho Park	.50
76	Gary Sheffield	1.00
77	Kevin Barker SP	3.00
78	Ron Belliard	.50
79	Jeromy Burnitz	.50
80	Geoff Jenkins	.75
81	Cristian Guzman	.50
82	Jacque Jones	.50
83	Corey Koskie	.50
84	Matt Lawton	.50
85	Peter Bergeron SP	3.00
86	Vladimir Guerrero	3.00
87	Andy Tracy SP	2.00
88	Jose Vidro	.50
89	Rondell White	.50
90	Edgardo Alfonzo	.75
91	Derek Bell	.50
92	Eric Cammack SP	2.00
93	Mike Piazza	5.00
94	Robin Ventura	.75
95	Roger Clemens	3.00
96	Orlando Hernandez	.75
97	Derek Jeter	5.00
98	Tino Martinez	.75
99	Alfonso Soriano SP	6.00
100	Bernie Williams	1.50
101	Eric Chavez	.50
102	Jason Giambi	.75
103	Ben Grieve	.75
104	Terrence Long SP	2.00
105	Mark Mulder SP	2.00
106	Adam Piatt SP	5.00
107	Bobby Abreu	.50
108	Rico Brogna	.50
109	Doug Glanville	.50
110	Mike Lieberthal	.50
111	Scott Rolen	1.50
112	Brian Giles	.50
113	Chad Hermansen SP	2.00
114	Jason Kendall	.50
115	Warren Morris	.50
116	Rick Ankiel SP	12.00
117	J.D. Drew	.50
118	Jim Edmonds	.75
119	Mark McGwire	8.00
120	Fernando Tatis	.75
121	Fernando Vina	.50
122	Tony Gwynn	3.00
123	Trevor Hoffman	.50
124	Ryan Klesko	.50
125	Eric Owens	.50
126	Barry Bonds	2.50
127	Ellis Burks	.50
128	Bobby Estalella	.50
129	Jeff Kent	.75
130	*Scott Linebrink SP*	2.00
131	Jay Buhner	.50
132	Stan Javier	.50
133	Edgar Martinez	.50
134	John Olerud	.75
135	Alex Rodriguez	6.00
136	*Kazuhiro Sasaki SP*	8.00
137	Jose Canseco	1.00
138	Vinny Castilla	.50
139	Fred McGriff	.75
140	Greg Vaughn	.75
141	Gabe Kapler	.75
142	*Mike Lamb SP*	3.00
143	Ruben Mateo	.50
144	Rafael Palmeiro	1.00
145	Ivan Rodriguez	2.00
146	Tony Batista	.50
147	Jose Cruz Jr.	.50
148	Carlos Delgado	1.50
149	Brad Fullmer	.50
150	Raul Mondesi	.75

2000 Pacific Revolution Red

A parallel to the 150-card base set these inserts have red foil in place of the gold from the base version. These are also serial numbered on the card front, limited to 299 sets.

	MT
Stars:	2-3X
SPs:	1X
Production 299 sets	

2000 Pacific Revolution Shadow

A parallel to the 150-card base set, these are identical to the base cards besides blue foil stamping replacing the gold foil and are serial numbered on the card front to 99 sets.

	MT
Stars:	4-8X
SPs:	2-3X
Production 99 sets	

2000 Pacific Revolution Season Opener

This 36-card set has a horizontal format with the set name, team logo, player name and Revolution logo stamped in gold foil. These are seeded 2:25 packs.

		MT
Complete Set (36):		175.00
Common Player:		2.00
Inserted 2:25		
1	Erubiel Durazo	2.00
2	Randy Johnson	5.00
3	Andruw Jones	3.00
4	Chipper Jones	10.00
5	Greg Maddux	10.00
6	Cal Ripken Jr.	15.00
7	Nomar Garciaparra	12.00
8	Pedro Martinez	5.00
9	Sammy Sosa	12.00
10	Frank Thomas	6.00
11	Magglio Ordonez	3.00
12	Ken Griffey Jr.	20.00
13	Barry Larkin	3.00
14	Kenny Lofton	3.00
15	Manny Ramirez	5.00
16	Jim Thome	3.00
17	Larry Walker	3.00

18	Juan Gonzalez	5.00
19	Jeff Bagwell	5.00
20	Craig Biggio	2.00
21	Carlos Beltran	2.00
22	Shawn Green	4.00
23	Vladimir Guerrero	8.00
24	Mike Piazza	12.00
25	Orlando Hernandez	2.00
26	Derek Jeter	12.00
27	Bernie Williams	4.00
28	Eric Chavez	2.00
29	Scott Rolen	4.00
30	Jim Edmonds	2.00
31	Tony Gwynn	8.00
32	Barry Bonds	5.00
33	Alex Rodriguez	15.00
34	Jose Canseco	3.00
35	Ivan Rodriguez	5.00
36	Rafael Palmeiro	3.00

2000 Pacific Revolution Triple Header

This 30-card set is broken down into three tiers with cards 1-10 spotlighting batting average leaders, 11-20 home run leaders and 21-30 strikeout leaders. The base versions are seeded 4:25 packs. A parallel version for each of the three groups is also inserted. Cards 1-20 are limited to 99 serial numbered sets while cards 21-30 are limited to 599 serial numbered sets.

		MT
Complete Set (30):		75.00
Common Player:		1.00
Inserted 4:25		
Parallel (1-10):		4-6X
99 sets produced		
Parallel (11-20):		4-6X
99 sets produced		
Parallel (21-30):		1-2X
599 sets produced		
1	Chipper Jones	4.00
2	Cal Ripken Jr.	6.00
3	Nomar Garciaparra	5.00
4	Frank Thomas	3.00
5	Larry Walker	1.00
6	Vladimir Guerrero	3.00
7	Mike Piazza	5.00
8	Derek Jeter	5.00
9	Tony Gwynn	3.00
10	Ivan Rodriguez	2.00
11	Sammy Sosa	5.00
12	Ken Griffey Jr.	8.00
13	Manny Ramirez	2.00
14	Jeff Bagwell	2.00
15	Shawn Green	1.00
16	Mark McGwire	8.00
17	Barry Bonds	2.00
18	Alex Rodriguez	6.00
19	Jose Canseco	1.00
20	Rafael Palmeiro	1.50
21	Randy Johnson	2.00
22	Tom Glavine	1.00
23	Greg Maddux	4.00
24	Mike Mussina	1.00
25	Pedro Martinez	2.00
26	Kerry Wood	1.00
27	Chuck Finley	1.00
28	Kevin Brown	1.00
29	Roger Clemens	3.00
30	Rick Ankiel	2.00

2000 Pacific Revolution Icons

These die-cut cards feature silver foil stamping and the players' team logo in the background. These are found on the average of 1:121 packs.

		MT
Complete Set (20):		500.00
Common Player:		8.00
Inserted 1:121		
1	Randy Johnson	15.00
2	Chipper Jones	30.00
3	Greg Maddux	30.00
4	Cal Ripken Jr.	50.00
5	Nomar Garciaparra	40.00
6	Pedro Martinez	15.00
7	Sammy Sosa	40.00
8	Frank Thomas	20.00
9	Ken Griffey Jr.	60.00
10	Juan Gonzalez	15.00
11	Jeff Bagwell	15.00
12	Vladimir Guerrero	25.00
13	Mike Piazza	40.00
14	Roger Clemens	20.00
15	Derek Jeter	40.00
16	Mark McGwire	60.00
17	Tony Gwynn	25.00
18	Barry Bonds	15.00
19	Alex Rodriguez	50.00
20	Ivan Rodriguez	15.00

2000 Pacific Revolution Foul Pole Net-Fusions

These inserts utilize net-fusion technology, with netting infused in the left and right portion. The player name and logo are stamped in gold foil. These are found on the average of 1:49 packs.

		MT
Complete Set (20):		250.00
Common Player:		4.00
Inserted 1:49		
1	Chipper Jones	15.00
2	Cal Ripken Jr.	25.00
3	Nomar Garciaparra	20.00
4	Pedro Martinez	8.00
5	Sammy Sosa	20.00
6	Frank Thomas	10.00
7	Ken Griffey Jr.	30.00
8	Manny Ramirez	8.00
9	Jeff Bagwell	8.00
10	Shawn Green	6.00
11	Vladimir Guerrero	12.00
12	Mike Piazza	20.00
13	Derek Jeter	20.00
14	Bernie Williams	6.00
15	Rick Ankiel	10.00
16	Mark McGwire	30.00
17	Tony Gwynn	12.00
18	Barry Bonds	8.00
19	Alex Rodriguez	25.00
20	Ivan Rodriguez	8.00

2000 Pacific Revolution On Deck

These inserts have a die-cut rounded bottom and feature the player in a simulated on-deck circle enhanced by green foil stamping. These are seeded 1:25 packs.

		MT
Complete Set (20):		140.00
Common Player:		3.00
Inserted 1:25		
1	Chipper Jones	10.00
2	Cal Ripken Jr.	15.00
3	Nomar Garciaparra	12.00
4	Sammy Sosa	12.00
5	Frank Thomas	6.00
6	Ken Griffey Jr.	20.00
7	Manny Ramirez	5.00
8	Larry Walker	3.00
9	Juan Gonzalez	5.00
10	Jeff Bagwell	5.00
11	Shawn Green	3.00
12	Vladimir Guerrero	8.00
13	Mike Piazza	12.00
14	Derek Jeter	12.00
15	Scott Rolen	5.00
16	Mark McGwire	20.00
17	Tony Gwynn	8.00
18	Alex Rodriguez	15.00
19	Jose Canseco	3.00
20	Ivan Rodriguez	5.00

2000 Pacific Revolution Game-Ball Signatures

This 25-card autographed set has a piece of baseball leather embedded into the front on which the player penned his signature.

		MT
Common Player:		10.00
1	Adam Kennedy	15.00
2	Randy Johnson	40.00
3	Rafael Furcal	20.00
4	Greg Maddux	100.00
5	Shane Andrews	10.00
6	Sean Casey	20.00
7	Travis Dawkins	15.00
8	Alex Gonzalez	10.00
9	Brad Penny	15.00
10	Shane Reynolds	15.00
11	Mark Quinn	15.00
12	Eric Gagne	15.00
13	Kevin Barker	15.00
14	Eric Milton	10.00
15	Alfonso Soriano	25.00
16	Mark Mulder	10.00
17	Adam Piatt	20.00
18	Brian Giles	15.00
19	Warren Morris	10.00
20	Rick Ankiel	75.00
21	Fernando Tatis	20.00
22	Barry Bonds	60.00
23	Alex Rodriguez	150.00
24	Ruben Mateo	15.00
25	Billy Koch	10.00

2000 Pacific Vanguard

		MT
Complete Set (100):		75.00
Common Player:		.25
Pack (4):		4.00
Wax Box (24):		85.00
1	Troy Glaus	1.25
2	Tim Salmon	.40
3	Mo Vaughn	.75
4	Albert Belle	.75
5	Mike Mussina	1.00
6	Cal Ripken Jr.	4.00
7	Nomar Garciaparra	3.00
8	Pedro Martinez	1.50
9	Troy O'Leary	.25
10	Wilton Veras	.25
11	Magglio Ordonez	.25
12	Chris Singleton	.25
13	Frank Thomas	1.50
14	Roberto Alomar	1.00
15	Russell Branyan	.25
16	Manny Ramirez	1.25
17	Jim Thome	.75
18	Omar Vizquel	.40
19	Tony Clark	.40
20	Juan Gonzalez	1.25
21	Dean Palmer	.25
22	Carlos Beltran	.25
23	Johnny Damon	.25
24	Jermaine Dye	.25

25	Mark Quinn	.25
26	Jacque Jones	.25
27	Corey Koskie	.25
28	Brad Radke	.25
29	Roger Clemens	2.00
30	Derek Jeter	3.00
31	Alfonso Soriano	.75
32	Bernie Williams	1.00
33	Eric Chavez	.25
34	Jason Giambi	.40
35	Ben Grieve	.40
36	Tim Hudson	.40
37	Mike Cameron	.25
38	Freddy Garcia	.25
39	Edgar Martinez	.25
40	Alex Rodriguez	4.00
41	Jose Canseco	1.25
42	Vinny Castilla	.40
43	Fred McGriff	.40
44	Rusty Greer	.25
45	Ruben Mateo	.40
46	Rafael Palmeiro	1.00
47	Ivan Rodriguez	1.25
48	Carlos Delgado	1.00
49	Shannon Stewart	.25
50	Vernon Wells	.25
51	Erubiel Durazo	.50
52	Randy Johnson	1.00
53	Matt Williams	.75
54	Andruw Jones	.75
55	Chipper Jones	2.50
56	Greg Maddux	2.50
57	Mark Grace	.50
58	Sammy Sosa	3.00
59	Kerry Wood	.75
60	Sean Casey	.75
61	Ken Griffey Jr.	5.00
62	Barry Larkin	.75
63	Todd Helton	1.25
64	Ben Petrick	.25
65	Larry Walker	1.00
66	Luis Castillo	.25
67	Alex Gonzalez	.25
68	Preston Wilson	.25
69	Jeff Bagwell	1.25
70	Craig Biggio	.75
71	Billy Wagner	.25
72	Kevin Brown	.50
73	Shawn Green	1.00
74	Gary Sheffield	.50
75	Kevin Barker	.25
76	Ron Belliard	.25
77	Jeromy Burnitz	.40
78	Michael Barrett	.25
79	Peter Bergeron	.25
80	Vladimir Guerrero	2.00
81	Edgardo Alfonzo	.50
82	Rey Ordonez	.25
83	Mike Piazza	3.00
84	Robin Ventura	.40
85	Bobby Abreu	.40
86	Mike Lieberthal	.25
87	Scott Rolen	1.25
88	Brian Giles	.40
89	Chad Hermansen	.25
90	Jason Kendall	.40
91	Rick Ankiel	3.00
92	J.D. Drew	.30
93	Mark McGwire	5.00
94	Fernando Tatis	.50
95	Ben Davis	.25
96	Tony Gwynn	2.50
97	Trevor Hoffman	.25
98	Barry Bonds	1.25
99	Ellis Burks	.25
100	Jeff Kent	.25

2000 Pacific Vanguard Green

	MT
A.L. (1-50):	8-15X
Production 99 sets	
N.L. (51-100):	5-10X
Production 199 sets	

2000 Pacific Vanguard Gold

	MT
A.L. (1-50):	5-10X
Production 199 sets R	
N.L. (51-100):	8-15X
Production 99 sets R	

2000 Pacific Vanguard Premiere Date

	MT
Stars:	6-12X
Production 135 sets H	

2000 Pacific Vanguard Purple

	MT
Production 10 sets	

2000 Pacific Vanguard Game Worn Jersey

		MT
Common Player:		60.00
Inserted 1:120		
1	Greg Maddux	100.00
2	Tony Gwynn	80.00
3	Alex Rodriguez	150.00
4	Frank Thomas	80.00
5	Chipper Jones	100.00

2000 Pacific Vanguard Cosmic Force

		MT
Complete Set (10):		220.00
Common Player:		6.00
Inserted 1:73		
1	Chipper Jones	18.00
2	Cal Ripken Jr.	30.00
3	Nomar Garciaparra	25.00
4	Sammy Sosa	25.00
5	Ken Griffey Jr.	35.00
6	Mike Piazza	25.00
7	Derek Jeter	25.00
8	Mark McGwire	35.00
9	Tony Gwynn	18.00
10	Alex Rodriguez	30.00

Modern cards in Near Mint condition are valued at about 75% of the Mint value shown here. Excellent-condition cards are worth 50%. Cards in lower grades are not generally collectible.

2000 Pacific Vanguard Diamond Architects

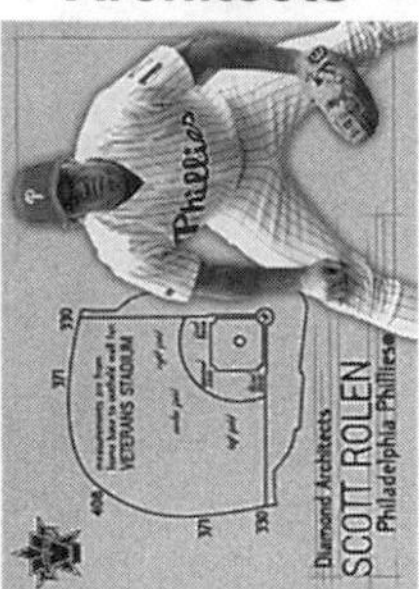

		MT
Complete Set (20):		125.00
Common Player:		2.00
Inserted 1:25		
1	Chipper Jones	8.00
2	Greg Maddux	8.00
3	Cal Ripken Jr.	12.00
4	Nomar Garciaparra	10.00
5	Sammy Sosa	10.00
6	Ken Griffey Jr.	15.00
7	Manny Ramirez	4.00
8	Larry Walker	3.00
9	Jeff Bagwell	4.00
10	Vladimir Guerrero	6.00
11	Mike Piazza	10.00
12	Roger Clemens	6.00
13	Derek Jeter	10.00
14	Bernie Williams	3.00
15	Scott Rolen	4.00
16	Mark McGwire	15.00
17	Tony Gwynn	8.00
18	Alex Rodriguez	12.00
19	Rafael Palmeiro	3.00
20	Ivan Rodriguez	4.00

The values of some parallel-card issues will have to be calculated based on figures presented in the heading for the regular-issue card set.

2000 Pacific Vanguard A.L. Vanguard Press

		MT
Complete Set (10):		20.00
Common Player:		1.00
Inserted 2:25		
1	Cal Ripken Jr.	5.00
2	Nomar Garciaparra	4.00
3	Pedro Martinez	1.50
4	Manny Ramirez	1.50
5	Carlos Beltran	1.00
6	Roger Clemens	2.00
7	Derek Jeter	4.00
8	Alex Rodriguez	5.00
9	Rafael Palmeiro	1.25
10	Ivan Rodriguez	1.50

2000 Pacific Vanguard N.L. Vanguard Press

		MT
Complete Set (10):		30.00
Common Player:		1.00
Inserted 2:37		
1	Chipper Jones	3.00
2	Greg Maddux	3.00
3	Sammy Sosa	4.00
4	Ken Griffey Jr.	6.00
5	Larry Walker	1.25
6	Jeff Bagwell	1.50
7	Vladimir Guerrero	2.50
8	Mike Piazza	4.00
9	Mark McGwire	6.00
10	Tony Gwynn	3.00

2000 Pacific Vanguard High Voltage

		MT
Complete Set (36):		30.00
Common Player:		.40
Inserted 1:1		
1	Mo Vaughn	.50
2	Erubiel Durazo	.40
3	Randy Johnson	.60
4	Andruw Jones	.60
5	Chipper Jones	1.50
6	Greg Maddux	1.50
7	Cal Ripken Jr.	2.50
8	Nomar Garciaparra	2.00
9	Pedro Martinez	.75
10	Sammy Sosa	2.00
11	Frank Thomas	1.00
12	Sean Casey	.50
13	Ken Griffey Jr.	3.00
14	Barry Larkin	.50
15	Manny Ramirez	.75
16	Jim Thome	.50
17	Larry Walker	.50
18	Jeff Bagwell	.75
19	Craig Biggio	.50
20	Carlos Beltran	.40
21	Shawn Green	.60
22	Vladimir Guerrero	1.00
23	Edgardo Alfonzo	.50
24	Mike Piazza	2.00
25	Roger Clemens	1.00

26	Derek Jeter	2.00
27	Bernie Williams	.60
28	Scott Rolen	.75
29	Brian Giles	.40
30	Rick Ankiel	2.00
31	Mark McGwire	3.00
32	Tony Gwynn	1.50
33	Barry Bonds	.75
34	Alex Rodriguez	2.50
35	Rafael Palmeiro	.50
36	Ivan Rodriguez	.75

1992 Pinnacle

Score entered the high-end card market with the release of this 620-card set. The cards feature black borders surrounding a white frame with a full-color action photo inside. The player extends beyond the natural background. The backs are horizontal and feature a closeup photo, statistics, team logo, biographical information and player information. Several subsets can be found within the set including "Idols, Sidelines, Grips, Shades" and "Technicians".

	MT
Complete Set (620):	45.00
Common Player:	.10
Series 1 or 2 Pack (16):	1.00
Series 1 or 2 Wax Box (36):	30.00

1	Frank Thomas	1.50
2	Benito Santiago	.10
3	Carlos Baerga	.10
4	Cecil Fielder	.15
5	Barry Larkin	.15
6	Ozzie Smith	.50
7	Willie McGee	.10
8	Paul Molitor	.50
9	Andy Van Slyke	.10
10	Ryne Sandberg	.75
11	Kevin Seitzer	.10
12	Len Dykstra	.15
13	Edgar Martinez	.10
14	Ruben Sierra	.10
15	Howard Johnson	.10
16	Dave Henderson	.10
17	Devon White	.10
18	Terry Pendleton	.10
19	Steve Finley	.10
20	Kirby Puckett	.75
21	Orel Hershiser	.10
22	Hal Morris	.10
23	Don Mattingly	.75
24	Delino DeShields	.15
25	Dennis Eckersley	.15
26	Ellis Burks	.10
27	Jay Buhner	.10
28	Matt Williams	.25
29	Lou Whitaker	.10
30	Alex Fernandez	.15
31	Albert Belle	.75
32	Todd Zeile	.10
33	Tony Pena	.10
34	Jay Bell	.10
35	Rafael Palmeiro	.30
36	Wes Chamberlain	.10
37	George Bell	.10
38	Robin Yount	.75
39	Vince Coleman	.10
40	Bruce Hurst	.10
41	Harold Baines	.10
42	Chuck Finley	.10
43	Ken Caminiti	.20
44	Ben McDonald	.10
45	Roberto Alomar	.60
46	Chili Davis	.10
47	Bill Doran	.10
48	Jerald Clark	.10
49	Jose Lind	.10
50	Nolan Ryan	2.00
51	Phil Plantier	.10
52	Gary DiSarcina	.10
53	Kevin Bass	.10
54	Pat Kelly	.10
55	Mark Wohlers	.10
56	Walt Weiss	.10
57	Lenny Harris	.10
58	Ivan Calderon	.10
59	Harold Reynolds	.10
60	George Brett	.75
61	Gregg Olson	.10
62	Orlando Merced	.10
63	Steve Decker	.10
64	John Franco	.10
65	Greg Maddux	1.50
66	Alex Cole	.10
67	Dave Hollins	.10
68	Kent Hrbek	.10
69	Tom Pagnozzi	.10
70	Jeff Bagwell	1.50
71	Jim Gantner	.10
72	Matt Nokes	.10
73	Brian Harper	.10
74	Andy Benes	.15
75	Tom Glavine	.25
76	Terry Steinbach	.10
77	Dennis Martinez	.10
78	John Olerud	.20
79	Ozzie Guillen	.10
80	Darryl Strawberry	.15
81	Gary Gaetti	.10
82	Dave Righetti	.10
83	Chris Hoiles	.10
84	Andujar Cedeno	.10
85	Jack Clark	.10
86	David Howard	.10
87	Bill Gullickson	.10
88	Bernard Gilkey	.15
89	Kevin Elster	.10
90	Kevin Maas	.10
91	Mark Lewis	.10
92	Greg Vaughn	.15
93	Bret Barberie	.10
94	Dave Smith	.10
95	Roger Clemens	.75
96	Doug Drabek	.10
97	Omar Vizquel	.15
98	Jose Guzman	.10
99	Juan Samuel	.10
100	Dave Justice	.25
101	Tom Browning	.10
102	Mark Gubicza	.10
103	Mickey Morandini	.10
104	Ed Whitson	.10
105	Lance Parrish	.10
106	Scott Erickson	.10
107	Jack McDowell	.10
108	Dave Stieb	.10
109	Mike Moore	.10
110	Travis Fryman	.10
111	Dwight Gooden	.15
112	Fred McGriff	.35
113	Alan Trammell	.15
114	Roberto Kelly	.10
115	Andre Dawson	.15
116	Bill Landrum	.10
117	Brian McRae	.10
118	B.J. Surhoff	.15
119	Chuck Knoblauch	.15
120	Steve Olin	.10
121	Robin Ventura	.30
122	Will Clark	.25
123	Tino Martinez	.15
124	Dale Murphy	.20
125	Pete O'Brien	.10
126	Ray Lankford	.10
127	Juan Gonzalez	.75
128	Ron Gant	.15
129	Marquis Grissom	.15
130	Jose Canseco	.40
131	Mike Greenwell	.10
132	Mark Langston	.10
133	Brett Butler	.10
134	Kelly Gruber	.10
135	Chris Sabo	.10
136	Mark Grace	.25
137	Tony Fernandez	.10
138	Glenn Davis	.10
139	Pedro Munoz	.10
140	Craig Biggio	.20
141	Pete Schourek	.10
142	Mike Boddicker	.10
143	Robby Thompson	.10
144	Mel Hall	.10
145	Bryan Harvey	.10
146	Mike LaValliere	.10
147	John Kruk	.10
148	Joe Carter	.15
149	Greg Olson	.10
150	Julio Franco	.10
151	Darryl Hamilton	.10
152	Felix Fermin	.10
153	Jose Offerman	.10
154	Paul O'Neill	.15
155	Tommy Greene	.10
156	Ivan Rodriguez	.60
157	Dave Stewart	.15
158	Jeff Reardon	.10
159	Felix Jose	.10
160	Doug Dascenzo	.10
161	Tim Wallach	.10
162	Dan Plesac	.10
163	Luis Gonzalez	.10
164	Mike Henneman	.10
165	Mike Devereaux	.10
166	Luis Polonia	.10
167	Mike Sharperson	.10
168	Chris Donnels	.10
169	Greg Harris	.10
170	Deion Sanders	.30
171	Mike Schooler	.10
172	Jose DeJesus	.10
173	Jeff Montgomery	.10
174	Milt Cuyler	.10
175	Wade Boggs	.45
176	Kevin Tapani	.10
177	Bill Spiers	.10
178	Tim Raines	.15
179	Randy Milligan	.10
180	Rob Dibble	.10
181	Kirt Manwaring	.10
182	Pascual Perez	.10
183	Juan Guzman	.15
184	John Smiley	.10
185	David Segui	.10
186	Omar Olivares	.10
187	Joe Slusarski	.10
188	Erik Hanson	.10
189	Mark Portugal	.10
190	Walt Terrell	.10
191	John Smoltz	.15
192	Wilson Alvarez	.15
193	Jimmy Key	.10
194	Larry Walker	.25
195	Lee Smith	.10
196	Pete Harnisch	.10
197	Mike Harkey	.10
198	Frank Tanana	.10
199	Terry Mulholland	.10
200	Cal Ripken, Jr.	2.50
201	Dave Magadan	.10
202	Bud Black	.10
203	Terry Shumpert	.10
204	Mike Mussina	.50
205	Mo Vaughn	.50
206	Steve Farr	.10
207	Darrin Jackson	.10
208	Jerry Browne	.10
209	Jeff Russell	.10
210	Mike Scioscia	.10
211	Rick Aguilera	.10
212	Jaime Navarro	.10
213	Randy Tomlin	.10
214	Bobby Thigpen	.10
215	Mark Gardner	.10
216	Norm Charlton	.10
217	Mark McGwire	3.00
218	Skeeter Barnes	.10
219	Bob Tewksbury	.10
220	Junior Felix	.10
221	Sam Horn	.10
222	Jody Reed	.10
223	Luis Sojo	.10
224	Jerome Walton	.10
225	Darryl Kile	.10
226	Mickey Tettleton	.10
227	Dan Pasqua	.10
228	Jim Gott	.10
229	Bernie Williams	.30
230	Shane Mack	.10
231	Steve Avery	.10
232	Dave Valle	.10
233	Mark Leonard	.10
234	Spike Owen	.10
235	Gary Sheffield	.25
236	Steve Chitren	.10
237	Zane Smith	.10
238	Tom Gordon	.10
239	Jose Oquendo	.10
240	Todd Stottlemyre	.10
241	Darren Daulton	.10
242	Tim Naehring	.10
243	Tony Phillips	.10
244	Shawon Dunston	.10
245	Manuel Lee	.10
246	Mike Pagliarulo	.10
247	Jim Thome (Rookie Prospect)	.30
248	Luis Mercedes (Rookie Prospect)	.15
249	Cal Eldred (Rookie Prospect)	.15
250	Derek Bell (Rookie Prospect)	.20
251	Arthur Rhodes (Rookie Prospect)	.15
252	Scott Cooper (Rookie Prospect)	.10
253	Roberto Hernandez (Rookie Prospect)	.15
254	Mo Sanford (Rookie Prospect)	.15
255	Scott Servais (Rookie Prospect)	.10
256	Eric Karros (Rookie Prospect)	.15
257	Andy Mota	.10
258	Keith Mitchell	.10
259	Joel Johnston (Rookie Prospect)	.10
260	John Wehner (Rookie Prospect)	.10
261	Gino Minutelli (Rookie Prospect)	.10
262	Greg Gagne	.10
263	Stan Royer (Rookie Prospect)	.15
264	Carlos Garcia (Rookie Prospect)	.15
265	Andy Ashby (Rookie Prospect)	.20
266	Kim Batiste (Rookie Prospect)	.10
267	Julio Valera (Rookie Prospect)	.10
268	Royce Clayton (Rookie Prospect)	.10
269	Gary Scott (Rookie Prospect)	.10
270	Kirk Dressendorfer (Rookie Prospect)	.10
271	Sean Berry (Rookie Prospect)	.15
272	Lance Dickson (Rookie Prospect)	.15
273	Rob Maurer (Rookie Prospect)	.10
274	Scott Brosius (Rookie Prospect)	.15
275	Dave Fleming (Rookie Prospect)	.10
276	Lenny Webster (Rookie Prospect)	.15
277	Mike Humphreys	.10
278	Freddie Benavides (Rookie Prospect)	.15
279	Harvey Pulliam (Rookie Prospect)	.10
280	Jeff Carter (Rookie Prospect)	.15
281	Jim Abbott, Nolan Ryan (Idols)	.25
282	Wade Boggs, George Brett (Idols)	.20
283	Ken Griffey Jr., Rickey Henderson (Idols)	.75
284	Dale Murphy, Wally Joyner (Idols)	.15

285 Chuck Knoblauch, Ozzie Smith (Idols) .15
286 Robin Ventura, Lou Gehrig (Idols) .35
287 Robin Yount (Sidelines - Motocross) .35
288 Bob Tewksbury (Sidelines - Cartoonist) .10
289 Kirby Puckett (Sidelines - Pool Player) .40
290 Kenny Lofton (Sidelines - Basketball Player) .50
291 Jack McDowell (Sidelines - Guitarist) .10
292 John Burkett (Sidelines - Bowler) .10
293 Dwight Smith (Sidelines - Singer) .10
294 Nolan Ryan (Sidelines - Cattle Rancher) 1.00
295 *Manny Ramirez* (1st Round Draft Pick) 6.00
296 *Cliff Floyd* (1st Round Draft Pick) .50
297 *Al Shirley* (1st Round Draft Pick) .10
298 *Brian Barber* (1st Round Draft Pick) .15
299 *Jon Farrell* (1st Round Draft Pick) .15
300 *Scott Ruffcorn* (1st Round Draft Pick) .25
301 *Tyrone Hill* (1st Round Draft Pick) .15
302 *Benji Gil* (1st Round Draft Pick) .25
303 *Tyler Green* (1st Round Draft Pick) .30
304 Allen Watson (Shades) .15
305 Jay Buhner (Shades) .15
306 Roberto Alomar (Shades) .35
307 Chuck Knoblauch (Shades) .15
308 Darryl Strawberry (Shades) .10
309 Danny Tartabull (Shades) .15
310 Bobby Bonilla (Shades) .10
311 Mike Felder .10
312 Storm Davis .10
313 Tim Teufel .10
314 Tom Brunansky .10
315 Rex Hudler .10
316 Dave Otto .10
317 Jeff King .10
318 Dan Gladden .10
319 Bill Pecota .10
320 Franklin Stubbs .10
321 Gary Carter .20
322 Melido Perez .10
323 Eric Davis .15
324 Greg Myers .10
325 Pete Incaviglia .10
326 Von Hayes .10
327 Greg Swindell .10
328 Steve Sax .10
329 Chuck McElroy .10
330 Gregg Jefferies .20
331 Joe Oliver .10
332 Paul Faries .10
333 David West .10
334 Craig Grebeck .10
335 Chris Hammond .10
336 Billy Ripken .10
337 Scott Sanderson .10
338 Dick Schofield .10
339 Bob Milacki .10
340 Kevin Reimer .10
341 Jose DeLeon .10
342 Henry Cotto .10
343 Daryl Boston .10
344 Kevin Gross .10
345 Milt Thompson .10
346 Luis Rivera .10
347 Al Osuna .10
348 Rob Deer .10
349 Tim Leary .10
350 Mike Stanton .10
351 Dean Palmer .10
352 Trevor Wilson .10
353 Mark Eichhorn .10
354 Scott Aldred .10
355 Mark Whiten .15
356 Leo Gomez .10
357 Rafael Belliard .10
358 Carlos Quintana .10
359 Mark Davis .10
360 Chris Nabholz .10
361 Carlton Fisk .25
362 Joe Orsulak .10
363 Eric Anthony .10
364 Greg Hibbard .10
365 Scott Leius .10
366 Hensley Meulens .10
367 Chris Bosio .10
368 Brian Downing .10
369 Sammy Sosa 2.00
370 Stan Belinda .10
371 Joe Grahe .10
372 Luis Salazar .10
373 Lance Johnson .10
374 Kal Daniels .10
375 Dave Winfield .50
376 Brook Jacoby .10
377 Mariano Duncan .10
378 Ron Darling .10
379 Randy Johnson .50
380 Chito Martinez .10
381 Andres Galarraga .15
382 Willie Randolph .10
383 Charles Nagy .10
384 Tim Belcher .10
385 Duane Ward .10
386 Vicente Palacios .10
387 Mike Gallego .10
388 Rich DeLucia .10
389 Scott Radinsky .10
390 Damon Berryhill .10
391 Kirk McCaskill .10
392 Pedro Guerrero .10
393 Kevin Mitchell .10
394 Dickie Thon .10
395 Bobby Bonilla .15
396 Bill Wegman .10
397 Dave Martinez .10
398 Rick Sutcliffe .10
399 Larry Andersen .10
400 Tony Gwynn 1.00
401 Rickey Henderson .45
402 Greg Cadaret .10
403 Keith Miller .10
404 Bip Roberts .10
405 Kevin Brown .15
406 Mitch Williams .10
407 Frank Viola .10
408 Darren Lewis .10
409 Bob Walk .10
410 Bob Walk .10
411 Todd Frohwirth .10
412 Brian Hunter .10
413 Ron Karkovice .10
414 Mike Morgan .10
415 Joe Hesketh .10
416 Don Slaught .10
417 Tom Henke .10
418 Kurt Stillwell .10
419 Hector Villanueva .10
420 Glenallen Hill .10
421 Pat Borders .10
422 Charlie Hough .10
423 Charlie Leibrandt .10
424 Eddie Murray .35
425 Jesse Barfield .10
426 Mark Lemke .10
427 Kevin McReynolds .10
428 Gilberto Reyes .10
429 Ramon Martinez .15
430 Steve Buechele .10
431 David Wells .15
432 Kyle Abbott (Rookie Prospect) .15
433 John Habyan .10
434 Kevin Appier .10
435 Gene Larkin .10
436 Sandy Alomar, Jr. .15
437 Mike Jackson .10
438 Todd Benzinger .10
439 Teddy Higuera .10
440 Reggie Sanders (Rookie Prospect) .15
441 Mark Carreon .10
442 Bret Saberhagen .10
443 Gene Nelson .10
444 Jay Howell .10
445 Roger McDowell .10
446 Sid Bream .10
447 Mackey Sasser .10
448 Bill Swift .10
449 Hubie Brooks .10
450 David Cone .15
451 Bobby Witt .10
452 Brady Anderson .15
453 Lee Stevens .10
454 Luis Aquino .10
455 Carney Lansford .10
456 Carlos Hernandez (Rookie Prospect) .15
457 Danny Jackson .10
458 Gerald Young .10
459 Tom Candiotti .10
460 Billy Hatcher .10
461 John Wetteland .15
462 Mike Bordick .10
463 Don Robinson .10
464 Jeff Johnson .10
465 Lonnie Smith .10
466 Paul Assenmacher .10
467 Alvin Davis .10
468 Jim Eisenreich .10
469 Brent Mayne .10
470 Jeff Brantley .10
471 Tim Burke .10
472 *Pat Mahomes* (Rookie Prospect) .25
473 Ryan Bowen .10
474 Bryn Smith .10
475 Mike Flanagan .10
476 Reggie Jefferson (Rookie Prospect) .15
477 Jeff Blauser .10
478 Craig Lefferts .10
479 Todd Worrell .10
480 Scott Scudder .10
481 Kirk Gibson .10
482 Kenny Rogers .10
483 Jack Morris .10
484 Russ Swan .10
485 Mike Huff .10
486 Ken Hill .10
487 Geronimo Pena .10
488 Charlie O'Brien .10
489 Mike Maddux .10
490 Scott Livingstone (Rookie Prospect) .15
491 Carl Willis .10
492 Kelly Downs .10
493 Dennis Cook .10
494 Joe Magrane .10
495 Bob Kipper .10
496 Jose Mesa .10
497 Charlie Hayes .10
498 Joe Girardi .10
499 Doug Jones .10
500 Barry Bonds .75
501 Bill Krueger .10
502 Glenn Braggs .10
503 Eric King .10
504 Frank Castillo .10
505 Mike Gardiner .10
506 Cory Snyder .10
507 Steve Howe .10
508 Jose Rijo .10
509 Sid Fernandez .10
510 *Archi Cianfrocco* (Rookie Prospect) .15
511 Mark Guthrie .10
512 Bob Ojeda .10
513 John Doherty (Rookie Prospect) .15
514 Dante Bichette .10
515 Juan Berenguer .10
516 Jeff Robinson .10
517 Mike MacFarlane .10
518 Matt Young .10
519 Otis Nixon .10
520 Brian Holman .10
521 Chris Haney .10
522 *Jeff Kent* (Rookie Prospect) .50
523 *Chad Curtis* (Rookie Prospect) .50
524 Vince Horsman .10
525 Rod Nichols .10
526 *Peter Hoy* (Rookie Prospect) .10
527 Shawn Boskie .10
528 Alejandro Pena .10
529 Dave Burba (Rookie Prospect) .10
530 Ricky Jordan .10
531 David Silvestri (Rookie Prospect) .15
532 John Patterson (Rookie Prospect) .20
533 Jeff Branson (Rookie Prospect) .15
534 Derrick May (Rookie Prospect) .15
535 Esteban Beltre (Rookie Prospect) .10
536 Jose Melendez .10
537 Wally Joyner .10
538 Eddie Taubensee (Rookie Prospect) .15
539 Jim Abbott .15
540 *Brian Williams* (Rookie Prospect) .15
541 Donovan Osborne (Rookie Prospect) .10
542 Patrick Lennon (Rookie Prospect) .10
543 *Mike Groppuso* (Rookie Prospect) .10
544 *Jarvis Brown* (Rookie Prospect) .10
545 *Shawn Livesy* (1st Round Draft Pick) .20
546 Jeff Ware (1st Round Draft Pick) .15
547 Danny Tartabull .10
548 *Bobby Jones* (1st Round Draft Pick) .60
549 Ken Griffey, Jr. 3.00
550 *Rey Sanchez* (Rookie Prospect) .25
551 *Pedro Astacio* (Rookie Prospect) .25
552 *Juan Guerrero* (Rookie Prospect) .10
553 *Jacob Brumfield* (Rookie Prospect) .15
554 *Ben Rivera* (Rookie Prospect) .10
555 *Brian Jordan* (Rookie Prospect) 1.00
556 Denny Neagle (Rookie Prospect) .10
557 Cliff Brantley (Rookie Prospect) .15
558 Anthony Young (Rookie Prospect) .10
559 *John VanderWal* (Rookie Prospect) .15
560 *Monty Fariss* (Rookie Prospect) .10
561 *Russ Springer* (Rookie Prospect) .20
562 *Pat Listach* (Rookie Prospect) .15
563 Pat Hentgen (Rookie Prospect) .10
564 Andy Stankiewicz (Rookie Prospect) .10
565 Mike Perez (Rookie Prospect) .15
566 Mike Bielecki .10
567 Butch Henry (Rookie Prospect) .10
568 *Dave Nilsson* (Rookie Prospect) .30
569 *Scott Hatteberg* (Rookie Prospect) .20
570 Ruben Amaro, Jr. (Rookie Prospect) .15
571 Todd Hundley (Rookie Prospect) .15
572 Moises Alou (Rookie Prospect) .20
573 Hector Fajardo (Rookie Prospect) .15
574 Todd Van Poppel (Rookie Prospect) .15

575	Willie Banks (Rookie Prospect)	.15
576	Bob Zupcic (Rookie Prospect)	.10
577	*J.J. Johnson* (1st Round Draft Pick)	.15
578	John Burkett	.10
579	Trever Miller (1st Round Draft Pick)	.15
580	Scott Bankhead	.10
581	Rich Amaral (Rookie Prospect)	.10
582	Kenny Lofton (Rookie Prospect)	.50
583	Matt Stairs (Rookie Prospect)	.20
584	Don Mattingly, Rod Carew (Idols)	.25
585	Jack Morris, Steve Avery (Idols)	.10
586	Roberto Alomar, Sandy Alomar (Idols)	.25
587	Scott Sanderson, Catfish Hunter (Idols)	.10
588	Dave Justice, Willie Stargell (Idols)	.30
589	Rex Hudler, Roger Staubach (Idols)	.10
590	David Cone, Jackie Gleason (Idols)	.10
591	Willie Davis, Tony Gwynn (Idols)	.15
592	Orel Hershiser (Sidelines)	.15
593	John Wetteland (Sidelines)	.15
594	Tom Glavine (Sidelines)	.15
595	Randy Johnson (Sidelines)	.20
596	Jim Gott (Sidelines)	.10
597	Donald Harris	.10
598	*Shawn Hare*	.15
599	Chris Gardner	.10
600	Rusty Meacham	.10
601	Benito Santiago (Shades)	.10
602	Eric Davis (Shades)	.15
603	Jose Lind (Shades)	.10
604	Dave Justice (Shades)	.30
605	Tim Raines (Shades)	.15
606	Randy Tomlin (Grips)	.10
607	Jack McDowell (Grips)	.10
608	Greg Maddux (Grips)	.30
609	Charles Nagy (Grips)	.10
610	Tom Candiotti (Grips)	.10
611	David Cone (Grips)	.10
612	Steve Avery (Grips)	.10
613	*Rod Beck*	.30
614	Rickey Henderson (Technician)	.25
615	Benito Santiago (Technician)	.10
616	Ruben Sierra (Technician)	.10
617	Ryne Sandberg (Technician)	.40
618	Nolan Ryan (Technician)	.75
619	Brett Butler (Technician)	.10
620	Dave Justice (Technician)	.30

1992 Pinnacle Rookie Idols

Carrying on with the Idols subset theme in the regular issue, these Series II foil-pack inserts feature 18 of the year's rookie prospects sharing cards with their baseball heroes. Both front and back are horizontal in format and include photos of both the rookie and his idol.

		MT
Complete Set (18):		95.00
Common Player:		2.00
1	Reggie Sanders, Eric Davis	2.00
2	Hector Fajardo, Jim Abbott	2.00
3	Gary Cooper, George Brett	10.00
4	Mark Wohlers, Roger Clemens	8.00
5	Luis Mercedes, Julio Franco	2.00
6	Willie Banks, Dwight Gooden	2.00
7	Kenny Lofton, Rickey Henderson	10.00
8	Keith Mitchell, Dave Henderson	2.00
9	Kim Batiste, Barry Larkin	2.00
10	Thurman Munson, Todd Hundley	7.50
11	Eddie Zosky, Cal Ripken Jr.	20.00
12	Todd Van Poppel, Nolan Ryan	20.00
13	Ryne Sandberg, Jim Thome	10.00
14	Dave Fleming, Bobby Murcer	2.00
15	Royce Clayton, Ozzie Smith	7.50
16	Don Harris, Darryl Strawberry	2.00
17	Alan Trammell, Chad Curtis	2.00
18	Derek Bell, Dave Winfield	4.00

1992 Pinnacle Rookies

Styled after the regular 1992 Score Pinnacle cards, this 30-card boxed set features the top rookies of 1992. The cards have a player action photo which is borderless on the top and sides. Beneath the photo a team color-coded strip carries the player's name in gold foil, with a round gold-bordered team logo at left. A black strip at bottom has the notation "1992 Rookie". Horizontal-format backs follow a similar design and include a bit of player information, Pinnacle's anti-counterfeiting strip and some gold-foil enhancements.

		MT
Complete Set (30):		6.00
Common Player:		.15
1	Luis Mercedes	.25
2	Scott Cooper	.15
3	Kenny Lofton	2.00
4	John Doherty	.20
5	Pat Listach	.20
6	Andy Stankiewicz	.15
7	Derek Bell	.45
8	Gary DiSarcina	.15
9	Roberto Hernandez	.25
10	Joel Johnston	.15
11	Pat Mahomes	.25
12	Todd Van Poppel	.15
13	Dave Fleming	.15
14	Monty Fariss	.15
15	Gary Scott	.15
16	Moises Alou	.50
17	Todd Hundley	.35
18	Kim Batiste	.15
19	Denny Neagle	.20
20	Donovan Osborne	.15
21	Mark Wohlers	.15
22	Reggie Sanders	.30
23	Brian Williams	.15
24	Eric Karros	.75
25	Frank Seminara	.15
26	Royce Clayton	.15
27	Dave Nilsson	.30
28	Matt Stairs	.20
29	Chad Curtis	.35
30	Carlos Hernandez	.15

1992 Pinnacle Slugfest

Each specially marked Slugfest jumbo pack of '92 Pinnacle contained one of these horizontal-format cards of the game's top hitters. The player's name is printed in gold foil at the bottom of the card, along with a red and white Slugfest logo. Backs, which are vertical in orientation, have a color player photo, a career summary and a few lifetime stats.

		MT
Complete Set (15):		35.00
Common Player:		.50
1	Cecil Fielder	.75
2	Mark McGwire	10.00
3	Jose Canseco	1.50
4	Barry Bonds	3.00
5	Dave Justice	1.00
6	Bobby Bonilla	.75
7	Ken Griffey, Jr.	10.00
8	Ron Gant	.75
9	Ryne Sandberg	3.00
10	Ruben Sierra	.50
11	Frank Thomas	7.50
12	Will Clark	2.00
13	Kirby Puckett	4.00
14	Cal Ripken, Jr.	6.00
15	Jeff Bagwell	4.00

1992 Pinnacle Team Pinnacle

The most sought-after and valuable of the 1992 Pinnacle insert cards is this 12-piece set of "two-headed" cards. An American and a National League superstar at each position are featured on each card, with two cards each for starting and relief pitchers. The ultra-realistic artwork of Chris Greco is featured on the cards, which were inserted into Series I foil packs.

		MT
Complete Set (12):		60.00
Common Player:		2.50
1	Roger Clemens, Ramon Martinez	6.00
2	Jim Abbott, Steve Avery	2.00
3	Benito Santiago, Ivan Rodriguez	3.00
4	Frank Thomas, Will Clark	7.50
5	Roberto Alomar, Ryne Sandberg	9.00
6	Robin Ventura, Matt Williams	4.00
7	Cal Ripken, Jr., Barry Larkin	12.50
8	Danny Tartabull, Barry Bonds	5.00
9	Brett Butler, Ken Griffey Jr.	15.00
10	Ruben Sierra, Dave Justice	4.00
11	Dennis Eckersley, Rob Dibble	2.00
12	Scott Radinsky, John Franco	2.00

1992 Pinnacle Team 2000

Young stars who were projected to be the game's superstars in the year 2000 were chosen for this 80-card insert set found three at a time in jumbo packs. Cards #1-40 were included in Series I packaging, while cards #41-80 were inserted with Series II Pinnacle. Cards feature gold foil highlights on both front and back.

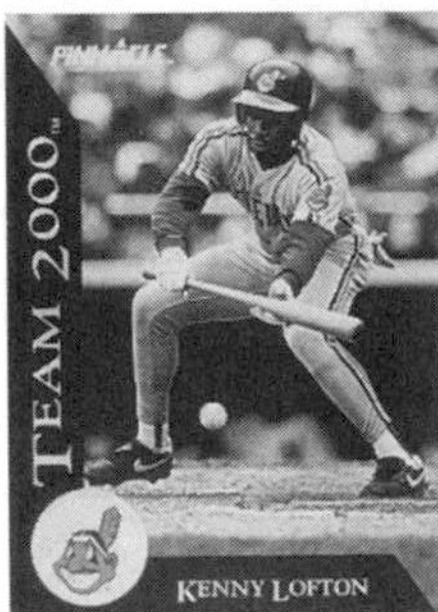

		MT
Complete Set (80):		30.00
Common Player:		.10
1	Mike Mussina	1.00
2	Phil Plantier	.10
3	Frank Thomas	2.50
4	Travis Fryman	.10
5	Kevin Appier	.10
6	Chuck Knoblauch	.50
7	Pat Kelly	.10
8	Ivan Rodriguez	1.25
9	Dave Justice	.25
10	Jeff Bagwell	2.00
11	Marquis Grissom	.15
12	Andy Benes	.10
13	Gregg Olson	.10
14	Kevin Morton	.10
15	Tim Naehring	.10
16	Dave Hollins	.10
17	Sandy Alomar Jr.	.20
18	Albert Belle	1.50
19	Charles Nagy	.15
20	Brian McRae	.10
21	Larry Walker	.65
22	Delino DeShields	.10
23	Jeff Johnson	.10
24	Bernie Williams	1.00
25	Jose Offerman	.10
26	Juan Gonzalez	1.50
27	Juan Guzman	.10
28	Eric Anthony	.10
29	Brian Hunter	.10
30	John Smoltz	.30
31	Deion Sanders	.25
32	Greg Maddux	2.50
33	Andujar Cedeno	.10
34	Royce Clayton	.10
35	Kenny Lofton	1.00
36	Cal Eldred	.10
37	Jim Thome	.60
38	Gary DiSarcina	.10
39	Brian Jordan	.50
40	Chad Curtis	.10
41	Ben McDonald	.10
42	Jim Abbott	.15
43	Robin Ventura	.25
44	Milt Cuyler	.10
45	Gregg Jefferies	.15
46	Scott Radinsky	.10
47	Ken Griffey, Jr.	5.00
48	Roberto Alomar	1.50
49	Ramon Martinez	.15
50	Bret Barberie	.10
51	Ray Lankford	.15
52	Leo Gomez	.10
53	Tommy Greene	.10
54	Mo Vaughn	1.00
55	Sammy Sosa	3.00
56	Carlos Baerga	.10
57	Mark Lewis	.10
58	Tom Gordon	.10
59	Gary Sheffield	.65
60	Scott Erickson	.10
61	Pedro Munoz	.10
62	Tino Martinez	.15
63	Darren Lewis	.10
64	Dean Palmer	.10
65	John Olerud	.25
66	Steve Avery	.10
67	Pete Harnisch	.10
68	Luis Gonzalez	.15
69	Kim Batiste	.10
70	Reggie Sanders	.15
71	Luis Mercedes	.10
72	Todd Van Poppel	.10
73	Gary Scott	.10
74	Monty Fariss	.10
75	Kyle Abbott	.10
76	Eric Karros	.15
77	Mo Sanford	.10
78	Todd Hundley	.50
79	Reggie Jefferson	.10
80	Pat Mahomes	.15

1993 Pinnacle Promos

On six of the eight cards issued to premiere Pinnacle's '93 set, the difference between the promo version and the issued version is so slight it can easily go unnoticed - the "TM" in the upper-right corner on front is larger on the promo than on the regular card. Promo cards #3 and 5 are easier to spot because the team logos on back of the promos are the old Expos and Mariners logos, rather than the new versions found on issued cards.

		MT
Complete Set (8):		50.00
Common Player:		5.00
1	Gary Sheffield	10.00
2	Cal Eldred	5.00
3	Larry Walker	9.00
4	Deion Sanders	10.00
5	Dave Fleming	5.00
6	Carlos Baerga	5.00
7	Bernie Williams	9.00
8	John Kruk	5.00

1993 Pinnacle

This 620-card set offers many of the same features which made the first Pinnacle set so popular in 1992. Subsets are titled Rookies, Now & Then (which shows the player as he looks now and as a rookie), Idols (active players and their heroes on the same card), Hometown Heroes (players who are playing with their hometown team), Draft Picks and Rookies. More than 100 rookies and 10 draft picks are featured. All regular cards have an action photo, a black border and the Pinnacle name stamped in gold. Series I cards feature portraits of players on the two new expansion teams; Series II cards feature action shots of them. Team Pinnacle insert cards return, while Rookie Team Pinnacle cards make their debut. Other insert sets are titled Team 2001, Slugfest and Tribute, which features five cards each of Nolan Ryan and George Brett.

		MT
Complete Set (620):		45.00
Complete Series 1 (310):		20.00
Complete Series 2 (310):		25.00
Common Player:		.05
Series 1 or 2 Pack (15):		1.00
Series 1 or 2 Wax Box (36):		30.00
1	Gary Sheffield	.30
2	Cal Eldred	.10
3	Larry Walker	.25
4	Deion Sanders	.15
5	Dave Fleming	.05
6	Carlos Baerga	.05
7	Bernie Williams	.40
8	John Kruk	.05
9	Jimmy Key	.05
10	Jeff Bagwell	1.00
11	Jim Abbott	.05
12	Terry Steinbach	.05
13	Bob Tewksbury	.05
14	Eric Karros	.10
15	Ryne Sandberg	.75
16	Will Clark	.30
17	Edgar Martinez	.10
18	Eddie Murray	.30
19	Andy Van Slyke	.05
20	Cal Ripken, Jr.	2.50
21	Ivan Rodriguez	.60
22	Barry Larkin	.20
23	Don Mattingly	1.00
24	Gregg Jefferies	.05
25	Roger Clemens	1.00
26	Cecil Fielder	.10
27	Kent Hrbek	.05
28	Robin Ventura	.15
29	Rickey Henderson	.30
30	Roberto Alomar	.60
31	Luis Polonia	.05
32	Andujar Cedeno	.05
33	Pat Listach	.05
34	Mark Grace	.20
35	Otis Nixon	.05
36	Felix Jose	.05
37	Mike Sharperson	.05
38	Dennis Martinez	.05
39	Willie McGee	.05
40	Kenny Lofton	.60
41	Randy Johnson	.40
42	Andy Benes	.05
43	Bobby Bonilla	.10
44	Mike Mussina	.60
45	Len Dykstra	.10
46	Ellis Burks	.05
47	Chris Sabo	.05
48	Jay Bell	.05
49	Jose Canseco	.35
50	Craig Biggio	.20
51	Wally Joyner	.05
52	Mickey Tettleton	.05
53	Tim Raines	.10
54	Brian Harper	.05
55	Rene Gonzales	.05
56	Mark Langston	.05
57	Jack Morris	.05
58	Mark McGwire	3.00
59	Ken Caminiti	.20
60	Terry Pendleton	.05
61	Dave Nilsson	.05
62	Tom Pagnozzi	.05
63	Mike Morgan	.05
64	Darryl Strawberry	.10
65	Charles Nagy	.05
66	Ken Hill	.05
67	Matt Williams	.25
68	Jay Buhner	.10
69	Vince Coleman	.05
70	Brady Anderson	.10
71	Fred McGriff	.30
72	Ben McDonald	.05
73	Terry Mulholland	.05
74	Randy Tomlin	.05
75	Nolan Ryan	2.50
76	Frank Viola	.05
77	Jose Rijo	.05
78	Shane Mack	.05
79	Travis Fryman	.15
80	Jack McDowell	.05
81	Mark Gubicza	.05
82	Matt Nokes	.05
83	Bert Blyleven	.05
84	Eric Anthony	.05
85	Mike Bordick	.05
86	John Olerud	.15
87	B.J. Surhoff	.05
88	Bernard Gilkey	.05
89	Shawon Dunston	.05
90	Tom Glavine	.15
91	Brett Butler	.05
92	Moises Alou	.15
93	Albert Belle	.75
94	Darren Lewis	.05
95	Omar Vizquel	.05
96	Dwight Gooden	.10
97	Gregg Olson	.05
98	Tony Gwynn	1.00
99	Darren Daulton	.05
100	Dennis Eckersley	.05
101	Rob Dibble	.05
102	Mike Greenwell	.05
103	Jose Lind	.05
104	Julio Franco	.05
105	Tom Gordon	.05
106	Scott Livingstone	.05
107	Chuck Knoblauch	.20
108	Frank Thomas	1.50
109	Melido Perez	.05
110	Ken Griffey, Jr.	3.00
111	Harold Baines	.05
112	Gary Gaetti	.05
113	Pete Harnisch	.05
114	David Wells	.10
115	Charlie Leibrandt	.05
116	Ray Lankford	.10
117	Kevin Seitzer	.05
118	Robin Yount	.45
119	Lenny Harris	.05
120	Chris James	.05
121	Delino DeShields	.05
122	Kirt Manwaring	.05
123	Glenallen Hill	.05
124	Hensley Meulens	.05
125	Darrin Jackson	.05
126	Todd Hundley	.15
127	Dave Hollins	.10
128	Sam Horn	.05
129	Roberto Hernandez	.05
130	Vicente Palacios	.05
131	George Brett	.75
132	Dave Martinez	.05
133	Kevin Appier	.05
134	Pat Kelly	.05
135	Pedro Munoz	.05
136	Mark Carreon	.05
137	Lance Johnson	.05
138	Devon White	.05
139	Julio Valera	.05
140	Eddie Taubensee	.05
141	Willie Wilson	.05
142	Stan Belinda	.05
143	John Smoltz	.15
144	Darryl Hamilton	.05
145	Sammy Sosa	1.50
146	Carlos Hernandez	.05
147	Tom Candiotti	.05
148	Mike Felder	.05
149	Rusty Meacham	.05
150	Ivan Calderon	.05
151	Pete O'Brien	.05
152	Erik Hanson	.05
153	Billy Ripken	.05
154	Kurt Stillwell	.05
155	Jeff Kent	.05
156	Mickey Morandini	.05
157	Randy Milligan	.05

158 Reggie Sanders .10
159 Luis Rivera .05
160 Orlando Merced .05
161 Dean Palmer .05
162 Mike Perez .05
163 Scott Erikson .05
164 Kevin McReynolds .05
165 Kevin Maas .05
166 Ozzie Guillen .05
167 Rob Deer .05
168 Danny Tartabull .05
169 Lee Stevens .05
170 Dave Henderson .05
171 Derek Bell .05
172 Steve Finley .05
173 Greg Olson .05
174 Geronimo Pena .05
175 Paul Quantrill .05
176 Steve Buechele .05
177 Kevin Gross .05
178 Tim Wallach .05
179 Dave Valle .05
180 Dave Silvestri .05
181 Bud Black .05
182 Henry Rodriguez .05
183 Tim Teufel .05
184 Mark McLemore .05
185 Bret Saberhagen .05
186 Chris Hoiles .05
187 Ricky Jordan .05
188 Don Slaught .05
189 Mo Vaughn .60
190 Joe Oliver .05
191 Juan Gonzalez .75
192 Scott Leius .05
193 Milt Cuyler .05
194 Chris Haney .05
195 Ron Karkovice .05
196 Steve Farr .05
197 John Orton .05
198 Kelly Gruber .05
199 Ron Darling .05
200 Ruben Sierra .05
201 Chuck Finley .05
202 Mike Moore .05
203 Pat Borders .05
204 Sid Bream .05
205 Todd Zeile .05
206 Rick Wilkins .05
207 Jim Gantner .05
208 Frank Castillo .05
209 Dave Hansen .05
210 Trevor Wilson .05
211 Sandy Alomar, Jr. .15
212 Sean Berry .05
213 Tino Martinez .25
214 Chito Martinez .05
215 Dan Walters .05
216 John Franco .05
217 Glenn Davis .05
218 Mariano Duncan .05
219 Mike LaValliere .05
220 Rafael Palmeiro .20
221 Jack Clark .05
222 Hal Morris .05
223 Ed Sprague .05
224 John Valentin .10
225 Sam Militello .05
226 Bob Wickman .05
227 Damion Easley .10
228 John Jaha .10
229 Bob Ayrault .05
230 Mo Sanford (Expansion Draft) .05
231 Walt Weiss (Expansion Draft) .05
232 Dante Bichette (Expansion Draft) .35
233 Steve Decker (Expansion Draft) .05
234 Jerald Clark (Expansion Draft) .05
235 Bryan Harvey (Expansion Draft) .05
236 Joe Girardi (Expansion Draft) .05
237 Dave Magadan (Expansion Draft) .05
238 David Nied (Rookie Prospect) .05
239 *Eric Wedge* (Rookie Prospect) .05
240 Rico Brogna (Rookie Prospect) .10
241 J.T. Bruett (Rookie Prospect) .05
242 Jonathan Hurst (Rookie Prospect) .05
243 Bret Boone (Rookie Prospect) .25
244 Manny Alexander (Rookie Prospect) .15
245 Scooter Tucker (Rookie Prospect) .05
246 Troy Neel (Rookie Prospect) .10
247 Eddie Zosky (Rookie Prospect) .05
248 Melvin Nieves (Rookie Prospect) .05
249 Ryan Thompson (Rookie Prospect) .15
250 Shawn Barton (Rookie Prospect) .10
251 Ryan Klesko (Rookie Prospect) .50
252 Mike Piazza (Rookie Prospect) 2.00
253 Steve Hosey (Rookie Prospect) .10
254 Shane Reynolds (Rookie Prospect) .15
255 Dan Wilson (Rookie Prospect) .15
256 Tom Marsh (Rookie Prospect) .05
257 Barry Manuel (Rookie Prospect) .05
258 Paul Miller (Rookie Prospect) .05
259 Pedro Martinez (Rookie Prospect) .25
260 Steve Cooke (Rookie Prospect) .10
261 Johnny Guzman (Rookie Prospect) .05
262 Mike Butcher (Rookie Prospect) .10
263 Bien Figueroa (Rookie Prospect) .10
264 Rich Rowland (Rookie Prospect) .05
265 Shawn Jeter (Rookie Prospect) .10
266 Gerald Williams (Rookie Prospect) .15
267 Derek Parks (Rookie Prospect) .05
268 Henry Mercedes (Rookie Prospect) .10
269 *David Hulse* (Rookie Prospect) .10
270 *Tim Pugh* (Rookie Prospect) .10
271 William Suero (Rookie Prospect) .05
272 Ozzie Canseco (Rookie Prospect) .05
273 Fernando Ramsey (Rookie Prospect) .10
274 Bernardo Brito (Rookie Prospect) .05
275 Dave Mlicki (Rookie Prospect) .10
276 Tim Salmon (Rookie Prospect) .60
277 Mike Raczka (Rookie Prospect) .05
278 *Ken Ryan* (Rookie Prospect) .25
279 Rafael Bournigal (Rookie Prospect) .10
280 Wil Cordero (Rookie Prospect) .15
281 Billy Ashley (Rookie Prospect) .10
282 Paul Wagner (Rookie Prospect) .10
283 Blas Minor (Rookie Prospect) .10
284 Rick Trlicek (Rookie Prospect) .05
285 Willie Greene (Rookie Prospect) .05
286 Ted Wood (Rookie Prospect) .05
287 Phil Clark (Rookie Prospect) .05
288 Jesse Levis (Rookie Prospect) .10
289 Tony Gwynn (Now & Then) .40
290 Nolan Ryan (Now & Then) 1.00
291 Dennis Martinez (Now & Then) .05
292 Eddie Murray (Now & Then) .15
293 Robin Yount (Now & Then) .30
294 George Brett (Now & Then) .40
295 Dave Winfield (Now & Then) .15
296 Bert Blyleven (Now & Then) .05
297 Jeff Bagwell (Idols - Carl Yastrzemski) .40
298 John Smoltz (Idols - Jack Morris) .10
299 Larry Walker (Idols - Mike Bossy) .20
300 Gary Sheffield (Idols - Barry Larkin) .15
301 Ivan Rodriguez (Idols - Carlton Fisk) .25
302 Delino DeShields (Idols - Malcolm X) .05
303 Tim Salmon (Idols - Dwight Evans) .25
304 Bernard Gilkey (Hometown Heroes) .05
305 Cal Ripken, Jr. (Hometown Heroes) 1.00
306 Barry Larkin (Hometown Heroes) .10
307 Kent Hrbek (Hometown Heroes) .05
308 Rickey Henderson (Hometown Heroes) .10
309 Darryl Strawberry (Hometown Heroes) .05
310 John Franco (Hometown Heroes) .05
311 Todd Stottlemyre .05
312 Luis Gonzalez .10
313 Tommy Greene .05
314 Randy Velarde .05
315 Steve Avery .05
316 Jose Oquendo .05
317 Rey Sanchez .05
318 Greg Vaughn .10
319 Orel Hershiser .05
320 Paul Sorrento .05
321 Royce Clayton .05
322 John Vander Wal .05
323 Henry Cotto .05
324 Pete Schourek .05
325 David Segui .05
326 Arthur Rhodes .05
327 Bruce Hurst .05
328 Wes Chamberlain .05
329 Ozzie Smith .45
330 Scott Cooper .05
331 Felix Fermin .05
332 Mike Macfarlane .05
333 Dan Gladden .05
334 Kevin Tapani .05
335 Steve Sax .05
336 Jeff Montgomery .05
337 Gary DiSarcina .05
338 Lance Blankenship .05
339 Brian Williams .05
340 Duane Ward .05
341 Chuck McElroy .05
342 Joe Magrane .05
343 Jaime Navarro .05
344 Dave Justice .25
345 Jose Offerman .05
346 Marquis Grissom .10
347 Bill Swift .05
348 Jim Thome .50
349 Archi Cianfrocco .05
350 Anthony Young .05
351 Leo Gomez .05
352 Bill Gullickson .05
353 Alan Trammell .10
354 Dan Pasqua .05
355 Jeff King .05
356 Kevin Brown .10
357 Tim Belcher .05
358 Bip Roberts .05
359 Brent Mayne .05
360 Rheal Cormier .05
361 Mark Guthrie .05
362 Craig Grebeck .05
363 Andy Stankiewicz .05
364 Juan Guzman .05
365 Bobby Witt .05
366 Mark Portugal .05
367 Brian McRae .05
368 Mark Lemke .05
369 Bill Wegman .05
370 Donovan Osborne .05
371 Derrick May .05
372 Carl Willis .05
373 Chris Nabholz .05
374 Mark Lewis .05
375 John Burkett .05
376 Luis Mercedes .05
377 Ramon Martinez .15
378 Kyle Abbott .05
379 Mark Wohlers .05
380 Bob Walk .05
381 Kenny Rogers .05
382 Tim Naehring .05
383 Alex Fernandez .05
384 Keith Miller .05
385 Mike Henneman .05
386 Rick Aguilera .05
387 George Bell .05
388 Mike Gallego .05
389 Howard Johnson .05
390 Kim Batiste .05
391 Jerry Browne .05
392 Damon Berryhill .05
393 Ricky Bones .05
394 Omar Olivares .05
395 Mike Harkey .05
396 Pedro Astacio .05
397 John Wetteland .05
398 Rod Beck .05
399 Thomas Howard .05
400 Mike Devereaux .05
401 Tim Wakefield .05
402 Curt Schilling .10
403 Zane Smith .05
404 Bob Zupcic .05
405 Tom Browning .05
406 Tony Phillips .05
407 John Doherty .05
408 Pat Mahomes .05
409 John Habyan .05
410 Steve Olin .05
411 Chad Curtis .10
412 Joe Grahe .05
413 John Patterson .05
414 Brian Hunter .05
415 Doug Henry .05
416 Lee Smith .05
417 Bob Scanlan .05
418 Kent Mercker .05
419 Mel Rojas .05
420 Mark Whiten .05
421 Carlton Fisk .20
422 Candy Maldonado .05
423 Doug Drabek .05
424 Wade Boggs .25
425 Mark Davis .05
426 Kirby Puckett .75
427 Joe Carter .10
428 Paul Molitor .45
429 Eric Davis .10
430 Darryl Kile .05
431 Jeff Parrett (Expansion Draft) .05
432 Jeff Blauser .05
433 Dan Plesac .05
434 Andres Galarraga (Expansion Draft) .15
435 Jim Gott .05
436 Jose Mesa .05
437 Ben Rivera .05
438 Dave Winfield .25
439 Norm Charlton .05
440 Chris Bosio .05
441 Wilson Alvarez .05
442 Dave Stewart .05
443 Doug Jones .05
444 Jeff Russell .05
445 Ron Gant .10
446 Paul O'Neill .15
447 Charlie Hayes (Expansion Draft) .05
448 Joe Hesketh .05
449 Chris Hammond .05
450 Hipolito Pichardo .05
451 Scott Radinsky .05
452 Bobby Thigpen .05
453 Xavier Hernandez .10
454 Lonnie Smith .05

455 *Jamie Arnold* (1st Draft Pick) .10
456 B.J. Wallace (1st Draft Pick) .15
457 *Derek Jeter* (Rookie Prospect) 18.00
458 *Jason Kendall* (Rookie Prospect) 2.00
459 Rick Helling (Rookie Prospect) .05
460 *Derek Wallace* (Rookie Prospect) .10
461 *Sean Lowe* (Rookie Prospect) .10
462 *Shannon Stewart* (Rookie Prospect) 1.00
463 *Benji Grigsby* (Rookie Prospect) .10
464 *Todd Steverson* (Rookie Prospect) .15
465 *Dan Serafini* (Rookie Prospect) .10
466 Michael Tucker (Rookie Prospect) .10
467 Chris Roberts (Rookie Prospect) .10
468 *Pete Janicki* (1st Draft Pick) .15
469 *Jeff Schmidt* (1st Draft Pick) .15
470 Don Mattingly (Now & Then) .40
471 Cal Ripken, Jr. (Now & Then) 1.00
472 Jack Morris (Now & Then) .05
473 Terry Pendleton (Now & Then) .05
474 Dennis Eckersley (Now & Then) .10
475 Carlton Fisk (Now & Then) .10
476 Wade Boggs (Now & Then) .20
477 Len Dykstra (Idols - Ken Stabler) .10
478 Danny Tartabull (Idols - Jose Tartabull) .10
479 Jeff Conine (Idols - Dale Murphy) .10
480 Gregg Jefferies (Idols - Ron Cey) .15
481 Paul Molitor (Idols - Harmon Killebrew) .20
482 John Valentin (Idols - Dave Concepcion) .10
483 Alex Arias (Idols - Dave Winfield) .10
484 Barry Bonds (Hometown Heroes) .50
485 Doug Drabek (Hometown Heroes) .05
486 Dave Winfield (Hometown Heroes) .15
487 Brett Butler (Hometown Heroes) .10
488 Harold Baines (Hometown Heroes) .10
489 David Cone (Hometown Heroes) .15
490 Willie McGee (Hometown Heroes) .10
491 Robby Thompson .05
492 Pete Incaviglia .05
493 Manuel Lee .05
494 Rafael Belliard .05
495 Scott Fletcher .05
496 Jeff Frye .05
497 Andre Dawson .15
498 Mike Scioscia .05
499 Spike Owen .05
500 Sid Fernandez .05
501 Joe Orsulak .05
502 Benito Santiago (Expansion Draft) .05
503 Dale Murphy .15
504 Barry Bonds .75
505 Jose Guzman .05
506 Tony Pena .05
507 Greg Swindell .05
508 Mike Pagliarulo .05
509 Lou Whitaker .05
510 Greg Gagne .05
511 Butch Henry (Expansion Draft) .05
512 Jeff Brantley .05
513 Jack Armstrong (Expansion Draft) .05
514 Danny Jackson .05
515 Junior Felix (Expansion Draft) .05
516 Milt Thompson .05
517 Greg Maddux 2.00
518 Eric Young (Expansion Draft) .05
519 Jody Reed .05
520 Roberto Kelly .05
521 Darren Holmes (Expansion Draft) .05
522 Craig Lefferts .05
523 Charlie Hough (Expansion Draft) .05
524 Bo Jackson .15
525 Bill Spiers .05
526 Orestes Destrade (Expansion Draft) .05
527 Greg Hibbard .05
528 Roger McDowell .05
529 Cory Snyder .05
530 Harold Reynolds .05
531 Kevin Reimer .05
532 Rick Sutcliffe .05
533 Tony Fernandez .05
534 Tom Brunansky .05
535 Jeff Reardon .05
536 Chili Davis .05
537 Bob Ojeda .05
538 Greg Colbrunn .05
539 Phil Plantier .05
540 Brian Jordan .10
541 Pete Smith .05
542 Frank Tanana .05
543 John Smiley .05
544 David Cone .10
545 Daryl Boston (Expansion Draft) .05
546 Tom Henke .05
547 Bill Krueger .05
548 Freddie Benavides (Expansion Draft) .05
549 Randy Myers .05
550 Reggie Jefferson .05
551 Kevin Mitchell .05
552 Dave Stieb .05
553 Bret Barberie (Expansion Draft) .05
554 Tim Crews .05
555 Doug Dascenzo .05
556 Alex Cole (Expansion Draft) .05
557 Jeff Innis .05
558 Carlos Garcia .15
559 Steve Howe .05
560 Kirk McCaskill .05
561 Frank Seminara .05
562 Cris Carpenter (Expansion Draft) .05
563 Mike Stanley .05
564 Carlos Quintana .05
565 Mitch Williams .05
566 Juan Bell .05
567 Eric Fox .05
568 Al Leiter .10
569 Mike Stanton .05
570 Scott Kamieniecki .05
571 Ryan Bowen (Expansion Draft) .05
572 Andy Ashby (Expansion Draft) .10
573 Bob Welch .05
574 Scott Sanderson .05
575 Joe Kmak (Rookie Prospect) .05
576 Scott Pose (Rookie Prospect/ Expansion Draft) .15
577 Ricky Gutierrez (Rookie Prospect) .15
578 Mike Trombley (Rookie Prospect) .10
579 *Sterling Hitchcock* (Rookie Prospect) .25
580 Rodney Bolton (Rookie Prospect) .10
581 Tyler Green (Rookie Prospect) .15
582 Tim Costo (Rookie Prospect) .10
583 *Tim Laker* (Rookie Prospect) .15
584 *Steve Reed* (Rookie Prospect/ Expansion Draft) .10
585 *Tom Kramer* (Rookie Prospect) .15
586 Robb Nen (Rookie Prospect) .10
587 *Jim Tatum* (Rookie Prospect) .10
588 Frank Bolick (Rookie Prospect) .15
589 Kevin Young (Rookie Prospect) .15
590 *Matt Whiteside* (Rookie Prospect) .15
591 Cesar Hernandez (Rookie Prospect) .15
592 *Mike Mohler* (Rookie Prospect) .15
593 Alan Embree (Rookie Prospect) .15
594 Terry Jorgensen (Rookie Prospect) .05
595 *John Cummings* (Rookie Prospect) .25
596 Domingo Martinez (Rookie Prospect) .10
597 Benji Gil (Rookie Prospect) .10
598 *Todd Pratt* (Rookie Prospect) .15
599 *Rene Arocha* (Rookie Prospect) .25
600 Dennis Moeller (Rookie Prospect) .10
601 Jeff Conine (Rookie Prospect/ Expansion Draft) .25
602 Trevor Hoffman (Rookie Prospect/ Expansion Draft) .15
603 Daniel Smith (Rookie Prospect) .10
604 Lee Tinsley (Rookie Prospect) .10
605 Dan Peltier (Rookie Prospect) .10
606 Billy Brewer (Rookie Prospect) .10
607 *Matt Walbeck* (Rookie Prospect) .20
608 Richie Lewis (Rookie Prospect/ Expansion Draft) .10
609 *J.T. Snow* (Rookie Prospect) .75
610 *Pat Gomez* (Rookie Prospect) .15
611 Phil Hiatt (Rookie Prospect) .10
612 Alex Arias (Rookie Prospect/ Expansion Draft) .15
613 Kevin Rogers (Rookie Prospect) .10
614 Al Martin (Rookie Prospect) .15
615 Greg Gohr (Rookie Prospect) .10
616 *Grame Lloyd* (Rookie Prospect) .15
617 Kent Bottenfield (Rookie Prospect) .15
618 Chuck Carr (Rookie Prospect/ Expansion Draft) .15
619 *Darrell Sherman* (Rookie Prospect) .10
620 *Mike Lansing* (Rookie Prospect) .25

1993 Pinnacle Expansion Opening Day

This nine-card set features 18 players for the two N.L. expansion teams: the Florida Marlins and Colorado Rockies. Each card side shows a projected Opening Day starter for each team. Cards were available one per every Series II hobby box. Complete sets were available through a special mail-in offer.

		MT
Complete Set (9):		5.00
Common Player:		.40
1	Charlie Hough, David Nied	.75
2	Benito Santiago, Joe Girardi	.50
3	Orestes Destrade, Andres Galarraga	1.50
4	Bret Barberie, Eric Young	.50
5	Dave Magadan, Charlie Hayes	.75
6	Walt Weiss, Freddie Benevides	.50
7	Jeff Conine, Jerald Clark	.75
8	Scott Pose, Alex Cole	.40
9	Junior Felix, Dante Bichette	.75

1993 Pinnacle Rookie Team Pinnacle

These 10 cards were randomly inserted into Score Pinnacle Series II packs. Rookie Team Pinnacle is written in gold foil on both sides of the card. Cards are numbered 1 of 10, etc., and use the special Dufex process. Each card shows two players painted by artist Christopher Greco. Stated odds of finding a Rookie Team Pinnacle insert were given as one in 90 packs.

	MT
Complete Set (10):	90.00
Common Player:	5.00

1	Pedro Martinez, Mike Trombley	12.00
2	Kevin Rogers, Sterling Hitchcock	5.00
3	Mike Piazza, Jesse Levis	50.00
4	Ryan Klesko, J.T. Snow	12.00
5	John Patterson, Bret Boone	5.00
6	Domingo Martinez, Kevin Young	5.00
7	Wil Cordero, Manny Alexander	6.00
8	Steve Hosey, Tim Salmon	15.00
9	Ryan Thompson, Gerald Williams	6.00
10	Melvin Nieves, David Hulse	5.00

1993 Pinnacle Slugfest

Baseball's top sluggers are featured in this 30-card insert set. Cards were available one per Series II jumbo packs. Slugfest is written in gold foil on the card front.

		MT
Complete Set (30):		45.00
Common Player:		.50
1	Juan Gonzalez	3.00
2	Mark McGwire	15.00
3	Cecil Fielder	.75
4	Joe Carter	.75
5	Fred McGriff	1.50
6	Barry Bonds	3.50
7	Gary Sheffield	1.00
8	Dave Hollins	.50
9	Frank Thomas	6.00
10	Danny Tartabull	.50
11	Albert Belle	3.00
12	Ruben Sierra	.50
13	Larry Walker	1.50
14	Jeff Bagwell	3.50
15	Dave Justice	.75
16	Kirby Puckett	5.00
17	John Kruk	.50
18	Howard Johnson	.50
19	Darryl Strawberry	.75
20	Will Clark	1.50
21	Kevin Mitchell	.50
22	Mickey Tettleton	.50
23	Don Mattingly	5.00
24	Jose Canseco	1.50
25	Sam Millitello	.50
26	Andre Dawson	.75
27	Ryne Sandberg	3.00
28	Ken Griffey, Jr.	15.00
29	Carlos Baerga	.50
30	Travis Fryman	.75

1993 Pinnacle Team Pinnacle

These cards were randomly inserted in Pinnacle Series I packs; cards were included one in about every 24 packs. Each card features two players painted by artist Christopher Greco. An eleventh card, featuring relief pitchers, was available only via a mail-in offer.

		MT
Complete Set (11):		90.00
Common Player:		6.00
1	Greg Maddux, Mike Mussina	25.00
2	Tom Glavine, John Smiley	4.00
3	Darren Daulton, Ivan Rodriguez	8.00
4	Fred McGriff, Frank Thomas	20.00
5	Delino DeShields, Carlos Baerga	3.00
6	Gary Sheffield, Edgar Martinez	6.00
7	Ozzie Smith, Pat Listach	7.50
8	Barry Bonds, Juan Gonzalez	15.00
9	Kirby Puckett, Andy Van Slyke	12.00
10	Larry Walker, Joe Carter	5.00
11	Rick Aguilera, Rob Dibble	3.00

1993 Pinnacle Team 2001

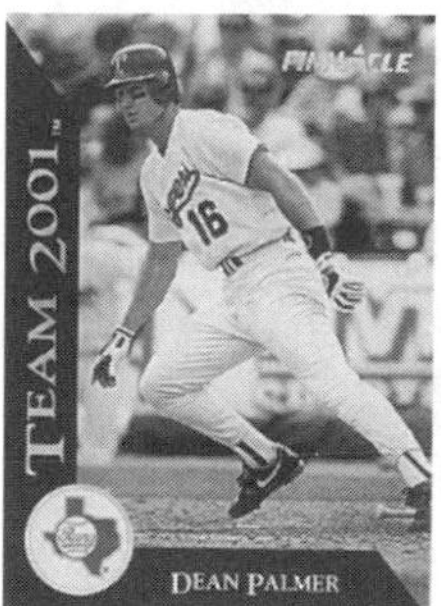

This insert set features 30 players who are expected to be stars in the year 2001. Cards were randomly inserted into 27-card jumbo packs from Series I.

		MT
Complete Set (30):		25.00
Common Player:		.40
1	Wil Cordero	.40
2	Cal Eldred	.40
3	Mike Mussina	2.00
4	Chuck Knoblauch	1.00
5	Melvin Nieves	.40
6	Tim Wakefield	.40
7	Carlos Baerga	.40
8	Bret Boone	.40
9	Jeff Bagwell	4.00
10	Travis Fryman	.75
11	Royce Clayton	.40
12	Delino DeShields	.40
13	Juan Gonzalez	2.50
14	Pedro Martinez	1.50
15	Bernie Williams	2.00
16	Billy Ashley	.40
17	Marquis Grissom	.75
18	Kenny Lofton	2.00
19	Ray Lankford	.40
20	Tim Salmon	1.50
21	Steve Hosey	.40
22	Charles Nagy	.40
23	Dave Fleming	.40
24	Reggie Sanders	.40
25	Sam Millitello	.40
26	Eric Karros	.75
27	Ryan Klesko	1.00
28	Dean Palmer	.40
29	Ivan Rodriguez	3.00
30	Sterling Hitchcock	.40

1993 Pinnacle Tribute

These two future Hall of Famers each have five-card sets devoted to their career achievements. Each card commemorates a milestone reached by George Brett or Nolan Ryan. Cards were random inserts in 1993 Score Pinnacle Series II packs, about one per every 24 packs. Fronts have a gold-foil stamped "Tribute" vertically at right.

		MT
Complete Set (10):		60.00
George Brett Card (1-5):		5.00
Nolan Ryan Card (6-10):		10.00
1	Kansas City Royalty (George Brett)	6.00
2	The Chase for .400 (George Brett)	6.00
3	Pine Tar Pandemonium - "The Bat"	6.00
4	MVP and a World Series, Too (George Brett)	6.00
5	3,000 or Bust (George Brett)	6.00
6	The Rookie (Nolan Ryan)	10.00
7	Angel of No Mercy (Nolan Ryan)	10.00
8	Astronomical Success (Nolan Ryan)	10.00
9	5,000 Ks (Nolan Ryan)	10.00
10	No-Hitter No. 7 (Nolan Ryan)	10.00

1994 Pinnacle Samples

Basically the same as the issued versions, these promo cards differ in the presence of a diagonal "SAMPLE" overprint on front and back. Cello-wrapped packs of hobby and retail versions were produced, with appropriate header cards.

		MT
Complete Set (12):		35.00
Common Player:		2.50
2	Carlos Baerga	2.50
3	Sammy Sosa	10.00
5	John Olerud	3.00
7	Moises Alou	3.00
8	Steve Avery	2.50
10	Cecil Fielder	2.50
11	Greg Maddux	10.00
269	Jeff Granger	2.50
---	Jeff Granger (Museum) (blank-back)	2.50
---	Jeff Granger (Museum) (black print on back)	2.50
TR1	Paul Molitor (Tribute)	7.50
---	Hobby version header card	.25
---	Retail version header card	.25

1994 Pinnacle

Typical of each card company's 1994 mid-priced brand, Pinnacle features full bleed photos, gold-foil stamping and UV coating. On front, player and team names appear in a shield-and-bar motif in the lower-left corner. On horizontal backs, the front photo is reproduced as a subdued background photo, over which are printed recent stats and a few biographical details. A different player photo is featured at left. Pinnacle's trademarks appear at lower-right, while the brand's optical-variable anti-counterfeiting device is at bottom center. Subsets include major award winners, Rookie Prospects and Draft Picks which are appropriately noted with gold-foil lettering on front. The issue was produced in two series of 270 cards each.

		MT
Complete Set (540):		35.00
Complete Series 1 (270):		20.00
Complete Series 2 (270):		15.00
Common Player:		.10
Series 1 or 2 Pack (14):		2.00
Series 1 or 2 Wax Box (24):		38.00
1	Frank Thomas	1.25
2	Carlos Baerga	.10
3	Sammy Sosa	1.50
4	Tony Gwynn	1.00
5	John Olerud	.25
6	Ryne Sandberg	.75
7	Moises Alou	.15
8	Steve Avery	.10
9	Tim Salmon	.40
10	Cecil Fielder	.15
11	Greg Maddux	1.50
12	Barry Larkin	.40
13	Mike Devereaux	.10
14	Charlie Hayes	.10
15	Albert Belle	.50
16	Andy Van Slyke	.10
17	Mo Vaughn	.50
18	Brian McRae	.10
19	Cal Eldred	.10
20	Craig Biggio	.25
21	Kirby Puckett	1.00
22	Derek Bell	.10
23	Don Mattingly	1.00
24	John Burkett	.10
25	Roger Clemens	1.00
26	Barry Bonds	.75
27	Paul Molitor	.40
28	Mike Piazza	2.00
29	Robin Ventura	.20
30	Jeff Conine	.15
31	Wade Boggs	.30
32	Dennis Eckersley	.10
33	Bobby Bonilla	.10
34	Len Dykstra	.10
35	Manny Alexander	.10
36	Ray Lankford	.10
37	Greg Vaughn	.15
38	Chuck Finley	.10
39	Todd Benzinger	.10
40	Dave Justice	.40
41	Rob Dibble	.10
42	Tom Henke	.10
43	David Nied	.10
44	Sandy Alomar Jr.	.15
45	Pete Harnisch	.10
46	Jeff Russell	.10
47	Terry Mulholland	.10
48	Kevin Appier	.10
49	Randy Tomlin	.10
50	Cal Ripken, Jr.	2.50
51	Andy Benes	.10
52	Jimmy Key	.10
53	Kirt Manwaring	.10
54	Kevin Tapani	.10
55	Jose Guzman	.10
56	Todd Stottlemyre	.10
57	Jack McDowell	.10
58	Orel Hershiser	.10
59	Chris Hammond	.10
60	Chris Nabholz	.10
61	Ruben Sierra	.10
62	Dwight Gooden	.10
63	John Kruk	.10
64	Omar Vizquel	.10
65	Tim Naehring	.10
66	Dwight Smith	.10
67	Mickey Tettleton	.10
68	J.T. Snow	.20
69	Greg McMichael	.10
70	Kevin Mitchell	.10
71	Kevin Brown	.15
72	Scott Cooper	.10
73	Jim Thome	.40
74	Joe Girardi	.10
75	Eric Anthony	.10
76	Orlando Merced	.10
77	Felix Jose	.10
78	Tommy Greene	.10
79	Bernard Gilkey	.10
80	Phil Plantier	.10
81	Danny Tartabull	.10
82	Trevor Wilson	.10
83	Chuck Knoblauch	.15
84	Rick Wilkins	.10
85	Devon White	.10
86	Lance Johnson	.10
87	Eric Karros	.15
88	Gary Sheffield	.25
89	Wil Cordero	.10
90	Ron Darling	.10
91	Darren Daulton	.10
92	Joe Orsulak	.10
93	Steve Cooke	.10
94	Darryl Hamilton	.10
95	Aaron Sele	.15
96	John Doherty	.10
97	Gary DiSarcina	.10
98	Jeff Blauser	.10
99	John Smiley	.10
100	Ken Griffey, Jr.	3.00
101	Dean Palmer	.10
102	Felix Fermin	.10
103	Jerald Clark	.10
104	Doug Drabek	.10
105	Curt Schilling	.15
106	Jeff Montgomery	.10
107	Rene Arocha	.10
108	Carlos Garcia	.10
109	Wally Whitehurst	.10
110	Jim Abbott	.15
111	Royce Clayton	.10
112	Chris Hoiles	.10
113	Mike Morgan	.10
114	Joe Magrane	.10
115	Tom Candiotti	.10
116	Ron Karkovice	.10
117	Ryan Bowen	.10
118	Rod Beck	.10
119	John Wetteland	.10
120	Terry Steinbach	.10
121	Dave Hollins	.10
122	Jeff Kent	.10
123	Ricky Bones	.10
124	Brian Jordan	.10
125	Chad Kreuter	.10
126	John Valentin	.10
127	Billy Hathaway	.10
128	Wilson Alvarez	.10
129	Tino Martinez	.10
130	Rodney Bolton	.10
131	David Segui	.10
132	Wayne Kirby	.10
133	Eric Young	.10
134	Scott Servais	.10
135	Scott Radinsky	.10
136	Bret Barberie	.10
137	John Roper	.10
138	Ricky Gutierrez	.10
139	Bernie Williams	.50
140	Bud Black	.10
141	Jose Vizcaino	.10
142	Gerald Williams	.10
143	Duane Ward	.10
144	Danny Jackson	.10
145	Allen Watson	.10
146	Scott Fletcher	.10
147	Delino DeShields	.10
148	Shane Mack	.10
149	Jim Eisenreich	.10
150	Troy Neel	.15
151	Jay Bell	.10
152	B.J. Surhoff	.10
153	Mark Whiten	.10
154	Mike Henneman	.10
155	Todd Hundley	.15
156	Greg Myers	.10
157	Ryan Klesko	.20
158	Dave Fleming	.10
159	Mickey Morandini	.10
160	Blas Minor	.10
161	Reggie Jefferson	.10
162	David Hulse	.10
163	Greg Swindell	.10
164	Roberto Hernandez	.10
165	Brady Anderson	.10
166	Jack Armstrong	.10
167	Phil Clark	.10
168	Melido Perez	.10
169	Darren Lewis	.10
170	Sam Horn	.10
171	Mike Harkey	.10
172	Juan Guzman	.10
173	Bob Natal	.10
174	Deion Sanders	.25
175	Carlos Quintana	.10
176	Mel Rojas	.10
177	Willie Banks	.10
178	Ben Rivera	.10
179	Kenny Lofton	.60
180	Leo Gomez	.10
181	Roberto Mejia	.10
182	Mike Perez	.10
183	Travis Fryman	.15
184	Ben McDonald	.10
185	Steve Frey	.10
186	Kevin Young	.10
187	Dave Magadan	.10
188	Bobby Munoz	.10
189	Pat Rapp	.10
190	Jose Offerman	.10
191	Vinny Castilla	.15
192	Ivan Calderon	.10
193	Ken Caminiti	.20
194	Benji Gil	.10
195	Chuck Carr	.10
196	Derrick May	.10
197	Pat Kelly	.10
198	Jeff Brantley	.10
199	Jose Lind	.10
200	Steve Buechele	.10
201	Wes Chamberlain	.10
202	Eduardo Perez	.10
203	Bret Saberhagen	.10
204	Gregg Jefferies	.10
205	Darrin Fletcher	.10
206	Kent Hrbek	.10
207	Kim Batiste	.10
208	Jeff King	.10
209	Donovan Osborne	.10
210	Dave Nilsson	.10
211	Al Martin	.10
212	Mike Moore	.10
213	Sterling Hitchcock	.15
214	Geronimo Pena	.10
215	Kevin Higgins	.10
216	Norm Charlton	.10
217	Don Slaught	.10
218	Mitch Williams	.10
219	Derek Lilliquist	.10
220	Armando Reynoso	.10
221	Kenny Rogers	.10
222	Doug Jones	.10
223	Luis Aquino	.10
224	Mike Oquist	.10
225	Darryl Scott	.10
226	Kurt Abbott	.10
227	Andy Tomberlin	.10
228	Norberto Martin	.10
229	Pedro Castellano	.10
230	*Curtis Pride*	.25
231	Jeff McNeely	.15
232	Scott Lydy	.10
233	Darren Oliver	.10
234	Danny Bautista	.10
235	Butch Huskey	.10
236	Chipper Jones	1.50
237	Eddie Zambrano	.10
238	Jean Domingo	.10
239	Javier Lopez	.30
240	Nigel Wilson	.15
241	*Drew Denson*	.15
242	Raul Mondesi	.25
243	Luis Ortiz	.10
244	Manny Ramirez	.75
245	Greg Blosser	.10
246	Rondell White	.20
247	Steve Karsay	.10
248	Scott Stahoviak	.10
249	Jose Valentin	.10
250	Marc Newfield	.10
251	Keith Kessinger	.10
252	Carl Everett	.10
253	John O'Donoghue	.10
254	Turk Wendell	.10
255	Scott Ruffcorn	.10
256	Tony Tarasco	.10
257	Andy Cook	.10
258	Matt Mieske	.10
259	Luis Lopez	.10
260	Ramon Caraballo	.10
261	Salomon Torres	.10
262	*Brooks Kieschnick*	.40
263	*Daron Kirkreit*	.15
264	*Bill Wagner*	.40
265	*Matt Drews*	.15
266	Scott Christman	.10
267	*Torii Hunter*	.15
268	*Jamey Wright*	.25
269	Jeff Granger	.10
270	*Trot Nixon*	.75
271	Randy Myers	.10
272	Trevor Hoffman	.15
273	Bob Wickman	.10
274	Willie McGee	.10
275	Hipolito Pichardo	.10
276	Bobby Witt	.10
277	Gregg Olson	.10
278	Randy Johnson	.75
279	Robb Nen	.10
280	Paul O'Neill	.20
281	Lou Whitaker	.10
282	Chad Curtis	.10
283	Doug Henry	.10
284	Tom Glavine	.25
285	Mike Greenwell	.10
286	Roberto Kelly	.10
287	Roberto Alomar	.60
288	Charlie Hough	.10
289	Alex Fernandez	.15
290	Jeff Bagwell	.75
291	Wally Joyner	.10
292	Andujar Cedeno	.10
293	Rick Aguilera	.10
294	Darryl Strawberry	.15
295	Mike Mussina	.40
296	Jeff Gardner	.10
297	Chris Gwynn	.10
298	Matt Williams	.30
299	Brent Gates	.15
300	Mark McGwire	3.00
301	Jim Deshaies	.10
302	Edgar Martinez	.10
303	Danny Darwin	.10
304	Pat Meares	.10
305	Benito Santiago	.10
306	Jose Canseco	.40
307	Jim Gott	.10
308	Paul Sorrento	.10
309	Scott Kamieniecki	.10
310	Larry Walker	.40
311	Mark Langston	.10
312	John Jaha	.10
313	Stan Javier	.10
314	Hal Morris	.10
315	Robby Thompson	.10
316	Pat Hentgen	.10
317	Tom Gordon	.10
318	Joey Cora	.10
319	Luis Alicea	.10
320	Andre Dawson	.20
321	Darryl Kile	.10
322	Jose Rijo	.10
323	Luis Gonzalez	.15
324	Billy Ashley	.10
325	David Cone	.20
326	Bill Swift	.10
327	Phil Hiatt	.10
328	Craig Paquette	.10
329	Bob Welch	.10
330	Tony Phillips	.10
331	Archi Cianfrocco	.10
332	Dave Winfield	.25
333	David McCarty	.15
334	Al Leiter	.15
335	Tom Browning	.10
336	Mark Grace	.20
337	Jose Mesa	.10
338	Mike Stanley	.10
339	Roger McDowell	.10
340	Damion Easley	.10
341	Angel Miranda	.10
342	John Smoltz	.10
343	Jay Buhner	.10
344	Bryan Harvey	.10
345	Joe Carter	.15
346	Dante Bichette	.25
347	Jason Bere	.10
348	Frank Viola	.10
349	Ivan Rodriguez	.75
350	Juan Gonzalez	.75
351	Steve Finley	.10
352	Mike Felder	.10
353	Ramon Martinez	.15
354	Greg Gagne	.10
355	Ken Hill	.10
356	Pedro Munoz	.10

357	Todd Van Poppel	.10
358	Marquis Grissom	.15
359	Milt Cuyler	.10
360	Reggie Sanders	.15
361	Scott Erickson	.10
362	Billy Hatcher	.10
363	Gene Harris	.10
364	Rene Gonzales	.10
365	Kevin Rogers	.10
366	Eric Plunk	.10
367	Todd Zeile	.10
368	John Franco	.10
369	Brett Butler	.10
370	Bill Spiers	.10
371	Terry Pendleton	.10
372	Chris Bosio	.10
373	Orestes Destrade	.10
374	Dave Stewart	.10
375	Darren Holmes	.10
376	Doug Strange	.10
377	Brian Turang	.15
378	Carl Willis	.10
379	Mark McLemore	.10
380	Bobby Jones	.15
381	Scott Sanders	.10
382	Kirk Rueter	.15
383	Randy Velarde	.10
384	Fred McGriff	.35
385	Charles Nagy	.10
386	Rich Amaral	.10
387	Geronimo Berroa	.10
388	Eric Davis	.10
389	Ozzie Smith	.40
390	Alex Arias	.10
391	Brad Ausmus	.10
392	Cliff Floyd	.15
393	Roger Salkeld	.10
394	Jim Edmonds	.20
395	Jeromy Burnitz	.15
396	Dave Staton	.10
397	Rob Butler	.10
398	Marcos Armas	.10
399	Darrell Whitmore	.10
400	Ryan Thompson	.15
401	*Ross Powell*	.10
402	Joe Oliver	.10
403	Paul Carey	.10
404	Bob Hamelin	.10
405	Chris Turner	.10
406	Nate Minchey	.10
407	*Lonnie Maclin*	.10
408	Harold Baines	.10
409	Brian Williams	.15
410	Johnny Ruffin	.10
411	*Julian Tavarez*	.20
412	Mark Hutton	.10
413	Carlos Delgado	.60
414	Chris Gomez	.10
415	Mike Hampton	.10
416	Alex Diaz	.10
417	Jeffrey Hammonds	.10
418	Jayhawk Owens	.10
419	J.R. Phillips	.10
420	*Cory Bailey*	.15
421	Denny Hocking	.10
422	Jon Shave	.10
423	Damon Buford	.15
424	Troy O'Leary	.10
425	Tripp Cromer	.10
426	Albie Lopez	.10
427	Tony Fernandez	.10
428	Ozzie Guillen	.10
429	Alan Trammell	.10
430	*John Wasdin*	.25
431	Marc Valdes	.10
432	*Brian Anderson*	.40
433	*Matt Brunson*	.25
434	*Wayne Gomes*	.25
435	*Jay Powell*	.25
436	*Kirk Presley*	.40
437	*Jon Ratliff*	.25
438	*Derrek Lee*	.75
439	Tom Pagnozzi	.10
440	Kent Mercker	.10
441	*Phil Leftwich*	.20
442	Jamie Moyer	.10
443	John Flaherty	.10
444	Mark Wohlers	.10
445	Jose Bautista	.10
446	Andres Galarraga	.40
447	Mark Lemke	.10
448	Tim Wakefield	.10
449	Pat Listach	.10
450	Rickey Henderson	.25
451	Mike Gallego	.10
452	Bob Tewksbury	.10
453	Kirk Gibson	.10
454	Pedro Astacio	.10
455	Mike Lansing	.10
456	Sean Berry	.10
457	Bob Walk	.10
458	Chili Davis	.10
459	Ed Sprague	.10
460	Kevin Stocker	.10
461	Mike Stanton	.10
462	Tim Raines	.15
463	Mike Bordick	.10
464	David Wells	.15
465	Tim Laker	.10
466	Cory Snyder	.10
467	Alex Cole	.10
468	Pete Incaviglia	.10
469	Roger Pavlik	.10
470	Greg W. Harris	.10
471	Xavier Hernandez	.10
472	Erik Hanson	.10
473	Jesse Orosco	.10
474	Greg Colbrunn	.10
475	Harold Reynolds	.10
476	Greg Harris	.10
477	Pat Borders	.10
478	Melvin Nieves	.10
479	Mariano Duncan	.10
480	Greg Hibbard	.10
481	Tim Pugh	.10
482	Bobby Ayala	.10
483	Sid Fernandez	.10
484	Tim Wallach	.10
485	Randy Milligan	.10
486	Walt Weiss	.10
487	Matt Walbeck	.20
488	Mike Macfarlane	.10
489	Jerry Browne	.10
490	Chris Sabo	.10
491	Tim Belcher	.10
492	Spike Owen	.10
493	Rafael Palmeiro	.40
494	Brian Harper	.10
495	Eddie Murray	.20
496	Ellis Burks	.10
497	Karl Rhodes	.10
498	Otis Nixon	.10
499	Lee Smith	.10
500	Bip Roberts	.10
501	Pedro Martinez	.10
502	Brian L. Hunter	.15
503	Tyler Green	.15
504	Bruce Hurst	.10
505	Alex Gonzalez	.15
506	Mark Portugal	.10
507	Bob Ojeda	.10
508	Dave Henderson	.10
509	Bo Jackson	.20
510	Bret Boone	.15
511	Mark Eichhorn	.10
512	Luis Polonia	.10
513	Will Clark	.35
514	Dave Valle	.10
515	Dan Wilson	.10
516	Dennis Martinez	.10
517	Jim Leyritz	.10
518	Howard Johnson	.10
519	Jody Reed	.10
520	Julio Franco	.10
521	Jeff Reardon	.10
522	Willie Greene	.10
523	Shawon Dunston	.10
524	Keith Mitchell	.10
525	Rick Helling	.10
526	Mark Kiefer	.10
527	*Chan Ho Park*	.75
528	Tony Longmire	.15
529	Rich Becker	.10
530	Tim Hyers	.10
531	Darrin Jackson	.10
532	Jack Morris	.10
533	Rick White	.10
534	Mike Kelly	.15
535	James Mouton	.10
536	Steve Trachsel	.10
537	Tony Eusebio	.10
538	Kelly Stinnett	.10
539	Paul Spoljaric	.10
540	Darren Dreifort	.15

1994 Pinnacle Artist's Proof

A specially designated version of the regular Pinnacle set, described as the first day's production of the first 1,000 of each card, was issued as a random pack insert. Cards feature a small gold-foil "Artist's Proof" rectangle embossed above the player/team name shield on front. In all other respects the cards are identical to the regular-issue versions.

	MT
Complete Set (540):	1600.
Common Player:	1.00
Stars:	20X
Young Stars/RCs:	15X

(See 1994 Pinnacle for checklist and base card values.)

1994 Pinnacle Museum Collection

Each card in the 1994 Pinnacle set was produced in a parallel "Museum Collection" version. The inserts were produced utilizing the company's Dufex foil-printing technology on front, with rays emanating from the Pinnacle logo. Backs are virtually identical to the regular-issue version except for the substitution of a "1994 Museum Collection" logo for the optical-variable anti-counterfeiting bar at bottom-center. Museums were random package inserts, appearing at the rate of about once per four packs.

	MT
Complete Set (540):	500.00
Common Player:	1.00
Stars:	8X
Young Stars/RCs:	5X

(See 1994 Pinnacle for checklist and base card values.)

1994 Pinnacle Rookie Team Pinnacle

The very popular Rookie Team Pinnacle insert card tradition continued in 1994 with a series of nine "two-headed" cards featuring the top prospect from each league at each position. The cards again feature the ultra-realistic artwork of Chris Greco. Each side is enhanced with gold-foil presentations of the player's name, the Pinnacle logo and the Rookie Team Pinnacle logo. The inserts were packaged, on average, one per 90 packs of hobby foil only.

		MT
Complete Set (9):		50.00
Common Player:		2.50
1	Carlos Delgado, Javier Lopez	15.00
2	Bob Hamelin, J.R. Phillips	3.00
3	Jon Shave, Keith Kessinger	2.50
4	Butch Huskey, Luis Ortiz	2.50
5	Chipper Jones, Kurt Abbott	18.00
6	Rondell White, Manny Ramirez	15.00
7	Cliff Floyd, Jeffrey Hammonds	4.00
8	Marc Newfield, Nigel Wilson	2.50
9	Salomon Torres, Mark Hutton	2.50

1994 Pinnacle Run Creators

This insert set, exclusive to Pinnacle jumbo packaging, features the top 44 performers of the previous season in the arcane statistic of "runs created." Fronts have an action player photo on which the stadium background has been muted in soft-focus red or blue. The player's last name appears at right in gold foil; the logo, "The Run Creators" is in one of the lower corners. Backs are printed in teal with a color team logo at center, beneath the stats that earned the player's inclusion in the series. The player's runs created are in gold foil above the write-up. Cards are numbered with an "RC" prefix.

		MT
Complete Set (44):		45.00
Common Player:		.75
1	John Olerud	1.00
2	Frank Thomas	3.00
3	Ken Griffey, Jr.	8.00
4	Paul Molitor	1.00
5	Rafael Palmeiro	1.00
6	Roberto Alomar	1.50
7	Juan Gonzalez	2.00
8	Albert Belle	1.50
9	Travis Fryman	.75
10	Rickey Henderson	1.00
11	Tony Phillips	.75
12	Mo Vaughn	1.50
13	Tim Salmon	.75
14	Kenny Lofton	1.50
15	Carlos Baerga	.75
16	Greg Vaughn	.75
17	Jay Buhner	.75
18	Chris Hoiles	.75
19	Mickey Tettleton	.75
20	Kirby Puckett	2.50
21	Danny Tartabull	.75
22	Devon White	.75
23	Barry Bonds	2.00
24	Lenny Dykstra	.75
25	John Kruk	.75
26	Fred McGriff	1.50
27	Gregg Jefferies	.75
28	Mike Piazza	5.00
29	Jeff Blauser	.75
30	Andres Galarraga	1.00
31	Darren Daulton	.75
32	Dave Justice	1.50
33	Craig Biggio	.75
34	Mark Grace	1.00
35	Tony Gwynn	3.00
36	Jeff Bagwell	2.00
37	Jay Bell	.75
38	Marquis Grissom	.75
39	Matt Williams	1.00
40	Charlie Hayes	.75
41	Dante Bichette	1.00
42	Bernard Gilkey	.75
43	Brett Butler	.75
44	Rick Wilkins	.75

1994 Pinnacle Team Pinnacle

The double-sided Team Pinnacle insert set features 18 of the top players in the game. Team Pinnacle shows two card fronts, one on each side. They were inserted into 1994 Pinnacle Baseball Series II at a rate of one every 90 packs.

		MT
Complete Set (9):		90.00
Common Player:		4.00
1	Jeff Bagwell, Frank Thomas	10.00
2	Carlos Baerga, Robby Thompson	4.00
3	Matt Williams, Dean Palmer	5.00
4	Cal Ripken, Jr., Jay Bell	20.00
5	Ivan Rodriguez, Mike Piazza	15.00
6	Len Dykstra, Ken Griffey, Jr.	25.00
7	Juan Gonzalez, Barry Bonds	8.00
8	Tim Salmon, Dave Justice	5.00
9	Greg Maddux, Jack McDowell	12.00

1994 Pinnacle Tribute

A hobby-only insert set, found approximately one per 18 foil packs, this nine-card series honors players who reached significant season or career milestones or otherwise had special achievements in 1993. Fronts feature full-bleed action photos. At left is a black strip with "TRIBUTE" in gold foil. A colored strip at bottom has the player name in gold foil and a short description of why he is being feted beneath. The Pinnacle logo is in gold foil at top. The same gold-foil enhancements are found on back, along with a portrait photo. In a black box at bottom are details of the tribute. The Pinnacle optical-variable anti-counterfeiting device is at bottom center. Card numbers are prefixed with "TR".

		MT
Complete Set (18):		60.00
Common Player:		1.50
1	Paul Molitor	3.00
2	Jim Abbott	1.50
3	Dave Winfield	2.00
4	Bo Jackson	1.50
5	Dave Justice	2.00
6	Len Dykstra	1.50
7	Mike Piazza	10.00
8	Barry Bonds	4.00
9	Randy Johnson	4.00
10	Ozzie Smith	3.00
11	Mark Whiten	1.50
12	Greg Maddux	8.00
13	Cal Ripken, Jr.	12.50
14	Frank Thomas	6.00
15	Juan Gonzalez	4.00
16	Roberto Alomar	2.50
17	Ken Griffey, Jr.	15.00
18	Lee Smith	1.50

1995 Pinnacle Series 1 Samples

This eight-card cello-wrapped sample set was sent to dealers to preview the 1995 Pinnacle Series I cards. The cards are identical to regular-issue Pinnacle cards except they carry a white diagonal "SAMPLE" notation on front and back.

		MT
Complete Set (9):		35.00
Common Player:		3.00
16	Mickey Morandini	3.00
22US	Wil Cordero (Upstart) (card not included in most packs)	10.00
119	Gary Sheffield	4.00
122	Ivan Rodriguez	4.00
132	Alex Rodriguez (Rookie)	10.00
208	Bo Jackson	3.00
223	Jose Rijo	3.00
224	Ryan Klesko	3.00
----	Header card	.15

1995 Pinnacle

The 1995 Pinnacle set was produced in two series of 225 base cards each, plus inserts. Fronts have borderless photos with a large embossed gold foil "wave" at bottom containing the player's last name and team logo. Backs are horizontally formatted and have a portrait photo at left, an action photo at right and a few sentences about the player at center. Stats at the bottom offer previous year, career and career-best numbers. Subsets with the base cards include rookie specials in Series I and II which have a design featuring a green stripe at one side or bottom with the player's name in gold and a special round gold-foil logo. A similar design, with red stripes, is used for Series I cards only featuring Draft Picks. In Series II, a 30-card Swing Men subset has a blue vortex background design and special gold-foil identifier. Basic pack configurations offered 12-card ($2.49) and 15-card ($2.99) counts in both retail and hobby versions, each with some unique inserts.

		MT
Complete Set (450):		30.00
Common Player:		.10
Unlisted Stars:		.20 to .35
Hobby Pack (12):		2.00
Hobby Wax Box (24):		40.00
Retail Pack (12):		2.00
Retail Wax Box (36):		50.00
1	Jeff Bagwell	1.00
2	Roger Clemens	.75
3	Mark Whiten	.10
4	Shawon Dunston	.10
5	Bobby Bonilla	.10
6	Kevin Tapani	.10
7	Eric Karros	.15
8	Cliff Floyd	.10
9	Pat Kelly	.10
10	Jeffrey Hammonds	.10
11	Jeff Conine	.10
12	Fred McGriff	.25
13	Chris Bosio	.10
14	Mike Mussina	.40
15	Danny Bautista	.10
16	Mickey Morandini	.10
17	Chuck Finley	.10
18	Jim Thome	.40
19	Luis Ortiz	.10
20	Walt Weiss	.10
21	Don Mattingly	1.00
22	Bob Hamelin	.10
23	Melido Perez	.10
24	Kevin Mitchell	.10
25	John Smoltz	.25
26	Hector Carrasco	.10
27	Pat Hentgen	.10
28	Derrick May	.10
29	Mike Kingery	.10
30	Chuck Carr	.10
31	Billy Ashley	.10
32	Todd Hundley	.15
33	Luis Gonzalez	.10
34	Marquis Grissom	.10
35	Jeff King	.10
36	Eddie Williams	.10
37	Tom Pagnozzi	.10
38	Chris Hoiles	.10
39	Sandy Alomar	.15
40	Mike Greenwell	.10
41	Lance Johnson	.10
42	Junior Felix	.10
43	Felix Jose	.10
44	Scott Leius	.10
45	Ruben Sierra	.10
46	Kevin Seitzer	.10
47	Wade Boggs	.25

No.	Player	Price
48	Reggie Jefferson	.10
49	Jose Canseco	.30
50	Dave Justice	.20
51	John Smiley	.10
52	Joe Carter	.15
53	Rick Wilkins	.10
54	Ellis Burks	.10
55	Dave Weathers	.10
56	Pedro Astacio	.10
57	Ryan Thompson	.10
58	James Mouton	.10
59	Mel Rojas	.10
60	Orlando Merced	.10
61	Matt Williams	.30
62	Bernard Gilkey	.10
63	J.R. Phillips	.10
64	Lee Smith	.10
65	Jim Edmonds	.15
66	Darrin Jackson	.10
67	Scott Cooper	.10
68	Ron Karkovice	.10
69	Chris Gomez	.10
70	Kevin Appier	.10
71	Bobby Jones	.10
72	Doug Drabek	.10
73	Matt Mieske	.10
74	Sterling Hitchcock	.10
75	John Valentin	.10
76	Reggie Sanders	.10
77	Wally Joyner	.10
78	Turk Wendell	.10
79	Wendell Hayes	.10
80	Bret Barberie	.10
81	Troy Neel	.10
82	Ken Caminiti	.25
83	Milt Thompson	.10
84	Paul Sorrento	.10
85	Trevor Hoffman	.10
86	Jay Bell	.10
87	Mark Portugal	.10
88	Sid Fernandez	.10
89	Charles Nagy	.10
90	Jeff Montgomery	.10
91	Chuck Knoblauch	.20
92	Jeff Frye	.10
93	Tony Gwynn	1.00
94	John Olerud	.15
95	David Nied	.10
96	Chris Hammond	.10
97	Edgar Martinez	.10
98	Kevin Stocker	.10
99	Jeff Fassero	.10
100	Curt Schilling	.15
101	Dave Clark	.10
102	Delino DeShields	.10
103	Leo Gomez	.10
104	Dave Hollins	.10
105	Tim Naehring	.10
106	Otis Nixon	.10
107	Ozzie Guillen	.10
108	Jose Lind	.10
109	Stan Javier	.10
110	Greg Vaughn	.15
111	Chipper Jones	2.00
112	Ed Sprague	.10
113	Mike Macfarlane	.10
114	Steve Finley	.10
115	Ken Hill	.10
116	Carlos Garcia	.10
117	Lou Whitaker	.10
118	Todd Zeile	.10
119	Gary Sheffield	.40
120	Ben McDonald	.10
121	Pete Harnisch	.10
122	Ivan Rodriguez	.60
123	Wilson Alvarez	.10
124	Travis Fryman	.15
125	Pedro Munoz	.10
126	Mark Lemke	.10
127	Jose Valentin	.10
128	Ken Griffey Jr.	3.00
129	Omar Vizquel	.10
130	Milt Cuyler	.10
131	Steve Traschel	.25
132	Alex Rodriguez	2.50
133	Garret Anderson	.15
134	Armando Benitez	.10
135	Shawn Green	.20
136	Jorge Fabregas	.10
137	Orlando Miller	.10
138	Rikkert Faneyte	.10
139	Ismael Valdes	.10
140	Jose Oliva	.10
141	Aaron Small	.10
142	Tim Davis	.10
143	Ricky Bottalacio	.10
144	Mike Matheny	.10
145	Roberto Petagine	.10
146	Fausto Cruz	.10
147	Bryce Florie	.10
148	Jose Lima	.10
149	John Hudek	.10
150	Duane Singleton	.10
151	John Mabry	.10
152	Robert Eenhoorn	.10
153	Jon Lieber	.10
154	Garey Ingram	.10
155	Paul Shuey	.10
156	Mike Lieberthal	.10
157	Steve Dunn	.10
158	Charles Johnson	.15
159	Ernie Young	.10
160	Jose Martinez	.10
161	Kurt Miller	.10
162	Joey Eischen	.10
163	Dave Stevens	.10
164	Brian Hunter	.15
165	Jeff Cirillo	.10
166	Mark Smith	.10
167	*McKay Christensen*	.20
168	C.J. Nitkowski	.10
169	*Antone Williamson*	.50
170	Paul Konerko	2.00
171	*Scott Elarton*	.35
172	Jacob Shumate	.10
173	Terrence Long	.15
174	*Mark Johnson*	.25
175	Ben Grieve	2.00
176	*Jayson Peterson*	.20
177	Checklist	.10
178	Checklist	.10
179	Checklist	.10
180	Checklist	.10
181	Brian Anderson	.15
182	Steve Buechele	.10
183	Mark Clark	.10
184	Cecil Fielder	.15
185	Steve Avery	.10
186	Devon White	.10
187	Craig Shipley	.10
188	Brady Anderson	.15
189	Kenny Lofton	.60
190	Alex Cole	.10
191	Brent Gates	.10
192	Dean Palmer	.10
193	Alex Gonzalez	.15
194	Steve Cooke	.10
195	Ray Lankford	.10
196	Mark McGwire	3.00
197	Marc Newfield	.10
198	Pat Rapp	.10
199	Darren Lewis	.10
200	Carlos Baerga	.10
201	Rickey Henderson	.25
202	Kurt Abbott	.10
203	Kirt Manwaring	.10
204	Cal Ripken Jr.	2.50
205	Darren Daulton	.10
206	Greg Colbrunn	.10
207	Darryl Hamilton	.10
208	Bo Jackson	.15
209	Tony Phillips	.10
210	Geronimo Berroa	.10
211	Rich Becker	.10
212	Tony Tarasco	.10
213	Karl Rhodes	.10
214	Phil Plantier	.10
215	J.T. Snow	.20
216	Mo Vaughn	.50
217	Greg Gagne	.10
218	Rickey Bones	.10
219	Mike Bordick	.10
220	Chad Curtis	.10
221	Royce Clayton	.10
222	Roberto Alomar	.60
223	Jose Rijo	.10
224	Ryan Klesko	.25
225	Mark Langston	.10
226	Frank Thomas	1.50
227	Juan Gonzalez	.75
228	Ron Gant	.15
229	Javier Lopez	.20
230	Sammy Sosa	2.00
231	Kevin Brown	.15
232	Gary DiSarcina	.10
233	Albert Belle	.75
234	Jay Buhner	.15
235	Pedro Martinez	.15
236	Bob Tewksbury	.10
237	Mike Piazza	2.00
238	Darryl Kile	.10
239	Bryan Harvey	.10
240	Andres Galarraga	.20
241	Jeff Blauser	.10
242	Jeff Kent	.10
243	Bobby Munoz	.10
244	Greg Maddux	2.00
245	Paul O'Neill	.15
246	Lenny Dykstra	.10
247	Todd Van Poppel	.10
248	Bernie Williams	.40
249	Glenallen Hill	.10
250	Duane Ward	.10
251	Dennis Eckersley	.10
252	Pat Mahomes	.10
253	Rusty Greer (photo actually Jeff Frye)	.10
254	Roberto Kelly	.10
255	Randy Myers	.10
256	Scott Ruffcorn	.10
257	Robin Ventura	.15
258	Eduardo Perez	.10
259	Aaron Sele	.10
260	Paul Molitor	.35
261	Juan Guzman	.10
262	Darren Oliver	.10
263	Mike Stanley	.10
264	Tom Glavine	.20
265	Rico Brogna	.10
266	Craig Biggio	.15
267	Darrell Whitmore	.10
268	Jimmy Key	.10
269	Will Clark	.30
270	David Cone	.15
271	Brian Jordan	.15
272	Barry Bonds	.75
273	Danny Tartabull	.10
274	Ramon Martinez	.10
275	Al Martin	.10
276	Fred McGriff (Swing Men)	.25
277	Carlos Delgado (Swing Men)	.40
278	Juan Gonzalez (Swing Men)	.40
279	Shawn Green (Swing Men)	.15
280	Carlos Baerga (Swing Men)	.10
281	Cliff Floyd (Swing Men)	.10
282	Ozzie Smith (Swing Men)	.25
283	Alex Rodriguez (Swing Men)	1.50
284	Kenny Lofton (Swing Men)	.40
285	Dave Justice (Swing Men)	.20
286	Tim Salmon (Swing Men)	.15
287	Manny Ramirez (Swing Men)	1.00
288	Will Clark (Swing Men)	.20
289	Garret Anderson (Swing Men)	.10
290	Billy Ashley (Swing Men)	.10
291	Tony Gwynn (Swing Men)	.50
292	Raul Mondesi (Swing Men)	.25
293	Rafael Palmeiro (Swing Men)	.15
294	Matt Williams (Swing Men)	.10
295	Don Mattingly (Swing Men)	.50
296	Kirby Puckett (Swing Men)	.50
297	Paul Molitor (Swing Men)	.20
298	Albert Belle (Swing Men)	.40
299	Barry Bonds (Swing Men)	.40
300	Mike Piazza (Swing Men)	.75
301	Jeff Bagwell (Swing Men)	.50
302	Frank Thomas (Swing Men)	.75
303	Chipper Jones (Swing Men)	.75
304	Ken Griffey Jr. (Swing Men)	2.00
305	Cal Ripken Jr. (Swing Men)	1.50
306	Eric Anthony	.10
307	Todd Benzinger	.10
308	Jacob Brumfield	.10
309	Wes Chamberlain	.10
310	Tino Martinez	.10
311	Roberto Mejia	.10
312	Jose Offerman	.10
313	David Segui	.10
314	Eric Young	.10
315	Rey Sanchez	.10
316	Raul Mondesi	.50
317	Bret Boone	.10
318	Andre Dawson	.15
319	Brian McRae	.10
320	Dave Nilsson	.10
321	Moises Alou	.15
322	Don Slaught	.10
323	Dave McCarty	.10
324	Mike Huff	.10
325	Rick Aguilera	.10
326	Rod Beck	.10
327	Kenny Rogers	.10
328	Andy Benes	.10
329	Allen Watson	.10
330	Randy Johnson	.35
331	Willie Greene	.10
332	Hal Morris	.10
333	Ozzie Smith	.35
334	Jason Bere	.10
335	Scott Erickson	.10
336	Dante Bichette	.35
337	Willie Banks	.10
338	Eric Davis	.10
339	Rondell White	.20
340	Kirby Puckett	.75
341	Deion Sanders	.20
342	Eddie Murray	.40
343	Mike Harkey	.10
344	Joey Hamilton	.10
345	Roger Salkeld	.10
346	Wil Cordero	.10
347	John Wetteland	.10
348	Geronimo Pena	.10
349	Kirk Gibson	.10
350	Manny Ramirez	1.00
351	William Van Landingham	.10
352	B.J. Surhoff	.10
353	Ken Ryan	.10
354	Terry Steinbach	.10
355	Bret Saberhagen	.10
356	John Jaha	.10
357	Joe Girardi	.10
358	Steve Karsay	.10
359	Alex Fernandez	.15
360	Salomon Torres	.10
361	John Burkett	.10
362	Derek Bell	.10
363	Tom Henke	.10
364	Gregg Jefferies	.10
365	Jack McDowell	.10
366	Andujar Cedeno	.10
367	Dave Winfield	.20
368	Carl Everett	.10
369	Danny Jackson	.10
370	Jeromy Burnitz	.10
371	Mark Grace	.20
372	Larry Walker	.25
373	Bill Swift	.10
374	Dennis Martinez	.10
375	Mickey Tettleton	.10
376	Mel Nieves	.10
377	Cal Eldred	.10
378	Orel Hershiser	.10
379	David Wells	.15
380	Gary Gaetti	.10
381	Tim Raines	.10
382	Barry Larkin	.20
383	Jason Jacome	.10
384	Tim Wallach	.10
385	Robby Thompson	.10
386	Frank Viola	.10
387	Dave Stewart	.10
388	Bip Roberts	.10
389	Ron Darling	.10
390	Carlos Delgado	.25
391	Tim Salmon	.20
392	Alan Trammell	.10
393	Kevin Foster	.10
394	Jim Abbott	.10
395	John Kruk	.10
396	Andy Van Slyke	.10
397	Dave Magadan	.10
398	Rafael Palmeiro	.25

399	Mike Devereaux	.10
400	Benito Santiago	.10
401	Brett Butler	.10
402	John Franco	.10
403	Matt Walbeck	.10
404	Terry Pendleton	.10
405	Chris Sabo	.10
406	Andrew Lorraine	.10
407	Dan Wilson	.10
408	Mike Lansing	.10
409	Ray McDavid	.10
410	Shane Andrews	.10
411	Tom Gordon	.10
412	Chad Ogea	.10
413	James Baldwin	.10
414	Russ Davis	.10
415	Ray Holbert	.10
416	Ray Durham	.15
417	Matt Nokes	.10
418	Rodney Henderson	.10
419	Gabe White	.10
420	Todd Hollandsworth	.10
421	Midre Cummings	.10
422	Harold Baines	.10
423	Troy Percival	.10
424	Joe Vitiello	.10
425	Andy Ashby	.10
426	Michael Tucker	.10
427	Mark Gubicza	.10
428	Jim Bullinger	.10
429	Jose Malave	.10
430	Pete Schourek	.10
431	Bobby Ayala	.10
432	Marvin Freeman	.10
433	Pat Listach	.10
434	Eddie Taubensee	.10
435	Steve Howe	.10
436	Kent Mercker	.10
437	Hector Fajardo	.10
438	Scott Kamieniecki	.10
439	Robb Nen	.10
440	Mike Kelly	.10
441	Tom Candiotti	.10
442	Albie Lopez	.10
443	Jeff Granger	.10
444	Rich Aude	.10
445	Luis Polonia	.10
446	A.L. Checklist (Frank Thomas)	.50
447	A.L. Checklist (Ken Griffey Jr.)	1.00
448	N.L. Checklist (Mike Piazza)	.50
449	N.L. Checklist (Jeff Bagwell)	.40
450	Insert Checklist (Frank Thomas, Ken Griffey Jr., Mike Piazza, Jeff Bagwell)	.50

1995 Pinnacle Artist's Proof

Said to represent the first 1,000 of each card printed, the Artist's Proof chase set is a parallel issue with a counterpart for each of the regular-issue cards. The proofs differ in the use of silver, rather than gold foil for front graphic highlights, and the inclusion of a rectangular silver-foil "ARTIST'S PROOF" logo on front. The AP inserts were reported seeded at an average rate of one per 26 packs.

	MT
Complete Set (450):	1650.
Common Player:	2.00
Stars:	15X
Young Stars/RCs:	10X

(See 1995 Pinnacle for checklist and base card values.)

1995 Pinnacle Museum Collection

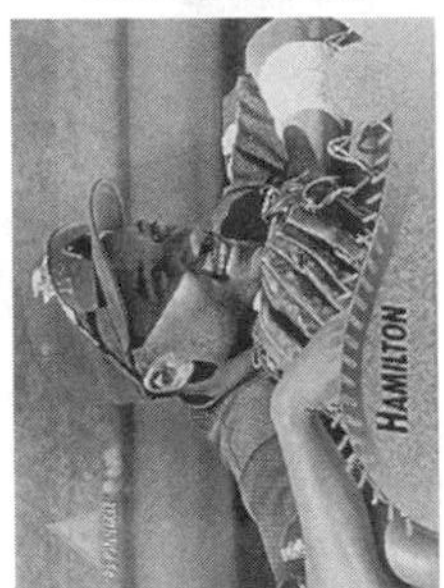

Pinnacle's Dufex foil-printing technology on the card fronts differentiates the cards in this parallel insert set from the corresponding cards in the regular issue. Backs have a rectangular "1995 Museum Collection" logo at the lower-left. Museum inserts are found at an average rate of one per four packs. Because of production difficulties, trade cards had to be issued in place of seven of the rookie cards in Series 2. Those redemption cards were valid only through Dec. 31, 1995.

	MT
Complete Set (450):	450.00
Common Player:	.75
Stars:	8X
Young Stars/RCs:	4X

(See 1995 Pinnacle for checklist and base card values.)

1995 Pinnacle E.T.A. '95

This hobby-only chase card set identifies six players who were picked to arrive in the major leagues for a 1995 debut. Both front and back have borderless action photos on which the background has been subdued and posterized. Gold-foil headlines on each side of the card give the player's credentials. These inserts are found on average of once per 24 packs.

		MT
Complete Set (6):		20.00
Common Player:		1.00
1	Ben Grieve	15.00
2	Alex Ochoa	1.50
3	Joe Vitiello	1.00
4	Johnny Damon	6.00
5	Trey Beamon	2.00
6	Brooks Kieschnick	1.50

1995 Pinnacle Gate Attraction

Series II jumbo packs are the exclusive source for this chase set. Printed on metallic foil, the cards have a color photo at top and a second photo at bottom that is shown in gold tones only. A "Gate Attraction" seal is in the lower-left corner. Backs have a large portrait photo on a color-streaked background, plus a few words about the player.

		MT
Complete Set (18):		60.00
Common Player:		1.00
1	Ken Griffey Jr.	12.00
2	Frank Thomas	6.00
3	Cal Ripken Jr.	10.00
4	Jeff Bagwell	5.00
5	Mike Piazza	7.50
6	Barry Bonds	3.00
7	Kirby Puckett	3.50
8	Albert Belle	3.00
9	Tony Gwynn	6.00
10	Raul Mondesi	1.00
11	Will Clark	1.50
12	Don Mattingly	3.50
13	Roger Clemens	5.00
14	Paul Molitor	3.00
15	Matt Williams	1.00
16	Greg Maddux	7.00
17	Kenny Lofton	2.00
18	Cliff Floyd	1.00

1995 Pinnacle New Blood

Both hobby and retail packs of Series II Pinnacle hide this insert set of young stars, at an average rate of one card per 90 packs. A player photo appears in the red and silver foil-printed background, and there is a color action photo in the foreground. Conventionally printed backs feature the same photos, but with their prominence reversed. A few words of text describe the player's star potential.

		MT
Complete Set (9):		55.00
Common Player:		2.00
1	Alex Rodriguez	25.00
2	Shawn Green	7.50
3	Brian Hunter	3.00
4	Garret Anderson	2.00
5	Charles Johnson	5.00
6	Chipper Jones	20.00
7	Carlos Delgado	4.00
8	Billy Ashley	2.00
9	J.R. Phillips	2.00

1995 Pinnacle Performers

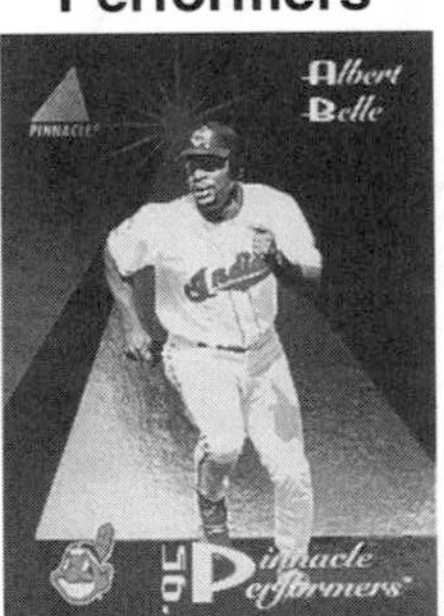

Series I jumbos were the only place to find this chase set. Fronts have a deep red background with a golden pyramid at center and a silver apex, all in foil printing. A color player action photo is in the center foreground. The reverse repeats the front photo in the background, in one color, and has a second color photo, along with a few words about the player.

		MT
Complete Set (18):		90.00
Common Player:		2.00
1	Frank Thomas	10.00
2	Albert Belle	6.00
3	Barry Bonds	7.50
4	Juan Gonzalez	6.00
5	Andres Galarraga	2.50
6	Raul Mondesi	2.50
7	Paul Molitor	5.00
8	Tim Salmon	2.00
9	Mike Piazza	15.00
10	Gregg Jefferies	2.00
11	Will Clark	3.00
12	Greg Maddux	12.50
13	Manny Ramirez	8.00
14	Kirby Puckett	7.50
15	Shawn Green	5.00
16	Rafael Palmeiro	3.00
17	Paul O'Neill	2.50
18	Jason Bere	2.00

1995 Pinnacle Red Hot

These Series II inserts are found at an average rate of one per 16 packs and feature top veterans stars. Fronts have a large action photo on right, over a background of foil-printed red and yellow flames. A vertical strip at left of graduated red tones has a player portrait photo and the "RED HOT" flame logo, again printed on foil. Backs are conventionally printed and have a black background with large flaming "RED HOT" letters and a color player photo.

		MT
Complete Set (25):		80.00
Common Player:		1.50
1	Cal Ripken Jr.	12.00
2	Ken Griffey Jr.	15.00
3	Frank Thomas	6.00
4	Jeff Bagwell	6.00
5	Mike Piazza	10.00
6	Barry Bonds	4.00
7	Albert Belle	4.00
8	Tony Gwynn	6.00
9	Kirby Puckett	5.00
10	Don Mattingly	5.00
11	Matt Williams	1.50
12	Greg Maddux	10.00
13	Raul Mondesi	2.00
14	Paul Molitor	3.00
15	Manny Ramirez	5.00
16	Joe Carter	1.50
17	Will Clark	2.00
18	Roger Clemens	5.00
19	Tim Salmon	1.50
20	Dave Justice	1.50
21	Kenny Lofton	3.00
22	Deion Sanders	1.50
23	Roberto Alomar	3.00
24	Cliff Floyd	1.50
25	Carlos Baerga	1.50

1995 Pinnacle Team Pinnacle

This nine-card Series I insert set becomes an 18-card challenge if the collector decides to hunt for both versions of each card. As in the past the Team Pinnacle cards picture National and American League counterparts at each position on different sides of the same card. In 1995 each card is printed with one side in Pinnacle's Dufex foil technology, and the other side conventionally printed. Thus card #1 can be found with Mike Mussina in Dufex and Greg Maddux conventionally printed, or with Maddux in Dufex and Mussina conventional. Team Pinnacle cards are found inserted at an average rate of only one per 90 packs.

		MT
Complete Set (9):		180.00
Common Player:		6.00
1	Mike Mussina, Greg Maddux	25.00
2	Carlos Delgado, Mike Piazza	25.00
3	Frank Thomas, Jeff Bagwell	20.00
4	Roberto Alomar, Craig Biggio	10.00
5	Cal Ripken Jr., Ozzie Smith	30.00
6	Travis Fryman, Matt Williams	6.00
7	Ken Griffey Jr., Barry Bonds	40.00
8	Albert Belle, Dave Justice	10.00
9	Kirby Puckett, Tony Gwynn	20.00

1995 Pinnacle Team Pinnacle Pin Trade Cards

In one of the hobby's first major attempts to cross-promote pin- and card-collecting, Series 2 Pinnacle packs offered a special insert set of cards which could be redeemed for a collector's pin of the same player. Seeded at the rate of one per 48 regular packs and one per 36 jumbo packs, the pin redemption cards were valid until Nov. 15, 1995. Payment of $2 handling fee was required for redemption.

		MT
Complete Set (18):		75.00
Common Player:		2.00
1	Greg Maddux	6.00
2	Mike Mussina	2.00
3	Mike Piazza	6.00
4	Carlos Delgado	2.00
5	Jeff Bagwell	4.00
6	Frank Thomas	5.00
7	Craig Biggio	2.00
8	Roberto Alomar	3.00
9	Ozzie Smith	3.00
10	Cal Ripken Jr.	8.00
11	Matt Williams	3.00
12	Travis Fryman	2.00
13	Barry Bonds	5.00
14	Ken Griffey Jr.	10.00
15	Dave Justice	2.00
16	Albert Belle	4.00
17	Tony Gwynn	5.00
18	Kirby Puckett	4.00

1995 Pinnacle Team Pinnacle Collector Pins

Redemption cards in Series 2 packs could be traded in (until Nov. 15, 1995) for an enameled pin of the player pictured on the trade card. Pins are about 1-3/8" x 1-1/4". A raised relief portrait of the player is at center with his name in pennants above and his team logo at bottom, along with the Pinnacle logo. Backs are gold-tone with a post-and-button style of pinback. The unnumbered pins are listed here in the same sequence as the redemption cards.

		MT
Complete Set (18):		150.00
Common Player:		4.00
(1)	Greg Maddux	12.00
(2)	Mike Mussina	4.00
(3)	Mike Piazza	12.00
(4)	Carlos Delgado	4.00
(5)	Jeff Bagwell	8.00
(6)	Frank Thomas	8.00
(7)	Craig Biggio	4.00
(8)	Roberto Alomar	8.00
(9)	Ozzie Smith	6.00
(10)	Cal Ripken Jr.	16.00
(11)	Matt Williams	6.00
(12)	Travis Fryman	4.00
(13)	Barry Bonds	10.00
(14)	Ken Griffey Jr.	16.00
(15)	Dave Justice	4.00
(16)	Albert Belle	8.00
(17)	Tony Gwynn	10.00
(18)	Kirby Puckett	10.00

1995 Pinnacle Upstarts

Thirty of the most dominant young players in the game were featured in this insert series. Cards are printed with most of the photo's background covered by the legs of a large blue and gold star device, which includes the team logo at its red center. A blue circular "'95 UPSTARTS" logo at bottom-left has the player name in gold. These cards are exclusive to Series I, found at an average rate of one per eight packs.

		MT
Complete Set (30):		35.00
Common Player:		.50
1	Frank Thomas	6.00
2	Roberto Alomar	2.00
3	Mike Piazza	9.00
4	Javier Lopez	.60
5	Albert Belle	4.50
6	Carlos Delgado	.75
7	Rusty Greer	.50
8	Tim Salmon	.75
9	Raul Mondesi	.65
10	Juan Gonzalez	4.00
11	Manny Ramirez	4.50
12	Sammy Sosa	10.00
13	Jeff Kent	.50
14	Melvin Nieves	.50
15	Rondell White	.65
16	Shawn Green	1.50
17	Bernie Williams	1.50
18	Aaron Sele	.50
19	Jason Bere	.50
20	Joey Hamilton	.50
21	Mike Kelly	.50
22	Wil Cordero	.50
23	Moises Alou	.60
24	Roberto Kelly	.50
25	Deion Sanders	1.50
26	Steve Karsay	.50
27	Bret Boone	.50
28	Willie Greene	.50
29	Billy Ashley	.50
30	Brian Anderson	.50

1995 Pinnacle White Hot

Similar in format to the Red Hot inserts, and featuring the same players, the hobby-only White Hot cards are a chase set of a chase set. Seeded once per 36 packs on average (more than twice as scarce as the Red Hots), the White Hot cards have fronts totally printed in the Dufex process, with predominantly blue and white background colors, while the backs are highlighted by blue foil printing in the "WHITE HOT" background lettering on black background.

		MT
Complete Set (25):		200.00
Common Player:		4.00
1	Cal Ripken Jr.	25.00
2	Ken Griffey Jr.	30.00
3	Frank Thomas	15.00
4	Jeff Bagwell	12.00
5	Mike Piazza	20.00
6	Barry Bonds	8.00
7	Albert Belle	8.00
8	Tony Gwynn	15.00
9	Kirby Puckett	10.00
10	Don Mattingly	10.00
11	Matt Williams	4.00
12	Greg Maddux	20.00
13	Raul Mondesi	4.00
14	Paul Molitor	6.00
15	Manny Ramirez	8.00
16	Joe Carter	4.00
17	Will Clark	6.00
18	Roger Clemens	8.00
19	Tim Salmon	4.00
20	Dave Justice	4.00
21	Kenny Lofton	6.00
22	Deion Sanders	6.00
23	Roberto Alomar	6.00
24	Cliff Floyd	4.00
25	Carlos Baerga	4.00

1996 Pinnacle

Pinnacle issued a 399-card regular-issue set with borderless front photos highlighted by prismatic gold-foil graphics in the shape of a triangle at bottom. The player's name is in black in the triangle. Backs have another player photo along with stats and data. Parallel Starburst and Starburst Artist's Proof sets contain only 200 of the cards in the base issue. Series I inserts include a Cal Ripken Jr. "Tribute" card, numbered "1 of 1" (seeded one per every 150 packs). The other five Series I inserts are Team Pinnacle, Pinnacle Power, Team Tomorrow, Essence of the Game and First Rate. Series II inserts the Christie Brinkley Collection, Project Stardom, Skylines, Slugfest and Team Spirit. Pinnacle was sold in 10-card hobby and retail foil packs, and 18-card jumbo packs.

		MT
Complete Set (400):		35.00
Common Player:		.10
Series 1 or 2 Pack (10):		2.50
Series 1 or 2 Wax Box (24):		45.00
1	Greg Maddux	1.50
2	Bill Pulsipher	.10
3	Dante Bichette	.20
4	Mike Piazza	2.00
5	Garret Anderson	.10
6	Steve Finley	.10
7	Andy Benes	.10
8	Chuck Knoblauch	.15
9	Tom Gordon	.10
10	Jeff Bagwell	.75
11	Wil Cordero	.10
12	John Mabry	.10
13	Jeff Frye	.10
14	Travis Fryman	.15
15	John Wetteland	.10
16	Jason Bates	.10
17	Danny Tartabull	.10
18	Charles Nagy	.10
19	Robin Ventura	.15
20	Reggie Sanders	.10
21	Dave Clark	.10
22	Jaime Navarro	.10
23	Joey Hamilton	.10
24	Al Leiter	.15
25	Deion Sanders	.25
26	Tim Salmon	.20
27	Tino Martinez	.15
28	Mike Greenwell	.10
29	Phil Plantier	.10
30	Bobby Bonilla	.10
31	Kenny Rogers	.10
32	Chili Davis	.10
33	Joe Carter	.15
34	Mike Mussina	.40
35	Matt Mieske	.10
36	Jose Canseco	.40
37	Brad Radke	.10
38	Juan Gonzalez	.75
39	David Segui	.10
40	Alex Fernandez	.10
41	Jeff Kent	.10
42	Todd Zeile	.10
43	Darryl Strawberry	.10
44	Jose Rijo	.10
45	Ramon Martinez	.10
46	Manny Ramirez	.75
47	Gregg Jefferies	.10
48	Bryan Rekar	.10
49	Jeff King	.10
50	John Olerud	.15
51	Marc Newfield	.10
52	Charles Johnson	.15
53	Robby Thompson	.10
54	Brian Hunter	.10
55	Mike Blowers	.10
56	Keith Lockhart	.10
57	Ray Lankford	.10
58	Tim Wallach	.10
59	Ivan Rodriguez	.75
60	Ed Sprague	.10
61	Paul Molitor	.30
62	Eric Karros	.10
63	Glenallen Hill	.10
64	Jay Bell	.10
65	Tom Pagnozzi	.10
66	Greg Colbrunn	.10
67	Edgar Martinez	.10
68	Paul Sorrento	.10
69	Kirt Manwaring	.10
70	Pete Schourek	.10
71	Orlando Merced	.10
72	Shawon Dunston	.10
73	Ricky Bottalico	.10
74	Brady Anderson	.15
75	Steve Ontiveros	.10
76	Jim Abbott	.10
77	Carl Everett	.10
78	Mo Vaughn	.40
79	Pedro Martinez	.75
80	Harold Baines	.10
81	Alan Trammell	.10
82	Steve Avery	.10
83	Jeff Cirillo	.10
84	John Valentin	.10
85	Bernie Williams	.50
86	Andre Dawson	.15
87	Dave Winfield	.25
88	B.J. Surhoff	.10
89	Jeff Blauser	.10
90	Barry Larkin	.15
91	Cliff Floyd	.15
92	Sammy Sosa	1.50
93	Andres Galarraga	.15
94	Dave Nilsson	.10
95	James Mouton	.10
96	Marquis Grissom	.10
97	Matt Williams	.25
98	John Jaha	.10
99	Don Mattingly	1.00
100	Tim Naehring	.10
101	Kevin Appier	.10
102	Bobby Higginson	.10
103	Andy Pettitte	.30
104	Ozzie Smith	.40
105	Kenny Lofton	.30
106	Ken Caminiti	.15
107	Walt Weiss	.10
108	Jack McDowell	.10
109	Brian McRae	.10
110	Gary Gaetti	.10
111	Curtis Goodwin	.10
112	Dennis Martinez	.10
113	Omar Vizquel	.10
114	Chipper Jones	1.50
115	Mark Gubicza	.10
116	Ruben Sierra	.10
117	Eddie Murray	.40
118	Chad Curtis	.10
119	Hal Morris	.10
120	Ben McDonald	.10
121	Marty Cordova	.10
122	Ken Griffey Jr.	2.50
123	Gary Sheffield	.20
124	Charlie Hayes	.10
125	Shawn Green	.30
126	Jason Giambi	.15
127	Mark Langston	.10
128	Mark Whiten	.10
129	Greg Vaughn	.15
130	Mark McGwire	3.00
131	Hideo Nomo	.50
132	Eric Karros, Raul Mondesi, Hideo Nomo, Mike Piazza	.50
133	Jason Bere	.10
134	Ken Griffey Jr. (The Naturals)	1.50
135	Frank Thomas (The Naturals)	.50
136	Cal Ripken Jr. (The Naturals)	1.25
137	Albert Belle (The Naturals)	.20
138	Mike Piazza (The Naturals)	1.00
139	Dante Bichette (The Naturals)	.15
140	Sammy Sosa (The Naturals)	.75
141	Mo Vaughn (The Naturals)	.20
142	Tim Salmon (The Naturals)	.15
143	Reggie Sanders (The Naturals)	.10
144	Cecil Fielder (The Naturals)	.10
145	Jim Edmonds (The Naturals)	.10
146	Rafael Palmeiro (The Naturals)	.10
147	Edgar Martinez (The Naturals)	.10
148	Barry Bonds (The Naturals)	.40
149	Manny Ramirez (The Naturals)	.50
150	Larry Walker (The Naturals)	.15
151	Jeff Bagwell (The Naturals)	.50
152	Ron Gant (The Naturals)	.10
153	Andres Galarraga (The Naturals)	.10
154	Eddie Murray (The Naturals)	.20
155	Kirby Puckett (The Naturals)	.50
156	Will Clark (The Naturals)	.15
157	Don Mattingly (The Naturals)	.50
158	Mark McGwire (The Naturals)	1.50
159	Dean Palmer (The Naturals)	.10
160	Matt Williams (The Naturals)	.15
161	Fred McGriff (The Naturals)	.20
162	Joe Carter (The Naturals)	.10
163	Juan Gonzalez (The Naturals)	.40
164	Alex Ochoa	.10
165	Ruben Rivera	.15
166	Tony Clark	.15
167	Brian Barber	.10
168	Matt Lawton	.10
169	Terrell Wade	.10
170	Johnny Damon	.20
171	Derek Jeter	2.00
172	Phil Nevin	.10
173	Robert Perez	.10
174	C.J. Nitkowski	.10
175	Joe Vitiello	.10
176	Roger Cedeno	.10
177	Ron Coomer	.10
178	Chris Widger	.10
179	Jimmy Haynes	.10
180	*Mike Sweeney*	1.00
181	Howard Battle	.10
182	John Wasdin	.10
183	Jim Pittsley	.10
184	Bob Wolcott	.10
185	LaTroy Hawkins	.10
186	Nigel Wilson	.10
187	Dustin Hermanson	.20
188	Chris Snopek	.10
189	Mariano Rivera	.20
190	Jose Herrera	.10
191	Chris Stynes	.10
192	Larry Thomas	.10
193	David Bell	.10
194	(Frank Thomas) (checklist)	.50
195	(Ken Griffey Jr.) (checklist)	1.00
196	(Cal Ripken Jr.) (checklist)	.75
197	(Jeff Bagwell) (checklist)	.25
198	(Mike Piazza) (checklist)	.50
199	(Barry Bonds) (checklist)	.40
200	(Garrett Anderson, Chipper Jones) (checklist)	.35
201	Frank Thomas	1.00
202	Michael Tucker	.10
203	Kirby Puckett	.75
204	Alex Gonzalez	.10
205	Tony Gwynn	1.00
206	Moises Alou	.10
207	Albert Belle	.40
208	Barry Bonds	.75

#	Player	MT
209	Fred McGriff	.40
210	Dennis Eckersley	.10
211	Craig Biggio	.20
212	David Cone	.15
213	Will Clark	.25
214	Cal Ripken Jr.	2.50
215	Wade Boggs	.25
216	Pete Schourek	.10
217	Darren Daulton	.10
218	Carlos Baerga	.10
219	Larry Walker	.30
220	Denny Neagle	.10
221	Jim Edmonds	.15
222	Lee Smith	.10
223	Jason Isringhausen	.15
224	Jay Buhner	.15
225	John Olerud	.15
226	Jeff Conine	.10
227	Dean Palmer	.10
228	Jim Abbott	.10
229	Raul Mondesi	.25
230	Tom Glavine	.15
231	Kevin Seitzer	.10
232	Lenny Dykstra	.10
233	Brian Jordan	.10
234	Rondell White	.10
235	Bret Boone	.10
236	Randy Johnson	.50
237	Paul O'Neill	.15
238	Jim Thome	.40
239	Edgardo Alfonzo	.15
240	Terry Pendleton	.10
241	Harold Baines	.10
242	Roberto Alomar	.60
243	Mark Grace	.20
244	Derek Bell	.10
245	Vinny Castilla	.10
246	Cecil Fielder	.15
247	Roger Clemens	1.00
248	Orel Hershiser	.10
249	J.T. Snow	.10
250	Rafael Palmeiro	.30
251	Bret Saberhagen	.10
252	Todd Hollandsworth	.10
253	Ryan Klesko	.25
254	Greg Maddux (Hardball Heroes)	.75
255	Ken Griffey Jr. (Hardball Heroes)	1.50
256	Hideo Nomo (Hardball Heroes)	.25
257	Frank Thomas (Hardball Heroes)	.75
258	Cal Ripken Jr. (Hardball Heroes)	1.25
259	Jeff Bagwell (Hardball Heroes)	.50
260	Barry Bonds (Hardball Heroes)	.40
261	Mo Vaughn (Hardball Heroes)	.25
262	Albert Belle (Hardball Heroes)	.20
263	Sammy Sosa (Hardball Heroes)	.50
264	Reggie Sanders (Hardball Heroes)	.10
265	Mike Piazza (Hardball Heroes)	1.00
266	Chipper Jones (Hardball Heroes)	.75
267	Tony Gwynn (Hardball Heroes)	.50
268	Kirby Puckett (Hardball Heroes)	.40
269	Wade Boggs (Hardball Heroes)	.15
270	Will Clark (Hardball Heroes)	.15
271	Gary Sheffield (Hardball Heroes)	.15
272	Dante Bichette (Hardball Heroes)	.15
273	Randy Johnson (Hardball Heroes)	.30
274	Matt Williams (Hardball Heroes)	.15
275	Alex Rodriguez (Hardball Heroes)	2.50
276	Tim Salmon (Hardball Heroes)	.20
277	Johnny Damon (Hardball Heroes)	.20
278	Manny Ramirez (Hardball Heroes)	.40
279	Derek Jeter (Hardball Heroes)	1.00
280	Eddie Murray (Hardball Heroes)	.20
281	Ozzie Smith (Hardball Heroes)	.25
282	Garret Anderson (Hardball Heroes)	.10
283	Raul Mondesi (Hardball Heroes)	.20
284	Terry Steinbach	.10
285	Carlos Garcia	.10
286	Dave Justice	.25
287	Eric Anthony	.10
288	Benji Gil	.10
289	Bob Hamelin	.10
290	Dwayne Hosey	.10
291	Andy Pettitte	.25
292	Rod Beck	.10
293	Shane Andrews	.10
294	Julian Tavarez	.10
295	Willie Greene	.10
296	Ismael Valdes	.10
297	Glenallen Hill	.10
298	Troy Percival	.10
299	Ray Durham	.10
300	Jeff Conine (.300 Series)	.10
301.8	Ken Griffey Jr. (.300 Series)	1.50
302	Will Clark (.300 Series)	.20
303	Mike Greenwell (.300 Series)	.10
304.9	Carlos Baerga (.300 Series)	.15
305.3	Paul Molitor (.300 Series)	.20
305.6	Jeff Bagwell (.300 Series)	.50
306	Mark Grace (.300 Series)	.15
307	Don Mattingly (.300 Series)	.50
308	Hal Morris (.300 Series)	.10
309	Butch Huskey	.10
310	Ozzie Guillen	.10
311	Erik Hanson	.10
312	Kenny Lofton (.300 Series)	.20
313	Edgar Martinez (.300 Series)	.10
314	Kurt Abbott	.10
315	John Smoltz	.20
316	Ariel Prieto	.10
317	Mark Carreon	.10
318	Kirby Puckett (.300 Series)	.40
319	Carlos Perez	.10
320	Gary DiSarcina	.10
321	Trevor Hoffman	.15
322	Mike Piazza (.300 Series)	1.00
323	Frank Thomas (.300 Series)	.50
324	Juan Acevedo	.10
325	Bip Roberts	.10
326	Javier Lopez	.15
327	Benito Santiago	.10
328	Mark Lewis	.10
329	Royce Clayton	.10
330	Tom Gordon	.10
331	Ben McDonald	.10
332	Dan Wilson	.10
333	Ron Gant	.15
334	Wade Boggs (.300 Series)	.20
335	Paul Molitor	.25
336	Tony Gwynn (.300 Series)	.50
337	Sean Berry	.10
338	Rickey Henderson	.25
339	Wil Cordero	.10
340	Kent Mercker	.10
341	Kenny Rogers	.10
342	Ryne Sandberg	.75
343	Charlie Hayes	.10
344	Andy Benes	.10
345	Sterling Hitchcock	.10
346	Bernard Gilkey	.10
347	Julio Franco	.10
348	Ken Hill	.10
349	Russ Davis	.10
350	Mike Blowers	.10
351	B.J. Surhoff	.10
352	Lance Johnson	.10
353	Darryl Hamilton	.10
354	Shawon Dunston	.10
355	Rick Aguilera	.10
356	Danny Tartabull	.10
357	Todd Stottlemyre	.10
358	Mike Bordick	.10
359	Jack McDowell	.10
360	Todd Zeile	.10
361	Tino Martinez	.10
362	Greg Gagne	.10
363	Mike Kelly	.10
364	Tim Raines	.15
365	Ernie Young	.10
366	Mike Stanley	.10
367	Wally Joyner	.10
368	Karim Garcia	.10
369	Paul Wilson	.15
370	Sal Fasano	.10
371	Jason Schmidt	.10
372	*Livan Hernandez*	.25
373	George Arias	.10
374	Steve Gibralter	.10
375	Jermaine Dye	.10
376	Jason Kendall	.15
377	Brooks Kieschnick	.10
378	Jeff Ware	.10
379	Alan Benes	.15
380	Rey Ordonez	.20
381	Jay Powell	.10
382	*Osvaldo Fernandez*	.15
383	*Wilton Guerrero*	.25
384	Eric Owens	.10
385	George Williams	.10
386	Chan Ho Park	.15
387	Jeff Suppan	.10
388	*F.P. Santangelo*	.25
389	Terry Adams	.10
390	Bob Abreu	.15
391	*Quinton McCracken*	.15
392	*Mike Busby*	.10
393	(Cal Ripken Jr.) (checklist)	1.00
394	(Ken Griffey Jr.) (checklist)	1.25
395	(Frank Thomas) (checklist)	.40
396	(Chipper Jones) (checklist)	.60
397	(Greg Maddux) (checklist)	.75
398	(Mike Piazza) (checklist)	.60
399	(Ken Griffey Jr., Frank Thomas, Cal Ripken Jr., Greg Maddux, Chipper Jones, Mike Piazza) (checklist)	.50

1996 Pinnacle Foil Series 2

The 200 cards from Series 2 were paralleled in a special foil edition which was sold at retail outlets only in five-card $2.99 packs. Fronts have a metallic foil background to differentiate them from the regular-issue Series 2 Pinnacle version.

	MT
Complete Set (200):	25.00
Common Player:	.25
Stars:	1.5X

(See 1996 Pinnacle #201-399 for checklist and base card values.)

1996 Pinnacle Cal Ripken Tribute

A special Cal Ripken Tribute card was issued in Series 1 Pinnacle packs at a rate of 1:150. Front features an etched metallic foil background, a gold-foil facsimile autograph and a "2,131+ Consecutive Games Played" starburst. Back has a photo of the scoreboard on that historic occasion, and a photo of Ripken being driven around Camden Yards in a red Corvette. The card is numbered "1 of 1", but it is not unique.

		MT
1 of 1	Cal Ripken Jr.	25.00

1996 Pinnacle Christie Brinkley Collection

Supermodel Christie Brinkley exclusively took photos for these 1996 Pinnacle Series II inserts. The 16 cards capture players from the 1995 World Series participants during a spring training photo session. Cards were seeded one per every 23 hobby packs or 32 retail packs.

		MT
Complete Set (16):		30.00
Common Player:		1.50
1	Greg Maddux	8.00
2	Ryan Klesko	1.50
3	Dave Justice	2.00
4	Tom Glavine	2.00
5	Chipper Jones	8.00
6	Fred McGriff	2.50
7	Javier Lopez	2.00
8	Marquis Grissom	1.50
9	Jason Schmidt	1.50
10	Albert Belle	4.50
11	Manny Ramirez	5.00
12	Carlos Baerga	1.50
13	Sandy Alomar	1.50
14	Jim Thome	2.00
15	Julio Franco	1.50
16	Kenny Lofton	4.00

1996 Pinnacle Essence of the Game

Essence of the Game is an 18-card insert set found only in hobby packs at a one per 23 packs rate in Series 1. Cards are printed on clear plastic with the front photo also appearing in an inverted fashion on back. Micro-etched Dufex printing technology is utilized on the front of the cards.

		MT
Complete Set (18):		90.00
Common Player:		1.50
1	Cal Ripken Jr.	12.00
2	Greg Maddux	8.00
3	Frank Thomas	5.00
4	Matt Williams	2.00
5	Chipper Jones	8.00
6	Reggie Sanders	1.50
7	Ken Griffey Jr.	15.00
8	Kirby Puckett	5.00
9	Hideo Nomo	2.00
10	Mike Piazza	8.00
11	Jeff Bagwell	4.00
12	Mo Vaughn	2.50
13	Albert Belle	4.00
14	Tim Salmon	1.50
15	Don Mattingly	4.00
16	Will Clark	2.00
17	Eddie Murray	2.00
18	Barry Bonds	4.00

1996 Pinnacle First Rate

Retail-exclusive First Rate showcases 18 former first round draft picks now in the majors. Printed in Dufex foil throughout, a red swirl pattern covers the left 2/3 of the card front. Backs show the player again, within a large numeral "1". These inserts are found at an average rate of one per 23 packs in Series 1.

		MT
Complete Set (18):		120.00
Common Player:		2.50
1	Ken Griffey Jr.	25.00
2	Frank Thomas	10.00
3	Mo Vaughn	6.00
4	Chipper Jones	15.00
5	Alex Rodriguez	20.00
6	Kirby Puckett	8.00
7	Gary Sheffield	4.00
8	Matt Williams	3.00
9	Barry Bonds	8.00
10	Craig Biggio	2.50
11	Robin Ventura	2.50
12	Michael Tucker	2.50
13	Derek Jeter	15.00
14	Manny Ramirez	8.00
15	Barry Larkin	2.50
16	Shawn Green	5.00
17	Will Clark	4.00
18	Mark McGwire	25.00

1996 Pinnacle Pinnacle Power

Pinnacle Powers inserts are seeded at the rate of one per 47 packs in both hobby and retail Series 1. Twenty different sluggers are featured on a two-layered front. The bottom layer is silver Dufex foil with solid black on top; a color action photo of the player is at center, giving the card a die-cut appearance.

		MT
Complete Set (20):		50.00
Common Player:		1.00
1	Frank Thomas	4.00
2	Mo Vaughn	2.50
2p	Mo Vaughn (promo)	2.00
3	Ken Griffey Jr.	12.50
4	Matt Williams	1.00
5	Barry Bonds	3.00
6	Reggie Sanders	1.00
7	Mike Piazza	7.50
8	Jim Edmonds	1.00
9	Dante Bichette	1.00
10	Sammy Sosa	6.00
11	Jeff Bagwell	5.00
12	Fred McGriff	2.00
13	Albert Belle	3.00
14	Tim Salmon	1.00
15	Joe Carter	1.00
16	Manny Ramirez	3.00
17	Eddie Murray	2.00
18	Cecil Fielder	1.00
19	Larry Walker	2.00
20	Juan Gonzalez	3.00

1996 Pinnacle Project Stardom

These 1996 Pinnacle inserts cards feature young players on their way to stardom. The cards, which use Dufex technology, are seeded one per every 35 packs of Series II hobby packs.

		MT
Complete Set (18):		120.00
Common Player:		2.50
1	Paul Wilson	2.50
2	Derek Jeter	25.00
3	Karim Garcia	2.50
4	Johnny Damon	3.00
5	Alex Rodriguez	30.00
6	Chipper Jones	25.00
7	Todd Walker	2.50
8	Bob Abreu	3.00
9	Alan Benes	2.50
10	Richard Hidalgo	4.00
11	Brooks Kieschnick	2.50
12	Garret Anderson	3.00
13	Livan Hernandez	2.50
14	Manny Ramirez	10.00
15	Jermaine Dye	3.00
16	Todd Hollandsworth	3.00
17	Raul Mondesi	5.00
18	Ryan Klesko	3.50

1996 Pinnacle Skylines

These 1996 Pinnacle inserts feature cards printed on a clear plastic stock. The cards were seeded one per every 29 Series II magazine packs, and one per 50 retail packs.

		MT
Complete Set (18):		350.00
Common Player:		8.00
1	Ken Griffey Jr.	65.00
2	Frank Thomas	25.00
3	Greg Maddux	30.00
4	Cal Ripken Jr.	50.00
5	Albert Belle	20.00
6	Mo Vaughn	15.00
7	Mike Piazza	35.00
8	Wade Boggs	17.50
9	Will Clark	12.00
10	Barry Bonds	20.00
11	Gary Sheffield	12.00
12	Hideo Nomo	12.00
13	Tony Gwynn	25.00
14	Kirby Puckett	35.00
15	Chipper Jones	35.00
16	Jeff Bagwell	20.00
17	Manny Ramirez	20.00
18	Raul Mondesi	8.00

1996 Pinnacle Slugfest

These 1996 Pinnacle Series II inserts feature 18 of the game's heaviest hitters on all-foil Dufex cards. The cards were seeded one per every 35 retail packs.

		MT
Complete Set (18):		150.00
Common Player:		3.00
1	Frank Thomas	15.00
2	Ken Griffey Jr.	30.00
3	Jeff Bagwell	15.00
4	Barry Bonds	10.00
5	Mo Vaughn	6.00
6	Albert Belle	8.00
7	Mike Piazza	25.00
8	Matt Williams	5.00
9	Dante Bichette	4.00
10	Sammy Sosa	20.00
11	Gary Sheffield	6.00
12	Reggie Sanders	3.00
13	Manny Ramirez	12.50
14	Eddie Murray	5.00
15	Juan Gonzalez	8.00
16	Dean Palmer	3.00
17	Rafael Palmeiro	4.00
18	Cecil Fielder	3.00

1996 Pinnacle Starburst

For 1996 Pinnacle abbreviated its parallel insert

set to just half of the cards from the base issue. Only 200 select players are included in the Starburst Dufex-printed parallel set found on average of once per seven hobby packs and once per 10 retail packs. An Artist's Proof version of the Starbursts, a parallel set within a parallel set, are inserted once per 47 (hobby) or 67 (retail) packs. On these super-premium inserts the Artist's Proof logo is repeated throughout the Dufex background.

	MT
Complete Set (200):	400.00
Complete Series 1 (100):	200.00
Complete Series 2 (100):	200.00
Common Player:	.50
Complete Artist's Proof Set (200):	1200.
Artist's Proofs:	3X to 4X

#	Player	MT
1	Greg Maddux	12.00
2	Bill Pulsipher	.50
3	Dante Bichette	2.50
4	Mike Piazza	12.00
5	Garret Anderson	.50
6	Chuck Knoblauch	.75
7	Jeff Bagwell	5.00
8	Wil Cordero	.50
9	Travis Fryman	.50
10	Reggie Sanders	.50
11	Deion Sanders	2.00
12	Tim Salmon	3.00
13	Tino Martinez	1.00
14	Bobby Bonilla	.50
15	Joe Carter	1.00
16	Mike Mussina	3.00
17	Jose Canseco	3.00
18	Manny Ramirez	5.00
19	Gregg Jefferies	.50
20	Charles Johnson	.50
21	Brian Hunter	.50
22	Ray Lankford	.50
23	Ivan Rodriguez	4.00
24	Paul Molitor	3.00
25	Eric Karros	.50
26	Edgar Martinez	.50
27	Shawon Dunston	.50
28	Mo Vaughn	2.50
29	Pedro Martinez	1.50
30	Marty Cordova	.50
31	Ken Caminiti	1.50
32	Gary Sheffield	1.50
33	Shawn Green	1.50
34	Cliff Floyd	.50
35	Andres Galarraga	1.50
36	Matt Williams	2.00
37	Don Mattingly	6.00
38	Kevin Appier	.50
39	Ozzie Smith	4.00
40	Kenny Lofton	2.50
41	Ken Griffey Jr.	20.00
42	Jack McDowell	.50
43	Gary Gaetti	.50
44	Dennis Martinez	.50
45	Chipper Jones	12.00
46	Eddie Murray	3.00
47	Bernie Williams	2.50
48	Andre Dawson	.75
49	Dave Winfield	.75
50	B.J. Surhoff	.50
51	Barry Larkin	1.00
52	Alan Trammell	.50
53	Sammy Sosa	12.00
54	Hideo Nomo	3.00
55	Mark McGwire	20.00
56	Jay Bell	.50
57	Juan Gonzalez	5.00
58	Chili Davis	.50
59	Robin Ventura	.75
60	John Mabry	.50
61	Ken Griffey Jr. (Naturals)	10.00
62	Frank Thomas (Naturals)	3.00
63	Cal Ripken Jr. (Naturals)	8.00
64	Albert Belle (Naturals)	3.00
65	Mike Piazza (Naturals)	6.00
66	Dante Bichette (Naturals)	1.00
67	Sammy Sosa (Naturals)	5.00
68	Mo Vaughn (Naturals)	1.00
69	Tim Salmon (Naturals)	1.00
70	Reggie Sanders (Naturals)	.50
71	Cecil Fielder (Naturals)	1.00
72	Jim Edmonds (Naturals)	.50
73	Rafael Palmeiro (Naturals)	1.50
74	Edgar Martinez (Naturals)	.50
75	Barry Bonds (Naturals)	3.00
76	Manny Ramirez (Naturals)	3.00
77	Larry Walker (Naturals)	.50
78	Jeff Bagwell (Naturals)	3.00
79	Ron Gant (Naturals)	.50
80	Andres Galarraga (Naturals)	.50
81	Eddie Murray (Naturals)	1.50
82	Kirby Puckett (Naturals)	3.00
83	Will Clark (Naturals)	1.50
84	Don Mattingly (Naturals)	3.00
85	Mark McGwire (Naturals)	15.00
86	Dean Palmer (Naturals)	.50
87	Matt Williams (Naturals)	1.50
88	Fred McGriff (Naturals)	1.50
89	Joe Carter (Naturals)	.50
90	Juan Gonzalez (Naturals)	2.50
91	Alex Ochoa	.50
92	Ruben Rivera	.50
93	Tony Clark	3.00
94	Pete Schourek	.50
95	Terrell Wade	.50
96	Johnny Damon	.75
97	Derek Jeter	12.00
98	Phil Nevin	.50
99	Robert Perez	.50
100	Dustin Hermanson	.50
101	Frank Thomas	6.00
102	Michael Tucker	.50
103	Kirby Puckett	5.00
104	Alex Gonzalez	.50
105	Tony Gwynn	10.00
106	Moises Alou	.50
107	Albert Belle	5.00
108	Barry Bonds	5.00
109	Fred McGriff	2.50
110	Dennis Eckersley	.50
111	Craig Biggio	.75
112	David Cone	.75
113	Will Clark	2.00
114	Cal Ripken Jr.	15.00
115	Wade Boggs	2.50
116	Pete Schourek	.50
117	Darren Daulton	.50
118	Carlos Baerga	.50
119	Larry Walker	2.00
120	Denny Neagle	.50
121	Jim Edmonds	.50
122	Lee Smith	.50
123	Jason Isringhausen	.50
124	Jay Buhner	1.00
125	John Olerud	.75
126	Jeff Conine	.50
127	Dean Palmer	.50
128	Jim Abbott	.50
129	Raul Mondesi	2.00
130	Tom Glavine	.75
131	Kevin Seitzer	.50
132	Lenny Dykstra	.50
133	Brian Jordan	.50
134	Rondell White	.50
135	Bret Boone	.50
136	Randy Johnson	4.00
137	Paul O'Neill	.75
138	Jim Thome	3.00
139	Edgardo Alfonzo	.75
140	Terry Pendleton	.50
141	Harold Baines	.50
142	Roberto Alomar	4.00
143	Mark Grace	1.50
144	Derek Bell	.50
145	Vinny Castilla	.50
146	Cecil Fielder	1.00
147	Roger Clemens	6.00
148	Orel Hershiser	.50
149	J.T. Snow	.50
150	Rafael Palmeiro	1.50
151	Bret Saberhagen	.50
152	Todd Hollandsworth	.50
153	Ryan Klesko	3.00
154	Greg Maddux (Hardball Heroes)	6.00
155	Ken Griffey Jr. (Hardball Heroes)	10.00
156	Hideo Nomo (Hardball Heroes)	2.00
157	Frank Thomas (Hardball Heroes)	3.00
158	Cal Ripken Jr. (Hardball Heroes)	8.00
159	Jeff Bagwell (Hardball Heroes)	3.00
160	Barry Bonds (Hardball Heroes)	3.00
161	Mo Vaughn (Hardball Heroes)	2.50
162	Albert Belle (Hardball Heroes)	3.00
163	Sammy Sosa (Hardball Heroes)	5.00
164	Reggie Sanders (Hardball Heroes)	.50
165	Mike Piazza (Hardball Heroes)	6.00
166	Chipper Jones (Hardball Heroes)	5.00
167	Tony Gwynn (Hardball Heroes)	4.00
168	Kirby Puckett (Hardball Heroes)	3.00
169	Wade Boggs (Hardball Heroes)	1.50
170	Will Clark (Hardball Heroes)	1.50
171	Gary Sheffield (Hardball Heroes)	1.50
172	Dante Bichette (Hardball Heroes)	1.00
173	Randy Johnson (Hardball Heroes)	2.00
174	Matt Williams (Hardball Heroes)	1.00
175	Alex Rodriguez (Hardball Heroes)	8.00
176	Tim Salmon (Hardball Heroes)	1.00
177	Johnny Damon (Hardball Heroes)	.50
178	Manny Ramirez (Hardball Heroes)	3.00
179	Derek Jeter (Hardball Heroes)	6.00
180	Eddie Murray (Hardball Heroes)	2.00
181	Ozzie Smith (Hardball Heroes)	3.00
182	Garret Anderson (Hardball Heroes)	.50
183	Raul Mondesi (Hardball Heroes)	1.00
184	Jeff Conine (.300 Series)	.50
185	Ken Griffey Jr. (.300 Series)	10.00
186	Will Clark (.300 Series)	1.50
187	Mike Greenwell (.300 Series)	.50
188	Carlos Baerga (.300 Series)	.50
189	Paul Molitor (.300 Series)	1.50
190	Jeff Bagwell (.300 Series)	3.00
191	Mark Grace (.300 Series)	.50
192	Don Mattingly (.300 Series)	3.00
193	Hal Morris (.300 Series)	.50
194	Kenny Lofton (.300 Series)	2.00
195	Edgar Martinez (.300 Series)	.50
196	Kirby Puckett (.300 Series)	3.00
197	Mike Piazza (.300 Series)	6.00
198	Frank Thomas (.300 Series)	3.00
199	Wade Boggs (.300 Series)	1.50
200	Tony Gwynn (.300 Series)	4.00

1996 Pinnacle Team Spirit

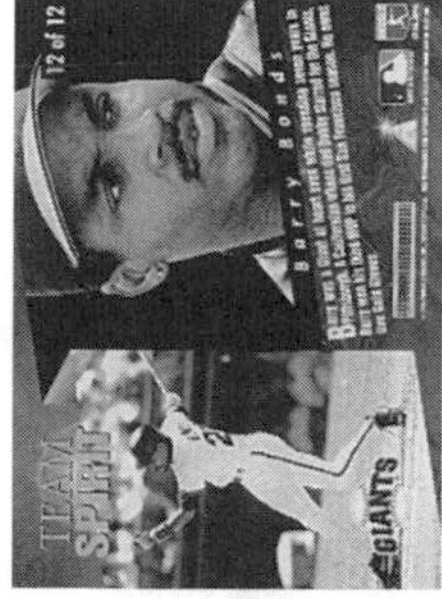

One in every 72 1996 Pinnacle Series II hobby packs or every 103 retail packs has one of these die-cut insert cards. Each card has a holographic baseball design behind an embossed glossy action photo of the player on a flat black background. Backs are conventionally printed.

		MT
Complete Set (12):		200.00
Common Player:		7.50
1	Greg Maddux	25.00
2	Ken Griffey Jr.	40.00
3	Derek Jeter	25.00
4	Mike Piazza	25.00
5	Cal Ripken Jr.	30.00
6	Frank Thomas	20.00
7	Jeff Bagwell	15.00
8	Mo Vaughn	7.50
9	Albert Belle	10.00
10	Chipper Jones	25.00
11	Johnny Damon	7.50
12	Barry Bonds	10.00

1996 Pinnacle Team Pinnacle

Team Pinnacle inserts offer 18 players in a double-sided nine-card set. Each card can be found with Dufex printing on one side and regular gold-foil printing on the other. Inserted one per 72 packs of Series 1, Team Pinnacle pairs up an American League player and a National Leaguer at the same position on each card.

		MT
Complete Set (9):		100.00
Common Player:		4.00
1	Frank Thomas, Jeff Bagwell	15.00
2	Chuck Knoblauch, Craig Biggio	5.00

3	Jim Thome, Matt Williams	5.00
4	Barry Larkin, Cal Ripken Jr.	20.00
5	Barry Bonds, Tim Salmon	8.00
6	Ken Griffey Jr., Reggie Sanders	25.00
7	Albert Belle, Sammy Sosa	15.00
8	Ivan Rodriguez, Mike Piazza	15.00
9	Greg Maddux, Randy Johnson	15.00

1996 Pinnacle Team Tomorrow

Team Tomorrow showcases 10 young superstars on a horizontal Dufex design. While the player appears twice on the card front, the left side is merely a close-up of the same shot appearing on the right. These inserts are exclusive to Series 1 jumbo packs, found on average at the rate of one per 19 packs.

		MT
Complete Set (10):		50.00
Common Player:		1.50
1	Ruben Rivera	1.50
2	Johnny Damon	2.00
3	Raul Mondesi	2.50
4	Manny Ramirez	9.00
5	Hideo Nomo	4.00
6	Chipper Jones	15.00
7	Garret Anderson	1.50
8	Alex Rodriguez	20.00
9	Derek Jeter	15.00
10	Karim Garcia	4.00

1996 Pinnacle/ Aficionado

Pinnacle's 1996 Aficionado set gives every card its own character; each card is printed as an all-wood card with a maple wood grain. The 200 regular issue cards include 160 cards in sepia-tone, giving each an antique-looking finish. The horizontal card front also has a rainbow holographic foil image of the player featured. His name is in foil in a panel at the bottom. The back has positional comparison statistics that show how each player compares with the league average at that position and the league average at that position in different eras. There are also 60 four-color cards, which include 25 four-color rookie cards, and a 10-card Global Reach subset. This subset, which honors baseball's international flavor, features Aficionado's new heliogram printing process. Artist's Proof parallel cards, seeded one per every 35 packs, were also created. These cards mirror the regular issue and use a unique gold foil stamp on them. There were also three insert sets created: Slick Picks, Rivals and Magic Numbers.

		MT
Complete Set (200):		50.00
Common Player:		.20
Veteran Star Artist's Proofs:		15X
Young Star Artist's Proofs:		10X
Pack (5):		2.00
Wax Box (16):		28.00
1	Jack McDowell	.20
2	Jay Bell	.20
3	Rafael Palmeiro	.35
4	Wally Joyner	.20
5	Ozzie Smith	.75
6	Mark McGwire	5.00
7	Kevin Seitzer	.20
8	Fred McGriff	.50
9	Roger Clemens	1.50
9s	Roger Clemens (marked "SAMPLE")	5.00
10	Randy Johnson	.75
11	Cecil Fielder	.25
12	David Cone	.35
13	Chili Davis	.20
14	Andres Galarraga	.40
15	Joe Carter	.25
16	Ryne Sandberg	1.25
17	Paul O'Neill	.40
18	Cal Ripken Jr.	4.00
19	Wade Boggs	.50
20	Greg Gagne	.20
21	Edgar Martinez	.20
22	Greg Maddux	3.00
23	Ken Caminiti	.60
24	Kirby Puckett	1.50
25	Craig Biggio	.40
26	Will Clark	.40
27	Ron Gant	.25
28	Eddie Murray	.50
29	Lance Johnson	.20
30	Tony Gwynn	2.50
31	Dante Bichette	.40
32	Darren Daulton	.20
33	Danny Tartabull	.20
34	Jeff King	.20
35	Tom Glavine	.35
36	Rickey Henderson	.40
37	Jose Canseco	.35
38	Barry Larkin	.40
39	Dennis Martinez	.20
40	Ruben Sierra	.20
41	Bobby Bonilla	.30
42	Jeff Conine	.20
43	Lee Smith	.20
44	Charlie Hayes	.20
45	Walt Weiss	.20
46	Jay Buhner	.30
47	Kenny Rogers	.20
48	Paul Molitor	.50
49	Hal Morris	.20
50	Todd Stottlemyre	.20
51	Mike Stanley	.20
52	Mark Grace	.40
53	Lenny Dykstra	.20
54	Andre Dawson	.25
55	Dennis Eckersley	.20
56	Ben McDonald	.20
57	Ray Lankford	.20
58	Mo Vaughn	1.00
59	Frank Thomas	2.50
60	Julio Franco	.20
61	Jim Abbott	.20
62	Greg Vaughn	.25
63	Marquis Grissom	.30
64	Tino Martinez	.30
65	Kevin Appier	.20
66	Matt Williams	.40
67	Sammy Sosa	2.50
68	Larry Walker	.60
69	Ivan Rodriguez	.75
70	Eric Karros	.20
71	Bernie Williams	.60
72	Carlos Baerga	.20
73	Jeff Bagwell	1.50
74	Pete Schourek	.20
75	Ken Griffey Jr.	5.00
76	Bernard Gilkey	.20
77	Albert Belle	1.25
78	Chuck Knoblauch	.40
79	John Smoltz	.30
80	Barry Bonds	1.25
81	Vinny Castilla	.25
82	John Olerud	.30
83	Mike Mussina	1.00
84	Alex Fernandez	.25
85	Shawon Dunston	.20
86	Travis Fryman	.20
87	Moises Alou	.35
88	Dean Palmer	.20
89	Gregg Jefferies	.20
90	Jim Thome	.30
91	Dave Justice	.40
92	B.J. Surhoff	.20
93	Ramon Martinez	.25
94	Gary Sheffield	.60
95	Andy Benes	.20
96	Reggie Sanders	.20
97	Roberto Alomar	1.00
98	Omar Vizquel	.20
99	Juan Gonzalez	1.50
100	Robin Ventura	.25
101	Jason Isringhausen	.20
102	Greg Colbrunn	.20
103	Brian Jordan	.20
104	Shawn Green	.40
105	Brian Hunter	.20
106	Rondell White	.30
107	Ryan Klesko	.30
107s	Ryan Klesko (marked "SAMPLE")	3.00
108	Sterling Hitchcock	.20
109	Manny Ramirez	1.50
110	Bret Boone	.20
111	Michael Tucker	.20
112	Julian Tavarez	.20
113	Benji Gil	.20
114	Kenny Lofton	1.00
115	Mike Kelly	.20
116	Ray Durham	.20
117	Trevor Hoffman	.25
118	Butch Huskey	.20
119	Phil Nevin	.20
120	Pedro Martinez	.40
121	Wil Cordero	.20
122	Tim Salmon	.40
123	Jim Edmonds	.30
124	Mike Piazza	3.00
125	Rico Brogna	.20
126	John Mabry	.20
127	Chipper Jones	3.00
128	Johnny Damon	.20
129	Raul Mondesi	.35
130	Denny Neagle	.20
131	Marc Newfield	.20
132	Hideo Nomo	.75
133	Joe Vitiello	.20
134	Garret Anderson	.20
135	Dave Nilsson	.20
136	Alex Rodriguez	4.00
137	Russ Davis	.20
138	Frank Rodriguez	.20
139	Royce Clayton	.20
140	John Valentin	.20
141	Marty Cordova	.20
142	Alex Gonzalez	.20
143	Carlos Delgado	.50
144	Willie Greene	.20
145	Cliff Floyd	.20
146	Bobby Higginson	.40
147	J.T. Snow	.20
148	Derek Bell	.20
149	Edgardo Alfonzo	.25
150	Charles Johnson	.20
151	Hideo Nomo (Global Reach)	.25
152	Larry Walker (Global Reach)	.30
153	Bob Abreu (Global Reach)	.20
154	Karim Garcia (Global Reach)	.40
155	Dave Nilsson (Global Reach)	.20
156	Chan Ho Park (Global Reach)	.25
157	Dennis Martinez (Global Reach)	.20
158	Sammy Sosa (Global Reach)	1.00
159	Rey Ordonez (Global Reach)	.40
160	Roberto Alomar (Global Reach)	.50
161	George Arias	.20
162	Jason Schmidt	.20
163	Derek Jeter	3.00
164	Chris Snopek	.20
165	Todd Hollandsworth	.20
166	Sal Fasano	.20
167	Jay Powell	.20
168	Paul Wilson	.30
169	Jim Pittsley	.20
170	LaTroy Hawkins	.20
171	Bob Abreu	.30
172	*Mike Grace*	.20
173	Karim Garcia	.75
174	Richard Hidalgo	.20
175	Felipe Crespo	.20
176	Terrell Wade	.20
177	Steve Gibralter	.20
178	Jermaine Dye	.20
179	Alan Benes	.30
180	*Wilton Guerrero*	.50
181	Brooks Kieschnick	.20
182	Roger Cedeno	.20
183	*Osvaldo Fernandez*	.20
184	*Matt Lawton*	1.00
185	George Williams	.20
186	Jimmy Haynes	.20
187	*Mike Busby*	.20
188	Chan Ho Park	.40
189	Marc Barcelo	.20
190	Jason Kendall	.20
191	Rey Ordonez	.50
192	Tyler Houston	.20
193	John Wasdin	.20
194	Jeff Suppan	.20
195	Jeff Ware	.20
196	Checklist	.20
197	Checklist	.20
198	Checklist	.20
199	Checklist	.20
200	Checklist	.20

1996 Pinnacle/ Aficionado First Pitch Previews

This parallel set differs from the regularly issued version in that there is a "FIRST PITCH / PREVIEW" label printed on the front on the end opposite the heliogram player portrait. Also, whereas on the regular cards, the player portrait is in silver metallic composition, the First Pitch Preview cards have the portrait in gold. These cards were most often obtained by visiting Pinnacle's site on the Internet and answering a trivia question.

	MT
Complete Set (200):	750.00
Common Player:	2.50

(Star cards valued at 8X-10X regular Aficionado edition.)

1996 Pinnacle/ Aficionado Magic Numbers

This 1996 Pinnacle Aficionado insert set focuses on 10 of the game's best players by printing them directly on to a wooden card, each of which carries the distinct grain and color of natural wood. The cards, seeded one per every 72 packs, take current players and compare them with other players who have worn the same uniform number. These cards have the most exclusive ratio of the inserts.

		MT
Complete Set (10):		160.00
Common Player:		6.00
1	Ken Griffey Jr.	40.00
2	Greg Maddux	25.00
3	Frank Thomas	15.00
4	Mo Vaughn	8.00
5	Jeff Bagwell	12.00
6	Chipper Jones	25.00
7	Albert Belle	8.00
8	Cal Ripken Jr.	40.00
9	Matt Williams	6.00
10	Sammy Sosa	25.00

1996 Pinnacle/ Aficionado Rivals

These 1996 Pinnacle Aficionado inserts concentrate on the many matchups and rivalries that make baseball fun. Each card uses spot embossing on it. The cards are seeded one per every 24 packs.

		MT
Complete Set (24):		175.00
Common Player:		7.50
1	Ken Griffey Jr., Frank Thomas	20.00
2	Frank Thomas, Cal Ripken Jr.	15.00
3	Cal Ripken Jr., Mo Vaughn	10.00
4	Mo Vaughn, Ken Griffey Jr.	15.00
5	Ken Griffey Jr., Cal Ripken Jr.	25.00
6	Frank Thomas, Mo Vaughn	10.00
7	Cal Ripken Jr., Ken Griffey Jr.	25.00
8	Mo Vaughn, Frank Thomas	10.00
9	Ken Griffey Jr., Mo Vaughn	15.00
10	Frank Thomas, Ken Griffey Jr.	20.00
11	Cal Ripken Jr., Frank Thomas	15.00
12	Mo Vaughn, Cal Ripken Jr.	10.00
13	Mike Piazza, Jeff Bagwell	10.00
14	Jeff Bagwell, Barry Bonds	7.50
15	Jeff Bagwell, Mike Piazza	10.00
16	Tony Gwynn, Mike Piazza	10.00
17	Mike Piazza, Barry Bonds	10.00
18	Jeff Bagwell, Tony Gwynn	7.50
19	Barry Bonds, Mike Piazza	10.00
20	Tony Gwynn, Jeff Bagwell	7.50
21	Mike Piazza, Tony Gwynn	10.00
22	Barry Bonds, Jeff Bagwell	7.50
23	Tony Gwynn, Barry Bonds	7.50
24	Barry Bonds, Tony Gwynn	7.50

1996 Pinnacle/ Aficionado Slick Picks

This 1996 Pinnacle Aficionado insert set pictures 32 of the best players in baseball on cards which use Spectroetch printing. Each card also notes where that player was selected in the annual draft, emphasizing that there are numerous bargains available throughout the amateur draft. The cards were seeded one per every 10 packs, making them the easiest to obtain of the set's insert cards.

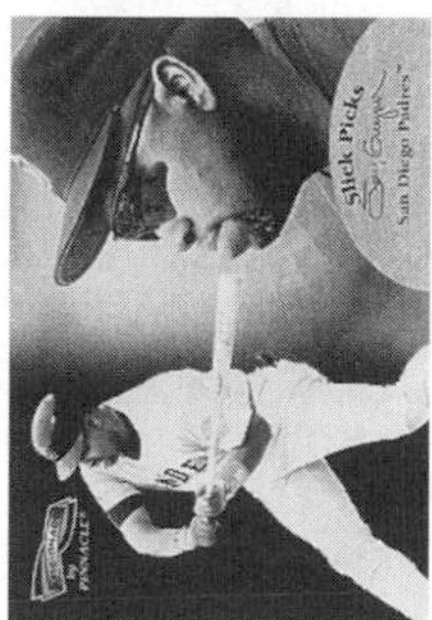

		MT
Complete Set (32):		175.00
Common Player:		2.00
1	Mike Piazza	12.00
2	Cal Ripken Jr.	15.00
3	Ken Griffey Jr.	20.00
4	Paul Wilson	2.00
5	Frank Thomas	10.00
6	Mo Vaughn	3.00
7	Barry Bonds	5.00
8	Albert Belle	5.00
9	Jeff Bagwell	8.00
10	Dante Bichette	3.00
11	Hideo Nomo	3.00
12	Raul Mondesi	3.00
13	Manny Ramirez	5.00
14	Greg Maddux	12.00
15	Tony Gwynn	10.00
16	Ryne Sandberg	5.00
17	Reggie Sanders	2.00
18	Derek Jeter	12.00
19	Johnny Damon	2.00
20	Alex Rodriguez	15.00
21	Ryan Klesko	3.00
22	Jim Thome	3.00
23	Kenny Lofton	3.00
24	Tino Martinez	2.00
25	Randy Johnson	4.00
26	Wade Boggs	3.00
27	Juan Gonzalez	5.00
28	Kirby Puckett	8.00
29	Tim Salmon	3.00
30	Chipper Jones	12.00
31	Garret Anderson	2.00
32	Eddie Murray	4.00

1997 Pinnacle

The '97 Pinnacle baseball set consists of 200 base cards. The card fronts consist of the player's name stamped within a foil baseball diamond-shape at the bottom of each card. Card backs contain summaries of the players' 1996 and lifetime statistics. Included within the base set is a 30-card Rookies subset, a 12-card Clout subset and three checklists. Inserts include two parallel sets (Artist's Proof and Museum Collection), Passport to the Majors, Shades, Team Pinnacle, Cardfrontations, and Home/Away. Cards were sold in 10-card packs for $2.49 each.

		MT
Complete Set (200):		20.00
Common Player:		.10
Pack (10):		2.00
Wax Box (24):		40.00
1	Cecil Fielder	.15
2	Garret Anderson	.10
3	Charles Nagy	.10
4	Darryl Hamilton	.10
5	Greg Myers	.10
6	Eric Davis	.15
7	Jeff Frye	.10
8	Marquis Grissom	.10
9	Curt Schilling	.15
10	Jeff Fassero	.10
11	Alan Benes	.15
12	Orlando Miller	.10
13	Alex Fernandez	.10
14	Andy Pettitte	.30
15	Andre Dawson	.15
16	Mark Grudzielanek	.10
17	Joe Vitiello	.10
18	Juan Gonzalez	.75
19	Mark Whiten	.10
20	Lance Johnson	.10
21	Trevor Hoffman	.10
22	Marc Newfield	.10
23	Jim Eisenreich	.10
24	Joe Carter	.15
25	Jose Canseco	.40
26	Bill Swift	.10
27	Ellis Burks	.10
28	Ben McDonald	.10
29	Edgar Martinez	.10
30	Jamie Moyer	.10
31	Chan Ho Park	.15
32	Carlos Delgado	.50
33	Kevin Mitchell	.10
34	Carlos Garcia	.10
35	Darryl Strawberry	.15
36	Jim Thome	.40
37	Jose Offerman	.10
38	Ryan Klesko	.20
39	Ruben Sierra	.10
40	Devon White	.10
41	Brian Jordan	.10
42	Tony Gwynn	1.00
43	Rafael Palmeiro	.40
44	Dante Bichette	.20
45	Scott Stahoviak	.10
46	Roger Cedeno	.10
47	Ivan Rodriguez	.75
48	Bob Abreu	.10
49	Darryl Kile	.10
50	Darren Dreifort	.10
51	Shawon Dunston	.10
52	Mark McGwire	3.00
53	Tim Salmon	.25
54	Gene Schall	.10
55	Roger Clemens	1.00
56	Rondell White	.20
57	Ed Sprague	.10
58	Craig Paquette	.10
59	David Segui	.10
60	Jaime Navarro	.10
61	Tom Glavine	.25
62	Jeff Brantley	.10
63	Kimera Bartee	.10
64	Fernando Vina	.10
65	Eddie Murray	.25
66	Lenny Dykstra	.10
67	Kevin Elster	.10
68	Vinny Castilla	.10
69	Todd Greene	.10
70	Brett Butler	.10
71	Robby Thompson	.10
72	Reggie Jefferson	.10
73	Todd Hundley	.15
74	Jeff King	.10
75	Ernie Young	.10
76	Jeff Bagwell	.75
77	Dan Wilson	.10

78 Paul Molitor .35
79 Kevin Seitzer .10
80 Kevin Brown .15
81 Ron Gant .15
82 Dwight Gooden .10
83 Todd Stottlemyre .10
84 Ken Caminiti .20
85 James Baldwin .10
86 Jermaine Dye .10
87 Harold Baines .10
88 Pat Hentgen .10
89 Frank Rodriguez .10
90 Mark Johnson .10
91 Jason Kendall .10
92 Alex Rodriguez 2.50
93 Alan Trammell .10
94 Scott Brosius .10
95 Delino DeShields .10
96 Chipper Jones 1.50
97 Barry Bonds .75
98 Brady Anderson .15
99 Ryne Sandberg .75
100 Albert Belle .40
101 Jeff Cirillo .10
102 Frank Thomas 1.00
103 Mike Piazza 2.00
104 Rickey Henderson .25
105 Rey Ordonez .20
106 Mark Grace .25
107 Terry Steinbach .10
108 Ray Durham .10
109 Barry Larkin .40
110 Tony Clark .20
111 Bernie Williams .60
112 John Smoltz .15
113 Moises Alou .15
114 Alex Gonzalez .10
115 Rico Brogna .10
116 Eric Karros .10
117 Jeff Conine .10
118 Todd Hollandsworth .10
119 Troy Percival .10
120 Paul Wilson .10
121 Orel Hershiser .10
122 Ozzie Smith .40
123 Dave Hollins .10
124 Ken Hill .10
125 Rick Wilkins .10
126 Scott Servais .10
127 Fernando Valenzuela .10
128 Mariano Rivera .20
129 Mark Loretta .10
130 Shane Reynolds .10
131 Darren Oliver .10
132 Steve Trachsel .10
133 Darren Bragg .10
134 Jason Dickson .10
135 Darren Fletcher .10
136 Gary Gaetti .10
137 Joey Cora .10
138 Terry Pendleton .10
139 Derek Jeter 2.50
140 Danny Tartabull .10
141 John Flaherty .10
142 B.J. Surhoff .10
143 Mark Sweeney .10
144 Chad Mottola .10
145 Andujar Cedeno .10
146 Tim Belcher .10
147 Mark Thompson .10
148 Rafael Bournigal .10
149 Marty Cordova .10
150 Osvaldo Fernandez .10
151 Mike Stanley .10
152 Ricky Bottalico .10
153 Donnie Wall .10
154 Omar Vizquel .10
155 Mike Mussina .50
156 Brant Brown .10
157 F.P. Santangelo .10
158 Ryan Hancock .10
159 Jeff D'Amico .10
160 Luis Castillo .10
161 Darin Erstad .50
162 Ugueth Urbina .10
163 Andruw Jones 1.00
164 Steve Gibralter .10
165 Robin Jennings .10
166 Mike Cameron .10
167 George Arias .10
168 Chris Stynes .10
169 Justin Thompson .10
170 Jamey Wright .10
171 Todd Walker .10
172 Nomar Garciaparra 2.00
173 Jose Paniagua .10
174 Marvin Benard .10
175 Rocky Coppinger .10
176 Quinton McCracken .10
177 Amaury Telemaco .10
178 Neifi Perez .10
179 Todd Greene .10
180 Jason Thompson .10
181 Wilton Guerrero .10
182 Edgar Renteria .10
183 Billy Wagner .15
184 Alex Ochoa .10
185 Billy McMillon .10
186 Kenny Lofton .30
187 Andres Galarraga (Clout) .20
188 Chuck Knoblauch (Clout) .15
189 Greg Maddux (Clout) 1.50
190 Mo Vaughn (Clout) .40
191 Cal Ripken Jr. (Clout) 2.50
192 Hideo Nomo (Clout) .40
193 Ken Griffey Jr. (Clout) 2.50
194 Sammy Sosa (Clout) 1.50
195 Jay Buhner (Clout) .15
196 Manny Ramirez (Clout) .75
197 Matt Williams (Clout) .25
198 Andruw Jones CL .50
199 Darin Erstad CL .40
200 Trey Beamon CL .10

1997 Pinnacle Artist's Proofs

	MT
Common Bronze (125):	5.00
Bronze Stars:	30X
Common Silver (50):	10.00
Silver Stars:	45X
Common Gold:	15.00
Gold Stars:	60X

(See 1997 Pinnacle for checklist and base card values.)

1997 Pinnacle Museum Collection

Each of the 200 cards in 1997 Pinnacle Series 1 was also issued in a graphically enhanced Museum Collection parallel set. The Museum cards utilize basically the same design as the regular-issue Pinnacle cards, but the front is printed in the company's Dufex gold-foil technology. On back, a small rectangular logo verifies the card's special status.

	MT
Complete Set (200):	500.00
Common Player:	1.00
Museum Stars:	10X

(See 1997 Pinnacle for checklist and regular-issue card values.)

1997 Pinnacle Cardfrontations

The 20-card, regular-sized, hobby-only set was inserted every 23 packs of 1997 Pinnacle baseball. The card fronts depict a player headshot imaged over a foil rainbow background. The same player is then pictured in action shots with the "Cardfrontation" logo in gold foil in the lower right half. The player's name appears in gold foil below the gold-foil team logo. The card backs depict another player's headshot with a short text describing interaction between the two players. The cards are numbered as "x of 20."

		MT
Complete Set (20):		180.00
Common Player:		3.00
1	Greg Maddux, Mike Piazza	20.00
2	Tom Glavine, Ken Caminiti	3.00
3	Randy Johnson, Cal Ripken Jr.	25.00
4	Kevin Appier, Mark McGwire	30.00
5	Andy Pettitte, Juan Gonzalez	8.00
6	Pat Hentgen, Albert Belle	5.00
7	Hideo Nomo, Chipper Jones	15.00
8	Ismael Valdes, Sammy Sosa	15.00
9	Mike Mussina, Manny Ramirez	8.00
10	David Cone, Jay Buhner	3.00
11	Mark Wohlers, Gary Sheffield	5.00
12	Alan Benes, Barry Bonds	8.00
13	Roger Clemens, Ivan Rodriguez	10.00
14	Mariano Rivera, Ken Griffey Jr.	25.00
15	Dwight Gooden, Frank Thomas	10.00
16	John Wetteland, Darin Erstad	5.00
17	John Smoltz, Brian Jordan	3.00
18	Kevin Brown, Jeff Bagwell	8.00
19	Jack McDowell, Alex Rodriguez	25.00
20	Charles Nagy, Bernie Williams	6.00

1997 Pinnacle Home/Away

The 24-card, regular-sized, die-cut set was inserted every 33 retail packs. The background on front and back is a facsimile of the player's home or road jersey. A color action photo is on front with gold-foil graphics. Backs have a few words about the player.

		MT
Complete Set (12):		200.00
Common Player:		5.00
1	Chipper Jones	20.00
2	Ken Griffey Jr.	30.00
3	Mike Piazza	20.00
4	Frank Thomas	12.00
5	Jeff Bagwell	12.00
6	Alex Rodriguez	25.00
7	Barry Bonds	10.00
8	Mo Vaughn	8.00
9	Derek Jeter	20.00
10	Mark McGwire	30.00
11	Cal Ripken Jr.	25.00
12	Albert Belle	8.00

1997 Pinnacle Passport to the Majors

The 25-card, regular-sized set was inserted every 36 packs of 1997 Pinnacle baseball. The cards fold out and resemble a mini passport.

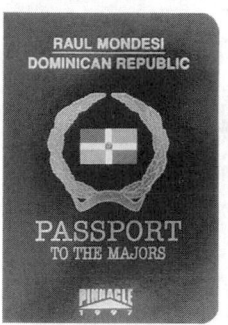

		MT
Complete Set (25):		150.00
Common Player:		3.00
1	Greg Maddux	12.00
1s	Greg Maddux ("SAMPLE" overprint)	5.00
2	Ken Griffey Jr.	20.00
3	Frank Thomas	8.00
4	Cal Ripken Jr.	20.00
5	Mike Piazza	15.00
6	Alex Rodriguez	20.00
7	Mo Vaughn	4.00
8	Chipper Jones	12.00
9	Roberto Alomar	5.00
10	Edgar Martinez	2.00
11	Javier Lopez	2.00
12	Ivan Rodriguez	6.00
13	Juan Gonzalez	6.00
14	Carlos Baerga	2.00
15	Sammy Sosa	15.00
16	Manny Ramirez	6.00
17	Raul Mondesi	3.00
18	Henry Rodriguez	2.00
19	Rafael Palmeiro	4.00
20	Rey Ordonez	2.00
21	Hideo Nomo	4.00
22	Makoto Suzuki	2.00
23	Chan Ho Park	2.00
24	Larry Walker	4.00
25	Ruben Rivera	2.00

1997 Pinnacle Shades

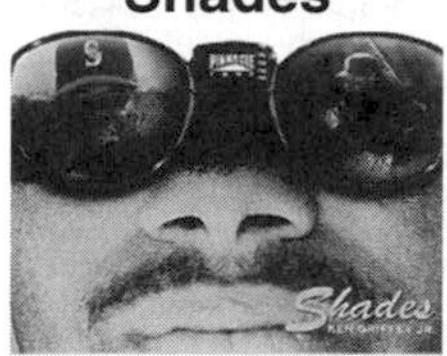

The 10-card, regular-sized set was inserted every 23 retail packs of Pinnacle baseball. The horizontal cards are die-cut at the top of a pair of sunglasses whose lenses contain color portrait and action pictures of the player. The player face beneath the shades is printed on silver foil stock. Backs have a mirror-image of the front photos in the lenses and a baseball diamond in the background.

		MT
Complete Set (10):		75.00
Common Player:		3.00
1	Ken Griffey Jr.	20.00
2	Juan Gonzalez	5.00
3	John Smoltz	3.00
4	Gary Sheffield	3.00
5	Cal Ripken Jr.	15.00
6	Mo Vaughn	3.00
7	Brian Jordan	3.00
8	Mike Piazza	12.00
9	Frank Thomas	10.00
10	Alex Rodriguez	15.00

1997 Pinnacle Team Pinnacle

The 10-card, regular-sized set features top National League players from a position on one side with the best American League players on the other. One side of the card is in Dufex printing and there is actually two versions of each card, as either side can feature the Dufex foil. Team Pinnacle is inserted every 90 packs.

		MT
Complete Set (10):		125.00
Common Player:		6.00
1	Frank Thomas, Jeff Bagwell	20.00
2	Chuck Knoblauch, Eric Young	6.00
3	Ken Caminiti, Jim Thome	7.50
4	Alex Rodriguez, Chipper Jones	25.00
5	Mike Piazza, Ivan Rodriguez	20.00
6	Albert Belle, Barry Bonds	9.00
7	Ken Griffey Jr., Ellis Burks	30.00
8	Juan Gonzalez, Gary Sheffield	8.00
9	John Smoltz, Andy Pettitte	7.50
10	All Players	20.00

1997 New Pinnacle Samples

This group of sample cards was sent to dealers to introduce the New Pinnacle brand which took the place of a second series of Pinnacle in 1997. Cards are virtually identical to the issued versions except for the large diagonal black-and-white "SAMPLE" overprint on front and back.

		MT
Complete Set (6):		30.00
Common Player:		5.00
2	Sammy Sosa	10.00
45	Mike Piazza	10.00
57	Jeff Bagwell	5.00
81	Alex Rodriguez	10.00
127	Ryan Klesko	5.00
175	Andruw Jones	5.00

1997 New Pinnacle

In lieu of a second series of Pinnacle Baseball, the company offered collectors New Pinnacle, a 200-card set sold in 10-card packs for $2.99. Two parallel versions of the 200-card set exist in Museum Collection and Artist's Proof. Other inserts include Press Plates, Spellbound, Keeping the Pace and Interleague Encounter. Collectors who obtained four Press Plates of the same player's card back or front were eligible to win cash prizes.

		MT
Complete Set (200):		25.00
Common Player:		.10
Pack (10):		2.00
Wax Box (18):		30.00
1	Ken Griffey Jr.	2.50
2	Sammy Sosa	2.00
3	Greg Maddux	1.50
4	Matt Williams	.30
5	Jason Isringhausen	.10
6	Gregg Jefferies	.10
7	Chili Davis	.10
8	Paul O'Neill	.20
9	Larry Walker	.30
10	Ellis Burks	.10
11	Cliff Floyd	.10
12	Albert Belle	.40
13	Javier Lopez	.20
14	David Cone	.20
15	Jose Canseco	.40
16	Todd Zeile	.10
17	Bernard Gilkey	.10
18	Andres Galarraga	.25
19	Chris Snopek	.10
20	Tim Salmon	.25
21	Roger Clemens	1.00
22	Reggie Sanders	.10
23	John Jaha	.10
24	Andy Pettitte	.30
25	Kenny Lofton	.30
26	Robb Nen	.10
27	John Wetteland	.10
28	Bobby Bonilla	.10
29	Hideo Nomo	.50
30	Cecil Fielder	.15
31	Garret Anderson	.10
32	Pat Hentgen	.10
33	David Justice	.30
34	Billy Wagner	.10
35	Al Leiter	.20
36	Mark Wohlers	.10
37	Rondell White	.10
38	Charles Johnson	.10
39	Mark Grace	.20
40	Pedro Martinez	.75
41	Tom Goodwin	.10
42	Manny Ramirez	.75
43	Greg Vaughn	.15
44	Brian Jordan	.10
45	Mike Piazza	2.00
46	Roberto Hernandez	.10
47	Wade Boggs	.30
48	Scott Sanders	.10
49	Alex Gonzalez	.10
50	Kevin Brown	.15
51	Bob Higginson	.10
52	Ken Caminiti	.20
53	Derek Jeter	2.50
54	Carlos Baerga	.10
55	Jay Buhner	.15
56	Tim Naehring	.10
57	Jeff Bagwell	.75
58	Steve Finley	.10
59	Kevin Appier	.10
60	Jay Bell	.10
61	Ivan Rodriguez	.75
62	Terrell Wade	.10
63	Rusty Greer	.10
64	Juan Guzman	.10
65	Fred McGriff	.25
66	Tino Martinez	.20
67	Ray Lankford	.10
68	Juan Gonzalez	.75
69	Ron Gant	.10
70	Jack McDowell	.10
71	Tony Gwynn	1.00
72	Joe Carter	.10
73	Wilson Alvarez	.10
74	Jason Giambi	.40
75	Brian Hunter	.10
76	Michael Tucker	.10
77	Andy Benes	.10
78	Brady Anderson	.15
79	Ramon Martinez	.10
80	Troy Percival	.10
81	Alex Rodriguez	2.50
82	Jim Thome	.40
83	Denny Neagle	.10
84	Rafael Palmeiro	.40
85	Jose Valentin	.10
86	Marc Newfield	.10
87	Mariano Rivera	.20
88	Alan Benes	.15
89	Jimmy Key	.10
90	Joe Randa	.10
91	Cal Ripken Jr.	2.50
92	Craig Biggio	.20
93	Dean Palmer	.10
94	Gary Sheffield	.35
95	Ismael Valdez	.10
96	John Valentin	.10
97	Johnny Damon	.10
98	Mo Vaughn	.40
99	Paul Sorrento	.10
100	Randy Johnson	.75
101	Raul Mondesi	.20
102	Roberto Alomar	.60
103	Royce Clayton	.10
104	Mark Grudzielanek	.10
105	Wally Joyner	.10
106	Wil Cordero	.10
107	Will Clark	.25
108	Chuck Knoblauch	.20
109	Derek Bell	.10
110	Henry Rodriguez	.10
111	Edgar Renteria	.10
112	Travis Fryman	.20
113	Eric Young	.10
114	Sandy Alomar Jr.	.15
115	Darin Erstad	.50
116	Barry Larkin	.40
117	Barry Bonds	.75
118	Frank Thomas	1.00

119	Carlos Delgado	.50
120	Jason Kendall	.10
121	Todd Hollandsworth	.10
122	Jim Edmonds	.20
123	Chipper Jones	1.50
124	Jeff Fassero	.10
125	Deion Sanders	.20
126	Matt Lawton	.10
127	Ryan Klesko	.20
128	Mike Mussina	.50
129	Paul Molitor	.50
130	Dante Bichette	.20
131	Bill Pulsipher	.10
132	Todd Hundley	.20
133	J.T. Snow	.10
134	Chuck Finley	.10
135	Shawn Green	.20
136	Charles Nagy	.10
137	Willie Greene	.10
138	Marty Cordova	.10
139	Eddie Murray	.30
140	Ryne Sandberg	.75
141	Alex Fernandez	.10
142	Mark McGwire	3.00
143	Eric Davis	.10
144	Jermaine Dye	.10
145	Ruben Sierra	.10
146	Damon Buford	.10
147	John Smoltz	.15
148	Alex Ochoa	.10
149	Moises Alou	.15
150	Rico Brogna	.10
151	Terry Steinbach	.10
152	Jeff King	.10
153	Carlos Garcia	.10
154	Tom Glavine	.25
155	Edgar Martinez	.10
156	Kevin Elster	.10
157	Darryl Hamilton	.10
158	Jason Dickson	.10
159	Kevin Orie	.10
160	*Bubba Trammell*	.25
161	Jose Guillen	.15
162	Brant Brown	.10
163	Wendell Magee	.10
164	Scott Spiezio	.10
165	Todd Walker	.10
166	*Rod Myers*	.10
167	Damon Mashore	.10
168	Wilton Guerrero	.10
169	Vladimir Guerrero	1.00
170	Nomar Garciaparra	2.00
171	Shannon Stewart	.10
172	Scott Rolen	.50
173	Bob Abreu	.10
174	*Danny Patterson*	.20
175	Andruw Jones	.50
176	*Brian Giles*	1.50
177	Dmitri Young	.10
178	Cal Ripken Jr. (East Meets West)	1.25
179	Chuck Knoblauch (East Meets West)	.10
180	Alex Rodriguez (East Meets West)	1.25
181	Andres Galarraga (East Meets West)	.15
182	Pedro Martinez (East Meets West)	.40
183	Brady Anderson (East Meets West)	.10
184	Barry Bonds (East Meets West)	.40
185	Ivan Rodriguez (East Meets West)	.30
186	Gary Sheffield (East Meets West)	.20
187	Denny Neagle (East Meets West)	.10
188	Mark McGwire (Aura)	1.50
189	Ellis Burks (Aura)	.10
190	Alex Rodriguez (Aura)	1.25
191	Mike Piazza (Aura)	1.00
192	Barry Bonds (Aura)	.40
193	Albert Belle (Aura)	.20
194	Chipper Jones (Aura)	1.00
195	Juan Gonzalez (Aura)	.40
196	Brady Anderson (Aura)	.10
197	Frank Thomas (Aura)	.50
198	Checklist (Vladimir Guerrero)	.50
199	Checklist (Todd Walker)	.10
200	Checklist (Scott Rolen)	.25

1997 New Pinnacle Artist's Proof

This 200-card parallel set features a special AP seal and foil treatment and is fractured into three levels of scarcity - Red (125 cards), Blue (50 cards) and Green (25 cards). Cards were inserted at a rate of 1:39 packs. The 200-card parallel set was randomly inserted (about 1:50) in packs of 1997 Pinnacle. Of the 200 cards, 125 were done in bronze foil (common), 50 in silver (uncommon) and 25 gold (rare). "Artist's Proof" is stamped along the lower edge.

	MT
Common Red Artist's Proof:	5.00
Red Artist's Proofs:	15X
Common Blue Artist's Proof:	15.00
Blue Artist's Proofs:	40X
Common Green Artist's Proof:	30.00
Green Artist's Proofs:	60X

(See 1997 New Pinnacle for checklist and base values.)

1997 New Pinnacle Museum Collection

Dufex printing on gold-foil backgrounds differentiates the Musuem Collection parallel of New Pinnacle from the regular-issue cards. Museums were inserted at an average rate of one per nine packs.

	MT
Complete Set (200):	500.00
Common Player:	1.00
Museum Stars:	15X

(See 1997 New Pinnacle for checklist and base card values.)

1997 New Pinnacle Interleague Encounter

Inserted 1:240 packs, this 10-card set showcases 20 American League and National League rivals with the date of their first interleague match-up on double-sided mirror mylar cards.

		MT
Complete Set (10):		300.00
Common Player:		10.00
1	Albert Belle, Brian Jordan	15.00
2	Andruw Jones, Brady Anderson	25.00
3	Ken Griffey Jr., Tony Gwynn	60.00
4	Cal Ripken Jr., Chipper Jones	50.00
5	Mike Piazza, Ivan Rodriguez	30.00
6	Derek Jeter, Vladimir Guerrero	30.00
7	Greg Maddux, Mo Vaughn	30.00
8	Alex Rodriguez, Hideo Nomo	50.00
9	Juan Gonzalez, Barry Bonds	25.00
10	Frank Thomas, Jeff Bagwell	30.00

1997 New Pinnacle Keeping the Pace

The top sluggers who are considered candidates to break Roger Maris' single-season record of 61 home runs are featured in this 18-card insert set. Cards feature Dot Matrix holographic borders and backgrounds on front. Backs present career stats of an all-time great and project future numbers for the current player. The cards were inserted 1:89 packs.

		MT
Complete Set (18):		500.00
Common Player:		4.00
1	Juan Gonzalez	20.00
2	Greg Maddux	50.00
3	Ivan Rodriguez	20.00
4	Ken Griffey Jr.	75.00
5	Alex Rodriguez	60.00
6	Barry Bonds	20.00
7	Frank Thomas	35.00
8	Chuck Knoblauch	10.00
9	Derek Jeter	50.00
10	Roger Clemens	25.00
11	Kenny Lofton	10.00
12	Tony Gwynn	35.00
13	Troy Percival	4.00
14	Cal Ripken Jr.	60.00
15	Andy Pettitte	10.00
16	Hideo Nomo	10.00
17	Randy Johnson	15.00
18	Mike Piazza	50.00

1997 New Pinnacle Press Plates

Just when collectors thought they had seen every type of pack insert chase card imaginable, New Pinnacle proved them wrong by cutting up and inserting into packs (about one per 1,250) the metal plates used to print the regular cards in the set. There are black, blue, red and yellow plates for the front and back of each card. Rather than touting the collector value of the plates, Pinnacle created a treasure hunt by offering $20,000-35,000 to anybody assembling a complete set of four plates for either the front or back of any card. The $35,000, which would have been awarded for completion prior to Aug. 22, was unclaimed. The amount decreased to $20,000 for any set redeemed by the end of 1997.

MT

(Because of the unique nature of each press plate, no current market value can be quoted.)

1997 New Pinnacle Spellbound

Each of the 50 cards in this insert features a letter of the alphabet as the basic card design. The letters can be used to spell out the names of nine players featured in the set. Cards featured micro-etched foil and are inserted 1:19 packs. Cards of Griffey, Ripken and the Jones were inserted only in hobby packs; retail packs have cards of Belle, Thomas, Piazza and the Rodriguezes. Values shown are per card; multiply by number of cards to determine a player's set value.

	MT
Complete Set (50):	500.00
1-5AB Albert Belle	5.00
1-6AJ Andruw Jones	8.00
1-4AR Alex Rodriguez	15.00
1-7CJ Chipper Jones	15.00
1-6CR Cal Ripken Jr.	20.00
1-5FT Frank Thomas	10.00
1-5IR Ivan Rodriguez	6.00
1-6KG Ken Griffey Jr.	25.00
1-6MP Mike Piazza	15.00

1997 Pinnacle Certified

This 150-card base features a mirror-like mylar finish and a peel-off protector on each card front. Backs feature the player's 1996 statistics against each opponent. There are four different parallel sets, each with varying degrees of scarcity - Certified Red (1:5), Mirror Red (1:99), Mirror Blue (1:199) and Mirror Gold (1:299). Other inserts include Lasting Impressions, Certified Team, and Certified Gold Team. Cards were sold in six-card packs for a suggested price of $4.99.

		MT
Complete Set (150):		40.00
Common Player:		.15
Jose Cruz Jr. Redemption:		25.00
Pack (6):		5.00
Wax Box (20):		75.00
1	Barry Bonds	1.00
2	Mo Vaughn	.50
3	Matt Williams	.40
4	Ryne Sandberg	1.00
5	Jeff Bagwell	1.00
6	Alan Benes	.15
7	John Wetteland	.15
8	Fred McGriff	.40
9	Craig Biggio	.25
10	Bernie Williams	.75
11	Brian L. Hunter	.15
12	Sandy Alomar Jr.	.25
13	Ray Lankford	.15
14	Ryan Klesko	.25
15	Jermaine Dye	.15
16	Andy Benes	.15
17	Albert Belle	.50
18	Tony Clark	.25
19	Dean Palmer	.15
20	Bernard Gilkey	.15
21	Ken Caminiti	.25
22	Alex Rodriguez	3.00
23	Tim Salmon	.40
24	Larry Walker	.50
25	Barry Larkin	.40
26	Mike Piazza	2.50
27	Brady Anderson	.20
28	Cal Ripken Jr.	3.00
29	Charles Nagy	.15
30	Paul Molitor	.75
31	Darin Erstad	.75
32	Rey Ordonez	.15
33	Wally Joyner	.15
34	David Cone	.25
35	Sammy Sosa	2.50
36	Dante Bichette	.25
37	Eric Karros	.15
38	Omar Vizquel	.15
39	Roger Clemens	1.50
40	Joe Carter	.15
41	Frank Thomas	1.50
42	Javier Lopez	.20
43	Mike Mussina	.50
44	Gary Sheffield	.50
45	Tony Gwynn	1.50
46	Jason Kendall	.15
47	Jim Thome	.50
48	Andres Galarraga	.40
49	Mark McGwire	4.00
50	Troy Percival	.15
51	Derek Jeter	3.00
52	Todd Hollandsworth	.15
53	Ken Griffey Jr.	3.00
54	Randy Johnson	1.00
55	Pat Hentgen	.15
56	Rusty Greer	.15
57	John Jaha	.15
58	Kenny Lofton	.40
59	Chipper Jones	2.00
60	Robb Nen	.15
61	Rafael Palmeiro	.50
62	Mariano Rivera	.25
63	Hideo Nomo	.75
64	Greg Vaughn	.20
65	Ron Gant	.15
66	Eddie Murray	.40
67	John Smoltz	.15
68	Manny Ramirez	1.00
69	Juan Gonzalez	1.00
70	F.P. Santangelo	.15
71	Moises Alou	.20
72	Alex Ochoa	.15
73	Chuck Knoblauch	.25
74	Raul Mondesi	.30
75	J.T. Snow	.15
76	Rickey Henderson	.40
77	Bobby Bonilla	.15
78	Wade Boggs	.40
79	Ivan Rodriguez	1.00
80	Brian Jordan	.15
81	Al Leiter	.20
82	Jay Buhner	.25
83	Greg Maddux	2.00
84	Edgar Martinez	.20
85	Kevin Brown	.20
86	Eric Young	.15
87	Todd Hundley	.20
88	Ellis Burks	.15
89	Marquis Grissom	.15
90	Jose Canseco	.50
91	Henry Rodriguez	.15
92	Andy Pettitte	.40
93	Mark Grudzielanek	.15
94	Dwight Gooden	.15
95	Roberto Alomar	.75
96	Paul Wilson	.15
97	Will Clark	.30
98	Rondell White	.15
99	Charles Johnson	.15
100	Jim Edmonds	.25
101	Jason Giambi	.50
102	Billy Wagner	.15
103	Edgar Renteria	.15
104	Johnny Damon	.15
105	Jason Isringhausen	.15
106	Andruw Jones	1.00
107	Jose Guillen	.15
108	Kevin Orie	.15
109	*Brian Giles*	5.00
110	Danny Patterson	.15
111	Vladimir Guerrero	1.50
112	Scott Rolen	.75
113	Damon Mashore	.15
114	Nomar Garciaparra	2.50
115	Todd Walker	.15
116	Wilton Guerrero	.15
117	Bob Abreu	.15
118	Brooks Kieschnick	.15
119	Pokey Reese	.15
120	Todd Greene	.15
121	Dmitri Young	.15
122	Raul Casanova	.15
123	Glendon Rusch	.15
124	Jason Dickson	.15
125	Jorge Posada	.25
126	*Rod Myers*	.15
127	*Bubba Trammell*	.50
128	Scott Spiezio	.15
129	*Hideki Irabu*	1.00
130	Wendell Magee	.15
131	Bartolo Colon	.15
132	Chris Holt	.15
133	Calvin Maduro	.15
134	Ray Montgomery	.15
135	Shannon Stewart	.15
136	Ken Griffey Jr. (Certified Stars)	1.50
137	Vladimir Guerrero (Certified Stars)	.75
138	Roger Clemens (Certified Stars)	.75
139	Mark McGwire (Certified Stars)	2.00
140	Albert Belle (Certified Stars)	.25
141	Derek Jeter (Certified Stars)	1.50
142	Juan Gonzalez (Certified Stars)	.50
143	Greg Maddux (Certified Stars)	1.00
144	Alex Rodriguez (Certified Stars)	1.50
145	Jeff Bagwell (Certified Stars)	.50
146	Cal Ripken Jr. (Certified Stars)	1.50
147	Tony Gwynn (Certified Stars)	.75
148	Frank Thomas (Certified Stars)	.75
149	Hideo Nomo (Certified Stars)	.40
150	Andruw Jones (Certified Stars)	.50

1997 Pinnacle Certified Red

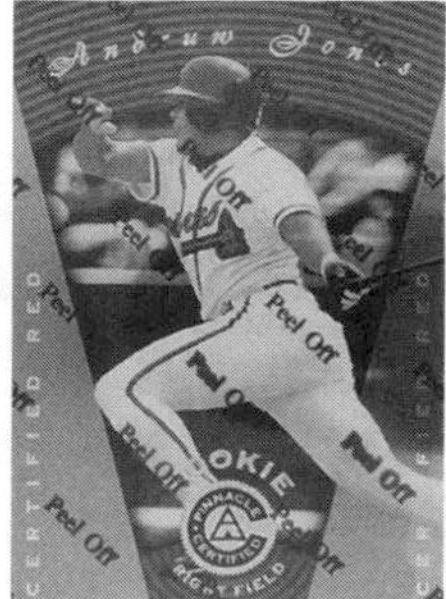

This parallel set features a red tint to the triangular mylar background left and right of the photo on the front. "CERTIFIED RED" is printed vertically on both edges. Backs are identical to regular Certified cards. A peel-off protection coating is on the front of the card. Cards were inserted 1:5 packs.

	MT
Common Certified Red:	1.00
Certified Red Stars:	5X

(See 1997 Pinnacle Certified for checklist and base values.)

1997 Pinnacle Certified Mirror Red

This parallel set features a red design element on the front of each card. Cards were inserted 1:99 packs.

	MT
Common Mirror Red:	4.00
Mirror Red Stars:	20X

(See 1997 Pinnacle Certified for checklist and base values.)

1997 Pinnacle Certified Mirror Blue

This parallel set features a blue design element on the front of each card. Cards were inserted 1:199 packs.

	MT
Common Mirror Blue:	8.00
Mirror Blue Stars:	35X

(See 1997 Pinnacle Certified for checklist and base values.)

1997 Pinnacle Certified Mirror Gold

This parallel set features a holographic gold design on the front of each card. Cards were inserted 1:299 packs.

	MT
Common Mirror Gold:	20.00
Mirror Gold Stars:	60X

(See 1997 Pinnacle Certified for checklist and base values.)

1997 Pinnacle Certified Mirror Black

The exact nature of these cards is undetermined. They may have been intentionally created and "secretly" seeded in packs as an insert or they may have been test cards which were mistakenly inserted. They are not marked in any fashion. The cards are said to reflect in bright green under direct light. It is commonly believed that each "Mirror Black" card exists in only a single piece, but that has not been verified. Neither is it confirmed that a Mirror Black parallel exists for each of the 151 cards in the base set. Even the most undistinguished player's card can sell for $100 or more due to the scarcity of the type.

	MT
Common Player:	100.00

(Star cards valued at 150-250X base value.)

1997 Pinnacle Certified Lasting Impression

This 20-card insert features a die-cut design and a mirror mylar finish and pictures some of baseball's top veteran stars. Backs are conventionally printed and include a color portrait photo and a few words about the player. Cards were inserted 1:19 packs.

		MT
Complete Set (20):		110.00
Common Player:		2.00
1	Cal Ripken Jr.	15.00
2	Ken Griffey Jr.	20.00
3	Mo Vaughn	3.00
4	Brian Jordan	2.00
5	Mark McGwire	20.00
6	Chuck Knoblauch	3.00
7	Sammy Sosa	10.00
8	Brady Anderson	2.00
9	Frank Thomas	9.00
10	Tony Gwynn	9.00
11	Roger Clemens	5.00
12	Alex Rodriguez	15.00
13	Paul Molitor	4.00
14	Kenny Lofton	3.00
15	John Smoltz	2.00
16	Roberto Alomar	4.00
17	Randy Johnson	4.00
18	Ryne Sandberg	5.00
19	Manny Ramirez	8.00
20	Mike Mussina	4.00

1997 Pinnacle Certified Team

The top 20 players in the game are honored on cards with frosted silver mylar printing. Cards were inserted 1:19 packs. A parallel version of this set, Certified Gold Team, has a gold mylar design with each card numbered to 500; while a super-premium parallel, Mirror Gold, is numbered to 25.

		MT
Complete Set (20):		150.00
Common Player:		2.00
Gold:		2X
Mirror Gold:		10X
1	Frank Thomas	9.00
2	Jeff Bagwell	9.00
3	Derek Jeter	12.50
4	Chipper Jones	12.50
5	Alex Rodriguez	15.00
6	Ken Caminiti	2.00
7	Cal Ripken Jr.	15.00
8	Mo Vaughn	4.00
9	Ivan Rodriguez	5.00
10	Mike Piazza	12.50
11	Juan Gonzalez	5.00
12	Barry Bonds	5.00
13	Ken Griffey Jr.	20.00
14	Andruw Jones	7.50
15	Albert Belle	5.00
16	Gary Sheffield	3.00
17	Andy Pettitte	4.00
18	Hideo Nomo	3.00
19	Greg Maddux	12.50
19s	Greg Maddux (Gold Team "SAMPLE")	5.00
20	John Smoltz	2.00

1997 Totally Certified Samples

This trio of promo cards previews the high-tech, all-numbered Totally Certified issue. The samples are similar in format to the issued versions except they carry a large, black "SAMPLE" overprint diagonally on front and back. Also, backs have a gold-foil "PROMO" instead of the individual serial number.

		MT
Complete Set (3):		15.00
Common Player:		3.00
18	Tony Clark (Platinum Red)	3.00
39	Roger Clemens (Platinum Blue)	6.00
41	Frank Thomas (Platinum Gold)	5.00

1997 Totally Certified Platinum Red

Totally Certified doesn't have a true base set. Instead, the product consists of three different 150-card parallel sets. Packs consisted of three cards for $6.99 each. The first of three parallels is the Platinum Red set, inserted two per pack, and featuring micro-etched holographic mylar stock with red accents and foil stamping. Each card in the Red set is sequentially-numbered to 3,999.

		MT
Complete Set (150):		250.00
Common Player:		.70
Minor Stars:		1.50
Pack (3):		10.00
Wax Box (20):		150.00
1	Barry Bonds	4.00
2	Mo Vaughn	3.00
3	Matt Williams	1.50
4	Ryne Sandberg	4.00
5	Jeff Bagwell	6.00
6	Alan Benes	.75
7	John Wetteland	.75
8	Fred McGriff	1.25
9	Craig Biggio	1.25
10	Bernie Williams	3.00
11	Brian Hunter	.75
12	Sandy Alomar Jr.	1.00
13	Ray Lankford	.75
14	Ryan Klesko	1.50
15	Jermaine Dye	.75
16	Andy Benes	.75
17	Albert Belle	5.00
18	Tony Clark	3.00
19	Dean Palmer	.75
20	Bernard Gilkey	.75
21	Ken Caminiti	2.00
22	Alex Rodriguez	12.50
23	Tim Salmon	1.50
24	Larry Walker	2.50
25	Barry Larkin	1.50
26	Mike Piazza	10.00
27	Brady Anderson	.75
28	Cal Ripken Jr.	12.50
29	Charles Nagy	.75
30	Paul Molitor	3.00
31	Darin Erstad	5.00
32	Rey Ordonez	.75
33	Wally Joyner	.75
34	David Cone	.75
35	Sammy Sosa	7.50
36	Dante Bichette	1.50
37	Eric Karros	.75
38	Omar Vizquel	.75
39	Roger Clemens	6.00
40	Joe Carter	.75
41	Frank Thomas	6.00
42	Javier Lopez	.75
43	Mike Mussina	3.00
44	Gary Sheffield	2.00
45	Tony Gwynn	7.50
46	Jason Kendall	.75
47	Jim Thome	3.00
48	Andres Galarraga	2.00
49	Mark McGwire	15.00
50	Troy Percival	.75
51	Derek Jeter	10.00
52	Todd Hollandsworth	.75
53	Ken Griffey Jr.	15.00
54	Randy Johnson	3.00
55	Pat Hentgen	.75
56	Rusty Greer	.75
57	John Jaha	.75
58	Kenny Lofton	3.00
59	Chipper Jones	10.00
60	Robb Nen	.75
61	Rafael Palmeiro	1.50
62	Mariano Rivera	1.25
63	Hideo Nomo	2.50
64	Greg Vaughn	.75
65	Ron Gant	.75
66	Eddie Murray	2.00
67	John Smoltz	1.50
68	Manny Ramirez	5.00
69	Juan Gonzalez	4.00
70	F.P. Santangelo	.75
71	Moises Alou	1.25
72	Alex Ochoa	.75
73	Chuck Knoblauch	1.50
74	Raul Mondesi	1.50
75	J.T. Snow	.75
76	Rickey Henderson	1.00
77	Bobby Bonilla	1.00
78	Wade Boggs	2.00
79	Ivan Rodriguez	4.00

80	Brian Jordan	.75
81	Al Leiter	.75
82	Jay Buhner	1.00
83	Greg Maddux	10.00
84	Edgar Martinez	.75
85	Kevin Brown	.75
86	Eric Young	.75
87	Todd Hundley	1.25
88	Ellis Burks	.75
89	Marquis Grissom	.75
90	Jose Canseco	1.50
91	Henry Rodriguez	.75
92	Andy Pettitte	3.00
93	Mark Grudzielanek	.75
94	Dwight Gooden	.75
95	Roberto Alomar	3.00
96	Paul Wilson	.75
97	Will Clark	1.50
98	Rondell White	1.25
99	Charles Johnson	.75
100	Jim Edmonds	1.00
101	Jason Giambi	.75
102	Billy Wagner	.75
103	Edgar Renteria	.75
104	Johnny Damon	.75
105	Jason Isringhausen	.75
106	Andruw Jones	7.50
107	Jose Guillen	3.00
108	Kevin Orie	.75
109	*Brian Giles*	20.00
110	Danny Patterson	.75
111	Vladimir Guerrero	6.00
112	Scott Rolen	7.50
113	Damon Mashore	.75
114	Nomar Garciaparra	10.00
115	Todd Walker	2.50
116	Wilton Guerrero	.75
117	Bob Abreu	.75
118	Brooks Kieschnick	.75
119	Pokey Reese	.75
120	Todd Greene	.75
121	Dmitri Young	.75
122	Raul Casanova	.75
123	Glendon Rusch	.75
124	Jason Dickson	.75
125	Jorge Posada	.75
126	Rod Myers	.75
127	Bubba Trammell	1.50
128	Scott Spiezio	.75
129	Hideki Irabu	2.50
130	Wendell Magee	.75
131	Bartolo Colon	.75
132	Chris Holt	.75
133	Calvin Maduro	.75
134	Ray Montgomery	.75
135	Shannon Stewart	.75
136	Ken Griffey Jr. (Certified Stars)	7.50
137	Vladimir Guerrero (Certified Stars)	3.00
138	Roger Clemens (Certified Stars)	3.00
139	Mark McGwire (Certified Stars)	7.50
140	Albert Belle (Certified Stars)	2.50
141	Derek Jeter (Certified Stars)	5.00
142	Juan Gonzalez (Certified Stars)	2.00
143	Greg Maddux (Certified Stars)	4.50
144	Alex Rodriguez (Certified Stars)	6.00
145	Jeff Bagwell (Certified Stars)	3.00
146	Cal Ripken Jr. (Certified Stars)	6.00
147	Tony Gwynn (Certified Stars)	4.00
148	Frank Thomas (Certified Stars)	3.00
149	Hideo Nomo (Certified Stars)	1.00
150	Andruw Jones (Certified Stars)	4.00

1997 Totally Certified Platinum Blue

Featuring blue accents and foil stamping, the Platinum Blue cards are sequentially numbered on back in gold foil to 1,999 and inserted per pack.

	MT
Complete Set (150):	500.00
Common Player:	2.00
Platinum Blue Stars:	2X

(See 1997 Totally Certified Platinum Red for checklist and base card values.)

1997 Totally Certified Platinum Gold

The most difficult to find of the Totally Certified cards, the Platinum Gold versions are sequentially-numbered to 30 per card and inserted 1:79 packs.

	MT
Common Player:	25.00
Platinum Gold Stars:	20X

(See 1997 Totally Certified Platinum Red for checklist and base card values.)

1997 Pinnacle Inside

The first baseball card set to be sold within a sealed tin can, Inside Baseball consisted of a 150-card base set featuring both a color and black-and-white photo of the player on the front of the card. Included in the base set were 20 Rookies cards and three checklists. Inserts include the Club Edition and Diamond Edition parallel sets, Dueling Dugouts and Fortysomething. In addition, 24 different cans, each featuring a different player, were available. Cans containing one pack of 10 cards were sold for $2.99 each.

		MT
Complete Set (150):		35.00
Common Player:		.10
Pack (10):		3.00
Wax Box (48):		120.00
1	David Cone	.20
2	Sammy Sosa	2.00
3	Joe Carter	.10
4	Juan Gonzalez	1.00
5	Hideo Nomo	.50
6	Moises Alou	.15
7	Marc Newfield	.10
8	Alex Rodriguez	3.00
9	Kimera Bartee	.10
10	Chuck Knoblauch	.25
11	Jason Isringhausen	.10
12	Jermaine Allensworth	.10
13	Frank Thomas	1.50
14	Paul Molitor	.75
15	John Mabry	.10
16	Greg Maddux	2.00
17	Rafael Palmeiro	.40
18	Brian Jordan	.10
19	Ken Griffey Jr.	3.00
20	Brady Anderson	.15
21	Ruben Sierra	.10
22	Travis Fryman	.20
23	Cal Ripken Jr.	3.00
24	Will Clark	.40
25	Todd Hollandsworth	.10
26	Kevin Brown	.15
27	Mike Piazza	2.50
28	Craig Biggio	.20
29	Paul Wilson	.10
30	Andres Galarraga	.40
31	Chipper Jones	2.00
32	Jason Giambi	.50
33	Ernie Young	.10
34	Marty Cordova	.10
35	Albert Belle	.50
36	Roger Clemens	1.50
37	Ryne Sandberg	1.00
38	Henry Rodriguez	.10
39	Jay Buhner	.15
40	Raul Mondesi	.20
41	Jeff Fassero	.10
42	Edgar Martinez	.15
43	Trey Beamon	.10
44	Mo Vaughn	.50
45	Gary Sheffield	.35
46	Ray Durham	.10
47	Brett Butler	.10
48	Ivan Rodriguez	1.00
49	Fred McGriff	.25
50	Dean Palmer	.10
51	Rickey Henderson	.25
52	Andy Pettitte	.40
53	Bobby Bonilla	.10
54	Shawn Green	.25
55	Tino Martinez	.20
56	Tony Gwynn	1.50
57	Tom Glavine	.25
58	Eric Young	.10
59	Kevin Appier	.10
60	Barry Bonds	1.00
61	Wade Boggs	.40
62	Jason Kendall	.10
63	Jeff Bagwell	1.00
64	Jeff Conine	.10
65	Greg Vaughn	.15
66	Eric Karros	.10
67	Manny Ramirez	1.00
68	John Smoltz	.15
69	Terrell Wade	.10
70	John Wetteland	.10
71	Kenny Lofton	.40
72	Jim Thome	.50
73	Bill Pulsipher	.10
74	Darryl Strawberry	.20
75	Roberto Alomar	.75
76	Bobby Higginson	.10
77	James Baldwin	.10
78	Mark McGwire	4.00
79	Jose Canseco	.50
80	Mark Grudzielanek	.10
81	Ryan Klesko	.20
82	Javier Lopez	.15
83	Ken Caminiti	.20
84	Dave Nilsson	.10
85	Tim Salmon	.15
86	Cecil Fielder	.10
87	Derek Jeter	3.00
88	Garret Anderson	.10
89	Dwight Gooden	.10
90	Carlos Delgado	.75
91	Ugueth Urbina	.10
92	Chan Ho Park	.15
93	Eddie Murray	.40
94	Alex Ochoa	.10
95	Rusty Greer	.10
96	Mark Grace	.20
97	Pat Hentgen	.10
98	John Jaha	.10
99	Charles Johnson	.10
100	Jermaine Dye	.10
101	Quinton McCracken	.10
102	Troy Percival	.10
103	Shane Reynolds	.10
104	Rondell White	.15
105	Charles Nagy	.10
106	Alan Benes	.10
107	Tom Goodwin	.10
108	Ron Gant	.10
109	Dan Wilson	.10
110	Darin Erstad	.50
111	Matt Williams	.25
112	Barry Larkin	.40
113	Mariano Rivera	.25
114	Larry Walker	.40
115	Jim Edmonds	.20
116	Michael Tucker	.10
117	Todd Hundley	.15
118	Alex Fernandez	.10
119	J.T. Snow	.10
120	Ellis Burks	.10
121	Steve Finley	.10
122	Mike Mussina	.60
123	Curtis Pride	.10
124	Derek Bell	.10
125	Dante Bichette	.20
126	Terry Steinbach	.10
127	Randy Johnson	1.00
128	Andruw Jones	1.00
129	Vladimir Guerrero	1.50
130	Ruben Rivera	.10
131	Billy Wagner	.15
132	Scott Rolen	.75
133	Rey Ordonez	.15
134	Karim Garcia	.15
135	George Arias	.10
136	Todd Greene	.10
137	Robin Jennings	.10
138	Raul Casanova	.10
139	Josh Booty	.10
140	Edgar Renteria	.10
141	Chad Mottola	.10
142	Dmitri Young	.10
143	Tony Clark	.20
144	Todd Walker	.10
145	Kevin Brown	.15
146	Nomar Garciaparra	2.50
147	Neifi Perez	.10
148	Derek Jeter, Todd Hollandsworth	.40
149	Pat Hentgen, John Smoltz	.10
150	Juan Gonzalez, Ken Caminiti	.25

1997 Pinnacle Inside Club Edition

A 150-card parallel set featuring a special silver foil design and "CLUB EDITION" notation on back, these cards were inserted 1:7 can of Inside.

	MT
Complete Club Edition Set (150):	300.00
Common Club Edition:	.75
Stars:	5X

(See 1997 Pinnacle Inside for checklist and base values.)

1997 Pinnacle Inside Diamond Edition

A second parallel set, this time featuring a special die-cut design and gold holographic stamping. Cards were inserted 1:63 packs.

	MT
Common Diamond Edition:	5.00
Stars:	25X

(See 1997 Pinnacle Inside for checklist and base values.)

1997 Pinnacle Inside Cans

In addition to the cards, collectors had the option of collecting the 24 different player cans which are the packs" in which the cards were sold. About the size of a can of peas (3" diameter, 4-1/2" tall, the cans feature several color and black-and-white reproductions of the player's Inside card. The package had to be opened with a can opener to access the cards. Values shown are for empty cans which have been opened from the bottom; top-opened cans have little collectible value.

		MT
Complete Set (24):		20.00
Common Can:		.50
Sealed Cans:		2X
1	Ken Griffey Jr.	2.50
2	Juan Gonzalez	.75
3	Frank Thomas	1.25
4	Cal Ripken Jr.	2.00
5	Derek Jeter	1.50
6	Andruw Jones	1.50
7	Alex Rodriguez	2.00
8	Mike Piazza	1.50
9	Mo Vaughn	.75
10	Jeff Bagwell	1.00
11	Ken Caminiti	.50
12	Andy Pettitte	.75
13	Barry Bonds	.75
14	Mark McGwire	2.50
15	Ryan Klesko	.50
16	Manny Ramirez	.75
17	Ivan Rodriguez	.50
18	Chipper Jones	1.50
19	Albert Belle	.75
20	Tony Gwynn	1.25
21	Kenny Lofton	.65
22	Greg Maddux	1.25
23	Hideo Nomo	.50
24	John Smoltz	.50

1997 Pinnacle Inside Dueling Dugouts

This 20-card insert set features a veteran player on one side, a rising star on the other, and a spinning wheel that reveals their respective achievements in various statistical categories. Cards were inserted 1:23 packs.

		MT
Complete Set (20):		300.00
Common Player:		5.00
1	Alex Rodriguez, Cal Ripken Jr.	50.00
2	Jeff Bagwell, Ken Caminiti	20.00
3	Barry Bonds, Albert Belle	15.00
4	Mike Piazza, Ivan Rodriguez	25.00
5	Chuck Knoblauch, Roberto Alomar	7.50
6	Ken Griffey Jr., Andruw Jones	50.00
7	Chipper Jones, Jim Thome	25.00
8	Frank Thomas, Mo Vaughn	20.00
9	Fred McGriff, Mark McGwire	45.00
10	Brian Jordan, Tony Gwynn	20.00
11	Barry Larkin, Derek Jeter	20.00
12	Kenny Lofton, Bernie Williams	5.00
13	Juan Gonzalez, Manny Ramirez	15.00
14	Will Clark, Rafael Palmeiro	7.50
15	Greg Maddux, Roger Clemens	20.00
16	John Smoltz, Andy Pettitte	5.00
17	Mariano Rivera, John Wetteland	5.00
18	Hideo Nomo, Mike Mussina	5.00
19	Todd Hollandsworth, Darin Erstad	10.00
20	Vladimir Guerrero, Karim Garcia	15.00

1997 Pinnacle Inside Forty something

The top home run hitters in the game are pictured in this 16-card set. Cards were inserted 1:47 packs.

		MT
Complete Set (16):		150.00
Common Player:		4.00
1	Juan Gonzalez	10.00
2	Barry Bonds	10.00
3	Ken Caminiti	5.00
4	Mark McGwire	40.00
5	Todd Hundley	4.00
6	Albert Belle	10.00
7	Ellis Burks	4.00
8	Jay Buhner	4.00
9	Brady Anderson	4.00
10	Vinny Castilla	4.00
11	Mo Vaughn	7.50
12	Ken Griffey Jr.	40.00
13	Sammy Sosa	20.00
14	Andres Galarraga	4.00
15	Gary Sheffield	5.00
16	Frank Thomas	20.00

1997 Pinnacle Mint Collection

The 30-card Mint Collection set came in three-card packs that also contained two coins. The cards came in two versions: die-cut and foil. Three foil versions appear with Bronze Act as the common with Silver (1:15) and Gold (1:48) also appearing. The coins that come with each pack arrive in brass, silver and gold and can be matched up with the corresponding player die-cut card. The card fronts feature a player action shot on the left side with a shadowed headshot on the right. On the die-cut versions, the coin-size hole is in the lower right quadrant while the foil team stamp for the common cards is in the same location. The card backs are numbered as "x of 30" and deliver a short text.

		MT
Complete Set (30):		20.00
Common Player:		.25
Bronze Cards:		2X
Silver Cards:		5X
Gold Cards:		10X
Wax Box:		50.00
1	Ken Griffey Jr.	3.50
2	Frank Thomas	1.50
3	Alex Rodriguez	2.50
4	Cal Ripken Jr.	2.50
5	Mo Vaughn	.50
6	Juan Gonzalez	1.00
7	Mike Piazza	2.00
8	Albert Belle	.75
9	Chipper Jones	2.00
10	Andruw Jones	1.50
11	Greg Maddux	1.75
12	Hideo Nomo	.25
13	Jeff Bagwell	1.25
14	Manny Ramirez	1.00
15	Mark McGwire	3.50
16	Derek Jeter	2.00
17	Sammy Sosa	1.50
18	Barry Bonds	.75
19	Chuck Knoblauch	.25
20	Dante Bichette	.25
21	Tony Gwynn	1.25
22	Ken Caminiti	.40
23	Gary Sheffield	.40
24	Tim Salmon	.25
25	Ivan Rodriguez	.50
26	Henry Rodriguez	.25
27	Barry Larkin	.25
28	Ryan Klesko	.40
29	Brian Jordan	.25
30	Jay Buhner	.25

1997 Pinnacle Mint Collection Coins

Two coins from the 30-coin set were included in each three-card pack of 1997 Pinnacle Mint Collection. Brass coins are common while nickel-silver coins were inserted every 20 packs and gold-plated coins were inserted every 48 packs. Redemption cards for solid silver coins were found every 2,300 packs and a redemption card for a solid gold coin was inserted in 47,200 packs. Only one of each 24K gold coin was produced. The front of the coins feature the player's portrait while the backs have a baseball diamond with "Limited Edition, Pinnacle Mint Collection 1997" printed.

		MT
Complete Set (30):		50.00
Common Brass Coin:		.50
Nickel Coins:		4X
Gold Plated Coins:		10X
Silver Coins:		200X
24K Gold Coins:		Value undermined
1	Ken Griffey Jr.	5.00
2	Frank Thomas	2.00
3	Alex Rodriguez	4.00
4	Cal Ripken Jr.	4.00
5	Mo Vaughn	.75
6	Juan Gonzalez	1.50
7	Mike Piazza	3.00
8	Albert Belle	1.25
9	Chipper Jones	3.00
10	Andruw Jones	2.50
11	Greg Maddux	3.00
12	Hideo Nomo	.50
13	Jeff Bagwell	2.00
14	Manny Ramirez	1.50
15	Mark McGwire	5.00
16	Derek Jeter	3.00
17	Sammy Sosa	2.50
18	Barry Bonds	1.25
19	Chuck Knoblauch	.50
20	Dante Bichette	.75
21	Tony Gwynn	2.00
22	Ken Caminiti	.75
23	Gary Sheffield	.75
24	Tim Salmon	.50
25	Ivan Rodriguez	1.00
26	Henry Rodriguez	.50
27	Barry Larkin	.50
28	Ryan Klesko	.75
29	Brian Jordan	.50
30	Jay Buhner	.50

1997 Pinnacle X-Press

The 150-card set features 115 base cards, a 22-card Rookies subset, 10 Peak Performers and three checklist cards. Each of the regular cards features a horizontal design with two photos of each player on the front of the card and his name across the bottom. There are a number of inserts within this product, including Swing for the Fences (regular player cards as well as base and booster cards that can be used to accumulate points for a sweepstakes), Men of Summer, Far & Away, Melting Pot, Metal Works silver and Metal Works Gold. Cards were sold in eight-card packs for $1.99 each. X-Press Metal Works boxes were also available for $14.99 and contained a regular pack, one metal card and a master deck used to play the Swing for the Fences game.

		MT
Complete Set (150):		12.00
Common Player:		.05
Men of Summer:		8X
Pack (8):		1.25
Wax Box (24):		25.00
1	Larry Walker	.25
2	Andy Pettitte	.25
3	Matt Williams	.20
4	Juan Gonzalez	.50
5	Frank Thomas	.75
6	Kenny Lofton	.25
7	Ken Griffey Jr.	1.50
8	Andres Galarraga	.20
9	Greg Maddux	1.00
10	Hideo Nomo	.25
11	Cecil Fielder	.10
12	Jose Canseco	.25
13	Tony Gwynn	.75
14	Eddie Murray	.20
15	Alex Rodriguez	1.50
16	Mike Piazza	1.25
17	Ken Hill	.05
18	Chuck Knoblauch	.15
19	Ellis Burks	.05
20	Rafael Palmeiro	.20
21	Vinny Castilla	.05
22	Rusty Greer	.05
23	Chipper Jones	1.00
24	Rey Ordonez	.05
25	Mariano Rivera	.10
26	Garret Anderson	.05
27	Edgar Martinez	.10
28	Dante Bichette	.15
29	Todd Hundley	.10
30	Barry Bonds	.50
31	Barry Larkin	.20
32	Derek Jeter	1.50
33	Marquis Grissom	.10
34	David Justice	.25
35	Ivan Rodriguez	.50
36	Jay Buhner	.10
37	Fred McGriff	.20
38	Brady Anderson	.10
39	Tony Clark	.15
40	Eric Young	.05
41	Charles Nagy	.05
42	Mark McGwire	2.00
43	Paul O'Neill	.15
44	Tino Martinez	.10
45	Ryne Sandberg	.50
46	Bernie Williams	.40
47	Albert Belle	.30
48	Jeff Cirillo	.05
49	Tim Salmon	.15
50	Steve Finley	.05
51	Lance Johnson	.05
52	John Smoltz	.10
53	Javier Lopez	.10
54	Roger Clemens	.75
55	Kevin Appier	.05
56	Ken Caminiti	.10
57	Cal Ripken Jr.	1.50
58	Moises Alou	.15
59	Marty Cordova	.05
60	David Cone	.15
61	Manny Ramirez	.50
62	Ray Durham	.05
63	Jermaine Dye	.05
64	Craig Biggio	.15
65	Will Clark	.20
66	Omar Vizquel	.05
67	Bernard Gilkey	.05
68	Greg Vaughn	.10
69	Wade Boggs	.25
70	Dave Nilsson	.05
71	Mark Grace	.20
72	Dean Palmer	.05
73	Sammy Sosa	1.00
74	Mike Mussina	.40
75	Alex Fernandez	.05
76	Henry Rodriguez	.05
77	Travis Fryman	.10
78	Jeff Bagwell	.50
79	Pat Hentgen	.05
80	Gary Sheffield	.20
81	Jim Edmonds	.15
82	Darin Erstad	.40
83	Mark Grudzielanek	.05
84	Jim Thome	.30
85	Bobby Higginson	.10
86	Al Martin	.05
87	Jason Giambi	.20
88	Mo Vaughn	.30
89	Jeff Conine	.05
90	Edgar Renteria	.05
91	Andy Ashby	.05
92	Ryan Klesko	.10
93	John Jaha	.05
94	Paul Molitor	.40
95	Brian Hunter	.05
96	Randy Johnson	.50
97	Joey Hamilton	.05
98	Billy Wagner	.05
99	John Wetteland	.05
100	Jeff Fassero	.05
101	Rondell White	.15
102	Kevin Brown	.15
103	Andy Benes	.10
104	Raul Mondesi	.15
105	Todd Hollandsworth	.05
106	Alex Ochoa	.05
107	Bobby Bonilla	.10
108	Brian Jordan	.05
109	Tom Glavine	.25
110	Ron Gant	.10
111	Jason Kendall	.05
112	Roberto Alomar	.40
113	Troy Percival	.05
114	Michael Tucker	.05
115	Joe Carter	.10
116	Andruw Jones	.40
117	Nomar Garciaparra	1.25
118	Todd Walker	.05
119	Jose Guillen	.05
120	*Bubba Trammell*	.20
121	Wilton Guerrero	.05
122	Bob Abreu	.05
123	Vladimir Guerrero	.75
124	Dmitri Young	.05
125	Kevin Orie	.05
126	Glendon Rusch	.05
127	Brooks Kieschnick	.05
128	Scott Spiezio	.05
129	*Brian Giles*	1.50
130	Jason Dickson	.05
131	Damon Mashore	.05
132	Wendell Magee	.05
133	Matt Morris	.05
134	Scott Rolen	.40
135	Shannon Stewart	.05
136	*Deivi Cruz*	.25
137	*Hideki Irabu*	.75
138	Larry Walker (Peak Performers)	.15
139	Ken Griffey Jr. (Peak Performers)	.75
140	Frank Thomas (Peak Performers)	.40
141	Ivan Rodriguez (Peak Performers)	.20
142	Randy Johnson (Peak Performers)	.20
143	Mark McGwire (Peak Performers)	1.00
144	Tino Martinez (Peak Performers)	.10
145	Tony Clark (Peak Performers)	.10
146	Mike Piazza (Peak Performers)	.60
147	Alex Rodriguez (Peak Performers)	.75
148	Checklist (Roger Clemens)	.25
149	Checklist (Greg Maddux)	.50
150	Checklist (Hideo Nomo)	.20

1997 Pinnacle X-Press Men of Summer

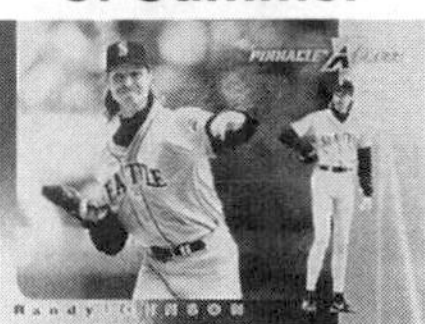

This parallel set of the 150 cards in the base X-Press issue differs in that the fronts are printed on foil backgrounds and the backs have a notation "MEN OF SUMMER" printed in gold vertically at top.

	MT
Complete Set (150):	200.00
Common Player:	.75

(See 1997 Pinnacle X-Press for checklist and base card values.)

1997 Pinnacle X-Press Far & Away

This 18-card insert highlights the top home run hitters in baseball and is printed with Dufex technology. Cards were inserted 1:19 packs.

		MT
Complete Set (18):		100.00
Common Player:		1.50
1	Albert Belle	5.00
2	Mark McGwire	20.00
3	Frank Thomas	10.00
4	Mo Vaughn	5.00
5	Jeff Bagwell	8.00
6	Juan Gonzalez	5.00
7	Mike Piazza	12.00
8	Andruw Jones	10.00
9	Chipper Jones	12.00
10	Gary Sheffield	2.50
11	Sammy Sosa	10.00
12	Darin Erstad	7.00
13	Jay Buhner	1.50
14	Ken Griffey Jr.	20.00
15	Ken Caminiti	1.50
16	Brady Anderson	1.50
17	Manny Ramirez	7.00
18	Alex Rodriguez	15.00

1997 Pinnacle X-Press Melting Pot

This 20-card insert showcases the talents of major leaguers from various countries. Fronts have color player photos on a background which combines shiny silver foil and textured foil in the design of the player's native flag. Backs have another photo and are ink-jet numbered in a white stripe at bottom in an edition of 500 each. Stated insertion rate was one per 288 packs.

		MT
Complete Set (20):		450.00
Common Player:		7.50
1	Jose Guillen	15.00
2	Vladimir Guerrero	30.00
3	Andruw Jones	40.00
4	Larry Walker	10.00
5	Manny Ramirez	20.00
6	Ken Griffey Jr.	75.00
7	Alex Rodriguez	60.00
7p	Alex Rodriguez (overprinted "SAMPLE")	5.00
8	Frank Thomas	35.00
9	Juan Gonzalez	20.00
10	Ivan Rodriguez	15.00
11	Hideo Nomo	10.00
12	Rafael Palmeiro	7.50
13	Dave Nilsson	7.50
14	Nomar Garciaparra	40.00
15	Wilton Guerrero	7.50
16	Sammy Sosa	45.00
17	Edgar Renteria	7.50
18	Cal Ripken Jr.	60.00
19	Derek Jeter	45.00
20	Rey Ordonez	7.50

1997 Pinnacle X-Press Metal Works

Each Home Plate Box of X-Press contains one heavy bronze Metal Works "card." The 2-3/8" x 3-1/2" slabs have a player portrait on front. Backs have a few words about the player. Redemption cards for silver-plated parallels were inserted 1:470 packs, while a silver slab was found 1:54 Home Plate Boxes. Silver Metal Works are serially numbered to 400 each. Redemption cards for gold-plated Metal Works cards, numbered in an edition of 200 each, were inserted 1:950 packs or one per 108 Home Plate Boxes.

		MT
Complete Set (20):		100.00
Common Player:		2.00
Silver:		30X
Gold:		50X
1	Ken Griffey Jr.	15.00
2	Frank Thomas	6.00
3	Andruw Jones	3.00
4	Alex Rodriguez	10.00
5	Derek Jeter	7.50
6	Cal Ripken Jr.	10.00
7	Mike Piazza	7.50
8	Chipper Jones	7.50
9	Juan Gonzalez	4.00
10	Greg Maddux	7.50
11	Tony Gwynn	6.00
12	Jeff Bagwell	3.00
13	Albert Belle	3.00
14	Mark McGwire	15.00
15	Nomar Garciaparra	7.50
16	Mo Vaughn	2.00
17	Andy Pettitte	2.00
18	Manny Ramirez	4.00
19	Kenny Lofton	2.00
20	Roger Clemens	4.00

1997 Pinnacle X-Press Swing for the Fences

These inserts allow collectors to play an interactive game based on the number of home runs hit by the home run champions of each league. Player Cards feature 60 different players and were inserted 1:2 packs. Base Cards feature a number between 20-42 printed on them and are found one in every master deck. Booster Cards feature a plus-or-minus point total (i.e. +7, -2) that can be used to add or subtract points to get to the winning home run total. Booster Cards are found 1:2 packs, while Base Cards are found one per master deck. Collectors who accumulated the winning home run totals were eligible to win prizes ranging from autographs to a trip to the 1998 All-Star Game. The unnumbered cards are checklisted here in alphabetical order.

		MT
Complete Set (60):		40.00
Common Player:		.25
(1)	Sandy Alomar Jr.	.50
(2)	Moises Alou	.35
(3)	Brady Anderson	.25
(4)	Jeff Bagwell	1.00
(5)	Derek Bell	.25
(6)	Jay Bell	.25
(7)	Albert Belle	1.00
(8)	Geronimo Berroa	.25
(9)	Dante Bichette	.35
(10)	Barry Bonds	1.00
(11)	Bobby Bonilla	.25
(12)	Jay Buhner	.25
(13)	Ellis Burks	.25
(14)	Ken Caminiti	.50
(15)	Jose Canseco	.75
(16)	Joe Carter	.25
(17)	Vinny Castilla	.25
(18)	Tony Clark	.50
(19)	Carlos Delgado	.50
(20)	Jim Edmonds	.25
(21)	Cecil Fielder	.25
(22)	Andres Galarraga	.50
(23)	Ron Gant	.25
(24)	Bernard Gilkey	.25
(25)	Juan Gonzalez	1.50
(26)	Ken Griffey Jr. (AL WINNER)	10.00
(27)	Vladimir Guerrero	1.50
(28)	Todd Hundley	.25
(29)	John Jaha	.25
(30)	Andruw Jones	2.00
(31)	Chipper Jones	2.50
(32)	David Justice	.50
(33)	Jeff Kent	.25
(34)	Ryan Klesko	.25
(35)	Barry Larkin	.25
(36)	Mike Lieberthal	.25
(37)	Javy Lopez	.25
(38)	Edgar Martinez	.25
(39)	Tino Martinez	.25
(40)	Fred McGriff	.25
(41)	Mark McGwire (AL/NL WINNER)	10.00
(42)	Raul Mondesi	.25
(43)	Tim Naehring	.25
(44)	Dave Nillson	.25
(45)	Rafael Palmeiro	.50
(46)	Dean Palmer	.25
(47)	Mike Piazza	2.50
(48)	Cal Ripken Jr.	4.00
(49)	Henry Rodriguez	.25
(50)	Tim Salmon	.25
(51)	Gary Sheffield	.45
(52)	Sammy Sosa	2.50
(53)	Terry Steinbach	.25
(54)	Frank Thomas	2.00
(55)	Jim Thome	.25
(56)	Mo Vaughn	.45
(57)	Larry Walker (NL Winner)	3.00
(58)	Rondell White	.25
(59)	Matt Williams	.25
(60)	Todd Zeile	.25

1997 Pinnacle XPressSwing /Fences Gold

Collectors who correctly matched Swing for the Fences insert game cards of the final 1997 season American and National home run champions with proper point cards equal to the number of home runs each hit could exchange them for a random assortment of 10 upgraded cards featuring gold-foil highlights and a premium card stock. The first 1,000 redemptions received an autographed Andruw Jones gold card. The redemption period ended March 1, 1998.

	MT
Complete Set (60):	150.00
Common Player:	1.00
Stars:	4X
Andruw Jones Autograph:	150.00

(See 1997 Pinnacle X-Press Swing for the Fences for checklist and base values.)

1998 Pinnacle

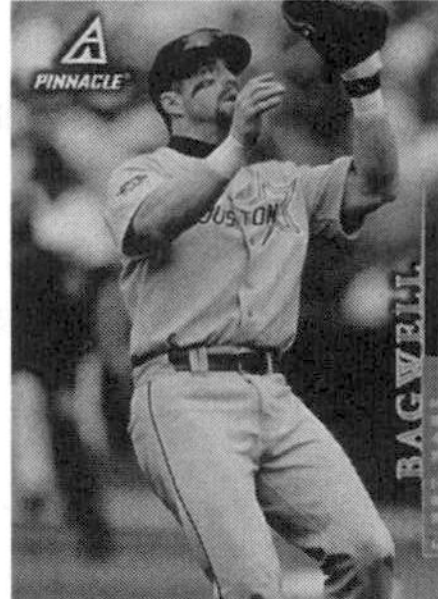

Pinnacle Baseball consists of a 200-card base set. The regular cards feature full-bleed photos on front. Three different backs were produced for each card: home stats, away stats and seasonal stats. The set includes 157 regular cards, 24 Rookies, six Field of Vision, 10 Goin'

Jake cards and three checklists. Parallel sets include Artist's Proofs, Press Plates and Museum Collection. Inserts include Epix, Hit it Here, Spellbound and Uncut.

		MT
Complete Set (200):		20.00
Common Player:		.10
Pack (10):		2.00
Wax Box (18):		30.00
1	Tony Gwynn (All-Star)	1.00
2	Pedro Martinez (All-Star)	.75
3	Kenny Lofton (All-Star)	.20
4	Curt Schilling (All-Star)	.15
5	Shawn Estes (All-Star)	.10
6	Tom Glavine (All-Star)	.20
7	Mike Piazza (All-Star)	2.00
8	Ray Lankford (All-Star)	.10
9	Barry Larkin (All-Star)	.20
10	Tony Womack (All-Star)	.10
11	Jeff Blauser (All-Star)	.10
12	Rod Beck (All-Star)	.10
13	Larry Walker (All-Star)	.30
14	Greg Maddux (All-Star)	1.50
15	Mark Grace (All-Star)	.20
16	Ken Caminiti (All-Star)	.10
17	Bobby Jones (All-Star)	.10
18	Chipper Jones (All-Star)	1.50
19	Javier Lopez (All-Star)	.15
20	Moises Alou (All-Star)	.10
21	Royce Clayton (All-Star)	.10
22	Darryl Kile (All-Star)	.10
23	Barry Bonds (All-Star)	.75
24	Steve Finley (All-Star)	.10
25	Andres Galarraga (All-Star)	.25
26	Denny Neagle (All-Star)	.10
27	Todd Hundley (All-Star)	.10
28	Jeff Bagwell	.75
29	Andy Pettitte	.35
30	Darin Erstad	.50
31	Carlos Delgado	.50
32	Matt Williams	.25
33	Will Clark	.30
34	Vinny Castilla	.10
35	Brad Radke	.10
36	John Olerud	.20
37	Andruw Jones	.75
38	Jason Giambi	.40
39	Scott Rolen	.50
40	Gary Sheffield	.30
41	Jimmy Key	.10
42	Kevin Appier	.10
43	Wade Boggs	.25
44	Hideo Nomo	.50
45	Manny Ramirez	.75
46	Wilton Guerrero	.10
47	Travis Fryman	.20
48	Chili Davis	.10
49	Jeromy Burnitz	.10
50	Craig Biggio	.20
51	Tim Salmon	.25
52	Jose Cruz Jr.	.15
53	Sammy Sosa	1.50
54	Hideki Irabu	.20
55	Chan Ho Park	.15
56	Robin Ventura	.15
57	Jose Guillen	.10
58	Deion Sanders	.25
59	Jose Canseco	.50
60	Jay Buhner	.15
61	Rafael Palmeiro	.40
62	Vladimir Guerrero	1.00
63	Mark McGwire	3.00
64	Derek Jeter	2.50
65	Bobby Bonilla	.15
66	Raul Mondesi	.20
67	Paul Molitor	.40
68	Joe Carter	.15
69	Marquis Grissom	.10
70	Juan Gonzalez	.75
71	Kevin Orie	.10
72	Rusty Greer	.10
73	Henry Rodriguez	.10
74	Fernando Tatis	.20
75	John Valentin	.10
76	Matt Morris	.10
77	Ray Durham	.10
78	Geronimo Berroa	.10
79	Scott Brosius	.10
80	Willie Greene	.10
81	Rondell White	.20
82	Doug Drabek	.10
83	Derek Bell	.10
84	Butch Huskey	.10
85	Doug Jones	.10
86	Jeff Kent	.10
87	Jim Edmonds	.20
88	Mark McLemore	.10
89	Todd Zeile	.10
90	Edgardo Alfonzo	.20
91	Carlos Baerga	.10
92	Jorge Fabregas	.10
93	Alan Benes	.10
94	Troy Percival	.10
95	Edgar Renteria	.10
96	Jeff Fassero	.10
97	Reggie Sanders	.10
98	Dean Palmer	.10
99	J.T. Snow	.10
100	Dave Nilsson	.10
101	Dan Wilson	.10
102	Robb Nen	.10
103	Damion Easley	.10
104	Kevin Foster	.10
105	Jose Offerman	.10
106	Steve Cooke	.10
107	Matt Stairs	.10
108	Darryl Hamilton	.10
109	Steve Karsay	.10
110	Gary DiSarcina	.10
111	Dante Bichette	.20
112	Billy Wagner	.10
113	David Segui	.10
114	Bobby Higginson	.10
115	Jeffrey Hammonds	.10
116	Kevin Brown	.20
117	Paul Sorrento	.10
118	Mark Leiter	.10
119	Charles Nagy	.10
120	Danny Patterson	.10
121	Brian McRae	.10
122	Jay Bell	.10
123	Jamie Moyer	.10
124	Carl Everett	.15
125	Greg Colbrunn	.10
126	Jason Kendall	.10
127	Luis Sojo	.10
128	Mike Lieberthal	.10
129	Reggie Jefferson	.10
130	Cal Eldred	.10
131	Orel Hershiser	.10
132	Doug Glanville	.10
133	Willie Blair	.10
134	Neifi Perez	.10
135	Sean Berry	.10
136	Chuck Finley	.10
137	Alex Gonzalez	.10
138	Dennis Eckersley	.15
139	Kenny Rogers	.10
140	Troy O'Leary	.10
141	Roger Bailey	.10
142	Yamil Benitez	.10
143	Wally Joyner	.10
144	Bobby Witt	.10
145	Pete Schourek	.10
146	Terry Steinbach	.10
147	B.J. Surhoff	.10
148	Esteban Loaiza	.10
149	Heathcliff Slocumb	.10
150	Ed Sprague	.10
151	Gregg Jefferies	.10
152	Scott Erickson	.10
153	Jaime Navarro	.10
154	David Wells	.15
155	Alex Fernandez	.10
156	Tim Belcher	.10
157	Mark Grudzielanek	.10
158	Scott Hatteberg	.10
159	Paul Konerko	.15
160	Ben Grieve	.25
161	Abraham Nunez	.10
162	Shannon Stewart	.10
163	Jaret Wright	.10
164	Derrek Lee	.10
165	Todd Dunwoody	.10
166	*Steve Woodard*	.25
167	Ryan McGuire	.10
168	Jeremi Gonzalez	.10
169	Mark Kotsay	.10
170	Brett Tomko	.10
171	Bobby Estalella	.10
172	Livan Hernandez	.10
173	Todd Helton	.75
174	Garrett Stephenson	.10
175	Pokey Reese	.10
176	Tony Saunders	.10
177	Antone Williamson	.10
178	Bartolo Colon	.15
179	Karim Garcia	.10
180	Juan Encarnacion	.10
181	Jacob Cruz	.10
182	Alex Rodriguez (Field of Vision)	1.00
183	Cal Ripken Jr., Roberto Alomar (Field of Vision)	1.00
184	Roger Clemens (Field of Vision)	.50
185	Derek Jeter (Field of Vision)	1.00
186	Frank Thomas (Field of Vision)	.50
187	Ken Griffey Jr. (Field of Vision)	1.00
188	Mark McGwire (Goin' Jake)	1.50
189	Tino Martinez (Goin' Jake)	.10
190	Larry Walker (Goin' Jake)	.15
191	Brady Anderson (Goin' Jake)	.10
192	Jeff Bagwell (Goin' Jake)	.50
193	Ken Griffey Jr. (Goin' Jake)	1.00
194	Chipper Jones (Goin' Jake)	.50
195	Ray Lankford (Goin' Jake)	.10
196	Jim Thome (Goin' Jake)	.20
197	Nomar Garciaparra (Goin' Jake)	.75
198	Checklist (1997 HR Contest)	.10
199	Checklist (1997 HR Contest Winner)	.10
200	Checklist (Overall View of the Park)	.10
9	Ken Griffey Jr. (All-Star, overprinted "SAMPLE" on back)	3.00
24	Frank Thomas (All-Star, overprinted "SAMPLE" on back)	1.50

1998 Pinnacle Artist's Proofs

Artist's Proofs is a 100-card partial parallel of the Pinnacle base set. The gold-foil Dufex cards were renumbered with a "PP" prefix and inserted one per 39 packs. A red AP seal appears on front.

		MT
Complete Set (100):		800.00
Common Artist's Proof:		3.00
1	Tony Gwynn (All-Star)	25.00
2	Pedro Martinez (All-Star)	10.00
3	Kenny Lofton (All-Star)	10.00
4	Curt Schilling (All-Star)	3.00
5	Shawn Estes (All-Star)	3.00
6	Tom Glavine (All-Star)	6.00
7	Mike Piazza (All-Star)	40.00
8	Ray Lankford (All-Star)	3.00
9	Barry Larkin (All-Star)	3.00
10	Tony Womack (All-Star)	3.00
11	Jeff Blauser (All-Star)	3.00
12	Rod Beck (All-Star)	3.00
13	Larry Walker (All-Star)	8.00
14	Greg Maddux (All-Star)	40.00
15	Mark Grace (All-Star)	6.00
16	Ken Caminiti (All-Star)	6.00
17	Bobby Jones (All-Star)	3.00
18	Chipper Jones (All-Star)	40.00
19	Javier Lopez (All-Star)	4.00
20	Moises Alou (All-Star)	4.00
21	Royce Clayton (All-Star)	3.00
22	Darryl Kile (All-Star)	3.00
23	Barry Bonds (All-Star)	15.00
24	Steve Finley (All-Star)	3.00
25	Andres Galarraga (All-Star)	3.00
26	Denny Neagle (All-Star)	3.00
27	Todd Hundley (All-Star)	3.00
28	Jeff Bagwell	25.00
29	Andy Pettitte	10.00
30	Darin Erstad	12.00
31	Carlos Delgado	4.00
32	Matt Williams	4.00
33	Will Clark	5.00
34	Brad Radke	3.00
35	John Olerud	5.00
36	Andruw Jones	20.00
37	Scott Rolen	20.00
38	Gary Sheffield	5.00
39	Jimmy Key	3.00
40	Wade Boggs	5.00
41	Hideo Nomo	10.00
42	Manny Ramirez	15.00
43	Wilton Guerrero	3.00
44	Travis Fryman	3.00
45	Craig Biggio	5.00
46	Tim Salmon	4.00
47	Jose Cruz Jr.	4.00
48	Sammy Sosa	45.00
49	Hideki Irabu	10.00
50	Jose Guillen	6.00
51	Deion Sanders	4.00
52	Jose Canseco	5.00
53	Jay Buhner	3.00
54	Rafael Palmeiro	5.00
55	Vladimir Guerrero	20.00
56	Mark McGwire	60.00
57	Derek Jeter	40.00
58	Bobby Bonilla	3.00
59	Raul Mondesi	5.00
60	Paul Molitor	10.00
61	Joe Carter	3.00
62	Marquis Grissom	3.00
63	Juan Gonzalez	20.00
64	Dante Bichette	4.00
65	Shannon Stewart (Rookie)	3.00
66	Jaret Wright (Rookie)	20.00
67	Derrek Lee (Rookie)	3.00
68	Todd Dunwoody (Rookie)	5.00

69	Steve Woodard (Rookie)	3.00
70	Ryan McGuire (Rookie)	4.00
71	Jeremi Gonzalez (Rookie)	3.00
72	Mark Kotsay (Rookie)	10.00
73	Brett Tomko (Rookie)	3.00
74	Bobby Estalella (Rookie)	5.00
75	Livan Hernandez (Rookie)	5.00
76	Todd Helton (Rookie)	15.00
77	Garrett Stephenson (Rookie)	3.00
78	Pokey Reese (Rookie)	3.00
79	Tony Saunders (Rookie)	5.00
80	Antone Williamson (Rookie)	3.00
81	Bartolo Colon (Rookie)	6.00
82	Karim Garcia (Rookie)	5.00
83	Juan Encarnacion (Rookie)	8.00
84	Jacob Cruz (Rookie)	6.00
85	Alex Rodriguez (Field of Vision)	30.00
86	Cal Ripken Jr., Roberto Alomar (Field of Vision)	25.00
87	Roger Clemens (Field of Vision)	12.00
88	Derek Jeter (Field of Vision)	30.00
89	Frank Thomas (Field of Vision)	15.00
90	Ken Griffey Jr. (Field of Vision)	35.00
91	Mark McGwire (Goin' Jake)	35.00
92	Tino Martinez (Goin' Jake)	3.00
93	Larry Walker (Goin' Jake)	5.00
94	Brady Anderson (Goin' Jake)	3.00
95	Jeff Bagwell (Goin' Jake)	12.00
96	Ken Griffey Jr. (Goin' Jake)	35.00
97	Chipper Jones (Goin' Jake)	20.00
98	Ray Lankford (Goin' Jake)	3.00
99	Jim Thome (Goin' Jake)	3.00
100	Nomar Garciaparra (Goin' Jake)	20.00

1998 Pinnacle Power Packs Supers

Two dozen regular and subset (Goin' Jake, Field of Vision) cards from Pinnacle are paralleled in this super-size (3-1/2" x 5") version which was included along with 21 regular cards in a $5.99 "Power Pack". Other than being four times the size of the regular card, these supers differ only in their numbering which specifies "x of 24" on back.

		MT
Complete Set (24):		20.00
Common Player:		.50
1	Alex Rodriguez (Field of Vision)	2.50
2	Cal Ripken Jr., Roberto Alomar (Field of Vision)	2.00
3	Roger Clemens (Field of Vision)	1.00
4	Derek Jeter (Field of Vision)	2.00
5	Frank Thomas (Field of Vision)	1.50
5s	Frank Thomas (FoV, "SAMPLE" overprint on back)	2.00
6	Ken Griffey Jr. (Field of Vision)	3.00
7	Mark McGwire (Goin' Jake)	3.00
8	Tino Martinez (Goin' Jake)	.50
9	Larry Walker (Goin' Jake)	.75
10	Brady Anderson (Goin' Jake)	.50
11	Jeff Bagwell (Goin' Jake)	1.00
12	Ken Griffey Jr. (Goin' Jake)	3.00
13	Chipper Jones (Goin' Jake)	2.00
14	Ray Lankford (Goin' Jake)	.50
15	Jim Thome (Goin' Jake)	.50
16	Nomar Garciaparra (Goin' Jake)	2.00
17	Mike Piazza	2.00
18	Andruw Jones	1.00
19	Greg Maddux	1.50
20	Tony Gwynn	1.00
21	Larry Walker	.75
22	Jeff Bagwell	1.00
23	Chipper Jones	2.00
24	Scott Rolen	.75

1998 Pinnacle Epix

This cross-brand insert was included in Pinnacle, Score, Pinnacle Certified and Zenith. Twenty-four cards were seeded in Pinnacle packs (1:21). The four-tiered set highlights a memorable Game, Season, Moment and Play in a player's career. The holographic foil cards came in three colors: orange, purple and emerald.

		MT
Common Player:		3.00
Purples:		1.5X
Emeralds:		2.5X
1	Ken Griffey Jr. G	20.00
2	Juan Gonzalez G	5.00
3	Jeff Bagwell G	5.00
4	Ivan Rodriguez G	8.00
5	Nomar Garciaparra G	12.00
6	Ryne Sandberg G	5.00
7	Frank Thomas S	15.00
8	Derek Jeter S	25.00
9	Tony Gwynn S	20.00
10	Albert Belle S	10.00
11	Scott Rolen S	8.00
12	Barry Larkin S	5.00
13	Alex Rodriguez M	30.00
14	Cal Ripken Jr. M	35.00
15	Chipper Jones M	30.00
16	Roger Clemens M	20.00
17	Mo Vaughn M	10.00
18	Mark McGwire M	60.00
19	Mike Piazza P	8.00
20	Andruw Jones P	3.00
21	Greg Maddux P	8.00
22	Barry Bonds P	5.00
23	Paul Molitor P	4.00
24	Eddie Murray P	3.00

1998 Pinnacle Hit It Here

Hit it Here is a 10-card insert seeded one per 17 packs. The micro-etched silver foil cards feature a color player photo with a red "Hit it Here" target on the left. Each card has a serial number. If the pictured player hit for the cycle on Opening Day 1998, the collector with the correct serially numbered card would win $1 million.

		MT
Complete Set (10):		40.00
Common Player:		1.00
Inserted 1:17		
1	Larry Walker	2.00
2	Ken Griffey Jr.	10.00
3	Mike Piazza	7.50
4	Frank Thomas	6.00
5	Barry Bonds	3.00
6	Albert Belle	2.50
7	Tino Martinez	1.00
8	Mark McGwire	10.00
9	Juan Gonzalez	2.50
10	Jeff Bagwell	2.50

1998 Pinnacle Spellbound

Spellbound is a 50-card insert seeded one per 17 packs of Pinnacle Baseball. Nine players were featured in the set. The cards featured a photo of the player with a letter from his first or last name in the background. Each player had enough cards to spell either his first or last name.

	MT
Complete Set (50):	350.00
Com. Mark McGwire (1MM-7MM)	20.00
Com. Roger Clemens (1RC-6RC)	8.00
Com. Frank Thomas (1FT-7FT)	7.50
Com. Scott Rolen (1SR-5SR)	5.00
Com. Ken Griffey Jr. (1KG-7KG)	20.00
Com. Larry Walker (1LW-6LW)	5.00
Com. Nomar Garciaparra (39-43)	10.00
Com. Cal Ripken Jr. (1CR-3CR)	12.00
Com. Tony Gwynn (1TG-4TG)	8.00
Inserted 1:17	

(Cards are contiguously numbered " ... of 50")

1998 Pinnacle Inside

Pinnacle Inside Baseball featured cards in a can. The 150 base cards featured full-bleed photos on the front with stats on the right and the player's name and position at the bottom. The Club Edition parallel (1:7) is printed on silver foil board and the Diamond Edition parallel (1:67) is printed on prismatic foil board. Each pack of cards was packaged inside a collectible can. Inserts include Behind the Numbers and Stand Up Guys.

		MT
Complete Set (150):		30.00
Common Player:		.15
Pack (10):		2.00
Wax Box (48):		75.00
1	Darin Erstad	.75
2	Derek Jeter	3.00
3	Alex Rodriguez	3.00
4	Bobby Higginson	.15
5	Nomar Garciaparra	2.50
6	Kenny Lofton	.40
7	Ivan Rodriguez	1.00
8	Cal Ripken Jr.	3.00
9	Todd Hundley	.15
10	Chipper Jones	2.00
11	Barry Larkin	.40
12	Roberto Alomar	.75
13	Mo Vaughn	.50
14	Sammy Sosa	2.50
15	Sandy Alomar Jr.	.25
16	Albert Belle	.50
17	Scott Rolen	.75
18	Pokey Reese	.15
19	Ryan Klesko	.25
20	Andres Galarraga	.40
21	Justin Thompson	.15
22	Gary Sheffield	.40
23	David Justice	.40
24	Ken Griffey Jr.	3.00
25	Andruw Jones	1.00
26	Jeff Bagwell	1.00
27	Vladimir Guerrero	1.50
28	Mike Piazza	2.50
29	Chuck Knoblauch	.25
30	Rondell White	.25
31	Greg Maddux	2.00
32	Andy Pettitte	.40
33	Larry Walker	.40
34	Bobby Estalella	.15
35	Frank Thomas	1.50
36	Tony Womack	.15
37	Tony Gwynn	1.50
38	Barry Bonds	1.00
39	Randy Johnson	1.00
40	Mark McGwire	4.00
41	Juan Gonzalez	1.00
42	Tim Salmon	.30
43	John Smoltz	.15
44	Rafael Palmeiro	.40
45	Mark Grace	.30
46	Mike Cameron	.15
47	Jim Thome	.40
48	Neifi Perez	.15
49	Kevin Brown	.25
50	Craig Biggio	.25
51	Bernie Williams	.75
52	Hideo Nomo	.50
53	Bob Abreu	.15
54	Edgardo Alfonzo	.20
55	Wade Boggs	.50
56	Jose Guillen	.15
57	Ken Caminiti	.20
58	Paul Molitor	.75
59	Shawn Estes	.15
60	Edgar Martinez	.20
61	Livan Hernandez	.15
62	Ray Lankford	.15
63	Rusty Greer	.15
64	Jim Edmonds	.25
65	Tom Glavine	.30
66	Alan Benes	.15
67	Will Clark	.25
68	Garret Anderson	.15
69	Javier Lopez	.25
70	Mike Mussina	.60
71	Kevin Orie	.15
72	Matt Williams	.40
73	Bobby Bonilla	.15
74	Ruben Rivera	.15
75	Jason Giambi	.40
76	Todd Walker	.15
77	Tino Martinez	.20
78	Matt Morris	.15
79	Fernando Tatis	.25
80	Todd Greene	.15
81	Fred McGriff	.25
82	Brady Anderson	.25
83	Mark Kotsay	.15
84	Raul Mondesi	.25
85	Moises Alou	.25
86	Roger Clemens	1.50
87	Wilton Guerrero	.15
88	Shannon Stewart	.15
89	Chan Ho Park	.25
90	Carlos Delgado	.75
91	Jose Cruz Jr.	.25
92	Shawn Green	.25
93	Robin Ventura	.25
94	Reggie Sanders	.15
95	Orel Hershiser	.15
96	Dante Bichette	.25
97	Charles Johnson	.15
98	Pedro Martinez	1.00
99	Mariano Rivera	.25
100	Joe Randa	.15
101	Jeff Kent	.15
102	Jay Buhner	.20
103	Brian Jordan	.15
104	Jason Kendall	.15
105	Scott Spiezio	.15
106	Desi Relaford	.15
107	Bernard Gilkey	.15
108	Manny Ramirez	1.00
109	Tony Clark	.25
110	Eric Young	.15
111	Johnny Damon	.15
112	Glendon Rusch	.15
113	Ben Grieve	.40
114	Homer Bush	.15
115	Miguel Tejada	.25
116	Lou Collier	.15
117	Derrek Lee	.15
118	Jacob Cruz	.15
119	Raul Ibanez	.15
120	Ryan McGuire	.15
121	Antone Williamson	.15
122	Abraham Nunez	.15
123	Jeff Abbott	.15
124	Brett Tomko	.15
125	Richie Sexson	.15
126	Todd Helton	1.00
127	Juan Encarnacion	.15
128	Richard Hidalgo	.15
129	Paul Konerko	.20
130	Brad Fullmer	.25
131	Jeremi Gonzalez	.15
132	Jaret Wright	.15
133	Derek Jeter (Inside Tips)	1.50
134	Frank Thomas (Inside Tips)	.75
135	Nomar Garciaparra (Inside Tips)	1.00
136	Kenny Lofton (Inside Tips)	.20
137	Jeff Bagwell (Inside Tips)	.50
138	Todd Hundley (Inside Tips)	.15
139	Alex Rodriguez (Inside Tips)	1.50
140	Ken Griffey Jr. (Inside Tips)	1.50
141	Sammy Sosa (Inside Tips)	1.00
142	Greg Maddux (Inside Tips)	1.00
143	Albert Belle (Inside Tips)	.25
144	Cal Ripken Jr. (Inside Tips)	1.50
145	Mark McGwire (Inside Tips)	2.00
146	Chipper Jones (Inside Tips)	1.00
147	Charles Johnson (Inside Tips)	.15
148	Checklist (Ken Griffey Jr.)	1.00
149	Checklist (Jose Cruz Jr.)	.15
150	Checklist (Larry Walker)	.20

1998 Pinnacle Inside Club Edition

This parallel set is virtually identical to the regular Inside cards, except for the addition of a "CLUB EDITION" notice to the right of the player's first name, and the use of gold foil highlights instead of silver on front.

	MT
Complete Set (150):	400.00
Common Player:	1.00
Club Edition Stars:	4-8X
Inserted 1:7	

(See 1998 Pinnacle Inside for checklist and base card values.)

1998 Pinnacle Inside Diamond Edition

Diamond Edition cards paralleled all 150 cards in Pinnacle Inside. The fronts had the insert name and they were printed on a prismatic foil and inserted one per 67 packs.

	MT
Common Card:	4.00
Diamond Edition Stars:	15-30X
Inserted 1:67	

(See 1998 Pinnacle Inside for checklist and base card values.)

1998 Pinnacle Inside Behind the Numbers

Behind the Numbers is a 20-card insert seeded one per 23 cans. The card front features an action photo printed in front of the player's number. The card is die-cut around the large metallic foil numerals. The back has a portrait photo and text explaining why the player wears that number.

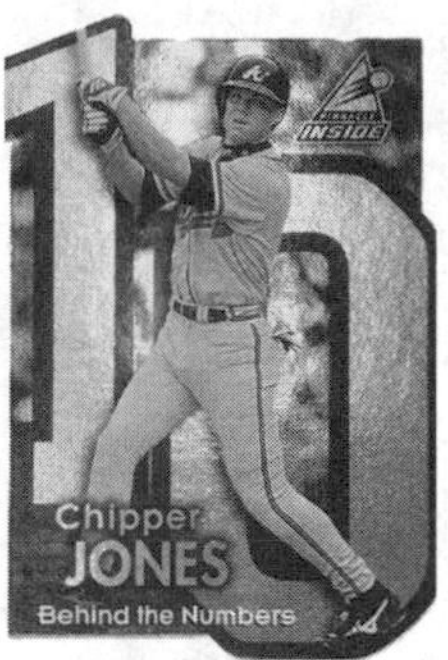

		MT
Complete Set (20):		240.00
Common Player:		3.00
Inserted 1:23		
1	Ken Griffey Jr.	25.00
2	Cal Ripken Jr.	25.00
3	Alex Rodriguez	25.00
4	Jose Cruz Jr.	3.00
5	Mike Piazza	20.00
6	Nomar Garciaparra	20.00
7	Scott Rolen	6.00
8	Andruw Jones	8.00
9	Frank Thomas	10.00
10	Mark McGwire	30.00
11	Ivan Rodriguez	8.00
12	Greg Maddux	15.00
13	Roger Clemens	10.00
14	Derek Jeter	25.00
15	Tony Gwynn	10.00
16	Ben Grieve	4.00
17	Jeff Bagwell	8.00
18	Chipper Jones	15.00
19	Hideo Nomo	6.00
20	Sandy Alomar Jr.	3.00

1998 Pinnacle Inside Cans

Ten-card packs of Pinnacle Inside were packaged in collectible cans. The 24 cans featured a player photo or team logo. Cans were created to honor the Florida Marlins' world championship and the expansion Arizona and Tampa Bay teams. Gold parallel versions of the cans were found one every 47 cans.

		MT
Complete Set (23):		20.00
Common Can:		.40
Sealed Cans:		3.00
Gold Cans:		3X
1	Ken Griffey Jr.	2.50

2	Frank Thomas	1.50
3	Alex Rodriguez	2.00
4	Andruw Jones	1.25
5	Mike Piazza	1.50
6	Ben Grieve	.75
7	Hideo Nomo	.50
8	Vladimir Guerrero	.75
9	Roger Clemens	1.00
10	Tony Gwynn	1.25
11	Mark McGwire	2.50
12	Cal Ripken Jr.	2.00
13	Jose Cruz Jr.	.40
14	Greg Maddux	1.50
15	Chipper Jones	1.50
16	Derek Jeter	1.50
17	Juan Gonzalez	.75
18	Nomar Garciaparra (AL ROY)	1.50
19	Scott Rolen (NL ROY)	1.00
20	Florida Marlins World Series Winner	.50
21	Larry Walker (NL MVP)	.50
22	Tampa Bay Devil Rays	.40
23	Arizona Diamondbacks	.40

1998 Pinnacle Inside Stand Up Guys

This 50-card insert was seeded one per can. Each card has a match; the two cards join together in the center to form a stand-up collectible featuring four Major League players.

		MT
Complete Set (50):		40.00
Common Player:		.25
Inserted 1:1		
1a	Ken Griffey Jr.	
1b	Cal Ripken Jr.	2.00
1c	Tony Gwynn	
1d	Mike Piazza	1.25
2a	Andruw Jones	
2b	Alex Rodriguez	1.50
2c	Scott Rolen	
2d	Nomar Garciaparra	1.25
3a	Andruw Jones	
3b	Greg Maddux	1.25
3c	Javier Lopez	.25
3d	Chipper Jones	1.25
4a	Jay Buhner	.25
4b	Randy Johnson	.40
4c	Ken Griffey Jr.	2.00
4d	Alex Rodriguez	1.50
5a	Frank Thomas	1.00
5b	Jeff Bagwell	.75
5c	Mark McGwire	2.00
5d	Mo Vaughn	.40
6a	Nomar Garciaparra	1.25
6b	Derek Jeter	1.25
6c	Alex Rodriguez	1.50
6d	Barry Larkin	.25
7a	Mike Piazza	1.25
7b	Ivan Rodriguez	.50
7c	Charles Johnson	.25
7d	Javier Lopez	.25
8a	Cal Ripken Jr.	1.50
8b	Chipper Jones	1.25
8c	Ken Caminiti	.25
8d	Scott Rolen	.75
9a	Jose Cruz Jr.	.25
9b	Vladimir Guerrero	.75
9c	Andruw Jones	.75
9d	Jose Guillen	.25
10a	Larry Walker	.40
10b	Dante Bichette	.25
10c	Ellis Burks	.25
10d	Neifi Perez	.25
11a	Juan Gonzalez	.50
11b	Sammy Sosa	1.50
11c	Vladimir Guerrero	.75
11d	Manny Ramirez	.50
12a	Greg Maddux	1.25
12b	Roger Clemens	.75
12c	Hideo Nomo	.50
12d	Randy Johnson	.50
13a	Ben Grieve	.50
13b	Paul Konerko	.50
13c	Jose Cruz Jr.	.25
13d	Fernando Tatis	.25
14a	Ryne Sandberg	.50
14b	Chuck Knoblauch	.40
14c	Roberto Alomar	.40
14d	Craig Biggio	.25
15a	Cal Ripken Jr.	1.50
15b	Brady Anderson	.25
15c	Rafael Palmeiro	.25
15d	Roberto Alomar	.40
16a	Darin Erstad	.50
16b	Jim Edmonds	.25
16c	Tim Salmon	.40
16d	Garret Anderson	.25
17a	Mike Piazza	1.25
17b	Hideo Nomo	.40
17c	Raul Mondesi	.25
17d	Eric Karros	.25
18a	Ivan Rodriguez	.50
18b	Juan Gonzalez	.50
18c	Will Clark	.40
18d	Rusty Greer	.25
19a	Derek Jeter	1.25
19b	Bernie Williams	.35
19c	Tino Martinez	.30
19d	Andy Pettitte	.40
20a	Kenny Lofton	.40
20b	Ken Griffey Jr.	2.00
20c	Brady Anderson	.25
20d	Bernie Williams	.35
21a	Paul Molitor	.40
21b	Eddie Murray	.35
21c	Ryne Sandberg	.50
21d	Rickey Henderson	.35
22a	Tony Clark	.40
22b	Frank Thomas	1.00
22c	Jeff Bagwell	.75
22d	Mark McGwire	2.00
23a	Manny Ramirez	.50
23b	Jim Thome	.40
23c	David Justice	.25
23d	Sandy Alomar Jr.	.25
24a	Barry Bonds	.50
24b	Albert Belle	.50
24c	Jeff Bagwell	.75
24d	Dante Bichette	.25
25a	Ken Griffey Jr.	2.00
25b	Frank Thomas	1.00
25c	Alex Rodriguez	1.50
25d	Andruw Jones	.75

1998 Pinnacle Mint Collection

Mint Collection consists of 30 cards and 30 matching coins with numerous parallels of each. The cards come in four different versions. The base card features a player photo on the left with a circular bronze foil team logo on the right. The base cards were inserted one per hobby pack and two per retail pack. Die-cut versions removed the team logo and were inserted two per hobby and one per retail packs. Silver Mint Team (1:15 hobby, 1:23 retail) and Gold Mint Team (1:47 hobby, 1:71 retail) parallels were printed on silver foil and gold foil board, respectively.

		MT
Complete Set (30):		20.00
Common Die-Cut:		.25
Bronze:		1.5X
Inserted 1:1 H		
Silver:		8X
Inserted 1:15 H		
Gold:		12X
Inserted 1:47 H		
Pack (1):		3.00
Wax Box (21):		70.00
1	Jeff Bagwell	1.00
2	Albert Belle	.75
3	Barry Bonds	.75
4	Tony Clark	.50
5	Roger Clemens	1.00
6	Juan Gonzalez	.75
7	Ken Griffey Jr.	2.50
8	Tony Gwynn	1.25
9	Derek Jeter	1.50
10	Randy Johnson	.40
11	Chipper Jones	1.50
12	Greg Maddux	1.50
13	Tino Martinez	.25
14	Mark McGwire	2.50
15	Hideo Nomo	.50
16	Andy Pettitte	.35
17	Mike Piazza	1.50
18	Cal Ripken Jr.	2.00
19	Alex Rodriguez	2.50
20	Ivan Rodriguez	.75
21	Sammy Sosa	1.50
22	Frank Thomas	1.25
23	Mo Vaughn	.40
24	Larry Walker	.40
25	Jose Cruz Jr.	.25
26	Nomar Garciaparra	1.50
27	Vladimir Guerrero	1.00
28	Livan Hernandez	.25
29	Andruw Jones	1.25
30	Scott Rolen	1.00

1998 Pinnacle Mint Collection Coins

Two base coins were included in each pack of Mint Collection. The coins feature the player's image, name and number on the front along with his team's name and logo. The back has the Mint Collection logo. Seven parallels were included: Nickel-Silver (1:41), Bronze Proof (numbered to 500), Silver Proof (numbered to 250), Gold Proof (numbered to 100), Gold-Plated (1:199), Solid Silver (1:288 hobby, 1:960 retail) and Solid Gold by redemption (1-of-1).

		MT
Complete Set (30):		60.00
Common Brass Coin:		.50
Nickel:		6X
Inserted 1:41		
Silver:		25X
Inserted 1:288 H, 1:960 R		
Gold Plated: 20X		
Inserted 1:		199
1	Jeff Bagwell	2.50
2	Albert Belle	1.50
3	Barry Bonds	1.50
4	Tony Clark	1.00
5	Roger Clemens	2.50
6	Juan Gonzalez	1.50
7	Ken Griffey Jr.	6.00
8	Tony Gwynn	3.00
9	Derek Jeter	4.00
10	Randy Johnson	1.00
11	Chipper Jones	4.00
12	Greg Maddux	4.00
13	Tino Martinez	1.00
14	Mark McGwire	6.00
15	Hideo Nomo	1.00
16	Andy Pettitte	1.00
17	Mike Piazza	4.00
18	Cal Ripken Jr.	5.00
19	Alex Rodriguez	5.00
20	Ivan Rodriguez	1.50
21	Sammy Sosa	3.00
22	Frank Thomas	2.50
23	Mo Vaughn	1.50
24	Larry Walker	1.00
25	Jose Cruz Jr.	.75
26	Nomar Garciaparra	4.00
27	Vladimir Guerrero	2.50
28	Livan Hernandez	.75
29	Andruw Jones	3.00
30	Scott Rolen	2.50

1998 Pinnacle Mint Collection Proof Coins

Special serially numbered editions of three versions of the Mint Collection coins were issued as random pack inserts. Brass proofs are numbered within an edition of 500. Nickel proofs are numbered to 250. Gold-plated proofs are numbered to 100 each.

	MT
Common Brass Proof:	8.00
Brass Proof Stars:	10X
Common Nickel Proof:	12.00
Nickel Proof Stars:	15X
Common Gold-plated Proof:	30.00
Gold-plated Proof Stars:	40X

(See 1998 Pinnacle Mint Collection Coins for checklist and base coin values.)

1998 Pinnacle Mint Collection Mint Gems

Mint Gems is a six-card insert printed on silver foil board. The cards were inserted 1:31 hobby packs and 1:47 retail. The oversized Mint Gems coins are twice the size of the regular coins. The six coins were inserted 1:31 hobby packs.

		MT
Complete Set (6)		50.00
Common Player:		4.00
Coins:		1X
1	Ken Griffey Jr.	20.00
2	Larry Walker	4.00
3	Roger Clemens	8.00
4	Pedro Martinez	4.00
5	Nomar Garciaparra	12.00
6	Scott Rolen	10.00

1998 Pinnacle Performers

Pinnacle Performers consists of a 150-card base set. The Peak Performers parallel adds silver foil to the base cards and was inserted 1:7. Inserts in the home run-themed product include Big Bang, Launching Pad, Player's Card and Power Trip.

		MT
Complete Set (150):		15.00
Common Player:		.10
Pack (10):		1.00
Wax Box (48):		30.00
1	Ken Griffey Jr.	1.50
2	Frank Thomas	.75
3	Cal Ripken Jr.	1.50
4	Alex Rodriguez	1.50
5	Greg Maddux	1.00
6	Mike Piazza	1.25
7	Chipper Jones	1.00
8	Tony Gwynn	.75
9	Derek Jeter	1.50
10	Jeff Bagwell	.50
11	Juan Gonzalez	.50
12	Nomar Garciaparra	1.25
13	Andruw Jones	.40
14	Hideo Nomo	.25
15	Roger Clemens	.75
16	Mark McGwire	2.00
17	Scott Rolen	.40
18	Vladimir Guerrero	.75
19	Barry Bonds	.50
20	Darin Erstad	.40
21	Albert Belle	.30
22	Kenny Lofton	.25
23	Mo Vaughn	.25
24	Tony Clark	.15
25	Ivan Rodriguez	.50
26	Jose Cruz Jr.	.15
27	Larry Walker	.25
28	Jaret Wright	.10
29	Andy Pettitte	.20
30	Roberto Alomar	.40
31	Randy Johnson	.50
32	Manny Ramirez	.50
33	Paul Molitor	.40
34	Mike Mussina	.40
35	Jim Thome	.30
36	Tino Martinez	.20
37	Gary Sheffield	.25
38	Chuck Knoblauch	.25
39	Bernie Williams	.40
40	Tim Salmon	.20
41	Sammy Sosa	1.25
42	Wade Boggs	.40
43	Will Clark	.30
44	Andres Galarraga	.25
45	Raul Mondesi	.25
46	Rickey Henderson	.20
47	Jose Canseco	.30
48	Pedro Martinez	.50
49	Jay Buhner	.20
50	Ryan Klesko	.15
51	Barry Larkin	.25
52	Charles Johnson	.10
53	Tom Glavine	.20
54	Edgar Martinez	.10
55	Fred McGriff	.20
56	Moises Alou	.15
57	Dante Bichette	.15
58	Jim Edmonds	.20
59	Mark Grace	.25
60	Chan Ho Park	.15
61	Justin Thompson	.10
62	John Smoltz	.20
63	Craig Biggio	.20
64	Ken Caminiti	.15
65	Richard Hidalgo	.10
66	Carlos Delgado	.40
67	David Justice	.25
68	J.T. Snow	.10
69	Jason Giambi	.25
70	Garret Anderson	.10
71	Rondell White	.20
72	Matt Williams	.25
73	Brady Anderson	.15
74	Eric Karros	.15
75	Javier Lopez	.10
76	Pat Hentgen	.10
77	Todd Hundley	.10
78	Ray Lankford	.10
79	Denny Neagle	.10
80	Sandy Alomar Jr.	.15
81	Jason Kendall	.10
82	Omar Vizquel	.10
83	Kevin Brown	.20
84	Kevin Appier	.10
85	Al Martin	.10
86	Rusty Greer	.10
87	Bobby Bonilla	.10
88	Shawn Estes	.10
89	Rafael Palmeiro	.30
90	Edgar Renteria	.10
91	Alan Benes	.10
92	Bobby Higginson	.10
93	Mark Grudzielanek	.10
94	Jose Guillen	.10
95	Neifi Perez	.10
96	Jeff Abbott	.10
97	Todd Walker	.10
98	Eric Young	.10
99	Brett Tomko	.10
100	Mike Cameron	.10
101	Karim Garcia	.10
102	Brian Jordan	.10
103	Jeff Suppan	.10
104	Robin Ventura	.20
105	Henry Rodriguez	.10
106	Shannon Stewart	.10
107	Kevin Orie	.10
108	Bartolo Colon	.10
109	Bob Abreu	.10
110	Vinny Castilla	.10
111	Livan Hernandez	.10
112	Derrek Lee	.10
113	Mark Kotsay	.10
114	Todd Greene	.10
115	Edgardo Alfonzo	.15
116	A.J. Hinch	.40
117	Paul Konerko	.15
118	Todd Helton	.50
119	Miguel Tejada	.20
120	Fernando Tatis	.20
121	Ben Grieve	.20
122	Travis Lee	.10
123	Kerry Wood	.20
124	Eli Marrero	.10
125	David Ortiz	.10
126	Juan Encarnacion	.10
127	Brad Fullmer	.10
128	Richie Sexson	.10
129	Aaron Boone	.10
130	Enrique Wilson	.10
131	Javier Valentin	.10
132	Abraham Nunez	.10
133	Ricky Ledee	.10
134	Carl Pavano	.10
135	Bobby Estalella	.10
136	Homer Bush	.10
137	Brian Rose	.10
138	Ken Griffey Jr. (Far and Away)	.75
139	Frank Thomas (Far and Away)	.40
140	Cal Ripken Jr. (Far and Away)	.75
141	Alex Rodriguez (Far and Away)	.75
142	Greg Maddux (Far and Away)	.50
143	Chipper Jones (Far and Away)	.50
144	Mike Piazza (Far and Away)	.50
145	Tony Gwynn (Far and Away)	.40
146	Derek Jeter (Far and Away)	.60
147	Jeff Bagwell (Far and Away)	.40
148	Checklist (Hideo Nomo)	.10
149	Checklist (Roger Clemens)	.40
150	Checklist (Greg Maddux)	.50

1998 Pinnacle Performers Peak Performers

This 150-card parallel set is printed on silver foil vs. the white cardboard stock used on regular-issue cards. The parallel set name is printed down the right side in gold letters and they were seeded one per seven packs.

	MT
Complete Set (150):	150.00
Common Player:	.50
Peak Performers Stars:	4-6X
Inserted 1:7	

(See 1998 Pinnacle Performers for checklist and base card values.)

1998 Pinnacle Performers Big Bang

This 20-card insert features top power hitters. The micro-etched cards are sequentially numbered to 2,500. Each player has a Seasonal Outburst parallel, with a red overlay and numbered to that player's best seasonal home run total.

		MT
Complete Set (20):		175.00
Common Player:		4.00
Production 2,500 sets		
1	Ken Griffey Jr.	25.00
2	Frank Thomas	12.00
3	Mike Piazza	15.00
4	Chipper Jones	15.00
5	Alex Rodriguez	20.00
6	Nomar Garciaparra	15.00
7	Jeff Bagwell	10.00
8	Cal Ripken Jr.	18.00
9	Albert Belle	6.00
10	Mark McGwire	25.00
10s	Mark McGwire (SAMPLE overprint on back)	15.00
11	Juan Gonzalez	8.00
12	Larry Walker	4.00
13	Tino Martinez	4.00
14	Jim Thome	4.00
15	Manny Ramirez	8.00
16	Barry Bonds	6.00
17	Mo Vaughn	4.00
18	Jose Cruz Jr.	4.00
19	Tony Clark	5.00

1998 Pinnacle Performers Big Bang Season Outburst

Season Outburst parallels the Big Bang insert. The cards have a red overlay and are sequentially numbered to each player's season-high home run total.

		MT
Common Player:		25.00
#'d to player's 1997 home run total		
1	Ken Griffey Jr. (56)	175.00
2	Frank Thomas (35)	60.00
3	Mike Piazza (40)	100.00
4	Chipper Jones (21)	200.00

5	Alex Rodriguez (23)	220.00
6	Nomar Garciaparra (30)	125.00
7	Jeff Bagwell (43)	40.00
8	Cal Ripken Jr. (17)	300.00
9	Albert Belle (30)	40.00
10	Mark McGwire (58)	250.00
11	Juan Gonzalez (42)	60.00
12	Larry Walker (49)	30.00
13	Tino Martinez (44)	30.00
14	Jim Thome (40)	30.00
15	Manny Ramirez (26)	80.00
16	Barry Bonds (40)	50.00
17	Mo Vaughn (35)	40.00
18	Jose Cruz Jr. (26)	25.00
19	Tony Clark (32)	25.00
20	Andruw Jones (18)	75.00

1998 Pinnacle Performers Launching Pad

Launching Pad is a 20-card insert seeded one per nine packs. It features top sluggers on foil-on-foil cards with an outer space background.

		MT
Complete Set (20):		50.00
Common Player:		1.00
Inserted 1:9		
1	Ben Grieve	1.00
2	Ken Griffey Jr.	6.00
3	Derek Jeter	6.00
4	Frank Thomas	2.50
5	Travis Lee	1.00
6	Vladimir Guerrero	2.50
7	Tony Gwynn	2.50
8	Jose Cruz Jr.	1.00
9	Cal Ripken Jr.	6.00
10	Chipper Jones	4.00
11	Scott Rolen	1.50
12	Andruw Jones	2.00
13	Ivan Rodriguez	2.00
14	Todd Helton	2.00
15	Nomar Garciaparra	5.00
16	Mark McGwire	8.00
17	Gary Sheffield	1.50
18	Bernie Williams	1.50
19	Alex Rodriguez	6.00
20	Mike Piazza	5.00

1998 Pinnacle Performers Power Trip

This 10-card insert was seeded 1:21. Printed on silver foil, each card is sequentially-numbered to 10,000. Cards backs have details about one of the player's power-hitting highlights of the previous season.

		MT
Complete Set (10):		55.00
Common Player:		3.00
Production 10,000 sets		
1	Frank Thomas	4.00
2	Alex Rodriguez	8.00
3	Nomar Garciaparra	6.00
4	Jeff Bagwell	3.00
5	Cal Ripken Jr.	7.50
6	Mike Piazza	6.00
7	Chipper Jones	6.00
8	Ken Griffey Jr.	10.00
9	Mark McGwire	10.00
10	Juan Gonzalez	2.50

1998 Pinnacle Performers Swing for the Fences

Pinnacle Performers included the "Swing for the Fences" sweepstakes. Fifty players were featured on cards with numbers on an all-red background. Fifty Home Run Points cards were also inserted, with each card featuring a point total on the front. Collectors who found the player cards of the AL and NL home run leaders, as well as enough point cards to match each of their season totals, were eligible to win prizes. A player or point card was inserted in each pack.

		MT
Complete Set (50):		25.00
Common Player:		.25
Inserted 1:1		
1	Brady Anderson	.25
2	Albert Belle	.75
3	Jay Buhner	.35
4	Jose Canseco	.45
5	Tony Clark	.60
6	Jose Cruz Jr.	.60
7	Jim Edmonds	.25
8	Cecil Fielder	.25
9	Travis Fryman	.25
10	Nomar Garciaparra	2.00
11	Juan Gonzalez	1.00
12	Ken Griffey Jr.	3.50
13	David Justice	.40
14	Travis Lee	1.25
15	Edgar Martinez	.25
16	Tino Martinez	.35
17	Rafael Palmeiro	.40
18	Manny Ramirez	.75
19	Cal Ripken Jr.	2.50
20	Alex Rodriguez	2.50
21	Tim Salmon	.35
22	Frank Thomas	2.00
23	Jim Thome	.45
24	Mo Vaughn	.45
25	Bernie Williams	.45
26	Fred McGriff	.30
27	Jeff Bagwell	1.00
28	Dante Bichette	.40
29	Barry Bonds	.75
30	Ellis Burks	.25
31	Ken Caminiti	.25
32	Vinny Castilla	.25
33	Andres Galarraga	.40
34	Vladimir Guerrero	.75
35	Todd Helton	.60
36	Todd Hundley	.25
37	Andruw Jones	.75
38	Chipper Jones	2.00
39	Eric Karros	.25
40	Ryan Klesko	.35
41	Ray Lankford	.25
42	Mark McGwire	3.50
43	Raul Mondesi	.30
44	Mike Piazza	2.00
45	Scott Rolen	.90
46	Gary Sheffield	.40
47	Sammy Sosa	1.50
48	Larry Walker	.50
49	Matt Williams	.40
50	WILDCARD	.25

1998 Pinnacle Plus

Pinnacle Plus consists of a 200-card base set. Five subsets are included: Field of Vision, Naturals, All-Stars, Devil Rays and Diamondbacks. Artist's Proof is a 60-card partial parallel of the base set, inserted 1:35 packs. Gold Artist's Proof cards are numbered to 100 and Mirror Artist's Proofs are 1-of-1 inserts. Inserts include Lasting Memories, Yardwork, A Piece of the Game, All-Star Epix, Team Pinnacle, Gold Team Pinnacle, Pinnabilia and Certified Souvenir.

		MT
Complete Set (200):		25.00
Common Player:		.10
Nolan Ryan Auto. Baseball (1,000)		85.00
1	Roberto Alomar (All-star)	.50
2	Sandy Alomar Jr. (All-star)	.15
3	Brady Anderson (All-star)	.10
4	Albert Belle (All-star)	.75
5	Jeff Cirillo (All-star)	.10
6	Roger Clemens (All-star)	1.00
7	David Cone (All-star)	.20
8	Nomar Garciaparra (All-star)	2.00
9	Ken Griffey Jr. (All-star)	3.00
10	Jason Dickson (All-star)	.10
11	Edgar Martinez (All-star)	.10
12	Tino Martinez (All-star)	.25
13	Randy Johnson (All-star)	.50
14	Mark McGwire (All-star)	3.00
15	David Justice (All-star)	.25
16	Mike Mussina (All-star)	.50
17	Chuck Knoblauch (All-star)	.30
18	Joey Cora (All-star)	.10
19	Pat Hentgen (All-star)	.10
20	Randy Myers (All-star)	.10
21	Cal Ripken Jr. (All-star)	2.50
22	Mariano Rivera (All-star)	.20
23	Jose Rosado (All-star)	.10
24	Frank Thomas (All-star)	1.00
25	Alex Rodriguez (All-star)	2.50
26	Justin Thompson (All-star)	.10
27	Ivan Rodriguez (All-star)	.75
28	Bernie Williams (All-star)	.40
29	Pedro Martinez	.50
30	Tony Clark	.40
31	Garret Anderson	.10
32	Travis Fryman	.10
33	Mike Piazza	2.00
33s	Mike Piazza ("SAMPLE" overprint on back)	3.00
34	Carl Pavano	.10
35	*Kevin Millwood*	2.50
36	Miguel Tejada	.25
37	Willie Blair	.10
38	Devon White	.10
39	Andres Galarraga	.30
40	Barry Larkin	.20
41	Al Leiter	.15
42	Moises Alou	.20
43	Eric Young	.10
44	John Jaha	.10
45	Bernard Gilkey	.10
46	Freddy Garcia	.10
47	Ruben Rivera	.10
48	Robb Nen	.10
49	Ray Lankford	.10
50	Kenny Lofton	.60
51	Joe Carter	.10

52	Jason McDonald	.10
53	Quinton McCracken	.10
54	Kerry Wood	.75
55	Mike Lansing	.10
56	Chipper Jones	2.00
57	Barry Bonds	.75
58	Brad Fullmer	.25
59	Jeff Bagwell	1.00
60	Rondell White	.20
61	Geronimo Berroa	.10
62	*Magglio Ordonez*	1.00
63	Dwight Gooden	.10
64	Brian Hunter	.10
65	Todd Walker	.20
66	*Frank Catalanotto*	.20
67	Tony Saunders	.10
68	Travis Lee	.75
69	Michael Tucker	.10
70	Reggie Sanders	.10
71	Derrek Lee	.10
72	Larry Walker	.25
72s	Larry Walker ("SAMPLE" overprint on back)	2.50
73	Marquis Grissom	.10
74	Craig Biggio	.20
75	Kevin Brown	.20
76	J.T. Snow	.10
77	Eric Davis	.10
78	Jeff Abbott	.10
79	Jermaine Dye	.10
80	Otis Nixon	.10
81	Curt Schilling	.20
82	Enrique Wilson	.10
83	Tony Gwynn	1.50
84	Orlando Cabrera	.10
85	Ramon Martinez	.10
86	Greg Vaughn	.20
87	Alan Benes	.10
88	Dennis Eckersley	.10
89	Jim Thome	.40
90	Juan Encarnacion	.25
91	Jeff King	.10
92	Shannon Stewart	.10
93	Roberto Hernandez	.10
94	Raul Ibanez	.10
95	Darryl Kile	.10
96	Charles Johnson	.10
97	Rich Becker	.10
98	Hal Morris	.10
99	Ismael Valdes	.10
100	Orel Hershiser	.10
101	Mo Vaughn	.60
102	Aaron Boone	.10
103	Jeff Conine	.10
104	Paul O'Neill	.25
105	Tom Candiotti	.10
106	Wilson Alvarez	.10
107	Mike Stanley	.10
108	Carlos Delgado	.40
109	Tony Batista	.10
110	Dante Bichette	.25
111	Henry Rodriguez	.10
112	Karim Garcia	.15
113	Shane Reynolds	.10
114	Ken Caminiti	.20
115	Jose Silva	.10
116	Juan Gonzalez	.75
117	Brian Jordan	.10
118	Jim Leyritz	.10
119	Manny Ramirez	1.00
120	Fred McGriff	.20
121	Brooks Kieschnick	.10
122	Sean Casey	.25
123	John Smoltz	.20
124	Rusty Greer	.10
125	Cecil Fielder	.10
126	Mike Cameron	.20
127	Reggie Jefferson	.10
128	Bobby Higginson	.10
129	Kevin Appier	.10
130	Robin Ventura	.15
131	Ben Grieve	1.00
132	Wade Boggs	.40
133	Jose Cruz Jr.	.15
134	Jeff Suppan	.10
135	Vinny Castilla	.20
136	Sammy Sosa	2.00
137	Mark Wohlers	.10
138	Jay Bell	.10
139	Brett Tomko	.10
140	Gary Sheffield	.25
141	Tim Salmon	.25
142	Jaret Wright	.75
143	Kenny Rogers	.10
144	Brian Anderson	.10
145	Darrin Fletcher	.10
146	John Flaherty	.10
147	Dmitri Young	.10
148	Andruw Jones	.75
149	Matt Williams	.25
150	Bobby Bonilla	.10
151	Mike Hampton	.10
152	Al Martin	.10
153	Mark Grudzielanek	.10
154	Dave Nilsson	.10
155	Roger Cedeno	.10
156	Greg Maddux	2.00
157	Mark Kotsay	.40
158	Steve Finley	.10
159	Wilson Delgado	.10
160	Ron Gant	.10
161	Jim Edmonds	.10
162	Jeff Blauser	.10
163	Dave Burba	.10
164	Pedro Astacio	.10
165	Livan Hernandez	.10
166	Neifi Perez	.10
167	Ryan Klesko	.15
168	Fernando Tatis	.10
169	Richard Hidalgo	.10
170	Carlos Perez	.10
171	Bob Abreu	.10
172	Francisco Cordova	.10
173	Todd Helton	.75
174	Doug Glanville	.10
175	Brian Rose	.10
176	Yamil Benitez	.10
177	Darin Erstad	.75
178	Scott Rolen	.75
179	John Wetteland	.10
180	Paul Sorrento	.10
181	Walt Weiss	.10
182	Vladimir Guerrero	1.00
183	Ken Griffey Jr. (The Naturals)	1.50
184	Alex Rodriguez (The Naturals)	1.25
185	Cal Ripken Jr. (The Naturals)	1.25
186	Frank Thomas (The Naturals)	.50
187	Chipper Jones (The Naturals)	.75
188	Hideo Nomo (The Naturals)	.30
189	Nomar Garciaparra (The Naturals)	1.00
190	Mike Piazza (The Naturals)	1.00
191	Greg Maddux (The Naturals)	1.00
192	Tony Gwynn (The Naturals)	.75
193	Mark McGwire (The Naturals)	1.50
194	Roger Clemens (The Naturals)	.50
195	Mike Piazza (Field of Vision)	1.00
196	Mark McGwire (Field of Vision)	1.50
197	Chipper Jones (Field of Vision)	.75
198	Larry Walker (Field of Vision)	.20
199	Hideo Nomo (Field of Vision)	.30
200	Barry Bonds (Field of Vision)	.40

1998 Pinnacle Plus Artist's Proofs

Artist's Proofs is a 60-card partial parallel of the Pinnacle Plus base set. The dot matrix hologram cards were inserted 1:35. Gold Artist's Proofs added a gold finish and are sequentially numbered to 100. Mirror Artist's Proofs are a "1-of-1" insert.

		MT
Complete Set (60):		550.00
Common Player:		2.50
Inserted 1:35		
Golds:		25-40X
Production 100 sets		
1	Roberto Alomar (All-Star)	12.00
2	Albert Belle (All-Star)	15.00
3	Roger Clemens (All-Star)	25.00
4	Nomar Garciaparra (All-Star)	40.00
5	Ken Griffey Jr. (All-Star)	60.00
6	Tino Martinez (All-Star)	6.00
7	Randy Johnson (All-Star)	10.00
8	Mark McGwire (All-Star)	60.00
9	David Justice (All-Star)	4.00
10	Chuck Knoblauch (All-Star)	5.00
11	Cal Ripken Jr. (All-Star)	50.00
12	Frank Thomas (All-Star)	35.00
13	Alex Rodriguez (All-Star)	50.00
14	Ivan Rodriguez (All-Star)	15.00
15	Bernie Williams (All-Star)	10.00
16	Pedro Martinez	10.00
17	Tony Clark	10.00
18	Mike Piazza	40.00
19	Miguel Tejada	5.00
20	Andres Galarraga	5.00
21	Barry Larkin	3.50
22	Kenny Lofton	10.00
23	Chipper Jones	40.00
24	Barry Bonds	15.00
25	Brad Fullmer	4.00
26	Jeff Bagwell	20.00
27	Todd Walker	4.00
28	Travis Lee	12.00
29	Larry Walker	5.00
30	Craig Biggio	3.50
31	Tony Gwynn	30.00
32	Jim Thome	4.00
33	Juan Encarnacion	4.00
34	Mo Vaughn	10.00
35	Karim Garcia	4.00
36	Ken Caminiti	4.00
37	Juan Gonzalez	25.00
38	Manny Ramirez	15.00
39	Fred McGriff	4.00
40	Rusty Greer	2.50
41	Bobby Higginson	2.50
42	Ben Grieve	12.00
43	Wade Boggs	5.00
44	Jose Cruz Jr.	3.00
45	Sammy Sosa	40.00
46	Gary Sheffield	4.00
47	Tim Salmon	3.50
48	Jaret Wright	12.00
49	Andruw Jones	15.00
50	Matt Williams	4.00
51	Greg Maddux	35.00
52	Jim Edmonds	2.50
53	Livan Hernandez	2.50
54	Neifi Perez	2.50
55	Fernando Tatis	3.00
56	Richard Hidalgo	2.50
57	Todd Helton	12.00
58	Darin Erstad	15.00
59	Scott Rolen	15.00
60	Vladimir Guerrero	18.00

1998 Pinnacle Plus All-Star Epix

The All-Star Epix insert is part of the cross-brand Epix set. This 12-card set honors the All-Star Game achievements of baseball's stars on cards with dot matrix holograms. All-Star Epix was seeded 1:21.

		MT
Complete Set (12):		175.00
Common Player:		4.00
Purples:		1.5X
Emeralds:		2.5X
Overall Odds 1:21		
13	Alex Rodriguez	30.00
14	Cal Ripken Jr.	30.00
15	Chipper Jones	20.00
16	Roger Clemens	15.00
17	Mo Vaughn	6.00
18	Mark McGwire	40.00
19	Mike Piazza	20.00
20	Andruw Jones	12.00
21	Greg Maddux	15.00
22	Barry Bonds	10.00
23	Paul Molitor	9.00
24	Hideo Nomo	4.00

1998 Pinnacle Plus A Piece of the Game

Inserted 1:17 hoby packs (1:19 retail), this 10-card insert features baseball's top players on micro-etched foil cards.

		MT
Complete Set (10):		75.00
Common Player:		3.00
Inserted 1:19		
1	Ken Griffey Jr.	15.00
2	Frank Thomas	6.00
3	Alex Rodriguez	10.00
4	Chipper Jones	8.00
5	Cal Ripken Jr.	10.00
6	Mike Piazza	8.00
7	Greg Maddux	7.50
8	Juan Gonzalez	4.00
9	Nomar Garciaparra	8.00
10	Larry Walker	3.00

1998 Pinnacle Plus Lasting Memories

Lasting Memories is a 30-card insert seeded 1:5. Printed on foil board, the cards feature a player photo with a sky background.

		MT
Complete Set (30):		40.00
Common Player:		.50
Inserted 1:5		
1	Nomar Garciaparra	3.00
2	Ken Griffey Jr.	4.00
3	Livan Hernandez	.50
4	Hideo Nomo	.75
5	Ben Grieve	.50
6	Scott Rolen	1.00
7	Roger Clemens	2.00
8	Cal Ripken Jr.	4.00
9	Mo Vaughn	.75
10	Frank Thomas	1.50
11	Mark McGwire	5.00
12	Barry Larkin	.75
13	Matt Williams	.50
14	Jose Cruz Jr.	.50
15	Andruw Jones	1.00
16	Mike Piazza	3.00
17	Jeff Bagwell	1.25
18	Chipper Jones	2.50
19	Juan Gonzalez	1.25
20	Kenny Lofton	.75
21	Greg Maddux	2.50
22	Ivan Rodriguez	1.25
23	Alex Rodriguez	4.00
24	Derek Jeter	4.00
25	Albert Belle	.75
26	Barry Bonds	1.25
27	Larry Walker	.75
28	Sammy Sosa	3.00
29	Tony Gwynn	1.50
30	Randy Johnson	1.25

1998 Pinnacle Plus Team Pinnacle

Team Pinnacle is a 15-card, double-sided insert. Printed on mirror-mylar, the cards were inserted 1:71. The hobby-only Gold Team Pinnacle parallel was inserted 1:199 packs.

		MT
Complete Set (15):		300.00
Common Player:		10.00
Inserted 1:71		
Golds:		1.5-2X
Inserted 1:199		
1	Mike Piazza, Ivan Rodriguez	30.00
2	Mark McGwire, Mo Vaughn	60.00
3	Roberto Alomar, Craig Biggio	10.00
4	Alex Rodriguez, Barry Larkin	40.00
5	Cal Ripken Jr., Chipper Jones	40.00
6	Ken Griffey Jr., Larry Walker	60.00
7	Juan Gonzalez, Tony Gwynn	25.00
8	Albert Belle, Barry Bonds	12.00
9	Kenny Lofton, Andruw Jones	12.00
10	Tino Martinez, Jeff Bagwell	15.00
11	Frank Thomas, Andres Galarraga	20.00
12	Roger Clemens, Greg Maddux	30.00
13	Pedro Martinez, Hideo Nomo	10.00
14	Nomar Garciaparra, Scott Rolen	30.00
15	Ben Grieve, Paul Konerko	15.00

1998 Pinnacle Plus Yardwork

Yardwork is a 15-card insert seeded one per 19 packs. It features the top home run hitters in Major League Baseball.

		MT
Complete Set (15):		20.00
Common Player:		.50
Inserted 1:9		
1	Mo Vaughn	.75
2	Frank Thomas	1.50
3	Albert Belle	.75
4	Nomar Garciaparra	3.00
5	Tony Clark	.50
6	Tino Martinez	.50
7	Ken Griffey Jr.	4.00
8	Juan Gonzalez	1.25
9	Sammy Sosa	3.00
10	Jose Cruz Jr.	.50
11	Jeff Bagwell	1.25
12	Mike Piazza	3.00
13	Larry Walker	.75
14	Mark McGwire	5.00
15	Barry Bonds	1.25

1998 Pinnacle Snapshots

One of Pinnacle's last issues was a team-oriented presentation of large-format (4" x 6") cards called Snapshots. Like their namesake, the focus on this issue is on candid photos rather than posed portraits or game-action pictures. The cards are printed on thin high-gloss cardboard stock resembling photo paper. Fronts, many of them horizontally formatted, are borderless and have no graphic enhancement. Backs are lightly printed with Pinnacle and licensor logos and a card number expressed "x of 18". The player's name is nowhere to be found.

MT

(See individual teams for checklists and values.)

1998 Pinnacle Snapshots Angels

		MT
Complete Set (18):		6.00
Common Player:		.25
1	Jason Dickson	.35
2	Gary DiSarcina	.25
3	Garret Anderson	.35
4	Shigetosi Hasegawa	.35
5	Ken Hill	.25
6	Todd Greene	.35
7	Tim Salmon	.50
8	Jim Edmonds	.50
9	Garret Anderson	.35
10	Dave Hollins	.25
11	Todd Greene	.35
12	Troy Percival	.25
13	Gary DiSarcina	.25
14	Cecil Fielder	.35
15	Darin Erstad	1.00
16	Chuck Finley	.35
17	Jim Edmonds	.50
18	Jason Dickson	.35

1998 Pinnacle Snapshots Braves

		MT
Complete Set (18):		10.00
Common Player:		.25
1	Ryan Klesko	.45
2	Walt Weiss	.25
3	Tom Glavine	.50
4	Randall Simon	.25
5	John Smoltz	.50
6	Chipper Jones	2.00
7	Javier Lopez	.75
8	Greg Maddux	2.00
9	Andruw Jones	1.50
10	Michael Tucker	.25
11	Andres Galarraga	.45
12	Andres Galarraga	.45
13	Greg Maddux	2.00
14	Wes Helms	.50
15	Bruce Chen	.35
16	Denny Neagle	.25
17	Mark Wohlers	.25
18	Kevin Millwood	1.00

1998 Pinnacle Snapshots Devil Rays

		MT
Complete Set (18):		6.00
Common Player:		.25
1	Kevin Stocker	.25
2	Paul Sorrento	.25
3	John Flaherty	.25
4	Wade Boggs	1.50
5	Rich Butler	.25
6	Wilson Alvarez	.25
7	Bubba Trammell	.50
8	David Martinez	.25
9	Brooks Kieschnick	.25
10	Tony Saunders	.25
11	Esteban Yan	.25
12	Quinton McCracken	.25
13	Albie Lopez	.25
14	Roberto Hernandez	.35
15	Fred McGriff	.75
16	Bubba Trammell	.50
17	Brooks Kieschnick	.25
18	Fred McGriff	.75

1998 Pinnacle Snapshots Diamondbacks

		MT
Complete Set (18):		6.50
Common Player:		.25
1	Travis Lee	1.00
2	Matt Williams	.75
3	Jay Bell	.45
4	Devon White	.35
5	Andy Benes	.35
6	Tony Batista	.25
7	Jay Bell	.45
8	Edwin Diaz	.25
9	Devon White	.35
10	Bob Wolcott	.25
11	Karim Garcia	.75
12	Yamil Benitez	.25
13	Jorge Fabregas	.25
14	Jeff Suppan	.25
15	Ben Ford	.25
16	Brian Anderson	.50
17	Travis Lee	1.00
18	Matt Williams	.75

1998 Pinnacle Snapshots Cardinals

		MT
Complete Set (18):		9.00
Common Player:		.25
1	Alan Benes	.35
2	Ron Gant	.45
3	Donovan Osborne	.25
4	Eli Marrero	.25
5	Mark McGwire	3.00
6	Delino DeShields	.25
7	Tom Pagnozzi	.25
8	Delino DeShields	.25

		MT
9	Mark McGwire	3.00
10	Royce Clayton	.25
11	Brian Jordan	.50
12	Ray Lankford	.50
13	Brian Jordan	.50
14	Matt Morris	.35
15	John Mabry	.25
16	Luis Ordaz	.25
17	Ron Gant	.50
18	Todd Stottlemyre	.25

1998 Pinnacle Snapshots Cubs

		MT
Complete Set (18):		9.00
Common Player:		.25
1	Mark Grace	1.00
2	Manny Alexander	.25
3	Jeremi Gonzalez	.35
4	Brant Brown	.50
5	Mark Grace	1.00
6	Lance Johnson	.25
7	Mark Clark	.35
8	Kevin Foster	.25
9	Brant Brown	.50
10	Kevin Foster	.25
11	Kevin Tapani	.25
12	Sammy Sosa	2.50
13	Sammy Sosa	2.50
14	Pat Cline	.35
15	Kevin Orie	.25
16	Steve Trachsel	.35
17	Lance Johnson	.25
18	Robin Jennings	.25

1998 Pinnacle Snapshots Dodgers

		MT
Complete Set (18):		8.00
Common Player:		.25
1	Mike Piazza	2.00
2	Eric Karros	.45
3	Raul Mondesi	.60
4	Wilton Guerrero	.25
5	Darren Dreifort	.25
6	Roger Cedeno	.35
7	Todd Zeile	.25
8	Paul Konerko	.50
9	Todd Hollandsworth	.25
10	Ismael Valdes	.25
11	Hideo Nomo	.75
12	Ramon Martinez	.45
13	Chan Ho Park	.75
14	Eric Young	.35
15	Dennis Reyes	.25
16	Eric Karros	.45
17	Mike Piazza	2.00
18	Raul Mondesi	.60

1998 Pinnacle Snapshots Indians

		MT
Complete Set (18):		7.00
Common Player:		.25
1	Manny Ramirez	1.00
2	Travis Fryman	.35
3	Jaret Wright	1.00
4	Brian Giles	.45
5	Bartolo Colon	.45
6	Kenny Lofton	.75
7	David Justice	.75
8	Brian Giles	.45
9	Sandy Alomar Jr.	.50
10	Jose Mesa	.25
11	Jim Thome	.50
12	Sandy Alomar Jr.	.50
13	Omar Vizquel	.35
14	Geronimo Berroa	.25
15	John Smiley	.25
16	Chad Ogea	.25
17	Charles Nagy	.40
18	Enrique Wilson	.35

1998 Pinnacle Snapshots Mariners

		MT
Complete Set (18):		10.00
Common Player:		.25
1	Alex Rodriguez	2.00
2	Jay Buhner	.35
3	Russ Davis	.25
4	Joey Cora	.25
5	Joey Cora	.25
6	Jay Buhner	.35
7	Ken Griffey Jr.	3.00
8	Raul Ibanez	.45
9	Rich Amaral	.25
10	Shane Monahan	.25
11	Alex Rodriguez	2.00
12	Dan Wilson	.25
13	Bob Wells	.25
14	Randy Johnson	1.00
15	Randy Johnson	1.00
16	Jeff Fassero	.25
17	Ken Cloude	.25
18	Edgar Martinez	.25

1998 Pinnacle Snapshots Mets

		MT
Complete Set (18):		6.00
Common Player:		.25
1	Rey Ordonez	.75
2	Todd Hundley	.40
3	Preston Wilson	.40
4	Rich Becker	.25
5	Bernard Gilkey	.25
6	Rey Ordonez	.75
7	Butch Huskey	.35
8	Carlos Baerga	.25
9	Edgardo Alfonzo	.75
10	Bill Pulsipher	.25
11	John Franco	.25
12	Todd Pratt	.25
13	Brian McRae	.25
14	Bobby Jones	.25
15	John Olerud	.60
16	Todd Hundley	.40
17	Jay Payton	.25
18	Paul Wilson	.25

1998 Pinnacle Snapshots Orioles

		MT
Complete Set (18):		9.00
Common Player:		.25
1	Cal Ripken Jr.	2.50
2	Rocky Coppinger	.25
3	Eric Davis	.35
4	Chris Hoiles	.25
5	Mike Mussina	.75
6	Joe Carter	.75
7	Rafael Palmeiro	.75
8	B.J. Surhoff	.35
9	Jimmy Key	.25
10	Scott Erickson	.35
11	Armando Benitez	.25
12	Roberto Alomar	.75
13	Cal Ripken Jr.	2.50
14	Mike Bordick	.25
15	Roberto Alomar	.75
16	Jeffrey Hammonds	.25
17	Rafael Palmeiro	.75
18	Brady Anderson	.40

1998 Pinnacle Snapshots Rangers

		MT
Complete Set (18):		6.00
Common Player:		.25
1	Ivan Rodriguez	.75
2	Fernando Tatis	.45
3	Danny Patterson	.25
4	Will Clark	.50
5	Kevin Elster	.25
6	Rusty Greer	.25
7	Darren Oliver	.25
8	John Burkett	.25
9	Tom Goodwin	.25
10	Roberto Kelly	.25
11	Aaron Sele	.25
12	Rick Helling	.25
13	Mark McLemore	.25
14	Lee Stevens	.25
15	John Wetteland	.25
16	Will Clark	.50
17	Juan Gonzalez	1.50
18	Roger Pavlik	.25

1998 Pinnacle Snapshots Red Sox

		MT
Complete Set (18):		6.50
Common Player:		.25
1	Tim Naehring	.25
2	Brian Rose	.25
3	Darren Bragg	.25
4	Pedro Martinez	.75
5	Mo Vaughn	.75
6	Jim Leyritz	.25
7	Troy O'Leary	.25
8	Mo Vaughn	.75
9	Nomar Garciaparra	2.00
10	Michael Coleman	.25
11	Tom Gordon	.25
12	Tim Naehring	.25
13	Nomar Garciaparra	2.00
14	John Valentin	.35
15	Steve Avery	.25
16	Damon Buford	.35
17	Troy O'Leary	.25
18	Bret Saberhagen	.35

1998 Pinnacle Snapshots Rockies

		MT
Complete Set (18):		6.00
Common Player:		.25
1	Larry Walker	.75
2	Pedro Astacio	.25
3	Jamey Wright	.25
4	Darryl Kile	.25
5	Kirt Manwaring	.25
6	Todd Helton	1.00
7	Mike Lansing	.25
8	Neifi Perez	.35
9	Dante Bichette	.75
10	Derrick Gibson	.50
11	Neifi Perez	.35
12	Darryl Kile	.25
13	Larry Walker	.75
14	Roger Bailey	.25
15	Ellis Burks	.35
16	Dante Bichette	.75
17	Derrick Gibson	.50
18	Ellis Burks	.35

1998 Pinnacle Snapshots Yankees

		MT
Complete Set (18):		10.00
Common Player:		.25
1	Andy Pettitte	.60
2	Darryl Strawberry	.40
3	Joe Girardi	.25
4	Derek Jeter	2.00
5	Andy Pettitte	.60
6	Tim Raines	.35
7	Mariano Rivera	.40
8	Tino Martinez	.35
9	Derek Jeter	2.00
10	Hideki Irabu	.75
11	Tino Martinez	.35
12	David Cone	.40
13	Bernie Williams	.50
14	David Cone	.40
15	Bernie Williams	.50
16	Chuck Knoblauch	.35
17	Paul O'Neill	.35
18	David Wells	.35

1988 Score Promo Cards

While these Score promotional sample cards carry a 1988 copyright date on back, they were actually released to hobby dealers late in 1987. They can be easily differentiated from regular-issue 1988 cards by the use of zeros in the stats lines on back for 1987 and career figures. Most of the promos are otherwise identical to the issued versions of the same players. These were among the first promo cards to be widely distributed within the hobby.

		MT
Complete Set (6):		30.00
Common Player:		5.00
30	Mark Langston	7.50
48	Tony Pena	5.00
71	Keith Moreland	5.00
72	Barry Larkin	10.00
121	Dennis Boyd	5.00
149	Denny Walling	5.00

1988 Score

A fifth member joined the group of nationally distributed baseball cards in 1988. Titled "Score," the cards are characterized by extremely sharp color photography and printing. Card backs are full-color also and carry a player portrait along with a brief biography, player data and statistics. The 660 cards in the set are standard 2-1/2" x 3-1/2" format. The fronts come with one of six different border colors which are equally divided at 110 cards per color. The Score set was produced by Major League Marketing, the same company that marketed the "triple-action" Sportflics card sets.

		MT
Complete Set (660):		15.00
Common Player:		.05
Plastic Pack (17):		.65
Plastic Wax Box (36):		11.50
1	Don Mattingly	.50
2	Wade Boggs	.25
3	Tim Raines	.10
4	Andre Dawson	.15
5	Mark McGwire	1.50
6	Kevin Seitzer	.05
7	Wally Joyner	.10
8	Jesse Barfield	.05
9	Pedro Guerrero	.05
10	Eric Davis	.10
11	George Brett	.35
12	Ozzie Smith	.25
13	Rickey Henderson	.20
14	Jim Rice	.10
15	*Matt Nokes*	.05
16	Mike Schmidt	.40
17	Dave Parker	.10
18	Eddie Murray	.20
19	Andres Galarraga	.10
20	Tony Fernandez	.05
21	Kevin McReynolds	.05
22	B.J. Surhoff	.10
23	Pat Tabler	.05
24	Kirby Puckett	.45
25	Benny Santiago	.05
26	Ryne Sandberg	.40
27	Kelly Downs	.05
28	Jose Cruz	.05
29	Pete O'Brien	.05
30	Mark Langston	.05
31	Lee Smith	.05
32	Juan Samuel	.05
33	Kevin Bass	.05
34	R.J. Reynolds	.05
35	Steve Sax	.05
36	John Kruk	.05
37	Alan Trammell	.10
38	Chris Bosio	.05
39	Brook Jacoby	.05
40	Willie McGee	.05
41	Dave Magadan	.05
42	Fred Lynn	.05
43	Kent Hrbek	.10
44	Brian Downing	.05
45	Jose Canseco	.25
46	Jim Presley	.05
47	Mike Stanley	.05
48	Tony Pena	.05
49	David Cone	.15
50	Rick Sutcliffe	.05
51	Doug Drabek	.05
52	Bill Doran	.05
53	Mike Scioscia	.05
54	Candy Maldonado	.05
55	Dave Winfield	.20
56	Lou Whitaker	.05
57	Tom Henke	.05
58	Ken Gerhart	.05
59	Glenn Braggs	.05
60	Julio Franco	.05
61	Charlie Leibrandt	.05
62	Gary Gaetti	.05
63	Bob Boone	.05
64	*Luis Polonia*	.10
65	Dwight Evans	.05
66	Phil Bradley	.05
67	Mike Boddicker	.05
68	Vince Coleman	.05
69	Howard Johnson	.05
70	Tim Wallach	.05
71	Keith Moreland	.05
72	Barry Larkin	.15
73	Alan Ashby	.10
74	Rick Rhoden	.05
75	Darrell Evans	.10
76	Dave Stieb	.05
77	Dan Plesac	.05
78	Will Clark	.25
79	Frank White	.05
80	Joe Carter	.10
81	Mike Witt	.05
82	Terry Steinbach	.05
83	Alvin Davis	.05
84	Tom Herr	.05
85	Vance Law	.05
86	Kal Daniels	.05
87	Rick Honeycutt	.05
88	Alfredo Griffin	.05
89	Bret Saberhagen	.10
90	Bert Blyleven	.05
91	Jeff Reardon	.05
92	Cory Snyder	.05
93	Greg Walker	.05
94	*Joe Magrane*	.10
95	Rob Deer	.05
96	Ray Knight	.05
97	Casey Candaele	.05
98	John Cerutti	.05
99	Buddy Bell	.05
100	Jack Clark	.05
101	Eric Bell	.05
102	Willie Wilson	.10
103	Dave Schmidt	.05
104	Dennis Eckersley	.10
105	Don Sutton	.15
106	Danny Tartabull	.05
107	Fred McGriff	.25
108	*Les Straker*	.05
109	Lloyd Moseby	.05
110	Roger Clemens	.35
111	Glenn Hubbard	.05
112	*Ken Williams*	.05
113	Ruben Sierra	.05
114	Stan Jefferson	.05
115	Milt Thompson	.05
116	Bobby Bonilla	.10
117	Wayne Tolleson	.05
118	Matt Williams	.20
119	Chet Lemon	.05
120	Dale Sveum	.05
121	Dennis Boyd	.05
122	Brett Butler	.05
123	Terry Kennedy	.05
124	Jack Howell	.05
125	Curt Young	.05
126a	Dale Valle (first name incorrect)	.25
126b	Dave Valle (correct spelling)	.05
127	Curt Wilkerson	.05
128	Tim Teufel	.05
129	Ozzie Virgil	.05
130	Brian Fisher	.05
131	Lance Parrish	.05
132	Tom Browning	.05
133a	Larry Anderson (incorrect spelling)	.25
133b	Larry Andersen (correct spelling)	.05
134a	Bob Brenley (incorrect spelling)	.25
134b	Bob Brenly (correct spelling)	.05
135	Mike Marshall	.05
136	Gerald Perry	.05
137	Bobby Meacham	.05
138	Larry Herndon	.05
139	*Fred Manrique*	.05
140	Charlie Hough	.05
141	Ron Darling	.05
142	Herm Winningham	.05
143	Mike Diaz	.05
144	*Mike Jackson*	.05
145	Denny Walling	.05
146	Rob Thompson	.05
147	Franklin Stubbs	.05
148	Albert Hall	.05
149	Bobby Witt	.05
150	Lance McCullers	.05
151	Scott Bradley	.05
152	Mark McLemore	.05
153	Tim Laudner	.05
154	Greg Swindell	.05
155	Marty Barrett	.05
156	Mike Heath	.05
157	Gary Ward	.05
158a	Lee Mazilli (incorrect spelling)	.25
158b	Lee Mazzilli (correct spelling)	.05
159	Tom Foley	.05
160	Robin Yount	.30
161	Steve Bedrosian	.05
162	Bob Walk	.05
163	Nick Esasky	.05
164	*Ken Caminiti*	.75
165	Jose Uribe	.05
166	Dave Anderson	.05
167	Ed Whitson	.05
168	Ernie Whitt	.05
169	Cecil Cooper	.05
170	Mike Pagliarulo	.05
171	Pat Sheridan	.05
172	Chris Bando	.05
173	Lee Lacy	.05
174	Steve Lombardozzi	.05
175	Mike Greenwell	.05
176	Greg Minton	.05
177	Moose Haas	.05
178	Mike Kingery	.05
179	Greg Harris	.05
180	Bo Jackson	.20
181	Carmelo Martinez	.05
182	Alex Trevino	.05
183	Ron Oester	.05
184	Danny Darwin	.05
185	Mike Krukow	.05
186	Rafael Palmeiro	.20
187	Tim Burke	.05
188	Roger McDowell	.05
189	Garry Templeton	.05
190	Terry Pendleton	.05
191	Larry Parrish	.05
192	Rey Quinones	.05
193	Joaquin Andujar	.05
194	Tom Brunansky	.05
195	Donnie Moore	.05
196	Dan Pasqua	.05
197	Jim Gantner	.05
198	Mark Eichhorn	.05
199	John Grubb	.05
200	*Bill Ripken*	.05
201	*Sam Horn*	.05
202	Todd Worrell	.05
203	Terry Leach	.05
204	Garth Iorg	.05
205	Brian Dayett	.05
206	Bo Diaz	.05
207	Craig Reynolds	.05
208	Brian Holton	.05
209	Marvelle Wynne (Marvell)	.05
210	Dave Concepcion	.05
211	Mike Davis	.05
212	Devon White	.10
213	Mickey Brantley	.05
214	Greg Gagne	.05
215	Oddibe McDowell	.05
216	Jimmy Key	.05
217	Dave Bergman	.05
218	Calvin Schiraldi	.05
219	Larry Sheets	.05
220	Mike Easler	.05
221	Kurt Stillwell	.05
222	*Chuck Jackson*	.05
223	Dave Martinez	.05
224	Tim Leary	.05
225	Steve Garvey	.15
226	Greg Mathews	.05
227	Doug Sisk	.05
228	Dave Henderson	.05
229	Jimmy Dwyer	.05
230	Larry Owen	.05
231	Andre Thornton	.05
232	Mark Salas	.05
233	Tom Brookens	.05
234	Greg Brock	.05
235	Rance Mulliniks	.05
236	Bob Brower	.05
237	Joe Niekro	.05
238	Scott Bankhead	.05
239	Doug DeCinces	.05
240	Tommy John	.10
241	Rich Gedman	.05
242	Ted Power	.05
243	*Dave Meads*	.05
244	Jim Sundberg	.05
245	Ken Oberkfell	.05
246	Jimmy Jones	.05
247	Ken Landreaux	.05
248	Jose Oquendo	.05
249	*John Mitchell*	.05
250	Don Baylor	.10
251	Scott Fletcher	.05
252	Al Newman	.05
253	Carney Lansford	.05
254	Johnny Ray	.05
255	Gary Pettis	.05
256	Ken Phelps	.05
257	Rick Leach	.05
258	Tim Stoddard	.05
259	Ed Romero	.05
260	Sid Bream	.05
261a	Tom Neidenfuer (incorrect spelling)	.25
261b	Tom Niedenfuer (correct spelling)	.05
262	Rick Dempsey	.05
263	Lonnie Smith	.05
264	Bob Forsch	.05
265	Barry Bonds	.50
266	Willie Randolph	.05
267	Mike Ramsey	.05
268	Don Slaught	.05
269	Mickey Tettleton	.05
270	Jerry Reuss	.05
271	Marc Sullivan	.05
272	Jim Morrison	.05
273	Steve Balboni	.05
274	Dick Schofield	.05
275	John Tudor	.05
276	*Gene Larkin*	.05
277	Harold Reynolds	.05
278	Jerry Browne	.05
279	Willie Upshaw	.05
280	Ted Higuera	.05
281	Terry McGriff	.05
282	Terry Puhl	.05
283	*Mark Wasinger*	.05
284	Luis Salazar	.05
285	Ted Simmons	.05
286	John Shelby	.05
287	*John Smiley*	.15
288	Curt Ford	.05
289	Steve Crawford	.05
290	Dan Quisenberry	.05
291	Alan Wiggins	.05
292	Randy Bush	.05
293	John Candelaria	.05
294	Tony Phillips	.05
295	Mike Morgan	.05
296	Bill Wegman	.05
297a	Terry Franconia (incorrect spelling)	.25
297b	Terry Francona (correct spelling)	.05
298	Mickey Hatcher	.05
299	Andres Thomas	.05
300	Bob Stanley	.05
301	*Alfredo Pedrique*	.05
302	Jim Lindeman	.05
303	Wally Backman	.05
304	Paul O'Neill	.15
305	Hubie Brooks	.05
306	Steve Buechele	.05
307	Bobby Thigpen	.05
308	George Hendrick	.05
309	John Moses	.05
310	Ron Guidry	.10
311	Bill Schroeder	.05
312	*Jose Nunez*	.05
313	Bud Black	.05
314	Joe Sambito	.05
315	Scott McGregor	.05
316	Rafael Santana	.05
317	Frank Williams	.05
318	Mike Fitzgerald	.05
319	Rick Mahler	.05
320	Jim Gott	.05
321	Mariano Duncan	.05
322	Jose Guzman	.05
323	Lee Guetterman	.05
324	Dan Gladden	.05
325	Gary Carter	.10
326	Tracy Jones	.05
327	Floyd Youmans	.05
328	Bill Dawley	.05
329	*Paul Noce*	.05
330	Angel Salazar	.05
331	Goose Gossage	.10
332	George Frazier	.05

333 Ruppert Jones .05
334 Billy Jo Robidoux .05
335 Mike Scott .05
336 Randy Myers .05
337 Bob Sebra .05
338 Eric Show .05
339 Mitch Williams .05
340 Paul Molitor .30
341 Gus Polidor .05
342 Steve Trout .05
343 Jerry Don Gleaton .05
344 Bob Knepper .05
345 Mitch Webster .05
346 John Morris .05
347 Andy Hawkins .05
348 Dave Leiper .05
349 Ernest Riles .05
350 Dwight Gooden .15
351 Dave Righetti .05
352 Pat Dodson .05
353 John Habyan .05
354 Jim Deshaies .05
355 Butch Wynegar .05
356 Bryn Smith .05
357 Matt Young .05
358 *Tom Pagnozzi* .05
359 Floyd Rayford .05
360 Darryl Strawberry .10
361 Sal Butera .05
362 Domingo Ramos .05
363 Chris Brown .05
364 Jose Gonzalez .05
365 Dave Smith .05
366 Andy McGaffigan .05
367 Stan Javier .05
368 Henry Cotto .05
369 Mike Birkbeck .05
370 Len Dykstra .05
371 Dave Collins .05
372 Spike Owen .05
373 Geno Petralli .05
374 Ron Karkovice .05
375 Shane Rawley .05
376 *DeWayne Buice* .05
377 *Bill Pecota* .05
378 Leon Durham .05
379 Ed Olwine .05
380 Bruce Hurst .05
381 Bob McClure .05
382 Mark Thurmond .05
383 Buddy Biancalana .05
384 Tim Conroy .05
385 Tony Gwynn .30
386 Greg Gross .05
387 *Barry Lyons* .05
388 Mike Felder .05
389 Pat Clements .05
390 Ken Griffey .10
391 Mark Davis .05
392 Jose Rijo .05
393 Mike Young .05
394 Willie Fraser .05
395 Dion James .05
396 *Steve Shields* .05
397 Randy St. Claire .05
398 Danny Jackson .05
399 Cecil Fielder .10
400 Keith Hernandez .05
401 Don Carman .05
402 *Chuck Crim* .05
403 Rob Woodward .05
404 Junior Ortiz .05
405 Glenn Wilson .05
406 Ken Howell .05
407 Jeff Kunkel .05
408 Jeff Reed .05
409 Chris James .05
410 Zane Smith .05
411 Ken Dixon .05
412 Ricky Horton .05
413 Frank DiPino .05
414 *Shane Mack* .10
415 Danny Cox .05
416 Andy Van Slyke .05
417 Danny Heep .05
418 John Cangelosi .05
419a John Christiansen (incorrect spelling) .25
419b John Christensen (correct spelling) .05
420 *Joey Cora* .10
421 Mike LaValliere .05
422 Kelly Gruber .05
423 Bruce Benedict .05
424 Len Matuszek .05
425 Kent Tekulve .05
426 Rafael Ramirez .05
427 Mike Flanagan .05
428 Mike Gallego .05
429 Juan Castillo .05
430 Neal Heaton .05
431 Phil Garner .05
432 *Mike Dunne* .05
433 Wallace Johnson .05
434 Jack O'Connor .05
435 Steve Jeltz .05
436 *Donnell Nixon* .05
437 Jack Lazorko .05
438 *Keith Comstock* .05
439 Jeff Robinson .05
440 Graig Nettles .10
441 Mel Hall .05
442 *Gerald Young* .05
443 Gary Redus .05
444 Charlie Moore .05
445 Bill Madlock .05
446 Mark Clear .05
447 Greg Booker .05
448 Rick Schu .05
449 Ron Kittle .05
450 Dale Murphy .10
451 Bob Dernier .05
452 Dale Mohorcic .05
453 Rafael Belliard .05
454 Charlie Puleo .05
455 Dwayne Murphy .05
456 Jim Eisenreich .05
457 David Palmer .05
458 Dave Stewart .10
459 Pascual Perez .05
460 Glenn Davis .05
461 Dan Petry .05
462 Jim Winn .05
463 Darrell Miller .05
464 Mike Moore .05
465 Mike LaCoss .05
466 Steve Farr .05
467 Jerry Mumphrey .05
468 Kevin Gross .05
469 Bruce Bochy .05
470 Orel Hershiser .10
471 Eric King .05
472 *Ellis Burks* .30
473 Darren Daulton .05
474 Mookie Wilson .05
475 Frank Viola .05
476 Ron Robinson .05
477 Bob Melvin .05
478 Jeff Musselman .05
479 Charlie Kerfeld .05
480 Richard Dotson .05
481 Kevin Mitchell .05
482 Gary Roenicke .05
483 Tim Flannery .05
484 Rich Yett .05
485 Pete Incaviglia .05
486 Rick Cerone .05
487 Tony Armas .05
488 Jerry Reed .05
489 Davey Lopes .05
490 Frank Tanana .05
491 Mike Loynd .05
492 Bruce Ruffin .05
493 Chris Speier .05
494 Tom Hume .05
495 Jesse Orosco .05
496 *Robby Wine, Jr.* .05
497 *Jeff Montgomery* .20
498 Jeff Dedmon .05
499 Luis Aguayo .05
500 Reggie Jackson (1968-75) .20
501 Reggie Jackson (1976) .20
502 Reggie Jackson (1977-81) .20
503 Reggie Jackson (1982-86) .20
504 Reggie Jackson (1987) .20
505 Billy Hatcher .05
506 Ed Lynch .05
507 Willie Hernandez .05
508 Jose DeLeon .05
509 Joel Youngblood .05
510 Bob Welch .05
511 Steve Ontiveros .05
512 Randy Ready .05
513 Juan Nieves .05
514 Jeff Russell .05
515 Von Hayes .05
516 Mark Gubicza .05
517 Ken Dayley .05
518 Don Aase .05
519 Rick Reuschel .05
520 *Mike Henneman* .15
521 Rick Aguilera .05
522 Jay Howell .05
523 Ed Correa .05
524 Manny Trillo .05
525 Kirk Gibson .05
526 *Wally Ritchie* .05
527 Al Nipper .05
528 Atlee Hammaker .05
529 Shawon Dunston .05
530 Jim Clancy .05
531 Tom Paciorek .05
532 Joel Skinner .05
533 Scott Garrelts .05
534 Tom O'Malley .05
535 John Franco .05
536 *Paul Kilgus* .05
537 Darrell Porter .05
538 Walt Terrell .05
539 *Bill Long* .05
540 George Bell .05
541 Jeff Sellers .05
542 *Joe Boever* .05
543 Steve Howe .05
544 Scott Sanderson .05
545 Jack Morris .10
546 *Todd Benzinger* .10
547 Steve Henderson .05
548 Eddie Milner .05
549 *Jeff Robinson* .05
550 Cal Ripken, Jr. .60
551 Jody Davis .05
552 Kirk McCaskill .05
553 Craig Lefferts .05
554 Darnell Coles .05
555 Phil Niekro .25
556 Mike Aldrete .05
557 Pat Perry .05
558 Juan Agosto .05
559 Rob Murphy .05
560 Dennis Rasmussen .05
561 Manny Lee .05
562 *Jeff Blauser* .10
563 Bob Ojeda .05
564 Dave Dravecky .05
565 Gene Garber .05
566 Ron Roenicke .05
567 *Tommy Hinzo* .05
568 *Eric Nolte* .05
569 Ed Hearn .05
570 *Mark Davidson* .05
571 *Jim Walewander* .05
572 Donnie Hill .05
573 Jamie Moyer .05
574 Ken Schrom .05
575 Nolan Ryan .60
576 Jim Acker .05
577 Jamie Quirk .05
578 *Jay Aldrich* .05
579 Claudell Washington .05
580 Jeff Leonard .05
581 Carmen Castillo .05
582 Daryl Boston .05
583 *Jeff DeWillis* .05
584 *John Marzano* .05
585 Bill Gullickson .05
586 Andy Allanson .05
587 Lee Tunnell .05
588 Gene Nelson .05
589 Dave LaPoint .05
590 Harold Baines .10
591 Bill Buckner .05
592 Carlton Fisk .15
593 Rick Manning .05
594 *Doug Jones* .10
595 Tom Candiotti .05
596 Steve Lake .05
597 *Jose Lind* .10
598 *Ross Jones* .05
599 Gary Matthews .05
600 Fernando Valenzuela .10
601 Dennis Martinez .10
602 *Les Lancaster* .10
603 Ozzie Guillen .05
604 Tony Bernazard .05
605 Chili Davis .10
606 Roy Smalley .05
607 Ivan Calderon .05
608 Jay Tibbs .05
609 Guy Hoffman .05
610 Doyle Alexander .05
611 Mike Bielecki .05
612 *Shawn Hillegas* .05
613 Keith Atherton .05
614 Eric Plunk .05
615 Sid Fernandez .05
616 Dennis Lamp .05
617 Dave Engle .05
618 Harry Spilman .05
619 Don Robinson .05
620 *John Farrell* .05
621 *Nelson Liriano* .05
622 Floyd Bannister .05
623 *Randy Milligan* .10
624 *Kevin Elster* .10
625 *Jody Reed* .15
626 *Shawn Abner* .05
627 *Kirt Manwaring* .10
628 *Pete Stanicek* .05
629 *Rob Ducey* .05
630 Steve Kiefer .05
631 *Gary Thurman* .05
632 *Darrel Akerfelds* .05
633 Dave Clark .05
634 *Roberto Kelly* .15
635 *Keith Hughes* .05
636 *John Davis* .05
637 *Mike Devereaux* .10
638 *Tom Glavine* .75
639 *Keith Miller* .05
640 *Chris Gwynn* .05
641 *Tim Crews* .05
642 *Mackey Sasser* .05
643 *Vicente Palacios* .05
644 Kevin Romine .05
645 *Gregg Jefferies* .25
646 *Jeff Treadway* .05
647 *Ron Gant* .25
648 Rookie Sluggers (Mark McGwire, Matt Nokes) .75
649 Speed and Power (Tim Raines, Eric Davis) .10
650 Game Breakers (Jack Clark, Don Mattingly) .20
651 Super Shortstops (Tony Fernandez, Cal Ripken, Jr., Alan Trammell) .25
652 Vince Coleman (Highlight) .05
653 Kirby Puckett (Highlight) .30
654 Benito Santiago (Highlight) .05
655 Juan Nieves (Highlight) .05
656 Steve Bedrosian (Highlight) .05
657 Mike Schmidt (Highlight) .20
658 Don Mattingly (Highlight) .30
659 Mark McGwire (Highlight) .75
660 Paul Molitor (Highlight) .15

1988 Score Glossy

With production of a reported 5,000 sets, there is a significant premium attached to the glossy version of Score's debut baseball card issue. The specially packaged collector's edition features cards with a high-gloss front finish and was sold only as a complete set.

	MT
Complete Set (660):	200.00
Common Player:	.50
Stars:	15X

(See 1988 Score for checklist and base card values.)

1988 Score Box Panels

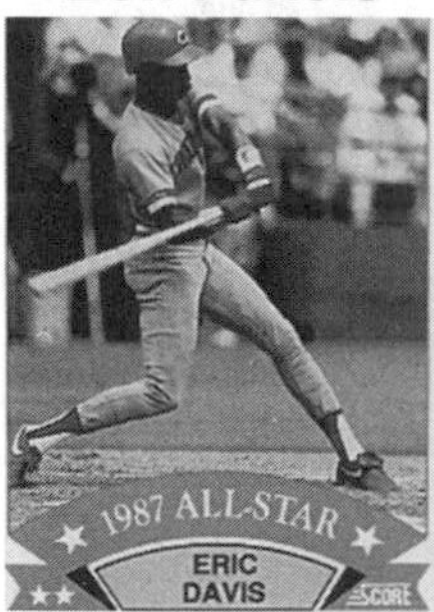

This 18-card set, produced by Major League Marketing and manufactured by Optigraphics, is the premiere box-bottom set issued under the Score trademark. The set features 1987 major league All-star players in full-color action poses, framed by a white border. A "1987 All-Star" banner (red or purple) curves above an orange player name block beneath the player photo. Card backs are printed in red, blue, gold and black and carry the card number, player name and position and league logo. Six colorful "Great Moments in Baseball" trivia cards are also included in this set.

		MT
Complete Panel Set:		8.00
Complete Singles Set (18):		3.00
Common Panel:		1.50
Common Single Player:		.15
Panel 1		1.50
1	Terry Kennedy	.15
3	Willie Randolph	.15
15	Eric Davis	.25
Panel 2		3.50
3	Don Mattingly	.75
5	Cal Ripken, Jr.	2.00
11	Jack Clark	.15
Panel 3		1.75
4	Wade Boggs	.60
9	Bret Saberhagen	.20
12	Ryne Sandberg	.60
Panel 4		1.75
6	George Bell	.15
13	Mike Schmidt	.65
18	Mike Scott	.15
Panel 5		1.75
7	Rickey Henderson	.50
16	Andre Dawson	.25
17	Darryl Strawberry	.20
	Panel 6	2.50
8	Dave Winfield	.40
10	Gary Carter	.20
14	Ozzie Smith	.50

1988 Score Traded/Rookie

This 110-card set featuring rookies and traded veterans is similar in design to the 1988 Score set, except for a change in border color. Individual standard-size player cards (2-1/2" x 3-1/2") feature a bright orange border framing action photos highlighted by a thin white outline. The player name (in white) is centered in the bottom margin, flanked by three yellow stars lower left and a yellow Score logo lower right. The backs carry full-color player portraits on a cream-colored background, plus team name and logo, personal information and a purple stats chart that lists year-by-year and major league totals. A brief player profile follows the stats chart and, on some cards, information is included about the player's trade or acquisition. The boxed update set also includes 10 Magic Motion 3-D trivia cards. The cards are numbered with a "T" suffix.

		MT
Complete Set (110):		40.00
Common Player:		.20
1	Jack Clark	.20
2	Danny Jackson	.20
3	Brett Butler	.20
4	Kurt Stillwell	.20
5	Tom Brunansky	.20
6	Dennis Lamp	.20
7	Jose DeLeon	.20
8	Tom Herr	.20
9	Keith Moreland	.20
10	Kirk Gibson	.25
11	Bud Black	.20
12	Rafael Ramirez	.20
13	Luis Salazar	.20
14	Goose Gossage	.25
15	Bob Welch	.20
16	Vance Law	.20
17	Ray Knight	.20
18	Dan Quisenberry	.20
19	Don Slaught	.20
20	Lee Smith	.25
21	Rick Cerone	.20
22	Pat Tabler	.20
23	Larry McWilliams	.20
24	Rick Horton	.20
25	Graig Nettles	.20
26	Dan Petry	.20
27	Jose Rijo	.20
28	Chili Davis	.25
29	Dickie Thon	.20
30	Mackey Sasser	.20
31	Mickey Tettleton	.20
32	Rick Dempsey	.20
33	Ron Hassey	.20
34	Phil Bradley	.20
35	Jay Howell	.20
36	Bill Buckner	.20
37	Alfredo Griffin	.20
38	Gary Pettis	.20
39	Calvin Schiraldi	.20
40	John Candelaria	.20
41	Joe Orsulak	.20
42	Willie Upshaw	.20
43	Herm Winningham	.20
44	Ron Kittle	.20
45	Bob Dernier	.20
46	Steve Balboni	.20
47	Steve Shields	.20
48	Henry Cotto	.20
49	Dave Henderson	.20
50	Dave Parker	.25
51	Mike Young	.20
52	Mark Salas	.20
53	Mike Davis	.20
54	Rafael Santana	.20
55	Don Baylor	.35
56	Dan Pasqua	.20
57	Ernest Riles	.20
58	Glenn Hubbard	.20
59	Mike Smithson	.20
60	Richard Dotson	.20
61	Jerry Reuss	.20
62	Mike Jackson	.20
63	Floyd Bannister	.20
64	Jesse Orosco	.20
65	Larry Parrish	.20
66	Jeff Bittiger	.20
67	Ray Hayward	.20
68	Ricky Jordan	.20
69	Tommy Gregg	.20
70	*Brady Anderson*	3.00
71	Jeff Montgomery	.25
72	Darryl Hamilton	1.00
73	Cecil Espy	.20
74	Greg Briley	.20
75	Joey Meyer	.20
76	Mike Macfarlane	.25
77	Oswald Peraza	.20
78	Jack Armstrong	.20
79	Don Heinkel	.20
80	*Mark Grace*	8.00
81	Steve Curry	.20
82	Damon Berryhill	.20
83	Steve Ellsworth	.20
84	Pete Smith	.20
85	*Jack McDowell*	.75
86	Rob Dibble	.25
87	Bryan Harvey	.25
88	John Dopson	.25
89	Dave Gallagher	.20
90	Todd Stottlemyre	2.00
91	Mike Schooler	.20
92	Don Gordon	.20
93	Sil Campusano	.20
94	Jeff Pico	.20
95	*Jay Buhner*	3.00
96	Nelson Santovenia	.20
97	Al Leiter	3.00
98	Luis Alicea	.25
99	Pat Borders	.50
100	Chris Sabo	.25
101	Tim Belcher	.25
102	Walt Weiss	1.00
103	*Craig Biggio*	10.00
104	Don August	.20
105	*Roberto Alomar*	20.00
106	Todd Burns	.20
107	John Costello	.20
108	Melido Perez	.25
109	Darrin Jackson	.50
110	Orestes Destrade	.20

1988 Score Traded/Rookie Glossy

Among the scarcest of the major card companies' high-gloss collector's editions of the late 1980s is the 1988 Score Rookie/Traded issue. Production of the regular-finish set was limited in itself and the glossy version is moreso, adding a significant premium value.

	MT
Complete Set (110):	250.00
Common Player:	.50
Stars:	3X

(See 1988 Score Traded/Rookie for checklist and base card values.)

1988 Score Young Superstar Series 1

This 40-card set of 2-1/2" x 3-1/2" cards is divided into five separate 8-card subsets. Similar to the company's regular issue, these cards are distinguished by excellent full-color photography on both front and back. The glossy player photos are centered on a white background and framed by a vivid blue and green border. A player name banner beneath the photo includes the name, position and uniform number. The card backs feature color player portraits beneath a hot pink player name/Score logo banner. Hot pink also frames the personal stats (in green), career stats (in black) and career biography (in blue). The backs also include quotes from well-known baseball authorities discussing player performance. This set was distributed via a write-in offer printed on 1988 Score 17-card package wrappers.

		MT
Complete Set (40):		7.00
Common Player:		.10
1	Mark McGwire	3.00
2	Benito Santiago	.10
3	Sam Horn	.10
4	Chris Bosio	.10
5	Matt Nokes	.10
6	Ken Williams	.10
7	Dion James	.10
8	B.J. Surhoff	.15
9	Joe Margrane	.10
10	Kevin Seitzer	.10
11	Stanley Jefferson	.10
12	Devon White	.30
13	Nelson Liriano	.10
14	Chris James	.10
15	Mike Henneman	.10
16	Terry Steinbach	.20
17	John Kruk	.10
18	Matt Williams	.75
19	Kelly Downs	.10
20	Bill Ripken	.10
21	Ozzie Guillen	.10
22	Luis Polonia	.10
23	Dave Magadan	.10
24	Mike Greenwell	.10
25	Will Clark	.75
26	Mike Dunne	.10

27 Wally Joyner .50
28 Robby Thompson .10
29 Ken Caminiti .25
30 Jose Canseco 1.00
31 Todd Benzinger .10
32 Pete Incaviglia .10
33 John Farrell .10
34 Casey Candaele .10
35 Mike Aldrete .10
36 Ruben Sierra .10
37 Ellis Burks .15
38 Tracy Jones .10
39 Kal Daniels .10
40 Cory Snyder .10

1988 Score Young Superstar Series 2

This set of 40 standard-size cards and five Magic trivia cards is part of a double series issued by Score. Each series is divided into five smaller sets of eight baseball cards and one trivia card. The design on both series is similar, except for border color. Series I has blue and green borders. Series II has red and blue borders framing full-color player photos. Backs carry color portrait photos and stats in a variety of colors. Young Superstar series were offered via a write-in offer on '88 Score wrappers. For each 8-card subset, collectors were instructed to send two Score wrappers and $1. Complete sets were offered by a number of hobby dealers nationwide.

MT
Complete Set (40): 7.00
Common Player: .10
1 Don Mattingly 1.50
2 Glenn Braggs .10
3 Dwight Gooden .15
4 Jose Lind .10
5 Danny Tartabull .10
6 Tony Fernandez .10
7 Julio Franco .10
8 Andres Galarraga .25
9 Bobby Bonilla .15
10 Eric Davis .15
11 Gerald Young .10
12 Barry Bonds 2.00
13 Jerry Browne .10
14 Jeff Blauser .10
15 Mickey Brantley .10
16 Floyd Youmans .10
17 Bret Saberhagen .25
18 Shawon Dunston .15
19 Len Dykstra .10
20 Darryl Strawberry .20
21 Rick Aguilera .10
22 Ivan Calderon .10
23 Roger Clemens 1.00
24 Vince Coleman .10
25 Gary Thurman .10
26 Jeff Treadway .10
27 Oddibe McDowell .10
28 Fred McGriff .50
29 Mark McLemore .10
30 Jeff Musselman .10
31 Mitch Williams .10
32 Dan Plesac .10
33 Juan Nieves .10
34 Barry Larkin .30
35 Greg Mathews .10
36 Shane Mack .10
37 Scott Bankhead .10
38 Eric Bell .10
39 Greg Swindell .10
40 Kevin Elster .10

1989 Score

This set of 660 cards plus 56 Magic Motion trivia cards is the second annual basic issue from Score. Full-color player photos highlight 651 individual players and 9 season highlights, including the first Wrigley Field night game. Action photos are framed by thin brightly colored borders (green, cyan blue, purple, orange, red, royal blue) with a baseball diamond logo/player name beneath the photo. Full-color player close-ups (1-5/16" x 1-5/8") are printed on the pastel-colored backs, along with personal information, stats and career highlights. The cards measure 2-1/2" x 3-1/2".

MT
Complete Set (660): 10.00
Common Player: .05
Plastic Pack
(16 - 2nd print): .75
Wax Box
(36 - 2nd print): 13.50
1 Jose Canseco .25
2 Andre Dawson .10
3 Mark McGwire 1.50
4 Benny Santiago .05
5 Rick Reuschel .05
6 Fred McGriff .20
7 Kal Daniels .05
8 Gary Gaetti .05
9 Ellis Burks .10
10 Darryl Strawberry .15
11 Julio Franco .05
12 Lloyd Moseby .05
13 *Jeff Pico* .05
14 Johnny Ray .05
15 Cal Ripken, Jr. .60
16 Dick Schofield .05
17 Mel Hall .05
18 Bill Ripken .05
19 Brook Jacoby .05
20 Kirby Puckett .35
21 Bill Doran .05
22 Pete O'Brien .05
23 Matt Nokes .05
24 Brian Fisher .05
25 Jack Clark .05
26 Gary Pettis .05
27 Dave Valle .05
28 Willie Wilson .05
29 Curt Young .05
30 Dale Murphy .10
31 Barry Larkin .15
32 Dave Stewart .10
33 Mike LaValliere .05
34 Glenn Hubbard .05
35 Ryne Sandberg .25
36 Tony Pena .05
37 Greg Walker .05
38 Von Hayes .05
39 Kevin Mitchell .05
40 Tim Raines .10
41 Keith Hernandez .05
42 Keith Moreland .05
43 Ruben Sierra .05
44 Chet Lemon .05
45 Willie Randolph .05
46 Andy Allanson .05
47 Candy Maldonado .05
48 Sid Bream .05
49 Denny Walling .05
50 Dave Winfield .15
51 Alvin Davis .05
52 Cory Snyder .05
53 Hubie Brooks .05
54 Chili Davis .05
55 Kevin Seitzer .05
56 Jose Uribe .05
57 Tony Fernandez .05
58 Tim Teufel .05
59 Oddibe McDowell .05
60 Les Lancaster .05
61 Billy Hatcher .05
62 Dan Gladden .05
63 Marty Barrett .05
64 Nick Esasky .05
65 Wally Joyner .10
66 Mike Greenwell .05
67 Ken Williams .05
68 Bob Horner .05
69 Steve Sax .05
70 Rickey Henderson .20
71 Mitch Webster .05
72 Rob Deer .05
73 Jim Presley .05
74 Albert Hall .05
75a George Brett
("At age 33 ...") 1.00
75b George Brett
("At age 35 ...") .30
76 Brian Downing .05
77 Dave Martinez .05
78 Scott Fletcher .05
79 Phil Bradley .05
80 Ozzie Smith .25
81 Larry Sheets .05
82 Mike Aldrete .05
83 Darnell Coles .05
84 Len Dykstra .05
85 Jim Rice .10
86 Jeff Treadway .05
87 Jose Lind .05
88 Willie McGee .05
89 Mickey Brantley .05
90 Tony Gwynn .40
91 R.J. Reynolds .05
92 Milt Thompson .05
93 Kevin McReynolds .05
94 Eddie Murray .25
95 Lance Parrish .05
96 Ron Kittle .05
97 Gerald Young .05
98 Ernie Whitt .05
99 Jeff Reed .05
100 Don Mattingly .40
101 Gerald Perry .05
102 Vance Law .05
103 John Shelby .05
104 *Chris Sabo* .15
105 Danny Tartabull .05
106 Glenn Wilson .05
107 Mark Davidson .05
108 Dave Parker .10
109 Eric Davis .10
110 Alan Trammell .10
111 Ozzie Virgil .05
112 Frank Tanana .05
113 Rafael Ramirez .05
114 Dennis Martinez .10
115 Jose DeLeon .05
116 Bob Ojeda .05
117 Doug Drabek .05
118 Andy Hawkins .05
119 Greg Maddux .50
120 Cecil Fielder
(reversed negative) .20
121 Mike Scioscia .05
122 Dan Petry .05
123 Terry Kennedy .05
124 Kelly Downs .05
125 Greg Gross .05
126 Fred Lynn .05
127 Barry Bonds .50
128 Harold Baines .10
129 Doyle Alexander .05
130 Kevin Elster .05
131 Mike Heath .05
132 Teddy Higuera .05
133 Charlie Leibrandt .05
134 Tim Laudner .05
135a Ray Knight
(photo reversed) .40
135b Ray Knight
(correct photo) .05
136 Howard Johnson .05
137 Terry Pendleton .05
138 Andy McGaffigan .05
139 Ken Oberkfell .05
140 Butch Wynegar .05
141 Rob Murphy .05
142 *Rich Renteria* .05
143 Jose Guzman .05
144 Andres Galarraga .15
145 Rick Horton .05
146 Frank DiPino .05
147 Glenn Braggs .05
148 John Kruk .05
149 Mike Schmidt .30
150 Lee Smith .05
151 Robin Yount .25
152 Mark Eichhorn .05
153 DeWayne Buice .05
154 B.J. Surhoff .05
155 Vince Coleman .05
156 Tony Phillips .05
157 Willie Fraser .05
158 Lance McCullers .05
159 Greg Gagne .05
160 Jesse Barfield .05
161 Mark Langston .05
162 Kurt Stillwell .05
163 Dion James .05
164 Glenn Davis .05
165 Walt Weiss .05
166 Dave Concepcion .05
167 Alfredo Griffin .05
168 *Don Heinkel* .05
169 Luis Rivera .05
170 Shane Rawley .05
171 Darrell Evans .10
172 Robby Thompson .05
173 Jody Davis .05
174 Andy Van Slyke .05
175 Wade Boggs .25
176 Garry Templeton .05
177 Gary Redus .05
178 Craig Lefferts .05
179 Carney Lansford .05
180 Ron Darling .05
181 Kirk McCaskill .05
182 Tony Armas .05
183 Steve Farr .05
184 Tom Brunansky .05
185 *Bryan Harvey* .10
186 Mike Marshall .05
187 Bo Diaz .05
188 Willie Upshaw .05
189 Mike Pagliarulo .05
190 Mike Krukow .05
191 Tommy Herr .05
192 Jim Pankovits .05
193 Dwight Evans .05
194 Kelly Gruber .05
195 Bobby Bonilla .10
196 Wallace Johnson .05
197 Dave Stieb .05
198 *Pat Borders* .25
199 Rafael Palmeiro .20
200 Dwight Gooden .10
201 Pete Incaviglia .05
202 Chris James .05
203 Marvell Wynne .05
204 Pat Sheridan .05

205	Don Baylor	.10
206	Paul O'Neill	.15
207	Pete Smith	.05
208	Mark McLemore	.05
209	Henry Cotto	.05
210	Kirk Gibson	.05
211	Claudell Washington	.05
212	Randy Bush	.05
213	Joe Carter	.10
214	Bill Buckner	.05
215	Bert Blyleven	.05
216	Brett Butler	.05
217	Lee Mazzilli	.05
218	Spike Owen	.05
219	Bill Swift	.05
220	Tim Wallach	.05
221	David Cone	.15
222	Don Carman	.05
223	Rich Gossage	.10
224	Bob Walk	.05
225	Dave Righetti	.05
226	Kevin Bass	.05
227	Kevin Gross	.05
228	Tim Burke	.05
229	Rick Mahler	.05
230	Lou Whitaker	.05
231	*Luis Alicea*	.10
232	Roberto Alomar	.30
233	Bob Boone	.05
234	Dickie Thon	.05
235	Shawon Dunston	.05
236	Pete Stanicek	.05
237	Craig Biggio	.50
238	Dennis Boyd	.05
239	Tom Candiotti	.05
240	Gary Carter	.10
241	Mike Stanley	.05
242	Ken Phelps	.05
243	Chris Bosio	.05
244	Les Straker	.05
245	Dave Smith	.05
246	John Candelaria	.05
247	Joe Orsulak	.05
248	Storm Davis	.05
249	Floyd Bannister	.05
250	Jack Morris	.05
251	Bret Saberhagen	.10
252	Tom Niedenfuer	.05
253	Neal Heaton	.05
254	Eric Show	.05
255	Juan Samuel	.05
256	Dale Sveum	.05
257	Jim Gott	.05
258	Scott Garrelts	.05
259	Larry McWilliams	.05
260	Steve Bedrosian	.05
261	Jack Howell	.05
262	Jay Tibbs	.05
263	Jamie Moyer	.05
264	Doug Sisk	.05
265	Todd Worrell	.05
266	John Farrell	.05
267	Dave Collins	.05
268	Sid Fernandez	.05
269	Tom Brookens	.05
270	Shane Mack	.05
271	Paul Kilgus	.05
272	Chuck Crim	.05
273	Bob Knepper	.05
274	Mike Moore	.05
275	Guillermo Hernandez	.05
276	Dennis Eckersley	.10
277	Graig Nettles	.05
278	Rich Dotson	.05
279	Larry Herndon	.05
280	Gene Larkin	.05
281	Roger McDowell	.05
282	Greg Swindell	.05
283	Juan Agosto	.05
284	Jeff Robinson	.05
285	Mike Dunne	.05
286	Greg Mathews	.05
287	Kent Tekulve	.05
288	Jerry Mumphrey	.05
289	Jack McDowell	.10
290	Frank Viola	.05
291	Mark Gubicza	.05
292	Dave Schmidt	.05
293	Mike Henneman	.05
294	Jimmy Jones	.05
295	Charlie Hough	.05
296	Rafael Santana	.05
297	Chris Speier	.05
298	Mike Witt	.05
299	Pascual Perez	.05
300	Nolan Ryan	.60
301	Mitch Williams	.05
302	Mookie Wilson	.05
303	Mackey Sasser	.05
304	John Cerutti	.05
305	Jeff Reardon	.05
306	Randy Myers	.05
307	Greg Brock	.05
308	Bob Welch	.05
309	Jeff Robinson	.05
310	Harold Reynolds	.05
311	Jim Walewander	.05
312	Dave Magadan	.05
313	Jim Gantner	.05
314	Walt Terrell	.05
315	Wally Backman	.05
316	Luis Salazar	.05
317	Rick Rhoden	.05
318	Tom Henke	.05
319	*Mike Macfarlane*	.15
320	Dan Plesac	.05
321	Calvin Schiraldi	.05
322	Stan Javier	.05
323	Devon White	.10
324	Scott Bradley	.05
325	Bruce Hurst	.05
326	Manny Lee	.05
327	Rick Aguilera	.05
328	Bruce Ruffin	.05
329	Ed Whitson	.05
330	Bo Jackson	.15
331	Ivan Calderon	.05
332	Mickey Hatcher	.05
333	Barry Jones	.05
334	Ron Hassey	.05
335	Bill Wegman	.05
336	Damon Berryhill	.05
337	Steve Ontiverso	.05
338	Dan Pasqua	.05
339	Bill Pecota	.05
340	Greg Cadaret	.05
341	Scott Bankhead	.05
342	Ron Guidry	.10
343	Danny Heep	.05
344	Bob Brower	.05
345	Rich Gedman	.05
346	*Nelson Santovenia*	.05
347	George Bell	.05
348	Ted Power	.05
349	Mark Grant	.05
350a	Roger Clemens (778 wins)	2.00
350b	Roger Clemens (78 wins)	.30
351	Bill Long	.05
352	Jay Bell	.05
353	Steve Balboni	.05
354	Bob Kipper	.05
355	Steve Jeltz	.05
356	Jesse Orosco	.05
357	Bob Dernier	.05
358	Mickey Tettleton	.05
359	Duane Ward	.05
360	Darrin Jackson	.05
361	Rey Quinones	.05
362	Mark Grace	.20
363	Steve Lake	.05
364	Pat Perry	.05
365	Terry Steinbach	.05
366	Alan Ashby	.10
367	Jeff Montgomery	.05
368	Steve Buechele	.05
369	Chris Brown	.05
370	Orel Hershiser	.10
371	Todd Benzinger	.05
372	Ron Gant	.15
373	Paul Assenmacher	.05
374	Joey Meyer	.05
375	Neil Allen	.05
376	Mike Davis	.05
377	Jeff Parrett	.05
378	Jay Howell	.05
379	Rafael Belliard	.05
380	Luis Polonia	.05
381	Keith Atherton	.05
382	Kent Hrbek	.10
383	Bob Stanley	.05
384	Dave LaPoint	.05
385	Rance Mulliniks	.05
386	Melido Perez	.05
387	Doug Jones	.05
388	Steve Lyons	.05
389	Alejandro Pena	.05
390	Frank White	.05
391	Pat Tabler	.05
392	Eric Plunk	.05
393	Mike Maddux	.05
394	Allan Anderson	.05
395	Bob Brenly	.05
396	Rick Cerone	.05
397	Scott Terry	.05
398	Mike Jackson	.05
399	Bobby Thigpen	.05
400	Don Sutton	.10
401	Cecil Espy	.05
402	Junior Ortiz	.05
403	Mike Smithson	.05
404	Bud Black	.05
405	Tom Foley	.05
406	Andres Thomas	.05
407	Rick Sutcliffe	.05
408	Brian Harper	.05
409	John Smiley	.05
410	Juan Nieves	.05
411	Shawn Abner	.05
412	Wes Gardner	.05
413	Darren Daulton	.05
414	Juan Berenguer	.05
415	Charles Hudson	.05
416	Rick Honeycutt	.05
417	Greg Booker	.05
418	Tim Belcher	.05
419	Don August	.05
420	Dale Mohorcic	.05
421	Steve Lombardozzi	.05
422	Atlee Hammaker	.05
423	Jerry Don Gleaton	.05
424	Scott Bailes	.05
425	Bruce Sutter	.05
426	Randy Ready	.05
427	Jerry Reed	.05
428	Bryn Smith	.05
429	Tim Leary	.05
430	Mark Clear	.05
431	Terry Leach	.05
432	John Moses	.05
433	Ozzie Guillen	.05
434	Gene Nelson	.05
435	Gary Ward	.05
436	Luis Aguayo	.05
437	Fernando Valenzuela	.05
438	Jeff Russell	.05
439	Cecilio Guante	.05
440	Don Robinson	.05
441	Rick Anderson	.05
442	Tom Glavine	.25
443	Daryl Boston	.05
444	Joe Price	.05
445	Stewart Cliburn	.05
446	Manny Trillo	.05
447	Joel Skinner	.05
448	Charlie Puleo	.05
449	Carlton Fisk	.10
450	Will Clark	.25
451	Otis Nixon	.05
452	Rick Schu	.05
453	Todd Stottlemyre	.10
454	Tim Birtsas	.05
455	*Dave Gallagher*	.05
456	Barry Lyons	.05
457	Fred Manrique	.05
458	Ernest Riles	.05
459	*Doug Jennings*	.05
460	Joe Magrane	.05
461	Jamie Quirk	.05
462	*Jack Armstrong*	.05
463	Bobby Witt	.05
464	Keith Miller	.05
465	*Todd Burns*	.05
466	*John Dopson*	.05
467	Rich Yett	.05
468	Craig Reynolds	.05
469	Dave Bergman	.05
470	Rex Hudler	.05
471	Eric King	.05
472	Joaquin Andujar	.05
473	*Sil Campusano*	.05
474	Terry Mulholland	.05
475	Mike Flanagan	.05
476	Greg Harris	.05
477	Tommy John	.10
478	Dave Anderson	.05
479	Fred Toliver	.05
480	Jimmy Key	.05
481	Donell Nixon	.05
482	Mark Portugal	.05
483	Tom Pagnozzi	.05
484	Jeff Kunkel	.05
485	Frank Williams	.05
486	Jody Reed	.05
487	Roberto Kelly	.05
488	Shawn Hillegas	.05
489	Jerry Reuss	.05
490	Mark Davis	.05
491	Jeff Sellers	.05
492	Zane Smith	.05
493	Al Newman	.05
494	Mike Young	.05
495	Larry Parrish	.05
496	Herm Winningham	.05
497	Carmen Castillo	.05
498	Joe Hesketh	.05
499	Darrell Miller	.05
500	Mike LaCoss	.05
501	Charlie Lea	.05
502	Bruce Benedict	.05
503	Chuck Finley	.05
504	Brad Wellman	.05
505	Tim Crews	.05
506	Ken Gerhart	.05
507a	Brian Holton (Born: 1/25/65, Denver)	.15
507b	Brian Holton (Born: 11/29/59, McKeesport)	.05
508	Dennis Lamp	.05
509	Bobby Meacham	.05
510	Tracy Jones	.05
511	Mike Fitzgerald	.05
512	*Jeff Bittiger*	.05
513	Tim Flannery	.05
514	Ray Hayward	.05
515	Dave Leiper	.05
516	Rod Scurry	.05
517	Carmelo Martinez	.05
518	Curtis Wilkerson	.05
519	Stan Jefferson	.05
520	Dan Quisenberry	.05
521	Lloyd McClendon	.05
522	Steve Trout	.05
523	Larry Andersen	.05
524	Don Aase	.05
525	Bob Forsch	.05
526	Geno Petralli	.05
527	Angel Salazar	.05
528	*Mike Schooler*	.05
529	Jose Oquendo	.05
530	Jay Buhner	.15
531	Tom Bolton	.05
532	Al Nipper	.05
533	Dave Henderson	.05
534	*John Costello*	.05
535	Donnie Moore	.05
536	Mike Laga	.05
537	Mike Gallego	.05
538	Jim Clancy	.05
539	Joel Youngblood	.05
540	Rick Leach	.05
541	Kevin Romine	.05
542	Mark Salas	.05
543	Greg Minton	.05
544	Dave Palmer	.05
545	Dwayne Murphy	.05
546	Jim Deshaies	.05
547	Don Gordon	.05
548	*Ricky Jordan*	.10
549	Mike Boddicker	.05
550	Mike Scott	.05
551	Jeff Ballard	.05
552a	Jose Rijo (uniform number #24 on card back)	.15
552b	Jose Rijo (uniform number #27 on card back)	.10
553	Danny Darwin	.05
554	Tom Browning	.05
555	Danny Jackson	.05
556	Rick Dempsey	.05
557	Jeffrey Leonard	.05
558	Jeff Musselman	.05
559	Ron Robinson	.05
560	John Tudor	.05
561	Don Slaught	.05
562	Dennis Rasmussen	.05
563	Brady Anderson	.15
564	Pedro Guerrero	.05
565	Paul Molitor	.25
566	*Terry Clark*	.05
567	Terry Puhl	.05
568	Mike Campbell	.05
569	Paul Mirabella	.05
570	Jeff Hamilton	.05
571	*Oswald Peraza*	.05
572	Bob McClure	.05
573	*Jose Bautista*	.10

574 Alex Trevino .05
575 John Franco .05
576 *Mark Parent* .05
577 Nelson Liriano .05
578 Steve Shields .05
579 Odell Jones .05
580 Al Leiter .10
581 Dave Stapleton .05
582 1988 World Series (Jose Canseco, Kirk Gibson, Orel Hershiser, Dave Stewart) .10
583 Donnie Hill .05
584 Chuck Jackson .05
585 Rene Gonzales .05
586 Tracy Woodson .05
587 Jim Adduci .05
588 Mario Soto .05
589 Jeff Blauser .05
590 Jim Traber .05
591 Jon Perlman .05
592 Mark Williamson .05
593 Dave Meads .05
594 Jim Eisenreich .05
595a *Paul Gibson* (player in background adjusting cup) .15
595b *Paul Gibson* (hand airbrushed away) .05
596 Mike Birkbeck .05
597 Terry Francona .05
598 Paul Zuvella .05
599 Franklin Stubbs .05
600 Gregg Jefferies .10
601 John Cangelosi .05
602 Mike Sharperson .05
603 Mike Diaz .05
604 *Gary Varsho* .05
605 *Terry Blocker* .05
606 Charlie O'Brien .05
607 Jim Eppard .05
608 John Davis .05
609 Ken Griffey, Sr. .10
610 Buddy Bell .05
611 Ted Simmons .05
612 Matt Williams .25
613 Danny Cox .05
614 Al Pedrique .05
615 Ron Oester .05
616 John Smoltz .15
617 Bob Melvin .05
618 *Rob Dibble* .15
619 Kirt Manwaring .05
620 Felix Fermin .05
621 *Doug Dascenzo* .05
622 *Bill Brennan* .05
623 *Carlos Quintana* .05
624 *Mike Harkey* .05
625 *Gary Sheffield* 1.00
626 *Tom Prince* .05
627 *Steve Searcy* .05
628 *Charlie Hayes* .25
629 *Felix Jose* .05
630 *Sandy Alomar* .75
631 *Derek Lilliquist* .05
632 Geronimo Berroa .05
633 *Luis Medina* .05
634 *Tom Gordon* .15
635 *Ramon Martinez* .50
636 *Craig Worthington* .05
637 Edgar Martinez .15
638 *Chad Krueter* .05
639 *Ron Jones* .05
640 *Van Snider* .05
641 *Lance Blankenship* .10
642 *Dwight Smith* .05
643 *Cameron Drew* .05
644 *Jerald Clark* .10
645 *Randy Johnson* 3.00
646 *Norm Charlton* .10
647 Todd Frohwirth .05
648 *Luis de los Santos* .05
649 *Tim Jones* .05
650 *Dave West* .10
651 *Bob Milacki* .10
652 1988 Highlight (Wrigley Field) .05
653 1988 Highlight (Orel Hershiser) .10
654a 1988 Highlight (Wade Boggs) ("...sixth consecutive seaason..." on back) 2.00
654b 1988 Highlight (Wade Boggs) ("season" corrected) .10
655 1988 Highlight (Jose Canseco) .15
656 1988 Highlight (Doug Jones) .05
657 1988 Highlight (Rickey Henderson) .10
658 1988 Highlight (Tom Browning) .05
659 1988 Highlight (Mike Greenwell) .05

1989 Score Traded

Score issued its second consecutive traded set in 1989 to supplement and update its regular set. The 110-card traded set features the same basic card design as the regular 1989 Score set. The set consists of rookies and traded players pictured with correct teams. The set was sold by hobby dealers in a special box that included an assortment of "Magic Motion" trivia cards. Cards are numbered with a "T" suffix.

		MT
Complete Set (110):		30.00
Common Player:		.06
1	Rafael Palmeiro	.50
2	Nolan Ryan	2.50
3	Jack Clark	.10
4	Dave LaPoint	.10
5	Mike Moore	.10
6	Pete O'Brien	.10
7	Jeffrey Leonard	.10
8	Rob Murphy	.10
9	Tom Herr	.10
10	Claudell Washington	.10
11	Mike Pagliarulo	.10
12	Steve Lake	.10
13	Spike Owen	.10
14	Andy Hawkins	.10
15	Todd Benzinger	.10
16	Mookie Wilson	.10
17	Bert Blyleven	.10
18	Jeff Treadway	.10
19	Bruce Hurst	.10
20	Steve Sax	.10
21	Juan Samuel	.10
22	Jesse Barfield	.10
23	Carmelo Castillo	.10
24	Terry Leach	.10
25	Mark Langston	.10
26	Eric King	.10
27	Steve Balboni	.10
28	Len Dykstra	.10
29	Keith Moreland	.10
30	Terry Kennedy	.10
31	Eddie Murray	.30
32	Mitch Williams	.10
33	Jeff Parrett	.10
34	Wally Backman	.10
35	Julio Franco	.10
36	Lance Parrish	.10
37	Nick Esasky	.10
38	Luis Polonia	.10
39	Kevin Gross	.10
40	John Dopson	.10
41	Willie Randolph	.10
42	Jim Clancy	.10
43	Tracy Jones	.10
44	Phil Bradley	.10
45	Milt Thompson	.10
46	Chris James	.10
47	Scott Fletcher	.10
48	Kal Daniels	.10
49	Steve Bedrosian	.10
50	Rickey Henderson	.40
51	Dion James	.10
52	Tim Leary	.10
53	Roger McDowell	.10
54	Mel Hall	.10
55	Dickie Thon	.10
56	Zane Smith	.10
57	Danny Heep	.10
58	Bob McClure	.10
59	Brian Holton	.10
60	Randy Ready	.10
61	Bob Melvin	.10
62	Harold Baines	.15
63	Lance McCullers	.10
64	Jody Davis	.10
65	Darrell Evans	.15
66	Joel Youngblood	.10
67	Frank Viola	.10
68	Mike Aldrete	.10
69	Greg Cadaret	.10
70	John Kruk	.10
71	Pat Sheridan	.10
72	Oddibe McDowell	.10
73	Tom Brookens	.10
74	Bob Boone	.10
75	Walt Terrell	.10
76	Joel Skinner	.10
77	Randy Johnson	4.00
78	Felix Fermin	.10
79	Rick Mahler	.10
80	Rich Dotson	.10
81	Cris Carpenter	.10
82	Bill Spiers	.10
83	Junior Felix	.10
84	Joe Girardi	.15
85	Jerome Walton	.10
86	Greg Litton	.10
87	Greg Harris	.10
88	Jim Abbott	.15
89	Kevin Brown	1.50
90	John Wetteland	.20
91	Gary Wayne	.10
92	Rich Monteleone	.10
93	Bob Geren	.10
94	Clay Parker	.10
95	Steve Finley	1.00
96	Gregg Olson	.10
97	Ken Patterson	.10
98	*Ken Hill*	.25
99	Scott Scudder	.10
100	*Ken Griffey, Jr.*	20.00
101	Jeff Brantley	.10
102	Donn Pall	.10
103	Carlos Martinez	.10
104	Joe Oliver	.10
105	Omar Vizquel	1.00
106	*Albert Belle*	4.00
107	Kenny Rogers	.20
108	Mark Carreon	.15
109	Rolando Roomes	.10
110	Pete Harnisch	.25

1989 Score Young Superstars Series 1

These standard-size cards (2-1/2" x 3-1/2") display color action photos with a high-gloss finish. Fronts feature a red and blue border surrounding the photo with the team logo in the lower right. A red band beneath the photo provides the setting for the player ID including name, position, and uniform number. Backs feature a red "Young Superstar" headline above a portrait photo. Above the headline appears the player's personal information and statistics in orange and black. To the right photo a condensed scouting report and career hightlights are revealed. The card number and related logos appear on the bottom portion. Five trivia cards featuring "A Year to Remember" accompanied the series. Each trivia card relates to a highlight from the past 56 years. This set was distributed via a write-in offer with Score card wrappers.

		MT
Complete Set (42):		5.00
Common Player:		.10
1	Gregg Jefferies	.25
2	Jody Reed	.10
3	Mark Grace	.50
4	Dave Gallagher	.10
5	Bo Jackson	.25
6	Jay Buhner	.15
7	Melido Perez	.10
8	Bobby Witt	.10
9	David Cone	.15
10	Chris Sabo	.10
11	Pat Borders	.10
12	Mark Grant	.10
13	Mike Macfarlane	.10
14	Mike Jackson	.10
15	Ricky Jordan	.10
16	Ron Gant	.30
17	Al Leiter	.15
18	Jeff Parrett	.10
19	Pete Smith	.10
20	Walt Weiss	.10
21	Doug Drabek	.10
22	Kirt Manwaring	.10
23	Keith Miller	.10
24	Damon Berryhill	.10
25	Gary Sheffield	.40
26	Brady Anderson	.15
27	Mitch Williams	.10
28	Roberto Alomar	.50
29	Bobby Thigpen	.10
30	Bryan Harvey	.10
31	Jose Rijo	.10
32	Dave West	.10
33	Joey Meyer	.10
34	Allan Anderson	.10
35	Rafael Palmeiro	.35
36	Tim Belcher	.10
37	John Smiley	.10
38	Mackey Sasser	.10
39	Greg Maddux	1.00
40	Ramon Martinez	.20
41	Randy Myers	.10
42	Scott Bankhead	.10

1989 Score Young Superstars Series 2

Score followed up with a second series of Young Superstars in 1989. The second series also included 42 cards and featured the same design as the first series. The set was also distributed via a write-in offer with Score card wrappers.

		MT
Complete Set (42):		6.00
Common Player:		.10
1	Sandy Alomar	.35
2	Tom Gordon	.10
3	Ron Jones	.10
4	Todd Burns	.10
5	Paul O'Neill	.20
6	Gene Larkin	.10
7	Eric King	.10
8	Jeff Robinson	.10
9	Bill Wegman	.10
10	Cecil Espy	.10
11	Jose Guzman	.10
12	Kelly Gruber	.10
13	Duane Ward	.10
14	Mark Gubicza	.10
15	Norm Charlton	.10
16	Jose Oquendo	.10
17	Geronimo Berroa	.10
18	Ken Griffey Jr.	5.00
19	Lance McCullers	.10
20	Todd Stottlemyre	.10
21	Craig Worthington	.10
22	Mike Devereaux	.10
23	Tom Glavine	.20
24	Dale Sveum	.10
25	Roberto Kelly	.10
26	Luis Medina	.10
27	Steve Searcy	.10
28	Don August	.10
29	Shawn Hillegas	.10
30	Mike Campbell	.10
31	Mike Harkey	.10
32	Randy Johnson	.45
33	Craig Biggio	.35
34	Mike Schooler	.10
35	Andres Thomas	.10
36	Jerome Walton	.10
37	Cris Carpenter	.10
38	Kevin Mitchell	.10
39	Eddie Williams	.10
40	Chad Kreuter	.10
41	Danny Jackson	.10
42	Kurt Stillwell	.10

1990 Score

The regular Score set increased to 704 cards in 1990. Included were a series of cards picturing first-round draft picks, an expanded subset of rookie cards, four World Series specials, five Highlight cards, and a 13-card "Dream Team" series featuring the game's top players pictured on old tobacco-style cards. For the first time in a Score set, team logos are displayed on the card fronts Card backs include a full-color portrait photo with player data. A one-paragraph write-up of each player was again provided by former Sports Illustrated editor Les Woodcock. The Score set was again distributed with "Magic Motion" trivia cards, this year using "Baseball's Most Valuable Players" as its theme.

		MT
Complete Set (704):		12.00
Common Player:		.05
Plastic Pack (16):		1.10
Plastic Wax Box (36):		22.50
1	Don Mattingly	.30
2	Cal Ripken, Jr.	.60
3	Dwight Evans	.05
4	Barry Bonds	.40
5	Kevin McReynolds	.05
6	Ozzie Guillen	.05
7	Terry Kennedy	.05
8	Bryan Harvey	.05
9	Alan Trammell	.10
10	Cory Snyder	.05
11	Jody Reed	.05
12	Roberto Alomar	.30
13	Pedro Guerrero	.05
14	Gary Redus	.05
15	Marty Barrett	.05
16	Ricky Jordan	.05
17	Joe Magrane	.05
18	Sid Fernandez	.05
19	Rich Dotson	.05
20	Jack Clark	.05
21	Bob Walk	.05
22	Ron Karkovice	.05
23	Lenny Harris	.05
24	Phil Bradley	.05
25	Andres Galarraga	.15
26	Brian Downing	.05
27	Dave Martinez	.05
28	Eric King	.05
29	Barry Lyons	.05
30	Dave Schmidt	.05
31	Mike Boddicker	.05
32	Tom Foley	.05
33	Brady Anderson	.10
34	Jim Presley	.05
35	Lance Parrish	.05
36	Von Hayes	.05
37	Lee Smith	.05
38	Herm Winningham	.05
39	Alejandro Pena	.05
40	Mike Scott	.05
41	Joe Orsulak	.05
42	Rafael Ramirez	.05
43	Gerald Young	.05
44	Dick Schofield	.05
45	Dave Smith	.05
46	Dave Magadan	.05
47	Dennis Martinez	.05
48	Greg Minton	.05
49	Milt Thompson	.05
50	Orel Hershiser	.10
51	Bip Roberts	.05
52	Jerry Browne	.05
53	Bob Ojeda	.05
54	Fernando Valenzuela	.05
55	Matt Nokes	.05
56	Brook Jacoby	.05
57	Frank Tanana	.05
58	Scott Fletcher	.05
59	Ron Oester	.05
60	Bob Boone	.05
61	Dan Gladden	.05
62	Darnell Coles	.05
63	Gregg Olson	.05
64	Todd Burns	.05
65	Todd Benzinger	.05
66	Dale Murphy	.15
67	Mike Flanagan	.05
68	Jose Oquendo	.05
69	Cecil Espy	.05
70	Chris Sabo	.05
71	Shane Rawley	.05
72	Tom Brunansky	.05
73	Vance Law	.05
74	B.J. Surhoff	.05
75	Lou Whitaker	.05
76	Ken Caminiti	.10
77	Nelson Liriano	.05
78	Tommy Gregg	.05
79	Don Slaught	.05
80	Eddie Murray	.20
81	Joe Boever	.05
82	Charlie Leibrandt	.05
83	Jose Lind	.05
84	Tony Phillips	.05
85	Mitch Webster	.05
86	Dan Plesac	.05
87	Rick Mahler	.05
88	Steve Lyons	.05
89	Tony Fernandez	.05
90	Ryne Sandberg	.30
91	Nick Esasky	.05
92	Luis Salazar	.05
93	Pete Incaviglia	.05
94	Ivan Calderon	.05
95	Jeff Treadway	.05
96	Kurt Stillwell	.05
97	Gary Sheffield	.25
98	Jeffrey Leonard	.05
99	Andres Thomas	.05
100	Roberto Kelly	.10
101	Alvaro Espinoza	.05
102	Greg Gagne	.05
103	John Farrell	.05
104	Willie Wilson	.05
105	Glenn Braggs	.05
106	Chet Lemon	.05
107	Jamie Moyer	.05
108	Chuck Crim	.05
109	Dave Valle	.05
110	Walt Weiss	.05
111	Larry Sheets	.05
112	Don Robinson	.05
113	Danny Heep	.05
114	Carmelo Martinez	.05
115	Dave Gallagher	.05
116	Mike LaValliere	.05
117	Bob McClure	.05
118	Rene Gonzales	.05
119	Mark Parent	.05
120	Wally Joyner	.10
121	Mark Gubicza	.05
122	Tony Pena	.05
123	Carmen Castillo	.05
124	Howard Johnson	.05
125	Steve Sax	.05
126	Tim Belcher	.05
127	Tim Burke	.05
128	Al Newman	.05
129	Dennis Rasmussen	.05
130	Doug Jones	.05
131	Fred Lynn	.05
132	Jeff Hamilton	.05
133	German Gonzalez	.05
134	John Morris	.05
135	Dave Parker	.10
136	Gary Pettis	.05
137	Dennis Boyd	.05
138	Candy Maldonado	.05
139	Rick Cerone	.05
140	George Brett	.30
141	Dave Clark	.05
142	Dickie Thon	.05
143	Junior Ortiz	.05
144	Don August	.05
145	Gary Gaetti	.05
146	Kirt Manwaring	.05
147	Jeff Reed	.05
148	Jose Alvarez	.05
149	Mike Schooler	.05
150	Mark Grace	.25
151	Geronimo Berroa	.05
152	Barry Jones	.05
153	Geno Petralli	.05
154	Jim Deshaies	.05
155	Barry Larkin	.15
156	Alfredo Griffin	.05
157	Tom Henke	.05
158	Mike Jeffcoat	.05
159	Bob Welch	.05
160	Julio Franco	.05
161	Henry Cotto	.05
162	Terry Steinbach	.05
163	Damon Berryhill	.05
164	Tim Crews	.05
165	Tom Browning	.05
166	Frd Manrique	.05
167	Harold Reynolds	.05
168a	Ron Hassey (uniform #27 on back)	.05
168b	Ron Hassey (uniform #24 on back)	.50
169	Shawon Dunston	.05
170	Bobby Bonilla	.10
171	Tom Herr	.05
172	Mike Heath	.05
173	Rich Gedman	.05
174	Bill Ripken	.05
175	Pete O'Brien	.05
176a	Lloyd McClendon (uniform number 1 on back)	1.00
176b	Lloyd McClendon (uniform number 10 on back)	.05
177	Brian Holton	.05
178	Jeff Blauser	.05
179	Jim Eisenreich	.05
180	Bert Blyleven	.05
181	Rob Murphy	.05
182	Bill Doran	.05
183	Curt Ford	.05
184	Mike Henneman	.05
185	Eric Davis	.10
186	Lance McCullers	.05
187	*Steve Davis*	.05
188	Bill Wegman	.05
189	Brian Harper	.05
190	Mike Moore	.05
191	Dale Mohorcic	.05
192	Tim Wallach	.05
193	Keith Hernandez	.05
194	Dave Righetti	.05
195a	Bret Saberhagen ("joke" on card back)	.25
195b	Bret Saberhagen ("joker" on card back)	.30
196	Paul Kilgus	.05
197	Bud Black	.05
198	Juan Samuel	.05
199	Kevin Seitzer	.05
200	Darryl Strawberry	.10
201	Dave Steib	.05
202	Charlie Hough	.05
203	Jack Morris	.05
204	Rance Mulliniks	.05
205	Alvin Davis	.05
206	Jack Howell	.05
207	Ken Patterson	.05
208	Terry Pendleton	.05
209	Craig Lefferts	.05
210	Kevin Brown	.05
211	Dan Petry	.05
212	Dave Leiper	.05
213	Daryl Boston	.05
214	Kevin Hickey	.05
215	Mike Krukow	.05
216	Terry Francona	.05
217	Kirk McCaskill	.05
218	Scott Bailes	.05
219	Bob Forsch	.05
220	Mike Aldrete	.05

No.	Player	Price
221	Steve Buechele	.05
222	Jesse Barfield	.05
223	Juan Berenguer	.05
224	Andy McGaffigan	.05
225	Pete Smith	.05
226	Mike Witt	.05
227	Jay Howell	.05
228	Scott Bradley	.05
229	*Jerome Walton*	.10
230	Greg Swindell	.05
231	Atlee Hammaker	.05
232a	Mike Devereaux (RF)	.05
232b	Mike Devereaux (CF)	.10
233	Ken Hill	.15
234	Craig Worthington	.05
235	Scott Terry	.05
236	Brett Butler	.05
237	Doyle Alexander	.05
238	Dave Anderson	.05
239	Bob Milacki	.05
240	Dwight Smith	.05
241	Otis Nixon	.05
242	Pat Tabler	.05
243	Derek Lilliquist	.05
244	Danny Tartabull	.05
245	Wade Boggs	.30
246	Scott Garrelts	.05
247	Spike Owen	.05
248	Norm Charlton	.05
249	Gerald Perry	.05
250	Nolan Ryan	.60
251	Kevin Gross	.05
252	Randy Milligan	.05
253	Mike LaCoss	.05
254	Dave Bergman	.05
255	Tony Gwynn	.30
256	Felix Fermin	.05
257	Greg Harris	.05
258	*Junior Felix*	.10
259	Mark Davis	.05
260	Vince Coleman	.05
261	Paul Gibson	.05
262	Mitch Williams	.05
263	Jeff Russell	.05
264	Omar Vizquel	.25
265	Andre Dawson	.15
266	Storm Davis	.05
267	Guillermo Hernandez	.05
268	Mike Felder	.05
269	Tom Candiotti	.05
270	Bruce Hurst	.05
271	Fred McGriff	.25
272	Glenn Davis	.05
273	John Franco	.05
274	Rich Yett	.05
275	Craig Biggio	.15
276	Gene Larkin	.05
277	Rob Dibble	.05
278	Randy Bush	.05
279	Kevin Bass	.05
280a	Bo Jackson ("Watham" on back)	.15
280b	Bo Jackson ("Wathan" on back)	1.00
281	Wally Backman	.05
282	Larry Andersen	.05
283	Chris Bosio	.05
284	Juan Agosto	.05
285	Ozzie Smith	.30
286	George Bell	.05
287	Rex Hudler	.05
288	Pat Borders	.05
289	Danny Jackson	.05
290	Carlton Fisk	.15
291	Tracy Jones	.05
292	Allan Anderson	.05
293	Johnny Ray	.05
294	Lee Guetterman	.05
295	Paul O'Neill	.15
296	Carney Lansford	.05
297	Tom Brookens	.05
298	Claudell Washington	.05
299	Hubie Brooks	.05
300	Will Clark	.25
301	*Kenny Rogers*	.20
302	Darrell Evans	.10
303	Greg Briley	.05
304	Donn Pall	.05
305	Teddy Higuera	.05
306	Dan Pasqua	.05
307	Dave Winfield	.25
308	Dennis Powell	.05
309	Jose DeLeon	.05
310	Roger Clemens	.40
311	Melido Perez	.05
312	Devon White	.10
313	Dwight Gooden	.10
314	*Carlos Martinez*	.10
315	Dennis Eckersley	.05
316	Clay Parker	.05
317	Rick Honeycutt	.05
318	Tim Laudner	.05
319	Joe Carter	.10
320	Robin Yount	.30
321	Felix Jose	.05
322	Mickey Tettleton	.05
323	Mike Gallego	.05
324	Edgar Martinez	.05
325	Dave Henderson	.05
326	Chili Davis	.05
327	Steve Balboni	.05
328	Jody Davis	.05
329	Shawn Hillegas	.05
330	Jim Abbott	.10
331	John Dopson	.05
332	Mark Williamson	.05
333	Jeff Robinson	.05
334	John Smiley	.05
335	Bobby Thigpen	.05
336	Garry Templeton	.05
337	Marvell Wynne	.05
338a	Ken Griffey, Sr. (uniform #25 on card back)	.25
338b	Ken Griffey, Sr. (uniform #30 on card back)	2.00
339	*Steve Finley*	.25
340	Ellis Burks	.10
341	Frank Williams	.05
342	Mike Morgan	.05
343	Kevin Mitchell	.05
344	Joel Youngblood	.05
345	Mike Greenwell	.05
346	Glenn Wilson	.05
347	John Costello	.05
348	Wes Gardner	.05
349	Jeff Ballard	.05
350	Mark Thurmond	.05
351	Randy Myers	.05
352	Shawn Abner	.05
353	Jesse Orosco	.05
354	Greg Walker	.05
355	Pete Harnisch	.10
356	Steve Farr	.05
357	Dave LaPoint	.05
358	Willie Fraser	.05
359	Mickey Hatcher	.05
360	Rickey Henderson	.25
361	Mike Fitzgerald	.05
362	Bill Schroeder	.05
363	Mark Carreon	.05
364	Ron Jones	.05
365	Jeff Montgomery	.05
366	Bill Krueger	.05
367	John Cangelosi	.05
368	Jose Gonzalez	.05
369	*Greg Hibbard*	.10
370	John Smoltz	.15
371	*Jeff Brantley*	.10
372	Frank White	.05
373	Ed Whitson	.05
374	Willie McGee	.05
375	Jose Canseco	.25
376	Randy Ready	.05
377	Don Aase	.05
378	Tony Armas	.05
379	Steve Bedrosian	.05
380	Chuck Finley	.05
381	Kent Hrbek	.10
382	Jim Gantner	.05
383	Mel Hall	.05
384	Mike Marshall	.05
385	Mark McGwire	1.00
386	Wayne Tolleson	.05
387	Brian Holton	.05
388	*John Wetteland*	.20
389	Darren Daulton	.05
390	Rob Deer	.05
391	John Moses	.05
392	Todd Worrell	.05
393	Chuck Cary	.05
394	Stan Javier	.05
395	Willie Randolph	.05
396	Bill Buckner	.05
397	Robby Thompson	.05
398	Mike Scioscia	.05
399	Lonnie Smith	.05
400	Kirby Puckett	.30
401	Mark Langston	.05
402	Danny Darwin	.05
403	Greg Maddux	.50
404	Lloyd Moseby	.05
405	Rafael Palmeiro	.20
406	Chad Kreuter	.05
407	Jimmy Key	.05
408	Tim Birtsas	.05
409	Tim Raines	.10
410	Dave Stewart	.10
411	*Eric Yelding*	.15
412	*Kent Anderson*	.05
413	Les Lancaster	.05
414	Rick Dempsey	.05
415	Randy Johnson	.25
416	Gary Carter	.10
417	Rolando Roomes	.05
418	Dan Schatzeder	.05
419	Bryn Smith	.05
420	Ruben Sierra	.05
421	Steve Jeltz	.05
422	Ken Oberkfell	.05
423	Sid Bream	.05
424	Jim Clancy	.05
425	Kelly Gruber	.05
426	Rick Leach	.05
427	Len Dykstra	.05
428	Jeff Pico	.05
429	John Cerutti	.05
430	David Cone	.15
431	Jeff Kunkel	.05
432	Luis Aquino	.05
433	Ernie Whitt	.05
434	Bo Diaz	.05
435	Steve Lake	.05
436	Pat Perry	.05
437	Mike Davis	.05
438	Cecilio Guante	.05
439	Duane Ward	.05
440	Andy Van Slyke	.05
441	Gene Nelson	.05
442	Luis Polonia	.05
443	Kevin Elster	.05
444	Keith Moreland	.05
445	Roger McDowell	.05
446	Ron Darling	.05
447	Ernest Riles	.05
448	Mookie Wilson	.05
449a	*Bill Spiers* (66 missing for year of birth)	1.00
449b	*Bill Spiers* (1966 for birth year)	.15
450	Rick Sutcliffe	.05
451	Nelson Santovenia	.05
452	Andy Allanson	.05
453	Bob Melvin	.05
454	Benny Santiago	.05
455	Jose Uribe	.05
456	Bill Landrum	.05
457	Bobby Witt	.05
458	Kevin Romine	.05
459	Lee Mazzilli	.05
460	Paul Molitor	.30
461	Ramon Martinez	.15
462	Frank DiPino	.05
463	Walt Terrell	.05
464	*Bob Geren*	.05
465	Rick Reuchel	.05
466	Mark Grant	.05
467	John Kruk	.05
468	Gregg Jefferies	.15
469	R.J. Reynolds	.05
470	Harold Baines	.05
471	Dennis Lamp	.05
472	Tom Gordon	.05
473	Terry Puhl	.05
474	Curtis Wilkerson	.05
475	Dan Quisenberry	.05
476	Oddibe McDowell	.05
477a	Zane Smith (Career ERA 3.93)	1.50
477b	Zane Smith	.05
478	Franklin Stubbs	.05
479	Wallace Johnson	.05
480	Jay Tibbs	.05
481	Tom Glavine	.15
482	Manny Lee	.05
483	Joe Hesketh	.05
484	Mike Bielecki	.05
485	Greg Brock	.05
486	Pascual Perez	.05
487	Kirk Gibson	.05
488	Scott Sanderson	.05
489	Domingo Ramos	.05
490	Kal Daniels	.05
491a	David Wells (reversed negative on back photo)	3.00
491b	David Wells (corrected)	.10
492	Jerry Reed	.05
493	Eric Show	.05
494	Mike Pagliarulo	.05
495	Ron Robinson	.05
496	Brad Komminsk	.05
497	*Greg Litton*	.05
498	Chris James	.05
499	Luis Quinones	.05
500	Frank Viola	.05
501	Tim Teufel	.05
502	Terry Leach	.05
503	Matt Williams	.25
504	Tim Leary	.05
505	Doug Drabek	.05
506	Mariano Duncan	.05
507	Charlie Hayes	.05
508	Albert Belle	.30
509	Pat Sheridan	.05
510	Mackey Sasser	.05
511	Jose Rijo	.05
512	Mike Smithson	.05
513	Gary Ward	.05
514	Dion James	.05
515	Jim Gott	.05
516	Drew Hall	.05
517	Doug Bair	.05
518	*Scott Scudder*	.10
519	Rick Aguilera	.05
520	Rafael Belliard	.05
521	Jay Buhner	.10
522	Jeff Reardon	.05
523	Steve Rosenberg	.05
524	Randy Velarde	.05
525	Jeff Musselman	.05
526	Bill Long	.05
527	*Gary Wayne*	.05
528	*Dave Johnson*	.05
529	Ron Kittle	.05
530	Erik Hanson	.05
531	Steve Wilson	.05
532	Joey Meyer	.05
533	Curt Young	.05
534	Kelly Downs	.05
535	Joe Girardi	.05
536	Lance Blankenship	.05
537	Greg Mathews	.05
538	Donell Nixon	.05
539	Mark Knudson	.05
540	*Jeff Wetherby*	.05
541	Darrin Jackson	.05
542	Terry Mulholland	.05
543	Eric Hetzel	.05
544	*Rick Reed*	.05
545	Dennis Cook	.05
546	Mike Jackson	.05
547	Brian Fisher	.05
548	*Gene Harris*	.05
549	Jeff King	.10
550	Dave Dravecky (Salute)	.10
551	Randy Kutcher	.05
552	Mark Portugal	.05
553	*Jim Corsi*	.05
554	Todd Stottlemyre	.05
555	Scott Bankhead	.05
556	Ken Dayley	.05
557	*Rick Wrona*	.15
558	*Sammy Sosa*	5.00
559	Keith Miller	.05
560	Ken Griffey, Jr.	1.00
561a	Ryne Sandberg (Highlight, 3B on front)	5.00
561b	Ryne Sandberg (Highlight, no position)	.25
562	Billy Hatcher	.05
563	Jay Bell	.05
564	*Jack Daugherty*	.05
565	*Rich Monteleone*	.05
566	Bo Jackson (All-Star MVP)	.25
567	*Tony Fossas*	.05
568	*Roy Smith*	.05
569	*Jaime Navarro*	.10
570	Lance Johnson	.05
571	*Mike Dyer*	.05
572	*Kevin Ritz*	.10
573	Dave West	.05
574	*Gary Mielke*	.05
575	Scott Lusader	.05

576 *Joe Oliver* .10
577 Sandy Alomar, Jr. .15
578 Andy Benes .15
579 Tim Jones .05
580 *Randy McCament* .05
581 Curt Schilling .10
582 *John Orton* .05
583a *Milt Cuyler* (998 games) 2.00
583b *Milt Cuyler* (98 games) .10
584 *Eric Anthony* .25
585 *Greg Vaughn* .30
586 Deion Sanders .20
587 Jose DeJesus .05
588 *Chip Hale* .10
589 *John Olerud* .50
590 *Steve Olin* .10
591 *Marquis Grissom* .40
592 *Moises Alou* .25
593 Mark Lemke .05
594 *Dean Palmer* .25
595 Robin Ventura .15
596 Tino Martinez .10
597 *Mike Huff* .05
598 *Scott Hemond* .10
599 *Wally Whitehurst* .10
600 *Todd Zeile* .15
601 Glenallen Hill .10
602 Hal Morris .10
603 Juan Bell .05
604 *Bobby Rose* .05
605 *Matt Merullo* .10
606 *Kevin Maas* .05
607 *Randy Nosek* .05
608a *Billy Bates* ("12 triples" mentioned in second-last line ine) .05
608b Billy Bates (triples not mentioned) .50
609 *Mike Stanton* .10
610 *Goose Gozzo* .10
611 *Charles Nagy* .40
612 *Scott Coolbaugh* .05
613 *Jose Vizcaino* .25
614 *Greg Smith* .05
615 *Jeff Huson* .10
616 *Mickey Weston* .05
617 *John Pawlowski* .05
618a *Joe Skalski* (uniform #27 on card back) .15
618b *Joe Skalski* (uniform #67 on card back) 2.00
619 *Bernie Williams* 1.50
620 *Shawn Holman* .05
621 *Gary Eave* .05
622 *Darrin Fletcher* .15
623 *Pat Combs* .10
624 *Mike Blowers* .10
625 Kevin Appier .05
626 *Pat Austin* .05
627 *Kelly Mann* .05
628 *Matt Kinzer* .05
629 *Chris Hammond* .15
630 *Dean Wilkins* .10
631 *Larry Walker* .50
632 *Blaine Beatty* .10
633a Tom Barrett (uniform #29 on card back) .10
633b Tom Barrett (uniform #14 on card back) 2.00
634 *Stan Belinda* .10
635 *Tex Smith* .05
636 *Hensley Meulens* .10
637 *Juan Gonzalez* 1.00
638 *Lenny Webster* .10
639 *Mark Gardner* .10
640 *Tommy Greene* .15
641 *Mike Hartley* .05
642 *Phil Stephenson* .05
643 *Kevin Mmahat* .10
644 *Ed Whited* .05
645 *Delino DeShields* .25
646 Kevin Blankenship .10
647 *Paul Sorrento* .15
648 *Mike Roesler* .10
649 *Jason Grimsley* .10
650 *Dave Justice* .75
651 *Scott Cooper* .10
652 Dave Eiland .05
653 *Mike Munoz* .05
654 *Jeff Fischer* .05
655 *Terry Jorgenson* .05
656 *George Canale* .05
657 *Brian DuBois* .05
658 Carlos Quintana .05
659 Luis de los Santos .05
660 Jerald Clark .05
661 *Donald Harris* (1st Round Pick) .10
662 *Paul Coleman* (1st Round Pick) .20
663 *Frank Thomas* (1st Round Pick) 3.00
664 *Brent Mayne* (1st Round Pick) .10
665 *Eddie Zosky* (1st Round Pick) .10
666 *Steve Hosey* (1st Round Pick) .15
667 *Scott Bryant* (1st Round Pick) .10
668 *Tom Goodwin* (1st Round Pick) .10
669 *Cal Eldred* (1st Round Pick) .25
670 *Earl Cunningham* (1st Round Pick) .10
671 *Alan Zinter* (1st Round Pick) .15
672 *Chuck Knoblauch* (1st Round Pick) .50
672 (a)Chuck Knoblauch (3,000 autographed cards with a special hologram on back were inserted into 1992 rack packs) 50.00
673 *Kyle Abbott* (1st Round Pick) .10
674 *Roger Salkeld* (1st Round Pick) .15
675 *Mo Vaughn* (1st Round Pick) .75
676 *Kiki Jones* (1st Round Pick) .10
677 *Tyler Houston* (1st Round Pick) .10
678 *Jeff Jackson* (1st Round Pick) .10
679 *Greg Gohr* (1st Round Pick) .10
680 *Ben McDonald* (1st Round Pick) .25
681 *Greg Blosser* (1st Round Pick) .15
682 *Willie Green* (Greene) 1st Round Pick) .15
683 Wade Boggs (Dream Team) .15
684 Will Clark (Dream Team) .20
685 Tony Gwynn (Dream Team) .25
686 Rickey Henderson (Dream Team) .15
687 Bo Jackson (Dream Team) .15
688 Mark Langston (Dream Team) .10
689 Barry Larkin (Dream Team) .15
690 Kirby Puckett (Dream Team) .25
691 Ryne Sandberg (Dream Team) .25
692 Mike Scott (Dream Team) .10
693 Terry Steinbach (Dream Team) .10
694 Bobby Thigpen (Dream Team) .05
695 Mitch Williams (Dream Team) .10
696 Nolan Ryan (Highlight) .50
697 Bo Jackson (FB/BB) .40
698 Rickey Henderson (ALCS MVP) .15
699 Will Clark (NLCS MVP) .15
700 World Series Games 1-2 .10
701 Lights Out: Candlestick .15
702 World Series Game 3 .10
703 World Series Wrap-up .20
704 Wade Boggs (Highlight) .10

1990 Score Rookie Dream Team

This 10-card "Rookie Dream Team" set, in the same format as those found in the regular-issue 1990 Score, was available only in factory sets for the hobby trade. Factory sets for general retail outlets did not include these cards, nor were they available in Score packs. Cards carry a "B" prefix to their numbers.

		MT
Complete Set (10):		4.00
Common Player:		.25
1	A. Bartlett Giamatti	.25
2	Pat Combs	.25
3	Todd Zeile	.30
4	Luis de los Santos	.25
5	Mark Lemke	.25
6	Robin Ventura	1.50
7	Jeff Huson	.25
8	Greg Vaughn	.40
9	Marquis Grissom	1.50
10	Eric Anthony	.25

1990 Score Traded

This 110-card set features players with new teams as well as 1990 Major League rookies. The cards feature full-color action photos framed in yellow with an orange border. The player's ID appears in green below the photo. The team logo is displayed next to the player's name. The card backs feature posed player photos and follow the style of the regular 1990 Score issue. The cards are numbered 1T-110T. Young hockey phenom Eric Lindros is featured trying out for the Toronto Blue Jays.

		MT
Complete Set (110):		5.00
Common Player:		.05
1	Dave Winfield	.25
2	Kevin Bass	.05
3	Nick Esasky	.05
4	Mitch Webster	.05
5	Pascual Perez	.05
6	Gary Pettis	.05
7	Tony Pena	.05
8	Candy Maldonado	.05
9	Cecil Fielder	.10
10	Carmelo Martinez	.05
11	Mark Langston	.05
12	Dave Parker	.15
13	Don Slaught	.05
14	Tony Phillips	.05
15	John Franco	.05
16	Randy Myers	.05
17	Jeff Reardon	.05
18	Sandy Alomar, Jr.	.25
19	Joe Carter	.15
20	Fred Lynn	.05
21	Storm Davis	.05
22	Craig Lefferts	.05
23	Pete O'Brien	.05
24	Dennis Boyd	.05
25	Lloyd Moseby	.05
26	Mark Davis	.05
27	Tim Leary	.05
28	Gerald Perry	.05
29	Don Aase	.05
30	Ernie Whitt	.05
31	Dale Murphy	.25
32	Alejandro Pena	.05
33	Juan Samuel	.05
34	Hubie Brooks	.05
35	Gary Carter	.10
36	Jim Presley	.05
37	Wally Backman	.05
38	Matt Nokes	.05
39	Dan Petry	.05
40	Franklin Stubbs	.05
41	Jeff Huson	.05
42	Billy Hatcher	.05
43	Terry Leach	.05
44	Phil Bradley	.05
45	Claudell Washington	.05
46	Luis Polonia	.05
47	Daryl Boston	.05
48	Lee Smith	.05
49	Tom Brunansky	.05
50	Mike Witt	.05
51	Willie Randolph	.05
52	Stan Javier	.05
53	Brad Komminsk	.05
54	John Candelaria	.05
55	Bryn Smith	.05
56	Glenn Braggs	.05
57	Keith Hernandez	.05
58	Ken Oberkfell	.05
59	Steve Jeltz	.05
60	Chris James	.05
61	Scott Sanderson	.05
62	Bill Long	.05
63	Rick Cerone	.05
64	Scott Bailes	.05
65	Larry Sheets	.05
66	Junior Ortiz	.05
67	Francisco Cabrera	.05
68	Gary DiSarcina	.10
69	Greg Olson	.05
70	Beau Allred	.05
71	Oscar Azocar	.05
72	Kent Mercker	.10
73	John Burkett	.10

74	*Carlos Baerga*	.35
75	Dave Hollins	.35
76	*Todd Hundley*	.75
77	Rick Parker	.05
78	Steve Cummings	.05
79	Bill Sampen	.05
80	Jerry Kutzler	.05
81	Derek Bell	.30
82	Kevin Tapani	.20
83	Jim Leyritz	.10
84	*Ray Lankford*	.75
85	Wayne Edwards	.05
86	Frank Thomas	3.00
87	Tim Naehring	.05
88	Willie Blair	.10
89	Alan Mills	.10
90	Scott Radinsky	.10
91	Howard Farmer	.05
92	Julio Machado	.05
93	Rafael Valdez	.05
94	Shawn Boskie	.10
95	David Segui	.20
96	Chris Hoiles	.10
97	D.J. Dozier	.05
98	Hector Villanueva	.05
99	Eric Gunderson	.05
100	*Eric Lindros*	1.50
101	Dave Otto	.05
102	Dana Kiecker	.05
103	Tim Drummond	.05
104	Mickey Pina	.05
105	Craig Grebeck	.10
106	*Bernard Gilkey*	.40
107	Tim Layana	.05
108	Scott Chiamparino	.05
109	Steve Avery	.05
110	Terry Shumpert	.05

1990 Score Young Superstars Set 1

For the third consecutive year, Score produced Young Superstars boxed sets. The 1990 versions contain 42 player cards plus five Magic-Motion trivia cards. The cards are similar to previous Young Superstar sets, with action photography on the front and a glossy finish. Card backs have a color portrait, major league statistics and scouting reports. Besides the boxed set, cards from Set I were inserted into rack packs.

		MT
Complete Set (42):		5.00
Common Player:		.15
1	Bo Jackson	.25
2	Dwight Smith	.15
3	Joey Belle	.50
4	Gregg Olson	.15
5	Jim Abbott	.25
6	Felix Fermin	.15
7	Brian Holman	.15
8	Clay Parker	.15
9	Junior Felix	.15
10	Joe Oliver	.15
11	Steve Finley	.15
12	Greg Briley	.15
13	Greg Vaughn	.20
14	Bill Spiers	.15
15	Eric Yelding	.15
16	Jose Gonzalez	.15
17	Mark Carreon	.15
18	Greg Harris	.15
19	Felix Jose	.15
20	Bob Milacki	.15
21	Kenny Rogers	.15
22	Rolando Roomes	.15
23	Bip Roberts	.15
24	Jeff Brantley	.15
25	Jeff Ballard	.15
26	John Dopson	.15
27	Ken Patterson	.15
28	Omar Vizquel	.25
29	Kevin Brown	.15
30	Derek Lilliquist	.15
31	David Wells	.25
32	Ken Hill	.15
33	Greg Litton	.15
34	Rob Ducey	.15
35	Carlos Martinez	.15
36	John Smoltz	.45
37	Lenny Harris	.15
38	Charlie Hayes	.15
39	Tommy Gregg	.15
40	John Wetteland	.15
41	Jeff Huson	.15
42	Eric Anthony	.15

1990 Score Young Superstars Set 2

Available only as a boxed set via a mail-order offer, Set II of 1990 Score Young Superstars is identical in format to Set I, with the exception that the graphic elements on the front of Set II cards are in red and green, while in Set I they are in blue and magenta.

		MT
Complete Set (42):		25.00
Common Player:		.15
1	Todd Zeile	.25
2	Ben McDonald	.15
3	Delino DeShields	.20
4	Pat Combs	.15
5	John Olerud	.40
6	Marquis Grissom	.50
7	Mike Stanton	.15
8	Robin Ventura	.60
9	Larry Walker	.50
10	Dante Bichette	.50
11	Jack Armstrong	.15
12	Jay Bell	.15
13	Andy Benes	.25
14	Joey Cora	.15
15	Rob Dibble	.15
16	Jeff King	.15
17	Jeff Hamilton	.15
18	Erik Hanson	.15
19	Pete Harnisch	.15
20	Greg Hibbard	.15
21	Stan Javier	.15
22	Mark Lemke	.15
23	Steve Olin	.15
24	Tommy Greene	.15
25	Sammy Sosa	24.00
26	Gary Wayne	.15
27	Deion Sanders	.60
28	Steve Wilson	.15
29	Joe Girardi	.15
30	John Orton	.15
31	Kevin Tapani	.15
32	Carlos Baerga	.20
33	Glenallen Hill	.15
34	Mike Blowers	.15
35	Dave Hollins	.20
36	Lance Blankenship	.15
37	Hal Morris	.15
38	Lance Johnson	.15
39	Chris Gwynn	.15
40	Doug Dascenzo	.15
41	Jerald Clark	.15
42	Carlos Quintana	.15

1991 Score

Score introduced a two series format in 1991. The first series includes cards 1-441. Score cards once again feature multiple border colors within the set, several subsets (Master Blaster, K-Man, Highlights and Riflemen), full-color action photos on the front and portraits on the flip side. Score eliminated display of the player's uniform number on the 1991 cards. Black-and-white Dream Team cards, plus Prospects and #1 Draft Picks highlight the 1991 set. The second series was released in February of 1991.

		MT
Complete Set (893):		10.00
Common Player:		.05
Pack (16):		.40
Wax Box (36):		10.00
1	Jose Canseco	.35
2	Ken Griffey, Jr.	1.50
3	Ryne Sandberg	.25
4	Nolan Ryan	.75
5	Bo Jackson	.15
6	Bret Saberhagen	.10
7	Will Clark	.20
8	Ellis Burks	.10
9	Joe Carter	.10
10	Rickey Henderson	.25
11	Ozzie Guillen	.05
12	Wade Boggs	.25
13	Jerome Walton	.05
14	John Franco	.05
15	Ricky Jordan	.05
16	Wally Backman	.05
17	Rob Dibble	.05
18	Glenn Braggs	.05
19	Cory Snyder	.05
20	Kal Daniels	.05
21	Mark Langston	.05
22	Kevin Gross	.05
23	Don Mattingly	.30
24	Dave Righetti	.05
25	Roberto Alomar	.30
26	Robby Thompson	.05
27	Jack McDowell	.05
28	Bip Roberts	.05
29	Jay Howell	.05
30	Dave Steib	.05
31	Johnny Ray	.05
32	Steve Sax	.05
33	Terry Mulholland	.05
34	Lee Guetterman	.05
35	Tim Raines	.10
36	Scott Fletcher	.05
37	Lance Parrish	.05
38	Tony Phillips	.05
39	Todd Stottlemyre	.05
40	Alan Trammell	.10
41	Todd Burns	.05
42	Mookie Wilson	.05
43	Chris Bosio	.05
44	Jeffrey Leonard	.05
45	Doug Jones	.05
46	Mike Scott	.05
47	Andy Hawkins	.05
48	Harold Reynolds	.05
49	Paul Molitor	.20
50	John Farrell	.05
51	Danny Darwin	.05
52	Jeff Blauser	.05
53	John Tudor	.05
54	Milt Thompson	.05
55	Dave Justice	.30
56	*Greg Olson*	.05
57	*Willie Blair*	.10
58	*Rick Parker*	.10
59	*Shawn Boskie*	.15
60	Kevin Tapani	.05
61	Dave Hollins	.10
62	*Scott Radinsky*	.10
63	Francisco Cabrera	.05
64	*Tim Layana*	.10
65	*Jim Leyritz*	.15
66	Wayne Edwards	.05
67	Lee Stevens	.10
68	*Bill Sampen*	.10
69	*Craig Grebeck*	.10
70	John Burkett	.10
71	*Hector Villanueva*	.05
72	*Oscar Azocar*	.05
73	*Alan Mills*	.15
74	Carlos Baerga	.10
75	Charles Nagy	.10
76	Tim Drummond	.05
77	*Dana Kiecker*	.05
78	*Tom Edens*	.05
79	Kent Mercker	.05
80	Steve Avery	.05
81	Lee Smith	.05
82	Dave Martinez	.05
83	Dave Winfield	.15
84	Bill Spiers	.05
85	Dan Pasqua	.05
86	Randy Milligan	.05
87	Tracy Jones	.05
88	Greg Myers	.05
89	Keith Hernandez	.05
90	Todd Benzinger	.05
91	Mike Jackson	.05
92	Mike Stanley	.05
93	Candy Maldonado	.05
94	John Kruk	.05
95	Cal Ripken, Jr.	.75
96	Willie Fraser	.05
97	Mike Felder	.05
98	Bill Landrum	.05
99	Chuck Crim	.05
100	Chuck Finley	.05
101	Kirt Manwaring	.05
102	Jaime Navarro	.05
103	Dickie Thon	.05
104	Brian Downing	.05
105	Jim Abbott	.10
106	Tom Brookens	.05
107	Darryl Hamilton	.05
108	Bryan Harvey	.05
109	Greg Harris	.05
110	Greg Swindell	.05

111 Juan Berenguer .05
112 Mike Heath .05
113 Scott Bradley .05
114 Jack Morris .05
115 Barry Jones .05
116 Kevin Romine .05
117 Garry Templeton .05
118 Scott Sanderson .05
119 Roberto Kelly .05
120 George Brett .30
121 Oddibe McDowell .05
122 Jim Acker .05
123 Bill Swift .05
124 Eric King .05
125 Jay Buhner .10
126 Matt Young .05
127 Alvaro Espinoza .05
128 Greg Hibbard .05
129 Jeff Robinson .05
130 Mike Greenwell .05
131 Dion James .05
132 Donn Pall .05
133 Lloyd Moseby .05
134 Randy Velarde .05
135 Allan Anderson .05
136 Mark Davis .05
137 Eric Davis .10
138 Phil Stephenson .05
139 Felix Fermin .05
140 Pedro Guerrero .05
141 Charlie Hough .05
142 Mike Henneman .05
143 Jeff Montgomery .05
144 Lenny Harris .05
145 Bruce Hurst .05
146 Eric Anthony .05
147 Paul Assenmacher .05
148 Jesse Barfield .05
149 Carlos Quintana .05
150 Dave Stewart .10
151 Roy Smith .05
152 Paul Gibson .05
153 Mickey Hatcher .05
154 Jim Eisenreich .05
155 Kenny Rogers .05
156 Dave Schmidt .05
157 Lance Johnson .05
158 Dave West .05
159 Steve Balboni .05
160 Jeff Brantley .05
161 Craig Biggio .20
162 Brook Jacoby .05
163 Dan Gladden .05
164 Jeff Reardon .05
165 Mark Carreon .05
166 Mel Hall .05
167 Gary Mielke .05
168 Cecil Fielder .10
169 Darrin Jackson .05
170 Rick Aguilera .05
171 Walt Weiss .05
172 Steve Farr .05
173 Jody Reed .05
174 Mike Jeffcoat .05
175 Mark Grace .15
176 Larry Sheets .05
177 Bill Gullickson .05
178 Chris Gwynn .05
179 Melido Perez .05
180 Sid Fernandez .05
181 Tim Burke .05
182 Gary Pettis .05
183 Rob Murphy .05
184 Craig Lefferts .05
185 Howard Johnson .05
186 Ken Caminiti .15
187 Tim Belcher .05
188 Greg Cadaret .05
189 Matt Williams .20
190 Dave Magadan .05
191 Geno Petralli .05
192 Jeff Robinson .05
193 Jim Deshaies .05
194 Willie Randolph .05
195 George Bell .05
196 Hubie Brooks .05
197 Tom Gordon .05
198 Mike Fitzgerald .05
199 Mike Pagliarulo .05
200 Kirby Puckett .25
201 Shawon Dunston .05
202 Dennis Boyd .05
203 Junior Felix .05
204 Alejandro Pena .05
205 Pete Smith .05
206 Tom Glavine .10
207 Luis Salazar .05
208 John Smoltz .15
209 Doug Dascenzo .05
210 Tim Wallach .05
211 Greg Gagne .05
212 Mark Gubicza .05
213 Mark Parent .05
214 Ken Oberkfell .05
215 Gary Carter .10
216 Rafael Palmeiro .10
217 Tom Niedenfuer .05
218 Dave LaPoint .05
219 Jeff Treadway .05
220 Mitch Williams .05
221 Jose DeLeon .05
222 Mike LaValliere .05
223 Darrel Akerfelds .05
224 Kent Anderson .05
225 Dwight Evans .05
226 Gary Redus .05
227 Paul O'Neill .15
228 Marty Barrett .05
229 Tom Browning .05
230 Terry Pendleton .05
231 Jack Armstrong .05
232 Mike Boddicker .05
233 Neal Heaton .05
234 Marquis Grissom .10
235 Bert Blyleven .05
236 Curt Young .05
237 Don Carman .05
238 Charlie Hayes .05
239 Mark Knudson .05
240 Todd Zeile .10
241 Larry Walker .25
242 Jerald Clark .05
243 Jeff Ballard .05
244 Jeff King .05
245 Tom Brunansky .05
246 Darren Daulton .05
247 Scott Terry .05
248 Rob Deer .05
249 Brady Anderson .10
250 Len Dykstra .05
251 Greg Harris .05
252 Mike Hartley .05
253 Joey Cora .05
254 Ivan Calderon .05
255 Ted Power .05
256 Sammy Sosa .75
257 Steve Buechele .05
258 Mike Devereaux .05
259 Brad Komminsk .05
260 Teddy Higuera .05
261 Shawn Abner .05
262 Dave Valle .05
263 Jeff Huson .05
264 Edgar Martinez .05
265 Carlton Fisk .10
266 Steve Finley .05
267 John Wetteland .10
268 Kevin Appier .05
269 Steve Lyons .05
270 Mickey Tettleton .05
271 Luis Rivera .05
272 Steve Jeltz .05
273 R.J. Reynolds .05
274 Carlos Martinez .05
275 Dan Plesac .05
276 Mike Morgan .05
277 Jeff Russell .05
278 Pete Incaviglia .05
279 Kevin Seitzer .05
280 Bobby Thigpen .05
281 Stan Javier .05
282 Henry Cotto .05
283 Gary Wayne .05
284 Shane Mack .05
285 Brian Holman .05
286 Gerald Perry .05
287 Steve Crawford .05
288 Nelson Liriano .05
289 Don Aase .05
290 Randy Johnson .25
291 Harold Baines .05
292 Kent Hrbek .05
293 Les Lancaster .05
294 Jeff Musselman .05
295 Kurt Stillwell .05
296 Stan Belinda .05
297 Lou Whitaker .05
298 Glenn Wilson .05
299 Omar Vizquel .10
300 Ramon Martinez .10
301 Dwight Smith .05
302 Tim Crews .05
303 Lance Blankenship .05
304 Sid Bream .05
305 Rafael Ramirez .05
306 Steve Wilson .05
307 Mackey Sasser .05
308 Franklin Stubbs .05
309 Jack Daugherty .05
310 Eddie Murray .20
311 Bob Welch .05
312 Brian Harper .05
313 Lance McCullers .05
314 Dave Smith .05
315 Bobby Bonilla .10
316 Jerry Don Gleaton .05
317 Greg Maddux .75
318 Keith Miller .05
319 Mark Portugal .05
320 Robin Ventura .15
321 Bob Ojeda .05
322 Mike Harkey .05
323 Jay Bell .05
324 Mark McGwire 1.50
325 Gary Gaetti .05
326 Jeff Pico .05
327 Kevin McReynolds .05
328 Frank Tanana .05
329 Eric Yelding .05
330 Barry Bonds .40
331 *Brian McRae* .20
332 *Pedro Munoz* .10
333 *Daryl Irvine* .10
334 Chris Hoiles .05
335 *Thomas Howard* .10
336 *Jeff Schulz* .05
337 Jeff Manto .05
338 Beau Allred .05
339 *Mike Bordick* .15
340 Todd Hundley .10
341 *Jim Vatcher* .05
342 Luis Sojo .05
343 *Jose Offerman* .15
344 *Pete Coachman* .10
345 Mike Benjamin .05
346 *Ozzie Canseco* .05
347 Tim McIntosh .05
348 *Phil Plantier* .10
349 *Terry Shumpert* .05
350 Darren Lewis .10
351 *David Walsh* .05
352 *Scott Chiamparino* .05
353 *Julio Valera* .10
354 *Anthony Telford* .10
355 Kevin Wickander .05
356 *Tim Naehring* .05
357 *Jim Poole* .05
358 *Mark Whiten* .10
359 *Terry Wells* .05
360 *Rafael Valdez* .05
361 *Mel Stottlemyre* .05
362 *David Segui* .10
363 Paul Abbott .05
364 *Steve Howard* .05
365 *Karl Rhodes* .10
366 *Rafael Novoa* .10
367 *Joe Grahe* .10
368 *Darren Reed* .15
369 Jeff McKnight .05
370 Scott Leius .10
371 *Mark Dewey* .05
372 *Mark Lee* .05
373 *Rosario Rodriguez* .05
374 Chuck McElroy .05
375 *Mike Bell* .05
376 Mickey Morandini .05
377 *Bill Haselman* .05
378 *Dave Pavlas* .05
379 Derrick May .05
380 *Jeromy Burnitz* (1st Draft Pick) .25
381 *Donald Peters* (1st Draft Pick) .10
382 *Alex Fernandez* (1st Draft Pick) .25
383 *Mike Mussina* (1st Draft Pick) 1.25
384 *Daniel Smith* (1st Draft Pick) .10
385 *Lance Dickson* (1st Draft Pick) .15
386 *Carl Everett* (1st Draft Pick) .75
387 *Thomas Nevers* (1st Draft Pick) .15
388 *Adam Hyzdu* (1st Draft Pick) .15
389 *Todd Van Poppel* (1st Draft Pick) .10
390 *Rondell White* (1st Draft Pick) .50
391 *Marc Newfield* (1st Draft Pick) .10
392 Julio Franco (AS) .05
393 Wade Boggs (AS) .10
394 Ozzie Guillen (AS) .05
395 Cecil Fielder (AS) .10
396 Ken Griffey, Jr. (AS) .50
397 Rickey Henderson (AS) .15
398 Jose Canseco (AS) .10
399 Roger Clemens (AS) .15
400 Sandy Alomar,Jr. (AS) .10
401 Bobby Thigpen (AS) .05
402 Bobby Bonilla (Master Blaster) .05
403 Eric Davis (Master Blaster) .10
404 Fred McGriff (Master Blaster) .10
405 Glenn Davis (Master Blaster) .05
406 Kevin Mitchell (Master Blaster) .05
407 Rob Dibble (K-Man) .05
408 Ramon Martinez (K-Man) .10
409 David Cone (K-Man) .10
410 Bobby Witt (K-Man) .05
411 Mark Langston (K-Man) .05
412 Bo Jackson (Rifleman) .15
413 Shawon Dunston (Rifleman) .05
414 Jesse Barfield (Rifleman) .05
415 Ken Caminiti (Rifleman) .10
416 Benito Santiago (Rifleman) .05
417 Nolan Ryan (Highlight) .35
418 Bobby Thigpen (HL) .05
419 Ramon Martinez (HL) .05
420 Bo Jackson (HL) .15
421 Carlton Fisk (HL) .10
422 Jimmy Key .05
423 Junior Noboa .05
424 Al Newman .05
425 Pat Borders .05
426 Von Hayes .05
427 Tim Teufel .05
428 Eric Plunk .05
429 John Moses .05
430 Mike Witt .05
431 Otis Nixon .05
432 Tony Fernandez .05
433 Rance Mulliniks .05
434 Dan Petry .05
435 Bob Geren .05
436 Steve Frey .05
437 Jamie Moyer .05
438 Junior Ortiz .05
439 Tom O'Malley .05
440 Pat Combs .05
441 Jose Canseco (Dream Team) .30
442 Alfredo Griffin .05
443 Andres Galarraga .10
444 Bryn Smith .05
445 Andre Dawson .10
446 Juan Samuel .05
447 Mike Aldrete .05
448 Ron Gant .10
449 Fernando Valenzuela .05
450 Vince Coleman .05
451 Kevin Mitchell .05
452 Spike Owen .05
453 Mike Bielecki .05
454 Dennis Martinez .05
455 Brett Butler .05
456 Ron Darling .05
457 Dennis Rasmussen .05
458 Ken Howell .05
459 Steve Bedrosian .05
460 Frank Viola .05
461 Jose Lind .05
462 Chris Sabo .05
463 Dante Bichette .10

No.	Player	Price
464	Rick Mahler	.05
465	John Smiley	.05
466	Devon White	.10
467	John Orton	.05
468	Mike Stanton	.05
469	Billy Hatcher	.05
470	Wally Joyner	.10
471	Gene Larkin	.05
472	Doug Drabek	.05
473	Gary Sheffield	.10
474	David Wells	.10
475	Andy Van Slyke	.05
476	Mike Gallego	.05
477	B.J. Surhoff	.05
478	Gene Nelson	.05
479	Mariano Duncan	.05
480	Fred McGriff	.20
481	Jerry Browne	.05
482	Alvin Davis	.05
483	Bill Wegman	.05
484	Dave Parker	.10
485	Dennis Eckersley	.10
486	Erik Hanson	.05
487	Bill Ripken	.05
488	Tom Candiotti	.05
489	Mike Schooler	.05
490	Gregg Olson	.05
491	Chris James	.05
492	Pete Harnisch	.05
493	Julio Franco	.05
494	Greg Briley	.05
495	Ruben Sierra	.05
496	Steve Olin	.05
497	Mike Fetters	.05
498	Mark Williamson	.05
499	Bob Tewksbury	.05
500	Tony Gwynn	.30
501	Randy Myers	.05
502	Keith Comstock	.05
503	Craig Worthington	.05
504	Mark Eichhorn	.05
505	Barry Larkin	.10
506	Dave Johnson	.05
507	Bobby Witt	.05
508	Joe Orsulak	.05
509	Pete O'Brien	.05
510	Brad Arnsberg	.05
511	Storm Davis	.05
512	Bob Milacki	.05
513	Bill Pecota	.05
514	Glenallen Hill	.05
515	Danny Tartabull	.05
516	Mike Moore	.05
517	Ron Robinson	.05
518	Mark Gardner	.05
519	Rick Wrona	.05
520	Mike Scioscia	.05
521	Frank Wills	.05
522	Greg Brock	.05
523	Jack Clark	.05
524	Bruce Ruffin	.05
525	Robin Yount	.25
526	Tom Foley	.05
527	Pat Perry	.05
528	Greg Vaughn	.10
529	Wally Whitehurst	.05
530	Norm Charlton	.05
531	Marvell Wynne	.05
532	Jim Gantner	.05
533	Greg Litton	.05
534	Manny Lee	.05
535	Scott Bailes	.05
536	Charlie Leibrandt	.05
537	Roger McDowell	.05
538	Andy Benes	.10
539	Rick Honeycutt	.05
540	Dwight Gooden	.10
541	Scott Garrelts	.05
542	Dave Clark	.05
543	Lonnie Smith	.05
544	Rick Rueschel	.05
545	Delino DeShields	.05
546	Mike Sharperson	.05
547	Mike Kingery	.05
548	Terry Kennedy	.05
549	David Cone	.15
550	Orel Hershiser	.10
551	Matt Nokes	.05
552	Eddie Williams	.05
553	Frank DiPino	.05
554	Fred Lynn	.05
555	Alex Cole	.05
556	Terry Leach	.05
557	Chet Lemon	.05
558	Paul Mirabella	.05
559	Bill Long	.05
560	Phil Bradley	.05
561	Duane Ward	.05
562	Dave Bergman	.05
563	Eric Show	.05
564	Xavier Hernandez	.05
565	Jeff Parrett	.05
566	Chuck Cary	.05
567	Ken Hill	.05
568	Bob Welch	.05
569	John Mitchell	.05
570	Travis Fryman	.10
571	Derek Lilliquist	.05
572	Steve Lake	.05
573	*John Barfield*	.05
574	Randy Bush	.05
575	Joe Magrane	.05
576	Edgar Diaz	.05
577	Casy Candaele	.05
578	Jesse Orosco	.05
579	Tom Henke	.05
580	Rick Cerone	.05
581	Drew Hall	.05
582	Tony Castillo	.05
583	Jimmy Jones	.05
584	Rick Reed	.05
585	Joe Girardi	.05
586	*Jeff Gray*	.05
587	Luis Polonia	.05
588	Joe Klink	.05
589	Rex Hudler	.05
590	Kirk McCaskill	.05
591	Juan Agosto	.05
592	Wes Gardner	.05
593	*Rich Rodriguez*	.05
594	Mitch Webster	.05
595	Kelly Gruber	.05
596	Dale Mohorcic	.05
597	Willie McGee	.05
598	Bill Krueger	.05
599	Bob Walk	.05
600	Kevin Maas	.05
601	Danny Jackson	.05
602	Craig McMurtry	.05
603	Curtis Wilkerson	.05
604	Adam Peterson	.05
605	Sam Horn	.05
606	Tommy Gregg	.05
607	Ken Dayley	.05
608	Carmelo Castillo	.05
609	John Shelby	.05
610	Don Slaught	.05
611	Calvin Schiraldi	.05
612	Dennis Lamp	.05
613	Andres Thomas	.05
614	Jose Gonzales	.05
615	Randy Ready	.05
616	Kevin Bass	.05
617	Mike Marshall	.05
618	Daryl Boston	.05
619	Andy McGaffigan	.05
620	Joe Oliver	.05
621	Jim Gott	.05
622	Jose Oquendo	.05
623	Jose DeJesus	.05
624	Mike Brumley	.05
625	John Olerud	.25
626	Ernest Riles	.05
627	Gene Harris	.05
628	Jose Uribe	.05
629	Darnell Coles	.05
630	Carney Lansford	.05
631	Tim Leary	.05
632	Tim Hulett	.05
633	Kevin Elster	.05
634	Tony Fossas	.05
635	Francisco Oliveras	.05
636	Bob Patterson	.05
637	Gary Ward	.05
638	Rene Gonzales	.05
639	Don Robinson	.05
640	Darryl Strawberry	.10
641	Dave Anderson	.05
642	Scott Scudder	.05
643	*Reggie Harris*	.10
644	Dave Henderson	.05
645	Ben McDonald	.05
646	Bob Kipper	.05
647	Hal Morris	.05
648	Tim Birtsas	.05
649	Steve Searcy	.05
650	Dale Murphy	.15
651	Ron Oester	.05
652	Mike LaCoss	.05
653	Ron Jones	.05
654	Kelly Downs	.05
655	Roger Clemens	.35
656	Herm Winningham	.05
657	Trevor Wilson	.05
658	Jose Rijo	.05
659	Dann Bilardello	.05
660	Gregg Jefferies	.15
661	Doug Drabek (All-Star)	.05
662	Randy Myers (AS)	.05
663	Benito Santiago (AS)	.05
664	Will Clark (AS)	.15
665	Ryne Sandberg (AS)	.15
666	Barry Larkin (AS)	.10
667	Matt Williams (AS)	.05
668	Barry Bonds (AS)	.20
669	Eric Davis	.10
670	Bobby Bonilla (AS)	.05
671	*Chipper Jones* (1st Draft Pick)	3.00
672	*Eric Christopherson* (1st Draft Pick)	.10
673	*Robbie Beckett* (1st Draft Pick)	.25
674	*Shane Andrews* (1st Draft Pick)	.45
675	*Steve Karsay* (1st Draft Pick)	.25
676	*Aaron Holbert* (1st Draft Pick)	.10
677	*Donovan Osborne* (1st Draft Pick)	.10
678	*Todd Ritchie* (1st Draft Pick)	.15
679	*Ron Walden* (1st Draft Pick)	.10
680	*Tim Costo* (1st Draft Pick)	.20
681	*Dan Wilson* (1st Draft Pick)	.15
682	*Kurt Miller* (1st Draft Pick)	.15
683	*Mike Lieberthal* (1st Draft Pick)	.25
684	Roger Clemens (K-Man)	.15
685	Dwight Gooden (K-Man)	.10
686	Nolan Ryan (K-Man)	.30
687	Frank Viola (K-Man)	.05
688	Erik Hanson (K-Man)	.05
689	Matt Williams (Master Blaster)	.05
690	Jose Canseco (Master Blaster)	.10
691	Darryl Strawberry (Master Blaster)	.10
692	Bo Jackson (Master Blaster)	.10
693	Cecil Fielder (Master Blaster)	.05
694	Sandy Alomar, Jr. (Rifleman)	.10
695	Cory Snyder (Rifleman)	.05
696	Eric Davis (Rifleman)	.05
697	Ken Griffey, Jr. (Rifleman)	.50
698	Andy Van Slyke (Rifleman)	.05
699	Mark Langston, Mike Witt (No-hitter)	.05
700	Randy Johnson (No-hitter)	.15
701	Nolan Ryan (No-hitter)	.30
702	Dave Stewart (No-hitter)	.05
703	Fernando Valenzuela (No-hitter)	.05
704	Andy Hawkins (No-hitter)	.05
705	Melido Perez (No-hitter)	.05
706	Terry Mulholland (No-hitter)	.05
707	Dave Stieb (No-hitter)	.05
708	*Brian Barnes*	.05
709	*Bernard Gilkey*	.20
710	*Steve Decker*	.10
711	*Paul Faries*	.10
712	*Paul Marak*	.10
713	*Wes Chamberlain*	.10
714	*Kevin Belcher*	.10
715	Dan Boone	.05
716	*Steve Adkins*	.10
717	*Geronimo Pena*	.10
718	*Howard Farmer*	.10
719	*Mark Leonard*	.05
720	Tom Lampkin	.05
721	*Mike Gardiner*	.10
722	*Jeff Conine*	.40
723	*Efrain Valdez*	.05
724	Chuck Malone	.05
725	*Leo Gomez*	.10
726	*Paul McClellan*	.05
727	*Mark Leiter*	.05
728	*Rich DeLucia*	.15
729	Mel Rojas	.05
730	*Hector Wagner*	.05
731	*Ray Lankford*	.25
732	*Turner Ward*	.10
733	*Gerald Alexander*	.05
734	*Scott Anderson*	.05
735	Tony Perezchica	.05
736	Jimmy Kremers	.05
737	American Flag	.25
738	*Mike York*	.05
739	Mike Rochford	.05
740	Scott Aldred	.05
741	*Rico Brogna*	.15
742	*Dave Burba*	.10
743	*Ray Stephens*	.05
744	*Eric Gunderson*	.10
745	*Troy Afenir*	.05
746	Jeff Shaw	.10
747	*Orlando Merced*	.15
748	*Omar Oliveras*	.05
749	Jerry Kutzler	.05
750	Mo Vaughn	.30
751	*Matt Stark*	.05
752	*Randy Hennis*	.05
753	*Andujar Cedeno*	.10
754	Kelvin Torve	.05
755	Joe Kraemer	.05
756	*Phil Clark*	.05
757	*Ed Vosberg*	.05
758	*Mike Perez*	.10
759	*Scott Lewis*	.10
760	*Steve Chitren*	.10
761	*Ray Young*	.05
762	*Andres Santana*	.05
763	*Rodney McCray*	.05
764	*Sean Berry*	.10
765	Brent Mayne	.05
766	*Mike Simms*	.05
767	*Glenn Sutko*	.05
768	Gary Disarcina	.05
769	George Brett (HL)	.20
770	Cecil Fielder (HL)	.05
771	Jim Presley	.05
772	John Dopson	.05
773	Bo Jackson (Breaker)	.10
774	Brent Knackert	.05
775	Bill Doran	.05
776	Dick Schofield	.05
777	Nelson Santovenia	.05
778	Mark Guthrie	.05
779	Mark Lemke	.05
780	Terry Steinbach	.05
781	Tom Bolton	.05
782	*Randy Tomlin*	.10
783	Jeff Kunkel	.05
784	Felix Jose	.05
785	Rick Sutcliffe	.05
786	John Cerutti	.05
787	Jose Vizcaino	.05
788	Curt Schilling	.10
789	Ed Whitson	.05
790	Tony Pena	.05
791	John Candelaria	.05
792	Carmelo Martinez	.05
793	Sandy Alomar, Jr.	.15
794	*Jim Neidlinger*	.05
795	Red's October (Barry Larkin, Chris Sabo)	.10
796	Paul Sorrento	.05
797	Tom Pagnozzi	.05
798	Tino Martinez	.10
799	Scott Ruskin	.05
800	Kirk Gibson	.05
801	Walt Terrell	.05
802	John Russell	.05
803	Chili Davis	.05
804	Chris Nabholz	.05
805	Juan Gonzalez	.50
806	Ron Hassey	.05
807	Todd Worrell	.05
808	Tommy Greene	.05
809	Joel Skinner	.05
810	Benito Santiago	.05
811	Pat Tabler	.05
812	*Scott Erickson*	.10
813	Moises Alou	.20

814	Dale Sveum	.05
815	Ryne Sandberg (Man of the Year)	.20
816	Rick Dempsey	.05
817	Scott Bankhead	.05
818	Jason Grimsley	.05
819	Doug Jennings	.05
820	Tom Herr	.05
821	Rob Ducey	.05
822	Luis Quinones	.05
823	Greg Minton	.05
824	Mark Grant	.05
825	Ozzie Smith	.20
826	Dave Eiland	.05
827	Danny Heep	.05
828	Hensley Meulens	.05
829	Charlie O'Brien	.05
830	Glenn Davis	.05
831	John Marzano	.05
832	Steve Ontiveros	.05
833	Ron Karkovice	.05
834	Jerry Goff	.05
835	Ken Griffey, Sr.	.10
836	Kevin Reimer	.05
837	Randy Kutcher	.05
838	Mike Blowers	.05
839	Mike Macfarlane	.05
840	Frank Thomas	.75
841	Ken Griffey Sr., Ken Griffey Jr.	.50
842	Jack Howell	.05
843	Mauro Gozzo	.05
844	Gerald Young	.05
845	Zane Smith	.05
846	Kevin Brown	.05
847	Sil Campusano	.05
848	Larry Andersen	.05
849	Cal Ripken, Jr. (Franchise)	.15
850	Roger Clemens (Franchise)	.15
851	Sandy Alomar, Jr. (Franchise)	.05
852	Alan Trammell (Franchise)	.05
853	George Brett (Franchise)	.15
854	Robin Yount (Franchise)	.10
855	Kirby Puckett (Franchise)	.10
856	Don Mattingly (Franchise)	.10
857	Rickey Henderson (Franchise)	.10
858	Ken Griffey, Jr. (Franchise)	.50
859	Ruben Sierra (Franchise)	.05
860	John Olerud (Franchise)	.20
861	Dave Justice (Franchise)	.15
862	Ryne Sandberg (Franchise)	.15
863	Eric Davis (Franchise)	.05
864	Darryl Strawberry (Franchise)	.05
865	Tim Wallach (Franchise)	.05
866	Dwight Gooden (Franchise)	.05
867	Len Dykstra (Franchise)	.05
868	Barry Bonds (Franchise)	.25
869	Todd Zeile (Franchise)	.05
870	Benito Santiago (Franchise)	.05
871	Will Clark (Franchise)	.10
872	Craig Biggio (Franchise)	.05
873	Wally Joyner (Franchise)	.05
874	Frank Thomas (Franchise)	.45
875	Rickey Henderson (MVP)	.10
876	Barry Bonds (MVP)	.25
877	Bob Welch (Cy Young)	.05
878	Doug Drabek (Cy Young)	.05
879	Sandy Alomar, Jr. (ROY)	.10
880	Dave Justice (ROY)	.25
881	Damon Berryhill	.05
882	Frank Viola (Dream Team)	.05
883	Dave Stewart (Dream Team)	.10
884	Doug Jones (Dream Team)	.05
885	Randy Myers (Dream Team)	.05
886	Will Clark (Dream Team)	.20
887	Roberto Alomar (Dream Team)	.25
888	Barry Larkin (Dream Team)	.10
889	Wade Boggs (Dream Team)	.20
890	Rickey Henderson (Dream Team)	.15
891	Kirby Puckett (Dream Team)	.40
892	Ken Griffey, Jr. (Dream Team)	.75
893	Benito Santiago (Dream Team)	.10

1991 Score Cooperstown

This seven-card set was included as an insert in every factory set. The card fronts are white, with an oval-vignetted player portrait. The backs have green borders surrounding a yellow background which contains a summary of the player's career.

		MT
Complete Set (7):		7.50
Common Player:		.50
B1	Wade Boggs	1.00
B2	Barry Larkin	.50
B3	Ken Griffey, Jr.	5.00
B4	Rickey Henderson	.50
B5	George Brett	2.00
B6	Will Clark	.50
B7	Nolan Ryan	4.00

1991 Score Hot Rookies

These standard-size cards were inserted one per every 100-card 1991 Score blister pack. Action photos with white borders are featured on the front, and "Hot Rookie" is written in yellow at the top. The background is shaded from yellow to orange. The backs are numbered and each has a color mug shot and a career summary.

		MT
Complete Set (10):		18.00
Common Player:		.50
1	Dave Justice	2.00
2	Kevin Maas	.50
3	Hal Morris	.75
4	Frank Thomas	4.00
5	Jeff Conine	1.00
6	Sandy Alomar Jr.	1.00
7	Ray Lankford	.75
8	Steve Decker	.50
9	Juan Gonzalez	3.00
10	Jose Offerman	.50

1991 Score Mickey Mantle

This special set recalls Mickey Mantle's career as a Yankee. Card fronts are glossy and have red and white borders. The card's caption appears at the bottom in a blue stripe. The backs have a photo and a summary of the caption, plus the card number and serial number. Dealers and media members received the sets, which were limited to 5,000, in a fin-fold plastic wrapper. A total of 2,500 of the cards were numbered and autographed.

		MT
Complete Set (7):		150.00
Common Card:		30.00
Autographed Card:		500.00
1	The Rookie	30.00
2	Triple Crown	30.00
3	World Series	30.00
4	Going, Going, Gone	30.00
5	Speed and Grace	30.00
6	A True Yankee	30.00
7	Twilight	30.00

1991 Score Traded

This 110-card set features players with new teams as well as 1991 Major League rookies. The cards are designed in the same style as the regular 1991 Score issue. The cards once again feature a "T" designation along with the card number. The complete set was sold at hobby shops in a special box.

		MT
Complete Set (110):		5.00
Common Player:		.05
1	Bo Jackson	.15
2	Mike Flanagan	.05
3	Pete Incaviglia	.05
4	Jack Clark	.05
5	Hubie Brooks	.05
6	Ivan Calderon	.05
7	Glenn Davis	.05
8	Wally Backman	.05
9	Dave Smith	.05
10	Tim Raines	.15
11	Joe Carter	.10
12	Sid Bream	.05
13	George Bell	.05
14	Steve Bedrosian	.05
15	Willie Wilson	.05
16	Darryl Strawberry	.10
17	Danny Jackson	.05
18	Kirk Gibson	.05
19	Willie McGee	.05
20	Junior Felix	.05
21	Steve Farr	.05
22	Pat Tabler	.05
23	Brett Butler	.05
24	Danny Darwin	.05
25	Mickey Tettleton	.05
26	Gary Carter	.10
27	Mitch Williams	.05
28	Candy Maldonado	.05
29	Otis Nixon	.05
30	Brian Downing	.05
31	Tom Candiotti	.05
32	John Candelaria	.05
33	Rob Murphy	.05
34	Deion Sanders	.25
35	Willie Randolph	.05
36	Pete Harnisch	.05
37	Dante Bichette	.10
38	Garry Templeton	.05
39	Gary Gaetti	.05
40	John Cerutti	.05
41	Rick Cerone	.05
42	Mike Pagliarulo	.05
43	Ron Hassey	.05
44	Roberto Alomar	.30
45	Mike Boddicker	.05
46	Bud Black	.05
47	Rob Deer	.05
48	Devon White	.10
49	Luis Sojo	.05
50	Terry Pendleton	.05
51	Kevin Gross	.05
52	Mike Huff	.05
53	Dave Righetti	.05
54	Matt Young	.05

55	Ernest Riles	.05
56	Bill Gullickson	.05
57	Vince Coleman	.05
58	Fred McGriff	.15
59	Franklin Stubbs	.05
60	Eric King	.05
61	Cory Snyder	.05
62	Dwight Evans	.05
63	Gerald Perry	.05
64	Eric Show	.05
65	Shawn Hillegas	.05
66	Tony Fernandez	.05
67	Tim Teufel	.05
68	Mitch Webster	.05
69	Mike Heath	.05
70	Chili Davis	.05
71	Larry Andersen	.05
72	Gary Varsho	.05
73	Juan Berenguer	.05
74	Jack Morris	.05
75	Barry Jones	.05
76	Rafael Belliard	.05
77	Steve Buechele	.05
78	Scott Sanderson	.05
79	Bob Ojeda	.05
80	Curt Schilling	.10
81	Brian Drahman	.05
82	*Ivan Rodriguez*	3.00
83	David Howard	.05
84	Heath Slocumb	.05
85	Mike Timlin	.05
86	Darryl Kile	.10
87	Pete Schourek	.10
88	Bruce Walton	.05
89	Al Osuna	.05
90	Gary Scott	.05
91	Doug Simons	.05
92	Chris Jones	.05
93	Chuck Knoblauch	.50
94	Dana Allison	.05
95	Erik Pappas	.05
96	*Jeff Bagwell*	3.00
97	Kirk Dressendorfer	.05
98	Freddie Benavides	.05
99	*Luis Gonzalez*	.50
100	Wade Taylor	.05
101	Ed Sprague	.05
102	Bob Scanlan	.05
103	Rick Wilkins	.05
104	Chris Donnels	.05
105	Joe Slusarski	.05
106	Mark Lewis	.10
107	Pat Kelly	.05
108	John Briscoe	.05
109	Luis Lopez	.05
110	Jeff Johnson	.05

1992 Score/Pinnacle Promo Panels

Score debuted both its base-brand (Score) and premium-brand (Pinnacle) sets at one time in 1992 with this issue of four-card panels. Each panel measures 1/16" short each way of 5" x 7" and features Score cards in the upper-left and lower-right, with Pinnacle samples at upper-right and lower-left. Backs have a very light gray overprint, "FOR PROMOTIONAL PURPOSES ONLY NOT FOR RESALE". Cards cut from the panels would be otherwise indistinguishable from the issued versions. Panels are checklisted here alphabetically according to the lowest-numbered Score player. S prefix to the card number indicates Score, P is for Pinnacle. The prefixes do not appear on the cards.

		MT
Complete Set (25):		150.00
Common Panel:		3.00
(1)	S2 Nolan Ryan, S13 Lonnie Smith, P7 Willie McGee, P18 Terry Pendleton	35.00
(2)	S3 Will Clark, S12 Mark Langston, P8 Paul Molitor, P17 Devon White	7.50
(3)	S4 Dave Justice, S19 Mark Carreon, P1 Frank Thomas, P16 Dave Henderson	6.00
(4)	S5 Dave Henderson, S15 Roberto Alomar, P10 Ryne Sandberg, P20 Kirby Puckett	15.00
(5)	S9 Darryl Strawberry, S14 Jeff Montgomery, P6 Ozzie Smith, P11 Kevin Seitzer	7.50
(6)	S22 Chuck Crim, S33 Jimmy Jones, P27 Jay Buhner, P38 Robin Yount	7.50
(7)	S23 Don Mattingly, S32 Dave Winfield, P28 Matt Williams, P37 George Bell	10.00
(8)	S24 Dickie Thon, S39 Gary Gaetti, P21 Orel Hershiser, P36 Wes Chamberlain	3.00
(9)	S25 Ron Gant, S35 Andres Galarraga, P30 Alex Fernandez, P40 Bruce Hurst	3.00
(10)	S29 Melido Perez, S34 Kevin Gross, P26 Ellis Burks, P31 Albert Belle	4.50
(11)	S42 Rick Aguilera, S53 Doug Jones, P47 Bill Doran, P58 Ivan Calderon	3.00
(12)	S43 Mike Gallego, S52 Todd Zeile, P48 Jerald Clark, P57 Lenny Harris	3.00
(13)	S44 Eric Davis, S59 Randy Ready, P41 Harold Baines, P56 Walt Weiss	3.00
(14)	S45 George Bell, S55 Rafael Palmeiro, P50 Nolan Ryan, P60 George Brett	45.00
(15)	S49 David Wells, S54 Bob Walk, P46 Chili Davis, P51 Phil Plantier	4.50
(16)	S62 Jack McDowell, S73 Juan Samuel, P67 Dave Hollins, P78 John Olerud	4.50
(17)	S63 Jim Acker, S72 Carlton Fisk, P68 Kent Hrbek, P77 Dennis Martinez	4.50
(18)	S64 Jay Buhner, S79 Kirk McCaskill, P61 Gregg Olson, P76 Terry Steinbach	3.00
(19)	S65 Travis Fryman, S75 Andre Dawson, P70 Jeff Bagwell, P80 Darryl Strawberry	4.50
(20)	S69 Ken Caminiti, S74 Todd Stottlemyre, P66 Alex Cole, P71 Jim Gantner	3.00
(21)	S82 Alex Fernandez, S93 Shawn Hillegas, P87 Bill Gullickson, P98 Jose Guzman	3.00
(22)	S83 Ivan Calderon, S92 Ozzie Guillen, P88 Bernard Gilkey, P97 Omar Vizquel	3.00
(23)	S84 Brent Mayne, S99 Tom Bolton, P81 Gary Gaetti, P96 Doug Drabek	3.00
(24)	S85 Jody Reed, S95 Vince Coleman, P90 Kevin Maas, P100 Dave Justice	3.00
(25)	S89 Hensley Meulens, S94 Chili Davis, P86 David Howard, P91 Mark Lewis	3.00

1992 Score Promos

The six known Score promo cards differ from the issued versions in 1992 only in the lack of 1991 and career stats on the back and changes in the career summaries on some of the cards. The promos of Sandberg and Mack were distributed at a St. Louis baseball card show in November, 1991, and are somewhat scarcer than the others.

		MT
Complete Set (6):		66.00
Common Player:		6.00
1	Ken Griffey Jr.	24.00
4	Dave Justice	12.00
122	Robin Ventura	8.00
200	Ryne Sandberg	18.00
241	Steve Avery	6.00
284	Shane Mack	6.00

1992 Score

Score used a two series format for the second consecutive year in 1992. Cards 1-442 are featured in the first series. Fronts feature full-color game action photos. Backs feature color head shots of the players, team logo and career stats on a vertical layout. Several subsets are included in 1992, including a five-card Joe DiMaggio set. DiMaggio autographed cards were also inserted into random packs. Cards 736-772 can be found with or without a "Rookie Prospects" banner on the card front.

		MT
Complete Set (893):		15.00
Common Player:		.05
C. Knoblauch Auto/3,000		50.00
Series 1 or 2 Pack (16):		.40
Series 1 or 2 Wax Box (36):		10.00
1	Ken Griffey, Jr.	1.50
2	Nolan Ryan	.90
3	Will Clark	.25
4	Dave Justice	.20
5	Dave Henderson	.05
6	Bret Saberhagen	.10
7	Fred McGriff	.15
8	Erik Hanson	.05
9	Darryl Strawberry	.10
10	Dwight Gooden	.10
11	Juan Gonzalez	.50
12	Mark Langston	.05
13	Lonnie Smith	.05
14	Jeff Montgomery	.05
15	Roberto Alomar	.25
16	Delino DeShields	.05
17	Steve Bedrosian	.05
18	Terry Pendleton	.05
19	Mark Carreon	.05
20	Mark McGwire	1.50
21	Roger Clemens	.25
22	Chuck Crim	.05
23	Don Mattingly	.50
24	Dickie Thon	.05
25	Ron Gant	.10
26	Milt Cuyler	.05
27	Mike Macfarlane	.05
28	Dan Gladden	.05
29	Melido Perez	.05
30	Willie Randolph	.05
31	Albert Belle	.30
32	Dave Winfield	.15
33	Jimmy Jones	.05
34	Kevin Gross	.05
35	Andres Galarraga	.10
36	Mike Devereaux	.05
37	Chris Bosio	.05
38	Mike LaValliere	.05
39	Gary Gaetti	.05
40	Felix Jose	.05
41	Alvaro Espinoza	.05
42	Rick Aguilera	.05

43 Mike Gallego .05
44 Eric Davis .10
45 George Bell .05
46 Tom Brunansky .05
47 Steve Farr .05
48 Duane Ward .05
49 David Wells .10
50 Cecil Fielder .10
51 Walt Weiss .05
52 Todd Zeile .10
53 Doug Jones .05
54 Bob Walk .05
55 Rafael Palmeiro .10
56 Rob Deer .05
57 Paul O'Neill .15
58 Jeff Reardon .05
59 Randy Ready .05
60 Scott Erickson .05
61 Paul Molitor .25
62 Jack McDowell .05
63 Jim Acker .05
64 Jay Buhner .10
65 Travis Fryman .10
66 Marquis Grissom .10
67 Mike Harkey .05
68 Luis Polonia .05
69 Ken Caminiti .20
70 Chris Sabo .05
71 Gregg Olson .05
72 Carlton Fisk .10
73 Juan Samuel .05
74 Todd Stottlemyre .05
75 Andre Dawson .10
76 Alvin Davis .05
77 Bill Doran .05
78 B.J. Surhoff .05
79 Kirk McCaskill .05
80 Dale Murphy .15
81 Jose DeLeon .05
82 Alex Fernandez .20
83 Ivan Calderon .05
84 Brent Mayne .05
85 Jody Reed .05
86 Randy Tomlin .05
87 Randy Milligan .05
88 Pascual Perez .05
89 Hensley Meulens .05
90 Joe Carter .10
91 Mike Moore .05
92 Ozzie Guillen .05
93 Shawn Hillegas .05
94 Chili Davis .05
95 Vince Coleman .05
96 Jimmy Key .05
97 Billy Ripken .05
98 Dave Smith .05
99 Tom Bolton .05
100 Barry Larkin .10
101 Kenny Rogers .05
102 Mike Boddicker .05
103 Kevin Elster .05
104 Ken Hill .05
105 Charlie Leibrandt .05
106 Pat Combs .05
107 Hubie Brooks .05
108 Julio Franco .05
109 Vicente Palacios .05
110 Kal Daniels .05
111 Bruce Hurst .05
112 Willie McGee .05
113 Ted Power .05
114 Milt Thompson .05
115 Doug Drabek .05
116 Rafael Belliard .05
117 Scott Garrelts .05
118 Terry Mulholland .05
119 Jay Howell .05
120 Danny Jackson .05
121 Scott Ruskin .05
122 Robin Ventura .15
123 Bip Roberts .05
124 Jeff Russell .05
125 Hal Morris .05
126 Teddy Higuera .05
127 Luis Sojo .05
128 Carlos Baerga .10
129 Jeff Ballard .05
130 Tom Gordon .05
131 Sid Bream .05
132 Rance Mulliniks .05
133 Andy Benes .10
134 Mickey Tettleton .05
135 Rich DeLucia .05
136 Tom Pagnozzi .05
137 Harold Baines .05
138 Danny Darwin .05
139 Kevin Bass .05
140 Chris Nabholz .05
141 Pete O'Brien .05
142 Jeff Treadway .05
143 Mickey Morandini .05
144 Eric King .05
145 Danny Tartabull .05
146 Lance Johnson .05
147 Casey Candaele .05
148 Felix Fermin .05
149 Rich Rodriguez .05
150 Dwight Evans .05
151 Joe Klink .05
152 Kevin Reimer .05
153 Orlando Merced .05
154 Mel Hall .05
155 Randy Myers .05
156 Greg Harris .05
157 Jeff Brantley .05
158 Jim Eisenreich .05
159 Luis Rivera .05
160 Cris Carpenter .05
161 Bruce Ruffin .05
162 Omar Vizquel .10
163 Gerald Alexander .05
164 Mark Guthrie .05
165 Scott Lewis .05
166 Bill Sampen .05
167 Dave Anderson .05
168 Kevin McReynolds .05
169 Jose Vizcaino .05
170 Bob Geren .05
171 Mike Morgan .05
172 Jim Gott .05
173 Mike Pagliarulo .05
174 Mike Jeffcoat .05
175 Craig Lefferts .05
176 Steve Finley .05
177 Wally Backman .05
178 Kent Mercker .05
179 John Cerutti .05
180 Jay Bell .05
181 Dale Sveum .05
182 Greg Gagne .05
183 Donnie Hill .05
184 Rex Hudler .05
185 Pat Kelly .05
186 Jeff Robinson .05
187 Jeff Gray .05
188 Jerry Willard .05
189 Carlos Quintana .05
190 Dennis Eckersley .05
191 Kelly Downs .05
192 Gregg Jefferies .10
193 Darrin Fletcher .05
194 Mike Jackson .05
195 Eddie Murray .20
196 Billy Landrum .05
197 Eric Yelding .05
198 Devon White .10
199 Larry Walker .15
200 Ryne Sandberg .25
201 Dave Magadan .05
202 Steve Chitren .05
203 Scott Fletcher .05
204 Dwayne Henry .05
205 Scott Coolbaugh .05
206 Tracy Jones .05
207 Von Hayes .05
208 Bob Melvin .05
209 Scott Scudder .05
210 Luis Gonzalez .10
211 Scott Sanderson .05
212 *Chris Donnels* .05
213 *Heath Slocumb* .05
214 Mike Timlin .05
215 Brian Harper .05
216 Juan Berenguer .05
217 Mike Henneman .05
218 Bill Spiers .05
219 Scott Terry .05
220 Frank Viola .05
221 Mark Eichhorn .05
222 Ernest Riles .05
223 Ray Lankford .10
224 Pete Harnisch .05
225 Bobby Bonilla .10
226 Mike Scioscia .05
227 Joel Skinner .05
228 Brian Holman .05
229 Gilberto Reyes .05
230 Matt Williams .20
231 Jaime Navarro .05
232 Jose Rijo .05
233 Atlee Hammaker .05
234 Tim Teufel .05
235 John Kruk .05
236 Kurt Stillwell .05
237 Dan Pasqua .05
238 Tim Crews .05
239 Dave Gallagher .05
240 Leo Gomez .05
241 Steve Avery .05
242 Bill Gullickson .05
243 Mark Portugal .05
244 Lee Guetterman .05
245 Benny Santiago .05
246 Jim Gantner .05
247 Robby Thompson .05
248 Terry Shumpert .05
249 *Mike Bell* .05
250 Harold Reynolds .05
251 Mike Felder .05
252 Bill Pecota .05
253 Bill Krueger .05
254 Alfredo Griffin .05
255 Lou Whitaker .05
256 Roy Smith .05
257 Jerald Clark .05
258 Sammy Sosa .75
259 Tim Naehring .05
260 Dave Righetti .05
261 Paul Gibson .05
262 Chris James .05
263 Larry Andersen .05
264 Storm Davis .05
265 Jose Lind .05
266 Greg Hibbard .05
267 Norm Charlton .05
268 Paul Kilgus .05
269 Greg Maddux .75
270 Ellis Burks .10
271 Frank Tanana .05
272 Gene Larkin .05
273 Ron Hassey .05
274 Jeff Robinson .05
275 Steve Howe .05
276 Daryl Boston .05
277 Mark Lee .05
278 *Jose Segura* .05
279 Lance Blankenship .05
280 Don Slaught .05
281 Russ Swan .05
282 Bob Tewksbury .05
283 Geno Petralli .05
284 Shane Mack .05
285 Bob Scanlan .05
286 Tim Leary .05
287 John Smoltz .10
288 Pat Borders .05
289 Mark Davidson .05
290 Sam Horn .05
291 Lenny Harris .05
292 Franklin Stubbs .05
293 Thomas Howard .05
294 Steve Lyons .05
295 Francisco Oliveras .05
296 Terry Leach .05
297 Barry Jones .05
298 Lance Parrish .05
299 Wally Whitehurst .05
300 Bob Welch .05
301 Charlie Hayes .05
302 Charlie Hough .05
303 Gary Redus .05
304 Scott Bradley .05
305 Jose Oquendo .05
306 Pete Incaviglia .05
307 Marvin Freeman .05
308 Gary Pettis .05
309 Joe Slusarski .05
310 Kevin Seitzer .05
311 Jeff Reed .05
312 Pat Tabler .05
313 Mike Maddux .05
314 Bob Milacki .05
315 Eric Anthony .05
316 Dante Bichette .15
317 Steve Decker .05
318 Jack Clark .05
319 Doug Dascenzo .05
320 Scott Leius .10
321 Jim Lindeman .05
322 Bryan Harvey .05
323 Spike Owen .05
324 Roberto Kelly .05
325 Stan Belinda .05
326 Joey Cora .05
327 Jeff Innis .05
328 Willie Wilson .05
329 Juan Agosto .05
330 Charles Nagy .10
331 Scott Bailes .05
332 *Pete Schourek* .10
333 Mike Flanagan .05
334 Omar Olivares .05
335 Dennis Lamp .05
336 Tommy Greene .05
337 Randy Velarde .05
338 Tom Lampkin .05
339 John Russell .05
340 Bob Kipper .05
341 Todd Burns .05
342 Ron Jones .05
343 Dave Valle .05
344 Mike Heath .05
345 John Olerud .25
346 Gerald Young .05
347 Ken Patterson .05
348 Les Lancaster .05
349 Steve Crawford .05
350 John Candelaria .05
351 Mike Aldrete .05
352 Mariano Duncan .05
353 Julio Machado .05
354 Ken Williams .05
355 Walt Terrell .05
356 Mitch Williams .05
357 Al Newman .05
358 Bud Black .05
359 Joe Hesketh .05
360 Paul Assenmacher .05
361 Bo Jackson .10
362 Jeff Blauser .05
363 Mike Brumley .05
364 Jim Deshaies .05
365 Brady Anderson .10
366 Chuck McElroy .05
367 Matt Merullo .05
368 Tim Belcher .05
369 Luis Aquino .05
370 Joe Oliver .05
371 Greg Swindell .05
372 Lee Stevens .05
373 Mark Knudson .05
374 Bill Wegman .05
375 Jerry Don Gleaton .05
376 Pedro Guerrero .05
377 Randy Bush .05
378 Greg Harris .05
379 Eric Plunk .05
380 Jose DeJesus .05
381 Bobby Witt .05
382 Curtis Wilkerson .05
383 Gene Nelson .05
384 Wes Chamberlain .05
385 Tom Henke .05
386 Mark Lemke .05
387 Greg Briley .05
388 Rafael Ramirez .05
389 Tony Fossas .05
390 Henry Cotto .05
391 Tim Hulett .05
392 Dean Palmer .05
393 Glenn Braggs .05
394 Mark Salas .05
395 *Rusty Meacham* .10
396 *Andy Ashby* .25
397 *Jose Melendez* .05
398 *Warren Newson* .10
399 *Frank Castillo* .05
400 *Chito Martinez* .05
401 Bernie Williams .20
402 Derek Bell .10
403 *Javier Ortiz* .05
404 *Tim Sherrill* .10
405 *Rob MacDonald* .05
406 Phil Plantier .05
407 Troy Afenir .05
408 *Gino Minutelli* .05
409 *Reggie Jefferson* .10
410 *Mike Remlinger* .10
411 *Carlos Rodriguez* .10
412 *Joe Redfield* .05
413 Alonzo Powell .05
414 *Scott Livingstone* .10
415 *Scott Kamieniecki* .10
416 *Tim Spehr* .10
417 *Brian Hunter* .10
418 *Ced Landrum* .05
419 *Bret Barberie* .10
420 Kevin Morton .05
421 *Doug Henry* .10
422 *Doug Piatt* .15
423 *Pat Rice* .10
424 Juan Guzman .05
425 Nolan Ryan (No-Hit) .30

426 Tommy Greene (No-Hit) .10
427 Bob Milacki, Mike Flanagan, Mark Williamson, Gregg Olson (No-Hit) .10
428 Wilson Alvarez (No-Hit) .10
429 Otis Nixon (Highlight) .05
430 Rickey Henderson (Highlight) .10
431 Cecil Fielder (All-Star) .05
432 Julio Franco (AS) .05
433 Cal Ripken, Jr. (AS) .25
434 Wade Boggs (AS) .10
435 Joe Carter (AS) .05
436 Ken Griffey, Jr. (AS) .60
437 Ruben Sierra (AS) .05
438 Scott Erickson (AS) .05
439 Tom Henke (AS) .05
440 Terry Steinbach (AS) .05
441 Rickey Henderson (Dream Team) .10
442 Ryne Sandberg (Dream Team) .25
443 Otis Nixon .05
444 Scott Radinsky .05
445 Mark Grace .15
446 Tony Pena .05
447 Billy Hatcher .05
448 Glenallen Hill .05
449 Chris Gwynn .05
450 Tom Glavine .10
451 John Habyan .05
452 Al Osuna .05
453 Tony Phillips .05
454 Greg Cadaret .05
455 Rob Dibble .05
456 Rick Honeycutt .05
457 Jerome Walton .05
458 Mookie Wilson .05
459 Mark Gubicza .05
460 Craig Biggio .20
461 Dave Cochrane .05
462 Keith Miller .05
463 Alex Cole .05
464 Pete Smith .05
465 Brett Butler .05
466 Jeff Huson .05
467 Steve Lake .05
468 Lloyd Moseby .05
469 Tim McIntosh .05
470 Dennis Martinez .05
471 Greg Myers .05
472 Mackey Sasser .05
473 Junior Ortiz .05
474 Greg Olson .05
475 Steve Sax .05
476 Ricky Jordan .05
477 Max Venable .05
478 Brian McRae .05
479 Doug Simons .05
480 Rickey Henderson .15
481 Gary Varsho .05
482 Carl Willis .05
483 *Rick Wilkins* .10
484 Donn Pall .05
485 Edgar Martinez .05
486 Tom Foley .05
487 Mark Williamson .05
488 Jack Armstrong .05
489 Gary Carter .10
490 Ruben Sierra .05
491 Gerald Perry .05
492 Rob Murphy .05
493 Zane Smith .05
494 *Darryl Kile* .10
495 Kelly Gruber .05
496 Jerry Browne .05
497 Darryl Hamilton .05
498 Mike Stanton .05
499 Mark Leonard .05
500 Jose Canseco .15
501 Dave Martinez .05
502 Jose Guzman .05
503 Terry Kennedy .05
504 *Ed Sprague* .10
505 Frank Thomas .75
506 Darren Daulton .05
507 Kevin Tapani .05
508 Luis Salazar .05
509 Paul Faries .05
510 Sandy Alomar, Jr. .15
511 Jeff King .05
512 Gary Thurman .05
513 Chris Hammond .05
514 *Pedro Munoz* .10
515 Alan Trammell .10
516 Geronimo Pena .05
517 Rodney McCray .05
518 Manny Lee .05
519 Junior Felix .05
520 Kirk Gibson .05
521 Darrin Jackson .05
522 John Burkett .05
523 Jeff Johnson .05
524 Jim Corsi .05
525 Robin Yount .25
526 Jamie Quirk .05
527 Bob Ojeda .05
528 Mark Lewis .05
529 Bryn Smith .05
530 Kent Hrbek .05
531 Dennis Boyd .05
532 Ron Karkovice .05
533 Don August .05
534 Todd Frohwirth .05
535 Wally Joyner .10
536 Dennis Rasmussen .05
537 Andy Allanson .05
538 Rich Gossage .05
539 John Marzano .05
540 Cal Ripken, Jr. 1.00
541 Bill Swift .05
542 Kevin Appier .05
543 Dave Bergman .05
544 Bernard Gilkey .10
545 Mike Greenwell .05
546 Jose Uribe .05
547 Jesse Orosco .05
548 Bob Patterson .05
549 Mike Stanley .05
550 Howard Johnson .05
551 Joe Orsulak .05
552 Dick Schofield .05
553 Dave Hollins .05
554 David Segui .05
555 Barry Bonds .40
556 Mo Vaughn .25
557 Craig Wilson .05
558 Bobby Rose .05
559 Rod Nichols .05
560 Len Dykstra .05
561 Craig Grebeck .05
562 Darren Lewis .10
563 Todd Benzinger .05
564 Ed Whitson .05
565 Jesse Barfield .05
566 Lloyd McClendon .05
567 Dan Plesac .05
568 Danny Cox .05
569 Skeeter Barnes .05
570 Bobby Thigpen .05
571 Deion Sanders .10
572 Chuck Knoblauch .10
573 Matt Nokes .05
574 Herm Winningham .05
575 Tom Candiotti .05
576 Jeff Bagwell .50
577 Brook Jacoby .05
578 Chico Walker .05
579 Brian Downing .05
580 Dave Stewart .05
581 Francisco Cabrera .05
582 Rene Gonzales .05
583 Stan Javier .05
584 Randy Johnson .25
585 Chuck Finley .05
586 Mark Gardner .05
587 Mark Whiten .05
588 Garry Templeton .05
589 Gary Sheffield .15
590 Ozzie Smith .25
591 Candy Maldonado .05
592 Mike Sharperson .05
593 Carlos Martinez .05
594 Scott Bankhead .05
595 Tim Wallach .05
596 Tino Martinez .10
597 Roger McDowell .05
598 Cory Snyder .05
599 Andujar Cedeno .05
600 Kirby Puckett .30
601 Rick Parker .05
602 Todd Hundley .10
603 Greg Litton .05
604 Dave Johnson .05
605 John Franco .05
606 Mike Fetters .05
607 Luis Alicea .05
608 Trevor Wilson .05
609 Rob Ducey .05
610 Ramon Martinez .10
611 Dave Burba .05
612 Dwight Smith .05
613 Kevin Maas .05
614 John Costello .05
615 Glenn Davis .05
616 Shawn Abner .05
617 Scott Hemond .05
618 Tom Prince .05
619 Wally Ritchie .05
620 Jim Abbott .05
621 Charlie O'Brien .05
622 Jack Daugherty .05
623 Tommy Gregg .05
624 Jeff Shaw .05
625 Tony Gwynn .35
626 Mark Leiter .05
627 Jim Clancy .05
628 Tim Layana .05
629 Jeff Schaefer .05
630 Lee Smith .05
631 Wade Taylor .05
632 Mike Simms .05
633 Terry Steinbach .05
634 Shawon Dunston .05
635 Tim Raines .10
636 Kirt Manwaring .05
637 Warren Cromartie .05
638 Luis Quinones .05
639 Greg Vaughn .10
640 Kevin Mitchell .05
641 Chris Hoiles .05
642 Tom Browning .05
643 Mitch Webster .05
644 Steve Olin .05
645 Tony Fernandez .05
646 Juan Bell .05
647 Joe Boever .05
648 Carney Lansford .05
649 Mike Benjamin .05
650 George Brett .25
651 Tim Burke .05
652 Jack Morris .05
653 Orel Hershiser .10
654 Mike Schooler .05
655 Andy Van Slyke .05
656 Dave Stieb .05
657 Dave Clark .05
658 Ben McDonald .05
659 John Smiley .05
660 Wade Boggs .20
661 Eric Bullock .05
662 Eric Show .05
663 Lenny Webster .05
664 Mike Huff .05
665 Rick Sutcliffe .05
666 Jeff Manto .05
667 Mike Fitzgerald .05
668 Matt Young .05
669 Dave West .05
670 Mike Hartley .05
671 Curt Schilling .10
672 Brian Bohanon .05
673 Cecil Espy .05
674 Joe Grahe .05
675 Sid Fernandez .05
676 Edwin Nunez .05
677 Hector Villanueva .05
678 Sean Berry .05
679 Dave Eiland .05
680 David Cone .10
681 Mike Bordick .05
682 Tony Castillo .05
683 John Barfield .05
684 Jeff Hamilton .05
685 Ken Dayley .05
686 Carmelo Martinez .05
687 Mike Capel .05
688 Scott Chiamparino .05
689 Rich Gedman .05
690 Rich Monteleone .05
691 Alejandro Pena .05
692 Oscar Azocar .05
693 Jim Poole .05
694 Mike Gardiner .05
695 Steve Buechele .05
696 Rudy Seanez .05
697 Paul Abbott .05
698 Steve Searcy .05
699 Jose Offerman .05
700 Ivan Rodriguez .30
701 Joe Girardi .05
702 Tony Perezchica .05
703 Paul McClellan .05
704 *David Howard* .10
705 Dan Petry .05
706 Jack Howell .05
707 Jose Mesa .05
708 Randy St. Claire .05
709 Kevin Brown .05
710 Ron Darling .05
711 Jason Grimsley .05
712 John Orton .05
713 Shawn Boskie .05
714 Pat Clements .05
715 Brian Barnes .05
716 *Luis Lopez* .05
717 Bob McClure .05
718 Mark Davis .05
719 Dann Billardello .05
720 Tom Edens .05
721 Willie Fraser .05
722 Curt Young .05
723 Neal Heaton .05
724 Craig Worthington .05
725 Mel Rojas .05
726 Daryl Irvine .05
727 Roger Mason .05
728 Kirk Dressendorfer .05
729 Scott Aldred .05
730 Willie Blair .05
731 Allan Anderson .05
732 Dana Kiecker .05
733 Jose Gonzalez .05
734 Brian Drahman .05
735 Brad Komminsk .05
736 *Arthur Rhodes* .10
737 *Terry Mathews* .05
738 *Jeff Fassero* .05
739 *Mike Magnante* .05
740 *Kip Gross* .05
741 *Jim Hunter* .05
742 *Jose Mota* .05
743 Joe Bitker .05
744 *Tim Mauser* .05
745 *Ramon Garcia* .05
746 *Rod Beck* .25
747 *Jim Austin* .05
748 *Keith Mitchell* .05
749 *Wayne Rosenthal* .05
750 *Bryan Hickerson* .05
751 *Bruce Egloff* .05
752 *John Wehner* .05
753 Darren Holmes .05
754 Dave Hansen .05
755 Mike Mussina .25
756 *Anthony Young* .05
757 Ron Tingley .05
758 *Ricky Bones* .05
759 *Mark Wohlers* .10
760 Wilson Alvarez .10
761 *Harvey Pulliam* .05
762 *Ryan Bowen* .10
763 Terry Bross .05
764 *Joel Johnston* .05
765 *Terry McDaniel* .05
766 *Esteban Beltre* .05
767 *Rob Maurer* .05
768 Ted Wood .05
769 *Mo Sanford* .10
770 *Jeff Carter* .05
771 *Gil Heredia* .10
772 Monty Fariss .05
773 Will Clark (AS) .10
774 Ryne Sandberg (AS) .15
775 Barry Larkin (AS) .10
776 Howard Johnson (AS) .05
777 Barry Bonds (AS) .25
778 Brett Butler (AS) .05
779 Tony Gwynn (AS) .15
780 Ramon Martinez (AS) .05
781 Lee Smith (AS) .05
782 Mike Scioscia (AS) .05
783 Dennis Martinez (Highlight) .05
784 Dennis Martinez (No-Hit) .05
785 Mark Gardner (No-Hit) .05
786 Bret Saberhagen (No-Hit) .05
787 Kent Mercker, Mark Wohlers, Alejandro Pena (No-Hit) .05
788 Cal Ripken (MVP) .25
789 Terry Pendleton (MVP) .05

790	Roger Clemens (CY)	.15
791	Tom Glavine (CY)	.05
792	Chuck Knoblauch (ROY)	.10
793	Jeff Bagwell (ROY)	.25
794	Cal Ripken, Jr. (Man of the Year)	.25
795	David Cone (Highlight)	.05
796	Kirby Puckett (Highlight)	.15
797	Steve Avery (Highlight)	.05
798	Jack Morris (Highlight)	.05
799	*Allen Watson*	.25
800	*Manny Ramirez*	4.00
801	*Cliff Floyd*	.40
802	*Al Shirley*	.05
803	*Brian Barber*	.05
804	*Jon Farrell*	.05
805	*Brent Gates*	.25
806	*Scott Ruffcorn*	.20
807	*Tyrone Hill*	.10
808	*Benji Gil*	.10
809	*Aaron Sele*	.30
810	*Tyler Green*	.25
811	Chris Jones	.05
812	Steve Wilson	.05
813	*Cliff Young*	.10
814	*Don Wakamatsu*	.05
815	*Mike Humphreys*	.05
816	*Scott Servais*	.05
817	*Rico Rossy*	.05
818	*John Ramos*	.05
819	Rob Mallicoat	.05
820	*Milt Hill*	.10
821	Carlos Carcia	.05
822	Stan Royer	.10
823	*Jeff Plympton*	.10
824	*Braulio Castillo*	.10
825	*David Haas*	.05
826	*Luis Mercedes*	.10
827	Eric Karros	.15
828	*Shawn Hare*	.10
829	Reggie Sanders	.10
830	Tom Goodwin	.05
831	*Dan Gakeler*	.05
832	*Stacy Jones*	.05
833	*Kim Batiste*	.05
834	Cal Eldred	.05
835	*Chris George*	.05
836	*Wayne Housie*	.05
837	*Mike Ignasiak*	.05
838	*Josias Manzanillo*	.05
839	*Jim Olander*	.05
840	*Gary Cooper*	.05
841	Royce Clayton	.05
842	Hector Fajardo	.05
843	Blaine Beatty	.05
844	*Jorge Pedre*	.05
845	Kenny Lofton	.30
846	Scott Brosius	.15
847	*Chris Cron*	.05
848	Denis Boucher	.05
849	Kyle Abbott	.10
850	Bob Zupcic	.05
851	*Rheal Cormier*	.15
852	*Jim Lewis*	.05
853	Anthony Telford	.05
854	*Cliff Brantley*	.05
855	*Kevin Campbell*	.05
856	*Craig Shipley*	.05
857	Chuck Carr	.05
858	*Tony Eusebio*	.10
859	Jim Thome	.25
860	*Vinny Castilla*	1.00
861	Dann Howitt	.05
862	*Kevin Ward*	.05
863	*Steve Wapnick*	.05
864	Rod Brewer	.05
865	Todd Van Poppel	.10
866	*Jose Hernandez*	.05
867	*Amalio Carreno*	.05
868	*Calvin Jones*	.05
869	*Jeff Gardner*	.05
870	*Jarvis Brown*	.05
871	*Eddie Taubensee*	.10
872	*Andy Mota*	.10
873	Chris Haney (Front photo actually Scott Ruskin)	.05
874	Roberto Hernandez	.10
875	*Laddie Renfroe*	.05
876	Scott Cooper	.05
877	*Armando Reynoso*	.05
878	Ty Cobb (Memorabilia)	.30
879	Babe Ruth (Memorabilia)	.40
880	Honus Wagner (Memorabilia)	.20
881	Lou Gehrig (Memorabilia)	.30
882	Satchel Paige (Memorabilia)	.20
883	Will Clark (Dream Team)	.20
884	Cal Ripken, Jr. (Dream Team)	.35
885	Wade Boggs (Dream Team)	.20
886	Kirby Puckett (Dream Team)	.30
887	Tony Gwynn (Dream Team)	.30
888	Craig Biggio (Dream Team)	.10
889	Scott Erickson (Dream Team)	.05
890	Tom Glavine (Dream Team)	.15
891	Rob Dibble (Dream Team)	.05
892	Mitch Williams (Dream Team)	.05
893	Frank Thomas (Dream Team)	.50

1992 Score Factory Inserts

Available exclusively in factory sets these 17 cards are divided into four subsets commemorating the 1991 World Series, potential Hall of Famers, the career of Joe DiMaggio and Carl Yastrzemski's 1967 Triple Crown season. Cards carry a "B" prefix to the card number.

		MT
Complete Set (17):		7.50
Common World Series (1-7):		.15
Common Cooperstown (8-11):		.70
Common DiMaggio (12-14):		.35
Common Yastrzemski (15-17):		.20
1	World Series Game 1 (Greg Gagne)	.15
2	World Series Game 2 (Scott Leius)	.15
3	World Series Game 3 (David Justice, Brian Harper)	.15
4	World Series Game 4 (Lonnie Smith, Brian Harper)	.15
5	World Series Game 5 (David Justice)	.30
6	World Series Game 6 (Kirby Puckett)	.60
7	World Series Game 7 (Gene Larkin)	.15
8	Carlton Fisk (Cooperstown)	.45
9	Ozzie Smith (Cooperstown)	.75
10	Dave Winfield (Cooperstown)	.75
11	Robin Yount (Cooperstown)	.75
12	Joe DiMaggio (The Hard Hitter)	.75
13	Joe DiMaggio (The Stylish Fielder)	.75
14	Joe DiMaggio (The Champion Player)	.75
15	Carl Yastrzemski (The Impossible Dream)	.20
16	Carl Yastrzemski (The Triple Crown)	.20
17	Carl Yastrzemski (The World Series)	.20

1992 Score The Franchise

This four-card set, in both autographed and unautographed form, was a random insert in various premium packaging of Score's 1992 Series II cards. Each of the four cards was produced in an edition of 150,000, with 2,000 of each player's card being autographed and 500 of the triple-player card carrying the autographs of all three superstars.

		MT
Complete Set (4):		30.00
Common Player:		6.00
Musial Autograph:		150.00
Mantle Autograph:		400.00
Yastrzemski Autograph:		100.00
Triple Autograph:		1000.
1	Stan Musial	8.00
2	Mickey Mantle	12.00
3	Carl Yastrzemski	6.00
4	Stan Musial, Mickey Mantle, Carl Yastrzemski	9.00

1992 Score Hot Rookies

This 10-card rookie issue was produced as an insert in special blister packs of 1992 Score cards sold at retail outlets. Action photos on front and portraits on back are set against white backgrounds with orange highlights. Cards are standard 2-1/2" x 3-1/2".

		MT
Complete Set (10):		10.00
Common Player:		.70
1	Cal Eldred	.50
2	Royce Clayton	1.00
3	Kenny Lofton	5.00
4	Todd Van Poppel	.50
5	Scott Cooper	.50
6	Todd Hundley	1.50
7	Tino Martinez	2.00
8	Anthony Telford	.50
9	Derek Bell	1.50
10	Reggie Jefferson	.50

1992 Score Impact Players

Jumbo packs of 1992 Score Series I and II cards contained five of these special inserts labeled "90's Impact Players". Front action photos contrast with portrait photos on the backs, which are color-coded by team. Cards #1-45 were packaged with Series I, cards #46-90 were included in Series II packs.

		MT
Complete Set (90):		20.00
Common Player:		.10
1	Chuck Knoblauch	.25
2	Jeff Bagwell	1.00
3	Juan Guzman	.10
4	Milt Cuyler	.10
5	Ivan Rodriguez	.60
6	Rich DeLucia	.10
7	Orlando Merced	.10
8	Ray Lankford	.20
9	Brian Hunter	.10
10	Roberto Alomar	.60
11	Wes Chamberlain	.10
12	Steve Avery	.10
13	Scott Erickson	.10
14	Jim Abbott	.15
15	Mark Whiten	.10
16	Leo Gomez	.10
17	Doug Henry	.10
18	Brent Mayne	.10
19	Charles Nagy	.15
20	Phil Plantier	.10
21	Mo Vaughn	.60
22	Craig Biggio	.20
23	Derek Bell	.20
24	Royce Clayton	.15
25	Gary Cooper	.10
26	Scott Cooper	.10
27	Juan Gonzalez	.75
28	Ken Griffey, Jr.	3.00
29	Larry Walker	.45
30	John Smoltz	.20
31	Todd Hundley	.15
32	Kenny Lofton	.60
33	Andy Mota	.10
34	Todd Zeile	.10

35	Arthur Rhodes	.10
36	Jim Thome	.25
37	Todd Van Poppel	.10
38	Mark Wohlers	.10
39	Anthony Young	.10
40	Sandy Alomar Jr.	.15
41	John Olerud	.25
42	Robin Ventura	.25
43	Frank Thomas	1.00
44	Dave Justice	.50
45	Hal Morris	.10
46	Ruben Sierra	.10
47	Travis Fryman	.10
48	Mike Mussina	.20
49	Tom Glavine	.15
50	Barry Larkin	.20
51	Will Clark	.30
52	Jose Canseco	.45
53	Bo Jackson	.25
54	Dwight Gooden	.15
55	Barry Bonds	1.00
56	Fred McGriff	.40
57	Roger Clemens	.75
58	Benito Santiago	.10
59	Darryl Strawberry	.15
60	Cecil Fielder	.15
61	John Franco	.10
62	Matt Williams	.25
63	Marquis Grissom	.15
64	Danny Tartabull	.10
65	Ron Gant	.20
66	Paul O'Neill	.15
67	Devon White	.10
68	Rafael Palmeiro	.25
69	Tom Gordon	.10
70	Shawon Dunston	.10
71	Rob Dibble	.10
72	Eddie Zosky	.10
73	Jack McDowell	.10
74	Len Dykstra	.10
75	Ramon Martinez	.15
76	Reggie Sanders	.20
77	Greg Maddux	1.50
78	Ellis Burks	.20
79	John Smiley	.10
80	Roberto Kelly	.10
81	Ben McDonald	.10
82	Mark Lewis	.10
83	Jose Rijo	.10
84	Ozzie Guillen	.10
85	Lance Dickson	.10
86	Kim Batiste	.10
87	Gregg Olson	.10
88	Andy Benes	.15
89	Cal Eldred	.10
90	David Cone	.15

1992 Score Joe DiMaggio

Colorized vintage photos are featured on the front and back of each of five Joe DiMaggio tribute cards which were issued as random inserts in 1992 Score Series 1 packs. A limited number (1,800) of each card were autographed. Curiously, the cards carry a 1993 copyright date.

		MT
Complete Set (5):		100.00
Common Card:		25.00
Autographed Card:		300.00
1	Joe DiMaggio (The Minors)	25.00
2	Joe DiMaggio (The Rookie)	25.00
3	Joe DiMaggio (The MVP)	25.00
4	Joe DiMaggio (The Streak)	25.00
5	Joe DiMaggio (The Legend)	25.00

1992 Score Rookie & Traded

This 110-card set features traded players, free agents and top rookies from 1992. The cards are styled after the regular 1992 Score cards. Cards 80-110 feature the rookies. The set was released as a boxed set and was available only through hobby dealers.

		MT
Complete Set (110):		15.00
Common Player:		.05
1	Gary Sheffield	.40
2	Kevin Seitzer	.05
3	Danny Tartabull	.05
4	Steve Sax	.05
5	Bobby Bonilla	.05
6	Frank Viola	.05
7	Dave Winfield	.40
8	Rick Sutcliffe	.05
9	Jose Canseco	.75
10	Greg Swindell	.05
11	Eddie Murray	.40
12	Randy Myers	.05
13	Wally Joyner	.10
14	Kenny Lofton	1.50
15	Jack Morris	.05
16	Charlie Hayes	.05
17	Pete Incaviglia	.05
18	Kevin Mitchell	.05
19	Kurt Stillwell	.05
20	Bret Saberhagen	.10
21	Steve Buechele	.05
22	John Smiley	.05
23	Sammy Sosa	4.00
24	George Bell	.05
25	Curt Schilling	.20
26	Dick Schofield	.05
27	David Cone	.20
28	Dan Gladden	.05
29	Kirk McCaskill	.05
30	Mike Gallego	.05
31	Kevin McReynolds	.05
32	Bill Swift	.05
33	Dave Martinez	.05
34	Storm Davis	.05
35	Willie Randolph	.05
36	Melido Perez	.05
37	Mark Carreon	.05
38	Doug Jones	.05
39	Gregg Jefferies	.20
40	Mike Jackson	.05
41	Dickie Thon	.05
42	Eric King	.05
43	Herm Winningham	.05
44	Derek Lilliquist	.05
45	Dave Anderson	.05
46	Jeff Reardon	.05
47	Scott Bankhead	.05
48	Cory Snyder	.05
49	Al Newman	.05
50	Keith Miller	.05
51	Dave Burba	.05
52	Bill Pecota	.05
53	Chuck Crim	.05
54	Mariano Duncan	.05
55	Dave Gallagher	.05
56	Chris Gwynn	.05
57	Scott Ruskin	.05
58	Jack Armstrong	.05
59	Gary Carter	.10
60	Andres Galarraga	.50
61	Ken Hill	.05
62	Eric Davis	.10
63	Ruben Sierra	.05
64	Darrin Fletcher	.05
65	Tim Belcher	.05
66	Mike Morgan	.05
67	Scott Scudder	.05
68	Tom Candiotti	.05
69	Hubie Brooks	.05
70	Kal Daniels	.05
71	Bruce Ruffin	.05
72	Billy Hatcher	.05
73	Bob Melvin	.05
74	Lee Guetterman	.05
75	Rene Gonzales	.05
76	Kevin Bass	.05
77	Tom Bolton	.05
78	John Wetteland	.05
79	Bip Roberts	.05
80	Pat Listach	.05
81	John Doherty	.05
82	Sam Militello	.05
83	*Brian Jordan*	1.50
84	Jeff Kent	2.00
85	Dave Fleming	.10
86	Jeff Tackett	.05
87	*Chad Curtis*	.50
88	Eric Fox	.05
89	Denny Neagle	.05
90	Donovan Osborne	.05
91	Carlos Hernandez	.05
92	Tim Wakefield	.10
93	Tim Salmon	2.00
94	Dave Nilsson	.10
95	Mike Perez	.05
96	Pat Hentgen	.10
97	Frank Seminara	.05
98	Ruben Amaro, Jr.	.10
99	Archi Cianfrocco	.05
100	Andy Stankiewicz	.05
101	Jim Bullinger	.10
102	Pat Mahomes	.10
103	Hipolito Pichardo	.05
104	Bret Boone	.50
105	John Vander Wal	.10
106	Vince Horsman	.05
107	James Austin	.05
108	Brian Williams	.05
109	Dan Walters	.05
110	Wil Cordero	.50

1993 Score

Score's 1993 cards have white borders surrounding color action photographs. The player's name is at the bottom of the card, while his team's name and position appears on the left side in a color band. Backs have color portraits, statistics and text. Subsets feature rookies, award winners, draft picks, highlights, World Series highlights, all-star caricatures, dream team players, and the Man of the Year (Kirby Puckett). Insert sets include: Boys of Summer, the Franchise and Stat Leaders, which feature Select's card design.

		MT
Complete Set (660):		30.00
Common Player:		.05
Pack (16):		.75
Wax Box (36):		18.00
1	Ken Griffey, Jr.	2.00
2	Gary Sheffield	.20
3	Frank Thomas	1.00
4	Ryne Sandberg	.40
5	Larry Walker	.20
6	Cal Ripken, Jr.	1.50
7	Roger Clemens	.75
8	Bobby Bonilla	.05
9	Carlos Baerga	.10
10	Darren Daulton	.05
11	Travis Fryman	.10
12	Andy Van Slyke	.05
13	Jose Canseco	.30
14	Roberto Alomar	.35
15	Tom Glavine	.10
16	Barry Larkin	.15
17	Gregg Jefferies	.10
18	Craig Biggio	.15
19	Shane Mack	.05
20	Brett Butler	.05
21	Dennis Eckersley	.05
22	Will Clark	.20
23	Don Mattingly	.50
24	Tony Gwynn	.75
25	Ivan Rodriguez	.40
26	Shawon Dunston	.05
27	Mike Mussina	.25
28	Marquis Grissom	.10
29	Charles Nagy	.10
30	Len Dykstra	.05
31	Cecil Fielder	.10
32	Jay Bell	.05
33	B.J. Surhoff	.05
34	Bob Tewksbury	.05
35	Danny Tartabull	.05
36	Terry Pendleton	.05
37	Jack Morris	.05
38	Hal Morris	.05
39	Luis Polonia	.05
40	Ken Caminiti	.15
41	Robin Ventura	.15
42	Darryl Strawberry	.10
43	Wally Joyner	.10
44	Fred McGriff	.15
45	Kevin Tapani	.05
46	Matt Williams	.15
47	Robin Yount	.25
48	Ken Hill	.05
49	Edgar Martinez	.05
50	Mark Grace	.15
51	Juan Gonzalez	.50
52	Curt Schilling	.10
53	Dwight Gooden	.10
54	Chris Hoiles	.05
55	Frank Viola	.05
56	Ray Lankford	.10
57	George Brett	.40
58	Kenny Lofton	.20
59	Nolan Ryan	1.25
60	Mickey Tettleton	.05
61	John Smoltz	.10
62	Howard Johnson	.05
63	Eric Karros	.10
64	Rick Aguilera	.05
65	Steve Finley	.05
66	Mark Langston	.05
67	Bill Swift	.05

No.	Player	Value
68	John Olerud	.15
69	Kevin McReynolds	.05
70	Jack McDowell	.05
71	Rickey Henderson	.20
72	Brian Harper	.05
73	Mike Morgan	.05
74	Rafael Palmeiro	.20
75	Dennis Martinez	.05
76	Tino Martinez	.10
77	Eddie Murray	.20
78	Ellis Burks	.10
79	John Kruk	.05
80	Gregg Olson	.05
81	Bernard Gilkey	.10
82	Milt Cuyler	.05
83	Mike LaValliere	.05
84	Albert Belle	.30
85	Bip Roberts	.05
86	Melido Perez	.05
87	Otis Nixon	.05
88	Bill Spiers	.05
89	Jeff Bagwell	.50
90	Orel Hershiser	.10
91	Andy Benes	.10
92	Devon White	.10
93	Willie McGee	.05
94	Ozzie Guillen	.05
95	Ivan Calderon	.05
96	Keith Miller	.05
97	Steve Buechele	.05
98	Kent Hrbek	.05
99	Dave Hollins	.05
100	Mike Bordick	.05
101	Randy Tomlin	.05
102	Omar Vizquel	.05
103	Lee Smith	.05
104	Leo Gomez	.05
105	Jose Rijo	.05
106	Mark Whiten	.05
107	Dave Justice	.15
108	Eddie Taubensee	.05
109	Lance Johnson	.05
110	Felix Jose	.05
111	Mike Harkey	.05
112	Randy Milligan	.05
113	Anthony Young	.05
114	Rico Brogna	.05
115	Bret Saberhagen	.05
116	Sandy Alomar, Jr.	.10
117	Terry Mulholland	.05
118	Darryl Hamilton	.05
119	Todd Zeile	.10
120	Bernie Williams	.40
121	Zane Smith	.05
122	Derek Bell	.10
123	Deion Sanders	.15
124	Luis Sojo	.05
125	Joe Oliver	.05
126	Craig Grebeck	.05
127	Andujar Cedeno	.05
128	Brian McRae	.05
129	Jose Offerman	.05
130	Pedro Munoz	.05
131	Bud Black	.05
132	Mo Vaughn	.25
133	Bruce Hurst	.05
134	Dave Henderson	.05
135	Tom Pagnozzi	.05
136	Erik Hanson	.05
137	Orlando Merced	.05
138	Dean Palmer	.05
139	John Franco	.05
140	Brady Anderson	.10
141	Ricky Jordan	.05
142	Jeff Blauser	.05
143	Sammy Sosa	1.25
144	Bob Walk	.05
145	Delino DeShields	.05
146	Kevin Brown	.10
147	Mark Lemke	.05
148	Chuck Knoblauch	.20
149	Chris Sabo	.05
150	Bobby Witt	.05
151	Luis Gonzalez	.10
152	Ron Karkovice	.05
153	Jeff Brantley	.05
154	Kevin Appier	.05
155	Darrin Jackson	.05
156	Kelly Gruber	.05
157	Royce Clayton	.05
158	Chuck Finley	.05
159	Jeff King	.05
160	Greg Vaughn	.10
161	Geronimo Pena	.05
162	Steve Farr	.05
163	Jose Oquendo	.05
164	Mark Lewis	.05
165	John Wetteland	.05
166	Mike Henneman	.05
167	Todd Hundley	.10
168	Wes Chamberlain	.05
169	Steve Avery	.05
170	Mike Devereaux	.05
171	Reggie Sanders	.10
172	Jay Buhner	.10
173	Eric Anthony	.05
174	John Burkett	.05
175	Tom Candiotti	.05
176	Phil Plantier	.05
177	Doug Henry	.05
178	Scott Leius	.05
179	Kirt Manwaring	.05
180	Jeff Parrett	.05
181	Don Slaught	.05
182	Scott Radinsky	.05
183	Luis Alicea	.05
184	Tom Gordon	.05
185	Rick Wilkins	.05
186	Todd Stottlemyre	.05
187	Moises Alou	.15
188	Joe Grahe	.05
189	Jeff Kent	.05
190	Bill Wegman	.05
191	Kim Batiste	.05
192	Matt Nokes	.05
193	Mark Wohlers	.05
194	Paul Sorrento	.05
195	Chris Hammond	.05
196	Scott Livingstone	.05
197	Doug Jones	.05
198	Scott Cooper	.05
199	Ramon Martinez	.10
200	Dave Valle	.05
201	Mariano Duncan	.05
202	Ben McDonald	.05
203	Darren Lewis	.05
204	Kenny Rogers	.05
205	Manuel Lee	.05
206	Scott Erickson	.05
207	Dan Gladden	.05
208	Bob Welch	.05
209	Greg Olson	.05
210	Dan Pasqua	.05
211	Tim Wallach	.05
212	Jeff Montgomery	.05
213	Derrick May	.05
214	Ed Sprague	.05
215	David Haas	.05
216	Darrin Fletcher	.05
217	Brian Jordan	.10
218	Jaime Navarro	.05
219	Randy Velarde	.05
220	Ron Gant	.10
221	Paul Quantrill	.05
222	Damion Easley	.05
223	Charlie Hough	.05
224	*Brad Brink*	.05
225	*Barry Manual*	.05
226	*Kevin Koslofski*	.05
227	*Ryan Thompson*	.10
228	*Mike Munoz*	.05
229	*Dan Wilson*	.10
230	*Peter Hoy*	.05
231	*Pedro Astacio*	.20
232	*Matt Stairs*	.15
233	*Jeff Reboulet*	.15
234	*Manny Alexander*	.10
235	*Willie Banks*	.05
236	*John Jaha*	.15
237	*Scooter Tucker*	.05
238	*Russ Springer*	.05
239	*Paul Miller*	.05
240	*Dan Peltier*	.05
241	*Ozzie Canseco*	.05
242	*Ben Rivera*	.05
243	*John Valentin*	.20
244	Henry Rodriguez	.10
245	*Derek Parks*	.10
246	*Carlos Garcia*	.10
247	*Tim Pugh*	.10
248	*Melvin Nieves*	.10
249	*Rich Amaral*	.05
250	*Willie Greene*	.15
251	*Tim Scott*	.05
252	*Dave Silvestri*	.10
253	*Rob Mallicoat*	.05
254	*Donald Harris*	.10
255	*Craig Colbert*	.05
256	Jose Guzman	.05
257	*Domingo Martinez*	.05
258	*William Suero*	.05
259	*Juan Guerrero*	.05
260	*J.T. Snow*	.50
261	Tony Pena	.05
262	*Tim Fortugno*	.05
263	*Tom Marsh*	.05
264	*Kurt Knudsen*	.05
265	*Tim Costo*	.10
266	*Steve Shifflett*	.05
267	*Billy Ashley*	.10
268	Jerry Nielsen	.05
269	*Pete Young*	.05
270	*Johnny Guzman*	.05
271	*Greg Colbrunn*	.10
272	Jeff Nelson	.05
273	*Kevin Young*	.10
274	Jeff Frye	.05
275	*J.T. Bruett*	.05
276	*Todd Pratt*	.05
277	*Mike Butcher*	.05
278	*John Flaherty*	.10
279	*John Patterson*	.10
280	*Eric Hillman*	.05
281	*Bien Figueros*	.05
282	*Shane Reynolds*	.10
283	*Rich Rowland*	.05
284	*Steve Foster*	.05
285	*Dave Mlicki*	.05
286	Mike Piazza	1.00
287	*Mike Trombley*	.10
288	*Jim Pena*	.05
289	*Bob Ayrault*	.05
290	*Henry Mercedes*	.10
291	Bob Wickman	.05
292	*Jacob Brumfield*	.05
293	*David Hulse*	.10
294	Ryan Klesko	.15
295	Doug Linton	.05
296	Steve Cooke	.05
297	Eddie Zosky	.05
298	*Gerald Williams*	.10
299	*Jonathan Hurst*	.10
300	*Larry Carter*	.05
301	*William Pennyfeather*	.05
302	*Cesar Hernandez*	.05
303	*Steve Hosey*	.10
304	*Blas Minor*	.10
305	*Jeff Grotewold*	.10
306	*Bernardo Brito*	.05
307	*Rafael Bournigal*	.10
308	*Jeff Branson*	.10
309	*Tom Quinlan*	.05
310	*Pat Gomez*	.10
311	*Sterling Hitchcock*	.10
312	Kent Bottenfield	.05
313	Alan Trammell	.10
314	*Cris Colon*	.05
315	*Paul Wagner*	.05
316	*Matt Maysey*	.05
317	Mike Stanton	.05
318	*Rick Trlicek*	.05
319	*Kevin Rogers*	.10
320	*Mark Clark*	.10
321	Pedro Martinez	.50
322	*Al Martin*	.15
323	Mike Macfarlane	.05
324	*Rey Sanchez*	.10
325	*Roger Pavlik*	.05
326	Troy Neel	.10
327	*Kerry Woodson*	.05
328	*Wayne Kirby*	.10
329	*Ken Ryan*	.15
330	*Jesse Levis*	.05
331	James Austin	.05
332	Dan Walters	.05
333	Brian Williams	.05
334	Wil Cordero	.10
335	Bret Boone	.10
336	Hipolito Pichardo	.05
337	Pat Mahomes	.05
338	Andy Stankiewicz	.05
339	Jim Bullinger	.05
340	Archi Cianfrocco	.05
341	Ruben Amaro, Jr.	.05
342	Frank Seminara	.05
343	Pat Hentgen	.05
344	Dave Nilsson	.05
345	Mike Perez	.05
346	Tim Salmon	.25
347	*Tim Wakefield*	.15
348	Carlos Hernandez	.05
349	Donovan Osborne	.05
350	Denny Naegle	.05
351	Sam Militello	.05
352	Eric Fox	.05
353	John Doherty	.05
354	Chad Curtis	.05
355	Jeff Tackett	.05
356	Dave Fleming	.05
357	Pat Listach	.05
358	Kevin Wickander	.05
359	John VanderWal	.05
360	Arthur Rhodes	.05
361	Bob Scanlan	.05
362	Bob Zupcic	.05
363	Mel Rojas	.05
364	Jim Thome	.25
365	Bill Pecota	.05
366	Mark Carreon	.05
367	Mitch Williams	.05
368	Cal Eldred	.05
369	Stan Belinda	.05
370	Pat Kelly	.05
371	Pheal Cormier	.05
372	Juan Guzman	.05
373	Damon Berryhill	.05
374	Gary DiSarcina	.05
375	Norm Charlton	.05
376	Roberto Hernandez	.05
377	Scott Kamieniecki	.05
378	Rusty Meacham	.05
379	Kurt Stillwell	.05
380	Lloyd McClendon	.05
381	Mark Leonard	.05
382	Jerry Browne	.05
383	Glenn Davis	.05
384	Randy Johnson	.40
385	Mike Greenwell	.05
386	Scott Chiamparino	.05
387	George Bell	.05
388	Steve Olin	.05
389	Chuck McElroy	.05
390	Mark Gardner	.05
391	Rod Beck	.05
392	Dennis Rasmussen	.05
393	Charlie Leibrandt	.05
394	Julio Franco	.05
395	Pete Harnisch	.05
396	Sid Bream	.05
397	Milt Thompson	.05
398	Glenallen Hill	.05
399	Chico Walker	.05
400	Alex Cole	.05
401	Trevor Wilson	.05
402	Jeff Conine	.10
403	Kyle Abbott	.05
404	Tom Browning	.05
405	Jerald Clark	.05
406	Vince Horsman	.05
407	Kevin Mitchell	.05
408	Pete Smith	.05
409	Jeff Innis	.05
410	Mike Timlin	.05
411	Charlie Hayes	.05
412	Alex Fernandez	.10
413	Jeff Russell	.05
414	Jody Reed	.05
415	Mickey Morandini	.05
416	Darnell Coles	.05
417	Xavier Hernandez	.05
418	Steve Sax	.05
419	Joe Girardi	.05
420	Mike Fetters	.05
421	Danny Jackson	.05
422	Jim Gott	.05
423	Tim Belcher	.05
424	Jose Mesa	.05
425	Junior Felix	.05
426	Thomas Howard	.05
427	Julio Valera	.05
428	Dante Bichette	.15
429	Mike Sharperson	.05
430	Darryl Kile	.05
431	Lonnie Smith	.05
432	Monty Fariss	.05
433	Reggie Jefferson	.05
434	Bob McClure	.05
435	Craig Lefferts	.05
436	Duane Ward	.05
437	Shawn Abner	.05
438	Roberto Kelly	.05
439	Paul O'Neill	.15
440	Alan Mills	.05
441	Roger Mason	.05
442	Gary Pettis	.05
443	Steve Lake	.05
444	Gene Larkin	.05
445	Larry Anderson	.05
446	Doug Dascenzo	.05
447	Daryl Boston	.05
448	John Candelaria	.05
449	Storm Davis	.05
450	Tom Edens	.05
451	Mike Maddux	.05

452 Tim Naehring .05
453 John Orton .05
454 Joey Cora .05
455 Chuck Crim .05
456 Dan Plesac .05
457 Mike Bielecki .05
458 *Terry Jorgensen* .05
459 John Habyan .05
460 Pete O'Brien .05
461 Jeff Treadway .05
462 Frank Castillo .05
463 Jimmy Jones .05
464 Tommy Greene .05
465 Tracy Woodson .05
466 Rich Rodriguez .05
467 Joe Hesketh .05
468 Greg Myers .05
469 Kirk McCaskill .05
470 Ricky Bones .05
471 Lenny Webster .05
472 Francisco Cabrera .05
473 Turner Ward .05
474 Dwayne Henry .05
475 Al Osuna .05
476 Craig Wilson .05
477 Chris Nabholz .05
478 Rafael Belliard .05
479 Terry Leach .05
480 Tim Teufel .05
481 Dennis Eckersley (Award Winner) .05
482 Barry Bonds (Award Winner) .20
483 Dennis Eckersley (Award Winner) .05
484 Greg Maddux (Award Winner) .50
485 Pat Listach (ROY) .05
486 Eric Karros (ROY) .15
487 *Jamie Arnold* .10
488 B.J. Wallace .10
489 *Derek Jeter* 10.00
490 *Jason Kendall* .50
491 Rick Helling .05
492 *Derek Wallace* .15
493 *Sean Lowe* .10
494 *Shannon Stewart* .50
495 *Benji Grigsby* .15
496 *Todd Steverson* .15
497 *Dan Serafini* .15
498 Michael Tucker .10
499 Chris Roberts (Draft Pick) .10
500 *Pete Janicki* (Draft Pick) .10
501 *Jeff Schmidt* .10
502 Edgar Martinez (All-Star) .05
503 Omar Vizquel (AS) .05
504 Ken Griffey, Jr. (AS) 1.00
505 Kirby Puckett (AS) .25
506 Joe Carter (AS) .05
507 Ivan Rodriguez (AS) .15
508 Jack Morris (AS) .05
509 Dennis Eckersley (AS) .05
510 Frank Thomas (AS) .50
511 Roberto Alomar (AS) .15
512 Mickey Morandini (Highlight) .05
513 Dennis Eckersley (Highlight) .05
514 Jeff Reardon (Highlight) .05
515 Danny Tartabull (Highlight) .05
516 Bip Roberts (Highlight) .05
517 George Brett (Highlight) .20
518 Robin Yount (Highlight) .15
519 Kevin Gross (Highlight) .05
520 Ed Sprague (World Series Highlight) .05
521 Dave Winfield (World Series Highlight) .10
522 Ozzie Smith (AS) .15
523 Barry Bonds (AS) .15
524 Andy Van Slyke (AS) .05
525 Tony Gwynn (AS) .25
526 Darren Daulton (AS) .05
527 Greg Maddux (AS) .50
528 Fred McGriff (AS) .05
529 Lee Smith (AS) .05
530 Ryne Sandberg (AS) .25
531 Gary Sheffield (AS) .15
532 Ozzie Smith (Dream Team) .15
533 Kirby Puckett (Dream Team) .25
534 Gary Sheffield (Dream Team) .15
535 Andy Van Slyke (Dream Team) .05
536 Ken Griffey, Jr. (Dream Team) 1.00
537 Ivan Rodriguez (Dream Team) .10
538 Charles Nagy (Dream Team) .05
539 Tom Glavine (Dream Team) .10
540 Dennis Eckersley (Dream Team) .05
541 Frank Thomas (Dream Team) .50
542 Roberto Alomar (Dream Team) .15
543 Sean Barry .05
544 Mike Schooler .05
545 Chuck Carr .05
546 Lenny Harris .05
547 Gary Scott .05
548 Derek Lilliquist .05
549 Brian Hunter .05
550 Kirby Puckett (MOY) .25
551 Jim Eisenreich .05
552 Andre Dawson .10
553 David Nied .05
554 Spike Owen .05
555 Greg Gagne .05
556 Sid Fernandez .05
557 Mark McGwire 2.00
558 Bryan Harvey .05
559 Harold Reynolds .05
560 Barry Bonds .50
561 *Eric Wedge* .05
562 Ozzie Smith .35
563 Rick Sutcliffe .05
564 Jeff Reardon .05
565 *Alex Arias* .05
566 Greg Swindell .05
567 Brook Jacoby .05
568 Pete Incaviglia .05
569 *Butch Henry* .10
570 Eric Davis .10
571 Kevin Seitzer .05
572 Tony Fernandez .05
573 *Steve Reed* .10
574 Cory Snyder .05
575 Joe Carter .10
576 Greg Maddux 1.00
577 Bert Blyleven .05
578 Kevin Bass .05
579 Carlton Fisk .10
580 Doug Drabek .05
581 Mark Gubicza .05
582 Bobby Thigpen .05
583 Chili Davis .05
584 Scott Bankhead .05
585 Harold Baines .05
586 *Eric Young* .20
587 Lance Parrish .05
588 Juan Bell .05
589 Bob Ojeda .05
590 Joe Orsulak .05
591 Benito Santiago .05
592 Wade Boggs .30
593 Robby Thompson .05
594 Erik Plunk .05
595 Hensley Meulens .05
596 Lou Whitaker .05
597 Dale Murphy .10
598 Paul Molitor .35
599 Greg W. Harris .05
600 Darren Holmes .05
601 Dave Martinez .05
602 Tom Henke .05
603 Mike Benjamin .05
604 Rene Gonzales .05
605 Roger McDowell .05
606 Kirby Puckett .75
607 Randy Myers .05
608 Ruben Sierra .05
609 Wilson Alvarez .05
610 Dave Segui .05
611 Juan Samuel .05
612 Tom Brunansky .05
613 Willie Randolph .05
614 Tony Phillips .05
615 Candy Maldonado .05
616 Chris Bosio .05
617 Bret Barberie .05
618 Scott Sanderson .05
619 Ron Darling .05
620 Dave Winfield .15
621 Mike Felder .05
622 Greg Hibbard .05
623 Mike Scioscia .05
624 John Smiley .05
625 Alejandro Pena .05
626 Terry Steinbach .05
627 Freddie Benavides .05
628 Kevin Reimer .05
629 Braulio Castillo .05
630 Dave Stieb .05
631 Dave Magadan .05
632 Scott Fletcher .05
633 Cris Carpenter .05
634 Kevin Maas .05
635 Todd Worrell .05
636 Rob Deer .05
637 Dwight Smith .05
638 Chito Martinez .05
639 Jimmy Key .05
640 Greg Harris .05
641 Mike Moore .05
642 Pat Borders .05
643 Bill Gullickson .05
644 Gary Gaetti .05
645 David Howard .05
646 Jim Abbott .05
647 Willie Wilson .05
648 David Wells .10
649 Andres Galarraga .10
650 Vince Coleman .05
651 Rob Dibble .05
652 Frank Tanana .05
653 Steve Decker .05
654 David Cone .10
655 Jack Armstrong .05
656 Dave Stewart .05
657 Billy Hatcher .05
658 Tim Raines .10
659 Walt Weiss .05
660 Jose Lind .05

1993 Score Boys of Summer

These cards were available as inserts only in Score 35-card Super Packs, about one in every four packs. Borderless fronts have a color action photo of the player superimposed over the sun. The player's name is in black script in a green strip at bottom, along with a subset logo. On back is a player portrait, again with the sun as a background. Subset, company, team and major league logos are in color on the right, and there is a short career summary on the green background at bottom.

		MT
Complete Set (30):		50.00
Common Player:		.75
1	Billy Ashley	.75
2	Tim Salmon	6.00
3	Pedro Martinez	10.00
4	Luis Mercedes	.75
5	Mike Piazza	30.00
6	Troy Neel	1.00
7	Melvin Nieves	.75
8	Ryan Klesko	2.00
9	Ryan Thompson	1.00
10	Kevin Young	.75
11	Gerald Williams	1.50
12	Willie Greene	1.50
13	John Patterson	.75
14	Carlos Garcia	1.50
15	Eddie Zosky	.75
16	Sean Berry	1.00
17	Rico Brogna	1.00
18	Larry Carter	.75
19	Bobby Ayala	.75
20	Alan Embree	.75
21	Donald Harris	.75
22	Sterling Hitchcock	1.00
23	David Nied	.75
24	Henry Mercedes	.75
25	Ozzie Canseco	.75
26	David Hulse	.75
27	Al Martin	1.00
28	Dan Wilson	1.00
29	Paul Miller	.75
30	Rich Rowland	.75

1993 Score The Franchise

These glossy inserts have full-bleed color action photos against a darkened background so that the player stands out. Cards could be found in 16-card packs only; odds of finding one are 1 in every 24 packs. The fronts have gold-foil highlights.

		MT
Complete Set (28):		100.00
Common Player:		1.00
1	Cal Ripken, Jr.	25.00
2	Roger Clemens	10.00
3	Mark Langston	1.00
4	Frank Thomas	15.00
5	Carlos Baerga	1.00
6	Cecil Fielder	1.00
7	Gregg Jefferies	1.00
8	Robin Yount	7.50
9	Kirby Puckett	12.00
10	Don Mattingly	12.00
11	Dennis Eckersley	1.00
12	Ken Griffey, Jr.	30.00
13	Juan Gonzalez	8.00
14	Roberto Alomar	5.00
15	Terry Pendleton	1.00
16	Ryne Sandberg	7.50
17	Barry Larkin	3.00

18	Jeff Bagwell	12.00
19	Brett Butler	1.00
20	Larry Walker	4.00
21	Bobby Bonilla	1.00
22	Darren Daulton	1.00
23	Andy Van Slyke	1.00
24	Ray Lankford	1.00
25	Gary Sheffield	4.00
26	Will Clark	2.00
27	Bryan Harvey	1.00
28	David Nied	1.00

1993 Score Gold Dream Team

This 11-player insert set consists of the same players in the regular set's Dream Team subset, except the cards are gold-foil stamped. There is an unnumbered header card in the set, which was available only via a mail-in offer.

		MT
Complete Set (12):		6.00
Common Player:		.25
1	Ozzie Smith	.75
2	Kirby Puckett	1.25
3	Gary Sheffield	.50
4	Andy Van Slyke	.25
5	Ken Griffey, Jr.	2.50
6	Ivan Rodriguez	.50
7	Charles Nagy	.25
8	Tom Glavine	.40
9	Dennis Eckersley	.40
10	Frank Thomas	1.50
11	Roberto Alomar	.50
---	Header card	.05

1994 Score Samples

Regular and Gold Rush versions of the first eight cards in the 1994 Score set were produced in a special promo version to familiarize buyers with the new issue. Cards have all zeroes in place of the 1993 stats and are overprinted on front and back with a diagonal black "SAMPLE". The samples were distributed in 11-card cello packs containing eight regular sample cards, one of the Gold Rush samples, a Barry Larkin Dream Team promo card and a header.

		MT
Complete Set (18):		120.00
Common Player:		1.50
1	Barry Bonds	4.50
1	Barry Bonds (Gold Rush)	15.00
2	John Olerud	2.00
2	John Olerud (Gold Rush)	6.00
3	Ken Griffey Jr.	7.50
3	Ken Griffey Jr. (Gold Rush)	35.00
4	Jeff Bagwell	4.00
4	Jeff Bagwell (Gold Rush)	15.00
5	John Burkett	1.50
5	John Burkett (Gold Rush)	5.00
6	Jack McDowell	1.50
6	Jack McDowell (Gold Rush)	5.00
7	Albert Belle	2.50
7	Albert Belle (Gold Rush)	7.50
8	Andres Galarraga	1.50
8	Andres Galarraga (Gold Rush)	6.00
5	Barry Larkin (Dream Team)	4.50
--	Hobby Header Card	.03
--	Retail Header Card	.03

1994 Score

Score's 1994 set, with a new design and UV coating, was issued in two series of 330 cards each. The cards, which use more action photos than before, have dark blue borders with the player's name in a team color-coded strip at the bottom. A special Gold Rush card, done for each card in the set, is included in every pack. Series I includes American League checklists, which are printed on the backs of cards depicting panoramic views of each team's ballpark. Series II has the National League team checklists. Insert sets include Dream Team players, and National (Series I packs) and American League Gold Stars (Series II packs), which use the Gold Rush process and appear once every 18 packs.

		MT
Complete Set (660):		20.00
Common Player:		.05
Gold Rush:		3X
Series 1 or 2 Pack (14):		1.25
Series 1 or 2 Wax Box (36):		36.00
1	Barry Bonds	.40
2	John Olerud	.15
3	Ken Griffey, Jr.	1.50
4	Jeff Bagwell	.50
5	John Burkett	.05
6	Jack McDowell	.05
7	Albert Belle	.20
8	Andres Galarraga	.20
9	Mike Mussina	.15
10	Will Clark	.15
11	Travis Fryman	.10
12	Tony Gwynn	.75
13	Robin Yount	.20
14	Dave Magadan	.05
15	Paul O'Neill	.10
16	Ray Lankford	.10
17	Damion Easley	.05
18	Andy Van Slyke	.05
19	Brian McRae	.05
20	Ryne Sandberg	.30
21	Kirby Puckett	.35
22	Dwight Gooden	.10
23	Don Mattingly	.50
24	Kevin Mitchell	.05
25	Roger Clemens	.50
26	Eric Karros	.10
27	Juan Gonzalez	.40
28	John Kruk	.05
29	Gregg Jefferies	.05
30	Tom Glavine	.15
31	Ivan Rodriguez	.40
32	Jay Bell	.05
33	Randy Johnson	.40
34	Darren Daulton	.05
35	Rickey Henderson	.20
36	Eddie Murray	.15
37	Brian Harper	.05
38	Delino DeShields	.05
39	Jose Lind	.05
40	Benito Santiago	.05
41	Frank Thomas	.50
42	Mark Grace	.15
43	Roberto Alomar	.25
44	Andy Benes	.05
45	Luis Polonia	.05
46	Brett Butler	.05
47	Terry Steinbach	.05
48	Craig Biggio	.15
49	Greg Vaughn	.10
50	Charlie Hayes	.05
51	Mickey Tettleton	.05
52	Jose Rijo	.05
53	Carlos Baerga	.10
54	Jeff Blauser	.05
55	Leo Gomez	.05
56	Bob Tewksbury	.05
57	Mo Vaughn	.20
58	Orlando Merced	.05
59	Tino Martinez	.10
60	Len Dykstra	.05
61	Jose Canseco	.25
62	Tony Fernandez	.05
63	Donovan Osborne	.05
64	Ken Hill	.05
65	Kent Hrbek	.05
66	Bryan Harvey	.05
67	Wally Joyner	.05
68	Derrick May	.05
69	Lance Johnson	.05
70	Willie McGee	.05
71	Mark Langston	.05
72	Terry Pendleton	.05
73	Joe Carter	.10
74	Barry Larkin	.20
75	Jimmy Key	.05
76	Joe Girardi	.05
77	B.J. Surhoff	.05
78	Pete Harnisch	.05
79	Lou Whitaker	.05
80	Cory Snyder	.05
81	Kenny Lofton	.25
82	Fred McGriff	.15
83	Mike Greenwell	.05
84	Mike Perez	.05
85	Cal Ripken, Jr.	1.00
86	Don Slaught	.05
87	Omar Vizquel	.05
88	Curt Schilling	.10
89	Chuck Knoblauch	.10
90	Moises Alou	.10
91	Greg Gagne	.05
92	Bret Saberhagen	.05
93	Ozzie Guillen	.05
94	Matt Williams	.20
95	Chad Curtis	.05
96	Mike Harkey	.05
97	Devon White	.10
98	Walt Weiss	.05
99	Kevin Brown	.10
100	Gary Sheffield	.15
101	Wade Boggs	.20
102	Orel Hershiser	.10
103	Tony Phillips	.05
104	Andujar Cedeno	.05
105	Bill Spiers	.05
106	Otis Nixon	.05
107	Felix Fermin	.05
108	Bip Roberts	.05
109	Dennis Eckersley	.05
110	Dante Bichette	.15
111	Ben McDonald	.05
112	Jim Poole	.05
113	John Dopson	.05
114	Rob Dibble	.05
115	Jeff Treadway	.05
116	Ricky Jordan	.05
117	Mike Henneman	.05
118	Willie Blair	.05
119	Doug Henry	.05
120	Gerald Perry	.05
121	Greg Myers	.05
122	John Franco	.05
123	Roger Mason	.05
124	Chris Hammond	.05
125	Hubie Brooks	.05
126	Kent Mercker	.05
127	Jim Abbott	.05
128	Kevin Bass	.05
129	Rick Aguilera	.05
130	Mitch Webster	.05
131	Eric Plunk	.05
132	Mark Carreon	.05
133	Dave Stewart	.05
134	Willie Wilson	.05
135	Dave Fleming	.05
136	Jeff Tackett	.05
137	Geno Petralli	.05
138	Gene Harris	.05
139	Scott Bankhead	.05
140	Trevor Wilson	.05
141	Alvaro Espinoza	.05
142	Ryan Bowen	.05
143	Mike Moore	.05
144	Bill Pecota	.05
145	Jaime Navarro	.05
146	Jack Daugherty	.05
147	Bob Wickman	.05
148	Chris Jones	.05
149	Todd Stottlemyre	.05
150	Brian Williams	.05
151	Chuck Finley	.05
152	Lenny Harris	.05
153	Alex Fernandez	.10
154	Candy Maldonado	.05
155	Jeff Montgomery	.05
156	David West	.05
157	Mark Williamson	.05
158	Milt Thompson	.05
159	Ron Darling	.05
160	Stan Belinda	.05
161	Henry Cotto	.05
162	Mel Rojas	.05
163	Doug Strange	.05
164	Rene Arocha (1993 Rookie)	.10
165	Tim Hulett	.05
166	Steve Avery	.05
167	Jim Thome	.15
168	Tom Browning	.05
169	Mario Diaz	.05
170	Steve Reed (1993 Rookie)	.05
171	Scott Livingstone	.05
172	Chris Donnels	.05
173	John Jaha	.05
174	Carlos Hernandez	.05
175	Dion James	.05
176	Bud Black	.05
177	Tony Castillo	.05
178	Jose Guzman	.05
179	Torey Lovullo	.05
180	John Vander Wal	.05
181	Mike LaValliere	.05
182	Sid Fernandez	.05
183	Brent Mayne	.05
184	Terry Mulholland	.05
185	Willie Banks	.05
186	Steve Cooke (1993 Rookie)	.05
187	Brent Gates (1993 Rookie)	.10
188	Erik Pappas (1993 Rookie)	.10

No.	Player	Price
189	Bill Haselman (1993 Rookie)	.05
190	Fernando Valenzuela	.05
191	Gary Redus	.05
192	Danny Darwin	.05
193	Mark Portugal	.05
194	Derek Lilliquist	.05
195	Charlie O'Brien	.05
196	Matt Nokes	.05
197	Danny Sheaffer	.05
198	Bill Gullickson	.05
199	Alex Arias (1993 Rookie)	.10
200	Mike Fetters	.05
201	Brian Jordan	.10
202	Joe Grahe	.05
203	Tom Candiotti	.05
204	Jeremy Stanton	.05
205	Mike Stanton	.05
206	David Howard	.05
207	Darren Holmes	.05
208	Rick Honeycutt	.05
209	Danny Jackson	.05
210	Rich Amaral (1993 Rookie)	.05
211	Blas Minor (1993 Rookie)	.10
212	Kenny Rogers	.05
213	Jim Leyritz	.05
214	Mike Morgan	.05
215	Dan Gladden	.05
216	Randy Velarde	.05
217	Mitch Williams	.05
218	Hipolito Pichardo	.05
219	Dave Burba	.05
220	Wilson Alvarez	.05
221	Bob Zupcic	.05
222	Francisco Cabrera	.05
223	Julio Valera	.05
224	Paul Assenmacher	.05
225	Jeff Branson	.05
226	Todd Frohwirth	.05
227	Armando Reynoso	.05
228	Rich Rowland (1993 Rookie)	.05
229	Freddie Benavides	.05
230	Wayne Kirby (1993 Rookie)	.05
231	Darryl Kile	.05
232	Skeeter Barnes	.05
233	Ramon Martinez	.10
234	Tom Gordon	.05
235	Dave Gallagher	.05
236	Ricky Bones	.05
237	Larry Andersen	.05
238	Pat Meares (1993 Rookie)	.05
239	Zane Smith	.05
240	Tim Leary	.05
241	Phil Clark	.05
242	Danny Cox	.05
243	Mike Jackson	.05
244	Mike Gallego	.05
245	Lee Smith	.05
246	Todd Jones (1993 Rookie)	.05
247	Steve Bedrosian	.05
248	Troy Neel	.05
249	Jose Bautista	.05
250	Steve Frey	.05
251	Jeff Reardon	.05
252	Stan Javier	.05
253	Mo Sanford (1993 Rookie)	.05
254	Steve Sax	.05
255	Luis Aquino	.05
256	Domingo Jean (1993 Rookie)	.05
257	Scott Servais	.05
258	Brad Pennington (1993 Rookie)	.05
259	Dave Hansen	.05
260	Goose Gossage	.05
261	Jeff Fassero	.05
262	Junior Ortiz	.05
263	Anthony Young	.05
264	Chris Bosio	.05
265	Ruben Amaro, Jr.	.05
266	Mark Eichhorn	.05
267	Dave Clark	.05
268	Gary Thurman	.05
269	Les Lancaster	.05
270	Jamie Moyer	.05
271	Ricky Gutierrez (1993 Rookie)	.10
272	Greg Harris	.05
273	Mike Benjamin	.05
274	Gene Nelson	.05
275	Damon Berryhill	.05
276	Scott Radinsky	.05
277	Mike Aldrete	.05
278	Jerry DiPoto (1993 Rookie)	.05
279	Chris Haney	.05
280	Richie Lewis (1993 Rookie)	.05
281	Jarvis Brown	.05
282	Juan Bell	.05
283	Joe Klink	.05
284	Graeme Lloyd (1993 Rookie)	.05
285	Casey Candaele	.05
286	Bob MacDonald	.05
287	Mike Sharperson	.05
288	Gene Larkin	.05
289	Brian Barnes	.05
290	David McCarty (1993 Rookie)	.10
291	Jeff Innis	.05
292	Bob Patterson	.05
293	Ben Rivera	.05
294	John Habyan	.05
295	Rich Rodriguez	.05
296	Edwin Nunez	.05
297	Rod Brewer	.05
298	Mike Timlin	.05
299	Jesse Orosco	.05
300	Gary Gaetti	.05
301	Todd Benzinger	.05
302	Jeff Nelson	.05
303	Rafael Belliard	.05
304	Matt Whiteside	.05
305	Vinny Castilla	.10
306	Matt Turner	.05
307	Eduardo Perez	.05
308	Joel Johnston	.05
309	Chris Gomez	.05
310	Pat Rapp	.05
311	Jim Tatum	.05
312	Kirk Rueter	.05
313	John Flaherty	.05
314	Tom Kramer	.05
315	Mark Whiten (Highlights)	.05
316	Chris Bosio (Highlights)	.05
317	Orioles Checklist	.05
318	Red Sox Checklist	.05
319	Angels Checklist	.05
320	White Sox Checklist	.05
321	Indians Checklist	.05
322	Tigers Checklist	.05
323	Royals Checklist	.05
324	Brewers Checklist	.05
325	Twins Checklist	.05
326	Yankees Checklist	.05
327	Athletics Checklist	.05
328	Mariners Checklist	.05
329	Rangers Checklist	.05
330	Blue Jays Checklist	.05
331	Frank Viola	.05
332	Ron Gant	.10
333	Charles Nagy	.10
334	Roberto Kelly	.05
335	Brady Anderson	.10
336	Alex Cole	.05
337	Alan Trammell	.10
338	Derek Bell	.10
339	Bernie Williams	.25
340	Jose Offerman	.05
341	Bill Wegman	.05
342	Ken Caminiti	.15
343	Pat Borders	.05
344	Kirt Manwaring	.05
345	Chili Davis	.05
346	Steve Buechele	.05
347	Robin Ventura	.15
348	Teddy Higuera	.05
349	Jerry Browne	.05
350	Scott Kamieniecki	.05
351	Kevin Tapani	.05
352	Marquis Grissom	.05
353	Jay Buhner	.05
354	Dave Hollins	.05
355	Dan Wilson	.05
356	Bob Walk	.05
357	Chris Hoiles	.05
358	Todd Zeile	.05
359	Kevin Appier	.05
360	Chris Sabo	.05
361	David Segui	.05
362	Jerald Clark	.05
363	Tony Pena	.05
364	Steve Finley	.05
365	Roger Pavlik	.05
366	John Smoltz	.10
367	Scott Fletcher	.05
368	Jody Reed	.05
369	David Wells	.10
370	Jose Vizcaino	.05
371	Pat Listach	.05
372	Orestes Destrade	.05
373	Danny Tartabull	.05
374	Greg W. Harris	.05
375	Juan Guzman	.05
376	Larry Walker	.20
377	Gary DiSarcina	.05
378	Bobby Bonilla	.05
379	Tim Raines	.10
380	Tommy Greene	.05
381	Chris Gwynn	.05
382	Jeff King	.05
383	Shane Mack	.05
384	Ozzie Smith	.20
385	*Eddie Zambrano*	.05
386	Mike Devereaux	.05
387	Erik Hanson	.05
388	Scott Cooper	.05
389	Dean Palmer	.05
390	John Wetteland	.05
391	Reggie Jefferson	.05
392	Mark Lemke	.05
393	Cecil Fielder	.05
394	Reggie Sanders	.10
395	Darryl Hamilton	.05
396	Daryl Boston	.05
397	Pat Kelly	.05
398	Joe Orsulak	.05
399	Ed Sprague	.05
400	Eric Anthony	.05
401	Scott Sanderson	.05
402	Jim Gott	.05
403	Ron Karkovice	.05
404	Phil Plantier	.05
405	David Cone	.10
406	Robby Thompson	.05
407	Dave Winfield	.15
408	Dwight Smith	.05
409	Ruben Sierra	.05
410	Jack Armstrong	.05
411	Mike Felder	.05
412	Wil Cordero	.05
413	Julio Franco	.05
414	Howard Johnson	.05
415	Mark McLemore	.05
416	Pete Incaviglia	.05
417	John Valentin	.05
418	Tim Wakefield	.05
419	Jose Mesa	.05
420	Bernard Gilkey	.10
421	Kirk Gibson	.05
422	Dave Justice	.10
423	Tom Brunansky	.05
424	John Smiley	.05
425	Kevin Maas	.05
426	Doug Drabek	.05
427	Paul Molitor	.20
428	Darryl Strawberry	.10
429	Tim Naehring	.05
430	Bill Swift	.05
431	Ellis Burks	.05
432	Greg Hibbard	.05
433	Felix Jose	.05
434	Bret Barberie	.05
435	Pedro Munoz	.05
436	Darrin Fletcher	.05
437	Bobby Witt	.05
438	Wes Chamberlain	.05
439	Mackey Sasser	.05
440	Mark Whiten	.05
441	Harold Reynolds	.05
442	Greg Olson	.05
443	Billy Hatcher	.05
444	Joe Oliver	.05
445	Sandy Alomar Jr.	.10
446	Tim Wallach	.05
447	Karl Rhodes	.05
448	Royce Clayton	.05
449	Cal Eldred	.05
450	Rick Wilkins	.05
451	Mike Stanley	.05
452	Charlie Hough	.05
453	Jack Morris	.05
454	*Jon Ratliff*	.05
455	Rene Gonzales	.05
456	Eddie Taubensee	.05
457	Roberto Hernandez	.05
458	Todd Hundley	.10
459	Mike MacFarlane	.05
460	Mickey Morandini	.05
461	Scott Erickson	.05
462	Lonnie Smith	.05
463	Dave Henderson	.05
464	Ryan Klesko	.10
465	Edgar Martinez	.05
466	Tom Pagnozzi	.05
467	Charlie Leibrandt	.05
468	*Brian Anderson*	.10
469	Harold Baines	.05
470	Tim Belcher	.05
471	Andre Dawson	.10
472	Eric Young	.05
473	Paul Sorrento	.05
474	Luis Gonzalez	.10
475	Rob Deer	.05
476	Mike Piazza	1.00
477	Kevin Reimer	.05
478	Jeff Gardner	.05
479	Melido Perez	.05
480	Darren Lewis	.05
481	Duane Ward	.05
482	Rey Sanchez	.05
483	Mark Lewis	.05
484	Jeff Conine	.05
485	Joey Cora	.05
486	*Trot Nixon*	.25
487	Kevin McReynolds	.05
488	Mike Lansing	.05
489	Mike Pagliarulo	.05
490	Mariano Duncan	.05
491	Mike Bordick	.05
492	Kevin Young	.05
493	Dave Valle	.05
494	*Wayne Gomes*	.10
495	Rafael Palmeiro	.25
496	Deion Sanders	.15
497	Rick Sutcliffe	.05
498	Randy Milligan	.05
499	Carlos Quintana	.05
500	Chris Turner	.05
501	Thomas Howard	.05
502	Greg Swindell	.05
503	Chad Kreuter	.05
504	Eric Davis	.05
505	Dickie Thon	.05
506	*Matt Drews*	.10
507	Spike Owen	.05
508	Rod Beck	.05
509	Pat Hentgen	.05
510	Sammy Sosa	1.00
511	J.T. Snow	.05
512	Chuck Carr	.05
513	Bo Jackson	.10
514	Dennis Martinez	.05
515	Phil Hiatt	.05
516	Jeff Kent	.05
517	*Brooks Kieschnick*	.20
518	*Kirk Presley*	.15
519	Kevin Seitzer	.05
520	Carlos Garcia	.05
521	Mike Blowers	.05
522	Luis Alicea	.05
523	David Hulse	.05
524	Greg Maddux	.75
525	Gregg Olson	.05
526	Hal Morris	.05
527	Daron Kirkreit	.05
528	David Nied	.05
529	Jeff Russell	.05
530	Kevin Gross	.05
531	John Doherty	.05
532	*Matt Brunson*	.10
533	Dave Nilsson	.05
534	Randy Myers	.05
535	Steve Farr	.05
536	*Billy Wagner*	.20
537	Darnell Coles	.05
538	Frank Tanana	.05
539	Tim Salmon	.10
540	Kim Batiste	.05
541	George Bell	.05
542	Tom Henke	.05
543	Sam Horn	.05
544	Doug Jones	.05
545	Scott Leius	.05
546	Al Martin	.05
547	Bob Welch	.05
548	*Scott Christman*	.05
549	Norm Charlton	.05
550	Mark McGwire	1.50
551	Greg McMichael	.05
552	Tim Costo	.05
553	Rodney Bolton	.05

554	Pedro Martinez	.40
555	Marc Valdes	.05
556	Darrell Whitmore	.05
557	Tim Bogar	.05
558	Steve Karsay	.05
559	Danny Bautista	.05
560	Jeffrey Hammonds	.10
561	Aaron Sele	.05
562	Russ Springer	.05
563	Jason Bere	.05
564	Billy Brewer	.05
565	Sterling Hitchcock	.05
566	Bobby Munoz	.05
567	Craig Paquette	.05
568	Bret Boone	.05
569	Dan Peltier	.05
570	Jeromy Burnitz	.05
571	*John Wasdin*	.10
572	Chipper Jones	.75
573	*Jamey Wright*	.10
574	Jeff Granger	.05
575	*Jay Powell*	.10
576	Ryan Thompson	.05
577	Lou Frazier	.05
578	Paul Wagner	.05
579	Brad Ausmus	.05
580	Jack Voigt	.05
581	Kevin Rogers	.05
582	Damon Buford	.10
583	Paul Quantrill	.05
584	Marc Newfield	.05
585	*Derrek Lee*	.20
586	Shane Reynolds	.05
587	Cliff Floyd	.10
588	Jeff Schwarz	.05
589	*Ross Powell*	.05
590	Gerald Williams	.05
591	Mike Trombley	.05
592	Ken Ryan	.05
593	John O'Donoghue	.05
594	Rod Correia	.05
595	Darrell Sherman	.05
596	Steve Scarsone	.05
597	Sherman Obando	.05
598	Kurt Abbott	.05
599	Dave Telgheder	.05
600	Rick Trlicek	.05
601	Carl Everett	.10
602	Luis Ortiz	.05
603	*Larry Luebbers*	.05
604	Kevin Roberson	.05
605	Butch Huskey	.10
606	Benji Gil	.05
607	Todd Van Poppel	.05
608	Mark Hutton	.05
609	Chip Hale	.05
610	Matt Maysey	.05
611	Scott Ruffcorn	.05
612	Hilly Hathaway	.05
613	Allen Watson	.05
614	Carlos Delgado	.25
615	Roberto Mejia	.05
616	Turk Wendell	.05
617	Tony Tarasco	.05
618	Raul Mondesi	.20
619	Kevin Stocker	.10
620	Javier Lopez	.15
621	*Keith Kessinger*	.10
622	Bob Hamelin	.05
623	John Roper	.05
624	Len Dykstra (World Series)	.05
625	Joe Carter (World Series)	.05
626	Jim Abbott (Highlight)	.05
627	Lee Smith (Highlight)	.05
628	Ken Griffey, Jr. (HL)	.75
629	Dave Winfield (Highlight)	.05
630	Darryl Kile (Highlight)	.05
631	Frank Thomas (MVP)	.45
632	Barry Bonds (MVP)	.15
633	Jack McDowell (Cy Young)	.05
634	Greg Maddux (Cy Young)	.50
635	Tim Salmon (ROY)	.10
636	Mike Piazza (ROY)	.50
637	*Brian Turang*	.10
638	Rondell White	.15
639	Nigel Wilson	.05
640	*Torii Hunter*	.10
641	Salomon Torres	.05
642	Kevin Higgins	.05
643	Eric Wedge	.05
644	Roger Salkeld	.05
645	Manny Ramirez	.50
646	Jeff McNeely	.05
647	Braves Checklist	.05
648	Cubs Checklist	.05
649	Reds Checklist	.05
650	Rockies Checklist	.05
651	Marlins Checklist	.05
652	Astros Checklist	.05
653	Dodgers Checklist	.05
654	Expos Checklist	.05
655	Mets Checklist	.05
656	Phillies Checklist	.05
657	Pirates Checklist	.05
658	Cardinals Checklist	.05
659	Padres Checklist	.05
660	Giants Checklist	.05

1994 Score Gold Rush

Opting to include one insert card in each pack of its 1994 product, Score created a "Gold Rush" version of each card in its regular set. Gold Rush cards are basically the same as their counterparts with a few enhancements. Card fronts are printed on foil with a gold border and a Score Gold Rush logo in one of the upper corners. The background of the photo has been metalized, allowing the color player portion to stand out in sharp contrast. Backs are identical to the regular cards except for the appearance of a large Gold Rush logo under the typography.

	MT
Complete Set (660):	150.00
Common Player:	.25
Stars:	3X

(See 1994 Score for checklist and base card values.)

1994 Score Boys of Summer

A heavy emphasis on rookies and recent rookies is noted in this 1994 Score insert set. Released in two series, cards #1-30 with Score's Series I and #31-60 packaged with Series II, card fronts feature a color action photo on which the background has been rendered in a blurred watercolor effect. A hot-color aura separates the player from the background. The player's name appears vertically in gold foil. Backs have backgrounds in reds and orange with a portrait-style player photo on one side and a large "Boys of Summer" logo on the other. A short description of the player's talents appears at center.

		MT
Complete Set (60):		65.00
Common Player:		.50
1	Jeff Conine	1.00
2	Aaron Sele	.75
3	Kevin Stocker	.50
4	Pat Meares	.50
5	Jeromy Burnitz	1.00
6	Mike Piazza	10.00
7	Allen Watson	.50
8	Jeffrey Hammonds	.75
9	Kevin Roberson	.50
10	Hilly Hathaway	.50
11	Kirk Reuter	.50
12	Eduardo Perez	.50
13	Ricky Gutierrez	.50
14	Domingo Jean	.50
15	David Nied	.50
16	Wayne Kirby	.50
17	Mike Lansing	1.00
18	Jason Bere	.50
19	Brent Gates	1.00
20	Javier Lopez	3.00
21	Greg McMichael	.50
22	David Hulse	.50
23	Roberto Mejia	.50
24	Tim Salmon	2.50
25	Rene Arocha	.50
26	Bret Boone	1.00
27	David McCarty	.50
28	Todd Van Poppel	.50
29	Lance Painter	.50
30	Erik Pappas	.50
31	Chuck Carr	.50
32	Mark Hutton	.50
33	Jeff McNeely	.50
34	Willie Greene	.50
35	Nigel Wilson	.50
36	Rondell White	2.50
37	Brian Turang	.50
38	Manny Ramirez	5.00
39	Salomon Torres	.50
40	Melvin Nieves	.50
41	Ryan Klesko	1.00
42	Keith Kessinger	.50
43	Eric Wedge	.50
44	Bob Hamelin	.50
45	Carlos Delgado	4.00
46	Marc Newfield	.50
47	Raul Mondesi	4.00
48	Tim Costo	.50
49	Pedro Martinez	5.00
50	Steve Karsay	.75
51	Danny Bautista	.50
52	Butch Huskey	1.00
53	Kurt Abbott	.75
54	Darrell Sherman	.50
55	Damon Buford	1.00
56	Ross Powell	.50
57	Darrell Whitmore	.50
58	Chipper Jones	10.00
59	Jeff Granger	.50
60	Cliff Floyd	1.00

1994 Score The Cycle

Leaders in the previous season's production of singles, doubles, triples and home runs are featured in this insert set which was packaged with Series II Score. Player action photos pop out of a circle at center and are surrounded by dark blue borders. "The Cycle" in printed in green at top. The player's name is in gold foil at bottom, printed over an infield diagram in a green strip. The stat which earned the player inclusion in the set is in gold foil at bottom right. On back are the rankings for the statistical category. Cards are numbered with a "TC" prefix.

		MT
Complete Set (20):		160.00
Common Player:		5.00
1	Brett Butler	5.00
2	Kenny Lofton	12.00
3	Paul Molitor	10.00
4	Carlos Baerga	5.00
5	Gregg Jefferies, Tony Phillips	5.00
6	John Olerud	6.00
7	Charlie Hayes	5.00
8	Len Dykstra	5.00
9	Dante Bichette	8.00
10	Devon White	5.00
11	Lance Johnson	5.00
12	Joey Cora, Steve Finley	5.00
13	Tony Fernandez	5.00
14	David Hulse, Brett Butler	5.00
15	Jay Bell, Brian McRae, Mickey Morandini	5.00
16	Juan Gonzalez, Barry Bonds	20.00
17	Ken Griffey, Jr.	60.00
18	Frank Thomas	20.00
19	Dave Justice	8.00
20	Matt Williams, Albert Belle	12.00

1994 Score Dream Team

Score's 1994 "Dream Team," one top player at each position, was featured in a 10-card insert set. The stars were decked out in vintage uniforms and equipment for the photos. Green and black bars at top and bottom frame the photo, and all printing on the front is in gold foil. Backs have a white background with green highlights. A color player portrait photo is featured, along with a brief justification for the player's selection to the squad. Cards are UV coated on both sides. Stated odds of finding a Dream Team insert were given as one per 72 packs.

		MT
Complete Set (10):		75.00
Common Player:		4.00
1	Mike Mussina	8.00
2	Tom Glavine	6.00
3	Don Mattingly	20.00
4	Carlos Baerga	4.00
5	Barry Larkin	7.50
6	Matt Williams	7.50
7	Juan Gonzalez	20.00
8	Andy Van Slyke	4.00
9	Larry Walker	7.50
10	Mike Stanley	4.00

1994 Score Gold Stars

Limited to inclusion in hobby packs, Score's 60-card "Gold Stars" insert set features 30 National League players, found in Series I packs, and 30 American Leaguers inserted with Series II. Stated odds of finding a Gold Stars card were listed on the wrapper as one in 18 packs. A notation on the cards' back indicates that no more than 6,500 sets of Gold Stars were produced. The high-tech cards feature a color player action photo, the full-bleed background of which has been converted to metallic tones. Backs have a graduated gold background with a portrait-style color player photo.

		MT
Complete Set (60):		200.00
Common Player:		1.00
1	Barry Bonds	8.00
2	Orlando Merced	1.00
3	Mark Grace	3.00
4	Darren Daulton	1.00
5	Jeff Blauser	1.00
6	Deion Sanders	3.00
7	John Kruk	1.00
8	Jeff Bagwell	8.00
9	Gregg Jefferies	1.00
10	Matt Williams	3.00
11	Andres Galarraga	4.00
12	Jay Bell	1.00
13	Mike Piazza	20.00
14	Ron Gant	1.00
15	Barry Larkin	3.00
16	Tom Glavine	2.00
17	Len Dykstra	1.00
18	Fred McGriff	2.00
19	Andy Van Slyke	1.00
20	Gary Sheffield	2.50
21	John Burkett	1.00
22	Dante Bichette	4.00
23	Tony Gwynn	15.00
24	Dave Justice	2.00
25	Marquis Grissom	1.50
26	Bobby Bonilla	1.00
27	Larry Walker	4.00
28	Brett Butler	1.00
29	Robby Thompson	1.00
30	Jeff Conine	1.00
31	Joe Carter	1.00
32	Ken Griffey, Jr.	30.00
33	Juan Gonzalez	8.00
34	Rickey Henderson	2.00
35	Bo Jackson	1.50
36	Cal Ripken, Jr.	25.00
37	John Olerud	2.00
38	Carlos Baerga	1.00
39	Jack McDowell	1.00
40	Cecil Fielder	1.00
41	Kenny Lofton	6.00
42	Roberto Alomar	6.00
43	Randy Johnson	8.00
44	Tim Salmon	4.00
45	Frank Thomas	10.00
46	Albert Belle	6.00
47	Greg Vaughn	1.50
48	Travis Fryman	1.00
49	Don Mattingly	8.00
50	Wade Boggs	4.00
51	Mo Vaughn	6.00
52	Kirby Puckett	8.00
53	Devon White	1.00
54	Tony Phillips	1.00
55	Brian Harper	1.00
56	Chad Curtis	1.00
57	Paul Molitor	6.00
58	Ivan Rodriguez	8.00
59	Rafael Palmeiro	4.00
60	Brian McRae	1.00

1994 Score Rookie/Traded Samples

To introduce the various types of card which would be included in the 1994 Score Rookie/Traded set, the company produced this sample set. Cards are virtually identical to the issued versions except for the overprint "SAMPLE" running diagonally on front and back. The Rafael Palmeiro "Changing Places" sample card does not feature the red foil logo found on issued cards.

		MT
Complete Set (11):		20.00
Common Player:		2.00
1RT	Lee Smith	1.00
2CP	Rafael Palmeiro (Changing Places)	2.00
2RT	Will Clark	4.00
2SU	Manny Ramirez (Super Rookie)	5.00
3RT	Bo Jackson (Gold Rush)	2.00
4RT	Ellis Burks	1.00
5RT	Eddie Murray	4.00
6RT	Delino DeShields	1.00
102RT	Carlos Delgado	2.00
---	September Call-Up Winner Card	1.00
---	Hobby header card	1.00
---	Retail header card	1.00

1994 Score Rookie/Traded

Score Rookie & Traded completed the 1994 Score baseball issue with a 165-card update set. These were available in both retail and hobby packs. Score issued Super Rookies and Changing Places insert sets, as well as a Traded Redemption card and a parallel Gold Rush set. Basic cards features red front borders. Team logos are in a bottom corner in a gold polygon. One of the upper corners contains a green polygon with a gold Score logo. Most cards #71-163 feature a square multi-colored "Rookie '94" logo in a lower corner. Backs of all cards have a purple background. Traded players' card backs are vertical and contain two additional photos. Backs of the rookie cards are horizontal and feature a portrait photo at left. The "Rookie '94" logo is repeated in the upper-right corner. This is in reverse of the card fronts, on which traded players have a single photo and rookie cards have both portrait and action photos.

		MT
Complete Set (165):		8.00
Common Player:		.05
Pack (10):		1.00
Wax Box (36):		25.00
1	Will Clark	.25
2	Lee Smith	.05
3	Bo Jackson	.15
4	Ellis Burks	.10
5	Eddie Murray	.20
6	Delino DeShields	.05
7	Erik Hanson	.05
8	Rafael Palmeiro	.30
9	Luis Polonia	.05
10	Omar Vizquel	.10
11	Kurt Abbott	.05
12	Vince Coleman	.05
13	Rickey Henderson	.40
14	Terry Mulholland	.05
15	Greg Hibbard	.05
16	Walt Weiss	.05
17	Chris Sabo	.05
18	Dave Henderson	.05
19	Rick Sutcliffe	.05
20	Harold Reynolds	.05
21	Jack Morris	.05
22	Dan Wilson	.05
23	Dave Magadan	.05
24	Dennis Martinez	.05
25	Wes Chamberlain	.05
26	Otis Nixon	.05
27	Eric Anthony	.05
28	Randy Milligan	.05
29	Julio Franco	.05
30	Kevin McReynolds	.05
31	Anthony Young	.05
32	Brian Harper	.05
33	Lenny Harris	.05
34	Eddie Taubensee	.05
35	David Segui	.05
36	Stan Javier	.05
37	Felix Fermin	.05
38	Darrin Jackson	.05
39	Tony Fernandez	.05
40	Jose Vizcaino	.05
41	Willie Banks	.05
42	Brian Hunter	.05
43	Reggie Jefferson	.05
44	Junior Felix	.05
45	Jack Armstrong	.05
46	Bip Roberts	.05
47	Jerry Browne	.05
48	Marvin Freeman	.05
49	Jody Reed	.05
50	Alex Cole	.05
51	Sid Fernandez	.05
52	Pete Smith	.05
53	Xavier Hernandez	.05
54	Scott Sanderson	.05
55	Turner Ward	.05
56	Rex Hudler	.05
57	Deion Sanders	.25
58	Sid Bream	.05
59	Tony Pena	.05
60	Bret Boone	.05
61	Bobby Ayala	.05
62	Pedro Martinez	1.00
63	Howard Johnson	.05
64	Mark Portugal	.05
65	Roberto Kelly	.05
66	Spike Owen	.05
67	Jeff Treadway	.05
68	Mike Harkey	.05
69	Doug Jones	.05
70	Steve Farr	.05
71	Billy Taylor	.05
72	Manny Ramirez	1.50
73	Bob Hamelin	.05
74	Steve Karsay	.05
75	Ryan Klesko	.15
76	Cliff Floyd	.10
77	Jeffrey Hammonds	.10
78	Javier Lopez	.20
79	Roger Salkeld	.05
80	Hector Carrasco	.05
81	Gerald Williams	.05
82	Raul Mondesi	.75
83	Sterling Hitchcock	.05
84	Danny Bautista	.05
85	Chris Turner	.05
86	Shane Reynolds	.05
87	Rondell White	.20
88	Salomon Torres	.05
89	Turk Wendell	.05
90	Tony Tarasco	.05
91	Shawn Green	.40

92	Greg Colbrunn	.05
93	Eddie Zambrano	.05
94	Rich Becker	.05
95	Chris Gomez	.05
96	John Patterson	.05
97	Derek Parks	.05
98	Rich Rowland	.05
99	James Mouton	.10
100	Tim Hyers	.10
101	Jose Valentin	.05
102	Carlos Delgado	.50
103	Robert Esenhoorn	.05
104	John Hudek	.10
105	Domingo Cedeno	.05
106	Denny Hocking	.10
107	Greg Pirkl	.05
108	Mark Smith	.05
109	Paul Shuey	.05
110	Jorge Fabregas	.05
111	Rikkert Faneyte	.05
112	Rob Butler	.05
113	Darren Oliver	.05
114	Troy O'Leary	.05
115	Scott Brow	.05
116	Tony Eusebio	.05
117	Carlos Reyes	.05
118	J.R. Phillips	.05
119	Alex Diaz	.05
120	Charles Johnson	.15
121	Nate Minchey	.05
122	Scott Sanders	.05
123	Daryl Boston	.05
124	Joey Hamilton	.30
125	Brian Anderson	.25
126	Dan Miceli	.05
127	Tom Brunansky	.05
128	Dave Staton	.05
129	Mike Oquist	.05
130	John Mabry	.15
131	Norberto Martin	.05
132	Hector Fajardo	.05
133	Mark Hutton	.05
134	Fernando Vina	.05
135	Lee Tinsley	.05
136	*Chan Ho Park*	.50
137	Paul Spoljaric	.05
138	Matias Carrillo	.05
139	Mark Kiefer	.05
140	Stan Royer	.05
141	Bryan Eversgerd	.05
143	Joe Hall	.05
144	Johnny Ruffin	.05
145	Alex Gonzalez	.25
146	Keith Lockhart	.05
147	Tom Marsh	.05
148	Tony Longmire	.05
149	Keith Mitchell	.05
150	Melvin Nieves	.05
151	Kelly Stinnett	.15
152	Miguel Jimenez	.05
153	Jeff Juden	.05
154	Matt Walbeck	.05
155	Marc Newfield	.05
156	Matt Mieske	.05
157	Marcus Moore	.05
158	*Jose Lima*	2.50
159	Mike Kelly	.05
160	Jim Edmonds	.40
161	Steve Trachsel	.25
162	Greg Blosser	.05
163	Mark Acre	.10
164	AL Checklist	.05
165	NL Checklist	.05

1994 Score Rookie/Traded Gold Rush

Each pack of Score Rookie and Traded cards included one Gold Rush parallel version of one of the set's cards. The insert cards feature fronts that are printed directly on gold foil and include a Gold Rush logo in an upper corner.

	MT
Complete Set (165):	45.00
Common Player:	.25
Stars:	2X

(See 1994 Score Rookie/Traded for checklist and base card values.)

1994 Score Rookie/Traded Changing Places

Changing Places documented the relocation of 10 veteran superstars. Cards were inserted into one of every 36 retail or hobby packs. Fronts have a color photo of the player in his new uniform and are enhanced with red foil. Backs have a montage of color and black-and-white photos and a few words about the trade.

		MT
Complete Set (10):		20.00
Common Player:		1.00
1	Will Clark	4.00
2	Rafael Palmeiro	4.00
3	Roberto Kelly	1.00
4	Bo Jackson	2.00
5	Otis Nixon	1.00
6	Rickey Henderson	4.00
7	Ellis Burks	1.00
8	Lee Smith	1.00
9	Delino DeShields	1.00
10	Deion Sanders	4.00

1994 Score Rookie/Traded Super Rookies

Super Rookies is an 18-card set honoring baseball's brightest young stars. Super Rookies appear only in hobby packs at a rate of one every 36 packs. Fronts are printed on foil, with a multi-colored border. Backs feature another photo, most of which is rendered in single-color blocks, along with a few words about the player and a large Super Rookie logo. Cards are numbered with an SU prefix.

		MT
Complete Set (18):		50.00
Common Player:		1.50
1	Carlos Delgado	3.00
2	Manny Ramirez	15.00
3	Ryan Klesko	3.00
4	Raul Mondesi	8.00
5	Bob Hamelin	1.50
6	Steve Karsay	1.50
7	Jeffrey Hammonds	2.00
8	Cliff Floyd	2.00
9	Kurt Abbott	2.00
10	Marc Newfield	1.50
11	Javier Lopez	5.00
12	Rich Becker	1.50
13	Greg Pirkl	1.50
14	Rondell White	4.00
15	James Mouton	1.50
16	Tony Tarasco	1.50
17	Brian Anderson	2.00
18	Jim Edmonds	6.00

1994 Score Rookie/Traded Redemption Card

The Score Rookie and Traded Redemption card was inserted at a rate of one every 240 packs. It gave collectors a chance to mail in for the best rookie in the annual September call-up: Alex Rodriguez

	MT
September Call-Up redemption card (expired)	12.00
Alex Rodriguez	450.00

1995 Score Samples

This cello-wrapped 10-card sample set of 1995 Score cards was sent to dealers to preview the issue. Cards are identical to the regular-issue versions except they have a diagonal white "SAMPLE" printed on front and back.

		MT
Complete Set (10):		30.00
Common Player:		2.00
2	Roberto Alomar	3.00
4	Jose Canseco	4.00
5	Matt Williams	3.00
5HG	Cal Ripken, Jr. (Hall of Gold)	10.00
8DP	McKay Christensen ('94 Draft Pick)	1.00
221	Jeff Bagwell	5.00
223	Albert Belle	4.00
224	Chuck Carr	1.00
288	Jorge Fabreges (Rookie)	2.50
	Header card	.50

1995 Score

Score 1995 Baseball is composed of 605 cards, issued in two series; the first comprising 330 cards, the second, 275. Basic cards have photos placed on a dirt-like background with a green strip running up each side. The player's name, position, and team logo is given in white letters on a blue strip across the bottom. Backs resemble the fronts, except with a smaller, portrait photo of the player, which leaves room for statistics and biographical information. Score had a parallel set of Gold Rush cards, along with several other series of inserts. Eleven players in Series II can be found in two team variations as the result of a redemption program for updated cards.

		MT
Complete Set (605):		20.00
Common Player:		.05
Gold Rush:		3X
Platinums:		6X
Series 1 or 2 Pack (12):		.75
Series 1 or 2 Wax Box (36):		20.00
1	Frank Thomas	.75
2	Roberto Alomar	.40
3	Cal Ripken, Jr.	1.50
4	Jose Canseco	.25
5	Matt Williams	.25
6	Esteban Beltre	.05
7	Domingo Cedeno	.05
8	John Valentin	.05
9	Glenallen Hill	.05
10	Rafael Belliard	.05
11	Randy Myers	.05
12	Mo Vaughn	.30

No.	Player	Price
13	Hector Carrasco	.05
14	Chili Davis	.05
15	Dante Bichette	.15
16	Darren Jackson	.05
17	Mike Piazza	1.25
18	Junior Felix	.05
19	Moises Alou	.10
20	Mark Gubicza	.05
21	Bret Saberhagen	.05
22	Len Dykstra	.05
23	Steve Howe	.05
24	Mark Dewey	.05
25	Brian Harper	.05
26	Ozzie Smith	.30
27	Scott Erickson	.05
28	Tony Gwynn	.75
29	Bob Welch	.05
30	Barry Bonds	.50
31	Leo Gomez	.05
32	Greg Maddux	1.00
33	Mike Greenwell	.05
34	Sammy Sosa	1.25
35	Darnell Coles	.05
36	Tommy Greene	.05
37	Will Clark	.20
38	Steve Ontiveros	.05
39	Stan Javier	.05
40	Bip Roberts	.05
41	Paul O'Neill	.10
42	Bill Haselman	.05
43	Shane Mack	.05
44	Orlando Merced	.05
45	Kevin Seitzer	.05
46	Trevor Hoffman	.10
47	Greg Gagne	.05
48	Jeff Kent	.05
49	Tony Phillips	.05
50	Ken Hill	.05
51	Carlos Baerga	.10
52	Henry Rodriguez	.05
53	Scott Sanderson	.05
54	Jeff Conine	.05
55	Chris Turner	.05
56	Ken Caminiti	.15
57	Harold Baines	.05
58	Charlie Hayes	.05
59	Roberto Kelly	.05
60	John Olerud	.15
61	Tim Davis	.05
62	Rich Rowland	.05
63	Rey Sanchez	.05
64	Junior Ortiz	.05
65	Ricky Gutierrez	.05
66	Rex Hudler	.05
67	Johnny Ruffin	.05
68	Jay Buhner	.10
69	Tom Pagnozzi	.05
70	Julio Franco	.05
71	Eric Young	.05
72	Mike Bordick	.05
73	Don Slaught	.05
74	Goose Gossage	.05
75	Lonnie Smith	.05
76	Jimmy Key	.05
77	Dave Hollins	.05
78	Mickey Tettleton	.05
79	Luis Gonzalez	.10
80	Dave Winfield	.15
81	Ryan Thompson	.05
82	Felix Jose	.05
83	Rusty Meacham	.05
84	Darryl Hamilton	.05
85	John Wetteland	.05
86	Tom Brunansky	.05
87	Mark Lemke	.05
88	Spike Owen	.05
89	Shawon Dunston	.05
90	Wilson Alvarez	.05
91	Lee Smith	.05
92	Scott Kamieniecki	.05
93	Jacob Brumfield	.05
94	Kirk Gibson	.05
95	Joe Girardi	.05
96	Mike Macfarlane	.05
97	Greg Colbrunn	.05
98	Ricky Bones	.05
99	Delino DeShields	.05
100	Pat Meares	.05
101	Jeff Fassero	.05
102	Jim Leyritz	.05
103	Gary Redus	.05
104	Terry Steinbach	.05
105	Kevin McReynolds	.05
106	Felix Fermin	.05
107	Danny Jackson	.05
108	Chris James	.05
109	Jeff King	.05
110	Pat Hentgen	.05
111	Gerald Perry	.05
112	Tim Raines	.10
113	Eddie Williams	.05
114	Jamie Moyer	.05
115	Bud Black	.05
116	Chris Gomez	.05
117	Luis Lopez	.05
118	Roger Clemens	.75
119	Javier Lopez	.20
120	Dave Nilsson	.05
121	Karl Rhodes	.05
122	Rick Aguilera	.05
123	Tony Fernandez	.05
124	Bernie Williams	.40
125	James Mouton	.05
126	Mark Langston	.05
127	Mike Lansing	.05
128	Tino Martinez	.10
129	Joe Orsulak	.05
130	David Hulse	.05
131	Pete Incaviglia	.05
132	Mark Clark	.05
133	Tony Eusebio	.05
134	Chuck Finley	.05
135	Lou Frazier	.05
136	Craig Grebeck	.05
137	Kelly Stinnett	.05
138	Paul Shuey	.05
139	David Nied	.05
140	Billy Brewer	.05
141	Dave Weathers	.05
142	Scott Leius	.05
143	Brian Jordan	.10
144	Melido Perez	.05
145	Tony Tarasco	.05
146	Dan Wilson	.05
147	Rondell White	.20
148	Mike Henneman	.05
149	Brian Johnson	.10
150	Tom Henke	.05
151	John Patterson	.05
152	Bobby Witt	.05
153	Eddie Taubensee	.05
154	Pat Borders	.05
155	Ramon Martinez	.10
156	Mike Kingery	.05
157	Zane Smith	.05
158	Benito Santiago	.05
159	Matias Carrillo	.05
160	Scott Brosius	.05
161	Dave Clark	.05
162	Mark McLemore	.05
163	Curt Schilling	.10
164	J.T. Snow	.10
165	Rod Beck	.10
166	Scott Fletcher	.05
167	Bob Tewksbury	.05
168	Mike LaValliere	.05
169	Dave Hansen	.05
170	Pedro Martinez	.40
171	Kirk Rueter	.05
172	Jose Lind	.05
173	Luis Alicea	.05
174	Mike Moore	.05
175	Andy Ashby	.10
176	Jody Reed	.05
177	Darryl Kile	.05
178	Carl Willis	.05
179	Jeromy Burnitz	.10
180	Mike Gallego	.05
181	*W. Van Landingham*	.10
182	Sid Fernandez	.05
183	Kim Batiste	.05
184	Greg Myers	.05
185	Steve Avery	.05
186	Steve Farr	.05
187	Robb Nen	.05
188	Dan Pasqua	.05
189	Bruce Ruffin	.05
190	Jose Valentin	.05
191	Willie Banks	.05
192	Mike Aldrete	.05
193	Randy Milligan	.05
194	Steve Karsay	.10
195	Mike Stanley	.05
196	Jose Mesa	.05
197	Tom Browning	.05
198	John Vander Wal	.05
199	Kevin Brown	.10
200	Mike Oquist	.05
201	Greg Swindell	.05
202	Eddie Zambrano	.05
203	Joe Boever	.05
204	Gary Varsho	.05
205	Chris Gwynn	.05
206	David Howard	.05
207	Jerome Walton	.05
208	Danny Darwin	.05
209	Darryl Strawberry	.10
210	Todd Van Poppel	.05
211	Scott Livingstone	.05
212	Dave Fleming	.05
213	Todd Worrell	.05
214	Carlos Delgado	.40
215	Bill Pecota	.05
216	Jim Lindeman	.05
217	Rick White	.05
218	Jose Oquendo	.05
219	Tony Castillo	.05
220	Fernando Vina	.05
221	Jeff Bagwell	.50
222	Randy Johnson	.50
223	Albert Belle	.50
224	Chuck Carr	.05
225	Mark Leiter	.05
226	Hal Morris	.05
227	Robin Ventura	.15
228	Mike Munoz	.05
229	Jim Thome	.20
230	Mario Diaz	.05
231	John Doherty	.05
232	Bobby Jones	.05
233	Raul Mondesi	.25
234	Ricky Jordan	.05
235	John Jaha	.05
236	Carlos Garcia	.05
237	Kirby Puckett	.75
238	Orel Hershiser	.10
239	Don Mattingly	.75
240	Sid Bream	.05
241	Brent Gates	.05
242	Tony Longmire	.05
243	Robby Thompson	.05
244	Rick Sutcliffe	.05
245	Dean Palmer	.05
246	Marquis Grissom	.05
247	Paul Molitor	.30
248	Mark Carreon	.05
249	Jack Voight	.05
250	Greg McMichael	.05
251	Damon Berryhill	.05
252	Brian Dorsett	.05
253	Jim Edmonds	.15
254	Barry Larkin	.15
255	Jack McDowell	.05
256	Wally Joyner	.10
257	Eddie Murray	.25
258	Lenny Webster	.05
259	Milt Cuyler	.05
260	Todd Benzinger	.05
261	Vince Coleman	.05
262	Todd Stottlemyre	.05
263	Turner Ward	.05
264	Ray Lankford	.10
265	Matt Walbeck	.05
266	Deion Sanders	.15
267	Gerald Williams	.05
268	Jim Gott	.05
269	Jeff Frye	.05
270	Jose Rijo	.05
271	Dave Justice	.20
272	Ismael Valdes	.10
273	Ben McDonald	.05
274	Darren Lewis	.05
275	Graeme Lloyd	.05
276	Luis Ortiz	.05
277	Julian Tavarez	.05
278	Mark Dalesandro	.05
279	Brett Merriman	.05
280	Ricky Bottalico	.05
281	Robert Eenhoorn	.05
282	Rikkert Faneyte	.05
283	Mike Kelly	.05
284	Mark Smith	.05
285	Turk Wendell	.05
286	Greg Blosser	.05
287	Garey Ingram	.05
288	Jorge Fabregas	.05
289	Blaise Ilsley	.05
290	Joe Hall	.05
291	Orlando Miller	.05
292	Jose Lima	.10
293	Greg O'Halloran	.05
294	Mark Kiefer	.05
295	Jose Oliva	.05
296	Rich Becker	.05
297	Brian Hunter	.10
298	Dave Silvestri	.05
299	*Armando Benitez*	.15
300	Darren Dreifort	.05
301	John Mabry	.05
302	Greg Pirkl	.05
303	J.R. Phillips	.05
304	Shawn Green	.20
305	Roberto Petagine	.05
306	Keith Lockhart	.05
307	Jonathon Hurst	.05
308	Paul Spoljaric	.05
309	Mike Lieberthal	.10
310	Garret Anderson	.10
311	John Johnston	.05
312	Alex Rodriguez	1.50
313	Kent Mercker	.05
314	John Valentin	.05
315	Kenny Rogers	.05
316	Fred McGriff	.20
317	Atlanta Braves, Baltimore Orioles	.05
318	Chicago Cubs, Boston Red Sox	.05
319	Cincinnati Reds, California Angels	.05
320	Colorado Rockies, Chicago White Sox	.05
321	Cleveland Indians, Florida Marlins	.05
322	Houston Astros, Detroit Tigers	.05
323	Los Angels Dodgers, Kansas City Royals	.05
324	Montreal Expos, Milwaukee Brewers	.05
325	New York Mets, Minnesota Twins	.05
326	Philadelphia Phillies, New York Yankees	.05
327	Pittsburgh Pirates, Oakland Athletics	.05
328	San Diego Padres, Seattle Mariners	.05
329	San Francisco Giants, Texas Rangers	.05
330	St. Louis Cardinals, Toronto Blue Jays	.05
331	Pedro Munoz	.05
332	Ryan Klesko	.20
333a	Andre Dawson (Red Sox)	.15
333b	Andre Dawson (Marlins)	.20
334	Derrick May	.05
335	Aaron Sele	.05
336	Kevin Mitchell	.05
337	Steve Traschel	.10
338	Andres Galarraga	.20
339a	Terry Pendleton (Braves)	.05
339b	Terry Pendleton (Marlins)	.15
340	Gary Sheffield	.30
341	Travis Fryman	.05
342	Bo Jackson	.10
343	Gary Gaetti	.05
344a	Brett Butler (Dodgers)	.10
344b	Brett Butler (Mets)	.15
345	B. J. Surhoff	.05
346a	Larry Walker (Expos)	.25
346b	Larry Walker (Rockies)	.25
347	Kevin Tapani	.05
348	Rick Wilkins	.05
349	Wade Boggs	.20
350	Mariano Duncan	.05
351	Ruben Sierra	.05
352a	Andy Van Slyke (Pirates)	.05
352b	Andy Van Slyke (Orioles)	.15
353	Reggie Jefferson	.05
354	Gregg Jefferies	.10
355	Tim Naehring	.05
356	John Roper	.05
357	Joe Carter	.10
358	Kurt Abbott	.05
359	Lenny Harris	.05
360	Lance Johnson	.05
361	Brian Anderson	.10
362	Jim Eisenreich	.05
363	Jerry Browne	.05
364	Mark Grace	.15
365	Devon White	.10
366	Reggie Sanders	.10
367	Ivan Rodriguez	.50
368	Kirt Manwaring	.05
369	Pat Kelly	.05

370 Ellis Burks .10
371 Charles Nagy .10
372 Kevin Bass .05
373 Lou Whitaker .05
374 Rene Arocha .05
375 Derrick Parks .05
376 Mark Whiten .05
377 Mark McGwire 2.00
378 Doug Drabek .05
379 Greg Vaughn .10
380 Al Martin .05
381 Ron Darling .05
382 Tim Wallach .05
383 Alan Trammell .10
384 Randy Velarde .05
385 Chris Sabo .05
386 Wil Cordero .05
387 Darrin Fletcher .05
388 David Segui .05
389 Steve Buechele .05
390 Otis Nixon .05
391 Jeff Brantley .05
392a Chad Curtis (Angels) .05
392b Chad Curtis (Tigers) .15
393 Cal Eldred .05
394 Jason Bere .05
395 Bret Barberie .05
396 Paul Sorrento .05
397 Steve Finley .05
398 Cecil Fielder .10
399 Eric Karros .10
400 Jeff Montgomery .05
401 Cliff Floyd .10
402 Matt Mieske .05
403 Brian Hunter .05
404 Alex Cole .05
405 Kevin Stocker .05
406 Eric Davis .10
407 Marvin Freeman .05
408 Dennis Eckersley .05
409 Todd Zeile .10
410 Keith Mitchell .05
411 Andy Benes .05
412 Juan Bell .05
413 Royce Clayton .05
414 Ed Sprague .05
415 Mike Mussina .25
416 Todd Hundley .15
417 Pat Listach .05
418 Joe Oliver .05
419 Rafael Palmeiro .20
420 Tim Salmon .15
421 Brady Anderson .10
422 Kenny Lofton .25
423 Craig Biggio .15
424 Bobby Bonilla .05
425 Kenny Rogers .05
426 Derek Bell .05
427a Scott Cooper (Red Sox) .05
427b Scott Cooper (Cardinals) .25
428 Ozzie Guillen .05
429 Omar Vizquel .05
430 Phil Plantier .05
431 Chuck Knoblauch .10
432 Darren Daulton .05
433 Bob Hamelin .05
434 Tom Glavine .15
435 Walt Weiss .05
436 Jose Vizcaino .05
437 Ken Griffey Jr. 1.50
438 Jay Bell .05
439 Juan Gonzalez .50
440 Jeff Blauser .05
441 Rickey Henderson .20
442 Bobby Ayala .05
443a David Cone (Royals) .10
443b David Cone (Blue Jays) .25
444 Pedro Martinez .05
445 Manny Ramirez .50
446 Mark Portugal .05
447 Damion Easley .05
448 Gary DiSarcina .05
449 Roberto Hernandez .05
450 Jeffrey Hammonds .10
451 Jeff Treadway .05
452a Jim Abbott (Yankees) .10
452b Jim Abbott (White Sox) .25
453 Carlos Rodriguez .05
454 Joey Cora .05
455 Bret Boone .05
456 Danny Tartabull .05
457 John Franco .05
458 Roger Salkeld .05
459 Fred McGriff .30
460 Pedro Astacio .05
461 Jon Lieber .05
462 Luis Polonia .05
463 Geronimo Pena .05
464 Tom Gordon .05
465 Brad Ausmus .05
466 Willie McGee .05
467 Doug Jones .05
468 John Smoltz .15
469 Troy Neel .05
470 Luis Sojo .05
471 John Smiley .05
472 Rafael Bournigal .05
473 Billy Taylor .05
474 Juan Guzman .05
475 Dave Magadan .05
476 Mike Devereaux .05
477 Andujar Cedeno .05
478 Edgar Martinez .05
479 Troy Neel .05
480 Allen Watson .05
481 Ron Karkovice .05
482 Joey Hamilton .05
483 Vinny Castilla .10
484 Kevin Gross .05
485 Bernard Gilkey .10
486 John Burkett .05
487 Matt Nokes .05
488 Mel Rojas .05
489 Craig Shipley .05
490 Chip Hale .05
491 Bill Swift .05
492 Pat Rapp .05
493a Brian McRae (Royals) .05
493b Brian McRae (Cubs) .20
494 Mickey Morandini .05
495 Tony Pena .05
496 Danny Bautista .05
497 Armando Reynoso .05
498 Ken Ryan .05
499 Billy Ripken .05
500 Pat Mahomes .05
501 Mark Acre .05
502 Geronimo Berroa .05
503 Norberto Martin .05
504 Chad Kreuter .05
505 Howard Johnson .05
506 Eric Anthony .05
507 Mark Wohlers .05
508 Scott Sanders .05
509 Pete Harnisch .05
510 Wes Chamberlain .05
511 Tom Candiotti .05
512 Albie Lopez .05
513 Denny Neagle .05
514 Sean Berry .05
515 Billy Hatcher .05
516 Todd Jones .05
517 Wayne Kirby .05
518 Butch Henry .05
519 Sandy Alomar Jr. .10
520 Kevin Appier .05
521 Robert Mejia .05
522 Steve Cooke .05
523 Terry Shumpert .05
524 Mike Jackson .05
525 Kent Mercker .05
526 David Wells .10
527 Juan Samuel .05
528 Salomon Torres .05
529 Duane Ward .05
530a Rob Dibble (Reds) .05
530b Rob Dibble (White Sox) .25
531 Mike Blowers .05
532 Mark Eichhorn .05
533 Alex Diaz .05
534 Dan Miceli .05
535 Jeff Branson .05
536 Dave Stevens .05
537 Charlie O'Brien .05
538 Shane Reynolds .05
539 Rich Amaral .05
540 Rusty Greer .05
541 Alex Arias .05
542 Eric Plunk .05
543 John Hudek .05
544 Kirk McCaskill .05
545 Jeff Reboulet .05
546 Sterling Hitchcock .05
547 Warren Newson .05
548 Bryan Harvey .05
549 Mike Huff .05
550 Lance Parrish .05
551 Ken Griffey Jr . (Hitters Inc.) .75
552 Matt Williams (Hitters Inc.) .15
553 Roberto Alomar (Hitters Inc.) .20
554 Jeff Bagwell (Hitters Inc.) .35
555 Dave Justice (Hitters Inc.) .10
556 Cal Ripken Jr. (Hitters Inc.) .75
557 Albert Belle (Hitters Inc.) .20
558 Mike Piazza (Hitters Inc.) .50
559 Kirby Puckett (Hitters Inc.) .40
560 Wade Boggs (Hitters Inc.) .15
561 Tony Gwynn (Hitters Inc.) .40
562 Barry Bonds (Hitters Inc.) .25
563 Mo Vaughn (Hitters Inc.) .20
564 Don Mattingly (Hitters Inc.) .50
565 Carlos Baerga (Hitters Inc.) .05
566 Paul Molitor (Hitters Inc.) .20
567 Raul Mondesi (Hitters Inc.) .15
568 Manny Ramirez (Hitters Inc.) .40
569 Alex Rodriguez (Hitters Inc.) .75
570 Will Clark (Hitters Inc.) .15
571 Frank Thomas (Hitters Inc.) .50
572 Moises Alou (Hitters Inc.) .05
573 Jeff Conine (Hitters Inc.) .05
574 Joe Ausanio .05
575 Charles Johnson .10
576 Ernie Young .05
577 Jeff Granger .05
578 Robert Perez .05
579 Melvin Nieves .05
580 Gar Finnvold .05
581 Duane Singleton .05
582 Chan Ho Park .15
583 Fausto Cruz .05
584 Dave Staton .05
585 Denny Hocking .05
586 Nate Minchey .05
587 Marc Newfield .05
588 Jayhawk Owens .05
589 Darren Bragg .05
590 Kevin King .05
591 Kurt Miller .05
592 Aaron Small .05
593 Troy O'Leary .05
594 Phil Stidham .05
595 Steve Dunn .05
596 Cory Bailey .10
597 Alex Gonzalez .10
598 Jim Bowie .05
599 Jeff Cirillo .10
600 Mark Hutton .05
601 Russ Davis .05
602 Team Checklist .05
603 Team Checklist .05
604 Team Checklist .05
605 Team Checklist .05
---- "You Trade 'em" redemption card (Expired Dec. 31, 1995) .50

1995 Score Airmail

Young ballplayers with a propensity for hitting the long ball are featured in this insert set found only in Series II jumbo packs. Cards have a player batting action photo set in sky-and-clouds background. A gold-foil stamp in the upper-left corner identifies the series. Backs have a background photo of sunset and dark clouds, with a player portrait photo in the foreground. A few stats and sentences describe the player's power hitting potential. Cards have an AM prefix to the number. Stated odds for insertion rate are an average of one Airmail chase card per 24 packs.

		MT
Complete Set (18):		40.00
Common Player:		1.00
1	Bob Hamelin	1.00
2	John Mabry	1.00
3	Marc Newfield	1.00
4	Jose Oliva	1.00
5	Charles Johnson	3.00
6	Russ Davis	1.00
7	Ernie Young	1.00
8	Billy Ashley	1.00
9	Ryan Klesko	3.00
10	J.R. Phillips	1.00
11	Cliff Floyd	2.00
12	Carlos Delgado	6.00
13	Melvin Nieves	1.00
14	Raul Mondesi	5.00
15	Manny Ramirez	8.00
16	Mike Kelly	1.00
17	Alex Rodriguez	20.00
18	Rusty Greer	1.50

1995 Score Double Gold Champions

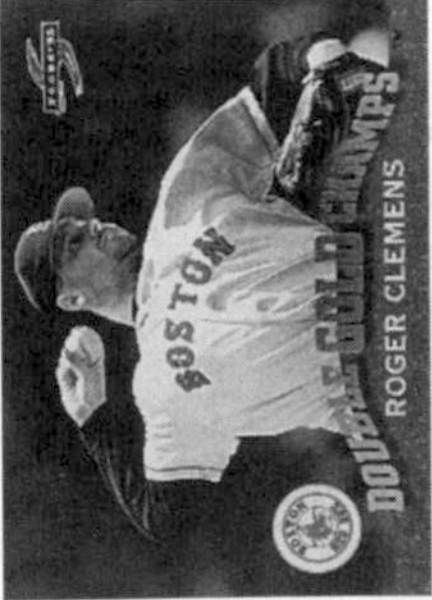

A dozen veteran players, who have won at least two of the game's top awards are designated as "Double Gold Champs," in this Series II hobby insert set. Fronts have horizontal action photos at top, with a speckled red border at bottom. Vertical backs have a portrait photo and a list of the major awards won by the player. Cards have a GC prefix to the number. These chase cards were reportedly inserted at an average rate of one per 36.

		MT
Complete Set (11):		60.00
Common Player:		3.00
1	Frank Thomas	10.00
2	Ken Griffey Jr.	20.00
3	Barry Bonds	6.00
4	Tony Gwynn	8.00
5	Don Mattingly	8.00
6	Greg Maddux	10.00
7	Roger Clemens	8.00
8	Kenny Lofton	3.00
9	Jeff Bagwell	6.00
10	Matt Williams	3.00
11	Kirby Puckett	6.00

1995 Score Draft Picks

These cards were randomly included in 1995 Score hobby packs at a rate of one per every 36 packs. The cards showcase 18 of baseball's potential superstars and document their professional beginnings. The card front has the player's team logo and name in the lower-right corner. " '94 Draft Pick" appears in the upper-right corner. The front also has a mug shot and an action shot of the player. The card back has a portrait and career summary and is numbered with a DP prefix.

		MT
Complete Set (18):		20.00
Common Player:		1.00
1	McKay Christensen	1.00
2	Brett Wagner	1.00
3	Paul Wilson	1.00
4	C.J. Nitkowski	1.00
5	Josh Booty	1.00
6	Antone Williamson	1.00
7	Paul Konerko	5.00
8	Scott Elarton	1.50
9	Jacob Shumate	1.00
10	Terrence Long	1.50
11	Mark Johnson	1.00
12	Ben Grieve	6.00
13	Doug Million	1.00
14	Jayson Peterson	1.00
15	Dustin Hermanson	1.50
16	Matt Smith	1.00
17	Kevin Witt	1.00
18	Brian Buchanon	1.00

1995 Score Dream Team Gold

The Major Leagues' top players at each position are featured in this Series I insert set. Fronts are printed entirely on rainbow holographic foil and feature a large and a small player action photo. Backs have a single-color version of one of the front photos as well as a color portrait photo in a circle at center, all in conventional printing technology. Card numbers have a DG prefix.

		MT
Complete Set (12):		120.00
Common Player:		2.00
1	Frank Thomas	17.50
2	Roberto Alomar	6.00
3	Cal Ripken Jr.	25.00
4	Matt Williams	4.00
5	Mike Piazza	20.00
6	Albert Belle	8.00
7	Ken Griffey Jr.	30.00
8	Tony Gwynn	15.00
9	Paul Molitor	7.50
10	Jimmy Key	2.00
11	Greg Maddux	17.50
12	Lee Smith	2.00

1995 Score Hall of Gold

Hall of Gold inserts picture 110 of the top players on gold foil cards. Each card front has the Hall of Gold logo in an upper corner, plus a color action photo of the player, and his name and team logo at the bottom. The card back is numbered using an "HG" prefix and includes another color photo of the player, his team's name, his position, and a career summary. Cards were inserted one per every six regular 1995 Score packs and one per every two jumbo packs. Updated versions of five traded players were issued in Series II, available only via mail-in offer with a trade card found randomly inserted in packs.

		MT
Complete Set (110):		80.00
Common Player:		.20
1	Ken Griffey Jr.	8.00
2	Matt Williams	.40
3	Roberto Alomar	1.50
4	Jeff Bagwell	3.00
5	Dave Justice	.40
6	Cal Ripken Jr.	6.50
7	Randy Johnson	.50
8	Barry Larkin	.40
9	Albert Belle	2.50
10	Mike Piazza	5.00
11	Kirby Puckett	2.50
12	Moises Alou	.25
13	Jose Canseco	.60
14	Tony Gwynn	3.00
15	Roger Clemens	3.00
16	Barry Bonds	2.50
17	Mo Vaughn	1.50
18	Greg Maddux	4.50
19	Dante Bichette	.60
20	Will Clark	.60
21	Len Dykstra	.20
22	Don Mattingly	2.50
23	Carlos Baerga	.20
24	Ozzie Smith	.75
25	Paul Molitor	.75
26	Paul O'Neill	.25
27	Deion Sanders	.80
28	Jeff Conine	.20
29	John Olerud	.25
30	Jose Rijo	.20
31	Sammy Sosa	4.00
32	Robin Ventura	.25
33	Raul Mondesi	.80
34	Eddie Murray	.60
35	Marquis Grissom	.20
36	Darryl Strawberry	.20
37	Dave Nilsson	.20
38	Manny Ramirez	3.00
39	Delino DeShields	.20
40	Lee Smith	.20
41	Alex Rodriguez	6.00
42	Julio Franco	.20
43	Bret Saberhagen	.20
44	Ken Hill	.20
45	Roberto Kelly	.20
46	Hal Morris	.20
47	Jimmy Key	.20
48	Terry Steinbach	.20
49	Mickey Tettleton	.20
50	Tony Phillips	.20
51	Carlos Garcia	.20
52	Jim Edmonds	.40
53	Rod Beck	.20
54	Shane Mack	.20
55	Ken Caminiti	.30
56	Frank Thomas	4.00
57	Kenny Lofton	1.50
58	Jack McDowell	.20
59	Jason Bere	.20
60	Joe Carter	.20
61	Gary Sheffield	.40
62	Andres Galarraga	.25
63	Gregg Jefferies	.20
64	Bobby Bonilla	.20
65	Tom Glavine	.25
66	John Smoltz	.30
67	Fred McGriff	.50
68	Craig Biggio	.30
69	Reggie Sanders	.20
70	Kevin Mitchell	.20
71a	Larry Walker (Expos)	.50
71b	Larry Walker (Rockies)	2.00
72	Carlos Delgado	.30
73	Andujar Cedeno	.20
74	Ivan Rodriguez	.60
75	Ryan Klesko	.40
76a	John Kruk (Phillies)	.20
76b	John Kruk (White Sox)	.60
77a	Brian McRae (Royals)	.20
77b	Brian McRae (Cubs)	.60
78	Tim Salmon	.40
79	Travis Fryman	.20
80	Chuck Knoblauch	.25
81	Jay Bell	.20
82	Cecil Fielder	.25
83	Cliff Floyd	.20
84	Ruben Sierra	.20
85	Mike Mussina	1.00
86	Mark Grace	.45
87	Dennis Eckersley	.20
88	Dennis Martinez	.20
89	Rafael Palmeiro	.25
90	Ben McDonald	.20
91	Dave Hollins	.20
92	Steve Avery	.20
93a	David Cone (Royals)	.25
93b	David Cone (Blue Jays)	.60
94	Darren Daulton	.20
95	Bret Boone	.20
96	Wade Boggs	.50
97	Doug Drabek	.20
98	Derek Bell	.20
99	Jim Thome	.60
100	Chili Davis	.20
101	Jeffrey Hammonds	.20
102	Rickey Henderson	.30
103	Brett Butler	.20
104	Tim Wallach	.20
105	Wil Cordero	.20
106	Mark Whiten	.20
107	Bob Hamelin	.20
108	Rondell White	.25
109	Devon White	.20
110a	Tony Tarasco (Braves)	.20
110b	Tony Tarasco (Expos)	.45
----	Redemption trade card (Expired Dec. 31, 1995)	.25

1995 Score Rookie Dream Team

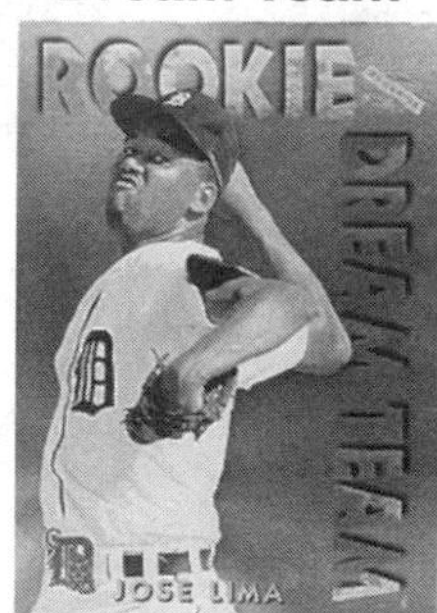

These Series II inserts feature a dozen of 1995's best rookie prospects. Fronts are printed on a silver-foil background. The words "ROOKIE DREAM TEAM" are formed of sky-and-cloud images within the letters. Horizontal backs repeat the motif and include another player photo in a vignette at center. Card numbers have an RDT prefix.

		MT
Complete Set (12):		45.00
Common Player:		1.00
1	J.R. Phillips	1.00
2	Alex Gonzalez	4.00
3	Alex Rodriguez	25.00
4	Jose Oliva	1.00
5	Charles Johnson	3.00
6	Shawn Green	5.00
7	Brian Hunter	3.00
8	Garret Anderson	3.00
9	Julian Tavarez	1.00
10	Jose Lima	5.00
11	Armando Benitez	1.50
12	Ricky Bottalico	2.50

1995 Score Rookie Greatness

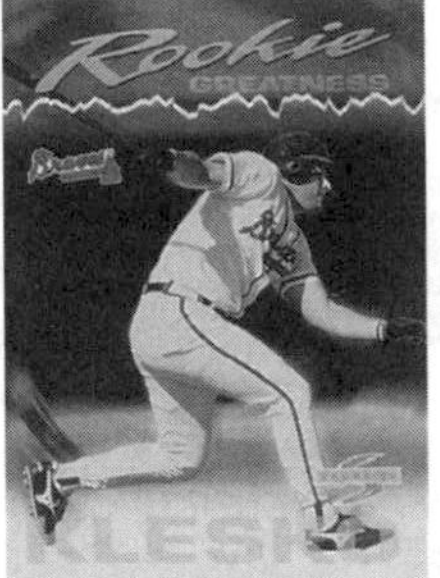

This single-card insert set is the toughest pull among the 1995 Score chase cards. Honoring slugging Braves star Ryan Klesko, the card is inserted at the rate of one per 720 retail packs. An even scarcer autographed version of the card in an edition of just over 6,000 was also created for insertion into hobby packs.

		MT
Complete Set (2):		45.00
RG1	Ryan Klesko	12.50
SG1	Ryan Klesko (autographed)	37.00

1995 Score Score Rules

Series I jumbo packs were the only sources for "Score Rules" insert set of rookie and veteran stars. A color player photo at left has a team logo toward the bottom, beneath which is a gold-foil "tie tack" device with the league initials and position. At top-right is a baseball which appears to be dripping orange and green goop down the card. The player's last name is presented vertically with a sepia photo of the player within the letters. Backs repeat the green baseball and ooze motif, with three progressive color proof versions of the sepia front photo and a few sentences about the star. Cards are numbered with an "SR" prefix.

		MT
Complete Set (30):		100.00
Common Player:		1.50
1	Ken Griffey, Jr.	20.00
2	Frank Thomas	10.00
3	Mike Piazza	12.00
4	Jeff Bagwell	10.00
5	Alex Rodriguez	15.00
6	Albert Belle	5.00
7	Matt Williams	2.00
8	Roberto Alomar	3.00
9	Barry Bonds	6.00
10	Raul Mondesi	3.00
11	Jose Canseco	2.50
12	Kirby Puckett	8.00
13	Fred McGriff	2.50
14	Kenny Lofton	4.00
15	Greg Maddux	12.00
16	Juan Gonzalez	5.00
17	Cliff Floyd	1.50
18	Cal Ripken, Jr.	15.00
19	Will Clark	2.50
20	Tim Salmon	2.50
21	Paul O'Neill	1.50
22	Jason Bere	1.50
23	Tony Gwynn	10.00
24	Manny Ramirez	6.00
25	Don Mattingly	9.00
26	Dave Justice	2.00
27	Javier Lopez	1.50
28	Ryan Klesko	2.00
29	Carlos Delgado	2.00
30	Mike Mussina	3.00

1995 Score Ad Prize Cards

In a series of ads in hobby and public media, Score offered a pair of special cards as prizes in a mail-in offer. Cards feature the same basic design as 1995 Score, but are printed on platinum foil on front. Backs are conventionally printed with a portrait photo and a few words about the player.

		MT
Complete Set (2):		50.00
Common Player:		15.00
AD1	Alex Rodriguez	35.00
AD2	Ivan Rodriguez	15.00

1996 Score Samples

Score premiered its 1996 base brand offering with a cello pack of nine cards, including one of its new Dugout Collection inserts. The samples are virtually identical to the issued versions except that all 1995 and career stats are stated as zeros and the word "SAMPLE" is printed in white letters diagonally across front and back. Each of the cards can be found as a Dugout Collection version, making them eight times scarcer than the other samples.

		MT
Complete Set (16):		80.00
Common Player:		3.00
3	Ryan Klesko	3.00
3	Ryan Klesko (Dugout Collection)	6.00
4	Jim Edmonds	3.00
4	Jim Edmonds (Dugout Collection)	6.00
5	Barry Larkin	3.00
5	Barry Larkin (Dugout Collection)	6.00
6	Jim Thome	3.00
6	Jim Thome (Dugout Collection)	8.00
7	Raul Mondesi	4.00
7	Raul Mondesi (Dugout Collection)	12.00
110	Derek Bell	3.00
110	Derek Bell (Dugout Collection)	6.00
240	Derek Jeter	9.00
240	Derek Jeter (Dugout Collection)	25.00
241	Michael Tucker	3.00
241	Michael Tucker (Dugout Collection)	6.00

1996 Score

Large, irregularly shaped action photos are featured on the fronts of the basic cards in the 1996 Score issue. Backs feature a portrait photo (in most cases) at left and a full slate of major and minor league stats at right, along with a few words about the player. Slightly different design details and a "ROOKIE" headline identify that subset within the regular issue. A wide variety of insert cards was produced, most of them exclusive to one type of packaging.

		MT
Complete Set (510):		20.00
Complete Series 1 (275):		13.50
Complete Series 2 (235):		11.00
Common Player:		.05
Series 1 or 2 Pack (10):		.75
Series 1 or 2 Wax Bo (36):		20.00
1	Will Clark	.20
2	Rich Becker	.05
3	Ryan Klesko	.10
4	Jim Edmonds	.15
5	Barry Larkin	.15
6	Jim Thome	.20
7	Raul Mondesi	.20
8	Don Mattingly	.60
9	Jeff Conine	.10
10	Rickey Henderson	.20
11	Chad Curtis	.05
12	Darren Daulton	.05
13	Larry Walker	.20
14	Carlos Garcia	.05
15	Carlos Baerga	.05
16	Tony Gwynn	.60
17	Jon Nunally	.05
18	Deion Sanders	.20
19	Mark Grace	.20
20	Alex Rodriguez	1.50
21	Frank Thomas	.75
22	Brian Jordan	.10
23	J.T. Snow	.10
24	Shawn Green	.15
25	Tim Wakefield	.05
26	Curtis Goodwin	.05
27	John Smoltz	.10
28	Devon White	.10
29	Brian Hunter	.10
30	Rusty Greer	.05
31	Rafael Palmeiro	.20
32	Bernard Gilkey	.10
33	John Valentin	.05
34	Randy Johnson	.40
35	Garret Anderson	.10
36	Rikkert Faneyte	.05
37	Ray Durham	.05
38	Bip Roberts	.05
39	Jaime Navarro	.05
40	Mark Johnson	.05
41	Darren Lewis	.05
42	Tyler Green	.05
43	Bill Pulsipher	.05
44	Jason Giambi	.25
45	Kevin Ritz	.05
46	Jack McDowell	.05
47	Felipe Lira	.05
48	Rico Brogna	.05
49	Terry Pendleton	.05
50	Rondell White	.10
51	Andre Dawson	.10
52	Kirby Puckett	.60
53	Wally Joyner	.10

54 B.J. Surhoff .05
55 Chan Ho Park .10
56 Greg Vaughn .10
57 Roberto Alomar .30
58 Dave Justice .20
59 Kevin Seitzer .05
60 Cal Ripken Jr. 1.50
61 Ozzie Smith .20
62 Mo Vaughn .30
63 Ricky Bones .05
64 Gary DiSarcina .05
65 Matt Williams .20
66 Wilson Alvarez .05
67 Lenny Dykstra .05
68 Brian McRae .05
69 Todd Stottlemyre .05
70 Bret Boone .05
71 Sterling Hitchcock .05
72 Albert Belle .30
73 Todd Hundley .10
74 Vinny Castilla .10
75 Moises Alou .10
76 Cecil Fielder .10
77 Brad Radke .05
78 Quilvio Veras .05
79 Eddie Murray .25
80 James Mouton .05
81 Pat Listach .05
82 Mark Gubicza .05
83 Dave Winfield .15
84 Fred McGriff .25
85 Darryl Hamilton .05
86 Jeffrey Hammonds .05
87 Pedro Munoz .05
88 Craig Biggio .15
89 Cliff Floyd .05
90 Tim Naehring .05
91 Brett Butler .05
92 Kevin Foster .05
93 Patrick Kelly .05
94 John Smiley .05
95 Terry Steinbach .05
96 Orel Hershiser .10
97 Darrin Fletcher .05
98 Walt Weiss .05
99 John Wetteland .05
100 Alan Trammell .10
101 Steve Avery .05
102 Tony Eusebio .05
103 Sandy Alomar .10
104 Joe Girardi .05
105 Rick Aguilera .05
106 Tony Tarasco .05
107 Chris Hammond .05
108 Mike McFarlane .05
109 Doug Drabek .05
110 Derek Bell .05
111 Ed Sprague .05
112 Todd Hollandsworth .05
113 Otis Nixon .05
114 Keith Lockhart .05
115 Donovan Osborne .05
116 Dave Magadan .05
117 Edgar Martinez .05
118 Chuck Carr .05
119 J.R. Phillips .05
120 Sean Bergman .05
121 Andujar Cedeno .05
122 Eric Young .10
123 Al Martin .05
124 Ken Hill .05
125 Jim Eisenreich .05
126 Benito Santiago .05
127 Ariel Prieto .05
128 Jim Bullinger .05
129 Russ Davis .05
130 Jim Abbott .05
131 Jason Isringhausen .10
132 Carlos Perez .05
133 David Segui .05
134 Troy O'Leary .05
135 Pat Meares .05
136 Chris Hoiles .05
137 Ismael Valdes .10
138 Jose Oliva .05
139 Carlos Delgado .40
140 Tom Goodwin .05
141 Bob Tewksbury .05
142 Chris Gomez .05
143 Jose Oquendo .05
144 Mark Lewis .05
145 Salomon Torres .05
146 Luis Gonzalez .10
147 Mark Carreon .05
148 Lance Johnson .05
149 Melvin Nieves .05
150 Lee Smith .05
151 Jacob Brumfield .05
152 Armando Benitez .05
153 Curt Schilling .10
154 Javier Lopez .10
155 Frank Rodriguez .05
156 Alex Gonzalez .10
157 Todd Worrell .05
158 Benji Gil .05
159 Greg Gagne .05
160 Tom Henke .05
161 Randy Myers .05
162 Joey Cora .05
163 Scott Ruffcorn .05
164 William VanLandingham .05
165 Tony Phillips .05
166 Eddie Williams .05
167 Bobby Bonilla .05
168 Denny Neagle .05
169 Troy Percival .05
170 Billy Ashley .05
171 Andy Van Slyke .05
172 Jose Offerman .05
173 Mark Parent .05
174 Edgardo Alfonzo .10
175 Trevor Hoffman .10
176 David Cone .10
177 Dan Wilson .05
178 Steve Ontiveros .05
179 Dean Palmer .05
180 Mike Kelly .05
181 Jim Leyritz .05
182 Ron Karkovice .05
183 Kevin Brown .10
184 *Jose Valentin* .05
185 Jorge Fabregas .05
186 Jose Mesa .05
187 Brent Mayne .05
188 Carl Everett .05
189 Paul Sorrento .05
190 Pete Shourek .05
191 Scott Kamieniecki .05
192 Roberto Hernandez .05
193 Randy Johnson (Radar Rating) .05
194 Greg Maddux (Radar Rating) .40
195 Hideo Nomo (Radar Rating) .15
196 David Cone (Radar Rating) .05
197 Mike Mussina (Radar Rating) .10
198 Andy Benes (Radar Rating) .05
199 Kevin Appier (Radar Rating) .05
200 John Smoltz (Radar Rating) .05
201 John Wetteland (Radar Rating) .05
202 Mark Wohlers (Radar Rating) .05
203 Stan Belinda .05
204 Brian Anderson .05
205 Mike Devereaux .05
206 Mark Wohlers .05
207 Omar Vizquel .05
208 Jose Rijo .05
209 Willie Blair .05
210 Jamie Moyer .05
211 Craig Shipley .05
212 Shane Reynolds .05
213 Chad Fonville .05
214 Jose Vizcaino .05
215 Sid Fernandez .05
216 Andy Ashby .10
217 Frank Castillo .05
218 Kevin Tapani .05
219 Kent Mercker .05
220 Karim Garcia .05
221 Chris Snopek .05
222 Tim Unroe .05
223 Johnny Damon .10
224 LaTroy Hawkins .10
225 Mariano Rivera .15
226 Jose Alberro .05
227 Angel Martinez .05
228 Jason Schmidt .05
229 Tony Clark .10
230 Kevin Jordan .05
231 Mark Thompson .05
232 Jim Dougherty .05
333 Roger Cedeno .10
234 Ugueth Urbina .10
235 Ricky Otero .05
236 Mark Smith .05
237 Brian Barber .05
238 Marc Kroon .05
239 Joe Rosselli .05
240 Derek Jeter 1.50
241 Michael Tucker .05
242 *Joe Borowski* .05
243 Joe Vitiello .05
244 Orlando Palmeiro .05
245 James Baldwin .05
246 Alan Embree .05
247 Shannon Penn .05
248 Chris Stynes .05
249 Oscar Munoz .05
250 Jose Herrera .05
251 Scott Sullivan .05
252 Reggie Williams .05
253 Mark Grudzielanek .05
254 Kevin Jordan .05
255 Terry Bradshaw .05
256 *F.P. Santangelo* .05
257 Doug Johns .05
258 George Williams .05
259 Larry Thomas .05
260 Rudy Pemberton .05
261 Jim Pittsley .05
262 Les Norman .05
263 Ruben Rivera .10
264 *Cesar Devarez* .05
265 Greg Zaun .05
266 Eric Owens .05
267 John Frascatore .05
268 Shannon Stewart .05
269 Checklist .05
270 Checklist .05
271 Checklist .05
272 Checklist .05
273 Checklist .05
274 Checklist .05
275 Checklist .05
276 Greg Maddux 1.00
277 Pedro Martinez .50
278 Bobby Higginson .05
279 Ray Lankford .10
280 Shawon Dunston .05
281 Gary Sheffield .20
282 Ken Griffey Jr. 1.50
283 Paul Molitor .20
284 Kevin Appier .05
285 Chuck Knoblauch .10
286 Alex Fernandez .10
287 Steve Finley .05
288 Jeff Blauser .05
289 Charles Johnson .10
290 John Franco .05
291 Mark Langston .05
292 Bret Saberhagen .05
293 John Mabry .05
294 Ramon Martinez .10
295 Mike Blowers .05
296 Paul O'Neill .15
297 Dave Nilsson .05
298 Dante Bichette .10
299 Marty Cordova .10
300 Jay Bell .05
301 Mike Mussina .25
302 Ivan Rodriguez .50
303 Jose Canseco .30
304 Jeff Bagwell .50
305 Manny Ramirez .50
306 Dennis Martinez .05
307 Charlie Hayes .05
308 Joe Carter .10
309 Travis Fryman .05
310 Mark McGwire 2.00
311 Reggie Sanders .10
312 Julian Tavarez .05
313 Jeff Montgomery .05
314 Andy Benes .05
315 John Jaha .05
316 Jeff Kent .05
317 Mike Piazza 1.25
318 Erik Hanson .05
319 Kenny Rogers .05
320 Hideo Nomo .30
321 Gregg Jefferies .10
322 Chipper Jones 1.00
323 Jay Buhner .10
324 Dennis Eckersley .05
325 Kenny Lofton .30
326 Robin Ventura .15
327 Tom Glavine .15
328 Tim Salmon .10
329 Andres Galarraga .15
330 Hal Morris .05
331 Brady Anderson .10
332 Chili Davis .05
333 Roger Clemens .60
334 Marquis Grissom .10
335 Jeff (Mike) Greenwell .05
336 Sammy Sosa 1.25
337 Ron Gant .10
338 Ken Caminiti .10
339 Danny Tartabull .05
340 Barry Bonds .50
341 Ben McDonald .05
342 Ruben Sierra .05
343 Bernie Williams .40
344 Wil Cordero .05
345 Wade Boggs .20
346 Gary Gaetti .05
347 Greg Colbrunn .05
348 Juan Gonzalez .50
349 Marc Newfield .05
350 Charles Nagy .10
351 Robby Thompson .05
352 Roberto Petagine .05
353 Darryl Strawberry .10
354 Tino Martinez .10
355 Eric Karros .10
356 Cal Ripken Jr. .75
357 Cecil Fielder .10
358 Kirby Puckett .25
359 Jim Edmonds .10
360 Matt Williams .10
361 Alex Rodriguez .75
362 Barry Larkin .15
363 Rafael Palmeiro .20
364 David Cone .10
365 Roberto Alomar .20
366 Eddie Murray .10
367 Randy Johnson .20
368 Ryan Klesko .10
369 Raul Mondesi .15
370 Mo Vaughn .25
371 Will Clark .10
372 Carlos Baerga .10
373 Frank Thomas .40
374 Larry Walker .10
375 Garret Anderson .10
376 Edgar Martinez .05
377 Don Mattingly .30
378 Tony Gwynn .30
379 Albert Belle .20
380 Jason Isringhausen .10
381 Ruben Rivera .10
382 Johnny Damon .10
383 Karim Garcia .05
384 Derek Jeter .75
385 David Justice .10
386 Royce Clayton .05
387 Mark Whiten .05
388 Mickey Tettleton .05
389 Steve Trachsel .05
390 Danny Bautista .05
391 Midre Cummings .05
392 Scott Leius .05
393 Manny Alexander .05
394 Brent Gates .05
395 Rey Sanchez .05
396 Andy Pettitte .20
397 Jeff Cirillo .05
398 Kurt Abbott .05
399 Lee Tinsley .05
400 Paul Assenmacher .05
401 Scott Erickson .05
402 Todd Zeile .05
403 Tom Pagnozzi .05
404 Ozzie Guillen .05
405 Jeff Frye .05
406 Kirt Manwaring .05
407 Chad Ogea .05
408 Harold Baines .05
409 Jason Bere .05
410 Chuck Finley .05
411 Jeff Fassero .05
412 Joey Hamilton .05
413 John Olerud .15
414 Kevin Stocker .05
415 Eric Anthony .05
416 Aaron Sele .05
417 Chris Bosio .05
418 Michael Mimbs .05
419 Orlando Miller .05
420 Stan Javier .05
421 Matt Mieske .05
422 Jason Bates .05
423 Orlando Merced .05
424 John Flaherty .05
425 Reggie Jefferson .05
426 Scott Stahoviak .05
427 John Burkett .05
428 Rod Beck .05
429 Bill Swift .05

430	Scott Cooper	.05
431	Mel Rojas	.05
432	Todd Van Poppel	.05
433	Bobby Jones	.05
434	Mike Harkey	.05
435	Sean Berry	.05
436	Glenallen Hill	.05
437	Ryan Thompson	.05
438	Luis Alicea	.05
439	Esteban Loaiza	.10
440	Jeff Reboulet	.05
441	Vince Coleman	.05
442	Ellis Burks	.10
443	Allen Battle	.05
444	Jimmy Key	.05
445	Ricky Bottalico	.05
446	Delino DeShields	.05
447	Albie Lopez	.05
448	Mark Petkovsek	.05
449	Tim Raines	.10
450	Bryan Harvey	.05
451	Pat Hentgen	.05
452	Tim Laker	.05
453	Tom Gordon	.05
454	Phil Plantier	.05
455	Ernie Young	.05
456	Pete Harnisch	.05
457	Roberto Kelly	.05
458	Mark Portugal	.05
459	Mark Leiter	.05
460	Tony Pena	.05
461	Roger Pavlik	.05
462	Jeff King	.05
463	Bryan Rekar	.05
464	Al Leiter	.10
465	Phil Nevin	.05
466	Jose Lima	.10
467	Mike Stanley	.05
468	David McCarty	.05
469	Herb Perry	.05
470	Geronimo Berroa	.05
471	David Wells	.10
472	Vaughn Eshelman	.05
473	Greg Swindell	.05
474	Steve Sparks	.05
475	Luis Sojo	.05
476	Derrick May	.05
477	Joe Oliver	.05
478	Alex Arias	.05
479	Brad Ausmus	.05
480	Gabe White	.05
481	Pat Rapp	.05
482	Damon Buford	.10
483	Turk Wendell	.05
484	Jeff Brantley	.05
485	Curtis Leskanic	.05
486	Robb Nen	.05
487	Lou Whitaker	.05
488	Melido Perez	.05
489	Luis Polonia	.05
490	Scott Brosius	.05
491	Robert Perez	.05
492	*Mike Sweeney*	1.00
493	Mark Loretta	.05
494	Alex Ochoa	.05
495	*Matt Lawton*	.50
496	Shawn Estes	.05
497	John Wasdin	.05
498	Marc Kroon	.05
499	Chris Snopek	.05
500	Jeff Suppan	.05
501	Terrell Wade	.05
502	*Marvin Benard*	.05
503	Chris Widger	.05
504	Quinton McCracken	.05
505	Bob Wolcott	.05
506	C.J. Nitkowski	.05
507	Aaron Ledesma	.05
508	Scott Hatteberg	.05
509	Jimmy Haynes	.05
510	Howard Battle	.05

1996 Score All-Stars

An exclusive insert found only in 20-card Series 2 jumbo packs at an average rate of one per nine packs, these inserts feature the game's top stars printed in a rainbow holographic-foil technology.

		MT
Complete Set (20):		60.00
Common Player:		.75
1	Frank Thomas	5.00
2	Albert Belle	3.00
3	Ken Griffey Jr.	12.00
4	Cal Ripken Jr.	9.00
5	Mo Vaughn	2.00
6	Matt Williams	1.50
7	Barry Bonds	3.00
8	Dante Bichette	.75
9	Tony Gwynn	5.00
10	Greg Maddux	7.50
11	Randy Johnson	2.00
12	Hideo Nomo	1.50
13	Tim Salmon	1.50
14	Jeff Bagwell	4.00
15	Edgar Martinez	.75
16	Reggie Sanders	.75
17	Larry Walker	1.50
18	Chipper Jones	7.50
19	Manny Ramirez	3.00
20	Eddie Murray	1.50

1996 Score Big Bats

Gold-foil printing highlights cards of 20 of the game's top hitters found in this retail-packaging exclusive insert set. Stated odds of picking a Big Bats card are one in 31 packs.

		MT
Complete Set (20):		100.00
Common Player:		2.00
1	Cal Ripken Jr.	15.00
2	Ken Griffey Jr.	20.00
3	Frank Thomas	10.00
4	Jeff Bagwell	7.50
5	Mike Piazza	12.00
6	Barry Bonds	6.00
7	Matt Williams	2.50
8	Raul Mondesi	2.50
9	Tony Gwynn	7.50
10	Albert Belle	5.00
11	Manny Ramirez	6.00
12	Carlos Baerga	2.00
13	Mo Vaughn	4.00
14	Derek Bell	2.00
15	Larry Walker	2.50
16	Kenny Lofton	4.00
17	Edgar Martinez	2.00
18	Reggie Sanders	2.00
19	Eddie Murray	3.00
20	Chipper Jones	12.00

1996 Score Cal Ripken Tribute

The toughest pick among the 1996 Score inserts is this special card marking Cal Ripken's 2,131st consecutive game. The insertion rate is one per 300 packs hobby and retail, one per 150 jumbo packs.

		MT
2131	Cal Ripken Jr. (Tribute)	16.00

1996 Score Diamond Aces

Thirty of the top veterans and young stars are included in this jumbo-only insert set, seeded at a rate of one per eight packs.

		MT
Complete Set (30):		125.00
Common Player:		2.50
1	Hideo Nomo	4.00
2	Brian Hunter	2.00
3	Ray Durham	2.00
4	Frank Thomas	8.00
5	Cal Ripken Jr.	15.00
6	Barry Bonds	5.00
7	Greg Maddux	10.00
8	Chipper Jones	10.00
9	Raul Mondesi	2.00
10	Mike Piazza	12.00
11	Derek Jeter	15.00
12	Bill Pulsipher	2.00
13	Larry Walker	3.00
14	Ken Griffey Jr.	15.00
15	Alex Rodriguez	15.00
16	Manny Ramirez	5.00
17	Mo Vaughn	3.00
18	Reggie Sanders	2.00
19	Derek Bell	2.00
20	Jim Edmonds	3.00
21	Albert Belle	3.00
22	Eddie Murray	2.00
23	Tony Gwynn	6.00
24	Jeff Bagwell	5.00
25	Carlos Baerga	2.00
26	Matt Williams	3.00
27	Garret Anderson	2.50
28	Todd Hollandsworth	2.00
29	Johnny Damon	3.00
30	Tim Salmon	3.00

Player names in *Italic* type indicate a rookie card.

1996 Score Dream Team

The hottest player at each position is honored in the Dream Team insert set. Once again featured on holographic foil printing technology, the cards are found in all types of Score packaging at a rate of once per 72 packs.

		MT
Complete Set (9):		75.00
Common Player:		3.00
1	Cal Ripken Jr.	20.00
2	Frank Thomas	8.00
3	Carlos Baerga	3.00
4	Matt Williams	4.00
5	Mike Piazza	15.00
6	Barry Bonds	6.00
7	Ken Griffey Jr.	20.00
8	Manny Ramirez	6.00
9	Greg Maddux	12.00

1996 Score Dugout Collection

The concept of a partial parallel set, including the stars and rookies but not the journeymen and bench warmers, was initiated with Score's "Dugout Collection," with fewer than half of the cards from the regular series chosen for inclusion. The white borders of the regular cards are replaced with copper-foil and background printing is also done on foil in this special version. On back is a special "Dugout Collection '96" logo. Advertised insertion rate of the copper-version cards is one per three packs.

		MT
Complete Set (220):		75.00
Complete Series 1 (1-110):		40.00
Complete Series 2 (1-110):		40.00
Common Player:		.25
Artist's Proofs:		4X
	SERIES 1	
1	(Will Clark)	.60
2	(Rich Becker)	.25
3	(Ryan Klesko)	.35
4	(Jim Edmonds)	.35
5	(Barry Larkin)	.30
6	(Jim Thome)	.40
7	(Raul Mondesi)	.40
8	(Don Mattingly)	.75
9	(Jeff Conine)	.25
10	(Rickey Henderson)	.35
11	(Chad Curtis)	.25
12	(Darren Daulton)	.25
13	(Larry Walker)	.40
14	(Carlos Baerga)	.25
15	(Tony Gwynn)	1.50
16	(Jon Nunnally)	.25
17	(Deion Sanders)	.35
18	(Mark Grace)	.40
19	(Alex Rodriguez)	4.00
20	(Frank Thomas)	2.00
21	(Brian Jordan)	.25
22	(J.T. Snow)	.30
23	(Shawn Green)	.40
24	(Tim Wakefield)	.25
25	(Curtis Goodwin)	.25
26	(John Smoltz)	.30
27	(Devon White)	.25
28	(Brian Hunter)	.25
29	(Rusty Greer)	.25
30	(Rafael Palmeiro)	.35
31	(Bernard Gilkey)	.25
32	(John Valentin)	.25
33	(Randy Johnson)	.45
34	(Garret Anderson)	.25
35	(Ray Durham)	.25
36	(Bip Roberts)	.25
37	(Tyler Green)	.25
38	(Bill Pulsipher)	.25
39	(Jason Giambi)	.25
40	(Jack McDowell)	.25
41	(Rico Brogna)	.25
42	(Terry Pendleton)	.25
43	(Rondell White)	.35
44	(Andre Dawson)	.35
45	(Kirby Puckett)	1.50
46	(Wally Joyner)	.25
47	(B.J. Surhoff)	.25
48	(Randy Velarde)	.25
49	(Greg Vaughn)	.30
50	(Roberto Alomar)	.50
51	(David Justice)	.40
52	(Cal Ripken Jr.)	4.00
53	(Ozzie Smith)	1.25
54	(Mo Vaughn)	.60
55	(Gary DiSarcina)	.25
56	(Matt Williams)	.40
57	(Lenny Dykstra)	.25
58	(Bret Boone)	.25
59	(Albert Belle)	1.50
60	(Vinny Castilla)	.30
61	(Moises Alou)	.25
62	(Cecil Fielder)	.25
63	(Brad Radke)	.25
64	(Quilvio Veras)	.25
65	(Eddie Murray)	.40
66	(Dave Winfield)	.40
67	(Fred McGriff)	.35
68	(Craig Biggio)	.35
69	(Cliff Floyd)	.25
70	(Tim Naehring)	.25
71	(John Wetteland)	.25
72	(Alan Trammell)	.35
73	(Steve Avery)	.25
74	(Rick Aguilera)	.25
75	(Derek Bell)	.25
76	(Todd Hollandsworth)	.25
77	(Edgar Martinez)	.25
78	(Mark Lemke)	.25
79	(Ariel Prieto)	.25
80	(Russ Davis)	.25
81	(Jim Abbott)	.25
82	(Jason Isringhausen)	.25
83	(Carlos Perez)	.25
84	(David Segui)	.25
85	(Troy O'Leary)	.25
86	(Ismael Valdes)	.25
87	(Carlos Delgado)	.30
88	(Lee Smith)	.25
89	(Javy Lopez)	.30
90	(Frank Rodriguez)	.25
91	(Alex Gonzalez)	.30
92	(Benji Gil)	.25
93	(Greg Gagne)	.25
94	(Randy Myers)	.25
95	(Bobby Bonilla)	.25
96	(Billy Ashley)	.25
97	(Andy Van Slyke)	.25
98	(Edgardo Alfonzo)	.30
99	(David Cone)	.30
100	(Dean Palmer)	.25
101	(Jose Mesa)	.25
102	(Karim Garcia)	.50
103	(Johnny Damon)	.35
104	(LaTroy Hawkins)	.25
105	(Mark Smith)	.25
106	(Derek Jeter)	4.00
107	(Michael Tucker)	.25
108	(Joe Vitiello)	.25
109	(Ruben Rivera)	.25
110	(Greg Zaun)	.25
	SERIES 2	
1	Greg Maddux	2.50
2	Pedro Martinez	.35
3	Bobby Higginson	.35
4	Ray Lankford	.25
5	Shawon Dunston	.25
6	Gary Sheffield	.60
7	Ken Griffey Jr.	5.00
8	Paul Molitor	1.25
9	Kevin Appier	.25
10	Chuck Knoblauch	.45
11	Alex Fernandez	.30
12	Steve Finley	.25
13	Jeff Blauser	.25
14	Charles Johnson	.35
15	John Franco	.25
16	Mark Langston	.25
17	Bret Saberhagen	.35
18	John Mabry	.25
19	Ramon Martinez	.30
20	Mike Blowers	.25
21	Paul O'Neill	.30
22	Dave Nilsson	.25
23	Dante Bichette	.40
24	Marty Cordova	.25
25	Jay Bell	.25
26	Mike Mussina	.35
27	Ivan Rodriguez	.40
28	Jose Canseco	.40
29	Jeff Bagwell	.75
30	Manny Ramirez	.60
31	Dennis Martinez	.25
32	Charlie Hayes	.25
33	Joe Carter	.25
34	Travis Fryman	.25
35	Mark McGwire	5.00
36	Reggie Sanders	.25
37	Julian Tavarez	.25
38	Jeff Montgomery	.25
39	Andy Benes	.25
40	John Jaha	.25
41	Jeff Kent	.25
42	Mike Piazza	2.50
43	Erik Hanson	.25
44	Kenny Rogers	.25
45	Hideo Nomo	1.00
46	Gregg Jefferies	.25
47	Chipper Jones	2.50
48	Jay Buhner	.35
49	Dennis Eckersley	.25
50	Kenny Lofton	.35
51	Robin Ventura	.30
52	Tom Glavine	.30
53	Tim Salmon	.35
54	Andres Galarraga	.30
55	Hal Morris	.25
56	Brady Anderson	.30
57	Chili Davis	.25
58	Roger Clemens	.65
59	Marquis Grissom	.30
60	Mike Greenwell	.25
61	Sammy Sosa	2.00
62	Ron Gant	.25
63	Ken Caminiti	.30
64	Danny Tartabull	.25
65	Barry Bonds	1.50
66	Ben McDonald	.25
67	Ruben Sierra	.25
68	Bernie Williams	.45
69	Wil Cordero	.25
70	Wade Boggs	.45
71	Gary Gaetti	.25
72	Greg Colbrunn	.25
73	Juan Gonzalez	.75
74	Marc Newfield	.25
75	Charles Nagy	.25
76	Robby Thompson	.25
77	Roberto Petagine	.25
78	Darryl Strawberry	.35
79	Tino Martinez	.25
80	Eric Karros	.25
81	Cal Ripken Jr. (Star Struck)	3.00
82	Cecil Fielder (Star Struck)	.25
83	Kirby Puckett (Star Struck)	1.00
84	Jim Edmonds (Star Struck)	.25
85	Matt Williams (Star Struck)	.25
86	Alex Rodriguez (Star Struck)	3.00
87	Barry Larkin (Star Struck)	.25
88	Rafael Palmeiro (Star Struck)	.25
89	David Cone (Star Struck)	.25
90	Roberto Alomar (Star Struck)	.35
91	Eddie Murray (Star Struck)	.30
92	Randy Johnson (Star Struck)	.35
93	Ryan Klesko (Star Struck)	.30
94	Raul Mondesi (Star Struck)	.30
95	Mo Vaughn (Star Struck)	.60
96	Will Clark (Star Struck)	.30
97	Carlos Baerga (Star Struck)	.25
98	Frank Thomas (Star Struck)	2.00
99	Larry Walker (Star Struck)	.30
100	Garret Anderson (Star Struck)	.25
101	Edgar Martinez (Star Struck)	.25
102	Don Mattingly (Star Struck)	.75
103	Tony Gwynn (Star Struck)	.75
104	Albert Belle (Star Struck)	1.50
105	Jason Isringhausen (Star Struck)	.25
106	Ruben Rivera (Star Struck)	.25
107	Johnny Damon (Star Struck)	.25
108	Karim Garcia (Star Struck)	.35
109	Derek Jeter (Star Struck)	2.50
110	David Justice (Star Struck)	.35

1996 Score Dugout Collection Artist's Proofs

A parallel set within a parallel set, the Artist's Proof logo added to the copper-foil design of the Dugout Collection cards raises the odds of finding one to just once in 36 packs.

	MT
(Artist's Proofs stars valued at 3X-5X of regular Dugout Collection versions)	
Complete Set (220):	600.00
Common Player:	1.50
Artist's Proof Stars:	4X
(See 1996 Score Dugout Collection for checklist and base card values.)	

> The values of some parallel-card issues will have to be calculated based on figures presented in the heading for the regular-issue card set.

1996 Score Future Franchise

Future Franchise is the most difficult insert to pull from packs of Series 2, at the rate of once per 72 packs, on average. Sixteen young stars are showcased on holographic gold-foil printing in the set.

		MT
Complete Set (16):		110.00
Common Player:		3.00
1	Jason Isringhausen	3.00
2	Chipper Jones	25.00
3	Derek Jeter	25.00
4	Alex Rodriguez	35.00
5	Alex Ochoa	3.00
6	Manny Ramirez	15.00
7	Johnny Damon	4.00
8	Ruben Rivera	3.00
9	Karim Garcia	7.50
10	Garret Anderson	3.00
11	Marty Cordova	3.00
12	Bill Pulsipher	3.00
13	Hideo Nomo	6.00
14	Marc Newfield	3.00
15	Charles Johnson	4.00
16	Raul Mondesi	5.00

1996 Score Gold Stars

Appearing once in every 15 packs of Series 2, Gold Stars are labeled with a stamp in the upper-left corner. The set contains 30 top current stars printed on gold-foil and seeded at the average rate of one per 15 packs.

		MT
Complete Set (30):		50.00
Common Player:		.75
1	Ken Griffey Jr.	9.00
2	Frank Thomas	5.00
3	Reggie Sanders	.75
4	Tim Salmon	1.00
5	Mike Piazza	6.00
6	Tony Gwynn	4.00
7	Gary Sheffield	1.00
8	Matt Williams	1.00
9	Bernie Williams	1.00
10	Jason Isringhausen	.75
11	Albert Belle	2.50
12	Chipper Jones	6.00
13	Edgar Martinez	.75
14	Barry Larkin	1.00
15	Barry Bonds	2.50
16	Jeff Bagwell	4.00
17	Greg Maddux	6.00
18	Mo Vaughn	2.00
19	Ryan Klesko	1.00
20	Sammy Sosa	6.00
21	Darren Daulton	.75
22	Ivan Rodriguez	1.50
23	Dante Bichette	1.00
24	Hideo Nomo	1.00
25	Cal Ripken Jr.	7.50
26	Rafael Palmeiro	1.00
27	Larry Walker	1.00
28	Carlos Baerga	.75
29	Randy Johnson	1.50
30	Manny Ramirez	4.00

1996 Score Numbers Game

Some of the 1995 season's most impressive statistical accomplishments are featured in this chase set. Cards are enhanced with gold foil and found in all types of Score packs at an average rate of one per 15 packs.

		MT
Complete Set (30):		60.00
Common Player:		.75
1	Cal Ripken Jr.	8.00
2	Frank Thomas	3.00
3	Ken Griffey Jr.	8.00
4	Mike Piazza	6.00
5	Barry Bonds	2.50
6	Greg Maddux	5.00
7	Jeff Bagwell	2.50
8	Derek Bell	.75
9	Tony Gwynn	3.00
10	Hideo Nomo	1.00
11	Raul Mondesi	1.00
12	Manny Ramirez	2.50
13	Albert Belle	1.50
14	Matt Williams	1.00
15	Jim Edmonds	1.00
16	Edgar Martinez	.75
17	Mo Vaughn	1.50
18	Reggie Sanders	.75
19	Chipper Jones	5.00
20	Larry Walker	1.00
21	Juan Gonzalez	2.50
22	Kenny Lofton	1.00
23	Don Mattingly	3.00
24	Ivan Rodriguez	2.50
25	Randy Johnson	2.50
26	Derek Jeter	6.00
27	J.T. Snow	.75
28	Will Clark	1.00
29	Rafael Palmeiro	1.50
30	Alex Rodriguez	8.00

1996 Score Power Pace

Power Pace is exclusive to retail packs in Series 2, where they are found on average every 31 packs. Eighteen top power hitters are featured in this issue in a gold-foil design.

		MT
Complete Set (18):		60.00
Common Player:		1.50
1	Mark McGwire	15.00
2	Albert Belle	2.50
3	Jay Buhner	1.50
4	Frank Thomas	5.00
5	Matt Williams	2.00
6	Gary Sheffield	2.00
7	Mike Piazza	12.00
8	Larry Walker	2.00
9	Mo Vaughn	2.50
10	Rafael Palmeiro	2.00
11	Dante Bichette	1.50
12	Ken Griffey Jr.	12.00
13	Barry Bonds	4.00
14	Manny Ramirez	4.00
15	Sammy Sosa	10.00
16	Tim Salmon	1.50
17	Dave Justice	1.50
18	Eric Karros	1.50

1996 Score Reflexions

Appearing only in hobby packs this insert set pairs 20 veteran stars with 20 up-and-coming players in a foil-printed format. Odds of finding a Reflexions insert are stated as one per 31 packs.

		MT
Complete Set (20):		80.00
Common Player:		1.00
1	Cal Ripken Jr., Chipper Jones	12.00
2	Ken Griffey Jr., Alex Rodriguez	12.00
3	Frank Thomas, Mo Vaughn	5.00
4	Kenny Lofton, Brian Hunter	2.00
5	Don Mattingly, J.T. Snow	5.00
6	Manny Ramirez, Raul Mondesi	4.00
7	Tony Gwynn, Garret Anderson	5.00
8	Roberto Alomar, Carlos Baerga	3.00
9	Andre Dawson, Larry Walker	2.00
10	Barry Larkin, Derek Jeter	10.00
11	Barry Bonds, Reggie Sanders	4.00
12	Mike Piazza, Albert Belle	10.00
13	Wade Boggs, Edgar Martinez	1.00
14	David Cone, John Smoltz	1.00
15	Will Clark, Jeff Bagwell	4.00
16	Mark McGwire, Cecil Fielder	15.00
17	Greg Maddux, Mike Mussina	8.00
18	Randy Johnson, Hideo Nomo	4.00
19	Jim Thome, Dean Palmer	1.00
20	Chuck Knoblauch, Craig Biggio	1.50

1996 Score Titantic Taters

One of the more creative names in the 1996 insert lineup, Titanic Taters are found one in every 31 packs of Series 2 hobby. Gold-foil fronts feature 18 of the game's heaviest hitters.

		MT
Complete Set (18):		80.00
Common Player:		2.00
1	Albert Belle	5.00
2	Frank Thomas	10.00
3	Mo Vaughn	4.00
4	Ken Griffey Jr.	20.00
5	Matt Williams	2.50
6	Mark McGwire	20.00
7	Dante Bichette	2.50
8	Tim Salmon	2.50
9	Jeff Bagwell	7.50
10	Rafael Palmeiro	2.50
11	Mike Piazza	15.00
12	Cecil Fielder	2.00
13	Larry Walker	2.50
14	Sammy Sosa	12.00
15	Manny Ramirez	7.50
16	Gary Sheffield	2.50
17	Barry Bonds	5.00
18	Jay Buhner	2.00

1997 Score

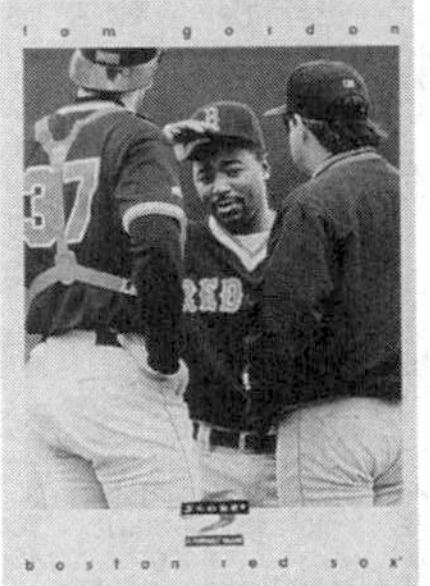

A total of 551 cards make up the base set, with 330 cards sold in Series I and 221 making up Series II. The basic card design features a color action photo surrounded by a white border. The player's name is above the photo, with the team name underneath. Backs feature text and statistics against a white background with the image of the team logo ghosted into the background. Two parallel insert sets - Artist's Proof and Showcase Series - were part of each series. Other inserts in Series I were Pitcher Perfect, The Franchise, The Glowing Franchise, Titanic Taters (retail exclusive), Stellar Season (magazine packs only), and The Highlight Zone (hobby exclusive). Series II inserts were Blastmasters, Heart of the Order and Stand and Deliver. Cards were sold in 10-card packs for 99 cents each.

	MT
Complete Set (551):	35.00
Complete Series 1 Set (330):	20.00
Complete Series 2 Set (221):	15.00
Common Player:	.05
Series 1 or 2 Pack (10):	1.00
Series 1 or 2 Wax Box (36):	25.00

1	Jeff Bagwell	.50
2	Mickey Tettleton	.05
3	Johnny Damon	.15
4	Jeff Conine	.05
5	Bernie Williams	.40
6	Will Clark	.20
7	Ryan Klesko	.15
8	Cecil Fielder	.10
9	Paul Wilson	.05
10	Gregg Jefferies	.05
11	Chili Davis	.05
12	Albert Belle	.30
13	Ken Hill	.05
14	Cliff Floyd	.05
15	Jaime Navarro	.05
16	Ismael Valdes	.05
17	Jeff King	.05
18	Chris Bosio	.05
19	Reggie Sanders	.05
20	Darren Daulton	.05
21	Ken Caminiti	.15
22	Mike Piazza	1.25
23	Chad Mottola	.05
24	Darin Erstad	.40
25	Dante Bichette	.15
26	Frank Thomas	.75
27	Ben McDonald	.05
28	Raul Casanova	.05
29	Kevin Ritz	.05
30	Garret Anderson	.05
31	Jason Kendall	.05
32	Billy Wagner	.10
33	David Justice	.25
34	Marty Cordova	.05
35	Derek Jeter	1.50
36	Trevor Hoffman	.10
37	Geronimo Berroa	.05
38	Walt Weiss	.05
39	Kirt Manwaring	.05
40	Alex Gonzalez	.10
41	Sean Berry	.05
42	Kevin Appier	.05
43	Rusty Greer	.05
44	Pete Incaviglia	.05
45	Rafael Palmeiro	.20
46	Eddie Murray	.25
47	Moises Alou	.10
48	Mark Lewis	.05
49	Hal Morris	.05
50	Edgar Renteria	.15
51	Rickey Henderson	.20
52	Pat Listach	.05
53	John Wasdin	.05
54	James Baldwin	.05
55	Brian Jordan	.05
56	Edgar Martinez	.10
57	Wil Cordero	.05
58	Danny Tartabull	.05
59	Keith Lockhart	.05
60	Rico Brogna	.05
61	Ricky Bottalico	.05
62	Terry Pendleton	.05
63	Bret Boone	.05
64	Charlie Hayes	.05
65	Marc Newfield	.05
66	Sterling Hitchcock	.05
67	Roberto Alomar	.40
68	John Jaha	.05
69	Greg Colbrunn	.05
70	Sal Fasano	.05
71	Brooks Kieschnick	.05
72	Pedro Martinez	.50
73	Kevin Elster	.05
74	Ellis Burks	.05
75	Chuck Finley	.05
76	John Olerud	.10
77	Jay Bell	.05
78	Allen Watson	.05
79	Darryl Strawberry	.05
80	Orlando Miller	.05
81	Jose Herrera	.05
82	Andy Pettitte	.25
83	Juan Guzman	.05
84	Alan Benes	.05
85	Jack McDowell	.05
86	Ugueth Urbina	.05
87	Rocky Coppinger	.05
88	Jeff Cirillo	.05
89	Tom Glavine	.15
90	Robby Thompson	.05
91	Barry Bonds	.50
92	Carlos Delgado	.40
93	Mo Vaughn	.30
94	Ryne Sandberg	.40
95	Alex Rodriguez	1.50
96	Brady Anderson	.10
97	Scott Brosius	.05
98	Dennis Eckersley	.05
99	Brian McRae	.05
100	Rey Ordonez	.15
101	John Valentin	.05
102	Brett Butler	.05
103	Eric Karros	.10
104	Harold Baines	.05
105	Javier Lopez	.15
106	Alan Trammell	.05
107	Jim Thome	.25
108	Frank Rodriguez	.05
109	Bernard Gilkey	.05
110	Reggie Jefferson	.05
111	Scott Stahoviak	.05
112	Steve Gibralter	.05
113	Todd Hollandsworth	.05
114	Ruben Rivera	.10
115	Dennis Martinez	.05
116	Mariano Rivera	.25
117	John Smoltz	.10
118	John Mabry	.05
119	Tom Gordon	.05
120	Alex Ochoa	.05
121	Jamey Wright	.05
122	Dave Nilsson	.05
123	Bobby Bonilla	.05
124	Al Leiter	.10
125	Rick Aguilera	.05
126	Jeff Brantley	.05
127	Kevin Brown	.10
128	George Arias	.05
129	Darren Oliver	.05
130	Bill Pulsipher	.05
131	Roberto Hernandez	.05
132	Delino DeShields	.05
133	Mark Grudzielanek	.05
134	John Wetteland	.05
135	Carlos Baerga	.05
136	Paul Sorrento	.05
137	Leo Gomez	.05
138	Andy Ashby	.05
139	Julio Franco	.05
140	Brian Hunter	.05
141	Jermaine Dye	.10
142	Tony Clark	.15
143	Ruben Sierra	.05
144	Donovan Osborne	.05
145	Mark McLemore	.05
146	Terry Steinbach	.05
147	Bob Wells	.05
148	Chan Ho Park	.10
149	Tim Salmon	.15
150	Paul O'Neill	.15
151	Cal Ripken Jr.	1.50
152	Wally Joyner	.05
153	Omar Vizquel	.05
154	Mike Mussina	.40
155	Andres Galarraga	.15
156	Ken Griffey Jr.	1.50
157	Kenny Lofton	.25
158	Ray Durham	.05
159	Hideo Nomo	.25
160	Ozzie Guillen	.05
161	Roger Pavlik	.05
162	Manny Ramirez	.50
163	Mark Lemke	.05
164	Mike Stanley	.05
165	Chuck Knoblauch	.10
166	Kimera Bartee	.05
167	Wade Boggs	.20
168	Jay Buhner	.10
169	Eric Young	.05
170	Jose Canseco	.25
171	Dwight Gooden	.05
172	Fred McGriff	.20
173	Sandy Alomar Jr.	.10
174	Andy Benes	.05
175	Dean Palmer	.05
176	Larry Walker	.25
177	Charles Nagy	.10
178	David Cone	.10
179	Mark Grace	.15
180	Robin Ventura	.10
181	Roger Clemens	.60
182	Bobby Witt	.05
183	Vinny Castilla	.10
184	Gary Sheffield	.15
185	Dan Wilson	.05
186	Roger Cedeno	.05
187	Mark McGwire	2.00
188	Darren Bragg	.05
189	Quinton McCracken	.05
190	Randy Myers	.05
191	Jeromy Burnitz	.05
192	Randy Johnson	.50
193	Chipper Jones	1.00
194	Greg Vaughn	.10
195	Travis Fryman	.15
196	Tim Naehring	.05
197	B.J. Surhoff	.05
198	Juan Gonzalez	.50
199	Terrell Wade	.05
200	Jeff Frye	.05
201	Joey Cora	.05
202	Raul Mondesi	.15
203	Ivan Rodriguez	.50
204	Armando Reynoso	.05
205	Jeffrey Hammonds	.05
206	Darren Dreifort	.05
207	Kevin Seitzer	.05
208	Tino Martinez	.15
209	Jim Bruske	.05
210	Jeff Suppan	.05
211	Mark Carreon	.05
212	Wilson Alvarez	.05
213	John Burkett	.05
214	Tony Phillips	.05
215	Greg Maddux	1.00
216	Mark Whiten	.05
217	Curtis Pride	.05
218	Lyle Mouton	.05
219	Todd Hundley	.10
220	Greg Gagne	.05
221	Rich Amaral	.05
222	Tom Goodwin	.05
223	Chris Hoiles	.05
224	Jayhawk Owens	.05
225	Kenny Rogers	.05
226	Mike Greenwell	.05
227	Mark Wohlers	.05
228	Henry Rodriguez	.05
229	Robert Perez	.05
230	Jeff Kent	.05
231	Darryl Hamilton	.05
232	Alex Fernandez	.10
233	Ron Karkovice	.05
234	Jimmy Haynes	.05
235	Craig Biggio	.15
236	Ray Lankford	.05
237	Lance Johnson	.05
238	Matt Williams	.20
239	Chad Curtis	.05
240	Mark Thompson	.05
241	Jason Giambi	.25
242	Barry Larkin	.15
243	Paul Molitor	.25
244	Sammy Sosa	1.00
245	Kevin Tapani	.05
246	Marquis Grissom	.05
247	Joe Carter	.10
248	Ramon Martinez	.10
249	Tony Gwynn	.75
250	Andy Fox	.05
251	Troy O'Leary	.05
252	Warren Newson	.05
253	Troy Percival	.05
254	Jamie Moyer	.05
255	Danny Graves	.05
256	David Wells	.10
257	Todd Zeile	.05
258	Raul Ibanez	.05
259	Tyler Houston	.05
260	LaTroy Hawkins	.05
261	Joey Hamilton	.05
262	Mike Sweeney	.05
263	Brant Brown	.05
264	Pat Hentgen	.05
265	Mark Johnson	.05
266	Robb Nen	.05
267	Justin Thompson	.05
268	Ron Gant	.05
269	Jeff D'Amico	.05
270	Shawn Estes	.05
271	Derek Bell	.05
272	Fernando Valenzuela	.05
273	Luis Castillo	.10
274	Ray Montgomery	.05
275	Ed Sprague	.05
276	F.P. Santangelo	.05
277	Todd Greene	.05
278	Butch Huskey	.05
279	Steve Finley	.05
280	Eric Davis	.05
281	Shawn Green	.15
282	Al Martin	.05
283	Michael Tucker	.05
284	Shane Reynolds	.05
285	Matt Mieske	.05
286	Jose Rosado	.05
287	Mark Langston	.05
288	Ralph Milliard	.05
289	Mike Lansing	.05
290	Scott Servais	.05
291	Royce Clayton	.05
292	Mike Grace	.05
293	James Mouton	.05
294	Charles Johnson	.05
295	Gary Gaetti	.05
296	Kevin Mitchell	.05
297	Carlos Garcia	.05
298	Desi Relaford	.05
299	Jason Thompson	.05
300	Osvaldo Fernandez	.05
301	Fernando Vina	.05
302	Jose Offerman	.05
303	Yamil Benitez	.05
304	J.T. Snow	.05
305	Rafael Bournigal	.05
306	Jason Isringhausen	.05
307	Bob Higginson	.05
308	*Nerio Rodriguez*	.15
309	*Brian Giles*	1.50
310	Andruw Jones	.50
311	Billy McMillon	.05
312	Arquimedez Pozo	.05
313	Jermaine Allensworth	.05
314	Luis Andujar	.05
315	Angel Echevarria	.05
316	Karim Garcia	.05
317	Trey Beamon	.05
318	Makoto Suzuki	.05
319	Robin Jennings	.05
320	Dmitri Young	.05
321	*Damon Mashore*	.05
322	Wendell Magee	.05
323	*Dax Jones*	.05
324	Todd Walker	.05
325	Marvin Benard	.05
326	*Brian Raabe*	.05
327	Marcus Jensen	.05
328	Checklist	.05
329	Checklist	.05
330	Checklist	.05
331	Norm Charlton	.05
332	Bruce Ruffin	.05
333	John Wetteland	.05
334	Marquis Grissom	.05
335	Sterling Hitchcock	.05
336	John Olerud	.10
337	David Wells	.10
338	Chili Davis	.05
339	Mark Lewis	.05
340	Kenny Lofton	.25
341	Alex Fernandez	.10
342	Ruben Sierra	.05
343	Delino DeShields	.05
344	John Wasdin	.05
345	Dennis Martinez	.05
346	Kevin Elster	.05
347	Bobby Bonilla	.05
348	Jaime Navarro	.05
349	Chad Curtis	.05
350	Terry Steinbach	.05
351	Ariel Prieto	.05
352	Jeff Kent	.05
353	Carlos Garcia	.05
354	Mark Whiten	.05
355	Todd Zeile	.05
356	Eric Davis	.05
357	Greg Colbrunn	.05
358	Moises Alou	.10
359	Allen Watson	.05
360	Jose Canseco	.25
361	Matt Williams	.25
362	Jeff King	.05
363	Darryl Hamilton	.05
364	Mark Clark	.05
365	J.T. Snow	.05

366 Kevin Mitchell .05
367 Orlando Miller .05
368 Rico Brogna .05
369 Mike James .05
370 Brad Ausmus .05
371 Darryl Kile .05
372 Edgardo Alfonzo .10
373 Julian Tavarez .05
374 Darren Lewis .05
375 Steve Karsay .05
376 Lee Stevens .05
377 Albie Lopez .05
378 Orel Hershiser .05
379 Lee Smith .05
380 Rick Helling .05
381 Carlos Perez .05
382 Tony Tarasco .05
383 Melvin Nieves .05
384 Benji Gil .05
385 Devon White .05
386 Armando Benitez .05
387 Bill Swift .05
388 John Smiley .05
389 Midre Cummings .05
390 Tim Belcher .05
391 Tim Raines .05
392 Todd Worrell .05
393 Quilvio Veras .05
394 Matt Lawton .05
395 Aaron Sele .05
396 Bip Roberts .05
397 Denny Neagle .05
398 Tyler Green .05
399 Hipolito Pichardo .05
400 Scott Erickson .05
401 Bobby Jones .05
402 Jim Edmonds .15
403 Chad Ogea .05
404 Cal Eldred .05
405 Pat Listach .05
406 Todd Stottlemyre .05
407 Phil Nevin .05
408 Otis Nixon .05
409 Billy Ashley .05
410 Jimmy Key .05
411 Mike Timlin .05
412 Joe Vitiello .05
413 Rondell White .10
414 Jeff Fassero .05
415 Rex Hudler .05
416 Curt Schilling .10
417 Rich Becker .05
418 William VanLandingham .05
419 Chris Snopek .05
420 David Segui .05
421 Eddie Murray .25
422 Shane Andrews .05
423 Gary DiSarcina .05
424 Brian Hunter .05
425 Willie Greene .05
426 Felipe Crespo .05
427 Jason Bates .05
428 Albert Belle .30
429 Rey Sanchez .05
430 Roger Clemens .75
431 Deion Sanders .20
432 Ernie Young .05
433 Jay Bell .05
434 Jeff Blauser .05
435 Lenny Dykstra .05
436 Chuck Carr .05
437 Russ Davis .05
438 Carl Everett .05
439 Damion Easley .05
440 Pat Kelly .05
441 Pat Rapp .05
442 David Justice .25
443 Graeme Lloyd .05
444 Damon Buford .05
445 Jose Valentin .05
446 Jason Schmidt .05
447 Dave Martinez .05
448 Danny Tartabull .05
449 Jose Vizcaino .05
450 Steve Avery .05
451 Mike Devereaux .05
452 Jim Eisenreich .05
453 Mark Leiter .05
454 Roberto Kelly .05
455 Benito Santiago .05
456 Steve Trachsel .05
457 Gerald Williams .05
458 Pete Schourek .05
459 Esteban Loaiza .05
460 Mel Rojas .05
461 Tim Wakefield .05
462 Tony Fernandez .05
463 Doug Drabek .05
464 Joe Girardi .05
465 Mike Bordick .05
466 Jim Leyritz .05
467 Erik Hanson .05
468 Michael Tucker .05
469 *Tony Womack* .40
470 Doug Glanville .05
471 Rudy Pemberton .05
472 Keith Lockhart .05
473 Nomar Garciaparra 1.25
474 Scott Rolen .50
475 Jason Dickson .05
476 Glendon Rusch .05
477 Todd Walker .05
478 Dmitri Young .05
479 *Rod Myers* .05
480 Wilton Guerrero .10
481 Jorge Posada .05
482 Brant Brown .05
483 *Bubba Trammell* .25
484 Jose Guillen .10
485 Scott Spiezio .05
486 Bob Abreu .05
487 Chris Holt .05
488 *Deivi Cruz* .25
489 Vladimir Guerrero .75
490 Julio Santana .05
491 Ray Montgomery .05
492 Kevin Orie .05
493 Todd Hundley (Goin' Yard) .10
494 Tim Salmon (Goin' Yard) .15
495 Albert Belle (Goin' Yard) .25
496 Manny Ramirez (Goin' Yard) .25
497 Rafael Palmeiro (Goin' Yard) .10
498 Juan Gonzalez (Goin' Yard) .25
499 Ken Griffey Jr. (Goin' Yard) .75
500 Andruw Jones (Goin' Yard) .25
501 Mike Piazza (Goin' Yard) .60
502 Jeff Bagwell (Goin' Yard) .25
503 Bernie Williams (Goin' Yard) .20
504 Barry Bonds (Goin' Yard) .25
505 Ken Caminiti (Goin' Yard) .10
506 Darin Erstad (Goin' Yard) .25
507 Alex Rodriguez (Goin' Yard) .75
508 Frank Thomas (Goin' Yard) .40
509 Chipper Jones (Goin' Yard) .50
510 Mo Vaughn (Goin' Yard) .25
511 Mark McGwire (Goin' Yard) 1.00
512 Fred McGriff (Goin' Yard) .15
513 Jay Buhner (Goin' Yard) .05
514 Jim Thome (Goin' Yard) .15
515 Gary Sheffield (Goin' Yard) .15
516 Dean Palmer (Goin' Yard) .05
517 Henry Rodriguez (Goin' Yard) .05
518 Andy Pettitte (Rock & Fire) .25
519 Mike Mussina (Rock & Fire) .20
520 Greg Maddux (Rock & Fire) .50
521 John Smoltz (Rock & Fire) .10
522 Hideo Nomo (Rock & Fire) .15
523 Troy Percival (Rock & Fire) .05
524 John Wetteland (Rock & Fire) .05
525 Roger Clemens (Rock & Fire) .25
526 Charles Nagy (Rock & Fire) .05
527 Mariano Rivera (Rock & Fire) .10
528 Tom Glavine (Rock & Fire) .10
529 Randy Johnson (Rock & Fire) .20
530 Jason Isringhausen (Rock & Fire) .05
531 Alex Fernandez (Rock & Fire) .05
532 Kevin Brown (Rock & Fire) .05
533 Chuck Knoblauch (True Grit) .10
534 Rusty Greer (True Grit) .05
535 Tony Gwynn (True Grit) .40
536 Ryan Klesko (True Grit) .10
537 Ryne Sandberg (True Grit) .25
538 Barry Larkin (True Grit) .10
539 Will Clark (True Grit) .10
540 Kenny Lofton (True Grit) .15
541 Paul Molitor (True Grit) .15
542 Roberto Alomar (True Grit) .20
543 Rey Ordonez (True Grit) .05
544 Jason Giambi (True Grit) .05
545 Derek Jeter (True Grit) .60
546 Cal Ripken Jr. (True Grit) .75
547 Ivan Rodriguez (True Grit) .20
548 Checklist (Ken Griffey Jr.) .50
549 Checklist (Frank Thomas) .25
550 Checklist (Mike Piazza) .50
551a *Hideki Irabu* (SP) (English on back; factory sets/retail packs) 1.00
551b *Hideki Irabu* (SP) (Japanese back; Hobby Reserve packs) 1.00

1997 Score Artist's Proofs

Specially marked Artist's Proof cards were random inserts in Series 1 and 2 retail packs.

	MT
Complete Set (551):	1600.
Complete Series 1 (330)	900.00
Complete Series 2 (221)	700.00
Common Player:	1.50
Artist's Proof Stars:	15X

(See 1997 Score for checklist and base card values.)

1997 Score Showcase

A silver metallic-foil background distinguishes the cards in this parallel set, inserted at a rate of about one per seven packs of both hobby and retail.

	MT
Complete Set (551):	450.00
Common Player:	.50
Showcase Stars:	4X

(See 1997 Score for checklist and base card values.)

1997 Score Showcase Artist's Proofs

This is a parallel of the Showcase parallel set covering all 551 cards of the base '97 Score set. The Artist's Proofs cards carry over the silver foil background of the Showcase cards on front with a rainbow-wave effect, and are marked with a round red "ARTIST'S PROOF" logo.

	MT
Complete Set (330):	1500.
Common Player:	2.00
Showcase Artist's Proof Stars:	15X

(See 1997 Score for checklist and base card values.)

1997 Score Premium Stock

This is an upscale version of Score's regular Series 1 1997 issue, designated for hobby sales only. The cards are basically the same as the regular issue, except for the use of gray borders on front and an embossed gold-foil "Premium Stock" logo.

	MT
Complete Set (330):	30.00
Common Player:	.10

Premium Stock Stars:	1,5X

(See 1997 Score #1-330 for checklist and base card values.)

1997 Score Hobby Reserve

This is a hobby-only parallel version of Score Series 2, similar in concept to the Series 1 Premium Stock. Cards are identical to the regular Series 2 cards except for the addition of a gold Hobby Reserve foil seal on front.

	MT
Complete Set (221):	30.00
Common Player:	.10
Hobby Reserve Stars:	1.5X

(See 1997 Score #331-551 for checklist and base card values.)

1997 Score Reserve Collection

This was a hobby-only parallel version of Score Series 2, Cards are similar to regular Series 2 Score except for the use of a textured ray-like silver-foil background on front and a Reserve Collection underprint on back. Cards are numbered with an "HR" prefix. Average insertion rate was one per 11 packs.

	MT
Complete Set (221):	450.00
Common Player:	2.00
Reserve Collection Stars:	10X

(See 1997 Score #331-551 for checklist and base card values.)

1997 Score Blast Masters

This 18-card set was inserted into every 35 Series II retail packs and every 23 hobby packs. The set displays the top power hitters in the game over a prismatic gold foil background. The word "Blast" is printed across the top, while "Master" is printed across the bottom, both in red. Backs are predominantly black with a color player photo at center.

		MT
Complete Set (18):		95.00
Common Player:		1.50
1	Mo Vaughn	4.00
2	Mark McGwire	20.00
3	Juan Gonzalez	5.00
4	Albert Belle	4.50
5	Barry Bonds	4.50
6	Ken Griffey Jr.	20.00
7	Andruw Jones	7.50
8	Chipper Jones	12.50
9	Mike Piazza	12.50
10	Jeff Bagwell	7.50
11	Dante Bichette	1.50
12	Alex Rodriguez	15.00
13	Gary Sheffield	2.00
14	Ken Caminiti	1.50
15	Sammy Sosa	12.50
16	Vladimir Guerrero	8.00
17	Brian Jordan	1.50
18	Tim Salmon	2.00

1997 Score The Franchise

There were two versions made for these 1997 Score Series 1 inserts - regular and The Glowing Franchise, which has glow-in-the-dark highlights. The regular version is seeded one per 72 packs; glow-in-the-dark cards are seeded one per 240 packs.

		MT
Complete Set (9):		95.00
Common Player:		3.00
Glowing:		5X
1	Ken Griffey Jr.	25.00
2	John Smoltz	3.00
3	Cal Ripken Jr.	20.00
4	Chipper Jones	15.00
5	Mike Piazza	15.00
6	Albert Belle	8.00
7	Frank Thomas	10.00
8	Sammy Sosa	12.50
9	Roberto Alomar	6.00

1997 Score Heart of the Order

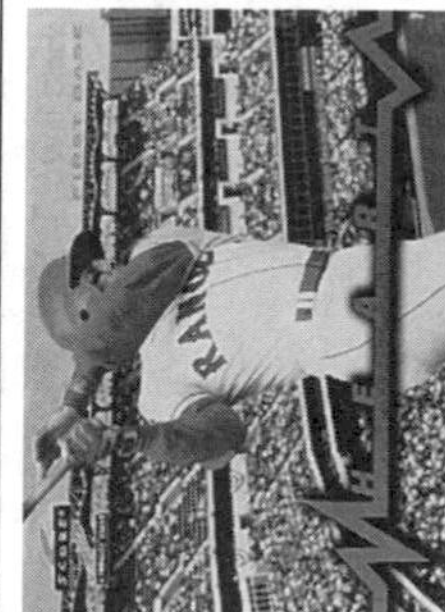

This 36-card set was distributed in Series II retail and hobby packs, with cards 1-18 in retail (one per 23 packs) and cards 19-36 in hobby (one per 15). The cards are printed in a horizontal format, with some of the top hitters in the game included in the insert. Fronts are highlighted in red metallic foil. Backs have a color portrait photo and a few words about the player.

		MT
Complete Set (36):		100.00
Complete Retail Set (1-18):		60.00
Complete Hobby Set (19-36):		40.00
Common Player:		1.00
1	Ivan Rodriguez	2.50
2	Will Clark	1.25
3	Juan Gonzalez	3.00
4	Frank Thomas	6.00
5	Albert Belle	3.00
6	Robin Ventura	1.25
7	Alex Rodriguez	10.00
8	Ken Griffey Jr.	12.00
9	Jay Buhner	1.00
10	Roberto Alomar	2.50
11	Rafael Palmeiro	1.25
12	Cal Ripken Jr.	9.00
13	Manny Ramirez	5.00
14	Matt Williams	1.50
15	Jim Thome	2.00
16	Derek Jeter	7.50
17	Wade Boggs	1.50
18	Bernie Williams	2.00
19	Chipper Jones	7.50
20	Andruw Jones	5.00
21	Ryan Klesko	1.00
22	Wilton Guerrero	1.00
23	Mike Piazza	7.50
24	Raul Mondesi	1.50
25	Tony Gwynn	6.00
26	Ken Caminiti	1.25
27	Greg Vaughn	1.00
28	Brian Jordan	1.00
29	Ron Gant	1.00
30	Dmitri Young	1.00
31	Darin Erstad	4.50
32	Jim Edmonds	1.00
33	Tim Salmon	1.25
34	Chuck Knoblauch	1.25
35	Paul Molitor	2.50
36	Todd Walker	3.00

1997 Score Highlight Zone

Exclusive to 1997 Score Series I hobby packs are these Highlight Zone inserts, seeded one per every 35 packs. Within the 18-card set, card numbers 1-9 are in regular hobby packs, while numbers 10-18 are found only in premium stock packs.

		MT
Complete Set (18):		120.00
Common Player:		2.00
1	Frank Thomas	10.00
2	Ken Griffey Jr.	20.00
3	Mo Vaughn	4.00
4	Albert Belle	5.00
5	Mike Piazza	12.00
6	Barry Bonds	5.00
7	Greg Maddux	12.00
8	Sammy Sosa	12.00
9	Jeff Bagwell	8.00
10	Alex Rodriguez	15.00
11	Chipper Jones	12.00
12	Brady Anderson	2.00
13	Ozzie Smith	5.00
14	Edgar Martinez	2.00
15	Cal Ripken Jr.	15.00
16	Ryan Klesko	2.00
17	Randy Johnson	5.00
18	Eddie Murray	4.00

1997 Score Pitcher Perfect

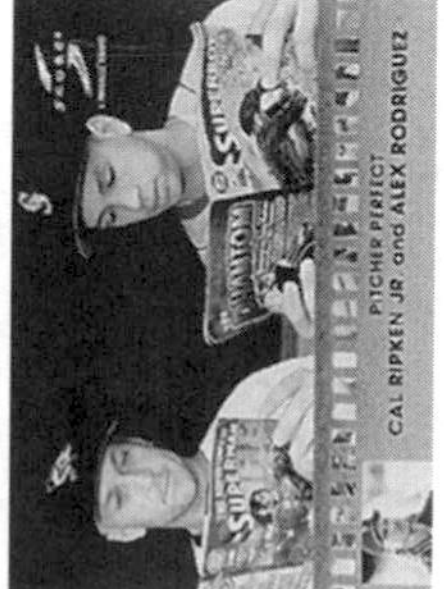

Seattle Mariners' star pitcher and accomplished photographer Randy

Johnson makes his picks for the top talent in this 1997 Score Series I insert set. Fronts have player photos with a gold-foil film-strip graphic at bottom featuring player names and a portrait of The Big Unit. Backs have additional color photos in a film-strip design and a few words about the player.

		MT
Complete Set (15):		70.00
Common Player:		1.50
1	Cal Ripken Jr.	12.00
2	Alex Rodriguez	12.00
3	Cal Ripken Jr., Alex Rodriguez	12.00
4	Edgar Martinez	1.50
5	Ivan Rodriguez	4.00
6	Mark McGwire	15.00
7	Tim Salmon	2.00
8	Chili Davis	1.50
9	Joe Carter	2.00
10	Frank Thomas	6.00
11	Will Clark	2.00
12	Mo Vaughn	3.00
13	Wade Boggs	4.00
14	Ken Griffey Jr.	15.00
15	Randy Johnson	2.00

1997 Score Stand & Deliver

This 24-card insert was printed on a silver foil background, with the series name and team logo in gold foil across the bottom. Cards were found in Series II packs one per 71 retail, one per 41 hobby. Card numbers 21-24 (Florida Marlins) were designated as the winning group, meaning the first 225 collectors that mailed in the complete four card set received a gold upgrade version of the set framed in glass.

		MT
Complete Set (24):		275.00
Common Player:		3.00
1	Andruw Jones	12.00
2	Greg Maddux	25.00
3	Chipper Jones	25.00
4	John Smoltz	4.00
5	Ken Griffey Jr.	40.00
6	Alex Rodriguez	40.00
7	Jay Buhner	3.00
8	Randy Johnson	12.00
9	Derek Jeter	30.00
10	Andy Pettitte	6.00
11	Bernie Williams	10.00
12	Mariano Rivera	3.00
13	Mike Piazza	30.00
14	Hideo Nomo	10.00
15	Raul Mondesi	4.00
16	Todd Hollandsworth	3.00
17	Manny Ramirez	12.00
18	Jim Thome	8.00
19	David Justice	6.00
20	Matt Williams	6.00
21	Juan Gonzalez	12.00
22	Jeff Bagwell	12.00
23	Cal Ripken Jr.	40.00
24	Frank Thomas	15.00

1997 Score Stellar Season

These 1997 Score Series I inserts were seeded one per every 17 magazine packs.

		MT
Complete Set (18):		70.00
Common Player:		2.00
1	Juan Gonzalez	4.00
2	Chuck Knoblauch	2.00
3	Jeff Bagwell	4.00
4	John Smoltz	1.50
5	Mark McGwire	15.00
6	Ken Griffey Jr.	12.00
7	Frank Thomas	5.00
8	Alex Rodriguez	12.00
9	Mike Piazza	10.00
10	Albert Belle	2.50
11	Roberto Alomar	3.00
12	Sammy Sosa	10.00
13	Mo Vaughn	2.50
14	Brady Anderson	1.50
15	Henry Rodriguez	1.50
16	Eric Young	1.50
17	Gary Sheffield	2.00
18	Ryan Klesko	2.00

1997 Score Titanic Taters

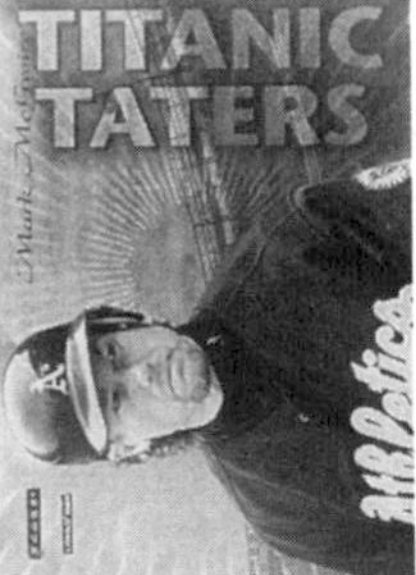

Some of the game's most powerful hitters are featured on these 1997 Score Series I inserts. The cards were seeded one per every 35 retail packs.

		MT
Complete Set (18):		100.00
Common Player:		2.00
1	Mark McGwire	25.00
2	Mike Piazza	15.00
3	Ken Griffey Jr.	20.00
4	Juan Gonzalez	6.00
5	Frank Thomas	8.00
6	Albert Belle	4.00
7	Sammy Sosa	15.00
8	Jeff Bagwell	6.00
9	Todd Hundley	2.00
10	Ryan Klesko	2.00
11	Brady Anderson	2.00
12	Mo Vaughn	4.00
13	Jay Buhner	2.00
14	Greg Vaughn	2.00
15	Barry Bonds	6.00
16	Gary Sheffield	4.00
17	Alex Rodriguez	20.00
18	Cecil Fielder	2.00

1997 Score Team Collection

Team sets consisting of 15 players each were produced for 10 different teams. Each card is similar in design to the regular 1997 Score set except for a special foil stamping at the bottom of the card that corresponds with team colors. In a parallel "Platinum" version, seeded one per six packs, the background and team foil on front are replaced with silver prismatic foil. A top of the line parallel set, "Premier" utilizes gold foil highlights on fronts and is found one per 31 packs. Team Collection was sold in five-card, single-team packs with a suggested retail price of about $1.29. It was reported that 100 cases of each team were issued.

		MT
Complete Set (150):		60.00
Common Player:		.25
Braves Wax Box:		80.00
Orioles Wax Box:		70.00
Red Sox Wax Box:		60.00
White Sox Wax Box:		70.00
Indians Wax Box:		70.00
Rockies Wax Box:		55.00
Dodgers Wax Box:		70.00
Yankees Wax Box:		75.00
Mariners Wax Box:		120.00
Rangers Wax Box:		60.00
	Atlanta Braves	8.00
1	Ryan Klesko	.25
2	David Justice	.35
3	Terry Pendleton	.25
4	Tom Glavine	.35
5	Javier Lopez	.35
6	John Smoltz	.35
7	Jermaine Dye	.30
8	Mark Lemke	.25
9	Fred McGriff	.40
10	Chipper Jones	2.50
11	Terrell Wade	.25
12	Greg Maddux	2.50
13	Mark Wohlers	.25
14	Marquis Grissom	.25
15	Andruw Jones	2.00
	Baltimore Orioles	5.00
1	Rafael Palmeiro	.35
2	Eddie Murray	.50
3	Roberto Alomar	1.00
4	Rocky Coppinger	.25
5	Brady Anderson	.35
6	Bobby Bonilla	.25
7	Cal Ripken Jr.	3.00
8	Mike Mussina	.50
9	Nerio Rodriguez	.25
10	Randy Myers	.25
11	B.J. Surhoff	.25
12	Jeffrey Hammonds	.25
13	Chris Hoiles	.25
14	Jimmy Haynes	.25
15	David Wells	.25
	Boston Red Sox	4.00
1	Wil Cordero	.25
2	Mo Vaughn	1.00
3	John Valentin	.25
4	Reggie Jefferson	.25
5	Tom Gordon	.25
6	Mike Stanley	.25
7	Jose Canseco	.40
8	Roger Clemens	.75
9	Darren Bragg	.25
10	Jeff Frye	.25
11	Jeff Suppan	.25
12	Mike Greenwell	.25
13	Arquimedez Pozo	.25
14	Tim Naehring	.25
15	Troy O'Leary	.25
	Chicago White Sox	6.00
1	Frank Thomas	2.00
2	James Baldwin	.25
3	Danny Tartabull	.25
4	Jeff Darwin	.25
5	Harold Baines	.25
6	Roberto Hernandez	.25
7	Ray Durham	.25
8	Robin Ventura	.30
9	Wilson Alvarez	.25
10	Lyle Mouton	.25
11	Alex Fernandez	.30
12	Ron Karkovice	.25
13	Kevin Tapani	.25
14	Tony Phillips	.25
15	Mike Cameron	.25
	Cleveland Indians	6.00
1	Albert Belle	1.50
2	Jack McDowell	.25
3	Jim Thome	.60
4	Dennis Martinez	.25
5	Julio Franco	.25
6	Omar Vizquel	.25
7	Kenny Lofton	1.00
8	Manny Ramirez	1.50
9	Sandy Alomar Jr.	.30
10	Charles Nagy	.25
11	Kevin Seitzer	.25
12	Mark Carreon	.25
13	Jeff Kent	.25
14	Danny Graves	.25
15	Brian Giles	.25
	Colorado Rockies	4.00
1	Dante Bichette	.40
2	Kevin Ritz	.25
3	Walt Weiss	.25
4	Ellis Burks	.25
5	Jamey Wright	.25
6	Andres Galarraga	.35
7	Eric Young	.25
8	Larry Walker	.50
9	Vinny Castilla	.25
10	Quinton McCracken	.25
11	Armando Reynoso	.25
12	Jayhawk Owens	.25
13	Mark Thompson	.25
14	John Burke	.25
15	Bruce Ruffin	.25
	Los Angeles Dodgers	6.00
1	Ismael Valdez	.25
2	Mike Piazza	2.50
3	Todd Hollandsworth	.25

4	Delino DeShields	.25
5	Chan Ho Park	.30
6	Roger Cedeno	.25
7	Raul Mondesi	.40
8	Darren Dreifort	.25
9	Jim Bruske	.25
10	Greg Gagne	.25
11	Chad Curtis	.25
12	Ramon Martinez	.25
13	Brett Butler	.25
14	Eric Karros	.25
15	Hideo Nomo	.50
	New York Yankees	6.00
1	Bernie Williams	.75
2	Cecil Fielder	.25
3	Derek Jeter	2.50
4	Darryl Strawberry	.25
5	Andy Pettitte	1.00
6	Ruben Rivera	.30
7	Mariano Rivera	.40
8	John Wetteland	.25
9	Paul O'Neill	.30
10	Wade Boggs	.50
11	Dwight Gooden	.25
12	David Cone	.35
13	Tino Martinez	.25
14	Kenny Rogers	.25
15	Andy Fox	.25
	Seattle Mariners	12.00
1	Chris Bosio	.25
2	Edgar Martinez	.25
3	Alex Rodriguez	3.00
4	Paul Sorrento	.25
5	Bob Wells	.25
6	Ken Griffey Jr.	4.00
7	Jay Buhner	.30
8	Dan Wilson	.25
9	Randy Johnson	.40
10	Joey Cora	.25
11	Mark Whiten	.25
12	Rich Amaral	.25
13	Raul Ibanez	.25
14	Jamie Moyer	.25
15	Makoto Suzuki	.25
	Texas Rangers	5.00
1	Mickey Tettleton	.25
2	Will Clark	.40
3	Ken Hill	.25
4	Rusty Greer	.25
5	Kevin Elster	.25
6	Darren Oliver	.25
7	Mark McLemore	.25
8	Roger Pavlik	.25
9	Dean Palmer	.25
10	Bobby Witt	.25
11	Juan Gonzalez	1.50
12	Ivan Rodriguez	.50
13	Darryl Hamilton	.25
14	John Burkett	.25
15	Warren Newson	.25

1997 Score Team Collection Platinum Team

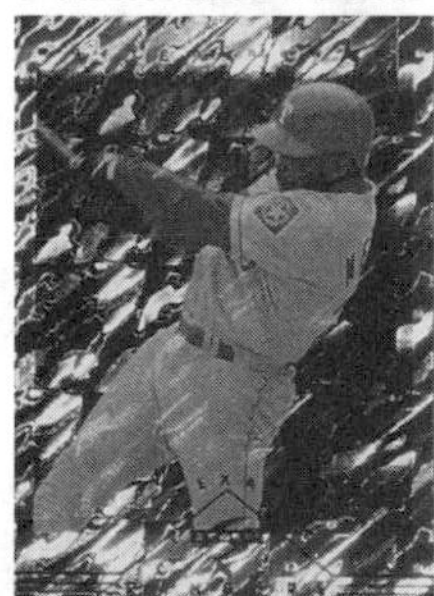

Team sets consisting of 15 players each were produced for 10 different teams. Each card is similar in design to the regular 1997 Score set except for a special foil stamping at the bottom of the card that corresponds with team colors. In a parallel "Platinum" version, seeded one per six packs, the background and team foil on front are replaced with silver prismatic foil. Backs are overprinted in gold script, "Platinum Team." Team Collection was sold in five-card, single-team packs with a suggested retail price of about $1.29. It was reported that 100 cases of each team were issued.

	MT
Complete Set (150):	250.00
Common Player:	2.00
Platinum Stars:	4X

(See 1997 Score Team Collection for checklists and base card values.)

1997 Score Team Collection Premier Club

Team sets consisting of 15 players each were produced for 10 different teams. Each card is similar in design to the regular 1997 Score set except for a special foil stamping at the bottom of the card that corresponds with team colors. In a top of the line parallel "Premier Club" version, seeded one per 31 packs, the background and team foil on front are replaced with gold prismatic foil, and backs are overprinted "Premier Club" in gold script. Team Collection was sold in five-card, single-team packs with a suggested retail price of about $1.29. It was reported that 100 cases of each team were issued.

	MT
Complete Set (150):	900.00
Common Player:	6.00
Premier Club Stars:	15X

(See 1997 Score Team Collection for checklists and base card values.)

1998 Score Samples

Half a dozen top stars were picked to introduce 1998 Score in this series of promo cards. Cards are virtually identical to the issued version except for the large black overprinted "SAMPLE" on back and the use of zeroes to replace 1997 stats.

		MT
Complete Set (6):		15.00
Common Player:		2.00
10	Alex Rodriguez	3.00
24	Mike Piazza	2.50
34	Ken Griffey Jr.	4.00
43	Cal Ripken Jr.	3.00
51	Chipper Jones	2.50
60	Carlos Delgado	2.00

1998 Score

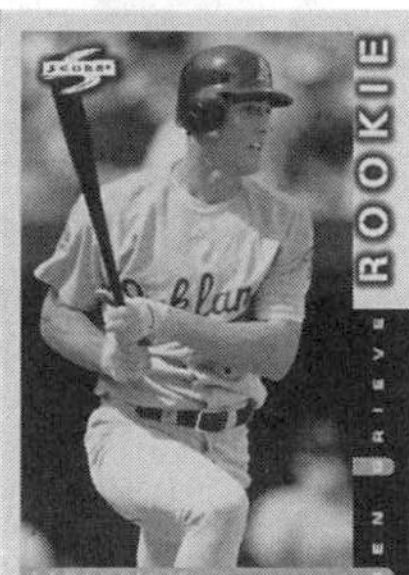

The cards in the 270-card base set feature a color photo inside a black and white border. The player's name is printed in the left border. The entire base set is paralleled in the silver-foil Showcase Series (1:5). The Artist's Proof partial parallel gives a prismatic foil treatment to 165 base cards and was seeded 1:23. Inserts included All-Stars, Complete Players and Epix.

		MT
Complete Set (270):		25.00
Common Player:		.05
Pack (10):		1.00
Wax Box (36):		25.00
1	Andruw Jones	.50
2	Dan Wilson	.05
3	Hideo Nomo	.25
4	Chuck Carr	.05
5	Barry Bonds	.50
6	Jack McDowell	.05
7	Albert Belle	.30
8	Francisco Cordova	.05
9	Greg Maddux	1.00
10	Alex Rodriguez	1.50
11	Steve Avery	.05
12	Chuck McElroy	.05
13	Larry Walker	.20
14	Hideki Irabu	.15
15	Roberto Alomar	.40
16	Neifi Perez	.05
17	Jim Thome	.30
18	Rickey Henderson	.20
19	Andres Galarraga	.20
20	Jeff Fassero	.05
21	Kevin Young	.05
22	Derek Jeter	1.50
23	Andy Benes	.05
24	Mike Piazza	1.25
25	Todd Stottlemyre	.05
26	Michael Tucker	.05
27	Denny Neagle	.05
28	Javier Lopez	.10
29	Aaron Sele	.05
30	Ryan Klesko	.10
31	Dennis Eckersley	.05
32	Quinton McCracken	.05
33	Brian Anderson	.05
34	Ken Griffey Jr.	1.50
35	Shawn Estes	.05
36	Tim Wakefield	.05
37	Jimmy Key	.05
38	Jeff Bagwell	.50
39	Edgardo Alfonzo	.10
40	Mike Cameron	.05
41	Mark McGwire	2.00
42	Tino Martinez	.15
43	Cal Ripken Jr.	1.50
44	Curtis Goodwin	.05
45	Bobby Ayala	.05
46	Sandy Alomar Jr.	.10
47	Bobby Jones	.05
48	Omar Vizquel	.05
49	Roger Clemens	.75
50	Tony Gwynn	.75
51	Chipper Jones	1.00
52	Ron Coomer	.05
53	Dmitri Young	.05
54	Brian Giles	.05
55	Steve Finley	.05
56	David Cone	.10
57	Andy Pettitte	.20
58	Wilton Guerrero	.05
59	Deion Sanders	.15
60	Carlos Delgado	.40
61	Jason Giambi	.25
62	Ozzie Guillen	.05
63	Jay Bell	.05
64	Barry Larkin	.20
65	Sammy Sosa	1.00
66	Bernie Williams	.40
67	Terry Steinbach	.05
68	Scott Rolen	.50
69	Melvin Nieves	.05
70	Craig Biggio	.15
71	Todd Greene	.05
72	Greg Gagne	.05
73	Shigetosi Hasegawa	.05
74	Mark McLemore	.05
75	Darren Bragg	.05
76	Brett Butler	.05
77	Ron Gant	.05
78	Mike Difelice	.05
79	Charles Nagy	.05
80	Scott Hatteberg	.05
81	Brady Anderson	.15
82	Jay Buhner	.10
83	Todd Hollandsworth	.05
84	Geronimo Berroa	.05
85	Jeff Suppan	.05
86	Pedro Martinez	.50
87	Roger Cedeno	.05
88	Ivan Rodriguez	.50
89	Jaime Navarro	.05
90	Chris Hoiles	.05
91	Nomar Garciaparra	1.25
92	Rafael Palmeiro	.20
93	Darin Erstad	.40
94	Kenny Lofton	.25
95	Mike Timlin	.05
96	Chris Clemons	.05
97	Vinny Castilla	.10
98	Charlie Hayes	.05
99	Lyle Mouton	.05
100	Jason Dickson	.05
101	Justin Thompson	.05
102	Pat Kelly	.05
103	Chan Ho Park	.05
104	Ray Lankford	.05
105	Frank Thomas	.75
106	Jermaine Allensworth	.05
107	Doug Drabek	.05
108	Todd Hundley	.10
109	Carl Everett	.05
110	Edgar Martinez	.05
111	Robin Ventura	.10
112	John Wetteland	.05
113	Mariano Rivera	.15
114	Jose Rosado	.05
115	Ken Caminiti	.10
116	Paul O'Neill	.15
117	Tim Salmon	.20
118	Eduardo Perez	.05
119	Mike Jackson	.05
120	John Smoltz	.10
121	Brant Brown	.05

122 John Mabry .05
123 Chuck Knoblauch .20
124 Reggie Sanders .05
125 Ken Hill .05
126 Mike Mussina .40
127 Chad Curtis .05
128 Todd Worrell .05
129 Chris Widger .05
130 Damon Mashore .05
131 Kevin Brown .10
132 Bip Roberts .05
133 Tim Naehring .05
134 Dave Martinez .05
135 Jeff Blauser .05
136 David Justice .20
137 Dave Hollins .05
138 Pat Hentgen .05
139 Darren Daulton .05
140 Ramon Martinez .05
141 Raul Casanova .05
142 Tom Glavine .15
143 J.T. Snow .05
144 Tony Graffanino .05
145 Randy Johnson .50
146 Orlando Merced .05
147 Jeff Juden .05
148 Darryl Kile .05
149 Ray Durham .05
150 Alex Fernandez .05
151 Joey Cora .05
152 Royce Clayton .05
153 Randy Myers .05
154 Charles Johnson .05
155 Alan Benes .05
156 Mike Bordick .05
157 Heathcliff Slocumb .05
158 Roger Bailey .05
159 Reggie Jefferson .05
160 Ricky Bottalico .05
161 Scott Erickson .05
162 Matt Williams .20
163 Robb Nen .05
164 Matt Stairs .05
165 Ismael Valdes .05
166 Lee Stevens .05
167 Gary DiSarcina .05
168 Brad Radke .05
169 Mike Lansing .05
170 Armando Benitez .05
171 Mike James .05
172 Russ Davis .05
173 Lance Johnson .05
174 Joey Hamilton .05
175 John Valentin .05
176 David Segui .05
177 David Wells .05
178 Delino DeShields .05
179 Eric Karros .10
180 Jim Leyritz .05
181 Raul Mondesi .15
182 Travis Fryman .15
183 Todd Zeile .05
184 Brian Jordan .05
185 Rey Ordonez .10
186 Jim Edmonds .15
187 Terrell Wade .05
188 Marquis Grissom .10
189 Chris Snopek .05
190 Shane Reynolds .05
191 Jeff Frye .05
192 Paul Sorrento .05
193 James Baldwin .05
194 Brian McRae .05
195 Fred McGriff .15
196 Troy Percival .05
197 Rich Amaral .05
198 Juan Guzman .05
199 Cecil Fielder .05
200 Willie Blair .05
201 Chili Davis .05
202 Gary Gaetti .05
203 B.J. Surhoff .05
204 Steve Cooke .05
205 Chuck Finley .05
206 Jeff Kent .05
207 Ben McDonald .05
208 Jeffrey Hammonds .05
209 Tom Goodwin .05
210 Billy Ashley .05
211 Wil Cordero .05
212 Shawon Dunston .05
213 Tony Phillips .05
214 Jamie Moyer .05
215 John Jaha .05
216 Troy O'Leary .05
217 Brad Ausmus .05
218 Garret Anderson .05
219 Wilson Alvarez .05
220 Kent Mercker .05
221 Wade Boggs .25
222 Mark Wohlers .05
223 Kevin Appier .05
224 Tony Fernandez .05
225 Ugueth Urbina .05
226 Gregg Jefferies .05
227 Mo Vaughn .30
228 Arthur Rhodes .05
229 Jorge Fabregas .05
230 Mark Gardner .05
231 Shane Mack .05
232 Jorge Posada .05
233 Jose Cruz Jr. .10
234 Paul Konerko .15
235 Derrek Lee .05
236 *Steve Woodard* .15
237 Todd Dunwoody .10
238 Fernando Tatis .15
239 Jacob Cruz .10
240 *Pokey Reese* .25
241 Mark Kotsay .10
242 Matt Morris .05
243 *Antone Williamson* .05
244 Ben Grieve .20
245 Ryan McGuire .05
246 *Lou Collier* .05
247 Shannon Stewart .05
248 *Brett Tomko* .05
249 Bobby Estalella .05
250 *Livan Hernandez* .15
251 Todd Helton .50
252 Jaret Wright .05
253 Darryl Hamilton (Interleague Moments) .05
254 Stan Javier (Interleague Moments) .05
255 Glenallen Hill (Interleague Moments) .05
256 Mark Gardner (Interleague Moments) .05
257 Cal Ripken Jr. (Interleague Moments) .75
258 Mike Mussina (Interleague Moments) .20
259 Mike Piazza (Interleague Moments) .60
260 Sammy Sosa (Interleague Moments) .50
261 Todd Hundley (Interleague Moments) .05
262 Eric Karros (Interleague Moments) .05
263 Denny Neagle (Interleague Moments) .05
264 Jeromy Burnitz (Interleague Moments) .05
265 Greg Maddux (Interleague Moments) .50
266 Tony Clark (Interleague Moments) .10
267 Vladimir Guerrero (Interleague Moments).40
268 Checklist .05
269 Checklist .05
270 Checklist .05

1998 Score Artist's Proofs

This partial parallel reprinted 160 of the 270 cards in Score Baseball on a foil background with an Artist's Proof logo on the front. The cards were renumbered within the 160-card set and inserted one per 35 packs. Cards have a "PP" prefix to the number on back.

	MT
Complete Set (160):	400.00
Common Player:	1.50
Inserted 1:35	

1 Andruw Jones 7.50
2 Dan Wilson 2.50
3 Hideo Nomo 6.00
4 Neifi Perez 2.50
5 Jim Thome 5.00
6 Jeff Fassero 2.50
7 Derek Jeter 15.00
8 Andy Benes 2.50
9 Michael Tucker 2.50
10 Ryan Klesko 2.50
11 Dennis Eckersley 2.50
12 Jimmy Key 2.50
13 Edgardo Alfonzo 3.00
14 Mike Cameron 2.50
15 Omar Vizquel 2.50
16 Ron Coomer 2.50
17 Dmitri Young 2.50
18 Brian Giles 2.50
19 Steve Finley 2.50
20 Andy Pettitte 4.00
21 Wilton Guerrero 2.50
22 Deion Sanders 3.00
23 Carlos Delgado 6.00
24 Jason Giambi 2.50
25 David Cone 3.50
26 Jay Bell 2.50
27 Sammy Sosa 12.50
28 Barry Larkin 2.50
29 Scott Rolen 7.50
30 Todd Greene 2.50
31 Bernie Williams 4.00
32 Brett Butler 2.50
33 Ron Gant 2.50
34 Brady Anderson 2.50
35 Craig Biggio 3.50
36 Charles Nagy 2.50
37 Jay Buhner 2.50
38 Geronimo Berroa 2.50
39 Jeff Suppan 2.50
40 Rafael Palmeiro 4.00
41 Darin Erstad 7.50
42 Mike Timlin 2.50
43 Vinny Castilla 2.50
44 Carl Everett 2.50
45 Robin Ventura 3.00
46 John Wetteland 2.50
47 Paul O'Neill 3.00
48 Tim Salmon 2.50
49 Mike Jackson 2.50
50 John Smoltz 2.50
51 Brant Brown 2.50
52 Reggie Sanders 2.50
53 Ken Hill 2.50
54 Todd Worrell 2.50
55 Bip Roberts 2.50
56 Tim Naehring 2.50
57 Darren Daulton 2.50
58 Ramon Martinez 4.00
59 Raul Casanova 2.50
60 J.T. Snow 2.50
61 Jeff Juden 2.50
62 Royce Clayton 2.50
63 Charles Johnson 2.50
64 Alan Benes 2.50
65 Reggie Jefferson 2.50
66 Ricky Bottalico 2.50
67 Scott Erickson 2.50
68 Matt Williams 2.50
69 Robb Nen 2.50
70 Matt Stairs 2.50
71 Ismael Valdes 2.50
72 Brad Radke 2.50
73 Armando Benitez 2.50
74 Russ Davis 2.50
75 Lance Johnson 2.50
76 Joey Hamilton 2.50
77 John Valentin 2.50
78 David Segui 2.50
79 David Wells 2.50
80 Eric Karros 2.50
81 Raul Mondesi 4.00
82 Travis Fryman 2.50
83 Todd Zeile 2.50
84 Brian Jordan 2.50
85 Rey Ordonez 2.50
86 Jim Edmonds 2.50
87 Marquis Grissom 2.50
88 Shane Reynolds 2.50
89 Paul Sorrento 2.50
90 Brian McRae 2.50
91 Fred McGriff 3.50
92 Troy Percival 2.50
93 Juan Guzman 2.50
94 Cecil Fielder 2.50
95 Chili Davis 2.50
96 B.J. Surhoff 2.50
97 Chuck Finley 2.50
98 Jeff Kent 2.50
99 Ben McDonald 2.50
100 Jeffrey Hammonds 2.50
101 Tom Goodwin 2.50
102 Wil Cordero 2.50
103 Tony Phillips 2.50
104 John Jaha 2.50
105 Garret Anderson 2.50
106 Wilson Alvarez 2.50
107 Wade Boggs 7.50
108 Mark Wohlers 2.50
109 Kevin Appier 2.50
110 Mo Vaughn 4.00
111 Ray Durham 2.50
112 Alex Fernandez 2.50
113 Barry Bonds 10.00
114 Albert Belle 8.00
115 Greg Maddux 10.00
116 Alex Rodriguez 20.00
117 Larry Walker 4.00
118 Roberto Alomar 6.00
119 Andres Galarraga 2.50
120 Mike Piazza 12.50
121 Denny Neagle 2.50
122 Javier Lopez 2.50
123 Ken Griffey Jr. 25.00
124 Shawn Estes 4.00
125 Jeff Bagwell 10.00
126 Mark McGwire 25.00
127 Tino Martinez 2.50
128 Cal Ripken Jr. 20.00
129 Sandy Alomar Jr. 3.00
130 Bobby Jones 2.50
131 Roger Clemens 10.00
132 Tony Gwynn 10.00
133 Chipper Jones 15.00
134 Orlando Merced 2.50
135 Todd Stottlemyre 2.50
136 Delino DeShields 2.50
137 Pedro Martinez 4.00
138 Ivan Rodriguez 6.00
139 Nomar Garciaparra 12.50
140 Kenny Lofton 3.00
141 Jason Dickson 2.50
142 Justin Thompson 2.50
143 Ray Lankford 2.50
144 Frank Thomas 10.00
145 Todd Hundley 2.50
146 Edgar Martinez 2.50
147 Mariano Rivera 3.00
148 Jose Rosado 2.50
149 Ken Caminiti 3.50
150 Chuck Knoblauch 3.00
151 Mike Mussina 3.00
152 Kevin Brown 3.00
153 Jeff Blauser 2.50
154 David Justice 3.00
155 Pat Hentgen 2.50
156 Tom Glavine 3.00
157 Randy Johnson 4.00
158 Darryl Kile 2.50
159 Joey Cora 2.50
160 Randy Myers 2.50

1998 Score Showcase Series

This partial parallel reprinted 160 of the 270 cards in Score Baseball on silver foil. They were marked on the back and renumbered within the 160-card set. Showcase parallels were inserted one per seven packs. All Showcase Series cards except #1 have a "PP" prefix to the number.

		MT
Complete Set (160):		150.00
Common Player:		.50
Inserted 1:7		
1	Andruw Jones	1.50
2	Dan Wilson	.50
3	Hideo Nomo	1.00
4	Neifi Perez	.50
5	Jim Thome	2.00
6	Jeff Fassero	.50
7	Derek Jeter	5.00
8	Andy Benes	.50
9	Michael Tucker	.50
10	Ryan Klesko	.60
11	Dennis Eckersley	.50
12	Jimmy Key	.50
13	Edgardo Alfonzo	.60
14	Mike Cameron	.50
15	Omar Vizquel	.50
16	Ron Coomer	.50
17	Dmitri Young	.50
18	Brian Giles	.50
19	Steve Finley	.50
20	Andy Pettitte	.90
21	Wilton Guerrero	.50
22	Deion Sanders	.75
23	Carlos Delgado	.75
24	Jason Giambi	.50
25	David Cone	.60
26	Jay Bell	.50
27	Sammy Sosa	4.00
28	Barry Larkin	.90
29	Scott Rolen	1.50
30	Todd Greene	.50
31	Bernie Williams	.75
32	Brett Butler	.50
33	Ron Gant	.50
34	Brady Anderson	.50
35	Craig Biggio	.75
36	Charles Nagy	.50
37	Jay Buhner	.50
38	Geronimo Berroa	.50
39	Jeff Suppan	.50
40	Rafael Palmeiro	1.00
41	Darin Erstad	2.00
42	Mike Timlin	.50
43	Vinny Castilla	.50
44	Carl Everett	.50
45	Robin Ventura	.75
46	John Wetteland	.50
47	Paul O'Neill	.60
48	Tim Salmon	.60
49	Mike Jackson	.50
50	John Smoltz	.50
51	Brant Brown	.50
52	Reggie Sanders	.50
53	Ken Hill	.50
54	Todd Worrell	.50
55	Bip Roberts	.50
56	Tim Naehring	.50
57	Darren Daulton	.50
58	Ramon Martinez	.75
59	Raul Casanova	.50
60	J.T. Snow	.50
61	Jeff Juden	.50
62	Royce Clayton	.50
63	Charles Johnson	.50
64	Alan Benes	.50
65	Reggie Jefferson	.50
66	Ricky Bottalico	.50
67	Scott Erickson	.50
68	Matt Williams	.75
69	Robb Nen	.50
70	Matt Stairs	.50
71	Ismael Valdes	.50
72	Brad Radke	.50
73	Armando Benitez	.50
74	Russ Davis	.50
75	Lance Johnson	.50
76	Joey Hamilton	.50
77	John Valentin	.50
78	David Segui	.50
79	David Wells	.60
80	Eric Karros	.60
81	Raul Mondesi	.75
82	Travis Fryman	.50
83	Todd Zeile	.60
84	Brian Jordan	.60
85	Rey Ordonez	.50
86	Jim Edmonds	.50
87	Marquis Grissom	.50
88	Shane Reynolds	.50
89	Paul Sorrento	.50
90	Brian McRae	.50
91	Fred McGriff	.75
92	Troy Percival	.50
93	Juan Guzman	.50
94	Cecil Fielder	.50
95	Chili Davis	.50
96	B.J. Surhoff	.50
97	Chuck Finley	.50
98	Jeff Kent	.50
99	Ben McDonald	.50
100	Jeffrey Hammonds	.50
101	Tom Goodwin	.50
102	Wil Cordero	.50
103	Tony Phillips	.50
104	John Jaha	.50
105	Garret Anderson	.50
106	Wilson Alvarez	.50
107	Wade Boggs	2.00
108	Mark Wohlers	.50
109	Kevin Appier	.50
110	Mo Vaughn	1.00
111	Ray Durham	.50
112	Alex Fernandez	.50
113	Barry Bonds	4.00
114	Albert Belle	4.00
115	Greg Maddux	4.00
116	Alex Rodriguez	6.00
117	Larry Walker	1.50
118	Roberto Alomar	1.25
119	Andres Galarraga	.60
120	Mike Piazza	5.00
121	Denny Neagle	.50
122	Javier Lopez	.50
123	Ken Griffey Jr.	7.50
124	Shawn Estes	.50
125	Jeff Bagwell	3.00
126	Mark McGwire	7.50
127	Tino Martinez	.60
128	Cal Ripken Jr.	6.00
129	Sandy Alomar Jr.	.60
130	Bobby Jones	.50
131	Roger Clemens	2.00
132	Tony Gwynn	2.00
133	Chipper Jones	4.00
134	Orlando Merced	.50
135	Todd Stottlemyre	.50
136	Delino DeShields	.50
137	Pedro Martinez	.90
138	Ivan Rodriguez	1.25
139	Nomar Garciaparra	5.00
140	Kenny Lofton	.75
141	Jason Dickson	.50
142	Justin Thompson	.50
143	Ray Lankford	.50
144	Frank Thomas	3.00
145	Todd Hundley	.50
146	Edgar Martinez	.50
147	Mariano Rivera	.50
148	Jose Rosado	.50
149	Ken Caminiti	.75
150	Chuck Knoblauch	.75
151	Mike Mussina	.75
152	Kevin Brown	.75
153	Jeff Blauser	.50
154	David Justice	1.00
155	Pat Hentgen	.50
156	Tom Glavine	.60
157	Randy Johnson	1.00
158	Darryl Kile	.50
159	Joey Cora	.50
160	Randy Myers	.50

1998 Score All Score Team

For its 10th anniversary Score selected an all-star team and issued this insert set. Cards have player action photos on a silver-foil background with an anniversary logo at bottom. Backs have a portrait photo and a career summary. The cards were inserted one per 35 packs.

		MT
Complete Set (20):		100.00
Common Player:		2.00
Inserted 1:35		
1	Mike Piazza	12.00
2	Ivan Rodriguez	5.00
3	Frank Thomas	8.00
4	Mark McGwire	20.00
5	Ryne Sandberg	4.00
6	Roberto Alomar	4.00
7	Cal Ripken Jr.	15.00
8	Barry Larkin	2.00
9	Paul Molitor	3.00
10	Travis Fryman	2.00
11	Kirby Puckett	5.00
12	Tony Gwynn	10.00
13	Ken Griffey Jr.	20.00
14	Juan Gonzalez	5.00
15	Barry Bonds	5.00
16	Andruw Jones	4.00
17	Roger Clemens	8.00
18	Randy Johnson	3.00
19	Greg Maddux	10.00
20	Dennis Eckersley	2.00

1998 Score Complete Players

Complete Players is a 30-card insert featuring 10 players who can do it all. Each player had three cards displaying their variety of skills. The cards feature holographic foil highlights on fronts. Backs form a three-piece vertical picture of the player. Values shown are for each of the three cards (A, B, C) per player. The cards were inserted about one per 23 packs. Cards can be found with either gold or silver holographic foil.

		MT
Complete Set (30):		150.00
Common Player:		1.50
Inserted 1:23		
three cards per player		
1	Ken Griffey Jr.	8.00
2	Mark McGwire	10.00
3	Derek Jeter	8.00
4	Cal Ripken Jr.	8.00
5	Mike Piazza	6.00
6	Darin Erstad	1.50
7	Frank Thomas	3.00
8	Andruw Jones	3.00
9	Nomar Garciaparra	6.00
10	Manny Ramirez	2.50

1998 Score Epix

Epix is a cross-brand insert, with 24 cards appearing in Score. The cards are printed on 20-point stock with holographic foil technology. The cards honor the top Play, Game, Season and Moment in a player's career and come in Orange, Purple and Emerald versions. Game cards were inserted 1:141, Plays 1:171, Seasons 1:437 and Moments 1:757.

		MT
Common Card:		3.00
Purple:		1.5X
Emeralds:		2.5X
1	Ken Griffey Jr. P	15.00
2	Juan Gonzalez P	4.00
3	Jeff Bagwell P	3.00
4	Ivan Rodriguez P	3.00
5	Nomar Garciaparra P	10.00
6	Ryne Sandberg P	3.00
7	Frank Thomas G	8.00
8	Derek Jeter G	15.00
9	Tony Gwynn G	12.00
10	Albert Belle G	5.00
11	Scott Rolen G	6.00
12	Barry Larkin G	3.00
13	Alex Rodriguez S	40.00
14	Cal Ripken Jr. S	40.00
15	Chipper Jones S	30.00
16	Roger Clemens S	25.00
17	Mo Vaughn S	8.00
18	Mark McGwire S	60.00
19	Mike Piazza M	50.00
20	Andruw Jones M	15.00
21	Greg Maddux M	45.00
22	Barry Bonds M	20.00
23	Paul Molitor M	15.00
24	Eddie Murray M	15.00

1998 Score First Pitch

These inserts were a 1:11 pack find in Score's All-Star edition. Fronts have portrait photos printed in the center of textured foil background of red and silver. The basic design is repeated on back, with career highlights and team logo instead of a photo.

		MT
Complete Set (20):		50.00
Common Player:		1.00
Inserted 1:11 All-Star Edition		
1	Ken Griffey Jr.	6.00
2	Frank Thomas	3.00
3	Alex Rodriguez	6.00
4	Cal Ripken Jr.	6.00
5	Chipper Jones	4.00

6	Juan Gonzalez	2.00
7	Derek Jeter	5.00
8	Mike Piazza	5.00
9	Andruw Jones	2.00
10	Nomar Garciaparra	5.00
11	Barry Bonds	2.00
12	Jeff Bagwell	2.00
13	Scott Rolen	1.50
14	Hideo Nomo	1.00
15	Roger Clemens	3.00
16	Mark McGwire	8.00
17	Greg Maddux	4.00
18	Albert Belle	1.00
19	Ivan Rodriguez	2.00
20	Mo Vaughn	1.00

1998 Score Loaded Lineup

This insert series was packaged on average of one card per 45 packs of Score's All-Star edition. Fronts have action photos printed on a copper and silver textured metallic-foil background. Backs have a portrait photo, career highlights, the Loaded Lineup batting order and stats for the player's best season. Cards have an "LL" prefix to their number.

		MT
Complete Set (10):		60.00
Common Player:		2.50
Inserted 1:45 All-Star Edition		
LL1	Chuck Knoblauch	2.50
LL2	Tony Gwynn	8.00
LL3	Frank Thomas	8.00
LL4	Ken Griffey Jr.	15.00
LL5	Mike Piazza	10.00
LL6	Barry Bonds	4.00
LL7	Cal Ripken Jr.	12.00
LL8	Paul Molitor	3.00
LL9	Nomar Garciaparra	10.00
LL10	Greg Maddux	10.00

1998 Score New Season

		MT
Complete Set (15):		60.00
Common Player:		2.00
Inserted 1:23 All-Star Edition		
NS1	Kenny Lofton	3.00
NS2	Nomar Garciaparra	8.00
NS3	Todd Helton	2.50
NS4	Miguel Tejada	2.00
NS5	Jaret Wright	4.00
NS6	Alex Rodriguez	10.00
NS7	Vladimir Guerrero	5.00
NS8	Ken Griffey Jr.	12.00
NS9	Ben Grieve	4.00
NS10	Travis Lee	3.00
NS11	Jose Cruz Jr.	2.00
NS12	Paul Konerko	2.00
NS13	Frank Thomas	7.00
NS14	Chipper Jones	8.00
NS15	Cal Ripken Jr.	10.00

1998 Score Rookie & Traded

Score Rookie/Traded consists of a 270-card base set. The base cards have a white and gray border with the player's name on the left. The Showcase Series parallels 110 base cards and was inserted 1:7. Artist's Proofs is a 50-card partial parallel done on prismatic foil and inserted 1:35. Inserts included All-Star Epix, Complete Players and Star Gazing.

		MT
Complete Set (270):		25.00
Common SP (1-50):		.25
Common Player (51-270):		.10
Paul Konerko Auto. (500):		25.00
Pack (10):		1.00
Wax Box (36):		30.00
1	Tony Clark	.40
2	Juan Gonzalez	.75
3	Frank Thomas	1.25
4	Greg Maddux	2.00
5	Barry Larkin	.30
6	Derek Jeter	2.00
7	Randy Johnson	.50
8	Roger Clemens	1.00
9	Tony Gwynn	1.50
10	Barry Bonds	.75
11	Jim Edmonds	.25
12	Bernie Williams	.40
13	Ken Griffey Jr.	3.00
14	Tim Salmon	.40
15	Mo Vaughn	.60
16	David Justice	.40
17	Jose Cruz Jr.	.25
18	Andruw Jones	.75
19	Sammy Sosa	1.25
20	Jeff Bagwell	1.00
21	Scott Rolen	1.00
22	Darin Erstad	.75
23	Andy Pettitte	.40
24	Mike Mussina	.40
25	Mark McGwire	3.00
26	Hideo Nomo	.40
27	Chipper Jones	2.00
28	Cal Ripken Jr.	2.50
29	Chuck Knoblauch	.40
30	Alex Rodriguez	2.50
31	Jim Thome	.50
32	Mike Piazza	2.00
33	Ivan Rodriguez	.75
34	Roberto Alomar	.50
35	Nomar Garciaparra	2.00
36	Albert Belle	.75
37	Vladimir Guerrero	1.00
38	Raul Mondesi	.25
39	Larry Walker	.40
40	Manny Ramirez	.75
41	Tino Martinez	.40
42	Craig Biggio	.35
43	Jay Buhner	.40
44	Kenny Lofton	.60
45	Pedro Martinez	.60
46	Edgar Martinez	.25
47	Gary Sheffield	.30
48	Jose Guillen	.25
49	Ken Caminiti	.35
50	Bobby Higginson	.25
51	Alan Benes	.10
52	Shawn Green	.15
53	Ron Coomer	.10
54	Charles Nagy	.10
55	Steve Karsay	.10
56	Matt Morris	.10
57	Bobby Jones	.10
58	Jason Kendall	.10
59	Jeff Conine	.10
60	Joe Girardi	.10
61	Mark Kotsay	.30
62	Eric Karros	.15
63	Bartolo Colon	.15
64	Mariano Rivera	.20
65	Alex Gonzalez	.15
66	Scott Spiezio	.10
67	Luis Castillo	.10
68	Joey Cora	.10
69	Mark McLemore	.10
70	Reggie Jefferson	.10
71	Lance Johnson	.10
72	Damian Jackson	.10
73	Jeff D'Amico	.10
74	David Ortiz	.10
75	J.T. Snow	.10
76	Todd Hundley	.15
77	Billy Wagner	.15
78	Vinny Castilla	.20
79	Ismael Valdes	.10
80	Neifi Perez	.10
81	Derek Bell	.10
82	Ryan Klesko	.25
83	Rey Ordonez	.15
84	Carlos Garcia	.10
85	Curt Schilling	.20
86	Robin Ventura	.20
87	Pat Hentgen	.10
88	Glendon Rusch	.10
89	Hideki Irabu	.40
90	Antone Williamson	.10
91	Denny Neagle	.10
92	Kevin Orie	.10
93	Reggie Sanders	.10
94	Brady Anderson	.10
95	Andy Benes	.10
96	John Valentin	.10
97	Bobby Bonilla	.10
98	Walt Weiss	.10
99	Robin Jennings	.10
100	Marty Cordova	.10
101	Brad Ausmus	.10
102	Brian Rose	.10
103	Calvin Maduro	.10
104	Raul Casanova	.10
105	Jeff King	.10
106	Sandy Alomar	.20
107	Tim Naehring	.10
108	Mike Cameron	.10
109	Omar Vizquel	.10
110	Brad Radke	.10
111	Jeff Fassero	.10
112	Deivi Cruz	.10
113	Dave Hollins	.10
114	Dean Palmer	.10
115	Esteban Loaiza	.10
116	Brian Giles	.10
117	Steve Finley	.10
118	Jose Canseco	.25
119	Al Martin	.10
120	Eric Young	.10
121	Curtis Goodwin	.10
122	Ellis Burks	.10
123	Mike Hampton	.10
124	Lou Collier	.10
125	John Olerud	.20
126	Ramon Martinez	.10
127	Todd Dunwoody	.10
128	Jermaine Allensworth	.10
129	Eduardo Perez	.10
130	Dante Bichette	.25
131	Edgar Renteria	.10
132	Bob Abreu	.10
133	Rondell White	.20
134	Michael Coleman	.10
135	Jason Giambi	.10
136	Brant Brown	.10
137	Michael Tucker	.10
138	Dave Nilsson	.10
139	Benito Santiago	.10
140	Ray Durham	.10
141	Jeff Kent	.10
142	Matt Stairs	.10
143	Kevin Young	.10
144	Eric Davis	.10
145	John Wetteland	.10
146	Esteban Yan	.10
147	Wilton Guerrero	.10
148	Moises Alou	.20
149	Edgardo Alfonzo	.15
150	Andy Ashby	.10
151	Todd Walker	.20
152	Jermaine Dye	.10
153	Brian Hunter	.10
154	Shawn Estes	.10
155	Bernard Gilkey	.10
156	Tony Womack	.10
157	John Smoltz	.20
158	Delino DeShields	.10
159	Jacob Cruz	.10
160	Javier Valentin	.10
161	Chris Hoiles	.10
162	Garret Anderson	.10
163	Dan Wilson	.10
164	Paul O'Neill	.20
165	Matt Williams	.25
166	Travis Fryman	.10
167	Javier Lopez	.10
168	Ray Lankford	.10
169	Bobby Estalella	.10
170	Henry Rodriguez	.10
171	Quinton McCracken	.10
172	Jaret Wright	.50
173	Darryl Kile	.10
174	Wade Boggs	.30
175	Orel Hershiser	.10
176	B.J. Surhoff	.10
177	Fernando Tatis	.20
178	Carlos Delgado	.25
179	Jorge Fabregas	.10
180	Tony Saunders	.10
181	Devon White	.10
182	Dmitri Young	.10
183	Ryan McGuire	.10
184	Mark Bellhorn	.10
185	Joe Carter	.15
186	Kevin Stocker	.10
187	Mike Lansing	.10
188	Jason Dickson	.10
189	Charles Johnson	.10
190	Will Clark	.25
191	Shannon Stewart	.10
192	Johnny Damon	.10
193	Todd Greene	.10
194	Carlos Baerga	.10
195	David Cone	.20
196	Pokey Reese	.10
197	Livan Hernandez	.10
198	Tom Glavine	.20
199	Geronimo Berroa	.10
200	Darryl Hamilton	.10
201	Terry Steinbach	.10
202	Robb Nen	.10
203	Ron Gant	.10
204	Rafael Palmeiro	.25
205	Rickey Henderson	.20
206	Justin Thompson	.10
207	Jeff Suppan	.10
208	Kevin Brown	.20
209	Jimmy Key	.10
210	Brian Jordan	.10
211	Aaron Sele	.10
212	Fred McGriff	.20
213	Jay Bell	.10
214	Andres Galarraga	.20
215	Mark Grace	.25
216	Brett Tomko	.10
217	Francisco Cordova	.10
218	Rusty Greer	.10
219	Bubba Trammell	.10
220	Derrek Lee	.10
221	Brian Anderson	.10
222	Mark Grudzielanek	.10
223	Marquis Grissom	.10
224	Gary DiSarcina	.10
225	Jim Leyritz	.10
226	Jeffrey Hammonds	.10
227	Karim Garcia	.15
228	Chan Ho Park	.30
229	Brooks Kieschnick	.10
230	Trey Beamon	.10
231	Kevin Appier	.10
232	Wally Joyner	.10
233	Richie Sexson	.10

234	*Frank Catalanotto*	.20
235	Rafael Medina	.10
236	Travis Lee	.60
237	Eli Marrero	.10
238	Carl Pavano	.20
239	Enrique Wilson	.10
240	Richard Hidalgo	.10
241	Todd Helton	.50
242	Ben Grieve	.75
243	Mario Valdez	.10
244	*Magglio Ordonez*	.75
245	Juan Encarnacion	.10
246	Russell Branyan	.10
247	Sean Casey	.25
248	Abraham Nunez	.10
249	Brad Fullmer	.25
250	Paul Konerko	.25
251	Miguel Tejada	.30
252	*Mike Lowell*	.30
253	Ken Griffey Jr. (Spring Training)	1.00
254	Frank Thomas (Spring Training)	.60
255	Alex Rodriguez (Spring Training)	.75
256	Jose Cruz Jr. (Spring Training)	.10
257	Jeff Bagwell (Spring Training)	.30
258	Chipper Jones (Spring Training)	.60
259	Mo Vaughn (Spring Training)	.20
260	Nomar Garciaparra (Spring Training)	.60
261	Jim Thome (Spring Training)	.20
262	Derek Jeter (Spring Training)	.60
263	Mike Piazza (Spring Training)	.60
264	Tony Gwynn (Spring Training)	.50
265	Scott Rolen (Spring Training)	.30
266	Andruw Jones (Spring Training)	.25
267	Cal Ripken Jr. (Spring Training)	.75
268	Checklist (Ken Griffey Jr.)	.75
269	Checklist (Cal Ripken Jr.)	.60
270	Checklist (Jose Cruz Jr.)	.10

1998 Score Rookie & Traded Artist's Proofs

This partial parallel reprints 160 (the same cards as the Showcase Series) of the 270 cards in Score Rookie & Traded. The cards are printed on a foil surface and feature an Artist's Proof logo on front. The cards were renumbered within the 160-card set and inserted one per 35 packs.

	MT
Complete Set (160):	600.00
Common Player:	1.50
Artist's Proof Stars:	10X

(See 1998 Score Rookie & Traded Showcase for checklist and base card values.)

1998 Score Rookie & Traded Showcase Series

The Showcase Series is a partial parallel reprint of 160 of the 270 cards in Rookie & Traded. The cards are printed on a silver-foil surface, marked on the back and renumbered (with an "RTPP" prefix) within the 160-card set. Showcase parallels were inserted one per seven packs.

		MT
Complete Set (160):		125.00
Common Player:		.75
1	Tony Clark	1.50
2	Juan Gonzalez	4.50
3	Frank Thomas	5.00
4	Greg Maddux	6.00
5	Barry Larkin	1.00
6	Derek Jeter	6.00
7	Randy Johnson	1.50
8	Roger Clemens	3.50
9	Tony Gwynn	4.50
10	Barry Bonds	2.50
11	Jim Edmonds	.75
12	Bernie Williams	1.50
13	Ken Griffey Jr.	9.00
14	Tim Salmon	1.00
15	Mo Vaughn	1.50
16	David Justice	1.50
17	Jose Cruz Jr.	.75
18	Andruw Jones	2.50
19	Sammy Sosa	5.00
20	Jeff Bagwell	3.50
21	Scott Rolen	3.00
22	Darin Erstad	2.00
23	Andy Pettitte	1.00
24	Mike Mussina	1.50
25	Mark McGwire	9.00
26	Hideo Nomo	1.50
27	Chipper Jones	6.00
28	Cal Ripken Jr.	7.50
29	Chuck Knoblauch	1.50
30	Alex Rodriguez	7.50
31	Jim Thome	1.50
32	Mike Piazza	6.00
33	Ivan Rodriguez	2.50
34	Roberto Alomar	2.00
35	Nomar Garciaparra	6.00
36	Albert Belle	2.00
37	Vladimir Guerrero	2.00
38	Raul Mondesi	1.00
39	Larry Walker	1.50
40	Manny Ramirez	3.00
41	Tino Martinez	1.00
42	Craig Biggio	1.00
43	Jay Buhner	.75
44	Kenny Lofton	1.00
45	Pedro Martinez	2.00
46	Edgar Martinez	.75
47	Gary Sheffield	.75
48	Jose Guillen	.75
49	Ken Caminiti	1.00
50	Bobby Higginson	1.00
51	Alan Benes	.75
52	Shawn Green	1.50
53	Matt Morris	.75
54	Jason Kendall	1.00
55	Mark Kotsay	.75
56	Bartolo Colon	1.00
57	Damian Jackson	.75
58	David Ortiz	.75
59	J.T. Snow	.75
60	Todd Hundley	.75
61	Neifi Perez	.75
62	Ryan Klesko	1.00
63	Robin Ventura	1.00
64	Pat Hentgen	.75
65	Antone Williamson	.75
66	Kevin Orie	.75
67	Brady Anderson	.75
68	Bobby Bonilla	.75
69	Brian Rose	.75
70	Sandy Alomar Jr.	1.00
71	Mike Cameron	.75
72	Omar Vizquel	.75
73	Steve Finley	.75
74	Jose Canseco	1.50
75	Al Martin	.75
76	Eric Young	.75
77	Ellis Burks	.75
78	Todd Dunwoody	.75
79	Dante Bichette	.75
80	Edgar Renteria	.75
81	Bobby Abreu	.75
82	Rondell White	.75
83	Michael Coleman	.75
84	Jason Giambi	.75
85	Wilton Guerrero	.75
86	Moises Alou	1.00
87	Todd Walker	.75
88	Shawn Estes	.75
89	John Smoltz	1.00
90	Jacob Cruz	.75
91	Javier Valentin	.75
92	Garret Anderson	.75
93	Paul O'Neill	1.00
94	Matt Williams	1.50
95	Travis Fryman	.75
96	Javier Lopez	1.00
97	Ray Lankford	.75
98	Bobby Estalella	.75
99	Jaret Wright	1.50
100	Wade Boggs	1.50
101	Fernando Tatis	1.00
102	Carlos Delgado	1.50
103	Joe Carter	.75
104	Jason Dickson	.75
105	Charles Johnson	.75
106	Will Clark	1.50
107	Shannon Stewart	.75
108	Todd Greene	.75
109	Pokey Reese	.75
110	Livan Hernandez	.75
111	Tom Glavine	1.00
112	Rafael Palmeiro	1.25
113	Justin Thompson	.75
114	Jeff Suppan	.75
115	Kevin Brown	1.50
116	Brian Jordan	.75
117	Fred McGriff	1.00
118	Andres Galarraga	.75
119	Mark Grace	1.50
120	Rusty Greer	.75
121	Bubba Trammell	.75
122	Derrek Lee	.75
123	Brian Anderson	.75
124	Karim Garcia	.75
125	Chan Ho Park	.75
126	Richie Sexson	.75
127	Frank Catalanotto	.75
128	Rafael Medina	.75
129	Travis Lee	1.00
130	Eli Marrero	.75
131	Carl Pavano	.75
132	Enrique Wilson	.75
133	Richard Hidalgo	.75
134	Todd Helton	.75
135	Ben Grieve	1.00
136	Mario Valdez	.75
137	Magglio Ordonez	.75
138	Juan Encarnacion	.75
139	Russell Branyan	.75
140	Sean Casey	1.25
141	Abraham Nunez	.75
142	Brad Fullmer	1.00
143	Paul Konerko	1.00
144	Miguel Tejada	1.00
145	Mike Lowell	.75
146	Ken Griffey Jr. (Spring Training)	3.00
147	Frank Thomas (Spring Training)	1.00
148	Alex Rodriguez (Spring Training)	2.00
149	Jose Cruz Jr. (Spring Training)	.75
150	Jeff Bagwell (Spring Training)	1.50
151	Chipper Jones (Spring Training)	2.00
152	Mo Vaughn (Spring Training)	1.00
153	Nomar Garciaparra (Spring Training)	1.50
154	Jim Thome (Spring Training)	.75
155	Derek Jeter (Spring Training)	2.00
156	Mike Piazza (Spring Training)	2.00
157	Tony Gwynn (Spring Training)	2.00
158	Scott Rolen (Spring Training)	1.50
159	Andruw Jones (Spring Training)	1.00
160	Cal Ripken Jr. (Spring Training)	2.50

1998 Score Rookie & Traded All-Star Epix

All-Star Epix is a 12-card insert seeded 1:61. The cards honor the top All-Star Game moments of 12 star players. The dot matrix hologram cards were printed in orange, purple and emerald versions.

		MT
Complete Set (12):		475.00
Common Player:		15.00
Purples:		2X
Emeralds:		4X
1	Ken Griffey Jr.	100.00
2	Juan Gonzalez	25.00
3	Jeff Bagwell	30.00
4	Ivan Rodriguez	25.00
5	Nomar Garciaparra	60.00
6	Ryne Sandberg	25.00
7	Frank Thomas	50.00
8	Derek Jeter	60.00
9	Tony Gwynn	50.00
10	Albert Belle	25.00
11	Scott Rolen	30.00
12	Barry Larkin	15.00

1998 Score Rookie & Traded Complete Players

Complete Players is a 30-card insert seeded one per 11 packs. The set highlights 10 players who can do it all on the field. Each player has three cards showcasing one of their talents. The cards feature holographic foil stamping. Values shown are for each card (A, B and C) in the player set trios.

		MT
Complete Set (30):		90.00
Common Player:		1.50
Inserted 1:11		
1	Ken Griffey Jr.	9.00
2	Larry Walker	1.50
3	Alex Rodriguez	7.00
4	Jose Cruz	1.50
5	Jeff Bagwell	3.00
6	Greg Maddux	5.00
7	Ivan Rodriguez	2.50
8	Roger Clemens	3.00
9	Chipper Jones	5.00
10	Hideo Nomo	1.50

1998 Score Rookie & Traded Star Gazing

Printed on micro-etched foil board, Star Gazing features 20 top players and was seeded 1:35.

		MT
Complete Set (20):		150.00
Common Player:		3.00
Inserted 1:35		
1	Ken Griffey Jr.	20.00
2	Frank Thomas	10.00
3	Chipper Jones	12.00
4	Mark McGwire	20.00
5	Cal Ripken Jr.	15.00
6	Mike Piazza	12.00
7	Nomar Garciaparra	12.00
8	Derek Jeter	15.00
9	Juan Gonzalez	5.00
10	Vladimir Guerrero	8.00
11	Alex Rodriguez	15.00
12	Tony Gwynn	10.00
13	Andruw Jones	5.00
14	Scott Rolen	7.00
15	Jose Cruz	3.00
16	Mo Vaughn	3.00
17	Bernie Williams	4.00
18	Greg Maddux	12.00
19	Tony Clark	3.00
20	Ben Grieve	6.00

1993 Select Promos

Zeroes in the stats lines on the back of the card distinguish the promo cards for Score's premiere issue of its Select brand name. The promo cards were distributed to introduce dealers and collectors to the new mid-range set.

		MT
Complete Set (5):		40.00
Common Player:		2.50
22	Robin Yount	15.00
24	Don Mattingly	20.00
26	Sandy Alomar Jr.	5.00
41	Gary Sheffield	10.00
75	John Smiley	2.50

1993 Select

This 400-card set from Score is designed for the mid-priced card market. The card fronts feature green borders on two sides of the card with the photo filling the remaining portion of the card front. The backs feature an additional photo, player information and statistics. Cards numbered 271-360 are devoted to rookies and draft picks.

		MT
Complete Set (405):		20.00
Common Player:		.05
Pack (15):		1.25
Wax Box (36):		30.00
1	Barry Bonds	.50
2	Ken Griffey, Jr.	1.50
3	Will Clark	.25
4	Kirby Puckett	.50
5	Tony Gwynn	.75
6	Frank Thomas	.75
7	Tom Glavine	.20
8	Roberto Alomar	.40
9	Andre Dawson	.15
10	Ron Darling	.05
11	Bobby Bonilla	.10
12	Danny Tartabull	.05
13	Darren Daulton	.05
14	Roger Clemens	.75
15	Ozzie Smith	.50
16	Mark McGwire	2.00
17	Terry Pendleton	.05
18	Cal Ripken, Jr.	1.50
19	Fred McGriff	.20
20	Cecil Fielder	.10
21	Darryl Strawberry	.10
22	Robin Yount	.40
23	Barry Larkin	.20
24	Don Mattingly	.75
25	Craig Biggio	.15
26	Sandy Alomar Jr.	.15
27	Larry Walker	.30
28	Junior Felix	.05
29	Eddie Murray	.15
30	Robin Ventura	.15
31	Greg Maddux	1.00
32	Dave Winfield	.15
33	John Kruk	.05
34	Wally Joyner	.05
35	Andy Van Slyke	.05
36	Chuck Knoblauch	.20
37	Tom Pagnozzi	.05
38	Dennis Eckersley	.05
39	Dave Justice	.25
40	Juan Gonzalez	.50
41	Gary Sheffield	.35
42	Paul Molitor	.40
43	Delino DeShields	.05
44	Travis Fryman	.10
45	Hal Morris	.05
46	Gregg Olson	.05
47	Ken Caminiti	.15
48	Wade Boggs	.25
49	Orel Hershiser	.10
50	Albert Belle	.30
51	Bill Swift	.05
52	Mark Langston	.05
53	Joe Girardi	.05
54	Keith Miller	.05
55	Gary Carter	.10
56	Brady Anderson	.10
57	Dwight Gooden	.10
58	Julio Franco	.05
59	Len Dykstra	.05
60	Mickey Tettleton	.05
61	Randy Tomlin	.05
62	B.J. Surhoff	.05
63	Todd Zeile	.05
64	Roberto Kelly	.05
65	Rob Dibble	.05
66	Leo Gomez	.05
67	Doug Jones	.05
68	Ellis Burks	.10
69	Mike Scioscia	.05
70	Charles Nagy	.10
71	Cory Snyder	.05
72	Devon White	.10
73	Mark Grace	.20
74	Luis Polonia	.05
75	John Smiley	.05
76	Carlton Fisk	.15
77	Luis Sojo	.05
78	George Brett	.75
79	Mitch Williams	.05
80	Kent Hrbek	.05
81	Jay Bell	.05
82	Edgar Martinez	.05
83	Lee Smith	.05
84	Deion Sanders	.15
85	Bill Gullickson	.05
86	Paul O'Neill	.15
87	Kevin Seitzer	.05
88	Steve Finley	.10
89	Mel Hall	.05
90	Nolan Ryan	2.00
91	Eric Davis	.10
92	Mike Mussina	.40
93	Tony Fernandez	.05
94	Frank Viola	.05
95	Matt Williams	.25
96	Joe Carter	.10
97	Ryne Sandberg	.50
98	Jim Abbott	.05
99	Marquis Grissom	.10
100	George Bell	.05
101	Howard Johnson	.05
102	Kevin Appier	.05
103	Dale Murphy	.10
104	Shane Mack	.05
105	Jose Lind	.05
106	Rickey Henderson	.20
107	Bob Tewksbury	.05
108	Kevin Mitchell	.05
109	Steve Avery	.05
110	Candy Maldonado	.05
111	Bip Roberts	.05
112	Lou Whitaker	.05
113	Jeff Bagwell	.50
114	Dante Bichette	.15
115	Brett Butler	.05
116	Melido Perez	.05
117	Andy Benes	.10
118	Randy Johnson	.50
119	Willie McGee	.05
120	Jody Reed	.05
121	Shawon Dunston	.05
122	Carlos Baerga	.10
123	Bret Saberhagen	.10
124	John Olerud	.15
125	Ivan Calderon	.05
126	Bryan Harvey	.05
127	Terry Mulholland	.05
128	Ozzie Guillen	.05
129	Steve Buechele	.05
130	Kevin Tapani	.05
131	Felix Jose	.05
132	Terry Steinbach	.05
133	Ron Gant	.10
134	Harold Reynolds	.05
135	Chris Sabo	.05
136	Ivan Rodriguez	.50
137	Eric Anthony	.05
138	Mike Henneman	.05
139	Robby Thompson	.05
140	Scott Fletcher	.05
141	Bruce Hurst	.05
142	Kevin Maas	.05
143	Tom Candiotti	.05
144	Chris Hoiles	.05
145	Mike Morgan	.05
146	Mark Whiten	.05
147	Dennis Martinez	.05
148	Tony Pena	.05
149	Dave Magadan	.05
150	Mark Lewis	.05
151	Mariano Duncan	.05
152	Gregg Jefferies	.05
153	Doug Drabek	.05
154	Brian Harper	.05
155	Ray Lankford	.10
156	Carney Lansford	.05
157	Mike Sharperson	.05
158	Jack Morris	.05
159	Otis Nixon	.05
160	Steve Sax	.05
161	Mark Lemke	.05
162	Rafael Palmeiro	.25
163	Jose Rijo	.05
164	Omar Vizquel	.05
165	Sammy Sosa	1.25
166	Milt Cuyler	.05
167	John Franco	.05
168	Darryl Hamilton	.05
169	Ken Hill	.05
170	Mike Devereaux	.05
171	Don Slaught	.05
172	Steve Farr	.05
173	Bernard Gilkey	.10
174	Mike Fetters	.05
175	Vince Coleman	.05
176	Kevin McReynolds	.05
177	John Smoltz	.10
178	Greg Gagne	.05
179	Greg Swindell	.05
180	Juan Guzman	.05
181	Kal Daniels	.05
182	Rick Sutcliffe	.05
183	Orlando Merced	.05
184	Bill Wegman	.05
185	Mark Gardner	.05
186	Rob Deer	.05
187	Dave Hollins	.05
188	Jack Clark	.05
189	Brian Hunter	.05
190	Tim Wallach	.05
191	Tim Belcher	.05
192	Walt Weiss	.05
193	Kurt Stillwell	.05
194	Charlie Hayes	.05
195	Willie Randolph	.05
196	Jack McDowell	.05
197	Jose Offerman	.05
198	Chuck Finley	.05
199	Darrin Jackson	.05
200	Kelly Gruber	.05
201	John Wetteland	.05
202	Jay Buhner	.10
203	Mike LaValliere	.05
204	Kevin Brown	.10
205	Luis Gonzalez	.10
206	Rick Aguilera	.05
207	Norm Charlton	.05
208	Mike Bordick	.05
209	Charlie Leibrandt	.05
210	Tom Brunansky	.05
211	Tom Henke	.05
212	Randy Milligan	.05
213	Ramon Martinez	.10
214	Mo Vaughn	.30
215	Randy Myers	.05
216	Greg Hibbard	.05
217	Wes Chamberlain	.05
218	Tony Phillips	.05
219	Pete Harnisch	.05
220	Mike Gallego	.05
221	Bud Black	.05
222	Greg Vaughn	.10
223	Milt Thompson	.05
224	Ben McDonald	.05
225	Billy Hatcher	.05
226	Paul Sorrento	.05
227	Mark Gubicza	.05
228	Mike Greenwell	.05
229	Curt Schilling	.10
230	Alan Trammell	.10
231	Zane Smith	.05
232	Bobby Thigpen	.05
233	Greg Olson	.05
234	Joe Orsulak	.05
235	Joe Oliver	.05
236	Tim Raines	.10
237	Juan Samuel	.05
238	Chili Davis	.05
239	Spike Owen	.05
240	Dave Stewart	.05

241	Jim Eisenreich	.05
242	Phil Plantier	.05
243	Sid Fernandez	.05
244	Dan Gladden	.05
245	Mickey Morandini	.05
246	Tino Martinez	.15
247	Kirt Manwaring	.05
248	Dean Palmer	.05
249	Tom Browning	.05
250	Brian McRae	.05
251	Scott Leius	.05
252	Bert Blyleven	.05
253	Scott Erickson	.05
254	Bob Welch	.05
255	Pat Kelly	.05
256	Felix Fermin	.05
257	Harold Baines	.10
258	Duane Ward	.05
259	Bill Spiers	.05
260	Jaime Navarro	.05
261	Scott Sanderson	.05
262	Gary Gaetti	.05
263	Bob Ojeda	.05
264	Jeff Montgomery	.05
265	Scott Bankhead	.05
266	Lance Johnson	.05
267	Rafael Belliard	.05
268	Kevin Reimer	.05
269	Benito Santiago	.05
270	Mike Moore	.05
271	Dave Fleming	.05
272	Moises Alou	.15
273	Pat Listach	.05
274	Reggie Sanders	.10
275	Kenny Lofton	.25
276	Donovan Osborne	.05
277	Rusty Meacham	.05
278	Eric Karros	.15
279	Andy Stankiewicz	.05
280	Brian Jordan	.10
281	Gary DiSarcina	.05
282	Mark Wohlers	.05
283	Dave Nilsson	.05
284	Anthony Young	.05
285	Jim Bullinger	.05
286	Derek Bell	.10
287	Brian Williams	.10
288	Julio Valera	.05
289	Dan Walters	.05
290	Chad Curtis	.05
291	Michael Tucker	.05
292	Bob Zupcic	.05
293	Todd Hundley	.10
294	Jeff Tackett	.05
295	Greg Colbrunn	.05
296	Cal Eldred	.05
297	Chris Roberts	.05
298	John Doherty	.05
299	Denny Neagle	.05
300	Arthur Rhodes	.05
301	Mark Clark	.05
302	Scott Cooper	.05
303	*Jamie Arnold*	.10
304	Jim Thome	.25
305	Frank Seminara	.05
306	Kurt Knudsen	.05
307	Tim Wakefield	.05
308	John Jaha	.05
309	Pat Hentgen	.05
310	B.J. Wallace	.05
311	Roberto Hernandez	.05
312	Hipolito Pichardo	.05
313	Eric Fox	.05
314	Willie Banks	.05
315	Sam Millitello	.05
316	Vince Horsman	.05
317	Carlos Hernandez	.05
318	Jeff Kent	.15
319	Mike Perez	.05
320	Scott Livingstone	.05
321	Jeff Conine	.10
322	James Austin	.05
323	John Vander Wal	.05
324	Pat Mahomes	.05
325	Pedro Astacio	.10
326	Bret Boone	.10
327	Matt Stairs	.10
328	Damion Easley	.10
329	Ben Rivera	.05
330	Reggie Jefferson	.10
331	Luis Mercedes	.05
332	Kyle Abbott	.10
333	Eddie Taubensee	.05
334	Tim McIntosh	.05
335	Phil Clark	.05
336	Wil Cordero	.10
337	Russ Springer	.05
338	Craig Colbert	.05
339	Tim Salmon	.30
340	Braulio Castillo	.05
341	Donald Harris	.05
342	Eric Young	.10
343	Bob Wickman	.05
344	John Valentin	.10
345	Dan Wilson	.05
346	Steve Hosey	.10
347	Mike Piazza	1.25
348	Willie Greene	.10
349	Tom Goodwin	.05
350	Eric Hillman	.05
351	*Steve Reed*	.10
352	*Dan Serafini*	.15
353	*Todd Steverson*	.15
354	Benji Grigsby	.05
355	*Shannon Stewart*	.75
356	Sean Lowe	.10
357	Derek Wallace	.10
358	Rick Helling	.05
359	*Jason Kendall*	2.00
360	*Derek Jeter*	18.00
361	David Cone	.15
362	Jeff Reardon	.05
363	Bobby Witt	.05
364	Jose Canseco	.30
365	Jeff Russell	.05
366	Ruben Sierra	.05
367	Alan Mills	.05
368	Matt Nokes	.05
369	Pat Borders	.05
370	Pedro Munoz	.05
371	Danny Jackson	.05
372	Geronimo Pena	.05
373	Craig Lefferts	.05
374	Joe Grahe	.05
375	Roger McDowell	.05
376	Jimmy Key	.05
377	Steve Olin	.05
378	Glenn Davis	.05
379	Rene Gonzales	.05
380	Manuel Lee	.05
381	Ron Karkovice	.05
382	Sid Bream	.05
383	Gerald Williams	.05
384	Lenny Harris	.05
385	*J.T. Snow*	.75
386	Dave Stieb	.05
387	Kirk McCaskill	.05
388	Lance Parrish	.05
389	Craig Greback	.05
390	Rick Wilkins	.05
391	Manny Alexander	.05
392	Mike Schooler	.05
393	Bernie Williams	.40
394	Kevin Koslofski	.05
395	Willie Wilson	.05
396	Jeff Parrett	.05
397	Mike Harkey	.05
398	Frank Tanana	.05
399	Doug Henry	.05
400	Royce Clayton	.05
401	Eric Wedge	.05
402	Derrick May	.05
403	Carlos Garcia	.05
404	Henry Rodriguez	.10
405	Ryan Klesko	.15

1993 Select Aces

Cards from this set feature 24 of the top pitchers from 1992 and were included one per every 27-card Super Pack. The fronts have a picture of the player in action against an Ace card background. Backs have text and a portrait in the middle of a card suit for an Ace.

		MT
Complete Set (24):		50.00
Common Player:		1.50
1	Roger Clemens	12.50
2	Tom Glavine	4.00
3	Jack McDowell	1.50
4	Greg Maddux	15.00
5	Jack Morris	1.50
6	Dennis Martinez	1.50
7	Kevin Brown	4.00
8	Dwight Gooden	2.00
9	Kevin Appier	1.50
10	Mike Morgan	1.50
11	Juan Guzman	1.50
12	Charles Nagy	2.00
13	John Smiley	1.50
14	Ken Hill	1.50
15	Bob Tewksbury	1.50
16	Doug Drabek	1.50
17	John Smoltz	4.00
18	Greg Swindell	1.50
19	Bruce Hurst	1.50
20	Mike Mussina	8.00
21	Cal Eldred	1.50
22	Melido Perez	1.50
23	Dave Fleming	1.50
24	Kevin Tapani	1.50

1993 Select Rookies

Top newcomers in 1992 are featured in this 21-card insert set. Cards were randomly inserted in 15-card hobby packs. The fronts, printed on metallic foil, have a Score Select Rookies logo on the front. The backs have text and a player portrait.

		MT
Complete Set (21):		35.00
Common Player:		1.00
1	Pat Listach	1.00
2	Moises Alou	3.00
3	Reggie Sanders	2.00
4	Kenny Lofton	8.00
5	Eric Karros	2.00
6	Brian Williams	1.00
7	Donovan Osborne	1.00
8	Sam Militello	1.00
9	Chad Curtis	1.50
10	Bob Zupcic	1.00
11	Tim Salmon	8.00
12	Jeff Conine	2.50
13	Pedro Astacio	1.50
14	Arthur Rhodes	1.00
15	Cal Eldred	1.00
16	Tim Wakefield	1.00
17	Andy Stankiewicz	1.00
18	Wil Cordero	1.50
19	Todd Hundley	4.00
20	Dave Fleming	1.00
21	Bret Boone	1.50

1993 Select Stars

The top 24 players from 1992 are featured in this insert set. Cards were randomly inserted in 15-card retail packs. Fronts are printed on metallic foil.

		MT
Complete Set (24):		75.00
Common Player:		1.00
Minor Stars:		2.00
1	Fred McGriff	1.50
2	Ryne Sandberg	5.00
3	Ozzie Smith	5.00
4	Gary Sheffield	2.00
5	Darren Daulton	1.00
6	Andy Van Slyke	1.00
7	Barry Bonds	6.00
8	Tony Gwynn	10.00
9	Greg Maddux	12.50
10	Tom Glavine	1.50
11	John Franco	1.00
12	Lee Smith	1.00
13	Cecil Fielder	1.00
14	Roberto Alomar	3.50
15	Cal Ripken, Jr.	15.00
16	Edgar Martinez	1.00
17	Ivan Rodriguez	4.00
18	Kirby Puckett	9.00
19	Ken Griffey, Jr.	20.00
20	Joe Carter	1.00
21	Roger Clemens	9.00
22	Dave Fleming	1.00
22s	Dave Fleming (blank-back sample card)	5.00
23	Paul Molitor	4.50
24	Dennis Eckersley	1.00

1993 Select Stat Leaders

This 90-card set features 1992 American League and National League leaders in various statistical categories.

Each card front indicates the league and the category in which the player finished at or near the top. The backs have a list of the leaders; the pictured player's name is in larger type size. Cards were inserted one per foil pack.

		MT
Complete Set (90):		10.00
Common Player:		.10
1	Edgar Martinez	.10
2	Kirby Puckett	.50
3	Frank Thomas	.50
4	Gary Sheffield	.20
5	Andy Van Slyke	.10
6	John Kruk	.10
7	Kirby Puckett	.50
8	Carlos Baerga	.10
9	Paul Molitor	.25
10	Andy Van Slyke, Terry Pendleton	.10
11	Ryne Sandberg	.40
12	Mark Grace	.20
13	Frank Thomas	.50
14	Don Mattingly	.50
15	Ken Griffey, Jr.	1.00
16	Andy Van Slyke	.10
17	Mariano Duncan, Jerald Clark, Ray Lankford	.10
18	Marquis Grissom, Terry Pendleton	.10
19	Lance Johnson	.10
20	Mike Devereaux	.10
21	Brady Anderson	.15
22	Deion Sanders	.20
23	Steve Finley	.10
24	Andy Van Slyke	.10
25	Juan Gonzalez	.25
26	Mark McGwire	.75
27	Cecil Fielder	.10
28	Fred McGriff	.20
29	Barry Bonds	.40
30	Gary Sheffield	.20
31	Cecil Fielder	.10
32	Joe Carter	.10
33	Frank Thomas	.50
34	Darren Daulton	.10
35	Terry Pendleton	.10
36	Fred McGriff	.20
37	Tony Phillips	.10
38	Frank Thomas	.50
39	Roberto Alomar	.25
40	Barry Bonds	.40
41	Dave Hollins	.10
42	Andy Van Slyke	.10
43	Mark McGwire	.75
44	Edgar Martinez	.10
45	Frank Thomas	.50
46	Barry Bonds	.40
47	Gary Sheffield	.20
48	Fred McGriff	.20
49	Frank Thomas	.50
50	Danny Tartabull	.10
51	Roberto Alomar	.25
52	Barry Bonds	.40
53	John Kruk	.10
54	Brett Butler	.10
55	Kenny Lofton	.30
56	Pat Listach	.10
57	Brady Anderson	.15
58	Marquis Grissom	.15
59	Delino DeShields	.10
60	Steve Finley, Bip Roberts	.10
61	Jack McDowell	.10
62	Kevin Brown	.15
63	Melido Perez	.10
64	Terry Mulholland	.10
65	Curt Schilling	.15
66	John Smoltz, Doug Drabek, Greg Maddux	.35
67	Dennis Eckersley	.10
68	Rick Aguilera	.10
69	Jeff Montgomery	.10
70	Lee Smith	.10
71	Randy Myers	.10
72	John Wetteland	.10
73	Randy Johnson	.25
74	Melido Perez	.10
75	Roger Clemens	.40
76	John Smoltz	.15
77	David Cone	.15
78	Greg Maddux	.60
79	Roger Clemens	.40
80	Kevin Appier	.10
81	Mike Mussina	.30
82	Bill Swift	.10
83	Bob Tewksbury	.10
84	Greg Maddux	.60
85	Kevin Brown	.15
86	Jack McDowell	.10
87	Roger Clemens	.40
88	Tom Glavine	.15
89	Ken Hill, Bob Tewksbury	.10
90	Dennis Martinez, Mike Morgan	.10

1993 Select Triple Crown

This three-card set commemorates the Triple Crown seasons of Hall of Famers Mickey Mantle, Frank Robinson and Carl Yastrzemski. Cards were randomly inserted in 15-card hobby packs. Card fronts have a green metallic-look textured border, with the player's name at top in gold, and "Triple Crown" in gold at bottom. There are other silver and green highlights around the photo, which feature the player set against a metallized background. Dark green backs have a player photo and information on his Triple Crown season.

		MT
Complete Set (3):		60.00
Common Player:		12.50
1	Mickey Mantle	45.00
2	Frank Robinson	12.50
3	Carl Yastrzemski	12.50

1993 Select Rookie/Traded

Production of this 150-card set was limited to 1,950 numbered cases. Several future Hall of Famers and six dozen top rookies are featured in the set. Cards were available in packs rather than collated sets and include randomly inserted FX cards, which feature Nolan Ryan (two per 24-box case), Tim Salmon and Mike Piazza (one per 576 packs) and All-Star Rookie Team members (one per 58 packs).

		MT
Complete Set (150):		15.00
Common Player:		.15
Pack (12):		2.50
Wax Box (24):		45.00
1	Rickey Henderson	.30
2	Rob Deer	.15
3	Tim Belcher	.15
4	Gary Sheffield	.40
5	Fred McGriff	.30
6	Mark Whiten	.15
7	Jeff Russell	.15
8	Harold Baines	.15
9	Dave Winfield	.30
10	Ellis Burks	.15
11	Andre Dawson	.20
12	Gregg Jefferies	.15
13	Jimmy Key	.15
14	Harold Reynolds	.15
15	Tom Henke	.15
16	Paul Molitor	.75
17	Wade Boggs	.35
18	David Cone	.30
19	Tony Fernandez	.15
20	Roberto Kelly	.15
21	Paul O'Neill	.30
22	Jose Lind	.15
23	Barry Bonds	2.50
24	Dave Stewart	.15
25	Randy Myers	.15
26	Benito Santiago	.15
27	Tim Wallach	.15
28	Greg Gagne	.15
29	Kevin Mitchell	.15
30	Jim Abbott	.15
31	Lee Smith	.15
32	*Bobby Munoz*	.20
33	*Mo Sanford*	.25
34	John Roper	.15
35	*David Hulse*	.20
36	Pedro Martinez	2.00
37	*Chuck Carr*	.15
38	*Armando Reynoso*	.25
39	Ryan Thompson	.25
40	*Carlos Garcia*	.20
41	Matt Whiteside	.15
42	Benji Gil	.15
43	*Rodney Bolton*	.15
44	J.T. Snow	.50
45	David McCarty	.15
46	*Paul Quantrill*	.15
47	Al Martin	.15
48	Lance Painter	.15
49	*Lou Frazier*	.15
50	Eduardo Perez	.15
51	Kevin Young	.15
52	Mike Trombley	.15
53	*Sterling Hitchcock*	.35
54	*Tim Bogar*	.25
55	*Hilly Hathaway*	.25
56	*Wayne Kirby*	.15
57	*Craig Paquette*	.15
58	Bret Boone	.25
59	*Greg McMichael*	.20
60	*Mike Lansing*	.35
61	Brent Gates	.25
62	Rene Arocha	.20
63	Ricky Gutierrez	.25
64	*Kevin Rogers*	.20
65	*Ken Ryan*	.25
66	Phil Hiatt	.15
67	*Pat Meares*	.25
68	Troy Neel	.20
69	Steve Cooke	.15
70	*Sherman Obando*	.15
71	*Blas Minor*	.15
72	*Angel Miranda*	.15
73	*Tom Kramer*	.20
74	*Chip Hale*	.20
75	*Brad Pennington*	.25
76	*Graeme Lloyd*	.15
77	*Darrell Whitmore*	.20
78	David Nied	.15
79	Todd Van Poppel	.15
80	*Chris Gomez*	.25
81	Jason Bere	.15
82	Jeffrey Hammonds	.25
83	*Brad Ausmus*	.20
84	Kevin Stocker	.15
85	Jeromy Burnitz	.25
86	Aaron Sele	.25
87	*Roberto Mejia*	.15
88	*Kirk Rueter*	.25
89	*Kevin Roberson*	.25
90	*Allen Watson*	.35
91	Charlie Leibrandt	.15
92	Eric Davis	.15
93	Jody Reed	.15
94	Danny Jackson	.15
95	Gary Gaetti	.15
96	Norm Charlton	.15
97	Doug Drabek	.15
98	Scott Fletcher	.15
99	Greg Swindell	.15
100	John Smiley	.15
101	Kevin Reimer	.15
102	Andres Galarraga	.20
103	Greg Hibbard	.15
104	Chris Hammond	.15
105	Darnell Coles	.15
106	Mike Felder	.15
107	Jose Guzman	.15
108	Chris Bosio	.15
109	Spike Owen	.15
110	Felix Jose	.15
111	Cory Snyder	.15
112	Craig Lefferts	.15
113	David Wells	.20
114	Pete Incaviglia	.15
115	Mike Pagliarulo	.15
116	Dave Magadan	.15
117	Charlie Hough	.15
118	Ivan Calderon	.15
119	Manuel Lee	.15
120	Bob Patterson	.15
121	Bob Ojeda	.15
122	Scott Bankhead	.15
123	Greg Maddux	4.00
124	Chili Davis	.15
125	Milt Thompson	.15
126	Dave Martinez	.15
127	Frank Tanana	.15
128	Phil Plantier	.15
129	Juan Samuel	.15
130	Eric Young	.25
131	Joe Orsulak	.15
132	Derek Bell	.15
133	Darrin Jackson	.15
134	Tom Brunansky	.15
135	Jeff Reardon	.15
136	*Kevin Higgins*	.15
137	*Joel Johnston*	.15
138	*Rick Trlicek*	.15
139	*Richie Lewis*	.25
140	*Jeff Gardner*	.20
141	*Jack Voigt*	.15
142	*Rod Correia*	.15
143	*Billy Brewer*	.15
144	*Terry Jorgensen*	.15
145	*Rich Amaral*	.15
146	*Sean Berry*	.30
147	*Dan Peltier*	.20
148	*Paul Wagner*	.35
149	*Damon Buford*	.75
150	Wil Cordero	.15

1993 Select Rookie/Traded All-Star Rookies

These cards were randomly inserted into the Score Select Rookie/Traded packs, making them among the scarcest of the year's many "chase" cards. Card fronts feature metallic foil printing. Backs have a few words about the player. Stated odds of finding an All-Star Rookie Team insert card are one per 58 packs.

		MT
Complete Set (10):		100.00
Common Player:		3.00
1	Jeff Conine	5.00
2	Brent Gates	3.00
3	Mike Lansing	5.00
4	Kevin Stocker	4.00
5	Mike Piazza	75.00
6	Jeffrey Hammonds	4.00
7	David Hulse	3.00
8	Tim Salmon	20.00
9	Rene Arocha	3.00
10	Greg McMichael	3.00

1993 Select Rookie/Traded Inserts

Three cards honoring the 1993 Rookies of the Year and retiring superstar Nolan Ryan were issued as random inserts in the Select Rookie/Traded packs. Cards are printed with metallic foil front backgrounds. Stated odds of finding a Piazza or Salmon card are about one per 24-box case; Ryan cards are found on average two per case.

		MT
Complete Set (3):		150.00
Common Player:		25.00
1NR	Nolan Ryan	75.00
1ROY	Tim Salmon	20.00
2ROY	Mike Piazza	75.00

1994 Select Promos

To introduce its 1994 offering to dealers and collectors, Score Select created an eight-card promo set. Cards are identical in format to regular-issue cards with the exception of the word "SAMPLE" overprinted diagonally on front and back. The promos included five of the regular-run cards, a Rookie Prospect card and one each of its Rookie Surge '94 and Crown Contenders insert sets. The promos were cello-packaged with a header card describing the set and chase cards.

		MT
Complete Set (8):		25.00
Common Player:		2.00
3	Paul Molitor	4.00
17	Kirby Puckett	6.00
19	Randy Johnson	4.00
24	John Kruk	2.00
51	Jose Lind	2.00
197	Ryan Klesko (Rookie Prospect)	4.00
1CC	Lenny Dykstra (Crown Contenders)	3.00
1RS	Cliff Floyd (Rookie Surge '94)	5.00
----	Header card	.10

1994 Select

Both series of this premium brand from the Score/Pinnacle lineup offered 210 regular cards for a combined 420 cards, and seven insert sets. The announced press runs for Series I and II was 4,950 20-box cases. Cards have a horizontal format with a color action photo at right and a second action photo at left done in a single team color-coded hue. The player's last name is dropped out of a vertical gold-foil strip between the two photos, with his first name in white at top-center. Backs are vertically oriented with yet another color action photo at center. In a vertical bar at right, matching the color-coding on front and printed over the photo are 1993 and career stats, a "Select Stat," and a few sentences about the player. The appropriate logos and Pinnacle's optical-variable counterfeiting device are at bottom-center. Thirty of the final 33 cards in the first series are a "1994 Rookie Prospect" subset, so noted in a special gold-foil logo on front.

		MT
Complete Set (420):		25.00
Complete Series 1 (210):		15.00
Complete Series 2 (210):		10.00
Common Player:		.10
Series 1 Pack (12):		1.50
Series 1 Wax Box (24):		30.00
Series 2 Pack (12):		1.00
Series 2 Wax Box (24):		20.00
1	Ken Griffey, Jr.	3.00
2	Greg Maddux	1.50
3	Paul Molitor	.60
4	Mike Piazza	2.00
5	Jay Bell	.10
6	Frank Thomas	1.00
7	Barry Larkin	.25
8	Paul O'Neill	.20
9	Darren Daulton	.10
10	Mike Greenwell	.10
11	Chuck Carr	.10
12	Joe Carter	.15
13	Lance Johnson	.10
14	Jeff Blauser	.10
15	Chris Hoiles	.10
16	Rick Wilkins	.10
17	Kirby Puckett	1.00
18	Larry Walker	.40
19	Randy Johnson	.75
20	Bernard Gilkey	.10
21	Devon White	.15
22	Randy Myers	.10
23	Don Mattingly	1.00
24	John Kruk	.10
25	Ozzie Guillen	.10
26	Jeff Conine	.10
27	Mike Macfarlane	.10
28	Dave Hollins	.10
29	Chuck Knoblauch	.15
30	Ozzie Smith	.60
31	Harold Baines	.10
32	Ryne Sandberg	.65
33	Ron Karkovice	.10
34	Terry Pendleton	.10
35	Wally Joyner	.10
36	Mike Mussina	.40
37	Felix Jose	.10
38	Derrick May	.10
39	Scott Cooper	.10
40	Jose Rijo	.10
41	Robin Ventura	.20
42	Charlie Hayes	.10
43	Jimmy Key	.10
44	Eric Karros	.10
45	Ruben Sierra	.10
46	Ryan Thompson	.10
47	Brian McRae	.10
48	Pat Hentgen	.10
49	John Valentin	.10
50	Al Martin	.10
51	Jose Lind	.10
52	Kevin Stocker	.10
53	Mike Gallego	.10
54	Dwight Gooden	.15
55	Brady Anderson	.15
56	Jeff King	.10
57	Mark McGwire	3.00
58	Sammy Sosa	1.50
59	Ryan Bowen	.10
60	Mark Lemke	.10
61	Roger Clemens	1.00
62	Brian Jordan	.10
63	Andres Galarraga	.40
64	Kevin Appier	.10
65	Don Slaught	.10
66	Mike Blowers	.10
67	Wes Chamberlain	.10
68	Troy Neel	.10
69	John Wetteland	.10
70	Joe Girardi	.10
71	Reggie Sanders	.10
72	Edgar Martinez	.10
73	Todd Hundley	.15
74	Pat Borders	.10
75	Roberto Mejia	.10
76	David Cone	.15
77	Tony Gwynn	1.00
78	Jim Abbott	.10
79	Jay Buhner	.10
80	Mark McLemore	.10
81	Wil Cordero	.10
82	Pedro Astacio	.10
83	Bob Tewksbury	.10
84	Dave Winfield	.25
85	Jeff Kent	.10
86	Todd Van Poppel	.10
87	Steve Avery	.10
88	Mike Lansing	.10
89	Len Dykstra	.10
90	Jose Guzman	.10
91	Brian Hunter	.10
92	Tim Raines	.15
93	Andre Dawson	.15
94	Joe Orsulak	.10
95	Ricky Jordan	.10
96	Billy Hatcher	.10
97	Jack McDowell	.10
98	Tom Pagnozzi	.10
99	Darryl Strawberry	.15
100	Mike Stanley	.10
101	Bret Saberhagen	.10
102	Willie Greene	.10
103	Bryan Harvey	.10
104	Tim Bogar	.10
105	Jack Voight	.10
106	Brad Ausmus	.10
107	Ramon Martinez	.10
108	Mike Perez	.10
109	Jeff Montgomery	.10
110	Danny Darwin	.10
111	Wilson Alvarez	.10
112	Kevin Mitchell	.10
113	David Nied	.10
114	Rich Amaral	.10
115	Stan Javier	.10
116	Mo Vaughn	.50
117	Ben McDonald	.10
118	Tom Gordon	.10
119	Carlos Garcia	.10
120	Phil Plantier	.10
121	Mike Morgan	.10
122	Pat Meares	.10
123	Kevin Young	.10
124	Jeff Fassero	.10
125	Gene Harris	.10
126	Bob Welch	.10
127	Walt Weiss	.10
128	Bobby Witt	.10
129	Andy Van Slyke	.10
130	Steve Cooke	.10
131	Mike Devereaux	.10
132	Joey Cora	.10
133	Bret Barberie	.10

No.	Player	Price
134	Orel Hershiser	.10
135	Ed Sprague	.10
136	Shawon Dunston	.10
137	Alex Arias	.10
138	Archi Cianfrocco	.10
139	Tim Wallach	.10
140	Bernie Williams	.50
141	Karl Rhodes	.10
142	Pat Kelly	.10
143	Dave Magadan	.10
144	Kevin Tapani	.10
145	Eric Young	.10
146	Derek Bell	.10
147	Dante Bichette	.25
148	Geronimo Pena	.10
149	Joe Oliver	.10
150	Orestes Destrade	.10
151	Tim Naehring	.10
152	Ray Lankford	.10
153	Phil Clark	.10
154	David McCarty	.10
155	Tommy Greene	.10
156	Wade Boggs	.50
157	Kevin Gross	.10
158	Hal Morris	.10
159	Moises Alou	.15
160	Rick Aguilera	.10
161	Curt Schilling	.15
162	Chip Hale	.10
163	Tino Martinez	.15
164	Mark Whiten	.10
165	Dave Stewart	.10
166	Steve Buechele	.10
167	Bobby Jones	.10
168	Darrin Fletcher	.10
169	John Smiley	.10
170	Cory Snyder	.10
171	Scott Erickson	.10
172	Kirk Rueter	.10
173	Dave Fleming	.10
174	John Smoltz	.10
175	Ricky Gutierrez	.10
176	Mike Bordick	.10
177	*Chan Ho Park*	.35
178	Alex Gonzalez	.20
179	Steve Karsay	.15
180	Jeffrey Hammonds	.10
181	Manny Ramirez	.75
182	Salomon Torres	.10
183	Raul Mondesi	.30
184	James Mouton	.10
185	Cliff Floyd	.15
186	Danny Bautista	.10
187	*Kurt Abbott*	.25
188	Javier Lopez	.15
189	John Patterson	.10
190	Greg Blosser	.10
191	Bob Hamelin	.10
192	Tony Eusebio	.10
193	Carlos Delgado	.50
194	Chris Gomez	.10
195	Kelly Stinnett	.10
196	Shane Reynolds	.10
197	Ryan Klesko	.20
198	Jim Edmonds	.25
199	James Hurst	.10
200	Dave Staton	.10
201	Rondell White	.30
202	Keith Mitchell	.10
203	Darren Oliver	.10
204	Mike Matheny	.10
205	Chris Turner	.10
206	Matt Mieske	.10
207	N.L. team checklist	.10
208	N.L. team checklist	.10
209	A.L. team checklist	.10
210	A.L. team checklist	.10
211	Barry Bonds	.75
212	Juan Gonzalez	.75
213	Jim Eisenreich	.10
214	Ivan Rodriguez	.75
215	Tony Phillips	.10
216	John Jaha	.10
217	Lee Smith	.10
218	Bip Roberts	.10
219	Dave Hansen	.10
220	Pat Listach	.10
221	Willie McGee	.10
222	Damion Easley	.10
223	Dean Palmer	.10
224	Mike Moore	.10
225	Brian Harper	.10
226	Gary DiSarcina	.10
227	Delino DeShields	.10
228	Otis Nixon	.10
229	Roberto Alomar	.65
230	Mark Grace	.30
231	Kenny Lofton	.40
232	Gregg Jefferies	.10
233	Cecil Fielder	.10
234	Jeff Bagwell	1.00
235	Albert Belle	.50
236	Dave Justice	.35
237	Tom Henke	.10
238	Bobby Bonilla	.10
239	John Olerud	.15
240	Robby Thompson	.10
241	Dave Valle	.10
242	Marquis Grissom	.15
243	Greg Swindell	.10
244	Todd Zeile	.10
245	Dennis Eckersley	.10
246	Jose Offerman	.10
247	Greg McMichael	.10
248	Tim Belcher	.10
249	Cal Ripken, Jr.	2.50
250	Tom Glavine	.20
251	Luis Polonia	.10
252	Bill Swift	.10
253	Juan Guzman	.10
254	Rickey Henderson	.25
255	Terry Mulholland	.10
256	Gary Sheffield	.20
257	Terry Steinbach	.10
258	Brett Butler	.10
259	Jason Bere	.10
260	Doug Strange	.10
261	Kent Hrbek	.10
262	Graeme Lloyd	.10
263	Lou Frazier	.10
264	Charles Nagy	.10
265	Bret Boone	.10
266	Kirk Gibson	.10
267	Kevin Brown	.15
269	Matt Williams	.35
270	Greg Gagne	.10
271	Mariano Duncan	.10
272	Jeff Russell	.10
273	Eric Davis	.10
274	Shane Mack	.10
275	Jose Vizcaino	.10
276	Jose Canseco	.40
277	Roberto Hernandez	.10
278	Royce Clayton	.10
279	Carlos Baerga	.10
280	Pete Incaviglia	.10
281	Brent Gates	.10
282	Jeromy Burnitz	.10
283	Chili Davis	.10
284	Pete Harnisch	.10
285	Alan Trammell	.10
286	Eric Anthony	.10
287	Ellis Burks	.10
288	Julio Franco	.10
289	Jack Morris	.10
290	Erik Hanson	.10
291	Chuck Finley	.10
292	Reggie Jefferson	.10
293	Kevin McReynolds	.10
294	Greg Hibbard	.10
295	Travis Fryman	.15
296	Craig Biggio	.20
297	Kenny Rogers	.10
298	Dave Henderson	.10
299	Jim Thome	.30
300	Rene Arocha	.10
301	Pedro Munoz	.10
302	David Hulse	.10
303	Greg Vaughn	.15
304	Darren Lewis	.10
305	Deion Sanders	.25
306	Danny Tartabull	.10
307	Darryl Hamilton	.10
308	Andujar Cedeno	.10
309	Tim Salmon	.30
310	Tony Fernandez	.10
311	Alex Fernandez	.10
312	Roberto Kelly	.10
313	Harold Reynolds	.10
314	Chris Sabo	.10
315	Howard Johnson	.10
316	Mark Portugal	.10
317	Rafael Palmeiro	.40
318	Pete Smith	.10
319	Will Clark	.30
320	Henry Rodriguez	.10
321	Omar Vizquel	.10
322	David Segui	.10
323	Lou Whitaker	.10
324	Felix Fermin	.10
325	Spike Owen	.10
326	Darryl Kile	.10
327	Chad Kreuter	.10
328	Rod Beck	.10
329	Eddie Murray	.40
330	B.J. Surhoff	.10
331	Mickey Tettleton	.10
332	Pedro Martinez	.75
333	Roger Pavlik	.10
334	Eddie Taubensee	.10
335	John Doherty	.10
336	Jody Reed	.10
337	Aaron Sele	.10
338	Leo Gomez	.10
339	Dave Nilsson	.10
340	Rob Dibble	.10
341	John Burkett	.10
342	Wayne Kirby	.10
343	Dan Wilson	.10
344	Armando Reynoso	.10
345	Chad Curtis	.10
346	Dennis Martinez	.10
347	Cal Eldred	.10
348	Luis Gonzalez	.10
349	Doug Drabek	.10
350	Jim Leyritz	.10
351	Mark Langston	.10
352	Darrin Jackson	.10
353	Sid Fernandez	.10
354	Benito Santiago	.10
355	Kevin Seitzer	.10
356	Bo Jackson	.20
357	David Wells	.15
358	Paul Sorrento	.10
359	Ken Caminiti	.15
360	Eduardo Perez	.10
361	Orlando Merced	.10
362	Steve Finley	.10
363	Andy Benes	.10
364	Manuel Lee	.10
365	Todd Benzinger	.10
366	Sandy Alomar Jr.	.15
367	Rex Hudler	.10
368	Mike Henneman	.10
369	Vince Coleman	.10
370	Kirt Manwaring	.10
371	Ken Hill	.10
372	Glenallen Hill	.10
373	Sean Berry	.10
374	Geronimo Berroa	.10
375	Duane Ward	.10
376	Allen Watson	.10
377	Marc Newfield	.10
378	Dan Miceli	.10
379	Denny Hocking	.10
380	Mark Kiefer	.10
381	Tony Tarasco	.10
382	Tony Longmire	.10
383	*Brian Anderson*	.40
384	Fernando Vina	.10
385	Hector Carrasco	.10
386	Mike Kelly	.10
387	Greg Colbrunn	.10
388	Roger Salkeld	.10
389	Steve Trachsel	.15
390	Rich Becker	.10
391	*Billy Taylor*	.10
392	Rich Rowland	.10
393	Carl Everett	.10
394	Johnny Ruffin	.10
395	*Keith Lockhart*	.10
396	J.R. Phillips	.10
397	Sterling Hitchcock	.10
398	Jorge Fabregas	.10
399	Jeff Granger	.10
400	*Eddie Zambrano*	.10
401	*Rikkert Faneyte*	.10
402	Gerald Williams	.10
403	Joey Hamilton	.10
404	*Joe Hall*	.10
405	*John Hudek*	.15
406	Roberto Petagine	.10
407	Charles Johnson	.15
408	Mark Smith	.10
409	Jeff Juden	.10
410	*Carlos Pulido*	.10
411	Paul Shuey	.10
412	Rob Butler	.10
413	Mark Acre	.10
414	Greg Pirkl	.10
415	Melvin Nieves	.10
416	*Tim Hyers*	.10
417	N.L. checklist	.10
418	N.L. checklist	.10
419	A.L. checklist	.10
420	A.L. checklist	.10

1994 Select Crown Contenders

Candidates for the major baseball annual awards are featured in this subset. Horizontal-format cards have a color player photo printed on a holographic foil background. Backs are vertically oriented with a player portrait photo and justification for the player's inclusion in the set. Cards are numbered with a "CC" prefix and feature a special optical-variable anti-counterfeiting device at bottom-center. According to stated odds of one card on average in every 24 packs it has been estimated that fewer than 12,000 of each Crown Contenders card was produced.

		MT
Complete Set (10):		70.00
Common Player:		1.50
1	Len Dykstra	1.50
2	Greg Maddux	10.00
3	Roger Clemens	6.00
4	Randy Johnson	5.00
5	Frank Thomas	8.00
6	Barry Bonds	5.00
7	Juan Gonzalez	5.00
8	John Olerud	3.00
9	Mike Piazza	15.00
10	Ken Griffey, Jr.	20.00

1994 Select MVP

Paul Molitor was the 1994 Select MVP and is featured in this one card set. Molitor is pictured in front of three distinct foil designs across the rest of the card.

	MT
MVP1 Paul Molitor	10.00

1994 Select Rookie of the Year

Carlos Delgado was the 1994 Select Rookie of the Year. Delgado is pictured on top of a glowing foil background with his initials in large capital letters in the background and Rookie of the Year printed across the bottom.

	MT
RY1 Carlos Delgado	6.00

1994 Select Rookie Surge

Each series of 1994 Score Select offered a chase card set of nine top rookies. Fronts feature action photos set against a rainbow-colored metallic foil background. Backs have a portrait photo and a few words about the player. Cards are numbered with an "RS" prefix and were inserted at an average rate of one per 48 packs.

		MT
Complete Set (18):		75.00
Complete Series 1 (9):		30.00
Complete Series 2 (9):		45.00
Common Player:		1.50
1	Cliff Floyd	3.00
2	Bob Hamelin	1.50
3	Ryan Klesko	3.00
4	Carlos Delgado	15.00
5	Jeffrey Hammonds	2.50
6	Rondell White	4.00
7	Salomon Torres	1.50
8	Steve Karsay	2.00
9	Javier Lopez	6.00
10	Manny Ramirez	20.00
11	Tony Tarasco	1.50
12	Kurt Abbott	2.00
13	Chan Ho Park	8.00
14	Rich Becker	1.50
15	James Mouton	1.50
16	Alex Gonzalez	3.00
17	Raul Mondesi	6.00
18	Steve Trachsel	2.00

1994 Select Salute

With odds of finding one of these cards stated at one per 360 packs, it is estimated that only about 4,000 of each of this two-card chase set were produced.

		MT
Complete Set (2):		45.00
1	Cal Ripken, Jr.	40.00
2	Dave Winfield	5.00

1994 Select Skills

Select Skills is a 10-card insert that was randomly inserted into every 24 packs. Ten specific skills were designated and matched with the player whom, in the opinion of Select officials, demonstrated that particular skill the best in baseball. Each card is printed on a foil background with the player name running along the lower right side of the card and the skill that they are being featured for along the bottom.

		MT
Complete Set (10):		50.00
Common Player:		3.00
1	Randy Johnson	10.00
2	Barry Larkin	4.00
3	Len Dykstra	3.00
4	Kenny Lofton	6.00
5	Juan Gonzalez	8.00
6	Barry Bonds	10.00
7	Marquis Grissom	3.00
8	Ivan Rodriguez	10.00
9	Larry Walker	4.00
10	Travis Fryman	3.00

1995 Select Samples

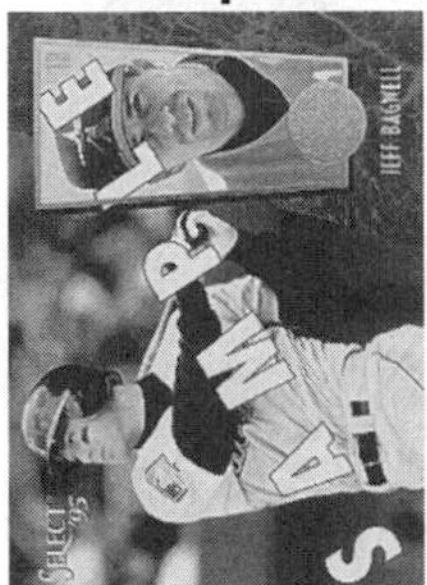

Pinnacle's hobby-only Select brand issue for 1995 was previewed with this four-card cello-packed sample set. Three player cards are in the basic format of the regular-issue Select cards, except they have a large white "SAMPLE" printed diagonally across the front and back. The fourth card in the sample pack is a header card advertising the features of the issue.

		MT
Complete Set (4):		20.00
Common Player:		5.00
34	Roberto Alomar	5.00
37	Jeff Bagwell	9.00
241	Alex Rodriguez	12.00
--	Header card	.15

1995 Select

The 250 regular-issue cards in Pinnacle's mid-price brand baseball set feature three basic formats. Veteran players' cards are presented in a horizontal design which features an action photo at left. At right is a portrait in a trapezoidal gold-foil frame set against a team color-coordinated marbled background. The team logo beneath the portrait and the player's name below that are printed in gold foil. Backs feature a black-and-white photo with a few career highlights, 1994 and Major League cumulative stats, and a "Select Stat" printed in red. The colored marble effect is carried over from the front. The Select Rookie cards which are grouped toward the end of the set are vertical in format and feature a borderless player photo with a gold-foil band at bottom which includes the player name and team logo, along with waves of gold emanating from the logo. Backs have a small, narrow color photo at left, with a large sepia version of the same photo ghosted at center and overprinted with a career summary. At bottom are 1994 and career stats. Ending the set are a series of "Show Time" cards of top prospects. Cards feature large gold-foil "Show Time" and team logos at bottom, with a facsimile autograph printed above. The player photo is shown as if at a curtain raising, with spotlight effects behind. Backs repeat the curtain and spotlight motif and feature another player photo, with autograph above. Production of this hobby-only product was stated as 4,950 cases, which translates to about 110,000 of each regular-issue card. A special card (#251) of Hideo Nomo was added to the set later. It was not issued in foil packs, but distributed to dealers who had purchased Select cases.

		MT
Complete Set (251):		15.00
Common Player:		.10
Pack (12):		2.00
Wax Box (24):		40.00
1	Cal Ripken Jr.	1.50
2	Robin Ventura	.15
3	Al Martin	.10
4	Jeff Frye	.10
5	Darryl Strawberry	.15
6	Chan Ho Park	.15
7	Steve Avery	.10
8	Bret Boone	.10
9	Danny Tartabull	.10
10	Dante Bichette	.15
11	Rondell White	.20
12	Dave McCarty	.10
13	Bernard Gilkey	.10
14	Mark McGwire	2.00
15	Ruben Sierra	.10
16	Wade Boggs	.40
17	Mike Piazza	1.25
18	Jeffrey Hammonds	.10
19	Mike Mussina	.35
20	Darryl Kile	.10
21	Greg Maddux	1.00

22 Frank Thomas .75
23 Kevin Appier .10
24 Jay Bell .10
25 Kirk Gibson .10
26 Pat Hentgen .10
27 Joey Hamilton .10
28 Bernie Williams .40
29 Aaron Sele .10
30 Delino DeShields .10
31 Danny Bautista .10
32 Jim Thome .30
33 Rikkert Faneyte .10
34 Roberto Alomar .40
35 Paul Molitor .40
36 Allen Watson .10
37 Jeff Bagwell .50
38 Jay Buhner .15
39 Marquis Grissom .10
40 Jim Edmonds .20
41 Ryan Klesko .15
42 Fred McGriff .20
43 Tony Tarasco .10
44 Darren Daulton .10
45 Marc Newfield .10
46 Barry Bonds .50
47 Bobby Bonilla .10
48 Greg Pirkl .10
49 Steve Karsay .10
50 Bob Hamelin .10
51 Javier Lopez .15
52 Barry Larkin .20
53 Kevin Young .10
54 Sterling Hitchcock .10
55 Tom Glavine .20
56 Carlos Delgado .40
57 Darren Oliver .10
58 Cliff Floyd .15
59 Tim Salmon .20
60 Albert Belle .30
61 Salomon Torres .10
62 Gary Sheffield .30
63 Ivan Rodriguez .50
64 Charles Nagy .10
65 Eduardo Perez .10
66 Terry Steinbach .10
67 Dave Justice .25
68 Jason Bere .10
69 Dave Nilsson .10
70 Brian Anderson .10
71 Billy Ashley .10
72 Roger Clemens .75
73 Jimmy Key .10
74 Wally Joyner .10
75 Andy Benes .10
76 Ray Lankford .10
77 Jeff Kent .10
78 Moises Alou .15
79 Kirby Puckett .50
80 Joe Carter .15
81 Manny Ramirez .50
82 J.R. Phillips .10
83 Matt Mieske .10
84 John Olerud .15
85 Andres Galarraga .20
86 Juan Gonzalez .50
87 Pedro Martinez .50
88 Dean Palmer .10
89 Ken Griffey Jr. 1.50
90 Brian Jordan .15
91 Hal Morris .10
92 Lenny Dykstra .10
93 Wil Cordero .10
94 Tony Gwynn .75
95 Alex Gonzalez .10
96 Cecil Fielder .10
97 Mo Vaughn .30
98 John Valentin .10
99 Will Clark .25
100 Geronimo Pena .10
101 Don Mattingly .75
102 Charles Johnson .15
103 Raul Mondesi .20
104 Reggie Sanders .10
105 Royce Clayton .10
106 Reggie Jefferson .10
107 Craig Biggio .15
108 Jack McDowell .10
109 James Mouton .10
110 Mike Greenwell .10
111 David Cone .15
112 Matt Williams .25
113 Garret Anderson .10
114 Carlos Garcia .10
115 Alex Fernandez .10
116 Deion Sanders .25
117 Chili Davis .10
118 Mike Kelly .10
119 Jeff Conine .10
120 Kenny Lofton .25
121 Rafael Palmeiro .25
122 Chuck Knoblauch .15
123 Ozzie Smith .50
124 Carlos Baerga .10
125 Brett Butler .10
126 Sammy Sosa 1.25
127 Ellis Burks .10
128 Bret Saberhagen .10
129 Doug Drabek .10
130 Dennis Martinez .10
131 Paul O'Neill .15
132 Travis Fryman .15
133 Brent Gates .10
134 Rickey Henderson .30
135 Randy Johnson .50
136 Mark Langston .10
137 Greg Colbrunn .10
138 Jose Rijo .10
139 Bryan Harvey .10
140 Dennis Eckersley .10
141 Ron Gant .15
142 Carl Everett .10
143 Jeff Granger .10
144 Ben McDonald .10
145 Kurt Abbott .10
146 Jim Abbott .10
147 Jason Jacome .10
148 Rico Brogna .10
149 Cal Eldred .10
150 Rich Becker .10
151 Pete Harnisch .10
152 Roberto Petagine .10
153 Jacob Brumfield .10
154 Todd Hundley .15
155 Roger Cedeno .10
156 Harold Baines .10
157 Steve Dunn .10
158 Tim Belk .10
159 Marty Cardova .10
160 Russ Davis .10
161 Jose Malave .10
162 Brian Hunter .10
163 Andy Pettitte .20
164 Brooks Kieschnick .10
165 Midre Cummings .10
166 Frank Rodriguez .10
167 Chad Mottola .10
168 Brian Barber .10
169 Tim Unroe .10
170 Shane Andrews .10
171 Kevin Flora .10
172 Ray Durham .15
173 Chipper Jones 1.00
174 Butch Huskey .10
175 Ray McDavid .10
176 Jeff Cirillo .10
177 Terry Pendleton .10
178 Scott Ruffcorn .10
179 Ray Holbert .10
180 Joe Randa .10
181 Jose Oliva .10
182 Andy Van Slyke .10
183 Albie Lopez .10
184 Chad Curtis .10
185 Ozzie Guillen .10
186 Chad Ogea .10
187 Dan Wilson .10
188 Tony Fernandez .10
189 John Smoltz .15
190 Willie Greene .10
191 Darren Lewis .10
192 Orlando Miller .10
193 Kurt Miller .10
194 Andrew Lorraine .10
195 Ernie Young .10
196 Jimmy Haynes .10
197 *Raul Casanova* .20
198 Joe Vitiello .10
199 Brad Woodall .10
200 Juan Acevedo .10
201 Michael Tucker .10
202 Shawn Green .25
203 Alex Rodriguez 1.50
204 Julian Tavarez .10
205 Jose Lima .10
206 Wilson Alvarez .10
207 Rich Aude .10
208 Armando Benitez .10
209 Dwayne Hosey .10
210 Gabe White .10
211 Joey Eischen .10
212 Bill Pulsipher .10
213 Robby Thompson .10
214 Toby Borland .10
215 Rusty Greer .10
216 Fausto Cruz .10
217 Luis Ortiz .10
218 Duane Singleton .10
219 Troy Percival .10
220 Gregg Jefferies .10
221 Mark Grace .25
222 Mickey Tettleton .10
223 Phil Plantier .10
224 Larry Walker .20
225 Ken Caminiti .15
226 Dave Winfield .25
227 Brady Anderson .15
228 Kevin Brown .15
229 Andujar Cedeno .10
230 Roberto Kelly .10
231 Jose Canseco .40
231 (Scott Ruffcorn) (Showtime) .10
232 Billy Ashley (Showtime) .10
234 J.R. Phillips (Showtime) .10
235 Chipper Jones (Showtime) .50
236 Charles Johnson (Showtime) .10
237 Midre Cummings (Showtime) .10
238 Brian Hunter (Showtime) .10
239 Garret Anderson (Showtime) .10
240 Shawn Green (Showtime) .20
241 Alex Rodriguez (Showtime) .75
242 Checklist #1 (Frank Thomas) .40
243 Checklist #2 (Ken Griffey Jr.) .75
244 Checklist #3 (Albert Belle) .30
245 Checklist #4 (Cal Ripken Jr.) .75
246 Checklist #5 (Barry Bonds) .25
247 Checklist #6 (Raul Mondesi) .15
248 Checklist #7 (Mike Piazza) .50
249 Checklist #8 (Jeff Bagwell) .50
250 Checklist #9 (Jeff Bagwell, Frank Thomas, Ken Griffey Jr., Mike Piazza) .40
251 Hideo Nomo 1.00

1995 Select Artist's Proofs

Among the scarcest and most valuable of 1995's baseball card inserts are the Select Artist's Proof parallel set. While an AP card is found on average once per 24 packs, the limited print run of the basic Select set means that only about 475 of each of the 250 regular-issue cards in the Select set were made in this edition. The AP inserts have a gold-foil "ARTIST'S PROOF" line at bottom, and other gold-foil highlights are embossed, rather than merely stamped on, as on regular Select cards.

	MT
Complete Set (250):	1200.
Common Player:	2.00
Artist's Proof Stars:	25X

(See 1995 Select for checklist and base card values.)

1995 Select Big Sticks

With fronts printed in what Pinnacle describes as "holographic Gold Rush technology," the Big Sticks chase card issue offers a dozen of the game's big hitters in action photos superimposed over their team logo. Conventionally printed backs have another player photo, along with a summary of career highlights and description of the player's power potential. Stated odds of pulling a Big Sticks chase card are one per 48 packs, on average. Cards are numbered with a "BS" prefix.

		MT
Complete Set (12):		80.00
Common Player:		3.00
1	Frank Thomas	8.00
2	Ken Griffey Jr.	20.00
3	Cal Ripken Jr.	20.00
4	Mike Piazza	15.00
5	Don Mattingly	10.00
6	Will Clark	4.00
7	Tony Gwynn	8.00
8	Jeff Bagwell	6.00
9	Barry Bonds	6.00
10	Paul Molitor	5.00
11	Matt Williams	3.00
12	Albert Belle	4.00

1995 Select Can't Miss

A mix of rookies and sophomore standouts, along with a few players of slightly longer service are presented in this chase set. Cards feature color player action photos printed on a metallic red background, with their last name in gold foil at lower-left. An umpire on the "Can't Miss" logo is at upper-left. Backs repeat the logo, have a tall, narrow player photo, a few biographical details and a paragraph of career summary. Cards are numbered with a "CM" prefix.

		MT
Complete Set (12):		60.00
Common Player:		2.00
1	Cliff Floyd	3.00
2	Ryan Klesko	3.00
3	Charles Johnson	3.00
4	Raul Mondesi	3.00
5	Manny Ramirez	8.00
6	Billy Ashley	2.00
7	Alex Gonzalez	2.00
8	Carlos Delgado	6.00
9	Garret Anderson	2.00
10	Alex Rodriguez	20.00
11	Chipper Jones	15.00
12	Shawn Green	4.00

1995 Select Sure Shots

Ten of Select's picks for future stardom are featured in this chase set, the toughest find of any of the 1995 Select inserts, at an average rate of one per 90 packs. Card fronts feature player action photos set against a gold "Dufex" foil printed background with a Sure Shots logo vertically at left. Backs have a blue background with a few words about the player and a portrait photo at left. Cards are numbered with a "SS" prefix.

		MT
Complete Set (10):		20.00
Common Player:		2.00
1	Ben Grieve	8.00
2	Kevin Witt	1.00
3	Mark Farris	1.00
4	Paul Konerko	5.00
5	Dustin Hermanson	1.50
6	Ramon Castro	1.00
7	McKay Christensen	1.00
8	Brian Buchanan	1.00
9	Paul Wilson	1.00
10	Terrence Long	2.00

1995 Select Certified Samples

Pinnacle's hobby-only Select brand issue for 1995 was previewed with this four-card cello-packed sample set. Three player cards are in the basic format of the regular-issue Select cards, except they have a large which "SAMPLE" printed diagonally across the front and back. The fourth card in the sample pack is a header card advertising the features of the issue.

		MT
Complete Set (8):		27.00
Common Player:		3.00
2	Reggie Sanders	3.00
10	Mo Vaughn	4.50
39	Mike Piazza	7.50
50	Mark McGwire	9.00
75	Roberto Alomar	5.00
89	Larry Walker	4.50
110	Ray Durham	3.00
3 of 12	Cal Ripken Jr. (Gold Team)	12.00

1995 Select Certified

The concepts of hobby-only distribution and limited production which were the hallmarks of Pinnacle's Select brand were carried a step further with the post-season release of Select Certified baseball. Printed on double-thich cardboard stock card fronts feature all metallic-foil printing protected by a double laminated gloss coat. Backs have key player stats against each team in the league. The final 44 cards in the set are distinguished with a special Rookie logo and with gold added to the silver foil in the photo background.

		MT
Complete Set (135):		40.00
Common Player:		.20
Pack (6):		4.00
Wax Box (20):		70.00
1	Barry Bonds	1.00
2	Reggie Sanders	.20
3	Terry Steinbach	.20
4	Eduardo Perez	.20
5	Frank Thomas	2.00
6	Wil Cordero	.20
7	John Olerud	.40
8	Deion Sanders	.40
9	Mike Mussina	.75
10	Mo Vaughn	.75
11	Will Clark	.50
12	Chili Davis	.20
13	Jimmy Key	.20
14	Eddie Murray	.50
15	Bernard Gilkey	.20
16	David Cone	.35
17	Tim Salmon	.40
18	(Not issued, see #2131)	
19	Steve Ontiveros	.20
20	Andres Galarraga	.40
21	Don Mattingly	1.25
22	Kevin Appier	.20
23	Paul Molitor	.75
24	Edgar Martinez	.20
25	Andy Benes	.20
26	Rafael Palmeiro	.40
27	Barry Larkin	.35
28	Gary Sheffield	.75
29	Wally Joyner	.20
30	Wade Boggs	.50
31	Rico Brogna	.20
32	Eddie Murray (Murray Tribute)	.75
33	Kirby Puckett	1.50
34	Bobby Bonilla	.20
35	Hal Morris	.20
36	Moises Alou	.30
37	Javier Lopez	.30
38	Chuck Knoblauch	.40
39	Mike Piazza	3.00
40	Travis Fryman	.20
41	Rickey Henderson	.50
42	Jim Thome	.60
43	Carlos Baerga	.20
44	Dean Palmer	.20
45	Kirk Gibson	.20
46	Bret Saberhagen	.20
47	Cecil Fielder	.20
48	Manny Ramirez	1.50
49	Derek Bell	.20
50	Mark McGwire	5.00
51	Jim Edmonds	.35
52	Robin Ventura	.30
53	Ryan Klesko	.40
54	Jeff Bagwell	1.50
55	Ozzie Smith	.75
56	Albert Belle	1.00
57	Darren Daulton	.20
58	Jeff Conine	.20
59	Greg Maddux	2.50
60	Lenny Dykstra	.20
61	Randy Johnson	.75
62	Fred McGriff	.40
63	Ray Lankford	.20
64	Dave Justice	.40
65	Paul O'Neill	.40
66	Tony Gwynn	2.00
67	Matt Williams	.50
68	Dante Bichette	.40
69	Craig Biggio	.40
70	Ken Griffey Jr.	5.00
71	J.T. Snow	.20
72	Cal Ripken Jr.	4.00
73	Jay Bell	.20
74	Joe Carter	.35
75	Roberto Alomar	.75
76	Benji Gil	.20
77	Ivan Rodriguez	1.00
78	Raul Mondesi	.50
79	Cliff Floyd	.25
80	Eric Karros, Mike Piazza, Raul Mondesi (Dodger Dynasty)	.75
81	Royce Clayton	.20
82	Billy Ashley	.20
83	Joey Hamilton	.20
84	Sammy Sosa	2.50
85	Jason Bere	.20
86	Dennis Martinez	.20
87	Greg Vaughn	.25
88	Roger Clemens	1.50
89	Larry Walker	.50
90	Mark Grace	.50
91	Kenny Lofton	.75
92	*Carlos Perez*	.40
93	Roger Cedeno	.20
94	Scott Ruffcorn	.20
95	Jim Pittsley	.20
96	Andy Pettitte	.75
97	James Baldwin	.20
98	*Hideo Nomo*	3.00
99	Ismael Valdes	.20
100	Armando Benitez	.20
101	Jose Malave	.20
102	*Bobby Higginson*	1.50
103	LaTroy Hawkins	.35
104	Russ Davis	.20
105	Shawn Green	.35
106	Joe Vitiello	.20
107	Chipper Jones	3.00
108	Shane Andrews	.20
109	Jose Oliva	.20
110	Ray Durham	.35
111	Jon Nunnally	.20
112	Alex Gonzalez	.40
113	Vaughn Eshelman	.20
114	Marty Cordova	.20
115	*Mark Grudzielanek*	.75
116	Brian Hunter	.20
117	Charles Johnson	.40
118	Alex Rodriguez	4.00
119	David Bell	.20
120	Todd Hollandsworth	.20
121	Joe Randa	.20
122	Derek Jeter	3.00
123	Frank Rodriguez	.20
124	Curtis Goodwin	.20
125	Bill Pulsipher	.20
126	John Mabry	.20
127	Julian Tavarez	.20
128	Edgardo Alfonzo	.25
129	Orlando Miller	.20
130	Juan Acevedo	.20
131	Jeff Cirillo	.20
132	Roberto Petagine	.20
133	Antonio Osuna	.20
134	Michael Tucker	.20
135	Garret Anderson	.20
2131	Cal Ripken Jr. (Consecutive Game Record)	4.00

1995 Select Certified Mirror Gold

Inserted at an average rate of one per nine packs, this parallel set is a gold-foil version of the regular Select Certified set. Backs have a "MIRROR GOLD" notation at bottom.

	MT
Complete Set (135):	750.00
Common Player:	2.00
Mirror Gold Stars:	9X

(See 1995 Select Certified for checklist and base card values.)

1995 Select Certified Checklists

The seven checklists issued with Select Certified are not numbered as part of the set. They are found one per foil pack and are printed on much thinner card stock than the regular-issue cards.

		MT
Complete Set (7):		2.00
Common Player:		.35
1	Ken Griffey Jr. (A.L., #3-41)	.75
2	Frank Thomas (A.L., #42-95)	.50
3	Cal Ripken Jr. (A.L., #96-135)	.60
4	Jeff Bagwell (N.L., #1-58)	.40
5	Mike Piazza (N.L., #59-92)	.50
6	Barry Bonds (N.L., #93-133)	.40
7	Manny Ramirez, Raul Mondesi (Chase cards)	.40

1995 Select Certified Future

A striking new all-metal, brushed-foil printing technology was used in the production of this chase set of 10 rookie players with "unlimited future potential." Stated odds of finding a Certified Future insert card were one in 19 packs.

		MT
Complete Set (10):		60.00
Common Player:		2.50
1	Chipper Jones	15.00
2	Curtis Goodwin	2.50
3	Hideo Nomo	4.50
4	Shawn Green	6.50
5	Ray Durham	3.00
6	Todd Hollandsworth	2.50
7	Brian Hunter	3.00
8	Carlos Delgado	9.00
9	Michael Tucker	2.50
10	Alex Rodriguez	25.00

1995 Select Certified Gold Team

A dozen of the top position players in the league were selected for appearance in this insert set. Cards are printed in a special double-sided, all-gold Dufex technology. An action photo is featured on the front, a portrait on back. Odds of picking a Gold Team card were stated as one in 41 packs.

		MT
Complete Set (12):		220.00
Common Player:		8.00
1	Ken Griffey Jr.	50.00
2	Frank Thomas	25.00
3	Cal Ripken Jr.	40.00
4	Jeff Bagwell	20.00
5	Mike Piazza	30.00
6	Barry Bonds	12.00
7	Matt Williams	8.00
8	Don Mattingly	20.00
9	Will Clark	8.00
10	Tony Gwynn	25.00
11	Kirby Puckett	25.00
12	Jose Canseco	8.00

1995 Select Certified Potential Unlimited

Dufex printing with textured foil highlights and transparent inks is featured in this chase set which was produced in an edition of no more the 1,975 sets, as witnessed by the numbering on card backs. Approximate odds of finding a Potential Unlimited card are one per 29 packs. A super-scarce edition of 903 cards each featuring "microetch" foil printing technology was issued at the rate of one per 70 packs.

		MT
Complete Set (20):		200.00
Common Player:		5.00
Comp. Numbered 903 Set		300.00
903's:		1.5X
1	Cliff Floyd	6.00
2	Manny Ramirez	25.00
3	Raul Mondesi	8.00
4	Scott Ruffcorn	5.00
5	Billy Ashley	5.00
6	Alex Gonzalez	7.50
7	Midre Cummings	5.00
8	Charles Johnson	6.00
9	Garret Anderson	5.00
10	Hideo Nomo	15.00
11	Chipper Jones	35.00
12	Curtis Goodwin	5.00
13	Frank Rodriguez	5.00
14	Shawn Green	10.00
15	Ray Durham	5.00
16	Todd Hollandsworth	5.00
17	Brian Hunter	5.00
18	Carlos Delgado	8.00
19	Michael Tucker	5.00
20	Alex Rodriguez	60.00

1996 Select

Select's 1996 baseball set has 200 cards in it, including 35 rookies, five checklists and 10 Lineup Leaders subset cards. All 200 cards are also reprinted as part of an Artist's Proof parallel set, using a holographic Artist's Proof logo. Cards were seeded one per every 35 packs; there were approximately 435 sets produced. Three insert sets were also created: Claim to Fame, En Fuego and Team Nucleus.

		MT
Complete Set (200):		15.00
Common Player:		.10
Pack (10):		2.00
Wax Box (24):		45.00
1	Wade Boggs	.30
2	Shawn Green	.20
3	Andres Galarraga	.15
4	Bill Pulsipher	.10
5	Chuck Knoblauch	.10
6	Ken Griffey Jr.	3.00
7	Greg Maddux	1.50
8	Manny Ramirez	1.00
9	Ivan Rodriguez	.50
10	Tim Salmon	.25
11	Frank Thomas	1.00
12	Jeff Bagwell	1.00
13	Travis Fryman	.15
14	Kenny Lofton	.75
15	Matt Williams	.25
16	Jay Bell	.10
17	Ken Caminiti	.15
18	Ray Lankford	.10
19	Cal Ripken Jr.	2.50
20	Roger Clemens	.60
21	Carlos Baerga	.10
22	Mike Piazza	2.00
23	Gregg Jefferies	.10
24	Reggie Sanders	.10
25	Rondell White	.15
26	Sammy Sosa	1.50
27	Kevin Appier	.10
28	Kevin Seitzer	.10
29	Gary Sheffield	.15
30	Mike Mussina	.40
31	Mark McGwire	3.00
32	Barry Larkin	.20
33	Marc Newfield	.10
34	Ismael Valdes	.10
35	Marty Cordova	.10
36	Albert Belle	.75
37	Johnny Damon	.25
38	Garret Anderson	.10
39	Cecil Fielder	.15
40	John Mabry	.10
41	Chipper Jones	2.00
42	Omar Vizquel	.10
43	Jose Rijo	.10
44	Charles Johnson	.10
45	Alex Rodriquez	2.50
46	Rico Brogna	.10
47	Joe Carter	.15
48	Mo Vaughn	.75
49	Moises Alou	.15
50	Raul Mondesi	.30
51	Robin Ventura	.20
52	Jim Thome	.40
53	Dave Justice	.20
54	Jeff King	.10
55	Brian Hunter	.15
56	Juan Gonzalez	.75
57	John Olerud	.15
58	Rafael Palmeiro	.20
59	Tony Gwynn	1.00
60	Eddie Murray	.35
61	Jason Isringhausen	.25
62	Dante Bichette	.20
63	Randy Johnson	.35

64	Kirby Puckett	1.00
65	Jim Edmonds	.15
66	David Cone	.15
67	Ozzie Smith	.30
68	Fred McGriff	.35
69	Darren Daulton	.10
70	Edgar Martinez	.10
71	J.T. Snow	.10
72	Butch Huskey	.10
73	Hideo Nomo	.40
74	Pedro Martinez	.20
75	Bobby Bonilla	.10
76	Jeff Conine	.10
77	Ryan Klesko	.20
78	Bernie Williams	.35
79	Andre Dawson	.15
80	Trevor Hoffman	.15
81	Mark Grace	.20
82	Benji Gil	.10
83	Eric Karros	.10
84	Pete Schourek	.10
85	Edgardo Alfonzo	.15
86	Jay Buhner	.15
87	Vinny Castilla	.10
88	Bret Boone	.10
89	Ray Durham	.10
90	Brian Jordan	.10
91	Jose Canseco	.25
92	Paul O'Neill	.15
93	Chili Davis	.10
94	Tom Glavine	.15
95	Julian Tavarez	.10
96	Derek Bell	.10
97	Will Clark	.25
98	Larry Walker	.25
99	Denny Neagle	.10
100	Alex Fernandez	.10
101	Barry Bonds	.60
102	Ben McDonald	.10
103	Andy Pettitte	.75
104	Tino Martinez	.10
105	Sterling Hitchcock	.10
106	Royce Clayton	.10
107	Jim Abbott	.10
108	Rickey Henderson	.25
109	Ramon Martinez	.10
110	Paul Molitor	.35
111	Dennis Eckersley	.10
112	Alex Gonzalez	.10
113	Marquis Grissom	.10
114	Greg Vaughn	.15
115	Lance Johnson	.10
116	Todd Stottlemyre	.10
117	Jack McDowell	.10
118	Ruben Sierra	.10
119	Brady Anderson	.15
120	Julio Franco	.10
121	Brooks Kieshnick	.10
122	Roberto Alomar	.50
123	Greg Gagne	.10
124	Wally Joyner	.10
125	John Smoltz	.20
126	John Valentin	.10
127	Russ Davis	.10
128	Joe Vitiello	.10
129	Shawon Dunston	.10
130	Frank Rodriguez	.10
131	Charlie Hayes	.10
132	Andy Benes	.10
133	B.J. Surhoff	.10
134	Dave Nilsson	.10
135	Carlos Delgado	.40
136	Walt Weiss	.10
137	Mike Stanley	.10
138	Greg Colbrunn	.10
139	Mike Kelly	.10
140	Ryne Sandberg	.50
141	Lee Smith	.10
142	Dennis Martinez	.10
143	Bernard Gilkey	.10
144	Lenny Dykstra	.10
145	Danny Tartabull	.10
146	Dean Palmer	.10
147	Craig Biggio	.20
148	Juan Acevedo	.10
149	Michael Tucker	.10
150	Bobby Higginson	.15
151	Ken Griffey Jr. (Line Up Leaders)	1.25
152	Frank Thomas (Line Up Leaders)	.50
153	Cal Ripken Jr. (Line Up Leaders)	1.00
154	Albert Belle (Line Up Leaders)	.40
155	Mike Piazza (Line Up Leaders)	.60
156	Barry Bonds (Line Up Leaders)	.25
157	Sammy Sosa (Line Up Leaders)	.75
158	Mo Vaughn (Line Up Leaders)	.25
159	Greg Maddux (Line Up Leaders)	.75
160	Jeff Bagwell (Line Up Leaders)	.50
161	Derek Jeter	2.00
162	Paul Wilson	.10
163	Chris Snopek	.10
164	Jason Schmidt	.10
165	Jimmy Haynes	.10
166	George Arias	.10
167	Steve Gibralter	.10
168	Bob Wolcott	.10
169	Jason Kendall	.10
170	Greg Zaun	.10
171	Quinton McCracken	.10
172	Alan Benes	.15
173	Rey Ordonez	.40
174	Ugueth Urbina	.10
175	*Osvaldo Fernandez*	.20
176	Marc Barcelo	.10
177	Sal Fasano	.10
178	*Mike Grace*	.10
179	Chan Ho Park	.15
180	Robert Perez	.10
181	Todd Hollandsworth	.10
182	*Wilton Guerrero*	.25
183	John Wasdin	.10
184	Jim Pittsley	.10
185	LaTroy Hawkins	.10
186	Jay Powell	.10
187	Felipe Crespo	.10
188	Jermaine Dye	.15
189	Bob Abreu	.10
190	*Matt Luke*	.15
191	Richard Hidalgo	.10
192	Karim Garcia	.35
193	Tavo Alvarez	.10
194	*Andy Fox*	.10
195	Terrell Wade	.10
196	Frank Thomas (checklist)	.40
197	Ken Griffey Jr. (checklist)	1.00
198	Greg Maddux (checklist)	.60
199	Mike Piazza (checklist)	.50
200	Cal Ripken Jr. (checklist)	.75

1996 Select Artist's Proofs

Approximately once per 35 packs, a card from this parallel chase set is encountered among 1996 Select. Reported production was 435 sets. The Artist's Proof cards are distinguished by a holographic logo testifying to their status on the front of the card.

	MT
Complete Set (200):	1200.
Common Player:	2.00
Artist's Proof Stars:	20X

(See 1996 Select for checklist and base card values.)

1996 Select Claim to Fame

Twenty different stars are featured on these 1996 Select insert cards. Each card is numbered "1 of 2100" and uses an external die-cut design. The cards were seeded one per every 72 packs.

		MT
Complete Set (20):		250.00
Common Player:		3.00
1	Cal Ripken Jr.	30.00
2	Greg Maddux	25.00
3	Ken Griffey Jr.	40.00
4	Frank Thomas	20.00
5	Mo Vaughn	6.00
6	Albert Belle	10.00
7	Jeff Bagwell	15.00
8	Sammy Sosa	25.00
8s	Sammy Sosa (overprinted "SAMPLE")	15.00
9	Reggie Sanders	3.00
10	Hideo Nomo	6.00
11	Chipper Jones	25.00
12	Mike Piazza	25.00
13	Matt Williams	5.00
14	Tony Gwynn	20.00
15	Johnny Damon	3.00
16	Dante Bichette	3.00
17	Kirby Puckett	10.00
18	Barry Bonds	10.00
19	Randy Johnson	8.00
20	Eddie Murray	4.00

1996 Select En Fuego

ESPN announcer Dan Patrick is featured on his own card in this set, inspired by his Sportscenter catch phrase "en fuego," which means "on fire." Patrick's teammate, Keith Olberman, wrote the card backs. The 25 cards, printed on all-foil Dufex stock, are seeded one per every 48 packs of 1996 Select baseball.

		MT
Complete Set (25):		180.00
Common Player:		3.00
1	Ken Griffey Jr.	25.00
2	Frank Thomas	12.00
3	Cal Ripken Jr.	20.00
4	Greg Maddux	15.00
5	Jeff Bagwell	8.00
6	Barry Bonds	6.00
7	Mo Vaughn	4.00
8	Albert Belle	6.00
9	Sammy Sosa	15.00
10	Reggie Sanders	3.00
11	Mike Piazza	15.00
12	Chipper Jones	15.00
13	Tony Gwynn	12.00
14	Kirby Puckett	6.00
15	Wade Boggs	4.00
16	Dan Patrick	3.00
17	Gary Sheffield	3.00
18	Dante Bichette	4.00
19	Randy Johnson	5.00
20	Matt Williams	3.00
21	Alex Rodriguez	20.00
22	Tim Salmon	3.00
23	Johnny Damon	3.00
24	Manny Ramirez	8.00
25	Hideo Nomo	4.00

1996 Select Team Nucleus

This 1996 Select insert set pays tribute to the three top players from each Major League Baseball team; each card features the three teammates on it. The cards are printed on a clear plastic, utilizing a holographic micro-etched design. They are seeded one per every 18 packs.

		MT
Complete Set (28):		80.00
Common Player:		2.00
1	Albert Belle, Manny Ramirez, Carlos Baerga	6.00
2	Ray Lankford, Brian Jordan, Ozzie Smith	4.00
3	Jay Bell, Jeff King, Denny Neagle	2.00
4	Dante Bichette, Andres Galarraga, Larry Walker	3.00
5	Mark McGwire, Mike Bordick, Terry Steinbach	10.00

6	Bernie Williams, Wade Boggs, David Cone	5.00
7	Joe Carter, Alex Gonzalez, Shawn Green	3.00
8	Roger Clemens, Mo Vaughn, Jose Canseco	5.00
9	Ken Griffey Jr., Edgar Martinez, Randy Johnson	15.00
10	Gregg Jefferies, Darren Daulton, Lenny Dykstra	2.00
11	Mike Piazza, Raul Mondesi, Hideo Nomo	9.00
12	Greg Maddux, Chipper Jones, Ryan Klesko	9.00
13	Cecil Fielder, Travis Fryman, Phil Nevin	2.00
14	Ivan Rodriguez, Will Clark, Juan Gonzalez	3.00
15	Ryne Sandberg, Sammy Sosa, Mark Grace	10.00
16	Gary Sheffield, Charles Johnson, Andre Dawson	3.00
17	Johnny Damon, Michael Tucker, Kevin Appier	2.00
18	Barry Bonds, Matt Williams, Rod Beck	3.00
19	Kirby Puckett, Chuck Knoblauch, Marty Cordova	3.00
20	Cal Ripken Jr., Bobby Bonilla, Mike Mussina	9.00
21	Jason Isringhausen, Bill Pulsipher, Rico Brogna	2.50
22	Tony Gwynn, Ken Caminiti, Marc Newfield	5.00
23	Tim Salmon, Garret Anderson, Jim Edmonds	2.50
24	Moises Alou, Rondell White, Cliff Floyd	2.50
25	Barry Larkin, Reggie Sanders, Bret Boone	2.00
26	Jeff Bagwell, Craig Biggio, Derek Bell	7.50
27	Frank Thomas, Robin Ventura, Alex Fernandez	6.00
28	John Jaha, Greg Vaughn, Kevin Seitzer	2.00

1996 Select Certified

This hobby-exclusive set has 144 cards in its regular issue, plus six parallel versions and two insert sets. The parallel sets are: Certified Red (one per five packs), Certified Blue (one per 50), Artist's Proofs (one per 12), Mirror Red (one per 100), Mirror Blue (one per 200), and Mirror Gold (one per 300). Breaking down the numbers, there are 1,800 Certified Red sets, 180 Certified Blue, 500 Artist's Proofs, 90 Mirror Red 45 Mirror Blue and 30 Mirror Gold sets. The insert sets are Interleague Preview cards and Select Few. Cards #135-144 are a "Pastime Power" subset.

		MT
Complete Set (144):		40.00
Common Player:		.20
Pack (6):		4.00
Wax Box (20):		70.00
1	Frank Thomas	1.50
2	Tino Martinez	.25
3	Gary Sheffield	.75
4	Kenny Lofton	.75
5	Joe Carter	.25
6	Alex Rodriguez	3.00
7	Chipper Jones	2.00
8	Roger Clemens	1.50
9	Jay Bell	.20
10	Eddie Murray	.40
11	Will Clark	.50
12	Mike Mussina	.75
13	Hideo Nomo	.75
14	Andres Galarraga	.35
15	Marc Newfield	.20
16	Jason Isringhausen	.20
17	Randy Johnson	1.00
18	Chuck Knoblauch	.40
19	J.T. Snow	.20
20	Mark McGwire	4.00
21	Tony Gwynn	1.50
22	Albert Belle	.75
23	Gregg Jefferies	.20
24	Reggie Sanders	.20
25	Bernie Williams	1.00
26	Ray Lankford	.20
27	Johnny Damon	.20
28	Ryne Sandberg	1.25
29	Rondell White	.40
30	Mike Piazza	2.50
31	Barry Bonds	1.25
32	Greg Maddux	2.00
33	Craig Biggio	.35
34	John Valentin	.20
35	Ivan Rodriguez	1.25
36	Rico Brogna	.20
37	Tim Salmon	.35
38	Sterling Hitchcock	.20
39	Charles Johnson	.20
40	Travis Fryman	.40
41	Barry Larkin	.50
42	Tom Glavine	.40
43	Marty Cordova	.20
44	Shawn Green	.50
45	Ben McDonald	.20
46	Robin Ventura	.30
47	Ken Griffey Jr.	3.00
48	Orlando Merced	.20
49	Paul O'Neill	.40
50	Ozzie Smith	1.00
51	Manny Ramirez	1.25
52	Ismael Valdes	.20
53	Cal Ripken Jr.	3.00
54	Jeff Bagwell	1.50
55	Greg Vaughn	.25
56	Juan Gonzalez	1.25
57	Raul Mondesi	.40
58	Carlos Baerga	.20
59	Sammy Sosa	2.50
60	Mike Kelly	.20
61	Edgar Martinez	.20
62	Kirby Puckett	1.00
63	Cecil Fielder	.25
64	David Cone	.30
65	Moises Alou	.35
66	Fred McGriff	.40
67	Mo Vaughn	.75
68	Edgardo Alfonzo	.25
69	Jim Thome	.75
70	Rickey Henderson	.40
71	Dante Bichette	.40
72	Lenny Dykstra	.20
73	Benji Gil	.20
74	Wade Boggs	.50
75	Jim Edmonds	.40
76	Michael Tucker	.20
77	Carlos Delgado	1.00
78	Butch Huskey	.20
79	Billy Ashley	.20
80	Dean Palmer	.20
81	Paul Molitor	.50
82	Ryan Klesko	.35
83	Brian Hunter	.20
84	Jay Buhner	.25
85	Larry Walker	.60
86	Mike Bordick	.20
87	Matt Williams	.40
88	Jack McDowell	.20
89	Hal Morris	.20
90	Brian Jordan	.20
91	Andy Pettitte	.75
92	Melvin Nieves	.20
93	Pedro Martinez	1.50
94	Mark Grace	.40
95	Garret Anderson	.20
96	Andre Dawson	.30
97	Ray Durham	.20
98	Jose Canseco	.75
99	Roberto Alomar	1.00
100	Derek Jeter	3.00
101	Alan Benes	.20
102	Karim Garcia	.25
103	*Robin Jennings*	.20
104	Bob Abreu	.20
105	Sal Fasano (Card front has Livan Hernandez' name)	.20
106	Steve Gibralter	.20
107	Jermaine Dye	.20
108	Jason Kendall	.20
109	*Mike Grace*	.20
110	Jason Schmidt	.20
111	Paul Wilson	.20
112	Rey Ordonez	.35
113	*Wilton Guerrero*	.50
114	Brooks Kieschnick	.20
115	George Arias	.20
116	*Osvaldo Fernandez*	.20
117	Todd Hollandsworth	.20
118	John Wasdin	.20
119	Eric Owens	.20
120	Chan Ho Park	.25
121	Mark Loretta	.20
122	Richard Hidalgo	.20
123	Jeff Suppan	.20
124	Jim Pittsley	.20
125	LaTroy Hawkins	.20
126	Chris Snopek	.20
127	Justin Thompson	.20
128	Jay Powell	.20
129	Alex Ochoa	.20
130	Felipe Crespo	.20
131	*Matt Lawton*	.20
132	Jimmy Haynes	.20
133	Terrell Wade	.20
134	Ruben Rivera	.25
135	Frank Thomas (Pastime Power)	.75
136	Ken Griffey Jr. (Pastime Power)	1.50
137	Greg Maddux (Pastime Power)	1.00
138	Mike Piazza (Pastime Power)	1.25
139	Cal Ripken Jr. (Pastime Power)	1.50
140	Albert Belle (Pastime Power)	.40
141	Mo Vaughn (Pastime Power)	.40
142	Chipper Jones (Pastime Power)	1.00
143	Hideo Nomo (Pastime Power)	.40
144	Ryan Klesko (Pastime Power)	.25

1996 Select Certified Artist's Proofs

Only 500 cards each of this parallel issue were produced, seeded one in every dozen packs. The cards are identical to the regular-issue Select Certified except for the presence on front of a prismatic gold Artist's Proof logo.

	MT
Complete Set (144):	1000.
Common Player:	2.00
Artist's Proof Stars:	10X

(See 1996 Select Certified for checklist and base card values.)

1996 Select Certified Red, Blue

These 1996 Select Certified insert cards were the most common of the parallel cards issued; they were seeded one per five packs. There were 1,800 Certified Red sets produced, with the number of Certified Blue sets at 180. Cards are essentially the same as regular-issue Select Certified except for the color of the foil background on front.

	MT
Complete Set, Red (144):	500.00
Common Player, Red:	1.00
Red Stars:	2.5X
Complete Set, Blue (144):	3000.
Common Player, Blue:	5.00
Blue Stars:	20X

(See 1996 Select Certified for checklist and base card values.)

1996 Select Certified Mirror Red, Blue, Gold

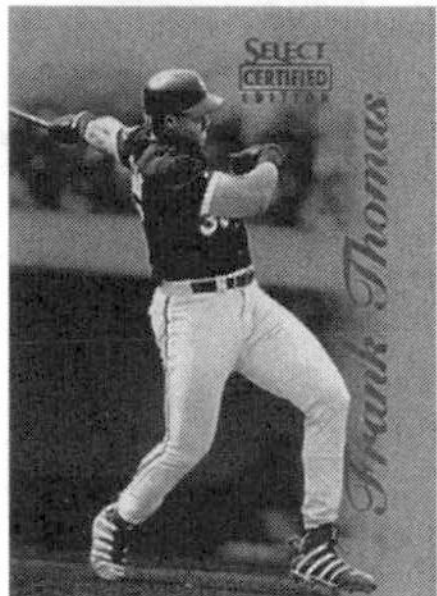

These 1996 Select Certified inserts are the scarcest of the set. Only 30 Mirror Gold sets were made, with 60 Mirror Blue sets and 90 Mirror Red. Due to the improbability of completing the collection, no complete set price is given.

	MT
Common Mirror Red:	12.00
Mirror Red Stars:	25X
Common Mirror Blue:	25.00
Mirror Blue Stars:	40X
Common Mirror Gold:	60.00
Mirror Gold Stars:	120X

(See 1996 Select Certified for checklist and base card values.)

1996 Select Certified Interleague Preview

These 1996 Select Certified insert cards feature 21 prospective matchups from when interleague play begins. The cards were seeded one per every 42 packs.

		MT
Complete Set (25):		125.00
Common Player:		3.00
1	Ken Griffey Jr., Hideo Nomo	15.00
2	Greg Maddux, Mo Vaughn	10.00
3	Frank Thomas, Sammy Sosa	12.00
4	Mike Piazza, Jim Edmonds	10.00
5	Ryan Klesko, Roger Clemens	6.00
6	Derek Jeter, Rey Ordonez	10.00
7	Johnny Damon, Ray Lankford	3.00
8	Manny Ramirez, Reggie Sanders	5.00
9	Barry Bonds, Jay Buhner	4.00
10	Jason Isringhausen, Wade Boggs	3.00
11	David Cone, Chipper Jones	10.00
12	Jeff Bagwell, Will Clark	4.00
13	Tony Gwynn, Randy Johnson	7.50
14	Cal Ripken Jr., Tom Glavine	12.50
15	Kirby Puckett, Alan Benes	4.00
16	Gary Sheffield, Mike Mussina	3.00
17	Raul Mondesi, Tim Salmon	3.00
18	Rondell White, Carlos Delgado	3.00
19	Cecil Fielder, Ryne Sandberg	4.00
20	Kenny Lofton, Brian Hunter	3.00
21	Paul Wilson, Paul O'Neill	3.00
22	Ismael Valdes, Edgar Martinez	3.00
23	Matt Williams, Mark McGwire	15.00
24	Albert Belle, Barry Larkin	4.00
25	Brady Anderson, Marquis Grissom	3.00

1996 Select Certified Select Few

Eighteen top players are featured on these 1996 Select Certified inserts, which utilize holographic technology with a dot matrix hologram. Cards were seeded one per every 60 packs.

		MT
Complete Set (18):		190.00
Common Player:		4.00
1	Sammy Sosa	20.00
2	Derek Jeter	20.00
3	Ken Griffey Jr.	30.00
4	Albert Belle	8.00
5	Cal Ripken Jr.	25.00
6	Greg Maddux	20.00
7	Frank Thomas	15.00
8	Mo Vaughn	6.00
9	Chipper Jones	20.00
10	Mike Piazza	20.00
11	Ryan Klesko	4.00
12	Hideo Nomo	6.00
13	Alan Benes	4.00
14	Manny Ramirez	10.00
15	Gary Sheffield	6.00
16	Barry Bonds	8.00
17	Matt Williams	4.00
18	Johnny Damon	4.00

1997 Select Samples

The 1997 edition of Select was previewed with the issue of several regular-issue cards carrying a large black "SAMPLE" overprint on front and back. The Rodriguez sample, untrimmed and larger than standard size, was not distributed in the cello packs with the other three cards.

		MT
Complete Set (4):		30.00
Common Player:		5.00
3	Tony Gwynn	5.00
23	Greg Maddux	5.00
47	Ken Griffey Jr.	9.00
53	Alex Rodriguez	12.00

1997 Select

The Series 1 base set is made up of 150 cards printed on a thick 16-point stock. Each card features a distinctive silver-foil treatment and either red (100 cards) or blue (50 cards) foil accent. Blue-foiled cards were short-printed at a ratio of 1:2 compared to the red-foil cards. Blue-foil cards are indicated with a (B) in the checklist. Subsets include 40 Rookies, eight Super Stars and two checklists. Inserts include two parallel sets, (Artist's Proof and Registered Gold), Tools of the Trade, Mirror Blue Tools of the Trade, and Rookie Revolution. The cards were sold only at hobby shops in six-card packs for $2.99 each. A high-number series was issued with each card bearing a "Select Company" notation.

		MT
Complete Set (200):		65.00
Complete Series 1 (150):		40.00
Common Red Player:		.10
Common Blue Player:		.25
Registered Golds:		4X
Complete High Series [(50):		25.00
Common High Series:		.25
Pack (6):		2.00
Wax Box (24):		45.00
1	Juan Gonzalez (B)	1.50
2	Mo Vaughn (B)	1.00
3	Tony Gwynn	1.50
4	Manny Ramirez (B)	1.50
5	Jose Canseco	.60
6	David Cone	.15
7	Chan Ho Park	.15
8	Frank Thomas (B)	1.50
9	Todd Hollandsworth	.10
10	Marty Cordova	.10
11	Gary Sheffield (B)	.50
12	John Smoltz (B)	.75
13	Mark Grudzielanek	.10
14	Sammy Sosa (B)	3.00
15	Paul Molitor	.40
16	Kevin Brown	.15
17	Albert Belle (B)	1.50
18	Eric Young	.15
19	John Wetteland	.10
20	Ryan Klesko (B)	.60
21	Joe Carter	.15
22	Alex Ochoa	.10
23	Greg Maddux (B)	4.00
24	Roger Clemens (B)	3.00
25	Ivan Rodriguez (B)	1.50
26	Barry Bonds (B)	1.50
27	Kenny Lofton (B)	1.00
28	Javy Lopez	.25
29	Hideo Nomo (B)	1.50
30	Rusty Greer	.10
31	Rafael Palmeiro	.30
32	Mike Piazza (B)	4.00
33	Ryne Sandberg	.75
34	Wade Boggs	.75
35	Jim Thome (B)	.75
36	Ken Caminiti (B)	.75
37	Mark Grace	.30
38	Brian Jordan (B)	.25
39	Craig Biggio	.30
40	Henry Rodriguez	.10
41	Dean Palmer	.10
42	Jason Kendall	.15
43	Bill Pulsipher	.10
44	Tim Salmon (B)	.75
45	Marc Newfield	.10
46	Pat Hentgen	.10
47	Ken Griffey Jr. (B)	6.00
48	Paul Wilson	.10
49	Jay Buhner (B)	.25
50	Rickey Henderson	.75
51	Jeff Bagwell (B)	1.50
52	Cecil Fielder	.15
53	Alex Rodriguez (B)	4.00
54	John Jaha	.10
55	Brady Anderson (B)	.15
56	Andres Galarraga	.60
57	Raul Mondesi	.30
58	Andy Pettitte	.40
59	Roberto Alomar (B)	1.25
60	Derek Jeter (B)	4.00
61	Charles Johnson	.15
62	Travis Fryman	.15
63	Chipper Jones (B)	3.00

64	Edgar Martinez	.10
65	Bobby Bonilla	.10
66	Greg Vaughn	.15
67	Bobby Higginson	.15
68	Garret Anderson	.10
69	Chuck Knoblauch (B)	1.25
70	Jermaine Dye	.10
71	Cal Ripken Jr. (B)	5.00
72	Jason Giambi	.15
73	Trey Beamon	.10
74	Shawn Green	.30
75	Mark McGwire (B)	6.00
76	Carlos Delgado	.20
77	Jason Isringhausen	.10
78	Randy Johnson (B)	1.25
79	Troy Percival (B)	.25
80	Ron Gant	.10
81	Ellis Burks	.10
82	Mike Mussina (B)	1.25
83	Todd Hundley	.15
84	Jim Edmonds	.15
85	Charles Nagy	.15
86	Dante Bichette (B)	.60
87	Mariano Rivera	.15
88	Matt Williams (B)	.60
89	Rondell White	.15
90	Steve Finley	.10
91	Alex Fernandez	.15
92	Barry Larkin	.20
93	Tom Goodwin	.10
94	Will Clark	.50
95	Michael Tucker	.10
96	Derek Bell	.10
97	Larry Walker	.40
98	Alan Benes	.10
99	Tom Glavine	.15
100	Darin Erstad (B)	2.00
101	Andruw Jones (B)	2.00
102	Scott Rolen	1.50
103	Todd Walker (B)	1.25
104	Dmitri Young	.10
105	Vladimir Guerrero (B)	2.50
106	Nomar Garciaparra	2.00
107	*Danny Patterson*	.10
108	Karim Garcia	.20
109	Todd Greene	.10
110	Ruben Rivera	.15
111	Raul Casanova	.10
112	Mike Cameron	.10
113	Bartolo Colon	.15
114	*Rod Myers*	.10
115	Todd Dunn	.10
116	Torii Hunter	.10
117	Jason Dickson	.20
118	*Gene Kingsale*	.20
119	Rafael Medina	.10
120	Raul Ibanez	.10
121	*Bobby Henley*	.20
122	Scott Spiezio	.10
123	*Bobby Smith*	.20
124	J.J. Johnson	.10
125	*Bubba Trammell*	1.00
126	Jeff Abbott	.10
127	Neifi Perez	.10
128	Derrek Lee	.10
129	*Kevin Brown*	.20
130	Mendy Lopez	.10
131	Kevin Orie	.10
132	Ryan Jones	.10
133	Juan Encarnacion	.40
134	Jose Guillen (B)	1.25
135	Greg Norton	.10
136	Richie Sexson	.15
137	Jay Payton	.10
138	Bob Abreu	.10
139	*Ronnie Belliard*	.25
140	Wilton Guerrero (B)	.25
141	Alex Rodriguez (Select Stars) (B)	2.00
142	Juan Gonzalez (Select Stars) (B)	.75
143	Ken Caminiti (Select Stars) (B)	.50
144	Frank Thomas (Select Stars) (B)	1.50
145	Ken Griffey Jr. (Select Stars) (B)	3.00
146	John Smoltz (Select Stars) (B)	.50
147	Mike Piazza (Select Stars) (B)	2.00
148	Derek Jeter (Select Stars) (B)	2.00
149	Frank Thomas (checklist)	.75
150	Ken Griffey Jr. (checklist)	1.50
151	*Jose Cruz Jr.*	1.50
152	Moises Alou	1.50
153	*Hideki Irabu*	1.00
154	Glendon Rusch	.25
155	Ron Coomer	.25
156	*Jeremi Gonzalez*	.50
157	*Fernando Tatis*	5.00
158	John Olerud	.75
159	Rickey Henderson	.75
160	Shannon Stewart	.50
161	Kevin Polcovich	.25
162	Jose Rosado	.25
163	Ray Lankford	.25
164	David Justice	.75
165	*Mark Kotsay*	.60
166	*Deivi Cruz*	.25
167	Billy Wagner	.45
168	Jacob Cruz	.50
169	Matt Morris	.35
170	Brian Banks	.25
171	Brett Tomko	.25
172	Todd Helton	1.00
173	Eric Young	.35
174	Bernie Williams	1.00
175	Jeff Fassero	.25
176	Ryan McGuire	.35
177	Darryl Kile	.25
178	*Kelvim Escobar*	.50
179	Dave Nilsson	.25
180	Geronimo Berroa	.25
181	Livan Hernandez	.35
182	*Tony Womack*	.40
183	Deion Sanders	.40
184	Jeff Kent	.25
185	Brian Hunter	.25
186	Jose Malave	.25
187	*Steve Woodard*	.50
188	Brad Radke	.50
189	Todd Dunwoody	.75
190	Joey Hamilton	.25
191	Denny Naegle	.25
192	Bobby Jones	.25
193	Tony Clark	1.50
194	*Jaret Wright*	3.00
195	Matt Stairs	.50
196	Francisco Cordova	.25
197	Justin Thompson	.25
198	Pokey Reese	.50
199	Garrett Stephenson	.25
200	Carl Everett	.25

1997 Select Artist's Proofs

Featuring a holographic foil background and special Artist's Proof logo on front, this parallel of the 150-card Series 1 Select was a random pack insert at an average pull rate of 1:71 for reds and 1:355 for blues.

	MT
Complete Set (150):	3000.
Common Red:	4.00
Common Blue:	10.00
Artist's Proof Stars:	20X

(See 1997 Select #1-150 for checklist and base card values.)

1997 Select Registered Gold

This parallel insert set, like the regular issue, can be found with 100 red-foil and 50 blue-foil enhanced cards. They differ from the regular issue in the use of gold foil instead of silver on the right side of the front. Also, the inserts have "Registered Gold" printed vertically on the right side of the photo. Backs are identical to the regular issue. Red-foil Registered Gold cards are found on average of once every 11 packs; blue-foiled cards are a 1-in-47 pick.

	MT
Complete Set (150):	600.00
Common Red Gold:	1.00
Common Blue Gold:	2.00

(See 1997 Select #1-150 for checklist and base card values.)

1997 Select Company

Select Company was intended to be a one-per-pack parallel found in '97 high series. The cards have the front background photo replaced with textured silver metallic foil and "Select Company" printed vertically at right-center. While all high-number (151-200) cards have the "Select Company" notation erroneously printed on front, only those cards with silver-foil backgrounds are true parallels.

	MT
Complete Set (200):	150.00
Common Player:	.50
Red Stars:	3X
Blue Stars:	1.5X
High-Series Stars:	1.5X

(See 1997 Select for checklist and base card values.)

1997 Select Autographs

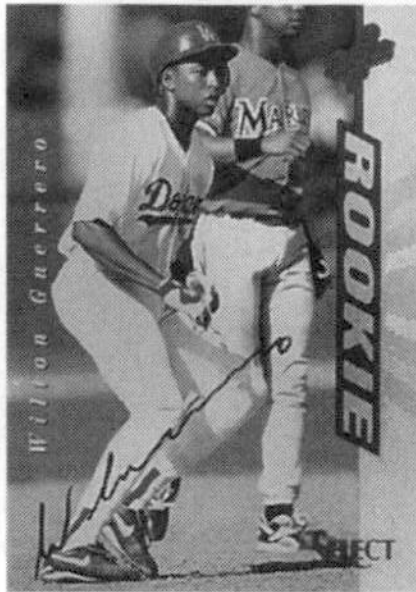

Four top candidates for the 1997 Rookie of the Year Award - Wilton Guerrero, Jose Guillen, Andruw Jones and Todd Walker - each signed a limited number of their Select Rookie cards. Jones signed 2,500 cards while each of the other players signed 3,000 each.

		MT
Complete Set (4):		50.00
Common Autograph:		8.00
AU1	Wilton Guerrero	8.00
AU2	Jose Guillen	10.00
AU3	Andruw Jones	30.00
AU4	Todd Walker	10.00

1997 Select Rookie Revolution

This 20-card insert highlights some of the top young stars in the game. Cards feature a silver micro-etched mylar design on front. Backs are sequentially numbered and contain a few words about the player. Odds of finding a card are 1:56 packs.

		MT
Complete Set (20):		50.00
Common Player:		1.00
1	Andruw Jones	7.50
2	Derek Jeter	12.50
3	Todd Hollandsworth	1.00
4	Edgar Renteria	2.50
5	Jason Kendall	4.00
6	Rey Ordonez	5.00
7	F.P. Santangelo	1.50
8	Jermaine Dye	1.50
9	Alex Ochoa	1.50

10	Vladimir Guerrero	10.00
11	Dmitri Young	1.00
12	Todd Walker	3.00
13	Scott Rolen	7.50
14	Nomar Garciaparra	12.50
15	Ruben Rivera	1.50
16	Darin Erstad	6.00
17	Todd Greene	1.50
18	Mariano Rivera	6.00
19	Trey Beamon	1.00
20	Karim Garcia	2.00

1997 Select Tools of the Trade

A 25-card insert featuring a double-front design salutes a top veteran player on one side and a promising youngster on the other. Cards feature a silver-foil card stock with gold-foil stamping. Cards were inserted 1:9 packs. A parallel to this set - Blue Mirror Tools of the Trade - features blue-foil stock with an insert ratio of 1:240 packs.

		MT
Complete Set (25):		125.00
Common Player:		2.00
Mirror Blues:		4X
1	Ken Griffey Jr., Andruw Jones	15.00
2	Greg Maddux, Andy Pettitte	8.00
3	Cal Ripken Jr., Chipper Jones	10.00
4	Mike Piazza, Jason Kendall	8.00
5	Albert Belle, Karim Garcia	5.00
6	Mo Vaughn, Dmitri Young	3.00
7	Juan Gonzalez, Vladimir Guerrero	5.00
8	Tony Gwynn, Jermaine Dye	6.00
9	Barry Bonds, Alex Ochoa	4.00
10	Jeff Bagwell, Jason Giambi	4.00
11	Kenny Lofton, Darin Erstad	5.00
12	Gary Sheffield, Manny Ramirez	4.00
13	Tim Salmon, Todd Hollandsworth	2.00
14	Sammy Sosa, Ruben Rivera	8.00
15	Paul Molitor, George Arias	3.00
16	Jim Thome, Todd Walker	2.00
17	Wade Boggs, Scott Rolen	6.00
18	Ryne Sandberg, Chuck Knoblauch	4.00
19	Mark McGwire, Frank Thomas	15.00
20	Ivan Rodriguez, Charles Johnson	4.00
21	Brian Jordan, Trey Beamon	2.00
22	Roger Clemens, Troy Percival	5.00
23	John Smoltz, Mike Mussina	3.00
24	Alex Rodriguez, Rey Ordonez	10.00
25	Derek Jeter, Nomar Garciaparra	10.00

1998 Select Selected Samples

Selected promos were released in two-card cello packs prior to Pinnacle's bankruptcy. Fronts have color action photos on bright metallic-foil backgrounds was a large "S". Backs have a smaller version of the front photo along with career highlights and a large overprinted "SAMPLE".

		MT
Complete Set (10):		40.00
Common Player:		4.00
1	Vladimir Guerrero	5.00
2	Nomar Garciaparra	6.00
3	Ben Grieve	4.00
4	Travis Lee	3.00
5	Jose Cruz Jr.	4.00
6	Alex Rodriguez	8.00
7	Todd Helton	4.00
8	Derek Jeter	6.00
9	Scott Rolen	4.00
10	Jaret Wright	3.00

1995 SkyBox E-Motion Promo

To introduce its new super-premium baseball card line, SkyBox debuted a Cal Ripken promo card at the 1995 National Sports Collectors Convention. The card is virtually identical to Ripken's card in the regular issue, except for diagonal overprinting on each side which reads, "Promotional Sample".

		MT
8	Cal Ripken Jr. (Class)	4.00

1995 SkyBox E-Motion

This is a super-premium debut issue from the newly merged Fleer/SkyBox company. Printed on double-thick cardboard, card fronts have borderless photos marred by the presence of four gold-foil "viewfinder" corner marks. The player's last name and team are printed in gold foil near the bottom. On each card there is a large silver-foil word printed in block letters; either a nickname or an emotion or attribute associated with the player. Backs have two more player photos, 1994 and career stats and a few biographical bits. Eight-cards packs were issued with a suggested retail price of $4.99.

		MT
Complete Set (200):		40.00
Common Player:		.15
Pack (8):		1.50
Wax Box (36):		50.00
1	Brady Anderson	.25
2	Kevin Brown	.20
3	Curtis Goodwin	.15
4	Jeffrey Hammonds	.15
5	Ben McDonald	.15
6	Mike Mussina	.75
7	Rafael Palmeiro	.25
8	Cal Ripken Jr.	3.00
9	Jose Canseco	.40
10	Roger Clemens	1.50
11	Vaughn Eshelman	.15
12	Mike Greenwell	.15
13	Erik Hanson	.15
14	Tim Naehring	.15
15	Aaron Sele	.15
16	John Valentin	.15
17	Mo Vaughn	.75
18	Chili Davis	.15
19	Gary DiSarcina	.15
20	Chuck Finley	.15
21	Tim Salmon	.30
22	Lee Smith	.15
23	J.T. Snow	.15
24	Jim Abbott	.15
25	Jason Bere	.15
26	Ray Durham	.15
27	Ozzie Guillen	.15
28	Tim Raines	.15
29	Frank Thomas	1.50
30	Robin Ventura	.25
31	Carlos Baerga	.15
32	Albert Belle	1.00
33	Orel Hershiser	.15
34	Kenny Lofton	.75
35	Dennis Martinez	.15
36	Eddie Murray	.60
37	Manny Ramirez	1.00
38	Julian Tavarez	.15
39	Jim Thome	.50
40	Dave Winfield	.30
41	Chad Curtis	.15
42	Cecil Fielder	.15
43	Travis Fryman	.15
44	Kirk Gibson	.15
45	*Bob Higginson*	1.50
46	Alan Trammell	.15
47	Lou Whitaker	.15
48	Kevin Appier	.15
49	Gary Gaetti	.15
50	Jeff Montgomery	.15
51	Jon Nunnally	.10
52	Ricky Bones	.15
53	Cal Eldred	.15
54	Joe Oliver	.15
55	Kevin Seitzer	.15
56	Marty Cordova	.15
57	Chuck Knoblauch	.25
58	Kirby Puckett	1.50
59	Wade Boggs	.50
60	Derek Jeter	2.00
61	Jimmy Key	.15
62	Don Mattingly	1.50
63	Jack McDowell	.15
64	Paul O'Neill	.20
65	Andy Pettitte	.75
66	Ruben Rivera	.50
67	Mike Stanley	.15
68	John Wetteland	.15
69	Geronimo Berroa	.15
70	Dennis Eckersley	.15
71	Rickey Henderson	.30
72	Mark McGwire	4.00
73	Steve Ontiveros	.15
74	Ruben Sierra	.15
75	Terry Steinbach	.15
76	Jay Buhner	.20
77	Ken Griffey Jr.	4.00
78	Randy Johnson	.60
79	Edgar Martinez	.15
80	Tino Martinez	.20
81	Marc Newfield	.15
82	Alex Rodriguez	3.00
83	Will Clark	.40
84	Benji Gil	.15
85	Juan Gonzalez	1.00
86	Rusty Greer	.15
87	Dean Palmer	.15
88	Ivan Rodriguez	.75
89	Kenny Rogers	.15
90	Roberto Alomar	.75
91	Joe Carter	.15
92	David Cone	.25
93	Alex Gonzalez	.15
94	Shawn Green	.25
95	Pat Hentgen	.15
96	Paul Molitor	.40
97	John Olerud	.20
98	Devon White	.15
99	Steve Avery	.15
100	Tom Glavine	.25
101	Marquis Grissom	.15
102	Chipper Jones	2.00
103	Dave Justice	.25
104	Ryan Klesko	.35
105	Javier Lopez	.25
106	Greg Maddux	2.00
107	Fred McGriff	.40
108	John Smoltz	.30
109	Shawon Dunston	.15
110	Mark Grace	.25

111	Brian McRae	.15
112	Randy Myers	.15
113	Sammy Sosa	2.00
114	Steve Trachsel	.15
115	Bret Boone	.15
116	Ron Gant	.25
117	Barry Larkin	.25
118	Deion Sanders	.25
119	Reggie Sanders	.15
120	Pete Schourek	.15
121	John Smiley	.15
122	Jason Bates	.15
123	Dante Bichette	.50
124	Vinny Castilla	.15
125	Andres Galarraga	.25
126	Larry Walker	.40
127	Greg Colbrunn	.15
128	Jeff Conine	.15
129	Andre Dawson	.20
130	Chris Hammond	.15
131	Charles Johnson	.15
132	Gary Sheffield	.60
133	Quilvio Veras	.15
134	Jeff Bagwell	1.25
135	Derek Bell	.15
136	Craig Biggio	.25
137	Jim Dougherty	.15
138	John Hudek	.15
139	Orlando Miller	.15
140	Phil Plantier	.15
141	Eric Karros	.20
142	Ramon Martinez	.15
143	Raul Mondesi	.50
144	*Hideo Nomo*	2.00
145	Mike Piazza	2.00
146	Ismael Valdes	.15
147	Todd Worrell	.15
148	Moises Alou	.15
149	*Yamil Benitez*	.15
150	Wil Cordero	.15
151	Jeff Fassero	.15
152	Cliff Floyd	.15
153	Pedro Martinez	.40
154	*Carlos Perez*	.25
155	Tony Tarasco	.15
156	Rondell White	.15
157	Edgardo Alfonzo	.15
158	Bobby Bonilla	.15
159	Rico Brogna	.15
160	Bobby Jones	.15
161	Bill Pulsipher	.15
162	Bret Saberhagen	.15
163	Ricky Bottalico	.15
164	Darren Daulton	.15
165	Lenny Dykstra	.15
166	Charlie Hayes	.15
167	Dave Hollins	.15
168	Gregg Jefferies	.15
169	*Michael Mimbs*	.40
170	Curt Schilling	.15
171	Heathcliff Slocumb	.15
172	Jay Bell	.15
173	*Micah Franklin*	.15
174	*Mark Johnson*	.40
175	Jeff King	.15
176	Al Martin	.15
177	Dan Miceli	.15
178	Denny Neagle	.15
179	Bernard Gilkey	.15
180	Ken Hill	.15
181	Brian Jordan	.20
182	Ray Lankford	.15
183	Ozzie Smith	.75
184	Andy Benes	.15
185	Ken Caminiti	.25
186	Steve Finley	.15
187	Tony Gwynn	1.50
188	Joey Hamilton	.20
189	Melvin Nieves	.15
190	Scott Sanders	.15
191	Rod Beck	.15
192	Barry Bonds	.75
193	Royce Clayton	.15
194	Glenallen Hill	.15
195	Darren Lewis	.15
196	Mark Portugal	.15
197	Matt Williams	.40
198	Checklist	.05
199	Checklist	.05
200	Checklist	.05

1995 SkyBox E-Motion Cal Ripken Jr. Timeless

A white background with a clockface and gold-foil "TIMELESS" logo are the standard elements of this insert tribute to Cal Ripken, Jr. Each card front features a large color photo and a smaller sepia photo contemporary to some phase of his career. The first 10 cards in the set chronicle Ripken's career through 1994. A special mail-in offer provided five more cards featuring highlights of his 1995 season.

		MT
Complete Set (15):		60.00
Common Player:		5.00
1	High School Pitcher	5.00
2	Role Model	5.00
3	Rookie of the Year	5.00
4	1st MVP Season	5.00
5	95 Consecutive Errorless Games	5.00
6	All-Star MVP	5.00
7	Conditioning	5.00
8	Shortstop HR Record	5.00
9	Literacy Work	5.00
10	2000th Consecutive Game	5.00
11	All-Star Selection	5.00
12	Record-tying Game	5.00
13	Record-breaking Game	5.00
14	2,153 and Counting	5.00
15	Birthday	5.00

1995 SkyBox E-Motion Masters

Ten of the game's top veterans are featured in this chase card set. A large close-up photo in a single team-related color in the background, with a color action photo in the foreground. Backs have a borderless color photo and a top to bottom color bar with some good words about the player. The Masters inserts are found at an average rate of one per eight packs.

		MT
Complete Set (10):		40.00
Common Player:		2.00
1	Barry Bonds	3.00
2	Juan Gonzalez	3.00
3	Ken Griffey Jr.	10.00
4	Tony Gwynn	4.00
5	Kenny Lofton	2.00
6	Greg Maddux	6.00
7	Raul Mondesi	2.00
8	Cal Ripken Jr.	10.00
9	Frank Thomas	4.00
10	Matt Williams	2.00

1995 SkyBox E-Motion N-Tense

A colored wave-pattern printed on metallic foil is the background for the action photo of one of baseball's top sluggers in this chase card set. A huge rainbow prismatic foil "N" appears in an upper corner. The player's name and team are at lower-right in gold foil. Backs are conventionally printed and repeat the front's patterned background, with another color player photo and a shaded box with a few career highlights.

		MT
Complete Set (12):		100.00
Common Player:		4.00
1	Jeff Bagwell	8.00
2	Albert Belle	5.00
3	Barry Bonds	8.00
4	Cecil Fielder	2.00
5	Ron Gant	2.00
6	Ken Griffey Jr.	25.00
7	Mark McGwire	30.00
8	Mike Piazza	20.00
9	Manny Ramirez	8.00
10	Frank Thomas	10.00
11	Mo Vaughn	5.00
12	Matt Williams	4.00

1995 SkyBox E-Motion Rookies

A bold colored background with outline white letters repeating the word "ROOKIE" is the frame for the central action photo in this insert series. The top of the photo is vignetted with a white circle that has the player's name in gold at left, and his team in white at right. Backs repeat the front background and include a player portrait photo and a few sentences about his potential. Rookie inserts are found at an average rate of one per five packs.

		MT
Complete Set (10):		24.00
Common Player:		1.00
1	Edgardo Alfonzo	2.00
2	Jason Bates	1.00
3	Marty Cordova	1.00
4	Ray Durham	1.50
5	Alex Gonzalez	2.00
6	Shawn Green	4.00
7	Charles Johnson	2.00
8	Chipper Jones	6.00
9	Hideo Nomo	4.00
10	Alex Rodriguez	8.00

1996 SkyBox E-Motion XL

Each card in SkyBox's 1996 E-Motion XL Baseball arrives on two layers of stock - a die-cut matte frame over a UV-coated card. The frames come in three colors - blue, green and maroon (but each player has only one color version). The 300-card set also includes four insert sets: Legion of Boom, D-Fense, N-Tense and Rare Breed.

		MT
Complete Set (300):		70.00
Common Player:		.20
Pack (7):		2.50
Wax Box (24):		50.00
1	Roberto Alomar	1.50
2	Brady Anderson	.30
3	Bobby Bonilla	.20
4	Jeffrey Hammonds	.20
5	Chris Hoiles	.20
6	Mike Mussina	1.00
7	Randy Myers	.20
8	Rafael Palmeiro	.40
9	Cal Ripken Jr.	5.00
10	B.J. Surhoff	.20
11	Jose Canseco	.50
12	Roger Clemens	2.00
13	Wil Cordero	.20
14	Mike Greenwell	.20
15	Dwayne Hosey	.20
16	Tim Naehring	.20
17	Troy O'Leary	.20
18	Mike Stanley	.20
19	John Valentin	.20
20	Mo Vaughn	1.00
21	Jim Abbott	.20
22	Garret Anderson	.20
23	George Arias	.20
24	Chili Davis	.20
25	Jim Edmonds	.30
26	Chuck Finley	.20
27	Todd Greene	.20
28	Mark Langston	.20
29	Troy Percival	.20
30	Tim Salmon	.40
31	Lee Smith	.20
32	J.T. Snow	.20
33	Harold Baines	.20
34	Jason Bere	.20
35	Ray Durham	.20
36	Alex Fernandez	.20
37	Ozzie Guillen	.20
38	Darren Lewis	.20
39	Lyle Mouton	.20
40	Tony Phillips	.20
41	Danny Tartabull	.20
42	Frank Thomas	2.50
43	Robin Ventura	.25
44	Sandy Alomar	.25
45	Carlos Baerga	.20
46	Albert Belle	1.50
47	Julio Franco	.20
48	Orel Hershiser	.20
49	Kenny Lofton	1.00
50	Dennis Martinez	.20
51	Jack McDowell	.20
52	Jose Mesa	.20
53	Eddie Murray	.75
54	Charles Nagy	.20
55	Manny Ramirez	2.00
55p	Manny Ramirez (over-printed "PROMO-TIONAL SAMPLE")	3.00
56	Jim Thome	1.00
57	Omar Vizquel	.20
58	Chad Curtis	.20
59	Cecil Fielder	.20
60	Travis Fryman	.20
61	Chris Gomez	.20
62	Felipe Lira	.20
63	Alan Trammell	.20
64	Kevin Appier	.20
65	Johnny Damon	.50
66	Tom Goodwin	.20
67	Mark Gubicza	.20
68	Jeff Montgomery	.20
69	Jon Nunnally	1.00
70	Bip Roberts	.20
71	Ricky Bones	.20
72	Chuck Carr	.20
73	John Jaha	.20
74	Ben McDonald	.20
75	Matt Mieske	.20
76	Dave Nilsson	.20
77	Kevin Seitzer	.20
78	Greg Vaughn	.20
79	Rick Aguilera	.20
80	Marty Cordova	.20
81	Roberto Kelly	.20
82	Chuck Knoblauch	.25
83	Pat Meares	.20
84	Paul Molitor	1.00
85	Kirby Puckett	2.00
86	Brad Radke	.20
87	Wade Boggs	.50
88	David Cone	.35
89	Dwight Gooden	.20
90	Derek Jeter	3.50
91	Tino Martinez	.30
92	Paul O'Neill	.25
93	Andy Pettitte	1.00
94	Tim Raines	.20
95	Ruben Rivera	.60
96	Kenny Rogers	.20
97	Ruben Sierra	.20
98	John Wetteland	.20
99	Bernie Williams	1.00
100	Allen Battle	.20
101	Geronimo Berroa	.20
102	Brent Gates	.20
103	Doug Johns	.20
104	Mark McGwire	7.00
105	Pedro Munoz	.20
106	Ariel Prieto	.20
107	Terry Steinbach	.20
108	Todd Van Poppel	.20
109	Chris Bosio	.20
110	Jay Buhner	.30
111	Joey Cora	.20
112	Russ Davis	.20
113	Ken Griffey Jr.	7.00
114	Sterling Hitchcock	.20
115	Randy Johnson	1.25
116	Edgar Martinez	.20
117	Alex Rodriguez	5.00
118	Paul Sorrento	.20
119	Dan Wilson	.20
120	Will Clark	.50
121	Juan Gonzalez	1.50
122	Rusty Greer	.20
123	Kevin Gross	.20
124	Ken Hill	.20
125	Dean Palmer	.20
126	Roger Pavlik	.20
127	Ivan Rodriguez	1.50
128	Mickey Tettleton	.20
129	Joe Carter	.30
130	Carlos Delgado	.75
131	Alex Gonzalez	.20
132	Shawn Green	.30
133	Erik Hanson	.20
134	Pat Hentgen	.20
135	Otis Nixon	.20
136	John Olerud	.30
137	Ed Sprague	.20
138	Steve Avery	.20
139	Jermaine Dye	.30
140	Tom Glavine	.40
141	Marquis Grissom	.20
142	Chipper Jones	3.50
143	David Justice	.40
144	Ryan Klesko	.35
145	Javier Lopez	.35
146	Greg Maddux	3.50
147	Fred McGriff	.75
148	Jason Schmidt	.20
149	John Smoltz	.75
150	Mark Wohlers	.20
151	Jim Bullinger	.20
152	Frank Castillo	.20
153	Kevin Foster	.20
154	Luis Gonzalez	.20
155	Mark Grace	.40
156	Brian McRae	.20
157	Jaime Navarro	.20
158	Rey Sanchez	.20
159	Ryne Sandberg	2.00
160	Sammy Sosa	3.00
161	Bret Boone	.20
162	Jeff Brantley	.20
163	Vince Coleman	.20
164	Steve Gibralter	.20
165	Curtis Goodwin	.20
166	Barry Larkin	.35
167	Hal Morris	.20
168	Mark Portugal	.20
169	Reggie Sanders	.20
170	Pete Schourek	.20
171	John Smiley	.20
172	Jason Bates	.20
173	Dante Bichette	.40
174	Ellis Burks	.20
175	Vinny Castilla	.20
176	Andres Galarraga	.40
177	Kevin Ritz	.20
178	Bill Swift	.20
179	Larry Walker	.40
180	Walt Weiss	.20
181	Eric Young	.20
182	Kurt Abbott	.20
183	Kevin Brown	.30
184	John Burkett	.20
185	Greg Colbrunn	.20
186	Jeff Conine	.20
187	Chris Hammond	.20
188	Charles Johnson	.20
189	Terry Pendleton	.20
190	Pat Rapp	.20
191	Gary Sheffield	1.00
192	Quilvio Veras	.20
193	Devon White	.20
194	Jeff Bagwell	2.50
195	Derek Bell	.20
196	Sean Berry	.20
197	Craig Biggio	.30
198	Doug Drabek	.20
199	Tony Eusebio	.20
200	Mike Hampton	.20
201	Brian Hunter	.30
202	Derrick May	.20
203	Orlando Miller	.20
204	Shane Reynolds	.20
205	Mike Blowers	.20
206	Tom Candiotti	.20
207	Delino DeShields	.20
208	Greg Gagne	.20
209	Karim Garcia	.75
210	Todd Hollandsworth	.20
211	Eric Karros	.20
212	Ramon Martinez	.20
213	Raul Mondesi	.40
214	Hideo Nomo	1.00
215	Mike Piazza	3.50
216	Ismael Valdes	.20
217	Todd Worrell	.20
218	Moises Alou	.20
219	Yamil Benitez	.20
220	Jeff Fassero	.20
221	Darrin Fletcher	.20
222	Cliff Floyd	.20
223	Pedro Martinez	.40
224	Carlos Perez	.20
225	Mel Rojas	.20
226	David Segui	.20
227	Rondell White	.20
228	Rico Brogna	.20
229	Carl Everett	.20
230	John Franco	.20
231	Bernard Gilkey	.20
232	Todd Hundley	.20
233	Jason Isringhausen	.30
234	Lance Johnson	.20
235	Bobby Jones	.20
236	Jeff Kent	.20
237	Rey Ordonez	.75
238	Bill Pulsipher	.20
239	Jose Vizcaino	.20
240	Paul Wilson	.35
241	Ricky Bottalico	.20
242	Darren Daulton	.20
243	Lenny Dykstra	.20
244	Jim Eisenreich	.20
245	Sid Fernandez	.20
246	Gregg Jefferies	.20
247	Mickey Morandini	.20
248	Benito Santiago	.20
249	Curt Schilling	.20
250	Mark Whiten	.20
251	Todd Zeile	.20
252	Jay Bell	.20
253	Carlos Garcia	.20
254	Charlie Hayes	.20
255	Jason Kendall	.20
256	Jeff King	.20
257	Al Martin	.20
258	Orlando Merced	.20
259	Dan Miceli	.20
260	Denny Neagle	.20
261	Alan Benes	.30
262	Andy Benes	.20
263	Royce Clayton	.20
264	Dennis Eckersley	.20
265	Gary Gaetti	.20
266	Ron Gant	.30
267	Brian Jordan	.20
268	Ray Lankford	.20
269	John Mabry	.20
270	Tom Pagnozzi	.20
271	Ozzie Smith	1.00
272	Todd Stottlemyre	.20
273	Andy Ashby	.20
274	Brad Ausmus	.20
275	Ken Caminiti	.40
276	Steve Finley	.20
277	Tony Gwynn	2.00
278	Joey Hamilton	.20
279	Rickey Henderson	.35
280	Trevor Hoffman	.25
281	Wally Joyner	.20
282	Jody Reed	.20
283	Bob Tewksbury	.20
284	Fernando Valenzuela	.20
285	Rod Beck	.20
286	Barry Bonds	1.50
287	Mark Carreon	.20
288	Shawon Dunston	.20
289	*Osvaldo Fernandez*	.30
290	Glenallen Hill	.20
291	Stan Javier	.20
292	Mark Leiter	.20
293	Kirt Manwaring	.20
294	Robby Thompson	.20
295	William VanLandingham	.20
296	Allen Watson	.20
297	Matt Williams	.50
298	Checklist	.10
299	Checklist	.10
300	Checklist	.10

1996 SkyBox E-Motion XL D-Fense

Ten top defensive players are featured on these 1996 SkyBox E-Motion XL insert cards. The cards were seeded at a rate of one per every four packs.

		MT
Complete Set (10):		20.00
Common Player:		.75
1	Roberto Alomar	1.00
2	Barry Bonds	2.00
3	Mark Grace	.75
4	Ken Griffey Jr.	7.50
5	Kenny Lofton	.75
6	Greg Maddux	4.00
7	Raul Mondesi	.75
8	Cal Ripken Jr.	5.00
9	Ivan Rodriguez	1.50
10	Matt Williams	.75

1996 SkyBox E-Motion XL Legion of Boom

The top power hitters in baseball are featured on these 1996 SkyBox E-Motion XL insert cards. The cards, exclusive to hobby packs at a ratio of one per every 36 packs, have translucent card backs.

		MT
Complete Set (12):		150.00
Common Player:		5.00
1	Albert Belle	6.00
2	Barry Bonds	10.00
3	Juan Gonzalez	10.00
4	Ken Griffey Jr.	30.00
5	Mark McGwire	40.00
6	Mike Piazza	25.00
7	Manny Ramirez	10.00
8	Tim Salmon	5.00
9	Sammy Sosa	25.00
10	Frank Thomas	15.00
11	Mo Vaughn	6.00
12	Matt Williams	5.00

1996 SkyBox E-Motion XL N-Tense

Ten top clutch performers are featured on these 1996 SkyBox E-Motion XL insert cards. The cards, which use an N-shaped die-cut design, were included one per every 12 packs.

		MT
Complete Set (10):		60.00
Common Player:		2.00
1	Albert Belle	3.50
2	Barry Bonds	4.50
3	Jose Canseco	2.50
4	Ken Griffey Jr.	15.00
5	Tony Gwynn	6.00
6	Randy Johnson	3.50
7	Greg Maddux	9.00
8	Cal Ripken Jr.	12.00
9	Frank Thomas	6.00
10	Matt Williams	2.00

1996 SkyBox E-Motion XL Rare Breed

These 1996 E-Motion XL inserts are the most difficult to find; they are seeded one per every 100 packs. The cards showcase top young stars on 3-D lenticular design, similar to the Hot Numbers in Fleer Flair basketball.

		MT
Complete Set (10):		110.00
Common Player:		5.00
1	Garret Anderson	6.00
2	Marty Cordova	6.00
3	Brian Hunter	6.00
4	Jason Isringhausen	6.00
5	Charles Johnson	6.00
6	Chipper Jones	40.00
7	Raul Mondesi	7.50
8	Hideo Nomo	12.00
9	Manny Ramirez	25.00
10	Rondell White	6.00

1997 SkyBox E-X2000 Sample

To introduce its innovative high-tech premium brand, SkyBox released this promo card. It is identical in format to the issued version, except it carries a "SAMPLE" notation instead of a card number on back.

	MT
Alex Rodriguez	10.00

1997 SkyBox E-X2000

The premiere issue of E-X2000 consists of 100 base cards designed with "SkyView" technology, utilizing a die-cut holofoil border and the player silhouetted in front of a transparent "window" featuring a variety of sky patterns. Inserts include two sequentially-numbered parallel sets - Credentials (1:50 packs) and Essential Credentials (1:200 packs) - as well as Emerald Autograph Exchange Cards, A Cut Above, Hall of Nothing, and Star Date. Cards were sold in two-card packs for $3.99 each.

		MT
Complete Set (100):		80.00
Common Player:		.50
Pack (2):		4.00
Wax Box (24):		80.00
1	Jim Edmonds	.75
2	Darin Erstad	2.00
3	Eddie Murray	.75
4	Roberto Alomar	1.50
5	Brady Anderson	.60
6	Mike Mussina	1.50
7	Rafael Palmeiro	1.50
8	Cal Ripken Jr.	6.00
9	Steve Avery	.50
10	Nomar Garciaparra	5.00
11	Mo Vaughn	1.00
12	Albert Belle	1.00
13	Mike Cameron	.50
14	Ray Durham	.50
15	Frank Thomas	3.00
16	Robin Ventura	.75
17	Manny Ramirez	2.00
18	Jim Thome	1.00
19	Matt Williams	.75
20	Tony Clark	.50
21	Travis Fryman	.60
22	Bob Higginson	.50
23	Kevin Appier	.50
24	Johnny Damon	.50
25	Jermaine Dye	.50
26	Jeff Cirillo	.50
27	Ben McDonald	.50
28	Chuck Knoblauch	.75
29	Paul Molitor	1.00
30	Todd Walker	.50
31	Wade Boggs	1.00
32	Cecil Fielder	.50
33	Derek Jeter	6.00
34	Andy Pettitte	.75
35	Ruben Rivera	.50
36	Bernie Williams	1.50
37	Jose Canseco	1.50
38	Mark McGwire	8.00
39	Jay Buhner	.50
40	Ken Griffey Jr.	6.00
41	Randy Johnson	2.00
42	Edgar Martinez	.50
43	Alex Rodriguez	6.00
44	Dan Wilson	.50
45	Will Clark	1.00
46	Juan Gonzalez	2.00
47	Ivan Rodriguez	2.00
48	Joe Carter	.50
49	Roger Clemens	3.00
50	Juan Guzman	.50
51	Pat Hentgen	.50
52	Tom Glavine	1.00
53	Andruw Jones	3.00
54	Chipper Jones	4.00
55	Ryan Klesko	.75
56	Kenny Lofton	.75
57	Greg Maddux	4.00
58	Fred McGriff	.75
59	John Smoltz	.50
60	Mark Wohlers	.50
61	Mark Grace	.75
62	Ryne Sandberg	2.00
63	Sammy Sosa	5.00
64	Barry Larkin	1.00
65	Deion Sanders	.75
66	Reggie Sanders	.50
67	Dante Bichette	.50
68	Ellis Burks	.50
69	Andres Galarraga	1.00
70	Moises Alou	.50
71	Kevin Brown	.60
72	Cliff Floyd	.50
73	Edgar Renteria	.50
74	Gary Sheffield	1.00
75	Bob Abreu	.50
76	Jeff Bagwell	2.00
77	Craig Biggio	.75
78	Todd Hollandsworth	.50
79	Eric Karros	.50
80	Raul Mondesi	.75
81	Hideo Nomo	1.50
82	Mike Piazza	5.00
83	Vladimir Guerrero	3.00
84	Henry Rodriguez	.50
85	Todd Hundley	.50
86	Rey Ordonez	.50
87	Alex Ochoa	.50
88	Gregg Jefferies	.50
89	Scott Rolen	2.00
90	Jermaine Allensworth	.50
91	Jason Kendall	.50
92	Ken Caminiti	.50
93	Tony Gwynn	3.00
94	Rickey Henderson	1.00
95	Barry Bonds	2.50
96	J.T. Snow	.50
97	Dennis Eckersley	.50
98	Ron Gant	.50
99	Brian Jordan	.50
100	Ray Lankford	.50

1997 SkyBox E-X2000 Credentials

This parallel set features different colored foils from the base cards, as well as different images on the "window." Cards are sequentially numbered on back within an issue of 299. Cards were inserted 1:50 packs.

	MT
Common Player:	4.00
Credentials Stars:	6X

(See E-X2000 for checklist, base card values)

1997 SkyBox E-X2000 Essential Credentials

A sequentially-numbered parallel set, found one per 200 packs, and limited to 99 total sets.

	MT
Common Player:	8.00
Essential Credentials Stars:	15X

(See 1997 SkyBox E-X2000 for checklist and base card values.)

1997 SkyBox E-X2000 Emerald Autograph Redemptions

Inserted 1:480 packs, these cards could be exchanged by mail prior to May 1, 1998, for autographed cards or memorabilia from one of six major leaguers.

		MT
Complete Set (6):		80.00
Common Player:		4.00
(1)	Darin Erstad	20.00
(2)	Todd Hollandsworth	6.00
(3)	Alex Ochoa	4.00
(4)	Alex Rodriguez	50.00
(5)	Scott Rolen	25.00
(6)	Todd Walker	6.00

1997 SkyBox E-X2000 Emerald Autographs

These authentically autographed versions of the players' E-X2000 cards were available (until May 1, 1998) by a mail-in exchange of redemption cards. The autographed cards are authenticated by the presence of an embossed SkyBox logo seal.

		MT
Complete Set (6):		400.00
Common Player:		16.00
2	Darin Erstad	80.00
30	Todd Walker	40.00
43	Alex Rodriguez	200.00
78	Todd Hollandsworth	20.00
86	Alex Ochoa	16.00
89	Scott Rolen	100.00

1997 SkyBox E-X2000 A Cut Above

Some of the game's elite players are featured in this 1:288 pack insert that features a die-cut design resembling a saw blade. Printed on silver-foil stock, the player's name and Cut Above logo are embossed on front. On back is another color photo and a few words about the player.

		MT
Complete Set (10):		100.00
Common Player:		4.00
1	Frank Thomas	12.50
2	Ken Griffey Jr.	30.00
3	Alex Rodriguez	25.00
4	Albert Belle	7.50
5	Juan Gonzalez	8.00
6	Mark McGwire	30.00
7	Mo Vaughn	4.00
8	Manny Ramirez	9.00
9	Barry Bonds	7.50
10	Fred McGriff	4.00

1997 SkyBox E-X2000 Hall or Nothing

This 20-card insert, featuring players who are candidates for the Hall of Fame, utilizes a die-cut design on plastic stock. Stately architectural details and brush bronze highlights frame the player picture on front. The player silhouette on back contains career information. Cards were inserted 1:20 packs.

		MT
Complete Set (20):		125.00
Common Player:		2.00
1	Frank Thomas	8.00
2	Ken Griffey Jr.	20.00
3	Eddie Murray	3.00
4	Cal Ripken Jr.	15.00
5	Ryne Sandberg	5.00
6	Wade Boggs	4.00
7	Roger Clemens	7.50
8	Tony Gwynn	10.00
9	Alex Rodriguez	15.00
10	Mark McGwire	20.00
11	Barry Bonds	6.00
12	Greg Maddux	10.00
13	Juan Gonzalez	5.00
14	Albert Belle	4.00
15	Mike Piazza	12.00
16	Jeff Bagwell	5.00
17	Dennis Eckersley	2.00
18	Mo Vaughn	3.00
19	Roberto Alomar	3.00
20	Kenny Lofton	2.00

1997 SkyBox E-X2000 Star Date 2000

A 15-card set highlighting young stars that are likely to be the game's top players in the year 2000. Cards were inserted 1:9 packs.

		MT
Complete Set (15):		40.00
Common Player:		1.50
1	Alex Rodriguez	10.00
2	Andruw Jones	4.50
3	Andy Pettitte	2.00
4	Brooks Kieschnick	1.50
5	Chipper Jones	7.50
6	Darin Erstad	4.00
7	Derek Jeter	7.50
8	Jason Kendall	3.00
9	Jermaine Dye	1.50
10	Neifi Perez	1.50
11	Scott Rolen	4.50
12	Todd Hollandsworth	1.50
13	Todd Walker	2.00
14	Tony Clark	3.00
15	Vladimir Guerrero	8.00

1998 SkyBox Dugout Axcess

Dugout Axcess was a 150-card set that attempted to provide collectors with an inside look at baseball. The cards were printed on "playing card" quality stock and used unique information and photography. The product arrived in 12-card packs with an Inside Axcess parallel set that was individually numbered to 50 sets. Six different inserts sets were available, including Double Header, Frequent Flyers, Dishwashers, Superheroes, Gronks and Autograph Redemptions.

		MT
Complete Set (150):		15.00
Common Player:		.10
Pack (12):		1.00
Wax Box (36):		30.00
1	Travis Lee	.15
2	Matt Williams	.20
3	Andy Benes	.10
4	Chipper Jones	1.00
5	Ryan Klesko	.15
6	Greg Maddux	1.00
7	Sammy Sosa	1.00
8	Henry Rodriguez	.10
9	Mark Grace	.20
10	Barry Larkin	.25
11	Bret Boone	.10
12	Reggie Sanders	.10
13	Vinny Castilla	.10
14	Larry Walker	.25
15	Darryl Kile	.10
16	Charles Johnson	.10
17	Edgar Renteria	.10
18	Gary Sheffield	.25
19	Jeff Bagwell	.50
20	Craig Biggio	.20
21	Moises Alou	.20
22	Mike Piazza	1.25
23	Hideo Nomo	.20
24	Raul Mondesi	.20
25	John Jaha	.10
26	Jeff Cirillo	.10
27	Jeromy Burnitz	.10
28	Mark Grudzielanek	.10
29	Vladimir Guerrero	.75
30	Rondell White	.15
31	Edgardo Alfonzo	.15
32	Rey Ordonez	.10
33	Bernard Gilkey	.10
34	Scott Rolen	.40
35	Curt Schilling	.15
36	Ricky Bottalico	.10
37	Tony Womack	.10
38	Al Martin	.10
39	Jason Kendall	.10
40	Ron Gant	.10
41	Mark McGwire	2.00
42	Ray Lankford	.10
43	Tony Gwynn	.75
44	Ken Caminiti	.15
45	Kevin Brown	.10
46	Barry Bonds	.50
47	J.T. Snow	.10
48	Shawn Estes	.10
49	Jim Edmonds	.20
50	Tim Salmon	.20
51	Jason Dickson	.10
52	Cal Ripken Jr.	1.50
53	Mike Mussina	.40
54	Roberto Alomar	.40
55	Mo Vaughn	.25

56	Pedro Martinez	.50
57	Nomar Garciaparra	1.25
58	Albert Belle	.25
59	Frank Thomas	.75
60	Robin Ventura	.20
61	Jim Thome	.30
62	Sandy Alomar Jr.	.20
63	Jaret Wright	.15
64	Bobby Higginson	.10
65	Tony Clark	.15
66	Justin Thompson	.10
67	Dean Palmer	.10
68	Kevin Appier	.10
69	Johnny Damon	.10
70	Paul Molitor	.30
71	Marty Cordova	.10
72	Brad Radke	.10
73	Derek Jeter	1.50
74	Bernie Williams	.40
75	Andy Pettitte	.20
76	Matt Stairs	.10
77	Ben Grieve	.20
78	Jason Giambi	.20
79	Randy Johnson	.50
80	Ken Griffey Jr.	1.50
81	Alex Rodriguez	1.50
82	Fred McGriff	.20
83	Wade Boggs	.25
84	Wilson Alvarez	.10
85	Juan Gonzalez	.50
86	Ivan Rodriguez	.50
87	Fernando Tatis	.20
88	Roger Clemens	.75
89	Jose Cruz Jr.	.15
90	Shawn Green	.20
91	Jeff Suppan (Little Dawgs)	.10
92	Eli Marrero (Little Dawgs)	.10
93	*Mike Lowell* (Little Dawgs)	.25
94	Ben Grieve (Little Dawgs)	.15
95	Cliff Politte (Little Dawgs)	.10
96	*Rolando Arrojo* (Little Dawgs)	.25
97	Mike Caruso (Little Dawgs)	.10
98	Miguel Tejada (Little Dawgs)	.10
99	Rod Myers (Little Dawgs)	.10
100	Juan Encarnacion (Little Dawgs)	.10
101	Enrique Wilson (Little Dawgs)	.10
102	Brian Giles (Little Dawgs)	.10
103	*Magglio Ordonez* (Little Dawgs)	.75
104	Brian Rose (Little Dawgs)	.10
105	*Ryan Jackson* (Little Dawgs)	.15
106	Mark Kotsay (Little Dawgs)	.10
107	Desi Relaford (Little Dawgs)	.10
108	A.J. Hinch (Little Dawgs)	.10
109	Eric Milton (Little Dawgs)	.10
110	Ricky Ledee (Little Dawgs)	.10
111	Karim Garcia (Little Dawgs)	.10
112	Derrek Lee (Little Dawgs)	.10
113	Brad Fullmer (Little Dawgs)	.10
114	Travis Lee (Little Dawgs)	.10
115	Greg Norton (Little Dawgs)	.10
116	Rich Butler (Little Dawgs)	.10
117	*Masato Yoshii* (Little Dawgs)	.25
118	Paul Konerko (Little Dawgs)	.20
119	Richard Hidalgo (Little Dawgs)	.10
120	Todd Helton (Little Dawgs)	.50
121	Nomar Garciaparra (7th Inning Sketch)	.50
122	Scott Rolen (7th Inning Sketch)	.20
123	Cal Ripken Jr. (7th Inning Sketch)	.75
124	Derek Jeter (7th Inning Sketch)	.60
125	Mike Piazza (7th Inning Sketch)	.50
126	Tony Gwynn (7th Inning Sketch)	.40
127	Mark McGwire (7th Inning Sketch)	1.00
128	Kenny Lofton (7th Inning Sketch)	.15
129	Greg Maddux (7th Inning Sketch)	.50
130	Jeff Bagwell (7th Inning Sketch)	.25
131	Randy Johnson (7th Inning Sketch)	.25
132	Alex Rodriguez (7th Inning Sketch)	.75
133	Mo Vaughn (Name Plates)	.20
134	Chipper Jones (Name Plates)	.50
135	Juan Gonzalez (Name Plates)	.25
136	Tony Clark (Name Plates)	.10
137	Fred McGriff (Name Plates)	.10
138	Roger Clemens (Name Plates)	.40
139	Ken Griffey Jr. (Name Plates)	.75
140	Ivan Rodriguez (Name Plates)	.25
141	Vinny Castilla (Trivia Card)	.10
142	Livan Hernandez (Trivia Card)	.10
143	Jose Cruz Jr. (Trivia Card)	.10
144	Andruw Jones (Trivia Card)	.20
145	Rafael Palmeiro (Trivia Card)	.20
146	Chuck Knoblauch (Trivia Card)	.10
147	Jay Buhner (Trivia Card)	.10
148	Andres Galarraga (Trivia Card)	.10
149	Frank Thomas (Trivia Card)	.40
150	Todd Hundley (Trivia Card)	.10

1998 SkyBox Dugout Axcess Inside Axcess

This 150-card parallel set was sequentially numbered to 50 sets, with each card containing a stamped logo on the front and serial numbering on the back.

	MT
Common Player:	10.00
Inside Axcess Stars:	60-75X

(See 1998 SkyBox Dugout Access for checklist and base card values.)

1998 SkyBox Dugout Axcess Dishwashers

This 10-card set was a tribute to the game's best pitchers who "clean the home plate of opposing batters." Cards were inserted one per eight packs.

		MT
Complete Set (10):		6.00
Common Player:		.25
Inserted 1:8		
D1	Greg Maddux	3.00
D2	Kevin Brown	.50
D3	Pedro Martinez	1.00
D4	Randy Johnson	1.00
D5	Curt Schilling	.40
D6	John Smoltz	.50
D7	Darryl Kile	.25
D8	Roger Clemens	2.00
D9	Andy Pettitte	.75
D10	Mike Mussina	.75

1998 SkyBox Dugout Axcess Double Header

Double Header featured 20 players on cards that doubled as game pieces. The game instructions were on the card and required two dice to play. These were inserted at a rate of two per pack.

		MT
Complete Set (20):		5.00
Common Player:		.20
Inserted 2:1		
DH1	Jeff Bagwell	.30
DH2	Albert Belle	.25
DH3	Barry Bonds	.25
DH4	Derek Jeter	.60
DH5	Tony Clark	.20
DH6	Nomar Garciaparra	.60
DH7	Juan Gonzalez	.30
DH8	Ken Griffey Jr.	1.00
DH9	Chipper Jones	.60
DH10	Kenny Lofton	.20
DH11	Mark McGwire	1.00
DH12	Mo Vaughn	.20
DH13	Mike Piazza	.60
DH14	Cal Ripken Jr.	.75
DH15	Ivan Rodriguez	.25
DH16	Scott Rolen	.30
DH17	Frank Thomas	.50
DH18	Tony Gwynn	.50
DH19	Travis Lee	.40
DH20	Jose Cruz Jr.	.20

1998 SkyBox Dugout Axcess Frequent Flyers

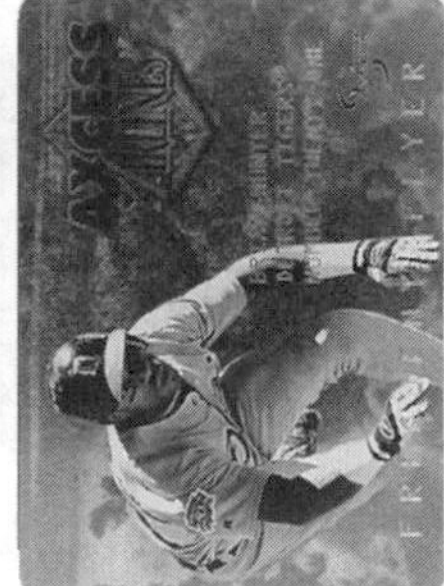

The game's top 10 base stealers were included in Frequent Flyers. This insert was designed to look like airline frequent flyer cards and was inserted one per four packs. Fronts have player action photos on a metallic-foil background of a cloudy sky. Backs have a portrait photo and a few words about the player's base-stealing ability. Cards are numbered with an "FF" prefix.

		MT
Complete Set (10):		3.00
Common Player:		.25
Inserted 1:4		
FF1	Brian Hunter	.25
FF2	Kenny Lofton	.50
FF3	Chuck Knoblauch	.40
FF4	Tony Womack	.25
FF5	Marquis Grissom	.25
FF6	Craig Biggio	.35
FF7	Barry Bonds	.75
FF8	Tom Goodwin	.25
FF9	Delino DeShields	.25
FF10	Eric Young	.25

1998 SkyBox Dugout Axcess Gronks

Gronks featured 10 of the top home run hitters and was a hobby exclusive insert. The name of the insert originated from shortstop Greg Gagne, and the cards were inserted in one per 72 packs.

		MT
Complete Set (10):		100.00
Common Player:		5.00
Inserted 1:72		
G1	Jeff Bagwell	12.50
G2	Albert Belle	7.50
G3	Juan Gonzalez	8.00
G4	Ken Griffey Jr.	30.00
G5	Mark McGwire	30.00
G6	Mike Piazza	20.00
G7	Frank Thomas	15.00
G8	Mo Vaughn	5.00
G9	Ken Caminiti	7.50
G10	Tony Clark	5.00

1998 SkyBox Dugout Axcess SuperHeroes

SuperHeroes combined 10 top superstars with the Marvel Comics superhero with whom they share a common trait in this 10-card insert set. Cards were inserted at a rate of one per 20 packs.

		MT
Complete Set (10):		50.00
Common Player:		2.00
Inserted 1:20		
SH1	Barry Bonds	4.00
SH2	Andres Galarraga	2.00
SH3	Ken Griffey Jr.	15.00
SH4	Chipper Jones	10.00
SH5	Andruw Jones	4.00
SH6	Hideo Nomo	2.00
SH7	Cal Ripken Jr.	12.00
SH8	Alex Rodriguez	12.00
SH9	Frank Thomas	6.00
SH10	Mo Vaughn	2.00

1998 SkyBox E-X2001 Sample

To preview its high-tech E-X2001 brand for 1998, SkyBox issued this sample card of A-Rod. Similar in format to the issued version, it is numbered "SAMPLE" on back and has a "PROMOTIONAL SAMPLE" overprint on back.

	MT
Alex Rodriguez	4.50

1998 SkyBox E-X2001

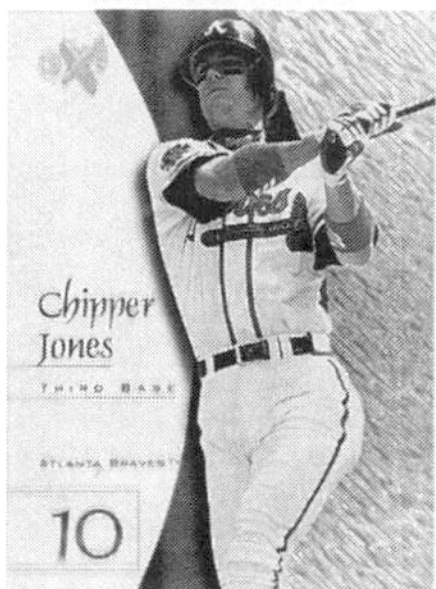

This super-premium set featured 100 players on a layered, die-cuct design utilizing mirror-image silhouetted photography and etched holofoil treatment over a clear, 20-point plastic card.

		MT
Complete Set (100):		90.00
Common Player:		.50
Kerry Wood Exchange:		15.00
Pack (2):		4.50
Wax Box (24):		90.00
1	Alex Rodriguez	6.00
2	Barry Bonds	2.00
3	Greg Maddux	4.00
4	Roger Clemens	3.00
5	Juan Gonzalez	2.00
6	Chipper Jones	4.00
7	Derek Jeter	6.00
8	Frank Thomas	3.00
9	Cal Ripken Jr.	6.00
10	Ken Griffey Jr.	6.00
11	Mark McGwire	8.00
12	Hideo Nomo	1.00
13	Tony Gwynn	3.00
14	Ivan Rodriguez	2.00
15	Mike Piazza	5.00
16	Roberto Alomar	1.50
17	Jeff Bagwell	2.00
18	Andruw Jones	2.00
19	Albert Belle	1.00
20	Mo Vaughn	1.00
21	Kenny Lofton	.75
22	Gary Sheffield	.75
23	Tony Clark	.50
24	Mike Mussina	1.50
25	Barry Larkin	.75
26	Moises Alou	.50
27	Brady Anderson	.50
28	Andy Pettitte	.75
29	Sammy Sosa	4.00
30	Raul Mondesi	.50
31	Andres Galarraga	1.00
32	Chuck Knoblauch	.75
33	Jim Thome	1.00
34	Craig Biggio	.50
35	Jay Buhner	.50
36	Rafael Palmeiro	1.00
37	Curt Schilling	.50
38	Tino Martinez	.75
39	Pedro Martinez	2.00
40	Jose Canseco	1.50
41	Jeff Cirillo	.50
42	Dean Palmer	.50
43	Tim Salmon	.75
44	Jason Giambi	1.00
45	Bobby Higginson	.50
46	Jim Edmonds	.75
47	David Justice	1.00
48	John Olerud	.75
49	Ray Lankford	.50
50	Al Martin	.50
51	Mike Lieberthal	.50
52	Henry Rodriguez	.50
53	Edgar Renteria	.50
54	Eric Karros	.60
55	Marquis Grissom	.50
56	Wilson Alvarez	.50
57	Darryl Kile	.50
58	Jeff King	.50
59	Shawn Estes	.50
60	Tony Womack	.50
61	Willie Greene	.50
62	Ken Caminiti	.50
63	Vinny Castilla	.50
64	Mark Grace	.75
65	Ryan Klesko	.75
66	Robin Ventura	.50
67	Todd Hundley	.50
68	Travis Fryman	.75
69	Edgar Martinez	.50
70	Matt Williams	.75
71	Paul Molitor	1.00
72	Kevin Brown	.60
73	Randy Johnson	2.00
74	Bernie Williams	1.50
75	Manny Ramirez	2.00
76	Fred McGriff	.75
77	Tom Glavine	.75
78	Carlos Delgado	1.50
79	Larry Walker	1.00
80	Hideki Irabu	.75
81	Ryan McGuire	.50
82	Justin Thompson	.50
83	Kevin Orie	.50
84	Jon Nunnally	.25
85	Mark Kotsay	.50
86	Todd Walker	.50
87	Jason Dickson	.50
88	Fernando Tatis	.50
89	Karim Garcia	.50
90	Ricky Ledee	.50
91	Paul Konerko	.75
92	Jaret Wright	.50
93	Darin Erstad	1.50
94	Livan Hernandez	.50
95	Nomar Garciaparra	5.00
96	Jose Cruz Jr.	.50
97	Scott Rolen	1.50
98	Ben Grieve	.75
99	Vladimir Guerrero	3.00
100	Travis Lee	.50

1998 SkyBox E-X2001 Kerry Wood

In an effort to get rookie pitching phenom Kerry Wood into its E-X2001 set, SkyBox created a cardboard, rather than plastic, trade card and inserted it at a rate of one per 50 packs. The trade card could be exchanged bu mail for a plastic version.

		MT
Complete Set (2):		10.00
---	Kerry Wood (cardboard trade card)	8.00
101	Kerry Wood (plastic redemption card)	5.00

1998 SkyBox E-X2001 Essential Credentials Future

Essential Credentials Future, along with Essential Credentials Now, paralleled all 100 cards in the base set. Production varied depending on the card number, with the exact production number of each player determined by subtracting his card number from 101. Number issued for each card is shown in parentheses. Because of rarity, the value of cards #93-100 cannot be determined.

		MT
Common Player:		15.00
1	Alex Rodriguez (100)	135.00
2	Barry Bonds (99)	50.00
3	Greg Maddux (98)	125.00
4	Roger Clemens (97)	75.00
5	Juan Gonzalez (96)	60.00
6	Chipper Jones (95)	125.00
7	Derek Jeter (94)	125.00
8	Frank Thomas (93)	75.00
9	Cal Ripken Jr. (92)	150.00
10	Ken Griffey Jr. (91)	225.00
11	Mark McGwire (90)	225.00
12	Hideo Nomo (89)	25.00
13	Tony Gwynn (88)	90.00
14	Ivan Rodriguez (87)	60.00
15	Mike Piazza (86)	130.00
16	Roberto Alomar (85)	40.00
17	Jeff Bagwell (84)	60.00
18	Andruw Jones (83)	45.00
19	Albert Belle (82)	40.00
20	Mo Vaughn (81)	40.00
21	Kenny Lofton (80)	40.00
22	Gary Sheffield (79)	25.00
23	Tony Clark (78)	25.00
24	Mike Mussina (77)	40.00
25	Barry Larkin (76)	30.00
26	Moises Alou (75)	30.00
27	Brady Anderson (74)	25.00
28	Andy Pettitte (73)	40.00
29	Sammy Sosa (72)	140.00
30	Raul Mondesi (71)	25.00
31	Andres Galarraga (70)	25.00
32	Chuck Knoblauch (69)	35.00
33	Jim Thome (68)	45.00
34	Craig Biggio (67)	50.00
35	Jay Buhner (66)	25.00
36	Rafael Palmeiro (65)	40.00

37	Curt Schilling (64)	30.00
38	Tino Martinez (63)	30.00
39	Pedro Martinez (62)	100.00
40	Jose Canseco (61)	50.00
41	Jeff Cirillo (60)	20.00
42	Dean Palmer (59)	20.00
43	Tim Salmon (58)	50.00
44	Jason Giambi (57)	30.00
45	Bobby Higginson (56)	30.00
46	Jim Edmonds (55)	30.00
47	David Justice (54)	35.00
48	John Olerud (53)	40.00
49	Ray Lankford (52)	20.00
50	Al Martin (51)	20.00
51	Mike Lieberthal (50)	25.00
52	Henry Rodriguez (49)	15.00
53	Edgar Renteria (48)	25.00
54	Eric Karros (47)	20.00
55	Marquis Grissom (46)	20.00
56	Wilson Alvarez (45)	15.00
57	Darryl Kile (44)	10.00
58	Jeff King (43)	10.00
59	Shawn Estes (42)	15.00
60	Tony Womack (41)	15.00
61	Willie Greene (40)	15.00
62	Ken Caminiti (39)	60.00
63	Vinny Castilla (38)	50.00
64	Mark Grace (37)	75.00
65	Ryan Klesko (36)	45.00
66	Robin Ventura (35)	50.00
67	Todd Hundley (34)	35.00
68	Travis Fryman (33)	35.00
69	Edgar Martinez (32)	30.00
70	Matt Williams (31)	45.00
71	Paul Molitor (30)	80.00
72	Kevin Brown (29)	50.00
73	Randy Johnson (28)	75.00
74	Bernie Williams (27)	65.00
75	Manny Ramirez (26)	125.00
76	Fred McGriff (25)	50.00
77	Tom Glavine (24)	50.00
78	Carlos Delgado (23)	75.00
79	Larry Walker (22)	75.00
80	Hideki Irabu (21)	50.00
81	Ryan McGuire (20)	30.00
82	Justin Thompson (19)	30.00
83	Kevin Orie (18)	30.00
84	Jon Nunnally (17)	10.00
85	Mark Kotsay (16)	40.00
86	Todd Walker (15)	50.00
87	Jason Dickson (14)	30.00
88	Fernando Tatis (13)	50.00
89	Karim Garcia (12)	50.00
90	Ricky Ledee (11)	50.00
91	Paul Konerko (10)	50.00
92	Jaret Wright (9)	65.00
93	Darin Erstad (8)	100.00
94	Livan Hernandez (7)	75.00
95	Nomar Garciaparra (6)	300.00
96	Jose Cruz (5)	75.00
97	Scott Rolen (4)	250.00
98	Ben Grieve (3)	250.00
99	Vladimir Guerrero (2)	925.00
100	Travis Lee (1)	600.00

1998 SkyBox E-X2001 Essential Credentials Now

Essential Credentials Now parallels all 100 cards in the E-X2001 base set. Production for each card was limited to that player's card number, as shown in parentheses. Values for cards #1-15 are not valued due to rarity.

		MT
	Common Player:	15.00
1	Alex Rodriguez (1)	1750.
2	Barry Bonds (2)	1000.
3	Greg Maddux (3)	450.00
4	Roger Clemens (4)	300.00
5	Juan Gonzalez (5)	300.00
6	Chipper Jones (6)	250.00
7	Derek Jeter (7)	350.00
8	Frank Thomas (8)	250.00
9	Cal Ripken Jr. (9)	450.00
10	Ken Griffey Jr. (10)	650.00
11	Mark McGwire (11)	600.00
12	Hideo Nomo (12)	125.00
13	Tony Gwynn (13)	150.00
14	Ivan Rodriguez (14)	125.00
15	Mike Piazza (15)	150.00
16	Roberto Alomar (16)	90.00
17	Jeff Bagwell (17)	125.00
18	Andruw Jones (18)	100.00
19	Albert Belle (19)	90.00
20	Mo Vaughn (20)	90.00
21	Kenny Lofton (21)	75.00
22	Gary Sheffield (22)	75.00
23	Tony Clark (23)	50.00
24	Mike Mussina (24)	75.00
25	Barry Larkin (25)	50.00
26	Moises Alou (26)	40.00
27	Brady Anderson (27)	40.00
28	Andy Pettitte (28)	50.00
29	Sammy Sosa (29)	250.00
30	Raul Mondesi (30)	40.00
31	Andres Galarraga (31)	50.00
32	Chuck Knoblauch (32)	50.00
33	Jim Thome (33)	50.00
34	Craig Biggio (34)	60.00
35	Jay Buhner (35)	30.00
36	Rafael Palmeiro (36)	45.00
37	Curt Schilling (37)	25.00
38	Tino Martinez (38)	40.00
39	Pedro Martinez (39)	100.00
40	Jose Canseco (40)	60.00
41	Jeff Cirillo (41)	20.00
42	Dean Palmer (42)	20.00
43	Tim Salmon (43)	30.00
44	Jason Giambi (44)	25.00
45	Bobby Higginson (45)	25.00
46	Jim Edmonds (46)	25.00
47	David Justice (47)	35.00
48	John Olerud (48)	35.00
49	Ray Lankford (49)	20.00
50	Al Martin (50)	10.00
51	Mike Lieberthal (51)	20.00
52	Henry Rodriguez (52)	10.00
53	Edgar Renteria (53)	15.00
54	Eric Karros (54)	15.00
55	Marquis Grissom (55)	15.00
56	Wilson Alvarez (56)	10.00
57	Darryl Kile (57)	10.00
58	Jeff King (58)	10.00
59	Shawn Estes (59)	10.00
60	Tony Womack (60)	10.00
61	Willie Greene (61)	10.00
62	Ken Caminiti (62)	25.00
63	Vinny Castilla (63)	20.00
64	Mark Grace (64)	25.00
65	Ryan Klesko (65)	15.00
66	Robin Ventura (66)	30.00
67	Todd Hundley (67)	15.00
68	Travis Fryman (68)	15.00
69	Edgar Martinez (69)	12.50
70	Matt Williams (70)	20.00
71	Paul Molitor (71)	40.00
72	Kevin Brown (72)	25.00
73	Randy Johnson (73)	40.00
74	Bernie Williams (74)	40.00
75	Manny Ramirez (75)	50.00
76	Fred McGriff (76)	25.00
77	Tom Glavine (77)	25.00
78	Carlos Delgado (78)	25.00
79	Larry Walker (79)	40.00
80	Hideki Irabu (80)	15.00
81	Ryan McGuire (81)	10.00
82	Justin Thompson (82)	10.00
83	Kevin Orie (83)	10.00
84	Jon Nunnally (84)	10.00
85	Mark Kotsay (85)	15.00
86	Todd Walker (86)	15.00
87	Jason Dickson (87)	10.00
88	Fernando Tatis (88)	30.00
89	Karim Garcia (89)	15.00
90	Ricky Ledee (90)	20.00
91	Paul Konerko (91)	30.00
92	Jaret Wright (92)	30.00
93	Darin Erstad (93)	40.00
94	Livan Hernandez (94)	15.00
95	Nomar Garciaparra (95)	150.00
96	Jose Cruz Jr. (96)	25.00
97	Scott Rolen (97)	60.00
98	Ben Grieve (98)	40.00
99	Vladimir Guerrero (99)	50.00
100	Travis Lee (100)	25.00

1998 SkyBox E-X2001 Cheap Seat Treats

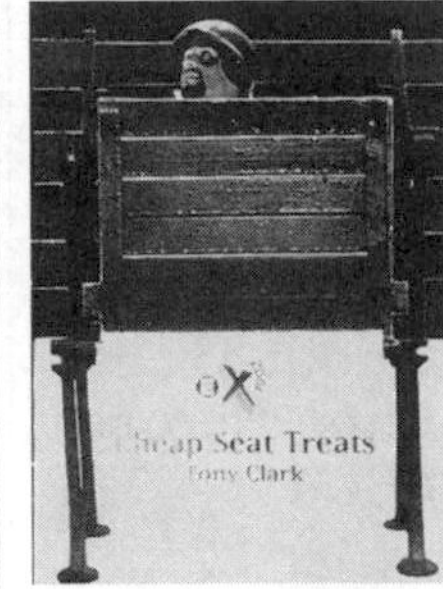

This 20-card die-cut insert arrived in the shape of a stadium seat. Inserted at one per 24 packs, Cheap Seat Treats included some of the top home run hitters and were numbered with a "CS" prefix.

		MT
	Complete Set (20):	100.00
	Common Player:	2.50
	Inserted 1:24	
1	Frank Thomas	8.00
2	Ken Griffey Jr.	20.00
3	Mark McGwire	25.00
4	Tino Martinez	2.50
5	Larry Walker	4.00
6	Juan Gonzalez	6.00
7	Mike Piazza	15.00
8	Jeff Bagwell	6.00
9	Tony Clark	2.50
10	Albert Belle	4.00
11	Andres Galarraga	4.00
12	Jim Thome	4.00
13	Mo Vaughn	3.00
14	Barry Bonds	6.00
15	Vladimir Guerrero	8.00
16	Scott Rolen	5.00
17	Travis Lee	2.50
18	David Justice	4.00
19	Jose Cruz Jr.	2.50
20	Andruw Jones	5.00

1998 SkyBox E-X2001 Destination: Cooperstown

Destination: Cooperstown captured a mixture of rising young stars and top veterans on die-cut cards that were inserted one per 720 packs. This insert included 15 players and was numbered with a "DC" prefix.

		MT
	Complete Set (15):	1200.
	Common Player:	15.00
	Inserted 1:720	
1	Alex Rodriguez	150.00
2	Frank Thomas	75.00
3	Cal Ripken Jr.	150.00
4	Roger Clemens	75.00
5	Greg Maddux	125.00
6	Chipper Jones	125.00
7	Ken Griffey Jr.	200.00
8	Mark McGwire	200.00
9	Tony Gwynn	100.00
10	Mike Piazza	125.00

11	Jeff Bagwell	60.00
12	Jose Cruz Jr.	15.00
13	Derek Jeter	125.00
14	Hideo Nomo	20.00
15	Ivan Rodriguez	50.00

1998 SkyBox E-X2001 Signature 2001

Seventeen top young and future stars signed cards for Signature 2001 inserts in E-X2001. The cards featured the player over a blue and white, sky-like background, with an embossed SkyBox seal of authenticity. Backs were horizontal and also included a Certificate of Authenticity. These cards were unnumbered and inserted one per 60 packs.

		MT
Complete Set (17):		300.00
Common Player:		8.00
Inserted 1:60		
1	Ricky Ledee	8.00
2	Derrick Gibson	8.00
3	Mark Kotsay	10.00
4	Kevin Millwood	20.00
5	Brad Fullmer	15.00
6	Todd Walker	8.00
7	Ben Grieve	20.00
8	Tony Clark	10.00
9	Jaret Wright	8.00
10	Randall Simon	8.00
11	Paul Konerko	12.00
12	Todd Helton	30.00
13	David Ortiz	8.00
14	Alex Gonzalez	8.00
15	Bobby Estalella	8.00
16	Alex Rodriguez	150.00
17	Mike Lowell	10.00

1998 SkyBox E-X2001 Star Date 2001

Star Date 2001 displays 15 of the top rising stars on an acetate space/planet background with gold-foil printing on front. This insert was seeded one per 12 packs and was numbered with a "SD" suffix.

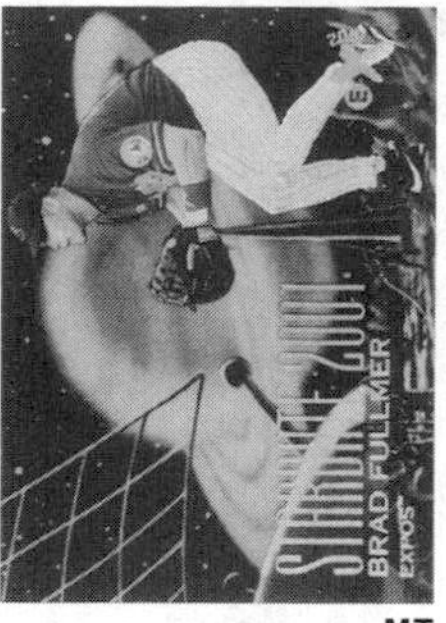

		MT
Complete Set (15):		30.00
Common Player:		1.00
Inserted 1:12		
1	Travis Lee	5.00
2	Jose Cruz Jr.	1.50
3	Paul Konerko	2.00
4	Bobby Estalella	1.00
5	Magglio Ordonez	3.00
6	Juan Encarnacion	1.00
7	Richard Hidalgo	1.00
8	Abraham Nunez	1.00
9	Sean Casey	3.00
10	Todd Helton	2.50
11	Brad Fullmer	2.00
12	Ben Grieve	7.50
13	Livan Hernandez	1.00
14	Jaret Wright	6.00
15	Todd Dunwoody	1.00

1999 SkyBox E-X Century

The 120-card base set features a clear plastic stock with the player name, logo and position stamped in holographic foil. Card backs have the featured player's vital information along with his '98 statistics and his major league totals. Cards 91-120 are part of a prospects subset and are short-printed seeded 1:2 packs. Three-card packs have a SRP of $5.99.

		MT
Complete Set (120):		75.00
Common Player:		.40
Common SP (91-120):		1.00
Inserted 1:2		
Pack (3):		5.00
Wax Box (18):		85.00
1	Scott Rolen	2.00
2	Nomar Garciaparra	4.50
3	Mike Piazza	4.50
4	Tony Gwynn	3.00
5	Sammy Sosa	4.50
6	Alex Rodriguez	6.00
7	Vladimir Guerrero	3.00
8	Chipper Jones	4.00
9	Derek Jeter	5.00
10	Kerry Wood	.75
11	Juan Gonzalez	2.00
12	Frank Thomas	3.00
13	Mo Vaughn	1.00
14	Greg Maddux	4.00
15	Jeff Bagwell	2.00
16	Mark McGwire	7.50
17	Ken Griffey Jr.	6.00
18	Roger Clemens	2.50
19	Cal Ripken Jr.	6.00
20	Travis Lee	.40
21	Todd Helton	2.00
22	Darin Erstad	2.00
23	Pedro Martinez	2.00
24	Barry Bonds	2.00
25	Andruw Jones	1.50
26	Larry Walker	1.00
27	Albert Belle	1.00
28	Ivan Rodriguez	2.00
29	Maggio Ordonez	.60
30	Andres Galarraga	.75
31	Mike Mussina	1.25
32	Randy Johnson	2.00
33	Tom Glavine	.60
34	Barry Larkin	.75
35	Jim Thome	.75
36	Gary Sheffield	.75
37	Bernie Williams	1.25
38	Carlos Delgado	1.50
39	Rafael Palmeiro	.60
40	Edgar Renteria	.40
41	Brad Fullmer	.40
42	David Wells	.40
43	Dante Bichette	.75
44	Jaret Wright	.40
45	Ricky Ledee	.40
46	Ray Lankford	.40
47	Mark Grace	.60
48	Jeff Cirillo	.40
49	Rondell White	.40
50	Jeromy Burnitz	.40
51	Sean Casey	.60
52	Rolando Arrojo	.40
53	Jason Giambi	.75
54	John Olerud	.50
55	Will Clark	.75
56	Raul Mondesi	.60
57	Scott Brosius	.40
58	Bartolo Colon	.40
59	Steve Finley	.40
60	Javy Lopez	.40
61	Tim Salmon	.50
62	Roberto Alomar	1.50
63	Vinny Castilla	.40
64	Craig Biggio	.75
65	Jose Guillen	.40
66	Greg Vaughn	.40
67	Jose Canseco	1.00
68	Shawn Green	.75
69	Curt Schilling	.50
70	Orlando Hernandez	.50
71	Jose Cruz Jr.	.40
72	Alex Gonzalez	.40
73	Tino Martinez	.50
74	Todd Hundley	.40
75	Brian Giles	.60
76	Cliff Floyd	.40
77	Paul O'Neill	.60
78	Ken Caminiti	.60
79	Ron Gant	.40
80	Juan Encarnacion	.40
81	Ben Grieve	1.00
82	Brian Jordan	.40
83	Rickey Henderson	.60
84	Tony Clark	.50
85	Shannon Stewart	.40
86	Robin Ventura	.50
87	Todd Walker	.40
88	Kevin Brown	.60
89	Moises Alou	.50
90	Manny Ramirez	2.00
91	Gabe Alvarez	1.00
92	Jeremy Giambi	1.00
93	Adrian Beltre	1.00
94	George Lombard	1.00
95	Ryan Minor	1.50
96	Kevin Witt	1.00
97	*Scott Hunter*	1.00
98	Carlos Guillen	1.00
99	Derrick Gibson	1.00
100	Trot Nixon	1.00
101	Troy Glaus	8.00
102	Armando Rios	1.00
103	Preston Wilson	1.00
104	*Pat Burrell*	10.00
105	J.D. Drew	1.00
106	Bruce Chen	1.00
107	Matt Clement	1.00
108	Carlos Beltran	1.00
109	Carlos Febles	1.00
110	Rob Fick	1.00
111	Russell Branyan	1.00
112	*Roosevelt Brown*	1.50
113	Corey Koskie	1.00
114	Mario Encarnacion	1.00
115	*Peter Tucci*	1.00
116	Eric Chavez	1.00
117	Gabe Kapler	1.50
118	Marlon Anderson	1.00
119	*A.J. Burnett*	1.50
120	Ryan Bradley	1.00
---	Checklist 1-96	.10
---	Checklist 97-120 /Inserts	.10

1999 SkyBox E-X Century Essential Credentials Future

A glossy silver design replaces the clear plastic portions seen on the base cards. Production varied depending on the card number, with the exact production number of each player determined by subtracting his card number from 121. Quantity issued is listed in parentheses. Cards #114-120 are not priced due to rarity.

		MT
Common Player:		15.00
1	Scott Rolen (120)	75.00
2	Nomar Garciaparra (119)	125.00
3	Mike Piazza (118)	125.00
4	Tony Gwynn (117)	100.00
5	Sammy Sosa (116)	125.00
6	Alex Rodriguez (115)	140.00
7	Vladimir Guerrero (114)	60.00
8	Chipper Jones (113)	125.00
9	Derek Jeter (112)	125.00
10	Kerry Wood (111)	50.00
11	Juan Gonzalez (110)	50.00
12	Frank Thomas (109)	75.00
13	Mo Vaughn (108)	50.00
14	Greg Maddux (107)	100.00
15	Jeff Bagwell (106)	60.00

16 Mark McGwire (105) 200.00
17 Ken Griffey Jr. (104) 200.00
18 Roger Clemens (103) 75.00
19 Cal Ripken Jr. (102) 140.00
20 Travis Lee (101) 30.00
21 Todd Helton (100) 40.00
22 Darin Erstad (99) 30.00
23 Pedro Martinez (98) 60.00
24 Barry Bonds (97) 60.00
25 Andruw Jones (96) 40.00
26 Larry Walker (95) 40.00
27 Albert Belle (94) 40.00
28 Ivan Rodriguez (93) 40.00
29 Magglio Ordonez (92) 40.00
30 Andres Galarraga (91) 30.00
31 Mike Mussina (90) 60.00
32 Randy Johnson (89) 60.00
33 Tom Glavine (88) 30.00
34 Barry Larkin (87) 25.00
35 Jim Thome (86) 30.00
36 Gary Sheffield (85) 30.00
37 Bernie Williams (84) 50.00
38 Carlos Delgado (83) 40.00
39 Rafael Palmeiro (82) 40.00
40 Edgar Renteria (81) 15.00
41 Brad Fullmer (80) 15.00
42 David Wells (79) 15.00
43 Dante Bichette (78) 30.00
44 Jaret Wright (77) 25.00
45 Ricky Ledee (76) 20.00
46 Ray Lankford (75) 10.00
47 Mark Grace (74) 30.00
48 Jeff Cirillo (73) 10.00
49 Rondell White (72) 15.00
50 Jeromy Burnitz (71) 10.00
51 Sean Casey (70) 50.00
52 Rolando Arrojo (69) 15.00
53 Jason Giambi (68) 15.00
54 John Olerud (67) 30.00
55 Will Clark (66) 50.00
56 Raul Mondesi (65) 30.00
57 Scott Brosius (64) 15.00
58 Bartolo Colon (63) 25.00
59 Steve Finley (62) 15.00
60 Javy Lopez (61) 25.00
61 Tim Salmon (60) 30.00
62 Roberto Alomar (59) 75.00
63 Vinny Castilla (58) 25.00
64 Craig Biggio (57) 60.00
65 Jose Guillen (56) 20.00
66 Greg Vaughn (55) 20.00
67 Jose Canseco (54) 70.00
68 Shawn Green (53) 30.00
69 Curt Schilling (52) 25.00
70 Orlando Hernandez (51) 75.00
71 Jose Cruz Jr. (50) 25.00
72 Alex Gonzalez (49) 20.00
73 Tino Martinez (48) 40.00
74 Todd Hundley (47) 20.00
75 Brian Giles (46) 20.00
76 Cliff Floyd (45) 20.00
77 Paul O'Neill (44) 35.00
78 Ken Caminiti (43) 40.00
79 Ron Gant (42) 30.00
80 Juan Encarnacion (41) 40.00
81 Ben Grieve (40) 70.00
82 Brian Jordan (39) 20.00
83 Rickey Henderson (38) 40.00
84 Tony Clark (37) 40.00
85 Shannon Stewart (36) 20.00
86 Robin Ventura (35) 30.00
87 Todd Walker (34) 25.00
88 Kevin Brown (33) 40.00
89 Moises Alou (32) 35.00
90 Manny Ramirez (31) 125.00
91 Gabe Alvarez (30) 25.00
92 Jeremy Giambi (29) 25.00
93 Adrian Beltre (28) 40.00
94 George Lombard (27) 35.00
95 Ryan Minor (26) 40.00
96 Kevin Witt (25) 25.00
97 Scott Hunter (24) 25.00
98 Carlos Guillen (23) 25.00
99 Derrick Gibson (22) 35.00
100 Trot Nixon (21) 25.00
101 Troy Glaus (20) 125.00
102 Armando Rios (19) 30.00
103 Preston Wilson (18) 40.00
104 Pat Burrell (17) 300.00
105 J.D. Drew (16) 100.00
106 Bruce Chen (15) 40.00
107 Matt Clement (14) 40.00
108 Carlos Beltran (13) 125.00
109 Carlos Febles (12) 40.00
110 Rob Fick (11) 40.00
111 Russell Branyan (10) 60.00
112 Roosevelt Brown (9) 100.00
113 Corey Koskie (8) 40.00
114 Mario Encarnacion (7) 60.00
115 Peter Tucci (6) 75.00
116 Eric Chavez (5) 125.00
117 Gabe Kapler (4) 125.00
118 Marlon Anderson (3) 150.00
119 A.J. Burnett (2) 150.00
120 Ryan Bradley (1) 200.00

1999 SkyBox E-X Century Essential Credentials Now

Like Future, this is a parallel of the base set, with production of each card limited to that player's card number. These cards have a glossy gold look. Cards #1-9 are not priced due to rarity.

MT

Common Player: 15.00
1 Scott Rolen (1) 600.00
2 Nomar Garciaparra (2) 300.00
3 Mike Piazza (3) 300.00
4 Tony Gwynn (4) 250.00
5 Sammy Sosa (5) 450.00
6 Alex Rodriguez (6) 400.00
7 Vladimir Guerrero (7) 200.00
8 Chipper Jones (8) 300.00
9 Derek Jeter (9) 300.00
10 Kerry Wood (10) 170.00
11 Juan Gonzalez (11) 225.00
12 Frank Thomas (12) 250.00
13 Mo Vaughn (13) 100.00
14 Greg Maddux (14) 200.00
15 Jeff Bagwell (15) 175.00
16 Mark McGwire (16) 800.00
17 Ken Griffey Jr. (17) 800.00
18 Roger Clemens (18) 200.00
19 Cal Ripken Jr. (19) 500.00
20 Travis Lee (20) 60.00
21 Todd Helton (21) 80.00
22 Darin Erstad (22) 60.00
23 Pedro Martinez (23) 80.00
24 Barry Bonds (24) 150.00
25 Andruw Jones (25) 120.00
26 Larry Walker (26) 80.00
27 Albert Belle (27) 120.00
28 Ivan Rodriguez (28) 100.00
29 Magglio Ordonez (29) 50.00
30 Andres Galarraga (30) 60.00
31 Mike Mussina (31) 90.00
32 Randy Johnson (32) 100.00
33 Tom Glavine (33) 40.00
34 Barry Larkin (34) 30.00
35 Jim Thome (35) 40.00
36 Gary Sheffield (36) 30.00
37 Bernie Williams (37) 75.00
38 Carlos Delgado (38) 50.00
39 Rafael Palmeiro (39) 60.00
40 Edgar Renteria (40) 25.00
41 Brad Fullmer (41) 20.00
42 David Wells (42) 20.00
43 Dante Bichette (43) 40.00
44 Jaret Wright (44) 25.00
45 Ricky Ledee (45) 20.00
46 Ray Lankford (46) 15.00
47 Mark Grace (47) 40.00
48 Jeff Cirillo (48) 15.00
49 Rondell White (49) 25.00
50 Jeromy Burnitz (50) 15.00
51 Sean Casey (51) 50.00
52 Rolando Arrojo (52) 15.00
53 Jason Giambi (53) 15.00
54 John Olerud (54) 25.00
55 Will Clark (55) 50.00
56 Raul Mondesi (56) 40.00
57 Scott Brosius (57) 15.00
58 Bartolo Colon (58) 20.00
59 Steve Finley (59) 15.00
60 Javy Lopez (60) 20.00
61 Tim Salmon (61) 20.00
62 Roberto Alomar (62) 75.00
63 Vinny Castilla (63) 20.00
64 Craig Biggio (64) 50.00
65 Jose Guillen (65) 15.00
66 Greg Vaughn (66) 15.00
67 Jose Canseco (67) 60.00
68 Shawn Green (68) 25.00
69 Curt Schilling (69) 20.00
70 Orlando Hernandez (70) 40.00
71 Jose Cruz Jr. (71) 15.00
72 Alex Gonzalez (72) 15.00
73 Tino Martinez (73) 20.00
74 Todd Hundley (74) 20.00
75 Brian Giles (75) 15.00
76 Cliff Floyd (76) 15.00
77 Paul O'Neill (77) 25.00
78 Ken Caminiti (78) 30.00
79 Ron Gant (79) 15.00
80 Juan Encarnacion (80) 20.00
81 Ben Grieve (81) 20.00
82 Brian Jordan (82) 15.00
83 Rickey Henderson (83) 30.00
84 Tony Clark (84) 40.00
85 Shannon Stewart (85) 15.00
86 Robin Ventura (86) 20.00
87 Todd Walker (87) 20.00
88 Kevin Brown (88) 30.00
89 Moises Alou (89) 20.00
90 Manny Ramirez (90) 60.00
91 Gabe Alvarez (91) 15.00
92 Jeremy Giambi (92) 15.00
93 Adrian Beltre (93) 25.00
94 George Lombard (94) 20.00
95 Ryan Minor (95) 25.00
96 Kevin Witt (96) 15.00
97 Scott Hunter (97) 15.00
98 Carlos Guillen (98) 15.00
99 Derrick Gibson (99) 20.00
100 Trot Nixon (100) 15.00
101 Troy Glaus (101) 40.00
102 Armando Rios (102) 15.00
103 Preston Wilson (103) 20.00
104 Pat Burrell (104) 125.00
105 J.D. Drew (105) 40.00
106 Bruce Chen (106) 15.00
107 Matt Clement (107) 15.00
108 Carlos Beltran (108) 40.00
109 Carlos Febles (109) 25.00
110 Rob Fick (110) 15.00
111 Russell Branyan (111) 20.00
112 Roosevelt Brown (112) 25.00
113 Corey Koskie (113) 15.00
114 Mario Encarnacion (114) 20.00
115 Peter Tucci (115) 15.00
116 Eric Chavez (116) 30.00
117 Gabe Kapler (117) 40.00
118 Marlon Anderson (118) 15.00
119 A.J. Burnett (119) 30.00
120 Ryan Bradley (120) 15.00

1999 SkyBox E-X Century Authen-Kicks

Authen-Kicks is a game-used insert that embeds game-worn shoe swatches from the featured player. Each is done in a horizontal format and is sequentially hand-numbered. The number of swatch cards differs from player to player, and is indicated here in parentheses. Autographed versions of two colors of J.D. Drew shoes were also produced.

		MT
Common Player:		20.00
(1)	J.D. Drew (160)	70.00
(1ab)	J.D. Drew (autographed black) (8)	600.00
(1ar)	J.D. Drew (autographed red) (8)	600.00
(2)	Travis Lee (175)	20.00
(3)	Kevin Millwood (160)	30.00
(4)	Bruce Chen (205)	20.00
(5)	Troy Glaus (205)	100.00
(6)	Todd Helton (205)	75.00
(7)	Ricky Ledee (180)	20.00
(8)	Scott Rolen (205)	75.00
(9)	Jeremy Giambi (205)	20.00

1999 SkyBox E-X Century E-X Quisite

15 of baseball's top young players are showcased, with a black background and interior die-cutting around the player image. These are seeded 1:18 packs.

		MT
Complete Set (15):		50.00
Common Player:		2.00
Inserted 1:18		
1	Troy Glaus	10.00
2	J.D. Drew	3.00
3	Pat Burrell	15.00
4	Russell Branyan	2.00
5	Kerry Wood	3.00
6	Eric Chavez	6.00
7	Ben Grieve	2.00
8	Gabe Kapler	7.50
9	Adrian Beltre	4.00
10	Todd Helton	5.00
11	Roosevelt Brown	4.00
12	Marlon Anderson	2.00
13	Jeremy Giambi	4.00
14	Magglio Ordonez	2.50
15	Travis Lee	6.00

1999 SkyBox E-X Century Favorites for Fenway

This 20-card set pays tribute to one of baseball's favorite ballparks, Fenway Park the venue for the 1999 All-Star Game. These have a photo of the featured player with an image of Fenway Park in the background on a horizontal format. These are seeded 1:36 packs.

		MT
Complete Set (20):		325.00
Common Player:		5.00
Inserted 1:36		
1	Mo Vaughn	5.00
2	Nomar Garciaparra	25.00
3	Frank Thomas	20.00
4	Ken Griffey Jr.	40.00
5	Roger Clemens	15.00
6	Alex Rodriguez	30.00
7	Derek Jeter	25.00
8	Juan Gonzalez	10.00
9	Cal Ripken Jr.	30.00
10	Ivan Rodriguez	8.00
11	J.D. Drew	6.00
12	Barry Bonds	10.00
13	Tony Gwynn	20.00
14	Vladimir Guerrero	15.00
15	Chipper Jones	25.00
16	Kerry Wood	8.00
17	Mike Piazza	25.00
18	Sammy Sosa	25.00
19	Scott Rolen	12.00
20	Mark McGwire	40.00

1999 SkyBox E-X Century Milestones of the Century

This 10-card set spotlights the top statistical performances from the 1998 season, sequentially numbered to that performance in a multi-layered design.

		MT
Complete Set (10):		1350.
Common Player:		15.00
Numbered to featured milestone		
1	Kerry Wood (20)	75.00
2	Mark McGwire (70)	300.00
3	Sammy Sosa (66)	150.00
4	Ken Griffey Jr. (350)	75.00
5	Roger Clemens (98)	100.00
6	Cal Ripken Jr. (17)	500.00
7	Alex Rodriguez (40)	200.00
8	Barry Bonds (400)	15.00
9	N.Y. Yankees (114)	100.00
10	Travis Lee (98)	50.00

1999 SkyBox Molten Metal

Distributed exclusively to the hobby, the 150-card set consists of three subsets: Metal Smiths, Heavy Metal and Supernatural. Metal Smiths (1-100) show baseball's top players, Heavy Metal (101-130) focus on power hitters and Supernatural (131-150) focus on rookies. Base cards feature silver foil stamping on a 24-point stock with holofoil and wet-laminate overlays. Molten Metal was released in six-card packs with a SRP of $4.99. A special version of the issue was sold only at the 20th Nat'l Sports Collectors Convention in Atlanta, July 19-24. The show version includes autograph redemption cards for show guests and a die-cut series of 30 current and former Braves favorites. Each of the show version cards has a small National Convention logo printed on back; they currently carry no premium.

		MT
Complete Set (150):		120.00
Common Metalsmiths (1-100):		.25
Inserted 4:1		
Common Heavy Metal (101-130):		.40
Inserted 1:1		
Common Supernatural (131-150):		1.00
Inserted 1:2		
Pack (6):		3.50
Wax Box (24):		85.00
1	Larry Walker	1.00
2	Jose Canseco	1.00
3	Brian Jordan	.25
4	Rafael Palmeiro	.75
5	Edgar Renteria	.25
6	Dante Bichette	.50
7	Mark Kotsay	.25
8	Denny Neagle	.25
9	Ellis Burks	.25
10	Paul O'Neill	.35
11	Miguel Tejada	.40
12	Ken Caminiti	.35
13	David Cone	.35
14	Jason Kendall	.35
15	Ruben Rivera	.25
16	Todd Walker	.25
17	Bobby Higginson	.25
18	Derrek Lee	.25
19	Rondell White	.35
20	Pedro J. Martinez	1.25
21	Jeff Kent	.25
22	Randy Johnson	1.00
23	Matt Williams	.50
24	Sean Casey	.40
25	Eric Davis	.25
26	Ryan Klesko	.25
27	Curt Schilling	.35
28	Geoff Jenkins	.25
29	Armand Abreu	.25
30	Vinny Castilla	.35
31	Will Clark	.75
32	Ray Durham	.25
33	Ray Lankford	.25
34	Richie Sexson	.25
35	Derrick Gibson	.25
36	Mark Grace	.50
37	Greg Vaughn	.25
38	Bartolo Colon	.25
39	Steve Finley	.25
40	Chuck Knoblauch	.50
41	Ricky Ledee	.25
42	John Smoltz	.25
43	Moises Alou	.40
44	Jim Edmonds	.25
45	Cliff Floyd	.25
46	Javy Lopez	.25
47	Jim Thome	.50
48	J.T. Snow	.25
49	Sandy Alomar Jr.	.25
50	Andy Pettitte	.35
51	Juan Encarnacion	.25
52	Travis Fryman	.25
53	Eli Marrero	.25
54	Jeff Cirillo	.25
55	Brady Anderson	.25
56	Jose Cruz Jr.	.40
57	Edgar Martinez	.25
58	Garret Anderson	.25
59	Paul Konerko	.25
60	Eric Milton	.25
61	Jason Giambi	.25
62	Tom Glavine	.35
63	Justin Thompson	.25
64	Brad Fullmer	.25
65	Marquis Grissom	.25
66	Fernando Tatis	.35
67	Carlos Beltran	.25
68	Charles Johnson	.25
69	Raul Mondesi	.40
70	Richard Hildalgo	.25
71	Barry Larkin	.35
72	David Wells	.25
73	Jay Buhner	.25
74	Matt Clement	.25
75	Eric Karros	.25
76	Carl Pavano	.25
77	Mariano Rivera	.40
78	Livan Hernandez	.25
79	A.J. Hinch	.25
80	Tino Martinez	.40
81	Rusty Greer	.25
82	Jose Guillen	.25
83	Robin Ventura	.40
84	Kevin Brown	.40
85	Chan Ho Park	.25
86	John Olerud	.40
87	Johnny Damon	.25
88	Todd Hundley	.25
89	Fred McGriff	.40
90	Wade Boggs	.75
91	Mike Cameron	.25
92	Gary Sheffield	.35
93	Rickey Henderson	.40
94	Pat Hentgen	.25
95	Omar Vizquel	.25
96	Craig Biggio	.60
97	Mike Caruso	.25
98	Neifi Perez	.25
99	Mike Mussina	.75
100	Carlos Delgado	.50
101	Andruw Jones (Heavy Metal)	1.50
102	*Pat Burrell* (Heavy Metal)	5.00
103	Orlando Hernandez (Heavy Metal)	1.50
104	Darin Erstad (Heavy Metal)	1.25
105	Roberto Alomar (Heavy Metal)	1.00
106	Tim Salmon (Heavy Metal)	.75
107	Albert Belle (Heavy Metal)	1.50
108	*Chad Allen* (Heavy Metal)	1.50
109	Travis Lee (Heavy Metal)	1.50
110	*Jesse Garcia* (Heavy Metal)	1.00
111	Tony Clark (Heavy Metal)	.50

112	Ivan Rodriguez (Heavy Metal)	1.50
113	Troy Glaus (Heavy Metal)	1.50
114	*A.J. Burnett* (Heavy Metal)	3.00
115	David Justice (Heavy Metal)	.50
116	Adrian Beltre (Heavy Metal)	.75
117	Eric Chavez (Heavy Metal)	.75
118	Kenny Lofton (Heavy Metal)	1.00
119	Michael Barrett (Heavy Metal)	.75
120	*Jeff Weaver* (Heavy Metal)	4.00
121	Manny Ramirez (Heavy Metal)	2.00
122	Barry Bonds (Heavy Metal)	1.50
123	Bernie Williams (Heavy Metal)	.75
124	*Freddy Garcia* (Heavy Metal)	6.00
125	*Scott Hunter* (Heavy Metal)	1.00
126	Jeremy Giambi (Heavy Metal)	.40
127	*Masao Kida* (Heavy Metal)	1.00
128	Todd Helton (Heavy Metal)	1.00
129	Mike Figga (Heavy Metal)	.40
130	Mo Vaughn (Heavy Metal)	.75
131	J.D. Drew (Supernaturals)	1.50
132	Cal Ripken Jr. (Supernaturals)	6.00
133	Ken Griffey Jr. (Supernaturals)	8.00
134	Mark McGwire (Supernaturals)	8.00
135	Nomar Garciaparra (Supernaturals)	6.00
136	Greg Maddux (Supernaturals)	6.00
137	Mike Piazza (Supernaturals)	6.00
138	Alex Rodriguez (Supernaturals)	8.00
139	Frank Thomas (Supernaturals)	5.00
140	Juan Gonzalez (Supernaturals)	2.00
141	Tony Gwynn (Supernaturals)	5.00
142	Derek Jeter (Supernaturals)	6.00
143	Chipper Jones (Supernaturals)	6.00
144	Scott Rolen (Supernaturals)	3.00
145	Sammy Sosa (Supernaturals)	5.00
146	Kerry Wood (Supernaturals)	2.00
147	Roger Clemens (Supernaturals)	3.00
148	Jeff Bagwell (Supernaturals)	2.00
149	Vladimir Guerrero (Supernaturals)	4.00
150	Ben Grieve (Supernaturals)	1.00

1999 SkyBox Molten Metal Fusion

Fusion is a 50-card partial parallel that is paralleled three times: Fusion, Sterling Fusion and Titanium Fusion. The three parallels consist of the two subsets Heavy Metal and Supernatural. Fusion Heavy Metals (1-30) are seeded 1:12 packs and Supernatural Fusions are seeded 1:24 packs. Fusions are laser die-cut with additional silver-foil stamping. Sterling Fusions are limited to 500 numbered sets with each card laser die-cut on a blue background with blue foil stamping. Titanium Fusions are limited to 50 sequentially numbered sets with gold background and enhanced with gold foil highlights.

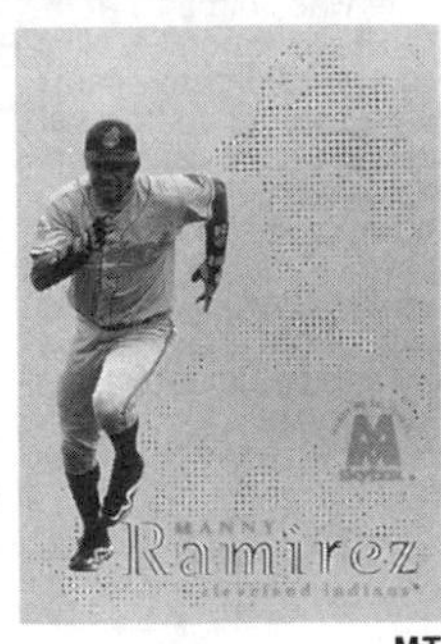

		MT
Complete Set (50):		500.00
Common Heavy Metal (1-30):		2.00
Inserted 1:12		
Common Supernatural (31-50):		5.00
Inserted 1:24		
Sterling (1-30):		2X
Sterling (31-50):		1.5X
Production 500 sets		
Titanium (1-30):		8X
Titanium (31-50):		6X
Production 50 sets		
1	Andruw Jones	5.00
2	Pat Burrell	20.00
3	Orlando Hernandez	5.00
4	Darin Erstad	5.00
5	Roberto Alomar	4.00
6	Tim Salmon	3.00
7	Albert Belle	4.00
8	Chad Allen	2.00
9	Travis Lee	4.00
10	Jesse Garcia	2.00
11	Tony Clark	2.00
12	Ivan Rodriguez	4.00
13	Troy Glaus	8.00
14	A.J. Burnett	5.00
15	David Justice	2.00
16	Adrian Beltre	3.00
17	Eric Chavez	3.00
18	Kenny Lofton	2.00
19	Michael Barrett	2.00
20	Jeff Weaver	6.00
21	Manny Ramirez	8.00
22	Barry Bonds	6.00
23	Bernie Williams	4.00
24	Freddy Garcia	15.00
25	Scott Hunter	2.00
26	Jeremy Giambi	2.00
27	Masao Kida	2.00
28	Todd Helton	5.00
29	Mike Figga	2.00
30	Mo Vaughn	2.00
31	J.D. Drew	5.00
32	Cal Ripken Jr.	30.00
33	Ken Griffey Jr.	40.00
34	Mark McGwire	40.00
35	Nomar Garciaparra	25.00
36	Greg Maddux	25.00
37	Mike Piazza	25.00
38	Alex Rodriguez	30.00
39	Frank Thomas	20.00
40	Juan Gonzalez	10.00
41	Tony Gwynn	20.00
42	Derek Jeter	25.00
43	Chipper Jones	25.00
44	Scott Rolen	10.00
45	Sammy Sosa	25.00
46	Kerry Wood	6.00
47	Roger Clemens	15.00
48	Jeff Bagwell	10.00
49	Vladimir Guerrero	20.00
50	Ben Grieve	5.00

1999 SkyBox Molten Metal Fusion - Sterling

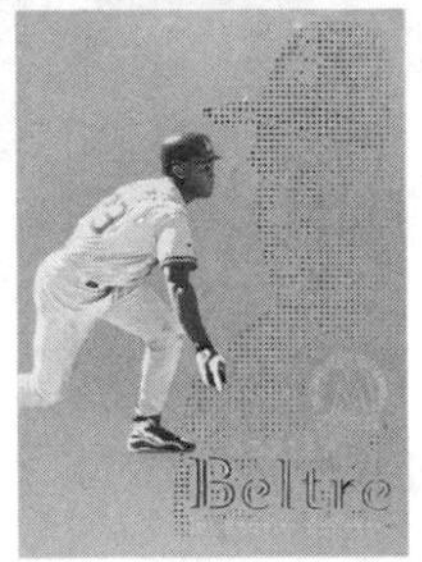

Sterling Fusions are limited to 500 numbered sets with each card laser die-cut on a blue background with blue foil graphic highlights. A special version of the issue was sold only at the 20th Nat'l Sports Collectors Convention in Atlanta, July 19-24. Each of the show-version cards has a small National Convention logo printed on back; they currently carry no premium.

	MT
Complete Set (50):	750.00
Common Player:	4.00
Sterling Stars:	1.5X

(See 1999 Molten Metal Fusion for checklist and base card values.)

1999 SkyBox Molten Metal Fusion - Titanium

Titanium Fusions are limited to 50 sequentially numbered sets with gold background and enhanced with gold foil highlights. A special version of the issue was sold only at the 20th Nat'l Sports Collectors Convention in Atlanta, July 19-24. Each of the show-version cards has a small National Convention logo printed on back; they currently carry no premium.

	MT
Common Player:	15.00
Titanium Stars:	6X

(See 1999 SkyBox Molten Metal Fusion for checklist and base card values.)

1999 SkyBox Molten Metal Oh Atlanta!

This 30-card set features players who are either current or former Atlanta Braves like Chipper Jones and Dave Justice. These inserts are seeded one per pack and was produced in conjunction with the 20th annual National Sports Collectors Convention in Atlanta.

		MT
Complete Set (30):		50.00
Common Player:		1.00
Inserted 1:1		
1	Kenny Lofton	3.00
2	Kevin Millwood	6.00
3	Bret Boone	1.00
4	Otis Nixon	1.00
5	Vinny Castilla	1.00
6	Brian Jordan	1.00
7	Chipper Jones	15.00
8	Dave Justice	3.00
9	Micah Bowie	1.00
10	Fred McGriff	2.00
11	Ron Gant	1.00
12	Andruw Jones	6.00
13	Kent Mercker	1.00
14	Greg McMichael	1.00
15	Steve Avery	1.00
16	Marquis Grissom	1.00
17	Jason Schmidt	1.00
18	Ryan Klesko	1.50
19	Charlie O'Brien	1.00
20	Terry Pendleton	1.00
21	Denny Neagle	1.00
22	Greg Maddux	15.00
23	Tom Glavine	2.00
24	Javy Lopez	1.50
25	John Rocker	1.50
26	Walt Weiss	1.00
27	John Smoltz	1.50
28	Michael Tucker	1.00
29	Odalis Perez	1.00
30	Andres Galarraga	2.00

1999 SkyBox Molten Metal Xplosion

This is a 150-card parallel set, which is seeeded 1:2 packs. These are made of actual metal that have added etching and some foil stamping.

	MT
Complete Set (150):	500.00
Common Player:	1.00
Metalsmith Stars (1-100):	5X
Heavy Metal Stars (101-130):	4X
Supernatural Stars (131-150):	3X
Inserted 1:2	

(See 1999 SkyBox Molten Metal for checklist and base card values.)

1999 SkyBox Premium

The base set consists of 300 cards, base cards feature full bleed fronts with gold-foil stamped player and team names. Card backs have complete year-by-year stats along with a close-up photo. The Rookie subset (223-272) also have a short-printed parallel version as well. Different photos are used but they have the same card number and card back. The short-print versions are seeded 1:8 packs and have an action photo front while the non-seeded cards have a close-up photo.

	MT
Complete Set (300):	30.00
Complete Set w/sp's (350):	200.00
Common Player:	.15
Common SP (223-272):	1.00
SPs inserted 1:8	
Star Rubies:	50x to 90x
Production 50 sets	
SP Star Rubies:	10x to 20x
Production 15 sets	
Pack (8):	3.00
Wax Box (24):	65.00

No.	Player	MT
1	Alex Rodriguez	3.00
2	Sidney Ponson	.15
3	Shawn Green	.25
4	Dan Wilson	.15
5	Rolando Arrojo	.15
6	Roberto Alomar	.50
7	Matt Anderson	.15
8	David Segui	.15
9	Alex Gonzalez	.15
10	Edgar Renteria	.15
11	Benito Santiago	.15
12	Todd Stottlemyre	.15
13	Rico Brogna	.15
14	Troy Glaus	.75
15	Al Leiter	.15
16	Pedro J. Martinez	1.00
17	Paul O'Neill	.25
18	Manny Ramirez	1.00
19	Scott Rolen	.75
20	Curt Schilling	.25
21	Bobby Abreu	.15
22	Robb Nen	.15
23	Andy Pettitte	.40
24	John Wetteland	.15
25	Bobby Bonilla	.15
26	Darin Erstad	.60
27	Shawn Estes	.15
28	John Franco	.15
29	Nomar Garciaparra	2.00
30	Rick Helling	.15
31	David Justice	.25
32	Chuck Knoblauch	.25
33	Quinton McCracken	.15
34	Kenny Rogers	.15
35	Brian Giles	.15
36	Armando Benitez	.15
37	Trevor Hoffman	.15
38	Charles Johnson	.15
39	Travis Lee	.50
40	Tom Glavine	.25
41	Rondell White	.25
42	Orlando Hernandez	.40
43	Mickey Morandini	.15
44	Darryl Kile	.15
45	Greg Vaughn	.25
46	Gregg Jefferies	.15
47	Mark McGwire	4.00
48	Kerry Wood	.40
49	Jeromy Burnitz	.15
50	Ron Gant	.15
51	Vinny Castilla	.15
52	Doug Glanville	.15
53	Juan Guzman	.15
54	Dustin Hermanson	.15
55	Jose Hernandez	.15
56	Bob Higginson	.15
57	A.J. Hinch	.15
58	Randy Johnson	.50
59	Eli Marrero	.15
60	Rafael Palmeiro	.50
61	Carl Pavano	.15
62	Brett Tomko	.15
63	Jose Guillen	.15
64	Mike Lieberthal	.15
65	Jim Abbott	.15
66	Dante Bichette	.25
67	Jeff Cirillo	.15
68	Eric Davis	.20
69	Delino DeShields	.15
70	Steve Finley	.15
71	Mark Grace	.25
72	Jason Kendall	.25
73	Jeff Kent	.15
74	Desi Relaford	.15
75	Ivan Rodriguez	.75
76	Shannon Stewart	.15
77	Geoff Jenkins	.15
78	Ben Grieve	.60
79	Cliff Floyd	.15
80	Jason Giambi	.15
81	Rod Beck	.15
82	Derek Bell	.15
83	Will Clark	.40
84	David Dellucci	.15
85	Joey Hamilton	.15
86	Livan Hernandez	.15
87	Barry Larkin	.20
88	Matt Mantei	.15
89	Dean Palmer	.15
90	Chan Ho Park	.25
91	Jim Thome	.40
92	Miguel Tejada	.15
93	Justin Thompson	.15
94	David Wells	.15
95	Bernie Williams	.50
96	Jeff Bagwell	.75
97	Derrek Lee	.15
98	Devon White	.15
99	Jeff Shaw	.15
100	Brad Radke	.15
101	Mark Grudzielanek	.15
102	Javy Lopez	.25
103	Mike Sirotka	.15
104	Robin Ventura	.25
105	Andy Ashby	.15
106	Juan Gonzalez	1.00
107	Albert Belle	.75
108	Andy Benes	.15
109	Jay Buhner	.15
110	Ken Caminiti	.25
111	Roger Clemens	1.25
112	Mike Hampton	.15
113	Pete Harnisch	.15
114	Mike Piazza	2.00
115	J.T. Snow	.15
116	John Olerud	.25
117	Tony Womack	.15
118	Todd Zeile	.15
119	Tony Gwynn	1.50
120	Brady Anderson	.15
121	Sean Casey	.50
122	Jose Cruz Jr.	.25
123	Carlos Delgado	.50
124	Edgar Martinez	.15
125	Jose Mesa	.15
126	Shane Reynolds	.25
127	John Valentin	.15
128	Mo Vaughn	.50
129	Kevin Young	.15
130	Jay Bell	.15
131	Aaron Boone	.15
132	John Smoltz	.15
133	Mike Stanley	.15
134	Bret Saberhagen	.15
135	Tim Salmon	.25
136	Mariano Rivera	.25
137	Ken Griffey Jr.	4.00
138	Jose Offerman	.15
139	Troy Percival	.15
140	Greg Maddux	2.00
141	Frank Thomas	1.50
142	Steve Avery	.15
143	Kevin Millwood	.40
144	Sammy Sosa	2.00
145	Larry Walker	.60
146	Matt Williams	.30
147	Mike Caruso	.15
148	Todd Helton	.75
149	Andruw Jones	.50
150	Ray Lankford	.15
151	Craig Biggio	.40
152	Ugueth Urbina	.15
153	Wade Boggs	.40
154	Derek Jeter	2.00
155	Wally Joyner	.15
156	Mike Mussina	.50
157	Gregg Olson	.15
158	Henry Rodriguez	.15
159	Reggie Sanders	.15
160	Fernando Tatis	.40
161	Dmitri Young	.15
162	Rick Aguilera	.15
163	Marty Cordova	.15
164	Johnny Damon	.15
165	Ray Durham	.15
166	Brad Fullmer	.15
167	Chipper Jones	2.00
168	Bobby Smith	.15
169	Omar Vizquel	.15
170	Todd Hundley	.15
171	David Cone	.25
172	Royce Clayton	.15
173	Ryan Klesko	.15
174	Jeff Montgomery	.15
175	Magglio Ordonez	.25
176	Billy Wagner	.15
177	Masato Yoshii	.15
178	Jason Christiansen	.15
179	Chuck Finley	.15
180	Tom Gordon	.15
181	Wilton Guerrero	.15
182	Rickey Henderson	.25
183	Sterling Hitchcock	.15
184	Kenny Lofton	.50
185	Tino Martinez	.20
186	Fred McGriff	.30
187	Matt Stairs	.15
188	Neifi Perez	.15
189	Bob Wickman	.15
190	Barry Bonds	.75
191	Jose Canseco	.50
192	Damion Easley	.15
193	Jim Edmonds	.15
194	Juan Encarnacion	.25
195	Travis Fryman	.25
196	Tom Goodwin	.15
197	Rusty Greer	.15
198	Roberto Hernandez	.15
199	B.J. Surhoff	.15
200	Scott Brosius	.15
201	Brian Jordan	.15
202	Paul Konerko	.25
203	Ismael Valdes	.15
204	Eric Milton	.15
205	Adrian Beltre	.40
206	Tony Clark	.40
207	Bartolo Colon	.15
208	Cal Ripken Jr.	3.00
209	Moises Alou	.25
210	Wilson Alvarez	.15
211	Kevin Brown	.25
212	Orlando Cabrera	.15
213	Vladimir Guerrero	1.50
214	Jose Rosado	.15
215	Raul Mondesi	.25
216	Dave Nilsson	.15
217	Carlos Perez	.15
218	Jason Schmidt	.15
219	Richie Sexson	.25
220	Gary Sheffield	.25
221	Fernando Vina	.15
222	Todd Walker	.15
223	*Scott Sauerbeck*	.25
223	*Scott Sauerbeck (sp)*	1.00
224	*Pascual Matos*	.40
224	*Pascual Matos (sp)*	1.50
225	*Kyle Farnsworth*	.25
225	*Kyle Farnsworth (sp)*	1.00
226	*Freddy Garcia*	1.00
226	*Freddy Garcia (sp)*	4.00
227	*David Lundquist*	.25
227	*David Lundquist (sp)*	1.00
228	*Jolbert Cabrera*	.25
228	*Jolbert Cabrera (sp)*	1.00
229	*Dan Perkins*	.25
229	*Dan Perkins (sp)*	1.00
230	Warren Morris	.15
230	Warren Morris (sp)	1.00
231	Carlos Febles	.15
231	Carlos Febles (sp)	1.00
232	*Brett Hinchliffe*	.25
232	*Brett Hinchliffe (sp)*	1.00
233	*Jason Phillips*	.25
233	*Jason Phillips (sp)*	1.00
234	*Glen Barker*	.25
234	*Glen Barker (sp)*	1.00
235	*Jose Macias*	.40
235	*Jose Macias (sp)*	1.50
236	*Joe Mays*	.25
236	*Joe Mays (sp)*	1.00
237	*Chad Allen*	.25
237	*Chad Allen (sp)*	1.00
238	*Miguel Del Toro*	.25
238	*Miguel Del Toro (sp)*	1.00
239	Chris Singleton	.40
239	Chris Singleton (sp)	1.50
240	*Jesse Garcia*	.25
240	*Jesse Garcia (sp)*	1.00
241	Kris Benson	.15
241	Kris Benson (sp)	1.00
242	*Clay Bellinger*	.40
242	*Clay Bellinger (sp)*	1.50
243	Scott Williamson	.15
243	Scott Williamson (sp)	1.00
244	*Masao Kida*	.25
244	*Masao Kida (sp)*	1.00
245	*Guillermo Garcia*	.25
245	*Guillermo Garcia (sp)*	1.00
246	*A.J. Burnett*	.75
246	*A.J. Burnett (sp)*	3.00
247	*Bo Porter*	.25
247	*Bo Porter (sp)*	1.00
248	*Pat Burrell*	3.00
248	*Pat Burrell (sp)*	15.00
249	Carlos Lee	.15
249	Carlos Lee (sp)	1.00
250	*Jeff Weaver*	.50
250	*Jeff Weaver (sp)*	2.00
251	Ruben Mateo	.25
251	Ruben Mateo (sp)	1.00
252	J.D. Drew	.40
252	J.D. Drew (sp)	3.00
253	Jeremy Giambi	.15
253	Jeremy Giambi (sp)	1.00
254	*Gary Bennett*	.15
254	*Gary Bennett (sp)*	1.00
255	*Edwards Guzman*	.15

255	*Edwards Guzman (sp)*	1.00
256	Ramon Martinez	.15
256	Ramon Martinez (sp)	1.00
257	*Giomar Guevara*	.25
257	*Giomar Guevara (sp)*	1.00
258	*Joe McEwing*	.40
258	*Joe McEwing (sp)*	1.50
259	*Tom Davey*	.25
259	*Tom Davey (sp)*	1.00
260	Gabe Kapler	.40
260	Gabe Kapler (sp)	1.50
261	*Ryan Rupe*	.25
261	*Ryan Rupe (sp)*	1.00
262	*Kelly Dransfeldt*	.25
262	*Kelly Dransfeldt (sp)*	1.00
263	Michael Barrett	.15
263	Michael Barrett (sp)	1.00
264	Eric Chavez	.20
264	Eric Chavez (sp)	1.00
265	*Orber Moreno*	.25
265	*Orber Moreno (sp)*	1.00
266	Marlon Anderson	.15
266	Marlon Anderson (sp)	1.00
267	Carlos Beltran	.25
267	Carlos Beltran (sp)	1.00
268	Doug Mientkiewicz	.25
268	Doug Mientkiewicz (sp)	1.00
269	Roy Halladay	.15
269	Roy Halladay (sp)	1.00
270	Torii Hunter	.15
270	Torii Hunter (sp)	1.00
271	Stan Spencer	.15
271	Stan Spencer (sp)	1.00
272	Alex Gonzalez	.15
272	Alex Gonzalez (sp)	1.00
273	Mark McGwire (Spring Fling)	2.00
274	Scott Rolen (Spring Fling)	.40
275	Jeff Bagwell (Spring Fling)	.40
276	Derek Jeter (Spring Fling)	1.00
277	Tony Gwynn (Spring Fling)	.75
278	Frank Thomas (Spring Fling)	.50
279	Sammy Sosa (Spring Fling)	1.00
280	Nomar Garciaparra (Spring Fling)	1.00
281	Cal Ripken Jr. (Spring Fling)	1.25
282	Albert Belle (Spring Fling)	.40
283	Kerry Wood (Spring Fling)	.25
284	Greg Maddux (Spring Fling)	1.00
285	Barry Bonds (Spring Fling)	.40
286	Juan Gonzalez (Spring Fling)	.50
287	Ken Griffey Jr. (Spring Fling)	1.50
288	Alex Rodriguez (Spring Fling)	1.50
289	Ben Grieve (Spring Fling)	.30
290	Travis Lee (Spring Fling)	.25
291	Mo Vaughn (Spring Fling)	.30
292	Mike Piazza (Spring Fling)	1.00
293	Roger Clemens (Spring Fling)	.60
294	J.D. Drew (Spring Fling)	.50
295	Randy Johnson (Spring Fling)	.25
296	Chipper Jones (Spring Fling)	1.00
297	Vladimir Guerrero (Spring Fling)	.75
298	Checklist (Nomar Garciaparra)	.75
299	Checklist (Ken Griffey Jr.)	1.00
300	Checklist (Mark McGwire)	1.00

1999 SkyBox Premium Autographics

This 54-card autographed set feature an embossed SkyBox Seal of Authenticity stamp and are seeded 1:68 packs. Cards are commonly found signed in black ink. Blue-ink versions, serially numbered to 50 each, were also produced.

	MT
Common Player:	8.00
Inserted 1:68	
Blue Ink:	2X
Production 50 sets	
Roberto Alomar	40.00
Paul Bako	8.00
Michael Barrett	12.00
Kris Benson	12.00
Micah Bowie	8.00
Roosevelt Brown	10.00
A.J. Burnett	15.00
Pat Burrell	60.00
Ken Caminiti	15.00
Royce Clayton	8.00
Edgard Clemente	8.00
Bartolo Colon	15.00
J.D. Drew	30.00
Damion Easley	8.00
Derrin Ebert	8.00
Mario Encarnacion	12.00
Juan Encarnacion	15.00
Troy Glaus	40.00
Tom Glavine	25.00
Juan Gonzalez	60.00
Shawn Green	40.00
Wilton Guerrero	8.00
Jose Guillen	8.00
Tony Gwynn	90.00
Mark Harriger	8.00
Bobby Higginson	12.00
Todd Hollandsworth	8.00
Scott Hunter	8.00
Gabe Kapler	20.00
Scott Karl	8.00
Mike Kinkade	8.00
Ray Lankford	12.00
Barry Larkin	25.00
Matt Lawton	8.00
Ricky Ledee	15.00
Travis Lee	15.00
Eli Marrero	8.00
Ruben Mateo	25.00
Joe McEwing	12.00
Doug Mientkiewicz	8.00
Russ Ortiz	8.00
Jim Parque	8.00
Robert Person	8.00
Alex Rodriguez	150.00
Scott Rolen	40.00
Benj Sampson	8.00
Luis Saturria	8.00
Curt Schilling	20.00
David Segui	8.00
Fernando Tatis	20.00
Peter Tucci	8.00
Javier Vasquez	8.00
Robin Ventura	25.00

1999 SkyBox Premium Diamond Debuts

This 15-card set features the best rookies of 1999 on a silver rainbow holo-foil card stock. These are seeded 1:49 packs. Card backs are numbered with a "DD" suffix.

		MT
Complete Set (15):		80.00
Common Player:		4.00
Inserted 1:49		
1	Eric Chavez	7.50
2	Kyle Farnsworth	4.00
3	Ryan Rupe	4.00
4	Jeremy Giambi	4.00
5	Marlon Anderson	4.00
6	J.D. Drew	5.00
7	Carlos Febles	5.00
8	Joe McEwing	6.00
9	Jeff Weaver	15.00
10	Alex Gonzalez	4.00
11	Chad Allen	4.00
12	Michael Barrett	6.00
13	Gabe Kapler	7.50
14	Carlos Lee	6.00
15	Edwards Guzman	4.00

1999 SkyBox Premium Intimidation Nation

This 15-card set highlights the top performers in baseball and features gold rainbow holo-foil stamping. These are limited to 99 sequentially numbered sets. Card backs are numbered with a "IN" suffix.

		MT
Complete Set (15):		700.00
Common Player:		20.00
Production 99 sets		
1	Cal Ripken Jr.	80.00
2	Tony Gwynn	30.00
3	Nomar Garciaparra	60.00
4	Frank Thomas	30.00
5	Mike Piazza	60.00
6	Mark McGwire	100.00
7	Scott Rolen	20.00
8	Chipper Jones	50.00
9	Greg Maddux	50.00
10	Ken Griffey Jr.	80.00
11	Juan Gonzalez	25.00
12	Derek Jeter	80.00
13	J.D. Drew	20.00
14	Roger Clemens	40.00
15	Alex Rodriguez	80.00

1999 SkyBox Premium Live Bats

This 15-card set spotlights baseball's top hitters and feature red foil stamping. Card backs are numbered with a "LB" suffix and are seeded 1:7 packs.

		MT
Complete Set (15):		25.00
Common Player:		.50
Inserted 1:7		
1	Juan Gonzalez	1.00
2	Mark McGwire	4.00
3	Jeff Bagwell	1.00
4	Frank Thomas	1.75
5	Mike Piazza	2.50
6	Nomar Garciaparra	2.50
7	Alex Rodriguez	3.00
8	Scott Rolen	.75
9	Travis Lee	.50
10	Tony Gwynn	1.75
11	Derek Jeter	2.50
12	Ben Grieve	.50
13	Chipper Jones	2.50
14	Ken Griffey Jr.	4.00
15	Cal Ripken Jr.	3.00

1999 SkyBox Premium Show Business

This 15-card set features some of the best players in the "show" on double foil-stamped card fronts. Card backs are numbered with a "SB" suffix and are seeded 1:70 packs.

		MT
Complete Set (15):		220.00
Common Player:		5.00
Inserted 1:70		
1	Mark McGwire	30.00
2	Tony Gwynn	15.00
3	Nomar Garciaparra	20.00
4	Juan Gonzalez	8.00
5	Roger Clemens	10.00
6	Chipper Jones	15.00
7	Cal Ripken Jr.	25.00
8	Alex Rodriguez	25.00
9	Orlando Hernandez	5.00
10	Greg Maddux	15.00
11	Mike Piazza	20.00
12	Frank Thomas	10.00
13	Ken Griffey Jr.	30.00
14	Scott Rolen	8.00
15	Derek Jeter	20.00

1999 SkyBox Premium Soul of The Game

This 15-card set features rainbow foil stamping and the name Soul of the Game prominently stamped, covering the entire card behind the player photo. Card backs are numbered with a "SG" suffix and are seeded 1:14 packs.

		MT
Complete Set (15):		55.00
Common Player:		2.00
Inserted 1:14		
1	Alex Rodriguez	6.00
2	Vladimir Guerrero	3.00
3	Chipper Jones	4.00
4	Derek Jeter	5.00
5	Tony Gwynn	3.00
6	Scott Rolen	2.00
7	Juan Gonzalez	2.00
8	Mark McGwire	8.00
9	Ken Griffey Jr.	8.00
10	Jeff Bagwell	2.00
11	Cal Ripken Jr.	6.00
12	Frank Thomas	3.00
13	Mike Piazza	5.00
14	Nomar Garciaparra	5.00
15	Sammy Sosa	5.00

1999 SkyBox Thunder

Skybox Thunder consists of a 300-card base set with three pa rallels and six inserts. The base set is inserted at varying odds. In hobby packs, regular-player cards #'s 1-140 come 4 -5 per pack; veteran stars on cards #'s 141-240 come 2 per p ack; and superstars on cards #'s 241-300 are seeded one per pack. For retail packs the odds were : #'s 1-141 (3-4 per pa ck); #'s 141-240 (2 per pack); and #'s 241-300 (1 per pack). The parallel sets include Rave (# to 150 sets) and Sup er Rave (# to 25), which are both hobby exclusive. The Rant parallel set is retail exclusive (1:2). The inserts are Unlea shed (1:6), www.batterz.com (1:18), In Depth (1:24), Hip-No-Tiz ed (1:36), Turbo-Charged (1:72), and Dial "1" (1:300).

		MT
Complete Set (300):		35.00
Common Player (1-140):		.10
Common Player (141-240):		.15
Common Player (241-300):		.25
Raves (1-140):		30x to 50x
Raves (141-240):		15x to 30x
Raves (241-300):		15x to 25x
Production 150 sets		
SuperRaves (1-140):		100x to 200x
SuperRaves (141-240):		50x to 120x
SuperRaves (241-300):		40x to 90x
Production 25 sets		
Rant (141-240):		2x to 5x
Rant (241-300):		1.5x to 3x
Inserted 1:2 R		
Pack (8):		1.75
Wax Box (36):		45.00
1	John Smoltz	.20
2	Garret Anderson	.10
3	Matt Williams	.25
4	Daryle Ward	.10
5	Andy Ashby	.10
6	Miguel Tejada	.20
7	Dmitri Young	.10
8	Roberto Alomar	.50
9	Kevin Brown	.20
10	Eric Young	.10
11	Odalis Perez	.10
12	Preston Wilson	.15
13	Jeff Abbott	.10
14	Bret Boone	.10
15	Mendy Lopez	.10
16	B.J. Surhoff	.10
17	Steve Woodard	.10
18	Ron Coomer	.10
19	Rondell White	.20
20	Edgardo Alfonzo	.15
21	Kevin Millwood	.60
22	Jose Canseco	.40
23	Blake Stein	.10
24	Quilvio Veras	.10
25	Chuck Knoblauch	.40
26	David Segui	.10
27	Eric Davis	.10
28	Francisco Cordova	.10
29	Randy Winn	.10
30	Will Clark	.30
31	Billy Wagner	.15
32	Kevin Witt	.10
33	Jim Edmonds	.20
34	Todd Stottlemyre	.10
35	Shane Andrews	.10
36	Michael Tucker	.10
37	Sandy Alomar Jr.	.10
38	Neifi Perez	.10
39	Jaret Wright	.25
40	Devon White	.10
41	Edgar Renteria	.10
42	Shane Reynolds	.10
43	Jeff King	.10
44	Darren Dreifort	.10
45	Fernando Vina	.10
46	Marty Cordova	.10
47	Ugueth Urbina	.10
48	Bobby Bonilla	.20
49	Omar Vizquel	.10
50	Tom Gordon	.10
51	Ryan Christenson	.10
52	Aaron Boone	.10
53	Jamie Moyer	.10
54	Brian Giles	.10
55	Kevin Tapani	.10
56	Scott Brosius	.10
57	Ellis Burks	.10
58	Al Leiter	.10
59	Royce Clayton	.10
60	Chris Carpenter	.10
61	Bubba Trammell	.10
62	Tom Glavine	.20
63	Shannon Stewart	.10
64	Todd Zeile	.10
65	J.T. Snow	.10
66	Matt Clement	.10
67	Matt Stairs	.10
68	Ismael Valdes	.10
69	Todd Walker	.10
70	Jose Lima	.10
71	Mike Caruso	.10
72	Brett Tomko	.10
73	Mike Lansing	.10
74	Justin Thompson	.10
75	Damion Easley	.10
76	Derrek Lee	.10
77	Derek Bell	.10
78	Brady Anderson	.10
79	Charles Johnson	.10
80	*Rafael Roque*	.10
81	Corey Koskie	.10
82	Fernando Seguignol	.50
83	Jay Tessmer	.10
84	Jason Giambi	.10
85	Mike Lieberthal	.10
86	Jose Guillen	.10
87	Jim Leyritz	.10
88	Shawn Estes	.10
89	Ray Lankford	.10
90	Paul Sorrento	.10
91	Javy Lopez	.20
92	John Wetteland	.10
93	Sean Casey	.15
94	Chuck Finley	.10
95	Trot Nixon	.10
96	Ray Durham	.10
97	Reggie Sanders	.10
98	Bartolo Colon	.10
99	Henry Rodriguez	.10
100	Rolando Arrojo	.10
101	Geoff Jenkins	.10
102	Darryl Kile	.10
103	Mark Kotsay	.10
104	Craig Biggio	.40
105	Omar Daal	.10
106	Carlos Febles	.10
107	Eric Karros	.10
108	Matt Lawton	.10
109	Carl Pavano	.10
110	Brian McRae	.10
111	Mariano Rivera	.20
112	Jay Buhner	.15
113	Doug Glanville	.10
114	Jason Kendall	.10
115	Wally Joyner	.10
116	Jeff Kent	.10
117	Shane Monahan	.10
118	Eli Marrero	.10
119	Bobby Smith	.10
120	Shawn Green	.15
121	Kirk Rueter	.10
122	Tom Goodwin	.10
123	Andy Benes	.10
124	Ed Sprague	.10
125	Mike Mussina	.50
126	Jose Offerman	.10
127	Mickey Morandini	.10
128	Paul Konerko	.25
129	Denny Neagle	.10
130	Travis Fryman	.10
131	John Rocker	.10
132	*Rob Fick*	.10
133	Livan Hernandez	.10
134	Ken Caminiti	.20
135	Johnny Damon	.10
136	Jeff Kubenka	.10
137	Marquis Grissom	.10
138	Doug Mientkiewicz	.10
139	Dustin Hermanson	.25
140	Carl Everett	.10
141	Hideo Nomo	.20
142	Jorge Posada	.15
143	Rickey Henderson	.25
144	Robb Nen	.15
145	Ron Gant	.25
146	Aramis Ramirez	.25
147	Trevor Hoffman	.15
148	Bill Mueller	.15
149	Edgar Martinez	.15
150	Fred McGriff	.30
151	Rusty Greer	.15
152	Tom Evans	.15
153	Todd Greene	.15
154	Jay Bell	.15
155	Mike Lowell	.25
156	Orlando Cabrera	.15
157	Troy O'Leary	.15
158	Jose Hernandez	.15
159	Magglio Ordonez	.25
160	Barry Larkin	.30
161	David Justice	.30
162	Derrick Gibson	.15
163	Luis Gonzalez	.15
164	Alex Gonzalez	.15
165	Scott Elarton	.15
166	Dermal Brown	.15
167	Eric Milton	.15
168	Raul Mondesi	.40
169	Jeff Cirillo	.15
170	Benj Sampson	.15
171	John Olerud	.25
172	Andy Pettitte	.40
173	A.J. Hinch	.15
174	Rico Brogna	.15
175	Jason Schmidt	.15
176	Dean Palmer	.25
177	Matt Morris	.15
178	Quinton McCracken	.15
179	Rick Helling	.15
180	Walt Weiss	.15
181	Troy Percival	.15
182	Tony Batista	.15
183	Brian Jordan	.15
184	Jerry Hairston	.15
185	Bret Saberhagen	.15
186	Mark Grace	.30
187	Brian Simmons	.15
188	Pete Harnisch	.15
189	Kenny Lofton	.75
190	Vinny Castilla	.25
191	Bobby Higginson	.15
192	Joey Hamilton	.15
193	Cliff Floyd	.15
194	Andres Galarraga	.40
195	Chan Ho Park	.40
196	Jeromy Burnitz	.15
197	David Ortiz	.15
198	Wilton Guerrero	.15
199	Rey Ordonez	.15
200	Paul O'Neill	.30
201	Kenny Rogers	.15
202	Marlon Anderson	.15
203	Tony Womack	.15
204	Robin Ventura	.25
205	Russ Ortiz	.15
206	Mike Frank	.15
207	Fernando Tatis	.15
208	Miguel Cairo	.15
209	Ivan Rodriguez	1.00
210	Carlos Delgado	.30
211	Tim Salmon	.30
212	Brian Anderson	.15
213	Ryan Klesko	.20
214	Scott Erickson	.15
215	Mike Stanley	.15
216	Brant Brown	.15
217	Rod Beck	.15
218	*Guillermo Garcia*	.15
219	David Wells	.15
220	Dante Bichette	.40
221	Armando Benitez	.15
222	Todd Dunwoody	.15
223	Kelvim Escobar	.15
224	Richard Hidalgo	.15
225	Angel Pena	.15
226	Ronnie Belliard	.15
227	Brad Radke	.15
228	Brad Fullmer	.30
229	Jay Payton	.15
230	Tino Martinez	.30
231	Scott Spiezio	.15
232	Bobby Abreu	.15
233	John Valentin	.15
234	Kevin Young	.15
235	Steve Finley	.15
236	David Cone	.30
237	Armando Rios	.15
238	Russ Davis	.15
239	Wade Boggs	.45
240	Aaron Sele	.15
241	Jose Cruz Jr.	.50
242	George Lombard	.25
243	Todd Helton	.75
244	Andruw Jones	1.25
245	Troy Glaus	1.50
246	Manny Ramirez	2.00
247	Ben Grieve	1.25
247p	Ben Grieve ("PROMOTIONAL SAMPLE")	3.00
248	Richie Sexson	.25
249	Juan Encarnacion	.50
250	Randy Johnson	.75
251	Gary Sheffield	.35
252	Rafael Palmeiro	.50
253	Roy Halladay	.40
254	Mike Piazza	3.00
255	Tony Gwynn	2.50
256	Juan Gonzalez	1.50
257	Jeremy Giambi	.25
258	Ben Davis	.25
259	Russ Branyon	.25
260	Pedro Martinez	1.00
261	Frank Thomas	2.50

262 Calvin Pickering .25
263 Chipper Jones 3.00
264 Ryan Minor .25
265 Roger Clemens 2.00
266 Sammy Sosa 3.00
267 Mo Vaughn .75
268 Carlos Beltran .25
269 Jim Thome .75
270 Mark McGwire 6.00
271 Travis Lee .60
272 Darin Erstad 1.25
273 Derek Jeter 3.00
274 Greg Maddux 3.00
275 Ricky Ledee .50
276 Alex Rodriguez 5.00
277 Vladimir Guerrero 2.50
278 Greg Vaughn .35
279 Scott Rolen 1.25
280 Carlos Guillen .25
281 Jeff Bagwell 1.25
282 Bruce Chen .25
283 Tony Clark .75
284 Albert Belle 1.25
285 Cal Ripken Jr. 4.50
286 Barry Bonds 1.25
287 Curt Schilling .35
288 Eric Chavez 1.00
289 Larry Walker .75
290 Orlando Hernandez 1.50
291 Moises Alou .40
292 Ken Griffey Jr. 6.00
293 Kerry Wood .75
294 Nomar Garciaparra 3.00
295 Gabe Kapler 1.25
296 Bernie Williams .75
297 Matt Anderson .25
298 Adrian Beltre .50
299 J.D. Drew .75
300 Ryan Bradley .25
--- Checklist 1-230
--- Checklist 231-300 and inserts
--- Video Game Sweepstakes form (Derek Jeter)

1999 SkyBox Thunder Rant

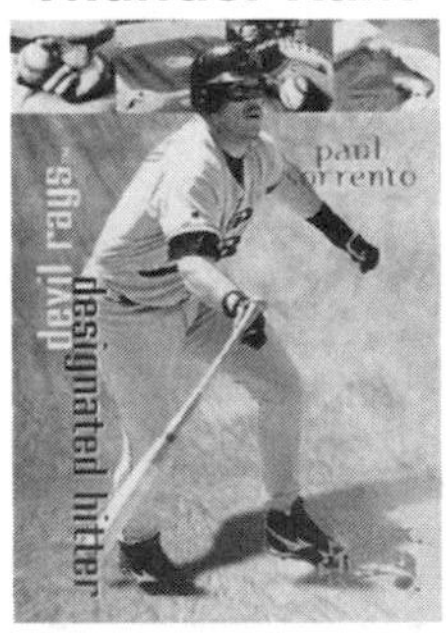

A retail-only parallel of the 300-card base set, Rant substitutes purple metallic foil highlights for the regular-issue's silver on front, and a has a "RANT" notation at upper-right on back, also in purple. The stated insertion rate for the parallel is one per two retail packs.

	MT
Complete Set (300):	250.00
Common Player:	.25
Rant Stars:	5X

(See 1999 SkyBox Thunder for checklist and base card values.)

1999 SkyBox Thunder Dial "1"

Designed to look like a mobile phone, this insert set featur ed 10 cards of long distance hitters. The set consisted of b lack plastic cards with rounded corners, and were seeded one card per every 300 packs.

		MT
Complete Set (10):		425.00
Common Player:		15.00
Inserted 1:300		
1D	Nomar Garciaparra	50.00
2D	Juan Gonzalez	30.00
3D	Ken Griffey Jr.	90.00
4D	Chipper Jones	50.00
5D	Mark McGwire	90.00
6D	Mike Piazza	50.00
7D	Manny Ramirez	30.00
8D	Alex Rodriguez	75.00
9D	Sammy Sosa	50.00
10D	Mo Vaughn	15.00

1999 SkyBox Thunder Hip-No-Tized

This insert set consisted of 15 cards, featuring both hitters and pitchers. The cards were seeded one card in every 36 packs, and consist of mesmerizing patterned holo-foil stamping.

		MT
Complete Set (15):		100.00
Common Player:		3.00
Inserted 1:36		
1H	J.D. Drew	3.00
2H	Nomar Garciaparra	10.00
3H	Juan Gonzalez	4.00
4H	Ken Griffey Jr.	15.00
5H	Derek Jeter	10.00
6H	Randy Johnson	4.00
7H	Chipper Jones	8.00
8H	Mark McGwire	15.00
9H	Mike Piazza	10.00
10H	Cal Ripken Jr.	12.00
11H	Alex Rodriguez	12.00
12H	Sammy Sosa	10.00
13H	Frank Thomas	5.00
14H	Jim Thome	3.00
15H	Kerry Wood	4.00

1999 SkyBox Thunder In Depth

This insert set consists of 10 cards, featuring baseball's elite players. The cards are highlighted with gold rainbow holo-foil and gold metallic ink. The insertion rate for this insert was one card in every 24 packs.

		MT
Complete Set (10):		60.00
Common Player:		2.50
Inserted 1:240		
1ID	Albert Belle	3.00
2ID	Barry Bonds	4.00
3ID	Roger Clemens	6.00
4ID	Juan Gonzalez	4.00
5ID	Ken Griffey Jr.	15.00
6ID	Mark McGwire	15.00
7ID	Mike Piazza	10.00
8ID	Sammy Sosa	10.00
9ID	Mo Vaughn	2.50
10ID	Kerry Wood	4.00

1999 SkyBox Thunder Turbo Charged

This 10-card insert set consisted of the top home run hitters. The players were featured on platic see-through cards with rainbow holofoil. One card was included in every 72 packs.

		MT
Complete Set (10):		120.00
Common Player:		5.00
Inserted 1:72		
1TC	Jose Canseco	5.00
2TC	Juan Gonzalez	6.00
3TC	Ken Griffey Jr.	25.00
4TC	Vladimir Guerrero	12.00
5TC	Mark McGwire	25.00
6TC	Mike Piazza	15.00
7TC	Manny Ramirez	10.00
8TC	Alex Rodriguez	20.00
9TC	Sammy Sosa	15.00
10TC	Mo Vaughn	5.00

1999 SkyBox Thunder Unleashed

This insert set contained 15 cards designed to resemble a cereal box. The players featured included the best young talent in baseball. The cards were silver-foil stamped, and offered facsimile signatures of each player. One card was included with every six packs.

		MT
Complete Set (15):		20.00
Common Player:		.75
Inserted 1:6		
1U	Carlos Beltran	.75
2U	Adrian Beltre	1.25
3U	Eric Chavez	2.00
4U	J.D. Drew	1.00
5U	Juan Encarnacion	1.00
6U	Jeremy Giambi	1.00
7U	Troy Glaus	2.50
8U	Ben Grieve	1.00
9U	Todd Helton	2.00
10U	Orlando Hernandez	3.00
11U	Gabe Kapler	3.00
12U	Travis Lee	1.50
13U	Calvin Pickering	.75
14U	Richie Sexson	.75
15U	Kerry Wood	1.00

1999 SkyBox Thunder www.Batterz. com

www.batterz.com is a 10 card insert set that was seeded one card per every 18 packs. The game's best hitters are in ther e own home site in this computer-inspired set.

		MT
Complete Set (10):		50.00
Common Player:		1.00
Inserted 1:18		
1WB	J.D. Drew	2.00
2WB	Nomar Garciaparra	6.00
3WB	Ken Griffey Jr.	10.00
4WB	Tony Gwynn	4.00
5WB	Derek Jeter	6.00
6WB	Mark McGwire	10.00
7WB	Alex Rodriguez	8.00
8WB	Scott Rolen	2.00
9WB	Sammy Sosa	5.00
10WB	Bernie Williams	1.00

2000 E-X

Released as a 90-card set the card fronts have a holofoil card front, with the E-X logo and player name stamped in silver foil. Card backs have a player image, 1999 stats and the featured players' career totals.

		MT
Complete Set (90):		300.00
Common Player:		.25
Common Prospect (61-90):		5.00
Production 3,499 sets		
Pack:		4.00
Wax Box:		90.00
1	Alex Rodriguez	5.00
2	Jeff Bagwell	1.50
3	Mike Piazza	4.00
4	Tony Gwynn	2.50
5	Ken Griffey Jr.	6.00
6	Juan Gonzalez	1.50
7	Vladimir Guerrero	3.00
8	Cal Ripken Jr.	5.00
9	Mo Vaughn	1.00
10	Chipper Jones	3.00
11	Derek Jeter	4.00
12	Nomar Garciaparra	4.00
13	Mark McGwire	6.00
14	Sammy Sosa	4.00
15	Pedro Martinez	1.50
16	Greg Maddux	3.00
17	Frank Thomas	2.00
18	Shawn Green	1.00
19	Carlos Beltran	.40
20	Roger Clemens	2.00
21	Randy Johnson	1.50
22	Bernie Williams	1.00
23	Carlos Delgado	1.00
24	Manny Ramirez	1.50
25	Freddy Garcia	.25
26	Barry Bonds	1.50
27	Tim Hudson	.50
28	Larry Walker	.75
29	Raul Mondesi	.50
30	Ivan Rodriguez	1.50
31	Magglio Ordonez	.50
32	Scott Rolen	1.50
33	Mike Mussina	.75
34	J.D. Drew	.40
35	Tom Glavine	.40
36	Barry Larkin	.50
37	Jim Thome	.75
38	Erubiel Durazo	.25
39	Curt Schilling	.40
40	Orlando Hernandez	.40
41	Rafael Palmeiro	1.00
42	Gabe Kapler	.25
43	Mark Grace	.50
44	Jeff Cirillo	.25
45	Jeromy Burnitz	.25
46	Sean Casey	.25
47	Kevin Millwood	.25
48	Vinny Castilla	.25
49	Jose Canseco	1.00
50	Roberto Alomar	1.00
51	Craig Biggio	.50
52	Preston Wilson	.25
53	Jeff Weaver	.25
54	Robin Ventura	.40
55	Ben Grieve	.50
56	Troy Glaus	1.50
57	Jacque Jones	.25
58	Brian Giles	.25
59	Kevin Brown	.40
60	Todd Helton	1.50
61	Ben Petrick (Prospects)	5.00
62	Chad Hermansen (Prospects)	5.00
63	Kevin Barker (Prospects)	5.00
64	Matt LeCroy (Prospects)	5.00
65	Brad Penny (Prospects)	5.00
66	D.T. Cromer (Prospects)	5.00
67	Steve Lomasney (Prospects)	5.00
68	Cole Liniak (Prospects)	5.00
69	B.J. Ryan (Prospects)	5.00
70	Wilton Veras (Prospects)	10.00
71	*Aaron McNeal* (Prospects)	12.00
72	Nick Johnson (Prospects)	15.00
73	Adam Piatt (Prospects)	10.00
74	Adam Kennedy (Prospects)	6.00
75	Cesar King (Prospects)	5.00
76	Peter Bergeron (Prospects)	6.00
77	Rob Bell (Prospects)	5.00
78	Wily Pena (Prospects)	20.00
79	Ruben Mateo (Prospects)	5.00
80	Kip Wells (Prospects)	6.00
81	Alex Escobar (Prospects)	5.00
82	*Danys Baez* (Prospects)	10.00
83	Travis Dawkins (Prospects)	5.00
84	Mark Quinn (Prospects)	6.00
85	Jimmy Anderson (Prospects)	5.00
86	Rick Ankiel (Prospects)	30.00
87	Alfonso Soriano (Prospects)	12.00
88	Pat Burrell (Prospects)	15.00
89	Eric Munson (Prospects)	15.00
90	Josh Beckett (Prospects)	18.00

2000 E-X Essential Credentials Now

Like Future, this is a parallel of the base set, with the production of cards 1-60 limited to that player's card number. Production for cards 61-90 can be determined by subtracting 60 from the card number. Quantity issued is listed in parantheses.

		MT
Common Player:		15.00
1	Alex Rodriguez (1)	
2	Jeff Bagwell (2)	
3	Mike Piazza (3)	
4	Tony Gwynn (4)	
5	Ken Griffey Jr. (5)	
6	Juan Gonzalez (6)	
7	Vladimir Guerrero (7)	
8	Cal Ripken Jr. (8)	
9	Mo Vaughn (9)	
10	Chipper Jones (10)	
11	Derek Jeter (11)	
12	Nomar Garciaparra (12)	
13	Mark McGwire (13)	
14	Sammy Sosa (14)	
15	Pedro Martinez (15)	
16	Greg Maddux (16)	
17	Frank Thomas (17)	
18	Shawn Green (18)	
19	Carlos Beltran (19)	
20	Roger Clemens (20)	200.00
21	Randy Johnson (21)	125.00
22	Bernie Williams (22)	125.00
23	Carlos Delgado (23)	90.00
24	Manny Ramirez (24)	100.00
25	Freddy Garcia (25)	30.00
26	Barry Bonds (26)	125.00
27	Tim Hudson (27)	40.00
28	Larry Walker (28)	75.00
29	Raul Mondesi (29)	50.00
30	Ivan Rodriguez (30)	125.00
31	Magglio Ordonez (31)	50.00
32	Scott Rolen (32)	100.00
33	Mike Mussina (33)	75.00
34	J.D. Drew (34)	35.00
35	Tom Glavine (35)	35.00
36	Barry Larkin (36)	40.00
37	Jim Thome (37)	40.00
38	Erubiel Durazo (38)	20.00
39	Curt Schilling (39)	25.00
40	Orlando Hernandez (40)	25.00
41	Rafael Palmeiro (41)	40.00
42	Gabe Kapler (42)	20.00
43	Mark Grace (43)	25.00
44	Jeff Cirillo (44)	20.00
45	Jeromy Burnitz (45)	15.00
46	Sean Casey (46)	15.00
47	Kevin Millwood (47)	15.00
48	Vinny Castilla (48)	15.00
49	Jose Canseco (49)	40.00
50	Roberto Alomar (50)	40.00
51	Craig Biggio (51)	25.00
52	Preston Wilson (52)	10.00
53	Jeff Weaver (53)	10.00
54	Robin Ventura (54)	15.00
55	Ben Grieve (55)	20.00
56	Troy Glaus (56)	20.00
57	Jacque Jones (57)	10.00
58	Brian Giles (58)	10.00
59	Kevin Brown (59)	15.00
60	Todd Helton (60)	40.00
61	Ben Petrick (1) (Prospects)	
62	Chad Hermansen (2) (Prospects)	
63	Kevin Barker (3) (Prospects)	
64	Matt LeCroy (4) (Prospects)	
65	Brad Penny (5) (Prospects)	
66	D.T. Cromer (6) (Prospects)	
67	Steve Lomasney (7) (Prospects)	
68	Cole Liniak (8) (Prospects)	
69	B.J. Ryan (9) (Prospects)	
70	Wilton Veras (10) (Prospects)	
71	Aaron McNeal (11) (Prospects)	
72	Nick Johnson (12) (Prospects)	
73	Adam Piatt (13) (Prospects)	
74	Adam Kennedy (14) (Prospects)	
75	Cesar King (15) (Prospects)	
76	Peter Bergeron (16) (Prospects)	
77	Rob Bell (17) (Prospects)	
78	Wily Pena (18) (Prospects)	100.00
79	Ruben Mateo (19) (Prospects)	20.00
80	Kip Wells (20) (Prospects)	20.00
81	Alex Escobar (21) (Prospects)	20.00
82	Danys Baez (22) (Prospects)	75.00
83	Travis Dawkins (23) (Prospects)	15.00
84	Mark Quinn (24) (Prospects)	15.00
85	Jimmy Anderson (25) (Prospects)	15.00
86	Rick Ankiel (26) (Prospects)	180.00
87	Alfonso Soriano (27) (Prospects)	65.00
88	Pat Burrell (28) (Prospects)	100.00
89	Eric Munson (29) (Prospects)	75.00
90	Josh Beckett (30) (Prospects)	75.00

2000 E-X Essential Credentials Future

Production varied for these parallel inserts depending on the card number, with the exact production number for cards 1-60 determined by subtracting the card number from 61. Cards 61-90 are determined by subtracting the card number from 91. Quantity issued is listed in parantheses.

		MT
Common Player:		15.00
1	Alex Rodriguez (60)	160.00
2	Jeff Bagwell (59)	60.00
3	Mike Piazza (58)	150.00
4	Tony Gwynn (57)	100.00
5	Ken Griffey Jr. (56)	250.00
6	Juan Gonzalez (55)	60.00
7	Vladimir Guerrero (54)	75.00
8	Cal Ripken Jr. (53)	180.00
9	Mo Vaughn (52)	50.00
10	Chipper Jones (51)	125.00
11	Derek Jeter (50)	160.00
12	Nomar Garciaparra (49)	150.00
13	Mark McGwire (48)	275.00
14	Sammy Sosa (47)	150.00
15	Pedro Martinez (46)	70.00
16	Greg Maddux (45)	125.00
17	Frank Thomas (44)	80.00
18	Shawn Green (43)	50.00
19	Carlos Beltran (42)	25.00
20	Roger Clemens (41)	80.00
21	Randy Johnson (40)	60.00
22	Bernie Williams (39)	50.00
23	Carlos Delgado (38)	50.00
24	Manny Ramirez (37)	60.00
25	Freddy Garcia (36)	25.00
26	Barry Bonds (35)	70.00
27	Tim Hudson (34)	30.00
28	Larry Walker (33)	50.00
29	Raul Mondesi (32)	30.00
30	Ivan Rodriguez (31)	80.00
31	Magglio Ordonez (30)	25.00
32	Scott Rolen (29)	60.00
33	Mike Mussina (28)	40.00
34	J.D. Drew (27)	30.00
35	Tom Glavine (26)	40.00
36	Barry Larkin (25)	40.00
37	Jim Thome (24)	40.00
38	Erubiel Durazo (23)	25.00
39	Curt Schilling (22)	25.00
40	Orlando Hernandez (21)	20.00
41	Rafael Palmeiro (20)	60.00
42	Gabe Kapler (19)	25.00
43	Mark Grace (18)	30.00
44	Jeff Cirillo (17)	20.00
45	Jeromy Burnitz (16)	20.00
46	Sean Casey (15)	20.00
47	Kevin Millwood (14)	20.00
48	Vinny Castilla (13)	25.00
49	Jose Canseco (12)	80.00
50	Roberto Alomar (11)	80.00
51	Craig Biggio (10)	50.00
52	Preston Wilson (9)	
53	Jeff Weaver (8)	
54	Robin Ventura (7)	
55	Ben Grieve (6)	
56	Troy Glaus (5)	
57	Jacque Jones (4)	
58	Brian Giles (3)	
59	Kevin Brown (2)	
60	Todd Helton (1)	
61	Ben Petrick (30) (Prospects)	15.00
62	Chad Hermansen (29) (Prospects)	15.00
63	Kevin Barker (28) (Prospects)	15.00
64	Matt LeCroy (27) (Prospects)	15.00
65	Brad Penny (26) (Prospects)	15.00
66	D.T. Cromer (25) (Prospects)	15.00
67	Steve Lomasney (24) (Prospects)	15.00
68	Cole Liniak (23) (Prospects)	15.00
69	B.J. Ryan (22) (Prospects)	20.00
70	Wilton Veras (21) (Prospects)	75.00
71	Aaron McNeal (20) (Prospects)	90.00
72	Nick Johnson (19) (Prospects)	125.00
73	Adam Piatt (18) (Prospects)	100.00
74	Adam Kennedy (17) (Prospects)	35.00
75	Cesar King (16) (Prospects)	25.00
76	Peter Bergeron (15) (Prospects)	35.00
77	Rob Bell (14) (Prospects)	25.00
78	Wily Pena (13) (Prospects)	150.00
79	Ruben Mateo (12) (Prospects)	25.00
80	Kip Wells (11) (Prospects)	25.00
81	Alex Escobar (10) (Prospects)	35.00
82	Danys Baez (9) (Prospects)	
83	Travis Dawkins (8) (Prospects)	
84	Mark Quinn (7) (Prospects)	
85	Jimmy Anderson (6) (Prospects)	
86	Rick Ankiel (5) (Prospects)	
87	Alfonso Soriano (4) (Prospects)	
88	Pat Burrell (3) (Prospects)	
89	Eric Munson (2) (Prospects)	
90	Josh Beckett (1) (Prospects)	

2000 E-X Autographics

	MT
Common Player:	10.00
Inserted 1:24	
Bob Abreu	20.00
Moises Alou	15.00
Rick Ankiel	75.00
Michael Barrett	10.00
Josh Beckett	25.00
Rob Bell	15.00
Adrian Beltre	20.00
Carlos Beltran	20.00
Wade Boggs	60.00
Barry Bonds	75.00
Kent Bottenfield	10.00
Milton Bradley	15.00
Pat Burrell	40.00
Chris Carpenter	10.00
Sean Casey	20.00
Eric Chavez	15.00
Will Clark	40.00
Johnny Damon	15.00
Mike Darr	10.00
Ben Davis	10.00
Russ Davis	10.00
Carlos Delgado	50.00
Jason Dewey	10.00
Octavio Dotel	10.00
J.D. Drew	40.00
Ray Durham	15.00
Damion Easley	10.00
Kelvim Escobar	10.00
Carlos Febles	10.00
Freddy Garcia	10.00
Jeremy Giambi	10.00
Todd Greene	10.00
Jason Grilli	10.00
Vladimir Guerrero	60.00
Tony Gwynn	75.00
Jerry Hairston	10.00
Mike Hampton	15.00
Todd Helton	40.00
Trevor Hoffman	10.00
Tim Hudson	20.00
John Jaha	10.00
Derek Jeter	200.00
D'Angelo Jimenez	10.00
Randy Johnson	75.00
Jason Kendall	15.00
Adam Kennedy	10.00
Cesar King	10.00
Paul Konerko	15.00
Mark Kotsay	10.00
Ray Lankford	15.00
Jason LaRue	10.00
Matt Lawton	10.00
Carlos Lee	10.00
Mike Lieberthal	10.00
Cole Liniak	10.00
Steve Lomasney	10.00
Jose Macias	10.00
Greg Maddux	150.00
Edgar Martinez	20.00
Pedro Martinez	75.00
Ruben Mateo	15.00
Gary Matthews Jr.	10.00
Aaron McNeal	10.00
Raul Mondesi	20.00
Orber Moreno	10.00
Warren Morris	10.00
Eric Munson	20.00
Heath Murray	10.00
Mike Mussina	30.00
Joe Nathan	15.00
Rafael Palmeiro	40.00
Jim Parque	10.00
Angel Pena	10.00
Wily Pena	25.00
Pokey Reese	15.00
Matt Riley	10.00
Cal Ripken Jr.	200.00
Alex Rodriguez	175.00
Scott Rolen	40.00
Jimmy Rollins	10.00
B.J. Ryan	10.00
Randall Simon	10.00
Chris Singleton	15.00
Alfonso Soriano	20.00
Shannon Stewart	15.00
Mike Sweeney	15.00
Miguel Tejada	15.00
Wilton Veras	25.00
Frank Thomas	75.00
Billy Wagner	15.00
Jeff Weaver	10.00
Rondell White	15.00
Scott Williamson	10.00
Randy Wolf	15.00
Jaret Wright	10.00
Ed Yarnall	15.00
Kevin Young	10.00

2000 E-X E-Xciting

Die-cut in the shape of a jersey card fronts have a holograpic appearance with silver foil stamping. These were seeded 1:24 packs. Card backs are numbered with an "XT" suffix.

		MT
Complete Set (10):		75.00
Common Player:		4.00
Inserted 1:24		
1	Mark McGwire	20.00
2	Ken Griffey Jr.	20.00
3	Randy Johnson	5.00
4	Sammy Sosa	12.00
5	Manny Ramirez	5.00
6	Jose Canseco	4.00
7	Derek Jeter	12.00
8	Scott Rolen	5.00
9	Juan Gonzalez	5.00
10	Barry Bonds	5.00

2000 E-X Genuine Coverage

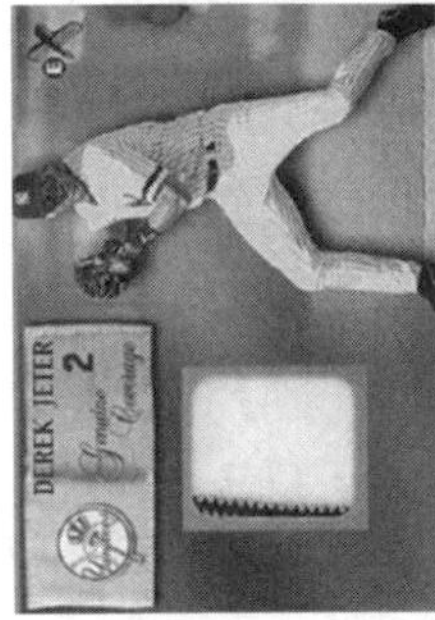

		MT
Common Player:		25.00
Inserted 1:144		
1	Alex Rodriguez	180.00
2	Tom Glavine	40.00
3	Cal Ripken Jr.	180.00
4	Edgar Martinez	40.00
5	Raul Mondesi	30.00
6	Carlos Beltran	25.00
7	Chipper Jones	75.00
8	Barry Bonds	75.00
9	Heath Murray	25.00
10	Tim Hudson	40.00
11	Mike Mussina	35.00
12	Derek Jeter	180.00

2000 E-X E-Xceptional Red

Die-cut in a shape similar to an oval, these inserts have a cloth like feel with silver foil stamping with a red background. Card backs are numbered consecutively "1 Of 15XC" and so on. These are seeded 1:14 packs. Two parallels are also inserted: Blues are seeded 1:288 packs and Greens are limited to 999 serial numbered sets.

		MT
Complete Set (15):		190.00
Common Player:		6.00
Inserted 1:14		
Blue:		2-3X
Inserted 1:288		
Green:		1-1.5X
Production 999 sets		
1	Ken Griffey Jr.	30.00
2	Derek Jeter	20.00
3	Nomar Garciaparra	20.00
4	Mark McGwire	30.00
5	Sammy Sosa	20.00
6	Mike Piazza	20.00
7	Alex Rodriguez	25.00
8	Cal Ripken Jr.	25.00
9	Chipper Jones	15.00
10	Pedro Martinez	8.00
11	Jeff Bagwell	8.00
12	Greg Maddux	15.00
13	Roger Clemens	10.00
14	Tony Gwynn	12.00
15	Frank Thomas	10.00

2000 E-X E-Xplosive

These inserts have a traditional format, with a holographic star like image in the background and "explosive" running down the top left side. Card backs are numbered with an "XP" suffix and are serial numbered on the bottom portion in an edition of 2,499 sets.

		MT
Complete Set (20):		150.00
Common Player:		4.00
Production 2,499 sets		
1	Tony Gwynn	8.00
2	Alex Rodriguez	15.00
3	Pedro Martinez	5.00
4	Sammy Sosa	12.00
5	Cal Ripken Jr.	15.00
6	Adam Piatt	4.00
7	Pat Burrell	6.00
8	J.D. Drew	4.00
9	Mike Piazza	12.00
10	Shawn Green	4.00
11	Troy Glaus	5.00
12	Randy Johnson	5.00
13	Juan Gonzalez	5.00
14	Chipper Jones	10.00
15	Ivan Rodriguez	5.00
16	Nomar Garciaparra	12.00
17	Ken Griffey Jr.	20.00
18	Nick Johnson	5.00
19	Mark McGwire	20.00
20	Frank Thomas	8.00

2000 E-X Generation E-X

This 15-card set spotlights the top young players in the game and were seeded 1:8 packs. Card fronts have silver foil stamping over a background resembling a sky. These were seeded 1:8 packs. Card backs are numbered with a "GX" suffix.

		MT
Complete Set (15):		50.00
Common Player:		1.50
Inserted 1:8		
1	Rick Ankiel	10.00
2	Josh Beckett	4.00
3	Carlos Beltran	1.50
4	Pat Burrell	5.00
5	Freddy Garcia	1.50
6	Alex Rodriguez	12.00
7	Derek Jeter	10.00
8	Tim Hudson	2.00
9	Shawn Green	3.00
10	Eric Munson	3.00
11	Adam Piatt	2.50
12	Adam Kennedy	1.50
13	Nick Johnson	3.00
14	Alfonso Soriano	4.00
15	Nomar Garciaparra	10.00

2000 SkyBox Dominion

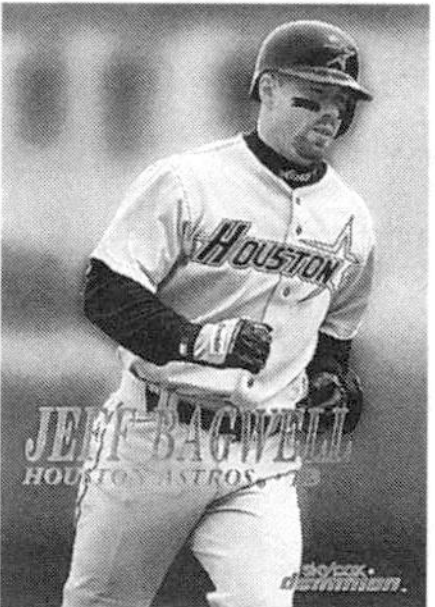

		MT
Complete Set (300):		35.00
Common Player:		.10
Pack (10):		1.25
Wax Box (36):		40.00
1	Mark McGwire, Ken Griffey Jr. (League Leaders)	.75
2	Mark McGwire, Manny Ramirez (League Leaders)	.50
3	Larry Walker, Nomar Garciaparra (League Leaders)	.25
4	Tony Womack, Brian Hunter (League Leaders)	.10
5	Mike Hampton, Pedro Martinez (League Leaders)	.25
6	Randy Johnson, Pedro Martinez (League Leaders)	.25
7	Randy Johnson, Pedro Martinez (League Leaders)	.25
8	Ugueth Urbina, Mariano Rivera (League Leaders)	.10
9	Vinny Castilla (Highlights)	.10
10	Orioles host Cuban National Team (Highlights)	.10
11	Jose Canseco (Highlights)	.25
12	Fernando Tatis (Highlights)	.10
13	Robin Ventura (Highlights)	.10
14	Roger Clemens (Highlights)	.40
15	Jose Jimenez (Highlights)	.10
16	David Cone (Highlights)	.10
17	Mark McGwire (Highlights)	.75
18	Cal Ripken Jr. (Highlights)	.50
19	Tony Gwynn (Highlights)	.25
20	Wade Boggs (Highlights)	.10
21	Ivan Rodriguez (Highlights)	.25
22	Chuck Finley (Highlights)	.10
23	Eric Milton (Highlights)	.10
24	Adrian Beltre (Highlights)	.10
25	Brad Radke	.10
26	Derek Bell	.10
27	Garret Anderson	.10
28	Ivan Rodriguez	.50
29	Jeff Kent	.10
30	Jeremy Giambi	.10
31	John Franco	.10
32	Jose Hernandez	.10
33	Jose Offerman	.10
34	Jose Rosado	.10
35	Kevin Appier	.10
36	Kris Benson	.10
37	Mark McGwire	2.00
38	Matt Williams	.25
39	Paul O'Neill	.20
40	Rickey Henderson	.25
41	Todd Greene	.10
42	Russ Ortiz	.10
43	Sean Casey	.25
44	Tony Womack	.10
45	Troy O'Leary	.10
46	Ugueth Urbina	.10
47	Tom Glavine	.20
48	Mike Mussina	.40
49	Carlos Febles	.10
50	Jon Lieber	.10
51	Juan Gonzalez	.50
52	Matt Clement	.10
53	Moises Alou	.10
54	Ray Durham	.10
55	Robb Nen	.10
56	Tino Martinez	.25
57	Troy Glaus	.50
58	Curt Schilling	.15
59	Mike Sweeney	.10
60	Steve Finley	.10
61	Roger Cedeno	.10
62	Bobby Jones	.10
63	John Smoltz	.15
64	Darin Erstad	.20
65	Carlos Delgado	.25
66	Ray Lankford	.10
67	Todd Stottlemyre	.10
68	Andy Ashby	.10
69	Bobby Abreu	.10
70	Chuck Finley	.10
71	Damion Easley	.10
72	Dustin Hermanson	.10
73	Frank Thomas	.60
74	Kevin Brown	.15
75	Kevin Millwood	.20
76	Mark Grace	.15
77	Matt Stairs	.10
78	Mike Hampton	.10
79	Omar Vizquel	.10
80	Preston Wilson	.10
81	Robin Ventura	.15
82	Todd Helton	.50
83	Tony Clark	.20
84	Al Leiter	.15
85	Alex Fernandez	.10
86	Bernie Williams	.40
87	Edgar Martinez	.15
88	Edgar Renteria	.10
89	Fred McGriff	.20
90	Jermaine Dye	.10
91	Joe McEwing	.10
92	John Halama	.10
93	Lee Stevens	.10
94	Matt Lawton	.10
95	Mike Piazza	1.25
96	Pete Harnisch	.10
97	Scott Karl	.10
98	Tony Fernandez	.10
99	Sammy Sosa	1.25
100	Bobby Higginson	.10
101	Tony Gwynn	1.00
102	J.D. Drew	.25
103	Roberto Hernandez	.20
104	Rondell White	.15
105	David Nilsson	.10
106	Shane Reynolds	.15
107	Jaret Wright	.10
108	Jeff Bagwell	.50
109	Jay Bell	.10
110	Kevin Tapani	.10
111	Michael Barrett	.10
112	Neifi Perez	.10
113	Pat Hentgen	.10
114	Roger Clemens	.75
115	Travis Fryman	.15
116	Aaron Sele	.10
117	Eric Davis	.15
118	Trevor Hoffman	.10
119	Chris Singleton	.10
120	Ryan Klesko	.15
121	Scott Rolen	.50
122	Jorge Posada	.15
123	Abraham Nunez	.10
124	Alex Gonzalez	.10
125	B.J. Surhoff	.10
126	Barry Bonds	.50
127	Billy Koch	.10
128	Billy Wagner	.10
129	Brad Ausmus	.10
130	Bret Boone	.10
131	Cal Ripken Jr.	1.25
132	Chad Allen	.10
133	Chris Carpenter	.10
134	Craig Biggio	.25
135	Dante Bichette	.15
136	Dean Palmer	.10
137	Derek Jeter	1.25
138	Ellis Burks	.10
139	Freddy Garcia	.10
140	Gabe Kapler	.10
141	Greg Maddux	1.00
142	Greg Vaughn	.25
143	Jason Kendall	.15
144	Jim Parque	.10
145	John Valentin	.10
146	Jose Vidro	.10
147	Ken Griffey Jr.	2.00
148	Kenny Lofton	.40
149	Kenny Rogers	.10
150	Kent Bottenfield	.10
151	Chuck Knoblauch	.20
152	Larry Walker	.40
153	Manny Ramirez	.50
154	Mickey Morandini	.10
155	Mike Cameron	.10
156	Mike Lieberthal	.10
157	Mo Vaughn	.40
158	Randy Johnson	.40
159	Rey Ordonez	.10
160	Roberto Alomar	.40
161	Scott Williamson	.10
162	Shawn Estes	.10
163	Tim Wakefield	.10
164	Tony Batista	.10

165	Will Clark	.25
166	Wade Boggs	.25
167	David Cone	.15
168	Doug Glanville	.10
169	Jeff Cirillo	.10
170	John Jaha	.10
171	Mariano Rivera	.20
172	Tom Gordon	.10
173	Wally Joyner	.10
174	Alex Gonzalez	.10
175	Andruw Jones	.25
176	Barry Larkin	.25
177	Bartolo Colon	.10
178	Brian Giles	.10
179	Carlos Lee	.10
180	Darren Dreifort	.10
181	Eric Chavez	.10
182	Henry Rodriguez	.10
183	Ismael Valdes	.10
184	Jason Giambi	.10
185	John Wetteland	.10
186	Juan Encarnacion	.10
187	Luis Gonzalez	.10
188	Reggie Sanders	.10
189	Richard Hidalgo	.10
190	Ryan Rupe	.10
191	Sean Berry	.10
192	Rick Helling	.10
193	Randy Wolf	.10
194	Cliff Floyd	.10
195	Jose Lima	.10
196	Chipper Jones	1.00
197	Charles Johnson	.10
198	Nomar Garciaparra	1.25
199	Magglio Ordonez	.20
200	Shawn Green	.40
201	Travis Lee	.15
202	Jose Canseco	.40
203	Fernando Tatis	.10
204	Bruce Aven	.10
205	Johnny Damon	.10
206	Gary Sheffield	.20
207	Ken Caminiti	.15
208	Ben Grieve	.20
209	Sidney Ponson	.10
210	Vinny Castilla	.10
211	Alex Rodriguez	1.50
212	Chris Widger	.10
213	Carl Pavano	.10
214	J.T. Snow	.10
215	Jim Thome	.25
216	Kevin Young	.10
217	Mike Sirotka	.10
218	Rafael Palmeiro	.25
219	Rico Brogna	.10
220	Todd Walker	.10
221	Todd Zelle	.10
222	Brian Rose	.10
223	Chris Fussell	.10
224	Corey Koskie	.10
225	Rich Aurilla	.10
226	Geoff Jenkins	.10
227	Pedro Martinez	.50
228	Todd Hundley	.10
229	Brian Jordan	.10
230	Cristian Guzman	.10
231	Raul Mondesi	.15
232	Tim Hudson	.10
233	Albert Belle	.40
234	Andy Pettitte	.20
235	Brady Anderson	.15
236	Brian Bohannon	.10
237	Carlos Beltran	.15
238	Doug Mientkiewicz	.10
239	Jason Schmidt	.10
240	Jeff Zimmerman	.10
241	John Olerud	.20
242	Paul Byrd	.10
243	Vladimir Guerrero	.75
244	Warren Morris	.10
245	Eric Karros	.10
246	Jeff Weaver	.10
247	Jeromy Burnitz	.10
248	David Bell	.10
249	Rusty Greer	.10
250	Kevin Stocker	.10
251	Shea Hillenbrand (Prospect)	.20
252	Alfonso Soriano (Prospect)	1.50
253	Micah Bowie (Prospect)	.20
254	Gary Matthews Jr. (Prospect)	.20
255	Lance Berkman (Prospect)	.20
256	Pat Burrell (Prospect)	1.00
257	Ruben Mateo (Prospect)	.25
258	Kip Wells (Prospect)	.25
259	Wilton Veras (Prospect)	.50
260	Ben Davis (Prospect)	.20
261	Eric Munson (Prospect)	.40
262	Ramon Hernandez (Prospect)	.20
263	Tony Armas, Jr. (Prospect)	.25
264	Erubiel Durazo (Prospect)	.25
265	Chad Meyers (Prospect)	.25
266	Rick Ankiel (Prospect)	4.00
267	Ramon Ortiz (Prospect)	.25
268	Adam Kennedy (Prospect)	.20
269	Vernon Wells (Prospect)	.20
270	Chad Hermansen (Prospect)	.20
271	Norm Hutchins, Trent Durrington (Prospects)	.25
272	Gabe Molina, B.J. Ryan (Prospects)	.25
273	Juan Pena, Tomokazu Ohka (Prospects)	.25
274	Pat Daneker, Aaron Myette (Prospects)	.25
275	Jason Rakers, Russell Branyan (Prospects)	.25
276	Beiker Graterol, Dave Borkowski (Prospects)	.25
277	Mark Quinn, Dan Reichert (Prospects)	.50
278	Mark Redman, Jacque Jones (Prospects)	.25
279	Ed Yarnall, Wily Pena (Prospects)	1.00
280	Chad Harville, Brett Laxton (Prospects)	.25
281	Aaron Scheffer, Gil Meche (Prospects)	.25
282	Jim Morris, Dan Wheeler (Prospects)	.25
283	Danny Kolb, Kelly Dransfeldt (Prospects)	.25
284	Peter Munro, Casey Blake (Prospects)	.25
285	Rob Ryan, Byung-Hyun Kim (Prospects)	.25
286	Derrin Ebert, Pascual Matos (Prospects)	.50
287	Richard Barker, Kyle Farnsworth (Prospects)	.25
288	Jason LaRue, Travis Dawkins (Prospects)	.50
289	Chris Sexton, Edgard Clemente (Prospects)	.25
290	Amaury Garcia, A.J. Burnett (Prospects)	.50
291	Carlos Hernandez, Daryle Ward (Prospects)	.50
292	Eric Gagne, Jeff Williams (Prospects)	.25
293	Kyle Peterson, Kevin Barker (Prospects)	.25
294	Fernando Seguignol, Guillermo Mota (Prospects)	.25
295	Melvin Mora, Octavio Dotel (Prospects)	.25
296	Anthony Shumaker, Cliff Politte (Prospects)	.25
297	Yamid Haad, Jimmy Anderson (Prospects)	.25
298	Rick Heiserman, Chad Hutchinson (Prospects)	.25
299	Mike Darr, Wiki Gonzalez (Prospects)	.25
300	Joe Nathan, Calvin Murray (Prospects)	.25

2000 SkyBox Dominion Autographics

		MT
Common Player:		15.00
Inserted 1:144		
1	Rick Ankiel	75.00
2	Peter Bergeron	15.00
3	Wade Boggs	100.00
4	Barry Bonds	80.00
5	Pat Burrell	40.00
6	Miguel Cairo	15.00
7	Mike Cameron	15.00
8	Ben Davis	15.00
9	Russ Davis	15.00
10	Einar Diaz	15.00
11	Scott Elarton	15.00
12	Jeremy Giambi	20.00
13	Todd Greene	15.00
14	Vladimir Guerrero	150.00
15	Tony Gwynn	125.00
16	Bobby Howry	15.00
17	Tim Hudson	20.00
18	Randy Johnson	60.00
19	Andruw Jones	40.00
20	Jacque Jones	15.00
21	Jason LaRue	15.00
22	Matt Lawton	15.00
23	Greg Maddux	200.00
24	Pedro Martinez	100.00
25	Pokey Reese	15.00
26	Alex Rodriguez	200.00
27	Ryan Rupe	15.00
28	J.T. Snow	15.00
29	Jose Vidro	15.00
30	Tony Womack	15.00
31	Ed Yarnall	20.00
32	Kevin Young	20.00

2000 SkyBox Dominion Double Play

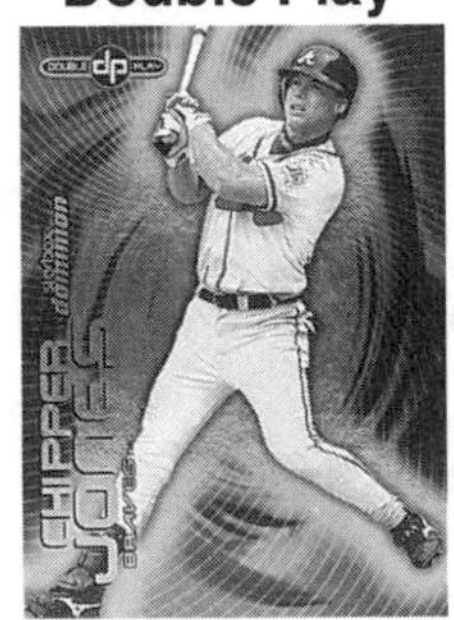

	MT
Complete Set (10):	25.00
Common Player:	1.50
Inserted 1:9	
Plus:	2x-4x
Inserted 1:90	
WarpTek:	12x to 20x
Inserted 1:900	

1	Nomar Garciaparra	4.00
2	Pedro Martinez	1.50
3	Chipper Jones	3.00
4	Mark McGwire	6.00
5	Cal Ripken Jr.	4.00
6	Roger Clemens	2.00
7	Juan Gonzalez	1.50
8	Tony Gwynn	3.00
9	Sammy Sosa	4.00
10	Mike Piazza	4.00

2000 SkyBox Dominion Eye on October

		MT
Complete Set (15):		75.00
Common Player:		2.00
Inserted 1:24		
Plus:		2x to 5x
Inserted 1:240		
1	Ken Griffey Jr.	12.00
2	Mark McGwire	12.00
3	Derek Jeter	8.00
4	Juan Gonzalez	3.00
5	Chipper Jones	6.00
6	Sammy Sosa	8.00
7	Greg Maddux	6.00
8	Frank Thomas	3.00
9	Nomar Garciaparra	8.00
10	Shawn Green	2.00
11	Cal Ripken Jr.	8.00
12	Manny Ramirez	3.00
13	Scott Rolen	3.00
14	Mike Piazza	8.00
15	Alex Rodriguez	10.00

2000 SkyBox Dominion Hats Off

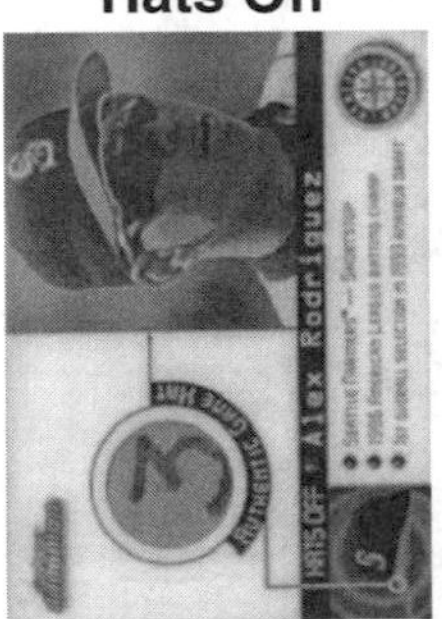

		MT
Common Player:		40.00
Inserted 1:468 H		
1	Wade Boggs	100.00
2	Barry Bonds	120.00
3	J.D. Drew	50.00
4	Shawn Green	100.00

5	Vladimir Guerrero	100.00
6	Randy Johnson	80.00
7	Andruw Jones	80.00
8	Greg Maddux	150.00
9	Pedro Martinez	125.00
10	Mike Mussina	80.00
11	Rafael Palmeiro	60.00
12	Alex Rodriguez	200.00
13	Scott Rolen	80.00
14	Tim Salmon	40.00
15	Robin Ventura	50.00

2000 SkyBox Dominion Milestones

		MT
Complete Set (6):		450.00
Common Player:		50.00
Inserted 1:1,999		
1	Mark McGwire	150.00
2	Roger Clemens	75.00
3	Tony Gwynn	75.00
4	Wade Boggs	40.00
5	Cal Ripken Jr.	120.00
6	Jose Canseco	60.00

2000 SkyBox Dominion New Era

		MT
Complete Set (20):		15.00
Common Player:		.50
Inserted 1:3		
Plus:		2x to 4x
Inserted 1:30		
WarpTek:		5x to 10x
Inserted 1:300		
1	Pat Burrell	2.00
2	Ruben Mateo	.50
3	Wilton Veras	.50
4	Eric Munson	.75
5	Jeff Weaver	.75
6	Tim Hudson	.75
7	Carlos Beltran	.50
8	Chris Singleton	.50
9	Lance Berkman	.50
10	Freddy Garcia	1.00
11	Erubiel Durazo	.75
12	Randy Wolf	.50
13	Shea Hillenbrand	.50
14	Kip Wells	.50
15	Alfonso Soriano	2.00
16	Rick Ankiel	5.00
17	Ramon Ortiz	.50
18	Adam Kennedy	.50
19	Vernon Wells	.50
20	Chad Hermansen	.50

Player names in *Italic* type indicate a rookie card.

2000 SkyBox

		MT
Complete Set (250):		40.00
Comp. Set w/SPs (300):		140.00
Common Player:		.10
Common SP (201-240):		2.00
Inserted 1:8		
Common SP (241-250):		1.00
Inserted 1:12		
Pack (10):		3.00
Wax Box (24):		65.00
1	Cal Ripken Jr.	2.50
2	Ivan Rodriguez	.75
3	Chipper Jones	1.50
4	Dean Palmer	.10
5	Devon White	.10
6	Ugueth Urbina	.10
7	Doug Glanville	.10
8	Damian Jackson	.10
9	Jose Canseco	.50
10	Billy Koch	.10
11	Brady Anderson	.20
12	Vladimir Guerrero	1.50
13	Dan Wilson	.10
14	Kevin Brown	.10
15	Eddie Taubensee	.10
16	Jose Lima	.10
17	Greg Maddux	1.50
18	Manny Ramirez	.75
19	Brad Fullmer	.10
20	Ron Gant	.10
21	Edgar Martinez	.20
22	Pokey Reese	.10
23	Jason Varitek	.10
24	Neifi Perez	.10
25	Shane Reynolds	.10
26	Robin Ventura	.20
27	Scott Rolen	.75
28	Trevor Hoffman	.10
29	John Valentin	.10
30	Shannon Stewart	.10
31	Troy Glaus	.75
32	Kerry Wood	.30
33	Jim Thome	.40
34	Rafael Roque	.10
35	Tino Martinez	.25
36	Jeffrey Hammonds	.10
37	Orlando Hernandez	.25
38	Kris Benson	.10
39	Fred McGriff	.25
40	Brian Jordan	.10
41	Trot Nixon	.10
42	Matt Clement	.10
43	Ray Durham	.10
44	Johnny Damon	.10
45	Todd Hollandsworth	.10
46	Edgardo Alfonzo	.20
47	Tim Hudson	.25
48	Tony Gwynn	1.00
49	Barry Bonds	.75
50	Andruw Jones	.50
51	Pedro Martinez	.75
52	Mike Hampton	.10
53	Miguel Tejada	.10
54	Kevin Young	.10
55	J.T. Snow	.10
56	Carlos Delgado	.50
57	Bobby Howry	.10
58	Andres Galarraga	.40
59	Paul Konerko	.10
60	Mike Cameron	.10
61	Jeremy Giambi	.10
62	Todd Hundley	.10
63	Al Leiter	.20
64	Matt Stairs	.10
65	Edgar Renteria	.10
66	Jeff Kent	.10
67	John Wetteland	.10
68	Nomar Garciaparra	2.00
69	Jeff Weaver	.10
70	Matt Williams	.40
71	Kyle Farnsworth	.10
72	Brad Radke	.10
73	Eric Chavez	.10
74	J.D. Drew	.25
75	Steve Finley	.10
76	Pete Harnisch	.10
77	Chad Kreuter	.10
78	Todd Pratt	.10
79	John Jaha	.10
80	Armando Rios	.10
81	Luis Gonzalez	.10
82	Ryan Minor	.10
83	Juan Gonzalez	.75
84	Rickey Henderson	.25
85	Jason Giambi	.20
86	Shawn Estes	.10
87	Chad Curtis	.10
88	Jeff Cirillo	.10
89	Juan Encarnacion	.10
90	Tony Womack	.10
91	Mike Mussina	.50
92	Jeff Bagwell	.75
93	Rey Ordonez	.10
94	Joe McEwing	.10
95	Robb Nen	.10
96	Will Clark	.40
97	Chris Singleton	.10
98	Jason Kendall	.10
99	Ken Griffey Jr.	3.00
100	Rusty Greer	.10
101	Charles Johnson	.10
102	Carlos Lee	.10
103	Brad Ausmus	.10
104	Preston Wilson	.10
105	Ronnie Belliard	.10
106	Mike Lieberthal	.10
107	Alex Rodriguez	2.50
108	Jay Bell	.10
109	Frank Thomas	1.00
110	Adrian Beltre	.20
111	Ron Coomer	.10
112	Ben Grieve	.20
113	Darryl Kile	.10
114	Erubiel Durazo	.10
115	Magglio Ordonez	.25
116	Gary Sheffield	.40
117	Joe Mays	.10
118	Fernando Tatis	.25
119	David Wells	.10
120	Tim Salmon	.20
121	Troy O'Leary	.10
122	Roberto Alomar	.50
123	Damion Easley	.10
124	Brant Brown	.10
125	Carlos Beltran	.10
126	Eric Karros	.20
127	Geoff Jenkins	.20
128	Roger Clemens	1.00
129	Warren Morris	.10
130	Eric Owens	.10
131	Jose Cruz Jr.	.10
132	Mo Vaughn	.50
133	Eric Young	.10
134	Kenny Lofton	.40
135	Marquis Grissom	.10
136	A.J. Burnett	.10
137	Bernie Williams	.50
138	Javy Lopez	.20
139	Jose Offerman	.10
140	Sean Casey	.10
141	Alex Gonzalez	.10
142	Carlos Febles	.10
143	Mike Piazza	2.00
144	Curt Schilling	.20
145	Ben Davis	.10
146	Rafael Palmeiro	.40
147	Scott Williamson	.10
148	Darin Erstad	.25
149	Joe Girardi	.10
150	Gerald Williams	.10
151	Richie Sexson	.10
152	Corey Koskie	.10
153	Paul O'Neill	.20
154	Chad Hermansen	.10
155	Randy Johnson	.75
156	Henry Rodriguez	.10
157	Bartolo Colon	.10
158	Tony Clark	.20
159	Mike Lowell	.10
160	Moises Alou	.20
161	Todd Walker	.10
162	Mariano Rivera	.20
163	Mark McGwire	3.00
164	Roberto Hernandez	.10
165	Larry Walker	.30
166	Albert Belle	.50
167	Barry Larkin	.30
168	Rolando Arrojo	.10
169	Mark Kotsay	.10
170	Ken Caminiti	.10
171	Dermal Brown	.10
172	Michael Barrett	.10
173	Jay Buhner	.20
174	Ruben Mateo	.10
175	Jim Edmonds	.20
176	Sammy Sosa	2.00
177	Omar Vizquel	.10
178	Todd Helton	.75
179	Kevin Barker	.10
180	Derek Jeter	2.00
181	Brian Giles	.10
182	Greg Vaughn	.20
183	Roy Halladay	.10
184	Tom Glavine	.25
185	Craig Biggio	.25
186	Jose Vidro	.10
187	Andy Ashby	.10
188	Freddy Garcia	.10
189	Garret Anderson	.10
190	Mark Grace	.25
191	Travis Fryman	.20
192	Jeromy Burnitz	.10
193	Jacque Jones	.10
194	David Cone	.20
195	Ryan Rupe	.10
196	John Smoltz	.10
197	Daryle Ward	.10
198	Rondell White	.20
199	Bobby Abreu	.20
200	Justin Thompson	.10
201	Norm Hutchins (Prospect)	.10
201	Norm Hutchins SP	2.00
202	Ramon Ortiz (Prospect)	.10
202	Ramon Ortiz SP	2.00
203	Dan Wheeler (Prospect)	.10
203	Dan Wheeler SP	2.00
204	Matt Riley (Prospect)	.40
204	Matt Riley SP	3.00
205	Steve Lomasney (Prospect)	.10
205	Steve Lomasney SP	2.00
206	Chad Meyers (Prospect)	.10
206	Chad Meyers SP	2.00
207	*Gary Glover* (Prospect)	.20
207	Gary Glover SP	2.00
208	Joe Crede (Prospect)	.10
208	Joe Crede SP	2.00
209	Kip Wells (Prospect)	.10
209	Kip Wells SP	2.00
210	Travis Dawkins (Prospect)	.10
210	Travis Dawkins SP	2.00
211	*Denny Stark* (Prospect)	.25
211	Denny Stark SP	2.00
212	Ben Petrick (Prospect)	.10
212	Ben Petrick SP	2.00
213	Eric Munson (Prospect)	.75
213	Eric Munson SP	4.00
214	Josh Beckett (Prospect)	.75
214	Josh Beckett SP	4.00
215	Pablo Ozuna (Prospect)	.10
215	Pablo Ozuna SP	2.00
216	Brad Penny (Prospect)	.10
216	Brad Penny SP	2.00
217	Julio Ramirez (Prospect)	.10
217	Julio Ramirez SP	2.00
218	Danny Peoples (Prospect)	.10
218	Danny Peoples SP	2.00
219	*Wilfredo Rodriguez* (Prospect)	.10
219	*Wilfredo Rodriguez SP*	3.00

220 Julio Lugo (Prospect) .10
220 Julio Lugo SP 2.00
221 Mark Quinn (Prospect) .10
221 Mark Quinn SP 2.00
222 Eric Gagne (Prospect) .10
222 Eric Gagne SP 2.00
223 Chad Green (Prospect) .10
223 Chad Green SP 2.00
224 Tony Armas, Jr. (Prospect) .10
224 Tony Armas, Jr. SP 2.00
225 Milton Bradley (Prospect) .10
225 Milton Bradley SP 3.00
226 Rob Bell (Prospect) .10
226 Rob Bell SP 2.00
227 Alfonso Soriano (Prospect) .25
227 Alfonso Soriano SP 4.00
228 Wily Pena (Prospect) .10
228 Wily Pena SP 5.00
229 Nick Johnson (Prospect) .10
229 Nick Johnson SP 4.00
230 Ed Yarnall (Prospect) .10
230 Ed Yarnall SP 2.00
231 Ryan Bradley (Prospect) .10
231 Ryan Bradley SP 2.00
232 Adam Piatt (Prospect) .10
232 Adam Piatt SP 4.00
233 Chad Harville (Prospect) .10
233 Chad Harville SP 2.00
234 Alex Sanchez (Prospect) .10
234 Alex Sanchez SP 2.00
235 Michael Coleman (Prospect) .10
235 Michael Coleman SP 2.00
236 Pat Burrell (Prospect) .40
236 Pat Burrell SP 8.00
237 *Wascar Serrano* (Prospect) .10
237 *Wascar Serrano SP* 3.00
238 Rick Ankiel (Prospect) .10
238 Rick Ankiel SP 10.00
239 *Mike Lamb* (Prospect) .10
239 *Mike Lamb SP* 5.00
240 Vernon Wells (Prospect) .10
240 Vernon Wells SP 2.00
241 Jorge Toca, Goefrey Tomlinson (Premium Pairs) .10
241 Jorge Toca, Goefrey Tomlinson SP 1.00
242 Shea Hillenbrand *,Josh Phelps* (Premium Pairs) .40
242 Shea Hillenbrand *,Josh Phelps SP* 1.50
243 Aaron Myette, Doug Davis (Premium Pairs) .10
243 Aaron Myette, Doug Davis SP 1.00
244 Brett Laxton, Robert Ramsay (Premium Pairs) .10
244 Brett Laxton, Robert Ramsay SP 1.00
245 B.J. Ryan, Corey Lee (Premium Pairs) .10
245 B.J. Ryan, Corey Lee SP 1.00
246 Chris Haas, Wilton Veras (Premium Pairs) .50
246 Chris Haas, Wilton Veras SP 2.00
247 Jimmy Anderson, Kyle Peterson (Premium Pairs) .10
247 Jimmy Anderson, Kyle Peterson SP 1.00
248 Jason Dewey, Giuseppe Chiaramonte (Premium Pairs) .10
248 Jason Dewey, Giuseppe Chiaramonte SP 1.00
249 Guillermo Mota, Orber Moreno (Premium Pairs) .10
249 Guillermo Mota, Orber Moreno SP 1.00
250 Steve Cox, *Julio Zuleta* (Premium Pairs) .25
250 Steve Cox *,Julio Zuleta SP* 1.50

2000 SkyBox Autographics

	MT
Common Player	10.00
Rick Ankiel	75.00
Michael Barrett	10.00
Josh Beckett	25.00
Rob Bell	15.00
Adrian Beltre	20.00
Peter Bergeron	20.00
Lance Berkman	15.00
Rico Brogna	10.00
Pat Burrell	40.00
Orlando Cabrera	10.00
Mike Cameron	10.00
Roger Cedeno	15.00
Eric Chavez	15.00
Bruce Chen	10.00
Johnny Damon	15.00
Ben Davis	10.00
Jason Dewey	10.00
Octavio Dotel	10.00
J.D. Drew	40.00
Erubiel Durazo	20.00
Jason Giambi	20.00
Doug Glanville	10.00
Troy Glaus	40.00
Alex Gonzalez	10.00
Shawn Green	40.00
Jason Grilli	10.00
Tony Gwynn	75.00
Mike Hampton	15.00
Tim Hudson	20.00
Norm Hutchins	10.00
John Jaha	10.00
Derek Jeter	200.00
D'Angelo Jimenez	10.00
Randy Johnson	75.00
Andruw Jones	30.00
Gabe Kapler	15.00
Jason Kendall	15.00
Adam Kennedy	10.00
Cesar King	10.00
Paul Konerko	15.00
Mark Kotsay	10.00
Carlos Lee	10.00
Mike Lieberthal	10.00
Steve Lomasney	10.00
Greg Maddux	150.00
Edgar Martinez	20.00
Aaron McNeal	10.00
Kevin Millwood	15.00
Raul Mondesi	20.00
Joe Nathan	15.00
Magglio Ordonez	25.00
Eric Owens	10.00
Rafael Palmeiro	40.00
Angel Pena	10.00
Wily Pena	25.00
Cal Ripken Jr.	200.00
Scott Rolen	40.00
Jimmy Rollins	10.00
B.J. Ryan	10.00
Tim Salmon	20.00
Chris Singleton	10.00
J.T. Snow	10.00
Mike Sweeney	15.00
Jose Vidro	20.00
Rondell White	15.00
Jaret Wright	10.00

2000 SkyBox E-Ticket

		MT
Complete Set (14):		25.00
Common Player:		.50
Inserted 1:4		
Star Ruby:		10-20X
Production 100 sets		
1	Alex Rodriguez	3.00
2	Derek Jeter	2.50
3	Nomar Garciaparra	2.50
4	Cal Ripken Jr.	3.00
5	Sean Casey	.50
6	Mark McGwire	4.00
7	Sammy Sosa	2.50
8	Ken Griffey Jr.	4.00
9	Tony Gwynn	2.00
10	Pedro Martinez	1.00
11	Chipper Jones	2.00
12	Vladimir Guerrero	2.00
13	Roger Clemens	1.50
14	Mike Piazza	2.50

2000 SkyBox Genuine Coverage HOBBY

		MT
Common Player:		50.00
Inserted 1:144		
1	Ivan Rodriguez	60.00
2	Jose Canseco	50.00
3	Frank Thomas	75.00
4	Manny Ramirez	60.00

2000 SkyBox Genuine Coverage

		MT
Common Player:		40.00
Inserted 1:399		
1	Troy Glaus	50.00
2	Cal Ripken Jr.	150.00
3	Alex Rodriguez	150.00
4	Mike Mussina	40.00
5	J.D. Drew	40.00
6	Robin Ventura	40.00
7	Matt Williams	50.00

2000 SkyBox Higher Level

		MT
Complete Set (10):		70.00
Common Player:		3.00
Inserted 1:24		
Star Ruby:		6-12X
Production 50 sets		
1	Cal Ripken Jr.	10.00
2	Derek Jeter	8.00
3	Nomar Garciaparra	8.00
4	Chipper Jones	6.00
5	Mike Piazza	8.00
6	Ivan Rodriguez	3.00
7	Ken Griffey Jr.	12.00
8	Sammy Sosa	8.00
9	Alex Rodriguez	10.00
10	Mark McGwire	12.00

2000 SkyBox Preeminence

		MT
Complete Set (10):		60.00
Common Player:		2.00
Inserted 1:24		
Star Ruby:		6-12X
Production 50 sets		
1	Pedro Martinez	3.00
2	Derek Jeter	8.00
3	Nomar Garciaparra	8.00
4	Alex Rodriguez	10.00
5	Mark McGwire	12.00
6	Sammy Sosa	8.00
7	Sean Casey	2.00
8	Mike Piazza	8.00
9	Chipper Jones	6.00
10	Ivan Rodriguez	3.00

Modern cards in Near Mint condition are valued at about 75% of the Mint value shown here. Excellent-condition cards are worth 50%. Cards in lower grades are not generally collectible.

2000 SkyBox SkyLines

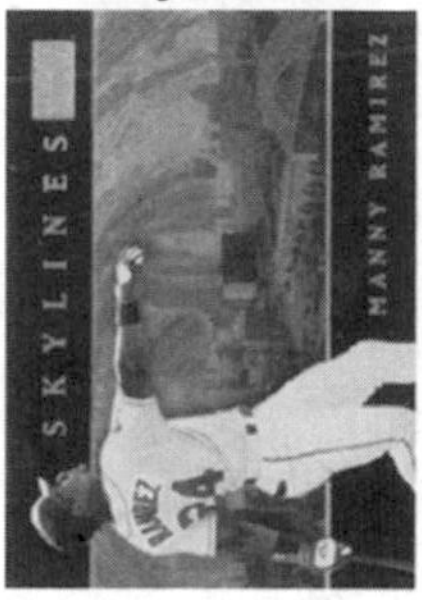

		MT
Complete Set (10):		35.00
Common Player:		1.00
Inserted 1:11		
Star Ruby:		15-25X
Production 50 sets		
1	Cal Ripken Jr.	5.00
2	Mark McGwire	6.00
3	Alex Rodriguez	5.00
4	Sammy Sosa	4.00
5	Derek Jeter	4.00
6	Mike Piazza	4.00
7	Nomar Garciaparra	4.00
8	Chipper Jones	3.00
9	Ken Griffey Jr.	6.00
10	Manny Ramirez	1.50

2000 SkyBox Speed Merchants

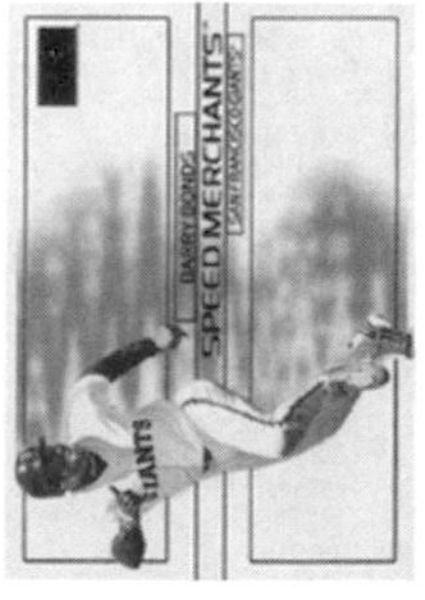

		MT
Complete Set (10):		20.00
Common Player:		.75
Inserted 1:8		
Star Ruby:		8-15X
Production 100 sets		
1	Derek Jeter	3.00
2	Sammy Sosa	3.00
3	Nomar Garciaparra	3.00
4	Alex Rodriguez	4.00
5	Randy Johnson	1.25
6	Ken Griffey Jr.	5.00
7	Pedro Martinez	1.25
8	Pat Burrell	2.00
9	Barry Bonds	1.25
10	Mark McGwire	5.00

The values of some parallel-card issues will have to be calculated based on figures presented in the heading for the regular-issue card set.

2000 SkyBox The Technique

		MT
Complete Set (15):		60.00
Common Player:		1.00
Inserted 1:11		
Star Ruby:		10-18X
Production 50 sets		
1	Alex Rodriguez	6.00
2	Tony Gwynn	3.00
3	Sean Casey	1.00
4	Mark McGwire	8.00
5	Sammy Sosa	5.00
6	Ken Griffey Jr.	8.00
7	Mike Piazza	5.00
8	Nomar Garciaparra	5.00
9	Derek Jeter	5.00
10	Vladimir Guerrero	4.00
11	Cal Ripken Jr.	6.00
12	Chipper Jones	4.00
13	Frank Thomas	3.00
14	Manny Ramirez	2.00
15	Jeff Bagwell	2.00

1993 SP

Upper Deck's first super-premium baseball card issue features 290 cards in the single-series set; 252 are individual player cards, while the remainder includes a Premier Prospects subset featuring top prospects (20 cards), 18 All-Stars and a Platinum Power insert set of 20 top home run hitters. Cards, which were available in 12-card foil packs, feature borderless color photos and UV coating on the front, plus a special logo using lenticular printing. Foil is also used intricately in the design. Backs have a large color photo and statistics. Cards are numbered and color-coded by team.

		MT
Complete Set (290):		150.00
Common Player:		.25
Pack (12):		10.00
Wax Box (24):		260.00
1	Roberto Alomar	1.50
2	Wade Boggs	.75
3	Joe Carter	.30
4	Ken Griffey, Jr.	6.00
5	Mark Langston	.25
6	John Olerud	.50
7	Kirby Puckett	3.00
8	Cal Ripken, Jr.	6.00
9	Ivan Rodriguez	2.00
10	Barry Bonds	2.50
11	Darren Daulton	.25
12	Marquis Grissom	.25
13	Dave Justice	.75
14	John Kruk	.25
15	Barry Larkin	.60
16	Terry Mulholland	.25
17	Ryne Sandberg	2.00
18	Gary Sheffield	.75
19	Chad Curtis	.25
20	Chili Davis	.25
21	Gary DiSarcina	.25
22	Damion Easley	.25
23	Chuck Finley	.25
24	Luis Polonia	.25
25	Tim Salmon	1.00
26	*J.T. Snow*	1.00
27	Russ Springer	.25
28	Jeff Bagwell	3.00
29	Craig Biggio	.40
30	Ken Caminiti	.40
31	Andujar Cedeno	.25
32	Doug Drabek	.25
33	Steve Finley	.25
34	Luis Gonzalez	.40
35	Pete Harnisch	.25
36	Darryl Kile	.25
37	Mike Bordick	.25
38	Dennis Eckersley	.25
39	Brent Gates	.25
40	Rickey Henderson	.50
41	Mark McGwire	8.00
42	Craig Paquette	.25
43	Ruben Sierra	.25
44	Terry Steinbach	.25
45	Todd Van Poppel	.25
46	Pat Borders	.25
47	Tony Fernandez	.25
48	Juan Guzman	.25
49	Pat Hentgen	.25
50	Paul Molitor	2.00
51	Jack Morris	.25
52	Ed Sprague	.25
53	Duane Ward	.25
54	Devon White	.25
55	Steve Avery	.25
56	Jeff Blauser	.25
57	Ron Gant	.35
58	Tom Glavine	.50
59	Greg Maddux	4.00
60	Fred McGriff	.50
61	Terry Pendleton	.25
62	Deion Sanders	.50
63	John Smoltz	.25
64	Cal Eldred	.25
65	Darryl Hamilton	.25
66	John Jaha	.25
67	Pat Listach	.25
68	Jaime Navarro	.25
69	Kevin Reimer	.25
70	B.J. Surhoff	.25
71	Greg Vaughn	.30
72	Robin Yount	1.50
73	*Rene Arocha*	.25
74	Bernard Gilkey	.25
75	Gregg Jefferies	.25
76	Ray Lankford	.25
77	Tom Pagnozzi	.25
78	Lee Smith	.25
79	Ozzie Smith	2.00
80	Bob Tewksbury	.25
81	Mark Whiten	.25
82	Steve Buechele	.25
83	Mark Grace	.40
84	Jose Guzman	.25
85	Derrick May	.25
86	Mike Morgan	.25
87	Randy Myers	.25
88	*Kevin Roberson*	.40
89	Sammy Sosa	5.00
90	Rick Wilkins	.25
91	Brett Butler	.25
92	Eric Davis	.25
93	Orel Hershiser	.25
94	Eric Karros	.40
95	Ramon Martinez	.25
96	Raul Mondesi	.75
97	Jose Offerman	.25
98	Mike Piazza	6.00
99	Darryl Strawberry	.35
100	Moises Alou	.35
101	Wil Cordero	.25
102	Delino DeShields	.25
103	Darrin Fletcher	.25
104	Ken Hill	.25
105	*Mike Lansing*	.40
106	Dennis Martinez	.25
107	Larry Walker	.75
108	John Wetteland	.25
109	Rod Beck	.25
110	John Burkett	.25
111	Will Clark	.75
112	Royce Clayton	.25
113	Darren Lewis	.25
114	Willie McGee	.25
115	Bill Swift	.25
116	Robby Thompson	.25
117	Matt Williams	.50
118	Sandy Alomar Jr.	.25
119	Carlos Baerga	.25
120	Albert Belle	1.00
121	Reggie Jefferson	.25
122	Kenny Lofton	.75
123	Wayne Kirby	.25
124	Carlos Martinez	.25
125	Charles Nagy	.25
126	Paul Sorrento	.25
127	Rich Amaral	.25
128	Jay Buhner	.30
129	Norm Charlton	.25
130	Dave Fleming	.25
131	Erik Hanson	.25
132	Randy Johnson	2.00
133	Edgar Martinez	.25
134	Tino Martinez	.40
135	Omar Vizquel	.40
136	Bret Barberie	.25
137	Chuck Carr	.25
138	Jeff Conine	.25
139	Orestes Destrade	.25
140	Chris Hammond	.25
141	Bryan Harvey	.25
142	Benito Santiago	.25
143	Walt Weiss	.25
144	*Darrell Whitmore*	.25
145	*Tim Bolger*	.25
146	Bobby Bonilla	.30
147	Jeromy Burnitz	.25
148	Vince Coleman	.25
149	Dwight Gooden	.30
150	Todd Hundley	.50
151	Howard Johnson	.25
152	Eddie Murray	.50
153	Bret Saberhagen	.25
154	Brady Anderson	.40
155	Mike Devereaux	.25
156	Jeffrey Hammonds	.25
157	Chris Hoiles	.25
158	Ben McDonald	.25
159	Mark McLemore	.25
160	Mike Mussina	1.50
161	Gregg Olson	.25
162	David Segui	.25
163	Derek Bell	.25
164	Andy Benes	.25
165	Archi Cianfrocco	.25
166	Ricky Gutierrez	.25
167	Tony Gwynn	3.00
168	Gene Harris	.25
169	Trevor Hoffman	.25
170	*Ray McDavid*	.25
171	Phil Plantier	.25
172	Mariano Duncan	.25
173	Len Dykstra	.25
174	Tommy Greene	.25
175	Dave Hollins	.25
176	Pete Incaviglia	.25
177	Mickey Morandini	.25
178	Curt Schilling	.40
179	Kevin Stocker	.25
180	Mitch Williams	.25
181	Stan Belinda	.25
182	Jay Bell	.25
183	Steve Cooke	.25
184	Carlos Garcia	.25
185	Jeff King	.25
186	Orlando Merced	.25
187	Don Slaught	.25

188	Andy Van Slyke	.25
189	Kevin Young	.25
190	Kevin Brown	.35
191	Jose Canseco	1.00
192	Julio Franco	.25
193	Benji Gil	.25
194	Juan Gonzalez	2.00
195	Tom Henke	.25
196	Rafael Palmeiro	.75
197	Dean Palmer	.25
198	Nolan Ryan	8.00
199	Roger Clemens	3.00
200	Scott Cooper	.25
201	Andre Dawson	.40
202	Mike Greenwell	.25
203	Carlos Quintana	.25
204	Jeff Russell	.25
205	Aaron Sele	.25
206	Mo Vaughn	1.00
207	Frank Viola	.25
208	Rob Dibble	.25
209	Roberto Kelly	.25
210	Kevin Mitchell	.25
211	Hal Morris	.25
212	Joe Oliver	.25
213	Jose Rijo	.25
214	Bip Roberts	.25
215	Chris Sabo	.25
216	Reggie Sanders	.25
217	Dante Bichette	.40
218	Jerald Clark	.25
219	Alex Cole	.25
220	Andres Galarraga	.40
221	Joe Girardi	.25
222	Charlie Hayes	.25
223	*Robert Mejia*	.25
224	Armando Reynoso	.25
225	Eric Young	.25
226	Kevin Appier	.25
227	George Brett	3.00
228	David Cone	.30
229	Phil Hiatt	.25
230	Felix Jose	.25
231	Wally Joyner	.25
232	Mike Macfarlane	.25
233	Brian McRae	.25
234	Jeff Montgomery	.25
235	Rob Deer	.25
236	Cecil Fielder	.25
237	Travis Fryman	.40
238	Mike Henneman	.25
239	Tony Phillips	.25
240	Mickey Tettleton	.25
241	Alan Trammell	.25
242	David Wells	.25
243	Lou Whitaker	.25
244	Rick Aguilera	.25
245	Scott Erickson	.25
246	Brian Harper	.25
247	Kent Hrbek	.25
248	Chuck Knoblauch	.40
249	Shane Mack	.25
250	David McCarty	.25
251	Pedro Munoz	.25
252	Dave Winfield	.35
253	Alex Fernandez	.25
254	Ozzie Guillen	.25
255	Bo Jackson	.25
256	Lance Johnson	.25
257	Ron Karkovice	.25
258	Jack McDowell	.25
259	Tim Raines	.25
260	Frank Thomas	3.00
261	Robin Ventura	.35
262	Jim Abbott	.25
263	Steve Farr	.25
264	Jimmy Key	.25
265	Don Mattingly	2.50
266	Paul O'Neill	.40
267	Mike Stanley	.25
268	Danny Tartabull	.25
269	Bob Wickman	.25
270	Bernie Williams	1.50
271	Jason Bere	.25
272	*Roger Cedeno*	4.00
273	*Johnny Damon*	10.00
274	*Russ Davis*	.50
275	Carlos Delgado	6.00
276	Carl Everett	1.50
277	Cliff Floyd	.50
278	Alex Gonzalez	.75
279	*Derek Jeter*	120.00
280	Chipper Jones	5.00
281	Javier Lopez	1.50
282	*Chad Mottola*	.40
283	Marc Newfield	.25
284	Eduardo Perez	.25
285	Manny Ramirez	8.00
286	*Todd Steverson*	.40
287	Michael Tucker	.25
288	Allen Watson	.25
289	Rondell White	.75
290	Dmitri Young	1.00

1993 SP Platinum Power

This 20-card insert set features 20 of the game's top home run hitters. The top of each insert card features a special die cut treatment. Backs are numbered with a PP prefix.

		MT
Complete Set (20):		90.00
Common Player:		2.00
1	Albert Belle	4.00
2	Barry Bonds	6.00
3	Joe Carter	2.00
4	Will Clark	4.50
5	Darren Daulton	2.00
6	Cecil Fielder	2.00
7	Ron Gant	2.50
8	Juan Gonzalez	5.00
9	Ken Griffey, Jr.	15.00
10	Dave Hollins	2.00
11	Dave Justice	3.00
12	Fred McGriff	3.00
13	Mark McGwire	20.00
14	Dean Palmer	2.00
15	Mike Piazza	15.00
16	Tim Salmon	3.00
17	Ryne Sandberg	5.00
18	Gary Sheffield	3.00
19	Frank Thomas	8.00
20	Matt Williams	3.00

1994 SP Promo

Virtually identical to the issued version of Ken Griffey, Jr.'s card in the regular SP set (#105) this differs in the card number on the back (#24) and the inclusion on front and back of the notice, "For Promotional Use Only".

		MT
24	Ken Griffey Jr.	8.00

1994 SP

The second edition of Upper Deck's top-shelf SP brand features each card with a front background printed on metallic foil; the first 20 cards in the set, a series of "Prospects," have front backgrounds of textured metallic foil. Backs are printed with standard processes and include a color player photo a few stats and typical copyright notice and logos. Each foil pack contains one card featuring a special die-cut treatment at top.

		MT
Complete Set (200):		125.00
Common Player:		.15
Pack (8):		9.00
Wax Box (32):		300.00
1	*Mike Bell*	.40
2	D.J. Boston	.25
3	Johnny Damon	.40
4	*Brad Fullmer*	4.00
5	Joey Hamilton	.40
6	Todd Hollandsworth	.40
7	Brian Hunter	.40
8	*LaTroy Hawkins*	.75
9	*Brooks Kieschnick*	.50
10	*Derrek Lee*	2.00
11	*Trot Nixon*	3.00
12	Alex Ochoa	.25
13	*Chan Ho Park*	3.00
14	*Kirk Presley*	.40
15	*Alex Rodriguez*	100.00
16	*Jose Silva*	.40
17	*Terrell Wade*	.50
18	*Billy Wagner*	1.00
19	*Glenn Williams*	1.00
20	Preston Wilson	1.50
21	Brian Anderson	.50
22	Chad Curtis	.15
23	Chili Davis	.15
24	Bo Jackson	.25
25	Mark Langston	.15
26	Tim Salmon	.40
27	Jeff Bagwell	1.50
28	Craig Biggio	.30
29	Ken Caminiti	.25
30	Doug Drabek	.15
31	John Hudek	.15
32	Greg Swindell	.15
33	Brent Gates	.15
34	Rickey Henderson	.40
35	Steve Karsay	.15
36	Mark McGwire	4.00
37	Ruben Sierra	.15
38	Terry Steinbach	.15
39	Roberto Alomar	.75
40	Joe Carter	.15
41	Carlos Delgado	.75
42	Alex Gonzalez	.25
43	Juan Guzman	.15
44	Paul Molitor	.75
45	John Olerud	.25
46	Devon White	.20
47	Steve Avery	.15
48	Jeff Blauser	.15
49	Tom Glavine	.40
50	Dave Justice	.50
51	Roberto Kelly	.15
52	Ryan Klesko	.40
53	Javier Lopez	.30
54	Greg Maddux	2.00
55	Fred McGriff	.40
56	Ricky Bones	.15
57	Cal Eldred	.15
58	Brian Harper	.15
59	Pat Listach	.15
60	B.J. Surhoff	.15
61	Greg Vaughn	.20
62	Bernard Gilkey	.15
63	Gregg Jefferies	.15
64	Ray Lankford	.15
65	Ozzie Smith	.75
66	Bob Tewksbury	.15
67	Mark Whiten	.15
68	Todd Zeile	.15
69	Mark Grace	.30
70	Randy Myers	.15
71	Ryne Sandberg	1.00
72	Sammy Sosa	2.50
73	Steve Trachsel	.20
74	Rick Wilkins	.15
75	Brett Butler	.15
76	Delino DeShields	.15
77	Orel Hershiser	.15
78	Eric Karros	.40
79	Raul Mondesi	.40
80	Mike Piazza	2.50
81	Tim Wallach	.15
82	Moises Alou	.25
83	Cliff Floyd	.15
84	Marquis Grissom	.15
85	Pedro Martinez	1.00
86	Larry Walker	.40
87	John Wetteland	.15
88	Rondell White	.35
89	Rod Beck	.15
90	Barry Bonds	1.00
91	John Burkett	.15
92	Royce Clayton	.15
93	Billy Swift	.15
94	Robby Thompson	.15
95	Matt Williams	.40
96	Carlos Baerga	.15
97	Albert Belle	.50
98	Kenny Lofton	.50
99	Dennis Martinez	.15
100	Eddie Murray	.40
101	Manny Ramirez	1.00
102	Eric Anthony	.15
103	Chris Bosio	.15
104	Jay Buhner	.15
105	Ken Griffey, Jr.	3.00
106	Randy Johnson	1.00
107	Edgar Martinez	.15
108	Chuck Carr	.15
109	Jeff Conine	.15
110	Carl Everett	.25
111	Chris Hammond	.15
112	Bryan Harvey	.15
113	Charles Johnson	.20
114	Gary Sheffield	.50
115	Bobby Bonilla	.20
116	Dwight Gooden	.25
117	Todd Hundley	.25
118	Bobby Jones	.20
119	Jeff Kent	.15
120	Bret Saberhagen	.15
121	Jeffrey Hammonds	.15
122	Chris Hoiles	.15
123	Ben McDonald	.15
124	Mike Mussina	.75
125	Rafael Palmeiro	.50
126	Cal Ripken, Jr.	3.00
127	Lee Smith	.15
128	Derek Bell	.15
129	Andy Benes	.20
130	Tony Gwynn	1.50
131	Trevor Hoffman	.20
132	Phil Plantier	.15
133	Bip Roberts	.15
134	Darren Daulton	.15
135	Len Dykstra	.15
136	Dave Hollins	.15
137	Danny Jackson	.15
138	John Kruk	.15
139	Kevin Stocker	.15
140	Jay Bell	.15
141	Carlos Garcia	.15
142	Jeff King	.15
143	Orlando Merced	.15
144	Andy Van Slyke	.15
145	Paul Wagner	.15
146	Jose Canseco	.50
147	Will Clark	.50
148	Juan Gonzalez	1.00
149	Rick Helling	.15
150	Dean Palmer	.15
151	Ivan Rodriguez	1.00
152	Roger Clemens	1.50
153	Scott Cooper	.15
154	Andre Dawson	.30
155	Mike Greenwell	.15
156	Aaron Sele	.20

157	Mo Vaughn	.50
158	Bret Boone	.15
159	Barry Larkin	.50
160	Kevin Mitchell	.15
161	Jose Rijo	.15
162	Deion Sanders	.25
163	Reggie Sanders	.20
164	Dante Bichette	.40
165	Ellis Burks	.20
166	Andres Galarraga	.40
167	Charlie Hayes	.15
168	David Nied	.15
169	Walt Weiss	.15
170	Kevin Appier	.15
171	David Cone	.20
172	Jeff Granger	.20
173	Felix Jose	.15
174	Wally Joyner	.15
175	Brian McRae	.15
176	Cecil Fielder	.20
177	Travis Fryman	.30
178	Mike Henneman	.15
179	Tony Phillips	.15
180	Mickey Tettleton	.15
181	Alan Trammell	.15
182	Rick Aguilera	.15
183	Rich Becker	.15
184	Scott Erickson	.15
185	Chuck Knoblauch	.25
186	Kirby Puckett	1.00
187	Dave Winfield	.30
188	Wilson Alvarez	.15
189	Jason Bere	.15
190	Alex Fernandez	.20
191	Julio Franco	.15
192	Jack McDowell	.15
193	Frank Thomas	1.50
194	Robin Ventura	.20
195	Jim Abbott	.15
196	Wade Boggs	.40
197	Jimmy Key	.15
198	Don Mattingly	1.50
199	Paul O'Neill	.30
200	Danny Tartabull	.15

1994 SP Die-Cut

Upper Deck SP Die-cuts are a 200-card parallel set inserted at the rate of one per foil pack. Each card has a die-cut top instead of the flat-top found on regular SP cards. Die-cuts also have a silver-foil Upper Deck hologram logo on back, in contrast to the gold-tone hologram found on regular SP; this is an effort to prevent fraudulent replication by any crook with a pair of scissors.

	MT
Complete Set (200):	150.00
Common Player:	.25

(Star cards valued at 1.5-3X corresponding cards in regular SP issue)

1994 SP Holoview Blue

Holoview F/X Blue is a 38-card set utilizing Holoview printing technology, which features 200 frames of video to produce a true, three-dimensional image on the bottom third of each card. The hologram is bordered in blue and there is a blue stripe running down the right side of the card. Backs are done with a blue background and feature a player photo over top of bold letters reading "Holo-View FX". This insert could be found in one per five packs of SP baseball.

		MT
Complete Set (38):		150.00
Common Player:		1.50
1	Roberto Alomar	4.00
2	Kevin Appier	1.50
3	Jeff Bagwell	5.00
4	Jose Canseco	4.00
5	Roger Clemens	8.00
6	Carlos Delgado	4.00
7	Cecil Fielder	1.50
8	Cliff Floyd	1.50
9	Travis Fryman	1.50
10	Andres Galarraga	4.00
11	Juan Gonzalez	5.00
12	Ken Griffey, Jr.	15.00
13	Tony Gwynn	8.00
14	Jeffrey Hammonds	1.50
15	Bo Jackson	2.00
16	Michael Jordan	25.00
17	Dave Justice	3.00
18	Steve Karsay	1.50
19	Jeff Kent	1.50
20	Brooks Kieschnick	1.50
21	Ryan Klesko	1.50
22	John Kruk	1.50
23	Barry Larkin	3.00
24	Pat Listach	1.50
25	Don Mattingly	6.00
26	Mark McGwire	20.00
27	Raul Mondesi	3.00
28	Trot Nixon	1.50
29	Mike Piazza	15.00
30	Kirby Puckett	5.00
31	Manny Ramirez	5.00
32	Cal Ripken, Jr.	15.00
33	Alex Rodriguez	40.00
34	Tim Salmon	3.00
35	Gary Sheffield	3.00
36	Ozzie Smith	5.00
37	Sammy Sosa	12.00
38	Andy Van Slyke	1.50

1994 SP Holoview Red

HoloView F/X Red is a parallel set to the Blue insert. Once again, this 38-card set utilizes Holoview printing technology. However, these cards have a red border surrounding the hologram and along the right side, as well as a red background on the back and a large "SPECIAL FX" under the player photo. Holoview red cards also have die-cut tops. Red cards are much scarcer than blue; the red being inserted once per 75 packs of SP baseball.

		MT
Complete Set (38):		1000.
Common Player:		4.00
1	Roberto Alomar	20.00
2	Kevin Appier	4.00
3	Jeff Bagwell	25.00
4	Jose Canseco	20.00
5	Roger Clemens	40.00
6	Carlos Delgado	20.00
7	Cecil Fielder	4.00
8	Cliff Floyd	4.00
9	Travis Fryman	4.00
10	Andres Galarraga	12.00
11	Juan Gonzalez	25.00
12	Ken Griffey, Jr.	80.00
13	Tony Gwynn	40.00
14	Jeffrey Hammonds	4.00
15	Bo Jackson	6.00
16	Michael Jordan	100.00
17	Dave Justice	15.00
18	Steve Karsay	4.00
19	Jeff Kent	4.00
20	Brooks Kieschnick	4.00
21	Ryan Klesko	5.00
22	John Kruk	4.00
23	Barry Larkin	10.00
24	Pat Listach	4.00
25	Don Mattingly	25.00
26	Mark McGwire	100.00
27	Raul Mondesi	10.00
28	Trot Nixon	8.00
29	Mike Piazza	60.00
30	Kirby Puckett	25.00
31	Manny Ramirez	25.00
32	Cal Ripken, Jr.	75.00
33	Alex Rodriguez	250.00
34	Tim Salmon	5.00
35	Gary Sheffield	15.00
36	Ozzie Smith	20.00
37	Sammy Sosa	50.00
38	Andy Van Slyke	4.00

1995 SP

Foil highlights and die-cut specialty cards are once again featured in Upper Deck's premium-brand SP baseball card issue. The 207-card set opens with four die-cut tribute cards, followed by 20 Premier Prospect die-cuts printed on metallic foil backgrounds with copper-foil highlights. Three checklists follow, also die-cut. The regular player cards in the set are arranged in team-alphabetical order within league. Card fronts feature photos which are borderless at top, bottom and right. On the left is a gold-highlighted metallic foil border of blue for N.L., red for A.L. Backs have a large photo at top, with a few stats and career highlights at bottom, along with a gold infield-shaped hologram. The SP insert program consists of a "SuperbaFoil" parallel set, in which each card's normal foil highlights are replaced with silver foil; a 48-card Special F/X set utilizing holographic portraits, and, a 20-card Platinum Power set. The hobby-only SP was issued in eight-card foil packs with a $3.99 suggested retail price.

		MT
Complete Set (207):		40.00
Common Player:		.15
Pack (8):		3.50
Wax Box (32):		80.00
1	Cal Ripken Jr. (Salute)	3.00
2	Nolan Ryan (Salute)	2.00
3	George Brett (Salute)	1.00
4	Mike Schmidt (Salute)	.75
5	Dustin Hermanson (Premier Prospects)	.25
6	Antonio Osuna (Premier Prospects)	.25
7	*Mark Grudzielanek* (Premier Prospects)	.75
8	Ray Durham (Premier Prospects)	.35
9	Ugueth Urbina (Premier Prospects)	.25
10	Ruben Rivera (Premier Prospects)	1.50
11	Curtis Goodwin (Premier Prospects)	.15
12	Jimmy Hurst (Premier Prospects)	.15
13	Jose Malave (Premier Prospects)	.15
14	*Hideo Nomo* (Premier Prospects)	2.00
15	Juan Acevedo (Premier Prospects)	.15
16	Tony Clark (Premier Prospects)	1.50
17	Jim Pittsley (Premier Prospects)	.15

18 *Freddy Garcia*
(Premier Prospects) .50
19 *Carlos Perez*
(Premier Prospects) .25
20 *Raul Casanova*
(Premier Prospects) .50
21 Quilvio Veras
(Premier Prospects) .25
22 Edgardo Alfonzo
(Premier Prospects) .50
23 Marty Cordova
(Premier Prospects) .25
24 C.J. Nitkowski
(Premier Prospects) .25
25 Checklist 1-69
(Wade Boggs) .25
26 Checklist 70-138
(Dave Winfield) .25
27 Checklist 139-207
(Eddie Murray) .50
28 Dave Justice .30
29 Marquis Grissom .15
30 Fred McGriff .50
31 Greg Maddux 2.50
32 Tom Glavine .30
33 Steve Avery .15
34 Chipper Jones 2.50
35 Sammy Sosa 2.50
36 Jaime Navarro .15
37 Randy Myers .15
38 Mark Grace .30
39 Todd Zeile .15
40 Brian McRae .15
41 Reggie Sanders .15
42 Ron Gant .15
43 Deion Sanders .25
44 Barry Larkin .25
45 Bret Boone .15
46 Jose Rijo .15
47 Jason Bates .15
48 Andres Galarraga .40
49 Bill Swift .15
50 Larry Walker .40
51 Vinny Castilla .15
52 Dante Bichette .40
53 Jeff Conine .15
54 John Burkett .15
55 Gary Sheffield .40
56 Andre Dawson .25
57 Terry Pendleton .15
58 Charles Johnson .20
59 Brian L. Hunter .20
60 Jeff Bagwell 1.25
61 Craig Biggio .35
62 Phil Nevin .15
63 Doug Drabek .15
64 Derek Bell .15
65 Raul Mondesi .50
66 Eric Karros .15
67 Roger Cedeno .15
68 Delino DeShields .15
69 Ramon Martinez .15
70 Mike Piazza 2.00
71 Billy Ashley .15
72 Jeff Fassero .15
73 Shane Andrews .15
74 Wil Cordero .15
75 Tony Tarasco .15
76 Rondell White .25
77 Pedro Martinez .25
78 Moises Alou .20
79 Rico Brogna .15
80 Bobby Bonilla .20
81 Jeff Kent .15
82 Brett Butler .15
83 Bobby Jones .15
84 Bill Pulsipher .15
85 Bret Saberhagen .15
86 Gregg Jefferies .15
87 Lenny Dykstra .15
88 Dave Hollins .15
89 Charlie Hayes .15
90 Darren Daulton .15
91 Curt Schilling .25
92 Heathcliff Slocumb .15
93 Carlos Garcia .15
94 Denny Neagle .15
95 Jay Bell .15
96 Orlando Merced .15
97 Dave Clark .15
98 Bernard Gilkey .15
99 Scott Cooper .15
100 Ozzie Smith .75
100 Ken Griffey Jr.
(promo card) 6.00
101 Tom Henke .15
102 Ken Hill .15
103 Brian Jordan .15
104 Ray Lankford .15
105 Tony Gwynn 1.25
106 Andy Benes .15
107 Ken Caminiti .35
108 Steve Finley .15
109 Joey Hamilton .20
110 Bip Roberts .15
111 Eddie Williams .15
112 Rod Beck .15
113 Matt Williams .40
114 Glenallen Hill .15
115 Barry Bonds 1.00
116 Robby Thompson .15
117 Mark Portugal .15
118 Brady Anderson .30
119 Mike Mussina .60
120 Rafael Palmeiro .30
121 Chris Hoiles .15
122 Harold Baines .15
123 Jeffrey Hammonds .15
124 Tim Naehring .15
125 Mo Vaughn .60
126 Mike Macfarlane .15
127 Roger Clemens 1.00
128 John Valentin .15
129 Aaron Sele .15
130 Jose Canseco .40
131 J.T. Snow .20
132 Mark Langston .15
133 Chili Davis .15
134 Chuck Finley .15
135 Tim Salmon .25
136 Tony Phillips .15
137 Jason Bere .15
138 Robin Ventura .25
139 Tim Raines .20
140a Frank Thomas
(5-yr. BA .326) 1.50
140b Frank Thomas
(5-yr. BA .303) 4.00
141 Alex Fernandez .20
142 Jim Abbott .15
143 Wilson Alvarez .15
144 Carlos Baerga .15
145 Albert Belle .75
146 Jim Thome .40
147 Dennis Martinez .15
148 Eddie Murray .60
149 Dave Winfield .35
150 Kenny Lofton .60
151 Manny Ramirez 1.00
152 Chad Curtis .15
153 Lou Whitaker .15
154 Alan Trammell .15
155 Cecil Fielder .20
156 Kirk Gibson .15
157 Michael Tucker .15
158 Jon Nunnally .15
159 Wally Joyner .15
160 Kevin Appier .15
161 Jeff Montgomery .15
162 Greg Gagne .15
163 Ricky Bones .15
164 Cal Eldred .15
165 Greg Vaughn .20
166 Kevin Seitzer .15
167 Jose Valentin .15
168 Joe Oliver .15
169 Rick Aguilera .15
170 Kirby Puckett 1.50
171 Scott Stahoviak .15
172 Kevin Tapani .15
173 Chuck Knoblauch .25
174 Rich Becker .15
175 Don Mattingly 1.50
176 Jack McDowell .15
177 Jimmy Key .15
178 Paul O'Neill .20
179 John Wetteland .15
180 Wade Boggs .50
181 Derek Jeter 3.00
182 Rickey Henderson .35
183 Terry Steinbach .15
184 Ruben Sierra .15
185 Mark McGwire 4.00
186 Todd Stottlemyre .15
187 Dennis Eckersley .15
188 Alex Rodriguez 3.00
189 Randy Johnson .50
190 Ken Griffey Jr. 3.00
190a Ken Griffey Jr.
(certified autograph)
200.00
190a
191 Tino Martinez .20
192 Jay Buhner .20
193 Edgar Martinez .15
194 Mickey Tettleton .15
195 Juan Gonzalez 1.50
196 Benji Gil .15
197 Dean Palmer .15
198 Ivan Rodriguez .75
199 Kenny Rogers .15
200 Will Clark .40
201 Roberto Alomar .75
202 David Cone .25
203 Paul Molitor .75
204 Shawn Green .25
205 Joe Carter .20
206 Alex Gonzalez .20
207 Pat Hentgen .15

1995 SP SuperbaFoil

This chase set parallels the 207 regular cards in the SP issue. Cards were found at the rate of one per eight-card foil pack. SuperbaFoil cards feature a silver-rainbow metallic foil in place of the gold, copper, red or blue foil highlights on regular-issue SP cards. On back, the SuperbaFoil inserts have a silver hologram instead of the gold version found on standard cards.

MT
Complete Set (207): 80.00
Common Player: .25
SuperbaFoil Stars: 2X
(See 1995 SP for checklist and base values.)

1995 SP Platinum Power

This die-cut insert set features the game's top power hitters in color action photos set against a background of two-toned gold rays emanating from the SP logo at lower-right. Player name, team and position are printed in white in a black band at bottom. Backs repeat the golden ray effect in the background and have a color photo at center. Career and 1994 stats are presented. An infield-shaped gold foil hologram is at lower-right. Cards have a "PP" prefix. Stated odds of finding one of the 20 Platinum Power inserts are one per five packs.

MT
Complete Set (20): 20.00
Common Player: .50
1 Jeff Bagwell 2.00
2 Barry Bonds 1.50
3 Ron Gant .50
4 Fred McGriff .75
5 Raul Mondesi .75
6 Mike Piazza 3.00
7 Larry Walker .75
8 Matt Williams .75
9 Albert Belle 1.00
10 Cecil Fielder .50
11 Juan Gonzalez 1.50
12 Ken Griffey Jr. 5.00
13 Mark McGwire 5.00
14 Eddie Murray 1.00
15 Manny Ramirez 2.00
16 Cal Ripken Jr. 4.00
17 Tim Salmon .60
18 Frank Thomas 3.00
19 Jim Thome .60
20 Mo Vaughn .75

1995 SP Special F/X

By far the preferred pick of the '95 SP insert program is the Special F/X set of 48. The cards have a color action photo on front, printed on a metallic foil background. A 3/4" square holographic portrait is printed on the front. Backs are printed in standard technology and include another photo and a few stats and career highlights. Stated odds of finding a Special F/X card are 1 per 75 packs, or about one per two boxes.

MT
Complete Set (48): 425.00
Common Player: 3.00
1 Jose Canseco 8.00
2 Roger Clemens 15.00
3 Mo Vaughn 10.00
4 Tim Salmon 4.00
5 Chuck Finley 3.00
6 Robin Ventura 4.00
7 Jason Bere 3.00
8 Carlos Baerga 3.00
9 Albert Belle 10.00
10 Kenny Lofton 8.00
11 Manny Ramirez 15.00
12 Jeff Montgomery 3.00
13 Kirby Puckett 12.00
14 Wade Boggs 7.50
15 Don Mattingly 15.00
16 Cal Ripken Jr. 40.00
17 Ruben Sierra 3.00
18 Ken Griffey Jr. 45.00

19 Randy Johnson 12.00
20 Alex Rodriguez 40.00
21 Will Clark 5.00
22 Juan Gonzalez 15.00
23 Roberto Alomar 8.00
24 Joe Carter 3.00
25 Alex Gonzalez 4.00
26 Paul Molitor 7.50
27 Ryan Klesko 4.00
28 Fred McGriff 4.00
29 Greg Maddux 25.00
30 Sammy Sosa 30.00
31 Bret Boone 3.00
32 Barry Larkin 4.00
33 Reggie Sanders 3.00
34 Dante Bichette 4.00
35 Andres Galarraga 6.00
36 Charles Johnson 3.00
37 Gary Sheffield 4.00
38 Jeff Bagwell 15.00
39 Craig Biggio 5.00
40 Eric Karros 3.00
41 Billy Ashley 3.00
42 Raul Mondesi 4.00
43 Mike Piazza 30.00
44 Rondell White 3.00
45 Bret Saberhagen 3.00
46 Tony Gwynn 20.00
47 Melvin Nieves 3.00
48 Matt Williams 4.00

1995 SP/ Championship

Championship was a version of Upper Deck's popular SP line designed for sale in retail outlets. The first 20 cards in the set are a "Diamond in the Rough" subset featuring hot rookies printed on textured metallic foil background. Regular player cards are arranged by team within league, alphabetically by city name. Each team set is led off with a "Pro Files" card of a star player; those card backs feature team season and post-season results. Each of the regular player cards has a borderless action photo on front, highlighted with a gold-foil SP Championship logo. The team name is in a blue-foil oval on National Leaguers' cards; red on American Leaguers. Backs have a portrait photo, a few stats and career highlights. Situated between the N.L. and A.L. cards in the checklist are a subset of 15 October Legends. A parallel set of cards with die-cut tops was inserted into the six-card foil packs at the rate of one per pack. A special card honoring Cal Ripken's consecutive-game record was issued as a super-scarce insert.

	MT
Complete Set (200):	40.00
Common Player:	.15
Pack (6):	2.00
Wax Box (44):	65.00

1 *Hideo Nomo* (Diamonds in the Rough) 2.00
2 Roger Cedeno (Diamonds in the Rough) .25
3 Curtis Goodwin (Diamonds in the Rough) .15
4 Jon Nunnally (Diamonds in the Rough) .15
5 Bill Pulsipher (Diamonds in the Rough) .25
6 C.J. Nitkowski (Diamonds in the Rough) .15
7 Dustin Hermanson (Diamonds in the Rough) .15
8 Marty Cordova (Diamonds in the Rough) .25
9 Ruben Rivera (Diamonds in the Rough) .75
10 *Ariel Prieto* (Diamonds in the Rough) .25
11 Edgardo Alfonzo (Diamonds in the Rough) .30
12 Ray Durham (Diamonds in the Rough) .25
13 Quilvio Veras (Diamonds in the Rough) .25
14 Ugueth Urbina (Diamonds in the Rough) .25
15 *Carlos Perez* (Diamonds in the Rough) .20
16 *Glenn Dishman* (Diamonds in the Rough) .25
17 Jeff Suppan (Diamonds in the Rough) .20
18 Jason Bates (Diamonds in the Rough) .15
19 Jason Isringhausen (Diamonds in the Rough) .50
20 Derek Jeter (Diamonds in the Rough) 3.00
21 Fred McGriff (Major League ProFiles) .40
22 Marquis Grissom .15
23 Fred McGriff .50
24 Tom Glavine .25
25 Greg Maddux 2.00
26 Chipper Jones 2.00
27 Sammy Sosa (Major League ProFiles) 1.50
28 Randy Myers .15
29 Mark Grace .25
30 Sammy Sosa 2.50
31 Todd Zeile .15
32 Brian McRae .15
33 Ron Gant (Major League ProFiles) .15
34 Reggie Sanders .15
35 Ron Gant .20
36 Barry Larkin .30
37 Bret Boone .15
38 John Smiley .15
39 Larry Walker (Major League ProFiles) .25
40 Andres Galarraga .25
41 Bill Swift .15
42 Larry Walker .35
43 Vinny Castilla .15
44 Dante Bichette .50
45 Jeff Conine (Major League ProFiles) .15
46 Charles Johnson .15
47 Gary Sheffield .30
48 Andre Dawson .20
49 Jeff Conine .15
50 Jeff Bagwell (Major League ProFiles) .40
51 Phil Nevin .15
52 Craig Biggio .25
53 Brian L. Hunter .20
54 Doug Drabek .15
55 Jeff Bagwell 1.25
56 Derek Bell .15
57 Mike Piazza (Major League ProFiles) .60
58 Raul Mondesi .40
59 Eric Karros .20
60 Mike Piazza 2.00
61 Ramon Martinez .20
62 Billy Ashley .15
63 Rondell White (Major League ProFiles) .20
64 Jeff Fassero .15
65 Moises Alou .20
66 Tony Tarasco .15
67 Rondell White .20
68 Pedro Martinez .25
69 Bobby Jones (Major League ProFiles) .15
70 Bobby Bonilla .20
71 Bobby Jones .15
72 Bret Saberhagen .15
73 Darren Daulton (Major League ProFiles) .15
74 Darren Daulton .15
75 Gregg Jefferies .15
76 Tyler Green .15
77 Heathcliff Slocumb .15
78 Lenny Dykstra .15
79 Jay Bell (Major League ProFiles) .15
80 Denny Neagle .15
81 Orlando Merced .15
82 Jay Bell .15
83 Ozzie Smith (Major League ProFiles) .30
84 Ken Hill .15
85 Ozzie Smith .50
86 Bernard Gilkey .15
87 Ray Lankford .15
88 Tony Gwynn (Major League ProFiles) .50
89 Ken Caminiti .25
90 Tony Gwynn 1.25
91 Joey Hamilton .15
92 Bip Roberts .15
93 Deion Sanders (Major League ProFiles) .25
94 Glenallen Hill .15
95 Matt Williams .30
96 Barry Bonds .75
97 Rod Beck .15
98 Eddie Murray (Checklist) .25
99 Cal Ripken Jr. (Checklist) 1.50
100 Roberto Alomar (October Legends) .40
101 George Brett (October Legends) .75
102 Joe Carter (Ocober Legends) .20
103 Will Clark (October Legends) .25
104 Dennis Eckersley (October Legends) .15
105 Whitey Ford (October Legends) .40
106 Steve Garvey (October Legends) .15
107 Kirk Gibson (October Legends) .15
108 Orel Hershiser (October Legends) .15
109 Reggie Jackson (October Legends) .50
110 Paul Molitor (October Legends) .25
111 Kirby Puckett (October Legends) .75
112 Mike Schmidt (October Legends) .50
113 Dave Stewart (October Legends) .15
114 Alan Trammell (October Legends) .15
115 Cal Ripken Jr. (Major League ProFiles) 1.50
116 Brady Anderson .20
117 Mike Mussina .50
118 Rafael Palmeiro .25
119 Chris Hoiles .15
120 Cal Ripken Jr. 2.50
121 Mo Vaughn (Major League ProFiles) .35
122 Roger Clemens .75
123 Tim Naehring .15
124 John Valentin .15
125 Mo Vaughn .60
126 Tim Wakefield .15
127 Jose Canseco .35
128 Rick Aguilera .15
129 Chili Davis (Major League ProFiles) .15
130 Lee Smith .15
131 Jim Edmonds .30
132 Chuck Finley .15
133 Chili Davis .15
134 J.T. Snow .15
135 Tim Salmon .30
136 Frank Thomas (Major League ProFiles) .75
137 Jason Bere .15
138 Robin Ventura .25
139 Tim Raines .20
140 Frank Thomas 1.50
141 Alex Fernandez .20
142 Eddie Murray (Major League ProFiles) .25
143 Carlos Baerga .15
144 Eddie Murray .40
145 Albert Belle .75
146 Jim Thome .30
147 Dennis Martinez .15
148 Dave Winfield .25
149 Kenny Lofton .60
150 Manny Ramirez .75
151 Cecil Fielder (Major League ProFiles) .20
152 Lou Whitaker .15
153 Alan Trammell .15
154 Kirk Gibson .15
155 Cecil Fielder .20
156 *Bobby Higginson* 1.50
157 Kevin Appier (Major League ProFiles) .15
158 Wally Joyner .15
159 Jeff Montgomery .15
160 Kevin Appier .15
161 Gary Gaetti .15
162 Greg Gagne .15
163 Ricky Bones (Major League ProFiles) .15
164 Greg Vaughn .20
165 Kevin Seitzer .15
166 Ricky Bones .15
167 Kirby Puckett (Major League ProFiles) .40
168 Pedro Munoz .15
169 Chuck Knoblauch .25
170 Kirby Puckett 1.00
171 Don Mattingly (Major League ProFiles) .50

172	Wade Boggs	.40
173	Paul O'Neill	.20
174	John Wetteland	.15
175	Don Mattingly	1.00
176	Jack McDowell	.15
177	Mark McGwire (Major League ProFiles)	2.00
178	Rickey Henderson	.30
179	Terry Steinbach	.15
180	Ruben Sierra	.15
181	Mark McGwire	3.00
182	Dennis Eckersley	.15
183	Ken Griffey Jr. (Major League ProFiles)	1.50
184	Alex Rodriguez	3.00
185	Ken Griffey Jr.	3.00
186	Randy Johnson	.60
187	Jay Buhner	.15
188	Edgar Martinez	.15
189	Will Clark (Major League ProFiles)	.25
190	Juan Gonzalez	1.25
191	Benji Gil	.15
192	Ivan Rodriguez	.60
193	Kenny Rogers	.15
194	Will Clark	.30
195	Paul Molitor (Major League ProFiles)	.25
196	Roberto Alomar	.60
197	David Cone	.20
198	Paul Molitor	.50
199	Shawn Green	.25
200	Joe Carter	.20
CR1	Cal Ripken Jr. (2,131 games tribute)	15.00
CR1	Cal Ripken Jr. die-cut	50.00

1995 SP/ Championship Die-Cuts

Each of the 200 cards in the regular SP championship issue, plus the 20 insert cards, can also be found in a parallel chase card set with die-cut tops. One die-cut card was found in each six-card foil pack, making them five times scarcer than the regular cards. To prevent regular cards from being fraudulently cut, factory-issue die-cuts have the Upper Deck hologram on back in silver tone, rather than the gold holograms found on regular cards.

	MT
Complete Set (200):	90.00
Common Player:	.25
Die-Cut Stars:	2X

(See 1995 SP/Championship for checklist and base values.)

1995 SP/ Championship Classic Performances

Vintage action photos are featured in this chase set marking great post-season performances of modern times. The cards have a wide red strip at top with "CLASSIC PERFORMANCES" in gold-foil; the player's name, team and the SP Championship embossed logo at bottom are also in gold. Backs have a portrait photo and description of the highlight along with stats from that series. Regular Classic Performances cards are found at a stated rate of one per 15 foil packs, with die-cut versions in every 75 packs, on average. The die-cuts have silver UD holograms on back as opposed to the gold hologram found on regular versions of the chase cards.

		MT
Complete Set (10):		40.00
Common Player:		2.50
Complete Die-Cut Set (10):		175.00
Common Die-Cuts:		10.00
CP1	Reggie Jackson (Game 6 of '77 WS)	3.00
CP1	Reggie Jackson (die-cut)	12.00
CP2	Nolan Ryan (Game 3 of '69 WS)	20.00
CP2	Nolan Ryan (die-cut)	75.00
CP3	Kirk Gibson (Game 1 of '88 WS)	2.50
CP3	Kirk Gibson (die-cut)	10.00
CP4	Joe Carter (Game 6 of '93 WS)	2.50
CP4	Joe Carter (die-cut)	10.00
CP5	George Brett (Game 3 of '80 ALCS)	6.00
CP5	George Brett (die-cut)	25.00
CP6	Roberto Alomar (Game 4 of '92 ALCS)	4.00
CP6	Roberto Alomar (die-cut)	16.00
CP7	Ozzie Smith (Game 5 of '85 NLCS)	4.00
CP7	Ozzie Smith (die-cut)	16.00
CP8	Kirby Puckett (Game 6 of '91 WS)	6.00
CP8	Kirby Puckett (die-cut)	24.00
CP9	Bret Saberhagen (Game 7 of '85 WS)	2.50
CP9	Bret Saberhagen (die-cut)	10.00
CP10	Steve Garvey (Game 4 of '84 NLCS)	2.50
CP10	Steve Garvey (die-cut)	10.00

1995 SP/ Championship Destination: Fall Classic

Colored foil background printing and copper-foil graphic highlights are featured on this insert set picturing players who, for the most part, had yet to make a post-season appearance prior to 1995's expanded playoffs. Found at a stated average rate of one per 40 foil packs, the cards have short career summaries and another photo on back. A die-cut version of the cards was also issued, with a silver UD hologram on back rather than the gold found on the standard chase cards. The die-cut Fall Classic cards were inserted at a rate of one per 75 packs.

		MT
Complete Set (9):		80.00
Common Player:		4.00
Complete Die-Cut Set (9):		200.00
Common Die-Cut:		10.00
1	Ken Griffey Jr.	25.00
1	Ken Griffey Jr. (die-cut)	60.00
2	Frank Thomas	10.00
2	Frank Thomas (die-cut)	25.00
3	Albert Belle	6.00
3	Albert Belle (die-cut)	15.00
4	Mike Piazza	15.00
4	Mike Piazza (die-cut)	40.00
5	Don Mattingly	10.00
5	Don Mattingly (die-cut)	25.00
6	Hideo Nomo	6.00
6	Hideo Nomo (die-cut)	15.00
7	Greg Maddux	15.00
7	Greg Maddux (die-cut)	40.00
8	Fred McGriff	4.00
8	Fred McGriff (die-cut)	10.00
9	Barry Bonds	8.00
9	Barry Bonds (die-cut)	20.00

1996 SP

This 188-card set, distributed through hobby-only channels, features tremendous photography, including two photos on the front, and six insert sets. The inserts sets are Heroes, Marquee Matchups Blue and Die-Cut Marquee Matchups Red, Holoview Special F/X Blue and Die-Cut Holoview Special F/X Red, and the continuation of the Cal Ripken Collection.

		MT
Complete Set (188):		40.00
Common Player:		.15
Pack (8):		4.00
Wax Box (30):		90.00
1	Rey Ordonez (Premier Prospects)	.50
2	George Arias (Premier Prospects)	.15
3	*Osvaldo Fernandez* (Premier Prospects)	.30
4	*Darin Erstad* (Premier Prospects)	15.00
5	Paul Wilson (Premier Prospects)	.30
6	Richard Hidalgo (Premier Prospects)	.15
7	Bob Wolcott (Premier Prospects)	.15
8	Jimmy Haynes (Premier Prospects)	.15
9	Edgar Renteria (Premier Prospects)	.35
10	Alan Benes (Premier Prospects)	.30
11	Chris Snopek (Premier Prospects)	.15
12	Billy Wagner (Premier Prospects)	.25
13	*Mike Grace* (Premier Prospects)	.20
14	Todd Greene (Premier Prospects)	.15
15	Karim Garcia (Premier Prospects)	.30
16	John Wasdin (Premier Prospects)	.15
17	Jason Kendall (Premier Prospects)	.25
18	Bob Abreu (Premier Prospects)	.40
19	Jermaine Dye (Premier Prospects)	.25

20	Jason Schmidt (Premier Prospects)	.15
21	Javy Lopez	.30
22	Ryan Klesko	.25
23	Tom Glavine	.25
24	John Smoltz	.25
25	Greg Maddux	2.00
26	Chipper Jones	2.00
27	Fred McGriff	.40
28	David Justice	.40
29	Roberto Alomar	.75
30	Cal Ripken Jr.	3.00
31	Jeffrey Hammonds	.15
32	Bobby Bonilla	.15
33	Mike Mussina	.75
34	Randy Myers	.15
35	Rafael Palmeiro	.40
36	Brady Anderson	.25
37	Tim Naehring	.15
38	Jose Canseco	.50
39	Roger Clemens	1.50
40	Mo Vaughn	.50
41	*Jose Valentin*	.20
42	Kevin Mitchell	.15
43	Chili Davis	.15
44	Garret Anderson	.15
45	Tim Salmon	.30
46	Chuck Finley	.15
47	Mark Langston	.15
48	Jim Abbott	.15
49	J.T. Snow	.15
50	Jim Edmonds	.25
51	Sammy Sosa	2.50
52	Brian McRae	.15
53	Ryne Sandberg	1.00
54	Mark Grace	.30
55	Jaime Navarro	.15
56	Harold Baines	.15
57	Robin Ventura	.20
58	Tony Phillips	.15
59	Alex Fernandez	.25
60	Frank Thomas	1.50
61	Ray Durham	.15
62	Bret Boone	.15
63	Barry Larkin	.40
64	Pete Schourek	.15
65	Reggie Sanders	.15
66	John Smiley	.15
67	Carlos Baerga	.15
68	Jim Thome	.50
69	Eddie Murray	.40
70	Albert Belle	.50
71	Dennis Martinez	.15
72	Jack McDowell	.15
73	Kenny Lofton	.50
74	Manny Ramirez	1.50
75	Dante Bichette	.35
76	Vinny Castilla	.15
77	Andres Galarraga	.35
78	Walt Weiss	.15
79	Ellis Burks	.15
80	Larry Walker	.40
81	Cecil Fielder	.20
82	Melvin Nieves	.15
83	Travis Fryman	.30
84	Chad Curtis	.15
85	Alan Trammell	.15
86	Gary Sheffield	.50
87	Charles Johnson	.15
88	Andre Dawson	.30
89	Jeff Conine	.15
90	Greg Colbrunn	.15
91	Derek Bell	.15
92	Brian Hunter	.15
93	Doug Drabek	.15
94	Craig Biggio	.25
95	Jeff Bagwell	1.50
96	Kevin Appier	.15
97	Jeff Montgomery	.15
98	Michael Tucker	.15
99	Bip Roberts	.15
100	Johnny Damon	.20
101	Eric Karros	.25
102	Raul Mondesi	.30
103	Ramon Martinez	.15
104	Ismael Valdes	.15
105	Mike Piazza	2.50
106	Hideo Nomo	.50
107	Chan Ho Park	.20
108	Ben McDonald	.15
109	Kevin Seitzer	.15
110	Greg Vaughn	.20
111	Jose Valentin	.15
112	Rick Aguilera	.15
113	Marty Cordova	.15
114	Brad Radke	.15
115	Kirby Puckett	1.50
116	Chuck Knoblauch	.25
117	Paul Molitor	.50
118	Pedro Martinez	1.00
119	Mike Lansing	.15
120	Rondell White	.15
121	Moises Alou	.20
122	Mark Grudzielanek	.15
123	Jeff Fassero	.15
124	Rico Brogna	.15
125	Jason Isringhausen	.15
126	Jeff Kent	.15
127	Bernard Gilkey	.15
128	Todd Hundley	.25
129	David Cone	.25
130	Andy Pettitte	.50
131	Wade Boggs	.40
132	Paul O'Neill	.30
133	Ruben Sierra	.15
134	John Wetteland	.15
135	Derek Jeter	3.00
136	Geronimo Pena	.15
137	Terry Steinbach	.15
138	Ariel Prieto	.15
139	Scott Brosius	.15
140	Mark McGwire	4.00
141	Lenny Dykstra	.15
142	Todd Zeile	.15
143	Benito Santiago	.15
144	Mickey Morandini	.15
145	Gregg Jefferies	.15
146	Denny Neagle	.15
147	Orlando Merced	.15
148	Charlie Hayes	.15
149	Carlos Garcia	.15
150	Jay Bell	.15
151	Ray Lankford	.15
152	Alan Benes	.20
153	Dennis Eckersley	.15
154	Gary Gaetti	.15
155	Ozzie Smith	.75
156	Ron Gant	.20
157	Brian Jordan	.15
158	Ken Caminiti	.25
159	Rickey Henderson	.40
160	Tony Gwynn	1.50
161	Wally Joyner	.15
162	Andy Ashby	.15
163	Steve Finley	.15
164	Glenallen Hill	.15
165	Matt Williams	.30
166	Barry Bonds	1.00
167	William VanLandingham	.15
168	Rod Beck	.15
169	Randy Johnson	1.00
170	Ken Griffey Jr.	3.00
170p	Ken Griffey Jr. (unmarked promo; bio on back says, "... against Cleveland" as opposed to "... against the Indians")	15.00
171	Alex Rodriguez	3.00
172	Edgar Martinez	.15
173	Jay Buhner	.15
174	Russ Davis	.15
175	Juan Gonzalez	1.00
176	Mickey Tettleton	.15
177	Will Clark	.50
178	Ken Hill	.15
179	Dean Palmer	.15
180	Ivan Rodriguez	1.00
181	Carlos Delgado	.75
182	Alex Gonzalez	.20
183	Shawn Green	.30
184	Erik Hanson	.15
185	Joe Carter	.20
186	Checklist (Hideo Nomo)	.25
187	Checklist (Cal Ripken Jr.)	1.50
188	Checklist (Ken Griffey Jr.)	1.50

1996 SP Baseball Heroes

This 1996 insert set is a continuation of the series which began in 1990. These cards, numbered 81-90, feature nine of today's top stars, plus a Ken Griffey Jr. header card (#81). The cards were seeded one per every 96 packs.

		MT
Complete Set (10):		175.00
Common Player:		8.00
81	Ken Griffey Jr. Header	30.00
82	Frank Thomas	20.00
83	Albert Belle	8.00
84	Barry Bonds	15.00
85	Chipper Jones	25.00
86	Hideo Nomo	10.00
87	Mike Piazza	30.00
88	Manny Ramirez	15.00
89	Greg Maddux	25.00
90	Ken Griffey Jr.	40.00

1996 SP Marquee Matchups Blue

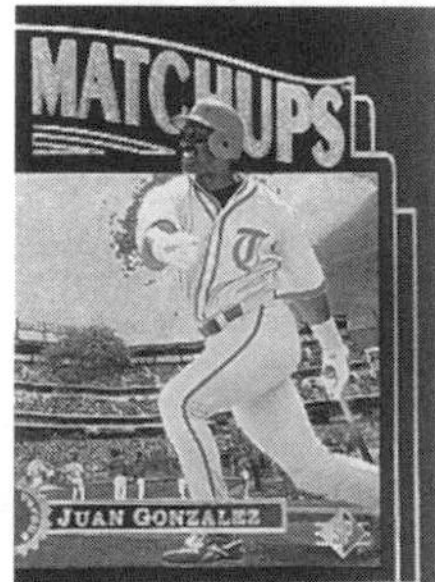

This 20-card Upper Deck SP insert set contains cards that allow collectors to match up the game's top players against each other, such as Greg Maddux against Cal Ripken Jr. The design and stadiums in the background match together when the two cards are next to each other. Blue versions are seeded one per every five packs. Red versions, with die-cut tops but otherwise identical to the blue, are found on average of once in 61 packs. Cards are numbered with a "MM" prefix.

		MT
Complete Set (20):		40.00
Common Player:		1.00
1	Ken Griffey Jr.	6.00
2	Hideo Nomo	1.50
3	Derek Jeter	6.00
4	Rey Ordonez	1.50
5	Tim Salmon	1.00
6	Mike Piazza	5.00
7	Mark McGwire	8.00
8	Barry Bonds	2.00
9	Cal Ripken Jr.	6.00
10	Greg Maddux	5.00
11	Albert Belle	1.50
12	Barry Larkin	1.00
13	Jeff Bagwell	3.00
14	Juan Gonzalez	2.00
15	Frank Thomas	3.00
16	Sammy Sosa	5.00
17	Mike Mussina	1.00
18	Chipper Jones	4.00
19	Roger Clemens	3.00
20	Fred McGriff	1.50

1996 SP Marquee Matchups Red

A parallel set to the blue Marquee Matchups, the red cards are found on average of one per 61 packs. Besides the red background printing, this version is distinguished from the more collon blue version by the die-cutting around the top. Cards are numbered with a "MM" prefix.

		MT
Complete Set (20):		200.00
Common Player:		3.00
1	Ken Griffey Jr.	35.00
2	Hideo Nomo	5.00
3	Derek Jeter	20.00
4	Rey Ordonez	5.00
5	Tim Salmon	4.00
6	Mike Piazza	20.00
7	Mark McGwire	35.00
8	Barry Bonds	8.00
9	Cal Ripken Jr.	25.00
10	Greg Maddux	20.00
11	Albert Belle	4.00
12	Barry Larkin	4.00
13	Jeff Bagwell	8.00
14	Juan Gonzalez	10.00
15	Frank Thomas	15.00
16	Sammy Sosa	20.00
17	Mike Mussina	6.00
18	Chipper Jones	20.00
19	Roger Clemens	10.00
20	Fred McGriff	4.00

1996 SP Ripken Collection

The last five cards of the Cal Ripken Jr. Collection, which began in Collector's Choice Series I, are featured in this Upper

Deck SP product. These five cards, numbered 18-22, cover Ripken's early days, including his 1982 Rookie of the Year Award, his Major League debut, and photos of him playing third base. Ripken Collection inserts are found one per every 45 packs.

		MT
Complete Set (5):		40.00
Common Ripken:		8.00
18	Cal Ripken Jr.	8.00
19	Cal Ripken Jr.	8.00
20	Cal Ripken Jr.	8.00
21	Cal Ripken Jr.	8.00
22	Cal Ripken Jr.	8.00

1996 SP SpecialFX

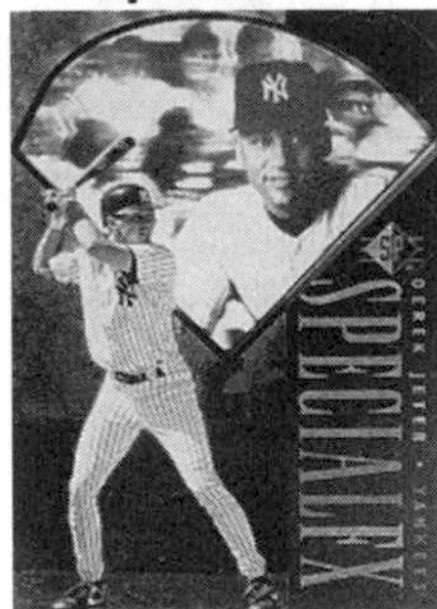

These 48 cards capture Upper Deck Holoview technology. Blue versions were seeded one per every five packs of 1996 Upper Deck SP baseball.

		MT
Complete Set (48):		120.00
Common Player:		1.50
1	Greg Maddux	7.50
2	Eric Karros	1.50
3	Mike Piazza	7.50
4	Raul Mondesi	1.75
5	Hideo Nomo	1.75
6	Jim Edmonds	1.50
7	Jason Isringhausen	1.50
8	Jay Buhner	1.50
9	Barry Larkin	1.50
10	Ken Griffey Jr.	12.00
11	Gary Sheffield	1.50
12	Craig Biggio	2.00
13	Paul Wilson	1.50
14	Rondell White	1.50
15	Chipper Jones	7.50
16	Kirby Puckett	3.50
17	Ron Gant	1.50
18	Wade Boggs	3.00
19	Fred McGriff	1.50
20	Cal Ripken Jr.	9.00
21	Jason Kendall	1.50
22	Johnny Damon	1.50
23	Kenny Lofton	2.00
24	Roberto Alomar	2.50
25	Barry Bonds	3.00
26	Dante Bichette	1.50
27	Mark McGwire	12.00
28	Rafael Palmeiro	2.00
29	Juan Gonzalez	3.00
30	Albert Belle	2.50
31	Randy Johnson	2.50
32	Jose Canseco	1.75
33	Sammy Sosa	6.00
34	Eddie Murray	2.00
35	Frank Thomas	5.00
36	Tom Glavine	1.50
37	Matt Williams	1.75
38	Roger Clemens	3.00
39	Paul Molitor	2.50
40	Tony Gwynn	6.00
41	Mo Vaughn	2.00
42	Tim Salmon	1.50
43	Manny Ramirez	3.00
44	Jeff Bagwell	5.00
45	Edgar Martinez	1.50
46	Rey Ordonez	1.50
47	Osvaldo Fernandez	1.50
48	Livan Hernandez	1.50

1996 SP SpecialFX Red

These 1996 Upper Deck SP red die-cut cards use Upper Deck's Holoview technology. They are scarcer than the blue versions; these being seeded one per every 75 packs.

		MT
Complete Set (48):		800.00
Common Player:		8.00
1	Greg Maddux	60.00
2	Eric Karros	8.00
3	Mike Piazza	60.00
4	Raul Mondesi	12.50
5	Hideo Nomo	15.00
6	Jim Edmonds	8.00
7	Jason Isringhausen	8.00
8	Jay Buhner	8.00
9	Barry Larkin	8.00
10	Ken Griffey Jr.	100.00
11	Gary Sheffield	10.00
12	Craig Biggio	10.00
13	Paul Wilson	8.00
14	Rondell White	8.00
15	Chipper Jones	60.00
16	Kirby Puckett	40.00
17	Ron Gant	8.00
18	Wade Boggs	10.00
19	Fred McGriff	10.00
20	Cal Ripken Jr.	80.00
21	Jason Kendall	8.00
22	Johnny Damon	8.00
23	Kenny Lofton	20.00
24	Roberto Alomar	20.00
25	Barry Bonds	25.00
26	Dante Bichette	10.00
27	Mark McGwire	100.00
28	Rafael Palmeiro	15.00
29	Juan Gonzalez	30.00
30	Albert Belle	25.00
31	Randy Johnson	20.00
32	Jose Canseco	15.00
33	Sammy Sosa	60.00
34	Eddie Murray	15.00
35	Frank Thomas	40.00
36	Tom Glavine	8.00
37	Matt Williams	12.50
38	Roger Clemens	25.00
39	Paul Molitor	20.00
40	Tony Gwynn	40.00
41	Mo Vaughn	20.00
42	Tim Salmon	10.00
43	Manny Ramirez	25.00
44	Jeff Bagwell	40.00
45	Edgar Martinez	8.00
46	Rey Ordonez	8.00
47	Osvaldo Fernandez	8.00
48	Livan Hernandez	8.00

1996 SPx

Upper Deck's 1996 SPX set has 60 players in it, which are each paralleled as a Gold version (one per every seven packs). Base cards feature a new look with a different perimeter die-cut design from those used in the past for basketball and football sets. A 10-card insert set, Bound for Glory, was also produced. Tribute cards were also made for Ken Griffey Jr. and Mike Piazza, with scarcer autographed versions also produced for each player.

		MT
Complete Set (60):		75.00
Common Player:		.75
Complete Gold Set (60):		300.00
Golds:		2.5X
Ken Griffey Jr. Autograph:		200.00
Mike Piazza Autograph:		150.00
Unlisted Stars:		1.50 to 2.00
Pack (1):		3.00
Wax Box (36):		100.00
1	Greg Maddux	4.00
2	Chipper Jones	4.00
3	Fred McGriff	1.00
4	Tom Glavine	1.00
5	Cal Ripken Jr.	6.00
6	Roberto Alomar	1.50
7	Rafael Palmeiro	1.00
8	Jose Canseco	1.50
9	Roger Clemens	3.00
10	Mo Vaughn	1.00
11	Jim Edmonds	1.00
12	Tim Salmon	1.00
13	Sammy Sosa	5.00
14	Ryne Sandberg	2.00
15	Mark Grace	1.00
16	Frank Thomas	3.00
17	Barry Larkin	1.00
18	Kenny Lofton	1.00
19	Albert Belle	1.00
20	Eddie Murray	.75
21	Manny Ramirez	2.00
22	Dante Bichette	.75
23	Larry Walker	1.00
24	Vinny Castilla	.75
25	Andres Galarraga	1.00
26	Cecil Fielder	.75
27	Gary Sheffield	1.00
28	Craig Biggio	.75
29	Jeff Bagwell	2.00
30	Derek Bell	.75
31	Johnny Damon	.75
32	Eric Karros	.75
33	Mike Piazza	5.00
34	Raul Mondesi	.75
35	Hideo Nomo	.75
36	Kirby Puckett	2.00
37	Paul Molitor	1.50
38	Marty Cordova	.75
39	Rondell White	.75
40	Jason Isringhausen	.75
41	Paul Wilson	.75
42	Rey Ordonez	.75
43	Derek Jeter	6.00
44	Wade Boggs	1.00
45	Mark McGwire	8.00
46	Jason Kendall	.75
47	Ron Gant	1.00
48	Ozzie Smith	2.00
49	Tony Gwynn	3.00
50	Ken Caminiti	.75
51	Barry Bonds	2.00
52	Matt Williams	.75
53	*Osvaldo Fernandez*	1.00
54	Jay Buhner	1.00
55	Ken Griffey Jr.	6.00
55p	Ken Griffey Jr. (overprinted "For Promotional Use Only")	10.00
56	Randy Johnson	2.00
57	Alex Rodriguez	6.00
58	Juan Gonzalez	2.00
59	Joe Carter	1.00
60	Carlos Delgado	1.50

1996 SPx Bound for Glory

Some of baseball's best players are highlighted on these 1996 Upper Deck SPX insert cards. The cards were seeded one per every 24 packs. Fronts of the die-cut cards feature a color photograph on a background of silver-foil holographic portrait and action photos. Backs have another portrait photo, stats, career highlights and logos.

		MT
Complete Set (10):		80.00
Common Player:		4.00
1	Ken Griffey Jr.	15.00
2	Frank Thomas	8.00
3	Barry Bonds	5.00
4	Cal Ripken Jr.	15.00
5	Greg Maddux	10.00
6	Chipper Jones	10.00
7	Roberto Alomar	4.00
8	Manny Ramirez	5.00
9	Tony Gwynn	6.00
10	Mike Piazza	12.00

1996 SPx Ken Griffey Jr. Commemorative

Seattle Mariners' star Ken Griffey Jr. has this tribute card in Upper Deck's 1996 SPX set. The card was seeded one per every 75 packs. Autographed versions were also produced; these cards were seeded one per every 2,000 packs.

		MT
KG1	Ken Griffey Jr.	15.00
KGA1	Ken Griffey Jr. (autographed)	300.00

1996 SPx Mike Piazza Tribute

Los Angeles Dodgers' star catcher Mike Piazza is featured on this 1996 Upper Deck SPX insert card. Normal versions of the card are found one per every 95 packs, making it scarcer than the Ken Griffey Jr. inserts. Autographed Piazza cards are seeded one per every 2,000 packs.

		MT
MP1	Mike Piazza	9.00
MP1	Mike Piazza (autographed)	200.00

1997 SP Sample

To preview its SP brand for 1997, Upper Deck issued a sample card of Ken Griffey, Jr. Similar in format to the issued cards, the promo bears card number 1 and is overprinted "SAMPLE" on back.

		MT
1	Ken Griffey Jr.	6.00

1997 SP

The fifth anniversary edition of SP Baseball features 184 regular cards sold in eight-card packs for $4.39. Card fronts feature the player's name in gold foil-stamping at bottom. Team name and position are vertically at one edge. Backs have two more photos along with "Best Year" and career stats. Inserts include Marquee Matchups, Special FX, Inside Info, Baseball Heroes, Game Film, SPx Force, and Autographed Vintage SP Cards.

	MT
Complete Set (184):	40.00
Common Player:	.15
Pack (8):	4.50
Wax Box (30):	100.00

1	Andruw Jones (Great Futures)	2.00
2	Kevin Orie (Great Futures)	.15
3	Nomar Garciaparra (Great Futures)	2.50
4	Jose Guillen (Great Futures)	1.50
5	Todd Walker (Great Futures)	1.00
6	Derrick Gibson (Great Futures)	.50
7	Aaron Boone (Great Futures)	.25
8	Bartolo Colon (Great Futures)	.45
9	Derrek Lee (Great Futures)	.25
10	Vladimir Guerrero (Great Futures)	2.00
11	Wilton Guerrero (Great Futures)	.15
12	Luis Castillo (Great Futures)	.15
13	Jason Dickson (Great Futures)	.15
14	*Bubba Trammell* (Great Futures)	1.50
15	*Jose Cruz Jr.* (Great Futures)	1.00
16	Eddie Murray	.50
17	Darin Erstad	1.50
18	Garret Anderson	.15
19	Jim Edmonds	.15
20	Tim Salmon	.40
21	Chuck Finley	.15
22	John Smoltz	.30
23	Greg Maddux	2.50
24	Kenny Lofton	.60
25	Chipper Jones	2.50
26	Ryan Klesko	.40
27	Javier Lopez	.15
28	Fred McGriff	.40
29	Roberto Alomar	.75
30	Rafael Palmeiro	.30
31	Mike Mussina	.75
32	Brady Anderson	.15
33	Rocky Coppinger	.15
34	Cal Ripken Jr.	4.00
35	Mo Vaughn	.60
36	Steve Avery	.15
37	Tom Gordon	.15
38	Tim Naehring	.15
39	Troy O'Leary	.15
40	Sammy Sosa	2.50
41	Brian McRae	.15
42	Mel Rojas	.15
43	Ryne Sandberg	1.00
44	Mark Grace	.30
45	Albert Belle	1.00
46	Robin Ventura	.20
47	Roberto Hernandez	.15
48	Ray Durham	.15
49	Harold Baines	.15
50	Frank Thomas	2.00
51	Bret Boone	.15
52	Reggie Sanders	.15
53	Deion Sanders	.25
54	Hal Morris	.15
55	Barry Larkin	.25
56	Jim Thome	.60
57	Marquis Grissom	.15
58	David Justice	.50
59	Charles Nagy	.15
60	Manny Ramirez	1.50
61	Matt Williams	.35
62	Jack McDowell	.15
63	Vinny Castilla	.15
64	Dante Bichette	.25
65	Andres Galarraga	.25
66	Ellis Burks	.15
67	Larry Walker	.50
68	Eric Young	.15
69	Brian L. Hunter	.15
70	Travis Fryman	.15
71	Tony Clark	1.00
72	Bobby Higginson	.15
73	Melvin Nieves	.15
74	Jeff Conine	.15
75	Gary Sheffield	.50
76	Moises Alou	.15
77	Edgar Renteria	.15
78	Alex Fernandez	.15
79	Charles Johnson	.15
80	Bobby Bonilla	.15
81	Darryl Kile	.15
82	Derek Bell	.15
83	Shane Reynolds	.15
84	Craig Biggio	.35
85	Jeff Bagwell	2.00
86	Billy Wagner	.15
87	Chili Davis	.15
88	Kevin Appier	.15
89	Jay Bell	.15
90	Johnny Damon	.15
91	Jeff King	.15
92	Hideo Nomo	.50
93	Todd Hollandsworth	.15
94	Eric Karros	.15
95	Mike Piazza	2.50
96	Ramon Martinez	.15
97	Todd Worrell	.15
98	Raul Mondesi	.40
99	Dave Nilsson	.15
100	John Jaha	.15
101	Jose Valentin	.15
102	Jeff Cirillo	.15
103	Jeff D'Amico	.15
104	Ben McDonald	.15
105	Paul Molitor	.50
106	Rich Becker	.15
107	Frank Rodriguez	.15
108	Marty Cordova	.15
109	Terry Steinbach	.15
110	Chuck Knoblauch	.30
111	Mark Grudzielanek	.15
112	Mike Lansing	.15
113	Pedro Martinez	.30
114	Henry Rodriguez	.15
115	Rondell White	.15
116	Rey Ordonez	.15
117	Carlos Baerga	.15
118	Lance Johnson	.15
119	Bernard Gilkey	.15
120	Todd Hundley	.30
121	John Franco	.15
122	Bernie Williams	.60
123	David Cone	.30
124	Cecil Fielder	.20
125	Derek Jeter	3.00
126	Tino Martinez	.25
127	Mariano Rivera	.25
128	Andy Pettitte	.60
129	Wade Boggs	.50
130	Mark McGwire	5.00
131	Jose Canseco	.40
132	Geronimo Berroa	.15
133	Jason Giambi	.15
134	Ernie Young	.15
135	Scott Rolen	1.50
136	Ricky Bottalico	.15
137	Curt Schilling	.15
138	Gregg Jefferies	.15
139	Mickey Morandini	.15
140	Jason Kendall	.15
141	Kevin Elster	.15
142	Al Martin	.15
143	Joe Randa	.15
144	Jason Schmidt	.15
145	Ray Lankford	.15
146	Brian Jordan	.15
147	Andy Benes	.15
148	Alan Benes	.20
149	Gary Gaetti	.15
150	Ron Gant	.15
151	Dennis Eckersley	.15
152	Rickey Henderson	.25
153	Joey Hamilton	.15
154	Ken Caminiti	.40
155	Tony Gwynn	2.00
156	Steve Finley	.15
157	Trevor Hoffman	.15
158	Greg Vaughn	.15
159	J.T. Snow	.15
160	Barry Bonds	1.00
161	Glenallen Hill	.15
162	William VanLandingham	.15
163	Jeff Kent	.15
164	Jay Buhner	.15
165	Ken Griffey Jr.	5.00
166	Alex Rodriguez	4.00
167	Randy Johnson	.75
168	Edgar Martinez	.15
169	Dan Wilson	.15
170	Ivan Rodriguez	.75
171	Roger Pavlik	.15
172	Will Clark	.30
173	Dean Palmer	.15
174	Rusty Greer	.15
175	Juan Gonzalez	1.50
176	John Wetteland	.15
177	Joe Carter	.15
178	Ed Sprague	.15
179	Carlos Delgado	.50
180	Roger Clemens	1.00
181	Juan Guzman	.15
182	Pat Hentgen	.15
183	Ken Griffey Jr.	4.00
184	*Hideki Irabu*	2.00

1997 SP Autographed Inserts

To celebrate the fifth anniversary of its premium

SP brand, Upper Deck went into the hobby market to buy nearly 3,000 previous years' cards for a special insert program in 1997 SP packs. Various SP cards from 1993-96 issues and inserts were autographed by star players and a numbered holographic seal added on back. The number of each particular card signed ranged widely from fewer than 10 to more than 100. Numbers in parentheses in the checklist are the quantity reported signed for that card. All cards were inserted into foil packs except those of Mo Vaughn, which were a mail-in redemption.

		MT
Common Autograph:		25.00
	1993 SP	
4	Ken Griffey Jr. (16)	2000.
28	Jeff Bagwell (7)	25.00
167	Tony Gwynn (17)	600.00
280	Chipper Jones (34)	400.00
	1993 SP Platinum Power	
PP9	Ken Griffey Jr. (5)	2000.
	1994 SP	
6	Todd Hollandsworth (167)	25.00
15	Alex Rodriguez (94)	1200.
105	Ken Griffey Jr. (103)	800.00
114	Gary Sheffield (130)	50.00
130	Tony Gwynn (367)	125.00
	1994 SP Holoview Blue	
13	Tony Gwynn (31)	400.00
	1994 SP Holoview Red	
35	Gary Sheffield (4)	100.00
	1995 SP	
34	Chipper Jones (60)	300.00
60	Jeff Bagwell (173)	100.00
75	Gary Sheffield (221)	30.00
105	Tony Gwynn (64)	300.00
188	Alex Rodriguez (63)	400.00
190	Ken Griffey Jr. (38)	1000.
195	Jay Buhner (57)	50.00
	1996 SP	
1	Rey Ordonez (111)	30.00
18	Gary Sheffield (58)	60.00
26	Chipper Jones (102)	250.00
40	Mo Vaughn (250)	50.00
95	Jeff Bagwell (292)	100.00
160	Tony Gwynn (20)	500.00
170	Ken Griffey Jr. (312)	400.00
171	Alex Rodriguez (73)	400.00
173	Jay Buhner (79)	40.00
	1996 SP Marquee Matchups	
MM13	Jeff Bagwell (23)	300.00
MM4	Rey Ordonez (40)	75.00
	1996 SP Special F/X	
8	Jay Buhner (27)	75.00

1997 SP Game Film

A 10-card insert utilizing pieces of actual game footage to highlight the top stars in the game. Only 500 of each card were available. Cards are numbered with a "GF" prefix.

		MT
Complete Set (10):		375.00
Common Player:		12.50
1	Alex Rodriguez	60.00
2	Frank Thomas	30.00
3	Andruw Jones	20.00
4	Cal Ripken Jr.	60.00
5	Mike Piazza	45.00
6	Derek Jeter	40.00
7	Mark McGwire	75.00
8	Chipper Jones	45.00
9	Barry Bonds	20.00
10	Ken Griffey Jr.	60.00

1997 SP Griffey Baseball Heroes

First started in 1990, this single-player insert continues with a salute to Ken Griffey Jr. Each card in the set is numbered to 2,000.

		MT
Complete Set (10):		150.00
Common Griffey Jr.:		20.00
91	Ken Griffey Jr.	20.00
92	Ken Griffey Jr.	20.00
93	Ken Griffey Jr.	20.00
94	Ken Griffey Jr.	20.00
95	Ken Griffey Jr.	20.00
96	Ken Griffey Jr.	20.00
97	Ken Griffey Jr.	20.00
98	Ken Griffey Jr.	20.00
99	Ken Griffey Jr.	20.00
100	Ken Griffey Jr.	20.00

1997 SP Inside Info

Each of the 25 cards in this insert feature a pull-out panel describing the player's major accomplishments. Both front and back are printed on metallic-foil stock. Cards were inserted one per box.

		MT
Complete Set (25):		200.00
Common Player:		3.00
1	Ken Griffey Jr.	20.00
2	Mark McGwire	25.00
3	Kenny Lofton	4.00
4	Paul Molitor	5.00
5	Frank Thomas	8.00
6	Greg Maddux	12.00
7	Mo Vaughn	4.00
8	Cal Ripken Jr.	20.00
9	Jeff Bagwell	6.00
10	Alex Rodriguez	20.00
11	John Smoltz	3.00
12	Manny Ramirez	6.00
13	Sammy Sosa	15.00
14	Vladimir Guerrero	8.00
15	Albert Belle	4.00
16	Mike Piazza	15.00
17	Derek Jeter	20.00
18	Scott Rolen	5.00
19	Tony Gwynn	8.00
20	Barry Bonds	6.00
21	Ken Caminiti	3.00
22	Chipper Jones	12.00
23	Juan Gonzalez	6.00
24	Roger Clemens	8.00
25	Andruw Jones	8.00

1997 SP Marquee Matchups

A 20-card die-cut set designed to highlight top interleague matchups. When the matching cards are put together, a third player is highlighted in the background. Cards were inserted 1:5 packs.

		MT
Complete Set (30):		50.00
Common Player:		1.00
MM1	Ken Griffey Jr.	9.00
MM2	Andres Galarraga	1.50
MM2	Juan Gonzalez	2.50
MM3	Barry Bonds	2.50
MM4	Mark McGwire	9.00
MM4	Jose Canseco	1.50
MM5	Mike Piazza	5.00
MM6	Tim Salmon	1.50
MM6	Hideo Nomo	1.50
MM7	Tony Gwynn	4.00
MM8	Alex Rodriguez	7.00
MM8	Ken Caminiti	1.00
MM9	Chipper Jones	5.00
MM10	Derek Jeter	5.00
MM10	Andruw Jones	2.50
MM11	Manny Ramirez	2.50
MM12	Jeff Bagwell	3.00
MM12	Matt Williams	1.50
MM13	Greg Maddux	5.00
MM14	Cal Ripken Jr.	6.00
MM14	Brady Anderson	1.00
MM15	Mo Vaughn	1.00
MM16	Gary Sheffield	1.00
MM16	Vladimir Guerrero	4.00
MM17	Jim Thome	1.00
MM18	Barry Larkin	1.00
MM18	Deion Sanders	1.00
MM19	Frank Thomas	4.00
MM20	Sammy Sosa	6.00
MM20	Albert Belle	2.00

1997 SP Special FX

Color 3-D motion portraits are front and center on these cards that also feature a die-cut design. The rest of the front includes color action photos printed on silver-foil stock.that also feature a die-cut design. Backs have another color photo. The Alex Rodriguez card features the 1996 die-cut design since it was not available in the '96 set and is numbered 49 of 49. Cards were inserted 1:9 packs.

		MT
Complete Set (48):		225.00
Common Player:		2.00
1	Ken Griffey Jr.	15.00
2	Frank Thomas	6.00
3	Barry Bonds	6.00
4	Albert Belle	3.00
5	Mike Piazza	12.00
6	Greg Maddux	10.00
7	Chipper Jones	10.00
8	Cal Ripken Jr.	15.00
9	Jeff Bagwell	5.00
10	Alex Rodriguez	15.00
11	Mark McGwire	20.00
12	Kenny Lofton	3.00
13	Juan Gonzalez	5.00
14	Mo Vaughn	4.00
15	John Smoltz	2.00
16	Derek Jeter	15.00
17	Tony Gwynn	6.00
18	Ivan Rodriguez	5.00
19	Barry Larkin	3.00
20	Sammy Sosa	12.00
21	Mike Mussina	4.00
22	Gary Sheffield	3.00
23	Brady Anderson	2.00
24	Roger Clemens	8.00
25	Ken Caminiti	2.00
26	Roberto Alomar	4.00
27	Hideo Nomo	4.00
28	Bernie Williams	4.00
29	Todd Hundley	2.00
30	Manny Ramirez	5.00
31	Eric Karros	3.00
32	Tim Salmon	3.00
33	Jay Buhner	3.00
34	Andy Pettitte	2.50
35	Jim Thome	3.00
36	Ryne Sandberg	5.00
37	Matt Williams	3.00
38	Ryan Klesko	3.00
39	Jose Canseco	4.00
40	Paul Molitor	4.00
41	Eddie Murray	3.00
42	Darin Erstad	5.00
43	Todd Walker	2.00
44	Wade Boggs	3.00
45	Andruw Jones	5.00
46	Scott Rolen	5.00
47	Vladimir Guerrero	6.00
48	not issued	
49	Alex Rodriguez	15.00

1997 SP SPx Force

Each of the 10 cards in this set feature four different players. Cards are individually numbered to 500. In addition, a number of players signed 100 versions of their SPx Force cards that are also randomly inserted into packs.

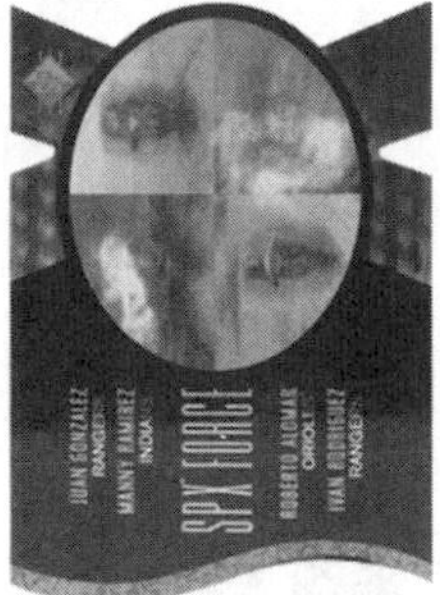

		MT
Complete Set (10):		250.00
Common Player:		15.00
1	Ken Griffey Jr., Jay Buhner, Andres Galarraga, Dante Bichette	40.00
2	Albert Belle, Brady Anderson, Mark McGwire, Cecil Fielder	50.00
3	Mo Vaughn, Ken Caminiti, Frank Thomas, Jeff Bagwell	20.00
4	Gary Sheffield, Sammy Sosa, Barry Bonds, Jose Canseco	30.00
5	Greg Maddux, Roger Clemens, John Smoltz, Randy Johnson	25.00
6	Alex Rodriguez, Derek Jeter, Chipper Jones, Rey Ordonez	50.00
7	Todd Hollandsworth, Mike Piazza, Raul Mondesi, Hideo Nomo	30.00
8	Juan Gonzalez, Manny Ramirez, Roberto Alomar, Ivan Rodriguez	15.00
9	Tony Gwynn, Wade Boggs, Eddie Murray, Paul Molitor	20.00
10	Andruw Jones, Vladimir Guerrero, Todd Walker, Scott Rolen	20.00

1997 SP SPx Force Autographs

Ten players signed cards for this insert, which was serially numbered to 100. The cards were randomly seeded in packs except the Mo Vaughn card which was available by redemption.

		MT
Common Player:		50.00
1	Ken Griffey Jr.	450.00
2	Albert Belle	75.00
3	Mo Vaughn	50.00
4	Gary Sheffield	50.00
5	Greg Maddux	250.00
6	Alex Rodriguez	400.00
7	Todd Hollandsworth	50.00
8	Roberto Alomar	80.00
9	Tony Gwynn	175.00
10	Andruw Jones	100.00

1997 SPx

Fifty cards, each featuring a perimeter die-cut design and a 3-D holoview photo, make up the SPx base set. Five different parallel sets - Steel (1:1 pack), Bronze (1:1), Silver (1:1), Gold (1:17) and Grand Finale (50 per card) - are found as inserts, as are Cornerstones of the Game, Bound for Glory and Bound for Glory Signature cards. Packs contain three cards and carried a suggested retail price of $5.99.

		MT
Complete Set (50):		60.00
Common Player:		.50
Steel:		2X
Bronze:		2X
Silver:		3X
Gold:		5X
Pack (3):		3.00
Wax Box (18):		50.00
1	Eddie Murray	1.25
2	Darin Erstad	3.00
3	Tim Salmon	1.00
4	Andruw Jones	3.00
5	Chipper Jones	4.00
6	John Smoltz	.50
7	Greg Maddux	4.00
8	Kenny Lofton	1.00
9	Roberto Alomar	1.25
10	Rafael Palmeiro	.50
11	Brady Anderson	.50
12	Cal Ripken Jr.	5.00
13	Nomar Garciaparra	3.00
14	Mo Vaughn	1.00
15	Ryne Sandberg	1.50
16	Sammy Sosa	4.00
17	Frank Thomas	3.00
18	Albert Belle	1.25
19	Barry Larkin	.50
20	Deion Sanders	.50
21	Manny Ramirez	2.00
22	Jim Thome	1.25
23	Dante Bichette	.50
24	Andres Galarraga	.50
25	Larry Walker	1.00
26	Gary Sheffield	1.00
27	Jeff Bagwell	2.50
28	Raul Mondesi	.50
29	Hideo Nomo	1.00
30	Mike Piazza	4.00
31	Paul Molitor	1.00
32	Todd Walker	1.00
33	Vladimir Guerrero	3.00
34	Todd Hundley	.50
35	Andy Pettitte	1.00
36	Derek Jeter	4.00
37	Jose Canseco	.50
38	Mark McGwire	7.50
39	Scott Rolen	2.50
40	Ron Gant	.50
41	Ken Caminiti	.50
42	Tony Gwynn	3.00
43	Barry Bonds	1.50
44	Jay Buhner	.50
45	Ken Griffey Jr.	7.50
45s	Ken Griffey Jr. (overprinted SAMPLE on back)	6.00
46	Alex Rodriguez	6.00
47	*Jose Cruz Jr.*	1.00
48	Juan Gonzalez	2.00
49	Ivan Rodriguez	1.25
50	Roger Clemens	2.00

1997 SPx Bound for Glory

A 20-card insert utilizing holoview technology and sequentially numbered to 1,500 per card. Five players (Andruw Jones, Gary Sheffield, Alex Rodriguez, Ken Griffey Jr. and Jeff Bagwell) signed versions of their cards as part of the Bound For Glory Supreme Signatures set.

		MT
Complete Set (20):		450.00
Common Player:		10.00
1	Andruw Jones	20.00
2	Chipper Jones	40.00
3	Greg Maddux	40.00
4	Kenny Lofton	10.00
5	Cal Ripken Jr.	50.00
6	Mo Vaughn	10.00
7	Frank Thomas	30.00
8	Albert Belle	12.50
9	Manny Ramirez	15.00
10	Gary Sheffield	10.00
11	Jeff Bagwell	25.00
12	Mike Piazza	40.00
13	Derek Jeter	40.00
14	Mark McGwire	60.00
15	Tony Gwynn	30.00
16	Ken Caminiti	10.00
17	Barry Bonds	20.00
18	Alex Rodriguez	50.00
19	Ken Griffey Jr.	60.00
20	Juan Gonzalez	15.00

1997 SPx Bound for Glory Supreme Signatures

This five-card set featured autographs from the players and was sequentially numbered to 250.

		MT
Complete Set (5):		1000.
Common Player:		60.00
1	Jeff Bagwell	200.00
2	Ken Griffey Jr.	450.00
3	Andruw Jones	150.00
4	Alex Rodriguez	350.00
5	Gary Sheffield	60.00

1997 SPx Cornerstones of the Game

A 20-card insert utilizing a double-front design highlighting 40 of the top players in the game. Each card is sequentially numbered to 500.

		MT
Complete Set (10):		300.00
Common Player:		20.00
1	Ken Griffey Jr., Barry Bonds	60.00
2	Frank Thomas, Albert Belle	20.00
3	Chipper Jones, Greg Maddux	40.00
4	Tony Gwynn, Paul Molitor	25.00
5	Andruw Jones, Vladimir Guerrero	25.00
6	Jeff Bagwell, Ryne Sandberg	20.00
7	Mike Piazza, Ivan Rodriguez	35.00
8	Cal Ripken Jr., Eddie Murray	40.00
9	Mo Vaughn, Mark McGwire	50.00
10	Alex Rodriguez, Derek Jeter	50.00

1998 SP Authentic Sample

This card of Upper Deck spokesman Ken Griffey, Jr., was issued to preview the new SP Authentic line. Design is similar to the issued version but the sample displays different photos, a different the card number and the word "SAMPLE" printed in large letters on back.

	MT
Ken Griffey Jr.	6.00

1998 SP Authentic

The SP Authentic base set consists of 198 cards, including the 30-card Future Watch subset and one checklist card. The base cards have a color photo inside a thick white border. Inserts include Chirography, Sheer Dominance and SP Authentics.

		MT
Complete Set (198):		50.00
Common Player:		.25
Pack (5):		5.00
Wax Box (24):		90.00
1	Travis Lee (Future Watch)	1.50

2	Mike Caruso (Future Watch)	.40
3	Kerry Wood (Future Watch)	1.00
4	Mark Kotsay (Future Watch)	.50
5	*Magglio Ordonez* (Future Watch)	5.00
6	Scott Elarton (Future Watch)	.25
7	Carl Pavano (Future Watch)	.25
8	A.J. Hinch (Future Watch)	.25
9	*Rolando Arrojo* (Future Watch)	.75
10	Ben Grieve (Future Watch)	1.50
11	Gabe Alvarez (Future Watch)	.25
12	*Mike Kinkade* (Future Watch)	1.50
13	Bruce Chen (Future Watch)	.25
14	Juan Encarnacion (Future Watch)	.40
15	Todd Helton (Future Watch)	1.25
16	Aaron Boone (Future Watch)	.25
17	Sean Casey (Future Watch)	.50
18	Ramon Hernandez (Future Watch)	.25
19	Daryle Ward (Future Watch)	.25
20	Paul Konerko (Future Watch)	.50
21	David Ortiz (Future Watch)	.25
22	Derrek Lee (Future Watch)	.25
23	Brad Fullmer (Future Watch)	.40
24	Javier Vazquez (Future Watch)	.25
25	Miguel Tejada (Future Watch)	1.00
26	David Dellucci (Future Watch)	.25
27	Alex Gonzalez (Future Watch)	.25
28	Matt Clement (Future Watch)	.25
29	Eric Milton (Future Watch)	.25
30	Russell Branyan (Future Watch)	.25
31	Chuck Finley	.25
32	Jim Edmonds	.25
33	Darren Erstad	1.25
34	Jason Dickson	.25
35	Tim Salmon	.40
36	Cecil Fielder	.25
37	Todd Greene	.25
38	Andy Benes	.25
39	Jay Bell	.25
40	Matt Williams	.50
41	Brian Anderson	.25
42	Karim Garcia	.40
43	Javy Lopez	.25
44	Tom Glavine	.50
45	Greg Maddux	3.00
46	Andruw Jones	1.25
47	Chipper Jones	3.00
48	Ryan Klesko	.30
49	John Smoltz	.40
50	Andres Galarraga	.50
51	Rafael Palmeiro	.50
52	Mike Mussina	1.00
53	Roberto Alomar	1.00
54	Joe Carter	.25
55	Cal Ripken Jr.	4.00
56	Brady Anderson	.25
57	Mo Vaughn	1.00
58	John Valentin	.25
59	Dennis Eckersley	.25
60	Nomar Garciaparra	3.00
61	Pedro J. Martinez	1.00
62	Jeff Blauser	.25
63	Kevin Orie	.25
64	Henry Rodriguez	.25
65	Mark Grace	.50
66	Albert Belle	1.25
67	Mike Cameron	.25
68	Robin Ventura	.25
69	Frank Thomas	2.50
70	Barry Larkin	.30
71	Brett Tomko	.25
72	Willie Greene	.25
73	Reggie Sanders	.25
74	Sandy Alomar Jr.	.40
75	Kenny Lofton	1.00
76	Jaret Wright	1.25
77	David Justice	.25
78	Omar Vizquel	.25
79	Manny Ramirez	1.50
80	Jim Thome	.60
81	Travis Fryman	.25
82	Neifi Perez	.25
83	Mike Lansing	.25
84	Vinny Castilla	.25
85	Larry Walker	.75
86	Dante Bichette	.40
87	Darryl Kile	.25
88	Justin Thompson	.25
89	Damion Easley	.25
90	Tony Clark	.75
91	Bobby Higginson	.25
92	Brian L. Hunter	.25
93	Edgar Renteria	.25
94	Craig Counsell	.25
95	Mike Piazza	3.00
96	Livan Hernandez	.25
97	Todd Zeile	.25
98	Richard Hidalgo	.25
99	Moises Alou	.40
100	Jeff Bagwell	1.50
101	Mike Hampton	.25
102	Craig Biggio	.50
103	Dean Palmer	.25
104	Tim Belcher	.25
105	Jeff King	.25
106	Jeff Conine	.25
107	Johnny Damon	.25
108	Hideo Nomo	.60
109	Raul Mondesi	.40
110	Gary Sheffield	.60
111	Ramon Martinez	.25
112	Chan Ho Park	.50
113	Eric Young	.25
114	Charles Johnson	.25
115	Eric Karros	.25
116	Bobby Bonilla	.25
117	Jeromy Burnitz	.25
118	Carl Eldred	.25
119	Jeff D'Amico	.25
120	Marquis Grissom	.25
121	Dave Nilsson	.25
122	Brad Radke	.25
123	Marty Cordova	.25
124	Ron Coomer	.25
125	Paul Molitor	1.00
126	Todd Walker	.50
127	Rondell White	.40
128	Mark Grudzielanek	.25
129	Carlos Perez	.25
130	Vladimir Guerrero	2.00
131	Dustin Hermanson	.25
132	Butch Huskey	.25
133	John Franco	.25
134	Rey Ordonez	.25
135	Todd Hundley	.25
136	Edgardo Alfonzo	.25
137	Bobby Jones	.25
138	John Olerud	.40
139	Chili Davis	.25
140	Tino Martinez	.40
141	Andy Pettitte	.60
142	Chuck Knoblauch	.40
143	Bernie Williams	1.00
144	David Cone	.40
145	Derek Jeter	3.00
146	Paul O'Neill	.40
147	Rickey Henderson	.50
148	Jason Giambi	.25
149	Kenny Rogers	.25
150	Scott Rolen	1.50
151	Curt Schilling	.40
152	Ricky Bottalico	.25
153	Mike Lieberthal	.25
154	Francisco Cordova	.25
155	Jose Guillen	.50
156	Jason Schmidt	.25
157	Jason Kendall	.25
158	Kevin Young	.25
159	Delino DeShields	.25
160	Mark McGwire	5.00
161	Ray Lankford	.25
162	Brian Jordan	.25
163	Ron Gant	.25
164	Todd Stottlemyre	.25
165	Ken Caminiti	.40
166	Kevin Brown	.40
167	Trevor Hoffman	.25
168	Steve Finley	.25
169	Wally Joyner	.25
170	Tony Gwynn	2.50
171	Shawn Estes	.25
172	J.T. Snow	.25
173	Jeff Kent	.25
174	Robb Nen	.25
175	Barry Bonds	1.25
176	Randy Johnson	1.00
177	Edgar Martinez	.25
178	Jay Buhner	.25
179	Alex Rodriguez	4.00
180	Ken Griffey Jr.	5.00
181	Ken Cloude	.25
182	Wade Boggs	.60
183	Tony Saunders	.25
184	Wilson Alvarez	.25
185	Fred McGriff	.40
186	Roberto Hernandez	.25
187	Kevin Stocker	.25
188	Fernando Tatis	.40
189	Will Clark	.50
190	Juan Gonzalez	1.50
191	Rusty Greer	.25
192	Ivan Rodriguez	1.25
193	Jose Canseco	.50
194	Carlos Delgado	.50
195	Roger Clemens	1.75
196	Pat Hentgen	.25
197	Randy Myers	.25
198	Checklist (Ken Griffey Jr.)	2.00

1998 SP Authentic Chirography

Chirography is a 30-card insert seeded one per 25 packs. The featured player signed his cards in the white border at the bottom.

		MT
Complete Set (30):		1600.
Common Card:		15.00
Inserted 1:25		
RA	Roberto Alomar	75.00
RB	Russell Branyan	15.00
SC	Sean Casey	30.00
TC	Tony Clark	30.00
RC	Roger Clemens	175.00
JC	Jose Cruz Jr.	15.00
DE	Darin Erstad	60.00
NG	Nomar Garciaparra	150.00
BG	Ben Grieve	60.00
KG	Ken Griffey Jr.	350.00
VG	Vladimir Guerrero	80.00
TG	Tony Gwynn	125.00
TH	Todd Helton	50.00
LH	Livan Hernandez	30.00
CJ	Charles Johnson	25.00
AJ	Andruw Jones	60.00
CHIP	Chipper Jones	120.00
PK	Paul Konerko	30.00
MK	Mark Kotsay	30.00
RL	Ray Lankford	25.00
TL	Travis Lee	50.00
PM	Paul Molitor	75.00
MM	Mike Mussina	60.00
AR	Alex Rodriguez	180.00
IR	Ivan Rodriguez	75.00
SR	Scott Rolen	60.00
DL	Gary Sheffield	35.00
MT	Miguel Tejada	40.00
JW	Jaret Wright	40.00
MV	Mo Vaughn	60.00

1998 SP Authentic Sheer Dominance

Sheer Dominance is a 42-card insert. The base set is inserted one per three packs. The Sheer Dominance Gold parallel is sequentially numbered to 2,000 and the Titanium parallel is numbered to 100. The cards feature a player photo inside a white border. The background color corresponds to the level of the insert.

		MT
Complete Set (42):		120.00
Common Player:		1.00
Inserted 1:3		
SD1	Ken Griffey Jr.	12.00
SD2	Rickey Henderson	1.50
SD3	Jaret Wright	3.00
SD4	Craig Biggio	1.50
SD5	Travis Lee	2.50
SD6	Kenny Lofton	1.50
SD7	Raul Mondesi	1.50
SD8	Cal Ripken Jr.	10.00
SD9	Matt Williams	1.50
SD10	Mark McGwire	12.00
SD11	Alex Rodriguez	10.00
SD12	Fred McGriff	1.00
SD13	Scott Rolen	4.00
SD14	Paul Molitor	2.50
SD15	Nomar Garciaparra	8.00
SD16	Vladimir Guerrero	4.00
SD17	Andruw Jones	3.00
SD18	Manny Ramirez	5.00
SD19	Tony Gwynn	6.00
SD20	Barry Bonds	3.00
SD21	Ben Grieve	4.00
SD22	Ivan Rodriguez	3.00
SD23	Jose Cruz Jr.	1.00
SD24	Pedro J. Martinez	2.50
SD25	Chipper Jones	8.00
SD26	Albert Belle	2.50
SD27	Todd Helton	3.00
SD28	Paul Konerko	1.50
SD29	Sammy Sosa	6.00
SD30	Frank Thomas	6.00
SD31	Greg Maddux	8.00
SD32	Randy Johnson	2.50
SD33	Larry Walker	2.00
SD34	Roberto Alomar	2.50
SD35	Roger Clemens	5.00
SD36	Mo Vaughn	1.50
SD37	Jim Thome	1.50
SD38	Jeff Bagwell	4.00

SD39 Tino Martinez 1.00
SD40 Mike Piazza 8.00
SD41 Derek Jeter 8.00
SD42 Juan Gonzalez 3.00

1998 SP Authentic Sheer Dominance Gold

Identical in format and using the same photos as the Silver version, the scarcer Sheer Dominance Gold card differs on front in its use of a gold-metallic foil background within the white border. Backs of the gold version are individually serial numbered within an edition of 2,000 each.

	MT
Complete Set (42):	500.00
Common Player:	3.00
Gold Stars:	6X

(Star and rookie cards valued at 3X Silver version.)

1998 SP Authentic Sheer Dominance Titanium

Sheer Dominance Titanium is a parallel of the 42-card Sheer Dominance insert. The cards are numbered to 100 and have a gray background with "Titanium" printed across it.

	MT
Common Player:	20.00
Titanium Stars:	25X

(See 1998 SP Authentic Sheer Dominance for checklist and base card values.)

1998 SP Authentic Trade Cards

Cards which could be traded (prior to the Aug. 1, 1999 cut-off) for special cards and autographed memorabilia were inserted into SP Authentic foil packs at an announced rate of one per 291 packs. Trade cards have a white background on front with a color player action photo and the name of the redemption item. Backs gives details for redemption. In some cases, because of their insertation-rate rarity, the cards are worth more than the redemption items. The unnumbered cards are listed here alphabetically.

		MT
Common Card:		20.00
(1)	Roberto Alomar (autographed ball 100)	30.00
(2)	Albert Belle (autographed ball 100)	30.00
(3)	Jay Buhner (jersey card 125)	20.00
(4)	Ken Griffey Jr. (autographed glove 30)	800.00
(5)	Ken Griffey Jr. (autographed jersey 30)	800.00
(6)	Ken Griffey Jr. (jersey card 125)	150.00
(7)	Ken Griffey Jr. (standee 200)	75.00
(8)	Ken Griffey Jr. (300th HR card 1000)	25.00
(9)	Tony Gwynn (jersey card 415)	25.00
(10)	Brian Jordan (autographed ball 50)	25.00
(11)	Greg Maddux (jersey card 125)	50.00
(12)	Raul Mondesi (autographed ball 100)	25.00
(13)	Alex Rodriguez (jersey card 125)	75.00
(14)	Gary Sheffield (jersey card 125)	20.00
(15)	Robin Ventura (autographed ball)	25.00

Player names in *Italic* type indicate a rookie card.

1998 SP Authentic Jersey Swatch

These 5" x 7" redemption cards were issued in exchange for Trade Cards found as random foil-packs inserts. Fronts have a player action photo on a white background. Backs have a congratulatory message of authenticity. Sandwiched between in a swatch of that player's uniform jersey. The large-format jersey cards were available in limited editions which are listed in parentheses, though all might not have been redeemed prior to the Aug. 1, 1999, cut-off date.

		MT
Complete Set (6):		1000.
Common Player:		50.00
(1)	Jay Buhner (125)	50.00
(2)	Ken Griffey Jr. (125)	450.00
(3)	Tony Gwynn (415)	125.00
(4)	Greg Maddux (125)	200.00
(5)	Alex Rodriguez (125)	300.00
(6)	Gary Sheffield (125)	75.00

1998 SP Authentic Ken Griffey Jr. 300th HR Redemption

This 5" x 7"version of Ken Griffey Jr.'s SP Authentic card was issued as a redemption for one of the 1000 Trade Cards which were foil-pack inserts.

	MT
KG300 Ken Griffey Jr.	30.00

1998 SPx Finite

SPx Finite is an all-sequentially numbered set issued in two 180-card series. The Series 1 base set consists of five subsets: 90 regular cards (numbered to 9,000), 30 Star Focus (7,000), 30 Youth Movement (5,000), 20 Power Explosion (4,000) and 10 Heroes of the Game (2,000). The set is paralleled in the Radiance and Spectrum sets. Radiance regular cards are numbered to 4,500, Star Focus to 3,500, Youth Movement to 2,500, Power Explosion to 1,000 and Heroes of the Game to 100. Spectrum regular cards are numbered to 2,250, Star Focus to 1,750, Youth Movement to 1,250, Power Explosion to 50 and Heroes of the Game to 1. The Series 2 base set has 90 regular cards (numbered to 9,000), 30 Power Passion (7,000), 30 Youth Movement (5,000), 20 Tradewinds (4,000) and 10 Cornerstones of the Game (2,000). Series 2 also has Radiance and Spectrum parallels. Radiance regular cards are numbered to 4,500, Power Passion to 3,500, Youth Movement to 2,500, Tradewinds to 1,000 and Cornerstones of the Game to 100. Spectrum regular cards are numbered to 2,250, Power Passion to 1,750, Youth Movement to 1,250, Tradewinds to 50 and Cornerstones of the Game to 1. The only insert is Home Run Hysteria.

		MT
Complete Set (360):		2000.
Common Youth Movement (#1-30, 181-210):		1.00
Radiance Youth Movement (2,500):		2x
Spectrum Youth Movement (1,250):		4x
Common Power Explosion (#31-50):		3.00
Radiance Power Explosion (1,000):		4x
Common Regular Card (#51-140, 241-330):		1.00
Radiance Regular Card (4,500):		2x
Spectrum Regular Card (2,250):		4x
Common Star Focus (#141-170):		1.50
Radiance Star Focus (3,500):		2x
Spectrum Star Focus (1,750):		4x
Common Heroes of the Game (#171-180):		12.00
Common Power Passion (#211-240):		1.50
Radiance Power Passion (3,500)		2x
Spectrum Power Passion (1,750)		4x
Common Tradewinds (#331-350):		2.50
Radiance Tradewinds (1,000)		4x
Common Cornerstones (#351-360):		12.00
Pack:		6.00
Wax Box:		110.00
1	Nomar Garciaparra (Youth Movement)	15.00
2	Miguel Tejada (Youth Movement)	2.50
3	Mike Cameron (Youth Movement)	1.00
4	Ken Cloude (Youth Movement)	2.00
5	Jaret Wright (Youth Movement)	10.00
6	Mark Kotsay (Youth Movement)	2.50
7	Craig Counsell (Youth Movement)	1.00
8	Jose Guillen (Youth Movement)	2.00
9	Neifi Perez (Youth Movement)	1.00
10	Jose Cruz Jr. (Youth Movement)	1.00
11	Brett Tomko (Youth Movement)	1.00
12	Matt Morris (Youth Movement)	1.50
13	Justin Thompson (Youth Movement)	1.00
14	Jeremi Gonzalez (Youth Movement)	1.00
15	Scott Rolen (Youth Movement)	10.00
16	Vladimir Guerrero (Youth Movement)	10.00
17	Brad Fullmer (Youth Movement)	2.50
18	Brian Giles (Youth Movement)	1.00
19	Todd Dunwoody (Youth Movement)	1.00
20	Ben Grieve (Youth Movement)	8.00
21	Juan Encarnacion (Youth Movement)	1.00
22	Aaron Boone (Youth Movement)	1.00
23	Richie Sexson (Youth Movement)	1.00
24	Richard Hidalgo (Youth Movement)	1.00

25	Andruw Jones (Youth Movement)	6.00
26	Todd Helton (Youth Movement)	6.00
27	Paul Konerko (Youth Movement)	3.00
28	Dante Powell (Youth Movement)	1.00
29	Elieser Marrero (Youth Movement)	1.00
30	Derek Jeter (Youth Movement)	15.00
31	Mike Piazza (Power Explosion)	15.00
32	Tony Clark (Power Explosion)	4.00
33	Larry Walker (Power Explosion)	3.00
34	Jim Thome (Power Explosion)	4.00
35	Juan Gonzalez (Power Explosion)	5.00
36	Jeff Bagwell (Power Explosion)	10.00
37	Jay Buhner (Power Explosion)	3.00
38	Tim Salmon (Power Explosion)	3.00
39	Albert Belle (Power Explosion)	6.00
40	Mark McGwire (Power Explosion)	12.00
41	Sammy Sosa (Power Explosion)	8.00
42	Mo Vaughn (Power Explosion)	6.00
43	Manny Ramirez (Power Explosion)	8.00
44	Tino Martinez (Power Explosion)	3.00
45	Frank Thomas (Power Explosion)	10.00
46	Nomar Garciaparra (Power Explosion)	15.00
47	Alex Rodriguez (Power Explosion)	18.00
48	Chipper Jones (Power Explosion)	15.00
49	Barry Bonds (Power Explosion)	6.00
50	Ken Griffey Jr. (Power Explosion)	25.00
51	Jason Dickson	1.00
52	Jim Edmonds	1.50
53	Darin Erstad	4.00
54	Tim Salmon	2.00
55	Chipper Jones	10.00
56	Ryan Klesko	2.00
57	Tom Glavine	1.50
58	Denny Neagle	1.00
59	John Smoltz	1.00
60	Javy Lopez	1.00
61	Roberto Alomar	3.00
62	Rafael Palmeiro	1.50
63	Mike Mussina	4.00
64	Cal Ripken Jr.	12.00
65	Mo Vaughn	4.00
66	Tim Naehring	1.00
67	John Valentin	1.00
68	Mark Grace	2.00
69	Kevin Orie	1.00
70	Sammy Sosa	6.00
71	Albert Belle	4.00
72	Frank Thomas	6.00
73	Robin Ventura	1.50
74	David Justice	2.00
75	Kenny Lofton	4.00
76	Omar Vizquel	1.00
77	Manny Ramirez	5.00
78	Jim Thome	2.50
79	Dante Bichette	2.00
80	Larry Walker	2.00
81	Vinny Castilla	1.50
82	Ellis Burks	1.00
83	Bobby Higginson	1.00
84	Brian L. Hunter	1.00
85	Tony Clark	2.50
86	Mike Hampton	1.00
87	Jeff Bagwell	6.00
88	Craig Biggio	2.00
89	Derek Bell	1.00
90	Mike Piazza	10.00
91	Ramon Martinez	1.00
92	Raul Mondesi	2.00
93	Hideo Nomo	2.00
94	Eric Karros	1.50
95	Paul Molitor	3.00
96	Marty Cordova	1.00
97	Brad Radke	1.00
98	Mark Grudzielanek	1.00
99	Carlos Perez	1.00
100	Rondell White	1.50
101	Todd Hundley	1.00
102	Edgardo Alfonzo	1.00
103	John Franco	1.00
104	John Olerud	1.50
105	Tino Martinez	2.00
106	David Cone	1.50
107	Paul O'Neill	1.50
108	Andy Pettitte	2.50
109	Bernie Williams	3.00
110	Rickey Henderson	1.50
111	Jason Giambi	1.00
112	Matt Stairs	1.00
113	Gregg Jefferies	1.00
114	Rico Brogna	1.00
115	Curt Schilling	1.50
116	Jason Schmidt	1.00
117	Jose Guillen	2.00
118	Kevin Young	1.00
119	Ray Lankford	1.00
120	Mark McGwire	8.00
121	Delino DeShields	1.00
122	Ken Caminiti	2.00
123	Tony Gwynn	8.00
124	Trevor Hoffman	1.00
125	Barry Bonds	4.00
126	Jeff Kent	1.00
127	Shawn Estes	1.00
128	J.T. Snow	1.00
129	Jay Buhner	2.00
130	Ken Griffey Jr.	15.00
131	Dan Wilson	1.00
132	Edgar Martinez	1.00
133	Alex Rodriguez	12.00
134	Rusty Greer	1.00
135	Juan Gonzalez	4.00
136	Fernando Tatis	1.00
137	Ivan Rodriguez	4.00
138	Carlos Delgado	1.50
139	Pat Hentgen	1.00
140	Roger Clemens	6.00
141	Chipper Jones (Star Focus)	12.00
142	Greg Maddux (Star Focus)	12.00
143	Rafael Palmeiro (Star Focus)	2.00
144	Mike Mussina (Star Focus)	4.00
145	Cal Ripken Jr. (Star Focus)	14.00
146	Nomar Garciaparra (Star Focus)	12.00
147	Mo Vaughn (Star Focus)	5.00
148	Sammy Sosa (Star Focus)	6.00
149	Albert Belle (Star Focus)	5.00
150	Frank Thomas (Star Focus)	6.00
151	Jim Thome (Star Focus)	4.00
152	Kenny Lofton (Star Focus)	5.00
153	Manny Ramirez (Star Focus)	6.00
154	Larry Walker (Star Focus)	2.50
155	Jeff Bagwell (Star Focus)	8.00
156	Craig Biggio (Star Focus)	1.50
157	Mike Piazza (Star Focus)	12.00
158	Paul Molitor (Star Focus)	4.00
159	Derek Jeter (Star Focus)	10.00
160	Tino Martinez (Star Focus)	2.50
161	Curt Schilling (Star Focus)	1.50
162	Mark McGwire (Star Focus)	10.00
163	Tony Gwynn (Star Focus)	10.00
164	Barry Bonds (Star Focus)	5.00
165	Ken Griffey Jr. (Star Focus)	18.00
166	Randy Johnson (Star Focus)	3.00
167	Alex Rodriguez (Star Focus)	12.00
168	Juan Gonzalez (Star Focus)	5.00
169	Ivan Rodriguez (Star Focus)	5.00
170	Roger Clemens (Star Focus)	8.00
171	Greg Maddux (Heroes of the Game)	30.00
172	Cal Ripken Jr. (Heroes of the Game)	40.00
173	Frank Thomas (Heroes of the Game)	20.00
174	Jeff Bagwell (Heroes of the Game)	20.00
175	Mike Piazza (Heroes of the Game)	30.00
176	Mark McGwire (Heroes of the Game)	25.00
177	Barry Bonds (Heroes of the Game)	12.00
178	Ken Griffey Jr. (Heroes of the Game)	50.00
179	Alex Rodriguez (Heroes of the Game)	40.00
180	Roger Clemens (Heroes of the Game)	20.00
181	Mike Caruso	1.00
182	David Ortiz	2.00
183	Gabe Alvarez	1.00
184	Gary Matthews Jr.	1.00
185	Kerry Wood	10.00
186	Carl Pavano	1.00
187	Alex Gonzalez	1.00
188	Masato Yoshii	2.00
189	Larry Sutton	1.00
190	Russell Branyan	1.00
191	Bruce Chen	1.00
192	Rolando Arrojo	2.50
193	Ryan Christenson	1.00
194	Cliff Politte	1.00
195	A.J. Hinch	1.00
196	Kevin Witt	1.00
197	Daryle Ward	1.00
198	Corey Koskie	1.00
199	Mike Lowell	1.00
200	Travis Lee	6.00
201	*Kevin Millwood*	25.00
202	Robert Smith	1.00
203	*Magglio Ordonez*	30.00
204	Eric Milton	1.00
205	Geoff Jenkins	1.00
206	Rich Butler	1.00
207	*Mike Kinkade*	1.00
208	Braden Looper	1.00
209	Matt Clement	1.00
210	Derrek Lee	1.00
211	Randy Johnson	3.00
212	John Smoltz	1.50
213	Roger Clemens	5.00
214	Curt Schilling	2.00
215	Pedro J. Martinez	4.00
216	Vinny Castilla	1.00
217	Jose Cruz Jr.	1.50
218	Jim Thome	2.50
219	Alex Rodriguez	12.00
220	Frank Thomas	5.00
221	Tim Salmon	2.00
222	Larry Walker	2.50
223	Albert Belle	4.00
224	Manny Ramirez	5.00
225	Mark McGwire	15.00
226	Mo Vaughn	4.00
227	Andres Galarraga	2.00
228	Scott Rolen	4.00
229	Travis Lee	4.00
230	Mike Piazza	10.00
231	Nomar Garciaparra	10.00
232	Andruw Jones	4.00
233	Barry Bonds	4.00
234	Jeff Bagwell	5.00
235	Juan Gonzalez	4.00
236	Tino Martinez	2.00
237	Vladimir Guerrero	6.00
238	Rafael Palmeiro	2.00
239	Russell Branyan	1.00
240	Ken Griffey Jr.	15.00
241	Cecil Fielder	1.00
242	Chuck Finley	1.00
243	Jay Bell	1.00
244	Andy Benes	1.00
245	Matt Williams	1.50
246	Brian Anderson	1.00
247	David Dellucci	1.00
248	Andres Galarraga	2.00
249	Andruw Jones	2.50
250	Greg Maddux	6.00
251	Brady Anderson	1.00
252	Joe Carter	1.00
253	Eric Davis	1.00
254	Pedro J. Martinez	2.50
255	Nomar Garciaparra	6.00
256	Dennis Eckersley	1.00
257	Henry Rodriguez	1.00
258	Jeff Blauser	1.00
259	Jaime Navarro	1.00
260	Ray Durham	1.00
261	Chris Stynes	1.00
262	Willie Greene	1.00
263	Reggie Sanders	1.00
264	Bret Boone	1.00
265	Barry Larkin	1.50
266	Travis Fryman	1.00
267	Charles Nagy	1.00
268	Sandy Alomar Jr.	1.00
269	Darryl Kile	1.00
270	Mike Lansing	1.00
271	Pedro Astacio	1.00
272	Damion Easley	1.00
273	Joe Randa	1.00
274	Luis Gonzalez	1.00
275	Mike Piazza	6.00
276	Todd Zeile	1.00
277	Edgar Renteria	1.00
278	Livan Hernandez	1.00
279	Cliff Floyd	1.00
280	Moises Alou	1.50
281	Billy Wagner	1.00
282	Jeff King	1.00
283	Hal Morris	1.00
284	Johnny Damon	1.00
285	Dean Palmer	1.00
286	Tim Belcher	1.00
287	Eric Young	1.00
288	Bobby Bonilla	1.00
289	Gary Sheffield	1.50
290	Chan Ho Park	1.50
291	Charles Johnson	1.00
292	Jeff Cirillo	1.00
293	Jeromy Burnitz	1.00
294	Jose Valentin	1.00
295	Marquis Grissom	1.00
296	Todd Walker	1.00
297	Terry Steinbach	1.00
298	Rick Aguilera	1.00
299	Vladimir Guerrero	3.00
300	Rey Ordonez	1.00
301	Butch Huskey	1.00
302	Bernard Gilkey	1.00
303	Mariano Rivera	1.50
304	Chuck Knoblauch	1.50
305	Derek Jeter	5.00
306	Ricky Bottalico	1.00
307	Bob Abreu	1.00
308	Scott Rolen	3.00
309	Al Martin	1.00
310	Jason Kendall	1.00
311	Brian Jordan	1.00
312	Ron Gant	1.00
313	Todd Stottlemyre	1.00
314	Greg Vaughn	1.00
315	J. Kevin Brown	1.00
316	Wally Joyner	1.00
317	Robb Nen	1.00
318	Orel Hershiser	1.00
319	Russ Davis	1.00
320	Randy Johnson	2.00
321	Quinton McCracken	1.00
322	Tony Saunders	1.00
323	Wilson Alvarez	1.00
324	Wade Boggs	1.50
325	Fred McGriff	1.50
326	Lee Stevens	1.00
327	John Wetteland	1.00
328	Jose Canseco	1.50
329	Randy Myers	1.00
330	Jose Cruz Jr.	2.00

331	Matt Williams	3.00
332	Andres Galarraga	4.00
333	Walt Weiss	2.50
334	Joe Carter	2.50
335	Pedro J. Martinez	5.00
336	Henry Rodriguez	2.50
337	Travis Fryman	2.50
338	Darryl Kile	2.50
339	Mike Lansing	2.50
340	Mike Piazza	12.00
341	Moises Alou	3.00
342	Charles Johnson	2.50
343	Chuck Knoblauch	4.00
344	Rickey Henderson	2.50
345	J. Kevin Brown	3.00
346	Orel Hershiser	2.50
347	Wade Boggs	3.00
348	Fred McGriff	3.00
349	Jose Canseco	3.00
350	Gary Sheffield	3.00
351	Travis Lee	8.00
352	Nomar Garciaparra	25.00
353	Frank Thomas	15.00
354	Cal Ripken Jr.	30.00
355	Mark McGwire	45.00
356	Mike Piazza	25.00
357	Alex Rodriguez	35.00
358	Barry Bonds	10.00
359	Tony Gwynn	20.00
360	Ken Griffey Jr.	45.00

1998 SPx Finite Home Run Hysteria

Home Run Hysteria is a 10-card insert in SPx Finite Series Two. The cards were sequentially numbered to 62.

		MT
Complete Set (10):		900.00
Common Player:		75.00
Production 62 sets		
HR1	Ken Griffey Jr.	250.00
HR2	Mark McGwire	250.00
HR3	Sammy Sosa	175.00
HR4	Albert Belle	60.00
HR5	Alex Rodriguez	175.00
HR6	Greg Vaughn	40.00
HR7	Andres Galarraga	50.00
HR8	Vinny Castilla	40.00
HR9	Juan Gonzalez	60.00
HR10	Chipper Jones	150.00

1998 SPx Finite Radiance Cornerstones

Radiance Cornerstones of the Game is a parallel of the 10-card subset. The cards have two images of the player on the front and are numbered to 100.

		MT
Common Player (100 sets):		15.00
351	Travis Lee	20.00
352	Nomar Garciaparra	100.00
353	Frank Thomas	75.00
354	Cal Ripken Jr.	140.00
355	Mark McGwire	175.00
356	Mike Piazza	100.00
357	Alex Rodriguez	140.00
358	Barry Bonds	40.00
359	Tony Gwynn	75.00
360	Ken Griffey Jr.	175.00

1998 SPx Finite Radiance Heroes of the Game

Radiance Heroes of the Game is a parallel of the 10-card subset. The cards have a horizontal layout and are numbered to 100.

		MT
Common Player:		40.00
Production 100 sets		
171	Greg Maddux	90.00
172	Cal Ripken Jr.	140.00
173	Frank Thomas	60.00
174	Jeff Bagwell	50.00
175	Mike Piazza	100.00
176	Mark McGwire	175.00
177	Barry Bonds	40.00
178	Ken Griffey Jr.	175.00
179	Alex Rodriguez	140.00
180	Roger Clemens	60.00

1998 SPx Finite Spectrum Power Explosion

Spectrum Power Explosion is a parallel of the 20-card subset in Series One. The horizontal cards have two images of the player and are numbered to 50.

		MT
Common Player:		40.00
Semistars:		75.00
Production 50 sets		
31	Mike Piazza	200.00
32	Tony Clark	40.00
33	Larry Walker	60.00
34	Jim Thome	30.00
35	Juan Gonzalez	200.00
36	Jeff Bagwell	75.00
37	Jay Buhner	30.00
38	Tim Salmon	30.00
39	Albert Belle	50.00
40	Mark McGwire	300.00
41	Sammy Sosa	200.00
42	Mo Vaughn	40.00
43	Manny Ramirez	75.00
44	Tino Martinez	40.00
45	Frank Thomas	100.00
46	Nomar Garciaparra	200.00
47	Alex Rodriguez	250.00
48	Chipper Jones	200.00
49	Barry Bonds	75.00
50	Ken Griffey Jr.	300.00

1998 SPx Finite Spectrum Tradewinds

Spectrum Tradewinds is a parallel of the 20-card subset in Series Two. The horizontal cards have two images of the player and are numbered to 50.

		MT
Common Player (50 sets):		30.00
331	Matt Williams	45.00
332	Andres Galarraga	50.00
333	Walt Weiss	30.00
334	Joe Carter	40.00
335	Pedro J. Martinez	100.00
336	Henry Rodriguez	30.00
337	Travis Fryman	30.00
338	Darryl Kile	30.00
339	Mike Lansing	30.00
340	Mike Piazza	200.00
341	Moises Alou	40.00
342	Charles Johnson	30.00
343	Chuck Knoblauch	45.00
344	Rickey Henderson	60.00
345	Kevin Brown	40.00
346	Orel Hershiser	30.00
347	Wade Boggs	60.00
348	Fred McGriff	60.00
349	Jose Canseco	75.00
350	Gary Sheffield	40.00

1999 SP Authentic Sample

UD spokesman Ken Griffey Jr. is featured on the promo card for '99 SP Authentic. In the same format as the issued version, the sample card has different photos on front and back, a different season summary on back and a large, black "SAMPLE" overprint on back.

		MT
1	Ken Griffey Jr.	6.00

1999 SP Authentic

SP Authentic Baseball was a 135-card set that sold in packs of 5 cards for $4.99 per pack. The set included a 30-card Future Watch subset and a 15-card Season to Remember subset. Both subsets were shorted-printed, with each card sequentially numbered to 2,700. The insert lineup included Ernie Banks 500 Club 'Piece of History' Bat cards. Each card features a piece of a Ernie Banks game-used bat. Only 350 of the cards were produced. Fourteen more of the cards were produced and autographed by Ernie Banks. Other insert sets included SP Chirography, The Home Run Chronicles, Epic Figures, Reflections, and SP Authentics.

		MT
Complete Set (135):		275.00
Common Player (1-90):		.25
Common Future Watch (91-120):		4.00
Production 2,700 sets		
Common Season to Remember (121-135):		4.00
Production 2,700 sets		
Pack (5):		4.00
Wax Box (24):		90.00
1	Mo Vaughn	.50
2	Jim Edmonds	.40
3	Darin Erstad	1.00
4	Travis Lee	.25
5	Matt Williams	.40
6	Randy Johnson	1.00
7	Chipper Jones	2.00
8	Greg Maddux	2.00
9	Andruw Jones	1.00
10	Andres Galarraga	.40
11	Tom Glavine	.40
12	Cal Ripken Jr.	3.00
13	Brady Anderson	.25
14	Albert Belle	.50
15	Nomar Garciaparra	2.50
16	Donnie Sadler	.25
17	Pedro Martinez	1.00
18	Sammy Sosa	2.50
19	Kerry Wood	.40
20	Mark Grace	.40
21	Mike Caruso	.25
22	Frank Thomas	1.50
23	Paul Konerko	.30
24	Sean Casey	.35
25	Barry Larkin	.40
26	Kenny Lofton	.50
27	Manny Ramirez	1.00
28	Jim Thome	.50
29	Bartolo Colon	.25
30	Jaret Wright	.25
31	Larry Walker	.50
32	Todd Helton	1.00
33	Tony Clark	.30
34	Dean Palmer	.25
35	Mark Kotsay	.25
36	Cliff Floyd	.25
37	Ken Caminiti	.25
38	Craig Biggio	.30
39	Jeff Bagwell	1.00
40	Moises Alou	.25
41	Johnny Damon	.25
42	Larry Sutton	.25
43	Kevin Brown	.35
44	Gary Sheffield	.35
45	Raul Mondesi	.40
46	Jeromy Burnitz	.25
47	Jeff Cirillo	.25
48	Todd Walker	.25
49	David Ortiz	.25
50	Brad Radtke	.25
51	Vladimir Guerrero	1.50
52	Rondell White	.35
53	Brad Fullmer	.25
54	Mike Piazza	2.50
55	Robin Ventura	.25
56	John Olerud	.40
57	Derek Jeter	3.00
58	Tino Martinez	.30
59	Bernie Williams	.75
60	Roger Clemens	1.50
61	Ben Grieve	.40
62	Miguel Tejada	.25
63	A.J. Hinch	.25

64	Scott Rolen	.75
65	Curt Schilling	.35
66	Doug Glanville	.25
67	Aramis Ramirez	.25
68	Tony Womack	.25
69	Jason Kendall	.25
70	Tony Gwynn	1.50
71	Wally Joyner	.25
72	Greg Vaughn	.35
73	Barry Bonds	1.00
74	Ellis Burks	.25
75	Jeff Kent	.25
76	Ken Griffey Jr.	3.00
77	Alex Rodriguez	3.00
78	Edgar Martinez	.25
79	Mark McGwire	4.00
80	Eli Marrero	.25
81	Matt Morris	.25
82	Rolando Arrojo	.25
83	Quinton McCracken	.25
84	Jose Canseco	.75
85	Ivan Rodriguez	1.00
86	Juan Gonzalez	1.00
87	Royce Clayton	.25
88	Shawn Green	.50
89	Jose Cruz Jr.	.25
90	Carlos Delgado	.75
91	Troy Glaus (Future Watch)	30.00
92	George Lombard (Future Watch)	4.00
93	Ryan Minor (Future Watch)	8.00
94	Calvin Pickering (Future Watch)	4.00
95	Jin Ho Cho (Future Watch)	8.00
96	Russ Branyon (Future Watch)	4.00
97	Derrick Gibson (Future Watch)	6.00
98	Gabe Kapler (Future Watch)	10.00
99	Matt Anderson (Future Watch)	6.00
100	Preston Wilson (Future Watch)	5.00
101	Alex Gonzalez (Future Watch)	6.00
102	Carlos Beltran (Future Watch)	4.00
103	Dee Brown (Future Watch)	4.00
104	Jeremy Giambi (Future Watch)	8.00
105	Angel Pena (Future Watch)	8.00
106	Geoff Jenkins (Future Watch)	6.00
107	Corey Koskie (Future Watch)	6.00
108	A.J. Pierzynski (Future Watch)	4.00
109	Michael Barrett (Future Watch)	8.00
110	Fernando Seguignol (Future Watch)	8.00
111	Mike Kinkade (Future Watch)	4.00
112	Ricky Ledee (Future Watch)	8.00
113	Mike Lowell (Future Watch)	6.00
114	Eric Chavez (Future Watch)	10.00
115	Matt Clement (Future Watch)	8.00
116	Shane Monahan (Future Watch)	8.00
117	J.D. Drew (Future Watch)	15.00
118	Bubba Trammell (Future Watch)	4.00
119	Kevin Witt (Future Watch)	6.00
120	Roy Halladay (Future Watch)	8.00
121	Mark McGwire (Season to Remember)	25.00
122	Mark McGwire, Sammy Sosa (Season to Remember)	20.00
123	Sammy Sosa (Season to Remember)	15.00
124	Ken Griffey Jr. (Season to Remember)	20.00
125	Cal Ripken Jr. (Season to Remember)	20.00
126	Juan Gonzalez (Season to Remember)	6.00
127	Kerry Wood (Season to Remember)	4.00
128	Trevor Hoffman (Season to Remember)	4.00
129	Barry Bonds (Season to Remember)	8.00
130	Alex Rodriguez (Season to Remember)	20.00
131	Ben Grieve (Season to Remember)	8.00
132	Tom Glavine (Season to Remember)	4.00
133	David Wells (Season to Remember)	4.00
134	Mike Piazza (Season to Remember)	15.00
135	Scott Brosius (Season to Remember)	4.00

1999 SP Authentic Chirography

Baseball's top players and future stars are included in this 39-card autograph insert set. The set was split into Level 1 and Level 2 versions. Level cards are not numbered, and were inserted one card per 24 packs. Level 2 cards are sequentially numbered to the featured player's jersey number.

		MT
Complete Set (39):		1850.
Common Player:		15.00
Inserted 1:24		
EC	Eric Chavez	40.00
GK	Gabe Kapler	75.00
GMj	Gary Matthews Jr.	25.00
CP	Calvin Pickering	25.00
CK	Corey Koskie	25.00
SM	Shane Monahan	20.00
RH	Richard Hidalgo	20.00
MK	Mike Kinkade	25.00
CB	Carlos Beltran	15.00
AG	Alex Gonzalez	25.00
BC	Bruce Chen	20.00
MA	Matt Anderson	25.00
RM	Ryan Minor	25.00
RL	Ricky Ledee	35.00
RR	Ruben Rivera	20.00
BF	Brad Fullmer	30.00
RB	Russ Branyon	20.00
ML	Mike Lowell	20.00
JG	Jeremy Giambi	50.00
GL	George Lombard	20.00
KW	Kevin Witt	25.00
TW	Todd Walker	25.00
SR	Scott Rolen	75.00
KW	Kerry Wood	50.00
BG	Ben Grieve	50.00
JR	Ken Griffey Jr.	300.00
CJ	Chipper Jones	150.00
IR	Ivan Rodriguez	75.00
TGl	Troy Glaus	50.00
TL	Travis Lee	50.00
VG	Vladimir Guerrero	75.00
GV	Greg Vaughn	20.00
JT	Jim Thome	25.00
JD	J.D. Drew	25.00
TH	Todd Helton	40.00
GM	Greg Maddux	200.00
NG	Nomar Garciaparra	175.00
TG	Tony Gwynn	125.00
CR	Cal Ripken Jr.	250.00

1999 SP Authentic Chirography Gold

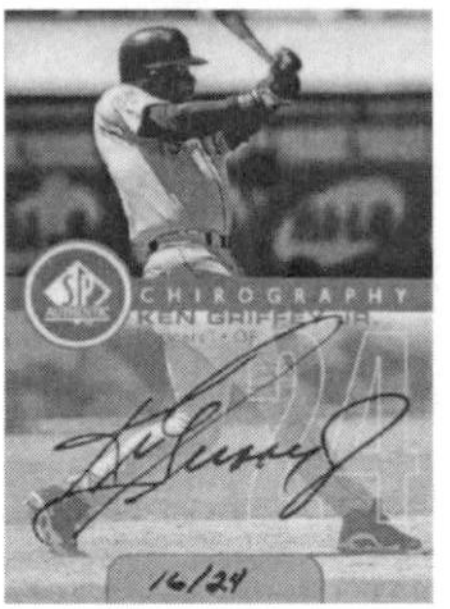

These Chirography parallels and can be identified by the gold tint on the card front and their sequential numbering; each featured player signed to his jersey number.

		MT
Common Player:		20.00
Inserted 1:24		
EC	Eric Chavez (30)	90.00
GK	Gabe Kapler (51)	40.00
GMj	Gary Matthews Jr. (68)	15.00
CP	Calvin Pickering (6)	150.00
CK	Corey Koskie (47)	25.00
SM	Shane Monahan (12)	60.00
RH	Richard Hidalgo (15)	75.00
MK	Mike Kinkade (33)	40.00
CB	Carlos Beltran (36)	60.00
AG	Alex Gonzalez (22)	50.00
BC	Bruce Chen (48)	45.00
MA	Matt Anderson (14)	50.00
RM	Ryan Minor (10)	150.00
RL	Ricky Ledee (38)	60.00
RR	Ruben Rivera (28)	40.00
BF	Brad Fullmer (20)	60.00
RB	Russ Branyon (66)	30.00
ML	Mike Lowell (60)	25.00
JG	Jeremy Giambi (15)	100.00
GL	George Lombard (26)	60.00
KW	Kevin Witt (6)	150.00
TW	Todd Walker (12)	100.00
SR	Scott Rolen (17)	250.00
KW	Kerry Wood (34)	60.00
BG	Ben Grieve (14)	125.00
JR	Ken Griffey Jr. (24)	1100.
CJ	Chipper Jones (10)	400.00
IR	Ivan Rodriguez (7)	250.00
TGl	Troy Glaus (14)	150.00
TL	Travis Lee (16)	75.00
VG	Vladimir Guerrero (27)	125.00
GV	Greg Vaughn (23)	40.00
JT	Jim Thome (25)	100.00
JD	J.D. Drew (8)	250.00
TH	Todd Helton (17)	160.00
GM	Greg Maddux (31)	400.00
NG	Nomar Garciaparra (5)	750.00
TG	Tony Gwynn (19)	500.00
CR	Cal Ripken Jr. (8)	1500.

1999 SP Authentic Epic Figures

This 30-card set highlights baseball's biggest talents, including Mark McGwire and Derek Jeter. The card fronts have two photos, with the larger photo done with a shadow look in the background. Fronts also feature a holographic look, while the card backs feature the player's career highlights. These are seeded one per seven packs.

		MT
Complete Set (30):		150.00
Common Player:		1.50
Inserted 1:7		
E01	Mo Vaughn	2.00
E02	Travis Lee	3.00
E03	Andres Galarraga	2.00
E04	Andruw Jones	5.00
E05	Chipper Jones	12.00
E06	Greg Maddux	12.00
E07	Cal Ripken Jr.	15.00
E08	Nomar Garciaparra	12.00
E09	Sammy Sosa	12.00
E10	Frank Thomas	10.00
E11	Kerry Wood	8.00
E12	Kenny Lofton	2.00
E13	Manny Ramirez	8.00

E14	Larry Walker	3.00
E15	Jeff Bagwell	5.00
E16	Paul Molitor	4.00
E17	Vladimir Guerrero	10.00
E18	Derek Jeter	12.00
E19	Tino Martinez	1.50
E20	Mike Piazza	12.00
E21	Ben Grieve	2.00
E22	Scott Rolen	4.00
E23	Mark McGwire	25.00
E24	Tony Gwynn	10.00
E25	Barry Bonds	5.00
E26	Ken Griffey Jr.	25.00
E27	Alex Rodriguez	20.00
E28	J.D. Drew	2.00
E29	Juan Gonzalez	10.00
E30	Kevin Brown	1.50

1999 SP Authentic Home Run Chronicles

This two-tiered 70-card set focuses on the amazing seasons of McGwire, Sosa and Griffey Jr. Other players help round out the 70-card set, but special emphasis has been placed on the trio. These are seeded one per pack. A die-cut version also exists, with each card serially numbered to 70.

	MT
Complete Set (70):	140.00
Common Player:	.50
Inserted 1:1	
Production 70 sets	
HR01Mark McGwire	10.00
HR02Sammy Sosa	2.00
HR03Ken Griffey Jr.	3.00
HR04Mark McGwire	4.00
HR05Mark McGwire	4.00
HR06Albert Belle	.75
HR07Jose Canseco	.50
HR08Juan Gonzalez	1.50
HR09Manny Ramirez	1.00
HR10Rafael Palmeiro	.50
HR11Mo Vaughn	.50
HR12Carlos Delgado	.50
HR13Nomar Garciaparra	2.00
HR14Barry Bonds	.75
HR15Alex Rodriguez	2.50
HR16Tony Clark	.50
HR17Jim Thome	.50
HR18Edgar Martinez	.50
HR19Frank Thomas	2.00
HR20Greg Vaughn	.50
HR21Vinny Castilla	.50
HR22Andres Galarraga	.50
HR23Moises Alou	.50
HR24Jeromy Burnitz	.50
HR25Vladimir Guerrero	1.00
HR26Jeff Bagwell	.75
HR27Chipper Jones	1.50
HR28Javier Lopez	.50
HR29Mike Piazza	2.00
HR30Andruw Jones	.75
HR31Henry Rodriguez	.50
HR32Jeff Kent	.50
HR33Ray Lankford	.50
HR34Scott Rolen	.75
HR35Raul Mondesi	.50
HR36Ken Caminiti	.50
HR37J.D. Drew	.75
HR38Troy Glaus	1.00
HR39Gabe Kapler	1.00
HR40Alex Rodriguez	2.50
HR41Ken Griffey Jr.	3.00
HR42Sammy Sosa	2.00
HR43Mark McGwire	4.00
HR44Sammy Sosa	2.00
HR45Mark McGwire	4.00
HR46Vinny Castilla	.50
HR47Sammy Sosa	2.00
HR48Mark McGwire	4.00
HR49Sammy Sosa	2.00
HR50Greg Vaughn	.50
HR51Sammy Sosa	2.00
HR52Mark McGwire	4.00
HR53Sammy Sosa	2.00
HR54Mark McGwire	4.00
HR55Sammy Sosa	2.00
HR56Ken Griffey Jr.	3.00
HR57Sammy Sosa	2.00
HR58Mark McGwire	4.00
HR59Sammy Sosa	2.00
HR60Mark McGwire	4.00
HR61Mark McGwire	10.00
HR62Mark McGwire	12.00
HR63Mark McGwire	4.00
HR64Mark McGwire	4.00
HR65Mark McGwire	4.00
HR66Sammy Sosa	10.00
HR67Mark McGwire	4.00
HR68Mark McGwire	4.00
HR69Mark McGwire	4.00
HR70Mark McGwire	20.00

1999 SP Authentic Home Run Chronicles Die-Cuts

Each of the 70 cards in the Home Run Chronicles insert set was also issued in a die-cut version. The die-cuts share the basic front and back design of the regular HR Chronicle cards but have portions of the upper-left and lower-right cut away. On back, each of the die-cuts features an ink-jetted serial number from within an edition of 70.

	MT
Complete Die-Cut Set (70):	1750.
HR Chronicle Die-Cuts:	15X

(See 1999 SP Authentics Home Run Chronicles for checklist, base values.)

1999 SP Authentic Reflections

Dot Matrix technology is utilized to provide a unique look at 30 of the best players in the game. Card fronts are horizontal with two small and one large photo. These are seeded 1:23 packs.

		MT
Complete Set (30):		375.00
Common Player:		2.50
Inserted 1:23		
R01	Mo Vaughn	2.50
R02	Travis Lee	4.00
R03	Andres Galarraga	3.50
R04	Andruw Jones	6.00
R05	Chipper Jones	12.00
R06	Greg Maddux	12.00
R07	Cal Ripken Jr.	20.00
R08	Nomar Garciaparra	15.00
R09	Sammy Sosa	15.00
R10	Frank Thomas	8.00
R11	Kerry Wood	4.00
R12	Kenny Lofton	2.50
R13	Manny Ramirez	6.00
R14	Larry Walker	3.50
R15	Jeff Bagwell	6.00
R16	Paul Molitor	4.00
R17	Vladimir Guerrero	8.00
R18	Derek Jeter	15.00
R19	Tino Martinez	2.50
R20	Mike Piazza	15.00
R21	Ben Grieve	4.00
R22	Scott Rolen	6.00
R23	Mark McGwire	25.00
R24	Tony Gwynn	8.00
R25	Barry Bonds	6.00
R26	Ken Griffey Jr.	20.00
R27	Alex Rodriguez	20.00
R28	J.D. Drew	3.00
R29	Juan Gonzalez	6.00
R30	Roger Clemens	9.00

1999 SP Authentic SP Authentics

These 1:864 pack inserts are redemption cards that could be redeemed for special pieces of memorabilia from either Ken Griffey Jr. or Mark McGwire. The redemption period ended March 1, 2000. Because of rarity any surviving unredeemed McGwire home run-game autographed tickets cannot be valued.

		MT
Complete Set (8):		600.00
Common Card:		25.00
(1)	Ken Griffey Jr. (autographed baseball) (75)	150.00
(2)	Ken Griffey Jr. (glove) (200)	50.00
(3)	Ken Griffey Jr. (home run cel card) (346)	25.00
(4)	Ken Griffey Jr. (autographed jersey) (25)	
(5)	Ken Griffey Jr. (autographed mini-helmet) (75)	150.00
(6)	Ken Griffey Jr. (Sports Illustrated Cover) (200)	25.00
(7)	Ken Griffey Jr. (autographed SI cover) (75)	150.00
(8)	Ken Griffey Jr. (standee) (300)	25.00
(9)	Mark McGwire (autographed 62HR ticket) (1)	
(10)	Mark McGwire (autographed 70HR ticket) (3)	

1999 SP Authentic 500 Club Piece of History

These cards feature a piece of game-used bat once swung by Ernie Banks. Approximately 350 cards exist. An autographed version of this card also exists, only 14 were produced.

		MT
		225.00
EB	Ernie Banks	250.00
EB	Ernie Banks Auto./14	650.00

1999 SP Signature Edition

		MT
Complete Set (180):		180.00
Common Player:		.50
Wax Box:		280.00
1	Nomar Garciaparra	5.00
2	Ken Griffey Jr.	8.00
3	J.D. Drew	.50
4	Alex Rodriguez	6.00
5	Juan Gonzalez	2.00
6	Mo Vaughn	1.00
7	Greg Maddux	5.00
8	Chipper Jones	5.00
9	Frank Thomas	2.00
10	Vladimir Guerrero	3.00
11	Mike Piazza	5.00
12	Eric Chavez	.75
13	Tony Gwynn	4.00
14	Orlando Hernandez	1.50
15	*Pat Burrell*	20.00
16	Darin Erstad	1.50
17	Greg Vaughn	.75
18	Russ Branyan	.50
19	Gabe Kapler	1.50
20	Craig Biggio	1.50
21	Troy Glaus	2.50
22	Pedro J. Martinez	1.00
23	Carlos Beltran	2.00
24	Derrek Lee	.50
25	Manny Ramirez	2.50
26	*Shea Hillenbrand*	2.00
27	Carlos Lee	.50
28	Angel Pena	.50

29	Rafael Roque	1.00
30	Octavio Dotel	.50
31	Jeromy Burnitz	.50
32	Jeremy Giambi	.50
33	Andruw Jones	1.50
34	Todd Helton	2.00
35	Scott Rolen	2.00
36	Jason Kendall	.50
37	Trevor Hoffman	.50
38	Barry Bonds	2.00
39	Ivan Rodriguez	2.00
40	Roy Halladay	.50
41	Rickey Henderson	1.00
42	Ryan Minor	.75
43	Brian Jordan	.50
44	Alex Gonzalez	.50
45	Raul Mondesi	.75
46	Corey Koskie	.50
47	Paul O'Neill	.75
48	Todd Walker	.50
49	Carlos Febles	1.00
50	Travis Fryman	.50
51	Albert Belle	2.00
52	Travis Lee	1.00
53	Bruce Chen	.50
54	Reggie Taylor	.50
55	Jerry Hairston Jr.	.50
56	Carlos Guillen	.50
57	Michael Barrett	.75
58	Jason Conti	.50
59	Joe Lawrence	.50
60	Jeff Cirillo	.50
61	Juan Melo	.50
62	Chad Hermansen	.50
63	Ruben Mateo	1.50
64	Ben Davis	.50
65	Mike Caruso	.50
66	Jason Giambi	.50
67	Jose Canseco	1.00
68	*Chad Hutchinson*	5.00
69	Mitch Meluskey	.50
70	Adrian Beltre	1.50
71	Mark Kotsay	.50
72	Juan Encarnacion	.50
73	Dermal Brown	.50
74	Kevin Witt	.50
75	Vinny Castilla	.50
76	Aramis Ramirez	.50
77	Marlon Anderson	.50
78	Mike Kinkade	.50
79	Kevin Barker	.50
80	Ron Belliard	.50
81	Chris Haas	.50
82	Bob Henley	.50
83	Fernando Seguignol	.50
84	Damon Minor	.50
85	*A.J. Burnett*	2.00
86	Calvin Pickering	.50
87	Mike Darr	.50
88	Cesar King	.50
89	Rob Bell	.50
90	Derrick Gibson	.50
91	*Ober Moreno*	1.50
92	Robert Fick	.50
93	*Doug Mientkiewicz*	1.50
94	A.J. Pierzynski	.50
95	Orlando Palmeiro	.50
96	Sidney Ponson	.50
97	*Ivanon Coffie*	.50
98	*Juan Pena*	1.00
99	Mark Karchner	1.50
100	Carlos Castillo	.50
101	Bryan Ward	1.00
102	Mario Valdez	.50
103	Billy Wagner	.50
104	Miguel Tejada	.75
105	Jose Cruz Jr.	.50
106	George Lombard	.50
107	Geoff Jenkins	.50
108	Ray Lankford	.50
109	Todd Stottlemyre	.50
110	Mike Lowell	.50
111	Matt Clement	.50
112	Scott Brosius	.50
113	Preston Wilson	.50
114	Bartolo Colon	.50
115	Rolando Arrojo	.50
116	Jose Guillen	.50
117	Ron Gant	.50
118	Ricky Ledee	.60
119	Carlos Delgado	1.50
120	Abraham Nunez	.50
121	John Olerud	1.00
122	Chan Ho Park	.75
123	Brad Radke	.50
124	Al Leiter	.50
125	Gary Matthews Jr.	.50
126	F.P. Santangelo	.50
127	Brad Fullmer	.50
128	Matt Anderson	.50
129	A.J. Hinch	.50
130	Sterling Hitchcock	.50
131	Edgar Martinez	.50
132	Fernando Tatis	1.00
133	Bobby Smith	.50
134	Paul Konerko	.75
135	Sean Casey	1.00
136	Donnie Sadler	.50
137	Denny Neagle	.50
138	Sandy Alomar	.50
139	Mariano Rivera	.75
140	Emil Brown	.50
141	J.T. Snow	.50
142	Eli Marrero	.50
143	Rusty Greer	.50
144	Johnny Damon	.50
145	Damion Easley	.50
146	Eric Milton	.50
147	Rico Brogna	.50
148	Ray Durham	.50
149	Wally Joyner	.50
150	Royce Clayton	.50
151	David Ortiz	.50
152	Wade Boggs	1.25
153	Ugueth Urbina	.50
154	Richard Hidalgo	.50
155	Bobby Abreu	.50
156	Robb Nen	.50
157	David Segui	.50
158	Sean Berry	.50
159	Kevin Tapani	.50
160	Jason Varitek	.50
161	Fernando Vina	.50
162	Jim Leyritz	.50
163	Enrique Wilson	.50
164	Jim Parque	.50
165	Doug Glanville	.50
166	Jesus Sanchez	.50
167	Nolan Ryan	6.00
168	Robin Yount	2.00
169	Stan Musial	4.00
170	Tom Seaver	2.00
171	Mike Schmidt	2.50
172	Willie Stargell	1.00
173	Rollie Fingers	.75
174	Willie McCovey	.75
175	Harmon Killebrew	1.00
176	Eddie Mathews	1.00
177	Reggie Jackson	2.50
178	Frank Robinson	2.00
179	Ken Griffey Sr.	.50
180	Eddie Murray	1.50

1999 SP Signature Edition Autographs

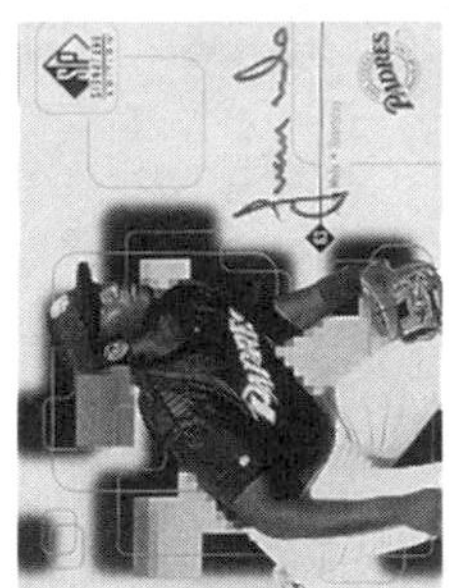

Authentically autographed cards of nearly 100 current stars, top prospects and Hall of Famers were featured as one-per-pack inserts in SP Signature Edition. Some players did not return their signed cards in time for pack inclusion and had to be obtained by returning an exchange card prior to the May 12, 2000, deadline.

		MT
	Common Player:	8.00
	Inserted 1:1	
BA	Bobby Abreu	15.00
SA	Sandy Alomar	10.00
MA	Marlon Anderson	8.00
KB	Kevin Barker	8.00
MB	Michael Barrett	8.00
RoB	Rob Bell	8.00
AB	Albert Belle	30.00
RBe	Ron Belliard	8.00
CBe	Carlos Beltran	10.00
ABe	Adrian Beltre	15.00
BB	Barry Bonds	75.00
RB	Russ Branyan	8.00
SB	Scott Brosius	8.00
DB	Dermal Brown	8.00
EB	Emil Brown	8.00
AJB	A.J. Burnett (exchange card)	15.00
AJB	A.J. Burnett (autographed)	20.00
PB	Pat Burrell	40.00
JoC	Jose Canseco	90.00
MC	Mike Caruso	8.00
SC	Sean Casey (exchange card)	8.00
SC	Sean Casey (autographed)	25.00
VC	Vinny Castilla (exchange card)	10.00
VC	Vinny Castilla (autographed)	15.00
CC	Carlos Castillo	8.00
EC	Eric Chavez	20.00
BC	Bruce Chen	12.00
JCi	Jeff Cirillo	8.00
RC	Royce Clayton	8.00
MCl	Matt Clement	8.00
IC	Ivanon Coffie	8.00
BCo	Bartolo Colon (exchange card)	12.00
BCo	Bartolo Colon (autographed)	15.00
JC	Jason Conti	8.00
JDa	Johnny Damon	12.00
BD	Ben Davis	8.00
CD	Carlos Delgado	30.00
OD	Octavio Dotel	12.00
JD	J.D. Drew	25.00
RD	Ray Durham	8.00
DEa	Damion Easley	8.00
JE	Juan Encarnacion	12.00
DE	Darin Erstad	25.00
CF	Carlos Febles	10.00
Rob	Robert Fick	8.00
Rol	Rollie Fingers	20.00
BF	Brad Fullmer	15.00
RGa	Ron Gant	15.00
NG	Nomar Garciaparra	120.00
JaG	Jason Giambi	25.00
DG	Derrick Gibson	8.00
DGl	Doug Glanville	8.00
TGl	Troy Glaus	30.00
AG	Alex Gonzalez	8.00
RGr	Rusty Greer	8.00
Jr.	Ken Griffey Jr.	225.00
Sr.	Ken Griffey Sr.	20.00
VG	Vladimir Guerrero	60.00
JG	Jose Guillen	12.00
TG	Tony Gwynn	80.00
CHa	Chris Haas	8.00
JHj	Jerry Hairston Jr.	8.00
RH	Roy Halladay	12.00
THe	Todd Helton	30.00
BH	Bob Henley	8.00
ED	Orlando Hernandez	40.00
CH	Chad Hermansen	15.00
ShH	Shea Hillenbrand	8.00
StH	Sterling Hitchcock	8.00
THo	Trevor Hoffman	12.00
CHu	Chad Hutchinson	15.00
RJ	Reggie Jackson	100.00
GJ	Geoff Jenkins	15.00
AJ	Andruw Jones	35.00
CJ	Chipper Jones	80.00
WJ	Wally Joyner	15.00
GK	Gabe Kapler	15.00
MKa	Mark Karchner	8.00
JK	Jason Kendall	15.00
HK	Harmon Killebrew	40.00
CKi	Cesar King	8.00
MKi	Mike Kinkade	8.00
PK	Paul Konerko	12.00
CK	Corey Koskie	12.00
MK	Mark Kotsay	12.00
RL	Ray Lankford	15.00
JLa	Joe Lawrence	8.00
CL	Carlos Lee	20.00
DL	Derrek Lee	8.00
AL	Al Leiter	12.00
JLe	Jim Leyritz	8.00
GL	George Lombard	8.00
GM	Greg Maddux	120.00
Eli	Eli Marrero	8.00
EM	Edgar Martinez	10.00
PM	Pedro J. Martinez (exchange card)	8.00
PM	Pedro J. Martinez (autographed)	140.00
RMa	Ruben Mateo (exchange card)	8.00
RMa	Ruben Mateo (autographed)	20.00
EMa	Eddie Mathews	40.00
GMj	Gary Matthews Jr.	12.00
WMc	Willie McCovey	40.00
JM	Juan Melo	8.00
MMe	Mitch Meluskey	8.00
DoM	Doug Mientkiewicz	8.00
EMi	Eric Milton	8.00
DaM	Damon Minor	8.00
RM	Ryan Minor	8.00
EMu	Eddie Murray	40.00
SM	Stan Musial	100.00
RN	Robb Nen	8.00
AN	Abraham Nunez	8.00
JO	John Olerud	20.00
PO	Paul O'Neill	20.00
DO	David Ortiz	8.00
OP	Orlando Palmeiro	8.00
JP	Jim Parque	8.00
AP	Angel Pena	8.00
MP	Mike Piazza (exchange card)	8.00
MP	Mike Piazza (autographed)	140.00
CP	Calvin Pickering	12.00
AJP	A.J. Pierzynski	8.00
SP	Sidney Ponson	8.00
BR	Brad Radke	8.00
ARa	Aramis Ramirez	8.00
MR	Manny Ramirez	50.00
MRi	Mariano Rivera	20.00
FR	Frank Robinson	30.00
AR	Alex Rodriguez	200.00
PG	Ivan Rodriguez	60.00
SR	Scott Rolen (exchange card)	8.00
SR	Scott Rolen (autographed)	30.00
RR	Rafael Roque	8.00
NR	Nolan Ryan	160.00
DS	Donnie Sadler	8.00
JS	Jesus Sanchez	8.00
MS	Mike Schmidt	75.00
TSe	Tom Seaver	75.00
DSe	David Segui	8.00
FS	Fernando Seguignol	8.00
BS	Bobby Smith	8.00
JT	J.T. Snow (exchange card)	8.00
JT	J.T. Snow (autographed)	12.00
POP	Willie Stargell (exchange card)	8.00
POP	Willie Stargell (autographed)	30.00
TSt	Todd Stottlemyre	12.00
FTa	Fernando Tatis	15.00
RT	Reggie Taylor	8.00
MT	Miguel Tejada	25.00
FT	Frank Thomas	80.00
MV	Mario Valdez	8.00
JV	Jason Varitek	8.00
GV	Greg Vaughn	15.00
MO	Mo Vaughn	30.00
FV	Fernando Vina	12.00
BWa	Billy Wagner	12.00
TW	Todd Walker	8.00
BW	Bryan Ward	8.00
EW	Enrique Wilson	8.00
KW	Kevin Witt	8.00
RY	Robin Yount	60.00

1999 SP Signature Edition Autographs Gold

This parallel edition of the Signature Series Autographs features special gold graphic highlights on front and cards serially numbered within an edition of 50 each (except A.J. Burnett). Cards of 11 in the checklist), while cards of several others had to be in the checklist, while cards of several others had to be obtained by sending in an exchange card, valid through May 12, 2000.

		MT
Common Player:		15.00
BA	Bobby Abreu	15.00
SA	Sandy Alomar	15.00
MA	Marlon Anderson	15.00
KB	Kevin Barker	15.00
MB	Michael Barrett	30.00
RoB	Rob Bell	15.00
AB	Albert Belle	80.00
RBe	Ron Belliard	15.00
CBe	Carlos Beltran	30.00
ABe	Adrian Beltre	30.00
CB	Craig Biggio (unsigned)	25.00
BB	Barry Bonds	180.00
RB	Russ Branyan	15.00
SB	Scott Brosius	15.00
DB	Dermal Brown	15.00
EB	Emil Brown	15.00
AJB	A.J. Burnett (exchange card)	30.00
AJB	A.J. Burnett (autographed edition of 20)	40.00
JB	Jeromy Burnitz (unsigned)	15.00
PB	Pat Burrell	150.00
JoC	Jose Canseco	120.00
MC	Mike Caruso	15.00
SC	Sean Casey	70.00
VC	Vinny Castilla (exchange card)	20.00
VC	Vinny Castilla (autographed)	30.00
CC	Carlos Castillo	15.00
EC	Eric Chavez	40.00
BC	Bruce Chen	24.00
JCi	Jeff Cirillo	15.00
RC	Royce Clayton	15.00
MCl	Matt Clement	15.00
IC	Ivanon Coffie	15.00
BCo	Bartolo Colon	30.00
JC	Jason Conti	15.00
JDa	Johnny Damon	15.00
MD	Mike Darr (unsigned)	15.00
BD	Ben Davis	15.00
CD	Carlos Delgado	30.00
OD	Octavio Dotel	24.00
JD	J.D. Drew	75.00
RD	Ray Durham	15.00
DEa	Damion Easley	15.00
JE	Juan Encarnacion	20.00
DE	Darin Erstad	50.00
CF	Carlos Febles	40.00
Rob	Robert Fick	15.00
Rol	Rollie Fingers	40.00
TF	Travis Fryman (unsigned)	15.00
BF	Brad Fullmer	30.00
RGa	Ron Gant	30.00
NG	Nomar Garciaparra	400.00
JaG	Jason Giambi	30.00
JeG	Jeremy Giambi (unsigned)	15.00
DG	Derrick Gibson	15.00
DGl	Doug Glanville	15.00
TGl	Troy Glaus	80.00
AG	Alex Gonzalez	15.00
JG	Juan Gonzalez (unsigned)	75.00
RGr	Rusty Greer	15.00
Jr.	Ken Griffey Jr.	800.00
Sr.	Ken Griffey Sr.	40.00
VG	Vladimir Guerrero	90.00
JG	Jose Guillen (unsigned)	15.00
TG	Tony Gwynn	150.00
CHa	Chris Haas	15.00
JHj	Jerry Hairston Jr.	15.00
RH	Roy Halladay	24.00
THe	Todd Helton	50.00
RH	Rickey Henderson (unsigned)	40.00
BH	Bob Henley	15.00
ED	Orlando Hernandez	80.00
CH	Chad Hermansen	30.00
ShH	Shea Hillenbrand	15.00
StH	Sterling Hitchcock	15.00
THo	Trevor Hoffman	24.00
CHu	Chad Hutchinson	50.00
RJ	Reggie Jackson	300.00
GJ	Geoff Jenkins	30.00
AJ	Andruw Jones	70.00
CJ	Chipper Jones	250.00
BJ	Brian Jordan (unsigned)	25.00
WJ	Wally Joyner	30.00
GK	Gabe Kapler	60.00
MKa	Mark Karchner	15.00
JK	Jason Kendall	30.00
HK	Harmon Killebrew	80.00
CKi	Cesar King	15.00
MKi	Mike Kinkade	15.00
PK	Paul Konerko	24.00
CK	Corey Koskie	24.00
MK	Mark Kotsay	24.00
RL	Ray Lankford	30.00
JLa	Joe Lawrence	15.00
CL	Carlos Lee	40.00
DL	Derrek Lee	15.00
TL	Travis Lee (unsigned)	20.00
AL	Al Leiter	24.00
JLe	Jim Leyritz	15.00
GL	George Lombard	15.00
GM	Greg Maddux	300.00
Eli	Eli Marrero	15.00
EM	Edgar Martinez	20.00
PM	Pedro Martinez (exchange card)	200.00
PM	Pedro Martinez (autographed)	250.00
RMa	Ruben Mateo (exchange card)	60.00
RMa	Ruben Mateo (autographed)	75.00
EMa	Eddie Mathews	100.00
GMj	Gary Matthews Jr.	24.00
WMc	Willie McCovey	80.00
JM	Juan Melo	15.00
MMe	Mitch Meluskey	15.00
DoM	Doug Mientkiewicz	15.00
EMi	Eric Milton	15.00
DaM	Damon Minor	15.00
RM	Ryan Minor	15.00
EMu	Eddie Murray	120.00
SM	Stan Musial	240.00
RN	Robb Nen	15.00
AN	Abraham Nunez	15.00
JO	John Olerud	40.00
PO	Paul O'Neill	40.00
DO	David Ortiz	15.00
OP	Orlando Palmeiro	15.00
JP	Jim Parque	15.00
AP	Angel Pena	15.00
MP	Mike Piazza (exchange card)	300.00
MP	Mike Piazza (autographed)	400.00
CP	Calvin Pickering	24.00
AJP	A.J. Pierzynski	15.00
SP	Sidney Ponson	15.00
BR	Brad Radke	15.00
ARa	Aramis Ramirez	15.00
MR	Manny Ramirez	120.00
MRi	Mariano Rivera	40.00
FR	Frank Robinson	100.00
AR	Alex Rodriguez	400.00
PG	Ivan Rodriguez	120.00
SR	Scott Rolen (exchange card)	90.00
SR	Scott Rolen (autographed)	100.00
RR	Rafael Roque	15.00
NR	Nolan Ryan	550.00
DS	Donnie Sadler	15.00
JS	Jesus Sanchez	15.00
MS	Mike Schmidt	300.00
TSe	Tom Seaver	180.00
DSe	David Segui	15.00
FS	Fernando Seguignol	15.00
BS	Bobby Smith	15.00
JT	J.T. Snow	15.00
POP	Willie Stargell	100.00
TSt	Todd Stottlemyre	15.00
FTa	Fernando Tatis	30.00
RT	Reggie Taylor	15.00
MT	Miguel Tejada	50.00
FT	Frank Thomas	240.00
MV	Mario Valdez	15.00
JV	Jason Varitek	15.00
GV	Greg Vaughn	15.00
MO	Mo Vaughn	50.00
FV	Fernando Vina	24.00
BWa	Billy Wagner	24.00
TW	Todd Walker	24.00
BW	Bryan Ward	15.00
EW	Enrique Wilson	15.00
KW	Kevin Witt	15.00
RY	Robin Yount	150.00

1999 SP Signature Edition Legendary Cuts

Each of the cards in this one-of-one insert series is unique, thus catalog values are impossible to assign.

		MT
Roy	Roy Campanella	
RC	Roy Campanella	
XX	Jimmie Foxx	
LG	Lefty Grove	
W	Walter Johnson	
MO	Mel Ott	
Mel1	Mel Ott	
Mel2	Mel Ott	
BR	Babe Ruth	

1999 SP Signature Edition 500 Club Piece of History

		MT
MO	Mel Ott (350)	250.00

1999 SPx

Formerly SPx Finite, this super-premium product showcases 80 of baseball's veteran players on regular cards and a 40-card rookie subset, which are serially numbered to 1,999. Two top rookies, J.D. Drew and Gabe Kapler autographed all 1,999 of their rookie subset cards. There are two parallels, SPx Radiance and SPx Spectrum. Radiance are serially numbered to 100 with Drew and Kapler signing all 100 of their cards. They are exclusive to Finite Radiance Hot Packs. Spectrums are limited to only one set and available only in Finite Spectrum Hot Packs. Packs consist of three cards with a S.R.P. of $5.99.

		MT
Complete Set (120):		575.00
Common Player:		.50
Common SPx Rookie (81-120):		4.00
Production 1,999 sets		
Pack (3):		6.00
Wax Box (18):		100.00
1	Mark McGwire #61	6.00
2	Mark McGwire #62	8.00
3	Mark McGwire #63	5.00
4	Mark McGwire #64	5.00
5	Mark McGwire #65	5.00
6	Mark McGwire #66	5.00
7	Mark McGwire #67	5.00
8	Mark McGwire #68	5.00
9	Mark McGwire #69	5.00
10	Mark McGwire #70	15.00
11	Mo Vaughn	1.50
12	Darin Erstad	2.50
13	Travis Lee	2.00
14	Randy Johnson	2.00
15	Matt Williams	1.25
16	Chipper Jones	6.00
17	Greg Maddux	6.00
18	Andruw Jones	2.50
19	Andres Galarraga	1.50
20	Cal Ripken Jr.	8.00
21	Albert Belle	2.50
22	Mike Mussina	2.00
23	Nomar Garciaparra	6.00
24	Pedro Martinez	2.00
25	John Valentin	.50
26	Kerry Wood	2.50
27	Sammy Sosa	6.00
28	Mark Grace	1.25
29	Frank Thomas	5.00
30	Mike Caruso	.50
31	Barry Larkin	.75
32	Sean Casey	1.00
33	Jim Thome	1.50
34	Kenny Lofton	1.50
35	Manny Ramirez	3.00
36	Larry Walker	1.50
37	Todd Helton	2.00
38	Vinny Castilla	.50
39	Tony Clark	1.50
40	Derrek Lee	.50
41	Mark Kotsay	.50
42	Jeff Bagwell	2.50
43	Craig Biggio	1.50
44	Moises Alou	.50
45	Larry Sutton	.50
46	Johnny Damon	.50
47	Gary Sheffield	.50
48	Raul Mondesi	1.00
49	Jeromy Burnitz	.50
50	Todd Walker	.75

51 David Ortiz .50
52 Vladimir Guerrero 4.00
53 Rondell White .50
54 Mike Piazza 6.00
55 Derek Jeter 6.00
56 Tino Martinez 1.00
57 David Wells .50
58 Ben Grieve 2.00
59 A.J. Hinch .50
60 Scott Rolen 2.50
61 Doug Glanville .50
62 Aramis Ramirez .50
63 Jose Guillen .50
64 Tony Gwynn 5.00
65 Greg Vaughn .50
66 Ruben Rivera .50
67 Barry Bonds 2.50
68 J.T. Snow .50
69 Alex Rodriguez 8.00
70 Ken Griffey Jr. 10.00
71 Jay Buhner .50
72 Mark McGwire 12.00
73 Fernando Tatis .50
74 Quinton McCracken .50
75 Wade Boggs 1.50
76 Ivan Rodriguez 2.50
77 Juan Gonzalez 2.50
78 Rafael Palmeiro 1.50
79 Jose Cruz Jr. .50
80 Carlos Delgado 1.00
81 Troy Glaus 30.00
82 Vladimir Nunez 4.00
83 George Lombard 8.00
84 Bruce Chen 6.00
85 Ryan Minor 15.00
86 Calvin Pickering 6.00
87 Jin Ho Cho 6.00
88 Russ Branyon 6.00
89 Derrick Gibson 5.00
90 Gabe Kapler (autographed) 75.00
91 Matt Anderson 8.00
92 Robert Fick 4.00
93 Juan Encarnacion 8.00
94 Preston Wilson 8.00
95 Alex Gonzalez 8.00
96 Carlos Beltran 10.00
97 Jeremy Giambi 15.00
98 Dee Brown 4.00
99 Adrian Beltre 10.00
100 Alex Cora 4.00
101 Angel Pena 8.00
102 Geoff Jenkins 6.00
103 Ronnie Belliard 6.00
104 Corey Koskie 6.00
105 A.J. Pierzynski 6.00
106 Michael Barrett 12.00
107 Fernando Seguignol 12.00
108 Mike Kinkade 10.00
109 Mike Lowell 8.00
110 Ricky Ledee 8.00
111 Eric Chavez 15.00
112 Abraham Nunez 6.00
113 Matt Clement 10.00
114 Ben Davis 6.00
115 Mike Darr 8.00
116 Ramon Martinez 8.00
117 Carlos Guillen 10.00
118 Shane Monahan 6.00
119 J.D. Drew (autographed) 40.00
120 Kevin Witt 6.00

1999 SPx Dominance

This 20-card set showcases the most dominant MLB superstars, including Derek Jeter and Alex Rodriguez. These are seeded 1:17 packs and numbered with a FB prefix.

MT
Complete Set (20): 200.00
Common Player: 4.00
Inserted 1:17
1 Chipper Jones 20.00
2 Greg Maddux 20.00
3 Cal Ripken Jr. 25.00
4 Nomar Garciaparra 20.00
5 Mo Vaughn 4.00
6 Sammy Sosa 20.00
7 Albert Belle 6.00
8 Frank Thomas 15.00
9 Jim Thome 4.00
10 Jeff Bagwell 8.00
11 Vladimir Guerrero 12.00
12 Mike Piazza 20.00
13 Derek Jeter 20.00
14 Tony Gwynn 15.00
15 Barry Bonds 8.00
16 Ken Griffey Jr. 30.00
17 Alex Rodriguez 25.00
18 Mark McGwire 30.00
19 J.D. Drew 4.00
20 Juan Gonzalez 8.00

1999 SPx Power Explosion

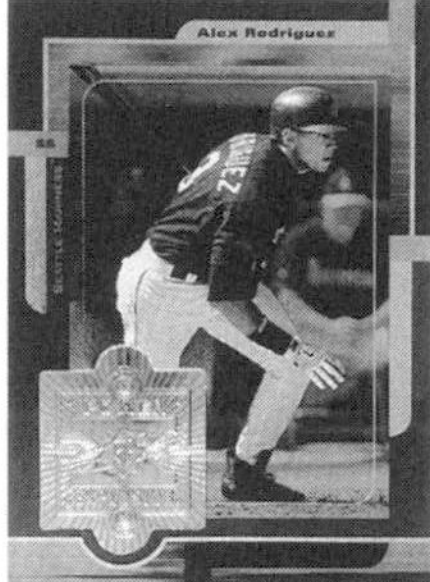

This 30-card set salutes the top power hitters in the game today, including Mark McGwire and Sammy Sosa. These are seeded 1:3 packs, and numbered with a PE prefix.

MT
Complete Set (30): 60.00
Common Player: .60
Inserted 1:3
1 Troy Glaus 1.50
2 Mo Vaughn 1.00
3 Travis Lee 1.25
4 Chipper Jones 3.50
5 Andres Galarraga 1.00
6 Brady Anderson .60
7 Albert Belle 1.50
8 Nomar Garciaparra 3.50
9 Sammy Sosa 3.50
10 Frank Thomas 2.50
11 Jim Thome .60
12 Manny Ramirez 2.00
13 Larry Walker 1.25
14 Tony Clark 1.25
15 Jeff Bagwell 1.50
16 Moises Alou .60
17 Ken Caminiti .60
18 Vladimir Guerrero 2.00
19 Mike Piazza 3.50
20 Tino Martinez .60
21 Ben Grieve 1.25
22 Scott Rolen 1.50
23 Greg Vaughn .60
24 Barry Bonds 1.50
25 Ken Griffey Jr. 6.00
26 Alex Rodriguez 5.00
27 Mark McGwire 6.00
28 J.D. Drew .75
29 Juan Gonzalez 1.50
30 Ivan Rodriguez 1.25

1999 SPx Premier Stars

This 30-card set captures baseball's most dominant players, including Randy Johnson and Ken Griffey Jr. Featured on a rainbow-foil design, these are seeded 1:17 packs and numbered with a PS prefix.

MT
Complete Set (30): 350.00
Common Player: 3.00
Inserted 1:17
1 Mark McGwire 35.00
2 Sammy Sosa 20.00
3 Frank Thomas 15.00
4 J.D. Drew 4.00
5 Kerry Wood 8.00
6 Moises Alou 3.00
7 Kenny Lofton 3.00
8 Jeff Bagwell 8.00
9 Tony Clark 6.00
10 Roberto Alomar 6.00
11 Cal Ripken Jr. 25.00
12 Derek Jeter 20.00
13 Mike Piazza 20.00
14 Jose Cruz Jr. 3.00
15 Chipper Jones 20.00
16 Nomar Garciaparra 20.00
17 Greg Maddux 20.00
18 Scott Rolen 8.00
19 Vladimir Guerrero 15.00
20 Albert Belle 5.00
21 Ken Griffey Jr. 35.00
22 Alex Rodriguez 25.00
23 Ben Grieve 6.00
24 Juan Gonzalez 8.00
25 Barry Bonds 8.00
26 Larry Walker 6.00
27 Tony Gwynn 15.00
28 Randy Johnson 6.00
29 Travis Lee 6.00
30 Mo Vaughn 3.00

1999 SPx Star Focus

This 30-card set focuses on the 30 brightest stars in the game. These are seeded 1:8 packs and numbered with a SF prefix.

MT
Complete Set (30): 150.00
Common Player: 2.00
Inserted 1:8
1 Chipper Jones 10.00
2 Greg Maddux 10.00
3 Cal Ripken Jr. 12.50
4 Nomar Garciaparra 10.00
5 Mo Vaughn 2.00
6 Sammy Sosa 10.00
7 Albert Belle 4.00
8 Frank Thomas 8.00
9 Jim Thome 2.00
10 Kenny Lofton 2.00
11 Manny Ramirez 6.00
12 Larry Walker 3.00
13 Jeff Bagwell 4.00
14 Craig Biggio 3.00
15 Randy Johnson 3.00
16 Vladimir Guerrero 6.00
17 Mike Piazza 10.00
18 Derek Jeter 10.00
19 Tino Martinez 2.00
20 Bernie Williams 2.00
21 Curt Schilling 2.00
22 Tony Gwynn 8.00
23 Barry Bonds 4.00
24 Ken Griffey Jr. 15.00
25 Alex Rodriguez 12.50
26 Mark McGwire 15.00
27 J.D. Drew 2.00
28 Juan Gonzalez 4.00
29 Ivan Rodriguez 3.00
30 Ben Grieve 3.00

1999 SPx Winning Materials

This eight-card set includes a piece of the featured player's game-worn jersey and game-used bat on each card. These are seeded 1:251 packs.

MT
Complete Set (8): 1300.
Common Player: 100.00
Inserted 1:251
VC Vinny Castilla 100.00
JD J.D. Drew 75.00
JR Ken Griffey Jr. 500.00
VG Vladimir Guerrero 175.00
TG Tony Gwynn 225.00
TH Todd Helton 125.00
TL Travis Lee 125.00
IR Ivan Rodriguez 150.00

1999 SPx 500 Club Piece of History

Each of these approximately 350 cards include a piece of game-used Louisville Slugger once swung by Wilie Mays. Mays also signed 24 of his Piece of History cards.

		MT
WM	Willie Mays (350)	350.00
WM	Willie Mays Auto./24	800.00

2000 SP Authentic

The 135-card base set is composed of 90 regular cards, 30 Future Watch subset cards (serial numbered to 2,500) and 15 SP Superstars (serial numbered to 2,500). The regular cards have a gold foiled stamped line around the player image with a matte finished white border around the player image. The player name is stamped in gold foil in the top portion and the SP Authentic logo is stamped in silver foil. Card backs have a small photo, a brief career note and up to the past five seasons of complete statistics. Five-card packs carried a $4.99 SRP.

		MT
Complete Set (135):		400.00
Common Player:		.20
Common (91-105):		4.00
Production 2,500 sets		
Common (106-135):		8.00
Production 2,500 sets		
Pack (5):		5.00
Box (24):		110.00
1	Mo Vaughn	.75
2	Troy Glaus	1.00
3	Jason Giambi	.30
4	Tim Hudson	.40
5	Eric Chavez	.30
6	Shannon Stewart	.20
7	Raul Mondesi	.30
8	Carlos Delgado	1.00
9	Jose Canseco	.60
10	Vinny Castilla	.20
11	Greg Vaughn	.30
12	Manny Ramirez	1.00
13	Roberto Alomar	.75
14	Jim Thome	.50
15	Richie Sexson	.20
16	Alex Rodriguez	3.00
17	Fred Garcia	.20
18	John Olerud	.40
19	Albert Belle	.60
20	Cal Ripken Jr.	3.00
21	Mike Mussina	.50
22	Ivan Rodriguez	1.00
23	Gabe Kapler	.40
24	Rafael Palmeiro	.50
25	Nomar Garciaparra	2.50
26	Pedro Martinez	1.00
27	Carl Everett	.20
28	Carlos Beltran	.20
29	Jermaine Dye	.20
30	Juan Gonzalez	1.00
31	Dean Palmer	.20
32	Corey Koskie	.20
33	Jacque Jones	.20
34	Frank Thomas	1.50
35	Paul Konerko	.20
36	Magglio Ordonez	.40
37	Bernie Williams	.75
38	Derek Jeter	2.50
39	Roger Clemens	1.50
40	Mariano Rivera	.40
41	Jeff Bagwell	1.00
42	Craig Biggio	.50
43	Jose Lima	.20
44	Moises Alou	.20
45	Chipper Jones	2.00
46	Greg Maddux	2.00
47	Andruw Jones	.75
48	Kevin Millwood	.20
49	Jeromy Burnitz	.20
50	Geoff Jenkins	.40
51	Mark McGwire	4.00
52	Fernando Tatis	.40
53	J.D. Drew	.40
54	Sammy Sosa	2.50
55	Kerry Wood	.50
56	Mark Grace	.40
57	Matt Williams	.50
58	Randy Johnson	1.00
59	Erubiel Durazo	.20
60	Gary Sheffield	.50
61	Kevin Brown	.40
62	Shawn Green	.50
63	Vladimir Guerrero	1.50
64	Michael Barrett	.20
65	Barry Bonds	1.00
66	Jeff Kent	.20
67	Russ Ortiz	.20
68	Preston Wilson	.20
69	Mike Lowell	.20
70	Mike Piazza	2.50
71	Mike Hampton	.20
72	Robin Ventura	.40
73	Edgardo Alfonzo	.40
74	Tony Gwynn	1.50
75	Ryan Klesko	.20
76	Trevor Hoffman	.20
77	Scott Rolen	.75
78	Bob Abreu	.30
79	Mike Lieberthal	.20
80	Curt Schilling	.30
81	Jason Kendall	.30
82	Brian Giles	.20
83	Kris Benson	.20
84	Ken Griffey Jr.	4.00
85	Sean Casey	.40
86	Pokey Reese	.20
87	Barry Larkin	.75
88	Larry Walker	.50
89	Todd Helton	1.00
90	Jeff Cirillo	.20
91	Ken Griffey Jr. (SP Superstars)	20.00
92	Mark McGwire (SP Superstars)	20.00
93	Chipper Jones (SP Superstars)	10.00
94	Derek Jeter (SP Superstars)	12.00
95	Shawn Green (SP Superstars)	4.00
96	Pedro Martinez (SP Superstars)	5.00
97	Mike Piazza (SP Superstars)	12.00
98	Alex Rodriguez (SP Superstars)	15.00
99	Jeff Bagwell (SP Superstars)	5.00
100	Cal Ripken Jr. (SP Superstars)	15.00
101	Sammy Sosa (SP Superstars)	12.00
102	Barry Bonds (SP Superstars)	5.00
103	Jose Canseco (SP Superstars)	4.00
104	Nomar Garciaparra (SP Superstars)	12.00
105	Ivan Rodriguez (SP Superstars)	5.00
106	Rick Ankiel (Future Watch)	50.00
107	Pat Burrell (Future Watch)	30.00
108	Vernon Wells (Future Watch)	8.00
109	Nick Johnson (Future Watch)	12.00
110	Kip Wells (Future Watch)	8.00
111	Matt Riley (Future Watch)	8.00
112	Alfonso Soriano (Future Watch)	12.00
113	Josh Beckett (Future Watch)	15.00
114	*Danys Baez* (Future Watch)	10.00
115	Travis Dawkins (Future Watch)	10.00
116	Eric Gagne (Future Watch)	8.00
117	*Mike Lamb* (Future Watch)	20.00
118	Eric Munson (Future Watch)	12.00
119	*Wilfredo Rodriguez* (Future Watch)	8.00
120	*Kazuhiro Sasaki* (Future Watch)	35.00
121	Chad Hutchinson (Future Watch)	8.00
122	Peter Bergeron (Future Watch)	10.00
123	*Wascar Serrano* (Future Watch)	10.00
124	Tony Armas, Jr. (Future Watch)	12.00
125	Ramon Ortiz (Future Watch)	8.00
126	Adam Kennedy (Future Watch)	10.00
127	Joe Crede (Future Watch)	12.00
128	Roosevelt Brown (Future Watch)	8.00
129	Mark Mulder (Future Watch)	8.00
130	Brad Penny (Future Watch)	8.00
131	Terrence Long (Future Watch)	10.00
132	Ruben Mateo (Future Watch)	10.00
133	Wily Mo Pena (Future Watch)	15.00
134	Rafael Furcal (Future Watch)	30.00
135	Mario Encarnacion (Future Watch)	8.00

2000 SP Authentic Limited

A parallel to the 135-card base set these have "SP Limited" printed down the right side of the front and are serial numbered on the card front in an edition of 100 sets.

	MT
Cards (1-90):	15-25X
Cards (91-105):	3-5X
Cards (106-135):	1-2X
Production 100 sets	

2000 SP Authentic Chirography

This autographed insert set has a horizontal format with two player images on the card front. The player signature appears in the top right portion over a silver, checkered background. The insert name and logo have a silver tint. Card backs are numbered with the featured players' first and last initial. Chirographies are seeded 1:23 packs.

		MT
Common Player:		10.00
Inserted 1:23		
RA	Rick Ankiel	50.00
CBe	Carlos Beltran	10.00
BB	Barry Bonds	60.00
PB	Pat Burrell	35.00
JC	Jose Canseco	50.00
SC	Sean Casey	15.00
RC	Roger Clemens	75.00
ED	Erubiel Durazo	10.00
TGl	Troy Glaus	35.00

VG	Vladimir Guerrero	60.00
TG	Tony Gwynn	60.00
DJ	Derek Jeter	150.00
NJ	Nick Johnson	20.00
CJ	Chipper Jones	75.00
AJ	Andruw Jones	35.00
BP	Ben Petrick	10.00
MQ	Mark Quinn	15.00
MR	Manny Ramirez	50.00
CR	Cal Ripken Jr.	175.00
AR	Alex Rodriguez	150.00
IR	Ivan Rodriguez	50.00
SR	Scott Rolen	25.00
AS	Alfonso Soriano	20.00
MV	Mo Vaughn	30.00
EY	Ed Yarnall	10.00

2000 SP Authentic Chirography Gold

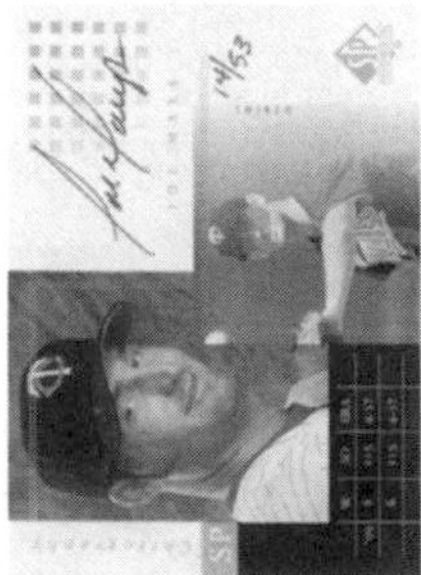

Golds use the same photos as the regular Chirography inserts and can be differentiated by the gold checkered background of the player signature in the upper right portion as well as the gold tint in the insert name and logo. Golds are also hand-numbered to the player's jersey number on the card front and are numbered with a "G" prefix on the card back before the players initials.

		MT
Common Player:		
RA	Rick Ankiel/66 EXCH	150.00
JB	Jeff Bagwell/5 EXCH	
JOB	John Bale/49	
CBe	Carlos Beltran/15	75.00
BB	Barry Bonds/25	275.00
PB	Pat Burrell/33 EXCH	150.00
JC	Jose Canseco /33	150.00
SC	Sean Casey/21	75.00
EC	Eric Chavez/3	
RC	Roger Clemens /22	325.00
JD	J.D. Drew	
ED	Erubiel Durazo/44	40.00
RF	Rafael Furcal/1	
JG	Jason Giambi/16	
TGl	Troy Glaus/14	
VG	Vladimir Guerrero /27	125.00
WG	Wilton Guerrero/4	
TG	Tony Gwynn/19	325.00
DJ	Derek Jeter/2	
NJ	Nick Johnson/63	40.00
AJ	Andruw Jones/25 EXCH	
CJ	Chipper Jones/10 EXCH	
JK	Josh Kalinowski/62	
SK	Sandy Koufax/32	
JL	Jose Lima/42 EXCH	
KL	Kenny Lofton/7	
JMA	Joe Mays/53	
JMO	Jim Morris/63	
EM	Eric Munson/17	
RP	Robert Person/31	
BP	Ben Petrick/15	40.00
MQ	Mark Quinn/14	
MR	Manny Ramirez/24 EXCH	175.00
MRI	Matt Riley/25	
CR	Cal Ripken Jr./8	
AR	Alex Rodriguez/3 EXCH	
IR	Ivan Rodriguez/7	
SR	Scott Rolen/17 EXCH	
AS	Alfonso Soriano /53	50.00
MV	Mo Vaughn/42	50.00
VW	Vernon Wells/3	
EY	Ed Yarnall/41	30.00

2000 SP Authentic Joe DiMaggio Game Jersey

This is DiMaggio's first Game Jersey insert and has three different versions. The first is limited to 500 total cards, the second version is Gold and numbered to 56. The rarest version has a DiMaggio cut signature along with a piece of his game-used jersey and is limited to only five total cards.

		MT
DiMaggio Jersey card		
JD	Joe DiMaggio jersey/500	600.00
JD	Joe DiMaggio jersey gold/56	1200.
JD	Joe DiMaggio jersey/auto/5	

2000 SP Authentic 3,000 Hit Club

A continuation of Upper Deck's cross brand salute to players who have reached the magical 3,000 hit milestone. 350 game- used bat cards and five bat/cut signature combos were issued for each player.

		MT
PW	Paul Waner bat/350	250.00
TS	Tris Speaker bat/350	250.00
PW	Paul Waner bat/auto/5	
TS	Tris Speaker bat/auto/5	

2000 SP Authentic Premier Performers

This 10-card set spotlights baseball's best on a silver holofoiled card front with the player name, insert name and logo stamped in gold foil. Card backs are numbered with an "PP" prefix and are found 1:12 packs.

		MT
Complete Set (10):		40.00
Common Player:		2.00
Inserted 1:12		
1	Mark McGwire	8.00
2	Alex Rodriguez	6.00
3	Cal Ripken Jr.	6.00
4	Nomar Garciaparra	5.00
5	Ken Griffey Jr.	8.00
6	Chipper Jones	4.00
7	Derek Jeter	5.00
8	Ivan Rodriguez	2.00
9	Vladimir Guerrero	3.00
10	Sammy Sosa	5.00

2000 SP Authentic Midsummer Classics

This 10-card set spotlights perennial All-Stars and has a silver holo-foiled front with gold foil etching and stamping. These are found 1:12 packs and are numbered on the card back with an "MC" prefix.

		MT
Complete Set (10):		
Common Player:		1.50
Inserted 1:12		
1	Cal Ripken Jr.	6.00
2	Roger Clemens	3.00
3	Jeff Bagwell	2.00
4	Barry Bonds	2.00
5	Jose Canseco	1.50
6	Frank Thomas	3.00
7	Mike Piazza	5.00
8	Tony Gwynn	3.00
9	Juan Gonzalez	2.00
10	Greg Maddux	4.00

2000 SP Authentic SP Supremacy

This seven-card set has a silver foiled card front with the insert name and logo stamped in gold foil. The inserts are found on the average of 1:23 packs and are numbered with an "S" prefix.

		MT
Complete Set (7):		20.00
Common Player:		2.00
Inserted 1:23		
1	Alex Rodriguez	8.00
2	Shawn Green	2.00
3	Pedro Martinez	2.50
4	Chipper Jones	5.00
5	Tony Gwynn	4.00
6	Ivan Rodriguez	2.50
7	Jeff Bagwell	2.50

2000 SP Authentic SP Cornerstones

Printed on a silver holofoiled card front a close-up image of the player appears in a baseball diamond shaped enclosed by gold foil etching. Another shadow image of the featured player appears in the background. The player name, insert name and logo are stamped in gold foil. These are seeded 1:23 packs and are numbered with a "C" prefix on the card back.

		MT
Complete Set (7):		40.00
Common Player:		2.00
Inserted 1:23		
1	Ken Griffey Jr.	10.00

2 Cal Ripken Jr. 8.00
3 Mike Piazza 6.00
4 Derek Jeter 6.00
5 Mark McGwire 10.00
6 Nomar Garciaparra 6.00
7 Sammy Sosa 6.00

2000 SP Authentic SP Buyback

This autographed set features previously issued SP cards that were re-purchased by Upper Deck. The cards are autographed by the featured player and hand-numbered on the card front. The number autographed and released by Upper Deck is listed after the player name. Buybacks are found 1:95 packs.

MT

Complete Set (140):
Common Player:
1 Jeff Bagwell Exch. 50.00
2 Craig Biggio '93/59 50.00
3 Craig Biggio '94/69 50.00
4 Craig Biggio '95/171 90.00
5 Craig Biggio '96/71 50.00
6 Craig Biggio '97/46 70.00
7 Craig Biggio '98/40 75.00
8 Craig Biggio '99/125 40.00
9 Barry Bonds '93/12
10 Barry Bonds '94/12
11 Barry Bonds '95/21
12 Barry Bonds '96
13 Barry Bonds '97
14 Barry Bonds '98/22
15 Barry Bonds '99/520 75.00
16 Jose Canseco '93/29 200.00
17 Jose Canseco '94/20 250.00
18 Jose Canseco '95
19 Jose Canseco '96/23 250.00
20 Jose Canseco '97/23 250.00
21 Jose Canseco '98/24 250.00
22 Jose Canseco '99/502 50.00
23 Sean Casey '98
24 Sean Casey '99/139 25.00
25 Roger Clemens '93/68 25.00
26 Roger Clemens '94/60 25.00
27 Roger Clemens '95/68 25.00
28 Roger Clemens '96/68
29 Roger Clemens '97/7
30 Roger Clemens '98/25 300.00
31 Roger Clemens '99/134 100.00
32 Jason Giambi '97/34 60.00
33 Jason Giambi '98/25 90.00
34 Tom Glavine '93/99 50.00
35 Tom Glavine '94/107 40.00
36 Tom Glavine '95/97 50.00
37 Tom Glavine '96/42 75.00
38 Tom Glavine '98/40 75.00
39 Tom Glavine '99/138 40.00
40 Shawn Green '96/55 60.00
41 Shawn Green '99/530 30.00
42 Ken Griffey Jr. Exch. 300.00
43 Tony Gwynn '93
44 Tony Gwynn '94
45 Tony Gwynn '95
46 Tony Gwynn '96
47 Tony Gwynn '97/24 300.00
48 Tony Gwynn '98
49 Tony Gwynn '99/129 80.00
50 Tony Gwynn '99/369 60.00
51 Derek Jeter '93
52 Derek Jeter '95/17
53 Derek Jeter '96
54 Derek Jeter '97
55 Derek Jeter '98/11
56 Derek Jeter '99/119 200.00
57 Randy Johnson '93/60 100.00
58 Randy Johnson '94/45 120.00
59 Randy Johnson '95/70 100.00
60 Randy Johnson '96/60 100.00
61 Randy Johnson '97
62 Randy Johnson '98
63 Randy Johnson '99/113 75.00
64 Andruw Jones Exch. 60.00
65 Chipper Jones Exch. 100.00
66 Kenny Lofton '94/100 30.00
67 Kenny Lofton '95/84 30.00
68 Kenny Lofton '96/34 60.00
69 Kenny Lofton '97/82 30.00
70 Kenny Lofton '98/21 100.00
71 Kenny Lofton '99/99 30.00
72 Javy Lopez '93/106 20.00
73 Javy Lopez '94/160 25.00
74 Javy Lopez '96/99 20.00
75 Javy Lopez '97/61 20.00
76 Javy Lopez '98
77 Greg Maddux '93/22 375.00
78 Greg Maddux '94/19 375.00
79 Greg Maddux '95
80 Greg Maddux '96
81 Greg Maddux '97/8
82 Greg Maddux '98/11
83 Greg Maddux '99/504 75.00
84 Paul O'Neill '93/110 25.00
85 Paul O'Neill '94/97 30.00
86 Paul O'Neill '95/142 25.00
87 Paul O'Neill '96/70 30.00
88 Paul O'Neill '98/23 75.00
89 Mario Ramirez Exch. 50.00
90 Cal Ripken Jr. '93/7
91 Cal Ripken Jr. '94/22 600.00
92 Cal Ripken Jr. '95/10
93 Cal Ripken Jr. '96/12
94 Cal Ripken Jr. '97/12
95 Cal Ripken Jr. '98/13
96 Cal Ripken Jr. '99/510 125.00
97 Alex Rodriguez Exch. 200.00
98 Ivan Rodriguez '93/29 150.00
99 Ivan Rodriguez '94
100 Ivan Rodriguez '95/18 200.00
101 Ivan Rodriguez '96/22 200.00
102 Ivan Rodriguez '97/14
103 Ivan Rodriguez '98/27 150.00
104 Ivan Rodriguez '99/2
105 Frank Thomas '93
106 Frank Thomas '94
107 Frank Thomas '95/5
108 Frank Thomas '96/10
109 Frank Thomas '97/20 300.00
110 Frank Thomas '98
111 Frank Thomas '99/100 120.00
112 Greg Vaughn '93/79 30.00
113 Greg Vaughn '94/75 30.00
114 Greg Vaughn '95/155 25.00
115 Greg Vaughn '96/113 25.00
116 Greg Vaughn '97
117 Greg Vaughn '99/527 15.00
118 Mo Vaughn '93/119 30.00
119 Mo Vaughn '94/96 40.00
120 Mo Vaughn '95/121 30.00
121 Mo Vaughn '96/114 30.00
122 Mo Vaughn '97/61 40.00
123 Mo Vaughn '98
124 Mo Vaughn '99/537 20.00
125 Robin Ventura '93/59 30.00
126 Robin Ventura '94/49 40.00
127 Robin Ventura '95/125 25.00
128 Robin Ventura '96/55 30.00
129 Robin Ventura '97/44 50.00
130 Robin Ventura '98/28 60.00
131 Robin Ventura '99/370 20.00
132 Matt Williams '93
133 Matt Williams '94/50 60.00
134 Matt Williams '95/137 40.00
135 Matt Williams '96/77 50.00
136 Matt Williams '97/54 50.00
137 Matt Williams '98/29 100.00
138 Matt Williams '99/529 25.00
139 Preston Wilson '94/249 20.00
140 Preston Wilson '99/195 20.00

2000 SP Authentic United Nations

Done on a horizontal format this 10-card set salutes the top international stars of the game. The featured players' country of origin flag is in the background of the player image. The card design features silver holofoil and silver foil etching and stamping. These are seeded 1:4 packs and are numbered with a "UN" prefix on the card back.

MT

Complete Set (10): 10.00
Common Player: .75
Inserted 1:4
1 Sammy Sosa (Dominican Rep.) 2.50
2 Ken Griffey Jr. (USA) 4.00
3 Orlando Hernandez (Cuba) .75
4 Andres Galarraga (Venezuela) 1.00
5 Kazuhiro Sasak (Japan) 2.00
6 Larry Walker (Canada) .75
7 Vinny Castilla (Mexico) .75
8 Andruw Jones (Neth. Antilles) 1.00
9 Ivan Rodriguez (Puerto Rico) 1.00
10 Chan Ho Park (So. Korea) .75

2000 SPx

The base set consists of 120-cards including 30 Rookie/ Young Star subset cards which has three tiers. The first five are numbered to 1,000, the next 22 are autographed and numbered to 1,500 and the final three are autographed and numbered to 500. Each base card has a holofoiled front with the SPx logo, player name and team name stamped in gold foil.

MT

Complete Set (120): 800.00
Common Player: .25
Common Rookie (91-120): 15.00
Pack (4): 7.00
Wax Box (18): 120.00
1 Troy Glaus 1.50

2	Mo Vaughn	.75
3	Ramon Ortiz	.25
4	Jeff Bagwell	1.25
5	Moises Alou	.40
6	Craig Biggio	.75
7	Jose Lima	.25
8	Jason Giambi	.50
9	John Jaha	.25
10	Matt Stairs	.25
11	Chipper Jones	2.50
12	Greg Maddux	2.50
13	Andres Galarraga	1.00
14	Andruw Jones	.75
15	Jeromy Burnitz	.40
16	Ron Belliard	.25
17	Carlos Delgado	1.00
18	David Wells	.25
19	Tony Batista	.25
20	Shannon Stewart	.25
21	Sammy Sosa	3.00
22	Mark Grace	.50
23	Henry Rodriguez	.25
24	Mark McGwire	5.00
25	J.D. Drew	.40
26	Luis Gonzalez	.25
27	Randy Johnson	1.00
28	Matt Williams	.75
29	Steve Finley	.25
30	Shawn Green	1.00
31	Kevin Brown	.50
32	Gary Sheffield	.50
33	Jose Canseco	1.25
34	Greg Vaughn	.50
35	Vladimir Guerrero	2.00
36	Michael Barrett	.25
37	Russ Ortiz	.25
38	Barry Bonds	1.25
39	Jeff Kent	.25
40	Richie Sexson	.25
41	Manny Ramirez	1.25
42	Jim Thome	.75
43	Roberto Alomar	1.00
44	Edgar Martinez	.40
45	Alex Rodriguez	4.00
46	John Olerud	.50
47	Alex Gonzalez	.25
48	Cliff Floyd	.25
49	Mike Piazza	3.00
50	Al Leiter	.40
51	Robin Ventura	.50
52	Edgardo Alfonzo	.50
53	Albert Belle	.75
54	Cal Ripken Jr.	4.00
55	B.J. Surhoff	.25
56	Tony Gwynn	2.50
57	Trevor Hoffman	.25
58	Brian Giles	.40
59	Jason Kendall	.40
60	Kris Benson	.25
61	Bob Abreu	.40
62	Scott Rolen	1.25
63	Curt Schilling	.40
64	Mike Lieberthal	.25
65	Sean Casey	.50
66	Dante Bichette	.50
67	Ken Griffey Jr.	5.00
68	Pokey Reese	.25
69	Mike Sweeney	.25
70	Carlos Febles	.25
71	Ivan Rodriguez	1.25
72	Ruben Mateo	.50
73	Rafael Palmeiro	1.00
74	Larry Walker	1.00
75	Todd Helton	1.00
76	Nomar Garciaparra	3.00
77	Pedro Martinez	1.25
78	Troy O'Leary	.25
79	Jacque Jones	.25
80	Corey Koskie	.25
81	Juan Gonzalez	1.25
82	Dean Palmer	.25
83	Juan Encarnacion	.25
84	Frank Thomas	1.50
85	Magglio Ordonez	.50
86	Paul Konerko	.50
87	Bernie Williams	1.00
88	Derek Jeter	3.00
89	Roger Clemens	2.00
90	Orlando Hernandez	.75
91	Vernon Wells AU-1,000	20.00
92	Rick Ankiel AU-1,000	125.00
93	Eric Chavez AU-1,000	20.00
94	Alfonso Soriano AU-1,000	30.00
95	Eric Gagne AU-1,000	20.00
96	Rob Bell AU-1,500	20.00
97	Matt Riley AU-1,500	20.00
98	Josh Beckett AU-1,500	40.00
99	Ben Petrick AU-1,500	20.00
100	*Rob Ramsay AU-1,500*	20.00
101	Scott Williamson AU-1,500	20.00
102	Doug Davis AU-1,500	20.00
103	Eric Munson AU-1,500	40.00
104	Pat Burrell AU-500	125.00
105	Jim Morris AU-1,500	20.00
106	Gabe Kapler AU-500	40.00
107	Lance Berkman 1,500	15.00
108	Erubiel Durazo AU-1,500	30.00
109	Tim Hudson AU-1,500	25.00
110	Ben Davis AU-1,500	20.00
111	Nick Johnson AU-1,500	40.00
112	Octavio Dotel AU-1,500	20.00
113	Jerry Hairston 1,500	15.00
114	Ruben Mateo 1,500	20.00
115	Chris Singleton 1,500	20.00
116	Bruce Chen AU-1,500	20.00
117	Derrick Gibson AU-1,500	20.00
118	Carlos Beltran AU-500	50.00
119	Fred Garcia AU-500	20.00
120	Preston Wilson AU-500	20.00

2000 SPx Radiance

A parallel to the 120-card base set these are serially numbered to 100. A one-of-one Spectrum parallel of each base card is also randomly seeded.

	MT
Stars (1-90):	10-20X
Common Yng Star (91-120):	10.00
Production 100 sets	

2000 SPx Highlight Heroes

This 10-card set has a horizontal format on a holofoiled front with gold foil stamping. Card backs are numbered with an "HH" prefix and inserted 1:16 packs.

		MT
Complete Set (10):		35.00
Common Player:		1.50
Inserted 1:16		
1	Pedro Martinez	2.50
2	Ivan Rodriguez	2.50
3	Carlos Beltran	1.50
4	Nomar Garciaparra	6.00
5	Ken Griffey Jr.	10.00
6	Randy Johnson	2.00
7	Chipper Jones	5.00
8	Scott Williamson	1.50
9	Larry Walker	2.00
10	Mark McGwire	10.00

2000 SPx Foundations

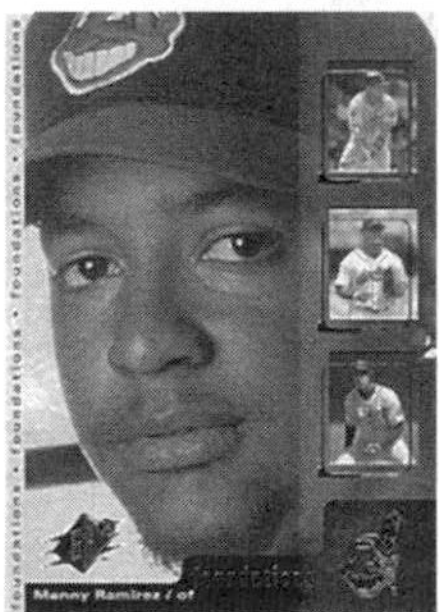

This 10-card set features a holofoiled front with gold foil stamping. Three miniature action shots appear to the right of a close-up shot of the featured player. Card backs are numbered with an "F" prefix and inserted 1:32 packs.

		MT
Complete Set (10):		80.00
Common Player:		4.00
Inserted 1:32		
1	Ken Griffey Jr.	20.00
2	Nomar Garciaparra	12.00
3	Cal Ripken Jr.	15.00
4	Chipper Jones	10.00
5	Mike Piazza	12.00
6	Derek Jeter	12.00
7	Manny Ramirez	5.00
8	Jeff Bagwell	5.00
9	Tony Gwynn	10.00
10	Larry Walker	4.00

2000 SPx Power Brokers

This 20-card set has a horizontal format with the background of the player photo having a kaleidoscope effect. The SPx logo is stamped in gold foil. Card backs are numbered with an "PB" prefix and are inserted 1:8 packs.

		MT
Complete Set (20):		60.00
Common Player:		1.50
Inserted 1:8		
1	Rafael Palmeiro	2.00
2	Carlos Delgado	2.00
3	Ken Griffey Jr.	10.00
4	Matt Stairs	1.50
5	Mike Piazza	6.00
6	Vladimir Guerrero	4.00
7	Chipper Jones	5.00
8	Mark McGwire	10.00
9	Matt Williams	2.00
10	Juan Gonzalez	2.50
11	Shawn Green	2.00
12	Sammy Sosa	6.00
13	Brian Giles	1.50
14	Jeff Bagwell	2.50
15	Alex Rodriguez	8.00
16	Frank Thomas	3.00
17	Larry Walker	2.00
18	Albert Belle	2.00
19	Dean Palmer	1.50
20	Mo Vaughn	2.00

2000 SPx SPx Signatures

These autographed inserts are seeded 1:112 packs.

		MT
Common Player:		15.00
Inserted 1:179		
JB	Jeff Bagwell	75.00
JC	Jose Canseco	90.00
SC	Sean Casey	30.00
RC	Roger Clemens	125.00
KG	Ken Griffey Jr.	275.00
VG	Vladimir Guerrero	80.00
TG	Tony Gwynn	80.00
OH	Orlando Hernandez	40.00
DJ	Derek Jeter	200.00
CJ	Chipper Jones	100.00
MR	Manny Ramirez	75.00
CR	Cal Ripken Jr.	225.00
IR	Ivan Rodriguez	75.00
SR	Scott Rolen	50.00

2000 SPx Untouchable Talents

These inserts have a holofoiled front and are numbered with a "UT" prefix. They are found on the average of 1:96 packs.

		MT
Complete Set (10):		220.00
Common Player:		10.00
Inserted 1:96		
1	Mark McGwire	50.00
2	Ken Griffey Jr.	50.00
3	Shawn Green	10.00
4	Ivan Rodriguez	15.00
5	Sammy Sosa	30.00
6	Derek Jeter	30.00
7	Sean Casey	10.00
8	Chipper Jones	25.00
9	Pedro Martinez	15.00
10	Vladimir Guerrero	20.00

2000 SPx SPxcitement

This 20-card set features a holofoiled front with gold foil stamping. Card backs are numbered with an "XC" prefix and are inserted 1:4 packs.

		MT
Complete Set (20):		35.00
Common Player:		1.00
Inserted 1:4		
1	Nomar Garciaparra	3.00
2	Mark McGwire	5.00
3	Derek Jeter	3.00
4	Cal Ripken Jr.	4.00
5	Barry Bonds	1.25
6	Alex Rodriguez	4.00
7	Scott Rolen	1.25
8	Pedro Martinez	1.25
9	Sean Casey	1.00
10	Sammy Sosa	3.00
11	Randy Johnson	1.00
12	Ivan Rodriguez	1.25
13	Frank Thomas	1.50
14	Greg Maddux	2.50
15	Tony Gwynn	2.50
16	Ken Griffey Jr.	5.00
17	Carlos Beltran	1.00
18	Mike Piazza	3.00
19	Chipper Jones	2.50
20	Craig Biggio	1.00

2000 SPx The Heart of the Order

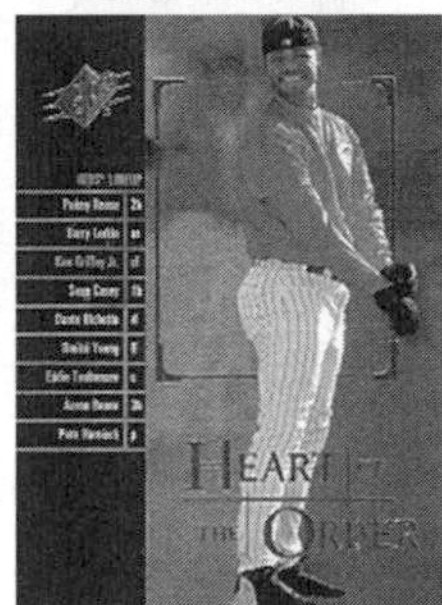

This 20-card set features a top hitter with his teams batting order to the left of his photo. The SPx logo and insert name are stamped in gold foil. Card backs are numbered with an "H" prefix and seeded 1:8 packs.

		MT
Complete Set (20):		60.00
Common Player:		1.50
Inserted 1:8		
1	Bernie Williams	2.00
2	Mike Piazza	6.00
3	Ivan Rodriguez	2.50
4	Mark McGwire	10.00
5	Manny Ramirez	2.50
6	Ken Griffey Jr.	10.00
7	Matt Williams	2.00
8	Sammy Sosa	6.00
9	Mo Vaughn	2.00
10	Carlos Delgado	2.00
11	Brian Giles	1.50
12	Chipper Jones	5.00
13	Sean Casey	1.50
14	Tony Gwynn	5.00
15	Barry Bonds	2.50
16	Carlos Beltran	1.50
17	Scott Rolen	2.50
18	Juan Gonzalez	2.50
19	Larry Walker	2.00
20	Vladimir Guerrero	4.00

2000 SPx Winning Materials

Five different tiers make up this memorabilia insert set with players having varying levels of their inserts in the set. Each insert has two pieces of memorabilia; combinations include jersey/bat, jersey/bat numbered to player's jersey number, jersey/cap, jersey/ball and ball/bat.

		MT
Common Player:		
AR	Alex Rodriguez bat/jersey	200.00
AR	Alex Rodriguez cap/jersey/100	300.00
AR	Alex Rodriguez ball/jersey/50	500.00
DJ	Derek Jeter bat/jersey	200.00
DJ	Derek Jeter ball/jersey/50	500.00
DJ	Derek Jeter bat/jersey/auto/2	
BB	Barry Bonds bat/jersey	125.00
BB	Barry Bonds cap/jersey/100	200.00
BB	Barry Bonds ball/jersey/auto/25	900.00
JB	Jeff Bagwell bat/jersey	100.00
JB	Jeff Bagwell cap/jersey/100	180.00
JB	Jeff Bagwell ball/jersey/50	300.00
KG	Ken Griffey Jr. bat/jersey	250.00
KG	Ken Griffey Jr. cap/jersey/100	450.00
KG	Ken Griffey Jr. jersey/bat/auto/24	3000.
TG	Tony Gwynn bat/jersey	125.00
TG	Tony Gwynn cap/jersey/100	200.00
BW	Bernie Williams bat/jersey	75.00
EC	Eric Chavez bat/jersey	40.00
EC	Eric Chavez cap/jersey/100	75.00
GM	Greg Maddux bat/jersey	125.00
IR	Ivan Rodriguez bat/jersey	90.00
JC	Jose Canseco bat/jersey	80.00
JL	Javy Lopez bat/jersey	50.00
JL	Javy Lopez cap/jersey/100	80.00
MM	Mark McGwire base/ball/500	450.00
MR	Manny Ramirez bat/jersey	75.00
MR	Manny Ramirez bat/jersey/auto./24	
MW	Matt Williams bat/jersey	50.00
PM	Pedro Martinez cap/jersey/100	250.00
PO	Paul O'Neill bat/jersey	50.00
VG	Vladimir Guerrero bat/jersey	100.00
VG	Vladimir Guerrero cap/jersey/100	200.00
VG	Vladimir Guerrero ball/jersey/50	250.00
TG	Troy Glaus bat/jersey	60.00

2000 SPx 3,000 Hit Club

A continuation of Upper Deck's cross brand insert program. This sets pays tribute to Ty Cobb with three variations. The collection includes 350 bat cards, three cut signatures and one bat/cut signature card.

		MT
TC-B	Ty Cobb bat/350	700.00
TC	Ty Cobb bat/cut/3	

1986 Sportflics

The premiere issue from Sportflics was distributed nationally by Amurol Division of Wrigley Gum Company. These high quality, three-phase "Magic Motion" cards depict three different photos per card, with each visible separately as the card is tilted. The 1986 issue features 200 full-color baseball cards plus 133 trivia cards. The cards come in the standard 2-1/2" x 3-1/2" size with the backs containing player stats and personal information. There are three different types of picture cards: 1) Tri-Star cards - 50 cards feature three players on one card; 2) Big Six cards - 10 cards which have six players in special categories; and 3) the Big Twelve card of 12 World Series players from the Kansas City Royals. The trivia cards are 1-3/4" x 2" and do not have player photos.

		MT
Complete Set (200):		10.00
Common Player:		.10
1	George Brett	2.00
2	Don Mattingly	3.00
3	Wade Boggs	1.25
4	Eddie Murray	1.00
5	Dale Murphy	.65
6	Rickey Henderson	.65
7	Harold Baines	.15
8	Cal Ripken, Jr.	5.00
9	Orel Hershiser	.15
10	Bret Saberhagen	.15
11	Tim Raines	.15
12	Fernando Valenzuela	.15
13	Tony Gwynn	1.50
14	Pedro Guerrero	.10
15	Keith Hernandez	.10
16	Ernest Riles	.10
17	Jim Rice	.15
18	Ron Guidry	.10
19	Willie McGee	.15
20	Ryne Sandberg	1.50
21	Kirk Gibson	.10
22	Ozzie Guillen	.10

23 Dave Parker .10
24 Vince Coleman .10
25 Tom Seaver .75
26 Brett Butler .10
27 Steve Carlton .65
28 Gary Carter .25
29 Cecil Cooper .10
30 Jose Cruz .10
31 Alvin Davis .10
32 Dwight Evans .10
33 Julio Franco .10
34 Damaso Garcia .10
35 Steve Garvey .40
36 Kent Hrbek .10
37 Reggie Jackson .75
38 Fred Lynn .10
39 Paul Molitor .75
40 Jim Presley .10
41 Dave Righetti .10
42a Robin Yount (Yankees logo on back) 150.00
42b Robin Yount (Brewers logo) 1.25
43 Nolan Ryan 5.00
44 Mike Schmidt 1.25
45 Lee Smith .10
46 Rick Sutcliffe .10
47 Bruce Sutter .10
48 Lou Whitaker .10
49 Dave Winfield .65
50 Pete Rose 3.00
51 N.L. MVPs (Steve Garvey, Pete Rose, Ryne Sandberg) .75
52 Slugging Stars (Harold Baines, George Brett, Jim Rice) .35
53 No-Hitters (Phil Niekro, Jerry Reuss, Mike Witt) .25
54 Big Hitters (Don Mattingly, Cal Ripken, Jr., Robin Yount) 2.00
55 Bullpen Aces (Goose Gossage, Dan Quisenberry, Lee Smith) .10
56 Rookies of the Year (Pete Rose, Steve Sax, Darryl Strawberry) 1.00
57 A.L. MVPs (Don Baylor, Reggie Jackson, Cal Ripken, Jr.) .50
58 Repeat Batting Champs (Bill Madlock, Dave Parker, Pete Rose) .45
59 Cy Young Winners (Mike Flanagan, Ron Guidry, LaMarr Hoyt) .10
60 Double Award Winners (Tom Seaver, Rick Sutcliffe, Fernando Valenzuela) .20
61 Home Run Champs (Tony Armas, Reggie Jackson, Jim Rice) .25
62 N.L. MVPs (Keith Hernandez, Dale Murphy, Mike Schmidt) .40
63 A.L. MVPs (George Brett, Fred Lynn, Robin Yount) .30
64 Comeback Players (Bert Blyleven, John Denny, Jerry Koosman) .10
65 Cy Young Relievers (Rollie Fingers, Willie Hernandez, Bruce Sutter) .10
66 Rookies of the Year (Andre Dawson, Bob Horner, Gary Matthews) .20
67 Rookies of the Year (Carlton Fisk, Ron Kittle, Tom Seaver) .20
68 Home Run Champs (George Foster, Dave Kingman, Mike Schmidt) .25
69 Double Award Winners (Rod Carew, Cal Ripken, Jr. , Pete Rose) 2.00
70 Cy Young Winners (Steve Carlton, Tom Seaver, Rick Sutcliffe) .25
71 Top Sluggers (Reggie Jackson, Fred Lynn, Robin Yount) .40
72 Rookies of the Year (Dave Righetti, Rick Sutcliffe, Fernando Valenzuela) .10
73 Rookies of the Year (Fred Lynn, Eddie Murray, Cal Ripken, Jr.) .50
74 Rookies of the Year (Rod Carew, Alvin Davis, Lou Whitaker) .20
75 Batting Champs (Wade Boggs, Carney Lansford, Don Mattingly) 1.00
76 Jesse Barfield .10
77 Phil Bradley .10
78 Chris Brown .10
79 Tom Browning .10
80 Tom Brunansky .10
81 Bill Buckner .10
82 Chili Davis .10
83 Mike Davis .10
84 Rich Gedman .10
85 Willie Hernandez .10
86 Ron Kittle .10
87 Lee Lacy .10
88 Bill Madlock .10
89 Mike Marshall .10
90 Keith Moreland .10
91 Graig Nettles .10
92 Lance Parrish .10
93 Kirby Puckett 2.50
94 Juan Samuel .10
95 Steve Sax .10
96 Dave Stieb .10
97 Darryl Strawberry .25
98 Willie Upshaw .10
99 Frank Viola .10
100 Dwight Gooden .25
101 Joaquin Andujar .10
102 George Bell .10
103 Bert Blyleven .10
104 Mike Boddicker .10
105 Britt Burns .10
106 Rod Carew .65
107 Jack Clark .10
108 Danny Cox .10
109 Ron Darling .10
110 Andre Dawson .25
111 Leon Durham .10
112 Tony Fernandez .10
113 Tom Herr .10
114 Teddy Higuera .10
115 Bob Horner .10
116 Dave Kingman .10
117 Jack Morris .10
118 Dan Quisenberry .10
119 Jeff Reardon .10
120 Bryn Smith .10
121 Ozzie Smith .75
122 John Tudor .10
123 Tim Wallach .10
124 Willie Wilson .10
125 Carlton Fisk .25
126 RBI Sluggers (Gary Carter, George Foster, Al Oliver) .10
127 Run Scorers (Keith Hernandez, Tim Raines, Ryne Sandberg) .25
128 Run Scorers (Paul Molitor, Cal Ripken, Jr., Willie Wilson) .50
129 No-Hitters (John Candelaria, Dennis Eckersley, Bob Forsch) .10
130 World Series MVPs (Ron Cey, Rollie Fingers, Pete Rose) .35
131 All-Star Game MVPs (Dave Concepcion, George Foster, Bill Madlock) .10
132 Cy Young Winners (Vida Blue, John Denny, Fernando Valenzuela) .10
133 Comeback Players (Doyle Alexander, Joaquin Andujar, Richard Dotson) .10
134 Big Winners (John Denny, Tom Seaver, Rick Sutcliffe) .10
135 Veteran Pitchers (Phil Niekro, Tom Seaver, Don Sutton) .25
136 Rookies of the Year (Vince Coleman, Dwight Gooden, Alfredo Griffin) .40
137 All-Star Game MVPs (Gary Carter, Steve Garvey, Fred Lynn) .20
138 Veteran Hitters (Tony Perez, Pete Rose, Rusty Staub) .50
139 Power Hitters (George Foster, Jim Rice, Mike Schmidt) .30
140 Batting Champs (Bill Buckner, Tony Gwynn, Al Oliver) .35
141 No-Hitters (Jack Morris, Dave Righetti, Nolan Ryan) .50
142 No-Hitters (Vida Blue, Bert Blyleven, Tom Seaver) .10
143 Strikeout Kings (Dwight Gooden, Nolan Ryan, Fernando Valenzuela) 1.25
144 Base Stealers (Dave Lopes, Tim Raines, Willie Wilson) .10
145 RBI Sluggers (Tony Armas, Cecil Cooper, Eddie Murray) .15
146 A.L. MVPs (Rod Carew, Rollie Fingers, Jim Rice) .15
147 World Series MVPs (Rick Dempsey, Reggie Jackson, Alan Trammell) .25
148 World Series MVPs (Pedro Guerrero, Darrell Porter, Mike Schmidt) .20
149 ERA Leaders (Mike Boddicker, Ron Guidry, Rick Sutcliffe) .10
150 Comeback Players (Reggie Jackson, Dave Kingman, Fred Lynn) .20
151 Buddy Bell .10
152 Dennis Boyd .10
153 Dave Concepcion .10
154 Brian Downing .10
155 Shawon Dunston .10
156 John Franco .10
157 Scott Garrelts .10
158 Bob James .10
159 Charlie Leibrandt .10
160 Oddibe McDowell .10
161 Roger McDowell .10
162 Mike Moore .10
163 Phil Niekro .50
164 Al Oliver .10
165 Tony Pena .10
166 Ted Power .10
167 Mike Scioscia .10
168 Mario Soto .10
169 Bob Stanley .10
170 Garry Templeton .10
171 Andre Thornton .10
172 Alan Trammell .20
173 Doug DeCinces .10
174 Greg Walker .10
175 Don Sutton .45
176 1985 Award Winners (Vince Coleman, Dwight Gooden, Ozzie Guillen, Don Mattingly, Willie McGee, Bret Saberhagen) .75
177 1985 Hot Rookies (Stewart Cliburn, Brian Fisher, Joe Hesketh, Joe Orsulak, Mark Salas, Larry Sheets) .10
178a Future Stars (Jose Canseco, Mark Funderburk, Mike Greenwell, Steve Lombardozzi, Billy Joe Robidoux, Danny Tartabull) 4.50
178b Future Stars (Jose Canseco, Mike Greenwell, Steve Lombardozzi, Billy Jo Robidoux, Danny Tartabull, Jim Wilson) 60.00
179 Gold Glove (George Brett, Ron Guidry, Keith Hernandez, Don Mattingly, Willie McGee, Dale Murphy) 1.00
180 .300 (Wade Boggs, George Brett, Rod Carew, Cecil Cooper, Don Mattingly, Willie Wilson) 1.00
181 .300 (Pedro Guerrero, Tony Gwynn, Keith Hernandez, Bill Madlock, Dave Parker, Pete Rose) .75
182 1985 Milestones (Rod Carew, Phil Niekro, Pete Rose, Nolan Ryan, Tom Seaver, Matt Tallman) 1.50
183 1985 Triple Crown (Wade Boggs, Darrell Evans, Don Mattingly, Willie McGee, Dale Murphy, Dave Parker) 1.00
184 1985 HL (Wade Boggs, Dwight Gooden, Rickey Henderson, Don Mattingly, Willie McGee, John Tudor) 1.00
185 1985 20-Game Winners (Joaquin Andujar, Tom Browning,

No.	Player	MT
	Dwight Gooden, Ron Guidry, Bret Saberhagen, John Tudor)	.35
186	World Series Champs (Steve Balboni, George Brett, Dane Iorg, Danny Jackson, Charlie Leibrandt, Darryl Motley, Dan Quisenberry, Bret Saberhagen, Lonnie Smith, Jim Sundberg, Frank White, Willie Wilson)	.40
187	Hubie Brooks	.10
188	Glenn Davis	.10
189	Darrell Evans	.10
190	Rich Gossage	.10
191	Andy Hawkins	.10
192	Jay Howell	.10
193	LaMarr Hoyt	.10
194	Davey Lopes	.10
195	Mike Scott	.10
196	Ted Simmons	.10
197	Gary Ward	.10
198	Bob Welch	.10
199	Mike Young	.10
200	Buddy Biancalana	.10

1986 Sportflics Rookies

The 1986 Rookies set offers 50 cards and features 47 individual rookie players. In addition, there are two Tri-Star cards; one highlights former Rookies of the Year and the other features three prominent players. There is one "Big Six" card featuring six superstars. The full-color photos on the 2-1/2" x 3-1/2" cards use Sportflics three-phase "Magic Motion" animation. The set was packaged in a collector box which also contained 34 trivia cards that measure 1-3/4" x 2". The set was distributed only by hobby dealers.

No.	Player	MT
	Complete Set (50):	8.00
	Common Player:	.10
1	John Kruk	.10
2	Edwin Correa	.10
3	Pete Incaviglia	.10
4	Dale Sveum	.10
5	Juan Nieves	.10
6	Will Clark	1.50
7	Wally Joyner	.75
8	Lance McCullers	.10
9	Scott Bailes	.10
10	Dan Plesac	.10
11	Jose Canseco	2.00
12	Bobby Witt	.10
13	Barry Bonds	4.00
14	Andres Thomas	.10
15	Jim Deshaies	.10
16	Ruben Sierra	.10
17	Steve Lombardozzi	.10
18	Cory Snyder	.10
19	Reggie Williams	.10
20	Mitch Williams	.10
21	Glenn Braggs	.10
22	Danny Tartabull	.10
23	Charlie Kerfeld	.10
24	Paul Assenmacher	.10
25	Robby Thompson	.10
26	Bobby Bonilla	.25
27	Andres Galarraga	.40
28	Billy Jo Robidoux	.10
29	Bruce Ruffin	.10
30	Greg Swindell	.10
31	John Cangelosi	.10
32	Jim Traber	.10
33	Russ Morman	.10
34	Barry Larkin	.30
35	Todd Worrell	.10
36	John Cerutti	.10
37	Mike Kingery	.10
38	Mark Eichhorn	.10
39	Scott Bankhead	.10
40	Bo Jackson	.30
41	Greg Mathews	.10
42	Eric King	.10
43	Kal Daniels	.10
44	Calvin Schiraldi	.10
45	Mickey Brantley	.10
46	Outstanding Rookie Seasons (Fred Lynn, Willie Mays, Pete Rose)	.60
47	Outstanding Rookie Seasons (Dwight Gooden, Tom Seaver, Fernando Valenzuela)	.25
48	Outstanding Rookie Seasons (Eddie Murray, Dave Righetti, Cal Ripken, Jr., Steve Sax, Darryl Strawberry, Lou Whitaker)	.50
49	Kevin Mitchell	.10
50	Mike Diaz	.10

1987 Sportflics

In its second year in the national market, Sportflics' basic issue was again a 200-card set of 2-1/2" x 3-1/2" "Magic Motion" cards, which offer three different photos on the same card, each visible in turn as the card is moved from top to bottom or side to side. Besides single-player cards, the '87 Sportflics set includes several three- and six-player cards, though not as many as in the 1986 set. The card backs feature a small player portrait photo on the single-player cards, an innovation for 1987.

No.	Player	MT
	Complete Set (200):	10.00
	Common Player:	.10
1	Don Mattingly	1.00
2	Wade Boggs	1.00
3	Dale Murphy	.50
4	Rickey Henderson	.50
5	George Brett	1.00
6	Eddie Murray	.75
7	Kirby Puckett	1.00
8	Ryne Sandberg	1.00
9	Cal Ripken, Jr.	4.00
10	Roger Clemens	1.00
11	Ted Higuera	.10
12	Steve Sax	.10
13	Chris Brown	.10
14	Jesse Barfield	.10
15	Kent Hrbek	.10
16	Robin Yount	1.00
17	Glenn Davis	.10
18	Hubie Brooks	.10
19	Mike Scott	.10
20	Darryl Strawberry	.25
21	Alvin Davis	.10
22	Eric Davis	.10
23	Danny Tartabull	.10
24a	Cory Snyder (Pat Tabler photo on back)	2.00
24b	Cory Snyder (Pat Tabler photo on back) (facing front, 1/4 swing on front)	2.00
24c	Cory Snyder (Snyder photo on back) (facing to side)	1.00
25	Pete Rose	1.00
26	Wally Joyner	.25
27	Pedro Guerrero	.10
28	Tom Seaver	.75
29	Bob Knepper	.10
30	Mike Schmidt	1.00
31	Tony Gwynn	1.00
32	Don Slaught	.10
33	Todd Worrell	.10
34	Tim Raines	.15
35	Dave Parker	.10
36	Bob Ojeda	.10
37	Pete Incaviglia	.10
38	Bruce Hurst	.10
39	Bobby Witt	.10
40	Steve Garvey	.35
41	Dave Winfield	.75
42	Jose Cruz	.10
43	Orel Hershiser	.10
44	Reggie Jackson	1.00
45	Chili Davis	.10
46	Robby Thompson	.10
47	Dennis Boyd	.10
48	Kirk Gibson	.10
49	Fred Lynn	.10
50	Gary Carter	.25
51	George Bell	.10
52	Pete O'Brien	.10
53	Ron Darling	.10
54	Paul Molitor	.75
55	Mike Pagliarulo	.10
56	Mike Boddicker	.10
57	Dave Righetti	.10
58	Len Dykstra	.15
59	Mike Witt	.10
60	Tony Bernazard	.10
61	John Kruk	.10
62	Mike Krukow	.10
63	Sid Fernandez	.10
64	Gary Gaetti	.10
65	Vince Coleman	.10
66	Pat Tabler	.10
67	Mike Scioscia	.10
68	Scott Garrelts	.10
69	Brett Butler	.10
70	Bill Buckner	.10
71a	Dennis Rasmussen (John Montefusco photo on back; mustache)	.25
71b	Dennis Rasmussen (correct photo on back, no mustache)	.10
72	Tim Wallach	.10
73	Bob Horner	.10
74	Willie McGee	.10
75	A.L. First Basemen (Wally Joyner, Don Mattingly, Eddie Murray)	.50
76	Jesse Orosco	.10
77	N.L. Relief Pitchers (Jeff Reardon, Dave Smith, Todd Worrell)	.10
78	Candy Maldonado	.10
79	N.L. Shortstops (Hubie Brooks, Shawon Dunston, Ozzie Smith)	.15
80	A.L. Left Fielders (George Bell, Jose Canseco, Jim Rice)	.25
81	Bert Blyleven	.10
82	Mike Marshall	.10
83	Ron Guidry	.10
84	Julio Franco	.10
85	Willie Wilson	.10
86	Lee Lacy	.10
87	Jack Morris	.10
88	Ray Knight	.10
89	Phil Bradley	.10
90	Jose Canseco	.75
91	Gary Ward	.10
92	Mike Easler	.10
93	Tony Pena	.10
94	Dave Smith	.10
95	Will Clark	.75
96	Lloyd Moseby	.10
97	Jim Rice	.10
98	Shawon Dunston	.10
99	Don Sutton	.45
100	Dwight Gooden	.15
101	Lance Parrish	.10
102	Mark Langston	.10
103	Floyd Youmans	.10
104	Lee Smith	.10
105	Willie Hernandez	.10
106	Doug DeCinces	.10
107	Ken Schrom	.10
108	Don Carman	.10
109	Brook Jacoby	.10
110	Steve Bedrosian	.10
111	A.L. Pitchers (Roger Clemens, Teddy Higuera , Jack Morris)	.25
112	A.L. Second Basemen (Marty Barrett, Tony Bernazard, Lou Whitaker)	.10
113	A.L. Shortstops (Tony Fernandez, Scott Fletcher, Cal Ripken, Jr.)	.25
114	A.L. Third Basemen (Wade Boggs, George Brett, Gary Gaetti)	.25
115	N.L. Third Basemen (Chris Brown, Mike Schmidt, Tim Wallach)	.20
116	N.L. Second Basemen (Bill Doran, Johnny Ray, Ryne Sandberg)	.15
117	N.L. Right Fielders (Kevin Bass, Tony Gwynn, Dave Parker)	.15
118	Hot Rookie Prospects (David Clark, Pat Dodson, Ty Gainey, Phil Lombardi, Benito Santiago), *(Terry Steinbach)*	.55
119	1986 Season Highlights (Dave Righetti, Mike Scott, Fernando Valenzuela)	.10
120	N.L. Pitchers (Dwight Gooden, Mike Scott, Fernando Valenzuela)	.10
121	Johnny Ray	.10
122	Keith Moreland	.10

123	Juan Samuel	.10
124	Wally Backman	.10
125	Nolan Ryan	4.00
126	Greg Harris	.10
127	Kirk McCaskill	.10
128	Dwight Evans	.10
129	Rick Rhoden	.10
130	Bill Madlock	.10
131	Oddibe McDowell	.10
132	Darrell Evans	.10
133	Keith Hernandez	.10
134	Tom Brunansky	.10
135	Kevin McReynolds	.10
136	Scott Fletcher	.10
137	Lou Whitaker	.10
138	Carney Lansford	.10
139	Andre Dawson	.25
140	Carlton Fisk	.25
141	Buddy Bell	.10
142	Ozzie Smith	.75
143	Dan Pasqua	.10
144	Kevin Mitchell	.10
145	Bret Saberhagen	.10
146	Charlie Kerfeld	.10
147	Phil Niekro	.45
148	John Candelaria	.10
149	Rich Gedman	.10
150	Fernando Valenzuela	.10
151	N.L. Catchers (Gary Carter, Tony Pena, Mike Scioscia)	.10
152	N.L. Left Fielders (Vince Coleman, Jose Cruz, Tim Raines)	.10
153	A.L. Right Fielders (Harold Baines, Jesse Barfield, Dave Winfield)	.10
154	A.L. Catchers (Rich Gedman, Lance Parrish, Don Slaught)	.10
155	N.L. Center Fielders (Kevin McReynolds, Dale Murphy, Eric Davis)	.15
156	'86 Highlights (Jim Deshaies, Mike Schmidt, Don Sutton)	.10
157	A.L. Speedburners (John Cangelosi, Rickey Henderson, Gary Pettis)	.10
158	Hot Rookie Prospects (Randy Asadoor, Casey Candaele, Dave Cochrane, Rafael Palmeiro, Tim Pyznarski, Kevin Seitzer)	.75
159	The Best of the Best (Roger Clemens, Dwight Gooden, Rickey Henderson, Don Mattingly, Dale Murphy, Eddie Murray)	1.00
160	Roger McDowell	.10
161	Brian Downing	.10
162	Bill Doran	.10
163	Don Baylor	.10
164	Alfredo Griffin	.10
165	Don Aase	.10
166	Glenn Wilson	.10
167	Dan Quisenberry	.10
168	Frank White	.10
169	Cecil Cooper	.10
170	Jody Davis	.10
171	Harold Baines	.10
172	Rob Deer	.10
173	John Tudor	.10
174	Larry Parrish	.10
175	Kevin Bass	.10
176	Joe Carter	.10
177	Mitch Webster	.10
178	Dave Kingman	.10
179	Jim Presley	.10
180	Mel Hall	.10
181	Shane Rawley	.10
182	Marty Barrett	.10
183	Damaso Garcia	.10
184	Bobby Grich	.10
185	Leon Durham	.10
186	Ozzie Guillen	.10
187	Tony Fernandez	.10
188	Alan Trammell	.10
189	Jim Clancy	.10
190	Bo Jackson	.35
191	Bob Forsch	.10
192	John Franco	.10
193	Von Hayes	.10
194	A.L. Relief Pitchers (Don Aase, Mark Eichhorn, Dave Righetti)	.10
195	N.L. First Basemen (Will Clark, Glenn Davis, Keith Hernandez)	.20
196	'86 Highlights (Roger Clemens, Joe Cowley, Bob Horner)	.15
197	The Best of the Best (Wade Boggs, George Brett, Hubie Brooks, Tony Gwynn, Tim Raines, Ryne Sandberg)	.80
198	A.L. Center Fielders (Rickey Henderson, Fred Lynn, Kirby Puckett)	.50
199	N.L. Speedburners (Vince Coleman, Tim Raines, Eric Davis)	.10
200	Steve Carlton	.45

1987 Sportflics Rookie Prospects

The Rookie Prospects set consists of 10 cards in standard 2-1/2" x 3-1/2" size. The card fronts feature Sportflics' "Magic Motion" process. Card backs contain a player photo plus a short biography and player personal and statistical information. The set was offered in two separately wrapped mylar packs of five cards to hobby dealers purchasing cases of Sportflics' Team Preview set. Twenty-four packs of "Rookie Prospects" cards were included with each case.

		MT
Complete Set (10):		6.00
Common Player:		.50
1	Terry Steinbach	.50
2	Rafael Palmeiro	2.00
3	Dave Magadan	.50
4	Marvin Freeman	.50
5	Brick Smith	.50
6	B.J. Surhoff	.60
7	John Smiley	.50
8	Alonzo Powell	.50
9	Benny Santiago	.50
10	Devon White	.75

1987 Sportflics Rookies

The Rookies set was issued in two series of 25 cards. The first was released in July with the second series following in October. The cards, which are the standard 2-1/2" x 3-1/2", feature Sportflics' special "Magic Motion" process. The card fronts contain a full-color photo and present three different pictures, depending on how the card is held. The backs also contain a full-color photo along with player statistics and a biography.

		MT
Complete Set (50):		15.00
Common Player:		.20
1	Eric Bell	.20
2	Chris Bosio	.20
3	Bob Brower	.20
4	Jerry Browne	.20
5	Ellis Burks	.45
6	Casey Candaele	.20
7	Ken Gerhart	.20
8	Mike Greenwell	.20
9	Stan Jefferson	.20
10	Dave Magadan	.20
11	Joe Magrane	.20
12	Fred McGriff	3.00
13	Mark McGwire	12.00
14	Mark McLemore	.25
15	Jeff Musselman	.20
16	Matt Nokes	.20
17	Paul O'Neill	.90
18	Luis Polonia	.20
19	Benny Santiago	.25
20	Kevin Seitzer	.20
21	John Smiley	.20
22	Terry Steinbach	.25
23	B.J. Surhoff	.25
24	Devon White	.60
25	Matt Williams	3.00
26	DeWayne Buice	.20
27	Willie Fraser	.20
28	Bill Ripken	.20
29	Mike Henneman	.20
30	Shawn Hillegas	.20
31	Shane Mack	.20
32	Rafael Palmeiro	2.50
33	Mike Jackson	.20
34	Gene Larkin	.20
35	Jimmy Jones	.20
36	Gerald Young	.10
37	Ken Caminiti	.75
38	Sam Horn	.20
39	David Cone	.75
40	Mike Dunne	.20
41	Ken Williams	.20
42	John Morris	.20
43	Jim Lindeman	.20
44	Mike Stanley	.20
45	Les Straker	.20
46	Jeff Robinson	.20
47	Todd Benzinger	.20
48	Jeff Blauser	.20
49	John Marzano	.20
50	Keith Miller	.20

1988 Sportflics

The design of the 1988 Sportflics set differs greatly from the previous two years. Besides increasing the number of cards in the set to 225, Sportflics included the player name, team and uniform number on the card front. The triple-action color photos are surrounded by a red border. The backs are re-designed, also. Full-color action photos, plus extensive statistics and informative biographies are utilized. Three highlights cards and three rookie prospects card are included in the set. The cards are the standard 2-1/2" x 3-1/2".

		MT
Complete Set (225):		20.00
Common Player:		.10
1	Don Mattingly	1.00
2	Tim Raines	.15
3	Andre Dawson	.25
4	George Bell	.10
5	Joe Carter	.10
6	Matt Nokes	.10
7	Dave Winfield	.75
8	Kirby Puckett	1.00
9	Will Clark	.75
10	Eric Davis	.15
11	Rickey Henderson	.65
12	Ryne Sandberg	1.00
13	Jesse Barfield	.10
14	Ozzie Guillen	.10
15	Bret Saberhagen	.12
16	Tony Gwynn	1.50
17	Kevin Seitzer	.10
18	Jack Clark	.10
19	Danny Tartabull	.10
20	Ted Higuera	.10
21	Charlie Leibrandt, Jr.	.10
22	Benny Santiago	.10
23	Fred Lynn	.10
24	Rob Thompson	.10
25	Alan Trammell	.10
26	Tony Fernandez	.10
27	Rick Sutcliffe	.10
28	Gary Carter	.20
29	Cory Snyder	.10
30	Lou Whitaker	.10
31	Keith Hernandez	.10
32	Mike Witt	.10
33	Harold Baines	.10
34	Robin Yount	1.50
35	Mike Schmidt	1.00

36 Dion James .10
37 Tom Candiotti .10
38 Tracy Jones .10
39 Nolan Ryan 2.50
40 Fernando Valenzuela .10
41 Vance Law .10
42 Roger McDowell .10
43 Carlton Fisk .20
44 Scott Garrelts .10
45 Lee Guetterman .10
46 Mark Langston .10
47 Willie Randolph .10
48 Bill Doran .10
49 Larry Parrish .10
50 Wade Boggs .65
51 Shane Rawley .10
52 Alvin Davis .10
53 Jeff Reardon .10
54 Jim Presley .10
55 Kevin Bass .10
56 Kevin McReynolds .10
57 B.J. Surhoff .10
58 Julio Franco .10
59 Eddie Murray .40
60 Jody Davis .10
61 Todd Worrell .10
62 Von Hayes .10
63 Billy Hatcher .10
64 John Kruk .10
65 Tom Henke .10
66 Mike Scott .10
67 Vince Coleman .10
68 Ozzie Smith .75
69 Ken Williams .10
70 Steve Bedrosian .10
71 Luis Polonia .10
72 Brook Jacoby .10
73 Ron Darling .10
74 Lloyd Moseby .10
75 Wally Joyner .10
76 Dan Quisenberry .10
77 Scott Fletcher .10
78 Kirk McCaskill .10
79 Paul Molitor 1.00
80 Mike Aldrete .10
81 Neal Heaton .10
82 Jeffrey Leonard .10
83 Dave Magadan .10
84 Danny Cox .10
85 Lance McCullers .10
86 Jay Howell .10
87 Charlie Hough .10
88 Gene Garber .10
89 Jesse Orosco .10
90 Don Robinson .10
91 Willie McGee .10
92 Bert Blyleven .10
93 Phil Bradley .10
94 Terry Kennedy .10
95 Kent Hrbek .10
96 Juan Samuel .10
97 Pedro Guerrero .10
98 Sid Bream .10
99 Devon White .10
100 Mark McGwire 3.00
101 Dave Parker .10
102 Glenn Davis .10
103 Greg Walker .10
104 Rick Rhoden .10
105 Mitch Webster .10
106 Lenny Dykstra .10
107 Gene Larkin .10
108 Floyd Youmans .10
109 Andy Van Slyke .10
110 Mike Scioscia .10
111 Kirk Gibson .10
112 Kal Daniels .10
113 Ruben Sierra .10
114 Sam Horn .10
115 Ray Knight .10
116 Jimmy Key .10
117 Bo Diaz .10
118 Mike Greenwell .10
119 Barry Bonds 1.50
120 Reggie Jackson .75
121 Mike Pagliarulo .10
122 Tommy John .10
123 Bill Madlock .10
124 Ken Caminiti .30
125 Gary Ward .10
126 Candy Maldonado .10
127 Harold Reynolds .10
128 Joe Magrane .10
129 Mike Henneman .10
130 Jim Gantner .10
131 Bobby Bonilla .10
132 John Farrell .10
133 Frank Tanana .10
134 Zane Smith .10
135 Dave Righetti .10
136 Rick Reuschel .10
137 Dwight Evans .10
138 Howard Johnson .10
139 Terry Leach .10
140 Casey Candaele .10
141 Tom Herr .10
142 Tony Pena .10
143 Lance Parrish .10
144 Ellis Burks .15
145 Pete O'Brien .10
146 Mike Boddicker .10
147 Buddy Bell .10
148 Bo Jackson .35
149 Frank White .10
150 George Brett 1.50
151 Tim Wallach .10
152 Cal Ripken, Jr. 2.50
153 Brett Butler .10
154 Gary Gaetti .10
155 Darryl Strawberry .20
156 Alfredo Griffin .10
157 Marty Barrett .10
158 Jim Rice .10
159 Terry Pendleton .10
160 Orel Hershiser .10
161 Larry Sheets .10
162 Dave Stewart .10
163 Shawon Dunston .10
164 Keith Moreland .10
165 Ken Oberkfell .10
166 Ivan Calderon .10
167 Bob Welch .10
168 Fred McGriff .50
169 Pete Incaviglia .10
170 Dale Murphy .25
171 Mike Dunne .10
172 Chili Davis .10
173 Milt Thompson .10
174 Terry Steinbach .10
175 Oddibe McDowell .10
176 Jack Morris .10
177 Sid Fernandez .10
178 Ken Griffey .10
179 Lee Smith .10
180 1987 Highlights (Juan Nieves, Kirby Puckett, Mike Schmidt) .25
181 Brian Downing .10
182 Andres Galarraga .25
183 Rob Deer .10
184 Greg Brock .10
185 Doug DeCinces .10
186 Johnny Ray .10
187 Hubie Brooks .10
188 Darrell Evans .10
189 Mel Hall .10
190 Jim Deshaies .10
191 Dan Plesac .10
192 Willie Wilson .10
193 Mike LaValliere .10
194 Tom Brunansky .10
195 John Franco .10
196 Frank Viola .10
197 Bruce Hurst .10
198 John Tudor .10
199 Bob Forsch .10
200 Dwight Gooden .15
201 Jose Canseco .75
202 Carney Lansford .10
203 Kelly Downs .10
204 Glenn Wilson .10
205 Pat Tabler .10
206 Mike Davis .10
207 Roger Clemens 1.00
208 Dave Smith .10
209 Curt Young .10
210 Mark Eichhorn .10
211 Juan Nieves .10
212 Bob Boone .10
213 Don Sutton .25
214 Willie Upshaw .10
215 Jim Clancy .10
216 Bill Ripken .10
217 Ozzie Virgil .10
218 Dave Concepcion .10
219 Alan Ashby .10
220 Mike Marshall .10
221 '87 Highlights (Vince Coleman, Mark McGwire, Paul Molitor) 2.00
222 '87 Highlights (Steve Bedrosian, Don Mattingly, Benito Santiago) .40
223 Hot Rookie Prospects (Shawn Abner), *(Jay Buhner*, Gary Thurman) .25
224 Hot Rookie Prospects (Tim Crews, John Davis, Vincente Palacios) .10
225 Hot Rookie Prospects (Keith Miller, Jody Reed, Jeff Treadway) .10

1989 Sportflics

This basic issue includes 225 standard-size player cards (2-1/2" x 3-1/2") and 153 trivia cards, all featuring the patented Magic Motion design. A 5-card sub-set of "Tri-Star" cards features a mix of veterans and rookies. The card fronts feature a white outer border and double color inner border in one of six color schemes. The inner border color changes when the card is tilted and the bottom border carries a double stripe of colors. The player name appears in the top border, player postition and uniform number appear, alternately, in the bottom border. The card backs contain crisp 1-7/8" by 1-3/4" player action shots, along with personal information, stats and career highlights. "The Unforgettables" trivia cards in this set salute members of the Hall of Fame.

MT
Complete Set (225): 20.00
Common Player: .10
1 Jose Canseco .60
2 Wally Joyner .20
3 Roger Clemens .75
4 Greg Swindell .10
5 Jack Morris .10
6 Mickey Brantley .10
7 Jim Presley .10
8 Pete O'Brien .10
9 Jesse Barfield .10
10 Frank Viola .10
11 Kevin Bass .10
12 Glenn Wilson .10
13 Chris Sabo .10
14 Fred McGriff .50
15 Mark Grace .25
16 Devon White .10
17 Juan Samuel .10
18 Lou Whitaker .10
19 Greg Walker .10
20 Roberto Alomar .50
21 Mike Schmidt .75
22 Benny Santiago .10
23 Dave Stewart .10
24 Dave Winfield .40
25 George Bell .10
26 Jack Clark .10
27 Doug Drabek .10
28 Ron Gant .15
29 Glenn Braggs .10
30 Rafael Palmeiro .25
31 Brett Butler .10
32 Ron Darling .10
33 Alvin Davis .10
34 Bob Walk .10
35 Dave Stieb .10
36 Orel Hershiser .10
37 John Farrell .10
38 Doug Jones .10
39 Kelly Downs .10
40 Bob Boone .10
41 Gary Sheffield .60
42 Doug Dascenzo .10
43 Chad Krueter .10
44 Ricky Jordan .10
45 Dave West .10
46 Danny Tartabull .10
47 Teddy Higuera .10
48 Gary Gaetti .10
49 Dave Parker .10
50 Don Mattingly 1.00
51 David Cone .10
52 Kal Daniels .10
53 Carney Lansford .10
54 Mike Marshall .10
55 Kevin Seitzer .10
56 Mike Henneman .10
57 Bill Doran .10
58 Steve Sax .10
59 Lance Parrish .10
60 Keith Hernandez .10
61 Jose Uribe .10
62 Jose Lind .10
63 Steve Bedrosian .10
64 George Brett .75
65 Kirk Gibson .10
66 Cal Ripken, Jr. 2.00
67 Mitch Webster .10
68 Fred Lynn .10
69 Eric Davis .10
70 Bo Jackson .50
71 Kevin Elster .10
72 Rick Reuschel .10
73 Tim Burke .10
74 Mark Davis .10
75 Claudell Washington .10
76 Lance McCullers .10
77 Mike Moore .10
78 Robby Thompson .10
79 Roger McDowell .10
80 Danny Jackson .10
81 Tim Leary .10
82 Bobby Witt .10
83 Jim Gott .10
84 Andy Hawkins .10
85 Ozzie Guillen .10
86 John Tudor .10
87 Todd Burns .10
88 Dave Gallagher .10
89 Jay Buhner .10
90 Gregg Jefferies .25
91 Bob Welch .10
92 Charlie Hough .10
93 Tony Fernandez .10
94 Ozzie Virgil .10
95 Andre Dawson .25
96 Hubie Brooks .10
97 Kevin McReynolds .10
98 Mike LaValliere .10
99 Terry Pendleton .10
100 Wade Boggs .75
101 Dennis Eckersley .10
102 Mark Gubicza .10
103 Frank Tanana .10
104 Joe Carter .10
105 Ozzie Smith .40
106 Dennis Martinez .10
107 Jeff Treadway .10
108 Greg Maddux 1.00
109 Bret Saberhagen .10
110 Dale Murphy .25
111 Rob Deer .10
112 Pete Incaviglia .10
113 Vince Coleman .10
114 Tim Wallach .10
115 Nolan Ryan 2.00

116	Walt Weiss	.10
117	Brian Downing	.10
118	Melido Perez	.10
119	Terry Steinbach	.10
120	Mike Scott	.10
121	Tim Belcher	.10
122	Mike Boddicker	.10
123	Len Dykstra	.10
124	Fernando Valenzuela	.10
125	Gerald Young	.10
126	Tom Henke	.10
127	Dave Henderson	.10
128	Dan Plesac	.10
129	Chili Davis	.10
130	Bryan Harvey	.10
131	Don August	.10
132	Mike Harkey	.10
133	Luis Polonia	.10
134	Craig Worthington	.10
135	Joey Meyer	.10
136	Barry Larkin	.20
137	Glenn Davis	.10
138	Mike Scioscia	.10
139	Andres Galarraga	.20
140	Doc Gooden	.15
141	Keith Moreland	.10
142	Kevin Mitchell	.10
143	Mike Greenwell	.10
144	Mel Hall	.10
145	Rickey Henderson	.35
146	Barry Bonds	1.00
147	Eddie Murray	.40
148	Lee Smith	.10
149	Julio Franco	.10
150	Tim Raines	.10
151	Mitch Williams	.10
152	Tim Laudner	.10
153	Mike Pagliarulo	.10
154	Floyd Bannister	.10
155	Gary Carter	.25
156	Kirby Puckett	.75
157	Harold Baines	.10
158	Dave Righetti	.10
159	Mark Langston	.10
160	Tony Gwynn	.75
161	Tom Brunansky	.10
162	Vance Law	.10
163	Kelly Gruber	.10
164	Gerald Perry	.10
165	Harold Reynolds	.10
166	Andy Van Slyke	.10
167	Jimmy Key	.10
168	Jeff Reardon	.10
169	Milt Thompson	.10
170	Will Clark	.65
171	Chet Lemon	.10
172	Pat Tabler	.10
173	Jim Rice	.10
174	Billy Hatcher	.10
175	Bruce Hurst	.10
176	John Franco	.10
177	Van Snider	.10
178	Ron Jones	.10
179	Jerald Clark	.10
180	Tom Browning	.10
181	Von Hayes	.10
182	Bobby Bonilla	.10
183	Todd Worrell	.10
184	John Kruk	.10
185	Scott Fletcher	.10
186	Willie Wilson	.10
187	Jody Davis	.10
188	Kent Hrbek	.10
189	Ruben Sierra	.10
190	Shawon Dunston	.10
191	Ellis Burks	.15
192	Brook Jacoby	.10
193	Jeff Robinson	.10
194	Rich Dotson	.10
195	Johnny Ray	.10
196	Cory Snyder	.10
197	Mike Witt	.10
198	Marty Barrett	.10
199	Robin Yount	.75
200	Mark McGwire	2.50
201	Ryne Sandberg	.75
202	John Candelaria	.10
203	Matt Nokes	.10
204	Dwight Evans	.10
205	Darryl Strawberry	.25
206	Willie McGee	.10
207	Bobby Thigpen	.10
208	B.J. Surhoff	.10
209	Paul Molitor	.40
210	Jody Reed	.10
211	Doyle Alexander	.10
212	Dennis Rasmussen	.10
213	Kevin Gross	.10
214	Kirk McCaskill	.10
215	Alan Trammell	.10
216	Damon Berryhill	.10
217	Rick Sutcliffe	.10
218	Don Slaught	.10
219	Carlton Fisk	.25
220	Allan Anderson	.10
221	'88 Highlights (Wade Boggs, Jose Canseco, Mike Greenwell)	.50
222	'88 Highlights (Tom Browning, Dennis Eckersley, Orel Hershiser)	.10
223	Hot Rookie Prospects (Sandy Alomar, Gregg Jefferies, Gary Sheffield)	1.00
224	Hot Rookie Prospects (Randy Johnson, Ramon Martinez, Bob Milacki)	2.00
225	Hot Rookie Prospects (Geronimo Berroa, Cameron Drew, Ron Jones)	.10

1990 Sportflics

The Sportflics set for 1990 again contains 225 cards. The cards feature the unique "Magic Motion" effect which displays either of two different photos depending on how the card is tilted. (Previous years' sets had used three photos per card.) The two-photo "Magic Motion" sequence is designed to depict sequential game-action, showing a batter following through on his swing, a pitcher completing his motion, etc. Sportflics also added a moving red and yellow "marquee" border on the cards to complement the animation effect. The player's name, which appears below the animation, remains stationary. The set includes 19 special rookie cards. The backs contain a color player photo, team logo, player information and stats. The cards were distributed in non-transparent mylar packs with small MVP trivia cards.

		MT
Complete Set (225):		18.00
Common Player:		.10
1	Kevin Mitchell	.10
2	Wade Boggs	.75
3	Cory Snyder	.10
4	Paul O'Neill	.20
5	Will Clark	.50
6	Tony Fernandez	.10
7	Ken Griffey, Jr.	3.00
8	Nolan Ryan	2.00
9	Rafael Palmeiro	.25
10	Jesse Barfield	.10
11	Kirby Puckett	.75
12	Steve Sax	.10
13	Fred McGriff	.40
14	Gregg Jefferies	.20
15	Mark Grace	.25
16	Devon White	.10
17	Juan Samuel	.10
18	Robin Yount	.75
19	Glenn Davis	.10
20	Jeffrey Leonard	.10
21	Chili Davis	.10
22	Craig Biggio	.25
23	Jose Canseco	.60
24	Derek Lilliquist	.10
25	Chris Bosio	.10
26	Dave Steib	.10
27	Bobby Thigpen	.10
28	Jack Clark	.10
29	Kevin Ritz	.10
30	Tom Gordon	.10
31	Bryan Harvey	.10
32	Jim Deshaies	.10
33	Terry Steinbach	.10
34	Tom Glavine	.15
35	Bob Welch	.10
36	Charlie Hayes	.10
37	Jeff Reardon	.10
38	Joe Orsulak	.10
39	Scott Garrelts	.10
40	Bob Boone	.10
41	Scott Bankhead	.10
42	Tom Henke	.10
43	Greg Briley	.10
44	Teddy Higuera	.10
45	Pat Borders	.10
46	Kevin Seitzer	.10
47	Bruce Hurst	.10
48	Ozzie Guillen	.10
49	Wally Joyner	.15
50	Mike Greenwell	.10
51	Gary Gaetti	.10
52	Gary Sheffield	.40
53	Dennis Martinez	.10
54	Ryne Sandberg	.60
55	Mike Scott	.10
56	Todd Benzinger	.10
57	Kelly Gruber	.10
58	Jose Lind	.10
59	Allan Anderson	.10
60	Robby Thompson	.10
61	John Smoltz	.15
62	Mark Davis	.10
63	Tom Herr	.10
64	Randy Johnson	.45
65	Lonnie Smith	.10
66	Pedro Guerrero	.10
67	Jerome Walton	.10
68	Ramon Martinez	.10
69	Tim Raines	.10
70	Matt Williams	.40
71	Joe Oliver	.10
72	Nick Esasky	.10
73	Kevin Brown	.15
74	Walt Weiss	.10
75	Roger McDowell	.10
76	Jose DeLeon	.10
77	Brian Downing	.10
78	Jay Howell	.10
79	Jose Uribe	.10
80	Ellis Burks	.15
81	Sammy Sosa	2.50
82	Johnny Ray	.10
83	Danny Darwin	.10
84	Carney Lansford	.10
85	Jose Oquendo	.10
86	John Cerutti	.10
87	Dave Winfield	.40
88	Dave Righetti	.10
89	Danny Jackson	.10
90	Andy Benes	.20
91	Tom Browning	.10
92	Pete O'Brien	.10
93	Roberto Alomar	.50
94	Bret Saberhagen	.10
95	Phil Bradley	.10
96	Doug Jones	.10
97	Eric Davis	.10
98	Tony Gwynn	1.00
99	Jim Abbott	.10
100	Cal Ripken, Jr.	2.00
101	Andy Van Slyke	.10
102	Dan Plesac	.10
103	Lou Whitaker	.10
104	Steve Bedrosian	.10
105	Dave Gallagher	.10
106	Keith Hernandez	.10
107	Duane Ward	.10
108	Andre Dawson	.15
109	Howard Johnson	.10
110	Mark Langston	.10
111	Jerry Browne	.10
112	Alvin Davis	.10
113	Sid Fernandez	.10
114	Mike Devereaux	.10
115	Benny Santiago	.10
116	Bip Roberts	.10
117	Craig Worthington	.10
118	Kevin Elster	.10
119	Harold Reynolds	.10
120	Joe Carter	.10
121	Brian Harper	.10
122	Frank Viola	.10
123	Jeff Ballard	.10
124	John Kruk	.10
125	Harold Baines	.10
126	Tom Candiotti	.10
127	Kevin McReynolds	.10
128	Mookie Wilson	.10
129	Danny Tartabull	.10
130	Craig Lefferts	.10
131	Jose DeJesus	.10
132	John Orton	.10
133	Curt Schilling	.10
134	Marquis Grissom	.10
135	Greg Vaughn	.10
136	Brett Butler	.10
137	Rob Deer	.10
138	John Franco	.10
139	Keith Moreland	.10
140	Dave Smith	.10
141	Mark McGwire	3.00
142	Vince Coleman	.10
143	Barry Bonds	.75
144	Mike Henneman	.10
145	Doc Gooden	.15
146	Darryl Strawberry	.15
147	Von Hayes	.10
148	Andres Galarraga	.15
149	Roger Clemens	.75
150	Don Mattingly	1.00
151	Joe Magrane	.10
152	Dwight Smith	.10
153	Ricky Jordan	.10
154	Alan Trammell	.10
155	Brook Jacoby	.10
156	Lenny Dykstra	.10
157	Mike LaValliere	.10
158	Julio Franco	.10
159	Joey Belle	.75
160	Barry Larkin	.20
161	Rick Reuschel	.10
162	Nelson Santovenia	.10
163	Mike Scioscia	.10
164	Damon Berryhill	.10
165	Todd Worrell	.10
166	Jim Eisenreich	.10
167	Ivan Calderon	.10
168	Goose Gozzo	.10
169	Kirk McCaskill	.10
170	Dennis Eckersley	.10
171	Mickey Tettleton	.10
172	Chuck Finley	.10
173	Dave Magadan	.10
174	Terry Pendleton	.10
175	Willie Randolph	.10
176	Jeff Huson	.10
177	Todd Zeile	.10
178	Steve Olin	.10
179	Eric Anthony	.10
180	Scott Coolbaugh	.10
181	Rick Sutcliffe	.10
182	Tim Wallach	.10
183	Paul Molitor	.75
184	Roberto Kelly	.10
185	Mike Moore	.10
186	Junior Felix	.10
187	Mike Schooler	.10
188	Ruben Sierra	.10
189	Dale Murphy	.20
190	Dan Gladden	.10
191	John Smiley	.10
192	Jeff Russell	.10
193	Bert Blyleven	.10
194	Dave Stewart	.10

195	Bobby Bonilla	.10
196	Mitch Williams	.10
197	Orel Hershiser	.10
198	Kevin Bass	.10
199	Tim Burke	.10
200	Bo Jackson	.40
201	David Cone	.10
202	Gary Pettis	.10
203	Kent Hrbek	.10
204	Carlton Fisk	.15
205	Bob Geren	.10
206	Bill Spiers	.10
207	Oddibe McDowell	.10
208	Rickey Henderson	.40
209	Ken Caminiti	.15
210	Devon White	.10
211	Greg Maddux	1.00
212	Ed Whitson	.10
213	Carlos Martinez	.10
214	George Brett	.75
215	Gregg Olson	.10
216	Kenny Rogers	.10
217	Dwight Evans	.10
218	Pat Tabler	.10
219	Jeff Treadway	.10
220	Scott Fletcher	.10
221	Deion Sanders	.40
222	Robin Ventura	.15
223	Chip Hale	.10
224	Tommy Greene	.10
225	Dean Palmer	.10

1994 Sportflics 2000 Promos

To reintroduce its "Magic Motion" baseball cards to the hobby (last produced by Score in 1990), Pinnacle Brands produced a three-card promo set which it sent to dealers along with a header card explaining the issue. In the same format as the regular issue, though some different photos were used, the promos feature on front what Sportflics calls "state-of-the-art lenticular technology" to create an action effect when the card is moved. Backs are produced by standard printing techniques and are gold-foil highlighted and UV-coated. Each of the promo cards has a large black "SAMPLE" overprinted diagonally across front and back.

		MT
Complete Set (4):		12.00
Common Player:		4.00
1	Lenny Dykstra	1.00
7	Javy Lopez (Shakers)	4.00
193	Greg Maddux (Starflics)	10.00
	Header card	.40
7	Javy Lopez (Shakers)	16.00
----	Header card	.40

1994 Sportflics 2000

The concept of "Magic Motion" baseball cards returned to the hobby in 1994 after a three-year hiatus. Pinnacle Brands refined its "state-of-the-art lenticular technology" to produce cards which show alternating pictures when viewed from different angles on the basic cards, and to create a striking 3-D effect on its "Starflics" A.L. and N.L. all-star team subset. Backs use conventional printing techniques and are UV-coated and gold-foil highlighted, featuring a player photo and recent stats. Cards were sold in eight-card foil packs with a suggested retail price of $2.49.

		MT
Complete Set (193):		20.00
Common Player:		.10
Pack (8):		1.50
Wax Box (24):		30.00
1	Len Dykstra	.10
2	Mike Stanley	.10
3	Alex Fernandez	.10
4	Mark McGuire (McGwire)	3.00
5	Eric Karros	.10
6	Dave Justice	.15
7	Jeff Bagwell	.75
8	Darren Lewis	.10
9	David McCarty	.10
10	Albert Belle	.60
11	Ben McDonald	.10
12	Joe Carter	.10
13	Benito Santiago	.10
14	Rob Dibble	.10
15	Roger Clemens	.60
16	Travis Fryman	.10
17	Doug Drabek	.10
18	Jay Buhner	.10
19	Orlando Merced	.10
20	Ryan Klesko	.40
21	Chuck Finley	.10
22	Dante Bichette	.30
23	Wally Joyner	.10
24	Robin Yount	.60
25	Tony Gwynn	.75
26	Allen Watson	.10
27	Rick Wilkins	.10
28	Gary Sheffield	.30
29	John Burkett	.10
30	Randy Johnson	.30
31	Roberto Alomar	.50
32	Fred McGriff	.30
33	Ozzie Guillen	.10
34	Jimmy Key	.10
35	Juan Gonzalez	.75
36	Wil Cordero	.10
37	Aaron Sele	.10
38	Mark Langston	.10
39	David Cone	.10
40	John Jaha	.10
41	Ozzie Smith	.60
42	Kirby Puckett	1.00
43	Kenny Lofton	.45
44	Mike Mussina	.30
45	Ryne Sandberg	.75
46	Robby Thompson	.10
47	Bryan Harvey	.10
48	Marquis Grissom	.10
49	Bobby Bonilla	.10
50	Dennis Eckersley	.10
51	Curt Schilling	.10
52	Andy Benes	.10
53	Greg Maddux	2.00
54	Bill Swift	.10
55	Andres Galarraga	.20
56	Tony Phillips	.10
57	Darryl Hamilton	.10
58	Duane Ward	.10
59	Bernie Williams	.30
60	Steve Avery	.10
61	Eduardo Perez	.10
62	Jeff Conine	.10
63	Dave Winfield	.25
64	Phil Plantier	.10
65	Ray Lankford	.10
66	Robin Ventura	.10
67	Mike Piazza	2.00
68	Jason Bere	.10
69	Cal Ripken, Jr.	2.50
70	Frank Thomas	1.50
71	Carlos Baerga	.10
72	Darryl Kile	.10
73	Ruben Sierra	.10
74	Gregg Jefferies	.10
75	John Olerud	.10
76	Andy Van Slyke	.10
77	Larry Walker	.30
78	Cecil Fielder	.10
79	Andre Dawson	.15
80	Tom Glavine	.20
81	Sammy Sosa	1.00
82	Charlie Hayes	.10
83	Chuck Knoblauch	.15
84	Kevin Appier	.10
85	Dean Palmer	.10
86	Royce Clayton	.10
87	Moises Alou	.10
88	Ivan Rodriguez	.60
89	Tim Salmon	.35
90	Ron Gant	.10
91	Barry Bonds	.75
92	Jack McDowell	.10
93	Alan Trammell	.10
94	Dwight Gooden	.10
95	Jay Bell	.10
96	Devon White	.10
97	Wilson Alvarez	.10
98	Jim Thome	.20
99	Ramon Martinez	.10
100	Kent Hrbek	.10
101	John Kruk	.10
102	Wade Boggs	.45
103	Greg Vaughn	.10
104	Tom Henke	.10
105	Brian Jordan	.10
106	Paul Molitor	.45
107	Cal Eldred	.10
108	Deion Sanders	.30
109	Barry Larkin	.20
110	Mike Greenwell	.10
111	Jeff Blauser	.10
112	Jose Rijo	.10
113	Pete Harnisch	.10
114	Chris Hoiles	.10
115	Edgar Martinez	.10
116	Juan Guzman	.10
117	Todd Zeile	.10
118	Danny Tartabull	.10
119	Chad Curtis	.10
120	Mark Grace	.25
121	J.T. Snow	.10
122	Mo Vaughn	.45
123	Lance Johnson	.10
124	Eric Davis	.10
125	Orel Hershiser	.10
126	Kevin Mitchell	.10
127	Don Mattingly	1.00
128	Darren Daulton	.10
129	Rod Beck	.10
130	Charles Nagy	.10
131	Mickey Tettleton	.10
132	Kevin Brown	.10
133	Pat Hentgen	.10
134	Terry Mulholland	.10
135	Steve Finley	.10
136	John Smoltz	.15
137	Frank Viola	.10
138	Jim Abbott	.10
139	Matt Williams	.25
140	Bernard Gilkey	.10
141	Jose Canseco	.40
142	Mark Whiten	.10
143	Ken Griffey, Jr.	3.00
144	Rafael Palmeiro	.20
145	Dave Hollins	.10
146	Will Clark	.25
147	Paul O'Neill	.10
148	Bobby Jones	.10
149	Butch Huskey	.15
150	Jeffrey Hammonds	.10
151	Manny Ramirez	.75
152	Bob Hamelin	.10
153	Kurt Abbott	.10
154	Scott Stahoviak	.10
155	Steve Hosey	.10
156	Salomon Torres	.10
157	Sterling Hitchcock	.10
158	Nigel Wilson	.10
159	Luis Lopez	.10
160	Chipper Jones	2.00
161	Norberto Martin	.10
162	Raul Mondesi	.45
163	Steve Karsay	.10
164	J.R. Phillips	.10
165	Marc Newfield	.10
166	Mark Hutton	.10
167	Curtis Pride	.10
168	Carl Everett	.10
169	Scott Ruffcorn	.10
170	Turk Wendell	.10
171	Jeff McNeely	.10
172	Javier Lopez	.25
173	Cliff Floyd	.10
174	Rondell White	.20
175	Scott Lydy	.10
176	Frank Thomas	.75
177	Roberto Alomar	.40
178	Travis Fryman	.10
179	Cal Ripken, Jr.	1.25
180	Chris Hoiles	.10
181	Ken Griffey, Jr.	1.50
182	Juan Gonzalez	.50
183	Joe Carter	.10
184	Jack McDowell	.10
185	Fred McGriff	.25
186	Robby Thompson	.10
187	Matt Williams	.20
188	Jay Bell	.10
189	Mike Piazza	1.00
190	Barry Bonds	.50
191	Len Dykstra	.10
192	Dave Justice	.20
193	Greg Maddux	1.00

1994 Sportflics 2000 Commemora-tives

A pair of extra-rare commemorative chase cards was produced for the Sportflics 2000 set honoring Canada's veteran superstar Paul Molitor and its hottest rookie, Cliff Floyd. Cards, utilizing Magic Motion technology to alternate card-front pictures when the viewing angle changes, were inserted on average once in every 360 packs.

		MT
Complete Set (2):		12.50
1	Paul Molitor	10.00
2	Cliff Floyd	3.75

1994 Sportflics 2000 Movers

A dozen top veteran ballplayers were featured in the "Movers" insert set produced for inclusion in retail packaging of Sportflics 2000. The inserts feature the same Magic Motion features as the regular cards, showing different images on the card front when the card is viewed from different angles. The UV-coated, gold-foil highlighted backs are printed conventionally. A special "Movers" logo is found on both front and back. Stated odds of finding a Movers card are one in 24 packs.

		MT
Complete Set (12):		40.00
Common Player:		2.00
1	Gregg Jefferies	2.00
2	Ryne Sandberg	6.00
3	Cecil Fielder	2.00
4	Kirby Puckett	8.00
5	Tony Gwynn	8.00
6	Andres Galarraga	2.00
7	Sammy Sosa	12.00
8	Rickey Henderson	2.50
9	Don Mattingly	10.00
10	Joe Carter	2.00
11	Carlos Baerga	2.00
12	Len Dykstra	2.00

1994 Sportflics 2000 Shakers

Hobby packs are the exclusive source for this 12-card insert set of top rookies, found on average once every 24 packs. The chase cards utilize the Sportflics Magic Motion technology to create two different images on the card front when the card is viewed from different angles. Backs are printed conventionally but feature UV-coating and gold-foil highlights. The "Shakers" logo appears on both front and back.

		MT
Complete Set (12):		60.00
Common Player:		2.00
1	Kenny Lofton	6.00
2	Tim Salmon	3.00
3	Jeff Bagwell	12.00
4	Jason Bere	2.00
5	Salomon Torres	2.00
6	Rondell White	3.00
7	Javier Lopez	3.00
7s	Javier Lopez (overprinted "SAMPLE")	5.00
8	Dean Palmer	2.00
9	Jim Thome	3.00
10	J.T. Snow	2.50
11	Mike Piazza	15.00
12	Manny Ramirez	10.00

1994 Sportflics 2000 Rookie/Traded Promos

This nine-card set was issued to promote the Sportflics Rookie/Traded update set which was released as a hobby-only product. Cards are virtually identical to the corresponding cards in the R/T set except for the overprinted "SAMPLE" in white on front and back.

		MT
Complete Set (9):		8.00
Common Player:		1.00
1	Will Clark	2.50
14	Bret Boone	1.00
20	Ellis Burks	1.00
25	Deion Sanders	1.50
62	Chris Turner	1.00
82	Tony Tarasco	1.00
102	Rich Becker	1.00
GG1	Gary Sheffield (Going, Going, Gone)	2.00
---	Header card	.20

1994 Sportflics 2000 Rookie/Traded

Each of the 150 regular cards in the Sportflics 2000 Rookie & Traded issue was also produced in a parallel chase card set designated on front with a black and gold "Artist's Proof" logo. Stated odds of finding an AP cards were one per 24 packs. Fewer than 1,000 or each AP card were reportedly produced.

		MT
Complete Set (150):		25.00
Common Player:		.25
Pack (5):		3.00
Wax Box (24):		60.00
1	Will Clark	1.00
2	Sid Fernandez	.25
3	Joe Magrane	.25
4	Pete Smith	.25
5	Roberto Kelly	.25
6	Delino DeShields	.25
7	Brian Harper	.25
8	Darrin Jackson	.25
9	Omar Vizquel	.30
10	Luis Polonia	.25
11	Reggie Jefferson	.25
12	Geronimo Berroa	.25
13	Mike Harkey	.25
14	Bret Boone	.30
15	Dave Henderson	.25
16	Pedro Martinez	.60
17	Jose Vizcaino	.25
18	Xavier Hernandez	.25
19	Eddie Taubensee	.25
20	Ellis Burks	.30
21	Turner Ward	.25
22	Terry Mulholland	.25
23	Howard Johnson	.25
24	Vince Coleman	.25
25	Deion Sanders	1.50
26	Rafael Palmeiro	.75
27	Dave Weathers	.25
28	Kent Mercker	.25
29	Gregg Olson	.25
30	Cory Bailey	.25
31	Brian Hunter	1.50
32	Garey Ingram	.25
33	Daniel Smith	.25
34	Denny Hocking	.25
35	Charles Johnson	1.50
36	Otis Nixon	.25
37	Hector Fajardo	.25
38	Lee Smith	.25
39	Phil Stidham	.25
40	Melvin Nieves	.25
41	Julio Franco	.25
42	Greg Gohr	.25
43	Steve Dunn	.25
44	Tony Fernandez	.25
45	Toby Borland	.25
46	Paul Shuey	.25
47	Shawn Hare	.25
48	Shawn Green	2.00
49	*Julian Tavarez*	.25
50	Ernie Young	.50
51	Chris Sabo	.25
52	Greg O'Halloran	.25
53	Donnie Elliott	.25
54	Jim Converse	.25
55	Ray Holbert	.25
56	Keith Lockhart	.25
57	Tony Longmire	.25
58	Jorge Fabregas	.25
59	Ravelo Manzanillo	.25
60	Marcus Moore	.25
61	Carlos Rodriguez	.25
62	Mark Portugal	.25
63	Yorkis Perez	.25
64	Dan Miceli	.25
65	Chris Turner	.25
66	Mike Oquist	.25
67	Tom Quinlan	.25
68	Matt Walbeck	.25
69	Dave Staton	.25
70	*Bill Van Landingham*	.25
71	Dave Stevens	.25
72	Domingo Cedeno	.25
73	Alex Diaz	.25
74	Darren Bragg	.30
75	James Hurst	.25
76	Alex Gonzalez	.60
77	Steve Dreyer	.25
78	Robert Eenhoorn	.25
79	Derek Parks	.25
80	Jose Valentin	.25
81	Wes Chamberlain	.25
82	Tony Tarasco	.25
83	Steve Trachsel	.40
84	Willie Banks	.25
85	Rob Butler	.25
86	Miguel Jimenez	.25
87	Gerald Williams	.25
88	Aaron Small	.25
89	Matt Mieske	.25
90	Tim Hyers	.25
91	Eddie Murray	.75
92	Dennis Martinez	.25
93	Tony Eusebio	.25
94	*Brian Anderson*	1.00
95	Blaise Ilsley	.25
96	Johnny Ruffin	.25
97	Carlos Reyes	.25
98	Greg Pirkl	.25
99	Jack Morris	.25
100	John Mabry	.50
101	Mike Kelly	.25
102	Rich Becker	.25
103	Chris Gomez	.25
104	Jim Edmonds	1.50
105	Rich Rowland	.25
106	Damon Buford	.25
107	Mark Kiefer	.25
108	Matias Carrillo	.25
109	James Mouton	.25
110	Kelly Stinnett	.25
111	Billy Ashley	.25
112	*Fausto Cruz*	.35
113	Roberto Petagine	.25
114	Joe Hall	.25
115	*Brian Johnson*	.40
116	Kevin Jarvis	.25
117	Tim Davis	.25
118	John Patterson	.25
119	Stan Royer	.25
120	Jeff Juden	.25
121	Bryan Eversgerd	.25
122	*Chan Ho Park*	1.50
123	Shane Reynolds	.25
124	Danny Bautista	.25
125	Rikkert Faneyte	.25
126	Carlos Pulido	.25
127	Mike Matheny	.25
128	Hector Carrasco	.25
129	Eddie Zambrano	.25
130	Lee Tinsley	.25
131	Roger Salkeld	.25
132	Carlos Delgado	.75
133	Troy O'Leary	.25
134	Keith Mitchell	.25
135	Lance Painter	.25
136	Nate Minchey	.25
137	Eric Anthony	.25
138	Rafael Bournigal	.25
139	Joey Hamilton	1.50
140	Bobby Munoz	.25
141	Rex Hudler	.25
142	Alex Cole	.25
143	Stan Javier	.25
144	Jose Oliva	.25
145	Tom Brunansky	.25
146	Greg Colbrunn	.25
147	Luis Lopez	.25
148	*Alex Rodriguez*	15.00
149	Darryl Strawberry	.35
150	Bo Jackson	.40

1994 Sportflics 2000 Rookie/Traded Going, Going, Gone

A dozen of the game's top home run hitters are featured in this insert set. On front, simulated 3-D action photos depict the player's swing for the fences. Backs have a portrait photo and information about the player's home run prowess. A crossed bats and "Going, Going Gone" logo appear on both front and back. Cards are numbered with a "GG" prefix. Stated odds of finding one of these inserts were once in 18 packs.

		MT
Complete Set (12):		40.00
Common Player:		1.50
1	Gary Sheffield	2.50
2	Matt Williams	2.00
3	Juan Gonzalez	4.00
4	Ken Griffey Jr.	15.00
5	Mike Piazza	8.00
6	Frank Thomas	6.00
7	Tim Salmon	1.50
8	Barry Bonds	5.00
9	Fred McGriff	2.50
10	Cecil Fielder	1.50
11	Albert Belle	3.50
12	Joe Carter	1.50

1994 Sportflics 2000 Rookie/Traded Rookies of the Year

Sportflics' choices for Rookies of the Year were featured on this one-card insert set. Ryan Klesko (National League) and Manny Ramirez (American League) are shown on the card when viewed from different angles. Sportflics batted .000 in their guesses, however, as Raul Mondesi and Bob Hamelin were the actual R.O.Y. selections. This card was inserted at the average rate of once per 360 packs.

		MT
Complete Set (1):		
RO1	Ryan Klesko, Manny Ramirez	10.00

1994 Sportflics 2000 Rookie/Traded 3-D Rookies

Eighteen of 1994's premier rookies are featured in this insert set. Combining a 3-D look and Sportflics' "Magic Motion" technology, the horizontal-format Starflics rookie cards present a striking appearance. Backs feature a full-bleed color photo overprinted with gold foil. A notice on back gives the production run of the chase cards as "No more than 5,000 sets." Stated odds of finding a Starflics Rookie card were given as one per 36 packs. Cards are numbered with a "TR" prefix.

		MT
Complete Set (18):		100.00
Common Player:		3.00
1	John Hudek	3.00
2	Manny Ramirez	20.00
3	Jeffrey Hammonds	3.00
4	Carlos Delgado	6.00
5	Javier Lopez	10.00
6	Alex Gonzalez	4.00
7	Raul Mondesi	10.00
8	Bob Hamelin	3.00
9	Ryan Klesko	4.00
10	Brian Anderson	3.00
11	Alex Rodriguez	40.00
12	Cliff Floyd	3.00
13	Chan Ho Park	7.50
14	Steve Karsay	3.00
15	Rondell White	5.00
16	Shawn Green	6.00
17	Rich Becker	3.00
18	Charles Johnson	5.00

1995 Sportflix Samples

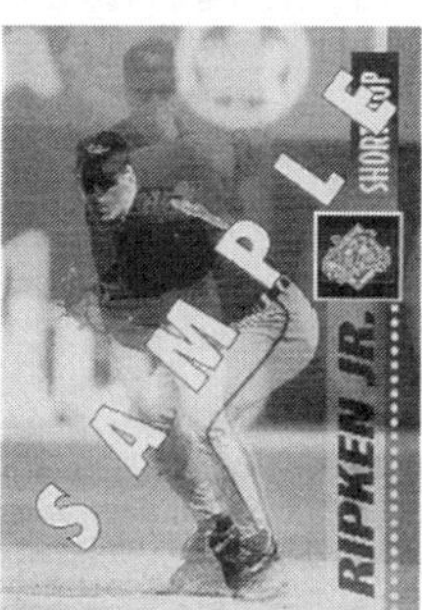

This nine-card promo pack was sent to Pinnacle's dealer network to introduce its revamped (new logo, spelling) magic-motion card set for 1995. The sample cards are identical in format to the regular-issue Sportflix cards except that a large white "SAMPLE" is printed diagonally on front and back of the promos.

		MT
Complete Set (9):		35.00
Common Player:		3.00
3	Fred McGriff	3.00
20	Frank Thomas	6.00
105	Manny Ramirez	5.00
122	Cal Ripken Jr.	9.00
128	Roberto Alomar	3.00
152	Russ Davis (Rookie)	3.00
162	Chipper Jones (Rookie)	7.50
DE2	Matt Williams (Detonators)	3.00
----	Advertising Card	.15

1995 Sportflix

With only 170 cards in the set, only the biggest stars and hottest rookies (25 of them in a specially designed subset) are included in this simulated 3-D issue. Fronts feature two borderless action photos which are alternately visible as the card's viewing angle is changed. Backs are conventionally printed and have a portrait photo, a few career stats and a couple of sentences about the player. The basic packaging options for '95 Sportflix were five- and eight card foils at $1.89 and $2.99, respectively.

		MT
Complete Set (170):		20.00
Common Player:		.15
Pack (5):		2.00
Wax Box (36):		50.00
1	Ken Griffey Jr.	3.00
2	Jeffrey Hammonds	.15
3	Fred McGriff	.25
4	Rickey Henderson	.35
5	Derrick May	.15
6	Robin Ventura	.25
7	Royce Clayton	.15
8	Paul Molitor	.45
9	Charlie Hayes	.15
10	David Nied	.15
11	Ellis Burks	.15
12	Bernard Gilkey	.15
13	Don Mattingly	.75
14	Albert Belle	.45
15	Doug Drabek	.15
16	Tony Gwynn	.75
17	Delino DeShields	.15
18	Bobby Bonilla	.15
19	Cliff Floyd	.15
20	Frank Thomas	1.00
21	Raul Mondesi	.40
22	Dave Nilsson	.15
23	Todd Zeile	.15
24	Bernie Williams	.45
25	Kirby Puckett	.75
26	David Cone	.20
27	Darren Daulton	.15
28	Marquis Grissom	.15
29	Randy Johnson	.40
30	Jeff Kent	.15
31	Orlando Merced	.15
32	Dave Justice	.25
33	Ivan Rodriguez	.50
34	Kirk Gibson	.15
35	Alex Fernandez	.15
36	Rick Wilkins	.15
37	Andy Benes	.15
38	Bret Saberhagen	.15
39	Billy Ashley	.15
40	Jose Rijo	.15
41	Matt Williams	.40
42	Lenny Dykstra	.15
43	Jay Bell	.15
44	Reggie Jefferson	.15
45	Greg Maddux	1.50
46	Gary Sheffield	.40
47	Bret Boone	.15
48	Jeff Bagwell	1.00
49	Ben McDonald	.15
50	Eric Karros	.15
51	Roger Clemens	.75
52	Sammy Sosa	1.00
53	Barry Bonds	.60
54	Joey Hamilton	.20
55	Brian Jordan	.15
56	Wil Cordero	.15
57	Aaron Sele	.15
58	Paul O'Neill	.20
59	Carlos Garcia	.15
60	Mike Mussina	.40
61	John Olerud	.20
62	Kevin Appier	.15
63	Matt Mieske	.15
64	Carlos Baerga	.15
65	Ryan Klesko	.25
66	Jimmy Key	.15
67	James Mouton	.15
68	Tim Salmon	.20
69	Hal Morris	.15
70	Albie Lopez	.15
71	Dave Hollins	.15
72	Greg Colbrunn	.15
73	Juan Gonzalez	.75
74	Wally Joyner	.15
75	Bob Hamelin	.15
76	Brady Anderson	.20
77	Deion Sanders	.25
78	Javier Lopez	.15
79	Brian McRae	.15
80	Craig Biggio	.25
81	Kenny Lofton	.40
82	Cecil Fielder	.15
83	Mike Piazza	1.50
84	Rafael Palmeiro	.30
85	Jim Thome	.40
86	Ruben Sierra	.15
87	Mark Langston	.15

88	John Valentin	.15
89	Shawon Dunston	.15
90	Travis Fryman	.15
91	Chuck Knoblauch	.30
92	Dean Palmer	.15
93	Robby Thompson	.15
94	Barry Larkin	.20
95	Darren Lewis	.15
96	Andres Galarraga	.25
97	Tony Phillips	.15
98	Mo Vaughn	.40
99	Pedro Martinez	.30
100	Chad Curtis	.15
101	Brent Gates	.15
102	Pat Hentgen	.15
103	Rico Brogna	.15
104	Carlos Delgado	.40
105	Manny Ramirez	.75
106	Mike Greenwell	.15
107	Wade Boggs	.35
108	Ozzie Smith	.45
109	Rusty Greer	.15
110	Willie Greene	.15
111	Chili Davis	.15
112	Reggie Sanders	.15
113	Roberto Kelly	.15
114	Tom Glavine	.25
115	Moises Alou	.25
116	Dennis Eckersley	.15
117	Danny Tartabull	.15
118	Jeff Conine	.15
119	Will Clark	.25
120	Joe Carter	.15
121	Mark McGwire	3.00
122	Cal Ripken Jr.	2.50
123	Danny Jackson	.15
124	Phil Plantier	.15
125	Dante Bichette	.25
126	Jack McDowell	.15
127	Jose Canseco	.35
128	Roberto Alomar	.50
129	Rondell White	.25
130	Ray Lankford	.15
131	Ryan Thompson	.15
132	Ken Caminiti	.25
133	Gregg Jefferies	.15
134	Omar Vizquel	.15
135	Mark Grace	.25
136	Derek Bell	.15
137	Mickey Tettleton	.15
138	Wilson Alvarez	.15
139	Larry Walker	.25
140	Bo Jackson	.20
141	Alex Rodriguez	2.50
142	Orlando Miller	.15
143	Shawn Green	.20
144	Steve Dunn	.15
145	Midre Cummings	.15
146	Chan Ho Park	.25
147	Jose Oliva	.15
148	Armando Benitez	.15
149	J.R. Phillips	.15
150	Charles Johnson	.25
151	Garret Anderson	.20
152	Russ Davis	.15
153	Brian Hunter	.15
154	Ernie Young	.15
155	Marc Newfield	.15
156	Greg Pirkl	.15
157	Scott Ruffcorn	.15
158	Rikkert Faneyte	.15
159	Duane Singleton	.15
160	Gabe White	.15
161	Alex Gonzalez	.15
162	Chipper Jones	1.50
163	Mike Kelly	.15
164	Kurt Miller	.15
165	Roberto Petagine	.15
166	Checklist (Jeff Bagwell)	.25
167	Checklist (Mike Piazza)	.40
168	Checklist (Ken Griffey Jr.)	1.00
169	Checklist (Frank Thomas)	.50
170	Checklist (Barry Bonds, Cal Ripken Jr.)	.75

1995 Sportflix Artist's Proofs

Each of the 170 cards in the regular Sportflix set can be found with a special tombstone shaped black-and-gold "Artist's Proof" seal designating it as one of a parallel edition of 700 cards each. Cards are otherwise identical to the regular-issue version. AP cards were inserted at an average rate of one per 36 packs.

	MT
Complete Set (170):	600.00
Common Player:	1.00
Stars:	15X

(See 1995 Sportflix for checklist and base card values.)

1995 Sportflix Double Take

A see-through plastic background and A.L. and N.L. stars at the same position sharing the card with their shadows marks this chase set as the top of the line for '95 Sportflix. Found at an average rate of one per 48packs, the Double Take inserts represent a new level in "magic motion" card technology.

		MT
Complete Set (12):		65.00
Common Player:		2.00
1	Frank Thomas, Jeff Bagwell	6.00
2	Will Clark, Fred McGriff	3.00
3	Roberto Alomar, Jeff Kent	4.00
4	Wade Boggs, Matt Williams	3.00
5	Cal Ripken Jr., Ozzie Smith	12.00
6	Alex Rodriguez, Wil Cordero	8.00
7	Carlos Delgado, Mike Piazza	7.50
8	Kenny Lofton, Dave Justice	4.00
9	Ken Griffey Jr., Barry Bonds	15.00
10	Albert Belle, Raul Mondesi	4.00
11	Kirby Puckett, Tony Gwynn	6.00
12	Jimmy Key, Greg Maddux	6.00

1995 Sportflix ProMotion

Twelve of baseball's biggest stars morph into team logos on a bright team-color background in this chase series. Backs have a portrait photo and a few words about the players. The ProMotion inserts are a one per 18 pack pick in jumbo packs only.

		MT
Complete Set (12):		90.00
Common Player:		2.50
1	Ken Griffey Jr.	18.00
2	Frank Thomas	7.00
3	Cal Ripken Jr.	14.00
4	Jeff Bagwell	6.00
5	Mike Piazza	9.00
6	Matt Williams	3.00
7	Albert Belle	5.00
8	Jose Canseco	4.00
9	Don Mattingly	7.00
10	Barry Bonds	6.00
11	Will Clark	4.00
12	Kirby Puckett	7.00

1995 Sportflix 3D Hammer Team

Sledge hammers flying in formation through a cloud-studded sky are the background for this insert set featuring the game's heavy hitters. Backs have a portrait photo and a few words about the player's power hitting prowess. Hammer Team cards are picked on an average of once per four packs.

		MT
Complete Set (18):		20.00
Common Player:		.50
1	Ken Griffey Jr.	4.00
2	Frank Thomas	1.75
3	Jeff Bagwell	1.50
4	Mike Piazza	2.00
5	Cal Ripken Jr.	3.00
6	Albert Belle	1.00
7	Barry Bonds	1.50
8	Don Mattingly	1.75
9	Will Clark	.75
10	Tony Gwynn	1.50
11	Matt Williams	1.00
12	Kirby Puckett	1.50
13	Manny Ramirez	1.50
14	Fred McGriff	.75
15	Juan Gonzalez	1.00
16	Kenny Lofton	.75
17	Raul Mondesi	.75
18	Tim Salmon	.60

1995 Sportflix 3D Detonators

With the players up ona pedestal and fireworks in the background. this chase set lives up to its name, "Detonators." The cards feature a deep 3-D look on front. Backs have a close-up photo of the plauer in the pedestal's column. Detonator cards are pulled at an average rate of one per 16 packs.

		MT
Complete Set (9):		25.00
Common Player:		1.50
1	Jeff Bagwell	4.00
2	Matt Williams	2.00
3	Ken Griffey Jr.	10.00
4	Frank Thomas	5.00
5	Mike Piazza	6.00
6	Barry Bonds	4.00
7	Albert Belle	3.00
8	Cliff Floyd	1.50
9	Juan Gonzalez	2.50

1995 Sportflix/UC3 Samples

To introduce the new technology it was bringing to the insert cards in the Sportflix UC3 issue, the company sent a sample of the Clear Shots insert, along with a header card describing the entire UC3 issue, to card dealers and the media in June, 1995. A large, black, "SAMPLE" is overprinted diagonally on the front. A similarly marked Fred McGriff previewed the set's regular cards.

		MT
Complete Set (3):		12.00
3	Fred McGriff	4.00
CS8	Cliff Floyd	5.00
CS10	Alex Gonzalez	5.00
--	Header card	.05

1995 Sportflix/UC3

Using advanced technology to create a premium 3-D card brand and inserts, UC3 offers three distinctly different card formats in the base 147-card set, plus a parallel set and three insert sets. All cards have borderless fronts and feature a heavy ribbed plastic top layer. The first 95 cards are veteran players in a horizontal format. A central action photo is flanked at left by a large gold glove (National Leaguers) or baseball (A.L.), and at right by a blue and green vista from which flies one (N.L.) or three (A.L.) baseballs. Player identification is in red at upper-left, the UC3 logo at lower-left. Backs have another color photo and a few stats set against a background of the team logo. Cards #96-122 are a vertical-format Rookie subset. Player photos are set against a purple and green vista with a large bat, ball and glove behind the player. His name is at upper-right; team logo at lower-right. Horizontal backs are similar to the other cards. The final 25 cards of the set are a subset titled, "In-Depth." These vertically formatted cards feature eye-popping graphics on front in which the main player photo almost jumps from the background. The only graphics are the player's name at left and the UC3 logo at upper-left. Backs have a portrait photo at top, bathed in golden rays. A team logo is at center and an outer space design at bottom. There is a short paragraph describing the player at right.

		MT
Complete Set (147):		20.00
Common Player:		.10
Pack (5):		2.00
Wax Box (36):		55.00
1	Frank Thomas	1.50
2	Wil Cordero	.10
3	John Olerud	.15
4	Deion Sanders	.20
5	Mike Mussina	.40
6	Mo Vaughn	.40
7	Will Clark	.25
8	Chili Davis	.10
9	Jimmy Key	.10
10	John Valentin	.10
11	Tony Tarasco	.10
12	Alan Trammell	.10
13	David Cone	.10
14	Tim Salmon	.20
15	Danny Tartabull	.10
16	Aaron Sele	.10
17	Alex Fernandez	.10
18	Barry Bonds	.75
19	Andres Galarraga	.15
20	Don Mattingly	1.00
21	Kevin Appier	.10
22	Paul Molitor	.40
23	Omar Vizquel	.10
24	Andy Benes	.10
25	Rafael Palmeiro	.25
26	Barry Larkin	.15
27	Bernie Williams	.25
28	Gary Sheffield	.25
29	Wally Joyner	.15
30	Wade Boggs	.40
31	Rico Brogna	.10
32	Ken Caminiti	.15
33	Kirby Puckett	.75
34	Bobby Bonilla	.10
35	Hal Morris	.10
36	Moises Alou	.10
37	Jim Thome	.25
38	Chuck Knoblauch	.10
39	Mike Piazza	2.00
40	Travis Fryman	.10
41	Rickey Henderson	.35
42	Jack McDowell	.10
43	Carlos Baerga	.10
44	Gregg Jeffries	.10
45	Kirk Gibson	.10
46	Bret Saberhagen	.10
47	Cecil Fielder	.10
48	Manny Ramirez	.75
49	Marquis Grissom	.10
50	Dave Winfield	.15
51	Mark McGwire	3.00
52	Dennis Eckersley	.10
53	Robin Ventura	.15
54	Ryan Klesko	.40
55	Jeff Bagwell	1.00
56	Ozzie Smith	.40
57	Brian McRae	.10
58	Albert Belle	.60
59	Darren Daulton	.10
60	Jose Canseco	.35
61	Greg Maddux	2.00
62	Ben McDonald	.10
63	Lenny Dykstra	.10
64	Randy Johnson	.30
65	Fred McGriff	.35
66	Ray Lankford	.10
67	Dave Justice	.20
68	Paul O'Neill	.10
69	Tony Gwynn	.80
70	Matt Williams	.25
71	Dante Bichette	.30
72	Craig Biggio	.25
73	Ken Griffey Jr.	3.00
74	Juan Gonzalez	.75
75	Cal Ripken Jr.	2.50
76	Jay Bell	.10
77	Joe Carter	.10
78	Roberto Alomar	.60
79	Mark Langston	.10
80	Dave Hollins	.10
81	Tom Glavine	.15
82	Ivan Rodriguez	.30
83	Mark Whiten	.10
84	Raul Mondesi	.40
85	Kenny Lofton	.40
86	Ruben Sierra	.10
87	Mark Grace	.20
88	Royce Clayton	.10
89	Billy Ashley	.10
90	Larry Walker	.30
91	Sammy Sosa	1.00
92	Jason Bere	.10
93	Bob Hamelin	.10
94	Greg Vaughn	.10
95	Roger Clemens	.65
96	Scott Ruffcorn	.10
97	*Hideo Nomo*	1.50
98	Michael Tucker	.10
99	J.R. Phillips	.10
100	Roberto Petagine	.10
101	Chipper Jones	2.00
102	Armando Benitez	.10
103	Orlando Miller	.10
104	Carlos Delgado	.40
105	Jeff Cirillo	.10
106	Shawn Green	.20
107	Joe Rando	.10
108	Vaughn Eshelman	.10
109	Frank Rodriguez	.10
110	Russ Davis	.10
111	Todd Hollandsworth	.10
112	Mark Grudzielanek	.10
113	Jose Oliva	.10
114	Ray Durham	.15
115	Alex Rodriguez	2.50
116	Alex Gonzalez	.10
117	Midre Cummings	.10
118	Marty Cordova	.10
119	John Mabry	.10
120	Jason Jacome	.10
121	Joe Vitiello	.10
122	Charles Johnson	.10
123	Cal Ripken Jr. (In Depth)	1.25
124	Ken Griffey Jr. (In Depth)	1.50
125	Frank Thomas (In Depth)	.75
126	Mike Piazza (In Depth)	.50
127	Matt Williams (In Depth)	.15
128	Barry Bonds (In Depth)	.40
129	Greg Maddux (In Depth)	1.00
130	Randy Johnson (In Depth)	.15
131	Albert Belle (In Depth)	.35
132	Will Clark (In Depth)	.15
133	Tony Gwynn (In Depth)	.40
134	Manny Ramirez (In Depth)	.40
135	Raul Mondesi (In Depth)	.15
136	Mo Vaughn (In Depth)	.15
137	Mark McGwire (In Depth)	1.50
138	Kirby Puckett (In Depth)	.40
139	Don Mattingly (In Depth)	.50
140	Carlos Baerga (In Depth)	.10
141	Roger Clemens (In Depth)	.35
142	Fred McGriff (In Depth)	.15
143	Kenny Lofton (In Depth)	.35
144	Jeff Bagwell (In Depth)	.40
145	Larry Walker (In Depth)	.15
146	Joe Carter (In Depth)	.10
147	Rafael Palmeiro (In Depth)	.15

1995 Sportflix/UC3 Artist's Proof

This chase set parallels the 147 regular cards in the UC3 set with a version on which a round, gold "ARTIST'S PROOF" seal is printed on the front of the card. The AP cards are found on the average of one per box (36 packs).

	MT
Complete Set (147):	900.00
Common Player:	2.00
Stars:	15X

(See 1995 Sportflix UC3 for checklist and base card values.)

1995 Sportflix/UC3 Clear Shots

Seeded at the rate of about one per 24 packs, the 12 cards in this chase set feature top rookies in a technologically advanced format. The left two-thirds of the card are clear plastic, the right third is blue (American League) or red-purple (N.L.). At center is a circle which features the player photos, portrait and action, depending on the viewing angle. Also changing with the viewpoint are the words "CLEAR" and "SHOT" at top-right, and team and UC3 logos at bottom-right. The player's last name is in black at lower-left and appears to change size as the card is moved. Backs have a gray strip vertically at left with the card number, manufacturer and licensor logos and copyright information. Card numbers have a "CS" prefix.

		MT
Complete Set (12):		50.00
Common Player:		2.00
1	Alex Rodriguez	25.00
2	Shawn Green	4.50
3	Hideo Nomo	6.00
4	Charles Johnson	3.00
5	Orlando Miller	1.00
6	Billy Ashley	1.00
7	Carlos Delgado	3.00
8	Cliff Floyd	3.00
9	Chipper Jones	15.00
10	Alex Gonzalez	2.00
11	J.R. Phillips	1.00
12	Michael Tucker	1.00

1995 Sportflix/UC3 Cyclone Squad

The most commonly encountered (one per four packs, on average) of the UC3 chase cards are the 20-card Cyclone Squad, featuring the game's top batsmen. Cards have a player in a batting pose set against a dark copper background with two golden pinwheels behind him which appear to spin when the card is moved. Horizontal backs have a green toned photo of the player in his follow-through swing, with shock waves radiating from the lower-left corner. Cards have a CS prefix.

		MT
Complete Set (20):		15.00
Common Player:		.40
1	Frank Thomas	1.50
2	Ken Griffey Jr.	4.00
3	Jeff Bagwell	1.50
4	Cal Ripken Jr.	3.00
5	Barry Bonds	1.00
6	Mike Piazza	2.00
7	Matt Williams	.50
8	Kirby Puckett	1.50
9	Jose Canseco	.75
10	Will Clark	.50
11	Don Mattingly	1.50
12	Albert Belle	.75
13	Tony Gwynn	1.50
14	Raul Mondesi	.40
15	Bobby Bonilla	.40
16	Rafael Palmeiro	.50
17	Fred McGriff	.50
18	Tim Salmon	.40
19	Kenny Lofton	.75
20	Joe Carter	.40

1995 Sportflix/UC3 In Motion

Found on an average of once per 18 packs, the cards in this chase set feature maximim motion. When the card is held almost vertically a small eight-piece jigsaw puzzle photo of the player is visible against a light blue background. As the card is moved toward a horizontal postion, the pieces appear to become large and move together until the picture fills most of the card. The player's name is in orange at lower-left, with manufacturer's logos at top. Horizontal backs have a green background, two color player photos and a few words of career highlights. The In Motion card numbers are preceded by an "IM" prefix.

		MT
Complete Set (10):		25.00
Common Player:		.75
1	Cal Ripken Jr.	5.00
2	Ken Griffey Jr.	6.00
3	Frank Thomas	2.50
4	Mike Piazza	4.00
5	Barry Bonds	2.00
6	Matt Williams	.75
7	Kirby Puckett	2.00
8	Greg Maddux	4.00
9	Don Mattingly	2.00
10	Will Clark	.75

1996 Sportflix

Distributed in only retail locations, this 1996 Sportflix set has 144 cards, including 24-card UC3 and 21-card Rookies subsets. The set also has a parallel set, Artist's Proof; these cards are seeded one per every 48 packs. Four insert sets were also produced: Double Take, Hit Parade, Power Surge and ProMotion.

		MT
Complete Set (144):		25.00
Common Player:		.10
Complete Artist's Proof Set (144):		1000.
Common Artist's Proof:		2.50
AP Stars:		15X
Pack (5):		1.50
Wax Bpx (36):		40.00
1	Wade Boggs	.25
2	Tim Salmon	.20
3	Will Clark	.35
4	Dante Bichette	.25
5	Barry Bonds	.75
6	Kirby Puckett	1.00
7	Albert Belle	.60
8	Greg Maddux	2.00
9	Tony Gwynn	1.00
10	Mike Piazza	1.50
11	Ivan Rodriguez	.15
12	Marty Cordova	.15
13	Frank Thomas	1.00
14	Raul Mondesi	.35
15	Johnny Damon	.40
16	Mark McGwire	3.00
17	Lenny Dykstra	.10
18	Ken Griffey Jr.	3.00
19	Chipper Jones	1.50
20	Alex Rodriguez	2.50
21	Jeff Bagwell	1.00
22	Jim Edmonds	.15
23	Edgar Martinez	.10
24	David Cone	.10
25	Tom Glavine	.15
26	Eddie Murray	.25
27	Paul Molitor	.30
28	Ryan Klesko	.40
29	Rafael Palmeiro	.20
30	Manny Ramirez	.75
31	Mo Vaughn	.45
32	Rico Brogna	.10
33	Marc Newfield	.10
34	J.T. Snow	.10
35	Reggie Sanders	.10
36	Fred McGriff	.40
37	Craig Biggio	.20
38	Jeff King	.10
39	Kenny Lofton	.45
40	Gary Gaetti	.10
41	Eric Karros	.10
42	Jason Isringhausen	.15
43	B.J. Surhoff	.10
44	Michael Tucker	.10
45	Gary Sheffield	.20
46	Chili Davis	.10
47	Bobby Bonilla	.10
48	Hideo Nomo	.50
49	Ray Durham	.10
50	Phil Nevin	.10
51	Randy Johnson	.40
52	Bill Pulsipher	.10
53	Ozzie Smith	.40
54	Cal Ripken Jr.	2.50
55	Cecil Fielder	.10
56	Matt Williams	.30
57	Sammy Sosa	1.50
58	Roger Clemens	.40
59	Brian Hunter	.10
60	Barry Larkin	.20
61	Charles Johnson	.10
62	Dave Justice	.20
63	Garret Anderson	.10
64	Rondell White	.10
65	Derek Bell	.10
66	Andres Galarraga	.15
67	Moises Alou	.10
68	Travis Fryman	.10
69	Pedro Martinez	.20
70	Carlos Baerga	.10
71	John Valentin	.10
72	Larry Walker	.20
73	Roberto Alomar	.60
74	Mike Mussina	.50
75	Kevin Appier	.10
76	Bernie Williams	.20
77	Ray Lankford	.10
78	Gregg Jefferies	.10
79	Robin Ventura	.10
80	Kenny Rogers	.10
81	Paul O'Neill	.10
82	Mark Grace	.20
83	Deion Sanders	.25
84	Tino Martinez	.10
85	Joe Carter	.10
86	Pete Schourek	.10
87	Jack McDowell	.10
88	John Mabry	.10
89	Darren Daulton	.10
90	Jim Thome	.25
91	Jay Buhner	.10
92	Jay Bell	.10
93	Kevin Seitzer	.10
94	Jose Canseco	.35
95	Juan Gonzalez	.75
96	Jeff Conine	.10
97	Chipper Jones	.75
98	Ken Griffey Jr.	1.50
99	Frank Thomas	.50
100	Cal Ripken Jr.	1.50
101	Albert Belle	.50
102	Mike Piazza	.75
103	Dante Bichette	.15
104	Sammy Sosa	.75
105	Mo Vaughn	.25
106	Tim Salmon	.20
107	Reggie Sanders	.10
108	Gary Sheffield	.10
109	Ruben Rivera	.25
110	Rafael Palmeiro	.15
111	Edgar Martinez	.10
112	Barry Bonds	.40
113	Manny Ramirez	.40
114	Larry Walker	.15
115	Jeff Bagwell	.50
116	Matt Williams	.20
117	Mark McGwire	2.00
118	Johnny Damon	.25
119	Eddie Murray	.20
120	Jay Buhner	.10
121	Tim Unroe	.10
122	Todd Hollandsworth	.10
123	Tony Clark	.40
124	Roger Cedeno	.20
125	Jim Pittsley	.10
126	Ruben Rivera	.40
127	Bob Wolcott	.10
128	Chan Ho Park	.15
129	Chris Snopek	.15
130	Alex Ochoa	.10
131	Yamil Benitez	.10
132	Jimmy Haynes	.10
133	Dustin Hermanson	.10
134	Shawn Estes	.10
135	Howard Battle	.10
136	*Matt Lawton*	.50
137	Terrell Wade	.10
138	Jason Schmidt	.10
139	Derek Jeter	1.50
140	Shannon Stewart	.10
141	Chris Stynes	.10
142	Ken Griffey Jr. CL	1.50
143	Greg Maddux CL	1.00
144	Ripken Jr. CL	1.25

1996 Sportflix Double Take

These 1996 Sportflix insert cards each feature two players who are tops at a particular position. Tilting the card to change the angle of view brings each player into focus. The cards were seeded one per 22 packs.

		MT
Complete Set (12):		100.00
Common Player:		4.00
1	Barry Larkin, Cal Ripken Jr.	15.00
2	Roberto Alomar, Craig Biggio	4.00
3	Chipper Jones, Matt Williams	9.00
4	Ken Griffey Jr., Ruben Rivera	20.00
5	Greg Maddux, Hideo Nomo	9.00

6	Frank Thomas, Mo Vaughn	7.50
7	Mike Piazza, Ivan Rodriguez	9.00
8	Albert Belle, Barry Bonds	4.00
9	Alex Rodriguez, Derek Jeter	15.00
10	Kirby Puckett, Tony Gwynn	7.50
11	Manny Ramirez, Sammy Sosa	12.00
12	Jeff Bagwell, Rico Brogna	4.00

1996 Sportflix Hit Parade

Sixteen of baseball's most productive hitters are featured on these inserts. Horizontal fronts have a player portrait at right. In the background is a lenticular-motion scene of a generic player swinging the bat. Backs have an action photo and a few career highlights. The cards were seeded one per every 35 packs.

		MT
Complete Set (16):		60.00
Common Player:		1.50
1	Ken Griffey Jr.	10.00
2	Cal Ripken Jr.	9.00
3	Frank Thomas	5.00
4	Mike Piazza	7.00
5	Mo Vaughn	2.00
6	Albert Belle	2.50
7	Jeff Bagwell	4.00
8	Matt Williams	1.50
9	Sammy Sosa	5.00
9p	Sammy Sosa (overprinted "SAMPLE")	8.00
10	Kirby Puckett	5.00
11	Dante Bichette	1.50
12	Gary Sheffield	2.00
13	Tony Gwynn	4.00
14	Wade Boggs	2.50
15	Chipper Jones	7.00
16	Barry Bonds	5.00

1996 Sportflix Power Surge

This 1996 Sportflix insert set showcases 24 sluggers on a clear 3-D parallel rendition of the UC3 subset in the main issue. These cards are seeded one per every 35 packs.

		MT
Complete Set (25):		90.00
Common Player:		1.50
1	Chipper Jones	10.00
2	Ken Griffey Jr.	17.50
3	Frank Thomas	6.00
4	Cal Ripken Jr.	15.00
5	Albert Belle	5.00
6	Mike Piazza	10.00
7	Dante Bichette	2.00
8	Sammy Sosa	8.00
9	Mo Vaughn	1.50
10	Tim Salmon	1.50
11	Reggie Sanders	1.50
12	Gary Sheffield	1.50
13	Ruben Rivera	1.50
14	Rafael Palmeiro	2.00
15	Edgar Martinez	1.50
16	Barry Bonds	6.00
17	Manny Ramirez	5.00
18	Larry Walker	2.00
19	Jeff Bagwell	6.00
20	Matt Williams	1.50
21	Mark McGwire	17.50
22	Johnny Damon	2.00
23	Eddie Murray	2.00
24	Jay Buhner	1.50
25	Kirby Puckett	6.00

1996 Sportflix ProMotion

These 1996 Sportflix inserts were seeded one per every 17 packs. The cards' "morphing" technology turns baseball equipment, such as bats, balls and gloves, into 20 of the top veteran superstars using multi-phase animation.

		MT
Complete Set (20):		60.00
Common Player:		.50
1	Cal Ripken Jr.	8.00
2	Greg Maddux	6.00
3	Mo Vaughn	1.00
4	Albert Belle	3.00
5	Mike Piazza	6.00
6	Ken Griffey Jr.	10.00
7	Frank Thomas	5.00
8	Jeff Bagwell	4.00
9	Hideo Nomo	2.00
10	Chipper Jones	6.00
11	Tony Gwynn	4.00
12	Don Mattingly	5.00
13	Dante Bichette	1.00
14	Matt Williams	1.00
15	Manny Ramirez	3.00
16	Barry Bonds	4.00
17	Reggie Sanders	.50
18	Tim Salmon	.75
19	Ruben Rivera	.75
20	Garret Anderson	.50

1996 Sportflix Rookie Supers

Eight of the young players included in the Sportflix Rookies subset are featured in an enlarged version which was issued one per retail box. The cards measure 3" x 5" and are numbered "X of 8," on back, but are otherwise identical to the smaller version.

		MT
Complete Set (8):		35.00
Common player:		4.00
1	Jason Schmidt	4.00
2	Chris Snopek	4.00
3	Tony Clark	6.00
4	Todd Hollandsworth	4.00
5	Alex Ochoa	4.00
6	Derek Jeter	15.00
7	Howard Battle	4.00
8	Bob Wolcott	4.00

1997 Sports Illustrated

Fleer teamed up with Sports Illustrated to produce a 180-card World Series Fever set. The regular set is divided into six different subsets: 96 Player Cards, 27 Fresh Faces, 18 Inside Baseball, 18 SIber Vision, 12 covers and 9 Newsmakers. Inserts included the Extra Edition parallel set, Great Shots, Cooperstown Collection and Autographed Mini-Cover Redemption Cards. Cards were sold in six-card packs for $1.99 each.

		MT
Complete Set (180):		40.00
Common Player:		.10
Pack (6):		2.00
Wax Box (24):		42.00
1	Bob Abreu (Fresh Faces)	.20
2	Jaime Bluma (Fresh Faces)	.10
3	Emil Brown (Fresh Faces)	.10
4	Jose Cruz, Jr. (Fresh Faces)	.50
5	Jason Dickson (Fresh Faces)	.15
6	Nomar Garciaparra (Fresh Faces)	2.50
7	Todd Greene (Fresh Faces)	.20
8	Vladimir Guerrero (Fresh Faces)	1.50
9	Wilton Guerrero (Fresh Faces)	.10
10	Jose Guillen (Fresh Faces)	1.00
11	Hideki Irabu (Fresh Faces)	1.00
12	Russ Johnson (Fresh Faces)	.10
13	Andruw Jones (Fresh Faces)	2.00
14	Damon Mashore (Fresh Faces)	.10
15	Jason McDonald (Fresh Faces)	.10
16	Ryan McGuire (Fresh Faces)	.10
17	Matt Morris (Fresh Faces)	.10
18	Kevin Orie (Fresh Faces)	.10
19	Dante Powell (Fresh Faces)	.10
20	Pokey Reese (Fresh Faces)	.15
21	Joe Roa (Fresh Faces)	.10
22	Scott Rolen (Fresh Faces)	2.00
23	Glendon Rusch (Fresh Faces)	.10
24	Scott Spiezio (Fresh Faces)	.10
25	Bubba Trammell (Fresh Faces)	1.00
26	Todd Walker (Fresh Faces)	.75
27	Jamey Wright (Fresh Faces)	.10
28	Ken Griffey Jr. (Season Highlights)	2.00
29	Tino Martinez (Season Highlights)	.10
30	Roger Clemens (Season Highlights)	.50
31	Hideki Irabu (Season Highlights)	.75
32	Kevin Brown (Season Highlights)	.10
33	Chipper Jones, Cal Ripken Jr. (Season Highlights)	1.25
34	Sandy Alomar (Season Highlights)	.10
35	Ken Caminiti (Season Highlights)	.20
36	Randy Johnson (Season Highlights)	.40
37	Andy Ashby (Inside Baseball)	.10
38	Jay Buhner (Inside Baseball)	.10
39	Joe Carter (Inside Baseball)	.10
40	Darren Daulton (Inside Baseball)	.10
41	Jeff Fassero (Inside Baseball)	.10
42	Andres Galarraga (Inside Baseball)	.10
43	Rusty Greer (Inside Baseball)	.10
44	Marquis Grissom (Inside Baseball)	.10
45	Joey Hamilton (Inside Baseball)	.10
46	Jimmy Key (Inside Baseball)	.10
47	Ryan Klesko (Inside Baseball)	.25
48	Eddie Murray (Inside Baseball)	.40

49	Charles Nagy (Inside Baseball)	.10
50	Dave Nilsson (Inside Baseball)	.10
51	Ricardo Rincon (Inside Baseball)	.10
52	Billy Wagner (Inside Baseball)	.10
53	Dan Wilson (Inside Baseball)	.10
54	Dmitri Young (Inside Baseball)	.10
55	Roberto Alomar (S.I.BER Vision)	.60
56	Sandy Alomar Jr. (S.I.BER Vision)	.10
57	Scott Brosius (S.I.BER Vision)	.10
58	Tony Clark (S.I.BER Vision)	.50
59	Carlos Delgado (S.I.BER Vision)	.25
60	Jermaine Dye (S.I.BER Vision)	.10
61	Darin Erstad (S.I.BER Vision)	2.00
62	Derek Jeter (S.I.BER Vision)	1.50
63	Jason Kendall (S.I.BER Vision)	.10
64	Hideo Nomo (S.I.BER Vision)	.25
65	Rey Ordonez (S.I.BER Vision)	.10
66	Andy Pettitte (S.I.BER Vision)	.50
67	Manny Ramirez (S.I.BER Vision)	.60
68	Edgar Renteria (S.I.BER Vision)	.10
69	Shane Reynolds (S.I.BER Vision)	.10
70	Alex Rodriguez (S.I.BER Vision)	1.50
71	Ivan Rodriguez (S.I.BER Vision)	.40
72	Jose Rosado (S.I.BER Vision)	.10
73	John Smoltz	.20
74	Tom Glavine	.20
75	Greg Maddux	2.50
76	Chipper Jones	2.50
77	Kenny Lofton	.50
78	Fred McGriff	.30
79	Kevin Brown	.10
80	Alex Fernandez	.10
81	Al Leiter	.10
82	Bobby Bonilla	.10
83	Gary Sheffield	.30
84	Moises Alou	.20
85	Henry Rodriguez	.10
86	Mark Grudzielanek	.10
87	Pedro Martinez	.25
88	Todd Hundley	.20
89	Bernard Gilkey	.10
90	Bobby Jones	.10
91	Curt Schilling	.10
92	Ricky Bottalico	.10
93	Mike Lieberthal	.10
94	Sammy Sosa	2.00
95	Ryne Sandberg	1.00
96	Mark Grace	.35
97	Deion Sanders	.20
98	Reggie Sanders	.10
99	Barry Larkin	.20
100	Craig Biggio	.20
101	Jeff Bagwell	1.50
102	Derek Bell	.10
103	Brian Jordan	.10
104	Ray Lankford	.10
105	Ron Gant	.10
106	Al Martin	.10
107	Kevin Elster	.10
108	Jermaine Allensworth	.10
109	Vinny Castilla	.10
110	Dante Bichette	.20
111	Larry Walker	.30
112	Mike Piazza	2.50
113	Eric Karros	.10
114	Todd Hollandsworth	.10
115	Raul Mondesi	.25
116	Hideo Nomo	.50
117	Ramon Martinez	.10
118	Ken Caminiti	.25
119	Tony Gwynn	2.00
120	Steve Finley	.10
121	Barry Bonds	1.00
122	J.T. Snow	.10
123	Rod Beck	.10
124	Cal Ripken Jr.	3.00
125	Mike Mussina	.60
126	Brady Anderson	.10
127	Bernie Williams	.75
128	Derek Jeter	3.00
129	Tino Martinez	.15
130	Andy Pettitte	.75
131	David Cone	.20
132	Mariano Rivera	.20
133	Roger Clemens	1.50
134	Pat Hentgen	.10
135	Juan Guzman	.10
136	Bob Higginson	.10
137	Tony Clark	1.00
138	Travis Fryman	.10
139	Mo Vaughn	.50
140	Tim Naehring	.10
141	John Valentin	.10
142	Matt Williams	.25
143	David Justice	.30
144	Jim Thome	.60
145	Chuck Knoblauch	.25
146	Paul Molitor	.40
147	Marty Cordova	.10
148	Frank Thomas	1.50
149	Albert Belle	.75
150	Robin Ventura	.10
151	John Jaha	.10
152	Jeff Cirillo	.10
153	Jose Valentin	.10
154	Jay Bell	.10
155	Jeff King	.10
156	Kevin Appier	.10
157	Ken Griffey Jr.	4.00
158	Alex Rodriguez	3.00
158p	Alex Rodriguez (overprinted "PROMOTIONAL SAMPLE")	3.00
159	Randy Johnson	.60
160	Juan Gonzalez	1.00
161	Will Clark	.25
162	Dean Palmer	.10
163	Tim Salmon	.15
164	Jim Edmonds	.10
165	Jim Leyritz	.10
166	Jose Canseco	.30
167	Jason Giambi	.10
168	Mark McGwire	4.00
169	Barry Bonds	1.00
170	Alex Rodriguez	1.50
171	Roger Clemens	.75
172	Ken Griffey Jr.	2.00
173	Greg Maddux	1.25
174	Mike Piazza	1.25
175	Will Clark, Mark McGwire	2.00
176	Hideo Nomo	.25
177	Cal Ripken Jr.	1.50
178	Ken Griffey Jr., Frank Thomas	.75
179	Alex Rodriguez, Derek Jeter	1.50
180	John Wetteland	.10

1997 Sports Illustrated Extra Edition

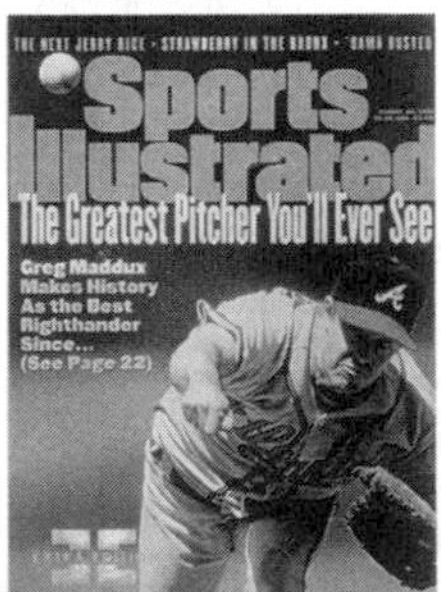

Each of the regular cards in the premiere Fleer SI issue is also found in a parallel set designated on front in gold holographic foil as "Extra Edition". Backs of the cards carry a serial number from within a production of 500 of each card.

	MT
Complete Set (180):	1200.
Common Player:	2.50
Extra Edition Stars:	15X

(See 1997 Sports Illustrated for checklist and base card values.)

1997 Sports Illustrated Autographed Mini-Covers

Six different players autographed 250 magazine mini-covers that were available through randomly seeded redemption cards. The players who autographed cards were Hank Aaron, Willie Mays, Frank Robinson, Kirby Puckett, Cal Ripken Jr., and Alex Rodriguez.

	MT
Complete Set (6):	800.00
Common Player:	60.00
Alex Rodriguez	200.00
Cal Ripken Jr.	250.00
Kirby Puckett	125.00
Willie Mays	150.00
Frank Robinson	60.00
Hank Aaron	150.00

1997 Sports Illustrated Box Topper

This special version of A-Rod's card was packaged one per box of foil packs. It was intended to be inserted into die-cuts on the box to create a sample display for the new issue. The card measures 2-1/2" x 4-1/16". The back is in black-and-white with instructions on how to insert the card into the box.

	MT
Alex Rodriguez	6.00

1997 Sports Illustrated Cooperstown Collection

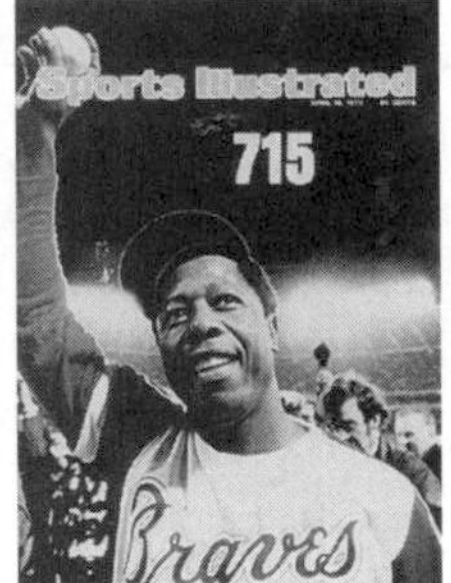

This 12-card insert (found 1:12 packs) lets collectors relive classic SI baseball covers with a description of each issue on the back.

		MT
Complete Set (12):		60.00
Common Player:		5.00
1	Hank Aaron	15.00
2	Yogi Berra	8.00
3	Lou Brock	5.00
4	Rod Carew	5.00
5	Juan Marichal	5.00
6	Al Kaline	5.00
7	Joe Morgan	5.00
8	Brooks Robinson	10.00
9	Willie Stargell	5.00
10	Kirby Puckett	12.00
11	Willie Mays	15.00
12	Frank Robinson	8.00

1997 Sports Illustrated Great Shots

A 25-card insert, found one per pack, designed to highlight Sports Illustrated's classic photography. Each card in the set folds out to a 5" x 7" format to showcase a larger photo.

		MT
Complete Set (25):		5.00
Common Player:		.10
(1)	Roberto Alomar	.20
(2)	Andy Ashby	.10
(3)	Albert Belle	.25
(4)	Barry Bonds	.25
(5)	Jay Buhner	.10
(6)	Vinny Castilla, Andres Galarraga	.10

(7) Darren Daulton .10
(8) Juan Gonzalez .25
(9) Ken Griffey Jr. 1.00
(10) Derek Jeter .60
(11) Randy Johnson .15
(12) Chipper Jones .60
(13) Eric Karros .10
(14) Ryan Klesko .15
(15) Kenny Lofton .20
(16) Greg Maddux .45
(17) Mark McGwire 1.00
(18) Mike Piazza .60
(19) Cal Ripken Jr. .75
(20) Alex Rodriguez .75
(21) Ryne Sandberg .35
(22) Deion Sanders .15
(23) John Smoltz .10
(24) Frank Thomas .50
(25) Mo Vaughn .20

1998 Sports Illustrated Then & Now

Then and Now was the first of three Sports Illustrated Baseball releases in 1998. It contained 150 cards and sold in six-card packs, with five cards and a mini- poster. Fronts carried photos of active and retired players, as well as rookies. There was only one subset - A Place in History (37-53) - and it compared statistics between current players and retired greats. The product arrived with an Extra Edition parallel set, Art of the Game, Autograph Redemptions, Covers and Great Shots inserts. There was also an Alex Rodriguez checklist/ mini-poster seeded every 12th pack.

	MT
Complete Set (150):	25.00
Common Player:	.10
Pack (5):	2.00
Wax Box (24):	38.00

1 Luis Aparicio (Legends of the Game) .10
2 Richie Ashburn (Legends of the Game) .10
3 Ernie Banks (Legends of the Game) .75
4 Yogi Berra (Legends of the Game) .75
5 Lou Boudreau (Legends of the Game) .10
6 Lou Brock (Legends of the Game) .25
7 Jim Bunning (Legends of the Game) .10
8 Rod Carew (Legends of the Game) .25
9 Bob Feller (Legends of the Game) .25
10 Rollie Fingers (Legends of the Game) .10
11 Bob Gibson (Legends of the Game) .50
12 Fergie Jenkins (Legends of the Game) .10
13 Al Kaline (Legends of the Game) .25
14 George Kell (Legends of the Game) .10
15 Harmon Killebrew (Legends of the Game) .50
16 Ralph Kiner (Legends of the Game) .10
17 Tommy Lasorda (Legends of the Game) .10
18 Juan Marichal (Legends of the Game) .10
19 Eddie Mathews (Legends of the Game) .40
20 Willie Mays (Legends of the Game) 1.50
21 Willie McCovey (Legends of the Game) .10
22 Joe Morgan (Legends of the Game) .10
23 Gaylord Perry (Legends of the Game) .10
24 Kirby Puckett (Legends of the Game) 1.00
25 Pee Wee Reese (Legends of the Game) .10
26 Phil Rizzuto (Legends of the Game) .25
27 Robin Roberts (Legends of the Game) .10
28 Brooks Robinson (Legends of the Game) .75
29 Frank Robinson (Legends of the Game) .50
30 Red Schoendienst (Legends of the Game) .10
31 Enos Slaughter (Legends of the Game) .10
32 Warren Spahn (Legends of the Game) .50
33 Willie Stargell (Legends of the Game) .20
34 Earl Weaver (Legends of the Game) .10
35 Billy Williams (Legends of the Game) .20
36 Early Wynn (Legends of the Game) .10
37 Rickey Henderson (A Place in History) .15
38 Greg Maddux (A Place in History) 1.50
39 Mike Mussina (A Place in History) .50
40 Cal Ripken Jr. (A Place in History) 2.00
41 Albert Belle (A Place in History) .60
42 Frank Thomas (A Place in History) 1.50
43 Jeff Bagwell (A Place in History) .75
44 Paul Molitor (A Place in History) .45
45 Chuck Knoblauch (A Place in History) .25
46 Todd Hundley (A Place in History) .10
47 Bernie Williams (A Place in History) .40
48 Tony Gwynn (A Place in History) 1.00
49 Barry Bonds (A Place in History) .60
50 Ken Griffey Jr. (A Place in History) 2.50
51 Randy Johnson (A Place in History) .50
52 Mark McGwire (A Place in History) 2.50
53 Roger Clemens (A Place in History) .75
54 Jose Cruz Jr. (A Place in History) .25
55 Roberto Alomar (Legends of Today) .50
56 Sandy Alomar (Legends of Today) .10
57 Brady Anderson (Legends of Today) .10
58 Kevin Appier (Legends of Today) .10
59 Jeff Bagwell (Legends of Today) .75
60 Albert Belle (Legends of Today) .60
61 Dante Bichette (Legends of Today) .20
62 Craig Biggio (Legends of Today) .25
63 Barry Bonds (Legends of Today) .60
64 Kevin Brown (Legends of Today) .10
65 Jay Buhner (Legends of Today) .10
66 Ellis Burks (Legends of Today) .10
67 Ken Caminiti (Legends of Today) .25
68 Jose Canseco (Legends of Today) .25
69 Joe Carter (Legends of Today) .10
70 Vinny Castilla (Legends of Today) .10
71 Tony Clark (Legends of Today) .40
72 Roger Clemens (Legends of Today) .75
73 David Cone (Legends of Today) .20
74 Jose Cruz Jr. (Legends of Today) .25
75 Jason Dickson (Legends of Today) .10
76 Jim Edmonds (Legends of Today) .10
77 Scott Erickson (Legends of Today) .10
78 Darin Erstad (Legends of Today) .60
79 Alex Fernandez (Legends of Today) .10
80 Steve Finley (Legends of Today) .10
81 Travis Fryman (Legends of Today) .10
82 Andres Galarraga (Legends of Today) .25
83 Nomar Garciaparra (Legends of Today) 1.50
84 Tom Glavine (Legends of Today) .20
85 Juan Gonzalez (Legends of Today) .75
86 Mark Grace (Legends of Today) .25
87 Willie Greene (Legends of Today) .10
88 Ken Griffey Jr. (Legends of Today) 2.50
89 Vladimir Guerrero (Legends of Today) 1.00
90 Tony Gwynn (Legends of Today) 1.00
91 Livan Hernandez (Legends of Today) .10
92 Bobby Higginson (Legends of Today) .10
93 Derek Jeter (Legends of Today) 1.50
94 Charles Johnson (Legends of Today) .10
95 Randy Johnson (Legends of Today) .40
96 Andruw Jones (Legends of Today) 1.00
97 Chipper Jones (Legends of Today) 1.50
98 David Justice (Legends of Today) .25
99 Eric Karros (Legends of Today) .10
100 Jason Kendall (Legends of Today) .10
101 Jimmy Key (Legends of Today) .10
102 Darryl Kile (Legends of Today) .10
103 Chuck Knoblauch (Legends of Today) .25
104 Ray Lankford (Legends of Today) .10
105 Barry Larkin (Legends of Today) .15
106 Kenny Lofton (Legends of Today) .45
107 Greg Maddux (Legends of Today) 1.50
108 Al Martin (Legends of Today) .10
109 Edgar Martinez (Legends of Today) .10
110 Pedro Martinez (Legends of Today) .25
111 Ramon Martinez (Legends of Today) .10
112 Tino Martinez (Legends of Today) .15
113 Mark McGwire (Legends of Today) 2.50
114 Raul Mondesi (Legends of Today) .25
115 Matt Morris (Legends of Today) .10
116 Charles Nagy (Legends of Today) .10
117 Denny Neagle (Legends of Today) .10
118 Hideo Nomo (Legends of Today) .50
119 Dean Palmer (Legends of Today) .10
120 Andy Pettitte (Legends of Today) .50
121 Mike Piazza (Legends of Today) 1.50
122 Manny Ramirez (Legends of Today) .75
123 Edgar Renteria (Legends of Today) .10
124 Cal Ripken Jr. (Legends of Today) 2.00
125 Alex Rodriguez (Legends of Today) 2.00
126 Henry Rodriguez (Legends of Today) .10
127 Ivan Rodriguez (Legends of Today) .60
128 Scott Rolen (Legends of Today) 1.00
129 Tim Salmon (Legends of Today) .15
130 Curt Schilling (Legends of Today) .10
131 Gary Sheffield (Legends of Today) .20
132 John Smoltz (Legends of Today) .20
133 Sammy Sosa (Legends of Today) 2.00
134 Frank Thomas (Legends of Today) 1.50

135	Jim Thome (Legends of Today)	.50
136	Mo Vaughn (Legends of Today)	.45
137	Robin Ventura (Legends of Today)	.10
138	Larry Walker (Legends of Today)	.25
139	Bernie Williams (Legends of Today)	.40
140	Matt Williams (Legends of Today)	.25
141	Jaret Wright (Legends of Today)	1.00
142	Michael Coleman (Legends of the Future)	.10
143	Juan Encarnacion (Legends of the Future)	.20
144	Brad Fullmer (Legends of the Future)	.25
145	Ben Grieve (Legends of the Future)	1.00
146	Todd Helton (Legends of the Future)	.75
147	Paul Konerko (Legends of the Future)	.75
148	Derrek Lee (Legends of the Future)	.20
149	*Magglio Ordonez* (Legends of the Future)	1.00
150	Enrique Wilson (Legends of the Future)	.10

Player names in *Italic* type indicate a rookie card.

1998 Sports Illustrated Then & Now Extra Edition

This 150-card set paralleled the base set and was distinguished by an "Extra Edition" foil stamp on the front. There were 500 sets of Extra Edition and the cards were individually numbered on the back.

	MT
Common Extra Edition:	2.00
Extra Edition Stars:	15X
Production 500 sets	

(See 1998 Sports Illustrated Then & Now for checklist and base card values.)

1998 Sports Illustrated Then & Now Art of the Game

Art of the Game was an eight-card insert featuring reproductions of original artwork of current and retired baseball stars done by eight popular sports artists. Cards are numbered with a "AG" prefix and inserted one per nine packs.

		MT
Complete Set (8):		22.00
Common Player:		1.50
Inserted 1:9		
1	It's Gone	5.00
2	Alex Rodriguez	5.00
3	Mike Piazza	4.00
4	Brooks Robinson	2.50
5	David Justice (All-Star)	2.00
6	Cal Ripken Jr.	5.00
7	The Prospect and the Prospector	1.50
8	Barry Bonds	2.50

1998 Sports Illustrated Then & Now Autographs

Six autograph redemption cards were randomly inserted into packs of Then & Now and could be exchanged prior to Nov. 1, 1999. The signed cards were produced in the following quantities: Clemens 250, Gibson 500, Gwynn 250, Killebrew 500, Mays 250 and Rolen 250. Four of the six cards use the same fronts as the Covers insert; Gibson and Rolen cards each feature unique card fronts.

	MT
Common Autograph:	70.00
Redemption Cards: 25%	
Bob Gibson (500)	50.00
Tony Gwynn (250)	125.00
Roger Clemens (250)	150.00
Scott Rolen (250)	60.00
Willie Mays (250)	200.00
Harmon Killebrew (500)	50.00

1998 Sports Illustrated Then & Now Covers

This 12-card insert features color shots of six actual Sports Illustrated covers, including six current players and six retired players. The cards are numbered with a "C" prefix and were seeded one per 18 packs.

		MT
Complete Set (12):		75.00
Common Player:		4.00
Inserted 1:18		
1	Lou Brock (10/16/67)	4.00
2	Kirby Puckett (4/6/92)	8.00
3	Harmon Killebrew (4/8/63 - inside)	4.00
4	Eddie Mathews (8/16/54)	10.00
5	Willie Mays (5/22/72)	10.00
6	Frank Robinson (10/6/69)	6.00
7	Cal Ripken Jr. (9/11/95)	12.00
8	Roger Clemens (5/12/86)	8.00
9	Ken Griffey Jr. (10/16/95)	15.00
10	Mark McGwire (6/1/92)	15.00
11	Tony Gwynn (7/28/97)	8.00
12	Ivan Rodriguez (8/11/97)	5.00

1998 Sports Illustrated Then & Now Great Shots!

This 25-card set featured 5" x 7" fold-out mini-posters using Sports Illustrated photos. Great Shots were inserted one per pack and contained a mix of retired and current players.

		MT
Complete Set (25):		5.00
Common Player:		.10
Inserted 1:1		
1	Ken Griffey Jr.	1.50
2	Frank Thomas	.50
3	Alex Rodriguez	1.00
4	Andruw Jones	.40
5	Chipper Jones	.60
6	Cal Ripken Jr.	.75
7	Mark McGwire	1.50
8	Derek Jeter	.60
9	Greg Maddux	.60
10	Jeff Bagwell	.40
11	Mike Piazza	.60
12	Scott Rolen	.40
13	Nomar Garciaparra	.60
14	Jose Cruz Jr.	.10
15	Charles Johnson	.10
16	Fergie Jenkins	.10
17	Lou Brock	.10
18	Bob Gibson	.10
19	Harmon Killebrew	.10
20	Juan Marichal	.10
21	Brooks Robinson	.25
22	Rod Carew	.20
23	Yogi Berra	.25
24	Willie Mays	.50
25	Kirby Puckett	.50

1998 Sports Illustrated Then & Now Road to Cooperstown

Road to Cooperstown features 10 current players who are having Hall of Fame careers. The insert name is printed across the back in bold, gold letters. Cards are numbered with a "RC" prefix and were inserted one per 24 packs.

		MT
Complete Set (10):		80.00
Common Player:		3.00
Inserted 1:24		
1	Barry Bonds	5.00
2	Roger Clemens	8.00
3	Ken Griffey Jr.	20.00
4	Tony Gwynn	10.00
5	Rickey Henderson	3.00
6	Greg Maddux	12.00
7	Paul Molitor	4.00
8	Mike Piazza	12.00
9	Cal Ripken Jr.	15.00
10	Frank Thomas	10.00

1998 Sports Illustrated

The second of three Sports Illustrated releases of 1998 from Fleer contained 200 cards and featured exclusive Sports Illustrated photography and commentary. Cards arrived in six-card packs and carried a Sports Illustrated logo in a top corner. The set included a Travis Lee One to Watch cards (#201) that was inserted just before going to press. Subsets included: Baseball's Best (129-148), One to Watch (149-176), and '97 in Review (177-200). Inserts sets include: Extra Edition and First Edition parallels, Autographs, Covers, Editor's Choice and Opening Day Mini Posters.

		MT
Complete Set (201):		40.00
Common Player:		.10
Pack (6):		2.00
Wax Box (24):		42.00
1	Edgardo Alfonzo	.10
2	Roberto Alomar	.50
3	Sandy Alomar	.10
4	Moises Alou	.20
5	Brady Anderson	.20
6	Garret Anderson	.10
7	Kevin Appier	.10
8	Jeff Bagwell	1.00
9	Jay Bell	.10
10	Albert Belle	.75
11	Dante Bichette	.25
12	Craig Biggio	.20
13	Barry Bonds	.75
14	Bobby Bonilla	.10
15	Kevin Brown	.20
16	Jay Buhner	.10
17	Ellis Burks	.10
18	Mike Cameron	.20
19	Ken Caminiti	.20
20	Jose Canseco	.25
21	Joe Carter	.10
22	Vinny Castilla	.10
23	Jeff Cirillo	.10
24	Tony Clark	.50
25	Will Clark	.25
26	Roger Clemens	1.00
27	David Cone	.20
28	Jose Cruz Jr.	.20
29	Carlos Delgado	.25
30	Jason Dickson	.10
31	Dennis Eckersley	.10
32	Jim Edmonds	.20
33	Scott Erickson	.10
34	Darin Erstad	.75
35	Shawn Estes	.10
36	Jeff Fassero	.10
37	Alex Fernandez	.10
38	Chuck Finley	.10
39	Steve Finley	.10
40	Travis Fryman	.10
41	Andres Galarraga	.25
42	Ron Gant	.20
43	Nomar Garciaparra	1.50
44	Jason Giambi	.10
45	Tom Glavine	.20
46	Juan Gonzalez	1.00
47	Mark Grace	.25
48	Willie Green	.10
49	Rusty Greer	.10
50	Ben Grieve	1.00
51	Ken Griffey Jr.	4.00
52	Mark Grudzielanek	.10
53	Vladimir Guerrero	1.50
54	Juan Guzman	.10
55	Tony Gwynn	1.50
56	Joey Hamilton	.10
57	Rickey Henderson	.25
58	Pat Hentgen	.10
59	Livan Hernandez	.10
60	Bobby Higginson	.10
61	Todd Hundley	.20
62	Hideki Irabu	.25
63	John Jaha	.10
64	Derek Jeter	2.00
65	Charles Johnson	.10
66	Randy Johnson	.50
67	Andruw Jones	.75
68	Bobby Jones	.10
69	Chipper Jones	2.00
70	Brian Jordan	.10
71	David Justice	.25
72	Eric Karros	.10
73	Jeff Kent	.10
74	Jimmy Key	.10
75	Darryl Kile	.10
76	Jeff King	.10
77	Ryan Klesko	.20
78	Chuck Knoblauch	.25
79	Ray Lankford	.10
80	Barry Larkin	.20
81	Kenny Lofton	.45
82	Greg Maddux	2.00
83	Al Martin	.10
84	Edgar Martinez	.10
85	Pedro Martinez	.25
86	Tino Martinez	.20
87	Mark McGwire	4.00
88	Paul Molitor	.50
89	Raul Mondesi	.25
90	Jamie Moyer	.10
91	Mike Mussina	.60
92	Tim Naehring	.10
93	Charles Nagy	.10
94	Denny Neagle	.10
95	Dave Nilsson	.10
96	Hideo Nomo	.50
97	Rey Ordonez	.10
98	Dean Palmer	.10
99	Rafael Palmeiro	.20
100	Andy Pettitte	.50
101	Mike Piazza	2.00
102	Brad Radke	.10
103	Manny Ramirez	.75
104	Edgar Renteria	.10
105	Cal Ripken Jr.	2.50
106	Alex Rodriguez	3.00
106p	Alex Rodriguez ("PROMOTIONAL SAMPLE")	3.00
107	Henry Rodriguez	.10
108	Ivan Rodriguez	.75
109	Scott Rolen	1.00
110	Tim Salmon	.25
111	Curt Schilling	.25
112	Gary Sheffield	.25
113	John Smoltz	.20
114	J.T. Snow	.10
115	Sammy Sosa	2.00
116	Matt Stairs	.10
117	Shannon Stewart	.10
118	Frank Thomas	1.00
119	Jim Thome	.40
120	Justin Thompson	.20
121	Mo Vaughn	.45
122	Robin Ventura	.20
123	Larry Walker	.40
124	Rondell White	.20
125	Bernie Williams	.60
126	Matt Williams	.25
127	Tony Womack	.10
128	Jaret Wright	1.75
129	Edgar Renteria (Baseball's Best)	.10
130	Kenny Lofton (Baseball's Best)	.40
131	Tony Gwynn (Baseball's Best)	.75
132	Mark McGwire (Baseball's Best)	2.00
133	Craig Biggio (Baseball's Best)	.10
134	Charles Johnson (Baseball's Best)	.10
135	J.T. Snow (Baseball's Best)	.10
136	Ken Caminiti (Baseball's Best)	.10
137	Vladimir Guerrero (Baseball's Best)	.75
138	Jim Edmonds (Baseball's Best)	.10
139	Randy Johnson (Baseball's Best)	.25
140	Darryl Kile (Baseball's Best)	.10
141	John Smoltz (Baseball's Best)	.10
142	Greg Maddux (Baseball's Best)	1.00
143	Andy Pettitte (Baseball's Best)	.25
144	Ken Griffey Jr. (Baseball's Best)	1.50
145	Mike Piazza (Baseball's Best)	1.00
146	Todd Greene (Baseball's Best)	.10
147	Vinny Castilla (Baseball's Best)	.10
148	Derek Jeter (Baseball's Best)	1.00
149	Robert Machado (One to Watch)	.10
150	Mike Gulan (One to Watch)	.10
151	Randall Simon (One to Watch)	.20
152	Michael Coleman (One to Watch)	.10
153	Brian Rose (One to Watch)	.25
154	*Scott Eyre* (One to Watch)	.25
155	*Magglio Ordonez* (One to Watch)	1.00
156	Todd Helton (One to Watch)	.75
157	Juan Encarnacion (One to Watch)	.10
158	Mark Kotsay (One to Watch)	.50
159	Josh Booty (One to Watch)	.10
160	*Melvin Rosario* (One to Watch)	.25
161	Shane Halter (One to Watch)	.10
162	Paul Konerko (One to Watch)	1.00
163	*Henry Blanco* (One to Watch)	.20
164	Antone Williamson (One to Watch)	.10
165	Brad Fullmer (One to Watch)	.20
166	Ricky Ledee (One to Watch)	.50
167	Ben Grieve (One to Watch)	.60
168	*Frank Catalanotto* (One to Watch)	.20
169	Bobby Estalella (One to Watch)	.10
170	Dennis Reyes (One to Watch)	.10
171	Kevin Polcovich (One to Watch)	.10
172	Jacob Cruz (One to Watch)	.10
173	Ken Cloude (One to Watch)	.10
174	Eli Marrero (One to Watch)	.10
175	Fernando Tatis (One to Watch)	.10
176	Tom Evans (One to Watch)	.10
177	Everett, Garciaparra (97 in Review)	.75
178	Eric Davis (97 in Review)	.10
179	Roger Clemens (97 in Review)	.50
180	Butler, Murray (97 in Review)	.10
181	Frank Thomas (97 in Review)	.75
182	Curt Schilling (97 in Review)	.10
183	Jeff Bagwell (97 in Review)	.50
184	McGwire, Griffey (97 in Review)	1.50
185	Kevin Brown (97 in Review)	.10
186	Cordova, Rincon (97 in Review)	.10
187	Charles Johnson (97 in Review)	.10
188	Hideki Irabu (97 in Review)	.20
189	Tony Gwynn (97 in Review)	.75
190	Sandy Alomar (97 in Review)	.10
191	Ken Griffey Jr. (97 in Review)	1.50
192	Larry Walker (97 in Review)	.20
193	Roger Clemens (97 in Review)	.50
194	Pedro Martinez (97 in Review)	.20
195	Nomar Garciaparra (97 in Review)	.75
196	Scott Rolen (97 in Review)	.50
197	Brian Anderson (97 in Review)	.10
198	Tony Saunders (97 in Review)	.10
199	Fla. Celebration (97 in Review)	.10
200	Livan Hernandez (97 in Review)	.10
201	Travis Lee (One to Watch) (SP)	2.00

1998 Sports Illustrated Extra Edition

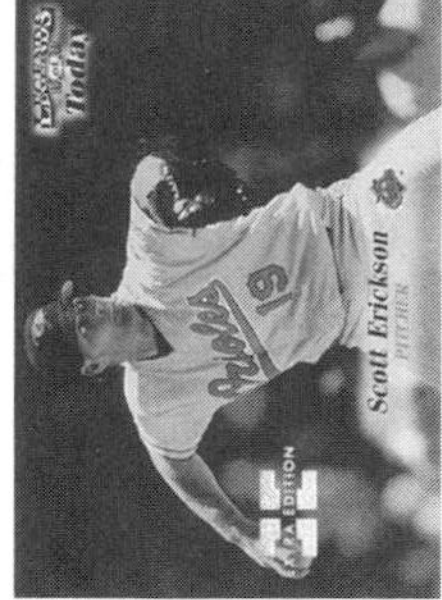

Extra Edition is a 201-card parallel set that includes a holofoil stamp on the front and sequential numbering to 250 on the back. There is also a First Edition version of these that was identical on the front, but contains the text "The Only 1 of 1 First Edition" in purple lettering on the card back.

	MT
Common Player:	4.00
Extra Edition Stars:	20X

(See 1998 Sports Illustrated for checklist and base card values.)

1998 Sports Illustrated Autographs

This six-card insert featured autographs of players with the following production: Brock 500, Cruz Jr. 250, Fingers 500, Grieve 250, Konerko 250 and Robinson 500. The Konerko and Greive cards were available through redemptions until Nov. 1, 1999.

	MT
Common Player:	30.00
Lou Brock (500)	50.00
Jose Cruz Jr. (250)	20.00
Rollie Fingers (500)	20.00
Ben Grieve (exchange card) (250)	10.00
Ben Grieve (signed card)	30.00
Paul Konerko (exchange card) (250)	20.00
Paul Konerko (signed card)	20.00
Brooks Robinson (250)	75.00

1998 Sports Illustrated Covers

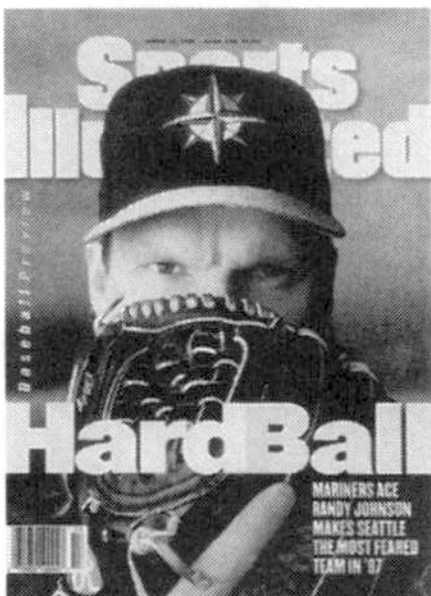

This 10-card insert set pictures actual Sports Illustrated covers on trading cards. The cards are numbered with a "C" prefix and inserted one per nine packs.

		MT
Complete Set (10):		30.00
Common Player:		2.00
Inserted 1:9		
1	Griffey, Piazza	7.00
2	Derek Jeter	5.00
3	Ken Griffey Jr.	8.00
4	Cal Ripken Jr.	6.00
5	Manny Ramirez	3.50
6	Jay Buhner	2.00
7	Matt Williams	2.00
8	Randy Johnson	2.00
9	Deion Sanders	2.00
10	Jose Canseco	2.00

1998 Sports Illustrated Editor's Choice

Editor's Choice includes 10 top players in 1998 as profiled by the editors of Sports Illustrated. Cards are numbered with an "EC" prefix and seeded one per 24 packs.

		MT
Complete Set (10):		100.00
Common Player:		4.00
Inserted 1:24		
1	Ken Griffey Jr.	20.00
2	Alex Rodriguez	15.00
3	Frank Thomas	10.00
4	Mark McGwire	20.00
5	Greg Maddux	12.00
6	Derek Jeter	12.00
7	Cal Ripken Jr.	15.00
8	Nomar Garciaparra	12.00
9	Jeff Bagwell	8.00
10	Jose Cruz Jr.	4.00

1998 Sports Illustrated Mini-Posters

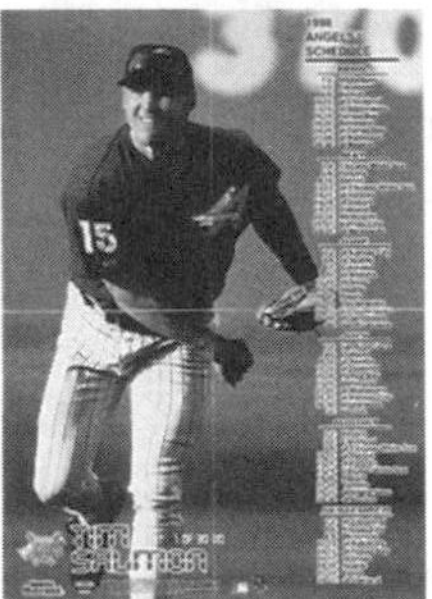

Thirty 5" x 7" mini-posters were available at a rate of one per pack. The posters took the top player or two from each team and added their 1998 schedule. Backs were blank so the cards are numbered on the front with an "OD" prefix.

		MT
Complete Set (30):		8.00
Common Player:		.15
Inserted 1:1		
1	Tim Salmon	.25
2	Travis Lee	.40
3	John Smoltz, Greg Maddux	.75
4	Cal Ripken Jr.	1.50
5	Nomar Garciaparra	.75
6	Sammy Sosa	.50
7	Frank Thomas	.75
8	Barry Larkin	.15
9	David Justice	.15
10	Larry Walker	.25
11	Tony Clark	.40
12	Livan Hernandez	.15
13	Jeff Bagwell	.60
14	Kevin Appier	.15
15	Mike Piazza	1.00
16	Fernando Vina	.15
17	Chuck Knoblauch	.25
18	Vladimir Guerrero	.50
19	Rey Ordonez	.15
20	Bernie Williams	.30
21	Matt Stairs	.15
22	Curt Schilling	.15
23	Tony Womack	.15
24	Mark McGwire	2.00
25	Tony Gwynn	.75
26	Barry Bonds	.50
27	Ken Griffey Jr.	2.00
28	Fred McGriff	.25
29	Juan Gonzalez, Alex Rodriguez	1.00
30	Roger Clemens	.75

1998 Sports Illustrated World Series Fever

The third and final Sports Illustrated release of 1998 contained 150 cards and focused on the World Series while recapping memorable moments from the season. The set also included many stars of tomorrow, like Kerry Wood, Orlando Hernandez, Ben Grieve and Travis Lee. Once again, all the photos were taken from Sports Illustrated archives. The set has two subsets - 10 Magnificent Moments and 20 Cover Collection. The set is paralleled twice in Extra and First Edition parallel sets, and has three insert sets - MVP Collection, Reggie Jackson's Picks and Autumn Excellence.

		MT
Complete Set (150):		40.00
Common Player:		.10
Pack (6):		2.00
Wax Box (24):		38.00
1	Mickey Mantle (Covers)	3.00
2	1957 World Series Preview (Covers)	.20
3	1958 World Series Preview (Covers)	.20
4	1959 World Series Preview (Covers)	.20
5	1962 World Series (Covers)	.20
6	Lou Brock (Covers)	.30
7	Brooks Robinson (Covers)	.75
8	Frank Robinson (Covers)	.50
9	1974 World Series (Covers)	.20
10	Reggie Jackson (Covers)	.50
11	1985 World Series (Covers)	.20
12	1987 World Series (Covers)	.20
13	Orel Hershiser (Covers)	.10
14	Rickey Henderson (Covers)	.10
15	1991 World Series (Covers)	.20
16	1992 World Series (Covers)	.10
17	Joe Carter (Covers)	.10
18	1995 World Series (Covers)	.20
19	1996 World Series (Covers)	.40
20	Edgar Renteria (Covers)	.10
21	Bill Mazeroski (Magnificent Moments)	.10
22	Joe Carter (Magnificent Moments)	.10
23	Carlton Fisk (Magnificent Moments)	.10
24	Bucky Dent (Magnificent Moments)	.10
25	Mookie Wilson (Magnificent Moments)	.10
26	Enos Slaughter (Magnificent Moments)	.10
27	Mickey Lolich (Magnificent Moments)	.10
28	Bobby Richardson (Magnificent Moments)	.10
29	Kirk Gibson (Magnificent Moments)	.10
30	Edgar Renteria (Magnificent Moments)	.10
31	Albert Belle	.60
32	Kevin Brown	.10
33	Brian Rose	.10
34	Ron Gant	.15
35	Jeromy Burnitz	.10
36	Andres Galarraga	.40
37	Jim Edmonds	.10
38	Jose Cruz Jr.	.20
39	Mark Grudzielanek	.10
40	Shawn Estes	.10
41	Mark Grace	.25
42	Nomar Garciaparra	2.00
43	Juan Gonzalez	.75
44	Tom Glavine	.20
45	Brady Anderson	.10
46	Tony Clark	.50
47	Jeff Cirillo	.10
48	Dante Bichette	.25
49	Ben Grieve	1.00
50	Ken Griffey Jr.	3.00
51	Edgardo Alfonzo	.10
52	Roger Clemens	1.00
53	Pat Hentgen	.10
54	Todd Helton	.75
55	Andy Benes	.10
56	Tony Gwynn	1.50
57	Andruw Jones	.75
58	Bobby Higginson	.10
59	Bobby Jones	.10
60	Darryl Kile	.10
61	Chan Ho Park	.25
62	Charles Johnson	.10
63	Rusty Greer	.10
64	Travis Fryman	.10
65	Derek Jeter	2.00
66	Jay Buhner	.10
67	Chuck Knoblauch	.40
68	David Justice	.40
69	Brian Hunter	.10
70	Eric Karros	.10
71	Edgar Martinez	.10

72 Chipper Jones 2.00
73 Barry Larkin .15
74 Mike Lansing .10
75 Craig Biggio .25
76 Al Martin .10
77 Barry Bonds .75
78 Randy Johnson .50
79 Ryan Klesko .25
80 Mark McGwire 3.00
81 Fred McGriff .25
82 Javy Lopez .10
83 Kenny Lofton .50
84 Sandy Alomar Jr. .10
85 Matt Morris .10
86 Paul Konerko .25
87 Ray Lankford .10
88 Kerry Wood .75
89 Roberto Alomar .50
90 Greg Maddux 2.00
91 Travis Lee .75
92 Moises Alou .25
93 Dean Palmer .10
94 Hideo Nomo .40
95 Ken Caminiti .20
96 Pedro Martinez .75
97 Raul Mondesi .25
98 Denny Neagle .10
99 Tino Martinez .30
100 Mike Mussina .60
101 Kevin Appier .10
102 Vinny Castilla .20
103 Jeff Bagwell 1.00
104 Paul O'Neill .20
105 Rey Ordonez .10
106 Vladimir Guerrero 1.25
107 Rafael Palmeiro .25
108 Alex Rodriguez 2.50
109 Andy Pettitte .50
110 Carl Pavano .20
111 Henry Rodriguez .10
112 Gary Sheffield .25
113 Curt Schilling .20
114 John Smoltz .20
115 Reggie Sanders .10
116 Scott Rolen 1.00
117 Mike Piazza 2.00
118 Manny Ramirez 1.00
119 Cal Ripken Jr. 2.50
120 Brad Radke .10
121 Tim Salmon .30
122 Brett Tomko .10
123 Robin Ventura .10
124 Mo Vaughn .50
125 A.J. Hinch .10
126 Derrek Lee .10
127 *Orlando Hernandez* 3.00
128 Aramis Ramirez .50
129 Frank Thomas 1.50
130 J.T. Snow .10
131 *Magglio Ordonez* .75
132 Bobby Bonilla .10
133 Marquis Grissom .10
134 Jim Thome .40
135 Justin Thompson .10
136 Matt Williams .30
137 Matt Stairs .10
138 Wade Boggs .40
139 Chuck Finley .10
140 Jaret Wright .75
141 Ivan Rodriguez .75
142 Brad Fullmer .25
143 Bernie Williams .40
144 Jason Giambi .10
145 Larry Walker .40
146 Tony Womack .10
147 Sammy Sosa 2.00
148 Rondell White .20
149 Todd Stottlemyre .10
150 Shane Reynolds .10

1998 Sports Illustrated WS Fever Extra Edition

Extra Edition parallels the entire 150-card base set and is identified by a gold foil stamp on the card front and sequential numbering to 98 sets on the back. World Series Fever also includes one-of-one parallel versions called First Edition. These have the same fronts, but are numbered 1 of 1 on back.

	MT
Common Player:	5.00
Stars:	30X
Production 98 sets	

(See 1998 Sports Illustrated World Series Fever for checklist and base values.)

1998 Sports Illustrated WS Fever Autumn Excellence

Autumn Excellence honors players with the most select World Series records. The 10-card set was seeded one per 24 packs, while rarer Gold versions were seeded one per 240 packs.

	MT
Complete Set (10):	60.00
Common Player:	2.00
Inserted 1:24	
Golds:	4X
Inserted 1:240	

AE1 Willie Mays 7.50
AE2 Kirby Puckett 6.00
AE3 Babe Ruth 20.00
AE4 Reggie Jackson 5.00
AE5 Whitey Ford 2.00
AE6 Lou Brock 2.00
AE7 Mickey Mantle 15.00
AE8 Yogi Berra 5.00
AE9 Bob Gibson 4.00
AE10 Don Larsen 4.00

1998 Sports Illustrated WS Fever MVP Collection

This 10-card insert set features select MVPs from the World Series. Card fronts contain a shot of the player over a white border with the year in black letters and the insert and player's name in blue foil. MVP Collection inserts were seeded one per four packs and numbered with a "MC" prefix.

	MT
Complete Set (10):	7.50
Common Player:	.75
Inserted 1:4	

1 Frank Robinson 1.50
2 Brooks Robinson 2.00
3 Willie Stargell .75
4 Bret Saberhagen .75
5 Rollie Fingers .75
6 Orel Hershiser .75
7 Paul Molitor 2.00
8 Tom Glavine .75
9 John Wetteland .75
10 Livan Hernandez .75

1998 Sports Illustrated WS Fever Reggie Jackson Picks

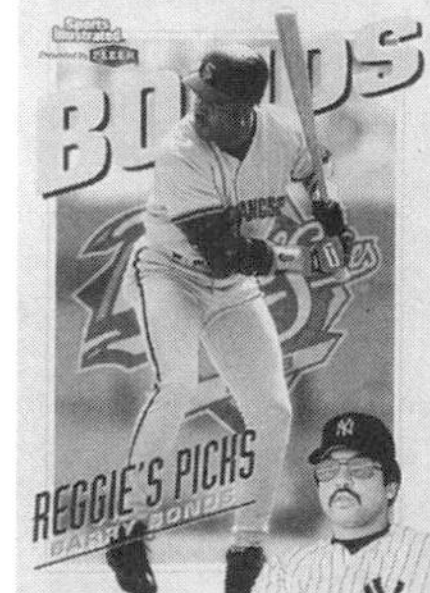

Reggie Jackson's Picks contains top players that Jackson believes have what it takes to perform on center stage in the World Series. Fronts have a shot of the player with his name in the background, and a head shot of Reggie Jackson in the bottom right corner. These were numbered with a "RP" prefix and inserted one per 12 packs.

	MT
Complete Set (15):	70.00
Common Player:	1.50
Inserted 1:12	

1 Paul O'Neill 1.50
2 Barry Bonds 3.00
3 Ken Griffey Jr. 12.50
4 Juan Gonzalez 3.00
5 Greg Maddux 7.50
6 Mike Piazza 7.50
7 Larry Walker 2.00
8 Mo Vaughn 1.50
9 Roger Clemens 4.00
10 John Smoltz 1.50
11 Alex Rodriguez 10.00
12 Frank Thomas 5.00
13 Mark McGwire 12.50
14 Jeff Bagwell 4.00
15 Randy Johnson 2.50

1999 Sports Illustrated

The Sports Illustrated Baseball by Fleer set consists of a 180-card base set. The base set is composed of 107 player cards, and four subsets. They include Team 2000, Postseason Review, Award Winners, and Season Highlights. Cards come in six-card packs with an SRP of $1.99. The set also includes five insert sets, along with hobby exclusive autographed J.D. Drew cards numbered to 250. The insert sets include: Headliners (1:4), Ones to Watch (1:12), Fabulous 40's (1:20), Fabulous 40's Extra (hobby exclusive), and The Dominators (1:90 and 1:180).

	MT
Complete Set (180):	30.00
Common Player:	.10
Pack (6):	2.00
Wax Box (24):	40.00

1 Yankees (Postseason Review) .25
2 Scott Brosius (Postseason Review) .10
3 David Wells (Postseason Review) .10
4 Sterling Hitchcock (Postseason Review) .10
5 David Justice (Postseason Review) .25
6 David Cone (Postseason Review) .20
7 Greg Maddux (Postseason Review) 1.00
8 Jim Leyritz (Postseason Review) .10
9 Gary Gaetti (Postseason Review) .10
10 Mark McGwire (Award Winners) 1.50
11 Sammy Sosa (Award Winners) 1.00
12 Larry Walker (Award Winners) .25
13 Tony Womack (Award Winners) .10
14 Tom Glavine (Award Winners) .10
15 Curt Schilling (Award Winners) .10
16 Greg Maddux (Award Winners) 1.00

17 Trevor Hoffman (Award Winners) .10
18 Kerry Wood (Award Winners) .50
19 Tom Glavine (Award Winners) .10
20 Sammy Sosa (Award Winners) 1.00
21 Travis Lee (Season Highlights) .30
22 Roberto Alomar (Season Highlights) .25
23 Roger Clemens (Season Highlights) .75
24 Barry Bonds (Season Highlights) .40
25 Paul Molitor (Season Highlights) .30
26 Todd Stottlemyre (Season Highlights) .10
27 Chris Hoiles (Season Highlights) .10
28 Albert Belle (Season Highlights) .40
29 Tony Clark (Season Highlights) .25
30 Kerry Wood (Season Highlights) .50
31 David Wells (Season Highlights) .10
32 Dennis Eckersley (Season Highlights) .10
33 Mark McGwire (Season Highlights) 1.50
34 Cal Ripken Jr. (Season Highlights) 1.25
35 Ken Griffey Jr. (Season Highlights) 1.50
36 Alex Rodriguez (Season Highlights) 1.25
37 Craig Biggio (Season Highlights) .20
38 Sammy Sosa (Season Highlights) 1.00
39 Dennis Martinez (Season Highlights) .10
40 Curt Schilling (Season Highlights) .20
41 Orlando Hernandez (Season Highlights) .50
42 Troy Glaus, *Ben Molina*, Todd Greene ("Team" 2000) .75
43 Mitch Meluskey, Daryle Ward, Mike Grzanich ("Team" 2000) .15
44 Eric Chavez, Mike Neill, *Steve Connelly* ("Team" 2000) .50
45 Roy Halladay, Tom Evans, Kevin Witt ("Team" 2000) .25
46 George Lombard, Adam Butler, Bruce Chen ("Team" 2000) .10
47 Ronnie Belliard, Valerio de los Santos, *Rafael Roque* ("Team" 2000) .25
48 J.D. Drew, Placido Polanco, *Mark Little* ("Team" 2000) .25
49 Jason Maxwell, *Jose Nieves*, Jeremi Gonzalez ("Team" 2000) .20
50 Scott McClain, Kerry Robinson, *Mike Duvall* ("Team" 2000) .25
51 Ben Ford, *Bryan Corey*, Danny Klassen ("Team" 2000) .25
52 Angel Pena, Jeff Kubenka, Paul LoDuca ("Team" 2000) .10
53 Kirk Bullinger, Fernando Seguignol, Tim Young ("Team" 2000) .10
54 Ramon Martinez, Wilson Delgado, Armando Rios ("Team" 2000) .10
55 Russ Branyon, *Jolbert Cabrera*, Jason Rakers ("Team" 2000) .20
56 *Carlos Guillen*, *David Holdridge*, *Giomar Guevara* ("Team" 2000) .25
57 Alex Gonzalez, Joe Fontenot, Preston Wilson ("Team" 2000) .25
58 Mike Kinkade, Jay Payton, Masato Yoshii ("Team" 2000) .10
59 Willis Otanez, Ryan Minor, Calvin Pickering ("Team" 2000) .20
60 Ben Davis, Matt Clement, Stan Spencer ("Team" 2000) .10
61 Marlon Anderson, Mike Welch, *Gary Bennett* ("Team" 2000) .25
62 Abraham Nunez, *Sean Lawrence*, Aramis Ramirez ("Team" 2000) .10
63 Jonathan Johnson, *Rob Sasser*, *Scott Sheldon* ("Team" 2000) .25
64 *Keith Glauber*, *Guillermo Garcia*, Eddie Priest ("Team" 2000) .25
65 Brian Barkley, Jin Ho Cho, Donnie Sadler ("Team" 2000) .15
66 Derrick Gibson, Mark Strittmatter, *Edgard Clemente* ("Team" 2000) .15
67 Jeremy Giambi, Dermal Brown, *Chris Hatcher* ("Team" 2000) .25
68 *Rob Fick*, Gabe Kapler, Marino Santana ("Team" 2000) .75
69 Corey Koskie, A.J. Pierzynski, Benj Sampson ("Team" 2000) .20
70 Brian Simmons, Mark Johnson, Craig Wilson ("Team" 2000) .10
71 Ryan Bradley, Mike Lowell, Jay Tessmer ("Team" 2000) .10
72 Ben Grieve .75
73 Shawn Green .20
74 Rafael Palmeiro .25
75 Juan Gonzalez .75
76 Mike Piazza 2.00
77 Devon White .10
78 Jim Thome .30
79 Barry Larkin .15
80 Scott Rolen .75
81 Raul Mondesi .25
82 Jason Giambi .10
83 Jose Canseco .40
84 Tony Gwynn 1.50
85 Cal Ripken Jr. 2.50
86 Andy Pettitte .30
87 Carlos Delgado .25
88 Jeff Cirillo .10
89 Bret Saberhagen .10
90 John Olerud .20
91 Ron Coomer .10
92 Todd Helton .75
93 Ray Lankford .10
94 Tim Salmon .25
95 Fred McGriff .20
96 Matt Stairs .10
97 Ken Griffey Jr. 3.00
98 Chipper Jones 2.00
99 Mark Grace .20
100 Ivan Rodriguez .75
101 Jeromy Burnitz .10
102 Kenny Rogers .10
103 Kevin Millwood .40
104 Vinny Castilla .20
105 Jim Edmonds .15
106 Craig Biggio .40
107 Andres Galarraga .40
108 Sammy Sosa 2.00
109 Juan Encarnacion .25
110 Larry Walker .50
111 John Smoltz .20
112 Randy Johnson .50
113 Bobby Higginson .10
114 Albert Belle .75
115 Jaret Wright .40
116 Edgar Renteria .10
117 Andruw Jones .75
118 Barry Bonds .75
119 Rondell White .20
120 Jamie Moyer .10
121 Darin Erstad .75
122 Al Leiter .20
123 Mark McGwire 3.00
124 Mo Vaughn .50
125 Livan Hernandez .10
126 Jason Kendall .10
127 Frank Thomas .75
128 Denny Neagle .10
129 Johnny Damon .10
130 Derek Bell .10
131 Jeff Kent .10
132 Tony Womack .10
133 Trevor Hoffman .10
134 Gary Sheffield .25
135 Tino Martinez .20
136 Travis Fryman .10
137 Rolando Arrojo .20
138 Dante Bichette .25
139 Nomar Garciaparra 2.00
140 Moises Alou .20
141 Chuck Knoblauch .40
142 Robin Ventura .10
143 Scott Erickson .10
144 David Cone .20
145 Greg Vaughn .20
146 Wade Boggs .35
147 Mike Mussina .50
148 Tony Clark .40
149 Alex Rodriguez 2.50
150 Javy Lopez .20
151 Bartolo Colon .10
152 Derek Jeter 2.00
153 Greg Maddux 2.00
154 Kevin Brown .20
155 Curt Schilling .20
156 Jeff King .10
157 Bernie Williams .50
158 Roberto Alomar .50
159 Travis Lee .60
160 Kerry Wood .75
160p Kerry Wood ("PROMOTIONAL SAMPLE") 1.00
161 Jeff Bagwell .75
162 Roger Clemens 1.00
163 Matt Williams .20
164 Chan Ho Park .25
165 Damion Easley .10
166 Manny Ramirez 1.00
167 Quinton McCracken .10
168 Todd Walker .25
169 Eric Karros .20
170 Will Clark .40
171 Edgar Martinez .10
172 Cliff Floyd .10
173 Vladimir Guerrero 1.25
174 Tom Glavine .25
175 Pedro Martinez .50
176 Chuck Finley .10
177 Dean Palmer .10
178 Omar Vizquel .10
179 Checklist .10
180 Checklist .10

1999 Sports Illustrated Diamond Dominators

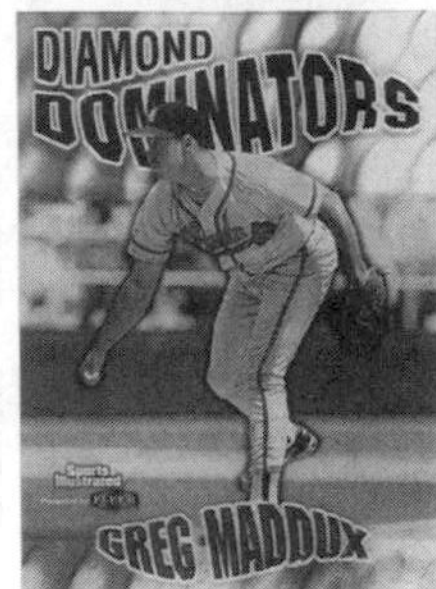

This 10-card insert set features five hitters and five pitchers on embossed cards. The hitters are seeded 1 in every 180 packs, while the pitchers are seeded 1 in every 90 packs.

		MT
Complete Set (10):		325.00
Common Player:		7.50
Pitchers inserted 1:90		
Hitters inserted 1:180		
1DD	Kerry Wood	10.00
2DD	Roger Clemens	20.00
3DD	Randy Johnson	7.50
4DD	Greg Maddux	30.00
5DD	Pedro Martinez	7.50
6DD	Ken Griffey Jr.	75.00
7DD	Sammy Sosa	55.00
8DD	Nomar Garciaparra	45.00
9DD	Mark McGwire	75.00
10DD	Alex Rodriguez	60.00

1999 Sports Illustrated Fabulous 40s

This 13-card insert set consists of the players that hit 40 or more homers during the 1998 season. The cards are sculpture embossed and foil-stamped, with the player's home run total also on the card. One card comes with every 20 packs.

		MT
Complete Set (13):		75.00
Common Player:		2.50
Inserted 1:20		
1FF	Mark McGwire	20.00

2FF	Sammy Sosa	12.00
3FF	Ken Griffey Jr.	20.00
4FF	Greg Vaughn	2.50
5FF	Albert Belle	4.50
6FF	Jose Canseco	4.50
7FF	Vinny Castilla	2.50
8FF	Juan Gonzalez	5.00
9FF	Manny Ramirez	7.50
10FF	Andres Galarraga	3.00
11FF	Rafael Palmeiro	3.00
12FF	Alex Rodriguez	15.00
13FF	Mo Vaughn	3.00

1999 Sports Illustrated Fabulous 40s Extra

The insert set parallels the 13 cards in the Fabulous 40s insert set. The cards are hobby exclusive, and contained silver pattern holofoil. Each players cards are hand-numbered to the total number of home runs he hit in 1998.

		MT
Common Player:		30.00
Numbered to amount of HRs		
1FF	Mark McGwire (70)	180.00
2FF	Sammy Sosa (66)	80.00
3FF	Ken Griffey Jr. (56)	125.00
4FF	Greg Vaughn (50)	20.00
5FF	Albert Belle (49)	25.00
6FF	Jose Canseco (46)	50.00
7FF	Vinny Castilla (46)	20.00
8FF	Juan Gonzalez (45)	50.00
9FF	Manny Ramirez (45)	60.00
10FF	Andres Galarraga (44)	20.00
11FF	Rafael Palmeiro (43)	30.00
12FF	Alex Rodriguez (42)	120.00
13FF	Mo Vaughn (40)	25.00

1999 Sports Illustrated Headliners

Headliners is a 25-card insert set that features silver foil stamped, team-color coded cards. One card comes with every four packs.

		MT
Complete Set (25):		45.00
Common Player:		.75
Inserted 1:4		
1H	Vladimir Guerrero	2.00
2H	Randy Johnson	.75
3H	Mo Vaughn	.75
4H	Chipper Jones	3.00
5H	Jeff Bagwell	1.25
6H	Juan Gonzalez	1.50
7H	Mark McGwire	5.00
8H	Cal Ripken Jr.	3.50
9H	Frank Thomas	1.50
10H	Manny Ramirez	1.70
11H	Ken Griffey Jr.	5.00
12H	Scott Rolen	1.25
13H	Alex Rodriguez	4.00
14H	Barry Bonds	1.25
15H	Roger Clemens	1.75
16H	Darin Erstad	1.25
17H	Nomar Garciaparra	3.00
18H	Mike Piazza	3.00
19H	Greg Maddux	3.00
20H	Ivan Rodriguez	1.25
21H	Derek Jeter	3.00
22H	Sammy Sosa	3.00
23H	Andruw Jones	1.25
24H	Pedro Martinez	.75
25H	Kerry Wood	1.00

1999 Sports Illustrated Ones To Watch

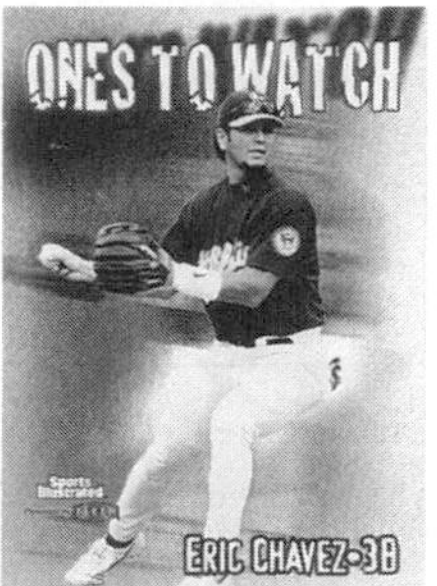

This 15-card insert set features the game's top rookies and young stars. The cards have 100%-foil background, and are team-color coded. One card was inserted in every 12 packs.

		MT
Complete Set (15):		20.00
Common Player:		.75
Inserted 1:12		
1OW	J.D. Drew	1.00
2OW	Marlon Anderson	.75
3OW	Roy Halladay	1.50
4OW	Ben Grieve	2.00
5OW	Todd Helton	1.50
6OW	Gabe Kapler	3.00
7OW	Troy Glaus	3.00
8OW	Ben Davis	.75
9OW	Eric Chavez	2.50
10OW	Richie Sexson	.75
11OW	Fernando Seguignol	1.50
12OW	Kerry Wood	2.00
13OW	Bobby Smith	.75
14OW	Ryan Minor	.75
15OW	Jeremy Giambi	1.25
	J.D. Drew Auto. (250)	40.00

1991 Stadium Club

One of the most popular sets of 1991, this 600-card issue was released in two 300-card series. The cards were available in foil packs only. No factory sets were available. The cards feature borderless high gloss photos on the front and a player evaluation and card photo on the back. Stadium Club cards were considered scarce in many areas, this driving up the price per pack. A special Stadium Club membership package was made available for $29.95 with 10 proof of purchase seals from wrappers.

		MT
Complete Set (600):		80.00
Complete Series 1 (300):		50.00
Complete Series 2 (300):		30.00
Common Player:		.20
Series 1 Pack (13):		2.50
Series 1 Wax Box (36):		65.00
Series 2 Pack (13):		1.75
Series 2 Wax Box (36):		45.00
1	Dave Stewart	.20
2	Wally Joyner	.30
3	Shawon Dunston	.20
4	Darren Daulton	.20
5	Will Clark	.75
6	Sammy Sosa	6.00
7	Dan Plesac	.20
8	Marquis Grissom	.30
9	Erik Hanson	.20
10	Geno Petralli	.20
11	Jose Rijo	.20
12	Carlos Quintana	.20
13	Junior Ortiz	.20
14	Bob Walk	.20
15	Mike Macfarlane	.20
16	Eric Yelding	.20
17	Bryn Smith	.20
18	Bip Roberts	.20
19	Mike Scioscia	.20
20	Mark Williamson	.20
21	Don Mattingly	2.00
22	John Franco	.20
23	Chet Lemon	.20
24	Tom Henke	.20
25	Jerry Browne	.20
26	Dave Justice	1.00
27	Mark Langston	.20
28	Damon Berryhill	.20
29	Kevin Bass	.20
30	Scott Fletcher	.20
31	Moises Alou	.40
32	Dave Valle	.20
33	Jody Reed	.20
34	Dave West	.20
35	Kevin McReynolds	.20
36	Pat Combs	.20
37	Eric Davis	.20
38	Bret Saberhagen	.25
39	Stan Javier	.20
40	Chuck Cary	.20
41	Tony Phillips	.20
42	Lee Smith	.20
43	Tim Teufel	.20
44	Lance Dickson	.20
45	Greg Litton	.20
46	Teddy Higuera	.20
47	Edgar Martinez	.20
48	Steve Avery	.20
49	Walt Weiss	.20
50	David Segui	.20
51	Andy Benes	.35
52	Karl Rhodes	.20
53	Neal Heaton	.20
54	Dan Gladden	.20
55	Luis Rivera	.20
56	Kevin Brown	.20
57	Frank Thomas	5.00
58	Terry Mulholland	.20
59	Dick Schofield	.20
60	Ron Darling	.20
61	Sandy Alomar, Jr.	.30
62	Dave Stieb	.20
63	Alan Trammell	.30
64	Matt Nokes	.20
65	Lenny Harris	.20
66	Milt Thompson	.20
67	Storm Davis	.20
68	Joe Oliver	.20
69	Andres Galarraga	.45
70	Ozzie Guillen	.20
71	Ken Howell	.20
72	Garry Templeton	.20
73	Derrick May	.20
74	Xavier Hernandez	.20
75	Dave Parker	.25
76	Rick Aguilera	.20
77	Robby Thompson	.20
78	Pete Incaviglia	.20
79	Bob Welch	.20
80	Randy Milligan	.20
81	Chuck Finley	.20
82	Alvin Davis	.20
83	Tim Naehring	.20
84	Jay Bell	.20
85	Joe Magrane	.20
86	Howard Johnson	.20
87	Jack McDowell	.20
88	Kevin Seitzer	.20
89	Bruce Ruffin	.20
90	Fernando Valenzuela	.25
91	Terry Kennedy	.20
92	Barry Larkin	.45
93	Larry Walker	.75
94	Luis Salazar	.20
95	Gary Sheffield	.60
96	Bobby Witt	.20
97	Lonnie Smith	.20
98	Bryan Harvey	.20
99	Mookie Wilson	.20
100	Dwight Gooden	.25
101	Lou Whitaker	.20
102	Ron Karkovice	.20
103	Jesse Barfield	.20
104	Jose DeJesus	.20
105	Benito Santiago	.20
106	Brian Holman	.20
107	Rafael Ramirez	.20
108	Ellis Burks	.30
109	Mike Bielecki	.20
110	Kirby Puckett	2.00
111	Terry Shumpert	.20
112	Chuck Crim	.20
113	Todd Benzinger	.20
114	Brian Barnes	.20
115	Carlos Baerga	.20
116	Kal Daniels	.20
117	Dave Johnson	.20
118	Andy Van Slyke	.20
119	John Burkett	.20
120	Rickey Henderson	.50
121	Tim Jones	.20
122	Daryl Irvine	.20
123	Ruben Sierra	.20
124	Jim Abbott	.20
125	Daryl Boston	.20
126	Greg Maddux	4.00
127	Von Hayes	.20
128	Mike Fitzgerald	.20
129	Wayne Edwards	.20
130	Greg Briley	.20
131	Rob Dibble	.20
132	Gene Larkin	.20
133	David Wells	.25
134	Steve Balboni	.20
135	Greg Vaughn	.25
136	Mark Davis	.20
137	Dave Rohde	.20
138	Eric Show	.20
139	Bobby Bonilla	.20
140	Dana Kiecker	.20
141	Gary Pettis	.20

142	Dennis Boyd	.20
143	Mike Benjamin	.20
144	Luis Polonia	.20
145	Doug Jones	.20
146	Al Newman	.20
147	Alex Fernandez	.40
148	Bill Doran	.20
149	Kevin Elster	.20
150	Len Dykstra	.20
151	Mike Gallego	.20
152	Tim Belcher	.20
153	Jay Buhner	.20
154	Ozzie Smith	1.00
155	Jose Canseco	.75
156	Gregg Olson	.20
157	Charlie O'Brien	.20
158	Frank Tanana	.20
159	George Brett	2.00
160	Jeff Huson	.20
161	Kevin Tapani	.20
162	Jerome Walton	.20
163	Charlie Hayes	.20
164	Chris Bosio	.20
165	Chris Sabo	.20
166	Lance Parrish	.20
167	Don Robinson	.20
168	Manuel Lee	.20
169	Dennis Rasmussen	.20
170	Wade Boggs	1.50
171	Bob Geren	.20
172	Mackey Sasser	.20
173	Julio Franco	.20
174	Otis Nixon	.20
175	Bert Blyleven	.20
176	Craig Biggio	.75
177	Eddie Murray	.60
178	Randy Tomlin	.20
179	Tino Martinez	.35
180	Carlton Fisk	.80
181	Dwight Smith	.20
182	Scott Garrelts	.20
183	Jim Gantner	.20
184	Dickie Thon	.20
185	John Farrell	.20
186	Cecil Fielder	.20
187	Glenn Braggs	.20
188	Allan Anderson	.20
189	Kurt Stillwell	.20
190	Jose Oquendo	.20
191	Joe Orsulak	.20
192	Ricky Jordan	.20
193	Kelly Downs	.20
194	Delino DeShields	.20
195	Omar Vizquel	.20
196	Mark Carreon	.20
197	Mike Harkey	.20
198	Jack Howell	.20
199	Lance Johnson	.20
200	Nolan Ryan	6.00
201	John Marzano	.20
202	Doug Drabek	.20
203	Mark Lemke	.20
204	Steve Sax	.20
205	Greg Harris	.20
206	B.J. Surhoff	.20
207	Todd Burns	.20
208	Jose Gonzalez	.20
209	Mike Scott	.20
210	Dave Magadan	.20
211	Dante Bichette	.75
212	Trevor Wilson	.20
213	Hector Villanueva	.20
214	Dan Pasqua	.20
215	Greg Colbrunn	.20
216	Mike Jeffcoat	.20
217	Harold Reynolds	.20
218	Paul O'Neill	.35
219	Mark Guthrie	.20
220	Barry Bonds	1.50
221	Jimmy Key	.20
222	Billy Ripken	.20
223	Tom Pagnozzi	.20
224	Bo Jackson	.40
225	Sid Fernandez	.20
226	Mike Marshall	.20
227	John Kruk	.20
228	Mike Fetters	.20
229	Eric Anthony	.20
230	Ryne Sandberg	1.50
231	Carney Lansford	.20
232	Melido Perez	.20
233	Jose Lind	.20
234	Darryl Hamilton	.20
235	Tom Browning	.20
236	Spike Owen	.20
237	Juan Gonzalez	3.00
238	Felix Fermin	.20
239	Keith Miller	.20
240	Mark Gubicza	.20
241	Kent Anderson	.20
242	Alvaro Espinoza	.20
243	Dale Murphy	.40
244	Orel Hershiser	.30
245	Paul Molitor	1.25
246	Eddie Whitson	.20
247	Joe Girardi	.20
248	Kent Hrbek	.25
249	Bill Sampen	.20
250	Kevin Mitchell	.20
251	Mariano Duncan	.20
252	Scott Bradley	.20
253	Mike Greenwell	.20
254	Tom Gordon	.20
255	Todd Zeile	.25
256	Bobby Thigpen	.20
257	Gregg Jefferies	.30
258	Kenny Rogers	.20
259	Shane Mack	.20
260	Zane Smith	.20
261	Mitch Williams	.20
262	Jim DeShaies	.20
263	Dave Winfield	.50
264	Ben McDonald	.20
265	Randy Ready	.20
266	Pat Borders	.20
267	Jose Uribe	.20
268	Derek Lilliquist	.20
269	Greg Brock	.20
270	Ken Griffey, Jr.	8.00
271	Jeff Gray	.20
272	Danny Tartabull	.20
273	Dennis Martinez	.20
274	Robin Ventura	.35
275	Randy Myers	.20
276	Jack Daugherty	.20
277	Greg Gagne	.20
278	Jay Howell	.20
279	Mike LaValliere	.20
280	Rex Hudler	.20
281	Mike Simms	.20
282	Kevin Maas	.20
283	Jeff Ballard	.20
284	Dave Henderson	.20
285	Pete O'Brien	.20
286	Brook Jacoby	.20
287	Mike Henneman	.20
288	Greg Olson	.20
289	Greg Myers	.20
290	Mark Grace	.40
291	Shawn Abner	.20
292	Frank Viola	.20
293	Lee Stevens	.20
294	Jason Grimsley	.20
295	Matt Williams	.40
296	Ron Robinson	.20
297	Tom Brunansky	.20
298	Checklist	.20
299	Checklist	.20
300	Checklist	.20
301	Darryl Strawberry	.40
302	Bud Black	.20
303	Harold Baines	.25
304	Roberto Alomar	1.00
305	Norm Charlton	.20
306	Gary Thurman	.20
307	Mike Felder	.20
308	Tony Gwynn	3.00
309	Roger Clemens	3.00
310	Andre Dawson	.40
311	Scott Radinsky	.20
312	Bob Melvin	.20
313	Kirk McCaskill	.20
314	Pedro Guerrero	.20
315	Walt Terrell	.20
316	Sam Horn	.20
317	*Wes Chamberlain*	.20
318	*Pedro Munoz*	.20
319	Roberto Kelly	.20
320	Mark Portugal	.20
321	Tim McIntosh	.20
322	Jesse Orosco	.20
323	Gary Green	.20
324	Greg Harris	.20
325	Hubie Brooks	.20
326	Chris Nabholz	.20
327	Terry Pendleton	.20
328	Eric King	.20
329	Chili Davis	.20
330	Anthony Telford	.20
331	Kelly Gruber	.20
332	Dennis Eckersley	.20
333	Mel Hall	.20
334	Bob Kipper	.20
335	Willie McGee	.20
336	Steve Olin	.20
337	Steve Buechele	.20
338	Scott Leius	.20
339	Hal Morris	.20
340	Jose Offerman	.25
341	Kent Mercker	.20
342	Ken Griffey	.20
343	Pete Harnisch	.20
344	Kirk Gibson	.20
345	Dave Smith	.20
346	Dave Martinez	.20
347	Atlee Hammaker	.20
348	Brian Downing	.20
349	Todd Hundley	.35
350	Candy Maldonado	.20
351	Dwight Evans	.20
352	Steve Searcy	.20
353	Gary Gaetti	.20
354	Jeff Reardon	.20
355	Travis Fryman	.30
356	Dave Righetti	.20
357	Fred McGriff	.60
358	Don Slaught	.20
359	Gene Nelson	.20
360	Billy Spiers	.20
361	Lee Guetterman	.20
362	Darren Lewis	.20
363	Duane Ward	.20
364	Lloyd Moseby	.20
365	John Smoltz	.60
366	Felix Jose	.20
367	David Cone	.30
368	Wally Backman	.20
369	Jeff Montgomery	.20
370	Rich Garces	.20
371	Billy Hatcher	.20
372	Bill Swift	.20
373	Jim Eisenreich	.20
374	Rob Ducey	.20
375	Tim Crews	.20
376	Steve Finley	.20
377	Jeff Blauser	.20
378	Willie Wilson	.20
379	Gerald Perry	.20
380	Jose Mesa	.20
381	Pat Kelly	.20
382	Matt Merullo	.20
383	Ivan Calderon	.20
384	Scott Chiamparino	.20
385	Lloyd McClendon	.20
386	Dave Bergman	.20
387	Ed Sprague	.20
388	*Jeff Bagwell*	10.00
389	Brett Butler	.20
390	Larry Andersen	.20
391	Glenn Davis	.20
392	Alex Cole (photo is Otis Nixon)	.20
393	Mike Heath	.20
394	Danny Darwin	.20
395	Steve Lake	.20
396	Tim Layana	.20
397	Terry Leach	.20
398	Bill Wegman	.20
399	Mark McGwire	8.00
400	Mike Boddicker	.20
401	Steve Howe	.20
402	Bernard Gilkey	.20
403	Thomas Howard	.20
404	Rafael Belliard	.20
405	Tom Candiotti	.20
406	Rene Gonzalez	.20
407	Chuck McElroy	.20
408	Paul Sorrento	.20
409	Randy Johnson	1.00
410	Brady Anderson	.30
411	Dennis Cook	.20
412	Mickey Tettleton	.20
413	Mike Stanton	.20
414	Ken Oberkfell	.20
415	Rick Honeycutt	.20
416	Nelson Santovenia	.20
417	Bob Tewksbury	.20
418	Brent Mayne	.20
419	Steve Farr	.20
420	Phil Stephenson	.20
421	Jeff Russell	.20
422	Chris James	.20
423	Tim Leary	.20
424	Gary Carter	.30
425	Glenallen Hill	.20
426	Matt Young	.20
427	Sid Bream	.20
428	Greg Swindell	.20
429	Scott Aldred	.20
430	Cal Ripken, Jr.	6.00
431	Bill Landrum	.20
432	Ernie Riles	.20
433	Danny Jackson	.20
434	Casey Candaele	.20
435	Ken Hill	.20
436	Jaime Navarro	.20
437	Lance Blankenship	.20
438	Randy Velarde	.20
439	Frank DiPino	.20
440	Carl Nichols	.20
441	Jeff Robinson	.20
442	Deion Sanders	.45
443	Vincente Palacios	.20
444	Devon White	.25
445	John Cerutti	.20
446	Tracy Jones	.20
447	Jack Morris	.20
448	Mitch Webster	.20
449	Bob Ojeda	.20
450	Oscar Azocar	.20
451	Luis Aquino	.20
452	Mark Whiten	.20
453	Stan Belinda	.20
454	Ron Gant	.30
455	Jose DeLeon	.20
456	Mark Salas	.20
457	Junior Felix	.20
458	Wally Whitehurst	.20
459	*Phil Plantier*	.35
460	Juan Berenguer	.20
461	Franklin Stubbs	.20
462	Joe Boever	.20
463	Tim Wallach	.20
464	Mike Moore	.20
465	Albert Belle	1.50
466	Mike Witt	.20
467	Craig Worthington	.20
468	Jerald Clark	.20
469	Scott Terry	.20
470	Milt Cuyler	.20
471	John Smiley	.20
472	Charles Nagy	.25
473	Alan Mills	.20
474	John Russell	.20
475	Bruce Hurst	.20
476	Andujar Cedeno	.20
477	Dave Eiland	.20
478	*Brian McRae*	.75
479	Mike LaCoss	.20
480	Chris Gwynn	.20
481	Jamie Moyer	.20
482	John Olerud	.30
483	Efrain Valdez	.20
484	Sil Campusano	.20
485	Pascual Perez	.20
486	Gary Redus	.20
487	Andy Hawkins	.20
488	Cory Snyder	.20
489	Chris Hoiles	.20
490	Ron Hassey	.20
491	Gary Wayne	.20
492	Mark Lewis	.20
493	Scott Coolbaugh	.20
494	Gerald Young	.20
495	Juan Samuel	.20
496	Willie Fraser	.20
497	Jeff Treadway	.20
498	Vince Coleman	.20
499	Cris Carpenter	.20
500	Jack Clark	.20
501	Kevin Appier	.20
502	Rafael Palmeiro	.50
503	Hensley Meulens	.20
504	George Bell	.20
505	Tony Pena	.20
506	Roger McDowell	.20
507	Luis Sojo	.20
508	Mike Schooler	.20
509	Robin Yount	1.50
510	Jack Armstrong	.20
511	Rick Cerone	.20
512	Curt Wilkerson	.20
513	Joe Carter	.20
514	Tim Burke	.20
515	Tony Fernandez	.20
516	Ramon Martinez	.25
517	Tim Hulett	.20
518	Terry Steinbach	.20
519	Pete Smith	.20
520	Ken Caminiti	.30
521	Shawn Boskie	.20
522	Mike Pagliarulo	.20
523	Tim Raines	.30
524	Alfredo Griffin	.20

525	Henry Cotto	.20
526	Mike Stanley	.20
527	Charlie Leibrandt	.20
528	Jeff King	.20
529	Eric Plunk	.20
530	Tom Lampkin	.20
531	Steve Bedrosian	.20
532	Tom Herr	.20
533	Craig Lefferts	.20
534	Jeff Reed	.20
535	Mickey Morandini	.20
536	Greg Cadaret	.20
537	Ray Lankford	.30
538	John Candelaria	.20
539	Rob Deer	.20
540	Brad Arnsberg	.20
541	Mike Sharperson	.20
542	Jeff Robinson	.20
543	Mo Vaughn	2.00
544	Jeff Parrett	.20
545	Willie Randolph	.20
546	Herm Winningham	.20
547	Jeff Innis	.20
548	Chuck Knoblauch	2.00
549	Tommy Greene	.20
550	Jeff Hamilton	.20
551	Barry Jones	.20
552	Ken Dayley	.20
553	Rick Dempsey	.20
554	Greg Smith	.20
555	Mike Devereaux	.20
556	Keith Comstock	.20
557	Paul Faries	.20
558	Tom Glavine	.60
559	Craig Grebeck	.20
560	Scott Erickson	.20
561	Joel Skinner	.20
562	Mike Morgan	.20
563	Dave Gallagher	.20
564	Todd Stottlemyre	.20
565	Rich Rodriguez	.20
566	*Craig Wilson*	.20
567	Jeff Brantley	.20
568	Scott Kamieniecki	.20
569	Steve Decker	.20
570	Juan Agosto	.20
571	Tommy Gregg	.20
572	Kevin Wickander	.20
573	Jamie Quirk	.20
574	Jerry Don Gleaton	.20
575	Chris Hammond	.20
576	*Luis Gonzalez*	.60
577	Russ Swan	.20
578	*Jeff Conine*	2.00
579	Charlie Hough	.20
580	Jeff Kunkel	.20
581	Darrel Akerfelds	.20
582	Jeff Manto	.20
583	Alejandro Pena	.20
584	Mark Davidson	.20
585	Bob MacDonald	.20
586	Paul Assenmacher	.20
587	Dan Wilson	.20
588	Tom Bolton	.20
589	Brian Harper	.20
590	John Habyan	.20
591	John Orton	.20
592	Mark Gardner	.20
593	Turner Ward	.20
594	Bob Patterson	.20
595	Edwin Nunez	.20
596	Gary Scott	.20
597	Scott Bankhead	.20
598	Checklist	.20
599	Checklist	.20
600	Checklist	.20

1992 Stadium Club

This 900-card set was released in three 100-card series. Like the 1991 issue, the cards feature borderless high-gloss photos on the front. The flip sides feature the player's first Topps card and a player evaluation. Topps released updated cards in the third series for traded player and free agents. Several players appear on two cards. Special Members Choice cards are included in the set. Series III features special inserts of the last three number one draft picks: Phil Nevin, Brien Taylor and Chipper Jones.

		MT
Complete Set (900):		60.00
Common Player:		.10
Series 1, 2, 3 Pack (15):		1.00
Series 1, 2, 3 Wax Box (36):		28.00
1	Cal Ripken, Jr.	4.00
2	Eric Yelding	.10
3	Geno Petralli	.10
4	Wally Backman	.10
5	Milt Cuyler	.10
6	Kevin Bass	.10
7	Dante Bichette	.30
8	Ray Lankford	.10
9	Mel Hall	.10
10	Joe Carter	.10
11	Juan Samuel	.10
12	Jeff Montgomery	.10
13	Glenn Braggs	.10
14	Henry Cotto	.10
15	Deion Sanders	.30
16	Dick Schofield	.10
17	David Cone	.15
18	Chili Davis	.10
19	Tom Foley	.10
20	Ozzie Guillen	.10
21	Luis Salazar	.10
22	Terry Steinbach	.10
23	Chris James	.10
24	Jeff King	.10
25	Carlos Quintana	.10
26	Mike Maddux	.10
27	Tommy Greene	.10
28	Jeff Russell	.10
29	Steve Finley	.10
30	Mike Flanagan	.10
31	Darren Lewis	.10
32	Mark Lee	.10
33	Willie Fraser	.10
34	Mike Henneman	.10
35	Kevin Maas	.10
36	Dave Hansen	.10
37	Erik Hanson	.10
38	Bill Doran	.10
39	Mike Boddicker	.10
40	Vince Coleman	.10
41	Devon White	.15
42	Mark Gardner	.10
43	Scott Lewis	.10
44	Juan Berenguer	.10
45	Carney Lansford	.10
46	Curt Wilkerson	.10
47	Shane Mack	.10
48	Bip Roberts	.10
49	Greg Harris	.10
50	Ryne Sandberg	.50
51	Mark Whiten	.10
52	Jack McDowell	.10
53	Jimmy Jones	.10
54	Steve Lake	.10
55	Bud Black	.10
56	Dave Valle	.10
57	Kevin Reimer	.10
58	Rich Gedman	.10
59	Travis Fryman	.10
60	Steve Avery	.10
61	Francisco de la Rosa	.10
62	Scott Hemond	.10
63	Hal Morris	.10
64	Hensley Meulens	.10
65	Frank Castillo	.10
66	Gene Larkin	.10
67	Jose DeLeon	.10
68	Al Osuna	.10
69	Dave Cochrane	.10
70	Robin Ventura	.25
71	John Cerutti	.10
72	Kevin Gross	.10
73	Ivan Calderon	.10
74	Mike Macfarlane	.10
75	Stan Belinda	.10
76	Shawn Hillegas	.10
77	Pat Borders	.10
78	Jim Vatcher	.10
79	Bobby Rose	.10
80	Roger Clemens	.75
81	Craig Worthington	.10
82	Jeff Treadway	.10
83	Jamie Quirk	.10
84	Randy Bush	.10
85	Anthony Young	.10
86	Trevor Wilson	.10
87	Jaime Navarro	.10
88	Les Lancaster	.10
89	Pat Kelly	.10
90	Alvin Davis	.10
91	Larry Andersen	.10
92	Rob Deer	.10
93	Mike Sharperson	.10
94	Lance Parrish	.10
95	Cecil Espy	.10
96	Tim Spehr	.10
97	Dave Stieb	.10
98	Terry Mulholland	.10
99	Dennis Boyd	.10
100	Barry Larkin	.15
101	Ryan Bowen	.10
102	Felix Fermin	.10
103	Luis Alicea	.10
104	Tim Hulett	.10
105	Rafael Belliard	.10
106	Mike Gallego	.10
107	Dave Righetti	.10
108	Jeff Schaefer	.10
109	Ricky Bones	.10
110	Scott Erickson	.10
111	Matt Nokes	.10
112	Bob Scanlan	.10
113	Tom Candiotti	.10
114	Sean Berry	.10
115	Kevin Morton	.10
116	Scott Fletcher	.10
117	B.J. Surhoff	.10
118	Dave Magadan	.10
119	Bill Gullickson	.10
120	Marquis Grissom	.10
121	Lenny Harris	.10
122	Wally Joyner	.15
123	Kevin Brown	.10
124	Braulio Castillo	.10
125	Eric King	.10
126	Mark Portugal	.10
127	Calvin Jones	.10
128	Mike Heath	.10
129	Todd Van Poppel	.10
130	Benny Santiago	.10
131	Gary Thurman	.10
132	Joe Girardi	.10
133	Dave Eiland	.10
134	Orlando Merced	.10
135	Joe Orsulak	.10
136	John Burkett	.10
137	Ken Dayley	.10
138	Ken Hill	.10
139	Walt Terrell	.10
140	Mike Scioscia	.10
141	Junior Felix	.10
142	Ken Caminiti	.20
143	Carlos Baerga	.10
144	Tony Fossas	.10
145	Craig Grebeck	.10
146	Scott Bradley	.10
147	Kent Mercker	.10
148	Derrick May	.10
149	Jerald Clark	.10
150	George Brett	.75
151	Luis Quinones	.10
152	Mike Pagliarulo	.10
153	Jose Guzman	.10
154	Charlie O'Brien	.10
155	Darren Holmes	.10
156	Joe Boever	.10
157	Rich Monteleone	.10
158	Reggie Harris	.10
159	Roberto Alomar	.60
160	Robby Thompson	.10
161	Chris Hoiles	.10
162	Tom Pagnozzi	.10
163	Omar Vizquel	.10
164	John Candelaria	.10
165	Terry Shumpert	.10
166	Andy Mota	.10
167	Scott Bailes	.10
168	Jeff Blauser	.10
169	Steve Olin	.10
170	Doug Drabek	.10
171	Dave Bergman	.10
172	Eddie Whitson	.10
173	Gilberto Reyes	.10
174	Mark Grace	.20
175	Paul O'Neill	.15
176	Greg Cadaret	.10
177	Mark Williamson	.10
178	Casey Candaele	.10
179	Candy Maldonado	.10
180	Lee Smith	.10
181	Harold Reynolds	.10
182	Dave Justice	.20
183	Lenny Webster	.10
184	Donn Pall	.10
185	Gerald Alexander	.10
186	Jack Clark	.10
187	Stan Javier	.10
188	Ricky Jordan	.10
189	Franklin Stubbs	.10
190	Dennis Eckersley	.10
191	Danny Tartabull	.10
192	Pete O'Brien	.10
193	Mark Lewis	.10
194	Mike Felder	.10
195	Mickey Tettleton	.10
196	Dwight Smith	.10
197	Shawn Abner	.10
198	Jim Leyritz	.10
199	Mike Devereaux	.10
200	Craig Biggio	.25
201	Kevin Elster	.10
202	Rance Mulliniks	.10
203	Tony Fernandez	.10
204	Allan Anderson	.10
205	Herm Winningham	.10
206	Tim Jones	.10
207	Ramon Martinez	.15
208	Teddy Higuera	.10
209	John Kruk	.10
210	Jim Abbott	.10
211	Dean Palmer	.10
212	Mark Davis	.10
213	Jay Buhner	.10
214	Jesse Barfield	.10
215	Kevin Mitchell	.10
216	Mike LaValliere	.10
217	Mark Wohlers	.10
218	Dave Henderson	.10
219	Dave Smith	.10
220	Albert Belle	.75
221	Spike Owen	.10
222	Jeff Gray	.10
223	Paul Gibson	.10
224	Bobby Thigpen	.10
225	Mike Mussina	.60
226	Darrin Jackson	.10
227	Luis Gonzalez	.15
228	Greg Briley	.10
229	Brent Mayne	.10
230	Paul Molitor	.50
231	Al Leiter	.15
232	Andy Van Slyke	.10
233	Ron Tingley	.10
234	Bernard Gilkey	.10
235	Kent Hrbek	.10
236	Eric Karros	.10
237	Randy Velarde	.10
238	Andy Allanson	.10
239	Willie McGee	.10
240	Juan Gonzalez	1.00
241	Karl Rhodes	.10
242	Luis Mercedes	.10
243	Billy Swift	.10
244	Tommy Gregg	.10
245	David Howard	.10
246	Dave Hollins	.10
247	Kip Gross	.10
248	Walt Weiss	.10
249	Mackey Sasser	.10
250	Cecil Fielder	.10

No.	Player	Value
251	Jerry Browne	.10
252	Doug Dascenzo	.10
253	Darryl Hamilton	.10
254	Dann Bilardello	.10
255	Luis Rivera	.10
256	Larry Walker	.40
257	Ron Karkovice	.10
258	Bob Tewksbury	.10
259	Jimmy Key	.10
260	Bernie Williams	.60
261	Gary Wayne	.10
262	Mike Simms	.10
263	John Orton	.10
264	Marvin Freeman	.10
265	Mike Jeffcoat	.10
266	Roger Mason	.10
267	Edgar Martinez	.10
268	Henry Rodriguez	.10
269	Sam Horn	.10
270	Brian McRae	.10
271	Kirt Manwaring	.10
272	Mike Bordick	.10
273	Chris Sabo	.10
274	Jim Olander	.10
275	Greg Harris	.10
276	Dan Gakeler	.10
277	Bill Sampen	.10
278	Joel Skinner	.10
279	Curt Schilling	.15
280	Dale Murphy	.25
281	Lee Stevens	.10
282	Lonnie Smith	.10
283	Manuel Lee	.10
284	Shawn Boskie	.10
285	Kevin Seitzer	.10
286	Stan Royer	.10
287	John Dopson	.10
288	Scott Bullett	.10
289	Ken Patterson	.10
290	Todd Hundley	.15
291	Tim Leary	.10
292	Brett Butler	.10
293	Gregg Olson	.10
294	Jeff Brantley	.10
295	Brian Holman	.10
296	Brian Harper	.10
297	Brian Bohanon	.10
298	Checklist 1-100	.10
299	Checklist 101-200	.10
300	Checklist 201-300	.10
301	Frank Thomas	2.00
302	Lloyd McClendon	.10
303	Brady Anderson	.15
304	Julio Valera	.10
305	Mike Aldrete	.10
306	Joe Oliver	.10
307	Todd Stottlemyre	.10
308	Rey Sanchez	.10
309	Gary Sheffield	.25
310	Andujar Cedeno	.10
311	Kenny Rogers	.10
312	Bruce Hurst	.10
313	Mike Schooler	.10
314	Mike Benjamin	.10
315	Chuck Finley	.10
316	Mark Lemke	.10
317	Scott Livingstone	.10
318	Chris Nabholz	.10
319	Mike Humphreys	.10
320	Pedro Guerrero	.10
321	Willie Banks	.10
322	Tom Goodwin	.10
323	Hector Wagner	.10
324	Wally Ritchie	.10
325	Mo Vaughn	.60
326	Joe Klink	.10
327	Cal Eldred	.10
328	Daryl Boston	.10
329	Mike Huff	.10
330	Jeff Bagwell	1.50
331	Bob Milacki	.10
332	Tom Prince	.10
333	Pat Tabler	.10
334	Ced Landrum	.10
335	Reggie Jefferson	.10
336	Mo Sanford	.10
337	Kevin Ritz	.10
338	Gerald Perry	.10
339	Jeff Hamilton	.10
340	Tim Wallach	.10
341	Jeff Huson	.10
342	Jose Melendez	.10
343	Willie Wilson	.10
344	Mike Stanton	.10
345	Joel Johnston	.10
346	Lee Guetterman	.10
347	Francisco Olivares	.10
348	Dave Burba	.10
349	Tim Crews	.10
350	Scott Leius	.10
351	Danny Cox	.10
352	Wayne Housie	.10
353	Chris Donnels	.10
354	Chris George	.10
355	Gerald Young	.10
356	Roberto Hernandez	.10
357	Neal Heaton	.10
358	Todd Frohwirth	.10
359	Jose Vizcaino	.10
360	Jim Thome	.60
361	Craig Wilson	.10
362	Dave Haas	.10
363	Billy Hatcher	.10
364	John Barfield	.10
365	Luis Aquino	.10
366	Charlie Leibrandt	.10
367	Howard Farmer	.10
368	Bryn Smith	.10
369	Mickey Morandini	.10
370	Jose Canseco (Members Choice, should have been #597)	.50
371	Jose Uribe	.10
372	Bob MacDonald	.10
373	Luis Sojo	.10
374	Craig Shipley	.10
375	Scott Bankhead	.10
376	Greg Gagne	.10
377	Scott Cooper	.10
378	Jose Offerman	.10
379	Billy Spiers	.10
380	John Smiley	.10
381	Jeff Carter	.10
382	Heathcliff Slocumb	.10
383	Jeff Tackett	.10
384	John Kiely	.10
385	John Vander Wal	.10
386	Omar Olivares	.10
387	Ruben Sierra	.10
388	Tom Gordon	.10
389	Charles Nagy	.10
390	Dave Stewart	.10
391	Pete Harnisch	.10
392	Tim Burke	.10
393	Roberto Kelly	.10
394	Freddie Benavides	.10
395	Tom Glavine	.20
396	Wes Chamberlain	.10
397	Eric Gunderson	.10
398	Dave West	.10
399	Ellis Burks	.10
400	Ken Griffey, Jr.	5.00
401	Thomas Howard	.10
402	Juan Guzman	.10
403	Mitch Webster	.10
404	Matt Merullo	.10
405	Steve Buechele	.10
406	Danny Jackson	.10
407	Felix Jose	.10
408	Doug Piatt	.10
409	Jim Eisenreich	.10
410	Bryan Harvey	.10
411	Jim Austin	.10
412	Jim Poole	.10
413	Glenallen Hill	.10
414	Gene Nelson	.10
415	Ivan Rodriguez	.75
416	Frank Tanana	.10
417	Steve Decker	.10
418	Jason Grimsley	.10
419	Tim Layana	.10
420	Don Mattingly	1.25
421	Jerome Walton	.10
422	Rob Ducey	.10
423	Andy Benes	.15
424	John Marzano	.10
425	Gene Harris	.10
426	Tim Raines	.15
427	Bret Barberie	.10
428	Harvey Pulliam	.10
429	Cris Carpenter	.10
430	Howard Johnson	.10
431	Orel Hershiser	.15
432	Brian Hunter	.10
433	Kevin Tapani	.10
434	Rick Reed	.10
435	Ron Witmeyer	.10
436	Gary Gaetti	.10
437	Alex Cole	.10
438	Chito Martinez	.10
439	Greg Litton	.10
440	Julio Franco	.10
441	Mike Munoz	.10
442	Erik Pappas	.10
443	Pat Combs	.10
444	Lance Johnson	.10
445	Ed Sprague	.10
446	Mike Greenwell	.10
447	Milt Thompson	.10
448	Mike Magnante	.10
449	Chris Haney	.10
450	Robin Yount	1.00
451	Rafael Ramirez	.10
452	Gino Minutelli	.10
453	Tom Lampkin	.10
454	Tony Perezchica	.10
455	Dwight Gooden	.15
456	Mark Guthrie	.10
457	Jay Howell	.10
458	Gary DiSarcina	.10
459	John Smoltz	.15
460	Will Clark	.50
461	Dave Otto	.10
462	Rob Maurer	.10
463	Dwight Evans	.10
464	Tom Brunansky	.10
465	*Shawn Hare*	.10
466	Geronimo Pena	.10
467	Alex Fernandez	.15
468	Greg Myers	.10
469	Jeff Fassero	.10
470	Len Dykstra	.10
471	Jeff Johnson	.10
472	Russ Swan	.10
473	Archie Corbin	.10
474	Chuck McElroy	.10
475	Mark McGwire	5.00
476	Wally Whitehurst	.10
477	Tim McIntosh	.10
478	Sid Bream	.10
479	Jeff Juden	.10
480	Carlton Fisk	.15
481	Jeff Plympton	.10
482	Carlos Martinez	.10
483	Jim Gott	.10
484	Bob McClure	.10
485	Tim Teufel	.10
486	Vicente Palacios	.10
487	Jeff Reed	.10
488	Tony Phillips	.10
489	Mel Rojas	.10
490	Ben McDonald	.10
491	Andres Santana	.10
492	Chris Beasley	.10
493	Mike Timlin	.10
494	Brian Downing	.10
495	Kirk Gibson	.10
496	Scott Sanderson	.10
497	Nick Esasky	.10
498	*Johnny Guzman*	.10
499	Mitch Williams	.10
500	Kirby Puckett	1.00
501	Mike Harkey	.10
502	Jim Gantner	.10
503	Bruce Egloff	.10
504	Josias Manzanillo	.10
505	Delino DeShields	.10
506	Rheal Cormier	.10
507	Jay Bell	.10
508	Rich Rowland	.10
509	Scott Servais	.10
510	Terry Pendleton	.10
511	Rich DeLucia	.10
512	Warren Newson	.10
513	Paul Faries	.10
514	Kal Daniels	.10
515	Jarvis Brown	.10
516	Rafael Palmeiro	.25
517	Kelly Downs	.10
518	Steve Chitren	.10
519	Moises Alou	.20
520	Wade Boggs	.40
521	Pete Schourek	.10
522	Scott Terry	.10
523	Kevin Appier	.10
524	Gary Redus	.10
525	George Bell	.10
526	Jeff Kaiser	.10
527	Alvaro Espinoza	.10
528	Luis Polonia	.10
529	Darren Daulton	.10
530	Norm Charlton	.10
531	John Olerud	.20
532	Dan Plesac	.10
533	Billy Ripken	.10
534	Rod Nichols	.10
535	Joey Cora	.10
536	Harold Baines	.10
537	Bob Ojeda	.10
538	Mark Leonard	.10
539	Danny Darwin	.10
540	Shawon Dunston	.10
541	Pedro Munoz	.10
542	Mark Gubicza	.10
543	Kevin Baez	.10
544	Todd Zeile	.15
545	Don Slaught	.10
546	Tony Eusebio	.10
547	Alonzo Powell	.10
548	Gary Pettis	.10
549	Brian Barnes	.10
550	Lou Whitaker	.10
551	Keith Mitchell	.10
552	Oscar Azocar	.10
553	Stu Cole	.10
554	Steve Wapnick	.10
555	Derek Bell	.15
556	Luis Lopez	.10
557	Anthony Telford	.10
558	Tim Mauser	.10
559	Glenn Sutko	.10
560	Darryl Strawberry	.15
561	Tom Bolton	.10
562	Cliff Young	.10
563	Bruce Walton	.10
564	Chico Walker	.10
565	John Franco	.10
566	Paul McClellan	.10
567	Paul Abbott	.10
568	Gary Varsho	.10
569	Carlos Maldonado	.10
570	Kelly Gruber	.10
571	Jose Oquendo	.10
572	Steve Frey	.10
573	Tino Martinez	.15
574	Bill Haselman	.10
575	Eric Anthony	.10
576	John Habyan	.10
577	Jeffrey McNeely	.10
578	Chris Bosio	.10
579	Joe Grahe	.10
580	Fred McGriff	.40
581	Rick Honeycutt	.10
582	Matt Williams	.60
583	Cliff Brantley	.10
584	Rob Dibble	.10
585	Skeeter Barnes	.10
586	Greg Hibbard	.10
587	Randy Milligan	.10
588	Checklist 301-400	.10
589	Checklist 401-500	.10
590	Checklist 501-600	.10
591	Frank Thomas (Members Choice)	1.00
592	Dave Justice (Members Choice)	.20
593	Roger Clemens (Members Choice)	.40
594	Steve Avery (Members Choice)	.10
595	Cal Ripken, Jr. (Members Choice)	2.00
596	Barry Larkin (Members Choice)	.15
597	Not issued (See #370)	
598	Will Clark (Members Choice)	.30
599	Cecil Fielder (Members Choice)	.10
600	Ryne Sandberg (Members Choice)	.40
601	Chuck Knoblauch (Members Choice)	.20
602	Dwight Gooden (Members Choice)	.15
603	Ken Griffey, Jr. (Members Choice)	2.50
604	Barry Bonds (Members Choice)	.45
605	Nolan Ryan (Members Choice)	1.50
606	Jeff Bagwell (Members Choice)	1.00
607	Robin Yount (Members Choice)	.50
608	Bobby Bonilla (Members Choice)	.10
609	George Brett (Members Choice)	.50
610	Howard Johnson (Members Choice)	.10
611	Esteban Beltre	.10
612	Mike Christopher	.10

613	Troy Afenir	.10
614	Mariano Duncan	.10
615	Doug Henry	.10
616	Doug Jones	.10
617	Alvin Davis	.10
618	Craig Lefferts	.10
619	Kevin McReynolds	.10
620	Barry Bonds	.75
621	Turner Ward	.10
622	Joe Magrane	.10
623	Mark Parent	.10
624	Tom Browning	.10
625	John Smiley	.10
626	Steve Wilson	.10
627	Mike Gallego	.10
628	Sammy Sosa	1.50
629	Rico Rossy	.10
630	Royce Clayton	.10
631	Clay Parker	.10
632	Pete Smith	.10
633	Jeff McKnight	.10
634	Jack Daugherty	.10
635	Steve Sax	.10
636	Joe Hesketh	.10
637	Vince Horsman	.10
638	Eric King	.10
639	Joe Boever	.10
640	Jack Morris	.10
641	Arthur Rhodes	.10
642	Bob Melvin	.10
643	Rick Wilkins	.10
644	Scott Scudder	.10
645	Bip Roberts	.10
646	Julio Valera	.10
647	Kevin Campbell	.10
648	Steve Searcy	.10
649	Scott Kamieniecki	.10
650	Kurt Stillwell	.10
651	Bob Welch	.10
652	Andres Galarraga	.15
653	Mike Jackson	.10
654	Bo Jackson	.15
655	Sid Fernandez	.10
656	Mike Bielecki	.10
657	Jeff Reardon	.10
658	Wayne Rosenthal	.10
659	Eric Bullock	.10
660	Eric Davis	.10
661	Randy Tomlin	.10
662	Tom Edens	.10
663	Rob Murphy	.10
664	Leo Gomez	.10
665	Greg Maddux	2.00
666	Greg Vaughn	.15
667	Wade Taylor	.10
668	Brad Arnsberg	.10
669	Mike Moore	.10
670	Mark Langston	.10
671	Barry Jones	.10
672	Bill Landrum	.10
673	Greg Swindell	.10
674	Wayne Edwards	.10
675	Greg Olson	.10
676	*Bill Pulsipher*	.60
677	Bobby Witt	.10
678	Mark Carreon	.10
679	Patrick Lennon	.10
680	Ozzie Smith	.50
681	John Briscoe	.10
682	Matt Young	.10
683	Jeff Conine	.15
684	Phil Stephenson	.10
685	Ron Darling	.10
686	Bryan Hickerson	.10
687	Dale Sveum	.10
688	Kirk McCaskill	.10
689	Rich Amaral	.10
690	Danny Tartabull	.10
691	Donald Harris	.10
692	Doug Davis	.10
693	John Farrell	.10
694	Paul Gibson	.10
695	Kenny Lofton	1.00
696	Mike Fetters	.10
697	Rosario Rodriguez	.10
698	Chris Jones	.10
699	Jeff Manto	.10
700	Rick Sutcliffe	.10
701	Scott Bankhead	.10
702	Donnie Hill	.10
703	Todd Worrell	.10
704	Rene Gonzales	.10
705	Rick Cerone	.10
706	Tony Pena	.10
707	Paul Sorrento	.10
708	Gary Scott	.10
709	Junior Noboa	.10
710	Wally Joyner	.15
711	Charlie Hayes	.10
712	Rich Rodriguez	.10
713	Rudy Seanez	.10
714	Jim Bullinger	.10
715	Jeff Robinson	.10
716	Jeff Branson	.10
717	Andy Ashby	.15
718	Dave Burba	.10
719	Rich Gossage	.10
720	Randy Johnson	.50
721	David Wells	.15
722	Paul Kilgus	.10
723	Dave Martinez	.10
724	Denny Neagle	.10
725	Andy Stankiewicz	.10
726	Rick Aguilera	.10
727	Junior Ortiz	.10
728	Storm Davis	.10
729	Don Robinson	.10
730	Ron Gant	.15
731	Paul Assenmacher	.10
732	Mark Gardiner	.10
733	Milt Hill	.10
734	Jeremy Hernandez	.10
735	Ken Hill	.10
736	Xavier Hernandez	.10
737	Gregg Jefferies	.15
738	Dick Schofield	.10
739	Ron Robinson	.10
740	Sandy Alomar	.15
741	Mike Stanley	.10
742	Butch Henry	.10
743	Floyd Bannister	.10
744	Brian Drahman	.10
745	Dave Winfield	.50
746	Bob Walk	.10
747	Chris James	.10
748	Don Prybylinski	.10
749	Dennis Rasmussen	.10
750	Rickey Henderson	.35
751	Chris Hammond	.10
752	Bob Kipper	.10
753	Dave Rohde	.10
754	Hubie Brooks	.10
755	Bret Saberhagen	.15
756	Jeff Robinson	.10
757	*Pat Listach*	.10
758	Bill Wegman	.10
759	John Wetteland	.10
760	Phil Plantier	.10
761	Wilson Alvarez	.10
762	Scott Aldred	.10
763	*Armando Reynoso*	.15
764	Todd Benzinger	.10
765	Kevin Mitchell	.10
766	Gary Sheffield	.25
767	Allan Anderson	.10
768	Rusty Meacham	.10
769	Rick Parker	.10
770	Nolan Ryan	3.00
771	Jeff Ballard	.10
772	Cory Snyder	.10
773	Denis Boucher	.10
774	Jose Gonzales	.10
775	Juan Guerrero	.10
776	Ed Nunez	.10
777	Scott Ruskin	.10
778	Terry Leach	.10
779	Carl Willis	.10
780	Bobby Bonilla	.10
781	Duane Ward	.10
782	Joe Slusarski	.10
783	David Segui	.10
784	Kirk Gibson	.10
785	Frank Viola	.10
786	Keith Miller	.10
787	Mike Morgan	.10
788	Kim Batiste	.10
789	Sergio Valdez	.10
790	Eddie Taubensee	.10
791	Jack Armstrong	.10
792	Scott Fletcher	.10
793	Steve Farr	.10
794	Dan Pasqua	.10
795	Eddie Murray	.25
796	John Morris	.10
797	Francisco Cabrera	.10
798	Mike Perez	.10
799	Ted Wood	.10
800	Jose Rijo	.10
801	Danny Gladden	.10
802	Arci Cianfrocco	.10
803	Monty Fariss	.10
804	Roger McDowell	.10
805	Randy Myers	.10
806	Kirk Dressendorfer	.10
807	Zane Smith	.10
808	Glenn Davis	.10
809	Torey Lovullo	.10
810	Andre Dawson	.15
811	Bill Pecota	.10
812	Ted Power	.10
813	Willie Blair	.10
814	Dave Fleming	.10
815	Chris Gwynn	.10
816	Jody Reed	.10
817	Mark Dewey	.10
818	Kyle Abbott	.10
819	Tom Henke	.10
820	Kevin Seitzer	.10
821	Al Newman	.10
822	Tim Sherrill	.10
823	Chuck Crim	.10
824	Darren Reed	.10
825	Tony Gwynn	.75
826	Steve Foster	.10
827	Steve Howe	.10
828	Brook Jacoby	.10
829	Rodney McCray	.10
830	Chuck Knoblauch	.15
831	John Wehner	.10
832	Scott Garrelts	.10
833	Alejandro Pena	.10
834	Jeff Parrett	.10
835	Juan Bell	.10
836	Lance Dickson	.10
837	Darryl Kile	.10
838	Efrain Valdez	.10
839	*Bob Zupcic*	.10
840	George Bell	.10
841	Dave Gallagher	.10
842	Tim Belcher	.10
843	Jeff Shaw	.10
844	Mike Fitzgerald	.10
845	Gary Carter	.15
846	John Russell	.10
847	*Eric Hillman*	.15
848	Mike Witt	.10
849	Curt Wilkerson	.10
850	Alan Trammell	.15
851	Rex Hudler	.10
852	*Michael Walkden*	.10
853	Kevin Ward	.10
854	Tim Naehring	.10
855	Bill Swift	.10
856	Damon Berryhill	.10
857	Mark Eichhorn	.10
858	Hector Villanueva	.10
859	Jose Lind	.10
860	Denny Martinez	.10
861	Bill Krueger	.10
862	Mike Kingery	.10
863	Jeff Innis	.10
864	Derek Lilliquist	.10
865	Reggie Sanders	.15
866	Ramon Garcia	.10
867	Bruce Ruffin	.10
868	Dickie Thon	.10
869	Melido Perez	.10
870	Ruben Amaro	.10
871	Alan Mills	.10
872	Matt Sinatro	.10
873	Eddie Zosky	.10
874	Pete Incaviglia	.10
875	Tom Candiotti	.10
876	Bob Patterson	.10
877	Neal Heaton	.10
878	*Terrel Hansen*	.10
879	Dave Eiland	.10
880	Von Hayes	.10
881	Tim Scott	.10
882	Otis Nixon	.10
883	Herm Winningham	.10
884	Dion James	.10
885	Dave Wainhouse	.10
886	Frank DiPino	.10
887	Dennis Cook	.10
888	Jose Mesa	.10
889	Mark Leiter	.10
890	Willie Randolph	.10
891	Craig Colbert	.10
892	Dwayne Henry	.10
893	Jim Lindeman	.10
894	Charlie Hough	.10
895	Gil Heredia	.10
896	Scott Chiamparino	.10
897	Lance Blankenship	.10
898	Checklist 601-700	.10
899	Checklist 701-800	.10
900	Checklist 801-900	.10

1992 Stadium Club First Draft Picks

Issued as inserts with Stadium Club Series III, this three-card set features the No. 1 draft picks of 1990-92. Fronts have a full-bleed photo with S.C. logo and player name in the lower-right corner. At bottom-lerft in a red strip is a gold-foil stamping, "#1 Draft Pick of the '90's". An orage circle at upper-right has the year the player was the No. 1 choice. The basic red-and-black back has a color photo, a few biographical and draft details and a gold facsimile autograph among other gold-foil highlights.

		MT
Complete Set (3):		12.00
Common Player:		1.00
1	Chipper Jones	10.00
2	Brien Taylor	1.00
3	Phil Nevin	1.00

1992 Stadium Club Master Photos

Uncropped versions of the photos which appear on regular Stadium Club cards are featured on these large-format (5" x 7") cards. The photos are set against a white background and trimmed with holographic foil. Backs are blank and the cards are unnumbered.

Members of Topps' Stadium Club received a Master Photo in their members' packs for 1992. The cards were also available as inserts in special boxes of Stadium Club cards sold at Wal-Mart stores.

		MT
Complete Set (15):		45.00
Common Player:		1.00
(1)	Wade Boggs	3.00
(2)	Barry Bonds	4.00
(3)	Jose Canseco	3.00
(4)	Will Clark	2.50
(5)	Cecil Fielder	1.00
(6)	Dwight Gooden	2.00
(7)	Ken Griffey, Jr.	9.00
(8)	Rickey Henderson	2.00
(9)	Lance Johnson	1.00
(10)	Cal Ripken, Jr.	7.50
(11)	Nolan Ryan	7.50
(12)	Deion Sanders	2.50
(13)	Darryl Strawberry	2.00
(14)	Danny Tartabull	1.00
(15)	Frank Thomas	6.00

1992 Stadium Club Special Edition (SkyDome)

This 200-card special Stadium Club set from Topps was uniquely packaged in a plastic replica of the Toronto SkyDome, the home of the 1991 All-Star Game. Featured in the set are members of Team USA, All-Stars, draft picks, top prospects and hight cards from the World Series between the Twins and Braves. The cards are styled much like the regular Stadium Club cards. Some cards have been found with incorrect gold-foil identifiers as well as the correct version.

		MT
Complete Set (200):		35.00
Common Player:		.10
1	*Terry Adams*	.10
2	Tommy Adams	.10
3	Rick Aguilera	.10
4	Ron Allen	.10
5	Roberto Alomar (All-Star)	.50
6	Sandy Alomar	.20
7	Greg Anthony	.10
8	James Austin	.10
9	Steve Avery	.10
10	Harold Baines	.10
11	*Brian Barber*	.15
12	Jon Barnes	.10
13	George Bell	.10
14	Doug Bennett	.10
15	Sean Bergman	.10
16	Craig Biggio	.10
17	Bill Bliss	.30
18	Wade Boggs (AS)	.30
19	Bobby Bonilla (AS)	.10
20	Russell Brock	.10
21	Tarrik Brock	.10
22	Tom Browning	.10
23	Brett Butler	.10
24	Ivan Calderon	.10
25	Joe Carter	.10
26	Joe Caruso	.10
27	Dan Cholowsky	.10
28	Will Clark (AS)	.20
29	Roger Clemens (AS)	.50
30	Shawn Curran	.10
31	Chris Curtis	.10
32	Chili Davis	.10
33	Andre Dawson	.15
34	Joe DeBerry	.10
35	John Dettmer	.10
36	Rob Dibble	.10
37	*John Donati*	.10
38	Dave Doorneweerd	.10
39	Darren Dreifort	.10
40	Mike Durant	.10
41	Chris Durkin	.10
42	Dennis Eckersley	.10
43	*Brian Edmondson*	.10
44	*Vaughn Eshelman*	.25
45	*Shawn Estes*	1.50
46	*Jorge Fabregas*	.15
47	Jon Farrell	.10
48	Cecil Fielder (AS)	.10
49	Carlton Fisk	.15
50	Tim Flannelly	.10
51	*Cliff Floyd*	1.50
52	Julio Franco	.10
53	Greg Gagne	.10
54	*Chris Gambs*	.10
55	Ron Gant	.15
56	Brent Gates	.15
57	Dwayne Gerald	.10
58	Jason Giambi	3.00
59	*Benji Gil*	.20
60	Mark Gipner	.10
61	Danny Gladden	.10
62	Tom Glavine	.20
63	Jimmy Gonzalez	.10
64	Jeff Granger	.10
65	Dan Grapenthien	.10
66	Dennis Gray	.10
67	*Shawn Green*	8.00
68	Tyler Green	.15
69	Todd Greene	1.00
70	Ken Griffey, Jr. (AS)	2.50
71	Kelly Gruber	.10
72	Ozzie Guillen	.10
73	Tony Gwynn (AS)	.50
74	Shane Halter	.10
75	Jeffrey Hammonds	.15
76	Larry Hanlon	.10
77	Pete Harnisch	.10
78	Mike Harrison	.10
79	Bryan Harvey	.10
80	Scott Hatteberg	.15
81	Rick Helling	.10
82	Dave Henderson	.10
83	Rickey Henderson (AS)	.25
84	Tyrone Hill	.10
85	*Todd Hollandsworth*	1.00
86	Brian Holliday	.10
87	Terry Horn	.10
88	Jeff Hostetler	.10
89	Kent Hrbek	.10
90	Mark Hubbard	.10
91	Charles Johnson	1.00
92	Howard Johnson	.10
93	Todd Johnson	.10
94	*Bobby Jones*	.75
95	Dan Jones	.10
96	Felix Jose	.10
97	Dave Justice	.30
98	Jimmy Key	.10
99	*Marc Kroom*	.10
100	John Kruk	.10
101	Mark Langston	.10
102	Barry Larkin	.20
103	Mike LaValliere	.10
104a	Scott Leius (1991 N.L. All-Star - error)	.10
104b	Scott Leius (1991 World Series - correct)	.10
105	Mark Lemke	.10
106	Donnie Leshnock	.10
107	Jimmy Lewis	.10
108	Shawn Livesy	.10
109	Ryan Long	.10
110	Trevor Mallory	.10
111	Denny Martinez	.10
112	Justin Mashore	.10
113	Jason McDonald	.10
114	Jack McDowell	.10
115	Tom McKinnon	.10
116	Billy McKinnon	.10
117	*Buck McNabb*	.10
118	Jim Mecir	.10
119	Dan Melendez	.10
120	*Shawn Miller*	.10
121	Trever Miller	.15
122	Paul Molitor	.40
123	Vincent Moore	.10
124	Mike Morgan	.10
125	Jack Morris (World Series)	.10
126	Jack Morris (All-Star)	.10
127	Sean Mulligan	.10
128	Eddie Murray	.30
129	Mike Neill	.10
130	Phil Nevin	.10
131	Mark O'Brien	.10
132	*Alex Ochoa*	.25
133	*Chad Ogea*	.20
134	Greg Olson	.10
135	Paul O'Neill	.15
136	Jared Osentowski	.10
137	Mike Pagliarulo	.10
138	Rafael Palmeiro	.20
139	Rodney Pedraza	.10
140	Tony Phillips	.10
141	*Scott Pisciotta*	.10
142	Chris Pritchett	.10
143	Jason Pruitt	.10
144a	Kirby Puckett (1991 N.L. All-Star - error)	.75
144b	Kirby Puckett (1991 World Series - correct)	.75
145	Kirby Puckett (AS)	.75
146	*Manny Ramirez*	20.00
147	Eddie Ramos	.10
148	Mark Ratekin	.10
149	Jeff Reardon	.10
150	Sean Rees	.10
151	*Calvin Reese*	2.00
152	*Desmond Relaford*	.20
153	Eric Richardson	.10
154	Cal Ripken, Jr. (AS)	2.00
155	Chris Roberts	.15
156	Mike Robertson	.10
157	Steve Rodriguez	.10
158	Mike Rossiter	.10
159	Scott Ruffcorn	.10
160a	Chris Sabo (1991 World Series - error)	.10
160b	Chris Sabo (1991 N.L. All-Star - correct)	.10
161	Juan Samuel	.10
162	Ryne Sandberg (AS)	.50
163	Scott Sanderson	.10
164	Benito Santiago	.10
165	*Gene Schall*	.10
166	Chad Schoenvogel	.10
167	*Chris Seelbach*	.10
168	*Aaron Sele*	.75
169	Basil Shabazz	.10
170	*Al Shirley*	.10
171	Paul Shuey	.10
172	Ruben Sierra	.10
173	John Smiley	.10
174	Lee Smith	.10
175	Ozzie Smith	.30
176	Tim Smith	.10
177	Zane Smith	.10
178	John Smoltz	.15
179	Scott Stahoviak	.10
180	Kennie Steenstra	.10
181	Kevin Stocker	.10
182	*Chris Stynes*	.10
183	Danny Tartabull	.10
184	Brien Taylor	.10
185	Todd Taylor	.10
186	Larry Thomas	.10
187a	*Ozzie Timmons*	.10
187b	David Tuttle (should be #188)	.10
188	Not issued	
189	Andy Van Slyke	.10
190a	Frank Viola (1991 World Series - error)	.10
190b	Frank Viola (1991 N.L. All-Star - correct)	.10
191	Michael Walkden	.10
192	Jeff Ware	.10
193	*Allen Watson*	.15
194	Steve Whitaker	.10
195a	Jerry Willard (1991 Draft Pick - error)	.10
195b	Jerry Willard (1991 World Series - correct)	.10
196	Craig Wilson	.10
197	Chris Wimmer	.15
198	*Steve Wojciechowski*	.10
199	Joel Wolfe	.10
200	Ivan Zweig	.10

1993 Stadium Club

Topps' premium set for 1993 was issued in three series, two 300-card series and a final series of 150. Boxes contained 24 packs this year, compared to 36 in the past. Packs had 14 cards and an insert card. Each box had a 5" x 7" Master Photo card.

		MT
Complete Set (750):		60.00
Complete Series 1 (300):		20.00
Complete Series 2 (300):		30.00
Complete Series 3 (150):		10.00
Common Player:		.10
First Day Production:		15X
Series 1, 2, 3 Pack (15):		1.50
Series 1, 2, 3 Wax Box (24):		25.00
1	Pat Borders	.10
2	Greg Maddux	2.50
3	Daryl Boston	.10
4	Bob Ayrault	.10
5	Tony Phillips	.10
6	Damion Easley	.10
7	Kip Gross	.10
8	Jim Thome	.40
9	Tim Belcher	.10
10	Gary Wayne	.10
11	Sam Militello	.10
12	Mike Magnante	.10
13	Tim Wakefield	.10
14	Tim Hulett	.10
15	Rheal Cormier	.10
16	Juan Guerrero	.10
17	Rich Gossage	.10
18	Tim Laker	.10
19	Darrin Jackson	.10

No.	Player	Price
20	Jack Clark	.10
21	Roberto Hernandez	.10
22	Dean Palmer	.10
23	Harold Reynolds	.10
24	Dan Plesac	.10
25	Brent Mayne	.10
26	Pat Hentgen	.10
27	Luis Sojo	.10
28	Ron Gant	.15
29	Paul Gibson	.10
30	Bip Roberts	.10
31	Mickey Tettleton	.10
32	Randy Velarde	.10
33	Brian McRae	.10
34	Wes Chamberlain	.10
35	Wayne Kirby	.10
36	Rey Sanchez	.10
37	Jesse Orosco	.10
38	Mike Stanton	.10
39	Royce Clayton	.10
40	Cal Ripken, Jr.	2.50
41	John Dopson	.10
42	Gene Larkin	.10
43	Tim Raines	.15
44	Randy Myers	.10
45	Clay Parker	.10
46	Mike Scioscia	.10
47	Pete Incaviglia	.10
48	Todd Van Poppel	.10
49	Ray Lankford	.15
50	Eddie Murray	.30
51	Barry Bonds	.75
52	Gary Thurman	.10
53	Bob Wickman	.10
54	Joey Cora	.10
55	Kenny Rogers	.10
56	Mike Devereaux	.10
57	Kevin Seitzer	.10
58	Rafael Belliard	.10
59	David Wells	.15
60	Mark Clark	.10
61	Carlos Baerga	.10
62	Scott Brosius	.10
63	Jeff Grotewold	.10
64	Rick Wrona	.10
65	Kurt Knudsen	.10
66	Lloyd McClendon	.10
67	Omar Vizquel	.10
68	Jose Vizcaino	.10
69	Rob Ducey	.10
70	Casey Candaele	.10
71	Ramon Martinez	.15
72	Todd Hundley	.20
73	John Marzano	.10
74	Derek Parks	.10
75	Jack McDowell	.10
76	Tim Scott	.10
77	Mike Mussina	.40
78	Delino DeShields	.10
79	Chris Bosio	.10
80	Mike Bordick	.10
81	Rod Beck	.10
82	Ted Power	.10
83	John Kruk	.10
84	Steve Shifflett	.10
85	Danny Tartabull	.10
86	Mike Greenwell	.10
87	Jose Melendez	.10
88	Craig Wilson	.10
89	Melvin Nieves	.10
90	Ed Sprague	.10
91	Willie McGee	.10
92	Joe Orsulak	.10
93	Jeff King	.10
94	Dan Pasqua	.10
95	Brian Harper	.10
96	Joe Oliver	.10
97	Shane Turner	.10
98	Lenny Harris	.10
99	Jeff Parrett	.10
100	Luis Polonia	.10
101	Kent Bottenfield	.10
102	Albert Belle	.75
103	Mike Maddux	.10
104	Randy Tomlin	.10
105	Andy Stankiewicz	.10
106	Rico Rossy	.10
107	Joe Hesketh	.10
108	Dennis Powell	.10
109	Derrick May	.10
110	Pete Harnisch	.10
111	Kent Mercker	.10
112	Scott Fletcher	.10
113	Rex Hudler	.10
114	Chico Walker	.10
115	Rafael Palmeiro	.20
116	Mark Leiter	.10
117	Pedro Munoz	.10
118	Jim Bullinger	.10
119	Ivan Calderon	.10
120	Mike Timlin	.10
121	Rene Gonzales	.10
122	Greg Vaughn	.15
123	Mike Flanagan	.10
124	Mike Hartley	.10
125	Jeff Montgomery	.10
126	Mike Gallego	.10
127	Don Slaught	.10
128	Charlie O'Brien	.10
129	Jose Offerman	.10
130	Mark Wohlers	.10
131	Eric Fox	.10
132	Doug Strange	.10
133	Jeff Frye	.10
134	Wade Boggs	.40
135	Lou Whitaker	.10
136	Craig Grebeck	.10
137	Rich Rodriguez	.10
138	Jay Bell	.10
139	Felix Fermin	.10
140	Denny Martinez	.10
141	Eric Anthony	.10
142	Roberto Alomar	.50
143	Darren Lewis	.10
144	Mike Blowers	.10
145	Scott Bankhead	.10
146	Jeff Reboulet	.10
147	Frank Viola	.10
148	Bill Pecota	.10
149	Carlos Hernandez	.10
150	Bobby Witt	.10
151	Sid Bream	.10
152	Todd Zeile	.10
153	Dennis Cook	.10
154	Brian Bohanon	.10
155	Pat Kelly	.10
156	Milt Cuyler	.10
157	Juan Bell	.10
158	Randy Milligan	.10
159	Mark Gardner	.10
160	Pat Tabler	.10
161	Jeff Reardon	.10
162	Ken Patterson	.10
163	Bobby Bonilla	.10
164	Tony Pena	.10
165	Greg Swindell	.10
166	Kirk McCaskill	.10
167	Doug Drabek	.10
168	Franklin Stubbs	.10
169	Ron Tingley	.10
170	Willie Banks	.10
171	Sergio Valdez	.10
172	Mark Lemke	.10
173	Robin Yount	.60
174	Storm Davis	.10
175	Dan Walters	.10
176	Steve Farr	.10
177	Curt Wilkerson	.10
178	Luis Alicea	.10
179	Russ Swan	.10
180	Mitch Williams	.10
181	Wilson Alvarez	.10
182	Carl Willis	.10
183	Craig Biggio	.25
184	Sean Berry	.10
185	Trevor Wilson	.10
186	Jeff Tackett	.10
187	Ellis Burks	.10
188	Jeff Branson	.10
189	Matt Nokes	.10
190	John Smiley	.10
191	Danny Gladden	.10
192	Mike Boddicker	.10
193	Roger Pavlik	.10
194	Paul Sorrento	.10
195	Vince Coleman	.10
196	Gary DiSarcina	.10
197	Rafael Bournigal	.10
198	Mike Schooler	.10
199	Scott Ruskin	.10
200	Frank Thomas	1.50
201	Kyle Abbott	.10
202	Mike Perez	.10
203	Andre Dawson	.15
204	Bill Swift	.10
205	Alejandro Pena	.10
206	Dave Winfield	.40
207	Andujar Cedeno	.10
208	Terry Steinbach	.10
209	Chris Hammond	.10
210	Todd Burns	.10
211	Hipolito Pichardo	.10
212	John Kiely	.10
213	Tim Teufel	.10
214	Lee Guetterman	.10
215	Geronimo Pena	.10
216	Brett Butler	.10
217	Bryan Hickerson	.10
218	Rick Trlicek	.10
219	Lee Stevens	.10
220	Roger Clemens	1.00
221	Carlton Fisk	.15
222	Chili Davis	.10
223	Walt Terrell	.10
224	Jim Eisenreich	.10
225	Ricky Bones	.10
226	Henry Rodriguez	.10
227	Ken Hill	.10
228	Rick Wilkins	.10
229	Ricky Jordan	.10
230	Bernard Gilkey	.10
231	Tim Fortugno	.10
232	Geno Petralli	.10
233	Jose Rijo	.10
234	Jim Leyritz	.10
235	Kevin Campbell	.10
236	Al Osuna	.10
237	Pete Smith	.10
238	Pete Schourek	.10
239	Moises Alou	.20
240	Donn Pall	.10
241	Denny Neagle	.10
242	Dan Peltier	.10
243	Scott Scudder	.10
244	Juan Guzman	.10
245	Dave Burba	.10
246	Rick Sutcliffe	.10
247	Tony Fossas	.10
248	Mike Munoz	.10
249	Tim Salmon	.30
250	Rob Murphy	.10
251	Roger McDowell	.10
252	Lance Parrish	.10
253	Cliff Brantley	.10
254	Scott Leius	.10
255	Carlos Martinez	.10
256	Vince Horsman	.10
257	Oscar Azocar	.10
258	Craig Shipley	.10
259	Ben McDonald	.10
260	Jeff Brantley	.10
261	Damon Berryhill	.10
262	Joe Grahe	.10
263	Dave Hansen	.10
264	Rich Amaral	.10
265	*Tim Pugh*	.20
266	Dion James	.10
267	Frank Tanana	.10
268	Stan Belinda	.10
269	Jeff Kent	.10
270	Bruce Ruffin	.10
271	Xavier Hernandez	.10
272	Darrin Fletcher	.10
273	Tino Martinez	.10
274	Benny Santiago	.10
275	Scott Radinsky	.10
276	Mariano Duncan	.10
277	Kenny Lofton	.50
278	Dwight Smith	.10
279	Joe Carter	.10
280	Tim Jones	.10
281	Jeff Huson	.10
282	Phil Plantier	.10
283	Kirby Puckett	1.00
284	Johnny Guzman	.10
285	Mike Morgan	.10
286	Chris Sabo	.10
287	Matt Williams	.30
288	Checklist 1-100	.10
289	Checklist 101-200	.10
290	Checklist 201-300	.10
291	Dennis Eckersley (Members Choice)	.10
292	Eric Karros (Members Choice)	.10
293	Pat Listach (Members Choice)	.10
294	Andy Van Slyke (Members Choice)	.10
295	Robin Ventura (Members Choice)	.10
296	Tom Glavine (Members Choice)	.10
297	Juan Gonzalez (Members Choice)	.50
298	Travis Fryman (Members Choice)	.10
299	Larry Walker (Members Choice)	.20
300	Gary Sheffield (Members Choice)	.20
301	Chuck Finley	.10
302	Luis Gonzalez	.10
303	Darryl Hamilton	.10
304	Bien Figueroa	.10
305	Ron Darling	.10
306	Jonathan Hurst	.10
307	Mike Sharperson	.10
308	Mike Christopher	.10
309	Marvin Freeman	.10
310	Jay Buhner	.10
311	Butch Henry	.10
312	Greg Harris	.10
313	Darren Daulton	.10
314	Chuck Knoblauch	.25
315	Greg Harris	.10
316	John Franco	.10
317	John Wehner	.10
318	Donald Harris	.10
319	Benny Santiago	.10
320	Larry Walker	.30
321	Randy Knorr	.10
322	*Ramon D. Martinez*	.10
323	Mike Stanley	.10
324	Bill Wegman	.10
325	Tom Candiotti	.10
326	Glenn Davis	.10
327	Chuck Crim	.10
328	Scott Livingstone	.10
329	Eddie Taubensee	.10
330	George Bell	.10
331	Edgar Martinez	.10
332	Paul Assenmacher	.10
333	Steve Hosey	.10
334	Mo Vaughn	.50
335	Bret Saberhagen	.10
336	Mike Trombley	.10
337	Mark Lewis	.10
338	Terry Pendleton	.10
339	Dave Hollins	.10
340	Jeff Conine	.15
341	Bob Tewksbury	.10
342	Billy Ashley	.10
343	Zane Smith	.10
344	John Wetteland	.10
345	Chris Hoiles	.10
346	Frank Castillo	.10
347	Bruce Hurst	.10
348	Kevin McReynolds	.10
349	Dave Henderson	.10
350	Ryan Bowen	.10
351	Sid Fernandez	.10
352	Mark Whiten	.10
353	Nolan Ryan	2.50
354	Rick Aguilera	.10
355	Mark Langston	.10
356	Jack Morris	.10
357	Rob Deer	.10
358	Dave Fleming	.10
359	Lance Johnson	.10
360	Joe Millette	.10
361	Wil Cordero	.10
362	Chito Martinez	.10
363	Scott Servais	.10
364	Bernie Williams	.60
365	Pedro Martinez	.75
366	Ryne Sandberg	.60
367	Brad Ausmus	.10
368	Scott Cooper	.10
369	Rob Dibble	.10
370	Walt Weiss	.10
371	Mark Davis	.10
372	Orlando Merced	.10
373	Mike Jackson	.10
374	Kevin Appier	.10
375	Esteban Beltre	.10
376	Joe Slusarski	.10
377	William Suero	.10
378	Pete O'Brien	.10
379	Alan Embree	.10
380	Lenny Webster	.10
381	Eric Davis	.10
382	Duane Ward	.10
383	John Habyan	.10
384	Jeff Bagwell	1.00
385	Ruben Amaro	.10
386	Julio Valera	.10
387	Robin Ventura	.25
388	Archi Cianfrocco	.10
389	Skeeter Barnes	.10
390	Tim Costo	.10
391	Luis Mercedes	.10
392	Jeremy Hernandez	.10

No.	Player	Price
393	Shawon Dunston	.10
394	Andy Van Slyke	.10
395	Kevin Maas	.10
396	Kevin Brown	.10
397	J.T. Bruett	.10
398	Darryl Strawberry	.10
399	Tom Pagnozzi	.10
400	Sandy Alomar	.15
401	Keith Miller	.10
402	Rich DeLucia	.10
403	Shawn Abner	.10
404	Howard Johnson	.10
405	Mike Benjamin	.10
406	*Roberto Mejia*	.15
407	Mike Butcher	.10
408	Deion Sanders	.20
409	Todd Stottlemyre	.10
410	Scott Kamieniecki	.10
411	Doug Jones	.10
412	John Burkett	.10
413	Lance Blankenship	.10
414	Jeff Parrett	.10
415	Barry Larkin	.15
416	Alan Trammell	.10
417	Mark Kiefer	.10
418	Gregg Olson	.10
419	Mark Grace	.25
420	Shane Mack	.10
421	Bob Walk	.10
422	Curt Schilling	.15
423	Erik Hanson	.10
424	George Brett	.60
425	Reggie Jefferson	.10
426	Mark Portugal	.10
427	Ron Karkovice	.10
428	Matt Young	.10
429	Troy Neel	.10
430	Hector Fajardo	.10
431	Dave Righetti	.10
432	Pat Listach	.10
433	Jeff Innis	.10
434	Bob MacDonald	.10
435	Brian Jordan	.10
436	Jeff Blauser	.10
437	*Mike Myers*	.10
438	Frank Seminara	.10
439	Rusty Meacham	.10
440	Greg Briley	.10
441	Derek Lilliquist	.10
442	John Vander Wal	.10
443	Scott Erickson	.10
444	Bob Scanlan	.10
445	Todd Frohwirth	.10
446	Tom Goodwin	.10
447	William Pennyfeather	.10
448	Travis Fryman	.15
449	Mickey Morandini	.10
450	Greg Olson	.10
451	Trevor Hoffman	.15
452	Dave Magadan	.10
453	Shawn Jeter	.10
454	Andres Galarraga	.25
455	Ted Wood	.10
456	Freddie Benavides	.10
457	Junior Felix	.10
458	Alex Cole	.10
459	John Orton	.10
460	Eddie Zosky	.10
461	Dennis Eckersley	.10
462	Lee Smith	.10
463	John Smoltz	.20
464	Ken Caminiti	.15
465	Melido Perez	.10
466	Tom Marsh	.10
467	Jeff Nelson	.10
468	Jesse Levis	.10
469	Chris Nabholz	.10
470	Mike Mcfarlane	.10
471	Reggie Sanders	.15
472	Chuck McElroy	.10
473	Kevin Gross	.10
474	*Matt Whiteside*	.15
475	Cal Eldred	.10
476	Dave Gallagher	.10
477	Len Dykstra	.10
478	Mark McGwire	3.00
479	David Segui	.10
480	Mike Henneman	.10
481	Bret Barberie	.10
482	Steve Sax	.10
483	Dave Valle	.10
484	Danny Darwin	.10
485	Devon White	.10
486	Eric Plunk	.10
487	Jim Gott	.10
488	Scooter Tucker	.10
489	Omar Oliveres	.10
490	Greg Myers	.10
491	Brian Hunter	.10
492	Kevin Tapani	.10
493	Rich Monteleone	.10
494	Steve Buechele	.10
495	Bo Jackson	.20
496	Mike LaValliere	.10
497	Mark Leonard	.10
498	Daryl Boston	.10
499	Jose Canseco	.25
500	Brian Barnes	.10
501	Randy Johnson	.50
502	Tim McIntosh	.10
503	Cecil Fielder	.10
504	Derek Bell	.15
505	Kevin Koslofski	.10
506	Darren Holmes	.10
507	Brady Anderson	.15
508	John Valentin	.15
509	Jerry Browne	.10
510	Fred McGriff	.25
511	Pedro Astacio	.10
512	Gary Gaetti	.10
513	*John Burke*	.10
514	Dwight Gooden	.15
515	Thomas Howard	.10
516	*Darrell Whitmore*	.20
517	Ozzie Guillen	.10
518	Darryl Kile	.10
519	Rich Rowland	.10
520	Carlos Delgado	.60
521	Doug Henry	.10
522	Greg Colbrunn	.10
523	Tom Gordon	.10
524	Ivan Rodriguez	.75
525	Kent Hrbek	.10
526	Eric Young	.10
527	Rod Brewer	.10
528	Eric Karros	.10
529	Marquis Grissom	.10
530	Rico Brogna	.10
531	Sammy Sosa	1.50
532	Bret Boone	.10
533	Luis Rivera	.10
534	Hal Morris	.10
535	Monty Fariss	.10
536	Leo Gomez	.10
537	Wally Joyner	.15
538	Tony Gwynn	1.00
539	Mike Williams	.10
540	Juan Gonzalez	1.00
541	Ryan Klesko	.50
542	Ryan Thompson	.15
543	Chad Curtis	.15
544	Orel Hershiser	.10
545	Carlos Garcia	.10
546	Bob Welch	.10
547	Vinny Castilla	.15
548	Ozzie Smith	.60
549	Luis Salazar	.10
550	Mark Guthrie	.10
551	Charles Nagy	.10
552	Alex Fernandez	.15
553	Mel Rojas	.10
554	Orestes Destrade	.10
555	Mark Gubicza	.10
556	Steve Finley	.10
557	Don Mattingly	1.00
558	Rickey Henderson	.40
559	Tommy Greene	.10
560	Arthur Rhodes	.10
561	Alfredo Griffin	.10
562	Will Clark	.25
563	Bob Zupcic	.10
564	Chuck Carr	.10
565	Henry Cotto	.10
566	Billy Spiers	.10
567	Jack Armstrong	.10
568	Kurt Stillwell	.10
569	David McCarty	.10
570	Joe Vitiello	.10
571	Gerald Williams	.10
572	Dale Murphy	.20
573	Scott Aldred	.10
574	Bill Gullickson	.10
575	Bobby Thigpen	.10
576	Glenallen Hill	.10
577	Dwayne Henry	.10
578	Calvin Jones	.10
579	Al Martin	.15
580	Ruben Sierra	.10
581	Andy Benes	.10
582	Anthony Young	.10
583	Shawn Boskie	.10
584	*Scott Pose*	.15
585	Mike Piazza	2.50
586	Donovan Osborne	.10
587	James Austin	.10
588	Checklist 301-400	.10
589	Checklist 401-500	.10
590	Checklist 501-600	.10
591	Ken Griffey, Jr. (Members Choice)	2.00
592	Ivan Rodriguez (Members Choice)	.40
593	Carlos Baerga (Members Choice)	.10
594	Fred McGriff (Members Choice)	.20
595	Mark McGwire (Members Choice)	2.00
596	Roberto Alomar (Members Choice)	.40
597	Kirby Puckett (Members Choice)	.40
598	Marquis Grissom (Members Choice)	.10
599	John Smoltz (Members Choice)	.10
600	Ryne Sandberg (Members Choice)	.40
601	Wade Boggs	.40
602	Jeff Reardon	.10
603	Billy Ripken	.10
604	Bryan Harvey	.10
605	Carlos Quintana	.10
606	Greg Hibbard	.10
607	Ellis Burks	.10
608	Greg Swindell	.10
609	Dave Winfield	.30
610	Charlie Hough	.10
611	Chili Davis	.10
612	Jody Reed	.10
613	Mark Williamson	.10
614	Phil Plantier	.10
615	Jim Abbott	.10
616	Dante Bichette	.35
617	Mark Eichhorn	.10
618	Gary Sheffield	.25
619	*Richie Lewis*	.10
620	Joe Girardi	.10
621	Jaime Navarro	.10
622	Willie Wilson	.10
623	Scott Fletcher	.10
624	Bud Black	.10
625	Tom Brunansky	.10
626	Steve Avery	.10
627	Paul Molitor	.60
628	Gregg Jefferies	.15
629	Dave Stewart	.10
630	Javier Lopez	.35
631	Greg Gagne	.10
632	Bobby Kelly	.10
633	Mike Fetters	.10
634	Ozzie Canseco	.10
635	Jeff Russell	.10
636	Pete Incaviglia	.10
637	Tom Henke	.10
638	Chipper Jones	1.50
639	Jimmy Key	.10
640	Dave Martinez	.10
641	Dave Stieb	.10
642	Milt Thompson	.10
643	Alan Mills	.10
644	Tony Fernandez	.10
645	Randy Bush	.10
646	Joe Magrane	.10
647	Ivan Calderon	.10
648	Jose Guzman	.10
649	John Olerud	.25
650	Tom Glavine	.20
651	Julio Franco	.10
652	Armando Reynoso	.10
653	Felix Jose	.10
654	Ben Rivera	.10
655	Andre Dawson	.20
656	Mike Harkey	.10
657	Kevin Seitzer	.10
658	Lonnie Smith	.10
659	Norm Charlton	.10
660	Dave Justice	.40
661	Fernando Valenzuela	.10
662	Dan Wilson	.10
663	Mark Gardner	.10
664	Doug Dascenzo	.10
665	Greg Maddux	2.50
666	Harold Baines	.10
667	Randy Myers	.10
668	Harold Reynolds	.10
669	Candy Maldonado	.10
670	Al Leiter	.15
671	Jerald Clark	.10
672	Doug Drabek	.10
673	Kirk Gibson	.10
674	*Steve Reed*	.10
675	Mike Felder	.10
676	Ricky Gutierrez	.10
677	Spike Owen	.10
678	Otis Nixon	.10
679	Scott Sanderson	.10
680	Mark Carreon	.10
681	Troy Percival	.10
682	Kevin Stocker	.10
683	*Jim Converse*	.10
684	Barry Bonds	.75
685	Greg Gohr	.10
686	Tim Wallach	.10
687	Matt Mieske	.10
688	Robby Thompson	.10
689	Brien Taylor	.10
690	Kirt Manwaring	.10
691	*Mike Lansing*	.25
692	Steve Decker	.10
693	Mike Moore	.10
694	Kevin Mitchell	.10
695	Phil Hiatt	.10
696	*Tony Tarasco*	.10
697	Benji Gil	.10
698	Jeff Juden	.10
699	Kevin Reimer	.10
700	Andy Ashby	.15
701	John Jaha	.15
702	*Tim Bogar*	.20
703	David Cone	.15
704	Willie Greene	.15
705	*David Hulse*	.15
706	Cris Carpenter	.10
707	Ken Griffey, Jr.	3.00
708	Steve Bedrosian	.10
709	Dave Nilsson	.10
710	Paul Wagner	.10
711	B.J. Surhoff	.10
712	*Rene Arocha*	.15
713	Manny Lee	.10
714	Brian Williams	.10
715	*Sherman Obando*	.15
716	Terry Mulholland	.10
717	Paul O'Neill	.20
718	David Nied	.10
719	*J.T. Snow*	.75
720	Nigel Wilson	.10
721	Mike Bielecki	.10
722	Kevin Young	.10
723	Charlie Leibrandt	.10
724	Frank Bolick	.10
725	*Jon Shave*	.15
726	Steve Cooke	.10
727	*Domingo Martinez*	.15
728	Todd Worrell	.10
729	Jose Lind	.10
730	*Jim Tatum*	.10
731	Mike Hampton	.10
732	Mike Draper	.10
733	Henry Mercedes	.15
734	*John Johnstone*	.15
735	Mitch Webster	.10
736	Russ Springer	.10
737	Rob Natal	.10
738	Steve Howe	.10
739	*Darrell Sherman*	.15
740	Pat Mahomes	.10
741	Alex Arias	.10
742	Damon Buford	.15
743	Charlie Hayes	.10
744	Guillermo Velasquez	.10
745	Checklist 601-750	.10
746	Frank Thomas (Members Choice)	1.00
747	Barry Bonds (Members Choice)	.35
748	Roger Clemens (Members Choice)	.50
749	Joe Carter (Members Choice)	.10
750	Greg Maddux (Members Choice)	1.00

1993 Stadium Club 1st Day Production

Inserted at the rate of about one per box, with an estimated production of 2,000 apiece, 1st Day Production cards are a parallel of 1993 TSC on which an embossed silver holographic foil logo has been added. Because of the considerably higher value of the 1st Day parallels, collectors should be aware that fakes can be created by cutting the logo off a common player's card and attaching it to a superstar card.

	MT
Complete Set (750):	1600.
Complete Series 1 (1-300)	600.00
Complete Series 2 (301-600):	700.00
Complete Series 3 (601-750):	400.00
Common Player:	1.00
1st Day Stars:	15X

(See 1993 Stadium Club for checklist and base card values.)

1993 Stadium Club I Inserts

Four bonus cards were produced as special inserts in Series I Stadium Club packs. Two of the full-bleed, gold-foil enhanced cards honor Robin Yount and George Brett for achieving the 3,000-hit mark, while the other two commemorate the first picks in the 1993 expansion draft by the Colorado Rockies (David Nied) and Marlins (Nigel Wilson).

		MT
Complete Set (4):		5.00
Common Player:		.75
1	Robin Yount (3,000 hits)	2.00
2	George Brett (3,000 hits)	3.00
3	David Nied (#1 pick)	.75
4	Nigel Wilson (#1 pick)	.75

1993 Stadium Club II Inserts

Cross-town and regional rivals were featured in this four-card insert set found, on average, one per 24 packs of Series II Stadium Club. Each of the two-faced cards is typical S.C. quality with gold-foil stamping and UV coating front and back.

		MT
Complete Set (4):		10.00
Common Card:		2.00
1	Pacific Terrific (Will Clark, Mark McGwire)	3.50
2	Broadway Stars (Dwight Gooden, Don Mattingly)	2.00
3	Second City Sluggers (Ryne Sandberg, Frank Thomas)	3.00
4	Pacific Terrific (Ken Griffey, Jr., Darryl Strawberry)	3.50

1993 Stadium Club III Inserts

Team "firsts" - first game, first pitch, first batter, etc. - for the 1993 expansion Florida Marlins and Colorado Rockies are featured on this pair of inserts found in Series III Stadium Club packs. Fronts featured game-action photos with the player's name in gold foil. On back is a stadium scene with the team first overprinted in black. At top the team name and Stadium Club logo are in gold foil.

		MT
Complete Set (2):		1.00
Common Player:		.50
1	David Nied	.50
2	Charlie Hough	.50

1993 Stadium Club Master Photos

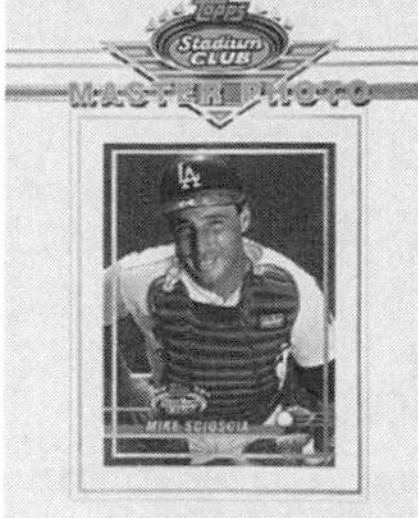

Each box of 1993 Stadium Club packs included one Master Photo premium insert. Prize cards good for three Master Photos in a mail-in offer were also included in each of the three series. The 5" x 7" Master Photos feature wide white borders and a large Stadium Club logo at top, highlighted by prismatic foil. The same foil is used as a border for a larger-format version of the player's regular S.C. card at the center of the Master Photo. A "Members Only" version of each of the 1993 Master Photos was available as a premium with the purchase of a Members Only Stadium Club set. the Members Only Master Photos have a gold-foil seal in the upper-right corner.

		MT
Complete Set (30):		25.00
Common Player:		.25
Series I		
(1)	Carlos Baerga	.25
(2)	Delino DeShields	.25
(3)	Brian McRae	.25
(4)	Sam Militello	.25
(5)	Joe Oliver	.25
(6)	Kirby Puckett	2.00
Series II		
(13)	George Brett	2.00
(14)	Jose Canseco	.75
(15)	Will Clark	.75
(16)	Travis Fryman	.25
(17)	Dwight Gooden	.50
(18)	Mark Grace	.75
Series III		
(25)	Barry Bonds	2.00
(26)	Ken Griffey, Jr.	5.00
(27)	Greg Maddux	3.00
(28)	David Nied	.25
(29)	J.T. Snow	.50
(30)	Brien Taylor	.25

1993 Stadium Club Special (Murphy)

Though the packaging and the cards themselves identify this 200-card set as a 1992 issue, it was not released until 1993 and is thought of by the hobby at large as a 1993 set. The set is sold in a plastic replica of Jack Murphy Stadium in San Diego, venue for the 1993 All-Star Game. Fifty-six of the cards feature players from that contest and are so identified by a line of gold-foil on the card front and an All-Star logo on back. Twenty-five members of the 1992 Team U.S.A. Olympic baseball squad are also included in the set, with appropriate logos and notations front and back. There are 19 cards depicting action and stars of the the 1992 League Championships and World Series. The other 100 cards in the set are 1992 draft picks. All cards have the same basic format as the regular-issue 1992 Topps Stadium Club cards, full-bleed photos on front and back, UV coating on both sides and gold-foil highlights on front. Besides the 200 standard-size cards, the Special Edition set included a dozen "Master Photos," 5" x 7" white-bordered premium cards.

	MT
Complete Set (200):	120.00
Common Player:	.10

1	Dave Winfield	.20
2	Juan Guzman	.10
3	Tony Gwynn	2.00
4	Chris Roberts	.20
5	Benny Santiago	.10
6	Sherard Clinkscales	.10
7	*Jonathan Nunnally*	.40
8	Chuck Knoblauch	.30
9	*Bob Wolcott*	.10
10	Steve Rodriguez	.10
11	*Mark Williams*	.10
12	*Danny Clyburn*	.15
13	Darren Dreifort	.15
14	Andy Van Slyke	.10
15	Wade Boggs	.45
16	Scott Patton	.10
17	Gary Sheffield	.25
18	Ron Villone	.10
19	Roberto Alomar	.50
20	Marc Valdes	.10
21	Daron Kirkreit	.10
22	Jeff Granger	.15
23	Levon Largusa	.10
24	Jimmy Key	.10
25	Kevin Pearson	.10
26	Michael Moore	.10
27	*Preston Wilson*	8.00
28	Kirby Puckett	1.00
29	*Tim Crabtree*	.15
30	Bip Roberts	.10
31	Kelly Gruber	.10
32	Tony Fernandez	.10
33	Jason Angel	.10
34	Calvin Murray	.10
35	Chad McConnell	.15
36	Jason Moler	.10
37	Mark Lemke	.10
38	Tom Knauss	.10
39	Larry Mitchell	.10
40	Doug Mirabelli	.10
41	Everett Stull II	.10
42	Chris Wimmer	.10
43	*Dan Serafini*	.10
44	Ryne Sandberg	.60
45	Steve Lyons	.10
46	Ryan Freeburg	.10
47	Ruben Sierra	.10
48	David Mysel	.10
49	Joe Hamilton	.15
50	Steve Rodriguez	.10
51	Tim Wakefield	.10
52	Scott Gentile	.10
53	Doug Jones	.10
54	Willie Brown	.10
55	*Chad Mottola*	.20
56	Ken Griffey, Jr.	6.00
57	Jon Lieber	.10
58	Denny Martinez	.10
59	Joe Petcka	.10
60	Benji Simonton	.10
61	Brett Backlund	.10
62	Damon Berryhill	.10
63	Juan Guzman	.10
64	Doug Hecker	.10
65	Jamie Arnold	.10
66	Bob Tewksbury	.10
67	Tim Leger	.10
68	Todd Etler	.10
69	Lloyd McClendon	.10
70	Kurt Ehmann	.10
71	Rick Magdaleno	.10
72	Tom Pagnozzi	.10
73	Jeffrey Hammonds	.15
74	Joe Carter	.10
75	Chris Holt	.10
76	Charles Johnson	.60
77	Bob Walk	.10
78	Fred McGriff	.20
79	Tom Evans	.10
80	Scott Klingenbeck	.10
81	Chad McConnell	.15
82	Chris Eddy	.10
83	Phil Nevin	.10
84	John Kruk	.10
85	Tony Sheffield	.10
86	John Smoltz	.20
87	Trevor Humphry	.10
88	Charles Nagy	.15
89	Sean Runyan	.10
90	Mike Gulan	.10
91	Darren Daulton	.10
92	Otis Nixon	.10
93	Nomar Garciaparra	40.00
94	Larry Walker	.35
95	Hut Smith	.10
96	Rick Helling	.10
97	Roger Clemens	1.50
98	Ron Gant	.15
99	Kenny Felder	.10
100	Steve Murphy	.10
101	Mike Smith	.10
102	Terry Pendleton	.10
103	Tim Davis	.10
104	Jeff Patzke	.10
105	Craig Wilson	.10
106	Tom Glavine	.20
107	Mark Langston	.10
108	Mark Thompson	.10
109	*Eric Owens*	.10
110	Keith Johnson	.10
111	Robin Ventura	.20
112	Ed Sprague	.10
113	*Jeff Schmidt*	.10
114	Don Wengert	.10
115	Craig Biggio	.20
116	Kenny Carlyle	.10
117	*Derek Jeter*	60.00
118	Manuel Lee	.10
119	Jeff Haas	.10
120	Roger Bailey	.10
121	Sean Lowe	.10
122	Rick Aguilera	.10
123	Sandy Alomar	.20
124	Derek Wallace	.10
125	B.J. Wallace	.10
126	Greg Maddux	2.00
127	Tim Moore	.10
128	Lee Smith	.10
129	Todd Steverson	.15
130	Chris Widger	.15
131	Paul Molitor	.60
132	Chris Smith	.10
133	*Chris Gomez*	.20
134	Jimmy Baron	.10
135	John Smoltz	.15
136	Pat Borders	.10
137	Donnie Leshnock	.10
138	Gus Gandarillos	.10
139	Will Clark	.25
140	*Ryan Luzinski*	.10
141	Cal Ripken, Jr.	3.00
142	B.J. Wallace	.10
143	*Trey Beamon*	.40
144	Norm Charlton	.10
145	Mike Mussina	.35
146	Billy Owens	.10
147	Ozzie Smith	.60
148	*Jason Kendall*	8.00
149	*Mike Matthews*	.10
150	David Spykstra	.10
151	Benji Grigsby	.10
152	Sean Smith	.10
153	Mark McGwire	4.00
154	David Cone	.20
155	*Shon Walker*	.15
156	Jason McDowell	.10
157	Jack McDowell	.10
158	Paxton Briley	.10
159	Edgar Martinez	.10
160	Brian Sackinsky	.10
161	Barry Bonds	.75
162	Roberto Kelly	.10
163	Jeff Alkire	.10
164	Mike Sharperson	.10
165	Jamie Taylor	.10
166	John Saffer	.10
167	Jerry Browne	.10
168	Travis Fryman	.10
169	Brady Anderson	.15
170	Chris Roberts	.20
171	Lloyd Peever	.10
172	Francisco Cabrera	.10
173	Ramiro Martinez	.10
174	Jeff Alkire	.10
175	Ivan Rodriguez	.60
176	Kevin Brown	.15
177	Chad Roper	.10
178	Rod Henderson	.10
179	Dennis Eckersley	.10
180	*Shannon Stewart*	8.00
181	DeShawn Warren	.10
182	Lonnie Smith	.10
183	Willie Adams	.10
184	Jeff Montgomery	.10
185	Damon Hollins	.10
186	Byron Matthews	.10
187	Harold Baines	.10
188	Rick Greene	.10
189	Carlos Baerga	.10
190	Brandon Cromer	.10
191	Roberto Alomar	.50
192	Rich Ireland	.10
193	Steve Montgomery	.10
194	Brant Brown	1.50
195	Ritchie Moody	.10
196	Michael Tucker	.10
197	*Jason Varitek*	.75
198	David Manning	.10
199	Marquis Riley	.10
200	Jason Giambi	.25

1993 Stadium Club Special Master Photos

Each 1993 Stadium Club Special (Jack Murphy Stadium) set included 12 Master Photos replicating cards from the set. there were nine All-Stars, two '92 rookies and a Team USA player among the Master Photos. Gold-tone prismatic foil highlights the 5" x 7" cards, decorating the large logo at top and separating the card photo from the wide white border. Backs have Stadium Club and MLB logos and copyright information printed in black. The unnumbered cards are checklisted here in alphabetical order.

		MT
Complete Set (12):		5.00
Common Player:		.25
(1)	Sandy Alomar	.35
(2)	Tom Glavine	.35
(3)	Ken Griffey, Jr.	3.00
(4)	Tony Gwynn	1.50
(5)	Chuck Knoblauch	.60
(6)	Chad Mottola	.25
(7)	Kirby Puckett	2.00
(8)	Chris Roberts	.40
(9)	Ryne Sandberg	1.50
(10)	Gary Sheffield	.75
(11)	Larry Walker	.75
(12)	Preston Wilson	.75

1994 Stadium Club Pre-production

These sample cards introducing the 1994 Stadium Club set differ from their regular-issue counterparts only in the inclusion of a line of type vertically on the back-right, "Pre-Production Sample."

		MT
Complete Set (9):		7.00
Common Player:		.50
6	Al Martin	.50
15	Junior Ortiz	.50
36	Tim Salmon	1.50
56	Jerry Spradlin	.50
122	Tom Pagnozzi	.50
123	Ron Gant	.75
125	Dennis Eckersley	.75
135	Jose Lind	.50
238	Barry Bonds	3.00

1994 Stadium Club

Issued in three series to a total of 720 cards, Topps' mid-price brand features a hip look and a wide range of insert specials. The regular cards feature a borderless photo with the player's name presented in a unique typewriter/label maker style at bottom. The player's last name and Topps Stadium Club logo at top are in red foil. Backs feature another player photo, some personal data and a headlined career summary. Various stats and skills rankings complete the data. Subsets within the issue include cards annotated with Major League debut dates, 1993 awards won, home run club cards, cards featuring two or three players, and Final Tribute cards for George Brett and Nolan Ryan.

	MT
Complete Set (720):	50.00
Common Player:	.10

Series 1, 2, 3 Pack (12): 1.00
Series 1, 2, 3 Wax Box (24): 20.00
1 Robin Yount .50
2 Rick Wilkins .10
3 Steve Scarsone .10
4 Gary Sheffield .40
5 George Brett .75
6 Al Martin .10
7 Joe Oliver .10
8 Stan Belinda .10
9 Denny Hocking .10
10 Roberto Alomar .60
11 Luis Polonia .10
12 Scott Hemond .10
13 Joey Reed .10
14 Mel Rojas .10
15 Junior Ortiz .10
16 Harold Baines .10
17 Brad Pennington .10
18 Jay Bell .10
19 Tom Henke .10
20 Jeff Branson .10
21 Roberto Mejia .10
22 Pedro Munoz .10
23 Matt Nokes .10
24 Jack McDowell .10
25 Cecil Fielder .10
26 Tony Fossas .10
27 Jim Eisenreich .10
28 Anthony Young .10
29 Chuck Carr .10
30 Jeff Treadway .10
31 Chris Nabholz .10
32 Tom Candiotti .10
33 Mike Maddux .10
34 Nolan Ryan 2.50
35 Luis Gonzalez .15
36 Tim Salmon .25
37 Mark Whiten .10
38 Roger McDowell .10
39 Royce Clayton .10
40 Troy Neel .10
41 Mike Harkey .10
42 Darrin Fletcher .10
43 Wayne Kirby .10
44 Rich Amaral .10
45 Robb Nen .10
46 Tim Teufel .10
47 Steve Cooke .10
48 Jeff McNeely .10
49 Jeff Montgomery .10
50 Skeeter Barnes .10
51 Scott Stahoviak .10
52 Pat Kelly .10
53 Brady Anderson .20
54 Mariano Duncan .10
55 Brian Bohanon .10
56 Jerry Spradlin .10
57 Ron Karkovice .10
58 Jeff Gardner .10
59 Bobby Bonilla .10
60 Tino Martinez .20
61 Todd Benzinger .10
62 *Steve Trachsel* .35
63 Brian Jordan .15
64 Steve Bedrosian .10
65 Brent Gates .10
66 Shawn Green .50
67 Sean Berry .10
68 Joe Klink .10
69 Fernando Valenzuela .10
70 Andy Tomberlin .10
71 Tony Pena .10
72 Eric Young .10
73 Chris Gomez .10
74 Paul O'Neill .20
75 Ricky Gutierrez .10
76 Brad Holman .10
77 Lance Painter .10
78 Mike Butcher .10
79 Sid Bream .10
80 Sammy Sosa 1.50
81 Felix Fermin .10
82 Todd Hundley .20
83 Kevin Higgins .10
84 Todd Pratt .10
85 Ken Griffey, Jr. 3.00
86 John O'Donoghue .10
87 Rick Renteria .10
88 John Burkett .10
89 Jose Vizcaino .10
90 Kevin Seitzer .10
91 Bobby Witt .10
92 Chris Turner .10
93 Omar Vizquel .10
94 Dave Justice .25
95 David Segui .10
96 Dave Hollins .10
97 Doug Strange .10
98 Jerald Clark .10
99 Mike Moore .10
100 Joey Cora .10
101 Scott Kamieniecki .10
102 Andy Benes .15
103 Chris Bosio .10
104 Rey Sanchez .10
105 John Jaha .10
106 Otis Nixon .10
107 Rickey Henderson .40
108 Jeff Bagwell 1.00
109 Gregg Jefferies .15
110 Topps Trios (Roberto Alomar, Paul Molitor, John Olerud) .25
111 Topps Trios (Ron Gant, David Justice, Fred McGriff) .25
112 Topps Trios (Juan Gonzalez, Rafael Palmeiro, Dean Palmer) .25
113 Greg Swindell .10
114 Bill Hasleman .10
115 Phil Plantier .10
116 Ivan Rodriguez .75
117 Kevin Tapani .10
118 Mike LaValliere .10
119 Tim Costo .10
120 Mickey Morandini .10
121 Brett Butler .10
122 Tom Pagnozzi .10
123 Ron Gant .15
124 Damion Easley .10
125 Dennis Eckersley .10
126 Matt Mieske .10
127 Cliff Floyd .10
128 *Julian Tavarez* .10
129 Arthur Rhodes .10
130 Dave West .10
131 Tim Naehring .10
132 Freddie Benavides .10
133 Paul Assenmacher .10
134 David McCarty .10
135 Jose Lind .10
136 Reggie Sanders .15
137 Don Slaught .10
138 Andujar Cedeno .10
139 Rob Deer .10
140 Mike Piazza 2.00
141 Moises Alou .15
142 Tom Foley .10
143 Benny Santiago .10
144 Sandy Alomar .15
145 Carlos Hernandez .10
146 Luis Alicea .10
147 Tom Lampkin .10
148 Ryan Klesko .20
149 Juan Guzman .10
150 Scott Servais .10
151 Tony Gwynn 1.00
152 Tim Wakefield .10
153 David Nied .10
154 Chris Haney .10
155 Danny Bautista .10
156 Randy Velarde .10
157 Darrin Jackson .10
158 *J.R. Phillips* .25
159 Greg Gagne .10
160 Luis Aquino .10
161 John Vander Wal .10
162 Randy Myers .10
163 Ted Power .10
164 Scott Brosius .10
165 Len Dykstra .10
166 Jacob Brumfield .10
167 Bo Jackson .20
168 Eddie Taubensee .10
169 Carlos Baerga .10
170 Tim Bogar .10
171 Jose Canseco .40
172 Greg Blosser .10
173 Chili Davis .10
174 Randy Knorr .10
175 Mike Perez .10
176 Henry Rodriguez .10
177 *Brian Turang* .15
178 Roger Pavlik .10
179 Aaron Sele .15
180 Tale of 2 Players (Fred McGriff, Gary Sheffield) .20
181 Tale of 2 Players (J.T. Snow, Tim Salmon) .20
182 Roberto Hernandez .10
183 Jeff Reboulet .10
184 John Doherty .10
185 Danny Sheaffer .10
186 Bip Roberts .10
187 Denny Martinez .10
188 Darryl Hamilton .10
189 Eduardo Perez .10
190 Pete Harnisch .10
191 Rick Gossage .10
192 Mickey Tettleton .10
193 Lenny Webster .10
194 Lance Johnson .10
195 Don Mattingly 1.00
196 Gregg Olson .10
197 Mark Gubicza .10
198 Scott Fletcher .10
199 Jon Shave .10
200 Tim Mauser .10
201 Jeromy Burnitz .10
202 Rob Dibble .10
203 Will Clark .40
204 Steve Buechele .10
205 Brian Williams .10
206 Carlos Garcia .10
207 Mark Clark .10
208 Rafael Palmeiro .40
209 Eric Davis .10
210 Pat Meares .10
211 Chuck Finley .10
212 Jason Bere .10
213 Gary DiSarcina .10
214 Tony Fernandez .10
215 B.J. Surhoff .10
216 Lee Guetterman .10
217 Tim Wallach .10
218 Kirt Manwaring .10
219 Albert Belle .50
220 Dwight Gooden .15
221 Archi Cianfrocco .10
222 Terry Mulholland .10
223 Hipolito Pichardo .10
224 Kent Hrbek .10
225 Criag Grebeck .10
226 Todd Jones .10
227 Mike Bordick .10
228 John Olerud .25
229 Jeff Blauser .10
230 Alex Arias .10
231 Bernard Gilkey .10
232 Denny Neagle .10
233 *Pedro Borbon* .10
234 Dick Schofield .10
235 Matias Carrillo .10
236 Juan Bell .10
237 Mike Hampton .10
238 Barry Bonds .75
239 Cris Carpenter .10
240 Eric Karros .20
241 Greg McMichael .10
242 Pat Hentgen .10
243 Tim Pugh .10
244 Vinny Castilla .10
245 Charlie Hough .10
246 Bobby Munoz .10
247 Kevin Baez .10
248 Todd Frohwirth .10
249 Charlie Hayes .10
250 Mike Macfarlane .10
251 Danny Darwin .10
252 Ben Rivera .10
253 Dave Henderson .10
254 Steve Avery .10
255 Tim Belcher .10
256 Dan Plesac .10
257 Jim Thome .40
258 Albert Belle (35+ HR Hitter) .30
259 Barry Bonds (35+ HR Hitter) .35
260 Ron Gant (35+ HR Hitter) .10
261 Juan Gonzalez (35+ HR Hitter) .50
262 Ken Griffey, Jr. (35+ HR Hitter) 1.50
263 Dave Justice (35+ HR Hitter) .20
264 Fred McGriff (35+ HR Hitter) .20
265 Rafael Palmeiro (35+ HR Hitter) .10
266 Mike Piazza (35+ HR Hitter) .75
267 Frank Thomas (35+ HR Hitter) 1.00
268 Matt Williams (35+ HR Hitter) .10
269a Checklist 1-135 .10
269b Checklist 271-408 .10
270a Checklist 136-270 .10
270b Checklist 409-540 .10
271 Mike Stanley .10
272 Tony Tarasco .10
273 Teddy Higuera .10
274 Ryan Thompson .10
275 Rick Aguilera .10
276 Ramon Martinez .15
277 Orlando Merced .10
278 Guillermo Velasquez .10
279 Mark Hutton .10
280 Larry Walker .40
281 Kevin Gross .10
282 Jose Offerman .10
283 Jim Leyritz .10
284 Jamie Moyer .10
285 Frank Thomas 1.00
286 Derek Bell .10
287 Derrick May .10
288 Dave Winfield .30
289 Curt Schilling .10
290 Carlos Quintana .10
291 Bob Natal .10
292 David Cone .15
293 Al Osuna .10
294 Bob Hamelin .10
295 Chad Curtis .10
296 Danny Jackson .10
297 Bob Welch .10
298 Felix Jose .10
299 Jay Buhner .10
300 Joe Carter .10
301 Kenny Lofton .40
302 *Kirk Rueter* .15
303 Kim Batiste .10
304 Mike Morgan .10
305 Pat Borders .10
306 Rene Arocha .10
307 Ruben Sierra .10
308 Steve Finley .10
309 Travis Fryman .10
310 Zane Smith .10
311 Willie Wilson .10
312 Trevor Hoffman .15
313 Terry Pendleton .10
314 Salomon Torres .10
315 Robin Ventura .15
316 Randy Tomlin .10
317 Dave Stewart .10
318 Mike Benjamin .10
319 Matt Turner .10
320 Manny Ramirez 1.00
321 Kevin Young .10
322 Ken Caminiti .15
323 Joe Girardi .10
324 Jeff McKnight .10
325 Gene Harris .10
326 Devon White .10
327 Darryl Kile .10
328 Craig Paquette .10
329 Cal Eldred .10
330 Bill Swift .10
331 Alan Trammell .10
332 Armando Reynoso .10
333 Brent Mayne .10
334 Chris Donnels .10
335 Darryl Strawberry .15
336 Dean Palmer .10
337 Frank Castillo .10
338 Jeff King .10
339 John Franco .10
340 Kevin Appier .10
341 Lance Blankenship .10
342 Mark McLemore .10
343 Pedro Astacio .10
344 Rich Batchelor .10
345 Ryan Bowen .10
346 Terry Steinbach .10
347 Troy O'Leary .10
348 Willie Blair .10
349 Wade Boggs .35
350 Tim Raines .15
351 Scott Livingstone .10
352 Rod Carreia .10
353 Ray Lankford .15
354 Pat Listach .10
355 Milt Thompson .10

356 Miguel Jimenez .10
357 Marc Newfield .10
358 Mark McGwire 3.00
359 Kirby Puckett .75
360 Kent Mercker .10
361 John Kruk .10
362 Jeff Kent .10
363 Hal Morris .10
364 Edgar Martinez .10
365 Dave Magadan .10
366 Dante Bichette .20
367 Chris Hammond .10
368 Bret Saberhagen .10
369 Billy Ripken .10
370 Bill Gullickson .10
371 Andre Dawson .15
372 Bobby Kelly .10
373 Cal Ripken, Jr. 2.50
374 Craig Biggio .25
375 Dan Pasqua .10
376 Dave Nilsson .10
377 Duane Ward .10
378 Greg Vaughn .15
379 Jeff Fassero .10
380 Jerry Dipoto .10
381 John Patterson .10
382 Kevin Brown .10
383 Kevin Roberson .10
384 Joe Orsulak .10
385 Hilly Hathaway .10
386 Mike Greenwell .10
387 Orestes Destrade .10
388 Mike Gallego .10
389 Ozzie Guillen .10
390 Raul Mondesi .40
391 Scott Lydy .10
392 Tom Urbani .10
393 Wil Cordero .10
394 Tony Longmire .10
395 Todd Zeile .10
396 Scott Cooper .10
397 Ryne Sandberg .60
398 Ricky Bones .10
399 Phil Clark .10
400 Orel Hershiser .15
401 Mike Henneman .10
402 Mark Lemke .10
403 Mark Grace .25
404 Ken Ryan .10
405 John Smoltz .15
406 Jeff Conine .10
407 Greg Harris .10
408 Doug Drabek .10
409 Dave Fleming .10
410 Danny Tartabull .10
411 Chad Kreuter .10
412 Brad Ausmus .10
413 Ben McDonald .10
414 Barry Larkin .25
415 Bret Barberie .10
416 Chuck Knoblauch .20
417 Ozzie Smith .50
418 Ed Sprague .10
419 Matt Williams .25
420 Jeremy Hernandez .10
421 Jose Bautista .10
422 Kevin Mitchell .10
423 Manuel Lee .10
424 Mike Devereaux .10
425 Omar Olivares .10
426 Rafael Belliard .10
427 Richie Lewis .10
428 Ron Darling .10
429 Shane Mack .10
430 Tim Hulett .10
431 Wally Joyner .15
432 Wes Chamberlain .10
433 Tom Browning .10
434 Scott Radinsky .10
435 Rondell White .25
436 Rod Beck .10
437 Rheal Cormier .10
438 Randy Johnson .75
439 Pete Schourek .10
440 Mo Vaughn .40
441 Mike Timlin .10
442 Mark Langston .10
443 Lou Whitaker .10
444 Kevin Stocker .10
445 Ken Hill .10
446 John Wetteland .10
447 J.T. Snow .15
448 Erik Pappas .10
449 David Hulse .10
450 Darren Daulton .10
451 Chris Hoiles .10
452 Bryan Harvey .10
453 Darren Lewis .10
454 Andres Galarraga .40
455 Joe Hesketh .10
456 Jose Valentin .10
457 Dan Peltier .10
458 Joe Boever .10
459 Kevin Rogers .10
460 Craig Shipley .10
461 Alvaro Espinoza .10
462 Wilson Alvarez .10
463 Cory Snyder .10
464 Candy Maldonado .10
465 Blas Minor .10
466 Rod Bolton .10
467 Kenny Rogers .10
468 Greg Myers .10
469 Jimmy Key .10
470 Tony Castillo .10
471 Mike Stanton .10
472 Deion Sanders .25
473 Tito Navarro .10
474 Mike Gardiner .10
475 Steve Reed .10
476 John Roper .10
477 Mike Trombley .10
478 Charles Nagy .10
479 Larry Casian .10
480 Eric Hillman .10
481 Bill Wertz .10
482 Jeff Schwarz .10
483 John Valentin .10
484 Carl Willis .10
485 Gary Gaetti .10
486 Bill Pecota .10
487 John Smiley .10
488 Mike Mussina .40
489 *Mike Ignasiak* .15
490 Billy Brewer .10
491 Jack Voigt .10
492 Mike Munoz .10
493 Lee Tinsley .10
494 Bob Wickman .10
495 Roger Salkeld .10
496 Thomas Howard .10
497 Mark Davis .10
498 Dave Clark .10
499 Turk Wendell .10
500 Rafael Bournigal .10
501 Chip Hale .10
502 Matt Whiteside .10
503 Brian Koelling .10
504 Jeff Reed .10
505 Paul Wagner .10
506 Torey Lovullo .10
507 Curtis Leskanic .10
508 Derek Lilliquist .10
509 Joe Magrane .10
510 Mackey Sasser .10
511 Lloyd McClendon .10
512 *Jayhawk Owens* .15
513 *Woody Williams* .15
514 Gary Redus .10
515 Tim Spehr .10
516 Jim Abbott .10
517 Lou Frazier .10
518 Erik Plantenberg .10
519 Tim Worrell .10
520 Brian McRae .10
521 *Chan Ho Park* 1.50
522 Mark Wohlers .10
523 Geronimo Pena .10
524 Andy Ashby .10
525 Tale of 2 Players (Tim Raines, Andre Dawson) .10
526 Tale of 2 Players (Paul Molitor, Dave Winfield) .35
527 Joe Carter (RBI Leader) .10
528 Frank Thomas (HR Leader) .75
529 Ken Griffey, Jr. (TB Leader) 1.50
530 Dave Justice (HR Leader) .10
531 Gregg Jefferies (AVG Leader) .10
532 Barry Bonds (HR Leader) .35
533 John Kruk (Quick Start) .10
534 Roger Clemens (Quick Start) .20
535 Cecil Fielder (Quick Start) .10
536 Ruben Sierra (Quick Start) .10
537 Tony Gwynn (Quick Start) .40
538 Tom Glavine (Quick Start) .10
539 Not issued, see #269
540 Not issued, see #270
541 Ozzie Smith (Career Leader) .25
542 Eddie Murray (Career Leader) .20
543a Lee Smith (Career Leader) .10
543b Lonnie Smith (should be #643) .10
544 Greg Maddux 1.50
545 Denis Boucher .10
546 Mark Gardner .10
547 Bo Jackson .15
548 Eric Anthony .10
549 Delino DeShields .10
550 Turner Ward .10
551 Scott Sanderson .10
552 Hector Carrasco .10
553 Tony Phillips .10
554 Melido Perez .10
555 Mike Felder .10
556 Jack Morris .10
557 Rafael Palmeiro .40
558 Shane Reynolds .10
559 Pete Incaviglia .10
560 Greg Harris .10
561 Matt Walbeck .10
562 Todd Van Poppel .10
563 Todd Stottlemyre .10
564 Ricky Bones .10
565 Mike Jackson .10
566 Kevin McReynolds .10
567 Melvin Nieves .10
568 Juan Gonzalez .75
569 Frank Viola .10
570 Vince Coleman .10
571 *Brian Anderson* .50
572 Omar Vizquel .10
573 Bernie Williams .50
574 Tom Glavine .25
575 Mitch Williams .10
576 Shawon Dunston .10
577 Mike Lansing .10
578 Greg Pirkl .10
579 Sid Fernandez .10
580 Doug Jones .10
581 Walt Weiss .10
582 Tim Belcher .10
583 Alex Fernandez .10
584 Alex Cole .10
585 Greg Cadaret .10
586 Bob Tewksbury .10
587 Dave Hansen .10
588 *Kurt Abbott* .25
589 *Rick White* .15
590 Kevin Bass .10
591 Geronimo Berroa .10
592 Jaime Navarro .10
593 Steve Farr .10
594 Jack Armstrong .10
595 Steve Howe .10
596 Jose Rijo .10
597 Otis Nixon .10
598 Robby Thompson .10
599 Kelly Stinnett .10
600 Carlos Delgado .50
601 *Brian Johnson* .15
602 Gregg Olson .10
603 Jim Edmonds .20
604 Mike Blowers .10
605 Lee Smith .10
606 Pat Rapp .10
607 Mike Magnante .10
608 Karl Rhodes .10
609 Jeff Juden .10
610 Rusty Meacham .10
611 Pedro Martinez .75
612 Todd Worrell .10
613 Stan Javier .10
614 Mike Hampton .10
615 Jose Guzman .10
616 Xavier Hernandez .10
617 David Wells .10
618 John Habyan .10
619 Chris Nabholz .10
620 Bobby Jones .15
621 Chris James .10
622 Ellis Burks .15
623 Erik Hanson .10
624 Pat Meares .10
625 Harold Reynolds .10
626 Bob Hamelin (Rookie Rocker) .10
627 Manny Ramirez (Rookie Rocker) .50
628 Ryan Klesko (Rookie Rocker) .15
629 Carlos Delgado (Rookie Rocker) .25
630 Javier Lopez (Rookie Rocker) .20
631 Steve Karsay (Rookie Rocket) .15
632 Rick Helling (Rookie Rocket) .10
633 Steve Trachsel (Rookie Rocket) .15
634 Hector Carrasco (Rookie Rocket) .10
635 Andy Stankiewicz .10
636 Paul Sorrento .10
637 Scott Erickson .10
638 Chipper Jones 2.00
639 Luis Polonia .10
640 Howard Johnson .10
641 John Dopson .10
642 Jody Reed .10
643 Not issued, see #543
644 Mark Portugal .10
645 Paul Molitor .50
646 Paul Assenmacher .10
647 Hubie Brooks .10
648 Gary Wayne .10
649 Sean Berry .10
650 Roger Clemens 1.00
651 Brian Hunter .10
652 Wally Whitehurst .10
653 Allen Watson .10
654 Rickey Henderson .35
655 Sid Bream .10
656 Dan Wilson .10
657 Ricky Jordan .10
658 Sterling Hitchcock .10
659 Darrin Jackson .10
660 Junior Felix .10
661 Tom Brunansky .10
662 Jose Vizcaino .10
663 Mark Leiter .10
664 Gil Heredia .10
665 Fred McGriff .30
666 Will Clark .30
667 Al Leiter .10
668 James Mouton .10
669 Billy Bean .10
670 Scott Leius .10
671 Bret Boone .10
672 Darren Holmes .10
673 Dave Weathers .10
674 Eddie Murray .25
675 Felix Fermin .10
676 Chris Sabo .10
677 Billy Spiers .10
678 Aaron Sele .10
679 Juan Samuel .10
680 Julio Franco .10
681 Heathcliff Slocumb .10
682 Denny Martinez .10
683 Jerry Browne .10
684 *Pedro A. Martinez* .10
685 Rex Hudler .10
686 Willie McGee .10
687 Andy Van Slyke .10
688 Pat Mahomes .10
689 Dave Henderson .10
690 Tony Eusebio .10
691 Rick Sutcliffe .10
692 Willie Banks .10
693 Alan Mills .10
694 Jeff Treadway .10
695 Alex Gonzalez .15
696 David Segui .10
697 Rick Helling .10
698 Bip Roberts .10
699 *Jeff Cirillo* .15
700 Terry Mulholland .10
701 Marvin Freeman .10
702 Jason Bere .10
703 Javier Lopez .25
704 Greg Hibbard .10
705 Tommy Greene .10
706 Marquis Grissom .10
707 Brian Harper .10
708 Steve Karsay .10
709 Jeff Brantley .10
710 Jeff Russell .10
711 Bryan Hickerson .10
712 *Jim Pittsley* .20

713	Bobby Ayala	.10
714	John Smoltz (Fantastic Finisher)	.10
715	Jose Rijo (Fantastic Finisher)	.10
716	Greg Maddux (Fantastic Finisher)	.75
717	Matt Williams (Fantastic Finisher)	.25
718	Frank Thomas (Fantastic Finisher)	.75
719	Ryne Sandberg (Fantastic Finisher)	.40
720	Checklist	.10

1994 Stadium Club Golden Rainbow

Found at the rate of one per pack, Stadium Club "Golden Rainbow" cards were issued for each of the 720 cards in the regular set. These inserts are distinguished by the use of gold prismatic foil highlights for the S.C. logo and box with the player's last name, instead of the red foil found on regular S.C. cards.

	MT
Complete Set (720):	150.00
Common Player:	.50
Stars:	3X

(See 1994 Stadium Club for checklist and base card values.)

1994 Stadium Club 1st Day Issue

A special silver-foil embossment designating "1st Day Issue" was placed on fewer than 2,000 of each of the 720 regular cards in the '94 Stadium Club set. Inserted at the rate of one per 24 foil packs and one per 15 jumbo packs, the cards are otherwise identical to the regular TSC cards.

	MT
Complete Set (720):	2000.
Common Player:	2.00
Stars:	15x

(See 1994 Stadium Club for checklist and base card values.)

1994 Stadium Club Dugout Dirt

Cartoons of some of baseball's top stars are featured on the backs of this 12-card insert set. Fronts are virtually identical in format to regular S.C. cards, except the logo and box with the player's last name are in gold-foil, rather than red. Stated odds of finding a Dugout Dirt insert card were one per six packs, on average. Cards can also be found with a gold "Members Only" seal on front.

		MT
Complete Set (12):		12.00
Common Player:		.25
1	Mike Piazza (Catch of the Day)	2.00
2	Dave Winfield (The Road to 3,000)	.50
3	John Kruk (From Coal Mine to Gold Mine)	.25
4	Cal Ripken, Jr. (On Track)	3.00
5	Jack McDowell (Chin Music)	.25
6	Barry Bonds (The Bonds Market)	1.00
7	Ken Griffey, Jr. (Gold Gloves/ All-Star)	4.00
8	Tim Salmon (The Salmon Run)	.35
9	Frank Thomas (Big Hurt)	2.00
10	Jeff Kent (Super Kent)	.25
11	Randy Johnson (High Heat)	.50
12	Darren Daulton (Daulton's Gym)	.25

1994 Stadium Club Finest

This insert set was included only in Series III packs of Topps Stadium Club, at the rate of one card per six packs, on average. Cards utilize Topps Finest technology and feature a player action photo on front, set against a red-and-gold sunburst background. Backs have a player portrait photo, a few stats and appropriate logos. Cards can also be found with a "Members Only" logo on front.

		MT
Complete Set (10):		25.00
Common Player:		1.00
1	Jeff Bagwell	2.50
2	Albert Belle	2.00
3	Barry Bonds	2.50
4	Juan Gonzalez	4.00
5	Ken Griffey, Jr.	10.00
6	Marquis Grissom	1.00
7	David Justice	1.00
8	Mike Piazza	5.00
9	Tim Salmon	1.50
10	Frank Thomas	4.00

1994 Stadium Club Finest Jumbo

Found only as a one per tub insert in special Wal-Mart repackaging of baseball packs, these 5" x 7" versions of the Series III Stadium Club inserts are identical to the smaller version. Cards utilize Topps Finest technology and feature a player action photo on front, set against a red-and-gold sunburst background. Backs have a player portrait photo, a few stats and appropriate logos.

		MT
Complete Set (10):		125.00
Common Player:		10.00
1	Jeff Bagwell	15.00
2	Albert Belle	12.00
3	Barry Bonds	15.00
4	Juan Gonzalez	15.00
5	Ken Griffey, Jr.	30.00
6	Marquis Grissom	10.00
7	David Justice	12.00
8	Mike Piazza	25.00
9	Tim Salmon	10.00
10	Frank Thomas	15.00

1994 Stadium Club Super Teams

Withs its football card issue the previous year, Topps Stadium Club debuted the idea of an insert card set whose value rose and fell with the on-field performance of each team. Super Team cards were issued for each of the 28 major league teams and inserted at the rate of one per 24 regular packs and one per 15 jumbo packs. At the end of the 1995 season (the promotion was carried over when the 1994 season was ended prematurely by the players' strike), persons holding Super Team cards of the divisions winners, league champions and World Champions could redeem the cards for prizes. Division winning team cards could be redeemed for a set of 10 S.C. cards of that team with a special division winner embossed logo. League champion cards could be redeemed for a set of 10 Master Photos of the team with a special league logo embossed. Persons with a Super Team card of the eventual World Series champion could trade the card in for a complete set of Stadium Club cards embossed with a World's Champion logo. Each of the Super Team cards features a small group of players on the front with the Super Team Card and S.C. logos in gold foil, and the team name in prismatic foil. Backs contain redemption rules. A version of the Super Team cards was distributed with "Members Only" sets containing such an indicia on front and team roster on back.

		MT
Complete Set (28):		50.00
Common Team:		1.50
Expired Jan. 31, 1996		
1	Atlanta Braves	10.00
2	Chicago Cubs	1.50
3	Cincinnati Reds	2.50
4	Colorado Rockies	2.00
5	Florida Marlins	1.50
6	Houston Astros	2.00
7	Los Angeles Dodgers	3.00
8	Montreal Expos	2.00
9	New York Mets	1.50
10	Philadelphia Phillies	1.50
11	Pittsburgh Pirates	1.50
12	St. Louis Cardinals	1.50
13	San Diego Padres	1.50
14	San Francisco Giants	2.50
15	Baltimore Orioles	2.50
16	Boston Red Sox	2.00
17	California Angels	1.50
18	Chicago White Sox	3.00
19	Cleveland Indians	4.00
20	Detroit Tigers	1.50
21	Kansas City Royals	2.00
22	Milwaukee Brewers	1.50
23	Minnesota Twins	2.00
24	New York Yankees	2.00
25	Oakland Athletics	2.00
26	Seattle Mariners	4.00
27	Texas Rangers	2.00
28	Toronto Blue Jays	2.00

1994 Stadium Club Superstar Sampler

A small, round black-and-white "Topps Superstar Sampler" logo printed on the back is all that distinguishes these cards from regular-issue S.C. cards. This version of 45 of the top stars from the Stadium Club set was issued only in three-card cello packs inserted into 1994 Topps retail factory sets. The packs also contained the same player's cards from the Bowman and Finest sets, similarly marked.

		MT
Complete Set (45):		200.00
Common Player:		2.50
4	Gary Sheffield	3.50
10	Roberto Alomar	5.00
24	Jack McDowell	2.50
25	Cecil Fielder	2.50
36	Tim Salmon	3.00
59	Bobby Bonilla	2.50
85	Ken Griffey Jr.	25.00
94	Dave Justice	3.50
108	Jeff Bagwell	8.00
109	Gregg Jefferies	3.00
127	Cliff Floyd	2.50
140	Mike Piazza	15.00
151	Tony Gwynn	7.50
165	Len Dykstra	2.50
169	Carlos Baerga	2.50
171	Jose Canseco	6.00
195	Don Mattingly	10.00
203	Will Clark	3.50
208	Rafael Palmeiro	3.50
219	Albert Belle	5.00
228	John Olerud	3.00
238	Barry Bonds	10.00
280	Larry Walker	3.50
285	Frank Thomas	15.00
300	Joe Carter	2.50
320	Manny Ramirez	6.00
359	Kirby Puckett	7.50
373	Cal Ripken Jr.	20.00
390	Raul Mondesi	3.50
397	Ryne Sandberg	10.00
403	Mark Grace	4.50
414	Barry Larkin	3.00
419	Matt Williams	3.00
438	Randy Johnson	3.50
440	Mo Vaughn	3.00
450	Darren Daulton	2.50
454	Andres Galarraga	3.00
544	Greg Maddux	15.00
568	Juan Gonzalez	7.50
574	Tom Glavine	3.00
645	Paul Molitor	4.50
650	Roger Clemens	6.00
665	Fred McGriff	3.50
687	Andy Van Slyke	2.50
706	Marquis Grissom	2.50

1994 Stadium Club Draft Picks

Produced well after the end of the strike-truncated 1994 baseball season, this set was largely ignored by the hobby at the time of issue. The full-bleed card fronts feature up-close and personal poses of 1994's top draft picks in major league uniforms, giving the hobby a good first look at tomorrow's stars. A home plate design in an upper corner has "Draft '94 Pick" in gold-foil. The player's name is printed in gold foil down one of the sides. Backs are horizontally arranged and have a parti-colored background that includes standard scouting report phrases. There is another color portrait of the player at one end with his name and position printed above. At the opposite end are the team by which the player was drafted, a few biographical details, some amateur and pro career highlights and a box detailing how the team's other recent draft picks at that round have fared.

		MT
Complete Set (90):		22.00
Common Player:		.25
1	Jacob Shumate	.30
2	C.J. Nitkowski	.40
3	Doug Million	.25
4	Matt Smith	.35
5	Kevin Lovinger	.25
6	Alberto Castillo	.25
7	Mike Russell	.25
8	Dan Lock	.25
9	Tom Szimanski	.25
10	Aaron Boone	.45
11	Jayson Peterson	.25
12	Mark Johnson	.40
13	Cade Gaspar	.25
14	George Lombard	.75
15	Russ Johnson	.40
16	Travis Miller	.35
17	Jay Payton	.75
18	Brian Buchanan	.35
19	Jacob Cruz	.75
20	Gary Rath	.25
21	Ramon Castro	.25
22	Tommy Davis	.25
23	Tony Terry	.25
24	Jerry Whittaker	.25
25	Mike Darr	.50
26	Doug Webb	.25
27	Jason Camilli	.25
28	Brad Rigby	.25
29	Ryan Nye	.25
30	Carl Dale	.25
31	Andy Taulbee	.25
32	Trey Moore	.25
33	John Crowther	.25
34	Joe Giuliano	.25
35	Brian Rose	.25
36	Paul Failla	.25
37	Brian Meadows	.25
38	Oscar Robles	.25
39	Mike Metcalff	.25
40	Larry Barnes	.25
41	Paul Ottavinia	.25
42	Chris McBride	.25
43	Ricky Stone	.25
44	Billy Blythe	.25
45	Eddie Priest	.25
46	Scott Forster	.25
47	Eric Pickett	.25
48	Matt Beaumont	.25
49	Darrell Nicolas	.25
50	Mike Hampton	.25
51	Paul O'Malley	.25
52	Steve Shoemaker	.25
53	Jason Sikes	.25
54	Bryan Farson	.25
55	Yates Hall	.25
56	Troy Brohawn	.25
57	Dan Hower	.25
58	Clay Caruthers	.25
59	Pepe McNeal	.25
60	Ray Ricken	.25
61	Scott Shores	.25
62	Eddie Brooks	.25
63	Dave Kauflin	.25
64	David Meyer	.25
65	Geoff Blum	.25
66	Roy Marsh	.25
67	Ryan Beeney	.25
68	Derek Dukart	.25
69	Nomar Garciaparra	7.00
70	Jason Kelley	.25
71	Jesse Ibarra	.25
72	Bucky Buckles	.25
73	Mark Little	.25
74	Heath Murray	.25
75	Greg Morris	.25
76	Mike Halperin	.25
77	Wes Helms	.65
78	Ray Brown	.25
79	Kevin Brown	.65
80	Paul Konerko	1.00
81	Mike Thurman	.25
82	Paul Wilson	.65
83	Terrence Long	.50
84	Ben Grieve	2.00
85	Mark Farris	.50
86	Bret Wagner	.25
87	Dustin Hermanson	.60
88	Kevin Witt	.25
89	Corey Pointer	.25
90	Tim Grieve	.30

1994 Stadium Club Draft Picks First Day Issue

Identical to the regular-issue S.C. Draft Picks cards except for a silver-foil First Day Issue logo on front, this parallel set was found on the average of one card per six packs of S.C. Draft Picks.

	MT
Complete Set (90):	150.00
Common Player:	1.50
Stars:	6X

(See 1994 Stadium Club Draft Picks for checklist and base card values.)

1995 Stadium Club

Topps' upscale brand was issued for 1995 in three series of, respectively, 270, 225 and 135 cards. Fronts have borderless color photos with a gold-foil device at bottom holding the team logo. Also in gold are the player's name at bottom and the Stadium Club logo at top. Backs have another player photo at left with a pair of computer-enhanced close-ups above it. At right are bar graphs detailing the player's '94 stats and his skills rankings. A number of specially designed subsets - "Best Seat in the House, Cover Story, MLB Debut," etc., are spread throughout the issue, which also includes a full slate of chase cards depending on the series and packaging.

	MT
Complete Set (630):	55.00
Complete Series 1 (270):	20.00
Complete Series 2 (225):	20.00
Complete High Series (135):	15.00
Common Player:	.10
First Day Production (1-270) Comp. Set:	225.00
Common First Day Production:	.50
Stars:	10X
Ser. 2 Packs and 10 pe Factory Set	
Series 1 or 2 Pack (14):	2.25
Series 1 or 2 Wax Box (24):	40.00
Series 3 Pack (13):	2.50
Series 3 Wax Box (24):	45.00

No.	Player	MT
1	Cal Ripken Jr.	2.50
2	Bo Jackson	.15
3	Bryan Harvey	.10
4	Curt Schilling	.15
5	Bruce Ruffin	.10
6	Travis Fryman	.20
7	Jim Abbott	.10
8	David McCarty	.10
9	Gary Gaetti	.10
10	Roger Clemens	1.00
11	Carlos Garcia	.10
12	Lee Smith	.10
13	Bobby Ayala	.10
14	Charles Nagy	.15
15	Lou Frazier	.10
16	Rene Arocha	.10
17	Carlos Delgado	.75
18	Steve Finley	.10
19	Ryan Klesko	.30
20	Cal Eldred	.10
21	Rey Sanchez	.10
22	Ken Hill	.10
23	Benny Santiago	.10
24	Julian Tavarez	.10
25	Jose Vizcaino	.10
26	Andy Benes	.10
27	Mariano Duncan	.10
28	Checklist A	.10
29	Shawon Dunston	.10
30	Rafael Palmeiro	.40
31	Dean Palmer	.10
32	Andres Galarraga	.25
33	Joey Cora	.10
34	Mickey Tettleton	.10
35	Barry Larkin	.40
36	Carlos Baerga	.10
37	Orel Hershiser	.15
38	Jody Reed	.10
39	Paul Molitor	.40
40	Jim Edmonds	.25
41	Bob Tewksbury	.10
42	John Patterson	.10
43	Ray McDavid	.10
44	Zane Smith	.10
45	Bret Saberhagen	.10
46	Greg Maddux	1.00
47	Frank Thomas	1.00
48	Carlos Baerga	.10
49	Billy Spiers	.10
50	Stan Javier	.10
51	Rex Hudler	.10
52	Denny Hocking	.10
53	Todd Worrell	.10
54	Mark Clark	.10
55	Hipilito Pichardo	.10
56	Bob Wickman	.10
57	Raul Mondesi	.30
58	Steve Cooke	.10
59	Rod Beck	.10
60	Tim Davis	.10
61	Jeff Kent	.10
62	John Valentin	.10
63	Alex Arias	.10
64	Steve Reed	.10
65	Ozzie Smith	.50
66	Terry Pendleton	.10
67	Kenny Rogers	.10
68	Vince Coleman	.10
69	Tom Pagnozzi	.10
70	Roberto Alomar	.60
71	Darrin Jackson	.10
72	Dennis Eckersley	.10
73	Jay Buhner	.10
74	Darren Lewis	.10
75	Dave Weathers	.10
76	Matt Walbeck	.10
77	Brad Ausmus	.10
78	Danny Bautista	.10
79	Bob Hamelin	.10
80	Steve Traschel	.20
81	Ken Ryan	.10
82	Chris Turner	.10
83	David Segui	.10
84	Ben McDonald	.10
85	Wade Boggs	.35
86	John Vander Wal	.10
87	Sandy Alomar	.15
88	Ron Karkovice	.10
89	Doug Jones	.10
90	Gary Sheffield	.30
91	Ken Caminiti	.15
92	Chris Bosio	.10
93	Kevin Tapani	.10
94	Walt Weiss	.10
95	Erik Hanson	.10
96	Ruben Sierra	.10
97	Nomar Garciaparra	2.50
98	Terrence Long	.10
99	Jacob Shumate	.10
100	Paul Wilson	.15
101	Kevin Witt	.10
102	Paul Konerko	.20
103	Ben Grieve	1.00
104	*Mark Johnson*	.25
105	*Cade Gaspar*	.10
106	Mark Farris	.25
107	Dustin Hermanson	.15
108	*Scott Elarton*	.75
109	Doug Million	.10
110	Matt Smith	.10
111	*Brian Buchanan*	.20
112	*Jayson Peterson*	.20
113	Bret Wagner	.10
114	C.J. Nitkowski	.15
115	*Ramon Castro*	.15
116	Rafael Bournigal	.10
117	Jeff Fassero	.10
118	Bobby Bonilla	.15
119	Ricky Gutierrez	.10
120	Roger Pavlik	.10
121	Mike Greenwell	.10
122	Deion Sanders	.20
123	Charlie Hayes	.10
124	Paul O'Neill	.25
125	Jay Bell	.10
126	Royce Clayton	.10
127	Willie Banks	.10
128	Mark Wohlers	.10
129	Todd Jones	.10
130	Todd Stottlemyre	.10
131	Will Clark	.40
132	Wilson Alvarez	.10
133	Chili Davis	.10
134	Dave Burba	.10
135	Chris Hoiles	.10
136	Jeff Blauser	.10
137	Jeff Reboulet	.10
138	Bret Saberhagen	.10
139	Kirk Rueter	.10
140	Dave Nilsson	.10
141	Pat Borders	.10
142	Ron Darling	.10
143	Derek Bell	.10
144	Dave Hollins	.10
145	Juan Gonzalez	.75
146	Andre Dawson	.25
147	Jim Thome	.30
148	Larry Walker	.30
149	Mike Piazza	1.75
150	Mike Perez	.10
151	Steve Avery	.10
152	Dan Wilson	.10
153	Andy Van Slyke	.10
154	Junior Felix	.10
155	Jack McDowell	.10
156	Danny Tartabull	.10
157	Willie Blair	.10
158	William Van Landingham	.10
159	Robb Nen	.10
160	Lee Tinsley	.10
161	Ismael Valdes	.10
162	Juan Guzman	.10
163	Scott Servais	.10
164	Cliff Floyd	.15
165	Allen Watson	.10
166	Eddie Taubensee	.10
167	Scott Hemond	.10
168	Jeff Tackett	.10
169	Chad Curtis	.10
170	Rico Brogna	.10
171	Luis Polonia	.10
172	Checklist B	.10
173	Lance Johnson	.10
174	Sammy Sosa	1.50
175	Mike MacFarlane	.10
176	Darryl Hamilton	.10
177	Rick Aguilera	.10
178	Dave West	.10
179	Mike Gallego	.10
180	Marc Newfield	.10
181	Steve Buechele	.10
182	David Wells	.10
183	Tom Glavine	.25
184	Joe Girardi	.10
185	Craig Biggio	.25
186	Eddie Murray	.25
187	Kevin Gross	.10
188	Sid Fernandez	.10
189	John Franco	.10
190	Bernard Gilkey	.15
191	Matt Williams	.35
192	Darrin Fletcher	.10
193	Jeff Conine	.10
194	Ed Sprague	.10
195	Eduardo Perez	.10
196	Scott Livingstone	.10
197	Ivan Rodriguez	.75
198	Orlando Merced	.10
199	Ricky Bones	.10
200	Javier Lopez	.20
201	Miguel Jimenez	.10
202	Terry McGriff	.10
203	Mike Lieberthal	.15
204	David Cone	.15
205	Todd Hundley	.15
206	Ozzie Guillen	.10
207	Alex Cole	.10
208	Tony Phillips	.10
209	Jim Eisenreich	.10
210	Greg Vaughn	.15
211	Barry Larkin	.20
212	Don Mattingly	.50
213	Mark Grace	.15
214	Jose Canseco	.50
215	Joe Carter	.10
216	David Cone	.15
217	Sandy Alomar	.15
218	Al Martin	.10
219	Roberto Kelly	.10
220	Paul Sorrento	.10
221	Tony Fernandez	.10
222	Stan Belinda	.10
223	Mike Stanley	.10
224	Doug Drabek	.10
225	Todd Van Poppel	.10
226	Matt Mieske	.10
227	Tino Martinez	.15
228	Andy Ashby	.10
229	Midre Cummings	.10
230	Jeff Frye	.10
231	Hal Morris	.10
232	Jose Lind	.10
233	Shawn Green	.30
234	Rafael Belliard	.10
235	Randy Myers	.10
236	Frank Thomas	.50
237	Darren Daulton	.10
238	Sammy Sosa	.75
239	Cal Ripken Jr.	1.25
240	Jeff Bagwell	.40
241	Ken Griffey Jr.	2.50
242	Brett Butler	.10
243	Derrick May	.10
244	Pat Listach	.10
245	Mike Bordick	.10
246	Mark Langston	.10
247	Randy Velarde	.10
248	Julio Franco	.10
249	Chuck Knoblauch	.15
250	Bill Gullickson	.10
251	Dave Henderson	.10
252	Bret Boone	.10
253	Al Martin	.10
254	Armando Benitez	.10
255	Wil Cordero	.10
256	Al Leiter	.20
257	Luis Gonzalez	.20
258	Charlie O'Brien	.10
259	Tim Wallach	.10
260	Scott Sanders	.10
261	Tom Henke	.10
262	Otis Nixon	.10
263	Darren Daulton	.10
264	Manny Ramirez	1.00
265	Bret Barberie	.10
266	Mel Rojas	.10
267	John Burkett	.10
268	Brady Anderson	.20
269	John Roper	.10
270	Shane Reynolds	.10
271	Barry Bonds	.75
272	Alex Fernandez	.10
273	Brian McRae	.10
274	Todd Zeile	.10
275	Greg Swindell	.10
276	Johnny Ruffin	.10
277	Troy Neel	.10
278	Eric Karros	.10
279	John Hudek	.10
280	Thomas Howard	.10
281	Joe Carter	.10
282	Mike Devereaux	.10
283	Butch Henry	.10
284	Reggie Jefferson	.10
285	Mark Lemke	.10
286	Jeff Montgomery	.10
287	Ryan Thompson	.10
288	Paul Shuey	.10
289	Mark McGwire	3.00
290	Bernie Williams	.50
291	Mickey Morandini	.10
292	Scott Leius	.10
293	David Hulse	.10
294	Greg Gagne	.10
295	Moises Alou	.15
296	Geronimo Berroa	.10
297	Eddie Zambrano	.10
298	Alan Trammell	.15
299	Don Slaught	.10
300	Jose Rijo	.10
301	Joe Ausanio	.10
302	Tim Raines	.10
303	Melido Perez	.10
304	Kent Mercker	.10
305	James Mouton	.10
306	Luis Lopez	.10
307	Mike Kingery	.10
308	Willie Greene	.10
309	Cecil Fielder	.10
310	Scott Kamieniecki	.10
311	Mike Greenwell (Best Seat in the House)	.10
312	Bobby Bonilla (Best Seat in the House)	.10
313	Andres Galarraga (Best Seat in the House)	.10
314	Cal Ripken Jr. (Best Seat in the House)	1.25
315	Matt Williams (Best Seat in the House)	.25
316	Tom Pagnozzi (Best Seat in the House)	.10
317	Len Dykstra (Best Seat in the House)	.10
318	Frank Thomas (Best Seat in the House)	.50
319	Kirby Puckett (Best Seat in the House)	.40

No.	Player	Price
320	Mike Piazza (Best Seat in the House)	.75
321	Jason Jacome	.10
322	Brian Hunter	.10
323	Brent Gates	.10
324	Jim Converse	.10
325	Damion Easley	.10
326	Dante Bichette	.15
327	Kurt Abbott	.10
328	Scott Cooper	.10
329	Mike Henneman	.10
330	Orlando Miller	.10
331	John Kruk	.10
332	Jose Oliva	.10
333	Reggie Sanders	.10
334	Omar Vizquel	.20
335	Devon White	.10
336	Mike Morgan	.10
337	J.R. Phillips	.10
338	Gary DiSarcina	.10
339	Joey Hamilton	.15
340	Randy Johnson	.75
341	Jim Leyritz	.10
342	Bobby Jones	.10
343	Jaime Navarro	.10
344	Bip Roberts	.10
345	Steve Karsay	.10
346	Kevin Stocker	.10
347	Jose Canseco	.30
348	Bill Wegman	.10
349	Rondell White	.20
350	Mo Vaughn	.40
351	Joe Orsulak	.10
352	Pat Meares	.10
353	Albie Lopez	.10
354	Edgar Martinez	.10
355	Brian Jordan	.10
356	Tommy Greene	.10
357	Chuck Carr	.10
358	Pedro Astacio	.10
359	Russ Davis	.10
360	Chris Hammond	.10
361	Gregg Jefferies	.10
362	Shane Mack	.10
363	Fred McGriff	.30
364	Pat Rapp	.10
365	Bill Swift	.10
366	Checklist	.10
367	Robin Ventura	.15
368	Bobby Witt	.10
369	Karl Rhodes	.10
370	Eddie Williams	.10
371	John Jaha	.10
372	Steve Howe	.10
373	Leo Gomez	.10
374	Hector Fajardo	.10
375	Jeff Bagwell	.75
376	Mark Acre	.10
377	Wayne Kirby	.10
378	Mark Portugal	.10
379	Jesus Tavarez	.10
380	Jim Lindeman	.10
381	Don Mattingly	1.00
382	Trevor Hoffman	.15
383	Chris Gomez	.10
384	Garret Anderson	.10
385	Bobby Munoz	.10
386	Jon Lieber	.10
387	Rick Helling	.10
388	Marvin Freeman	.10
389	Juan Castillo	.10
390	Jeff Cirillo	.10
391	Sean Berry	.10
392	Hector Carrasco	.10
393	Mark Grace	.25
394	Pat Kelly	.10
395	Tim Naehring	.10
396	Greg Pirkl	.10
397	John Smoltz	.15
398	Robby Thompson	.10
399	Rick White	.10
400	Frank Thomas	1.00
401	Jeff Conine (Cover Story)	.10
402	Jose Valentin (Cover Story)	.10
403	Carlos Baerga (Cover Story)	.10
404	Rick Aguilera (Cover Story)	.10
405	Wilson Alvarez (Cover Story)	.10
406	Juan Gonzalez (Cover Story)	.40
407	Barry Larkin (Cover Story)	.10
408	Ken Hill (Cover Story)	.10
409	Chuck Carr (Cover Story)	.10
410	Tim Raines (Cover Story)	.10
411	Bryan Eversgerd	.10
412	Phil Plantier	.10
413	Josias Manzanillo	.10
414	Roberto Kelly	.10
415	Rickey Henderson	.30
416	John Smiley	.10
417	Kevin Brown	.10
418	Jimmy Key	.10
419	Wally Joyner	.15
420	Roberto Hernandez	.10
421	Felix Fermin	.10
422	Checklist	.10
423	Greg Vaughn	.15
424	Ray Lankford	.15
425	Greg Maddux	1.50
426	Mike Mussina	.40
427	Geronimo Pena	.10
428	David Nied	.10
429	Scott Erickson	.10
430	Kevin Mitchell	.10
431	Mike Lansing	.10
432	Brian Anderson	.15
433	Jeff King	.10
434	Ramon Martinez	.15
435	Kevin Seitzer	.10
436	Salomon Torres	.10
437	Brian Hunter	.10
438	Melvin Nieves	.10
439	Mike Kelly	.10
440	Marquis Grissom	.10
441	Chuck Finley	.10
442	Len Dykstra	.10
443	Ellis Burks	.10
444	Harold Baines	.10
445	Kevin Appier	.10
446	Dave Justice	.30
447	Darryl Kile	.10
448	John Olerud	.15
449	Greg McMichael	.10
450	Kirby Puckett	.75
451	Jose Valentin	.10
452	Rick Wilkins	.10
453	Arthur Rhodes	.10
454	Pat Hentgen	.10
455	Tom Gordon	.10
456	Tom Candiotti	.10
457	Jason Bere	.10
458	Wes Chamberlain	.10
459	Greg Colbrunn	.10
460	John Doherty	.10
461	Kevin Foster	.10
462	Mark Whiten	.10
463	Terry Steinbach	.10
464	Aaron Sele	.15
465	Kirt Manwaring	.10
466	Darren Hall	.10
467	Delino DeShields	.10
468	Andujar Cedeno	.10
469	Billy Ashley	.10
470	Kenny Lofton	.40
471	Pedro Munoz	.10
472	John Wetteland	.10
473	Tim Salmon	.20
474	Denny Neagle	.10
475	Tony Gwynn	1.00
476	Vinny Castilla	.10
477	Steve Dreyer	.10
478	Jeff Shaw	.10
479	Chad Ogea	.10
480	Scott Ruffcorn	.10
481	Lou Whitaker	.10
482	J.T. Snow	.10
483	Rich Rowland	.10
484	Dennis Martinez	.10
485	Pedro Martinez	.75
486	Rusty Greer	.10
487	Dave Fleming	.10
488	John Dettmer	.10
489	Albert Belle	.50
490	Ravelo Manzanillo	.10
491	Henry Rodriguez	.10
492	Andrew Lorraine	.15
493	Dwayne Hosey	.10
494	Mike Blowers	.10
495	Turner Ward	.10
496	Fred McGriff (Extreme Corps)	.20
497	Sammy Sosa (Extreme Corps)	.75
498	Barry Larkin (Extreme Corps)	.10
499	Andres Galarraga (Extreme Corps)	.10
500	Gary Sheffield (Extreme Corps)	.10
501	Jeff Bagwell (Extreme Corps)	.40
502	Mike Piazza (Extreme Corps)	.60
503	Moises Alou (Extreme Corps)	.10
504	Bobby Bonilla (Extreme Corps)	.10
505	Darren Daulton (Extreme Corps)	.10
506	Jeff King (Extreme Corps)	.10
507	Ray Lankford (Extreme Corps)	.10
508	Tony Gwynn (Extreme Corps)	.50
509	Barry Bonds (Extreme Corps)	.40
510	Cal Ripken Jr. (Extreme Corps)	1.25
511	Mo Vaughn (Extreme Corps)	.30
512	Tim Salmon (Extreme Corps)	.10
513	Frank Thomas (Extreme Corps)	.75
514	Albert Belle (Extreme Corps)	.40
515	Cecil Fielder (Extreme Corps)	.10
516	Kevin Appier (Extreme Corps)	.10
517	Greg Vaughn (Extreme Corps)	.10
518	Kirby Puckett (Extreme Corps)	.40
519	Paul O'Neill (Extreme Corps)	.10
520	Ruben Sierra (Extreme Corps)	.10
521	Ken Griffey Jr. (Extreme Corps)	1.25
522	Will Clark (Extreme Corps)	.25
523	Joe Carter (Extreme Corps)	.10
524	Antonio Osuna	.10
525	Glenallen Hill	.10
526	Alex Gonzalez	.10
527	Dave Stewart	.10
528	Ron Gant	.15
529	Jason Bates	.10
530	Mike Macfarlane	.10
531	Esteban Loaiza	.15
532	Joe Randa	.10
533	Dave Winfield	.25
534	Danny Darwin	.10
535	Pete Harnisch	.10
536	Joey Cora	.10
537	Jaime Navarro	.10
538	Marty Cordova	.15
539	Andujar Cedeno	.10
540	Mickey Tettleton	.10
541	Andy Van Slyke	.10
542	*Carlos Perez*	.20
543	Chipper Jones	2.00
544	Tony Fernandez	.10
545	Tom Henke	.10
546	Pat Borders	.10
547	Chad Curtis	.10
548	Ray Durham	.15
549	Joe Oliver	.10
550	Jose Mesa	.10
551	Steve Finley	.10
552	Otis Nixon	.10
553	Jacob Brumfield	.10
554	Bill Swift	.10
555	Quilvio Veras	.10
556	*Hideo Nomo*	1.50
557	Joe Vitiello	.10
558	Mike Perez	.10
559	Charlie Hayes	.10
560	*Brad Radke*	.20
561	Darren Bragg	.10
562	Orel Hershiser	.15
563	Edgardo Alfonzo	.15
564	Doug Jones	.10
565	Andy Pettitte	.30
566	Benito Santiago	.10
567	John Burkett	.10
568	Brad Clontz	.10
569	Jim Abbott	.10
570	Joe Rosselli	.10
571	*Mark Grudzielanek*	.75
572	Dustin Hermanson	.10
573	Benji Gil	.10
574	Mark Whiten	.10
575	Mike Ignasiak	.10
576	Kevin Ritz	.10
577	Paul Quantrill	.10
578	Andre Dawson	.15
579	Jerald Clark	.10
580	Frank Rodriguez	.10
581	Mark Kiefer	.10
582	Trevor Wilson	.10
583	*Gary Wilson*	.10
584	Andy Stankiewicz	.10
585	Felipe Lira	.10
586	*Mike Mimbs*	.15
587	Jon Nunnally	.10
588	*Tomas Perez*	.15
589	Checklist	.10
590	Todd Hollandsworth	.15
591	Roberto Petagine	.10
592	Mariano Rivera	.10
593	Mark McLemore	.10
594	Bobby Witt	.10
595	Jose Offerman	.10
596	Jason Christiansen	.10
597	Jeff Manto	.10
598	Jim Dougherty	.10
599	Juan Acevedo	.10
600	Troy O'Leary	.10
601	Ron Villone	.10
602	Tripp Cromer	.10
603	Steve Scarsone	.10
604	Lance Parrish	.10
605	Ozzie Timmons	.10
606	Ray Holbert	.10
607	Tony Phillips	.10
608	Phil Plantier	.10
609	Shane Andrews	.10
610	Heathcliff Slocumb	.10
611	*Bobby Higginson*	1.00
612	Bob Tewksbury	.10
613	Terry Pendleton	.10
614	Scott Cooper (Trans-Action)	.10
615	John Wetteland (Trans-Action)	.10
616	Ken Hill (Trans-Action)	.10
617	Marquis Grissom (Trans-Action)	.10
618	Larry Walker (Trans-Action)	.25
619	Derek Bell (Trans-Action)	.10
620	David Cone (Trans-Action)	.10
621	Ken Caminiti (Trans-Action)	.10
622	Jack McDowell (Trans-Action)	.10
623	Vaughn Eshelman (Trans-Action)	.10
624	Brian McRae (Trans-Action)	.10
625	Gregg Jefferies (Trans-Action)	.10
626	Kevin Brown (Trans-Action)	.10
627	Lee Smith (Trans-Action)	.10
628	Tony Tarasco (Trans-Action)	.10
629	Brett Butler (Trans-Action)	.10
630	Jose Canseco (Trans-Action)	.35

1995 Stadium Club 1st Day Pre-production

Stadium Club 1st Day Preproduction cards were randomly packed into one every 36 packs of Topps Series I baseball. The set of nine cards is only found in hobby packs.

		MT
Complete Set (9):		34.00
Common Player:		3.00
29	Shawon Dunston	2.00
39	Paul Molitor	7.50
79	Bob Hamelin	2.00
96	Ruben Sierra	2.00
131	Will Clark	4.00
149	Mike Piazza	12.00
153	Andy Van Slyke	2.00
166	Jeff Tackett	2.00
197	Ivan Rodriguez	6.00

1995 Stadium Club 1st Day Issue

Series II hobby packs of Topps baseball featured a chase set of Stadium Club 1st Day Issue cards, #1-270. The FDI cards have a small gold embossed seal on front. Cards were seeded on an average of one per six packs. Ten FDI cards were also randomly inserted in each Factory set.

	MT
Complete Set (270):	225.00
Common Player:	.50
Stars:	10X

(See 1995 Stadium Club #1-270 for checklist and base card values.)

1995 Stadium Club Clear Cut

Among the most technically advanced of 1995's insert cards is the Clear Cut chase set found in Series I and II packs. Cards feature a color player action photo printed on see-through plastic. There is a rainbow-hued trapezoid behind the player with an overall background tinted in blue, green and gold. The player's name is in white in a vertical blue bar at right. Backs have a few stats and data in a blue bar vertically at left. Each of the cards can also be found in a version with the round Members Only seal embossed into the plastic at lower-left.

		MT
Complete Set (28):		80.00
Common Player:		1.00
1	Mike Piazza	10.00
2	Ruben Sierra	1.00
3	Tony Gwynn	6.00
4	Frank Thomas	8.00
5	Fred McGriff	2.50
6	Rafael Palmeiro	3.00
7	Bobby Bonilla	1.00
8	Chili Davis	1.00
9	Hal Morris	1.00
10	Jose Canseco	3.00
11	Jay Bell	1.00
12	Kirby Puckett	6.00
13	Gary Sheffield	2.00
14	Bob Hamelin	1.00
15	Jeff Bagwell	6.00
16	Albert Belle	4.00
17	Sammy Sosa	10.00
18	Ken Griffey Jr.	15.00
19	Todd Zeile	1.00
20	Mo Vaughn	2.00
21	Moises Alou	1.25
22	Paul O'Neill	1.50
23	Andres Galarraga	1.25
24	Greg Vaughn	1.00
25	Len Dykstra	1.00
26	Joe Carter	1.00
27	Barry Bonds	5.00
28	Cecil Fielder	1.00

1995 Stadium Club Crunch Time

Series I rack packs were the exclusive provenance of these cards featuring baseball's top run creators. Fronts are printed on rainbow prismatic foil. The central color action photo is repeated as an enlarged background photo, along with a team logo. At bottom in gold foil are the player name and Crunch Time logo. Backs have a positive and a negative image of the same photo as background to a pie chart and stats relative to the player's runs-created stats.

		MT
Complete Set (20):		30.00
Common Player:		1.00
1	Jeff Bagwell	2.50
2	Kirby Puckett	3.00
3	Frank Thomas	4.00
4	Albert Belle	1.50
5	Julio Franco	1.00
6	Jose Canseco	1.50
7	Paul Molitor	2.00
8	Joe Carter	1.00
9	Ken Griffey Jr.	8.00
10	Larry Walker	1.50
11	Dante Bichette	1.00
12	Carlos Baerga	1.00
13	Fred McGriff	1.50
14	Ruben Sierra	1.00
15	Will Clark	1.50
16	Moises Alou	1.00
17	Rafael Palmeiro	1.50
18	Travis Fryman	1.00
19	Barry Bonds	2.50
20	Cal Ripken Jr.	6.00

1995 Stadium Club Crystal Ball

Multi-colored swirls around a clear central circle with the player's photo, all printed on foil, are the front design for this Series III insert. Backs have a portrait photo in a floating crystal ball image at one side. At the other end are year-by-year minor league stats and a few words about each of the player's seasons. This insert was also produced in an edition of 4,000 bearing a gold-foil "Members Only" seal, sold in complete Stadium Club Members Only factory sets.

		MT
Complete Set (15):		55.00
Common Player:		2.00
1	Chipper Jones	20.00
2	Dustin Hermanson	2.00
3	Ray Durham	3.00
4	Phil Nevin	2.00
5	Billy Ashley	2.00
6	Shawn Green	6.00
7	Jason Bates	2.00
8	Benji Gil	2.00
9	Marty Cordova	2.00
10	Quilvio Veras	2.00
11	Mark Grudzielanek	3.00
12	Ruben Rivera	2.00
13	Bill Pulsipher	2.00
14	Derek Jeter	25.00
15	LaTroy Hawkins	2.00

1995 Stadium Club Power Zone

The performance in several parks around the league is chronicled on the back of these Series III inserts. Fronts are printed on foil and feature a player swinging into an exploding asteroid. His name is printed vertically down one side in prismatic glitter foil. Backs also have a portrait photo and a baseball with a weird red and green vapor trail. A special edition of 4,000 each of these inserts was included with the purchase of Stadium Club Members Only factory sets; those cards have an embossed gold-foil seal on front.

		MT
Complete Set (12):		55.00
Common Player:		1.50
1	Jeff Bagwell	6.00
2	Albert Belle	4.00
3	Barry Bonds	5.00
4	Joe Carter	1.50
5	Cecil Fielder	1.50
6	Andres Galarraga	1.50
7	Ken Griffey Jr.	15.00
8	Paul Molitor	3.00
9	Fred McGriff	2.00
10	Rafael Palmeiro	2.50
11	Frank Thomas	6.00
12	Matt Williams	1.50

1995 Stadium Club Ring Leaders

With a background that looks like an explosion at a jewelry factory, these cards feature players who have won championship, All-Star or other award rings. Fronts are foil-printed with a player action photo on a background of flying rings and stars, and, - for some reason - an attacking eagle. Backs repeat the background motif, have a player portrait in an oval frame at top-left, photos of some of his rings and a list of rings won. Cards were random inserts in both Series I and II; complete sets could also be won in Stadium Clug's phone card insert contest. A version with the Members Only gold seal was also issued for each.

		MT
Complete Set (40):		165.00
Common Player:		1.25
1	Jeff Bagwell	9.00
2	Mark McGwire	20.00
3	Ozzie Smith	5.00
4	Paul Molitor	5.00
5	Darryl Strawberry	1.50
6	Eddie Murray	3.00
7	Tony Gwynn	9.00
8	Jose Canseco	3.00
9	Howard Johnson	1.25
10	Andre Dawson	1.25
11	Matt Williams	2.00
12	Tim Raines	1.25
13	Fred McGriff	2.00
14	Ken Griffey Jr.	20.00
15	Gary Sheffield	2.00
16	Dennis Eckersley	1.25
17	Kevin Mitchell	1.25
18	Will Clark	1.75
19	Darren Daulton	1.25
20	Paul O'Neill	1.50
21	Julio Franco	1.25
22	Albert Belle	6.00
23	Juan Gonzalez	5.00
24	Kirby Puckett	9.00
25	Joe Carter	1.25
26	Frank Thomas	10.00
27	Cal Ripken Jr.	17.50
28	John Olerud	2.00
29	Ruben Sierra	1.25
30	Barry Bonds	5.00
31	Cecil Fielder	1.25
32	Roger Clemens	5.00
33	Don Mattingly	12.00
34	Terry Pendleton	1.25
35	Rickey Henderson	2.50
36	Dave Winfield	2.50
37	Edgar Martinez	1.25
38	Wade Boggs	3.00
39	Willie McGee	1.25
40	Andres Galarraga	1.25

1995 Stadium Club Super Skills

These random hobby pack inserts in both Series I and II are printed on rainbow prismatic foil which features as a background an enlarged version of the front photo. The S.C. and Super Skills logos are printed in gold foil in opposite corners, while the player's name is in blue at bottom-right. Backs repeat the enlarged background image of a close-up foreground photo, while a few choice words about the player's particular specialties are in white at left. Each card can also be found in a version featuring the Members Only gold-foil seal on front.

		MT
Complete Set (20):		55.00
Complete Series 1 (9):		25.00
Complete Series 2 (11):		30.00
Common Player:		1.50
1	Roberto Alomar	5.00
2	Barry Bonds	7.50
3	Jay Buhner	2.00
4	Chuck Carr	1.50
5	Don Mattingly	10.00
6	Raul Mondesi	3.00
7	Tim Salmon	2.00
8	Deion Sanders	2.50
9	Devon White	1.50
10	Mark Whiten	1.50
11	Ken Griffey Jr.	25.00
12	Marquis Grissom	2.00
13	Paul O'Neill	2.00
14	Kenny Lofton	3.00
15	Larry Walker	2.50
16	Scott Cooper	1.50
17	Barry Larkin	2.00
18	Matt Williams	2.00
19	John Wetteland	1.50
20	Randy Johnson	4.00

1995 Stadium Club Virtual Reality

A partial parallel set found one per foil pack, two per rack pack, these cards share the basic front and back with the corresponding card in the regular S.C. issue. On front, however, is a "Virtual Reality" seal around the team logo at bottom (gold foil in Series I, silver-foil in Series II). Backs differ in that instead of actual 1994 season stats, they present a bar graph of computer projected stats representing full 162-game season instead of the strike-shortened reality. Each of these inserts can also be found in a version bearing the round gold- (Series I) or silver-foil (Series II) Members Only seal on the front.

		MT
Complete Set (270):		80.00
Complete Series I (135):		40.00
Complete Series II (135):		40.00
Common Player:		.25
1	Cal Ripken Jr.	7.50
2	Travis Fryman	.25
3	Jim Abbott	.25
4	Gary Gaetti	.25
5	Roger Clemens	2.00
6	Carlos Garcia	.25
7	Lee Smith	.25
8	Bobby Ayala	.25
9	Charles Nagy	.25
10	Rene Arocha	.25
11	Carlos Delgado	.75
12	Steve Finley	.25
13	Ryan Klesko	.50
14	Cal Eldred	.25
15	Rey Sanchez	.25
16	Ken Hill	.25
17	Jose Vizcaino	.25
18	Andy Benes	.25
19	Shawon Dunston	.25
20	Rafael Palmeiro	.50
21	Dean Palmer	.25
22	Joey Cora	.25
23	Mickey Tettleton	.25
24	Barry Larkin	.35
25	Carlos Baerga	.25
26	Orel Hershiser	.25
27	Jody Reed	.25
28	Paul Molitor	1.50
29	Jim Edmonds	.25
30	Bob Tewksbury	.25
31	Ray McDavid	.25
32	Stan Javier	.25
33	Todd Worrell	.25
34	Bob Wickman	.25
35	Raul Mondesi	1.00
36	Rod Beck	.25
37	Jeff Kent	.25
38	John Valentin	.25
39	Ozzie Smith	1.50
40	Terry Pendleton	.25
41	Kenny Rogers	.25
42	Vince Coleman	.25
43	Roberto Alomar	1.50
44	Darrin Jackson	.25
45	Dennis Eckersley	.25
46	Jay Buhner	.25
47	Dave Weathers	.25
48	Danny Bautista	.25
49	Bob Hamelin	.25
50	Steve Trachsel	.25
51	Ben McDonald	.25
52	Wade Boggs	.75
53	Sandy Alomar	.30
54	Ron Karkovice	.25
55	Doug Jones	.25
56	Gary Sheffield	1.00
57	Ken Caminiti	.75
58	Kevin Tapani	.25
59	Ruben Sierra	.25
60	Bobby Bonilla	.25
61	Deion Sanders	1.00
62	Charlie Hayes	.25
63	Paul O'Neill	.30
64	Jay Bell	.25
65	Todd Jones	.25
66	Todd Stottlemyre	.25
67	Will Clark	1.00
68	Wilson Alvarez	.25
69	Chili Davis	.25
70	Chris Hoiles	.25
71	Bret Saberhagen	.25
72	Dave Nilsson	.25
73	Derek Bell	.25
74	Juan Gonzalez	2.50
75	Andre Dawson	.35
76	Jim Thome	.60
77	Larry Walker	.60
78	Mike Piazza	5.00
79	Dan Wilson	.25
80	Junior Felix	.25
81	Jack McDowell	.25
82	Danny Tartabull	.25
83	William Van Landingham	.25
84	Robb Nen	.25
85	Ismael Valdes	.25
86	Juan Guzman	.25
87	Cliff Floyd	.25
88	Rico Brogna	.25
89	Luis Polonia	.25
90	Lance Johnson	.25
91	Sammy Sosa	5.00
92	Dave West	.25
93	Tom Glavine	.35
94	Joe Girardi	.25
95	Craig Biggio	.35
96	Eddie Murray	.75
97	Kevin Gross	.25
98	John Franco	.25
99	Matt Williams	.75
100	Darrin Fletcher	.25
101	Jeff Conine	.25
102	Ed Sprague	.25
103	Ivan Rodriguez	1.50
104	Orlando Merced	.25
105	Ricky Bones	.25
106	David Cone	.40
107	Todd Hundley	.40
108	Alex Cole	.25
109	Tony Phillips	.25
110	Jim Eisenreich	.25
111	Paul Sorrento	.25
112	Mike Stanley	.25
113	Doug Drabek	.25
114	Matt Mieske	.25
115	Tino Martinez	.30
116	Midre Cummings	.25
117	Hal Morris	.25
118	Shawn Green	.35
119	Randy Myers	.25
120	Ken Griffey Jr.	10.00
121	Brett Butler	.25
122	Julio Franco	.25
123	Chuck Knoblauch	.50
124	Bret Boone	.25
125	Wil Cordero	.25
126	Luis Gonzalez	.25
127	Tim Wallach	.25
128	Scott Sanders	.25
129	Tom Henke	.25
130	Otis Nixon	.25
131	Darren Daulton	.25
132	Manny Ramirez	2.00
133	Bret Barberie	.25
134	Brady Anderson	.35
135	Shane Reynolds	.25
136	Barry Bonds	2.00
137	Alex Fernandez	.25
138	Brian McRae	.25
139	Todd Zeile	.25
140	Greg Swindell	.25
141	Troy Neel	.25
142	Eric Karros	.25
143	John Hudek	.25
144	Joe Carter	.25
145	Mike Devereaux	.25
146	Butch Henry	.25
147	Mark Lemke	.25
148	Jeff Montgomery	.25
149	Ryan Thompson	.25
150	Bernie Williams	.75
151	Scott Leius	.25
152	Greg Gagne	.25
153	Moises Alou	.25
154	Geronimo Berroa	.25
155	Alan Trammell	.25
156	Don Slaught	.25
157	Jose Rijo	.25
158	Tim Raines	.25
159	Melido Perez	.25
160	Kent Mercker	.25
161	James Mouton	.25
162	Luis Lopez	.25
163	Mike Kingery	.25
164	Cecil Fielder	.25
165	Scott Kamieniecki	.25
166	Brent Gates	.25
167	Jason Jacome	.25
168	Dante Bichette	.75
169	Kurt Abbott	.25
170	Mike Henneman	.25

171	John Kruk	.25
172	Jose Oliva	.25
173	Reggie Sanders	.35
174	Omar Vizquel	.25
175	Devon White	.25
176	Mark McGwire	10.00
177	Gary DiSarcina	.25
178	Joey Hamilton	.25
179	Randy Johnson	1.00
180	Jim Leyritz	.25
181	Bobby Jones	.25
182	Bip Roberts	.25
183	Jose Canseco	.75
184	Mo Vaughn	1.00
185	Edgar Martinez	.25
186	Tommy Greene	.25
187	Chuck Carr	.25
188	Pedro Astacio	.25
189	Shane Mack	.25
190	Fred McGriff	.75
191	Pat Rapp	.25
192	Bill Swift	.25
193	Robin Ventura	.35
194	Bobby Witt	.25
195	Steve Howe	.25
196	Leo Gomez	.25
197	Hector Fajardo	.25
198	Jeff Bagwell	2.50
199	Rondell White	.40
200	Don Mattingly	2.50
201	Trevor Hoffman	.25
202	Chris Gomez	.25
203	Bobby Munoz	.25
204	Marvin Freeman	.25
205	Sean Berry	.25
206	Mark Grace	.40
207	Pat Kelly	.25
208	Eddie Williams	.25
209	Frank Thomas	4.00
210	Bryan Eversgerd	.25
211	Phil Plantier	.25
212	Roberto Kelly	.25
213	Rickey Henderson	.50
214	John Smiley	.25
215	Kevin Brown	.30
216	Jimmy Key	.25
217	Wally Joyner	.25
218	Roberto Hernandez	.25
219	Felix Fermin	.25
220	Greg Vaughn	.25
221	Ray Lankford	.30
222	Greg Maddux	5.00
223	Mike Mussina	1.00
224	David Nied	.25
225	Scott Erickson	.25
226	Kevin Mitchell	.25
227	Brian Anderson	.25
228	Jeff King	.25
229	Ramon Martinez	.25
230	Kevin Seitzer	.25
231	Marquis Grissom	.25
232	Chuck Finley	.25
233	Len Dykstra	.25
234	Ellis Burks	.25
235	Harold Baines	.25
236	Kevin Appier	.25
237	Dave Justice	.40
238	Darryl Kile	.25
239	John Olerud	.35
240	Greg McMichael	.25
241	Kirby Puckett	2.00
242	Jose Valentin	.25
243	Rick Wilkins	.25
244	Pat Hentgen	.25
245	Tom Gordon	.25
246	Tom Candiotti	.25
247	Jason Bere	.25
248	Wes Chamberlain	.25
249	Jeff Cirillo	.25
250	Kevin Foster	.25
251	Mark Whiten	.25
252	Terry Steinbach	.25
253	Aaron Sele	.25
254	Kirt Manwaring	.25
255	Delino DeShields	.25
256	Andujar Cedeno	.25
257	Kenny Lofton	1.00
258	John Wetteland	.25
259	Tim Salmon	.40
260	Denny Neagle	.25
261	Tony Gwynn	2.50
262	Lou Whitaker	.25
263	J.T. Snow	.25
264	Dennis Martinez	.25
265	Pedro Martinez	.40
266	Rusty Greer	.25
267	Dave Fleming	.25
268	John Dettmer	.25
269	Albert Belle	1.50
270	Henry Rodriguez	.25

1995 Stadium Club VR Extremist

A huge silver-blue metallic baseball separates the player from the background of the photo in this Series II insert found only in rack packs. A blue sky and clouds provides the front border. The player rises out of the clouds in a back photo in the foreground of which are some pie-in-the-sky stats. The metallic baseball is also repeated on the back, with the player's name in orange script on the sweet spot. Each card was also issued in the Members Only boxed set in a version with a round silver-foil Members Only seal on front. Cards are numbered with a "VRE" prefix.

		MT
Complete Set (10):		80.00
Common Player:		2.00
1	Barry Bonds	8.00
2	Ken Griffey Jr.	30.00
3	Jeff Bagwell	8.00
4	Albert Belle	6.00
5	Frank Thomas	12.00
6	Tony Gwynn	10.00
7	Kenny Lofton	4.00
8	Deion Sanders	4.00
9	Ken Hill	2.00
10	Jimmy Key	2.00

1996 Stadium Club

Consisting of 450 cards in a pair of 225-card series, Stadium Club continued Topps' 1996 tribute to Mickey Mantle with 19 Retrospective inserts. Cards feature full-bleed photos with gold-foil graphic highlights. Backs offer a TSC Skills Matrix along with another player photo, some biographical data and stats. Team TSC is the only subset with 45 cards each in Series 1 and 2. Stadium Club was issued in retail and hobby packs, with inserts found at differing ratios in each type of packaging.

		MT
Complete Set (450):		60.00
Common Player:		.10
Series 1 or 2 Pack (10):		2.00
Series 1 or 2 Wax Box (24):		40.00
1	Hideo Nomo (Extreme Player)	.50
2	Paul Molitor	.40
3	Garret Anderson (Extreme Player)	.15
4	Jose Mesa (Extreme Player)	.10
5	Vinny Castilla (Extreme Player)	.15
6	Mike Mussina (Extreme Player)	.40
7	Ray Durham (Extreme Player)	.10
8	Jack McDowell (Extreme Player)	.10
9	Juan Gonzalez (EP)	1.00
10	Chipper Jones (Extreme Player)	2.00
11	Deion Sanders (Extreme Player)	.25
12	Rondell White (Extreme Player)	.15
13	Tom Henke (Extreme Player)	.10
14	Derek Bell (Extreme Player)	.10
15	Randy Myers (Extreme Player)	.10
16	Randy Johnson (Extreme Player)	.40
17	Len Dykstra (Extreme Player)	.10
18	Bill Pulsipher (Extreme Player)	.10
19	Greg Colbrunn	.10
20	David Wells	.15
21	Chad Curtis (Extreme Player)	.10
22	Roberto Hernandez (Extreme Player)	.10
23	Kirby Puckett (Extreme Player)	1.00
24	Joe Vitiello	.10
25	Roger Clemens (Extreme Player)	1.50
26	Al Martin	.10
27	Chad Ogea	.10
28	David Segui	.10
29	Joey Hamilton	.10
30	Dan Wilson	.10
31	Chad Fonville (Extreme Player)	.15
32	Bernard Gilkey (Extreme Player)	.15
33	Kevin Seitzer	.10
34	Shawn Green (Extreme Player)	.25
35	Rick Aguilera (Extreme Player)	.10
36	Gary DiSarcina	.10
37	Jaime Navarro	.10
38	Doug Jones	.10
39	Brent Gates	.10
40	Dean Palmer (Extreme Player)	.10
41	Pat Rapp	.10
42	Tony Clark	.25
43	Bill Swift	.10
44	Randy Velarde	.10
45	Matt Williams (Extreme Player)	.30
46	John Mabry	.10
47	Mike Fetters	.10
48	Orlando Miller	.10
49	Tom Glavine (Extreme Player)	.25
50	Delino DeShields (Extreme Player)	.10
51	Scott Erickson	.10
52	Andy Van Slyke	.10
53	Jim Bullinger	.10
54	Lyle Mouton	.10
55	Bret Saberhagen	.10
56	Benito Santiago (Extreme Player)	.10
57	Dan Miceli	.10
58	Carl Everett	.10
59	Rod Beck (Extreme Player)	.10
60	Phil Nevin	.10
61	Jason Giambi	.40
62	Paul Menhart	.10
63	Eric Karros (Extreme Player)	.15
64	Allen Watson	.10
65	Jeff Cirillo	.10
66	Lee Smith (Extreme Player)	.10
67	Sean Berry	.10
68	Luis Sojo	.10
69	Jeff Montgomery (Extreme Player)	.10
70	Todd Hundley (Extreme Player)	.20
71	John Burkett	.10
72	Mark Gubicza	.10
73	Don Mattingly (Extreme Player)	1.00
74	Jeff Brantley	.10
75	Matt Walbeck	.10
76	Steve Parris	.10
77	Ken Caminiti (Extreme Player)	.20
78	Kirt Manwaring	.10
79	Greg Vaughn	.10
80	Pedro Martinez (Extreme Player)	1.00
81	Benji Gil	.10
82	Heathcliff Slocumb (Extreme Player)	.10
83	Joe Girardi (Extreme Player)	.10
84	Sean Bergman	.10
85	Matt Karchner	.10
86	Butch Huskey	.10
87	Mike Morgan	.10
88	Todd Worrell (Extreme Player)	.10
89	Mike Bordick	.10
90	Bip Roberts (Extreme Player)	.10
91	Mike Hampton	.10
92	Troy O'Leary	.10
93	Wally Joyner	.15
94	Dave Stevens	.10
95	Cecil Fielder (Extreme Player)	.15
96	Wade Boggs (Extreme Player)	.30
97	Hal Morris	.10
98	Mickey Tettleton (Extreme Player)	.10
99	Jeff Kent (Extreme Player)	.10
100	Denny Martinez	.10
101	Luis Gonzalez (Extreme Player)	.15
102	John Jaha	.10
103	Javy Lopez (Extreme Player)	.20
104	Mark McGwire (Extreme Player)	4.00
105	Ken Griffey Jr. (EP)	3.00
106	Darren Daulton (Extreme Player)	.10
107	Bryan Rekar	.10
108	Mike Macfarlane (Extreme Player)	.10
109	Gary Gaetti (Extreme Player)	.10

110 Shane Reynolds (Extreme Player) .10
111 Pat Meares .10
112 Jason Schmidt .10
113 Otis Nixon .10
114 John Franco (Extreme Player) .10
115 Marc Newfield .10
116 Andy Benes (Extreme Player) .10
117 Ozzie Guillen .10
118 Brian Jordan (Extreme Player) .15
119 Terry Pendleton (Extreme Player) .10
120 Chuck Finley (Extreme Player) .10
121 Scott Stahoviak .10
122 Sid Fernandez .10
123 Derek Jeter (Extreme Player) 2.50
124 John Smiley (Extreme Player) .10
125 David Bell .10
126 Brett Butler (Extreme Player) .10
127 Doug Drabek (Extreme Player) .10
128 J.T. Snow (Extreme Player) .10
129 Joe Carter (Extreme Player) .15
130 Dennis Eckersley (Extreme Player) .10
131 Marty Cordova (Extreme Player) .20
132 Greg Maddux (Extreme Player) 2.00
133 Tom Goodwin .10
134 Andy Ashby .10
135 Paul Sorrento (Extreme Player) .10
136 Ricky Bones .10
137 Shawon Dunston (Extreme Player) .15
138 Moises Alou (Extreme Player) .15
139 Mickey Morandini .10
140 Ramon Martinez (Extreme Player) .15
141 Royce Clayton (Extreme Player) .10
142 Brad Ausmus .10
143 Kenny Rogers (Extreme Player) .10
144 Tim Naehring (Extreme Player) .10
145 Chris Gomez (Extreme Player) .10
146 Bobby Bonilla (Extreme Player) .10
147 Wilson Alvarez .10
148 Johnny Damon (Extreme Player) .20
149 Pat Hentgen .10
150 Andres Galarraga (Extreme Player) .20
151 David Cone (Extreme Player) .15
152 Lance Johnson (Extreme Player) .10
153 Carlos Garcia .10
154 Doug Johns .10
155 Midre Cummings .10
156 Steve Sparks .10
157 *Sandy Martinez* .10
158 William Van Landingham .10
159 Dave Justice (Extreme Player) .40
160 Mark Grace (Extreme Player) .25
161 Robb Nen (Extreme Player) .10
162 Mike Greenwell (Extreme Player) .10
163 Brad Radke .10
164 Edgardo Alfonzo .20
165 Mark Leiter .10
166 Walt Weiss .10
167 Mel Rojas (Extreme Player) .10
168 Bret Boone (Extreme Player) .10
169 Ricky Bottalico .10
170 Bobby Higginson .10
171 Trevor Hoffman .15
172 Jay Bell (Extreme Player) .10
173 Gabe White .10
174 Curtis Goodwin .10
175 Tyler Green .10
176 Roberto Alomar (Extreme Player) .75
177 Sterling Hitchcock .10
178 Ryan Klesko (Extreme Player) .25
179 *Donne Wall* .10
180 Brian McRae .10
181 Will Clark (Team TSC) .40
182 Frank Thomas (Team TSC) 1.50
183 Jeff Bagwell (Team TSC) 1.50
184 Mo Vaughn (Team TSC) .50
185 Tino Martinez (Team TSC) .15
186 Craig Biggio (Team TSC) .15
187 Chuck Knoblauch (Team TSC) .25
188 Carlos Baerga (Team TSC) .15
189 Quilvio Veras (Team TSC) .10
190 Luis Alicea (Team TSC) .10
191 Jim Thome (Team TSC) .40
192 Mike Blowers (Team TSC) .10
193 Robin Ventura (Team TSC) .15
194 Jeff King (Team TSC) .10
195 Tony Phillips (Team TSC) .10
196 John Valentin (Team TSC) .10
197 Barry Larkin (Team TSC) .40
198 Cal Ripken Jr. (Team TSC) 3.00
199 Omar Vizquel (Team TSC) .20
200 Kurt Abbott (Team TSC) .10
201 Albert Belle (Team TSC) .75
202 Barry Bonds (Team TSC) .75
203 Ron Gant (Team TSC) .10
204 Dante Bichette (Team TSC) .25
205 Jeff Conine (Team TSC) .10
206 Jim Edmonds (Team TSC) .25
207 Stan Javier (Team TSC) .10
208 Kenny Lofton (Team TSC) .50
209 Ray Lankford (Team TSC) .15
210 Bernie Williams (Team TSC) .75
211 Jay Buhner (Team TSC) .15
212 Paul O'Neill (Team TSC) .20
213 Tim Salmon (Team TSC) .25
214 Reggie Sanders (Team TSC) .10
215 Manny Ramirez (Team TSC) .75
216 Mike Piazza (Team TSC) 2.50
217 Mike Stanley (Team TSC) .10
218 Tony Eusebio (Team TSC) .10
219 Chris Hoiles (Team TSC) .10
220 Ron Karkovice (Team TSC) .10
221 Edgar Martinez (Team TSC) .10
222 Chili Davis (Team TSC) .10
223 Jose Canseco (Team TSC) .50
224 Eddie Murray (Team TSC) .40
225 Geronimo Berroa (Team TSC) .10
226 Chipper Jones (Team TSC) 2.00
227 Garret Anderson (Team TSC) .20
228 Marty Cordova (Team TSC) .20
229 Jon Nunnally (Team TSC) .10
230 Brian Hunter (Team TSC) .10
231 Shawn Green (Team TSC) .25
232 Ray Durham (Team TSC) .10
233 Alex Gonzalez (Team TSC) .10
234 Bobby Higginson (Team TSC) .15
235 Randy Johnson (Team TSC) .75
236 Al Leiter (Team TSC) .20
237 Tom Glavine (Team TSC) .25
238 Kenny Rogers (Team TSC) .10
239 Mike Hampton (Team TSC) .10
240 David Wells (Team TSC) .10
241 Jim Abbott (Team TSC) .10
242 Denny Neagle (Team TSC) .10
243 Wilson Alvarez (Team TSC) .10
244 John Smiley (Team TSC) .10
245 Greg Maddux (Team TSC) 2.00
246 Andy Ashby (Team TSC) .10
247 Hideo Nomo (Team TSC) .50
248 Pat Rapp (Team TSC) .10
249 Tim Wakefield (Team TSC) .10
250 John Smoltz (Team TSC) .15
251 Joey Hamilton (Team TSC) .10
252 Frank Castillo (Team TSC) .10
253 Denny Martinez (Team TSC) .10
254 Jaime Navarro (Team TSC) .10
255 Karim Garcia (Team TSC) .10
256 Bob Abreu (Team TSC) .30
257 Butch Huskey (Team TSC) .15
258 Ruben Rivera (Team TSC) .10
259 Johnny Damon (Team TSC) .15
260 Derek Jeter (Team TSC) 2.50
261 Dennis Eckersley (Team TSC) .10
262 Jose Mesa (Team TSC) .10
263 Tom Henke (Team TSC) .10
264 Rick Aguilera (Team TSC) .10
265 Randy Myers (Team TSC) .10
266 John Franco (Team TSC) .10
267 Jeff Brantley (Team TSC) .10
268 John Wetteland (Team TSC) .10
269 Mark Wohlers (Team TSC) .10
270 Rod Beck (Team TSC) .10
271 Barry Larkin .40
272 Paul O'Neill .25
273 Bobby Jones .10
274 Will Clark .40
275 Steve Avery .10
276 Jim Edmonds .30
277 John Olerud .25
278 Carlos Perez .10
279 Chris Hoiles .10
280 Jeff Conine .10
281 Jim Eisenreich .10
282 Jason Jacome .10
283 Ray Lankford .15
284 John Wasdin .10
285 Frank Thomas 1.50
286 Jason Isringhausen .15
287 Glenallen Hill .10
288 Esteban Loaiza .15
289 Bernie Williams .75
290 Curtis Leskanic .10
291 Scott Cooper .10
292 Curt Schilling .10
293 Eddie Murray .40
294 Rick Krivda .10
295 Domingo Cedeno .10
296 Jeff Fassero .10
297 Albert Belle .75
298 Craig Biggio .20
299 Fernando Vina .10
300 Edgar Martinez .10
301 Tony Gwynn 1.00
302 Felipe Lira .10
303 Mo Vaughn .50
304 Alex Fernandez .15
305 Keith Lockhart .10
306 Roger Pavlik .10
307 Lee Tinsley .10
308 Omar Vizquel .25
309 Scott Servais .10
310 Danny Tartabull .10
311 Chili Davis .10
312 Cal Eldred .10
313 Roger Cedeno .15
314 Chris Hammond .10
315 Rusty Greer .10
316 Brady Anderson .20
317 Ron Villone .10
318 Mark Carreon .10
319 Larry Walker .30
320 Pete Harnisch .10
321 Robin Ventura .15
322 Tim Belcher .10
323 Tony Tarasco .10
324 Juan Guzman .10
325 Kenny Lofton .50
326 Kevin Foster .10
327 Wil Cordero .10
328 Troy Percival .10
329 Turk Wendell .10
330 Thomas Howard .10
331 Carlos Baerga .10
332 B.J. Surhoff .10
333 Jay Buhner .10
334 Andujar Cedeno .10
335 Jeff King .10
336 Dante Bichette .25
337 Alan Trammell .15
338 Scott Leius .10
339 Chris Snopek .10
340 Roger Bailey .10
341 Jacob Brumfield .10
342 Jose Canseco .50
343 Rafael Palmeiro .40
344 Quilvio Veras .10
345 Darrin Fletcher .10
346 Carlos Delgado .75
347 Tony Eusebio .10
348 Ismael Valdes .10
349 Terry Steinbach .10
350 Orel Hershiser .10
351 Kurt Abbott .10
352 Jody Reed .10
353 David Howard .10
354 Ruben Sierra .10
355 John Ericks .10
356 Buck Showalter .10
357 Jim Thome .40
358 Geronimo Berroa .10
359 Robby Thompson .10
360 Jose Vizcaino .10
361 Jeff Frye .10
362 Kevin Appier .10
363 Pat Kelly .10
364 Ron Gant .15
365 Luis Alicea .10
366 Armando Benitez .10
367 Rico Brogna .10

368	Manny Ramirez	1.00
369	Mike Lansing	.10
370	Sammy Sosa	2.00
371	Don Wengert	.10
372	Dave Nilsson	.10
373	Sandy Alomar	.15
374	Joey Cora	.10
375	Larry Thomas	.10
376	John Valentin	.10
377	Kevin Ritz	.10
378	Steve Finley	.10
379	Frank Rodriguez	.10
380	Ivan Rodriguez	1.00
381	Alex Ochoa	.10
382	Mark Lemke	.10
383	Scott Brosius	.10
384	James Mouton	.10
385	Mark Langston	.10
386	Ed Sprague	.10
387	Joe Oliver	.10
388	Steve Ontiveros	.10
389	Rey Sanchez	.10
390	Mike Henneman	.10
391	*Jose Valentin*	.10
392	Tom Candiotti	.10
393	Damon Buford	.10
394	Erik Hanson	.10
395	Mark Smith	.10
396	Pete Schourek	.10
397	John Flaherty	.10
398	Dave Martinez	.10
399	Tommy Greene	.10
400	Gary Sheffield	.40
401	Glenn Dishman	.10
402	Barry Bonds	1.00
403	Tom Pagnozzi	.10
404	Todd Stottlemyre	.10
405	Tim Salmon	.25
406	John Hudek	.10
407	Fred McGriff	.30
408	Orlando Merced	.10
409	Brian Barber	.10
410	Ryan Thompson	.10
411	Mariano Rivera	.25
412	Eric Young	.10
413	Chris Bosio	.10
414	Chuck Knoblauch	.20
415	Jamie Moyer	.10
416	Chan Ho Park	.15
417	Mark Portugal	.10
418	Tim Raines	.10
419	Antonio Osuna	.10
420	Todd Zeile	.10
421	Steve Wojciechowski	.10
422	Marquis Grissom	.15
423	Norm Charlton	.10
424	Cal Ripken Jr.	3.00
425	Gregg Jefferies	.15
426	Mike Stanton	.10
427	Tony Fernandez	.10
428	Jose Rijo	.10
429	Jeff Bagwell	1.00
430	Raul Mondesi	.30
431	Travis Fryman	.25
432	Ron Karkovice	.10
433	Alan Benes	.15
434	Tony Phillips	.10
435	Reggie Sanders	.15
436	Andy Pettitte	.40
437	*Matt Lawton*	.75
438	Jeff Blauser	.10
439	Michael Tucker	.10
440	Mark Loretta	.10
441	Charlie Hayes	.10
442	Mike Piazza	2.50
443	Shane Andrews	.10
444	Jeff Suppan	.10
445	Steve Rodriguez	.10
446	Mike Matheny	.10
447	Trenidad Hubbard	.10
448	Denny Hocking	.10
449	Mark Grudzielanek	.10
450	Joe Randa	.10

1996 Stadium Club Bash & Burn

Inserted in one per 24 retail packs and one per 48 hobby packs of Series II, Bash & Burn includes 10 players on double-fronted cards. Both sides are foil-etched with the Bash side highlighting home runs and runs batted in for 1995 and career, and the Burn side featured stolen base and runs scored leaders for 1995 and career. Cards are numbered with a "B&B" prefix.

		MT
Complete Set (10):		30.00
Common Player:		1.00
1	Sammy Sosa	15.00
2	Barry Bonds	6.00
3	Reggie Sanders	3.00
4	Craig Biggio	2.50
5	Raul Mondesi	3.00
6	Ron Gant	1.00
7	Ray Lankford	1.00
8	Glenallen Hill	1.00
9	Chad Curtis	1.00
10	John Valentin	1.00

1996 Stadium Club Extreme Player

A special interactive version of 179 players' cards in 1996 Stadium Club was issued as an insert set across Series 1 and 2. Specially stamped with an "Extreme Player" logo in bronze (1 per 12 packs average), silver (1:24) or gold (1:48), the cards have backs which detail a contest by which the player's on-field performance was used to rank each by position. At season's end, cards of the winning players at each position could be redeemed for special prizes.

		MT
Complete Bronze Set (179):		200.00
Common Bronze:		.50
Silvers:		1.5X
Golds:		3X
1	(Hideo Nomo)	6.00
3	Garret Anderson	1.00
4	Jose Mesa	.50
5	Vinny Castilla	.50
6	Mike Mussina	3.00
7	Ray Durham	.50
8	Jack McDowell	.50
9	Juan Gonzalez	8.00
10	Chipper Jones	15.00
11	Deion Sanders	2.00
12	Rondell White	.50
13	Tom Henke	.50
14	Derek Bell	.50
15	Randy Myers	.50
16	Randy Johnson	4.00
17	Len Dykstra	.50
18	Bill Pulsipher	.50
21	Chad Curtis	.50
22	Roberto Hernandez	.50
23	Kirby Puckett	7.00
25	Roger Clemens	4.00
31	Chad Fonville	.50
32	Bernard Gilkey	1.00
34	Shawn Green	1.00
35	Rick Aguilera	.50
40	Dean Palmer	.50
45	Matt Williams	1.50
49	Tom Glavine	2.00
50	Delino DeShields	.50
56	Benito Santiago	.50
59	Rod Beck	.50
63	Eric Karros	.50
66	Lee Smith	.50
69	Jeff Montgomery	.50
70	Todd Hundley	2.00
73	Don Mattingly	8.00
77	Ken Caminiti	1.50
80	Pedro Martinez	1.50
82	Heathcliff Slocumb	.50
83	Joe Girardi	.50
88	Todd Worrell	.50
90	Bip Roberts	.50
95	Cecil Fielder	.50
96	Wade Boggs	4.00
98	Mickey Tettleton	.50
99	Jeff Kent	.50
101	Luis Gonzalez	.50
103	Javier Lopez	1.50
104	Mark McGwire	25.00
105	Ken Griffey Jr.	25.00
106	Darren Daulton	.50
108	Mike Macfarlane	.50
109	Gary Gaetti	.50
110	Shane Reynolds	.50
114	John Franco	.50
116	Andy Benes	.50
118	Brian Jordan	.50
119	Terry Pendleton	.50
120	Chuck Finley	.50
123	Derek Jeter	15.00
124	John Smiley	.50
126	Brett Butler	.50
127	Doug Drabek	.50
128	J.T. Snow	.50
129	Joe Carter	.50
130	Dennis Eckersley	.50
131	Marty Cordova	.50
132	Greg Maddux	15.00
135	Paul Sorrento	.50
137	Shawon Dunston	.50
138	Moises Alou	.50
140	Ramon Martinez	.50
141	Royce Clayton	.50
143	Kenny Rogers	.50
144	Tim Naehring	.50
145	Chris Gomez	.50
146	Bobby Bonilla	.50
148	Johnny Damon	1.50
150	Andres Galarraga	.75
151	David Cone	1.50
152	Lance Johnson	.50
159	Dave Justice	2.00
160	Mark Grace	2.50
161	Robb Nen	.50
162	Mike Greenwell	.50
167	Mel Rojas	.50
168	Bret Boone	.50
172	Jay Bell	.50
176	Roberto Alomar	6.00
178	Ryan Klesko	3.00
271	Barry Larkin	1.00
272	Paul O'Neill	.75
274	Will Clark	2.50
275	Steve Avery	.50
276	Jim Edmonds	1.00
277	John Olerud	2.00
279	Chris Hoiles	.50
280	Jeff Conine	.50
283	Ray Lankford	.50
285	Frank Thomas	12.50
286	Jason Isringhausen	.50
287	Glenallen Hill	.50
289	Bernie Williams	2.00
290	Eddie Murray	1.50
296	Jeff Fassero	.50
297	Albert Belle	6.00
298	Craig Biggio	1.00
300	Edgar Martinez	.50
301	Tony Gwynn	10.00
303	Mo Vaughn	1.50
304	Alex Fernandez	.50
308	Omar Vizquel	.50
310	Danny Tartabull	.50
316	Brady Anderson	1.00
319	Larry Walker	1.50
321	Robin Ventura	.75
325	Kenny Lofton	1.50
327	Wil Cordero	.50
328	Troy Percival	1.00
331	Carlos Baerga	.50
333	Jay Buhner	.50
335	Jeff King	.50
336	Dante Bichette	1.50
337	Alan Trammell	.50
342	Jose Canseco	2.00
343	Rafael Palmeiro	1.00
344	Quilvio Veras	.50
345	Darrin Fletcher	.50
347	Tony Eusebio	.50
348	Ismael Valdes	.50
349	Terry Steinbach	.50
350	Orel Hershiser	.50
351	Kurt Abbott	.50
354	Ruben Sierra	.50
357	Jim Thome	1.50
358	Geronimo Berroa	.50
359	Robby Thompson	.50
360	Jose Vizcaino	.50
362	Kevin Appier	.50
364	Ron Gant	.50
367	Rico Brogna	.50
368	Manny Ramirez	7.50
370	Sammy Sosa	15.00
373	Sandy Alomar	.75
378	Steve Finley	.50
380	Ivan Rodriguez	1.25
382	Mark Lemke	.50
385	Mark Langston	.50
386	Ed Sprague	.50
388	Steve Ontiveros	.50
392	Tom Candiotti	.50
394	Erik Hanson	.50
396	Pete Schourek	.50
400	Gary Sheffield	1.50
402	Barry Bonds	8.00
403	Tom Pagnozzi	.50
404	Todd Stottlemyre	.50
405	Tim Salmon	1.50
407	Fred McGriff	2.00
408	Orlando Merced	.50
412	Eric Young	.50
414	Chuck Knoblauch	2.00
417	Mark Portugal	.50
418	Tim Raines	.50
420	Todd Zeile	.50
422	Marquis Grissom	.50
423	Norm Charlton	.50
424	Cal Ripken Jr.	20.00
425	Gregg Jefferies	.50
428	Jose Rijo	.50
429	Jeff Bagwell	8.00
430	Raul Mondesi	2.00
431	Travis Fryman	.50
434	Tony Phillips	.50
435	Reggie Sanders	.50
436	Andy Pettitte	3.00
438	Jeff Blauser	.50
441	Charlie Hayes	.50
442	Mike Piazza	15.00

1996 Stadium Club Mega Heroes

Ten herois players are matched with a comic book-style illustration depicting their nickname in the Mega Heroes insert set. Printed on foil-board in a defraction technology, the cards are found, on average, once per 48 Series I hobby packs and twice as often in retail packs.

		MT
Complete Set (10):		40.00
Common Player:		2.00
1	Frank Thomas	7.50
2	Ken Griffey Jr.	15.00
3	Hideo Nomo	4.50
4	Ozzie Smith	5.00
5	Will Clark	2.50
6	Jack McDowell	2.00
7	Andres Galarraga	2.00
8	Roger Clemens	6.00
9	Deion Sanders	3.00
10	Mo Vaughn	4.00

1996 Stadium Club Metalists

Eight players who have won two or more major awards in their careers are featured in this Series II insert. Cards are printed on foilboard and feature intricate laser-cut designs that depict the player's face. Metalist inserts are found one per 96 retail and one per 48 hobby packs, on average. Cards are numbered with a "M" prefix.

		MT
Complete Set (8):		45.00
Common Player:		1.50
1	Jeff Bagwell	6.00
2	Barry Bonds	6.00
3	Jose Canseco	2.50
4	Roger Clemens	4.50
5	Dennis Eckersley	1.50
6	Greg Maddux	12.00
7	Cal Ripken Jr.	15.00
8	Frank Thomas	7.50

1996 Stadium Club Mickey Mantle Retrospective

Following the success of the Mantle reprints in Topps baseball, Stadium Club produced a series of 19 Mickey Mantle Retrospective inserts; nine black-and-white cards in Series 1 and 10 color cards in Series 2. The cards chronicle Mantle's career and provide insights from baseball contemporaries. Throughout both series, the Mantle cards are found on an average of once per 24 Series 1 packs and once per 12 Series 2 packs. Cards are numbered with an "MM" prefix.

		MT
Complete Set (19):		150.00
Complete Series 1 (9):		100.00
Complete Series 2 (10):		50.00
Common Series 1:		12.00
Common Series 2:		7.50
1	Mickey Mantle (1950, minor league)	12.00
2	Mickey Mantle (1951)	12.00
3	Mickey Mantle (1951)	12.00
4	Mickey Mantle (1953)	12.00
5	Mickey Mantle (1954) (w/ Yogi Berra)	12.00
6	Mickey Mantle (1956)	12.00
7	Mickey Mantle (1957)	12.00
8	Mickey Mantle (1958) (w/ Casey Stengel)	12.00
9	Mickey Mantle (1959)	12.00
10	Mickey Mantle (1960) (w/ Elston Howard)	7.50
11	Mickey Mantle (1961)	7.50
12	Mickey Mantle (1961) (w/ Roger Maris)	12.00
13	Mickey Mantle (1962)	7.50
14	Mickey Mantle (1963)	7.50
15	Mickey Mantle (1964)	7.50
16	Mickey Mantle	7.50
17	Mickey Mantle (1968)	7.50
18	Mickey Mantle (1969)	7.50
19	Mickey Mantle (In Memoriam)	7.50

1996 Stadium Club Midsummer Matchups

These inserts salute 1995 National League and American League All-Stars on back-to-back etched-foil cards. Players are matched by position in the 10-card set. Average insertion rate is one per 48 hobby packs and one per 24 retail packs in Series I. Cards are numbered with a "M" prefix.

		MT
Complete Set (10):		60.00
Common Player:		2.50
1	Hideo Nomo, Randy Johnson	4.00
2	Mike Piazza, Ivan Rodriguez	12.00
3	Fred McGriff, Frank Thomas	7.50
4	Craig Biggio, Carlos Baerga	2.50
5	Vinny Castilla, Wade Boggs	3.00
6	Barry Larkin, Cal Ripken Jr.	15.00
7	Barry Bonds, Albert Belle	6.00
8	Len Dykstra, Kenny Lofton	2.50
9	Tony Gwynn, Kirby Puckett	7.00
10	Ron Gant, Edgar Martinez	2.50

1996 Stadium Club Power Packed

Topps' Power Matrix technology is used to showcase 15 of the biggest, strongest players in this Series II insert set. Card backs feature a diagram of the player's home park with baseball graphics measuring this home runs during the 1995 season. The inserts are a one in 48 packs pick, on average, both hobby and retail. Cards are numbered with a "PP" prefix.

		MT
Complete Set (15):		75.00
Common Player:		2.00
1	Albert Belle	4.00
2	Mark McGwire	20.00
3	Jose Canseco	4.00
4	Mike Piazza	12.00
5	Ron Gant	3.00
6	Ken Griffey Jr.	15.00
7	Mo Vaughn	3.00
8	Cecil Fielder	2.00
9	Tim Salmon	3.00
10	Frank Thomas	7.50
11	Juan Gonzalez	5.00
12	Andres Galarraga	3.00
13	Fred McGriff	4.00
14	Jay Buhner	2.00
15	Dante Bichette	2.00

1996 Stadium Club Power Streak

The best power hitters in baseball are featured in Power Matrix technology on these Series I inserts. Average insertion rate is one per 24 hobby and 48 retail packs. Cards are numbered with a "PS" prefix.

		MT
Complete Set (15):		60.00
Common Player:		2.00
1	Randy Johnson	4.00
2	Hideo Nomo	4.00
3	Albert Belle	4.00
4	Dante Bichette	3.00
5	Jay Buhner	2.00
6	Frank Thomas	6.00

7	Mark McGwire	20.00
8	Rafael Palmeiro	3.00
9	Mo Vaughn	3.00
10	Sammy Sosa	10.00
11	Larry Walker	3.00
12	Gary Gaetti	2.00
13	Tim Salmon	2.50
14	Barry Bonds	5.00
15	Jim Edmonds	3.00

1996 Stadium Club Prime Cuts

The purest swings in baseball are the focus on these laser-cut, defraction-foil inserts found in Series 1 packs at an average rate of one per 36 hobby and 72 retail packs. Cards are numbered with a "PC" prefix.

		MT
Complete Set (8):		45.00
Common Player:		3.00
1	Albert Belle	3.00
2	Barry Bonds	5.00
3	Ken Griffey Jr.	15.00
4	Tony Gwynn	6.00
5	Edgar Martinez	3.00
6	Rafael Palmeiro	3.00
7	Mike Piazza	12.00
8	Frank Thomas	6.00

1996 Stadium Club TSC Awards

TSC Awards insert cards allowed Topps' experts to honor best performances, newcomer, comeback, etc. The cards are found in Series II packs at an average rate of one per 24 retail and 48 hobby packs.

		MT
Complete Set (10):		40.00
Common Player:		1.00
1	Cal Ripken Jr.	10.00
2	Albert Belle	4.50
3	Tom Glavine	1.50
4	Jeff Conine	1.50
5	Ken Griffey Jr.	15.00
6	Hideo Nomo	2.50
7	Greg Maddux	7.50
8	Chipper Jones	7.50
9	Randy Johnson	3.00
10	Jose Mesa	1.00

1997 Stadium Club

Stadium Club totalled 390 cards in 1997, issued in two Series of 195 cards each. In Series 1 (Feb.), cards #181-195 are a rookie subset called TSC 2000. In Series 2 (April), cards #376-390 form a subset called Stadium Slugger. Each of these subsets was short-printed and inserted about one per two packs. TSC is printed on an improved 20-point stock with Topps' Super Color process.

		MT
Complete Set (390):		80.00
Common Player:		.10
Series 1 or 2 Pack (9):		2.50
Series 1 or 2 Wax Box (24):		50.00
1	Chipper Jones	1.50
2	Gary Sheffield	.40
3	Kenny Lofton	.40
4	Brian Jordan	.10
5	Mark McGwire	3.00
6	Charles Nagy	.10
7	Tim Salmon	.20
8	Cal Ripken Jr.	2.50
9	Jeff Conine	.10
10	Paul Molitor	.40
11	Mariano Rivera	.20
12	Pedro Martinez	.75
13	Jeff Bagwell	.75
14	Bobby Bonilla	.15
15	Barry Bonds	.75
16	Ryan Klesko	.25
17	Barry Larkin	.40
18	Jim Thome	.30
19	Jay Buhner	.10
20	Juan Gonzalez	.75
21	Mike Mussina	.40
22	Kevin Appier	.10
23	Eric Karros	.20
24	Steve Finley	.10
25	Ed Sprague	.10
26	Bernard Gilkey	.10
27	Tony Phillips	.10
28	Henry Rodriguez	.10
29	John Smoltz	.20
30	Dante Bichette	.20
31	Mike Piazza	2.00
32	Paul O'Neill	.20
33	Billy Wagner	.15
34	Reggie Sanders	.10
35	John Jaha	.10
36	Eddie Murray	.40
37	Eric Young	.10
38	Roberto Hernandez	.10
39	Pat Hentgen	.10
40	Sammy Sosa	1.50
41	Todd Hundley	.10
42	Mo Vaughn	.50
43	Robin Ventura	.15
44	Mark Grudzielanek	.10
45	Shane Reynolds	.10
46	Andy Pettitte	.40
47	Fred McGriff	.25
48	Rey Ordonez	.20
49	Will Clark	.30
50	Ken Griffey Jr.	2.50
51	Todd Worrell	.10
52	Rusty Greer	.10
53	Mark Grace	.25
54	Tom Glavine	.30
55	Derek Jeter	2.50
56	Rafael Palmeiro	.40
57	Bernie Williams	.60
58	Marty Cordova	.10
59	Andres Galarraga	.25
60	Ken Caminiti	.20
61	Garret Anderson	.10
62	Denny Martinez	.10
63	Mike Greenwell	.10
64	David Segui	.10
65	Julio Franco	.10
66	Rickey Henderson	.25
67	Ozzie Guillen	.10
68	Pete Harnisch	.10
69	Chan Ho Park	.20
70	Harold Baines	.10
71	Mark Clark	.10
72	Steve Avery	.10
73	Brian Hunter	.10
74	Pedro Astacio	.10
75	Jack McDowell	.10
76	Gregg Jefferies	.10
77	Jason Kendall	.10
78	Todd Walker	.10
79	B.J. Surhoff	.10
80	Moises Alou	.20
81	Fernando Vina	.10
82	Darryl Strawberry	.20
83	Jose Rosado	.10
84	Chris Gomez	.10
85	Chili Davis	.10
86	Alan Benes	.10
87	Todd Hollandsworth	.10
88	Jose Vizcaino	.10
89	Edgardo Alfonzo	.20
90	Ruben Rivera	.20
91	Donovan Osborne	.10
92	Doug Glanville	.10
93	Gary DiSarcina	.10
94	Brooks Kieschnick	.10
95	Bobby Jones	.10
96	Raul Casanova	.10
97	Jermaine Allensworth	.10
98	Kenny Rogers	.10
99	Mark McLemore	.10
100	Jeff Fassero	.10
101	Sandy Alomar	.15
102	Chuck Finley	.10
103	Eric Owens	.10
104	Billy McMillon	.10
105	Dwight Gooden	.10
106	Sterling Hitchcock	.10
107	Doug Drabek	.10
108	Paul Wilson	.10
109	Chris Snopek	.10
110	Al Leiter	.20
111	Bob Tewksbury	.10
112	Todd Greene	.10
113	Jose Valentin	.10
114	Delino DeShields	.10
115	Mike Bordick	.10
116	Pat Meares	.10
117	Mariano Duncan	.10
118	Steve Trachsel	.10
119	Luis Castillo	.15
120	Andy Benes	.10
121	Donne Wall	.10
122	Alex Gonzalez	.10
123	Dan Wilson	.10
124	Omar Vizquel	.20
125	Devon White	.10
126	Darryl Hamilton	.10
127	Orlando Merced	.10
128	Royce Clayton	.10
129	William VanLandingham	.10
130	Terry Steinbach	.10
131	Jeff Blauser	.10
132	Jeff Cirillo	.10
133	Roger Pavlik	.10
134	Danny Tartabull	.10
135	Jeff Montgomery	.10
136	Bobby Higginson	.10
137	Mike Grace	.10
138	Kevin Elster	.10
139	*Brian Giles*	1.50
140	Rod Beck	.10
141	Ismael Valdes	.10
142	Scott Brosius	.10
143	Mike Fetters	.10
144	Gary Gaetti	.10
145	Mike Lansing	.10
146	Glenallen Hill	.10
147	Shawn Green	.40
148	Mel Rojas	.10
149	Joey Cora	.10
150	John Smiley	.10
151	Marvin Benard	.10
152	Curt Schilling	.10
153	Dave Nilsson	.10
154	Edgar Renteria	.20
155	Joey Hamilton	.10
156	Carlos Garcia	.10
157	Nomar Garciaparra	2.00
158	Kevin Ritz	.10
159	Keith Lockhart	.10
160	Justin Thompson	.10
161	Terry Adams	.10
162	Jamey Wright	.10
163	Otis Nixon	.10
164	Michael Tucker	.10
165	Mike Stanley	.10
166	Ben McDonald	.10
167	John Mabry	.10
168	Troy O'Leary	.10
169	Mel Nieves	.10
170	Bret Boone	.10
171	Mike Timlin	.10
172	Scott Rolen	1.00
173	Reggie Jefferson	.10
174	Neifi Perez	.10
175	Brian McRae	.10
176	Tom Goodwin	.10
177	Aaron Sele	.10
178	Benny Santiago	.10
179	Frank Rodriguez	.10
180	Eric Davis	.10
181	Andruw Jones (TSC 2000)	1.50
182	Todd Walker (TSC 2000)	.40
183	Wes Helms (TSC 2000)	.40
184	*Nelson Figueroa* (TSC 2000)	.40
185	Vladimir Guerrero (TSC 2000)	2.50
186	Billy McMillon (TSC 2000)	.40
187	Todd Helton (TSC 2000)	2.00
188	Nomar Garciaparra (TSC 2000)	4.00
189	Katsuhiro Maeda (TSC 2000)	.40
190	Russell Branyan (TSC 2000)	.60
191	Glendon Rusch (TSC 2000)	.25
192	Bartolo Colon (TSC 2000)	.40
193	Scott Rolen (TSC 2000)	1.50
194	Angel Echevarria (TSC 2000)	.15
195	Bob Abreu (TSC 2000)	.25
196	Greg Maddux	1.50
197	Joe Carter	.10
198	Alex Ochoa	.10
199	Ellis Burks	.10
200	Ivan Rodriguez	.75
201	Marquis Grissom	.10
202	Trevor Hoffman	.15
203	Matt Williams	.25
204	Carlos Delgado	.75
205	Ramon Martinez	.10
206	Chuck Knoblauch	.20
207	Juan Guzman	.10

No.	Player	MT
208	Derek Bell	.10
209	Roger Clemens	1.00
210	Vladimir Guerrero	1.00
211	Cecil Fielder	.10
212	Hideo Nomo	.50
213	Frank Thomas	1.00
214	Greg Vaughn	.10
215	Javy Lopez	.20
216	Raul Mondesi	.25
217	Wade Boggs	.40
218	Carlos Baerga	.10
219	Tony Gwynn	1.00
220	Tino Martinez	.20
221	Vinny Castilla	.20
222	Lance Johnson	.10
223	David Justice	.40
224	Rondell White	.20
225	Dean Palmer	.10
226	Jim Edmonds	.20
227	Albert Belle	.50
228	Alex Fernandez	.20
229	Ryne Sandberg	.75
230	Jose Mesa	.10
231	David Cone	.20
232	Troy Percival	.10
233	Edgar Martinez	.10
234	Jose Canseco	.40
235	Kevin Brown	.20
236	Ray Lankford	.10
237	Karim Garcia	.10
238	J.T. Snow	.10
239	Dennis Eckersley	.10
240	Roberto Alomar	.60
241	John Valentin	.10
242	Ron Gant	.15
243	Geronimo Berroa	.10
244	Manny Ramirez	1.00
245	Travis Fryman	.20
246	Denny Neagle	.10
247	Randy Johnson	.75
248	Darin Erstad	.75
249	Mark Wohlers	.10
250	Ken Hill	.10
251	Larry Walker	.30
252	Craig Biggio	.20
253	Brady Anderson	.20
254	John Wetteland	.10
255	Andruw Jones	.75
256	Turk Wendell	.10
257	Jason Isringhausen	.10
258	Jaime Navarro	.10
259	Sean Berry	.10
260	Albie Lopez	.10
261	Jay Bell	.10
262	Bobby Witt	.10
263	Tony Clark	.20
264	Tim Wakefield	.10
265	Brad Radke	.10
266	Tim Belcher	.10
267	Mark Lewis	.10
268	Roger Cedeno	.10
269	Tim Naehring	.10
270	Kevin Tapani	.10
271	Joe Randa	.10
272	Randy Myers	.10
273	Dave Burba	.10
274a	Mike Sweeney	.10
274b	Tom Pagnozzi (should be #374)	.10
275	Danny Graves	.10
276	Chad Mottola	.10
277	Ruben Sierra	.10
278	Norm Charlton	.10
279	Scott Servais	.10
280	Jacob Cruz	.10
281	Mike Macfarlane	.10
282	Rich Becker	.10
283	Shannon Stewart	.10
284	Gerald Williams	.10
285	Jody Reed	.10
286	Jeff D'Amico	.10
287	Walt Weiss	.10
288	Jim Leyritz	.10
289	Francisco Cordova	.15
290	F.P. Santangelo	.10
291	Scott Erickson	.10
292	Hal Morris	.10
293	Ray Durham	.10
294	Andy Ashby	.10
295	Darryl Kile	.10
296	Jose Paniagua	.10
297	Mickey Tettleton	.10
298	Joe Girardi	.10
299	Rocky Coppinger	.10
300	Bob Abreu	.10
301	John Olerud	.20
302	Paul Shuey	.10
303	Jeff Brantley	.10
304	Bob Wells	.10
305	Kevin Seitzer	.10
306	Shawon Dunston	.10
307	Jose Herrera	.10
308	Butch Huskey	.10
309	Jose Offerman	.10
310	Rick Aguilera	.10
311	Greg Gagne	.10
312	John Burkett	.10
313	Mark Thompson	.10
314	Alvaro Espinoza	.10
315	Todd Stottlemyre	.10
316	Al Martin	.10
317	James Baldwin	.10
318	Cal Eldred	.10
319	Sid Fernandez	.10
320	Mickey Morandini	.10
321	Robb Nen	.10
322	Mark Lemke	.10
323	Pete Schourek	.10
324	Marcus Jensen	.10
325	Rich Aurilia	.10
326	Jeff King	.10
327	Scott Stahoviak	.10
328	Ricky Otero	.10
329	Antonio Osuna	.10
330	Chris Hoiles	.10
331	Luis Gonzalez	.20
332	Wil Cordero	.10
333	Johnny Damon	.10
334	Mark Langston	.10
335	Orlando Miller	.10
336	Jason Giambi	.40
337	Damian Jackson	.10
338	David Wells	.10
339	Bip Roberts	.10
340	Matt Ruebel	.10
341	Tom Candiotti	.10
342	Wally Joyner	.10
343	Jimmy Key	.10
344	Tony Batista	.10
345	Paul Sorrento	.10
346	Ron Karkovice	.10
347	Wilson Alvarez	.10
348	John Flaherty	.10
349	Rey Sanchez	.10
350	John Vander Wal	.10
351a	Jermaine Dye	.15
351b	Brant Brown (should be #361)	.25
352	Mike Hampton	.20
353	Greg Colbrunn	.10
354	Heathcliff Slocumb	.10
355	Ricky Bottalico	.10
356	Marty Janzen	.10
357	Orel Hershiser	.10
358	Rex Hudler	.10
359	Amaury Telemaco	.10
360	Darrin Fletcher	.10
361	Not issued - see #351	
362	Russ Davis	.10
363	Allen Watson	.10
364	Mike Lieberthal	.10
365	Dave Stevens	.10
366	Jay Powell	.10
367	Tony Fossas	.10
368	Bob Wolcott	.10
369	Mark Loretta	.10
370	Shawn Estes	.10
371	Sandy Martinez	.10
372	Wendell Magee Jr.	.10
373	John Franco	.10
374	Not issued - see #274	
375	Willie Adams	.10
376	Chipper Jones (Stadium Sluggers)	3.00
377	Mo Vaughn (Stadium Sluggers)	1.00
378	Frank Thomas (Stadium Sluggers)	2.00
379	Albert Belle (Stadium Sluggers)	1.00
380	Andres Galarraga (Stadium Sluggers)	.25
381	Gary Sheffield (Stadium Sluggers)	.25
382	Jeff Bagwell (Stadium Sluggers)	1.50
383	Mike Piazza (Stadium Sluggers)	4.00
384	Mark McGwire (Stadium Sluggers)	6.00
385	Ken Griffey Jr. (Stadium Sluggers)	5.00
386	Barry Bonds (Stadium Sluggers)	1.50
387	Juan Gonzalez (Stadium Sluggers)	1.50
388	Brady Anderson (Stadium Sluggers)	.20
389	Ken Caminiti (Stadium Sluggers)	.25
390	Jay Buhner (Stadium Sluggers)	.15

1997 Stadium Club Co-Signers

Each Series of Stadium Club included five different Co-Signers, with an insertion ratio of one per 168 hobby packs. These double-sided cards featured authentic autographs from each star, one per side.

		MT
Complete Set (10):		400.00
Common Card:		15.00
CO1	Andy Pettitte, Derek Jeter	150.00
CO2	Paul Wilson, Todd Hundley	15.00
CO3	Jermaine Dye, Mark Wohlers	15.00
CO4	Scott Rolen, Gregg Jefferies	75.00
CO5	Todd Hollandsworth, Jason Kendall	20.00
CO6	Alan Benes, Robin Ventura	25.00
CO7	Eric Karros, Raul Mondesi	35.00
CO8	Rey Ordonez, Nomar Garciaparra	125.00
CO9	Rondell White, Marty Cordova	20.00
CO10	Tony Gwynn, Karim Garcia	100.00

1997 Stadium Club Firebrand Redemption

Because of production problems with its "Laser-Etched Wood" technology, Stadium Club was unable to package the Firebrand insert cards with the rest of the issue. Instead, a redemption card was substituted. The redemption card pictures the Firebrand card on its horizontal front; the back has details for exchanging the redemption card for the actual wood-printed, die-cut version. The exchange offer ended Sept. 30, 1997.

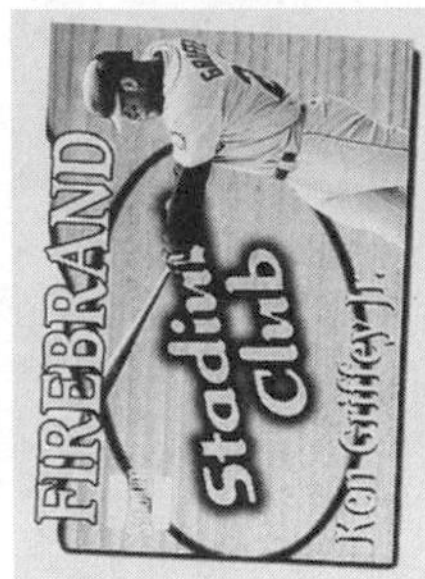

		MT
Complete Set (12):		85.00
Common Player:		3.00
F1	Jeff Bagwell	8.00
F2	Albert Belle	4.00
F3	Barry Bonds	5.00
F4	Andres Galarraga	3.00
F5	Ken Griffey Jr.	15.00
F6	Brady Anderson	3.00
F7	Mark McGwire	15.00
F8	Chipper Jones	12.50
F9	Frank Thomas	10.00
F10	Mike Piazza	12.50
F11	Mo Vaughn	3.00
F12	Juan Gonzalez	4.00

1997 Stadium Club Firebrand

This 12-card insert was found only in packs sold at retail chains. Cards were inserted 1:36 packs. The hortizontal format cards are printed on thin wood stock, die-cut at top. Fronts are trimmed in gold foil. Cards are numbered with a "F" prefix.

		MT
Complete Set (12):		120.00
Common Player:		3.00
1	Jeff Bagwell	8.00
2	Albert Belle	6.00
3	Barry Bonds	8.00
4	Andres Galarraga	4.00
5	Ken Griffey Jr.	25.00
6	Brady Anderson	3.00
7	Mark McGwire	30.00
8	Chipper Jones	15.00
9	Frank Thomas	10.00
10	Mike Piazza	20.00
11	Mo Vaughn	4.00
12	Juan Gonzalez	8.00

1997 Stadium Club Instavision

Instavision features holographic cards with exciting moments from the 1996 playoffs and World Series. Inserted one per 24 hobby packs and one per 36 retail packs, these cards are printed on a horizontal, plastic card. Cards carry an "I" prefix, with the first 10 found in Series I and the final 12 in Series II.

		MT
Complete Set (22):		50.00
Complete Series 1 Set (10):		20.00
Complete Series 2 Set (12):		30.00
Common Player:		1.50
11	Eddie Murray	2.00
12	Paul Molitor	4.00
13	Todd Hundley	2.00
14	Roger Clemens	5.00
15	Barry Bonds	4.00
16	Mark McGwire	12.50
17	Brady Anderson	1.50
18	Barry Larkin	2.50
19	Ken Caminiti	2.50
110	Hideo Nomo	3.00
111	Bernie Williams	2.00
112	Juan Gonzalez	4.00
113	Andy Pettitte	3.00
114	Albert Belle	3.00
115	John Smoltz	2.00
116	Brian Jordan	1.50
117	Derek Jeter	10.00
118	Ken Caminiti	2.00
119	John Wetteland	1.50
120	Brady Anderson	1.50
121	Andruw Jones	5.00
122	Jim Leyritz	1.50

1997 Stadium Club Millenium

Millennium was a 40-card insert that was released with 20 cards in Series I and Series II. The set featured 40 top prospects and rookies on a silver foil, holographic front, with a Future Forecast section on the back. Cards carried an "M" prefix and were numbered consecutively M1-M40. Millennium inserts were found every 24 hobby packs and every 36 retail packs.

		MT
Complete Set (40):		190.00
Complete Series 1 Set (20):		90.00
Complete Series 2 Set (20):		100.00
Common Player:		2.00
1	Derek Jeter	25.00
2	Mark Grudzielanek	2.00
3	Jacob Cruz	2.50
4	Ray Durham	2.00
5	Tony Clark	4.00
6	Chipper Jones	25.00
7	Luis Castillo	2.00
8	Carlos Delgado	12.00
9	Brant Brown	2.00
10	Jason Kendall	3.00
11	Alan Benes	3.00
12	Rey Ordonez	3.00
13	Justin Thompson	3.00
14	Jermaine Allensworth	2.00
15	Brian Hunter	2.00
16	Marty Cordova	2.00
17	Edgar Renteria	4.00
18	Karim Garcia	2.50
19	Todd Greene	2.00
20	Paul Wilson	2.00
21	Andruw Jones	15.00
22	Todd Walker	4.00
23	Alex Ochoa	2.00
24	Bartolo Colon	4.00
25	Wendell Magee Jr.	3.00
26	Jose Rosado	2.00
27	Katsuhiro Maeda	2.00
28	Bob Abreu	5.00
29	Brooks Kieschnick	2.00
30	Derrick Gibson	3.00
31	Mike Sweeney	4.00
32	Jeff D'Amico	4.00
33	Chad Mottola	2.00
34	Chris Snopek	2.00
35	Jaime Bluma	2.00
36	Vladimir Guerrero	20.00
37	Nomar Garciaparra	25.00
38	Scott Rolen	12.00
39	Dmitri Young	2.00
40	Neifi Perez	3.00

1997 Stadium Club Patent Leather

Patent Leather featured 13 of the top gloves in baseball on a leather, die-cut card. The cards carry a "PL" prefix and are inerted one per 36 retail packs.

		MT
Complete Set (13):		100.00
Common Player:		5.00
1	Ivan Rodriguez	10.00
2	Ken Caminiti	4.00
3	Barry Bonds	10.00
4	Ken Griffey Jr.	30.00
5	Greg Maddux	20.00
6	Craig Biggio	5.00
7	Andres Galarraga	6.00
8	Kenny Lofton	6.00
9	Barry Larkin	6.00
10	Mark Grace	6.00
11	Rey Ordonez	4.00
12	Roberto Alomar	8.00
13	Derek Jeter	25.00

1997 Stadium Club Pure Gold

Pure Gold featured 20 of the top players in baseball on gold, embossed foil cards. Cards carry a "PG" prefix and were inserted every 72 hobby packs and every 108 retail packs. The first 10 cards were in Series I packs, while the final 10 cards are exclusive to Series II.

		MT
Complete Set (20):		250.00
Complete Series 1 Set (10):		100.00
Complete Series 2 Set (10):		150.00
Common Player:		3.00
1	Brady Anderson	5.00
2	Albert Belle	6.00
3	Dante Bichette	5.00
4	Barry Bonds	10.00
5	Jay Buhner	5.00
6	Tony Gwynn	15.00
7	Chipper Jones	20.00
8	Mark McGwire	40.00
9	Gary Sheffield	7.00
10	Frank Thomas	15.00
11	Juan Gonzalez	10.00
12	Ken Caminiti	5.00
13	Kenny Lofton	6.00
14	Jeff Bagwell	10.00
15	Ken Griffey Jr.	30.00
16	Cal Ripken Jr.	30.00
17	Mo Vaughn	6.00
18	Mike Piazza	25.00
19	Derek Jeter	30.00
20	Andres Galarraga	6.00

1997 Stadium Club TSC Matrix

TSC Matrix consists of 120 cards from Series I and II reprinted with Power Matrix technology. In each Series, 60 of the 190 cards were selected for inclusion in TSC Matrix and inserted every 12 hobby packs and every 18 retail packs. Each insert carries the TSC Matrix logo in a top corner of the card.

		MT
Common Player:		1.00
1	Chipper Jones	15.00
2	Gary Sheffield	3.00
3	Kenny Lofton	5.00
4	Brian Jordan	1.00
5	Mark McGwire	30.00
6	Charles Nagy	1.00
7	Tim Salmon	1.50
8	Cal Ripken Jr.	25.00
9	Jeff Conine	1.00
10	Paul Molitor	5.00
11	Mariano Rivera	2.00
12	Pedro Martinez	8.00
13	Jeff Bagwell	8.00
14	Bobby Bonilla	1.00
15	Barry Bonds	8.00
16	Ryan Klesko	1.50
17	Barry Larkin	2.00
18	Jim Thome	3.00
19	Jay Buhner	1.00
20	Juan Gonzalez	8.00
21	Mike Mussina	4.00
22	Kevin Appier	1.00
23	Eric Karros	1.00
24	Steve Finley	1.00
25	Ed Sprague	1.00
26	Bernard Gilkey	1.00
27	Tony Phillips	1.00
28	Henry Rodriguez	1.00
29	John Smoltz	1.00
30	Dante Bichette	2.00
31	Mike Piazza	20.00
32	Paul O'Neill	1.50
33	Billy Wagner	1.00
34	Reggie Sanders	1.00
35	John Jaha	1.00
36	Eddie Murray	3.00
37	Eric Young	1.00
38	Roberto Hernandez	1.00
39	Pat Hentgen	1.00
40	Sammy Sosa	20.00
41	Todd Hundley	1.00
42	Mo Vaughn	5.00
43	Robin Ventura	1.00
44	Mark Grudzielanek	1.00
45	Shane Reynolds	1.00
46	Andy Pettitte	2.50
47	Fred McGriff	2.50
48	Rey Ordonez	1.00
49	Will Clark	2.50
50	Ken Griffey Jr.	25.00
51	Todd Worrell	1.00
52	Rusty Greer	1.00
53	Mark Grace	2.50
54	Tom Glavine	1.50

55 Derek Jeter 25.00
56 Rafael Palmeiro 3.00
57 Bernie Williams 6.00
58 Marty Cordova 1.00
59 Andres Galarraga 2.00
60 Ken Caminiti 1.00
196 Greg Maddux 15.00
197 Joe Carter 1.00
198 Alex Ochoa 1.00
199 Ellis Burks 1.00
200 Ivan Rodriguez 8.00
201 Marquis Grissom 1.00
202 Trevor Hoffman 1.00
203 Matt Williams 2.00
204 Carlos Delgado 6.00
205 Ramon Martinez 1.00
206 Chuck Knoblauch 1.50
207 Juan Guzman 1.00
208 Derek Bell 1.00
209 Roger Clemens 10.00
210 Vladimir Guerrero 10.00
211 Cecil Fielder 1.00
212 Hideo Nomo 4.00
213 Frank Thomas 10.00
214 Greg Vaughn 1.00
215 Javy Lopez 1.50
216 Raul Mondesi 2.00
217 Wade Boggs 3.00
218 Carlos Baerga 1.00
219 Tony Gwynn 10.00
220 Tino Martinez 1.50
221 Vinny Castilla 1.00
222 Lance Johnson 1.00
223 David Justice 2.00
224 Rondell White 1.00
225 Dean Palmer 1.00
226 Jim Edmonds 1.50
227 Albert Belle 5.00
228 Alex Fernandez 1.00
229 Ryne Sandberg 10.00
230 Jose Mesa 1.00
231 David Cone 1.50
232 Troy Percival 1.00
233 Edgar Martinez 1.00
234 Jose Canseco 5.00
235 Kevin Brown 1.50
236 Ray Lankford 1.00
237 Karim Garcia 1.00
238 J.T. Snow 1.00
239 Dennis Eckersley 1.00
240 Roberto Alomar 6.00
241 John Valentin 1.00
242 Ron Gant 1.00
243 Geronimo Berroa 1.00
244 Manny Ramirez 8.00
245 Travis Fryman 1.50
246 Denny Neagle 1.00
247 Randy Johnson 8.00
248 Darin Erstad 10.00
249 Mark Wohlers 1.00
250 Ken Hill 1.00
251 Larry Walker 2.00
252 Craig Biggio 1.50
253 Brady Anderson 1.50
254 John Wetteland 1.00
255 Andruw Jones 8.00

1998 Stadium Club

Stadium Club was issued in two separate series for 1998, with 200 odd-numbered cards in Series I and 200 even-numbered cards in Series II. Retail packs contained six cards and an SRP of $2, hobby packs contained nine cards and an SRP of $3 and HTA packs contained 15 cards and an SRP of $5. Three subets were included in the set, with Future Stars (361-379) and Draft Picks (381-399) both being odd-numbered and Traded (356-400) being even- numbered. Inserts in Series I include: First Day Issue parallels (retail), One of a Kind parallels (hobby), Printing Plates parallels (HTA), Bowman Previews, Co-Signers (hobby), In the Wings, Never Comprimise, and Triumvirates (retail). Inserts in Series II include: First Day Issue parallels (retail), One of a Kind parallels (hobby), Printing Plates parallels (HTA), Bowman Prospect Previews, Co-Signers (hobby), Playing with Passion, Royal Court and Triumvirates (retail).

	MT
Complete Set (400):	75.00
Complete Series 1 (200):	40.00
Complete Series 2 (200):	35.00
Common Player:	.10
Cal Ripken Screen Play Sound Chip:	12.50
Hobby Pack (10):	3.00
Retail Pack (7):	2.00
Home Team Adv. Pack (16):	5.00
Wax Box (24):	65.00

1 Chipper Jones 1.50
2 Frank Thomas 1.00
3 Vladimir Guerrero 1.00
4 Ellis Burks .10
5 John Franco .10
6 Paul Molitor .50
7 Rusty Greer .10
8 Todd Hundley .10
9 Brett Tomko .10
10 Eric Karros .20
11 Mike Cameron .10
12 Jim Edmonds .25
13 Bernie Williams .50
14 Denny Neagle .10
15 Jason Dickson .10
16 Sammy Sosa 2.00
17 Brian Jordan .10
18 Jose Vidro .10
19 Scott Spiezio .10
20 Jay Buhner .15
21 Jim Thome .40
22 Sandy Alomar .20
23 Devon White .10
24 Roberto Alomar .60
25 John Flaherty .10
26 John Wetteland .10
27 Willie Greene .10
28 Gregg Jefferies .10
29 Johnny Damon .10
30 Barry Larkin .40
31 Chuck Knoblauch .20
32 Mo Vaughn .40
33 Tony Clark .20
34 Marty Cordova .10
35 Vinny Castilla .10
36 Jeff King .10
37 Reggie Jefferson .10
38 Mariano Rivera .20
39 Jermaine Allensworth .10
40 Livan Hernandez .10
41 Heathcliff Slocumb .10
42 Jacob Cruz .10
43 Barry Bonds .75
44 Dave Magadan .10
45 Chan Ho Park .15
46 Jeremi Gonzalez .10
47 Jeff Cirillo .10
48 Delino DeShields .10
49 Craig Biggio .25
50 Benito Santiago .10
51 Mark Clark .10
52 Fernando Vina .10
53 F.P. Santangelo .10
54 *Pep Harris* .25
55 Edgar Renteria .10
56 Jeff Bagwell .75
57 Jimmy Key .10
58 Bartolo Colon .10
59 Curt Schilling .20
60 Steve Finley .10
61 Andy Ashby .10
62 John Burkett .10
63 Orel Hershiser .10
64 Pokey Reese .10
65 Scott Servais .10
66 Todd Jones .10
67 Javy Lopez .20
68 Robin Ventura .20
69 Miguel Tejada .25
70 Raul Casanova .10
71 Reggie Sanders .10
72 Edgardo Alfonzo .20
73 Dean Palmer .10
74 Todd Stottlemyre .10
75 David Wells .10
76 Troy Percival .10
77 Albert Belle .40
78 Pat Hentgen .10
79 Brian Hunter .10
80 Richard Hidalgo .10
81 Darren Oliver .10
82 Mark Wohlers .10
83 Cal Ripken Jr. 2.50
84 Hideo Nomo .40
85 Derrek Lee .15
86 Stan Javier .10
87 Rey Ordonez .10
88 Randy Johnson .75
89 Jeff Kent .10
90 Brian McRae .10
91 Manny Ramirez .75
92 Trevor Hoffman .10
93 Doug Glanville .10
94 Todd Walker .10
95 Andy Benes .10
96 Jason Schmidt .10
97 Mike Matheny .10
98 Tim Naehring .10
99 Jeff Blauser .10
100 Jose Rosado .10
101 Roger Clemens 1.00
102 Pedro Astacio .10
103 Mark Bellhorn .10
104 Paul O'Neill .25
105 Darin Erstad .75
106 Mike Lieberthal .10
107 Wilson Alvarez .10
108 Mike Mussina .50
109 George Williams .10
110 Cliff Floyd .10
111 Shawn Estes .10
112 Mark Grudzielanek .10
113 Tony Gwynn 1.00
114 Alan Benes .15
115 Terry Steinbach .10
116 Greg Maddux 1.50
117 Andy Pettitte .25
118 Dave Nilsson .10
119 Deivi Cruz .10
120 Carlos Delgado .60
121 Scott Hatteberg .10
122 John Olerud .20
123 Moises Alou .20
124 Garret Anderson .10
125 Royce Clayton .10
126 Dante Powell .10
127 Tom Glavine .25
128 Gary DiSarcina .10
129 Terry Adams .10
130 Raul Mondesi .25
131 Dan Wilson .10
132 Al Martin .10
133 Mickey Morandini .10
134 Rafael Palmeiro .40
135 Juan Encarnacion .15
136 Jim Pittsley .10
137 *Magglio Ordonez* 2.50
138 Will Clark .30
139 Todd Helton .75
140 Kelvim Escobar .10
141 Esteban Loaiza .10
142 John Jaha .10
143 Jeff Fassero .10
144 Harold Baines .10
145 Butch Huskey .10
146 Pat Meares .10
147 Brian Giles .20
148 Ramiro Mendoza .10
149 John Smoltz .15
150 Felix Martinez .10
151 Jose Valentin .10
152 Brad Rigby .10
153 Ed Sprague .10
154 Mike Hampton .10
155 Mike Lansing .10
156 Ray Lankford .10
157 Bobby Bonilla .10
158 Bill Mueller .10
159 Jeffrey Hammonds .10
160 Charles Nagy .10
161 Rich Loiselle .10
162 Al Leiter .15
163 Larry Walker .25
164 Chris Hoiles .10
165 Jeff Montgomery .10
166 Francisco Cordova .10
167 James Baldwin .10
168 Mark McLemore .10
169 Kevin Appier .10
170 Jamey Wright .10
171 Nomar Garciaparra 2.00
172 Matt Franco .10
173 Armando Benitez .10
174 Jeromy Burnitz .10
175 Ismael Valdes .10
176 Lance Johnson .10
177 Paul Sorrento .10
178 Rondell White .20
179 Kevin Elster .10
180 Jason Giambi .40
181 Carlos Baerga .10
182 Russ Davis .10
183 Ryan McGuire .10
184 Eric Young .10
185 Ron Gant .10
186 Manny Alexander .10
187 Scott Karl .10
188 Brady Anderson .10
189 Randall Simon .10
190 Tim Belcher .10
191 Jaret Wright .15
192 Dante Bichette .20
193 John Valentin .10
194 Darren Bragg .10
195 Mike Sweeney .10
196 Craig Counsell .10
197 Jaime Navarro .10
198 Todd Dunn .10
199 Ken Griffey Jr. 2.50
200 Juan Gonzalez .75
201 Billy Wagner .10
202 Tino Martinez .20
203 Mark McGwire 3.00
204 Jeff D'Amico .10
205 Rico Brogna .10
206 Todd Hollandsworth .10
207 Chad Curtis .10
208 Tom Goodwin .10
209 Neifi Perez .10
210 Derek Bell .10
211 Quilvio Veras .10
212 Greg Vaughn .10
213 Roberto Hernandez .10
214 Arthur Rhodes .10
215 Cal Eldred .10
216 Bill Taylor .10
217 Todd Greene .10
218 Mario Valdez .10
219 Ricky Bottalico .10
220 Frank Rodriguez .10
221 Rich Becker .10
222 Roberto Duran .10
223 Ivan Rodriguez .75
224 Mike Jackson .10
225 Deion Sanders .20
226 Tony Womack .10
227 Mark Kotsay .15
228 Steve Trachsel .10
229 Ryan Klesko .20
230 Ken Cloude .10
231 Luis Gonzalez .15

232 Gary Gaetti .10
233 Michael Tucker .10
234 Shawn Green .25
235 Ariel Prieto .10
236 Kirt Manwaring .10
237 Omar Vizquel .25
238 Matt Beech .10
239 Justin Thompson .10
240 Bret Boone .10
241 Derek Jeter 2.50
242 Ken Caminiti .20
243 Jay Bell .10
244 Kevin Tapani .10
245 Jason Kendall .10
246 Jose Guillen .10
247 Mike Bordick .10
248 Dustin Hermanson .10
249 Darrin Fletcher .10
250 Dave Hollins .10
251 Ramon Martinez .15
252 Hideki Irabu .15
253 Mark Grace .25
254 Jason Isringhausen .10
255 Jose Cruz Jr. .15
256 Brian Johnson .10
257 Brad Ausmus .10
258 Andruw Jones .75
259 Doug Jones .10
260 Jeff Shaw .10
261 Chuck Finley .10
262 Gary Sheffield .30
263 David Segui .10
264 John Smiley .10
265 Tim Salmon .20
266 J.T. Snow Jr. .10
267 Alex Fernandez .10
268 Matt Stairs .10
269 B.J. Surhoff .10
270 Keith Foulke .10
271 Edgar Martinez .10
272 Shannon Stewart .10
273 Eduardo Perez .10
274 Wally Joyner .10
275 Kevin Young .10
276 Eli Marrero .10
277 Brad Radke .10
278 Jamie Moyer .10
279 Joe Girardi .10
280 Troy O'Leary .10
281 Aaron Sele .10
282 Jose Offerman .10
283 Scott Erickson .10
284 Sean Berry .10
285 Shigetosi Hasegawa .10
286 Felix Heredia .10
287 Willie McGee .10
288 Alex Rodriguez 2.50
289 Ugueth Urbina .10
290 Jon Lieber .10
291 Fernando Tatis .10
292 Chris Stynes .10
293 Bernard Gilkey .10
294 Joey Hamilton .10
295 Matt Karchner .10
296 Paul Wilson .10
297 Mel Nieves .10
298 *Kevin Millwood* 1.00
299 Quinton McCracken .10
300 Jerry DiPoto .10
301 Jermaine Dye .10
302 Travis Lee .10
303 Ron Coomer .10
304 Matt Williams .25
305 Bobby Higginson .10
306 Jorge Fabregas .10
307 Hal Morris .10
308 Jay Bell .10
309 Joe Randa .10
310 Andy Benes .10
311 Sterling Hitchcock .10
312 Jeff Suppan .10
313 Shane Reynolds .10
314 Willie Blair .10
315 Scott Rolen .75
316 Wilson Alvarez .10
317 David Justice .40
318 Fred McGriff .25
319 Bobby Jones .10
320 Wade Boggs .40
321 Tim Wakefield .10
322 Tony Saunders .10
323 David Cone .20
324 Roberto Hernandez .10
325 Jose Canseco .40
326 Kevin Stocker .10
327 Gerald Williams .10
328 Quinton McCracken .10
329 Mark Gardner .10
330 Ben Grieve (Prime Rookie) .40
331 Kevin Brown .20
332 *Mike Lowell* (Prime Rookie) .40
333 Jed Hansen .10
334 Abraham Nunez (Prime Rookie) .15
335 John Thomson .10
336 Derrek Lee (Prime Rookie) .10
337 Mike Piazza 2.00
338 Brad Fullmer (Prime Rookie) .10
339 Ray Durham .10
340 Kerry Wood (Prime Rookie) .25
341 *Kevin Polcovich* .10
342 Russ Johnson (Prime Rookie) .10
343 Darryl Hamilton .10
344 David Ortiz (Prime Rookie) .15
345 Kevin Orie .10
346 Sean Casey (Prime Rookie) .25
347 Juan Guzman .10
348 Ruben Rivera (Prime Rookie) .10
349 Rick Aguilera .10
350 Bobby Estalella (Prime Rookie) .10
351 Bobby Witt .10
352 Paul Konerko (Prime Rookie) .15
353 Matt Morris .10
354 Carl Pavano (Prime Rookie) .10
355 Todd Zeile .10
356 Kevin Brown (Transaction) .10
357 Alex Gonzalez .10
358 Chuck Knoblauch (Transaction) .20
359 Joey Cora .10
360 Mike Lansing (Transaction) .10
361 Adrian Beltre (Future Stars) .25
362 Dennis Eckersley (Transaction) .10
363 A.J. Hinch (Future Stars) .15
364 Kenny Lofton (Transaction) .25
365 Alex Gonzalez (Future Stars) .10
366 Henry Rodriguez (Transaction) .10
367 *Mike Stoner* (Future Stars) .75
368 Darryl Kile (Transaction) .10
369 Carl Pavano (Future Stars) .10
370 Walt Weiss (Transaction) .10
371 Kris Benson (Future Stars) .20
372 Cecil Fielder (Transaction) .10
373 Dermal Brown (Future Stars) .15
374 Rod Beck (Transaction) .10
375 Eric Milton (Future Stars) .15
376 Travis Fryman (Transaction) .10
377 Preston Wilson (Future Stars) .10
378 Chili Davis (Transaction) .10
379 Travis Lee (Future Stars) .15
380 Jim Leyritz (Transaction) .10
381 Vernon Wells (Draft Picks) .15
382 Joe Carter (Transaction) .10
383 J.J. Davis (Draft Picks) .15
384 Marquis Grissom (Transaction) .10
385 *Mike Cuddyer* (Draft Picks) .50
386 Rickey Henderson (Transaction) .20
387 *Chris Enochs* (Draft Picks) .50
388 Andres Galarraga (Transaction) .25
389 Jason Dellaero (Draft Picks) .15
390 Robb Nen (Transaction) .10
391 Mark Mangum (Draft Picks) .10
392 Jeff Blauser (Transaction) .10
393 Adam Kennedy (Draft Picks) .15
394 Bob Abreu (Transaction) .10
395 *Jack Cust* (Draft Picks) 1.50
396 Jose Vizcaino (Transaction) .10
397 Jon Garland (Draft Picks) .20
398 Pedro Martinez (Transaction) .50
399 Aaron Akin (Draft Picks) .10
400 Jeff Conine (Transaction) .10

1998 Stadium Club First Day Issue

	MT
Common Player:	5.00
Stars:	30X

Production 200 sets
(See 1998 Stadium Club for checklist and base card values.)

1998 Stadium Club One of a Kind

This hobby-only parallel set includes all 400 cards from Series 1 and 2 printed on a silver mirror-board stock. Cards are sequentially numbered to 150 and inserted one per 21 Series 1 packs and one per 24 Series 2 packs.

	MT
Common Player:	5.00
Stars:	40X

Production 150 sets
(See 1998 Stadium Club for checklist and base card values.)

1998 Stadium Club Bowman Preview

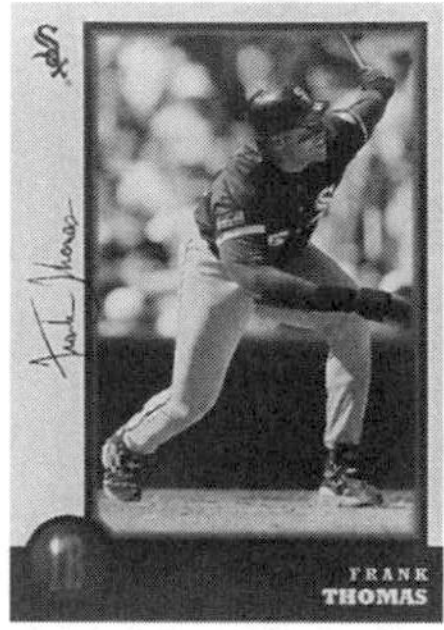

This Series I insert gave collectors a sneak peak at Bowman's 50th anniversary set, with 10 top veterans displayed on the 1998 Bowman design. The cards were inserted one per 12 packs and numbered with a "BP" prefix.

	MT
Complete Set (10):	40.00
Common Player:	1.00
Inserted 1:12	
BP1 Nomar Garciaparra	6.50
BP2 Scott Rolen	4.50
BP3 Ken Griffey Jr.	10.00
BP4 Frank Thomas	5.00
BP5 Larry Walker	1.25
BP6 Mike Piazza	6.50
BP7 Chipper Jones	6.50
BP8 Tino Martinez	1.00
BP9 Mark McGwire	10.00
BP10 Barry Bonds	3.00

1998 Stadium Club Bowman Prospect Preview

Bowman Prospect Previews were inserted into Series II retail and hobby packs at a rate of one per 12 and HTA packs at one per four. The 10-card insert previews the upcoming 1998 Bowman set and includes top prospects that are expected to make an impact in 1998.

	MT
Complete Set (10):	15.00
Common Player:	1.00
Inserted 1:12	
BP1 Ben Grieve	4.00
BP2 Brad Fullmer	1.50
BP3 Ryan Anderson	5.00
BP4 Mark Kotsay	1.50
BP5 Bobby Estalella	1.25
BP6 Juan Encarnacion	1.50
BP7 Todd Helton	3.00
BP8 Mike Lowell	1.00
BP9 A.J. Hinch	1.25
BP10 Richard Hidalgo	1.00

1998 Stadium Club Co-Signers

Co-Signers were inserted into both Series 1 and 2 hobby and HTA packs. The complete set is 36 cards and contains two top players on one side along with both autographs. They were available in three levels of scarcity: Series 1 Group A 1:4,372 hobby and 1:2,623 HTA; Series 1 Group B 1:1,457 hobby and HTA 1:874; Series 1 Group C 1:121 hobby and 1:73 HTA; Series 2 Group A 1:4,702 hobby and 1:2,821 HTA; Series 2 Group B 1:1,567 hobby and 1:940 HTA, Series 2 Group C 1:1,131 hobby and 1:78 HTA.

	MT
Common Player:	25.00
Group A 1:4,372	
Group B 1:1,457	
Group C 1:121	
CS1 Nomar Garciaparra, Scott Rolen (A)	700.00
CS2 Nomar Garciaparra, Derek Jeter (B)	300.00
CS3 Nomar Garciaparra, Eric Karros (C)	100.00
CS4 Scott Rolen, Derek Jeter (C)	150.00
CS5 Scott Rolen, Eric Karros (B)	150.00
CS6 Derek Jeter, Eric Karros (A)	500.00
CS7 Travis Lee, Jose Cruz Jr. (B)	40.00
CS8 Travis Lee, Mark Kotsay (C)	25.00
CS9 Travis Lee, Paul Konerko (A)	75.00
CS10 Jose Cruz Jr., Mark Kotsay (A)	50.00
CS11 Jose Cruz Jr., Paul Konerko (C)	25.00
CS12 Mark Kotsay, Paul Konerko (B)	60.00
CS13 Tony Gwynn, Larry Walker (A)	500.00
CS14 Tony Gwynn, Mark Grudzielanek (C)	100.00
CS15 Tony Gwynn, Andres Galarraga (B)	150.00
CS16 Larry Walker, Mark Grudzielanek (B)	75.00
CS17 Larry Walker, Andres Galarraga (C)	100.00
CS18 Mark Grudzielanek, Andres Galarraga (A)	50.00
CS19 Sandy Alomar, Roberto Alomar (A)	400.00
CS20 Sandy Alomar, Andy Pettitte (C)	40.00
CS21 Sandy Alomar, Tino Martinez (B)	75.00
CS22 Roberto Alomar, Andy Pettitte (B)	125.00
CS23 Roberto Alomar, Tino Martinez (C)	60.00
CS24 Andy Pettitte, Tino Martinez (A)	150.00
CS25 Tony Clark, Todd Hundley (A)	100.00
CS26 Tony Clark, Tim Salmon (B)	75.00
CS27 Tony Clark, Robin Ventura (C)	50.00
CS28 Todd Hundley, Tim Salmon (C)	50.00
CS29 Todd Hundley, Robin Ventura (B)	50.00
CS30 Tim Salmon, Robin Ventura (A)	100.00
CS31 Roger Clemens, Randy Johnson (B)	225.00
CS32 Roger Clemens, Jaret Wright (A)	400.00
CS33 Roger Clemens, Matt Morris (C)	100.00
CS34 Randy Johnson, Jaret Wright (C)	80.00
CS35 Randy Johnson, Matt Morris (A)	150.00
CS36 Jaret Wright, Matt Morris (B)	50.00

1998 Stadium Club In the Wings

In the Wings was a Series I insert found every 36 packs. It included 15 future stars on uniluster technology.

	MT
Complete Set (15):	45.00
Common Player:	1.50
Inserted 1:36	
W1 Juan Encarnacion	2.50
W2 Brad Fullmer	3.00
W3 Ben Grieve	8.00
W4 Todd Helton	10.00
W5 Richard Hidalgo	3.00
W6 Russ Johnson	1.50
W7 Paul Konerko	6.00
W8 Mark Kotsay	2.50
W9 Derrek Lee	1.50
W10 Travis Lee	2.50
W11 Eli Marrero	1.50
W12 David Ortiz	1.50
W13 Randall Simon	1.50
W14 Shannon Stewart	2.50
W15 Fernando Tatis	3.00

1998 Stadium Club Never Compromise

Never Compromise was a 20-card insert found in packs of Series I. Cards were inserted one per 12 packs and numbered with a "NC" prefix.

	MT
Complete Set (20):	80.00
Common Player:	1.00
Inserted 1:12	
NC1 Cal Ripken Jr.	10.00
NC2 Ivan Rodriguez	3.00
NC3 Ken Griffey Jr.	10.00
NC4 Frank Thomas	4.00
NC5 Tony Gwynn	4.00
NC6 Mike Piazza	8.00
NC7 Randy Johnson	3.00
NC8 Greg Maddux	6.00
NC9 Roger Clemens	4.00
NC10 Derek Jeter	10.00
NC11 Chipper Jones	6.00
NC12 Barry Bonds	3.00
NC13 Larry Walker	2.00
NC14 Jeff Bagwell	3.00
NC15 Barry Larkin	1.50
NC16 Ken Caminiti	1.00
NC17 Mark McGwire	12.00
NC18 Manny Ramirez	3.00
NC19 Tim Salmon	1.00
NC20 Paul Molitor	2.50

1998 Stadium Club Playing with Passion

This Series II insert displayed 10 players with a strong desire to win. The cards were inserted one per 12 packs and numbered with a "P" prefix.

	MT
Complete Set (10):	30.00
Common Player:	1.00
Inserted 1:12	
P1 Bernie Williams	1.00
P2 Jim Edmonds	1.00
P3 Chipper Jones	4.00
P4 Cal Ripken Jr.	5.00
P5 Craig Biggio	1.00
P6 Juan Gonzalez	2.50
P7 Alex Rodriguez	5.00
P8 Tino Martinez	1.00
P9 Mike Piazza	4.00
P10 Ken Griffey Jr.	7.00

1998 Stadium Club Royal Court

Fifteen players were showcased on uniluster technology for this Series II insert. The set is broken up into 10 Kings (veterans) and five Princes (rookies) and inserted one per 36 packs.

	MT
Complete Set (15):	160.00
Common Player:	3.00
Inserted 1:36	
RC1 Ken Griffey Jr.	25.00
RC2 Frank Thomas	10.00
RC3 Mike Piazza	20.00
RC4 Chipper Jones	15.00
RC5 Mark McGwire	30.00
RC6 Cal Ripken Jr.	25.00
RC7 Jeff Bagwell	10.00
RC8 Barry Bonds	8.00
RC9 Juan Gonzalez	8.00
RC10 Alex Rodriguez	25.00
RC11 Travis Lee	3.00
RC12 Paul Konerko	3.00
RC13 Todd Helton	8.00
RC14 Ben Grieve	5.00
RC15 Mark Kotsay	3.00

1998 Stadium Club Triumvirate

Triumvirates were included in both series of Stadium Club and were available only in retail packs. Series 1 has 24 players, with three players from eight different teams, while Series 2 has 30 players, with three players from 10 different positions. The cards are all die-cut and fit together to form three-card panels. Three different versions of each card were available - Luminous (regular) versions were seeded one per 48 packs, Luminescent versions were seeded one per 192 packs and Illuminator versions were seeded one per 384 packs.

		MT
Complete Set (54):		600.00
Complete Series 1 (24):		250.00
Complete Series 2 (30):		350.00
Common Player:		4.00
Luminous 1:48		
Luminescents 1:192:		2X
Illuminators 1:384:		4X
T1a	Chipper Jones	30.00
T1b	Andruw Jones	12.00
T1c	Kenny Lofton	6.00
T2a	Derek Jeter	30.00
T2b	Bernie Williams	8.00
T2c	Tino Martinez	4.00
T3a	Jay Buhner	4.00
T3b	Edgar Martinez	4.00
T3c	Ken Griffey Jr.	40.00
T4a	Albert Belle	8.00
T4b	Robin Ventura	4.00
T4c	Frank Thomas	20.00
T5a	Brady Anderson	4.00
T5b	Cal Ripken Jr.	40.00
T5c	Rafael Palmeiro	8.00
T6a	Mike Piazza	30.00
T6b	Raul Mondesi	5.00
T6c	Eric Karros	4.00
T7a	Vinny Castilla	4.00
T7b	Andres Galarraga	5.00
T7c	Larry Walker	5.00
T8a	Jim Thome	6.00
T8b	Manny Ramirez	12.00
T8c	David Justice	5.00
T9a	Mike Mussina	8.00
T9b	Greg Maddux	25.00
T9c	Randy Johnson	12.00
T10a	Mike Piazza	30.00
T10b	Sandy Alomar	4.00
T10c	Ivan Rodriguez	12.00
T11a	Mark McGwire	50.00
T11b	Tino Martinez	4.00
T11c	Frank Thomas	20.00
T12a	Roberto Alomar	10.00
T12b	Chuck Knoblauch	4.00
T12c	Craig Biggio	4.00
T13a	Cal Ripken Jr.	40.00
T13b	Chipper Jones	25.00
T13c	Ken Caminiti	4.00
T14a	Derek Jeter	30.00
T14b	Nomar Garciaparra	30.00
T14c	Alex Rodriguez	40.00
T15a	Barry Bonds	12.00
T15b	David Justice	6.00
T15c	Albert Belle	8.00
T16a	Bernie Williams	8.00
T16b	Ken Griffey Jr.	40.00
T16c	Ray Lankford	4.00
T17a	Tim Salmon	4.00
T17b	Larry Walker	6.00
T17c	Tony Gwynn	20.00
T18a	Paul Molitor	10.00
T18b	Edgar Martinez	4.00
T18c	Juan Gonzalez	12.00

1999 Stadium Club

Released in two series with Series 1 170-cards and Series 2 185-cards. Base cards feature a full bleed design on 20-pt. stock with an embossed holographic logo. Draft Pick and Prospect subset cards are short-printed, seeded in every three packs. Card backs have 1998 statistics and personal information. Hobby packs consist of six cards with a S.R.P. of $2.

		MT
Complete Set (355):		115.00
Complete Series 1 Set (170):		65.00
Complete Series 2 Set (185):		55.00
Common Player:		.15
Common Prospect (141-148):		1.00
Inserted 1:3		
Common Draft Pick (149-160):		1.00
Inserted 1:3		
Common SP (311-335, 346-355):		1.00
Common SP (336-345):		2.00
Pack (6):		2.00
Wax Box (24):		40.00
1	Alex Rodriguez	2.50
2	Chipper Jones	2.00
3	Rusty Greer	.15
4	Jim Edmonds	.20
5	Ron Gant	.15
6	Kevin Polcovich	.15
7	Darryl Strawberry	.25
8	Bill Mueller	.15
9	Vinny Castilla	.15
10	Wade Boggs	.40
11	Jose Lima	.15
12	Darren Dreifort	.15
13	Jay Bell	.15
14	Ben Grieve	.75
15	Shawn Green	.25
16	Andres Galarraga	.60
17	Bartolo Colon	.15
18	Francisco Cordova	.15
19	Paul O'Neill	.30
20	Trevor Hoffman	.15
21	Darren Oliver	.15
22	John Franco	.15
23	Eli Marrero	.15
24	Roberto Hernandez	.15
25	Craig Biggio	.30
26	Brad Fullmer	.25
27	Scott Erickson	.15
28	Tom Gordon	.15
29	Brian Hunter	.15
30	Raul Mondesi	.25
31	Rick Reed	.15
32	Jose Canseco	.40
33	Robb Nen	.15
34	Turner Ward	.15
35	Bret Boone	.15
36	Jose Offerman	.15
37	Matt Lawton	.15
38	David Wells	.15
39	Bob Abreu	.15
40	Jeromy Burnitz	.15
41	Deivi Cruz	.15
42	Mike Cameron	.15
43	Rico Brogna	.15
44	Dmitri Young	.15
45	Chuck Knoblauch	.30
46	Johnny Damon	.15
47	Brian Meadows	.15
48	Jeremi Gonzalez	.15
49	Gary DiSarcina	.15
50	Frank Thomas	1.50
51	F.P. Santangelo	.15
52	Tom Candiotti	.15
53	Shane Reynolds	.15
54	Rod Beck	.15
55	Rey Ordonez	.15
56	Todd Helton	.75
57	Mickey Morandini	.15
58	Jorge Posada	.15
59	Mike Mussina	.50
60	Bobby Bonilla	.15
61	David Segui	.15
62	Brian McRae	.15
63	Fred McGriff	.25
64	Brett Tomko	.15
65	Derek Jeter	2.00
66	Sammy Sosa	2.50
67	Kenny Rogers	.15
68	Dave Nilsson	.15
69	Eric Young	.15
70	Mark McGwire	3.00
71	Kenny Lofton	.45
72	Tom Glavine	.20
73	Joey Hamilton	.15
74	John Valentin	.15
75	Mariano Rivera	.25
76	Ray Durham	.15
77	Tony Clark	.50
78	Livan Hernandez	.15
79	Rickey Henderson	.30
80	Vladimir Guerrero	1.25
81	J.T. Snow Jr.	.15
82	Juan Guzman	.15
83	Darryl Hamilton	.15
84	Matt Anderson	.25
85	Travis Lee	.75
86	Joe Randa	.15
87	Dave Dellucci	.15
88	Moises Alou	.20
89	Alex Gonzalez	.15
90	Tony Womack	.15
91	Neifi Perez	.15
92	Travis Fryman	.15
93	Masato Yoshii	.15
94	Woody Williams	.15
95	Ray Lankford	.15
96	Roger Clemens	1.00
97	Dustin Hermanson	.15
98	Joe Carter	.15
99	Jason Schmidt	.15
100	Greg Maddux	2.00
101	Kevin Tapani	.15
102	Charles Johnson	.15
103	Derrek Lee	.15
104	Pete Harnisch	.15
105	Dante Bichette	.40
106	Scott Brosius	.15
107	Mike Caruso	.15
108	Eddie Taubensee	.15
109	Jeff Fassero	.15
110	Marquis Grissom	.15
111	Jose Hernandez	.15
112	Chan Ho Park	.25
113	Wally Joyner	.15
114	Bobby Estalella	.15
115	Pedro Martinez	.50
116	Shawn Estes	.15
117	Walt Weiss	.15
118	John Mabry	.15
119	Brian Johnson	.15
120	Jim Thome	.35
121	Bill Spiers	.15
122	John Olerud	.25
123	Jeff King	.15
124	Tim Belcher	.15
125	John Wetteland	.15
126	Tony Gwynn	1.50
127	Brady Anderson	.15
128	Randy Winn	.15
129	Devon White	.15
130	Eric Karros	.15
131	Kevin Millwood	.40
132	Andy Benes	.15
133	Andy Ashby	.15
134	Ron Comer	.15
135	Juan Gonzalez	.75
136	Randy Johnson	.50
137	Aaron Sele	.15
138	Edgardo Alfonzo	.15
139	B.J. Surhoff	.15
140	Jose Vizcaino	.15
141	*Chad Moeller* (Prospect)	1.00
142	*Mike Zwicka* (Prospect)	1.00
143	Angel Pena (Prospect)	1.00
144	*Nick Johnson* (Prospect)	4.00
145	*Giuseppe Chiaramonte* (Prospect)	1.50
146	*Kit Pellow* (Prospect)	1.00
147	*Clayton Andrews* (Prospect)	1.00
148	*Jerry Hairston Jr.* (Prospect)	1.50
149	*Jason Tyner* (Draft Pick)	1.50
150	*Chip Ambres* (Draft Pick)	1.00
151	*Pat Burrell* (Draft Pick)	10.00
152	*Josh McKinley* (Draft Pick)	1.00
153	*Choo Freeman* (Draft Pick)	1.50
154	*Rick Elder* (Draft Pick)	2.00
155	*Eric Valent* (Draft Pick)	2.00
156	*Jeff Winchester* (Draft Pick)	1.50
157	*Mike Nannini* (Draft Pick)	1.00
158	*Mamon Tucker* (Draft Pick)	1.00
159	*Nate Bump* (Draft Pick)	1.00
160	*Andy Brown* (Draft Pick)	1.50
161	Troy Glaus (Future Star)	1.00
162	Adrian Beltre (Future Star)	.40
163	Mitch Meluskey (Future Star)	1.00
164	Alex Gonzalez (Future Star)	.20
165	George Lombard (Future Star)	.20
166	Eric Chavez (Future Star)	.50
167	Ruben Mateo (Future Star)	.75
168	Calvin Pickering (Future Star)	.20
169	Gabe Kapler (Future Star)	1.50
170	Bruce Chen (Future Star)	.15
171	Darin Erstad	.75
172	Sandy Alomar	.25
173	Miguel Cairo	.15

174 Jason Kendall .25
175 Cal Ripken Jr. 2.50
176 Darryl Kile .15
177 David Cone .25
178 Mike Sweeney .15
179 Royce Clayton .15
180 Curt Schilling .30
181 Barry Larkin .30
182 Eric Milton .15
183 Ellis Burks .15
184 A.J. Hinch .15
185 Garret Anderson .15
186 Sean Bergman .15
187 Shannon Stewart .15
188 Bernard Gilkey .15
189 Jeff Blauser .15
190 Andruw Jones .75
191 Omar Daal .15
192 Jeff Kent .15
193 Mark Kotsay .15
194 Dave Burba .15
195 Bobby Higginson .15
196 Hideki Irabu .30
197 Jamie Moyer .15
198 Doug Glanville .15
199 Quinton McCracken .15
200 Ken Griffey Jr. 3.00
201 Mike Lieberthal .15
202 Carl Everett .15
203 Omar Vizquel .15
204 Mike Lansing .15
205 Manny Ramirez 1.50
206 Ryan Klesko .25
207 Jeff Montgomery .15
208 Chad Curtis .15
209 Rick Helling .15
210 Justin Thompson .15
211 Tom Goodwin .15
212 Todd Dunwoody .15
213 Kevin Young .15
214 Tony Saunders .15
215 Gary Sheffield .25
216 Jaret Wright .15
217 Quilvio Veras .15
218 Marty Cordova .15
219 Tino Martinez .40
220 Scott Rolen .75
221 Fernando Tatis .15
222 Damion Easley .15
223 Aramis Ramirez .15
224 Brad Radke .15
225 Nomar Garciaparra 2.00
226 Magglio Ordonez .15
227 Andy Pettitte .40
228 David Ortiz .15
229 Todd Jones .15
230 Larry Walker .50
231 Tim Wakefield .15
232 Jose Guillen .15
233 Gregg Olson .15
234 Ricky Gutierrez .15
235 Todd Walker .25
236 Abraham Nunez .15
237 Sean Casey .40
238 Greg Norton .15
239 Bret Saberhagen .15
240 Bernie Williams .45
241 Tim Salmon .30
242 Jason Giambi .15
243 Fernando Vina .15
244 Darrin Fletcher .15
245 Greg Vaughn .30
246 Dennis Reyes .15
247 Hideo Nomo .25
248 Reggie Sanders .15
249 Mike Hampton .15
250 Kerry Wood .75
251 Ismael Valdes .15
252 Pat Hentgen .15
253 Scott Spiezio .15
254 Chuck Finley .15
255 Troy Glaus .50
256 Bobby Jones .15
257 Wayne Gomes .15
258 Rondell White .25
259 Todd Zeile .15
260 Matt Williams .30
261 Henry Rodriguez .25
262 Matt Stairs .15
263 Jose Valentin .15
264 David Justice .40
265 Javy Lopez .25
266 Matt Morris .15
267 Steve Trachsel .15
268 Edgar Martinez .15
269 Al Martin .15
270 Ivan Rodriguez .75
271 Carlos Delgado .40
272 Mark Grace .35
273 Ugueth Urbina .15
274 Jay Buhner .15
275 Mike Piazza 2.00
276 Rick Aguilera .15
277 Javier Valentin .15
278 Brian Anderson .15
279 Cliff Floyd .15
280 Barry Bonds .75
281 Troy O'Leary .15
282 Seth Greisinger .15
283 Mark Grudzielanek .15
284 Jose Cruz Jr. .25
285 Jeff Bagwell .75
286 John Smoltz .25
287 Jeff Cirillo .15
288 Richie Sexson .15
289 Charles Nagy .15
290 Pedro Martinez .50
291 Juan Encarnacion .25
292 Phil Nevin .15
293 Terry Steinbach .15
294 Miguel Tejada .25
295 Dan Wilson .15
296 Chris Peters .15
297 Brian Moehler .15
298 Jason Christiansen .15
299 Kelly Stinnett .15
300 Dwight Gooden .25
301 Randy Velarde .15
302 Kirt Manwaring .15
303 Jeff Abbott .15
304 Dave Hollins .15
305 Kerry Ligtenberg .15
306 Aaron Boone .15
307 Carlos Hernandez .15
308 Mike DiFelice .15
309 Brian Meadows .15
310 Tim Bogar .15
311 Greg Vaughn (Transaction) 1.00
312 Brant Brown (Transaction) 1.00
313 Steve Finley (Transaction) 1.00
314 Bret Boone (Transaction) 1.00
315 Albert Belle (Transaction) 1.50
316 Robin Ventura (Transaction) 1.00
317 Eric Davis (Transaction) 1.00
318 Todd Hundley (Transaction) 1.00
319 Jose Offerman (Transaction) 1.00
320 Kevin Brown (Transaction) 1.50
321 Denny Neagle (Transaction) 1.00
322 Brian Jordan (Transaction) 1.00
323 Brian Giles (Transaction) 1.00
324 Bobby Bonilla (Transaction) 1.00
325 Roberto Alomar (Transaction) 1.50
326 Ken Caminiti (Transaction) 1.25
327 Todd Stottlemyre (Transaction) 1.00
328 Randy Johnson (Transaction) 1.50
329 Luis Gonzalez (Transaction) 1.00
330 Rafael Palmeiro (Transaction) 1.50
331 Devon White (Transaction) 1.00
332 Will Clark (Transaction) 1.50
333 Dean Palmer (Transaction) 1.00
334 Gregg Jefferies (Transaction) 1.00
335 Mo Vaughn (Transaction) 1.25
336 *Brad Lidge* (Draft Pick) 1.00
337 *Chris George* (Draft Pick) 1.50
338 *Austin Kearns* (Draft Pick) 4.00
339 *Matt Belisle* (Draft Pick) 2.00
340 *Nate Cornejo* (Draft Pick) 1.00
341 *Matt Holiday* (Draft Pick) 1.50
342 *J.M. Gold* (Draft Pick) 1.00
343 *Matt Roney* (Draft Pick) 1.00
344 *Seth Etherton* (Draft Pick) 1.00
345 *Adam Everett* (Draft Pick) 1.50
346 Marlon Anderson (Future Star) 1.00
347 Ron Belliard (Future Star) 1.00
348 Fernando Seguignol (Future Star) 1.00
349 Michael Barrett (Future Star) 1.00
350 Dernell Stenson (Future Star) 1.00
351 Ryan Anderson (Future Star) 1.00
352 Ramon Hernandez (Future Star) 1.00
353 Jeremy Giambi (Future Star) 1.00
354 Ricky Ledee (Future Star) 1.00
355 Carlos Lee (Future Star) 1.00

1999 Stadium Club First Day Issue

A parallel of the 355-card set inserted exclusively in retail packs, Series I (1-170) are serially numbered to 170 at a rate of 1:75 packs. Series 2 (171-355) are serially numbered to 200 and inserted at a rate of 1:60 packs.

	MT
Common Player:	3.00
Stars:	15X
SP Stars:	4X

(See 1999 Stadium Club for checklist and base card values.)

1999 Stadium Club One of a Kind

This insert set parallels the 355-card base set. Cards feature a mirror-board look and are serially numbered to 150. Inserted exclusively in hobby packs, insertion rate for Series 1 is 1:53 and Series 2 is 1:48 packs.

	MT
Common Player:	3.00
Stars:	15X
SP Stars:	4X

(See 1999 Stadium Club for checklist and base card values.)

1999 Stadium Club Autographs

This 10-card autographed set was issued in Series 1 and 2 with five players signing in each series. Available exclusively in retail chains, Series 1 autographs were seeded 1:1,107 packs, while series 2 were inserted in every 877 packs. Each autograph is marked with the Topps Certified Autograph Issue stamp. Card numbers have an "SCA" prefix.

		MT
Complete Set (10):		550.00
Complete Series 1 (5):		325.00
Complete Series 2 (5):		225.00
Common Player:		25.00
Inserted 1:1,107		
1	Alex Rodriguez	150.00
2	Chipper Jones	100.00
3	Barry Bonds	50.00
4	Tino Martinez	25.00
5	Ben Grieve	30.00
6	Juan Gonzalez	60.00
7	Vladimir Guerrero	65.00
8	Albert Belle	30.00
9	Kerry Wood	30.00
10	Todd Helton	50.00

1999 Stadium Club Chrome

This 40-card set was inserted in series 1 and 2 packs, with 1-20 in first series packs and 21-40 in Series 2. Chrome appropriately utilizes chromium technology. The insertion rate is 1:24 packs with Refractor parallel versions also seeded 1:96 packs.

Card numbers have an "SCC" prefix.

		MT
Complete Set (40):		125.00
Complete Series 1 (20):		65.00
Complete Series 2 (20):		65.00
Common Player:		1.00
Inserted 1:24		
Refractors:		2X
Inserted 1:96		
1	Nomar Garciaparra	6.00
2	Kerry Wood	1.50
3	Jeff Bagwell	2.50
4	Ivan Rodriguez	2.50
5	Albert Belle	2.00
6	Gary Sheffield	1.50
7	Andruw Jones	1.50
8	Kevin Brown	1.00
9	David Cone	1.00
10	Darin Erstad	2.00
11	Manny Ramirez	3.00
12	Larry Walker	1.50
13	Mike Piazza	6.00
14	Ken Caminiti	1.00
15	Pedro Martinez	2.50
16	Greg Vaughn	1.00
17	Barry Bonds	3.00
18	Mo Vaughn	1.50
19	Bernie Williams	1.50
20	Ken Griffey Jr.	10.00
21	Alex Rodriguez	8.00
22	Chipper Jones	5.00
23	Ben Grieve	1.50
24	Frank Thomas	4.00
25	Derek Jeter	6.00
26	Sammy Sosa	6.00
27	Mark McGwire	10.00
28	Vladimir Guerrero	4.00
29	Greg Maddux	5.00
30	Juan Gonzalez	2.50
31	Troy Glaus	2.50
32	Adrian Beltre	1.50
33	Mitch Meluskey	1.00
34	Alex Gonzalez	1.00
35	George Lombard	1.50
36	Eric Chavez	1.50
37	Ruben Mateo	1.50
38	Calvin Pickering	1.00
39	Gabe Kapler	1.50
40	Bruce Chen	1.00

1999 Stadium Club Co-Signers

Co-Signers feature two autographs on each card and also for the first time includes one level of four autographs per card. Co-Signers are grouped into categories A, B, C and D. Group A Co-Signers are autographed by four players, while B-D are signed by two players. Insertion odds are as follows: Group D, 1:254; C, 1:3,014; B, 1:9,043; A, 1:45,213. Each card features the Topps Certified Autograph Issue stamp.

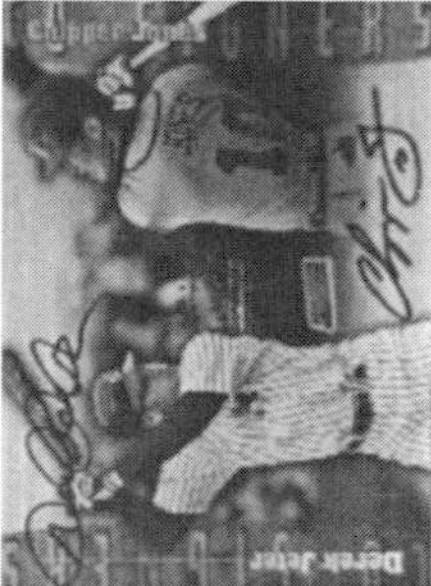

		MT
Common Group A:		
Inserted 1:18,085		
Common Group B:		50.00
Inserted 1:9043		
Common Group C:		25.00
Inserted 1:3014		
Common Group D:		15.00
Inserted 1:254		
CS1	Ben Grieve, Richie Sexson (D)	50.00
CS2	Todd Helton, Troy Glaus (D)	80.00
CS3	Alex Rodriguez, Scott Rolen (D)	200.00
CS4	Derek Jeter, Chipper Jones (D)	200.00
CS5	Cliff Floyd, Eli Marrero (D)	15.00
CS6	Jay Buhner, Kevin Young (D)	15.00
CS7	Ben Grieve, Troy Glaus (C)	50.00
CS8	Todd Helton, Richie Sexson (C)	50.00
CS9	Alex Rodriguez, Chipper Jones (C)	300.00
CS10	Derek Jeter, Scott Rolen (C)	200.00
CS11	Cliff Floyd, Kevin Young (C)	25.00
CS12	Jay Buhner, Eli Marrero (B)	50.00
CS13	Ben Grieve, Todd Helton (B)	150.00
CS14	Richie Sexson, Troy Glaus (B)	100.00
CS15	Alex Rodriguez, Derek Jeter (B)	450.00
CS16	Chipper Jones, Scott Rolen (B)	250.00
CS17	Cliff Floyd, Jay Buhner (B)	50.00
CS18	Eli Marrero, Kevin Young (B)	50.00
CS19	Ben Grieve, Todd Helton, Richie Sexson, Troy Glaus (A)	300.00
CS20	Alex Rodriguez, Derek Jeter, Chipper Jones, Scott Rolen (A)	2500.
CS21	Cliff Floyd, Jay Buhner, Eli Marrero, Kevin Young (A)	150.00
CS22	Edgardo Alfonzo, Jose Guillen (D)	45.00
CS23	Mike Lowell, Ricardo Rincon (D)	25.00
CS24	Juan Gonzalez, Vinny Castilla (D)	100.00
CS25	Moises Alou, Roger Clemens (D)	75.00
CS26	Scott Spezio, Tony Womack (D)	15.00
CS27	Fernando Vina, Quilvio Veras (D)	15.00
CS28	Edgardo Alfonzo, Ricardo Rincon (C)	30.00
CS29	Jose Guillen, Mike Lowell (C)	30.00
CS30	Juan Gonzalez, Moises Alou (C)	150.00
CS31	Roger Clemens, Vinny Castilla (C)	150.00
CS32	Scott Spezio, Fernando Vina (C)	25.00
CS33	Tony Womack, Quilvio Veras (B)	50.00
CS34	Edgardo Alfonzo, Mike Lowell (B)	60.00
CS35	Jose Guillen, Ricardo Rincon (B)	60.00
CS36	Juan Gonzalez, Roger Clemens (B)	300.00
CS37	Moises Alou, Vinny Castilla (B)	75.00
CS38	Scott Spezio, Quilvio Veras (B)	50.00
CS39	Tony Womack, Fernando Vina (B)	50.00
CS40	Edgardo Alfonzo, Jose Guillen, Mike Lowell, Ricardo Rincon (A)	200.00
CS41	Juan Gonzalez, Moises Alou, Roger Clemens, Vinny Castilla (A)	1500.
CS42	Scott Spezio, Tony Womack, Fernando Vina, Quilvio Veras (A)	200.00

1999 Stadium Club Never Compromise

Topps selected players who bring hard work and devotion to the field every game are highlighted, including Cal Ripken Jr. The first 10 cards in the set are inserted in series I packs while the remaining 10 are seeded in series II at a rate of 1:12 packs.

		MT
Complete Set (20):		65.00
Complete Series 1 (10):		40.00
Complete Series 2 (10):		25.00
Common Player:		1.50
Inserted 1:12		
NC1	Mark McGwire	8.00
NC2	Sammy Sosa	5.00
NC3	Ken Griffey Jr.	8.00
NC4	Greg Maddux	4.00
NC5	Barry Bonds	2.00
NC6	Alex Rodriguez	6.00
NC7	Darin Erstad	1.50
NC8	Roger Clemens	3.00
NC9	Nomar Garciaparra	5.00
NC10	Derek Jeter	5.00
NC11	Cal Ripken Jr.	6.00
NC12	Mike Piazza	5.00
NC13	Greg Vaughn	1.50
NC14	Andres Galarraga	1.50
NC15	Vinny Castilla	1.50
NC16	Jeff Bagwell	2.00
NC17	Chipper Jones	4.00
NC18	Eric Chavez	1.50
NC19	Orlando Hernandez	1.50
NC20	Troy Glaus	2.50

1999 Stadium Club Triumvirate

Three of these inserts "fuse" together to form a set of three cards, forming a Triumvirate. 48 players, 24 from each series, are available in three different technologies, Luminous, Luminescent and Illuminator. The insert ratio is as follows: Luminous (1:36), Luminescent (1:144) and Illuminator (1:288).

		MT
Complete Set (48):		350.00
Complete Series 1 (24):		165.00
Complete Series 2 (24):		185.00
Common Player:		3.00
Inserted 1:36		
Luminescents:		2X
Inserted 1:144		
Illuminators:		4X
Inserted 1:288		
T1A	Greg Vaughn	3.00
T1B	Ken Caminiti	3.00
T1C	Tony Gwynn	12.50
T2A	Andruw Jones	6.50
T2B	Chipper Jones	15.00
T2C	Andres Galarraga	4.50
T3A	Jay Buhner	3.00
T3B	Ken Griffey Jr.	25.00
T3C	Alex Rodriguez	20.00
T4A	Derek Jeter	15.00
T4B	Tino Martinez	3.00
T4C	Bernie Williams	4.50
T5A	Brian Jordan	3.00

T5B Ray Lankford 3.00
T5C Mark McGwire 25.00
T6A Jeff Bagwell 8.00
T6B Craig Biggio 5.00
T6C Randy Johnson 5.00
T7A Nomar Garciaparra 15.00
T7B Pedro Martinez 5.00
T7C Mo Vaughn 4.00
T8A Mark Grace 5.00
T8B Sammy Sosa 15.00
T8C Kerry Wood 4.50
T9A Alex Rodriguez 20.00
T9B Nomar Garciaparra 15.00
T9C Derek Jeter 15.00
T10A Todd Helton 6.50
T10B Travis Lee 5.00
T10C Pat Burrell 12.50
T11A Greg Maddux 15.00
T11B Kerry Wood 4.50
T11C Tom Glavine 3.00
T12A Chipper Jones 15.00
T12B Vinny Castilla 3.00
T12C Scott Rolen 6.50
T13A Juan Gonzalez 8.00
T13B Ken Griffey Jr. 25.00
T13C Ben Grieve 6.50
T14A Sammy Sosa 15.00
T14B Vladimir Guerrero 10.00
T14C Barry Bonds 8.00
T15A Frank Thomas 10.00
T15B Jim Thome 4.00
T15C Tino Martinez 3.00
T16A Mark McGwire 25.00
T16B Andres Galarraga 4.50
T16C Jeff Bagwell 8.00

1999 Stadium Club Video Replay

Utilizing lenticular technology, these inserts capture highlights, such as McGwire's 70th home run, from the '98 season. By tilting the card, successive images show the selected highlight almost come to life. Video Replays are in inserted in series II packs at a rate of 1:12.

	MT
Complete Set (5):	20.00
Common Player:	2.00
Inserted 1:12	
VR1 Mark McGwire	7.50
VR2 Sammy Sosa	5.00
VR3 Ken Griffey Jr.	7.50
VR4 Kerry Wood	2.00
VR5 Alex Rodriguez	5.00

2000 Stadium Club

Released in one series, the base set consists of 250 cards, embossed and printed on 20-pt. stock with silver holofoil stamping. Card backs have a small photo, with the player's vital information and 1999 season statistical breakdown. The 20-card Draft Pick subset (#231-250) are short-printed, seeded 1:5 packs.

	MT
Complete Set (250):	200.00
Common Player:	.15
Common SP (201-250):	2.00
Inserted 1:5	
Pack (6):	2.00
Wax Box (24):	45.00

1 Nomar Garciaparra 2.00
2 Brian Jordan .15
3 Mark Grace .25
4 Jeromy Burnitz .25
5 Shane Reynolds .25
6 Alex Gonzalez .15
7 Jose Offerman .15
8 Orlando Hernandez .25
9 Mike Caruso .15
10 Tony Clark .30
11 Sean Casey .50
12 Johnny Damon .15
13 Dante Bichette .25
14 Kevin Young .15
15 Juan Gonzalez .75
16 Chipper Jones 1.50
17 Quilvio Veras .15
18 Trevor Hoffman .15
19 Roger Cedeno .15
20 Ellis Burks .15
21 Richie Sexson .15
22 Gary Sheffield .40
23 Delino DeShields .15
24 Wade Boggs .50
25 Ray Lankford .15
26 Kevin Appier .15
27 Roy Halladay .15
28 Harold Baines .15
29 Todd Zeile .15
30 Barry Larkin .40
31 Ron Coomer .15
32 Jorge Posada .25
33 Magglio Ordonez .25
34 Brian Giles .15
35 Jeff Kent .15
36 Henry Rodriguez .15
37 Fred McGriff .25
38 Shawn Green .50
39 Derek Bell .15
40 Ben Grieve .30
41 Dave Nilsson .15
42 Mo Vaughn .50
43 Rondell White .25
44 Doug Glanville .15
45 Paul O'Neill .25
46 Carlos Lee .15
47 Vinny Castilla .20
48 Mike Sweeney .15
49 Rico Brogna .15
50 Alex Rodriguez 2.50
51 Luis Castillo .15
52 Kevin Brown .25
53 Jose Vidro .15
54 John Smoltz .15
55 Garret Anderson .15
56 Matt Stairs .15
57 Omar Vizquel .15
58 Tom Goodwin .15
59 Scott Brosius .15
60 Robin Ventura .25
61 B.J. Surhoff .15
62 Andy Ashby .15
63 Chris Widger .15
64 Tim Hudson .40
65 Javy Lopez .15
66 Tim Salmon .25
67 Warren Morris .15
68 John Wetteland .15
69 Gabe Kapler .25
70 Bernie Williams .50
71 Rickey Henderson .40
72 Andruw Jones .50
73 Eric Young .15
74 Bob Abreu .15
75 David Cone .25
76 Rusty Greer .15
77 Ron Belliard .15
78 Troy Glaus .75
79 Mike Hampton .15
80 Miguel Tejada .15
81 Jeff Cirillo .15
82 Todd Hundley .15
83 Roberto Alomar .50
84 Charles Johnson .15
85 Rafael Palmeiro .40
86 Doug Mientkiewicz .15
87 Mariano Rivera .25
88 Neifi Perez .15
89 Jermaine Dye .15
90 Ivan Rodriguez .75
91 Jay Buhner .15
92 Pokey Reese .15
93 John Olerud .25
94 Brady Anderson .20
95 Manny Ramirez .75
96 Keith Osik .15
97 Mickey Morandini .15
98 Matt Williams .40
99 Eric Karros .25
100 Ken Griffey Jr. 3.00
101 Bret Boone .15
102 Ryan Klesko .15
103 Craig Biggio .40
104 John Jaha .15
105 Vladimir Guerrero 1.25
106 Devon White .15
107 Tony Womack .15
108 Marvin Benard .15
109 Kenny Lofton .40
110 Preston Wilson .15
111 Al Leiter .25
112 Reggie Sanders .15
113 Scott Williamson .15
114 Deivi Cruz .15
115 Carlos Beltran .15
116 Ray Durham .15
117 Ricky Ledee .15
118 Torii Hunter .15
119 John Valentin .15
120 Scott Rolen .75
121 Jason Kendall .25
122 Dave Martinez .15
123 Jim Thome .40
124 David Bell .15
125 Jose Canseco .75
126 Jose Lima .15
127 Carl Everett .15
128 Kevin Millwood .25
129 Bill Spiers .15
130 Omar Daal .15
131 Miguel Cairo .15
132 Mark Grudzielanek .15
133 David Justice .25
134 Russ Ortiz .15
135 Mike Piazza 2.00
136 Brian Meadows .15
137 Tony Gwynn 1.50
138 Cal Ripken Jr. 2.00
139 Kris Benson .15
140 Larry Walker .50
141 Cristian Guzman .15
142 Tino Martinez .25
143 Chris Singleton .15
144 Lee Stevens .15
145 Rey Ordonez .15
146 Russ Davis .15
147 J.T. Snow Jr. .15
148 Luis Gonzalez .15
149 Marquis Grissom .15
150 Greg Maddux 1.50
151 Fernando Tatis .25
152 Jason Giambi .15
153 Carlos Delgado .50
154 Joe McEwing .15
155 Raul Mondesi .25
156 Rich Aurilia .15
157 Alex Fernandez .15
158 Albert Belle .60
159 Pat Meares .15
160 Mike Lieberthal .15
161 Mike Cameron .15
162 Juan Encarnacion .15
163 Chuck Knoblauch .30
164 Pedro Martinez .75
165 Randy Johnson .50
166 Shannon Stewart .15
167 Jeff Bagwell .75
168 Edgar Renteria .15
169 Barry Bonds .75
170 Steve Finley .15
171 Brian Hunter .15
172 Tom Glavine .25
173 Mark Kotsay .15
174 Tony Fernandez .15
175 Sammy Sosa 2.00
176 Geoff Jenkins .15
177 Adrian Beltre .15
178 Jay Bell .15
179 Mike Bordick .15
180 Ed Sprague .15
181 Dave Roberts .15
182 Greg Vaughn .25
183 Brian Daubach .15
184 Damion Easley .15
185 Carlos Febles .15
186 Kevin Tapani .15
187 Frank Thomas .75
188 Roger Clemens 1.00
189 Mike Benjamin .15
190 Curt Schilling .25
191 Edgardo Alfonzo .25
192 Mike Mussina .50
193 Todd Helton .75
194 Todd Jones .15
195 Dean Palmer .15
196 John Flaherty .15
197 Derek Jeter 2.00
198 Todd Walker .15
199 Brad Ausmus .15
200 Mark McGwire 3.00
201 Erubiel Durazo (Future Stars) 2.00
202 Nick Johnson (Future Stars) 2.50
203 Ruben Mateo (Future Stars) 2.00
204 Lance Berkman (Future Stars) 2.00
205 Pat Burrell (Future Stars) 8.00
206 Pablo Ozuna (Future Stars) 2.00
207 Roosevelt Brown (Future Stars) 2.00
208 Alfonso Soriano (Future Stars) 2.50
209 A.J. Burnett (Future Stars) 2.50
210 Rafael Furcal (Future Stars) 10.00
211 Scott Morgan (Future Stars) 2.00
212 Adam Piatt (Future Stars) 4.00
213 Dee Brown (Future Stars) 2.00
214 Corey Patterson (Future Stars) 8.00
215 Mickey Lopez (Future Stars) 2.00
216 Rob Ryan (Future Stars) 2.00
217 Sean Burroughs (Future Stars) 2.50
218 Jack Cust (Future Stars) 3.00
219 John Patterson (Future Stars) 2.00
220 Kit Pellow (Future Stars) 2.00
221 Chad Hermansen (Future Stars) 2.00
222 Daryle Ward (Future Stars) 2.00
223 Jayson Werth (Future Stars) 2.00
224 Jason Standridge (Future Stars) 2.00
225 Mark Mulder (Future Stars) 2.00

226	Peter Bergeron (Future Stars)	2.00
227	Willi Mo Pena (Future Stars)	2.50
228	Aramis Ramirez (Future Stars)	2.00
229	*John Sneed* (Future Stars)	3.00
230	Wilton Veras (Future Stars)	2.00
231	Josh Hamilton (Draft Picks)	8.00
232	Eric Munson (Draft Picks)	3.00
233	*Bobby Bradley* (Draft Picks)	6.00
234	*Larry Bigbie* (Draft Picks)	3.00
235	*B.J. Garbe* (Draft Picks)	6.00
236	*Brett Myers* (Draft Picks)	4.00
237	*Jason Stumm* (Draft Picks)	4.00
238	*Corey Myers* (Draft Picks)	3.00
239	*Ryan Christianson* (Draft Picks)	4.00
240	David Walling (Draft Picks)	2.00
241	Josh Girdley (Draft Picks)	2.00
242	Omar Ortiz (Draft Picks)	2.00
243	Jason Jennings (Draft Picks)	2.00
244	*Kyle Snyder* (Draft Picks)	2.00
245	Jay Gehrke (Draft Picks)	2.00
246	*Mike Paradis* (Draft Picks)	2.00
247	*Chance Caple* (Draft Picks)	3.00
248	*Ben Christiansen* (Draft Picks)	5.00
249	*Brad Baker* (Draft Picks)	5.00
250	*Rick Asadoorian* (Draft Picks)	12.00

2000 Stadium Club First Day Issue

Identifiable by the "First Day Issue" stamp, this retail exclusive parallel set is limited to 150 sequentially numbered sets.

	MT
Stars:	20x-30x
Short-prints:	3x-5x
Production 150 sets R	

(See 2000 Stadium Club for checklist and base card values.)

2000 Stadium Club One of a Kind

This 250-card set is a parallel to the base set, is hobby exclusive and limited to 150 serially numbered sets.

	MT
Stars:	20x-30x
Short-prints:	3x-5x
Production 150 sets H	

(See 2000 Stadium Club for checklist and base card values.)

2000 Stadium Club Co-Signers

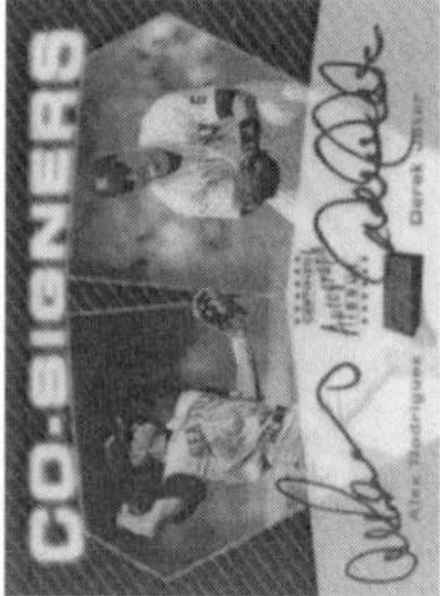

This 15-card hobby exclusive set features two signatures on the card front, with the Topps "Certified Autograph Issue" stamp as well as the Topps 3M sticker to ensure its authenticity. The cards are divided into three groupings with the following odds:

		MT
Common Player:		40.00
Group A 1:10,184		
Group B 1:5,092		
Group C 1:508		
1	Alex Rodriguez, Derek Jeter	800.00
2	Derek Jeter, Omar Vizquel	250.00
3	Alex Rodriguez, Rey Ordonez	250.00
4	Derek Jeter, Rey Ordonez	250.00
5	Omar Vizquel, Alex Rodriguez	250.00
6	Rey Ordonez, Omar Vizquel	50.00
7	Wade Boggs, Robin Ventura	80.00
8	Randy Johnson, Mike Mussina	120.00
9	Pat Burrell, Magglio Ordonez	60.00
10	Chad Hermansen, Pat Burrell	60.00
11	Magglio Ordonez, Chad Hermansen	40.00
12	Josh Hamilton, Corey Myers	60.00
13	B.J. Garbe, Josh Hamilton	80.00
14	Corey Myers, B.J. Garbe	60.00
15	Tino Martinez, Fred McGriff	50.00

2000 Stadium Club Capture the Action

This 20-card set is divided into 3 categories: Rookies, Stars and Legends. These were seeded 1:12 packs and have the insert head, player name and logo stamped in silver foil. They are numbered with a "CA" prefix on the backs. A hobby exclusive parallel version is also available. They are serially numbered to 100 and features a replica of the actual photo slide used to create the card and is viewable from both sides.

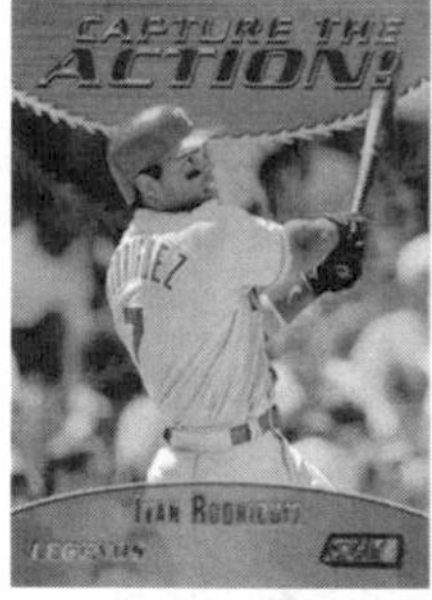

		MT
Complete Set (20):		80.00
Common Player:		1.50
Inserted 1:12		
Game View Stars:		8x-15x
Yng stars:		3x-6x
Production 100 sets H		
1	Josh Hamilton	8.00
2	Pat Burrell	5.00
3	Erubiel Durazo	5.00
4	Alfonso Soriano	6.00
5	A.J. Burnett	1.50
6	Alex Rodriguez	8.00
7	Sean Casey	1.50
8	Derek Jeter	6.00
9	Vladimir Guerrero	4.00
10	Nomar Garciaparra	6.00
11	Mike Piazza	6.00
12	Ken Griffey Jr.	10.00
13	Sammy Sosa	6.00
14	Juan Gonzalez	2.50
15	Mark McGwire	10.00
16	Ivan Rodriguez	2.50
17	Barry Bonds	2.50
18	Wade Boggs	1.50
19	Tony Gwynn	5.00
20	Cal Ripken Jr.	8.00

2000 Stadium Club Bats of Brilliance

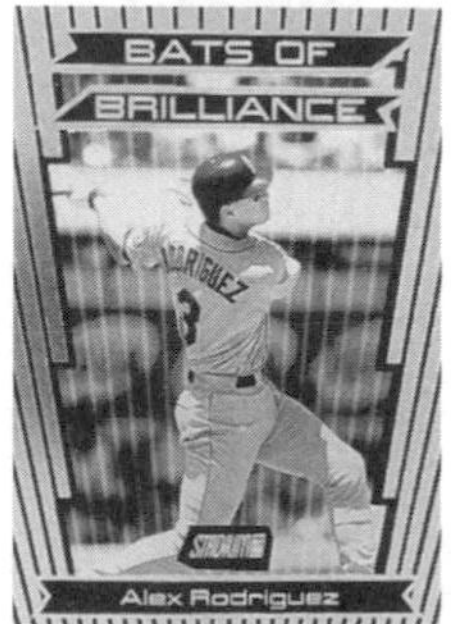

This insert set focused on 10 of baseball's top hitters. Card fronts have a silver foil border over a black backdrop. Backs highlight the player's statistics from 1999 and his career statistics. They are numbered with a "BB" prefix and are seeded 1:12 packs. A die-cut parallel is also randomly seeded 1:60 packs.

		MT
Complete Set (10):		30.00
Common Player:		1.50
Inserted 1:12		
1	Mark McGwire	6.00
2	Sammy Sosa	4.00
3	Jose Canseco	1.50
4	Jeff Bagwell	1.50
5	Ken Griffey Jr.	5.00
6	Nomar Garciaparra	4.00
7	Mike Piazza	4.00
8	Alex Rodriguez	5.00
9	Vladimir Guerrero	2.50
10	Chipper Jones	3.00

2000 Stadium Club Lone Star Signatures

This 16-card autographed set features the Topps "Certified Autograph Issue" stamp to verify its authenticity. The cards are divided into four groupings with the following odds: Group 1, 1:1,979 hobby; Group 2, 1:2,374 hobby; Group 3, 1:1,979 hobby; and Group 4, 1:424 hobby.

		MT
Common Player:		20.00
Group 1 1:1,979		
Group 2 1:2,374		
Group 3 1:1,979		
Group 4 1:424		
1	Derek Jeter	250.00
2	Alex Rodriguez	250.00
3	Wade Boggs	75.00
4	Robin Ventura	40.00
5	Randy Johnson	60.00
6	Mike Mussina	60.00
7	Tino Martinez	40.00
8	Fred McGriff	30.00
9	Omar Vizquel	30.00
10	Rey Ordonez	30.00
11	Pat Burrell	40.00
12	Chad Hermansen	20.00
13	Magglio Ordonez	20.00
14	Josh Hamilton	60.00
15	Corey Myers	30.00
16	B.J. Garbe	50.00

2000 Stadium Club 3 X 3

Ten groups of three top-notch players are arranged by position on three different laser-cut technologies. The three players can be "fused" together to form one oversize card. The three versions are luminous (1:18), luminescent (1:72) and illuminator (1:144).

		MT
Complete Set (30):		120.00
Common Player:		1.50
Inserted 1:18		
Luminescent:		2x
Inserted 1:72		
Illuminator:		3x-4x
Inserted 1:144		
1A	Randy Johnson	3.00
1B	Pedro Martinez	4.00
1C	Greg Maddux	8.00
2A	Mike Piazza	10.00
2B	Ivan Rodriguez	4.00
2C	Mike Lieberthal	1.50
3A	Mark McGwire	15.00
3B	Jeff Bagwell	4.00
3C	Sean Casey	2.00
4A	Craig Biggio	2.00
4B	Roberto Alomar	2.50
4C	Jay Bell	1.50
5A	Chipper Jones	8.00
5B	Matt Williams	2.00
5C	Robin Ventura	2.00
6A	Alex Rodriguez	12.00
6B	Derek Jeter	10.00
6C	Nomar Garciaparra	10.00
7A	Barry Bonds	4.00
7B	Luis Gonzalez	1.50
7C	Dante Bichette	1.50
8A	Ken Griffey Jr.	15.00
8B	Bernie Williams	3.00
8C	Andruw Jones	3.00
9A	Manny Ramirez	4.00
9B	Sammy Sosa	10.00
9C	Juan Gonzalez	4.00
10A	Jose Canseco	4.00
10B	Frank Thomas	4.00
10C	Rafael Palmeiro	2.50

2000 Stadium Club Onyx Extreme

This 10-card set features black styrene technology with silver foil stamping and are seeded 1:12 packs. A die-cut parallel is also randomly inserted 1:60 hobby packs.

		MT
Complete Set (10):		20.00
Common Player:		1.00
Inserted 1:12		
Die-cuts:		2x-3x
Inserted 1:60		
1	Ken Griffey Jr.	6.00
2	Derek Jeter	4.00
3	Vladimir Guerrero	2.50
4	Nomar Garciaparra	4.00
5	Barry Bonds	1.50
6	Alex Rodriguez	5.00
7	Sammy Sosa	4.00
8	Ivan Rodriguez	1.50
9	Larry Walker	1.00
10	Andruw Jones	1.00

2000 Stadium Club Scenes

Available only in hobby and Home Team Advantage boxes, these broaden the view of the featured player and have a format sized 2 1/2" x 4 11/16". These are boxtoppers, seeded one per box.

		MT
Complete Set (9):		30.00
Common Player:		1.00
Inserted 1:box		
1	Mark McGwire	6.00
2	Alex Rodriguez	5.00
3	Cal Ripken Jr.	5.00
4	Sammy Sosa	4.00
5	Derek Jeter	4.00
6	Ken Griffey Jr.	6.00
7	Raul Mondesi	1.00
8	Chipper Jones	3.00
9	Nomar Garciaparra	4.00

2000 Stadium Club Souvenirs

These memorabilia inserts feature die-cut technology that incorporates an actual piece of a game-used uniform. Each card back contains the Topps 3M sticker to ensure its authenticity. The insert rate is 2:339 hobby packs and 2:136 HTA packs.

		MT
Complete Set (3):		160.00
Common Player:		40.00
Inserted 2:339		
1	Wade Boggs	100.00
2	Randy Johnson	50.00
3	Robin Ventura	40.00

2000 Stadium Club Chrome Preview

This 20-card set features Topps Chromium technology, previewing the debut of Stadium Club Chrome, a later release. The insertion odds are 1:24 packs. A Refractor parallel version is also available seeded 1:120 packs.

		MT
Complete Set (20):		100.00
Common Player:		2.00
Inserted 1:24		
Refractors:		2x-3x
Inserted 1:120		
1	Nomar Garciaparra	10.00
2	Juan Gonzalez	4.00
3	Chipper Jones	8.00
4	Alex Rodriguez	12.00
5	Ivan Rodriguez	4.00
6	Manny Ramirez	4.00
7	Ken Griffey Jr.	15.00
8	Vladimir Guerrero	6.00
9	Mike Piazza	10.00
10	Pedro Martinez	4.00
11	Jeff Bagwell	4.00
12	Barry Bonds	4.00
13	Sammy Sosa	10.00
14	Derek Jeter	10.00
15	Mark McGwire	15.00
16	Erubiel Durazo	2.00
17	Nick Johnson	4.00
18	Pat Burrell	5.00
19	Alfonso Soriano	5.00
20	Adam Piatt	3.00

2000 Stadium Club Chrome

The 250-card base set uses the same photography and is identical to 2000 Stadium Club besides the utilization of Chromium technology. Five-card packs had a $4 SRP.

		MT
Complete Set (250):		120.00
Common Player:		.25
Pack (11):		3.00
Wax Box (36):		65.00
1	Nomar Garciaparra	3.00
2	Brian Jordan	.25
3	Mark Grace	.40
4	Jeromy Burnitz	.40
5	Shane Reynolds	.25
6	Alex Gonzalez	.25
7	Jose Offerman	.25
8	Orlando Hernandez	.40
9	Mike Caruso	.25
10	Tony Clark	.50
11	Sean Casey	.50
12	Johnny Damon	.25
13	Dante Bichette	.40
14	Kevin Young	.25
15	Juan Gonzalez	1.00
16	Chipper Jones	2.50
17	Quilvio Veras	.25
18	Trevor Hoffman	.25
19	Roger Cedeno	.25
20	Ellis Burks	.25
21	Richie Sexson	.25
22	Gary Sheffield	.50
23	Delino DeShields	.25
24	Wade Boggs	.75
25	Ray Lankford	.25
26	Kevin Appier	.25
27	Roy Halladay	.25
28	Harold Baines	.25
29	Todd Zeile	.25
30	Barry Larkin	.50
31	Ron Coomer	.25
32	Jorge Posada	.40
33	Magglio Ordonez	.40
34	Brian Giles	.25
35	Jeff Kent	.25
36	Henry Rodriguez	.25
37	Fred McGriff	.40
38	Shawn Green	.75
39	Derek Bell	.25
40	Ben Grieve	.50
41	Dave Nilsson	.25
42	Mo Vaughn	.75
43	Rondell White	.40
44	Doug Glanville	.25
45	Paul O'Neill	.40
46	Carlos Lee	.25
47	Vinny Castilla	.40
48	Mike Sweeney	.25
49	Rico Brogna	.25
50	Alex Rodriguez	4.00
51	Luis Castillo	.25
52	Kevin Brown	.40
53	Jose Vidro	.25
54	John Smoltz	.25
55	Garret Anderson	.25
56	Matt Stairs	.25
57	Omar Vizquel	.25
58	Tom Goodwin	.25
59	Scott Brosius	.25
60	Robin Ventura	.40
61	B.J. Surhoff	.25
62	Andy Ashby	.25
63	Chris Widger	.25
64	Tim Hudson	.40
65	Javy Lopez	.40
66	Tim Salmon	.40
67	Warren Morris	.25
68	John Wetteland	.25
69	Gabe Kapler	.40
70	Bernie Williams	.75
71	Rickey Henderson	.50
72	Andruw Jones	.50
73	Eric Young	.25
74	Bobby Abreu	.25
75	David Cone	.25
76	Rusty Greer	.25
77	Ron Belliard	.25
78	Troy Glaus	1.00
79	Mike Hampton	.25
80	Miguel Tejada	.25
81	Jeff Cirillo	.25
82	Todd Hundley	.25
83	Roberto Alomar	.75
84	Charles Johnson	.25
85	Rafael Palmeiro	.75
86	Doug Mientkiewicz	.25
87	Mariano Rivera	.40
88	Neifi Perez	.25
89	Jermaine Dye	.25
90	Ivan Rodriguez	1.00
91	Jay Buhner	.25

92	Pokey Reese	.25
93	John Olerud	.40
94	Brady Anderson	.40
95	Manny Ramirez	1.00
96	Keith Osik	.25
97	Mickey Morandini	.25
98	Matt Williams	.50
99	Eric Karros	.25
100	Ken Griffey Jr.	4.00
101	Bret Boone	.25
102	Ryan Klesko	.25
103	Craig Biggio	.50
104	John Jaha	.25
105	Vladimir Guerrero	1.50
106	Devon White	.25
107	Tony Womack	.25
108	Marvin Benard	.25
109	Kenny Lofton	.75
110	Preston Wilson	.25
111	Al Leiter	.40
112	Reggie Sanders	.25
113	Scott Williamson	.25
114	Deivi Cruz	.25
115	Carlos Beltran	.25
116	Ray Durham	.25
117	Ricky Ledee	.25
118	Torii Hunter	.25
119	John Valentin	.25
120	Scott Rolen	1.00
121	Jason Kendall	.40
122	Dave Martinez	.25
123	Jim Thome	.75
124	David Bell	.25
125	Jose Canseco	1.00
126	Jose Lima	.25
127	Carl Everett	.40
128	Kevin Millwood	.40
129	Bill Spiers	.25
130	Omar Daal	.25
131	Miguel Cairo	.25
132	Mark Grudzielanek	.25
133	David Justice	.40
134	Russ Ortiz	.25
135	Mike Piazza	3.00
136	Brian Meadows	.25
137	Tony Gwynn	2.00
138	Cal Ripken Jr.	4.00
139	Kris Benson	.25
140	Larry Walker	.75
141	Cristian Guzman	.25
142	Tino Martinez	.50
143	Chris Singleton	.25
144	Lee Stevens	.25
145	Rey Ordonez	.25
146	Russ Davis	.25
147	J.T. Snow Jr.	.25
148	Luis Gonzalez	.40
149	Marquis Grissom	.25
150	Greg Maddux	2.00
151	Fernando Tatis	.40
152	Jason Giambi	.40
153	Carlos Delgado	1.00
154	Joe McEwing	.25
155	Raul Mondesi	.40
156	Rich Aurilia	.25
157	Alex Fernandez	.25
158	Albert Belle	.75
159	Pat Meares	.25
160	Mike Lieberthal	.25
161	Mike Cameron	.25
162	Juan Encarnacion	.25
163	Chuck Knoblauch	.40
164	Pedro Martinez	1.00
165	Randy Johnson	1.00
166	Shannon Stewart	.25
167	Jeff Bagwell	1.00
168	Edgar Renteria	.25
169	Barry Bonds	1.00
170	Steve Finley	.25
171	Brian Hunter	.25
172	Tom Glavine	.50
173	Mark Kotsay	.25
174	Tony Fernandez	.25
175	Sammy Sosa	2.50
176	Geoff Jenkins	.40
177	Adrian Beltre	.40
178	Jay Bell	.25
179	Mike Bordick	.25
180	Ed Sprague	.25
181	Dave Roberts	.25
182	Greg Vaughn	.50
183	Brian Daubach	.25
184	Damion Easley	.25
185	Carlos Febles	.25
186	Kevin Tapani	.25
187	Frank Thomas	1.50
188	Roger Clemens	1.50
189	Mike Benjamin	.25
190	Curt Schilling	.40
191	Edgardo Alfonzo	.40
192	Mike Mussina	.75
193	Todd Helton	1.00
194	Todd Jones	.25
195	Dean Palmer	.25
196	John Flaherty	.25
197	Derek Jeter	4.00
198	Todd Walker	.25
199	Brad Ausmus	.25
200	Mark McGwire	5.00
201	Erubiel Durazo (Future Stars)	1.00
202	Nick Johnson (Future Stars)	3.00
203	Ruben Mateo (Future Stars)	1.50
204	Lance Berkman (Future Stars)	1.50
205	Pat Burrell (Future Stars)	3.00
206	Pablo Ozuna (Future Stars)	1.00
207	Roosevelt Brown (Future Stars)	1.00
208	Alfonso Soriano (Future Stars)	4.00
209	A.J. Burnett (Future Stars)	1.50
210	Rafael Furcal (Future Stars)	6.00
211	Scott Morgan (Future Stars)	1.00
212	Adam Piatt (Future Stars)	1.50
213	Dee Brown (Future Stars)	1.00
214	Corey Patterson (Future Stars)	8.00
215	Mickey Lopez (Future Stars)	1.00
216	Rob Ryan (Future Stars)	1.00
217	Sean Burroughs (Future Stars)	3.00
218	Jack Cust (Future Stars)	1.00
219	John Patterson (Future Stars)	1.50
220	Kit Pellow (Future Stars)	1.00
221	Chad Hermansen (Future Stars)	1.00
222	Daryle Ward (Future Stars)	1.50
223	Jayson Werth (Future Stars)	1.00
224	Jason Standridge (Future Stars)	1.00
225	Mark Mulder (Future Stars)	1.00
226	Peter Bergeron (Future Stars)	1.50
227	Willi Mo Pena (Future Stars)	4.00
228	Aramis Ramirez (Future Stars)	1.00
229	John Sneed (Future Stars)	2.50
230	Wilton Veras (Future Stars)	1.50
231	Josh Hamilton (Draft Picks)	5.00
232	Eric Munson (Draft Picks)	4.00
233	*Bobby Bradley* (Draft Picks)	6.00
234	*Larry Bigbie* (Draft Picks)	2.00
235	*B.J. Garbe* (Draft Picks)	4.00
236	*Brett Myers* (Draft Picks)	2.00
237	*Jason Stumm* (Draft Picks)	2.00
238	*Corey Myers* (Draft Picks)	3.00
239	*Ryan Christianson* (Draft Picks)	2.00
240	David Walling (Draft Picks)	1.00
241	Josh Girdley (Draft Picks)	1.00
242	Omar Ortiz (Draft Picks)	1.00
243	Jason Jennings (Draft Picks)	1.00
244	Kyle Snyder (Draft Picks)	1.00
245	Jay Gehrke (Draft Picks)	1.00
246	Mike Paradis (Draft Picks)	1.00
247	*Chance Caple* (Draft Picks)	2.00
248	*Ben Christensen* (Draft Picks)	2.00
249	*Brad Baker* (Draft Picks)	2.00
250	*Rick Asadoorian* (Draft Picks)	8.00

2000 Stadium Club Chrome Refractor

A parallel to the 250-card base set these utilize Refractor technology and have a mirror sheen to them when held up to a light source. "Refractor" is also written under the card number on the card back. Refractors are seeded 1:12 packs.

	MT
Stars:	5-10X
Rookies:	2-5X
Inserted 1:12	

2000 Stadium Club Chrome First Day Issue

A parallel to the 250-card base set. Card fronts are identical besides "First Day Issue" printed three times over the player name and Stadium Club Chrome logo. Card backs are serial numbered in an edition of 100. A Refractor First Day Issue parallel is also randomly inserted, limited to 25 serial numbered sets.

	MT
Stars:	15-25X
Rookies:	5-10X
Production 100 sets	
Refractor:	40-75X
Rookies:	20-30X
Production 25 sets	

2000 Stadium Club Chrome Clear Shots

Printed on a clear, acetate stock this 10-card insert set will depict the front of the player on the card front and the back on the card back. Card backs are numbered with a "CS" prefix. Clear Shots are inserted 1:24 packs. A die-cut Refractor parallel version is also randomly seeded 1:120 packs.

		MT
Complete Set (10):		45.00
Common Player:		2.50
Inserted 1:24		
Refractor:		2-3X
Inserted 1:120		
1	Derek Jeter	8.00
2	Bernie Williams	2.50
3	Roger Clemens	5.00
4	Chipper Jones	6.00
5	Greg Maddux	6.00
6	Andruw Jones	2.50
7	Juan Gonzalez	3.00
8	Manny Ramirez	3.00
9	Ken Griffey Jr.	12.00
10	Josh Hamilton	6.00

2000 Stadium Club Chrome Capture the Action

This 20-card set is divided into three groups: Rookies, Stars and Legends. Card backs are numbered with a "CA" prefix. These are found 1:18 packs. A Refractor parallel version is also randomly seeded 1:90 packs and also have "Refractor" written under the card number on the back.

		MT
Complete Set (20):		150.00
Common Player:		3.00
Inserted 1:18		
Refractors:		2-3X
Inserted 1:90		
1	Josh Hamilton	12.00
2	Pat Burrell	10.00
3	Erubiel Durazo	6.00
4	Alfonso Soriano	10.00
5	A.J. Burnett	3.00
6	Alex Rodriguez	15.00
7	Sean Casey	3.00
8	Derek Jeter	12.00
9	Vladimir Guerrero	8.00
10	Nomar Garciaparra	12.00
11	Mike Piazza	12.00
12	Ken Griffey Jr.	20.00
13	Sammy Sosa	12.00
14	Juan Gonzalez	5.00
15	Mark McGwire	20.00
16	Ivan Rodriguez	5.00
17	Barry Bonds	5.00
18	Wade Boggs	3.00
19	Tony Gwynn	10.00
20	Cal Ripken Jr.	15.00

2000 Stadium Club Chrome Eyes of the Game

Printed on a clear, acetate stock this 10-card set focuses on the facial expression of the featured player. Two images are on the front with the background image a close-up shot of the player's facial expression. These were seeded 1:16. Card backs are numbered with an "EG" prefix. A Refractor parallel is randomly inserted in 1:80 packs and has "Refractor" written under the card number on the back.

		MT
Complete Set (10):		50.00
Common Player:		2.00
Inserted 1:16		
Refractors:		2-3X
Inserted 1:80		
1	Randy Johnson	2.50
2	Mike Piazza	6.00
3	Nomar Garciaparra	6.00
4	Mark McGwire	10.00
5	Alex Rodriguez	8.00
6	Derek Jeter	6.00
7	Tony Gwynn	5.00
8	Sammy Sosa	6.00
9	Larry Walker	2.00
10	Ken Griffey Jr.	10.00

2000 Stadium Club Chrome True Colors

This 10-card set focuses on players that Topps that deemed performed best when the game's on the line. These were inserted 1:32 and are numbered with a "TC" prefix on the card back. A Refractor parallel is randomly inserted 1:160 packs.

		MT
Complete Set (10):		80.00
Common Player:		3.00
Inserted 1:32		
Refractors:		2-3X
Inserted 1:160		
1	Sammy Sosa	10.00
2	Nomar Garciaparra	10.00
3	Alex Rodriguez	12.00
4	Derek Jeter	10.00
5	Mark McGwire	15.00
6	Chipper Jones	8.00
7	Mike Piazza	10.00
8	Ken Griffey Jr.	12.00
9	Manny Ramirez	4.00
10	Vladimir Guerrero	6.00

2000 Stadium Club Chrome Visionaries

This 20-card set spotlights young prospects who are deemed destined for stardom. Card backs are numbered with a "V" prefix. These are found 1:18 packs. A Refractor parallel version is also seeded 1:90 packs. "Refractor" is written under the card number on the back.

		MT
Complete Set (20):		100.00
Common Player:		3.00
Inserted 1:18		
Refractors:		2X
Inserted 1:90		
1	Alfonso Soriano	10.00
2	Josh Hamilton	12.00
3	A.J. Burnett	3.00
4	Pat Burrell	10.00
5	Ruben Salazar	3.00
6	Aaron Rowand	3.00
7	Adam Piatt	5.00
8	Nick Johnson	8.00
9	Rafael Furcal	8.00
10	Jack Cust	3.00
11	Corey Patterson	15.00
12	Sean Burroughs	8.00
13	Pablo Ozuna	3.00
14	Dee Brown	3.00
15	John Patterson	3.00
16	Willi Mo Pena	8.00
17	Mark Mulder	4.00
18	Eric Munson	8.00
19	Alex Escobar	3.00
20	Rob Ryan	3.00

1991 Studio Preview

Each 1991 Donruss set packaged for the retail trade included a pack of four cards previewing the debut Studio set. The cards are in the same format as the regular set, 2-1/2" x 3-1/2" with evocative black-and-white photos bordered in maroon on front, and a biographical write-up on the back.

		MT
Complete Set (18):		75.00
Common Player:		3.00
1	Juan Bell	3.00
2	Roger Clemens	15.00
3	Dave Parker	3.00
4	Tim Raines	4.50
5	Kevin Seitzer	3.00
6	Teddy Higuera	3.00
7	Bernie Williams	8.00
8	Harold Baines	4.50
9	Gary Pettis	3.00
10	Dave Justice	8.00
11	Eric Davis	4.00
12	Andujar Cedeno	3.00
13	Tom Foley	3.00
14	Dwight Gooden	6.00
15	Doug Drabek	3.00
16	Steve Decker	3.00
17	Joe Torre	4.50
18	Header card	.50

1991 Studio

Donruss introduced this 264-card set in 1991. The cards feature maroon borders surrounding black and white posed player photos. The card backs are printed in black and white and feature personal data, career highlights, hobbies and interests and the player's hero. The cards were released in foil packs only and feature a special Rod Carew puzzle.

		MT
Complete Set (264):		15.00
Common Player:		.10
Pack (10):		1.00
Wax Box (48):		25.00
1	Glenn Davis	.10
2	Dwight Evans	.10
3	Leo Gomez	.10
4	Chris Hoiles	.10
5	Sam Horn	.10
6	Ben McDonald	.10
7	Randy Milligan	.10
8	Gregg Olson	.10
9	Cal Ripken, Jr.	2.00
10	David Segui	.10
11	Wade Boggs	.50
12	Ellis Burks	.10
13	Jack Clark	.10
14	Roger Clemens	.75
15	Mike Greenwell	.10
16	Tim Naehring	.10
17	Tony Pena	.10
18	*Phil Plantier*	.10
19	Jeff Reardon	.10
20	Mo Vaughn	.75
21	Jimmy Reese	.15
22	Jim Abbott	.10
23	Bert Blyleven	.10
24	Chuck Finley	.10
25	Gary Gaetti	.10
26	Wally Joyner	.15

No.	Player	Price
27	Mark Langston	.10
28	Kirk McCaskill	.10
29	Lance Parrish	.10
30	Dave Winfield	.40
31	Alex Fernandez	.15
32	Carlton Fisk	.35
33	Scott Fletcher	.10
34	Greg Hibbard	.10
35	Charlie Hough	.10
36	Jack McDowell	.10
37	Tim Raines	.15
38	Sammy Sosa	2.00
39	Bobby Thigpen	.10
40	Frank Thomas	2.00
41	Sandy Alomar	.15
42	John Farrell	.10
43	Glenallen Hill	.10
44	Brook Jacoby	.10
45	Chris James	.10
46	Doug Jones	.10
47	Eric King	.10
48	Mark Lewis	.10
49	Greg Swindell	.10
50	Mark Whiten	.10
51	Milt Cuyler	.10
52	Rob Deer	.10
53	Cecil Fielder	.10
54	Travis Fryman	.10
55	Bill Gullickson	.10
56	Lloyd Moseby	.10
57	Frank Tanana	.10
58	Mickey Tettleton	.10
59	Alan Trammell	.20
60	Lou Whitaker	.10
61	Mike Boddicker	.10
62	George Brett	.50
63	Jeff Conine	.25
64	Warren Cromartie	.10
65	Storm Davis	.10
66	Kirk Gibson	.10
67	Mark Gubicza	.10
68	*Brian McRae*	.40
69	Bret Saberhagen	.15
70	Kurt Stillwell	.10
71	Tim McIntosh	.10
72	Candy Maldonado	.10
73	Paul Molitor	.50
74	Willie Randolph	.10
75	Ron Robinson	.10
76	Gary Sheffield	.25
77	Franklin Stubbs	.10
78	B.J. Surhoff	.10
79	Greg Vaughn	.15
80	Robin Yount	.50
81	Rick Aguilera	.10
82	Steve Bedrosian	.10
83	Scott Erickson	.10
84	Greg Gagne	.10
85	Dan Gladden	.10
86	Brian Harper	.10
87	Kent Hrbek	.10
88	Shane Mack	.10
89	Jack Morris	.10
90	Kirby Puckett	.60
91	Jesse Barfield	.10
92	Steve Farr	.10
93	Steve Howe	.10
94	Roberto Kelly	.10
95	Tim Leary	.10
96	Kevin Maas	.10
97	Don Mattingly	.75
98	Hensley Meulens	.10
99	Scott Sanderson	.10
100	Steve Sax	.10
101	Jose Canseco	.35
102	Dennis Eckersley	.10
103	Dave Henderson	.10
104	Rickey Henderson	.40
105	Rick Honeycutt	.10
106	Mark McGwire	4.00
107	Dave Stewart	.10
108	Eric Show	.10
109	*Todd Van Poppel*	.10
110	Bob Welch	.10
111	Alvin Davis	.10
112	Ken Griffey, Jr.	4.00
113	Ken Griffey, Sr.	.10
114	Erik Hanson	.10
115	Brian Holman	.10
116	Randy Johnson	.45
117	Edgar Martinez	.10
118	Tino Martinez	.20
119	Harold Reynolds	.10
120	David Valle	.10
121	Kevin Belcher	.10
122	Scott Chiamparino	.10
123	Julio Franco	.10
124	Juan Gonzalez	1.00
125	Rich Gossage	.10
126	Jeff Kunkel	.10
127	Rafael Palmeiro	.25
128	Nolan Ryan	2.00
129	Ruben Sierra	.10
130	Bobby Witt	.10
131	Roberto Alomar	.50
132	Tom Candiotti	.10
133	Joe Carter	.10
134	Ken Dayley	.10
135	Kelly Gruber	.10
136	John Olerud	.20
137	Dave Stieb	.10
138	Turner Ward	.10
139	Devon White	.15
140	Mookie Wilson	.10
141	Steve Avery	.10
142	Sid Bream	.10
143	Nick Esasky	.10
144	Ron Gant	.15
145	Tom Glavine	.25
146	Dave Justice	.25
147	Kelly Mann	.10
148	Terry Pendleton	.10
149	John Smoltz	.20
150	Jeff Treadway	.10
151	George Bell	.10
152	Shawn Boskie	.10
153	Andre Dawson	.15
154	Lance Dickson	.10
155	Shawon Dunston	.10
156	Joe Girardi	.10
157	Mark Grace	.25
158	Ryne Sandberg	.50
159	Gary Scott	.10
160	Dave Smith	.10
161	Tom Browning	.10
162	Eric Davis	.15
163	Rob Dibble	.10
164	Mariano Duncan	.10
165	Chris Hammond	.10
166	Billy Hatcher	.10
167	Barry Larkin	.20
168	Hal Morris	.10
169	Paul O'Neill	.15
170	Chris Sabo	.10
171	Eric Anthony	.10
172	*Jeff Bagwell*	4.00
173	Craig Biggio	.25
174	Ken Caminitti	.25
175	Jim Deshaies	.10
176	Steve Finley	.10
177	Pete Harnisch	.10
178	Darryl Kile	.10
179	Curt Schilling	.15
180	Mike Scott	.10
181	Brett Butler	.10
182	Gary Carter	.15
183	Orel Hershiser	.15
184	Ramon Martinez	.15
185	Eddie Murray	.40
186	Jose Offerman	.15
187	Bob Ojeda	.10
188	Juan Samuel	.10
189	Mike Scioscia	.10
190	Darryl Strawberry	.15
191	Moises Alou	.15
192	Brian Barnes	.10
193	Oil Can Boyd	.10
194	Ivan Calderon	.10
195	Delino DeShields	.10
196	Mike Fitzgerald	.10
197	Andres Galarraga	.20
198	Marquis Grissom	.15
199	Bill Sampen	.10
200	Tim Wallach	.10
201	Daryl Boston	.10
202	Vince Coleman	.10
203	John Franco	.10
204	Dwight Gooden	.15
205	Tom Herr	.10
206	Gregg Jefferies	.10
207	Howard Johnson	.10
208	Dave Magadan	.10
209	Kevin McReynolds	.10
210	Frank Viola	.10
211	Wes Chamberlain	.10
212	Darren Daulton	.10
213	Len Dykstra	.10
214	Charlie Hayes	.10
215	Ricky Jordan	.10
216	Steve Lake	.10
217	Roger McDowell	.10
218	Mickey Morandini	.10
219	Terry Mulholland	.10
220	Dale Murphy	.25
221	Jay Bell	.10
222	Barry Bonds	.75
223	Bobby Bonilla	.15
224	Doug Drabek	.10
225	Bill Landrum	.10
226	Mike LaValliere	.10
227	Jose Lind	.10
228	Don Slaught	.10
229	John Smiley	.10
230	Andy Van Slyke	.10
231	Bernard Gilkey	.15
232	Pedro Guerrero	.10
233	Rex Hudler	.10
234	Ray Lankford	.15
235	Joe Magrane	.10
236	Jose Oquendo	.10
237	Lee Smith	.10
238	Ozzie Smith	.50
239	Milt Thompson	.10
240	Todd Zeile	.10
241	Larry Andersen	.10
242	Andy Benes	.15
243	Paul Faries	.10
244	Tony Fernandez	.10
245	Tony Gwynn	.75
246	Atlee Hammaker	.10
247	Fred McGriff	.30
248	Bip Roberts	.10
249	Benito Santiago	.10
250	Ed Whitson	.10
251	Dave Anderson	.10
252	Mike Benjamin	.10
253	John Burkett	.10
254	Will Clark	.35
255	Scott Garrelts	.10
256	Willie McGee	.10
257	Kevin Mitchell	.10
258	Dave Righetti	.10
259	Matt Williams	.25
260	Black & Decker (Bud Black, Steve Decker)	.20
261	Checklist	.05
262	Checklist	.05
263	Checklist	.05
264	Checklist	.05

1992 Studio Preview

To introduce its 1992 Studio brand, Leaf produced 22 preview cards in format virtually identical to the issued versions of the same cards. The only differences are the appearance of the word "PREVIEW" in the lower-right corner of the card front, in place of the player's position, and the number "X of 22 / Preview Card" on the back where regular cards have the card number in the upper-right corner. The cards were distributed on a very limited basis to members of the Donruss dealers' network.

		MT
Complete Set (22):		1050.
Common Player:		25.00
1	Ruben Sierra	25.00
2	Kirby Puckett	75.00
3	Ryne Sandberg	55.00
4	John Kruk	25.00
5	Cal Ripken, Jr.	90.00
6	Robin Yount	65.00
7	Dwight Gooden	30.00
8	David Justice	45.00
9	Don Mattingly	75.00
10	Wally Joyner	25.00
11	Will Clark	45.00
12	Rob Dibble	25.00
13	Roberto Alomar	35.00
14	Wade Boggs	55.00
15	Barry Bonds	65.00
16	Jeff Bagwell	60.00
17	Mark McGwire	100.00
18	Frank Thomas	60.00
19	Brett Butler	25.00
20	Ozzie Smith	60.00
21	Jim Abbott	25.00
22	Tony Gwynn	75.00

1992 Studio

Donruss introduced the Studio line in 1991 and released another 264-card set entitled Leaf Studio for 1992. The cards feature a color player closeup with a large, rough-textured black-and-white photo of the player in the background. Tan borders surround the photos. The cards were only released in foil packs. Special Heritage insert cards featuring top players in vintage uniforms could be found in foil and jumbo packs.

		MT
Complete Set (264):		15.00
Common Player:		.05
Pack (12):		.50
Wax Box (36):		15.00
1	Steve Avery	.05
2	Sid Bream	.05
3	Ron Gant	.10
4	Tom Glavine	.15
5	Dave Justice	.25
6	Mark Lemke	.05
7	Greg Olson	.05
8	Terry Pendleton	.05
9	Deion Sanders	.30
10	John Smoltz	.15
11	Doug Dascenzo	.05
12	Andre Dawson	.15
13	Joe Girardi	.05
14	Mark Grace	.25
15	Greg Maddux	1.50
16	Chuck McElroy	.05
17	Mike Morgan	.05
18	Ryne Sandberg	.50
19	Gary Scott	.05

20 Sammy Sosa 1.50
21 Norm Charlton .05
22 Rob Dibble .05
23 Barry Larkin .15
24 Hal Morris .05
25 Paul O'Neill .15
26 Jose Rijo .05
27 Bip Roberts .05
28 Chris Sabo .05
29 Reggie Sanders .20
30 Greg Swindell .05
31 Jeff Bagwell 1.00
32 Craig Biggio .20
33 Ken Caminiti .20
34 Andujar Cedeno .05
35 Steve Finley .05
36 Pete Harnisch .05
37 Butch Henry .05
38 Doug Jones .05
39 Darryl Kile .05
40 Eddie Taubensee .05
41 Brett Butler .05
42 Tom Candiotti .05
43 Eric Davis .10
44 Orel Hershiser .10
45 Eric Karros .10
46 Ramon Martinez .15
47 Jose Offerman .05
48 Mike Scioscia .05
49 Mike Sharperson .05
50 Darryl Strawberry .15
51 Bret Barbarie .05
52 Ivan Calderon .05
53 Gary Carter .15
54 Delino DeShields .05
55 Marquis Grissom .10
56 Ken Hill .05
57 Dennis Martinez .05
58 Spike Owen .05
59 Larry Walker .25
60 Tim Wallach .05
61 Bobby Bonilla .10
62 Tim Burke .05
63 Vince Coleman .05
64 John Franco .05
65 Dwight Gooden .10
66 Todd Hundley .15
67 Howard Johnson .05
68 Eddie Murray .35
69 Bret Saberhagen .10
70 Anthony Young .05
71 Kim Batiste .05
72 Wes Chamberlain .05
73 Darren Daulton .05
74 Mariano Duncan .05
75 Len Dykstra .05
76 John Kruk .05
77 Mickey Morandini .05
78 Terry Mulholland .05
79 Dale Murphy .25
80 Mitch Williams .05
81 Jay Bell .05
82 Barry Bonds .60
83 Steve Buechele .05
84 Doug Drabek .05
85 Mike LaValliere .05
86 Jose Lind .05
87 Denny Neagle .05
88 Randy Tomlin .05
89 Andy Van Slyke .05
90 Gary Varsho .05
91 Pedro Guerrero .05
92 Rex Hudler .05
93 Brian Jordan .10
94 Felix Jose .05
95 Donovan Osborne .05
96 Tom Pagnozzi .05
97 Lee Smith .05
98 Ozzie Smith .40
99 Todd Worrell .05
100 Todd Zeile .10
101 Andy Benes .10
102 Jerald Clark .05
103 Tony Fernandez .05
104 Tony Gwynn .75
105 Greg Harris .05
106 Fred McGriff .30
107 Benito Santiago .05
108 Gary Sheffield .25
109 Kurt Stillwell .05
110 Tim Teufel .05
111 Kevin Bass .05
112 Jeff Brantley .05
113 John Burkett .05
114 Will Clark .25
115 Royce Clayton .05
116 Mike Jackson .05
117 Darren Lewis .05
118 Bill Swift .05
119 Robby Thompson .05
120 Matt Williams .20
121 Brady Anderson .20
122 Glenn Davis .05
123 Mike Devereaux .05
124 Chris Hoiles .05
125 Sam Horn .05
126 Ben McDonald .05
127 Mike Mussina .30
128 Gregg Olson .05
129 Cal Ripken, Jr. 2.00
130 Rick Sutcliffe .05
131 Wade Boggs .40
132 Roger Clemens .65
133 Greg Harris .05
134 Tim Naehring .05
135 Tony Pena .05
136 Phil Plantier .05
137 Jeff Reardon .05
138 Jody Reed .05
139 Mo Vaughn .40
140 Frank Viola .05
141 Jim Abbott .05
142 Hubie Brooks .05
143 *Chad Curtis* .20
144 Gary DiSarcina .05
145 Chuck Finley .05
146 Bryan Harvey .05
147 Von Hayes .05
148 Mark Langston .10
149 Lance Parrish .05
150 Lee Stevens .05
151 George Bell .05
152 Alex Fernandez .10
153 Greg Hibbard .05
154 Lance Johnson .05
155 Kirk McCaskill .05
156 Tim Raines .10
157 Steve Sax .05
158 Bobby Thigpen .05
159 Frank Thomas 1.50
160 Robin Ventura .25
161 Sandy Alomar, Jr. .15
162 Jack Armstrong .05
163 Carlos Baerga .05
164 Albert Belle .50
165 Alex Cole .05
166 Glenallen Hill .05
167 Mark Lewis .05
168 Kenny Lofton .40
169 Paul Sorrento .05
170 Mark Whiten .05
171 Milt Cuyler (color photo actually Lou Whitaker) .05
172 Rob Deer .05
173 Cecil Fielder .10
174 Travis Fryman .10
175 Mike Henneman .05
176 Tony Phillips .05
177 Frank Tanana .05
178 Mickey Tettleton .05
179 Alan Trammell .10
180 Lou Whitaker .05
181 George Brett .65
182 Tom Gordon .05
183 Mark Gubicza .05
184 Gregg Jefferies .10
185 Wally Joyner .10
186 Brent Mayne .05
187 Brian McRae .10
188 Kevin McReynolds .05
189 Keith Miller .05
190 Jeff Montgomery .05
191 Dante Bichette .20
192 Ricky Bones .05
193 Scott Fletcher .05
194 Paul Molitor .50
195 Jaime Navarro .05
196 Franklin Stubbs .05
197 B.J. Surhoff .05
198 Greg Vaughn .10
199 Bill Wegman .05
200 Robin Yount .50
201 Rick Aguilera .05
202 Scott Erickson .05
203 Greg Gagne .05
204 Brian Harper .05
205 Kent Hrbek .05
206 Scott Leius .05
207 Shane Mack .05
208 Pat Mahomes .05
209 Kirby Puckett .65
210 John Smiley .05
211 Mike Gallego .05
212 Charlie Hayes .05
213 Pat Kelly .05
214 Roberto Kelly .05
215 Kevin Maas .05
216 Don Mattingly .75
217 Matt Nokes .05
218 Melido Perez .05
219 Scott Sanderson .05
220 Danny Tartabull .05
221 Harold Baines .10
222 Jose Canseco .35
223 Dennis Eckersley .05
224 Dave Henderson .05
225 Carney Lansford .05
226 Mark McGwire 3.00
227 Mike Moore .05
228 Randy Ready .05
229 Terry Steinbach .05
230 Dave Stewart .05
231 Jay Buhner .05
232 Ken Griffey, Jr. 3.00
233 Erik Hanson .05
234 Randy Johnson .25
235 Edgar Martinez .05
236 Tino Martinez .15
237 Kevin Mitchell .05
238 Pete O'Brien .05
239 Harold Reynolds .05
240 David Valle .05
241 Julio Franco .05
242 Juan Gonzalez .75
243 Jose Guzman .05
244 Rafael Palmeiro .25
245 Dean Palmer .05
246 Ivan Rodriguez .50
247 Jeff Russell .05
248 Nolan Ryan 1.50
249 Ruben Sierra .05
250 Dickie Thon .05
251 Roberto Alomar .40
252 Derek Bell .15
253 Pat Borders .05
254 Joe Carter .10
255 Kelly Gruber .05
256 Juan Guzman .05
257 Jack Morris .05
258 John Olerud .20
259 Devon White .15
260 Dave Winfield .40
261 Checklist .05
262 Checklist .05
263 Checklist .05
264 History card .05

1992 Studio Heritage

Superstars of 1992 were photographed in vintage-style uniforms in this 14-card insert set found in packages of Studio's 1992 issue. Cards #1-8 could be found in standard foil packs while #9-14 were inserted in Studio jumbos. Cards featured a sepia-tone photo bordered in turquoise and highlighted with copper foil. Cards carry a "BC" prefix to the card number on back.

MT
Complete Set (14): 22.00
Common Player: 1.00
1 Ryne Sandberg 1.50
2 Carlton Fisk 1.00
3 Wade Boggs 1.50
4 Jose Canseco 1.50
5 Don Mattingly 3.00
6 Darryl Strawberry 1.00
7 Cal Ripken, Jr. 5.00
8 Will Clark 1.00
9 Andre Dawson 1.00
10 Andy Van Slyke 1.00
11 Paul Molitor 1.50
12 Jeff Bagwell 2.00
13 Darren Daulton 1.00
14 Kirby Puckett 3.00

1993 Studio

This 220-card set features full-bleed photos. The player's portrait appears against one of several backgrounds featuring his team's uniform. His signature and the Studio logo are printed in gold foil. Backs have an extreme closeup partial portrait of the player and insights into his personality.

MT
Complete Set (220): 20.00
Common Player: .10
Pack (12): 1.00
Wax Box (36): 25.00
1 Dennis Eckersley .10
2 Chad Curtis .10
3 Eric Anthony .10
4 Roberto Alomar .50
5 Steve Avery .10
6 Cal Eldred .10
7 Bernard Gilkey .10
8 Steve Buechele .10
9 Brett Butler .10
10 Terry Mulholland .10
11 Moises Alou .15
12 Barry Bonds .75
13 Sandy Alomar Jr. .15
14 Chris Bosio .10
15 Scott Sanderson .10
16 Bobby Bonilla .10
17 Brady Anderson .15
18 Derek Bell .10
19 Wes Chamberlain .10
20 Jay Bell .10
21 Kevin Brown .15
22 Roger Clemens 1.00
23 Roberto Kelly .10
24 Dante Bichette .20
25 George Brett .75
26 Rob Deer .10
27 Brian Harper .10
28 George Bell .10
29 Jim Abbott .10
30 Dave Henderson .10
31 Wade Boggs .35

32	Chili Davis	.10
33	Ellis Burks	.10
34	Jeff Bagwell	1.00
35	Kent Hrbek	.10
36	Pat Borders	.10
37	Cecil Fielder	.10
38	Sid Bream	.10
39	Greg Gagne	.10
40	Darryl Hamilton	.10
41	Jerald Clark	.10
42	Mark Grace	.20
43	Barry Larkin	.15
44	John Burkett	.10
45	Scott Cooper	.10
46	*Mike Lansing*	.25
47	Jose Canseco	.25
48	Will Clark	.25
49	Carlos Garcia	.10
50	Carlos Baerga	.10
51	Darren Daulton	.10
52	Jay Buhner	.10
53	Andy Benes	.10
54	Jeff Conine	.10
55	Mike Devereaux	.10
56	Vince Coleman	.10
57	Terry Steinbach	.10
58	*J.T. Snow*	.75
59	Greg Swindell	.10
60	Devon White	.10
61	John Smoltz	.15
62	Todd Zeile	.10
63	Rick Wilkins	.10
64	Tim Wallach	.10
65	John Wetteland	.10
66	Matt Williams	.30
67	Paul Sorrento	.10
68	David Valle	.10
69	Walt Weiss	.10
70	John Franco	.10
71	Nolan Ryan	2.50
72	Frank Viola	.10
73	Chris Sabo	.10
74	David Nied	.10
75	Kevin McReynolds	.10
76	Lou Whitaker	.10
77	Dave Winfield	.30
78	Robin Ventura	.15
79	Spike Owen	.10
80	Cal Ripken, Jr.	2.50
81	Dan Walter	.10
82	Mitch Williams	.10
83	Tim Wakefield	.10
84	Rickey Henderson	.30
85	Gary DiSarcina	.10
86	Craig Biggio	.20
87	Joe Carter	.10
88	Ron Gant	.15
89	John Jaha	.10
90	Gregg Jefferies	.10
91	Jose Guzman	.10
92	Eric Karros	.10
93	Wil Cordero	.10
94	Royce Clayton	.10
95	Albert Belle	.60
96	Ken Griffey, Jr.	3.00
97	Orestes Destrade	.10
98	Tony Fernandez	.10
99	Leo Gomez	.10
100	Tony Gwynn	1.00
101	Len Dykstra	.10
102	Jeff King	.10
103	Julio Franco	.10
104	Andre Dawson	.15
105	Randy Milligan	.10
106	Alex Cole	.10
107	Phil Hiatt	.10
108	Travis Fryman	.10
109	Chuck Knoblauch	.15
110	Bo Jackson	.15
111	Pat Kelly	.10
112	Bret Saberhagen	.10
113	Ruben Sierra	.10
114	Tim Salmon	.30
115	Doug Jones	.10
116	Ed Sprague	.10
117	Terry Pendleton	.10
118	Robin Yount	.50
119	Mark Whiten	.10
120	Checklist	.10
121	Sammy Sosa	1.50
122	Darryl Strawberry	.15
123	Larry Walker	.25
124	Robby Thompson	.10
125	Carlos Martinez	.10
126	Edgar Martinez	.10
127	Benito Santiago	.10
128	Howard Johnson	.10
129	Harold Reynolds	.10
130	Craig Shipley	.10
131	Curt Schilling	.10
132	Andy Van Slyke	.10
133	Ivan Rodriguez	.50
134	Mo Vaughn	.50
135	Bip Roberts	.10
136	Charlie Hayes	.10
137	Brian McRae	.10
138	Mickey Tettleton	.10
139	Frank Thomas	1.50
140	Paul O'Neill	.15
141	Mark McGwire	3.00
142	Damion Easley	.10
143	Ken Caminiti	.20
144	Juan Guzman	.10
145	Tom Glavine	.15
146	Pat Listach	.10
147	Lee Smith	.10
148	Derrick May	.10
149	Ramon Martinez	.10
150	Delino DeShields	.10
151	Kirt Manwaring	.10
152	Reggie Jefferson	.10
153	Randy Johnson	.40
154	Dave Magadan	.10
155	Dwight Gooden	.15
156	Chris Hoiles	.10
157	Fred McGriff	.20
158	Dave Hollins	.10
159	Al Martin	.10
160	Juan Gonzalez	.75
161	Mike Greenwell	.10
162	Kevin Mitchell	.10
163	Andres Galarraga	.20
164	Wally Joyner	.15
165	Kirk Gibson	.10
166	Pedro Munoz	.10
167	Ozzie Guillen	.10
168	Jimmy Key	.10
169	Kevin Seitzer	.10
170	Luis Polonia	.10
171	Luis Gonzalez	.10
172	Paul Molitor	.50
173	Dave Justice	.20
174	B.J. Surhoff	.10
175	Ray Lankford	.10
176	Ryne Sandberg	.50
177	Jody Reed	.10
178	Marquis Grissom	.10
179	Willie McGee	.10
180	Kenny Lofton	.50
181	Junior Felix	.10
182	Jose Offerman	.10
183	John Kruk	.10
184	Orlando Merced	.10
185	Rafael Palmeiro	.25
186	Billy Hatcher	.10
187	Joe Oliver	.10
188	Joe Girardi	.10
189	Jose Lind	.10
190	Harold Baines	.10
191	Mike Pagliarulo	.10
192	Lance Johnson	.10
193	Don Mattingly	1.00
194	Doug Drabek	.10
195	John Olerud	.20
196	Greg Maddux	2.00
197	Greg Vaughn	.15
198	Tom Pagnozzi	.10
199	Willie Wilson	.10
200	Jack McDowell	.10
201	Mike Piazza	2.00
202	Mike Mussina	.40
203	Charles Nagy	.10
204	Tino Martinez	.15
205	Charlie Hough	.10
206	Todd Hundley	.20
207	Gary Sheffield	.20
208	Mickey Morandini	.10
209	Don Slaught	.10
210	Dean Palmer	.10
211	Jose Rijo	.10
212	Vinny Castilla	.10
213	Tony Phillips	.10
214	Kirby Puckett	.75
215	Tim Raines	.15
216	Otis Nixon	.10
217	Ozzie Smith	.50
218	Jose Vizcaino	.10
220	Checklist	.10

1993 Studio Frank Thomas

This five-card set is devoted to Frank Thomas. Cards were randomly included in all types of 1993 Leaf Studio packs. Topics covered on the cards include Thomas' childhood, his baseball memories, his family, his performance and being a role model.

		MT
Complete Set (5):		20.00
Common Player:		4.00
1	Childhood	4.00
2	Baseball Memories	4.00
3	Importance of Family	4.00
4	Performance	4.00
5	On Being a Role Model	4.00

1993 Studio Heritage

All types of 1993 Leaf Studio packs were candidates for having one of 12 Heritage cards inserted in them. The fronts feature the player posing in an old-time uniform, framed in turquiose with copper highlights. The backs have a mug shot surrounded by an ornate frame and describe the uniform on the front. Team trivia is also included.

		MT
Complete Set (12):		20.00
Common Player:		1.00
1	George Brett	4.00
2	Juan Gonzalez	3.00
3	Roger Clemens	3.00
4	Mark McGwire	12.00
5	Mark Grace	1.50
6	Ozzie Smith	2.50
7	Barry Larkin	1.00
8	Frank Thomas	5.00
9	Carlos Baerga	1.00
10	Eric Karros	1.00
11	J.T. Snow	1.00
12	John Kruk	1.00

1993 Studio Silhouettes

These insert cards were randomly included in jumbo packs only. The card fronts feature a ghosted image of the player against an action silhouette on a gray background. The player's name is in bronze foil at bottom. Backs have a player action photo and description of career highlights.

		MT
Complete Set (10):		25.00
Common Player:		1.00
1	Frank Thomas	4.00
2	Barry Bonds	2.50
3	Jeff Bagwell	4.00
4	Juan Gonzalez	3.00
5	Travis Fryman	1.00
6	J.T. Snow	1.00
7	John Kruk	1.00
8	Jeff Blauser	1.00
9	Mike Piazza	6.00
10	Nolan Ryan	7.50

1993 Studio Superstars on Canvas

Ten players are featured on these insert cards, which were available in hobby and retail packs. The cards show player portraits which mix photography and artwork.

		MT
Complete Set (10):		25.00
Common Player:		1.00
1	Ken Griffey, Jr.	12.00
2	Jose Canseco	1.50
3	Mark McGwire	12.00
4	Mike Mussina	2.00
5	Joe Carter	1.00
6	Frank Thomas	6.00
7	Darren Daulton	1.00
8	Mark Grace	1.50
9	Andres Galarraga	1.00
10	Barry Bonds	3.00

1994 Studio Promotional Samples

To introduce its "locker-room look" issue for 1994 Leaf's Studio brand produced this three-star sample set and distributed it to its hobby dealer network. The cards are basically the same as the regular-issue cards of those players except for the addition of a "Promotional Sample" overprinted diagonally on front and back. The "Up Close" biographies on the cards' backs are different between the promos and the regular cards and there is a slight difference in front photo cropping on the Gonzalez card.

		MT
Complete Set (3):		15.00
Common Player:		4.00
83	Barry Bonds	5.00
154	Juan Gonzalez	4.00
209	Frank Thomas	5.00

1994 Studio

Studio baseball from Donruss returned in mid-August, 1994, with a three-time MVP spokesman, several jazzy and short-printed inserts subsets and a reduced overall production figure that represents a sharp drop from 1993. Barry Bonds is the MVP whose mug adorns Studio counter boxes and advertisements. According to Donruss officials, production was limited to 8,000 cases of 20 boxes each, which represents a 35 percent decrease from 1993 and works out to about 315,000 of each card. Only 2,000 cases were earmarked for retail distribution and no jumbo packs were produced. Studio 1994 features 220 cards issued in one series, once again with close-up personal portraits of the top stars in the game. Each card is foil-stamped with a borderless design and UV coating front and back. The front of the card features the player in the foreground with his locker in the background. As in the previous three Studio offerings, the backs of the cards contain personal information about the players.

		MT
Complete Set (220):		15.00
Common Player:		.10
Pack (12):		1.00
Wax Box (36):		25.00
1	Dennis Eckersley	.10
2	Brent Gates	.10
3	Rickey Henderson	.35
4	Mark McGwire	3.00
5	Troy Neel	.10
6	Ruben Sierra	.10
7	Terry Steinbach	.10
8	Chad Curtis	.10
9	Chili Davis	.10
10	Gary DiSarcina	.10
11	Damion Easley	.10
12	Bo Jackson	.25
13	Mark Langston	.10
14	Eduardo Perez	.10
15	Tim Salmon	.20
16	Jeff Bagwell	.75
17	Craig Biggio	.25
18	Ken Caminiti	.20
19	Andujar Cedeno	.10
20	Doug Drabek	.10
21	Steve Finley	.10
22	Luis Gonzalez	.10
23	Darryl Kile	.10
24	Roberto Alomar	.60
25	Pat Borders	.10
26	Joe Carter	.10
27	Carlos Delgado	.50
28	Pat Hentgen	.10
29	Paul Molitor	.50
30	John Olerud	.20
31	Ed Sprague	.10
32	Devon White	.10
33	Steve Avery	.10
34	Tom Glavine	.20
35	David Justice	.20
36	Roberto Kelly	.10
37	Ryan Klesko	.20
38	Javier Lopez	.10
39	Greg Maddux	1.50
40	Fred McGriff	.25
41	Terry Pendleton	.10
42	Ricky Bones	.10
43	Darryl Hamilton	.10
44	Brian Harper	.10
45	John Jaha	.10
46	Dave Nilsson	.10
47	Kevin Seitzer	.10
48	Greg Vaughn	.15
49	Turner Ward	.10
50	Bernard Gilkey	.10
51	Gregg Jefferies	.10
52	Ray Lankford	.10
53	Tom Pagnozzi	.10
54	Ozzie Smith	.50
55	Bob Tewksbury	.10
56	Mark Whiten	.10
57	Todd Zeile	.10
58	Steve Buechele	.10
59	Shawon Dunston	.10
60	Mark Grace	.25
61	Derrick May	.10
62	Tuffy Rhodes	.10
63	Ryne Sandberg	.60
64	Sammy Sosa	1.50
65	Rick Wilkins	.10
66	Brett Butler	.10
67	Delino DeShields	.10
68	Orel Hershiser	.10
69	Eric Karros	.10
70	Raul Mondesi	.30
71	Jose Offerman	.10
72	Mike Piazza	2.00
73	Tim Wallach	.10
74	Moises Alou	.15
75	Sean Berry	.10
76	Wil Cordero	.10
77	Cliff Floyd	.10
78	Marquis Grissom	.10
79	Ken Hill	.10
80	Larry Walker	.25
81	John Wetteland	.10
82	Rod Beck	.10
83	Barry Bonds	.75
84	Royce Clayton	.10
85	Darren Lewis	.10
86	Willie McGee	.10
87	Bill Swift	.10
88	Robby Thompson	.10
89	Matt Williams	.25
90	Sandy Alomar Jr.	.15
91	Carlos Baerga	.10
92	Albert Belle	.60
93	Kenny Lofton	.50
94	Eddie Murray	.30
95	Manny Ramirez	.75
96	Paul Sorrento	.10
97	Jim Thome	.25
98	Rich Amaral	.10
99	Eric Anthony	.10
100	Jay Buhner	.10
101	Ken Griffey, Jr.	3.00
102	Randy Johnson	.75
103	Edgar Martinez	.10
104	Tino Martinez	.20
105	*Kurt Abbott*	.15
106	Bret Barberie	.10
107	Chuck Carr	.10
108	Jeff Conine	.10
109	Chris Hammond	.10
110	Bryan Harvey	.10
111	Benito Santiago	.10
112	Gary Sheffield	.30
113	Bobby Bonilla	.10
114	Dwight Gooden	.15
115	Todd Hundley	.10
116	Bobby Jones	.10
117	Jeff Kent	.10
118	Kevin McReynolds	.10
119	Bret Saberhagen	.10
120	Ryan Thompson	.10
121	Harold Baines	.10
122	Mike Devereaux	.10
123	Jeffrey Hammonds	.10
124	Ben McDonald	.10
125	Mike Mussina	.30
126	Rafael Palmeiro	.40
127	Cal Ripken, Jr.	2.50
128	Lee Smith	.10
129	Brad Ausmus	.10
130	Derek Bell	.10
131	Andy Benes	.10
132	Tony Gwynn	1.00
133	Trevor Hoffman	.10
134	Scott Livingstone	.10
135	Phil Plantier	.10
136	Darren Daulton	.10
137	Mariano Duncan	.10
138	Len Dykstra	.10
139	Dave Hollins	.10
140	Pete Incaviglia	.10
141	Danny Jackson	.10
142	John Kruk	.10
143	Kevin Stocker	.10
144	Jay Bell	.10
145	Carlos Garcia	.10
146	Jeff King	.10
147	Al Martin	.10
148	Orlando Merced	.10
149	Don Slaught	.10
150	Andy Van Slyke	.10
151	Kevin Brown	.15
152	Jose Canseco	.40
153	Will Clark	.25
154	Juan Gonzalez	.75
155	David Hulse	.10
156	Dean Palmer	.10
157	Ivan Rodriguez	.75
158	Kenny Rogers	.10
159	Roger Clemens	1.00
160	Scott Cooper	.10
161	Andre Dawson	.15
162	Mike Greenwell	.10
163	Otis Nixon	.10
164	Aaron Sele	.10
165	John Valentin	.10
166	Mo Vaughn	.50
167	Bret Boone	.10
168	Barry Larkin	.25
169	Kevin Mitchell	.10
170	Hal Morris	.10
171	Jose Rijo	.10
172	Deion Sanders	.20
173	Reggie Sanders	.10
174	John Smiley	.10
175	Dante Bichette	.30
176	Ellis Burks	.10
177	Andres Galarraga	.40
178	Joe Girardi	.10
179	Charlie Hayes	.10
180	Roberto Mejia	.10
181	Walt Weiss	.10
182	David Cone	.15
183	Gary Gaetti	.10
184	Greg Gagne	.10
185	Felix Jose	.10
186	Wally Joyner	.10
187	Mike Macfarlane	.10
188	Brian McRae	.10
189	Eric Davis	.10
190	Cecil Fielder	.10
191	Travis Fryman	.15
192	Tony Phillips	.10
193	Mickey Tettleton	.10
194	Alan Trammell	.10
195	Lou Whitaker	.10
196	Kent Hrbek	.10
197	Chuck Knoblauch	.15
198	Shane Mack	.10
199	Pat Meares	.10
200	Kirby Puckett	.75
201	Matt Walbeck	.10
202	Dave Winfield	.25
203	Wilson Alvarez	.10
204	Alex Fernandez	.10
205	Julio Franco	.10
206	Ozzie Guillen	.10
207	Jack McDowell	.10
208	Tim Raines	.10
209	Frank Thomas	1.50
210	Robin Ventura	.15
211	Jim Abbott	.10
212	Wade Boggs	.35
213	Pat Kelly	.10
214	Jimmy Key	.10
215	Don Mattingly	1.00
216	Paul O'Neill	.15
217	Mike Stanley	.10
218	Danny Tartabull	.10
219	Checklist	.10
220	Checklist	.10

1994 Studio Editor's Choice

Printed in similitude to a strip of color slide film, each of the cards in this insert set feature a complete player photo at center, with partial "frames" at top and bottom. Printed on acetate, the back of the card shows a reversed image of the front. Stated odds of finding an Editor's Choice insert card are about one per box of 36 packs.

		MT
Complete Set (8):		35.00
Common Player:		1.00
1	Barry Bonds	5.00
2	Frank Thomas	6.00
3	Ken Griffey, Jr.	15.00
4	Andres Galarraga	2.50
5	Juan Gonzalez	4.00
6	Tim Salmon	2.00
7	Paul O'Neill	1.00
8	Mike Piazza	8.00

1994 Studio Heritage

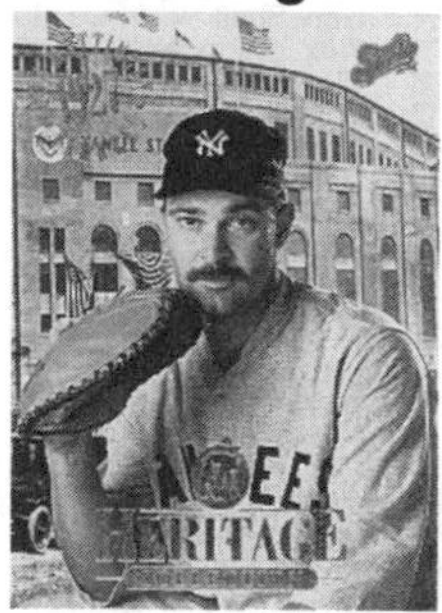

Besides picturing today's players in vintage uniforms, the 1994 Studio Heritage inserts have the player portraits set against sepia-toned photos of old ballparks. Fronts are enhanced by copper-foil logos and by a round device at upper-left containing the player's name, team and year represented. Backs have a second color player photo and a short write-up about the team represented. Unlike the other cards in the set, the Heritage cards are printed on a porous cardboard stock to enhance the image of antiquity. Stated odds of finding a Heritage Collection insert card are one in nine packs.

		MT
Complete Set (8):		15.00
Common Player:		1.00
1	Barry Bonds	2.50
2	Frank Thomas	4.00
3	Joe Carter	1.00
4	Don Mattingly	3.00
5	Ryne Sandberg	2.50
6	Javier Lopez	1.50
7	Gregg Jefferies	1.00
8	Mike Mussina	1.50

1994 Studio Silver Stars

Each of the 10 players in this insert set was produced in an edition of 10,000 cards. Printed on acetate, fronts feature action photos set against a clear plastic background with a silver-foil seal at bottom. Within the player silhouette on back, a second photo is printed. The back also features a black-and-white version of the seal, including the card's unique serial number. Stated odds of picking a Silver Series Star are one per 60 packs, on average.

		MT
Complete Set (10):		60.00
Common Player:		2.00
1	Tony Gwynn	8.00
2	Barry Bonds	5.00
3	Frank Thomas	6.00
4	Ken Griffey, Jr.	15.00
5	Joe Carter	2.00
6	Mike Piazza	10.00
7	Cal Ripken, Jr.	12.00
8	Greg Maddux	8.00
9	Juan Gonzalez	4.00
10	Don Mattingly	5.00

1994 Studio Gold Stars

The scarcest of the 1994 Studio chase cards, only 5,000 cards of each of the 10 players were produced. Printed on acetate, fronts feature an action photo set against a clear plastic background. At bottom is a large gold-foil seal. Backs have another player photo, within the silhouette of the front photo, and a black-and-white version of the seal, including the card's unique serial number. According to the series wrapper, odds of finding a Gold Series Star card are one in 120 packs.

		MT
Complete Set (10):		240.00
Common Player:		8.00
1	Tony Gwynn	25.00
2	Barry Bonds	15.00
3	Frank Thomas	20.00
4	Ken Griffey, Jr.	60.00
5	Joe Carter	8.00
6	Mike Piazza	40.00
7	Cal Ripken, Jr.	50.00
8	Greg Maddux	30.00
9	Juan Gonzalez	15.00
10	Don Mattingly	20.00

1995 Studio

Known since its inception as a brand name for its innovative design, Studio did not disappoint in 1995, unveiling a baseball card with a credit card look. In horizontal format the cards feature embossed stats and data on front, plus a team logo hologram. Backs have a color player photo, facsimile autograph and simulated magnetic data strip to carry through the credit card impression.

		MT
Complete Set (200):		40.00
Common Player:		.10
Pack (5):		1.50
Wax Box (36):		40.00
1	Frank Thomas	1.50
2	Jeff Bagwell	1.00
3	Don Mattingly	1.50
4	Mike Piazza	2.00
5	Ken Griffey Jr.	4.00
6	Greg Maddux	2.00
7	Barry Bonds	.75
8	Cal Ripken Jr.	2.50
9	Jose Canseco	.35
10	Paul Molitor	.50
11	Kenny Lofton	.50
12	Will Clark	.30
13	Tim Salmon	.25
14	Joe Carter	.10
15	Albert Belle	.60
16	Roger Clemens	1.00
17	Roberto Alomar	.60
18	Alex Rodriguez	3.00
19	Raul Mondesi	.40
20	Deion Sanders	.25
21	Juan Gonzalez	1.00
22	Kirby Puckett	1.00
23	Fred McGriff	.30
24	Matt Williams	.25
25	Tony Gwynn	.75
26	Cliff Floyd	.10
27	Travis Fryman	.10
28	Shawn Green	.15
29	Mike Mussina	.35
30	Bob Hamelin	.10
31	Dave Justice	.20
32	Manny Ramirez	1.00
33	David Cone	.15
34	Marquis Grissom	.10
35	Moises Alou	.15
36	Carlos Baerga	.10
37	Barry Larkin	.20
38	Robin Ventura	.15
39	Mo Vaughn	.50
40	Jeffrey Hammonds	.10
41	Ozzie Smith	.50
42	Andres Galarraga	.15
43	Carlos Delgado	.50
44	Lenny Dykstra	.10
45	Cecil Fielder	.10
46	Wade Boggs	.35
47	Gregg Jefferies	.10
48	Randy Johnson	.30
49	Rafael Palmeiro	.20
50	Craig Biggio	.20
51	Steve Avery	.10
52	Ricky Bottalico	.10
53	Chris Gomez	.10
54	Carlos Garcia	.10
55	Brian Anderson	.10
56	Wilson Alvarez	.10
57	Roberto Kelly	.10
58	Larry Walker	.25
59	Dean Palmer	.10
60	Rick Aguilera	.10
61	Javy Lopez	.10
62	Shawon Dunston	.10
63	William Van Landingham	.10
64	Jeff Kent	.10
65	David McCarty	.10
66	Armando Benitez	.10
67	Brett Butler	.10
68	Bernard Gilkey	.10
69	Joey Hamilton	.10
70	Chad Curtis	.10
71	Dante Bichette	.25
72	Chuck Carr	.10
73	Pedro Martinez	.15
74	Ramon Martinez	.10
75	Rondell White	.15
76	Alex Fernandez	.10
77	Dennis Martinez	.10
78	Sammy Sosa	1.50
79	Bernie Williams	.35
80	Lou Whitaker	.10
81	Kurt Abbott	.10
82	Tino Martinez	.15
83	Willie Greene	.10
84	Garret Anderson	.15
85	Jose Rijo	.10
86	Jeff Montgomery	.10
87	Mark Langston	.10
88	Reggie Sanders	.10
89	Rusty Greer	.10
90	Delino DeShields	.10
91	Jason Bere	.10
92	Lee Smith	.10
93	Devon White	.10
94	John Wetteland	.10
95	Luis Gonzalez	.10
96	Greg Vaughn	.10
97	Lance Johnson	.10
98	Alan Trammell	.10
99	Bret Saberhagen	.10
100	Jack McDowell	.10
101	Trevor Hoffman	.10
102	Dave Nilsson	.10
103	Bryan Harvey	.10
104	Chuck Knoblauch	.20
105	Bobby Bonilla	.10
106	Hal Morris	.10
107	Mark Whiten	.10
108	Phil Plantier	.10
109	Ryan Klesko	.20
110	Greg Gagne	.10
111	Ruben Sierra	.10
112	J.R. Phillips	.10
113	Terry Steinbach	.10
114	Jay Buhner	.10
115	Ken Caminiti	.25
116	Gary DiSarcina	.10
117	Ivan Rodriguez	.50
118	Bip Roberts	.10
119	Jay Bell	.10
120	Ken Hill	.10
121	Mike Greenwell	.10
122	Rick Wilkins	.10
123	Rickey Henderson	.30
124	Dave Hollins	.10
125	Terry Pendleton	.10
126	Rich Becker	.10
127	Billy Ashley	.10

128	Derek Bell	.10
129	Dennis Eckersley	.10
130	Andujar Cedeno	.10
131	John Jaha	.10
132	Chuck Finley	.10
133	Steve Finley	.10
134	Danny Tartabull	.10
135	Jeff Conine	.10
136	Jon Lieber	.10
137	Jim Abbott	.10
138	Steve Traschel	.10
139	Bret Boone	.10
140	Charles Johnson	.10
141	Mark McGwire	4.00
142	Eddie Murray	.40
143	Doug Drabek	.10
144	Steve Cooke	.10
145	Kevin Seitzer	.10
146	Rod Beck	.10
147	Eric Karros	.10
148	Tim Raines	.15
149	Joe Girardi	.10
150	Aaron Sele	.10
151	Robby Thompson	.10
152	Chan Ho Park	.15
153	Ellis Burks	.10
154	Brian McRae	.10
155	Jimmy Key	.10
156	Rico Brogna	.10
157	Ozzie Guillen	.10
158	Chili Davis	.10
159	Darren Daulton	.10
160	Chipper Jones	2.00
161	Walt Weiss	.10
162	Paul O'Neill	.15
163	Al Martin	.10
164	John Valentin	.10
165	Tim Wallach	.10
166	Scott Erickson	.10
167	Ryan Thompson	.10
168	Todd Zeile	.10
169	Scott Cooper	.10
170	Matt Mieske	.10
171	Allen Watson	.10
172	Brian Hunter	.10
173	Kevin Stocker	.10
174	Cal Eldred	.10
175	Tony Phillips	.10
176	Ben McDonald	.10
177	Mark Grace	.20
178	Midre Cummings	.10
179	Orlando Merced	.10
180	Jeff King	.10
181	Gary Sheffield	.40
182	Tom Glavine	.20
183	Edgar Martinez	.10
184	Steve Karsay	.10
185	Pat Listach	.10
186	Wil Cordero	.10
187	Brady Anderson	.15
188	Bobby Jones	.10
189	Andy Benes	.10
190	Ray Lankford	.10
191	John Doherty	.10
192	Wally Joyner	.15
193	Jim Thome	.20
194	Royce Clayton	.10
195	John Olerud	.15
196	Steve Buechele	.10
197	Harold Baines	.10
198	Geronimo Berroa	.10
199	Checklist	.10
200	Checklist	.10

1995 Studio Gold

The chase cards in 1995 Studio are plastic versions of some of the regular cards. The round-cornered plastic format of the inserts gives them an even greater similitude to credit cards. The first 50 numbers in the regular set are reproduced in a parallel Studio Gold plastic version, found one per pack, except for those packs which have a platinum card.

		MT
Complete Set (50):		30.00
Common Player:		.25
1	Frank Thomas	1.50
2	Jeff Bagwell	1.50
3	Don Mattingly	1.50
4	Mike Piazza	2.00
5	Ken Griffey Jr.	4.00
6	Greg Maddux	2.00
7	Barry Bonds	1.00
8	Cal Ripken Jr.	3.00
9	Jose Canseco	.50
10	Paul Molitor	1.00
11	Kenny Lofton	.75
12	Will Clark	.50
13	Tim Salmon	.35
14	Joe Carter	.25
15	Albert Belle	.75
16	Roger Clemens	1.50
17	Roberto Alomar	.75
18	Alex Rodriguez	3.00
19	Raul Mondesi	.50
20	Deion Sanders	.40
21	Juan Gonzalez	1.00
22	Kirby Puckett	1.50
23	Fred McGriff	.40
24	Matt Williams	.35
25	Tony Gwynn	1.50
26	Cliff Floyd	.25
27	Travis Fryman	.25
28	Shawn Green	.35
29	Mike Mussina	.60
30	Bob Hamelin	.25
31	Dave Justice	.50
32	Manny Ramirez	.75
33	David Cone	.25
34	Marquis Grissom	.25
35	Moises Alou	.25
36	Carlos Baerga	.25
37	Barry Larkin	.30
38	Robin Ventura	.30
39	Mo Vaughn	.60
40	Jeffrey Hammonds	.25
41	Ozzie Smith	1.00
42	Andres Galarraga	.35
43	Carlos Delgado	.50
44	Lenny Dykstra	.25
45	Cecil Fielder	.25
46	Wade Boggs	.50
47	Gregg Jefferies	.25
48	Randy Johnson	.50
49	Rafael Palmeiro	.40
50	Craig Biggio	.35

1995 Studio Platinum

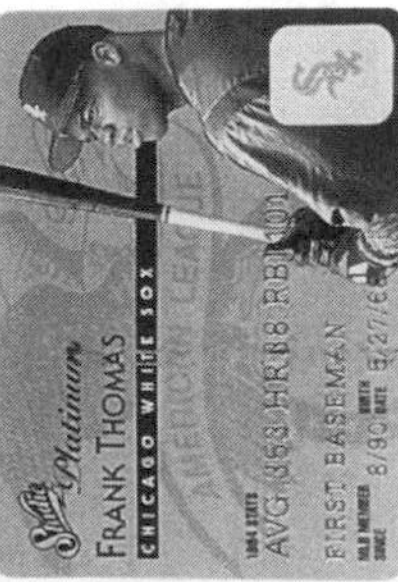

Found at the rate of one per 10 packs, Studio Platinum cards are silver-toned plastic versions of the first 25 cards from the regular set.

		MT
Complete Set (25):		100.00
Common Player:		1.50
1	Frank Thomas	6.00
2	Jeff Bagwell	6.00
3	Don Mattingly	5.00
4	Mike Piazza	8.00
5	Ken Griffey Jr.	15.00
6	Greg Maddux	8.00
7	Barry Bonds	4.00
8	Cal Ripken Jr.	12.00
9	Jose Canseco	2.00
10	Paul Molitor	4.00
11	Kenny Lofton	2.00
12	Will Clark	1.50
13	Tim Salmon	1.50
14	Joe Carter	1.50
15	Albert Belle	3.00
16	Roger Clemens	5.00
17	Roberto Alomar	2.00
18	Alex Rodriguez	12.00
19	Raul Mondesi	1.50
20	Deion Sanders	1.50
21	Juan Gonzalez	4.00
22	Kirby Puckett	5.00
23	Fred McGriff	1.50
24	Matt Williams	1.50
25	Tony Gwynn	6.00

1996 Studio

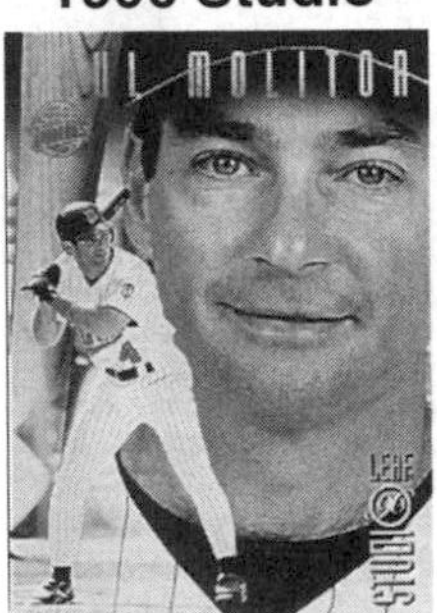

The 1996 Studio set is the first Donruss product to be released under the Pinnacle Brands flagship. The 150-card set has three parallel sets - Bronze Press Proofs (2,000 sets), Silver Press Proofs (found only in magazine packs, 100 sets), and Gold Press Proofs (500 sets). Three insert sets were also made - Hit Parade, Masterstrokes and Stained Glass Stars.

		MT
Complete Set (150):		15.00
Common Player:		.10
Pack (7):		2.50
Wax Box (24):		45.00
1	Cal Ripken Jr.	2.50
2	Alex Gonzalez	.10
3	Roger Cedeno	.15
4	Todd Hollandsworth	.10
5	Gregg Jefferies	.10
6	Ryne Sandberg	.75
7	Eric Karros	.10
8	Jeff Conine	.10
9	Rafael Palmeiro	.25
10	Bip Roberts	.10
11	Roger Clemens	1.00
12	Tom Glavine	.20
13	Jason Giambi	.15
14	Rey Ordonez	.40
15	Chan Ho Park	.15
16	Vinny Castilla	.10
17	Butch Huskey	.10
18	Greg Maddux	2.00
19	Bernard Gilkey	.10
20	Marquis Grissom	.10
21	Chuck Knoblauch	.20
22	Ozzie Smith	.75
23	Garret Anderson	.10
24	J.T. Snow	.10
25	John Valentin	.10
26	Barry Larkin	.20
27	Bobby Bonilla	.10
28	Todd Zeile	.10
29	Roberto Alomar	.65
30	Ramon Martinez	.10
31	Jeff King	.10
32	Dennis Eckersley	.10
33	Derek Jeter	2.00
34	Edgar Martinez	.10
35	Geronimo Berroa	.10
36	Hal Morris	.10
37	Troy Percival	.10
38	Jason Isringhausen	.15
39	Greg Vaughn	.10
40	Robin Ventura	.15
41	Craig Biggio	.20
42	Will Clark	.30
43	Sammy Sosa	1.50
44	Bernie Williams	.40
45	Kenny Lofton	.45
46	Wade Boggs	.30
47	Javy Lopez	.15
48	Reggie Sanders	.10
49	Jeff Bagwell	1.25
50	Fred McGriff	.35
51	Charles Johnson	.10
52	Darren Daulton	.10
53	Jose Canseco	.35
54	Cecil Fielder	.10
55	Raul Mondesi	.30
56	Tim Salmon	.25
57	Carlos Delgado	.50
58	David Cone	.15
59	Tim Raines	.10
60	Lyle Mouton	.10
61	Wally Joyner	.10
62	Bret Boone	.10
63	Hideo Nomo	.50
64	Gary Sheffield	.30
65	Alex Rodriguez	3.00
66	Russ Davis	.10
67	Checklist	.10
68	Marty Cordova	.10
69	Ruben Sierra	.10
70	Jose Mesa	.10
71	Matt Williams	.30
72	Chipper Jones	2.00
73	Randy Johnson	.40
74	Kirby Puckett	1.00
75	Jim Edmonds	.10
76	Barry Bonds	.75
77	David Segui	.10
78	Larry Walker	.30
79	Jason Kendall	.10
80	Mike Piazza	2.00
81	Brian Hunter	.10
82	Julio Franco	.10
83	Jay Bell	.10
84	Kevin Seitzer	.10
85	John Smoltz	.20
86	Joe Carter	.10
87	Ray Durham	.10
88	Carlos Baerga	.10
89	Ron Gant	.10
90	Orlando Merced	.10
91	Lee Smith	.10
92	Pedro Martinez	.15
93	Frank Thomas	1.50
94	Al Martin	.10
95	Chad Curtis	.10
96	Eddie Murray	.40
97	Rusty Greer	.10
98	Jay Buhner	.10
99	Rico Brogna	.10
100	Todd Hundley	.15
101	Moises Alou	.10
102	Chili Davis	.10
103	Ismael Valdes	.10
104	Mo Vaughn	.45
105	Juan Gonzalez	1.00
106	Mark Grudzielanek	.10
107	Derek Bell	.10
108	Shawn Green	.15
109	David Justice	.20
110	Paul O'Neill	.15
111	Kevin Appier	.10

112	Ray Lankford	.10
113	Travis Fryman	.10
114	Manny Ramirez	1.00
115	Brooks Kieschnick	.10
116	Ken Griffey Jr.	4.00
117	Jeffrey Hammonds	.10
118	Mark McGwire	4.00
119	Denny Neagle	.10
120	Quilvio Veras	.10
121	Alan Benes	.10
122	Rondell White	.10
123	*Osvaldo Fernandez*	.20
124	Andres Galarraga	.20
125	Johnny Damon	.20
126	Lenny Dykstra	.10
127	Jason Schmidt	.10
128	Mike Mussina	.50
129	Ken Caminiti	.25
130	Michael Tucker	.10
131	LaTroy Hawkins	.10
132	Checklist	.10
133	Delino DeShields	.10
134	Dave Nilsson	.10
135	Jack McDowell	.10
136	Joey Hamilton	.10
137	Dante Bichette	.20
138	Paul Molitor	.40
139	Ivan Rodriguez	.50
140	Mark Grace	.25
141	Paul Wilson	.20
142	Orel Hershiser	.10
143	Albert Belle	.60
144	Tino Martinez	.15
145	Tony Gwynn	1.00
146	George Arias	.10
147	Brian Jordan	.15
148	Brian McRae	.10
149	Rickey Henderson	.25
150	Ryan Klesko	.20

1996 Studio Press Proofs

The basic 150-card 1996 Studio set was also produced in three parallel press proof versions. Each is basically identical to the regular-issue cards except for appropriately colored foil highlights on front and a notation of edition size in the circle around the portrait photo on back. Bronze press proofs were issued in an edition of 2,000 each and were inserted at an average rate of one per six packs. Gold press proofs were an edition of 500 with an average insertion rate of one per 24 packs. The silver press proofs were inserted only into magazine packs and limited to just 100 cards of each.

	MT
Complete Set, Bronze (150):	400.00
Common Player, Bronze:	.75
Bronze Stars:	8X
Complete Set, Gold (150):	1200.
Common Player, Gold:	3.00
Gold Rookies, Stars:	30X
Common Player, Silver:	7.50
Silver Rookies, Stars:	60X

(See 1996 Studio for checklist, base card values)

1996 Studio Hit Parade

These die-cut inserts resemble an album with half of the record pulled out of the sleeve. Hit Parade cards, which feature top long ball hitters, were seeded one per every 36 packs. The cards were individually numbered up to 7,500. Each card can also be found in a sample version which has a "XXXX/5000" serial number on back.

		MT
Complete Set (10):		80.00
Common Player:		4.00
1	Tony Gwynn	10.00
2	Ken Griffey Jr.	25.00
3	Frank Thomas	10.00
4	Jeff Bagwell	8.00
5	Kirby Puckett	6.00
6	Mike Piazza	18.00
7	Barry Bonds	6.00
8	Albert Belle	5.00
9	Tim Salmon	4.00
10	Mo Vaughn	4.00

1996 Studio Masterstrokes

Only 5,000 each of these 1996 Studio insert cards were made. The cards simulate oil painting detail on an embossed canvas-feel front. Backs are glossy and individually serial numbered. They are found on average of once per 70 packs. Sample versions of each card overprinted as such on the back and numbered "PROMO/5000" are also known.

		MT
Complete Set (8):		100.00
Common Player:		5.00
1	Tony Gwynn	9.00
2	Mike Piazza	15.00
3	Jeff Bagwell	8.00
4	Manny Ramirez	8.00
5	Cal Ripken Jr.	20.00
6	Frank Thomas	8.00
7	Ken Griffey Jr.	25.00
8	Greg Maddux	12.50

1996 Studio Stained Glass Stars

Twelve superstars are featured on these clear, die-cut plastic cards which resemble stained glass windows. These 1996 Studio inserts were seeded one per every 30 packs.

		MT
Complete Set (12):		90.00
Common Player:		4.00
1	Cal Ripken Jr.	12.50
2	Ken Griffey Jr.	15.00
3	Frank Thomas	7.50
4	Greg Maddux	10.00
5	Chipper Jones	10.00
6	Mike Piazza	10.00
7	Albert Belle	3.00
8	Jeff Bagwell	9.00
9	Hideo Nomo	3.00
10	Barry Bonds	4.00
11	Manny Ramirez	8.00
12	Kenny Lofton	3.00

1997 Studio

Innovations in both product and packaging marked the seventh annual issue of Donruss' Studio brand. As in the past, the 165 cards in the base set rely on high-quality front photos to bring out the players' personalities. For '97, the photos are set against a background of variously shaded gray horizontal stripes. Backs have a second player photo, often an action shot, along with a short career summary. The "pack" for '97 Studio is something totally new to the hobby. An 8-1/2" x 12" cardboard envelope, complete with a zip strip opener in the style of an express-mail envelope, contains a cello pack of five standard-size cards plus either an 8" x 10" Studio Portrait card or an 8" x 10" version of the Master Strokes insert. Suggested retail price at issue was $2.49 per pack. Regular-size Master Strokes cards are one of several insert series which includes silver and gold press proofs and die-cut plastic Hard Hats.

		MT
Complete Set (165):		40.00
Common Player:		.10
Pack (5):		3.50
Wax Box (18):		60.00
1	Frank Thomas	1.50
2	Gary Sheffield	.25
3	Jason Isringhausen	.10
4	Ron Gant	.10
5	Andy Pettitte	.65
6	Todd Hollandsworth	.10
7	Troy Percival	.10
8	Mark McGwire	4.00
9	Barry Larkin	.20
10	Ken Caminiti	.20
11	Paul Molitor	.50
12	Travis Fryman	.10
13	Kevin Brown	.15
14	Robin Ventura	.15
15	Andres Galarraga	.20
16	Ken Griffey Jr.	4.00
17	Roger Clemens	1.00
18	Alan Benes	.10
19	David Justice	.25
20	Damon Buford	.10
21	Mike Piazza	2.00
22	Ray Durham	.10
23	Billy Wagner	.10
24	Dean Palmer	.10
25	David Cone	.20
26	Ruben Sierra	.10
27	Henry Rodriguez	.10
28	Ray Lankford	.10
29	Jamey Wright	.10
30	Brady Anderson	.15
31	Tino Martinez	.20
32	Manny Ramirez	1.00
33	Jeff Conine	.10
34	Dante Bichette	.20
35	Jose Canseco	.30
36	Mo Vaughn	.50
37	Sammy Sosa	1.50
38	Mark Grudzielanek	.10
39	Mike Mussina	.60
40	Bill Pulsipher	.10
41	Ryne Sandberg	.75
42	Rickey Henderson	.25
43	Alex Rodriguez	3.00
44	Eddie Murray	.40

45 Ernie Young .10
46 Joey Hamilton .10
47 Wade Boggs .35
48 Rusty Greer .10
49 Carlos Delgado .50
50 Ellis Burks .10
51 Cal Ripken Jr. 3.00
52 Alex Fernandez .10
53 Wally Joyner .10
54 James Baldwin .10
55 Juan Gonzalez 1.00
56 John Smoltz .15
57 Omar Vizquel .10
58 Shane Reynolds .10
59 Barry Bonds .75
60 Jason Kendall .10
61 Marty Cordova .10
62 Charles Johnson .10
63 John Jaha .10
64 Chan Ho Park .15
65 Jermaine Allensworth .10
66 Mark Grace .20
67 Tim Salmon .15
68 Edgar Martinez .10
69 Marquis Grissom .10
70 Craig Biggio .20
71 Bobby Higginson .10
72 Kevin Seitzer .10
73 Hideo Nomo .50
74 Dennis Eckersley .10
75 Bobby Bonilla .10
76 Dwight Gooden .10
77 Jeff Cirillo .10
78 Brian McRae .10
79 Chipper Jones 2.00
80 Jeff Fassero .10
81 Fred McGriff .25
82 Garret Anderson .10
83 Eric Karros .10
84 Derek Bell .10
85 Kenny Lofton .50
86 John Mabry .10
87 Pat Hentgen .10
88 Greg Maddux 2.00
89 Jason Giambi .10
90 Al Martin .10
91 Derek Jeter 2.00
92 Rey Ordonez .15
93 Will Clark .25
94 Kevin Appier .10
95 Roberto Alomar .50
96 Joe Carter .10
97 Bernie Williams .50
98 Albert Belle .60
99 Greg Vaughn .10
100 Tony Clark .50
101 Matt Williams .25
102 Jeff Bagwell 1.25
103 Reggie Sanders .10
104 Mariano Rivera .20
105 Larry Walker .35
106 Shawn Green .15
107 Alex Ochoa .10
108 Ivan Rodriguez .60
109 Eric Young .10
110 Javier Lopez .10
111 Brian Hunter .10
112 Raul Mondesi .25
113 Randy Johnson .60
114 Tony Phillips .10
115 Carlos Garcia .10
116 Moises Alou .15
117 Paul O'Neill .15
118 Jim Thome .30
119 Jermaine Dye .10
120 Wilson Alvarez .10
121 Rondell White .10
122 Michael Tucker .10
123 Mike Lansing .10
124 Tony Gwynn 1.25
125 Ryan Klesko .15
126 Jim Edmonds .10
127 Chuck Knoblauch .20
128 Rafael Palmeiro .20
129 Jay Buhner .10
130 Tom Glavine .20
131 Julio Franco .10
132 Cecil Fielder .10
133 Paul Wilson .10
134 Deion Sanders .20
135 Alex Gonzalez .10
136 Charles Nagy .10
137 Andy Ashby .10
138 Edgar Renteria .10
139 Pedro Martinez .20
140 Brian Jordan .10
141 Todd Hundley .20
142 Marc Newfield .10
143 Darryl Strawberry .10
144 Dan Wilson .10
145 *Brian Giles* 2.00
146 Bartolo Colon .10
147 Shannon Stewart .10
148 Scott Spiezio .10
149 Andruw Jones 1.50
150 Karim Garcia .10
151 Vladimir Guerrero 1.50
152 George Arias .10
153 Brooks Kieschnick .10
154 Todd Walker .50
155 Scott Rolen 1.50
156 Todd Greene .10
157 Dmitri Young .10
158 Ruben Rivera .10
159 Trey Beamon .10
160 Nomar Garciaparra 2.00
161 Bob Abreu .15
162 Darin Erstad 1.25
163 Ken Griffey Jr. (checklist) 1.00
164 Frank Thomas (checklist) .50
165 Alex Rodriguez (checklist) .75

1997 Studio Press Proofs

Each of the 165 cards in the base set of '97 Studio was also produced in a pair of Press Proof versions as random pack inserts. Fronts of the Press Proofs have either silver or gold holographic foil replacing the silver foil graphics found on regular cards, as well as foil strips down each side. Backs are identical to the regular issue. The silver Press Proofs were issued in an edition of 1,500 of each player; the golds are limited to 500 of each.

MT
Complete Set, Silver (165): 450.00
Common Player, Silver: 1.50
Silver Stars: 8X
Complete Set, Gold (165): 1600.
Common Player, Gold: 4.00
Gold Stars: 20X
(Silver stars valued at 8-15X regular cards; gold at 15-40X.)

1997 Studio Hard Hats

Die-cut plastic is used to represent a player's batting helmet in this set of '97 Studio inserts. A player action photo appears in the foreground with his name and other graphic elements in silver foil. Backs feature a small portrait photo, short career summary and a serial number from within the edition of 5,000 of each card.

MT
Complete Set (24): 160.00
Common Player: 2.00
1 Ivan Rodriguez 6.00
2 Albert Belle 5.00
3 Ken Griffey Jr. 25.00
4 Chuck Knoblauch 4.00
5 Frank Thomas 12.00
6 Cal Ripken Jr. 20.00
7 Todd Walker 4.00
8 Alex Rodriguez 20.00
9 Jim Thome 3.00
10 Mike Piazza 15.00
11 Barry Larkin 3.00
12 Chipper Jones 15.00
13 Derek Jeter 15.00
14 Jermaine Dye 2.00
15 Jason Giambi 2.00
16 Tim Salmon 4.00
17 Brady Anderson 2.00
18 Rondell White 2.00
19 Bernie Williams 4.00
20 Juan Gonzalez 8.00
21 Karim Garcia 4.00
22 Scott Rolen 8.00
23 Darin Erstad 6.00
24 Brian Jordan 2.00

1997 Studio Master Strokes

The look and feel of a painting on canvas is the effect presented by '97 Studio's Master Strokes inserts. Card fronts feature unique player action art and are highlighted by gold-foil graphics. Each card has a facsimile autograph on front. UV-coated backs are team-color coordinated and have a few sentences about the player. Gold-foil serial numbering identifies the card from an edition of 2,000 of each player.

MT
Complete Set (24): 450.00
Common Player: 7.50
1 Derek Jeter 25.00
2 Jeff Bagwell 15.00
3 Ken Griffey Jr. 50.00
4 Barry Bonds 15.00
5 Frank Thomas 15.00
6 Andy Pettitte 10.00
7 Mo Vaughn 7.50
8 Alex Rodriguez 40.00
9 Andruw Jones 12.50
10 Kenny Lofton 7.50
11 Cal Ripken Jr. 35.00
12 Greg Maddux 20.00
13 Manny Ramirez 15.00
14 Mike Piazza 25.00
14p Mike Piazza (promo) 7.50
15 Vladimir Guerrero 20.00
16 Albert Belle 10.00
17 Chipper Jones 25.00
18 Hideo Nomo 7.50
19 Sammy Sosa 25.00
20 Tony Gwynn 20.00
21 Gary Sheffield 7.50
22 Mark McGwire 50.00
23 Juan Gonzalez 15.00
24 Paul Molitor 10.00

1997 Studio Master Strokes 8x10

The look and feel of a painting on canvas is the effect presented by the 8" x 10" version of '97 Studio's Master Strokes inserts. Card fronts feature unique player action art and are highlighted by gold-foil graphics. Each card has a facsimile autograph on front. UV-coated backs are team-color coordinated and have a few sentences about the player. Gold-foil serial numbering identifies the card from an edition of 5,000 of each player - making the super-size version more than twice as common as the 2-1/2" x 3-1/2" version.

MT
Complete Set (24): 220.00
Common Player: 4.00
1 Derek Jeter 15.00
2 Jeff Bagwell 10.00
3 Ken Griffey Jr. 25.00
4 Barry Bonds 6.00
5 Frank Thomas 10.00
6 Andy Pettitte 5.00
7 Mo Vaughn 4.00
8 Alex Rodriguez 20.00
9 Andruw Jones 12.00
10 Kenny Lofton 4.00
11 Cal Ripken Jr. 20.00
12 Greg Maddux 15.00
13 Manny Ramirez 9.00
14 Mike Piazza 15.00
15 Vladimir Guerrero 10.00
16 Albert Belle 5.00
17 Chipper Jones 15.00
18 Hideo Nomo 4.00
19 Sammy Sosa 15.00
20 Tony Gwynn 10.00
21 Gary Sheffield 4.00
22 Mark McGwire 25.00
23 Juan Gonzalez 8.00
24 Paul Molitor 6.00

1997 Studio Portraits

Perhaps the most innovative feature of '97 Studio is the 8" x 10" Portrait cards which come one per pack (except when a pack contains a Master Strokes 8x10). Virtually identical to the player's regular-size Studio card, the jumbo version has the word "PORTRAIT" in black beneath the team name on front. Backs have different card numbers than the same player's card in the regular set. The Portrait cards are produced with a special UV coating on front to facilitate autographing. Pre-autographed cards of three youngsters in the series were included as random pack inserts.

		MT
Complete Set (24):		25.00
Common Player:		.50
1	Ken Griffey Jr.	4.00
1s	Frank Thomas (over-printed "SAMPLE")	.50
2	Frank Thomas	1.50
3	Alex Rodriguez	3.00
4	Andruw Jones	1.50
5	Cal Ripken Jr.	3.00
6	Greg Maddux	2.00
7	Mike Piazza	2.00
8	Chipper Jones	2.00
9	Albert Belle	1.00
10	Derek Jeter	2.00
11	Juan Gonzalez	1.00
12	Todd Walker	.75
12a	Todd Walker (autographed edition of 1,250)	40.00
13	Mark McGwire	4.00
14	Barry Bonds	.75
15	Jeff Bagwell	1.00
16	Manny Ramirez	1.00
17	Kenny Lofton	.50
18	Mo Vaughn	.50
19	Hideo Nomo	.50
20	Tony Gwynn	1.00
21	Vladimir Guerrero	1.50
21a	Vladimir Guerrero (autographed edition of 500)	100.00
22	Gary Sheffield	.50
23	Ryne Sandberg	.75
24	Scott Rolen	1.25
24a	Scott Rolen (autographed edition of 1,000)	75.00

1998 Studio

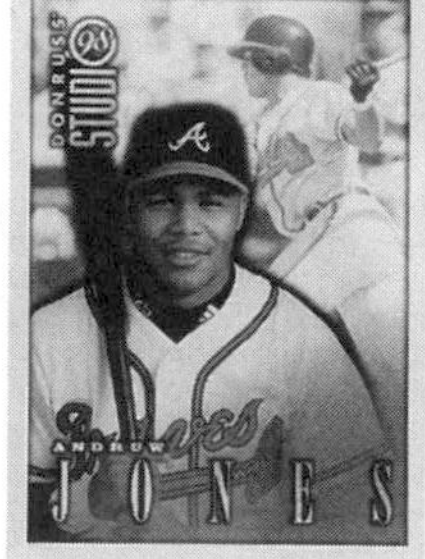

The Donruss Studio base set consists of 220 regular-sized cards and 36 8-x-10 portraits. The base cards feature a posed photo with an action shot in the background, surrounded by a white border. Silver Studio Proofs (numbered to 1,000) and Gold Studio Proofs (300) parallel the regular-size base set. Inserts included Freeze Frame, Hit Parade and Masterstrokes.

		MT
Complete Set (220):		35.00
Common Player:		.15
Pack (7 cards 1 8x10):		3.00
Wax Box (18):		45.00
1	Tony Clark	.40
2	Jose Cruz Jr.	.20
3	Ivan Rodriguez	.75
4	Mo Vaughn	.50
5	Kenny Lofton	.50
6	Will Clark	.25
7	Barry Larkin	.20
8	Jay Bell	.15
9	Kevin Young	.15
10	Francisco Cordova	.15
11	Justin Thompson	.15
12	Paul Molitor	.50
13	Jeff Bagwell	1.25
14	Jose Canseco	.35
15	Scott Rolen	1.00
16	Wilton Guerrero	.15
17	Shannon Stewart	.15
18	Hideki Irabu	.50
19	Michael Tucker	.15
20	Joe Carter	.15
21	Gabe Alvarez	.15
22	Ricky Ledee	.40
23	Karim Garcia	.20
24	Eli Marrero	.15
25	Scott Elarton	.15
26	Mario Valdez	.15
27	Ben Grieve	1.00
28	Paul Konerko	.40
29	*Esteban Yan*	.20
30	Esteban Loaiza	.15
31	Delino DeShields	.15
32	Bernie Williams	.40
33	Joe Randa	.15
34	Randy Johnson	.50
35	Brett Tomko	.15
36	*Todd Erdos*	.20
37	Bobby Higginson	.15
38	Jason Kendall	.15
39	Ray Lankford	.15
40	Mark Grace	.30
41	Andy Pettitte	.40
42	Alex Rodriguez	2.50
43	Hideo Nomo	.40
44	Sammy Sosa	2.00
45	J.T. Snow	.15
46	Jason Varitek	.25
47	Vinny Castilla	.15
48	Neifi Perez	.15
49	Todd Walker	.15
50	Mike Cameron	.15
51	Jeffrey Hammonds	.15
52	Deivi Cruz	.15
53	Brian Hunter	.15
54	Al Martin	.15
55	Ron Coomer	.15
56	Chan Ho Park	.15
57	Pedro Martinez	.40
58	Darin Erstad	.75
59	Albert Belle	.60
60	Nomar Garciaparra	2.00
61	Tony Gwynn	1.50
62	Mike Piazza	2.00
63	Todd Helton	.75
64	David Ortiz	.30
65	Todd Dunwoody	.15
66	Orlando Cabrera	.15
67	Ken Cloude	.15
68	Andy Benes	.15
69	Mariano Rivera	.25
70	Cecil Fielder	.15
71	Brian Jordan	.15
72	Darryl Kile	.15
73	Reggie Jefferson	.15
74	Shawn Estes	.15
75	Bobby Bonilla	.15
76	Denny Neagle	.15
77	Robin Ventura	.25
78	Omar Vizquel	.15
79	Craig Biggio	.30
80	Moises Alou	.25
81	Garret Anderson	.15
82	Eric Karros	.15
83	Dante Bichette	.30
84	Charles Johnson	.15
85	Rusty Greer	.15
86	Travis Fryman	.15
87	Fernando Tatis	.25
88	Wilson Alvarez	.15
89	Carl Pavano	.15
90	Brian Rose	.15
91	Geoff Jenkins	.15
92	*Magglio Ordonez*	1.50
93	David Segui	.15
94	David Cone	.25
95	John Smoltz	.20
96	Jim Thome	.30
97	Gary Sheffield	.40
98	Barry Bonds	.75
99	Andres Galarraga	.40
100	Brad Fullmer	.40
101	Bobby Estalella	.15
102	Enrique Wilson	.15
103	*Frank Catalanotto*	.20
104	*Mike Lowell*	.40
105	Kevin Orie	.15
106	Matt Morris	.20
107	Pokey Reese	.15
108	Shawn Green	.20
109	Tony Womack	.15
110	Ken Caminiti	.25
111	Roberto Alomar	.50
112	Ken Griffey Jr.	3.00
113	Cal Ripken Jr.	2.50
114	Lou Collier	.15
115	Larry Walker	.40
116	Fred McGriff	.30
117	Jim Edmonds	.20
118	Edgar Martinez	.15
119	Matt Williams	.30
120	Ismael Valdes	.15
121	Bartolo Colon	.20
122	Jeff Cirillo	.15
123	*Steve Woodard*	.25
124	*Kevin Millwood*	4.00
125	Derrick Gibson	.15
126	Jacob Cruz	.15
127	Russell Branyan	.15
128	Sean Casey	.40
129	Derrek Lee	.15
130	Paul O'Neill	.25
131	Brad Radke	.15
132	Kevin Appier	.15
133	John Olerud	.25
134	Alan Benes	.15
135	Todd Greene	.15
136	*Carlos Mendoza*	.35
137	Wade Boggs	.40
138	Jose Guillen	.25
139	Tino Martinez	.30
140	Aaron Boone	.15
141	Abraham Nunez	.15
142	Preston Wilson	.15
143	Randall Simon	.20
144	Dennis Reyes	.15
145	Mark Kotsay	.30
146	Richard Hidalgo	.15
147	Travis Lee	.60
148	*Hanley Frias*	.15
149	Ruben Rivera	.15
150	Rafael Medina	.15
151	Dave Nilsson	.15
152	Curt Schilling	.25
153	Brady Anderson	.15
154	Carlos Delgado	.50
155	Jason Giambi	.15
156	Pat Hentgen	.15
157	Tom Glavine	.25
158	Ryan Klesko	.20
159	Chipper Jones	2.00
160	Juan Gonzalez	.75
161	Mark McGwire	3.00
162	Vladimir Guerrero	1.25
163	Derek Jeter	2.00
164	Manny Ramirez	1.00
165	Mike Mussina	.60
166	Rafael Palmeiro	.30
167	Henry Rodriguez	.15
168	Jeff Suppan	.15
169	Eric Milton	.15
170	Scott Spiezio	.15
171	Wilson Delgado	.15
172	Bubba Trammell	.15
173	Ellis Burks	.15
174	Jason Dickson	.15
175	Butch Huskey	.15
176	Edgardo Alfonzo	.15
177	Eric Young	.15
178	Marquis Grissom	.15
179	Lance Johnson	.15
180	Kevin Brown	.25
181	Sandy Alomar Jr.	.25
182	Todd Hundley	.15
183	Rondell White	.20
184	Javier Lopez	.20
185	Damian Jackson	.15
186	Raul Mondesi	.40
187	Rickey Henderson	.35
188	David Justice	.40
189	Jay Buhner	.15
190	Jaret Wright	1.00
191	Miguel Tejada	.40
192	Ron Wright	.15
193	Livan Hernandez	.15
194	A.J. Hinch	.50
195	Richie Sexson	.15
196	Bob Abreu	.15
197	Luis Castillo	.15
198	Michael Coleman	.15
199	Greg Maddux	2.00
200	Frank Thomas	1.50
201	Andruw Jones	.75
202	Roger Clemens	1.25
203	Tim Salmon	.30
204	Chuck Knoblauch	.40
205	Wes Helms	.15
206	Juan Encarnacion	.15
207	Russ Davis	.15
208	John Valentin	.15
209	Tony Saunders	.15
210	Mike Sweeney	.15
211	Steve Finley	.15
212	*David Dellucci*	.50
213	Edgar Renteria	.15
214	Jeremi Gonzalez	.15
215	Checklist (Jeff Bagwell)	.60
216	Checklist (Mike Piazza)	1.00
217	Checklist (Greg Maddux)	1.00
218	Checklist (Cal Ripken Jr.)	1.25
219	Checklist (Frank Thomas)	.75
220	Checklist (Ken Griffey Jr.)	1.50

1998 Studio Silver Proofs

This parallel set includes all 220 cards in Studio baseball. Cards are identified by a silver holographic strip around the borders. Silver versions are limited to 1,000 sets.

	MT
Complete Set (220):	850.00
Common Player:	1.50
Silver Stars:	8X

(See 1998 Studio for checklist, base card values.)

1998 Studio Gold Proofs

Gold proofs is a parallel of the 220-card base set. Card fronts feature gold holo-foil highlights. Backs are sequentially numbered to 300 each.

	MT
Complete Set (220):	2500.
Common Player:	4.00
Stars:	25X

(See 1998 Studio for checklist and base card values.)

1998 Studio Autographs

Three top rookies signed a number of 8x10s for this product. Lee signed 500 while the other two autographed 1,000 each.

		MT
1	Travis Lee (500)	15.00
2	Todd Helton (1000)	40.00
3	Ben Grieve (1000)	25.00

1998 Studio Freeze Frame

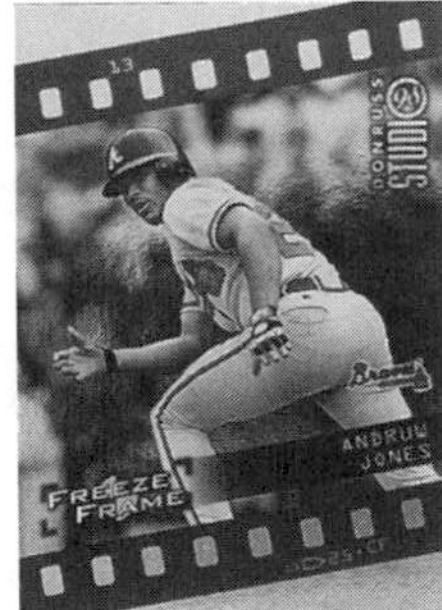

Freeze Frame is a 30-card insert sequentially numbered to 5,000. The cards are designed to look like a piece of film with a color action photo. The first 500 of each card are die-cut.

		MT
Complete Set (30):		245.00
Common Player:		3.00
Production 4,500 sets		
Die-Cuts:		8X
Production 500 sets		
1	Ken Griffey Jr.	20.00
2	Derek Jeter	15.00
3	Ben Grieve	6.00
4	Cal Ripken Jr.	17.50
5	Alex Rodriguez	18.00
6	Greg Maddux	15.00
7	David Justice	4.50
8	Mike Piazza	15.00
9	Chipper Jones	15.00
10	Randy Johnson	4.50
11	Jeff Bagwell	9.00
12	Nomar Garciaparra	15.00
13	Andruw Jones	6.00
14	Frank Thomas	9.00
15	Scott Rolen	6.00
16	Barry Bonds	6.00
17	Kenny Lofton	4.00
18	Ivan Rodriguez	5.00
19	Chuck Knoblauch	4.00
20	Jose Cruz Jr.	3.00
21	Bernie Williams	4.00
22	Tony Gwynn	12.00
23	Juan Gonzalez	5.00
24	Gary Sheffield	3.00
25	Roger Clemens	7.50
26	Travis Lee	4.50
27	Brad Fullmer	6.00
28	Tim Salmon	3.00
29	Raul Mondesi	3.00
30	Roberto Alomar	4.00

1998 Studio Hit Parade

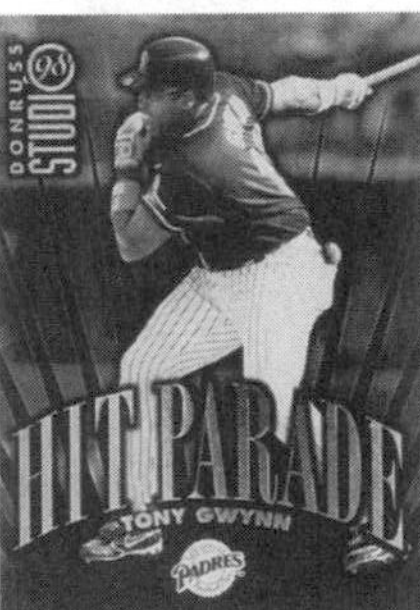

These 20 cards are printed on micro-etched foil board. This set honors baseball's top hitters and is sequentially numbered to 5,000.

		MT
Complete Set (20):		140.00
Common Player:		4.00
Production 5,000 sets		
1	Tony Gwynn	12.00
2	Larry Walker	4.00
3	Mike Piazza	15.00
4	Frank Thomas	10.00
5	Manny Ramirez	9.00
6	Ken Griffey Jr.	25.00
7	Todd Helton	6.00
8	Vladimir Guerrero	10.00
9	Albert Belle	5.00
10	Jeff Bagwell	10.00
11	Juan Gonzalez	8.00
12	Jim Thome	4.00
13	Scott Rolen	8.00
14	Tino Martinez	4.00
15	Mark McGwire	25.00
16	Barry Bonds	6.00
17	Tony Clark	4.00
18	Mo Vaughn	4.00
19	Darin Erstad	6.00
20	Paul Konerko	4.00

1998 Studio Masterstrokes

Printed on a canvas-like material, these 20 cards are numbered to 1,000.

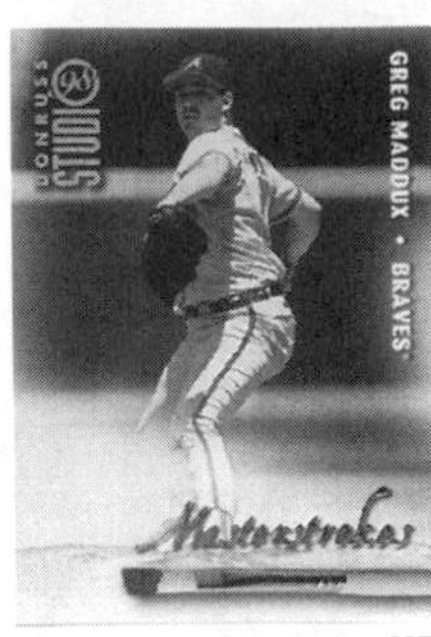

		MT
Complete Set (20):		650.00
Common Player:		10.00
Production 1,000 sets		
1	Travis Lee	20.00
2	Kenny Lofton	10.00
3	Mo Vaughn	10.00
4	Ivan Rodriguez	15.00
5	Roger Clemens	30.00
6	Mark McGwire	75.00
7	Hideo Nomo	10.00
8	Andruw Jones	20.00
9	Nomar Garciaparra	50.00
10	Juan Gonzalez	20.00
11	Jeff Bagwell	25.00
12	Derek Jeter	50.00
13	Tony Gwynn	40.00
14	Chipper Jones	50.00
15	Mike Piazza	50.00
16	Greg Maddux	50.00
17	Alex Rodriguez	60.00
18	Cal Ripken Jr.	60.00
19	Frank Thomas	25.00
20	Ken Griffey Jr.	75.00

1998 Studio Sony MLB 99

Twenty Sony MLB '99 sweepstakes cards were inserted one per two Studio packs. The fronts feature a color action shot and the backs have sweepstakes rules and a MLB '99 tip.

		MT
Complete Set (20):		10.00
Common Player:		.25
1	Cal Ripken Jr.	2.00
2	Nomar Garciaparra	1.50
3	Barry Bonds	.60
4	Mike Mussina	.50
5	Pedro Martinez	.40
6	Derek Jeter	1.50
7	Andruw Jones	.60
8	Kenny Lofton	.40
9	Gary Sheffield	.25
10	Raul Mondesi	.25
11	Jeff Bagwell	.75
12	Tim Salmon	.25
13	Tom Glavine	.25
14	Ben Grieve	.75
15	Matt Williams	.25
16	Juan Gonzalez	1.00
17	Mark McGwire	3.00
18	Bernie Williams	.40
19	Andres Galarraga	.25
20	Jose Cruz Jr.	.25

1998 Studio 8x10 Portraits

One Studio 8-x-10 was included in each pack. The cards were blown-up versions of the regular-size base cards, which were inserted seven per pack. The large portraits are paralleled in the Gold Proofs set, which adds gold holo-foil to the cards. Gold Proofs are numbered to 300.

		MT
Complete Set (36):		40.00
Common Player:		.50
Inserted 1:1		
1	Travis Lee	1.50
2	Todd Helton	1.50
3	Ben Grieve	1.50
4	Paul Konerko	.75
5	Jeff Bagwell	2.00
6	Derek Jeter	3.00
7	Ivan Rodriguez	1.50
8	Cal Ripken Jr.	4.00
9	Mike Piazza	3.00
10	Chipper Jones	3.00
11	Frank Thomas	2.50
12	Tony Gwynn	2.50
13	Nomar Garciaparra	3.00
14	Juan Gonzalez	1.50
15	Greg Maddux	3.00
16	Hideo Nomo	.75
17	Scott Rolen	1.50
18	Barry Bonds	1.50
19	Ken Griffey Jr.	5.00
20	Alex Rodriguez	4.00
21	Roger Clemens	2.00
22	Mark McGwire	5.00
23	Jose Cruz Jr.	.50
24	Andruw Jones	1.50
25	Tino Martinez	.50
26	Mo Vaughn	.75
27	Vladimir Guerrero	2.00
28	Tony Clark	1.00
29	Andy Pettitte	1.00
30	Jaret Wright	1.50
31	Paul Molitor	1.00
32	Darin Erstad	1.50
33	Larry Walker	.50
34	Chuck Knoblauch	.50
35	Barry Larkin	.50
36	Kenny Lofton	.75

1998 Studio 8x10 Portraits Gold Proofs

This parallel of the 8x10 base set adds gold holo-foil treatments to the 36 cards, which are sequentially numbered to 300 and randomly inserted in packs.

	MT
Complete Set (36):	600.00
Common Player:	8.00
Stars:	20X

(See 1998 Studio 8X10 Portraits for checklist and base card values.)

1995 Summit

A late-season release, Summit introduced the Score label to a premium brand card. Printed on extra heavy cardboard stock and UV coated on both sides the veteran player cards (#1-111) feature horizontal or vertical action photos with the player's name and team logo printed in gold-foil on front. Backs have a player portrait photo along with his 1994 stats in monthly charted form. The rookie cards subset (#112-173) have a large black "ROOKIE" on top-front while the back has a short career summary instead of stats. Other subsets include "BAT SPEED" (#174-188), honoring top hitters, and "SPECIAL DELIVERY" (#189-193), featuring top pitchers. Each are designated on front with special gold-foil logos. Seven checklists close out the regular 200-card set. The Summit issued featured a four-tiered chase card program, including a parallel "Nth Degree" set. Summit was a hobby-only issue sold in 7-card foil packs.

		MT
Complete Set (200):		20.00
Common Player:		.10
Pack (7):		2.00
Wax Box (24):		30.00
1	Ken Griffey Jr.	3.00
2	Alex Fernandez	.15
3	Fred McGriff	.35
4	Ben McDonald	.10
5	Rafael Palmeiro	.15
6	Tony Gwynn	1.00
7	Jim Thome	.30
8	Ken Hill	.10
9	Barry Bonds	.75
10	Barry Larkin	.20
11	Albert Belle	.60
12	Billy Ashley	.10
13	Matt Williams	.25
14	Andy Benes	.10
15	Midre Cummings	.10
16	J.R. Phillips	.10
17	Edgar Martinez	.10
18	Manny Ramirez	.75
19	Jose Canseco	.35
20	Chili Davis	.10
21	Don Mattingly	1.00
22	Bernie Williams	.40
23	Tom Glavine	.20
24	Robin Ventura	.15
25	Jeff Conine	.10
26	Mark Grace	.20
27	Mark McGwire	3.00
28	Carlos Delgado	.50
29	Greg Colbrunn	.10
30	Greg Maddux	2.00
31	Craig Biggio	.25
32	Kirby Puckett	1.00
33	Derek Bell	.10
34	Lenny Dykstra	.10
35	Tim Salmon	.20
36	Deion Sanders	.20
37	Moises Alou	.15
38	Ray Lankford	.10
39	Willie Greene	.10
40	Ozzie Smith	.50
41	Roger Clemens	.75
42	Andres Galarraga	.20
43	Gary Sheffield	.30
44	Sammy Sosa	1.50
45	Larry Walker	.30
46	Kevin Appier	.10
47	Raul Mondesi	.30
48	Kenny Lofton	.50
49	Darryl Hamilton	.10
50	Roberto Alomar	.60
51	Hal Morris	.10
52	Cliff Floyd	.10
53	Brent Gates	.10
54	Rickey Henderson	.35
55	John Olerud	.15
56	Gregg Jefferies	.10
57	Cecil Fielder	.10
58	Paul Molitor	.50
59	Bret Boone	.10
60	Greg Vaughn	.10
61	Wally Joyner	.15
62	Jeffrey Hammonds	.10
63	James Mouton	.10
64	Omar Vizquel	.10
65	Wade Boggs	.35
66	Terry Steinbach	.10
67	Wil Cordero	.10
68	Joey Hamilton	.10
69	Rico Brogna	.10
70	Darren Daulton	.10
71	Chuck Knoblauch	.20
72	Bob Hamelin	.10
73	Carl Everett	.10
74	Joe Carter	.10
75	Dave Winfield	.35
76	Bobby Bonilla	.10
77	Paul O'Neill	.15
78	Javier Lopez	.15
79	Cal Ripken Jr.	2.50
80	David Cone	.15
81	Bernard Gilkey	.10
82	Ivan Rodriguez	.50
83	Dean Palmer	.10
84	Jason Bere	.10
85	Will Clark	.25
86	Scott Cooper	.10
87	Royce Clayton	.10
88	Mike Piazza	2.00
89	Ryan Klesko	.30
90	Juan Gonzalez	1.00
91	Travis Fryman	.10
92	Frank Thomas	1.50
93	Eduardo Perez	.10
94	Mo Vaughn	.50
95	Jay Bell	.10
96	Jeff Bagwell	1.00
97	Randy Johnson	.35
98	Jimmy Key	.10
99	Dennis Eckersley	.10
100	Carlos Baerga	.10
101	Eddie Murray	.35
102	Mike Mussina	.40
103	Brian Anderson	.10
104	Jeff Cirillo	.10
105	Dante Bichette	.25
106	Bret Saberhagen	.10
107	Jeff Kent	.10
108	Ruben Sierra	.10
109	Kirk Gibson	.10
110	Reggie Sanders	.15
111	Dave Justice	.20
112	Benji Gil	.10
113	Vaughn Eshelman	.10
114	*Carlos Perez*	.20
115	Chipper Jones	2.00
116	Shane Andrews	.10
117	Orlando Miller	.10
118	Scott Ruffcorn	.10
119	Jose Oliva	.10
120	Joe Vitiello	.10
121	Jon Nunnally	.10
122	Garret Anderson	.15
123	Curtis Goodwin	.10
124	*Mark Grudzielanek*	.35
125	Alex Gonzalez	.15
126	David Bell	.10
127	Dustin Hermanson	.10
128	Dave Nilsson	.10
129	Wilson Heredia	.10
130	Charles Johnson	.15
131	Frank Rodriguez	.10
132	Alex Ochoa	.10
133	Alex Rodriguez	2.50
134	*Bobby Higginson*	1.50
135	Edgardo Alfonzo	.15
136	Armando Benitez	.10
137	Rich Aude	.10
138	Tim Naehring	.10
139	Joe Randa	.10
140	Quilvio Veras	.10
141	*Hideo Nomo*	2.00
142	Ray Holbert	.10
143	Michael Tucker	.10
144	Chad Mottola	.10
145	John Valentin	.10
146	James Baldwin	.10
147	Esteban Loaiza	.10
148	Marty Cordova	.15
149	*Juan Acevedo*	.10
150	*Tim Unroe*	.10
151	Brad Clontz	.10
152	Steve Rodriguez	.10
153	Rudy Pemberton	.10
154	Ozzie Timmons	.10
155	Ricky Otero	.10
156	Allen Battle	.10
157	Joe Roselli	.10
158	Roberto Petagine	.10
159	Todd Hollandsworth	.10
160	Shannon Penn	.10
161	Antonio Osuna	.10
162	Russ Davis	.10
163	Jason Giambi	.10
164	Terry Bradshaw	.10
165	Ray Durham	.10
166	Todd Steverson	.10
167	Tim Belk	.10
168	Andy Pettitte	.60
169	Roger Cedeno	.10
170	Jose Parra	.10
171	Scott Sullivan	.10
172	LaTroy Hawkins	.10
173	Jeff McCurry	.10
174	Ken Griffey Jr. (Bat Speed)	1.50
175	Frank Thomas (Bat Speed)	.75
176	Cal Ripken Jr. (Bat Speed)	1.25
177	Jeff Bagwell (Bat Speed)	.50
178	Mike Piazza (Bat Speed)	.60
179	Barry Bonds (Bat Speed)	.35
180	Matt Williams (Bat Speed)	.20
181	Don Mattingly (Bat Speed)	.50
182	Will Clark (Bat Speed)	.20
183	Tony Gwynn (Bat Speed)	.40
184	Kirby Puckett (Bat Speed)	.50
185	Jose Canseco (Bat Speed)	.20
186	Paul Molitor (Bat Speed)	.25
187	Albert Belle (Bat Speed)	.40
188	Joe Carter (Bat Speed)	.10
189	Greg Maddux (Special Delivery)	1.00
190	Roger Clemens (Special Delivery)	.40
191	David Cone (Special Delivery)	.10
192	Mike Mussina (Special Delivery)	.20
193	Randy Johnson (Special Delivery)	.15
194	Checklist (Frank Thomas)	.50
195	Checklist (Ken Griffey Jr.)	.75
196	Checklist (Cal Ripken Jr.)	.60
197	Checklist (Jeff Bagwell)	.30
198	Checklist (Mike Piazza)	.40
199	Checklist (Barry Bonds)	.25
200	Checklist (Mo Vaughn, Matt Williams)	.20

1995 Summit Nth Degree

	MT
Complete Set (200):	400.00
Common Player:	1.00
Stars:	8X

(See 1995 Summit for checklist, base card values.)

1995 Summit Big Bang

The game's top sluggers are featured in this insert set. The front is printed on prismatic metallic foil, a process which Score calls "Spectroetch," with large and small action photos. Backs are conventionally printed and have a large photo with a career highlight printed beneath. The toughest of the Summit chase cards, these are found on the average of once every two boxes (72 packs). Cards are numbered with a "BB" prefix.

		MT
Complete Set (20):		250.00
Common Player:		3.00
1	Ken Griffey Jr.	50.00
2	Frank Thomas	20.00
3	Cal Ripken Jr.	40.00
4	Jeff Bagwell	20.00
5	Mike Piazza	30.00
6	Barry Bonds	12.00
7	Matt Williams	4.00
8	Don Mattingly	15.00
9	Will Clark	4.00
10	Tony Gwynn	25.00
11	Kirby Puckett	20.00
12	Jose Canseco	6.00
13	Paul Molitor	10.00
14	Albert Belle	10.00
15	Joe Carter	3.00
16	Rafael Palmeiro	4.00
17	Fred McGriff	4.00
18	Dave Justice	3.00
19	Tim Salmon	3.00
20	Mo Vaughn	3.00

1995 Summit New Age

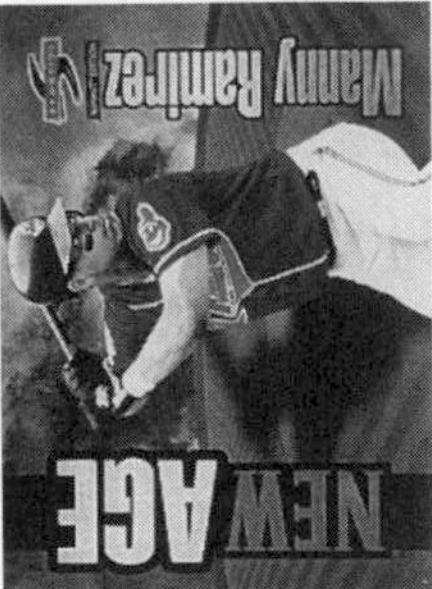

Printed on metallic foil in a horizontal format, the New Age inserts were seeded at a rate of about one per 18 packs. Red and silver colors predominate on front, while the backs are printed in standard technology and feature a second photo and a short career summary of the players who were generally in their second or third Major League season in 1995.

		MT
Complete Set (15):		50.00
Common Player:		1.00
1	Cliff Floyd	1.00
2	Manny Ramirez	10.00
3	Raul Mondesi	5.00
4	Alex Rodriguez	30.00
5	Billy Ashley	1.00
6	Alex Gonzalez	2.00
7	Michael Tucker	1.00
8	Charles Johnson	3.00
9	Carlos Delgado	5.00
10	Benji Gil	1.00
11	Chipper Jones	25.00
12	Todd Hollandsworth	1.50
13	Frank Rodriguez	1.00
14	Shawn Green	5.00
15	Ray Durham	2.00

1995 Summit 21 Club

Metallic foil printing on front and back distinguishes this set of chase cards. A large red-foil "21 / CLUB" logo on each side identifies the theme of this set as players who professed to be that age during the 1955 baseball season. The players are pictured in action pose on front and a portrait on back. On average the 21 Club cards are seeded one per box (36 packs). Cards are numbered with a "TC" prefix.

		MT
Complete Set (9):		30.00
Common Player:		3.00
1	Bob Abreu	6.00
2	Pokey Reese	4.00
3	Edgardo Alfonzo	6.00
4	Jim Pittsley	3.00
5	Ruben Rivera	4.00
6	Chan Ho Park	8.00
7	Julian Tavarez	3.00
8	Ismael Valdes	4.00
9	Dmitri Young	3.00

1996 Summit

Pinnacle's 1996 Summit baseball has 200 cards, including 35 rookies, four checklists and 10 Deja Vu subset cards. Each card is also reprinted in three parallel versions - Above and Beyond (one per seven packs), Artist's Proofs (one in 36) and a retail-only silver foil-bordered version. Above and Beyond cards use an all-prismatic foil design; Artist's Proof cards have holographic foil stamping. Five insert sets were produced: Big Bang; Mirage (a parallel set to Big Bang); Hitters, Inc.; Ballparks; and Positions (found one per every 50 magazine packs).

		MT
Complete Set (200):		20.00
Common Player:		.10
Pack (7):		2.00
Wax Box (18):		30.00
1	Mike Piazza	2.00
2	Matt Williams	.30
3	Tino Martinez	.20
4	Reggie Sanders	.10
5	Ray Durham	.10
6	Brad Radke	.10
7	Jeff Bagwell	1.25
8	Ron Gant	.15
9	Lance Johnson	.10
10	Kevin Seitzer	.10
11	Dante Bichette	.25
12	Ivan Rodriguez	.60
13	Jim Abbott	.10
14	Greg Colbrunn	.10
15	Rondell White	.10
16	Shawn Green	.20
17	Gregg Jefferies	.10
18	Omar Vizquel	.10
19	Cal Ripken Jr.	3.00
20	Mark McGwire	4.00
21	Wally Joyner	.10
22	Chili Davis	.10
23	Jose Canseco	.35
24	Royce Clayton	.10
25	Jay Bell	.10
26	Travis Fryman	.10
27	Jeff King	.10
28	Todd Hundley	.20
29	Joe Vitiello	.10
30	Russ Davis	.10
31	Mo Vaughn	.50
32	Raul Mondesi	.30
33	Ray Lankford	.10
34	Mike Stanley	.10
35	B.J. Surhoff	.10
36	Greg Vaughn	.10
37	Todd Stottlemyre	.10
38	Carlos Delgado	.40
39	Kenny Lofton	.50
40	Hideo Nomo	.60
41	Sterling Hitchcock	.10
42	Pete Schourek	.10
43	Edgardo Alfonzo	.15
44	Ken Hill	.10
45	Ken Caminiti	.25
46	Bobby Higginson	.15
47	Michael Tucker	.10
48	David Cone	.20
49	Cecil Fielder	.10
50	Brian Hunter	.10
51	Charles Johnson	.10
52	Bobby Bonilla	.10
53	Eddie Murray	.40
54	Kenny Rogers	.10
55	Jim Edmonds	.15
56	Trevor Hoffman	.10
57	Kevin Mitchell	.10
58	Ruben Sierra	.10
59	Benji Gil	.10
60	Juan Gonzalez	1.00
61	Larry Walker	.40
62	Jack McDowell	.10
63	Shawon Dunston	.10
64	Andy Benes	.10
65	Jay Buhner	.10
66	Rickey Henderson	.25
67	Alex Gonzalez	.10
68	Mike Kelly	.10
69	Fred McGriff	.35
70	Ryne Sandberg	.75
71	Ernie Young	.10
72	Kevin Appier	.10
73	Moises Alou	.10
74	John Jaha	.10
75	J.T. Snow	.10
76	Jim Thome	.20
77	Kirby Puckett	1.00
78	Hal Morris	.10
79	Robin Ventura	.15
80	Ben McDonald	.10
81	Tim Salmon	.20
82	Albert Belle	.75
83	Marquis Grissom	.10
84	Alex Rodriguez	3.00
85	Manny Ramirez	1.00
86	Ken Griffey Jr.	4.00
87	Sammy Sosa	1.50
88	Frank Thomas	1.00
89	Lee Smith	.10
90	Marty Cordova	.15
91	Greg Maddux	2.00
92	Lenny Dykstra	.10
93	Butch Huskey	.10
94	Garret Anderson	.10
95	Mike Bordick	.10
96	Dave Justice	.20
97	Chad Curtis	.10
98	Carlos Baerga	.10
99	Jason Isringhausen	.10
100	Gary Sheffield	.30
101	Roger Clemens	1.25
102	Ozzie Smith	.50
103	Ramon Martinez	.10
104	Paul O'Neill	.15
105	Will Clark	.25
106	Tom Glavine	.15
107	Barry Bonds	.75
108	Barry Larkin	.20
109	Derek Bell	.10
110	Randy Johnson	.40
111	Jeff Conine	.10
112	John Mabry	.10
113	Julian Tavarez	.10
114	Gary DiSarcina	.10
115	Andres Galarraga	.20
116	Marc Newfield	.10
117	Frank Rodriguez	.10
118	Brady Anderson	.15
119	Mike Mussina	.40
120	Orlando Merced	.10
121	Melvin Nieves	.10
122	Brian Jordan	.15
123	Rafael Palmeiro	.20
124	Johnny Damon	.15
125	Wil Cordero	.10
126	Chipper Jones	2.00
127	Eric Karros	.10
128	Darren Daulton	.10
129	Vinny Castilla	.10
130	Joe Carter	.10
131	Bernie Williams	.50
132	Bernard Gilkey	.10
133	Bret Boone	.10
134	Tony Gwynn	1.25
135	Dave Nilsson	.10
136	Ryan Klesko	.20
137	Paul Molitor	.40
138	John Olerud	.15
139	Craig Biggio	.20
140	John Valentin	.10
141	Chuck Knoblauch	.20
142	Edgar Martinez	.10
143	Rico Brogna	.10
144	Dean Palmer	.10
145	Mark Grace	.25
146	Roberto Alomar	.75
147	Alex Fernandez	.15
148	Andre Dawson	.10
149	Wade Boggs	.35
150	Mark Lewis	.10
151	Gary Gaetti	.10
152	Paul Wilson, Roger Clemens (Deja Vu)	.30
153	Rey Ordonez, Ozzie Smith (Deja Vu)	.50
154	Derek Jeter, Cal Ripken Jr. (Deja Vu)	1.00
155	Alan Benes, Andy Benes (Deja Vu)	.10
156	Jason Kendall, Mike Piazza (Deja Vu)	.75
157	Ryan Klesko, Frank Thomas (Deja Vu)	.50
158	Johnny Damon, Ken Griffey Jr. (Deja Vu)	1.00
159	Karim Garcia, Sammy Sosa (Deja Vu)	1.00
160	Raul Mondesi, Tim Salmon (Deja Vu)	.20
161	Chipper Jones, Matt Williams (Deja Vu)	.75
162	Rey Ordonez	.40
163	Bob Wolcott	.10
164	Brooks Kieschnick	.10
165	Steve Gibralter	.10
166	Bob Abreu	.20
167	Greg Zaun	.10
168	Tavo Alvarez	.10
169	Sal Fasano	.10
170	George Arias	.10
171	Derek Jeter	2.00
172	*Livan Hernandez*	2.00
173	Alan Benes	.15
174	George Williams	.10
175	John Wasdin	.10
176	Chan Ho Park	.15
177	Paul Wilson	.20
178	Jeff Suppan	.20
179	Quinton McCracken	.10
180	*Wilton Guerrero*	.75
181	Eric Owens	.10
182	Felipe Crespo	.10
183	LaTroy Hawkins	.10
184	Jason Schmidt	.10
185	Terrell Wade	.10
186	*Mike Grace*	.30
187	Chris Snopek	.10
188	Jason Kendall	.20
189	Todd Hollandsworth	.15
190	Jim Pittsley	.10
191	Jermaine Dye	.15
192	*Mike Busby*	.10
193	Richard Hidalgo	.10
194	Tyler Houston	.10
195	Jimmy Haynes	.10
196	Karim Garcia	.40
197	Ken Griffey Jr. (Checklist)	2.00
198	Frank Thomas (Checklist)	.50
199	Greg Maddux (Checklist)	1.00
200	Cal Ripken Jr. (Checklist)	1.50

1996 Summit Above & Beyond

These 200 insert cards parallel Pinnacle's 1996 Summit set, using all-prismatic foil for each card. The cards were seeded one per every four packs.

	MT
Complete Set (200):	400.00
Common Player:	1.00
Stars:	8X

(See 1996 Summit for checklist, base card values.)

1996 Summit Artist's Proof

Holographic-foil highlights and an "ARTIST'S PROOF" notation on the front photo distinguish the cards in this parallel edition. The AP cards are found once per 36 packs.

	MT
Complete Set (200):	1500.
Common Player:	2.50
Stars:	25X

(See 1996 Summit for checklist, base card values.)

1996 Summit Ballparks

These 18 cards feature images of players superimposed over their respective teams' ballparks. The cards were seeded one per every 18 packs of 1996 Pinnacle Summit baseball.

		MT
Complete Set (18):		125.00
Common Player:		2.50
1	Cal Ripken Jr.	15.00
2	Albert Belle	6.00
3	Dante Bichette	2.50
4	Mo Vaughn	2.50
5	Ken Griffey Jr.	20.00
6	Derek Jeter	12.50
7	Juan Gonzalez	6.00
8	Greg Maddux	12.50
9	Frank Thomas	10.00
10	Ryne Sandberg	6.00
11	Mike Piazza	12.50
12	Johnny Damon	4.00
13	Barry Bonds	6.00
14	Jeff Bagwell	9.00
15	Paul Wilson	2.50
16	Tim Salmon	2.50
17	Kirby Puckett	8.00
18	Tony Gwynn	9.00

1996 Summit Big Bang

Sixteen of the biggest hitters are featured on these 1996 Pinnacle Summit insert cards. The cards, seeded one per every 72 packs, use Spectroetched backgrounds with foil highlights.

		MT
Complete Set (16):		500.00
Common Player:		10.00
Mirages:		1X
1	Frank Thomas	50.00
2	Ken Griffey Jr.	120.00
3	Albert Belle	20.00
4	Mo Vaughn	10.00
5	Barry Bonds	30.00
6	Cal Ripken Jr.	90.00
7	Jeff Bagwell	35.00
8	Mike Piazza	75.00
9	Ryan Klesko	10.00
10	Manny Ramirez	30.00
11	Tim Salmon	10.00
12	Dante Bichette	10.00
13	Sammy Sosa	60.00
14	Raul Mondesi	10.00
15	Chipper Jones	75.00
16	Garret Anderson	10.00

1996 Summit Big Bang Mirage

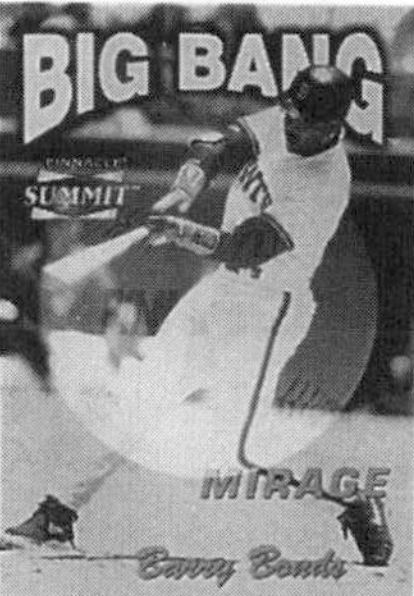

These 18 cards form a parallel version to Pinnacle's Big Bang inserts. The cards, found one per every 72 packs, use an all-new technology that creates a floating background behind the player's image. By holding the card in direct sunlight or an incandescent bulb, a collector can see three dimensions and a floating baseball that seems to levitate in the background. Mirage cards are serially numbered in an edition of 600 each.

		MT
Complete Set (16):		500.00
Common Player:		10.00
1	Frank Thomas	50.00
2	Ken Griffey Jr.	120.00
3	Albert Belle	20.00
4	Mo Vaughn	10.00
5	Barry Bonds	30.00
6	Cal Ripken Jr.	90.00
7	Jeff Bagwell	35.00
8	Mike Piazza	75.00
9	Ryan Klesko	10.00
10	Manny Ramirez	30.00
11	Tim Salmon	10.00
12	Dante Bichette	10.00
13	Sammy Sosa	60.00
14	Raul Mondesi	10.00
15	Chipper Jones	75.00
16	Garret Anderson	10.00

1996 Summit Hitters, Inc.

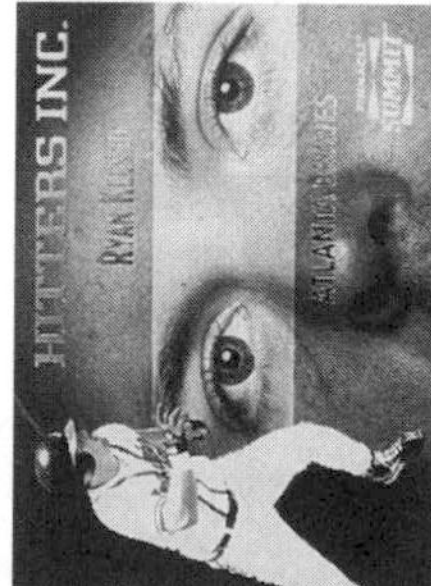

This 1996 Pinnacle Summit set honors 16 top hitters. The cards, seeded one per every 36 packs, puts an embossed highlight on an enlarged photo of the player's eyes.

		MT
Complete Set (16):		200.00
Common Player:		5.00
1	Tony Gwynn	15.00
2	Mo Vaughn	5.00
3	Tim Salmon	5.00
4	Ken Griffey Jr.	40.00
5	Sammy Sosa	25.00
6	Frank Thomas	15.00
7	Wade Boggs	10.00
8	Albert Belle	10.00
9	Cal Ripken Jr.	30.00
10	Manny Ramirez	12.00
11	Ryan Klesko	5.00
11p	Ryan Klesko (overprinted "SAMPLE")	4.50
12	Dante Bichette	5.00
13	Mike Piazza	25.00
14	Chipper Jones	25.00
15	Ryne Sandberg	10.00
16	Matt Williams	5.00

1996 Summit Positions

This insert issue features top players at each position. It is an exclusive magazine pack find, seeded about one per 50 packs. Fronts have action photos of three top players at the position on a baseball infield background at top. Close-ups of those photo appear at bottom, separated by a gold-foil strip. Backs have narrow action photos of each player, a few stats and a serial number from within an edition of 1,500 each.

		MT
Complete Set (9):		225.00
Common Card:		12.00
1	Jeff Bagwell, Mo Vaughn, Frank Thomas (First Base)	15.00
2	Roberto Alomar, Craig Biggio, Chuck Knoblauch (Second Base)	12.00
3	Matt Williams, Jim Thome, Chipper Jones (Third Base)	20.00
4	Barry Larkin, Cal Ripken Jr., Alex Rodriguez (Short Stop)	50.00
5	Mike Piazza, Ivan Rodriguez, Charles Johnson (Catcher)	30.00
6	Hideo Nomo, Greg Maddux, Randy Johnson (Pitcher)	20.00
7	Barry Bonds, Albert Belle, Ryan Klesko (Left Field)	15.00
8	Johnny Damon, Jim Edmonds,	

Ken Griffey Jr. (Center Field) 40.00
9 Manny Ramirez, Gary Sheffield, Sammy Sosa (Right Field) 35.00

1996 Summit Foil

This parallel issue was an exclusive in Summit retail packaging. The black borders of the regular Summit versions have been replaced on these cards by silver foil.

	MT
Complete Set (200):	50.00
Common Player:	.25
Stars:	2X

(See 1996 Summit for checklist and base card values.)

1981 Topps

This is another 726-card set of 2-1/2" x 3-1/2" cards from Topps. The cards have the usual color photo with all cards from the same team sharing the same color borders. Player names appear under the photo with team and position on a baseball cap at lower-left. The Topps logo returned in a small baseball in the lower-right. Card backs include the usual stats along with a headline and a cartoon if there was room. Specialty cards include previous season record-breakers, highlights of the playoffs and World Series, along with the final appearance of team cards. Eleven cards on each of the six press sheets were double-printed.

	MT
Complete Set (726):	50.00
Common Player:	.10
Pack (15 - H.T.W.):	3.50
Wax Box (36 - H.T.W.):	77.50

1 Batting Leaders (George Brett, Bill Buckner) .75
2 Home Run Leaders (Reggie Jackson, Ben Oglivie, Mike Schmidt) .75
3 RBI Leaders (Cecil Cooper, Mike Schmidt) .30
4 Stolen Base Leaders (Rickey Henderson, Ron LeFlore) .50
5 Victory Leaders (Steve Carlton, Steve Stone) .15
6 Strikeout Leaders (Len Barker, Steve Carlton) .15
7 ERA Leaders (Rudy May, Don Sutton) .10
8 Leading Firemen (Rollie Fingers, Tom Hume, Dan Quisenberry) .10
9 Pete LaCock (DP) .10
10 Mike Flanagan .10
11 Jim Wohlford (DP) .10
12 Mark Clear .10
13 *Joe Charboneau* .25
14 *John Tudor* .20
15 Larry Parrish .10
16 Ron Davis .10
17 Cliff Johnson .10
18 Glenn Adams .10
19 Jim Clancy .10
20 Jeff Burroughs .10
21 Ron Oester .10
22 Danny Darwin .10
23 Alex Trevino .10
24 Don Stanhouse .10
25 Sixto Lezcano .10
26 U.L. Washington .10
27 Champ Summers (DP) .10
28 Enrique Romo .10
29 Gene Tenace .10
30 Jack Clark .10
31 Checklist 1-121 (DP) .10
32 Ken Oberkfell .10
33 Rick Honeycutt .10
34 Aurelio Rodriguez .10
35 Mitchell Page .10
36 Ed Farmer .10
37 Gary Roenicke .10
38 Win Remmerswaal .10
39 Tom Veryzer .10
40 Tug McGraw .10
41 Rangers Future Stars (Bob Babcock, John Butcher, Jerry Don Gleaton) .10
42 Jerry White (DP) .10
43 Jose Morales .10
44 Larry McWilliams .10
45 Enos Cabell .10
46 Rick Bosetti .10
47 Ken Brett .10
48 Dave Skaggs .10
49 Bob Shirley .10
50 Dave Lopes .10
51 Bill Robinson (DP) .10
52 Hector Cruz .10
53 Kevin Saucier .10
54 Ivan DeJesus .10
55 Mike Norris .10
56 Buck Martinez .10
57 Dave Roberts .10
58 Joel Youngblood .10
59 Dan Petry .10
60 Willie Randolph .10
61 Butch Wynegar .10
62 Joe Pettini .10
63 Steve Renko (DP) .10
64 Brian Asselstine .10
65 Scott McGregor .10
66 Royals Future Stars (Manny Castillo, Tim Ireland, Mike Jones) .10
67 Ken Kravec .10
68 Matt Alexander (DP) .10
69 Ed Halicki .10
70 Al Oliver (DP) .10
71 Hal Dues .10
72 Barry Evans (DP) .10
73 Doug Bair .10
74 Mike Hargrove .10
75 Reggie Smith .10
76 Mario Mendoza .10
77 Mike Barlow .10
78 Steve Dillard .10
79 Bruce Robbins .10
80 Rusty Staub .15
81 Dave Stapleton .10
82 Astros Future Stars (Danny Heep, Alan Knicely, Bobby Sprowl) (DP) .10
83 Mike Proly .10
84 Johnnie LeMaster .10
85 Mike Caldwell .10
86 Wayne Gross .10
87 Rick Camp .10
88 Joe Lefebvre .10
89 Darrell Jackson .10
90 Bake McBride .10
91 Tim Stoddard (DP) .10
92 Mike Easler .10
93 Ed Glynn (DP) .10
94 Harry Spilman (DP) .10
95 Jim Sundberg .10
96 A's Future Stars (Dave Beard), *(Ernie Camacho,* Pat Dempsey) .10
97 Chris Speier .10
98 Clint Hurdle .10
99 Eric Wilkins .10
100 Rod Carew 2.00
101 Benny Ayala .10
102 Dave Tobik .10
103 Jerry Martin .10
104 Terry Forster .10
105 Jose Cruz .15
106 Don Money .10
107 Rich Wortham .10
108 Bruce Benedict .10
109 Mike Scott .10
110 Carl Yastrzemski 2.00
111 Greg Minton .10
112 White Sox Future Stars (Rusty Kuntz, Fran Mullins, Leo Sutherland) .10
113 Mike Phillips .10
114 Tom Underwood .10
115 Roy Smalley .10
116 Joe Simpson .10
117 Pete Falcone .10
118 Kurt Bevacqua .10
119 Tippy Martinez .10
120 Larry Bowa .10
121 Larry Harlow .10
122 John Denny .10
123 Al Cowens .10
124 Jerry Garvin .10
125 Andre Dawson .90
126 *Charlie Leibrandt* .40
127 Rudy Law .10
128 Gary Allenson (DP) .10
129 Art Howe .10
130 Larry Gura .10
131 *Keith Moreland* .20
132 Tommy Boggs .10
133 Jeff Cox .10
134 Steve Mura .10
135 Gorman Thomas .10
136 Doug Capilla .10
137 Hosken Powell .10
138 *Rich Dotson* (DP) .20
139 Oscar Gamble .10
140 Bob Forsch .10
141 Miguel Dilone .10
142 Jackson Todd .10
143 Dan Meyer .10
144 Allen Ripley .10
145 Mickey Rivers .10
146 Bobby Castillo .10
147 Dale Berra .10
148 Randy Niemann .10
149 Joe Nolan .10
150 Mark Fidrych .15
151 Claudell Washington (DP) .10
152 John Urrea .10
153 Tom Poquette .10
154 Rick Langford .10
155 Chris Chambliss .10
156 Bob McClure .10
157 John Wathan .10
158 Fergie Jenkins .90
159 Brian Doyle .10
160 Garry Maddox .10
161 Dan Graham .10
162 Doug Corbett .10
163 Billy Almon .10
164 *Lamarr Hoyt (LaMarr)* .15
165 Tony Scott .10
166 Floyd Bannister .10
167 Terry Whitfield .10
168 Don Robinson (DP) .10
169 John Mayberry .10
170 Ross Grimsley .10
171 Gene Richards .10
172 Gary Woods .10
173 Bump Wills .10
174 Doug Rau .10
175 Dave Collins .10
176 Mike Krukow .10
177 Rick Peters .10
178 Jim Essian (DP) .10
179 Rudy May .10
180 Pete Rose 3.00
181 Elias Sosa .10
182 Bob Grich .10
183 Dick Davis (DP) .10
184 Jim Dwyer .10
185 Dennis Leonard .10
186 Wayne Nordhagen .10
187 Mike Parrott .10
188 Doug DeCinces .10
189 Craig Swan .10
190 Cesar Cedeno .10
191 Rick Sutcliffe .10
192 Braves Future Stars *(Terry Harper,* Ed Miller), *(Rafael Ramirez)* .10
193 Pete Vuckovich .10
194 *Rod Scurry* .10
195 Rich Murray .10
196 Duffy Dyer .10
197 Jim Kern .10
198 Jerry Dybzinski .10
199 Chuck Rainey .10
200 George Foster .15
201 Johnny Bench (Record Breaker) .45
202 Steve Carlton (Record Breaker) .35
203 Bill Gullickson (Record Breaker) .10
204 Ron LeFlore, Rodney Scott (Record Breaker) .10
205 Pete Rose (Record Breaker) 1.50
206 Mike Schmidt (Record Breaker) 1.00
207 Ozzie Smith (Record Breaker) 1.00
208 Willie Wilson (Record Breaker) .10
209 Dickie Thon (DP) .10
210 Jim Palmer 1.50
211 Derrel Thomas .10
212 Steve Nicosia .10
213 *Al Holland* .10
214 Angels Future Stars (Ralph Botting, Jim Dorsey, John Harris) .10
215 Larry Hisle .10
216 John Henry Johnson .10
217 Rich Hebner .10
218 Paul Splittorff .10
219 Ken Landreaux .10
220 Tom Seaver 2.00
221 Bob Davis .10
222 Jorge Orta .10
223 Roy Lee Jackson .10
224 Pat Zachry .10
225 Ruppert Jones .10
226 Manny Sanguillen (DP) .10
227 Fred Martinez .10
228 Tom Paciorek .10
229 Rollie Fingers .90
230 George Hendrick .10
231 Joe Beckwith .10

232 Mickey Klutts .10
233 Skip Lockwood .10
234 Lou Whitaker .20
235 Scott Sanderson .10
236 Mike Ivie .10
237 Charlie Moore .10
238 Willie Hernandez .10
239 Rick Miller (DP) .10
240 Nolan Ryan 12.00
241 Checklist 122-242 (DP) .10
242 Chet Lemon .10
243 Sal Butera .10
244 Cardinals Future Stars (*Tito Landrum*, Al Olmsted, Andy Rincon) .10
245 Ed Figueroa .10
246 Ed Ott (DP) .10
247 Glenn Hubbard (DP) .10
248 Joey McLaughlin .10
249 Larry Cox .10
250 Ron Guidry .20
251 Tom Brookens .10
252 Victor Cruz .10
253 Dave Bergman .10
254 Ozzie Smith 7.50
255 Mark Littell .10
256 Bombo Rivera .10
257 Rennie Stennett .10
258 *Joe Price* .10
259 Mets Future Stars (Juan Berenguer), (*Hubie Brooks*), (*Mookie Wilson*) .75
260 Ron Cey .15
261 Rickey Henderson 7.00
262 Sammy Stewart .10
263 Brian Downing .10
264 Jim Norris .10
265 John Candelaria .10
266 Tom Herr .10
267 Stan Bahnsen .10
268 Jerry Royster .10
269 Ken Forsch .10
270 Greg Luzinski .10
271 Bill Castro .10
272 Bruce Kimm .10
273 Stan Papi .10
274 Craig Chamberlain .10
275 Dwight Evans .10
276 Dan Spillner .10
277 Alfredo Griffin .10
278 Rick Sofield .10
279 Bob Knepper .10
280 Ken Griffey .10
281 Fred Stanley .10
282 Mariners Future Stars (Rick Anderson, Greg Biercevicz, Rodney Craig) .10
283 Billy Sample .10
284 Brian Kingman .10
285 Jerry Turner .10
286 Dave Frost .10
287 Lenn Sakata .10
288 Bob Clark .10
289 Mickey Hatcher .10
290 Bob Boone (DP) .10
291 Aurelio Lopez .10
292 Mike Squires .10
293 *Charlie Lea* .15
294 Mike Tyson (DP) .10
295 Hal McRae .10
296 Bill Nahorodny (DP) .10
297 Bob Bailor .10
298 Buddy Solomon .10
299 Elliott Maddox .10
300 Paul Molitor 5.00
301 Matt Keough .10
302 Dodgers Future Stars (*Jack Perconte*), (*Mike Scioscia*), (*Fernando Valenzuela*) 2.00
303 Johnny Oates .10
304 John Castino .10
305 Ken Clay .10
306 Juan Beniquez (DP) .10
307 Gene Garber .10
308 Rick Manning .10
309 *Luis Salazar* .10
310 Vida Blue (DP) .10
311 Freddie Patek .10
312 Rick Rhoden .10
313 Luis Pujols .10
314 Rich Dauer .10
315 *Kirk Gibson* 3.00
316 Craig Minetto .10
317 Lonnie Smith .10
318 Steve Yeager .10
319 Rowland Office .10
320 Tom Burgmeier .10
321 *Leon Durham* .15
322 Neil Allen .10
323 Jim Morrison (DP) .10
324 Mike Willis .10
325 Ray Knight .10
326 Biff Pocoroba .10
327 Moose Haas .10
328 Twins Future Stars (*Dave Engle*, Greg Johnston, Gary Ward) .15
329 Joaquin Andujar .10
330 Frank White .10
331 Dennis Lamp .10
332 Lee Lacy (DP) .10
333 Sid Monge .10
334 Dane Iorg .10
335 Rick Cerone .10
336 Eddie Whitson .10
337 Lynn Jones .10
338 Checklist 243-363 .10
339 John Ellis .10
340 Bruce Kison .10
341 Dwayne Murphy .10
342 Eric Rasmussen (DP) .10
343 Frank Taveras .10
344 Byron McLaughlin .10
345 Warren Cromartie .10
346 Larry Christenson (DP) .10
347 *Harold Baines* 8.00
348 Bob Sykes .10
349 Glenn Hoffman .10
350 J.R. Richard .15
351 Otto Velez .10
352 Dick Tidrow (DP) .10
353 Terry Kennedy .10
354 Mario Soto .10
355 Bob Horner .10
356 Padres Future Stars (George Stablein, Craig Stimac, Tom Tellmann) .10
357 Jim Slaton .10
358 Mark Wagner .10
359 Tom Hausman .10
360 Willie Wilson .15
361 Joe Strain .10
362 Bo Diaz .10
363 Geoff Zahn .10
364 *Mike Davis* .10
365 Graig Nettles (DP) .15
366 Mike Ramsey .10
367 Denny Martinez .10
368 Leon Roberts .10
369 Frank Tanana .10
370 Dave Winfield 4.00
371 Charlie Hough .10
372 Jay Johnstone .10
373 Pat Underwood .10
374 Tom Hutton .10
375 Dave Concepcion .10
376 Ron Reed .10
377 Jerry Morales .10
378 Dave Rader .10
379 Lary Sorensen .10
380 Willie Stargell 1.00
381 Cubs Future Stars (Carlos Lezcano, Steve Macko, Randy Martz) .10
382 *Paul Mirabella* .10
383 Eric Soderholm (DP) .10
384 Mike Sadek .10
385 Joe Sambito .10
386 Dave Edwards .10
387 Phil Niekro .90
388 Andre Thornton .10
389 Marty Pattin .10
390 Cesar Geronimo .10
391 Dave Lemanczyk (DP) .10
392 Lance Parrish .10
393 Broderick Perkins .10
394 Woodie Fryman .10
395 Scot Thompson .10
396 Bill Campbell .10
397 Julio Cruz .10
398 Ross Baumgarten .10
399 Orioles Future Stars (*Mike Boddicker*, Mark Corey), (*Floyd Rayford*) .20
400 Reggie Jackson 2.00
401 A.L. Championships (Royals Sweep Yankees) .75
402 N.L. Championships (Phillies Squeak Past Astros) .35
403 World Series (Phillies Beat Royals In 6) .25
404 World Series Summary (Phillies Win First World Series) .25
405 Nino Espinosa .10
406 Dickie Noles .10
407 Ernie Whitt .10
408 Fernando Arroyo .10
409 Larry Herndon .10
410 Bert Campaneris .10
411 Terry Puhl .10
412 *Britt Burns* .10
413 Tony Bernazard .10
414 John Pacella (DP) .10
415 Ben Oglivie .10
416 Gary Alexander .10
417 Dan Schatzeder .10
418 Bobby Brown .10
419 Tom Hume .10
420 Keith Hernandez .10
421 Bob Stanley .10
422 Dan Ford .10
423 Shane Rawley .10
424 Yankees Future Stars (Tim Lollar, Bruce Robinson, Dennis Werth) .10
425 Al Bumbry .10
426 Warren Brusstar .10
427 John D'Acquisto .10
428 John Stearns .10
429 Mick Kelleher .10
430 Jim Bibby .10
431 Dave Roberts .10
432 Len Barker .10
433 Rance Mulliniks .10
434 Roger Erickson .10
435 Jim Spencer .10
436 Gary Lucas .10
437 Mike Heath (DP) .10
438 John Montefusco .10
439 Denny Walling .10
440 Jerry Reuss .10
441 Ken Reitz .10
442 Ron Pruitt .10
443 Jim Beattie (DP) .10
444 Garth Iorg .10
445 Ellis Valentine .10
446 Checklist 364-484 .10
447 Junior Kennedy (DP) .10
448 Tim Corcoran .10
449 Paul Mitchell .10
450 Dave Kingman (DP) .10
451 Indians Future Stars (Chris Bando, Tom Brennan, Sandy Wihtol) .10
452 Renie Martin .10
453 Rob Wilfong (DP) .10
454 Andy Hassler .10
455 Rick Burleson .10
456 *Jeff Reardon* 1.50
457 Mike Lum .10
458 Randy Jones .10
459 Greg Gross .10
460 Rich Gossage .10
461 Dave McKay .10
462 Jack Brohamer .10
463 Milt May .10
464 Adrian Devine .10
465 Bill Russell .10
466 Bob Molinaro .10
467 Dave Stieb .15
468 Johnny Wockenfuss .10
469 Jeff Leonard .10
470 Manny Trillo .10
471 Mike Vail .10
472 Dyar Miller (DP) .10
473 Jose Cardenal .10
474 Mike LaCoss .10
475 Buddy Bell .10
476 Jerry Koosman .10
477 Luis Gomez .10
478 Juan Eichelberger .10
479 Expos Future Stars (*Bobby Pate*), (*Tim Raines*), (*Roberto Ramos*) 4.00
480 Carlton Fisk .90
481 Bob Lacey (DP) .10
482 Jim Gantner .10
483 Mike Griffin .10
484 Max Venable (DP) .10
485 Garry Templeton .10
486 Marc Hill .10
487 Dewey Robinson .10
488 *Damaso Garcia* .10
489 John Littlefield (photo actually Mark Riggins) .10
490 Eddie Murray 5.00
491 Gordy Pladson .10
492 Barry Foote .10
493 Dan Quisenberry .10
494 *Bob Walk* .20
495 Dusty Baker .15
496 Paul Dade .10
497 Fred Norman .10
498 Pat Putnam .10
499 Frank Pastore .10
500 Jim Rice .25
501 Tim Foli (DP) .10
502 Giants Future Stars (Chris Bourjos, Al Hargesheimer, Mike Rowland) .10
503 Steve McCatty .10
504 Dale Murphy .90
505 Jason Thompson .10
506 Phil Huffman .10
507 Jamie Quirk .10
508 Rob Dressler .10
509 Pete Mackanin .10
510 Lee Mazzilli .10
511 Wayne Garland .10
512 Gary Thomasson .10
513 Frank LaCorte .10
514 George Riley .10
515 Robin Yount 4.00
516 Doug Bird .10
517 Richie Zisk .10
518 Grant Jackson .10
519 John Tamargo (DP) .10
520 Steve Stone .10
521 Sam Mejias .10
522 Mike Colbern .10
523 John Fulgham .10
524 Willie Aikens .10
525 Mike Torrez .10
526 Phillies Future Stars (Marty Bystrom, Jay Loviglio, Jim Wright) .10
527 Danny Goodwin .10
528 Gary Matthews .10
529 Dave LaRoche .10
530 Steve Garvey .75
531 John Curtis .10
532 Bill Stein .10
533 Jesus Figueroa .10
534 *Dave Smith* .15
535 Omar Moreno .10
536 Bob Owchinko (DP) .10
537 Ron Hodges .10
538 Tom Griffin .10
539 Rodney Scott .10
540 Mike Schmidt (DP) 4.00
541 Steve Swisher .10
542 Larry Bradford (DP) .10
543 Terry Crowley .10
544 Rich Gale .10
545 Johnny Grubb .10
546 Paul Moskau .10
547 Mario Guerrero .10
548 Dave Goltz .10
549 Jerry Remy .10
550 Tommy John .20
551 Pirates Future Stars (*Vance Law*), (*Tony Pena*), (*Pascual Perez*) .75
552 Steve Trout .10
553 Tim Blackwell .10
554 Bert Blyleven .10
555 Cecil Cooper .10
556 Jerry Mumphrey .10
557 Chris Knapp .10
558 Barry Bonnell .10
559 Willie Montanez .10
560 Joe Morgan .90
561 Dennis Littlejohn .10
562 Checklist 485-605 .10
563 Jim Kaat .25
564 Ron Hassey (DP) .10
565 Burt Hooton .10
566 Del Unser .10
567 Mark Bomback .10
568 Dave Revering .10

569 Al Williams (DP) .10
570 Ken Singleton .10
571 Todd Cruz .10
572 Jack Morris .25
573 Phil Garner .10
574 Bill Caudill .10
575 Tony Perez .30
576 Reggie Cleveland .10
577 Blue Jays Future Stars (Luis Leal, Brian Milner), *(Ken Schrom)* .10
578 *Bill Gullickson* .20
579 Tim Flannery .10
580 Don Baylor .15
581 Roy Howell .10
582 Gaylord Perry .90
583 Larry Milbourne .10
584 Randy Lerch .10
585 Amos Otis .10
586 Silvio Martinez .10
587 Jeff Newman .10
588 Gary Lavelle .10
589 Lamar Johnson .10
590 Bruce Sutter .10
591 John Lowenstein .10
592 Steve Comer .10
593 Steve Kemp .10
594 Preston Hanna (DP) .10
595 Butch Hobson .10
596 Jerry Augustine .10
597 Rafael Landestoy .10
598 George Vukovich (DP) .10
599 Dennis Kinney .10
600 Johnny Bench 3.00
601 Don Aase .10
602 Bobby Murcer .10
603 John Verhoeven .10
604 Rob Picciolo .10
605 Don Sutton .90
606 Reds Future Stars (Bruce Berenyi, Geoff Combe, Paul Householder) (DP) .10
607 Dave Palmer .10
608 Greg Pryor .10
609 Lynn McGlothen .10
610 Darrell Porter .10
611 Rick Matula (DP) .10
612 Duane Kuiper .10
613 Jim Anderson .10
614 Dave Rozema .10
615 Rick Dempsey .10
616 Rick Wise .10
617 Craig Reynolds .10
618 John Milner .10
619 Steve Henderson .10
620 Dennis Eckersley .50
621 Tom Donohue .10
622 Randy Moffitt .10
623 Sal Bando .10
624 Bob Welch .10
625 Bill Buckner .15
626 Tigers Future Stars (Dave Steffen, Jerry Ujdur, Roger Weaver) .10
627 Luis Tiant .10
628 Vic Correll .10
629 Tony Armas .10
630 Steve Carlton 2.00
631 Ron Jackson .10
632 Alan Bannister .10
633 Bill Lee .10
634 Doug Flynn .10
635 Bobby Bonds .10
636 Al Hrabosky .10
637 Jerry Narron .10
638 Checklist 606 .10
639 Carney Lansford .10
640 Dave Parker .50
641 Mark Belanger .10
642 Vern Ruhle .10
643 *Lloyd Moseby* .20
644 Ramon Aviles (DP) .10
645 Rick Reuschel .10
646 Marvis Foley .10
647 Dick Drago .10
648 Darrell Evans .15
649 Manny Sarmiento .10
650 Bucky Dent .10
651 Pedro Guerrero .10
652 John Montague .10
653 Bill Fahey .10
654 Ray Burris .10
655 Dan Driessen .10
656 Jon Matlack .10
657 Mike Cubbage (DP) .10
658 Milt Wilcox .10
659 Brewers Future Stars (John Flinn, Ed Romero, Ned Yost) .10
660 Gary Carter .75
661 Orioles Team (Earl Weaver) .25
662 Red Sox Team (Ralph Houk) .15
663 Angels Team (Jim Fregosi) .10
664 White Sox Team (Tony LaRussa) .25
665 Indians Team (Dave Garcia) .10
666 Tigers Team (Sparky Anderson) .30
667 Royals Team (Jim Frey) .10
668 Brewers Team (Bob Rodgers) .10
669 Twins Team (John Goryl) .10
670 Yankees Team (Gene Michael) .25
671 A's Team (Billy Martin) .25
672 Mariners Team (Maury Wills) .15
673 Rangers Team (Don Zimmer) .15
674 Blue Jays Team (Bobby Mattick) .10
675 Braves Team (Bobby Cox) .25
676 Cubs Team (Joe Amalfitano) .15
677 Reds Team (John McNamara) .10
678 Astros Team (Bill Virdon) .10
679 Dodgers Team (Tom Lasorda) .40
680 Expos Team (Dick Williams) .15
681 Mets Team (Joe Torre) .25
682 Phillies Team (Dallas Green) .25
683 Pirates Team (Chuck Tanner) .15
684 Cardinals Team (Whitey Herzog) .25
685 Padres Team (Frank Howard) .15
686 Giants Team (Dave Bristol) .10
687 Jeff Jones .10
688 Kiko Garcia .10
689 Red Sox Future Stars *(Bruce Hurst*, Keith MacWhorter), *(Reid Nichols)* .60
690 Bob Watson .10
691 Dick Ruthven .10
692 Lenny Randle .10
693 *Steve Howe* .20
694 Bud Harrelson (DP) .10
695 Kent Tekulve .10
696 Alan Ashby .10
697 Rick Waits .10
698 Mike Jorgensen .10
699 Glenn Abbott .10
700 George Brett 6.00
701 Joe Rudi .10
702 George Medich .10
703 Alvis Woods .10
704 Bill Travers (DP) .10
705 Ted Simmons .10
706 Dave Ford .10
707 Dave Cash .10
708 Doyle Alexander .10
709 Alan Trammell (DP) .50
710 Ron LeFlore (DP) .10
711 Joe Ferguson .10
712 Bill Bonham .10
713 Bill North .10
714 Pete Redfern .10
715 Bill Madlock .10
716 Glenn Borgmann .10
717 Jim Barr (DP) .10
718 Larry Biittner .10
719 Sparky Lyle .10
720 Fred Lynn .10
721 Toby Harrah .10
722 Joe Niekro .10
723 Bruce Bochte .10
724 Lou Piniella .10
725 Steve Rogers .10
726 Rick Monday .10

1981 Topps Traded

The 132 cards in this extension set are numbered from 727 to 858, technically making them a high-numbered series of the regular Topps set. The set was not packaged in gum packs, but rather placed in a specially designed red box and sold through baseball card dealers only. While many complained about the method, the fact remains, even at higher prices, the set has done well for its owners as it features not only mid-season trades, but also single-player rookie cards of some of the hottest prospects. The cards measure 2-1/2" x 3-1/2".

MT
Complete Set (132): 30.00
Common Player: .20
727 Danny Ainge 6.00
728 Doyle Alexander .20
729 Gary Alexander .20
730 Billy Almon .20
731 Joaquin Andujar .20
732 Bob Bailor .20
733 Juan Beniquez .20
734 Dave Bergman .20
735 Tony Bernazard .20
736 Larry Biittner .20
737 Doug Bird .20
738 Bert Blyleven .30
739 Mark Bomback .20
740 Bobby Bonds .25
741 Rick Bosetti .20
742 Hubie Brooks .35
743 Rick Burleson .20
744 Ray Burris .20
745 Jeff Burroughs .20
746 Enos Cabell .20
747 Ken Clay .20
748 Mark Clear .20
749 Larry Cox .20
750 Hector Cruz .20
751 Victor Cruz .20
752 Mike Cubbage .20
753 Dick Davis .20
754 Brian Doyle .20
755 Dick Drago .20
756 Leon Durham .20
757 Jim Dwyer .20
758 Dave Edwards .20
759 Jim Essian .20
760 Bill Fahey .20
761 Rollie Fingers 2.50
762 Carlton Fisk 7.50
763 Barry Foote .20
764 Ken Forsch .20
765 Kiko Garcia .20
766 Cesar Geronimo .20
767 Gary Gray .20
768 Mickey Hatcher .20
769 Steve Henderson .20
770 Marc Hill .20
771 Butch Hobson .20
772 Rick Honeycutt .20
773 Roy Howell .20
774 Mike Ivie .20
775 Roy Lee Jackson .20
776 Cliff Johnson .20
777 Randy Jones .20
778 Ruppert Jones .20
779 Mick Kelleher .20
780 Terry Kennedy .20
781 Dave Kingman .20
782 Bob Knepper .20
783 Ken Kravec .20
784 Bob Lacey .20
785 Dennis Lamp .20
786 Rafael Landestoy .20
787 Ken Landreaux .20
788 Carney Lansford .20
789 Dave LaRoche .20
790 Joe Lefebvre .20
791 Ron LeFlore .20
792 Randy Lerch .20
793 Sixto Lezcano .20
794 John Littlefield .20
795 Mike Lum .20
796 Greg Luzinski .50
797 Fred Lynn .20
798 Jerry Martin .20
799 Buck Martinez .20
800 Gary Matthews .20
801 Mario Mendoza .20
802 Larry Milbourne .20
803 Rick Miller .20
804 John Montefusco .20
805 Jerry Morales .20
806 Jose Morales .20
807 Joe Morgan 3.00
808 Jerry Mumphrey .20
809 Gene Nelson .20
810 Ed Ott .20
811 Bob Owchinko .20
812 Gaylord Perry 2.50
813 Mike Phillips .20
814 Darrell Porter .20
815 Mike Proly .20
816 Tim Raines 12.00
817 Lenny Randle .20
818 Doug Rau .20
819 Jeff Reardon 1.00
820 Ken Reitz .20
821 Steve Renko .20
822 Rick Reuschel .20
823 Dave Revering .20
824 Dave Roberts .20
825 Leon Roberts .20
826 Joe Rudi .20
827 Kevin Saucier .20
828 Tony Scott .20
829 Bob Shirley .20
830 Ted Simmons .20
831 Lary Sorensen .20
832 Jim Spencer .20
833 Harry Spilman .20
834 Fred Stanley .20
835 Rusty Staub .45
836 Bill Stein .20
837 Joe Strain .20
838 Bruce Sutter .20
839 Don Sutton 2.50
840 Steve Swisher .20
841 Frank Tanana .20
842 Gene Tenace .20
843 Jason Thompson .20
844 Dickie Thon .20
845 Bill Travers .20
846 Tom Underwood .20
847 John Urrea .20
848 Mike Vail .20
849 Ellis Valentine .20
850 Fernando Valenzuela 2.00
851 Pete Vuckovich .20
852 Mark Wagner .20
853 Bob Walk .20
854 Claudell Washington .20
855 Dave Winfield 12.00
856 Geoff Zahn .20
857 Richie Zisk .20
858 Checklist 727-858 .10

1982 Topps

At 792 cards, this was the largest issue produced up to that time, eliminating the need for double- printed cards. The 2-1/2" x 3-1/2" cards feature a front color photo with a pair of stripes down the left side. Under the player's photo are found his name, team and position. A facsimile autograph runs across the front of the picture. Specialty cards include great performances of the previous season, All-Stars, statistical leaders and "In Action" cards (indicated by "IA" in listings below). Managers and hitting/pitching leaders have cards, while rookies are shown as "Future Stars" on group cards.

		MT
Complete Set (792):		100.00
Common Player:		.10
Pack (15):		6.25
Wax Box (36):		180.00
1	Steve Carlton (1981 Highlight)	.25
2	Ron Davis (1981 Highlight)	.10
3	Tim Raines (1981 Highlight)	.15
4	Pete Rose (1981 Highlight)	.75
5	Nolan Ryan (1981 Highlight)	3.00
6	Fernando Valenzuela (1981 Highlight)	.10
7	Scott Sanderson	.10
8	Rich Dauer	.10
9	Ron Guidry	.15
10	Ron Guidry (In Action)	.10
11	Gary Alexander	.10
12	Moose Haas	.10
13	Lamar Johnson	.10
14	Steve Howe	.10
15	Ellis Valentine	.10
16	Steve Comer	.10
17	Darrell Evans	.15
18	Fernando Arroyo	.10
19	Ernie Whitt	.10
20	Garry Maddox	.10
21	Orioles Future Stars *(Bob Bonner)*, *(Cal Ripken, Jr.)*, *(Jeff Schneider)*	60.00
22	Jim Beattie	.10
23	Willie Hernandez	.10
24	Dave Frost	.10
25	Jerry Remy	.10
26	Jorge Orta	.10
27	Tom Herr	.10
28	John Urrea	.10
29	Dwayne Murphy	.10
30	Tom Seaver	1.50
31	Tom Seaver (In Action)	1.00
32	Gene Garber	.10
33	Jerry Morales	.10
34	Joe Sambito	.10
35	Willie Aikens	.10
36	Rangers Batting/ Pitching Leaders (George Medich, Al Oliver)	.10
37	Dan Graham	.10
38	Charlie Lea	.10
39	Lou Whitaker	.20
40	Dave Parker	.20
41	Dave Parker (In Action)	.10
42	Rick Sofield	.10
43	Mike Cubbage	.10
44	Britt Burns	.10
45	Rick Cerone	.10
46	Jerry Augustine	.10
47	Jeff Leonard	.10
48	Bobby Castillo	.10
49	Alvis Woods	.10
50	Buddy Bell	.10
51	Chicago Cubs Future Stars *(Jay Howell)*, *(Carlos Lezcano)*, *(Ty Waller)*	.40
52	Larry Andersen	.10
53	Greg Gross	.10
54	Ron Hassey	.10
55	Rick Burleson	.10
56	Mark Littell	.10
57	Craig Reynolds	.10
58	John D'Acquisto	.10
59	*Rich Gedman*	.10
60	Tony Armas	.10
61	Tommy Boggs	.10
62	Mike Tyson	.10
63	Mario Soto	.10
64	Lynn Jones	.10
65	Terry Kennedy	.10
66	Astros Batting/ Pitching Leaders (Art Howe, Nolan Ryan)	.75
67	Rich Gale	.10
68	Roy Howell	.10
69	Al Williams	.10
70	Tim Raines	1.00
71	Roy Lee Jackson	.10
72	Rick Auerbach	.10
73	Buddy Solomon	.10
74	Bob Clark	.10
75	Tommy John	.30
76	Greg Pryor	.10
77	Miguel Dilone	.10
78	George Medich	.10
79	Bob Bailor	.10
80	Jim Palmer	1.00
81	Jim Palmer (In Action)	.30
82	Bob Welch	.10
83	Yankees Future Stars *(Steve Balboni)*, *(Andy McGaffigan)*, *(Andre Robertson)*	.15
84	Rennie Stennett	.10
85	Lynn McGlothen	.10
86	Dane Iorg	.10
87	Matt Keough	.10
88	Biff Pocoroba	.10
89	Steve Henderson	.10
90	Nolan Ryan	12.00
91	Carney Lansford	.10
92	Brad Havens	.10
93	Larry Hisle	.10
94	Andy Hassler	.10
95	Ozzie Smith	3.00
96	Royals Batting/ Pitching Leaders (George Brett, Larry Gura)	.35
97	Paul Moskau	.10
98	Terry Bulling	.10
99	Barry Bonnell	.10
100	Mike Schmidt	3.00
101	Mike Schmidt (In Action)	1.25
102	Dan Briggs	.10
103	Bob Lacey	.10
104	Rance Mulliniks	.10
105	Kirk Gibson	.20
106	Enrique Romo	.10
107	Wayne Krenchicki	.10
108	Bob Sykes	.10
109	Dave Revering	.10
110	Carlton Fisk	1.00
111	Carlton Fisk (In Action)	.65
112	Billy Sample	.10
113	Steve McCatty	.10
114	Ken Landreaux	.10
115	Gaylord Perry	.60
116	Jim Wohlford	.10
117	Rawly Eastwick	.10
118	Expos Future Stars *(Terry Francona)*, *(Brad Mills)*, *(Bryn Smith)*	.20
119	Joe Pittman	.10
120	Gary Lucas	.10
121	Ed Lynch	.10
122	Jamie Easterly	.10
123	Danny Goodwin	.10
124	Reid Nichols	.10
125	Danny Ainge	1.00
126	Braves Batting/ Pitching Leaders (Rick Mahler, Claudell Washington)	.10
127	Lonnie Smith	.10
128	Frank Pastore	.10
129	Checklist 1-132	.10
130	Julio Cruz	.10
131	Stan Bahnsen	.10
132	Lee May	.10
133	Pat Underwood	.10
134	Dan Ford	.10
135	Andy Rincon	.10
136	Lenn Sakata	.10
137	George Cappuzzello	.10
138	Tony Pena	.10
139	Jeff Jones	.10
140	Ron LeFlore	.10
141	Indians Future Stars (Chris Bando, Tom Brennan), *(Von Hayes)*	.20
142	Dave LaRoche	.10
143	Mookie Wilson	.10
144	Fred Breining	.10
145	Bob Horner	.10
146	Mike Griffin	.10
147	Denny Walling	.10
148	Mickey Klutts	.10
149	Pat Putnam	.10
150	Ted Simmons	.10
151	Dave Edwards	.10
152	Ramon Aviles	.10
153	Roger Erickson	.10
154	Dennis Werth	.10
155	Otto Velez	.10
156	A's Batting/ Pitching Leaders (Rickey Henderson, Steve McCatty)	.15
157	Steve Crawford	.10
158	Brian Downing	.10
159	Larry Biittner	.10
160	Luis Tiant	.10
161	Batting Leaders (Carney Lansford, Bill Madlock)	.10
162	Home Run Leaders (Tony Armas, Dwight Evans, Bobby Grich, Eddie Murray, Mike Schmidt)	.25
163	RBI Leaders (Eddie Murray, Mike Schmidt)	.50
164	Stolen Base Leaders (Rickey Henderson, Tim Raines)	.50
165	Victory Leaders (Denny Martinez, Steve McCatty, Jack Morris, Tom Seaver, Pete Vuckovich)	.20
166	Strikeout Leaders (Len Barker, Fernando Valenzuela)	.10
167	ERA Leaders (Steve McCatty, Nolan Ryan)	1.50
168	Leading Relievers (Rollie Fingers, Bruce Sutter)	.20
169	Charlie Leibrandt	.10
170	Jim Bibby	.10
171	Giants Future Stars *(Bob Brenly)*, *(Chili Davis)*, *(Bob Tufts)*	3.00
172	Bill Gullickson	.10
173	Jamie Quirk	.10
174	Dave Ford	.10
175	Jerry Mumphrey	.10
176	Dewey Robinson	.10
177	John Ellis	.10
178	Dyar Miller	.10
179	Steve Garvey	.75
180	Steve Garvey (In Action)	.30
181	Silvio Martinez	.10
182	Larry Herndon	.10
183	Mike Proly	.10
184	Mick Kelleher	.10
185	Phil Niekro	1.00
186	Cardinals Batting/ Pitching Leaders (Bob Forsch, Keith Hernandez)	.10
187	Jeff Newman	.10
188	Randy Martz	.10
189	Glenn Hoffman	.10
190	J.R. Richard	.15
191	*Tim Wallach*	2.50
192	Broderick Perkins	.10
193	Darrell Jackson	.10
194	Mike Vail	.10
195	Paul Molitor	4.00
196	Willie Upshaw	.10
197	Shane Rawley	.10
198	Chris Speier	.10
199	Don Aase	.10
200	George Brett	5.00
201	George Brett (In Action)	2.50
202	Rick Manning	.10
203	Blue Jays Future Stars *(Jesse Barfield)*, Brian Milner, Boomer Wells)	.50
204	Gary Roenicke	.10
205	Neil Allen	.10
206	Tony Bernazard	.10
207	Rod Scurry	.10
208	Bobby Murcer	.10
209	Gary Lavelle	.10
210	Keith Hernandez	.10
211	Dan Petry	.10
212	Mario Mendoza	.10
213	*Dave Stewart*	4.00
214	Brian Asselstine	.10
215	Mike Krukow	.10
216	White Sox Batting/ Pitching Leaders (Dennis Lamp, Chet Lemon)	.10
217	Bo McLaughlin	.10
218	Dave Roberts	.10
219	John Curtis	.10
220	Manny Trillo	.10
221	Jim Slaton	.10
222	Butch Wynegar	.10
223	Lloyd Moseby	.10
224	Bruce Bochte	.10
225	Mike Torrez	.10
226	Checklist 133-264	.10
227	Ray Burris	.10
228	Sam Mejias	.10
229	Geoff Zahn	.10
230	Willie Wilson	.10
231	Phillies Future Stars *(Mark Davis)*, *(Bob Dernier)*, *(Ozzie Virgil)*	.20
232	Terry Crowley	.10
233	Duane Kuiper	.10
234	Ron Hodges	.10
235	Mike Easler	.10
236	John Martin	.10
237	Rusty Kuntz	.10
238	Kevin Saucier	.10
239	Jon Matlack	.10
240	Bucky Dent	.10
241	Bucky Dent (In Action)	.10
242	Milt May	.10
243	Bob Owchinko	.10
244	Rufino Linares	.10
245	Ken Reitz	.10
246	Mets Batting/ Pitching Leaders (Hubie Brooks, Mike Scott)	.10
247	Pedro Guerrero	.10
248	Frank LaCorte	.10
249	Tim Flannery	.10
250	Tug McGraw	.10
251	Fred Lynn	.10
252	Fred Lynn (In Action)	.10
253	Chuck Baker	.10
254	*George Bell*	1.00
255	Tony Perez	.25

256 Tony Perez (In Action) .10
257 Larry Harlow .10
258 Bo Diaz .10
259 Rodney Scott .10
260 Bruce Sutter .10
261 Tigers Future Stars (Howard Bailey, Marty Castillo, Dave Rucker) .10
262 Doug Bair .10
263 Victor Cruz .10
264 Dan Quisenberry .10
265 Al Bumbry .10
266 Rick Leach .10
267 Kurt Bevacqua .10
268 Rickey Keeton .10
269 Jim Essian .10
270 Rusty Staub .15
271 Larry Bradford .10
272 Bump Wills .10
273 Doug Bird .10
274 *Bob Ojeda* .60
275 Bob Watson .10
276 Angels Batting/ Pitching Leaders (Rod Carew, Ken Forsch) .25
277 Terry Puhl .10
278 John Littlefield .10
279 Bill Russell .10
280 Ben Oglivie .10
281 John Verhoeven .10
282 Ken Macha .10
283 Brian Allard .10
284 Bob Grich .10
285 Sparky Lyle .10
286 Bill Fahey .10
287 Alan Bannister .10
288 Garry Templeton .10
289 Bob Stanley .10
290 Ken Singleton .10
291 Pirates Future Stars (Vance Law, Bob Long), *(Johnny Ray)* .15
292 Dave Palmer .10
293 Rob Picciolo .10
294 Mike LaCoss .10
295 Jason Thompson .10
296 Bob Walk .10
297 Clint Hurdle .10
298 Danny Darwin .10
299 Steve Trout .10
300 Reggie Jackson 3.00
301 Reggie Jackson (In Action) 1.50
302 Doug Flynn .10
303 Bill Caudill .10
304 Johnnie LeMaster .10
305 Don Sutton .65
306 Don Sutton (In Action) .20
307 Randy Bass .10
308 Charlie Moore .10
309 Pete Redfern .10
310 Mike Hargrove .10
311 Dodgers Batting/ Pitching Leaders (Dusty Baker, Burt Hooton) .10
312 Lenny Randle .10
313 John Harris .10
314 Buck Martinez .10
315 Burt Hooton .10
316 Steve Braun .10
317 Dick Ruthven .10
318 Mike Heath .10
319 Dave Rozema .10
320 Chris Chambliss .10
321 Chris Chambliss (In Action) .10
322 Garry Hancock .10
323 Bill Lee .10
324 Steve Dillard .10
325 Jose Cruz .10
326 Pete Falcone .10
327 Joe Nolan .10
328 Ed Farmer .10
329 U.L. Washington .10
330 Rick Wise .10
331 Benny Ayala .10
332 Don Robinson .10
333 Brewers Future Stars (*Frank DiPino*, Marshall Edwards, Chuck Porter) .10
334 Aurelio Rodriguez .10
335 Jim Sundberg .10
336 Mariners Batting/ Pitching Leaders (Glenn Abbott, Tom Paciorek) .10
337 Pete Rose (All-Star) 1.25
338 Dave Lopes (All-Star) .10
339 Mike Schmidt (All-Star) 1.00
340 Dave Concepcion (All-Star) .10
341 Andre Dawson (All-Star) .25
342a George Foster (All-Star no autograph) 2.50
342b George Foster (All-Star autograph on front) .15
343 Dave Parker (All-Star) .10
344 Gary Carter (All-Star) .15
345 Fernando Valenzuela (All-Star) .10
346 Tom Seaver (All-Star) .75
347 Bruce Sutter (All-Star) .10
348 Derrel Thomas .10
349 George Frazier .10
350 Thad Bosley .10
351 Reds Future Stars (Scott Brown, Geoff Combe, Paul Householder) .10
352 Dick Davis .10
353 Jack O'Connor .10
354 Roberto Ramos .10
355 Dwight Evans .10
356 Denny Lewallyn .10
357 Butch Hobson .10
358 Mike Parrott .10
359 Jim Dwyer .10
360 Len Barker .10
361 Rafael Landestoy .10
362 Jim Wright .10
363 Bob Molinaro .10
364 Doyle Alexander .10
365 Bill Madlock .10
366 Padres Batting/ Pitching Leaders (Juan Eichelberger, Luis Salazar) .10
367 Jim Kaat .20
368 Alex Trevino .10
369 Champ Summers .10
370 Mike Norris .10
371 Jerry Don Gleaton .10
372 Luis Gomez .10
373 *Gene Nelson* .10
374 Tim Blackwell .10
375 Dusty Baker .15
376 Chris Welsh .10
377 Kiko Garcia .10
378 Mike Caldwell .10
379 Rob Wilfong .10
380 Dave Stieb .10
381 Red Sox Future Stars (Bruce Hurst, Dave Schmidt, Julio Valdez) .25
382 Joe Simpson .10
383a Pascual Perez (no position on front) 8.00
383b Pascual Perez ("Pitcher" on front) .10
384 Keith Moreland .10
385 Ken Forsch .10
386 Jerry White .10
387 Tom Veryzer .10
388 Joe Rudi .10
389 George Vukovich .10
390 Eddie Murray 4.00
391 Dave Tobik .10
392 Rick Bosetti .10
393 Al Hrabosky .10
394 Checklist 265-396 .10
395 Omar Moreno .10
396 Twins Batting/ Pitching Leaders (Fernando Arroyo, John Castino) .10
397 Ken Brett .10
398 Mike Squires .10
399 Pat Zachry .10
400 Johnny Bench 1.50
401 Johnny Bench (In Action) .40
402 Bill Stein .10
403 Jim Tracy .10
404 Dickie Thon .10
405 Rick Reuschel .10
406 Al Holland .10
407 Danny Boone .10
408 Ed Romero .10
409 Don Cooper .10
410 Ron Cey .10
411 Ron Cey (In Action) .10
412 Luis Leal .10
413 Dan Meyer .10
414 Elias Sosa .10
415 Don Baylor .15
416 Marty Bystrom .10
417 Pat Kelly .10
418 Rangers Future Stars (John Butcher, Bobby Johnson), *(Dave Schmidt)* .10
419 Steve Stone .15
420 George Hendrick .10
421 Mark Clear .10
422 Cliff Johnson .10
423 Stan Papi .10
424 Bruce Benedict .10
425 John Candelaria .10
426 Orioles Batting/ Pitching Leaders (Eddie Murray, Sammy Stewart) .25
427 Ron Oester .10
428 Lamarr Hoyt (LaMarr) .10
429 John Wathan .10
430 Vida Blue .10
431 Vida Blue (In Action) .10
432 Mike Scott .10
433 Alan Ashby .10
434 Joe Lefebvre .10
435 Robin Yount 3.50
436 Joe Strain .10
437 Juan Berenguer .10
438 Pete Mackanin .10
439 *Dave Righetti* .90
440 Jeff Burroughs .10
441 Astros Future Stars (Danny Heep, Billy Smith, Bobby Sprowl) .10
442 Bruce Kison .10
443 Mark Wagner .10
444 Terry Forster .10
445 Larry Parrish .10
446 Wayne Garland .10
447 Darrell Porter .10
448 Darrell Porter (In Action) .10
449 *Luis Aguayo* .10
450 Jack Morris .10
451 Ed Miller .10
452 *Lee Smith* 8.00
453 Art Howe .10
454 Rick Langford .10
455 Tom Burgmeier .10
456 Cubs Batting & Pitching Ldrs. (Bill Buckner, Randy Martz) .10
457 Tim Stoddard .10
458 Willie Montanez .10
459 Bruce Berenyi .10
460 Jack Clark .10
461 Rich Dotson .10
462 Dave Chalk .10
463 Jim Kern .10
464 Juan Bonilla .10
465 Lee Mazzilli .10
466 Randy Lerch .10
467 Mickey Hatcher .10
468 Floyd Bannister .10
469 Ed Ott .10
470 John Mayberry .10
471 Royals Future Stars (*Atlee Hammaker*, Mike Jones, Darryl Motley) .15
472 Oscar Gamble .10
473 Mike Stanton .10
474 Ken Oberkfell .10
475 Alan Trammell .45
476 Brian Kingman .10
477 Steve Yeager .10
478 Ray Searage .10
479 Rowland Office .10
480 Steve Carlton 1.00
481 Steve Carlton (In Action) .40
482 Glenn Hubbard .10
483 Gary Woods .10
484 Ivan DeJesus .10
485 Kent Tekulve .10
486 Yankees Batting & Pitching Ldrs. (Tommy John, Jerry Mumphrey) .10
487 Bob McClure .10
488 Ron Jackson .10
489 Rick Dempsey .10
490 Dennis Eckersley .20
491 Checklist 397-528 .10
492 Joe Price .10
493 Chet Lemon .10
494 Hubie Brooks .10
495 Dennis Leonard .10
496 Johnny Grubb .10
497 Jim Anderson .10
498 Dave Bergman .10
499 Paul Mirabella .10
500 Rod Carew 1.00
501 Rod Carew (In Action) .40
502 Braves Future Stars *(Steve Bedrosian)*, *(Brett Butler*, Larry Owen) 2.00
503 Julio Gonzalez .10
504 Rick Peters .10
505 Graig Nettles .10
506 Graig Nettles (In Action) .10
507 Terry Harper .10
508 *Jody Davis* .15
509 Harry Spilman .10
510 Fernando Valenzuela .20
511 Ruppert Jones .10
512 Jerry Dybzinski .10
513 Rick Rhoden .10
514 Joe Ferguson .10
515 Larry Bowa .10
516 Larry Bowa (In Action) .10
517 Mark Brouhard .10
518 Garth Iorg .10
519 Glenn Adams .10
520 Mike Flanagan .10
521 Billy Almon .10
522 Chuck Rainey .10
523 Gary Gray .10
524 Tom Hausman .10
525 Ray Knight .10
526 Expos Batting & Pitching Ldrs. (Warren Cromartie, Bill Gullickson) .10
527 John Henry Johnson .10
528 Matt Alexander .10
529 Allen Ripley .10
530 Dickie Noles .10
531 A's Future Stars (Rich Bordi, Mark Budaska, Kelvin Moore) .10
532 Toby Harrah .10
533 Joaquin Andujar .10
534 Dave McKay .10
535 Lance Parrish .10
536 Rafael Ramirez .10
537 Doug Capilla .10
538 Lou Piniella .10
539 Vern Ruhle .10
540 Andre Dawson .80
541 Barry Evans .10
542 Ned Yost .10
543 Bill Robinson .10
544 Larry Christenson .10
545 Reggie Smith .10
546 Reggie Smith (In Action) .10
547 Rod Carew (All-Star) .25
548 Willie Randolph (All-Star) .10
549 George Brett (All-Star) 1.50
550 Bucky Dent (All-Star) .10
551 Reggie Jackson (All-Star) .80
552 Ken Singleton (All-Star) .10
553 Dave Winfield (All-Star) .60

554 Carlton Fisk (All-Star) .20
555 Scott McGregor (All-Star) .10
556 Jack Morris (All-Star) .10
557 Rich Gossage (All-Star) .10
558 John Tudor .10
559 Indians Batting & Pitching Ldrs. (Bert Blyleven, Mike Hargrove) .10
560 Doug Corbett .10
561 Cardinals Future Stars (Glenn Brummer, Luis DeLeon, Gene Roof) .10
562 Mike O'Berry .10
563 Ross Baumgarten .10
564 Doug DeCinces .10
565 Jackson Todd .10
566 Mike Jorgensen .10
567 Bob Babcock .10
568 Joe Pettini .10
569 Willie Randolph .10
570 Willie Randolph (In Action) .10
571 Glenn Abbott .10
572 Juan Beniquez .10
573 Rick Waits .10
574 Mike Ramsey .10
575 Al Cowens .10
576 Giants Batting & Pitching Ldrs. (Vida Blue, Milt May) .10
577 Rick Monday .10
578 Shooty Babitt .10
579 *Rick Mahler* .10
580 Bobby Bonds .10
581 Ron Reed .10
582 Luis Pujols .10
583 Tippy Martinez .10
584 Hosken Powell .10
585 Rollie Fingers .40
586 Rollie Fingers (In Action) .15
587 Tim Lollar .10
588 Dale Berra .10
589 Dave Stapleton .10
590 Al Oliver .10
591 Al Oliver (In Action) .10
592 Craig Swan .10
593 Billy Smith .10
594 Renie Martin .10
595 Dave Collins .10
596 Damaso Garcia .10
597 Wayne Nordhagen .10
598 Bob Galasso .10
599 White Sox Future Stars (Jay Loviglio, Reggie Patterson, Leo Sutherland) .10
600 Dave Winfield 2.50
601 Sid Monge .10
602 Freddie Patek .10
603 Rich Hebner .10
604 Orlando Sanchez .10
605 Steve Rogers .10
606 Blue Jays Batting & Pitching Ldrs. (John Mayberry, Dave Stieb) .10
607 Leon Durham .10
608 Jerry Royster .10
609 Rick Sutcliffe .10
610 Rickey Henderson 3.50
611 Joe Niekro .10
612 Gary Ward .10
613 Jim Gantner .10
614 Juan Eichelberger .10
615 Bob Boone .10
616 Bob Boone (In Action) .10
617 Scott McGregor .10
618 Tim Foli .10
619 Bill Campbell .10
620 Ken Griffey .10
621 Ken Griffey (In Action) .10
622 Dennis Lamp .10
623 Mets Future Stars (Ron Gardenhire), (*Terry Leach*), (*Tim Leary*) .20
624 Fergie Jenkins .65
625 Hal McRae .10
626 Randy Jones .10
627 Enos Cabell .10
628 Bill Travers .10
629 Johnny Wockenfuss .10
630 Joe Charboneau .10
631 Gene Tenace .10
632 Bryan Clark .10
633 Mitchell Page .10
634 Checklist 529-660 .10
635 Ron Davis .10
636 Phillies Batting & Pitching Ldrs. (Steve Carlton, Pete Rose) .50
637 Rick Camp .10
638 John Milner .10
639 Ken Kravec .10
640 Cesar Cedeno .10
641 Steve Mura .10
642 Mike Scioscia .10
643 Pete Vuckovich .10
644 John Castino .10
645 Frank White .10
646 Frank White (In Action) .10
647 Warren Brusstar .10
648 Jose Morales .10
649 Ken Clay .10
650 Carl Yastrzemski 1.50
651 Carl Yastrzemski (In Action) .60
652 Steve Nicosia .10
653 Angels Future Stars (*Tom Brunansky*), (*Luis Sanchez*), (*Daryl Sconiers*) .40
654 Jim Morrison .10
655 Joel Youngblood .10
656 Eddie Whitson .10
657 Tom Poquette .10
658 Tito Landrum .10
659 Fred Martinez .10
660 Dave Concepcion .10
661 Dave Concepcion (In Action) .10
662 Luis Salazar .10
663 Hector Cruz .10
664 Dan Spillner .10
665 Jim Clancy .10
666 Tigers Batting & Pitching Ldrs. (Steve Kemp, Dan Petry) .10
667 Jeff Reardon .50
668 Dale Murphy 1.25
669 Larry Milbourne .10
670 Steve Kemp .10
671 Mike Davis .10
672 Bob Knepper .10
673 Keith Drumright .10
674 Dave Goltz .10
675 Cecil Cooper .10
676 Sal Butera .10
677 Alfredo Griffin .10
678 Tom Paciorek .10
679 Sammy Stewart .10
680 Gary Matthews .10
681 Dodgers Future Stars (*Mike Marshall*), (*Ron Roenicke*), (*Steve Sax*) .75
682 Jesse Jefferson .10
683 Phil Garner .10
684 Harold Baines .30
685 Bert Blyleven .10
686 Gary Allenson .10
687 Greg Minton .10
688 Leon Roberts .10
689 Lary Sorensen .10
690 Dave Kingman .10
691 Dan Schatzeder .10
692 Wayne Gross .10
693 Cesar Geronimo .10
694 Dave Wehrmeister .10
695 Warren Cromartie .10
696 Pirates Batting & Pitching Ldrs. (Bill Madlock, Buddy Solomon) .10
697 John Montefusco .10
698 Tony Scott .10
699 Dick Tidrow .10
700 George Foster .10
701 George Foster (In Action) .10
702 Steve Renko .10
703 Brewers Batting & Pitching Ldrs. (Cecil Cooper, Pete Vuckovich) .10
704 Mickey Rivers .10
705 Mickey Rivers (In Action) .10
706 Barry Foote .10
707 Mark Bomback .10
708 Gene Richards .10
709 Don Money .10
710 Jerry Reuss .10
711 Mariners Future Stars (*Dave Edler*), (*Dave Henderson*), (*Reggie Walton*) .50
712 Denny Martinez .10
713 Del Unser .10
714 Jerry Koosman .10
715 Willie Stargell .80
716 Willie Stargell (In Action) .30
717 Rick Miller .10
718 Charlie Hough .10
719 Jerry Narron .10
720 Greg Luzinski .15
721 Greg Luzinski (In Action) .10
722 Jerry Martin .10
723 Junior Kennedy .10
724 Dave Rosello .10
725 Amos Otis .10
726 Amos Otis (In Action) .10
727 Sixto Lezcano .10
728 Aurelio Lopez .10
729 Jim Spencer .10
730 Gary Carter .75
731 Padres Future Stars (Mike Armstrong, Doug Gwosdz, Fred Kuhaulua) .10
732 Mike Lum .10
733 Larry McWilliams .10
734 Mike Ivie .10
735 Rudy May .10
736 Jerry Turner .10
737 Reggie Cleveland .10
738 Dave Engle .10
739 Joey McLaughlin .10
740 Dave Lopes .10
741 Dave Lopes (In Action) .10
742 Dick Drago .10
743 John Stearns .10
744 *Mike Witt* .50
745 Bake McBride .10
746 Andre Thornton .10
747 John Lowenstein .10
748 Marc Hill .10
749 Bob Shirley .10
750 Jim Rice .15
751 Rick Honeycutt .10
752 Lee Lacy .10
753 Tom Brookens .10
754 Joe Morgan .75
755 Joe Morgan (In Action) .20
756 Reds Batting & Pitching Ldrs. (Ken Griffey, Tom Seaver) .30
757 Tom Underwood .10
758 Claudell Washington .10
759 Paul Splittorff .10
760 Bill Buckner .10
761 Dave Smith .10
762 Mike Phillips .10
763 Tom Hume .10
764 Steve Swisher .10
765 Gorman Thomas .10
766 Twins Future Stars (*Lenny Faedo*), (*Kent Hrbek*), (*Tim Laudner*) 2.00
767 Roy Smalley .10
768 Jerry Garvin .10
769 Richie Zisk .10
770 Rich Gossage .15
771 Rich Gossage (In Action) .10
772 Bert Campaneris .10
773 John Denny .10
774 Jay Johnstone .10
775 Bob Forsch .10
776 Mark Belanger .10
777 Tom Griffin .10
778 Kevin Hickey .10
779 Grant Jackson .10
780 Pete Rose 3.00
781 Pete Rose (In Action) 1.50
782 Frank Taveras .10
783 *Greg Harris* .15
784 Milt Wilcox .10
785 Dan Driessen .10
786 Red Sox Batting & Pitching Ldrs. (Carney Lansford, Mike Torrez) .10
787 Fred Stanley .10
788 Woodie Fryman .10
789 Checklist 661-792 .10
790 Larry Gura .10
791 Bobby Brown .10
792 Frank Tanana .10

1982 Topps Traded

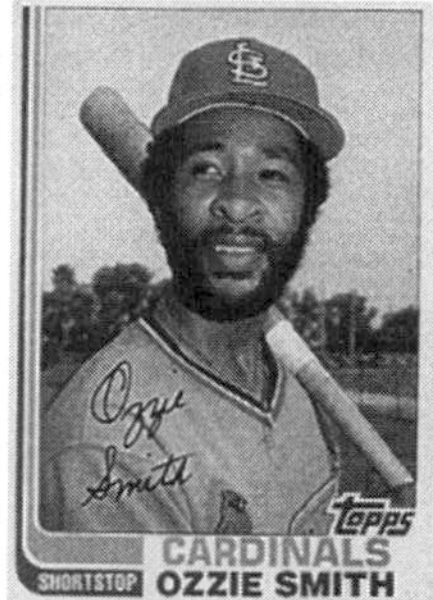

Topps released its second straight 132-card Traded set in September of 1982. Again, the 2-1/2" x 3-1/2" cards feature not only players who had been traded during the season, but also promising rookies who were given their first individual cards. The cards follow the basic design of the regular issues, but have their backs printed in red rather than the regular-issue green. As in 1981, the cards were not available in normal retail outlets and could only be purchased through regular baseball card dealers. Unlike the previous year, the cards are numbered 1-132 with the letter "T" following the number.

MT
Complete Set (132): 250.00
Common Player: .20
1T Doyle Alexander .20
2T Jesse Barfield .20
3T Ross Baumgarten .20
4T Steve Bedrosian .20
5T Mark Belanger .20
6T Kurt Bevacqua .20
7T Tim Blackwell .20
8T Vida Blue .20
9T Bob Boone .30
10T Larry Bowa .20
11T Dan Briggs .20
12T Bobby Brown .20
13T Tom Brunansky .20
14T Jeff Burroughs .20
15T Enos Cabell .20
16T Bill Campbell .20
17T Bobby Castillo .20
18T Bill Caudill .20
19T Cesar Cedeno .20
20T Dave Collins .20
21T Doug Corbett .20
22T Al Cowens .20
23T Chili Davis 1.00
24T Dick Davis .20
25T Ron Davis .20
26T Doug DeCinces .20
27T Ivan DeJesus .20
28T Bob Dernier .20
29T Bo Diaz .20
30T Roger Erickson .20
31T Jim Essian .20

32T Ed Farmer .20
33T Doug Flynn .20
34T Tim Foli .20
35T Dan Ford .20
36T George Foster .20
37T Dave Frost .20
38T Rich Gale .20
39T Ron Gardenhire .20
40T Ken Griffey .25
41T Greg Harris .20
42T Von Hayes .20
43T Larry Herndon .20
44T Kent Hrbek 4.00
45T Mike Ivie .20
46T Grant Jackson .20
47T Reggie Jackson 12.00
48T Ron Jackson .20
49T Fergie Jenkins 2.50
50T Lamar Johnson .20
51T Randy Johnson .20
52T Jay Johnstone .20
53T Mick Kelleher .20
54T Steve Kemp .20
55T Junior Kennedy .20
56T Jim Kern .20
57T Ray Knight .20
58T Wayne Krenchicki .20
59T Mike Krukow .20
60T Duane Kuiper .20
61T Mike LaCoss .20
62T Chet Lemon .20
63T Sixto Lezcano .20
64T Dave Lopes .20
65T Jerry Martin .20
66T Renie Martin .20
67T John Mayberry .20
68T Lee Mazzilli .20
69T Bake McBride .20
70T Dan Meyer .20
71T Larry Milbourne .20
72T Eddie Milner .20
73T Sid Monge .20
74T John Montefusco .20
75T Jose Morales .20
76T Keith Moreland .20
77T Jim Morrison .20
78T Rance Mulliniks .20
79T Steve Mura .20
80T Gene Nelson .20
81T Joe Nolan .20
82T Dickie Noles .20
83T Al Oliver .20
84T Jorge Orta .20
85T Tom Paciorek .20
86T Larry Parrish .20
87T Jack Perconte .20
88T Gaylord Perry 2.50
89T Rob Picciolo .20
90T Joe Pittman .20
91T Hosken Powell .20
92T Mike Proly .20
93T Greg Pryor .20
94T Charlie Puleo .20
95T Shane Rawley .20
96T Johnny Ray .20
97T Dave Revering .20
98T Cal Ripken, Jr. 200.00
99T Allen Ripley .20
100T Bill Robinson .20
101T Aurelio Rodriguez .20
102T Joe Rudi .20
103T Steve Sax 1.00
104T Dan Schatzeder .20
105T Bob Shirley .20
106T Eric Show .20
107T Roy Smalley .20
108T Lonnie Smith .20
109T Ozzie Smith 25.00
110T Reggie Smith .20
111T Lary Sorensen .20
112T Elias Sosa .20
113T Mike Stanton .20
114T Steve Stroughter .20
115T Champ Summers .20
116T Rick Sutcliffe .20
117T Frank Tanana .20
118T Frank Taveras .20
119T Garry Templeton .20
120T Alex Trevino .20
121T Jerry Turner .20
122T Ed Vande Berg .20
123T Tom Veryzer .20
124T Ron Washington .20
125T Bob Watson .20
126T Dennis Werth .20
127T Eddie Whitson .20
128T Rob Wilfong .20
129T Bump Wills .20
130T Gary Woods .20
131T Butch Wynegar .20
132T Checklist 1-132 .20

1983 Topps

The 1983 Topps set totals 792 cards. Missing among the regular 2-1/2" x 3-1/2" cards are some form of future stars cards, as Topps was saving them for the now-established late season "Traded" set. The 1983 cards carry a large color photo as well as a smaller color photo on the front, quite similar in design to the 1963 set. Team colors frame the card, which, at the bottom, have the player's name, position and team. At the upper right-hand corner is a Topps Logo. The backs are horizontal and include statistics, personal information and 1982 highlights. Specialty cards include record-breaking perfor- mances, league leaders, All-Stars, numbered check-lists "Team Leaders" and "Super Veteran" cards which are horizontal with a current and first-season picture of the honored player.

	MT
Complete Set (792):	125.00
Common Player:	.08
Pack (15):	9.25
Wax Box (36):	265.00
Crimp-end Test Pack (15):	9.50
Crimp-end Test Wax Box (36):	270.00

1 Tony Armas (Record Breaker) .08
2 Rickey Henderson (Record Breaker) .75
3 Greg Minton (Record Breaker) .08
4 Lance Parrish (Record Breaker) .08
5 Manny Trillo (Record Breaker) .08
6 John Wathan (Record Breaker) .08
7 Gene Richards .08
8 Steve Balboni .08
9 Joey McLaughlin .08
10 Gorman Thomas .08
11 Billy Gardner .08
12 Paul Mirabella .08
13 Larry Herndon .08
14 Frank LaCorte .08
15 Ron Cey .08
16 George Vukovich .08
17 Kent Tekulve .08
18 Kent Tekulve (Super Veteran) .08
19 Oscar Gamble .08
20 Carlton Fisk .75
21 Orioles Batting & Pitching Ldrs. (Eddie Murray, Jim Palmer) .25
22 Randy Martz .08
23 Mike Heath .08
24 Steve Mura .08
25 Hal McRae .08
26 Jerry Royster .08
27 Doug Corbett .08
28 Bruce Bochte .08
29 Randy Jones .08
30 Jim Rice .15
31 Bill Gullickson .08
32 Dave Bergman .08
33 Jack O'Connor .08
34 Paul Householder .08
35 Rollie Fingers .65
36 Rollie Fingers (Super Veteran) .15
37 Darrell Johnson .08
38 Tim Flannery .08
39 Terry Puhl .08
40 Fernando Valenzuela .15
41 Jerry Turner .08
42 Dale Murray .08
43 Bob Dernier .08
44 Don Robinson .08
45 John Mayberry .08
46 Richard Dotson .08
47 Dave McKay .08
48 Lary Sorensen .08
49 *Willie McGee* 1.50
50 Bob Horner .08
51 Cubs Batting & Pitching Ldrs. (Leon Durham, Fergie Jenkins) .08
52 *Onix Concepcion* .08
53 Mike Witt .08
54 Jim Maler .08
55 Mookie Wilson .08
56 Chuck Rainey .08
57 Tim Blackwell .08
58 Al Holland .08
59 Benny Ayala .08
60 Johnny Bench 1.50
61 Johnny Bench (Super Veteran) .60
62 Bob McClure .08
63 Rick Monday .08
64 Bill Stein .08
65 Jack Morris .08
66 Bob Lillis .08
67 Sal Butera .08
68 *Eric Show* .15
69 Lee Lacy .08
70 Steve Carlton 1.00
71 Steve Carlton (Super Veteran) .30
72 Tom Paciorek .08
73 Allen Ripley .08
74 Julio Gonzalez .08
75 Amos Otis .08
76 Rick Mahler .08
77 Hosken Powell .08
78 Bill Caudill .08
79 Mick Kelleher .08
80 George Foster .08
81 Yankees Batting & Pitching Ldrs. (Jerry Mumphrey, Dave Righetti) .08
82 Bruce Hurst .08
83 *Ryne Sandberg* 27.50
84 Milt May .08
85 Ken Singleton .08
86 Tom Hume .08
87 Joe Rudi .08
88 Jim Gantner .08
89 Leon Roberts .08
90 Jerry Reuss .08
91 Larry Milbourne .08
92 Mike LaCoss .08
93 John Castino .08
94 Dave Edwards .08
95 Alan Trammell .50
96 Dick Howser .08
97 Ross Baumgarten .08
98 Vance Law .08
99 Dickie Noles .08
100 Pete Rose 3.00
101 Pete Rose (Super Veteran) 1.50
102 Dave Beard .08
103 Darrell Porter .08
104 Bob Walk .08
105 Don Baylor .15
106 Gene Nelson .08
107 Mike Jorgensen .08
108 Glenn Hoffman .08
109 Luis Leal .08
110 Ken Griffey .08
111 Expos Batting & Pitching Ldrs. (Al Oliver, Steve Rogers) .08
112 Bob Shirley .08
113 Ron Roenicke .08
114 Jim Slaton .08
115 Chili Davis .50
116 Dave Schmidt .08
117 Alan Knicely .08
118 Chris Welsh .08
119 Tom Brookens .08
120 Len Barker .08
121 Mickey Hatcher .08
122 Jimmy Smith .08
123 George Frazier .08
124 Marc Hill .08
125 Leon Durham .08
126 Joe Torre .15
127 Preston Hanna .08
128 Mike Ramsey .08
129 Checklist 1-132 .08
130 Dave Stieb .08
131 Ed Ott .08
132 Todd Cruz .08
133 Jim Barr .08
134 Hubie Brooks .08
135 Dwight Evans .08
136 Willie Aikens .08
137 Woodie Fryman .08
138 Rick Dempsey .08
139 Bruce Berenyi .08
140 Willie Randolph .08
141 Indians Batting & Pitching Ldrs. (Toby Harrah, Rick Sutcliffe) .08
142 Mike Caldwell .08
143 Joe Pettini .08
144 Mark Wagner .08
145 Don Sutton .75
146 Don Sutton (Super Veteran) .20
147 Rick Leach .08
148 Dave Roberts .08
149 Johnny Ray .08
150 Bruce Sutter .08
151 Bruce Sutter (Super Veteran) .08
152 Jay Johnstone .08
153 Jerry Koosman .08
154 Johnnie LeMaster .08
155 Dan Quisenberry .08
156 Billy Martin .15
157 Steve Bedrosian .08
158 Rob Wilfong .08
159 Mike Stanton .08
160 Dave Kingman .08
161 Dave Kingman (Super Veteran) .08
162 Mark Clear .08
163 Cal Ripken, Jr. 15.00
164 Dave Palmer .08
165 Dan Driessen .08
166 John Pacella .08
167 Mark Brouhard .08
168 Juan Eichelberger .08
169 Doug Flynn .08
170 Steve Howe .08
171 Giants Batting & Pitching Ldrs. (Bill Laskey, Joe Morgan) .08
172 Vern Ruhle .08
173 Jim Morrison .08
174 Jerry Ujdur .08
175 Bo Diaz .08
176 Dave Righetti .08
177 Harold Baines .60
178 Luis Tiant .08
179 Luis Tiant (Super Veteran) .08
180 Rickey Henderson 3.00
181 Terry Felton .08
182 Mike Fischlin .08
183 *Ed Vande Berg* .08
184 Bob Clark .08
185 Tim Lollar .08
186 Whitey Herzog .08
187 Terry Leach .08
188 Rick Miller .08
189 Dan Schatzeder .08
190 Cecil Cooper .08
191 Joe Price .08
192 Floyd Rayford .08
193 Harry Spilman .08
194 Cesar Geronimo .08
195 Bob Stoddard .08
196 Bill Fahey .08
197 *Jim Eisenreich* .50
198 Kiko Garcia .08
199 Marty Bystrom .08
200 Rod Carew 1.00

No.	Card	Value
201	Rod Carew (Super Veteran)	.35
202	Blue Jays Batting & Pitching Ldrs. (Damaso Garcia, Dave Stieb)	.08
203	Mike Morgan	.08
204	Junior Kennedy	.08
205	Dave Parker	.15
206	Ken Oberkfell	.08
207	Rick Camp	.08
208	Dan Meyer	.08
209	*Mike Moore*	.40
210	Jack Clark	.08
211	John Denny	.08
212	John Stearns	.08
213	Tom Burgmeier	.08
214	Jerry White	.08
215	Mario Soto	.08
216	Tony LaRussa	.08
217	Tim Stoddard	.08
218	Roy Howell	.08
219	Mike Armstrong	.08
220	Dusty Baker	.08
221	Joe Niekro	.08
222	Damaso Garcia	.08
223	John Montefusco	.08
224	Mickey Rivers	.08
225	Enos Cabell	.08
226	Enrique Romo	.08
227	Chris Bando	.08
228	Joaquin Andujar	.08
229	Phillies Batting/Pitching Leaders (Steve Carlton, Bo Diaz)	.15
230	Fergie Jenkins	.75
231	Fergie Jenkins (Super Veteran)	.20
232	Tom Brunansky	.08
233	Wayne Gross	.08
234	Larry Andersen	.08
235	Claudell Washington	.08
236	Steve Renko	.08
237	Dan Norman	.08
238	*Bud Black*	.55
239	Dave Stapleton	.08
240	Rich Gossage	.08
241	Rich Gossage (Super Veteran)	.08
242	Joe Nolan	.08
243	Duane Walker	.08
244	Dwight Bernard	.08
245	Steve Sax	.08
246	George Bamberger	.08
247	Dave Smith	.08
248	Bake McBride	.08
249	Checklist 133-264	.08
250	Bill Buckner	.08
251	*Alan Wiggins*	.08
252	Luis Aguayo	.08
253	Larry McWilliams	.08
254	Rick Cerone	.08
255	Gene Garber	.08
256	Gene Garber (Super Veteran)	.08
257	Jesse Barfield	.08
258	Manny Castillo	.08
259	Jeff Jones	.08
260	Steve Kemp	.08
261	Tigers Batting & Pitching Ldrs. (Larry Herndon, Dan Petry)	.08
262	Ron Jackson	.08
263	Renie Martin	.08
264	Jamie Quirk	.08
265	Joel Youngblood	.08
266	Paul Boris	.08
267	Terry Francona	.08
268	*Storm Davis*	.08
269	Ron Oester	.08
270	Dennis Eckersley	.75
271	Ed Romero	.08
272	Frank Tanana	.08
273	Mark Belanger	.08
274	Terry Kennedy	.08
275	Ray Knight	.08
276	Gene Mauch	.08
277	Rance Mulliniks	.08
278	Kevin Hickey	.08
279	Greg Gross	.08
280	Bert Blyleven	.15
281	Andre Robertson	.08
282	Reggie Smith	.08
283	Reggie Smith (Super Veteran)	.08
284	Jeff Lahti	.08
285	Lance Parrish	.08
286	Rick Langford	.08
287	Bobby Brown	.08
288	*Joe Cowley*	.08
289	Jerry Dybzinski	.08
290	Jeff Reardon	.20
291	Pirates Batting & Pitching Ldrs. (John Candelaria, Bill Madlock)	.08
292	Craig Swan	.08
293	Glenn Gulliver	.08
294	Dave Engle	.08
295	Jerry Remy	.08
296	Greg Harris	.08
297	Ned Yost	.08
298	Floyd Chiffer	.08
299	George Wright	.08
300	Mike Schmidt	3.50
301	Mike Schmidt (Super Veteran)	1.00
302	Ernie Whitt	.08
303	Miguel Dilone	.08
304	Dave Rucker	.08
305	Larry Bowa	.08
306	Tom Lasorda	.25
307	Lou Piniella	.08
308	Jesus Vega	.08
309	Jeff Leonard	.08
310	Greg Luzinski	.08
311	Glenn Brummer	.08
312	Brian Kingman	.08
313	Gary Gray	.08
314	Ken Dayley	.08
315	Rick Burleson	.08
316	Paul Splittorff	.08
317	Gary Rajsich	.08
318	John Tudor	.08
319	Lenn Sakata	.08
320	Steve Rogers	.08
321	Brewers Batting & Pitching Ldrs. (Pete Vuckovich, Robin Yount)	.20
322	Dave Van Gorder	.08
323	Luis DeLeon	.08
324	Mike Marshall	.08
325	Von Hayes	.08
326	Garth Iorg	.08
327	Bobby Castillo	.08
328	Craig Reynolds	.08
329	Randy Niemann	.08
330	Buddy Bell	.08
331	Mike Krukow	.08
332	*Glenn Wilson*	.08
333	Dave LaRoche	.08
334	Dave LaRoche (Super Veteran)	.08
335	Steve Henderson	.08
336	Rene Lachemann	.08
337	Tito Landrum	.08
338	Bob Owchinko	.08
339	Terry Harper	.08
340	Larry Gura	.08
341	Doug DeCinces	.08
342	Atlee Hammaker	.08
343	Bob Bailor	.08
344	Roger LaFrancois	.08
345	Jim Clancy	.08
346	Joe Pittman	.08
347	Sammy Stewart	.08
348	Alan Bannister	.08
349	Checklist 265-396	.08
350	Robin Yount	3.00
351	Reds Batting & Pitching Ldrs. (Cesar Cedeno, Mario Soto)	.08
352	Mike Scioscia	.08
353	Steve Comer	.08
354	Randy S. Johnson	.08
355	Jim Bibby	.08
356	Gary Woods	.08
357	*Len Matuszek*	.08
358	Jerry Garvin	.08
359	Dave Collins	.08
360	Nolan Ryan	12.00
361	Nolan Ryan (Super Veteran)	5.00
362	Bill Almon	.08
363	*John Stuper*	.08
364	Brett Butler	.50
365	Dave Lopes	.08
366	Dick Williams	.08
367	Bud Anderson	.08
368	Richie Zisk	.08
369	Jesse Orosco	.08
370	Gary Carter	.25
371	Mike Richardt	.08
372	Terry Crowley	.08
373	Kevin Saucier	.08
374	Wayne Krenchicki	.08
375	Pete Vuckovich	.08
376	Ken Landreaux	.08
377	Lee May	.08
378	Lee May (Super Veteran)	.08
379	Guy Sularz	.08
380	Ron Davis	.08
381	Red Sox Batting & Pitching Ldrs. (Jim Rice, Bob Stanley)	.08
382	Bob Knepper	.08
383	Ozzie Virgil	.08
384	*Dave Dravecky*	.50
385	Mike Easler	.08
386	Rod Carew (All-Star)	.40
387	Bob Grich (All-Star)	.08
388	George Brett (All-Star)	1.25
389	Robin Yount (All-Star)	.60
390	Reggie Jackson (All-Star)	.75
391	Rickey Henderson (All-Star)	.50
392	Fred Lynn (All-Star)	.08
393	Carlton Fisk (All-Star)	.15
394	Pete Vuckovich (All-Star)	.08
395	Larry Gura (All-Star)	.08
396	Dan Quisenberry (All-Star)	.08
397	Pete Rose (All-Star)	1.00
398	Manny Trillo (All-Star)	.08
399	Mike Schmidt (All-Star)	1.00
400	Dave Concepcion (All-Star)	.08
401	Dale Murphy (All-Star)	.20
402	Andre Dawson (All-Star)	.40
403	Tim Raines (All-Star)	.25
404	Gary Carter (All-Star)	.20
405	Steve Rogers (All-Star)	.08
406	Steve Carlton (All-Star)	.50
407	Bruce Sutter (All-Star)	.08
408	Rudy May	.08
409	Marvis Foley	.08
410	Phil Niekro	.75
411	Phil Niekro (Super Veteran)	.25
412	Rangers Batting & Pitching Ldrs. (Buddy Bell, Charlie Hough)	.08
413	Matt Keough	.08
414	Julio Cruz	.08
415	Bob Forsch	.08
416	Joe Ferguson	.08
417	Tom Hausman	.08
418	Greg Pryor	.08
419	Steve Crawford	.08
420	Al Oliver	.08
421	Al Oliver (Super Veteran)	.08
422	George Cappuzzello	.08
423	*Tom Lawless*	.08
424	Jerry Augustine	.08
425	Pedro Guerrero	.08
426	Earl Weaver	.20
427	Roy Lee Jackson	.08
428	Champ Summers	.08
429	Eddie Whitson	.08
430	Kirk Gibson	.25
431	*Gary Gaetti*	.75
432	Porfirio Altamirano	.08
433	Dale Berra	.08
434	Dennis Lamp	.08
435	Tony Armas	.08
436	Bill Campbell	.08
437	Rick Sweet	.08
438	*Dave LaPoint*	.08
439	Rafael Ramirez	.08
440	Ron Guidry	.20
441	Astros Batting & Pitching Ldrs. (Ray Knight, Joe Niekro)	.08
442	Brian Downing	.08
443	Don Hood	.08
444	Wally Backman	.08
445	Mike Flanagan	.08
446	Reid Nichols	.08
447	Bryn Smith	.08
448	Darrell Evans	.08
449	*Eddie Milner*	.08
450	Ted Simmons	.08
451	Ted Simmons (Super Veteran)	.08
452	Lloyd Moseby	.08
453	Lamar Johnson	.08
454	Bob Welch	.08
455	Sixto Lezcano	.08
456	Lee Elia	.08
457	Milt Wilcox	.08
458	Ron Washington	.08
459	Ed Farmer	.08
460	Roy Smalley	.08
461	Steve Trout	.08
462	Steve Nicosia	.08
463	Gaylord Perry	.65
464	Gaylord Perry (Super Veteran)	.20
465	Lonnie Smith	.08
466	Tom Underwood	.08
467	Rufino Linares	.08
468	Dave Goltz	.08
469	Ron Gardenhire	.08
470	Greg Minton	.08
471	Royals Batting & Pitching Ldrs. (Vida Blue, Willie Wilson)	.08
472	Gary Allenson	.08
473	John Lowenstein	.08
474	Ray Burris	.08
475	Cesar Cedeno	.08
476	Rob Picciolo	.08
477	Tom Niedenfuer	.08
478	Phil Garner	.08
479	Charlie Hough	.08
480	Toby Harrah	.08
481	Scot Thompson	.08
482	*Tony Gwynn*	60.00
483	Lynn Jones	.08
484	Dick Ruthven	.08
485	Omar Moreno	.08
486	Clyde King	.08
487	Jerry Hairston	.08
488	Alfredo Griffin	.08
489	Tom Herr	.08
490	Jim Palmer	.90
491	Jim Palmer (Super Veteran)	.20
492	Paul Serna	.08
493	Steve McCatty	.08
494	Bob Brenly	.08
495	Warren Cromartie	.08
496	Tom Veryzer	.08
497	Rick Sutcliffe	.08
498	*Wade Boggs*	30.00
499	Jeff Little	.08
500	Reggie Jackson	2.00
501	Reggie Jackson (Super Veteran)	.75
502	Braves Batting & Pitching Ldrs. (Dale Murphy, Phil Niekro)	.30
503	Moose Haas	.08
504	Don Werner	.08
505	Garry Templeton	.08
506	*Jim Gott*	.25
507	Tony Scott	.08
508	Tom Filer	.08
509	Lou Whitaker	.08
510	Tug McGraw	.08
511	Tug McGraw (Super Veteran)	.08
512	Doyle Alexander	.08
513	Fred Stanley	.08
514	Rudy Law	.08
515	Gene Tenace	.08
516	Bill Virdon	.08
517	Gary Ward	.08
518	Bill Laskey	.08
519	Terry Bulling	.08
520	Fred Lynn	.08
521	Bruce Benedict	.08
522	Pat Zachry	.08
523	Carney Lansford	.08
524	Tom Brennan	.08
525	Frank White	.08
526	Checklist 397-528	.08
527	Larry Biittner	.08
528	Jamie Easterly	.08
529	Tim Laudner	.08
530	Eddie Murray	3.00
531	Athletics Batting & Pitching Ldrs.	

(Rickey Henderson, Rick Langford) .15
532 Dave Stewart .50
533 Luis Salazar .08
534 John Butcher .08
535 Manny Trillo .08
536 Johnny Wockenfuss .08
537 Rod Scurry .08
538 Danny Heep .08
539 Roger Erickson .08
540 Ozzie Smith 3.00
541 Britt Burns .08
542 Jody Davis .08
543 Alan Fowlkes .08
544 Larry Whisenton .08
545 Floyd Bannister .08
546 Dave Garcia .08
547 Geoff Zahn .08
548 Brian Giles .08
549 *Charlie Puleo* .08
550 Carl Yastrzemski 1.00
551 Carl Yastrzemski (Super Veteran) .50
552 Tim Wallach .20
553 Denny Martinez .08
554 Mike Vail .08
555 Steve Yeager .08
556 Willie Upshaw .08
557 Rick Honeycutt .08
558 Dickie Thon .08
559 Pete Redfern .08
560 Ron LeFlore .08
561 Cardinals Batting & Pitching Ldrs. (Joaquin Andujar, Lonnie Smith) .08
562 Dave Rozema .08
563 Juan Bonilla .08
564 Sid Monge .08
565 Bucky Dent .08
566 Manny Sarmiento .08
567 Joe Simpson .08
568 Willie Hernandez .08
569 Jack Perconte .08
570 Vida Blue .08
571 Mickey Klutts .08
572 Bob Watson .08
573 Andy Hassler .08
574 Glenn Adams .08
575 Neil Allen .08
576 Frank Robinson .15
577 Luis Aponte .08
578 David Green .08
579 Rich Dauer .08
580 Tom Seaver 1.50
581 Tom Seaver (Super Veteran) .50
582 Marshall Edwards .08
583 Terry Forster .08
584 Dave Hostetler .08
585 Jose Cruz .08
586 *Frank Viola* 1.50
587 Ivan DeJesus .08
588 Pat Underwood .08
589 Alvis Woods .08
590 Tony Pena .08
591 White Sox Batting & Pitching Ldrs. (LaMarr Hoyt, Greg Luzinski) .08
592 Shane Rawley .08
593 Broderick Perkins .08
594 Eric Rasmussen .08
595 Tim Raines .60
596 Randy S. Johnson .08
597 Mike Proly .08
598 Dwayne Murphy .08
599 Don Aase .08
600 George Brett 4.00
601 Ed Lynch .08
602 Rich Gedman .08
603 Joe Morgan .75
604 Joe Morgan (Super Veteran) .15
605 Gary Roenicke .08
606 Bobby Cox .08
607 Charlie Leibrandt .08
608 Don Money .08
609 Danny Darwin .08
610 Steve Garvey .75
611 Bert Roberge .08
612 Steve Swisher .08
613 Mike Ivie .08
614 Ed Glynn .08
615 Garry Maddox .08
616 Bill Nahorodny .08
617 Butch Wynegar .08
618 LaMarr Hoyt .08
619 Keith Moreland .08
620 Mike Norris .08
621 Mets Batting & Pitching Ldrs. (Craig Swan, Mookie Wilson) .08
622 Dave Edler .08
623 Luis Sanchez .08
624 Glenn Hubbard .08
625 Ken Forsch .08
626 Jerry Martin .08
627 Doug Bair .08
628 Julio Valdez .08
629 Charlie Lea .08
630 Paul Molitor 3.00
631 Tippy Martinez .08
632 Alex Trevino .08
633 Vicente Romo .08
634 Max Venable .08
635 Graig Nettles .08
636 Graig Nettles (Super Veteran) .08
637 Pat Corrales .08
638 Dan Petry .08
639 Art Howe .08
640 Andre Thornton .08
641 Billy Sample .08
642 Checklist 529-660 .08
643 Bump Wills .08
644 Joe Lefebvre .08
645 Bill Madlock .08
646 Jim Essian .08
647 Bobby Mitchell .08
648 Jeff Burroughs .08
649 Tommy Boggs .08
650 George Hendrick .08
651 Angels Batting & Pitching Ldrs. (Rod Carew, Mike Witt) .08
652 Butch Hobson .08
653 Ellis Valentine .08
654 Bob Ojeda .08
655 Al Bumbry .08
656 Dave Frost .08
657 Mike Gates .08
658 Frank Pastore .08
659 Charlie Moore .08
660 Mike Hargrove .08
661 Bill Russell .08
662 Joe Sambito .08
663 Tom O'Malley .08
664 Bob Molinaro .08
665 Jim Sundberg .08
666 Sparky Anderson .15
667 Dick Davis .08
668 Larry Christenson .08
669 Mike Squires .08
670 Jerry Mumphrey .08
671 Lenny Faedo .08
672 Jim Kaat .20
673 Jim Kaat (Super Veteran) .08
674 Kurt Bevacqua .08
675 Jim Beattie .08
676 Biff Pocoroba .08
677 Dave Revering .08
678 Juan Beniquez .08
679 Mike Scott .08
680 Andre Dawson .75
681 Dodgers Batting & Pitching Ldrs. (Pedro Guerrero, Fernando Valenzuela) .08
682 Bob Stanley .08
683 Dan Ford .08
684 Rafael Landestoy .08
685 Lee Mazzilli .08
686 Randy Lerch .08
687 U.L. Washington .08
688 Jim Wohlford .08
689 Ron Hassey .08
690 Kent Hrbek .75
691 Dave Tobik .08
692 Denny Walling .08
693 Sparky Lyle .08
694 Sparky Lyle (Super Veteran) .08
695 Ruppert Jones .08
696 Chuck Tanner .08
697 Barry Foote .08
698 Tony Bernazard .08
699 Lee Smith 1.50
700 Keith Hernandez .08
701 Batting Leaders (Al Oliver, Willie Wilson) .08
702 Home Run Leaders (Reggie Jackson, Dave Kingman, Gorman Thomas) .15
703 Runs Batted In Leaders (Hal McRae, Dale Murphy, Al Oliver) .08
704 Stolen Base Leaders (Rickey Henderson, Tim Raines) .20
705 Victory Leaders (Steve Carlton, LaMarr Hoyt) .08
706 Strikeout Leaders (Floyd Bannister, Steve Carlton) .08
707 Earned Run Average Leaders (Steve Rogers, Rick Sutcliffe) .08
708 Leading Firemen (Dan Quisenberry, Bruce Sutter) .08
709 Jimmy Sexton .08
710 Willie Wilson .08
711 Mariners Batting & Pitching Ldrs. (Jim Beattie, Bruce Bochte) .08
712 Bruce Kison .08
713 Ron Hodges .08
714 Wayne Nordhagen .08
715 Tony Perez .15
716 Tony Perez (Super Veteran) .08
717 Scott Sanderson .08
718 Jim Dwyer .08
719 Rich Gale .08
720 Dave Concepcion .08
721 John Martin .08
722 Jorge Orta .08
723 Randy Moffitt .08
724 Johnny Grubb .08
725 Dan Spillner .08
726 Harvey Kuenn .08
727 Chet Lemon .08
728 Ron Reed .08
729 Jerry Morales .08
730 Jason Thompson .08
731 Al Williams .08
732 Dave Henderson .08
733 Buck Martinez .08
734 Steve Braun .08
735 Tommy John .25
736 Tommy John (Super Veteran) .08
737 Mitchell Page .08
738 Tim Foli .08
739 Rick Ownbey .08
740 Rusty Staub .08
741 Rusty Staub (Super Veteran) .08
742 Padres Batting & Pitching Ldrs. (Terry Kennedy, Tim Lollar) .08
743 Mike Torrez .08
744 Brad Mills .08
745 Scott McGregor .08
746 John Wathan .08
747 Fred Breining .08
748 Derrel Thomas .08
749 Jon Matlack .08
750 Ben Oglivie .08
751 Brad Havens .08
752 Luis Pujols .08
753 Elias Sosa .08
754 Bill Robinson .08
755 John Candelaria .08
756 Russ Nixon .08
757 Rick Manning .08
758 Aurelio Rodriguez .08
759 Doug Bird .08
760 Dale Murphy .75
761 Gary Lucas .08
762 Cliff Johnson .08
763 Al Cowens .08
764 Pete Falcone .08
765 Bob Boone .08
766 Barry Bonnell .08
767 Duane Kuiper .08
768 Chris Speier .08
769 Checklist 661-792 .08
770 Dave Winfield 2.50
771 Twins Batting & Pitching Ldrs. (Bobby Castillo, Kent Hrbek) .08
772 Jim Kern .08
773 Larry Hisle .08
774 Alan Ashby .08
775 Burt Hooton .08
776 Larry Parrish .08
777 John Curtis .08
778 Rich Hebner .08
779 Rick Waits .08
780 Gary Matthews .08
781 Rick Rhoden .08
782 Bobby Murcer .08
783 Bobby Murcer (Super Veteran) .08
784 Jeff Newman .08
785 Dennis Leonard .08
786 Ralph Houk .08
787 Dick Tidrow .08
788 Dane Iorg .08
789 Bryan Clark .08
790 Bob Grich .08
791 Gary Lavelle .08
792 Chris Chambliss .08

1983 Topps Traded

These 2-1/2" x 3-1/2" cards mark a continuation of the traded set introduced in 1981. The 132 cards retain the basic design of the year's regular issue, with their numbering being 1-132 with the "T" suffix. Cards in the set include traded players, new managers and promising rookies. Sold only through dealers, the set was in heavy demand as it contained the first cards of Darryl Strawberry, Ron Kittle, Julio Franco and Mel Hall. While some of those cards were very hot in 1983, it seems likely that some of the rookies may not live up to their initial promise.

		MT
Complete Set (132):		25.00
Common Player:		.10
1T	Neil Allen	.10
2T	Bill Almon	.10
3T	Joe Altobelli	.10
4T	Tony Armas	.10
5T	Doug Bair	.10
6T	Steve Baker	.10
7T	Floyd Bannister	.10
8T	Don Baylor	.50
9T	Tony Bernazard	.10
10T	Larry Biittner	.10
11T	Dann Bilardello	.10
12T	Doug Bird	.10
13T	Steve Boros	.10
14T	Greg Brock	.10
15T	Mike Brown	.10
16T	Tom Burgmeier	.10
17T	Randy Bush	.10
18T	Bert Campaneris	.10
19T	Ron Cey	.10
20T	Chris Codiroli	.10
21T	Dave Collins	.10
22T	Terry Crowley	.10
23T	Julio Cruz	.10
24T	Mike Davis	.10
25T	Frank DiPino	.10
26T	Bill Doran	.25

27T Jerry Dybzinski .10
28T Jamie Easterly .10
29T Juan Eichelberger .10
30T Jim Essian .10
31T Pete Falcone .10
32T Mike Ferraro .10
33T Terry Forster .10
34T *Julio Franco* 3.00
35T Rich Gale .10
36T Kiko Garcia .10
37T Steve Garvey 2.00
38T Johnny Grubb .10
39T Mel Hall .25
40T Von Hayes .25
41T Danny Heep .10
42T Steve Henderson .10
43T Keith Hernandez .15
44T Leo Hernandez .10
45T Willie Hernandez .10
46T Al Holland .10
47T Frank Howard .15
48T Bobby Johnson .10
49T Cliff Johnson .10
50T Odell Jones .10
51T Mike Jorgensen .10
52T Bob Kearney .10
53T Steve Kemp .10
54T Matt Keough .10
55T Ron Kittle .10
56T Mickey Klutts .10
57T Alan Knicely .10
58T Mike Krukow .10
59T Rafael Landestoy .10
60T Carney Lansford .10
61T Joe Lefebvre .10
62T Bryan Little .10
63T Aurelio Lopez .10
64T Mike Madden .10
65T Rick Manning .10
66T Billy Martin .40
67T Lee Mazzilli .10
68T Andy McGaffigan .10
69T Craig McMurtry .10
70T John McNamara .10
71T Orlando Mercado .10
72T Larry Milbourne .10
73T Randy Moffitt .10
74T Sid Monge .10
75T Jose Morales .10
76T Omar Moreno .10
77T Joe Morgan 4.00
78T Mike Morgan .10
79T Dale Murray .10
80T Jeff Newman .10
81T Pete O'Brien .25
82T Jorge Orta .10
83T Alejandro Pena .10
84T Pascual Perez .15
85T Tony Perez 1.50
86T Broderick Perkins .10
87T *Tony Phillips* 3.00
88T Charlie Puleo .10
89T Pat Putnam .10
90T Jamie Quirk .10
91T Doug Rader .10
92T Chuck Rainey .10
93T Bobby Ramos .10
94T Gary Redus .10
95T Steve Renko .10
96T Leon Roberts .10
97T Aurelio Rodriguez .10
98T Dick Ruthven .10
99T Daryl Sconiers .10
100T Mike Scott .10
101T Tom Seaver 7.50
102T John Shelby .10
103T Bob Shirley .10
104T Joe Simpson .10
105T Doug Sisk .10
106T Mike Smithson .10
107T Elias Sosa .10
108T *Darryl Strawberry* 10.00
109T Tom Tellmann .10
110T Gene Tenace .10
111T Gorman Thomas .10
112T Dick Tidrow .10
113T Dave Tobik .10
114T Wayne Tolleson .10
115T Mike Torrez .10
116T Manny Trillo .10
117T Steve Trout .10
118T Lee Tunnell .10
119T Mike Vail .10
120T Ellis Valentine .10
121T Tom Veryzer .10
122T George Vukovich .10
123T Rick Waits .10
124T Greg Walker .10
125T Chris Welsh .10
126T Len Whitehouse .10
127T Eddie Whitson .10
128T Jim Wohlford .10
129T Matt Young .10
130T Joel Youngblood .10
131T Pat Zachry .10
132T Checklist 1-132 .10

1983 Topps All-Star Glossy Set of 40

This set was a "consolation prize" in a scratch-off contest in regular packs of 1983 cards. The 2-1/2" x 3-1/2" cards have a large color photo surrounded by a yellow frame on the front. In very small type on a white border is printed the player's name. Backs carry the player's name, team, position and the card number along with a Topps identification. A major feature is that the surface of the front is glossy, which most collectors find very attractive. With many top stars, the set is a popular one, but the price has not moved too far above the issue price.

		MT
Complete Set (40):		13.00
Common Player:		.15
1	Carl Yastrzemski	.75
2	Mookie Wilson	.15
3	Andre Thornton	.15
4	Keith Hernandez	.15
5	Robin Yount	.60
6	Terry Kennedy	.15
7	Dave Winfield	.50
8	Mike Schmidt	.75
9	Buddy Bell	.15
10	Fernando Valenzuela	.15
11	Rich Gossage	.15
12	Bob Horner	.15
13	Toby Harrah	.15
14	Pete Rose	1.00
15	Cecil Cooper	.15
16	Dale Murphy	.35
17	Carlton Fisk	.30
18	Ray Knight	.15
19	Jim Palmer	.45
20	Gary Carter	.25
21	Richard Zisk	.15
22	Dusty Baker	.15
23	Willie Wilson	.15
24	Bill Buckner	.15
25	Dave Stieb	.15
26	Bill Madlock	.15
27	Lance Parrish	.15
28	Nolan Ryan	1.50
29	Rod Carew	.60
30	Al Oliver	.15
31	George Brett	.75
32	Jack Clark	.15
33	Rickey Henderson	.60
34	Dave Concepcion	.15
35	Kent Hrbek	.15
36	Steve Carlton	.50
37	Eddie Murray	.60
38	Ruppert Jones	.15
39	Reggie Jackson	.75
40	Bruce Sutter	.15

1983 Topps 1952 Reprint Set

The first of several reprint/retro sets in different sports issued by Topps, the 402-card reprinting of its classic 1952 baseball card set was controversial at the time of issue, but has since gained hobby acceptance and market value. To avoid possible confusion of the reprints for originals, the reprints were done in the now-standard 2-1/2" x 3-1/2" format instead of the original 2-5/8" x 3-3/4". Backs, printed in red, carry a line "Topps 1952 Reprint Series" at bottom, though there is no indication of the year of reprinting. Fronts have a semi-gloss finish, which also differs from the originals. Because of inability to come to terms with five of the players from the original 1952 Topps set, they were not included in the reprint series. Those cards which weren't issued are: #20 Billy Loes, #22 Dom DiMaggio, #159 Saul Rogovin, #196 Solly Hemus, and #289 Tommy Holmes. The '52 reprints were available only as a complete boxed set with a retail price of about $40 at issue.

		MT
Complete Sealed Boxed Set:		450.00
Complete Set (402):		300.00
Common Player:		.25
Minor Stars:		.50
Typical Hall of Famers:		2.00
Superstar Hall of Famers:		8.00
311	Mickey Mantle	75.00
407	Eddie Mathews (sample card)	12.00

(See 1952 Topps for checklist)

1984 Topps

Another 792-card regular set from Topps. For the second straight year, the 2-1/2" x 3-1/2" cards featured a color action photo on the front along with a small portrait photo in the lower left. The team name runs in big letters down the left side, while the player's name and position runs under the large action photo. In the upper right-hand corner is the Topps logo. Backs have a team logo in the upper right corner, along with statistics, personal information and a few highlights. The backs have an unusual and hard-to-read red and purple coloring. Specialty cards include past season highlights, team leaders, major league statistical leaders, All-Stars, active career leaders and numbered checklists. Again, promising rookies were saved for the traded set. Late in 1984, Topps introduced a specially boxed "Tiffany" edition of the 1984 set, with the cards printed on white cardboard with a glossy finish. A total of 10,000 sets were produced. Prices for Tiffany edition super-stars can run from six to eight times the value of the "regular" edition, while common cards sell in the 40¢ range.

		MT
Complete Set (792):		40.00
Common Player:		.08
Pack (15):		2.00
Wax Box (36):		40.00
1	Steve Carlton (1983 Highlight)	.25
2	Rickey Henderson (1983 Highlight)	.40
3	Dan Quisenberry (1983 Highlight)	.08
4	Steve Carlton, Gaylord Perry, Nolan Ryan (1983 Highlight)	.75
5	Bob Forsch, Dave Righetti, Mike Warren (1983 Highlight)	.08
6	Johnny Bench, Gaylord Perry, Carl Yastrzemski (1983 Highlight)	.30
7	Gary Lucas	.08
8	*Don Mattingly*	10.00
9	Jim Gott	.08
10	Robin Yount	2.00
11	Twins Batting & Pitching Leaders (Kent Hrbek, Ken Schrom)	.08
12	Billy Sample	.08
13	Scott Holman	.08
14	Tom Brookens	.08
15	Burt Hooton	.08

No.	Card	Value
16	Omar Moreno	.08
17	John Denny	.08
18	Dale Berra	.08
19	*Ray Fontenot*	.08
20	Greg Luzinski	.08
21	Joe Altobelli	.08
22	Bryan Clark	.08
23	Keith Moreland	.08
24	John Martin	.08
25	Glenn Hubbard	.08
26	Bud Black	.08
27	Daryl Sconiers	.08
28	Frank Viola	.08
29	Danny Heep	.08
30	Wade Boggs	4.00
31	Andy McGaffigan	.08
32	Bobby Ramos	.08
33	Tom Burgmeier	.08
34	Eddie Milner	.08
35	Don Sutton	.35
36	Denny Walling	.08
37	Rangers Batting & Pitching Leaders (Buddy Bell, Rick Honeycutt)	.08
38	Luis DeLeon	.08
39	Garth Iorg	.08
40	Dusty Baker	.08
41	Tony Bernazard	.08
42	Johnny Grubb	.08
43	Ron Reed	.08
44	Jim Morrison	.08
45	Jerry Mumphrey	.08
46	Ray Smith	.08
47	Rudy Law	.08
48	Julio Franco	.45
49	John Stuper	.08
50	Chris Chambliss	.08
51	Jim Frey	.08
52	Paul Splittorff	.08
53	Juan Beniquez	.08
54	Jesse Orosco	.08
55	Dave Concepcion	.08
56	Gary Allenson	.08
57	Dan Schatzeder	.08
58	Max Venable	.08
59	Sammy Stewart	.08
60	Paul Molitor	2.00
61	*Chris Codiroli*	.08
62	Dave Hostetler	.08
63	Ed Vande Berg	.08
64	Mike Scioscia	.08
65	Kirk Gibson	.08
66	Astros Batting & Pitching Leaders (Jose Cruz, Nolan Ryan)	.25
67	Gary Ward	.08
68	Luis Salazar	.08
69	Rod Scurry	.08
70	Gary Matthews	.08
71	Leo Hernandez	.08
72	Mike Squires	.08
73	Jody Davis	.08
74	Jerry Martin	.08
75	Bob Forsch	.08
76	Alfredo Griffin	.08
77	Brett Butler	.08
78	Mike Torrez	.08
79	Rob Wilfong	.08
80	Steve Rogers	.08
81	Billy Martin	.15
82	Doug Bird	.08
83	Richie Zisk	.08
84	Lenny Faedo	.08
85	Atlee Hammaker	.08
86	*John Shelby*	.08
87	Frank Pastore	.08
88	Rob Picciolo	.08
89	*Mike Smithson*	.08
90	Pedro Guerrero	.08
91	Dan Spillner	.08
92	Lloyd Moseby	.08
93	Bob Knepper	.08
94	Mario Ramirez	.08
95	Aurelio Lopez	.08
96	Royals Batting & Pitching Leaders (Larry Gura, Hal McRae)	.08
97	LaMarr Hoyt	.08
98	Steve Nicosia	.08
99	*Craig Lefferts*	.25
100	Reggie Jackson	1.50
101	Porfirio Altamirano	.08
102	Ken Oberkfell	.08
103	Dwayne Murphy	.08
104	Ken Dayley	.08
105	Tony Armas	.08
106	Tim Stoddard	.08
107	Ned Yost	.08
108	Randy Moffitt	.08
109	Brad Wellman	.08
110	Ron Guidry	.08
111	Bill Virdon	.08
112	Tom Niedenfuer	.08
113	Kelly Paris	.08
114	Checklist 1-132	.08
115	Andre Thornton	.08
116	George Bjorkman	.08
117	Tom Veryzer	.08
118	Charlie Hough	.08
119	Johnny Wockenfuss	.08
120	Keith Hernandez	.08
121	*Pat Sheridan*	.08
122	Cecilio Guante	.08
123	Butch Wynegar	.08
124	Damaso Garcia	.08
125	Britt Burns	.08
126	Braves Batting & Pitching Leaders (Craig McMurtry, Dale Murphy)	.08
127	Mike Madden	.08
128	Rick Manning	.08
129	Bill Laskey	.08
130	Ozzie Smith	2.00
131	Batting Leaders (Wade Boggs, Bill Madlock)	.25
132	Home Run Leaders (Jim Rice, Mike Schmidt)	.30
133	RBI Leaders (Cecil Cooper, Dale Murphy, Jim Rice)	.20
134	Stolen Base Leaders (Rickey Henderson, Tim Raines)	.25
135	Victory Leaders (John Denny, LaMarr Hoyt)	.08
136	Strikeout Leaders (Steve Carlton, Jack Morris)	.08
137	Earned Run Average Leaders (Atlee Hammaker, Rick Honeycutt)	.08
138	Leading Firemen (Al Holland, Dan Quisenberry)	.08
139	Bert Campaneris	.08
140	Storm Davis	.08
141	Pat Corrales	.08
142	Rich Gale	.08
143	Jose Morales	.08
144	*Brian Harper*	.35
145	Gary Lavelle	.08
146	Ed Romero	.08
147	Dan Petry	.08
148	Joe Lefebvre	.08
149	Jon Matlack	.08
150	Dale Murphy	.50
151	Steve Trout	.08
152	Glenn Brummer	.08
153	Dick Tidrow	.08
154	Dave Henderson	.08
155	Frank White	.08
156	Athletics Batting & Pitching Leaders (Tim Conroy, Rickey Henderson)	.15
157	Gary Gaetti	.08
158	John Curtis	.08
159	Darryl Cias	.08
160	Mario Soto	.08
161	*Junior Ortiz*	.08
162	Bob Ojeda	.08
163	Lorenzo Gray	.08
164	Scott Sanderson	.08
165	Ken Singleton	.08
166	Jamie Nelson	.08
167	Marshall Edwards	.08
168	Juan Bonilla	.08
169	Larry Parrish	.08
170	Jerry Reuss	.08
171	Frank Robinson	.15
172	Frank DiPino	.08
173	*Marvell Wynne*	.08
174	Juan Berenguer	.08
175	Graig Nettles	.08
176	Lee Smith	.08
177	Jerry Hairston	.08
178	Bill Krueger	.08
179	Buck Martinez	.08
180	Manny Trillo	.08
181	Roy Thomas	.08
182	Darryl Strawberry	1.50
183	Al Williams	.08
184	Mike O'Berry	.08
185	Sixto Lezcano	.08
186	Cardinals Batting & Pitching Leaders (Lonnie Smith, John Stuper)	.08
187	Luis Aponte	.08
188	Bryan Little	.08
189	*Tim Conroy*	.08
190	Ben Oglivie	.08
191	Mike Boddicker	.08
192	*Nick Esasky*	.08
193	Darrell Brown	.08
194	Domingo Ramos	.08
195	Jack Morris	.08
196	Don Slaught	.08
197	Garry Hancock	.08
198	*Bill Doran*	.15
199	Willie Hernandez	.08
200	Andre Dawson	.60
201	Bruce Kison	.08
202	Bobby Cox	.08
203	Matt Keough	.08
204	*Bobby Meacham*	.08
205	Greg Minton	.08
206	*Andy Van Slyke*	.75
207	Donnie Moore	.08
208	*Jose Oquendo*	.15
209	Manny Sarmiento	.08
210	Joe Morgan	.30
211	Rick Sweet	.08
212	Broderick Perkins	.08
213	Bruce Hurst	.08
214	Paul Householder	.08
215	Tippy Martinez	.08
216	White Sox Batting & Pitching Leaders (Richard Dotson, Carlton Fisk)	.08
217	Alan Ashby	.08
218	Rick Waits	.08
219	Joe Simpson	.08
220	Fernando Valenzuela	.08
221	Cliff Johnson	.08
222	Rick Honeycutt	.08
223	Wayne Krenchicki	.08
224	Sid Monge	.08
225	Lee Mazzilli	.08
226	Juan Eichelberger	.08
227	Steve Braun	.08
228	John Rabb	.08
229	Paul Owens	.08
230	Rickey Henderson	1.75
231	Gary Woods	.08
232	Tim Wallach	.08
233	Checklist 133-264	.08
234	Rafael Ramirez	.08
235	*Matt Young*	.08
236	Ellis Valentine	.08
237	John Castino	.08
238	Reid Nichols	.08
239	Jay Howell	.08
240	Eddie Murray	1.50
241	Billy Almon	.08
242	Alex Trevino	.08
243	Pete Ladd	.08
244	Candy Maldonado	.08
245	Rick Sutcliffe	.08
246	Mets Batting & Pitching Leaders (Tom Seaver, Mookie Wilson)	.25
247	Onix Concepcion	.08
248	*Bill Dawley*	.08
249	Jay Johnstone	.08
250	Bill Madlock	.08
251	Tony Gwynn	6.00
252	Larry Christenson	.08
253	Jim Wohlford	.08
254	Shane Rawley	.08
255	Bruce Benedict	.08
256	Dave Geisel	.08
257	Julio Cruz	.08
258	Luis Sanchez	.08
259	Sparky Anderson	.15
260	Scott McGregor	.08
261	Bobby Brown	.08
262	*Tom Candiotti*	.25
263	Jack Fimple	.08
264	Doug Frobel	.08
265	*Donnie Hill*	.08
266	Steve Lubratich	.08
267	*Carmelo Martinez*	.08
268	Jack O'Connor	.08
269	Aurelio Rodriguez	.08
270	*Jeff Russell*	.20
271	Moose Haas	.08
272	Rick Dempsey	.08
273	Charlie Puleo	.08
274	Rick Monday	.08
275	Len Matuszek	.08
276	Angels Batting & Pitching Leaders (Rod Carew, Geoff Zahn)	.20
277	Eddie Whitson	.08
278	Jorge Bell	.20
279	Ivan DeJesus	.08
280	Floyd Bannister	.08
281	Larry Milbourne	.08
282	Jim Barr	.08
283	Larry Biittner	.08
284	Howard Bailey	.08
285	Darrell Porter	.08
286	Lary Sorensen	.08
287	Warren Cromartie	.08
288	Jim Beattie	.08
289	Randy S. Johnson	.08
290	Dave Dravecky	.08
291	Chuck Tanner	.08
292	Tony Scott	.08
293	Ed Lynch	.08
294	U.L. Washington	.08
295	Mike Flanagan	.08
296	Jeff Newman	.08
297	Bruce Berenyi	.08
298	Jim Gantner	.08
299	John Butcher	.08
300	Pete Rose	2.00
301	Frank LaCorte	.08
302	Barry Bonnell	.08
303	Marty Castillo	.08
304	Warren Brusstar	.08
305	Roy Smalley	.08
306	Dodgers Batting & Pitching Leaders (Pedro Guerrero, Bob Welch)	.08
307	Bobby Mitchell	.08
308	Ron Hassey	.08
309	Tony Phillips	.25
310	Willie McGee	.08
311	Jerry Koosman	.08
312	Jorge Orta	.08
313	Mike Jorgensen	.08
314	Orlando Mercado	.08
315	Bob Grich	.08
316	Mark Bradley	.08
317	Greg Pryor	.08
318	Bill Gullickson	.08
319	Al Bumbry	.08
320	Bob Stanley	.08
321	Harvey Kuenn	.08
322	Ken Schrom	.08
323	Alan Knicely	.08
324	*Alejandro Pena*	.15
325	Darrell Evans	.15
326	Bob Kearney	.08
327	Ruppert Jones	.08
328	Vern Ruhle	.08
329	Pat Tabler	.08
330	John Candelaria	.08
331	Bucky Dent	.08
332	*Kevin Gross*	.15
333	Larry Herndon	.08
334	Chuck Rainey	.08
335	Don Baylor	.15
336	Mariners Batting & Pitching Leaders (Pat Putnam, Matt Young)	.08
337	Kevin Hagen	.08
338	Mike Warren	.08
339	Roy Lee Jackson	.08
340	Hal McRae	.08
341	Dave Tobik	.08
342	Tim Foli	.08
343	Mark Davis	.08
344	Rick Miller	.08
345	Kent Hrbek	.25
346	Kurt Bevacqua	.08
347	Allan Ramirez	.08
348	Toby Harrah	.08
349	Bob L. Gibson	.08
350	George Foster	.08
351	Russ Nixon	.08
352	Dave Stewart	.08
353	Jim Anderson	.08
354	Jeff Burroughs	.08
355	Jason Thompson	.08
356	Glenn Abbott	.08
357	Ron Cey	.08
358	Bob Dernier	.08
359	*Jim Acker*	.08
360	Willie Randolph	.08
361	Dave Smith	.08
362	David Green	.08
363	Tim Laudner	.08
364	Scott Fletcher	.15
365	Steve Bedrosian	.08
366	Padres Batting & Pitching Leaders	

No.	Player	Price
	(Dave Dravecky, Terry Kennedy)	.08
367	Jamie Easterly	.08
368	Hubie Brooks	.08
369	Steve McCatty	.08
370	Tim Raines	.50
371	Dave Gumpert	.08
372	Gary Roenicke	.08
373	Bill Scherrer	.08
374	Don Money	.08
375	Dennis Leonard	.08
376	*Dave Anderson*	.08
377	Danny Darwin	.08
378	Bob Brenly	.08
379	Checklist 265-396	.08
380	Steve Garvey	.45
381	Ralph Houk	.08
382	Chris Nyman	.08
383	Terry Puhl	.08
384	*Lee Tunnell*	.08
385	Tony Perez	.15
386	George Hendrick (All-Star)	.08
387	Johnny Ray (All-Star)	.08
388	Mike Schmidt (All-Star)	.50
389	Ozzie Smith (All-Star)	.40
390	Tim Raines (All-Star)	.25
391	Dale Murphy (All-Star)	.20
392	Andre Dawson (All-Star)	.25
393	Gary Carter (All-Star)	.15
394	Steve Rogers (All-Star)	.08
395	Steve Carlton (All-Star)	.25
396	Jesse Orosco (All-Star)	.08
397	Eddie Murray (All-Star)	.40
398	Lou Whitaker (All-Star)	.08
399	George Brett (All-Star)	.75
400	Cal Ripken, Jr. (All-Star)	2.00
401	Jim Rice (All-Star)	.08
402	Dave Winfield (All-Star)	.30
403	Lloyd Moseby (All-Star)	.08
404	Ted Simmons (All-Star)	.08
405	LaMarr Hoyt (All-Star)	.08
406	Ron Guidry (All-Star)	.08
407	Dan Quisenberry (All-Star)	.08
408	Lou Piniella	.08
409	*Juan Agosto*	.08
410	Claudell Washington	.08
411	Houston Jimenez	.08
412	Doug Rader	.08
413	*Spike Owen*	.20
414	Mitchell Page	.08
415	Tommy John	.15
416	Dane Iorg	.08
417	Mike Armstrong	.08
418	Ron Hodges	.08
419	John Henry Johnson	.08
420	Cecil Cooper	.08
421	Charlie Lea	.08
422	Jose Cruz	.08
423	Mike Morgan	.08
424	Dann Bilardello	.08
425	Steve Howe	.08
426	Orioles Batting & Pitching Leaders (Mike Boddicker, Cal Ripken, Jr.)	1.00
427	Rick Leach	.08
428	Fred Breining	.08
429	*Randy Bush*	.08
430	Rusty Staub	.08
431	Chris Bando	.08
432	*Charlie Hudson*	.08
433	Rich Hebner	.08
434	Harold Baines	.15
435	Neil Allen	.08
436	Rick Peters	.08
437	Mike Proly	.08
438	Biff Pocoroba	.08
439	Bob Stoddard	.08
440	Steve Kemp	.08
441	Bob Lillis	.08
442	Byron McLaughlin	.08
443	Benny Ayala	.08
444	Steve Renko	.08
445	Jerry Remy	.08
446	Luis Pujols	.08
447	Tom Brunansky	.08
448	Ben Hayes	.08
449	Joe Pettini	.08
450	Gary Carter	.30
451	Bob Jones	.08
452	Chuck Porter	.08
453	Willie Upshaw	.08
454	Joe Beckwith	.08
455	Terry Kennedy	.08
456	Cubs Batting & Pitching Leaders (Fergie Jenkins, Keith Moreland)	.08
457	Dave Rozema	.08
458	Kiko Garcia	.08
459	Kevin Hickey	.08
460	Dave Winfield	1.50
461	Jim Maler	.08
462	Lee Lacy	.08
463	Dave Engle	.08
464	Jeff Jones	.08
465	Mookie Wilson	.08
466	Gene Garber	.08
467	Mike Ramsey	.08
468	Geoff Zahn	.08
469	Tom O'Malley	.08
470	Nolan Ryan	7.00
471	Dick Howser	.08
472	Mike Brown	.08
473	Jim Dwyer	.08
474	Greg Bargar	.08
475	*Gary Redus*	.15
476	Tom Tellmann	.08
477	Rafael Landestoy	.08
478	Alan Bannister	.08
479	Frank Tanana	.08
480	Ron Kittle	.08
481	*Mark Thurmond*	.08
482	Enos Cabell	.08
483	Fergie Jenkins	.25
484	Ozzie Virgil	.08
485	Rick Rhoden	.08
486	Yankees Batting & Pitching Leaders (Don Baylor, Ron Guidry)	.08
487	Ricky Adams	.08
488	Jesse Barfield	.08
489	Dave Von Ohlen	.08
490	Cal Ripken, Jr.	7.00
491	Bobby Castillo	.08
492	Tucker Ashford	.08
493	Mike Norris	.08
494	Chili Davis	.08
495	Rollie Fingers	.25
496	Terry Francona	.08
497	Bud Anderson	.08
498	Rich Gedman	.08
499	Mike Witt	.08
500	George Brett	2.00
501	Steve Henderson	.08
502	Joe Torre	.08
503	Elias Sosa	.08
504	Mickey Rivers	.08
505	Pete Vuckovich	.08
506	Ernie Whitt	.08
507	Mike LaCoss	.08
508	Mel Hall	.08
509	Brad Havens	.08
510	Alan Trammell	.15
511	Marty Bystrom	.08
512	Oscar Gamble	.08
513	Dave Beard	.08
514	Floyd Rayford	.08
515	Gorman Thomas	.08
516	Expos Batting & Pitching Leaders (Charlie Lea, Al Oliver)	.08
517	John Moses	.08
518	*Greg Walker*	.08
519	Ron Davis	.08
520	Bob Boone	.08
521	Pete Falcone	.08
522	Dave Bergman	.08
523	Glenn Hoffman	.08
524	Carlos Diaz	.08
525	Willie Wilson	.08
526	Ron Oester	.08
527	Checklist 397-528	.08
528	Mark Brouhard	.08
529	*Keith Atherton*	.08
530	Dan Ford	.08
531	Steve Boros	.08
532	Eric Show	.08
533	Ken Landreaux	.08
534	Pete O'Brien	.08
535	Bo Diaz	.08
536	Doug Bair	.08
537	Johnny Ray	.08
538	Kevin Bass	.08
539	George Frazier	.08
540	George Hendrick	.08
541	Dennis Lamp	.08
542	Duane Kuiper	.08
543	*Craig McMurtry*	.08
544	Cesar Geronimo	.08
545	Bill Buckner	.08
546	Indians Batting & Pitching Leaders (Mike Hargrove, Lary Sorensen)	.08
547	Mike Moore	.08
548	Ron Jackson	.08
549	*Walt Terrell*	.20
550	Jim Rice	.15
551	Scott Ullger	.08
552	Ray Burris	.08
553	Joe Nolan	.08
554	Ted Power	.08
555	Greg Brock	.08
556	Joey McLaughlin	.08
557	Wayne Tolleson	.08
558	Mike Davis	.08
559	Mike Scott	.08
560	Carlton Fisk	.60
561	Whitey Herzog	.08
562	Manny Castillo	.08
563	Glenn Wilson	.08
564	Al Holland	.08
565	Leon Durham	.08
566	Jim Bibby	.08
567	Mike Heath	.08
568	Pete Filson	.08
569	Bake McBride	.08
570	Dan Quisenberry	.08
571	Bruce Bochy	.08
572	Jerry Royster	.08
573	Dave Kingman	.08
574	Brian Downing	.08
575	Jim Clancy	.08
576	Giants Batting & Pitching Leaders (Atlee Hammaker, Jeff Leonard)	.08
577	Mark Clear	.08
578	Lenn Sakata	.08
579	Bob James	.08
580	Lonnie Smith	.08
581	*Jose DeLeon*	.08
582	Bob McClure	.08
583	Derrel Thomas	.08
584	Dave Schmidt	.08
585	Dan Driessen	.08
586	Joe Niekro	.08
587	Von Hayes	.08
588	Milt Wilcox	.08
589	Mike Easler	.08
590	Dave Stieb	.08
591	Tony LaRussa	.08
592	Andre Robertson	.08
593	Jeff Lahti	.08
594	Gene Richards	.08
595	Jeff Reardon	.08
596	Ryne Sandberg	4.00
597	Rick Camp	.08
598	Rusty Kuntz	.08
599	*Doug Sisk*	.08
600	Rod Carew	.75
601	John Tudor	.08
602	John Wathan	.08
603	Renie Martin	.08
604	John Lowenstein	.08
605	Mike Caldwell	.08
606	Blue Jays Batting & Pitching Leaders (Lloyd Moseby, Dave Stieb)	.08
607	Tom Hume	.08
608	Bobby Johnson	.08
609	Dan Meyer	.08
610	Steve Sax	.08
611	Chet Lemon	.08
612	Harry Spilman	.08
613	Greg Gross	.08
614	Len Barker	.08
615	Garry Templeton	.08
616	Don Robinson	.08
617	Rick Cerone	.08
618	Dickie Noles	.08
619	Jerry Dybzinski	.08
620	Al Oliver	.08
621	Frank Howard	.08
622	Al Cowens	.08
623	Ron Washington	.08
624	Terry Harper	.08
625	Larry Gura	.08
626	Bob Clark	.08
627	Dave LaPoint	.08
628	Ed Jurak	.08
629	Rick Langford	.08
630	Ted Simmons	.08
631	Denny Martinez	.08
632	Tom Foley	.08
633	Mike Krukow	.08
634	Mike Marshall	.08
635	Dave Righetti	.08
636	Pat Putnam	.08
637	Phillies Batting & Pitching Leaders (John Denny, Gary Matthews)	.08
638	George Vukovich	.08
639	Rick Lysander	.08
640	Lance Parrish	.08
641	Mike Richardt	.08
642	Tom Underwood	.08
643	Mike Brown	.08
644	Tim Lollar	.08
645	Tony Pena	.08
646	Checklist 529-660	.08
647	Ron Roenicke	.08
648	Len Whitehouse	.08
649	Tom Herr	.08
650	Phil Niekro	.50
651	John McNamara	.08
652	Rudy May	.08
653	Dave Stapleton	.08
654	Bob Bailor	.08
655	Amos Otis	.08
656	Bryn Smith	.08
657	Thad Bosley	.08
658	Jerry Augustine	.08
659	Duane Walker	.08
660	Ray Knight	.08
661	Steve Yeager	.08
662	Tom Brennan	.08
663	Johnnie LeMaster	.08
664	Dave Stegman	.08
665	Buddy Bell	.08
666	Tigers Batting & Pitching Leaders (Jack Morris, Lou Whitaker)	.08
667	Vance Law	.08
668	Larry McWilliams	.08
669	Dave Lopes	.08
670	Rich Gossage	.08
671	Jamie Quirk	.08
672	Ricky Nelson	.08
673	Mike Walters	.08
674	Tim Flannery	.08
675	Pascual Perez	.08
676	Brian Giles	.08
677	Doyle Alexander	.08
678	Chris Speier	.08
679	Art Howe	.08
680	Fred Lynn	.08
681	Tom Lasorda	.25
682	Dan Morogiello	.08
683	*Marty Barrett*	.08
684	Bob Shirley	.08
685	Willie Aikens	.08
686	Joe Price	.08
687	Roy Howell	.08
688	George Wright	.08
689	Mike Fischlin	.08
690	Jack Clark	.08
691	*Steve Lake*	.08
692	Dickie Thon	.08
693	Alan Wiggins	.08
694	Mike Stanton	.08
695	Lou Whitaker	.08
696	Pirates Batting & Pitching Leaders (Bill Madlock, Rick Rhoden)	.08
697	Dale Murray	.08
698	Marc Hill	.08
699	Dave Rucker	.08
700	Mike Schmidt	2.00
701	NL Active Career Batting Leaders (Bill Madlock, Dave Parker, Pete Rose)	.25
702	NL Active Career Hit Leaders (Tony Perez, Pete Rose, Rusty Staub)	.25
703	NL Active Career Home Run Leaders (Dave Kingman, Tony Perez, Mike Schmidt)	.15

704 NL Active Career RBI Leaders (Al Oliver, Tony Perez, Rusty Staub) .08
705 NL Active Career Stolen Bases Leaders (Larry Bowa, Cesar Cedeno, Joe Morgan) .08
706 NL Active Career Victory Leaders (Steve Carlton, Fergie Jenkins, Tom Seaver) .08
707 NL Active Career Strikeout Leaders (Steve Carlton, Nolan Ryan, Tom Seaver) .35
708 NL Active Career ERA Leaders (Steve Carlton, Steve Rogers, Tom Seaver) .08
709 NL Active Career Save Leaders (Gene Garber, Tug McGraw, Bruce Sutter) .08
710 AL Active Career Batting Leaders (George Brett, Rod Carew, Cecil Cooper) .30
711 AL Active Career Hit Leaders (Bert Campaneris, Rod Carew, Reggie Jackson) .15
712 AL Active Career Home Run Leaders (Reggie Jackson, Greg Luzinski, Graig Nettles) .20
713 AL Active Career RBI Leaders (Reggie Jackson, Graig Nettles, Ted Simmons) .15
714 AL Active Career Stolen Bases Leaders (Bert Campaneris, Dave Lopes, Omar Moreno) .08
715 AL Active Career Victory Leaders (Tommy John, Jim Palmer, Don Sutton) .08
716 AL Active Strikeout Leaders (Bert Blyleven, Jerry Koosman, Don Sutton) .08
717 AL Active Career ERA Leaders (Rollie Fingers, Ron Guidry, Jim Palmer) .08
718 AL Active Career Save Leaders (Rollie Fingers, Rich Gossage, Dan Quisenberry) .08
719 Andy Hassler .08
720 Dwight Evans .08
721 Del Crandall .08
722 Bob Welch .08
723 Rich Dauer .08
724 Eric Rasmussen .08
725 Cesar Cedeno .08
726 Brewers Batting & Pitching Leaders (Moose Haas, Ted Simmons) .08
727 Joel Youngblood .08
728 Tug McGraw .08
729 Gene Tenace .08
730 Bruce Sutter .08
731 Lynn Jones .08
732 Terry Crowley .08
733 Dave Collins .08
734 Odell Jones .08
735 Rick Burleson .08
736 Dick Ruthven .08
737 Jim Essian .08
738 *Bill Schroeder* .08
739 Bob Watson .08
740 Tom Seaver 1.00
741 Wayne Gross .08
742 Dick Williams .08
743 Don Hood .08
744 Jamie Allen .08
745 Dennis Eckersley .08
746 Mickey Hatcher .08
747 Pat Zachry .08
748 Jeff Leonard .08
749 Doug Flynn .08
750 Jim Palmer 1.00
751 Charlie Moore .08
752 Phil Garner .08
753 Doug Gwosdz .08
754 Kent Tekulve .08
755 Garry Maddox .08
756 Reds Batting & Pitching Leaders (Ron Oester, Mario Soto) .08
757 Larry Bowa .08
758 Bill Stein .08
759 Richard Dotson .08
760 Bob Horner .08
761 John Montefusco .08
762 Rance Mulliniks .08
763 Craig Swan .08
764 Mike Hargrove .08
765 Ken Forsch .08
766 Mike Vail .08
767 Carney Lansford .08
768 Champ Summers .08
769 Bill Caudill .08
770 Ken Griffey .08
771 Billy Gardner .08
772 Jim Slaton .08
773 Todd Cruz .08
774 Tom Gorman .08
775 Dave Parker .08
776 Craig Reynolds .08
777 Tom Paciorek .08
778 *Andy Hawkins* .15
779 Jim Sundberg .08
780 Steve Carlton 1.00
781 Checklist 661-792 .08
782 Steve Balboni .08
783 Luis Leal .08
784 Leon Roberts .08
785 Joaquin Andujar .08
786 Red Sox Batting & Pitching Leaders (Wade Boggs, Bob Ojeda) .30
787 Bill Campbell .08
788 Milt May .08
789 Bert Blyleven .08
790 Doug DeCinces .08
791 Terry Forster .08
792 Bill Russell .08

1984 Topps Tiffany

In 1984 Topps introduced a specially boxed, limited edition version of its baseball card set. Sold only through hobby dealers, the cards differed from regular-issue 1984 Topps cards in their use of white cardboard stock and the application of a high-gloss finish to the front of the card. Production was limited to a reported 10,000 sets. The nickname "Tiffany" was coined by collectors to identify the glossy collectors edition.

	MT
Complete Set (792):	200.00
Common Player:	.15
Stars:	6X

(See 1984 Topps for checklist and base card values.)

1984 Topps Traded

The popular Topps Traded set returned for its fourth year in 1984 with another 132-card set. The 2-1/2" x 3-1/2" cards have an identical design to the regular Topps cards except that the back cardboard is white and card numbers carry a "T" suffix. As before, the set was sold only through hobby dealers. Also as before, players who changed teams, new managers and promising rookies are included in the set. A glossy-finish "Tiffany" version of the set was also issued.

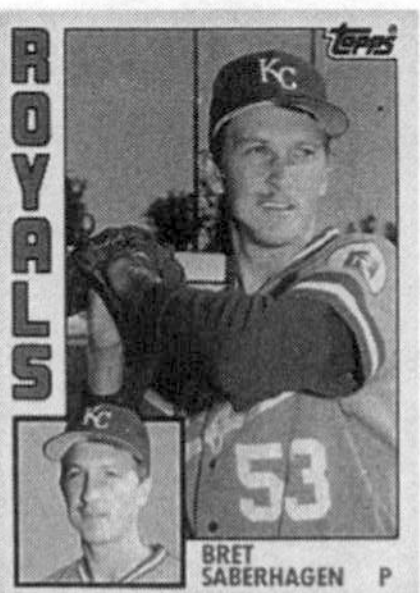

	MT
Complete Set (132):	35.00
Common Player:	.25

1T Willie Aikens .25
2T Luis Aponte .25
3T Mike Armstrong .25
4T Bob Bailor .25
5T Dusty Baker .50
6T Steve Balboni .25
7T Alan Bannister .25
8T Dave Beard .25
9T Joe Beckwith .25
10T Bruce Berenyi .25
11T Dave Bergman .25
12T Tony Bernazard .25
13T Yogi Berra .60
14T Barry Bonnell .25
15T Phil Bradley .25
16T Fred Breining .25
17T Bill Buckner .25
18T Ray Burris .25
19T John Butcher .25
20T Brett Butler .25
21T Enos Cabell .25
22T Bill Campbell .25
23T Bill Caudill .25
24T Bob Clark .25
25T Bryan Clark .25
26T Jaime Cocanower .25
27T *Ron Darling* 1.00
28T Alvin Davis .25
29T Ken Dayley .25
30T Jeff Dedmon .25
31T Bob Dernier .25
32T Carlos Diaz .25
33T Mike Easler .25
34T Dennis Eckersley 4.00
35T Jim Essian .25
36T Darrell Evans .35
37T Mike Fitzgerald .25
38T Tim Foli .25
39T George Frazier .25
40T Rich Gale .25
41T Barbaro Garbey .25
42T *Dwight Gooden* 4.00
43T Rich Gossage .40
44T Wayne Gross .25
45T Mark Gubicza .90
46T Jackie Gutierrez .25
47T Mel Hall .25
48T Toby Harrah .25
49T Ron Hassey .25
50T Rich Hebner .25
51T Willie Hernandez .25
52T Ricky Horton .25
53T Art Howe .25
54T Dane Iorg .25
55T Brook Jacoby .25
56T Mike Jeffcoat .25
57T Dave Johnson .25
58T Lynn Jones .25
59T Ruppert Jones .25
60T Mike Jorgensen .25
61T Bob Kearney .25
62T *Jimmy Key* 3.00
63T Dave Kingman .25
64T Jerry Koosman .25
65T Wayne Krenchicki .25
66T Rusty Kuntz .25
67T Rene Lachemann .25
68T Frank LaCorte .25
69T Dennis Lamp .25
70T *Mark Langston* 3.00
71T Rick Leach .25
72T Craig Lefferts .25
73T Gary Lucas .25
74T Jerry Martin .25
75T Carmelo Martinez .25
76T Mike Mason .25
77T Gary Matthews .25
78T Andy McGaffigan .25
79T Larry Milbourne .25
80T Sid Monge .25
81T Jackie Moore .25
82T Joe Morgan 3.00
83T Graig Nettles .25
84T Phil Niekro 3.00
85T Ken Oberkfell .25
86T Mike O'Berry .25
87T Al Oliver .25
88T Jorge Orta .25
89T Amos Otis .25
90T Dave Parker 1.50
91T Tony Perez 1.00
92T Gerald Perry .50
93T Gary Pettis .25
94T Rob Picciolo .25
95T Vern Rapp .25
96T Floyd Rayford .25
97T Randy Ready .25
98T Ron Reed .25
99T Gene Richards .25
100T *Jose Rijo* 1.50
101T Jeff Robinson .25
102T Ron Romanick .25
103T Pete Rose 8.00
104T *Bret Saberhagen* 6.00
105T Juan Samuel .50
106T Scott Sanderson .25
107T Dick Schofield .25
108T Tom Seaver 6.00
109T Jim Slaton .25
110T Mike Smithson .25
111T Lary Sorensen .25
112T Tim Stoddard .25
113T Champ Summers .25
114T Jim Sundberg .25
115T Rick Sutcliffe .25
116T Craig Swan .25
117T Tim Teufel .35
118T Derrel Thomas .25
119T Gorman Thomas .25
120T Alex Trevino .25
121T Manny Trillo .25
122T John Tudor .25
123T Tom Underwood .25
124T Mike Vail .25
125T Tom Waddell .25
126T Gary Ward .25
127T Curt Wilkerson .25
128T Frank Williams .25
129T Glenn Wilson .25
130T Johnny Wockenfuss .25
131T Ned Yost .25
132T Checklist 1-132 .25

1984 Topps Traded Tiffany

Following up on its inaugural Tiffany collectors edition, Topps produced a special glossy version of its Traded set for 1984, as well. Cards in this special boxed set differ from regular Traded cards only in the use of white cardboard stock with a high-gloss finish coat on front.

	MT
Complete Set (132):	50.00
Common Player:	.15
Stars:	4X

(See 1984 Topps Traded for checklist and base card values.)

1984 Topps All-Star Glossy Set of 22

These 2-1/2" x 3-1/2" cards were a result of the success of Topps' efforts the previous year with glossy cards on a mail-in basis. The set is divided evenly between the two leagues. Each All-Star Game starter for both leagues, the managers and the honorary team captains have an All-Star Glossy card. Cards feature a large color photo on the front with an All-Star banner across the top and the league emblem in the lower-left. Player identification appears below the photo. Backs have a name, team, position and card number along with the phrase "1983 All-Star Game Commemorative Set". The '84 Glossy All-Stars were distributed one card per rack pack.

		MT
Complete Set (22):		4.00
Common Player:		.10
1	Harvey Kuenn	.10
2	Rod Carew	.50
3	Manny Trillo	.10
4	George Brett	.75
5	Robin Yount	.75
6	Jim Rice	.25
7	Fred Lynn	.10
8	Dave Winfield	.50
9	Ted Simmons	.10
10	Dave Stieb	.10
11	Carl Yastrzemski	.50
12	Whitey Herzog	.10
13	Al Oliver	.10
14	Steve Sax	.10
15	Mike Schmidt	.75
16	Ozzie Smith	.50
17	Tim Raines	.35
18	Andre Dawson	.35
19	Dale Murphy	.35
20	Gary Carter	.35
21	Mario Soto	.10
22	Johnny Bench	.60

1984 Topps All-Star Glossy Set of 40

For the second straight year in 1984, Topps produced a 40-card All-Star "Collector's Edition" set as a "consolation prize" for its sweepstakes game. By collecting game cards and sending them in with a bit of cash, the collector could receive one of eight different five-card series. As the previous year, the 2-1/2" x 3-1/2" cards feature a nearly full-frame color photo on its glossy finish front. Backs are printed in red and blue.

		MT
Complete Set (40):		16.00
Common Player:		.15
1	Pete Rose	2.00
2	Lance Parrish	.15
3	Steve Rogers	.15
4	Eddie Murray	.90
5	Johnny Ray	.15
6	Rickey Henderson	.75
7	Atlee Hammaker	.15
8	Wade Boggs	.90
9	Gary Carter	.30
10	Jack Morris	.15
11	Darrell Evans	.15
12	George Brett	1.50
13	Bob Horner	.15
14	Ron Guidry	.15
15	Nolan Ryan	4.00
16	Dave Winfield	.50
17	Ozzie Smith	.75
18	Ted Simmons	.15
19	Bill Madlock	.15
20	Tony Armas	.15
21	Al Oliver	.15
22	Jim Rice	.25
23	George Hendrick	.15
24	Dave Stieb	.15
25	Pedro Guerrero	.15
26	Rod Carew	.60
27	Steve Carlton	.50
28	Dave Righetti	.15
29	Darryl Strawberry	.30
30	Lou Whitaker	.15
31	Dale Murphy	.35
32	LaMarr Hoyt	.15
33	Jesse Orosco	.15
34	Cecil Cooper	.15
35	Andre Dawson	.25
36	Robin Yount	1.00
37	Tim Raines	.25
38	Dan Quisenberry	.15
39	Mike Schmidt	1.50
40	Carlton Fisk	.25

1985 Topps

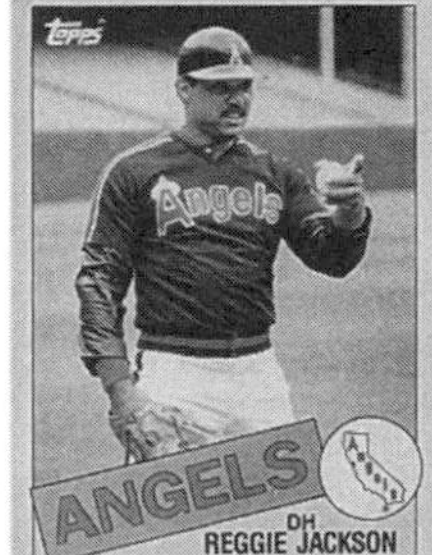

Holding the line at 792 cards, Topps initiated major design changes in its 2-1/2" x 3-1/2" cards in 1985. The use of two photos on the front was discontinued in favor of one large photo. The Topps logo appears in the upper-left corner. At bottom is a diagonal box with the team name. It joins a team logo, and below that point runs the player's position and name. The backs feature statistics, biographical information and a trivia question. Some interesting specialty sets were introduced in 1985, including the revival of the father/son theme from 1976, a subset of the 1984 U.S. Olympic Baseball Team members and a set featuring #1 draft choices since the inception of the baseball draft in 1965. Large numbers of uncut sheets were made available within the hobby, originally selling around $60 for a set of six.

		MT
Complete Set (792):		200.00
Complete Set, Uncut Sheets (6):		450.00
Common Player:		.05
Pack (15):		11.00
Wax Box (36):		340.00
1	Carlton Fisk (Record Breaker)	.25
2	Steve Garvey (Record Breaker)	.05
3	Dwight Gooden (Record Breaker)	.25
4	Cliff Johnson (Record Breaker)	.05
5	Joe Morgan (Record Breaker)	.05
6	Pete Rose (Record Breaker)	.50
7	Nolan Ryan (Record Breaker)	1.50
8	Juan Samuel (Record Breaker)	.05
9	Bruce Sutter (Record Breaker)	.05
10	Don Sutton (Record Breaker)	.05
11	Ralph Houk	.05
12	Dave Lopes	.05
13	Tim Lollar	.05
14	Chris Bando	.05
15	Jerry Koosman	.05
16	Bobby Meacham	.05
17	Mike Scott	.05
18	Mickey Hatcher	.05
19	George Frazier	.05
20	Chet Lemon	.05
21	Lee Tunnell	.05
22	Duane Kuiper	.05
23	Bret Saberhagen	1.25
24	Jesse Barfield	.05
25	Steve Bedrosian	.05
26	Roy Smalley	.05
27	Bruce Berenyi	.05
28	Dann Bilardello	.05
29	Odell Jones	.05
30	Cal Ripken, Jr.	4.00
31	Terry Whitfield	.05
32	Chuck Porter	.05
33	Tito Landrum	.05
34	Ed Nunez	.05
35	Graig Nettles	.05
36	Fred Breining	.05
37	Reid Nichols	.05
38	Jackie Moore	.05
39	Johnny Wockenfuss	.05
40	Phil Niekro	.40
41	Mike Fischlin	.05
42	Luis Sanchez	.05
43	Andre David	.05
44	Dickie Thon	.05
45	Greg Minton	.05
46	Gary Woods	.05
47	Dave Rozema	.05
48	Tony Fernandez	.15
49	Butch Davis	.05
50	John Candelaria	.05
51	Bob Watson	.05
52	Jerry Dybzinski	.05
53	Tom Gorman	.05
54	Cesar Cedeno	.05
55	Frank Tanana	.05
56	Jim Dwyer	.05
57	Pat Zachry	.05
58	Orlando Mercado	.05
59	Rick Waits	.05
60	George Hendrick	.05
61	Curt Kaufman	.05
62	Mike Ramsey	.05
63	Steve McCatty	.05
64	*Mark Bailey*	.05
65	Bill Buckner	.05
66	Dick Williams	.05
67	*Rafael Santana*	.05
68	Von Hayes	.05
69	*Jim Winn*	.05
70	Don Baylor	.10
71	Tim Laudner	.05
72	Rick Sutcliffe	.05
73	Rusty Kuntz	.05
74	Mike Krukow	.05
75	Willie Upshaw	.05
76	Alan Bannister	.05
77	Joe Beckwith	.05
78	Scott Fletcher	.05
79	Rick Mahler	.05
80	Keith Hernandez	.05
81	Lenn Sakata	.05
82	Joe Price	.05
83	Charlie Moore	.05
84	Spike Owen	.05
85	Mike Marshall	.05
86	Don Aase	.05
87	David Green	.05
88	Bryn Smith	.05
89	Jackie Gutierrez	.05
90	Rich Gossage	.05
91	Jeff Burroughs	.05
92	Paul Owens	.05
93	*Don Schulze*	.05
94	Toby Harrah	.05
95	Jose Cruz	.05
96	Johnny Ray	.05
97	Pete Filson	.05
98	Steve Lake	.05
99	Milt Wilcox	.05
100	George Brett	2.00
101	Jim Acker	.05
102	Tommy Dunbar	.05
103	Randy Lerch	.05
104	Mike Fitzgerald	.05
105	Ron Kittle	.05
106	Pascual Perez	.05
107	Tom Foley	.05
108	Darnell Coles	.05
109	Gary Roenicke	.05
110	Alejandro Pena	.05
111	Doug DeCinces	.05
112	Tom Tellmann	.05
113	Tom Herr	.05
114	Bob James	.05
115	Rickey Henderson	1.00
116	Dennis Boyd	.10
117	Greg Gross	.05
118	Eric Show	.05
119	Pat Corrales	.05
120	Steve Kemp	.05
121	Checklist 1-132	.05
122	Tom Brunansky	.05
123	Dave Smith	.05
124	Rich Hebner	.05
125	Kent Tekulve	.05
126	Ruppert Jones	.05
127	*Mark Gubicza*	.25
128	Ernie Whitt	.05
129	Gene Garber	.05
130	Al Oliver	.05
131	Father - Son (Buddy Bell, Gus Bell)	.10
132	Father - Son (Dale Berra, Yogi Berra)	.20
133	Father - Son (Bob Boone, Ray Boone)	.10
134	Father - Son (Terry Francona, Tito Francona)	.05
135	Father - Son (Bob Kennedy, Terry Kennedy)	.05

No.	Card	Price
136	Father - Son (Bill Kunkel, Jeff Kunkel)	.05
137	Father - Son (Vance Law, Vern Law)	.10
138	Father - Son (Dick Schofield, Dick Schofield, Jr.)	.05
139	Father - Son (Bob Skinner, Joel Skinner)	.05
140	Father - Son (Roy Smalley, Jr., Roy Smalley III)	.05
141	Father - Son (Dave Stenhouse, Mike Stenhouse)	.05
142	Father - Son (Dizzy Trout, Steve Trout)	.05
143	Father - Son (Ozzie Virgil, Ozzie Virgil)	.05
144	Ron Gardenhire	.05
145	*Alvin Davis*	.05
146	Gary Redus	.05
147	Bill Swaggerty	.05
148	Steve Yeager	.05
149	Dickie Noles	.05
150	Jim Rice	.10
151	Moose Haas	.05
152	Steve Braun	.05
153	Frank LaCorte	.05
154	Argenis Salazar	.05
155	Yogi Berra	.10
156	Craig Reynolds	.05
157	Tug McGraw	.05
158	Pat Tabler	.05
159	Carlos Diaz	.05
160	Lance Parrish	.05
161	Ken Schrom	.05
162	*Benny Distefano*	.05
163	Dennis Eckersley	.10
164	Jorge Orta	.05
165	Dusty Baker	.05
166	Keith Atherton	.05
167	Rufino Linares	.05
168	Garth Iorg	.05
169	Dan Spillner	.05
170	George Foster	.05
171	Bill Stein	.05
172	Jack Perconte	.05
173	Mike Young	.05
174	Rick Honeycutt	.05
175	Dave Parker	.05
176	Bill Schroeder	.05
177	Dave Von Ohlen	.05
178	Miguel Dilone	.05
179	Tommy John	.10
180	Dave Winfield	1.00
181	Roger Clemens	25.00
182	Tim Flannery	.05
183	Larry McWilliams	.05
184	Carmen Castillo	.05
185	Al Holland	.05
186	Bob Lillis	.05
187	Mike Walters	.05
188	Greg Pryor	.05
189	Warren Brusstar	.05
190	Rusty Staub	.05
191	Steve Nicosia	.05
192	Howard Johnson	.10
193	Jimmy Key	1.00
194	Dave Stegman	.05
195	Glenn Hubbard	.05
196	Pete O'Brien	.05
197	Mike Warren	.05
198	Eddie Milner	.05
199	Denny Martinez	.05
200	Reggie Jackson	.75
201	Burt Hooton	.05
202	Gorman Thomas	.05
203	Bob McClure	.05
204	Art Howe	.05
205	Steve Rogers	.05
206	Phil Garner	.05
207	Mark Clear	.05
208	Champ Summers	.05
209	Bill Campbell	.05
210	Gary Matthews	.05
211	Clay Christiansen	.05
212	George Vukovich	.05
213	Billy Gardner	.05
214	John Tudor	.05
215	Bob Brenly	.05
216	Jerry Don Gleaton	.05
217	Leon Roberts	.05
218	Doyle Alexander	.05
219	Gerald Perry	.05
220	Fred Lynn	.05
221	Ron Reed	.05
222	Hubie Brooks	.05
223	Tom Hume	.05
224	Al Cowens	.05
225	Mike Boddicker	.05
226	Juan Beniquez	.05
227	Danny Darwin	.05
228	Dion James	.05
229	Dave LaPoint	.05
230	Gary Carter	.25
231	Dwayne Murphy	.05
232	Dave Beard	.05
233	Ed Jurak	.05
234	Jerry Narron	.05
235	Garry Maddox	.05
236	Mark Thurmond	.05
237	Julio Franco	.10
238	Jose Rijo	.10
239	Tim Teufel	.05
240	Dave Stieb	.05
241	Jim Frey	.05
242	Greg Harris	.05
243	Barbaro Garbey	.05
244	Mike Jones	.05
245	Chili Davis	.10
246	Mike Norris	.05
247	Wayne Tolleson	.05
248	Terry Forster	.05
249	Harold Baines	.05
250	Jesse Orosco	.05
251	Brad Gulden	.05
252	Dan Ford	.05
253	*Sid Bream*	.10
254	Pete Vuckovich	.05
255	Lonnie Smith	.05
256	Mike Stanton	.05
257	Brian Little (Bryan)	.05
258	Mike Brown	.05
259	Gary Allenson	.05
260	Dave Righetti	.05
261	Checklist 133-264	.05
262	*Greg Booker*	.05
263	Mel Hall	.05
264	Joe Sambito	.05
265	Juan Samuel	.10
266	Frank Viola	.10
267	*Henry Cotto*	.05
268	Chuck Tanner	.05
269	*Doug Baker*	.05
270	Dan Quisenberry	.05
271	Tim Foli (#1 Draft Pick)	.05
272	Jeff Burroughs (#1 Draft Pick)	.05
273	Bill Almon (#1 Draft Pick)	.05
274	Floyd Bannister (#1 Draft Pick)	.05
275	Harold Baines (#1 Draft Pick)	.10
276	Bob Horner (#1 Draft Pick)	.10
277	Al Chambers (#1 Draft Pick)	.05
278	Darryl Strawberry (#1 Draft Pick)	.30
279	Mike Moore (#1 Draft Pick)	.10
280	*Shawon Dunston* (#1 Draft Pick)	.40
281	*Tim Belcher* (#1 Draft Pick)	.30
282	*Shawn Abner* (#1 Draft Pick)	.05
283	Fran Mullins	.05
284	Marty Bystrom	.05
285	Dan Driessen	.05
286	Rudy Law	.05
287	Walt Terrell	.05
288	*Jeff Kunkel*	.05
289	Tom Underwood	.05
290	Cecil Cooper	.05
291	Bob Welch	.05
292	Brad Komminsk	.05
293	*Curt Young*	.05
294	*Tom Nieto*	.05
295	Joe Niekro	.05
296	Ricky Nelson	.05
297	Gary Lucas	.05
298	Marty Barrett	.05
299	Andy Hawkins	.05
300	Rod Carew	.40
301	John Montefusco	.05
302	Tim Corcoran	.05
303	*Mike Jeffcoat*	.05
304	Gary Gaetti	.05
305	Dale Berra	.05
306	Rick Reuschel	.05
307	Sparky Anderson	.10
308	John Wathan	.05
309	Mike Witt	.05
310	Manny Trillo	.05
311	Jim Gott	.05
312	Marc Hill	.05
313	Dave Schmidt	.05
314	Ron Oester	.05
315	Doug Sisk	.05
316	John Lowenstein	.05
317	*Jack Lazorko*	.05
318	Ted Simmons	.05
319	Jeff Jones	.05
320	Dale Murphy	.25
321	*Ricky Horton*	.05
322	Dave Stapleton	.05
323	Andy McGaffigan	.05
324	Bruce Bochy	.05
325	John Denny	.05
326	Kevin Bass	.05
327	Brook Jacoby	.05
328	Bob Shirley	.05
329	Ron Washington	.05
330	Leon Durham	.05
331	Bill Laskey	.05
332	Brian Harper	.05
333	Willie Hernandez	.05
334	Dick Howser	.05
335	Bruce Benedict	.05
336	Rance Mulliniks	.05
337	Billy Sample	.05
338	Britt Burns	.05
339	Danny Heep	.05
340	Robin Yount	.75
341	Floyd Rayford	.05
342	Ted Power	.05
343	Bill Russell	.05
344	Dave Henderson	.05
345	Charlie Lea	.05
346	*Terry Pendleton*	.75
347	Rick Langford	.05
348	Bob Boone	.05
349	Domingo Ramos	.05
350	Wade Boggs	1.50
351	Juan Agosto	.05
352	Joe Morgan	.40
353	Julio Solano	.05
354	Andre Robertson	.05
355	Bert Blyleven	.05
356	Dave Meier	.05
357	Rich Bordi	.05
358	Tony Pena	.05
359	Pat Sheridan	.05
360	Steve Carlton	.45
361	Alfredo Griffin	.05
362	Craig McMurtry	.05
363	Ron Hodges	.05
364	Richard Dotson	.05
365	Danny Ozark	.05
366	Todd Cruz	.05
367	Keefe Cato	.05
368	Dave Bergman	.05
369	*R.J. Reynolds*	.10
370	Bruce Sutter	.05
371	Mickey Rivers	.05
372	Roy Howell	.05
373	Mike Moore	.05
374	Brian Downing	.05
375	Jeff Reardon	.05
376	Jeff Newman	.05
377	Checklist 265-396	.05
378	Alan Wiggins	.05
379	Charles Hudson	.05
380	Ken Griffey	.05
381	Roy Smith	.05
382	Denny Walling	.05
383	Rick Lysander	.05
384	Jody Davis	.05
385	Jose DeLeon	.05
386	*Dan Gladden*	.30
387	*Buddy Biancalana*	.05
388	Bert Roberge	.05
389	Rod Dedeaux (Team USA)	.05
390	Sid Akins (Team USA)	.05
391	Flavio Alfaro (Team USA)	.05
392	Don August (Team USA)	.10
393	*Scott Bankhead* (Team USA)	.10
394	Bob Caffrey (Team USA)	.05
395	Mike Dunne (Team USA)	.10
396	Gary Green (Team USA)	.10
397	John Hoover (Team USA)	.05
398	*Shane Mack* (Team USA)	.25
399	John Marzano (Team USA)	.10
400	Oddibe McDowell (Team USA)	.10
401	*Mark McGwire* (Team USA)	175.00
402	Pat Pacillo (Team USA)	.05
403	*Cory Snyder* (Team USA)	.30
404	*Billy Swift* (Team USA)	.40
405	Tom Veryzer	.05
406	Len Whitehouse	.05
407	Bobby Ramos	.05
408	Sid Monge	.05
409	Brad Wellman	.05
410	Bob Horner	.05
411	Bobby Cox	.05
412	Bud Black	.05
413	Vance Law	.05
414	Gary Ward	.05
415	Ron Darling	.05
416	Wayne Gross	.05
417	*John Franco*	.45
418	Ken Landreaux	.05
419	Mike Caldwell	.05
420	Andre Dawson	.60
421	Dave Rucker	.05
422	Carney Lansford	.05
423	Barry Bonnell	.05
424	*Al Nipper*	.05
425	Mike Hargrove	.05
426	Verne Ruhle	.05
427	Mario Ramirez	.05
428	Larry Andersen	.05
429	Rick Cerone	.05
430	Ron Davis	.05
431	U.L. Washington	.05
432	Thad Bosley	.05
433	Jim Morrison	.05
434	Gene Richards	.05
435	Dan Petry	.05
436	Willie Aikens	.05
437	Al Jones	.05
438	Joe Torre	.10
439	Junior Ortiz	.05
440	Fernando Valenzuela	.10
441	Duane Walker	.05
442	Ken Forsch	.05
443	George Wright	.05
444	Tony Phillips	.05
445	Tippy Martinez	.05
446	Jim Sundberg	.05
447	Jeff Lahti	.05
448	Derrel Thomas	.05
449	*Phil Bradley*	.10
450	Steve Garvey	.25
451	Bruce Hurst	.05
452	John Castino	.05
453	Tom Waddell	.05
454	Glenn Wilson	.05
455	Bob Knepper	.05
456	Tim Foli	.05
457	Cecilio Guante	.05
458	Randy S. Johnson	.05
459	Charlie Leibrandt	.05
460	Ryne Sandberg	2.50
461	Marty Castillo	.05
462	Gary Lavelle	.05
463	Dave Collins	.05
464	*Mike Mason*	.05
465	Bob Grich	.05
466	Tony LaRussa	.10
467	Ed Lynch	.05
468	Wayne Krenchicki	.05
469	Sammy Stewart	.05
470	Steve Sax	.05
471	Pete Ladd	.05
472	Jim Essian	.05
473	Tim Wallach	.05
474	Kurt Kepshire	.05
475	Andre Thornton	.05
476	*Jeff Stone*	.05
477	Bob Ojeda	.05
478	Kurt Bevacqua	.05
479	Mike Madden	.05
480	Lou Whitaker	.10
481	Dale Murray	.05
482	Harry Spilman	.05
483	Mike Smithson	.05
484	Larry Bowa	.05
485	Matt Young	.05
486	Steve Balboni	.05
487	*Frank Williams*	.05
488	Joel Skinner	.05
489	Bryan Clark	.05
490	Jason Thompson	.05
491	Rick Camp	.05
492	Dave Johnson	.05
493	*Orel Hershiser*	1.50
494	Rich Dauer	.05

#	Player	MT
495	Mario Soto	.05
496	Donnie Scott	.05
497	Gary Pettis	.05
498	Ed Romero	.05
499	Danny Cox	.05
500	Mike Schmidt	1.50
501	Dan Schatzeder	.05
502	Rick Miller	.05
503	Tim Conroy	.05
504	Jerry Willard	.05
505	Jim Beattie	.05
506	*Franklin Stubbs*	.05
507	Ray Fontenot	.05
508	John Shelby	.05
509	Milt May	.05
510	Kent Hrbek	.05
511	Lee Smith	.10
512	Tom Brookens	.05
513	Lynn Jones	.05
514	Jeff Cornell	.05
515	Dave Concepcion	.05
516	Roy Lee Jackson	.05
517	Jerry Martin	.05
518	Chris Chambliss	.05
519	Doug Rader	.05
520	LaMarr Hoyt	.05
521	Rick Dempsey	.05
522	Paul Molitor	.75
523	Candy Maldonado	.05
524	Rob Wilfong	.05
525	Darrell Porter	.05
526	Dave Palmer	.05
527	Checklist 397-528	.05
528	Bill Krueger	.05
529	Rich Gedman	.05
530	Dave Dravecky	.05
531	Joe Lefebvre	.05
532	Frank DiPino	.05
533	Tony Bernazard	.05
534	Brian Dayett	.05
535	Pat Putnam	.05
536	Kirby Puckett	7.00
537	Don Robinson	.05
538	Keith Moreland	.05
539	Aurelio Lopez	.05
540	Claudell Washington	.05
541	Mark Davis	.05
542	Don Slaught	.05
543	Mike Squires	.05
544	Bruce Kison	.05
545	Lloyd Moseby	.05
546	Brent Gaff	.05
547	Pete Rose	1.00
548	Larry Parrish	.05
549	Mike Scioscia	.05
550	Scott McGregor	.05
551	Andy Van Slyke	.05
552	Chris Codiroli	.05
553	Bob Clark	.05
554	Doug Flynn	.05
555	Bob Stanley	.05
556	Sixto Lezcano	.05
557	Len Barker	.05
558	Carmelo Martinez	.05
559	Jay Howell	.05
560	Bill Madlock	.05
561	Darryl Motley	.05
562	Houston Jimenez	.05
563	Dick Ruthven	.05
564	Alan Ashby	.05
565	Kirk Gibson	.05
566	Ed Vande Berg	.05
567	Joel Youngblood	.05
568	Cliff Johnson	.05
569	Ken Oberkfell	.05
570	Darryl Strawberry	.30
571	Charlie Hough	.05
572	Tom Paciorek	.05
573	*Jay Tibbs*	.05
574	Joe Altobelli	.05
575	Pedro Guerrero	.05
576	Jaime Cocanower	.05
577	Chris Speier	.05
578	Terry Francona	.05
579	*Ron Romanick*	.05
580	Dwight Evans	.05
581	Mark Wagner	.05
582	Ken Phelps	.05
583	Bobby Brown	.05
584	Kevin Gross	.05
585	Butch Wynegar	.05
586	Bill Scherrer	.05
587	Doug Frobel	.05
588	Bobby Castillo	.05
589	Bob Dernier	.05
590	Ray Knight	.05
591	Larry Herndon	.05
592	*Jeff Robinson*	.05
593	Rick Leach	.05
594	Curt Wilkerson	.05
595	Larry Gura	.05
596	Jerry Hairston	.05
597	Brad Lesley	.05
598	Jose Oquendo	.05
599	Storm Davis	.05
600	Pete Rose	1.00
601	Tom Lasorda	.20
602	*Jeff Dedmon*	.05
603	Rick Manning	.05
604	Daryl Sconiers	.05
605	Ozzie Smith	.75
606	Rich Gale	.05
607	Bill Almon	.05
608	Craig Lefferts	.05
609	Broderick Perkins	.05
610	Jack Morris	.05
611	Ozzie Virgil	.05
612	Mike Armstrong	.05
613	Terry Puhl	.05
614	Al Williams	.05
615	Marvell Wynne	.05
616	Scott Sanderson	.05
617	Willie Wilson	.05
618	Pete Falcone	.05
619	Jeff Leonard	.05
620	Dwight Gooden	1.00
621	Marvis Foley	.05
622	Luis Leal	.05
623	Greg Walker	.05
624	Benny Ayala	.05
625	Mark Langston	1.00
626	German Rivera	.05
627	*Eric Davis*	.45
628	Rene Lachemann	.05
629	Dick Schofield	.05
630	Tim Raines	.15
631	Bob Forsch	.05
632	Bruce Bochte	.05
633	Glenn Hoffman	.05
634	Bill Dawley	.05
635	Terry Kennedy	.05
636	Shane Rawley	.05
637	Brett Butler	.05
638	*Mike Pagliarulo*	.10
639	Ed Hodge	.05
640	Steve Henderson	.05
641	Rod Scurry	.05
642	Dave Owen	.05
643	Johnny Grubb	.05
644	Mark Huismann	.05
645	Damaso Garcia	.05
646	Scot Thompson	.05
647	Rafael Ramirez	.05
648	Bob Jones	.05
649	Sid Fernandez	.05
650	Greg Luzinski	.05
651	Jeff Russell	.05
652	Joe Nolan	.05
653	Mark Brouhard	.05
654	Dave Anderson	.05
655	Joaquin Andujar	.05
656	Chuck Cottier	.05
657	Jim Slaton	.05
658	Mike Stenhouse	.05
659	Checklist 529-660	.05
660	Tony Gwynn	3.00
661	Steve Crawford	.05
662	Mike Heath	.05
663	Luis Aguayo	.05
664	*Steve Farr*	.20
665	Don Mattingly	3.00
666	Mike LaCoss	.05
667	Dave Engle	.05
668	Steve Trout	.05
669	Lee Lacy	.05
670	Tom Seaver	.40
671	Dane Iorg	.05
672	Juan Berenguer	.05
673	Buck Martinez	.05
674	Atlee Hammaker	.05
675	Tony Perez	.10
676	*Albert Hall*	.05
677	Wally Backman	.05
678	Joey McLaughlin	.05
679	Bob Kearney	.05
680	Jerry Reuss	.05
681	Ben Oglivie	.05
682	Doug Corbett	.05
683	Whitey Herzog	.05
684	Bill Doran	.05
685	Bill Caudill	.05
686	Mike Easler	.05
687	Bill Gullickson	.05
688	Len Matuszek	.05
689	Luis DeLeon	.05
690	Alan Trammell	.10
691	Dennis Rasmussen	.05
692	Randy Bush	.05
693	Tim Stoddard	.05
694	Joe Carter	3.00
695	Rick Rhoden	.05
696	John Rabb	.05
697	Onix Concepcion	.05
698	Jorge Bell	.10
699	Donnie Moore	.05
700	Eddie Murray	1.25
701	Eddie Murray (All-Star)	.40
702	Damaso Garcia (All-Star)	.05
703	George Brett (All-Star)	.50
704	Cal Ripken, Jr. (All-Star)	2.00
705	Dave Winfield (All-Star)	.50
706	Rickey Henderson (All-Star)	.25
707	Tony Armas (All-Star)	.05
708	Lance Parrish (All-Star)	.05
709	Mike Boddicker (All-Star)	.05
710	Frank Viola (All-Star)	.05
711	Dan Quisenberry (All-Star)	.05
712	Keith Hernandez (All-Star)	.05
713	Ryne Sandberg (All-Star)	.60
714	Mike Schmidt (All-Star)	.45
715	Ozzie Smith (All-Star)	.25
716	Dale Murphy (All-Star)	.15
717	Tony Gwynn (All-Star)	.75
718	Jeff Leonard (All-Star)	.05
719	Gary Carter (All-Star)	.10
720	Rick Sutcliffe (All-Star)	.05
721	Bob Knepper (All-Star)	.05
722	Bruce Sutter (All-Star)	.05
723	Dave Stewart	.05
724	Oscar Gamble	.05
725	Floyd Bannister	.05
726	Al Bumbry	.05
727	Frank Pastore	.05
728	Bob Bailor	.05
729	Don Sutton	.30
730	Dave Kingman	.05
731	Neil Allen	.05
732	John McNamara	.05
733	Tony Scott	.05
734	John Henry Johnson	.05
735	Garry Templeton	.05
736	Jerry Mumphrey	.05
737	Bo Diaz	.05
738	Omar Moreno	.05
739	Ernie Camacho	.05
740	Jack Clark	.05
741	John Butcher	.05
742	Ron Hassey	.05
743	Frank White	.05
744	Doug Bair	.05
745	Buddy Bell	.05
746	Jim Clancy	.05
747	Alex Trevino	.05
748	Lee Mazzilli	.05
749	Julio Cruz	.05
750	Rollie Fingers	.25
751	Kelvin Chapman	.05
752	Bob Owchinko	.05
753	Greg Brock	.05
754	Larry Milbourne	.05
755	Ken Singleton	.05
756	Rob Picciolo	.05
757	Willie McGee	.05
758	Ray Burris	.05
759	Jim Fanning	.05
760	Nolan Ryan	5.00
761	Jerry Remy	.05
762	Eddie Whitson	.05
763	Kiko Garcia	.05
764	Jamie Easterly	.05
765	Willie Randolph	.05
766	Paul Mirabella	.05
767	Darrell Brown	.05
768	Ron Cey	.05
769	Joe Cowley	.05
770	Carlton Fisk	.45
771	Geoff Zahn	.05
772	Johnnie LeMaster	.05
773	Hal McRae	.05
774	Dennis Lamp	.05
775	Mookie Wilson	.05
776	Jerry Royster	.05
777	Ned Yost	.05
778	Mike Davis	.05
779	Nick Esasky	.05
780	Mike Flanagan	.05
781	Jim Gantner	.05
782	Tom Niedenfuer	.05
783	Mike Jorgensen	.05
784	Checklist 661-792	.05
785	Tony Armas	.05
786	Enos Cabell	.05
787	Jim Wohlford	.05
788	Steve Comer	.05
789	Luis Salazar	.05
790	Ron Guidry	.10
791	Ivan DeJesus	.05
792	Darrell Evans	.10

1985 Topps Tiffany

In its second year of producing a high-gloss collectors edition of its regular baseball card set, Topps cut production to a reported 5,000 sets. Other than the use of white cardboard stock and the glossy front coating, the cards in this specially boxed set are identical to regular 1985 Topps cards.

	MT
Complete Unopened Set (792):	1250.
Complete Set, Opened (792):	700.00
Common Player:	.25
Stars:	4X

(See 1985 Topps for checklist and base card values.)

1985 Topps Traded

Topps continued the annual Traded set tradition with another 132-card set. The 2-1/2" x 3-1/2" cards follow the pattern of being virtually identical in design to the regular cards of that year. Sold only through hobby dealers, the set features traded veterans and promising rookies. A glossy-finish "Tiffany" edition of the set was also issued. Cards are numbered with a "T" suffix.

	MT
Complete Set (132):	8.00
Common Player:	.10
Wax Test Pack (8):	3.25
Wax Test Wax Box (36):	75.00

#	Player	MT
1	Don Aase	.10
2	Bill Almon	.10

3	Benny Ayala	.10
4	Dusty Baker	.15
5	George Bamberger	.10
6	Dale Berra	.10
7	Rich Bordi	.10
8	Daryl Boston	.10
9	Hubie Brooks	.10
10	Chris Brown	.10
11	Tom Browning	.50
12	Al Bumbry	.10
13	Ray Burris	.10
14	Jeff Burroughs	.10
15	Bill Campbell	.10
16	Don Carman	.10
17	Gary Carter	.45
18	Bobby Castillo	.10
19	Bill Caudill	.10
20	Rick Cerone	.10
21	Bryan Clark	.10
22	Jack Clark	.10
23	Pat Clements	.10
24	*Vince Coleman*	.60
25	Dave Collins	.10
26	Danny Darwin	.10
27	Jim Davenport	.10
28	Jerry Davis	.10
29	Brian Dayett	.10
30	Ivan DeJesus	.10
31	Ken Dixon	.10
32	Mariano Duncan	.50
33	John Felske	.10
34	Mike Fitzgerald	.10
35	Ray Fontenot	.10
36	Greg Gagne	.35
37	Oscar Gamble	.10
38	Scott Garrelts	.15
39	Bob L. Gibson	.10
40	Jim Gott	.10
41	David Green	.10
42	Alfredo Griffin	.10
43	*Ozzie Guillen*	1.25
44	Eddie Haas	.10
45	Terry Harper	.10
46	Toby Harrah	.10
47	Greg Harris	.10
48	Ron Hassey	.10
49	Rickey Henderson	2.00
50	Steve Henderson	.10
51	George Hendrick	.10
52	Joe Hesketh	.10
53	Teddy Higuera	.10
54	Donnie Hill	.10
55	Al Holland	.10
56	Burt Hooton	.10
57	Jay Howell	.10
58	Ken Howell	.15
59	LaMarr Hoyt	.10
60	Tim Hulett	.10
61	Bob James	.10
62	Steve Jeltz	.10
63	Cliff Johnson	.10
64	Howard Johnson	.25
65	Ruppert Jones	.10
66	Steve Kemp	.10
67	Bruce Kison	.10
68	Alan Knicely	.10
69	Mike LaCoss	.10
70	Lee Lacy	.10
71	Dave LaPoint	.10
72	Gary Lavelle	.10
73	Vance Law	.10
74	Johnnie LeMaster	.10
75	Sixto Lezcano	.10
76	Tim Lollar	.10
77	Fred Lynn	.15
78	Billy Martin	.25
79	Ron Mathis	.10
80	Len Matuszek	.10
81	Gene Mauch	.10
82	Oddibe McDowell	.10
83	Roger McDowell	.50
84	John McNamara	.10
85	Donnie Moore	.10
86	Gene Nelson	.10
87	Steve Nicosia	.10
88	Al Oliver	.10
89	Joe Orsulak	.15
90	Rob Picciolo	.10
91	Chris Pittaro	.10
92	Jim Presley	.10
93	Rick Reuschel	.10
94	Bert Roberge	.10
95	Bob Rodgers	.10
96	Jerry Royster	.10
97	Dave Rozema	.10
98	Dave Rucker	.10
99	Vern Ruhle	.10
100	Paul Runge	.10
101	Mark Salas	.10
102	Luis Salazar	.10
103	Joe Sambito	.10
104	Rick Schu	.10
105	Donnie Scott	.10
106	Larry Sheets	.10
107	Don Slaught	.10
108	Roy Smalley	.10
109	Lonnie Smith	.10
110	Nate Snell	.10
111	Chris Speier	.10
112	Mike Stenhouse	.10
113	Tim Stoddard	.10
114	Jim Sundberg	.10
115	Bruce Sutter	.10
116	Don Sutton	1.00
117	Kent Tekulve	.10
118	Tom Tellmann	.10
119	Walt Terrell	.10
120	*Mickey Tettleton*	1.00
121	Derrel Thomas	.10
122	Rich Thompson	.10
123	Alex Trevino	.10
124	John Tudor	.10
125	Jose Uribe	.10
126	Bobby Valentine	.10
127	Dave Von Ohlen	.10
128	U.L. Washington	.10
129	Earl Weaver	.25
130	Eddie Whitson	.10
131	Herm Winningham	.10
132	Checklist 1-132	.10

1985 Topps Traded Tiffany

This specially boxed collectors version of the Topps Traded sets features cards that differ only in the use of a high-gloss finish coat on the fronts.

	MT
Complete Set (132):	40.00
Common Player:	.25
Stars:	4X

(See 1985 Topps Traded for checklist and base card values.)

1985 Topps All-Star Glossy Set of 22

This was the second straight year for this set of 22 cards featuring the starting players, honorary captains and managers in the All-Star Game. The set is virtually identical to that of the previous year in design with a color photo, All-Star banner, league emblem, and player ID on the front. Fronts have a high-gloss finish. The cards were available as inserts in Topps rack packs.

		MT
Complete Set (22):		3.00
Common Player:		.10
1	Paul Owens	.10
2	Steve Garvey	.30
3	Ryne Sandberg	.60
4	Mike Schmidt	.75
5	Ozzie Smith	.50
6	Tony Gwynn	.75
7	Dale Murphy	.30
8	Darryl Strawberry	.30
9	Gary Carter	.30
10	Charlie Lea	.10
11	Willie McCovey	.35
12	Joe Altobelli	.10
13	Rod Carew	.40
14	Lou Whitaker	.10
15	George Brett	.75
16	Cal Ripken, Jr.	1.00
17	Dave Winfield	.35
18	Chet Lemon	.10
19	Reggie Jackson	.45
20	Lance Parrish	.10
21	Dave Stieb	.10
22	Hank Greenberg	.25

1985 Topps All-Star Glossy Set of 40

Similar to previous years' glossy sets, the 1985 All-Star "Collector's Edition" set of 40 could be obtained through the mail in eight five-card subsets. To obtain the 2-1/2" x 3-1/2" cards, collectors had to accumulate sweepstakes insert cards from Topps packs, and pay 75U postage and handling. Under the circumstances, the complete set of 40 cards was not inexpensive.

		MT
Complete Set (40):		8.00
Common Player:		.10
1	Dale Murphy	.30
2	Jesse Orosco	.10
3	Bob Brenly	.10
4	Mike Boddicker	.10
5	Dave Kingman	.10
6	Jim Rice	.25
7	Frank Viola	.10
8	Alvin Davis	.10
9	Rick Sutcliffe	.10
10	Pete Rose	1.50
11	Leon Durham	.10
12	Joaquin Andujar	.10
13	Keith Hernandez	.10
14	Dave Winfield	.40
15	Reggie Jackson	.50
16	Alan Trammell	.25
17	Bert Blyleven	.10
18	Tony Armas	.10
19	Rich Gossage	.10
20	Jose Cruz	.10
21	Ryne Sandberg	.75
22	Bruce Sutter	.10
23	Mike Schmidt	1.00
24	Cal Ripken, Jr.	2.00
25	Dan Petry	.10
26	Jack Morris	.10
27	Don Mattingly	1.00
28	Eddie Murray	.60
29	Tony Gwynn	.75
30	Charlie Lea	.10
31	Juan Samuel	.10
32	Phil Niekro	.25
33	Alejandro Pena	.10
34	Harold Baines	.10
35	Dan Quisenberry	.10
36	Gary Carter	.20
37	Mario Soto	.10
38	Dwight Gooden	.25
39	Tom Brunansky	.10
40	Dave Stieb	.10

1986 Topps

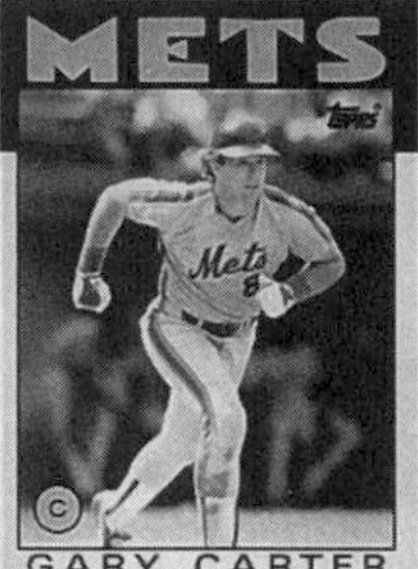

The 1986 Topps set consists of 792 cards. Fronts of the 2-1/2" x 3-1/2" cards feature color photos with the Topps logo in the upper right-hand corner while the player's position is in the lower left-hand corner. Above the picture is the team name, while below it is the player's name. The borders are a departure from previous practice, as the top 7/8" is black, while the remainder is white. Once again, a 5,000-set glossy-finish "Tiffany" edition was produced.

		MT
Complete Set (792):		25.00
Common Player:		.05
Wax Box:		30.00
1	Pete Rose	.50
2	Pete Rose (Special 1963-66)	.25
3	Pete Rose (Special 1967-70)	.25
4	Pete Rose (Special 1971-74)	.25
5	Pete Rose (Special 1975-78)	.25
6	Pete Rose (Special 1972-82)	.25
7	Pete Rose (Special 1983-85)	.25
8	Dwayne Murphy	.05
9	Roy Smith	.05
10	Tony Gwynn	1.00
11	Bob Ojeda	.05
12	*Jose Uribe*	.05
13	Bob Kearney	.05
14	Julio Cruz	.05
15	Eddie Whitson	.05
16	Rick Schu	.05
17	Mike Stenhouse	.05
18	Brent Gaff	.05
19	Rich Hebner	.05
20	Lou Whitaker	.05
21	George Bamberger	.05
22	Duane Walker	.05
23	*Manny Lee*	.05
24	Len Barker	.05
25	Willie Wilson	.05
26	Frank DiPino	.05
27	Ray Knight	.05
28	Eric Davis	.10
29	Tony Phillips	.05
30	Eddie Murray	.40
31	Jamie Easterly	.05
32	Steve Yeager	.05
33	Jeff Lahti	.05
34	Ken Phelps	.05

No.	Player	Value
35	Jeff Reardon	.05
36	Tigers Leaders (Lance Parrish)	.05
37	Mark Thurmond	.05
38	Glenn Hoffman	.05
39	Dave Rucker	.05
40	Ken Griffey	.10
41	Brad Wellman	.05
42	Geoff Zahn	.05
43	Dave Engle	.05
44	*Lance McCullers*	.05
45	Damaso Garcia	.05
46	Billy Hatcher	.05
47	Juan Berenguer	.05
48	Bill Almon	.05
49	Rick Manning	.05
50	Dan Quisenberry	.05
51	Not issued, see #57	
52	Chris Welsh	.05
53	*Len Dykstra*	.50
54	John Franco	.05
55	Fred Lynn	.05
56	Tom Niedenfuer	.05
57a	Bill Doran	.05
57b	Bobby Wine (supposed to be #51)	.05
58	Bill Krueger	.05
59	Andre Thornton	.05
60	Dwight Evans	.05
61	Karl Best	.05
62	Bob Boone	.05
63	Ron Roenicke	.05
64	Floyd Bannister	.05
65	Dan Driessen	.05
66	Cardinals Leaders (Bob Forsch)	.05
67	Carmelo Martinez	.05
68	Ed Lynch	.05
69	Luis Aguayo	.05
70	Dave Winfield	.40
71	Ken Schrom	.05
72	Shawon Dunston	.05
73	Randy O'Neal	.05
74	Rance Mulliniks	.05
75	Jose DeLeon	.05
76	Dion James	.05
77	Charlie Leibrandt	.05
78	Bruce Benedict	.05
79	Dave Schmidt	.05
80	Darryl Strawberry	.20
81	Gene Mauch	.05
82	Tippy Martinez	.05
83	Phil Garner	.05
84	Curt Young	.05
85	Tony Perez	.25
86	Tom Waddell	.05
87	Candy Maldonado	.05
88	Tom Nieto	.05
89	Randy St. Claire	.05
90	Garry Templeton	.05
91	Steve Crawford	.05
92	Al Cowens	.05
93	Scot Thompson	.05
94	Rich Bordi	.05
95	Ozzie Virgil	.05
96	Blue Jay Leaders (Jim Clancy)	.05
97	Gary Gaetti	.10
98	Dick Ruthven	.05
99	Buddy Biancalana	.05
100	Nolan Ryan	2.00
101	Dave Bergman	.05
102	*Joe Orsulak*	.15
103	Luis Salazar	.05
104	Sid Fernandez	.05
105	Gary Ward	.05
106	Ray Burris	.05
107	Rafael Ramirez	.05
108	Ted Power	.05
109	Len Matuszek	.05
110	Scott McGregor	.05
111	Roger Craig	.05
112	Bill Campbell	.05
113	U.L. Washington	.05
114	Mike Brown	.05
115	Jay Howell	.05
116	Brook Jacoby	.05
117	Bruce Kison	.05
118	Jerry Royster	.05
119	Barry Bonnell	.05
120	Steve Carlton	.30
121	Nelson Simmons	.05
122	Pete Filson	.05
123	Greg Walker	.05
124	Luis Sanchez	.05
125	Dave Lopes	.05
126	Mets Leaders (Mookie Wilson)	.05
127	*Jack Howell*	.05
128	John Wathan	.05
129	Jeff Dedmon	.05
130	Alan Trammell	.15
131	Checklist 1-132	.05
132	Razor Shines	.05
133	Andy McGaffigan	.05
134	Carney Lansford	.05
135	Joe Niekro	.05
136	Mike Hargrove	.05
137	Charlie Moore	.05
138	Mark Davis	.05
139	Daryl Boston	.05
140	John Candelaria	.05
141a	Chuck Cottier	.05
141b	Bob Rodgers (supposed to be #171)	.05
142	Bob Jones	.05
143	Dave Van Gorder	.05
144	Doug Sisk	.05
145	Pedro Guerrero	.05
146	Jack Perconte	.05
147	Larry Sheets	.05
148	Mike Heath	.05
149	Brett Butler	.05
150	Joaquin Andujar	.05
151	Dave Stapleton	.05
152	Mike Morgan	.05
153	Ricky Adams	.05
154	Bert Roberge	.05
155	Bob Grich	.05
156	White Sox Leaders (Richard Dotson)	.05
157	Ron Hassey	.05
158	Derrel Thomas	.05
159	Orel Hershiser	.15
160	Chet Lemon	.05
161	Lee Tunnell	.05
162	Greg Gagne	.05
163	Pete Ladd	.05
164	Steve Balboni	.05
165	Mike Davis	.05
166	Dickie Thon	.05
167	Zane Smith	.05
168	Jeff Burroughs	.05
169	George Wright	.05
170	Gary Carter	.20
171	Not issued, see #141	
172	Jerry Reed	.05
173	Wayne Gross	.05
174	Brian Snyder	.05
175	Steve Sax	.05
176	Jay Tibbs	.05
177	Joel Youngblood	.05
178	Ivan DeJesus	.05
179	*Stu Cliburn*	.05
180	Don Mattingly	.75
181	Al Nipper	.05
182	Bobby Brown	.05
183	Larry Andersen	.05
184	Tim Laudner	.05
185	Rollie Fingers	.20
186	Astros Leaders (Jose Cruz)	.05
187	Scott Fletcher	.05
188	Bob Dernier	.05
189	Mike Mason	.05
190	George Hendrick	.05
191	Wally Backman	.05
192	Milt Wilcox	.05
193	Daryl Sconiers	.05
194	Craig McMurtry	.05
195	Dave Concepcion	.05
196	Doyle Alexander	.05
197	Enos Cabell	.05
198	Ken Dixon	.05
199	Dick Howser	.05
200	Mike Schmidt	.75
201	Vince Coleman (Record Breaker)	.05
202	Dwight Gooden (Record Breaker)	.05
203	Keith Hernandez (Record Breaker)	.05
204	Phil Niekro (Record Breaker)	.15
205	Tony Perez (Record Breaker)	.10
206	Pete Rose (Record Breaker)	.25
207	Fernando Valenzuela (Record Breaker)	.05
208	Ramon Romero	.05
209	Randy Ready	.05
210	Calvin Schiraldi	.05
211	Ed Wojna	.05
212	Chris Speier	.05
213	Bob Shirley	.05
214	Randy Bush	.05
215	Frank White	.05
216	A's Leaders (Dwayne Murphy)	.05
217	Bill Scherrer	.05
218	Randy Hunt	.05
219	Dennis Lamp	.05
220	Bob Horner	.05
221	Dave Henderson	.05
222	Craig Gerber	.05
223	Atlee Hammaker	.05
224	Cesar Cedeno	.05
225	Ron Darling	.05
226	Lee Lacy	.05
227	Al Jones	.05
228	Tom Lawless	.05
229	Bill Gullickson	.05
230	Terry Kennedy	.05
231	Jim Frey	.05
232	Rick Rhoden	.05
233	Steve Lyons	.05
234	Doug Corbett	.05
235	Butch Wynegar	.05
236	Frank Eufemia	.05
237	Ted Simmons	.05
238	Larry Parrish	.05
239	Joel Skinner	.05
240	Tommy John	.10
241	Tony Fernandez	.05
242	Rich Thompson	.05
243	Johnny Grubb	.05
244	Craig Lefferts	.05
245	Jim Sundberg	.05
246	Phillies Leaders (Steve Carlton)	.10
247	Terry Harper	.05
248	Spike Owen	.05
249	Rob Deer	.05
250	Dwight Gooden	.25
251	Rich Dauer	.05
252	Bobby Castillo	.05
253	Dann Bilardello	.05
254	*Ozzie Guillen*	.30
255	Tony Armas	.05
256	Kurt Kepshire	.05
257	Doug DeCinces	.05
258	*Tim Burke*	.05
259	Dan Pasqua	.05
260	Tony Pena	.05
261	Bobby Valentine	.05
262	Mario Ramirez	.05
263	Checklist 133-264	.05
264	Darren Daulton	.15
265	Ron Davis	.05
266	Keith Moreland	.05
267	Paul Molitor	.75
268	Mike Scott	.05
269	Dane Iorg	.05
270	Jack Morris	.05
271	Dave Collins	.05
272	Tim Tolman	.05
273	Jerry Willard	.05
274	Ron Gardenhire	.05
275	Charlie Hough	.05
276	Yankees Leaders (Willie Randolph)	.05
277	Jaime Cocanower	.05
278	Sixto Lezcano	.05
279	Al Pardo	.05
280	Tim Raines	.12
281	Steve Mura	.05
282	Jerry Mumphrey	.05
283	Mike Fischlin	.05
284	Brian Dayett	.05
285	Buddy Bell	.05
286	Luis DeLeon	.05
287	*John Christensen*	.05
288	Don Aase	.05
289	Johnnie LeMaster	.05
290	Carlton Fisk	.30
291	Tom Lasorda	.20
292	Chuck Porter	.05
293	Chris Chambliss	.05
294	Danny Cox	.05
295	Kirk Gibson	.05
296	Geno Petralli	.05
297	Tim Lollar	.05
298	Craig Reynolds	.05
299	Bryn Smith	.05
300	George Brett	.75
301	Dennis Rasmussen	.05
302	Greg Gross	.05
303	Curt Wardle	.05
304	*Mike Gallego*	.12
305	Phil Bradley	.05
306	Padres Leaders (Terry Kennedy)	.05
307	Dave Sax	.05
308	Ray Fontenot	.05
309	John Shelby	.05
310	Greg Minton	.05
311	Dick Schofield	.05
312	Tom Filer	.05
313	Joe DeSa	.05
314	Frank Pastore	.05
315	Mookie Wilson	.05
316	Sammy Khalifa	.05
317	Ed Romero	.05
318	Terry Whitfield	.05
319	Rick Camp	.05
320	Jim Rice	.10
321	Earl Weaver	.20
322	Bob Forsch	.05
323	Jerry Davis	.05
324	Dan Schatzeder	.05
325	Juan Beniquez	.05
326	Kent Tekulve	.05
327	Mike Pagliarulo	.05
328	Pete O'Brien	.05
329	Kirby Puckett	2.00
330	Rick Sutcliffe	.05
331	Alan Ashby	.05
332	Darryl Motley	.05
333	Tom Henke	.05
334	Ken Oberkfell	.05
335	Don Sutton	.25
336	Indians Leaders (Andre Thornton)	.05
337	Darnell Coles	.05
338	Jorge Bell	.10
339	Bruce Berenyi	.05
340	Cal Ripken, Jr.	2.00
341	Frank Williams	.05
342	Gary Redus	.05
343	Carlos Diaz	.05
344	Jim Wohlford	.05
345	Donnie Moore	.05
346	Bryan Little	.05
347	*Teddy Higuera*	.10
348	Cliff Johnson	.05
349	Mark Clear	.05
350	Jack Clark	.05
351	Chuck Tanner	.05
352	Harry Spilman	.05
353	Keith Atherton	.05
354	Tony Bernazard	.05
355	Lee Smith	.10
356	Mickey Hatcher	.05
357	Ed Vande Berg	.05
358	Rick Dempsey	.05
359	Mike LaCoss	.05
360	Lloyd Moseby	.05
361	Shane Rawley	.05
362	Tom Paciorek	.05
363	Terry Forster	.05
364	Reid Nichols	.05
365	Mike Flanagan	.05
366	Reds Leaders (Dave Concepcion)	.05
367	Aurelio Lopez	.05
368	Greg Brock	.05
369	Al Holland	.05
370	*Vince Coleman*	.35
371	Bill Stein	.05
372	Ben Oglivie	.05
373	*Urbano Lugo*	.05
374	Terry Francona	.05
375	Rich Gedman	.05
376	Bill Dawley	.05
377	Joe Carter	.15
378	Bruce Bochte	.05
379	Bobby Meacham	.05
380	LaMarr Hoyt	.05
381	Ray Miller	.05
382	*Ivan Calderon*	.05
383	*Chris Brown*	.05
384	Steve Trout	.05
385	Cecil Cooper	.05
386	*Cecil Fielder*	.75
387	Steve Kemp	.05
388	Dickie Noles	.05
389	Glenn Davis	.05
390	Tom Seaver	.35
391	Julio Franco	.10
392	John Russell	.05
393	Chris Pittaro	.05
394	Checklist 265-396	.05
395	Scott Garrelts	.05
396	Red Sox Leaders (Dwight Evans)	.05
397	*Steve Buechele*	.20
398	*Earnie Riles*	.05
399	Bill Swift	.05
400	Rod Carew	.30
401	Fernando Valenzuela (Turn Back the Clock)	.05
402	Tom Seaver (Turn Back the Clock)	.15
403	Willie Mays (Turn Back the Clock)	.20
404	Frank Robinson (Turn Back the Clock)	.15

No.	Card	Price
405	Roger Maris (Turn Back the Clock)	.25
406	Scott Sanderson	.05
407	Sal Butera	.05
408	Dave Smith	.05
409	*Paul Runge*	.05
410	Dave Kingman	.10
411	Sparky Anderson	.10
412	Jim Clancy	.05
413	Tim Flannery	.05
414	Tom Gorman	.05
415	Hal McRae	.05
416	Denny Martinez	.05
417	R.J. Reynolds	.05
418	Alan Knicely	.05
419	Frank Wills	.05
420	Von Hayes	.05
421	Dave Palmer	.05
422	Mike Jorgensen	.05
423	Dan Spillner	.05
424	Rick Miller	.05
425	Larry McWilliams	.05
426	Brewers Leaders (Charlie Moore)	.05
427	Joe Cowley	.05
428	Max Venable	.05
429	Greg Booker	.05
430	Kent Hrbek	.10
431	George Frazier	.05
432	Mark Bailey	.05
433	Chris Codiroli	.05
434	Curt Wilkerson	.05
435	Bill Caudill	.05
436	Doug Flynn	.05
437	Rick Mahler	.05
438	Clint Hurdle	.05
439	Rick Honeycutt	.05
440	Alvin Davis	.05
441	Whitey Herzog	.05
442	Ron Robinson	.05
443	Bill Buckner	.05
444	Alex Trevino	.05
445	Bert Blyleven	.05
446	Lenn Sakata	.05
447	Jerry Don Gleaton	.05
448	*Herm Winningham*	.05
449	Rod Scurry	.05
450	Graig Nettles	.05
451	Mark Brown	.05
452	Bob Clark	.05
453	Steve Jeltz	.05
454	Burt Hooton	.05
455	Willie Randolph	.05
456	Braves Leaders (Dale Murphy)	.10
457	Mickey Tettleton	.10
458	Kevin Bass	.05
459	Luis Leal	.05
460	Leon Durham	.05
461	Walt Terrell	.05
462	Domingo Ramos	.05
463	Jim Gott	.05
464	Ruppert Jones	.05
465	Jesse Orosco	.05
466	Tom Foley	.05
467	Bob James	.05
468	Mike Scioscia	.05
469	Storm Davis	.05
470	Bill Madlock	.05
471	Bobby Cox	.05
472	Joe Hesketh	.05
473	Mark Brouhard	.05
474	John Tudor	.05
475	Juan Samuel	.05
476	Ron Mathis	.05
477	Mike Easler	.05
478	Andy Hawkins	.05
479	*Bob Melvin*	.05
480	*Oddibe McDowell*	.05
481	Scott Bradley	.05
482	Rick Lysander	.05
483	George Vukovich	.05
484	Donnie Hill	.05
485	Gary Matthews	.05
486	Angels Leaders (Bob Grich)	.05
487	Bret Saberhagen	.25
488	Lou Thornton	.05
489	Jim Winn	.05
490	Jeff Leonard	.05
491	Pascual Perez	.05
492	Kelvin Chapman	.05
493	Gene Nelson	.05
494	Gary Roenicke	.05
495	Mark Langston	.10
496	Jay Johnstone	.05
497	John Stuper	.05
498	Tito Landrum	.05
499	Bob L. Gibson	.05
500	Rickey Henderson	.40
501	Dave Johnson	.05
502	Glen Cook	.05
503	Mike Fitzgerald	.05
504	Denny Walling	.05
505	Jerry Koosman	.05
506	Bill Russell	.05
507	*Steve Ontiveros*	.10
508	Alan Wiggins	.05
509	Ernie Camacho	.05
510	Wade Boggs	.50
511	Ed Nunez	.05
512	Thad Bosley	.05
513	Ron Washington	.05
514	Mike Jones	.05
515	Darrell Evans	.05
516	Giants Leaders (Greg Minton)	.05
517	*Milt Thompson*	.05
518	Buck Martinez	.05
519	Danny Darwin	.05
520	Keith Hernandez	.05
521	Nate Snell	.05
522	Bob Bailor	.05
523	Joe Price	.05
524	Darrell Miller	.05
525	Marvell Wynne	.05
526	Charlie Lea	.05
527	Checklist 397-528	.05
528	Terry Pendleton	.10
529	Marc Sullivan	.05
530	Rich Gossage	.10
531	Tony LaRussa	.05
532	*Don Carman*	.05
533	Billy Sample	.05
534	Jeff Calhoun	.05
535	Toby Harrah	.05
536	Jose Rijo	.05
537	Mark Salas	.05
538	Dennis Eckersley	.10
539	Glenn Hubbard	.05
540	Dan Petry	.05
541	Jorge Orta	.05
542	Don Schulze	.05
543	Jerry Narron	.05
544	Eddie Milner	.05
545	Jimmy Key	.10
546	Mariners Leaders (Dave Henderson)	.05
547	*Roger McDowell*	.12
548	Mike Young	.05
549	Bob Welch	.05
550	Tom Herr	.05
551	Dave LaPoint	.05
552	Marc Hill	.05
553	Jim Morrison	.05
554	Paul Householder	.05
555	Hubie Brooks	.05
556	John Denny	.05
557	Gerald Perry	.05
558	Tim Stoddard	.05
559	Tommy Dunbar	.05
560	Dave Righetti	.05
561	Bob Lillis	.05
562	Joe Beckwith	.05
563	Alejandro Sanchez	.05
564	Warren Brusstar	.05
565	Tom Brunansky	.05
566	Alfredo Griffin	.05
567	Jeff Barkley	.05
568	Donnie Scott	.05
569	Jim Acker	.05
570	Rusty Staub	.10
571	Mike Jeffcoat	.05
572	Paul Zuvella	.05
573	Tom Hume	.05
574	Ron Kittle	.05
575	Mike Boddicker	.05
576	Expos Leaders (Andre Dawson)	.10
577	Jerry Reuss	.05
578	Lee Mazzilli	.05
579	Jim Slaton	.05
580	Willie McGee	.05
581	Bruce Hurst	.05
582	Jim Gantner	.05
583	Al Bumbry	.05
584	*Brian Fisher*	.05
585	Garry Maddox	.05
586	Greg Harris	.05
587	Rafael Santana	.05
588	Steve Lake	.05
589	Sid Bream	.05
590	Bob Knepper	.05
591	Jackie Moore	.05
592	Frank Tanana	.05
593	Jesse Barfield	.05
594	Chris Bando	.05
595	Dave Parker	.15
596	Onix Concepcion	.05
597	Sammy Stewart	.05
598	Jim Presley	.05
599	*Rick Aguilera*	.25
600	Dale Murphy	.15
601	Gary Lucas	.05
602	*Mariano Duncan*	.25
603	Bill Laskey	.05
604	Gary Pettis	.05
605	Dennis Boyd	.05
606	Royals Leaders (Hal McRae)	.05
607	Ken Dayley	.05
608	Bruce Bochy	.05
609	Barbaro Garbey	.05
610	Ron Guidry	.05
611	Gary Woods	.05
612	Richard Dotson	.05
613	Roy Smalley	.05
614	Rick Waits	.05
615	Johnny Ray	.05
616	Glenn Brummer	.05
617	Lonnie Smith	.05
618	Jim Pankovits	.05
619	Danny Heep	.05
620	Bruce Sutter	.05
621	John Felske	.05
622	Gary Lavelle	.05
623	Floyd Rayford	.05
624	Steve McCatty	.05
625	Bob Brenly	.05
626	Roy Thomas	.05
627	Ron Oester	.05
628	*Kirk McCaskill*	.15
629	*Mitch Webster*	.05
630	Fernando Valenzuela	.05
631	Steve Braun	.05
632	Dave Von Ohlen	.05
633	Jackie Gutierrez	.05
634	Roy Lee Jackson	.05
635	Jason Thompson	.05
636	Cubs Leaders (Lee Smith)	.05
637	Rudy Law	.05
638	John Butcher	.05
639	Bo Diaz	.05
640	Jose Cruz	.05
641	Wayne Tolleson	.05
642	Ray Searage	.05
643	Tom Brookens	.05
644	Mark Gubicza	.12
645	Dusty Baker	.05
646	Mike Moore	.05
647	Mel Hall	.05
648	Steve Bedrosian	.05
649	Ronn Reynolds	.05
650	Dave Stieb	.05
651	Billy Martin	.10
652	Tom Browning	.05
653	Jim Dwyer	.05
654	Ken Howell	.05
655	Manny Trillo	.05
656	Brian Harper	.05
657	Juan Agosto	.05
658	Rob Wilfong	.05
659	Checklist 529-660	.05
660	Steve Garvey	.15
661	Roger Clemens	4.00
662	Bill Schroeder	.05
663	Neil Allen	.05
664	Tim Corcoran	.05
665	Alejandro Pena	.05
666	Rangers Leaders (Charlie Hough)	.05
667	Tim Teufel	.05
668	Cecilio Guante	.05
669	Ron Cey	.05
670	Willie Hernandez	.05
671	Lynn Jones	.05
672	Rob Picciolo	.05
673	Ernie Whitt	.05
674	Pat Tabler	.05
675	Claudell Washington	.05
676	Matt Young	.05
677	Nick Esasky	.05
678	Dan Gladden	.05
679	Britt Burns	.05
680	George Foster	.05
681	Dick Williams	.05
682	Junior Ortiz	.05
683	Andy Van Slyke	.05
684	Bob McClure	.05
685	Tim Wallach	.05
686	Jeff Stone	.05
687	Mike Trujillo	.05
688	Larry Herndon	.05
689	Dave Stewart	.12
690	Ryne Sandberg	.75
691	Mike Madden	.05
692	Dale Berra	.05
693	Tom Tellmann	.05
694	Garth Iorg	.05
695	Mike Smithson	.05
696	Dodgers Leaders (Bill Russell)	.05
697	Bud Black	.05
698	Brad Komminsk	.05
699	Pat Corrales	.05
700	Reggie Jackson	.25
701	Keith Hernandez (All-Star)	.05
702	Tom Herr (All-Star)	.05
703	Tim Wallach (All-Star)	.05
704	Ozzie Smith (All-Star)	.15
705	Dale Murphy (All-Star)	.10
706	Pedro Guerrero (All-Star)	.05
707	Willie McGee (All-Star)	.05
708	Gary Carter (All-Star)	.10
709	Dwight Gooden (All-Star)	.10
710	John Tudor (All-Star)	.05
711	Jeff Reardon (All-Star)	.05
712	Don Mattingly (All-Star)	.40
713	Damasco Garcia (All-Star)	.05
714	George Brett (All-Star)	.35
715	Cal Ripken, Jr. (All-Star)	.75
716	Rickey Henderson (All-Star)	.20
717	Dave Winfield (All-Star)	.20
718	George Bell (All-Star)	.05
719	Carlton Fisk (All-Star)	.15
720	Bret Saberhagen (All-Star)	.15
721	Ron Guidry (All-Star)	.10
722	Dan Quisenberry (All-Star)	.05
723	Marty Bystrom	.05
724	Tim Hulett	.05
725	Mario Soto	.05
726	Orioles Leaders (Rick Dempsey)	.05
727	David Green	.05
728	Mike Marshall	.05
729	Jim Beattie	.05
730	Ozzie Smith	.30
731	Don Robinson	.05
732	*Floyd Youmans*	.05
733	Ron Romanick	.05
734	Marty Barrett	.05
735	Dave Dravecky	.05
736	Glenn Wilson	.05
737	Pete Vuckovich	.05
738	Andre Robertson	.05
739	Dave Rozema	.05
740	Lance Parrish	.05
741	Pete Rose	.50
742	Frank Viola	.05
743	Pat Sheridan	.05
744	Lary Sorensen	.05
745	Willie Upshaw	.05
746	Denny Gonzalez	.05
747	Rick Cerone	.05
748	Steve Henderson	.05
749	Ed Jurak	.05
750	Gorman Thomas	.05
751	Howard Johnson	.05
752	Mike Krukow	.05
753	Dan Ford	.05
754	*Pat Clements*	.05
755	Harold Baines	.10
756	Pirates Leaders (Rick Rhoden)	.05
757	Darrell Porter	.05
758	Dave Anderson	.05
759	Moose Haas	.05
760	Andre Dawson	.30
761	Don Slaught	.05
762	Eric Show	.05
763	Terry Puhl	.05
764	Kevin Gross	.05
765	Don Baylor	.10
766	Rick Langford	.05
767	Jody Davis	.05
768	Vern Ruhle	.05
769	*Harold Reynolds*	.25
770	Vida Blue	.05
771	John McNamara	.05
772	Brian Downing	.05
773	Greg Pryor	.05
774	Terry Leach	.05
775	Al Oliver	.05
776	Gene Garber	.05
777	Wayne Krenchicki	.05
778	Jerry Hairston	.05

779	Rick Reuschel	.05
780	Robin Yount	.50
781	Joe Nolan	.05
782	Ken Landreaux	.05
783	Ricky Horton	.05
784	Alan Bannister	.05
785	Bob Stanley	.05
786	Twins Leaders (Mickey Hatcher)	.05
787	Vance Law	.05
788	Marty Castillo	.05
789	Kurt Bevacqua	.05
790	Phil Niekro	.30
791	Checklist 661-792	.05
792	Charles Hudson	.05

1986 Topps Tiffany

A total of only 5,000 of these specially boxed collectors edition sets was reported produced. Sold only through hobby dealers the cards differ from the regular-issue 1986 Topps cards only in the use of white cardboard stock and the application of a high-gloss finish on the cards' fronts.

	MT
Complete Set (792):	125.00
Common Player:	.25

(Star cards valued at 4X-6X corresponding cards in regular 1986 Topps issue)

1986 Topps Traded

This 132-card set of 2-1/2" x 3-1/2" cards was, at issue, one of the most popular sets of recent times. As always, the set features traded veterans, and a better than usual crop of rookies. As in the previous two years, a glossy-finish "Tiffany" edition of 5,000 Traded sets was produced.

		MT
	Complete Set (132):	20.00
	Common Player:	.10
1T	Andy Allanson	.10
2T	Neil Allen	.10
3T	Joaquin Andujar	.10
4T	Paul Assenmacher	.10
5T	Scott Bailes	.10
6T	Don Baylor	.15
7T	Steve Bedrosian	.10
8T	Juan Beniquez	.10
9T	Juan Berenguer	.10
10T	Mike Bielecki	.10
11T	*Barry Bonds*	15.00
12T	*Bobby Bonilla*	.50
13T	Juan Bonilla	.10
14T	Rich Bordi	.10
15T	Steve Boros	.10
16T	Rick Burleson	.10
17T	Bill Campbell	.10
18T	Tom Candiotti	.10
19T	John Cangelosi	.10
20T	*Jose Canseco*	5.00
21T	Carmen Castillo	.10
22T	Rick Cerone	.10
23T	John Cerutti	.10
24T	*Will Clark*	1.50
25T	Mark Clear	.10
26T	Darnell Coles	.10
27T	Dave Collins	.10
28T	Tim Conroy	.10
29T	Joe Cowley	.10
30T	Joel Davis	.10
31T	Rob Deer	.10
32T	John Denny	.10
33T	Mike Easler	.10
34T	Mark Eichhorn	.15
35T	Steve Farr	.10
36T	Scott Fletcher	.10
37T	Terry Forster	.10
38T	Terry Francona	.10
39T	Jim Fregosi	.10
40T	Andres Galarraga	1.50
41T	Ken Griffey	.15
42T	Bill Gullickson	.10
43T	Jose Guzman	.10
44T	Moose Haas	.10
45T	Billy Hatcher	.10
46T	Mike Heath	.10
47T	Tom Hume	.10
48T	*Pete Incaviglia*	.20
49T	Dane Iorg	.10
50T	*Bo Jackson*	1.00
51T	*Wally Joyner*	.40
52T	Charlie Kerfeld	.10
53T	Eric King	.10
54T	Bob Kipper	.10
55T	Wayne Krenchicki	.10
56T	*John Kruk*	.35
57T	Mike LaCoss	.10
58T	Pete Ladd	.10
59T	Mike Laga	.10
60T	Hal Lanier	.10
61T	Dave LaPoint	.10
62T	Rudy Law	.10
63T	Rick Leach	.10
64T	Tim Leary	.10
65T	Dennis Leonard	.10
66T	Jim Leyland	.10
67T	Steve Lyons	.10
68T	Mickey Mahler	.10
69T	Candy Maldonado	.10
70T	Roger Mason	.10
71T	Bob McClure	.10
72T	Andy McGaffigan	.10
73T	Gene Michael	.10
74T	*Kevin Mitchell*	.25
75T	Omar Moreno	.10
76T	Jerry Mumphrey	.10
77T	Phil Niekro	.25
78T	Randy Niemann	.10
79T	Juan Nieves	.10
80T	Otis Nixon	.10
81T	Bob Ojeda	.10
82T	Jose Oquendo	.10
83T	Tom Paciorek	.10
84T	Dave Palmer	.10
85T	Frank Pastore	.10
86T	Lou Piniella	.10
87T	Dan Plesac	.10
88T	Darrell Porter	.10
89T	Rey Quinones	.10
90T	Gary Redus	.10
91T	Bip Roberts	.10
92T	Billy Jo Robidoux	.10
93T	Jeff Robinson	.10
94T	Gary Roenicke	.10
95T	Ed Romero	.10
96T	Argenis Salazar	.10
97T	Joe Sambito	.10
98T	Billy Sample	.10
99T	Dave Schmidt	.10
100T	Ken Schrom	.10
101T	Tom Seaver	.50
102T	Ted Simmons	.10
103T	Sammy Stewart	.10
104T	Kurt Stillwell	.10
105T	Franklin Stubbs	.10
106T	Dale Sveum	.10
107T	Chuck Tanner	.10
108T	Danny Tartabull	.10
109T	Tim Teufel	.10
110T	Bob Tewksbury	.15
111T	Andres Thomas	.10
112T	Milt Thompson	.10
113T	Robby Thompson	.10
114T	Jay Tibbs	.10
115T	Wayne Tolleson	.10
116T	Alex Trevino	.10
117T	Manny Trillo	.10
118T	Ed Vande Berg	.10
119T	Ozzie Virgil	.10
120T	Bob Walk	.10
121T	Gene Walter	.10
122T	Claudell Washington	.10
123T	Bill Wegman	.10
124T	Dick Williams	.10
125T	Mitch Williams	.15
126T	Bobby Witt	.15
127T	Todd Worrell	.15
128T	George Wright	.10
129T	Ricky Wright	.10
130T	Steve Yeager	.10
131T	Paul Zuvella	.10
132T	Checklist	.10

1986 Topps Traded Tiffany

This collectors edition differs from the regular 1986 Topps Traded set only in the use of a high-gloss front finish. The set was sold only through hobby channels in a specially design box.

	MT
Complete Set (132):	200.00
Common Player:	.25

(Star cards valued at 3X-4X corresponding cards in regular Topps Traded)

1986 Topps All-Star Glossy Set of 22

As in previous years, Topps continued to make the popular glossy-surfaced cards as an insert in rack packs. The All-Star Glossy set of 2-1/2" x 3-1/2" cards shows little design change from previous years. Cards feature a front color photo and All-Star banner at the top. The bottom has the player's name and position. The set includes the All-Star starting teams as well as the managers and honorary captains.

		MT
	Complete Set (22):	4.00
	Common Player:	.20
1	Sparky Anderson	.20
2	Eddie Murray	.50
3	Lou Whitaker	.20
4	George Brett	.80
5	Cal Ripken, Jr.	1.00
6	Jim Rice	.25
7	Rickey Henderson	.50
8	Dave Winfield	.50
9	Carlton Fisk	.50
10	Jack Morris	.20
11	A.L. All-Star Team	.20
12	Dick Williams	.20
13	Steve Garvey	.30
14	Tom Herr	.20
15	Graig Nettles	.20
16	Ozzie Smith	.50
17	Tony Gwynn	.75
18	Dale Murphy	.40
19	Darryl Strawberry	.25
20	Terry Kennedy	.20
21	LaMarr Hoyt	.20
22	N.L. All-Star Team	.20

Player names in *Italic* type indicate a rookie card.

1986 Topps Mini League Leaders

Topps had long experimented with bigger cards, but in 1986, they also decided to try smaller ones. These 2-1/8" x 2-15/16" cards feature top players in a number of categories. Sold in plastic packs as a regular Topps issue, the 66-card set is attractive as well as innovative. The cards feature color photos and a minimum of added information on the fronts where only the player's name and Topps logo appear. Backs limited information as well, but do feature enough to justify the player's inclusion in a set of league leaders.

		MT
	Complete Set (66):	6.00
	Common Player:	.10
1	Eddie Murray	.35
2	Cal Ripken, Jr.	1.00
3	Wade Boggs	.50
4	Dennis Boyd	.10
5	Dwight Evans	.10
6	Bruce Hurst	.10
7	Gary Pettis	.10
8	Harold Baines	.15
9	Floyd Bannister	.10
10	Britt Burns	.10
11	Carlton Fisk	.35
12	Brett Butler	.10
13	Darrell Evans	.10
14	Jack Morris	.10
15	Lance Parrish	.10
16	Walt Terrell	.10
17	Steve Balboni	.10
18	George Brett	.75
19	Charlie Leibrandt	.10
20	Bret Saberhagen	.15
21	Lonnie Smith	.10
22	Willie Wilson	.10
23	Bert Blyleven	.10
24	Mike Smithson	.10
25	Frank Viola	.10
26	Ron Guidry	.10
27	Rickey Henderson	.35
28	Don Mattingly	.90
29	Dave Winfield	.30
30	Mike Moore	.10
31	Gorman Thomas	.10
32	Toby Harrah	.10
33	Charlie Hough	.10
34	Doyle Alexander	.10
35	Jimmy Key	.10
36	Dave Stieb	.10
37	Dale Murphy	.30
38	Keith Moreland	.10
39	Ryne Sandberg	.50
40	Tom Browning	.10
41	Dave Parker	.10
42	Mario Soto	.10
43	Nolan Ryan	1.00
44	Pedro Guerrero	.10
45	Orel Hershiser	.15
46	Mike Scioscia	.10

47	Fernando Valenzuela	.10
48	Bob Welch	.10
49	Tim Raines	.15
50	Gary Carter	.15
51	Sid Fernandez	.10
52	Dwight Gooden	.25
53	Keith Hernandez	.10
54	Juan Samuel	.10
55	Mike Schmidt	.75
56	Glenn Wilson	.10
57	Rick Reuschel	.10
58	Joaquin Andujar	.10
59	Jack Clark	.10
60	Vince Coleman	.10
61	Danny Cox	.10
62	Tom Herr	.10
63	Willie McGee	.10
64	John Tudor	.10
65	Tony Gwynn	.75
66	Checklist	.10

1987 Topps

The design of Topps' set of 792 2-1/2" x 3-1/2" cards is closely akin to the 1962 set in that the player photo is set against a woodgrain border. Instead of a rolling corner, as in 1962, the player photos in '87 feature a couple of clipped corners at top left and bottom right, where the team logo and player name appear. The player's position is not given on the front of the card. For the first time in several years, the trophy which designates members of Topps All-Star Rookie Team returned to the card design. As in the previous three years, Topps issued a glossy-finish "Tiffany" edition of their 792-card set. However, it was speculated that as many as 30,000 sets were produced as opposed to the 5,000 sets printed in 1985 and 1986.

		MT
Complete Set (792):		12.00
Common Player:		.05
Pack (15):		1.00
Wax Box (36):		18.50
1	Roger Clemens (Record Breaker)	.30
2	Jim Deshaies (Record Breaker)	.05
3	Dwight Evans (Record Breaker)	.05
4	Dave Lopes (Record Breaker)	.05
5	Dave Righetti (Record Breaker)	.05
6	Ruben Sierra (Record Breaker)	.05
7	Todd Worrell (Record Breaker)	.05
8	Terry Pendleton	.05
9	Jay Tibbs	.05
10	Cecil Cooper	.05
11	Indians Leaders (Jack Aker, Chris Bando, Phil Niekro)	.10
12	*Jeff Sellers*	.05
13	Nick Esasky	.05
14	Dave Stewart	.05
15	Claudell Washington	.05
16	Pat Clements	.05
17	Pete O'Brien	.05
18	Dick Howser	.05
19	Matt Young	.05
20	Gary Carter	.10
21	Mark Davis	.05
22	Doug DeCinces	.05
23	Lee Smith	.05
24	Tony Walker	.05
25	Bert Blyleven	.05
26	Greg Brock	.05
27	Joe Cowley	.05
28	Rick Dempsey	.05
29	Jimmy Key	.05
30	Tim Raines	.15
31	Braves Leaders (Glenn Hubbard, Rafael Ramirez)	.05
32	Tim Leary	.05
33	Andy Van Slyke	.05
34	Jose Rijo	.05
35	Sid Bream	.05
36	*Eric King*	.05
37	Marvell Wynne	.05
38	Dennis Leonard	.05
39	Marty Barrett	.05
40	Dave Righetti	.05
41	Bo Diaz	.05
42	Gary Redus	.05
43	Gene Michael	.05
44	Greg Harris	.05
45	Jim Presley	.05
46	Danny Gladden	.05
47	Dennis Powell	.05
48	Wally Backman	.05
49	Terry Harper	.05
50	Dave Smith	.05
51	Mel Hall	.05
52	Keith Atherton	.05
53	Ruppert Jones	.05
54	Bill Dawley	.05
55	Tim Wallach	.05
56	Brewers Leaders (Jamie Cocanower, Paul Molitor, Charlie Moore, Herm Starrette)	.10
57	*Scott Nielsen*	.05
58	Thad Bosley	.05
59	Ken Dayley	.05
60	Tony Pena	.05
61	*Bobby Thigpen*	.05
62	Bobby Meacham	.05
63	Fred Toliver	.05
64	Harry Spilman	.05
65	Tom Browning	.05
66	Marc Sullivan	.05
67	Bill Swift	.05
68	Tony LaRussa	.05
69	Lonnie Smith	.05
70	Charlie Hough	.05
71	*Mike Aldrete*	.05
72	Walt Terrell	.05
73	Dave Anderson	.05
74	Dan Pasqua	.05
75	Ron Darling	.05
76	Rafael Ramirez	.05
77	Bryan Oelkers	.05
78	Tom Foley	.05
79	Juan Nieves	.05
80	*Wally Joyner*	.35
81	Padres Leaders (Andy Hawkins, Terry Kennedy)	.05
82	*Rob Murphy*	.05
83	Mike Davis	.05
84	Steve Lake	.05
85	Kevin Bass	.05
86	Nate Snell	.05
87	Mark Salas	.05
88	Ed Wojna	.05
89	Ozzie Guillen	.05
90	Dave Stieb	.05
91	Harold Reynolds	.05
92a	Urbano Lugo (no trademark on front)	.10
92b	Urbano Lugo (trademark on front)	.05
93	Jim Leyland	.05
94	Calvin Schiraldi	.05
95	Oddibe McDowell	.05
96	Frank Williams	.05
97	Glenn Wilson	.05
98	Bill Scherrer	.05
99	Darryl Motley	.05
100	Steve Garvey	.15
101	*Carl Willis*	.05
102	Paul Zuvella	.05
103	Rick Aguilera	.05
104	Billy Sample	.05
105	Floyd Youmans	.05
106	Blue Jays Leaders (George Bell, Willie Upshaw)	.05
107	John Butcher	.05
108	Jim Gantner (photo reversed)	.05
109	R.J. Reynolds	.05
110	John Tudor	.05
111	Alfredo Griffin	.05
112	Alan Ashby	.05
113	Neil Allen	.05
114	Billy Beane	.05
115	Donnie Moore	.05
116	*Mike Stanley*	.05
117	Jim Beattie	.05
118	Bobby Valentine	.05
119	Ron Robinson	.05
120	Eddie Murray	.40
121	*Kevin Romine*	.05
122	Jim Clancy	.05
123	John Kruk	.10
124	Ray Fontenot	.05
125	Bob Brenly	.05
126	*Mike Loynd*	.05
127	Vance Law	.05
128	Checklist 1-132	.05
129	Rick Cerone	.05
130	Dwight Gooden	.10
131	Pirates Leaders (Sid Bream, Tony Pena)	.05
132	*Paul Assenmacher*	.05
133	Jose Oquendo	.05
134	*Rich Yett*	.05
135	Mike Easler	.05
136	Ron Romanick	.05
137	Jerry Willard	.05
138	Roy Lee Jackson	.05
139	*Devon White*	.40
140	Bret Saberhagen	.10
141	Herm Winningham	.05
142	Rick Sutcliffe	.05
143	Steve Boros	.05
144	Mike Scioscia	.05
145	Charlie Kerfeld	.05
146	*Tracy Jones*	.05
147	Randy Niemann	.05
148	Dave Collins	.05
149	Ray Searage	.05
150	Wade Boggs	.40
151	Mike LaCoss	.05
152	Toby Harrah	.05
153	*Duane Ward*	.25
154	Tom O'Malley	.05
155	Eddie Whitson	.05
156	Mariners Leaders (Bob Kearney, Phil Regan, Matt Young)	.05
157	Danny Darwin	.05
158	Tim Teufel	.05
159	Ed Olwine	.05
160	Julio Franco	.05
161	Steve Ontiveros	.05
162	*Mike LaValliere*	.10
163	Kevin Gross	.05
164	Sammy Khalifa	.05
165	Jeff Reardon	.05
166	Bob Boone	.05
167	*Jim Deshaies*	.10
168	Lou Piniella	.05
169	Ron Washington	.05
170	Bo Jackson (Future Stars)	.40
171	*Chuck Cary*	.05
172	Ron Oester	.05
173	Alex Trevino	.05
174	Henry Cotto	.05
175	Bob Stanley	.05
176	Steve Buechele	.05
177	Keith Moreland	.05
178	Cecil Fielder	.10
179	Bill Wegman	.05
180	Chris Brown	.05
181	Cardinals Leaders (Mike LaValliere, Ozzie Smith, Ray Soff)	.10
182	Lee Lacy	.05
183	Andy Hawkins	.05
184	Bobby Bonilla	.15
185	Roger McDowell	.05
186	Bruce Benedict	.05
187	Mark Huismann	.05
188	Tony Phillips	.05
189	Joe Hesketh	.05
190	Jim Sundberg	.05
191	Charles Hudson	.05
192	Cory Snyder	.05
193	Roger Craig	.05
194	Kirk McCaskill	.05
195	Mike Pagliarulo	.05
196	Randy O'Neal	.05
197	Mark Bailey	.05
198	Lee Mazzilli	.05
199	Mariano Duncan	.05
200	Pete Rose	.40
201	*John Cangelosi*	.05
202	Ricky Wright	.05
203	*Mike Kingery*	.05
204	Sammy Stewart	.05
205	Graig Nettles	.05
206	Twins Leaders (Tim Laudner, Frank Viola)	.05
207	George Frazier	.05
208	John Shelby	.05
209	Rick Schu	.05
210	Lloyd Moseby	.05
211	John Morris	.05
212	Mike Fitzgerald	.05
213	*Randy Myers*	.25
214	Omar Moreno	.05
215	Mark Langston	.05
216	*B.J. Surhoff* (Future Stars)	.15
217	Chris Codiroli	.05
218	Sparky Anderson	.15
219	Cecilio Guante	.05
220	Joe Carter	.10
221	Vern Ruhle	.05
222	Denny Walling	.05
223	Charlie Leibrandt	.05
224	Wayne Tolleson	.05
225	Mike Smithson	.05
226	Max Venable	.05
227	*Jamie Moyer*	.05
228	Curt Wilkerson	.05
229	*Mike Birkbeck*	.05
230	Don Baylor	.10
231	Giants Leaders (Bob Brenly, Mike Krukow)	.05
232	*Reggie Williams*	.05
233	*Russ Morman*	.05
234	Pat Sheridan	.05
235	Alvin Davis	.05
236	Tommy John	.10
237	Jim Morrison	.05
238	Bill Krueger	.05
239	Juan Espino	.05
240	Steve Balboni	.05
241	Danny Heep	.05
242	Rick Mahler	.05
243	Whitey Herzog	.05
244	Dickie Noles	.05
245	Willie Upshaw	.05
246	Jim Dwyer	.05
247	Jeff Reed	.05
248	Gene Walter	.05
249	Jim Pankovits	.05
250	Teddy Higuera	.05
251	Rob Wilfong	.05
252	Denny Martinez	.05
253	Eddie Milner	.05
254	*Bob Tewksbury*	.20
255	Juan Samuel	.05
256	Royals Leaders (George Brett, Frank White)	.15
257	Bob Forsch	.05
258	Steve Yeager	.05
259	*Mike Greenwell*	.25
260	Vida Blue	.05
261	Ruben Sierra	.10
262	Jim Winn	.05
263	Stan Javier	.05
264	Checklist 133-264	.05
265	Darrell Evans	.05
266	*Jeff Hamilton*	.05
267	Howard Johnson	.05
268	Pat Corrales	.05
269	Cliff Speck	.05
270	Jody Davis	.05
271	Mike Brown	.05
272	Andres Galarraga	.40
273	Gene Nelson	.05
274	*Jeff Hearron*	.05
275	LaMarr Hoyt	.05
276	Jackie Gutierrez	.05
277	Juan Agosto	.05
278	Gary Pettis	.05

279 *Dan Plesac* .05
280 Jeffrey Leonard .05
281 Reds Leaders (Bo Diaz, Bill Gullickson, Pete Rose) .10
282 Jeff Calhoun .05
283 *Doug Drabek* .25
284 John Moses .05
285 Dennis Boyd .05
286 Mike Woodard .05
287 Dave Von Ohlen .05
288 Tito Landrum .05
289 Bob Kipper .05
290 Leon Durham .05
291 *Mitch Williams* .25
292 Franklin Stubbs .05
293 Bob Rodgers .05
294 Steve Jeltz .05
295 Len Dykstra .10
296 *Andres Thomas* .05
297 Don Schulze .05
298 Larry Herndon .05
299 Joel Davis .05
300 Reggie Jackson .25
301 *Luis Aquino* .05
302 Bill Schroeder .05
303 Juan Berenguer .05
304 Phil Garner .05
305 John Franco .05
306 Red Sox Leaders (Rich Gedman, John McNamara, Tom Seaver) .10
307 *Lee Guetterman* .05
308 Don Slaught .05
309 Mike Young .05
310 Frank Viola .05
311 Rickey Henderson (Turn Back the Clock) .15
312 Reggie Jackson (Turn Back the Clock) .10
313 Roberto Clemente (Turn Back the Clock) .45
314 Carl Yastrzemski (Turn Back the Clock) .10
315 Maury Wills (Turn Back the Clock) .05
316 Brian Fisher .05
317 Clint Hurdle .05
318 Jim Fregosi .05
319 *Greg Swindell* .10
320 Barry Bonds 1.50
321 Mike Laga .05
322 Chris Bando .05
323 *Al Newman* .05
324 Dave Palmer .05
325 Garry Templeton .05
326 Mark Gubicza .05
327 *Dale Sveum* .05
328 Bob Welch .05
329 Ron Roenicke .05
330 Mike Scott .05
331 Mets Leaders (Gary Carter, Keith Hernandez, Dave Johnson, Darryl Strawberry) .10
332 Joe Price .05
333 Ken Phelps .05
334 *Ed Correa* .05
335 Candy Maldonado .05
336 *Allan Anderson* .05
337 Darrell Miller .05
338 Tim Conroy .05
339 Donnie Hill .05
340 Roger Clemens .75
341 Mike Brown .05
342 Bob James .05
343 Hal Lanier .05
344a Joe Niekro (copyright outside yellow on back) .25
344b Joe Niekro (copyright inside yellow on back) .05
345 Andre Dawson .15
346 Shawon Dunston .05
347 Mickey Brantley .05
348 Carmelo Martinez .05
349 Storm Davis .05
350 Keith Hernandez .05
351 Gene Garber .05
352 Mike Felder .05
353 Ernie Camacho .05
354 Jamie Quirk .05
355 Don Carman .05
356 White Sox Leaders (Ed Brinkman, Julio Cruz) .05
357 *Steve Fireovid* .05
358 Sal Butera .05
359 Doug Corbett .05
360 Pedro Guerrero .05
361 Mark Thurmond .05
362 *Luis Quinones* .05
363 Jose Guzman .05
364 Randy Bush .05
365 Rick Rhoden .05
366 Mark McGwire 5.00
367 Jeff Lahti .05
368 John McNamara .05
369 Brian Dayett .05
370 Fred Lynn .05
371 *Mark Eichhorn* .05
372 Jerry Mumphrey .05
373 Jeff Dedmon .05
374 Glenn Hoffman .05
375 Ron Guidry .10
376 Scott Bradley .05
377 John Henry Johnson .05
378 Rafael Santana .05
379 John Russell .05
380 Rich Gossage .05
381 Expos Leaders (Mike Fitzgerald, Bob Rodgers) .05
382 Rudy Law .05
383 Ron Davis .05
384 Johnny Grubb .05
385 Orel Hershiser .10
386 Dickie Thon .05
387 *T.R. Bryden* .05
388 Geno Petralli .05
389 Jeff Robinson .05
390 Gary Matthews .05
391 Jay Howell .05
392 Checklist 265-396 .05
393 Pete Rose .35
394 Mike Bielecki .05
395 Damaso Garcia .05
396 Tim Lollar .05
397 Greg Walker .05
398 Brad Havens .05
399 Curt Ford .05
400 George Brett .50
401 Billy Jo Robidoux .05
402 Mike Trujillo .05
403 Jerry Royster .05
404 Doug Sisk .05
405 Brook Jacoby .05
406 Yankees Leaders (Rickey Henderson, Don Mattingly) .25
407 Jim Acker .05
408 John Mizerock .05
409 Milt Thompson .05
410 Fernando Valenzuela .05
411 Darnell Coles .05
412 Eric Davis .05
413 Moose Haas .05
414 Joe Orsulak .05
415 *Bobby Witt* .10
416 Tom Nieto .05
417 Pat Perry .05
418 Dick Williams .05
419 *Mark Portugal* .10
420 Will Clark .75
421 Jose DeLeon .05
422 Jack Howell .05
423 Jaime Cocanower .05
424 Chris Speier .05
425 Tom Seaver .30
426 Floyd Rayford .05
427 Ed Nunez .05
428 Bruce Bochy .05
429 *Tim Pyznarski* (Future Stars) .05
430 Mike Schmidt .50
431 Dodgers Leaders (Tom Niedenfuer, Ron Perranoski, Alex Trevino) .05
432 Jim Slaton .05
433 *Ed Hearn* .05
434 Mike Fischlin .05
435 Bruce Sutter .05
436 *Andy Allanson* .05
437 Ted Power .05
438 *Kelly Downs* .05
439 Karl Best .05
440 Willie McGee .05
441 *Dave Leiper* .05
442 Mitch Webster .05
443 John Felske .05
444 Jeff Russell .05
445 Dave Lopes .05
446 *Chuck Finley* .25
447 Bill Almon .05
448 *Chris Bosio* .10
449 *Pat Dodson* (Future Stars) .05
450 Kirby Puckett .50
451 Joe Sambito .05
452 Dave Henderson .05
453 *Scott Terry* .05
454 Luis Salazar .05
455 Mike Boddicker .05
456 A's Leaders (Carney Lansford, Tony LaRussa, Mickey Tettleton, Dave Von Ohlen) .05
457 Len Matuszek .05
458 Kelly Gruber .05
459 Dennis Eckersley .10
460 Darryl Strawberry .10
461 Craig McMurtry .05
462 Scott Fletcher .05
463 Tom Candiotti .05
464 Butch Wynegar .05
465 Todd Worrell .05
466 Kal Daniels .05
467 Randy St. Claire .05
468 George Bamberger .05
469 *Mike Diaz* .05
470 Dave Dravecky .05
471 Ronn Reynolds .05
472 Bill Doran .05
473 Steve Farr .05
474 Jerry Narron .05
475 Scott Garrelts .05
476 Danny Tartabull .05
477 Ken Howell .05
478 Tim Laudner .05
479 *Bob Sebra* .05
480 Jim Rice .10
481 Phillies Leaders (Von Hayes, Juan Samuel, Glenn Wilson) .05
482 Daryl Boston .05
483 Dwight Lowry .05
484 Jim Traber .05
485 Tony Fernandez .05
486 Otis Nixon .05
487 Dave Gumpert .05
488 Ray Knight .05
489 Bill Gullickson .05
490 Dale Murphy .15
491 *Ron Karkovice* .10
492 Mike Heath .05
493 Tom Lasorda .10
494 *Barry Jones* .05
495 Gorman Thomas .05
496 Bruce Bochte .05
497 *Dale Mohorcic* .05
498 Bob Kearney .05
499 *Bruce Ruffin* .05
500 Don Mattingly .50
501 Craig Lefferts .05
502 Dick Schofield .05
503 Larry Andersen .05
504 Mickey Hatcher .05
505 Bryn Smith .05
506 Orioles Leaders (Rich Bordi, Rick Dempsey, Earl Weaver) .10
507 Dave Stapleton .05
508 *Scott Bankhead* .05
509 Enos Cabell .05
510 Tom Henke .05
511 Steve Lyons .05
512 *Dave Magadan* (Future Stars) .20
513 Carmen Castillo .05
514 Orlando Mercado .05
515 Willie Hernandez .05
516 Ted Simmons .05
517 Mario Soto .05
518 Gene Mauch .05
519 Curt Young .05
520 Jack Clark .05
521 Rick Reuschel .05
522 Checklist 397-528 .05
523 Earnie Riles .05
524 Bob Shirley .05
525 Phil Bradley .05
526 Roger Mason .05
527 Jim Wohlford .05
528 Ken Dixon .05
529 *Alvaro Espinoza* .05
530 Tony Gwynn .50
531 Astros Leaders (Yogi Berra, Hal Lanier, Denis Menke, Gene Tenace) .05
532 Jeff Stone .05
533 Argenis Salazar .05
534 Scott Sanderson .05
535 Tony Armas .05
536 *Terry Mulholland* .25
537 Rance Mulliniks .05
538 Tom Niedenfuer .05
539 Reid Nichols .05
540 Terry Kennedy .05
541 *Rafael Belliard* .05
542 Ricky Horton .05
543 Dave Johnson .05
544 Zane Smith .05
545 Buddy Bell .05
546 Mike Morgan .05
547 Rob Deer .05
548 *Bill Mooneyham* .05
549 Bob Melvin .05
550 Pete Incaviglia .25
551 Frank Wills .05
552 Larry Sheets .05
553 *Mike Maddux* .05
554 Buddy Biancalana .05
555 Dennis Rasmussen .05
556 Angels Leaders (Bob Boone, Marcel Lachemann, Mike Witt) .05
557 *John Cerutti* .05
558 Greg Gagne .05
559 Lance McCullers .05
560 Glenn Davis .05
561 *Rey Quinones* .05
562 *Bryan Clutterbuck* .05
563 John Stefero .05
564 Larry McWilliams .05
565 Dusty Baker .05
566 Tim Hulett .05
567 *Greg Mathews* .05
568 Earl Weaver .10
569 Wade Rowdon .05
570 Sid Fernandez .05
571 Ozzie Virgil .05
572 Pete Ladd .05
573 Hal McRae .05
574 Manny Lee .05
575 Pat Tabler .05
576 Frank Pastore .05
577 Dann Bilardello .05
578 Billy Hatcher .05
579 Rick Burleson .05
580 Mike Krukow .05
581 Cubs Leaders (Ron Cey, Steve Trout) .05
582 Bruce Berenyi .05
583 Junior Ortiz .05
584 Ron Kittle .05
585 *Scott Bailes* .05
586 Ben Oglivie .05
587 Eric Plunk .05
588 Wallace Johnson .05
589 Steve Crawford .05
590 Vince Coleman .05
591 Spike Owen .05
592 Chris Welsh .05
593 Chuck Tanner .05
594 Rick Anderson .05
595 Keith Hernandez (All-Star) .05
596 Steve Sax (All-Star) .05
597 Mike Schmidt (All-Star) .20
598 Ozzie Smith (All-Star) .10
599 Tony Gwynn (All-Star) .20
600 Dave Parker (All-Star) .05
601 Darryl Strawberry (All-Star) .05
602 Gary Carter (All-Star) .05
603a Dwight Gooden (All-Star, no trademark on front) .25
603b Dwight Gooden (All-Star, trademark on front) .10
604 Fernando Valenzuela (All-Star) .05
605 Todd Worrell (All-Star) .05
606a Don Mattingly (All-Star, no trademark on front) .75
606b Don Mattingly (All-Star, trademark on front) .25
607 Tony Bernazard (All-Star) .05

No.	Player	MT
608	Wade Boggs (All-Star)	.20
609	Cal Ripken, Jr. (All-Star)	.60
610	Jim Rice (All-Star)	.05
611	Kirby Puckett (All-Star)	.40
612	George Bell (All-Star)	.05
613	Lance Parrish (All-Star)	.05
614	Roger Clemens (All-Star)	.20
615	Teddy Higuera (All-Star)	.05
616	Dave Righetti (All-Star)	.05
617	Al Nipper	.05
618	Tom Kelly	.05
619	Jerry Reed	.05
620	Jose Canseco	1.00
621	Danny Cox	.05
622	*Glenn Braggs*	.10
623	*Kurt Stillwell*	.05
624	Tim Burke	.05
625	Mookie Wilson	.05
626	Joel Skinner	.05
627	Ken Oberkfell	.05
628	Bob Walk	.05
629	Larry Parrish	.05
630	John Candelaria	.05
631	Tigers Leaders (Sparky Anderson, Mike Heath, Willie Hernandez)	.05
632	Rob Woodward	.05
633	Jose Uribe	.05
634	*Rafael Palmeiro*	1.50
635	Ken Schrom	.05
636	Darren Daulton	.10
637	*Bip Roberts*	.15
638	Rich Bordi	.05
639	Gerald Perry	.05
640	Mark Clear	.05
641	Domingo Ramos	.05
642	Al Pulido	.05
643	Ron Shepherd	.05
644	John Denny	.05
645	Dwight Evans	.05
646	Mike Mason	.05
647	Tom Lawless	.05
648	*Barry Larkin*	.75
649	Mickey Tettleton	.10
650	Hubie Brooks	.05
651	Benny Distefano	.05
652	Terry Forster	.05
653	Kevin Mitchell	.05
654	Checklist 529-660	.05
655	Jesse Barfield	.05
656	Rangers Leaders (Bobby Valentine, Rickey Wright)	.05
657	Tom Waddell	.05
658	*Robby Thompson*	.15
659	Aurelio Lopez	.05
660	Bob Horner	.05
661	Lou Whitaker	.05
662	Frank DiPino	.05
663	Cliff Johnson	.05
664	Mike Marshall	.05
665	Rod Scurry	.05
666	Von Hayes	.05
667	Ron Hassey	.05
668	Juan Bonilla	.05
669	Bud Black	.05
670	Jose Cruz	.05
671a	Ray Soff (no "D*" before copyright line)	.20
671b	Ray Soff ("D*" before copyright line)	.05
672	Chili Davis	.05
673	Don Sutton	.20
674	Bill Campbell	.05
675	Ed Romero	.05
676	Charlie Moore	.05
677	Bob Grich	.05
678	Carney Lansford	.05
679	Kent Hrbek	.05
680	Ryne Sandberg	.50
681	George Bell	.05
682	Jerry Reuss	.05
683	Gary Roenicke	.05
684	Kent Tekulve	.05
685	Jerry Hairston	.05
686	Doyle Alexander	.05
687	Alan Trammell	.10
688	Juan Beniquez	.05
689	Darrell Porter	.05
690	Dane Iorg	.05
691	Dave Parker	.10
692	Frank White	.05
693	Terry Puhl	.05
694	Phil Niekro	.25
695	Chico Walker	.05
696	Gary Lucas	.05
697	Ed Lynch	.05
698	Ernie Whitt	.05
699	Ken Landreaux	.05
700	Dave Bergman	.05
701	Willie Randolph	.05
702	Greg Gross	.05
703	Dave Schmidt	.05
704	Jesse Orosco	.05
705	Bruce Hurst	.05
706	Rick Manning	.05
707	Bob McClure	.05
708	Scott McGregor	.05
709	Dave Kingman	.05
710	Gary Gaetti	.05
711	Ken Griffey	.05
712	Don Robinson	.05
713	Tom Brookens	.05
714	Dan Quisenberry	.05
715	Bob Dernier	.05
716	Rick Leach	.05
717	Ed Vande Berg	.05
718	Steve Carlton	.20
719	Tom Hume	.05
720	Richard Dotson	.05
721	Tom Herr	.05
722	Bob Knepper	.05
723	Brett Butler	.05
724	Greg Minton	.05
725	George Hendrick	.05
726	Frank Tanana	.05
727	Mike Moore	.05
728	Tippy Martinez	.05
729	Tom Paciorek	.05
730	Eric Show	.05
731	Dave Concepcion	.05
732	Manny Trillo	.05
733	Bill Caudill	.05
734	Bill Madlock	.05
735	Rickey Henderson	.25
736	Steve Bedrosian	.05
737	Floyd Bannister	.05
738	Jorge Orta	.05
739	Chet Lemon	.05
740	Rich Gedman	.05
741	Paul Molitor	.25
742	Andy McGaffigan	.05
743	Dwayne Murphy	.05
744	Roy Smalley	.05
745	Glenn Hubbard	.05
746	Bob Ojeda	.05
747	Johnny Ray	.05
748	Mike Flanagan	.05
749	Ozzie Smith	.40
750	Steve Trout	.05
751	Garth Iorg	.05
752	Dan Petry	.05
753	Rick Honeycutt	.05
754	Dave LaPoint	.05
755	Luis Aguayo	.05
756	Carlton Fisk	.20
757	Nolan Ryan	.75
758	Tony Bernazard	.05
759	Joel Youngblood	.05
760	Mike Witt	.05
761	Greg Pryor	.05
762	Gary Ward	.05
763	Tim Flannery	.05
764	Bill Buckner	.05
765	Kirk Gibson	.05
766	Don Aase	.05
767	Ron Cey	.05
768	Dennis Lamp	.05
769	Steve Sax	.05
770	Dave Winfield	.20
771	Shane Rawley	.05
772	Harold Baines	.05
773	Robin Yount	.30
774	Wayne Krenchicki	.05
775	Joaquin Andujar	.05
776	Tom Brunansky	.05
777	Chris Chambliss	.05
778	Jack Morris	.05
779	Craig Reynolds	.05
780	Andre Thornton	.05
781	Atlee Hammaker	.05
782	Brian Downing	.05
783	Willie Wilson	.05
784	Cal Ripken, Jr.	.75
785	Terry Francona	.05
786	Jimy Williams	.05
787	Alejandro Pena	.05
788	Tim Stoddard	.05
789	Dan Schatzeder	.05
790	Julio Cruz	.05
791	Lance Parrish	.05
792	Checklist 661-792	.05

1987 Topps Tiffany

Produced in much greater quantity (reportedly 30,000 sets) than the previous years' sets, this specially boxed collectors edition differs from the regular 1987 Topps cards only in its use of white cardboard stock and a high-gloss finish on the cards' fronts.

	MT
Complete Set (792):	110.00
Common Player:	.15

(Star cards valued at 3X-5X corresponding cards in regular 1987 Topps)

1987 Topps Traded

The Topps Traded set consists of 132 cards as did all Traded sets issued by Topps since 1981. Cards measure the standard 2-1/2" x 3-1/2" and are identical in design to the regular edition set. The purpose of the set is to update player trades and feature rookies not included in the regular issue. As they had done the previous three years, Topps produced a glossy-coated "Tiffany" edition of the Traded set. Cards are numbered with a "T" suffix.

No.	Player	MT
	Complete Set (132):	8.00
	Common Player:	.08
1	Bill Almon	.08
2	Scott Bankhead	.08
3	Eric Bell	.08
4	Juan Beniquez	.08
5	Juan Berenguer	.08
6	Greg Booker	.08
7	Thad Bosley	.08
8	Larry Bowa	.08
9	Greg Brock	.08
10	Bob Brower	.08
11	Jerry Browne	.10
12	Ralph Bryant	.08
13	DeWayne Buice	.08
14	Ellis Burks	.50
15	Ivan Calderon	.08
16	Jeff Calhoun	.08
17	Casey Candaele	.08
18	John Cangelosi	.08
19	Steve Carlton	.30
20	Juan Castillo	.08
21	Rick Cerone	.08
22	Ron Cey	.08
23	John Christensen	.08
24	Dave Cone	.50
25	Chuck Crim	.08
26	Storm Davis	.08
27	Andre Dawson	.25
28	Rick Dempsey	.08
29	Doug Drabek	.15
30	Mike Dunne	.08
31	Dennis Eckersley	.25
32	Lee Elia	.08
33	Brian Fisher	.08
34	Terry Francona	.08
35	Willie Fraser	.08
36	Billy Gardner	.08
37	Ken Gerhart	.08
38	Danny Gladden	.08
39	Jim Gott	.08
40	Cecilio Guante	.08
41	Albert Hall	.08
42	Terry Harper	.08
43	Mickey Hatcher	.08
44	Brad Havens	.08
45	Neal Heaton	.08
46	Mike Henneman	.20
47	Donnie Hill	.08
48	Guy Hoffman	.08
49	Brian Holton	.08
50	Charles Hudson	.08
51	Danny Jackson	.08
52	Reggie Jackson	.25
53	Chris James	.08
54	Dion James	.08
55	Stan Jefferson	.08
56	Joe Johnson	.08
57	Terry Kennedy	.08
58	Mike Kingery	.08
59	Ray Knight	.08
60	Gene Larkin	.10
61	Mike LaValliere	.08
62	Jack Lazorko	.08
63	Terry Leach	.08
64	Tim Leary	.08
65	Jim Lindeman	.08
66	Steve Lombardozzi	.08
67	Bill Long	.08
68	Barry Lyons	.08
69	Shane Mack	.10
70	*Greg Maddux*	5.00
71	Bill Madlock	.08
72	Joe Magrane	.08
73	Dave Martinez	.08
74	Fred McGriff	.50
75	Mark McLemore	.15
76	Kevin McReynolds	.10
77	Dave Meads	.08
78	Eddie Milner	.08
79	Greg Minton	.08
80	John Mitchell	.08
81	Kevin Mitchell	.10
82	Charlie Moore	.08
83	Jeff Musselman	.08
84	Gene Nelson	.08
85	Graig Nettles	.08
86	Al Newman	.08
87	Reid Nichols	.08
88	Tom Niedenfuer	.08
89	Joe Niekro	.08
90	Tom Nieto	.08
91	Matt Nokes	.10
92	Dickie Noles	.08
93	Pat Pacillo	.08
94	Lance Parrish	.10
95	Tony Pena	.08
96	Luis Polonia	.08
97	Randy Ready	.08
98	Jeff Reardon	.08
99	Gary Redus	.08
100	Jeff Reed	.08
101	Rick Rhoden	.08
102	Cal Ripken, Sr.	.08
103	Wally Ritchie	.08
104	Jeff Robinson	.08
105	Gary Roenicke	.08
106	Jerry Royster	.08
107	Mark Salas	.08
108	Luis Salazar	.08
109	Benny Santiago	.25
110	Dave Schmidt	.08
111	Kevin Seitzer	.10
112	John Shelby	.08
113	Steve Shields	.08
114	John Smiley	.20
115	Chris Speier	.08
116	Mike Stanley	.10
117	Terry Steinbach	.25
118	Les Straker	.08
119	Jim Sundberg	.08
120	Danny Tartabull	.10
121	Tom Trebelhorn	.08
122	Dave Valle	.08
123	Ed Vande Berg	.08
124	Andy Van Slyke	.08
125	Gary Ward	.08
126	Alan Wiggins	.08

#	Player	MT
127	Bill Wilkinson	.08
128	Frank Williams	.08
129	*Matt Williams*	.75
130	Jim Winn	.08
131	Matt Young	.08
132	Checklist 1T-132T	.08

1987 Topps Traded Tiffany

The cards in this specially boxed limited edition version of the Traded set differ from the regular-issue cards only in the application of a high-gloss finish to the cards' fronts. Production was reported as 30,000 sets.

	MT
Complete Set (132):	50.00
Common Player:	.25

(Star cards valued at 2X-3X corresponding cards in regular Topps Traded)

1987 Topps All-Star Glossy Set of 22

For the fourth consecutive year, Topps produced an All-Star Game commemorative set of 22 cards. The glossy cards, 2-1/2" x 3-1/2", were included in rack packs. Using the same basic design as in previous efforts with a few minor changes, the 1987 edition features American and National League logos on the card fronts. Cards #1-12 feature representatives from the American League, while #13-22 are National Leaguers.

		MT
Complete Set (22):		4.00
Common Player:		.15
1	Whitey Herzog	.15
2	Keith Hernandez	.15
3	Ryne Sandberg	.50
4	Mike Schmidt	.70
5	Ozzie Smith	.50
6	Tony Gwynn	.75
7	Dale Murphy	.25
8	Darryl Strawberry	.20
9	Gary Carter	.25
10	Dwight Gooden	.20
11	Fernando Valenzuela	.15
12	Dick Howser	.15
13	Wally Joyner	.25
14	Lou Whitaker	.15
15	Wade Boggs	.40
16	Cal Ripken, Jr.	1.00
17	Dave Winfield	.40
18	Rickey Henderson	.35
19	Kirby Puckett	.50
20	Lance Parrish	.15
21	Roger Clemens	.50
22	Teddy Higuera	.15

1987 Topps Glossy Rookies

The 1987 Topps Glossy Rookies set of 22 cards was introduced with Topps' new 100-card "Jumbo Packs". Intended for sale in supermarkets, the jumbo packs contained one glossy card. Measuring the standard 2-1/2" x 3-1/2" size, the special insert cards feature the top rookies from the previous season.

		MT
Complete Set (22):		4.00
Common Player:		.10
1	Andy Allanson	.10
2	John Cangelosi	.10
3	Jose Canseco	2.00
4	Will Clark	1.50
5	Mark Eichhorn	.10
6	Pete Incaviglia	.15
7	Wally Joyner	.30
8	Eric King	.10
9	Dave Magadan	.10
10	John Morris	.10
11	Juan Nieves	.10
12	Rafael Palmeiro	1.50
13	Billy Jo Robidoux	.10
14	Bruce Ruffin	.10
15	Ruben Sierra	.10
16	Cory Snyder	.10
17	Kurt Stillwell	.10
18	Dale Sveum	.10
19	Danny Tartabull	.10
20	Andres Thomas	.10
21	Robby Thompson	.10
22	Todd Worrell	.10

1987 Topps Mini League Leaders

Returning for 1987, the Topps "Major League Leaders" set was increased in size from 66 to 76 cards. The 2-1/8" x 3" cards feature woodgrain borders that encompass a white-bordered color photo. Backs are printed in yellow, orange and brown and list the player's official ranking based on his 1986 American or National League statistics. The players featured are those who finished the top five in their leagues' various batting and pitching categories. The cards were sold in plastic-wrapped packs, seven cards plus a game card per pack.

		MT
Complete Set (77):		4.00
Common Player:		.05
1	Bob Horner	.05
2	Dale Murphy	.15
3	Lee Smith	.05
4	Eric Davis	.05
5	John Franco	.05
6	Dave Parker	.05
7	Kevin Bass	.05
8	Glenn Davis	.05
9	Bill Doran	.05
10	Bob Knepper	.05
11	Mike Scott	.05
12	Dave Smith	.05
13	Mariano Duncan	.05
14	Orel Hershiser	.05
15	Steve Sax	.05
16	Fernando Valenzuela	.05
17	Tim Raines	.10
18	Jeff Reardon	.05
19	Floyd Youmans	.05
20	Gary Carter	.10
21	Ron Darling	.05
22	Sid Fernandez	.05
23	Dwight Gooden	.05
24	Keith Hernandez	.05
25	Bob Ojeda	.05
26	Darryl Strawberry	.10
27	Steve Bedrosian	.05
28	Von Hayes	.05
29	Juan Samuel	.05
30	Mike Schmidt	.40
31	Rick Rhoden	.05
32	Vince Coleman	.05
33	Danny Cox	.05
34	Todd Worrell	.05
35	Tony Gwynn	.40
36	Mike Krukow	.05
37	Candy Maldonado	.05
38	Don Aase	.05
39	Eddie Murray	.20
40	Cal Ripken, Jr.	1.00
41	Wade Boggs	.30
42	Roger Clemens	.45
43	Bruce Hurst	.05
44	Jim Rice	.10
45	Wally Joyner	.10
46	Donnie Moore	.05
47	Gary Pettis	.05
48	Mike Witt	.05
49	John Cangelosi	.05
50	Tom Candiotti	.05
51	Joe Carter	.05
52	Pat Tabler	.05
53	Kirk Gibson	.05
54	Willie Hernandez	.05
55	Jack Morris	.05
56	Alan Trammell	.05
57	George Brett	.45
58	Willie Wilson	.05
59	Rob Deer	.05
60	Teddy Higuera	.05
61	Bert Blyleven	.05
62	Gary Gaetti	.05
63	Kirby Puckett	.40
64	Rickey Henderson	.20
65	Don Mattingly	.45
66	Dennis Rasmussen	.05
67	Dave Righetti	.05
68	Jose Canseco	.30
69	Dave Kingman	.05
70	Phil Bradley	.05
71	Mark Langston	.05
72	Pete O'Brien	.05
73	Jesse Barfield	.05
74	George Bell	.05
75	Tony Fernandez	.05
76	Tom Henke	.05
77	Checklist	.05

1988 Topps

The 1988 Topps set features a clean, attractive design of a player photo surrounded by a thin colored frame which is encompassed by a white border. The player's name appears in the lower-right corner in a diagonal colored strip. The team nickname is in large letters at the top of the card. Backs feature black print on orange and gray stock and include the usual player personal and career statistics. Many of the cards contain a new feature titled "This Way To The Clubhouse", which explains how the player joined his current team. The 792-card set includes a number of special subsets including "Future Stars," "Turn Back The Clock," All-Star teams, All-Star rookie selections, and Record Breakers.

		MT
Complete Set (792):		15.00
Common Player:		.05
Pack (15):		.55
Wax Box (36):		10.00
1	Vince Coleman (Record Breakers)	.05
2	Don Mattingly (Record Breakers)	.15
3a	Mark McGwire (Record Breakers, white triangle by left foot)	1.00
3b	Mark McGwire (Record Breakers, no white triangle)	.50
4a	Eddie Murray (Record Breakers, no mention of record on front)	.25
4b	Eddie Murray (Record Breakers, record in box on front)	.20
5	Joe Niekro, Phil Niekro (Record Breakers)	.10
6	Nolan Ryan (Record Breakers)	.40
7	Benito Santiago (Record Breakers)	.05

8 Kevin Elster (Future Stars) .05
9 Andy Hawkins .05
10 Ryne Sandberg .40
11 Mike Young .05
12 Bill Schroeder .05
13 Andres Thomas .05
14 Sparky Anderson .10
15 Chili Davis .05
16 Kirk McCaskill .05
17 Ron Oester .05
18a *Al Leiter* (Future Stars, no "NY" on shirt, photo actually Steve George) .40
18b *Al Leiter* (Future Stars, "NY" on shirt, correct photo) .20
19 *Mark Davidson* .05
20 Kevin Gross .05
21 Red Sox Leaders (Wade Boggs, Spike Owen) .10
22 Greg Swindell .05
23 Ken Landreaux .05
24 Jim Deshaies .05
25 Andres Galarraga .25
26 Mitch Williams .05
27 R.J. Reynolds .05
28 *Jose Nunez* .05
29 Argenis Salazar .05
30 Sid Fernandez .05
31 Bruce Bochy .05
32 Mike Morgan .05
33 Rob Deer .05
34 Ricky Horton .05
35 Harold Baines .05
36 Jamie Moyer .05
37 Ed Romero .05
38 Jeff Calhoun .05
39 Gerald Perry .05
40 Orel Hershiser .05
41 Bob Melvin .05
42 *Bill Landrum* .05
43 Dick Schofield .05
44 Lou Piniella .05
45 Kent Hrbek .05
46 Darnell Coles .05
47 Joaquin Andujar .05
48 Alan Ashby .05
49 Dave Clark .05
50 Hubie Brooks .05
51 Orioles Leaders (Eddie Murray, Cal Ripken, Jr.) .25
52 Don Robinson .05
53 Curt Wilkerson .05
54 Jim Clancy .05
55 Phil Bradley .05
56 Ed Hearn .05
57 *Tim Crews* .05
58 Dave Magadan .05
59 Danny Cox .05
60 Rickey Henderson .15
61 *Mark Knudson* .05
62 Jeff Hamilton .05
63 Jimmy Jones .05
64 *Ken Caminiti* .50
65 Leon Durham .05
66 Shane Rawley .05
67 Ken Oberkfell .05
68 Dave Dravecky .05
69 *Mike Hart* .05
70 Roger Clemens .50
71 Gary Pettis .05
72 Dennis Eckersley .05
73 Randy Bush .05
74 Tom Lasorda .10
75 Joe Carter .10
76 Denny Martinez .05
77 Tom O'Malley .05
78 Dan Petry .05
79 Ernie Whitt .05
80 Mark Langston .05
81 Reds Leaders (John Franco, Ron Robinson) .05
82 *Darrel Akerfelds* .05
83 Jose Oquendo .05
84 Cecilio Guante .05
85 Howard Johnson .05
86 Ron Karkovice .05
87 Mike Mason .05
88 Earnie Riles .05
89 *Gary Thurman* .05
90 Dale Murphy .15
91 *Joey Cora* .20
92 Len Matuszek .05
93 Bob Sebra .05
94 *Chuck Jackson* .05

95 Lance Parrish .05
96 *Todd Benzinger* .10
97 Scott Garrelts .05
98 *Rene Gonzales* .05
99 Chuck Finley .05
100 Jack Clark .05
101 Allan Anderson .05
102 Barry Larkin .20
103 Curt Young .05
104 Dick Williams .05
105 Jesse Orosco .05
106 *Jim Walewander* .05
107 Scott Bailes .05
108 Steve Lyons .05
109 Joel Skinner .05
110 Teddy Higuera .05
111 Expos Leaders (Hubie Brooks, Vance Law) .05
112 *Les Lancaster* .05
113 Kelly Gruber .05
114 Jeff Russell .05
115 Johnny Ray .05
116 Jerry Don Gleaton .05
117 *James Steels* .05
118 Bob Welch .05
119 *Robbie Wine* .05
120 Kirby Puckett .40
121 Checklist 1-132 .05
122 Tony Bernazard .05
123 Tom Candiotti .05
124 Ray Knight .05
125 Bruce Hurst .05
126 Steve Jeltz .05
127 Jim Gott .05
128 Johnny Grubb .05
129 Greg Minton .05
130 Buddy Bell .05
131 Don Schulze .05
132 Donnie Hill .05
133 Greg Mathews .05
134 Chuck Tanner .05
135 Dennis Rasmussen .05
136 Brian Dayett .05
137 Chris Bosio .05
138 Mitch Webster .05
139 Jerry Browne .05
140 Jesse Barfield .05
141 Royals Leaders (George Brett, Bret Saberhagen) .20
142 Andy Van Slyke .05
143 Mickey Tettleton .05
144 *Don Gordon* .05
145 Bill Madlock .05
146 *Donell Nixon* .05
147 Bill Buckner .05
148 Carmelo Martinez .05
149 Ken Howell .05
150 Eric Davis .05
151 Bob Knepper .05
152 *Jody Reed* .15
153 John Habyan .05
154 Jeff Stone .05
155 Bruce Sutter .05
156 Gary Matthews .05
157 Atlee Hammaker .05
158 Tim Hulett .05
159 *Brad Arnsberg* .05
160 Willie McGee .05
161 Bryn Smith .05
162 Mark McLemore .05
163 Dale Mohorcic .05
164 Dave Johnson .05
165 Robin Yount .25
166 *Rick Rodriguez* .05
167 Rance Mulliniks .05
168 Barry Jones .05
169 *Ross Jones* .05
170 Rich Gossage .05
171 Cubs Leaders (Shawon Dunston, Manny Trillo) .05
172 *Lloyd McClendon* .05
173 Eric Plunk .05
174 Phil Garner .05
175 Kevin Bass .05
176 Jeff Reed .05
177 Frank Tanana .05
178 Dwayne Henry .05
179 Charlie Puleo .05
180 Terry Kennedy .05
181 Dave Cone .20
182 Ken Phelps .05
183 Tom Lawless .05
184 Ivan Calderon .05
185 Rick Rhoden .05
186 Rafael Palmeiro .30
187 Steve Kiefer .05
188 John Russell .05
189 *Wes Gardner* .05

190 Candy Maldonado .05
191 John Cerutti .05
192 Devon White .05
193 Brian Fisher .05
194 Tom Kelly .05
195 Dan Quisenberry .05
196 Dave Engle .05
197 Lance McCullers .05
198 Franklin Stubbs .05
199 *Dave Meads* .05
200 Wade Boggs .25
201 Rangers Leaders (Steve Buechele, Pete Incaviglia, Pete O'Brien, Bobby Valentine) .05
202 Glenn Hoffman .05
203 Fred Toliver .05
204 Paul O'Neill .20
205 *Nelson Liriano* .05
206 Domingo Ramos .05
207 *John Mitchell* .05
208 Steve Lake .05
209 Richard Dotson .05
210 Willie Randolph .05
211 Frank DiPino .05
212 Greg Brock .05
213 Albert Hall .05
214 Dave Schmidt .05
215 Von Hayes .05
216 Jerry Reuss .05
217 Harry Spilman .05
218 Dan Schatzeder .05
219 Mike Stanley .05
220 Tom Henke .05
221 Rafael Belliard .05
222 Steve Farr .05
223 Stan Jefferson .05
224 Tom Trebelhorn .05
225 Mike Scioscia .05
226 Dave Lopes .05
227 Ed Correa .05
228 Wallace Johnson .05
229 Jeff Musselman .05
230 Pat Tabler .05
231 Pirates Leaders (Barry Bonds, Bobby Bonilla) .20
232 Bob James .05
233 Rafael Santana .05
234 Ken Dayley .05
235 Gary Ward .05
236 Ted Power .05
237 Mike Heath .05
238 *Luis Polonia* .10
239 Roy Smalley .05
240 Lee Smith .05
241 Damaso Garcia .05
242 Tom Niedenfuer .05
243 Mark Ryal .05
244 Jeff Robinson .05
245 Rich Gedman .05
246 *Mike Campbell* (Future Stars) .05
247 Thad Bosley .05
248 Storm Davis .05
249 Mike Marshall .05
250 Nolan Ryan .75
251 Tom Foley .05
252 Bob Brower .05
253 Checklist 133-264 .05
254 Lee Elia .05
255 Mookie Wilson .05
256 Ken Schrom .05
257 Jerry Royster .05
258 Ed Nunez .05
259 Ron Kittle .05
260 Vince Coleman .05
261 Giants Leaders (Will Clark, Candy Maldonado, Kevin Mitchell, Robby Thompson, Jose Uribe) .10
262 Drew Hall .05
263 Glenn Braggs .05
264 *Les Straker* .05
265 Bo Diaz .05
266 Paul Assenmacher .05
267 *Billy Bean* .05
268 Bruce Ruffin .05
269 *Ellis Burks* .25
270 Mike Witt .05
271 Ken Gerhart .05
272 Steve Ontiveros .05
273 Garth Iorg .05
274 Junior Ortiz .05
275 Kevin Seitzer .05
276 Luis Salazar .05
277 Alejandro Pena .05
278 Jose Cruz .05

279 Randy St. Claire .05
280 Pete Incaviglia .05
281 Jerry Hairston .05
282 Pat Perry .05
283 Phil Lombardi .05
284 Larry Bowa .05
285 Jim Presley .05
286 *Chuck Crim* .05
287 Manny Trillo .05
288 *Pat Pacillo* .05
289 Dave Bergman .05
290 Tony Fernandez .05
291 Astros Leaders (Kevin Bass, Billy Hatcher) .05
292 Carney Lansford .05
293 *Doug Jones* .15
294 *Al Pedrique* .05
295 Bert Blyleven .05
296 Floyd Rayford .05
297 Zane Smith .05
298 Milt Thompson .05
299 Steve Crawford .05
300 Don Mattingly .50
301 Bud Black .05
302 Jose Uribe .05
303 Eric Show .05
304 George Hendrick .05
305 Steve Sax .05
306 Billy Hatcher .05
307 Mike Trujillo .05
308 Lee Mazzilli .05
309 *Bill Long* .05
310 Tom Herr .05
311 Scott Sanderson .05
312 Joey Meyer (Future Stars) .05
313 Bob McClure .05
314 Jimy Williams .05
315 Dave Parker .10
316 Jose Rijo .05
317 Tom Nieto .05
318 Mel Hall .05
319 Mike Loynd .05
320 Alan Trammell .05
321 White Sox Leaders (Harold Baines, Carlton Fisk) .10
322 *Vicente Palacios* .05
323 Rick Leach .05
324 Danny Jackson .05
325 Glenn Hubbard .05
326 Al Nipper .05
327 Larry Sheets .05
328 *Greg Cadaret* .05
329 Chris Speier .05
330 Eddie Whitson .05
331 Brian Downing .05
332 Jerry Reed .05
333 Wally Backman .05
334 Dave LaPoint .05
335 Claudell Washington .05
336 Ed Lynch .05
337 Jim Gantner .05
338 Brian Holton .05
339 Kurt Stillwell .05
340 Jack Morris .05
341 Carmen Castillo .05
342 Larry Andersen .05
343 Greg Gagne .05
344 Tony LaRussa .05
345 Scott Fletcher .05
346 Vance Law .05
347 Joe Johnson .05
348 Jim Eisenreich .05
349 Bob Walk .05
350 Will Clark .25
351 Cardinals Leaders (Tony Pena, Red Schoendienst) .05
352 *Billy Ripken* .05
353 Ed Olwine .05
354 Marc Sullivan .05
355 Roger McDowell .05
356 Luis Aguayo .05
357 Floyd Bannister .05
358 Rey Quinones .05
359 Tim Stoddard .05
360 Tony Gwynn .30
361 Greg Maddux 1.00
362 Juan Castillo .05
363 Willie Fraser .05
364 Nick Esasky .05
365 Floyd Youmans .05
366 Chet Lemon .05
367 Tim Leary .05
368 *Gerald Young* .05
369 Greg Harris .05
370 Jose Canseco .40
371 Joe Hesketh .05
372 Matt Williams .75

No.	Player	Value
373	Checklist 265-396	.05
374	Doc Edwards	.05
375	Tom Brunansky	.05
376	*Bill Wilkinson*	.05
377	*Sam Horn*	.05
378	*Todd Frohwirth*	.05
379	Rafael Ramirez	.05
380	*Joe Magrane*	.05
381	Angels Leaders (Jack Howell, Wally Joyner)	.05
382	*Keith Miller*	.05
383	Eric Bell	.05
384	Neil Allen	.05
385	Carlton Fisk	.25
386	Don Mattingly (All-Star)	.15
387	Willie Randolph (All-Star)	.05
388	Wade Boggs (All-Star)	.15
389	Alan Trammell (All-Star)	.05
390	George Bell (All-Star)	.05
391	Kirby Puckett (All-Star)	.20
392	Dave Winfield (All-Star)	.10
393	Matt Nokes (All-Star)	.05
394	Roger Clemens (All-Star)	.15
395	Jimmy Key (All-Star)	.05
396	Tom Henke (All-Star)	.05
397	Jack Clark (All-Star)	.05
398	Juan Samuel (All-Star)	.05
399	Tim Wallach (All-Star)	.05
400	Ozzie Smith (All-Star)	.15
401	Andre Dawson (All-Star)	.10
402	Tony Gwynn (All-Star)	.15
403	Tim Raines (All-Star)	.05
404	Benny Santiago (All-Star)	.05
405	Dwight Gooden (All-Star)	.10
406	Shane Rawley (All-Star)	.05
407	Steve Bedrosian (All-Star)	.05
408	Dion James	.05
409	Joel McKeon	.05
410	Tony Pena	.05
411	Wayne Tolleson	.05
412	Randy Myers	.10
413	John Christensen	.05
414	John McNamara	.05
415	Don Carman	.05
416	Keith Moreland	.05
417	*Mark Ciardi*	.05
418	Joel Youngblood	.05
419	Scott McGregor	.05
420	Wally Joyner	.10
421	Ed Vande Berg	.05
422	Dave Concepcion	.05
423	*John Smiley*	.20
424	Dwayne Murphy	.05
425	Jeff Reardon	.05
426	Randy Ready	.05
427	*Paul Kilgus*	.05
428	John Shelby	.05
429	Tigers Leaders (Kirk Gibson, Alan Trammell)	.05
430	Glenn Davis	.05
431	Casey Candaele	.05
432	Mike Moore	.05
433	*Bill Pecota*	.05
434	Rick Aguilera	.05
435	Mike Pagliarulo	.05
436	Mike Bielecki	.05
437	*Fred Manrique*	.05
438	*Rob Ducey*	.05
439	Dave Martinez	.05
440	Steve Bedrosian	.05
441	Rick Manning	.05
442	*Tom Bolton*	.05
443	Ken Griffey	.05
444	Cal Ripken, Sr.	.05
445	Mike Krukow	.05
446	Doug DeCinces	.05
447	*Jeff Montgomery*	.20
448	Mike Davis	.05
449	*Jeff Robinson*	.05
450	Barry Bonds	.50
451	Keith Atherton	.05
452	Willie Wilson	.05
453	Dennis Powell	.05
454	Marvell Wynne	.05
455	*Shawn Hillegas*	.05
456	Dave Anderson	.05
457	Terry Leach	.05
458	Ron Hassey	.05
459	Yankees Leaders (Willie Randolph, Dave Winfield)	.05
460	Ozzie Smith	.25
461	Danny Darwin	.05
462	Don Slaught	.05
463	Fred McGriff	.25
464	Jay Tibbs	.05
465	Paul Molitor	.25
466	Jerry Mumphrey	.05
467	Don Aase	.05
468	Darren Daulton	.05
469	Jeff Dedmon	.05
470	Dwight Evans	.05
471	Donnie Moore	.05
472	Robby Thompson	.05
473	Joe Niekro	.05
474	Tom Brookens	.05
475	Pete Rose	.30
476	Dave Stewart	.05
477	Jamie Quirk	.05
478	Sid Bream	.05
479	Brett Butler	.05
480	Dwight Gooden	.10
481	Mariano Duncan	.05
482	Mark Davis	.05
483	*Rod Booker*	.05
484	Pat Clements	.05
485	Harold Reynolds	.05
486	*Pat Keedy*	.05
487	Jim Pankovits	.05
488	Andy McGaffigan	.05
489	Dodgers Leaders (Pedro Guerrero, Fernando Valenzuela)	.05
490	Larry Parrish	.05
491	B.J. Surhoff	.05
492	Doyle Alexander	.05
493	Mike Greenwell	.05
494	*Wally Ritchie*	.05
495	Eddie Murray	.20
496	Guy Hoffman	.05
497	Kevin Mitchell	.05
498	Bob Boone	.05
499	Eric King	.05
500	Andre Dawson	.10
501	Tim Birtsas	.05
502	Danny Gladden	.05
503	*Junior Noboa*	.05
504	Bob Rodgers	.05
505	Willie Upshaw	.05
506	John Cangelosi	.05
507	Mark Gubicza	.05
508	Tim Teufel	.05
509	Bill Dawley	.05
510	Dave Winfield	.15
511	Joel Davis	.05
512	Alex Trevino	.05
513	Tim Flannery	.05
514	Pat Sheridan	.05
515	Juan Nieves	.05
516	Jim Sundberg	.05
517	Ron Robinson	.05
518	Greg Gross	.05
519	Mariners Leaders (Phil Bradley, Harold Reynolds)	.05
520	Dave Smith	.05
521	Jim Dwyer	.05
522	*Bob Patterson*	.05
523	Gary Roenicke	.05
524	Gary Lucas	.05
525	Marty Barrett	.05
526	Juan Berenguer	.05
527	Steve Henderson	.05
528a	Checklist 397-528 (#455 is Steve Carlton)	.05
528b	Checklist 397-528 (#455 is Shawn Hillegas)	.05
529	Tim Burke	.05
530	Gary Carter	.10
531	Rich Yett	.05
532	Mike Kingery	.05
533	*John Farrell*	.05
534	John Wathan	.05
535	Ron Guidry	.05
536	John Morris	.05
537	Steve Buechele	.05
538	Bill Wegman	.05
539	Mike LaValliere	.05
540	Bret Saberhagen	.10
541	Juan Beniquez	.05
542	*Paul Noce*	.05
543	Kent Tekulve	.05
544	Jim Traber	.05
545	Don Baylor	.10
546	John Candelaria	.05
547	*Felix Fermin*	.05
548	*Shane Mack*	.10
549	Braves Leaders (Ken Griffey, Dion James, Dale Murphy, Gerald Perry)	.05
550	Pedro Guerrero	.05
551	Terry Steinbach	.05
552	Mark Thurmond	.05
553	Tracy Jones	.05
554	Mike Smithson	.05
555	Brook Jacoby	.05
556	*Stan Clarke*	.05
557	Craig Reynolds	.05
558	Bob Ojeda	.05
559	*Ken Williams*	.05
560	Tim Wallach	.05
561	Rick Cerone	.05
562	Jim Lindeman	.05
563	Jose Guzman	.05
564	Frank Lucchesi	.05
565	Lloyd Moseby	.05
566	*Charlie O'Brien*	.05
567	Mike Diaz	.05
568	Chris Brown	.05
569	Charlie Leibrandt	.05
570	Jeffrey Leonard	.05
571	*Mark Williamson*	.05
572	Chris James	.05
573	Bob Stanley	.05
574	Graig Nettles	.05
575	Don Sutton	.10
576	*Tommy Hinzo*	.05
577	Tom Browning	.05
578	Gary Gaetti	.05
579	Mets Leaders (Gary Carter, Kevin McReynolds)	.05
580	Mark McGwire	1.50
581	Tito Landrum	.05
582	*Mike Henneman*	.15
583	Dave Valle	.05
584	Steve Trout	.05
585	Ozzie Guillen	.05
586	Bob Forsch	.05
587	Terry Puhl	.05
588	*Jeff Parrett*	.05
589	Geno Petralli	.05
590	George Bell	.05
591	Doug Drabek	.05
592	Dale Sveum	.05
593	Bob Tewksbury	.05
594	Bobby Valentine	.05
595	Frank White	.05
596	John Kruk	.05
597	Gene Garber	.05
598	Lee Lacy	.05
599	Calvin Schiraldi	.05
600	Mike Schmidt	.25
601	Jack Lazorko	.05
602	Mike Aldrete	.05
603	Rob Murphy	.05
604	Chris Bando	.05
605	Kirk Gibson	.05
606	Moose Haas	.05
607	Mickey Hatcher	.05
608	Charlie Kerfeld	.05
609	Twins Leaders (Gary Gaetti, Kent Hrbek)	.05
610	Keith Hernandez	.05
611	Tommy John	.05
612	Curt Ford	.05
613	Bobby Thigpen	.05
614	Herm Winningham	.05
615	Jody Davis	.05
616	*Jay Aldrich*	.05
617	Oddibe McDowell	.05
618	Cecil Fielder	.10
619	*Mike Dunne*	.05
620	Cory Snyder	.05
621	Gene Nelson	.05
622	Kal Daniels	.05
623	Mike Flanagan	.05
624	Jim Leyland	.05
625	Frank Viola	.05
626	Glenn Wilson	.05
627	*Joe Boever*	.05
628	Dave Henderson	.05
629	Kelly Downs	.05
630	Darrell Evans	.05
631	Jack Howell	.05
632	*Steve Shields*	.05
633	*Barry Lyons*	.05
634	Jose DeLeon	.05
635	Terry Pendleton	.05
636	Charles Hudson	.05
637	*Jay Bell*	.25
638	Steve Balboni	.05
639	Brewers Leaders (Glenn Braggs, Tony Muser)	.05
640	Garry Templeton	.05
641	Rick Honeycutt	.05
642	Bob Dernier	.05
643	*Rocky Childress*	.05
644	Terry McGriff	.05
645	*Matt Nokes*	.10
646	Checklist 529-660	.05
647	Pascual Perez	.05
648	Al Newman	.05
649	*DeWayne Buice*	.05
650	Cal Ripken, Jr.	.60
651	*Mike Jackson*	.10
652	Bruce Benedict	.05
653	Jeff Sellers	.05
654	Roger Craig	.05
655	Len Dykstra	.10
656	Lee Guetterman	.05
657	Gary Redus	.05
658	Tim Conroy	.05
659	Bobby Meacham	.05
660	Rick Reuschel	.05
661	Nolan Ryan (Turn Back the Clock)	.35
662	Jim Rice (Turn Back the Clock)	.05
663	Ron Blomberg (Turn Back the Clock)	.05
664	Bob Gibson (Turn Back the Clock)	.10
665	Stan Musial (Turn Back the Clock)	.15
666	Mario Soto	.05
667	Luis Quinones	.05
668	Walt Terrell	.05
669	Phillies Leaders (Lance Parrish, Mike Ryan)	.05
670	Dan Plesac	.05
671	Tim Laudner	.05
672	*John Davis*	.05
673	Tony Phillips	.05
674	Mike Fitzgerald	.05
675	Jim Rice	.10
676	Ken Dixon	.05
677	Eddie Milner	.05
678	Jim Acker	.05
679	Darrell Miller	.05
680	Charlie Hough	.05
681	Bobby Bonilla	.10
682	Jimmy Key	.05
683	Julio Franco	.05
684	Hal Lanier	.05
685	Ron Darling	.05
686	Terry Francona	.05
687	Mickey Brantley	.05
688	Jim Winn	.05
689	*Tom Pagnozzi*	.05
690	Jay Howell	.05
691	Dan Pasqua	.05
692	Mike Birkbeck	.05
693	Benny Santiago	.05
694	*Eric Nolte*	.05
695	Shawon Dunston	.15
696	Duane Ward	.05
697	Steve Lombardozzi	.05
698	Brad Havens	.05
699	Padres Leaders (Tony Gwynn, Benny Santiago)	.15
700	George Brett	.40
701	Sammy Stewart	.05
702	Mike Gallego	.05
703	Bob Brenly	.05
704	Dennis Boyd	.05
705	Juan Samuel	.05
706	Rick Mahler	.05
707	Fred Lynn	.05
708	Gus Polidor	.05
709	George Frazier	.05
710	Darryl Strawberry	.10
711	Bill Gullickson	.05
712	John Moses	.05
713	Willie Hernandez	.05
714	Jim Fregosi	.05
715	Todd Worrell	.05
716	Lenn Sakata	.05
717	Jay Baller	.05
718	Mike Felder	.05
719	Denny Walling	.05
720	Tim Raines	.10
721	Pete O'Brien	.05

722 Manny Lee .05
723 Bob Kipper .05
724 Danny Tartabull .05
725 Mike Boddicker .05
726 Alfredo Griffin .05
727 Greg Booker .05
728 Andy Allanson .05
729 Blue Jays Leaders (George Bell, Fred McGriff) .10
730 John Franco .05
731 Rick Schu .05
732 Dave Palmer .05
733 Spike Owen .05
734 Craig Lefferts .05
735 Kevin McReynolds .05
736 Matt Young .05
737 Butch Wynegar .05
738 Scott Bankhead .05
739 Daryl Boston .05
740 Rick Sutcliffe .05
741 Mike Easler .05
742 Mark Clear .05
743 Larry Herndon .05
744 Whitey Herzog .05
745 Bill Doran .05
746 *Gene Larkin* .10
747 Bobby Witt .05
748 Reid Nichols .05
749 Mark Eichhorn .05
750 Bo Jackson .20
751 Jim Morrison .05
752 Mark Grant .05
753 Danny Heep .05
754 Mike LaCoss .05
755 Ozzie Virgil .05
756 Mike Maddux .05
757 *John Marzano* .05
758 *Eddie Williams* .05
759 A's Leaders (Jose Canseco, Mark McGwire) .75
760 Mike Scott .05
761 Tony Armas .05
762 Scott Bradley .05
763 Doug Sisk .05
764 Greg Walker .05
765 Neal Heaton .05
766 Henry Cotto .05
767 *Jose Lind* (Future Stars) .15
768 Dickie Noles .05
769 Cecil Cooper .05
770 Lou Whitaker .05
771 Ruben Sierra .05
772 Sal Butera .05
773 Frank Williams .05
774 Gene Mauch .05
775 Dave Stieb .05
776 Checklist 661-792 .05
777 Lonnie Smith .05
778a *Keith Comstock* (white team letters) .40
778b *Keith Comstock* (blue team letters) .15
779 *Tom Glavine* .75
780 Fernando Valenzuela .05
781 *Keith Hughes* .05
782 *Jeff Ballard* .05
783 Ron Roenicke .05
784 Joe Sambito .05
785 Alvin Davis .05
786 Joe Price .05
787 Bill Almon .05
788 Ray Searage .05
789 Indians Leaders (Joe Carter, Cory Snyder) .10
790 Dave Righetti .05
791 Ted Simmons .05
792 John Tudor .05

1988 Topps Tiffany

Sharing a checklist with the regular issue 1988 Topps baseball set, this specially boxed, limited-edition (25,000 sets) features cards printed on white cardboard stock with high-gloss front finish. Topps offered the sets directly to the public in ads in USA Today and Sporing News at a price of $99.

MT
Complete Set (792): 85.00
Common Player: .15
(Star cards valued at 3X-5X corresponding cards in regular 1988 Topps issue)

1988 Topps Box Panels

After a one-year hiatus during which they appeared on the sides of Topps wax pack display boxes, Topps retail box cards returned to box bottoms in 1988. The series includes 16 standard-size baseball cards, four cards per each of four different display boxes. Card fronts follow the same design as the 1988 Topps basic issue; full-color player photos, framed in yellow, surrounded by a white border; diagonal player name lower-right; team name in large letters at the top. Card backs are "numbered" A through P and are printed in black and orange.

MT
Complete Panel Set (4):3.00
Complete Singles Set (16):1.50
Common Panel:.50
Common Single Player:.05
Panel .50
A Don Baylor .05
B Steve Bedrosian .05
C Juan Beniquez .05
D Bob Boone .05
Panel .70
E Darrell Evans .05
F Tony Gwynn .50
G John Kruk .05
H Marvell Wynne .05
Panel .60
I Joe Carter .10
J Eric Davis .05
K Howard Johnson .05
L Darryl Strawberry .10
Panel 2.00
M Rickey Henderson .20
N Nolan Ryan 1.00
O Mike Schmidt .35
P Kent Tekulve .05

Panel .50
A Don Baylor .08
B Steve Bedrosian .06
C Juan Beniquez .04
D Bob Boone .06
Panel .70
E Darrell Evans .06
F Tony Gwynn .15
G John Kruk .13
H Marvell Wynne .04
Panel .60
I Joe Carter .13
J Eric Davis .13
K Howard Johnson .06
L Darryl Strawberry .10
Panel 2.00
M Rickey Henderson .25
N Nolan Ryan .40
O Mike Schmidt .20
P Kent Tekulve .04

1988 Topps Traded

In addition to new players and traded veterans, 21 members of the U.S.A. Olympic Baseball team are showcased in this 132-card set, numbered 1T-132T. The 2-1/2" x 3-1/2" cards follow the same design as the basic Topps issue - white borders, large full-color photos, team name (or U.S.A.) in large bold letters at the top of the card face, player name on a diagonal stripe across the lower-right corner. Topps had issued its traded series each year since 1981 in boxed complete sets available only through hobby dealers.

MT
Complete Set (132):12.00
Common Player:.05
1 *Jim Abbott* (USA) .25
2 Juan Agosto .05
3 Luis Alicea .05
4 *Roberto Alomar* 3.00
5 *Brady Anderson* 1.00
6 Jack Armstrong .05
7 Don August .05
8 Floyd Bannister .05
9 Bret Barberie (USA) .20
10 Jose Bautista .05
11 Don Baylor .15
12 Tim Belcher .05
13 Buddy Bell .05
14 *Andy Benes* (USA) .50
15 Damon Berryhill .05
16 Bud Black .05
17 Pat Borders .05
18 Phil Bradley .05
19 Jeff Branson (USA) .05
20 Tom Brunansky .05
21 *Jay Buhner* .75
22 Brett Butler .10
23 Jim Campanis (USA) .10
24 Sil Campusano .05
25 John Candelaria .05
26 Jose Cecena .05
27 Rick Cerone .05
28 Jack Clark .05
29 Kevin Coffman .05
30 Pat Combs (USA) .10
31 Henry Cotto .05
32 Chili Davis .05
33 Mike Davis .05
34 Jose DeLeon .05
35 Richard Dotson .05
36 Cecil Espy .05
37 Tom Filer .05
38 Mike Fiore (USA) .05
39 *Ron Gant* .50
40 Kirk Gibson .05
41 Rich Gossage .05
42 *Mark Grace* 1.50
43 Alfredo Griffin .05
44 Ty Griffin (USA) .10
45 Bryan Harvey .10
46 Ron Hassey .05
47 Ray Hayward .05
48 Dave Henderson .05
49 Tom Herr .05
50 Bob Horner .05
51 Ricky Horton .05
52 Jay Howell .05
53 Glenn Hubbard .05
54 Jeff Innis .10
55 Danny Jackson .05
56 Darrin Jackson .10
57 Roberto Kelly .10
58 Ron Kittle .05
59 Ray Knight .05
60 Vance Law .05
61 Jeffrey Leonard .05
62 Mike Macfarlane .10
63 Scotti Madison .05
64 Kirt Manwaring .10
65 Mark Marquess (USA) .05
66 *Tino Martinez* (USA) 2.00
67 Billy Masse (USA) .05
68 *Jack McDowell* .25
69 Jack McKeon .05
70 Larry McWilliams .05
71 Mickey Morandini (USA) .25
72 Keith Moreland .05
73 Mike Morgan .05
74 Charles Nagy (USA) .50
75 Al Nipper .05
76 Russ Nixon .05
77 Jesse Orosco .05
78 Joe Orsulak .05
79 Dave Palmer .05
80 Mark Parent .10
81 Dave Parker .10
82 Dan Pasqua .10
83 Melido Perez .05
84 Steve Peters .05
85 Dan Petry .05
86 Gary Pettis .05
87 Jeff Pico .05
88 Jim Poole (USA) .10
89 Ted Power .05
90 Rafael Ramirez .05
91 Dennis Rasmussen .05
92 Jose Rijo .05
93 Earnie Riles .05
94 Luis Rivera .05
95 Doug Robbins (USA) .05
96 Frank Robinson .15
97 Cookie Rojas .05
98 Chris Sabo .10
99 Mark Salas .05
100 Luis Salazar .05
101 Rafael Santana .05
102 Nelson Santovenia .05
103 Mackey Sasser .05
104 Calvin Schiraldi .05
105 Mike Schooler .05
106 Scott Servais (USA) .10
107 Dave Silvestri (USA) .10
108 Don Slaught .05
109 Joe Slusarski (USA) .10
110 Lee Smith .10
111 Pete Smith .10
112 Jim Snyder .05
113 Ed Sprague (USA) .40
114 Pete Stanicek .05
115 Kurt Stillwell .05
116 Todd Stottlemyre .25
117 Bill Swift .05
118 Pat Tabler .05
119 Scott Terry .05
120 Mickey Tettleton .10
121 Dickie Thon .05
122 Jeff Treadway .05
123 Willie Upshaw .05
124 *Robin Ventura* 4.00
125 Ron Washington .05
126 Walt Weiss .25
127 Bob Welch .05
128 David Wells 1.00
129 Glenn Wilson .05
130 Ted Wood (USA) .05
131 Don Zimmer .05
132 Checklist 1T-132T .05

1988 Topps Traded Tiffany

The high-gloss front surface is all that distinguishes this limited-edition, hobby-only collectors version from the regular Topps Traded boxed set.

	MT
Complete Set (132):	55.00
Common Player:	.15

(Star cards valued at 3X-4X corresponding cards in regular Topps Traded issue)

1988 Topps All-Star Glossy Set of 22

The fifth edition of Topps' special All-Star inserts was included in the company's 1988 rack packs. The 1987 American and National League All-Star lineup, plus honorary captains Jim Hunter and Billy Williams, are featured on the 2-1/2" x 3-1/2" cards. The glossy full-color fronts contain player photos centered between a red and yellow "1987 All-Star" logo at top and the player name (also red and yellow) which is printed in the bottom margin. A league logo is in the lower-left corner. Card backs are printed in red and blue on a white background, with the title and All-Star logo emblem printed above the player name and card number.

		MT
Complete Set (22):3.00		
Common Player:.15		
1	John McNamara	.15
2	Don Mattingly	1.00
3	Willie Randolph	.15
4	Wade Boggs	.65
5	Cal Ripken, Jr.	1.50
6	George Bell	.15
7	Rickey Henderson	.50
8	Dave Winfield	.40
9	Terry Kennedy	.15
10	Bret Saberhagen	.15
11	Catfish Hunter	.15
12	Davey Johnson	.15
13	Jack Clark	.15
14	Ryne Sandberg	.65
15	Mike Schmidt	.75
16	Ozzie Smith	.50
17	Eric Davis	.15
18	Andre Dawson	.20
19	Darryl Strawberry	.15
20	Gary Carter	.20
21	Mike Scott	.15
22	Billy Williams	.15

1988 Topps Big Baseball

Topps Big Baseball cards (2-5/8" x 3-3/4") were issued in three series, 88 cards per series (a total set of 264 cards) sold in seven-card packs. The glossy cards are similar in format, both front and back, to the 1956 Topps set. Each card features a portrait and a game-action photo on the front, framed by a wide white border. A white outline highlights the portrait. The player's name appears at bottom on a splash of color that fades from yellow to orange to red to pink. On the card back, the player's name is printed in large red letters across the top, followed by his team name and position in black. Personal info is printed in a red rectangle beside a Topps baseball logo bearing the card number. A triple cartoon strip, in full-color, illustrates career highlights, performance, personal background, etc. A red, white and blue statistics box (pitching, batting, fielding) is printed across the bottom.

		MT
Complete Set (264):21.00		
Common Player:.05		
1	Paul Molitor	.50
2	Milt Thompson	.05
3	Billy Hatcher	.05
4	Mike Witt	.05
5	Vince Coleman	.05
6	Dwight Evans	.05
7	Tim Wallach	.05
8	Alan Trammell	.10
9	Will Clark	.50
10	Jeff Reardon	.05
11	Dwight Gooden	.15
12	Benny Santiago	.05
13	Jose Canseco	.50
14	Dale Murphy	.15
15	George Bell	.05
16	Ryne Sandberg	.60
17	Brook Jacoby	.05
18	Fernando Valenzuela	.05
19	Scott Fletcher	.05
20	Eric Davis	.10
21	Willie Wilson	.05
22	B.J. Surhoff	.05
23	Steve Bedrosian	.05
24	Dave Winfield	.45
25	Bobby Bonilla	.10
26	Larry Sheets	.05
27	Ozzie Guillen	.05
28	Checklist 1-88	.05
29	Nolan Ryan	2.00
30	Bob Boone	.05
31	Tom Herr	.05
32	Wade Boggs	.60
33	Neal Heaton	.05
34	Doyle Alexander	.05
35	Candy Maldonado	.05
36	Kirby Puckett	.85
37	Gary Carter	.10
38	Lance McCullers	.05
39a	Terry Steinbach (black Topps logo on front)	.15
39b	Terry Steinbach (white Topps logo on front)	.15
40	Gerald Perry	.05
41	Tom Henke	.05
42	Leon Durham	.05
43	Cory Snyder	.05
44	Dale Sveum	.05
45	Lance Parrish	.05
46	Steve Sax	.05
47	Charlie Hough	.05
48	Kal Daniels	.05
49	Bo Jackson	.25
50	Ron Guidry	.05
51	Bill Doran	.05
52	Wally Joyner	.10
53	Terry Pendleton	.05
54	Marty Barrett	.05
55	Andres Galarraga	.15
56	Larry Herndon	.05
57	Kevin Mitchell	.05
58	Greg Gagne	.05
59	Keith Hernandez	.05
60	John Kruk	.05
61	Mike LaValliere	.05
62	Cal Ripken, Jr.	2.00
63	Ivan Calderon	.05
64	Alvin Davis	.05
65	Luis Polonia	.05
66	Robin Yount	.45
67	Juan Samuel	.05
68	Andres Thomas	.05
69	Jeff Musselman	.05
70	Jerry Mumphrey	.05
71	Joe Carter	.10
72	Mike Scioscia	.05
73	Pete Incaviglia	.05
74	Barry Larkin	.15
75	Frank White	.05
76	Willie Randolph	.05
77	Kevin Bass	.05
78	Brian Downing	.05
79	Willie McGee	.05
80	Ellis Burks	.10
81	Hubie Brooks	.05
82	Darrell Evans	.05
83	Robby Thompson	.05
84	Kent Hrbek	.05
85	Ron Darling	.05
86	Stan Jefferson	.05
87	Teddy Higuera	.05
88	Mike Schmidt	.85
89	Barry Bonds	.75
90	Jim Presley	.05
91	Orel Hershiser	.05
92	Jesse Barfield	.05
93	Tom Candiotti	.05
94	Bret Saberhagen	.05
95	Jose Uribe	.05
96	Tom Browning	.05
97	Johnny Ray	.05
98	Mike Morgan	.05
100	Jim Sundberg	.05
101	Roger McDowell	.05
102	Randy Ready	.05
103	Mike Gallego	.05
104	Steve Buechele	.05
105	Greg Walker	.05
106	Jose Lind	.05
107	Steve Trout	.05
108	Rick Rhoden	.05
109	Jim Pankovits	.05
110	Ken Griffey	.05
111	Danny Cox	.05
112	Franklin Stubbs	.05
113	Lloyd Moseby	.05
114	Mel Hall	.05
115	Kevin Seitzer	.05
116	Tim Raines	.15
117	Juan Castillo	.05
118	Roger Clemens	.75
119	Mike Aldrete	.05
120	Mario Soto	.05
121	Jack Howell	.05
122	Rick Schu	.05
123	Jeff Robinson	.05
124	Doug Drabek	.05
125	Henry Cotto	.05
126	Checklist 89-176	.05
127	Gary Gaetti	.05
128	Rick Sutcliffe	.05
129	Howard Johnson	.05
130	Chris Brown	.05
131	Dave Henderson	.05
132	Curt Wilkerson	.05
133	Mike Marshall	.05
134	Kelly Gruber	.05
135	Julio Franco	.05
136	Kurt Stillwell	.05
137	Donnie Hill	.05
138	Mike Pagliarulo	.05
139	Von Hayes	.05
140	Mike Scott	.05
141	Bob Kipper	.05
142	Harold Reynolds	.05
143	Bob Brenly	.05
144	Dave Concepcion	.05
145	Devon White	.10
146	Jeff Stone	.05
147	Chet Lemon	.05
148	Ozzie Virgil	.05
149	Todd Worrell	.05
150	Mitch Webster	.05
151	Rob Deer	.05
152	Rich Gedman	.05
153	Andre Dawson	.10
154	Mike Davis	.05
155	Nelson Liriano	.05
156	Greg Swindell	.05
157	George Brett	.75
158	Kevin McReynolds	.05
159	Brian Fisher	.05
160	Mike Kingery	.05
161	Tony Gwynn	.75
162	Don Baylor	.05
163	Jerry Browne	.05
164	Dan Pasqua	.05
165	Rickey Henderson	.25
166	Brett Butler	.05
167	Nick Esasky	.05
168	Kirk McCaskill	.05
169	Fred Lynn	.05
170	Jack Morris	.05
171	Pedro Guerrero	.05
172	Dave Stieb	.05
173	Pat Tabler	.05
174	Floyd Bannister	.05
175	Rafael Belliard	.05
176	Mark Langston	.05
177	Greg Mathews	.05
178	Claudell Washington	.05
179	Mark McGwire	2.50
180	Bert Blyleven	.05
181	Jim Rice	.10
182	Mookie Wilson	.05
183	Willie Fraser	.05
184	Andy Van Slyke	.05
185	Matt Nokes	.05
186	Eddie Whitson	.05
187	Tony Fernandez	.05
188	Rick Reuschel	.05
189	Ken Phelps	.05
190	Juan Nieves	.05
191	Kirk Gibson	.05
192	Glenn Davis	.05
193	Zane Smith	.05
194	Jose DeLeon	.05
195	Gary Ward	.05
196	Pascual Perez	.05
197	Carlton Fisk	.25
198	Oddibe McDowell	.05
199	Mark Gubicza	.05
200	Glenn Hubbard	.05
201	Frank Viola	.05
202	Jody Reed	.05
203	Len Dykstra	.05
204	Dick Schofield	.05
205	Sid Bream	.05
206	Guillermo Hernandez	.05
207	Keith Moreland	.05
208	Mark Eichhorn	.05
209	Rene Gonzales	.05
210	Dave Valle	.05
211	Tom Brunansky	.05
212	Charles Hudson	.05
213	John Farrell	.05
214	Jeff Treadway	.05
215	Eddie Murray	.35
216	Checklist 177-264	.05
217	Greg Brock	.05
218	John Shelby	.05
219	Craig Reynolds	.05
220	Dion James	.05
221	Carney Lansford	.05
222	Juan Berenguer	.05

223 Luis Rivera .05
224 Harold Baines .10
225 Shawon Dunston .05
226 Luis Aguayo .05
227 Pete O'Brien .05
228 Ozzie Smith .50
229 Don Mattingly .90
230 Danny Tartabull .05
231 Andy Allanson .05
232 John Franco .05
233 Mike Greenwell .05
234 Bob Ojeda .05
235 Chili Davis .05
236 Mike Dunne .05
237 Jim Morrison .05
238 Carmelo Martinez .05
239 Ernie Whitt .05
240 Scott Garrelts .05
241 Mike Moore .05
242 Dave Parker .05
243 Tim Laudner .05
244 Bill Wegman .05
245 Bob Horner .05
246 Rafael Santana .05
247 Alfredo Griffin .05
248 Mark Bailey .05
249 Ron Gant .15
250 Bryn Smith .05
251 Lance Johnson .05
252 Sam Horn .05
253 Darryl Strawberry .15
254 Chuck Finley .05
255 Darnell Coles .05
256 Mike Henneman .05
257 Andy Hawkins .05
258 Jim Clancy .05
259 Atlee Hammaker .05
260 Glenn Wilson .05
261 Larry McWilliams .05
262 Jack Clark .05
263 Walt Weiss .05
264 Gene Larkin .05

1988 Topps Glossy Rookies

The Topps 1988 Rookies special insert cards follow the same basic design as the All-Star inserts. The set consists of 22 standard-size cards found one per pack in 100-card jumbo cellos. Large, glossy color player photos are printed on a white background below a red, yellow and blue "1987 Rookies" banner. A red and yellow player name appears beneath the photo. Red, white and blue card backs bear the title of the special insert set, the Rookies logo emblem, player name and card number.

MT
Complete Set (22):12.50
Common Player:.50
1 Billy Ripken .50
2 Ellis Burks 1.00
3 Mike Greenwell .60
4 DeWayne Buice .50
5 Devon White .60
6 Fred Manrique .50
7 Mike Henneman .50
8 Matt Nokes .50
9 Kevin Seitzer .50
10 B.J. Surhoff .60
11 Casey Candaele .50
12 Randy Myers .60
13 Mark McGwire 10.00
14 Luis Polonia .50
15 Terry Steinbach .60
16 Mike Dunne .50
17 Al Pedrique .50
18 Benny Santiago .60
19 Kelly Downs .50
20 Joe Magrane .50
21 Jerry Browne .50
22 Jeff Musselman .50

1988 Topps Mini League Leaders

The third consecutive issue of Topps mini-cards (2-1/8" x 3") includes 77 cards spotlighting the top five ranked pitchers and batters. This set is unique in that it was the first time Topps included full-color player photos on both the front and back. Glossy action shots on the card fronts fade into a white border with a Topps logo in an upper corner. The player's name is printed in bold black letters beneath the photo. Horizontal reverses feature circular player photos on a blue and white background with the card number, player name, personal information, 1987 ranking and lifetime/1987 stats printed in red, black and yellow lettering.

MT
Complete Set (77):4.00
Common Player:.10
1 Wade Boggs .65
2 Roger Clemens .75
3 Dwight Evans .10
4 DeWayne Downing .10
5 Brian Downing .10
6 Wally Joyner .15
7 Ivan Calderon .10
8 Carlton Fisk .40
9 Gary Redus .10
10 Darrell Evans .10
11 Jack Morris .10
12 Alan Trammell .15
13 Lou Whitaker .10
14 Bret Saberhagen .10
15 Kevin Seitzer .10
16 Danny Tartabull .10
17 Willie Wilson .10
18 Teddy Higuera .10
19 Paul Molitor .50
20 Dan Plesac .10
21 Robin Yount .65
22 Kent Hrbek .10
23 Kirby Puckett .75
24 Jeff Reardon .10
25 Frank Viola .10
26 Rickey Henderson .45
27 Don Mattingly .90
28 Willie Randolph .10
29 Dave Righetti .10
30 Jose Canseco .55
31 Mark McGwire 2.00
32 Dave Stewart .10
33 Phil Bradley .10
34 Mark Langston .10
35 Harold Reynolds .10
36 Charlie Hough .10
37 George Bell .10
38 Tom Henke .10
39 Jimmy Key .10
40 Dion James .10
41 Dale Murphy .15
42 Zane Smith .10
43 Andre Dawson .15
44 Lee Smith .10
45 Rick Sutcliffe .10
46 Eric Davis .10
47 John Franco .10
48 Dave Parker .10
49 Billy Hatcher .10
50 Nolan Ryan 1.50
51 Mike Scott .10
52 Pedro Guerrero .10
53 Orel Hershiser .10
54 Fernando Valenzuela .10
55 Bob Welch .10
56 Andres Galarraga .15
57 Tim Raines .15
58 Tim Wallach .10
59 Len Dykstra .10
60 Dwight Gooden .15
61 Howard Johnson .10
62 Roger McDowell .10
63 Darryl Strawberry .15
64 Steve Bedrosian .10
65 Shane Rawley .10
66 Juan Samuel .10
67 Mike Schmidt .65
68 Mike Dunne .10
69 Jack Clark .10
70 Vince Coleman .10
71 Willie McGee .15
72 Ozzie Smith .60
73 Todd Worrell .10
74 Tony Gwynn .70
75 John Kruk .10
76 Rick Rueschel .10
77 Checklist .10

1989 Topps

Ten top young players from the June, 1988, draft are featured on "#1 Draft Pick" cards in this full-color basic set of 792 standard-size baseball cards. An additional five cards salute 1989 Future Stars, 22 cards highlight All-Stars, seven contain Record Breakers, five are designated Turn Back The Clock, and six contain checklists. This set features the familiar white borders, but upper-left and lower-right photo corners have been rounded off. A curved name banner in bright red or blue is beneath the team name in large script in the lower-right corner. The card backs are printed in black on a red background and include personal information and complete minor and major league stats. Another new addition in this set is the special Monthly Scoreboard chart that lists monthly stats (April through September) in two of several categories (hits, run, home runs, stolen bases, RBIs, wins, strikeouts, games or saves).

MT
Complete Set (792): 10.00
Factory Set (792): 14.00
Common Player: .05
Wax Pack (15): .65
Wax Box (36): 12.00
1 George Bell (Record Breaker) .05
2 Wade Boggs (Record Breaker) .15
3 Gary Carter (Record Breaker) .05
4 Andre Dawson (Record Breaker) .05
5 Orel Hershiser (Record Breaker) .05
6 Doug Jones (Record Breaker) .05
7 Kevin McReynolds (Record Breaker) .05
8 *Dave Eiland* .05
9 Tim Teufel .05
10 Andre Dawson .10
11 Bruce Sutter .05
12 Dale Sveum .05
13 Doug Sisk .05
14 Tom Kelly .05
15 Robby Thompson .05
16 Ron Robinson .05
17 Brian Downing .05
18 Rick Rhoden .05
19 Greg Gagne .05
20 Steve Bedrosian .05
21 White Sox Leaders (Greg Walker) .05
22 Tim Crews .05
23 Mike Fitzgerald .05
24 Larry Andersen .05
25 Frank White .05
26 Dale Mohorcic .05
27 *Orestes Destrade* .05
28 Mike Moore .05
29 Kelly Gruber .05
30 Dwight Gooden .10
31 Terry Francona .05
32 Dennis Rasmussen .05
33 B.J. Surhoff .05
34 Ken Williams .05
35 John Tudor .05
36 Mitch Webster .05
37 Bob Stanley .05
38 Paul Runge .05
39 Mike Maddux .05
40 Steve Sax .05
41 Terry Mulholland .05
42 Jim Eppard .05
43 Guillermo Hernandez .05
44 Jim Snyder .05
45 Kal Daniels .05
46 Mark Portugal .05
47 Carney Lansford .05
48 Tim Burke .05
49 Craig Biggio .60
50 George Bell .05
51 Angels Leaders (Mark McLemore) .05
52 Bob Brenly .05
53 Ruben Sierra .05
54 Steve Trout .05
55 Julio Franco .05
56 Pat Tabler .05
57 Alejandro Pena .05
58 Lee Mazzilli .05
59 Mark Davis .05

No.	Card	Value
60	Tom Brunansky	.05
61	Neil Allen	.05
62	Alfredo Griffin	.05
63	Mark Clear	.05
64	Alex Trevino	.05
65	Rick Reuschel	.05
66	Manny Trillo	.05
67	Dave Palmer	.05
68	Darrell Miller	.05
69	Jeff Ballard	.05
70	Mark McGwire	1.50
71	Mike Boddicker	.05
72	John Moses	.05
73	Pascual Perez	.05
74	Nick Leyva	.05
75	Tom Henke	.05
76	*Terry Blocker*	.05
77	Doyle Alexander	.05
78	Jim Sundberg	.05
79	Scott Bankhead	.05
80	Cory Snyder	.05
81	Expos Leaders (Tim Raines)	.05
82	Dave Leiper	.05
83	Jeff Blauser	.05
84	*Bill Bene* (#1 Draft Pick)	.05
85	Kevin McReynolds	.05
86	Al Nipper	.05
87	Larry Owen	.05
88	*Darryl Hamilton*	.10
89	Dave LaPoint	.05
90	Vince Coleman	.05
91	Floyd Youmans	.05
92	Jeff Kunkel	.05
93	Ken Howell	.05
94	Chris Speier	.05
95	Gerald Young	.05
96	Rick Cerone	.05
97	Greg Mathews	.05
98	Larry Sheets	.05
99	*Sherman Corbett*	.05
100	Mike Schmidt	.25
101	Les Straker	.05
102	Mike Gallego	.05
103	Tim Birtsas	.05
104	Dallas Green	.05
105	Ron Darling	.05
106	Willie Upshaw	.05
107	Jose DeLeon	.05
108	Fred Manrique	.05
109	*Hipolito Pena*	.05
110	Paul Molitor	.25
111	Reds Leaders (Eric Davis)	.05
112	Jim Presley	.05
113	Lloyd Moseby	.05
114	Bob Kipper	.05
115	Jody Davis	.05
116	Jeff Montgomery	.05
117	Dave Anderson	.05
118	Checklist 1-132	.05
119	Terry Puhl	.05
120	Frank Viola	.05
121	Garry Templeton	.05
122	Lance Johnson	.05
123	Spike Owen	.05
124	Jim Traber	.05
125	Mike Krukow	.05
126	Sid Bream	.05
127	Walt Terrell	.05
128	Milt Thompson	.05
129	*Terry Clark*	.05
130	Gerald Perry	.05
131	Dave Otto	.05
132	Curt Ford	.05
133	Bill Long	.05
134	Don Zimmer	.05
135	Jose Rijo	.05
136	Joey Meyer	.05
137	Geno Petralli	.05
138	Wallace Johnson	.05
139	Mike Flanagan	.05
140	Shawon Dunston	.05
141	Indians Leaders (Brook Jacoby)	.05
142	Mike Diaz	.05
143	Mike Campbell	.05
144	Jay Bell	.05
145	Dave Stewart	.05
146	Gary Pettis	.05
147	DeWayne Buice	.05
148	Bill Pecota	.05
149	*Doug Dascenzo*	.05
150	Fernando Valenzuela	.05
151	Terry McGriff	.05
152	Mark Thurmond	.05
153	Jim Pankovits	.05
154	Don Carman	.05
155	Marty Barrett	.05
156	*Dave Gallagher*	.05
157	Tom Glavine	.20
158	Mike Aldrete	.05
159	Pat Clements	.05
160	Jeffrey Leonard	.05
161	*Gregg Olson* (#1 Draft Pick)	.10
162	John Davis	.05
163	Bob Forsch	.05
164	Hal Lanier	.05
165	Mike Dunne	.05
166	*Doug Jennings*	.05
167	*Steve Searcy* (Future Star)	.05
168	Willie Wilson	.05
169	Mike Jackson	.05
170	Tony Fernandez	.05
171	Braves Leaders (Andres Thomas)	.05
172	Frank Williams	.05
173	Mel Hall	.05
174	*Todd Burns*	.05
175	John Shelby	.05
176	Jeff Parrett	.05
177	*Monty Fariss* (#1 Draft Pick)	.10
178	Mark Grant	.05
179	Ozzie Virgil	.05
180	Mike Scott	.05
181	*Craig Worthington*	.05
182	Bob McClure	.05
183	Oddibe McDowell	.05
184	*John Costello*	.05
185	Claudell Washington	.05
186	Pat Perry	.05
187	Darren Daulton	.05
188	Dennis Lamp	.05
189	Kevin Mitchell	.05
190	Mike Witt	.05
191	*Sil Campusano*	.05
192	Paul Mirabella	.05
193	Sparky Anderson	.10
194	*Greg Harris*	.10
195	Ozzie Guillen	.05
196	Denny Walling	.05
197	Neal Heaton	.05
198	Danny Heep	.05
199	*Mike Schooler*	.05
200	George Brett	.30
201	Blue Jays Leaders (Kelly Gruber)	.05
202	*Brad Moore*	.05
203	Rob Ducey	.05
204	Brad Havens	.05
205	Dwight Evans	.05
206	Roberto Alomar	.50
207	Terry Leach	.05
208	Tom Pagnozzi	.05
209	*Jeff Bittiger*	.05
210	Dale Murphy	.10
211	Mike Pagliarulo	.05
212	Scott Sanderson	.05
213	Rene Gonzales	.05
214	Charlie O'Brien	.05
215	Kevin Gross	.05
216	Jack Howell	.05
217	Joe Price	.05
218	Mike LaValliere	.05
219	Jim Clancy	.05
220	Gary Gaetti	.05
221	Cecil Espy	.05
222	*Mark Lewis* (#1 Draft Pick)	.10
223	Jay Buhner	.15
224	Tony LaRussa	.05
225	*Ramon Martinez*	.25
226	Bill Doran	.05
227	John Farrell	.05
228	*Nelson Santovenia*	.05
229	Jimmy Key	.05
230	Ozzie Smith	.25
231	Padres Leaders (Roberto Alomar)	.15
232	Ricky Horton	.05
233	Gregg Jefferies (Future Star)	.25
234	Tom Browning	.05
235	John Kruk	.05
236	Charles Hudson	.05
237	Glenn Hubbard	.05
238	Eric King	.05
239	Tim Laudner	.05
240	Greg Maddux	.50
241	Brett Butler	.05
242	Ed Vande Berg	.05
243	Bob Boone	.05
244	Jim Acker	.05
245	Jim Rice	.10
246	Rey Quinones	.05
247	Shawn Hillegas	.05
248	Tony Phillips	.05
249	Tim Leary	.05
250	Cal Ripken, Jr.	.60
251	*John Dopson*	.05
252	Billy Hatcher	.05
253	*Jose Alvarez*	.05
254	Tom LaSorda	.15
255	Ron Guidry	.10
256	Benny Santiago	.05
257	Rick Aguilera	.05
258	Checklist 133-264	.05
259	Larry McWilliams	.05
260	Dave Winfield	.15
261	Cardinals Leaders (Tom Brunansky)	.05
262	*Jeff Pico*	.05
263	Mike Felder	.05
264	*Rob Dibble*	.10
265	Kent Hrbek	.05
266	Luis Aquino	.05
267	Jeff Robinson	.05
268	Keith Miller	.05
269	Tom Bolton	.05
270	Wally Joyner	.10
271	Jay Tibbs	.05
272	Ron Hassey	.05
273	Jose Lind	.05
274	Mark Eichhorn	.05
275	Danny Tartabull	.05
276	Paul Kilgus	.05
277	Mike Davis	.05
278	Andy McGaffigan	.05
279	Scott Bradley	.05
280	Bob Knepper	.05
281	Gary Redus	.05
282	*Cris Carpenter*	.10
283	Andy Allanson	.05
284	Jim Leyland	.05
285	John Candelaria	.05
286	Darrin Jackson	.05
287	Juan Nieves	.05
288	Pat Sheridan	.05
289	Ernie Whitt	.05
290	John Franco	.05
291	Mets Leaders (Darryl Strawberry)	.10
292	*Jim Corsi*	.05
293	Glenn Wilson	.05
294	Juan Berenguer	.05
295	Scott Fletcher	.05
296	Ron Gant	.10
297	*Oswald Peraza*	.05
298	Chris James	.05
299	*Steve Ellsworth*	.05
300	Darryl Strawberry	.10
301	Charlie Leibrandt	.05
302	Gary Ward	.05
303	Felix Fermin	.05
304	Joel Youngblood	.05
305	Dave Smith	.05
306	Tracy Woodson	.05
307	Lance McCullers	.05
308	Ron Karkovice	.05
309	Mario Diaz	.05
310	Rafael Palmeiro	.25
311	Chris Bosio	.05
312	Tom Lawless	.05
313	Denny Martinez	.05
314	Bobby Valentine	.05
315	Greg Swindell	.05
316	Walt Weiss	.05
317	*Jack Armstrong*	.05
318	Gene Larkin	.05
319	Greg Booker	.05
320	Lou Whitaker	.05
321	Red Sox Leaders (Jody Reed)	.05
322	John Smiley	.05
323	Gary Thurman	.05
324	*Bob Milacki*	.05
325	Jesse Barfield	.05
326	Dennis Boyd	.05
327	*Mark Lemke*	.05
328	Rick Honeycutt	.05
329	Bob Melvin	.05
330	Eric Davis	.10
331	Curt Wilkerson	.05
332	Tony Armas	.05
333	Bob Ojeda	.05
334	Steve Lyons	.05
335	Dave Righetti	.05
336	Steve Balboni	.05
337	Calvin Schiraldi	.05
338	Jim Adduci	.05
339	Scott Bailes	.05
340	Kirk Gibson	.05
341	Jim Deshaies	.05
342	Tom Brookens	.05
343	*Gary Sheffield* (Future Star)	1.50
344	Tom Trebelhorn	.05
345	Charlie Hough	.05
346	Rex Hudler	.05
347	John Cerutti	.05
348	Ed Hearn	.05
349	*Ron Jones*	.05
350	Andy Van Slyke	.05
351	Giants Leaders (Bob Melvin)	.05
352	Rick Schu	.05
353	Marvell Wynne	.05
354	Larry Parrish	.05
355	Mark Langston	.05
356	Kevin Elster	.05
357	Jerry Reuss	.05
358	*Ricky Jordan*	.05
359	Tommy John	.10
360	Ryne Sandberg	.30
361	Kelly Downs	.05
362	Jack Lazorko	.05
363	Rich Yett	.05
364	Rob Deer	.05
365	Mike Henneman	.05
366	Herm Winningham	.05
367	*Johnny Paredes*	.05
368	Brian Holton	.05
369	Ken Caminiti	.10
370	Dennis Eckersley	.10
371	Manny Lee	.05
372	Craig Lefferts	.05
373	Tracy Jones	.05
374	John Wathan	.05
375	Terry Pendleton	.05
376	Steve Lombardozzi	.05
377	Mike Smithson	.05
378	Checklist 265-396	.05
379	Tim Flannery	.05
380	Rickey Henderson	.10
381	Orioles Leaders (Larry Sheets)	.05
382	John Smoltz	.50
383	Howard Johnson	.05
384	Mark Salas	.05
385	Von Hayes	.05
386	Andres Galarraga (All-Star)	.10
387	Ryne Sandberg (All-Star)	.15
388	Bobby Bonilla (All-Star)	.05
389	Ozzie Smith (All-Star)	.15
390	Darryl Strawberry (All-Star)	.10
391	Andre Dawson (All-Star)	.05
392	Andy Van Slyke (All-Star)	.05
393	Gary Carter (All-Star)	.05
394	Orel Hershiser (All-Star)	.05
395	Danny Jackson (All-Star)	.05
396	Kirk Gibson (All-Star)	.05
397	Don Mattingly (All-Star)	.20
398	Julio Franco (All-Star)	.05
399	Wade Boggs (All-Star)	.15
400	Alan Trammell (All-Star)	.05
401	Jose Canseco (All-Star)	.20
402	Mike Greenwell (All-Star)	.05
403	Kirby Puckett (All-Star)	.20
404	Bob Boone (All-Star)	.05
405	Roger Clemens (All-Star)	.25
406	Frank Viola (All-Star)	.05
407	Dave Winfield (All-Star)	.10
408	Greg Walker	.05
409	Ken Dayley	.05
410	Jack Clark	.05
411	Mitch Williams	.05
412	Barry Lyons	.05
413	Mike Kingery	.05
414	Jim Fregosi	.05
415	Rich Gossage	.10
416	Fred Lynn	.05
417	Mike LaCoss	.05
418	Bob Dernier	.05
419	Tom Filer	.05
420	Joe Carter	.10
421	Kirk McCaskill	.05
422	Bo Diaz	.05
423	Brian Fisher	.05
424	Luis Polonia	.05
425	Jay Howell	.05
426	Danny Gladden	.05
427	Eric Show	.05

428 Craig Reynolds .05
429 Twins Leaders (Greg Gagne) .05
430 Mark Gubicza .05
431 Luis Rivera .05
432 *Chad Kreuter* .10
433 Albert Hall .05
434 *Ken Patterson* .10
435 Len Dykstra .05
436 Bobby Meacham .05
437 Andy Benes (#1 Draft Pick) .25
438 Greg Gross .05
439 Frank DiPino .05
440 Bobby Bonilla .10
441 Jerry Reed .05
442 Jose Oquendo .05
443 *Rod Nichols* .05
444 Moose Stubing .05
445 Matt Nokes .05
446 Rob Murphy .05
447 Donell Nixon .05
448 Eric Plunk .05
449 Carmelo Martinez .05
450 Roger Clemens .50
451 Mark Davidson .05
452 *Israel Sanchez* .05
453 Tom Prince .05
454 Paul Assenmacher .05
455 Johnny Ray .05
456 Tim Belcher .05
457 Mackey Sasser .05
458 *Donn Pall* .05
459 Mariners Leaders (Dave Valle) .05
460 Dave Stieb .05
461 Buddy Bell .05
462 Jose Guzman .05
463 Steve Lake .05
464 Bryn Smith .05
465 Mark Grace .25
466 Chuck Crim .05
467 Jim Walewander .05
468 Henry Cotto .05
469 *Jose Bautista* .05
470 Lance Parrish .05
471 *Steve Curry* .05
472 Brian Harper .05
473 Don Robinson .05
474 Bob Rodgers .05
475 Dave Parker .05
476 Jon Perlman .05
477 Dick Schofield .05
478 Doug Drabek .05
479 *Mike Macfarlane* .10
480 Keith Hernandez .05
481 Chris Brown .05
482 *Steve Peters* .05
483 Mickey Hatcher .05
484 Steve Shields .05
485 Hubie Brooks .05
486 Jack McDowell .05
487 Scott Lusader .05
488 Kevin Coffman .05
489 Phillies Leaders (Mike Schmidt) .15
490 *Chris Sabo* .15
491 Mike Birkbeck .05
492 Alan Ashby .05
493 Todd Benzinger .05
494 Shane Rawley .05
495 Candy Maldonado .05
496 Dwayne Henry .05
497 Pete Stanicek .05
498 Dave Valle .05
499 *Don Heinkel* .05
500 Jose Canseco .25
501 Vance Law .05
502 Duane Ward .05
503 Al Newman .05
504 Bob Walk .05
505 Pete Rose .30
506 Kirt Manwaring .05
507 Steve Farr .05
508 Wally Backman .05
509 Bud Black .05
510 Bob Horner .05
511 Richard Dotson .05
512 Donnie Hill .05
513 Jesse Orosco .05
514 Chet Lemon .05
515 Barry Larkin .25
516 Eddie Whitson .05
517 Greg Brock .05
518 Bruce Ruffin .05
519 Yankees Leaders (Willie Randolph) .05
520 Rick Sutcliffe .05
521 Mickey Tettleton .05
522 *Randy Kramer* .05
523 Andres Thomas .05
524 Checklist 397-528 .05
525 Chili Davis .05
526 Wes Gardner .05
527 Dave Henderson .05
528 *Luis Medina* .05
529 Tom Foley .05
530 Nolan Ryan .75
531 Dave Hengel .05
532 Jerry Browne .05
533 Andy Hawkins .05
534 Doc Edwards .05
535 Todd Worrell .05
536 Joel Skinner .05
537 Pete Smith .05
538 Juan Castillo .05
539 Barry Jones .05
540 Bo Jackson .20
541 Cecil Fielder .10
542 Todd Frohwirth .05
543 Damon Berryhill .05
544 Jeff Sellers .05
545 Mookie Wilson .05
546 Mark Williamson .05
547 Mark McLemore .05
548 Bobby Witt .05
549 Cubs Leaders (Jamie Moyer) .05
550 Orel Hershiser .05
551 Randy Ready .05
552 Greg Cadaret .05
553 Luis Salazar .05
554 Nick Esasky .05
555 Bert Blyleven .05
556 Bruce Fields .05
557 *Keith Miller* .05
558 Dan Pasqua .05
559 Juan Agosto .05
560 Tim Raines .10
561 Luis Aguayo .05
562 Danny Cox .05
563 Bill Schroeder .05
564 Russ Nixon .05
565 Jeff Russell .05
566 Al Pedrique .05
567 David Wells .10
568 Mickey Brantley .05
569 *German Jimenez* .05
570 Tony Gwynn .50
571 Billy Ripken .05
572 Atlee Hammaker .05
573 Jim Abbott (#1 Draft Pick) .15
574 Dave Clark .05
575 Juan Samuel .05
576 Greg Minton .05
577 Randy Bush .05
578 John Morris .05
579 Astros Leaders (Glenn Davis) .05
580 Harold Reynolds .05
581 Gene Nelson .05
582 Mike Marshall .05
583 *Paul Gibson* .05
584 Randy Velarde .05
585 Harold Baines .05
586 Joe Boever .05
587 Mike Stanley .05
588 *Luis Alicea* .10
589 Dave Meads .05
590 Andres Galarraga .25
591 Jeff Musselman .05
592 John Cangelosi .05
593 Drew Hall .05
594 Jimy Williams .05
595 Teddy Higuera .05
596 Kurt Stillwell .05
597 *Terry Taylor* .05
598 Ken Gerhart .05
599 Tom Candiotti .05
600 Wade Boggs .25
601 Dave Dravecky .05
602 Devon White .05
603 Frank Tanana .05
604 Paul O'Neill .20
605a Bob Welch (missing Complete Major League Pitching Record line) 1.00
605b Bob Welch (contains Complete Major League Pitching Record line) .05
606 Rick Dempsey .05
607 *Willie Ansley* (#1 Draft Pick) .05
608 Phil Bradley .05
609 Tigers Leaders (Frank Tanana) .05
610 Randy Myers .05
611 Don Slaught .05
612 Dan Quisenberry .05
613 *Gary Varsho* .05
614 Joe Hesketh .05
615 Robin Yount .25
616 *Steve Rosenberg* .05
617 *Mark Parent* .05
618 Rance Mulliniks .05
619 Checklist 529-660 .05
620 Barry Bonds .40
621 Rick Mahler .05
622 Stan Javier .05
623 Fred Toliver .05
624 Jack McKeon .05
625 Eddie Murray .15
626 Jeff Reed .05
627 Greg Harris .05
628 Matt Williams .25
629 Pete O'Brien .05
630 Mike Greenwell .05
631 Dave Bergman .05
632 *Bryan Harvey* .10
633 Daryl Boston .05
634 Marvin Freeman .05
635 Willie Randolph .05
636 Bill Wilkinson .05
637 Carmen Castillo .05
638 Floyd Bannister .05
639 Athletics Leaders (Walt Weiss) .05
640 Willie McGee .05
641 Curt Young .05
642 Argenis Salazar .05
643 *Louie Meadows* .05
644 Lloyd McClendon .05
645 Jack Morris .05
646 Kevin Bass .05
647 *Randy Johnson* 2.00
648 *Sandy Alomar* (Future Star) .25
649 Stewart Cliburn .05
650 Kirby Puckett .35
651 Tom Niedenfuer .05
652 Rich Gedman .05
653 *Tommy Barrett* .05
654 Whitey Herzog .05
655 Dave Magadan .05
656 Ivan Calderon .05
657 Joe Magrane .05
658 R.J. Reynolds .05
659 Al Leiter .05
660 Will Clark .20
661 Dwight Gooden (Turn Back the Clock) .10
662 Lou Brock (Turn Back the Clock) .05
663 Hank Aaron (Turn Back the Clock) .15
664 Gil Hodges (Turn Back the Clock) .05
665 Tony Oliva (Turn Back the Clock) .05
666 Randy St. Claire .05
667 Dwayne Murphy .05
668 Mike Bielecki .05
669 Dodgers Leaders (Orel Hershiser) .05
670 Kevin Seitzer .05
671 Jim Gantner .05
672 Allan Anderson .05
673 Don Baylor .10
674 Otis Nixon .05
675 Bruce Hurst .05
676 Ernie Riles .05
677 Dave Schmidt .05
678 Dion James .05
679 Willie Fraser .05
680 Gary Carter .10
681 Jeff Robinson .05
682 Rick Leach .05
683 *Jose Cecena* .05
684 Dave Johnson .05
685 Jeff Treadway .05
686 Scott Terry .05
687 Alvin Davis .05
688 Zane Smith .05
689 Stan Jefferson .05
690 Doug Jones .05
691 Roberto Kelly .05
692 Steve Ontiveros .05
693 *Pat Borders* .15
694 Les Lancaster .05
695 Carlton Fisk .25
696 Don August .05
697 Franklin Stubbs .05
698 Keith Atherton .05
699 Pirates Leaders (Al Pedrique) .05
700 Don Mattingly .35
701 Storm Davis .05
702 Jamie Quirk .05
703 Scott Garrelts .05
704 *Carlos Quintana* .05
705 Terry Kennedy .05
706 Pete Incaviglia .05
707 Steve Jeltz .05
708 Chuck Finley .05
709 Tom Herr .05
710 Dave Cone .20
711 *Candy Sierra* .05
712 Bill Swift .05
713 *Ty Griffin* (#1 Draft Pick) .05
714 Joe M. Morgan .05
715 Tony Pena .05
716 Wayne Tolleson .05
717 Jamie Moyer .05
718 Glenn Braggs .05
719 Danny Darwin .05
720 Tim Wallach .05
721 *Ron Tingley* .05
722 Todd Stottlemyre .05
723 Rafael Belliard .05
724 Jerry Don Gleaton .05
725 Terry Steinbach .05
726 Dickie Thon .05
727 Joe Orsulak .05
728 Charlie Puleo .05
729 Rangers Leaders (Steve Buechele) .05
730 Danny Jackson .05
731 Mike Young .05
732 Steve Buechele .05
733 *Randy Bockus* .05
734 Jody Reed .05
735 Roger McDowell .05
736 Jeff Hamilton .05
737 *Norm Charlton* .15
738 Darnell Coles .05
739 Brook Jacoby .05
740 Dan Plesac .05
741 Ken Phelps .05
742 *Mike Harkey* (Future Star) .05
743 Mike Heath .05
744 Roger Craig .05
745 Fred McGriff .15
746 *German Gonzalez* .05
747 Wil Tejada .05
748 Jimmy Jones .05
749 Rafael Ramirez .05
750 Bret Saberhagen .05
751 Ken Oberkfell .05
752 Jim Gott .05
753 Jose Uribe .05
754 Bob Brower .05
755 Mike Scioscia .05
756 *Scott Medvin* .05
757 Brady Anderson .20
758 Gene Walter .05
759 Brewers Leaders (Rob Deer) .05
760 Lee Smith .05
761 *Dante Bichette* .50
762 Bobby Thigpen .05
763 Dave Martinez .05
764 Robin Ventura (#1 Draft Pick) .75
765 Glenn Davis .05
766 Cecilio Guante .05
767 *Mike Capel* .05
768 Bill Wegman .05
769 Junior Ortiz .05
770 Alan Trammell .10
771 Ron Kittle .05
772 Ron Oester .05
773 Keith Moreland .05
774 Frank Robinson .15
775 Jeff Reardon .05
776 Nelson Liriano .05
777 Ted Power .05
778 Bruce Benedict .05
779 Craig McMurtry .05
780 Pedro Guerrero .05
781 *Greg Briley* .05
782 Checklist 661-792 .05
783 *Trevor Wilson* .10
784 *Steve Avery* (#1 Draft Pick) .20
785 Ellis Burks .10
786 Melido Perez .05
787 *Dave West* .10
788 Mike Morgan .05
789 Royals Leaders (Bo Jackson) .10
790 Sid Fernandez .05
791 Jim Lindeman .05
792 Rafael Santana .05

1989 Topps Tiffany

This special hobby-only edition shares the checklist with the regular 1989 Topps set. Cards are identical except for the use of white cardboard stock and the high-gloss front coating. Production has been reported as 25,000 sets.

	MT
Complete Set (792):	100.00
Common Player:	.10

(Star cards valued at 3x-4X corresponding cards in regular 1989 Topps issue)

1989 Topps Traded

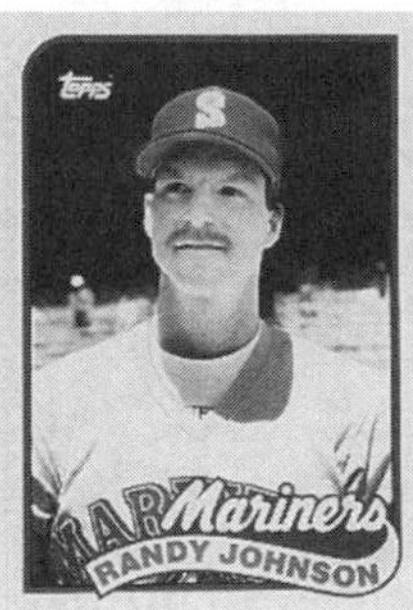

For the ninth straight year, Topps issued its annual 132-card "Traded" set at the end of the 1989 baseball season. The set, which was packaged in a special box and sold by hobby dealers, includes traded players and rookies who were not in the regular 1989 Topps set.

		MT
Complete Set (132):		25.00
Common Player:		.05
1T	Don Aase	.05
2T	Jim Abbott	.10
3T	Kent Anderson	.05
4T	Keith Atherton	.05
5T	Wally Backman	.05
6T	Steve Balboni	.05
7T	Jesse Barfield	.05
8T	Steve Bedrosian	.05
9T	Todd Benzinger	.05
10T	Geronimo Berroa	.10
11T	Bert Blyleven	.05
12T	Bob Boone	.05
13T	Phil Bradley	.05
14T	Jeff Brantley	.10
15T	Kevin Brown	.15
16T	Jerry Browne	.05
17T	Chuck Cary	.05
18T	Carmen Castillo	.05
19T	Jim Clancy	.05
20T	Jack Clark	.05
21T	Bryan Clutterbuck	.05
22T	Jody Davis	.05
23T	Mike Devereaux	.05
24T	Frank DiPino	.05
25T	Benny Distefano	.05
26T	John Dopson	.05
27T	Len Dykstra	.05
28T	Jim Eisenreich	.05
29T	Nick Esasky	.05
30T	Alvaro Espinoza	.05
31T	Darrell Evans	.05
32T	Junior Felix	.05
33T	Felix Fermin	.05
34T	Julio Franco	.05
35T	Terry Francona	.05
36T	Cito Gaston	.05
37T	Bob Geren (photo actually Mike Fennell)	.05
38T	*Tom Gordon*	.15
39T	Tommy Gregg	.05
40T	Ken Griffey	.10
41T	*Ken Griffey, Jr.*	20.00
42T	Kevin Gross	.05
43T	Lee Guetterman	.05
44T	Mel Hall	.05
45T	Erik Hanson	.15
46T	Gene Harris	.05
47T	Andy Hawkins	.05
48T	Rickey Henderson	.25
49T	Tom Herr	.05
50T	*Ken Hill*	.20
51T	Brian Holman	.05
52T	Brian Holton	.05
53T	Art Howe	.05
54T	Ken Howell	.05
55T	Bruce Hurst	.05
56T	Chris James	.05
57T	Randy Johnson	1.50
58T	Jimmy Jones	.05
59T	Terry Kennedy	.05
60T	Paul Kilgus	.05
61T	Eric King	.05
62T	Ron Kittle	.05
63T	John Kruk	.05
64T	Randy Kutcher	.05
65T	Steve Lake	.05
66T	Mark Langston	.10
67T	Dave LaPoint	.05
68T	Rick Leach	.05
69T	Terry Leach	.05
70T	Jim Levebvre	.05
71T	Al Leiter	.05
72T	Jeffrey Leonard	.05
73T	Derek Lilliquist	.05
74T	Rick Mahler	.05
75T	Tom McCarthy	.05
76T	Lloyd McClendon	.05
77T	Lance McCullers	.05
78T	Oddibe McDowell	.05
79T	Roger McDowell	.05
80T	Larry McWilliams	.05
81T	Randy Milligan	.05
82T	Mike Moore	.05
83T	Keith Moreland	.05
84T	Mike Morgan	.05
85T	Jamie Moyer	.05
86T	Rob Murphy	.05
87T	Eddie Murray	.25
88T	Pete O'Brien	.05
89T	Gregg Olson	.05
90T	Steve Ontiveros	.05
91T	Jesse Orosco	.05
92T	Spike Owen	.05
93T	Rafael Palmeiro	.40
94T	Clay Parker	.05
95T	Jeff Parrett	.05
96T	Lance Parrish	.05
97T	Dennis Powell	.05
98T	Rey Quinones	.05
99T	Doug Rader	.05
100T	Willie Randolph	.05
101T	Shane Rawley	.05
102T	Randy Ready	.05
103T	Bip Roberts	.05
104T	Kenny Rogers	.25
105T	Ed Romero	.05
106T	Nolan Ryan	1.50
107T	Luis Salazar	.05
108T	Juan Samuel	.05
109T	Alex Sanchez	.05
110T	*Deion Sanders*	.50
111T	Steve Sax	.05
112T	Rick Schu	.05
113T	Dwight Smith	.05
114T	Lonnie Smith	.05
115T	Billy Spiers	.10
116T	Kent Tekulve	.05
117T	Walt Terrell	.05
118T	Milt Thompson	.05
119T	Dickie Thon	.05
120T	Jeff Torborg	.05
121T	Jeff Treadway	.05
122T	*Omar Vizquel*	.50
123T	Jerome Walton	.05
124T	Gary Ward	.05
125T	Claudell Washington	.05
126T	Curt Wilkerson	.05
127T	Eddie Williams	.05
128T	Frank Williams	.05
129T	Ken Williams	.05
130T	Mitch Williams	.05
131T	Steve Wilson	.05
---	Topps Magazine subscription offer card	.05

1989 Topps Traded Tiffany

The Topps Traded set was issued in a specially boxed, hobby-only editions. Cards are identical to the regular-issue Topps Traded cards except for the application of a high-gloss to the fronts. Production has been reported as 15,000 sets.

	MT
Complete Set (132):	350.00
Common Player:	.15

(Star cards valued at 3X-4X corresponding cards in regular Topps Traded issue)

1989 Topps All-Star Glossy Set of 22

The glossy All-Stars were included in the Topps 1989 rack packs. Format was very similar to the sets produced since 1984. Besides the starting lineups of the 1988 All-Star Game, the set included the managers and honorary team captains, Bobby Doerr and Willie Stargell.

		MT
Complete Set (22):		2.50
Common Player:		.05
1	Tom Kelly	.05
2	Mark McGwire	1.50
3	Paul Molitor	.25
4	Wade Boggs	.30
5	Cal Ripken, Jr.	.90
6	Jose Canseco	.30
7	Rickey Henderson	.15
8	Dave Winfield	.15
9	Terry Steinbach	.05
10	Frank Viola	.05
11	Bobby Doerr	.05
12	Whitey Herzog	.05
13	Will Clark	.20
14	Ryne Sandberg	.40
15	Bobby Bonilla	.05
16	Ozzie Smith	.30
17	Vince Coleman	.05
18	Andre Dawson	.10
19	Darryl Strawberry	.10
20	Gary Carter	.10
21	Dwight Gooden	.10
22	Willie Stargell	.10

1989 Topps Big Baseball

Known by collectors as Topps "Big Baseball," the cards in this 330-card set measure 2-5/8" x 3-3/4" and are patterned after the 1956 Topps cards. The glossy card fronts are horizontally-designed and include two photos of each player, a portrait alongside an action photo. The backs include 1988 and career stats, but are dominated by a color cartoon featuring the player. Members of the 1988 Team U.S.A. Olympic baseball team are included in the set, which was issued in three series of 110 cards each.

		MT
Complete Set (330):		22.00
Common Player:		.05
1	Orel Hershiser	.10
2	Harold Reynolds	.05
3	Jody Davis	.05
4	Greg Walker	.05
5	Barry Bonds	.60
6	Bret Saberhagen	.10
7	Johnny Ray	.05
8	Mike Fiore	.05
9	Juan Castillo	.05
10	Todd Burns	.05
11	Carmelo Martinez	.05
12	Geno Petralli	.05
13	Mel Hall	.05
14	Tom Browning	.05
15	Fred McGriff	.15
16	Kevin Elster	.05
17	Tim Leary	.05
18	Jim Rice	.10
19	Bret Barberie	.10
20	Jay Buhner	.05
21	Atlee Hammaker	.05
22	Lou Whitaker	.05
23	Paul Runge	.05
24	Carlton Fisk	.20
25	Jose Lind	.05
26	Mark Gubicza	.05
27	Billy Ripken	.05
28	Mike Pagliarulo	.05
29	Jim Deshaies	.05
30	Mark McLemore	.05
31	Scott Terry	.05
32	Franklin Stubbs	.05
33	Don August	.05
34	Mark McGwire	1.50
35	Eric Show	.05
36	Cecil Espy	.05
37	Ron Tingley	.05
38	Mickey Brantley	.05
39	Paul O'Neill	.10
40	Ed Sprague	.10
41	Len Dykstra	.05
42	Roger Clemens	.60
43	Ron Gant	.10
44	Dan Pasqua	.05
45	Jeff Robinson	.05
46	George Brett	.70
47	Bryn Smith	.05
48	Mike Marshall	.05
49	Doug Robbins	.05
50	Don Mattingly	.90
51	Mike Scott	.05
52	Steve Jeltz	.05
53	Dick Schofield	.05
54	Tom Brunansky	.05

55	Gary Sheffield	.75
56	Dave Valle	.05
57	Carney Lansford	.05
58	Tony Gwynn	.75
59	Checklist	.05
60	Damon Berryhill	.05
61	Jack Morris	.05
62	Brett Butler	.05
63	Mickey Hatcher	.05
64	Bruce Sutter	.05
65	Robin Ventura	.50
66	Junior Oritiz	.05
67	Pat Tabler	.05
68	Greg Swindell	.05
69	Jeff Branson	.10
70	Manny Lee	.05
71	Dave Magadan	.05
72	Rich Gedman	.05
73	Tim Raines	.10
74	Mike Maddux	.05
75	Jim Presley	.05
76	Chuck Finley	.05
77	Jose Oquendo	.05
78	Rob Deer	.05
79	Jay Howell	.05
80	Terry Steinbach	.05
81	Eddie Whitson	.05
82	Ruben Sierra	.05
83	Bruce Benedict	.05
84	Fred Manrique	.05
85	John Smiley	.05
86	Mike Macfarlane	.05
87	Rene Gonzales	.05
88	Charles Hudson	.05
90	Les Straker	.05
91	Carmen Castillo	.05
92	Tracy Woodson	.05
93	Tino Martinez	.65
94	Herm Winningham	.05
95	Kelly Gruber	.05
96	Terry Leach	.05
97	Jody Reed	.05
98	Nelson Santovenia	.05
99	Tony Armas	.05
100	Greg Brock	.05
101	Dave Stewart	.05
102	Roberto Alomar	.25
103	Jim Sundberg	.05
104	Albert Hall	.05
105	Steve Lyons	.05
106	Sid Bream	.05
107	Danny Tartabull	.05
108	Rick Dempsey	.05
109	Rich Renteria	.05
110	Ozzie Smith	.25
111	Steve Sax	.05
112	Kelly Downs	.05
113	Larry Sheets	.05
114	Andy Benes	.50
115	Pete O'Brien	.05
116	Kevin McReynolds	.05
117	Juan Berenguer	.05
118	Billy Hatcher	.05
119	Rick Cerone	.05
120	Andre Dawson	.10
121	Storm Davis	.05
122	Devon White	.05
123	Alan Trammell	.05
124	Vince Coleman	.05
125	Al Leiter	.05
126	Dale Sveum	.05
127	Pete Incaviglia	.05
128	Dave Stieb	.05
129	Kevin Mitchell	.05
130	Dave Schmidt	.05
131	Gary Redus	.05
132	Ron Robinson	.05
133	Darnell Coles	.05
134	Benny Santiago	.05
135	John Farrell	.05
136	Willie Wilson	.05
137	Steve Bedrosian	.05
138	Don Slaught	.05
139	Darryl Strawberry	.15
140	Frank Viola	.05
141	Dave Silvestri	.10
142	Carlos Quintana	.05
143	Vance Law	.05
144	Dave Parker	.05
145	Tim Belcher	.05
146	Will Clark	.35
147	Mark Williamson	.05
148	Ozzie Guillen	.05
149	Kirk McCaskill	.05
150	Pat Sheridan	.05
151	Terry Pendleton	.05
152	Roberto Kelly	.05
153	Joey Meyer	.05
154	Mark Grant	.05
155	Joe Carter	.10
156	Steve Buechele	.05
157	Tony Fernandez	.05
158	Jeff Reed	.05
159	Bobby Bonilla	.10
160	Henry Cotto	.05
161	Kurt Stillwell	.05
162	Mickey Morandini	.15
163	Robby Thompson	.05
164	Rick Schu	.05
165	Stan Jefferson	.05
166	Ron Darling	.05
167	Kirby Puckett	.50
168	Bill Doran	.05
169	Dennis Lamp	.05
170	Ty Griffin	.10
171	Ron Hassey	.05
172	Dale Murphy	.10
173	Andres Galarraga	.10
174	Tim Flannery	.05
175	Cory Snyder	.05
176	Checklist	.05
177	Tommy Barrett	.05
178	Dan Petry	.05
179	Billy Masse	.05
180	Terry Kennedy	.05
181	Joe Orsulak	.05
182	Doyle Alexander	.05
183	Willie McGee	.05
184	Jim Gantner	.05
185	Keith Hernandez	.05
186	Greg Gagne	.05
187	Kevin Bass	.05
188	Mark Eichhorn	.05
189	Mark Grace	.30
190	Jose Canseco	.50
191	Bobby Witt	.05
192	Rafael Santana	.05
193	Dwight Evans	.05
194	Greg Booker	.05
195	Brook Jacoby	.05
196	Rafael Belliard	.05
197	Candy Maldonado	.05
198	Mickey Tettleton	.05
199	Barry Larkin	.10
200	Frank White	.05
201	Wally Joyner	.10
202	Chet Lemon	.05
203	Joe Magrane	.05
204	Glenn Braggs	.05
205	Scott Fletcher	.05
206	Gary Ward	.05
207	Nelson Liriano	.05
208	Howard Johnson	.05
209	Kent Hrbek	.05
210	Ken Caminiti	.10
211	Mike Greenwell	.05
212	Ryne Sandberg	.50
213	Joe Slusarski	.10
214	Donnell Nixon	.05
215	Tim Wallach	.05
216	John Kruk	.05
217	Charles Nagy	.25
218	Alvin Davis	.05
219	Oswald Peraza	.05
220	Mike Schmidt	.50
221	Spike Owen	.05
222	Mike Smithson	.05
223	Dion James	.05
224	Ernie Whitt	.05
225	Mike Davis	.05
226	Gene Larkin	.05
227	Pat Combs	.15
228	Jack Howell	.05
229	Ron Oester	.05
230	Paul Gibson	.05
231	Mookie Wilson	.05
232	Glenn Hubbard	.05
233	Shawon Dunston	.05
234	Otis Nixon	.05
235	Melido Perez	.05
236	Jerry Browne	.05
237	Rick Rhoden	.05
238	Bo Jackson	.20
239	Randy Velarde	.05
240	Jack Clark	.05
241	Wade Boggs	.60
242	Lonnie Smith	.05
243	Mike Flanagan	.05
244	Willie Randolph	.05
245	Oddibe McDowell	.05
246	Ricky Jordan	.05
247	Greg Briley	.05
248	Rex Hudler	.05
249	Robin Yount	.35
250	Lance Parrish	.05
251	Chris Sabo	.05
252	Mike Henneman	.05
253	Gregg Jefferies	.10
254	Curt Young	.05
255	Andy Van Slyke	.05
256	Rod Booker	.05
257	Rafael Palmeiro	.20
258	Jose Uribe	.05
259	Ellis Burks	.10
260	John Smoltz	.10
261	Tom Foley	.05
262	Lloyd Moseby	.05
263	Jim Poole	.10
264	Gary Gaetti	.05
265	Bob Dernier	.05
266	Harold Baines	.05
267	Tom Candiotti	.05
268	Rafael Ramirez	.05
269	Bob Boone	.05
270	Buddy Bell	.05
271	Rickey Henderson	.20
272	Willie Fraser	.05
273	Eric Davis	.05
274	Jeff Robinson	.05
275	Damaso Garcia	.05
276	Sid Fernandez	.05
277	Stan Javier	.05
278	Marty Barrett	.05
279	Gerald Perry	.05
280	Rob Ducey	.05
281	Mike Scioscia	.05
282	Randy Bush	.05
283	Tom Herr	.05
284	Glenn Wilson	.05
285	Pedro Guerrero	.05
286	Cal Ripken, Jr.	.95
287	Randy Johnson	.25
288	Julio Franco	.05
289	Ivan Calderon	.05
290	Rich Yett	.05
291	Scott Servais	.10
292	Bill Pecota	.05
293	Ken Phelps	.05
294	Chili Davis	.05
295	Manny Trillo	.05
296	Mike Boddicker	.05
297	Geronimo Berroa	.05
298	Todd Stottlemyre	.05
299	Kirk Gibson	.05
300	Wally Backman	.05
301	Hubie Brooks	.05
302	Von Hayes	.05
303	Matt Nokes	.05
304	Dwight Gooden	.10
305	Walt Weiss	.05
306	Mike LaValliere	.05
307	Cris Carpenter	.10
308	Ted Wood	.05
309	Jeff Russell	.05
310	Dave Gallagher	.05
311	Andy Allanson	.05
312	Craig Reynolds	.05
313	Kevin Seitzer	.05
314	Dave Winfield	.25
315	Andy McGaffigan	.05
316	Nick Esasky	.05
317	Jeff Blauser	.05
318	George Bell	.05
319	Eddie Murray	.25
320	Mark Davidson	.05
321	Juan Samuel	.05
322	Jim Abbott	.10
323	Kal Daniels	.05
324	Mike Brumley	.05
325	Gary Carter	.10
326	Dave Henderson	.05
327	Checklist	.05
328	Garry Templeton	.05
329	Pat Perry	.05
330	Paul Molitor	.25

1989 Topps Double Headers All-Stars

This scarce test issue was produced in two versions, an All-Stars set and a set of exclusively Mets and Yankees players. The "cards" are two-sided miniature (1-5/8" x 2-1/4") reproductions of the player's 1989 Topps card and his Topps rookie card, encased in a clear plastic stand.

		MT
Complete Set (24):		45.00
Common Player:		1.00
(1)	Alan Ashby	1.00
(2)	Wade Boggs	3.00
(3)	Bobby Bonilla	1.00
(4)	Jose Canseco	3.00
(5)	Will Clark	3.00
(6)	Roger Clemens	4.00
(7)	Andre Dawson	1.00
(8)	Dennis Eckersley	1.00
(9)	Carlton Fisk	2.00
(10)	John Franco	1.00
(11)	Julio Franco	1.00
(12)	Kirk Gibson	1.00
(13)	Mike Greenwell	1.00
(14)	Orel Hershiser	1.00
(15)	Danny Jackson	1.00
(16)	Don Mattingly	5.00
(17)	Mark McGwire	6.00
(18)	Kirby Puckett	5.00
(19)	Ryne Sandberg	3.00
(20)	Ozzie Smith	3.00
(21)	Darryl Strawberry	1.50
(22)	Alan Trammell	1.00
(23)	Andy Van Slyke	1.00
(24)	Frank Viola	1.00

1989 Topps Glossy Rookies Set of 22

Bearing the same design and style of the past two years, Topps featured the top first-year players from the 1988 season in this glossy set. The full-color player photo appears beneath the "1988 Rookies" banner. The player's name is displayed beneath the photo. The flip side features the "1988 Rookies Commemorative Set" logo followed by the player ID and card number. Glossy rookies were found only in 100-card jumbo cello packs.

	MT
Complete Set (22):	9.00
Common Player:	.30

1	Roberto Alomar	1.00
2	Brady Anderson	.50
3	Tim Belcher	.30
4	Damon Berryhill	.30
5	Jay Buhner	.50
6	Kevin Elster	.30
7	Cecil Espy	.30
8	Dave Gallagher	.30
9	Ron Gant	.50
10	Paul Gibson	.30
11	Mark Grace	1.50
12	Darrin Jackson	.30
13	Gregg Jefferies	.60
14	Ricky Jordan	.30
15	Al Leiter	.65
16	Melido Perez	.30
17	Chris Sabo	.30
18	Nelson Santovenia	.30
19	Mackey Sasser	.30
20	Gary Sheffield	1.00
21	Walt Weiss	.60
22	David Wells	.90

1989 Topps Mini League Leaders

This 77-card set features baseball's statistical leaders from the 1988 season. It is referred to as a "mini" set because of the cards' small (2-1/8" x 3") size. The glossy cards feature action photos that have a soft focus on all edges. The player's team and name appear along the bottom of the card. The back features a head-shot of the player along with his 1988 season ranking and stats.

		MT
Complete Set (77):		4.00
Common Player:		.10
1	Dale Murphy	.15
2	Gerald Perry	.10
3	Andre Dawson	.15
4	Greg Maddux	.90
5	Rafael Palmeiro	.25
6	Tom Browning	.10
7	Kal Daniels	.10
8	Eric Davis	.10
9	John Franco	.10
10	Danny Jackson	.10
11	Barry Larkin	.20
12	Jose Rijo	.10
13	Chris Sabo	.10
14	Nolan Ryan	1.00
15	Mike Scott	.10
16	Gerald Young	.10
17	Kirk Gibson	.10
18	Orel Hershiser	.10
19	Steve Sax	.10
20	John Tudor	.10
21	Hubie Brooks	.10
22	Andres Galarraga	.15
23	Otis Nixon	.10
24	Dave Cone	.15
25	Sid Fernandez	.10
26	Dwight Gooden	.15
27	Kevin McReynolds	.10
28	Darryl Strawberry	.15
29	Juan Samuel	.10
30	Bobby Bonilla	.10
31	Sid Bream	.10
32	Jim Gott	.10
33	Andy Van Slyke	.10
34	Vince Coleman	.10
35	Jose DeLeon	.10
36	Joe Magrane	.10
37	Ozzie Smith	.45
38	Todd Worrell	.10
39	Tony Gwynn	.65
40	Brett Butler	.10
41	Will Clark	.50
42	Rick Reuschel	.10
43	Checklist	.10
44	Eddie Murray	.30
45	Wade Boggs	.60
46	Roger Clemens	.65
47	Dwight Evans	.10
48	Mike Greenwell	.10
49	Bruce Hurst	.10
50	Johnny Ray	.10
51	Doug Jones	.10
52	Greg Swindell	.10
53	Gary Pettis	.10
54	George Brett	.75
55	Mark Gubicza	.10
56	Willie Wilson	.10
57	Teddy Higuera	.10
58	Paul Molitor	.45
59	Robin Yount	.50
60	Allan Anderson	.10
61	Gary Gaetti	.10
62	Kirby Puckett	.65
63	Jeff Reardon	.10
64	Frank Viola	.10
65	Jack Clark	.10
66	Rickey Henderson	.25
67	Dave Winfield	.35
68	Jose Canseco	.50
69	Dennis Eckersley	.10
70	Mark McGwire	1.50
71	Dave Stewart	.10
72	Alvin Davis	.10
73	Mark Langston	.10
74	Harold Reynolds	.10
75	George Bell	.10
76	Tony Fernandez	.10
77	Fred McGriff	.20

1990 Topps 1989 Major League Debut

This 150-card set chronicles the debut date of all 1989 Major League rookies. Two checklist cards are also included in this boxed set, listing the players in order of debut date, though the cards are numbered alphabetically. The card fronts resemble the 1990 Topps cards in style. A debut banner appears in an upper corner. The flip sides are horizontal and are printed in black on yellow stock, providing an overview of the player's first game. The set is packaged in a special collectors box and was only available through hobby dealers.

		MT
Complete Set (150):		45.00
Common Player:		.10
1	Jim Abbott	.15
2	Beau Allred	.10
3	Wilson Alvarez	.15
4	Kent Anderson	.10
5	Eric Anthony	.20
6	Kevin Appier	.20
7	Larry Arndt	.10
8	John Barfield	.10
9	Billy Bates	.10
10	Kevin Batiste	.10
11	Blaine Beatty	.10
12	Stan Belinda	.10
13	Juan Bell	.10
14	Joey Belle	2.00
15	Andy Benes	.20
16	Mike Benjamin	.10
17	Geronimo Berroa	.10
18	Mike Blowers	.10
19	Brian Brady	.10
20	Francisco Cabrera	.10
21	George Canale	.10
22	Jose Cano	.10
23	Steve Carter	.10
24	Pat Combs	.10
25	Scott Coolbaugh	.10
26	Steve Cummings	.10
27	Pete Dalena	.10
28	Jeff Datz	.10
29	Bobby Davidson	.10
30	Drew Denson	.10
31	Gary DiSarcina	.10
32	Brian DuBois	.10
33	Mike Dyer	.10
34	Wayne Edwards	.10
35	Junior Felix	.10
36	Mike Fetters	.10
37	Steve Finley	.20
38	Darren Fletcher	.15
39	LaVel Freeman	.10
40	Steve Frey	.10
41	Mark Gardner	.10
42	Joe Girardi	.20
43	Juan Gonzalez	3.00
44	Goose Gozzo	.10
45	Tommy Greene	.15
46	Ken Griffey, Jr.	9.00
47	Jason Grimsley	.10
48	Marquis Grissom	.75
49	Mark Guthrie	.10
50	Chip Hale	.10
51	John Hardy	.10
52	Gene Harris	.10
53	Mike Hartley	.10
54	Scott Hemond	.10
55	Xavier Hernandez	.10
56	Eric Hetzel	.10
57	Greg Hibbard	.10
58	Mark Higgins	.10
59	Glenallen Hill	.15
60	Chris Hoiles	.15
61	Shawn Holman	.10
62	Dann Howitt	.10
63	Mike Huff	.10
64	Terry Jorgenson	.10
65	Dave Justice	2.00
66	Jeff King	.15
67	Matt Kinzer	.10
68	Joe Kraemer	.10
69	Marcus Lawton	.10
70	Derek Lilliquist	.10
71	Scott Little	.10
72	Greg Litton	.10
73	Rick Lueken	.10
74	Julio Machado	.10
75	Tom Magrann	.10
76	Kelly Mann	.10
77	Randy McCament	.10
78	Ben McDonald	.10
79	Chuck McElroy	.10
80	Jeff McKnight	.10
81	Kent Mercker	.10
82	Matt Merullo	.10
83	Hensley Meulens	.10
84	Kevin Mmahat	.10
85	Mike Munoz	.10
86	Dan Murphy	.10
87	Jaime Navarro	.10
88	Randy Nosek	.10
89	John Olerud	.50
90	Steve Olin	.10
91	Joe Oliver	.10
92	Francisco Oliveras	.10
93	Greg Olson	.10
94	John Orton	.10
95	Dean Palmer	.10
96	Ramon Pena	.10
97	Jeff Peterek	.10
98	Marty Pevey	.10
99	Rusty Richards	.10
100	Jeff Richardson	.10
101	Rob Richie	.10
102	Kevin Ritz	.10
103	Rosario Rodriguez	.10
104	Mike Roesler	.10
105	Kenny Rogers	.15
106	Bobby Rose	.10
107	Alex Sanchez	.10
108	Deion Sanders	.60
109	Jeff Schaefer	.10
110	Jeff Schulz	.10
111	Mike Schwabe	.10
112	Dick Scott	.10
113	Scott Scudder	.10
114	Rudy Seanez	.10
115	Joe Skalski	.10
116	Dwight Smith	.10
117	Greg Smith	.10
118	Mike Smith	.10
119	Paul Sorrento	.10
120	Sammy Sosa	20.00
121	Billy Spiers	.10
122	Mike Stanton	.10
123	Phil Stephenson	.10
124	Doug Strange	.10
125	Russ Swan	.10
126	Kevin Tapani	.15
127	Stu Tate	.10
128	Greg Vaughn	.30
129	Robin Ventura	.40
130	Randy Veres	.10
131	Jose Vizcaino	.10
132	Omar Vizquel	.15
133	Larry Walker	1.00
134	Jerome Walton	.10
135	Gary Wayne	.10
136	Lenny Webster	.10
137	Mickey Weston	.10
138	Jeff Wetherby	.10
139	John Wetteland	.15
140	Ed Whited	.10
141	Wally Whitehurst	.10
142	Kevin Wickander	.10
143	Dean Wilkins	.10
144	Dana Williams	.10
145	Paul Wilmet	.10
146	Craig Wilson	.10
147	Matt Winters	.10
148	Eric Yelding	.10
149	Clint Zavaras	.10
150	Todd Zeile	.15
----	Checklist (1 of 2)	.05
----	Checklist (2 of 2)	.05

1990 Topps

The 1990 Topps set again included 792 cards, and sported a newly-designed front that featured six different color schemes. The set led off with a special four-card salute to Nolan Ryan, and features other specials including All-Stars, Number 1 Draft Picks, Record Breakers, managers, rookies, and "Turn Back the Clock" cards. The set also includes a special card commemorating A. Bartlett Giamatti, the late baseball commissioner. Backs are printed in black on a chartreuse background. The set features 725 different individual player cards, the most ever, including 138 players' first appearance in a regular Topps set.

MT
Complete Set (792): 18.00
Common Player: .05
Wax Pack (16): 1.20
Wax Box (36): 24.50
1 Nolan Ryan .50
2 Nolan Ryan (Mets) .20
3 Nolan Ryan (Angels) .20
4 Nolan Ryan (Astros) .20
5 Nolan Ryan (Rangers) .20
6 Vince Coleman (Record Breaker) .05
7 Rickey Henderson (Record Breaker) .10
8 Cal Ripken, Jr. (Record Breaker) .25
9 Eric Plunk .05
10 Barry Larkin .10
11 Paul Gibson .05
12 Joe Girardi .05
13 Mark Williamson .05
14 *Mike Fetters* .10
15 Teddy Higuera .05
16 *Kent Anderson* .05
17 Kelly Downs .05
18 Carlos Quintana .05
19 Al Newman .05
20 Mark Gubicza .05
21 Jeff Torborg .05
22 Bruce Ruffin .05
23 Randy Velarde .05
24 Joe Hesketh .05
25 Willie Randolph .05
26 Don Slaught .05
27 Rick Leach .05
28 Duane Ward .05
29 John Cangelosi .05
30 David Cone .20
31 Henry Cotto .05
32 John Farrell .05
33 Greg Walker .05
34 *Tony Fossas* .05
35 Benito Santiago .05
36 John Costello .05
37 Domingo Ramos .05
38 Wes Gardner .05
39 Curt Ford .05
40 Jay Howell .05
41 Matt Williams .20
42 Jeff Robinson .05
43 Dante Bichette .10
44 *Roger Salkeld* (#1 Draft Pick) .15
45 Dave Parker .05
46 Rob Dibble .05
47 Brian Harper .05
48 Zane Smith .05
49 Tom Lawless .05
50 Glenn Davis .05
51 Doug Rader .05
52 *Jack Daugherty* .10
53 Mike LaCoss .05
54 Joel Skinner .05
55 Darrell Evans .05
56 Franklin Stubbs .05
57 Greg Vaughn .10
58 Keith Miller .05
59 Ted Power .05
60 George Brett .25
61 Deion Sanders .25
62 Ramon Martinez .10
63 Mike Pagliarulo .05
64 Danny Darwin .05
65 Devon White .05
66 *Greg Litton* .05
67 Scott Sanderson .05
68 Dave Henderson .05
69 Todd Frohwirth .05
70 Mike Greenwell .05
71 Allan Anderson .05
72 *Jeff Huson* .10
73 Bob Milacki .05
74 *Jeff Jackson* (#1 Draft Pick) .05
75 Doug Jones .05
76 Dave Valle .05
77 Dave Bergman .05
78 Mike Flanagan .05
79 Ron Kittle .05
80 Jeff Russell .05
81 Bob Rodgers .05
82 Scott Terry .05
83 Hensley Meulens .05
84 Ray Searage .05
85 Juan Samuel .05
86 Paul Kilgus .05
87 *Rick Luecken* .05
88 Glenn Braggs .05
89 *Clint Zavaras* .05
90 Jack Clark .05
91 *Steve Frey* .10
92 Mike Stanley .05
93 Shawn Hillegas .05
94 Herm Winningham .05
95 Todd Worrell .05
96 Jody Reed .05
97 Curt Schilling .10
98 Jose Gonzalez .05
99 *Rich Monteleone* .05
100 Will Clark .30
101 Shane Rawley .05
102 Stan Javier .05
103 Marvin Freeman .05
104 Bob Knepper .05
105 Randy Myers .05
106 Charlie O'Brien .05
107 Fred Lynn .05
108 Rod Nichols .05
109 Roberto Kelly .05
110 Tommy Helms .05
111 Ed Whited .05
112 Glenn Wilson .05
113 Manny Lee .05
114 Mike Bielecki .05
115 Tony Pena .05
116 Floyd Bannister .05
117 Mike Sharperson .05
118 Erik Hanson .05
119 Billy Hatcher .05
120 John Franco .05
121 Robin Ventura .15
122 Shawn Abner .05
123 Rich Gedman .05
124 Dave Dravecky .05
125 Kent Hrbek .05
126 Randy Kramer .05
127 Mike Devereaux .05
128 Checklist 1-132 .05
129 Ron Jones .05
130 Bert Blyleven .05
131 Matt Nokes .05
132 Lance Blankenship .05
133 Ricky Horton .05
134 *Earl Cunningham* (#1 Draft Pick) .05
135 Dave Magadan .05
136 Kevin Brown .20
137 *Marty Pevey* .05
138 Al Leiter .10
139 Greg Brock .05
140 Andre Dawson .10
141 John Hart .05
142 *Jeff Wetherby* .05
143 Rafael Belliard .05
144 Bud Black .05
145 Terry Steinbach .05
146 *Rob Richie* .05
147 Chuck Finley .05
148 Edgar Martinez .10
149 Steve Farr .05
150 Kirk Gibson .05
151 Rick Mahler .05
152 Lonnie Smith .05
153 Randy Milligan .05
154 Mike Maddux .05
155 Ellis Burks .10
156 Ken Patterson .05
157 Craig Biggio .25
158 Craig Lefferts .05
159 Mike Felder .05
160 Dave Righetti .05
161 Harold Reynolds .05
162 *Todd Zeile* .20
163 Phil Bradley .05
164 *Jeff Juden* (#1 Draft Pick) .15
165 Walt Weiss .05
166 Bobby Witt .05
167 Kevin Appier .10
168 Jose Lind .05
169 Richard Dotson .05
170 George Bell .05
171 Russ Nixon .05
172 Tom Lampkin .05
173 Tim Belcher .05
174 Jeff Kunkel .05
175 Mike Moore .05
176 Luis Quinones .05
177 Mike Henneman .05
178 Chris James .05
179 Brian Holton .05
180 Rock Raines .10
181 Juan Agosto .05
182 Mookie Wilson .05
183 Steve Lake .05
184 Danny Cox .05
185 Ruben Sierra .05
186 Dave LaPoint .05
187 *Rick Wrona* .05
188 Mike Smithson .05
189 Dick Schofield .05
190 Rick Reuschel .05
191 Pat Borders .05
192 Don August .05
193 Andy Benes .15
194 Glenallen Hill .10
195 Tim Burke .05
196 Gerald Young .05
197 Doug Drabek .05
198 Mike Marshall .05
199 *Sergio Valdez* .05
200 Don Mattingly .35
201 Cito Gaston .05
202 Mike Macfarlane .05
203 *Mike Roesler* .05
204 Bob Dernier .05
205 Mark Davis .05
206 Nick Esasky .05
207 Bob Ojeda .05
208 Brook Jacoby .05
209 Greg Mathews .05
210 Ryne Sandberg .30
211 John Cerutti .05
212 Joe Orsulak .05
213 Scott Bankhead .05
214 Terry Francona .05
215 Kirk McCaskill .05
216 Ricky Jordan .05
217 Don Robinson .05
218 Wally Backman .05
219 Donn Pall .05
220 Barry Bonds .40
221 *Gary Mielke* .05
222 Kurt Stillwell .05
223 Tommy Gregg .05
224 *Delino DeShields* .25
225 Jim Deshaies .05
226 Mickey Hatcher .05
227 *Kevin Tapani* .25
228 Dave Martinez .05
229 David Wells .10
230 Keith Hernandez .05
231 Jack McKeon .05
232 Darnell Coles .05
233 Ken Hill .10
234 Mariano Duncan .05
235 Jeff Reardon .05
236 Hal Morris .05
237 *Kevin Ritz* .10
238 Felix Jose .05
239 Eric Show .05
240 Mark Grace .15
241 Mike Krukow .05
242 Fred Manrique .05
243 Barry Jones .05
244 Bill Schroeder .05
245 Roger Clemens .40
246 Jim Eisenreich .05
247 Jerry Reed .05
248 Dave Anderson .05
249 *Mike Smith* .05
250 Jose Canseco .40
251 Jeff Blauser .05
252 Otis Nixon .05
253 Mark Portugal .05
254 Francisco Cabrera .05
255 Bobby Thigpen .05
256 Marvell Wynne .05
257 Jose DeLeon .05
258 Barry Lyons .05
259 Lance McCullers .05
260 Eric Davis .10
261 Whitey Herzog .05
262 Checklist 133-264 .05
263 *Mel Stottlemyre, Jr.* .10
264 Bryan Clutterbuck .05
265 Pete O'Brien .05
266 German Gonzalez .05
267 Mark Davidson .05
268 Rob Murphy .05
269 Dickie Thon .05
270 Dave Stewart .05
271 Chet Lemon .05
272 Bryan Harvey .05
273 Bobby Bonilla .10
274 *Goose Gozzo* .05
275 Mickey Tettleton .05
276 Gary Thurman .05
277 Lenny Harris .05
278 Pascual Perez .05
279 Steve Buechele .05
280 Lou Whitaker .05
281 Kevin Bass .05
282 Derek Lilliquist .05
283 Albert Belle .60
284 *Mark Gardner* .10
285 Willie McGee .05
286 Lee Guetterman .05
287 Vance Law .05
288 Greg Briley .05
289 Norm Charlton .05
290 Robin Yount .30
291 Dave Johnson .05
292 Jim Gott .05
293 Mike Gallego .05
294 Craig McMurtry .05
295 Fred McGriff .25
296 Jeff Ballard .05
297 Tom Herr .05
298 Danny Gladden .05
299 Adam Peterson .05
300 Bo Jackson .20
301 Don Aase .05
302 *Marcus Lawton* .05
303 Rick Cerone .05
304 Marty Clary .05
305 Eddie Murray .25
306 Tom Niedenfuer .05
307 Bip Roberts .05
308 Jose Guzman .05
309 *Eric Yelding* .20
310 Steve Bedrosian .05
311 Dwight Smith .05
312 Dan Quisenberry .05
313 Gus Polidor .05
314 *Donald Harris* (#1 Draft Pick) .10
315 Bruce Hurst .05
316 Carney Lansford .05
317 *Mark Guthrie* .05
318 Wallace Johnson .05
319 Dion James .05
320 Dave Steib .05
321 Joe M. Morgan .05
322 Junior Ortiz .05
323 Willie Wilson .05
324 Pete Harnisch .05
325 Robby Thompson .05
326 *Tom McCarthy* .05
327 Ken Williams .05
328 Curt Young .05
329 Oddibe McDowell .05
330 Ron Darling .05
331 *Juan Gonzalez* 1.50
332 Paul O'Neill .15
333 Bill Wegman .05
334 Johnny Ray .05
335 Andy Hawkins .05
336 Ken Griffey, Jr. 2.00
337 Lloyd McClendon .05
338 Dennis Lamp .05
339 Dave Clark .05
340 Fernando Valenzuela .05
341 Tom Foley .05
342 Alex Trevino .05
343 Frank Tanana .05
344 *George Canale* .05
345 Harold Baines .05
346 Jim Presley .05
347 *Junior Felix* .05
348 *Gary Wayne* .05
349 *Steve Finley* .15
350 Bret Saberhagen .05
351 Roger Craig .05
352 Bryn Smith .05
353 Sandy Alomar .10
354 *Stan Belinda* .10
355 Marty Barrett .05
356 Randy Ready .05
357 Dave West .05
358 Andres Thomas .05
359 Jimmy Jones .05
360 Paul Molitor .25
361 *Randy McCament* .05
362 Damon Berryhill .05
363 Dan Petry .05
364 Rolando Roomes .05
365 Ozzie Guillen .05
366 Mike Heath .05
367 Mike Morgan .05
368 Bill Doran .05
369 Todd Burns .05
370 Tim Wallach .05
371 Jimmy Key .05
372 Terry Kennedy .05
373 Alvin Davis .05
374 *Steve Cummings* .05
375 Dwight Evans .05
376 Checklist 265-396 .05
377 *Mickey Weston* .05

No.	Player	Value
378	Luis Salazar	.05
379	Steve Rosenberg	.05
380	Dave Winfield	.20
381	Frank Robinson	.10
382	Jeff Musselman	.05
383	John Morris	.05
384	*Pat Combs*	.05
385	Fred McGriff (All-Star)	.10
386	Julio Franco (All-Star)	.05
387	Wade Boggs (All-Star)	.15
388	Cal Ripken, Jr. (All-Star)	.40
389	Robin Yount (All-Star)	.15
390	Ruben Sierra (All-Star)	.05
391	Kirby Puckett (All-Star)	.20
392	Carlton Fisk (All-Star)	.15
393	Bret Saberhagen (All-Star)	.05
394	Jeff Ballard (All-Star)	.05
395	Jeff Russell (All-Star)	.05
396	A. Bartlett Giamatti	.20
397	Will Clark (All-Star)	.15
398	Ryne Sandberg (All-Star)	.20
399	Howard Johnson (All-Star)	.05
400	Ozzie Smith (All-Star)	.15
401	Kevin Mitchell (All-Star)	.05
402	Eric Davis (All-Star)	.05
403	Tony Gwynn (All-Star)	.20
404	Craig Biggio (All-Star)	.10
405	Mike Scott (All-Star)	.05
406	Joe Magrane (All-Star)	.05
407	Mark Davis (All-Star)	.05
408	Trevor Wilson	.10
409	Tom Brunansky	.05
410	Joe Boever	.05
411	Ken Phelps	.05
412	Jamie Moyer	.05
413	*Brian DuBois*	.10
414a	*Frank Thomas No Name* (#1 Draft Pick, no name on front)	800.00
414b	*Frank Thomas* (#1 Draft Pick, name on front)	3.00
415	Shawon Dunston	.05
416	*Dave Johnson*	.05
417	Jim Gantner	.05
418	Tom Browning	.05
419	*Beau Allred*	.05
420	Carlton Fisk	.20
421	Greg Minton	.05
422	Pat Sheridan	.05
423	Fred Toliver	.05
424	Jerry Reuss	.05
425	Bill Landrum	.05
426	Jeff Hamilton	.05
427	Carmem Castillo	.05
428	*Steve Davis*	.05
429	Tom Kelly	.05
430	Pete Incaviglia	.05
431	Randy Johnson	.30
432	Damaso Garcia	.05
433	*Steve Olin*	.05
434	Mark Carreon	.10
435	Kevin Seitzer	.05
436	Mel Hall	.05
437	Les Lancaster	.05
438	Greg Myers	.05
439	Jeff Parrett	.05
440	Alan Trammell	.05
441	Bob Kipper	.05
442	Jerry Browne	.05
443	Cris Carpenter	.05
444	*Kyle Abbott* (FDP)	.10
445	Danny Jackson	.05
446	Dan Pasqua	.05
447	Atlee Hammaker	.05
448	Greg Gagne	.05
449	Dennis Rasmussen	.05
450	Rickey Henderson	.20
451	Mark Lemke	.05
452	Luis de los Santos	.05
453	Jody Davis	.05
454	Jeff King	.10
455	Jeffrey Leonard	.05
456	Chris Gwynn	.05
457	Gregg Jefferies	.15
458	Bob McClure	.05
459	Jim Lefebvre	.05
460	Mike Scott	.05
461	*Carlos Martinez*	.05
462	Denny Walling	.05
463	Drew Hall	.05
464	*Jerome Walton*	.10
465	Kevin Gross	.05
466	Rance Mulliniks	.05
467	Juan Nieves	.05
468	Billy Ripken	.05
469	John Kruk	.05
470	Frank Viola	.05
471	Mike Brumley	.05
472	Jose Uribe	.05
473	Joe Price	.05
474	Rich Thompson	.05
475	Bob Welch	.05
476	Brad Komminsk	.05
477	Willie Fraser	.05
478	Mike LaValliere	.05
479	Frank White	.05
480	Sid Fernandez	.05
481	Garry Templeton	.05
482	*Steve Carter*	.05
483	Alejandro Pena	.05
484	Mike Fitzgerald	.05
485	John Candelaria	.05
486	Jeff Treadway	.05
487	Steve Searcy	.05
488	Ken Oberkfell	.05
489	Nick Leyva	.05
490	Dan Plesac	.05
491	*Dave Cochrane*	.05
492	Ron Oester	.05
493	*Jason Grimsley*	.10
494	Terry Puhl	.05
495	Lee Smith	.05
496	Cecil Espy	.05
497	Dave Schmidt	.05
498	Rick Schu	.05
499	Bill Long	.05
500	Kevin Mitchell	.05
501	Matt Young	.05
502	Mitch Webster	.05
503	Randy St. Claire	.05
504	Tom O'Malley	.05
505	Kelly Gruber	.05
506	Tom Glavine	.15
507	Gary Redus	.05
508	Terry Leach	.05
509	Tom Pagnozzi	.05
510	Dwight Gooden	.10
511	Clay Parker	.05
512	Gary Pettis	.05
513	Mark Eichhorn	.05
514	Andy Allanson	.05
515	Len Dykstra	.05
516	Tim Leary	.05
517	Roberto Alomar	.30
518	Bill Krueger	.05
519	Bucky Dent	.05
520	Mitch Williams	.05
521	Craig Worthington	.05
522	Mike Dunne	.05
523	Jay Bell	.05
524	Daryl Boston	.05
525	Wally Joyner	.10
526	Checklist 397-528	.05
527	Ron Hassey	.05
528	*Kevin Wickander*	.10
529	Greg Harris	.05
530	Mark Langston	.05
531	Ken Caminiti	.15
532	Cecilio Guante	.05
533	Tim Jones	.05
534	Louie Meadows	.05
535	John Smoltz	.15
536	*Bob Geren*	.05
537	Mark Grant	.05
538	*Billy Spiers*	.05
539	Neal Heaton	.05
540	Danny Tartabull	.05
541	Pat Perry	.05
542	Darren Daulton	.05
543	Nelson Liriano	.05
544	Dennis Boyd	.05
545	Kevin McReynolds	.05
546	Kevin Hickey	.05
547	Jack Howell	.05
548	Pat Clements	.05
549	Don Zimmer	.05
550	Julio Franco	.05
551	Tim Crews	.05
552	*Mike Smith*	.05
553	*Scott Scudder*	.05
554	Jay Buhner	.10
555	Jack Morris	.05
556	Gene Larkin	.05
557	*Jeff Innis*	.05
558	Rafael Ramirez	.05
559	Andy McGaffigan	.05
560	Steve Sax	.05
561	Ken Dayley	.05
562	Chad Kreuter	.05
563	Alex Sanchez	.05
564	*Tyler Houston* (#1 Draft Pick)	.10
565	Scott Fletcher	.05
566	Mark Knudson	.05
567	Ron Gant	.10
568	John Smiley	.05
569	Ivan Calderon	.05
570	Cal Ripken, Jr.	.75
571	Brett Butler	.05
572	Greg Harris	.05
573	Danny Heep	.05
574	Bill Swift	.05
575	Lance Parrish	.05
576	*Mike Dyer*	.05
577	Charlie Hayes	.05
578	Joe Magrane	.05
579	Art Howe	.05
580	Joe Carter	.10
581	Ken Griffey	.05
582	Rick Honeycutt	.05
583	Bruce Benedict	.05
584	*Phil Stephenson*	.05
585	Kal Daniels	.05
586	Ed Nunez	.05
587	Lance Johnson	.05
588	Rick Rhoden	.05
589	Mike Aldrete	.05
590	Ozzie Smith	.30
591	Todd Stottlemyre	.05
592	R.J. Reynolds	.05
593	Scott Bradley	.05
594	*Luis Sojo*	.05
595	Greg Swindell	.05
596	Jose DeJesus	.05
597	Chris Bosio	.05
598	Brady Anderson	.20
599	Frank Williams	.05
600	Darryl Strawberry	.10
601	Luis Rivera	.05
602	Scott Garrelts	.05
603	Tony Armas	.05
604	Ron Robinson	.05
605	Mike Scioscia	.05
606	Storm Davis	.05
607	Steve Jeltz	.05
608	*Eric Anthony*	.25
609	Sparky Anderson	.10
610	Pedro Guerrero	.05
611	Walt Terrell	.05
612	Dave Gallagher	.05
613	Jeff Pico	.05
614	Nelson Santovenia	.05
615	Rob Deer	.05
616	Brian Holman	.05
617	Geronimo Berroa	.05
618	Eddie Whitson	.05
619	Rob Ducey	.05
620	*Tony Castillo*	.05
621	Melido Perez	.05
622	Sid Bream	.05
623	Jim Corsi	.05
624	Darrin Jackson	.05
625	Roger McDowell	.05
626	Bob Melvin	.05
627	Jose Rijo	.05
628	Candy Maldonado	.05
629	Eric Hetzel	.05
630	Gary Gaetti	.05
631	*John Wetteland*	.25
632	Scott Lusader	.05
633	Dennis Cook	.05
634	Luis Polonia	.05
635	Brian Downing	.05
636	Jesse Orosco	.05
637	Craig Reynolds	.05
638	Jeff Montgomery	.05
639	Tony LaRussa	.05
640	Rick Sutcliffe	.05
641	*Doug Strange*	.05
642	Jack Armstrong	.05
643	Alfredo Griffin	.05
644	Paul Assenmacher	.05
645	Jose Oquendo	.05
646	Checklist 529-660	.05
647	Rex Hudler	.05
648	Jim Clancy	.05
649	*Dan Murphy*	.05
650	Mike Witt	.05
651	Rafael Santana	.05
652	Mike Boddicker	.05
653	John Moses	.05
654	*Paul Coleman* (#1 Draft Pick)	.05
655	Gregg Olson	.05
656	Mackey Sasser	.05
657	Terry Mulholland	.05
658	Donell Nixon	.05
659	Greg Cadaret	.05
660	Vince Coleman	.05
661	Dick Howser (Turn Back the Clock)	.05
662	Mike Schmidt (Turn Back the Clock)	.10
663	Fred Lynn (Turn Back the Clock)	.05
664	Johnny Bench (Turn Back the Clock)	.05
665	Sandy Koufax (Turn Back the Clock)	.15
666	Brian Fisher	.05
667	Curt Wilkerson	.05
668	*Joe Oliver*	.10
669	Tom Lasorda	.15
670	Dennis Eckersley	.05
671	Bob Boone	.05
672	Roy Smith	.05
673	Joey Meyer	.05
674	Spike Owen	.05
675	Jim Abbott	.10
676	Randy Kutcher	.05
677	Jay Tibbs	.05
678	Kirt Manwaring	.05
679	Gary Ward	.05
680	Howard Johnson	.05
681	Mike Schooler	.05
682	Dann Bilardello	.05
683	*Kenny Rogers*	.10
684	*Julio Machado*	.05
685	Tony Fernandez	.05
686	Carmelo Martinez	.05
687	Tim Birtsas	.05
688	Milt Thompson	.05
689	Rich Yett	.05
690	Mark McGwire	1.50
691	Chuck Cary	.05
692	*Sammy Sosa*	5.00
693	Calvin Schiraldi	.05
694	*Mike Stanton*	.05
695	Tom Henke	.05
696	B.J. Surhoff	.05
697	Mike Davis	.05
698	*Omar Vizquel*	.25
699	Jim Leyland	.05
700	Kirby Puckett	.25
701	*Bernie Williams*	1.50
702	Tony Phillips	.05
703	*Jeff Brantley*	.10
704	*Chip Hale*	.10
705	Claudell Washington	.05
706	Geno Petralli	.05
707	Luis Aquino	.05
708	Larry Sheets	.05
709	Juan Berneguer	.05
710	Von Hayes	.05
711	Rick Aguilera	.05
712	Todd Benzinger	.05
713	*Tim Drummond*	.10
714	*Marquis Grissom*	.25
715	Greg Maddux	.50
716	Steve Balboni	.05
717	Ron Kakovice	.05
718	Gary Sheffield	.20
719	*Wally Whitehurst*	.05
720	Andres Galarraga	.20
721	Lee Mazzilli	.05
722	Felix Fermin	.05
723	Jeff Robinson	.05
724	Juan Bell	.10
725	Terry Pendleton	.05
726	Gene Nelson	.05
727	Pat Tabler	.05
728	Jim Acker	.05
729	Bobby Valentine	.05
730	Tony Gwynn	.40
731	Don Carman	.05
732	Ernie Riles	.05
733	John Dopson	.05
734	Kevin Elster	.05
735	Charlie Hough	.05
736	Rick Dempsey	.05
737	Chris Sabo	.05
738	*Gene Harris*	.05
739	Dale Sveum	.05
740	Jesse Barfield	.05
741	Steve Wilson	.05
742	Ernie Whitt	.05
743	Tom Candiotti	.05
744	*Kelly Mann*	.05
745	Hubie Brooks	.05
746	Dave Smith	.05
747	Randy Bush	.05
748	Doyle Alexander	.05
749	Mark Parent	.05
750	Dale Murphy	.15

751	Steve Lyons	.05
752	Tom Gordon	.05
753	Chris Speier	.05
754	Bob Walk	.05
755	Rafael Palmeiro	.20
756	Ken Howell	.05
757	*Larry Walker*	.75
758	Mark Thurmond	.05
759	Tom Trebelhorn	.05
760	Wade Boggs	.25
761	Mike Jackson	.05
762	Doug Dascenzo	.05
763	Denny Martinez	.05
764	Tim Teufel	.05
765	Chili Davis	.05
766	Brian Meyer	.05
767	Tracy Jones	.05
768	Chuck Crim	.05
769	*Greg Hibbard*	.10
770	Cory Snyder	.05
771	Pete Smith	.05
772	Jeff Reed	.05
773	Dave Leiper	.05
774	*Ben McDonald*	.20
775	Andy Van Slyke	.05
776	Charlie Leibrandt	.05
777	Tim Laudner	.05
778	Mike Jeffcoat	.05
779	Lloyd Moseby	.05
780	Orel Hershiser	.05
781	Mario Diaz	.05
782	Jose Alvarez	.05
783	Checklist 661-792	.05
784	Scott Bailes	.05
785	Jim Rice	.10
786	Eric King	.05
787	Rene Gonzales	.05
788	Frank DiPino	.05
789	John Wathan	.05
790	Gary Carter	.15
791	Alvaro Espinoza	.05
792	Gerald Perry	.05

1990 Topps Tiffany

This specially boxed version of Topps' 1990 baseball card set was sold through hobby channels only. The checklist is identical to the regular-issue Topps set and the cards are nearly so. The Tiffany version features white cardboard stock and a high-gloss finish on the fronts.

	MT
Complete Set (792):	95.00
Common Player:	.10

(Star cards valued at 3X-4X corresponding cards in regular Topps issue)

1990 Topps Traded

For the first time, Topps "Traded" series cards were made available nationwide in retail wax packs. The 132-card set was also sold in complete boxed form as it has been in recent years. The wax pack traded cards feature gray backs, while the boxed set cards feature white backs. The cards are numbered 1T-132T and showcase rookies, players who changed teams and new managers.

		MT
Complete Set (132):		4.00
Common Player:		.05
1	Darrel Akerfelds	.05
2	Sandy Alomar, Jr.	.20
3	Brad Arnsberg	.05
4	Steve Avery	.10
5	Wally Backman	.05
6	*Carlos Baerga*	.10
7	Kevin Bass	.05
8	Willie Blair	.05
9	Mike Blowers	.05
10	Shawn Boskie	.10
11	Daryl Boston	.05
12	Dennis Boyd	.05
13	Glenn Braggs	.05
14	Hubie Brooks	.05
15	Tom Brunansky	.05
16	John Burkett	.15
17	Casey Candaele	.05
18	John Candelaria	.05
19	Gary Carter	.15
20	Joe Carter	.15
21	Rick Cerone	.05
22	Scott Coolbaugh	.05
23	Bobby Cox	.05
24	Mark Davis	.05
25	Storm Davis	.05
26	Edgar Diaz	.05
27	Wayne Edwards	.05
28	Mark Eichhorn	.05
29	Scott Erickson	.25
30	Nick Esasky	.05
31	Cecil Fielder	.15
32	John Franco	.05
33	*Travis Fryman*	.30
34	Bill Gullickson	.05
35	Darryl Hamilton	.05
36	Mike Harkey	.05
37	Bud Harrelson	.05
38	Billy Hatcher	.05
39	Keith Hernandez	.05
40	Joe Hesketh	.05
41	Dave Hollins	.15
42	Sam Horn	.05
43	Steve Howard	.05
44	*Todd Hundley*	.50
45	Jeff Huson	.05
46	Chris James	.05
47	Stan Javier	.05
48	*Dave Justice*	1.00
49	Jeff Kaiser	.05
50	Dana Kiecker	.05
51	Joe Klink	.05
52	Brent Knackert	.05
53	Brad Komminsk	.05
54	Mark Langston	.05
55	Tim Layana	.10
56	Rick Leach	.05
57	Terry Leach	.05
58	Tim Leary	.05
59	Craig Lefferts	.05
60	Charlie Leibrandt	.05
61	Jim Leyritz	.25
62	Fred Lynn	.05
63	Kevin Maas	.05
64	Shane Mack	.05
65	Candy Maldonado	.05
66	Fred Manrique	.05
67	Mike Marshall	.05
68	Carmelo Martinez	.05
69	John Marzano	.05
70	Ben McDonald	.05
71	Jack McDowell	.05
72	John McNamara	.05
73	Orlando Mercado	.05
74	Stump Merrill	.05
75	Alan Mills	.05
76	Hal Morris	.10
77	Lloyd Moseby	.05
78	Randy Myers	.10
79	Tim Naehring	.10
80	Junior Noboa	.05
81	Matt Nokes	.05
82	Pete O'Brien	.05
83	*John Olerud*	.75
84	Greg Olson	.05
85	Junior Ortiz	.05
86	Dave Parker	.10
87	Rick Parker	.10
88	Bob Patterson	.05
89	Alejandro Pena	.05
90	Tony Pena	.05
91	Pascual Perez	.05
92	Gerald Perry	.05
93	Dan Petry	.05
94	Gary Pettis	.05
95	Tony Phillips	.05
96	Lou Pinella	.05
97	Luis Polonia	.05
98	Jim Presley	.05
99	Scott Radinsky	.15
100	Willie Randolph	.05
101	Jeff Reardon	.05
102	Greg Riddoch	.05
103	Jeff Robinson	.05
104	Ron Robinson	.05
105	Kevin Romine	.05
106	Scott Ruskin	.05
107	John Russell	.05
108	Bill Sampen	.05
109	Juan Samuel	.05
110	Scott Sanderson	.05
111	Jack Savage	.05
112	Dave Schmidt	.05
113	Red Schoendienst	.10
114	Terry Shumpert	.05
115	Matt Sinatro	.05
116	Don Slaught	.05
117	Bryn Smith	.05
118	Lee Smith	.05
119	Paul Sorrento	.10
120	Franklin Stubbs	.05
121	Russ Swan	.05
122	Bob Tewksbury	.10
123	Wayne Tolleson	.05
124	John Tudor	.05
125	Randy Veres	.10
126	Hector Villanueva	.05
127	Mitch Webster	.05
128	Ernie Whitt	.05
129	Frank Wills	.05
130	Dave Winfield	.25
131	Matt Young	.05
132	Checklist	.05

1990 Topps Traded Tiffany

Identical to the regular Topps Traded issue except for the glossy front surface, this special hobby-only boxed set shares the same checklist.

	MT
Complete Set (132):	25.00
Common Player:	.15

(Star cards valued at 4X-6X corresponding cards in regular Topps Traded issue)

1990 Topps All-Star Glossy Set of 22

One glossy All-Star card was included in each 1990 Topps rack pack. The cards measure 2-1/2" x 3-1/2" and feature a similar style to past glossy All-Star cards. Special cards of All-Star team captains Carl Yastrzemski and Don Drysdale are included in the set.

		MT
Complete Set (22):		4.00
Common Player:		.10
1	Tom Lasorda	.15
2	Will Clark	.25
3	Ryne Sandberg	.40
4	Howard Johnson	.10
5	Ozzie Smith	.40
6	Kevin Mitchell	.10
7	Eric Davis	.10
8	Tony Gwynn	.50
9	Benny Santiago	.10
10	Rick Rueschel	.10
11	Don Drysdale	.20
12	Tony LaRussa	.10
13	Mark McGwire	1.50
14	Julio Franco	.10
15	Wade Boggs	.30
16	Cal Ripken, Jr.	.90
17	Bo Jackson	.25
18	Kirby Puckett	.50
19	Ruben Sierra	.10
20	Terry Steinbach	.10
21	Dave Stewart	.10
22	Carl Yastrzemski	.20

1990 Topps Big Baseball

For the third consecutive year, Topps issued a 330-card set of oversized cards (2-5/8" x 3-3/4") in three 110-card series. The cards are reminiscent of Topps cards from the mid-1950s in that they feature players in portrait and action shots. The 1990 set has action photos in freeze frames. As in previous years, the cards are printed on white card stock with a glossy finish on the front. The card backs include 1989 and career hitting, fielding and pitching stats and a player cartoon.

		MT
Complete Set (330):		18.00
Common Player:		.05
1	Dwight Evans	.05
2	Kirby Puckett	.65
3	Kevin Gross	.05
4	Ron Hassey	.05
5	Lloyd McClendon	.05
6	Bo Jackson	.25
7	Lonnie Smith	.05
8	Alvaro Espinoza	.05
9	Roberto Alomar	.25
10	Glenn Braggs	.05
11	David Cone	.10

12 Claudell Washington .05
13 Pedro Guerrero .05
14 Todd Benzinger .05
15 Jeff Russell .05
16 Terry Kennedy .05
17 Kelly Gruber .05
18 Alfredo Griffin .05
19 Mark Grace .25
20 Dave Winfield .20
21 Bret Saberhagen .10
22 Roger Clemens .45
23 Bob Walk .05
24 Dave Magadan .05
25 Spike Owen .05
26 Jody Davis .05
27 Kent Hrbek .05
28 Mark McGwire 2.00
29 Eddie Murray .25
30 Paul O'Neill .10
31 Jose DeLeon .05
32 Steve Lyons .05
33 Dan Plesac .05
34 Jack Howell .05
35 Greg Briley .05
36 Andy Hawkins .05
37 Cecil Espy .05
38 Rick Sutcliffe .05
39 Jack Clark .05
40 Dale Murphy .15
41 Mike Henneman .05
42 Rick Honeycutt .05
43 Willie Randolph .05
44 Marty Barrett .05
45 Willie Wilson .05
46 Wallace Johnson .05
47 Greg Brock .05
48 Tom Browning .05
49 Gerald Young .05
50 Dennis Eckersley .05
51 Scott Garrelts .05
52 Gary Redus .05
53 Al Newman .05
54 Darryl Boston .05
55 Ron Oester .05
56 Danny Tartabull .05
57 Gregg Jefferies .10
58 Tom Foley .05
59 Robin Yount .40
60 Pat Borders .05
61 Mike Greenwell .05
62 Shawon Dunston .05
63 Steve Buechele .05
64 Dave Stewart .05
65 Jose Oquendo .05
66 Ron Gant .15
67 Mike Scioscia .05
68 Randy Velarde .05
69 Charlie Hayes .05
70 Tim Wallach .05
71 Eric Show .05
72 Eric Davis .05
73 Mike Gallego .05
74 Rob Deer .05
75 Ryne Sandberg .50
76 Kevin Seitzer .05
77 Wade Boggs .45
78 Greg Gagne .05
79 John Smiley .05
80 Ivan Calderon .05
81 Pete Incaviglia .05
82 Orel Hershiser .05
83 Carney Lansford .05
84 Mike Fitzgerald .05
85 Don Mattingly .75
86 Chet Lemon .05
87 Rolando Roomes .05
88 Bill Spiers .05
89 Pat Tabler .05
90 Danny Heep .05
91 Andre Dawson .15
92 Randy Bush .05
93 Tony Gwynn .40
94 Tom Brunansky .05
95 Johnny Ray .05
96 Matt Williams .30
97 Barry Lyons .05
98 Jeff Hamilton .05
99 Tom Glavine .10
100 Ken Griffey, Sr. .05
101 Tom Henke .05
102 Dave Righetti .05
103 Paul Molitor .35
104 Mike LaValliere .05
105 Frank White .05
106 Bob Welch .05
107 Ellis Burks .05
108 Andres Galarraga .15
109 Mitch Williams .05
110 Checklist .05
111 Craig Biggio .10
112 Dave Steib .05
113 Ron Darling .05
114 Bert Blyleven .05
115 Dickie Thon .05
116 Carlos Martinez .05
117 Jeff King .05
118 Terry Steinbach .05
119 Frank Tanana .05
120 Mark Lemke .05
121 Chris Sabo .05
122 Glenn Davis .05
123 Mel Hall .05
124 Jim Gantner .05
125 Benito Santiago .05
126 Milt Thompson .05
127 Rafael Palmeiro .20
128 Barry Bonds .75
129 Mike Bielecki .05
130 Lou Whitaker .05
131 Bob Ojeda .05
132 Dion James .05
133 Denny Martinez .05
134 Fred McGriff .25
135 Terry Pendleton .05
136 Pat Combs .05
137 Kevin Mitchell .05
138 Marquis Grissom .15
139 Chris Bosio .05
140 Omar Vizquel .05
141 Steve Sax .05
142 Nelson Liriano .05
143 Kevin Elster .05
144 Dan Pasqua .05
145 Dave Smith .05
146 Craig Worthington .05
147 Dan Gladden .05
148 Oddibe McDowell .05
149 Bip Roberts .05
150 Randy Ready .05
151 Dwight Smith .05
152 Ed Whitson .05
153 George Bell .05
154 Tim Raines .10
155 Sid Fernandez .05
156 Henry Cotto .05
157 Harold Baines .05
158 Willie McGee .05
159 Bill Doran .05
160 Steve Balboni .05
161 Pete Smith .05
162 Frank Viola .05
163 Gary Sheffield .25
164 Bill Landrum .05
165 Tony Fernandez .05
166 Mike Heath .05
167 Jody Reed .05
168 Wally Joyner .10
169 Robby Thompson .05
170 Ken Caminiti .10
171 Nolan Ryan 1.75
172 Ricky Jordan .05
173 Lance Blankenship .05
174 Dwight Gooden .10
175 Ruben Sierra .05
176 Carlton Fisk .25
177 Garry Templeton .05
178 Mike Devereaux .05
179 Mookie Wilson .05
180 Jeff Blauser .05
181 Scott Bradley .05
182 Luis Salazar .05
183 Rafael Ramirez .05
184 Vince Coleman .05
185 Doug Drabek .05
186 Darryl Strawberry .10
187 Tim Burke .05
188 Jesse Barfield .05
189 Barry Larkin .20
190 Alan Trammell .05
191 Steve Lake .05
192 Derek Lilliquist .05
193 Don Robinson .05
194 Kevin McReynolds .05
195 Melido Perez .05
196 Jose Lind .05
197 Eric Anthony .05
198 B.J. Surhoff .05
199 John Olerud .25
200 Mike Moore .05
201 Mark Gubicza .05
202 Phil Bradley .05
203 Ozzie Smith .35
204 Greg Maddux .90
205 Julio Franco .05
206 Tom Herr .05
207 Scott Fletcher .05
208 Bobby Bonilla .10
209 Bob Geren .05
210 Junior Felix .05
211 Dick Schofield .05
212 Jim Deshaies .05
213 Jose Uribe .05
214 John Kruk .05
215 Ozzie Guillen .05
216 Howard Johnson .05
217 Andy Van Slyke .05
218 Tim Laudner .05
219 Manny Lee .05
220 Checklist .05
221 Cory Snyder .05
222 Billy Hatcher .05
223 Bud Black .05
224 Will Clark .30
225 Kevin Tapani .05
226 Mike Pagliarulo .05
227 Dave Parker .05
228 Ben McDonald .05
229 Carlos Baerga .05
230 Roger McDowell .05
231 Delino DeShields .05
232 Mark Langston .05
233 Wally Backman .05
234 Jim Eisenreich .05
235 Mike Schooler .05
236 Kevin Bass .05
237 John Farrell .05
238 Kal Daniels .05
239 Tony Phillips .05
240 Todd Stottlemyre .05
241 Greg Olson .05
242 Charlie Hough .05
243 Mariano Duncan .05
244 Billy Ripken .05
245 Joe Carter .05
246 Tim Belcher .05
247 Roberto Kelly .05
248 Candy Maldonado .05
249 Mike Scott .05
250 Ken Griffey, Jr. 2.00
251 Nick Esasky .05
252 Tom Gordon .05
253 John Tudor .05
254 Gary Gaetti .05
255 Neal Heaton .05
256 Jerry Browne .05
257 Jose Rijo .05
258 Mike Boddicker .05
259 Brett Butler .05
260 Andy Benes .10
261 Kevin Brown .15
262 Hubie Brooks .05
263 Randy Milligan .05
264 John Franco .05
265 Sandy Alomar .10
266 Dave Valle .05
267 Jerome Walton .05
268 Bob Boone .05
269 Ken Howell .05
270 Jose Canseco .35
271 Joe Magrane .05
272 Brian DuBois .05
273 Carlos Quintana .05
274 Lance Johnson .05
275 Steve Bedrosian .05
276 Brook Jacoby .05
277 Fred Lynn .05
278 Jeff Ballard .05
279 Otis Nixon .05
280 Chili Davis .05
281 Joe Oliver .05
282 Brian Holman .05
283 Juan Samuel .05
284 Rick Aguilera .05
285 Jeff Reardon .05
286 Sammy Sosa 1.50
287 Carmelo Martinez .05
288 Greg Swindell .05
289 Erik Hanson .05
290 Tony Pena .05
291 Pascual Perez .05
292 Rickey Henderson .20
293 Kurt Stillwell .05
294 Todd Zeile .15
295 Bobby Thigpen .05
296 Larry Walker .25
297 Rob Murphy .05
298 Mitch Webster .05
299 Devon White .05
300 Len Dykstra .05
301 Keith Hernandez .05
302 Gene Larkin .05
303 Jeffrey Leonard .05
304 Jim Presley .05
305 Lloyd Moseby .05
306 John Smoltz .10
307 Sam Horn .05
308 Greg Litton .05
309 Dave Henderson .05
310 Mark McLemore .05
311 Gary Pettis .05
312 Mark Davis .05
313 Cecil Fielder .10
314 Jack Armstrong .05
315 Alvin Davis .05
316 Doug Jones .05
317 Eric Yelding .10
318 Joe Orsulak .05
319 Chuck Finley .05
320 Glenn Wilson .05
321 Harold Reynolds .05
322 Teddy Higuera .05
323 Lance Parrish .05
324 Bruce Hurst .05
325 Dave West .05
326 Kirk Gibson .05
327 Cal Ripken, Jr. 1.75
328 Rick Reuschel .05
329 Jim Abbott .10
330 Checklist .05

1990 Topps Double Headers

For a second (and final) year, Topps produced an issue of mini cards encased in plastic stands and marketed as Double Headers. Each piece features a 1-5/8" x 2-1/4" reproduction of the player's Topps rookie card, backed by a reproduction of his card from the regular 1990 Topps set. The size of the DH set was increased from 24 in 1989 to 72 for 1990. The novelties were sold for 50 cents apiece. The unnumbered cards are checklisted here alphabetically.

	MT
Complete Set (72):	40.00
Common Player:	.25
(1) Jim Abbott	.25
(2) Jeff Ballard	.25
(3) George Bell	.25
(4) Wade Boggs	1.00
(5) Barry Bonds	2.00
(6) Bobby Bonilla	.25
(7) Ellis Burks	.25
(8) Jose Canseco	1.50
(9) Joe Carter	.25
(10) Will Clark	.75
(11) Roger Clemens	1.50
(12) Vince Coleman	.25
(13) Alvin Davis	.25
(14) Eric Davis	.25
(15) Glenn Davis	.25
(16) Mark Davis	.25
(17) Andre Dawson	.35
(18) Shawon Dunston	.25
(19) Dennis Eckersley	.25
(20) Sid Fernandez	.25
(21) Tony Fernandez	.25
(22) Chuck Finley	.25
(23) Carlton Fisk	.60
(24) Julio Franco	.25
(25) Gary Gaetti	.25
(26) Dwight Gooden	.30
(27) Mark Grace	.45
(28) Mike Greenwell	.25
(29) Ken Griffey, Jr.	4.00
(30) Pedro Guerrero	.25
(31) Tony Gwynn	1.50
(32) Von Hayes	.25

(33)	Rickey Henderson	.50
(34)	Orel Hershiser	.25
(35)	Bo Jackson	.35
(36)	Gregg Jefferies	.25
(37)	Howard Johnson	.25
(38)	Ricky Jordan	.25
(39)	Carney Lansford	.25
(40)	Barry Larkin	.30
(41)	Greg Maddux	2.00
(42)	Joe Magrane	.25
(43)	Don Mattingly	2.00
(44)	Fred McGriff	.60
(45)	Mark McGwire	4.00
(46)	Kevin McReynolds	.25
(47)	Kevin Mitchell	.25
(48)	Gregg Olson	.25
(49)	Kirby Puckett	1.50
(50)	Tim Raines	.30
(51)	Harold Reynolds	.25
(52)	Cal Ripken, Jr.	3.00
(53)	Nolan Ryan	3.00
(54)	Bret Saberhagen	.30
(55)	Ryne Sandberg	1.50
(56)	Benito Santiago	.25
(57)	Steve Sax	.25
(58)	Mike Scioscia	.25
(59)	Mike Scott	.25
(60)	Ruben Sierra	.25
(61)	Lonnie Smith	.25
(62)	Ozzie Smith	1.00
(63)	Dave Stewart	.25
(64)	Darryl Strawberry	.30
(65)	Greg Swindell	.25
(66)	Alan Trammell	.25
(67)	Frank Viola	.25
(68)	Tim Wallach	.25
(69)	Jerome Walton	.25
(70)	Lou Whitaker	.25
(71)	Mitch Williams	.25
(72)	Robin Yount	1.50

1990 Topps Glossy Rookies

While the size of the annual glossy rookies set increased to 33 cards from previous years' issues of 22, the format remained identical in 1990. Above the player photo is a colored banner with "1989 Rookies." The player's name appears in red in a yellow bar beneath the photo. Backs are printed in red and blue and contain a shield design with the notation, "1989 Rookies Commemorative Set". The player's name, position and team are listed below, along with a card number. Cards are numbered alphabetically in the set. The glossy rookies were found one per pack in jumbo (100-card) cello packs.

		MT
Complete Set (33):		25.00
Common Player:		.50
1	Jim Abbott	.50
2	Joey Belle	6.00
3	Andy Benes	.75
4	Greg Briley	.50
5	Kevin Brown	4.50
6	Mark Carreon	.50
7	Mike Devereaux	.50
8	Junior Felix	.50
9	Bob Geren	.50
10	Tom Gordon	.75
11	Ken Griffey, Jr.	15.00
12	Pete Harnisch	.50
13	Greg W. Harris	.50
14	Greg Hibbard	.50
15	Ken Hill	.50
16	Gregg Jefferies	.60
17	Jeff King	.50
18	Derek Lilliquist	.50
19	Carlos Martinez	.50
20	Ramon Martinez	.75
21	Bob Milacki	.50
22	Gregg Olson	.50
23	Donn Pall	.50
24	Kenny Rogers	.50
25	Gary Sheffield	1.50
26	Dwight Smith	.50
27	Billy Spiers	.50
28	Omar Vizquel	.60
29	Jerome Walton	.50
30	Dave West	.50
31	John Wetteland	.60
32	Steve Wilson	.50
33	Craig Worthington	.50

1990 Topps Mini League Leaders

The last in a five-year string of mini cards, the 1990 league leaders' set offers players who were in the top five in major batting and pitching stats during the 1989 season. Fronts of the 2-1/8" x 3" cards mimic the regular Topps' design for 1990; featuring an action photo with multi-colored borders. Backs offer a round player portrait photo and information about the statistical achievement, all printed in full color. Cards are numbered alphabetically within teams. The 1990 minis are considerably scarcer than the previous years' offerings.

		MT
Complete Set (88):		15.00
Common Player:		.10
1	Jeff Ballard	.10
2	Phil Bradley	.10
3	Wade Boggs	.50
4	Roger Clemens	.75
5	Nick Esasky	.10
6	Jody Reed	.10
7	Bert Blyleven	.10
8	Chuck Finley	.10
9	Kirk McCaskill	.10
10	Devon White	.10
11	Ivan Calderon	.10
12	Bobby Thigpen	.10
13	Joe Carter	.10
14	Gary Pettis	.10
15	Tom Gordon	.10
16	Bo Jackson	.25
17	Bret Saberhagen	.15
18	Kevin Seitzer	.10
19	Chris Bosio	.10
20	Paul Molitor	.50
21	Dan Plesac	.10
22	Robin Yount	.50
23	Kirby Puckett	1.00
24	Don Mattingly	1.00
25	Steve Sax	.10
26	Storm Davis	.10
27	Dennis Eckersley	.10
28	Rickey Henderson	.25
29	Carney Lansford	.10
30	Mark McGwire	3.00
31	Mike Moore	.10
32	Dave Stewart	.10
33	Alvin Davis	.10
34	Harold Reynolds	.10
35	Mike Schooler	.10
36	Cecil Espy	.10
37	Julio Franco	.10
38	Jeff Russell	.10
39	Nolan Ryan	2.00
40	Ruben Sierra	.10
41	George Bell	.10
42	Tony Fernandez	.10
43	Fred McGriff	.25
44	Dave Steib	.10
45	Checklist	.05
46	Lonnie Smith	.10
47	John Smoltz	.15
48	Mike Bielecki	.10
49	Mark Grace	.25
50	Greg Maddux	1.50
51	Ryne Sandberg	.75
52	Mitch Williams	.10
53	Eric Davis	.10
54	John Franco	.10
55	Glenn Davis	.10
56	Mike Scott	.10
57	Tim Belcher	.10
58	Orel Hershiser	.10
59	Jay Howell	.10
60	Eddie Murray	.30
61	Tim Burke	.10
62	Mark Langston	.10
63	Tim Raines	.15
64	Tim Wallach	.10
65	David Cone	.15
66	Sid Fernandez	.10
67	Howard Johnson	.10
68	Juan Samuel	.10
69	Von Hayes	.10
70	Barry Bonds	1.00
71	Bobby Bonilla	.10
72	Andy Van Slyke	.10
73	Vince Coleman	.10
74	Jose DeLeon	.10
75	Pedro Guerrero	.10
76	Joe Magrane	.10
77	Roberto Alomar	.25
78	Jack Clark	.10
79	Mark Davis	.10
80	Tony Gwynn	.65
81	Bruce Hurst	.10
82	Eddie Whitson	.10
83	Brett Butler	.10
84	Will Clark	.25
85	Scott Garrelts	.10
86	Kevin Mitchell	.10
87	Rick Reuschel	.10
88	Robby Thompson	.10

1991 Topps 1990 Major League Debut

This 171-card set features the players who made their Major League debut in 1990. The cards are styled like the 1991 Topps cards and are numbered in alphabetical order. The card backs are printed horizontally and feature information about the player's debut and statistics. The issue was sold only as a boxed set through hobby channels.

		MT
Complete Set (171):		25.00
Common Player:		.10
1	Paul Abbott	.10
2	Steve Adkins	.10
3	Scott Aldred	.10
4	Gerald Alexander	.10
5	Moises Alou	1.00
6	Steve Avery	.25
7	Oscar Azocar	.10
8	Carlos Baerga	.15
9	Kevin Baez	.10
10	Jeff Baldwin	.10
11	Brian Barnes	.15
12	Kevin Bearse	.10
13	Kevin Belcher	.20
14	Mike Bell	.10
15	Sean Berry	.20
16	Joe Bitker	.10
17	Willie Blair	.10
18	Brian Bohanon	.10
19	Mike Bordick	.25
20	Shawn Boskie	.25
21	Rod Brewer	.10
22	Kevin Brown	.25
23	Dave Burba	.10
24	Jim Campbell	.10
25	Ozzie Canseco	.20
26	Chuck Carr	.10
27	Larry Casian	.10
28	Andujar Cedeno	.25
29	Wes Chamberlain	.20
30	Scott Chiamparino	.10
31	Steve Chitren	.10
32	Pete Coachman	.10
33	Alex Cole	.10
34	Jeff Conine	.25
35	Scott Cooper	.25
36	Milt Cuyler	.10
37	Steve Decker	.10
38	Rich DeLucia	.10
39	Delino DeShields	.25
40	Mark Dewey	.10
41	Carlos Diaz	.10
42	Lance Dickson	.20
43	Narciso Elvira	.10
44	Luis Encarnacion	.10
45	Scott Erickson	.50
46	Paul Faries	.10
47	Howard Farmer	.10
48	Alex Fernandez	.25
49	Travis Fryman	.75
50	Rich Garces	.10
51	Carlos Garcia	.10
52	Mike Gardiner	.10
53	Bernard Gilkey	.25
54	Tom Gilles	.10
55	Jerry Goff	.10
56	Leo Gomez	.25
57	Luis Gonzalez	.75
58	Joe Grahe	.20
59	Craig Grebeck	.10
60	Kip Gross	.10
61	Eric Gunderson	.10
62	Chris Hammond	.20
63	Dave Hansen	.20
64	Reggie Harris	.10
65	Bill Haselman	.10
66	Randy Hennis	.10
67	Carlos Hernandez	.20
68	Howard Hilton	.10
69	Dave Hollins	.25
70	Darren Holmes	.20
71	John Hoover	.10
72	Steve Howard	.10
73	Thomas Howard	.10
74	Todd Hundley	.40
75	Daryl Irvine	.10
76	Chris Jelic	.10
77	Dana Kiecker	.10
78	Brent Knackert	.10

79 Jimmy Kremers .10
80 Jerry Kutzler .10
81 Ray Lankford 1.00
82 Tim Layana .10
83 Terry Lee .10
84 Mark Leiter .10
85 Scott Leius .25
86 Mark Leonard .10
87 Darren Lewis .25
88 Scott Lewis .10
89 Jim Leyritz .20
90 Dave Liddell .10
91 Luis Lopez .10
92 Kevin Maas .10
93 Bob MacDonald .10
94 Carlos Maldonado .10
95 Chuck Malone .10
96 Ramon Manon .10
97 Jeff Manto .10
98 Paul Marak .10
99 Tino Martinez 1.00
100 Derrick May .10
101 Brent Mayne .20
102 Paul McClellan .10
103 Rodney McCray .10
104 Tim McIntosh .10
105 Brian McRae .25
106 Jose Melendez .10
107 Orlando Merced .25
108 Alan Mills .10
109 Gino Minutelli .10
110 Mickey Morandini .15
111 Pedro Munoz .15
112 Chris Nabholz .10
113 Tim Naehring .20
114 Charles Nagy .25
115 Jim Neidlinger .10
116 Rafael Novoa .10
117 Jose Offerman .25
118 Omar Olivares .25
119 Javier Ortiz .10
120 Al Osuna .10
121 Rick Parker .10
122 Dave Pavlas .10
123 Geronimo Pena .10
124 Mike Perez .10
125 Phil Plantier .15
126 Jim Poole .10
127 Tom Quinlan .10
128 Scott Radinsky .10
129 Darren Reed .20
130 Karl Rhodes .10
131 Jeff Richardson .10
132 Rich Rodriguez .15
133 Dave Rohde .10
134 Mel Rojas .25
135 Vic Rosario .10
136 Rich Rowland .10
137 Scott Ruskin .10
138 Bill Sampen .10
139 Andres Santana .10
140 David Segui .25
141 Jeff Shaw .10
142 Tim Sherrill .10
143 Terry Shumpert .10
144 Mike Simms .10
145 Daryl Smith .10
146 Luis Sojo .10
147 Steve Springer .10
148 Ray Stephens .10
149 Lee Stevens .10
150 Mel Stottlemyre, Jr. .10
151 Glenn Sutko .10
152 Anthony Telford .15
153 Frank Thomas 6.00
154 Randy Tomlin .25
155 Brian Traxler .10
156 Efrain Valdez .10
157 Rafael Valdez .10
158 Julio Valera .10
159 Jim Vatcher .10
160 Hector Villanueva .10
161 Hector Wagner .10
162 Dave Walsh .10
163 Steve Wapnick .10
164 Colby Ward .10
165 Turner Ward .10
166 Terry Wells .10
167 Mark Whiten .10
168 Mike York .10
169 Cliff Young .10
170 Checklist .10
171 Checklist .10

1991 Topps

Topps celebrated its 40th anniversary in 1991 with the biggest promotional campaign in baseball card history. More than 300,000 vintage Topps cards (or certificates redeemable for valuable older cards) produced from 1952 to 1990 were randomly inserted in packs. Also a grand prize winner received a complete set from each year, and others received a single set from 1952-1990. The 1991 Topps card fronts feature the "Topps 40 Years of Baseball" logo in the upper-left corner. Colored borders frame the player photos. All players of the same team have cards with the same frame/border colors. Both action and posed shots appear in full-color on the card fronts. The flip sides are printed horizontally and feature complete statistics. Record Breakers and other special cards were once again included in the set. The cards measure 2-1/2" x 3-1/2".

	MT
Complete Set (792):	15.00
Common Player:	.05
Pack (15):	.35
Wax Box (36):	9.00

1 Nolan Ryan .75
2 George Brett (Record Breaker) .15
3 Carlton Fisk (Record Breaker) .10
4 Kevin Maas (Record Breaker) .05
5 Cal Ripken, Jr. (Record Breaker) .25
6 Nolan Ryan (Record Breaker) .25
7 Ryne Sandberg (Record Breaker) .15
8 Bobby Thigpen (Record Breaker) .05
9 Darrin Fletcher .10
10 Gregg Olson .05
11 Roberto Kelly .05
12 Paul Assenmacher .05
13 Mariano Duncan .05
14 Dennis Lamp .05
15 Von Hayes .05
16 Mike Heath .05
17 Jeff Brantley .05
18 Nelson Liriano .05
19 Jeff Robinson .05
20 Pedro Guerrero .05
21 Joe M. Morgan .05
22 Storm Davis .05
23 Jim Gantner .05
24 Dave Martinez .05
25 Tim Belcher .05
26 Luis Sojo .05
27 Bobby Witt .05
28 Alvaro Espinoza .05
29 Bob Walk .05
30 Gregg Jefferies .15
31 *Colby Ward* .05
32 *Mike Simms* .05
33 Barry Jones .05
34 Atlee Hammaker .05
35 Greg Maddux .50
36 Donnie Hill .05
37 Tom Bolton .05
38 Scott Bradley .05
39 *Jim Neidlinger* .05
40 Kevin Mitchell .05
41 Ken Dayley .05
42a *Chris Hoiles* (white inner photo frame) .20
42b *Chris Hoiles* (gray inner photo frame) .20
43 Roger McDowell .05
44 Mike Felder .05
45 Chris Sabo .05
46 Tim Drummond .05
47 Brook Jacoby .05
48 Dennis Boyd .05
49a Pat Borders (40 stolen bases in Kinston 1986) .20
49b Pat Borders (0 stolen bases in Kinston 1986) .10
50 Bob Welch .05
51 Art Howe .05
52 *Francisco Oliveras* .05
53 Mike Sharperson .05
54 Gary Mielke .05
55 Jeffrey Leonard .05
56 Jeff Parrett .05
57 Jack Howell .05
58 Mel Stottlemyre .05
59 Eric Yelding .05
60 Frank Viola .05
61 Stan Javier .05
62 Lee Guetterman .05
63 Milt Thompson .05
64 Tom Herr .05
65 Bruce Hurst .05
66 Terry Kennedy .05
67 Rick Honeycutt .05
68 Gary Sheffield .20
69 Steve Wilson .05
70 Ellis Burks .10
71 Jim Acker .05
72 Junior Ortiz .05
73 Craig Worthington .05
74 *Shane Andrews* (#1 Draft Pick) .20
75 Jack Morris .05
76 Jerry Browne .05
77 Drew Hall .05
78 Geno Petralli .05
79 Frank Thomas .50
80a Fernando Valenzuela (no diamond after 104 ER in 1990) .25
80b Fernando Valenzuela (diamond after 104 ER in 1990) .10
81 Cito Gaston .05
82 Tom Glavine .20
83 Daryl Boston .05
84 Bob McClure .05
85 Jesse Barfield .05
86 Les Lancaster .05
87 Tracy Jones .05
88 Bob Tewksbury .05
89 Darren Daulton .05
90 Danny Tartabull .05
91 *Greg Colbrunn* (Future Star) .10
92 Danny Jackson .05
93 Ivan Calderon .05
94 John Dopson .05
95 Paul Molitor .20
96 Trevor Wilson .05
97a Brady Anderson (3H, 2RBI in Sept. scoreboard) .25
97b Brady Anderson (14H, 3 RBI in Sept. scoreboard) .15
98 Sergio Valdez .05
99 Chris Gwynn .05
100a Don Mattingly (10 hits 1990) .50
100b Don Mattingly (101 hits in 1990) .45
101 Rob Ducey .05
102 Gene Larkin .05
103 *Tim Costo* (#1 Draft Pick) .10
104 Don Robinson .05
105 Kevin McReynolds .05
106 Ed Nunez .05
107 Luis Polonia .05
108 Matt Young .05
109 Greg Riddoch .05
110 Tom Henke .05
111 Andres Thomas .05
112 Frank DiPino .05
113 *Carl Everett* (#1 Draft Pick) 1.00
114 *Lance Dickson* (Future Star) .10
115 Hubie Brooks .05
116 Mark Davis .05
117 Dion James .05
118 *Tom Edens* .05
119 Carl Nichols .05
120 Joe Carter .10
121 Eric King .05
122 Paul O'Neill .15
123 Greg Harris .05
124 Randy Bush .05
125 Steve Bedrosian .05
126 *Bernard Gilkey* .20
127 Joe Price .05
128 Travis Fryman .10
129 Mark Eichhorn .05
130 Ozzie Smith .25
131a Checklist 1 (Phil Bradley #727) .05
131b Checklist 1 (Phil Bradley #717) .05
132 Jamie Quirk .05
133 Greg Briley .05
134 Kevin Elster .05
135 Jerome Walton .05
136 Dave Schmidt .05
137 Randy Ready .05
138 Jamie Moyer .05
139 Jeff Treadway .05
140 Fred McGriff .15
141 Nick Leyva .05
142 Curtis Wilkerson .05
143 John Smiley .05
144 Dave Henderson .05
145 Lou Whitaker .05
146 Dan Plesac .05
147 Carlos Baerga .05
148 Rey Palacios .05
149 *Al Osuna* .05
150 Cal Ripken, Jr. .75
151 Tom Browning .05
152 Mickey Hatcher .05
153 Bryan Harvey .05
154 Jay Buhner .10
155a Dwight Evans (diamond after 162 G 1982) .10
155b Dwight Evans (no diamond after 162 G 1982) .05
156 Carlos Martinez .05
157 John Smoltz .10
158 Jose Uribe .05
159 Joe Boever .05
160 Vince Coleman .05
161 Tim Leary .05
162 *Ozzie Canseco* .10
163 Dave Johnson .05
164 Edgar Diaz .05
165 Sandy Alomar .10
166 Harold Baines .05
167a *Randy Tomlin* ("Harriburg" 1989-90) .10
167b *Randy Tomlin* ("Harrisburg" 1989-90) .05
168 John Olerud .25
169 Luis Aquino .05
170 Carlton Fisk .20
171 Tony LaRussa .05
172 Pete Incaviglia .05
173 Jason Grimsley .05
174 Ken Caminiti .10
175 Jack Armstrong .05
176 John Orton .05
177 *Reggie Harris* .10
178 Dave Valle .05
179 Pete Harnisch .05
180 Tony Gwynn .40
181 Duane Ward .05
182 Junior Noboa .05
183 Clay Parker .05
184 Gary Green .05
185 Joe Magrane .05
186 Rod Booker .05
187 Greg Cadaret .05
188 Damon Berryhill .05
189 *Daryl Irvine* .05
190 Matt Williams .15
191 *Willie Blair* .05
192 Rob Deer .05
193 Felix Fermin .05
194 Xavier Hernandez .10

No.	Player	Price
195	Wally Joyner	.10
196	*Jim Vatcher*	.05
197	*Chris Nabholz*	.10
198	R.J. Reynolds	.05
199	Mike Hartley	.05
200	Darryl Strawberry	.10
201	Tom Kelly	.05
202	*Jim Leyritz*	.20
203	Gene Harris	.05
204	Herm Winningham	.05
205	*Mike Perez*	.10
206	Carlos Quintana	.05
207	Gary Wayne	.05
208	Willie Wilson	.05
209	Ken Howell	.05
210	Lance Parrish	.05
211	*Brian Barnes* (Future Star)	.10
212	Steve Finley	.05
213	Frank Wills	.05
214	Joe Girardi	.05
215	Dave Smith	.05
216	Greg Gagne	.05
217	Chris Bosio	.05
218	*Rick Parker*	.05
219	Jack McDowell	.05
220	Tim Wallach	.05
221	Don Slaught	.05
222	*Brian McRae*	.20
223	Allan Anderson	.05
224	Juan Gonzalez	.50
225	Randy Johnson	.30
226	Alfredo Griffin	.05
227	Steve Avery	.05
228	Rex Hudler	.05
229	Rance Mulliniks	.05
230	Sid Fernandez	.05
231	Doug Rader	.05
232	Jose DeJesus	.05
233	Al Leiter	.05
234	*Scott Erickson*	.20
235	Dave Parker	.10
236a	Frank Tanana (no diamond after 269 SO 1975)	.10
236b	Frank Tanana (diamond after 269 SO 1975)	.05
237	Rick Cerone	.05
238	Mike Dunne	.05
239	*Darren Lewis*	.20
240	Mike Scott	.05
241	Dave Clark	.05
242	Mike LaCoss	.05
243	Lance Johnson	.05
244	Mike Jeffcoat	.05
245	Kal Daniels	.05
246	Kevin Wickander	.05
247	Jody Reed	.05
248	Tom Gordon	.05
249	Bob Melvin	.05
250	Dennis Eckersley	.05
251	Mark Lemke	.05
252	*Mel Rojas*	.10
253	Garry Templeton	.05
254	*Shawn Boskie*	.10
255	Brian Downing	.05
256	Greg Hibbard	.05
257	Tom O'Malley	.05
258	Chris Hammond	.10
259	Hensley Meulens	.05
260	Harold Reynolds	.05
261	Bud Harrelson	.05
262	Tim Jones	.05
263	Checklist 2	.05
264	*Dave Hollins*	.20
265	Mark Gubicza	.05
266	Carmen Castillo	.05
267	Mark Knudson	.05
268	Tom Brookens	.05
269	Joe Hesketh	.05
270a	Mark McGwire (1987 SLG .618)	1.50
270b	Mark McGwire (1987 SLG 618)	1.50
271	*Omar Olivares*	.15
272	Jeff King	.05
273	Johnny Ray	.05
274	Ken Williams	.05
275	Alan Trammell	.05
276	Bill Swift	.05
277	Scott Coolbaugh	.05
278	*Alex Fernandez* (#1 Draft Pick)	.20
279a	Jose Gonzalez (photo of Billy Bean, left-handed batter)	.15
279b	Jose Gonzalez (correct photo, right-handed batter)	.10
280	Bret Saberhagen	.05
281	Larry Sheets	.05
282	Don Carman	.05
283	Marquis Grissom	.10
284	Bill Spiers	.05
285	Jim Abbott	.05
286	Ken Oberkfell	.05
287	Mark Grant	.05
288	Derrick May	.10
289	Tim Birtsas	.05
290	Steve Sax	.05
291	John Wathan	.05
292	Bud Black	.05
293	Jay Bell	.05
294	Mike Moore	.05
295	Rafael Palmeiro	.20
296	Mark Williamson	.05
297	Manny Lee	.05
298	Omar Vizquel	.05
299	*Scott Radinsky*	.15
300	Kirby Puckett	.25
301	Steve Farr	.05
302	Tim Teufel	.05
303	Mike Boddicker	.05
304	Kevin Reimer	.05
305	Mike Scioscia	.05
306a	Lonnie Smith (136 G 1990)	.10
306b	Lonnie Smith (135 G 1990)	.05
307	Andy Benes	.10
308	Tom Pagnozzi	.05
309	Norm Charlton	.05
310	Gary Carter	.10
311	Jeff Pico	.05
312	Charlie Hayes	.05
313	Ron Robinson	.05
314	Gary Pettis	.05
315	Roberto Alomar	.25
316	Gene Nelson	.05
317	Mike Fitzgerald	.05
318	Rick Aguilera	.05
319	Jeff McKnight	.05
320	Tony Fernandez	.05
321	Bob Rodgers	.05
322	*Terry Shumpert*	.05
323	Cory Snyder	.05
324a	Ron Kittle ("6 Home Runs" in career summary)	.10
324b	Ron Kittle ("7 Home Runs" in career summary)	.05
325	Brett Butler	.05
326	Ken Patterson	.05
327	Ron Hassey	.05
328	Walt Terrell	.05
329	Dave Justice	.25
330	Dwight Gooden	.10
331	Eric Anthony	.05
332	Kenny Rogers	.05
333	*Chipper Jones* (#1 Draft Pick)	4.00
334	Todd Benzinger	.05
335	Mitch Williams	.05
336	Matt Nokes	.05
337a	Keith Comstock (Mariners logo)	.05
337b	Keith Comstock (Cubs logo)	.10
338	Luis Rivera	.05
339	Larry Walker	.25
340	Ramon Martinez	.10
341	John Moses	.05
342	*Mickey Morandini*	.10
343	Jose Oquendo	.05
344	Jeff Russell	.05
345	Len Dykstra	.05
346	Jesse Orosco	.05
347	Greg Vaughn	.05
348	Todd Stottlemyre	.05
349	Dave Gallagher	.05
350	Glenn Davis	.05
351	Joe Torre	.05
352	Frank White	.05
353	Tony Castillo	.05
354	Sid Bream	.05
355	Chili Davis	.05
356	Mike Marshall	.05
357	Jack Savage	.05
358	Mark Parent	.05
359	Chuck Cary	.05
360	Tim Raines	.10
361	Scott Garrelts	.05
362	*Hector Villanueva*	.05
363	Rick Mahler	.05
364	Dan Pasqua	.05
365	Mike Schooler	.05
366a	Checklist 3 (Carl Nichols #19)	.05
366b	Checklist 3 (Carl Nichols #119)	.05
367	*Dave Walsh*	.05
368	Felix Jose	.05
369	Steve Searcy	.05
370	Kelly Gruber	.05
371	Jeff Montgomery	.05
372	Spike Owen	.05
373	Darrin Jackson	.05
374	*Larry Casian*	.10
375	Tony Pena	.05
376	Mike Harkey	.05
377	Rene Gonzales	.05
378a	*Wilson Alvarez* (no 1989 Port Charlotte stats)	.30
378b	*Wilson Alvarez* (1989 Port Charlotte stats)	.20
379	Randy Velarde	.05
380	Willie McGee	.05
381	Jim Leyland	.05
382	Mackey Sasser	.05
383	Pete Smith	.05
384	Gerald Perry	.05
385	Mickey Tettleton	.05
386	Cecil Fielder (All-Star)	.05
387	Julio Franco (All-Star)	.05
388	Kelly Gruber (All-Star)	.05
389	Alan Trammell (All-Star)	.05
390	Jose Canseco (All-Star)	.15
391	Rickey Henderson (All-Star)	.10
392	Ken Griffey, Jr. (All-Star)	.50
393	Carlton Fisk (All-Star)	.10
394	Bob Welch (All-Star)	.05
395	Chuck Finley (All-Star)	.05
396	Bobby Thigpen (All-Star)	.05
397	Eddie Murray (All-Star)	.10
398	Ryne Sandberg (All-Star)	.10
399	Matt Williams (All-Star)	.05
400	Barry Larkin (All-Star)	.05
401	Barry Bonds (All-Star)	.15
402	Darryl Strawberry (All-Star)	.05
403	Bobby Bonilla (All-Star)	.05
404	Mike Scoscia (All-Star)	.05
405	Doug Drabek (All-Star)	.05
406	Frank Viola (All-Star)	.05
407	John Franco (All-Star)	.05
408	Ernie Riles	.05
409	Mike Stanley	.05
410	Dave Righetti	.05
411	Lance Blankenship	.05
412	Dave Bergman	.05
413	Terry Mulholland	.05
414	Sammy Sosa	.75
415	Rick Sutcliffe	.05
416	Randy Milligan	.05
417	Bill Krueger	.05
418	Nick Esasky	.05
419	Jeff Reed	.05
420	Bobby Thigpen	.05
421	Alex Cole	.05
422	Rick Rueschel	.05
423	Rafael Ramirez	.05
424	Calvin Schiraldi	.05
425	Andy Van Slyke	.05
426	*Joe Grahe*	.10
427	Rick Dempsey	.05
428	*John Barfield*	.05
429	Stump Merrill	.05
430	Gary Gaetti	.05
431	Paul Gibson	.05
432	Delino DeShields	.05
433	Pat Tabler	.05
434	Julio Machado	.05
435	Kevin Maas	.05
436	Scott Bankhead	.05
437	Doug Dascenzo	.05
438	Vicente Palacios	.05
439	Dickie Thon	.05
440	George Bell	.05
441	Zane Smith	.05
442	Charlie O'Brien	.05
443	Jeff Innis	.05
444	Glenn Braggs	.05
445	Greg Swindell	.05
446	*Craig Grebeck*	.05
447	John Burkett	.05
448	Craig Lefferts	.05
449	Juan Berenguer	.05
450	Wade Boggs	.25
451	Neal Heaton	.05
452	Bill Schroeder	.05
453	Lenny Harris	.05
454a	Kevin Appier (no 1990 Omaha stats)	.15
454b	Kevin Appier (1990 Omaha stats)	.10
455	Walt Weiss	.05
456	Charlie Leibrandt	.05
457	Todd Hundley	.15
458	Brian Holman	.05
459	Tom Trebelhorn	.05
460	Dave Steib	.05
461a	Robin Ventura (gray inner photo frame at left)	.15
461b	Robin Ventura (red inner photo frame at left)	.15
462	Steve Frey	.05
463	Dwight Smith	.05
464	Steve Buechele	.05
465	Ken Griffey	.05
466	Charles Nagy	.10
467	Dennis Cook	.05
468	Tim Hulett	.05
469	Chet Lemon	.05
470	Howard Johnson	.05
471	*Mike Lieberthal* (#1 Draft Pick)	.50
472	Kirt Manwaring	.05
473	Curt Young	.05
474	*Phil Plantier*	.15
475	Teddy Higuera	.05
476	Glenn Wilson	.05
477	Mike Fetters	.05
478	Kurt Stillwell	.05
479	Bob Patterson	.05
480	Dave Magadan	.05
481	Eddie Whitson	.05
482	Tino Martinez	.15
483	Mike Aldrete	.05
484	Dave LaPoint	.05
485	Terry Pendleton	.05
486	Tommy Greene	.10
487	Rafael Belliard	.05
488	Jeff Manto	.10
489	Bobby Valentine	.05
490	Kirk Gibson	.05
491	*Kurt Miller* (#1 Draft Pick)	.15
492	Ernie Whitt	.05
493	Jose Rijo	.05
494	Chris James	.05
495	Charlie Hough	.05
496	Marty Barrett	.05
497	Ben McDonald	.05
498	Mark Salas	.05
499	Melido Perez	.05
500	Will Clark	.20
501	Mike Bielecki	.05
502	Carney Lansford	.05
503	Roy Smith	.05
504	*Julio Valera*	.05
505	Chuck Finley	.05
506	Darnell Coles	.05
507	Steve Jeltz	.05
508	*Mike York*	.05
509	Glenallen Hill	.05
510	John Franco	.05
511	Steve Balboni	.05
512	Jose Mesa	.05
513	Jerald Clark	.05
514	Mike Stanton	.05
515	Alvin Davis	.05
516	*Karl Rhodes*	.10
517	Joe Oliver	.05
518	Cris Carpenter	.05
519	Sparky Anderson	.10
520	Mark Grace	.20
521	Joe Orsulak	.05
522	Stan Belinda	.05
523	*Rodney McCray*	.05
524	Darrel Akerfelds	.05
525	Willie Randolph	.05
526a	Moises Alou (37 R 1990 Pirates)	.20
526b	Moises Alou (0 R 1990 Pirates)	.10
527a	Checklist 4 (Kevin McReynolds #719)	.05
527b	Checklist 4 (Kevin McReynolds #105)	.05
528	Denny Martinez	.05

529	*Mark Newfield* (#1 Draft Pick)	.15
530	Roger Clemens	.40
531	*Dave Rhode*	.10
532	Kirk McCaskill	.05
533	Oddibe McDowell	.05
534	Mike Jackson	.05
535	Ruben Sierra	.05
536	Mike Witt	.05
537	Jose Lind	.05
538	Bip Roberts	.05
539	Scott Terry	.05
540	George Brett	.30
541	Domingo Ramos	.05
542	Rob Murphy	.05
543	Junior Felix	.05
544	Alejandro Pena	.05
545	Dale Murphy	.10
546	Jeff Ballard	.05
547	Mike Pagliarulo	.05
548	Jaime Navarro	.05
549	John McNamara	.05
550	Eric Davis	.05
551	Bob Kipper	.05
552	Jeff Hamilton	.05
553	*Joe Klink*	.05
554	Brian Harper	.05
555	*Turner Ward*	.10
556	Gary Ward	.05
557	Wally Whitehurst	.05
558	Otis Nixon	.05
559	Adam Peterson	.05
560	Greg Smith	.05
561	Tim McIntosh (Future Star)	.10
562	Jeff Kunkel	.05
563	*Brent Knackert*	.10
564	Dante Bichette	.15
565	Craig Biggio	.25
566	*Craig Wilson*	.10
567	Dwayne Henry	.05
568	Ron Karkovice	.05
569	Curt Schilling	.05
570	Barry Bonds	.30
571	Pat Combs	.05
572	Dave Anderson	.05
573	*Rich Rodriguez*	.10
574	John Marzano	.05
575	Robin Yount	.20
576	Jeff Kaiser	.05
577	Bill Doran	.05
578	Dave West	.05
579	Roger Craig	.05
580	Dave Stewart	.05
581	Luis Quinones	.05
582	Marty Clary	.05
583	Tony Phillips	.05
584	Kevin Brown	.05
585	Pete O'Brien	.05
586	Fred Lynn	.05
587	Jose Offerman (Future Star)	.10
588a	Mark Whiten (hand inside left border)	.15
588b	Mark Whiten (hand over left border)	.20
589	*Scott Ruskin*	.10
590	Eddie Murray	.15
591	Ken Hill	.05
592	B.J. Surhoff	.05
593a	*Mike Walker* (No 1990 Canton-Akron stats)	.15
593b	*Mike Walker* (1990 Canton-Akron stats)	.15
594	*Rich Garces* (Future Star)	.10
595	Bill Landrum	.05
596	*Ronnie Walden* (#1 Draft Pick)	.10
597	Jerry Don Gleaton	.05
598	Sam Horn	.05
599a	Greg Myers (no 1990 Syracuse stats)	.10
599b	Greg Myers (1990 Syracuse stats)	.10
600	Bo Jackson	.15
601	Bob Ojeda	.05
602	Casey Candaele	.05
603a	*Wes Chamberlain* (photo of Louie Meadows, no bat)	.20
603b	*Wes Chamberlain* (correct photo, holding bat)	.10
604	Billy Hatcher	.05
605	Jeff Reardon	.05
606	Jim Gott	.05
607	Edgar Martinez	.05
608	Todd Burns	.05
609	Jeff Torborg	.05
610	Andres Galarraga	.20
611	Dave Eiland	.05
612	Steve Lyons	.05
613	Eric Show	.05
614	Luis Salazar	.05
615	Bert Blyleven	.05
616	Todd Zeile	.05
617	Bill Wegman	.05
618	Sil Campusano	.05
619	David Wells	.05
620	Ozzie Guillen	.05
621	Ted Power	.05
622	Jack Daugherty	.05
623	Jeff Blauser	.05
624	Tom Candiotti	.05
625	Terry Steinbach	.05
626	Gerald Young	.05
627	*Tim Layana*	.10
628	Greg Litton	.05
629	Wes Gardner	.05
630	Dave Winfield	.15
631	Mike Morgan	.05
632	Lloyd Moseby	.05
633	Kevin Tapani	.05
634	Henry Cotto	.05
635	Andy Hawkins	.05
636	Geronimo Pena	.05
637	Bruce Ruffin	.05
638	Mike Macfarlane	.05
639	Frank Robinson	.05
640	Andre Dawson	.10
641	Mike Henneman	.05
642	Hal Morris	.05
643	Jim Presley	.05
644	Chuck Crim	.05
645	Juan Samuel	.05
646	*Andujar Cedeno*	.05
647	Mark Portugal	.05
648	Lee Stevens	.05
649	*Bill Sampen*	.05
650	Jack Clark	.05
651	*Alan Mills*	.10
652	Kevin Romine	.05
653	*Anthony Telford*	.15
654	Paul Sorrento	.10
655	Erik Hanson	.05
656a	Checklist 5 (Vincente Palacios #348)	.05
656b	Checklist 5 (Palacios #433)	.05
656c	Checklist 5 (Palacios #438)	.05
657	Mike Kingery	.05
658	*Scott Aldred*	.05
659	*Oscar Azocar*	.05
660	Lee Smith	.05
661	Steve Lake	.05
662	Rob Dibble	.05
663	Greg Brock	.05
664	John Farrell	.05
665	Mike LaValliere	.05
666	Danny Darwin	.05
667	Kent Anderson	.05
668	Bill Long	.05
669	Lou Pinella	.05
670	Rickey Henderson	.20
671	Andy McGaffigan	.05
672	Shane Mack	.05
673	*Greg Olson*	.05
674a	Kevin Gross (no diamond after 89 BB 1988)	.10
674b	Kevin Gross (diamond after 89 BB 1988)	.10
675	Tom Brunansky	.05
676	*Scott Chiamparino*	.10
677	Billy Ripken	.05
678	Mark Davidson	.05
679	Bill Bathe	.05
680	David Cone	.15
681	*Jeff Schaefer*	.05
682	*Ray Lankford*	.20
683	Derek Lilliquist	.05
684	Milt Cuyler	.05
685	Doug Drabek	.05
686	Mike Gallego	.05
687a	John Cerutti (4.46 ERA 1990)	.05
687b	John Cerutti (4.76 ERA 1990)	.05
688	*Rosario Rodriguez*	.05
689	John Kruk	.05
690	Orel Hershiser	.05
691	Mike Blowers	.05
692a	*Efrain Valdez* (no text below stats)	.15
692b	*Efrain Valdez* (two lines of text below stats)	.15
693	Francisco Cabrera	.05
694	Randy Veres	.05
695	Kevin Seitzer	.05
696	Steve Olin	.05
697	Shawn Abner	.05
698	Mark Guthrie	.05
699	Jim Lefebvre	.05
700	Jose Canseco	.25
701	Pascual Perez	.05
702	*Tim Naehring*	.15
703	Juan Agosto	.05
704	Devon White	.05
705	Robby Thompson	.05
706a	Brad Arnsberg (68.2 IP Rangers 1990)	.05
706b	Brad Arnsberg (62.2 IP Rangers 1990)	.05
707	Jim Eisenreich	.05
708	John Mitchell	.05
709	Matt Sinatro	.05
710	Kent Hrbek	.05
711	Jose DeLeon	.05
712	Ricky Jordan	.05
713	Scott Scudder	.05
714	Marvell Wynne	.05
715	Tim Burke	.05
716	Bob Geren	.05
717	Phil Bradley	.05
718	Steve Crawford	.05
719	Keith Miller	.05
720	Cecil Fielder	.10
721	*Mark Lee*	.05
722	Wally Backman	.05
723	Candy Maldonado	.05
724	*David Segui*	.10
725	Ron Gant	.15
726	Phil Stephenson	.05
727	Mookie Wilson	.05
728	Scott Sanderson	.05
729	Don Zimmer	.05
730	Barry Larkin	.20
731	*Jeff Gray*	.05
732	Franklin Stubbs	.05
733	Kelly Downs	.05
734	John Russell	.05
735	Ron Darling	.05
736	Dick Schofield	.05
737	Tim Crews	.05
738	Mel Hall	.05
739	*Russ Swan*	.05
740	Ryne Sandberg	.25
741	Jimmy Key	.05
742	Tommy Gregg	.05
743	Bryn Smith	.05
744	Nelson Santovenia	.05
745	Doug Jones	.05
746	John Shelby	.05
747	Tony Fossas	.05
748	Al Newman	.05
749	Greg Harris	.05
750	Bobby Bonilla	.10
751	*Wayne Edwards*	.05
752	Kevin Bass	.05
753	*Paul Marak*	.05
754	Bill Pecota	.05
755	Mark Langston	.05
756	Jeff Huson	.05
757	Mark Gardner	.05
758	Mike Devereaux	.05
759	Bobby Cox	.05
760	Benny Santiago	.05
761	Larry Andersen	.05
762	Mitch Webster	.05
763	*Dana Kiecker*	.05
764	Mark Carreon	.05
765	Shawon Dunston	.05
766	Jeff Robinson	.05
767	*Dan Wilson* (#1 Draft Pick)	.15
768	Donn Pall	.05
769	*Tim Sherrill*	.05
770	Jay Howell	.05
771	Gary Redus	.05
772	Kent Mercker	.05
773	Tom Foley	.05
774	Dennis Rasmussen	.05
775	Julio Franco	.05
776	Brent Mayne	.10
777	John Candelaria	.05
778	Danny Gladden	.05
779	Carmelo Martinez	.05
780a	Randy Myers (Career losses 15)	.10
780b	Randy Myers (Career losses 19)	.10
781	Darryl Hamilton	.05
782	Jim Deshaies	.05
783	Joel Skinner	.05
784	Willie Fraser	.05
785	Scott Fletcher	.05
786	Eric Plunk	.05
787	Checklist 6	.05
788	Bob Milacki	.05
789	Tom Lasorda	.10
790	Ken Griffey, Jr.	1.00
791	Mike Benjamin	.05
792	Mike Greenwell	.05

1991 Topps Tiffany

Topps ended its annual run of special collectors edition boxed sets in 1991, producing the glossy sets in considerably more limited quantity than in previous years. Cards are identical to the regular 1991 Topps set except for the use of white cardboard stock and a high-gloss front finish.

	MT
Complete Set (792):	150.00
Common Player:	.10

(Star cards valued at 3X-4X corresponding regular issue Topps cards)

1991 Topps Traded

"Team USA" players are featured in the 1991 Topps Traded set. The cards feature the same style as the regular 1991 issue, including the 40th anniversary logo. The set includes 132 cards and showcases rookies and traded players along with "Team USA." The cards are numbered with a "T" designation in alphabetical order.

		MT
Complete Set (132):		10.00
Common Player:		.05
1	Juan Agosto	.05
2	Roberto Alomar	.25
3	Wally Backman	.05
4	*Jeff Bagwell*	3.00
5	Skeeter Barnes	.05
6	Steve Bedrosian	.05
7	Derek Bell	.25
8	George Bell	.05
9	Rafael Belliard	.05
10	Dante Bichette	.20
11	Bud Black	.05
12	Mike Boddicker	.05
13	Sid Bream	.05

14	Hubie Brooks	.05
15	Brett Butler	.10
16	Ivan Calderon	.05
17	John Candelaria	.05
18	Tom Candiotti	.05
19	Gary Carter	.10
20	Joe Carter	.10
21	Rick Cerone	.05
22	Jack Clark	.05
23	Vince Coleman	.05
24	Scott Coolbaugh	.05
25	Danny Cox	.05
26	Danny Darwin	.05
27	Chili Davis	.05
28	Glenn Davis	.05
29	Steve Decker	.10
30	Rob Deer	.05
31	Rich DeLucia	.05
32	*John Dettmer* (USA)	.05
33	Brian Downing	.05
34	*Darren Dreifort* (USA)	.75
35	Kirk Dressendorfer	.10
36	Jim Essian	.05
37	Dwight Evans	.05
38	Steve Farr	.05
39	Jeff Fassero	.10
40	Junior Felix	.05
41	Tony Fernandez	.05
42	Steve Finley	.05
43	Jim Fregosi	.05
44	Gary Gaetti	.05
45	*Jason Giambi* (USA)	6.00
46	Kirk Gibson	.05
47	Leo Gomez	.10
48	Luis Gonzalez	.75
49	*Jeff Granger* (USA)	.15
50	*Todd Greene* (USA)	.25
51	*Jeffrey Hammonds* (USA)	1.00
52	Mike Hargrove	.05
53	Pete Harnisch	.05
54	*Rick Helling* (USA)	.50
55	Glenallen Hill	.05
56	Charlie Hough	.05
57	Pete Incaviglia	.05
58	Bo Jackson	.20
59	Danny Jackson	.05
60	Reggie Jefferson	.15
61	*Charles Johnson* (USA)	.75
62	Jeff Johnson	.10
63	*Todd Johnson* (USA)	.10
64	Barry Jones	.05
65	Chris Jones	.05
66	Scott Kamieniecki	.05
67	*Pat Kelly*	.15
68	Darryl Kile	.10
69	Chuck Knoblauch	.40
70	Bill Krueger	.05
71	Scott Leius	.10
72	*Donnie Leshnock* (USA)	.10
73	Mark Lewis	.15
74	Candy Maldonado	.05
75	*Jason McDonald* (USA)	.10
76	Willie McGee	.05
77	Fred McGriff	.25
78	*Billy McMillon* (USA)	.10
79	Hal McRae	.05
80	*Dan Melendez* (USA)	.15
81	Orlando Merced	.15
82	Jack Morris	.05
83	*Phil Nevin* (USA)	1.00
84	Otis Nixon	.05
85	Johnny Oates	.05
86	Bob Ojeda	.05
87	Mike Pagliarulo	.05
88	Dean Palmer	.25
89	Dave Parker	.05
90	Terry Pendleton	.05
91	*Tony Phillips* (USA)	.10
92	Doug Piatt	.10
93	Ron Polk (U.S.A.)	.05
94	Tim Raines	.10
95	Willie Randolph	.05
96	Dave Righetti	.05
97	Ernie Riles	.05
98	*Chris Roberts* (USA)	.15
99	Jeff Robinson (Angels)	.05
100	Jeff Robinson (Orioles)	.05
101	*Ivan Rodriguez*	3.00
102	*Steve Rodriguez* (USA)	.10
103	Tom Runnells	.05
104	Scott Sanderson	.05
105	Bob Scanlan	.05
106	Pete Schourek	.15
107	Gary Scott	.05
108	*Paul Shuey* (USA)	.15
109	*Doug Simons*	.10
110	Dave Smith	.05
111	Cory Snyder	.05
112	Luis Sojo	.05
113	*Kennie Steenstra* (USA)	.10
114	Darryl Strawberry	.20
115	Franklin Stubbs	.05
116	*Todd Taylor* (USA)	.10
117	Wade Taylor	.10
118	Garry Templeton	.05
119	Mickey Tettleton	.05
120	Tim Teufel	.05
121	Mike Timlin	.10
122	*David Tuttle* (USA)	.10
123	Mo Vaughn	.25
124	*Jeff Ware* (USA)	.10
125	Devon White	.05
126	Mark Whiten	.05
127	Mitch Williams	.05
128	*Craig Wilson* (USA)	.10
129	Willie Wilson	.05
130	*Chris Wimmer* (USA)	.10
131	*Ivan Zweig* (USA)	.10
132	Checklist	.05

1991 Topps All-Star Glossy Set of 22

Continuing the same basic format used since 1984, these glossy-front rack-pak inserts honor the players, manager and honorary captains of the previous year's All-Star Game. Fronts have a league logo in the lower-left corner, a 1990 All-Star banner above the photo and a Topps 40th anniversary logo superimposed over the photo. Backs have a shield and star design and the legend "1990 All-Star Commemorative Set" above the player's name, position and card number. Backs are printed in red and blue.

		MT
Complete Set (22):		5.00
Common Player:		.10
1	Tony LaRussa	.10
2	Mark McGwire	1.50
3	Steve Sax	.10
4	Wade Boggs	.40
5	Cal Ripken, Jr.	.90
6	Rickey Henderson	.30
7	Ken Griffey, Jr.	1.50
8	Jose Canseco	.40
9	Sandy Alomar, Jr.	.15
10	Bob Welch	.10
11	Al Lopez	.10
12	Roger Craig	.10
13	Will Clark	.25
14	Ryne Sandberg	.45
15	Chris Sabo	.10
16	Ozzie Smith	.40
17	Kevin Mitchell	.10
18	Len Dykstra	.10
19	Andre Dawson	.15
20	Mike Scioscia	.10
21	Jack Armstrong	.10
22	Juan Marichal	.10

1991 Topps Desert Shield

As a special treat for U.S. armed services personnel serving in the Persian Gulf prior to and during the war with Iraq, Topps produced a special edition of its 1991 baseball card set featuring a gold-foil overprint honoring the military effort. Enough cards were produced to equal approximately 6,800 sets. While some cards actually reached the troops in the Middle East, many were shortstopped by military supply personnel stateside and sold into the hobby. Many of the cards sent to Saudi Arabia never returned to the U.S., however, making the supply of available cards somewhat scarce. At the peak of their popularity Desert Shield cards sold for price two to three times their current levels. The checklist cards in the set were not overprinted. At least two types of counterfeit overprint have been seen on genuine Topps cards in an attempt to cash in on the scarcity of these war "veterans."

	MT
Complete Set (792):	2000.
Common Player:	1.00

(Star cards valued at 100X corresponding cards in regular 1991 Topps issue)

1991 Topps Glossy Rookies

Similar in format to previous years' glossy rookies sets, this 33-card issue was available one per pack in 100-card jumbo cello packs. Card fronts have a colored "1990 Rookies" banner above the player photo, with the player's name in red in a yellow bar beneath. The Topps 40th anniversary logo appears in one of the upper corners of the photo. Backs are printed in red and blue and feature a "1990 Rookies Commemorative Set" shield logo. The player's name, position, team and card number are printed beneath. Cards are numbered alphabetically.

		MT
Complete Set (33):		11.00
Common Player:		.25
1	Sandy Alomar, Jr.	.35
2	Kevin Appier	.35
3	Steve Avery	.25
4	Carlos Baerga	.25
5	John Burkett	.25
6	Alex Cole	.25
7	Pat Combs	.25
8	Delino DeShields	.25
9	Travis Fryman	.25
10	Marquis Grissom	.50
11	Mike Harkey	.25
12	Glenallen Hill	.25
13	Jeff Huson	.25
14	Felix Jose	.25
15	Dave Justice	.90
16	Jim Leyritz	.30
17	Kevin Maas	.25
18	Ben McDonald	.25
19	Kent Mercker	.25
20	Hal Morris	.25
21	Chris Nabholz	.25
22	Tim Naehring	.25
23	Jose Offerman	.25
24	John Olerud	.50
25	Scott Radinsky	.25
26	Scott Ruskin	.25
27	Kevin Tapani	.25
28	Frank Thomas	3.00
29	Randy Tomlin	.25
30	Greg Vaughn	.45
31	Robin Ventura	.45
32	Larry Walker	.50
33	Todd Zeile	.25

1992 Topps

This 792-card set features white stock much like the 1991 issue. The card fronts feature full-color action and posed photos with a gray inner frame and the player name and position at bottom. Backs feature biographical information, statistics and stadium photos on player cards where space is available. All-Star cards and #1 Draft Pick cards are once again included. Topps brought back four-player rookie cards in 1992. Nine Top Prospect cards of this nature can be found within the set. "Match the Stats" game cards were inserted into packs of 1992 Topps cards. Special bonus cards were given away to winners of this insert game. This was the first Topps regular-issue baseball card set since 1951 which was sold without bubblegum.

		MT
Complete Set (792):		25.00
Common Player:		.05
Pack (14):		.50
Wax Box (36):		14.00
1	Nolan Ryan	.75
2	Rickey Henderson (Record Breaker)	.05
3	Jeff Reardon (Record Breaker)	.05
4	Nolan Ryan (Record Breaker)	.40
5	Dave Winfield (Record Breaker)	.05
6	*Brien Taylor* (Draft Pick)	.10
7	*Jim Olander*	.05
8	*Bryan Hickerson*	.05
9	John Farrell (Draft Pick)	.05
10	Wade Boggs	.20
11	Jack McDowell	.05
12	Luis Gonzalez	.10
13	Mike Scioscia	.05
14	Wes Chamberlain	.05
15	Denny Martinez	.05
16	Jeff Montgomery	.05
17	Randy Milligan	.05
18	Greg Cadaret	.05
19	Jamie Quirk	.05
20	Bip Roberts	.05
21	Buck Rodgers	.05
22	Bill Wegman	.05
23	Chuck Knoblauch	.15
24	Randy Myers	.05
25	Ron Gant	.10
26	Mike Bielecki	.05
27	Juan Gonzalez	.50
28	Mike Schooler	.05
29	Mickey Tettleton	.05
30	John Kruk	.05
31	Bryn Smith	.05
32	Chris Nabholz	.05
33	Carlos Baerga	.05
34	Jeff Juden	.05
35	Dave Righetti	.05
36	*Scott Ruffcorn* (Draft Pick)	.15
37	Luis Polonia	.05
38	Tom Candiotti	.05
39	Greg Olson	.05
40	Cal Ripken, Jr.	1.50
41	Craig Lefferts	.05
42	Mike Macfarlane	.05
43	Jose Lind	.05
44	Rick Aguilera	.05
45	Gary Carter	.10
46	Steve Farr	.05
47	Rex Hudler	.05
48	Scott Scudder	.05
49	Damon Berryhill	.05
50	Ken Griffey, Jr.	1.50
51	Tom Runnells	.05
52	Juan Bell	.05
53	Tommy Gregg	.05
54	David Wells	.05
55	Rafael Palmeiro	.20
56	Charlie O'Brien	.05
57	Donn Pall	.05
58	Top Prospects-Catchers (*Brad Ausmus*), (*Jim Campanis*), (*Dave Nilsson*), (*Doug Robbins*)	.15
59	Mo Vaughn	.30
60	Tony Fernandez	.05
61	Paul O'Neill	.15
62	Gene Nelson	.05
63	Randy Ready	.05
64	Bob Kipper	.05
65	Willie McGee	.05
66	*Scott Stahoviak* (Draft Pick)	.15
67	Luis Salazar	.05
68	Marvin Freeman	.05
69	Kenny Lofton	.40
70	Gary Gaetti	.05
71	Erik Hanson	.05
72	Eddie Zosky	.10
73	Brian Barnes	.05
74	Scott Leius	.05
75	Bret Saberhagen	.05
76	Mike Gallego	.05
77	Jack Armstrong	.05
78	Ivan Rodriguez	.40
79	Jesse Orosco	.05
80	Dave Justice	.20
81	*Ced Landrum*	.05
82	*Doug Simons*	.10
83	Tommy Greene	.05
84	Leo Gomez	.05
85	Jose DeLeon	.05
86	Steve Finley	.05
87	*Bob MacDonald*	.10
88	Darrin Jackson	.05
89	Neal Heaton	.05
90	Robin Yount	.20
91	Jeff Reed	.05
92	Lenny Harris	.05
93	Reggie Jefferson	.05
94	Sammy Sosa	1.00
95	Scott Bailes	.05
96	*Tom McKinnon* (Draft Pick)	.10
97	Luis Rivera	.05
98	Mike Harkey	.05
99	Jeff Treadway	.05
100	Jose Canseco	.25
101	Omar Vizquel	.05
102	*Scott Kamieniecki*	.10
103	Ricky Jordan	.05
104	Jeff Ballard	.05
105	Felix Jose	.05
106	Mike Boddicker	.05
107	Dan Pasqua	.05
108	*Mike Timlin*	.15
109	Roger Craig	.05
110	Ryne Sandberg	.25
111	Mark Carreon	.05
112	Oscar Azocar	.05
113	Mike Greenwell	.05
114	Mark Portugal	.05
115	Terry Pendleton	.05
116	Willie Randolph	.05
117	Scott Terry	.05
118	Chili Davis	.05
119	Mark Gardner	.05
120	Alan Trammell	.10
121	Derek Bell	.10
122	Gary Varsho	.05
123	Bob Ojeda	.05
124	*Shawn Livsey* (Draft Pick)	.10
125	Chris Hoiles	.05
126	Top Prospects-1st Baseman (Rico Brogna, John Jaha, Ryan Klesko, Dave Staton)	.25
127	Carlos Quintana	.05
128	Kurt Stillwell	.05
129	Melido Perez	.05
130	Alvin Davis	.05
131	Checklist 1	.05
132	Eric Show	.05
133	Rance Mulliniks	.05
134	Darryl Kile	.05
135	Von Hayes	.05
136	Bill Doran	.05
137	Jeff Robinson	.05
138	Monty Fariss	.05
139	Jeff Innis	.05
140	Mark Grace	.15
141	Jim Leyland	.05
142	Todd Van Poppel	.05
143	Paul Gibson	.05
144	Bill Swift	.05
145	Danny Tartabull	.05
146	Al Newman	.05
147	Cris Carpenter	.05
148	*Anthony Young*	.15
149	*Brian Bohanon*	.10
150	Roger Clemens	.50
151	Jeff Hamilton	.05
152	Charlie Leibrandt	.05
153	Ron Karkovice	.05
154	Hensley Meulens	.05
155	Scott Bankhead	.05
156	*Manny Ramirez* (Draft Pick)	2.00
157	Keith Miller	.05
158	Todd Frohwirth	.05
159	Darrin Fletcher	.05
160	Bobby Bonilla	.05
161	Casey Candaele	.05
162	Paul Faries	.05
163	Dana Kiecker	.05
164	Shane Mack	.05
165	Mark Langston	.05
166	Geronimo Pena	.05
167	Andy Allanson	.05
168	Dwight Smith	.05
169	Chuck Crim	.05
170	Alex Cole	.05
171	Bill Plummer	.05
172	Juan Berenguer	.05
173	Brian Downing	.05
174	Steve Frey	.05
175	Orel Hershiser	.05
176	*Ramon Garcia*	.10
177	Danny Gladden	.05
178	Jim Acker	.05
179	Top Prospects-2nd Baseman (*Cesar Bernhardt*), (*Bobby DeJardin*), (*Armando Moreno*), (*Andy Stankiewicz*)	.15
180	Kevin Mitchell	.05
181	Hector Villanueva	.05
182	Jeff Reardon	.05
183	Brent Mayne	.05
184	Jimmy Jones	.05
185	Benny Santiago	.05
186	*Cliff Floyd* (Draft Pick)	.40
187	Ernie Riles	.05
188	Jose Guzman	.05
189	Junior Felix	.05
190	Glenn Davis	.05
191	Charlie Hough	.05
192	*Dave Fleming*	.10
193	Omar Oliveras	.05
194	Eric Karros	.10
195	David Cone	.15
196	*Frank Castillo*	.05
197	Glenn Braggs	.05
198	Scott Aldred	.05
199	Jeff Blauser	.05
200	Len Dykstra	.05
201	Buck Showalter	.05
202	Rick Honeycutt	.05
203	Greg Myers	.05
204	Trevor Wilson	.05
205	Jay Howell	.05
206	Luis Sojo	.05
207	Jack Clark	.05
208	Julio Machado	.05
209	Lloyd McClendon	.05
210	Ozzie Guillen	.05
211	*Jeremy Hernandez*	.10
212	Randy Velarde	.05
213	Les Lancaster	.05
214	*Andy Mota*	.10
215	Rich Gossage	.05
216	*Brent Gates* (Draft Pick)	.20
217	Brian Harper	.05
218	Mike Flanagan	.05
219	Jerry Browne	.05
220	Jose Rijo	.05
221	Skeeter Barnes	.05
222	Jaime Navarro	.05
223	Mel Hall	.05
224	*Brett Barberie*	.10
225	Roberto Alomar	.25
226	Pete Smith	.05
227	Daryl Boston	.05
228	Eddie Whitson	.05
229	Shawn Boskie	.05
230	Dick Schofield	.05
231	*Brian Drahman*	.10
232	John Smiley	.05
233	Mitch Webster	.05
234	Terry Steinbach	.05
235	Jack Morris	.05
236	Bill Pecota	.05
237	*Jose Hernandez*	.10
238	Greg Litton	.05
239	Brian Holman	.05
240	Andres Galarraga	.15
241	Gerald Young	.05
242	Mike Mussina	.25
243	Alvaro Espinoza	.05
244	Darren Daulton	.05
245	John Smoltz	.15
246	*Jason Pruitt* (Draft Pick)	.10
247	Chuck Finley	.05
248	Jim Gantner	.05
249	Tony Fossas	.05
250	Ken Griffey	.05
251	Kevin Elster	.05
252	Dennis Rasmussen	.05
253	Terry Kennedy	.05
254	*Ryan Bowen*	.15
255	Robin Ventura	.20
256	Mike Aldrete	.05
257	Jeff Russell	.05
258	Jim Lindeman	.05
259	Ron Darling	.05
260	Devon White	.05
261	Tom Lasorda	.10
262	Terry Lee	.10
263	Bob Patterson	.05
264	Checklist 2	.05
265	Teddy Higuera	.05
266	Roberto Kelly	.05
267	Steve Bedrosian	.05
268	Brady Anderson	.10
269	*Ruben Amaro*	.10
270	Tony Gwynn	.50
271	Tracy Jones	.05
272	Jerry Don Gleaton	.05
273	Craig Grebeck	.05
274	*Bob Scanlan*	.10
275	Todd Zeile	.05
276	*Shawn Green* (Draft Pick)	1.50
277	Scott Chiamparino	.05
278	Darryl Hamilton	.05
279	Jim Clancy	.05
280	Carlos Martinez	.05
281	Kevin Appier	.05
282	*John Wehner*	.10
283	Reggie Sanders	.15
284	Gene Larkin	.05
285	Bob Welch	.05
286	Gilberto Reyes	.05
287	*Pete Schourek*	.15
288	Andujar Cedeno	.05
289	Mike Morgan	.05
290	Bo Jackson	.15
291	Phil Garner	.05
292	Ray Lankford	.10
293	Mike Henneman	.05
294	Dave Valle	.05
295	Alonzo Powell	.05
296	Tom Brunansky	.05
297	Kevin Brown	.05
298	Kelly Gruber	.05
299	Charles Nagy	.05
300	Don Mattingly	.40
301	Kirk McCaskill	.05
302	Joey Cora	.05
303	Dan Plesac	.05
304	Joe Oliver	.05
305	Tom Glavine	.15
306	*Al Shirley* (Draft Pick)	.10
307	Bruce Ruffin	.05
308	*Craig Shipley*	.05
309	Dave Martinez	.05
310	Jose Mesa	.05
311	Henry Cotto	.05
312	Mike LaValliere	.05
313	Kevin Tapani	.05
314	Jeff Huson	.05
315	Juan Samuel	.05
316	Curt Schilling	.10
317	Mike Bordick	.05
318	Steve Howe	.05
319	Tony Phillips	.05
320	George Bell	.05
321	Lou Pinella	.05
322	Tim Burke	.05
323	Milt Thompson	.05
324	Danny Darwin	.05
325	Joe Orsulak	.05
326	Eric King	.05
327	Jay Buhner	.10
328	*Joel Johnston*	.10
329	Franklin Stubbs	.05
330	Will Clark	.20
331	Steve Lake	.05
332	*Chris Jones*	.10
333	Pat Tabler	.05
334	Kevin Gross	.05
335	Dave Henderson	.05
336	*Greg Anthony* (Draft Pick)	.10
337	Alejandro Pena	.05
338	Shawn Abner	.05
339	Tom Browning	.05
340	Otis Nixon	.05
341	Bob Geren	.05
342	*Tim Spehr*	.10
343	*Jon Vander Wal*	.20
344	Jack Daugherty	.05
345	Zane Smith	.05
346	*Rheal Cormier*	.15

347 Kent Hrbek .05
348 *Rick Wilkins* .10
349 Steve Lyons .05
350 Gregg Olson .05
351 Greg Riddoch .05
352 Ed Nunez .05
353 *Braulio Castillo* .05
354 Dave Bergman .05
355 *Warren Newson* .10
356 Luis Quinones .05
357 Mike Witt .05
358 *Ted Wood* .10
359 Mike Moore .05
360 Lance Parrish .05
361 Barry Jones .05
362 *Javier Ortiz* .10
363 John Candelaria .05
364 Glenallen Hill .05
365 Duane Ward .05
366 Checklist 3 .05
367 Rafael Belliard .05
368 Bill Krueger .05
369 *Steve Whitaker* (Draft Pick) .10
370 Shawon Dunston .05
371 Dante Bichette .15
372 *Kip Gross* .05
373 Don Robinson .05
374 Bernie Williams .30
375 Bert Blyleven .05
376 *Chris Donnels* .10
377 *Bob Zupcic* .05
378 Joel Skinner .05
379 Steve Chitren .05
380 Barry Bonds .35
381 Sparky Anderson .10
382 Sid Fernandez .05
383 Dave Hollins .05
384 Mark Lee .05
385 Tim Wallach .05
386 Will Clark (All-Star) .10
387 Ryne Sandberg (All-Star) .10
388 Howard Johnson (All-Star) .05
389 Barry Larkin (All-Star) .05
390 Barry Bonds (All-Star) .10
391 Ron Gant (All-Star) .05
392 Bobby Bonilla (All-Star) .05
393 Craig Biggio (All-Star) .10
394 Denny Martinez (All-Star) .05
395 Tom Glavine (All-Star) .05
396 Lee Smith (All-Star) .05
397 Cecil Fielder (All-Star) .05
398 Julio Franco (All-Star) .05
399 Wade Boggs (All-Star) .10
400 Cal Ripken, Jr. (All-Star) .25
401 Jose Canseco (All-Star) .10
402 Joe Carter (All-Star) .05
403 Ruben Sierra (All-Star) .05
404 Matt Nokes (All-Star) .05
405 Roger Clemens (All-Star) .20
406 Jim Abbott (All-Star) .05
407 Bryan Harvey (All-Star) .05
408 Bob Milacki .05
409 Geno Petralli .05
410 Dave Stewart .05
411 Mike Jackson .05
412 Luis Aquino .05
413 Tim Teufel .05
414 Jeff Ware (Draft Pick) .10
415 Jim Deshaies .05
416 Ellis Burks .10
417 Allan Anderson .05
418 Alfredo Griffin .05
419 Wally Whitehurst .05
420 Sandy Alomar .10
421 Juan Agosto .05
422 Sam Horn .05
423 *Jeff Fassero* .10
424 *Paul McClellan* .10
425 Cecil Fielder .10
426 Tim Raines .10
427 *Eddie Taubensee* .20
428 Dennis Boyd .05
429 Tony LaRussa .05
430 Steve Sax .05
431 Tom Gordon .05
432 Billy Hatcher .05
433 Cal Eldred .05
434 Wally Backman .05
435 Mark Eichhorn .05
436 Mookie Wilson .05
437 *Scott Servais* .10
438 Mike Maddux .05
439 *Chico Walker* .05
440 Doug Drabek .05
441 Rob Deer .05
442 Dave West .05
443 Spike Owen .05
444 *Tyrone Hill* (Draft Pick) .10
445 Matt Williams .15
446 Mark Lewis .05
447 David Segui .05
448 Tom Pagnozzi .05
449 *Jeff Johnson* .10
450 Mark McGwire 1.50
451 Tom Henke .05
452 Wilson Alvarez .05
453 Gary Redus .05
454 Darren Holmes .05
455 Pete O'Brien .05
456 Pat Combs .05
457 Hubie Brooks .05
458 Frank Tanana .05
459 Tom Kelly .05
460 Andre Dawson .10
461 Doug Jones .05
462 Rich Rodriguez .05
463 *Mike Simms* .10
464 Mike Jeffcoat .05
465 Barry Larkin .10
466 Stan Belinda .05
467 Lonnie Smith .05
468 Greg Harris .05
469 Jim Eisenreich .05
470 Pedro Guerrero .05
471 Jose DeJesus .05
472 *Rich Rowland* .10
473 Top Prospects-3rd Baseman (*Frank Bolick*), (*Craig Paquette*), (*Tom Redington*), (*Paul Russo*) .15
474 *Mike Rossiter* (Draft Pick) .15
475 Robby Thompson .05
476 Randy Bush .05
477 Greg Hibbard .05
478 Dale Sveum .05
479 *Chito Martinez* .10
480 Scott Sanderson .05
481 Tino Martinez .10
482 Jimmy Key .05
483 Terry Shumpert .05
484 Mike Hartley .05
485 Chris Sabo .05
486 Bob Walk .05
487 John Cerutti .05
488 Scott Cooper .10
489 Bobby Cox .05
490 Julio Franco .05
491 Jeff Brantley .05
492 Mike Devereaux .05
493 Jose Offerman .05
494 Gary Thurman .05
495 Carney Lansford .05
496 Joe Grahe .05
497 *Andy Ashby* .15
498 Gerald Perry .05
499 Dave Otto .05
500 Vince Coleman .05
501 *Rob Mallicoat* .05
502 Greg Briley .05
503 Pascual Perez .05
504 *Aaron Sele* (Draft Pick) .40
505 Bobby Thigpen .05
506 Todd Benzinger .05
507 Candy Maldonado .05
508 Bill Gullickson .05
509 Doug Dascenzo .05
510 Frank Viola .05
511 Kenny Rogers .05
512 Mike Heath .05
513 Kevin Bass .05
514 *Kim Batiste* .10
515 Delino DeShields .05
516 *Ed Sprague* .10
517 Jim Gott .05
518 *Jose Melendez* .10
519 Hal McRae .05
520 Jeff Bagwell .50
521 Joe Hesketh .05
522 Milt Cuyler .05
523 Shawn Hillegas .05
524 Don Slaught .05
525 Randy Johnson .20
526 *Doug Piatt* .10
527 Checklist 4 .05
528 *Steve Foster* .15
529 Joe Girardi .05
530 Jim Abbott .05
531 Larry Walker .25
532 Mike Huff .05
533 Mackey Sasser .05
534 *Benji Gil* (Draft Pick) .20
535 Dave Stieb .05
536 Willie Wilson .05
537 *Mark Leiter* .05
538 Jose Uribe .05
539 Thomas Howard .05
540 Ben McDonald .05
541 *Jose Tolentino* .10
542 *Keith Mitchell* .05
543 Jerome Walton .05
544 *Cliff Brantley* .10
545 Andy Van Slyke .05
546 Paul Sorrento .05
547 Herm Winningham .05
548 Mark Guthrie .05
549 Joe Torre .05
550 Darryl Strawberry .15
551 Top Prospects-Shortstops (Manny Alexander, Alex Arias, Wil Cordero, Chipper Jones) 1.50
552 Dave Gallagher .05
553 Edgar Martinez .05
554 Donald Harris .05
555 Frank Thomas .75
556 Storm Davis .05
557 Dickie Thon .05
558 Scott Garrelts .05
559 Steve Olin .05
560 Rickey Henderson .15
561 Jose Vizcaino .05
562 *Wade Taylor* .10
563 Pat Borders .05
564 *Jimmy Gonzalez* (Draft Pick) .10
565 Lee Smith .05
566 Bill Sampen .05
567 Dean Palmer .05
568 Bryan Harvey .05
569 Tony Pena .05
570 Lou Whitaker .05
571 Randy Tomlin .05
572 Greg Vaughn .10
573 Kelly Downs .05
574 Steve Avery .05
575 Kirby Puckett .35
576 *Heathcliff Slocumb* .05
577 Kevin Seitzer .05
578 Lee Guetterman .05
579 Johnny Oates .05
580 Greg Maddux .75
581 Stan Javier .05
582 Vicente Palacios .05
583 Mel Rojas .05
584 *Wayne Rosenthal* .10
585 Lenny Webster .05
586 Rod Nichols .05
587 Mickey Morandini .05
588 Russ Swan .05
589 Mariano Duncan .05
590 Howard Johnson .05
591 Top Prospects-Outfielders (*Jacob Brumfield*), (*Jeremy Burnitz*), (*Alan Cockrell*, D.J. Dozier) .25
592 *Denny Neagle* .10
593 Steve Decker .05
594 *Brian Barber* (Draft Pick) .10
595 Bruce Hurst .05
596 Kent Mercker .05
597 *Mike Magnante* .05
598 Jody Reed .05
599 Steve Searcy .05
600 Paul Molitor .20
601 Dave Smith .05
602 Mike Fetters .05
603 *Luis Mercedes* .10
604 Chris Gwynn .05
605 Scott Erickson .05
606 Brook Jacoby .05
607 Todd Stottlemyre .05
608 Scott Bradley .05
609 Mike Hargrove .05
610 Eric Davis .05
611 *Brian Hunter* .05
612 Pat Kelly .05
613 Pedro Munoz .10
614 Al Osuna .05
615 Matt Merullo .05
616 Larry Andersen .05
617 Junior Ortiz .05
618 Top Prospects-Outfielders (*Cesar Hernandez*, Steve Hosey, Dan Peltier), (*Jeff McNeely*) .20
619 Danny Jackson .05
620 George Brett .40
621 *Dan Gakeler* .10
622 Steve Buechele .05
623 Bob Tewksbury .05
624 *Shawn Estes* (Draft Pick) .25
625 Kevin McReynolds .05
626 *Chris Haney* .05
627 Mike Sharperson .05
628 Mark Williamson .05
629 Wally Joyner .10
630 Carlton Fisk .20
631 *Armando Reynoso* .10
632 Felix Fermin .05
633 Mitch Williams .05
634 Manuel Lee .05
635 Harold Baines .05
636 Greg Harris .05
637 Orlando Merced .05
638 Chris Bosio .05
639 *Wayne Housie* .10
640 Xavier Hernandez .05
641 *David Howard* .10
642 Tim Crews .05
643 Rick Cerone .05
644 Terry Leach .05
645 Deion Sanders .15
646 Craig Wilson .05
647 Marquis Grissom .10
648 Scott Fletcher .05
649 Norm Charlton .05
650 Jesse Barfield .05
651 *Joe Slusarski* .10
652 Bobby Rose .05
653 Dennis Lamp .05
654 *Allen Watson* (Draft Pick) .20
655 Brett Butler .05
656 Top Prospects-Outfielders (*Rudy Pemberton*, Henry Rodriguez), (*Lee Tinsley*), (*Gerald Williams*) .25
657 Dave Johnson .05
658 Checklist 5 .05
659 Brian McRae .05
660 Fred McGriff .15
661 Bill Landrum .05
662 Juan Guzman .05
663 Greg Gagne .05
664 Ken Hill .05
665 *Dave Haas* .05
666 Tom Foley .05
667 *Roberto Hernandez* .10
668 Dwayne Henry .05
669 Jim Fregosi .05
670 Harold Reynolds .05
671 Mark Whiten .05
672 Eric Plunk .05
673 Todd Hundley .10
674 *Mo Sanford* .10
675 Bobby Witt .05
676 Top Prospects-Pitchers (*Pat Mahomes*), (*Sam Militello*, Roger Salkeld), (*Turk Wendell*) .15
677 John Marzano .05
678 Joe Klink .05
679 Pete Incaviglia .05
680 Dale Murphy .10
681 Rene Gonzales .05
682 Andy Benes .05
683 Jim Poole .05
684 *Trever Miller* (Draft Pick) .15
685 *Scott Livingstone* .15
686 Rich DeLucia .05
687 *Harvey Pulliam* .10
688 Tim Belcher .05
689 Mark Lemke .05
690 John Franco .05
691 Walt Weiss .05
692 Scott Ruskin .05
693 Jeff King .05
694 Mike Gardiner .05
695 Gary Sheffield .15
696 Joe Boever .05
697 Mike Felder .05

698	John Habyan	.05
699	Cito Gaston	.05
700	Ruben Sierra	.05
701	Scott Radinsky	.05
702	Lee Stevens	.05
703	*Mark Wohlers*	.10
704	Curt Young	.05
705	Dwight Evans	.05
706	Rob Murphy	.05
707	Gregg Jefferies	.05
708	Tom Bolton	.05
709	Chris James	.05
710	Kevin Maas	.05
711	*Ricky Bones*	.10
712	Curt Wilkerson	.05
713	Roger McDowell	.05
714	*Calvin Reese* (Draft Pick)	.20
715	Craig Biggio	.25
716	*Kirk Dressendorfer*	.10
717	Ken Dayley	.05
718	B.J. Surhoff	.10
719	Terry Mulholland	.05
720	Kirk Gibson	.05
721	Mike Pagliarulo	.05
722	Walt Terrell	.05
723	Jose Oquendo	.05
724	Kevin Morton	.05
725	Dwight Gooden	.10
726	Kirt Manwaring	.05
727	Chuck McElroy	.05
728	Dave Burba	.10
729	Art Howe	.05
730	Ramon Martinez	.10
731	Donnie Hill	.05
732	Nelson Santovenia	.05
733	Bob Melvin	.05
734	*Scott Hatteberg* (Draft Pick)	.10
735	Greg Swindell	.05
736	Lance Johnson	.05
737	Kevin Reimer	.05
738	Dennis Eckersley	.05
739	Rob Ducey	.05
740	Ken Caminiti	.10
741	Mark Gubicza	.05
742	Billy Spiers	.05
743	Darren Lewis	.05
744	Chris Hammond	.05
745	Dave Magadan	.05
746	Bernard Gilkey	.10
747	Willie Banks	.05
748	Matt Nokes	.05
749	Jerald Clark	.05
750	Travis Fryman	.05
751	Steve Wilson	.05
752	Billy Ripken	.05
753	Paul Assenmacher	.05
754	Charlie Hayes	.05
755	Alex Fernandez	.10
756	Gary Pettis	.05
757	Rob Dibble	.05
758	Tim Naehring	.05
759	Jeff Torborg	.05
760	Ozzie Smith	.25
761	Mike Fitzgerald	.05
762	John Burkett	.05
763	Kyle Abbott	.05
764	*Tyler Green* (Draft Pick)	.20
765	Pete Harnisch	.05
766	Mark Davis	.05
767	Kal Daniels	.05
768	Jim Thome	.50
769	Jack Howell	.05
770	Sid Bream	.05
771	*Arthur Rhodes*	.10
772	Garry Templeton	.05
773	Hal Morris	.05
774	Bud Black	.05
775	Ivan Calderon	.05
776	*Doug Henry*	.05
777	John Olerud	.20
778	Tim Leary	.05
779	Jay Bell	.05
780	Eddie Murray	.15
781	Paul Abbott	.05
782	Phil Plantier	.05
783	Joe Magrane	.05
784	Ken Patterson	.05
785	Albert Belle	.30
786	Royce Clayton	.10
787	Checklist 6	.05
788	Mike Stanton	.05
789	Bobby Valentine	.05
790	Joe Carter	.10
791	Danny Cox	.05
792	Dave Winfield	.15

1992 Topps Gold

Topps Gold cards share a checklist and format with the regular-issue 1992 Topps baseball issue except the color bars with the player's name and team printed beneath the photo have been replaced with gold foil. On back the light blue Topps logo printed beneath the stats has been replaced with a gold "ToppsGold" logo. Topps Gold cards were random inserts in all forms of packs. Additionally, factory sets of Gold cards were sold which included an autographed card of Yankees #1 draft pick Brien Taylor, and which had the checklist cards replaced with player cards. Several errors connected with the gold name/team strips are noted; no corrected versions were issued.

		MT
Complete Set (792):		120.00
Complete Factory Set (793):		130.00
Common Player:		.20
	(Star cards valued at 10X-15X corresponding cards in regular-issue 1992 Topps)	.20
86	Steve Finley (incorrect name, Mark Davidson, on gold strip)	.20
131	Terry Mathews	.20
264	Rod Beck	1.50
288	Andujar Cedeno (incorrect team, Yankees, listed on gold strip)	.60
366	Tony Perezchica	.20
465	Barry Larkin (incorrect team, Astros, listed on gold strip)	2.00
527	Terry McDaniel	.20
532	Mike Huff (incorrect team, Red Sox, listed on gold strip)	.20
658	John Ramos	.20
787	Brian Williams	.20
793	Brien Taylor (autographed edition of 12,000; factory sets only)	20.00

1992 Topps Gold Winners

A second gold-foil enhanced parallel version of the regular 1992 Topps issue was the Gold Winner cards awarded as prizes in a scratch-off contest found in each pack. Winner cards are identical to the Topps Gold cards except for the addition of a gold-foil "Winner" and star added above the team name. Due to a flaw in the dfesign of the scratch-off game cards, it was easy to win every time and the Winner cards had to be produced in quantities far greater than originally planned, making them rather common. Six checklist cards from the regular issue were replaced with player cards in the Winners edition.

		MT
Complete Set (792):		40.00
Common Player:		.15
	(Star cards valued at 5X-7X corresponding cards in regular 1992 Topps issue)	
131	Terry Mathews	.15
264	Rod Beck	.90
366	Tony Perezchica	.15
465a	Barry Larkin (team name incorrect, Astros)	.90
465b	Barry Larkin (team name correct, Reds)	.35
527	Terry McDaniel	.15
658	John Ramos	.15
787	Brian Williams	.15

1992 Topps Traded

Members of the United States baseball team are featured in this 132-card boxed set released by Topps. The cards are styled after the regular 1992 Topps cards and are numbered alphabetically. Several United States baseball players featured in this set were also featured in the 1991 Topps Traded set.

		MT
Complete Set (132):		125.00
Common Player:		.05
1	*Willie Adams* (USA)	.20
2	Jeff Alkire (USA)	.20
3	Felipe Alou	.05
4	Moises Alou	.50
5	Ruben Amaro	.05
6	Jack Armstrong	.05
7	Scott Bankhead	.05
8	Tim Belcher	.05
9	George Bell	.05
10	Freddie Benavides	.10
11	Todd Benzinger	.05
12	Joe Boever	.05
13	Ricky Bones	.05
14	Bobby Bonilla	.10
15	Hubie Brooks	.05
16	Jerry Browne	.05
17	Jim Bullinger	.05
18	Dave Burba	.05
19	Kevin Campbell	.10
20	Tom Candiotti	.05
21	Mark Carreon	.05
22	Gary Carter	.10
23	Archi Cianfrocco	.05
24	Phil Clark	.05
25	*Chad Curtis*	.50
26	Eric Davis	.10
27	Tim Davis (USA)	.10
28	Gary DiSarcina	.05
29	Darren Dreifort (USA)	.40
30	Mariano Duncan	.05
31	Mike Fitzgerald	.05
32	John Flaherty	.10
33	Darrin Fletcher	.10
34	Scott Fletcher	.05
35	Ron Fraser (USA)	.05
36	Andres Galarraga	.25
37	Dave Gallagher	.05
38	Mike Gallego	.05
39	*Nomar Garciaparra* (USA)	125.00
40	Jason Giambi (USA)	1.50
41	Danny Gladden	.05
42	Rene Gonzales	.05
43	Jeff Granger (USA)	.25
44	Rick Greene (USA)	.10
45	Jeffrey Hammonds (USA)	.50
46	Charlie Hayes	.05
47	Von Hayes	.05
48	Rick Helling (USA)	.10
49	Butch Henry	.10
50	Carlos Hernandez	.10
51	Ken Hill	.05
52	Butch Hobson	.05
53	Vince Horsman	.10
54	Pete Incaviglia	.05
55	Gregg Jefferies	.10
56	Charles Johnson (USA)	.50
57	Doug Jones	.05
58	*Brian Jordan*	4.00
59	Wally Joyner	.10
60	*Daron Kirkreit* (USA)	.20
61	Bill Krueger	.05
62	Gene Lamont	.05
63	Jim Lefebvre	.05
64	*Danny Leon*	.05
65	Pat Listach	.05
66	Kenny Lofton	.75
67	Dave Martinez	.05
68	Derrick May	.05
69	Kirk McCaskill	.05
70	*Chad McConnell* (USA)	.25
71	Kevin McReynolds	.05
72	Rusty Meacham	.05
73	Keith Miller	.05
74	Kevin Mitchell	.05
75	*Jason Moler* (USA)	.25
76	Mike Morgan	.05
77	Jack Morris	.05
78	*Calvin Murray* (USA)	.25
79	Eddie Murray	.20
80	Randy Myers	.05
81	Denny Neagle	.10
82	Phil Nevin (USA)	.40
83	Dave Nilsson	.10
84	Junior Ortiz	.05
85	Donovan Osborne	.05

86 Bill Pecota .05
87 Melido Perez .05
88 Mike Perez .05
89 Hipolito Pena .05
90 Willie Randolph .05
91 Darren Reed .10
92 Bip Roberts .05
93 Chris Roberts (USA) .25
94 Steve Rodriguez (USA) .10
95 Bruce Ruffin .05
96 Scott Ruskin .05
97 Bret Saberhagen .10
98 Rey Sanchez .10
99 Steve Sax .05
100 Curt Schilling .10
101 Dick Schofield .05
102 Gary Scott .05
103 Kevin Seitzer .05
104 Frank Seminara .10
105 Gary Sheffield .20
106 John Smiley .05
107 Cory Snyder .05
108 Paul Sorrento .05
109 Sammy Sosa 1.50
110 *Matt Stairs* 1.00
111 Andy Stankiewicz .10
112 Kurt Stillwell .05
113 Rick Sutcliffe .05
114 Bill Swift .05
115 Jeff Tackett .10
116 Danny Tartabull .05
117 Eddie Taubensee .15
118 Dickie Thon .05
119 *Michael Tucker* (USA) .50
120 Scooter Tucker .10
121 *Marc Valdes* (USA) .10
122 Julio Valera .10
123 *Jason Varitek* (USA) 2.00
124 *Ron Villone* (USA) .20
125 Frank Viola .05
126 *B.J. Wallace* (USA) .25
127 Dan Walters .10
128 Craig Wilson (USA) .10
129 Chris Wimmer (USA) .10
130 Dave Winfield .20
131 Herm Winningham .05
132 Checklist .05

1992 Topps Traded Gold

A reported 6,000 sets of 1992 Topps Traded were produced in a gold edition, with gold-foil strips on front bearing the player and team names. The cards are in all other respects identical to the regular boxed Traded issue.

	MT
Complete Set (132):	325.00
Common Player:	.25
Stars/Rookies:	2X

1992 Topps 1991 Major League Debut

This 194-card set highlights the debut date of 1991 Major League rookies. Two checklist cards are also included in this boxed set. The card fronts resemble the 1992 Topps cards. A debut banner appears in the lower-right corner of the card front. The set is packaged in an attractive collector box and the cards are numbered alphabetically. This set was available only through hobby dealers.

	MT
Complete Set (194):	30.00
Common Player:	.15

1 Kyle Abbott .15
2 Dana Allison .15
3 Rich Amaral .15
4 Ruben Amaro .15
5 Andy Ashby .30
6 Jim Austin .15
7 Jeff Bagwell 5.00
8 Jeff Banister .15
9 Willie Banks .15
10 Bret Barberie .15
11 Kim Batiste .15
12 Chris Beasley .15
13 Rod Beck .20
14 Derek Bell .40
15 Esteban Beltre .15
16 Freddie Benavides .15
17 Rickey Bones .15
18 Denis Boucher .15
19 Ryan Bowen .20
20 Cliff Brantley .20
21 John Briscoe .15
22 Scott Brosius .25
23 Terry Bross .15
24 Jarvis Brown .15
25 Scott Bullett .15
26 Kevin Campbell .15
27 Amalio Carreno .15
28 Matias Carrillo .15
29 Jeff Carter .15
30 Vinny Castilla 1.00
31 Braulio Castillo .15
32 Frank Castillo .15
33 Darrin Chapin .15
34 Mike Christopher .15
35 Mark Clark .20
36 Royce Clayton .30
37 Stu Cole .15
38 Gary Cooper .15
39 Archie Corbin .15
40 Rheal Cormier .20
41 Chris Cron .15
42 Mike Dalton .15
43 Mark Davis .15
44 Francisco de la Rosa .15
45 Chris Donnels .20
46 Brian Drahman .20
47 Tom Drees .15
48 Kirk Dressendorfer .15
49 Bruce Egloff .15
50 Cal Eldred .25
51 Jose Escobar .15
52 Tony Eusebio .20
53 Hector Fajardo .20
54 Monty Farriss .20
55 Jeff Fassero .30
56 Dave Fleming .20
57 Kevin Flora .15
58 Steve Foster .15
59 Dan Gakeler .15
60 Ramon Garcia .15
61 Chris Gardner .15
62 Jeff Gardner .20
63 Chris George .20
64 Ray Giannelli .15
65 Tom Goodwin .25
66 Mark Grater .15
67 Johnny Guzman .15
68 Juan Guzman .25
69 Dave Haas .15
70 Chris Haney .15
71 Shawn Hare .20
72 Donald Harris .20
73 Doug Henry .20
74 Pat Hentgen .40
75 Gil Heredia .20
76 Jeremy Hernandez .15
77 Jose Hernandez .15
78 Roberto Hernandez .20
79 Bryan Hickerson .20
80 Milt Hill .15
81 Vince Horsman .15
82 Wayne Housie .15
83 Chris Howard .15
84 David Howard .20
85 Mike Humphreys .15
86 Brian Hunter .15
87 Jim Hunter .15
88 Mike Ignasiak .15
89 Reggie Jefferson .25
90 Jeff Johnson .20
91 Joel Johnson .15
92 Calvin Jones .15
93 Chris Jones .20
94 Stacy Jones .15
95 Jeff Juden .15
96 Scott Kamieniecki .20
97 Eric Karros 1.00
98 Pat Kelly .20
99 John Kiely .15
100 Darryl Kile .40
101 Wayne Kirby .20
102 Garland Kiser .15
103 Chuck Knoblauch 1.00
104 Randy Knorr .15
105 Tom Kramer .15
106 Ced Landrum .15
107 Patrick Lennon .15
108 Jim Lewis .15
109 Mark Lewis .15
110 Doug Lindsey .15
111 Scott Livingstone .20
112 Kenny Lofton 1.50
113 Ever Magallanes .15
114 Mike Magnante .20
115 Barry Manuel .15
116 Josias Manzanillo .20
117 Chito Martinez .20
118 Terry Mathews .15
119 Rob Mauer .15
120 Tim Mauser .15
121 Terry McDaniel .15
122 Rusty Meacham .15
123 Luis Mercedes .20
124 Paul Miller .20
125 Keith Mitchell .15
126 Bobby Moore .15
127 Kevin Morton .20
128 Andy Mota .15
129 Jose Mota .15
130 Mike Mussina 3.00
131 Jeff Mutis .15
132 Denny Neagle .15
133 Warren Newson .20
134 Jim Olander .15
135 Erik Pappas .20
136 Jorge Pedre .15
137 Yorkis Perez .20
138 Mark Petkovsek .20
139 Doug Piatt .15
140 Jeff Plympton .15
141 Harvey Pulliam .15
142 John Ramos .15
143 Mike Remlinger .15
144 Laddie Renfroe .15
145 Armando Reynoso .20
146 Arthur Rhodes .15
147 Pat Rice .20
148 Nikco Riesgo .15
149 Carlos Rodriguez .15
150 Ivan Rodriguez 5.00
151 Wayne Rosenthal .15
152 Rico Rossy .15
153 Stan Royer .20
154 Rey Sanchez .20
155 Reggie Sanders .40
156 Mo Sanford .15
157 Bob Scanlan .20
158 Pete Schourek .20
159 Gary Scott .15
160 Tim Scott .15
161 Tony Scruggs .15
162 Scott Servais .20
163 Doug Simons .15
164 Heathcliff Slocumb .15
165 Joe Slusarski .20
166 Tim Spehr .20
167 Ed Sprague .25
168 Jeff Tackett .20
169 Eddie Taubensee .25
170 Wade Taylor .20
171 Jim Thome 2.50
172 Mike Timlin .25
173 Jose Tolentino .15
174 John Vander Wal .20
175 Todd Van Poppel .20
176 Mo Vaughn 1.50
177 Dave Wainhouse .15
178 Don Wakamatsu .15
179 Bruce Walton .15
180 Kevin Ward .15
181 Dave Weathers .15
182 Eric Wedge .15
183 John Wehner .15
184 Rick Wilkins .20
185 Bernie Williams 1.50
186 Brian Williams .15
187 Ron Witmeyer .15
188 Mark Wohlers .15
189 Ted Wood .15
190 Anthony Young .15
191 Eddie Zosky .20
192 Bob Zupcic .15
193 Checklist .15
194 Checklist .15

1993 Topps

Topps issued in a two-series format in 1993. Series I includes cards #1-396; Series II comprises #397-825. The card fronts feature full-color photos enclosed by a white border. The player's name and team appear at the bottom. The backs feature an additional player photo and biographical information at the top. The bottom box includes statistics and player information. The cards are numbered in red in a yellow flag on the back.

	MT
Complete Set (825):	30.00
Common Player:	.05
Series 1 or 2 Pack (15):	.75
Series 1 or 2 Wax Box (36):	20.00

1 Robin Yount .35
2 Barry Bonds .50
3 Ryne Sandberg .40
4 Roger Clemens .75
5 Tony Gwynn .75
6 *Jeff Tackett* .10
7 Pete Incaviglia .05
8 Mark Wohlers .05
9 Kent Hrbek .05
10 Will Clark .20
11 Eric Karros .10
12 Lee Smith .05
13 Esteban Beltre .05
14 Greg Briley .05
15 Marquis Grissom .10
16 Dan Plesac .05
17 Dave Hollins .05
18 Terry Steinbach .05
19 Ed Nunez .05
20 Tim Salmon .35
21 Luis Salazar .05
22 Jim Eisenreich .05
23 Todd Stottlemyre .05
24 Tim Naehring .05
25 John Franco .05
26 Skeeter Barnes .05
27 *Carlos Garcia* .15
28 Joe Orsulak .05
29 Dwayne Henry .05
30 Fred McGriff .20
31 Derek Lilliquist .05
32 Don Mattingly .60
33 B.J. Wallace (1992 Draft Pick) .15

No.	Player	Price
34	Juan Gonzalez	.50
35	John Smoltz	.15
36	Scott Servais	.05
37	Lenny Webster	.05
38	Chris James	.05
39	Roger McDowell	.05
40	Ozzie Smith	.40
41	Alex Fernandez	.10
42	Spike Owen	.05
43	Ruben Amaro	.05
44	Kevin Seitzer	.05
45	Dave Fleming	.05
46	*Eric Fox*	.05
47	Bob Scanlan	.05
48	Bert Blyleven	.05
49	Brian McRae	.05
50	Roberto Alomar	.30
51	Mo Vaughn	.30
52	Bobby Bonilla	.10
53	Frank Tanana	.05
54	Mike LaValliere	.05
55	Mark McLemore	.05
56	*Chad Mottola* (1992 Draft Pick)	.15
57	Norm Charlton	.05
58	Jose Melendez	.05
59	Carlos Martinez	.05
60	Roberto Kelly	.05
61	Gene Larkin	.05
62	Rafael Belliard	.05
63	Al Osuna	.05
64	Scott Chiamparino	.05
65	Brett Butler	.05
66	John Burkett	.05
67	Felix Jose	.05
68	Omar Vizquel	.05
69	*John Vander Wal*	.10
70	Roberto Hernandez	.05
71	Ricky Bones	.05
72	*Jeff Grotewold*	.10
73	Mike Moore	.05
74	Steve Buechele	.05
75	Juan Guzman	.05
76	Kevin Appier	.05
77	Junior Felix	.05
78	Greg Harris	.05
79	Dick Schofield	.05
80	Cecil Fielder	.10
81	Lloyd McClendon	.05
82	David Segui	.05
83	Reggie Sanders	.10
84	Kurt Stillwell	.05
85	Sandy Alomar	.10
86	John Habyan	.05
87	Kevin Reimer	.05
88	Mike Stanton	.05
89	Eric Anthony	.05
90	Scott Erickson	.05
91	Craig Colbert	.05
92	Tom Pagnozzi	.05
93	*Pedro Astacio*	.20
94	Lance Johnson	.05
95	Larry Walker	.30
96	Russ Swan	.05
97	Scott Fletcher	.05
98	*Derek Jeter* (1992 Draft Pick)	10.00
99	*Mike Williams*	.05
100	Mark McGwire	2.00
101	*Jim Bullinger*	.15
102	Brian Hunter	.05
103	Jody Reed	.05
104	*Mike Butcher*	.10
105	Gregg Jefferies	.05
106	Howard Johnson	.05
107	*John Kiely*	.10
108	Jose Lind	.05
109	Sam Horn	.05
110	Barry Larkin	.20
111	Bruce Hurst	.05
112	Brian Barnes	.05
113	Thomas Howard	.05
114	Mel Hall	.05
115	Robby Thompson	.05
116	Mark Lemke	.05
117	Eddie Taubensee	.05
118	David Hulse	.05
119	Pedro Munoz	.05
120	Ramon Martinez	.10
121	Todd Worrell	.05
122	Joey Cora	.05
123	Moises Alou	.20
124	Franklin Stubbs	.05
125	Pete O'Brien	.05
126	*Bob Ayrault*	.10
127	Carney Lansford	.05
128	Kal Daniels	.05
129	Joe Grahe	.05
130	Jeff Montgomery	.05
131	Dave Winfield	.15
132	*Preston Wilson* (1992 Draft Pick)	1.00
133	Steve Wilson	.05
134	Lee Guetterman	.05
135	Mickey Tettleton	.05
136	Jeff King	.05
137	Alan Mills	.05
138	Joe Oliver	.05
139	Gary Gaetti	.05
140	Gary Sheffield	.15
141	Dennis Cook	.05
142	Charlie Hayes	.05
143	Jeff Huson	.05
144	Kent Mercker	.05
145	*Eric Young*	.25
146	Scott Leius	.05
147	Bryan Hickerson	.05
148	Steve Finley	.05
149	Rheal Cormier	.05
150	Frank Thomas	.75
151	*Archi Cianfrocco*	.05
152	Rich DeLucia	.05
153	Greg Vaughn	.20
154	Wes Chamberlain	.05
155	Dennis Eckersley	.05
156	Sammy Sosa	1.00
157	Gary DiSarcina	.05
158	*Kevin Koslofski*	.10
159	*Doug Linton*	.10
160	Lou Whitaker	.05
161	Chad McDonnell (1992 Draft Pick)	.15
162	Joe Hesketh	.05
163	*Tim Wakefield*	.10
164	Leo Gomez	.05
165	Jose Rijo	.05
166	*Tim Scott*	.10
167	Steve Olin	.05
168	Kevin Maas	.05
169	Kenny Rogers	.05
170	Dave Justice	.25
171	Doug Jones	.05
172	*Jeff Reboulet*	.10
173	Andres Galarraga	.20
174	Randy Velarde	.05
175	Kirk McCaskill	.05
176	Darren Lewis	.05
177	Lenny Harris	.05
178	Jeff Fassero	.05
179	Ken Griffey, Jr.	2.00
180	Darren Daulton	.05
181	John Jaha	.05
182	Ron Darling	.05
183	Greg Maddux	1.00
184	*Damion Easley*	.10
185	Jack Morris	.05
186	Mike Magnante	.05
187	John Dopson	.05
188	Sid Fernandez	.05
189	Tony Phillips	.05
190	Doug Drabek	.05
191	*Sean Lowe* (1992 Draft Pick)	.10
192	Bob Milacki	.05
193	*Steve Foster*	.05
194	Jerald Clark	.05
195	Pete Harnisch	.05
196	Pat Kelly	.05
197	Jeff Frye	.10
198	Alejandro Pena	.05
199	Junior Ortiz	.05
200	Kirby Puckett	.50
201	Jose Uribe	.05
202	Mike Scioscia	.05
203	Bernard Gilkey	.05
204	Dan Pasqua	.05
205	Gary Carter	.10
206	Henry Cotto	.05
207	Paul Molitor	.40
208	Mike Hartley	.05
209	Jeff Parrett	.05
210	Mark Langston	.05
211	Doug Dascenzo	.05
212	Rick Reed	.05
213	Candy Maldonado	.05
214	Danny Darwin	.05
215	*Pat Howell*	.10
216	Mark Leiter	.05
217	Kevin Mitchell	.05
218	Ben McDonald	.05
219	Bip Roberts	.05
220	Benny Santiago	.05
221	Carlos Baerga	.05
222	Bernie Williams	.30
223	*Roger Pavlik*	.10
224	Sid Bream	.05
225	Matt Williams	.25
226	Willie Banks	.05
227	Jeff Bagwell	.50
228	Tom Goodwin	.05
229	Mike Perez	.05
230	Carlton Fisk	.20
231	John Wetteland	.05
232	Tino Martinez	.15
233	*Rick Greene* (1992 Draft Pick)	.10
234	Tim McIntosh	.05
235	Mitch Williams	.05
236	*Kevin Campbell*	.10
237	Jose Vizcaino	.05
238	Chris Donnels	.05
239	Mike Boddicker	.05
240	John Olerud	.20
241	Mike Gardiner	.05
242	Charlie O'Brien	.05
243	Rob Deer	.05
244	Denny Neagle	.05
245	Chris Sabo	.05
246	Gregg Olson	.05
247	Frank Seminara	.05
248	Scott Scudder	.05
249	Tim Burke	.05
250	Chuck Knoblauch	.25
251	Mike Bielecki	.05
252	Xavier Hernandez	.05
253	Jose Guzman	.05
254	Cory Snyder	.05
255	Orel Hershiser	.05
256	Wil Cordero	.10
257	Luis Alicea	.05
258	Mike Schooler	.05
259	Craig Grebeck	.05
260	Duane Ward	.05
261	Bill Wegman	.05
262	Mickey Morandini	.05
263	*Vince Horsman*	.10
264	Paul Sorrento	.05
265	Andre Dawson	.15
266	Rene Gonzales	.05
267	Keith Miller	.05
268	Derek Bell	.10
269	*Todd Steverson* (1992 Draft Pick)	.15
270	Frank Viola	.05
271	Wally Whitehurst	.05
272	*Kurt Knudsen*	.05
273	*Dan Walters*	.15
274	Rick Sutcliffe	.05
275	Andy Van Slyke	.05
276	Paul O'Neill	.15
277	Mark Whiten	.05
278	Chris Nabholz	.05
279	Todd Burns	.05
280	Tom Glavine	.15
281	*Butch Henry*	.10
282	Shane Mack	.05
283	Mike Jackson	.05
284	Henry Rodriguez	.10
285	Bob Tewksbury	.05
286	Ron Karkovice	.05
287	Mike Gallego	.05
288	Dave Cochrane	.05
289	Jesse Orosco	.05
290	Dave Stewart	.05
291	Tommy Greene	.05
292	Rey Sanchez	.05
293	Rob Ducey	.05
294	Brent Mayne	.05
295	Dave Stieb	.05
296	Luis Rivera	.05
297	Jeff Innis	.05
298	Scott Livingstone	.05
299	Bob Patterson	.05
300	Cal Ripken, Jr.	1.50
301	Cesar Hernandez	.05
302	Randy Myers	.05
303	Brook Jacoby	.05
304	Melido Perez	.05
305	Rafael Palmeiro	.20
306	Damon Berryhill	.05
307	*Dan Serafini* (1992 Draft Pick)	.10
308	Darryl Kile	.05
309	*J.T. Bruett*	.05
310	Dave Righetti	.05
311	Jay Howell	.05
312	Geronimo Pena	.05
313	Greg Hibbard	.05
314	Mark Gardner	.05
315	Edgar Martinez	.05
316	Dave Nilsson	.05
317	Kyle Abbott	.05
318	Willie Wilson	.05
319	Paul Assenmacher	.05
320	*Tim Fortugno*	.10
321	Rusty Meacham	.05
322	Pat Borders	.05
323	Mike Greenwell	.05
324	Willie Randolph	.05
325	Bill Gullickson	.05
326	Gary Varsho	.05
327	Tim Hulett	.05
328	Scott Ruskin	.05
329	Mike Maddux	.05
330	Danny Tartabull	.05
331	Kenny Lofton	.30
332	Geno Petralli	.05
333	Otis Nixon	.05
334	*Jason Kendall* (1992 Draft Pick)	1.50
335	Mark Portugal	.05
336	Mike Pagliarulo	.05
337	Kirt Manwaring	.05
338	Bob Ojeda	.05
339	*Mark Clark*	.10
340	John Kruk	.05
341	Mel Rojas	.05
342	Erik Hanson	.05
343	Doug Henry	.05
344	Jack McDowell	.05
345	Harold Baines	.05
346	Chuck McElroy	.05
347	Luis Sojo	.05
348	Andy Stankiewicz	.05
349	*Hipolito Pichardo*	.10
350	Joe Carter	.05
351	Ellis Burks	.05
352	Pete Schourek	.05
353	*Buddy Groom*	.10
354	Jay Bell	.05
355	Brady Anderson	.15
356	Freddie Benavides	.05
357	Phil Stephenson	.05
358	Kevin Wickander	.05
359	Mike Stanley	.05
360	Ivan Rodriguez	.50
361	Scott Bankhead	.05
362	Luis Gonzalez	.10
363	John Smiley	.05
364	Trevor Wilson	.05
365	Tom Candiotti	.05
366	Craig Wilson	.05
367	Steve Sax	.05
368	Delino Deshields	.10
369	Jaime Navarro	.05
370	Dave Valle	.05
371	Mariano Duncan	.05
372	Rod Nichols	.05
373	Mike Morgan	.05
374	Julio Valera	.05
375	Wally Joyner	.10
376	Tom Henke	.05
377	Herm Winningham	.05
378	Orlando Merced	.05
379	Mike Munoz	.05
380	Todd Hundley	.05
381	Mike Flanagan	.05
382	Tim Belcher	.05
383	Jerry Browne	.05
384	Mike Benjamin	.05
385	Jim Leyritz	.05
386	Ray Lankford	.10
387	Devon White	.05
388	Jeremy Hernandez	.05
389	Brian Harper	.05
390	Wade Boggs	.25
391	Derrick May	.05
392	Travis Fryman	.05
393	Ron Gant	.10
394	Checklist 1-132	.05
395	Checklist 133-264	.05
396	Checklist 265-396	.05
397	George Brett	.50
398	Bobby Witt	.05
399	Daryl Boston	.05
400	Bo Jackson	.15
401	Fred McGriff, Frank Thomas (All-Star)	.30
402	Ryne Sandberg, Carlos Baerga (All-Star)	.15
403	Gary Sheffield, Edgar Martinez (All-Star)	.05
404	Barry Larkin, Travis Fryman (All-Star)	.10
405	Andy Van Slyke, Ken Griffey, Jr. (All-Star)	.50
406	Larry Walker, Kirby Puckett (All-Star)	.25
407	Barry Bonds, Joe Carter (All-Star)	.15
408	Darren Daulton, Brian Harper (All-Star)	.05
409	Greg Maddux, Roger Clemens (All-Star)	.40

No.	Player	Price
410	Tom Glavine, Dave Fleming (All-Star)	.10
411	Lee Smith, Dennis Eckersley (All-Star)	.05
412	Jamie McAndrew	.05
413	Pete Smith	.05
414	Juan Guerrero	.05
415	Todd Frohwirth	.05
416	Randy Tomlin	.05
417	B.J. Surhoff	.10
418	Jim Gott	.05
419	Mark Thompson (1992 Draft Pick)	.10
420	Kevin Tapani	.05
421	Curt Schilling	.05
422	*J.T. Snow*	.50
423	Top Prospects 1B (Ryan Klesko, Ivan Cruz, Bubba Smith, Larry Sutton)	.25
424	John Valentin	.05
425	Joe Girardi	.05
426	*Nigel Wilson*	.15
427	Bob MacDonald	.05
428	Todd Zeile	.05
429	Milt Cuyler	.05
430	Eddie Murray	.20
431	Rich Amaral	.05
432	Pete Young	.05
433	Rockies Future Stars (Roger Bailey, Tom Schmidt)	.15
434	Jack Armstrong	.05
435	Willie McGee	.05
436	Greg Harris	.05
437	Chris Hammond	.05
438	*Ritchie Moody* (1992 Draft Pick)	.15
439	Bryan Harvey	.05
440	Ruben Sierra	.05
441	Marlins Future Stars (Don Lemon, Todd Pridy)	.10
442	Kevin McReynolds	.05
443	Terry Leach	.05
444	David Nied	.10
445	Dale Murphy	.15
446	Luis Mercedes	.05
447	*Keith Shepherd*	.10
448	Ken Caminiti	.15
449	James Austin	.05
450	Darryl Strawberry	.10
451	Top Prospects 2B (Ramon Caraballo, Jon Shave, Brent Gates), *(Quinton McCracken)*	.15
452	Bob Wickman	.05
453	Victor Cole	.05
454	*John Johnstone*	.10
455	Chili Davis	.05
456	Scott Taylor	.05
457	Tracy Woodson	.05
458	David Wells	.05
459	*Derek Wallace* (1992 Draft Pick)	.20
460	Randy Johnson	.35
461	*Steve Reed*	.05
462	Felix Fermin	.05
463	Scott Aldred	.05
464	Greg Colbrunn	.05
465	Tony Fernandez	.05
466	Mike Felder	.05
467	Lee Stevens	.05
468	Matt Whiteside	.05
469	Dave Hansen	.05
470	Rob Dibble	.05
471	Dave Gallagher	.05
472	Chris Gwynn	.05
473	Dave Henderson	.05
474	Ozzie Guillen	.05
475	Jeff Reardon	.05
476	Rockies Future Stars (Mark Voisard, Will Scalzitti)	.15
477	Jimmy Jones	.05
478	Greg Cadaret	.05
479	Todd Pratt	.20
480	Pat Listach	.05
481	*Ryan Luzinski* (1992 Draft Pick)	.10
482	Darren Reed	.05
483	*Brian Griffiths*	.10
484	John Wehner	.05
485	Glenn Davis	.05
486	*Eric Wedge*	.05
487	Jesse Hollins	.05
488	Manuel Lee	.05
489	*Scott Fredrickson*	.10
490	Omar Olivares	.05
491	Shawn Hare	.05
492	Tom Lampkin	.05
493	Jeff Nelson	.05
494	Top Prospects 3B (Kevin Young, Adell Davenport, Eduardo Perez, Lou Lucca)	.15
495	Ken Hill	.05
496	Reggie Jefferson	.05
497	Marlins Future Stars (Matt Petersen, Willie Brown)	.10
498	Bud Black	.05
499	Chuck Crim	.05
500	Jose Canseco	.50
501	Major League Managers (Johnny Oates, Bobby Cox)	.05
502	Major League Managers (Butch Hobson, Jim Lefebvre)	.05
503	Major League Managers (Buck Rodgers, Tony Perez)	.05
504	Major League Managers (Gene Lamont, Don Baylor)	.05
505	Major League Managers (Mike Hargrove, Rene Lachemann)	.05
506	Major League Managers (Sparky Anderson, Art Howe)	.10
507	Major League Managers (Hal McRae, Tommy Lasorda)	.15
508	Major League Manager (Phil Garner, Felipe Alou)	.05
509	Major League Managers (Tom Kelly, Jeff Torborg)	.05
510	Major League Managers (Buck Showalter, Jim Fregosi)	.05
511	Major League Managers (Tony LaRussa, Jim Leyland)	.05
512	Major League Managers (Lou Piniella, Joe Torre)	.05
513	Major League Managers (Toby Harrah, Jim Riggleman)	.05
514	Major League Managers (Cito Gaston, Dusty Baker)	.05
515	Greg Swindell	.05
516	Alex Arias	.05
517	Bill Pecota	.05
518	*Benji Grigsby* (1992 Draft Pick)	.15
519	David Howard	.05
520	Charlie Hough	.05
521	Kevin Flora	.05
522	Shane Reynolds	.10
523	*Doug Bochtler*	.10
524	Chris Hoiles	.05
525	Scott Sanderson	.05
526	Mike Sharperson	.05
527	Mike Fetters	.05
528	Paul Quantrill	.05
529	Top Propsects SS (Dave Silvestri, Chipper Jones, Benji Gil, Jeff Patzke)	1.50
530	Sterling Hitchcock	.05
531	Joe Millette	.05
532	Tom Brunansky	.05
533	Frank Castillo	.05
534	Randy Knorr	.05
535	Jose Oquendo	.05
536	Dave Haas	.05
537	Rockies Future Stars (Jason Hutchins, Ryan Turner)	.15
538	Jimmy Baron (1992 Draft Pick)	.10
539	Kerry Woodson	.05
540	Ivan Calderon	.05
541	Denis Boucher	.05
542	Royce Clayton	.10
543	Reggie Williams	.05
544	Steve Decker	.05
545	Dean Palmer	.05
546	Hal Morris	.05
547	*Ryan Thompson*	.10
548	Lance Blankenship	.05
549	Hensley Meulens	.05
550	Scott Radinsky	.05
551	*Eric Young*	.25
552	Jeff Blauser	.05
553	Andujar Cedeno	.05
554	Arthur Rhodes	.05
555	Terry Mulholland	.05
556	Darryl Hamilton	.05
557	Pedro Martinez	1.00
558	Marlins Future Stars (Ryan Whitman, Mark Skeels)	.15
559	*Jamie Arnold* (1992 Draft Pick)	.15
560	Zane Smith	.05
561	Matt Nokes	.05
562	Bob Zupcic	.05
563	Shawn Boskie	.05
564	Mike Timlin	.05
565	Jerald Clark	.05
566	Rod Brewer	.05
567	Mark Carreon	.05
568	Andy Benes	.05
569	Shawn Barton	.05
570	Tim Wallach	.05
571	Dave Mlicki	.05
572	Trevor Hoffman	.10
573	John Patterson	.05
574	DeShawn Warren (1992 Draft Pick)	.15
575	Monty Fariss	.05
576	Top Prospects OF (Darrell Sherman, Damon Buford, Cliff Floyd, Michael Moore)	.15
577	Tim Costo	.05
578	Dave Magadan	.05
579	Rockies Future Stars (Neil Garret, Jason Bates)	.15
580	Walt Weiss	.05
581	Chris Haney	.05
582	Shawn Abner	.05
583	Marvin Freeman	.05
584	Casey Candaele	.05
585	Ricky Jordan	.05
586	Jeff Tabaka	.05
587	Manny Alexander	.05
588	Mike Trombley	.05
589	Carlos Hernandez	.05
590	Cal Eldred	.05
591	Alex Cole	.05
592	Phil Plantier	.05
593	Brett Merriman	.05
594	Jerry Nielsen	.05
595	Shawon Dunston	.05
596	Jimmy Key	.05
597	Gerald Perry	.05
598	Rico Brogna	.05
599	Marlins Future Stars (Clemente Nunez, Dan Robinson)	.15
600	Bret Saberhagen	.10
601	Craig Shipley	.05
602	Henry Mercedes	.05
603	Jim Thome	.30
604	Rod Beck	.05
605	Chuck Finley	.05
606	J. Owens	.05
607	Dan Smith	.05
608	Bill Doran	.05
609	Lance Parrish	.05
610	Denny Martinez	.05
611	Tom Gordon	.05
612	Byron Mathews (1992 Draft Pick)	.10
613	Joel Adamson	.05
614	Brian Williams	.05
615	Steve Avery	.05
616	Top Prospects OF (Matt Mieske, Tracy Sanders, Midre Cummings, Ryan Freeburg)	.15
617	Craig Lefferts	.05
618	Tony Pena	.05
619	Billy Spiers	.05
620	Todd Benzinger	.05
621	Rockies Future Stars (Mike Kotarski, Greg Boyd)	.15
622	Ben Rivera	.05
623	Al Martin	.10
624	Sam Militello	.05
625	Rick Aguilera	.05
626	Danny Gladden	.05
627	Andres Berumen	.05
628	Kelly Gruber	.05
629	Cris Carpenter	.05
630	Mark Grace	.15
631	Jeff Brantley	.05
632	Chris Widger (1992 Draft Pick)	.20
633	Russian Angels (Rodolf Razjigaev, Evgenyi Puchkov, Ilya Bogatyrev)	.10
634	Mo Sanford	.05
635	Albert Belle	.40
636	Tim Teufel	.05
637	Greg Myers	.05
638	Brian Bohanon	.05
639	Mike Bordick	.05
640	Dwight Gooden	.10
641	Marlins Future Stars (Pat Leahy, Gavin Baugh)	.10
642	Milt Hill	.05
643	Luis Aquino	.05
644	Dante Bichette	.15
645	Bobby Thigpen	.05
646	Rich Scheid	.05
647	Brian Sackinsky (1992 Draft Pick)	.10
648	Ryan Hawblitzel	.05
649	Tom Marsh	.05
650	Terry Pendleton	.05
651	*Rafael Bournigal*	.10
652	Dave West	.05
653	Steve Hosey	.05
654	Gerald Williams	.05
655	Scott Cooper	.05
656	Gary Scott	.05
657	Mike Harkey	.05
658	Top Prospects OF (Jeromy Burnitz, Melvin Nieves, Rich Becker, Shon Walker)	.25
659	Ed Sprague	.05
660	Alan Trammell	.05
661	Rockies Future Stars (Garvin Alston, Mike Case)	.15
662	Donovan Osborne	.05
663	Jeff Gardner	.05
664	Calvin Jones	.05
665	Darrin Fletcher	.05
666	Glenallen Hill	.05
667	Jim Rosenbohm (1992 Draft Pick)	.10
668	Scott Lewis	.05
669	Kip Yaughn	.05
670	Julio Franco	.05
671	Dave Martinez	.05
672	Kevin Bass	.05
673	Todd Van Poppel	.10
674	Mark Gubicza	.05
675	Tim Raines	.10
676	Rudy Seanez	.05
677	Charlie Leibrandt	.05
678	Randy Milligan	.05
679	Kim Batiste	.05
680	Craig Biggio	.25
681	Darren Holmes	.05
682	John Candelaria	.05
683	Marlins Future Stars (Jerry Stafford, Eddie Christian)	.15
684	Pat Mahomes	.05
685	Bob Walk	.05
686	Russ Springer	.05
687	Tony Sheffield (1992 Draft Picks)	.10
688	Dwight Smith	.05
689	Eddie Zosky	.05
690	Bien Figueroa	.05
691	Jim Tatum	.05
692	Chad Kreuter	.05
693	Rich Rodriguez	.05
694	Shane Turner	.05
695	Kent Bottenfield	.05
696	Jose Mesa	.05
697	*Darrell Whitmore*	.10
698	Ted Wood	.05
699	Chad Curtis	.05

700	Nolan Ryan	1.50
701	Top Prospects C (Mike Piazza, Carlos Delgado, Brook Fordyce, Donnie Leshnock)	2.00
702	*Tim Pugh*	.15
703	Jeff Kent	.10
704	Rockies Future Stars (Jon Goodrich, Danny Figueroa)	.15
705	Bob Welch	.05
706	Sherard Clinkscales (1992 Draft Pick)	.05
707	Donn Pall	.05
708	Greg Olson	.05
709	Jeff Juden	.05
710	Mike Mussina	.30
711	Scott Chiamparino	.05
712	Stan Javier	.05
713	John Doherty	.05
714	Kevin Gross	.05
715	Greg Gagne	.05
716	Steve Cooke	.05
717	Steve Farr	.05
718	Jay Buhner	.10
719	Butch Henry	.05
720	David Cone	.15
721	Rick Wilkins	.05
722	Chuck Carr	.05
723	*Kenny Felder* (1992 Draft Pick)	.10
724	Guillermo Velasquez	.05
725	Billy Hatcher	.05
726	Marlins Future Stars (Mike Veneziale, Ken Kendrena)	.15
727	Jonathan Hurst	.05
728	Steve Frey	.05
729	Mark Leonard	.05
730	Charles Nagy	.05
731	Donald Harris	.05
732	Travis Buckley	.05
733	Tom Browning	.05
734	Anthony Young	.05
735	Steve Shifflett	.05
736	Jeff Russell	.05
737	Wilson Alvarez	.05
738	Lance Painter	.05
739	Dave Weathers	.05
740	Len Dykstra	.05
741	Mike Devereaux	.05
742	Top Prospects SP (Rene Arocha, Alan Embree), *(Tim Crabtree,* Brien Taylor)	.20
743	Dave Landaker (1992 Draft Pick)	.05
744	Chris George	.05
745	Eric Davis	.05
746	Rockies Future Stars *(Mark Strittmatter,* LaMarr Rogers)	.15
747	Carl Willis	.05
748	Stan Belinda	.05
749	Scott Kamieniecki	.05
750	Rickey Henderson	.25
751	Eric Hillman	.05
752	Pat Hentgen	.05
753	Jim Corsi	.05
754	Brian Jordan	.10
755	Bill Swift	.05
756	Mike Henneman	.05
757	Harold Reynolds	.05
758	Sean Berry	.05
759	Charlie Hayes	.05
760	Luis Polonia	.05
761	Darrin Jackson	.05
762	Mark Lewis	.05
763	Rob Maurer	.05
764	Willie Greene	.05
765	Vince Coleman	.05
766	Todd Revenig	.05
767	Rich Ireland (1992 Draft Pick)	.10
768	Mike MacFarlane	.05
769	Francisco Cabrera	.05
770	Robin Ventura	.25
771	Kevin Ritz	.05
772	Chito Martinez	.05
773	Cliff Brantley	.05
774	Curtis Leskanic	.05
775	Chris Bosio	.05
776	Jose Offerman	.05
777	Mark Guthrie	.05
778	Don Slaught	.05
779	Rich Monteleone	.05
780	Jim Abbott	.10
781	Jack Clark	.05
782	Marlins Future Stars (Rafael Mendoza, Dan Roman)	.15
783	Heathcliff Slocumb	.05
784	Jeff Branson	.05
785	Kevin Brown	.15
786	Top Prospects RP (Mike Christopher, Ken Ryan, Aaron Taylor, Gus Gandarillas)	.15
787	Mike Matthews (1992 Draft Pick)	.05
788	Mackey Sasser	.05
789	Jeff Conine	.10
790	George Bell	.05
791	Pat Rapp	.05
792	Joe Boever	.05
793	Jim Poole	.05
794	Andy Ashby	.10
795	Deion Sanders	.20
796	Scott Brosius	.10
797	Brad Pennington (Coming Attraction)	.10
798	Greg Blosser (Coming Attraction)	.10
799	*Jim Edmonds* (Coming Attraction)	1.50
800	Shawn Jeter (Coming Attraction)	.15
801	Jesse Levis (Coming Attraction)	.05
802	Phil Clark (Coming Attraction)	.10
803	Ed Pierce (Coming Attraction)	.05
804	*Jose Valentin* (Coming Attraction)	.25
805	Terry Jorgensen (Coming Attraction)	.05
806	Mark Hutton (Coming Attraction)	.05
807	Troy Neel (Coming Attraction)	.10
808	Bret Boone (Coming Attraction)	.20
809	Chris Colon (Coming Attraction)	.05
810	*Domingo Martinez* (Coming Attraction)	.10
811	Javier Lopez (Coming Attraction)	.30
812	Matt Walbeck (Coming Attraction)	.10
813	Dan Wilson (Coming Attraction)	.10
814	Scooter Tucker (Coming Attraction)	.10
815	*Billy Ashley* (Coming Attraction)	.05
816	*Tim Laker* (Coming Attraction)	.10
817	Bobby Jones (Coming Attraction)	.10
818	Brad Brink (Coming Attraction)	.05
819	William Pennyfeather (Coming Attraction)	.05
820	Stan Royer (Coming Attraction)	.10
821	Doug Brocail (Coming Attraction)	.10
822	Kevin Rogers (Coming Attraction)	.05
823	Checklist 397-528	.05
824	Checklist 541-691	.05
825	Checklist 692-825	.05

1993 Topps Gold

Expanding on the concept begun in 1992, Topps issued a "gold" version of each of its regular 1993 cards as a package insert. One Gold card was found in each wax pack; three per rack-pack and five per jumbo cello pack. Ten Gold cards were included in each factory set. Identical in format to the regular-issue 1993 Topps cards, the Gold version replaces the black or white Topps logo on front with a "ToppsGold" logo in gold-foil. The color bars and angled strips beneath the player photo which carry the player and team ID on regular cards are replaced with a gold-foil version on the insert cards. Backs are identical to the regular cards. The six checklist cards in the regular issue were replaced in the Gold version with cards of players who do not appear in the 1993 Topps set.

		MT
Complete Set (825):		70.00
Common Player:		.25
(Star cards valued at 3X-4X corresponding cards in regular 1993 Topps issue)		
394	Bernardo Brito	.25
395	Jim McNamara	.25
396	Rich Sauveur	.25
823	Keith Brown	.25
824	Russ McGinnis	.25
825	Mike Walker	.25

1993 Topps Black Gold

Randomly inserted in regular 1993 Topps packs, as well as 10 per factory set, Black Gold cards are found in both single-player versions and "Winner" cards. The single-player cards feature an action photo set against a black background and highlighted at top and bottom with gold foil. Backs have another player photo at left, again on a black background. A career summary is printed in a blue box at right. A "Topps Black Gold" logo appears at top-left, and the player's name is printed in gold foil in an art deco device at top-right. The Winner cards picture tiny versions of the Black Gold player cards for which they could be redeemed by mail.

		MT
Complete Set (44):		10.00
Common Player:		.25
Winner A (1-11):		.50
Winner B (12-22):		.50
Winner C (23-33):		.50
Winner D (34-44):		.50
Winner AB (1-22):		2.00
Winner CD (23-44):		2.00
Winner ABCD (1-44):		8.00
1	Barry Bonds	.75
2	Will Clark	.30
3	Darren Daulton	.25
4	Andre Dawson	.25
5	Delino DeShields	.25
6	Tom Glavine	.30
7	Marquis Grissom	.25
8	Tony Gwynn	.75
9	Eric Karros	.25
10	Ray Lankford	.25
11	Barry Larkin	.30
12	Greg Maddux	1.50
13	Fred McGriff	.30
14	Joe Oliver	.25
15	Terry Pendleton	.25
16	Bip Roberts	.25
17	Ryne Sandberg	.50
18	Gary Sheffield	.30
19	Lee Smith	.25
20	Ozzie Smith	.50
21	Andy Van Slyke	.25
22	Larry Walker	.40
23	Roberto Alomar	.40
24	Brady Anderson	.30
25	Carlos Baerga	.25
26	Joe Carter	.25
27	Roger Clemens	.75
28	Mike Devereaux	.25
29	Dennis Eckersley	.25
30	Cecil Fielder	.25
31	Travis Fryman	.25
32	Juan Gonzalez	.50
33	Ken Griffey Jr.	3.00
34	Brian Harper	.25
35	Pat Listach	.25
36	Kenny Lofton	.40
37	Edgar Martinez	.25
38	Jack McDowell	.25
39	Mark McGwire	2.50
40	Kirby Puckett	.65
41	Mickey Tettleton	.25
42	Frank Thomas	1.50
43	Robin Ventura	.35
44	Dave Winfield	.30

1993 Topps Traded

The 1993 Topps Traded baseball set features many players in their new uniforms as a result of trades, free agent signings and rookie call-ups. The set also features 35 expansion players from the Colorado Rockies and

Florida Marlins, as well as 22 Team USA members exclusive to Topps. The 132-card set is packed in a color deluxe printed box.

	MT
Complete Set (132):	45.00
Common Player:	.05
1 Barry Bonds	.50
2 Rich Renteria	.05
3 Aaron Sele	.30
4 *Carlton Loewer* (USA)	.75
5 Erik Pappas	.05
6 *Greg McMichael*	.15
7 Freddie Benavides	.05
8 Kirk Gibson	.10
9 Tony Fernandez	.05
10 *Jay Gainer* (USA)	.20
11 Orestes Destrade	.05
12 *A.J. Hinch* (USA)	1.00
13 Bobby Munoz	.05
14 Tom Henke	.05
15 Rob Butler	.05
16 Gary Wayne	.05
17 David McCarty	.15
18 Walt Weiss	.05
19 *Todd Helton* (USA)	35.00
20 Mark Whiten	.05
21 Ricky Gutierrez	.15
22 *Dustin Hermanson* (USA)	1.00
23 *Sherman Obando*	.10
24 Mike Piazza	3.00
25 Jeff Russell	.05
26 Jason Bere	.15
27 *Jack Voight*	.10
28 Chris Bosio	.05
29 Phil Hiatt	.15
30 *Matt Beaumont* (USA)	.10
31 Andres Galarraga	.40
32 Greg Swindell	.05
33 Vinny Castilla	.40
34 *Pat Clougherty* (USA)	.10
35 Greg Briley	.05
36 Dallas Green, Davey Johnson	.05
37 Tyler Green	.10
38 Craig Paquette	.05
39 Danny Sheaffer	.05
40 Jim Converse	.05
41 Terry Harvey	.05
42 Phil Plantier	.10
43 *Doug Saunders*	.10
44 Benny Santiago	.05
45 *Dante Powell* (USA)	.75
46 Jeff Parrett	.05
47 Wade Boggs	.50
48 Paul Molitor	.50
49 Turk Wendell	.05
50 David Wells	.10
51 Gary Sheffield	.25
52 Kevin Young	.15
53 Nelson Liriano	.05
54 Greg Maddux	1.50
55 Derek Bell	.10
56 *Matt Turner*	.20
57 *Charlie Nelson* (USA)	.10
58 Mike Hampton	.05
59 *Troy O'Leary*	1.00
60 Benji Gil	.15
61 *Mitch Lyden*	.15
62 J.T. Snow	.25
63 Damon Buford	.10
64 Gene Harris	.05
65 Randy Myers	.05
66 Felix Jose	.05
67 *Todd Dunn* (USA)	.10
68 Jimmy Key	.05
69 Pedro Castellano	.05
70 *Mark Merila* (USA)	.10
71 Rich Rodriguez	.05
72 Matt Mieske	.05
73 Pete Incaviglia	.05
74 Carl Everett	.25
75 Jim Abbott	.15
76 Luis Aquino	.05
77 *Rene Arocha*	.15
78 *Jon Shave*	.10
79 *Todd Walker* (USA)	1.00
80 Jack Armstrong	.05
81 Jeff Richardson	.05
82 Blas Minor	.05
83 Dave Winfield	.25
84 Paul O'Neill	.25
85 *Steve Reich* (USA)	.10
86 Chris Hammond	.05
87 *Hilly Hathaway*	.10
88 Fred McGriff	.25
89 *Dave Telgheder*	.10
90 *Richie Lewis*	.15
91 Brent Gates	.10
92 Andre Dawson	.15
93 *Andy Barkett* (USA)	.10
94 Doug Drabek	.05
95 Joe Klink	.05
96 Willie Blair	.05
97 *Danny Graves* (USA)	.75
98 Pat Meares	.05
99 Mike Lansing	.10
100 *Marcos Armas*	.10
101 *Darren Grass* (USA)	.10
102 Chris Jones	.05
103 *Ken Ryan*	.15
104 Ellis Burks	.10
105 Bobby Kelly	.05
106 Dave Magadan	.05
107 *Paul Wilson* (USA)	.20
108 Rob Natal	.05
109 Paul Wagner	.05
110 Jeromy Burnitz	.25
111 Monty Fariss	.05
112 Kevin Mitchell	.05
113 *Scott Pose*	.15
114 Dave Stewart	.05
115 *Russ Johnson* (USA)	.25
116 Armando Reynoso	.05
117 Geronimo Berroa	.05
118 *Woody Williams*	.25
119 *Tim Bogar*	.15
120 *Bob Scafa* (USA)	.15
121 Henry Cotto	.05
122 Gregg Jefferies	.10
123 Norm Charlton	.05
124 *Bret Wagner* (USA)	.05
125 David Cone	.25
126 Daryl Boston	.05
127 Tim Wallach	.05
128 *Mike Martin* (USA)	.10
129 *John Cummings*	.15
130 Ryan Bowen	.05
131 *John Powell* (USA)	.20
132 Checklist 1	.05

1994 Topps

Once again released in two series of 396 cards each, Topps' basic baseball issue for 1994 offers a standard mix of regular player cards, Future Stars, multi-player rookie cards and double-header All-Star cards. On most cards the player photo on front is framed in a home-plate shaped design. The player's name appears in script beneath the photo and a team color-coded strip at bottom carries the team name and position designation. On back is a player photo, a red box at top with biographical details and a marbled panel which carries the stats and a career highlight. Cards are UV coated on each side. Inserts include a gold-foil enhanced parallel card in every pack, plus random Black Gold cards.

	MT
Complete Set (792):	30.00
Complete Factory Set (808):	60.00
Common Player:	.05
Complete Gold Set (792):	75.00
Series 1 or 2 Pack (12):	.75
Series 1 or 2 Wax Box (36):	18.00
1 Mike Piazza (All-Star Rookie)	1.00
2 Bernie Williams	.40
3 Kevin Rogers	.05
4 Paul Carey (Future Star)	.10
5 Ozzie Guillen	.05
6 Derrick May	.05
7 Jose Mesa	.05
8 Todd Hundley	.05
9 Chris Haney	.05
10 John Olerud	.20
11 Andujar Cedeno	.05
12 John Smiley	.05
13 Phil Plantier	.05
14 Willie Banks	.05
15 Jay Bell	.05
16 Doug Henry	.05
17 Lance Blankenship	.05
18 Greg Harris	.05
19 Scott Livingstone	.05
20 Bryan Harvey	.05
21 Wil Cordero (All-Star Rookie)	.10
22 Roger Pavlik	.05
23 Mark Lemke	.05
24 Jeff Nelson	.05
25 Todd Zeile	.05
26 Billy Hatcher	.05
27 Joe Magrane	.05
28 Tony Longmire (Future Star)	.10
29 Omar Daal	.05
30 Kirt Manwaring	.05
31 Melido Perez	.05
32 Tim Hulett	.05
33 Jeff Schwarz	.05
34 Nolan Ryan	1.00
35 Jose Guzman	.05
36 Felix Fermin	.05
37 Jeff Innis	.05
38 Brent Mayne	.05
39 *Huck Flener*	.05
40 Jeff Bagwell	.50
41 Kevin Wickander	.05
42 Ricky Gutierrez	.05
43 Pat Mahomes	.05
44 Jeff King	.05
45 Cal Eldred	.05
46 Craig Paquette	.05
47 Richie Lewis	.05
48 Tony Phillips	.05
49 Armando Reynoso	.05
50 Moises Alou	.20
51 Manuel Lee	.05
52 Otis Nixon	.05
53 Billy Ashley (Future Star)	.10
54 Mark Whiten	.05
55 Jeff Russell	.05
56 Chad Curtis	.05
57 Kevin Stocker	.05
58 Mike Jackson	.05
59 Matt Nokes	.05
60 Chris Bosio	.05
61 Damon Buford	.05
62 Tim Belcher	.05
63 Glenallen Hill	.05
64 Bill Wertz	.05
65 Eddie Murray	.25
66 Tom Gordon	.05
67 Alex Gonzalez (Future Star)	.15
68 Eddie Taubensee	.05
69 Jacob Brumfield	.05
70 Andy Benes	.05
71 Rich Becker (Future Star)	.10
72 Steve Cooke (All-Star Rookie)	.05
73 Billy Spiers	.05
74 Scott Brosius	.10
75 Alan Trammell	.05
76 Luis Aquino	.05
77 Jerald Clark	.05
78 Mel Rojas	.05
79 OF Prospects (Billy Masse, Stanton Cameron, Tim Clark, Craig McClure)	.15
80 Jose Canseco	.40
81 Greg McMichael (All-Star Rookie)	.05
82 Brian Turang	.05
83 Tom Urban	.05
84 Garret Anderson (Future Star)	.15
85 Tony Pena	.05
86 Ricky Jordan	.05
87 Jim Gott	.05
88 Pat Kelly	.05
89 Bud Black	.05
90 Robin Ventura	.20
91 Rick Sutcliffe	.05
92 Jose Bautista	.05
93 Bob Ojeda	.05
94 Phil Hiatt	.05
95 Tim Pugh	.05
96 Randy Knorr	.05
97 Todd Jones (Future Star)	.05
98 Ryan Thompson	.05
99 Tim Mauser	.05
100 Kirby Puckett	.75
101 Mark Dewey	.05
102 B.J. Surhoff	.05
103 Sterling Hitchcock	.05
104 Alex Arias	.05
105 David Wells	.10
106 Daryl Boston	.05
107 Mike Stanton	.05
108 Gary Redus	.05
109a Delino DeShields (red "Expos, 2B")	.15
109b Delino DeShields (yellow "Expos, 2B")	.05
110 Lee Smith	.05
111 Greg Litton	.05
112 Frank Rodriguez (Future Star)	.10
113 Russ Springer	.05
114 Mitch Williams	.05
115 Eric Karros	.15
116 Jeff Brantley	.05
117 Jack Voight	.05
118 Jason Bere	.10
119 Kevin Roberson	.10
120 Jimmy Key	.05
121 Reggie Jefferson	.05
122 Jeremy Burnitz	.15
123 Billy Brewer (Future Star)	.05
124 Willie Canate	.05
125 Greg Swindell	.05
126 Hal Morris	.05
127 Brad Ausmus	.05
128 George Tsamis	.05
129 Denny Neagle	.05
130 Pat Listach	.05
131 Steve Karsay	.05
132 Bret Barberie	.05
133 Mark Leiter	.05
134 Greg Colbrunn	.05
135 David Nied	.05
136 Dean Palmer	.05
137 Steve Avery	.05
138 Bill Haselman	.05
139 Tripp Cromer (Future Star)	.10
140 Frank Viola	.05
141 Rene Gonzales	.05
142 Curt Schilling	.15
143 Tim Wallach	.05
144 Bobby Munoz	.05
145 Brady Anderson	.10
146 Rod Beck	.05
147 Mike LaValliere	.05
148 Greg Hibbard	.05
149 Kenny Lofton	.40
150 Dwight Gooden	.10
151 Greg Gagne	.05
152 Ray McDavid (Future Star)	.10
153 Chris Donnels	.05
154 Dan Wilson	.05
155 Todd Stottlemyre	.10
156 David McCarty	.05
157 Paul Wagner	.05
158 SS Prospects (Orlando Miller, Brandon Wilson, Derek Jeter, Mike Neal)	1.50
159 Mike Fetters	.05
160 Scott Lydy	.05
161 Darrell Whitmore	.05
162 Bob MacDonald	.05
163 Vinny Castilla	.10
164 Denis Boucher	.05

165 Ivan Rodriguez .50
166 Ron Gant .10
167 Tim Davis .05
168 Steve Dixon .05
169 Scott Fletcher .05
170 Terry Mulholland .05
171 Greg Myers .05
172 Brett Butler .05
173 Bob Wickman .05
174 Dave Martinez .05
175 Fernando Valenzuela .05
176 Craig Grebeck .05
177 Shawn Boskie .05
178 Albie Lopez .05
179 Butch Huskey (Future Star) .15
180 George Brett .50
181 Juan Guzman .05
182 Eric Anthony .05
183 Bob Dibble .05
184 Craig Shipley .05
185 Kevin Tapani .05
186 Marcus Moore .05
187 Graeme Lloyd .05
188 Mike Bordick .05
189 Chris Hammond .05
190 Cecil Fielder .05
191 Curtis Leskanic .05
192 Lou Frazier .05
193 Steve Dreyer .05
194 Javier Lopez (Future Star) .25
195 Edgar Martinez .05
196 Allen Watson .10
197 John Flaherty .05
198 Kurt Stillwell .05
199 Danny Jackson .05
200 Cal Ripken, Jr. 1.50
201 Mike Bell (Draft Pick) .05
202 *Alan Benes* (Draft Pick) .25
203 Matt Farner (Draft Pick) .05
204 *Jeff Granger* (Draft Pick) .15
205 *Brooks Kieschnick* (Draft Pick) .20
206 Jeremy Lee (Draft Pick) .05
207 *Charles Peterson* (Draft Pick) .05
208 Andy Rice (Draft Pick) .05
209 *Billy Wagner* (Draft Pick) .30
210 Kelly Wunsch (Draft Pick) .15
211 Tom Candiotti .05
212 Domingo Jean (Draft Pick) .05
213 John Burkett .05
214 George Bell .05
215 Dan Plesac .05
216 Manny Ramirez (Future Star) 1.00
217 Mike Maddux .05
218 Kevin McReynolds .05
219 Pat Borders .05
220 Doug Drabek .05
221 Larry Luebbers .05
222 Trevor Hoffman .10
223 Pat Meares .05
224 Danny Miceli (Future Star) .10
225 Greg Vaughn .15
226 Scott Hemond .05
227 Pat Rapp .05
228 Kirk Gibson .05
229 Lance Painter .05
230 Larry Walker .40
231 Benji Gil (Future Star) .10
232 Mark Wohlers .05
233 Rich Amaral .05
234 Erik Pappas .05
235 Scott Cooper .05
236 Mike Butcher .05
237 OF Prospects (*Curtis Pride*, Shawn Green, Mark Sweeney, Eddie Davis) .50
238 Kim Batiste .05
239 Paul Assenmacher .05
240 Will Clark .25
241 Jose Offerman .05
242 Todd Frohwirth .05
243 Tim Raines .10
244 Rick Wilkins .05
245 Bret Saberhagen .05
246 Thomas Howard .05
247 Stan Belinda .05
248 Rickey Henderson .30
249 Brian Williams .05
250 Barry Larkin .20
251 Jose Valentin (Future Star) .05
252 Lenny Webster .05
253 Blas Minor .05
254 Tim Teufel .05
255 Bobby Witt .05
256 Walt Weiss .05
257 Chad Kreuter .05
258 Roberto Mejia .05
259 Cliff Floyd (Future Star) .15
260 Julio Franco .05
261 Rafael Belliard .05
262 Marc Newfield .05
263 Gerald Perry .05
264 Ken Ryan .05
265 Chili Davis .05
266 Dave West .05
267 Royce Clayton .05
268 Pedro Martinez .50
269 Mark Hutton .05
270 Frank Thomas .75
271 Brad Pennington .05
272 Mike Harkey .05
273 Sandy Alomar .15
274 Dave Gallagher .05
275 Wally Joyner .10
276 Ricky Trlicek .05
277 Al Osuna .05
278 Calvin Reese (Future Star) .15
279 Kevin Higgins .05
280 Rick Aguilera .05
281 Orlando Merced .05
282 Mike Mohler .05
283 John Jaha .10
284 Robb Nen .05
285 Travis Fryman .10
286 Mark Thompson (Future Star) .05
287 Mike Lansing (All-Star Rookie) .10
288 Craig Lefferts .05
289 Damon Berryhill .05
290 Randy Johnson .50
291 Jeff Reed .05
292 Danny Darwin .05
293 J.T. Snow (All-Star Rookie) .10
294 Tyler Green .05
295 Chris Hoiles .05
296 Roger McDowell .05
297 Spike Owen .05
298 Salomon Torres (Future Star) .05
299 Wilson Alvarez .05
300 Ryne Sandberg .40
301 Derek Lilliquist .05
302 Howard Johnson .05
303 Greg Cadaret .05
304 Pat Hentgen .05
305 Craig Biggio .20
306 Scott Service .05
307 Melvin Nieves .05
308 Mike Trombley .05
309 Carlos Garcia (All-Star Rookie) .05
310 Robin Yount .35
311 Marcos Armas .05
312 Rich Rodriguez .05
313 Justin Thompson (Future Star) .05
314 Danny Sheaffer .05
315 Ken Hill .05
316 P Propsects (*Chad Ogea*), (*Duff Brumley*), (*Terrell Wade*), (*Chris Michalak*) .25
317 Cris Carpenter .05
318 Jeff Blauser .05
319 Ted Power .05
320 Ozzie Smith .40
321 John Dopson .05
322 Chris Turner .05
323 Pete Incaviglia .05
324 Alan Mills .05
325 Jody Reed .05
326 Rich Monteleone .05
327 Mark Carreon .05
328 Donn Pall .05
329 Matt Walbeck (Future Star) .05
330 Charles Nagy .05
331 Jeff McKnight .05
332 Jose Lind .05
333 Mike Timlin .05
334 Doug Jones .05
335 Kevin Mitchell .05
336 Luis Lopez .05
337 Shane Mack .05
338 Randy Tomlin .05
339 Matt Mieske .05
340 Mark McGwire 2.00
341 Nigel Wilson (Future Star) .05
342 Danny Gladden .05
343 Mo Sanford .05
344 Sean Berry .05
345 Kevin Brown .15
346 Greg Olson .05
347 Dave Magadan .05
348 Rene Arocha .05
349 Carlos Quintana .05
350 Jim Abbott .05
351 Gary DiSarcina .05
352 Ben Rivera .05
353 Carlos Hernandez .05
354 Darren Lewis .05
355 Harold Reynolds .05
356 Scott Ruffcorn (Future Star) .10
357 Mark Gubicza .05
358 Paul Sorrento .05
359 Anthony Young .05
360 Mark Grace .20
361 Rob Butler .05
362 Kevin Bass .05
363 Eric Helfand (Future Star) .05
364 Derek Bell .05
365 Scott Erickson .10
366 Al Martin .05
367 Ricky Bones .05
368 Jeff Branson .05
369 3B Prospects (Luis Ortiz, David Bell, Jason Giambi), (*George Arias*) .40
370a Benny Santiago .05
370b Mark McLemore (originally checklisted as #379) .05
371 John Doherty .05
372 Joe Girardi .05
373 Tim Scott .05
374 Marvin Freeman .05
375 Deion Sanders .25
376 Roger Salkeld .05
377 Bernard Gilkey .05
378 Tony Fossas .05
379 (Not issued, see #370)
380 Darren Daulton .05
381 Chuck Finley .05
382 Mitch Webster .05
383 Gerald Williams .05
384 Frank Thomas, Fred McGriff (All Star) .30
385 Roberto Alomar, Robby Thompson (All Star) .20
386 Wade Boggs, Matt Williams (All Star) .15
387 Cal Ripken, Jr., Jeff Blauser (All Star) .40
388 Ken Griffey, Jr., Len Dykstra (All Star) .50
389 Juan Gonzalez, Dave Justice (All Star) .30
390 Albert Belle, Barry Bonds (All Star) .30
391 Mike Stanley, Mike Piazza (All Star) .40
392 Jack McDowell, Greg Maddux (All Star) .25
393 Jimmy Key, Tom Glavine (All Star) .10
394 Jeff Montgomery, Randy Myers (All Star) .05
395 Checklist 1 .05
396 Checklist 2 .05
397 Tim Salmon (All-Star Rookie) .25
398 Todd Benzinger .05
399 Frank Castillo .05
400 Ken Griffey, Jr. 2.00
401 John Kruk .05
402 Dave Telgheder .05
403 Gary Gaetti .05
404 Jim Edmonds .15
405 Don Slaught .05
406 Jose Oquendo .05
407 Bruce Ruffin .05
408 Phil Clark .05
409 Joe Klink .05
410 Lou Whitaker .05
411 Kevin Seitzer .05
412 Darrin Fletcher .05
413 Kenny Rogers .05
414 Bill Pecota .05
415 Dave Fleming .05
416 Luis Alicea .05
417 Paul Quantrill .05
418 Damion Easley .05
419 Wes Chamberlain .05
420 Harold Baines .10
421 Scott Radinsky .05
422 Rey Sanchez .05
423 Junior Ortiz .05
424 Jeff Kent .05
425 Brian McRae .05
426 Ed Sprague .05
427 Tom Edens .05
428 Willie Greene .05
429 Bryan Hickerson .05
430 Dave Winfield .25
431 Pedro Astacio .05
432 Mike Gallego .05
433 Dave Burba .05
434 Bob Walk .05
435 Darryl Hamilton .05
436 Vince Horsman .05
437 Bob Natal .05
438 Mike Henneman .05
439 Willie Blair .05
440 Denny Martinez .05
441 Dan Peltier .05
442 Tony Tarasco .05
443 John Cummings .05
444 Geronimo Pena .05
445 Aaron Sele .10
446 Stan Javier .05
447 Mike Williams .05
448 1B Prospects (Greg Pirkl, Roberto Petagine, D.J. Boston, Shawn Wooten) .10
449 Jim Poole .05
450 Carlos Baerga .05
451 Bob Scanlan .05
452 Lance Johnson .05
453 Eric Hillman .05
454 Keith Miller .05
455 Dave Stewart .05
456 Pete Harnisch .05
457 Roberto Kelly .05
458 Tim Worrell .05
459 Pedro Munoz .05
460 Orel Hershiser .05
461 Randy Velarde .05
462 Trevor Wilson .05
463 Jerry Goff .05
464 Bill Wegman .05
465 Dennis Eckersley .10
466 Jeff Conine (All-Star Rookie) .10
467 Joe Boever .05
468 Dante Bichette .15
469 Jeff Shaw .05
470 Rafael Palmeiro .25
471 *Phil Leftwich* .10
472 Jay Buhner .10
473 Bob Tewksbury .05
474 Tim Naehring .05
475 Tom Glavine .15
476 Dave Hollins .05
477 Arthur Rhodes .05
478 Joey Cora .05
479 Mike Morgan .05
480 Albert Belle .40
481 John Franco .05
482 Hipolito Pichardo .05
483 Duane Ward .05
484 Luis Gonzalez .10
485 Joe Oliver .05
486 Wally Whitehurst .05
487 Mike Benjamin .05
488 Eric Davis .05
489 Scott Kamieniecki .05
490 Kent Hrbek .05
491 *John Hope* .15
492 Jesse Orosco .05
493 Troy Neel .05
494 Ryan Bowen .05
495 Mickey Tettleton .05
496 Chris Jones .05
497 John Wetteland .05
498 David Hulse .05
499 Greg Maddux 1.00
500 Bo Jackson .10

501 Donovan Osborne .05
502 Mike Greenwell .05
503 Steve Frey .05
504 Jim Eisenreich .05
505 Robby Thompson .05
506 Leo Gomez .05
507 Dave Staton .05
508 Wayne Kirby (All-Star Rookie) .05
509 Tim Bogar .05
510 David Cone .15
511 Devon White .05
512 Xavier Hernandez .05
513 Tim Costo .05
514 Gene Harris .05
515 Jack McDowell .05
516 Kevin Gross .05
517 Scott Leius .05
518 Lloyd McClendon .05
519 *Alex Diaz* .10
520 Wade Boggs .25
521 Bob Welch .05
522 Henry Cotto .05
523 Mike Moore .05
524 Tim Laker .05
525 Andres Galarraga .20
526 Jamie Moyer .05
527 2B Prospects (Norberto Martin, Ruben Santana, Jason Hardtke, Chris Sexton) .10
528 Sid Bream .05
529 Erik Hanson .05
530 Ray Lankford .05
531 Rob Deer .05
532 Rod Correia .05
533 Roger Mason .05
534 Mike Devereaux .05
535 Jeff Montgomery .05
536 Dwight Smith .05
537 Jeremy Hernandez .05
538 Ellis Burks .05
539 Bobby Jones .15
540 Paul Molitor .40
541 Jeff Juden .05
542 Chris Sabo .05
543 Larry Casian .05
544 Jeff Gardner .05
545 Ramon Martinez .10
546 Paul O'Neill .15
547 Steve Hosey .05
548 Dave Nilsson .05
549 Ron Darling .05
550 Matt Williams .20
551 Jack Armstrong .05
552 Bill Krueger .05
553 Freddie Benavides .05
554 Jeff Fassero .05
555 Chuck Knoblauch .15
556 Guillermo Velasquez .05
557 Joel Johnston .05
558 Tom Lampkin .05
559 Todd Van Poppel .05
560 Gary Sheffield .15
561 Skeeter Barnes .05
562 Darren Holmes .05
563 John Vander Wal .05
564 Mike Ignasiak .05
565 Fred McGriff .20
566 Luis Polonia .05
567 Mike Perez .05
568 John Valentin .05
569 Mike Felder .05
570 Tommy Greene .05
571 David Segui .05
572 Roberto Hernandez .05
573 Steve Wilson .05
574 Willie McGee .05
575 Randy Myers .05
576 Darrin Jackson .05
577 Eric Plunk .05
578 Mike MacFarlane .05
579 Doug Brocail .05
580 Steve Finley .05
581 John Roper .05
582 Danny Cox .05
583 Chip Hale .05
584 Scott Bullett .05
585 Kevin Reimer .05
586 Brent Gates .05
587 Matt Turner .05
588 Rich Rowland .05
589 Kent Bottenfield .05
590 Marquis Grissom .10
591 Doug Strange .05
592 Jay Howell .05
593 Omar Vizquel .10
594 Rheal Cormier .05
595 Andre Dawson .15
596 Hilly Hathaway .05
597 Todd Pratt .05
598 Mike Mussina .20
599 Alex Fernandez .10
600 Don Mattingly .75
601 Frank Thomas (Measures of Greatness) .30
602 Ryne Sandberg (Measures of Greatness) .20
603 Wade Boggs (Measures of Greatness) .15
604 Cal Ripken, Jr. (Measures of Greatness) .75
605 Barry Bonds (Measures of Greatness) .25
606 Ken Griffey, Jr. (Measures of Greatness) 1.00
607 Kirby Puckett (Measures of Greatness) .25
608 Darren Daulton (Measures of Greatness) .05
609 Paul Molitor (Measures of Greatness) .15
610 Terry Steinbach .05
611 Todd Worrell .05
612 Jim Thome .40
613 Chuck McElroy .05
614 John Habyan .05
615 Sid Fernandez .05
616 OF Prospects (Eddie Zambrano , Glenn Murray, Chad Mottola), *(Jermaine Allensworth)* .25
617 Steve Bedrosian .05
618 Rob Ducey .05
619 Tom Browning .05
620 Tony Gwynn .75
621 Carl Willis .05
622 Kevin Young .05
623 Rafael Novoa .05
624 Jerry Browne .05
625 Charlie Hough .05
626 Chris Gomez .05
627 Steve Reed .05
628 Kirk Rueter .05
629 Matt Whiteside .05
630 Dave Justice .25
631 Brad Holman .05
632 Brian Jordan .05
633 Scott Bankhead .05
634 Torey Lovullo .05
635 Len Dykstra .05
636 Ben McDonald .05
637 Steve Howe .05
638 Jose Vizcaino .05
639 Bill Swift .05
640 Darryl Strawberry .15
641 Steve Farr .05
642 Tom Kramer .05
643 Joe Orsulak .05
644 Tom Henke .05
645 Joe Carter .05
646 Ken Caminiti .15
647 Reggie Sanders .10
648 Andy Ashby .10
649 Derek Parks .05
650 Andy Van Slyke .05
651 Juan Bell .05
652 Roger Smithberg .05
653 Chuck Carr .05
654 Bill Gullickson .05
655 Charlie Hayes .05
656 Chris Nabholz .05
657 Karl Rhodes .05
658 Pete Smith .05
659 Bret Boone .05
660 Gregg Jefferies .10
661 Bob Zupcic .05
662 Steve Sax .05
663 Mariano Duncan .05
664 Jeff Tackett .05
665 Mark Langston .05
666 Steve Buechele .05
667 Candy Maldonado .05
668 Woody Williams .05
669 Tim Wakefield .05
670 Danny Tartabull .05
671 Charlie O'Brien .05
672 Felix Jose .05
673 Bobby Ayala .05
674 Scott Servais .05
675 Roberto Alomar .40
676 Pedro Martinez .05
677 Eddie Guardado .05
678 Mark Lewis .05
679 Jaime Navarro .05
680 Ruben Sierra .05
681 Rick Renteria .05
682 Storm Davis .05
683 Cory Snyder .05
684 Ron Karkovice .05
685 Juan Gonzalez .50
686 C Prospects (Chris Howard, Carlos Delgado, Jason Kendall, Paul Bako) .50
687 John Smoltz .15
688 Brian Dorsett .05
689 Omar Olivares .05
690 Mo Vaughn .30
691 Joe Grahe .05
692 Mickey Morandini .05
693 Tino Martinez .10
694 Brian Barnes .05
695 Mike Stanley .05
696 Mark Clark .05
697 Dave Hansen .05
698 Willie Wilson .05
699 Pete Schourek .05
700 Barry Bonds .45
701 Kevin Appier .05
702 Tony Fernandez .05
703 Darryl Kile .05
704 Archi Cianfrocco .05
705 Jose Rijo .05
706 Brian Harper .05
707 Zane Smith .05
708 Dave Henderson .05
709 Angel Miranda .05
710 Orestes Destrade .05
711 Greg Gohr .05
712 Eric Young .05
713 P Prospects (Todd Williams, Ron Watson, Kirk Bullinger, Mike Welch) .15
714 Tim Spehr .05
715 Hank Aaron (20th Anniversary #715) .50
716 Nate Minchey .05
717 Mike Blowers .05
718 Kent Mercker .05
719 Tom Pagnozzi .05
720 Roger Clemens .75
721 Eduardo Perez .05
722 Milt Thompson .05
723 Gregg Olson .05
724 Kirk McCaskill .05
725 Sammy Sosa 1.00
726 Alvaro Espinoza .05
727 Henry Rodriguez .05
728 Jim Leyritz .05
729 Steve Scarsone .05
730 Bobby Bonilla .10
731 Chris Gwynn .05
732 Al Leiter .10
733 Bip Roberts .05
734 Mark Portugal .05
735 Terry Pendleton .05
736 Dave Valle .05
737 Paul Kilgus .05
738 Greg Harris .05
739 *Jon Ratliff* (Draft Pick) .15
740 *Kirk Presley* (Draft Pick) .10
741 *Josue Estrada* (Draft Pick) .10
742 *Wayne Gomes* (Draft Pick) .20
743 *Pat Watkins* (Draft Pick) .15
744 *Jamey Wright* (Draft Pick) .20
745 *Jay Powell* (Draft Pick) .15
746 *Ryan McGuire* (Draft Pick) .15
747 *Marc Barcelo* (Draft Pick) .10
748 *Sloan Smith* (Draft Pick) .15
749 *John Wasdin* (Draft Pick) .15
750 Marc Valdes (Draft Pick) .10
751 *Dan Ehler* (Draft Pick) .10
752 *Andre King* (Draft Pick) .15
753 *Greg Keagle* (Draft Pick) .20
754 *Jason Myers* (Draft Pick) .10
755 *Dax Winslett* (Draft Pick) .10
756 *Casey Whitten* (Draft Pick) .15
757 *Tony Fuduric* (Draft Pick) .10
758 *Greg Norton* (Draft Pick) .10
759 *Jeff D'Amico* (Draft Pick) .10
760 *Ryan Hancock* (Draft Pick) .15
761 *David Cooper* (Draft Pick) .10
762 *Kevin Orie* (Draft Pick) .15
763 John O'Donoghue, Mike Oquist (Coming Attractions) .10
764 Cory Bailey, Scott Hatteberg (Coming Attractions) .10
765 Mark Holzemer, Paul Swingle (Coming Attractions) .10
766 James Baldwin, Rod Bolton (Coming Attractions) .15
767 *Jerry DiPoto* *,Julian Tavarez* (Coming Attractions) .20
768 Danny Bautista, Sean Bergman (Coming Attractions) .10
769 Bob Hamelin, Joe Vitiello (Coming Attractions) .20
770 Mark Kiefer, Troy O'Leary (Coming Attractions) .15
771 Denny Hocking, Oscar Munoz (Coming Attractions) .15
772 Russ Davis, Brien Taylor (Coming Attractions) .20
773 Kurt Abbott, Miguel Jimenez (Coming Attractions) .20
774 Kevin King, Eric Plantenberg (Coming Attractions) .15
775 Jon Shave, Desi Wilson (Coming Attractions) .15
776 Domingo Cedeno, Paul Spoljaric (Coming Attractions) .10
777 Chipper Jones, Ryan Klesko (Coming Attractions) .75
778 Steve Trachsel, Turk Wendell (Coming Attractions) .20
779 Johnny Ruffin, Jerry Spradlin (Coming Attractions) .10
780 Jason Bates, John Burke (Coming Attractions) .15
781 Carl Everett, Dave Weathers (Coming Attractions) .35
782 Gary Mota, James Mouton (Coming Attractions) .15
783 Raul Mondesi, Ben Van Ryn (Coming Attractions) .25
784 Gabe White, Rondell White (Coming Attractions) .25
785 Brook Fordyce, Bill Pulsipher (Coming Attractions) .20
786 Kevin Foster, Gene Schall (Coming Attractions) .10
787 Rich Aude, Midre Cummings (Coming Attractions) .15
788 Brian Barber, Richard Batchelor (Coming Attractions) .10
789 *Brian Johnson*, Scott Sanders (Coming Attractions) .10
790 Rikkert Faneyte, J.R. Phillips (Coming Attractions) .10
791 Checklist 3 .05
792 Checklist 4 .05

1994 Topps Gold

This premium parallel set was issued as inserts in virtually all forms of Topps packaging. Identical in all other ways to the regular Topps cards, the Gold version replaces the white or black Topps logo on front with a gold-foil "Topps Gold" logo, and prints either the player name or card title in gold foil. The four checklist cards from the regular issue are replaced with cards of players not found in the regular Topps set.

	MT
Complete Set (792):	75.00
Common Player:	.15

(Star cards valued at 4X-5X corresponding cards in regular Topps issue)

1994 Topps Black Gold

The Black Gold insert set returned for 1994 randomly included in all types of Topps packaging. Single Black Gold cards, as well as cards redeemable by mail for 11, 22 or 44 Black Gold cards, were produced. The basic single-player card features an action photo, the background of which has been almost completely blacked out. At top is the team name in black letters against a gold prismatic foil background. The player name at bottom is in the same gold foil. On back, bordered in white, is a background which fades from black at top to gray at the bottom and is gridded with white lines. To the left is another color player action photo. The Topps Black Gold logo and player name appear in gold foil; the latter printed on a simulated wooden board "hanging" from the top of the card. A second hanging plank has player stats and rankings from the 1993 season. The multi-card redemption cards come in two versions. The type found in packs has all 11, 22 or 44 of the cards pictured on front in miniature and redemption details printed on back. A second version, returned with the single cards won, has on back a checklist and non-redemption notice. Stated odds of winning Black Gold cards were one in 72 packs for single cards; one in 180 packs for 11-card winners and one in 720 packs (one per foil-pack case) for a 22-card winner.

		MT
Complete Set (44):		25.00
Complete Series 1 (22):		15.00
Complete Series 2 (22):		10.00
Common Player:		.25
1	Roberto Alomar	.50
2	Carlos Baerga	.25
3	Albert Belle	.65
4	Joe Carter	.25
5	Cecil Fielder	.25
6	Travis Fryman	.25
7	Juan Gonzalez	.75
8	Ken Griffey, Jr.	4.00
9	Chris Hoiles	.25
10	Randy Johnson	.40
11	Kenny Lofton	.40
12	Jack McDowell	.25
13	Paul Molitor	.50
14	Jeff Montgomery	.25
15	John Olerud	.30
16	Rafael Palmeiro	.40
17	Kirby Puckett	1.00
18	Cal Ripken, Jr.	3.00
19	Tim Salmon	.40
20	Mike Stanley	.25
21	Frank Thomas	.75
22	Robin Ventura	.30
23	Jeff Bagwell	1.00
24	Jay Bell	.25
25	Craig Biggio	.35
26	Jeff Blauser	.25
27	Barry Bonds	.75
28	Darren Daulton	.25
29	Len Dykstra	.25
30	Andres Galarraga	.25
31	Ron Gant	.25
32	Tom Glavine	.30
33	Mark Grace	.40
34	Marquis Grissom	.25
35	Gregg Jefferies	.25
36	Dave Justice	.35
37	John Kruk	.25
38	Greg Maddux	1.50
39	Fred McGriff	.40
40	Randy Myers	.25
41	Mike Piazza	2.00
42	Sammy Sosa	2.00
43	Robby Thompson	.25
44	Matt Williams	.30
---	Winner A	.75
---	Winner B	.75
---	Winner C	.75
---	Winner D	.75
---	Winner A/B	1.00
---	Winner C/D	1.00
---	Winner A/B/C/D	1.00

1994 Topps Traded

Topps Traded consists of 132 cards featuring many top prospects and rookies, as well as traded veterans. Also included with this boxed set was an eight-card Topps Finest subset, including six MVPs and two Rookie of the Year cards. Regular cards have the same design as the previously released 1994 Topps set. Players are featured on a white bordered card, with their name across the bottom in white. "Anatomy of a Trade" is a two-card subset that includes Roberto Kelly/Deion Sanders and Pedro Martinez/Delino DeShields on a split, puzzle-like front. There is also a Prospect card, showcasing a top prospect from AAA, AA and A, as well as a top-rated draft pick. In addition, there are 12 Draft Pick cards included in the Topps Traded set. Finally, there are two cards that pay tribute to Ryne Sandberg, one in a Phillies uniform, one with the Cubs.

		MT
Complete Set (132):		60.00
Comp. Factory Set (140):		70.00
Common Player:		.05
1	Paul Wilson (Draft Pick)	.25
2	Bill Taylor	.05
3	Dan Wilson	.10
4	Mark Smith	.05
5	Toby Borland	.10
6	Dave Clark	.05
7	Denny Martinez	.05
8	Dave Gallagher	.05
9	Josias Manzanillo	.05
10	Brian Anderson	.10
11	Damon Berryhill	.05
12	Alex Cole	.05
13	Jacob Shumate (Draft Pick)	.15
14	Oddibe McDowell	.05
15	Willie Banks	.05
16	Jerry Browne	.05
17	Donnie Elliott	.05
18	Ellis Burks	.05
19	Chuck McElroy	.05
20	Luis Polonia	.05
21	Brian Harper	.05
22	Mark Portugal	.05
23	Dave Henderson	.05
24	Mark Acre	.15
25	Julio Franco	.05
26	Darren Hall	.05
27	Eric Anthony	.05
28	Sid Fernandez	.05
29	Rusty Greer	5.00
30	Riccardo Ingram	.15
31	Gabe White	.10
32	Tim Belcher	.05
33	*Terrence Long* (Draft Pick)	1.50
34	Mark Dalesandro	.10
35	Mike Kelly	.05
36	Jack Morris	.05
37	Jeff Brantley	.05
38	Larry Barnes (Draft Pick)	.15
39	Brian Hunter	.10
40	Otis Nixon	.05
41	Bret Wagner (Draft pick)	.05
42	Anatomy of a Trade (Pedro Martinez, Delino DeShields)	.25
43	Heathcliff Slocumb	.05
44	*Ben Grieve* (Draft Pick)	30.00
45	John Hudek	.15
46	Shawon Dunston	.05
47	Greg Colbrunn	.05
48	Joey Hamilton	.25
49	Marvin Freeman	.05
50	Terry Mulholland	.05
51	Keith Mitchell	.05
52	Dwight Smith	.05
53	Shawn Boskie	.05
54	*Kevin Witt* (Draft Pick)	1.50
55	Ron Gant	.15
56	1994 Prospects (Trenidad Hubbard, Jason Schmidt, Larry Sutton, Stephen Larkin)	1.00
57	Jody Reed	.05
58	Rick Helling	.05
59	John Powell (Draft Pick)	.10
60	Eddie Murray	.35
61	Joe Hall	.10
62	Jorge Fabregas	.10
63	Mike Mordecai	.10
64	Ed Vosberg	.05
65	Rickey Henderson	.25
66	Tim Grieve (Draft pick)	.15
67	Jon Lieber	.05
68	Chris Howard	.05
69	Matt Walbeck	.05
70	Chan Ho Park	4.00
71	Bryan Eversgerd	.10
72	John Dettmer	.05
73	Erik Hanson	.05
74	Mike Thurman (Draft pick)	.15
75	Bobby Ayala	.05
76	Rafael Palmeiro	.40
77	Bret Boone	.15
78	Paul Shuey (Future Star)	.10
79	Kevin Foster	.10
80	Dave Magadan	.05
81	Bip Roberts	.05
82	Howard Johnson	.05
83	Xavier Hernandez	.05
84	Ross Powell	.05
85	*Doug Million* (Draft Pick)	.05
86	Geronimo Berroa	.05
87	*Mark Farris* (Draft Pick)	.25
88	Butch Henry	.05
89	Junior Felix	.05
90	Bo Jackson	.10
91	Hector Carrasco	.10
92	Charlie O'Brien	.05
93	Omar Vizquel	.10
94	David Segui	.10
95	Dustin Hermanson (Draft Pick)	.50
96	Gar Finnvold	.05
97	Dave Stevens	.05
98	Corey Pointer (Draft Pick)	.15
99	Felix Fermin	.05
100	Lee Smith	.05
101	Reid Ryan (Draft Pick)	.15
102	Bobby Munoz	.05
103	Anatomy of a Trade (Deion Sanders, Roberto Kelly)	.10
104	Turner Ward	.05
105	William Van Landingham	.05
106	Vince Coleman	.05
107	Stan Javier	.05

108 Darrin Jackson .05
109 C.J. Nitkowski (Draft Pick) .10
110 Anthony Young .05
111 Kurt Miller .05
112 *Paul Konerko* (Draft Pick) 10.00
113 Walt Weiss .05
114 Daryl Boston .05
115 Will Clark .40
116 *Matt Smith* (Draft Pick) .25
117 Mark Leiter .05
118 Gregg Olson .05
119 Tony Pena .05
120 Jose Vizcaino .05
121 Rick White .10
122 Rich Rowland .05
123 Jeff Reboulet .10
124 Greg Hibbard .05
125 Chris Sabo .05
126 Doug Jones .05
127 Tony Fernandez .05
128 Carlos Reyes .10
129 Kevin Brown (Draft Pick) .15
130 Commemorative (Ryne Sandberg) 1.00
131 Commemorative (Ryne Sandberg) 1.00
132 Checklist 1-132 .05

1994 Topps Traded Finest Inserts

Eight Topps Finest cards were included in the 1994 Topps Traded set. Cards picture the player on a blue and gold Finest card. Either Rookie of the Year or MVP is printed across the bottom on the opposite side of the player's name, indicating the player's candidacy for such an award in 1994. Backs offer a portrait photo, stats through the All-Star break and comments on the player's season to that point.

	MT
Complete Set (8):	8.00
Common Player:	1.50
1 Greg Maddux	1.50
2 Mike Piazza	2.00
3 Matt Williams	.25
4 Raul Mondesi	.50
5 Ken Griffey Jr.	3.00
6 Kenny Lofton	.50
7 Frank Thomas	1.50
8 Manny Ramirez	1.00

1995 Topps

Topps 1995 baseball arrived offering Cyberstats, which projected full-season statistics for the strike shortened year, as well as League Leaders and Stadium Club First Day Issue preproduction inserts. The entire Series I set was composed of 396 cards, including subsets like 1994 Draft Picks, Star Tracks, a Babe Ruth commemorative card and the Topps All-Stars, featuring two players per card at each position, as selected by Topps. Regular cards have a jagged white border around the color picture of the player, with his name in gold foil under the picture. Series II concluded the Cyberstats inserts and added 264 cards to the regular set. Subsets in Series II included a continuation of the Draft Picks from Series I, as well as two-player On Deck cards and four-player Prospects cards, arranged by position.

	MT
Complete Set (660):	40.00
Complete Series 1 (396):	20.00
Complete Series 2 (264):	20.00
Common Player:	.05
Series 1 or 2 Pack (15):	1.25
Series 1 or 2 Wax Box (36):	35.00

1 Frank Thomas 1.00
2 Mickey Morandini .05
3a Babe Ruth (100th Birthday, no gold "Topps" logo) 2.00
3b Babe Ruth (100th Birthday, gold "Topps" logo) 2.00
4 Scott Cooper .05
5 David Cone .15
6 Jacob Shumate (Draft Pick) .10
7 Trevor Hoffman .10
8 Shane Mack .05
9 Delino DeShields .05
10 Matt Williams .25
11 Sammy Sosa 1.50
12 Gary DiSarcina .05
13 Kenny Rogers .05
14 Jose Vizcaino .05
15 Lou Whitaker .05
16 Ron Darling .05
17 Dave Nilsson .05
18 Chris Hammond .05
19 Sid Bream .05
20 Denny Martinez .05
21 Orlando Merced .05
22 John Wetteland .05
23 Mike Devereaux .05
24 Rene Arocha .05
25 Jay Buhner .10
26 Darren Holmes .05
27 Hal Morris .05
28 *Brian Buchanan* (Draft Pick) .15
29 Keith Miller .05
30 Paul Molitor .40
31 Dave West .05
32 Tony Tarasco .05
33 Scott Sanders .05
34 Eddie Zambrano .05
35 Ricky Bones .05
36 John Valentin .05
37 Kevin Tapani .05
38 Tim Wallach .05
39 Darren Lewis .05
40 Travis Fryman .10
41 Mark Leiter .05
42 Jose Bautista .05
43 Pete Smith .05
44 Bret Barberie .05
45 Dennis Eckersley .10
46 Ken Hill .05
47 Chad Ogea (Star Track) .12
48 Pete Harnisch .05
49 James Baldwin (Future Star) .15
50 Mike Mussina .30
51 Al Martin .05
52 Mark Thompson (Star Track) .05
53 Matt Smith (Draft Pick) .10
54 Joey Hamilton (All Star Rookie) .10
55 Edgar Martinez .05
56 John Smiley .05
57 Rey Sanchez .05
58 Mike Timlin .05
59 Ricky Bottalico (Star Track) .10
60 Jim Abbott .05
61 Mike Kelly .05
62 Brian Jordan .15
63 Ken Ryan .10
64 Matt Mieske .05
65 Rick Aguilera .05
66 Ismael Valdes .05
67 Royce Clayton .05
68 Junior Felix .05
69 Harold Reynolds .05
70 Juan Gonzalez .75
71 Kelly Stinnett .05
72 Carlos Reyes .05
73 Dave Weathers .05
74 Mel Rojas .05
75 Doug Drabek .05
76 Charles Nagy .05
77 Tim Raines .10
78 Midre Cummings .05
79 1B Prospects (Gene Schall), *(Scott Talanoa)*, *(Harold Williams)*, *(Ray Brown)* .15
80 Rafael Palmeiro .25
81 Charlie Hayes .05
82 Ray Lankford .15
83 Tim Davis .05
84 *C.J. Nitkowski* (Draft Pick) .15
85 Andy Ashby .05
86 Gerald Williams .05
87 Terry Shumpert .05
88 Heathcliff Slocumb .05
89 Domingo Cedeno .05
90 Mark Grace .20
91 *Brad Woodall* (Star Track) .10
92 Gar Finnvold .05
93 Jaime Navarro .05
94 Carlos Hernandez .05
95 Mark Langston .05
96 Chuck Carr .05
97 Mike Gardiner .05
98 David McCarty .05
99 Cris Carpenter .05
100 Barry Bonds .60
101 David Segui .05
102 Scott Brosius .05
103 Mariano Duncan .05
104 Kenny Lofton .30
105 Ken Caminiti .20
106 Darrin Jackson .05
107 Jim Poole .05
108 Wil Cordero .05
109 Danny Miceli .05
110 Walt Weiss .05
111 Tom Pagnozzi .05
112 Terrence Long (Draft Pick) .05
113 Bret Boone .05
114 Daryl Boston .05
115 Wally Joyner .10
116 Rob Butler .05
117 Rafael Belliard .05
118 Luis Lopez .05
119 Tony Fossas .05
120 Len Dykstra .05
121 Mike Morgan .05
122 Denny Hocking .05
123 Kevin Gross .05
124 Todd Benzinger .05
125 John Doherty .05
126 Eduardo Perez .05
127 Dan Smith .05
128 Joe Orsulak .05
129 Brent Gates .05
130 Jeff Conine .10
131 Doug Henry .05
132 Paul Sorrento .05
133 Mike Hampton .05
134 Tim Spehr .05
135 Julio Franco .05
136 Mike Dyer .05
137 Chris Sabo .05
138 Rheal Cormier .05
139 Paul Konerko (Draft Pick) .75
140 Dante Bichette .15
141 Chuck McElroy .05
142 Mike Stanley .05
143 Bob Hamelin (All Star Rookie) .05
144 Tommy Greene .05
145 John Smoltz .15
146 Ed Sprague .05
147 Ray McDavid (Star Track) .10
148 Otis Nixon .05
149 Turk Wendell .05
150 Chris James .05
151 Derek Parks .05
152 Jose Offerman .05
153 Tony Clark (Future Star) .50
154 Chad Curtis .05
155 Mark Portugal .05
156 Bill Pulsipher (Future Star) .15
157 Troy Neel .05
158 Dave Winfield .15
159 Bill Wegman .05
160 Benny Santiago .05
161 Jose Mesa .05
162 Luis Gonzalez .10
163 Alex Fernandez .10
164 Freddie Benavides .05
165 Ben McDonald .05
166 Blas Minor .05
167 Bret Wagner (Draft Pick) .05
168 Mac Suzuki (Future Star) .10
169 Roberto Mejia .05
170 Wade Boggs .30
171 Calvin Reese (Future Star) .15
172 Hipolito Pichardo .05
173 Kim Batiste .05
174 Darren Hall .05
175 Tom Glavine .15
176 Phil Plantier .05
177 Chris Howard .05
178 Karl Rhodes .05
179 LaTroy Hawkins (Future Star) .15
180 Raul Mondesi (All Star Rookie) .40
181 Jeff Reed .05
182 Milt Cuyler .05
183 Jim Edmonds .15
184 Hector Fajardo .05
185 Jeff Kent .05
186 Wilson Alvarez .05
187 Geronimo Berroa .05
188 Billy Spiers .05
189 Derek Lilliquist .05
190 Craig Biggio .20
191 Roberto Hernandez .05
192 Bob Natal .05
193 Bobby Ayala .05
194 *Travis Miller* (Draft Pick) .20
195 Bob Tewksbury .05
196 Rondell White .15
197 Steve Cooke .05
198 Jeff Branson .05
199 Derek Jeter (Future Star) 2.00
200 Tim Salmon .25
201 Steve Frey .05
202 Kent Mercker .05
203 Randy Johnson .40
204 Todd Worrell .05
205 Mo Vaughn .30
206 Howard Johnson .05
207 John Wasdin (Future Star) .10

208 Eddie Williams .05
209 Tim Belcher .05
210 Jeff Montgomery .05
211 Kirt Manwaring .05
212 Ben Grieve (Draft Pick) 1.50
213 Pat Hentgen .05
214 Shawon Dunston .05
215 Mike Greenwell .05
216 Alex Diaz .05
217 Pat Mahomes .05
218 Dave Hanson .05
219 Kevin Rogers .05
220 Cecil Fielder .10
221 Andrew Lorraine (Star Track) .10
222 Jack Armstrong .05
223 Todd Hundley .15
224 Mark Acre .05
225 Darrell Whitmore .05
226 Randy Milligan .05
227 Wayne Kirby .05
228 Darryl Kile .05
229 Bob Zupcic .05
230 Jay Bell .05
231 Dustin Hermanson (Draft Pick) .15
232 Harold Baines .05
233 Alan Benes (Future Star) .15
234 Felix Fermin .05
235 Ellis Burks .05
236 Jeff Brantley .05
237 OF Prospects (Brian Hunter, Jose Malave, Shane Pullen), *(Karim Garcia)* .40
238 Matt Nokes .05
239 Ben Rivera .05
240 Joe Carter .10
241 Jeff Granger (Star Track) .05
242 Terry Pendleton .05
243 Melvin Nieves .05
244 Frank Rodriguez (Future Star) .10
245 Darryl Hamilton .05
246 Brooks Kieschnick (Future Star) .25
247 Todd Hollandsworth (Future Star) .15
248 Joe Rosselli (Future Star) .10
249 Bill Gullickson .05
250 Chuck Knoblauch .15
251 Kurt Miller (Star Track) .05
252 Bobby Jones .10
253 Lance Blankenship .05
254 Matt Whiteside .05
255 Darrin Fletcher .05
256 Eric Plunk .05
257 Shane Reynolds .10
258 Norberto Martin .05
259 Mike Thurman (Draft Pick) .05
260 Andy Van Slyke .05
261 Dwight Smith .05
262 Allen Watson .10
263 Dan Wilson .05
264 Brent Mayne .05
265 Bip Roberts .05
266 Sterling Hitchcock .05
267 Alex Gonzalez (Star Track) .15
268 Greg Harris .05
269 Ricky Jordan .05
270 Johnny Ruffin .05
271 Mike Stanton .05
272 Rich Rowland .05
273 Steve Trachsel .10
274 Pedro Munoz .05
275 Ramon Martinez .10
276 Dave Henderson .05
277 Chris Gomez (All Star Rookie) .10
278 Joe Grahe .05
279 Rusty Greer .05
280 John Franco .05
281 Mike Bordick .05
282 Jeff D'Amico (Future Star) .10
283 Dave Magadan .05
284 Tony Pena .05
285 Greg Swindell .05
286 Doug Million (Draft Pick) .05
287 Gabe White (Star Track) .15
288 Trey Beamon (Future Star) .15
289 Arthur Rhodes .05
290 Juan Guzman .05
291 Jose Oquendo .05
292 Willie Blair .05
293 Eddie Taubensee .05
294 Steve Howe .05
295 Greg Maddux 1.50
296 Mike MacFarlane .05
297 Curt Schilling .10
298 Phil Clark .05
299 Woody Williams .05
300 Jose Canseco .50
301 Aaron Sele .10
302 Carl Willis .05
303 Steve Buechele .05
304 Dave Burba .05
305 Orel Hershiser .05
306 Damion Easley .05
307 Mike Henneman .05
308 Josias Manzanillo .05
309 Kevin Seitzer .05
310 Ruben Sierra .05
311 Bryan Harvey .05
312 Jim Thome .25
313 *Ramon Castro* (Draft Pick) .15
314 Lance Johnson .05
315 Marquis Grissom .10
316 SP Prospects (Terrell Wade, Juan Acevedo, Matt Arrandale), *(Eddie Priest)* .10
317 Paul Wagner .05
318 Jamie Moyer .05
319 Todd Zeile .10
320 Chris Bosio .05
321 Steve Reed .05
322 Erik Hanson .05
323 Luis Polonia .05
324 Ryan Klesko .20
325 Kevin Appier .05
326 Jim Eisenreich .05
327 Randy Knorr .05
328 Craig Shipley .05
329 Tim Naehring .05
330 Randy Myers .05
331 Alex Cole .05
332 Jim Gott .05
333 Mike Jackson .05
334 John Flaherty .05
335 Chili Davis .05
336 Benji Gil (Star Track) .10
337a Jason Jacome (No Diamond Vision logo on back photo) .15
337b Jason Jacome (Diamond Vision logo on back photo) .15
338 Stan Javier .05
339 Mike Fetters .05
340 Rick Renteria .05
341 Kevin Witt (Draft Pick) .05
342 Scott Servais .05
343 Craig Grebeck .05
344 Kirk Rueter .05
345 Don Slaught .05
346 *Armando Benitez* (Star Track) .15
347 Ozzie Smith .40
348 Mike Blowers .05
349 Armando Reynoso .05
350 Barry Larkin .15
351 Mike Williams .05
352 Scott Kamieniecki .05
353 Gary Gaetti .05
354 Todd Stottlemyre .05
355 Fred McGriff .20
356 Tim Mauser .05
357 Chris Gwynn .05
358 Frank Castillo .05
359 Jeff Reboulet .10
360 Roger Clemens .75
361 Mark Carreon .05
362 Chad Kreuter .05
363 Mark Farris (Draft Pick) .10
364 Bob Welch .05
365 Dean Palmer .05
366 Jeromy Burnitz .05
367 B.J. Surhoff .05
368 Mike Butcher .05
369 RP Prospects (Brad Clontz, Steve Phoenix, Scott Gentile, Bucky Buckles) .10
370 Eddie Murray .20
371 Orlando Miller (Star Track) .05
372 Ron Karkovice .05
373 Richie Lewis .05
374 Lenny Webster .05
375 Jeff Tackett .05
376 Tom Urbani .05
377 Tino Martinez .15
378 Mark Dewey .05
379 Charlie O'Brien .05
380 Terry Mulholland .05
381 Thomas Howard .05
382 Chris Haney .05
383 Billy Hatcher .05
384 Jeff Bagwell, Frank Thomas (All Stars) .50
385 Bret Boone, Carlos Baerga (All Stars) .10
386 Matt Williams, Wade Boggs (All Stars) .15
387 Wil Cordero, Cal Ripken Jr. (All Stars) .50
388 Barry Bonds, Ken Griffey Jr. (All Stars) .75
389 Tony Gwynn, Albert Belle (All Stars) .40
390 Dante Bichette, Kirby Puckett (All Stars) .25
391 Mike Piazza, Mike Stanley (All Stars) .40
392 Greg Maddux, David Cone (All Stars) .40
393 Danny Jackson, Jimmy Key (All Stars) .05
394 John Franco, Lee Smith (All Stars) .05
395 Checklist 1-198 .05
396 Checklist 199-396 .05
397 Ken Griffey Jr. 3.00
398 *Rick Heiserman* (Draft Pick) .10
399 Don Mattingly .75
400 Henry Rodriguez .05
401 Lenny Harris .05
402 Ryan Thompson .05
403 Darren Oliver .05
404 Omar Vizquel .10
405 Jeff Bagwell .60
406 *Doug Webb* Draft Pick) .10
407 Todd Van Poppel .05
408 Leo Gomez .05
409 Mark Whiten .05
410 Pedro Martinez .05
411 Reggie Sanders .10
412 Kevin Foster .05
413 Danny Tartabull .05
414 Jeff Blauser .05
415 Mike Magnante .05
416 Tom Candiotti .05
417 Rod Beck .05
418 Jody Reed .05
419 Vince Coleman .05
420 Danny Jackson .05
421 *Ryan Nye* (Draft Pick) .15
422 Larry Walker .30
423 Russ Johnson (Draft Pick) .15
424 Pat Borders .05
425 Lee Smith .05
426 Paul O'Neill .15
427 Devon White .05
428 Jim Bullinger .05
429 SP Prospects (Greg Hansell, Brian Sackinsky, Carey Paige, Rob Welch) .10
430 Steve Avery .05
431 Tony Gwynn 1.00
432 Pat Meares .05
433 Bill Swift .05
434 David Wells .05
435 John Briscoe .05
436 Roger Pavlik .05
437 *Jayson Peterson* (Draft Pick) .15
438 Roberto Alomar .40
439 Billy Brewer .05
440 Gary Sheffield .20
441 Lou Frazier .05
442 Terry Steinbach .05
443 *Jay Payton* (Draft Pick) .25
444 Jason Bere .05
445 Denny Neagle .05
446 Andres Galarraga .15
447 Hector Carrasco .05
448 Bill Risley .05
449 Andy Benes .05
450 Jim Leyritz .05
451 Jose Oliva .05
452 Greg Vaughn .05
453 Rich Monteleone .05
454 Tony Eusebio .05
455 Chuck Finley .05
456 Kevin Brown .15
457 Joe Boever .05
458 Bobby Munoz .05
459 Bret Saberhagen .05
460 Kurt Abbott .05
461 Bobby Witt .05
462 Cliff Floyd .10
463 Mark Clark .05
464 Andujar Cedeno .05
465 Marvin Freeman .05
466 Mike Piazza 1.50
467 Willie Greene .05
468 Pat Kelly .05
469 Carlos Delgado .50
470 Willie Banks .05
471 Matt Walbeck .05
472 Mark McGwire 3.00
473 McKay Christensen (Draft Pick) .15
474 Alan Trammell .10
475 Tom Gordon .05
476 Greg Colbrunn .05
477 Darren Daulton .05
478 Albie Lopez .05
479 Robin Ventura .25
480 C Prospects *(Eddie Perez,* Jason Kendall), *(Einar Diaz,* Bret Hemphill) .20
481 Bryan Eversgerd .05
482 Dave Fleming .05
483 Scott Livingstone .05
484 Pete Schourek .05
485 Bernie Williams .30
486 Mark Lemke .05
487 Eric Karros .10
488 Scott Ruffcorn .05
489 Billy Ashley .05
490 Rico Brogna .05
491 John Burkett .05
492 *Cade Gaspar* (Draft Pick) .15
493 Jorge Fabregas .05
494 Greg Gagne .05
495 Doug Jones .05
496 Troy O'Leary .05
497 Pat Rapp .05
498 Butch Henry .05
499 John Olerud .20
500 John Hudek .05
501 Jeff King .05
502 Bobby Bonilla .10
503 Albert Belle .30
504 Rick Wilkins .05
505 John Jaha .05
506 Nigel Wilson .05
507 Sid Fernandez .05
508 Deion Sanders .20
509 Gil Heredia .05
510 *Scott Elarton* (Draft Pick) .75
511 Melido Perez .05
512 Greg McMichael .05
513 Rusty Meacham .05
514 Shawn Green .40
515 Carlos Garcia .05
516 Dave Stevens .05
517 Eric Young .05
518 Omar Daal .05
519 Kirk Gibson .05
520 Spike Owen .05
521 *Jacob Cruz* (Draft Pick) .40
522 Sandy Alomar .10
523 Steve Bedrosian .05
524 Ricky Gutierrez .05
525 Dave Veres .05
526 Gregg Jefferies .10
527 Jose Valentin .05
528 Robb Nen .05
529 Jose Rijo .05
530 Sean Berry .05
531 Mike Gallego .05
532 Roberto Kelly .05

533 Kevin Stocker .05
534 Kirby Puckett .75
535 Chipper Jones 1.00
536 Russ Davis .05
537 Jon Lieber .05
538 *Trey Moore* (Draft Pick) .10
539 Joe Girardi .05
540 2B Prospects (Quilvio Veras, Arquimedez Pozo, Miguel Cairo, Jason Camilli) .20
541 Tony Phillips .05
542 Brian Anderson .15
543 Ivan Rodriguez .75
544 Jeff Cirillo .05
545 Joey Cora .05
546 Chris Hoiles .05
547 Bernard Gilkey .10
548 Mike Lansing .05
549 Jimmy Key .05
550 Mark Wohlers .05
551 *Chris Clemons* (Draft Pick) .15
552 Vinny Castilla .15
553 Mark Guthrie .05
554 Mike Lieberthal .10
555 *Tommy Davis* (Draft Pick) .15
556 Robby Thompson .05
557 Danny Bautista .05
558 Will Clark .30
559 Rickey Henderson .25
560 Todd Jones .05
561 Jack McDowell .05
562 Carlos Rodriguez .05
563 Mark Eichhorn .05
564 Jeff Nelson .05
565 Eric Anthony .05
566 Randy Velarde .05
567 Javy Lopez .15
568 Kevin Mitchell .05
569 Steve Karsay .05
570 *Brian Meadows* (Draft Pick) .20
571 SS Propects (*Rey Ordonez*, Mike Metcalfe, Ray Holbert, Kevin Orie) 1.00
572 John Kruk .05
573 Scott Leius .05
574 John Patterson .05
575 Kevin Brown .15
576 Mike Moore .05
577 Manny Ramirez .75
578 Jose Lind .05
579 Derrick May .05
580 Cal Eldred .05
581 3B Prospects (David Bell, Joel Chelmis, Lino Diaz), (*Aaron Boone*) .15
582 J.T. Snow .10
583 Luis Sojo .05
584 Moises Alou .20
585 Dave Clark .05
586 Dave Hollins .05
587 Nomar Garciaparra (Draft Pick) 4.00
588 Cal Ripken Jr. 2.50
589 Pedro Astacio .05
590 J.R. Phillips .05
591 Jeff Frye .05
592 Bo Jackson .15
593 Steve Ontiveros .05
594 David Nied .05
595 Brad Ausmus .05
596 Carlos Baerga .05
597 James Mouton .05
598 Ozzie Guillen .05
599 OF Prospects (Ozzie Timmons, Curtis Goodwin, Johnny Damon), (*Jeff Abbott*) .20
600 Yorkis Perez .05
601 Rich Rodriguez .05
602 Mark McLemore .05
603 Jeff Fassero .05
604 John Roper .05
605 *Mark Johnson* (Draft Pick) .20
606 Wes Chamberlain .05
607 Felix Jose .05
608 Tony Longmire .05
609 Duane Ward .05
610 Brett Butler .05
611 William Van Landingham .05
612 Mickey Tettleton .05
613 Brady Anderson .15
614 Reggie Jefferson .05
615 Mike Kingery .05
616 Derek Bell .10
617 Scott Erickson .05
618 Bob Wickman .05
619 Phil Leftwich .05
620 Dave Justice .20
621 Paul Wilson (Draft Pick) .15
622 Pedro Martinez .75
623 Terry Mathews .05
624 Brian McRae .05
625 Bruce Ruffin .05
626 Steve Finley .05
627 Ron Gant .15
628 Rafael Bournigal .05
629 Darryl Strawberry .15
630 Luis Alicea .05
631 Mark Smith, Scott Klingenbeck (On Deck) .10
632 Cory Bailey, Scott Hatteberg (On Deck) .15
633 Todd Greene, Troy Percival (On Deck) .10
634 Rod Bolton, Olmedo Saenz (On Deck) .10
635 Herb Perry, Steve Kline (On Deck) .10
636 Sean Bergman, Shannon Penn (On Deck) .10
637 Joe Vitiello, Joe Randa (On Deck) .10
638 Jose Mercedes, Duane Singleton (On Deck) .05
639 Marty Cordova, Marc Barcelo (On Deck) .10
640 Ruben Rivera, Andy Pettitte (On Deck) 1.00
641 Willie Adams, Scott Spiezio (On Deck) .10
642 Eddie Diaz, Desi Relaford (On Deck) .10
643 Jon Shave, Terrell Lowery (On Deck) .10
644 Paul Spoljaric, Angel Martinez (On Deck) .05
645 Damon Hollins, Tony Graffanino (On Deck) .10
646 Darron Cox, Doug Glanville (On Deck) .10
647 Tim Belk, Pat Watkins (On Deck) .10
648 Rod Pedraza, Phil Schneider (On Deck) .10
649 Marc Valdes, Vic Darensbourg (On Deck) .10
650 Rick Huisman, Roberto Petagine (On Deck) .05
651 Ron Coomer, Roger Cedeno (On Deck) .20
652 *Carlos Perez*, Shane Andrews (On Deck) .30
653 Jason Isringhausen, Chris Roberts (On Deck) .10
654 Kevin Jordan, Wayne Gomes (On Deck) .10
655 Esteban Loaiza, Steve Pegues (On Deck) .10
656 John Frascatore, Terry Bradshaw (On Deck) .10
657 Bryce Florie, Andres Berumen (On Deck) .10
658 Keith Williams, Dan Carlson (On Deck) .10
659 Checklist .05
660 Checklist .05

1995 Topps Cyberstats

	MT
Complete Set (396):	60.00
Series 1 (198):	30.00
Series 2 (198):	30.00
Common Player:	.15

(Valued at 2x their regular Topps card.)

1995 Topps Cyberstat Season in Review

This special edition of Cyberstat cards was available only in Topps factory sets. Carrying forward the idea of computerized projections to complete the strike-shortened 1994 season, the Season in Review cards speculate on career milestones and the playoffs that never happened. The Season in Review cards have player action photos printed on a foil background resembling the U.S. flag. Names are in gold foil. Backs have a black background and a recap of the computer simulation.

	MT
Complete Set (7):	8.00
Common Player:	1.50

1 Barry Bonds (61 Home Runs) 3.00
2 Jose Canseco (AL West One-Game Playoff) 2.00
3 Juan Gonzalez (AL Divisional Playoffs) 3.00
4 Fred McGriff (NL Divisional Playoffs) 1.50
5 Carlos Baerga (ALCS MVP) 1.00
6 Ryan Klesko (NLCS MVP) 1.00
7 Kenny Lofton (World Series MVP) 1.50

1995 Topps League Leaders

League Leaders is a 50-card insert set found in one of every six retail packs only of both Series I and II. The set includes the top five players in each league across 10 statistical categories. Cards featured the statistical category running up the right side, with the player's name across the bottom. Photo backgrounds have been darkened and posterized to make the player action stand out. Backs have the player's stat rankings within his division and league, and a bar graph at bottom gives his performance in that statistical category for the previous five seasons.

	MT
Complete Set (50):	30.00
Complete Series 1 (25):	15.00
Complete Series 2 (25):	15.00
Common Player:	.25

1 Albert Belle .75
2 Kevin Mitchell .25
3 Wade Boggs .50
4 Tony Gwynn 1.50
5 Moises Alou .40
6 Andres Galarraga .40
7 Matt Williams .40
8 Barry Bonds 1.00
9 Frank Thomas 1.00
10 Jose Canseco .75
11 Jeff Bagwell 1.00
12 Kirby Puckett 1.00
13 Julio Franco .25
14 Albert Belle .75
15 Fred McGriff .40
16 Kenny Lofton .50
17 Otis Nixon .25
18 Brady Anderson .25
19 Deion Sanders .40
20 Chuck Carr .25
21 Pat Hentgen .25
22 Andy Benes .25
23 Roger Clemens 1.50
24 Greg Maddux 2.00
25 Pedro Martinez 1.00

26	Paul O'Neill	.40
27	Jeff Bagwell	1.00
28	Frank Thomas	1.00
29	Hal Morris	.25
30	Kenny Lofton	.50
31	Ken Griffey Jr.	4.00
32	Jeff Bagwell	1.00
33	Albert Belle	.75
34	Fred McGriff	.50
35	Cecil Fielder	.25
36	Matt Williams	.40
37	Joe Carter	.25
38	Dante Bichette	.45
39	Frank Thomas	1.00
40	Mike Piazza	2.00
41	Craig Biggio	.50
42	Vince Coleman	.25
43	Marquis Grissom	.25
44	Chuck Knoblauch	.45
45	Darren Lewis	.25
46	Randy Johnson	.50
47	Jose Rijo	.25
48	Chuck Finley	.25
49	Bret Saberhagen	.25
50	Kevin Appier	.25

1995 Topps Opening Day

This 10-card set featuring top performers on the belated opening day of the 1995 season was available exclusively in retail factory sets. Card fronts feature color action photos printed on textured foil in a U.S. flag-like design. A large colorful Opening Day logo appears in an upper corner while the player's key stats from that game appear in a foil box at lower-right. Backs have a portrait photo along with complete details and a stats line of the opening day performance.

		MT
Complete Set (10):		16.00
Common Player:		2.00
1	Kevin Appier	2.00
2	Dante Bichette	3.00
3	Ken Griffey Jr.	8.00
4	Todd Hundley	3.00
5	John Jaha	2.00
6	Fred McGriff	3.00
7	Raul Mondesi	3.00
8	Manny Ramirez	4.00
9	Danny Tartabull	2.00
10	Devon White	2.50

1995 Topps Total Bases Finest

Printed in Topps Finest technology, including a peel-off plastic protector coating on the front, these cards honor the 1994 statistical leaders in total bases. The cards have a silver waffle-texture background on front as a background to the color action photo. At bottom is a team logo and team-color bar with the player's name. Backs feature a portrait photo and the player's total base stats. These inserts are found in Series II Topps packs at an average rate of one per 36 packs (one box).

		MT
Complete Set (15):		60.00
Common Player:		1.00
1	Jeff Bagwell	4.00
2	Albert Belle	3.00
3	Ken Griffey Jr.	10.00
4	Frank Thomas	4.00
5	Matt Williams	1.50
6	Dante Bichette	1.50
7	Barry Bonds	4.00
8	Moises Alou	1.00
9	Andres Galarraga	1.00
10	Kenny Lofton	1.50
11	Rafael Palmeiro	2.00
12	Tony Gwynn	4.00
13	Kirby Puckett	4.00
14	Jose Canseco	2.00
15	Jeff Conine	1.00

1995 Topps Traded and Rookies

Traded players, free agents who signed with new teams and all the up-and-coming rookies are the meat of the 1995 Topps Traded and Rookies set, sold for the first time exclusively in foil pack form. Maintaining the same format used in Series 1 and 2 Topps, the updates also reused the Future Star, Draft Pick and Star Track subsets, along with four-player Prospects cards. New subsets included Rookie of the Year Candidates, All-Stars, On Deck and "At the Break," 10 cards chronicling star players' performances through the first half of the 1995 season. A double-thick, foil-printed version of the "At the Break" cards called "Power Boosters" were the only inserts in the Traded/Rookies set.

		MT
Complete Set (165):		50.00
Common Player:		.10
Pack (11):		4.00
Wax Box (36):		125.00
1	Frank Thomas (At The Break)	.40
2	Ken Griffey Jr. (At The Break)	1.50
3	Barry Bonds (At The Break)	.40
4	Albert Belle (At The Break)	.25
5	Cal Ripken Jr. (At The Break)	1.00
6	Mike Piazza (At The Break)	.75
7	Tony Gwynn (At The Break)	.40
8	Jeff Bagwell (At The Break)	.25
9	Mo Vaughn (At The Break)	.25
10	Matt Williams (At The Break)	.15
11	Ray Durham	.10
12	*Juan LeBron* (Draft Pick)	2.00
13	Shawn Green (Rookie of the Year Candidate)	.50
14	Kevin Gross	.10
15	Jon Nunnally	.10
16	*Brian Maxcy*	.10
17	Mark Kiefer	.10
18	*Carlos Beltran* (Draft Pick) (photo actually Juan Beltran)	6.00
19	*Mike Mimbs*	.10
20	Larry Walker	.40
21	Chad Curtis	.10
22	Jeff Barry	.10
23	Joe Oliver	.10
24	*Tomas Perez*	.10
25	*Michael Barrett* (Draft Pick)	2.50
26	Brian McRae	.10
27	Derek Bell	.10
28	Ray Durham (Rookie of the Year Candidate)	.10
29	Todd Williams	.10
30	*Ryan Jaroncyk* (Draft Pick)	.20
31	Todd Steverson	.10
32	Mike Devereaux	.10
33	Rheal Cormier	.10
34	Benny Santiago	.10
35	*Bobby Higginson*	1.50
36	Jack McDowell	.10
37	Mike Macfarlane	.10
38	*Tony McKnight* (Draft Pick)	.20
39	Brian Hunter (Rookie of the Year Candidate)	.15
40	*Hideo Nomo* (Star Track)	2.00
41	Brett Butler	.10
42	Donovan Osborne	.10
43	Scott Karl	.10
44	Tony Phillips	.10
45	Marty Cordova (Rookie of the Year Candidate)	.20
46	Dave Mlicki	.10
47	*Bronson Arroyo* (Draft Pick)	1.50
48	John Burkett	.10
49	*J.D. Smart* (Draft Pick)	.25
50	Mickey Tettleton	.10
51	Todd Stottlemyre	.15
52	Mike Perez	.10
53	Terry Mulholland	.10
54	Edgardo Alfonzo	.25
55	Zane Smith	.10
56	Jacob Brumfield	.10
57	Andujar Cedeno	.10
58	Jose Parra	.10
59	Manny Alexander	.10
60	Tony Tarasco	.10
61	Orel Hershiser	.10
62	Tim Scott	.10
63	*Felix Rodriguez*	.10
64	Ken Hill	.10
65	Marquis Grissom	.15
66	Lee Smith	.10
67	Jason Bates (Rookie of the Year Candidate)	.10
68	Felipe Lira	.10
69	*Alex Hernandez* (Draft Pick)	1.50
70	Tony Fernandez	.10
71	Scott Radinsky	.10
72	Jose Canseco	.50
73	*Mark Grudzielanek*	.50
74	*Ben Davis* (Draft Pick)	4.00
75	Jim Abbott	.10
76	Roger Bailey	.10
77	Gregg Jefferies	.10
78	Erik Hanson	.10
79	*Brad Radke*	1.00
80	Jaime Navarro	.10
81	John Wetteland	.10
82	*Chad Fonville*	.15
83	John Mabry	.10
84	Glenallen Hill	.10
85	Ken Caminiti	.20
86	Tom Goodwin	.10
87	Darren Bragg	.10
88	1995 Prospects (Pitchers) *(Pat Ahearne)*, *(Gary Rath)*, *(Larry Wimberly)*, *(Robbie Bell)*	3.00
89	Jeff Russell	.10
90	Dave Gallagher	.10
91	Steve Finley	.10
92	Vaughn Eshelman	.10
93	Kevin Jarvis	.10
94	Mark Gubicza	.10
95	Tim Wakefield	.10
96	Bob Tewksbury	.10
97	*Sid Roberson*	.10
98	Tom Henke	.10
99	Michael Tucker (Future Star)	.15
100	Jason Bates	.10
101	Otis Nixon	.10
102	Mark Whiten	.10
103	Dilson Torres	.10
104	*Melvin Bunch*	.10
105	Terry Pendleton	.10
106	*Corey Jenkins* (Draft Pick)	.20
107	On Deck *(Glenn Dishman)*, *(Rob Grable)*	.15
108	*Reggie Taylor* (Draft Pick)	2.00
109	Curtis Goodwin (Rookie of the Year Candidate)	.10
110	David Cone	.20
111	Antonio Osuna	.10
112	Paul Shuey	.10
113	Doug Jones	.10
114	Mark McLemore	.10
115	Kevin Ritz	.10
116	John Kruk	.10
117	Trevor Wilson	.10
118	Jerald Clark	.10
119	Julian Tavarez	.10
120	Tim Pugh	.10
121	Todd Zeile	.10
122	1995 Prospects (Fielders) *(Mark Sweeney*, George Arias), *(Richie Sexson)*, *(Brian Schneider)*	8.00
123	Bobby Witt	.10
124	Hideo Nomo (Rookie of the Year Candidate)	.40
125	Joey Cora	.10
126	*Jim Scharrer* (Draft Pick)	.10
127	Paul Quantrill	.10

128 Chipper Jones (Rookie of the Year Candidate) 1.00
129 *Kenny James* (Draft Pick) .10
130 On Deck (Lyle Mouton, Mariano Rivera) .10
131 Tyler Green (Rookie of the Year Candidate) .10
132 Brad Clontz .10
133 Jon Nunnally (Rookie of the Year Candidate) .10
134 Dave Magadan .10
135 Al Leiter .20
136 Bret Barberie .10
137 Bill Swift .10
138 Scott Cooper .10
139 Roberto Kelly .10
140 Charlie Hayes .10
141 Pete Harnisch .10
142 Rich Amaral .10
143 Rudy Seanez .10
144 Pat Listach .10
145 Quilvio Veras (Rookie of the Year Candidate) .15
146 *Jose Olmeda* (Draft Pick) .10
147 Roberto Petagine .10
148 Kevin Brown .20
149 Phil Plantier .10
150 *Carlos Perez* (Rookie of the Year Candidate) .40
151 Pat Borders .10
152 Tyler Green .10
153 Stan Belinda .10
154 Dave Stewart .10
155 Andre Dawson .15
156 Frank Thomas, Fred McGriff (All-Star) .25
157 Carlos Baerga, Craig Biggio (All-Star) .15
158 Wade Boggs, Matt Williams (All-Star) .10
159 Cal Ripken Jr., Ozzie Smith (All-Star) .50
160 Ken Griffey Jr., Tony Gwynn (All-Star) .75
161 Albert Belle, Barry Bonds (All-Star) .25
162 Kirby Puckett, Len Dykstra (All-Star) .25
163 Ivan Rodriguez, Mike Piazza (All-Star) .25
164 Randy Johnson, Hideo Nomo (All-Star) .25
165 Checklist .10

1995 Topps Traded and Rookies Power Boosters

Virtually identical to the first 10 cards of the 1995 Topps Traded and Rookies issue, the "At the Break" subset is the only insert found in Traded packs. Cards are printed on double-thick cardboard stock on metallized foil. The chase cards are found at an average rate of one per 36 packs.

		MT
Complete Set (10):		37.00
Common Player:		1.50
1	Frank Thomas	6.00
2	Ken Griffey Jr.	12.50
3	Barry Bonds	4.00
4	Albert Belle	3.00
5	Cal Ripken Jr.	10.00
6	Mike Piazza	7.50
7	Tony Gwynn	6.00
8	Jeff Bagwell	3.00
9	Mo Vaughn	1.50
10	Matt Williams	1.50

1995 Topps/DIII

Describing its cards as featuring "infinite depth perspectives" with game-action photos, Topps entered the 3-D card market with its Dimension III product. Utilizing "super thick laminated construction" to provide the illusion of depth, the cards feature borderless action photos on front. Backs are conventionally printed with a color portrait photo and several sets of stats that go beyond the usual to the provide a more in-depth look at the player's performance.

		MT
Complete Set (59):		27.50
Common Player:		.25
Retail Pack (3):		1.00
Retail Wax Box (24):		20.00
Hobby Pack (5):		1.25
Hobby Wax Box (24):		25.00
1	Dave Justice	.40
2	Cal Ripken Jr.	5.00
3	Ruben Sierra	.25
4	Roberto Alomar	1.00
5	Dennis Martinez	.25
6	Todd Zeile	.25
7	Albert Belle	1.00
8	Chuck Knoblauch	.50
9	Roger Clemens	1.00
10	Cal Eldred	.25
11	Dennis Eckersley	.25
12	Andy Benes	.25
13	Moises Alou	.35
14	Andres Galarraga	.35
15	Jim Thome	.40
16	Tim Salmon	.40
17	Carlos Garcia	.25
18	Scott Leius	.25
19	Jeff Montgomery	.25
20	Brian Anderson	.25
21	Will Clark	.50
22	Bobby Bonilla	.25
23	Mike Stanley	.25
24	Barry Bonds	1.50
25	Jeff Conine	.25
26	Paul O'Neill	.25
27	Mike Piazza	2.50
28	Tom Glavine	.35
29	Jim Edmonds	.35
30	Lou Whitaker	.25
31	Jeff Frye	.25
32	Ivan Rodriguez	.50
33	Bret Boone	.25
34	Mike Greenwell	.25
35	Mark Grace	.45
36	Darren Lewis	.25
37	Don Mattingly	2.50
38	Jose Rijo	.25
39	Robin Ventura	.35
40	Bob Hamelin	.25
41	Tim Wallach	.25
42	Tony Gwynn	1.50
43	Ken Griffey Jr.	6.00
44	Doug Drabek	.25
45	Rafael Palmeiro	.35
46	Dean Palmer	.25
47	Bip Roberts	.25
48	Barry Larkin	.25
49	Dave Nilsson	.25
50	Wil Cordero	.25
51	Travis Fryman	.25
52	Chuck Carr	.25
53	Rey Sanchez	.25
54	Walt Weiss	.25
55	Joe Carter	.25
56	Len Dykstra	.25
57	Orlando Merced	.25
58	Ozzie Smith	.75
59	Chris Gomez	.25

1995 Topps/DIII Zone

A barrage of baseballs in the background, behind a player action photo, are featured on the front of this DIII chase set.Backs have a blazing baseball across the top and a description and stats of the pictured player's hot streaks of the previous season -- those times when athletes are said to be "in the zone." The inserts are found on average of one per six packs.

		MT
Complete Set (6):		22.00
Common Player:		2.00
1	Frank Thomas	5.00
2	Kirby Puckett	3.50
3	Jeff Bagwell	3.00
4	Fred McGriff	2.50
5	Raul Mondesi	2.00
6	Kenny Lofton	2.00

1995 Topps/ Embossed

Taking the embossed sportscard idea which Action Packed developed years earlier to a new level, Topps Embossed baseball features the tactile image on both sides of the card. Fronts have a lightly textured border while the central player photo is deeply embossed. The player name is embossed in gold-foil letters at bottom. Backs have another embossed player photo and various levels of embossing around the borders and boxes which contain stats and trivia.

		MT
Complete Set (140):		20.00
Common Player:		.10
Wax Box:		40.00
1	Kenny Lofton	.50
2	Gary Sheffield	.20
3	Hal Morris	.10
4	Cliff Floyd	.15
5	Pat Hentgen	.10
6	Tony Gwynn	1.50
7	Jose Valentin	.10
8	Jason Bere	.10
9	Jeff Kent	.10
10	John Valentin	.10
11	Brian Anderson	.10
12	Deion Sanders	.40
13	Ryan Thompson	.10
14	Ruben Sierra	.10
15	Jay Bell	.10
16	Chuck Carr	.10
17	Brent Gates	.10
18	Bret Boone	.10
19	Paul Molitor	.25
20	Chili Davis	.10
21	Ryan Klesko	.20
22	Will Clark	.35
23	Greg Vaughn	.10
24	Moises Alou	.10
25	Ray Lankford	.10
26	Jose Rijo	.10
27	Bobby Jones	.10
28	Rick Wilkins	.10
29	Cal Eldred	.10
30	Juan Gonzalez	.75
31	Royce Clayton	.10
32	Bryan Harvey	.10
33	Dave Nilsson	.10
34	Chris Hoiles	.10
35	David Nied	.10
36	Javy Lopez	.15
37	Tim Wallach	.10
38	Bobby Bonilla	.10
39	Danny Tartabull	.10
40	Andy Benes	.10
41	Dean Palmer	.10
42	Chris Gomez	.10
43	Kevin Appier	.10
44	Brady Anderson	.15
45	Alex Fernandez	.10
46	Roberto Kelly	.10
47	Dave Hollins	.10
48	Chuck Finley	.10
49	Wade Boggs	.30
50	Travis Fryman	.10
51	Ken Griffey Jr.	3.00
52	John Olerud	.15
53	Delino DeShields	.10
54	Ivan Rodriguez	.25
55	Tommy Greene	.10
56	Tom Pagnozzi	.10
57	Bip Roberts	.10
58	Luis Gonzalez	.10
59	Rey Sanchez	.10
60	Ken Ryan	.10
61	Darren Daulton	.10
62	Rick Aguilera	.10
63	Wally Joyner	.10
64	Mike Greenwell	.10
65	Jay Buhner	.10
66	Craig Biggio	.10
67	Charles Nagy	.10
68	Devon White	.10
69	Randy Johnson	.25
70	Shawon Dunston	.10
71	Kirby Puckett	1.00
72	Paul O'Neill	.10
73	Tino Martinez	.15
74	Carlos Garcia	.10
75	Ozzie Smith	.60
76	Cecil Fielder	.10
77	Mike Stanley	.10
78	Lance Johnson	.10
79	Tony Phillips	.10
80	Bobby Munoz	.10
81	Kevin Tapani	.10
82	William Van Landingham	.10
83	Dante Bichette	.25
84	Tom Candiotti	.10
85	Wil Cordero	.10
86	Jeff Conine	.10
87	Joey Hamilton	.10
88	Mark Whiten	.10
89	Jeff Montgomery	.10
90	Andres Galarraga	.10
91	Roberto Alomar	.50
92	Orlando Merced	.10

93 Mike Mussina .30
94 Pedro Martinez .10
95 Carlos Baerga .10
96 Steve Trachsel .10
97 Lou Whitaker .10
98 David Cone .10
99 Chuck Knoblauch .15
100 Frank Thomas 2.00
101 Dave Justice .20
102 Raul Mondesi .30
103 Rickey Henderson .25
104 Doug Drabek .10
105 Sandy Alomar .10
106 Roger Clemens .60
107 Mark McGwire 3.00
108 Tim Salmon .25
109 Greg Maddux 1.50
110 Mike Piazza 2.00
111 Tom Glavine .10
112 Walt Weiss .10
113 Cal Ripken Jr. 2.50
114 Eddie Murray .40
115 Don Mattingly 1.50
116 Ozzie Guillen .10
117 Bob Hamelin .10
118 Jeff Bagwell 1.50
119 Eric Karros .10
120 Barry Bonds .75
121 Mickey Tettleton .10
122 Mark Langston .10
123 Robin Ventura .10
124 Bret Saberhagen .10
125 Albert Belle .75
126 Rafael Palmeiro .10
127 Fred McGriff .25
128 Jimmy Key .10
129 Barry Larkin .10
130 Tim Raines .10
131 Len Dykstra .10
132 Todd Zeile .10
133 Joe Carter .10
134 Matt Williams .25
135 Terry Steinbach .10
136 Manny Ramirez .75
137 John Wetteland .10
138 Rod Beck .10
139 Mo Vaughn .50
140 Darren Lewis .10

1995 Topps/ Embossed Golden Idols

The only insert in the Topps Embossed baseball set was a parallel set of the 140 cards rendered in gold tones on front and inserted at the rate of one per pack. Backs are identical to the regular version.

	MT
Complete Set (140):	70.00
Common Player:	.25

(Star cards valued at 2X-4X corresponding regular Embossed cards)

1996 Topps

At 440 cards, the basic Topps set for 1996 was the smallest regular-issue from the company since it adopted the 2-1/2" x 3-1/2" format in 1957. Honoring the late Mickey Mantle on card No. 7, Topps announced it would hereafter retire that card number. Subsets in the 220-card Series 1 are Star Power, Commemoratives, Draft Picks, Tribute, AAA Stars and Future Stars. Series 2 subsets repeat Star Power and Draft Picks and add Prospects, Now Appearing and Rookie All-Stars.

	MT
Complete Set (440):	40.00
Complete Series 1 (220):	25.00
Complete Series 2 (220):	15.00
Common Player:	.05
Series 1 Pack (12):	2.50
Series 1 Wax Box (36):	75.00
Series 2 Pack (12):	2.00
Series 2 Wax Box (36):	55.00

1 Tony Gwynn (Star Power) .25
2 Mike Piazza (Star Power) .40
3 Greg Maddux (Star Power) .50
4 Jeff Bagwell (Star Power) .30
5 Larry Walker (Star Power) .20
6 Barry Larkin (Star Power) .10
7 Mickey Mantle (Commemorative) 5.00
8 Tom Glavine (Star Power) .10
9 Craig Biggio (Star Power) .05
10 Barry Bonds (Star Power) .20
11 Heathcliff Slocumb (Star Power) .05
12 Matt Williams (Star Power) .15
13 Todd Helton (Draft Pick) 1.00
14 Mark Redman (Draft Pick) .15
15 Michael Barrett (Draft Pick) .50
16 Ben Davis (Draft Pick) .25
17 Juan LeBron (Draft Pick) .20
18 Tony McKnight (Draft Pick) .10
19 Ryan Jaroncyk (Draft Pick) .05
20 Corey Jenkins (Draft Pick) .15
21 Jim Scharrer (Draft Pick) .05
22 *Mark Bellhorn* (Draft Pick) .25
23 *Jarrod Washburn* (Draft Pick) .40
24 *Geoff Jenkins* (Draft Pick) 2.00
25 *Sean Casey* (Draft Pick) 10.00
26 *Brett Tomko* (Draft Pick) .20
27 Tony Fernandez .05
28 Rich Becker .05
29 Andujar Cedeno .05
30 Paul Molitor .25
31 Brent Gates .05
32 Glenallen Hill .05
33 Mike MacFarlane .05
34 Manny Alexander .05
35 Todd Zeile .05
36 Joe Girardi .05
37 Tony Tarasco .05
38 Tim Belcher .05
39 Tom Goodwin .05
40 Orel Hershiser .05
41 Tripp Cromer .05
42 Sean Bergman .05
43 Troy Percival .05
44 Kevin Stocker .05
45 Albert Belle .60
46 Tony Eusebio .05
47 Sid Roberson .05
48 Todd Hollandsworth .05
49 Mark Wohlers .05
50 Kirby Puckett .65
51 Darren Holmes .05
52 Ron Karkovice .05
53 Al Martin .05
54 Pat Rapp .05
55 Mark Grace .15
56 Greg Gagne .05
57 Stan Javier .05
58 Scott Sanders .05
59 J.T. Snow .05
60 David Justice .15
61 Royce Clayton .05
62 Kevin Foster .05
63 Tim Naehring .05
64 Orlando Miller .05
65 Mike Mussina .30
66 Jim Eisenreich .05
67 Felix Fermin .05
68 Bernie Williams .30
69 Robb Nen .05
70 Ron Gant .10
71 Felipe Lira .05
72 Jacob Brumfield .05
73 John Mabry .05
74 Mark Carreon .05
75 Carlos Baerga .05
76 Jim Dougherty .05
77 Ryan Thompson .05
78 Scott Leius .05
79 Roger Pavlik .05
80 Gary Sheffield .35
81 Julian Tavarez .05
82 Andy Ashby .05
83 Mark Lemke .05
84 Omar Vizquel .05
85 Darren Daulton .05
86 Mike Lansing .05
87 Rusty Greer .05
88 Dave Stevens .05
89 Jose Offerman .05
90 Tom Henke .05
91 Troy O'Leary .05
92 Michael Tucker .05
93 Marvin Freeman .05
94 Alex Diaz .05
95 John Wetteland .05
96 Cal Ripken Jr. (Tribute Card) 2.00
97 Mike Mimbs .05
98 Bobby Higginson .10
99 Edgardo Alfonzo .10
100 Frank Thomas .75
101 Steve Gibralter, Bob Abreu (AAA Stars) .15
102 Brian Givens, T.J. Mathews (AAA Stars) .05
103 Chris Pritchett, Trenidad Hubbard (AAA Stars) .10
104 Eric Owens, Butch Huskey (AAA Stars) .15
105 Doug Drabek .05
106 Tomas Perez .05
107 Mark Leiter .05
108 Joe Oliver .05
109 Tony Castillo .05
110 Checklist .05
111 Kevin Seitzer .05
112 Pete Schourek .05
113 Sean Berry .05
114 Todd Stottlemyre .05
115 Joe Carter .05
116 Jeff King .05
117 Dan Wilson .05
118 Kurt Abbott .05
119 Lyle Mouton .05
120 Jose Rijo .05
121 Curtis Goodwin .05
122 *Jose Valentin* .05
123 Ellis Burks .05
124 David Cone .10
125 Eddie Murray .25
126 Brian Jordan .10
127 Darrin Fletcher .05
128 Curt Schilling .05
129 Ozzie Guillen .05
130 Kenny Rogers .05
131 Tom Pagnozzi .05
132 Garret Anderson .05
133 Bobby Jones .05
134 Chris Gomez .05
135 Mike Stanley .05
136 Hideo Nomo .50
137 Jon Nunnally .05
138 Tim Wakefield .05
139 Steve Finley .05
140 Ivan Rodriguez .50
141 Quilvio Veras .05
142 Mike Fetters .05
143 Mike Greenwell .05
144 Bill Pulsipher .10
145 Mark McGwire 2.50
146 Frank Castillo .05
147 Greg Vaughn .05
148 Pat Hentgen .05
149 Walt Weiss .05
150 Randy Johnson .30
151 David Segui .05
152 Benji Gil .05
153 Tom Candiotti .05
154 Geronimo Berroa .05
155 John Franco .05
156 Jay Bell .05
157 Mark Gubicza .05
158 Hal Morris .05
159 Wilson Alvarez .05
160 Derek Bell .10
161 Ricky Bottalico .05
162 Bret Boone .05
163 Brad Radke .05
164 John Valentin .05
165 Steve Avery .05
166 Mark McLemore .05
167 Danny Jackson .05
168 Tino Martinez .10
169 Shane Reynolds .05
170 Terry Pendleton .05
171 Jim Edmonds .10
172 Esteban Loaiza .05
173 Ray Durham .05
174 Carlos Perez .05
175 Raul Mondesi .25
176 Steve Ontiveros .05
177 Chipper Jones 1.00
178 Otis Nixon .05
179 John Burkett .05
180 Gregg Jefferies .05
181 Denny Martinez .05
182 Ken Caminiti .15
183 Doug Jones .05
184 Brian McRae .05
185 Don Mattingly .75
186 Mel Rojas .05
187 Marty Cordova .05
188 Vinny Castilla .15
189 John Smoltz .15
190 Travis Fryman .10
191 Chris Hoiles .05
192 Chuck Finley .05
193 Ryan Klesko .15
194 Alex Fernandez .05
195 Dante Bichette .25
196 Eric Karros .10
197 Roger Clemens 1.00
198 Randy Myers .05
199 Tony Phillips .05
200 Cal Ripken Jr. 2.00
201 Rod Beck .05
202 Chad Curtis .05
203 Jack McDowell .05
204 Gary Gaetti .05
205 Ken Griffey Jr. 2.50
206 Ramon Martinez .10
207 Jeff Kent .05
208 Brad Ausmus .05
209 Devon White .05
210 Jason Giambi (Future Star) .15
211 Nomar Garciaparra (Future Star) 1.50

212 Billy Wagner (Future Star) .10
213 Todd Greene (Future Star) .15
214 Paul Wilson (Future Star) .15
215 Johnny Damon (Future Star) .10
216 Alan Benes (Future Star) .15
217 Karim Garcia (Future Star) .30
218 Dustin Hermanson (Future Star) .10
219 Derek Jeter (Future Star) 1.50
220 Checklist .05
221 Kirby Puckett (Star Power) .25
222 Cal Ripken Jr. (Star Power) .75
223 Albert Belle (Star Power) .25
224 Randy Johnson (Star Power) .15
225 Wade Boggs (Star Power) .10
226 Carlos Baerga (Star Power) .05
227 Ivan Rodriguez (Star Power) .25
228 Mike Mussina (Star Power) .15
229 Frank Thomas (Star Power) .30
230 Ken Griffey Jr. (Star Power) 1.00
231 Jose Mesa (Star Power) .05
232 *Matt Morris* (Draft Pick) .25
233 Craig Wilson (Draft Pick) .05
234 *Alvie Shepherd* (Draft Pick) .10
235 *Randy Winn* (Draft Pick) .05
236 *David Yocum* (Draft Pick) .15
237 *Jason Brester* (Draft Pick) .20
238 *Shane Monahan* (Draft Pick) .25
239 *Brian McNichol* (Draft Pick) .20
240 Reggie Taylor (Draft Pick) .05
241 Garrett Long (Draft Pick) .05
242 *Jonathan Johnson* (Draft Pick) .20
243 *Jeff Liefer* (Draft Pick) .25
244 *Brian Powell* (Draft Pick) .05
245 Brian Buchanan (Draft Pick) .10
246 Mike Piazza 1.25
247 Edgar Martinez .05
248 Chuck Knoblauch .15
249 Andres Galarraga .20
250 Tony Gwynn 1.00
251 Lee Smith .05
252 Sammy Sosa 1.50
253 Jim Thome .30
254 Frank Rodriguez .05
255 Charlie Hayes .05
256 Bernard Gilkey .10
257 John Smiley .05
258 Brady Anderson .15
259 Rico Brogna .05
260 Kirt Manwaring .05
261 Len Dykstra .05
262 Tom Glavine .15
263 Vince Coleman .05
264 John Olerud .15
265 Orlando Merced .05
266 Kent Mercker .05
267 Terry Steinbach .05
268 Brian Hunter .05
269 Jeff Fassero .05
270 Jay Buhner .10
271 Jeff Brantley .05
272 Tim Raines .05
273 Jimmy Key .05
274 Mo Vaughn .30
275 Andre Dawson .10
276 Jose Mesa .05
277 Brett Butler .05
278 Luis Gonzalez .10
279 Steve Sparks .05
280 Chili Davis .05
281 Carl Everett .10
282 Jeff Cirillo .10
283 Thomas Howard .05
284 Paul O'Neill .20
285 Pat Meares .05
286 Mickey Tettleton .05
287 Rey Sanchez .05
288 Bip Roberts .05
289 Roberto Alomar .40
290 Ruben Sierra .05
291 John Flaherty .05
292 Bret Saberhagen .10
293 Barry Larkin .15
294 Sandy Alomar .10
295 Ed Sprague .05
296 Gary DiSarcina .05
297 Marquis Grissom .10
298 John Frascatore .05
299 Will Clark .25
300 Barry Bonds .50
301 Ozzie Smith .40
302 Dave Nilsson .05
303 Pedro Martinez .50
304 Joey Cora .05
305 Rick Aguilera .05
306 Craig Biggio .25
307 Jose Vizcaino .05
308 Jeff Montgomery .05
309 Moises Alou .15
310 Robin Ventura .15
311 David Wells .05
312 Delino DeShields .05
313 Trevor Hoffman .05
314 Andy Benes .05
315 Deion Sanders .20
316 Jim Bullinger .05
317 John Jaha .05
318 Greg Maddux 1.00
319 Tim Salmon .20
320 Ben McDonald .05
321 *Sandy Martinez* .10
322 Dan Miceli .05
323 Wade Boggs .25
324 Ismael Valdes .05
325 Juan Gonzalez .75
326 Charles Nagy .05
327 Ray Lankford .10
328 Mark Portugal .05
329 Bobby Bonilla .10
330 Reggie Sanders .10
331 Jamie Brewington .05
332 Aaron Sele .05
333 Pete Harnisch .05
334 Cliff Floyd .05
335 Cal Eldred .05
336 Jason Bates (Now Appearing) .05
337 Tony Clark (Now Appearing) .25
338 Jose Herrera (Now Appearing) .05
339 Alex Ochoa (Now Appearing) .10
340 Mark Loretta (Now Appearing) .05
341 *Donne Wall* (Now Appearing) .05
342 Jason Kendall (Now Appearing) .10
343 Shannon Stewart (Now Appearing) .10
344 Brooks Kieschnick (Now Appearing) .10
345 Chris Snopek (Now Appearing) .10
346 Ruben Rivera (Now Appearing) .10
347 Jeff Suppan (Now Appearing) .05
348 Phil Nevin (Now Appearing) .05
349 John Wasdin (Now Appearing) .05
350 Jay Payton (Now Appearing) .05
351 Tim Crabtree (Now Appearing) .05
352 Rick Krivda (Now Appearing) .05
353 Bob Wolcott (Now Appearing) .05
354 Jimmy Haynes (Now Appearing) .05
355 Herb Perry .05
356 Ryne Sandberg .40
357 Harold Baines .05
358 Chad Ogea .05
359 Lee Tinsley .05
360 Matt Williams .25
361 Randy Velarde .05
362 Jose Canseco .50
363 Larry Walker .35
364 Kevin Appier .05
365 Darryl Hamilton .05
366 Jose Lima .05
367 Javy Lopez .15
368 Dennis Eckersley .10
369 Jason Isringhausen .10
370 Mickey Morandini .05
371 Scott Cooper .05
372 Jim Abbott .05
373 Paul Sorrento .05
374 Chris Hammond .05
375 Lance Johnson .05
376 Kevin Brown .10
377 Luis Alicea .05
378 Andy Pettitte .25
379 Dean Palmer .05
380 Jeff Bagwell .50
381 Jaime Navarro .05
382 Rondell White .10
383 Erik Hanson .05
384 Pedro Munoz .05
385 Heathcliff Slocumb .05
386 Wally Joyner .10
387 Bob Tewksbury .05
388 David Bell .05
389 Fred McGriff .25
390 Mike Henneman .05
391 Robby Thompson .05
392 Norm Charlton .05
393 Cecil Fielder .10
394 Benito Santiago .05
395 Rafael Palmeiro .20
396 Ricky Bones .05
397 Rickey Henderson .25
398 C.J. Nitkowski .05
399 Shawon Dunston .05
400 Manny Ramirez .75
401 Bill Swift .05
402 Chad Fonville .05
403 Joey Hamilton .05
404 Alex Gonzalez .05
405 Roberto Hernandez .05
406 Jeff Blauser .05
407 LaTroy Hawkins .05
408 Greg Colbrunn .05
409 Todd Hundley .10
410 Glenn Dishman .05
411 Joe Vitiello .05
412 Todd Worrell .05
413 Wil Cordero .05
414 Ken Hill .05
415 Carlos Garcia .05
416 Bryan Rekar .05
417 Shawn Green (Topps Rookie All-Star) .40
418 Tyler Green .05
419 Mike Blowers .05
420 Kenny Lofton .30
421 Denny Neagle .05
422 Jeff Conine .05
423 Mark Langston .05
424 Steve Cox, *Jesse Ibarra*, Derrek Lee, *Ron Wright* (Prospects) .25
425 *Jim Bonnici*, Billy Owens, Richie Sexson, *Daryle Ward* (Prospects) 3.00
426 Kevin Jordan, *Bobby Morris*, Desi Relaford, *Adam Riggs* (Prospects) .05
427 Tim Harkrider, Rey Ordonez, Neifi Perez, Enrique Wilson (Prospects) .25
428 Bartolo Colon, Doug Million, Rafael Orellano, *Ray Ricken* (Prospects) .10
429 Jeff D'Amico, *Marty Janzen*, Gary Rath, Clint Sodowsky (Prospects) .10
430 Matt Drews, *Rich Hunter*, *Matt Ruebel*, Bret Wagner (Prospects) .10
431 Jaime Bluma, *Dave Coggin*, Steve Montgomery, Brandon Reed (Prospects) .10
432 Mike Figga, *Raul Ibanez*, Paul Konerko, Julio Mosquera (Prospects) .20
433 Brian Barber, Marc Kroon, Marc Valdes, Don Wengert (Prospects) .05
434 George Arias, *Chris Haas*, Scott Rolen, Scott Spiezio (Prospects) 1.00
435 *Brian Banks*, Vladimir Guerrero, Andruw Jones, Billy McMillon (Prospects) 2.00
436 Roger Cedeno, Derrick Gibson, Ben Grieve, *Shane Spencer* (Prospects) 1.50
437 Anton French, Demond Smith, *Darond Stovall*, Keith Williams (Prospects) .20
438 *Michael Coleman*, Jacob Cruz, Richard Hidalgo, Charles Peterson (Prospects) .40
439 Trey Beamon, Yamil Benitez, Jermaine Dye, Angel Echevarria (Prospects) .15
440 Checklist .05

1996 Topps Classic Confrontations

Head-to-head stats among baseball's top pitchers and hitters are featured in this insert set. The cards were seeded one per pack in the special 50-cent packs sold exclusively at Wal-Mart during the T206 Honus Wagner card giveaway promotion. Fronts have player action poses against a granite background and are highlighted in gold foil. Backs have a portrait photo and stats.

		MT
Complete Set (15):		6.00
Common Player:		.25
1	Ken Griffey Jr.	1.50
2	Cal Ripken Jr.	1.00
3	Edgar Martinez	.25
4	Kirby Puckett	.75
5	Frank Thomas	.60
6	Barry Bonds	.50
7	Reggie Sanders	.25

8	Andres Galarraga	.25
9	Tony Gwynn	.75
10	Mike Piazza	1.00
11	Randy Johnson	.35
12	Mike Mussina	.25
13	Roger Clemens	.75
14	Tom Glavine	.25
15	Greg Maddux	.90

1996 Topps 5-Star Mystery Finest

The 5-Star Mystery Finest inserts have an opaque black film over the card front, like the regular Mystery Finest, but has the words "5-Star" in large letters across the background. They are inserted at the average rate of one per 36 packs.

		MT
Complete Set (5):		40.00
Common Player:		2.00
Refractors:		3X to 5X
M22	Hideo Nomo	3.00
M23	Cal Ripken Jr.	12.00
M24	Mike Piazza	12.00
M25	Ken Griffey Jr.	20.00
M26	Frank Thomas	5.00

1996 Topps Masters of the Game

Appearing at a one per 18 pack rate, these inserts are exclusive to Series 1 hobby packs.

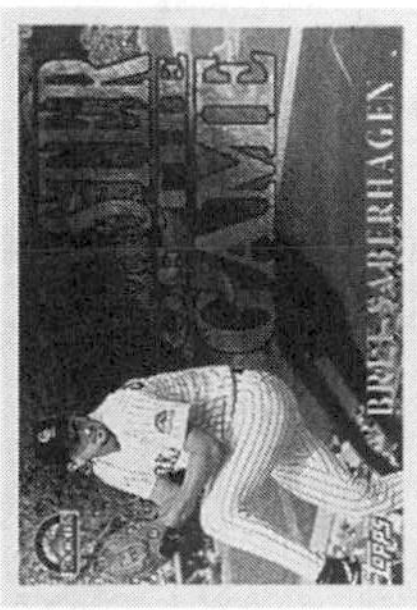

		MT
Complete Set (20):		25.00
Common Player:		.50
1	Dennis Eckersley	.50
2	Denny Martinez	.50
3	Eddie Murray	1.00
4	Paul Molitor	1.50
5	Ozzie Smith	1.50
6	Rickey Henderson	1.00
7	Tim Raines	.50
8	Lee Smith	.50
9	Cal Ripken Jr.	8.00
10	Chili Davis	.50
11	Wade Boggs	1.00
12	Tony Gwynn	4.00
13	Don Mattingly	2.00
14	Bret Saberhagen	.50
15	Kirby Puckett	1.50
16	Joe Carter	.50
17	Roger Clemens	3.00
18	Barry Bonds	3.00
19	Greg Maddux	5.00
20	Frank Thomas	2.00

1996 Topps Mickey Mantle Reprint Cards

One of Mickey Mantle's regular-issue Bowman or Topps cards from each year 1951-1969 was reproduced in 2-1/2" x 3-1/2" format as a Series 1 insert. Each card carries a gold-foil commemorative seal in one corner of the front. The reprints are found one per six retail packs and, in hobby, once per nine packs. The 1965-69 reprints were somewhat shortprinted (four 1965-69 cards for each five 1951-1964) and are 20% scarcer.

		MT
Complete Set (19):		100.00
Common Mantle:		5.00
Common SP Mantle (15-19):		8.00
1	1951 Bowman #253	10.00
2	1952 Topps #311	15.00
3	1953 Topps #82	6.00
4	1954 Bowman #65	5.00
5	1955 Bowman #202	5.00
6	1956 Topps #135	5.00
7	1957 Topps #95	5.00
8	1958 Topps #150	5.00
9	1959 Topps #10	5.00
10	1960 Topps #350	5.00
11	1961 Topps #300	5.00
12	1962 Topps #200	5.00
13	1963 Topps #200	5.00
14	1964 Topps #50	5.00
15	1965 Topps #350	8.00
16	1966 Topps #50	8.00
17	1967 Topps #150	8.00
18	1968 Topps #280	8.00
19	1969 Topps #500	8.00

1996 Topps/Finest Mickey Mantle

Nineteen of Mickey Mantle's regular-issue Bowman and Topps cards from 1951-1969 were printed in Finest technology for this Series 2 insert set. Each card's chrome front is protected with a peel-off plastic layer. Average insertion rate for the Mantle Finest reprints is one per 18 packs. The 1965-69 reprints were printed in a ratio of four for every five 1951-64 reprints, making them 20% scarcer.

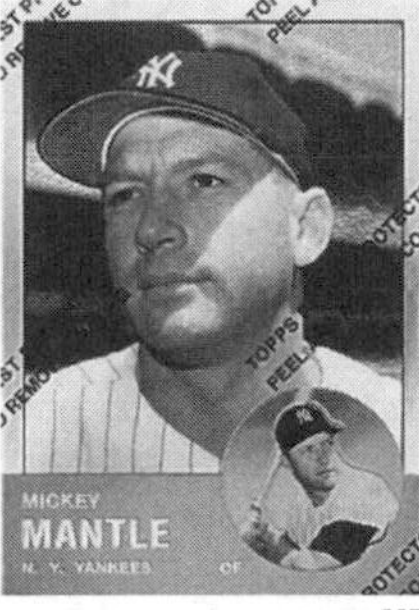

		MT
Complete Set (19):		140.00
Common Mantle:		6.00
Common Shortprint Mantle (15-19):		10.00
1	1951 Bowman #253	12.00
2	1952 Topps #311	20.00
3	1953 Topps #82	10.00
4	1954 Bowman #65	6.00
5	1955 Bowman #202	6.00
6	1956 Topps #135	6.00
7	1957 Topps #95	6.00
8	1958 Topps #150	6.00
9	1959 Topps #10	6.00
10	1960 Topps #350	6.00
11	1961 Topps #300	6.00
12	1962 Topps #200	6.00
13	1963 Topps #200	6.00
14	1964 Topps #50	6.00
15	1965 Topps #350	10.00
16	1966 Topps #50	10.00
17	1967 Topps #150	10.00
18	1968 Topps #280	10.00
19	1969 Topps #500	10.00

1996 Topps/Finest Mickey Mantle Refractors

Each of the 19 Mickey Mantle Finest reprints in Series 2 can also be found in an unmarked Refractor version. Average insertion rate of these superscarce inserts is one per 144 packs.

		MT
Complete Set (19):		725.00
Common Mantle:		40.00
Common SP Mantle (15-19):		48.00
1	1951 Bowman #253	80.00
2	1952 Topps #311	120.00
3	1953 Topps #82	48.00
4	1954 Bowman #65	40.00
5	1955 Bowman #202	40.00
6	1956 Topps #135	40.00
7	1957 Topps #95	40.00
8	1958 Topps #150	40.00
9	1959 Topps #10	40.00
10	1960 Topps #350	40.00
11	1961 Topps #300	40.00
12	1962 Topps #200	40.00
13	1963 Topps #200	40.00
14	1964 Topps #50	40.00
15	1965 Topps #350	48.00
16	1966 Topps #50	48.00
17	1967 Topps #150	48.00
18	1968 Topps #280	48.00
19	1969 Topps #500	48.00

1996 Topps Mickey Mantle Foundation Card

This black-and-white card was an insert exclusive to specially marked 1996 Topps factory sets. In standard 2-1/2" x 3-1/2" format, the card offers on its back information about the foundation and it work in health care and organ donation causes.

	MT
Mickey Mantle	6.00

1996 Topps Mickey Mantle Redemption

Each of the 19 Mantle reprint cards, minus the commemorative gold-foil stamp on front, was also issued in a sweepstakes set. Seeded one per 108 packs, these cards could be sent in for a chance to win the authentic Mantle card pictured on front. Between one and 10 genuine Mantles were awarded for each of the 19 years.

Cards entered in the sweepstakes were not returned when the contest ended Oct. 15, 1996. The sweepstakes cards are a Series 2 exclusive insert.

		MT
Complete Set (19):		200.00
Common Mantle:		10.00
1	1951 Bowman #253	25.00
2	1952 Topps #311	35.00
3	1953 Topps #82	15.00
4	1954 Bowman #65	10.00
5	1955 Bowman #202	10.00
6	1956 Topps #135	10.00
7	1957 Topps #95	10.00
8	1958 Topps #150	10.00
9	1959 Topps #10	10.00
10	1960 Topps #350	10.00
11	1961 Topps #300	10.00
12	1962 Topps #200	10.00
13	1963 Topps #200	10.00
14	1964 Topps #50	10.00
15	1965 Topps #350	10.00
16	1966 Topps #50	10.00
17	1967 Topps #150	10.00
18	1968 Topps #280	10.00
19	1969 Topps #500	10.00

1996 Topps Mickey Mantle Case Inserts

Inserted one per case of Series 2 Topps, these special versions of the 19 Mickey Mantle reprint cards come sealed in a soft plastic holder. The plastic sleeve has a gold-foil stamp at bottom-back which reads "FACTRORY TOPPS SEAL 1996". Like the other Mantle reprints, the 1965-69 cards are somewhat scarcer due to short-printing.

		MT
Complete Set (19):		700.00
Common Mantle:		40.00
Common SP Mantle (15-19):		50.00
1	1951 Bowman #253	60.00
2	1952 Topps #311	75.00
3	1953 Topps #82	50.00
4	1954 Bowman #65	40.00
5	1955 Bowman #202	40.00
6	1956 Topps #135	40.00
7	1957 Topps #95	40.00
8	1958 Topps #150	40.00
9	1959 Topps #10	40.00
10	1960 Topps #350	40.00
11	1961 Topps #300	40.00
12	1962 Topps #200	40.00
13	1963 Topps #200	40.00
14	1964 Topps #50	40.00
15	1965 Topps #350	50.00
16	1966 Topps #50	50.00
17	1967 Topps #150	50.00
18	1968 Topps #280	50.00
19	1969 Topps #500	50.00

1996 Topps Mystery Finest

Each Mystery Finest insert has an opaque black film over the card front, concealing the identity of the player until removed. The inserts are seeded at the rate of one per 36 packs.

		MT
Complete Set (21)		60.00
Common Player:		1.00
Refractors:		3X to 6X
M1	Hideo Nomo	1.50
M2	Greg Maddux	5.00
M3	Randy Johnson	1.50
M4	Chipper Jones	6.00
M5	Marty Cordova	1.00
M6	Garret Anderson	1.00
M7	Cal Ripken Jr.	7.50
M8	Kirby Puckett	2.50
M9	Tony Gwynn	4.00
M10	Manny Ramirez	3.00
M11	Jim Edmonds	1.00
M12	Mike Piazza	6.00
M13	Barry Bonds	3.00
M14	Raul Mondesi	1.00
M15	Sammy Sosa	6.00
M16	Ken Griffey Jr.	10.00
M17	Albert Belle	2.00
M18	Dante Bichette	1.00
M19	Mo Vaughn	1.50
M20	Jeff Bagwell	2.50
M21	Frank Thomas	4.00

1996 Topps Power Boosters

This insert set is printed in Topps' "Power Matrix" technology, replacing two regular cards when found on the average of once per 36 packs. The Power Boosters reproduce the Star Power and Draft Picks subsets on a double-thick card.

		MT
Complete Set (26):		110.00
Common Player:		1.25
1	Tony Gwynn (Star Power)	4.00
2	Mike Piazza (Star Power)	8.00
3	Greg Maddux (Star Power)	6.00
4	Jeff Bagwell (Star Power)	4.00
5	Larry Walker (Star Power)	2.00
6	Barry Larkin (Star Power)	1.50
8	Tom Glavine (Star Power)	1.50
9	Craig Biggio (Star Power)	2.00
10	Barry Bonds (Star Power)	4.00
11	Heathcliff Slocumb (Star Power)	1.50
12	Matt Williams (Star Power)	1.50
13	Todd Helton (Draft Pick)	10.00
14	Mark Redman (Draft Pick)	1.50
15	Michael Barrett (Draft Pick)	3.00
16	Ben Davis (Draft Pick)	4.00
17	Juan LeBron (Draft Pick)	1.50
18	Tony McKnight (Draft Pick)	1.50
19	Ryan Jaroncyk (Draft Pick)	1.50
20	Corey Jenkins (Draft Pick)	1.50
21	Jim Scharrer (Draft Pick)	1.50
22	Mark Bellhorn (Draft Pick)	1.50
23	Jarrod Washburn (Draft Pick)	1.50
24	Geoff Jenkins (Draft Pick)	20.00
25	Sean Casey (Draft Pick)	40.00
26	Brett Tomko (Draft Pick)	2.00

1996 Topps Profiles-AL

Ten cards from this insert issue can be found in each of Topps Series 1 and 2. Analyzing an up-and-coming star, the cards are found every 12th pack, on average.

		MT
Complete Set (20):		20.00
Complete Series 1 (10):		10.00
Complete Series 2 (10):		10.00
Common Player:		.50
1	Roberto Alomar	1.00
2	Carlos Baerga	.50
3	Albert Belle	.75
4	Cecil Fielder	.50
5	Ken Griffey Jr.	5.00
6	Randy Johnson	.60
7	Paul O'Neill	.50
8	Cal Ripken Jr.	3.00
9	Frank Thomas	1.50
10	Mo Vaughn	.50
11	Jay Buhner	.50
12	Marty Cordova	.50
13	Jim Edmonds	.50
14	Juan Gonzalez	1.50
15	Kenny Lofton	.50
16	Edgar Martinez	.50
17	Don Mattingly	1.50
18	Mark McGwire	5.00
19	Rafael Palmeiro	1.00
20	Tim Salmon	.75

1996 Topps Profiles-NL

Projected future stars of the National League are featured in this insert set. Ten players each are found in Series 1 and 2 packs at the rate of one per 12, on average.

		MT
Complete Set (20):		15.00
Complete Series 1 (10):		10.00
Complete Series 2 (10):		5.00
Common Player:		.50
1	Jeff Bagwell	1.50
2	Derek Bell	.50
3	Barry Bonds	1.50
4	Greg Maddux	3.00
5	Fred McGriff	.75
6	Raul Mondesi	.50
7	Mike Piazza	3.00
8	Reggie Sanders	.50
9	Sammy Sosa	3.00
10	Larry Walker	1.00
11	Dante Bichette	.75
12	Andres Galarraga	.75
13	Ron Gant	.50
14	Tom Glavine	.50
15	Chipper Jones	3.00
16	David Justice	.50
17	Barry Larkin	.50
18	Hideo Nomo	.75
19	Gary Sheffield	.75
20	Matt Williams	.75

1996 Topps Wrecking Crew

Printed on foilboard stock, cards of 15 players known for their hitting prowess are featured in this insert set. Found only in Series 2 hobby packs, the inserts are a one per 72 packs find, on average. Cards are numbered with a "WC" prefix.

		MT
Complete Set (15):		40.00
Common Player:		1.00
1	Jeff Bagwell	2.50
2	Albert Belle	2.00
3	Barry Bonds	2.50
4	Jose Canseco	2.00
5	Joe Carter	1.00
6	Cecil Fielder	1.00
7	Ron Gant	1.00
8	Juan Gonzalez	2.50
9	Ken Griffey Jr.	10.00
10	Fred McGriff	1.50
11	Mark McGwire	10.00
12	Mike Piazza	5.00
13	Frank Thomas	2.50
14	Mo Vaughn	1.50
15	Matt Williams	1.50

1996 Topps/ Chrome

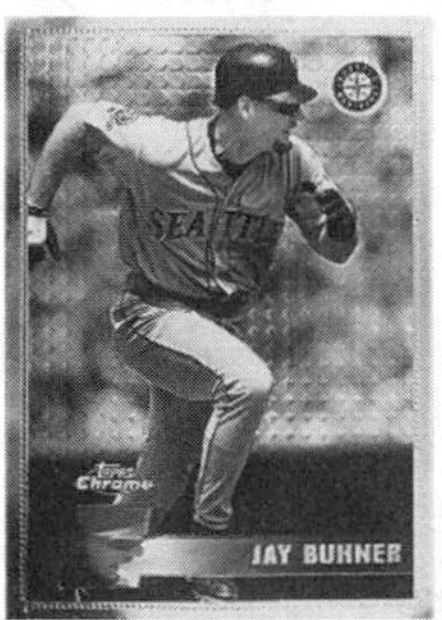

In conjunction with baseball's postseason, Topps introduced the premiere edition of Chrome Baseball. The set has 165 of the elite players from 1996 Topps Baseball Series I and II. Card #7 is a Mickey Mantle tribute card, similar to Topps' Series I card. There are four insert sets: Masters of the Game and Wrecking Crew, and scarcer Refractor versions for both types.

		MT
Complete Set (165):		75.00
Common Player:		.25
Complete Refractor Set (165):		2500.
Common Refractor:		5.00
Refractors:		4x to 8x
Pack (4):		5.00
Wax Box (24):		90.00
1	Tony Gwynn (Star Power)	2.00
2	Mike Piazza (Star Power)	2.50
3	Greg Maddux (Star Power)	2.50
4	Jeff Bagwell (Star Power)	1.50
5	Larry Walker (Star Power)	.75
6	Barry Larkin (Star Power)	.50
7	Mickey Mantle (Commemorative)	10.00
8	Tom Glavine (Star Power)	.40
9	Craig Biggio (Star Power)	.50
10	Barry Bonds (Star Power)	1.00
11	Heathcliff Slocumb (Star Power)	.25
12	Matt Williams (Star Power)	.50
13	Todd Helton (Draft Pick)	20.00
14	Paul Molitor	1.50
15	Glenallen Hill	.25
16	Troy Percival	.25
17	Albert Belle	1.50
18	Mark Wohlers	.25
19	Kirby Puckett	2.00
20	Mark Grace	.50
21	J.T. Snow	.25
22	David Justice	.50
23	Mike Mussina	1.50
24	Bernie Williams	1.50
25	Ron Gant	.25
26	Carlos Baerga	.25
27	Gary Sheffield	.75
28	Cal Ripken Jr. (Tribute Card)	6.00
29	Frank Thomas	2.50
30	Kevin Seitzer	.25
31	Joe Carter	.30
32	Jeff King	.25
33	David Cone	.40
34	Eddie Murray	.75
35	Brian Jordan	.25
36	Garret Anderson	.25
37	Hideo Nomo	.50
38	Steve Finley	.25
39	Ivan Rodriguez	2.00
40	Quilvio Veras	.25
41	Mark McGwire	8.00
42	Greg Vaughn	.25
43	Randy Johnson	1.50
44	David Segui	.25
45	Derek Bell	.25
46	John Valentin	.25
47	Steve Avery	.25
48	Tino Martinez	.25
49	Shane Reynolds	.50
50	Jim Edmonds	.40
51	Raul Mondesi	.60
52	Chipper Jones	5.00
53	Gregg Jefferies	.25
54	Ken Caminiti	.75
55	Brian McRae	.25
56	Don Mattingly	2.00
57	Marty Cordova	.25
58	Vinny Castilla	.40
59	John Smoltz	.60
60	Travis Fryman	.30
61	Ryan Klesko	.35
62	Alex Fernandez	.25
63	Dante Bichette	.50
64	Eric Karros	.30
65	Roger Clemens	3.00
66	Randy Myers	.25
67	Cal Ripken Jr.	6.00
68	Rod Beck	.25
69	Jack McDowell	.25
70	Ken Griffey Jr.	8.00
71	Ramon Martinez	.30
72	Jason Giambi (Future Star)	.50
73	Nomar Garciaparra (Future Star)	5.00
74	Billy Wagner (Future Star)	.50
75	Todd Greene (Future Star)	.25
76	Paul Wilson (Future Star)	.40
77	Johnny Damon (Future Star)	.25
78	Alan Benes (Future Star)	.50
79	Karim Garcia (Future Star)	.75
80	Derek Jeter (Future Star)	5.00
81	Kirby Puckett (Star Power)	1.00
82	Cal Ripken Jr. (Star Power)	3.00
83	Albert Belle (Star Power)	1.00
84	Randy Johnson (Star Power)	.50
85	Wade Boggs (Star Power)	.40
86	Carlos Baerga (Star Power)	.25
87	Ivan Rodriguez (Star Power)	1.00
88	Mike Mussina (Star Power)	.75
89	Frank Thomas (Star Power)	1.00
90	Ken Griffey Jr. (Star Power)	4.00
91	Jose Mesa (Star Power)	.25
92	*Matt Morris* (Draft Pick)	3.00
93	Mike Piazza	5.00
94	Edgar Martinez	.25
95	Chuck Knoblauch	.50
96	Andres Galarraga	.75
97	Tony Gwynn	4.00
98	Lee Smith	.25
99	Sammy Sosa	5.00
100	Jim Thome	.75
101	Bernard Gilkey	.25
102	Brady Anderson	.35
103	Rico Brogna	.25
104	Lenny Dykstra	.25
105	Tom Glavine	.50
106	John Olerud	.75
107	Terry Steinbach	.25
108	Brian Hunter	.25
109	Jay Buhner	.30
110	Mo Vaughn	1.50
111	Jose Mesa	.25
112	Brett Butler	.25
113	Chili Davis	.25
114	Paul O'Neill	.75
115	Roberto Alomar	1.50
116	Barry Larkin	.50
117	Marquis Grissom	.25
118	Will Clark	.50
119	Barry Bonds	2.00
120	Ozzie Smith	1.50
121	Pedro Martinez	2.50
122	Craig Biggio	1.00
123	Moises Alou	.50
124	Robin Ventura	.50
125	Greg Maddux	5.00
126	Tim Salmon	.50
127	Wade Boggs	.50
128	Ismael Valdes	.25
129	Juan Gonzalez	2.00
130	Ray Lankford	.25
131	Bobby Bonilla	.30
132	Reggie Sanders	.25
133	Alex Ochoa (Now Appearing)	.25
134	Mark Loretta (Now Appearing)	.25
135	Jason Kendall (Now Appearing)	.25
136	Brooks Kieschnick (Now Appearing)	.25
137	Chris Snopek (Now Appearing)	.25
138	Ruben Rivera (Now Appearing)	.50
139	Jeff Suppan (Now Appearing)	.25
140	John Wasdin (Now Appearing)	.25
141	Jay Payton (Now Appearing)	.40
142	Rick Krivda (Now Appearing)	.25
143	Jimmy Haynes (Now Appearing)	.25
144	Ryne Sandberg	1.50
145	Matt Williams	.50
146	Jose Canseco	1.50
147	Larry Walker	1.50
148	Kevin Appier	.25
149	Javy Lopez	.40
150	Dennis Eckersley	.25
151	Jason Isringhausen	.25
152	Dean Palmer	.25
153	Jeff Bagwell	2.00
154	Rondell White	.40
155	Wally Joyner	.25
156	Fred McGriff	.50
157	Cecil Fielder	.30
158	Rafael Palmeiro	1.00
159	Rickey Henderson	.50
160	Shawon Dunston	.25
161	Manny Ramirez	2.00
162	Alex Gonzalez	.25
163	Shawn Green	1.00
164	Kenny Lofton	1.50
165	Jeff Conine	.25

1996 Topps/ Chrome Wrecking Crew

Wrecking Crew insert cards were inserted one per every 24 packs of 1996 Topps Chrome Baseball. Refractor versions were also made for these cards; they are seeded one per every 72 packs. Cards are numbered with a "WC" prefix.

		MT
Complete Set (15):		45.00
Common Player:		1.50
Refractors:		1.5x to 2x
1	Jeff Bagwell	5.00
2	Albert Belle	2.00
3	Barry Bonds	3.00
4	Jose Canseco	2.00
5	Joe Carter	1.50
6	Cecil Fielder	1.50
7	Ron Gant	1.50
8	Juan Gonzalez	6.00
9	Ken Griffey Jr.	12.50
10	Fred McGriff	2.00
11	Mark McGwire	12.50
12	Mike Piazza	7.50
13	Frank Thomas	4.00
14	Mo Vaughn	2.00
15	Matt Williams	2.00

1996 Topps/ Chrome Masters of the Game

These 1996 Topps Chrome inserts were seeded one per every 12 packs. Each of the cards is also reprinted in a Refractor version; these cards are seeded one per every 36 packs.

	MT
Complete Set (20):	55.00
Common Player:	1.50

Refractors: 1.5x to 2x
1 Dennis Eckersley 1.50
2 Denny Martinez 1.50
3 Eddie Murray 3.00
4 Paul Molitor 3.50
5 Ozzie Smith 3.50
6 Rickey Henderson 2.00
7 Tim Raines 1.50
8 Lee Smith 1.50
9 Cal Ripken Jr. 11.00
10 Chili Davis 1.50
11 Wade Boggs 2.25
12 Tony Gwynn 7.50
13 Don Mattingly 6.00
14 Bret Saberhagen 1.50
15 Kirby Puckett 6.00
16 Joe Carter 2.25
17 Roger Clemens 6.00
18 Barry Bonds 4.50
19 Greg Maddux 9.00
20 Frank Thomas 4.50

1996 Topps/ Gallery

This 180-card set is printed on 24-point stock utilizing metallic inks and a high-definition printing process. Then a high-gloss film is applied to each card, followed by foil stamping. The regular set is broken down into five subsets - The Classics, The Modernists, The Futurists, The Masters and New Editions. Each theme has a different design. Gallery also has four insert sets. Player's Private Issue cards are a parallel set to the main issue; these cards are seeded one per every 12 packs. The backs are sequentially numbered from 0-999, with the first 100 cards sent to the players; the rest are inserted into packs. The backs are UV coated on the photo only, to allow for autographing. The other insert sets are Expressionists, Photo Gallery and a Mickey Mantle Masterpiece card.

MT
Complete Set (180): 35.00
Common Player: .25
Pack (8): 2.50
Wax Box (24): 50.00
1 Tom Glavine .50
2 Carlos Baerga .25
3 Dante Bichette .40
4 Mark Langston .25
5 Ray Lankford .25
6 Moises Alou .40
7 Marquis Grissom .25
8 Ramon Martinez .25
8p Ramon Martinez (unmarked promo, "Pitcher" spelled out under photo on back) 5.00
9 Steve Finley .25
10 Todd Hundley .25
11 Brady Anderson .25
12 John Valentin .25
13 Heathcliff Slocumb .25
14 Ruben Sierra .25
15 Jeff Conine .25
16 Jay Buhner .35
16p Jay Buhner (unmarked promo; height, weight and "Bats" on same line) 5.00
17 Sammy Sosa 3.00
18 Doug Drabek .25
19 Jose Mesa .25
20 Jeff King .25
21 Mickey Tettleton .25
22 Jeff Montgomery .25
23 Alex Fernandez .25
24 Greg Vaughn .25
25 Chuck Finley .25
26 Terry Steinbach .25
27 Rod Beck .25
28 Jack McDowell .25
29 Mark Wohlers .25
30 Lenny Dykstra .25
31 Bernie Williams .75
32 Travis Fryman .25
33 Jose Canseco 1.25
34 Ken Caminiti .40
35 Devon White .25
36 Bobby Bonilla .25
37 Paul Sorrento .25
38 Ryne Sandberg 1.00
39 Derek Bell .25
40 Bobby Jones .25
41 J.T. Snow .25
42 Denny Neagle .25
43 Tim Wakefield .25
44 Andres Galarraga .75
45 David Segui .25
46 Lee Smith .25
47 Mel Rojas .25
48 John Franco .25
49 Pete Schourek .25
50 John Wetteland .25
51 Paul Molitor .75
52 Ivan Rodriguez 1.50
53 Chris Hoiles .25
54 Mike Greenwell .25
55 Orel Hershiser .25
56 Brian McRae .25
57 Geronimo Berroa .25
58 Craig Biggio .75
59 David Justice .40
59p David Justice (unmarked promo; height,weight and "Bats" on same line) 5.00
60 Lance Johnson .25
61 Andy Ashby .25
62 Randy Myers .25
63 Gregg Jefferies .25
64 Kevin Appier .25
65 Rick Aguilera .25
66 Shane Reynolds .40
67 John Smoltz .40
68 Ron Gant .25
69 Eric Karros .25
70 Jim Thome .40
71 Terry Pendleton .25
72 Kenny Rogers .25
73 Robin Ventura .50
74 Dave Nilsson .25
75 Brian Jordan .25
76 Glenallen Hill .25
77 Greg Colbrunn .25
78 Roberto Alomar 1.00
79 Rickey Henderson .50
80 Carlos Garcia .25
81 Dean Palmer .25
82 Mike Stanley .25
83 Hal Morris .25
84 Wade Boggs .75
85 Chad Curtis .25
86 Roberto Hernandez .25
87 John Olerud .75
88 Frank Castillo .25
89 Rafael Palmeiro 1.00
90 Trevor Hoffman .25
91 Marty Cordova .25
92 Hideo Nomo .50
93 Johnny Damon .25
94 Bill Pulsipher .25
95 Garret Anderson .25
96 Ray Durham .25
97 Ricky Bottalico .25
98 Carlos Perez .25
99 Troy Percival .25
100 Chipper Jones 3.00
101 Esteban Loaiza .25
102 John Mabry .25
103 Jon Nunnally .15
104 Andy Pettitte .75
105 Lyle Mouton .25
106 Jason Isringhausen .25
107 Brian Hunter .25
108 Quilvio Veras .25
109 Jim Edmonds .25
110 Ryan Klesko .40
111 Pedro Martinez 1.50
112 Joey Hamilton .25
113 Vinny Castilla .40
114 Alex Gonzalez .25
115 Raul Mondesi .40
116 Rondell White .40
117 Dan Miceli .25
118 Tom Goodwin .25
119 Bret Boone .25
120 Shawn Green 1.00
121 Jeff Cirillo .25
122 Rico Brogna .25
123 Chris Gomez .25
124 Ismael Valdes .25
125 Javy Lopez .40
126 Manny Ramirez 1.50
127 Paul Wilson .25
128 Billy Wagner .25
129 Eric Owens .25
130 Todd Greene .25
131 Karim Garcia .25
132 Jimmy Haynes .25
133 Michael Tucker .25
134 John Wasdin .25
135 Brooks Kieschnick .25
136 Alex Ochoa .25
137 Ariel Prieto .25
138 Tony Clark .40
139 Mark Loretta .25
140 Rey Ordonez .50
141 Chris Snopek .25
142 Roger Cedeno .25
143 Derek Jeter 3.00
144 Jeff Suppan .25
145 Greg Maddux 2.50
146 Ken Griffey Jr. 5.00
147 Tony Gwynn 2.50
148 Darren Daulton .25
149 Will Clark .50
150 Mo Vaughn .75
151 Reggie Sanders .25
152 Kirby Puckett 1.50
153 Paul O'Neill .50
154 Tim Salmon .50
155 Mark McGwire 5.00
156 Barry Bonds 1.50
157 Albert Belle 1.00
158 Edgar Martinez .25
159 Mike Mussina .75
160 Cecil Fielder .25
161 Kenny Lofton .75
162 Randy Johnson 1.00
163 Juan Gonzalez 1.50
164 Jeff Bagwell 1.50
165 Joe Carter .25
166 Mike Piazza 3.00
167 Eddie Murray .50
168 Cal Ripken Jr. 3.00
169 Barry Larkin .50
170 Chuck Knoblauch .40
171 Chili Davis .25
172 Fred McGriff .50
173 Matt Williams .40
174 Roger Clemens 2.00
175 Frank Thomas 1.50
176 Dennis Eckersley .25
177 Gary Sheffield .40
178 David Cone .40
179 Larry Walker 1.00
180 Mark Grace .50

1996 Topps/ Gallery Players Private Issue

The first 999 examples of each of the base cards in the Gallery issue are designated on the front with a gold-foil stamp as "Players Private Issue." The first 100 of those cards were given to the depicted player, the others are randomly packed. Besides the logo on front, the PPI cards are identified on back with an individual serial number.

MT
Complete Set (180): 475.00
Common Player: 1.50
(Star cards valued at 8X to 15X regular Gallery versions)

1996 Topps/ Gallery Expressionists

These 1996 Topps Gallery inserts feature 20 team leaders printed on triple foil-stamped and texture-embossed cards. Cards are seeded one per every 24 packs.

MT
Complete Set (20): 45.00
Common Player: .75
1 Mike Piazza 6.00
2 J.T. Snow .75
3 Ken Griffey Jr. 10.00
4 Kirby Puckett 2.50
5 Carlos Baerga .75
6 Chipper Jones 6.00
7 Hideo Nomo .75
8 Mark McGwire 10.00
9 Gary Sheffield 1.00
10 Randy Johnson 2.00
11 Ray Lankford .75
12 Sammy Sosa 6.00
13 Denny Martinez .75
14 Jose Canseco 2.00
15 Tony Gwynn 5.00
16 Edgar Martinez .75
17 Reggie Sanders .75
18 Andres Galarraga 1.50
19 Albert Belle 2.50
20 Barry Larkin 1.00

1996 Topps/ Gallery Masterpiece

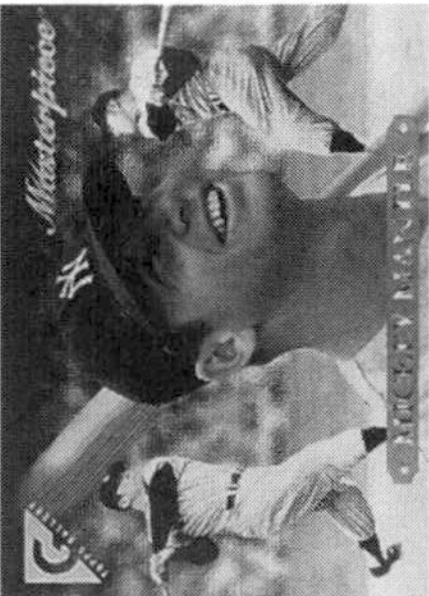

Topps continues its tribute to Mickey Mantle

with this 1996 Topps Gallery insert card. The card, seeded one per every 48 packs, has three photos of Mantle on the front, with his comprehensive career statistics on the back.

		MT
MP1	Mickey Mantle	10.00

1996 Topps/ Gallery Photo Gallery

Photo Gallery is a collection of 15 cards featuring photography of baseball's biggest stars and greatest moments from the last season. The text on the card includes details of the card's front and back photos. The cards are seeded one per every 30 packs. Cards are numbered with a "PG" prefix.

		MT
Complete Set (15):		30.00
Common Player:		1.00
1	Eddie Murray	1.00
2	Randy Johnson	2.00
3	Cal Ripken Jr.	7.50
4	Bret Boone	1.00
5	Frank Thomas	2.50
6	Jeff Conine	1.00
7	Johnny Damon	1.00
8	Roger Clemens	4.00
9	Albert Belle	2.00
10	Ken Griffey Jr.	10.00
11	Kirby Puckett	2.50
12	David Justice	1.50
13	Bobby Bonilla	1.00
14	Larry Walker, Andres Galarraga, Vinny Castilla, Dante Bichette	1.50
15	Mark Wohlers, Javier Lopez	1.00

1996 Topps/ Laser

Topps' 1996 Laser Baseball was the first set to use laser-cut technology on every card, creating surgically-precise laticework across the entire card. Every card in the 128-card regular issue set features one of four designs laser-cut into 20-point stock. One card from each of the four different designs is found in each four-card pack. Three different laser-cut insert sets were also produced: Bright Spots, Power Cuts and Stadium Stars. Cards 1-8 from each insert set were in Series 1 packs; cards 9-16 were seeded in Series 2 packs. A slightly oversize (1-5/8" x 3-5/8") checklist card in each pack helped protect the delicate die-cut details from damage.

		MT
Complete Set (128):		100.00
Complete Series 1 Set (64):		50.00
Complete Series 2 Set (64):		50.00
Common Player:		.25
Series 1 or 2 Pack (4):		3.00
Series 1 or 2 Wax Box (24):		60.00
1	Moises Alou	.75
2	Derek Bell	.25
3	Joe Carter	.25
4	Jeff Conine	.25
5	Darren Daulton	.25
6	Jim Edmonds	.25
7	Ron Gant	.35
8	Juan Gonzalez	2.00
9	Brian Jordan	.25
10	Ryan Klesko	.35
11	Paul Molitor	1.50
12	Tony Phillips	.25
13	Manny Ramirez	2.00
14	Sammy Sosa	5.00
15	Devon White	.25
16	Bernie Williams	1.00
17	Garret Anderson	.25
18	Jay Bell	.25
19	Craig Biggio	1.00
20	Bobby Bonilla	.25
21	Ken Caminiti	.40
22	Shawon Dunston	.25
23	Mark Grace	.75
23p	Mark Grace (unmarked promo, plain, rather than brushed, gold foil)	4.00
24	Gregg Jefferies	.25
25	Jeff King	.25
26	Javy Lopez	.25
27	Edgar Martinez	.25
28	Dean Palmer	.25
29	J.T. Snow	.25
30	Mike Stanley	.25
30p	Mike Stanley (unmarked promo; plain, rather than brushed, gold foil)	3.00
31	Terry Steinbach	.25
32	Robin Ventura	.75
33	Roberto Alomar	1.50
34	Jeff Bagwell	2.00
35	Dante Bichette	.75
36	Wade Boggs	.75
37	Barry Bonds	2.00
38	Jose Canseco	1.50
39	Vinny Castilla	.25
40	Will Clark	1.00
41	Marty Cordova	.25
42	Ken Griffey Jr.	8.00
43	Tony Gwynn	4.00
44	Rickey Henderson	.75
45	Chipper Jones	5.00
46	Mark McGwire	8.00
47	Brian McRae	.25
48	Ryne Sandberg	2.00
49	Andy Ashby	.25
50	Alan Benes	.25
51	Andy Benes	.25
52	Roger Clemens	3.00
53	Doug Drabek	.25
54	Dennis Eckersley	.25
55	Tom Glavine	.50
56	Randy Johnson	1.50
57	Mark Langston	.25
58	Denny Martinez	.25
59	Jack McDowell	.25
60	Hideo Nomo	.50
61	Shane Reynolds	.40
62	John Smoltz	.40
63	Paul Wilson	.25
64	Mark Wohlers	.25
65	Shawn Green	1.00
66	Marquis Grissom	.25
67	Dave Hollins	.25
68	Todd Hundley	.25
69	David Justice	.50
70	Eric Karros	.25
71	Ray Lankford	.25
72	Fred McGriff	.50
73	Hal Morris	.25
74	Eddie Murray	.50
75	Paul O'Neill	.50
76	Rey Ordonez	.50
77	Reggie Sanders	.25
78	Gary Sheffield	.50
79	Jim Thome	1.00
80	Rondell White	.50
81	Travis Fryman	.30
82	Derek Jeter	5.00
83	Chuck Knoblauch	.60
84	Barry Larkin	.50
85	Tino Martinez	.50
86	Raul Mondesi	1.00
87	John Olerud	.75
88	Rafael Palmeiro	1.00
89	Mike Piazza	5.00
90	Cal Ripken Jr.	6.00
91	Ivan Rodriguez	2.00
92	Frank Thomas	2.00
93	John Valentin	.25
94	Mo Vaughn	1.50
95	Quilvio Veras	.25
96	Matt Williams	.75
97	Brady Anderson	.40
98	Carlos Baerga	.25
99	Albert Belle	1.50
100	Jay Buhner	.35
101	Johnny Damon	.25
102	Chili Davis	.25
103	Ray Durham	.25
104	Lenny Dykstra	.25
105	Cecil Fielder	.25
106	Andres Galarraga	.75
107	Brian Hunter	.25
108	Kenny Lofton	1.50
109	Kirby Puckett	2.00
110	Tim Salmon	.50
111	Greg Vaughn	.30
112	Larry Walker	1.50
113	Rick Aguilera	.25
114	Kevin Appier	.25
115	Kevin Brown	.40
116	David Cone	.50
117	Alex Fernandez	.25
118	Chuck Finley	.25
119	Joey Hamilton	.25
120	Jason Isringhausen	.25
121	Greg Maddux	4.00
122	Pedro Martinez	2.00
123	Jose Mesa	.25
124	Jeff Montgomery	.25
125	Mike Mussina	1.50
126	Randy Myers	.25
127	Kenny Rogers	.25
128	Ismael Valdes	.25
	Series 1 checklist	.05
	Series 2 Checklist	.05

1996 Topps/ Laser Bright Spots

Top young stars are featured on these 1996 Topps Laser cards, which use etched silver and gold diffraction foil. The cards are seeded one per every 20 packs. Numbers 1-8 are in Series I packs; cards 9-16 are in Series II packs.

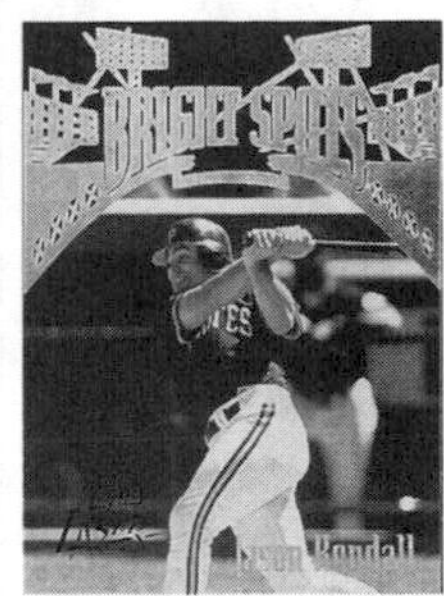

		MT
Complete Set (16):		35.00
Complete Series 1 Set (8):		15.00
Complete Series 2 Set (8):		20.00
Common Player:		1.50
1	Brian Hunter	1.50
2	Derek Jeter	7.50
3	Jason Kendall	2.50
4	Brooks Kieschnick	1.50
5	Rey Ordonez	2.00
6	Jason Schmidt	1.50
7	Chris Snopek	1.50
8	Bob Wolcott	1.50
9	Alan Benes	2.00
10	Marty Cordova	1.50
11	Jimmy Haynes	1.50
12	Todd Hollandsworth	1.50
13	Derek Jeter	7.50
14	Chipper Jones	6.00
15	Hideo Nomo	2.00
16	Paul Wilson	1.50

1996 Topps/ Laser Power Cuts

This 1996 Topps Laser insert set spotlights 16 of the game's top power hitters on etched foil and gold diffraction foil cards. These cards were seeded one per every 40 packs; numbers 1-8 were in Series I packs; cards 9-16 were in Series II packs.

		MT
Complete Set (8):		80.00
Complete Series 1 Set (8):		37.00
Complete Series 2 Set (8):		45.00
Common Player:		2.00
1	Albert Belle	5.00
2	Jay Buhner	2.00
3	Fred McGriff	2.00
4	Mike Piazza	12.50
5	Tim Salmon	2.50
6	Frank Thomas	7.50
7	Mo Vaughn	5.00

8	Matt Williams	2.50
9	Jeff Bagwell	6.00
10	Barry Bonds	6.00
11	Jose Canseco	3.00
12	Cecil Fielder	2.00
13	Juan Gonzalez	10.00
14	Ken Griffey Jr.	20.00
15	Sammy Sosa	12.50
16	Larry Walker	3.00

1996 Topps /Laser Stadium Stars

These 1996 Topps Laser cards are the most difficult to find; they are seeded one per every 60 packs. The 16 cards feature a laser-sculpted cover that folds back to reveal striated silver and gold etched diffraction foil on each card front. Cards 1-8 were in Series I packs; numbers 9-16 were Series II inserts.

		MT
Complete Set (8):		75.00
Complete Series 1 Set (8):		45.00
Complete Series 2 Set (8):		35.00
Common Player:		2.50
1	Carlos Baerga	2.50
2	Barry Bonds	5.00
3	Andres Galarraga	4.00
4	Ken Griffey Jr.	20.00
5	Barry Larkin	3.00
6	Raul Mondesi	2.50
7	Kirby Puckett	5.00
8	Cal Ripken Jr.	15.00
9	Will Clark	4.00
10	Roger Clemens	7.50
11	Tony Gwynn	10.00
12	Randy Johnson	3.00
13	Kenny Lofton	3.00
14	Edgar Martinez	2.50
15	Ryne Sandberg	5.00
16	Frank Thomas	7.50

1997 Topps

Topps' 1997 set includes the first-ever player cards of the expansion Diamondbacks and Devil Rays; 16 Mickey Mantle reprints; a special Jackie Robinson tribute card; 27 Willie Mays Topps and Bowman reprints; randomly-inserted Willie Mays autographed reprint cards; and Inter-League Finest and Finest Refractors cards. The base set has 275 cards in each series. Each card front has a gloss coating on the photo and a spot matte finish on the outside border. Gold foil stamping is also used. Card backs have informative text, complete player stats and biographies, and a second photo. The Jackie Robinson card pays tribute to the 50th anniversary of his breaking the color line. This card is #42 in the regular issue. Mantle reprints, seeded one per every 12 packs, feature the 16 remaining Mantle cards which were not reprinted in 1996 Topps baseball. The cards, each stamped with a gold foil logo, are numbered from #21 to #36. Willie Mays has 27 of his cards reprinted and seeded one per every eight packs. Each card also has a gold foil stamp. As a special hobby-exclusive bonus, 1,000 randomly-selected Mays reprints will be autographed and randomly inserted in packs. Five other insert sets were made: All-Stars, Inter-League Finest and Inter-League Finest Refractors, Sweet Strokes and Hobby Masters.

		MT
Complete Set (496):		40.00
Complete Series 1 Set (276):		20.00
Complete Series 2 Set (220):		20.00
Common Player:		.05
Ser. 1 or 2 Pack (11):		1.50
Ser. 1 or 2 Wax Box (36):		45.00
1	Barry Bonds	.50
2	Tom Pagnozzi	.05
3	Terrell Wade	.05
4	Jose Valentin	.05
5	Mark Clark	.05
6	Brady Anderson	.15
7	Not issued	
8	Wade Boggs	.25
9	Scott Stahoviak	.05
10	Andres Galarraga	.25
11	Steve Avery	.05
12	Rusty Greer	.05
13	Derek Jeter	1.50
14	Ricky Bottalico	.05
15	Andy Ashby	.05
16	Paul Shuey	.05
17	F.P. Santangelo	.05
18	Royce Clayton	.05
19	Mike Mohler	.05
20	Mike Piazza	1.50
21	Jaime Navarro	.05
22	Billy Wagner	.10
23	Mike Timlin	.05
24	Garret Anderson	.05
25	Ben McDonald	.05
26	Mel Rojas	.05
27	John Burkett	.05
28	Jeff King	.05
29	Reggie Jefferson	.05
30	Kevin Appier	.05
31	Felipe Lira	.05
32	Kevin Tapani	.05
33	Mark Portugal	.05
34	Carlos Garcia	.05
35	Joey Cora	.05
36	David Segui	.05
37	Mark Grace	.25
38	Erik Hanson	.05
39	Jeff D'Amico	.05
40	Jay Buhner	.05
41	B.J. Surhoff	.05
42	Jackie Robinson	3.00
43	Roger Pavlik	.05
44	Hal Morris	.05
45	Mariano Duncan	.05
46	Harold Baines	.10
47	Jorge Fabregas	.05
48	Jose Herrera	.05
49	Jeff Cirillo	.05
50	Tom Glavine	.15
51	Pedro Astacio	.05
52	Mark Gardner	.05
53	Arthur Rhodes	.05
54	Troy O'Leary	.05
55	Bip Roberts	.05
56	Mike Lieberthal	.05
57	Shane Andrews	.05
58	Scott Karl	.05
59	Gary DiSarcina	.05
60	Andy Pettitte	.25
61a	Kevin Elster	.05
61b	Mike Fetters (should be #84)	.05
62	Mark McGwire	2.50
63	Dan Wilson	.05
64	Mickey Morandini	.05
65	Chuck Knoblauch	.20
66	Tim Wakefield	.05
67	Raul Mondesi	.25
68	Todd Jones	.05
69	Albert Belle	.50
70	Trevor Hoffman	.05
71	Eric Young	.10
72	Robert Perez	.05
73	Butch Huskey	.05
74	Brian McRae	.05
75	Jim Edmonds	.10
76	Mike Henneman	.05
77	Frank Rodriguez	.05
78	Danny Tartabull	.05
79	Robby Nen	.05
80	Reggie Sanders	.10
81	Ron Karkovice	.05
82	Benny Santiago	.05
83	Mike Lansing	.05
84	Not issued - see #61b	
85	Craig Biggio	.25
86	Mike Bordick	.05
87	Ray Lankford	.10
88	Charles Nagy	.05
89	Paul Wilson	.05
90	John Wetteland	.05
91	Tom Candiotti	.05
92	Carlos Delgado	.40
93	Derek Bell	.10
94	Mark Lemke	.05
95	Edgar Martinez	.05
96	Rickey Henderson	.25
97	Greg Myers	.05
98	Jim Leyritz	.05
99	Mark Johnson	.05
100	Dwight Gooden (Season Highlights)	.05
101	Al Leiter (Season Highlights)	.05
102a	John Mabry (Season Highlights) (last line on back ends "... Mabry"))	.05
102b	John Mabry (Season Highlights) (last line on back ends "...walked.")	.05
103	Alex Ochoa (Season Highlights)	.05
104	Mike Piazza (Season Highlights)	.60
105	Jim Thome	.30
106	Ricky Otero	.05
107	Jamey Wright	.05
108	Frank Thomas	.50
109	Jody Reed	.05
110	Orel Hershiser	.10
111	Terry Steinbach	.05
112	Mark Loretta	.05
113	Turk Wendell	.05
114	Marvin Benard	.05
115	Kevin Brown	.05
116	Robert Person	.05
117	Joey Hamilton	.05
118	Francisco Cordova	.10
119	John Smiley	.05
120	Travis Fryman	.15
121	Jimmy Key	.05
122	Tom Goodwin	.05
123	Mike Greenwell	.05
124	Juan Gonzalez	.75
125	Pete Harnisch	.05
126	Roger Cedeno	.05
127	Ron Gant	.15
128	Mark Langston	.05
129	Tim Crabtree	.05
130	Greg Maddux	1.50
131	William VanLandingham	.05
132	Wally Joyner	.10
133	Randy Myers	.05
134	John Valentin	.10
135	Bret Boone	.05
136	Bruce Ruffin	.05
137	Chris Snopek	.05
138	Paul Molitor	.40
139	Mark McLemore	.05
140	Rafael Palmeiro	.25
141	Herb Perry	.05
142	Luis Gonzalez	.10
143	Doug Drabek	.05
144	Ken Ryan	.05
145	Todd Hundley	.10
146	Ellis Burks	.05
147	Ozzie Guillen	.05
148	Rich Becker	.05
149	Sterling Hitchcock	.05
150	Bernie Williams	.40
151	Mike Stanley	.05
152	Roberto Alomar	.40
153	Jose Mesa	.05
154	Steve Trachsel	.05
155	Alex Gonzalez	.05
156	Troy Percival	.05
157	John Smoltz	.20
158	Pedro Martinez	.50
159	Jeff Conine	.10
160	Bernard Gilkey	.05
161	Jim Eisenreich	.05
162	Mickey Tettleton	.05
163	Justin Thompson	.05
164	Jose Offerman	.05
165	Tony Phillips	.05
166	Ismael Valdes	.05
167	Ryne Sandberg	.50
168	Matt Mieske	.05
169	Geronimo Berroa	.05
170	Otis Nixon	.05
171	John Mabry	.05
172	Shawon Dunston	.05
173	Omar Vizquel	.10
174	Chris Holles	.05
175	Doc Gooden	.10
176	Wilson Alvarez	.05
177	Todd Hollandsworth	.10
178	Roger Salkeld	.05
179	Rey Sanchez	.05
180	Rey Ordonez	.15
181	Denny Martinez	.05
182	Ramon Martinez	.10
183	Dave Nilsson	.05
184	Marquis Grissom	.10
185	Randy Velarde	.05
186	Ron Coomer	.05
187	Tino Martinez	.15
188	Jeff Brantley	.05
189	Steve Finley	.05
190	Andy Benes	.10
191	Terry Adams	.05
192	Mike Blowers	.05
193	Russ Davis	.05
194	Darryl Hamilton	.05
195	Jason Kendall	.15
196	Johnny Damon	.10
197	Dave Martinez	.05
198	Mike Macfarlane	.05
199	Norm Charlton	.05
200	Doug Million, Damian Moss, Bobby Rodger (Prospect)	.20
201	Geoff Jenkins, Raul Ibanez, Mike Cameron (Prospect)	.25
202	Sean Casey, Jim Bonnici, Dmitri Young (Prospect)	1.00
203	Jed Hansen, Homer Bush, Felipe Crespo (Prospect)	.10

204 Kevin Orie, Gabe Alvarez, Aaron Boone (Prospect) .25
205 Ben Davis, Kevin Brown, Bobby Estalella (Prospect) .10
206 Billy McMillon, *Bubba Trammell*, Dante Powell (Prospect) .25
207 Jarrod Washburn, *Marc Wilkins*, Glendon Rusch (Prospect) .15
208 Brian Hunter .05
209 Jason Giambi .10
210 Henry Rodriguez .05
211 Edgar Renteria .20
212 Edgardo Alfonzo .15
213 Fernando Vina .05
214 Shawn Green .40
215 Ray Durham .05
216 Joe Randa .05
217 Armando Reynoso .05
218 Eric Davis .05
219 Bob Tewksbury .05
220 Jacob Cruz .05
221 Glenallen Hill .05
222 Gary Gaetti .05
223 Donne Wall .05
224 Brad Clontz .05
225 Marty Janzen .05
226 Todd Worrell .05
227 John Franco .05
228 David Wells .05
229 Gregg Jefferies .10
230 Tim Naehring .05
231 Thomas Howard .05
232 Roberto Hernandez .05
233 Kevin Ritz .05
234 Julian Tavarez .05
235 Ken Hill .05
236 Greg Gagne .05
237 Bobby Chouinard .05
238 Joe Carter .05
239 Jermaine Dye .05
240 Antonio Osuna .05
241 Julio Franco .05
242 Mike Grace .05
243 Aaron Sele .05
244 David Justice .20
245 Sandy Alomar .10
246 Jose Canseco .50
247 Paul O'Neill .20
248 Sean Berry .05
249 *Nick Bierbrodt*, *Kevin Sweeney* (Diamond Backs) .75
250 *Larry Rodriguez*, *Vladimir Nunez* (Diamond Backs) .25
251 Ron Hartman, David Hayman (Diamond Backs) .20
252 Alex Sanchez, Matt Quatraro (Devil Rays) .20
253 Ronni Seberino, *Pablo Ortega* (Devil Rays) .25
254 Rex Hudler .05
255 Orlando Miller .05
256 Mariano Rivera .25
257 Brad Radke .05
258 Bobby Higginson .05
259 Jay Bell .05
260 Mark Grudzielanek .05
261 Lance Johnson .05
262 Ken Caminiti .15
263 J.T. Snow .05
264 Gary Sheffield .20
265 Darrin Fletcher .05
266 Eric Owens .05
267 Luis Castillo .10
268 Scott Rolen .75
269 *Todd Noel*, John Oliver (Draft Pick) .25
270 *Robert Stratton*, *Corey Lee* (Draft Pick) .25
271 *Gil Meche*, *Matt Halloran* (Draft Pick) 1.00
272 *Eric Milton*, Dermal Brown (Draft Pick) .75
273 *Josh Garrett*, *Chris Reitsma* (Draft Pick) .25
274 *A.J. Zapp*, *Jason Marquis* (Draft Pick) .50
275 Checklist .05
276a Checklist .05
276b Chipper Jones (should be #277) 1.50
277 Not issued
278 Orlando Merced .05
279 Ariel Prieto .05
280 Al Leiter .15
281 Pat Meares .05
282 Darryl Strawberry .15
283 Jamie Moyer .05
284 Scott Servais .05
285 Delino DeShields .05
286 Danny Graves .05
287 Gerald Williams .05
288 Todd Greene .05
289 Rico Brogna .05
290 Derrick Gibson .05
291 Joe Girardi .05
292 Darren Lewis .05
293 Nomar Garciaparra 1.50
294 Greg Colbrunn .05
295 Jeff Bagwell .50
296 Brent Gates .05
297 Jose Vizcaino .05
298 Alex Ochoa .05
299 Sid Fernandez .05
300 Ken Griffey Jr. 2.50
301 Chris Gomez .05
302 Wendell Magee .05
303 Darren Oliver .05
304 Mel Nieves .05
305 Sammy Sosa 1.50
306 George Arias .05
307 Jack McDowell .05
308 Stan Javier .05
309 Kimera Bartee .05
310 James Baldwin .05
311 Rocky Coppinger .05
312 Keith Lockhart .05
313 C.J. Nitkowski .05
314 Allen Watson .05
315 Darryl Kile .05
316 Amaury Telemaco .05
317 Jason Isringhausen .05
318 Manny Ramirez .50
319 Terry Pendleton .05
320 Tim Salmon .15
321 Eric Karros .10
322 Mark Whiten .05
323 Rick Krivda .05
324 Brett Butler .05
325 Randy Johnson .30
326 Eddie Taubensee .05
327 Mark Leiter .05
328 Kevin Gross .05
329 Ernie Young .05
330 Pat Hentgen .05
331 Rondell White .15
332 Bobby Witt .05
333 Eddie Murray .30
334 Tim Raines .10
335 Jeff Fassero .05
336 Chuck Finley .05
337 Willie Adams .05
338 Chan Ho Park .15
339 Jay Powell .05
340 Ivan Rodriguez .50
341 Jermaine Allensworth .05
342 Jay Payton .15
343 T.J. Mathews .05
344 Tony Batista .05
345 Ed Sprague .05
346 Jeff Kent .05
347 Scott Erickson .05
348 Jeff Suppan .05
349 Pete Schourek .05
350 Kenny Lofton .40
351 Alan Benes .05
352 Fred McGriff .25
353 Charlie O'Brien .05
354 Darren Bragg .05
355 Alex Fernandez .05
356 Al Martin .05
357 Bob Wells .05
358 Chad Mottola .05
359 Devon White .05
360 David Cone .15
361 Bobby Jones .05
362 Scott Sanders .05
363 Karim Garcia .10
364 Kirt Manwaring .05
365 Chili Davis .05
366 Mike Hampton .05
367 Chad Ogea .05
368 Curt Schilling .15
369 Phil Nevin .05
370 Roger Clemens 1.00
371 Willie Greene .05
372 Kenny Rogers .05
373 Jose Rijo .05
374 Bobby Bonilla .05
375 Mike Mussina .40
376 Curtis Pride .05
377 Todd Walker .15
378 Jason Bere .05
379 Heathcliff Slocumb .05
380 Dante Bichette .20
381 Carlos Baerga .05
382 Livan Hernandez .05
383 Jason Schmidt .05
384 Kevin Stocker .05
385 Matt Williams .20
386 Bartolo Colon .15
387 Will Clark .25
388 Dennis Eckersley .10
389 Brooks Kieschnick .10
390 Ryan Klesko .15
391 Mark Carreon .05
392 Tim Worrell .05
393 Dean Palmer .05
394 Wil Cordero .05
395 Javy Lopez .15
396 Rich Aurilla .05
397 Greg Vaughn .15
398 Vinny Castilla .15
399 Jeff Montgomery .05
400 Cal Ripken Jr. 1.50
401 Walt Weiss .05
402 Brad Ausmus .05
403 Ruben Rivera .15
404 Mark Wohlers .05
405 Rick Aguilera .05
406 Tony Clark .20
407 Lyle Mouton .05
408 Bill Pulsipher .05
409 Jose Rosado .05
410 Tony Gwynn 1.00
411 Cecil Fielder .10
412 John Flaherty .05
413 Lenny Dykstra .05
414 Ugueth Urbina .05
415 Brian Jordan .15
416 Bob Abreu .10
417 Craig Paquette .05
418 Sandy Martinez .05
419 Jeff Blauser .05
420 Barry Larkin .10
421 Kevin Seitzer .05
422 Tim Belcher .05
423 Paul Sorrento .05
424 Cal Eldred .05
425 Robin Ventura .15
426 John Olerud .20
427 Bob Wolcott .05
428 Matt Lawton .05
429 Rod Beck .05
430 Shane Reynolds .15
431 Mike James .05
432 Steve Wojciechowski .05
433 Vladimir Guerrero 1.00
434 Dustin Hermanson .10
435 Marty Cordova .05
436 Marc Newfield .05
437 Todd Stottlemyre .05
438 Jeffrey Hammonds .05
439 Dave Stevens .05
440 Hideo Nomo .20
441 Mark Thompson .05
442 Mark Lewis .05
443 Quinton McCracken .05
444 Cliff Floyd .05
445 Denny Neagle .05
446 John Jaha .05
447 Mike Sweeney .05
448 John Wasdin .05
449 Chad Curtis .05
450 Mo Vaughn .40
451 Donovan Osborne .05
452 Ruben Sierra .05
453 Michael Tucker .05
454 Kurt Abbott .05
455 Andruw Jones .50
456 Shannon Stewart .05
457 Scott Brosius .05
458 Juan Guzman .05
459 Ron Villone .05
460 Moises Alou .15
461 Larry Walker .40
462 Eddie Murray (Season Highlights) .20
463 Paul Molitor (Season Highlights) .20
464 Hideo Nomo (Season Highlights) .25
465 Barry Bonds (Season Highlights) .40
466 Todd Hundley (Season Highlights) .05
467 Rheal Cormier .05
468 *Jason Conti* .50
469 Rod Barajas .05
470 Jared Sandberg, *Cedric Bowers* .50
471 Paul Wilders, *Chie Gunner* .20
472 Mike Decelle, *Marcus McCain* .20
473 Todd Zeile .05
474 Neifi Perez .05
475 Jeromy Burnitz .05
476 Trey Beamon .05
477 John Patterson, *Braden Looper* (Draft Picks) .50
478 *Danny Peoples*, *Jake Westbrook* (Draft Picks) .25
479 *Eric Chavez*, Adam Eaton (Draft Picks) 1.50
480 *Joe Lawrence*, Pete Tucci (Draft Picks) .50
481 Kris Benson, *Billy Koch* (Draft Picks) .50
482 John Nicholson, Andy Prater (Draft Picks) .25
483 *Mark Kotsay*, Mark Johnson (Draft Picks) .50
484 Armando Benitez .05
485 Mike Matheny .05
486 Jeff Reed .05
487 Mark Bellhorn, Russ Johnson, Enrique Wilson (Prospects) .05
488 Ben Grieve, Richard Hidalgo, *Scott Morgan* (Prospects) .75
489 Paul Konerko, Derrek Lee, Ron Wright (Prospects) .25
490 Wes Helms, *Bill Mueller*, Brad Seitzer (Prospects) .50
491 Jeff Abbott, Shane Monahan, Edgard Velazquez (Prospects) .20
492 *Jimmy Anderson*, Ron Blazier, Gerald Witasick, Jr. (Prospects) .25
493 Darin Blood, Heath Murray, Carl Pavano (Prospects) .05
494 Mark Redman, *Mike Villano*, Nelson Figueroa (Prospects) .20
495 Checklist .05
496 Checklist .05

1997 Topps All-Stars

Topps' 1997 All-Stars insert cards, printed on a dazzling rainbow foil-board, feature the top players from each position. There are 22 cards, 11 from each league, which showcase the top three players from each position as voted by Topps' sports department. On the front of each card is a photo of a "first team" all-star player; the back has a different photo of that player, who appears alongside the "second team" and "third team" selections. These cards are seeded one per every 18 1997 Topps Series I packs. Cards are numbered with an "AS" prefix.

		MT
Complete Set (22):		40.00
Common Player:		1.00
1	Ivan Rodriguez	3.00
2	Todd Hundley	1.00
3	Frank Thomas	5.00
4	Andres Galarraga	1.25
5	Chuck Knoblauch	1.25
6	Eric Young	1.25
7	Jim Thome	1.25
8	Chipper Jones	7.00
9	Cal Ripken Jr.	8.00
10	Barry Larkin	1.25
11	Albert Belle	3.00
12	Barry Bonds	3.00
13	Ken Griffey Jr.	10.00
14	Ellis Burks	1.00
15	Juan Gonzalez	3.00
16	Gary Sheffield	1.25
17	Andy Pettitte	1.25
18	Tom Glavine	1.25
19	Pat Hentgen	1.00
20	John Smoltz	1.25
21	Roberto Hernandez	1.00
22	Mark Wohlers	1.00

1997 Topps Awesome Impact

This flashy insert exclusive to Series 2 retail packaging features young players who have quickly made their mark in the big leagues. Fronts have player action photos against a background of silver primatic geometric shapes. Backs are horizontal with a player portrait photo, recent stats and a few words about the player's current and projected impact. Stated odds of finding this insert are one per 18 packs. Cards are numbered with an "AI" prefix.

		MT
Complete Set (20):		50.00
Common Player:		1.00
1	Jaime Bluma	1.00
2	Tony Clark	2.00
3	Jermaine Dye	1.00
4	Nomar Garciaparra	12.00
5	Vladimir Guerrero	10.00
6	Todd Hollandsworth	1.00
7	Derek Jeter	15.00
8	Andruw Jones	4.00
9	Chipper Jones	12.00
10	Jason Kendall	2.00
11	Brooks Kieschnick	1.00
12	Alex Ochoa	1.00
13	Rey Ordonez	1.50
14	Neifi Perez	1.00
15	Edgar Renteria	1.50
16	Mariano Rivera	1.50
17	Ruben Rivera	1.00
18	Scott Rolen	5.00
19	Billy Wagner	1.00
20	Todd Walker	1.00

1997 Topps Hobby Masters

These 10 cards lead the way as dealers' top selections. The cards, printed on 28-point diffraction foilboard, replace two regular cards in every 36th pack of 1997 Topps Series I product. Cards are numbered with a "HM" prefix.

		MT
Complete Set (20):		50.00
Complete Series 1 (10):		30.00
Complete Series 2 (10):		25.00
Common Player:		.75
1	Ken Griffey Jr.	8.00
2	Cal Ripken Jr.	6.00
3	Greg Maddux	4.00
4	Albert Belle	1.50
5	Tony Gwynn	3.00
6	Jeff Bagwell	2.00
7	Randy Johnson	2.00
8	Raul Mondesi	1.00
9	Juan Gonzalez	2.00
10	Kenny Lofton	1.00
11	Frank Thomas	3.00
12	Mike Piazza	5.00
13	Chipper Jones	4.00
14	Brady Anderson	.75
15	Ken Caminiti	.75
16	Barry Bonds	2.00
17	Mo Vaughn	1.00
18	Derek Jeter	5.00
19	Sammy Sosa	5.00
20	Andres Galarraga	1.00

1997 Topps Inter-League Match Ups

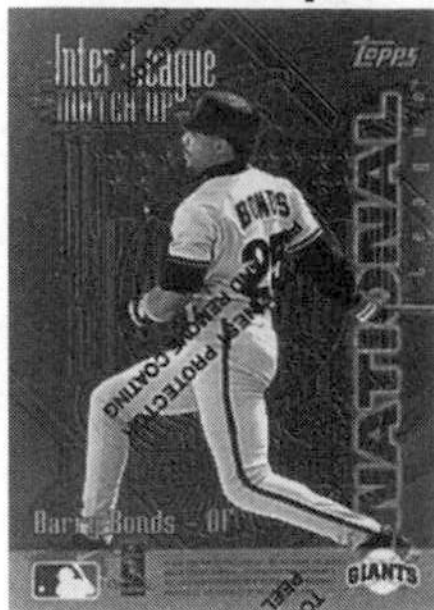

The double-sided Inter-League Finest and Inter-League Finest Refracators (seeded one in 36 and one in 216 Topps Series I packs respectively) feature top individual matchups from inter-league rivalries. One player from each major league team is represented, for a total of 28 players on 14 different cards. Each card is covered with a Finest clear protector. Cards are numbered with an "ILM" prefix.

		MT
Complete Set (14):		35.00
Common Player:		1.00
Refractors:		2X
1	Mark McGwire, Barry Bonds	7.50
2	Tim Salmon, Mike Piazza	5.00
3	Ken Griffey Jr., Dante Bichette	7.50
4	Juan Gonzalez, Tony Gwynn	4.00
5	Frank Thomas, Sammy Sosa	5.00
6	Albert Belle, Barry Larkin	2.00
7	Johnny Damon, Brian Jordan	1.00
8	Paul Molitor, Jeff King	1.50
9	John Jaha, Jeff Bagwell	2.50
10	Bernie Williams, Todd Hundley	1.00
11	Joe Carter, Henry Rodriguez	1.00
12	Cal Ripken Jr., Gregg Jefferies	6.00
13	Mo Vaughn, Chipper Jones	5.00
14	Travis Fryman, Gary Sheffield	1.00

1997 Topps Mickey Mantle Finest

The 16-card Mickey Mantle reprints insert that was found in Series I was re-issued in Series II in the Topps Finest technology. The Finest versions are found on average of every 24 packs.

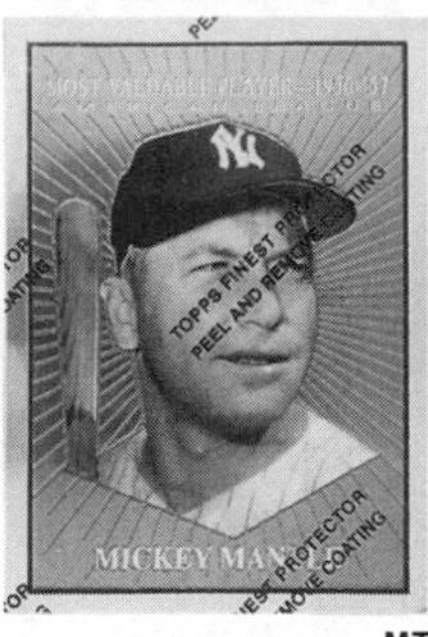

		MT
Complete Set (16):		90.00
Common Mantle:		6.00
21	1953 Bowman #44	6.00
22	1953 Bowman #59	9.00
23	1957 Topps #407	6.00
24	1958 Topps #418	6.00
25	1958 Topps #487	6.00
26	1959 Topps #461	6.00
27	1959 Topps #564	6.00
28	1960 Topps #160	6.00
29	1960 Topps #563	6.00
30	1961 Topps #406	6.00
31	1961 Topps #475	6.00
32	1961 Topps #578	6.00
33	1962 Topps #18	6.00
34	1962 Topps #318	6.00
35	1962 Topps #471	6.00
36	1964 Topps #331	6.00

1997 Topps Mickey Mantle Finest Refractors

Each of the 16 Mantle Finest reprints from Series II can also be found in a Refractor version. Refractors are found every 216 packs, on average.

		MT
Complete Set (16):		400.00
Common Mantle:		25.00
21	1953 Bowman #44	25.00
22	1953 Bowman #59	40.00
23	1957 Topps #407	25.00
24	1958 Topps #418	25.00
25	1958 Topps #487	25.00
26	1959 Topps #461	25.00
27	1959 Topps #564	25.00
28	1960 Topps #160	25.00
29	1960 Topps #563	25.00
30	1961 Topps #406	25.00
31	1961 Topps #475	25.00
32	1961 Topps #578	25.00
33	1962 Topps #18	25.00
34	1962 Topps #318	25.00
35	1962 Topps #471	25.00
36	1964 Topps #331	25.00

1997 Topps Mickey Mantle Reprints

All 16 remaining Mickey Mantle cards that were not reprinted in 1996 Topps Baseball are found in this insert, seeded every 12 packs of Series I Topps. The set starts off with No. 21 and runs through No. 36 since the '96 reprints were numbered 1-20.

		MT
Complete Set (16):		60.00
Common Card:		5.00
21	1953 Bowman #44	5.00
22	1953 Bowman #59	6.00
23	1957 Topps #407	5.00
24	1958 Topps #418	5.00
25	1958 Topps #487	5.00
26	1959 Topps #461	5.00
27	1959 Topps #564	5.00
28	1960 Topps #160	5.00
29	1960 Topps #563	5.00
30	1961 Topps #406	5.00
31	1961 Topps #475	5.00
32	1961 Topps #578	5.00
33	1962 Topps #18	5.00
34	1962 Topps #318	5.00
35	1962 Topps #471	5.00
36	1964 Topps #331	5.00

1997 Topps Season's Best

Season's Best features 25 players on prismatic illusion foilboard, and can be found every six packs. The set has the top five players from five statistical categories: home runs, RBIs, batting average, steals, and wins. Season's Best were found in packs of Topps Series II, and later reprinted on chromium stock as part of Topps Chrome.

		MT
Complete Set (25):		15.00
Common Player:		.25
1	Tony Gwynn	2.00
2	Frank Thomas	2.00
3	Ellis Burks	.25
4	Paul Molitor	.75
5	Chuck Knoblauch	.40
6	Mark McGwire	4.00
7	Brady Anderson	.25
8	Ken Griffey Jr.	4.00
9	Albert Belle	.75
10	Andres Galarraga	.50
11	Andres Galarraga	.50
12	Albert Belle	.75
13	Juan Gonzalez	1.00
14	Mo Vaughn	.60
15	Rafael Palmeiro	.50
16	John Smoltz	.25
17	Andy Pettitte	.25
18	Pat Hentgen	.25
19	Mike Mussina	.60
20	Andy Benes	.25
21	Kenny Lofton	.60
22	Tom Goodwin	.25
23	Otis Nixon	.25
24	Eric Young	.25
25	Lance Johnson	.25

1997 Topps Sweet Strokes

These retail-exclusive Sweet Strokes insert cards consist of 15 Power Matrix foil cards of the top hitters in the game. These players have the swings to produce game winning-hits. The cards were seeded one per every 12 1997 Topps Series I retail packs. Cards are numbered with a "SS" prefix.

		MT
Complete Set (15):		40.00
Common Player:		1.00
1	Roberto Alomar	2.00
2	Jeff Bagwell	4.00
3	Albert Belle	2.50
4	Barry Bonds	2.50
5	Mark Grace	1.50
6	Ken Griffey Jr.	12.00
7	Tony Gwynn	4.00
8	Chipper Jones	6.00
9	Edgar Martinez	1.00
10	Mark McGwire	12.00
11	Rafael Palmeiro	1.50
12	Mike Piazza	6.00
13	Gary Sheffield	1.50
14	Frank Thomas	4.00
15	Mo Vaughn	1.50

1997 Topps Team Timber

Team Timber was a 16-card insert that was exclusive to retail packs and inserted one per 36. The set displays the game's top sluggers on laminated litho wood cards. Cards are numbered with a "TT" prefix.

		MT
Complete Set (16):		50.00
Common Player:		1.00
1	Ken Griffey Jr.	10.00
2	Ken Caminiti	1.50
3	Bernie Williams	2.00
4	Jeff Bagwell	4.00
5	Frank Thomas	4.00
6	Andres Galarraga	1.00
7	Barry Bonds	3.00
8	Rafael Palmeiro	1.50
9	Brady Anderson	1.00
10	Juan Gonzalez	4.00
11	Mo Vaughn	2.00
12	Mark McGwire	10.00
13	Gary Sheffield	1.50
14	Albert Belle	2.50
15	Chipper Jones	6.50
16	Mike Piazza	6.50

1997 Topps Willie Mays Reprints

There are 27 different Willie Mays cards reprinted in Topps Series I and seeded every eight packs. The inserts form a collection of Topps and Bowman cards from throughout Mays' career and each is highlighted by a special commemorative gold foil stamp. Each of the Mays reprints can also be found in an autographed edition, bearing a special "Certified Autograph Issue" gold-foil logo.

		MT
Complete Set (27):		60.00
Common Card:		2.25
Autographed Card:		100.00
1	1951 Bowman #305	4.50
2	1952 Topps #261	3.00
3	1953 Topps #244	3.00
4	1954 Bowman #89	2.25
5	1954 Topps #90	2.25
6	1955 Bowman #184	2.25
7	1955 Topps #194	2.25
8	1956 Topps #130	2.25
9	1957 Topps #10	2.25
10	1958 Topps #5	2.25
11	1959 Topps #50	2.25
12	1960 Topps #200	2.25
13	1961 Topps #150	2.25
14	1961 Topps #579	2.25
15	1962 Topps #300	2.25
16	1963 Topps #300	2.25
17	1964 Topps #150	2.25
18	1965 Topps #250	2.25
19	1966 Topps #1	2.25
20	1967 Topps #200	2.25
21	1968 Topps #50	2.25
22	1969 Topps #190	2.25
23	1970 Topps #600	2.25
24	1971 Topps #600	2.25
25	1971 Topps #600	2.25
26	1972 Topps #49	2.25
27	1973 Topps #305	2.25

1997 Topps Willie Mays Finest

The introduction of Series II Topps offered collectors a chance to find Finest technology versions of each of the 27 commemorative reprint Topps and Bowman cards from throughout Mays' career. The Finest Mays reprints are found one in every 30 packs, on average.

		MT
Complete Set (27):		75.00
Common Card:		4.00
1	1951 Bowman #305	8.00
2	1952 Topps #261	6.00
3	1953 Topps #244	6.00
4	1954 Bowman #89	4.00
5	1954 Topps #90	4.00
6	1955 Bowman #184	4.00
7	1955 Topps #194	4.00
8	1956 Topps #130	4.00
9	1957 Topps #10	4.00
10	1958 Topps #5	4.00
11	1959 Topps #50	4.00
12	1960 Topps #200	4.00
13	1961 Topps #150	4.00
14	1961 Topps #579	4.00
15	1962 Topps #300	4.00
16	1963 Topps #300	4.00
17	1964 Topps #150	4.00
18	1965 Topps #250	4.00
19	1966 Topps #1	4.00
20	1967 Topps #200	4.00
21	1968 Topps #50	4.00
22	1969 Topps #190	4.00
23	1970 Topps #600	4.00
24	1971 Topps #600	4.00
25	1971 Topps #600	4.00
26	1972 Topps #49	4.00
27	1973 Topps #305	4.00

1997 Topps Willie Mays Finest Refractors

A high-end parallel set to the Willie Mays 27-card commemorative reprint issue is the Finest Refractor version issued in Series II. Refractors are found on average of once per 180 packs.

		MT
Complete Set (27):		250.00
Common Card:		10.00
1	1951 Bowman #305	25.00
2	1952 Topps #261	20.00
3	1953 Topps #244	20.00
4	1954 Bowman #89	15.00
5	1954 Topps #90	15.00
6	1955 Bowman #184	15.00
7	1955 Topps #194	15.00
8	1956 Topps #130	15.00
9	1957 Topps #10	15.00
10	1958 Topps #5	15.00
11	1959 Topps #50	15.00
12	1960 Topps #200	15.00
13	1961 Topps #150	15.00
14	1961 Topps #579	15.00
15	1962 Topps #300	15.00
16	1963 Topps #300	15.00
17	1964 Topps #150	15.00
18	1965 Topps #250	15.00
19	1966 Topps #1	15.00
20	1967 Topps #200	15.00
21	1968 Topps #50	15.00
22	1969 Topps #190	15.00
23	1970 Topps #600	15.00
24	1971 Topps #600	15.00
25	1971 Topps #600	15.00
26	1972 Topps #49	15.00
27	1973 Topps #305	15.00

1997 Topps Screenplays

Twenty of the game's top stars were featured in this multi-part collectible. The packaging is a 5-1/8" diameter lithographed steel can. The can was shrink-wrapped at the factory with a round checklist disc covering the color player photo on top of the can. The top has a woodgrain border around the photo and a gold facsimile autograph. The back of the topper disc has a career summary of the player. Inside the tin is a 2-1/2" x 3-1/2" plastic motion card with several seconds of game action shown as the angle of view changes. The cards is covered by a peel-off protective layer on front and back. Foam pieces in the package allow both the can and card to be displayed upright. Issue price was about $10 per can. The unnumbered cans are checklisted here alphabetically. Values shown are for can/card combinations.

		MT
Complete Set (20):		50.00
Common Player:		1.00
Pack (1):		8.00
Wax Box (21):		120.00
(1)	Jeff Bagwell	2.50
(2)	Albert Belle	2.50
(3)	Barry Bonds	2.50
(4)	Andres Galarraga	2.00
(5)	Nomar Garciaparra	5.00
(6)	Juan Gonzalez	2.50
(7)	Ken Griffey Jr.	7.50
(8)	Tony Gwynn	4.00
(9)	Derek Jeter	5.00
(10)	Randy Johnson	2.00
(11)	Andruw Jones	2.00
(12)	Chipper Jones	5.00
(13)	Kenny Lofton	2.00
(14)	Mark McGwire	7.50
(15)	Paul Molitor	2.00
(16)	Hideo Nomo	1.00
(17)	Cal Ripken Jr.	6.00
(18)	Sammy Sosa	5.00
(19)	Frank Thomas	2.50
(20)	Jim Thome	1.00

1997 Topps Screenplays Inserts

		MT
Complete Set (6):		75.00
Common Player:		9.25
1	Larry Walker	5.00
2	Cal Ripken Jr.	17.50
3	Chipper Jones	15.00
4	Frank Thomas	7.50
5	Mike Piazza	15.00
6	Ken Griffey Jr.	25.00

1997 Topps/ Chrome

Chrome Baseball reprinted the top 165 cards from Topps Series I and II baseball on a chromium, metallized stock. Chrome sold in four-card packs and included three insert sets: Diamond Duos, which was created exclusively for this product, Season's Best and Topps All-Stars, which were both reprinted from Topps products. Refractor versions of each card were found every 12 packs.

		MT
Complete Set (165):		70.00
Common Player:		.25
Common Refractors:		5.00
Star Refractors:		6X
Young Stars and RCs:		4X
Pack (4):		4.50
Wax Box (24):		85.00
1	Barry Bonds	2.00
2	Jose Valentin	.25
3	Brady Anderson	.35
4	Wade Boggs	.50
5	Andres Galarraga	.75
6	Rusty Greer	.25
7	Derek Jeter	5.00
8	Ricky Bottalico	.25
9	Mike Piazza	5.00
10	Garret Anderson	.25
11	Jeff King	.25
12	Kevin Appier	.25
13	Mark Grace	.40
14	Jeff D'Amico	.25
15	Jay Buhner	.30
16	Hal Morris	.25
17	Harold Baines	.25
18	Jeff Cirillo	.25
19	Tom Glavine	.40
20	Andy Pettitte	.60
21	Mark McGwire	8.00
22	Chuck Knoblauch	.50
23	Raul Mondesi	.50
24	Albert Belle	1.50
25	Trevor Hoffman	.25
26	Eric Young	.25
27	Brian McRae	.25
28	Jim Edmonds	.25
29	Robb Nen	.25
30	Reggie Sanders	.25
31	Mike Lansing	.25
32	Craig Biggio	1.00
33	Ray Lankford	.25
34	Charles Nagy	.25
35	Paul Wilson	.25
36	John Wetteland	.25
37	Derek Bell	.25
38	Edgar Martinez	.25
39	Rickey Henderson	.75
40	Jim Thome	.75
41	Frank Thomas	2.00
42	Jackie Robinson (Tribute)	6.00
43	Terry Steinbach	.25
44	Kevin Brown	.40
45	Joey Hamilton	.25
46	Travis Fryman	.30
47	Juan Gonzalez	2.00
48	Ron Gant	.30
49	Greg Maddux	4.00
50	Wally Joyner	.30
51	John Valentin	.25
42	Bret Boone	.25
53	Paul Molitor	1.00
54	Rafael Palmeiro	1.00
55	Todd Hundley	.25
56	Ellis Burks	.25
57	Bernie Williams	1.50
58	Roberto Alomar	1.50
59	Jose Mesa	.25
60	Troy Percival	.25
61	John Smoltz	.50
62	Jeff Conine	.25
63	Bernard Gilkey	.25
64	Mickey Tettleton	.25
65	Justin Thompson	.25
66	Tony Phillips	.25
67	Ryne Sandberg	1.50
68	Geronimo Berroa	.25
69	Todd Hollandsworth	.25
70	Rey Ordonez	.25
71	Marquis Grissom	.25
72	Tino Martinez	.30
73	Steve Finley	.25
74	Andy Benes	.25
75	Jason Kendall	.40
76	Johnny Damon	.25
77	Jason Giambi	.25
78	Henry Rodriguez	.25
79	Edgar Renteria	.25
80	Ray Durham	.25
81	Gregg Jefferies	.25
82	Roberto Hernandez	.25
83	Joe Carter	.30
84	Jermaine Dye	.25
85	Julio Franco	.25
86	David Justice	.50
87	Jose Canseco	1.50
88	Paul O'Neill	.50
89	Mariano Rivera	.40
90	Bobby Higginson	.25
91	Mark Grudzielanek	.25
92	Lance Johnson	.25
93	Ken Caminiti	.40
94	Gary Sheffield	.40
95	Luis Castillo	.25
96	Scott Rolen	2.50
97	Chipper Jones	5.00
98	Darryl Strawberry	.50
99	Nomar Garciaparra	5.00
100	Jeff Bagwell	2.00
101	Ken Griffey Jr.	8.00
102	Sammy Sosa	5.00
103	Jack McDowell	.25
104	James Baldwin	.25
105	Rocky Coppinger	.25
106	Manny Ramirez	2.00
107	Tim Salmon	.40
108	Eric Karros	.25
109	Brett Butler	.25
110	Randy Johnson	1.50
111	Pat Hentgen	.25
112	Rondell White	.40
113	Eddie Murray	.50
114	Ivan Rodriguez	2.00
115	Jermaine Allensworth	.25
116	Ed Sprague	.25
117	Kenny Lofton	1.00
118	Alan Benes	.25
119	Fred McGriff	.50
120	Alex Fernandez	.25
121	Al Martin	.25
122	Devon White	.25
123	David Cone	.40
124	Karim Garcia	.25
125	Chili Davis	.25
126	Roger Clemens	3.00
127	Bobby Bonilla	.25
128	Mike Mussina	1.00
129	Todd Walker	.40
130	Dante Bichette	.40
131	Carlos Baerga	.25
132	Matt Williams	.50
133	Will Clark	.50
134	Dennis Eckersley	.25
135	Ryan Klesko	.40
136	Dean Palmer	.25
137	Javy Lopez	.40
138	Greg Vaughn	.40
139	Vinny Castilla	.40
140	Cal Ripken Jr.	6.00
141	Ruben Rivera	.25
142	Mark Wohlers	.25
143	Tony Clark	1.00
144	Jose Rosado	.25
145	Tony Gwynn	4.00
146	Cecil Fielder	.25
147	Brian Jordan	.25
148	Bob Abreu	.25
149	Barry Larkin	.50
150	Robin Ventura	.40
151	John Olerud	.75
152	Rod Beck	.25
153	Vladimir Guerrero	4.00
154	Marty Cordova	.25
155	Todd Stottlemyre	.25
156	Hideo Nomo	.40
157	Denny Neagle	.25
158	John Jaha	.25
159	Mo Vaughn	1.00
160	Andruw Jones	1.50
161	Moises Alou	.40
162	Larry Walker	1.00
163	Eddie Murray (Season Highlights)	.50
164	Paul Molitor (Season Highlights)	.75
165	Checklist	.25

1997 Topps/ Chrome All-Stars

Topps Chrome All-Stars display the same 22

cards found in Topps Series I, however these are reprinted on a Chrome stock. Regular versions are seeded every 24 packs, while Refractor versions arrive every 72 packs. Cards are numbered with an "AS" prefix.

		MT
Complete Set (22):		90.00
Common Player:		2.00
Refractors:		3X
1	Ivan Rodriguez	5.00
2	Todd Hundley	3.00
3	Frank Thomas	6.00
4	Andres Galarraga	4.00
5	Chuck Knoblauch	2.00
6	Eric Young	2.00
7	Jim Thome	3.00
8	Chipper Jones	12.00
9	Cal Ripken Jr.	15.00
10	Barry Larkin	3.00
11	Albert Belle	4.00
12	Barry Bonds	5.00
13	Ken Griffey Jr.	20.00
14	Ellis Burks	2.00
15	Juan Gonzalez	5.00
16	Gary Sheffield	3.00
17	Andy Pettitte	3.00
18	Tom Glavine	3.00
19	Pat Hentgen	2.00
20	John Smoltz	2.00
21	Roberto Hernandez	2.00
22	Mark Wohlers	2.00

1997 Topps/ Chrome Diamond Duos

Diamond Duos is the only one of the three insert sets in Chrome Baseball that was developed exclusively for this product. The set has 10 cards featuring two superstar teammates on double-sided chromium cards. Diamond Duos are found every 36 packs, while Refractor versions are found every 108 packs. Cards are numbered with a "DD" prefix.

		MT
Complete Set (10):		70.00
Common Player:		3.00
Refractors:		2X
1	Chipper Jones, Andruw Jones	10.00
2	Derek Jeter, Bernie Williams	10.00
3	Ken Griffey Jr., Jay Buhner	20.00
4	Kenny Lofton, Manny Ramirez	5.00
5	Jeff Bagwell, Craig Biggio	5.00
6	Juan Gonzalez, Ivan Rodriguez	6.00
7	Cal Ripken Jr., Brady Anderson	15.00
8	Mike Piazza, Hideo Nomo	10.00
9	Andres Galarraga, Dante Bichette	3.00
10	Frank Thomas, Albert Belle	5.00

1997 Topps/ Chrome Season's Best

Season's Best includes the 25 players found in Topps Series II, but in a chromium version. The top five players from five statistical categories, including Leading Looters, Bleacher Reachers and Kings of Swing. Regular versions are seeded every 18 packs, with Refractors every 54 packs.

		MT
Complete Set (25):		100.00
Common Player:		2.00
Refractors:		3X
1	Tony Gwynn	10.00
2	Frank Thomas	5.00
3	Ellis Burks	2.00
4	Paul Molitor	4.00
5	Chuck Knoblauch	3.00
6	Mark McGwire	20.00
7	Brady Anderson	2.50
8	Ken Griffey Jr.	20.00
9	Albert Belle	4.00
10	Andres Galarraga	4.00
11	Andres Galarraga	4.00
12	Albert Belle	4.00
13	Juan Gonzalez	5.00
14	Mo Vaughn	4.00
15	Rafael Palmeiro	4.00
16	John Smoltz	2.00
17	Andy Pettitte	3.00
18	Pat Hentgen	2.00
19	Mike Mussina	4.00
20	Andy Benes	2.00
21	Kenny Lofton	4.00
22	Tom Goodwin	2.00
23	Otis Nixon	2.00
24	Eric Young	2.00
25	Lance Johnson	2.00

1997 Topps/ Gallery

The second year of Gallery features 180 cards printed on extra-thick 24-point stock. Card fronts feature a player photo surrounded by an embossed foil "frame" to give each card the look of a piece of artwork. Backs contain career stats and biographical information on each player. Inserts include Peter Max Serigraphs, Signature Series Serigraphs, Player's Private Issue (parallel set), Photo Gallery and Gallery of Heroes. Cards were sold exclusively in hobby shops in eight-card packs for $4 each.

		MT
Complete Set (180):		50.00
Common Player:		.15
Pack (8):		4.00
Wax Box (24):		70.00
1	Paul Molitor	1.00
2	Devon White	.15
3	Andres Galarraga	.50
4	Cal Ripken Jr.	3.00
5	Tony Gwynn	2.00
6	Mike Stanley	.15
7	Orel Hershiser	.15
8	Jose Canseco	1.00
9	Chili Davis	.15
10	Harold Baines	.15
11	Rickey Henderson	.25
12	Darryl Strawberry	.15
13	Todd Worrell	.15
14	Cecil Fielder	.15
15	Gary Gaetti	.15
16	Bobby Bonilla	.15
17	Will Clark	.50
18	Kevin Brown	.15
19	Tom Glavine	.40
20	Wade Boggs	.40
21	Edgar Martinez	.15
22	Lance Johnson	.15
23	Gregg Jefferies	.15
24	Bip Roberts	.15
25	Tony Phillips	.15
26	Greg Maddux	2.50
27	Mickey Tettleton	.15
28	Terry Steinbach	.15
29	Ryne Sandberg	1.00
30	Wally Joyner	.15
31	Joe Carter	.15
32	Ellis Burks	.15
33	Fred McGriff	.40
34	Barry Larkin	.25
35	John Franco	.15
36	Rafael Palmeiro	.50
37	Mark McGwire	5.00
38	Ken Caminiti	.25
39	David Cone	.25
40	Julio Franco	.15
41	Roger Clemens	2.00
42	Barry Bonds	1.25
43	Dennis Eckersley	.15
44	Eddie Murray	.50
45	Paul O'Neill	.20
46	Craig Biggio	.20
47	Roberto Alomar	1.00
48	Mark Grace	.40
49	Matt Williams	.40
50	Jay Buhner	.15
51	John Smoltz	.25
52	Randy Johnson	.75
53	Ramon Martinez	.15
54	Curt Schilling	.15
55	Gary Sheffield	.50
56	Jack McDowell	.15
57	Brady Anderson	.15
58	Dante Bichette	.30
59	Ron Gant	.20
60	Alex Fernandez	.25
61	Moises Alou	.15
62	Travis Fryman	.15
63	Dean Palmer	.15
64	Todd Hundley	.20
65	Jeff Brantley	.15
66	Bernard Gilkey	.15
67	Geronimo Berroa	.15
68	John Wetteland	.15
69	Robin Ventura	.20
70	Ray Lankford	.15
71	Kevin Appier	.15
72	Larry Walker	.75
73	Juan Gonzalez	1.00
74	Jeff King	.15
75	Greg Vaughn	.15
76	Steve Finley	.15
77	Brian McRae	.15
78	Paul Sorrento	.15
79	Ken Griffey Jr.	5.00
80	Omar Vizquel	.15
81	Jose Mesa	.15
82	Albert Belle	1.00
83	Glenallen Hill	.15
84	Sammy Sosa	3.00
85	Andy Benes	.15
86	David Justice	.40
87	Marquis Grissom	.15
88	John Olerud	.20
89	Tino Martinez	.20
90	Frank Thomas	1.50
91	Raul Mondesi	.40
92	Steve Trachsel	.15
93	Jim Edmonds	.15
94	Rusty Greer	.15
95	Joey Hamilton	.15
96	Ismael Valdes	.15
97	Dave Nilsson	.15
98	John Jaha	.15
99	Alex Gonzalez	.15
100	Javy Lopez	.25
101	Ryan Klesko	.25
102	Tim Salmon	.25
103	Bernie Williams	.75
104	Roberto Hernandez	.15
105	Chuck Knoblauch	.35
106	Mike Lansing	.15
107	Vinny Castilla	.15
108	Reggie Sanders	.15
109	Mo Vaughn	.75
110	Rondell White	.15
111	Ivan Rodriguez	1.25
112	Mike Mussina	.75
113	Carlos Baerga	.15
114	Jeff Conine	.15
115	Jim Thome	.50
116	Manny Ramirez	1.25
117	Kenny Lofton	.75
118	Wilson Alvarez	.15
119	Eric Karros	.15
120	Robb Nen	.15
121	Mark Wohlers	.15
122	Ed Sprague	.15
123	Pat Hentgen	.15
124	Juan Guzman	.15
125	Derek Bell	.15
126	Jeff Bagwell	1.25
127	Eric Young	.15
128	John Valentin	.15
129	Al Martin (photo actually Javy Lopez)	.25
130	Trevor Hoffman	.15
131	Henry Rodriguez	.15
132	Pedro Martinez	1.25
133	Mike Piazza	3.00
134	Brian Jordan	.15
135	Jose Valentin	.15
136	Jeff Cirillo	.15
137	Chipper Jones	3.00
138	Ricky Bottalico	.15
139	Hideo Nomo	.40
140	Troy Percival	.15
141	Rey Ordonez	.15
142	Edgar Renteria	.15
143	Luis Castillo	.15
144	Vladimir Guerrero	2.00
145	Jeff D'Amico	.15
146	Andruw Jones	.50
147	Darin Erstad	.50
148	Bob Abreu	.15
149	Carlos Delgado	.75
150	Jamey Wright	.15
151	Nomar Garciaparra	3.00
152	Jason Kendall	.25
153	Jermaine Allensworth	.15
154	Scott Rolen	1.25
155	Rocky Coppinger	.15
156	Paul Wilson	.15
157	Garret Anderson	.15
158	Mariano Rivera	.30
159	Ruben Rivera	.25
160	Andy Pettitte	.35
161	Derek Jeter	3.00
162	Neifi Perez	.15
163	Ray Durham	.15
164	James Baldwin	.15

165	Marty Cordova	.15
166	Tony Clark	.40
167	Michael Tucker	.15
168	Mike Sweeney	.15
169	Johnny Damon	.15
170	Jermaine Dye	.15
171	Alex Ochoa	.15
172	Jason Isringhausen	.15
173	Mark Grudzielanek	.15
174	Jose Rosado	.15
175	Todd Hollandsworth	.15
176	Alan Benes	.30
177	Jason Giambi	.15
178	Billy Wagner	.15
179	Justin Thompson	.15
180	Todd Walker	.25

1997 Topps/ Gallery Players Private Issue Parallel

A parallel version of the Gallery issue called Players Private Issue was produced as a 1:12 pack insert. The PPI cards differ from trhe regular version in the use of a "PPI-" prefix to the card number on front and the application of a small silver PPI seal in a lower corner. On back, the line "One of 250 Issued" has been added.

	MT
Complete Set (180):	1700.
Common Player:	5.00
Stars:	15X

1997 Topps/ Gallery of Heroes

This 10-card die-cut insert features a design resembling stained glass. Cards were inserted 1:36 packs. Cards are numbered with a "GH" prefix.

		MT
Complete Set (10):		135.00
Common Player:		6.00
1	Derek Jeter	20.00
2	Chipper Jones	20.00
3	Frank Thomas	7.50
4	Ken Griffey Jr.	30.00
5	Cal Ripken Jr.	22.50
6	Mark McGwire	30.00
7	Mike Piazza	20.00
8	Jeff Bagwell	7.50
9	Tony Gwynn	12.00
10	Mo Vaughn	6.00

1997 Topps/ Gallery Peter Max

Noted artist Peter Max has painted renditions of 10 superstar players and offered his commentary about those players on the backs. Cards were inserted 1:24 packs. In addition, Max-autographed cards signed and numbered from an edition of 40 are inserted 1:1,200 packs.

		MT
Complete Set (10):		50.00
Common Player:		2.00
Complete Autographed Set (10):		2000.
Common Autographed Player:		75.00
1	Ken Griffey Jr.	10.00
1	Ken Griffey Jr. (autographed)	275.00
2	Frank Thomas	4.00
2	Frank Thomas (autographed)	150.00
3	Albert Belle	3.00
3	Albert Belle (autographed)	75.00
4	Barry Bonds	3.00
4	Barry Bonds (autographed)	75.00
5	Derek Jeter	6.00
5	Derek Jeter (autographed)	175.00
6	Ken Caminiti	2.00
6	Ken Caminiti (autographed)	75.00
7	Mike Piazza	6.00
7	Mike Piazza (autographed)	200.00
8	Cal Ripken Jr.	7.50
8	Cal Ripken Jr. (autographed)	225.00
9	Mark McGwire	10.00
9	Mark McGwire (autographed)	275.00
10	Chipper Jones	6.00
10	Chipper Jones (autographed)	200.00

1997 Topps/ Gallery Photo Gallery

This 21-card set features full-bleed, high-gloss action photos of some of the game's top stars. Cards were inserted 1:24 packs. They are numbered with a "PG" prefix.

		MT
Complete Set (16):		130.00
Common Player:		3.00
1	World Series	8.00
2	Paul Molitor	7.00
3	Eddie Murray	5.00
4	Ken Griffey Jr.	30.00
5	Chipper Jones	15.00
6	Derek Jeter	20.00
7	Frank Thomas	12.00
8	Mark McGwire	30.00
9	Kenny Lofton	6.00
10	Gary Sheffield	5.00
11	Mike Piazza	20.00
12	Vinny Castilla	3.00
13	Andres Galarraga	4.00
14	Andy Pettitte	5.00
15	Robin Ventura	3.00
16	Barry Larkin	4.00

1997 Topps Stars

The premiere version of this product was sold only to hobby shops that were members of the Topps Home Team Advantage program. Each of the 125 regular cards in the set is printed on 20-point stock. Card fronts feature spot UV coating with a textured star pattern running down one side of the card. Inserts include the parallel Always Mint set, as well al '97 All-Stars, Future All-Stars, All-Star memories, and Autographed Rookie Reprints. Cards were sold in seven-card packs for $3 each.

		MT
Complete Set (125):		50.00
Common Player:		.15
Always Mint Stars, RCs:		10X
Pack (7):		5.50
Wax Box (24):		120.00
1	Larry Walker	.75
2	Tino Martinez	.25
3	Cal Ripken Jr.	3.00
4	Ken Griffey Jr.	4.00
5	Chipper Jones	2.50
6	David Justice	.25
7	Mike Piazza	2.50
8	Jeff Bagwell	1.00
9	Ron Gant	.25
10	Sammy Sosa	2.50
11	Tony Gwynn	2.00
12	Carlos Baerga	.15
13	Frank Thomas	1.00
14	Moises Alou	.25
15	Barry Larkin	.25
16	Ivan Rodriguez	1.00
17	Greg Maddux	2.00
18	Jim Edmonds	.20
19	Jose Canseco	.75
20	Rafael Palmeiro	.40
21	Paul Molitor	.75
22	Kevin Appier	.15
23	Raul Mondesi	.25
24	Lance Johnson	.15
25	Edgar Martinez	.15
26	Andres Galarraga	.40
27	Mo Vaughn	.60
28	Ken Caminiti	.25
29	Cecil Fielder	.15
30	Harold Baines	.15
31	Roberto Alomar	.60
32	Shawn Estes	.15
33	Tom Glavine	.25
34	Dennis Eckersley	.15
35	Manny Ramirez	1.00
36	John Olerud	.40
37	Juan Gonzalez	1.00
38	Chuck Knoblauch	.30
39	Albert Belle	.75
40	Vinny Castilla	.20
41	John Smoltz	.20
42	Barry Bonds	1.00
43	Randy Johnson	.60
44	Brady Anderson	.20
45	Jeff Blauser	.15
46	Craig Biggio	.40
47	Jeff Conine	.15
48	Marquis Grissom	.20
49	Mark Grace	.30
50	Roger Clemens	1.50
51	Mark McGwire	4.00
52	Fred McGriff	.25
53	Gary Sheffield	.30
54	Bobby Jones	.15
55	Eric Young	.15
56	Robin Ventura	.25
57	Wade Boggs	.25
58	Joe Carter	.15
59	Ryne Sandberg	.75
60	Matt Williams	.30
61	Todd Hundley	.20
62	Dante Bichette	.25
63	Chili Davis	.15
64	Kenny Lofton	.60
65	Jay Buhner	.15
66	Will Clark	.25
67	Travis Fryman	.20
68	Pat Hentgen	.15
69	Ellis Burks	.15
70	Mike Mussina	.60
71	Hideo Nomo	.25
72	Sandy Alomar	.20
73	Bobby Bonilla	.15
74	Rickey Henderson	.25
75	David Cone	.25
76	Terry Steinbach	.15
77	Pedro Martinez	1.25
78	Jim Thome	.50
79	Rod Beck	.15
80	Randy Myers	.15
81	Charles Nagy	.15
82	Mark Wohlers	.15
83	Paul O'Neill	.25
84	Curt Schilling	.25
85	Joey Cora	.15
86	John Franco	.15
87	Kevin Brown	.25
88	Benito Santiago	.15
89	Ray Lankford	.20
90	Bernie Williams	.60
91	Jason Dickson	.15

92	Jeff Cirillo	.15
93	Nomar Garciaparra	2.50
94	Mariano Rivera	.25
95	Javy Lopez	.20
96	*Tony Womack*	1.00
97	Jose Rosado	.15
98	Denny Neagle	.15
99	Darryl Kile	.15
100	Justin Thompson	.15
101	Juan Encarnacion	.25
102	Brad Fullmer	.15
103	*Kris Benson*	4.00
104	Todd Helton	1.00
105	Paul Konerko	.25
106	*Travis Lee*	3.00
107	Todd Greene	.15
108	*Mark Kotsay*	2.00
109	Carl Pavano	.20
110	*Kerry Wood*	8.00
111	*Jason Romano*	2.00
112	*Geoff Goetz*	.75
113	*Scott Hodges*	.75
114	*Aaron Akin*	.50
115	*Vernon Wells*	4.00
116	*Chris Stowe*	.50
117	*Brett Caradonna*	.75
118	*Adam Kennedy*	3.00
119	*Jayson Werth*	2.00
120	*Glenn Davis*	.75
121	*Troy Cameron*	1.00
122	*J.J. Davis*	2.00
123	*Jason Dellaero*	.75
124	*Jason Standridge*	2.00
125	*Lance Berkman*	6.00

1997 Topps Stars All-Star Memories

This 10-card insert features stars who have had memorable performances in previous All-Star Games. Cards feature a laser-cut cascade of stars on a foilboard stock. Backs have another photo and a description of the All-Star memory. The cards were inserted 1:24 packs. Cards are numbered with an "ASM" prefix.

		MT
Complete Set (10):		50.00
Common Player:		2.00
1	Cal Ripken Jr.	15.00
2	Jeff Conine	2.00
3	Mike Piazza	12.00
4	Randy Johnson	4.00
5	Ken Griffey Jr.	20.00
6	Fred McGriff	3.00
7	Moises Alou	2.50
8	Hideo Nomo	2.50
9	Larry Walker	4.00
10	Sandy Alomar	2.00

1997 Topps Stars Autographed Rookie Reprints

Fourteen different Hall of Famers autographed reprinted versions of their Topps rookie cards as a one-per-30-pack insert. Each card features a special certified stamp. Richie Ashburn was to have been card #2, but he died before he could autograph them.

		MT
Complete Set (14):		300.00
Common Player:		20.00
(1)	Luis Aparicio	35.00
(3)	Jim Bunning	25.00
(4)	Bob Feller	35.00
(5)	Rollie Fingers	20.00
(6)	Monte Irvin	20.00
(7)	Al Kaline	40.00
(8)	Ralph Kiner	25.00
(9)	Eddie Mathews	40.00
(10)	Hal Newhouser	20.00
(11)	Gaylord Perry	20.00
(12)	Robin Roberts	20.00
(13)	Brooks Robinson	40.00
(14)	Enos Slaughter	20.00
(15)	Earl Weaver	35.00

1997 Topps Stars Future All-Stars

This 15-card set showcases the top candidates to make their All-Star Game debut in 1998. Cards feature a prismatic rainbow foil background and were inserted 1:12 packs. Cards are numbered with a "FAS" prefix.

		MT
Complete Set (15):		40.00
Common Player:		2.00
1	Derek Jeter	12.00
2	Andruw Jones	4.00
3	Vladimir Guerrero	8.00
4	Scott Rolen	5.00
5	Jose Guillen	2.00
6	Jose Cruz, Jr.	2.00
7	Darin Erstad	3.00
8	Tony Clark	3.00
9	Scott Spiezio	2.00
10	Kevin Orie	2.00
11	Calvin Reese	2.00
12	Billy Wagner	2.00
13	Matt Morris	2.00
14	Jeremi Gonzalez	2.00
15	Hideki Irabu	2.00

1997 Topps Stars 1997 All-Stars

This 20-card insert honors participants of the 1997 All-Star Game in Cleveland. Cards were inserted 1:24 packs. Fronts are printed on prismatic foil with hundreds of stars in the background. On back is another player photo and his All-Star Game 1997 and career stats. Cards are numbered with an "AS" prefix.

		MT
Complete Set (20):		200.00
Common Player:		6.00
1	Greg Maddux	30.00
2	Randy Johnson	8.00
3	Tino Martinez	6.00
4	Jeff Bagwell	15.00
5	Ivan Rodriguez	12.00
6	Mike Piazza	30.00
7	Cal Ripken Jr.	40.00
8	Ken Caminiti	6.00
9	Tony Gwynn	25.00
10	Edgar Martinez	6.00
11	Craig Biggio	6.00
12	Roberto Alomar	10.00
13	Larry Walker	8.00
14	Brady Anderson	6.00
15	Barry Bonds	12.00
16	Ken Griffey Jr.	50.00
17	Ray Lankford	6.00
18	Paul O'Neill	6.00
19	Jeff Blauser	6.00
20	Sandy Alomar	6.00

1998 Topps

Topps was issued in two series in 1998 that totalled 503 cards, with 282 in Series I and 220 in Series II. Cards featured a gold border instead of the traditional white used in past years and the product featured Roberto Clemente inserts and a tribute card No. 21 in the base set. Series Highlights, Expansion Team Prospects, Interleague Highlights, Season Highlights, Prospects and Draft Picks. Subsets in Series II included: Expansion Teams, InterLeague Preview, Season Highlights, Prospects and Draft Picks. Every card in the set is paralleled in a Minted in Cooperstown insert that was stamped on-site at the Baseball Hall of Fame in Cooperstown. Inserts in Series I include: Roberto Clemente Reprints, Clemente Finest, Clemente Tribute, Memorabilila Madness, Etch a Sketch, Mystery Finest, Flashback and Baby Boomers. Inserts in Series II included: Clemente Reprints, Clemente Finest, 1998 Rookie Class, Mystery Finest, Milestones, Focal Points, and Clout 9.

		MT
Complete Set (503):		40.00
Complete Series 1 (282):		20.00
Complete Series 2 (220):		20.00
Common Player:		.05
Minted:		10X
Inserted 1:8		
Series 1 or 2 Pack (11):		1.00
Series 1 or 2 Wax Box (36):		35.00
1	Tony Gwynn	1.25
2	Larry Walker	.25
3	Billy Wagner	.05
4	Denny Neagle	.05
5	Vladimir Guerrero	1.00
6	Kevin Brown	.15
7	NOT ISSUED	
8	Mariano Rivera	.15
9	Tony Clark	.25
10	Deion Sanders	.15
11	Francisco Cordova	.05
12	Matt Williams	.20
13	Carlos Baerga	.05
14	Mo Vaughn	.40
15	Bobby Witt	.05
16	Matt Stairs	.05
17	Chan Ho Park	.10
18	Mike Bordick	.05
19	Michael Tucker	.05
20	Frank Thomas	.75
21	Roberto Clemente	1.50
22	Dmitri Young	.05
23	Steve Trachsel	.05
24	Jeff Kent	.05
25	Scott Rolen	.75
26	John Thomson	.05
27	Joe Vitiello	.05
28	Eddie Guardado	.05
29	Charlie Hayes	.05
30	Juan Gonzalez	.75
31	Garret Anderson	.05
32	John Jaha	.05
33	Omar Vizquel	.05
34	Brian Hunter	.05
35	Jeff Bagwell	.75
36	Mark Lemke	.05
37	Doug Glanville	.05
38	Dan Wilson	.05
39	Steve Cooke	.05
40	Chili Davis	.05
41	Mike Cameron	.05
42	F.P. Santangelo	.05
43	Brad Ausmus	.05
44	Gary DiSarcina	.05
45	Pat Hentgen	.05
46	Wilton Guerrero	.05
47	Devon White	.05
48	Danny Patterson	.05
49	Pat Meares	.05
50	Rafael Palmeiro	.25
51	Mark Gardner	.05
52	Jeff Blauser	.05
53	Dave Hollins	.05

54 Carlos Garcia .05
55 Ben McDonald .05
56 John Mabry .05
57 Trevor Hoffman .05
58 Tony Fernandez .05
59 Rich Loiselle .05
60 Mark Leiter .05
61 Pat Kelly .05
62 John Flaherty .05
63 Roger Bailey .05
64 Tom Gordon .05
65 Ryan Klesko .15
66 Darryl Hamilton .05
67 Jim Eisenreich .05
68 Butch Huskey .05
69 Mark Grudzielanek .05
70 Marquis Grissom .10
71 Mark McLemore .05
72 Gary Gaetti .05
73 Greg Gagne .05
74 Lyle Mouton .05
75 Jim Edmonds .10
76 Shawn Green .50
77 Greg Vaughn .10
78 Terry Adams .05
79 *Kevin Polcovich* .20
80 Troy O'Leary .05
81 Jeff Shaw .05
82 Rich Becker .05
83 David Wells .05
84 Steve Karsay .05
85 Charles Nagy .05
86 B.J. Surhoff .05
87 Jamey Wright .05
88 James Baldwin .05
89 Edgardo Alfonzo .15
90 Jay Buhner .10
91 Brady Anderson .15
92 Scott Servais .05
93 Edgar Renteria .05
94 Mike Lieberthal .10
95 Rick Aguilera .05
96 Walt Weiss .05
97 Deivi Cruz .05
98 Kurt Abbott .05
99 Henry Rodriguez .05
100 Mike Piazza 1.50
101 Bill Taylor .05
102 Todd Zeile .05
103 Rey Ordonez .05
104 Willie Greene .05
105 Tony Womack .05
106 Mike Sweeney .05
107 Jeffrey Hammonds .05
108 Kevin Orie .05
109 Alex Gonzalez .05
110 Jose Canseco .50
111 Paul Sorrento .05
112 Joey Hamilton .05
113 Brad Radke .05
114 Steve Avery .05
115 Esteban Loaiza .05
116 Stan Javier .05
117 Chris Gomez .05
118 Royce Clayton .05
119 Orlando Merced .05
120 Kevin Appier .05
121 Mel Nieves .05
122 Joe Girardi .05
123 Rico Brogna .05
124 Kent Mercker .05
125 Manny Ramirez .75
126 Jeromy Burnitz .05
127 Kevin Foster .05
128 Matt Morris .05
129 Jason Dickson .05
130 Tom Glavine .15
131 Wally Joyner .05
132 Rick Reed .05
133 Todd Jones .05
134 Dave Martinez .05
135 Sandy Alomar .05
136 Mike Lansing .05
137 Sean Berry .05
138 Doug Jones .05
139 Todd Stottlemyre .05
140 Jay Bell .05
141 Jaime Navarro .05
142 Chris Hoiles .05
143 Joey Cora .05
144 Scott Spiezio .05
145 Joe Carter .05
146 Jose Guillen .15
147 Damion Easley .05
148 Lee Stevens .05
149 Alex Fernandez .05
150 Randy Johnson .40
151 J.T. Snow .10
152 Chuck Finley .05
153 Bernard Gilkey .05
154 David Segui .05
155 Dante Bichette .15
156 Kevin Stocker .05
157 Carl Everett .15
158 Jose Valentin .05
159 Pokey Reese .05
160 Derek Jeter 1.50
161 Roger Pavlik .05
162 Mark Wohlers .05
163 Ricky Bottalico .05
164 Ozzie Guillen .05
165 Mike Mussina .40
166 Gary Sheffield .15
167 Hideo Nomo .25
168 Mark Grace .20
169 Aaron Sele .05
170 Darryl Kile .10
171 Shawn Estes .05
172 Vinny Castilla .10
173 Ron Coomer .05
174 Jose Rosado .05
175 Kenny Lofton .40
176 Jason Giambi .10
177 Hal Morris .05
178 Darren Bragg .05
179 Orel Hershiser .05
180 Ray Lankford .05
181 Hideki Irabu .15
182 Kevin Young .05
183 Javy Lopez .15
184 Jeff Montgomery .05
185 Mike Holtz .05
186 George Williams .05
187 Cal Eldred .05
188 Tom Candiotti .05
189 Glenallen Hill .05
190 Brian Giles .05
191 Dave Mlicki .05
192 Garrett Stephenson .05
193 Jeff Frye .05
194 Joe Oliver .05
195 Bob Hamelin .05
196 Luis Sojo .05
197 LaTroy Hawkins .05
198 Kevin Elster .05
199 Jeff Reed .05
200 Dennis Eckersley .05
201 Bill Mueller .05
202 Russ Davis .05
203 Armando Benitez .05
204 Quilvio Veras .05
205 Tim Naehring .05
206 Quinton McCracken .05
207 Raul Casanova .05
208 Matt Lawton .05
209 Luis Alicea .05
210 Luis Gonzalez .10
211 Allen Watson .05
212 Gerald Williams .05
213 David Bell .05
214 Todd Hollandsworth .05
215 Wade Boggs .15
216 Jose Mesa .05
217 Jamie Moyer .05
218 Darren Daulton .05
219 Mickey Morandini .05
220 Rusty Greer .10
221 Jim Bullinger .05
222 Jose Offerman .05
223 Matt Karchner .05
224 Woody Williams .05
225 Mark Loretta .05
226 Mike Hampton .05
227 Willie Adams .05
228 Scott Hatteberg .05
229 Rich Amaral .05
230 Terry Steinbach .05
231 Glendon Rusch .05
232 Bret Boone .05
233 Robert Person .05
234 Jose Hernandez .05
235 Doug Drabek .05
236 Jason McDonald .05
237 Chris Widger .05
238 *Tom Martin* .05
239 Dave Burba .05
240 Pete Rose II .05
241 Bobby Ayala .05
242 Tim Wakefield .05
243 Dennis Springer .05
244 Tim Belcher .05
245 Jon Garland, Geoff Goetz (Draft Pick) .15
246 Glenn Davis, Lance Berkman (Draft Pick) .25
247 Vernon Wells, Aaron Akin (Draft Pick) .25
248 Adam Kennedy, Jason Romano (Draft Pick) .10
249 Jason Dellaero, Troy Cameron (Draft Pick) .20
250 Alex Sanchez *Jared Sandberg* (Expansion Team Prospects) .20
251 Pablo Ortega, Jim Manias (Expansion Team Prospects) .15
252 Jason Conti, *Mike Stoner* (Expansion Team Prospects) .40
253 John Patterson, Larry Rodriguez (Expansion Team Prospects) .20
254 Adrian Beltre, *Ryan Minor*, Aaron Boone (Prospect) .75
255 Ben Grieve, Brian Buchanan, Dermal Brown (Prospect) .50
256 Carl Pavano, Kerry Wood, Gil Meche (Prospect) .50
257 David Ortiz, Daryle Ward, Richie Sexson (Prospect) .15
258 Randy Winn, Juan Encarnacion, Andrew Vessel (Prospect) .15
259 Kris Benson, Travis Smith, Courtney Duncan (Prospect) .15
260 Chad Hermansen, Brent Butler, *Warren Morris* (Prospect) .50
261 Ben Davis, Elieser Marrero, Ramon Hernandez (Prospect) .10
262 Eric Chavez, Russell Branyan, Russ Johnson (Prospect) .15
263 Todd Dunwoody, John Barnes, *Ryan Jackson* (Prospect) .25
264 Matt Clement, Roy Halladay, *Brian Fuentes* (Prospect) .25
265 Randy Johnson (Season Highlight) .10
266 Kevin Brown (Season Highlight) .05
267 Ricardo Rincon, Francisco Cordova (Season Highlight) .05
268 Nomar Garciaparra (Season Highlight) .65
269 Tino Martinez (Season Highlight) .05
270 Chuck Knoblauch (Interleague) .05
271 Pedro Martinez (Interleague) .40
272 Denny Neagle (Interleague) .05
273 Juan Gonzalez (Interleague) .40
274 Andres Galarraga (Interleague) .05
275 Checklist .05
276 Checklist .05
277 Moises Alou (World Series) .05
278 Sandy Alomar (World Series) .05
279 Gary Sheffield (World Series) .05
280 Matt Williams (World Series) .05
281 Livan Hernandez (World Series) .05
282 Chad Ogea (World Series) .05
283 Marlins Win (World Series) .05
284 Tino Martinez .10
285 Roberto Alomar .50
286 Jeff King .05
287 Brian Jordan .05
288 Darin Erstad .15
289 Ken Caminiti .20
290 Jim Thome .30
291 Paul Molitor .50
292 Ivan Rodriguez .75
293 Bernie Williams .40
294 Todd Hundley .10
295 Andres Galarraga .40
296 Greg Maddux 1.25
297 Edgar Martinez .05
298 Ron Gant .10
299 Derek Bell .05
300 Roger Clemens 1.00
301 Rondell White .15
302 Barry Larkin .15
303 Robin Ventura .20
304 Jason Kendall .15
305 Chipper Jones 1.50
306 John Franco .05
307 Sammy Sosa 1.50
308 Troy Percival .05
309 Chuck Knoblauch .15
310 Ellis Burks .05
311 Al Martin .05
312 Tim Salmon .20
313 Moises Alou .15
314 Lance Johnson .05
315 Justin Thompson .10
316 Will Clark .25
317 Barry Bonds .60
318 Craig Biggio .25
319 John Smoltz .15
320 Cal Ripken Jr. 2.00
321 Ken Griffey Jr. 2.50
322 Paul O'Neill .15
323 Todd Helton .50
324 John Olerud .25
325 Mark McGwire 2.50
326 Jose Cruz Jr. .10
327 Jeff Cirillo .05
328 Dean Palmer .05
329 John Wetteland .05
330 Steve Finley .05
331 Albert Belle .50
332 Curt Schilling .10
333 Raul Mondesi .20
334 Andruw Jones .40
335 Nomar Garciaparra 1.50
336 David Justice .20
337 Andy Pettitte .20
338 Pedro Martinez .75
339 Travis Miller .05
340 Chris Stynes .05
341 Gregg Jefferies .05
342 Jeff Fassero .05
343 Craig Counsell .05
344 Wilson Alvarez .05
345 Bip Roberts .05
346 Kelvim Escobar .05
347 Mark Bellhorn .05
348 *Cory Lidle* .05
349 Fred McGriff .15
350 Chuck Carr .05
351 Bob Abreu .05
352 Juan Guzman .05
353 Fernando Vina .05
354 Andy Benes .05
355 Dave Nilsson .05
356 Bobby Bonilla .05
357 Ismael Valdes .05
358 Carlos Perez .05
359 Kirk Rueter .05
360 Bartolo Colon .15
361 Mel Rojas .05
362 Johnny Damon .05
363 Geronimo Berroa .05
364 Reggie Sanders .05
365 Jermaine Allensworth .05
366 Orlando Cabrera .05
367 Jorge Fabregas .05
368 Scott Stahoviak .05
369 Ken Cloude .05
370 Donovan Osborne .05
371 Roger Cedeno .05
372 Neifi Perez .05
373 Chris Holt .05
374 Cecil Fielder .05
375 Marty Cordova .05
376 Tom Goodwin .05
377 Jeff Suppan .05
378 Jeff Brantley .05
379 Mark Langston .05
380 Shane Reynolds .10
381 Mike Fetters .05

#	Player	MT
382	Todd Greene	.05
383	Ray Durham	.05
384	Carlos Delgado	.50
385	Jeff D'Amico	.05
386	Brian McRae	.05
387	Alan Benes	.10
388	Heathcliff Slocumb	.05
389	Eric Young	.05
390	Travis Fryman	.05
391	David Cone	.10
392	Otis Nixon	.05
393	Jeremi Gonzalez	.05
394	Jeff Juden	.05
395	Jose Vizcaino	.05
396	Ugueth Urbina	.05
397	Ramon Martinez	.10
398	Robb Nen	.05
399	Harold Baines	.05
400	Delino DeShields	.05
401	John Burkett	.05
402	Sterling Hitchcock	.05
403	Mark Clark	.05
404	Terrell Wade	.05
405	Scott Brosius	.05
406	Chad Curtis	.05
407	Brian Johnson	.05
408	Roberto Kelly	.05
409	*Dave Dellucci*	.05
410	Michael Tucker	.05
411	Mark Kotsay	.10
412	Mark Lewis	.05
413	Ryan McGuire	.05
414	Shawon Dunston	.05
415	Brad Rigby	.05
416	Scott Erickson	.05
417	Bobby Jones	.05
418	Darren Oliver	.05
419	John Smiley	.05
420	T.J. Mathews	.05
421	Dustin Hermanson	.05
422	Mike Timlin	.05
423	Willie Blair	.05
424	Manny Alexander	.05
425	Bob Tewksbury	.05
426	Pete Schourek	.05
427	Reggie Jefferson	.05
428	Ed Sprague	.05
429	Jeff Conine	.05
430	Roberto Hernandez	.05
431	Tom Pagnozzi	.05
432	Jaret Wright	.20
433	Livan Hernandez	.10
434	Andy Ashby	.05
435	Todd Dunn	.05
436	Bobby Higginson	.05
437	Rod Beck	.05
438	Jim Leyritz	.05
439	Matt Williams	.20
440	Brett Tomko	.05
441	Joe Randa	.05
442	Chris Carpenter	.05
443	Dennis Reyes	.05
444	Al Leiter	.10
445	Jason Schmidt	.05
446	Ken Hill	.05
447	Shannon Stewart	.05
448	Enrique Wilson	.05
449	Fernando Tatis	.15
450	Jimmy Key	.05
451	Darrin Fletcher	.05
452	John Valentin	.05
453	Kevin Tapani	.05
454	Eric Karros	.10
455	Jay Bell	.05
456	Walt Weiss	.05
457	Devon White	.05
458	Carl Pavano	.05
459	Mike Lansing	.05
460	John Flaherty	.05
461	Richard Hidalgo	.05
462	Quinton McCracken	.05
463	Karim Garcia	.10
464	Miguel Cairo	.05
465	Edwin Diaz	.05
466	Bobby Smith	.05
467	Yamil Benitez	.05
468	*Rich Butler*	.25
469	*Ben Ford*	.05
470	Bubba Trammell	.05
471	Brent Brede	.05
472	Brooks Kieschnick	.05
473	Carlos Castillo	.05
474	Brad Radke (Season Highlight)	.05
475	Roger Clemens (Season Highlight)	.50
476	Curt Schilling (Season Highlight)	.05
477	John Olerud (Season Highlight)	.05
478	Mark McGwire (Season Highlight)	1.25
479	Mike Piazza, Ken Griffey Jr. (Interleague)	1.00
480	Jeff Bagwell, Frank Thomas (Interleague)	.50
481	Chipper Jones, Nomar Garciaparra (Interleague)	.75
482	Larry Walker, Juan Gonzalez (Interleague)	.40
483	Gary Sheffield, Tino Martinez (Interleague)	.05
484	Derrick Gibson, Michael Coleman, Norm Hutchins (Prospect)	.10
485	Braden Looper, Cliff Politte, Brian Rose (Prospect)	.15
486	Eric Milton, Jason Marquis, Corey Lee (Prospect)	.15
487	A.J. Hinch, Mark Osborne, *Robert Fick* (Prospect)	.50
488	Aramis Ramirez, Alex Gonzalez, Sean Casey (Prospect)	.60
489	*Donnie Bridges*, *Tim Drew* (Draft Pick)	.40
490	*Ntema Ndungidi*, *Darnell McDonald* (Draft Pick)	.50
491	*Ryan Anderson*, Mark Mangum (Draft Pick)	.75
492	J.J. Davis, *Troy Glaus* (Draft Pick)	2.00
493	Jayson Werth, *Dan Reichert* (Draft Pick)	.25
494	*John Curtice*, *Mike Cuddyer* (Draft Pick)	.50
495	*Jack Cust*, Jason Standridge (Draft Pick)	.50
496	Brian Anderson (Expansion Team Prospect)	.05
497	Tony Saunders (Expansion Team Prospect)	.05
498	Vladimir Nunez *Jhensy Sandoval* (Expansion Team Prospect)	.10
499	Brad Penny, Nick Bierbrodt (Expansion Team Prospect)	.15
500	*Dustin Carr*, *Luis Cruz* (Expansion Team Prospect)	.20
501	*Marcus McCain*, *Cedrick Bowers* (Expansion Team Prospect)	.20
502	Checklist	.05
503	Checklist	.05
504	Alex Rodriguez	2.00

1998 Topps Baby Boomers

This 15-card retail exclusive insert was seeded one per 36 packs of Series I. It featured some of the top young players in the game and was numbered with a "BB" prefix.

		MT
Complete Set (15):		30.00
Common Player:		.75
Inserted 1:36 retail		
1	Derek Jeter	5.00
2	Scott Rolen	2.00
3	Nomar Garciaparra	5.00
4	Jose Cruz Jr.	.75
5	Darin Erstad	2.00
6	Todd Helton	3.00
7	Tony Clark	1.00
8	Jose Guillen	.75
9	Andruw Jones	1.50
10	Vladimir Guerrero	4.00
11	Mark Kotsay	.75
12	Todd Greene	.75
13	Andy Pettitte	.75
14	Justin Thompson	.75
15	Alan Benes	.75

1998 Topps Clout 9

Clout 9 captured nine players known for their statistical supremacy. Cards were numbered with a "C" prefix and inserted one per 72 packs of Series II.

		MT
Complete Set (9):		50.00
Common Player:		3.00
Inserted 1:72		
1	Edgar Martinez	3.00
2	Mike Piazza	12.00
3	Frank Thomas	7.50
4	Craig Biggio	4.00
5	Vinny Castilla	3.00
6	Jeff Blauser	3.00
7	Barry Bonds	7.50
8	Ken Griffey Jr.	20.00
9	Larry Walker	4.00

1998 Topps Etch-A-Sketch

Etch-a-Sketch featured nine different players depicted by nationally acclaimed artist George Vlosich III. Known as "The Etch-a-Sketch Kid," Vlosich created each one of these Series I inserts, which were inserted at a rate of one per 36 packs. Cards are numbered with an "ES" prefix.

		MT
Complete Set (9):		30.00
Common Player:		1.50
Inserted 1:36		
1	Albert Belle	2.00
2	Barry Bonds	3.00
3	Ken Griffey Jr.	10.00
4	Greg Maddux	5.00
5	Hideo Nomo	1.50
6	Mike Piazza	6.00
7	Cal Ripken Jr.	8.00
8	Frank Thomas	3.00
9	Mo Vaughn	2.00

1998 Topps Flashback

This double-sided insert showed "then and now" photos of 10 top major leaguers. One side contained a shot of the player in 1998, while the other side showed him at the beginning of his major league career. Flashback inserts were seeded one per 72 packs and numbered with a "FB" prefix.

		MT
Complete Set (10):		70.00
Common Player:		3.00
Inserted 1:72		
1	Barry Bonds	8.00
2	Ken Griffey Jr.	25.00
3	Paul Molitor	4.00
4	Randy Johnson	4.00
5	Cal Ripken Jr.	15.00
6	Tony Gwynn	12.00
7	Kenny Lofton	4.00
8	Gary Sheffield	4.00
9	Deion Sanders	3.00
10	Brady Anderson	3.00

1998 Topps Focal Point

This hobby exclusive insert contained 15 top players and focused on the skills that have made that player great. Focal Point inserts were available in Series II packs and seeded one per 36 packs, and were numbered with a "FP" prefix.

		MT
Complete Set (15):		80.00
Common Player:		2.00
Inserted 1:36		
1	Juan Gonzalez	5.00
2	Nomar Garciaparra	12.00
3	Jose Cruz Jr.	2.00
4	Cal Ripken Jr.	15.00
5	Ken Griffey Jr.	20.00
6	Ivan Rodriguez	5.00
7	Larry Walker	4.00
8	Barry Bonds	5.00
9	Roger Clemens	6.00
10	Frank Thomas	5.00
11	Chuck Knoblauch	2.00
12	Mike Piazza	12.00
13	Greg Maddux	10.00
14	Vladimir Guerrero	8.00
15	Andruw Jones	4.00

1998 Topps Hallbound

Hall Bound featured 15 top players who are considered locks to be inducted into the Hall of Fame when there career is over. This insert was exclusive to Series I hobby packs and seeded one per 36 packs. Cards are numbered with a "HB" prefix.

		MT
Complete Set (15):		75.00
Common Player:		1.50
1	Paul Molitor	3.00
2	Tony Gwynn	8.00
3	Wade Boggs	2.00
4	Roger Clemens	6.00
5	Dennis Eckersley	1.50
6	Cal Ripken Jr.	12.00
7	Greg Maddux	8.00
8	Rickey Henderson	2.00
9	Ken Griffey Jr.	15.00
10	Frank Thomas	6.00
11	Mark McGwire	15.00
12	Barry Bonds	5.00
13	Mike Piazza	10.00
14	Juan Gonzalez	4.00
15	Randy Johnson	3.00

1998 Topps Inter-League Mystery Finest

Five of the 1997 season's most intriguing inter-league matchups are showcased with four cards each in Inter-League Mystery Finest. Regular versions of this Series 1 insert are seeded one per 36 packs, while Refractor versions are seeded one per 144 packs. Cards are numbered with an "ILM" prefix.

		MT
Complete Set (20):		100.00
Common Player:		1.50
Inserted 1:36		
Refractors:		5X
Inserted 1:144		
1	Chipper Jones	12.00
2	Cal Ripken Jr.	15.00
3	Greg Maddux	10.00
4	Rafael Palmeiro	3.00
5	Todd Hundley	1.50
6	Derek Jeter	12.00
7	John Olerud	2.50
8	Tino Martinez	2.00
9	Larry Walker	4.00
10	Ken Griffey Jr.	20.00
11	Andres Galarraga	2.00
12	Randy Johnson	4.00
13	Mike Piazza	12.00
14	Jim Edmonds	1.50
15	Eric Karros	2.00
16	Tim Salmon	3.00
17	Sammy Sosa	12.00
18	Frank Thomas	9.00
19	Mark Grace	3.00
20	Albert Belle	4.00

1998 Topps Milestones

Milestones features 10 records that could be broken in during the 1998 season and the player's who have the best shot at breaking them. This retail exclusive insert is seeded one per 36 packs and is numbered with a "MS" prefix.

		MT
Complete Set (10):		60.00
Common Player:		1.50
MS1	Barry Bonds	5.00
MS2	Roger Clemens	5.00
MS3	Dennis Eckersley	1.50
MS4	Juan Gonzalez	4.00
MS5	Ken Griffey Jr.	15.00
MS6	Tony Gwynn	7.50
MS7	Greg Maddux	10.00
MS8	Mark McGwire	15.00
MS9	Cal Ripken Jr.	12.00
MS10	Frank Thomas	6.00

1998 Topps Mystery Finest

This 20-card insert set features top players on bordered and borderless designs, with Refractor versions of each. Exclusive to Series 2 packs, bordered cards are seeded 1:36 packs, borderless are seeded 1:72 packs, bordered Refractors are 1:108 and borderless Refractors are seeded 1:288 packs. Mystery Finest inserts are numbered with a "M" prefix.

		MT
Complete Set (20):		125.00
Common Player:		2.50
Inserted 1:36		
Borderless 1:72:		1.5X
Bordered Refractors 1:108:		3X
Borderless Refractors 1:288:		5X
1	Nomar Garciaparra	12.00
2	Chipper Jones	12.00
3	Scott Rolen	5.00
4	Albert Belle	4.00
5	Mo Vaughn	3.00
6	Jose Cruz Jr.	2.50
7	Mark McGwire	20.00
8	Derek Jeter	12.00
9	Tony Gwynn	10.00
10	Frank Thomas	7.50
11	Tino Martinez	3.00
12	Greg Maddux	10.00
13	Juan Gonzalez	5.00
14	Larry Walker	4.00
15	Mike Piazza	12.00
16	Cal Ripken Jr.	15.00
17	Jeff Bagwell	6.00
18	Andruw Jones	4.00
19	Barry Bonds	6.00
20	Ken Griffey Jr.	20.00

1998 Topps Rookie Class

Rookie Class features 10 young stars from 1998 and was exclusive to Series II packs. The cards were inserted one per 12 packs and numbered with a "R" prefix.

		MT
Complete Set (10):		9.00
Common Player:		.50
Inserted 1:12		
1	Travis Lee	1.00
2	Richard Hidalgo	.75
3	Todd Helton	2.50
4	Paul Konerko	1.50
5	Mark Kotsay	1.00
6	Derrek Lee	.50
7	Eli Marrero	.50
8	Fernando Tatis	1.00
9	Juan Encarnacion	.60
10	Ben Grieve	2.00

1998 Topps Roberto Clemente Finest

Clemente Finest inserts were included in both Series I and II at a rate of one per 72 packs. There were a total of 19 different, with odd numbers in Series I and even numbers in Series II. The insert helped honor the memory of the 25th anniversary of his death.

		MT
Complete Set (19):		150.00
Common Card:		10.00
Inserted 1:72		
Refractors:		2.5X
Inserted 1:288		
1	1955	15.00
2	1956	10.00
3	1957	10.00
4	1958	10.00
5	1959	10.00
6	1960	10.00
7	1961	10.00
8	1962	10.00
9	1963	10.00
10	1964	10.00
11	1965	10.00
12	1966	10.00
13	1967	10.00
14	1968	10.00
15	1969	10.00
16	1970	10.00
17	1971	10.00
18	1972	10.00
19	1973	10.00

1998 Topps Roberto Clemente Reprints

Nineteen different Topps Clemente cards were reprinted with a gold foil stamp and included 1998 Topps. Odd numbers were included in Series I, while even numbers were inserted into Series II, both at a rate of one per 18 packs. The insert was created to honor the memory of the 25th anniversary of Clemente's death.

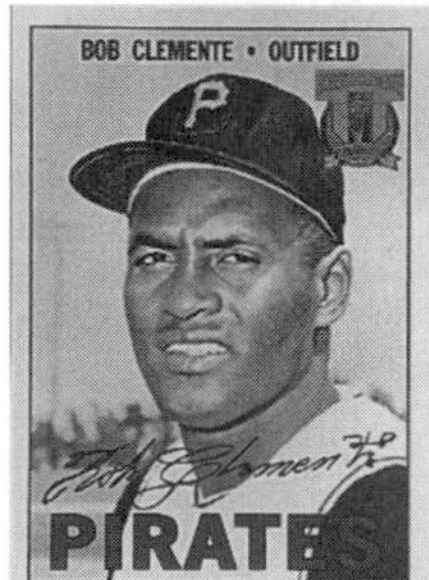

		MT
Complete Set (19):		70.00
Common Clemente:		4.00
Inserted 1:18		
1	1955	10.00
2	1956	4.00
3	1957	4.00
4	1958	4.00
5	1959	4.00
6	1960	4.00
7	1961	4.00
8	1962	4.00
9	1963	4.00
10	1964	4.00
11	1965	4.00
12	1966	4.00
13	1967	4.00
14	1968	4.00
15	1969	4.00
16	1970	4.00
17	1971	4.00
18	1972	4.00
19	1973	4.00

1998 Topps Roberto Clemente Tribute

Five Clemente Tribute cards were produced for Series I and inserted in one per 12 packs. The set features some classic photos of Clemente and honor his memory in the 25th anniversary of his death. Clemente Tribute cards are numbered with a "RC" prefix.

		MT
Complete Set (5):		6.00
Common Clemente:		1.50
Inserted 1:12		
1	Roberto Clemente	1.50
2	Roberto Clemente	1.50
3	Roberto Clemente	1.50
4	Roberto Clemente	1.50
5	Roberto Clemente	1.50

1998 Topps Opening Day

Topps Opening Day was a retail exclusive product included 165 cards, with 110 from Series I and 55 from Series II. The 55 cards from Series II were available in this product prior to the cards being released. Opening Day cards featured a silver border vs. the gold border in the base set, and included a silver Opening Day stamp.

		MT
Complete Set (165):		15.00
Common Player:		.05
1	Tony Gwynn	1.00
2	Larry Walker	.40
3	Billy Wagner	.10
4	Denny Neagle	.05
5	Vladimir Guerrero	.75
6	Kevin Brown	.15
7	Mariano Rivera	.15
8	Tony Clark	.25
9	Deion Sanders	.10
10	Matt Williams	.15
11	Carlos Baerga	.05
12	Mo Vaughn	.40
13	Chan Ho Park	.10
14	Frank Thomas	.75
15	John Jaha	.05
16	Steve Trachsel	.05
17	Jeff Kent	.05
18	Scott Rolen	.60
19	Juan Gonzalez	.75
20	Garret Anderson	.05
21	Roberto Clemente	1.50
22	Omar Vizquel	.05
23	Brian Hunter	.05
24	Jeff Bagwell	.50
25	Chili Davis	.05
26	Mike Cameron	.10
27	Pat Hentgen	.05
28	Wilton Guerrero	.05
29	Devon White	.05
30	Rafael Palmeiro	.25
31	Jeff Blauser	.05
32	Dave Hollins	.05
33	Trevor Hoffman	.10
34	Ryan Klesko	.10
35	Butch Huskey	.05
36	Mark Grudzielanek	.05
37	Marquis Grissom	.05
38	Jim Edmonds	.15
39	Greg Vaughn	.10
40	David Wells	.05
41	Charles Nagy	.05
42	B.J. Surhoff	.05
43	Edgardo Alfonzo	.15
44	Jay Buhner	.05
45	Brady Anderson	.15
46	Edgar Renteria	.05
47	Rick Aguilera	.05
48	Henry Rodriguez	.05
49	Mike Piazza	1.25
50	Todd Zeile	.05
51	Rey Ordonez	.10
52	Tony Womack	.05
53	Mike Sweeney	.05
54	Jeffrey Hammonds	.05
55	Kevin Orie	.05
56	Alex Gonzalez	.05
57	Jose Canseco	.40
58	Joey Hamilton	.05
59	Brad Radke	.05
60	Kevin Appier	.05
61	Manny Ramirez	.50
62	Jeromy Burnitz	.05
63	Matt Morris	.05
64	Jason Dickson	.05
65	Tom Glavine	.15
66	Wally Joyner	.05
67	Todd Jones	.05
68	Sandy Alomar	.10
69	Mike Lansing	.05
70	Todd Stottlemyre	.05
71	Jay Bell	.05
72	Joey Cora	.05
73	Scott Spiezio	.05
74	Joe Carter	.05
75	Jose Guillen	.10
76	Damion Easley	.05
77	Alex Fernandez	.05
78	Randy Johnson	.40
79	J.T. Snow	.15
80	Bernard Gilkey	.05
81	David Segui	.05
82	Dante Bichette	.15
83	Derek Jeter	1.25
84	Mark Wohlers	.05
85	Ricky Bottalico	.05
86	Mike Mussina	.40
87	Gary Sheffield	.15
88	Hideo Nomo	.20
89	Mark Grace	.20
90	Darryl Kile	.05
91	Shawn Estes	.15
92	Vinny Castilla	.10
93	Jose Rosado	.05
94	Kenny Lofton	.40
95	Jason Giambi	.05
96	Ray Lankford	.05
97	Hideki Irabu	.15
98	Javy Lopez	.05
99	Jeff Montgomery	.05
100	Dennis Eckersley	.05
101	Armando Benitez	.05
102	Tim Naehring	.05
103	Luis Gonzalez	.05
104	Todd Hollandsworth	.05
105	Wade Boggs	.20
106	Mickey Morandini	.05
107	Rusty Greer	.10
108	Terry Steinbach	.05
109	Pete Rose II	.25
110	Checklist	.05
111	Tino Martinez	.20
112	Roberto Alomar	.40
113	Jeff King	.05
114	Brian Jordan	.05
115	Darin Erstad	.25
116	Ken Caminiti	.15
117	Jim Thome	.30
118	Paul Molitor	.40
119	Ivan Rodriguez	.50
120	Bernie Williams	.40
121	Todd Hundley	.15
122	Andres Galarraga	.25
123	Greg Maddux	1.00
124	Edgar Martinez	.05
125	Ron Gant	.10
126	Derek Bell	.05
127	Roger Clemens	.75
128	Rondell White	.15
129	Barry Larkin	.20
130	Robin Ventura	.15
131	Jason Kendall	.10
132	Chipper Jones	1.25
133	John Franco	.05
134	Sammy Sosa	1.25
135	Chuck Knoblauch	.20
136	Ellis Burks	.05
137	Al Martin	.05
138	Tim Salmon	.20
139	Moises Alou	.15
140	Lance Johnson	.05
141	Justin Thompson	.05
142	Will Clark	.15
143	Barry Bonds	.50
144	Craig Biggio	.25
145	John Smoltz	.15
146	Cal Ripken Jr.	1.50
147	Ken Griffey Jr.	2.50
148	Paul O'Neill	.15
149	Todd Helton	.50
150	John Olerud	.15
151	Mark McGwire	2.50
152	Jose Cruz Jr.	.10
153	Jeff Cirillo	.05
154	Dean Palmer	.05
155	John Wetteland	.05
156	Eric Karros	.10
157	Steve Finley	.05
158	Albert Belle	.50
159	Curt Schilling	.10
160	Raul Mondesi	.15
161	Andruw Jones	.40
162	Nomar Garciaparra	1.25
163	David Justice	.15
164	Andy Pettitte	.10
165	Pedro Martinez	.60

1998 Topps Chrome

All 502 cards from Topps Series I and II were reprinted in chromium versions for Topps Chrome. Chrome was released in two series, with Series I containing 282 cards and Series II including 220 cards. Four-card packs were sold for a suggested retail price of $3, while cards included a Topps Chrome logo. Chrome also included a sampling of the inserts from Topps, along with Refractor versions of every card and insert. Series I inserts included: Flashbacks, Baby Boomers and Hall Bound. Series II inserts included: Milestones, '98 Rookie Class and Clout 9.

		MT
Complete Set (502):		300.00
Complete Series 1 (282):		150.00
Complete Series 2 (220)		150.00
Common Player:		.25
Pack (4):		3.00
Series 1 Wax Box (24):		60.00
Series 2 Wax Box (24):		60.00
1	Tony Gwynn	4.00
2	Larry Walker	1.50
3	Billy Wagner	.25
4	Denny Neagle	.25
5	Vladimir Guerrero	2.50
6	Kevin Brown	.50
7	Not Issued	
8	Mariano Rivera	.75
9	Tony Clark	.75
10	Deion Sanders	.75
11	Francisco Cordova	.25
12	Matt Williams	1.00
13	Carlos Baerga	.25
14	Mo Vaughn	1.50
15	Bobby Witt	.25
16	Matt Stairs	.25
17	Chan Ho Park	.50
18	Mike Bordick	.25
19	Michael Tucker	.25
20	Frank Thomas	2.00
21	Roberto Clemente (Tribute)	5.00
22	Dmitri Young	.25

No.	Player	Price
23	Steve Trachsel	.25
24	Jeff Kent	.25
25	Scott Rolen	2.00
26	John Thomson	.25
27	Joe Vitiello	.25
28	Eddie Guardado	.25
29	Charlie Hayes	.25
30	Juan Gonzalez	2.00
31	Garret Anderson	.25
32	John Jaha	.25
33	Omar Vizquel	.25
34	Brian Hunter	.25
35	Jeff Bagwell	2.00
36	Mark Lemke	.25
37	Doug Glanville	.25
38	Dan Wilson	.25
39	Steve Cooke	.25
40	Chili Davis	.25
41	Mike Cameron	.25
42	F.P. Santangelo	.25
43	Brad Ausmus	.25
44	Gary DiSarcina	.25
45	Pat Hentgen	.25
46	Wilton Guerrero	.25
47	Devon White	.25
48	Danny Patterson	.25
49	Pat Meares	.25
50	Rafael Palmeiro	1.00
51	Mark Gardner	.25
52	Jeff Blauser	.25
53	Dave Hollins	.25
54	Carlos Garcia	.25
55	Ben McDonald	.25
56	John Mabry	.25
57	Trevor Hoffman	.25
58	Tony Fernandez	.25
59	Rich Loiselle	.25
60	Mark Leiter	.25
61	Pat Kelly	.25
62	John Flaherty	.25
63	Roger Bailey	.25
64	Tom Gordon	.25
65	Ryan Klesko	.40
66	Darryl Hamilton	.25
67	Jim Eisenreich	.25
68	Butch Huskey	.25
69	Mark Grudzielanek	.25
70	Marquis Grissom	.25
71	Mark McLemore	.25
72	Gary Gaetti	.25
73	Greg Gagne	.25
74	Lyle Mouton	.25
75	Jim Edmonds	.25
76	Shawn Green	1.00
77	Terry Vaughn	.25
78	Terry Adams	.25
79	*Kevin Polcovich*	.60
80	Troy O'Leary	.25
81	Jeff Shaw	.25
82	Rich Becker	.25
83	David Wells	.25
84	Steve Karsay	.25
85	Charles Nagy	.25
86	B.J. Surhoff	.25
87	Jamey Wright	.25
88	James Baldwin	.25
89	Edgardo Alfonzo	.75
90	Jay Buhner	.75
91	Brady Anderson	.50
92	Scott Servais	.25
93	Edgar Renteria	.25
94	Mike Lieberthal	.25
95	Rick Aguilera	.25
96	Walt Weiss	.25
97	Deivi Cruz	.25
98	Kurt Abbott	.25
99	Henry Rodriguez	.25
100	Mike Piazza	5.00
101	Bill Taylor	.25
102	Todd Zeile	.25
103	Rey Ordonez	.25
104	Willie Greene	.25
105	Tony Womack	.25
106	Mike Sweeney	.25
107	Jeffrey Hammonds	.25
108	Kevin Orie	.25
109	Alex Gonzalez	.25
110	Jose Canseco	2.00
111	Paul Sorrento	.25
112	Joey Hamilton	.25
113	Brad Radke	.25
114	Steve Avery	.25
115	Esteban Loaiza	.25
116	Stan Javier	.25
117	Chris Gomez	.25
118	Royce Clayton	.25
119	Orlando Merced	.25
120	Kevin Appier	.25
121	Mel Nieves	.25
122	Joe Girardi	.25
123	Rico Brogna	.25
124	Kent Mercker	.25
125	Manny Ramirez	2.00
126	Jeromy Burnitz	.25
127	Kevin Foster	.25
128	Matt Morris	.50
129	Jason Dickson	.25
130	Tom Glavine	.50
131	Wally Joyner	.25
132	Rick Reed	.25
133	Todd Jones	.25
134	Dave Martinez	.25
135	Sandy Alomar	.50
136	Mike Lansing	.25
137	Sean Berry	.25
138	Doug Jones	.25
139	Todd Stottlemyre	.25
140	Jay Bell	.25
141	Jaime Navarro	.25
142	Chris Hoiles	.25
143	Joey Cora	.25
144	Scott Spiezio	.25
145	Joe Carter	.50
146	Jose Guillen	.50
147	Damion Easley	.25
148	Lee Stevens	.25
149	Alex Fernandez	.25
150	Randy Johnson	1.50
151	J.T. Snow	.50
152	Chuck Finley	.25
153	Bernard Gilkey	.25
154	David Segui	.25
155	Dante Bichette	.75
156	Kevin Stocker	.25
157	Carl Everett	.50
158	Jose Valentin	.50
159	Pokey Reese	.25
160	Derek Jeter	5.00
161	Roger Pavlik	.25
162	Mark Wohlers	.25
163	Ricky Bottalico	.25
164	Ozzie Guillen	.25
165	Mike Mussina	1.50
166	Gary Sheffield	.75
167	Hideo Nomo	.75
168	Mark Grace	.75
169	Aaron Sele	.25
170	Darryl Kile	.25
171	Shawn Estes	.25
172	Vinny Castilla	.50
173	Ron Coomer	.25
174	Jose Rosado	.25
175	Kenny Lofton	1.50
176	Jason Giambi	.25
177	Hal Morris	.25
178	Darren Bragg	.25
179	Orel Hershiser	.25
180	Ray Lankford	.25
181	Hideki Irabu	.75
182	Kevin Young	.25
183	Javy Lopez	.25
184	Jeff Montgomery	.25
185	Mike Holtz	.25
186	George Williams	.25
187	Cal Eldred	.25
188	Tom Candiotti	.25
189	Glenallen Hill	.25
190	Brian Giles	.25
191	Dave Mlicki	.25
192	Garrett Stephenson	.25
193	Jeff Frye	.25
194	Joe Oliver	.25
195	Bob Hamelin	.25
196	Luis Sojo	.25
197	LaTroy Hawkins	.25
198	Kevin Elster	.25
199	Jeff Reed	.25
200	Dennis Eckersley	.50
201	Bill Mueller	.25
202	Russ Davis	.25
203	Armando Benitez	.25
204	Quilvio Veras	.25
205	Tim Naehring	.25
206	Quinton McCracken	.25
207	Raul Casanova	.25
208	Matt Lawton	.25
209	Luis Alicea	.25
210	Luis Gonzalez	.25
211	Allen Watson	.25
212	Gerald Williams	.25
213	David Bell	.25
214	Todd Hollandsworth	.25
215	Wade Boggs	1.00
216	Jose Mesa	.25
217	Jamie Moyer	.25
218	Darren Daulton	.25
219	Mickey Morandini	.25
220	Rusty Greer	.50
221	Jim Bullinger	.25
222	Jose Offerman	.25
223	Matt Karchner	.25
224	Woody Williams	.25
225	Mark Loretta	.25
226	Mike Hampton	.25
227	Willie Adams	.25
228	Scott Hatteberg	.25
229	Rich Amaral	.25
230	Terry Steinbach	.25
231	Glendon Rusch	.25
232	Bret Boone	.25
233	Robert Person	.25
234	Jose Hernandez	.25
235	Doug Drabek	.25
236	Jason McDonald	.25
237	Chris Widger	.25
238	*Tom Martin*	.25
239	Dave Burba	.25
240	Pete Rose	.25
241	Bobby Ayala	.25
242	Tim Wakefield	.25
243	Dennis Springer	.25
244	Tim Belcher	.25
245	Jon Garland, Geoff Goetz (Draft Pick)	1.50
246	Glenn Davis, Lance Berkman (Draft Pick)	1.00
247	Vernon Wells, Aaron Akin (Draft Pick)	1.00
248	Adam Kennedy, Jason Romano (Draft Pick)	1.00
249	Jason Dellaero, Troy Cameron (Draft Pick)	1.00
250	Alex Sanchez, *Jared Sandberg* (Expansion)	1.50
251	Pablo Ortega, *James Manias* (Expansion)	1.00
252	Jason Conti, *Mike Stoner* (Expansion)	4.00
253	John Patterson, Larry Rodriguez (Expansion)	1.00
254	Adrian Beltre, *Ryan Minor*, Aaron Boone (Prospect)	6.00
255	Ben Grieve, Brian Buchanan, Dermal Brown (Prospect)	3.00
256	Carl Pavano, Kerry Wood, Gil Meche (Prospect)	3.00
257	David Ortiz, Daryle Ward, Richie Sexson (Prospect)	1.00
258	Randy Winn, Juan Encarnacion, Andrew Vessel (Prospect)	1.00
259	Kris Benson, Travis Smith, Courtney Duncan (Prospect)	2.00
260	Chad Hermansen, Brent Butler, *Warren Morris* (Prospect)	5.00
261	Ben Davis, Elieser Marrero, Ramon Hernandez (Prospect)	1.00
262	Eric Chavez, Russell Branyan, Russ Johnson (Prospect)	1.00
263	Todd Dunwoody, John Barnes, *Ryan Jackson* (Prospect)	2.50
264	Matt Clement, Roy Halladay, Brian Fuentes (Prospect)	2.00
265	Randy Johnson (Season Highlight)	.75
266	Kevin Brown (Season Highlight)	.40
267	Francisco Cordova, Ricardo Rincon (Season Highlight)	.25
268	Nomar Garciaparra (Season Highlight)	3.00
269	Tino Martinez (Season Highlight)	.50
270	Chuck Knoblauch (Inter-League)	.50
271	Pedro Martinez (Inter-League)	1.00
272	Denny Neagle (Inter-League)	.25
273	Juan Gonzalez (Inter-League)	1.00
274	Andres Galarraga (Inter-League)	.50
275	Checklist	.25
276	Checklist	.25
277	Moises Alou (World Series)	.25
278	Sandy Alomar (World Series)	.25
279	Gary Sheffield (World Series)	.50
280	Matt Williams (World Series)	.50
281	Livan Hernandez (World Series)	.50
282	Chad Ogea (World Series)	.25
283	Marlins Win (World Series)	.75
284	Tino Martinez	.75
285	Roberto Alomar	1.50
286	Jeff King	.25
287	Brian Jordan	.25
288	Darin Erstad	.75
289	Ken Caminiti	.50
290	Jim Thome	1.00
291	Paul Molitor	1.50
292	Ivan Rodriguez	2.00
293	Bernie Williams	1.50
294	Todd Hundley	.50
295	Andres Galarraga	.75
296	Greg Maddux	4.00
297	Edgar Martinez	.50
298	Ron Gant	.50
299	Derek Bell	.25
300	Roger Clemens	3.00
301	Rondell White	.50
302	Barry Larkin	1.00
303	Robin Ventura	.75
304	Jason Kendall	.40
305	Chipper Jones	5.00
306	John Franco	.25
307	Sammy Sosa	5.00
308	Troy Percival	.25
309	Chuck Knoblauch	.75
310	Ellis Burks	.25
311	Al Martin	.25
312	Tim Salmon	.75
313	Moises Alou	.50
314	Lance Johnson	.25
315	Justin Thompson	.25
316	Will Clark	.75
317	Barry Bonds	2.00
318	Craig Biggio	1.00
319	John Smoltz	.50
320	Cal Ripken Jr.	6.00
321	Ken Griffey Jr.	8.00
322	Paul O'Neill	.75
323	Todd Helton	2.00
324	John Olerud	.75
325	Mark McGwire	10.00
326	Jose Cruz Jr.	.40
327	Jeff Cirillo	.25
328	Dean Palmer	.25
329	John Wetteland	.25
330	Steve Finley	.25
331	Albert Belle	2.00
332	Curt Schilling	.50
333	Raul Mondesi	.50
334	Andruw Jones	1.00
335	Nomar Garciaparra	5.00
336	David Justice	.75
337	Andy Pettitte	1.00
338	Pedro Martinez	2.50
339	Travis Miller	.25
340	Chris Stynes	.25
341	Gregg Jefferies	.25
342	Jeff Fassero	.25
343	Craig Counsell	.25
344	Wilson Alvarez	.25
345	Bip Roberts	.25
346	Kelvim Escobar	.25
347	Mark Bellhorn	.25
348	Cory Lidle	.25
349	Fred McGriff	.50
350	Chuck Carr	.25
351	Bob Abreu	.40
352	Juan Guzman	.25
353	Fernando Vina	.25
354	Andy Benes	.50
355	Dave Nilsson	.25
356	Bobby Bonilla	.50
357	Ismael Valdes	.25
358	Carlos Perez	.25

359	Kirk Rueter	.25
360	Bartolo Colon	.25
361	Mel Rojas	.25
362	Johnny Damon	.25
363	Geronimo Berroa	.25
364	Reggie Sanders	.25
365	Jermaine Allensworth	.25
366	Orlando Cabrera	.25
367	Jorge Fabregas	.25
368	Scott Stahoviak	.25
369	Ken Cloude	.50
370	Donovan Osborne	.25
371	Roger Cedeno	.25
372	Neifi Perez	.25
373	Chris Holt	.25
374	Cecil Fielder	.50
375	Marty Cordova	.25
376	Tom Goodwin	.25
377	Jeff Suppan	.25
378	Jeff Brantley	.25
379	Mark Langston	.25
380	Shane Reynolds	.50
381	Mike Fetters	.25
382	Todd Greene	.25
383	Ray Durham	.25
384	Carlos Delgado	1.00
385	Jeff D'Amico	.25
386	Brian McRae	.25
387	Alan Benes	.50
388	Heathcliff Slocumb	.25
389	Eric Young	.25
390	Travis Fryman	.50
391	David Cone	.75
392	Otis Nixon	.25
393	Jeremi Gonzalez	.25
394	Jeff Juden	.25
395	Jose Vizcaino	.25
396	Ugueth Urbina	.25
397	Ramon Martinez	.50
398	Robb Nen	.25
399	Harold Baines	.25
400	Delino DeShields	.25
401	John Burkett	.25
402	Sterling Hitchcock	.25
403	Mark Clark	.25
404	Terrell Wade	.25
405	Scott Brosius	.25
406	Chad Curtis	.25
407	Brian Johnson	.25
408	Roberto Kelly	.25
409	*Dave Dellucci*	2.00
410	Michael Tucker	.25
411	Mark Kotsay	.75
412	Mark Lewis	.25
413	Ryan McGuire	.25
414	Shawon Dunston	.25
415	Brad Rigby	.25
416	Scott Erickson	.25
417	Bobby Jones	.25
418	Darren Oliver	.25
419	John Smiley	.25
420	T.J. Mathews	.25
421	Dustin Hermanson	.25
422	Mike Timlin	.25
423	Willie Blair	.25
424	Manny Alexander	.25
425	Bob Tewksbury	.25
426	Pete Schourek	.25
427	Reggie Jefferson	.25
428	Ed Sprague	.25
429	Jeff Conine	.25
430	Roberto Hernandez	.25
431	Tom Pagnozzi	.25
432	Jaret Wright	.60
433	Livan Hernandez	.25
434	Andy Ashby	.25
435	Todd Dunn	.25
436	Bobby Higginson	.25
437	Rod Beck	.25
438	Jim Leyritz	.25
439	Matt Williams	.75
440	Brett Tomko	.25
441	Joe Randa	.25
442	Chris Carpenter	.25
443	Dennis Reyes	.25
444	Al Leiter	.40
445	Jason Schmidt	.25
446	Ken Hill	.25
447	Shannon Stewart	.25
448	Enrique Wilson	.25
449	Fernando Tatis	.75
450	Jimmy Key	.25
451	Darrin Fletcher	.25
452	John Valentin	.25
453	Kevin Tapani	.25
454	Eric Karros	.50
455	Jay Bell	.25
456	Walt Weiss	.25
457	Devon White	.25
458	Carl Pavano	.50
459	Mike Lansing	.25
460	John Flaherty	.25
461	Richard Hidalgo	.25
462	Quinton McCracken	.25
463	Karim Garcia	.50
464	Miguel Cairo	.25
465	Edwin Diaz	.25
466	Bobby Smith	.25
467	Yamil Benitez	.25
468	*Rich Butler*	1.50
469	*Ben Ford*	.50
470	Bubba Trammell	.25
471	Brent Brede	.25
472	Brooks Kieschnick	.25
473	Carlos Castillo	.25
474	Brad Radke (Season Highlight)	.25
475	Roger Clemens (Season Highlight)	1.50
476	Curt Schilling (Season Highlight)	.25
477	John Olerud (Season Highlight)	.40
478	Mark McGwire (Season Highlight)	5.00
479	Mike Piazza, Ken Griffey Jr. (Interleague)	4.00
480	Jeff Bagwell, Frank Thomas (Interleague)	1.00
481	Chipper Jones, Nomar Garciaparra (Interleague)	2.50
482	Larry Walker, Juan Gonzalez (Interleague)	1.00
483	Gary Sheffield, Tino Martinez (Interleague)	.50
484	Derrick Gibson, Michael Coleman, Norm Hutchins (Prospect)	.50
485	Braden Looper, Cliff Politte, Brian Rose (Prospect)	1.00
486	Eric Milton, Jason Marquis, Corey Lee (Prospect)	1.00
487	A.J. Hinch, Mark Osborne, *Robert Fick* (Prospect)	3.00
488	Aramis Ramirez, Alex Gonzalez, Sean Casey (Prospect)	6.00
489	*Donnie Bridges*, *Tim Drew* (Draft Pick)	2.50
490	*Ntema Ndungidi*, *Darnell McDonald* (Draft Pick)	6.00
491	*Ryan Anderson*, Mark Mangum (Draft Pick)	6.00
492	J.J. Davis, *Troy Glaus* (Draft Pick)	15.00
493	Jayson Werth, Dan Reichert (Draft Pick)	2.00
494	*John Curtice*, *Mike Cuddyer* (Draft Pick)	5.00
495	*Jack Cust*, Jason Standridge (Draft Pick)	6.00
496	Brian Anderson (Expansion Team Prospect)	.25
497	Tony Saunders (Expansion Team Prospect)	.50
498	Vladimir Nunez, *Jhensy Sandoval* (Expansion Team Prospect)	.50
499	Brad Penny, Nick Bierbrodt (Expansion Team Prospect)	1.00
500	*Dustin Carr*, *Luis Cruz* (Expansion Team Prospect)	2.00
501	*Marcus McCain*, *Cedrick Bowers* (Expansion Team Prospect)	.25
502	Checklist	.25
503	Checklist	.25
504	Alex Rodriguez	5.00

1998 Topps Chrome Refractors

Each card in the regular Topps Series 1 and Series 2 Chrome issue could also be found in a refractor version seeded approximately one per 12 packs. Refractor versions are so designated above the card number of back.

	MT
Common Player:	4.00

(Stars and rookies valued at 5-8X regular Chrome version.)

1998 Topps Chrome Baby Boomers

This 15-card insert featured players with less than three years of experience. Cards were inserted one per 24 packs, with Refractor versions found every 72 packs of Series I. Cards were numbered with a "BB" prefix.

		MT
Complete Set (15):		60.00
Common Player:		2.00
Inserted 1:24		
Refractors:		4X
Inserted 1:72		
1	Derek Jeter	15.00
2	Scott Rolen	6.00
3	Nomar Garciaparra	12.00
4	Jose Cruz Jr.	2.00
5	Darin Erstad	3.00
6	Todd Helton	5.00
7	Tony Clark	3.00
8	Jose Guillen	3.00
9	Andruw Jones	4.00
10	Vladimir Guerrero	10.00
11	Mark Kotsay	3.00
12	Todd Greene	2.00
13	Andy Pettitte	3.00
14	Justin Thompson	2.00
15	Alan Benes	2.00

1998 Topps Chrome Clout 9

This nine-card insert included players for their statistical supremacy. Clout 9 cards were found in Series II packs at a rate of one per 24 packs, with Refractor versions every 72 packs. Cards are numbered with a "C" prefix.

		MT
Complete Set (9):		70.00
Common Player:		3.00
Inserted 1:24		
Refractors:		4X
Inserted 1:72		
1	Edgar Martinez	3.00
2	Mike Piazza	20.00
3	Frank Thomas	10.00
4	Craig Biggio	5.00
5	Vinny Castilla	4.00
6	Jeff Blauser	3.00
7	Barry Bonds	10.00
8	Ken Griffey Jr.	30.00
9	Larry Walker	5.00

1998 Topps Chrome Flashback

This 10-card double-sided insert features top players as they looked in 1998 on one side, and how they looked when they first appeared in the majors on the other side. Flashback inserts were seeded one per 24 packs of Series I, with Refractors every 72 packs. This insert was numbered with a "FB" prefix.

		MT
Complete Set (10):		50.00
Common Player:		3.00
Inserted 1:24		
Refractors:		4X
Inserted 1:72		
1	Barry Bonds	8.00
2	Ken Griffey Jr.	20.00
3	Paul Molitor	4.00
4	Randy Johnson	4.00
5	Cal Ripken Jr.	12.00
6	Tony Gwynn	10.00
7	Kenny Lofton	3.00
8	Gary Sheffield	3.00
9	Deion Sanders	3.00
10	Brady Anderson	3.00

1998 Topps Chrome Hallbound

Hall Bound highlighted 15 players destined for the Hall of Fame on die-cut cards. Inserted at a rate of one per 24 packs of Series I, with Refractors every 72 packs, these were numbered with a "HB" prefix.

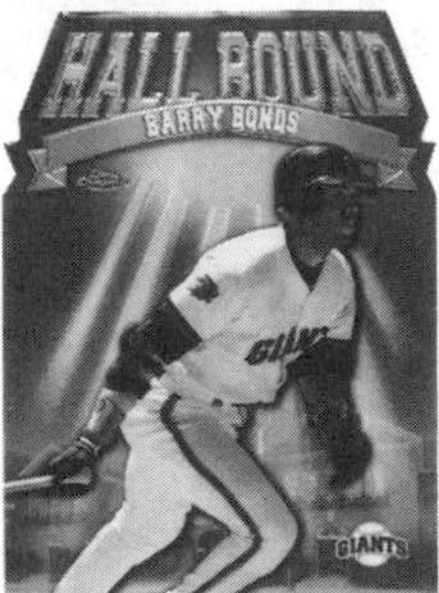

	MT
Complete Set (15):	125.00
Common Player:	3.00
Inserted 1:24	
Refractors:	4X
Inserted 1:72	
1 Paul Molitor	5.00
2 Tony Gwynn	12.00
3 Wade Boggs	4.00
4 Roger Clemens	10.00
5 Dennis Eckersley	3.00
6 Cal Ripken Jr.	20.00
7 Greg Maddux	12.00
8 Rickey Henderson	3.00
9 Ken Griffey Jr.	30.00
10 Frank Thomas	10.00
11 Mark McGwire	30.00
12 Barry Bonds	8.00
13 Mike Piazza	15.00
14 Juan Gonzalez	8.00
15 Randy Johnson	5.00

1998 Topps Chrome Milestones

Ten superstars who were within reach of major records for the 1998 season are featured in Milestones. This Series II insert was seeded one per 24 packs, with Refractor versions seeded one per 72 packs. Milestones were numbered with a "MS" prefix.

	MT
Complete Set (10):	120.00
Common Player:	3.00
Inserted 1:24	
Refractors:	4X
Inserted 1:72	
1 Barry Bonds	8.00
2 Roger Clemens	10.00
3 Dennis Eckersley	3.00
4 Juan Gonzalez	8.00
5 Ken Griffey Jr.	30.00
6 Tony Gwynn	15.00
7 Greg Maddux	12.00
8 Mark McGwire	30.00
9 Cal Ripken Jr.	25.00
10 Frank Thomas	8.00

1998 Topps Chrome Rookie Class

This insert featured 10 players with less than one year of major league experience. Inserted in Series II packs at a rate of one per 12 packs, with Refractors every 24 packs, '98 Rookie Class inserts were numbered with a "R" prefix.

	MT
Complete Set (10):	20.00
Common Player:	1.50
Inserted 1:12	
Refractors:	2.5X
Inserted 1:24	
1 Travis Lee	3.00
2 Richard Hidalgo	1.50
3 Todd Helton	5.00
4 Paul Konerko	3.00
5 Mark Kotsay	2.00
6 Derrek Lee	2.00
7 Eli Marrero	1.50
8 Fernando Tatis	3.00
9 Juan Encarnacion	1.50
10 Ben Grieve	4.00

1998 Topps Gallery

Gallery returned in 1998 with a 150-card set broken up into five different subsets - Exhibitions, Impressions, Expressionists, Portraits and Permanent Collection. The set was paralleled twice - first in a Player's Private Issue set and, second in Gallery Proofs. Gallery cards were made to look like works of art instead of simply a photo of the player on cardboard, and were sold in six-card packs. Inserts in this single-series product include: Photo Gallery, Gallery of Heroes and Awards Gallery.

	MT
Complete Set (150):	50.00
Common Player:	.20
Pack (6):	2.50
Wax Box (24):	55.00
1 Andruw Jones	1.00
2 Fred McGriff	.40
3 Wade Boggs	.40
4 Pedro Martinez	1.50
5 Matt Williams	.50
6 Wilson Alvarez	.20
7 Henry Rodriguez	.20
8 Jay Bell	.20
9 Marquis Grissom	.20
10 Darryl Kile	.20
11 Chuck Knoblauch	.30
12 Kenny Lofton	.75
13 Quinton McCracken	.20
14 Andres Galarraga	.75
15 Brian Jordan	.20
16 Mike Lansing	.20
17 Travis Fryman	.30
18 Tony Saunders	.20
19 Moises Alou	.40
20 Travis Lee	.50
21 Garret Anderson	.20
22 Ken Caminiti	.35
23 Pedro Astacio	.20
24 Ellis Burks	.20
25 Albert Belle	.75
26 Alan Benes	.25
27 Jay Buhner	.20
28 Derek Bell	.20
29 Jeromy Burnitz	.20
30 Kevin Appier	.20
31 Jeff Cirillo	.20
32 Bernard Gilkey	.20
33 David Cone	.40
34 Jason Dickson	.20
35 Jose Cruz Jr.	.30
36 Marty Cordova	.20
37 Ray Durham	.20
38 Jaret Wright	.35
39 Billy Wagner	.20
40 Roger Clemens	2.00
41 Juan Gonzalez	1.50
42 Jeremi Gonzalez	.20
43 Mark Grudzielanek	.20
44 Tom Glavine	.40
45 Barry Larkin	.30
46 Lance Johnson	.20
47 Bobby Higginson	.20
48 Mike Mussina	.75
49 Al Martin	.20
50 Mark McGwire	5.00
51 Todd Hundley	.20
52 Ray Lankford	.20
53 Jason Kendall	.30
54 Javy Lopez	.30
55 Ben Grieve	.50
56 Randy Johnson	.75
57 Jeff King	.20
58 Mark Grace	.40
59 Rusty Greer	.20
60 Greg Maddux	2.50
61 Jeff Kent	.20
62 Rey Ordonez	.25
63 Hideo Nomo	.40
64 Charles Nagy	.20
65 Rondell White	.40
66 Todd Helton	1.25
67 Jim Thome	.75
68 Denny Neagle	.20
69 Ivan Rodriguez	1.25
70 Vladimir Guerrero	2.00
71 Jorge Posada	.20
72 J.T. Snow Jr.	.20
73 Reggie Sanders	.20
74 Scott Rolen	1.25
75 Robin Ventura	.40
76 Mariano Rivera	.40
77 Cal Ripken Jr.	4.00
78 Justin Thompson	.20
79 Mike Piazza	3.00
80 Kevin Brown	.40
81 Sandy Alomar	.40
82 Craig Biggio	.75
83 Vinny Castilla	.40
84 Eric Young	.20
85 Bernie Williams	.65
86 Brady Anderson	.20
87 Bobby Bonilla	.20
88 Tony Clark	.40
89 Dan Wilson	.20
90 John Wetteland	.20
91 Barry Bonds	1.50
92 Chan Ho Park	.40
93 Carlos Delgado	.75
94 David Justice	.40
95 Chipper Jones	3.00
96 Shawn Estes	.20
97 Jason Giambi	.20
98 Ron Gant	.20
99 John Olerud	.50
100 Frank Thomas	1.50
101 Jose Guillen	.20
102 Brad Radke	.20
103 Troy Percival	.20
104 John Smoltz	.40
105 Edgardo Alfonzo	.40
106 Dante Bichette	.40
107 Larry Walker	.75
108 John Valentin	.20
109 Roberto Alomar	.75
110 Mike Cameron	.20
111 Eric Davis	.20
112 Johnny Damon	.20
113 Darin Erstad	.40
114 Omar Vizquel	.20
115 Derek Jeter	3.00
116 Tony Womack	.20
117 Edgar Renteria	.20
118 Raul Mondesi	.40
119 Tony Gwynn	2.50
120 Ken Griffey Jr.	5.00
121 Jim Edmonds	.20
122 Brian Hunter	.20
123 Neifi Perez	.20
124 Dean Palmer	.20
125 Alex Rodriguez	4.00
126 Tim Salmon	.40
127 Curt Schilling	.20
128 Kevin Orie	.20
129 Andy Pettitte	.30
130 Gary Sheffield	.40
131 Jose Rosado	.20
132 Manny Ramirez	1.50
133 Rafael Palmeiro	.75
134 Sammy Sosa	3.00
135 Jeff Bagwell	1.25
136 Delino DeShields	.20
137 Ryan Klesko	.40
138 Mo Vaughn	.75
139 Steve Finley	.20
140 Nomar Garciaparra	3.00
141 Paul Molitor	.75
142 Pat Hentgen	.20
143 Eric Karros	.25
144 Bobby Jones	.20
145 Tino Martinez	.25
146 Matt Morris	.20
147 Livan Hernandez	.25
148 Edgar Martinez	.20
149 Paul O'Neill	.40
150 Checklist	.20

1998 Topps Gallery Player's Private Issue

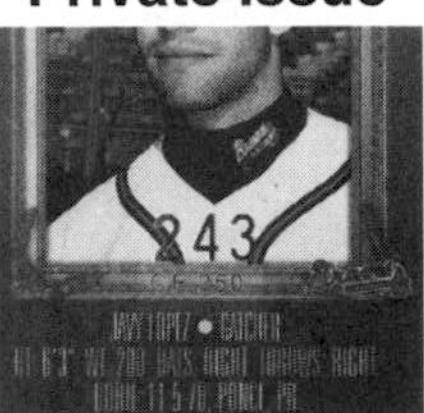

Players Private Issue inserts parallel the 150-card base set with a distinct design and embossing. The average insertion rate is one per 12 packs.

	MT
Common Player:	5.00
Stars:	25X
Young Stars/RCs	15X
Production 250 sets	

1998 Topps Gallery Awards Gallery

Awards Gallery featured 10 players who earned the highest honors in the game on a horizontal design. Fronts featured a shot of the player and the award he won on silver foilboard. These were inserted every 24 packs and numbered with an "AG" prefix.

		MT
Complete Set (10):		80.00
Common Player:		3.00
Inserted 1:24		
1	Ken Griffey Jr.	25.00
2	Larry Walker	5.00
3	Roger Clemens	8.00
4	Pedro Martinez	6.00
5	Nomar Garciaparra	15.00
6	Scott Rolen	6.00
7	Frank Thomas	8.00
8	Tony Gwynn	12.00
9	Mark McGwire	25.00
10	Livan Hernandez	3.00

1998 Topps Gallery Photo Gallery

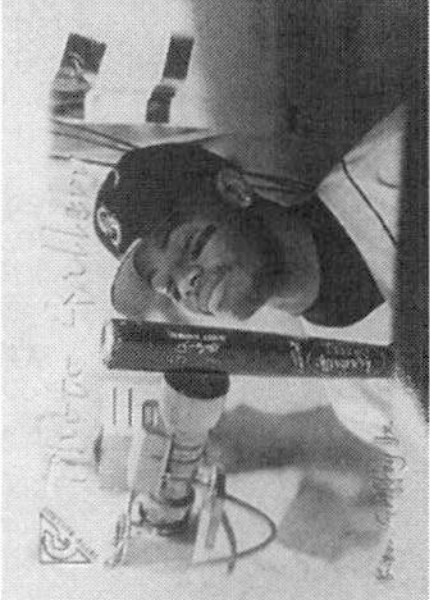

This 10-card insert captured unique shots of players on a silver foilboard design. Photo Gallery inserts were seeded one per 24 packs and numbered with a "PG" prefix.

		MT
Complete Set (10):		90.00
Common Player:		3.00
Inserted 1:24		
1	Alex Rodriguez	20.00
2	Frank Thomas	10.00
3	Derek Jeter	15.00
4	Cal Ripken Jr.	20.00
5	Ken Griffey Jr.	25.00
6	Mike Piazza	15.00
7	Nomar Garciaparra	15.00
8	Tim Salmon	3.00
9	Jeff Bagwell	10.00
10	Barry Bonds	10.00

1998 Topps Gallery of Heroes

Gallery of Heroes is a 15-card insert printed on colored, die-cut plastic that resembles a stained glass window. Cards were inserted one per 24 packs and numbered with a "GH" prefix. More is less in the case in the jumbo (3-1/4" x 4-1/2") version of the cards which were inserted one per hobby box. Cards are numbered with a "GH" prefix.

		MT
Complete Set (15):		150.00
Common Player:		2.50
Inserted 1:24		
Jumbo Version (1:24):		75%
1	Ken Griffey Jr.	25.00
2	Derek Jeter	15.00
3	Barry Bonds	7.00
4	Alex Rodriguez	20.00
5	Frank Thomas	7.00
6	Nomar Garciaparra	15.00
7	Mark McGwire	25.00
8	Mike Piazza	15.00
9	Cal Ripken Jr.	17.50
10	Jose Cruz Jr.	2.50
11	Jeff Bagwell	7.00
12	Chipper Jones	15.00
13	Juan Gonzalez	7.00
14	Hideo Nomo	3.50
15	Greg Maddux	12.50

1998 Topps Gold Label Class 1 (Fielding, Follow-thru)

Topps debuted its Gold Label brand with 100 cards printed on 30-point "spectral-reflective stock" with gold foil stamping and two shots of the player on each card front. Cards arrived in Gold Label, Black Label and Red Label versions, each with varying levels of scarcity. The rarity of the cards was determined by the photo and foil stamping on the cards. In the foreground of each card front, the photograph is the same, but in the background one of three shots is featured. Class 1, fielding, are considered base cards; Class 2: running (inserted 1:4 packs) and Class 3, hitting (inserted 1:8 packs) are seeded levels. For pitching the levels are: Class 1, set position (base); Class 2, throwing (inserted 1:4 packs) and Class 3, follow-through (inserted 1:8 packs). Black Label cards are scarcer, while Red Label cards are scarcer yet. In addition, 1 of 1 cards exist for each Class and version. Class 1 cards have matte gold-foil graphic highlights on front. Black Label Class 1 cards were inserted one per eight packs. Red Label Class 1 cards are a 1:99 insert and are serially numbered to 100.

		MT
Complete Set (100):		50.00
Gold Label		
Common Player:		.25
Black Label		
Common Player:		1.00
Black Label Stars/RCs:		6X
Red Label		
Common Player:		5.00
Red Label Stars/RCs:		15X
Pack (5):		6.00
Wax Box (24):		150.00
1	Kevin Brown	.30
2	Greg Maddux	2.50
3	Albert Belle	.75
4	Andres Galarraga	.75
5	Craig Biggio	.50
6	Matt Williams	.40
7	Derek Jeter	3.00
8	Randy Johnson	1.25
9	Jay Bell	.25
10	Jim Thome	.40
11	Roberto Alomar	.75
12	Tom Glavine	.40
13	Reggie Sanders	.25
14	Tony Gwynn	2.00
15	Mark McGwire	5.00
16	Jeromy Burnitz	.25
17	Andruw Jones	.50
18	Jay Buhner	.30
19	Robin Ventura	.30
20	Jeff Bagwell	1.25
21	Roger Clemens	1.50
22	*Masato Yoshii*	.40
23	Travis Fryman	.30
24	Rafael Palmeiro	.75
25	Alex Rodriguez	4.00
26	Sandy Alomar	.25
27	Chipper Jones	2.50
28	Rusty Greer	.25
29	Cal Ripken Jr.	4.00
30	Tony Clark	.40
31	Derek Bell	.25
32	Fred McGriff	.40
33	Paul O'Neill	.40
34	Moises Alou	.30
35	Henry Rodriguez	.25
36	Steve Finley	.25
37	Marquis Grissom	.25
38	Jason Giambi	.25
39	Javy Lopez	.25
40	Damion Easley	.25
41	Mariano Rivera	.30
42	Mo Vaughn	.75
43	Mike Mussina	.60
44	Jason Kendall	.25
45	Pedro Martinez	1.50
46	Frank Thomas	1.50
47	Jim Edmonds	.40
48	Hideki Irabu	.30
49	Eric Karros	.25
50	Juan Gonzalez	1.25
51	Ellis Burks	.25
52	Dean Palmer	.25
53	Scott Rolen	1.00
54	Raul Mondesi	.30
55	Quinton McCraken	.25
56	John Olerud	.40
57	Ken Caminiti	.30
58	Brian Jordan	.25
59	Wade Boggs	.40
60	Mike Piazza	3.00
61	Darin Erstad	.40
62	Curt Schilling	.30
63	David Justice	.40
64	Kenny Lofton	.60
65	Barry Bonds	1.50
66	Ray Lankford	.25
67	Brian Hunter	.25
68	Chuck Knoblauch	.30
69	Vinny Castilla	.25
70	Vladimir Guerrero	2.00
71	Tim Salmon	.30
72	Larry Walker	.60
73	Paul Molitor	.50
74	Barry Larkin	.50
75	Edgar Martinez	.25
76	Bernie Williams	1.00
77	Dante Bichette	.30
78	Nomar Garciaparra	3.00
79	Ben Grieve	.40
80	Ivan Rodriguez	1.25
81	Todd Helton	1.25
82	Ryan Klesko	.25
83	Sammy Sosa	2.50
84	Travis Lee	.25
85	Jose Cruz	.25
86	Mark Kotsay	.25
87	Richard Hidalgo	.25
88	Rondell White	.25
89	Greg Vaughn	.25
90	Gary Sheffield	.40
91	Paul Konerko	.25
92	Mark Grace	.35
93	*Kevin Millwood*	3.00
94	Manny Ramirez	1.25
95	Tino Martinez	.40
96	Brad Fullmer	.25
97	Todd Walker	.35
98	Carlos Delgado	1.00
99	Kerry Wood	.40
100	Ken Griffey Jr.	5.00

1998 Topps Gold Label Class 2 (Running, Set Position)

Class 2 Gold Label and parallels feature background photos on front of position players running and pitchers in the set position. Class 2 cards have sparkling silver-foil graphic highlights on front and were inserted one per two packs. Black Label Class 2 cards were inserted one per 16 packs. Red Label Class 2 cards are a 1:198 insert and are serially numbered to 50.

	MT
Complete Set (100):	100.00
Gold Label	
Common Player:	.50
Gold Label Stars/RCs:	2.5X
Black Label	
Common Player:	2.00
Black Label Stars/RCs:	6X
Red Label	
Common Player:	10.00
Red Label Stars/RCs:	25X

(See 1998 Topps Gold Label Class 1 for checklist and base card values.)

1998 Topps Gold Label Class 3 (Hitting, Throwing)

Class 3 Gold Label and parallels feature background photos on front of position players hitting and pitchers throwing. Class 3 cards have sparkling gold-foil graphic highlights on front and were inserted one per four packs. Black Label Class 3 cards were inserted one per 32 packs. Red Label Class 2 cards are a 1:396 insert and are serially numbered to 25.

	MT
Complete Set (100):	200.00
Common Player:	1.00
Gold Label Stars/RCs:	4X
Black Label	
Common Player:	3.00
Black Label Stars/RCs	8X
Red Label	
Common Player:	10.00
Red Label Stars/RCs:	40X

(See 1998 Topps Gold Label Class 1 for checklist and base card values.)

1998 Topps Gold Label Home Run Race

Home Run Race of '98 was a four-card insert set. Each of the current players' cards features a background photo of Roger Maris, while the fourth card features two shots of Maris. Gold, Black and Red Label versions are identified by the different foil-stamp logos. Gold cards were inserted 1:12 packs, Black Label cards were inserted 1:48 packs and Red Label cards were sequentially numbered to 61 and inserted 1:4,055 packs. The Home Run Race inserts are exclusive to Topps Home Team Advantage boxes.

		MT
Complete Set (4):		40.00
Common Player:		10.00
Black Label:		2X
Red Label:		15X
HR1	Roger Maris	8.00
HR2	Mark McGwire	15.00
HR3	Ken Griffey Jr.	15.00
HR4	Sammy Sosa	8.00

1998 Topps Stars

Topps Stars adopted an all-sequential numbering format in 1998 with a 150-card set. Every card was available in a bronze (numbered to 9,799), red (9,799), silver (4,399), gold (2,299) and gold rainbow format (99) with different color foil to distinguish the groups. Players were each judged in five categories: arm strength, hit for average, power, defense and speed. Inserts in the product include: Galaxy, Luminaries, Supernovas, Rookie Reprints and Rookie Reprint Autographs. All regular-issue cards and inserts were individually numbered except the Rookie Reprints.

		MT
Complete Set, Red or Bronze (150):		75.00
Common Player, Red or Bronze:		.25
Production 9,799 sets each		
Pack (6):		3.00
Wax Box (24):		70.00
1	Greg Maddux	5.00
2	Darryl Kile	.25
3	Rod Beck	.25
4	Ellis Burks	.25
5	Gary Sheffield	.50
6	David Ortiz	.25
7	Marquis Grissom	.30
8	Tony Womack	.25
9	Mike Mussina	1.50
10	Bernie Williams	1.50
11	Andy Benes	.25
12	Rusty Greer	.30
13	Carlos Delgado	1.50
14	Jim Edmonds	.30
15	Raul Mondesi	.50
16	Andres Galarraga	1.00
17	Wade Boggs	.60
18	Paul O'Neill	.75
19	Edgar Renteria	.25
20	Tony Clark	.75
21	Vladimir Guerrero	3.00
22	Moises Alou	.50
23	Bernard Gilkey	.25
24	Lance Johnson	.25
25	Ben Grieve	.75
26	Sandy Alomar	.25
27	Ray Durham	.25
28	Shawn Estes	.25
29	David Segui	.25
30	Javy Lopez	.35
31	Steve Finley	.25
32	Rey Ordonez	.25
33	Derek Jeter	6.00
34	Henry Rodriguez	.25
35	Mo Vaughn	1.50
36	Richard Hidalgo	.25
37	Omar Vizquel	.25
38	Johnny Damon	.25
39	Brian Hunter	.25
40	Matt Williams	.60
41	Chuck Finley	.25
42	Jeromy Burnitz	.25
43	Livan Hernandez	.25
44	Delino DeShields	.25
45	Charles Nagy	.25
46	Scott Rolen	2.50
47	Neifi Perez	.25
48	John Wetteland	.25
49	Eric Milton	.25
50	Mike Piazza	6.00
51	Cal Ripken Jr.	7.50
52	Mariano Rivera	.50
53	Butch Huskey	.25
54	Quinton McCracken	.25
55	Jose Cruz Jr.	.25
56	Brian Jordan	.25
57	Hideo Nomo	.50
58	Masato Yoshii	.25
59	Cliff Floyd	.25
60	Jose Guillen	.50
61	Jeff Shaw	.25
62	Edgar Martinez	.25
63	Rondell White	.50
64	Hal Morris	.25
65	Barry Larkin	.60
66	Eric Young	.25
67	Ray Lankford	.25
68	Derek Bell	.25
69	Charles Johnson	.25
70	Robin Ventura	.50
71	Chuck Knoblauch	.60
72	Kevin Brown	.50
73	Jose Valentin	.25
74	Jay Buhner	.25
75	Tony Gwynn	5.00
76	Andy Pettitte	.30
77	Edgardo Alfonzo	.50
78	Kerry Wood	.75
79	Darin Erstad	.40
80	Paul Konerko	.50
81	Jason Kendall	.30
82	Tino Martinez	.30
83	Brad Radke	.25
84	Jeff King	.25
85	Travis Lee	.50
86	Jeff Kent	.25
87	Trevor Hoffman	.25
88	David Cone	.35
89	Jose Canseco	2.00
90	Juan Gonzalez	2.50
91	Todd Hundley	.25
92	John Valentin	.25
93	Sammy Sosa	6.00
94	Jason Giambi	.25
95	Chipper Jones	6.00
96	Jeff Blauser	.25
97	Brad Fullmer	.30
98	Derrek Lee	.25
99	Denny Neagle	.25
100	Ken Griffey Jr.	9.00
101	David Justice	.50
102	Tim Salmon	.40
103	J.T. Snow	.25
104	Fred McGriff	.50
105	Brady Anderson	.30
106	Larry Walker	1.50
107	Jeff Cirillo	.25
108	Andruw Jones	1.00
109	Manny Ramirez	2.50
110	Justin Thompson	.25
111	Vinny Castilla	.50
112	Chan Ho Park	.50
113	Mark Grudzielanek	.25
114	Mark Grace	.50
115	Ken Caminiti	.50
116	Ryan Klesko	.30
117	Rafael Palmeiro	.75
118	Pat Hentgen	.25
119	Eric Karros	.30
120	Randy Johnson	1.50
121	Roberto Alomar	1.50
122	John Olerud	.75
123	Paul Molitor	1.50
124	Dean Palmer	.25
125	Nomar Garciaparra	6.00
126	Curt Schilling	.40
127	Jay Bell	.25
128	Craig Biggio	1.50
129	Marty Cordova	.25
130	Ivan Rodriguez	2.50
131	Todd Helton	1.50
132	Jim Thome	.75
133	Albert Belle	1.50
134	Mike Lansing	.25
135	Mark McGwire	9.00
136	Roger Clemens	4.00
137	Tom Glavine	.50
138	Ron Gant	.25
139	Alex Rodriguez	8.00
140	Jeff Bagwell	2.50
141	John Smoltz	.50
142	Kenny Lofton	1.50
143	Dante Bichette	.50
144	Pedro Martinez	2.50
145	Barry Bonds	2.50
146	Travis Fryman	.35
147	Bobby Jones	.25
148	Bobby Higginson	.25
149	Reggie Sanders	.25
150	Frank Thomas	2.50

1998 Topps Stars Silver

	MT
Common Silver:	.75
Silver Stars:	1.5X
Production 4,399 sets	

1998 Topps Stars Gold

	MT
Common Gold:	1.00
Gold Stars:	2.5X
Production 2,299 sets	

1998 Topps Stars Gold Rainbow

	MT
Common Gold Rainbow:	8.00
Gold Rainbow Stars:	15X
Production 99 sets	

1998 Topps Stars Galaxy

Galaxy featured 10 players who possess all five skills featured in Topps Stars Baseball. Four versions were available and sequentially numbered, including: Bronze (numbered to 100, inserted 1:682 packs), Silver (numbered to 75, inserted 1:910), Gold (numbered to 50, inserted 1:1,364) and Gold Rainbow (numbered to 5, inserted 1:13,643).

		MT
Complete Set (10):		500.00
Common Player:		10.00
Production 100 sets		
Silvers:		1.5X
Production 75 sets		
Golds:		2X
Production 50 sets		
G1	Barry Bonds	40.00
G2	Jeff Bagwell	40.00
G3	Nomar Garciaparra	100.00
G4	Chipper Jones	100.00
G5	Ken Griffey Jr.	175.00
G6	Sammy Sosa	100.00
G7	Larry Walker	30.00
G8	Alex Rodriguez	135.00
G9	Craig Biggio	25.00
G10	Raul Mondesi	10.00

1998 Topps Stars Luminaries

Luminaries feature three top players in each "tool" group. The 15-card insert has four parallel sequentially numbered versions inserted as follows: bronze (numbered to 100, inserted 1:455), silver (numbered to 75, inserted 1:606), gold (numbered to 50, inserted 1:910) and gold rainbow (numbered to 5, inserted 1:9,095).

		MT
Complete Set (15):		750.00
Common Player:		10.00
Production 100 sets		
Silver:		1.5X
Production 75 sets		
Gold:		1.5X
Production 50 sets		
Gold Rainbow: Values undetermined		
Production 5 sets		
L1	Ken Griffey Jr.	125.00
L2	Mark McGwire	150.00
L3	Juan Gonzalez	40.00
L4	Tony Gwynn	50.00
L5	Frank Thomas	50.00
L6	Mike Piazza	100.00
L7	Chuck Knoblauch	10.00
L8	Kenny Lofton	20.00
L9	Barry Bonds	40.00
L10	Matt Williams	10.00

L11	Raul Mondesi	15.00
L12	Ivan Rodriguez	40.00
L13	Alex Rodriguez	125.00
L14	Nomar Garciaparra	90.00
L15	Ken Caminiti	10.00

1998 Topps Stars Rookie Reprints

Topps reprinted the rookie cards of five Hall of Famers in Rookie Reprints. The cards are inserted one per 24 packs and have UV coating.

	MT
Complete Set (5):	20.00
Common Player:	3.00
Johnny Bench	6.00
Whitey Ford	3.00
Joe Morgan	3.00
Mike Schmidt	8.00
Carl Yastrzemski	6.00

1998 Topps Stars Rookie Reprints Autographs

Autographed versions of all five Rookie Reprint inserts were available and seeded one per 273 packs. Each card arrive with a Topps "Certified Autograph Issue" stamp to ensure its authenticity.

	MT
Complete Set (5):	300.00
Common Player:	40.00
Johnny Bench	75.00
Whitey Ford	40.00
Joe Morgan	40.00
Mike Schmidt	100.00
Carl Yastrzemski	75.00

1998 Topps Stars Supernovas

Supernovas was a 10-card insert in Topps Stars and included rookies and prospects who either have all five tools focused on in the product, or excel dramatically in one of the five. Four sequentially numbered levels were available, with insert rates as follows: bronze (numbered to 100, inserted 1:682), silver (numbered to 75, inserted 1:910), gold (numbered to 50, inserted 1:1,364) and gold rainbow (numbered to 5, inserted 1:13,643).

		MT
Complete Set (10):		175.00
Common Player:		10.00
Production 100 sets		
Silver:		1.5X
Production 75 sets		
Gold:		2X
Production 50 sets		
S1	Ben Grieve	40.00
S2	Travis Lee	20.00
S3	Todd Helton	40.00

S4	Adrian Beltre	20.00
S5	Derrek Lee	10.00
S6	David Ortiz	10.00
S7	Brad Fullmer	15.00
S8	Mark Kotsay	15.00
S9	Paul Konerko	15.00
S10	Kerry Wood	40.00

1998 Topps Stars N' Steel

Stars 'N Steel was a 44-card set printed on four-colored textured film laminate bonded to a sheet of 25-gauge metal. Regular cards featured a silver colored border while gold versions were also available and seeded one per 12 packs. Stars 'N Steel was available only to Home Team Advantage members and was packaged in three-card packs that arrived in sturdy, tri-fold stand-up display unit. A second parallel version was also available featuring gold holographic technology and was seeded one per 40 packs.

		MT
Complete Set (44):		150.00
Common Player:		2.00
Golds:		3X
Holographics:		10X
Pack (3):		10.00
Wax Box (12):		100.00
1	Roberto Alomar	5.00
2	Jeff Bagwell	8.00
3	Albert Belle	5.00
4	Dante Bichette	2.00
5	Barry Bonds	8.00
6	Jay Buhner	2.00
7	Ken Caminiti	2.00
8	Vinny Castilla	2.00
9	Roger Clemens	10.00
10	Jose Cruz Jr.	2.00
11	Andres Galarraga	3.00
12	Nomar Garciaparra	15.00
13	Juan Gonzalez	8.00
14	Mark Grace	4.00
15	Ken Griffey Jr.	25.00
16	Tony Gwynn	12.00
17	Todd Hundley	2.00
18	Derek Jeter	15.00
19	Randy Johnson	4.00
20	Andruw Jones	4.00
21	Chipper Jones	15.00
22	David Justice	2.00
23	Ray Lankford	2.00
24	Barry Larkin	2.00
25	Kenny Lofton	4.00
26	Greg Maddux	12.00
27	Edgar Martinez	2.00
28	Tino Martinez	2.00
29	Mark McGwire	25.00
30	Paul Molitor	5.00
31	Rafael Palmeiro	4.00
32	Mike Piazza	15.00
33	Manny Ramirez	6.00
34	Cal Ripken Jr.	20.00
35	Ivan Rodriguez	5.00
36	Scott Rolen	5.00
37	Tim Salmon	2.00
38	Gary Sheffield	2.00
39	Sammy Sosa	15.00
40	Frank Thomas	7.50
41	Jim Thome	4.00
42	Mo Vaughn	4.00
43	Larry Walker	5.00
44	Bernie Williams	4.00

1998 Topps Super Chrome

This 36-card oversized set featured some of the top players from Chrome on 4-1/8" x 5-3/4" cards. The product sold in three-card packs and featured the same photography as Topps and Topps Chrome before it, but added a Super Chrome logo. Refractor versions of each card were also available, inserted one per 12 packs.

		MT
Complete Set (36):		30.00
Common Player:		.25
Refractors:		8X
Inserted 1:12		
Pack (3):		5.00
Wax Box (12):		50.00
1	Tony Gwynn	2.00
2	Larry Walker	.50
3	Vladimir Guerrero	1.50
4	Mo Vaughn	.75
5	Frank Thomas	1.50
6	Barry Larkin	.40
7	Scott Rolen	1.00
8	Juan Gonzalez	1.50
9	Jeff Bagwell	1.00
10	Ryan Klesko	.25
11	Mike Piazza	2.50
12	Randy Johnson	.50
13	Derek Jeter	2.50
14	Gary Sheffield	.40
15	Hideo Nomo	.40
16	Tino Martinez	.25
17	Ivan Rodriguez	.75
18	Bernie Williams	.50
19	Greg Maddux	2.00
20	Roger Clemens	1.50
21	Roberto Clemente	1.50
22	Chipper Jones	2.50
23	Sammy Sosa	2.50
24	Tony Clark	.50
25	Barry Bonds	1.00
26	Craig Biggio	.25
27	Cal Ripken Jr.	3.00
28	Ken Griffey Jr.	4.00
29	Todd Helton	1.00
30	Mark McGwire	4.00
31	Jose Cruz	.75
32	Albert Belle	.75
33	Andruw Jones	1.00
34	Nomar Garciaparra	2.00
35	Andy Pettitte	.50
36	Alex Rodriguez	3.00

1998 Topps TEK

A myriad of collecting methods was created with this innovative product which features 90 different players each printed on an acetate stock with 90 different background patterns. A parallel series utilizing Diffraction technology was inserted at the rate of one per six packs. Each of the 8,100 different cards was created in the same quantity, so there is no differentiation in value among patterns.

		MT
Complete Set (90):		125.00
Common Player:		.25
Pack (4):		5.00
Wax Box (20):		70.00
1	Ben Grieve	1.00
2	Kerry Wood	1.00
3	Barry Bonds	2.50
4	John Olerud	.75
5	Ivan Rodriguez	2.50
6	Frank Thomas	2.50
7	Bernie Williams	1.50
8	Dante Bichette	.75
9	Alex Rodriguez	8.00
10	Tom Glavine	.50
11	Eric Karros	.40
12	Craig Biggio	.75
13	Mark McGwire	10.00
14	Derek Jeter	6.00
15	Nomar Garciaparra	5.00
16	Brady Anderson	.25
17	Vladimir Guerrero	4.00
18	David Justice	.75
19	Chipper Jones	6.00
20	Jim Edmonds	.25
21	Roger Clemens	4.00
22	Mark Kotsay	.25
23	Tony Gwynn	5.00
24	Todd Walker	.40
25	Tino Martinez	.50
26	Andruw Jones	1.50
27	Sandy Alomar	.25
28	Sammy Sosa	6.00
29	Gary Sheffield	.50
30	Ken Griffey Jr.	10.00
31	Aramis Ramirez	.35
32	Curt Schilling	.50
33	Robin Ventura	.50
34	Larry Walker	1.50
35	Darin Erstad	.75
36	Todd Dunwoody	.25
37	Paul O'Neill	.60
38	Vinny Castilla	.50
39	Randy Johnson	2.00
40	Rafael Palmeiro	1.00
41	Pedro Martinez	3.00
42	Derek Bell	.25
43	Carlos Delgado	.75
44	Matt Williams	.60
45	Kenny Lofton	1.50
46	Edgar Renteria	.25
47	Albert Belle	2.00
48	Jeromy Burnitz	.25
49	Adrian Beltre	.75
50	Greg Maddux	5.00
51	Cal Ripken Jr.	7.50
52	Jason Kendall	.40
53	Ellis Burks	.25
54	Paul Molitor	1.50
55	Moises Alou	.50
56	Raul Mondesi	.50
57	Barry Larkin	.50
58	Tony Clark	.75
59	Travis Lee	.75
60	Juan Gonzalez	2.50
61	*Troy Glaus*	4.00
62	Jose Cruz Jr.	.35
63	Paul Konerko	.50
64	Edgar Martinez	.25
65	Javy Lopez	.50
66	Manny Ramirez	2.50
67	Roberto Alomar	1.50
68	Ken Caminiti	.50
69	Todd Helton	2.00
70	Chuck Knoblauch	.50
71	Kevin Brown	.50

72 Tim Salmon .50
73 *Orlando Hernandez* 4.00
74 Jeff Bagwell 2.50
75 Brian Jordan .25
76 Derrek Lee .25
77 Brad Fullmer .35
78 Mark Grace .75
79 Jeff King .25
80 Mike Mussina 1.50
81 Jay Buhner .25
82 Quinton McCracken .25
83 A.J. Hinch .25
84 Richard Hidalgo .25
85 Andres Galarraga .75
86 Mike Piazza 6.00
87 Mo Vaughn 1.50
88 Scott Rolen 2.50
89 Jim Thome .75
90 Ray Lankford .25

1998 Topps TEK Diffraction

Not only can each of the 90 cards in Topps TEK be found in 90 different background patterns, but each can be found in a parallel edition printed with diffraction foil. The parallels are inserted on an average of one per six packs. Like the regular issue TEKs, all patterns were produced equally and there is no value differentiation among them.

	MT
Complete Set (90):	600.00
Common Player:	3.00
Stars/RCs:	4X

(See 1998 Topps TEK for checklist and base card values.)

1999 Topps

Released in two series, the 462-card set includes two home run record subsets, featuring McGwire and Sosa. McGwire's subset card #220 has 70 different versions, commemorating each of his home runs, including where it was hit, the pitcher, date and estimated distance. Sosa's subset card #461 has 66 different versions. Other subsets include World Series Highlights, Prospects, Draft Picks and Season Highlights. Each pack contains 11 cards with an SRP of $1.29. MVPs are the only parallel. They feature a special Topps MVP logo; 100 cards of each player exist. If the player on the card was named a weekly Topps MVP, collectors won a special set of redemption cards.

	MT
Complete Set (462):	55.00
Complete Series 1 (241):	30.00
Complete Series 2 (221):	25.00
Common Player:	.10
Complete Hobby Set (462):	60.00
Complete X-Mas Set (463):	60.00
MVP Stars:	60X
Young Stars/RCs:	40X
Series 1 Hobby Pack (11):	2.25
Series 2 Hobby Pack (11):	1.50
Series 1 Hobby Wax Box (36):	70.00
Series 2 Hobby Wax Box (36):	35.00
Retail Wax Box (22):	60.00
Wax Box (24):	30.00

1 Roger Clemens 1.00
2 Andres Galarraga .30
3 Scott Brosius .10
4 John Flaherty .10
5 Jim Leyritz .10
6 Ray Durham .10
7 not issued
8 Joe Vizcaino .10
9 Will Clark .25
10 David Wells .10
11 Jose Guillen .15
12 Scott Hatteberg .10
13 Edgardo Alfonzo .25
14 Mike Bordick .10
15 Manny Ramirez .75
16 Greg Maddux 1.25
17 David Segui .10
18 Darryl Strawberry .20
19 Brad Radke .10
20 Kerry Wood .40
21 Matt Anderson .10
22 Derrek Lee .10
23 Mickey Morandini .10
24 Paul Konerko .20
25 Travis Lee .25
26 Ken Hill .10
27 Kenny Rogers .10
28 Paul Sorrento .10
29 Quilvio Veras .10
30 Todd Walker .15
31 Ryan Jackson .10
32 John Olerud .25
33 Doug Glanville .10
34 Nolan Ryan 2.50
35 Ray Lankford .10
36 Mark Loretta .10
37 Jason Dickson .10
38 Sean Bergman .10
39 Quinton McCracken .10
40 Bartolo Colon .15
41 Brady Anderson .15
42 Chris Stynes .10
43 Jorge Posada .10
44 Justin Thompson .10
45 Johnny Damon .10
46 Armando Benitez .10
47 Brant Brown .10
48 Charlie Hayes .10
49 Darren Dreifort .10
50 Juan Gonzalez .75
51 Chuck Knoblauch .25
52 Todd Helton (Rookie All-Star) .60
53 Rick Reed .10
54 Chris Gomez .10
55 Gary Sheffield .25
56 Rod Beck .10
57 Rey Sanchez .10
58 Garret Anderson .10
59 Jimmy Haynes .10
60 Steve Woodard .10
61 Rondell White .20
62 Vladimir Guerrero 1.00
63 Eric Karros .20
64 Russ Davis .10
65 Mo Vaughn .50
66 Sammy Sosa 1.50
67 Troy Percival .10
68 Kenny Lofton .40
69 Bill Taylor .10
70 Mark McGwire 3.00
71 Roger Cedeno .10
72 Javy Lopez .20
73 Damion Easley .10
74 Andy Pettitte .25
75 Tony Gwynn 1.25
76 Ricardo Rincon .10
77 F.P. Santangelo .10
78 Jay Bell .10
79 Scott Servais .10
80 Jose Canseco .40
81 Roberto Hernandez .10
82 Todd Dunwoody .10
83 John Wetteland .10
84 Mike Caruso (Rookie All-Star) .10
85 Derek Jeter 1.50
86 Aaron Sele .10
87 Jose Lima .10
88 Ryan Christenson .10
89 Jeff Cirillo .10
90 Jose Hernandez .10
91 Mark Kotsay (Rookie All-Star) .20
92 Darren Bragg .10
93 Albert Belle .50
94 Matt Lawton .10
95 Pedro Martinez .50
96 Greg Vaughn .20
97 Neifi Perez .10
98 Gerald Williams .10
99 Derek Bell .10
100 Ken Griffey Jr. 3.00
101 David Cone .20
102 Brian Johnson .10
103 Dean Palmer .10
104 Javier Valentin .10
105 Trevor Hoffman .10
106 Butch Huskey .10
107 Dave Martinez .10
108 Billy Wagner .10
109 Shawn Green .40
110 Ben Grieve (Rookie All-Star) .25
111 Tom Goodwin .10
112 Jaret Wright .20
113 Aramis Ramirez .15
114 Dmitri Young .10
115 Hideki Irabu .20
116 Roberto Kelly .10
117 Jeff Fassero .10
118 Mark Clark .10
119 Jason McDonald .10
120 Matt Williams .25
121 Dave Burba .10
122 Bret Saberhagen .10
123 Deivi Cruz .10
124 Chad Curtis .10
125 Scott Rolen .50
126 Lee Stevens .10
127 J.T. Snow Jr. .10
128 Rusty Greer .10
129 Brian Meadows .10
130 Jim Edmonds .20
131 Ron Gant .20
132 A.J. Hinch (Rookie All-Star) .10
133 Shannon Stewart .10
134 Brad Fullmer .15
135 Cal Eldred .10
136 Matt Walbeck .10
137 Carl Everett .15
138 Walt Weiss .10
139 Fred McGriff .20
140 Darin Erstad .25
141 Dave Nilsson .10
142 Eric Young .10
143 Dan Wilson .10
144 Jeff Reed .10
145 Brett Tomko .10
146 Terry Steinbach .10
147 Seth Greisinger .10
148 Pat Meares .10
149 Livan Hernandez .10
150 Jeff Bagwell .75
151 Bob Wickman .10
152 Omar Vizquel .10
153 Eric Davis .15
154 Larry Sutton .10
155 Magglio Ordonez (Rookie All-Star) .15
156 Eric Milton .10
157 Darren Lewis .10
158 Rick Aguilera .10
159 Mike Lieberthal .10
160 Robb Nen .10
161 Brian Giles .20
162 Jeff Brantley .10
163 Gary DiSarcina .10
164 John Valentin .10
165 David Dellucci .10
166 Chan Ho Park .15
167 Masato Yoshii .10
168 Jason Schmidt .10
169 LaTroy Hawkins .10
170 Bret Boone .10
171 Jerry DiPoto .10
172 Mariano Rivera .20
173 Mike Cameron .10
174 Scott Erickson .10
175 Charles Johnson .10
176 Bobby Jones .10
177 Francisco Cordova .10
178 Todd Jones .10
179 Jeff Montgomery .10
180 Mike Mussina .50
181 Bob Abreu .20
182 Ismael Valdes .10
183 Andy Fox .10
184 Woody Williams .10
185 Denny Neagle .10
186 Jose Valentin .10
187 Darrin Fletcher .10
188 Gabe Alvarez .10
189 Eddie Taubensee .10
190 Edgar Martinez .10
191 Jason Kendall .20
192 Darryl Kile .10
193 Jeff King .10
194 Rey Ordonez .10
195 Andruw Jones .25
196 Tony Fernandez .10
197 Jamey Wright .10
198 B.J. Surhoff .10
199 Vinny Castilla .20
200 David Wells (Season Highlight) .10
201 Mark McGwire (Season Highlight) 1.00
202 Sammy Sosa (Season Highlight) .75
203 Roger Clemens (Season Highlight) .50
204 Kerry Wood (Season Highlight) .25
205 Lance Berkman, Mike Frank, Gabe Kapler (Prospects) .25
206 *Alex Escobar*, Ricky Ledee, Mike Stoner (Prospects) .75
207 *Peter Bergeron*, Jeremy Giambi, George Lombard (Prospects) .40
208 Michael Barrett, Ben Davis, Robert Fick (Prospects) .15
209 Pat Cline, Ramon Hernandez, Jayson Werth (Prospects) .25
210 Bruce Chen, Chris Enochs, Ryan Anderson (Prospects) .25
211 Mike Lincoln, Octavio Dotel, Brad Penny (Prospects) .20
212 Chuck Abbott, Brent Butler, Danny Klassen (Prospects) .25
213 Chris Jones, *Jeff Urban* (Draft Pick) .25
214 *Arturo McDowell*, *Tony Torcato* (Draft Pick) .25

215 *Josh McKinley ,Jason Tyner* (Draft Pick) .40
216 *Matt Burch, Seth Etherton* (Draft Pick) .40
217 *Mamon Tucker, Rick Elder* (Draft Pick) .50
218 *J.M. Gold, Ryan Mills* (Draft Pick) .50
219 *Adam Brown ,Choo Freeman* (Draft Pick) .40
220 Home Run Record #1 (M. McGwire) 25.00
220 HR Record #2-60 (M. McGwire) 15.00
220 HR Record #61-62 (M. McGwire) 40.00
220 HR Record #63-69 (M. McGwire) 15.00
220 HR Record #70 (Mark McGwire) 90.00
221 Larry Walker (League Leader) .25
222 Bernie Williams (League Leader) .30
223 Mark McGwire (League Leader) 1.00
224 Ken Griffey Jr. (League Leader) 1.00
225 Sammy Sosa (League Leader) .75
226 Juan Gonzalez (League Leader) .40
227 Dante Bichette (League Leader) .25
228 Alex Rodriguez (League Leader) 1.00
229 Sammy Sosa (League Leader) 1.00
230 Derek Jeter (League Leader) .75
231 Greg Maddux (League Leader) .50
232 Roger Clemens (League Leader) .50
233 Ricky Ledee (World Series) .10
234 Chuck Knoblauch (World Series) .20
235 Bernie Williams (World Series) .25
236 Tino Martinez (World Series) .20
237 Orlando Hernandez (World Series) .25
238 Scott Brosius (World Series) .10
239 Andy Pettitte (World Series) .25
240 Mariano Rivera (World Series) .20
241 Checklist .10
242 Checklist .10
243 Tom Glavine .25
244 Andy Benes .10
245 Sandy Alomar .20
246 Wilton Guerrero .10
247 Alex Gonzalez .10
248 Roberto Alomar .40
249 Ruben Rivera .10
250 Eric Chavez .20
251 Ellis Burks .10
252 Richie Sexson .15
253 Steve Finley .10
254 Dwight Gooden .10
255 Dustin Hermanson .10
256 Kirk Rueter .10
257 Steve Trachsel .10
258 Gregg Jefferies .10
259 Matt Stairs .10
260 Shane Reynolds .15
261 Gregg Olson .10
262 Kevin Tapani .10
263 Matt Morris .10
264 Carl Pavano .10
265 Nomar Garciaparra 1.50
266 Kevin Young .10
267 Rick Helling .10
268 Mark Leiter .10
269 Brian McRae .10
270 Cal Ripken Jr. 2.00
271 Jeff Abbott .10
272 Tony Batista .10
273 Bill Simas .10
274 Brian Hunter .10
275 John Franco .10
276 Devon White .10
277 Rickey Henderson .25
278 Chuck Finley .10
279 Mike Blowers .10
280 Mark Grace .25
281 Randy Winn .10
282 Bobby Bonilla .20
283 David Justice .25
284 Shane Monahan .10
285 Kevin Brown .25
286 Todd Zeile .10
287 Al Martin .10
288 Troy O'Leary .10
289 Darryl Hamilton .10
290 Tino Martinez .25
291 David Ortiz .10
292 Tony Clark .25
293 Ryan Minor .25
294 Reggie Sanders .10
295 Wally Joyner .10
296 Cliff Floyd .10
297 Shawn Estes .10
298 Pat Hentgen .10
299 Scott Elarton .10
300 Alex Rodriguez 2.00
301 Ozzie Guillen .10
302 Manny Martinez .10
303 Ryan McGuire .10
304 Brad Ausmus .10
305 Alex Gonzalez .10
306 Brian Jordan .10
307 John Jaha .10
308 Mark Grudzielanek .10
309 Juan Guzman .10
310 Tony Womack .10
311 Dennis Reyes .10
312 Marty Cordova .10
313 Ramiro Mendoza .10
314 Robin Ventura .20
315 Rafael Palmeiro .30
316 Ramon Martinez .10
317 John Mabry .10
318 Dave Hollins .10
319 Tom Candiotti .10
320 Al Leiter .20
321 Rico Brogna .10
322 Jimmy Key .10
323 Bernard Gilkey .10
324 Jason Giambi .10
325 Craig Biggio .30
326 Troy Glaus .50
327 Delino DeShields .10
328 Fernando Vina .10
329 John Smoltz .20
330 Jeff Kent .10
331 Roy Halladay .15
332 Andy Ashby .10
333 Tim Wakefield .10
334 Tim Belcher .10
335 Bernie Williams .40
336 Desi Relaford .10
337 John Burkett .10
338 Mike Hampton .10
339 Royce Clayton .10
340 Mike Piazza 1.50
341 Jeremi Gonzalez .10
342 Mike Lansing .10
343 Jamie Moyer .10
344 Ron Coomer .10
345 Barry Larkin .30
346 Fernando Tatis .20
347 Chili Davis .10
348 Bobby Higginson .10
349 Hal Morris .10
350 Larry Walker .40
351 Carlos Guillen .10
352 Miguel Tejada .10
353 Travis Fryman .20
354 Jarrod Washburn .10
355 Chipper Jones 1.25
356 Todd Stottlemyre .15
357 Henry Rodriguez .10
358 Eli Marrero .10
359 Alan Benes .10
360 Tim Salmon .25
361 Luis Gonzalez .10
362 Scott Spiezio .10
363 Chris Carpenter .10
364 Bobby Howry .10
365 Raul Mondesi .20
366 Ugueth Urbina .10
367 Tom Evans .10
368 *Kerry Ligtenberg* .25
369 Adrian Beltre .25
370 Ryan Klesko .25
371 Wilson Alvarez .10
372 John Thomson .10
373 Tony Saunders .10
374 Mike Stanley .10
375 Ken Caminiti .20
376 Jay Buhner .20
377 Bill Mueller .10
378 Jeff Blauser .10
379 Edgar Renteria .10
380 Jim Thome .25
381 Joey Hamilton .10
382 Calvin Pickering .15
383 Marquis Grissom .10
384 Omar Daal .10
385 Curt Schilling .20
386 Jose Cruz Jr. .15
387 Chris Widger .10
388 Pete Harnisch .10
389 Charles Nagy .10
390 Tom Gordon .10
391 Bobby Smith .10
392 Derrick Gibson .10
393 Jeff Conine .10
394 Carlos Perez .10
395 Barry Bonds .50
396 Mark McLemore .10
397 Juan Encarnacion .20
398 Wade Boggs .25
399 Ivan Rodriguez .50
400 Moises Alou .25
401 Jeromy Burnitz .10
402 Sean Casey .25
403 Jose Offerman .10
404 Joe Fontenot .10
405 Kevin Millwood .20
406 Lance Johnson .10
407 Richard Hidalgo .10
408 Mike Jackson .10
409 Brian Anderson .10
410 Jeff Shaw .10
411 Preston Wilson .10
412 Todd Hundley .10
413 Jim Parque .10
414 Justin Baughman .10
415 Dante Bichette .20
416 Paul O'Neill .30
417 Miguel Cairo .10
418 Randy Johnson .40
419 Jesus Sanchez .10
420 Carlos Delgado .40
421 Ricky Ledee .25
422 Orlando Hernandez .15
423 Frank Thomas .75
424 Pokey Reese .10
425 Carlos Lee, Mike Lowell, *Kit Pellow* (Prospect) .25
426 Michael Cuddyer, Mark DeRosa, Jerry Hairston (Prospect) .10
427 Marlon Anderson, Ron Belliard, Orlando Cabrera (Prospect) .10
428 *Micah Bowie, Phil Norton,* Randy Wolf (Prospect) .25
429 Jack Cressend, Jason Rakers, John Rocker (Prospect) .20
430 Ruben Mateo, Scott Morgan, *Mike Zywica* (Prospect) .40
431 Jason LaRue, *Matt LeCroy,* Mitch Meluskey (Prospect) .15
432 Gabe Kapler, Armando Rios, Fernando Seguignol (Prospect) .20
433 Adam Kennedy *Mickey Lopez,* Jackie Rexrode (Prospect) .25
434 *Jose Fernandez,* Jeff Liefer, Chris Truby (Prospect) .25
435 Corey Koskie, Doug Mientkiewicz, Damon Minor (Prospect) .25
436 *Roosevelt Brown,* Dernell Stenson, Vernon Wells (Prospect) .25
437 *A.J. Burnett,* John Nicholson, Billy Koch (Prospect) .50
438 *Matt Belisle, Matt Roney* (Draft Pick) .50
439 *Austin Kearns, Chris George* (Draft Pick) .50
440 *Nate Bump, Nate Cornejo* (Draft Pick) .40
441 *Brad Lidge, Mike Nannini* (Draft Pick) .50
442 *Matt Holiday Jeff Winchester* (Draft Pick) .50
443 *Adam Everett, Chip Ambres* (Draft Pick) .50
444 *Pat Burrell, Eric Valent* (Draft Pick) 2.00
445 Roger Clemens (Strikeout Kings) .50
446 Kerry Wood (Strikeout Kings) .20
447 Curt Schilling (Strikeout Kings) .10
448 Randy Johnson (Strikeout Kings) .20
449 Pedro Martinez (Strikeout Kings) .25
450 Jeff Bagwell, Andres Galarraga, Mark McGwire (All-Topps) 1.00
451 John Olerud, Jim Thome, Tino Martinez (All-Topps) .20
452 Alex Rodriguez, Nomar Garciaparra, Derek Jeter (All-Topps) .50
453 Vinny Castilla, Chipper Jones, Scott Rolen (All-Topps) .25
454 Sammy Sosa, Ken Griffey Jr., Juan Gonzalez (All-Topps) .75
455 Barry Bonds, Manny Ramirez, Larry Walker (All-Topps) .40
456 Frank Thomas, Tim Salmon, David Justice (All-Topps) .40
457 Travis Lee, Todd Helton, Ben Grieve (All-Topps) .30
458 Vladimir Guerrero, Greg Vaughn, Bernie Williams (All-Topps) .50
459 Mike Piazza, Ivan Rodriguez, Jason Kendall (All-Topps) .40
460 Roger Clemens, Kerry Wood, Greg Maddux (All-Topps) .25
461 Home Run Parade #1 (Sammy Sosa) 8.00
461 HR Parade #2-60 (Sammy Sosa) 4.00
461 HR Parade #61-62 (Sammy Sosa) 15.00
461 HR Parade #63-65 (Sammy Sosa) 8.00
461 HR Parade #66 (Sammy Sosa) 20.00
462 Checklist .10
463 Checklist .10

1999 Topps MVP Promotion

Each of the 198 players cards in Series 1 and Series 2 was issued in a parallel version of 100 each for use in an MVP of the Week sweepstakes. Overprinted with a large gold-foil seal on front, the MVP cards have contest rules on back. The MVP cards were inserted at ratios of between 1:142 (HTA) and 1:515 (Hobby) packs. Cards of players who won MVP of the Week during the 1999 season could be redeemed for a special set of MVP cards prior to the Dec. 31, 1999 deadline.

	MT
Common Player:	4.00
Stars:	60X
Rookies:	40X

(See 1999 Topps for checklist and base card values.)

1999 Topps Autographs

Autographs were inserted exclusively in hobby packs in both Topps series I and II. Each series had eight cards with each one carrying the Topps Certified Autograph Issue stamp. Series I Autographs were seeded 1:532 packs while Series II were found 1:501 packs.

		MT
Complete Set (16):		700.00
Complete Series 1 (8):		450.00
Complete Series 2 (8):		250.00
Common Player:		25.00
Series 1 Inserted 1:532 H		
Series 2 Inserted 1:501 H		
A1	Roger Clemens	75.00
A2	Chipper Jones	80.00
A3	Scott Rolen	50.00
A4	Alex Rodriguez	120.00
A5	Andres Galarraga	30.00
A6	Rondell White	20.00
A7	Ben Grieve	30.00
A8	Troy Glaus	35.00
A9	Moises Alou	20.00
A10	Barry Bonds	75.00
A11	Vladimir Guerrero	60.00
A12	Andruw Jones	40.00
A13	Darin Erstad	25.00
A14	Shawn Green	35.00
A15	Eric Chavez	20.00
A16	Pat Burrell	50.00

1999 Topps All-Matrix

This 30-card set features holo-foil card fronts and features the top stars in the game. Each card is numbered with a "AM" prefix on card backs and are seeded 1:18 packs.

		MT
Complete Set (30):		90.00
Common Player:		1.50
Inserted 1:18		
AM1	Mark McGwire	15.00
AM2	Sammy Sosa	10.00
AM3	Ken Griffey Jr.	15.00
AM4	Greg Vaughn	1.50
AM5	Albert Belle	3.50
AM6	Vinny Castilla	1.50
AM7	Jose Canseco	4.00
AM8	Juan Gonzalez	4.00
AM9	Manny Ramirez	4.00
AM10	Andres Galarraga	3.00
AM11	Rafael Palmeiro	3.00
AM12	Alex Rodriguez	12.00
AM13	Mo Vaughn	2.00
AM14	Eric Chavez	2.00
AM15	Gabe Kapler	3.00
AM16	Calvin Pickering	1.50
AM17	Ruben Mateo	3.00
AM18	Roy Halladay	1.50
AM19	Jeremy Giambi	1.50
AM20	Alex Gonzalez	1.50
AM21	Ron Belliard	1.50
AM22	Marlon Anderson	1.50
AM23	Carlos Lee	1.50
AM24	Kerry Wood	2.50
AM25	Roger Clemens	6.00
AM26	Curt Schilling	1.50
AM27	Kevin Brown	2.00
AM28	Randy Johnson	2.00
AM29	Pedro Martinez	5.00
AM30	Orlando Hernandez	2.50

1999 Topps All-Topps Mystery Finest

This 33-card set features a black opaque covering that collectors peel off to reveal the player. Each card is numbered with a "M" prefix and inserted 1:36 packs. A parallel Refractor version is also randomly seeded and inserted 1:144 packs.

		MT
Complete Set (33):		250.00
Common Player:		3.00
Inserted 1:36		
Refractors:		2X
Inserted 1:144		
M1	Jeff Bagwell	8.00
M2	Andres Galarraga	5.00
M3	Mark McGwire	30.00
M4	John Olerud	4.00
M5	Jim Thome	5.00
M6	Tino Martinez	5.00
M7	Alex Rodriguez	25.00
M8	Nomar Garciaparra	15.00
M9	Derek Jeter	15.00
M10	Vinny Castilla	3.00
M11	Chipper Jones	15.00
M12	Scott Rolen	8.00
M13	Sammy Sosa	15.00
M14	Ken Griffey Jr.	30.00
M15	Juan Gonzalez	8.00
M16	Barry Bonds	8.00
M17	Manny Ramirez	8.00
M18	Larry Walker	6.00
M19	Frank Thomas	8.00
M20	Tim Salmon	4.00
M21	David Justice	4.00
M22	Travis Lee	4.00
M23	Todd Helton	6.00
M24	Ben Grieve	5.00
M25	Bernie Williams	5.00
M26	Greg Vaughn	3.00
M27	Vladimir Guerrero	12.00
M28	Mike Piazza	15.00
M29	Ivan Rodriguez	8.00
M30	Jason Kendall	3.00
M31	Roger Clemens	12.00
M32	Kerry Wood	6.00
M33	Greg Maddux	12.00

1999 Topps Lords of the Diamond

Inserted in every 18 packs this 15-card set features the top players in the game including Barry Bonds and Ken Griffey Jr. Card fronts include a holographic look with die-cutting across the top of the card on a silver background.

		MT
Complete Set (15):		50.00
Common Player:		1.00
Inserted 1:18		
LD1	Ken Griffey Jr.	10.00
LD2	Chipper Jones	6.00
LD3	Sammy Sosa	6.00
LD4	Frank Thomas	3.50
LD5	Mark McGwire	10.00
LD6	Jeff Bagwell	2.50
LD7	Alex Rodriguez	8.00
LD8	Juan Gonzalez	2.50
LD9	Barry Bonds	2.50
LD10	Nomar Garciaparra	6.00
LD11	Darin Erstad	1.50
LD12	Tony Gwynn	5.00
LD13	Andres Galarraga	1.00
LD14	Mike Piazza	6.00
LD15	Greg Maddux	5.00

1999 Topps Hall of Fame

Found exclusively in hobby packs, Hall of Fame Collection is a ten-card set featured on cards that silhouette their images against their respective Hall of Fame plaques. Featured players include Yogi Berra, Reggie Jackson and Ernie Banks among others. These were seeded 1:12 packs.

		MT
Complete Set (10):		20.00
Common Player:		1.00
Inserted 1:12 H		
HOF1	Mike Schmidt	4.00
HOF2	Brooks Robinson	2.00
HOF3	Stan Musial	3.00
HOF4	Willie McCovey	1.00
HOF5	Eddie Mathews	1.50
HOF6	Reggie Jackson	4.00
HOF7	Ernie Banks	2.50
HOF8	Whitey Ford	1.50
HOF9	Bob Feller	1.00
HOF10	Yogi Berra	2.50

1999 Topps New Breed

The next generation of stars are featured in this 15-card set that showcases the young talent on a silver foil card. These are seeded 1:18 packs.

		MT
Complete Set (15):		20.00
Common Player:		.50
Inserted 1:18		
NB1	Darin Erstad	1.00
NB2	Brad Fullmer	.75
NB3	Kerry Wood	1.50
NB4	Nomar Garciaparra	5.00
NB5	Travis Lee	1.00
NB6	Scott Rolen	2.00
NB7	Todd Helton	1.50
NB8	Vladimir Guerrero	3.00
NB9	Derek Jeter	5.00
NB10	Alex Rodriguez	7.50
NB11	Ben Grieve	1.50
NB12	Andruw Jones	1.50
NB13	Paul Konerko	.50
NB14	Aramis Ramirez	.50
NB15	Adrian Beltre	.75

1999 Topps Nolan Ryan Reprints

Topps reprinted all 27 of Nolan Ryan's basic Topps cards, with 14 odd numbers appearing in Series I and the remaining 13 even cards inserted into Series II packs. Each card is stamped with a gold Topps commemorative stamp on the front for identification. Reprints were seeded in every 18 packs. Nolan Ryan also autographed a number of the reprints for both series. Series I Ryan autographs are seeded 1:4,260 with Series II autographs found 1:5,007 packs. Ryan autographs were inserted exclusively in hobby packs.

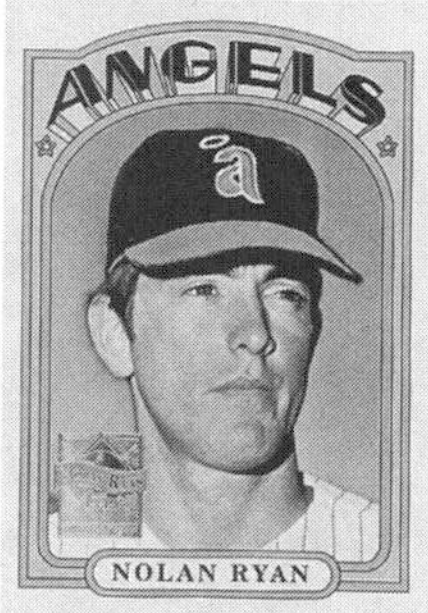

		MT
Complete Set (27):		100.00
Common Ryan:		5.00
Inserted 1:18		
Nolan Ryan Autograph:		200.00
1	Nolan Ryan (1968)	15.00
2	Nolan Ryan (1969)	10.00
3	Nolan Ryan (1970)	5.00
4	Nolan Ryan (1971)	5.00
5	Nolan Ryan (1972)	5.00
6	Nolan Ryan (1973)	5.00
7	Nolan Ryan (1974)	5.00
8	Nolan Ryan (1975)	5.00
9	Nolan Ryan (1976)	5.00
10	Nolan Ryan (1977)	5.00
11	Nolan Ryan (1978)	5.00
12	Nolan Ryan (1979)	5.00
13	Nolan Ryan (1980)	5.00
14	Nolan Ryan (1981)	5.00
15	Nolan Ryan (1982)	5.00
16	Nolan Ryan (1983)	5.00
17	Nolan Ryan (1984)	5.00
18	Nolan Ryan (1985)	5.00
19	Nolan Ryan (1986)	5.00
20	Nolan Ryan (1987)	5.00
21	Nolan Ryan (1988)	5.00
22	Nolan Ryan (1989)	5.00
23	Nolan Ryan (1990)	5.00
24	Nolan Ryan (1991)	5.00
25	Nolan Ryan (1992)	5.00
26	Nolan Ryan (1993)	5.00
27	Nolan Ryan (1994)	5.00

1999 Topps Nolan Ryan Finest Reprints

This 27-card set reprinted all 27 of Ryan's basic Topps cards. Odd numbers were distributed in Series I packs, with even numbers distributed in Series II packs. These are seeded 1:72 packs in both series I and II packs. A Refractor parallel version is inserted 1:288 packs.

		MT
Complete Set (27):		250.00
Common Card:		12.00
Inserted 1:72		
Refractors:		2X
Inserted 1:288		
1	1968	20.00
2	1969	12.00
3	1970	12.00
4	1971	12.00
5	1972	12.00
6	1973	12.00
7	1974	12.00
8	1975	12.00
9	1976	12.00
10	1977	12.00
11	1978	12.00
12	1979	12.00
13	1980	12.00
14	1981	12.00
15	1982	12.00
16	1983	12.00
17	1984	12.00
18	1985	12.00
19	1986	12.00
20	1987	12.00
21	1988	12.00
22	1989	12.00
23	1990	12.00
24	1991	12.00
25	1992	12.00
26	1992	12.00
27	1992	12.00

1999 Topps Picture Perfect

This 10-card set features a full bleed photo of baseball's biggest stars, including Derek Jeter and Ken Griffey Jr. These are found one per eight packs.

		MT
Complete Set (10):		12.00
Common Player:		.50
Inserted 1:8		
P1	Ken Griffey Jr.	5.00
P2	Kerry Wood	.75
P3	Pedro Martinez	1.00
P4	Mark McGwire	5.00
P5	Greg Maddux	2.00
P6	Sammy Sosa	2.50
P7	Greg Vaughn	.50
P8	Juan Gonzalez	1.00
P9	Jeff Bagwell	1.00
P10	Derek Jeter	2.50

1999 Topps Power Brokers

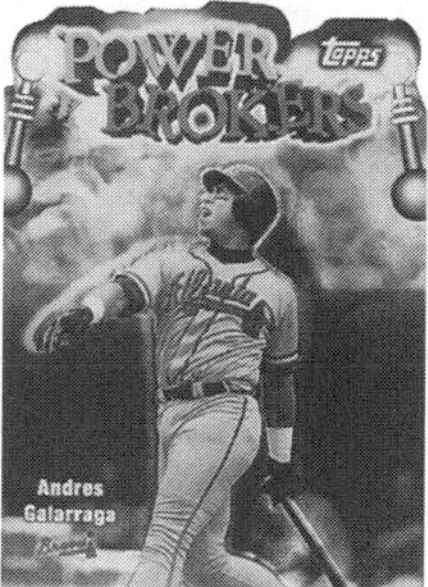

This 20-card set features baseball's biggest superstars including McGwire, Sosa and Chipper Jones. The cards are die-cut at the top and printed on Finest technology. Power Brokers are inserted in every 36 packs. A Refractor parallel version also exists, which are seeded 1:144 packs.

		MT
Complete Set (20):		100.00
Common Player:		1.25
Inserted 1:36		
Refractors:		2X
Inserted 1:144		
PB1	Mark McGwire	15.00
PB2	Andres Galarraga	2.00
PB3	Ken Griffey Jr.	15.00
PB4	Sammy Sosa	10.00
PB5	Juan Gonzalez	4.00
PB6	Alex Rodriguez	15.00
PB7	Frank Thomas	4.00
PB8	Jeff Bagwell	4.00
PB9	Vinny Castilla	1.25
PB10	Mike Piazza	10.00
PB11	Greg Vaughn	1.25
PB12	Barry Bonds	4.00
PB13	Mo Vaughn	2.50
PB14	Jim Thome	2.00
PB15	Larry Walker	2.00
PB16	Chipper Jones	10.00
PB17	Nomar Garciaparra	10.00
PB18	Manny Ramirez	4.00
PB19	Roger Clemens	6.00
PB20	Kerry Wood	3.00

1999 Topps Record Numbers

This 10-card set highlights achievements from the game's current stars, including Nomar Garciaparra's 30 game hitting streak, the longest by a rookie in major league history. These inserts are randomly seeded 1:8 packs, each card is numbered on the back with a "RN" prefix.

		MT
Complete Set (10):		20.00
Common Player:		.75
Inserted 1:8		
RN1	Mark McGwire	5.00
RN2	Mike Piazza	3.00
RN3	Curt Schilling	.50
RN4	Ken Griffey Jr.	5.00
RN5	Sammy Sosa	3.00
RN6	Nomar Garciaparra	4.00
RN7	Kerry Wood	1.00
RN8	Roger Clemens	1.50
RN9	Cal Ripken Jr.	4.00
RN10	Mark McGwire	5.00

1999 Topps Record Numbers Gold

This is a parallel of the Record Numbers insert set, each card features the appropriate sequential numbering based on the featured players' highlighted record. Each card is numbered with a "RN" prefix on the back.

		MT
Complete Set (10):		1200.
Common Player:		8.00
RN1	Mark McGwire (70)	250.00
RN2	Mike Piazza (362)	40.00
RN3	Curt Schilling (319)	8.00
RN4	Ken Griffey Jr. (350)	60.00
RN5	Sammy Sosa (20)	350.00
RN6	Nomar Garciaparra (30)	300.00
RN7	Kerry Wood (20)	100.00
RN8	Roger Clemens (20)	250.00
RN9	Cal Ripken Jr. (2,632)	25.00
RN10	Mark McGwire (162)	125.00

1999 Topps Traded and Rookies

Identical in design to the base 1999 Topps cards the 121- card set includes players involved in pre and mid-season transactions as well as top prospects and 1999 Draft Picks. Released in a boxed set, each set also includes one autographed card from the 75 rookie/draft pick cards in the set.

		MT
Complete Set (121):		30.00
Common Player:		.15
1	*Seth Etherton*	.20
2	*Mark Harriger*	.25
3	*Matt Wise*	.20
4	*Carlos Hernandez*	.20
5	*Julio Lugo*	.25
6	*Mike Nannini*	.20
7	*Justin Bowles*	.20
8	*Mark Mulder*	.50
9	*Roberto Vaz*	.20
10	*Felipe Lopez*	.75
11	*Matt Belisle*	.40
12	Micah Bowie	.15
13	*Ruben Quevedo*	.30
14	*Jose Garcia*	.20
15	*David Kelton*	.50
16	*Phillip Norton*	.25
17	*Corey Patterson*	3.00
18	*Ron Walker*	.20
19	*Paul Hoover*	.20
20	*Ryan Rupe*	.30
21	*J.D. Closser*	.25
22	*Rob Ryan*	.20
23	*Steve Colyer*	.20
24	*Bubba Crosby*	.20
25	*Luke Prokopec*	.40
26	*Matt Blank*	.25
27	*Josh McKinley*	.20
28	*Nate Bump*	.15
29	*Giuseppe Chiaramonte*	.25
30	*Arturo McDowell*	.30
31	*Tony Torcato*	.50
32	Dave Roberts	.15
33	*C.C. Sabathia*	1.00
34	*Sean Spencer*	.30
35	*Chip Ambres*	.25
36	*A.J. Burnett*	.40
37	*Mo Bruce*	.25
38	*Jason Tyner*	.40
39	*Mamon Tucker*	.25
40	*Sean Burroughs*	2.00
41	*Kevin Eberwein*	.25
42	*Junior Herndon*	.25
43	*Bryan Wolff*	.25
44	*Pat Burrell*	3.00
45	*Eric Valent*	.40
46	*Carlos Pena*	1.00
47	*Mike Zywica*	.15
48	*Adam Everett*	.25
49	*Juan Pena*	.25
50	*Adam Dunn*	1.00
51	*Austin Kearns*	1.50
52	*Jacobo Sequea*	.25
53	*Choo Freeman*	.25
54	*Jeff Winchester*	.15
55	*Matt Burch*	.15
56	*Chris George*	.50
57	*Scott Mullen*	.25
58	*Kit Pellow*	.25
59	*Mark Quinn*	1.00
60	*Nate Cornejo*	.25
61	*Ryan Mills*	.20
62	*Kevin Beirne*	.25
63	*Kip Wells*	.40
64	*Juan Rivera*	.50
65	*Alfonso Soriano*	1.00
66	*Josh Hamilton*	3.00
67	*Josh Girdley*	.40
68	*Kyle Snyder*	.20
69	*Mike Paradis*	.25
70	*Jason Jennings*	.25
71	*David Walling*	.40
72	*Omar Ortiz*	.25
73	*Jay Gehrke*	.25
74	*Casey Burns*	.25
75	*Carl Crawford*	.50
76	Reggie Sanders	.15
77	Will Clark	.25
78	David Wells	.15
79	Paul Konerko	.15
80	Armando Benitez	.15
81	Brant Brown	.15
82	Mo Vaughn	.25
83	Jose Canseco	.50
84	Albert Belle	.25
85	Dean Palmer	.15
86	Greg Vaughn	.25
87	Mark Clark	.15
88	Pat Meares	.15
89	Eric Davis	.15
90	Brian Giles	.15
91	Jeff Brantley	.15
92	Bret Boone	.15
93	Ron Gant	.15
94	Mike Cameron	.15
95	Charles Johnson	.15
96	Denny Neagle	.15
97	Brian Hunter	.15
98	Jose Hernandez	.15
99	Rick Aguilera	.15
100	Tony Batista	.15
101	Roger Cedeno	.15
102	Creighton Gubanich	.15
103	Tim Belcher	.15
104	Bruce Aven	.15
105	*Brian Daubach*	.40
106	Ed Sprague	.15
107	Michael Tucker	.15
108	Homer Bush	.15
109	Armando Reynoso	.15
110	Brook Fordyce	.15
111	Matt Mantei	.15
112	Jose Guillen	.15
113	Kenny Rogers	.15
114	Livan Hernandez	.15
115	Butch Huskey	.15
116	David Segui	.15
117	Darryl Hamilton	.15
118	Jim Leyritz	.15
119	Randy Velarde	.15
120	Bill Taylor	.15
121	Kevin Appier	.15

1999 Topps Traded and Rookies Autographs

These autographs have identical photos and design from the Traded and Rookies set. Seeded one per boxed set, each card has a "Topps Certified Autograph Issue" stamp ensuring its authenticity. 75 of the rookie/draft picks included in the 121-card boxed set signed.

		MT
Common Player:		5.00
Inserted 1:set		
1	Seth Etherton	5.00
2	Mark Harriger	5.00
3	Matt Wise	5.00
4	Carlos Hernandez	5.00
5	Julio Lugo	5.00
6	Mike Nannini	5.00
7	Justin Bowles	5.00
8	Mark Mulder	15.00
9	Roberto Vaz	5.00
10	Felipe Lopez	15.00
11	Matt Belisle	8.00
12	Micah Bowie	5.00
13	Ruben Quevedo	5.00
14	Jose Garcia	5.00
15	David Kelton	15.00
16	Phillip Norton	5.00
17	Corey Patterson	70.00
18	Ron Walker	5.00
19	Paul Hoover	5.00
20	Ryan Rupe	5.00
21	J.D. Closser	5.00
22	Rob Ryan	5.00
23	Steve Colyer	5.00
24	Bubba Crosby	5.00
25	Luke Prokopec	10.00
26	Matt Blank	5.00
27	Josh McKinley	5.00
28	Nate Bump	8.00
29	Giuseppe Chiaramonte	5.00
30	Arturo McDowell	5.00
31	Tony Torcato	5.00
32	Dave Roberts	5.00
33	C.C. Sabathia	20.00
34	Sean Spencer	5.00
35	Chip Ambres	10.00
36	A.J. Burnett	10.00
37	Mo Bruce	5.00
38	Jason Tyner	8.00
39	Mamon Tucker	5.00
40	Sean Burroughs	40.00
41	Kevin Eberwein	5.00
42	Junior Herndon	5.00
43	Bryan Wolff	5.00
44	Pat Burrell	50.00
45	Eric Valent	12.00
46	Carlos Pena	25.00
47	Mike Zywica	5.00
48	Adam Everett	10.00
49	Juan Pena	8.00
50	Adam Dunn	25.00
51	Austin Kearns	25.00
52	Jacobo Sequea	5.00
53	Choo Freeman	8.00
54	Jeff Winchester	10.00
55	Matt Burch	5.00
56	Chris George	8.00
57	Scott Mullen	5.00
58	Kit Pellow	5.00
59	Mark Quinn	20.00
60	Nate Cornejo	5.00
61	Ryan Mills	5.00
62	Kevin Beirne	5.00
63	Kip Wells	10.00
64	Juan Rivera	15.00
65	Alfonso Soriano	25.00
66	Josh Hamilton	60.00
67	Josh Girdley	10.00
68	Kyle Snyder	8.00
69	Mike Paradis	5.00
70	Jason Jennings	8.00
71	David Walling	10.00
72	Omar Ortiz	5.00
73	Jay Gehrke	5.00
74	Casey Burns	5.00
75	Carl Crawford	15.00

1999 Topps Super Chrome

Using identical photos from Topps Chrome Baseball, Topps super-sized 36 players to 4-1/8" x 5-3/4" card size. The cards are done on standard chromium technology. Each pack contains three oversized cards and sells for S.R.P. of $4.99. There also is a Refractor parallel set, which are seeded 1:12 packs.

		MT
Complete Set (36):		50.00
Common Player:		.50
Refractors:		4X
Inserted 1:12		
Pack (3):		5.00
Wax Box (12):		50.00
1	Roger Clemens	2.00
2	Andres Galarraga	.75
3	Manny Ramirez	1.50
4	Greg Maddux	3.00
5	Kerry Wood	1.50
6	Travis Lee	1.00
7	Nolan Ryan	5.00
8	Juan Gonzalez	1.50
9	Vladimir Guerrero	2.00
10	Sammy Sosa	3.00
11	Mark McGwire	6.00
12	Javy Lopez	.50
13	Tony Gwynn	2.50
14	Derek Jeter	3.00
15	Albert Belle	1.00
16	Pedro Martinez	1.00
17	Greg Vaughn	.50
18	Ken Griffey Jr.	6.00
19	Ben Grieve	1.25
20	Vinny Castilla	.50
21	Moises Alou	.50
22	Barry Bonds	1.25
23	Nomar Garciaparra	3.00
24	Chipper Jones	3.00
25	Mike Piazza	3.00
26	Alex Rodriguez	5.00
27	Ivan Rodriguez	1.25
28	Frank Thomas	3.00
29	Larry Walker	1.00
30	Troy Glaus	1.50
31	David Wells (Season Highlight)	.50
32	Roger Clemens (Season Highlight)	1.50
33	Kerry Wood (Season Highlight)	.75
34	Mark McGwire (Home Run Record)	8.00
35	Sammy Sosa (Home Run Parade)	4.00
36	World Series	.50

1999 Topps Opening Day

This retail exclusive product is comprised of 165 cards. Base cards have a silver border, and the Opening Day logo stamped with silver foil. Packs are pre-priced at $.99, each pack has seven cards. Hank Aaron autographs are randomly seeded and are stamped with the Topps "Certified Autograph Issue" stamp. The insertion rate for the autograph is 1:29,642 packs.

		MT
Complete Set (165):		30.00
Common Player:		.15
Hank Aaron Autograph:		200.00
Pack (7):		.99
Wax Box (24):		18.00
1	Hank Aaron	2.00
2a	Roger Clemens	1.00
2b	Andres Galarraga (should be #3)	.50
4	Scott Brosius	.15
5	Ray Durham	.15
6	Will Clark	.40
7	David Wells	.15
8	Jose Guillen	.15
9	Edgardo Alfonzo	.15
10	Manny Ramirez	1.00
11	Greg Maddux	2.00
12	David Segui	.15
13	Darryl Strawberry	.25
14	Brad Radke	.15
15	Kerry Wood	.75
16	Paul Konerko	.25
17	Travis Lee	.50
18	Kenny Rogers	.15
19	Todd Walker	.25

20 John Olerud .25
21 Nolan Ryan 3.00
22 Ray Lankford .15
23 Bartolo Colon .15
24 Brady Anderson .15
25 Jorge Posada .15
26 Justin Thompson .15
27 Juan Gonzalez .75
28 Chuck Knoblauch .40
29 Todd Helton .60
30 Gary Sheffield .30
31 Rod Beck .15
32 Garret Anderson .15
33 Rondell White .25
34 Vladimir Guerrero 1.25
35 Eric Karros .15
36 Mo Vaughn .60
37 Sammy Sosa 2.50
38 Kenny Lofton .60
39 Mark McGwire 4.00
40 Javy Lopez .25
41 Damion Easley .15
42 Andy Pettitte .40
43 Tony Gwynn 1.50
44 Jay Bell .15
45 Jose Canseco .40
46 John Wetteland .15
47 Mike Caruso .15
48 Derek Jeter 2.00
49 Aaron Sele .15
50 Jeff Cirillo .15
51 Mark Kotsay .15
52 Albert Belle .75
53 Matt Lawton .15
54 Pedro Martinez .50
55 Greg Vaughn .25
56 Neifi Perez .15
57 Derek Bell .15
58 Ken Griffey Jr. 4.00
59 David Cone .25
60 Dean Palmer .15
61 Trevor Hoffman .15
62 Billy Wagner .15
63 Shawn Green .15
64 Ben Grieve .75
65 Tom Goodwin .15
66 Jaret Wright .40
67 Dmitri Young .15
68 Hideki Irabu .25
69 Jeff Fassero .15
70 Matt Williams .30
71 Bret Saberhagen .15
72 Chad Curtis .15
73 Scott Rolen .75
74 J.T. Snow Jr. .15
75 Rusty Greer .15
76 Jim Edmonds .15
77 Ron Gant .15
78 A.J. Hinch .15
79 Shannon Stewart .15
80 Brad Fullmer .25
81 Walt Weiss .15
82 Fred McGriff .25
83 Darin Erstad .75
84 Eric Young .15
85 Livan Hernandez .15
86 Jeff Bagwell 1.00
87 Omar Vizquel .15
88 Eric Davis .15
89 Magglio Ordonez .15
90 John Valentin .15
91 Dave Dellucci .15
92 Chan Ho Park .25
93 Masato Yoshii .15
94 Bret Boone .15
95 Mariano Rivera .25
96 Bobby Jones .15
97 Francisco Cordova .15
98 Mike Mussina .50
99 Denny Neagle .15
100 Edgar Martinez .15
101 Jason Kendall .25
102 Jeff King .15
103 Rey Ordonez .15
104 Andruw Jones .75
105 Vinny Castilla .15
106 Troy Glaus 1.00
107 Tom Glavine .25
108 Moises Alou .25
109 Carlos Delgado .25
110 Raul Mondesi .25
111 Shane Reynolds .15
112 Jason Giambi .15
113 Jose Cruz Jr. .15
114 Craig Biggio .40
115 Tim Salmon .40
116 Chipper Jones 2.00
117 Andy Benes .15
118 John Smoltz .25
119 Jeromy Burnitz .15
120 Randy Johnson .50
121 Mark Grace .25
122 Henry Rodriguez .15
123 Ryan Klesko .15
124 Kevin Millwood .50
125 Sean Casey .15
126 Brian Jordan .15
127 Kevin Brown .25
128 Orlando Hernandez 1.50
129 Barry Bonds .75
130 David Justice .25
131 Carlos Perez .15
132 Andy Ashby .15
133 Paul O'Neill .30
134 Curt Schilling .25
135 Alex Rodriguez 3.00
136 Cliff Floyd .15
137 Rafael Palmeiro .30
138 Nomar Garciaparra 2.00
139 Mike Piazza 2.00
140 Roberto Alomar .50
141 Todd Hundley .15
142 Jeff Kent .15
143 Barry Larkin .25
144 Cal Ripken Jr. 3.00
145 Jay Buhner .25
146 Kevin Young .15
147 Ivan Rodriguez .75
148 Al Leiter .15
149 Sandy Alomar .15
150 Bernie Williams .50
151 Ellis Burks .15
152 Wally Joyner .15
153 Bobby Higginson .15
154 Tony Clark .50
155 Larry Walker .40
156 Frank Thomas 1.50
157 Tino Martinez .40
158 Jim Thome .40
159 Dante Bichette .25
160 David Wells (Season Highlights) .15
161 Roger Clemens (Season Highlights) .60
162 Kerry Wood (Season Highlights) .50
163 Mark McGwire (HR Record #70) 5.00
164 Sammy Sosa (HR Record #66) 3.00
165 Checklist .15

1999 Topps Chrome

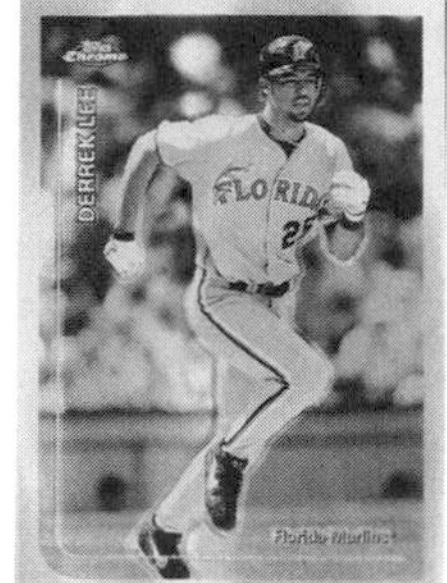

The 462-card base set is a chromium parallel version of Topps baseball. Included are the Mark McGwire #220 and Sammy Sosa #461 home run subset cards, which commemorate each of his home runs. Each pack contains four cards with a S.R.P. of $3.00 per pack.

	MT
Complete Set (461):	250.00
Series 1 Set (242):	125.00
Series 2 Set (221):	125.00
Common Player:	.40
Star Refractors:	10X
Young Stars/RCs:	6X
McGwire Refractors #220:	4X
Sosa Refractors #461:	4X
Inserted 1:12	
Series 1 Pack (4):	4.50
Series 1 Hobby Wax Box (24):	110.00
Series 2 Pack (4):	3.50
Series 2 Hobby Wax Box (24):	100.00

1 Roger Clemens 3.00
2 Andres Galarraga .75
3 Scott Brosius .40
4 John Flaherty .40
5 Jim Leyritz .40
6 Ray Durham .40
7 not issued
8 Joe Vizcaino .40
9 Will Clark 1.00
10 David Wells .40
11 Jose Guillen .40
12 Scott Hatteberg .40
13 Edgardo Alfonzo .60
14 Mike Bordick .40
15 Manny Ramirez 2.00
16 Greg Maddux 4.00
17 David Segui .40
18 Darryl Strawberry .75
19 Brad Radke .40
20 Kerry Wood .75
21 Matt Anderson .40
22 Derrek Lee .40
23 Mickey Morandini .40
24 Paul Konerko .60
25 Travis Lee .40
26 Ken Hill .40
27 Kenny Rogers .40
28 Paul Sorrento .40
29 Quilvio Veras .40
30 Todd Walker .40
31 Ryan Jackson .40
32 John Olerud .60
33 Doug Glanville .40
34 Nolan Ryan 8.00
35 Ray Lankford .40
36 Mark Loretta .40
37 Jason Dickson .40
38 Sean Bergman .40
39 Quinton McCracken .40
40 Bartolo Colon .50
41 Brady Anderson .50
42 Chris Stynes .40
43 Jorge Posada .60
44 Justin Thompson .40
45 Johnny Damon .40
46 Armando Benitez .40
47 Brant Brown .40
48 Charlie Hayes .40
49 Darren Dreifort .40
50 Juan Gonzalez 2.00
51 Chuck Knoblauch .60
52 Todd Helton (Rookie All-Star) 2.00
53 Rick Reed .40
54 Chris Gomez .40
55 Gary Sheffield .75
56 Rod Beck .40
57 Rey Sanchez .40
58 Garret Anderson .40
59 Jimmy Haynes .40
60 Steve Woodard .40
61 Rondell White .60
62 Vladimir Guerrero 3.00
63 Eric Karros .60
64 Russ Davis .40
65 Mo Vaughn 1.00
66 Sammy Sosa 5.00
67 Troy Percival .40
68 Kenny Lofton .75
69 Bill Taylor .40
70 Mark McGwire 10.00
71 Roger Cedeno .40
72 Javy Lopez .60
73 Damion Easley .40
74 Andy Pettitte .75
75 Tony Gwynn 3.00
76 Ricardo Rincon .40
77 F.P. Santangelo .40
78 Jay Bell .40
79 Scott Servais .40
80 Jose Canseco 1.50
81 Roberto Hernandez .40
82 Todd Dunwoody .40
83 John Wetteland .40
84 Mike Caruso (Rookie All-Star) .40
85 Derek Jeter 5.00
86 Aaron Sele .40
87 Jose Lima .40
88 Ryan Christenson .40
89 Jeff Cirillo .40
90 Jose Hernandez .40
91 Mark Kotsay (Rookie All-Star) .50
92 Darren Bragg .40
93 Albert Belle 1.00
94 Matt Lawton .40
95 Pedro Martinez 2.00
96 Greg Vaughn .60
97 Neifi Perez .40
98 Gerald Williams .40
99 Derek Bell .40
100 Ken Griffey Jr. 6.00
101 David Cone .50
102 Brian Johnson .40
103 Dean Palmer .40
104 Javier Valentin .40
105 Trevor Hoffman .40
106 Butch Huskey .40
107 Dave Martinez .40
108 Billy Wagner .40
109 Shawn Green 1.00
110 Ben Grieve (Rookie All-Star) .75
111 Tom Goodwin .40
112 Jaret Wright .40
113 Aramis Ramirez .40
114 Dmitri Young .40
115 Hideki Irabu .40
116 Roberto Kelly .40
117 Jeff Fassero .40
118 Mark Clark .40
119 Jason McDonald .40
120 Matt Williams .75
121 Dave Burba .40
122 Bret Saberhagen .40
123 Deivi Cruz .40
124 Chad Curtis .40
125 Scott Rolen 1.50
126 Lee Stevens .40
127 J.T. Snow Jr. .40
128 Rusty Greer .40
129 Brian Meadows .40
130 Jim Edmonds .75
131 Ron Gant .60
132 A.J. Hinch (Rookie All-Star) .40
133 Shannon Stewart .40
134 Brad Fullmer .50
135 Cal Eldred .40
136 Matt Walbeck .40
137 Carl Everett .40
138 Walt Weiss .40
139 Fred McGriff .60
140 Darin Erstad 1.00
141 Dave Nilsson .40
142 Eric Young .40
143 Dan Wilson .40
144 Jeff Reed .40
145 Brett Tomko .40
146 Terry Steinbach .40
147 Seth Greisinger .40
148 Pat Meares .40
149 Livan Hernandez .40
150 Jeff Bagwell 2.00
151 Bob Wickman .40
152 Omar Vizquel .60
153 Eric Davis .50
154 Larry Sutton .40
155 Magglio Ordonez (Rookie All-Star) .75
156 Eric Milton .40
157 Darren Lewis .40
158 Rick Aguilera .40
159 Mike Lieberthal .40
160 Robb Nen .40
161 Brian Giles .60
162 Jeff Brantley .40
163 Gary DiSarcina .40
164 John Valentin .40
165 David Dellucci .40
166 Chan Ho Park .60
167 Masato Yoshii .40
168 Jason Schmidt .40
169 LaTroy Hawkins .40
170 Bret Boone .40
171 Jerry DiPoto .40
172 Mariano Rivera .60
173 Mike Cameron .40
174 Scott Erickson .40
175 Charles Johnson .40
176 Bobby Jones .40
177 Francisco Cordova .40
178 Todd Jones .40
179 Jeff Montgomery .40
180 Mike Mussina 1.50
181 Bob Abreu .40
182 Ismael Valdes .40
183 Andy Fox .40
184 Woody Williams .40
185 Denny Neagle .40
186 Jose Valentin .40
187 Darrin Fletcher .40

188 Gabe Alvarez .40
189 Eddie Taubensee .40
190 Edgar Martinez .40
191 Jason Kendall .60
192 Darryl Kile .40
193 Jeff King .40
194 Rey Ordonez .40
195 Andruw Jones 1.00
196 Tony Fernandez .40
197 Jamey Wright .40
198 B.J. Surhoff .40
199 Vinny Castilla .40
200 David Wells (Season Highlight) .40
201 Mark McGwire (Season Highlight) 5.00
202 Sammy Sosa (Season Highlight) 2.00
203 Roger Clemens (Season Highlight) 1.50
204 Kerry Wood (Season Highlight) .50
205 Lance Berkman, Mike Frank, Gabe Kapler (Prospects) 1.00
206 *Alex Escobar*, Ricky Ledee, Mike Stoner (Prospects) 4.00
207 *Peter Bergeron*, Jeremy Giambi, George Lombard (Prospects) 1.50
208 Michael Barrett, Ben Davis, Robert Fick (Prospects) 1.00
209 Pat Cline, Ramon Hernandez, Jayson Werth (Prospects) 1.00
210 Bruce Chen, Chris Enochs, Ryan Anderson (Prospects) 1.00
211 Mike Lincoln, Octavio Dotel, Brad Penny (Prospects) 1.00
212 Chuck Abbott, Brent Butler, Danny Klassen (Prospects) 1.00
213 Chris Jones, *Jeff Urban* (Draft Pick) 1.00
214 *Arturo McDowell ,Tony Torcato* (Draft Pick) 2.00
215 *Josh McKinley ,Jason Tyner* (Draft Pick) 2.00
216 *Matt Burch, Seth Etherton* (Draft Pick) 1.00
217 *Mamon Tucker, Rick Elder* (Draft Pick) 1.50
218 *J.M. Gold, Ryan Mills* (Draft Pick) 1.00
219 *Adam Brown, Choo Freeman* (Draft Pick) 1.50
220 Mark McGwire HR #1 (Record Breaker) 60.00
220 Mark McGwire HR #2-60 30.00
220 McGwire HR #61-62 80.00
220 McGwire HR #63-69 50.00
220 McGwire HR #70 250.00
221 Larry Walker (League Leader) .50
222 Bernie Williams (League Leader) .75
223 Mark McGwire (League Leader) 6.00
224 Ken Griffey Jr. (League Leader) 4.00
225 Sammy Sosa (League Leader) 2.00
226 Juan Gonzalez (League Leader) 1.00
227 Dante Bichette (League Leader) .50
228 Alex Rodriguez (League Leader) 4.00
229 Sammy Sosa (League Leader) 2.00
230 Derek Jeter (League Leader) 3.00
231 Greg Maddux (League Leader) 2.00
232 Roger Clemens (League Leader) 1.50
233 Ricky Ledee (World Series) .40
234 Chuck Knoblauch (World Series) .40
235 Bernie Williams (World Series) .75
236 Tino Martinez (World Series) .50
237 Orlando Hernandez (World Series) .50
238 Scott Brosius (World Series) .40
239 Andy Pettitte (World Series) .50
240 Mariano Rivera (World Series) .60
241 Checklist .40
242 Checklist .40
243 Tom Glavine .75
244 Andy Benes .40
245 Sandy Alomar .60
246 Wilton Guerrero .40
247 Alex Gonzalez .40
248 Roberto Alomar 1.50
249 Ruben Rivera .40
250 Eric Chavez .40
251 Ellis Burks .40
252 Richie Sexson .50
253 Steve Finley .40
254 Dwight Gooden .60
255 Dustin Hermanson .40
256 Kirk Rueter .40
257 Steve Trachsel .40
258 Gregg Jefferies .40
259 Matt Stairs .40
260 Shane Reynolds .40
261 Gregg Olson .40
262 Kevin Tapani .40
263 Matt Morris .40
264 Carl Pavano .40
265 Nomar Garciaparra 5.00
266 Kevin Young .40
267 Rick Helling .40
268 Matt Franco .40
269 Brian McRae .40
270 Cal Ripken Jr. 6.00
271 Jeff Abbott .40
272 Tony Batista .40
273 Bill Simas .40
274 Brian Hunter .40
275 John Franco .40
276 Devon White .40
277 Rickey Henderson .75
278 Chuck Finley .40
279 Mike Blowers .40
280 Mark Grace .75
281 Randy Winn .40
282 Bobby Bonilla .50
283 David Justice .75
284 Shane Monahan .40
285 Kevin Brown .75
286 Todd Zeile .40
287 Al Martin .40
288 Troy O'Leary .40
289 Darryl Hamilton .40
290 Tino Martinez .60
291 David Ortiz .40
292 Tony Clark .50
293 Ryan Minor .40
294 Reggie Sanders .40
295 Wally Joyner .40
296 Cliff Floyd .40
297 Shawn Estes .40
298 Pat Hentgen .40
299 Scott Elarton .40
300 Alex Rodriguez 6.00
301 Ozzie Guillen .40
302 Hideo Martinez .40
303 Ryan McGuire .40
304 Brad Ausmus .40
305 Alex Gonzalez .40
306 Brian Jordan .40
307 John Jaha .40
308 Mark Grudzielanek .40
309 Juan Guzman .40
310 Tony Womack .40
311 Dennis Reyes .40
312 Marty Cordova .40
313 Ramiro Mendoza .40
314 Robin Ventura .60
315 Rafael Palmeiro 1.50
316 Ramon Martinez .40
317 Pedro Astacio .40
318 Dave Hollins .40
319 Tom Candiotti .40
320 Al Leiter .60
321 Rico Brogna .40
322 Reggie Jefferson .40
323 Bernard Gilkey .40
324 Jason Giambi 1.00
325 Craig Biggio .60
326 Troy Glaus 2.00
327 Delino DeShields .40
328 Fernando Vina .40
329 John Smoltz .40
330 Jeff Kent .50
331 Roy Halladay .75
332 Andy Ashby .40
333 Tim Wakefield .40
334 Roger Clemens 3.00
335 Bernie Williams 1.50
336 Desi Relaford .40
337 John Burkett .40
338 Mike Hampton .40
339 Royce Clayton .40
340 Mike Piazza 5.00
341 Jeremi Gonzalez .40
342 Mike Lansing .40
343 Jamie Moyer .40
344 Ron Coomer .40
345 Barry Larkin 1.00
346 Fernando Tatis .50
347 Chili Davis .40
348 Bobby Higginson .40
349 Hal Morris .40
350 Larry Walker 1.00
351 Carlos Guillen .40
352 Miguel Tejada .60
353 Travis Fryman .60
354 Jarrod Washburn .40
355 Chipper Jones 4.00
356 Todd Stottlemyre .60
357 Henry Rodriguez .40
358 Eli Marrero .40
359 Alan Benes .40
360 Tim Salmon .75
361 Luis Gonzalez .60
362 Scott Spiezio .40
363 Chris Carpenter .40
364 Bobby Howry .40
365 Raul Mondesi .75
366 Ugueth Urbina .40
367 Tom Evans .40
368 *Kerry Ligtenberg* .75
369 Adrian Beltre .75
370 Ryan Klesko .50
371 Wilson Alvarez .40
372 John Thomson .40
373 Tony Saunders .40
374 Mike Stanley .40
375 Ken Caminiti .60
376 Jay Buhner .60
377 Bill Mueller .40
378 Jeff Blauser .40
379 Edgar Renteria .40
380 Jim Thome 1.00
381 Joey Hamilton .40
382 Calvin Pickering .40
383 Marquis Grissom .40
384 Omar Daal .40
385 Curt Schilling .60
386 Jose Cruz Jr. .50
387 Chris Widger .40
388 Pete Harnisch .40
389 Charles Nagy .40
390 Tom Gordon .40
391 Bobby Smith .40
392 Derrick Gibson .40
393 Jeff Conine .40
394 Carlos Perez .40
395 Barry Bonds 2.00
396 Mark McLemore .40
397 Juan Encarnacion .40
398 Wade Boggs 1.00
399 Ivan Rodriguez 2.00
400 Moises Alou .60
401 Jeromy Burnitz .40
402 Sean Casey .60
403 Jose Offerman .40
404 Joe Fontenot .40
405 Kevin Millwood .50
406 Lance Johnson .40
407 Richard Hidalgo .40
408 Mike Jackson .40
409 Brian Anderson .40
410 Jeff Shaw .40
411 Preston Wilson .40
412 Todd Hundley .40
413 Jim Parque .40
414 Justin Baughman .40
415 Dante Bichette .60
416 Paul O'Neill .75
417 Miguel Cairo .40
418 Randy Johnson 2.00
419 Jesus Sanchez .40
420 Carlos Delgado 1.50
421 Ricky Ledee .40
422 Orlando Hernandez .60
423 Frank Thomas 2.50
424 Pokey Reese .40
425 Carlos Lee, Mike Lowell, *Kit Pellow* (Prospect) 1.00
426 Michael Cuddyer, Mark DeRosa ,*Jerry Hairston Jr.* (Prospect) 1.00
427 Marlon Anderson, Ron Belliard, Orlando Cabrera (Prospect) 1.00
428 *Micah Bowie, Phil Norton,* Randy Wolf (Prospect) 1.00
429 Jack Cressend, Jason Rakers, John Rocker (Prospect) 1.00
430 Ruben Mateo, Scott Morgan, *Mike Zywica* (Prospect) 1.00
431 Jason LaRue, *Matt LeCroy, Mitch Meluskey* (Prospect) 1.00
432 Gabe Kapler, *Armando Rios,* Fernando Seguignol (Prospect) 1.00
433 Adam Kennedy, *Mickey Lopez,* Jackie Rexrode (Prospect) 1.00
434 *Jose Fernandez,* Jeff Liefer, Chris Truby (Prospect) 1.00
435 Corey Koskie, *Doug Mientkiewicz,* Damon Minor (Prospect) 1.00
436 *Roosevelt Brown,* Dernell Stenson, Vernon Wells (Prospect) 1.00
437 *A.J. Burnett,* John Nicholson, Billy Koch (Prospect) 1.50
438 *Matt Belisle, Matt Roney* (Draft Pick) 1.50
439 *Austin Kearns, Chris George* (Draft Pick) 4.00
440 *Nate Bump, Nate Cornejo* (Draft Pick) 1.00
441 *Brad Lidge, Mike Nannini* (Draft Pick) 1.00
442 *Matt Holliday ,Jeff Winchester* (Draft Pick) 2.00
443 *Adam Everett,Chip Ambres* (Draft Pick) 1.00
444 *Pat Burrell,Eric Valent* (Draft Pick) 12.00
445 Roger Clemens (Strike-out Kings) 1.50
446 Kerry Wood (Strikeout Kings) .50
447 Curt Schilling (Strikeout Kings) .40
448 Randy Johnson (Strike-out Kings) 1.00
449 Pedro Martinez (Strike-out Kings) 1.00
450 Jeff Bagwell, Andres Galarraga, Mark McGwire (All-Topps) 4.00
451 John Olerud, Jim Thome,

	Tino Martinez (All-Topps)	.40
452	Alex Rodriguez, Nomar Garciaparra, Derek Jeter (All-Topps)	3.00
453	Vinny Castilla, Chipper Jones, Scott Rolen (All-Topps)	1.50
454	Sammy Sosa, Ken Griffey Jr., Juan Gonzalez (All-Topps)	3.00
455	Barry Bonds, Manny Ramirez, Larry Walker (All-Topps)	1.00
456	Frank Thomas, Tim Salmon, David Justice (All-Topps)	1.00
457	Travis Lee, Todd Helton, Ben Grieve (All-Topps)	1.00
458	Vladimir Guerrero, Greg Vaughn, Bernie Williams (All-Topps)	1.00
459	Mike Piazza, Ivan Rodriguez, Jason Kendall (All-Topps)	2.00
460	Roger Clemens, Kerry Wood, Greg Maddux (All-Topps)	1.00
461	Sammy Sosa #1 (Home Run Parade)	25.00
461	Sammy Sosa HR #2-60	12.00
461	S. Sosa HR #61-62	30.00
461	S. Sosa HR #63-65	15.00
461	S. Sosa HR #66	60.00
---	Checklist 1-100	.40
---	Checklist - inserts	.40

1999 Topps Chrome All-Etch

Inserted in Series II packs, All-Etch has three different levels of inserts, all printed on All-Etch technology. The three levels include '99 Rookie Rush which features rookies who have the best shot of winning '99 Rookie of the Year. Club 40 features 13 players who hit 40 homers or more from the '98 season and Club K features seven pitchers who are known for their strikeout abilities including Roger Clemens and Pedro Martinez. Each of these three levels are inserted 1:6 packs while the Refractor versions are all seeded 1:24 packs.

		MT
Complete Set (30):		60.00
Common Player:		1.00
Inserted 1:6		
Refractors:		2X
Inserted 1:24		
1	Mark McGwire	12.00
2	Sammy Sosa	6.00
3	Ken Griffey Jr.	12.00
4	Greg Vaughn	1.00
5	Albert Belle	2.00
6	Vinny Castilla	1.00
7	Jose Canseco	2.00
8	Juan Gonzalez	2.50
9	Manny Ramirez	3.00
10	Andres Galarraga	1.50
11	Rafael Palmeiro	1.50
12	Alex Rodriguez	8.00
13	Mo Vaughn	1.50
14	Eric Chavez	2.50
15	Gabe Kapler	3.00
16	Calvin Pickering	1.00
17	Ruben Mateo	2.50
18	Roy Halladay	1.50
19	Jeremy Giambi	1.50
20	Alex Gonzalez	1.00
21	Ron Belliard	1.00
22	Marlon Anderson	1.00
23	Carlos Lee	1.00
24	Kerry Wood	2.50
25	Roger Clemens	4.00
26	Curt Schilling	1.00
27	Kevin Brown	1.50
28	Randy Johnson	1.50
29	Pedro Martinez	2.00
30	Orlando Hernandez	2.50

1999 Topps Chrome Early Road to the Hall

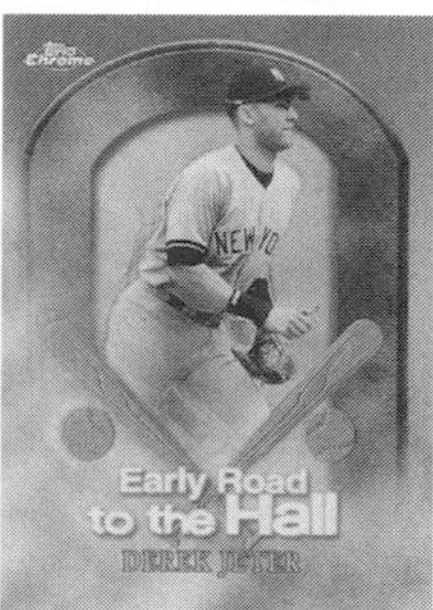

This insert set spotlights 10 players with less than 10 years in the Majors but are gunning towards their respective spots in Cooperstown. Utilizing Chromium technology featured players include Alex Rodriguez and Derek Jeter, with an insert rate of 1:12 packs. A Refractor parallel edition, numbered to 100 each, was a 1:944 hobby-pack insert.

		MT
Complete Set (10):		75.00
Common Player:		3.00
Inserted 1:12		
Refractors (#d to 100):		8X
ER1	Nomar Garciaparra	12.00
ER2	Derek Jeter	12.00
ER3	Alex Rodriguez	15.00
ER4	Juan Gonzalez	5.00
ER5	Ken Griffey Jr.	20.00
ER6	Chipper Jones	12.00
ER7	Vladimir Guerrero	8.00
ER8	Jeff Bagwell	6.00
ER9	Ivan Rodriguez	5.00
ER10	Frank Thomas	8.00

1999 Topps Chrome Lords of the Diamond

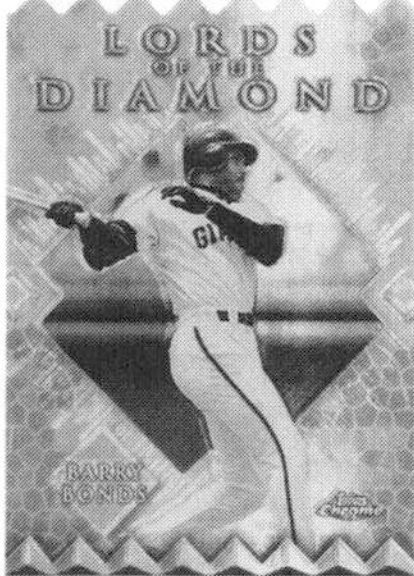

Parallel to the Topps version, the 15-card set features die-cutting across the card top and are seeded 1:8 in Series 1 packs. Refractor versions can be found 1:24 packs.

		MT
Complete Set (15):		60.00
Common Player:		1.00
Inserted 1:8		
Refractors:		2X
Inserted 1:24		
LD1	Ken Griffey Jr.	12.00
LD2	Chipper Jones	6.00
LD3	Sammy Sosa	8.00
LD4	Frank Thomas	4.00
LD5	Mark McGwire	12.00
LD6	Jeff Bagwell	3.00
LD7	Alex Rodriguez	8.00
LD8	Juan Gonzalez	2.50
LD9	Barry Bonds	3.00
LD10	Nomar Garciaparra	6.00
LD11	Darin Erstad	2.50
LD12	Tony Gwynn	5.00
LD13	Andres Galarraga	1.00
LD14	Mike Piazza	6.00
LD15	Greg Maddux	6.00

1999 Topps Chrome New Breed

A parallel version of Topps New Breed utilizing Chromium technology. The 15-card set features the top young stars in the game and are seeded 1:24 packs. A Refractor version also exists which are found 1:72 packs.

		MT
Complete Set (15):		35.00
Common Player:		.50
Inserted 1:24		
Refractors:		1.5X
Inserted 1:72		
NB1	Darin Erstad	2.50
NB2	Brad Fullmer	1.00
NB3	Kerry Wood	2.50
NB4	Nomar Garciaparra	6.00
NB5	Travis Lee	2.00
NB6	Scott Rolen	2.50
NB7	Todd Helton	2.00
NB8	Vladimir Guerrero	4.00
NB9	Derek Jeter	6.00
NB10	Alex Rodriguez	8.00
NB11	Ben Grieve	2.50
NB12	Andruw Jones	2.50
NB13	Paul Konerko	.50
NB14	Aramis Ramirez	.50
NB15	Adrian Beltre	.75

1999 Topps Chrome Fortune 15

Fortune 15 showcases the baseball's best players and hot rookies. They are inserted in Series 2 packs at a rate of 1:12. A Refractor version also exists found exclusively in hobby packs at a rate of 1:627 packs. Refractors are sequentially numbered to 100.

		MT
Complete Set (15):		100.00
Common Player:		2.50
Inserted 1:12		
Refractors:		8X
Production 100 sets H		
1	Alex Rodriguez	15.00
2	Nomar Garciaparra	10.00
3	Derek Jeter	10.00
4	Troy Glaus	5.00
5	Ken Griffey Jr.	20.00
6	Vladimir Guerrero	6.00
7	Kerry Wood	4.00
8	Eric Chavez	4.00
9	Greg Maddux	10.00
10	Mike Piazza	10.00
11	Sammy Sosa	10.00
12	Mark McGwire	20.00
13	Ben Grieve	4.00
14	Chipper Jones	10.00
15	Manny Ramirez	5.00

Modern cards in Near Mint condition are valued at about 75% of the Mint value shown here. Excellent-condition cards are worth 50%. Cards in lower grades are not generally collectible.

1999 Topps Chrome Record Numbers

This 10-card insert set salutes 10 record-setters who have earned a mark of distinction, including Cal Ripken Jr. for his record setting consecutive game streak. Inserted randomly in series II packs at a rate of 1:36 packs. Refractor parallel versions are seeded 1:144 packs.

		MT
Complete Set (10):		120.00
Common Player:		3.00
Inserted 1:36		
Refractors:		2X
Inserted 1:144		
1	Mark McGwire	25.00
2	Craig Biggio	3.00
3	Barry Bonds	6.00
4	Ken Griffey Jr.	25.00
5	Sammy Sosa	15.00
6	Alex Rodriguez	25.00
7	Kerry Wood	6.00
8	Roger Clemens	9.00
9	Cal Ripken Jr.	20.50
10	Mark McGwire	25.00

1999 Topps Gallery

This 150-card base set features a white textured border surrounding the player image with the player's name, team name and Topps Gallery logo stamped with gold foil. The first 100 cards in the set portray veteran players while the next 50 cards are broken down into three subsets: Masters, Artisans and Apprentices. Card backs have a monthly batting or pitching record from the '98 season, one player photo and vital information.

		MT
Complete Set (150):		120.00
Common Player (1-100):		.20
Common Player (101-150):		.50
Player's Private Issue:		10X
PPI SPs:		6X
Rookie SP:		3X
Production 250 sets		
Pack (6):		3.00
Wax Box (24):		60.00
1	Mark McGwire	4.00
2	Jim Thome	.75
3	Bernie Williams	.75
4	Larry Walker	.75
5	Juan Gonzalez	1.00
6	Ken Griffey Jr.	4.00
7	Raul Mondesi	.40
8	Sammy Sosa	2.50
9	Greg Maddux	2.00
10	Jeff Bagwell	1.00
11	Vladimir Guerrero	2.00
12	Scott Rolen	1.00
13	Nomar Garciaparra	2.50
14	Mike Piazza	2.50
15	Travis Lee	.40
16	Carlos Delgado	.75
17	Darin Erstad	.40
18	David Justice	.40
19	Cal Ripken Jr.	2.50
20	Derek Jeter	2.50
21	Tony Clark	.40
22	Barry Larkin	.50
23	Greg Vaughn	.40
24	Jeff Kent	.20
25	Wade Boggs	.50
26	Andres Galarraga	.50
27	Ken Caminiti	.30
28	Jason Kendall	.40
29	Todd Helton	1.00
30	Chuck Knoblauch	.50
31	Roger Clemens	1.50
32	Jeromy Burnitz	.20
33	Javy Lopez	.20
34	Roberto Alomar	.75
35	Eric Karros	.30
36	Ben Grieve	.50
37	Eric Davis	.30
38	Rondell White	.40
39	Dmitri Young	.20
40	Ivan Rodriguez	1.25
41	Paul O'Neill	.50
42	Jeff Cirillo	.20
43	Kerry Wood	.50
44	Albert Belle	1.00
45	Frank Thomas	1.00
46	Manny Ramirez	1.00
47	Tom Glavine	.40
48	Mo Vaughn	.75
49	Jose Cruz Jr.	.25
50	Sandy Alomar	.20
51	Edgar Martinez	.20
52	John Olerud	.40
53	Todd Walker	.20
54	Tim Salmon	.40
55	Derek Bell	.20
56	Matt Williams	.50
57	Alex Rodriguez	3.00
58	Rusty Greer	.20
59	Vinny Castilla	.40
60	Jason Giambi	.20
61	Mark Grace	.40
62	Jose Canseco	1.00
63	Gary Sheffield	.40
64	Brad Fullmer	.20
65	Trevor Hoffman	.20
66	Mark Kotsay	.20
67	Mike Mussina	.75
68	Johnny Damon	.20
69	Tino Martinez	.75
70	Curt Schilling	.40
71	Jay Buhner	.40
72	Kenny Lofton	.75
73	Randy Johnson	.75
74	Kevin Brown	.50
75	Brian Jordan	.20
76	Craig Biggio	.75
77	Barry Bonds	1.00
78	Tony Gwynn	2.00
79	Jim Edmonds	.20
80	Shawn Green	.75
81	Todd Hundley	.20
82	Cliff Floyd	.20
83	Jose Guillen	.20
84	Dante Bichette	.40
85	Moises Alou	.40
86	Chipper Jones	2.50
87	Ray Lankford	.20
88	Fred McGriff	.40
89	Rod Beck	.20
90	Dean Palmer	.30
91	Pedro Martinez	1.00
92	Andruw Jones	.75
93	Robin Ventura	.40
94	Ugueth Urbina	.20
95	Orlando Hernandez	.50
96	Sean Casey	.75
97	Denny Neagle	.20
98	Troy Glaus	1.00
99	John Smoltz	.30
100	Al Leiter	.30
101	Ken Griffey Jr.	6.00
102	Frank Thomas	1.50
103	Mark McGwire	6.00
104	Sammy Sosa	4.00
105	Chipper Jones	4.00
106	Alex Rodriguez	5.00
107	Nomar Garciaparra	4.00
108	Juan Gonzalez	1.50
109	Derek Jeter	4.00
110	Mike Piazza	4.00
111	Barry Bonds	1.50
112	Tony Gwynn	3.00
113	Cal Ripken Jr.	4.00
114	Greg Maddux	3.00
115	Roger Clemens	2.00
116	Brad Fullmer	.50
117	Kerry Wood	1.00
118	Ben Grieve	1.00
119	Todd Helton	1.00
120	Kevin Millwood	.50
121	Sean Casey	1.00
122	Vladimir Guerrero	2.50
123	Travis Lee	.50
124	Troy Glaus	1.00
125	Bartolo Colon	.50
126	Andruw Jones	1.00
127	Scott Rolen	1.50
128	*Alfonso Soriano*	5.00
129	*Nick Johnson*	8.00
130	*Matt Belisle*	1.00
131	*Jorge Toca*	3.00
132	*Masao Kida*	.50
133	*Carlos Pena*	2.50
134	Adrian Beltre	.50
135	Eric Chavez	.50
136	Carlos Beltran	.50
137	Alex Gonzalez	.50
138	Ryan Anderson	.50
139	Ruben Mateo	1.50
140	Bruce Chen	.50
141	*Pat Burrell*	10.00
142	Michael Barrett	.50
143	Carlos Lee	.50
144	*Mark Mulder*	2.50
145	*Choo Freeman*	2.00
146	Gabe Kapler	.50
147	Juan Encarnacion	.50
148	Jeremy Giambi	.50
149	*Jason Tyner*	1.50
150	George Lombard	.50
	Checklist folder 1 (1:3 packs)	.10
	Checklist folder 2 (1:3)	.10
	Checklist folder 3 (1:3)	.10
	Checklist folder 4 (1:12)	.25
	Checklist folder 5 (1:240)	3.00
	Checklist folder 6 (1:640)	6.00

1999 Topps Gallery Awards Gallery

This 10-card set features players who have earned the highest honors in baseball. Each insert commemorates the player's award by stamping his achievement on the bottom of the card front. Card fronts have silver borders surrounding the player's image. These are seeded 1:12 and card numbers have a "AG" prefix.

		MT
Complete Set (10):		50.00
Common Player:		2.00
Inserted 1:12		
AG1	Kerry Wood	3.00
AG2	Ben Grieve	3.00
AG3	Roger Clemens	5.00
AG4	Tom Glavine	2.00
AG5	Juan Gonzalez	4.00
AG6	Sammy Sosa	10.00
AG7	Ken Griffey Jr.	15.00
AG8	Mark McGwire	15.00
AG9	Bernie Williams	2.00
AG10	Larry Walker	3.00

1999 Topps Gallery Autograph Cards

Three of baseball's top young third baseman are featured in this autographed set, Eric Chavez, Troy Glaus and Adrian Beltre. The insertion odds are 1:209.

		MT
Complete Set (3):		55.00
Common Player:		40.00
Inserted 1:209		
GA1	Troy Glaus	30.00
GA2	Adrian Beltre	20.00
GA3	Eric Chavez	15.00

1999 Topps Gallery Gallery of Heroes

This 10-card set is done on card stock that simulates medieval stained glass. Gallery of Heroes are found 1:24 packs.

	MT
Complete Set (10):	90.00
Common Player:	3.00

Inserted 1:24

GH1	Mark McGwire	20.00
GH2	Sammy Sosa	12.00
GH3	Ken Griffey Jr.	20.00
GH4	Mike Piazza	12.00
GH5	Derek Jeter	12.00
GH6	Nomar Garciaparra	12.00
GH7	Kerry Wood	3.00
GH8	Ben Grieve	3.00
GH9	Chipper Jones	10.00
GH10	Alex Rodriguez	15.00

1999 Topps Gallery Exhibitions

This 20-card set is done on textured 24-point stock and features baseball's top stars. Exhibitions are seeded 1:48 packs.

		MT
Complete Set (20):		200.00
Common Player:		3.50
Inserted 1:48		
E1	Sammy Sosa	15.00
E2	Mark McGwire	25.00
E3	Greg Maddux	12.00
E4	Roger Clemens	10.00
E5	Ben Grieve	5.00
E6	Kerry Wood	5.00
E7	Ken Griffey Jr.	25.00
E8	Tony Gwynn	12.00
E9	Cal Ripken Jr.	20.00
E10	Frank Thomas	8.00
E11	Jeff Bagwell	7.50
E12	Derek Jeter	15.00
E13	Alex Rodriguez	18.00
E14	Nomar Garciaparra	15.00
E15	Manny Ramirez	6.00
E16	Vladimir Guerrero	12.00
E17	Darin Erstad	3.50
E18	Scott Rolen	6.00
E19	Mike Piazza	15.00
E20	Andres Galarraga	3.50

1999 Topps Gallery Heritage

Nineteen contemporary legends and Hall-of-Famer Hank Aaron are artistically depicted using the 1953 Topps design as a template. For a chance to bid on the original art used in the development of this insert set, collectors were able to enter the Topps Gallery Auction. Collectors could accumulate auction points found in Topps Gallery packs. Heritages are seeded 1:12 packs. A parallel called Heritage Proofs are also randomly inserted 1:48 packs and have a chrome styrene finish.

		MT
Complete Set (20):		400.00
Common Player:		8.00
Inserted 1:12		
Heritage Proofs:		2X
Inserted 1:48		
TH1	Hank Aaron	40.00
TH2	Ben Grieve	10.00
TH3	Nomar Garciaparra	30.00
TH4	Roger Clemens	20.00
TH5	Travis Lee	8.00
TH6	Tony Gwynn	25.00
TH7	Alex Rodriguez	35.00
TH8	Ken Griffey Jr.	50.00
TH9	Derek Jeter	30.00
TH10	Sammy Sosa	30.00
TH11	Scott Rolen	10.00
TH12	Chipper Jones	25.00
TH13	Cal Ripken Jr.	40.00
TH14	Kerry Wood	10.00
TH15	Barry Bonds	12.00
TH16	Juan Gonzalez	12.00
TH17	Mike Piazza	30.00
TH18	Greg Maddux	25.00
TH19	Frank Thomas	15.00
TH20	Mark McGwire	50.00

1999 Topps Gallery Heritage Proofs

Heritage Proofs are a parallel to the 1953-style inserts. Printed on chrome styrene, the proofs have a silver metallic background on front and the notation on bottom-back, "1953 TOPPS HERITAGE PROOF". The proof versions are found on average of one per 48 packs.

		MT
Complete Set (20):		750.00
Common Player:		12.00
TH1	Hank Aaron	50.00
TH2	Ben Grieve	20.00
TH3	Nomar Garciaparra	40.00
TH4	Roger Clemens	30.00
TH5	Travis Lee	12.00
TH6	Tony Gwynn	40.00
TH7	Alex Rodriguez	60.00
TH8	Ken Griffey Jr.	100.00
TH9	Derek Jeter	40.00
TH10	Sammy Sosa	40.00
TH11	Scott Rolen	20.00
TH12	Chipper Jones	60.00
TH13	Cal Ripken Jr.	60.00
TH14	Kerry Wood	20.00
TH15	Barry Bonds	30.00
TH16	Juan Gonzalez	30.00
TH17	Mike Piazza	40.00
TH18	Greg Maddux	40.00
TH19	Frank Thomas	30.00
TH20	Mark McGwire	100.00

1999 Topps Gold Label Class 1

This set consists of 100 cards on 35-point spectral-reflective rainbow stock with gold foil stamping. All cards are available in three versions each with the same foreground photo, but with different background photos that vary by category: Class 1 (fielding), Class 2 (running, 1:2), Class 3 (hitting, 1:4), In addition each variation has a different version of the player's team logo in the background. Variations for pitchers are Class 1, set position; Class 2, wind-up, and Class 3, throwing. Black Label parallels were inserted at the rate of between 1:8 and 1:12, depending on packaging. Red Label parallels, serially numbered to 100 each were inserted at rates from 1:118 to 1:148. A One to One parallel version also exists and is limited to one numbered card for each variation and color (Gold, Black and Red), for a total of 900 cards inserted about one per 1,500 packs.

		MT
Complete Set (100):		60.00
Common Gold Label:		.25
Common Black Label:		.50
Black Label Stars:		2X
Common Red Label:		4.00
Red Label Stars:		15X
Pack (5):		5.00
Wax Box (24):		110.00
1	Mike Piazza	3.00
2	Andres Galarraga	.75
3	Mark Grace	.40
4	Tony Clark	.40
5	Jim Thome	.75
6	Tony Gwynn	2.50
7	*Kelly Dransfeldt*	.50
8	Eric Chavez	.40
9	Brian Jordan	.25
10	Todd Hundley	.25
11	Rondell White	.40
12	Dmitri Young	.25
13	Jeff Kent	.25
14	Derek Bell	.25
15	Todd Helton	1.25
16	Chipper Jones	2.50
17	Albert Belle	1.00
18	Barry Larkin	.50
19	Dante Bichette	.40
20	Gary Sheffield	.40
21	Cliff Floyd	.25
22	Derek Jeter	3.00
23	Jason Giambi	.25
24	Ray Lankford	.25
25	Alex Rodriguez	4.00
26	Ruben Mateo	.50
27	Wade Boggs	.50
28	Carlos Delgado	1.00
29	Tim Salmon	.40
30	*Alfonso Soriano*	4.00
31	Javy Lopez	.25
32	Jason Kendall	.40
33	*Nick Johnson*	4.00
34	*A.J. Burnett*	.75
35	Troy Glaus	1.50
36	*Pat Burrell*	5.00
37	Jeff Cirillo	.25
38	David Justice	.40
39	Ivan Rodriguez	1.25
40	Bernie Williams	1.00
41	Jay Buhner	.40
42	Mo Vaughn	1.00
43	Randy Johnson	1.25
44	Pedro Martinez	1.25
45	Larry Walker	.75
46	Todd Walker	.25
47	Roberto Alomar	1.00
48	Kevin Brown	.40
49	Mike Mussina	1.00
50	Tom Glavine	.40
51	Curt Schilling	.40
52	Ken Caminiti	.40
53	Brad Fullmer	.25
54	*Bobby Seay*	.50
55	Orlando Hernandez	.75
56	Sean Casey	.50
57	Al Leiter	.25
58	Sandy Alomar	.25
59	Mark Kotsay	.25
60	Matt Williams	.50
61	Raul Mondesi	.40
62	*Joe Crede*	1.50
63	Jim Edmonds	.25
64	Jose Cruz Jr.	.25
65	Juan Gonzalez	1.25
66	Sammy Sosa	3.00
67	Cal Ripken Jr.	4.00
68	Vinny Castilla	.40
69	Craig Biggio	.75
70	Mark McGwire	5.00
71	Greg Vaughn	.40
72	Greg Maddux	2.50
73	Paul O'Neill	.40
74	Scott Rolen	1.25
75	Ben Grieve	.50
76	Vladimir Guerrero	1.50
77	John Olerud	.40
78	Eric Karros	.25
79	Jeromy Burnitz	.25
80	Jeff Bagwell	1.25
81	Kenny Lofton	.75
82	Manny Ramirez	1.25
83	Andruw Jones	.75
84	Travis Lee	.40
85	Darin Erstad	.40
86	Nomar Garciaparra	3.00
87	Frank Thomas	1.50
88	Moises Alou	.40
89	Tino Martinez	.50
90	*Carlos Pena*	1.50
91	Shawn Green	1.00
92	Rusty Greer	.25
93	*Matt Belisle*	.50
94	Adrian Beltre	.40
95	Roger Clemens	1.50
96	John Smoltz	.40
97	*Mark Mulder*	1.00
98	Kerry Wood	.75
99	Barry Bonds	1.50
100	Ken Griffey Jr.	5.00
	Checklist folder	.05

1999 Topps Gold Label Black Parallel

Blacks are a parallel of the 100-card base set and are identical besides the black foil stamping and their insertion ratio. Variation #1 are seeded 1:8 packs, #2 1:16 and #3 1:32.

	MT
Variation 1:	2x to 3x
Inserted 1:8	
Variation 2:	3x to 4x
Inserted 1:16	
Variation 3:	5x to 8x
Inserted 1:32	

1999 Topps Gold Label Red Parallel

A parallel to the 100-card base set these inserts can be idenified by their red foil stamping and sequential numbering. Variation #1 are numbered to 100, #2 numbered to 50 and #3 numbered to 25.

	MT
Variation 1:	10x to 20x
Production 100 sets	
Variation 2:	20x to 35x
Production 50 sets	
Variation 3:	40x to 60x
Production 25 sets	

1999 Topps Gold Label One to One

Depending on type of packaging, these rare parallels are found at the rate of only one per approximately 1,200-1,600 packs. Each of the three Classes in Gold, Red and Black versions can be found as a One to One insert, for a total of nine "unique" cards for each player in the base set and three in the Race to Aaron insert series. Backs of the One to One cards are printed in silver foil with a "1/1" foil serial number.

	MT
Common Player, Base Set:	50.00
Common Player, Race to Aaron:	150.00

(Star/rookie card values cannot be determined due to scarcity.)

1999 Topps Gold Label Race to Aaron

This 10-card set features the best current players who are chasing Hank Aaron's career home run and career RBI records. Each player is pictured in the foreground with Aaron silhouetted in the background on the card front. These are seeded 1:12 packs. Two parallel versions also exist: Black and Red. Blacks have black foil stamping and are seeded 1:48 packs. Reds have red foil stamping and are limited to 44 sequentially numbered sets.

		MT
Complete Set (10):		90.00
Common Player:		3.00
Blacks:		2X
Reds:		12X
1	Mark McGwire	20.00
2	Ken Griffey Jr.	20.00
3	Alex Rodriguez	15.00
4	Vladimir Guerrero	10.00
5	Albert Belle	3.00
6	Nomar Garciaparra	12.00
7	Ken Griffey Jr.	20.00
8	Alex Rodriguez	15.00
9	Juan Gonzalez	4.00
10	Barry Bonds	4.00

1999 Topps Stars

Topps Stars consists of 180 cards, on 20-point stock with foil stamping and metallic inks. Within the base set there are 150 base cards and 30 subset cards, Luminaries and Supernovas. Packs contain six cards; three base cards, two One-Star cards and one Two-Star card on the average.

		MT
Complete Set (180):		90.00
Common Player:		.25
Pack (6):		5.00
Wax Box (24):		100.00
1	Ken Griffey Jr.	5.00
2	Chipper Jones	2.50
3	Mike Piazza	2.50
4	Nomar Garciaparra	2.50
5	Derek Jeter	2.50
6	Frank Thomas	1.00
7	Ben Grieve	.75
8	Mark McGwire	5.00
9	Sammy Sosa	2.50
10	Alex Rodriguez	4.00
11	Troy Glaus	1.00
12	Eric Chavez	.50
13	Kerry Wood	.50
14	Barry Bonds	1.00
15	Vladimir Guerrero	1.50
16	Albert Belle	.75
17	Juan Gonzalez	1.00
18	Roger Clemens	1.50
19	Ruben Mateo	.75
20	Cal Ripken Jr.	3.75
21	Darin Erstad	.40
22	Jeff Bagwell	1.00
23	Roy Halladay	.25
24	Todd Helton	.75
25	Michael Barrett	.25
26	Manny Ramirez	1.00
27	Fernando Seguignol	.25
28	*Pat Burrell*	4.00
29	Andruw Jones	.75
30	Randy Johnson	.60
31	Jose Canseco	.60
32	Brad Fullmer	.25
33	*Alex Escobar*	1.25
34	*Alfonso Soriano*	2.00
35	Larry Walker	.60
36	Matt Clement	.25
37	Mo Vaughn	.50
38	Bruce Chen	.25
39	Travis Lee	.40
40	Adrian Beltre	.40
41	Alex Gonzalez	.25
42	*Jason Tyner*	.50
43	George Lombard	.25
44	Scott Rolen	1.00
45	*Mark Mulder*	1.25
46	Gabe Kapler	1.00
47	*Choo Freeman*	.60
48	Tony Gwynn	2.00
49	*A.J. Burnett*	1.00
50	*Matt Belisle*	.40
51	Greg Maddux	2.00
52	John Smoltz	.25
53	Mark Grace	.40
54	Wade Boggs	.40
55	Bernie Williams	.50
56	Pedro Martinez	1.00
57	Barry Larkin	.50
58	Orlando Hernandez	.40
59	Jason Kendall	.25
60	Mark Kotsay	.25
61	Jim Thome	.50
62	Gary Sheffield	.25
63	Preston Wilson	.25
64	Rafael Palmeiro	.60
65	David Wells	.25
66	Shawn Green	.75
67	Tom Glavine	.25
68	Jeromy Burnitz	.25
69	Kevin Brown	.40
70	Rondell White	.40
71	Roberto Alomar	.60
72	Cliff Floyd	.25
73	Craig Biggio	.60
74	Greg Vaughn	.25
75	Ivan Rodriguez	1.00
76	Vinny Castilla	.25
77	Todd Walker	.25
78	Paul Konerko	.25
79	*Andy Brown*	.40
80	Todd Hundley	.25
81	Dmitri Young	.25
82	Tony Clark	.50
83	*Nick Johnson*	2.50
84	Mike Caruso	.25
85	David Ortiz	.25
86	Matt Williams	.50
87	Raul Mondesi	.25
88	Kenny Lofton	.50
89	Miguel Tejada	.25
90	Dante Bichette	.40
91	Jorge Posada	.25
92	Carlos Beltran	.25
93	Carlos Delgado	.50
94	Javy Lopez	.25
95	Aramis Ramirez	.25
96	Neifi Perez	.25
97	Marlon Anderson	.25
98	David Cone	.25
99	Moises Alou	.25
100	John Olerud	.40
101	Tim Salmon	.25
102	Jason Giambi	.25
103	Sandy Alomar	.25
104	Curt Schilling	.25
105	Andres Galarraga	.50
106	Rusty Greer	.25
107	*Bobby Seay*	.40
108	Eric Young	.25
109	Brian Jordan	.25
110	Eric Davis	.25
111	Will Clark	.40
112	Andy Ashby	.25
113	Edgardo Alfonzo	.50
114	Paul O'Neill	.25
115	Denny Neagle	.25
116	Eric Karros	.25
117	Ken Caminiti	.25
118	Garret Anderson	.25
119	Todd Stottlemyre	.25
120	David Justice	.25
121	Francisco Cordova	.25
122	Robin Ventura	.25
123	Mike Mussina	.50
124	Hideki Irabu	.25
125	Justin Thompson	.25
126	Mariano Rivera	.25
127	Delino DeShields	.25
128	Steve Finley	.25
129	Jose Cruz Jr.	.25
130	Ray Lankford	.25
131	Jim Edmonds	.25
132	Charles Johnson	.25
133	Al Leiter	.25
134	Jose Offerman	.25
135	Eric Milton	.25
136	Dean Palmer	.25
137	Johnny Damon	.25
138	Andy Pettitte	.25
139	Ray Durham	.25
140	Ugueth Urbina	.25
141	Marquis Grissom	.25
142	Ryan Klesko	.25
143	Brady Anderson	.25
144	Bobby Higginson	.25
145	Chuck Knoblauch	.40
146	Rickey Henderson	.40
147	Kevin Millwood	.40
148	Fred McGriff	.25
149	Damion Easley	.25
150	Tino Martinez	.25
151	Greg Maddux (Luminaries)	1.00
152	Scott Rolen (Luminaries)	.50
153	Pat Burrell (Luminaries)	2.00
154	Roger Clemens (Luminaries)	.60
155	Albert Belle (Luminaries)	.40
156	Troy Glaus (Luminaries)	.50
157	Cal Ripken Jr. (Luminaries)	2.00
158	Alfonso Soriano (Luminaries)	1.00
159	Manny Ramirez (Luminaries)	.50
160	Eric Chavez (Luminaries)	.25
161	Kerry Wood (Luminaries)	.25
162	Tony Gwynn (Luminaries)	1.00
163	Barry Bonds (Luminaries)	.50
164	Ruben Mateo (Luminaries)	.40
165	Todd Helton (Luminaries)	.25
166	Darin Erstad (Luminaries)	.25
167	Jeff Bagwell (Luminaries)	.50
168	Juan Gonzalez (Luminaries)	.50
169	Mo Vaughn (Luminaries)	.25
170	Vladimir Guerrero (Luminaries)	.75
171	Nomar Garciaparra (Supernovas)	1.25
172	Derek Jeter (Supernovas)	1.25
173	Alex Rodriguez (Supernovas)	2.00
174	Ben Grieve (Supernovas)	.25
175	Mike Piazza (Supernovas)	1.25
176	Chipper Jones (Supernovas)	1.25
177	Frank Thomas (Supernovas)	.50
178	Ken Griffey Jr. (Supernovas)	2.00
179	Sammy Sosa (Supernovas)	1.50

180	Mark McGwire (Supernovas)	2.50
	Checklist 1 (1-45)	.05
	Checklist 2 (46-136)	.05
	Checklist 3 (137-150, inserts)	.05

1999 Topps Stars Foil

Metallic foil in the background and a serial number on back from within a specific edition identifies this parallel. Stated odds of insertion were one in 15 packs for parallels of the 180 base cards, numbered to 299 each. One-Star foil parallels are numbered to 249 and inserted 1:33. The Two-Star Foils are numbered to 199 each and found on average of one per 82 packs. With insertion odds of 1:410, the Three-Star Foil parallels are numbered within an edition of 99. At the top of the scarcity scale, the Foil Four-Star parallels are sequentially numbered to 49 and are a one per 650-pack find.

	MT
Complete Base Set (180):	125.00
Common Foil Player:	.25
Foil Stars:	4X
One-Star Foils:	10X
Two-Star Foils:	12X
Three-Star Foils:	15X
Four-Star Foils:	25X
(Stars/rookies valued about 3-8X base card values.)	

1999 Topps Stars One-Star

One-Star inserts include card numbers 1-100 from the base set and have silver foil stamping with one star on the bottom left portion of the card front. These are seeded two per pack. A foil One-Star parallel also is randomly seeded and sequentially numbered to 249 sets. These are a 1:33 pack insert.

		MT
Complete Set (100):		40.00
Common Player:		.25
Foils (249 each):		10X
1	Ken Griffey Jr.	4.00
2	Chipper Jones	2.00
3	Mike Piazza	2.50
4	Nomar Garciaparra	2.50
5	Derek Jeter	2.50
6	Frank Thomas	1.50
7	Ben Grieve	.75
8	Mark McGwire	5.00
9	Sammy Sosa	2.50
10	Alex Rodriguez	3.00
11	Troy Glaus	1.00
12	Eric Chavez	.50
13	Kerry Wood	.50
14	Barry Bonds	1.00
15	Vladimir Guerrero	1.50
16	Albert Belle	.75
17	Juan Gonzalez	2.00
18	Roger Clemens	1.50
19	Ruben Mateo	.75
20	Cal Ripken Jr.	3.00
21	Darin Erstad	.75
22	Jeff Bagwell	1.00
23	Roy Halladay	.25
24	Todd Helton	.75
25	Michael Barrett	.25
26	Manny Ramirez	1.00
27	Fernando Seguignol	.25
28	Pat Burrell	4.00
29	Andruw Jones	.75
30	Randy Johnson	.75
31	Jose Canseco	.75
32	Brad Fullmer	.25
33	Alex Escobar	2.00
34	Alfonso Soriano	1.50
35	Larry Walker	.75
36	Matt Clement	.25
37	Mo Vaughn	.75
38	Bruce Chen	.25
39	Travis Lee	.60
40	Adrian Beltre	.50
41	Alex Gonzalez	.25
42	Jason Tyner	.60
43	George Lombard	.25
44	Scott Rolen	1.00
45	Mark Mulder	2.00
46	Gabe Kapler	1.00
47	Choo Freeman	.50
48	Tony Gwynn	2.00
49	A.J. Burnett	1.00
50	Matt Belisle	.75
51	Greg Maddux	2.50
52	John Smoltz	.25
53	Mark Grace	.40
54	Wade Boggs	.40
55	Bernie Williams	.75
56	Pedro Martinez	1.00
57	Barry Larkin	.40
58	Orlando Hernandez	.40
59	Jason Kendall	.25
60	Mark Kotsay	.25
61	Jim Thome	.60
62	Gary Sheffield	.40
63	Preston Wilson	.25
64	Rafael Palmeiro	.75
65	David Wells	.25
66	Shawn Green	.60
67	Tom Glavine	.25
68	Jeromy Burnitz	.25
69	Kevin Brown	.40
70	Rondell White	.40
71	Roberto Alomar	.75
72	Cliff Floyd	.25
73	Craig Biggio	.60
74	Greg Vaughn	.40
75	Ivan Rodriguez	1.00
76	Vinny Castilla	.25
77	Todd Walker	.25
78	Paul Konerko	.25
79	*Andy Brown*	.50
80	Todd Hundley	.25
81	Dmitri Young	.25
82	Tony Clark	.50
83	*Nick Johnson*	2.00
84	Mike Caruso	.25
85	David Ortiz	.25
86	Matt Williams	.50
87	Raul Mondesi	.40
88	Kenny Lofton	.75
89	Miguel Tejada	.25
90	Dante Bichette	.40
91	Jorge Posada	.40
92	Carlos Beltran	.25
93	Carlos Delgado	.75
94	Javy Lopez	.25
95	Aramis Ramirez	.25
96	Neifi Perez	.25
97	Marlon Anderson	.25
98	David Cone	.25
99	Moises Alou	.25
100	John Olerud	.40

1999 Topps Stars Two-Star

Two-Stars are inserted one per pack and feature light gold metallic inks and foil stamping. Two-Stars include card numbers 1-50 from the base set. A Two-Star parallel is also randomly seeded and limited to 199 sequentially numbered sets.

		MT
Complete Set (50):		30.00
Common Player:		.25
Foils:		12X
1	Ken Griffey Jr.	4.00
2	Chipper Jones	2.00
3	Mike Piazza	2.50
4	Nomar Garciaparra	2.50
5	Derek Jeter	2.50
6	Frank Thomas	1.50
7	Ben Grieve	.75
8	Mark McGwire	5.00
9	Sammy Sosa	2.50
10	Alex Rodriguez	3.00
11	Troy Glaus	1.00
12	Eric Chavez	.60
13	Kerry Wood	.50
14	Barry Bonds	1.00
15	Vladimir Guerrero	1.50
16	Albert Belle	.75
17	Juan Gonzalez	2.00
18	Roger Clemens	1.50
19	Ruben Mateo	.75
20	Cal Ripken Jr.	3.00
21	Darin Erstad	.75
22	Jeff Bagwell	1.00
23	Roy Halladay	.25
24	Todd Helton	.75
25	Michael Barrett	.25
26	Manny Ramirez	1.00
27	Fernando Seguignol	.25
28	Pat Burrell	3.00
29	Andruw Jones	.75
30	Randy Johnson	.75
31	Jose Canseco	.75
32	Brad Fullmer	.25
33	Alex Escobar	2.00
34	Alfonso Soriano	2.00
35	Larry Walker	.75
36	Matt Clement	.25
37	Mo Vaughn	.75
38	Bruce Chen	.25
39	Travis Lee	.50
40	Adrian Beltre	.40
41	Alex Gonzalez	.25
42	Jason Tyner	.50
43	George Lombard	.25
44	Scott Rolen	1.00
45	Mark Mulder	2.00
46	Gabe Kapler	1.00
47	Choo Freeman	.50
48	Tony Gwynn	2.00
49	A.J. Burnett	1.00
50	Matt Belisle	.75

1999 Topps Stars Three-Star

Three-Star inserts are a partial parallel from the base set including cards 1-20. Inserted 1:5 packs, these cards feature refractive silver foil stamping along with gold metallic inks. A Three-Star parallel also is randomly inserted featuring gold stamping and limited to 99 serial numbered sets, inserted one per 410 packs.

		MT
Complete Set (20):		60.00
Common Player:		1.00
Foils (99 each):		15X
1	Ken Griffey Jr.	8.00
2	Chipper Jones	4.00
3	Mike Piazza	5.00
4	Nomar Garciaparra	5.00
5	Derek Jeter	5.00
6	Frank Thomas	3.00
7	Ben Grieve	1.50
8	Mark McGwire	10.00
9	Sammy Sosa	5.00
10	Alex Rodriguez	6.00
11	Troy Glaus	2.00
12	Eric Chavez	1.00
13	Kerry Wood	1.00
14	Barry Bonds	2.00
15	Vladimir Guerrero	3.00
16	Albert Belle	1.50
17	Juan Gonzalez	4.00
18	Roger Clemens	3.00
19	Ruben Mateo	1.50
20	Cal Ripken Jr.	6.00

1999 Topps Stars Four-Star

Four-Star inserts include cards numbered 1-10 from the base set and are seeded 1:10 packs. The cards feature dark metallic inks and refractive foil stamping on front. A Four-Star parallel is also randomly seeded and has gold metallic inks. Sequentially numbered to 49, it is inserted at the rate of one per 650 packs.

		MT
Complete Set (10):		40.00
Common Player:		1.50
Foils (49 each):		25X
1	Ken Griffey Jr.	8.00
2	Chipper Jones	4.00
3	Mike Piazza	5.00
4	Nomar Garciaparra	5.00
5	Derek Jeter	5.00
6	Frank Thomas	3.00
7	Ben Grieve	1.50
8	Mark McGwire	10.00
9	Sammy Sosa	5.00
10	Alex Rodriguez	6.00

1999 Topps Stars Bright Futures

This 10-card set features top prospects with a brilliant future ahead of them. Each card features foil stamping and is sequentially numbered to 1,999. Cards have a "BF" prefix to the number. A metallized foil parallel version is also randomly seeded (1:2702) and limited to 30 numbered sets.

	MT
Complete Set (10):	50.00
Common Player:	2.00
Production 1,999 sets	

Foil (30 each):		8X
1	Troy Glaus	8.00
2	Eric Chavez	4.00
3	Adrian Beltre	4.00
4	Michael Barrett	4.00
5	Fernando Seguignol	2.00
6	Alex Gonzalez	3.00
7	Matt Clement	2.00
8	Pat Burrell	15.00
9	Ruben Mateo	4.00
10	Alfonso Soriano	8.00

1999 Topps Stars Galaxy

This 10-card set highlights the top players in baseball with foil stamping and limited to 1,999 numbered sets, inserted at the rate of one per 41 packs. Each card is numbered on the back with a "G" prefix. A Galaxy parallel version is randomly seeded (1:2,702) and sequentially numbered to 30 sets.

		MT
Complete Set (10):		150.00
Common Player:		5.00
Production 1,999 sets		
Foil (30 each):		8X
1	Mark McGwire	30.00
2	Roger Clemens	10.00
3	Nomar Garciaparra	20.00
4	Alex Rodriguez	25.00
5	Kerry Wood	5.00
6	Ben Grieve	5.00
7	Derek Jeter	20.00
8	Vladimir Guerrero	12.00
9	Ken Griffey Jr.	30.00
10	Sammy Sosa	20.00

1999 Topps Stars Rookie Reprints

Topps reprinted five Hall of Famers' rookie cards. The rookie reprints are inserted 1:65 packs and limited to 2,500 numbered sets.

		MT
Complete Set (5):		50.00
Common Player:		10.00
Production 2,500 sets		
1	Frank Robinson	10.00
2	Ernie Banks	12.50
3	Yogi Berra	12.50
4	Bob Gibson	10.00
5	Tom Seaver	17.50

1999 Topps Stars Rookie Reprints Autographs

These foil stamped inserts feature the "Topps Certified Autograph Issue" stamp and are inserted 1:406 packs. The Ernie Banks autograph is inserted 1:812 packs.

		MT
Complete Set (5):		400.00
Common Player:		60.00
Inserted 1:406		
Banks inserted 1:812		
1	Frank Robinson	80.00
2	Ernie Banks	90.00
3	Yogi Berra	80.00
4	Bob Gibson	60.00
5	Tom Seaver	125.00

1999 Topps TEK

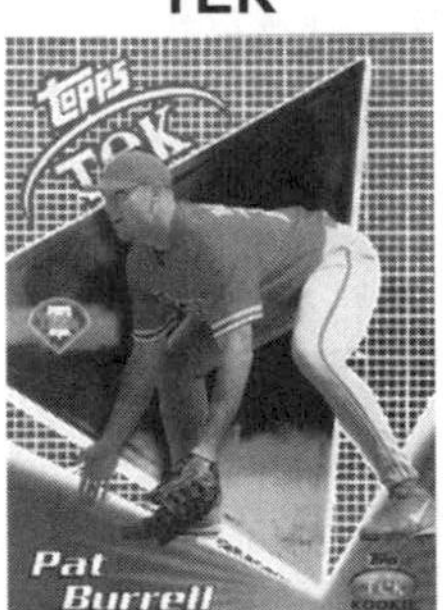

Topps TEK baseball contains 45 players, with all cards printed on a transparent, 27-point stock. Each player is featured in two different versions (A & B), which are noted on the card back. The versions are differentiated by type of player uniform (home is version A and away uniforms are version B). Each version also has 30 different baseball focused background patterns; as a result every player in the 45-card set has 60 total cards. There also is a Gold parallel set that has a gold design and all versions are paralleled. Each gold card is numbered to 10, with an insertion rate of 1:15 packs.

		MT
Complete Set (45):		80.00
Common Player:		.50
Gold (10 each variation):		8X
Pack (4):		5.00
Wax Box (20):		90.00
1	Ben Grieve	1.50
2	Andres Galarraga	1.50
3	Travis Lee	1.00
4	Larry Walker	2.00
5	Ken Griffey Jr.	10.00
6	Sammy Sosa	6.00
7	Mark McGwire	10.00
8	Roberto Alomar	2.00
9	Wade Boggs	1.00
10	Troy Glaus	2.00
11	Craig Biggio	1.50
12	Kerry Wood	1.50
13	Vladimir Guerrero	4.00
14	Albert Belle	2.50
15	Mike Piazza	6.00
16	Chipper Jones	5.00
17	Randy Johnson	2.00
18	Adrian Beltre	1.00
19	Barry Bonds	2.50
20	Jim Thome	1.50
21	Greg Vaughn	.75
22	Scott Rolen	2.50
23	Ivan Rodriguez	2.50
24	Derek Jeter	6.00
25	Cal Ripken Jr.	7.50
26	Mark Grace	.75
27	Bernie Williams	2.00
28	Darin Erstad	1.00
29	Eric Chavez	1.00
30	Tom Glavine	.75
31	Jeff Bagwell	2.50
32	Manny Ramirez	2.50
33	Tino Martinez	1.50
34	Todd Helton	1.50
35	Jason Kendall	.75
36	*Pat Burrell*	6.00
37	Tony Gwynn	5.00
38	Nomar Garciaparra	6.00
39	Frank Thomas	3.00
40	Orlando Hernandez	1.00
41	Juan Gonzalez	2.50
42	Alex Rodriguez	8.00
43	Greg Maddux	5.00
44	Mo Vaughn	2.00
45	Roger Clemens	3.00
	Version A checklist folder (orange)	.05
	Version B checklist folder (green)	.05

1999 Topps TEK Gold

Each of the two player versions on each of the 30 background patterns was paralleled in a gold insert version. Cards share the same front and back designs and photos but feature gold graphics. Each card is serially numbered within an edition of just 10. Insertion rate is one per 15 packs.

	MT
Gold Parallels	5X-8X

(See 1999 Topps TEK for checklist, base card values.)

1999 Topps TEK Teknicians

This 10-card set focuses on baseball's top stars on a clear, plastic stock utilizing metallic blue, silver and red inks. These are inserted 1:18 packs.

		MT
Complete Set (10):		90.00
Common Player:		2.00
Inserted 1:18		
T1	Ken Griffey Jr.	20.00
T2	Mark McGwire	20.00
T3	Kerry Wood	4.00
T4	Ben Grieve	4.00
T5	Sammy Sosa	12.00
T6	Derek Jeter	12.00
T7	Alex Rodriguez	15.00
T8	Roger Clemens	6.00
T9	Nomar Garciaparra	12.00
T10	Vladimir Guerrero	8.00

1999 Topps TEK Fantastek Phenoms

This 10-card set highlights top young prospects on a transparent plastic stock with silver and blue highlighting. These are inserted 1:18 packs.

		MT
Complete Set (10):		35.00
Common Player:		2.00
Inserted 1:18		
F1	Eric Chavez	3.00
F2	Troy Glaus	8.00
F3	Pat Burrell	15.00
F4	Alex Gonzalez	2.00
F5	Carlos Lee	2.00
F6	Ruben Mateo	3.00
F7	Carlos Beltran	2.00
F8	Adrian Beltre	4.00
F9	Bruce Chen	2.00
F10	Ryan Anderson	4.00

1999 Topps Stars 'N Steel

Using Serilusion technology, each borderless card features a four-colored textured film laminate bonded to a sheet of strong 25-gauge metal. Each pack contains three cards, packaged in a stand-up tri-fold display unit, at a SRP of $9.99. There are two parallels to the 44-card set, Gold and Holographics. Golds are seeded 1:12 packs, Holographics are found every 24 packs.

		MT
Complete Set (44):		125.00
Common Player:		2.00
Gold:		2X
Inserted 1:12		
Pack (3):		10.00
Wax Box (12):		120.00
1	Kerry Wood	4.00
2	Ben Grieve	4.00
3	Chipper Jones	12.00
4	Alex Rodriguez	20.00
5	Mo Vaughn	4.00
6	Bernie Williams	4.00
7	Juan Gonzalez	6.00
8	Vinny Castilla	2.00
9	Tony Gwynn	12.00
10	Manny Ramirez	6.00
11	Raul Mondesi	2.00
12	Roger Clemens	10.00
13	Darin Erstad	2.50
14	Barry Bonds	6.00
15	Cal Ripken Jr.	20.00
16	Barry Larkin	3.00
17	Scott Rolen	6.00
18	Albert Belle	4.00
19	Craig Biggio	4.00
20	Tony Clark	2.50
21	Mark McGwire	25.00
22	Andres Galarraga	3.00
23	Kenny Lofton	4.00
24	Pedro Martinez	6.00
25	Paul O'Neill	2.00
26	Ken Griffey Jr.	25.00
27	Travis Lee	2.50
28	Tim Salmon	3.00
29	Frank Thomas	6.00
30	Larry Walker	4.00
31	Moises Alou	2.00
32	Vladimir Guerrero	10.00
33	Ivan Rodriguez	6.00
34	Derek Jeter	15.00
35	Greg Vaughn	3.00
36	Gary Sheffield	3.00
37	Carlos Delgado	3.00
38	Greg Maddux	12.00
39	Sammy Sosa	15.00
40	Mike Piazza	15.00
41	Nomar Garciaparra	15.00
42	Dante Bichette	3.00
43	Jeff Bagwell	6.00
44	Jim Thome	3.00

1999 Topps Stars 'N Steel Gold Domed Holographics

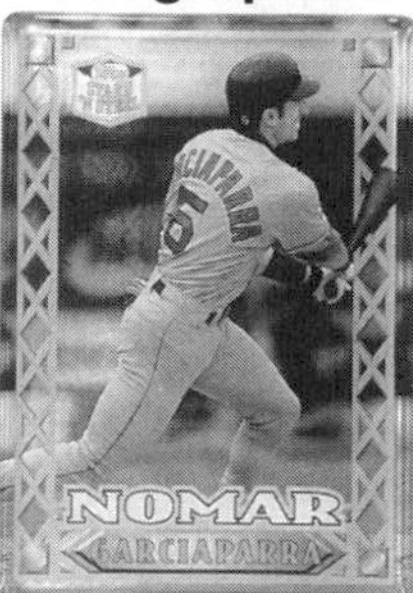

This parallel edition was inserted at a rate of one per box. Cards are basically the same as the regular-issue, except for the use of holographic foil highlights on front and the presence of a thick plastic dome which covers the front.

	MT
Complete Set (44):	1500.
Common Player:	6.00
Stars:	4X

(See 1999 Topps Stars 'N Steel for checklist and base card values.)

1999 Topps Chrome Traded and Rookies

Actually issued in 2000, this parallel of the Topps Traded set utilizing Chromium technology was issued only in complete set form.

		MT
Complete Set (121):		100.00
Common Player:		.40
1	*Seth Etherton*	1.50
2	*Mark Harriger*	1.50
3	*Matt Wise*	1.50
4	*Carlos Hernandez*	1.50
5	*Julio Lugo*	2.00
6	*Mike Nannini*	2.00
7	*Justin Bowles*	1.00
8	*Mark Mulder*	3.00
9	*Roberto Vaz*	1.50
10	*Felipe Lopez*	4.00
11	*Matt Belisle*	2.50
12	Micah Bowie	.40
13	*Ruben Quevedo*	2.00
14	*Jose Garcia*	1.50
15	*David Kelton*	3.00
16	*Phillip Norton*	1.00
17	*Corey Patterson*	15.00
18	*Ron Walker*	1.50
19	*Paul Hoover*	1.25
20	*Ryan Rupe*	2.00
21	*J.D. Closser*	1.50
22	*Rob Ryan*	1.00
23	*Steve Colyer*	1.50
24	*Bubba Crosby*	1.50
25	*Luke Prokopec*	3.00
26	*Matt Blank*	1.25
27	*Josh McKinley*	2.00
28	*Nate Bump*	1.50
29	*Giuseppe Chiaramonte*	2.50
30	*Arturo McDowell*	2.00
31	*Tony Torcato*	2.50
32	Dave Roberts	.75
33	*C.C. Sabathia*	5.00
34	*Sean Spencer*	1.50
35	*Chip Ambres*	2.00
36	*A.J. Burnett*	3.00
37	*Mo Bruce*	1.50
38	*Jason Tyner*	2.00
39	*Mamon Tucker*	2.00
40	*Sean Burroughs*	10.00
41	*Kevin Eberwein*	1.00
42	*Junior Herndon*	1.00
43	*Bryan Wolff*	1.00
44	*Pat Burrell*	15.00
45	*Eric Valent*	3.00
46	*Carlos Pena*	5.00
47	*Mike Zywica*	1.00
48	*Adam Everett*	2.00
49	*Juan Pena*	1.50
50	*Adam Dunn*	8.00
51	*Austin Kearns*	6.00
52	*Jacobo Sequea*	1.00
53	*Choo Freeman*	2.00
54	*Jeff Winchester*	2.00
55	*Matt Burch*	1.50
56	*Chris George*	2.00
57	*Scott Mullen*	1.00
58	*Kit Pellow*	1.50
59	*Mark Quinn*	4.00
60	*Nate Cornejo*	2.00
61	*Ryan Mills*	1.00
62	*Kevin Beirne*	1.00
63	*Kip Wells*	2.50
64	*Juan Rivera*	2.50
65	*Alfonso Soriano*	6.00
66	*Josh Hamilton*	20.00
67	*Josh Girdley*	2.50
68	*Kyle Snyder*	1.50
69	*Mike Paradis*	1.50
70	*Jason Jennings*	2.00
71	*David Walling*	2.00
72	*Omar Ortiz*	1.00
73	*Jay Gehrke*	1.50
74	*Casey Burns*	1.00
75	*Carl Crawford*	4.00
76	Reggie Sanders	.40
77	Will Clark	.75
78	David Wells	.40
79	Paul Konerko	.40
80	Armando Benitez	.40
81	Brant Brown	.40
82	Mo Vaughn	.75
83	Jose Canseco	1.50
84	Albert Belle	.75
85	Dean Palmer	.40
86	Greg Vaughn	.50
87	Mark Clark	.40
88	Pat Meares	.40
89	Eric Davis	.40
90	Brian Giles	.40
91	Jeff Brantley	.40
92	Bret Boone	.40
93	Ron Gant	.40
94	Mike Cameron	.40
95	Charles Johnson	.40
96	Denny Neagle	.40
97	Brian Hunter	.40
98	Jose Hernandez	.40
99	Rick Aguilera	.40
100	Tony Batista	.40
101	Roger Cedeno	.40
102	Creighton Gubanich	.40
103	Tim Belcher	.40
104	Bruce Aven	.40
105	*Brian Daubach*	2.00
106	Ed Sprague	.40
107	Michael Tucker	.40
108	Homer Bush	.40
109	Armando Reynoso	.40
110	Brook Fordyce	.40
111	Matt Mantei	.40
112	Jose Guillen	.40
113	Kenny Rogers	.40
114	Livan Hernandez	.40
115	Butch Huskey	.40
116	David Segui	.40
117	Darryl Hamilton	.40
118	Jim Leyritz	.40
119	Randy Velarde	.40
120	Bill Taylor	.40
121	Kevin Appier	.40

2000 Topps

Released in two series the card fronts have a silver border with the Topps logo, player name and position stamped with gold foil. Card backs have complete year-by-year statistics along with a small photo in the upper right portion and the player's vital information. Subsets within the first series 239-card set include Draft Picks, Prospects, Magic Moments, Season Highlights and 20th Century's Best. The Topps MVP promotion is a parallel of 200 of the base cards, excluding subsets, with a special Topps MVP logo. 100 cards of each player was produced and if the featured player is named MVP for a week, collectors win a prize.

		MT
Complete Set (478):		50.00
Complete Series I set (239):		25.00
Complete Series II set (239):		25.00
Common Player:		.10
MVP Stars:		30x to 60x
Yng Stars & RCs:		20x to 40x
Production 100 sets		
5 Versions for 236-240, 475-479		
Pack (11):		1.50
Wax Box (36):		45.00
1	Mark McGwire	2.50
2	Tony Gwynn	1.25
3	Wade Boggs	.25
4	Cal Ripken Jr.	2.00
5	Matt Williams	.25
6	Jay Buhner	.20
7	Not Issued	.10
8	Jeff Conine	.10
9	Todd Greene	.10
10	Mike Lieberthal	.10
11	Steve Avery	.10
12	Bret Saberhagen	.10
13	Magglio Ordonez	.20
14	Brad Radke	.10
15	Derek Jeter	1.25
16	Javy Lopez	.25
17	Russ David	.10
18	Armando Benitez	.10
19	B.J. Surhoff	.10
20	Darryl Kile	.10
21	Mark Lewis	.10
22	Mike Williams	.10
23	Mark McLemore	.10
24	Sterling Hitchcock	.10
25	Darin Erstad	.25
26	Ricky Gutierrez	.10
27	John Jaha	.10
28	Homer Bush	.10
29	Darrin Fletcher	.10
30	Mark Grace	.25
31	Fred McGriff	.25
32	Omar Daal	.10
33	Eric Karros	.20
34	Orlando Cabrera	.10
35	J.T. Snow Jr.	.10
36	Luis Castillo	.10
37	Rey Ordonez	.10
38	Bob Abreu	.10
39	Warren Morris	.10
40	Juan Gonzalez	.60
41	Mike Lansing	.10
42	Chili Davis	.10
43	Dean Palmer	.10
44	Hank Aaron	2.00

45 Jeff Bagwell .50
46 Jose Valentin .10
47 Shannon Stewart .10
48 Kent Bottenfield .10
49 Jeff Shaw .10
50 Sammy Sosa 1.25
51 Randy Johnson .40
52 Benny Agbayani .10
53 Dante Bichette .25
54 Pete Harnisch .10
55 Frank Thomas .60
56 Jorge Posada .10
57 Todd Walker .10
58 Juan Encarnacion .10
59 Mike Sweeney .10
60 Pedro Martinez .60
61 Lee Stevens .10
62 Brian Giles .10
63 Chad Ogea .10
64 Ivan Rodriguez .50
65 Roger Cedeno .10
66 David Justice .20
67 Steve Trachsel .10
68 Eli Marrero .10
69 Dave Nilsson .10
70 Ken Caminiti .20
71 Tim Raines .10
72 Brian Jordan .10
73 Jeff Blauser .10
74 Bernard Gilkey .10
75 John Flaherty .10
76 Brent Mayne .10
77 Jose Vidro .10
78 Jeff Fassero .10
79 Bruce Aven .10
80 John Olerud .25
81 Juan Guzman .10
82 Woody Williams .10
83 Ed Sprague .10
84 Joe Girardi .10
85 Barry Larkin .40
86 Mike Caruso .10
87 Bobby Higginson .10
88 Roberto Kelly .10
89 Edgar Martinez .20
90 Mark Kotsay .10
91 Paul Sorrento .10
92 Eric Young .10
93 Carlos Delgado .40
94 Troy Glaus .60
95 Ben Grieve .25
96 Jose Lima .10
97 Garret Anderson .10
98 Luis Gonzalez .10
99 Carl Pavano .10
100 Alex Rodriguez 1.25
101 Preston Wilson .10
102 Ron Gant .10
103 Harold Baines .10
104 Rickey Henderson .25
105 Gary Sheffield .25
106 Mickey Morandini .10
107 Jim Edmonds .10
108 Kris Benson .10
109 Adrian Beltre .25
110 Alex Fernandez .10
111 Dan Wilson .10
112 Mark Clark .10
113 Greg Vaughn .25
114 Neifi Perez .10
115 Paul O'Neill .25
116 Jermaine Dye .10
117 Todd Jones .10
118 Terry Steinbach .10
119 Greg Norton .10
120 Curt Schilling .20
121 Todd Zeile .10
122 Edgardo Alfonzo .25
123 Ryan McGuire .10
124 Stan Javier .10
125 John Smoltz .20
126 Bob Wickman .10
127 Richard Hidalgo .10
128 Chuck Finley .10
129 Billy Wagner .10
130 Todd Hundley .10
131 Dwight Gooden .10
132 Russ Ortiz .10
133 Mike Lowell .10
134 Reggie Sanders .10
135 John Valentin .10
136 Brad Ausmus .10
137 Chad Kreuter .10
138 David Cone .25
139 Brook Fordyce .10
140 Roberto Alomar .40
141 Charles Nagy .10
142 Brian Hunter .10
143 Mike Mussina .40
144 Robin Ventura .25
145 Kevin Brown .25
146 Pat Hentgen .10
147 Ryan Klesko .20
148 Derek Bell .10
149 Andy Sheets .10
150 Larry Walker .40
151 Scott Williamson .10
152 Jose Offerman .10
153 Doug Mientkiewicz .10
154 John Snyder .10
155 Sandy Alomar .25
156 Joe Nathan .10
157 Lance Johnson .10
158 Odalis Perez .10
159 Hideo Nomo .25
160 Steve Finley .10
161 Dave Martinez .10
162 Matt Walbeck .10
163 Bill Spiers .10
164 Fernando Tatis .25
165 Kenny Lofton .50
166 Paul Byrd .10
167 Aaron Sele .10
168 Eddie Taubensee .10
169 Reggie Jefferson .10
170 Roger Clemens 1.00
171 Francisco Cordova .10
172 Mike Bordick .10
173 Wally Joyner .10
174 Marvin Benard .10
175 Jason Kendall .10
176 Mike Stanley .10
177 Chad Allen .10
178 Carlos Beltran .15
179 Deivi Cruz .10
180 Chipper Jones 1.25
181 Vladimir Guerrero .75
182 Dave Burba .10
183 Tom Goodwin .10
184 Brian Daubach .10
185 Jay Bell .10
186 Roy Halladay .10
187 Miguel Tejada .10
188 Armando Rios .10
189 Fernando Vina .10
190 Eric Davis .10
191 Henry Rodriguez .10
192 Joe McEwing .10
193 Jeff Kent .10
194 Mike Jackson .10
195 Mike Morgan .10
196 Jeff Montgomery .10
197 Jeff Zimmerman .10
198 Tony Fernandez .10
199 Jason Giambi .10
200 Jose Canseco .50
201 Alex Gonzalez .10
202 Jack Cust, Mike Colangelo, Dee Brown .20
203 Felipe Lopez, Alfonso Soriano, Pablo Ozuna .40
204 Erubiel Durazo, Pat Burrell, Nick Johnson .50
205 *John Sneed*, Kip Wells, Matt Blank .40
206 *Josh Kalinowski*, *Michael Tejera*, Chris Mears .25
207 Roosevelt Brown, Corey Patterson, Lance Berkman .75
208 Kit Pellow, Kevin Barker, Russ Branyan .25
209 *B.J. Garbe*, *Larry Bigbie* 1.00
210 Eric Munson, *Bobby Bradley* 1.00
211 Josh Girdley, Kyle Snyder .40
212 *Chance Caple*, Jason Jennings .40
213 *Ryan Christiansen*, *Brett Myers* .40
214 *Jason Stumm*, *Rob Purvis* .50
215 David Walling, Mike Paradis .40
216 Omar Ortiz, Jay Gehrke .20
217 David Cone (Season Highlights) .10
218 Jose Jimenez (Season Highlights) .10
219 Chris Singleton (Season Highlights) .10
220 Fernando Tatis (Season Highlights) .10
221 Todd Helton (Season Highlights) .20
222 Kevin Millwood (Post-Season Highlights) .20
223 Todd Pratt (Post-Season Highlights) .10
224 Orlando Hernandez (Post-Season Highlights) .20
225 (Post-Season Highlights) .10
226 (Post-Season Highlights) .10
227 Bernie Williams (Post-Season Highlights) .40
228 Mariano Rivera (Post-Season Highlights) .20
229 Tony Gwynn (20th Century's Best) .50
230 Wade Boggs (20th Century's Best) .25
231 Tim Raines (20th Century's Best) .10
232 Mark McGwire (20th Century's Best) 2.00
233 Rickey Henderson (20th Century's Best) .25
234 Rickey Henderson (20th Century's Best) .25
235 Roger Clemens (20th Century's Best) .50
236 Mark McGwire (Magic Moments) 4.00
237 Hank Aaron (Magic Moments) 3.00
238 Cal Ripken Jr. (Magic Moments) 3.00
239 Wade Boggs (Magic Moments) .75
240 Tony Gwynn (Magic Moments) 2.00
Series 1 checklist (1-201) .05
Series 1 checklist (202-240, inserts) .05
241 Tom Glavine .25
242 David Wells .10
243 Kevin Appier .10
244 Troy Percival .10
245 Ray Lankford .10
246 Marquis Grissom .10
247 Randy Winn .10
248 Miguel Batista .10
249 Darren Dreifort .10
250 Barry Bonds .60
251 Harold Baines .10
252 Cliff Floyd .10
253 Freddy Garcia .20
254 Kenny Rogers .10
255 Ben Davis .10
256 Charles Johnson .10
257 John Burkett .10
258 Desi Relaford .10
259 Al Martin .10
260 Andy Pettitte .20
261 Carlos Lee .10
262 Matt Lawton .10
263 Andy Fox .10
264 Chan Ho Park .10
265 Billy Koch .10
266 Dave Roberts .10
267 Carl Everett .20
268 Orel Hershiser .10
269 Trot Nixon .10
270 Rusty Greer .10
271 Will Clark .25
272 Quilvio Veras .10
273 Rico Brogna .10
274 Devon White .10
275 Tim Hudson .25
276 Mike Hampton .10
277 Miguel Cairo .10
278 Darren Oliver .10
279 Jeff Cirillo .10
280 Al Leiter .20
281 Brant Brown .10
282 Carlos Febles .10
283 Pedro Astacio .10
284 Juan Guzman .10
285 Orlando Hernandez .25
286 Paul Konerko .20
287 Tony Clark .20
288 Aaron Boone .10
289 Ismael Valdes .10
290 Moises Alou .20
291 Kevin Tapani .10
292 John Franco .10
293 Todd Zeile .20
294 Jason Schmidt .10
295 Johnny Damon .10
296 Scott Brosius .10
297 Travis Fryman .20
298 Jose Vizcaino .10
299 Eric Chavez .20
300 Mike Piazza 1.50
301 Matt Clement .10
302 Cristian Guzman .10
303 Darryl Strawberry .20
304 Jeff Abbott .10
305 Brett Tomko .10
306 Mike Lansing .10
307 Eric Owens .10
308 Livan Hernandez .10
309 Rondell White .20
310 Todd Stottlemyre .20
311 Chris Carpenter .10
312 Ken Hill .10
313 Mark Loretta .10
314 John Rocker .10
315 Richie Sexson .10
316 Ruben Mateo .25
317 Ramon Martinez .10
318 Mike Sirotka .10
319 Jose Rosado .10
320 Matt Mantei .10
321 Kevin Millwood .20
322 Gary DiSarcina .10
323 Dustin Hermanson .10
324 Mike Stanton .10
325 Kirk Rueter .10
326 Damian Miller .10
327 Doug Glanville .10
328 Scott Rolen .60
329 Ray Durham .10
330 Butch Huskey .10
331 Mariano Rivera .20
332 Darren Lewis .10
333 Ramiro Mendoza .10
334 Mark Grudzielanek .10
335 Mike Cameron .10
336 Kelvim Escobar .10
337 Bret Boone .10
338 Mo Vaughn .40
339 Craig Biggio .40
340 Michael Barrett .10
341 Marlon Anderson .10
342 Bobby Jones .10
343 John Halama .10
344 Todd Ritchie .10
345 Chuck Knoblauch .20
346 Rick Reed .10
347 Kelly Stinnett .10
348 Tim Salmon .20
349 A.J. Hinch .10
350 Jose Cruz Jr. .10
351 Roberto Hernandez .10
352 Edgar Renteria .10
353 Jose Hernandez .10
354 Brad Fullmer .20
355 Trevor Hoffman .10
356 Troy O'Leary .10
357 Justin Thompson .10
358 Kevin Young .10
359 Hideki Irabu .10
360 Jim Thome .25
361 Todd Dunwoody .10
362 Octavio Dotel .10
363 Omar Vizquel .20
364 Raul Mondesi .20
365 Shane Reynolds .10
366 Bartolo Colon .20
367 Chris Widger .10
368 Gabe Kapler .20
369 Bill Simas .10
370 Tino Martinez .25
371 John Thomson .10
372 Delino DeShields .10
373 Carlos Perez .10
374 Eddie Perez .10
375 Jeromy Burnitz .20
376 Jimmy Haynes .10
377 Travis Lee .20
378 Darryl Hamilton .10
379 Jamie Moyer .10
380 Alex Gonzalez .10
381 John Wetteland .10
382 Vinny Castilla .20
383 Jeff Suppan .10
384 Chad Curtis .10
385 Robb Nen .10
386 Wilson Alvarez .10
387 Andres Galarraga .25
388 Mike Remlinger .10
389 Geoff Jenkins .20
390 Matt Stairs .10
391 Bill Mueller .10
392 Mike Lowell .10

393 Andy Ashby .10
394 Ruben Rivera .10
395 Todd Helton .25
396 Bernie Williams .50
397 Royce Clayton .10
398 Manny Ramirez .60
399 Kerry Wood .25
400 Ken Griffey Jr. 2.50
401 Enrique Wilson .10
402 Joey Hamilton .10
403 Shawn Estes .10
404 Ugueth Urbina .10
405 Albert Belle .40
406 Rick Helling .10
407 Steve Parris .10
408 Eric Milton .10
409 Dave Mlicki .10
410 Shawn Green .50
411 Jaret Wright .10
412 Tony Womack .10
413 Vernon Wells .10
414 Ron Belliard .10
415 Ellis Burks .10
416 Scott Erickson .10
417 Rafael Palmeiro .30
418 Damion Easley .10
419 Jamey Wright .10
420 Corey Koskie .10
421 Bobby Howry .10
422 Ricky Ledee .10
423 Dmitri Young .10
424 Sidney Ponson .10
425 Greg Maddux 1.25
426 Jose Guillen .10
427 Jon Lieber .10
428 Andy Benes .20
429 Randy Velarde .10
430 Sean Casey .25
431 Torii Hunter .10
432 Ryan Rupe .10
433 David Segui .10
434 Rich Aurilia .10
435 Nomar Garciaparra 1.50
436 Denny Neagle .10
437 Ron Coomer .10
438 Chris Singleton .10
439 Tony Batista .10
440 Andruw Jones .40
441 Adam Piatt, Aubrey Huff, Sean Burroughs (Prospects) .40
442 Rafael Furcal, Jason Dallero, Travis Dawkins (Prospects) .75
443 Wilton Veras, Joe Crede ,*Mike Lamb* (Prospects) .10
444 *Julio Zuleta*, Dernell Stenson, Jorge Toca (Prospects) .10
445 Tim Raines, Jr., Gary Mathews Jr., *Garry Maddox Jr.* (Prospects) .10
446 Matt Riley, Mark Mulder, C.C. Sabathia (Prospects) .10
447 *Scott Downs*, Chris George, Matt Belisle (Prospects) .10
448 Doug Mirabelli, Ben Petrick, Jayson Werth (Prospects) .10
449 Josh Hamilton, *Corey Myers* (Draft Picks) 1.00
450 *Ben Christensen*, *Brett Myers* (Draft Picks) .40
451 *Barry Zito*, *Ben Sheets* (Draft Picks) 1.50
452 *Ty Howington*, *Kurt Ainsworth* (Draft Picks) .25
453 *Rick Asadoorian*, *Vince Faison* (Draft Picks) 1.50
454 *Keith Reed*, *Jeff Heaverlo* (Draft Picks) .25
455 *Mike MacDougal*, Jay Gehrke (Draft Picks) .25
456 Mark McGwire (Season Highlights) 1.50
457 Cal Ripken Jr. (Season Highlights) 1.00
458 Wade Boggs (Season Highlights) .25
459 Tony Gwynn (Season Highlights) .75
460 Jesse Orosco (Season Highlights) .10
461 Nomar Garciaparra, Larry Walker (League Leaders) .50
462 Mark McGwire, Ken Griffey Jr. (League Leaders) 1.00
463 Mark McGwire, Manny Ramirez 0(League Leaders) .75
464 Randy Johnson, Pedro Martinez (League Leaders) .25
465 Randy Johnson, Pedro Martinez (League Leaders) .25
466 Luis Gonzalez, Derek Jeter (League Leaders) .50
467 Manny Ramirez, Larry Walker (League Leaders) .25
468 Tony Gwynn (20th Century's Best) 1.00
469 Mark McGwire (20th Century's Best) 2.00
470 Frank Thomas (20th Century's Best) .75
471 Harold Baines (20th Century's Best) .10
472 Roger Clemens (20th Century's Best) .75
473 John Franco (20th Century's Best) .10
474 John Franco (20th Century's Best) .10
475 Ken Griffey Jr. (Magic Moments) 4.00
476 Barry Bonds (Magic Moments) 1.00
477 Sammy Sosa (Magic Moments) 2.50
478 Derek Jeter (Magic Moments) 2.50
479 Alex Rodriguez (Magic Moments) 2.50

2000 Topps All-Star Rookie Team

		MT
Complete Set (10):		35.00
Common Player:		.50
Inserted 1:36		
1	Mark McGwire	8.00
2	Chuck Knoblauch	1.00
3	Chipper Jones	4.00
4	Cal Ripken Jr.	6.00
5	Manny Ramirez	2.00
6	Jose Canseco	2.00
7	Ken Griffey Jr.	8.00
8	Mike Piazza	5.00
9	Dwight Gooden	.50
10	Billy Wagner	.50

2000 Topps All-Topps Team

This insert set spotlights 10 National League (Series 1) and 10 A.L. (Series 2) players who are deemed the best at their respective position. On front, a Hall of Fame style plaque design features gold-foil highlights. Backs offer stat comparisons to contemporary players and Hall of Fame greats at their position. These were seeded 1:12 packs. Cards are numbered with an "AT" prefix.

		MT
Complete Set (20):		25.00
Common Player:		.50
Inserted 1:12		
1	Greg Maddux	2.00
2	Mike Piazza	2.50
3	Mark McGwire	4.00
4	Craig Biggio	.50
5	Chipper Jones	2.00
6	Barry Larkin	.50
7	Barry Bonds	1.00
8	Andruw Jones	.75
9	Sammy Sosa	2.50
10	Larry Walker	.75
11	Pedro Martinez	1.00
12	Ivan Rodriguez	1.00
13	Rafael Palmeiro	.75
14	Roberto Alomar	.75
15	Cal Ripken Jr.	3.00
16	Derek Jeter	2.50
17	Albert Belle	.75
18	Ken Griffey Jr.	4.00
19	Manny Ramirez	1.00
20	Jose Canseco	1.00

2000 Topps Autographs

Inserted exclusively in Series 1 and 2 hobby packs, each card features the "Topps Certified Autograph Issue" stamp and is autographed on the card front.

		MT
Common Player:		15.00
Group A 1:7,589		
Group B 1:4,553		
Group C 1:518		
Group D 1:911		
Group E 1:1,138		
1	Alex Rodriguez (A)	275.00
2	Tony Gwynn (A)	175.00
3	Vinny Castilla (B)	50.00
4	Sean Casey (B)	20.00
5	Shawn Green (C)	50.00
6	Rey Ordonez (C)	20.00
7	Matt Lawton (C)	15.00
8	Tony Womack (C)	15.00
9	Gabe Kapler (D)	20.00
10	Pat Burrell (D)	50.00
11	Preston Wilson (D)	25.00
12	Troy Glaus (D)	30.00
13	Carlos Beltran (D)	15.00
14	Josh Girdley (E)	15.00
15	B.J. Garbe (E)	25.00
16	Derek Jeter (A)	200.00
17	Cal Ripken Jr. (A)	250.00
18	Ivan Rodriguez (B)	75.00
19	Rafael Palmeiro (B)	50.00
20	Vladimir Guerrero (E)	80.00
21	Raul Mondesi (C)	20.00
22	Scott Rolen (C)	40.00
23	Billy Wagner (C)	15.00
24	Fernando Tatis (C)	25.00
25	Ruben Mateo (D)	20.00
26	Carlos Febles (D)	15.00
27	Mike Sweeney (E)	20.00
28	Alex Gonzalez (D)	15.00
29	Miguel Tejada (D)	20.00
30	Josh Hamilton (E)	40.00

2000 Topps Century Best

		MT
Common Player:		15.00
Ser. 1 1:869 H		
Ser. 2 1:362		
CB1	Tony Gwynn (339)	80.00
CB2	Wade Boggs (578)	35.00
CB3	Lance Johnson (117)	20.00
CB4	Mark McGwire (522)	90.00
CB5	Rickey Henderson (1,334)	20.00
CB6	Rickey Henderson (2,103)	15.00
CB7	Roger Clemens (247)	80.00
CB8	Tony Gwynn (3,067)	25.00
CB9	Mark McGwire (587)	90.00
CB10	Frank Thomas (440)	40.00
CB11	Harold Baines (1,583)	15.00
CB12	Roger Clemens (3,316)	25.00
CB13	John Franco (264)	25.00
CB14	John Franco (416)	20.00

The values of some parallel-card issues will have to be calculated based on figures presented in the heading for the regular-issue card set.

2000 Topps Combos

		MT
Complete Set (10):		40.00
Common Player:		1.00
Inserted 1:18		
1	Roberto Alomar, Manny Ramirez, Kenny Lofton, Jim Thome	2.00
2	Tom Glavine, Greg Maddux, John Smoltz	4.00
3	Derek Jeter, Bernie Williams, Tino Martinez	5.00
4	Ivan Rodriguez, Mike Piazza	5.00
5	Nomar Garciaparra, Alex Rodriguez, Derek Jeter	6.00
6	Sammy Sosa, Mark McGwire	8.00
7	Pedro Martinez, Randy Johnson	2.00
8	Barry Bonds, Ken Griffey Jr.	8.00
9	Chipper Jones, Ivan Rodriguez	4.00
10	Cal Ripken Jr., Tony Gwynn, Wade Boggs	6.00

2000 Topps Hank Aaron Chrome Reprints

This 23-card set reprints Aaron's regular issued Topps cards utilizing Chromium technology. Each card has a commemorative logo and are seeded 1:72 packs. A Refractor parallel version is also randomly inserted 1:288 packs and have Refractor printed underneath the number on the card back.

		MT
Complete Set (23):		200.00
Common Aaron:		8.00
Inserted 1:72		
Refractors:		2x to 3x
Inserted 1:288		
1	Hank Aaron - 1954	20.00
2	Hank Aaron - 1955	8.00
3	Hank Aaron - 1956	8.00
4	Hank Aaron - 1957	8.00
5	Hank Aaron - 1958	8.00
6	Hank Aaron - 1959	8.00
7	Hank Aaron - 1960	8.00
8	Hank Aaron - 1961	8.00
9	Hank Aaron - 1962	8.00
10	Hank Aaron - 1963	8.00
11	Hank Aaron - 1964	8.00
12	Hank Aaron - 1965	8.00
13	Hank Aaron - 1966	8.00
14	Hank Aaron - 1967	8.00
15	Hank Aaron - 1968	8.00
16	Hank Aaron - 1969	8.00
17	Hank Aaron - 1970	8.00
18	Hank Aaron - 1971	8.00
19	Hank Aaron - 1972	8.00
20	Hank Aaron - 1973	8.00
21	Hank Aaron - 1974	8.00
22	Hank Aaron - 1975	8.00
23	Hank Aaron - 1976	8.00

2000 Topps Hank Aaron Reprints

This 23-card set reprints all of Aaron's 23 regular-issued Topps cards and are seeded 1:18 packs.

		MT
Complete Set (23):		120.00
Common Aaron:		6.00
Inserted 1:18		
Autographed:		150.00
1	Hank Aaron - 1954	10.00
2	Hank Aaron - 1955	6.00
3	Hank Aaron - 1956	6.00
4	Hank Aaron - 1957	6.00
5	Hank Aaron - 1958	6.00
6	Hank Aaron - 1959	6.00
7	Hank Aaron - 1960	6.00
8	Hank Aaron - 1961	6.00
9	Hank Aaron - 1962	6.00
10	Hank Aaron - 1963	6.00
11	Hank Aaron - 1964	6.00
12	Hank Aaron - 1965	6.00
13	Hank Aaron - 1966	6.00
14	Hank Aaron - 1967	6.00
15	Hank Aaron - 1968	6.00
16	Hank Aaron - 1969	6.00
17	Hank Aaron - 1970	6.00
18	Hank Aaron - 1971	6.00
19	Hank Aaron - 1972	6.00
20	Hank Aaron - 1973	6.00
21	Hank Aaron - 1974	6.00
22	Hank Aaron - 1975	6.00
23	Hank Aaron - 1976	6.00

2000 Topps Hands of Gold

This seven-card insert set highlights players who have won at least five gold gloves. Each card is foil stamped and die-cut and is seeded 1:18 packs.

		MT
Complete Set (7):		10.00
Common Player:		.50
Inserted 1:18		
1	Barry Bonds	1.00
2	Ivan Rodriguez	1.00
3	Ken Griffey Jr.	4.00
4	Roberto Alomar	.75
5	Tony Gwynn	2.00
6	Omar Vizquel	.50
7	Greg Maddux	2.00

2000 Topps Mark McGwire 1985 Rookie Reprint

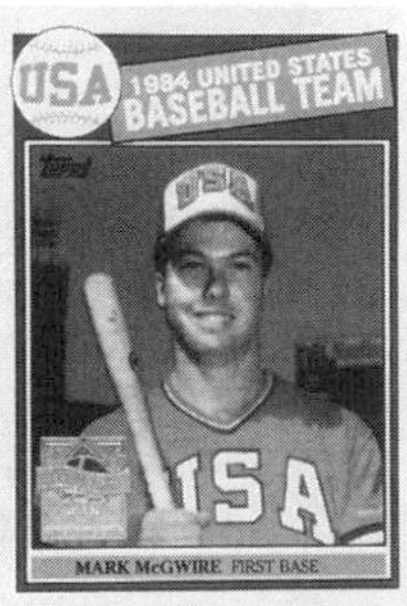

This insert pays tribute to baseball's reigning single season home run record holder by reprinting his '85 Topps Rookie card. Card fronts have a commemorative gold stamp and is seeded 1:36 packs.

	MT
Complete Set (1):	8.00
Mark McGwire	6.00

2000 Topps Own the Game

		MT
Complete Set (30):		75.00
Common Player:		.75
Inserted 1:12		
1	Derek Jeter	5.00
2	B.J. Surhoff	.75
3	Luis Gonzalez	.75
4	Manny Ramirez	2.00
5	Rafael Palmeiro	1.25
6	Mark McGwire	8.00
7	Mark McGwire	8.00
8	Sammy Sosa	5.00
9	Ken Griffey Jr.	8.00
10	Larry Walker	1.50
11	Nomar Garciaparra	5.00
12	Derek Jeter	5.00
13	Larry Walker	1.50
14	Mark McGwire	8.00
15	Manny Ramirez	2.00
16	Pedro Martinez	2.00
17	Randy Johnson	1.50
18	Kevin Millwood	1.00
19	Pedro Martinez	2.00
20	Randy Johnson	1.50
21	Kevin Brown	1.00
22	Chipper Jones	4.00
23	Ivan Rodriguez	2.00
24	Mariano Rivera	1.00
25	Scott Williamson	.75
26	Carlos Beltran	.75
27	Randy Johnson	1.50
28	Pedro Martinez	2.00
29	Sammy Sosa	5.00
30	Manny Ramirez	2.00

2000 Topps Perennial All-Stars

This 10-card set highlights 10 superstars who have consistently achieved All-Star recognition. Card fronts feature a silver holographic foil throughout, while card backs have the featured player's career

All-Star statistics. These were seeded 1:18 packs. Cards are numbered with a "PA" prefix.

		MT
Complete Set (10):		20.00
Common Player:		.50
Inserted 1:18		
1	Ken Griffey Jr.	4.00
2	Derek Jeter	2.50
3	Sammy Sosa	2.50
4	Cal Ripken Jr.	3.00
5	Mike Piazza	2.50
6	Nomar Garciaparra	2.50
7	Jeff Bagwell	1.00
8	Barry Bonds	1.00
9	Alex Rodriguez	3.00
10	Mark McGwire	4.00

2000 Topps Power Players

This 20-card set highlights the top power hitters in the game and are printed on a holographic silver foil front. They are numbered with a "P" prefix and are seeded 1:8 packs.

		MT
Complete Set (20):		25.00
Common Player:		.50
Inserted 1:8		
1	Juan Gonzalez	1.00
2	Ken Griffey Jr.	4.00
3	Mark McGwire	4.00
4	Nomar Garciaparra	2.50
5	Barry Bonds	1.00
6	Mo Vaughn	.75
7	Larry Walker	.75
8	Alex Rodriguez	3.00
9	Jose Canseco	1.00
10	Jeff Bagwell	1.00
11	Manny Ramirez	1.00
12	Albert Belle	.75
13	Frank Thomas	1.50
14	Mike Piazza	2.50
15	Chipper Jones	2.00
16	Sammy Sosa	2.50
17	Vladimir Guerrero	2.00
18	Scott Rolen	1.00
19	Raul Mondesi	.50
20	Derek Jeter	2.50

2000 Topps Stadium Relics

Inserted exclusively in Home-Team Advantage packs, this five-card set features historical baseball stadiums and the autograph of the players who made them sacred. Besides the player autograph, the cards also have a piece of base from the featured stadium embedded into each card. These were seeded 1:165 HTA packs and are numbered with a "SR" prefix.

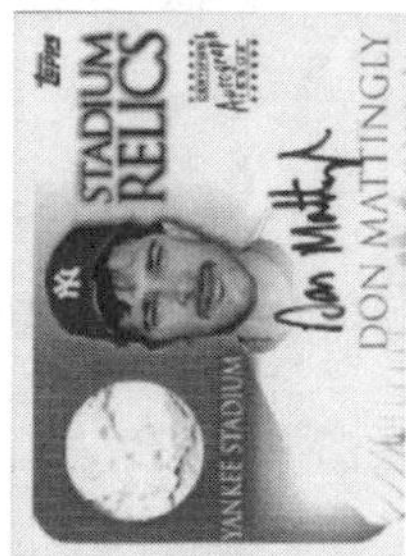

		MT
Common Player:		125.00
Inserted 1:165 HTA		
1	Don Mattingly	200.00
2	Carl Yastrzemski	140.00
3	Ernie Banks	140.00
4	Johnny Bench	150.00
5	Willie Mays	250.00
6	Mike Schmidt	180.00
7	Lou Brock	125.00
8	Al Kaline	125.00
9	Paul Molitor	125.00
10	Eddie Matthews	125.00

2000 Topps Supers

Each box of Topps foil packs includes one upwrapped box-topper card in an oversize (3-1/2" x 5") format. Except for its size, the super version differs from the same players' issued cards only in the numbering on back which designates each card "x of 8..

		MT
Complete Set (16):		35.00
Common Player:		1.00
Inserted 1:box		
	SERIES 1	
1	Mark McGwire	5.00
2	Hank Aaron	5.00
3	Derek Jeter	3.00
4	Sammy Sosa	3.00
5	Alex Rodriguez	3.00
6	Chipper Jones	4.00
7	Cal Ripken Jr.	4.00
8	Pedro Martinez	2.00
	SERIES 2	
1	Barry Bonds	1.50
2	Orlando Hernandez	1.00
3	Mike Piazza	3.00
4	Manny Ramirez	1.50
5	Ken Griffey Jr.	5.00
6	Rafael Palmeiro	1.00
7	Greg Maddux	2.50
8	Nomar Garciaparra	3.00

2000 Topps 21st Century Topps

Printed on a silver holographic foil front, this 10-card set highlights young players who are poised to thrive into the next millennium. These are seeded 1:18 packs and are numbered on the card backs with a "C" prefix.

		MT
Complete Set (10):		10.00
Common Player:		.50
Inserted 1:18		
1	Ben Grieve	.75
2	Alex Gonzalez	.50
3	Derek Jeter	3.00
4	Sean Casey	.75
5	Nomar Garciaparra	3.00
6	Alex Rodriguez	3.00
7	Scott Rolen	1.25
8	Andruw Jones	1.00
9	Vladimir Guerrero	2.00
10	Todd Helton	1.00

2000 Topps Traded and Rookies

		MT
Complete Set (135):		20.00
Common Player:		.10
Unopened Set (136):		30.00
1	*Mike MacDougal*	.10
2	*Andy Tracy*	.20
3	*Brandon Phillips*	.20
4	*Brandon Inge*	.40
5	*Robbie Morrison*	.25
6	*Josh Pressley*	.10
7	*Todd Moser*	.25
8	*Rob Purvis*	.50
9	*Chance Caple*	.10
10	Ben Sheets	2.50
11	*Russ Jacobson*	.10
12	*Brian Cole*	.50
13	*Brad Baker*	.25
14	*Alex Cintron*	.40
15	*Lyle Overbay*	.75
16	*Mike Edwards*	.10
17	*Sean McGowan*	.25
18	*Jose Molina*	.25
19	*Marcos Castillo*	.10
20	*Josue Espada*	.10
21	*Alex Gordon*	.10
22	*Rob Pugmire*	.10
23	*Jason Stumm*	.40
24	*Ty Howington*	.40
25	*Brett Myers*	.10
26	*Maicer Izturis*	.10
27	*John McDonald*	.10
28	*Wilfredo Rodriguez*	.50
29	*Carlos Zambrano*	.50
30	*Alejandro Diaz*	.20
31	*Geraldo Guzman*	.20
32	*J.R. House*	1.50
33	*Elvin Nina*	.10
34	*Juan Pierre*	.50
35	*Ben Johnson*	.20
36	*Jeff Bailey*	.20
37	*Miguel Olivo*	.10
38	*Francisco Rodriguez*	.25
39	*Tony Pena Jr.*	.25
40	*Miguel Cabrera*	.10
41	*Asdrubal Oropeza*	.10
42	*Junior Zamora*	.10
43	*Jovanny Cedeno*	.50
44	*John Sneed*	.10
45	*Josh Kalinowski*	.10
46	*Mike Young*	.25
47	*Rico Washington*	.10
48	*Chad Durbin*	.40
49	*Junior Brignac*	.25
50	*Carlos Hernandez*	.10
51	*Cesar Izturis*	.40
52	*Oscar Salazar*	.25
53	*Pat Strange*	.10
54	*Rick Asadoorian*	1.50
55	*Keith Reed*	.10
56	*Leo Estrella*	.10
57	*Wascar Serrano*	.10
58	*Richard Gomez*	.25
59	*Ramon Santiago*	.25
60	*Jovanny Sosa*	.25
61	*Aaron Rowand*	.50
62	*Junior Guerrero*	.25
63	*Luis Terrero*	.10
64	*Brian Sanches*	.10
65	*Scott Sobkowiak*	.10
66	*Gary Majewski*	.10
67	Barry Zito	2.50
68	*Ryan Christianson*	.10
69	*Cristian Guerrero*	2.00
70	*Tomas de la Rosa*	.10
71	*Andrew Beinbrink*	.25
72	*Ryan Knox*	.10
73	*Alex Graman*	.40
74	*Juan Guzman*	.10
75	*Ruben Salazar*	.50
76	*Luis Matos*	.25
77	*Tony Mota*	.10
78	*Doug Davis*	.25
79	*Ben Christensen*	.10
80	Mike Lamb	.10
81	*Adrian Gonzalez* (Draft Picks)	1.00
82	*Mike Stodolka* (Draft Picks)	.25
83	*Adam Johnson* (Draft Picks)	.25
84	*Matt Wheatland* (Draft Picks)	.40
85	*Corey Smith* (Draft Picks)	.40
86	*Rocco Baldelli* (Draft Picks)	1.00
87	*Keith Bucktrot* (Draft Picks)	.25
88	*Adam Wainwright* (Draft Picks)	.50
89	*Scott Thorman* (Draft Picks)	.50
90	*Tripper Johnson* (Draft Picks)	.25
91	Jim Edmonds	.25
92	Masato Yoshii	.10
93	Adam Kennedy	.10
94	Darryl Kile	.10
95	Mark McLemore	.10
96	Ricky Gutierrez	.10
97	Juan Gonzalez	.40
98	Melvin Mora	.10
99	Dante Bichette	.25
100	Lee Stevens	.10
101	Roger Cedeno	.10
102	John Olerud	.25
103	Eric Young	.10
104	Mickey Morandini	.10
105	Travis Lee	.10
106	Greg Vaughn	.10
107	Todd Zeile	.10
108	Chuck Finley	.10
109	Ismael Valdes	.10
110	Ron Henika	.10
111	Pat Hentgen	.10
112	Ryan Klesko	.10
113	Derek Bell	.10
114	Hideo Nomo	.40
115	Aaron Sele	.10
116	Fernando Vina	.10
117	Wally Joyner	.10
118	Brian Hunter	.10
119	Joe Girardi	.10
120	Omar Daal	.10
121	Brook Fordyce	.10
122	Jose Valentin	.10
123	Curt Schilling	.10
124	B.J. Surhoff	.10
125	Henry Rodriguez	.10
126	Mike Bordick	.10
127	David Justice	.50

128	Charles Johnson	.10
129	Will Clark	.25
130	Dwight Gooden	.10
131	David Segui	.10
132	Denny Neagle	.10
133	Andy Ashby	.10
134	Bruce Chen	.10
135	Jason Bere	.10

2000 Topps Traded and Rookies Autographs

		MT
Common Player:		5.00
Inserted 1:set		
1	Mike MacDougal	5.00
2	Andy Tracy	5.00
3	Brandon Phillips	5.00
4	Brandon Inge	10.00
5	Robbie Morrison	5.00
6	Josh Pressley	5.00
7	Todd Moser	5.00
8	Rob Purvis	10.00
9	Chance Caple	5.00
10	Ben Sheets	30.00
11	Russ Jacobson	5.00
12	Brian Cole	15.00
13	Brad Baker	10.00
14	Alex Cintron	10.00
15	Lyle Overbay	15.00
16	Mike Edwards	5.00
17	Sean McGowan	8.00
18	Jose Molina	5.00
19	Marcos Castillo	5.00
20	Josue Espada	5.00
21	Alex Gordon	10.00
22	Rob Pugmire	5.00
23	Jason Stumm	10.00
24	Ty Howington	8.00
25	Brett Myers	8.00
26	Maicer Izturis	5.00
27	John McDonald	5.00
28	Wilfredo Rodriguez	12.00
29	Carlos Zambrano	10.00
30	Alejandro Diaz	5.00
31	Geraldo Guzman	5.00
32	J.R. House	30.00
33	Elvin Nina	5.00
34	Juan Pierre	10.00
35	Ben Johnson	10.00
36	Jeff Bailey	5.00
37	Miguel Olivo	5.00
38	Francisco Rodriguez	10.00
39	Tony Pena Jr.	8.00
40	Miguel Cabrera	5.00
41	Asdrubal Oropeza	5.00
42	Junior Zamora	5.00
43	Jovanny Cedeno	10.00
44	John Sneed	5.00
45	Josh Kalinowski	5.00
46	Mike Young	5.00
47	Rico Washington	10.00
48	Chad Durbin	10.00
49	Junior Brignac	5.00
50	Carlos Hernandez	5.00
51	Cesar Izturis	5.00
52	Oscar Salazar	5.00
53	Pat Strange	15.00
54	Rick Asadoorian	35.00
55	Keith Reed	10.00
56	Leo Estrella	5.00
57	Wascar Serrano	10.00
58	Richard Gomez	10.00
59	Ramon Santiago	10.00
60	Jovanny Sosa	8.00
61	Aaron Rowand	15.00
62	Junior Guerrero	5.00
63	Luis Terrero	5.00
64	Brian Sanches	5.00
65	Scott Sobkowiak	5.00
66	Gary Majewski	5.00
67	Barry Zito	50.00
68	Ryan Christianson	8.00
69	Cristian Guerrero	35.00
70	Tomas de la Rosa	5.00
71	Andrew Beinbrink	5.00
72	Ryan Knox	5.00
73	Alex Graman	10.00
74	Juan Guzman	5.00
75	Ruben Salazar	15.00
76	Luis Matos	10.00
77	Tony Mota	5.00
78	Doug Davis	5.00
79	Ben Christensen	15.00
80	Mike Lamb	10.00

2000 Topps Opening Day

Essentially identical in design to 2000 Topps regular cards, Opening Day has a silver border with "2000 Opening Day" stamped in silver foil on the card front. The checklist is made up of cards from Series 1 and 2 from Topps base set with identical photos. The rookie reprint card of Hank Aaron was intended to carry card #110, but it does not appear, only the original '54 Topps card #128.

		MT
Complete Set (165):		40.00
Common Player:		.15
Pack (8):		1.00
Wax Box (36):		28.00
1	Mark McGwire	3.00
2	Tony Gwynn	1.50
3	Wade Boggs	.40
4	Cal Ripken Jr.	2.50
5	Matt Williams	.50
6	Jay Buhner	.15
7	Mike Lieberthal	.15
8	Magglio Ordonez	.25
9	Derek Jeter	2.00
10	Javy Lopez	.15
11	Armando Benitez	.15
12	Darin Erstad	.25
13	Mark Grace	.25
14	Eric Karros	.15
15	J.T. Snow Jr.	.15
16	Luis Castillo	.15
17	Rey Ordonez	.15
18	Bob Abreu	.15
19	Warren Morris	.15
20	Juan Gonzalez	1.00
21	Dean Palmer	.15
22	Hank Aaron	3.00
23	Jeff Bagwell	.75
24	Sammy Sosa	2.00
25	Randy Johnson	.50
26	Dante Bichette	.15
27	Frank Thomas	1.00
28	Pedro Martinez	.75
29	Brian Giles	.15
30	Ivan Rodriguez	.75
31	Roger Cedeno	.15
32	David Justice	.40
33	Ken Caminiti	.15
34	Brian Jordan	.15
35	John Olerud	.25
36	Pokey Reese	.15
37	Barry Larkin	.40
38	Edgar Martinez	.15
39	Carlos Delgado	.50
40	Troy Glaus	.40
41	Ben Grieve	.25
42	Jose Lima	.15
43	Luis Gonzalez	.15
44	Alex Rodriguez	2.00
45	Preston Wilson	.15
46	Rickey Henderson	.40
47	Gary Sheffield	.25
48	Jim Edmonds	.15
49	Greg Vaughn	.25
50	Neifi Perez	.15
51	Paul O'Neill	.25
52	Jermaine Dye	.15
53	Curt Schilling	.25
54	Edgardo Alfonzo	.15
55	John Smoltz	.15
56	Chuck Finley	.15
57	Billy Wagner	.15
58	David Cone	.25
59	Roberto Alomar	.50
60	Charles Nagy	.15
61	Mike Mussina	.50
62	Robin Ventura	.25
63	Kevin Brown	.15
64	Pat Hentgen	.15
65	Ryan Klesko	.15
66	Derek Bell	.15
67	Larry Walker	.50
68	Scott Williamson	.15
69	Jose Offerman	.15
70	Doug Mientkiewicz	.15
71	John Snyder	.15
72	Sandy Alomar	.15
73	Joe Nathan	.15
74	Steve Finley	.15
75	Dave Martinez	.15
76	Fernando Tatis	.15
77	Kenny Lofton	.40
78	Paul Byrd	.15
79	Aaron Sele	.15
80	Roger Clemens	1.00
81	Francisco Cordova	.15
82	Wally Joyner	.15
83	Jason Kendall	.25
84	Carlos Beltran	.15
85	Chipper Jones	1.50
86	Vladimir Guerrero	1.00
87	Tom Goodwin	.15
88	Brian Daubach	.15
89	Jay Bell	.15
90	Roy Halladay	.15
91	Miguel Tejada	.15
92	Eric Davis	.15
93	Henry Rodriguez	.15
94	Joe McEwing	.15
95	Jeff Kent	.15
96	Jeff Zimmerman	.15
97	Tony Fernandez	.15
98	Jason Giambi	.15
99	Jose Canseco	.75
100	Alex Gonzalez	.15
101	Erubiel Durazo, Pat Burrell, Nick Johnson	1.00
102	Corey Patterson, Roosevelt Brown, Lance Berkman (Prospects)	2.50
103	Eric Munson, *Bobby Bradley* (Draft Picks)	1.00
104	Josh Hamilton, *Corey Myers* (Draft Picks)	1.00
105	Mark McGwire (Magic Moments)	3.00
106	Hank Aaron (Magic Moments)	3.00
107	Cal Ripken Jr. (Magic Moments)	2.50
108	Wade Boggs (Magic Moments)	.40
109	Tony Gwynn (Magic Moments)	1.50
(110)	Hank Aaron (Rookie Reprint)	3.00
111	Tom Glavine	.40
112	Mo Vaughn	.50
113	Tino Martinez	.25
114	Craig Biggio	.40
115	Tim Hudson	.25
116	John Wetteland	.15
117	Ellis Burks	.15
118	David Wells	.15
119	Rico Brogna	.15
120	Greg Maddux	1.50
121	Jeromy Burnitz	.15
122	Raul Mondesi	.25
123	Rondell White	.25
124	Barry Bonds	.75
125	Orlando Hernandez	.40
126	Bartolo Colon	.15
127	Tim Salmon	.25
128	Kevin Young	.15
129	Troy O'Leary	.15
130	Jim Thome	.40
131	Ray Durham	.15
132	Tony Clark	.40
133	Mariano Rivera	.25
134	Omar Vizquel	.15
135	Ken Griffey Jr.	3.00
136	Shawn Green	.50
137	Cliff Floyd	.15
138	Al Leiter	.15
139	Mike Hampton	.15
140	Mike Piazza	2.00
141	Andy Pettitte	.25
142	Albert Belle	.50
143	Scott Rolen	.75
144	Rusty Greer	.15
145	Kevin Millwood	.25
146	Ivan Rodriguez	.75
147	Nomar Garciaparra	2.00
148	Denny Neagle	.15
149	Manny Ramirez	.75
150	Vinny Castilla	.15
151	Andruw Jones	.50
152	Johnny Damon	.15
153	Eric Milton	.15
154	Todd Helton	.50
155	Rafael Palmeiro	.40
156	Damion Easley	.15
157	Carlos Febles	.15
158	Paul Konerko	.25
159	Bernie Williams	.50
160	Ken Griffey Jr. (Magic Moments)	3.00
161	Barry Bonds (Magic Moments)	.75
162	Sammy Sosa (Magic Moments)	2.00
163	Derek Jeter (Magic Moments)	2.00
164	Alex Rodriguez (Magic Moments)	2.00
165	Checklist (Magic Moments)	.15

2000 Topps Opening Day Autograph

		MT
Complete Set (5):		250.00
Common Player:		40.00
1	Edgardo Alfonzo	50.00
2	Wade Boggs	100.00
3	Robin Ventura	40.00
4	Josh Hamilton	50.00
5	Vernon Wells	40.00

2000 Topps Chrome

The base set consists of 478 cards utilizing Topps Chromium technology and features the same photos and basic design as the 2000 Topps base set. Subsets include Prospects, Draft Picks, 20th Century's Best, Magic Moments and Post Season Highlights. A parallel Refractor version is also available 1:12 packs.

	MT
Complete Set (478):	320.00
Complete Series I Set (239):	150.00

Complete Series II Set (239): 160.00
Common Player: .40
5 versions for #236-240, 475-479
Pack (4): 3.00
Wax Box (24): 65.00
1 Mark McGwire 8.00
2 Tony Gwynn 4.00
3 Wade Boggs 1.00
4 Cal Ripken Jr. 6.00
5 Matt Williams 1.00
6 Jay Buhner .50
7 Not Issued
8 Jeff Conine .40
9 Todd Greene .40
10 Mike Lieberthal .40
11 Steve Avery .40
12 Bret Saberhagen .40
13 Magglio Ordonez .40
14 Brad Radke .40
15 Derek Jeter 5.00
16 Javy Lopez .50
17 Russ David .40
18 Armando Benitez .40
19 B.J. Surhoff .40
20 Darryl Kile .40
21 Mark Lewis .40
22 Mike Williams .40
23 Mark McLemore .40
24 Sterling Hitchcock .40
25 Darin Erstad .60
26 Ricky Gutierrez .40
27 John Jaha .40
28 Homer Bush .40
29 Darrin Fletcher .40
30 Mark Grace .75
31 Fred McGriff .75
32 Omar Daal .40
33 Eric Karros .60
34 Orlando Cabrera .40
35 J.T. Snow Jr. .40
36 Luis Castillo .40
37 Rey Ordonez .40
38 Bob Abreu .40
39 Warren Morris .40
40 Juan Gonzalez 2.00
41 Mike Lansing .40
42 Chili Davis .40
43 Dean Palmer .40
44 Hank Aaron 8.00
45 Jeff Bagwell 2.00
46 Jose Valentin .40
47 Shannon Stewart .40
48 Kent Bottenfield .40
49 Jeff Shaw .40
50 Sammy Sosa 5.00
51 Randy Johnson 1.50
52 Benny Agbayani .40
53 Dante Bichette .75
54 Pete Harnisch .40
55 Frank Thomas 2.00
56 Jorge Posada .75
57 Todd Walker .40
58 Juan Encarnacion .40
59 Mike Sweeney .40
60 Pedro Martinez 2.00
61 Lee Stevens .40
62 Brian Giles .40
63 Chad Ogea .40
64 Ivan Rodriguez 2.00
65 Roger Cedeno .40
66 David Justice .75
67 Steve Trachsel .40
68 Eli Marrero .40
69 Dave Nilsson .40
70 Ken Caminiti .60
71 Tim Raines .40
72 Brian Jordan .40
73 Jeff Blauser .40
74 Bernard Gilkey .40
75 John Flaherty .40
76 Brent Mayne .40
77 Jose Vidro .40
78 Jeff Fassero .40
79 Bruce Aven .40
80 John Olerud .75
81 Juan Guzman .40
82 Woody Williams .40
83 Ed Sprague .40
84 Joe Girardi .40
85 Barry Larkin 1.00
86 Mike Caruso .40
87 Bobby Higginson .40
88 Roberto Kelly .40
89 Edgar Martinez .20
90 Mark Kotsay .40
91 Paul Sorrento .40
92 Eric Young .40
93 Carlos Delgado 1.50
94 Troy Glaus 2.00
95 Ben Grieve .75
96 Jose Lima .40
97 Garret Anderson .40
98 Luis Gonzalez .40
99 Carl Pavano .40
100 Alex Rodriguez 6.00
101 Preston Wilson .40
102 Ron Gant .60
103 Harold Baines .40
104 Rickey Henderson 1.00
105 Gary Sheffield .75
106 Mickey Morandini .40
107 Jim Edmonds .40
108 Kris Benson .40
109 Adrian Beltre .60
110 Alex Fernandez .40
111 Dan Wilson .40
112 Mark Clark .40
113 Greg Vaughn .75
114 Neifi Perez .40
115 Paul O'Neill .75
116 Jermaine Dye .40
117 Todd Jones .40
118 Terry Steinbach .40
119 Greg Norton .40
120 Curt Schilling .60
121 Todd Zeile .40
122 Edgardo Alfonzo .75
123 Ryan McGuire .40
124 Stan Javier .40
125 John Smoltz .60
126 Bob Wickman .40
127 Richard Hidalgo .40
128 Chuck Finley .40
129 Billy Wagner .40
130 Todd Hundley .40
131 Dwight Gooden .60
132 Russ Ortiz .40
133 Mike Lowell .40
134 Reggie Sanders .40
135 John Valentin .40
136 Brad Ausmus .40
137 Chad Kreuter .40
138 David Cone .75
139 Brook Fordyce .40
140 Roberto Alomar 1.50
141 Charles Nagy .40
142 Brian Hunter .40
143 Mike Mussina 1.50
144 Robin Ventura .75
145 Kevin Brown .60
146 Pat Hentgen .40
147 Ryan Klesko .60
148 Derek Bell .40
149 Andy Sheets .40
150 Larry Walker 1.50
151 Scott Williamson .40
152 Jose Offerman .40
153 Doug Mientkiewicz .40
154 John Snyder .40
155 Sandy Alomar .25
156 Joe Nathan .40
157 Lance Johnson .40
158 Odalis Perez .40
159 Hideo Nomo .75
160 Steve Finley .40
161 Dave Martinez .40
162 Matt Walbeck .40
163 Bill Spiers .40
164 Fernando Tatis .75
165 Kenny Lofton 1.25
166 Paul Byrd .40
167 Aaron Sele .40
168 Eddie Taubensee .40
169 Reggie Jefferson .40
170 Roger Clemens 3.00
171 Francisco Cordova .40
172 Mike Bordick .40
173 Wally Joyner .40
174 Marvin Benard .40
175 Jason Kendall .60
176 Mike Stanley .40
177 Chad Allen .40
178 Carlos Beltran .40
179 Deivi Cruz .40
180 Chipper Jones 4.00
181 Vladimir Guerrero 3.00
182 Dave Burba .40
183 Tom Goodwin .40
184 Brian Daubach .40
185 Jay Bell .40
186 Roy Halladay .40
187 Miguel Tejada .40
188 Armando Rios .40
189 Fernando Vina .40
190 Eric Davis .60
191 Henry Rodriguez .40
192 Joe McEwing .40
193 Jeff Kent .40
194 Mike Jackson .40
195 Mike Morgan .40
196 Jeff Montgomery .40
197 Jeff Zimmerman .40
198 Tony Fernandez .40
199 Jason Giambi .40
200 Jose Canseco 2.00
201 Alex Gonzalez .40
202 Jack Cust, Mike Colangelo, Dee Brown 1.50
203 Felipe Lopez, Alfonso Soriano, Pablo Ozuna 3.00
204 Erubiel Durazo, Pat Burrell, Nick Johnson 3.00
205 *John Sneed*, Kip Wells, Matt Blank 1.50
206 *Josh Kalinowski*, *Michael Tejera*, Chris Mears 1.00
207 Roosevelt Brown, Corey Patterson, Lance Berkman 8.00
208 Kit Pellow, Kevin Barker, Russ Branyan 1.00
209 *B.J. Garbe*, *Larry Bigbie* 3.00
210 Eric Munson, *Bobby Bradley* 4.00
211 Josh Girdley, Kyle Snyder 1.50
212 *Chance Caple*, Jason Jennings 2.00
213 *Ryan Christiansen*, *Brett Myers* 4.00
214 *Jason Stumm*, *Rob Purvis* 8.00
215 David Walling, Mike Paradis 1.50
216 Omar Ortiz, Jay Gehrke .75
217 David Cone (Season Highlights) .75
218 Jose Jimenez (Season Highlights) .40
219 Chris Singleton (Season Highlights) .40
220 Fernando Tatis (Season Highlights) .75
221 Todd Helton (Season Highlights) 1.00
222 Kevin Millwood (Post-Season Highlights) .60
223 Todd Pratt (Post-Season Highlights) .40
224 Orlando Hernandez (Post-Season Highlights) .75
225 Post-Season Highlights .40
226 Post-Season Highlights .40
227 Bernie Williams (Post-Season Highlights) 1.00
228 Mariano Rivera (Post-Season Highlights) .75
229 Tony Gwynn (20th Century's Best) 2.00
230 Wade Boggs (20th Century's Best) 1.00
231 Tim Raines (20th Century's Best) .40
232 Mark McGwire (20th Century's Best) 8.00
233 Rickey Henderson (20th Century's Best) .75
234 Rickey Henderson (20th Century's Best) .75
235 Roger Clemens (20th Century's Best) 3.00
236 Mark McGwire (Magic Moments) 15.00
237 Hank Aaron (Magic Moments) 8.00
238 Cal Ripken Jr. (Magic Moments) 10.00
239 Wade Boggs (Magic Moments) 4.00
240 Tony Gwynn (Magic Moments) 8.00
Series 1 checklist (1-201) .05
Series 1 checklist (202-240, inserts) .05
241 Tom Glavine .75
242 David Wells .40
243 Kevin Appier .40
244 Troy Percival .40
245 Ray Lankford .40
246 Marquis Grissom .40
247 Randy Winn .40
248 Miguel Batista .40
249 Darren Dreifort .40
250 Barry Bonds 2.00
251 Harold Baines .40
252 Cliff Floyd .40
253 Freddy Garcia .75
254 Kenny Rogers .40
255 Ben Davis .40
256 Charles Johnson .40
257 John Burkett .40
258 Desi Relaford .40
259 Al Martin .40
260 Andy Pettitte .75
261 Carlos Lee .40
262 Matt Lawton .40
263 Andy Fox .40
264 Chan Ho Park .40
265 Billy Koch .40
266 Dave Roberts .40
267 Carl Everett .75
268 Orel Hershiser .40
269 Trot Nixon .40
270 Rusty Greer .40
271 Will Clark 1.00
272 Quilvio Veras .40
273 Rico Brogna .40
274 Devon White .40
275 Tim Hudson .75
276 Mike Hampton .40
277 Miguel Cairo .40
278 Darren Oliver .40
279 Jeff Cirillo .75
280 Al Leiter .60
281 Brant Brown .40
282 Carlos Febles .40
283 Pedro Astacio .40
284 Juan Guzman .40
285 Orlando Hernandez .75
286 Paul Konerko .75
287 Tony Clark .60
288 Aaron Boone .40
289 Ismael Valdes .40
290 Moises Alou .60
291 Kevin Tapani .40
292 John Franco .40
293 Todd Zeile .40
294 Jason Schmidt .40
295 Johnny Damon .40
296 Scott Brosius .40
297 Travis Fryman .60
298 Jose Vizcaino .40
299 Eric Chavez .75
300 Mike Piazza 5.00
301 Matt Clement .40
302 Cristian Guzman .40
303 Darryl Strawberry .75
304 Jeff Abbott .40
305 Brett Tomko .40
306 Mike Lansing .40
307 Eric Owens .40
308 Livan Hernandez .40
309 Rondell White .75
310 Todd Stottlemyre .75
311 Chris Carpenter .40
312 Ken Hill .40
313 Mark Loretta .40
314 John Rocker .40
315 Richie Sexson .40
316 Ruben Mateo .75
317 Ramon Martinez .40
318 Mike Sirotka .40
319 Jose Rosado .40
320 Matt Mantei .40
321 Kevin Millwood .75
322 Gary DiSarcina .40
323 Dustin Hermanson .40
324 Mike Stanton .40
325 Kirk Rueter .40
326 Damian Miller .40
327 Doug Glanville .40
328 Scott Rolen 2.00
329 Ray Durham .40
330 Butch Huskey .40
331 Mariano Rivera .75
332 Darren Lewis .40
333 Ramiro Mendoza .40
334 Mark Grudzielanek .40
335 Mike Cameron .40
336 Kelvin Escobar .40
337 Bret Boone .40

338 Mo Vaughn 1.50
339 Craig Biggio 1.00
340 Michael Barrett .40
341 Marlon Anderson .40
342 Bobby Jones .40
343 John Halama .40
344 Todd Ritchie .40
345 Chuck Knoblauch .75
346 Rick Reed .40
347 Kelly Stinnett .40
348 Tim Salmon .75
349 A.J. Hinch .40
350 Jose Cruz Jr. .40
351 Roberto Hernandez .40
352 Edgar Renteria .40
353 Jose Hernandez .40
354 Brad Fullmer .40
355 Trevor Hoffman .40
356 Troy O'Leary .40
357 Justin Thompson .40
358 Kevin Young .40
359 Hideki Irabu .40
360 Jim Thome 1.00
361 Todd Dunwoody .40
362 Octavio Dotel .40
363 Omar Vizquel .75
364 Raul Mondesi .75
365 Shane Reynolds .40
366 Bartolo Colon .40
367 Chris Widger .40
368 Gabe Kapler .75
369 Bill Simas .40
370 Tino Martinez 1.00
371 John Thomson .40
372 Delino DeShields .40
373 Carlos Perez .40
374 Eddie Perez .40
375 Jeromy Burnitz .75
376 Jimmy Haynes .40
377 Travis Lee .75
378 Darryl Hamilton .40
379 Jamie Moyer .40
380 Alex Gonzalez .40
381 John Wetteland .40
382 Vinny Castilla .60
383 Jeff Suppan .40
384 Chad Curtis .40
385 Robb Nen .40
386 Wilson Alvarez .40
387 Andres Galarraga 1.50
388 Mike Remlinger .40
389 Geoff Jenkins .75
390 Matt Stairs .40
391 Bill Mueller .40
392 Mike Lowell .40
393 Andy Ashby .40
394 Ruben Rivera .40
395 Todd Helton 2.00
396 Bernie Williams 1.50
397 Royce Clayton .40
398 Manny Ramirez 2.00
399 Kerry Wood 1.00
400 Ken Griffey Jr. 8.00
401 Enrique Wilson .40
402 Joey Hamilton .40
403 Shawn Estes .40
404 Ugueth Urbina .40
405 Albert Belle 1.50
406 Rick Helling .40
407 Steve Parris .40
408 Eric Milton .40
409 Dave Mlicki .40
410 Shawn Green 2.00
411 Jaret Wright .40
412 Tony Womack .40
413 Vernon Wells .75
414 Ron Belliard .40
415 Ellis Burks .40
416 Scott Erickson .40
417 Rafael Palmeiro 1.50
418 Damion Easley .40
419 Jamey Wright .40
420 Corey Koskie .40
421 Bobby Howry .40
422 Ricky Ledee .40
423 Dmitri Young .40
424 Sidney Ponson .40
425 Greg Maddux 4.00
426 Jose Guillen .40
427 Jon Lieber .40
428 Andy Benes .40
429 Randy Velarde .40
430 Sean Casey 1.00
431 Torii Hunter .40
432 Ryan Rupe .40
433 David Segui .40
434 Rich Aurilia .40
435 Nomar Garciaparra 5.00
436 Denny Neagle .40
437 Ron Coomer .40
438 Chris Singleton .40
439 Tony Batista 1.00
440 Andruw Jones 1.50
441 Adam Piatt, Aubrey Huff, Sean Burroughs (Prospects) 3.00
442 Rafael Furcal, Jason Dallero, Travis Dawkins (Prospects) 3.00
443 Wilton Veras, Joe Crede, *Mike Lamb* (Prospects) .40
444 *Julio Zuleta*, Dernell Stenson, Jorge Toca (Prospects) .40
445 Tim Raines, Jr., Gary Mathews Jr., *Garry Maddox Jr.* (Prospects) 2.00
446 Matt Riley, Mark Mulder, C.C. Sabathia (Prospects) .40
447 *Scott Downs*, Chris George, Matt Belisle (Prospects) 1.50
448 Doug Mirabelli, Ben Petrick, Jayson Werth (Prospects) .40
449 Josh Hamilton, *Corey Myers* (Draft Picks) 5.00
450 *Ben Christensen*, *Brett Myers* (Draft Picks) 3.00
451 *Barry Zito*, *Ben Sheets* (Draft Picks) 8.00
452 *Ty Howington*, *Kurt Ainsworth* (Draft Picks) 2.00
453 *Rick Asadoorian*, *Vince Faison* (Draft Picks) 10.00
454 *Keith Reed*, *Jeff Heaverlo* (Draft Picks) 2.00
455 *Mike MacDougal*, Jay Gehrke (Draft Picks) 1.50
456 Mark McGwire (Season Highlights) 4.00
457 Cal Ripken Jr. (Season Highlights) 3.00
458 Wade Boggs (Season Highlights) .75
459 Tony Gwynn (Season Highlights) 2.00
460 Jesse Orosco (Season Highlights) .40
461 Nomar Garciaparra, Larry Walker (League Leaders) 2.00
462 Mark McGwire, Ken Griffey Jr. (League Leaders) 4.00
463 Mark McGwire, Manny Ramirez (League Leaders) 3.00
464 Randy Johnson, Pedro Martinez (League Leaders) 1.00
465 Randy Johnson, Pedro Martinez (League Leaders) 1.00
466 Luis Gonzalez, Derek Jeter (League Leaders) 2.00
467 Manny Ramirez, Larry Walker (League Leaders) .75
468 Tony Gwynn (20th Century's Best) .40
469 Mark McGwire (20th Century's Best) 4.00
470 Frank Thomas (20th Century's Best) 1.50
471 Harold Baines (20th Century's Best) .40
472 Roger Clemens (20th Century's Best) 1.50
473 John Franco (20th Century's Best) .40
474 John Franco (20th Century's Best) .40
475 Ken Griffey Jr. (Magic Moments) 15.00
476 Barry Bonds (Magic Moments) 4.00
477 Sammy Sosa (Magic Moments) 10.00
478 Derek Jeter (Magic Moments) 10.00
479 Alex Rodriguez (Magic Moments) 12.00

2000 Topps Chrome Refractors

A parallel to the base set, Refractors have a reflective sheen to them when held up to light. They are seeded 1:12 packs and have "Refractor" written underneath the card number on the back.

	MT
Stars:	5-10X
Young Stars/RCs:	2-4X
Inserted 1:12	

(See 2000 Topps Chrome for checklist and base card values.)

2000 Topps Chrome All-Topps Team

These feature top National League players and picks a top player for each position. They have a brown border utilizing Topps Chromium technology. Card backs have a small photo along with statistical comparisons made to current and former greats for their respective position. Backs are numbered with an "AT" prefix and are seeded 1:32 packs. A Refractor parallel is inserted 1:160 packs.

		MT
Complete Set (20):		120.00
Complete Series I Set (10):		60.00
Complete Series II Set (10):		60.00
Common Player:		3.00
Inserted 1:32		
Refractors:		2-3X
Inserted 1:160		
1	Greg Maddux	10.00
2	Mike Piazza	12.00
3	Mark McGwire	20.00
4	Craig Biggio	3.00
5	Chipper Jones	10.00
6	Barry Larkin	4.00
7	Barry Bonds	5.00
8	Andruw Jones	4.00
9	Sammy Sosa	12.00
10	Larry Walker	4.00
11	Pedro Martinez	5.00
12	Ivan Rodriguez	5.00
13	Rafael Palmeiro	4.00
14	Roberto Alomar	4.00
15	Cal Ripken Jr.	15.00
16	Derek Jeter	12.00
17	Albert Belle	3.00
18	Ken Griffey Jr.	20.00
19	Manny Ramirez	5.00
20	Jose Canseco	5.00

2000 Topps Chrome Allegiance

Allegiance features 20 stars who have spent their entire career with one team. They are seeded 1:16 and are numbered with a "TA" prefix. There is also a hobby-exclusive Refractor parallel version, sequentially numbered to 100 and inserted 1:424 packs.

		MT
Complete Set (20):		100.00
Common Player:		2.00
Inserted 1:16		
1	Derek Jeter	12.00
2	Ivan Rodriguez	5.00
3	Alex Rodriguez	15.00
4	Cal Ripken Jr.	15.00
5	Mark Grace	2.00
6	Tony Gwynn	10.00
7	Juan Gonzalez	5.00
8	Frank Thomas	5.00
9	Manny Ramirez	5.00
10	Barry Larkin	4.00
11	Bernie Williams	4.00
12	Raul Mondesi	2.00
13	Vladimir Guerrero	8.00
14	Craig Biggio	3.00
15	Nomar Garciaparra	12.00
16	Andruw Jones	4.00
17	Jim Thome	3.00
18	Scott Rolen	5.00
19	Chipper Jones	10.00
20	Ken Griffey Jr.	20.00

2000 Topps Chrome Allegiance Refractors

A parallel to the Allegiance inserts, these were limited to 100 sequentially numbered sets and inserted 1:424 packs.

		MT
Common Player:		15.00
Production 100 sets		
1	Derek Jeter	100.00
2	Ivan Rodriguez	40.00
3	Alex Rodriguez	100.00
4	Cal Ripken Jr.	120.00
5	Mark Grace	15.00
6	Tony Gwynn	75.00
7	Juan Gonzalez	40.00
8	Frank Thomas	40.00
9	Manny Ramirez	40.00
10	Barry Larkin	30.00
11	Bernie Williams	30.00
12	Raul Mondesi	15.00
13	Vladimir Guerrero	60.00
14	Craig Biggio	30.00
15	Nomar Garciaparra	100.00
16	Andruw Jones	30.00
17	Jim Thome	25.00
18	Scott Rolen	40.00
19	Chipper Jones	75.00
20	Ken Griffey Jr.	150.00

2000 Topps Chrome All-Star Rookie Team

This 10-card set highlights players who lived up to the high expectations placed on them during their rookie season. These are seeded 1:16 packs and are numbered with an "RT" prefix on the card back. A Refractor parallel is also randomly inserted, seeded 1:80 packs. "Refractor" is printed under the card number on the back.

		MT
Complete Set (10):		40.00
Common Player:		1.00
Inserted 1:16		
Refractors:		2-3X
Inserted 1:80		
1	Mark McGwire	10.00
2	Chuck Knoblauch	1.50
3	Chipper Jones	5.00
4	Cal Ripken Jr.	8.00
5	Manny Ramirez	2.50
6	Jose Canseco	2.50
7	Ken Griffey Jr.	10.00
8	Mike Piazza	6.00
9	Dwight Gooden	1.50
10	Billy Wagner	1.00

2000 Topps Chrome Combos

Ten player combinations linked by a common element are featured in this set. Combos are found 1:16 packs and are numbered with a "TC" prefix on the card back. A Refractor parallel is randomly seeded 1:80 packs and have "Refractor" printed under the card number on the back.

		MT
Complete Set (10):		80.00
Common Player:		3.00
Inserted 1:16		
Refractors:		2-3X
Inserted 1:80		
1	Roberto Alomar, Manny Ramirez, Kenny Lofton, Jim Thome	4.00
2	Tom Glavine, Greg Maddux, John Smoltz	8.00
3	Derek Jeter, Bernie Williams, Tino Martinez	10.00
4	Ivan Rodriguez, Mike Piazza	10.00
5	Nomar Garciaparra, Alex Rodriguez, Derek Jeter	12.00
6	Sammy Sosa, Mark McGwire	15.00
7	Pedro Martinez, Randy Johnson	4.00
8	Barry Bonds, Ken Griffey Jr.	15.00
9	Chipper Jones, Ivan Rodriguez	8.00
10	Cal Ripken Jr., Tony Gwynn, Wade Boggs	12.00

2000 Topps Chrome Kings

This 10-card set spotlights hitters who have average 30 or more home runs per season during their career. Kings are seeded 1:32 packs and are numbered with a "CK" prefix on the card back. A Refractor parallel is also randomly inserted and are serially numbered to the featured player's career home run total.

		MT
Complete Set (10):		90.00
Common Player:		4.00
Inserted 1:32		
1	Mark McGwire	20.00
2	Sammy Sosa	12.00
3	Ken Griffey Jr.	20.00
4	Mike Piazza	12.00
5	Alex Rodriguez	15.00
6	Manny Ramirez	5.00
7	Barry Bonds	5.00
8	Nomar Garciaparra	12.00
9	Chipper Jones	10.00
10	Vladimir Guerrero	8.00

2000 Topps Chrome Millennium Stars

This 10-card set features stars who had less than three years major league experience in 2000. Millennium Stars are seeded 1:32 packs and are numbered with an "NMS" prefix. A Refractor parallel is randomly inserted in 1:160 packs and has "Refractor" printed under the card number on the back.

		MT
Complete Set (10):		50.00
Common Player:		4.00
Inserted 1:32		
Refractors:		2-3X
Inserted 1:160		
1	Nomar Garciaparra	12.00
2	Vladimir Guerrero	10.00
3	Sean Casey	4.00
4	Richie Sexson	3.00
5	Todd Helton	5.00
6	Carlos Beltran	3.00
7	Kevin Millwood	3.00
8	Ruben Mateo	3.00
9	Pat Burrell	8.00
10	Alfonso Soriano	8.00

2000 Topps Chrome Own the Game

This 30-card set spotlights statistical stars and 1999 Major League Baseball award winners. These were seeded 1:11 packs and are numbered with an "OTG" prefix on the card back. A Refractor parallel is randomly inserted 1:55 packs and has "Refractor" written under the card number on the back.

		MT
Complete Set (30):		160.00
Common Player:		2.00
Inserted 1:12		
Refractors:		2-3X
Inserted 1:55		
1	Derek Jeter	12.00
2	B.J. Surhoff	2.00
3	Luis Gonzalez	2.00
4	Manny Ramirez	5.00
5	Rafael Palmeiro	4.00
6	Mark McGwire	20.00
7	Mark McGwire	20.00
8	Sammy Sosa	12.00
9	Ken Griffey Jr.	20.00
10	Larry Walker	4.00
11	Nomar Garciaparra	12.00
12	Derek Jeter	12.00
13	Larry Walker	4.00
14	Mark McGwire	20.00
15	Manny Ramirez	5.00
16	Pedro Martinez	5.00
17	Randy Johnson	4.00
18	Kevin Millwood	3.00
19	Pedro Martinez	5.00
20	Randy Johnson	4.00
21	Kevin Brown	3.00
22	Chipper Jones	10.00
23	Ivan Rodriguez	5.00
24	Mariano Rivera	3.00
25	Scott Williamson	2.00
26	Carlos Beltran	2.00
27	Randy Johnson	4.00
28	Pedro Martinez	5.00
29	Sammy Sosa	12.00
30	Manny Ramirez	5.00

2000 Topps Chrome Mark McGwire 1985 Rookie Reprint

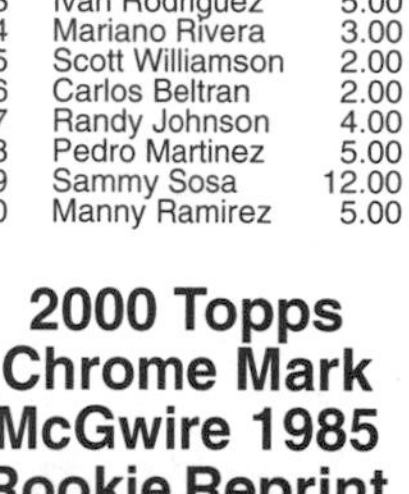

This insert is a chromium reprinted version of McGwire's 1985 Topps rookie card. Each card features a commemorative gold-foil stamp. The insertion rate is 1:32 packs. A hobby-exclusive Refractor version is also inserted, limited to 70 sequentially numbered sets and seeded 1:12,116 packs.

	MT
Complete Set (1):	10.00
Inserted 1:32	
Refractor:	250.00
Production 70 cards	
Mark McGwire	10.00

2000 Topps Chrome Power Players

Twenty of the leading power hitters are featured on a colorful design. They are seeded 1:8 packs and are numbered with a "P" prefix. A Refractor parallel is also randomly seeded 1:40 packs.

		MT
Complete Set (20):		75.00
Common Player:		1.00
Inserted 1:8		
Refractors:		2x-3x
Inserted 1:40		
1	Juan Gonzalez	3.00
2	Ken Griffey Jr.	12.00
3	Mark McGwire	12.00
4	Nomar Garciaparra	8.00
5	Barry Bonds	3.00
6	Mo Vaughn	2.00
7	Larry Walker	2.00
8	Alex Rodriguez	10.00
9	Jose Canseco	3.00
10	Jeff Bagwell	3.00
11	Manny Ramirez	3.00
12	Albert Belle	2.00
13	Frank Thomas	4.00
14	Mike Piazza	8.00
15	Chipper Jones	6.00
16	Sammy Sosa	8.00
17	Vladimir Guerrero	5.00
18	Scott Rolen	3.00
19	Raul Mondesi	1.00
20	Derek Jeter	8.00

2000 Topps Chrome 21st Century Topps

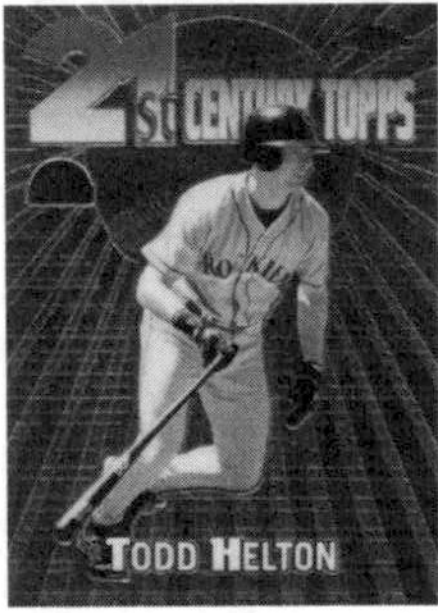

This 10-card set focuses on the top young stars in baseball heading into the next century. These were seeded 1:16 packs and are numbered with a "C" prefix on the card back. A Refractor parallel version is also seeded 1:80 packs.

		MT
Complete Set (10):		40.00
Common Player:		1.50
Inserted 1:16		
Refractors:		2x-3x
Inserted 1:80		
1	Ben Grieve	2.00
2	Alex Gonzalez	1.50
3	Derek Jeter	10.00
4	Sean Casey	2.50
5	Nomar Garciaparra	10.00
6	Alex Rodriguez	10.00
7	Scott Rolen	4.00
8	Andruw Jones	3.00
9	Vladimir Guerrero	4.00
10	Todd Helton	2.00

2000 Topps Chrome Traded and Rookies

		MT
Complete Set (135):		90.00
Common Player:		.25
1	*Mike MacDougal*	1.00
2	*Andy Tracy*	1.00
3	*Brandon Phillips*	1.00
4	*Brandon Inge*	2.00
5	*Robbie Morrison*	1.00
6	*Josh Pressley*	1.00
7	*Todd Moser*	1.00
8	*Rob Purvis*	2.00
9	*Chance Caple*	1.00
10	Ben Sheets	6.00
11	*Russ Jacobson*	1.00
12	*Brian Cole*	2.00
13	*Brad Baker*	1.00
14	*Alex Cintron*	2.00
15	*Lyle Overbay*	3.00
16	*Mike Edwards*	.75
17	*Sean McGowan*	1.00
18	*Jose Molina*	1.00
19	*Marcos Castillo*	.50
20	*Josue Espada*	.50
21	*Alex Gordon*	.75
22	*Rob Pugmire*	.75
23	*Jason Stumm*	2.00
24	*Ty Howington*	2.00
25	*Brett Myers*	.75
26	*Maicer Izturis*	1.00
27	*John McDonald*	1.00
28	*Wilfredo Rodriguez*	2.00
29	*Carlos Zambrano*	4.00
30	*Alejandro Diaz*	1.00
31	*Geraldo Guzman*	1.00
32	*J.R. House*	8.00
33	*Elvin Nina*	.75
34	*Juan Pierre*	1.50
35	*Ben Johnson*	1.00
36	*Jeff Bailey*	1.00
37	*Miguel Olivo*	.75
38	*Francisco Rodriguez*	1.00
39	*Tony Pena Jr.*	1.00
40	*Miguel Cabrera*	.75
41	*Asdrubal Oropeza*	.75
42	*Junior Zamora*	.75
43	*Jovanny Cedeno*	3.00
44	*John Sneed*	.75
45	*Josh Kalinowski*	1.00
46	*Mike Young*	1.00
47	*Rico Washington*	.75
48	*Chad Durbin*	2.00
49	*Junior Brignac*	1.00
50	*Carlos Hernandez*	.75
51	*Cesar Izturis*	2.00
52	*Oscar Salazar*	1.00
53	*Pat Strange*	.75
54	*Rick Asadoorian*	5.00
55	*Keith Reed*	.75
56	*Leo Estrella*	.75
57	*Wascar Serrano*	1.00
58	*Richard Gomez*	1.00
59	*Ramon Santiago*	1.00
60	*Jovanny Sosa*	1.00
61	*Aaron Rowand*	2.00
62	*Junior Guerrero*	1.00
63	*Luis Terrero*	.75
64	*Brian Sanches*	.75
65	*Scott Sobkowiak*	.75
66	*Gary Majewski*	.75
67	Barry Zito	5.00
68	*Ryan Christianson*	.75
69	*Cristian Guerrero*	8.00
70	*Tomas de la Rosa*	.75
71	*Andrew Beinbrink*	1.00
72	*Ryan Knox*	.75
73	*Alex Graman*	2.00
74	*Juan Guzman*	.75
75	*Ruben Salazar*	2.00
76	*Luis Matos*	.50
77	*Tony Mota*	.75
78	*Doug Davis*	1.00
79	*Ben Christensen*	.75
80	Mike Lamb	.50
81	*Adrian Gonzalez* (Draft Picks)	8.00
82	*Mike Stodolka* (Draft Picks)	1.00
83	*Adam Johnson* (Draft Picks)	2.00
84	*Matt Wheatland* (Draft Picks)	2.00
85	*Corey Smith* (Draft Picks)	1.50
86	*Rocco Baldelli* (Draft Picks)	4.00
87	*Keith Bucktrot* (Draft Picks)	1.00
88	*Adam Wainwright* (Draft Picks)	3.00
89	*Scott Thorman* (Draft Picks)	3.00
90	*Tripper Johnson* (Draft Picks)	1.00
91	Jim Edmonds	.50
92	Masato Yoshii	.25
93	Adam Kennedy	.25
94	Darryl Kile	.25
95	Mark McLemore	.25
96	Ricky Gutierrez	.25
97	Juan Gonzalez	1.00
98	Melvin Mora	.25
99	Dante Bichette	.50
100	Lee Stevens	.25
101	Roger Cedeno	.25
102	John Olerud	.40
103	Eric Young	.25
104	Mickey Morandini	.25
105	Travis Lee	.25
106	Greg Vaughn	.40
107	Todd Zeile	.25
108	Chuck Finley	.25
109	Ismael Valdes	.25
110	Ron Henika	.25
111	Pat Hentgen	.25
112	Ryan Klesko	.40
113	Derek Bell	.25
114	Hideo Nomo	1.00
115	Aaron Sele	.25
116	Fernando Vina	.25
117	Wally Joyner	.25
118	Brian Hunter	.25
119	Joe Girardi	.25
120	Omar Daal	.25
121	Brook Fordyce	.25
122	Jose Valentin	.25
123	Curt Schilling	.40
124	B.J. Surhoff	.25
125	Henry Rodriguez	.25
126	Mike Bordick	.25
127	David Justice	1.00
128	Charles Johnson	.25
129	Will Clark	.75
130	Dwight Gooden	.25
131	David Segui	.25
132	Denny Neagle	.25
133	Andy Ashby	.25
134	Bruce Chen	.25
135	Jason Bere	.25

2000 Topps Gallery

The base set consists of 150 cards. Cards 101-150 are broken down into two subsets Masters of the Game (20 cards) and Students of the Game (30 cards). The subset cards are found one per pack. Card fronts have a tan textured border around the player photo with the player name, team and Gallery logo stamped in gold foil. Card backs have a small photo, brief career note and the featured player's '99 statistics. Gallery was a hobby exclusive product. Five-card packs carried a $3 SRP.

		MT
Complete Set (150):		75.00
Common Player:		.15
Common (101-150):		.75
Inserted 1:1		
Pack (6):		3.00
Wax Box (24):		65.00
1	Nomar Garciaparra	2.00
2	Kevin Millwood	.25
3	Jay Bell	.15
4	Rusty Greer	.15
5	Bernie Williams	.60
6	Barry Larkin	.40
7	Carlos Beltran	.25
8	Damion Easley	.15
9	Magglio Ordonez	.25
10	Matt Williams	.40
11	Shannon Stewart	.15
12	Ray Lankford	.15
13	Vinny Castilla	.25
14	Miguel Tejada	.15
15	Craig Biggio	.40
16	Chipper Jones	1.50
17	Albert Belle	.50
18	Doug Glanville	.15
19	Brian Giles	.25
20	Shawn Green	.50
21	J.T. Snow Jr.	.15
22	Luis Gonzalez	.25
23	Carlos Delgado	.75
24	J.D. Drew	.25
25	Ivan Rodriguez	.75
26	Tino Martinez	.40
27	Erubiel Durazo	.25
28	Scott Rolen	.75
29	Gary Sheffield	.40
30	Manny Ramirez	.75
31	Luis Castillo	.15
32	Fernando Tatis	.25
33	Darin Erstad	.25
34	Tim Hudson	.25
35	Sammy Sosa	2.00
36	Jason Kendall	.25
37	Todd Walker	.15
38	Orlando Hernandez	.25
39	Pokey Reese	.15
40	Mike Piazza	2.00
41	B.J. Surhoff	.15
42	Tony Gwynn	1.50
43	Kevin Brown	.25
44	Preston Wilson	.15
45	Kenny Lofton	.40
46	Rondell White	.25
47	Frank Thomas	1.00
48	Neifi Perez	.15
49	Edgardo Alfonzo	.25
50	Ken Griffey Jr.	3.00
51	Barry Bonds	.75
52	Brian Jordan	.15
53	Raul Mondesi	.25
54	Troy Glaus	.75
55	Curt Schilling	.25
56	Mike Mussina	.50
57	Brian Daubach	.15
58	Roger Clemens	1.00
59	Carlos Febles	.15
60	Todd Helton	.75
61	Mark Grace	.25
62	Randy Johnson	.75
63	Jeff Bagwell	.75
64	Tom Glavine	.40
65	Adrian Beltre	.25
66	Rafael Palmeiro	.50
67	Paul O'Neill	.25
68	Robin Ventura	.25
69	Ray Durham	.15
70	Mark McGwire	3.00
71	Greg Vaughn	.40
72	Javy Lopez	.25
73	Jeromy Burnitz	.25
74	Mike Lieberthal	.15
75	Cal Ripken Jr.	2.50
76	Juan Gonzalez	.75
77	Sean Casey	.25
78	Jermaine Dye	.15
79	John Olerud	.25
80	Jose Canseco	.75
81	Eric Karros	.25
82	Roberto Alomar	.50
83	Ben Grieve	.25
84	Greg Maddux	1.50
85	Pedro Martinez	.75
86	Tony Clark	.15
87	Richie Sexson	.15
88	Cliff Floyd	.15
89	Eric Chavez	.15
90	Andruw Jones	.50
91	Vladimir Guerrero	1.25
92	Alex Gonzalez	.15
93	Jim Thome	.40
94	Bob Abreu	.25
95	Derek Jeter	2.00
96	Larry Walker	.50
97	John Smoltz	.15
98	Mo Vaughn	.50
99	Jason Giambi	.25
100	Alex Rodriguez	2.50
101	Mark McGwire (Masters of the Game)	5.00

102	Sammy Sosa (Masters of the Game)	3.00
103	Alex Rodriguez (Masters of the Game)	4.00
104	Derek Jeter (Masters of the Game)	3.00
105	Greg Maddux (Masters of the Game)	2.50
106	Jeff Bagwell (Masters of the Game)	1.25
107	Nomar Garciaparra (Masters of the Game)	3.00
108	Mike Piazza (Masters of the Game)	3.00
109	Pedro Martinez (Masters of the Game)	1.25
110	Chipper Jones (Masters of the Game)	2.50
111	Randy Johnson (Masters of the Game)	1.25
112	Barry Bonds (Masters of the Game)	1.25
113	Ken Griffey Jr. (Masters of the Game)	5.00
114	Manny Ramirez (Masters of the Game)	1.25
115	Ivan Rodriguez (Masters of the Game)	1.25
116	Juan Gonzalez (Masters of the Game)	1.25
117	Vladimir Guerrero (Masters of the Game)	2.00
118	Tony Gwynn (Masters of the Game)	2.50
119	Larry Walker (Masters of the Game)	1.00
120	Cal Ripken Jr. (Masters of the Game)	4.00
121	Josh Hamilton (Students of the Game)	3.00
122	Corey Patterson (Students of the Game)	3.00
123	Pat Burrell (Students of the Game)	3.00
124	Nick Johnson (Students of the Game)	1.00
125	Adam Piatt (Students of the Game)	1.50
126	Rick Ankiel (Students of the Game)	5.00
127	A.J. Burnett (Students of the Game)	1.00
128	Ben Petrick (Students of the Game)	.75
129	Rafael Furcal (Students of the Game)	4.00
130	Alfonso Soriano (Students of the Game)	1.00
131	Dee Brown (Students of the Game)	.75
132	Ruben Mateo (Students of the Game)	.75
133	Pablo Ozuna (Students of the Game)	.75
134	Sean Burroughs (Students of the Game)	1.50
135	Mark Mulder (Students of the Game)	.75
136	Jason Jennings (Students of the Game)	.75
137	Eric Munson (Students of the Game)	2.00
138	Vernon Wells (Students of the Game)	.75
139	*Brett Myers* (Students of the Game)	1.50
140	*Ben Christensen* (Students of the Game)	1.50
141	*Bobby Bradley* (Students of the Game)	3.00
142	*Ruben Salazar* (Students of the Game)	1.50
143	*Ryan Christianson* (Students of the Game)	1.50
144	*Corey Myers* (Students of the Game)	1.50
145	*Aaron Rowand* (Students of the Game)	2.00
146	*Julio Zuleta* (Students of the Game)	1.00
147	*Kurt Ainsworth* (Students of the Game)	1.00
148	*Scott Downs* (Students of the Game)	.75
149	*Larry Bigbie* (Students of the Game)	2.00
150	*Chance Caple* (Students of the Game)	1.00

2000 Topps Gallery Player's Private Issue

A parallel to the 150-card base set, Player's Private Issue cards differ from the base cards with silver foil stamping on the card front and "Players Private Issue" stamped in silver foil across the card bottom. Card backs are serially numbered in an edition of 250 sets.

	MT
Stars (1-100):	10-20X
SPs (101-150):	6-10X
Production 250 sets	

2000 Topps Gallery Autographs

This five-card set features top prospects. Each card is stamped with the Topps Certified Autograph Issue logo and the Topps Authentication sticker. Autographs are seeded 1:153 packs.

		MT
Complete Set (5):		180.00
Common Player:		20.00
Inserted 1:153		
RA	Rick Ankiel	80.00
RM	Ruben Mateo	20.00
CP	Corey Patterson	60.00
BP	Ben Petrick	20.00
VW	Vernon Wells	20.00

2000 Topps Gallery Gallery Exhibits

This 30-card set traces the history of art from medieval to contemporary. Card fronts have gold foil stamping and the card backs are numbered with a "GE" prefix and are found 1:18 packs.

		MT
Complete Set (30):		300.00
Common Player:		3.00
Inserted 1:18		
1	Mark McGwire	30.00
2	Jeff Bagwell	8.00
3	Mike Piazza	20.00
4	Alex Rodriguez	25.00
5	Nomar Garciaparra	20.00
6	Ivan Rodriguez	8.00
7	Chipper Jones	15.00
8	Cal Ripken Jr.	25.00
9	Tony Gwynn	15.00
10	Jose Canseco	8.00
11	Albert Belle	6.00
12	Greg Maddux	15.00
13	Barry Bonds	8.00
14	Ken Griffey Jr.	30.00
15	Juan Gonzalez	8.00
16	Rickey Henderson	4.00
17	Craig Biggio	5.00
18	Vladimir Guerrero	12.00
19	Rey Ordonez	3.00
20	Roberto Alomar	6.00
21	Derek Jeter	20.00
22	Manny Ramirez	8.00
23	Shawn Green	6.00
24	Sammy Sosa	20.00
25	Larry Walker	6.00
26	Pedro Martinez	8.00
27	Randy Johnson	8.00
28	Pat Burrell	10.00
29	Josh Hamilton	12.00
30	Corey Patterson	12.00

2000 Topps Gallery Topps Heritage

Twenty current players are artistically depicted using the 1954 Topps card design as a template. They are seeded 1:12 packs and are numbered on the card back with a "TGH" prefix. As an added bonus the original artwork used in the development of the set is available through the Topps Gallery Auction. Auction-points cards are found in every pack of Gallery.

		MT
Complete Set (20):		250.00
Common Player:		4.00
Inserted 1:12		
Proofs:		1-2X
Inserted 1:27		
1	Mark McGwire	30.00
2	Sammy Sosa	20.00
3	Greg Maddux	15.00
4	Mike Piazza	20.00
5	Ivan Rodriguez	8.00
6	Manny Ramirez	8.00
7	Jeff Bagwell	8.00
8	Sean Casey	4.00
9	Orlando Hernandez	4.00
10	Randy Johnson	8.00
11	Pedro Martinez	8.00
12	Vladimir Guerrero	12.00
13	Shawn Green	6.00
14	Ken Griffey Jr.	30.00
15	Alex Rodriguez	25.00
16	Nomar Garciaparra	20.00
17	Derek Jeter	20.00
18	Tony Gwynn	15.00
19	Chipper Jones	15.00
20	Cal Ripken Jr.	25.00

2000 Topps Gallery Lithos

Eight cards from the Topps Gallery set were issued in the form of limited edition lithographs by Bill Goff Inc. Measuring 18" x 25", the lithographs were each produced in an edition of 600, with 60 artist's proofs. Issue price on the lithos was $80 for single-player pieces and $100 for the multi-player prints.

		MT
Complete Set (8):		675.00
Common Player:		80.00
(1)	Shawn Green (1954 Topps Style)	80.00
(2)	Ken Griffey Jr. (1954 Topps Style)	80.00
(3)	Chipper Jones (1954 Topps Style)	80.00
(4)	Pedro Martinez (1954 Topps Style)	80.00
(5)	Alex Rodriguez (1954 Topps Style)	80.00
(6)	Ivan Rodriguez (1954 Topps Style)	80.00

(7)	Three of a Kind (Nomar Garciaparra, Alex Rodriguez, Derek Jeter)	100.00
(8)	Torre's Terrors (Paul O'Neill, Derek Jeter, Bernie Williams, Tino Martinez)	100.00

2000 Topps Gallery Proof Positive

This 10-card set features both positive and negative photography. Done on a horizontal format the inserts pair a current star with a top prospect at the same position. Printed on a clear polycarbonate stock they were inserted 1:48 packs and are numbered with a "P" prefix.

		MT
Complete Set (10):		125.00
Common Player:		6.00
Inserted 1:48		
1	Ken Griffey Jr., Ruben Mateo	25.00
2	Derek Jeter, Alfonso Soriano	15.00
3	Mark McGwire, Pat Burrell	25.00
4	Pedro Martinez, A.J. Burnett	6.00
5	Alex Rodriguez, Rafael Furcal	20.00
6	Sammy Sosa, Corey Patterson	15.00
7	Randy Johnson, Rick Ankiel	15.00
8	Chipper Jones, Adam Piatt	12.00
9	Nomar Garciaparra, Pablo Ozuna	15.00
10	Mike Piazza, Eric Munson	15.00

2000 Topps Gallery of Heroes

This 10-card set is printed on an acetate stock that simulates stained glass. Gallery of Heroes are found on the average of 1:24 packs and are numbered with a "GH" prefix on the card back.

		MT
Complete Set (10):		100.00
Common Player:		4.00
Inserted 1:24		
1	Alex Rodriguez	15.00
2	Chipper Jones	10.00
3	Pedro Martinez	5.00
4	Sammy Sosa	12.00
5	Mark McGwire	18.00
6	Nomar Garciaparra	12.00
7	Vladimir Guerrero	8.00
8	Ken Griffey Jr.	18.00
9	Mike Piazza	12.00
10	Derek Jeter	12.00

2000 Topps Gold Label Class 1

Each base card in the 100-card set has three different classes, each noted on the card back below the featured player's team logo. Each base card is also printed on 35-point rainbow styrene stock with gold-foil stamping. Besides the notation on the card back, Class 1's can also be identified by the action in the background photo. Hitters are hitting and pitchers are at the start of their wind-up. A Gold die-cut parallel is also randomly seeded and are serially numbered to 100.

		MT
Complete Set (100):		90.00
Common Player:		.25
Gold parallel:		10-20X
Production 100 sets		
Pack (3):		3.00
Wax Box (24):		65.00
1	Sammy Sosa	3.00
2	Greg Maddux	2.50
3	Dee Brown	.25
4	Rondell White	.25
5	Fernando Tatis	.25
6	Troy Glaus	1.50
7	Nick Johnson	.50
8	Albert Belle	.75
9	Scott Rolen	1.00
10	Rafael Palmeiro	1.00
11	Tony Gwynn	2.00
12	Kevin Brown	.50
13	Roberto Alomar	1.00
14	John Olerud	.50
15	Rick Ankiel	3.00
16	Chipper Jones	2.50
17	Craig Biggio	.50
18	Mark Mulder	.25
19	Carlos Delgado	1.00
20	Alex Gonzalez	.25
21	Gabe Kapler	.75
22	Derek Jeter	3.00
23	Carlos Beltran	.25
24	Todd Helton	1.25
25	Mark McGwire	5.00
26	Ben Grieve	.50
27	Rafael Furcal	.75
28	Vernon Wells	.25
29	Greg Vaughn	.50
30	Vladimir Guerrero	2.00
31	Mike Piazza	3.00
32	Roger Clemens	1.75
33	Barry Larkin	.75
34	Pedro Martinez	1.25
35	Matt Williams	.75
36	Mo Vaughn	.75
37	Tim Hudson	.50
38	Andruw Jones	.75
39	Vinny Castilla	.25
40	Frank Thomas	2.00
41	Pokey Reese	.25
42	Corey Patterson	1.50
43	Jeromy Burnitz	.25
44	Preston Wilson	.25
45	Juan Gonzalez	1.25
46	Brian Giles	.25
47	Todd Walker	.25
48	Magglio Ordonez	.25
49	Alfonso Soriano	.75
50	Ken Griffey Jr.	5.00
51	Michael Barrett	.25
52	Shawn Green	.50
53	Erubiel Durazo	.25
54	Adam Piatt	.25
55	Pat Burrell	1.25
56	Mike Mussina	.75
57	Bernie Williams	1.00
58	Sean Casey	.50
59	Randy Johnson	1.25
60	Jeff Bagwell	1.25
61	Eric Chavez	.25
62	Josh Hamilton	1.50
63	A.J. Burnett	.25
64	Jim Thome	.75
65	Raul Mondesi	.50
66	Jason Kendall	.40
67	Mike Lieberthal	.25
68	Robin Ventura	.40
69	Ivan Rodriguez	1.25
70	Larry Walker	.75
71	Eric Munson	.50
72	Brian Jordan	.25
73	Edgardo Alfonzo	.50
74	Curt Schilling	.40
75	Nomar Garciaparra	3.00
76	Mark Grace	.50
77	Shannon Stewart	.25
78	J.D. Drew	.25
79	Jack Cust	.25
80	Cal Ripken Jr.	4.00
81	Bob Abreu	.25
82	Ruben Mateo	.25
83	Orlando Hernandez	.50
84	Kris Benson	.25
85	Barry Bonds	1.25
86	Manny Ramirez	1.25
87	Jose Canseco	.75
88	Sean Burroughs	.50
89	Kevin Millwood	.25
90	Alex Rodriguez	4.00
91	*Brett Myers*	1.50
92	*Rick Asadoorian*	5.00
93	*Ben Christensen*	1.50
94	*Bobby Bradley*	2.50
95	*Corey Myers*	1.00
96	*Brad Baisley*	.75
97	*Aaron McNeal*	1.00
98	*Aaron Rowand*	.50
99	*Scott Downs*	1.00
100	*Michael Tejera*	1.00

2000 Topps Gold Label Class 2

Each base card in the 100-card set has three different classes, each noted on the card back below the featured player's team logo. Each base card is also printed on 35-point rainbow styrene stock with gold-foil stamping. Besides the notation on the card back, Class 2's can also be identified by the action in the background photo. Hitters are fielding and pitchers are in a throwing motion. A Gold die-cut parallel is also randomly seeded and are serially numbered to 100.

	MT
Same prices as Class 1	
Gold Parallel:	10-20X

2000 Topps Gold Label Class 3

Each base card in the 100-card set has three different classes, each noted on the card back below the featured player's team logo. Each base card is also printed on 35-point rainbow styrene stock with gold foil stamping. Besides the notation on the card back, Class 3's can also be identified by the action in the background photo. Hitters are running and pitchers are in their follow through. A Gold die-cut parallel is also randomly seeded and are serially numbered to 100.

	MT
Same prices as Class 1	
Gold parallel:	10-20X
Production 100 sets	

2000 Topps Gold Label Name Mismatches

Because of faulty alignment when the gold-foil logo and player name were applied to card fronts, some Gold Label cards are found with the wrong name on front. Because each of these error cards is rare or possibly unique, and the demand is dependent on the combination of photo and name, it is not possible to assign values.

MT
(Values undetermined.)

2000 Topps Gold Label Bullion

This 10-card set features three teammates superimposed over their team logo on a gold holo-foiled front with gold-foil stamping. They are seeded 1:53 packs and are numbered on the card back with a "B" prefix.

		MT
Complete Set (10):		125.00
Common Player:		4.00
Inserted 1:53		
1	Jim Thome, Manny Ramirez, Roberto Alomar	6.00
2	Derek Jeter, Orlando Hernandez, Bernie Williams	15.00
3	Chipper Jones, Andruw Jones, Greg Maddux	12.00
4	Alex Rodriguez, Jay Buhner, John Olerud	20.00
5	Nomar Garciaparra, Pedro Martinez, Brian Daubach	15.00
6	Mark McGwire, J.D. Drew, Rick Ankiel	25.00
7	Sammy Sosa, Mark Grace, Kerry Wood	15.00
8	Ken Griffey Jr., Sean Casey, Barry Larkin	25.00
9	Mike Piazza, Edgardo Alfonzo, Robin Ventura	15.00
10	Randy Johnson, Matt Williams, Erubiel Durazo	6.00

2000 Topps Gold Label End of the Rainbow

This 15-card set highlights some of baseball's top prospects on a silver holo foiled card front with gold-foil stamping. Card backs are numbered with an "ER" prefix and are seeded 1:11 packs.

		MT
Complete Set (15):		30.00
Common Player:		1.50
Inserted 1:11		
1	Pat Burrell	5.00
2	Corey Patterson	5.00
3	Josh Hamilton	5.00
4	Eric Munson	2.50
5	Sean Burroughs	2.50
6	Jack Cust	2.00
7	Rafael Furcal	2.50
8	Ruben Salazar	1.50
9	Brett Myers	1.50
10	Wes Anderson	1.50
11	Nick Johnson	2.50
12	Scott Downs	1.50
13	Choo Freeman	1.50
14	Brad Baisley	1.50
15	A.J. Burnett	1.50

2000 Topps Gold Label Prospector's Dream

These inserts feature 10 players whose success was projected early in their careers. Card fronts feature gold holofoil with the player name, Gold Label logo and insert name stamped in gold foil. Card backs are numbered with a "PD" prefix. They are inserted 1:26 packs.

		MT
Complete Set (10):		75.00
Common Player:		3.00
Inserted 1:26		
1	Mark McGwire	20.00
2	Alex Rodriguez	15.00
3	Nomar Garciaparra	12.00
4	Pat Burrell	5.00
5	Todd Helton	5.00
6	Derek Jeter	12.00
7	Adam Piatt	4.00
8	Chipper Jones	10.00
9	Shawn Green	4.00
10	Josh Hamilton	5.00

2000 Topps Gold Label The Treasury

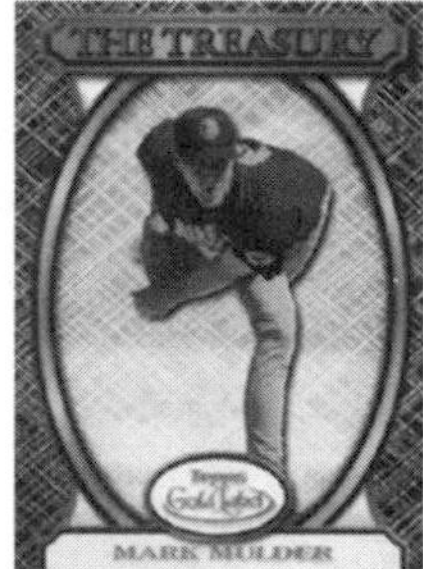

This 25-card set spotlights 15 veterans and 10 prospects on a silver holo foiled front with gold-foil stamping. They have an insertion ratio of 1:21 packs and are numbered on the card back with a "T" prefix.

		MT
Complete Set (25):		150.00
Common Player:		3.00
Inserted 1:21		
1	Ken Griffey Jr.	20.00
2	Derek Jeter	12.00
3	Chipper Jones	10.00
4	Manny Ramirez	5.00
5	Nomar Garciaparra	12.00
6	Sammy Sosa	12.00
7	Cal Ripken Jr.	15.00
8	Alex Rodriguez	15.00
9	Mike Piazza	12.00
10	Pedro Martinez	5.00
11	Vladimir Guerrero	6.00
12	Jeff Bagwell	5.00
13	Shawn Green	4.00
14	Greg Maddux	10.00
15	Mark McGwire	20.00
16	Josh Hamilton	5.00
17	Corey Patterson	5.00
18	Dee Brown	3.00
19	Rafael Furcal	4.00
20	Pat Burrell	5.00
21	Alfonso Soriano	4.00
22	Adam Piatt	4.00
23	A.J. Burnett	3.00
24	Mark Mulder	3.00
25	Ruben Mateo	3.00

2000 Topps HD

This super-premium product consists of 100 regular base cards comprised of 88 veterans and 12 rookies. The base cards feature hyper-color technology and are printed on very thick 50-pt. card stock. Card backs have a small photo, career highlights and complete year-by-year statistics. A Platinum parallel to the base set is also randomly seeded and are sequentially numbered to 99 sets.

		MT
Complete Set (100):		100.00
Common Player:		.50
Platinums:		10x to 20x
Production 99 sets		
Pack (4):		4.00
Wax Box (20):		70.00
1	Derek Jeter	5.00
2	Andruw Jones	1.25
3	Ben Grieve	.75
4	Carlos Beltran	.50
5	Randy Johnson	1.50
6	Javy Lopez	.50
7	Gary Sheffield	.75
8	John Olerud	.75
9	Vinny Castilla	.50
10	Barry Larkin	1.00
11	Tony Clark	.50
12	Roberto Alomar	1.25
13	Brian Jordan	.50
14	Wade Boggs	1.00
15	Carlos Febles	.50
16	Alfonso Soriano	1.00
17	A.J. Burnett	.50
18	Matt Williams	.75
19	Alex Gonzalez	.50
20	Larry Walker	.75
21	Jeff Bagwell	1.50
22	Al Leiter	.50
23	Ken Griffey Jr.	5.00
24	Ruben Mateo	.50
25	Mark Grace	.75
26	Carlos Delgado	1.25
27	Vladimir Guerrero	2.00
28	Kenny Lofton	.75
29	Rusty Greer	.50
30	Pedro Martinez	1.50
31	Todd Helton	1.50
32	Ray Lankford	.50
33	Jose Canseco	1.00
34	Raul Mondesi	.75
35	Mo Vaughn	1.00
36	Eric Chavez	.75
37	Manny Ramirez	1.50
38	Jason Kendall	.50
39	Mike Mussina	1.00
40	Dante Bichette	.50
41	Troy Glaus	1.50
42	Rickey Henderson	1.00
43	Pablo Ozuna	.50
44	Michael Barrett	.50
45	Tony Gwynn	2.00
46	John Smoltz	.50
47	Rafael Palmeiro	1.00
48	Curt Schilling	.50
49	Todd Walker	.50
50	Greg Vaughn	.50
51	Orlando Hernandez	.50
52	Jim Thome	1.00
53	Pat Burrell	1.00
54	Tim Salmon	.75
55	Tom Glavine	.75
56	Travis Lee	.50
57	Gabe Kapler	.50

58	Greg Maddux	3.00
59	Scott Rolen	1.00
60	Cal Ripken Jr.	5.00
61	Preston Wilson	.50
62	Ivan Rodriguez	1.50
63	Johnny Damon	.50
64	Bernie Williams	1.25
65	Barry Bonds	1.50
66	Sammy Sosa	3.00
67	Robin Ventura	.50
68	Tony Fernandez	.50
69	Jay Bell	.50
70	Mark McGwire	6.00
71	Jeromy Burnitz	.50
72	Chipper Jones	3.00
73	Josh Hamilton	1.00
74	Darin Erstad	.50
75	Alex Rodriguez	5.00
76	Sean Casey	.75
77	Tino Martinez	.50
78	Juan Gonzalez	1.50
79	Cliff Floyd	.50
80	Craig Biggio	.75
81	Shawn Green	1.00
82	Adrian Beltre	.50
83	Mike Piazza	4.00
84	Nomar Garciaparra	4.00
85	Kevin Brown	.75
86	Roger Clemens	2.00
87	Frank Thomas	2.00
88	Albert Belle	.75
89	Erubiel Durazo	.50
90	David Walling	.50
91	*John Sneed*	2.50
92	*Larry Bigbie*	2.00
93	*B.J. Garbe*	2.50
94	*Bobby Bradley*	4.00
95	*Ryan Christiansen*	1.50
96	*Jay Gerhke*	1.00
97	*Jason Stumm*	2.00
98	*Brett Myers*	1.50
99	*Chance Caple*	1.50
100	*Corey Myers*	2.00

2000 Topps HD Autographs

This two-card set features Cal Ripken Jr. and Derek Jeter. Card fronts include the Topps "Certified Autograph Issue" logo stamp as well as the Topps 3M authentication sticker to verify its authenticity. The insert rate for Jeter is 1:859 and Ripken Jr. 1:4,386.

		MT
Complete Set (2):		600.00
Jeter 1:859		
Ripken 1:4,386		
1	Derek Jeter	250.00
2	Cal Ripken Jr.	400.00

2000 Topps HD Ballpark Figures

This 10-card set features a baseball field designed die-cut. These are seeded 1:11 packs and are numbered with a "BF" prefix on the card back.

		MT
Complete Set (10):		50.00
Common Player:		1.50
Inserted 1:11		
1	Mark McGwire	12.00
2	Ken Griffey Jr.	12.00
3	Nomar Garciaparra	8.00
4	Derek Jeter	8.00
5	Sammy Sosa	8.00
6	Mike Piazza	8.00
7	Juan Gonzalez	3.00
8	Larry Walker	2.50
9	Ben Grieve	1.50
10	Barry Bonds	3.00

2000 Topps HD Image

This 10-card insert set highlights those batters with the best eyes at the plate. These were seeded 1:44 packs and are numbered with a "HD" prefix on the card back.

		MT
Complete Set (10):		150.00
Common Player:		5.00
Inserted 1:44		
1	Sammy Sosa	15.00
2	Mark McGwire	30.00
3	Derek Jeter	25.00
4	Albert Belle	5.00
5	Vladimir Guerrero	10.00
6	Ken Griffey Jr.	25.00
7	Mike Piazza	20.00
8	Alex Rodriguez	25.00
9	Barry Bonds	8.00
10	Nomar Garciaparra	20.00

2000 Topps HD On the Cutting Edge

This 10-card insert set is die-cut down the right hand side of the card highlighting the five-tool stars top five baseball attributes. These are inserted 1:22 packs and are numbered with a "CE" prefix on the card back.

		MT
Complete Set (10):		75.00
Common Player:		3.00
Inserted 1:22		
1	Andruw Jones	3.00
2	Nomar Garciaparra	12.00
3	Barry Bonds	5.00
4	Larry Walker	3.00
5	Vladimir Guerrero	8.00
6	Jeff Bagwell	5.00
7	Derek Jeter	12.00
8	Sammy Sosa	12.00
9	Alex Rodriguez	15.00
10	Ken Griffey Jr.	20.00

2000 Topps HD Clearly Refined

This 10-card set focuses on baseball's top young stars heading into the 2000 season. They are printed on high definition card stock and are seeded 1:20 packs. These are numbered with a "CR" prefix on the card back.

		MT
Complete Set (10):		30.00
Common Player:		2.00
Inserted 1:20		
1	Alfonso Soriano	3.00
2	Ruben Mateo	2.00
3	Josh Hamilton	6.00
4	Chad Hermansen	2.00
5	Ryan Anderson	3.00
6	Nick Johnson	3.00
7	Octavio Dotel	2.00
8	Peter Bergeron	2.00
9	Adam Piatt	4.00
10	Pat Burrell	8.00

2000 Topps Opening Day 2K

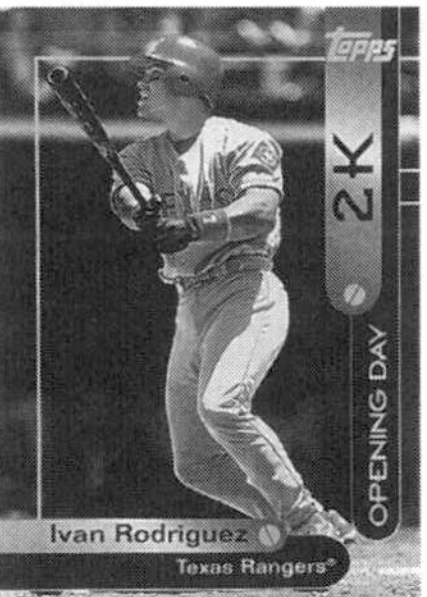

As part of a multi-manufacturer promotion, Topps issued eight cards of an "Opening Day 2K" set. Packages containing some of the 32 cards in the issue were distributed by MLB teams early in the season. The cards were also available exclusively as inserts in Topps Opening Day packs sold at K-Mart stores early in the season. The Topps OD2K cards have gold-foil graphic highlights on front. Backs have portrait photos, stats and are numbered with an "OD" prefix.

		MT
Complete Set (8):		6.00
Common Player:		.50
1	Mark McGwire	2.00
2	Barry Bonds	.75
3	Ivan Rodriguez	.75
4	Sean Casey	.65
5	Derek Jeter	1.00
6	Vladimir Guerrero	1.00
7	Preston Wilson	.65
8	Ben Grieve	.50

2000 Topps Stars

The base set consists of 200 cards, including a 50-card Spotlights subset (151-200). Card fronts have a shadow image of the featured player in the background of the player photo. The Topps Stars logo, player name, team logo and position are stamped in silver foil.

		MT
Complete Set (200):		35.00
Common Player:		.10
Pack (6):		2.75
Box (24):		60.00
1	Vladimir Guerrero	1.00
2	Eric Karros	.10
3	Omar Vizquel	.10
4	Ken Griffey Jr.	3.00
5	Preston Wilson	.10
6	Albert Belle	.50
7	Ryan Klesko	.10
8	Bob Abreu	.10
9	Warren Morris	.10
10	Rafael Palmeiro	.40
11	Nomar Garciaparra	2.00
12	Dante Bichette	.10
13	Jeff Cirillo	.10
14	Carlos Beltran	.10
15	Tony Clark	.10
16	Ray Durham	.10
17	Mark McGwire	3.00
18	Jim Thome	.40
19	Todd Walker	.10
20	Richie Sexson	.10
21	Adrian Beltre	.10
22	Jay Bell	.10
23	Craig Biggio	.25
24	Ben Grieve	.25
25	Greg Maddux	1.50
26	Fernando Tatis	.10
27	Jeromy Burnitz	.10
28	Vinny Castilla	.10
29	Mark Grace	.25
30	Derek Jeter	2.00
31	Larry Walker	.40
32	Ivan Rodriguez	.75
33	Curt Schilling	.20
34	*Mike Lamb*	.40
35	Kevin Brown	.20
36	Andruw Jones	.40
37	*Chris Mears*	.10
38	Bartolo Colon	.10
39	Edgardo Alfonzo	.25
40	Brady Anderson	.20

41 Andres Galarraga .50
42 Scott Rolen .50
43 Manny Ramirez .75
44 Carlos Delgado .75
45 David Cone .10
46 Carl Everett .10
47 Chipper Jones 1.50
48 Barry Bonds .75
49 Dean Palmer .10
50 Frank Thomas 1.00
51 Paul O'Neill .25
52 Mo Vaughn .40
53 Todd Helton .75
54 Jason Giambi .20
55 Brian Jordan .10
56 Luis Gonzalez .10
57 Alex Rodriguez 2.50
58 J.D. Drew .10
59 Javy Lopez .10
60 Tony Gwynn 1.25
61 Jason Kendall .20
62 Pedro Martinez .75
63 Matt Williams .40
64 Gary Sheffield .40
65 Roberto Alomar .50
66 *Lyle Overbay* .10
67 Jeff Bagwell .75
68 Tim Hudson .20
69 Sammy Sosa 2.00
70 *Keith Reed* .10
71 Robin Ventura .20
72 Cal Ripken Jr. 2.50
73 Alex Gonzalez .10
74 *Aaron McNeal* .10
75 Mike Lieberthal .10
76 Brian Giles .25
77 Kevin Millwood .10
78 Troy O'Leary .10
79 Raul Mondesi .20
80 John Olerud .20
81 David Justice .25
82 Erubiel Durazo .10
83 Shawn Green .40
84 Tino Martinez .20
85 Greg Vaughn .20
86 Tom Glavine .20
87 Jose Canseco .40
88 Kenny Lofton .25
89 Brian Daubach .10
90 Mike Piazza 2.00
91 Randy Johnson .75
92 Pokey Reese .10
93 Troy Glaus .50
94 Kerry Wood .25
95 Sean Casey .20
96 Magglio Ordonez .20
97 Bernie Williams .50
98 Juan Gonzalez .75
99 Barry Larkin .30
100 Orlando Hernandez .20
101 Roger Clemens 1.00
102 Bob Gibson (Retired Stars) .40
103 Gary Carter (Retired Stars) .10
104 Willie Stargell (Retired Stars) .10
105 Joe Morgan (Retired Stars) .40
106 Brooks Robinson (Retired Stars) .50
107 Ozzie Smith (Retired Stars) .50
108 Carl Yastrzemski (Retired Stars) .25
109 Al Kaline (Retired Stars) .40
110 Frank Robinson (Retired Stars) .50
111 Lance Berkman (Shining Prospects) .10
112 Adam Piatt (Shining Prospects) .40
113 Vernon Wells (Shining Prospects) .10
114 Rafael Furcal (Shining Prospects) .40
115 Rick Ankiel (Shining Prospects) 1.50
116 Corey Patterson (Shining Prospects) .75
117 Josh Hamilton (Shining Prospects) .75
118 Jack Cust (Shining Prospects) .40
119 Josh Girdley (Shining Prospects) .10
120 Pablo Ozuna (Shining Prospects) .10
121 Sean Burroughs (Shining Prospects) .40
122 Pat Burrell (Shining Prospects) .75
123 Chad Hermansen (Shining Prospects) .10
124 Ruben Mateo (Shining Prospects) .10
125 Ben Petrick (Shining Prospects) .10
126 Dee Brown (Shining Prospects) .10
127 Eric Munson (Shining Prospects) .10
128 Ruben Salazar (Shining Prospects) .10
129 Kip Wells (Shining Prospects) .10
130 Alfonso Soriano (Shining Prospects) .75
131 Mark Mulder (Shining Prospects) .10
132 Roosevelt Brown (Shining Prospects) .10
133 Nick Johnson (Shining Prospects) .40
134 Kyle Snyder (Shining Prospects) .10
135 David Walling (Shining Prospects) .10
136 *Geraldo Guzman* .50
137 *John Sneed* .50
138 *Ben Christensen* .75
139 *Corey Myers* 1.00
140 *Jose Ortiz* 6.00
141 *Ryan Christianson* 1.00
142 *Brett Myers* 1.00
143 *Bobby Bradley* 1.50
144 *Rick Asadoorian* 4.00
145 *Julio Zuleta* .40
146 *Ty Howington* .50
147 *Josh Kalinowski* .40
148 *B.J. Garbe* 1.50
149 *Scott Downs* .40
150 *Dan Wright* .50
151 Jeff Bagwell (Veterans) .40
152 Vladimir Guerrero (Veterans) .50
153 Mike Piazza (Veterans) 1.00
154 Juan Gonzalez (Veterans) .40
155 Ivan Rodriguez (Veterans) .40
156 Manny Ramirez (Veterans) .40
157 Sammy Sosa (Veterans) 1.00
158 Chipper Jones (Veterans) .75
159 Shawn Green (Veterans) .20
160 Ken Griffey Jr. (Veterans) 1.50
161 Cal Ripken Jr. (Veterans) 1.25
162 Nomar Garciaparra (Veterans) 1.00
163 Derek Jeter (Veterans) 1.00
164 Barry Bonds (Veterans) .40
165 Greg Maddux (Veterans) .75
166 Mark McGwire (Veterans) 1.50
167 Roberto Alomar (Veterans) .25
168 Alex Rodriguez (Veterans) 1.25
169 Randy Johnson (Veterans) .40
170 Tony Gwynn (Veterans) .60
171 Pedro Martinez (Veterans) .40
172 Bob Gibson (Retired Stars) .25
173 Gary Carter (Retired Stars) .10
174 Willie Stargell (Retired Stars) .25
175 Joe Morgan (Retired Stars) .25
176 Brooks Robinson (Retired Stars) .40
177 Ozzie Smith (Retired Stars) .50
178 Carl Yastrzemski (Retired Stars) .20
179 Al Kaline (Retired Stars) .25
180 Frank Robinson (Retired Stars) .40
181 Adam Piatt (Prospects) .20
182 Alfonso Soriano (Prospects) .40
183 Corey Patterson (Prospects) .40
184 Vernon Wells (Prospects) .10
185 Pat Burrell (Prospects) .40
186 Mark Mulder (Prospects) .10
187 Eric Munson (Prospects) .10
188 Rafael Furcal (Prospects) .20
189 Rick Ankiel (Prospects) .75
190 Ruben Mateo (Prospects) .10
191 Sean Burroughs (Prospects) .20
192 Josh Hamilton (Prospects) .40
193 Brett Myers .50
194 Ben Christensen .40
195 Ty Howington .25
196 Rick Asadoorian 2.00
197 Josh Kalinowski .20
198 Corey Myers .50
199 Ryan Christianson .50
200 John Sneed .25

2000 Topps Stars Blue

A parallel to the 200-card base set the player's shadow has blue tint and the Topps Stars logo, player name, team logo and position are stamped in blue foil. Cards 1-150 are serially numbered on the card back to 299 and cards 151-200 are serially numbered to 99.

	MT
Stars (1-150):	5-10X
Production 299 sets	
Stars (151-180):	20-30X
Rookies (181-200):	8-15X
Production 99 sets	

2000 Topps Stars Autographs

A combination of retired and current players make up this 13-card set. The set is broken down into two levels: A and B. Level A autographs are seeded 1:382 packs and Level B autographs are found 1:1,636 packs. Each card features the Topps "Certified Autograph Issue" stamp and the Topps "Genuine Issue" sticker on the card back. Card backs are numbered with the featured player's initials.

		MT
Common Player:		15.00
Group A 1:382		
Group B 1:1,636		
RA	Rick Ankiel A	60.00
GC	Gary Carter B	60.00
RF	Rafael Furcal A	40.00
BG	Bob Gibson A	60.00
DJ	Derek Jeter A	180.00
AK	Al Kaline B	250.00
KM	Kevin Millwood A	15.00
JM	Joe Morgan B	90.00
BR	Brooks Robinson B	90.00
FR	Frank Robinson B	75.00
OS	Ozzie Smith B	100.00
WS	Willie Stargell B	50.00
CY	Carl Yastrzemski B	100.00

2000 Topps Stars Game Gear Bats

A piece of the featured player's game-used bat is embedded into the card front and are seeded 1:175 packs.

		MT
Common Player:		15.00
Group A 1:2,289		
Group B 1:1,153		
Group C 1:409		
1	Rafael Furcal C	40.00
2	Sean Burroughs B	25.00
3	Corey Patterson B	40.00
4	Chipper Jones B	75.00
5	Vernon Wells C	15.00
6	Alfonso Soriano B	25.00
7	Eric Munson C	20.00
8	Ben Petrick B	15.00
9	Dee Brown A	20.00
10	Lance Berkman C	20.00

2000 Topps Stars Game Gear Jersey

A piece of the featured player's game-used jersey is embedded into the card front and are seeded 1:382 packs.

		MT
Common Player:		20.00
Inserted 1:382		
1	Kevin Millwood	30.00
2	Brad Penny	20.00
3	J.D. Drew	40.00

2000 Topps Stars All-Star Authority

This 14-card set features a gold and silver holofoiled front with gold etching. Card backs are numbered with an "AS" prefix. They are found on the the average of 1:13 packs.

		MT
Complete Set (14):		50.00
Common Player:		1.50
Inserted 1:13		
1	Mark McGwire	8.00
2	Sammy Sosa	5.00
3	Ken Griffey Jr.	8.00
4	Cal Ripken Jr.	6.00
5	Tony Gwynn	3.00
6	Barry Bonds	2.00
7	Mike Piazza	5.00
8	Pedro Martinez	2.00
9	Chipper Jones	4.00
10	Manny Ramirez	2.00
11	Alex Rodriguez	6.00
12	Derek Jeter	5.00
13	Nomar Garciaparra	5.00
14	Roberto Alomar	1.50

2000 Topps Stars Progression

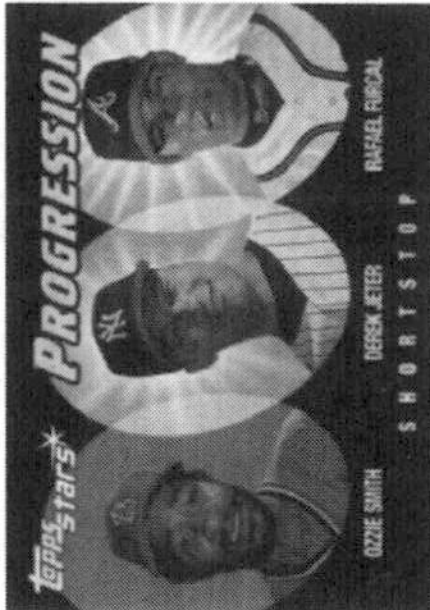

Each of the nine cards features three players on a horizontal format, progressing from past, present and future stars at each of the nine positions. They were seeded 1:13 packs and are numbered on the back with a "P" prefix.

		MT
Complete Set (9):		20.00
Common Player:		1.00
Inserted 1:13		
1	Bob Gibson, Pedro Martinez, Rick Ankiel	1.50
2	Gary Carter, Mike Piazza, Ben Petrick	4.00
3	Willie Stargell, Mark McGwire, Pat Burrell	6.00
4	Joe Morgan, Roberto Alomar, Ruben Salazar	1.00
5	Brooks Robinson, Chipper Jones, Sean Burroughs	3.00
6	Ozzie Smith, Derek Jeter, Rafael Furcal	4.00
7	Carl Yastrzemski, Barry Bonds,	1.50
8	Al Kaline, Ken Griffey Jr., Ruben Mateo	6.00
9	Frank Robinson, Manny Ramirez, Corey Patterson	1.50

2000 Topps Stars Walk of Fame

This 15-card set spotlights the top stars on a silver and gold holofoiled card front. Card backs feature comparative commentary with the all-time best at their respective positions and are numbered with a "WF" prefix. They are seeded 1:8 packs.

		MT
Complete Set (15):		40.00
Common Player:		1.00
Inserted 1:8		
1	Cal Ripken Jr.	5.00
2	Ken Griffey Jr.	5.00
3	Mark McGwire	6.00
4	Sammy Sosa	3.00
5	Alex Rodriguez	5.00
6	Derek Jeter	4.00
7	Nomar Garciaparra	4.00
8	Chipper Jones	3.00
9	Manny Ramirez	1.50
10	Mike Piazza	4.00
11	Vladimir Guerrero	2.00
12	Barry Bonds	1.50
13	Tony Gwynn	2.00
14	Roberto Alomar	1.00
15	Pedro Martinez	1.50

2000 Topps TEK

Forty-five players make up this set including 5 rookies (41-45). Each card is printed on a transparent, polycarbonate stock with patterns 1-15 featuring silver foil metalization. All 45 players are featured on 20 different player-focused background patterns. Card backs have two numbers, the first is the player's card number within the set and the second is the pattern number. Patterns 16-20 have color variations and have an insertion rate of 1:10 packs. Each pack contains 4 TEK cards with an SRP of $5.

		MT
Complete Set (45):		50.00
Common Player:		.40
Common Rookie (41-45):		1.00
2,000 serial numbered rookies		
Pack (4):		4.00
Box (20):		75.00
1	Mike Piazza	3.00
2	Chipper Jones	2.50
3	Juan Gonzalez	1.25
4	Ivan Rodriguez	1.25
5	Cal Ripken Jr.	4.00
6	A.J. Burnett	.40
7	Jim Thome	.75
8	Mo Vaughn	.75
9	Andruw Jones	.75
10	Mark McGwire	5.00
11	Jose Canseco	.75
12	Shawn Green	.75
13	Barry Bonds	1.25
14	Bernie Williams	1.00
15	Manny Ramirez	1.25
16	Greg Maddux	2.50
17	Carlos Beltran	.40
18	Pedro Martinez	1.25
19	Jeff Bagwell	1.25
20	Sammy Sosa	3.00
21	J.D. Drew	.40
22	Randy Johnson	1.25
23	Larry Walker	.75
24	Frank Thomas	2.00
25	Orlando Hernandez	.40
26	Scott Rolen	1.00
27	Tony Gwynn	2.00
28	Rick Ankiel	2.00
29	Roberto Alomar	1.00
30	Ken Griffey Jr.	5.00
31	Vladimir Guerrero	1.50
32	Derek Jeter	3.00
33	Nomar Garciaparra	3.00
34	Alex Rodriguez	4.00
35	Sean Casey	.40
36	Adam Piatt (Prospects)	.40
37	Corey Patterson (Prospects)	1.25
38	Josh Hamilton (Prospects)	1.25
39	Pat Burrell (Prospects)	1.25
40	Eric Munson (Prospects)	.40
41	*Ruben Salazar* (Rookies)	3.00
42	*John Sneed* (Rookies)	1.00
43	*Josh Girdley* (Rookies)	1.50
44	*Brett Myers* (Rookies)	3.00
45	*Rick Asadoorian* (Rookies)	8.00

2000 Topps TEK Color

Color variations make up patterns 16-20 of the base set and instead of metallic silver foil they have a different color background. They are seeded on the average of 1:10 packs.

	MT
Patterns 16-20:	1-2X
Inserted 1:10	

Player names in *Italic* type indicate a rookie card.

2000 Topps TEK Gold

This parallel to the base set has a rounded top corner and rounded bottom corner with a gold background. Each pattern is serially numbered on the card back in an edition of 10 sets.

	MT
Stars:	10-20X
Rookies:	5-10X
Production 10 sets	

2000 Topps TEK ArchiTEKs

Printed on a clear, polycarbonate card stock, the TEK logo and player name are stamped in gold foil. Card backs are numbered with an "A" prefix. They are found on the average of 1:5 packs.

		MT
Complete Set (18):		60.00
Common Player:		1.50
Inserted 1:5		
1	Nomar Garciaparra	5.00
2	Derek Jeter	5.00
3	Chipper Jones	4.00
4	Vladimir Guerrero	3.00
5	Mark McGwire	8.00
6	Ken Griffey Jr.	8.00
7	Mike Piazza	5.00
8	Jeff Bagwell	2.00
9	Larry Walker	1.50
10	Manny Ramirez	2.00
11	Alex Rodriguez	6.00
12	Sammy Sosa	5.00
13	Shawn Green	1.50
14	Juan Gonzalez	2.00
15	Barry Bonds	2.00
16	Pedro Martinez	2.00
17	Cal Ripken Jr.	6.00
18	Ivan Rodriguez	2.00

2000 Topps TEK DramaTEK Performers

Printed on a clear, polycarbonate stock, the insert name and TEK logo are stamped in blue foil. Card backs are numbered with a "DP" prefix and are seeded 1:10 packs.

		MT
Complete Set (9):		50.00
Common Player:		3.00
Inserted 1:10		
1	Mark McGwire	10.00
2	Sammy Sosa	6.00
3	Ken Griffey Jr.	10.00
4	Nomar Garciaparra	6.00
5	Chipper Jones	5.00
6	Mike Piazza	6.00
7	Alex Rodriguez	8.00
8	Derek Jeter	6.00
9	Vladimir Guerrero	3.00

2000 Topps TEK TEKtonics

This nine-card set features baseball's top hitters on a die-cut design on a clear, polycarbonate stock. Card backs are numbered with a "TT" prefix and are inserted 1:30 packs.

		MT
Complete Set (9):		100.00
Common Player:		5.00
Inserted 1:30		
1	Derek Jeter	12.00
2	Mark McGwire	20.00
3	Ken Griffey Jr.	15.00
4	Mike Piazza	12.00
5	Alex Rodriguez	12.00
6	Chipper Jones	10.00
7	Nomar Garciaparra	12.00
8	Sammy Sosa	10.00
9	Cal Ripken Jr.	15.00

2001 Topps

		MT
Complete Set (405):		40.00
Common Player:		.10
Pack (10):		1.75
Box (36):		55.00
1	Cal Ripken Jr.	1.50
2	Chipper Jones	1.00
3	Roger Cedeno	.10
4	Garret Anderson	.10
5	Robin Ventura	.20
6	Daryle Ward	.10
7	not issued	.10
8	Ron Gant	.20
9	Phil Nevin	.10
10	Jermaine Dye	.10
11	Chris Singleton	.10
12	Mike Stanton	.10
13	Brian Hunter	.10
14	Mike Redmond	.10
15	Jim Thome	.25
16	Brian Jordan	.10
17	Joe Girardi	.10
18	Steve Woodard	.10
19	Dustin Hermanson	.10
20	Shawn Green	.30
21	Todd Stottlemyre	.10
22	Dan Wilson	.10
23	Todd Pratt	.10
24	Derek Lowe	.10
25	Juan Gonzalez	.40
26	Clay Bellinger	.10
27	Jeff Fassero	.10
28	Pat Meares	.10
29	Eddie Taubensee	.10
30	Paul O'Neill	.25
31	Jeffrey Hammonds	.10
32	Pokey Reese	.10
33	Mike Mussina	.30
34	Rico Brogna	.10
35	Jay Buhner	.10
36	Steve Cox	.10
37	Quilvio Veras	.10
38	Marquis Grissom	.10
39	Shigetoshi Hasagawa	.10
40	Shane Reynolds	.10
41	Adam Piatt	.10
42	Luis Polonia	.10
43	Brook Fordyce	.10
44	Preston Wilson	.10
45	Ellis Burks	.10
46	Armando Rios	.10
47	Chuck Finley	.10
48	Dan Plesac	.10
49	Shannon Stewart	.10
50	Mark McGwire	2.00
51	Mark Loretta	.10
52	Gerald Williams	.10
53	Eric Young	.10
54	Peter Bergeron	.10
55	Dave Hansen	.10
56	Arthur Rhodes	.10
57	Bobby Jones	.10
58	Matt Clement	.10
59	Mike Benjamin	.10
60	Pedro Martinez	.50
61	Jose Canseco	.40
62	Matt Anderson	.10
63	Torii Hunter	.10
64	Carlos Lee	.10
65	David Cone	.10
66	Ray Sanchez	.10
67	Eric Chavez	.20
68	Rick Helling	.10
69	Manny Alexander	.10
70	John Franco	.10
71	Mike Bordick	.10
72	Andres Galarraga	.25
73	Jose Cruz Jr.	.10
74	Mike Matheny	.10
75	Randy Johnson	.50
76	Richie Sexson	.10
77	Vladimir Nunez	.10
78	Harold Baines	.10
79	Aaron Boone	.10
80	Darin Erstad	.40
81	Alex Gonzalez	.10
82	Gil Heredia	.10
83	Shane Andrews	.10
84	Todd Hundley	.10
85	Bill Mueller	.10
86	Mark McLemore	.10
87	Scott Spiezio	.10
88	Kevin McGlinchy	.10
89	Bubba Trammell	.10
90	Manny Ramirez	.50
91	Mike Lamb	.10
92	Scott Karl	.10
93	Brian Buchanan	.10
94	Chris Turner	.10
95	Mike Sweeney	.10
96	John Wetteland	.10
97	Rob Bell	.10
98	Pat Rapp	.10
99	John Burkett	.10
100	Derek Jeter	1.50
101	J.D. Drew	.25
102	Jose Offerman	.10
103	Rick Reed	.10
104	Will Clark	.30
105	Rickey Henderson	.25
106	Dave Berg	.10
107	Kirk Rueter	.10
108	Lee Stevens	.10
109	Jay Bell	.10
110	Fred McGriff	.20
111	Julio Zuleta	.10
112	Brian Anderson	.10
113	Orlando Cabrera	.10
114	Alex Fernandez	.10
115	Derek Bell	.10
116	Eric Owens	.10
117	Brian Bohannon	.10
118	Dennys Reyes	.10
119	Mike Stanley	.10
120	Jorge Posada	.20
121	Rich Becker	.10
122	Paul Konerko	.10
123	Mike Remlinger	.10
124	Travis Lee	.10
125	Ken Caminiti	.10
126	Kevin Barker	.10
127	Paul Quantrill	.10
128	Ozzie Guillen	.10
129	Kevin Tapani	.10
130	Mark Johnson	.10
131	Randy Wolf	.10
132	Michael Tucker	.10
133	Darren Lewis	.10
134	Joe Randa	.10
135	Jeff Cirillo	.10
136	David Ortiz	.10
137	Herb Perry	.10
138	Jeff Nelson	.10
139	Chris Stynes	.10
140	Johnny Damon	.10
141	Desi Relaford	.10
142	Jason Schmidt	.10
143	Charles Johnson	.10
144	Pat Burrell	.40
145	Gary Sheffield	.25
146	Tom Glavine	.25
147	Jason Isringhausen	.10
148	Chris Carpenter	.10
149	Jeff Suppan	.10
150	Ivan Rodriguez	.50
151	Luis Sojo	.10
152	Ron Villone	.10
153	Mike Sirotka	.10
154	Chuck Knoblauch	.20
155	Jason Kendall	.10
156	Dennis Cook	.10
157	Bobby Estalella	.10
158	Jose Guillen	.10
159	Thomas Howard	.10
160	Carlos Delgado	.50
161	Benji Gil	.10
162	Tim Bogar	.10
163	Kevin Elster	.10
164	Scott Downs	.10
165	Andy Benes	.10
166	Adrian Beltre	.10
167	David Bell	.10
168	Turk Wendell	.10
169	Pete Harnisch	.10
170	Roger Clemens	.75
171	Scott Williamson	.10
172	Kevin Jordan	.10
173	Brad Penny	.10
174	John Flaherty	.10
175	Troy Glaus	.50
176	Kevin Appier	.10
177	Walt Weiss	.10
178	Tyler Houston	.10
179	Michael Barrett	.10
180	Mike Hampton	.10
181	Francisco Cordova	.10
182	Mike Jackson	.10
183	David Segui	.10
184	Carlos Febles	.10
185	Roy Halladay	.10
186	Seth Etherton	.10
187	Charlie Hayes	.10
188	Fernando Tatis	.10
189	Steve Trachsel	.10
190	Livan Hernandez	.10
191	Joe Oliver	.10
192	Stan Javier	.10
193	B.J. Surhoff	.10
194	Rob Ducey	.10
195	Barry Larkin	.25
196	Danny Patterson	.10
197	Bobby Howry	.10
198	Dmitri Young	.10
199	Brian Hunter	.10
200	Alex Rodriguez	1.50
201	Hideo Nomo	.25
202	Luis Alicea	.10
203	Warren Morris	.10
204	Antonio Alfonseca	.10
205	Edgardo Alfonzo	.20
206	Mark Grudzielanek	.10
207	Fernando Vina	.10
208	Willie Greene	.10
209	Homer Bush	.10
210	Jason Giambi	.30
211	Mike Morgan	.10
212	Steve Karsay	.10
213	Matt Lawton	.10
214	Wendell Magee Jr.	.10
215	Rusty Greer	.10
216	Keith Lockhart	.10
217	Billy Koch	.10
218	Todd Hollandsworth	.10
219	Raul Ibanez	.10
220	Tony Gwynn	.75
221	Carl Everett	.20
222	Hector Carrasco	.10
223	Jose Valentin	.10
224	Deivi Cruz	.10

225 Bret Boone .10
226 Kurt Abbott .10
227 Melvin Mora .10
228 Danny Graves .10
229 Jose Jimenez .10
230 James Baldwin .10
231 C.J. Nitkowski .10
232 Jeff Zimmerman .10
233 Mike Lowell .10
234 Hideki Irabu .10
235 Greg Vaughn .20
236 Omar Daal .10
237 Darren Dreifort .10
238 Gil Meche .10
239 Damian Jackson .10
240 Frank Thomas .75
241 Travis Miller .10
242 Jeff Frye .10
243 Dave Magadan .10
244 Luis Castillo .10
245 Bartolo Colon .10
246 Steve Kline .10
247 Shawon Dunston .10
248 Rick Aguilera .10
249 Omar Olivares .10
250 Craig Biggio .20
251 Scott Schoeneweis .10
252 Dave Veres .10
253 Ramon Martinez .10
254 Jose Vidro .10
255 Todd Helton .50
256 Greg Norton .10
257 Jacque Jones .10
258 Jason Grimsley .10
259 Dan Reichert .10
260 Robb Nen .10
261 Mark Clark .10
262 Scott Hatteberg .10
263 Doug Brocail .10
264 Mark Johnson .10
265 Eric Davis .20
266 Terry Shumpert .10
267 Kevin Millar .10
268 Ismael Valdes .10
269 Richard Hidalgo .20
270 Randy Velarde .10
271 Bengie Molina .10
272 Tony Womack .10
273 Enrique Wilson .10
274 Jeff Brantley .10
275 Rick Ankiel .40
276 Terry Mulholland .10
277 Ron Belliard .10
278 Terrence Long .10
279 Alberto Castillo .10
280 Royce Clayton .10
281 Joe McEwing .10
282 Jason McDonald .10
283 Ricky Bottalico .10
284 Keith Foulke .10
285 Brad Radke .10
286 Gabe Kapler .10
287 Pedro Astacio .10
288 Armando Reynoso .10
289 Darryl Kile .10
290 Reggie Sanders .10
291 Esteban Yan .10
292 Joe Nathan .10
293 Jay Payton .10
294 Francisco Cordero .10
295 Gregg Jefferies .10
296 LaTroy Hawkins .10
297 Jeff Tam .10
298 Jacob Cruz .10
299 Chris Holt .10
300 Vladimir Guerrero .75
301 Marvin Benard .10
302 Matt Franco .10
303 Mike Williams .10
304 Sean Bergman .10
305 Juan Encarnacion .10
306 Russ Davis .10
307 Hanley Frias .10
308 Ramon Hernandez .10
309 Matt Walbeck .10
310 Bill Spiers .10
311 Bob Wickman .10
312 Sandy Alomar .10
313 Eddie Guardado .10
314 Shane Halter .10
315 Geoff Jenkins .20
316 Gerald Witasick .10
317 Damian Miller .10
318 Darrin Fletcher .10
319 Rafael Furcal .50
320 Mark Grace .25
321 Mark Mulder .10
322 Joe Torre (Managers) .10
323 Bobby Cox (Managers) .10
324 Mike Scioscia (Managers) .10
325 Mike Hargrove (Managers) .10
326 Jimy Williams (Managers) .10
327 Jerry Manuel (Managers) .10
328 Buck Showalter (Managers) .10
329 Charlie Manuel (Managers) .10
330 Don Baylor (Managers) .10
331 Phil Garner (Managers) .10
332 Jack McKeon (Managers) .10
333 Tony Muser (Managers) .10
334 Buddy Bell (Managers) .10
335 Tom Kelly (Managers) .10
336 John Boles (Managers) .10
337 Art Howe (Managers) .10
338 Larry Dierker (Managers) .10
339 Lou Pinella (Managers) .10
340 Davey Johnson (Managers) .10
341 Larry Rothschild (Managers) .10
342 Davey Lopes (Managers) .10
343 Johnny Oates (Managers) .10
344 Felipe Alou (Managers) .10
345 Jim Fregosi (Managers) .10
346 Bobby Valentine (Managers) .10
347 Terry Francona (Managers) .10
348 Gene Lamont (Managers) .10
349 Tony LaRussa (Managers) .10
350 Bruce Bochy (Managers) .10
351 Dusty Baker (Managers) .10
352 Adrian Gonzalez, Adam Johnson (Draft Picks) .75
353 Matt Wheatland, Brian Digby (Draft Picks) .40
354 Tripper Johnson, Scott Thorman (Draft Picks) .40
355 Phil Dumatrait, Adam Wainwright (Draft Picks) .40
356 Scott Heard, *David Parrish* (Draft Picks) .75
357 Rocco Baldelli, *Mark Folsom* (Draft Picks) .40
358 *Dominic Rich*, Aaron Herr (Draft Picks) .40
359 Mike Stodolka, Sean Burnett (Draft Picks) .25
360 Derek Thompson, Corey Smith (Draft Picks) .40
361 *Danny Borrell ,Jason Bourgeois* (Draft Picks) .40
362 Chin-Feng Chen, Corey Patterson, Josh Hamilton (Prospects) .75
363 Ryan Anderson, Barry Zito, C.C. Sabathia (Prospects) .75
364 Scott Sobkowiak, David Walling, Ben Sheets (Prospects) .50
365 Ty Howington, Josh Kalinowski, Josh Girdley (Prospects) .10
366 Hee Seop Choi, Aaron McNeal, Jason Hart (Prospects) .75
367 Bobby Bradley, Kurt Ainsworth, Chin-Hui Tsao (Prospects) .75
368 Mike Glendenning, Kenny Kelly *,Juan Silvestri* (Prospects) .25
369 J.R. House, Ramon Castro, Ben Davis (Prospects) .25
370 Chance Caple, *Rafael Soriano*, Pasqual Coco (Prospects) .40
371 Travis Hafner, Eric Munson, Bucky Jacobsen (Prospects) .25
372 Jason Conti, Chris Wakeland, Brian Cole (Prospects) .20
373 Scott Seabol, Aubrey Huff, Joe Crede (Prospects) .40
374 Adam Everett, *Jose Ortiz*, Keith Ginter (Prospects) .40
375 Carlos Hernandez, Geraldo Guzman, Adam Eaton (Prospects) .25
376 Bobby Kielty, Milton Bradley, Juan Rivera (Prospects) .25
377 Mark McGwire (Golden Moments) 1.00
378 Don Larsen (Golden Moments) .20
379 Bobby Thomson (Golden Moments) .10
380 Bill Mazeroski (Golden Moments) .10
381 Reggie Jackson (Golden Moments) .40
382 Kirk Gibson (Golden Moments) .10
383 Roger Maris (Golden Moments) .40
384 Cal Ripken Jr. (Golden Moments) .75
385 Hank Aaron (Golden Moments) .75
386 Joe Carter (Golden Moments) .10
387 Cal Ripken Jr. (Season Highlights) 1.00
388 Randy Johnson (Season Highlights) .30
389 Ken Griffey Jr. (Season Highlights) 1.00
390 Troy Glaus (Season Highlights) .30
391 Kazuhiro Sasaki (Season Highlights) .40
392 Sammy Sosa, Troy Glaus (League Leaders) .50
393 Todd Helton, Edgar Martinez (League Leaders) .25
394 Nomar Garciaparra, Todd Helton (League Leaders) .50
395 Barry Bonds, Jason Giambi (League Leaders) .25
396 Todd Helton, Manny Ramirez (League Leaders) .25
397 Todd Helton, Darin Erstad (League Leaders) .25
398 Kevin Brown, Pedro Martinez (League Leaders) .25
399 Randy Johnson, Pedro Martinez (League Leaders) .25
400 Will Clark (Playoff Highlights) .20
401 NY Mets Divisional Highlight .10
402 NY Yankees Divisional Highlight .10
403 Seattle Mariners Divisional Highlight .10
404 Mike Hampton (Playoff Highlights) .10
405 NY Yankees ALCS Highlight .75
406 World Series Highlight 1.00

2001 Topps Gold

	MT
Stars:	8-15X
Prospects and RCs:	6-12X
Inserted 1:17	

2001 Topps Autographs

MT

Complete Set (51):
Common Player:
Group A 1:22,866
Group B 1:3,054
Group C 1:1,431
Group D 1:18,339
Group E 1:13,737
Group F 1:11,015
Group G 1:625

HA Hank Aaron 200.00
DA Dick Allen 40.00
RA Rick Ankiel 40.00
RB Rocco Baldelli 25.00
EB Ernie Banks 125.00
GB George Bell
JB Johnny Bench
YB Yogi Berra 125.00
GB George Brett
LB Lou Brock 75.00
PB Pat Burrell 35.00
RC Rod Carew 90.00
MC Mike Cuellar 30.00
WD Willie Davis
CE Carl Erskine
WF Whitey Ford
RF Rafael Furcal 40.00
BG Bob Gibson
AG Adrian Gonzalez 35.00
DG Dick Groat
SH Scott Heard 25.00
WH Willie Hernandez 25.00
KH Ken Holtzman
RJ Reggie Jackson
AJ Adam Johnson 20.00
CJ Chipper Jones 90.00
SK Sandy Koufax 400.00
ML Mike Lamb 20.00
VL Vernon Law 30.00
JM Jason Marquis 20.00
GM Gary Matthews
WM Willie Mays 300.00
SM Stan Musial
BO Ben Oglivie
MO Magglio Ordonez 40.00
AP Andy Pafko 75.00
BR Brooks Robinson 100.00
JR Joe Rudi 30.00
NR Nolan Ryan
MS Mike Schmidt 160.00
TS Tom Seaver

MS	Mike Stodolka	15.00
RS	Ron Swoboda	30.00
KT	Kent Tekulve	
GT	Garry Templeton	30.00
JV	Jose Vidro	20.00
MW	Matt Wheatland	20.00
TW	Ted Williams	
WW	Wilbur Wood	
CY	Carl Yastrzemski	
TZ	Todd Zeile	20.00

2001 Topps A Look Ahead

		MT
Complete Set (10):		40.00
Common Player:		2.00
Inserted 1:25		
1	Vladimir Guerrero	3.00
2	Derek Jeter	8.00
3	Todd Helton	2.50
4	Alex Rodriguez	8.00
5	Ken Griffey Jr.	8.00
6	Nomar Garciaparra	6.00
7	Chipper Jones	5.00
8	Ivan Rodriguez	2.50
9	Pedro Martinez	2.50
10	Rick Ankiel	2.00

2001 Topps A Tradition Continues

		MT
Complete Set (30):		125.00
Common Player:		1.50
Inserted 1:17		
1	Chipper Jones	8.00
2	Cal Ripken Jr.	12.00
3	Mike Piazza	10.00
4	Ken Griffey Jr.	12.00
5	Randy Johnson	4.00
6	Derek Jeter	12.00
7	Scott Rolen	2.00
8	Nomar Garciaparra	10.00
9	Roberto Alomar	3.00
10	Greg Maddux	8.00
11	Ivan Rodriguez	4.00
12	Jeff Bagwell	4.00
13	Ivan Rodriguez	4.00
14	Pedro Martinez	4.00
15	Sammy Sosa	10.00
16	Jim Edmonds	2.50
17	Mo Vaughn	1.50
18	Barry Bonds	4.00
19	Larry Walker	1.50
20	Mark McGwire	15.00
21	Vladimir Guerrero	5.00
22	Andruw Jones	3.00
23	Todd Helton	4.00
24	Kevin Brown	1.50
25	Tony Gwynn	5.00
26	Manny Ramirez	4.00
27	Roger Clemens	5.00
28	Frank Thomas	5.00
29	Shawn Green	2.00
30	Jim Thome	2.00

2001 Topps Combos

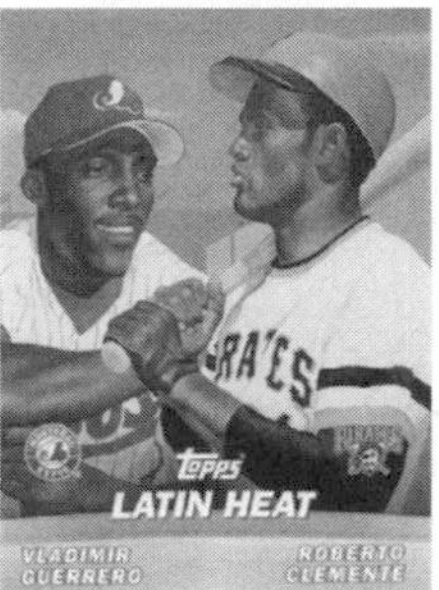

		MT
Complete Set (10):		30.00
Common Player:		2.00
Inserted 1:12		
1	Yogi Berra, Whitey Ford, Reggie Jackson, Don Mattingly, Derek Jeter	5.00
2	Brooks Robinson, Cal Ripken Jr.	5.00
3	Barry Bonds, Willie Mays	4.00
4	Bob Gibson, Pedro Martinez	2.00
5	Ivan Rodriguez, Johnny Bench	2.00
6	Ernie Banks, Alex Rodriguez	4.00
7	Sandy Koufax, Randy Johnson, Warren Spahn, Steve Carlton	4.00
8	Vladimir Guerrero, Roberto Clemente	4.00
9	Ted Williams, Carl Yastrzemski, Nomar Garciaparra	5.00
10	Joe Torre, Casey Stengel	2.00

2001 Topps Golden Anniversary

		MT
Complete Set (50):		150.00
Common Player:		1.00
Inserted 1:10		
1	Hank Aaron	6.00
2	Ernie Banks	2.50
3	Mike Schmidt	4.00
4	Willie Mays	5.00
5	Johnny Bench	2.50
6	Tom Seaver	2.50
7	Frank Robinson	1.50
8	Sandy Koufax	10.00
9	Bob Gibson	2.00
10	Ted Williams	8.00
11	Cal Ripken Jr.	10.00
12	Tony Gwynn	4.00
13	Mark McGwire	12.00
14	Ken Griffey Jr.	10.00
15	Greg Maddux	6.00
16	Roger Clemens	4.00
17	Barry Bonds	3.00
18	Rickey Henderson	1.00
19	Mike Piazza	8.00
20	Jose Canseco	2.00
21	Derek Jeter	10.00
22	Nomar Garciaparra	8.00
23	Alex Rodriguez	10.00
24	Sammy Sosa	8.00
25	Ivan Rodriguez	3.00
26	Vladimir Guerrero	4.00
27	Chipper Jones	6.00
28	Jeff Bagwell	3.00
29	Pedro Martinez	3.00
30	Randy Johnson	3.00
31	Pat Burrell	2.00
32	Josh Hamilton	2.00
33	Nick Johnson	1.00
34	Corey Patterson	2.00
35	Eric Munson	1.00
36	Sean Burroughs	1.00
37	Alfonso Soriano	1.00
38	Chin-Feng Chen	3.00
39	Barry Zito	4.00
40	Adrian Gonzalez	4.00
41	Mark McGwire	12.00
42	Nomar Garciaparra	8.00
43	Todd Helton	3.00
44	Matt Williams	1.00
45	Troy Glaus	3.00
46	Geoff Jenkins	1.00
47	Frank Thomas	4.00
48	Mo Vaughn	1.00
49	Barry Larkin	1.50
50	J.D. Drew	1.00

2001 Topps King of Kings

		MT
Complete Set (3):		
Common card:		100.00
Inserted 1:2,056		
1	Hank Aaron	275.00
2	Nolan Ryan	300.00
3	Rickey Henderson	100.00

2001 Topps King of Kings Golden Edition

		MT
Production 50 cards		
KKGE	Hank Aaron, Nolan Ryan, Rickey Henderson	750.00

2001 Topps Originals

		MT
Complete Set (5):		900.00
Common Player:		100.00
Game-used Jersey cards		
1	Roberto Clemente 1955	400.00
2	Carl Yastrzemski 1960	200.00
3	Mike Schmidt 1974	150.00
4	Wade Boggs 1983	100.00
5	Chipper Jones 1991	150.00

2001 Topps The Shot Heard Round the World Autograph

	MT
Complete Set (2):	
Common Player:	
Ralph Branca	
Bobby Thompson	

2001 Topps Through the Years

		MT
Complete Set (50):		200.00
Common Player:		3.00
Inserted 1:8		
1	Yogi Berra	4.00
2	Roy Campanella	4.00
3	Willie Mays	6.00
4	Andy Pafko	3.00
5	Jackie Robinson	10.00
6	Stan Musial	5.00
7	Duke Snider	3.00
8	Warren Spahn	4.00
9	Ted Williams	10.00
10	Eddie Matthews	3.00
11	Willie McCovey	3.00
12	Frank Robinson	3.00
13	Ernie Banks	4.00
14	Hank Aaron	8.00
15	Sandy Koufax	8.00
16	Bob Gibson	4.00
17	Harmon Killebrew	3.00
18	Whitey Ford	3.00
19	Roberto Clemente	8.00
20	Juan Marichal	3.00
21	Johnny Bench	4.00
22	Willie Stargell	3.00
23	Joe Morgan	3.00
24	Carl Yastrzemski	4.00
25	Reggie Jackson	4.00
26	Tom Seaver	4.00
27	Steve Carlton	3.00
28	Jim Palmer	3.00
29	Rod Carew	3.00
30	George Brett	6.00
31	Roger Clemens	4.00
32	Don Mattingly	6.00
33	Ryne Sandberg	3.00
34	Mike Schmidt	4.00
35	Cal Ripken Jr.	8.00
36	Tony Gwynn	3.00
37	Ozzie Smith	4.00
38	Wade Boggs	3.00
39	Nolan Ryan	10.00
40	Robin Yount	3.00
41	Mark McGwire	10.00
42	Ken Griffey Jr.	8.00
43	Sammy Sosa	6.00
44	Alex Rodriguez	8.00
45	Barry Bonds	3.00
46	Mike Piazza	6.00
47	Chipper Jones	5.00
48	Greg Maddux	5.00
49	Nomar Garciaparra	6.00
50	Derek Jeter	8.00

1992 Triple Play

This set was released only in wax pack form. Cards feature red borders. Boyhood photos, mascots and ballparks are among the featured cards. This set was designed to give collectors an alternative product to the high-end card sets. The cards are standard size.

		MT
Complete Set (264):		10.00
Common Player:		.05
Wax Box:		10.00
1	SkyDome	.05
2	Tom Foley	.05
3	Scott Erickson	.05
4	Matt Williams	.15
5	Dave Valle	.05
6	Andy Van Slyke (Little Hotshot)	.05
7	Tom Glavine	.10
8	Kevin Appier	.05
9	Pedro Guerrero	.05
10	Terry Steinbach	.05
11	Terry Mulholland	.05
12	Mike Boddicker	.05
13	Gregg Olson	.05
14	Tim Burke	.05
15	Candy Maldonado	.05
16	Orlando Merced	.05
17	Robin Ventura	.10
18	Eric Anthony	.05
19	Greg Maddux	.75
20	Erik Hanson	.05
21	Bob Ojeda	.05
22	Nolan Ryan	.50
23	Dave Righetti	.05
24	Reggie Jefferson	.05
25	Jody Reed	.05
26	Awesome Action (Steve Finley, Gary Carter)	.05
27	Chili Davis	.05
28	Hector Villanueva	.05
29	Cecil Fielder	.05
30	Hal Morris	.05
31	Barry Larkin	.10
32	Bobby Thigpen	.05
33	Andy Benes	.10
34	Harold Baines	.05
35	David Cone	.10
36	Mark Langston	.05
37	Bryan Harvey	.05
38	John Kruk	.05
39	Scott Sanderson	.05
40	Lonnie Smith	.05
41	Awesome Action (Rex Hudler)	.05
42	George Bell	.05
43	Steve Finley	.05
44	Mickey Tettleton	.05
45	Robby Thompson	.05
46	Pat Kelly	.05
47	Marquis Grissom	.10
48	Tony Pena	.05
49	Alex Cole	.05
50	Steve Buechele	.05
51	Ivan Rodriguez	.25
52	John Smiley	.05
53	Gary Sheffield	.15
54	Greg Olson	.05
55	Ramon Martinez	.10
56	B.J. Surhoff	.05
57	Bruce Hurst	.05
58	Todd Stottlemyre	.05
59	Brett Butler	.05
60	Glenn Davis	.05
61	Awesome Action (Glenn Braggs, Kirt Manwaring)	.05
62	Lee Smith	.05
63	Rickey Henderson	.15
64	Fun at the Ballpark (David Cone, Jeff Innis, John Franco)	.05
65	Rick Aguilera	.05
66	Kevin Elster	.05
67	Dwight Evans	.05
68	Andujar Cedeno	.05
69	Brian McRae	.05
70	Benito Santiago	.05
71	Randy Johnson	.20
72	Roberto Kelly	.05
73	Awesome Action (Juan Samuel)	.05
74	Alex Fernandez	.05
75	Felix Jose	.05
76	Brian Harper	.05
77	Scott Sanderson (Little Hotshot)	.05
78	Ken Caminiti	.10
79	Mo Vaughn	.15
80	Roger McDowell	.05
81	Robin Yount	.20
82	Dave Magadan	.05
83	Julio Franco	.05
84	Roberto Alomar	.25
85	Steve Avery	.05
86	Travis Fryman	.10
87	Fred McGriff	.15
88	Dave Stewart	.05
89	Larry Walker	.15
90	Chris Sabo	.05
91	Chuck Finley	.05
92	Dennis Martinez	.05
93	Jeff Johnson	.05
94	Len Dykstra	.05
95	Mark Whiten	.05
96	Wade Taylor	.05
97	Lance Dickson	.05
98	Kevin Tapani	.05
99	Awesome Action (Luis Polonia, Tony Phillips)	.05
100	Milt Cuyler	.05
101	Willie McGee	.05
102	Awesome Action (Tony Fernandez, Ryne Sandberg)	.05
103	Albert Belle	.25
104	Todd Hundley	.05
105	Ben McDonald	.05
106	Doug Drabek	.05
107	Tim Raines	.10
108	Joe Carter	.05
109	Reggie Sanders	.05
110	John Olerud	.10
111	Darren Lewis	.05
112	Juan Gonzalez	.30
113	Awesome Action (Andre Dawson)	.05
114	Mark Grace	.15
115	George Brett	.25
116	Barry Bonds	.30
117	Lou Whitaker	.05
118	Jose Oquendo	.05
119	Lee Stevens	.05
120	Phil Plantier	.05
121	Awesome Action (Devon White, Matt Merullo)	.05
122	Greg Vaughn	.10
123	Royce Clayton	.05
124	Bob Welch	.05
125	Juan Samuel	.05
126	Ron Gant	.10
127	Edgar Martinez	.05
128	Andy Ashby	.05
129	Jack McDowell	.05
130	Awesome Action (Dave Henderson, Jerry Browne)	.05
131	Leo Gomez	.05
132	Checklist 1-88	.05
133	Phillie Phanatic	.05
134	Bret Barbarie	.05
135	Kent Hrbek	.05
136	Hall of Fame	.05
137	Omar Vizquel	.05
138	The Famous Chicken	.05
139	Terry Pendleton	.05
140	Jim Eisenreich	.05
141	Todd Zeile	.05
142	Todd Van Poppel	.05
143	Darren Daulton	.05
144	Mike Macfarlane	.05
145	Luis Mercedes	.05
146	Trevor Wilson	.05
147	Dave Steib	.05
148	Andy Van Slyke	.05
149	Carlton Fisk	.20
150	Craig Biggio	.15
151	Joe Girardi	.05
152	Ken Griffey, Jr.	1.25
153	Jose Offerman	.05
154	Bobby Witt	.05
155	Will Clark	.20
156	Steve Olin	.05
157	Greg Harris	.05
158	Dale Murphy (Little Hotshot)	.05
159	Don Mattingly	.30
160	Shawon Dunston	.05
161	Bill Gullickson	.05
162	Paul O'Neill	.10
163	Norm Charlton	.05
164	Bo Jackson	.15
165	Tony Fernandez	.05
166	Dave Henderson	.05
167	Dwight Gooden	.10
168	Junior Felix	.05
169	Lance Parrish	.05
170	Pat Combs	.05
171	Chuck Knoblauch	.15
172	John Smoltz	.10
173	Wrigley Field	.05
174	Andre Dawson	.10
175	Pete Harnisch	.05
176	Alan Trammell	.10
177	Kirk Dressendorfer	.05
178	Matt Nokes	.05
179	Wil Cordero	.05
180	Scott Cooper	.05
181	Glenallen Hill	.05
182	John Franco	.05
183	Rafael Palmeiro	.15
184	Jay Bell	.05
185	Bill Wegman	.05
186	Deion Sanders	.15
187	Darryl Strawberry	.10
188	Jaime Navarro	.05
189	Darren Jackson	.05
190	Eddie Zosky	.05
191	Mike Scioscia	.05
192	Chito Martinez	.05
193	Awesome Action (Pat Kelly, Ron Tingley)	.05
194	Ray Lankford	.05
195	Dennis Eckersley	.05
196	Awesome Action (Ivan Calderon, Mike Maddux)	.05
197	Shane Mack	.05
198	Checklist 89-176	.05
199	Cal Ripken, Jr.	1.00
200	Jeff Bagwell	.40
201	David Howard	.05
202	Kirby Puckett	.30
203	Harold Reynolds	.05
204	Jim Abbott	.05
205	Mark Lewis	.05
206	Frank Thomas	.50
207	Rex Hudler	.05
208	Vince Coleman	.05
209	Delino DeShields	.05
210	Luis Gonzalez	.05
211	Wade Boggs	.15
212	Orel Hershiser	.05
213	Cal Eldred	.05
214	Jose Canseco	.30
215	Jose Guzman	.05
216	Roger Clemens	.35
217	Dave Justice	.15
218	Tony Phillips	.05
219	Tony Gwynn	.40
220	Mitch Williams	.05
221	Bill Sampen	.05
222	Billy Hatcher	.05
223	Gary Gaetti	.05
224	Tim Wallach	.05
225	Kevin Maas	.05
226	Kevin Brown	.10
227	Sandy Alomar	.10
228	John Habyan	.05
229	Ryne Sandberg	.25
230	Greg Gagne	.05
231	Autographs (Mark McGwire)	1.00
232	Mike LaValliere	.05
233	Mark Gubicza	.05
234	Lance Parrish (Little Hotshot)	.05
235	Carlos Baerga	.05
236	Howard Johnson	.05
237	Mike Mussina	.10
238	Ruben Sierra	.05
239	Lance Johnson	.05
240	Devon White	.05
241	Dan Wilson	.05
242	Kelly Gruber	.05
243	Brett Butler (Little Hotshot)	.05
244	Ozzie Smith	.25
245	Chuck McElroy	.05
246	Shawn Boskie	.05
247	Mark Davis	.05
248	Bill Landrum	.05
249	Frank Tanana	.05
250	Darryl Hamilton	.05
251	Gary DiSarcina	.05
252	Mike Greenwell	.05
253	Cal Ripken, Jr. (Little Hotshot)	.25
254	Paul Molitor	.15
255	Tim Teufel	.05
256	Chris Hoiles	.05
257	Rob Dibble	.05
258	Sid Bream	.05
259	Chito Martinez	.05
260	Dale Murphy	.15
261	Greg Hibbard	.05
262	Mark McGwire	1.00
263	Oriole Park	.05
264	Checklist 177-264	.05

1992 Triple Play Gallery of Stars

Two levels of scarcity are represented in this insert issue. Cards #1-6 (all cards have a GS prefix to the card number) feature in their new uniforms players who changed teams for 1993. Those inserts were found in the standard Triple Play foil packs and are somewhat more common than cards #7-12, which were found only in jumbo packs and which feature a better selection of established stars and rookies. All of the inserts feature the artwork of Dick Perez, with player portraits set against a colorful background. Silver-foil accents highlight the front design. Backs are red with a white "tombstone" containing a career summary.

		MT
Complete Set (12):		9.00
Common Player:		.40
1	Bobby Bonilla	.40
2	Wally Joyner	.40
3	Jack Morris	.40
4	Steve Sax	.40
5	Danny Tartabull	.40
6	Frank Viola	.40
7	Jeff Bagwell	1.00
8	Ken Griffey, Jr.	3.50
9	David Justice	.50
10	Ryan Klesko	.50
11	Cal Ripken, Jr.	2.50
12	Frank Thomas	1.25

1993 Triple Play

For the second year, Leaf-Donruss used the "Triple Play" brand name for its base-level card set aimed at the younger collector. The 264-card set was available in several types of retail packaging and included a number of special subsets, such as childhood photos (labeled LH - Little Hotshots - in the checklist) and insert sets. Checklist card #264 incorrectly shows card #129, Joe Robbie Stadium, as #259. There is a second card, "Equipment," which also bears #129. An "Action Baseball" scratch-off game card was included in each foil pack.

		MT
Complete Set (264):		10.00
Common Player:		.05
Wax Box:		14.00
1	Ken Griffey, Jr.	1.50
2	Roberto Alomar	.25
3	Cal Ripken, Jr.	1.00
4	Eric Karros	.10
5	Cecil Fielder	.05
6	Gary Sheffield	.15
7	Darren Daulton	.05
8	Andy Van Slyke	.05
9	Dennis Eckersley	.05
10	Ryne Sandberg	.30
11	Mark Grace (Little Hotshots)	.10
12	Awesome Action #1 (Luis Polonia, David Segui)	.05
13	Mike Mussina	.15
14	Vince Coleman	.05
15	Rafael Belliard	.05
16	Ivan Rodriguez	.25
17	Eddie Taubensee	.05
18	Cal Eldred	.05
19	Rick Wilkins	.05
20	Edgar Martinez	.05
21	Brian McRae	.05
22	Darren Holmes	.05
23	Mark Whiten	.05
24	Todd Zeile	.05
25	Scott Cooper	.05
26	Frank Thomas	.50
27	Wil Cordero	.05
28	Juan Guzman	.05
29	Pedro Astacio	.05
30	Steve Avery	.05
31	Barry Larkin	.15
32	President Clinton	.25
33	Scott Erickson	.05
34	Mike Devereaux	.05
35	Tino Martinez	.10
36	Brent Mayne	.05
37	Tim Salmon	.15
38	Dave Hollins	.05
39	Royce Clayton	.05
40	Shawon Dunston	.05
41	Eddie Murray	.15
42	Larry Walker	.15
43	Jeff Bagwell	.25
44	Milt Cuyler	.05
45	Mike Bordick	.05
46	Mike Greenwell	.05
47	Steve Sax	.05
48	Chuck Knoblauch	.10
49	Charles Nagy	.05
50	Tim Wakefield	.05
51	Tony Gwynn	.40
52	Rob Dibble	.05
53	Mickey Morandini	.05
54	Steve Hosey	.05
55	Mike Piazza	.75
56	Bill Wegman	.05
57	Kevin Maas	.05
58	Gary DiSarcina	.05
59	Travis Fryman	.10
60	Ruben Sierra	.05
61	Awesome Action #2 (Ken Caminiti)	.05
62	Brian Jordan	.05
63	Scott Chiamparino	.05
64	Awesome Action #3 (Mike Bordick, George Brett)	.05
65	Carlos Garcia	.05
66	Checklist 1-66	.05
67	John Smoltz	.10
68	Awesome Action #4 (Mark McGwire, Brian Harper)	.75
69	Kurt Stillwell	.05
70	Chad Curtis	.05
71	Rafael Palmeiro	.15
72	Kevin Young	.05
73	Glenn Davis	.05
74	Dennis Martinez	.05
75	Sam Militello	.05
76	Mike Morgan	.05
77	Frank Thomas (Little Hotshots)	.25
78	Staying Fit (Bip Roberts, Mike Devereaux)	.05
79	Steve Buechele	.05
80	Carlos Baerga	.05
81	Robby Thompson	.05
82	Kirk McCaskill	.05
83	Lee Smith	.05
84	Gary Scott	.05
85	Tony Pena	.05
86	Howard Johnson	.05
87	Mark McGwire	1.50
88	Bip Roberts	.05
89	Devon White	.05
90	John Franco	.05
91	Tom Browning	.05
92	Mickey Tettleton	.05
93	Jeff Conine	.05
94	Albert Belle	.20
95	Fred McGriff	.15
96	Nolan Ryan	1.00
97	Paul Molitor (Little Hotshots)	.15
98	Juan Bell	.05
99	Dave Fleming	.05
100	Craig Biggio	.15
101a	Andy Stankiewicz (white name on front)	.05
101b	Andy Stankiewicz (red name on front)	.25
102	Delino DeShields	.05
103	Damion Easley	.05
104	Kevin McReynolds	.05
105	David Nied	.05
106	Rick Sutcliffe	.05
107	Will Clark	.15
108	Tim Raines	.10
109	Eric Anthony	.05
110	Mike LaValliere	.05
111	Dean Palmer	.05
112	Eric Davis	.05
113	Damon Berryhill	.05
114	Felix Jose	.05
115	Ozzie Guillen	.05
116	Pat Listach	.05
117	Tom Glavine	.15
118	Roger Clemens	.40
119	Dave Henderson	.05
120	Don Mattingly	.50
121	Orel Hershiser	.05
122	Ozzie Smith	.20
123	Joe Carter	.05
124	Bret Saberhagen	.10
125	Mitch Williams	.05
126	Jerald Clark	.05
127	Mile High Stadium	.05
128	Kent Hrbek	.05
129a	Equipment (Curt Schilling, Mark Whiten)	.05
129b	Joe Robbie Stadium	.05
130	Gregg Jefferies	.05
131	John Orton	.05
132	Checklist 67-132	.05
133	Bret Boone	.05
134	Pat Borders	.05
135	Gregg Olson	.05
136	Brett Butler	.05
137	Rob Deer	.05
138	Darrin Jackson	.05
139	John Kruk	.05
140	Jay Bell	.05
141	Bobby Witt	.05
142	New Cubs (Dan Plesac, Randy Myers, Jose Guzman)	.05
143	Wade Boggs (Little Hotshots)	.15
144	Awesome Action #5 (Kenny Lofton)	.05
145	Ben McDonald	.05
146	Dwight Gooden	.10
147	Terry Pendleton	.05
148	Julio Franco	.05
149	Ken Caminiti	.10
150	Greg Vaughn	.10
151	Sammy Sosa	.75
152	David Valle	.05
153	Wally Joyner	.05
154	Dante Bichette	.10
155	Mark Lewis	.05
156	Bob Tewksbury	.05
157	Billy Hatcher	.05
158	Jack McDowell	.05
159	Marquis Grissom	.05
160	Jack Morris	.05
161	Ramon Martinez	.10
162	Deion Sanders	.10
163	Tim Belcher	.05
164	Mascots	.10
165	Scott Leius	.05
166	Brady Anderson	.10
167	Randy Johnson	.15
168	Mark Gubicza	.05
169	Chuck Finley	.05
170	Terry Mulholland	.05
171	Matt Williams	.10
172	Dwight Smith	.05
173	Bobby Bonilla	.05
174	Ken Hill	.05
175	Doug Jones	.05
176	Tony Phillips	.05
177	Terry Steinbach	.05
178	Frank Viola	.05
179	Robin Ventura	.10
180	Shane Mack	.05
181	Kenny Lofton	.20
182	Jeff King	.05
183	Tim Teufel	.05
184	Chris Sabo	.05
185	Lenny Dykstra	.05
186	Trevor Wilson	.05
187	Darryl Strawberry	.10
188	Robin Yount	.25
189	Bob Wickman	.05
190	Luis Polonia	.05
191	Alan Trammell	.10
192	Bob Welch	.05
193	Awesome Action #6	.05
194	Tom Pagnozzi	.05
195	Bret Barberie	.05
196	Awesome Action #7 (Mike Scioscia)	.05
197	Randy Tomlin	.05
198	Checklist 133-198	.05
199	Ron Gant	.10
200	Awesome Action #8 (Roberto Alomar)	.05
201	Andy Benes	.10
202	Pepper	.05
203	Steve Finley	.05
204	Steve Olin	.05
205	Chris Hoiles	.05
206	John Wetteland	.05
207	Danny Tartabull	.05
208	Bernard Gilkey	.05
209	Tom Glavine (Little Hotshots)	.05
210	Benito Santiago	.05
211	Mark Grace	.15
212	Glenallen Hill	.05
213	Jeff Brantley	.05
214	George Brett	.40
215	Mark Lemke	.05
216	Ron Karkovice	.05
217	Tom Brunansky	.05
218	Todd Hundley	.05
219	Rickey Henderson	.20
220	Joe Oliver	.05
221	Juan Gonzalez	.50
222	John Olerud	.15
223	Hal Morris	.05
224	Lou Whitaker	.05
225	Bryan Harvey	.05
226	Mike Gallego	.05
227	Willie McGee	.05
228	Jose Oquendo	.05
229	Darren Daulton (Little Hotshots)	.05
230	Curt Schilling	.05
231	Jay Buhner	.05
232	New Astros (Doug Drabek, Greg Swindell)	.05
233	Jaime Navarro	.05
234	Kevin Appier	.05
235	Mark Langston	.05
236	Jeff Montgomery	.05
237	Joe Girardi	.05
238	Ed Sprague	.05
239	Dan Walters	.05
240	Kevin Tapani	.05
241	Pete Harnisch	.05
242	Al Martin	.05
243	Jose Canseco	.25
244	Moises Alou	.10
245	Mark McGwire (Little Hotshots)	.75
246	Luis Rivera	.05
247	George Bell	.05
248	B.J. Surhoff	.05
249	Dave Justice	.15
250	Brian Harper	.05
251	Sandy Alomar, Jr.	.10
252	Kevin Brown	.10
253	New Dodgers (Tim Wallach, Jody Reed, Todd Worrell)	.05
254	Ray Lankford	.05
255	Derek Bell	.05
256	Joe Grahe	.05
257	Charlie Hayes	.05
258	New Yankees (Wade Boggs, Jim Abbott)	.15
259	Joe Robbie Stadium	.05
260	Kirby Puckett	.40
261	Fun at the Ballpark (Jay Bell, Vince Coleman)	.05
262	Bill Swift	.05
263	Fun at the Ballpark (Roger McDowell)	.05
264	Checklist 199-264	.05

1993 Triple Play Gallery

The Gallery of Stars cards were found as random inserts in Triple Play jumbo packs. The cards feature Dick Perez painted representations of the players.

		MT
Complete Set (10):		7.50
Common Player:		.40
1	Barry Bonds	1.50
2	Andre Dawson	.40
3	Wade Boggs	1.00
4	Greg Maddux	2.50
5	Dave Winfield	.75
6	Paul Molitor	1.50
7	Jim Abbott	.40
8	J.T. Snow	.40
9	Benito Santiago	.40
10	David Nied	.40

1993 Triple Play League Leaders

These "double-headed" cards feature one player on each side. The six cards were random inserts in Triple Play retail packs.

		MT
Complete Set (6):		7.00
Common Player:		.50
1	Barry Bonds, Dennis Eckersley	1.50
2	Greg Maddux, Dennis Eckersley	2.50
3	Eric Karros, Pat Listach	.50
4	Fred McGriff, Juan Gonzalez	2.00
5	Darren Daulton, Cecil Fielder	.50
6	Gary Sheffield, Edgar Martinez	.50

1993 Triple Play Nicknames

Popular nicknames of 10 of the game's top stars are featured in silver foil on this insert set found in Triple Play foil packs.

		MT
Complete Set (10):		18.00
Common Player:		1.00
1	Frank Thomas (Big Hurt)	2.00
2	Roger Clemens (Rocket)	2.00
3	Ryne Sandberg (Ryno)	1.50
4	Will Clark (Thrill)	1.50
5	Ken Griffey, Jr. (Junior)	6.00
6	Dwight Gooden (Doc)	1.00
7	Nolan Ryan (Express)	4.50
8	Deion Sanders (Prime Time)	1.00
9	Ozzie Smith (Wizard)	1.50
10	Fred McGriff (Crime Dog)	1.00

1994 Triple Play

Triple Play cards returned for a third year in 1994, this time with a borderless design. According to company officials, production was less than 1994 Donruss Series I baseball, which was roughly 17,500 20-box cases. In the regular-issue 300-card set, 10 players from each team were featured, along with a 17-card Rookie Review subset and several insert sets.

		MT
Complete Set (300):		14.00
Common Player:		.05
Wax Box:		22.00
1	Mike Bordick	.05
2	Dennis Eckersley	.05
3	Brent Gates	.05
4	Rickey Henderson	.20
5	Mark McGwire	1.50
6	Troy Neel	.05
7	Craig Paquette	.05
8	Ruben Sierra	.05
9	Terry Steinbach	.05
10	Bobby Witt	.05
11	Chad Curtis	.05
12	Chili Davis	.05
13	Gary DiSarcina	.05
14	Damion Easley	.05
15	Chuck Finley	.05
16	Joe Grahe	.05
17	Mark Langston	.05
18	Eduardo Perez	.05
19	Tim Salmon	.15
20	J.T. Snow	.10
21	Jeff Bagwell	.50
22	Craig Biggio	.20
23	Ken Caminiti	.10
24	Andujar Cedeno	.05
25	Doug Drabek	.05
26	Steve Finley	.05
27	Luis Gonzalez	.05
28	Pete Harnisch	.05
29	Darryl Kile	.05
30	Mitch Williams	.05
31	Roberto Alomar	.25
32	Joe Carter	.05
33	Juan Guzman	.05
34	Pat Hentgen	.05
35	Paul Molitor	.25
36	John Olerud	.15
37	Ed Sprague	.05
38	Dave Stewart	.05
39	Duane Ward	.05
40	Devon White	.05
41	Steve Avery	.05
42	Jeff Blauser	.05
43	Ron Gant	.10
44	Tom Glavine	.15
45	Dave Justice	.15
46	Greg Maddux	.75
47	Fred McGriff	.15
48	Terry Pendleton	.05
49	Deion Sanders	.15
50	John Smoltz	.10
51	Ricky Bones	.05
52	Cal Eldred	.05
53	Darryl Hamilton	.05
54	John Jaha	.05
55	Pat Listach	.05
56	Jaime Navarro	.05
57	Dave Nilsson	.05
58	B.J. Surhoff	.05
59	Greg Vaughn	.10
60	Robin Yount	.25
61	Bernard Gilkey	.05
62	Gregg Jefferies	.10
63	Brian Jordan	.05
64	Ray Lankford	.05
65	Tom Pagnozzi	.05
66	Ozzie Smith	.30
67	Bob Tewksbury	.05
68	Allen Watson	.05
69	Mark Whiten	.05
70	Todd Zeile	.05
71	Steve Buechele	.05
72	Mark Grace	.15
73	Jose Guzman	.05
74	Derrick May	.05
75	Mike Morgan	.05
76	Randy Myers	.05
77	Ryne Sandberg	.30
78	Sammy Sosa	1.00
79	Jose Vizcaino	.05
80	Rick Wilkins	.05
81	Pedro Astacio	.05
82	Brett Butler	.05
83	Delino DeShields	.05
84	Orel Hershiser	.05
85	Eric Karros	.05
86	Ramon Martinez	.10
87	Jose Offerman	.05
88	Mike Piazza	.60
89	Darryl Strawberry	.10
90	Tim Wallach	.05
91	Moises Alou	.10
92	Wil Cordero	.05
93	Jeff Fassero	.05
94	Darrin Fletcher	.05
95	Marquis Grissom	.10
96	Ken Hill	.05
97	Mike Lansing	.05
98	Kirk Rueter	.05
99	Larry Walker	.20
100	John Wetteland	.05
101	Rod Beck	.05
102	Barry Bonds	.40
103	John Burkett	.05
104	Royce Clayton	.05
105	Darren Lewis	.05
106	Kirt Manwaring	.05
107	Willie McGee	.05
108	Bill Swift	.05
109	Robby Thompson	.05
110	Matt Williams	.15
111	Sandy Alomar Jr.	.10
112	Carlos Baerga	.05
113	Albert Belle	.35
114	Wayne Kirby	.05
115	Kenny Lofton	.20
116	Jose Mesa	.05
117	Eddie Murray	.15
118	Charles Nagy	.05
119	Paul Sorrento	.05
120	Jim Thome	.15
121	Rich Amaral	.05
122	Eric Anthony	.05
123	Mike Blowers	.05
124	Chris Bosio	.05
125	Jay Buhner	.05
126	Dave Fleming	.05
127	Ken Griffey, Jr.	1.50
128	Randy Johnson	.25
129	Edgar Martinez	.05
130	Tino Martinez	.10
131	Bret Barberie	.05
132	Ryan Bowen	.05
133	Chuck Carr	.05
134	Jeff Conine	.10
135	Orestes Destrade	.05
136	Chris Hammond	.05
137	Bryan Harvey	.05
138	Dave Magadan	.05
139	Benito Santiago	.05
140	Gary Sheffield	.15
141	Bobby Bonilla	.05
142	Jeromy Burnitz	.05
143	Dwight Gooden	.10
144	Todd Hundley	.10
145	Bobby Jones	.05
146	Jeff Kent	.05
147	Joe Orsulak	.05
148	Bret Saberhagen	.05
149	Pete Schourek	.05
150	Ryan Thompson	.05
151	Brady Anderson	.10
152	Harold Baines	.05
153	Mike Devereaux	.05
154	Chris Hoiles	.05
155	Ben McDonald	.05
156	Mark McLemore	.05
157	Mike Mussina	.15
158	Rafael Palmeiro	.20
159	Cal Ripken, Jr.	1.00
160	Chris Sabo	.05
161	Brad Ausmus	.05
162	Derek Bell	.05
163	Andy Benes	.05
164	Doug Brocail	.05
165	Archi Cianfrocco	.05
166	Ricky Gutierrez	.05
167	Tony Gwynn	.50
168	Gene Harris	.05
169	Pedro Martinez	.50
170	Phil Plantier	.05
171	Darren Daulton	.05
172	Mariano Duncan	.05
173	Len Dykstra	.05
174	Tommy Greene	.05
175	Dave Hollins	.05
176	Danny Jackson	.05
177	John Kruk	.05
178	Terry Mulholland	.05
179	Curt Schilling	.10
180	Kevin Stocker	.05
181	Jay Bell	.05
182	Steve Cooke	.05
183	Carlos Garcia	.05
184	Joel Johnston	.05
185	Jeff King	.05
186	Al Martin	.05
187	Orlando Merced	.05
188	Don Slaught	.05
189	Andy Van Slyke	.05
190	Kevin Young	.05
191	Kevin Brown	.10
192	Jose Canseco	.30
193	Will Clark	.20
194	Juan Gonzalez	.40
195	Tom Henke	.05
196	David Hulse	.05
197	Dean Palmer	.05
198	Roger Pavlik	.05
199	Ivan Rodriguez	.40
200	Kenny Rogers	.05
201	Roger Clemens	.40
202	Scott Cooper	.05
203	Andre Dawson	.10
204	Mike Greenwell	.05
205	Billy Hatcher	.05
206	Jeff Russell	.05
207	Aaron Sele	.05
208	John Valentin	.05
209	Mo Vaughn	.25
210	Frank Viola	.05
211	Rob Dibble	.05
212	Willie Greene	.05
213	Roberto Kelly	.05
214	Barry Larkin	.15
215	Kevin Mitchell	.05
216	Hal Morris	.05
217	Joe Oliver	.05
218	Jose Rijo	.05
219	Reggie Sanders	.05
220	John Smiley	.05
221	Dante Bichette	.10
222	Ellis Burks	.05
223	Andres Galarraga	.15
224	Joe Girardi	.05
225	Charlie Hayes	.05
226	Darren Holmes	.05
227	Howard Johnson	.05
228	Roberto Mejia	.05
229	David Nied	.05
230	Armando Reynoso	.05
231	Kevin Appier	.05
232	David Cone	.10
233	Greg Gagne	.05
234	Tom Gordon	.05
235	Felix Jose	.05
236	Wally Joyner	.05
237	Jose Lind	.05
238	Brian McRae	.05
239	Mike MacFarlane	.05
240	Jeff Montgomery	.05
241	Eric Davis	.05
242	John Doherty	.05
243	Cecil Fielder	.05
244	Travis Fryman	.10
245	Bill Gullickson	.05
246	Mike Henneman	.05

247	Tony Phillips	.05
248	Mickey Tettleton	.05
249	Alan Trammell	.10
250	Lou Whitaker	.05
251	Rick Aguilera	.05
252	Scott Erickson	.05
253	Kent Hrbek	.05
254	Chuck Knoblauch	.10
255	Shane Mack	.05
256	Dave McCarty	.05
257	Pat Meares	.05
258	Kirby Puckett	.40
259	Kevin Tapani	.05
260	Dave Winfield	.20
261	Wilson Alvarez	.05
262	Jason Bere	.05
263	Alex Fernandez	.05
264	Ozzie Guillen	.05
265	Roberto Hernandez	.05
266	Lance Johnson	.05
267	Jack McDowell	.05
268	Tim Raines	.10
269	Frank Thomas	.50
270	Robin Ventura	.10
271	Jim Abbott	.05
272	Wade Boggs	.25
273	Mike Gallego	.05
274	Pat Kelly	.05
275	Jimmy Key	.05
276	Don Mattingly	.50
277	Paul O'Neill	.15
278	Mike Stanley	.05
279	Danny Tartabull	.05
280	Bernie Williams	.25
281	Chipper Jones	.60
282	Ryan Klesko	.15
283	Javier Lopez	.10
284	Jeffrey Hammonds	.10
285	Jeff McNeely	.05
286	Manny Ramirez	.50
287	Billy Ashley	.05
288	Raul Mondesi	.15
289	Cliff Floyd	.10
290	Rondell White	.10
291	Steve Karsay	.05
292	Midre Cummings	.10
293	Salomon Torres	.05
294	J.R. Phillips	.05
295	Marc Newfield	.05
296	Carlos Delgado	.25
297	Butch Huskey	.10
298	Checklist (Frank Thomas)	.05
299	Checklist (Barry Bonds)	.05
300	Checklist (Juan Gonzalez)	.05

1994 Triple Play Bomb Squad

Ten of the top major league home run hitters are included in this insert set. Fronts feature sepia-toned player photos within a wide brown frame. Gold foil enhances the typography. Backs have a white background with representations of vintage airplanes. A bar chart at left gives the player's home run totals by year. A small color portrait photo is at upper-right. Below are a few words about his homer history.

		MT
Complete Set (10):		15.00
Common Player:		.50
1	Frank Thomas	2.00
2	Cecil Fielder	.50
3	Juan Gonzalez	2.00
4	Barry Bonds	2.00
5	Dave Justice	.75
6	Fred McGriff	.75
7	Ron Gant	.50
8	Ken Griffey, Jr.	6.00
9	Albert Belle	1.50
10	Matt Williams	.50

1994 Triple Play Medalists

Statistical performance over the 1992-93 seasons was used to rank the players appearing in the Medalists insert set. Horizontal format cards have photos of the first, second and third place winners in appropriate boxes of gold, silver and bronze foil. "Medalists," the "medals" and "Triple Play 94" are embossed on the front. Backs have color action photos of each player along with team logos and a few stats.

		MT
Complete Set (15):		10.00
Common Player:		.50
1	A.L. Catchers (Chris Hoiles, Mickey Tettleton, Brian Harper)	.50
2	N.L. Catchers (Darren Daulton, Rick Wilkins, Kirt Manwaring)	.50
3	A.L. First Basemen (Frank Thomas, Rafael Palmeiro, John Olerud)	.75
4	N.L. First Basemen (Mark Grace, Fred McGriff, Jeff Bagwell)	1.50
5	A.L. Second Basemen (Roberto Alomar, Carlos Baerga, Lou Whitaker)	.50
6	N.L. Second Basemen (Ryne Sandberg, Craig Biggio, Robby Thompson)	1.00
7	A.L. Shortstops (Tony Fernandez, Cal Ripken, Jr., Alan Trammell)	2.00
8	N.L. Shortstops (Barry Larkin, Jay Bell, Jeff Blauser)	.50
9	A.L. Third Basemen (Robin Ventura, Travis Fryman, Wade Boggs)	.60
10	N.L. Third Basemen (Terry Pendleton, Dave Hollins, Gary Sheffield)	.50
11	A.L. Outfielders (Ken Griffey, Jr., Kirby Puckett, Albert Belle)	2.50
12	N.L. Outfielders (Barry Bonds, Andy Van Slyke, Len Dykstra)	.75
13	A.L. Starters (Jack McDowell, Kevin Brown, Randy Johnson)	.65
14	N.L. Starters (Greg Maddux, Jose Rijo, Billy Swift)	1.00
15	Designated Hitters (Paul Molitor, Dave Winfield, Harold Baines)	.60

1994 Triple Play Nicknames

Eight of baseball's most colorful team nicknames are featured in this insert set. Fronts feature a background photo representative of the nickname, with a player photo is superimposed over that. Backs have another player photo and a history of the team's nickname.

		MT
Complete Set (8):		15.00
Common Player:		1.50
1	Cecil Fielder	1.00
2	Ryne Sandberg	2.00
3	Gary Sheffield	1.00
4	Joe Carter	1.00
5	John Olerud	1.50
6	Cal Ripken, Jr.	4.00
7	Mark McGwire	6.00
8	Gregg Jefferies	1.00

1991 Ultra

This 400-card set was originally going to be called the Elite set, but Fleer chose to use the Ultra label. The card fronts feature gray borders surrounding full-color action photos. The backs feature three player photos and statistics. Hot Prospects and Great Performers are among the special cards featured within the set.

		MT
Complete Set (400):		20.00
Common Player:		.05
Wax Pack (14):		.75
Wax Box (36):		17.00
1	Steve Avery	.05
2	Jeff Blauser	.05
3	Francisco Cabrera	.05
4	Ron Gant	.20
5	Tom Glavine	.15
6	Tommy Gregg	.05
7	Dave Justice	.25
8	Oddibe McDowell	.05
9	Greg Olson	.05
10	Terry Pendleton	.05
11	Lonnie Smith	.05
12	John Smoltz	.15
13	Jeff Treadway	.05
14	Glenn Davis	.05
15	Mike Devereaux	.05
16	Leo Gomez	.05
17	Chris Hoiles	.05
18	Dave Johnson	.05
19	Ben McDonald	.05
20	Randy Milligan	.05
21	Gregg Olson	.05
22	Joe Orsulak	.05
23	Bill Ripken	.05
24	Cal Ripken, Jr.	2.00
25	David Segui	.05
26	Craig Worthington	.05
27	Wade Boggs	.25
28	Tom Bolton	.05
29	Tom Brunansky	.05
30	Ellis Burks	.05
31	Roger Clemens	1.00
32	Mike Greenwell	.05
33	Greg Harris	.05
34	Daryl Irvine	.05
35	Mike Marshall	.05
36	Tim Naehring	.05
37	Tony Pena	.05
38	*Phil Plantier*	.05
39	Carlos Quintana	.05
40	Jeff Reardon	.05
41	Jody Reed	.05
42	Luis Rivera	.05
43	Jim Abbott	.05
44	Chuck Finley	.05
45	Bryan Harvey	.05
46	Donnie Hill	.05
47	Jack Howell	.05
48	Wally Joyner	.05
49	Mark Langston	.05
50	Kirk McCaskill	.05
51	Lance Parrish	.05
52	Dick Schofield	.05
53	Lee Stevens	.05
54	Dave Winfield	.20
55	George Bell	.05
56	Damon Berryhill	.05
57	Mike Bielecki	.05
58	Andre Dawson	.15
59	Shawon Dunston	.05
60	Joe Girardi	.05
61	Mark Grace	.20
62	Mike Harkey	.05
63	Les Lancaster	.05
64	Greg Maddux	1.50
65	Derrick May	.05
66	Ryne Sandberg	.60
67	Luis Salazar	.05
68	Dwight Smith	.05
69	Hector Villanueva	.05
70	Jerome Walton	.05
71	Mitch Williams	.05
72	Carlton Fisk	.20

73 Scott Fletcher .05
74 Ozzie Guillen .05
75 Greg Hibbard .05
76 Lance Johnson .05
77 Steve Lyons .05
78 Jack McDowell .05
79 Dan Pasqua .05
80 Melido Perez .05
81 Tim Raines .10
82 Sammy Sosa 2.00
83 Cory Snyder .05
84 Bobby Thigpen .05
85 Frank Thomas 1.50
86 Robin Ventura .20
87 Todd Benzinger .05
88 Glenn Braggs .05
89 Tom Browning .05
90 Norm Charlton .05
91 Eric Davis .05
92 Rob Dibble .05
93 Bill Doran .05
94 Mariano Duncan .05
95 Billy Hatcher .05
96 Barry Larkin .25
97 Randy Myers .05
98 Hal Morris .05
99 Joe Oliver .05
100 Paul O'Neill .20
101a Jeff Reed .05
101b Beau Allred (Should be #104) .05
102 Jose Rijo .05
103a Chris Sabo .05
103b Carlos Baerga (Should be #106) .05
104 Not Issued (See #101b)
105 Sandy Alomar,Jr. .15
106 Not Issued (See #103b)
107 Albert Belle .50
108 Jerry Browne .05
109 Tom Candiotti .05
110 Alex Cole .05
111a John Farrell .05
111b Chris James (Should be #114) .05
112 Felix Fermin .05
113 Brook Jacoby .05
114 Not Issued (See #111b)
115 Doug Jones .05
116a Steve Olin .05
116b Mitch Webster (Should be #119) .05
117 Greg Swindell .05
118 Turner Ward .05
119 Not Issued (See #116b)
120 Dave Bergman .05
121 Cecil Fielder .05
122 Travis Fryman .15
123 Mike Henneman .05
124 Lloyd Moseby .05
125 Dan Petry .05
126 Tony Phillips .05
127 Mark Salas .05
128 Frank Tanana .05
129 Alan Trammell .10
130 Lou Whitaker .05
131 Eric Anthony .05
132 Craig Biggio .25
133 Ken Caminiti .20
134 Casey Candaele .05
135 Andujar Cedeno .05
136 Mark Davidson .05
137 Jim Deshaies .05
138 Mark Portugal .05
139 Rafael Ramirez .05
140 Mike Scott .05
141 Eric Yelding .05
142 Gerald Young .05
143 Kevin Appier .05
144 George Brett .50
145 *Jeff Conine* .40
146 Jim Eisenreich .05
147 Tom Gordon .05
148 Mark Gubicza .05
149 Bo Jackson .20
150 Brent Mayne .05
151 Mike Macfarlane .05
152 *Brian McRae* .35
153 Jeff Montgomery .05
154 Bret Saberhagen .05
155 Kevin Seitzer .05
156 Terry Shumpert .05
157 Kurt Stillwell .05
158 Danny Tartabull .05
159 Tim Belcher .05
160 Kal Daniels .05
161 Alfredo Griffin .05
162 Lenny Harris .05
163 Jay Howell .05
164 Ramon Martinez .10
165 Mike Morgan .05
166 Eddie Murray .30
167 Jose Offerman .05
168 Juan Samuel .05
169 Mike Scioscia .05
170 Mike Sharperson .05
171 Darryl Strawberry .15
172 Greg Brock .05
173 Chuck Crim .05
174 Jim Gantner .05
175 Ted Higuera .05
176 Mark Knudson .05
177 Tim McIntosh .05
178 Paul Molitor .30
179 Dan Plesac .05
180 Gary Sheffield .25
181 Bill Spiers .05
182 B.J. Surhoff .05
183 Greg Vaughn .10
184 Robin Yount .25
185 Rick Aguilera .05
186 Greg Gagne .05
187 Dan Gladden .05
188 Brian Harper .05
189 Kent Hrbek .05
190 Gene Larkin .05
191 Shane Mack .05
192 Pedro Munoz .05
193 Al Newman .05
194 Junior Ortiz .05
195 Kirby Puckett .60
196 Kevin Tapani .05
197 Dennis Boyd .05
198 Tim Burke .05
199 Ivan Calderon .05
200 Delino DeShields .05
201 Mike Fitzgerald .05
202 Steve Frey .05
203 Andres Galarraga .25
204 Marquis Grissom .10
205 Dave Martinez .05
206 Dennis Martinez .05
207 Junior Noboa .05
208 Spike Owen .05
209 Scott Ruskin .05
210 Tim Wallach .05
211 Daryl Boston .05
212 Vince Coleman .05
213 David Cone .20
214 Ron Darling .05
215 Kevin Elster .05
216 Sid Fernandez .05
217 John Franco .05
218 Dwight Gooden .10
219 Tom Herr .05
220 Todd Hundley .20
221 Gregg Jefferies .10
222 Howard Johnson .05
223 Dave Magadan .05
224 Kevin McReynolds .05
225 Keith Miller .05
226 Mackey Sasser .05
227 Frank Viola .05
228 Jesse Barfield .05
229 Greg Cadaret .05
230 Alvaro Espinoza .05
231 Bob Geren .05
232 Lee Guetterman .05
233 Mel Hall .05
234 Andy Hawkins .05
235 Roberto Kelly .05
236 Tim Leary .05
237 Jim Leyritz .05
238 Kevin Maas .05
239 Don Mattingly .75
240 Hensley Meulens .05
241 Eric Plunk .05
242 Steve Sax .05
243 Todd Burns .05
244 Jose Canseco .50
245 Dennis Eckersley .05
246 Mike Gallego .05
247 Dave Henderson .05
248 Rickey Henderson .30
249 Rick Honeycutt .05
250 Carney Lansford .05
251 Mark McGwire 3.00
252 Mike Moore .05
253 Terry Steinbach .05
254 Dave Stewart .05
255 Walt Weiss .05
256 Bob Welch .05
257 Curt Young .05
258 Wes Chamberlain .05
259 Pat Combs .05
260 Darren Daulton .05
261 Jose DeJesus .05
262 Len Dykstra .05
263 Charlie Hayes .05
264 Von Hayes .05
265 Ken Howell .05
266 John Kruk .05
267 Roger McDowell .05
268 Mickey Morandini .05
269 Terry Mulholland .05
270 Dale Murphy .10
271 Randy Ready .05
272 Dickie Thon .05
273 Stan Belinda .05
274 Jay Bell .05
275 Barry Bonds .60
276 Bobby Bonilla .05
277 Doug Drabek .05
278 *Carlos Garcia* .15
279 Neal Heaton .05
280 Jeff King .05
281 Bill Landrum .05
282 Mike LaValliere .05
283 Jose Lind .05
284 *Orlando Merced* .20
285 Gary Redus .05
286 Don Slaught .05
287 Andy Van Slyke .05
288 Jose DeLeon .05
289 Pedro Guerrero .05
290 Ray Lankford .05
291 Joe Magrane .05
292 Jose Oquendo .05
293 Tom Pagnozzi .05
294 Bryn Smith .05
295 Lee Smith .05
296 Ozzie Smith .40
297 Milt Thompson .05
298 *Craig Wilson* .05
299 Todd Zeile .10
300 Shawn Abner .05
301 Andy Benes .10
302 Paul Faries .05
303 Tony Gwynn 1.00
304 Greg Harris .05
305 Thomas Howard .05
306 Bruce Hurst .05
307 Craig Lefferts .05
308 Fred McGriff .35
309 Dennis Rasmussen .05
310 Bip Roberts .05
311 Benito Santiago .05
312 Garry Templeton .05
313 Ed Whitson .05
314 Dave Anderson .05
315 Kevin Bass .05
316 Jeff Brantley .05
317 John Burkett .05
318 Will Clark .25
319 Steve Decker .05
320 Scott Garrelts .05
321 Terry Kennedy .05
322 Mark Leonard .05
323 Darren Lewis .05
324 Greg Litton .05
325 Willie McGee .05
326 Kevin Mitchell .05
327 Don Robinson .05
328 Andres Santana .05
329 Robby Thompson .05
330 Jose Uribe .05
331 Matt Williams .15
332 Scott Bradley .05
333 Henry Cotto .05
334 Alvin Davis .05
335 Ken Griffey, Sr. .05
336 Ken Griffey, Jr. 3.00
337 Erik Hanson .05
338 Brian Holman .05
339 Randy Johnson .50
340 Edgar Martinez .05
341 Tino Martinez .20
342 Pete O'Brien .05
343 Harold Reynolds .05
344 David Valle .05
345 Omar Vizquel .05
346 Brad Arnsberg .05
347 Kevin Brown .15
348 Julio Franco .05
349 Jeff Huson .05
350 Rafael Palmeiro .40
351 Geno Petralli .05
352 Gary Pettis .05
353 Kenny Rogers .05
354 Jeff Russell .05
355 Nolan Ryan 2.00
356 Ruben Sierra .05
357 Bobby Witt .05
358 Roberto Alomar .40
359 Pat Borders .05
360 Joe Carter .05
361 Kelly Gruber .05
362 Tom Henke .05
363 Glenallen Hill .05
364 Jimmy Key .05
365 Manny Lee .05
366 Rance Mulliniks .05
367 John Olerud .25
368 Dave Stieb .05
369 Duane Ward .05
370 David Wells .10
371 Mark Whiten .05
372 Mookie Wilson .05
373 Willie Banks .05
374 Steve Carter .05
375 Scott Chiamparino .05
376 Steve Chitren .05
377 Darrin Fletcher .05
378 Rich Garces .05
379 Reggie Jefferson .05
380 *Eric Karros* .75
381 Pat Kelly .05
382 Chuck Knoblauch .25
383 Denny Neagle .05
384 Dan Opperman .05
385 John Ramos .05
386 *Henry Rodriguez* .50
387 Mo Vaughn .50
388 Gerald Williams .05
389 Mike York .05
390 Eddie Zosky .05
391 Barry Bonds (Great Performer) .30
392 Cecil Fielder (Great Performer) .05
393 Rickey Henderson (Great Performer) .10
394 Dave Justice (Great Performer) .20
395 Nolan Ryan (Great Performer) 1.00
396 Bobby Thigpen (Great Performer) .05
397 Checklist .05
398 Checklist .05
399 Checklist .05
400 Checklist .05

1991 Ultra Gold

A pair of action photos flanking and below a portrait in a home plate frame at top-center are featured on these cards. Background is a graduated gold coloring. The Fleer Ultra Team logo is in the upper-left corner. Backs have narrative career information. The Puckett and Sandberg cards feature incorrect historical information on the backs.

		MT
Complete Set (10):		7.50
Common Player:		.25
1	Barry Bonds	1.50
2	Will Clark	.50
3	Doug Drabek	.25
4	Ken Griffey, Jr.	4.00
5	Rickey Henderson	.50
6	Bo Jackson	.40
7	Ramon Martinez	.30
8	Kirby Puckett	1.25
9	Chris Sabo	.25
10	Ryne Sandberg	1.00

1991 Ultra Update

This 120-card set was produced as a supplement to the premier Fleer Ultra set. Cards feature the same style as the regular Fleer Ultra cards. The cards were sold only as complete sets in full color, shrinkwrapped boxes.

		MT
Complete Set (120):		50.00
Common Player:		.15
1	Dwight Evans	.15
2	Chito Martinez	.15
3	Bob Melvin	.15
4	*Mike Mussina*	6.00
5	Jack Clark	.15
6	Dana Kiecker	.15
7	Steve Lyons	.15
8	Gary Gaetti	.15
9	Dave Gallagher	.15
10	Dave Parker	.20
11	Luis Polonia	.15
12	Luis Sojo	.15
13	Wilson Alvarez	.15
14	Alex Fernandez	.15
15	Craig Grebeck	.15
16	Ron Karkovice	.15
17	Warren Newson	.15
18	Scott Radinsky	.15
19	Glenallen Hill	.15
20	Charles Nagy	.20
21	Mark Whiten	.15
22	Milt Cuyler	.15
23	Paul Gibson	.15
24	Mickey Tettleton	.15
25	Todd Benzinger	.15
26	Storm Davis	.15
27	Kirk Gibson	.15
28	Bill Pecota	.15
29	Gary Thurman	.15
30	Darryl Hamilton	.15
31	Jaime Navarro	.15
32	Willie Randolph	.15
33	Bill Wegman	.15
34	Randy Bush	.15
35	Chili Davis	.15
36	Scott Erickson	.25
37	Chuck Knoblauch	.50
38	Scott Leius	.15
39	Jack Morris	.15
40	John Habyan	.15
41	Pat Kelly	.15
42	Matt Nokes	.15
43	Scott Sanderson	.15
44	Bernie Williams	4.00
45	Harold Baines	.20
46	Brook Jacoby	.15
47	Ernest Riles	.15
48	Willie Wilson	.15
49	Jay Buhner	.15
50	Rich DeLucia	.15
51	Mike Jackson	.15
52	Bill Krueger	.15
53	Bill Swift	.15
54	Brian Downing	.15
55	Juan Gonzalez	8.00
56	Dean Palmer	1.00
57	Kevin Reimer	.15
58	*Ivan Rodriguez*	15.00
59	Tom Candiotti	.15
60	Juan Guzman	.15
61	Bob MacDonald	.15
62	Greg Myers	.15
63	Ed Sprague	.15
64	Devon White	.20
65	Rafael Belliard	.15
66	Juan Berenguer	.15
67	Brian Hunter	.15
68	Kent Mercker	.15
69	Otis Nixon	.15
70	Danny Jackson	.15
71	Chuck McElroy	.15
72	Gary Scott	.15
73	Heathcliff Slocumb	.15
74	Chico Walker	.15
75	Rick Wilkins	.15
76	Chris Hammond	.15
77	Luis Quinones	.15
78	Herm Winningham	.15
79	*Jeff Bagwell*	15.00
80	Jim Corsi	.15
81	Steve Finley	.15
82	*Luis Gonzalez*	2.00
83	Pete Harnisch	.15
84	Darryl Kile	.15
85	Brett Butler	.15
86	Gary Carter	.25
87	Tim Crews	.15
88	Orel Hershiser	.15
89	Bob Ojeda	.15
90	Bret Barberie	.15
91	Barry Jones	.15
92	Gilberto Reyes	.15
93	Larry Walker	1.50
94	Hubie Brooks	.15
95	Tim Burke	.15
96	Rick Cerone	.15
97	Jeff Innis	.15
98	Wally Backman	.15
99	Tommy Greene	.15
100	Ricky Jordan	.15
101	Mitch Williams	.15
102	John Smiley	.15
103	Randy Tomlin	.15
104	Gary Varsho	.15
105	Cris Carpenter	.15
106	Ken Hill	.15
107	Felix Jose	.15
108	*Omar Oliveras*	.75
109	Gerald Perry	.15
110	Jerald Clark	.15
111	Tony Fernandez	.15
112	Darrin Jackson	.15
113	Mike Maddux	.15
114	Tim Teufel	.15
115	Bud Black	.15
116	Kelly Downs	.15
117	Mike Felder	.15
118	Willie McGee	.15
119	Trevor Wilson	.15
120	Checklist	.15

1992 Ultra

Fleer released its second annual Ultra set in 1992. Card fronts feature full-color action photos with a marble accent at the card bottom. The flip sides are horizontal with two additional player photos. Many insert sets were randomly included in foil packs as premiums. These included rookie, All-Star and award winners, among others. A two-card Tony Gwynn send-away set was also available through an offer from Fleer. For $1 and 10 Ultra wrappers, collectors could receive the Gwynn cards. The set is numbered by team; cards #1-300 comprise Series I, cards #301-600 are Series II.

		MT
Complete Set (600):		30.00
Series 1 (300):		20.00
Series 2 (300):		10.00
Common Player:		.10
Series 1 Pack (14):		1.25
Series 1 Wax Box (36):		40.00
Series 2 Pack (14):		1.00
Series 2 Wax Box (36):		30.00
1	Glenn Davis	.10
2	Mike Devereaux	.10
3	Dwight Evans	.10
4	Leo Gomez	.10
5	Chris Hoiles	.10
6	Sam Horn	.10
7	Chito Martinez	.10
8	Randy Milligan	.10
9	Mike Mussina	.60
10	Billy Ripken	.10
11	Cal Ripken, Jr.	2.00
12	Tom Brunansky	.10
13	Ellis Burks	.10
14	Jack Clark	.10
15	Roger Clemens	1.00
16	Mike Greenwell	.10
17	Joe Hesketh	.10
18	Tony Pena	.10
19	Carlos Quintana	.10
20	Jeff Reardon	.10
21	Jody Reed	.10
22	Luis Rivera	.10
23	Mo Vaughn	.40
24	Gary DiSarcina	.10
25	Chuck Finley	.10
26	Gary Gaetti	.10
27	Bryan Harvey	.10
28	Lance Parrish	.10
29	Luis Polonia	.10
30	Dick Schofield	.10
31	Luis Sojo	.10
32	Wilson Alvarez	.10
33	Carlton Fisk	.40
34	Craig Grebeck	.10
35	Ozzie Guillen	.10
36	Greg Hibbard	.10
37	Charlie Hough	.10
38	Lance Johnson	.10
39	Ron Karkovice	.10
40	Jack McDowell	.10
41	Donn Pall	.10
42	Melido Perez	.10
43	Tim Raines	.15
44	Frank Thomas	1.00
45	Sandy Alomar, Jr.	.20
46	Carlos Baerga	.10
47	Albert Belle	.40
48	Jerry Browne	.10
49	Felix Fermin	.10
50	Reggie Jefferson	.10
51	Mark Lewis	.10
52	Carlos Martinez	.10
53	Steve Olin	.10
54	Jim Thome	.75
55	Mark Whiten	.10
56	Dave Bergman	.10
57	Milt Cuyler	.10
58	Rob Deer	.10
59	Cecil Fielder	.10
60	Travis Fryman	.25
61	Scott Livingstone	.10
62	Tony Phillips	.10
63	Mickey Tettleton	.10
64	Alan Trammell	.15
65	Lou Whitaker	.10
66	Kevin Appier	.10
67	Mike Boddicker	.10
68	George Brett	.75
69	Jim Eisenreich	.10
70	Mark Gubicza	.10
71	David Howard	.10
72	Joel Johnston	.10
73	Mike Macfarlane	.10
74	Brent Mayne	.10
75	Brian McRae	.10
76	Jeff Montgomery	.10
77	Terry Shumpert	.10
78	Don August	.10
79	Dante Bichette	.25
80	Ted Higuera	.10
81	Paul Molitor	.40
82	Jamie Navarro	.10
83	Gary Sheffield	.25
84	Bill Spiers	.10
85	B.J. Surhoff	.10
86	Greg Vaughn	.10
87	Robin Yount	.40
88	Rick Aguilera	.10
89	Chili Davis	.10
90	Scott Erickson	.10
91	Brian Harper	.10
92	Kent Hrbek	.10
93	Chuck Knoblauch	.15
94	Scott Leius	.10
95	Shane Mack	.10
96	Mike Pagliarulo	.10
97	Kirby Puckett	.75
98	Kevin Tapani	.10
99	Jesse Barfield	.10
100	Alvaro Espinoza	.10
101	Mel Hall	.10
102	Pat Kelly	.10
103	Roberto Kelly	.10
104	Kevin Maas	.10
105	Don Mattingly	1.00
106	Hensley Meulens	.10
107	Matt Nokes	.10
108	Steve Sax	.10
109	Harold Baines	.10
110	Jose Canseco	.50
111	Ron Darling	.10
112	Mike Gallego	.10
113	Dave Henderson	.10
114	Rickey Henderson	.40
115	Mark McGwire	3.00
116	Terry Steinbach	.10
117	Dave Stewart	.10
118	Todd Van Poppel	.10
119	Bob Welch	.10
120	Greg Briley	.10
121	Jay Buhner	.10
122	Rich DeLucia	.10
123	Ken Griffey, Jr.	3.00
124	Erik Hanson	.10
125	Randy Johnson	.40
126	Edgar Martinez	.10
127	Tino Martinez	.15
128	Pete O'Brien	.10
129	Harold Reynolds	.10
130	Dave Valle	.10
131	Julio Franco	.10
132	Juan Gonzalez	1.00
133	Jeff Huson	.10
134	Mike Jeffcoat	.10
135	Terry Mathews	.10
136	Rafael Palmeiro	.40
137	Dean Palmer	.10
138	Geno Petralli	.10
139	Ivan Rodriguez	.75
140	Jeff Russell	.10
141	Nolan Ryan	2.00
142	Ruben Sierra	.10
143	Roberto Alomar	.50
144	Pat Borders	.10
145	Joe Carter	.10
146	Kelly Gruber	.10
147	Jimmy Key	.10
148	Manny Lee	.10
149	Rance Mulliniks	.10
150	Greg Myers	.10
151	John Olerud	.25
152	Dave Stieb	.10
153	Todd Stottlemyre	.10
154	Duane Ward	.10
155	Devon White	.10
156	Eddie Zosky	.10
157	Steve Avery	.10
158	Rafael Belliard	.10
159	Jeff Blauser	.10
160	Sid Bream	.10
161	Ron Gant	.10
162	Tom Glavine	.25
163	Brian Hunter	.10
164	Dave Justice	.25
165	Mark Lemke	.10
166	Greg Olson	.10
167	Terry Pendleton	.10
168	Lonnie Smith	.10
169	John Smoltz	.15
170	Mike Stanton	.10
171	Jeff Treadway	.10
172	Paul Assenmacher	.10
173	George Bell	.10
174	Shawon Dunston	.10
175	Mark Grace	.20
176	Danny Jackson	.10
177	Les Lancaster	.10
178	Greg Maddux	1.50
179	Luis Salazar	.10
180	Rey Sanchez	.10
181	Ryne Sandberg	.50
182	Jose Vizcaino	.10
183	Chico Walker	.10
184	Jerome Walton	.10
185	Glenn Braggs	.10
186	Tom Browning	.10
187	Rob Dibble	.10
188	Bill Doran	.10
189	Chris Hammond	.10

190	Billy Hatcher	.10
191	Barry Larkin	.15
192	Hal Morris	.10
193	Joe Oliver	.10
194	Paul O'Neill	.25
195	Jeff Reed	.10
196	Jose Rijo	.10
197	Chris Sabo	.10
198	Jeff Bagwell	1.00
199	Craig Biggio	.20
200	Ken Caminiti	.25
201	Andujar Cedeno	.10
202	Steve Finley	.10
203	Luis Gonzalez	.10
204	Pete Harnisch	.10
205	Xavier Hernandez	.10
206	Darryl Kile	.10
207	Al Osuna	.10
208	Curt Schilling	.10
209	Brett Butler	.10
210	Kal Daniels	.10
211	Lenny Harris	.10
212	Stan Javier	.10
213	Ramon Martinez	.15
214	Roger McDowell	.10
215	Jose Offerman	.10
216	Juan Samuel	.10
217	Mike Scioscia	.10
218	Mike Sharperson	.10
219	Darryl Strawberry	.20
220	Delino DeShields	.10
221	Tom Foley	.10
222	Steve Frey	.10
223	Dennis Martinez	.10
224	Spike Owen	.10
225	Gilberto Reyes	.10
226	Tim Wallach	.10
227	Daryl Boston	.10
228	Tim Burke	.10
229	Vince Coleman	.10
230	David Cone	.25
231	Kevin Elster	.10
232	Dwight Gooden	.15
233	Todd Hundley	.10
234	Jeff Innis	.10
235	Howard Johnson	.10
236	Dave Magadan	.10
237	Mackey Sasser	.10
238	Anthony Young	.10
239	Wes Chamberlain	.10
240	Darren Daulton	.10
241	Len Dykstra	.10
242	Tommy Greene	.10
243	Charlie Hayes	.10
244	Dave Hollins	.10
245	Ricky Jordan	.10
246	John Kruk	.10
247	Mickey Morandini	.10
248	Terry Mulholland	.10
249	Dale Murphy	.20
250	Jay Bell	.10
251	Barry Bonds	.75
252	Steve Buechele	.10
253	Doug Drabek	.10
254	Mike LaValliere	.10
255	Jose Lind	.10
256	Lloyd McClendon	.10
257	Orlando Merced	.10
258	Don Slaught	.10
259	John Smiley	.10
260	Zane Smith	.10
261	Randy Tomlin	.10
262	Andy Van Slyke	.10
263	Pedro Guerrero	.10
264	Felix Jose	.10
265	Ray Lankford	.10
266	Omar Olivares	.10
267	Jose Oquendo	.10
268	Tom Pagnozzi	.10
269	Bryn Smith	.10
270	Lee Smith	.10
271	Ozzie Smith	.50
272	Milt Thompson	.10
273	Todd Zeile	.10
274	Andy Benes	.15
275	Jerald Clark	.10
276	Tony Fernandez	.10
277	Tony Gwynn	.75
278	Greg Harris	.10
279	Thomas Howard	.10
280	Bruce Hurst	.10
281	Mike Maddux	.10
282	Fred McGriff	.40
283	Benito Santiago	.10
284	Kevin Bass	.10
285	Jeff Brantley	.10
286	John Burkett	.10
287	Will Clark	.40
288	Royce Clayton	.10
289	Steve Decker	.10
290	Kelly Downs	.10
291	Mike Felder	.10
292	Darren Lewis	.10
293	Kirt Manwaring	.10
294	Willie McGee	.10
295	Robby Thompson	.10
296	Matt Williams	.30
297	Trevor Wilson	.10
298	Checklist 1-108 (Sandy Alomar, Jr.)	.10
299	Checklist 109-208 (Rey Sanchez)	.10
300	Checklist 209-300 (Nolan Ryan)	.15
301	Brady Anderson	.15
302	Todd Frohwirth	.10
303	Ben McDonald	.10
304	Mark McLemore	.10
305	Jose Mesa	.10
306	Bob Milacki	.10
307	Gregg Olson	.10
308	David Segui	.10
309	Rick Sutcliffe	.10
310	Jeff Tackett	.10
311	Wade Boggs	.40
312	Scott Cooper	.10
313	John Flaherty	.10
314	Wayne Housie	.10
315	Peter Hoy	.10
316	John Marzano	.10
317	Tim Naehring	.10
318	Phil Plantier	.10
319	Frank Viola	.10
320	Matt Young	.10
321	Jim Abbott	.10
322	Hubie Brooks	.10
323	*Chad Curtis*	.40
324	Alvin Davis	.10
325	Junior Felix	.10
326	Von Hayes	.10
327	Mark Langston	.10
328	Scott Lewis	.10
329	Don Robinson	.10
330	Bobby Rose	.10
331	Lee Stevens	.10
332	George Bell	.10
333	Esteban Beltre	.10
334	Joey Cora	.10
335	Alex Fernandez	.20
336	Roberto Hernandez	.10
337	Mike Huff	.10
338	Kirk McCaskill	.10
339	Dan Pasqua	.10
340	Scott Radinsky	.10
341	Steve Sax	.10
342	Bobby Thigpen	.10
343	Robin Ventura	.25
344	Jack Armstrong	.10
345	Alex Cole	.10
346	Dennis Cook	.10
347	Glenallen Hill	.10
348	Thomas Howard	.10
349	Brook Jacoby	.10
350	Kenny Lofton	.40
351	Charles Nagy	.10
352	Rod Nichols	.10
353	Junior Ortiz	.10
354	Dave Otto	.10
355	Tony Perezchica	.10
356	Scott Scudder	.10
357	Paul Sorrento	.10
358	Skeeter Barnes	.10
359	Mark Carreon	.10
360	John Doherty	.10
361	Dan Gladden	.10
362	Bill Gullickson	.10
363	Shawn Hare	.10
364	Mike Henneman	.10
365	Chad Kreuter	.10
366	Mark Leiter	.10
367	Mike Munoz	.10
368	Kevin Ritz	.10
369	Mark Davis	.10
370	Tom Gordon	.10
371	Chris Gwynn	.10
372	Gregg Jefferies	.15
373	Wally Joyner	.10
374	Kevin McReynolds	.10
375	Keith Miller	.10
376	Rico Rossy	.10
377	Curtis Wilkerson	.10
378	Ricky Bones	.10
379	Chris Bosio	.10
380	Cal Eldred	.10
381	Scott Fletcher	.10
382	Jim Gantner	.10
383	Darryl Hamilton	.10
384	Doug Henry	.10
385	*Pat Listach*	.10
386	Tim McIntosh	.10
387	Edwin Nunez	.10
388	Dan Plesac	.10
389	Kevin Seitzer	.10
390	Franklin Stubbs	.10
391	William Suero	.10
392	Bill Wegman	.10
393	Willie Banks	.10
394	Jarvis Brown	.10
395	Greg Gagne	.10
396	Mark Guthrie	.10
397	Bill Krueger	.10
398	*Pat Mahomes*	.25
399	Pedro Munoz	.10
400	John Smiley	.10
401	Gary Wayne	.10
402	Lenny Webster	.10
403	Carl Willis	.10
404	Greg Cadaret	.10
405	Steve Farr	.10
406	Mike Gallego	.10
407	Charlie Hayes	.10
408	Steve Howe	.10
409	Dion James	.10
410	Jeff Johnson	.10
411	Tim Leary	.10
412	Jim Leyritz	.10
413	Melido Perez	.10
414	Scott Sanderson	.10
415	Andy Stankiewicz	.10
416	Mike Stanley	.10
417	Danny Tartabull	.10
418	Lance Blankenship	.10
419	Mike Bordick	.10
420	*Scott Brosius*	.40
421	Dennis Eckersley	.10
422	Scott Hemond	.10
423	Carney Lansford	.10
424	Henry Mercedes	.10
425	Mike Moore	.10
426	Gene Nelson	.10
427	Randy Ready	.10
428	Bruce Walton	.10
429	Willie Wilson	.10
430	Rich Amaral	.10
431	Dave Cochrane	.10
432	Henry Cotto	.10
433	Calvin Jones	.10
434	Kevin Mitchell	.10
435	Clay Parker	.10
436	Omar Vizquel	.10
437	Floyd Bannister	.10
438	Kevin Brown	.20
439	John Cangelosi	.10
440	Brian Downing	.10
441	Monty Fariss	.10
442	Jose Guzman	.10
443	Donald Harris	.10
444	Kevin Reimer	.10
445	Kenny Rogers	.10
446	Wayne Rosenthal	.10
447	Dickie Thon	.10
448	Derek Bell	.10
449	Juan Guzman	.10
450	Tom Henke	.10
451	Candy Maldonado	.10
452	Jack Morris	.10
453	David Wells	.10
454	Dave Winfield	.35
455	Juan Berenguer	.10
456	Damon Berryhill	.10
457	Mike Bielecki	.10
458	Marvin Freeman	.10
459	Charlie Leibrandt	.10
460	Kent Mercker	.10
461	Otis Nixon	.10
462	Alejandro Pena	.10
463	Ben Rivera	.10
464	Deion Sanders	.20
465	Mark Wohlers	.10
466	Shawn Boskie	.10
467	Frank Castillo	.10
468	Andre Dawson	.15
469	Joe Girardi	.10
470	Chuck McElroy	.10
471	Mike Morgan	.10
472	Ken Patterson	.10
473	Bob Scanlan	.10
474	Gary Scott	.10
475	Dave Smith	.10
476	Sammy Sosa	1.50
477	Hector Villanueva	.10
478	Scott Bankhead	.10
479	Tim Belcher	.10
480	Freddie Benavides	.10
481	Jacob Brumfield	.10
482	Norm Charlton	.10
483	Dwayne Henry	.10
484	Dave Martinez	.10
485	Bip Roberts	.10
486	Reggie Sanders	.10
487	Greg Swindell	.10
488	Ryan Bowen	.10
489	Casey Candaele	.10
490	Juan Guerrero	.10
491	Pete Incaviglia	.10
492	Jeff Juden	.10
493	Rob Murphy	.10
494	Mark Portugal	.10
495	Rafael Ramirez	.10
496	Scott Servais	.10
497	Ed Taubensee	.10
498	Brian Williams	.10
499	Todd Benzinger	.10
500	John Candelaria	.10
501	Tom Candiotti	.10
502	Tim Crews	.10
503	Eric Davis	.10
504	Jim Gott	.10
505	Dave Hansen	.10
506	Carlos Hernandez	.10
507	Orel Hershiser	.10
508	Eric Karros	.15
509	Bob Ojeda	.10
510	Steve Wilson	.10
511	Moises Alou	.20
512	Bret Barberie	.10
513	Ivan Calderon	.10
514	Gary Carter	.15
515	Archi Cianfrocco	.10
516	Jeff Fassero	.10
517	Darrin Fletcher	.10
518	Marquis Grissom	.10
519	Chris Haney	.10
520	Ken Hill	.10
521	Chris Nabholz	.10
522	Bill Sampen	.10
523	John VanderWal	.10
524	David Wainhouse	.10
525	Larry Walker	.40
526	John Wetteland	.10
527	Bobby Bonilla	.10
528	Sid Fernandez	.10
529	John Franco	.10
530	Dave Gallagher	.10
531	Paul Gibson	.10
532	Eddie Murray	.35
533	Junior Noboa	.10
534	Charlie O'Brien	.10
535	Bill Pecota	.10
536	Willie Randolph	.10
537	Bret Saberhagen	.10
538	Dick Schofield	.10
539	Pete Schourek	.10
540	Ruben Amaro	.10
541	Andy Ashby	.15
542	Kim Batiste	.10
543	Cliff Brantley	.10
544	Mariano Duncan	.10
545	Jeff Grotewold	.10
546	Barry Jones	.10
547	Julio Peguero	.10
548	Curt Schilling	.10
549	Mitch Williams	.10
550	Stan Belinda	.10
551	Scott Bullett	.10
552	Cecil Espy	.10
553	Jeff King	.10
554	Roger Mason	.10
555	Paul Miller	.10
556	Denny Neagle	.10
557	Vocente Palacios	.10
558	Bob Patterson	.10
559	Tom Prince	.10
560	Gary Redus	.10
561	Gary Varsho	.10
562	Juan Agosto	.10
563	Cris Carpenter	.10
564	*Mark Clark*	.20
565	Jose DeLeon	.10
566	Rich Gedman	.10
567	Bernard Gilkey	.10
568	Rex Hudler	.10
569	Tim Jones	.10
570	Donovan Osborne	.10
571	Mike Perez	.10
572	Gerald Perry	.10
573	Bob Tewksbury	.10
574	Todd Worrell	.10
575	Dave Eiland	.10
576	Jeremy Hernandez	.10
577	Craig Lefferts	.10
578	Jose Melendez	.10
579	Randy Myers	.10
580	Gary Pettis	.10
581	Rich Rodriguez	.10
582	Gary Sheffield	.30
583	Craig Shipley	.10
584	Kurt Stillwell	.10
585	Tim Teufel	.10
586	*Rod Beck*	.25
587	Dave Burba	.10
588	Craig Colbert	.10
589	Bryan Hickerson	.10
590	Mike Jackson	.10

591	Mark Leonard	.10
592	Jim McNamara	.10
593	John Patterson	.10
594	Dave Righetti	.10
595	Cory Snyder	.10
596	Bill Swift	.10
597	Ted Wood	.10
598	Checklist 301-403 (Scott Sanderson)	.10
599	Checklist 404-498 (Junior Ortiz)	.10
600	Checklist 499-600 (Mike Morgan)	.10

1992 Ultra All-Rookies

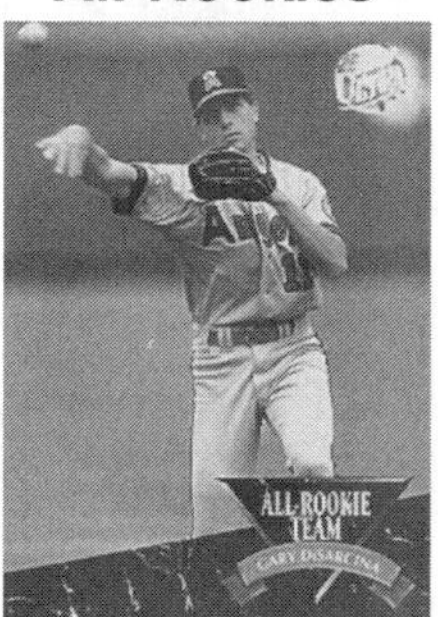

The 10 promising rookies in this set could be found on special cards inserted in Ultra Series 2 foil packs.

		MT
Complete Set (10):		8.00
Common Player:		.50
1	Eric Karros	2.00
2	Andy Stankiewicz	.50
3	Gary DiSarcina	.50
4	Archi Cianfrocco	.50
5	Jim McNamara	.50
6	Chad Curtis	1.50
7	Kenny Lofton	2.50
8	Reggie Sanders	1.00
9	Pat Mahomes	.50
10	Donovan Osborne	.50

1992 Ultra All-Stars

An All-Star team from each league, with two pitchers, could be assembled by collecting these inserts from Ultra Series 2 foil packs.

		MT
Complete Set (20):		25.00
Common Player:		.50
1	Mark McGwire	6.00
2	Roberto Alomar	1.00
3	Cal Ripken, Jr.	4.00
4	Wade Boggs	1.00
5	Mickey Tettleton	.50
6	Ken Griffey, Jr.	6.00
7	Roberto Kelly	.50
8	Kirby Puckett	1.50
9	Frank Thomas	2.00
10	Jack McDowell	.50
11	Will Clark	1.00
12	Ryne Sandberg	1.50
13	Barry Larkin	.60
14	Gary Sheffield	.75
15	Tom Pagnozzi	.50
16	Barry Bonds	2.00
17	Deion Sanders	.75
18	Darryl Strawberry	.60
19	David Cone	.75
20	Tom Glavine	.75

1992 Ultra Award Winners

The 25 cards in this insert issue were randomly packaged with Series 1 Ultra. One of the Cal Ripken cards (#21) can be found with a photo made from a reversed negative, as well as with the proper orientation. Neither version carries a premium.

		MT
Complete Set (26):		40.00
Common Player:		.60
1	Jack Morris	.60
2	Chuck Knoblauch	1.00
3	Jeff Bagwell	2.50
4	Terry Pendleton	.60
5	Cal Ripken, Jr.	5.00
6	Roger Clemens	2.50
7	Tom Glavine	.75
8	Tom Pagnozzi	.60
9	Ozzie Smith	1.50
10	Andy Van Slyke	.60
11	Barry Bonds	2.50
12	Tony Gwynn	3.50
13	Matt Williams	.60
14	Will Clark	.75
15	Robin Ventura	.75
16	Mark Langston	.60
18	Devon White	.60
19	Don Mattingly	2.50
20	Roberto Alomar	1.50
21a	Cal Ripken, Jr. (reversed negative)	5.00
21b	Cal Ripken, Jr. (correct)	5.00
22	Ken Griffey, Jr.	8.00
23	Kirby Puckett	2.00
24	Greg Maddux	4.00
25	Ryne Sandberg	1.50

1992 Ultra Tony Gwynn

This 12-card subset of Ultra's spokesman features 10 cards which were available as inserts in Series I foil packs, plus two cards labeled "Special No. 1" and "Special No. 2" which could only be obtained in a send-away offer. Some 2,000 of these cards carry a "certified" Gwynn autograph. Not part of the issue, but similar in format were a pair of extra Tony Gwynn cards. One pictures him with Fleer CEO Paul Mullan, the other shows him with the poster child for Casa de Amparo, a children's shelter in San Diego County.

		MT
Complete Set (12):		10.00
Common Card:		1.00
Certified Autograph Card:		90.00
	INSERT CARDS	1.00
1	Tony Gwynn (fielding)	1.00
2	Tony Gwynn (batting)	1.00
3	Tony Gwynn (fielding)	1.00
4	Tony Gwynn (batting)	1.00
5	Tony Gwynn (base-running)	1.00
6	Tony Gwynn (awards)	1.00
7	Tony Gwynn (bunting)	1.00
8	Tony Gwynn (batting)	1.00
9	Tony Gwynn (running)	1.00
10	Tony Gwynn (batting)	1.00
	SEND-AWAY CARDS	1.00
1	Tony Gwynn (batting)	4.00
2	Tony Gwynn (fielding)	4.00
	SPECIAL CARDS	1.00
---	Tony Gwynn, Paul Mullan	6.00
---	Tony Gwynn (Casa de Amparo)	15.00
1	Tony Gwynn (leaping at outfield wall)	1.00
2	Tony Gwynn (batting in brown warm-up jersey)	1.00
1	Tony Gwynn (batting)	1.00
2	Tony Gwynn (fielding)	1.00
---	Tony Gwynn, Paul Mullan	6.00
---	Casa de Amparo Salute (Tony Gwynn)	15.00

1993 Ultra

The first series of 300 cards retains Fleer's successful features from 1992, including additional gold foil stamping, UV coating, and team color-coded marbled bars on the fronts. The backs feature a stylized ballpark background, which creates a 3-D effect, stats and portrait and an action photo. Dennis Eckersley is featured in a limited-edition "Career Highlights" set and personally autographed more than 2,000 of his cards, to be randomly inserted into both series' packs. A 10-card Home Run Kings subset and 25-card Ultra Awards Winners subset were also randomly inserted in packs. Ultra Rookies cards are included in both series. Ultra's second series has three limited-edition subsets: Ultra All-Stars, Ultra All-Rookie Team, and Strikeout Kings, plus cards featuring Colorado Rockies and Florida Marlins players.

		MT
Complete Set (650):		30.00
Series 1 (300):		15.00
Series 2 (350):		15.00
Common Player:		.10
Series 1 or 2 Pack (14):		1.25
Series 1 or 2 Wax Box (36):		35.00
1	Steve Avery	.10
2	Rafael Belliard	.10
3	Damon Berryhill	.10
4	Sid Bream	.10
5	Ron Gant	.15
6	Tom Glavine	.20
7	Ryan Klesko	.25
8	Mark Lemke	.10
9	Javier Lopez	.25
10	Greg Olson	.10
11	Terry Pendleton	.10
12	Deion Sanders	.25
13	Mike Stanton	.10
14	Paul Assenmacher	.10
15	Steve Buechele	.10
16	Frank Castillo	.10
17	Shawon Dunston	.10
18	Mark Grace	.35
19	Derrick May	.10
20	Chuck McElroy	.10
21	Mike Morgan	.10
22	Bob Scanlan	.10
23	Dwight Smith	.10
24	Sammy Sosa	1.50
25	Rick Wilkins	.10
26	Tim Belcher	.10
27	Jeff Branson	.10
28	Bill Doran	.10
29	Chris Hammond	.10
30	Barry Larkin	.20
31	Hal Morris	.10
32	Joe Oliver	.10
33	Jose Rijo	.10
34	Bip Roberts	.10
35	Chris Sabo	.10
36	Reggie Sanders	.15

37	Craig Biggio	.40
38	Ken Caminiti	.20
39	Steve Finley	.10
40	Luis Gonzalez	.10
41	Juan Guerrero	.10
42	Pete Harnisch	.10
43	Xavier Hernandez	.10
44	Doug Jones	.10
45	Al Osuna	.10
46	Eddie Taubensee	.10
47	Scooter Tucker	.10
48	Brian Williams	.10
49	Pedro Astacio	.10
50	Rafael Bournigal	.10
51	Brett Butler	.10
52	Tom Candiotti	.10
53	Eric Davis	.10
54	Lenny Harris	.10
55	Orel Hershiser	.10
56	Eric Karros	.20
57	Pedro Martinez	1.00
58	Roger McDowell	.10
59	Jose Offerman	.10
60	Mike Piazza	3.00
61	Moises Alou	.20
62	Kent Bottenfield	.10
63	Archi Cianfrocco	.10
64	Greg Colbrunn	.10
65	Wil Cordero	.10
66	Delino DeShields	.10
67	Darrin Fletcher	.10
68	Ken Hill	.10
69	Chris Nabholz	.10
70	Mel Rojas	.10
71	Larry Walker	.40
72	Sid Fernandez	.10
73	John Franco	.10
74	Dave Gallagher	.10
75	Todd Hundley	.15
76	Howard Johnson	.10
77	Jeff Kent	.15
78	Eddie Murray	.25
79	Bret Saberhagen	.15
80	Chico Walker	.10
81	Anthony Young	.10
82	Kyle Abbott	.10
83	Ruben Amaro Jr.	.10
84	Juan Bell	.10
85	Wes Chamberlain	.10
86	Darren Daulton	.10
87	Mariano Duncan	.10
88	Dave Hollins	.10
89	Ricky Jordan	.10
90	John Kruk	.10
91	Mickey Morandini	.10
92	Terry Mulholland	.10
93	Ben Rivera	.10
94	Mike Williams	.10
95	Stan Belinda	.10
96	Jay Bell	.10
97	Jeff King	.10
98	Mike LaValliere	.10
99	Lloyd McClendon	.10
100	Orlando Merced	.10
101	Zane Smith	.10
102	Randy Tomlin	.10
103	Andy Van Slyke	.10
104	Tim Wakefield	.10
105	John Wehner	.10
106	Bernard Gilkey	.10
107	Brian Jordan	.15
108	Ray Lankford	.10
109	Donovan Osborne	.10
110	Tom Pagnozzi	.10
111	Mike Perez	.10
112	Lee Smith	.10
113	Ozzie Smith	.50
114	Bob Tewksbury	.10
115	Todd Zeile	.10
116	Andy Benes	.15
117	Greg Harris	.10
118	Darrin Jackson	.10
119	Fred McGriff	.25
120	Rich Rodriguez	.10
121	Frank Seminara	.10
122	Gary Sheffield	.25
123	Craig Shipley	.10
124	Kurt Stillwell	.10
125	Dan Walters	.10
126	Rod Beck	.10
127	Mike Benjamin	.10
128	Jeff Brantley	.10
129	John Burkett	.10
130	Will Clark	.25
131	Royce Clayton	.10
132	Steve Hosey	.10
133	Mike Jackson	.10
134	Darren Lewis	.10
135	Kirt Manwaring	.10
136	Bill Swift	.10
137	Robby Thompson	.10
138	Brady Anderson	.20
139	Glenn Davis	.10
140	Leo Gomez	.10
141	Chito Martinez	.10
142	Ben McDonald	.10
143	Alan Mills	.10
144	Mike Mussina	.50
145	Gregg Olson	.10
146	David Segui	.10
147	Jeff Tackett	.10
148	Jack Clark	.10
149	Scott Cooper	.10
150	Danny Darwin	.10
151	John Dopson	.10
152	Mike Greenwell	.10
153	Tim Naehring	.10
154	Tony Pena	.10
155	Paul Quantrill	.10
156	Mo Vaughn	.40
157	Frank Viola	.10
158	Bob Zupcic	.10
159	Chad Curtis	.10
160	Gary DiScarcina	.10
161	Damion Easley	.10
162	Chuck Finley	.10
163	Tim Fortugno	.10
164	Rene Gonzales	.10
165	Joe Grahe	.10
166	Mark Langston	.10
167	John Orton	.10
168	Luis Polonia	.10
169	Julio Valera	.10
170	Wilson Alvarez	.10
171	George Bell	.10
172	Joey Cora	.10
173	Alex Fernandez	.15
174	Lance Johnson	.10
175	Ron Karkovice	.10
176	Jack McDowell	.10
177	Scott Radinsky	.10
178	Tim Raines	.15
179	Steve Sax	.10
180	Bobby Thigpen	.10
181	Frank Thomas	1.50
182	Sandy Alomar Jr.	.20
183	Carlos Baerga	.10
184	Felix Fermin	.10
185	Thomas Howard	.10
186	Mark Lewis	.10
187	Derek Lilliquist	.10
188	Carlos Martinez	.10
189	Charles Nagy	.15
190	Scott Scudder	.10
191	Paul Sorrento	.10
192	Jim Thome	.40
193	Mark Whiten	.10
194	Milt Cuyler	.10
195	Rob Deer	.10
196	John Doherty	.10
197	Travis Fryman	.20
198	Dan Gladden	.10
199	Mike Henneman	.10
200	John Kiely	.10
201	Chad Kreuter	.10
202	Scott Livingstone	.10
203	Tony Phillips	.10
204	Alan Trammell	.15
205	Mike Boddicker	.10
206	George Brett	.75
207	Tom Gordon	.10
208	Mark Gubicza	.10
209	Gregg Jefferies	.15
210	Wally Joyner	.10
211	Kevin Koslofski	.10
212	Brent Mayne	.10
213	Brian McRae	.10
214	Kevin McReynolds	.10
215	Rusty Meacham	.10
216	Steve Shifflett	.10
217	James Austin	.10
218	Cal Eldred	.10
219	Darryl Hamilton	.10
220	Doug Henry	.10
221	John Jaha	.10
222	Dave Nilsson	.10
223	Jesse Orosco	.10
224	B.J. Surhoff	.10
225	Greg Vaughn	.15
226	Bill Wegman	.10
227	Robin Yount	.25
228	Rick Aguilera	.10
229	J.T. Bruett	.10
230	Scott Erickson	.10
231	Kent Hrbek	.10
232	Terry Jorgensen	.10
233	Scott Leius	.10
234	Pat Mahomes	.10
235	Pedro Munoz	.10
236	Kirby Puckett	1.00
237	Kevin Tapani	.10
238	Lenny Webster	.10
239	Carl Willis	.10
240	Mike Gallego	.10
241	John Habyan	.10
242	Pat Kelly	.10
243	Kevin Maas	.10
244	Don Mattingly	1.00
245	Hensley Meulens	.10
246	Sam Militello	.10
247	Matt Nokes	.10
248	Melido Perez	.10
249	Andy Stankiewicz	.10
250	Randy Velarde	.10
251	Bob Wickman	.10
252	Bernie Williams	.40
253	Lance Blankenship	.10
254	Mike Bordick	.10
255	Jerry Browne	.10
256	Ron Darling	.10
257a	Dennis Eckersley	.10
257b	Dennis Eckersley" (Wt. 195; no "MLBPA" on back - unmarked sample card)	3.00
257c	Dennis Eckersley (Wt, 195; no "Printed in USA" on back - unmarked sample card)	3.00
258	Rickey Henderson	.40
259	Vince Horsman	.10
260	Troy Neel	.10
261	Jeff Parrett	.10
262	Terry Steinbach	.10
263	Bob Welch	.10
264	Bobby Witt	.10
265	Rich Amaral	.10
266	Bret Boone	.20
267	Jay Buhner	.10
268	Dave Fleming	.10
269	Randy Johnson	.40
270	Edgar Martinez	.10
271	Mike Schooler	.10
272	Russ Swan	.10
273	Dave Valle	.10
274	Omar Vizquel	.10
275	Kerry Woodson	.10
276	Kevin Brown	.20
277	Julio Franco	.10
278	Jeff Frye	.10
279	Juan Gonzalez	1.00
280	Jeff Huson	.10
281	Rafael Palmeiro	.40
282	Dean Palmer	.10
283	Roger Pavlik	.10
284	Ivan Rodriguez	.75
285	Kenny Rogers	.10
286	Derek Bell	.10
287	Pat Borders	.10
288	Joe Carter	.10
289	Bob MacDonald	.10
290	Jack Morris	.10
291	John Olerud	.25
292	Ed Sprague	.10
293	Todd Stottlemyre	.10
294	Mike Timlin	.10
295	Duane Ward	.10
296	David Wells	.10
297	Devon White	.10
298	Checklist	.10
299	Checklist	.10
300	Checklist	.10
301	Steve Bedrosian	.10
302	Jeff Blauser	.10
303	Francisco Cabrera	.10
304	Marvin Freeman	.10
305	Brian Hunter	.10
306	Dave Justice	.25
307	Greg Maddux	1.50
308	*Greg McMichael*	.10
309	Kent Mercker	.10
310	Otis Nixon	.10
311	Pete Smith	.10
312	John Smoltz	.20
313	Jose Guzman	.10
314	Mike Harkey	.10
315	Greg Hibbard	.10
316	Candy Maldonado	.10
317	Randy Myers	.10
318	Dan Plesac	.10
319	Rey Sanchez	.10
320	Ryne Sandberg	.60
321	*Tommy Shields*	.10
322	Jose Vizcaino	.10
323	*Matt Walbeck*	.15
324	Willie Wilson	.10
325	Tom Browning	.10
326	Tim Costo	.10
327	Rob Dibble	.10
328	Steve Foster	.10
329	Roberto Kelly	.10
330	Randy Milligan	.10
331	Kevin Mitchell	.10
332	*Tim Pugh*	.15
333	Jeff Reardon	.10
334	*John Roper*	.10
335	Juan Samuel	.10
336	John Smiley	.10
337	San Wilson	.10
338	Scott Aldred	.10
339	Andy Ashby	.10
340	Freddie Benavides	.10
341	Dante Bichette	.20
342	Willie Blair	.10
343	Daryl Boston	.10
344	Vinny Castilla	.20
345	Jerald Clark	.10
346	Alex Cole	.10
347	Andres Galarraga	.25
348	Joe Girardi	.10
349	*Ryan Hawblitzel*	.10
350	Charlie Hayes	.10
351	Butch Henry	.10
352	Darren Holmes	.10
353	Dale Murphy	.20
354	David Nied	.10
355	Jeff Parrett	.10
356	*Steve Reed*	.15
357	Bruce Ruffin	.10
358	*Danny Sheaffer*	.15
359	Bryn Smith	.10
360	*Jim Tatum*	.10
361	Eric Young	.10
362	Gerald Young	.10
363	Luis Aquino	.10
364	*Alex Arias*	.10
365	Jack Armstrong	.10
366	Bret Barberie	.10
367	Ryan Bowen	.10
368	Greg Briley	.10
369	Cris Carpenter	.10
370	Chuck Carr	.10
371	*Jeff Conine*	.25
372	Steve Decker	.10
373	Orestes Destrade	.10
374	Monty Fariss	.10
375	Junior Felix	.10
376	Chris Hammond	.10
377	Bryan Harvey	.10
378	*Trevor Hoffman*	.25
379	Charlie Hough	.10
380	Joe Klink	.10
381	*Richie Lewis*	.10
382	Dave Magadan	.10
383	Bob McCLure	.10
384	*Scott Pose*	.15
385	*Rich Renteria*	.15
386	Benito Santiago	.10
387	Walt Weiss	.10
388	Nigel Wilson	.10
389	Eric Anthony	.10
390	Jeff Bagwell	1.25
391	Andujar Cedeno	.10
392	Doug Drabek	.10
393	Darryl Kile	.10
394	Mark Portugal	.10
395	Karl Rhodes	.10
396	Scott Servais	.10
397	Greg Swindell	.10
398	Tom Goodwin	.10
399	Kevin Gross	.10
400	Carlos Hernandez	.10
401	Ramon Martinez	.15
402	Raul Mondesi	.40
403	Jody Reed	.10
404	Mike Sharperson	.10
405	Cory Snyder	.10
406	Darryl Strawberry	.20
407	*Rick Trlicek*	.10
408	Tim Wallach	.10
409	Todd Worrell	.10
410	Tavo Alvarez	.10
411	*Sean Berry*	.15
412	*Frank Bolick*	.10
413	Cliff Floyd	.15
414	Mike Gardiner	.10
415	Marquis Grissom	.15
416	*Tim Laker*	.10
417	*Mike Lansing*	.25
418	Dennis Martinez	.10
419	John Vander Wal	.10
420	John Wetteland	.10
421	Rondell White	.15
422	Bobby Bonilla	.10
423	Jeromy Burnitz	.15
424	*Vince Burnitz*	.10
425	*Mike Draper*	.10
426	Tony Fernandez	.10
427	Dwight Gooden	.15
428	Jeff Innis	.10
429	Bobby Jones	.15
430	Mike Maddux	.10
431	Charlie O'Brien	.10

No.	Player	MT
432	Joe Orsulak	.10
433	Pete Schourek	.10
434	Frank Tanana	.10
435	*Ryan Thompson*	.15
436	Kim Batiste	.10
437	Mark Davis	.10
438	Jose DeLeon	.10
439	Len Dykstra	.10
440	Jim Eisenreich	.10
441	Tommy Greene	.10
442	Pete Incaviglia	.10
443	Danny Jackson	.10
444	*Todd Pratt*	.20
445	Curt Schilling	.15
446	Milt Thompson	.10
447	David West	.10
448	Mitch Williams	.10
449	Steve Cooke	.10
450	Carlos Garcia	.10
451	Al Martin	.15
452	*Blas Minor*	.15
453	Dennis Moeller	.10
454	Denny Neagle	.10
455	Don Slaught	.10
456	Lonnie Smith	.10
457	Paul Wagner	.10
458	Bob Walk	.10
459	Kevin Young	.10
460	*Rene Arocha*	.15
461	Brian Barber	.10
462	Rheal Cormier	.10
463	Gregg Jefferies	.15
464	Joe Magrane	.10
465	Omar Olivares	.10
466	Geronimo Pena	.10
467	Allen Watson	.10
468	Mark Whiten	.10
469	Derek Bell	.10
470	Phil Clark	.10
471	*Pat Gomez*	.20
472	Tony Gwynn	1.25
473	Jeremy Hernandez	.10
474	Bruce Hurst	.10
475	Phil Plantier	.10
476	*Scott Sanders*	.20
477	*Tim Scott*	.10
478	*Darrell Sherman*	.10
479	Guillermo Velasquez	.10
480	*Tim Worrell*	.10
481	Todd Benzinger	.10
482	Bud Black	.10
483	Barry Bonds	.75
484	Dave Burba	.10
485	Bryan Hickerson	.10
486	Dave Martinez	.10
487	Willie McGee	.10
488	Jeff Reed	.10
489	Kevin Rogers	.10
490	Matt Williams	.20
491	Trevor Wilson	.10
492	Harold Baines	.10
493	Mike Devereaux	.10
494	Todd Frohwirth	.10
495	Chris Hoiles	.10
496	Luis Mercedes	.10
497	*Sherman Obando*	.15
498	*Brad Pennington*	.15
499	Harold Reynolds	.10
500	Arthur Rhodes	.10
501	Cal Ripken, Jr.	2.50
502	Rick Sutcliffe	.10
503	Fernando Valenzuela	.10
504	Mark Williamson	.10
505	Scott Bankhead	.10
506	Greg Blosser	.10
507	Ivan Calderon	.10
508	Roger Clemens	1.25
509	Andre Clemens	.10
510	Scott Fletcher	.10
511	Greg Harris	.10
512	Billy Hatcher	.10
513	Bob Melvin	.10
514	Carlos Quintana	.10
515	Luis Rivera	.10
516	Jeff Russell	.10
517	*Ken Ryan*	.20
518	Chili Davis	.10
519	*Jim Edmonds*	2.00
520	Gary Gaetti	.10
521	Torey Lovullo	.10
522	*Tony Percival*	.10
523	Tim Salmon	.40
524	Scott Sanderson	.10
525	*J.T. Snow*	.75
526	Jerome Walton	.10
527	Jason Bere	.10
528	*Rod Bolton*	.10
529	Ellis Burks	.10
530	Carlton Fisk	.25
531	Craig Grebeck	.10
532	Ozzie Guillen	.10
533	Roberto Hernandez	.10
534	Bo Jackson	.25
535	Kirk McCaskill	.10
536	Dave Stieb	.10
537	Robin Ventura	.25
538	Albert Belle	.50
539	Mike Bielecki	.10
540	Glenallen Hill	.10
541	Reggie Jefferson	.10
542	Kenny Lofton	.40
543	*Jeff Mutis*	.15
544	Junior Ortiz	.10
545	Manny Ramirez	1.50
546	Jeff Treadway	.10
547	Kevin Wickander	.10
548	Cecil Fielder	.10
549	Kirk Gibson	.10
550	*Greg Gohr*	.10
551	David Haas	.10
552	Bill Krueger	.10
553	Mike Moore	.10
554	Mickey Tettleton	.10
555	Lou Whitaker	.10
556	Kevin Appier	.10
557	*Billy Brewer*	.10
558	David Cone	.25
559	Greg Gagne	.10
560	Mark Gardner	.10
561	Phil Hiatt	.10
562	Felix Jose	.10
563	Jose Lind	.10
564	Mike Macfarlane	.10
565	Keith Miller	.10
566	Jeff Montgomery	.10
567	Hipolito Pechardo	.10
568	Ricky Bones	.10
569	Tom Brunansky	.10
570	*Joe Kmak*	.10
571	Pat Listach	.10
572	*Graeme Lloyd*	.20
573	*Carlos Maldonado*	.10
574	Josias Manzanillo	.10
575	Matt Mieske	.10
576	Kevin Reimer	.10
577	Bill Spiers	.10
578	Dickie Thon	.10
579	Willie Banks	.10
580	Jim Deshaies	.10
581	Mark Guthrie	.10
582	Brian Harper	.10
583	Chuck Knoblauch	.25
584	Gene Larkin	.10
585	Shane Mack	.10
586	David McCarty	.10
587	Mike Pagliarulo	.10
588	Mike Trombley	.10
589	Dave Winfield	.25
590	Jim Abbott	.10
591	Wade Boggs	.30
592	*Russ Davis*	.20
593	Steve Farr	.10
594	Steve Howe	.10
595	*Mike Humphreys*	.10
596	Jimmy Key	.10
597	Jim Leyritz	.10
598	*Bobby Munoz*	.15
599	Paul O'Neill	.25
600	Spike Owen	.10
601	Mike Stanley	.10
602	Danny Tartabull	.10
603	Scott Brosius	.10
604	Storm Davis	.10
605	Eric Fox	.10
606	Goose Gossage	.10
607	Scott Hammond	.10
608	Dave Henderson	.10
609	Mark McGwire	3.00
610	*Mike Mohler*	.10
611	Edwin Nunez	.10
612	Kevin Seitzer	.10
613	Ruben Sierra	.10
614	Chris Bosio	.10
615	Norm Charlton	.10
616	*Jim Converse*	.10
617	*John Cummings*	.10
618	Mike Felder	.10
619	Ken Griffey, Jr.	3.00
620	Mike Hampton	.10
621	Erik Hanson	.10
622	Bill Haselman	.10
623	Tino Martinez	.20
624	Lee Tinsley	.10
625	*Fernando Vina*	.25
626	*David Wainhouse*	.15
627	Jose Canseco	.75
628	Benji Gil	.10
629	Tom Henke	.10
630	*David Hulse*	.20
631	Manuel Lee	.10
632	Craig Lefferts	.10
633	*Robb Nen*	.15
634	Gary Redus	.10
635	Bill Ripken	.10
636	Nolan Ryan	2.50
637	Dan Smith	.10
638	*Matt Whiteside*	.10
639	Roberto Alomar	.50
640	Juan Guzman	.10
641	Pat Hentgen	.15
642	Darrin Jackson	.10
643	Randy Knorr	.10
644	*Domingo Martinez*	.20
645	Paul Molitor	.40
646	Dick Schofield	.10
647	Dave Stewart	.10
648	Checklist	.10
649	Checklist	.10
650	Checklist	.10

1993 Ultra All-Rookies

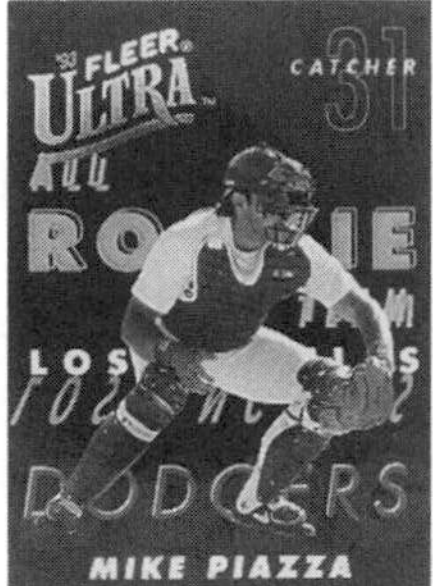

These insert cards are foil stamped on both sides and were randomly inserted into Series II packs. The cards have black fronts, with six different colors of type. The player's uniform number and position are located in the upper righthand corner. The player's name and Ultra logo are gold-foil stamped. Backs have a black background on which is a player photo and a career summary.

		MT
Complete Set (10):		15.00
Common Player:		1.00
1	Rene Arocha	.50
2	Jeff Conine	1.00
3	Phil Hiatt	.50
4	Mike Lansing	.75
5	Al Martin	.75
6	David Nied	.50
7	Mike Piazza	10.00
8	Tim Salmon	3.00
9	J.T. Snow	2.50
10	Kevin Young	.75

Player names in *Italic* type indicate a rookie card.

1993 Ultra All-Stars

This 20-card set features 10 of the top players from each league. Cards were randomly inserted into Series II packs and are foil stamped on both sides.

		MT
Complete Set (20):		45.00
Common Player:		.75
1	Darren Daulton	.75
2	Will Clark	1.50
3	Ryne Sandberg	3.00
4	Barry Larkin	1.00
5	Gary Sheffield	1.00
6	Barry Bonds	3.00
7	Ray Lankford	.75
8	Larry Walker	1.50
9	Greg Maddux	6.00
10	Lee Smith	.75
11	Ivan Rodriguez	3.00
12	Mark McGwire	10.00
13	Carlos Baerga	.75
14	Cal Ripken, Jr.	8.00
15	Edgar Martinez	.75
16	Juan Gonzalez	2.50
17	Ken Griffey, Jr.	10.00
18	Kirby Puckett	3.00
19	Frank Thomas	3.00
20	Mike Mussina	1.50

1993 Ultra Award Winners

This insert set features 18 Top Glove players (nine from each league), two rookies of the year, three MVPs (both leagues and World Series), both Cy Young Award winners and one Player of the Year. All cards are UV coated and foil stamped on both sides and were found in Series I packs. Fronts have a black background with "Fleer Ultra Award Winners" splashed around in trendy colors. The Ultra logo, player's name and his award are spelled out in gold foil. The horizontally arranged backs have much the same elements, plus a summary of the season's performance which led to the award. There is a close-up player photo, as well.

		MT
Complete Set (25):		40.00
Common Player:		.75
1	Greg Maddux	6.00
2	Tom Pagnozzi	.75
3	Mark Grace	1.00
4	Jose Lind	.75
5	Terry Pendleton	.75
6	Ozzie Smith	2.00
7	Barry Bonds	3.00
8	Andy Van Slyke	.75
9	Larry Walker	1.50
10	Mark Langston	.75
11	Ivan Rodriguez	3.00
12	Don Mattingly	3.00
13	Roberto Alomar	2.00
14	Robin Ventura	1.00
15	Cal Ripken, Jr.	8.00
16	Ken Griffey, Jr.	10.00
17	Kirby Puckett	3.00
18	Devon White	.75
19	Pat Listach	.75
20	Eric Karros	.75
21	Pat Borders	.75
22	Greg Maddux	6.00
23	Dennis Eckersley	.75
24	Barry Bonds	3.00
25	Gary Sheffield	1.00

1993 Ultra Dennis Eckersley Career Highlights

This limited-edition subset chronicles Dennis Eckersley's illustrious career. Cards, which are UV coated and silver foil-stamped on both sides, were randomly inserted into both series' packs. Eckersley autographed more than 2,000 of the cards, which were also randomly inserted into packs. By sending in 10 Fleer Ultra wrappers plus $1, collectors could receive two additional Eckersley cards which were not available in regular packs. Card fronts have a color action photo, the background of which has been colorized into shades of purple. A black marble strip at bottom has the city name and years he was with the team in silver foil. A large black marble box in one corner has the "Dennis Eckersley Career Highlights" logo in silver foil. On back, a purple box is dropped out of a color photo, and silver-foil typography describes some phrase of Eck's career.

		MT
Complete Set (12):		5.00
Common Card:		.50
Autographed Card:		40.00
1	"Perfection" (A's 1987-92)	.50
2	"The Kid" (Indians 1975-77)	.50
3	"The Warrior" (Indians 1975-77)	.50
4	"Beantown Blazer" (Red Sox 1978-84)	.50
5	"Eckspeak" (Red Sox 1978-84)	.50
6	"Down to Earth" (Red Sox 1978-84)	.50
7	"Wrigley Bound" (Cubs 1984-86)	.50
8	"No Relief" (A's 1987-92)	.50
9	"In Control" (A's 1987-92)	.50
10	"Simply the Best" (A's 1987-92)	.50
11	"Reign of Perfection" (A's 1987-92)	.50
12	"Leaving His Mark" (A's 1987-92)	.50

1993 Ultra Home Run Kings

This insert set features top home run kings. Cards, which are UV coated and have gold foil stamping on both sides, were inserts in Series I packs.

		MT
Complete Set (10):		15.00
Common Player:		1.00
1	Juan Gonzalez	2.50
2	Mark McGwire	10.00
3	Cecil Fielder	1.00
4	Fred McGriff	1.50
5	Albert Belle	2.00
6	Barry Bonds	3.00
7	Joe Carter	1.00
8	Gary Sheffield	1.00
9	Darren Daulton	1.00
10	Dave Hollins	1.00

1993 Ultra Performers

An Ultra Performers set of Fleer Ultra baseball cards was offered directly to collectors in 1993. The set, available only by mail, was limited to 150,000 sets. The cards featured gold-foil stamping and UV coating on each side and a six-photo design, including five on the front of the card. Each card was identified on the back by set serial number jet-printed in black in a strip at bottom.

		MT
Complete Set (10):		12.00
Common Player:		1.00
1	Barry Bonds	2.00
2	Juan Gonzalez	2.00
3	Ken Griffey, Jr.	6.00
4	Eric Karros	.75
5	Pat Listach	.75
6	Greg Maddux	3.00
7	David Nied	.75
8	Gary Sheffield	.75
9	J.T. Snow	.75
10	Frank Thomas	2.00

1993 Ultra Strikeout Kings

Five of baseball's top strikeout pitchers are featured in this second-series Ultra insert set. Cards are UV coated and foil stamped on both sides. Each card front has a picture of a pitcher winding up to throw. A baseball is in the background, with the pitcher in the forefront.

		MT
Complete Set (5):		15.00
Common Player:		1.00
1	Roger Clemens	4.00
2	Juan Guzman	1.00
3	Randy Johnson	2.50
4	Nolan Ryan	10.00
5	John Smoltz	1.50

1994 Ultra

Issued in two series of 300 cards each, Ultra for 1994 represented a new highwater mark in production values for a mid-priced brand. Each side of the basic cards is UV coated and gold-foil embossed. Fronts feature full-bleed action photos. At bottom the player name, team, position and Fleer Ultra logo appear in gold foil above a gold-foil strip. Some rookie cards are specially designated with a large gold "ROOKIE" above the Ultra logo. Backs feature a basic background that is team color coordinated. Three more player action photos are featured on the back, along with a team logo and a modicum of stats and personal data. There is a gold stripe along the left edge and the player's name and card number appear in gold in the lower-left corner. The set features seven types of insert cards, packaged one per pack.

		MT
Complete Set (600):		40.00
Complete Series I (300):		20.00
Complete Series II (300):		20.00
Common Player:		.10
Series 1 or 2 Pack (14):		1.50
Series 1 or 2 Wax Box (36):		40.00
1	Jeffrey Hammonds	.15
2	Chris Hoiles	.10
3	Ben McDonald	.10
4	Mark McLemore	.10
5	Alan Mills	.10
6	Jamie Moyer	.10
7	Brad Pennington	.10
8	Jim Poole	.10
9	Cal Ripken, Jr.	2.50
10	Jack Voigt	.10
11	Roger Clemens	1.00
12	Danny Darwin	.10
13	Andre Dawson	.20
14	Scott Fletcher	.10
15	Greg Harris	.10
16	Billy Hatcher	.10
17	Jeff Russell	.10
18	Aaron Sele	.15
19	Mo Vaughn	.50
20	Mike Butcher	.10
21	Rod Correia	.10
22	Steve Frey	.10
23	*Phil Leftwich*	.10
24	Torey Lovullo	.10
25	Ken Patterson	.10
26	Eduardo Perez	.10
27	Tim Salmon	.25
28	J.T. Snow	.20
29	Chris Turner	.10
30	Wilson Alvarez	.10
31	Jason Bere	.10
32	Joey Cora	.10
33	Alex Fernandez	.15
34	Roberto Hernandez	.10
35	Lance Johnson	.10
36	Ron Karkovice	.10
37	Kirk McCaskill	.10
38	Jeff Schwarz	.10
39	Frank Thomas	1.00
40	Sandy Alomar Jr.	.15
41	Albert Belle	.75

No.	Player	Value
42	Felix Fermin	.10
43	Wayne Kirby	.10
44	Tom Kramer	.10
45	Kenny Lofton	.50
46	Jose Mesa	.10
47	Eric Plunk	.10
48	Paul Sorrento	.10
49	Jim Thome	.40
50	Bill Wertz	.10
51	John Doherty	.10
52	Cecil Fielder	.10
53	Travis Fryman	.20
54	Chris Gomez	.10
55	Mike Henneman	.10
56	Chad Kreuter	.10
57	Bob MacDonald	.10
58	Mike Moore	.10
59	Tony Phillips	.10
60	Lou Whitaker	.10
61	Kevin Appier	.10
62	Greg Gagne	.10
63	Chris Gwynn	.10
64	Bob Hamelin	.10
65	Chris Haney	.10
66	Phil Hiatt	.10
67	Felix Jose	.10
68	Jose Lind	.10
69	Mike Macfarlane	.10
70	Jeff Montgomery	.10
71	Hipolito Pichardo	.10
72	Juan Bell	.10
73	Cal Eldred	.10
74	Darryl Hamilton	.10
75	Doug Henry	.10
76	Mike Ignasiak	.10
77	John Jaha	.15
78	Graeme Lloyd	.10
79	Angel Miranda	.10
80	Dave Nilsson	.10
81	Troy O'Leary	.10
82	Kevin Reimer	.10
83	Willie Banks	.10
84	Larry Casian	.10
85	Scott Erickson	.15
86	Eddie Guardado	.10
87	Kent Hrbek	.10
88	Terry Jorgensen	.10
89	Chuck Knoblauch	.25
90	Pat Meares	.10
91	Mike Trombley	.10
92	Dave Winfield	.20
93	Wade Boggs	.25
94	Scott Kamieniecki	.10
95	Pat Kelly	.10
96	Jimmy Key	.10
97	Jim Leyritz	.10
98	Bobby Munoz	.10
99	Paul O'Neill	.25
100	Melido Perez	.10
101	Mike Stanley	.10
102	Danny Tartabull	.10
103	Bernie Williams	.50
104	*Kurt Abbott*	.25
105	Mike Bordick	.10
106	Ron Darling	.10
107	Brent Gates	.10
108	Miguel Jimenez	.10
109	Steve Karsay	.10
110	Scott Lydy	.10
111	Mark McGwire	3.00
112	Troy Neel	.10
113	Craig Paquette	.10
114	Bob Welch	.10
115	Bobby Witt	.10
116	Rich Amaral	.10
117	Mike Blowers	.10
118	Jay Buhner	.10
119	Dave Fleming	.10
120	Ken Griffey, Jr.	3.00
121	Tino Martinez	.20
122	Marc Newfield	.10
123	Ted Power	.10
124	Mackey Sasser	.10
125	Omar Vizquel	.15
126	Kevin Brown	.20
127	Juan Gonzalez	.75
128	Tom Henke	.10
129	David Hulse	.10
130	Dean Palmer	.10
131	Roger Pavlik	.10
132	Ivan Rodriguez	.75
133	Kenny Rogers	.10
134	Doug Strange	.10
135	Pat Borders	.10
136	Joe Carter	.10
137	Darnell Coles	.10
138	Pat Hentgen	.10
139	Al Leiter	.15
140	Paul Molitor	.40
141	John Olerud	.25
142	Ed Sprague	.10
143	Dave Stewart	.10
144	Mike Timlin	.10
145	Duane Ward	.10
146	Devon White	.10
147	Steve Avery	.10
148	Steve Bedrosian	.10
149	Damon Berryhill	.10
150	Jeff Blauser	.10
151	Tom Glavine	.25
152	Chipper Jones	2.00
153	Mark Lemke	.10
154	Fred McGriff	.25
155	Greg McMichael	.10
156	Deion Sanders	.25
157	John Smoltz	.20
158	Mark Wohlers	.10
159	Jose Bautista	.10
160	Steve Buechele	.10
161	Mike Harkey	.10
162	Greg Hibbard	.10
163	Chuck McElroy	.10
164	Mike Morgan	.10
165	Kevin Roberson	.10
166	Ryne Sandberg	.75
167	Jose Vizcaino	.10
168	Rick Wilkins	.10
169	Willie Wilson	.10
170	Willie Greene	.10
171	Roberto Kelly	.10
172	Larry Luebbers	.10
173	Kevin Mitchell	.10
174	Joe Oliver	.10
175	John Roper	.10
176	Johnny Ruffin	.10
177	Reggie Sanders	.15
178	John Smiley	.10
179	Jerry Spradlin	.10
180	Freddie Benavides	.10
181	Dante Bichette	.25
182	Willie Blair	.10
183	Kent Bottenfield	.10
184	Jerald Clark	.10
185	Joe Girardi	.10
186	Roberto Mejia	.10
187	Steve Reed	.10
188	Armando Reynoso	.10
189	Bruce Ruffin	.10
190	Eric Young	.15
191	Luis Aquino	.10
192	Bret Barberie	.10
193	Ryan Bowen	.10
194	Chuck Carr	.10
195	Orestes Destrade	.10
196	Richie Lewis	.10
197	Dave Magadan	.10
198	Bob Natal	.10
199	Gary Sheffield	.25
200	Matt Turner	.10
201	Darrell Whitmore	.10
202	Eric Anthony	.10
203	Jeff Bagwell	1.00
204	Andujar Cedeno	.10
205	Luis Gonzalez	.15
206	Xavier Hernandez	.10
207	Doug Jones	.10
208	Darryl Kile	.10
209	Scott Servais	.10
210	Greg Swindell	.10
211	Brian Williams	.10
212	Pedro Astacio	.10
213	Brett Butler	.10
214	Omar Daal	.10
215	Jim Gott	.10
216	Raul Mondesi	.25
217	Jose Offerman	.10
218	Mike Piazza	2.00
219	Cory Snyder	.10
220	Tim Wallach	.10
221	Todd Worrell	.10
222	Moises Alou	.15
223	Sean Berry	.10
224	Wil Cordero	.10
225	Jeff Fassero	.10
226	Darrin Fletcher	.10
227	Cliff Floyd	.15
228	Marquis Grissom	.15
229	Ken Hill	.10
230	Mike Lansing	.10
231	Kirk Rueter	.10
232	John Wetteland	.10
233	Rondell White	.25
234	Tim Bogar	.10
235	Jeromy Burnitz	.10
236	Dwight Gooden	.20
237	Todd Hundley	.15
238	Jeff Kent	.10
239	Josias Manzanillo	.10
240	Joe Orsulak	.10
241	Ryan Thompson	.10
242	Kim Batiste	.10
243	Darren Daulton	.10
243a	Darren Daulton (promotional sample)	.50
244	Tommy Greene	.10
245	Dave Hollins	.10
246	Pete Incaviglia	.10
247	Danny Jackson	.10
248	Ricky Jordan	.10
249	John Kruk	.10
249a	John Kruk (promotional sample)	.50
250	Mickey Morandini	.10
251	Terry Mulholland	.10
252	Ben Rivera	.10
253	Kevin Stocker	.10
254	Jay Bell	.10
255	Steve Cooke	.10
256	Jeff King	.10
257	Al Martin	.10
258	Danny Micelli	.10
259	Blas Minor	.10
260	Don Slaught	.10
261	Paul Wagner	.10
262	Tim Wakefield	.10
263	Kevin Young	.10
264	Rene Arocha	.10
265	*Richard Batchelor*	.10
266	Gregg Jefferies	.15
267	Brian Jordan	.15
268	Jose Oquendo	.10
269	Donovan Osborne	.10
270	Erik Pappas	.10
271	Mike Perez	.10
272	Bob Tewksbury	.10
273	Mark Whiten	.10
274	Todd Zeile	.15
275	Andy Ashby	.10
276	Brad Ausmus	.10
277	Phil Clark	.10
278	Jeff Gardner	.10
279	Ricky Gutierrez	.10
280	Tony Gwynn	1.00
281	Tim Mauser	.10
282	Scott Sanders	.10
283	Frank Seminara	.10
284	Wally Whitehurst	.10
285	Rod Beck	.10
286	Barry Bonds	1.00
287	Dave Burba	.10
288	Mark Carreon	.10
289	Royce Clayton	.10
290	Mike Jackson	.10
291	Darren Lewis	.10
292	Kirt Manwaring	.10
293	Dave Martinez	.10
294	Billy Swift	.10
295	Salomon Torres	.10
296	Matt Williams	.25
297	Checklist 1-103 (Joe Orsulak)	.10
298	Checklist 104-201 (Pete Incaviglia)	.10
299	Checklist 202-300 (Todd Hundley)	.10
300	Checklist - Inserts (John Doherty)	.10
301	Brady Anderson	.25
302	Harold Baines	.10
303	Damon Buford	.10
304	Mike Devereaux	.10
305	Sid Fernandez	.10
306	Rick Krivda	.10
307	Mike Mussina	.50
308	Rafael Palmeiro	.50
309	Arthur Rhodes	.10
310	Chris Sabo	.10
311	Lee Smith	.10
312	*Gregg Zaun*	.15
313	Scott Cooper	.10
314	Mike Greenwell	.10
315	Tim Naehring	.10
316	Otis Nixon	.10
317	Paul Quantrill	.10
318	John Valentin	.15
319	Dave Valle	.10
320	Frank Viola	.10
321	*Brian Anderson*	.15
322	Garret Anderson	.10
323	Chad Curtis	.10
324	Chili Davis	.10
325	Gary DiSarcina	.10
326	Damion Easley	.10
327	Jim Edmonds	.20
328	Chuck Finley	.10
329	Joe Grahe	.10
330	Bo Jackson	.20
331	Mark Langston	.10
332	Harold Reynolds	.10
333	James Baldwin	.15
334	*Ray Durham*	.75
335	Julio Franco	.10
336	Craig Grebeck	.10
337	Ozzie Guillen	.10
338	Joe Hall	.10
339	Darrin Jackson	.10
340	Jack McDowell	.10
341	Tim Raines	.10
342	Robin Ventura	.20
343	Carlos Baerga	.10
344	Derek Lilliquist	.10
345	Dennis Martinez	.10
346	Jack Morris	.10
347	Eddie Murray	.20
348	Chris Nabholz	.10
349	Charles Nagy	.10
350	Chad Ogea	.10
351	Manny Ramirez	1.00
352	Omar Vizquel	.10
353	Tim Belcher	.10
354	Eric Davis	.10
355	Kirk Gibson	.10
356	Rick Greene	.10
357	Mickey Tettleton	.10
358	Alan Trammell	.15
359	David Wells	.10
360	Stan Belinda	.10
361	Vince Coleman	.10
362	David Cone	.15
363	Gary Gaetti	.10
364	Tom Gordon	.10
365	Dave Henderson	.10
366	Wally Joyner	.10
367	Brent Mayne	.10
368	Brian McRae	.10
369	Michael Tucker	.10
370	Ricky Bones	.10
371	Brian Harper	.10
372	Tyrone Hill	.10
373	Mark Kiefer	.10
374	Pat Listach	.10
375	*Mike Matheny*	.15
376	*Jose Mercedes*	.10
377	Jody Reed	.10
378	Kevin Seitzer	.10
379	B.J. Surhoff	.10
380	Greg Vaughn	.20
381	Turner Ward	.10
382	*Wes Weger*	.10
383	Bill Wegman	.10
384	Rick Aguilera	.10
385	Rich Becker	.10
386	Alex Cole	.10
387	Steve Dunn	.10
388	*Keith Garagozzo*	.10
389	*LaTroy Hawkins*	.20
390	Shane Mack	.10
391	David McCarty	.10
392	Pedro Munoz	.10
393	*Derek Parks*	.20
394	Kirby Puckett	1.00
395	Kevin Tapani	.10
396	Matt Walbeck	.10
397	Jim Abbott	.10
398	Mike Gallego	.10
399	Xavier Hernandez	.10
400	Don Mattingly	1.00
401	Terry Mulholland	.10
402	Matt Nokes	.10
403	Luis Polonia	.10
404	Bob Wickman	.10
405	Mark Acre	.10
406	*Fausto Cruz*	.20
407	Dennis Eckersley	.10
408	Rickey Henderson	.40
409	Stan Javier	.10
410	*Carlos Reyes*	.10
411	Ruben Sierra	.10
412	Terry Steinbach	.10
413	Bill Taylor	.10
414	Todd Van Poppel	.10
415	Eric Anthony	.10
416	Bobby Ayala	.10
417	Chris Bosio	.10
418	Tim Davis	.10
419	Randy Johnson	.75
420	Kevin King	.10
421	*Anthony Manahan*	.15
422	Edgar Martinez	.10
423	Keith Mitchell	.10
424	Roger Salkeld	.10
425	*Mac Suzuki*	.15
426	Dan Wilson	.10
427	*Duff Brumley*	.10
428	Jose Canseco	.50
429	Will Clark	.40
430	Steve Dreyer	.10
431	Rick Helling	.10
432	Chris James	.10
433	Matt Whiteside	.10
434	Roberto Alomar	.50
435	Scott Brow	.10
436	*Domingo Cedeno*	.15
437	Carlos Delgado	.75

438 Juan Guzman .10
439 Paul Spoljaric .10
440 Todd Stottlemyre .10
441 Woody Williams .10
442 Dave Justice .20
443 Mike Kelly .10
444 Ryan Klesko .15
445 Javier Lopez .15
446 Greg Maddux 1.50
447 Kent Mercker .10
448 Charlie O'Brien .10
449 Terry Pendleton .10
450 Mike Stanton .10
451 Tony Tarasco .10
452 *Terrell Wade* .10
453 Willie Banks .10
454 Shawon Dunston .10
455 Mark Grace .20
456 Jose Guzman .10
457 Jose Hernandez .10
458 Glenallen Hill .10
459 Blaise Ilsley .10
460 *Brooks Kieschnick* .40
461 Derrick May .10
462 Randy Myers .10
463 Karl Rhodes .10
464 Sammy Sosa 2.00
465 *Steve Trachsel* .25
466 Anthony Young .10
467 *Eddie Zambrano* .15
468 Bret Boone .10
469 Tom Browning .10
470 *Hector Carrasco* .15
471 Rob Dibble .10
472 Erik Hanson .10
473 Thomas Howard .10
474 Barry Larkin .40
475 Hal Morris .10
476 Jose Rijo .10
477 John Burke .10
478 Ellis Burks .10
479 Marvin Freeman .10
480 Andres Galarraga .40
481 Greg Harris .10
482 Charlie Hayes .10
483 Darren Holmes .10
484 Howard Johnson .10
485 *Marcus Moore* .15
486 David Nied .10
487 Mark Thompson .10
488 Walt Weiss .10
489 Kurt Abbott .10
490 Matias Carrillo .10
491 Jeff Conine .15
492 Chris Hammond .10
493 Bryan Harvey .10
494 Charlie Hough .10
495 *Yorkis Perez* .15
496 Pat Rapp .15
497 Benito Santiago .10
498 David Weathers .10
499 Craig Biggio .40
500 Ken Caminiti .25
501 Doug Drabek .10
502 *Tony Eusebio* .20
503 Steve Finley .10
504 Pete Harnisch .10
505 Brian Hunter .10
506 Domingo Jean .10
507 Todd Jones .10
508 Orlando Miller .10
509 James Mouton .10
510 Roberto Petagine .10
511 Shane Reynolds .10
512 Mitch Williams .10
513 Billy Ashley .10
514 Tom Candiotti .10
515 Delino DeShields .10
516 Kevin Gross .10
517 Orel Hershiser .10
518 Eric Karros .15
519 Ramon Martinez .15
520 *Chan Ho Park* .50
521 Henry Rodriguez .10
522 Joey Eischen .10
523 Rod Henderson .10
524 Pedro Martinez 1.00
525 Mel Rojas .10
526 Larry Walker .50
527 *Gabe White* .20
528 Bobby Bonilla .10
529 Jonathan Hurst .10
530 Bobby Jones .10
531 Kevin McReynolds .10
532 Bill Pulsipher .10
533 Bret Saberhagen .10
534 David Segui .10
535 Pete Smith .10
536 *Kelly Stinnett* .15
537 Dave Telgheder .10
538 *Quilvio Veras* .25
539 Jose Vizcaino .10
540 Pete Walker .10
541 Ricky Bottalico .10
542 Wes Chamberlain .10
543 Mariano Duncan .10
544 Len Dykstra .10
545 Jim Eisenreich .10
546 *Phil Geisler* .10
547 *Wayne Gomes* .15
548 Doug Jones .10
549 Jeff Juden .10
550 Mike Lieberthal .20
551 *Tony Longmire* .15
552 Tom Marsh .10
553 Bobby Munoz .10
554 Curt Schilling .10
555 Carlos Garcia .10
556 *Ravelo Manzanillo* .10
557 Orlando Merced .10
558 *Will Pennyfeather* .10
559 Zane Smith .10
560 Andy Van Slyke .10
561 Rick White .10
562 Luis Alicea .10
563 *Brian Barber* .15
564 *Clint Davis* .10
565 Bernard Gilkey .10
566 Ray Lankford .10
567 Tom Pagnozzi .10
568 Ozzie Smith .50
569 Rick Sutcliffe .10
570 Allen Watson .10
571 Dmitri Young .10
572 Derek Bell .10
573 Andy Benes .15
574 Archi Cianfrocco .10
575 Joey Hamilton .10
576 Gene Harris .10
577 Trevor Hoffman .15
578 *Tim Hyers* .15
579 *Brian Johnson* .15
580 *Keith Lockhart* .20
581 Pedro Martinez 1.00
582 Ray McDavid .10
583 Phil Plantier .10
584 Bip Roberts .10
585 Dave Staton .10
586 Todd Benzinger .10
587 John Burkett .10
588 Bryan Hickerson .10
589 Willie McGee .10
590 John Patterson .10
591 Mark Portugal .10
592 Kevin Rogers .10
593 *Joe Rosselli* .10
594 *Steve Soderstrom* .10
595 Robby Thompson .10
596 125th Anniversary card .10
597 Checklist .10
598 Checklist .10
599 Checklist .10
600 Checklist .10

1994 Ultra All-Rookie Team

A stylized sunrise landscape is the background for this insert set featuring top rookies and inserted into Ultra Series II packs at the rate of about one per 10. Backs repeat the motif with an action photo. Both sides are gold-foil enhanced and UV-coated.

		MT
Complete Set (10):		6.00
Common Player:		.50
1	Kurt Abbott	.50
2	Carlos Delgado	3.00
3	Cliff Floyd	.50
4	Jeffrey Hammonds	.50
5	Ryan Klesko	.75
6	Javier Lopez	1.00
7	Raul Mondesi	1.00
8	James Mouton	.50
9	Chan Ho Park	1.00
10	Dave Staton	.50

1994 Ultra All-Stars

Fleer's opinion of the top 20 players in 1994 are featured in this most common of the Series II Ultra insert sets. Silver-foil highlights enhance the chase cards, found, according to stated odds, once per three packs, on average. National Leaguers have purple backgrounds front and back, American Leaguers have red.

		MT
Complete Set (20):		15.00
Common Player:		.50
1	Chris Hoiles	.50
2	Frank Thomas	1.50
3	Roberto Alomar	.75
4	Cal Ripken, Jr.	3.00
5	Robin Ventura	.75
6	Albert Belle	1.00
7	Juan Gonzalez	1.00
8	Ken Griffey, Jr.	4.00
9	John Olerud	.75
10	Jack McDowell	.50
11	Mike Piazza	2.50
12	Fred McGriff	.75
13	Ryne Sandberg	1.00
14	Jay Bell	.50
15	Matt Williams	.60
16	Barry Bonds	1.00
17	Len Dykstra	.50
18	Dave Justice	.75
19	Tom Glavine	.60
20	Greg Maddux	2.00

1994 Ultra Award Winners

The most common of the Fleer Ultra insert sets for 1994 is the 25-card "Award Winners." Horizontal format cards feature front and back background with a gold-embossed look. A player action photo appears on the front. A gold-foil seal on the front has a symbolic player representation flanked by the pictured player's name and award. A gold Fleer Ultra logo is at top. Backs have a player portrait photo and a write-up about the award. The name of the award and the player's name appear in gold foil at the top. Stated odds of finding an Award Winners card were one in three packs.

		MT
Complete Set (25):		18.00
Common Player:		.40
1	Ivan Rodriguez	1.00
2	Don Mattingly	1.00
3	Roberto Alomar	.75
4	Robin Ventura	.60
5	Omar Vizquel	.40
6	Ken Griffey, Jr.	4.00
7	Kenny Lofton	.60
8	Devon White	.50
9	Mark Langston	.40
10	Kirt Manwaring	.40
11	Mark Grace	.60
12	Robby Thompson	.40
13	Matt Williams	.50
14	Jay Bell	.40
15	Barry Bonds	1.00
16	Marquis Grissom	.40
17	Larry Walker	.75
18	Greg Maddux	2.00
19	Frank Thomas	1.50
20	Barry Bonds	1.00
21	Paul Molitor	.75
22	Jack McDowell	.40
23	Greg Maddux	2.00
24	Tim Salmon	.50
25	Mike Piazza	3.00

1994 Ultra Firemen

Ten of the major leagues' leading relief pitchers are featured in this Ultra insert set. Cards have an action photo of the player superimposed over a background photo of a fire truck. A shield at top, in gold foil, has a smoke-eater's helmet, stylized flames and proclaims the player an "Ultra Fireman." Backs are horizontal in format and feature the pumper's control panel in the background photo. A color player portrait photo appears on one side, with a description of his relief role and successes in a whitened box. Fireman crads are found, on average, once per 11 packs, according to stated odds.

		MT
Complete Set (10):		5.00
Common Player:		.50
1	Jeff Montgomery	.50
2	Duane Ward	.50
3	Tom Henke	.50
4	Roberto Hernandez	.50
5	Dennis Eckersley	1.00
6	Randy Myers	.50
7	Rod Beck	.50
8	Bryan Harvey	.50
9	John Wetteland	.50
10	Mitch Williams	.50

1994 Ultra Hitting Machines

A heavy metal background of gears and iron-letter logo is featured in this insert set honoring the game's top hitters. The cards turn up about once in every five packs of Ultra Series II. Both front and back are highlighted in silver foil.

		MT
Complete Set (10):		10.00
Common Player:		.50
1	Roberto Alomar	1.00
2	Carlos Baerga	.50
3	Barry Bonds	1.25
4	Andres Galarraga	.75
5	Juan Gonzalez	1.00
6	Tony Gwynn	1.50
7	Paul Molitor	.75
8	John Olerud	.75
9	Mike Piazza	2.50
10	Frank Thomas	1.50

1994 Ultra Home Run Kings

One of two high-end insert sets in '94 Ultra is the 12-card "Home Run Kings" found exclusively in 14-card foil packs, on an average of once per 36-pack box. Featuring the technology Fleer calls "etched metallization," the cards have a black background with a red and blue foil representation of a batter. An action photo of a player taking a mighty cut or starting his home-run trot is featured. A large gold-foil "Home Run King" crown-and-shield device are in an upper corner, while the Ultra logo and player name are in gold foil at bottom. Backs have a white background with the red and blue batter symbol. The player's name appears in gold foil at the top, along with a portrait photo and a summary of his home run prowess.

		MT
Complete Set (12):		60.00
Common Player:		3.00
1	Juan Gonzalez	5.00
2	Ken Griffey, Jr.	20.00
3	Frank Thomas	8.00
4	Albert Belle	4.00
5	Rafael Palmeiro	3.00
6	Joe Carter	2.00
7	Barry Bonds	6.00
8	Dave Justice	2.50
9	Matt Williams	2.50
10	Fred McGriff	2.50
11	Ron Gant	2.00
12	Mike Piazza	12.00

1994 Ultra League Leaders

Arguably the least attractive of the '94 Fleer Ultra inserts are the 10 "League Leaders." Fronts feature a full-bleed action photo on which the bottom has been re-colored to a team hue giving the effect of teal, purple and magenta miasmas rising from the turf. An Ultra logo appear in gold foil in an upper corner, with the player's name in gold foil at about the dividing line between the natural color and colorized portions of the photo. A large "League Leader" appears in the bottom half of the photo, with the category led printed in the lower-left. Backs repeat the team color at top, fading to white at the bottom. In gold foil are "League Leader" and the category. A portrait-type player photo appears at bottom. Several paragraphs detail the league leading performance of the previous season.

		MT
Complete Set (10):		5.00
Common Player:		.50
1	John Olerud	.75
2	Rafael Palmeiro	.75
3	Kenny Lofton	.75
4	Jack McDowell	.50
5	Randy Johnson	1.00
6	Andres Galarraga	.75
7	Len Dykstra	.50
8	Chuck Carr	.50
9	Tom Glavine	.75
10	Jose Rijo	.50

1994 Ultra On-Base Leaders

One of the lesser-known, but most valuable, stats - on-base percentage - is featured in this subset found exclusively in 17-card packs, at the rate of about one per 37 packs. The fronts feature color photos against a stat-filled printed-foil background.

		MT
Complete Set (12):		100.00
Common Player:		5.00
1	Roberto Alomar	10.00
2	Barry Bonds	12.00
3	Len Dykstra	5.00
4	Andres Galarraga	8.00
5	Mark Grace	8.00
6	Ken Griffey, Jr.	40.00
7	Gregg Jefferies	5.00
8	Orlando Merced	5.00
9	Paul Molitor	10.00
10	John Olerud	8.00
11	Tony Phillips	5.00
12	Frank Thomas	15.00

1994 Ultra Phillies Finest

As a tribute to two of Fleer's home-team heroes, the Philadelphia-based card company created an Ultra insert set featuring 12 cards each of "Phillies Finest," John Kruk and Darren Daulton. Twenty of the cards were issued as Series 1 and 2 inserts, about one in every eight packs, while four were available only by a mail-in offer. Fronts feature action photos with large block letters popping out of the background. The Ultra logo and player name appear in gold foil. Backs have portrait photos and career summaries, with the player's name and card number in gold foil. Daulton and Kruk each autographed 1,000 of the inserts. Stated odds of finding the autographed cards were one in 11,000 packs. Values listed are per card.

		MT
Complete Set (24):		10.00
Common player:		.50
Autographed Daulton or Kruk:		25.00
1-5	Darren Daulton	.50
6-10	John Kruk	.50
11-15	Darren Daulton	.50
16-20	John Kruk	.50
9a	John Kruk (PROMOTIONAL SAMPLE)	3.00
	MAIL-IN CARDS	
1M, 3M	Darren Daulton	1.50
2M, 4M	John Kruk	1.50
1	Darren Daulton (holding mask and glove)	.50
2	Darren Daulton (power swing, home uniform)	.50
3	Darren Daulton (blocking home plate)	.50
4	Darren Daulton (home run trot, home uniform)	.50
1M	Darren Daulton (standing, throwing)	1.50
2M	John Kruk (ready to field)	1.50
3M	Darren Daulton (awaiting pitch)	1.50
4M	John Kruk (running)	1.50

1994 Ultra Rising Stars

An outer space background printed on metallic foil sets this chase set apart from most of the rest of the Ultra Series II inserts. The silver-foil enhanced cards of projected superstars of tomorrow are found on average once every 37 packs.

		MT
Complete Set (12):		65.00
Common Player:		4.00
1	Carlos Baerga	3.00
2	Jeff Bagwell	10.00
3	Albert Belle	8.00
4	Cliff Floyd	4.00
5	Travis Fryman	4.00
6	Marquis Grissom	3.00
7	Kenny Lofton	8.00
8	John Olerud	4.00
9	Mike Piazza	20.00
10	Kirk Rueter	3.00
11	Tim Salmon	8.00
12	Aaron Sele	3.00

1994 Ultra RBI Kings

Exclusive to the 19-card jumbo packs of Fleer Ultra are a series of 12 "RBI Kings" insert cards, found, according to stated odds, one per 36 packs. The horizontal-format card front uses Fleer's "etched metallized" technology to produce a sepia-toned background action photo, in front of which is a color player photo. An Ultra logo appears in gold foil in an upper corner while a fancy shield-and-scroll "RBI King" logo and the player's name are in gold at the bottom. Backs repeat the basic front motif and include a color player portrait photo, his name in gold foil and a paragraph justifying his selection as an RBI King.

		MT
Complete Set (12):		70.00
Common Player:		4.00
1	Albert Belle	6.00
2	Frank Thomas	10.00
3	Joe Carter	4.00
4	Juan Gonzalez	8.00
5	Cecil Fielder	4.00
6	Carlos Baerga	4.00
7	Barry Bonds	8.00
8	David Justice	5.00
9	Ron Gant	5.00
10	Mike Piazza	20.00
11	Matt Williams	5.00
12	Darren Daulton	5.00

1994 Ultra Second Year Standouts

Approximately once every 11 packs, the Ultra insert find is a "Second Year Standout" card. Ten of the game's sophomore stars are featured. Fronts feature a pair of action photos against a team-color background. Gold-foil highlights are the Ultra logo, the player's name and a "Second Year Standout" shield. The shield and player name are repeated in gold foil on the back, as is the team color background. There is a player portrait photo at bottom and a summary of the player's 1993 season.

		MT
Complete Set (10):		10.00
Common Player:		.50
1	Jason Bere	.75
2	Brent Gates	.50
3	Jeffrey Hammonds	.75
4	Tim Salmon	2.00
5	Aaron Sele	.75
6	Chuck Carr	.50
7	Jeff Conine	.75
8	Greg McMichael	.50
9	Mike Piazza	8.00
10	Kevin Stocker	.50

1994 Ultra Strikeout Kings

A gold-foil "Strikeout Kings" crown-and-shield logo is featured on the front of this chase set. Cards are found on average once per seven packs. Each of the cards features the K-king in sequential action photos. Backs have a larger action photo with a large version of the Strikeout King shield in the background.

		MT
Complete Set (5):		4.00
Common Player:		.75
1	Randy Johnson	1.25
2	Mark Langston	.75
3	Greg Maddux	2.50
4	Jose Rijo	.75
5	John Smoltz	1.00

1995 Ultra

A clean design enhanced with three different colors of metallic foil graphics is featured on the basic cards of 1995 Fleer Ultra. Two series of 250 cards each were issued with cards arranged alphabetically within team, also sequenced alphabetically. Fronts have a gold-foil Ultra logo in an upper corner, with the player's name and team logo in a team-color coded foil at bottom. There are no other graphic elements on the borderless photos. Backs have a large photo rendered in a single color, again team-coded. A postage-stamp sized color photo in one corner is flanked by a few vital stats in silver foil. Career and '94 stats are printed at bottom, enhanced by the foil color from the front. Cards were issued in 12-card retail and hobby packs at $1.99 and jumbo pre-priced ($2.69) magazine packs. Each pack contains one of the several insert series from the appropriate series.

		MT
Complete Set (450):		30.00
Series 1 (250):		20.00
Series 2 (200):		15.00
Common Player:		.10
Gold Medallion:		2X
Series 1 or 2 Pack (12):		2.00
Series 1 or 2 Wax Box (36):		50.00
1	Brady Anderson	.15
2	Sid Fernandez	.10
3	Jeffrey Hammonds	.10
4	Chris Hoiles	.10
5	Ben McDonald	.10
6	Mike Mussina	.50
7	Rafael Palmeiro	.40
8	Jack Voigt	.10
9	Wes Chamberlain	.10
10	Roger Clemens	1.25
11	Chris Howard	.10
12	Tim Naehring	.10
13	Otis Nixon	.10
14	Rich Rowland	.10
15	Ken Ryan	.10
16	John Valentin	.10
17	Mo Vaughn	.50
18	Brian Anderson	.10
19	Chili Davis	.10
20	Damion Easley	.10
21	Jim Edmonds	.10
22	Mark Langston	.10
23	Tim Salmon	.25
24	J.T. Snow	.15
25	Chris Turner	.10
26	Wilson Alvarez	.10
27	Joey Cora	.10
28	Alex Fernandez	.10
29	Roberto Hernandez	.10
30	Lance Johnson	.10
31	Ron Karkovice	.10
32	Kirk McCaskill	.10
33	Tim Raines	.15
34	Frank Thomas	1.25
35	Sandy Alomar	.15
36	Albert Belle	.75
37	Mark Clark	.10
38	Kenny Lofton	.50
39	Eddie Murray	.40
40	Eric Plunk	.10
41	Manny Ramirez	1.00
42	Jim Thome	.30
43	Omar Vizquel	.10
44	Danny Bautista	.10
45	Junior Felix	.10
46	Cecil Fielder	.10
47	Chris Gomez	.10
48	Chad Kreuter	.10
49	Mike Moore	.10
50	Tony Phillips	.10
51	Alan Trammell	.15
52	David Wells	.10
53	Kevin Appier	.10
54	Billy Brewer	.10
55	David Cone	.15
56	Greg Gagne	.10
57	Bob Hamelin	.10
58	Jose Lind	.10
59	Brent Mayne	.10
60	Brian McRae	.10
61	Terry Shumpert	.10
62	Ricky Bones	.10
63	Mike Fetters	.10
64	Darryl Hamilton	.10
65	John Jaha	.10
66	Graeme Lloyd	.10
67	Matt Mieske	.10
68	Kevin Seitzer	.10
69	Jose Valentin	.10
70	Turner Ward	.10
71	Rick Aguilera	.10
72	Rich Becker	.10
73	Alex Cole	.10
74	Scott Leius	.10
75	Pat Meares	.10
76	Kirby Puckett	.75
77	Dave Stevens	.10
78	Kevin Tapani	.10
79	Matt Walbeck	.10
80	Wade Boggs	.35
81	Scott Kamieniecki	.10
82	Pat Kelly	.10
83	Jimmy Key	.10
84	Paul O'Neill	.25
85	Luis Polonia	.10
86	Mike Stanley	.10
87	Danny Tartabull	.10
88	Bob Wickman	.10
89	Mark Acre	.10
90	Geronimo Berroa	.10
91	Mike Bordick	.10

No.	Player	Price
92	Ron Darling	.10
93	Stan Javier	.10
94	Mark McGwire	3.00
95	Troy Neel	.10
96	Ruben Sierra	.10
97	Terry Steinbach	.10
98	Eric Anthony	.10
99	Chris Bosio	.10
100	Dave Fleming	.10
101	Ken Griffey Jr.	3.00
102	Reggie Jefferson	.10
103	Randy Johnson	.40
104	Edgar Martinez	.10
105	Bill Risley	.10
106	Dan Wilson	.10
107	Cris Carpenter	.10
108	Will Clark	.35
109	Juan Gonzalez	1.00
110	Rusty Greer	.10
111	David Hulse	.10
112	Roger Pavlik	.10
113	Ivan Rodriguez	.75
114	Doug Strange	.10
115	Matt Whiteside	.10
116	Roberto Alomar	.50
117	Brad Cornett	.10
118	Carlos Delgado	.50
119	Alex Gonzalez	.10
120	Darren Hall	.10
121	Pat Hentgen	.10
122	Paul Molitor	.40
123	Ed Sprague	.10
124	Devon White	.10
125	Tom Glavine	.25
126	Dave Justice	.20
127	Roberto Kelly	.10
128	Mark Lemke	.10
129	Greg Maddux	1.50
130	Charles Johnson	.10
131	Kent Mercker	.10
132	Charlie O'Brien	.10
133	John Smoltz	.25
134	Willie Banks	.10
135	Steve Buechele	.10
136	Kevin Foster	.10
137	Glenallen Hill	.10
138	Ray Sanchez	.10
139	Sammy Sosa	2.00
140	Steve Trachsel	.10
141	Rick Wilkins	.10
142	Jeff Brantley	.10
143	Hector Carrasco	.10
144	Kevin Jarvis	.10
145	Barry Larkin	.15
146	Chuck McElroy	.10
147	Jose Rijo	.10
148	Johnny Ruffin	.10
149	Deion Sanders	.20
150	Eddie Taubensee	.10
151	Dante Bichette	.20
152	Ellis Burks	.10
153	Joe Girardi	.10
154	Charlie Hayes	.10
155	Mike Kingery	.10
156	Steve Reed	.10
157	Kevin Ritz	.10
158	Bruce Ruffin	.10
159	Eric Young	.15
160	Kurt Abbott	.10
161	Chuck Carr	.10
162	Chris Hammond	.10
163	Bryan Harvey	.10
164	Terry Mathews	.10
165	Yorkis Perez	.10
166	Pat Rapp	.10
167	Gary Sheffield	.20
168	Dave Weathers	.10
169	Jeff Bagwell	.75
170	Ken Caminiti	.20
171	Doug Drabek	.10
172	Steve Finley	.10
173	John Hudek	.10
174	Todd Jones	.10
175	James Mouton	.10
176	Shane Reynolds	.15
177	Scott Servais	.10
178	Tom Candiotti	.10
179	Omar Daal	.10
180	Darren Dreifort	.10
181	Eric Karros	.10
182	Ramon Martinez	.15
183	Raul Mondesi	.25
184	Henry Rodriguez	.10
185	Todd Worrell	.10
186	Moises Alou	.20
187	Sean Berry	.10
188	Wil Cordero	.10
189	Jeff Fassero	.10
190	Darrin Fletcher	.10
191	Butch Henry	.10
192	Ken Hill	.10
193	Mel Rojas	.10
194	John Wetteland	.10
195	Bobby Bonilla	.10
196	Rico Brogna	.10
197	Bobby Jones	.10
198	Jeff Kent	.10
199	Josias Manzanillo	.10
200	Kelly Stinnett	.10
201	Ryan Thompson	.10
202	Jose Vizcaino	.10
203	Lenny Dykstra	.10
204	Jim Eisenreich	.10
205	Dave Hollins	.10
206	Mike Lieberthal	.20
207	Mickey Morandini	.10
208	Bobby Munoz	.10
209	Curt Schilling	.10
210	Heathcliff Slocumb	.10
211	David West	.10
212	Dave Clark	.10
213	Steve Cooke	.10
214	Midre Cummings	.10
215	Carlos Garcia	.10
216	Jeff King	.10
217	Jon Lieber	.10
218	Orlando Merced	.10
219	Don Slaught	.10
220	Rick White	.10
221	Rene Arocha	.10
222	Bernard Gilkey	.10
223	Brian Jordan	.15
224	Tom Pagnozzi	.10
225	Vicente Palacios	.10
226	Geronimo Pena	.10
227	Ozzie Smith	.50
228	Allen Watson	.10
229	Mark Whiten	.10
230	Brad Ausmus	.10
231	Derek Bell	.10
232	Andy Benes	.10
233	Tony Gwynn	1.50
234	Joey Hamilton	.10
235	Luis Lopez	.10
236	Pedro A. Martinez	.10
237	Scott Sanders	.10
238	Eddie Williams	.10
239	Rod Beck	.10
240	Dave Burba	.10
241	Darren Lewis	.10
242	Kirt Manwaring	.10
243	Mark Portugal	.10
244	Darryl Strawberry	.20
245	Robby Thompson	.10
246	William VanLandingham	.10
247	Matt Williams	.20
248	Checklist	.10
249	Checklist	.10
250	Checklist	.10
251	Harold Baines	.10
252	Bret Barberie	.10
253	Armando Benitez	.10
254	Mike Devereaux	.10
255	Leo Gomez	.10
256	Jamie Moyer	.10
257	Arthur Rhodes	.10
258	Cal Ripken Jr.	2.00
259	Luis Alicea	.10
260	Jose Canseco	.75
261	Scott Cooper	.10
262	Andre Dawson	.20
263	Mike Greenwell	.10
264	Aaron Sele	.10
265	Garret Anderson	.10
266	Chad Curtis	.10
267	Gary DiSarcina	.10
268	Chuck Finley	.10
269	Rex Hudler	.10
270	Andrew Lorraine	.10
271	Spike Owen	.10
272	Lee Smith	.10
273	Jason Bere	.10
274	Ozzie Guillen	.10
275	Norberto Martin	.10
276	Scott Ruffcorn	.10
277	Robin Ventura	.25
278	Carlos Baerga	.10
279	Jason Grimsley	.10
280	Dennis Martinez	.10
281	Charles Nagy	.10
282	Paul Sorrento	.10
283	Dave Winfield	.25
284	John Doherty	.10
285	Travis Fryman	.15
286	Kirk Gibson	.10
287	Lou Whitaker	.10
288	Gary Gaetti	.10
289	Tom Gordon	.10
290	Mark Gubicza	.10
291	Wally Joyner	.10
292	Mike Macfarlane	.10
293	Jeff Montgomery	.10
294	Jeff Cirillo	.10
295	Cal Eldred	.10
296	Pat Listach	.10
297	Jose Mercedes	.10
298	Dave Nilsson	.10
299	Duane Singleton	.10
300	Greg Vaughn	.15
301	Scott Erickson	.15
302	Denny Hocking	.10
303	Chuck Knoblauch	.15
304	Pat Mahomes	.10
305	Pedro Munoz	.10
306	Erik Schullstrom	.10
307	Jim Abbott	.10
308	Tony Fernandez	.10
309	Sterling Hitchcock	.10
310	Jim Leyritz	.10
311	Don Mattingly	.75
312	Jack McDowell	.10
313	Melido Perez	.10
314	Bernie Williams	.40
315	Scott Brosius	.10
316	Dennis Eckersley	.10
317	Brent Gates	.10
318	Rickey Henderson	.50
319	Steve Karsay	.10
320	Steve Ontiveros	.10
321	Bill Taylor	.10
322	Todd Van Poppel	.10
323	Bob Welch	.10
324	Bobby Ayala	.10
325	Mike Blowers	.10
326	Jay Buhner	.10
327	Felix Fermin	.10
328	Tino Martinez	.15
329	Marc Newfield	.10
330	Greg Pirkl	.10
331	Alex Rodriguez	2.50
332	Kevin Brown	.20
333	John Burkett	.10
334	Jeff Frye	.10
335	Kevin Gross	.10
336	Dean Palmer	.10
337	Joe Carter	.10
338	Shawn Green	.50
339	Juan Guzman	.10
340	Mike Huff	.10
341	Al Leiter	.15
342	John Olerud	.25
343	Dave Stewart	.10
344	Todd Stottlemyre	.10
345	Steve Avery	.10
346	Jeff Blauser	.10
347	Chipper Jones	1.50
348	Mike Kelly	.10
349	Ryan Klesko	.15
350	Javier Lopez	.15
351	Fred McGriff	.20
352	Jose Oliva	.10
353	Terry Pendleton	.10
354	Mike Stanton	.10
355	Tony Tarasco	.10
356	Mark Wohlers	.10
357	Jim Bullinger	.10
358	Shawon Dunston	.10
359	Mark Grace	.25
360	Derrick May	.10
361	Randy Myers	.10
362	Karl Rhodes	.10
363	Bret Boone	.10
364	Brian Dorsett	.10
365	Ron Gant	.10
366	Brian R. Hunter	.10
367	Hal Morris	.10
368	Jack Morris	.10
369	John Roper	.10
370	Reggie Sanders	.10
371	Pete Schourek	.10
372	John Smiley	.10
373	Marvin Freeman	.10
374	Andres Galarraga	.25
375	Mike Munoz	.10
376	David Nied	.10
377	Walt Weiss	.10
378	Greg Colbrunn	.10
379	Jeff Conine	.10
380	Charles Johnson	.15
381	Kurt Miller	.10
382	Robb Nen	.10
383	Benito Santiago	.10
384	Craig Biggio	.40
385	Tony Eusebio	.10
386	Luis Gonzalez	.15
387	Brian L. Hunter	.10
388	Darryl Kile	.10
389	Orlando Miller	.10
390	Phil Plantier	.10
391	Greg Swindell	.10
392	Billy Ashley	.10
393	Pedro Astacio	.10
394	Brett Butler	.10
395	Delino DeShields	.10
396	Orel Hershiser	.10
397	Garey Ingram	.10
398	Chan Ho Park	.15
399	Mike Piazza	1.50
400	Ismael Valdes	.10
401	Tim Wallach	.10
402	Cliff Floyd	.10
403	Marquis Grissom	.15
404	Mike Lansing	.10
405	Pedro Martinez	1.00
406	Kirk Rueter	.10
407	Tim Scott	.10
408	Jeff Shaw	.10
409	Larry Walker	.50
410	Rondell White	.15
411	John Franco	.10
412	Todd Hundley	.10
413	Jason Jacome	.10
414	Joe Orsulak	.10
415	Bret Saberhagen	.15
416	David Segui	.10
417	Darren Daulton	.10
418	Mariano Duncan	.10
419	Tommy Greene	.10
420	Gregg Jefferies	.10
421	John Kruk	.10
422	Kevin Stocker	.10
423	Jay Bell	.10
424	Al Martin	.10
425	Denny Neagle	.10
426	Zane Smith	.10
427	Andy Van Slyke	.10
428	Paul Wagner	.10
429	Tom Henke	.10
430	Danny Jackson	.10
431	Ray Lankford	.10
432	John Mabry	.10
433	Bob Tewksbury	.10
434	Todd Zeile	.10
435	Andy Ashby	.10
436	Andujar Cedeno	.10
437	Donnie Elliott	.10
438	Bryce Florie	.10
439	Trevor Hoffman	.10
440	Melvin Nieves	.10
441	Bip Roberts	.10
442	Barry Bonds	.75
443	Royce Clayton	.10
444	Mike Jackson	.10
445	John Patterson	.10
446	J.R. Phillips	.10
447	Bill Swift	.10
448	Checklist	.10
449	Checklist	.10
450	Checklist	.10

1995 Ultra All-Rookies

Enlarged pieces of the central color action photo, set on a white background, make up the front design on these inserts. The player's name, card title and Ultra logo are printed in silver foil. Horizontal backs have another color photo, which is also repeated in single-color fashion. A career summary is printed over the larger photo. The All-Rookie inserts are found only in 12-

card packs, at the rate of about one per four packs.

		MT
Complete Set (10):		6.00
Common Player:		.40
Gold Medallion:		2X
1	Cliff Floyd	.50
2	Chris Gomez	.40
3	Rusty Greer	.50
4	Bob Hamelin	.50
5	Joey Hamilton	.50
6	John Hudek	.40
7	Ryan Klesko	.75
8	Raul Mondesi	1.00
9	Manny Ramirez	4.00
10	Steve Trachsel	.50

1995 Ultra All-Stars

Twenty of the top players in the majors were chosen as Ultra All-Stars in this Series II chase set. Fronts have a color player photo at left. At right is a second photo, printed in only one color. A large "ALL-STAR" is at bottom, with the player's name above and team below in silver foil. An Ultra logo is at left. Backs have another color photo, with a '94 season summary printed in a black panel at right. These cards were found one per five packs, on average.

		MT
Complete Set (20):		15.00
Common Player:		.25
Gold Medallion:		2X
1	Moises Alou	.25
2	Albert Belle	.75
3	Craig Biggio	.50
4	Wade Boggs	.50
5	Barry Bonds	1.00
6	David Cone	.25
7	Ken Griffey Jr.	5.00
8	Tony Gwynn	2.00
9	Chuck Knoblauch	.35
10	Barry Larkin	.35
11	Kenny Lofton	.60
12	Greg Maddux	2.50
13	Fred McGriff	.50
14	Paul O'Neill	.25
15	Mike Piazza	2.50
16	Kirby Puckett	1.50
17	Cal Ripken Jr.	3.00
18	Ivan Rodriguez	1.00
19	Frank Thomas	1.50
20	Matt Williams	.35

1995 Ultra Award Winners

Various official and unofficial award winners from the 1994 season are featured in this Series I insert set. Horizontal cards have a color player photo on the right side, with a single-color, vertically compressed action photo at left. The player's award is printed in a white strip at top, while his name and team logo, along with the Ultra logo, are at bottom. All front typography is in gold foil. Backs repeat the compressed photo at left, combined with another color photo at right. A season summary is printed over the photo at left. The Award Winners inserts were common to all types of packaging, found at the rate of about one per four packs.

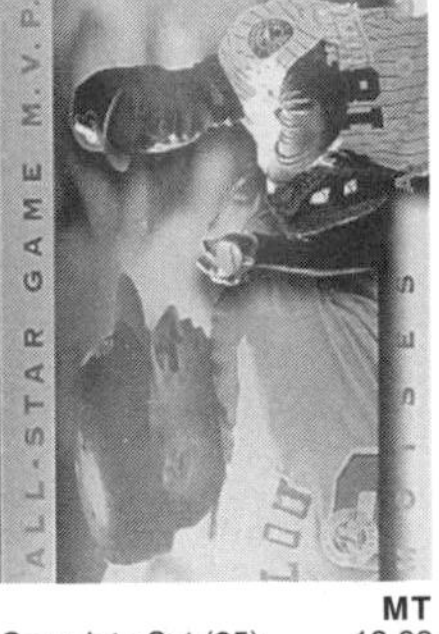

		MT
Complete Set (25):		18.00
Common Player:		.25
Gold Medallion:		2x
1	Ivan Rodriguez	1.25
2	Don Mattingly	1.50
3	Roberto Alomar	1.00
4	Wade Boggs	.40
5	Omar Vizquel	.25
6	Ken Griffey Jr.	5.00
7	Kenny Lofton	1.00
8	Devon White	.25
9	Mark Langston	.25
10	Tom Pagnozzi	.25
11	Jeff Bagwell	1.50
12	Craig Biggio	.50
13	Matt Williams	.40
14	Barry Larkin	.40
15	Barry Bonds	1.25
16	Marquis Grissom	.25
17	Darren Lewis	.25
18	Greg Maddux	2.50
19	Frank Thomas	1.50
20	Jeff Bagwell	1.50
21	David Cone	.35
22	Greg Maddux	2.50
23	Bob Hamelin	.25
24	Raul Mondesi	.40
25	Moises Alou	.25

1995 Ultra Gold Medallion

Less than 10% of the production run of Fleer Ultra (regular and insert sets) was produced in a special parallel Gold Medallion edition. On these special cards an embossed round gold seal replaces the Fleer Ultra logo in the upper corner. One Gold Medallion card was inserted into each Ultra foil pack.

	MT
Complete Set (450):	100.00
Series 1 (1-250):	60.00
Series 2 (251-450)	40.00
Common Player:	.25

(Star cards valued at 2X regular Fleer Ultra version.)

1995 Ultra Gold Medallion Rookies Mail-in

This set of 20 was available only by mailing in 10 Fleer Ultra wrappers plus $5.95. A reported 100,000 sets were produced. The cards are in the same format as the regular-issue Fleer Ultra. Each card has a team logo, player name and "ROOKIE" notation in gold foil at bottom, and the round Gold Medallion seal in an upper-corner of the borderless game-action photo front. Backs have two more action photos, a large one in one-color and a small one in full-color. Much of the typography on back is rendered in gold foil. Card numbers have an M prefix.

		MT
Complete Set (20):		9.00
Common Player:		.25
M-1	Manny Alexander	.25
M-2	Edgardo Alfonzo	1.50
M-3	Jason Bates	.25
M-4	Andres Berumen	.25
M-5	Darren Bragg	.25
M-6	Jamie Brewington	.25
M-7	Jason Christiansen	.25
M-8	Brad Clontz	.25
M-9	Marty Cordova	1.00
M-10	Johnny Damon	1.00
M-11	Vaughn Eshelman	.25
M-12	Chad Fonville	.25
M-13	Curtis Goodwin	.35
M-14	Tyler Green	.35
M-15	Bob Higginson	.50
M-16	Jason Isringhausen	.75
M-17	Hideo Nomo	4.00
M-18	Jon Nunnally	.50
M-19	Carlos Perez	.25
M-20	Julian Tavarez	.25

1995 Ultra Golden Prospects

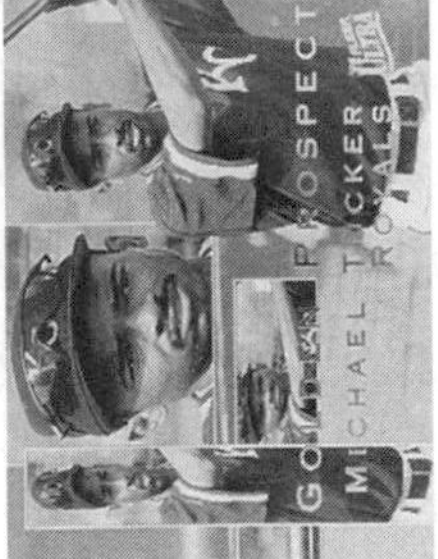

A hobby-pack exclusive, found at the rate of one per eight packs on average in Series I. Fronts feature a player photo at right, with three horizontally and vertically compressed versions of the same photo at right. The photo's background has been rendered in a single color. All typography - Ultra logo, card title, name and team - is in gold foil. Backs are also horizontal and have a color player photo and career summary.

		MT
Complete Set (10):		10.00
Common Player:		.35
Gold Medallion:		2X
1	James Baldwin	.50
2	Alan Benes	.35
3	Armando Benitez	.35
4	Ray Durham	.75
5	LaTroy Hawkins	.35
6	Brian Hunter	.35
7	Derek Jeter	4.00
8	Charles Johnson	.50
9	Alex Rodriguez	5.00
10	Michael Tucker	.35

1995 Ultra Hitting Machines

Various mechanical devices and dynamics make up the letters of "HITTING MACHINE" behind the color player action photo in this insert set. Both of those elements, along with the gold-foil player name, team and Ultra logo are in UV-coated contrast to the matte-finish gray background. Backs are also horizontal in format and feature a portrait photo at right, against a gray-streaked background. A career summary is printed at right. The Hitting Machines series is found only in Series II Ultra retail packs, at the rate of one card per eight packs, on average.

		MT
Complete Set (10):		15.00
Common Player:		.50
Gold Medallion:		2X
1	Jeff Bagwell	1.50
2	Albert Belle	1.00
3	Dante Bichette	.75
4	Barry Bonds	1.50
5	Jose Canseco	1.00
6	Ken Griffey Jr.	5.00
7	Tony Gwynn	2.50
8	Fred McGriff	.75
9	Mike Piazza	3.00
10	Frank Thomas	1.50

1995 Ultra Home Run Kings

Retail packaging of Fleer Ultra Series I was the hiding place for this sluggers' chase set. An average of one out of eight packs yielded a Home Run King insert. Fronts have a photo of the player's home run cut, while large letters "H," "R" and "K" are stacked vertically down one side. All front typography is in gold foil. Backs have another batting photo and a couple of sentences of recent career slugging prowess.

		MT
Complete Set (10):		25.00
Common Player:		.75
Gold Medallion:		2X
1	Ken Griffey Jr.	10.00
2	Frank Thomas	4.00
3	Albert Belle	2.00
4	Jose Canseco	2.50
5	Cecil Fielder	.75
6	Matt Williams	1.00
7	Jeff Bagwell	4.00
8	Barry Bonds	4.00
9	Fred McGriff	1.00
10	Andres Galarraga	1.00

1995 Ultra League Leaders

Top performers in major statistical categories are featured in this Series I insert. Cards were seeded in all types of Ultra packaging at the rate of about one card per three packs. Cards have a horizontal orientation with a color player action photo printed over a black logo of the appropriate league. American Leaguers' cards have a light brown overall background color, National Leaguers have dark green. The player's name, team and Ultra logos, and box with his league-leading category are printed in silver foil. The background from the front is carried over to the back, where a color portrait photo is at left, and a '94 season summary printed at right.

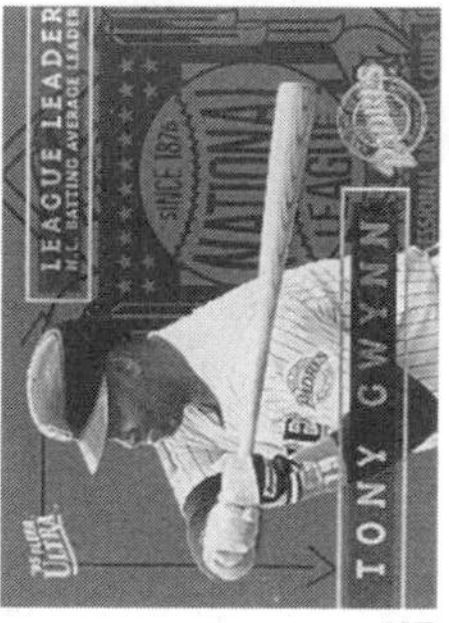

		MT
Complete Set (10):		4.00
Common Player:		.25
Gold Medallion:		2X
1	Paul O'Neill	.50
2	Kenny Lofton	.75
3	Jimmy Key	.25
4	Randy Johnson	.75
5	Lee Smith	.25
6	Tony Gwynn	1.50
7	Craig Biggio	.75
8	Greg Maddux	1.50
9	Andy Benes	.25
10	John Franco	.25

1995 Ultra On-Base Leaders

Numerous smaller versions in several sizes of the central action photo against a graduated color background from the front design of this Series II insert set. The player name, card title and Ultra logo are printed in gold foil down one side. Backs have a horizontal player photo with a large team logo at top, a smaller version at bottom and a 1994 season summary. One out of eight (on average) prepriced packs yielded an On-Base Leaders insert.

		MT
Complete Set (10):		40.00
Common Player:		2.50
Gold Medallion:		2X
1	Jeff Bagwell	6.00
2	Albert Belle	4.00
3	Craig Biggio	4.00
4	Wade Boggs	4.00
5	Barry Bonds	5.00
6	Will Clark	3.00
7	Tony Gwynn	8.00
8	Dave Justice	3.00
9	Paul O'Neill	3.00
10	Frank Thomas	6.00

1995 Ultra Power Plus

The scarcest of the Series I Ultra inserts are the Power Plus cards, printed on 100% etched foil and inserted at the rate of less than one per box. Fronts have a player action photo overprinted on a background of "POWER PLUS" logos in various metallic colors. A team logo and player name are at bottom in gold foil, as is the Ultra logo at top. Backs are conventionally printed and have a player photo on one side and season summary on the other.

		MT
Complete Set (6):		35.00
Common Player:		3.00
Gold Medallion:		2X
1	Albert Belle	4.00
2	Ken Griffey Jr.	15.00
3	Frank Thomas	5.00
4	Jeff Bagwell	5.00
5	Barry Bonds	4.00
6	Matt Williams	3.00

1995 Ultra Rising Stars

The top of the line among Series II chase cards is this set printed on 100% etched foil and seeded at the rate of less than one per box, on average. Horizontal-format cards have two player photos on a background of multi-colored rays. The Ultra logo, card title, player name and team are printed in gold foil. Backs repeat the colored rays, have another player photo and a career summary.

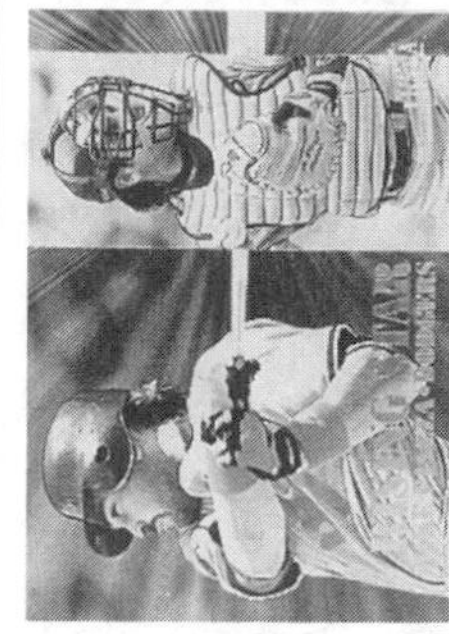

		MT
Complete Set (9):		45.00
Common Player:		2.50
Gold Medallion:		2X
1	Moises Alou	2.50
2	Jeff Bagwell	7.50
3	Albert Belle	5.00
4	Juan Gonzalez	8.00
5	Chuck Knoblauch	2.50
6	Kenny Lofton	5.00
7	Raul Mondesi	3.00
8	Mike Piazza	15.00
9	Frank Thomas	10.00

1995 Ultra RBI Kings

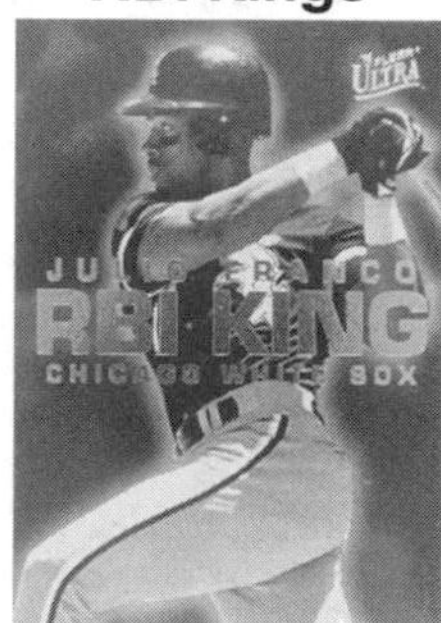

A bright aura surrounds the central player action photo on these cards, separating the player image from an indistinct colored background. At center is a large gold-foil "RBI KING" with the player's name above and team below. Backs have a similar design with a white box at bottom covering the player's RBI abilities. This set is found only in Series I jumbo packs, at an average rate of one per eight packs.

		MT
Complete Set (10):		40.00
Common Player:		2.00
Gold Medallion:		2X
1	Kirby Puckett	3.00
2	Joe Carter	2.00
3	Albert Belle	3.00
4	Frank Thomas	6.00
5	Julio Franco	2.00
6	Jeff Bagwell	5.00
7	Matt Williams	2.50

8	Dante Bichette	2.50
9	Fred McGriff	3.00
10	Mike Piazza	10.00

1995 Ultra Second Year Standouts

Fifteen of the game's sophomore stars are featured in this Series I insert set. Horizontal-format cards have player action photos front and back set against a background of orange and yellow rays. Besides the player name, card title and Ultra logo in gold-foil, the front features a pair of leafed branches flanking a team logo, all in embossed gold-foil. Backs have a career summary. The series was seeded at the average rate of one per six packs.

		MT
Complete Set (15):		8.00
Common Player:		.25
Gold Medallion:		2X
1	Cliff Floyd	.40
2	Chris Gomez	.25
3	Rusty Greer	.35
4	Darren Hall	.25
5	Bob Hamelin	.25
6	Joey Hamilton	.40
7	Jeffrey Hammonds	.35
8	John Hudek	.25
9	Ryan Klesko	.50
10	Raul Mondesi	1.00
11	Manny Ramirez	5.00
12	Bill Risley	.25
13	Steve Trachsel	.35
14	William Van Landingham	.25
15	Rondell White	1.00

1995 Ultra Strikeout Kings

A purple background with several types of concentric and overlapping circular designs in white are the background of this Series II chase set. An action color photo of the K-King is at center, while down one side are stacked photos of the grips used for various pitches. The player name, card title and Ultra logo are in silver foil. Backs have a portrait photo and career summary with purple circles behind and a black background. Stated odds of finding a Strikeout King card are one in five packs, on average.

		MT
Complete Set (6):		6.00
Common Player:		.50
Gold Medallion:		2X
1	Andy Benes	.50
2	Roger Clemens	1.50
3	Randy Johnson	1.00
4	Greg Maddux	3.00
5	Pedro Martinez	1.50
6	Jose Rijo	.50

1996 Ultra

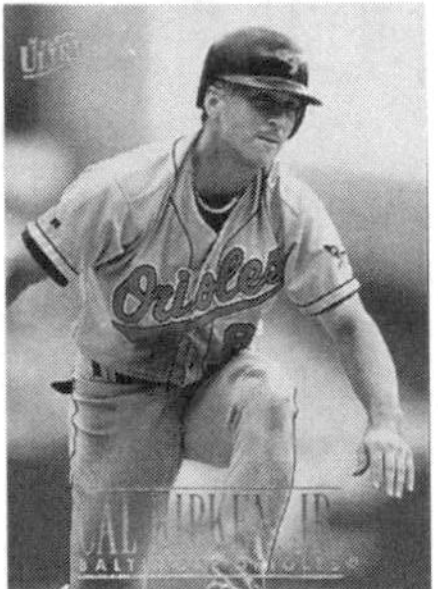

A 40% thicker cardboard stock and silver-foil highlights are featured in this year's edition. Fronts are very basic with a borderless action photo and silver-foil graphics. Backs feature a three-photo montage along with 1995 and career stats. The set was released in two 300-card series; each card is also reprinted as part of a limited-edition Gold Medallion parallel set. One Gold Medallion card is found in every pack. Each series has eight insert sets. Series I inserts are RBI Kings, Home Run Kings, Fresh Foundations, Diamond Producers, Power Plus, Season Crowns, Golden Prospects and Prime Leather. Series II inserts are Call to the Hall, Golden Prospects, Hitting Machines, On-Base Leaders, RESPECT, Rawhide, Rising Stars and Thunderclap. Checklist cards were also randomly inserted into packs from both series.

		MT
Complete Set (600):		55.00
Series 1 (300):		30.00
Series 2 (300):		25.00
Common Player:		.10
Series 1 or 2 Pack (12):		2.00
Series 1 or 2 Wax Box (24):		45.00
1	Manny Alexander	.10
2	Brady Anderson	.15
3	Bobby Bonilla	.10
4	Scott Erickson	.10
5	Curtis Goodwin	.10
6	Chris Hoiles	.10
7	Doug Jones	.10
8	Jeff Manto	.10
9	Mike Mussina	.50
10	Rafael Palmeiro	.40
11	Cal Ripken Jr.	2.50
12	Rick Aguilera	.10
13	Luis Alicea	.10
14	Stan Belinda	.10
15	Jose Canseco	.50
16	Roger Clemens	1.00
17	Mike Greenwell	.10
18	Mike Macfarlane	.10
19	Tim Naehring	.10
20	Troy O'Leary	.10
21	John Valentin	.10
22	Mo Vaughn	.40
23	Tim Wakefield	.10
24	Brian Anderson	.10
25	Garret Anderson	.10
26	Chili Davis	.10
27	Gary DiSarcina	.10
28	Jim Edmonds	.20
29	Jorge Fabregas	.10
30	Chuck Finley	.10
31	Mark Langston	.10
32	Troy Percival	.10
33	Tim Salmon	.25
34	Lee Smith	.10
35	Wilson Alvarez	.10
36	Ray Durham	.15
37	Alex Fernandez	.10
38	Ozzie Guillen	.10
39	Roberto Hernandez	.10
40	Lance Johnson	.10
41	Ron Karkovice	.10
42	Lyle Mouton	.10
43	Tim Raines	.10
44	Frank Thomas	1.00
45	Carlos Baerga	.10
46	Albert Belle	.40
47	Orel Hershiser	.10
48	Kenny Lofton	.30
49	Dennis Martinez	.10
50	Jose Mesa	.10
51	Eddie Murray	.40
52	Chad Ogea	.10
53	Manny Ramirez	.75
54	Jim Thome	.35
55	Omar Vizquel	.20
56	Dave Winfield	.25
57	Chad Curtis	.10
58	Cecil Fielder	.10
59	John Flaherty	.10
60	Travis Fryman	.20
61	Chris Gomez	.10
62	Bob Higginson	.10
63	Felipe Lira	.10
64	Brian Maxcy	.10
65	Alan Trammell	.15
66	Lou Whitaker	.10
67	Kevin Appier	.10
68	Gary Gaetti	.10
69	Tom Goodwin	.10
70	Tom Gordon	.10
71	Jason Jacome	.10
72	Wally Joyner	.10
73	Brent Mayne	.10
74	Jeff Montgomery	.10
75	Jon Nunnally	.10
76	Joe Vitiello	.10
77	Ricky Bones	.10
78	Jeff Cirillo	.10
79	Mike Fetters	.10
80	Darryl Hamilton	.10
81	David Hulse	.10
82	Dave Nilsson	.10
83	Kevin Seitzer	.10
84	Steve Sparks	.10
85	B.J. Surhoff	.10
86	Jose Valentin	.10
87	Greg Vaughn	.10
88	Marty Cordova	.10
89	Chuck Knoblauch	.20
90	Pat Meares	.10
91	Pedro Munoz	.10
92	Kirby Puckett	.75
93	Brad Radke	.10
94	Scott Stahoviak	.10
95	Dave Stevens	.10
96	Mike Trombley	.10
97	Matt Walbeck	.10
98	Wade Boggs	.25
99	Russ Davis	.10
100	Jim Leyritz	.10
101	Don Mattingly	1.00
102	Jack McDowell	.10
103	Paul O'Neill	.25
104	Andy Pettitte	.30
105	Mariano Rivera	.20
106	Ruben Sierra	.10
107	Darryl Strawberry	.15
108	John Wetteland	.10
109	Bernie Williams	.50
110	Geronimo Berroa	.10
111	Scott Brosius	.10
112	Dennis Eckersley	.10
113	Brent Gates	.10
114	Rickey Henderson	.40
115	Mark McGwire	3.00
116	Ariel Prieto	.10
117	Terry Steinbach	.10
118	Todd Stottlemyre	.10
119	Todd Van Poppel	.10
120	Steve Wojciechowski	.10
121	Rich Amaral	.10
122	Bobby Ayala	.10
123	Mike Blowers	.10
124	Chris Bosio	.10
125	Joey Cora	.10
126	Ken Griffey Jr.	2.50
127	Randy Johnson	.60
128	Edgar Martinez	.10
129	Tino Martinez	.15
130	Alex Rodriguez	2.50
131	Dan Wilson	.10
132	Will Clark	.30
133	Jeff Frye	.10
134	Benji Gil	.10
135	Juan Gonzalez	.75
136	Rusty Greer	.10
137	Mark McLemore	.10
138	Roger Pavlik	.10
139	Ivan Rodriguez	.75
140	Kenny Rogers	.10
141	Mickey Tettleton	.10
142	Roberto Alomar	.50
143	Joe Carter	.10
144	Tony Castillo	.10
145	Alex Gonzalez	.10
146	Shawn Green	.40
147	Pat Hentgen	.15
148	*Sandy Martinez*	.10
149	Paul Molitor	.40
150	John Olerud	.25
151	Ed Sprague	.10
152	Jeff Blauser	.10
153	Brad Clontz	.10
154	Tom Glavine	.25
155	Marquis Grissom	.15
156	Chipper Jones	1.50
157	David Justice	.25
158	Ryan Klesko	.15
159	Javier Lopez	.15
160	Greg Maddux	1.50
161	John Smoltz	.15
162	Mark Wohlers	.10
163	Jim Bullinger	.10
164	Frank Castillo	.10
165	Shawon Dunston	.10
166	Kevin Foster	.10
167	Luis Gonzalez	.20
168	Mark Grace	.25
169	Rey Sanchez	.10
170	Scott Servais	.10
171	Sammy Sosa	1.50
172	Ozzie Timmons	.10
173	Steve Trachsel	.10
174	Bret Boone	.10
175	Jeff Branson	.10
176	Jeff Brantley	.10
177	Dave Burba	.10
178	Ron Gant	.10
179	Barry Larkin	.25
180	Darren Lewis	.10
181	Mark Portugal	.10
182	Reggie Sanders	.10
183	Pete Schourek	.10
184	John Smiley	.10
185	Jason Bates	.10
186	Dante Bichette	.20
187	Ellis Burks	.10
188	Vinny Castilla	.15
189	Andres Galarraga	.30
190	Darren Holmes	.10
191	Armando Reynoso	.10
192	Kevin Ritz	.10
193	Bill Swift	.10
194	Larry Walker	.40
195	Kurt Abbott	.10
196	John Burkett	.10

197 Greg Colbrunn .10
198 Jeff Conine .15
199 Andre Dawson .20
200 Chris Hammond .10
201 Charles Johnson .15
202 Robb Nen .10
203 Terry Pendleton .10
204 Quilvio Veras .10
205 Jeff Bagwell .75
206 Derek Bell .10
207 Doug Drabek .10
208 Tony Eusebio .10
209 Mike Hampton .10
210 Brian Hunter .10
211 Todd Jones .10
212 Orlando Miller .10
213 James Mouton .10
214 Shane Reynolds .15
215 Dave Veres .10
216 Billy Ashley .10
217 Brett Butler .10
218 Chad Fonville .10
219 Todd Hollandsworth .10
220 Eric Karros .15
221 Ramon Martinez .15
222 Raul Mondesi .20
223 Hideo Nomo .25
224 Mike Piazza 2.00
225 Kevin Tapani .10
226 Ismael Valdes .10
227 Todd Worrell .10
228 Moises Alou .20
229 Wil Cordero .10
230 Jeff Fassero .10
231 Darrin Fletcher .10
232 Mike Lansing .10
233 Pedro Martinez 1.00
234 Carlos Perez .10
235 Mel Rojas .10
236 David Segui .10
237 Tony Tarasco .10
238 Rondell White .20
239 Edgardo Alfonzo .25
240 Rico Brogna .10
241 Carl Everett .10
242 Todd Hundley .15
243 Butch Huskey .10
244 Jason Isringhausen .15
245 Bobby Jones .10
246 Jeff Kent .10
247 Bill Pulsipher .10
248 Jose Vizcaino .10
249 Ricky Bottalico .10
250 Darren Daulton .10
251 Jim Eisenreich .10
252 Tyler Green .10
253 Charlie Hayes .10
254 Gregg Jefferies .15
255 Tony Longmire .10
256 Michael Mimbs .10
257 Mickey Morandini .10
258 Paul Quantrill .10
259 Heathcliff Slocumb .10
260 Jay Bell .10
261 Jacob Brumfield .10
262 *Angelo Encarnacion* .15
263 John Ericks .10
264 Mark Johnson .10
265 Esteban Loaiza .10
266 Al Martin .10
267 Orlando Merced .10
268 Dan Miceli .10
269 Denny Neagle .10
270 Brian Barber .10
271 Scott Cooper .10
272 Tripp Cromer .10
273 Bernard Gilkey .10
274 Tom Henke .10
275 Brian Jordan .10
276 John Mabry .10
277 Tom Pagnozzi .10
278 *Mark Petkovsek* .10
279 Ozzie Smith .50
280 Andy Ashby .10
281 Brad Ausmus .10
282 Ken Caminiti .15
283 Glenn Dishman .10
284 Tony Gwynn 1.00
285 Joey Hamilton .10
286 Trevor Hoffman .10
287 Phil Plantier .10
288 Jody Reed .10
289 Eddie Williams .10
290 Barry Bonds .75
291 Jamie Brewington .10
292 Mark Carreon .10
293 Royce Clayton .10
294 Glenallen Hill .10
295 Mark Leiter .10
296 Kirt Manwaring .10
297 J.R. Phillips .10
298 Deion Sanders .20
299 William VanLandingham .10
300 Matt Williams .20
301 Roberto Alomar .60
302 Armando Benitez .10
303 Mike Devereaux .10
304 Jeffrey Hammonds .10
305 Jimmy Haynes .10
306 *Scott McClain* .10
307 Kent Mercker .10
308 Randy Myers .10
309 B.J. Surhoff .10
310 Tony Tarasco .10
311 David Wells .10
312 Wil Cordero .10
313 Alex Delgado .10
314 Tom Gordon .10
315 Dwayne Hosey .10
316 Jose Malave .10
317 Kevin Mitchell .10
318 Jamie Moyer .10
319 Aaron Sele .10
320 Heathcliff Slocumb .10
321 Mike Stanley .10
322 Jeff Suppan .10
323 Jim Abbott .10
324 George Arias .10
325 Todd Greene .10
326 Bryan Harvey .10
327 J.T. Snow .15
328 Randy Velarde .10
329 Tim Wallach .10
330 Harold Baines .10
331 Jason Bere .10
332 Darren Lewis .10
333 Norberto Martin .10
334 Tony Phillips .10
335 Bill Simas .10
336 Chris Snopek .10
337 Kevin Tapani .10
338 Danny Tartabull .10
339 Robin Ventura .20
340 Sandy Alomar .15
341 Julio Franco .10
342 Jack McDowell .10
343 Charles Nagy .10
344 Julian Tavarez .10
345 Kimera Bartee .10
346 Greg Keagle .10
347 Mark Lewis .10
348 Jose Lima .10
349 Melvin Nieves .10
350 Mark Parent .10
351 Eddie Williams .10
352 Johnny Damon .15
353 Sal Fasano .10
354 Mark Gubicza .10
355 Bob Hamelin .10
356 Chris Haney .10
357 Keith Lockhart .10
358 Mike Macfarlane .10
359 Jose Offerman .10
360 Bip Roberts .10
361 Michael Tucker .10
362 Chuck Carr .10
363 Bobby Hughes .10
364 John Jaha .10
365 Mark Loretta .10
366 Mike Matheny .10
367 Ben McDonald .10
368 Matt Mieske .10
369 Angel Miranda .10
370 Fernando Vina .10
371 Rick Aguilera .10
372 Rich Becker .10
373 LaTroy Hawkins .10
374 Dave Hollins .10
375 Roberto Kelly .10
376 *Matt Lawton* .75
377 Paul Molitor .40
378 *Dan Naulty* .10
379 Rich Robertson .10
380 Frank Rodriguez .10
381 David Cone .20
382 Mariano Duncan .10
383 *Andy Fox* .10
384 Joe Girardi .10
385 Dwight Gooden .15
386 Derek Jeter 2.50
387 Pat Kelly .10
388 Jimmy Key .10
389 *Matt Luke* .10
390 Tino Martinez .15
391 Jeff Nelson .10
392 Melido Perez .10
393 Tim Raines .15
394 Ruben Rivera .10
395 Kenny Rogers .10
396 *Tony Batista* 4.00
397 Allen Battle .10
398 Mike Bordick .10
399 Steve Cox .10
400 Jason Giambi .10
401 Doug Johns .10
402 Pedro Munoz .10
403 Phil Plantier .10
404 Scott Spiezio .10
405 George Williams .10
406 Ernie Young .10
407 Darren Bragg .10
408 Jay Buhner .10
409 Norm Charlton .10
410 Russ Davis .10
411 Sterling Hitchcock .10
412 Edwin Hurtado .10
413 *Raul Ibanez* .10
414 Mike Jackson .10
415 Luis Sojo .10
416 Paul Sorrento .10
417 Bob Wolcott .10
418 Damon Buford .10
419 Kevin Gross .10
420 Darryl Hamilton .10
421 Mike Henneman .10
422 Ken Hill .10
423 Dean Palmer .10
424 Bobby Witt .10
425 Tilson Brito .10
426 Giovanni Carrara .10
427 Domingo Cedeno .10
428 Felipe Crespo .10
429 Carlos Delgado .60
430 Juan Guzman .10
431 Erik Hanson .10
432 *Marty Janzen* .10
433 Otis Nixon .10
434 Robert Perez .10
435 Paul Quantrill .10
436 Bill Risley .10
437 Steve Avery .10
438 Jermaine Dye .10
439 Mark Lemke .10
440 *Marty Malloy* .10
441 Fred McGriff .20
442 Greg McMichael .10
443 Wonderful Monds .10
444 Eddie Perez .10
445 Jason Schmidt .10
446 Terrell Wade .10
447 Terry Adams .10
448 Scott Bullett .10
449 *Robin Jennings* .10
450 Doug Jones .10
451 Brooks Kieschnick .10
452 Dave Magadan .10
453 *Jason Maxwell* .10
454 Brian McRae .10
455 Rodney Myers .10
456 Jaime Navarro .10
457 Ryne Sandberg .75
458 Vince Coleman .10
459 Eric Davis .10
460 Steve Gibralter .10
461 Thomas Howard .10
462 Mike Kelly .10
463 Hal Morris .10
464 Eric Owens .10
465 Jose Rijo .10
466 Chris Sabo .10
467 Eddie Taubensee .10
468 Trenidad Hubbard .10
469 Curt Leskanic .10
470 Quinton McCracken .10
471 Jayhawk Owens .10
472 Steve Reed .10
473 Bryan Rekar .10
474 Bruce Ruffin .10
475 Bret Saberhagen .10
476 Walt Weiss .10
477 Eric Young .10
478 Kevin Brown .20
479 Al Leiter .20
480 Pat Rapp .10
481 Gary Sheffield .30
482 Devon White .10
483 Bob Abreu .10
484 Sean Berry .10
485 Craig Biggio .20
486 Jim Dougherty .10
487 Richard Hidalgo .10
488 Darryl Kile .10
489 Derrick May .10
490 Greg Swindell .10
491 Rick Wilkins .10
492 Mike Blowers .10
493 Tom Candiotti .10
494 Roger Cedeno .10
495 Delino DeShields .10
496 Greg Gagne .10
497 Karim Garcia .10
498 *Wilton Guerrero* .25
499 Chan Ho Park .15
500 Israel Alcantara .10
501 Shane Andrews .10
502 Yamil Benitez .10
503 Cliff Floyd .10
504 Mark Grudzielanek .10
505 Ryan McGuire .10
506 Sherman Obando .10
507 Jose Paniagua .10
508 Henry Rodriguez .10
509 Kirk Rueter .10
510 Juan Acevedo .10
511 John Franco .10
512 Bernard Gilkey .10
513 Lance Johnson .10
514 Rey Ordonez .15
515 Robert Person .10
516 Paul Wilson .15
517 Toby Borland .10
518 *David Doster* .10
519 Lenny Dykstra .10
520 Sid Fernandez .10
521 *Mike Grace* .10
522 *Rich Hunter* .10
523 Benito Santiago .10
524 Gene Schall .10
525 Curt Schilling .15
526 *Kevin Sefcik* .10
527 Lee Tinsley .10
528 David West .10
529 Mark Whiten .10
530 Todd Zeile .10
531 Carlos Garcia .10
532 Charlie Hayes .10
533 Jason Kendall .15
534 Jeff King .10
535 Mike Kingery .10
536 Nelson Liriano .10
537 Dan Plesac .10
538 Paul Wagner .10
539 Luis Alicea .10
540 David Bell .10
541 Alan Benes .10
542 Andy Benes .15
543 *Mike Busby* .10
544 Royce Clayton .10
545 Dennis Eckersley .10
546 Gary Gaetti .10
547 Ron Gant .10
548 Aaron Holbert .10
549 Ray Lankford .10
550 T.J. Mathews .10
551 Willie McGee .10
552 *Miguel Mejia* .10
553 Todd Stottlemyre .10
554 Sean Bergman .10
555 Willie Blair .10
556 Andujar Cedeno .10
557 Steve Finley .10
558 Rickey Henderson .40
559 Wally Joyner .10
560 Scott Livingstone .10
561 Marc Newfield .10
562 Bob Tewksbury .10
563 Fernando Valenzuela .10
564 Rod Beck .10
565 Doug Creek .10
566 Shawon Dunston .10
567 *Osvaldo Fernandez* .20
568 Stan Javier .10
569 Marcus Jensen .10
570 Steve Scarsone .10
571 Robby Thompson .10
572 Allen Watson .10
573 Roberto Alomar (Ultra Stars) .25
574 Jeff Bagwell (Ultra Stars) .40
575 Albert Belle (Ultra Stars) .30
576 Wade Boggs (Ultra Stars) .20
577 Barry Bonds (Ultra Stars) .40
578 Juan Gonzalez (Ultra Stars) .40
579 Ken Griffey Jr. (Ultra Stars) 1.25
580 Tony Gwynn (Ultra Stars) .50
581 Randy Johnson (Ultra Stars) .30
582 Chipper Jones (Ultra Stars) .75
583 Barry Larkin (Ultra Stars) .10
584 Kenny Lofton (Ultra Stars) .20
585 Greg Maddux (Ultra Stars) .75

586	Raul Mondesi (Ultra Stars)	.10
587	Mike Piazza (Ultra Stars)	1.00
588	Cal Ripken Jr. (Ultra Stars)	1.25
589	Tim Salmon (Ultra Stars)	.20
590	Frank Thomas (Ultra Stars)	.50
591	Mo Vaughn (Ultra Stars)	.20
592	Matt Williams (Ultra Stars)	.10
593	Marty Cordova (Raw Power)	.10
594	Jim Edmonds (Raw Power)	.10
595	Cliff Floyd (Raw Power)	.10
596	Chipper Jones (Raw Power)	.75
597	Ryan Klesko (Raw Power)	.15
598	Raul Mondesi (Raw Power)	.20
599	Manny Ramirez (Raw Power)	.40
600	Ruben Rivera (Raw Power)	.15

1996 Ultra Gold Medallion

Limited to less than 10% of the regular edition's production, the Gold Medallion parallel set replaces the front photo's background with gold foil featuring a large embossed Fleer Ultra Gold Medallion seal at center. One Gold Medallion card is found in each foil pack.

	MT
Complete Set (600):	100.00
Common Player:	.25

(Star cards valued at 2X regular edition Fleer Ultra.)

1996 Ultra Call to the Hall

Ten probable future Hall of Famers are featured on these cards, which use classic style original illustrations of the players. The cards were seeded one per every 24 Series 2 packs.

		MT
Complete Set (10):		60.00
Common Player:		2.50
Gold Medallion Edition:		2X
1	Barry Bonds	5.00
2	Ken Griffey Jr.	15.00
3	Tony Gwynn	6.00
4	Rickey Henderson	3.00
5	Greg Maddux	10.00
6	Eddie Murray	3.00
7	Cal Ripken Jr.	12.00
8	Ryne Sandberg	5.00
9	Ozzie Smith	4.00
10	Frank Thomas	6.00

1996 Ultra Checklists

Fleer Ultra featured 10 checklist cards that were inserted every four packs. These cards featured a superstar player on the front and, throughout the set, a full checklist of all cards in the 1996 Ultra set on the back.

		MT
Complete Set (20):		20.00
Common Player:		.25
	SERIES 1	
1	Jeff Bagwell	.75
2	Barry Bonds	.75
3	Juan Gonzalez	.75
4	Ken Griffey Jr.	3.00
5	Chipper Jones	2.00
6	Mike Piazza	2.00
7	Manny Ramirez	1.00
8	Cal Ripken Jr.	2.50
9	Frank Thomas	1.50

The values of some parallel-card issues will have to be calculated based on figures presented in the heading for the regular-is-

1996 Ultra Diamond Dust

This card commemorates Cal Ripken's history-making 1995 record of playing in 2,131 consecutive regular-season games. Horizontal in format, the front has a color action photo of Ripken on a simulated leather background. Back has a photo of Ripken on the night he set the new record. Sandwiched between front and back is a dime-sized plastic capsule of dirt certified, according to the facsimile autograph on back of the team's head groundskeeper, to have been used on the infield at Oriole Park in Camden Yards during the 1995 season. Two versions of the card were made. A hand-numbered version limited to 2,131 was offered direct to dealers for $39.99. An unnumbered version was available to collectors as a wrapper redemption for $24.99.

	MT
Cal Ripken Jr. (numbered)	250.00
Cal Ripken Jr. (unnumbered)	150.00

1996 Ultra Diamond Producers

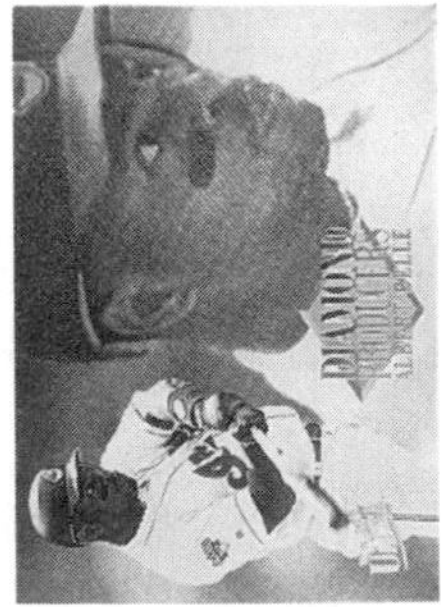

A horizontal layout and two versions of the same photo printed on holographic foil are featured in this insert set. Stated odds of finding a Diamond Producers card are one per every 20 Series I packs.

		MT
Complete Set (12):		60.00
Common Player:		2.00
Gold Medallions:		2X
1	Albert Belle	2.50
2	Barry Bonds	5.00
3	Ken Griffey Jr.	12.00
4	Tony Gwynn	5.00
5	Greg Maddux	8.00
6	Hideo Nomo	2.00
7	Mike Piazza	10.00
8	Kirby Puckett	4.00
9	Cal Ripken Jr.	12.00
10	Frank Thomas	5.00
11	Mo Vaughn	2.50
12	Matt Williams	2.00

1996 Ultra Fresh Foundations

Rising stars who can carry their teams' fortunes into the next century are featured in this foil-printed insert set, found on average of one card per every three Series I foil packs.

		MT
Complete Set (10):		5.00
Common Player:		.50
Gold Medallions:		2X
1	Garret Anderson	.50
2	Marty Cordova	.50
3	Jim Edmonds	.50
4	Brian Hunter	.50
5	Chipper Jones	1.50
6	Ryan Klesko	.75
7	Raul Mondesi	.75
8	Hideo Nomo	.75
9	Manny Ramirez	1.50
10	Rondell White	.50

1996 Ultra Golden Prospects, Series 1

A hobby-pack-only insert, these horizontal format cards have rainbow foil ballpark backgrounds and feature 1996's rookie crop. They are found on average of one per every five Series I packs.

		MT
Complete Set (10):		5.00
Common Player:		.25
Gold Medallions:		2X
1	Yamil Benitez	.30
2	Alberto Castillo	.25
3	Roger Cedeno	.50
4	Johnny Damon	.50
5	Micah Franklin	.25
6	Jason Giambi	.75
7	Jose Herrera	.25
8	Derek Jeter	4.00
9	Kevin Jordan	.25
10	Ruben Rivera	.75

1996 Ultra Golden Prospects, Series 2

The Golden Prospects insert series continued with 15 more young stars found exclusively in Series 2 hobby packs, though in much lower numbers than the Series 1 inserts.

		MT
Complete Set (15):		45.00
Common Player:		2.00
Gold Medallions:		2X
1	Bob Abreu	12.00
2	Israel Alcantara	2.00
3	Tony Batista	5.00
4	Mike Cameron	4.00
5	Steve Cox	2.00
6	Jermaine Dye	4.00
7	Wilton Guerrero	3.00
8	Richard Hidalgo	5.00
9	Raul Ibanez	3.00
10	Marty Janzen	2.00
11	Robin Jennings	2.00
12	Jason Maxwell	2.00
13	Scott McClain	2.00
14	Wonderful Monds	2.00
15	Chris Singleton	6.00

1996 Ultra Hitting Machines

These die-cut 1996 Fleer Ultra Series II insert cards showcase the heaviest hitters on cards featuring a machine-gear design. The cards were seeded one per every 288 Series II packs.

		MT
Complete Set (10):		200.00
Common Player:		8.00
Gold Medallion:		2X
1	Albert Belle	12.00
2	Barry Bonds	20.00
3	Juan Gonzalez	20.00
4	Ken Griffey Jr.	60.00
5	Edgar Martinez	8.00
6	Rafael Palmeiro	10.00
7	Mike Piazza	50.00
8	Tim Salmon	10.00
9	Frank Thomas	25.00
10	Matt Williams	10.00

1996 Ultra Home Run Kings

Printed on a thin wood veneer, these super-scarce inserts are seeded one per every 75 Series I packs. Because of quality control problems, the cards were initially released as exchange cards, with instructions on back for a mail-in redemption offer for the actual wooden card.

		MT
Complete Set (12):		50.00
Common Player:		4.00
Gold Medallions:		2X
1	Jeff Bagwell	5.00
2	Albert Belle	3.00
3	Dante Bichette	2.00
4	Barry Bonds	6.00
5	Ron Gant	2.00
6	Ken Griffey Jr.	15.00
7	Manny Ramirez	5.00
8	Tim Salmon	2.00
9	Frank Thomas	8.00
10	Mo Vaughn	3.00
11	Larry Walker	3.00
12	Matt Williams	3.00

1996 Ultra Home Run Kings Exchange Cards

Printed on a thin wood veneer, these super-scarce inserts are found at the rate of only one per 75 packs. Because of quality control problems, the cards were initially released as exchange cards, with instructions on back for a mail-in redemption offer for the actual wooden card. The redemption period expired Dec. 1, 1996.

		MT
Complete Set (12):		16.00
Common Player:		.75
Gold Medallions:		2X
1	Jeff Bagwell	2.00
2	Albert Belle	1.00
3	Dante Bichette	1.00
4	Barry Bonds	2.00
5	Ron Gant	.75
6	Ken Griffey Jr.	4.00
7	Manny Ramirez	1.00
8	Tim Salmon	.75
9	Frank Thomas	2.00
10	Mo Vaughn	.75
11	Larry Walker	.75
12	Matt Williams	.75

1996 Ultra On-Base Leaders

These 1996 Fleer Ultra Series II inserts feature 10 of the game's top on-base leaders. The cards were seeded one per every four packs.

		MT
Complete Set (10):		6.00
Common Player:		.50
Gold Medallion:		2X
1	Wade Boggs	.75
2	Barry Bonds	1.50
3	Tony Gwynn	1.50
4	Rickey Henderson	.75
5	Chuck Knoblauch	.50
6	Edgar Martinez	.50
7	Mike Piazza	2.50
8	Tim Salmon	.50
9	Frank Thomas	1.50
10	Jim Thome	.50

1996 Ultra Power Plus

Etched-foil backgrounds, multiple player photos and a horizontal format are featured in this chase set. Stated odds of finding one of the dozen Power Plus cards are one per every 10 Series I packs.

		MT
Complete Set (12):		20.00
Common Player:		.50
Gold Medallions:		2X
1	Jeff Bagwell	4.00
2	Barry Bonds	2.50
3	Ken Griffey Jr.	9.00
4	Raul Mondesi	.75
5	Rafael Palmeiro	1.00
6	Mike Piazza	6.00
7	Manny Ramirez	2.50
8	Tim Salmon	.75
9	Reggie Sanders	.50
10	Frank Thomas	4.00
11	Larry Walker	1.00
12	Matt Williams	.75

1996 Ultra Prime Leather

An embossed leather-feel background is featured on these cards of top fielders, seeded one per every eight Series I packs, on average.

		MT
Complete Set (18):		35.00
Common Player:		.75

Gold Medallions:		2X
1	Ivan Rodriguez	3.00
2	Will Clark	1.50
3	Roberto Alomar	2.00
4	Cal Ripken Jr.	7.50
5	Wade Boggs	1.00
6	Ken Griffey Jr.	9.00
7	Kenny Lofton	1.50
8	Kirby Puckett	3.00
9	Tim Salmon	.75
10	Mike Piazza	6.00
11	Mark Grace	.75
12	Craig Biggio	1.00
13	Barry Larkin	.75
14	Matt Williams	.75
15	Barry Bonds	3.00
16	Tony Gwynn	5.00
17	Brian McRae	.75
18	Raul Mondesi	.75

1996 Ultra R-E-S-P-E-C-T

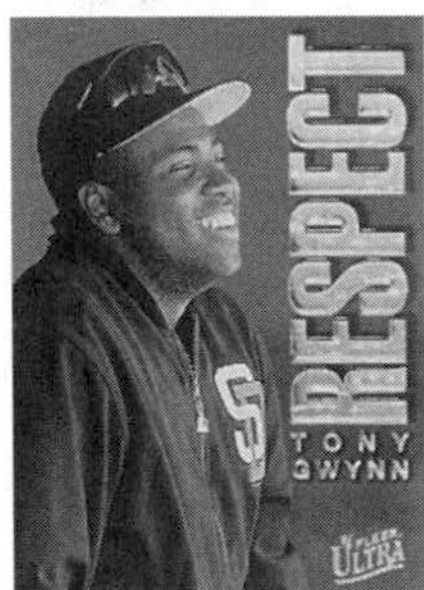

These cards feature 10 players held in high esteem by their major league peers. The cards were seeded one per every 18 1996 Ultra Series II packs.

		MT
Complete Set (10):		50.00
Common Player:		1.50
Gold Medallion:		2X
1	Joe Carter	1.50
2	Ken Griffey Jr.	15.00
3	Tony Gwynn	7.00
4	Greg Maddux	8.00
5	Eddie Murray	3.00
6	Kirby Puckett	4.00
7	Cal Ripken Jr.	10.00
8	Ryne Sandberg	4.00
9	Frank Thomas	6.00
10	Mo Vaughn	3.00

1996 Ultra Rawhide

Ten top fielders are featured on these 1996 Fleer Ultra Series II inserts. The cards were seeded one per every eight packs.

		MT
Complete Set (10):		15.00
Common Player:		1.00
Gold Medallion:		2X
1	Roberto Alomar	.75
2	Barry Bonds	1.50
3	Mark Grace	.75
4	Ken Griffey Jr.	6.00
5	Kenny Lofton	.75
6	Greg Maddux	2.50
7	Raul Mondesi	.75
8	Mike Piazza	3.00
9	Cal Ripken Jr.	4.00
10	Matt Williams	.75

1996 Ultra Rising Stars

Ten of baseball's best young players are spotlighted on these 1996 Fleer Ultra Series II inserts. Cards were seeded one per every four packs.

		MT
Complete Set (10):		5.00
Common Player:		.25
Gold Medallion:		2X
1	Garret Anderson	.35
2	Marty Cordova	.50
3	Jim Edmonds	.40
4	Cliff Floyd	.25
5	Brian Hunter	.35
6	Chipper Jones	2.50
7	Ryan Klesko	.40
8	Hideo Nomo	.75
9	Manny Ramirez	2.00
10	Rondell White	.50

1996 Ultra RBI Kings

Retail packs are the exclusive provenance of this 10-card set of top RBI men. Stated odds of finding an RBI King card are one per every five Series I packs.

		MT
Complete Set (10):		18.00
Common Player:		.40
Gold Medallions:		2X
1	Derek Bell	.50
2	Albert Belle	2.00
3	Dante Bichette	.75
4	Barry Bonds	3.00
5	Jim Edmonds	.50
6	Manny Ramirez	3.00
7	Reggie Sanders	.50
8	Sammy Sosa	10.00
9	Frank Thomas	4.00
10	Mo Vaughn	2.00

1996 Ultra Season Crowns

Large coats-of-arms printed on "Ultra Crystal" clear plastic are the background for player action photos in this insert set. Odds of one per every 10 Series II packs were stated.

		MT
Complete Set (10):		25.00
Common Player:		1.00
Gold Medallions:		2X
1	Barry Bonds	2.50
2	Tony Gwynn	5.00
3	Randy Johnson	2.00
4	Kenny Lofton	1.50
5	Greg Maddux	5.00
6	Edgar Martinez	1.00
7	Hideo Nomo	1.50
8	Cal Ripken Jr.	7.50
9	Frank Thomas	4.00
10	Tim Wakefield	1.00

1996 Ultra Thunderclap

The active career home run leaders are featured in this retail-exclusive Ultra insert set. Seeded only one per 72 packs, the Thunderclap cards have action photos on front with simulated lightning in the background and other graphic highlights rendered in holographic foil. Backs have a large portrait photo and career summary. Each of these scarce retail inserts can also be found in an even more elusive Gold Medallion version.

		MT
Complete Set (20):		260.00
Common Player:		4.50
Gold Medallion:		2X
1	Albert Belle	10.00
2	Barry Bonds	15.00
3	Bobby Bonilla	4.00
4	Jose Canseco	10.00
5	Joe Carter	4.00
6	Will Clark	8.00
7	Andre Dawson	4.00
8	Cecil Fielder	4.00
9	Andres Galarraga	6.00
10	Juan Gonzalez	15.00
11	Ken Griffey Jr.	50.00
12	Fred McGriff	6.00
13	Mark McGwire	55.00
14	Eddie Murray	6.00
15	Rafael Palmeiro	10.00
16	Kirby Puckett	15.00
17	Cal Ripken Jr.	45.00
18	Ryne Sandberg	15.00
19	Frank Thomas	20.00
20	Matt Williams	5.00

1997 Ultra

Ultra arrived in a 300-card Series I issue with two parallel sets, Gold and Platinum, which featured "G" and "P" prefixes on the card number, respectively. Cards were issued in 10-card packs. Player names and the Ultra logo are in silver holographic foil. Backs contains complete year-by-year statistics, plus two photos of the player. This also marked the first time that the Gold and Platinum parallel sets displayed a different photo than the base cards. Inserts in Ultra included: Rookie Reflections, Double Trouble, Checklists, Season Crowns, RBI Kings, Power Plus, Fielder's Choice, Diamond Producers, HR Kings and Baseball Rules.

		MT
Complete Set (553):		55.00
Series 1 (300):		30.00
Series 2 (253):		25.00
Common Player:		.10
Series 1 or 2 Pack (10):		2.00
Series 1 or 2 Wax Box (24):		45.00
1	Roberto Alomar	.50
2	Brady Anderson	.15
3	Rocky Coppinger	.10
4	Jeffrey Hammonds	.10

No.	Player	Price
5	Chris Hoiles	.10
6	Eddie Murray	.40
7	Mike Mussina	.50
8	Jimmy Myers	.10
9	Randy Myers	.10
10	Arthur Rhodes	.10
11	Cal Ripken Jr.	2.50
12	Jose Canseco	.50
13	Roger Clemens	1.00
14	Tom Gordon	.10
15	Jose Malave	.10
16	Tim Naehring	.10
17	Troy O'Leary	.10
18	Bill Selby	.10
19	Heathcliff Slocumb	.10
20	Mike Stanley	.10
21	Mo Vaughn	.40
22	Garret Anderson	.10
23	George Arias	.10
24	Chili Davis	.10
25	Jim Edmonds	.20
26	Darin Erstad	.40
27	Chuck Finley	.10
28	Todd Greene	.10
29	Troy Percival	.10
30	Tim Salmon	.20
31	Jeff Schmidt	.10
32	Randy Velarde	.10
33	Shad Williams	.10
34	Wilson Alvarez	.10
35	Harold Baines	.10
36	James Baldwin	.10
37	Mike Cameron	.10
38	Ray Durham	.10
39	Ozzie Guillen	.10
40	Roberto Hernandez	.10
41	Darren Lewis	.10
42	Jose Munoz	.10
43	Tony Phillips	.10
44	Frank Thomas	1.00
45	Sandy Alomar Jr.	.15
46	Albert Belle	.40
47	Mark Carreon	.10
48	Julio Franco	.10
49	Orel Hershiser	.10
50	Kenny Lofton	.30
51	Jack McDowell	.15
52	Jose Mesa	.10
53	Charles Nagy	.10
54	Manny Ramirez	.75
55	Julian Tavarez	.10
56	Omar Vizquel	.20
57	Raul Casanova	.10
58	Tony Clark	.15
59	Travis Fryman	.20
60	Bob Higginson	.10
61	Melvin Nieves	.10
62	Curtis Pride	.10
63	Justin Thompson	.10
64	Alan Trammell	.15
65	Kevin Appier	.10
66	Johnny Damon	.20
67	Keith Lockhart	.10
68	Jeff Montgomery	.10
69	Jose Offerman	.10
70	Bip Roberts	.10
71	Jose Rosado	.10
72	Chris Stynes	.10
73	Mike Sweeney	.10
74	Jeff Cirillo	.10
75	Jeff D'Amico	.10
76	John Jaha	.10
77	Scott Karl	.10
78	Mike Matheny	.10
79	Ben McDonald	.10
80	Matt Mieske	.10
81	Marc Newfield	.10
82	Dave Nilsson	.10
83	Jose Valentin	.10
84	Fernando Vina	.10
85	Rick Aguilera	.10
86	Marty Cordova	.10
87	Chuck Knôblauch	.20
88	Matt Lawton	.10
89	Pat Meares	.10
90	Paul Molitor	.40
91	Greg Myers	.10
92	Dan Naulty	.10
93	Kirby Puckett	1.00
94	Frank Rodriguez	.10
95	Wade Boggs	.20
96	Cecil Fielder	.15
97	Joe Girardi	.10
98	Dwight Gooden	.15
99	Derek Jeter	2.00
100	Tino Martinez	.20
101	*Ramiro Mendoza*	.50
102	Andy Pettitte	.30
103	Mariano Rivera	.20
104	Ruben Rivera	.10
105	Kenny Rogers	.10
106	Darryl Strawberry	.15
107	Bernie Williams	.50
108	Tony Batista	.20
109	Geronimo Berroa	.10
110	Bobby Chouinard	.10
111	Brent Gates	.10
112	Jason Giambi	.25
113	*Damon Mashore*	.10
114	Mark McGwire	3.00
115	Scott Spiezio	.10
116	John Wasdin	.10
117	Steve Wojciechowski	.10
118	Ernie Young	.10
119	Norm Charlton	.10
120	Joey Cora	.10
121	Ken Griffey Jr.	2.50
122	Sterling Hitchcock	.10
123	Raul Ibanez	.10
124	Randy Johnson	.75
125	Edgar Martinez	.15
126	Alex Rodriguez	2.50
127	Matt Wagner	.10
128	Bob Wells	.10
129	Dan Wilson	.10
130	Will Clark	.30
131	Kevin Elster	.10
132	Juan Gonzalez	.75
133	Rusty Greer	.10
134	Darryl Hamilton	.10
135	Mike Henneman	.10
136	Ken Hill	.10
137	Mark McLemore	.10
138	Dean Palmer	.20
139	Roger Pavlik	.10
140	Ivan Rodriguez	.75
141	Joe Carter	.20
142	Carlos Delgado	.50
143	Alex Gonzalez	.10
144	Juan Guzman	.10
145	Pat Hentgen	.10
146	Marty Janzen	.10
147	Otis Nixon	.10
148	Charlie O'Brien	.10
149	John Olerud	.20
150	Robert Perez	.10
151	Jermaine Dye	.15
152	Tom Glavine	.20
153	Andruw Jones	.75
154	Chipper Jones	1.50
155	Ryan Klesko	.20
156	Javier Lopez	.20
157	Greg Maddux	1.50
158	Fred McGriff	.25
159	Wonderful Monds	.10
160	John Smoltz	.15
161	Terrell Wade	.10
162	Mark Wohlers	.10
163	Brant Brown	.10
164	Mark Grace	.25
165	Tyler Houston	.10
166	Robin Jennings	.10
167	Jason Maxwell	.10
168	Ryne Sandberg	.75
169	Sammy Sosa	1.50
170	Amaury Telemaco	.10
171	Steve Trachsel	.10
172	*Pedro Valdes*	.10
173	Tim Belk	.10
174	Bret Boone	.10
175	Jeff Brantley	.10
176	Eric Davis	.15
177	Barry Larkin	.30
178	Chad Mottola	.10
179	Mark Portugal	.10
180	Reggie Sanders	.10
181	John Smiley	.10
182	Eddie Taubensee	.10
183	Dante Bichette	.20
184	Ellis Burks	.15
185	Andres Galarraga	.25
186	Curt Leskanic	.10
187	Quinton McCracken	.10
188	Jeff Reed	.10
189	Kevin Ritz	.10
190	Walt Weiss	.10
191	Jamey Wright	.10
192	Eric Young	.10
193	Kevin Brown	.20
194	Luis Castillo	.15
195	Jeff Conine	.10
196	Andre Dawson	.15
197	Charles Johnson	.10
198	Al Leiter	.20
199	Ralph Milliard	.10
200	Robb Nen	.10
201	Edgar Renteria	.15
202	Gary Sheffield	.30
203	Bob Abreu	.10
204	Jeff Bagwell	.75
205	Derek Bell	.10
206	Sean Berry	.10
207	Richard Hidalgo	.10
208	Todd Jones	.10
209	Darryl Kile	.10
210	Orlando Miller	.10
211	Shane Reynolds	.15
212	Billy Wagner	.10
213	Donne Wall	.10
214	Roger Cedeno	.10
215	Greg Gagne	.10
216	Karim Garcia	.10
217	Wilton Guerrero	.15
218	Todd Hollandsworth	.10
219	Ramon Martinez	.15
220	Raul Mondesi	.20
221	Hideo Nomo	.25
222	Chan Ho Park	.15
223	Mike Piazza	2.00
224	Ismael Valdes	.10
225	Moises Alou	.15
226	Derek Aucoin	.10
227	Yamil Benitez	.10
228	Jeff Fassero	.10
229	Darrin Fletcher	.10
230	Mark Grudzielanek	.10
231	Barry Manuel	.10
232	Pedro Martinez	1.00
233	Henry Rodriguez	.10
234	Ugueth Urbina	.10
235	Rondell White	.15
236	Carlos Baerga	.10
237	John Franco	.10
238	Bernard Gilkey	.10
239	Todd Hundley	.10
240	Butch Huskey	.10
241	Jason Isringhausen	.10
242	Lance Johnson	.10
243	Bobby Jones	.10
244	Alex Ochoa	.10
245	Rey Ordonez	.15
246	Paul Wilson	.10
247	Ron Blazier	.10
248	David Doster	.10
249	Jim Eisenreich	.10
250	Mike Grace	.10
251	Mike Lieberthal	.10
252	Wendell Magee	.10
253	Mickey Morandini	.10
254	Ricky Otero	.10
255	Scott Rolen	.50
256	Curt Schilling	.15
257	Todd Zeile	.10
258	Jermaine Allensworth	.10
259	Trey Beamon	.10
260	Carlos Garcia	.10
261	Mark Johnson	.10
262	Jason Kendall	.20
263	Jeff King	.10
264	Al Martin	.10
265	Denny Neagle	.10
266	Matt Ruebel	.10
267	*Marc Wilkins*	.10
268	Alan Benes	.10
269	Dennis Eckersley	.15
270	Ron Gant	.15
271	Aaron Holbert	.10
272	Brian Jordan	.10
273	Ray Lankford	.15
274	John Mabry	.10
275	T.J. Mathews	.10
276	Ozzie Smith	.50
277	Todd Stottlemyre	.15
278	Mark Sweeney	.10
279	Andy Ashby	.10
280	Steve Finley	.10
281	John Flaherty	.10
282	Chris Gomez	.10
283	Tony Gwynn	1.00
284	Joey Hamilton	.10
285	Rickey Henderson	.25
286	Trevor Hoffman	.10
287	Jason Thompson	.10
288	Fernando Valenzuela	.10
289	Greg Vaughn	.20
290	Barry Bonds	.75
291	Jay Canizaro	.10
292	Jacob Cruz	.10
293	Shawon Dunston	.10
294	Shawn Estes	.10
295	Mark Gardner	.10
296	Marcus Jensen	.10
297	*Bill Mueller*	.40
298	Chris Singleton	.10
299	Allen Watson	.10
300	Matt Williams	.25
301	Rod Beck	.10
302	Jay Bell	.10
303	Shawon Dunston	.10
304	Reggie Jefferson	.10
305	Darren Oliver	.10
306	Benito Santiago	.10
307	Gerald Williams	.10
308	Damon Buford	.10
309	Jeromy Burnitz	.10
310	Sterling Hitchcock	.10
311	Dave Hollins	.10
312	Mel Rojas	.10
313	Robin Ventura	.15
314	David Wells	.10
315	Cal Eldred	.10
316	Gary Gaetti	.10
317	John Hudek	.10
318	Brian Johnson	.10
319	Denny Neagle	.10
320	Larry Walker	.40
321	Russ Davis	.10
322	Delino DeShields	.10
323	Charlie Hayes	.10
324	Jermaine Dye	.10
325	John Ericks	.10
326	Jeff Fassero	.10
327	Nomar Garciaparra	2.00
328	Willie Greene	.10
329	Greg McMichael	.10
330	Damion Easley	.10
331	Ricky Bones	.10
332	John Burkett	.10
333	Royce Clayton	.10
334	Greg Colbrunn	.10
335	Tony Eusebio	.10
336	Gregg Jefferies	.10
337	Wally Joyner	.10
338	Jim Leyritz	.10
339	Paul O'Neill	.25
340	Bruce Ruffin	.10
341	Michael Tucker	.10
342	Andy Benes	.10
343	Craig Biggio	.20
344	Rex Hudler	.10
345	Brad Radke	.10
346	Deion Sanders	.25
347	Moises Alou	.15
348	Brad Ausmus	.10
349	Armando Benitez	.10
350	Mark Gubicza	.10
351	Terry Steinbach	.10
352	Mark Whiten	.10
353	Ricky Bottalico	.10
354	*Brian Giles*	2.50
355	Eric Karros	.20
356	Jimmy Key	.10
357	Carlos Perez	.10
358	Alex Fernandez	.10
359	J.T. Snow	.10
360	Bobby Bonilla	.15
361	Scott Brosius	.10
362	Greg Swindell	.10
363	Jose Vizcaino	.10
364	Matt Williams	.30
365	Darren Daulton	.10
366	Shane Andrews	.10
367	Jim Eisenreich	.10
368	Ariel Prieto	.10
369	Bob Tewksbury	.10
370	Mike Bordick	.10
371	Rheal Cormier	.10
372	Cliff Floyd	.10
373	David Justice	.30
374	John Wetteland	.10
375	Mike Blowers	.10
376	Jose Canseco	.50
377	Roger Clemens	1.00
378	Kevin Mitchell	.10
379	Todd Zeile	.10
380	Jim Thome	.50
381	Turk Wendell	.10
382	Rico Brogna	.10
383	Eric Davis	.15
384	Mike Lansing	.10
385	Devon White	.10
386	Marquis Grissom	.10
387	Todd Worrell	.10
388	Jeff Kent	.10
389	Mickey Tettleton	.10
390	Steve Avery	.10
391	David Cone	.20
392	Scott Cooper	.10
393	Lee Stevens	.10
394	Kevin Elster	.10
395	Tom Goodwin	.10
396	Shawn Green	.25
397	Pete Harnisch	.10
398	Eddie Murray	.40
399	Joe Randa	.10
400	Scott Sanders	.10
401	John Valentin	.10
402	Todd Jones	.10
403	Terry Adams	.10
404	Brian Hunter	.10
405	Pat Listach	.10

406 Kenny Lofton .30
407 Hal Morris .10
408 Ed Sprague .10
409 Rich Becker .10
410 Edgardo Alfonzo .25
411 Albert Belle .40
412 Jeff King .10
413 Kirt Manwaring .10
414 Jason Schmidt .10
415 Allen Watson .10
416 Lee Tinsley .10
417 Brett Butler .10
418 Carlos Garcia .10
419 Mark Lemke .10
420 Jaime Navarro .10
421 David Segui .10
422 Ruben Sierra .10
423 B.J. Surhoff .10
424 Julian Tavarez .10
425 Billy Taylor .10
426 Ken Caminiti .20
427 Chuck Carr .10
428 Benji Gil .10
429 Terry Mulholland .10
430 Mike Stanton .10
431 Wil Cordero .10
432 Chili Davis .10
433 Mariano Duncan .10
434 Orlando Merced .10
435 Kent Mercker .10
436 John Olerud .25
437 Quilvio Veras .10
438 Mike Fetters .10
439 Glenallen Hill .10
440 Bill Swift .10
441 Tim Wakefield .10
442 Pedro Astacio .10
443 Vinny Castilla .15
444 Doug Drabek .10
445 Alan Embree .10
446 Lee Smith .10
447 Darryl Hamilton .10
448 Brian McRae .10
449 Mike Timlin .10
450 Bob Wickman .10
451 Jason Dickson .10
452 Chad Curtis .10
453 Mark Leiter .10
454 Damon Berryhill .10
455 Kevin Orie .10
456 Dave Burba .10
457 Chris Holt .10
458 *Ricky Ledee* .75
459 Mike Devereaux .10
460 Pokey Reese .10
461 Tim Raines .15
462 Ryan Jones .10
463 Shane Mack .10
464 Darren Dreifort .10
465 Mark Parent .10
466 Mark Portugal .10
467 Dante Powell .10
468 Craig Grebeck .10
469 Ron Villone .10
470 Dmitri Young .10
471 Shannon Stewart .10
472 Rick Helling .10
473 Bill Haselman .10
474 Albie Lopez .10
475 Glendon Rusch .10
476 Derrick May .10
477 Chad Ogea .10
478 Kirk Reuter .10
479 Chris Hammond .10
480 Russ Johnson .10
481 James Mouton .10
482 Mike Macfarlane .10
483 Scott Ruffcorn .10
484 Jeff Frye .10
485 Richie Sexson .10
486 *Emil Brown* .25
487 Desi Wilson .10
488 Brent Gates .10
489 Tony Graffanino .10
490 Dan Miceli .10
491 *Orlando Cabrera* .25
492 *Tony Womack* .75
493 Jerome Walton .10
494 Mark Thompson .10
495 Jose Guillen .10
496 Willie Blair .10
497 *T.J. Staton* .25
498 Scott Kamieniecki .10
499 Vince Coleman .10
500 Jeff Abbott .10
501 Chris Widger .10
502 Kevin Tapani .10
503 *Carlos Castillo* .25
504 Luis Gonzalez .10
505 Tim Belcher .10
506 Armando Reynoso .10
507 Jamie Moyer .10
508 *Randall Simon* .60
509 Vladimir Guerrero 1.00
510 *Wady Almonte* .25
511 Dustin Hermanson .10
512 *Deivi Cruz* .50
513 Luis Alicea .10
514 *Felix Heredia* .25
515 Don Slaught .10
516 Shigetosi Hasegawa .10
517 Matt Walbeck .10
518 *David Arias* (last name actually Ortiz) 1.00
519 *Brady Raggio* .10
520 Rudy Pemberton .10
521 Wayne Kirby .10
522 Calvin Maduro .10
523 Mark Lewis .10
524 Mike Jackson .10
525 Sid Fernandez .10
526 Mike Bielecki .10
527 *Bubba Trammell* .25
528 *Brent Brede* .10
529 Matt Morris .10
530 Joe Borowski .10
531 Orlando Miller .10
532 Jim Bullinger .10
533 Robert Person .10
534 Doug Glanville .10
535 Terry Pendleton .10
536 Jorge Posada .20
537 *Marc Sagmoen* .10
538 *Fernando Tatis* 2.00
539 Aaron Sele .10
540 Brian Banks .10
541 Derrek Lee .10
542 John Wasdin .10
543 *Justin Towle* .40
544 Pat Cline .10
545 Dave Magadan .10
546 Jeff Blauser .10
547 Phil Nevin .10
548 Todd Walker .10
549 Elieser Marrero .10
550 Bartolo Colon .15
551 *Jose Cruz Jr.* .75
552 Todd Dunwoody .10
553 *Hideki Irabu* .50

1997 Ultra Gold Medallion Edition

A new concept in parallel editions was debuted by Ultra in Series I. While sharing the card numbers with regular-issue Ultra cards, the Gold Medallion Edition features a "G" prefix to the card number and gold-foil highlights on front. Unlike past parallels, however, the '97 Ultra Gold Medallion and Platinum Medallion inserts share a photograph which is entirely different from the regular Ultra base cards. Gold Medallion Edition cards are identified as such in the lower-right corner and were inserted at a rate of one per pack.

MT
Complete Set (553): 200.00
Common Player: .25
(Gold Medallion Edition stars valued at 2X regular Fleer Ultra.)

1997 Ultra Platinum Medallion Edition

A new concept in parallel editions was debuted by Ultra in Series I. While sharing the card numbers with regular-issue Ultra cards, the Platinum Medallion Edition features a "P" prefix to the card number and holographic-foil highlights on front. Unlike past parallels, however, the '97 Ultra Gold Medallion and Platinum Medallion inserts share a photograph which is entirely different from the regular Ultra base cards are identified as such in the lower-right corner and were inserted at a rate of one per 100 packs.

MT
Complete Set (553): 1200.
Common Player: 3.00
(Platinum Medallion Edition stars valued at 15X regular Fleer Ultra.)

1997 Ultra Baseball "Rules!"

Baseball Rules was a 10-card insert that was found only in retail packs at a rate of one per 36 packs. The cards are die-cut with a player in front of a mound of baseballs with embossed seams on the front, while each card back explains a baseball term or rule.

MT
Complete Set (10): 90.00
Common Player: 2.00
1 Barry Bonds 5.00
2 Ken Griffey Jr. 15.00
3 Derek Jeter 15.00
4 Chipper Jones 10.00
5 Greg Maddux 10.00
6 Mark McGwire 20.00
7 Troy Percival 2.00
8 Mike Piazza 12.00
9 Cal Ripken Jr. 15.00
10 Frank Thomas 8.00

1997 Ultra Checklists

There are 10 Checklist cards in each series of Ultra baseball covering all regular-issue cards and inserts. The front of the card features a superstar, while the back contains a portion of the set checklist. The cards have the player's name and "CHECKLIST" in bold, all caps across the bottom in silver foil.

MT
Complete Set (20): 15.00
Common Player: .25
SERIES 1
1 Dante Bichette .25
2 Barry Bonds .60
3 Ken Griffey Jr. 2.00
4 Greg Maddux 1.00
5 Mark McGwire 2.00
6 Mike Piazza 1.50
7 Cal Ripken Jr. 1.50
8 John Smoltz .25
9 Sammy Sosa 1.50
10 Frank Thomas 1.00
SERIES 2
1 Andruw Jones .75
2 Ken Griffey Jr. 2.00
3 Frank Thomas 1.00
4 Alex Rodriguez 1.50
5 Cal Ripken Jr. 1.50
6 Mike Piazza 1.50
7 Greg Maddux 1.00
8 Chipper Jones 1.50
9 Derek Jeter 1.50
10 Juan Gonzalez .50

1997 Ultra Diamond Producers

Printed on textured, uniform-like matterial, this 12-card insert contains some of the most consistent producers in baseball. Horizontal backs are conventionally printed with another color player photo on a pin-striped background and a few words about him. This was the most difficult insert Ultra foil-pack insert, with a ratio of one per 288.

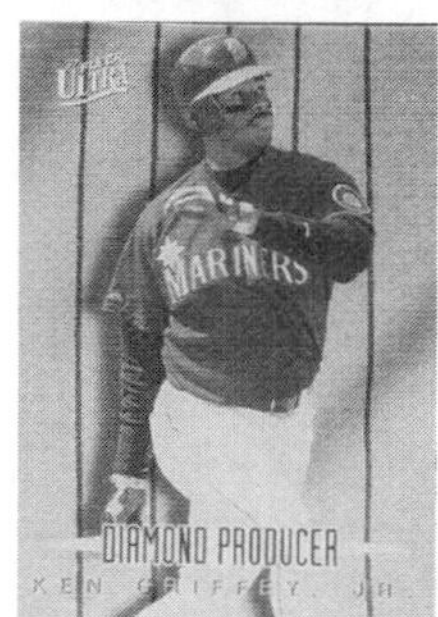

		MT
Complete Set (12):		375.00
Common Player:		10.00
1	Jeff Bagwell	20.00
2	Barry Bonds	20.00
3	Ken Griffey Jr.	60.00
4	Chipper Jones	35.00
5	Kenny Lofton	10.00
6	Greg Maddux	35.00
7	Mark McGwire	70.00
8	Mike Piazza	40.00
9	Cal Ripken Jr.	60.00
10	Alex Rodriguez	60.00
11	Frank Thomas	25.00
12	Matt Williams	10.00

1997 Ultra Double Trouble

Double Trouble is a 20-card, team color coded set pairing two stars from the same team on a horizontal front. These inserts were found every four packs.

		MT
Complete Set (20):		9.00
Common Player:		.15
1	Roberto Alomar, Cal Ripken Jr.	1.25
2	Mo Vaughn, Jose Canseco	.45
3	Jim Edmonds, Tim Salmon	.15
4	Harold Baines, Frank Thomas	.60
5	Albert Belle, Kenny Lofton	.30
6	Chuck Knoblauch, Marty Cordova	.15
7	Andy Pettitte, Derek Jeter	1.25
8	Jason Giambi, Mark McGwire	1.75
9	Ken Griffey Jr., Alex Rodriguez	2.50
10	Juan Gonzalez, Will Clark	.60
11	Greg Maddux, Chipper Jones	.90
12	Mark Grace, Sammy Sosa	1.00
13	Dante Bichette, Andres Galarraga	.15
14	Jeff Bagwell, Derek Bell	.45
15	Hideo Nomo, Mike Piazza	.90
16	Henry Rodriguez, Moises Alou	.15
17	Rey Ordonez, Alex Ochoa	.15
18	Ray Lankford, Ron Gant	.15
19	Tony Gwynn, Rickey Henderson	.90
20	Barry Bonds, Matt Williams	.45

1997 Ultra Fame Game

This eight-card hobby-exclusive insert showcases players who have displayed Hall of Fame potential. The player photo on front and Fame Game logo are embossed and highlighted in gold and silver foil. Backs have a color portrait photo and a few words about the player. Cards were inserted 1:8 packs.

		MT
Complete Set (18):		55.00
Common Player:		.75
1	Ken Griffey Jr.	10.00
2	Frank Thomas	4.00
3	Alex Rodriguez	10.00
4	Cal Ripken Jr.	8.00
5	Mike Piazza	6.00
6	Greg Maddux	5.00
7	Derek Jeter	6.00
8	Jeff Bagwell	3.00
9	Juan Gonzalez	2.50
10	Albert Belle	2.50
11	Tony Gwynn	4.00
12	Mark McGwire	10.00
13	Andy Pettitte	1.50
14	Kenny Lofton	1.50
15	Roberto Alomar	2.00
16	Ryne Sandberg	2.50
17	Barry Bonds	2.50
18	Eddie Murray	1.00

1997 Ultra Fielder's Choice

Fielder's Choice highlights 18 of the top defensive players in baseball. Fronts of the horizontal cards have a leather look and feel and are highlighted in gold foil. Backs are conventionally printed with another player photo and some words about his fielding ability. Fielder's Choice inserts were found every 144 packs.

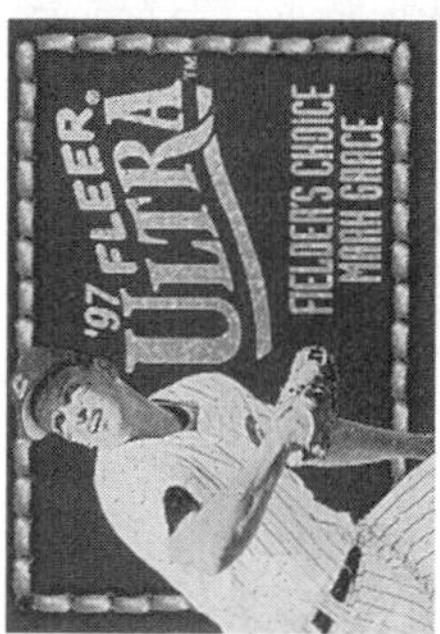

		MT
Complete Set (18):		240.00
Common Player:		3.00
1	Roberto Alomar	10.00
2	Jeff Bagwell	15.00
3	Wade Boggs	7.50
4	Barry Bonds	15.00
5	Mark Grace	5.00
6	Ken Griffey Jr.	50.00
7	Marquis Grissom	3.00
8	Charles Johnson	3.00
9	Chuck Knoblauch	3.00
10	Barry Larkin	6.00
11	Kenny Lofton	8.00
12	Greg Maddux	30.00
13	Raul Mondesi	3.00
14	Rey Ordonez	3.00
15	Cal Ripken Jr.	50.00
16	Alex Rodriguez	50.00
17	Ivan Rodriguez	15.00
18	Matt Williams	6.00

1997 Ultra Golden Prospects

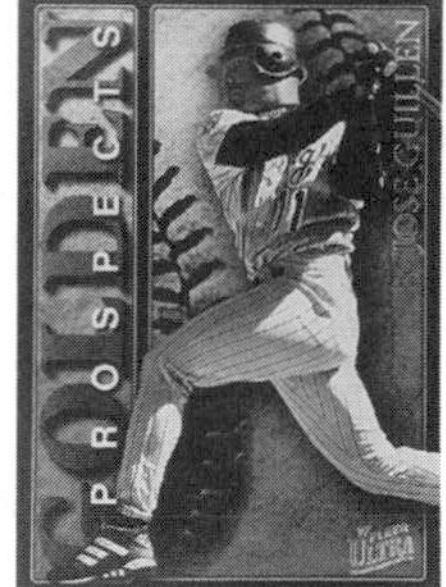

This 10-card set was exclusive to hobby shop packs and highlighted the top young players in baseball. Action photos on front and portraits on back are set on a sepia background. Cards were inserted 1:4 packs.

		MT
Complete Set (10):		4.00
Common Player:		.25
1	Andruw Jones	1.00
2	Vladimir Guerrero	2.00
3	Todd Walker	.50
4	Karim Garcia	.25
5	Kevin Orie	.25
6	Brian Giles	.25
7	Jason Dickson	.25
8	Jose Guillen	.25
9	Ruben Rivera	.40
10	Derrek Lee	.25

1997 Ultra Hitting Machines

This 36-card insert was only found in hobby packs and showcases the game's top hitters. Cards were inserted at a ratio of 1:36 packs.

		MT
Complete Set (18):		150.00
Common Player:		3.00
1	Andruw Jones	6.00
2	Ken Griffey Jr.	20.00
3	Frank Thomas	8.00
4	Alex Rodriguez	20.00
5	Cal Ripken Jr.	20.00
6	Mike Piazza	15.00
7	Derek Jeter	20.00
8	Albert Belle	4.00
9	Tony Gwynn	8.00
10	Jeff Bagwell	6.00
11	Mark McGwire	25.00
12	Kenny Lofton	4.00
13	Manny Ramirez	6.00
14	Roberto Alomar	4.00
15	Ryne Sandberg	6.00
16	Eddie Murray	3.00
17	Sammy Sosa	12.00
18	Ken Caminiti	3.00

1997 Ultra HR Kings

HR Kings are printed on clear plastic with transparent refractive holofoil crowns and other objects in the plastic. Backs contain a white silhouette of the player with career summary and logos within the figure. Stated odds of finding an HR King card were one per 36 packs.

		MT
Complete Set (12):		75.00
Common Player:		3.00
1	Albert Belle	3.00
2	Barry Bonds	5.00
3	Juan Gonzalez	5.00
4	Ken Griffey Jr.	15.00
5	Todd Hundley	2.00
6	Ryan Klesko	2.00
7	Mark McGwire	20.00
8	Mike Piazza	12.00
9	Sammy Sosa	10.00
10	Frank Thomas	6.00
11	Mo Vaughn	3.00
12	Matt Williams	2.50

1997 Ultra Leather Shop

Baseball's best fielders are honored in this 12-card hobby-exclusive insert. Cards were inserted at a ratio of 1:6 packs and feature an embossed grain-like finish on the fronts.

		MT
Complete Set (12):		15.00
Common Player:		.50
1	Ken Griffey Jr.	4.00
2	Alex Rodriguez	3.00
3	Cal Ripken Jr.	3.00
4	Derek Jeter	2.50
5	Juan Gonzalez	1.00
6	Tony Gwynn	2.00
7	Jeff Bagwell	1.25
8	Roberto Alomar	.75
9	Ryne Sandberg	1.00
10	Ken Caminiti	.50
11	Kenny Lofton	.75
12	John Smoltz	.50

1997 Ultra Power Plus Series 1

Series 1 Power Plus is a 12-card insert utilizing silver rainbow holofoil in the background, with the featured player in the foreground. Backs another action photo and the player's credentials. The insert captures power hitters that also excel in other areas of the game. Power Plus inserts can be found every 24 packs.

		MT
Complete Set (12):		80.00
Common Player:		2.50
1	Jeff Bagwell	4.00
2	Barry Bonds	4.00
3	Juan Gonzalez	4.00
4	Ken Griffey Jr.	15.00
5	Chipper Jones	10.00
6	Mark McGwire	15.00
7	Mike Piazza	10.00
8	Cal Ripken Jr.	12.00
9	Alex Rodriguez	12.00
10	Sammy Sosa	10.00
11	Frank Thomas	6.00
12	Matt Williams	3.00

1997 Ultra Power Plus Series 2

Similar in design to the Power Plus insert in Series I, this 12-card insert salutes the game's top sluggers and was found only in hobby packs. Cards were inserted at a ratio of 1:8 packs. Front design features gold holographic foil graphics. Backs have another photo and a description of the player's skills.

		MT
Complete Set (12):		30.00
Common Player:		1.00
1	Ken Griffey Jr.	6.00
2	Frank Thomas	2.50
3	Alex Rodriguez	5.00
4	Cal Ripken Jr.	5.00
5	Mike Piazza	4.00
6	Chipper Jones	4.00
7	Albert Belle	1.00
8	Juan Gonzalez	1.50
9	Jeff Bagwell	1.50
10	Mark McGwire	6.00
11	Mo Vaughn	1.00
12	Barry Bonds	1.50

1997 Ultra Rookie Reflections

Rookie Reflections features 10 of the 1996 season's top first-year stars. Cards are inserted every four packs. Front features an action photo on a black-and-silver starburst pattern. Horizontal backs have another photo and a career summary of the prospect.

		MT
Complete Set (10):		5.00
Common Player:		.25
1	James Baldwin	.25
2	Jermaine Dye	.25
3	Darin Erstad	.50
4	Todd Hollandsworth	.25
5	Derek Jeter	3.00
6	Jason Kendall	.40
7	Alex Ochoa	.25
8	Rey Ordonez	.50
9	Edgar Renteria	.25
10	Scott Rolen	1.00

1997 Ultra RBI Kings

Ten different players are featured in RBI Kings, which contain a metallic paisley background, with an English shield of armor and latin words in the background. RBI Kings were inserted every 18 packs of Series I.

		MT
Complete Set (10):		40.00
Common Player:		2.00
1	Jeff Bagwell	4.00
2	Albert Belle	3.00
3	Dante Bichette	2.00
4	Barry Bonds	4.00
5	Jay Buhner	2.00
6	Juan Gonzalez	4.00
7	Ken Griffey Jr.	15.00
8	Sammy Sosa	10.00
9	Frank Thomas	5.00
10	Mo Vaughn	3.00

1997 Ultra Season Crowns

Season Crowns were found at a rate of one per eight packs of Ultra I Baseball. This etched, silver-foil insert contained 12 statistical leaders and award winners from the 1996 season.

		MT
Complete Set (12):		10.00
Common Player:		.50
1	Albert Belle	.75
2	Dante Bichette	.50
3	Barry Bonds	1.00
4	Kenny Lofton	.75
5	Edgar Martinez	.50
6	Mark McGwire	3.50
7	Andy Pettitte	.50
8	Mike Piazza	2.00
9	Alex Rodriguez	3.00
10	John Smoltz	.50
11	Sammy Sosa	2.00
12	Frank Thomas	1.00

1997 Ultra Starring Role

Another hobby-exclusive insert, these 12 cards salute baseball's clutch performers and were found 1:288 packs.

		MT
Complete Set (12):		260.00
Common Player:		10.00
1	Andruw Jones	10.00
2	Ken Griffey Jr.	50.00
3	Frank Thomas	15.00
4	Alex Rodriguez	40.00
5	Cal Ripken Jr.	40.00
6	Mike Piazza	30.00
7	Greg Maddux	25.00
8	Chipper Jones	30.00
9	Derek Jeter	30.00
10	Juan Gonzalez	15.00
11	Albert Belle	10.00
12	Tony Gwynn	25.00

1997 Ultra Thunderclap

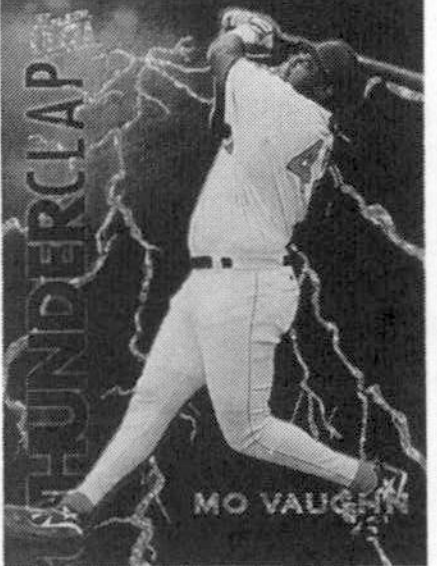

This 10-card hobby-exclusive insert showcases hitters who strike fear in opposing pitchers. Cards were inserted 1:18 packs. Fronts are highlighted by streaks of gold prismatic foil lightning in a story sky. Backs have another player photo and a few words about him.

		MT
Complete Set (10):		60.00
Common Player:		3.00
1	Barry Bonds	4.00
2	Mo Vaughn	3.00
3	Mark McGwire	15.00
4	Jeff Bagwell	4.00
5	Juan Gonzalez	5.00
6	Alex Rodriguez	12.00
7	Chipper Jones	9.00
8	Ken Griffey Jr.	15.00
9	Mike Piazza	9.00
10	Frank Thomas	5.00

1997 Ultra Top 30

This 30-card insert was found only in retail store packs and salutes the 30 most collectible players in the game. Cards were inserted one per pack. A Top 30 Gold Medallion parallel set was also produced and inserted 1:18 packs.

		MT
Complete Set (30):		35.00
Common Player:		.50
Gold Medallions:		5X
1	Andruw Jones	1.50
2	Ken Griffey Jr.	6.00
3	Frank Thomas	2.00
4	Alex Rodriguez	4.00
5	Cal Ripken Jr.	4.00
6	Mike Piazza	3.00
7	Greg Maddux	2.50
8	Chipper Jones	3.00
9	Derek Jeter	3.00
10	Juan Gonzalez	.75
11	Albert Belle	1.00
12	Tony Gwynn	2.50
13	Jeff Bagwell	1.50
14	Mark McGwire	6.00
15	Andy Pettitte	1.00
16	Mo Vaughn	1.00
17	Kenny Lofton	1.00
18	Manny Ramirez	1.50
19	Roberto Alomar	1.00
20	Ryne Sandberg	1.00
21	Hideo Nomo	.60
22	Barry Bonds	1.50
23	Eddie Murray	.75
24	Ken Caminiti	.50
25	John Smoltz	.50
26	Pat Hentgen	.50
27	Todd Hollandsworth	.50
28	Matt Williams	.60
29	Bernie Williams	1.00
30	Brady Anderson	.50

1998 Ultra

Ultra was released in two series and contained a total of 501 cards, with 250 in Series I and 251 in Series II. The product sold in 10-card packs for an SRP of $2.59 and three parallel sets - Gold Medallion, Platinum Medallion and Masterpieces. Series I has 210 regular cards, 25 Prospects (seeded 1:4 packs), 10 Season's Crowns (seeded 1:12) and five Checklists (1:8). Series II had 202 regular cards, 25 Pizzazz (seeded 1:4), 20 New Horizons and three checklists. Series II also added a Mike Piazza N.Y. Mets cards that was added to the set as card No. 501 and inserted every 20 packs. Inserts in Series I include: Big Shots, Double Trouble, Kid Gloves, Back to the Future, Artistic Talents, Fall Classics, Power Plus, Prime Leather, Diamond Producers, Diamond Ink and Million Dollar Moments. Series II included: Notables, Rocket to Stardom, Millennium Men, Win Now, Ticket Studs, Diamond Immortals, Diamond Ink, Top 30 and 750 sequentially numbered Alex Rodriguez autographed cards.

		MT
Complete Set (501):		175.00
Series 1 Set (250):		100.00
Series 2 Set (251):		75.00
Common Player:		.10
Alex Rodriguez Autograph (750):		125.00
Pack (10):		3.50
Wax Box (24):		70.00
1	Ken Griffey Jr.	2.50
2	Matt Morris	.10
3	Roger Clemens	1.00
4	Matt Williams	.25
5	Roberto Hernandez	.10
6	Rondell White	.10
7	Tim Salmon	.20
8	Brad Radke	.10
9	Brett Butler	.10
10	Carl Everett	.10
11	Chili Davis	.10
12	Chuck Finley	.10
13	Darryl Kile	.10
14	Deivi Cruz	.10
15	Gary Gaetti	.10
16	Matt Stairs	.10
17	Pat Meares	.10
18	Will Cunnane	.10
19	*Steve Woodard*	.30
20	Andy Ashby	.10
21	Bobby Higginson	.15
22	Brian Jordan	.10
23	Craig Biggio	.20
24	Jim Edmonds	.20
25	Ryan McGuire	.10
26	Scott Hatteberg	.10
27	Willie Greene	.10
28	Albert Belle	.50
29	Ellis Burks	.10
30	Hideo Nomo	.50
31	Jeff Bagwell	.75
32	Kevin Brown	.10
33	Nomar Garciaparra	2.00
34	Pedro Martinez	.75
35	Raul Mondesi	.25
36	Ricky Bottalico	.10
37	Shawn Estes	.10
38	Shawon Dunston	.10
39	Terry Steinbach	.10
40	Tom Glavine	.25
41	Todd Dunwoody	.10
42	Deion Sanders	.25
43	Gary Sheffield	.35
44	Mike Lansing	.10
45	Mike Lieberthal	.10
46	Paul Sorrento	.10
47	Paul O'Neill	.20
48	Tom Goodwin	.10
49	Andruw Jones	1.00
50	Barry Bonds	.75
51	Bernie Williams	.50
52	Jeremi Gonzalez	.10
53	Mike Piazza	2.00
54	Russ Davis	.10
55	Vinny Castilla	.10
56	Rod Beck	.10
57	Andres Galarraga	.20
58	Ben McDonald	.10
59	Billy Wagner	.10
60	Charles Johnson	.10
61	Fred McGriff	.25
62	Dean Palmer	.10
63	Frank Thomas	1.00
64	Ismael Valdes	.10
65	Mark Bellhorn	.10
66	Jeff King	.10
67	John Wetteland	.10
68	Mark Grace	.25
69	Mark Kotsay	.15
70	Scott Rolen	.75
71	Todd Hundley	.15
72	Todd Worrell	.10
73	Wilson Alvarez	.10
74	Bobby Jones	.10
75	Jose Canseco	.40
76	Kevin Appier	.10
77	Neifi Perez	.10
78	Paul Molitor	.50
79	Quilvio Veras	.10
80	Randy Johnson	.75
81	Glendon Rusch	.10
82	Curt Schilling	.10
83	Alex Rodriguez	2.50
84	Rey Ordonez	.10
85	Jeff Juden	.10
86	Mike Cameron	.10
87	Ryan Klesko	.25
88	Trevor Hoffman	.10
89	Chuck Knoblauch	.25
90	Larry Walker	.30
91	Mark McLemore	.10
92	B.J. Surhoff	.10
93	Darren Daulton	.10
94	Ray Durham	.10
95	Sammy Sosa	1.50
96	Eric Young	.10
97	Gerald Williams	.10
98	Javy Lopez	.15
99	John Smiley	.10
100	Juan Gonzalez	.75
101	Shawn Green	.30
102	Charles Nagy	.10
103	David Justice	.25
104	Joey Hamilton	.10
105	Pat Hentgen	.10
106	Raul Casanova	.10
107	Tony Phillips	.10
108	Tony Gwynn	1.00
109	Will Clark	.25
110	Jason Giambi	.40
111	Jay Bell	.10
112	Johnny Damon	.10
113	Alan Benes	.10
114	Jeff Suppan	.10
115	*Kevin Polcovich*	.25
116	Shigetosi Hasegawa	.10
117	Steve Finley	.10
118	Tony Clark	.20
119	David Cone	.20
120	Jose Guillen	.15
121	*Kevin Millwood*	1.00
122	Greg Maddux	1.50
123	Dave Nilsson	.10
124	Hideki Irabu	.50
125	Jason Kendall	.10
126	Jim Thome	.40
127	Delino DeShields	.10
128	Edgar Renteria	.15
129	Edgardo Alfonzo	.20
130	J.T. Snow	.10
131	Jeff Abbott	.10
132	Jeffrey Hammonds	.10
133	Rich Loiselle	.10
134	Vladimir Guerrero	1.00
135	Jay Buhner	.20
136	Jeff Cirillo	.10
137	Jeromy Burnitz	.10
138	Mickey Morandini	.10
139	Tino Martinez	.25
140	Jeff Shaw	.10
141	Rafael Palmeiro	.30
142	Bobby Bonilla	.20
143	Cal Ripken Jr.	2.50
144	*Chad Fox*	.25
145	Dante Bichette	.20
146	Dennis Eckersley	.20
147	Mariano Rivera	.20
148	Mo Vaughn	.40
149	Reggie Sanders	.10
150	Derek Jeter	2.00
151	Rusty Greer	.20
152	Brady Anderson	.20
153	Brett Tomko	.10
154	Jaime Navarro	.10
155	Kevin Orie	.10
156	Roberto Alomar	.60
157	Edgar Martinez	.15
158	John Olerud	.20
159	John Smoltz	.15
160	Ryne Sandberg	.75
161	Billy Taylor	.10
162	Chris Holt	.10
163	Damion Easley	.10
164	Darin Erstad	.75
165	Joe Carter	.20
166	Kelvim Escobar	.10
167	Ken Caminiti	.15
168	Pokey Reese	.10
169	Ray Lankford	.10
170	Livan Hernandez	.15
171	Steve Kline	.10
172	Tom Gordon	.10
173	Travis Fryman	.20
174	Al Martin	.10
175	Andy Pettitte	.30
176	Jeff Kent	.10
177	Jimmy Key	.10
178	Mark Grudzielanek	.10
179	Tony Saunders	.15
180	Barry Larkin	.25
181	Bubba Trammell	.15
182	Carlos Delgado	.60
183	Carlos Baerga	.10
184	Derek Bell	.10
185	Henry Rodriguez	.10
186	Jason Dickson	.10
187	Ron Gant	.10
188	Tony Womack	.10
189	Justin Thompson	.10
190	Fernando Tatis	.20
191	Mark Wohlers	.10
192	Takashi Kashiwada	.25
193	Garret Anderson	.10
194	Jose Cruz, Jr.	.25
195	Ricardo Rincon	.10
196	Tim Naehring	.10
197	Moises Alou	.20
198	Eric Karros	.10
199	John Jaha	.10
200	Marty Cordova	.10
201	Travis Lee	.15
202	Mark Davis	.10
203	Vladimir Nunez	.10
204	Stanton Cameron	.10
205	*Mike Stoner*	1.00
206	*Rolando Arrojo*	.40
207	Rick White	.10
208	Luis Polonia	.10
209	Greg Blosser	.10
210	Cesar Devarez	.10
211	Jeff Bagwell (Season Crown)	2.50
212	Barry Bonds (Season Crown)	2.50
213	Roger Clemens (Season Crown)	4.00
214	Nomar Garciaparra (Season Crown)	6.00
215	Ken Griffey Jr. (Season Crown)	10.00
216	Tony Gwynn (Season Crown)	4.00

217 Randy Johnson (Season Crown) 1.50
218 Mark McGwire (Season Crown) 12.00
219 Scott Rolen (Season Crown) 2.00
220 Frank Thomas (Season Crown) 3.00
221 Matt Perisho (Prospect) .10
222 Wes Helms (Prospect) .75
223 *David Dellucci* (Prospect) 1.00
224 Todd Helton (Prospect) 3.00
225 Brian Rose (Prospect) .75
226 Aaron Boone (Prospect) .25
227 Keith Foulke (Prospect) .50
228 Homer Bush (Prospect) .40
229 Shannon Stewart (Prospect) .25
230 Richard Hidalgo (Prospect) .75
231 Russ Johnson (Prospect) .50
232 *Henry Blanco* (Prospect) .40
233 Paul Konerko (Prospect) .75
234 Antone Williamson (Prospect) .50
235 *Shane Bowers* (Prospect) .50
236 Jose Vidro (Prospect) .25
237 Derek Wallace (Prospect) .25
238 Ricky Ledee (Prospect) .75
239 Ben Grieve (Prospect) 1.50
240 Lou Collier (Prospect) .50
241 Derrek Lee (Prospect) .75
242 Ruben Rivera (Prospect) .50
243 Jorge Velandia (Prospect) .25
244 Andrew Vessel (Prospect) .40
245 Chris Carpenter (Prospect) .50
246 Checklist (Ken Griffey Jr.) 1.00
247 Checklist (Andruw Jones) .50
248 Checklist (Alex Rodriguez) 1.00
249 Checklist (Frank Thomas) .50
250 Checklist (Cal Ripken Jr.) 1.00
251 Carlos Perez .10
252 Larry Sutton .10
253 Brad Rigby .10
254 Wally Joyner .10
255 Todd Stottlemyre .10
256 Nerio Rodriguez .10
257 Jeff Frye .10
258 Pedro Astacio .10
259 Cal Eldred .10
260 Chili Davis .10
261 Freddy Garcia .10
262 Bobby Witt .10
263 Michael Coleman .10
264 Mike Caruso .10
265 Mike Lansing .10
266 Dennis Reyes .10
267 F.P. Santangelo .10
268 Darryl Hamilton .10
269 Mike Fetters .10
270 Charlie Hayes .10
271 Royce Clayton .10
272 Doug Drabek .10
273 James Baldwin .10
274 Brian Hunter .10
275 Chan Ho Park .20
276 John Franco .10
277 David Wells .10
278 Eli Marrero .10
279 Kerry Wood .40
280 Donnie Sadler .10
281 *Scott Winchester* .25
282 Hal Morris .10
283 Brad Fullmer .25
284 Bernard Gilkey .10
285 Ramiro Mendoza .10
286 Kevin Brown .20
287 David Segui .10
288 Willie McGee .10
289 Darren Oliver .10
290 Antonio Alfonseca .10
291 Eric Davis .10
292 Mickey Morandini .10
293 *Frank Catalanotto* .20
294 Derrek Lee .10
295 Todd Zeile .10
296 Chuck Knoblauch .25
297 Wilson Delgado .10
298 Raul Ibanez .10
299 Orel Hershiser .10
300 Ozzie Guillen .10
301 Aaron Sele .10
302 Joe Carter .20
303 Darryl Kile .10
304 Shane Reynolds .10
305 Todd Dunn .10
306 Bob Abreu .10
307 Doug Strange .10
308 Jose Canseco .40
309 Lance Johnson .10
310 Harold Baines .10
311 Todd Pratt .10
312 Greg Colbrunn .10
313 *Masato Yoshii* .40
314 Felix Heredia .10
315 Dennis Martinez .10
316 Geronimo Berroa .10
317 Darren Lewis .10
318 Billy Ripken .10
319 Enrique Wilson .10
320 Alex Ochoa .10
321 Doug Glanville .10
322 Mike Stanley .10
323 Gerald Williams .10
324 Pedro Martinez .75
325 Jaret Wright .15
326 Terry Pendleton .10
327 LaTroy Hawkins .10
328 Emil Brown .10
329 Walt Weiss .10
330 Omar Vizquel .10
331 Carl Everett .10
332 Fernando Vina .10
333 Mike Blowers .10
334 Dwight Gooden .20
335 Mark Lewis .10
336 Jim Leyritz .10
337 Kenny Lofton .40
338 *John Halama* .30
339 Jose Valentin .10
340 Desi Relaford .10
341 Dante Powell .10
342 Ed Sprague .10
343 Reggie Jefferson .10
344 Mike Hampton .10
345 Marquis Grissom .10
346 Heathcliff Slocumb .10
347 Francisco Cordova .10
348 Ken Cloude .10
349 Benito Santiago .10
350 Denny Neagle .10
351 Sean Casey .25
352 Robb Nen .10
353 Orlando Merced .10
354 Adrian Brown .10
355 Gregg Jefferies .10
356 Otis Nixon .10
357 Michael Tucker .10
358 Eric Milton .10
359 Travis Fryman .10
360 Gary DiSarcina .10
361 Mario Valdez .10
362 Craig Counsell .10
363 Jose Offerman .10
364 Tony Fernandez .10
365 Jason McDonald .10
366 Sterling Hitchcock .10
367 Donovan Osborne .10
368 Troy Percival .10
369 Henry Rodriguez .10
370 Dmitri Young .10
371 Jay Powell .10
372 Jeff Conine .10
373 Orlando Cabrera .10
374 Butch Huskey .10
375 *Mike Lowell* .40
376 Kevin Young .10
377 Jamie Moyer .10
378 Jeff D'Amico .10
379 Scott Erickson .10
380 *Magglio Ordonez* 2.00
381 Melvin Nieves .10
382 Ramon Martinez .20
383 A.J. Hinch .15
384 Jeff Brantley .10
385 Kevin Elster .10
386 Allen Watson .10
387 Moises Alou .20
388 Jeff Blauser .10
389 Pete Harnisch .10
390 Shane Andrews .10
391 Rico Brogna .10
392 Stan Javier .10
393 David Howard .10
394 Darryl Strawberry .20
395 Kent Mercker .10
396 Juan Encarnacion .10
397 Sandy Alomar .20
398 Al Leiter .20
399 Tony Graffanino .10
400 Terry Adams .10
401 Bruce Aven .10
402 Derrick Gibson .10
403 Jose Cabrera .10
404 Rich Becker .10
405 David Ortiz .10
406 Brian McRae .10
407 Bobby Estalella .10
408 Bill Mueller .10
409 Dennis Eckersley .20
410 Sandy Martinez .10
411 Jose Vizcaino .10
412 Jermaine Allensworth .10
413 Miguel Tejada .20
414 Turner Ward .10
415 Glenallen Hill .10
416 Lee Stevens .10
417 Cecil Fielder .15
418 Ruben Sierra .10
419 Jon Nunnally .10
420 Rod Myers .10
421 Dustin Hermanson .10
422 James Mouton .10
423 Dan Wilson .10
424 Roberto Kelly .10
425 Antonio Osuna .10
426 Jacob Cruz .10
427 Brent Mayne .10
428 Matt Karchner .10
429 Damian Jackson .10
430 Roger Cedeno .10
431 Rickey Henderson .40
432 Joe Randa .10
433 Greg Vaughn .10
434 Andres Galarraga .40
435 Rod Beck .10
436 Curtis Goodwin .10
437 Brad Ausmus .10
438 Bob Hamelin .10
439 Todd Walker .10
440 Scott Brosius .10
441 Lenny Dykstra .10
442 Abraham Nunez .10
443 Brian Johnson .10
444 Randy Myers .10
445 Bret Boone .10
446 Oscar Henriquez .10
447 Mike Sweeney .10
448 Kenny Rogers .10
449 Mark Langston .10
450 Luis Gonzalez .10
451 John Burkett .10
452 Bip Roberts .10
453 Travis Lee (New Horizons) .40
454 Felix Rodriguez (New Horizons) .10
455 Andy Benes (New Horizons) .10
456 Willie Blair (New Horizons) .10
457 Brian Anderson (New Horizons) .10
458 Jay Bell (New Horizons) .10
459 Matt Williams (New Horizons) .25
460 Devon White (New Horizons) .10
461 Karim Garcia (New Horizons) .10
462 Jorge Fabregas (New Horizons) .10
463 Wilson Alvarez (New Horizons) .10
464 Roberto Hernandez (New Horizons) .10
465 Tony Saunders (New Horizons) .10
466 *Rolando Arrojo* (New Horizons) .40
467 Wade Boggs (New Horizons) .25
468 Fred McGriff (New Horizons) .25
469 Paul Sorrento (New Horizons) .10
470 Kevin Stocker (New Horizons) .10
471 Bubba Trammell (New Horizons) .25
472 Quinton McCracken (New Horizons) .10
473 Checklist (Ken Griffey Jr.) 1.00
474 Checklist (Cal Ripken Jr.) .75
475 Checklist (Frank Thomas) .40
476 Ken Griffey Jr. (Pizzazz) 6.00
477 Cal Ripken Jr. (Pizzazz) 5.00
478 Frank Thomas (Pizzazz) 2.00
479 Alex Rodriguez (Pizzazz) 5.00
480 Nomar Garciaparra (Pizzazz) 4.00
481 Derek Jeter (Pizzazz) 5.00
482 Andruw Jones (Pizzazz) 1.50
483 Chipper Jones (Pizzazz) 4.00
484 Greg Maddux (Pizzazz) 3.00
485 Mike Piazza (Pizzazz) 4.00
486 Juan Gonzalez (Pizzazz) 1.50
487 Jose Cruz (Pizzazz) .75
488 Jaret Wright (Pizzazz) .75
489 Hideo Nomo (Pizzazz) .75
490 Scott Rolen (Pizzazz) 1.50
491 Tony Gwynn (Pizzazz) 2.50
492 Roger Clemens (Pizzazz) 2.00
493 Darin Erstad (Pizzazz) .75
494 Mark McGwire (Pizzazz) 8.00
495 Jeff Bagwell (Pizzazz) 1.50
496 Mo Vaughn (Pizzazz) 1.00
497 Albert Belle (Pizzazz) 1.00
498 Kenny Lofton (Pizzazz) .75
499 Ben Grieve (Pizzazz) 1.00
500 Barry Bonds (Pizzazz) 1.50
501 Mike Piazza (mets) 3.00

1998 Ultra Gold Medallion

This parallel to the Ultra set is found seeded on a one per pack ratio. Cards are similar to the regular-issue Ultra except for a gold presentation of the embossed player name on front and a shower of gold specks in the photo background. Backs have a "G" suffix to the card number and a "GOLD MEDALLION EDITION" notation at bottom. The short-printed subset cards from the regular Ultra edition are not short-printed in Gold Medallion.

	MT
Complete Set (501):	300.00
Common Player:	.25
Stars/RCs:	2X
Checklists:	3X
Season Crowns: 50%	
Prospects: 50%	
Pizzazz:	1X

(See 1998 Ultra for checklist and base card values.)

1998 Ultra Platinum Medallion

Insertion odds on this super-scarce insert set are not given but each card is produced and serially numbered in an edition of only 100. Fronts are similar to regular Ultra cards except the photo is black-and-white and the name is rendered in silver prismatic foil. Backs are in color with the serial number printed in silver foil at bottom. Series 2 checklist cards #473-475 were never printed in the Platinum Medallion edition.

	MT
Common Player:	6.00
Stars/RCs:	30X
Checklists:	3X
Season Crowns:	6X
Prospects:	8X
Pizzazz:	8X

(See 1998 Ultra for checklist and base card values.)

1998 Ultra Artistic Talents

This 18-card insert featured top players in the game on a canvas-like surface with the insert name in silver holographic letters across the top. The backs are done in black and white and numbered with an "AT" suffix. Artistic Talents are inserted one per eight packs.

		MT
Complete Set (18):		60.00
Common Player:		1.50
Inserted 1:8		
1	Ken Griffey Jr.	8.00
2	Andruw Jones	2.00
3	Alex Rodriguez	6.00
4	Frank Thomas	4.00
5	Cal Ripken Jr.	6.00
6	Derek Jeter	5.00
7	Chipper Jones	5.00
8	Greg Maddux	4.00
9	Mike Piazza	5.00
10	Albert Belle	1.50
11	Darin Erstad	1.50
12	Juan Gonzalez	2.50
13	Jeff Bagwell	3.00
14	Tony Gwynn	4.00
15	Mark McGwire	8.00
16	Scott Rolen	2.00
17	Barry Bonds	2.00
18	Kenny Lofton	1.50

1998 Ultra Back to the Future

This 15-card insert was printed in a horizontal format with a baseball field background. Cards were numbered with a "BF" suffix and seeded one per six packs.

		MT
Complete Set (15):		15.00
Common Player:		.40
Inserted 1:6		
1	Andruw Jones	.75
2	Alex Rodriguez	5.00
3	Derek Jeter	3.00
4	Darin Erstad	.60
5	Mike Cameron	.40
6	Scott Rolen	1.50
7	Nomar Garciaparra	3.00
8	Hideki Irabu	.60
9	Jose Cruz, Jr.	.40
10	Vladimir Guerrero	2.00
11	Mark Kotsay	.60
12	Tony Womack	.40
13	Jason Dickson	.40
14	Jose Guillen	.60
15	Tony Clark	.75

1998 Ultra Big Shots

Big Shots was a 15-card insert displaying some of the top home run hitters in baseball. A generic stadium is pictured across the bottom with the insert name running up the left side. Cards were numbered with a "BS" suffix and inserted one per four Series I packs.

		MT
Complete Set (15):		10.00
Common Player:		.25
Inserted 1:4		
1	Ken Griffey Jr.	3.00
2	Frank Thomas	1.00
3	Chipper Jones	2.00
4	Albert Belle	.60
5	Juan Gonzalez	1.00
6	Jeff Bagwell	.75
7	Mark McGwire	3.00
8	Barry Bonds	.75
9	Manny Ramirez	.75
10	Mo Vaughn	.50
11	Matt Williams	.35
12	Jim Thome	.25
13	Tino Martinez	.25
14	Mike Piazza	2.00
15	Tony Clark	.25

1998 Ultra Diamond Immortals

This Series II insert showcased 15 top player on an intricate silver holographic foil design that frames each player. Cards were numbered with a "DI" suffix and inserted one per 288 packs.

		MT
Complete Set (15):		400.00
Common Player:		7.50
Inserted 1:288		
1	Ken Griffey Jr.	50.00
2	Frank Thomas	20.00
3	Alex Rodriguez	50.00
4	Cal Ripken Jr.	50.00
5	Mike Piazza	40.00
6	Mark McGwire	60.00
7	Greg Maddux	30.00
8	Andruw Jones	15.00
9	Chipper Jones	30.00
10	Derek Jeter	50.00
11	Tony Gwynn	20.00
12	Juan Gonzalez	15.00
13	Jose Cruz	7.50
14	Roger Clemens	20.00
15	Barry Bonds	15.00

1998 Ultra Diamond Producers

This 15-card insert captured players on a prismatic silver design, with a wood backdrop and a black felt frame around the border. Cards were seeded one per 288 Series I packs and numbered with a "DP" suffix.

		MT
Complete Set (15):		300.00
Common Player:		7.50
Inserted 1:288		
1	Ken Griffey Jr.	50.00
2	Andruw Jones	15.00
3	Alex Rodriguez	50.00
4	Frank Thomas	20.00
5	Cal Ripken Jr.	50.00
6	Derek Jeter	50.00
7	Chipper Jones	30.00
8	Greg Maddux	30.00
9	Mike Piazza	40.00
10	Juan Gonzalez	15.00
11	Jeff Bagwell	15.00
12	Tony Gwynn	20.00
13	Mark McGwire	60.00
14	Barry Bonds	15.00
15	Jose Cruz, Jr.	7.50

1998 Ultra Double Trouble

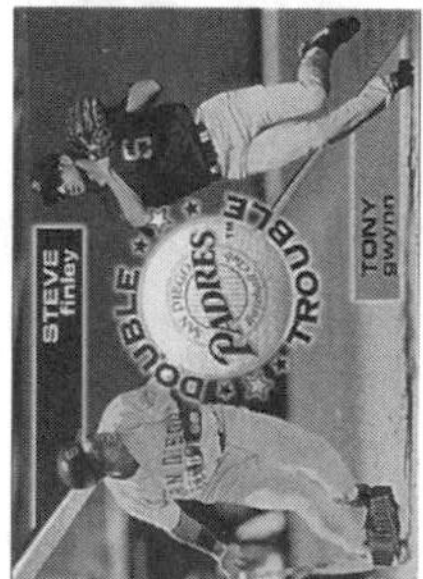

Double Trouble includes 20 cards and pairs two teammates on a horizontal format with the team's logo and the insert name featured in a silver holographic circle in the middle. These were numbered with a "DT" suffix and exclusive to Series I packs at a rate of one per four.

		MT
Complete Set (20):		10.00
Common Player:		.15
Inserted 1:4		
1	Ken Griffey Jr., Alex Rodriguez	2.00
2	Vladimir Guerrero, Pedro Martinez	.75
3	Andruw Jones, Kenny Lofton	.50
4	Chipper Jones, Greg Maddux	1.00

5	Derek Jeter, Tino Martinez	1.00
6	Frank Thomas, Albert Belle	.75
7	Cal Ripken Jr., Roberto Alomar	1.25
8	Mike Piazza, Hideo Nomo	.75
9	Darin Erstad, Jason Dickson	.15
10	Juan Gonzalez, Ivan Rodriguez	.75
11	Jeff Bagwell, Darryl Kile	.75
12	Tony Gwynn, Steve Finley	.75
13	Mark McGwire, Ray Lankford	2.00
14	Barry Bonds, Jeff Kent	.50
15	Andy Pettitte, Bernie Williams	.25
16	Mo Vaughn, Nomar Garciaparra	1.00
17	Matt Williams, Jim Thome	.15
18	Hideki Irabu, Mariano Rivera	.25
19	Roger Clemens, Jose Cruz, Jr.	.75
20	Manny Ramirez, David Justice	.60

1998 Ultra Fall Classics

This Series I insert pictures 15 stars over a green holographic bacground that contains the insert name in script. Fall Classics were inserted one per 18 packs and numbered with a "FC" suffix.

		MT
Complete Set (15):		100.00
Common Player:		3.00
Inserted 1:18		
1	Ken Griffey Jr.	15.00
2	Andruw Jones	4.00
3	Alex Rodriguez	12.00
4	Frank Thomas	7.50
5	Cal Ripken Jr.	12.00
6	Derek Jeter	10.00
7	Chipper Jones	10.00
8	Greg Maddux	8.00
9	Mike Piazza	10.00
10	Albert Belle	3.00
11	Juan Gonzalez	4.00
12	Jeff Bagwell	4.00
13	Tony Gwynn	8.00
14	Mark McGwire	15.00
15	Barry Bonds	4.00

1998 Ultra Kid Gloves

Kid Gloves featured top fielders in the game over an embossed glove background. Exclusive to Series I packs, they were inserted in one per eight packs and numbered with a "KG" suffix.

		MT
Complete Set (12):		15.00
Common Player:		.50
Inserted 1:8		
1	Andruw Jones	1.25
2	Alex Rodriguez	4.00
3	Derek Jeter	3.00
4	Chipper Jones	3.00
5	Darin Erstad	.75
6	Todd Walker	.50
7	Scott Rolen	1.50
8	Nomar Garciaparra	3.00
9	Jose Cruz, Jr.	.50
10	Charles Johnson	.50
11	Rey Ordonez	.50
12	Vladimir Guerrero	2.00

1998 Ultra Power Plus

This 10-card insert was exclusive to Series I packs and seeded one per 36 packs. Cards pictured the player over an embossed blue background featuring plus signs. These were numbered with a "PP" suffix.

		MT
Complete Set (10):		75.00
Common Player:		3.00
Inserted 1:36		
1	Ken Griffey Jr.	25.00
2	Andruw Jones	6.00
3	Alex Rodriguez	20.00
4	Frank Thomas	8.00
5	Mike Piazza	10.00
6	Albert Belle	4.00
7	Juan Gonzalez	8.00
8	Jeff Bagwell	6.00
9	Barry Bonds	6.00
10	Jose Cruz, Jr.	3.00

1998 Ultra Prime Leather

This 18-card insert features top fielders on a leather-like card stock, with a large baseball in the background. Cards are seeded one per 144 Series I packs and numbered with a "PL" suffix.

		MT
Complete Set (18):		350.00
Common Player:		8.00
Inserted 1:144		
1	Ken Griffey Jr.	50.00
2	Andruw Jones	10.00
3	Alex Rodriguez	50.00
4	Frank Thomas	20.00
5	Cal Ripken Jr.	50.00
6	Derek Jeter	40.00
7	Chipper Jones	30.00
8	Greg Maddux	30.00
9	Mike Piazza	40.00
10	Albert Belle	10.00
11	Darin Erstad	10.00
12	Juan Gonzalez	15.00
13	Jeff Bagwell	15.00
14	Tony Gwynn	20.00
15	Roberto Alomar	12.00
16	Barry Bonds	15.00
17	Kenny Lofton	8.00
18	Jose Cruz, Jr.	8.00

1998 Ultra Millennium Men

Millennium Men was a 15-card hobby-only insert exclusive to Series II packs. These tri-fold cards featured an embossed wax seal design and could be unfolded to reveal another shot of the player, team logo and statistics. They were numbered with a "MM" suffix and inserted every 35 packs.

		MT
Complete Set (15):		125.00
Common Player:		3.00
Inserted 1:35		
1	Jose Cruz	3.00
2	Ken Griffey Jr.	20.00
3	Cal Ripken Jr.	20.00
4	Derek Jeter	15.00
5	Andruw Jones	5.00
6	Alex Rodriguez	20.00
7	Chipper Jones	12.00
8	Scott Rolen	5.00
9	Nomar Garciaparra	15.00
10	Frank Thomas	8.00
11	Mike Piazza	15.00
12	Greg Maddux	12.00
13	Juan Gonzalez	6.00
14	Ben Grieve	4.00
15	Jaret Wright	3.00

1998 Ultra Notables

This 20-card insert pictured a player over a holographic background with either an American League or National League logo in the background. Notables were seeded one per four Series II packs and numbered with a "N" suffix.

		MT
Complete Set (20):		25.00
Common Player:		.50
Inserted 1:4		
1	Frank Thomas	1.50
2	Ken Griffey Jr.	5.00
3	Edgar Renteria	.50
4	Albert Belle	1.00
5	Juan Gonzalez	1.00
6	Jeff Bagwell	1.25
7	Mark McGwire	5.00
8	Barry Bonds	1.00
9	Scott Rolen	1.00
10	Mo Vaughn	.75
11	Andruw Jones	1.00
12	Chipper Jones	2.50
13	Tino Martinez	.50
14	Mike Piazza	2.50
15	Tony Clark	.50
16	Jose Cruz	.50
17	Nomar Garciaparra	2.50
18	Cal Ripken Jr.	3.50
19	Alex Rodriguez	4.00
20	Derek Jeter	2.50

1998 Ultra Rocket to Stardom

This 15-card insert set was exclusive to Series II packs and inserted in one per 20 packs. Cards were in black-and- white and were die-cut and embossed. The insert contained a collection of top young stars and was numbered with a "RS" suffix.

		MT
Complete Set (15):		25.00
Common Player:		1.00
Inserted 1:20		
1	Ben Grieve	3.00
2	Magglio Ordonez	8.00
3	Travis Lee	1.50
4	Carl Pavano	1.00
5	Brian Rose	1.00
6	Brad Fullmer	1.50
7	Michael Coleman	1.00
8	Juan Encarnacion	1.00
9	Karim Garcia	1.00
10	Todd Helton	4.00
11	Richard Hildalgo	1.00
12	Paul Konerko	1.50
13	Rod Myers	1.00
14	Jaret Wright	1.50
15	Miguel Tejada	2.00

1998 Ultra Ticket Studs

Fifteen players are featured on fold-out game ticket-like cards in Ticket Studs. The cards arrived folded across the middle and open to reveal a full-length shot of the player with prismatic team color stipes in over a white background that has section, seat and row numbers. Cards were inserted one per 144 Series II packs and are numbered with a "TS" suffix.

		MT
Complete Set (15):		400.00
Common Player:		5.00
Inserted 1:144		
1	Travis Lee	5.00
2	Tony Gwynn	20.00
3	Scott Rolen	12.00
4	Nomar Garciaparra	40.00
5	Mike Piazza	40.00
6	Mark McGwire	60.00
7	Ken Griffey Jr.	50.00
8	Juan Gonzalez	15.00
9	Jose Cruz	5.00
10	Frank Thomas	20.00
11	Derek Jeter	50.00
12	Chipper Jones	30.00
13	Cal Ripken Jr.	50.00
14	Andruw Jones	15.00
15	Alex Rodriguez	50.00

1998 Ultra Win Now

This Series II insert has 20 top players printed on plastic card stock, with a color shot of the player on the left side and a close-up shot on the right with black lines through it. Win Now cards were seeded one per 72 packs and numbered with a "WN" suffix.

		MT
Complete Set (20):		300.00
Common Player:		5.00
Inserted 1:72		
1	Alex Rodriguez	30.00
2	Andruw Jones	10.00
3	Cal Ripken Jr.	30.00
4	Chipper Jones	20.00
5	Darin Erstad	6.00
6	Derek Jeter	30.00
7	Frank Thomas	15.00
8	Greg Maddux	20.00
9	Hideo Nomo	5.00
10	Jeff Bagwell	12.00
11	Jose Cruz	5.00
12	Juan Gonzalez	10.00
13	Ken Griffey Jr.	30.00
14	Mark McGwire	40.00
15	Mike Piazza	25.00
16	Mo Vaughn	6.00
17	Nomar Garciaparra	25.00
18	Roger Clemens	15.00
19	Scott Rolen	8.00
20	Tony Gwynn	15.00

1998 Ultra Top 30

		MT
Complete Set (30):		30.00
Common Player:		.25
Inserted 1:1 R		
1	Barry Bonds	1.00
2	Ivan Rodriguez	1.00
3	Kenny Lofton	.75
4	Albert Belle	1.00
5	Mo Vaughn	.75
6	Jeff Bagwell	1.25
7	Mark McGwire	4.00
8	Darin Erstad	.50
9	Roger Clemens	1.50
10	Tony Gwynn	2.00
11	Scott Rolen	1.00
12	Hideo Nomo	.40
13	Juan Gonzalez	1.00
14	Mike Piazza	2.50
15	Greg Maddux	2.00
16	Chipper Jones	2.50
17	Andruw Jones	.75
18	Derek Jeter	2.50
19	Nomar Garciaparra	2.50
20	Alex Rodriguez	3.00
21	Frank Thomas	1.50
22	Cal Ripken Jr.	3.00
23	Ken Griffey Jr.	4.00
24	Jose Cruz Jr.	.25
25	Jaret Wright	.50
26	Travis Lee	.50
27	Wade Boggs	.40
28	Chuck Knoblauch	.25
29	Joe Carter	.25
30	Ben Grieve	.75

1999 Ultra

Base cards feature the full career stats by year in 15 categories and career highlights. There are short-printed subsets including Season Crowns (216-225) found 1:8 packs and Prospects (226-250) found 1:4 packs. Card fronts feature full bleed photography, and metallic foil stamping. There are three parallel versions Gold Medallion seeded 1 per pack with Prospects 1:40 and Season Crowns 1:80. Platinum Medallions are numbered to 99 with Prospects numbered to 65 and Season Crowns numbered to 50 sets. One of One Masterpiece parallels also exist. Packs consist of 10 cards with a SRP of $2.69.

		MT
Complete Set (250):		80.00
Common Player:		.10
Common Season Crown:		.50
Inserted 1:8		
Common Prospect:		.25
Inserted 1:4		
Pack (10):		3.00
Wax Box (24):		60.00
1	Greg Maddux	1.50
2	Greg Vaughn	.20
3	John Wetteland	.10
4	Tino Martinez	.20
5	Todd Walker	.10
6	Troy O'Leary	.10
7	Barry Larkin	.30
8	Mike Lansing	.10
9	Delino DeShields	.10
10	Brett Tomko	.10
11	Carlos Perez	.10
12	Mark Langston	.10
13	Jamie Moyer	.10
14	Jose Guillen	.10
15	Bartolo Colon	.10
16	Brady Anderson	.15
17	Walt Weiss	.10
18	Shane Reynolds	.15
19	David Segui	.10
20	Vladimir Guerrero	1.00
21	Freddy Garcia	.10
22	Carl Everett	.15
23	Jose Cruz Jr.	.20
24	David Ortiz	.10
25	Andruw Jones	.50
26	Darren Lewis	.10
27	Ray Lankford	.10
28	Wally Joyner	.10
29	Charles Johnson	.10
30	Derek Jeter	2.50
31	Sean Casey	.25
32	Bobby Bonilla	.15
33	Todd Zelle	.10
34	Todd Helton	.75
35	David Wells	.10
36	Darin Erstad	.40
37	Ivan Rodriguez	.75
38	Antonio Osuna	.10
39	Mickey Morandini	.10
40	Rusty Greer	.10
41	Rod Beck	.10
42	Larry Sutton	.10
43	Edgar Renteria	.10
44	Otis Nixon	.10
45	Eli Marrero	.10
46	Reggie Jefferson	.10
47	Trevor Hoffman	.10
48	Andres Galarraga	.40
49	Scott Brosius	.10
50	Vinny Castilla	.15
51	Bret Boone	.10
52	Masato Yoshii	.10
53	Matt Williams	.25
54	Robin Ventura	.20
55	Jay Powell	.10
56	Dean Palmer	.15
57	Eric Milton	.10
58	Willie McGee	.10
59	Tony Gwynn	1.00
60	Tom Gordon	.10
61	Dante Bichette	.20
62	Jaret Wright	.10
63	Devon White	.10
64	Frank Thomas	1.00
65	Mike Piazza	2.00
66	Jose Offerman	.10
67	Pat Meares	.10
68	Brian Meadows	.10
69	Nomar Garciaparra	2.00
70	Mark McGwire	3.00
71	Tony Graffanino	.10
72	Ken Griffey Jr.	2.50
73	Ken Caminiti	.15
74	Todd Jones	.10
75	A.J. Hinch	.10
76	Marquis Grissom	.10
77	Jay Buhner	.15
78	Albert Belle	.40
79	Brian Anderson	.10
80	Quinton McCracken	.10
81	Omar Vizquel	.20
82	Todd Stottlemyre	.15
83	Cal Ripken Jr.	2.50
84	Magglio Ordonez	.25
85	John Olerud	.25
86	Hal Morris	.10
87	Derrek Lee	.10
88	Doug Glanville	.10
89	Marty Cordova	.10
90	Kevin Brown	.20
91	Kevin Young	.10
92	Rico Brogna	.10
93	Wilson Alvarez	.10
94	Bob Wickman	.10
95	Jim Thome	.50
96	Mike Mussina	.50
97	Al Leiter	.15
98	Travis Lee	.10
99	Jeff King	.10
100	Kerry Wood	.20
101	Cliff Floyd	.10
102	Jose Valentin	.10
103	Manny Ramirez	1.00
104	Butch Huskey	.10
105	Scott Erickson	.15
106	Ray Durham	.10

107	Johnny Damon	.10
108	Craig Counsell	.10
109	Rolando Arrojo	.10
110	Bob Abreu	.10
111	Tony Womack	.10
112	Mike Stanley	.10
113	Kenny Lofton	.40
114	Eric Davis	.15
115	Jeff Conine	.10
116	Carlos Baerga	.10
117	Rondell White	.20
118	Billy Wagner	.10
119	Ed Sprague	.10
120	Jason Schmidt	.10
121	Edgar Martinez	.15
122	Travis Fryman	.20
123	Armando Benitez	.10
124	Matt Stairs	.10
125	Roberto Hernandez	.10
126	Jay Bell	.10
127	Justin Thompson	.10
128	John Jaha	.10
129	Mike Caruso	.10
130	Miguel Tejada	.20
131	Geoff Jenkins	.20
132	Wade Boggs	.25
133	Andy Benes	.10
134	Aaron Sele	.10
135	Bret Saberhagen	.10
136	Mariano Rivera	.20
137	Neifi Perez	.10
138	Paul Konerko	.20
139	Barry Bonds	.75
140	Garret Anderson	.10
141	Bernie Williams	.50
142	Gary Sheffield	.25
143	Rafael Palmeiro	.40
144	Orel Hershiser	.10
145	Craig Biggio	.20
146	Dmitri Young	.10
147	Damion Easley	.10
148	Henry Rodriguez	.10
149	Brad Radke	.10
150	Pedro Martinez	.75
151	Mike Lieberthal	.10
152	Jim Leyritz	.10
153	Chuck Knoblauch	.15
154	Darryl Kile	.10
155	Brian Jordan	.10
156	Chipper Jones	1.50
157	Pete Harnisch	.10
158	Moises Alou	.20
159	Ismael Valdes	.10
160	Stan Javier	.10
161	Mark Grace	.25
162	Jason Giambi	.40
163	Chuck Finley	.10
164	Juan Encarnacion	.10
165	Chan Ho Park	.15
166	Randy Johnson	.75
167	J.T. Snow	.10
168	Tim Salmon	.25
169	Brian Hunter	.10
170	Rickey Henderson	.25
171	Cal Eldred	.10
172	Curt Schilling	.20
173	Alex Rodriguez	2.50
174	Dustin Hermanson	.10
175	Mike Hampton	.10
176	Shawn Green	.40
177	Roberto Alomar	.50
178	Sandy Alomar Jr.	.20
179	Larry Walker	.30
180	Mo Vaughn	.40
181	Raul Mondesi	.25
182	Hideki Irabu	.20
183	Jim Edmonds	.25
184	Shawn Estes	.10
185	Tony Clark	.15
186	Dan Wilson	.10
187	Michael Tucker	.10
188	Jeff Shaw	.10
189	Mark Grudzielanek	.10
190	Roger Clemens	1.00
191	Juan Gonzalez	.75
192	Sammy Sosa	1.50
193	Troy Percival	.10
194	Robb Nen	.10
195	Bill Mueller	.10
196	Ben Grieve	.30
197	Luis Gonzalez	.15
198	Will Clark	.25
199	Jeff Cirillo	.10
200	Scott Rolen	.50
201	Reggie Sanders	.10
202	Fred McGriff	.25
203	Denny Neagle	.10
204	Brad Fullmer	.15
205	Royce Clayton	.10
206	Jose Canseco	.60
207	Jeff Bagwell	1.00
208	Hideo Nomo	.25
209	Karim Garcia	.10
210	Kenny Rogers	.10
211	Checklist (Kerry Wood)	.25
212	Checklist (Alex Rodriguez)	1.00
213	Checklist (Cal Ripken Jr.)	1.00
214	Checklist (Frank Thomas)	.50
215	Checklist (Ken Griffey Jr.)	1.50
216	Alex Rodriguez (Season Crowns)	5.00
217	Greg Maddux (Season Crowns)	3.00
218	Juan Gonzalez (Season Crowns)	1.50
219	Ken Griffey Jr. (Season Crowns)	5.00
220	Kerry Wood (Season Crowns)	1.00
221	Mark McGwire (Season Crowns)	6.00
222	Mike Piazza (Season Crowns)	4.00
223	Rickey Henderson (Season Crowns)	.50
224	Sammy Sosa (Season Crowns)	3.00
225	Travis Lee (Season Crowns)	.50
226	Gabe Alvarez (Prospects)	.50
227	Matt Anderson (Prospects)	.50
228	Adrian Beltre (Prospects)	1.50
229	Orlando Cabrera (Prospects)	.25
230	Orlando Hernandez (Prospects)	1.00
231	Aramis Ramirez (Prospects)	.50
232	Troy Glaus (Prospects)	6.00
233	Gabe Kapler (Prospects)	2.00
234	Jeremy Giambi (Prospects)	.75
235	Derrick Gibson (Prospects)	.25
236	Carlton Loewer (Prospects)	.25
237	Mike Frank (Prospects)	.25
238	Carlos Guillen (Prospects)	.25
239	Alex Gonzalez (Prospects)	.25
240	Enrique Wilson (Prospects)	.25
241	J.D. Drew (Prospects)	2.00
242	Bruce Chen (Prospects)	.25
243	Ryan Minor (Prospects)	.50
244	Preston Wilson (Prospects)	.25
245	Josh Booty (Prospects)	.25
246	Luis Ordaz (Prospects)	.25
247	George Lombard (Prospects)	.50
248	Matt Clement (Prospects)	.25
249	Eric Chavez (Prospects)	1.00
250	Corey Koskie (Prospects)	.50

1999 Ultra Gold Medallion

The basic cards (#1-215) in this parallel set are found one per pack, while the short-printed versions are seen one per 40 packs (Prospects) or one per 80 packs (Season Crowns). Sharing the photos and format of the regular-issue cards, these inserts have a gold-foil background on front. On back, "GOLD MEDALLION EDITION" is printed in gold foil.

	MT
Common Player (1-215):	.50
Stars/RCs	2X
Season Crowns (216-225):	4X
Prospects (226-250):	3X

(See 1999 Ultra for checklist and base card values.)

1999 Ultra Platinum Medallion

The basic cards (#1-215) in this parallel set are found in an individually serial numbered edition of 99. The short-printed cards were released in editions of 65 (Prospects) and 50 (Season Crowns). Sharing the photos and format of the regular-issue cards, these inserts have a silver-foil background on front. On back, "PLATINUM MEDALLION" is printed in silver foil along with the serial number.

	MT
Common Player (1-215):	6.00
Stars/RCs:	30X
Season Crowns (216-225):	30X
Prospects (226-250):	6X

(See 1999 Ultra for checklist and base card values.)

1999 Ultra The Book On

This 20-card set features insider scouting reports on the game's best players, utilizing embossing and gold foil stamping. These are found 1:6 packs.

		MT
Complete Set (20):		35.00
Common Player:		.50
Inserted 1:6		
1	Kerry Wood	1.00
2	Ken Griffey Jr.	4.00
3	Frank Thomas	1.50
4	Albert Belle	.75
5	Juan Gonzalez	1.25
6	Jeff Bagwell	1.25
7	Mark McGwire	5.00
8	Barry Bonds	1.25
9	Andruw Jones	1.00
10	Mo Vaughn	.75
11	Scott Rolen	1.00
12	Travis Lee	.50
13	Tony Gwynn	1.50
14	Greg Maddux	2.50
15	Mike Piazza	3.00
16	Chipper Jones	2.50
17	Nomar Garciaparra	3.00
18	Cal Ripken Jr.	4.00
19	Derek Jeter	4.00
20	Alex Rodriguez	4.00

1999 Ultra Damage Inc.

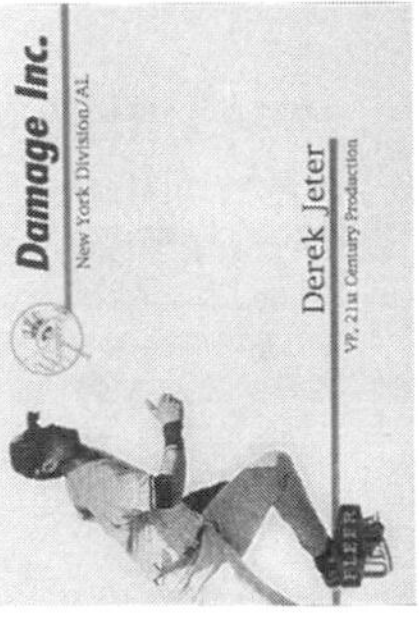

This 15-card insert set has a buisness card design, for players who mean business. These are seeded 1:72 packs.

		MT
Complete Set (15):		200.00
Common Player:		4.00
Inserted 1:72		
1	Alex Rodriguez	25.00
2	Greg Maddux	15.00
3	Cal Ripken Jr.	25.00
4	Chipper Jones	15.00
5	Derek Jeter	25.00
6	Frank Thomas	10.00
7	Juan Gonzalez	8.00
8	Ken Griffey Jr.	25.00
9	Kerry Wood	5.00
10	Mark McGwire	30.00
11	Mike Piazza	20.00
12	Nomar Garciaparra	20.00
13	Scott Rolen	6.00
14	Tony Gwynn	10.00
15	Travis Lee	4.00

1999 Ultra Diamond Producers

This die-cut set uses full-foil plastic with custom embossing. Baseball's biggest stars comprise this 10-card set, which are seeded 1:288 packs.

		MT
Complete Set (10):		325.00
Common Player:		10.00
Inserted 1:288		
1	Ken Griffey Jr.	50.00
2	Frank Thomas	20.00
3	Alex Rodriguez	50.00
4	Cal Ripken Jr.	50.00
5	Mike Piazza	40.00
6	Mark McGwire	60.00
7	Greg Maddux	30.00
8	Kerry Wood	10.00
9	Chipper Jones	30.00
10	Derek Jeter	40.00

1999 Ultra RBI Kings

Found exclusively in retail packs, this 30-card set showcases baseball's top run producers. These are seeded one per retail pack.

		MT
Complete Set (30):		25.00
Common Player:		.25
Inserted 1:1 R		
1	Rafael Palmeiro	.50
2	Mo Vaughn	.75
3	Ivan Rodriguez	1.00
4	Barry Bonds	1.00
5	Albert Belle	.75
6	Jeff Bagwell	1.50
7	Mark McGwire	4.00
8	Darin Erstad	.50
9	Manny Ramirez	1.50
10	Chipper Jones	2.50
11	Jim Thome	.40
12	Scott Rolen	1.00
13	Tony Gwynn	2.00
14	Juan Gonzalez	1.00
15	Mike Piazza	2.50
16	Sammy Sosa	3.00
17	Andruw Jones	.50
18	Derek Jeter	2.50
19	Nomar Garciaparra	2.50
20	Alex Rodriguez	3.00
21	Frank Thomas	1.50
22	Cal Ripken Jr.	3.00
23	Ken Griffey Jr.	4.00
24	Travis Lee	.40
25	Paul O'Neill	.25
26	Greg Vaughn	.25
27	Andres Galarraga	.50
28	Tino Martinez	.40
29	Jose Canseco	.75
30	Ben Grieve	.75

1999 Ultra Thunderclap

This set highlights the top hitters in the game, such as Nomar Garciaparra. Card fronts feature a lightning bolt in the background and are seeded 1:36 packs.

		MT
Complete Set (15):		100.00
Common Player:		2.00
Inserted 1:36		
1	Alex Rodriguez	12.00
2	Andruw Jones	4.00
3	Cal Ripken Jr.	12.00
4	Chipper Jones	8.00
5	Darin Erstad	3.00
6	Derek Jeter	12.00
7	Frank Thomas	5.00
8	Jeff Bagwell	4.00
9	Juan Gonzalez	4.00
10	Ken Griffey Jr.	12.00
11	Mark McGwire	15.00
12	Mike Piazza	10.00
13	Travis Lee	2.00
14	Nomar Garciaparra	10.00
15	Scott Rolen	3.00

1999 Ultra World Premiere

This 15-card set highlights rookies who made debuts in 1998, including J.D. Drew and Ben Grieve. These are seeded 1:18 packs.

		MT
Complete Set (15):		12.00
Common Player:		1.00
Inserted 1:18		
1	Gabe Alvarez	.75
2	Kerry Wood	1.50
3	Orlando Hernandez	2.00
4	Mike Caruso	.75
5	Matt Anderson	.75
6	Randall Simon	.75
7	Adrian Beltre	1.50
8	Scott Elarton	.75
9	Karim Garcia	.75
10	Mike Frank	.75
11	Richard Hidalgo	1.00
12	Paul Konerko	1.00
13	Travis Lee	.75
14	J.D. Drew	1.50
15	Miguel Tejada	1.00

2000 Ultra

The 300-card base set features a borderless design with silver holographic foil stamping on the card front. Card backs have an action image along with complete year-by-year statistics. The base set includes a 50-card short-printed Prospects (1:4) subset. A Masterpiece one-of-one parallel was produced.

		MT
Complete Set (300):		120.00
Common Player:		.10
Common Player (251-300):		.75
Inserted 1:4		
Pack (10):		3.00
Wax Box (24):		65.00
1	Alex Rodriguez	2.50
2	Shawn Green	.40
3	Magglio Ordonez	.40
4	Tony Gwynn	1.00
5	Joe McEwing	.10
6	Jose Rosado	.10
7	Sammy Sosa	1.50
8	Gary Sheffield	.30
9	Mickey Morandini	.10
10	Mo Vaughn	.40
11	Todd Hollandsworth	.10
12	Tom Gordon	.10
13	Charles Johnson	.10
14	Derek Bell	.10
15	Kevin Young	.10
16	Jay Buhner	.20
17	J.T. Snow	.10
18	Jay Bell	.10
19	John Rocker	.10
20	Ivan Rodriguez	.75
21	Pokey Reese	.10
22	Paul O'Neill	.20
23	Ronnie Belliard	.10
24	Ryan Rupe	.10
25	Travis Fryman	.20
26	Trot Nixon	.10
27	Wally Joyner	.10
28	Andy Pettitte	.25
29	Dan Wilson	.10
30	Orlando Hernandez	.25
31	Dmitri Young	.10
32	Edgar Renteria	.10
33	Eric Karros	.20
34	Fernando Seguignol	.10
35	Jason Kendall	.20
36	Jeff Shaw	.10
37	Matt Lawton	.10
38	Robin Ventura	.20
39	Scott Williamson	.10
40	Ben Grieve	.25
41	Billy Wagner	.10
42	Javy Lopez	.20
43	Joe Randa	.10
44	Neifi Perez	.10
45	David Justice	.40
46	Ray Durham	.10
47	Dustin Hermanson	.10
48	Andres Galarraga	.40
49	Brad Fullmer	.10
50	Nomar Garciaparra	2.00
51	David Cone	.20
52	David Nilsson	.10
53	David Wells	.10
54	Miguel Tejada	.10
55	Ismael Valdes	.10
56	Jose Lima	.10
57	Juan Encarnacion	.10
58	Fred McGriff	.25
59	Kenny Rogers	.10
60	Vladimir Guerrero	1.00
61	Benito Santiago	.10
62	Chris Singleton	.10
63	Carlos Lee	.10
64	Sean Casey	.20
65	Tom Goodwin	.10
66	Todd Hundley	.10
67	Ellis Burks	.10
68	Tim Hudson	.25
69	Matt Stairs	.10
70	Chipper Jones	1.50
71	Craig Biggio	.20
72	Brian Rose	.10
73	Carlos Delgado	.60
74	Eddie Taubensee	.10
75	John Smoltz	.20
76	Ken Caminiti	.20
77	Rafael Palmeiro	.50
78	Sidney Ponson	.10
79	Todd Helton	.75
80	Juan Gonzalez	.75
81	Bruce Aven	.10
82	Desi Relaford	.10
83	Johnny Damon	.10
84	Albert Belle	.50
85	Mark McGwire	3.00
86	Rico Brogna	.10
87	Tom Glavine	.25
88	Harold Baines	.10
89	Chad Allen	.10
90	Barry Bonds	.75
91	Mark Grace	.25
92	Paul Byrd	.10
93	Roberto Alomar	.50
94	Roberto Hernandez	.10
95	Steve Finley	.10
96	Bret Boone	.10
97	Charles Nagy	.10
98	Eric Chavez	.10
99	Jamie Moyer	.10
100	Ken Griffey Jr.	2.50
101	J.D. Drew	.25
102	Todd Stottlemyre	.10
103	Tony Fernandez	.10
104	Jeromy Burnitz	.10
105	Jeremy Giambi	.10
106	Livan Hernandez	.10
107	Marlon Anderson	.10
108	Troy Glaus	1.00
109	Troy O'Leary	.10
110	Scott Rolen	.50
111	Bernard Gilkey	.10
112	Brady Anderson	.20
113	Chuck Knoblauch	.20
114	Jeff Weaver	.20
115	B.J. Surhoff	.10
116	Alex Gonzalez	.10
117	Vinny Castilla	.10
118	Tim Salmon	.25
119	Brian Jordan	.10
120	Corey Koskie	.10
121	Dean Palmer	.10
122	Gabe Kapler	.25
123	Jim Edmonds	.20
124	John Jaha	.10
125	Mark Grudzielanek	.10
126	Mike Bordick	.10
127	Mike Lieberthal	.10
128	Pete Harnisch	.10
129	Russ Ortiz	.10
130	Kevin Brown	.20
131	Troy Percival	.10
132	Alex Gonzalez	.10
133	Bartolo Colon	.10
134	John Valentin	.10
135	Jose Hernandez	.10
136	Marquis Grissom	.10
137	Wade Boggs	.40
138	Dante Bichette	.25
139	Bobby Higginson	.10
140	Frank Thomas	1.00
141	Geoff Jenkins	.20
142	Jason Giambi	.40
143	Jeff Cirillo	.10
144	Sandy Alomar Jr.	.20

145 Luis Gonzalez .20
146 Preston Wilson .10
147 Carlos Beltran .10
148 Greg Vaughn .20
149 Carlos Febles .10
150 Jose Canseco .50
151 Kris Benson .10
152 Chuck Finley .10
153 Michael Barrett .10
154 Rey Ordonez .10
155 Adrian Beltre .25
156 Andruw Jones .50
157 Barry Larkin .40
158 Brian Giles .20
159 Carl Everett .10
160 Manny Ramirez .75
161 Darryl Kile .10
162 Edgar Martinez .15
163 Jeff Kent .10
164 Matt Williams .25
165 Mike Piazza 2.00
166 Pedro J. Martinez .75
167 Ray Lankford .10
168 Roger Cedeno .10
169 Ron Coomer .10
170 Cal Ripken Jr. 2.50
171 Jose Offerman .10
172 Kenny Lofton .30
173 Kent Bottenfield .10
174 Kevin Millwood .20
175 Omar Daal .10
176 Orlando Cabrera .10
177 Pat Hentgen .10
178 Tino Martinez .25
179 Tony Clark .20
180 Roger Clemens 1.00
181 Brad Radke .10
182 Darin Erstad .40
183 Jose Jimenez .10
184 Jim Thome .40
185 John Wetteland .10
186 Justin Thompson .10
187 John Hamala .10
188 Lee Stevens .10
189 Miguel Cairo .10
190 Mike Mussina .60
191 Raul Mondesi .20
192 Armando Rios .10
193 Trevor Hoffman .10
194 Tony Batista .10
195 Will Clark .40
196 Brad Ausmus .10
197 Chili Davis .10
198 Cliff Floyd .10
199 Curt Schilling .20
200 Derek Jeter 2.00
201 Henry Rodriguez .10
202 Jose Cruz Jr. .10
203 Omar Vizquel .20
204 Randy Johnson .75
205 Reggie Sanders .10
206 Al Leiter .20
207 Damion Easley .10
208 David Bell .10
209 Fernando Tatis .20
210 Kerry Wood .25
211 Kevin Appier .10
212 Mariano Rivera .25
213 Mike Caruso .10
214 Moises Alou .20
215 Randy Winn .10
216 Roy Halladay .10
217 Shannon Stewart .10
218 Todd Walker .10
219 Jim Parque .10
220 Travis Lee .10
221 Andy Ashby .10
222 Ed Sprague .10
223 Larry Walker .30
224 Rick Helling .10
225 Rusty Greer .10
226 Todd Zeile .10
227 Freddy Garcia .15
228 Hideo Nomo .40
229 Marty Cordova .10
230 Greg Maddux 1.50
231 Rondell White .20
232 Paul Konerko .20
233 Warren Morris .10
234 Bernie Williams .50
235 Bobby Abreu .10
236 John Olerud .25
237 Doug Glanville .10
238 Eric Young .10
239 Robb Nen .10
240 Jeff Bagwell .75
241 Sterling Hitchcock .10
242 Todd Greene .10
243 Bill Mueller .10
244 Rickey Henderson .25
245 Chan Ho Park .20
246 Jason Schmidt .10
247 Jeff Zimmerman .10
248 Jermaine Dye .10
249 Randall Simon .10
250 Richie Sexson .10
251 Micah Bowie .75
252 Joe Nathan .75
253 Chris Woodward .75
254 Lance Berkman .75
255 Ruben Mateo 1.00
256 Russell Branyan .75
257 Randy Wolf .75
258 A.J. Burnett 1.50
259 Mark Quinn 2.00
260 Buddy Carlyle .75
261 Ben Davis .75
262 Yamid Haad .75
263 Mike Colangelo .75
264 Rick Ankiel 10.00
265 Jacque Jones .75
266 Kelly Dransfeldt .75
267 Matt Riley .75
268 Adam Kennedy .75
269 Octavio Dotel .75
270 Francisco Cordero .75
271 Wilton Veras .75
272 Calvin Pickering .75
273 Alex Sanchez .75
274 Tony Armas, Jr. 1.00
275 Pat Burrell 8.00
276 Chad Meyers 1.00
277 Ben Petrick .75
278 Ramon Hernandez .75
279 Ed Yarnall 1.00
280 Erubiel Durazo .75
281 Vernon Wells .75
282 Gary Matthews .75
283 Kip Wells .75
284 Peter Bergeron 1.00
285 Travis Dawkins .75
286 Jorge Toca .75
287 Cole Liniak .75
288 Chad Hermansen .75
289 Eric Gagne .75
290 Chad Hutchinson .75
291 Eric Munson 1.50
292 (Wiki Gonzalez) .75
293 (Alfonso Soriano) 1.50
294 Trent Durrington .75
295 (Ben Molina) .75
296 Aaron Myette .75
297 (Willi Mo Pena) 2.00
298 Kevin Barker .75
299 (Geoff Blum) .75
300 Josh Beckett 4.00

2000 Ultra Gold Medallion

A parallel to the 300-card base set these have gold foil stamping over a metallic gold background. Cards 1-250 are seeded one per pack, Prospects 251-300 are seeded 1:24 packs. Card backs are numbered with a "G" suffix.

	MT
Stars:	2x
Young Stars:	1.5x
Inserted 1:1	
Prospects (251-300):	2x to 4x
Inserted 1:24	

(See 2000 Ultra for checklist and base card values.)

2000 Ultra Platinum Medallion

Platinum Medallion are a parallel to the 300-card base set and are die-cut like the Gold Medallion parallel inserts. Card fronts are stamped with silver foil over a metallic silver background. Card backs are serially numbered with cards 1-250 limited to 50 sets and Prospects limited to 25 numbered sets. Card backs are numbered with a "P" suffix.

	MT
Stars:	50x to 75x
Young Stars:	30x to 50x
Production 50 sets	
Prospects (251-300):	6x to 12x
Production 25 sets	

(See 2000 Ultra for checklist and base card values.)

2000 Ultra Club 3000

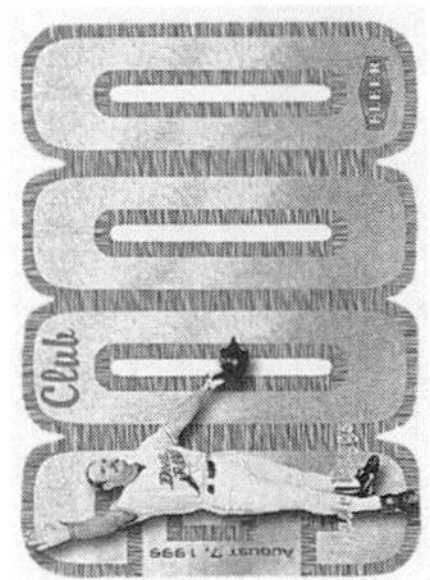

This three-card set is die-cut around the number 3,000 and commemorates 3,000 Hit Club members Wade Boggs, Tony Gwynn and Carl Yastrzemski. These were seeded 1:24 packs.

	MT
Complete Set (3):	10.00
Common Player:	3.00
Inserted 1:24	
Wade Boggs	4.00
Tony Gwynn	6.00
Carl Yastrzemski	3.00

2000 Ultra Club 3000 Memorabilia

Each featured player has a total of four different memorabilia-based inserts: hat, jersey, bat/jersey and bat/hat/jersey.

	MT
Common Card:	75.00
Wade Boggs bat (250)	90.00
Wade Boggs hat (100)	120.00
Wade Boggs jersey (440)	75.00
Wade Boggs bat/jersey (100)	150.00
W Boggs bat/hat/jersey (25)	400.00
Tony Gwynn bat (260)	150.00
Tony Gwynn hat (115)	200.00
Tony Gwynn jersey (450)	100.00
T Gwynn bat/jersey (100)	250.00
T Gwynn bat/jersey/hat (25)	700.00
C. Yaz (bat (250)	125.00
C. Yaz hat (100)	200.00
C. Yaz jersey (440)	100.00
C. Yaz bat/jersey (100)	200.00
C. Yaz bat/hat/jersey (25)	600.00

2000 Ultra Crunch Time

This 15-card insert set is printed on suede stock with gold-foil stamping. These were seeded 1:72 packs and numbered with a "CT" suffix on the card back.

		MT
Complete Set (15):		160.00
Common Player:		4.00
Inserted 1:72		
1	Nomar Garciaparra	15.00
2	Ken Griffey Jr.	20.00
3	Mark McGwire	25.00
4	Alex Rodriguez	20.00
5	Derek Jeter	20.00
6	Sammy Sosa	12.00
7	Mike Piazza	15.00
8	Cal Ripken Jr.	20.00
9	Frank Thomas	8.00
10	Juan Gonzalez	6.00
11	J.D. Drew	4.00
12	Greg Maddux	12.00
13	Tony Gwynn	8.00
14	Vladimir Guerrero	8.00
15	Ben Grieve	4.00

2000 Ultra Diamond Mine

These were printed on a silver-foil card front with Diamond Mine stamped in the background of the player image. These were inserted 1:6 packs and numbered with a "DM" suffix on the card back.

		MT
Complete Set (15):		25.00
Common Player:		1.00
Inserted 1:6		
1	Greg Maddux	2.00
2	Mark McGwire	4.00
3	Ken Griffey Jr.	3.00

4	Cal Ripken Jr.	3.00
5	Nomar Garciaparra	2.50
6	Mike Piazza	2.50
7	Alex Rodriguez	3.00
8	Frank Thomas	1.50
9	Juan Gonzalez	1.00
10	Derek Jeter	3.00
11	Tony Gwynn	1.50
12	Chipper Jones	2.00
13	Sammy Sosa	2.00
14	Roger Clemens	1.50
15	Vladimir Guerrero	1.50

2000 Ultra Feel the Game

These memorabilia-based inserts have a piece of game worn jersey or batting glove embedded into the card front.

	MT
Common Player:	25.00
Roberto Alomar	100.00
J.D. Drew	50.00
Tony Gwynn	100.00
Randy Johnson	75.00
Greg Maddux	120.00
Edgar Martinez	30.00
Pedro Martinez	100.00
Kevin Millwood	25.00
Cal Ripken Jr.	150.00
Alex Rodriguez	150.00
Scott Rolen	50.00
Curt Schilling	30.00
Chipper Jones	75.00
Frank Thomas	150.00
Robin Ventura	30.00

2000 Ultra Fresh Ink

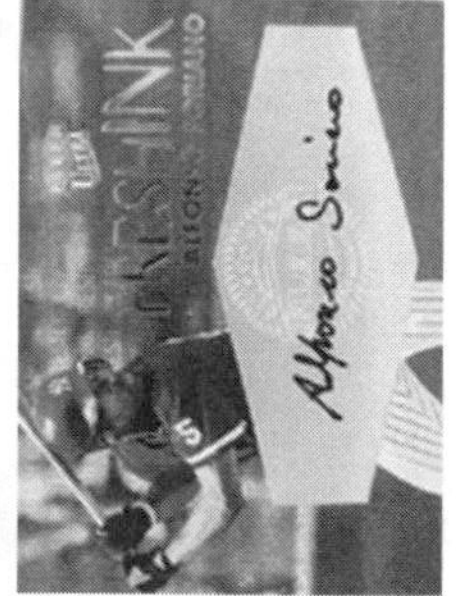

These autographed cards have the words "Fresh Ink" printed continually in the background image of the player. The signature is in a designated blank box intended for the autograph. Production numbers vary from player to player and are listed in parentheses after the player name.

		MT
	Common Player:	10.00
1	Bobby Abreu (400)	20.00
2	Chad Allen (1,000)	10.00
3	Marlon Anderson (1,000)	10.00
4	Glen Barker (1,000)	10.00
5	Michael Barrett (1,000)	10.00
6	Carlos Beltran (1,000)	20.00
7	Adrian Beltre (1,000)	20.00
8	Wade Boggs (250)	50.00
9	Barry Bonds (250)	75.00
10	Peter Bergeron (1,000)	10.00
11	Pat Burrell (500)	40.00
12	Roger Cedeno (500)	10.00
13	Eric Chavez (750)	20.00
14	Bruce Chen (600)	15.00
15	Johnny Damon (750)	15.00
16	Ben Davis (1,000)	10.00
17	Carlos Delgado (300)	50.00
18	Einar Diaz (1,000)	10.00
19	Octavio Dotel (1,000)	10.00
20	J.D. Drew (600)	40.00
21	Scott Elarton (1,000)	10.00
22	Freddy Garcia (500)	20.00
23	Jeremy Giambi (1,000)	10.00
24	Troy Glaus (500)	40.00
25	Shawn Green (350)	30.00
26	Tony Gwynn (250)	100.00
27	Richard Hidalgo (500)	15.00
28	Bobby Higginson (1,000)	10.00
29	Tim Hudson (1,000)	20.00
30	Norm Hutchins (1,000)	10.00
31	Derek Jeter (95)	300.00
32	Randy Johnson (150)	60.00
33	Gabe Kapler (750)	25.00
34	Jason Kendall (400)	20.00
35	Paul Konerko (500)	15.00
36	Matt Lawton (1,000)	10.00
37	Carlos Lee (1,000)	15.00
38	Jose Macias (1,000)	10.00
39	Greg Maddux (250)	160.00
40	Ruben Mateo (250)	20.00
41	Kevin Millwood (500)	15.00
42	Warren Morris (1,000)	10.00
43	Eric Munson (1,000)	20.00
44	Heath Murray (1,000)	10.00
45	Joe Nathan (1,000)	10.00
46	Magglio Ordonez (350)	20.00
47	Angel Pena (1,000)	10.00
48	Cal Ripken Jr. (350)	200.00
49	Alex Rodriguez (350)	150.00
50	Scott Rolen (250)	50.00
51	Ryan Rupe (1,000)	10.00
52	Curt Schilling (375)	20.00
53	Randall Simon (1,000)	10.00
54	Alfonso Soriano (1,000)	20.00
55	Shannon Stewart (300)	10.00
56	Miguel Tejada (1,000)	10.00
57	Frank Thomas (150)	140.00
58	Jeff Weaver (1,000)	15.00
59	Randy Wolf (1,000)	10.00
60	Ed Yarnall (1,000)	20.00
61	Kevin Young (1,000)	10.00
62	Tony Gwynn, Wade Boggs, Nolan Ryan (100)	700.00
63	Rick Ankiel (500)	75.00

2000 Ultra Swing Kings

Printed on a clear, plastic stock this 10-card set features the top hitters in the game. Card fronts also utilize silver-foil stamping. These were seeded 1:24 packs and are numbered on the card back with a "SK" suffix.

		MT
	Complete Set (10):	50.00
	Common Player:	3.00
	Inserted 1:24	
1	Cal Ripken Jr.	8.00
2	Nomar Garciaparra	6.00
3	Frank Thomas	3.00
4	Tony Gwynn	3.00
5	Ken Griffey Jr.	8.00
6	Chipper Jones	5.00
7	Mark McGwire	10.00
8	Sammy Sosa	5.00
9	Derek Jeter	8.00
10	Alex Rodriguez	8.00

2000 Ultra Ultra Talented

Available exclusively in hobby packs these were printed on a holofoil background with gold-foil stamping. Each card is serially numbered to 100 and are numbered on the card back with a "UT" suffix.

		MT
	Complete Set (10):	675.00
	Common Player:	15.00
	Production 100 sets	
1	Sammy Sosa	60.00
2	Derek Jeter	100.00
3	Alex Rodriguez	100.00
4	Mike Piazza	75.00
5	Ken Griffey Jr.	100.00
6	Nomar Garciaparra	75.00
7	Mark McGwire	120.00
8	Cal Ripken Jr.	100.00
9	Frank Thomas	40.00
10	J.D. Drew	15.00

2000 Ultra World Premiere

This insert set highlights ten young potential stars on a die-cut, silver-foil etched design. These were inserted 1:12 packs and are numbered with a "WP" suffix on the card back.

		MT
	Complete Set (10):	15.00
	Common Player:	.75
	Inserted 1:12	
1	Ruben Mateo	1.00
2	Lance Berkman	1.00
3	Octavio Dotel	.75
4	Joe McEwing	.75
5	Ben Davis	.75
6	Warren Morris	.75
7	Carlos Lee	.75
8	Rick Ankiel	8.00
9	Adam Kennedy	.75
10	Tim Hudson	3.00

1989 Upper Deck

This premiere "Collector's Choice" issue from Upper Deck contains 700 cards (2-1/2" x 3-1/2") with full-color photos on both sides. The first 26 cards feature Star Rookies. The set also includes 26 special portrait cards with team checklist backs and seven numberical checklist cards. Major 1988 award winners (Cy Young, Rookie of Year, MVP) are honored on 10 cards in the set, in addition to their individual player cards. There are also special cards for the Most Valuable Players in both League Championship series and the World Series. The card fronts feature player photos framed by a white border. A vertical brown and green artist's rendition of the runner's lane that leads from home plate to first base is found along the right margin. Backs carry full-color action poses that fill the card back, except for a compact (yet complete) stats chart. A high-number series, cards 701-800, featuring rookies and traded players, was released in mid-season in foil packs mixed within the complete set, in boxed complete sets and in high number set boxes.

	MT
Complete Set (800):	220.00
Unopened Fact. Set (800):	250.00
Complete Low Set (700):	210.00
Complete High Set (100):	15.00
Common Player:	.10
Low Foil Pack (15 - Final):	14.00
Low Foil Wax Box (36- Final):	360.00
High Foil Pack (15):	11.00
High Foil Wax Box (36):	250.00

1 *Ken Griffey, Jr.* 160.00
2 *Luis Medina* .10
3 *Tony Chance* .10
4 *Dave Otto* .10
5 *Sandy Alomar, Jr.* 1.50
6 *Rolando Roomes* .10
7 *David West* .10
8 *Cris Carpenter* .15
9 Gregg Jefferies .40
10 *Doug Dascenzo* .10
11 *Ron Jones* .10
12 *Luis de los Santos* .10
13a *Gary Sheffield* ("SS" upside-down) 6.00
13b *Gary Sheffield* ("SS" correct) 6.00
14 *Mike Harkey* .10
15 *Lance Blankenship* .15
16 *William Brennan* .10
17 John Smoltz .75
18 *Ramon Martinez* .75
19 *Mark Lemke* .20
20 *Juan Bell* .10
21 *Rey Palacios* .10
22 *Felix Jose* .15
23 *Van Snider* .10
24 *Dante Bichette* 2.00
25 *Randy Johnson* 15.00
26 *Carlos Quintana* .15
27 Star Rookie Checklist 1-26 .10
28 *Mike Schooler* .10
29 Randy St. Claire .10
30 *Jerald Clark* .15
31 Kevin Gross .10
32 *Dan Firova* .10
33 Jeff Calhoun .10
34 Tommy Hinzo .10
35 *Ricky Jordan* .20
36 Larry Parrish .10
37 Bret Saberhagen .15
38 Mike Smithson .10
39 Dave Dravecky .10
40 Ed Romero .10
41 Jeff Musselman .10
42 Ed Hearn .10
43 Rance Mulliniks .10
44 Jim Eisenreich .10
45 *Sil Campusano* .10
46 Mike Krukow .10
47 *Paul Gibson* .10
48 Mike LaCoss .10
49 Larry Herndon .10
50 Scott Garrelts .10
51 Dwayne Henry .10
52 Jim Acker .10
53 Steve Sax .10
54 Pete O'Brien .10
55 Paul Runge .10
56 Rick Rhoden .10
57 *John Dopson* .10
58 Casey Candaele .10
59 Dave Righetti .10
60 Joe Hesketh .10
61 Frank DiPino .10
62 Tim Laudner .10
63 Jamie Moyer .10
64 Fred Toliver .10
65 Mitch Webster .10
66 John Tudor .10
67 John Cangelosi .10
68 Mike Devereaux .10
69 Brian Fisher .10
70 Mike Marshall .10
71 Zane Smith .10
72a Brian Holton (ball not visible on card front, photo a ctually Shawn Hillegas) 1.50
72b Brian Holton (ball visible, correct photo) .10
73 Jose Guzman .10
74 Rick Mahler .10
75 John Shelby .10
76 Jim Deshaies .10
77 Bobby Meacham .10
78 Bryn Smith .10
79 Joaquin Andujar .10
80 Richard Dotson .10
81 Charlie Lea .10
82 Calvin Schiraldi .10
83 Les Straker .10
84 Les Lancaster .10
85 Allan Anderson .10
86 Junior Ortiz .10
87 Jesse Orosco .10
88 Felix Fermin .10
89 Dave Anderson .10
90 Rafael Belliard .10
91 Franklin Stubbs .10
92 Cecil Espy .10
93 Albert Hall .10
94 Tim Leary .10
95 Mitch Williams .10
96 Tracy Jones .10
97 Danny Darwin .10
98 Gary Ward .10
99 Neal Heaton .10
100 Jim Pankovits .10
101 Bill Doran .10
102 Tim Wallach .10
103 Joe Magrane .10
104 Ozzie Virgil .10
105 Alvin Davis .10
106 Tom Brookens .10
107 Shawon Dunston .10
108 Tracy Woodson .10
109 Nelson Liriano .10
110 Devon White .15
111 Steve Balboni .10
112 Buddy Bell .10
113 *German Jimenez* .10
114 Ken Dayley .10
115 Andres Galarraga .60
116 Mike Scioscia .10
117 Gary Pettis .10
118 Ernie Whitt .10
119 Bob Boone .10
120 Ryne Sandberg 1.00
121 Bruce Benedict .10
122 Hubie Brooks .10
123 Mike Moore .10
124 Wallace Johnson .10
125 Bob Horner .10
126 Chili Davis .10
127 Manny Trillo .10
128 Chet Lemon .10
129 John Cerutti .10
130 Orel Hershiser .10
131 Terry Pendleton .10
132 Jeff Blauser .10
133 Mike Fitzgerald .10
134 Henry Cotto .10
135 Gerald Young .10
136 Luis Salazar .10
137 Alejandro Pena .10
138 Jack Howell .10
139 Tony Fernandez .10
140 Mark Grace .60
141 Ken Caminiti 1.00
142 Mike Jackson .10
143 Larry McWilliams .10
144 Andres Thomas .10
145 Nolan Ryan 3.00
146 Mike Davis .10
147 DeWayne Buice .10
148 Jody Davis .10
149 Jesse Barfield .10
150 Matt Nokes .10
151 Jerry Reuss .10
152 Rick Cerone .10
153 Storm Davis .10
154 Marvell Wynne .10
155 Will Clark .75
156 Luis Aguayo .10
157 Willie Upshaw .10
158 Randy Bush .10
159 Ron Darling .10
160 Kal Daniels .10
161 Spike Owen .10
162 Luis Polonia .10
163 Kevin Mitchell .10
164 *Dave Gallagher* .10
165 Benito Santiago .10
166 Greg Gagne .10
167 Ken Phelps .10
168 Sid Fernandez .10
169 Bo Diaz .10
170 Cory Snyder .10
171 Eric Show .10
172 Robby Thompson .10
173 Marty Barrett .10
174 Dave Henderson .10
175 Ozzie Guillen .10
176 Barry Lyons .10
177 *Kelvin Torve* .10
178 Don Slaught .10
179 Steve Lombardozzi .10
180 *Chris Sabo* .20
181 Jose Uribe .10
182 Shane Mack .10
183 Ron Karkovice .10
184 Todd Benzinger .10
185 Dave Stewart .10
186 Julio Franco .10
187 Ron Robinson .10
188 Wally Backman .10
189 Randy Velarde .10
190 Joe Carter .20
191 Bob Welch .10
192 Kelly Paris .10
193 Chris Brown .10
194 Rick Reuschel .10
195 Roger Clemens 2.00
196 Dave Concepcion .10
197 Al Newman .10
198 Brook Jacoby .10
199 Mookie Wilson .10
200 Don Mattingly 1.50
201 Dick Schofield .10
202 Mark Gubicza .10
203 Gary Gaetti .10
204 Dan Pasqua .10
205 Andre Dawson .25
206 Chris Speier .10
207 Kent Tekulve .10
208 Rod Scurry .10
209 Scott Bailes .10
210 Rickey Henderson .50
211 Harold Baines .10
212 Tony Armas .10
213 Kent Hrbek .10
214 Darrin Jackson .10
215 George Brett 1.50
216 Rafael Santana .10
217 Andy Allanson .10
218 Brett Butler .10
219 Steve Jeltz .10
220 Jay Buhner .30
221 Bo Jackson .25
222 Angel Salazar .10
223 Kirk McCaskill .10
224 Steve Lyons .10
225 Bert Blyleven .10
226 Scott Bradley .10
227 Bob Melvin .10
228 Ron Kittle .10
229 Phil Bradley .10
230 Tommy John .10
231 Greg Walker .10
232 Juan Berenguer .10
233 Pat Tabler .10
234 *Terry Clark* .10
235 Rafael Palmeiro 1.00
236 Paul Zuvella .10
237 Willie Randolph .10
238 Bruce Fields .10
239 Mike Aldrete .10
240 Lance Parrish .10
241 Greg Maddux 3.00
242 John Moses .10
243 Melido Perez .10
244 Willie Wilson .10
245 Mark McLemore .10
246 Von Hayes .10
247 Matt Williams .75
248 John Candelaria .10
249 Harold Reynolds .10
250 Greg Swindell .10
251 Juan Agosto .10
252 Mike Felder .10
253 Vince Coleman .10
254 Larry Sheets .10
255 George Bell .10
256 Terry Steinbach .10
257 *Jack Armstrong* .10
258 Dickie Thon .10
259 Ray Knight .10
260 Darryl Strawberry .25
261 Doug Sisk .10
262 Alex Trevino .10
263 Jeff Leonard .10
264 Tom Henke .10
265 Ozzie Smith 1.00
266 Dave Bergman .10
267 Tony Phillips .10
268 Mark Davis .10
269 Kevin Elster .10
270 Barry Larkin .30
271 Manny Lee .10
272 Tom Brunansky .10
273 Craig Biggio 3.00
274 Jim Gantner .10
275 Eddie Murray .40
276 Jeff Reed .10
277 Tim Teufel .10
278 Rick Honeycutt .10
279 Guillermo Hernandez .10
280 John Kruk .10
281 *Luis Alicea* .20
282 Jim Clancy .10
283 Billy Ripken .10
284 Craig Reynolds .10
285 Robin Yount .50
286 Jimmy Jones .10
287 Ron Oester .10
288 Terry Leach .10
289 Dennis Eckersley .20
290 Alan Trammell .10
291 Jimmy Key .15
292 Chris Bosio .10
293 Jose DeLeon .10
294 Jim Traber .10
295 Mike Scott .10
296 Roger McDowell .10
297 Garry Templeton .10
298 Doyle Alexander .10
299 Nick Esasky .10
300 Mark McGwire 5.00
301 *Darryl Hamilton* .20
302 Dave Smith .10
303 Rick Sutcliffe .10
304 Dave Stapleton .10
305 Alan Ashby .10
306 Pedro Guerrero .10
307 Ron Guidry .10
308 Steve Farr .10
309 Curt Ford .10
310 Claudell Washington .10
311 Tom Prince .10
312 *Chad Kreuter* .15
313 Ken Oberkfell .10
314 Jerry Browne .10
315 R.J. Reynolds .10
316 Scott Bankhead .10
317 Milt Thompson .10
318 Mario Diaz .10
319 Bruce Ruffin .10
320 Dave Valle .10
321a *Gary Varsho* (batting righty on card back, photo actually Mike Bielecki) 2.00
321b *Gary Varsho* (batting lefty on card back, correct photo) .10
322 Paul Mirabella .10
323 Chuck Jackson .10
324 Drew Hall .10
325 Don August .10
326 *Israel Sanchez* .10
327 Denny Walling .10
328 Joel Skinner .10
329 Danny Tartabull .10
330 Tony Pena .10
331 Jim Sundberg .10
332 Jeff Robinson .10
333 Odibbe McDowell .10
334 Jose Lind .10
335 Paul Kilgus .10
336 Juan Samuel .10
337 Mike Campbell .10
338 Mike Maddux .10
339 Darnell Coles .10
340 Bob Dernier .10
341 Rafael Ramirez .10
342 Scott Sanderson .10

343 B.J. Surhoff .10
344 Billy Hatcher .10
345 Pat Perry .10
346 Jack Clark .10
347 Gary Thurman .10
348 *Timmy Jones* .10
349 Dave Winfield .25
350 Frank White .10
351 Dave Collins .10
352 Jack Morris .10
353 Eric Plunk .10
354 Leon Durham .10
355 Ivan DeJesus .10
356 *Brian Holman* .15
357a Dale Murphy (reversed negative) 25.00
357b Dale Murphy (corrected) .25
358 Mark Portugal .10
359 Andy McGaffigan .10
360 Tom Glavine 1.00
361 Keith Moreland .10
362 Todd Stottlemyre .20
363 Dave Leiper .10
364 Cecil Fielder .15
365 Carmelo Martinez .10
366 Dwight Evans .10
367 Kevin McReynolds .10
368 Rich Gedman .10
369 Len Dykstra .10
370 Jody Reed .10
371 Jose Canseco 1.00
372 Rob Murphy .10
373 Mike Henneman .10
374 Walt Weiss .10
375 *Rob Dibble* .15
376 Kirby Puckett 1.00
377 Denny Martinez .10
378 Ron Gant .30
379 Brian Harper .10
380 *Nelson Santovenia* .10
381 Lloyd Moseby .10
382 Lance McCullers .10
383 Dave Stieb .10
384 Tony Gwynn 1.50
385 Mike Flanagan .10
386 Bob Ojeda .10
387 Bruce Hurst .10
388 Dave Magadan .10
389 Wade Boggs .25
390 Gary Carter .15
391 Frank Tanana .10
392 Curt Young .10
393 Jeff Treadway .10
394 Darrell Evans .10
395 Glenn Hubbard .10
396 Chuck Cary .10
397 Frank Viola .10
398 Jeff Parrett .10
399 *Terry Blocker* .10
400 Dan Gladden .10
401 *Louie Meadows* .10
402 Tim Raines .15
403 Joey Meyer .10
404 Larry Andersen .10
405 Rex Hudler .10
406 Mike Schmidt 1.50
407 John Franco .10
408 Brady Anderson .75
409 Don Carman .10
410 Eric Davis .10
411 Bob Stanley .10
412 Pete Smith .10
413 Jim Rice .15
414 Bruce Sutter .10
415 Oil Can Boyd .10
416 Ruben Sierra .10
417 Mike LaValliere .10
418 Steve Buechele .10
419 Gary Redus .10
420 Scott Fletcher .10
421 Dale Sveum .10
422 Bob Knepper .10
423 Luis Rivera .10
424 Ted Higuera .10
425 Kevin Bass .10
426 Ken Gerhart .10
427 Shane Rawley .10
428 Paul O'Neill .25
429 Joe Orsulak .10
430 Jackie Gutierrez .10
431 Gerald Perry .10
432 Mike Greenwell .10
433 Jerry Royster .10
434 Ellis Burks .30
435 Ed Olwine .10
436 Dave Rucker .10
437 Charlie Hough .10
438 Bob Walk .10
439 Bob Brower .10
440 Barry Bonds 1.50
441 Tom Foley .10
442 Rob Deer .10
443 Glenn Davis .10
444 Dave Martinez .10
445 Bill Wegman .10
446 Lloyd McClendon .10
447 Dave Schmidt .10
448 Darren Daulton .10
449 Frank Williams .10
450 Don Aase .10
451 Lou Whitaker .10
452 Goose Gossage .10
453 Ed Whitson .10
454 Jim Walewander .10
455 Damon Berryhill .10
456 Tim Burke .10
457 Barry Jones .10
458 Joel Youngblood .10
459 Floyd Youmans .10
460 Mark Salas .10
461 Jeff Russell .10
462 Darrell Miller .10
463 Jeff Kunkel .10
464 *Sherman Corbett* .10
465 Curtis Wilkerson .10
466 Bud Black .10
467 Cal Ripken, Jr. 3.00
468 John Farrell .10
469 Terry Kennedy .10
470 Tom Candiotti .10
471 Roberto Alomar 1.50
472 Jeff Robinson .10
473 Vance Law .10
474 Randy Ready .10
475 Walt Terrell .10
476 Kelly Downs .10
477 *Johnny Paredes* .10
478 Shawn Hillegas .10
479 Bob Brenly .10
480 Otis Nixon .10
481 Johnny Ray .10
482 Geno Petralli .10
483 Stu Cliburn .10
484 Pete Incaviglia .10
485 Brian Downing .10
486 Jeff Stone .10
487 Carmen Castillo .10
488 Tom Niedenfuer .10
489 Jay Bell .10
490 Rick Schu .10
491 *Jeff Pico* .10
492 *Mark Parent* .15
493 Eric King .10
494 Al Nipper .10
495 Andy Hawkins .10
496 Daryl Boston .10
497 Ernie Riles .10
498 Pascual Perez .10
499 Bill Long .10
500 Kirt Manwaring .10
501 Chuck Crim .10
502 Candy Maldonado .10
503 Dennis Lamp .10
504 Glenn Braggs .10
505 Joe Price .10
506 Ken Williams .10
507 Bill Pecota .10
508 Rey Quinones .10
509 *Jeff Bittiger* .10
510 Kevin Seitzer .10
511 Steve Bedrosian .10
512 Todd Worrell .10
513 Chris James .10
514 Jose Oquendo .10
515 David Palmer .10
516 John Smiley .10
517 Dave Clark .10
518 Mike Dunne .10
519 Ron Washington .10
520 Bob Kipper .10
521 Lee Smith .15
522 Juan Castillo .10
523 Don Robinson .10
524 Kevin Romine .10
525 Paul Molitor .50
526 Mark Langston .15
527 Donnie Hill .10
528 Larry Owen .10
529 Jerry Reed .10
530 Jack McDowell .10
531 Greg Mathews .10
532 John Russell .10
533 Dan Quisenberry .10
534 Greg Gross .10
535 Danny Cox .10
536 Terry Francona .10
537 Andy Van Slyke .10
538 Mel Hall .10
539 Jim Gott .10
540 Doug Jones .10
541 Criag Lefferts .10
542 Mike Boddicker .10
543 Greg Brock .10
544 Atlee Hammaker .10
545 Tom Bolton .10
546 *Mike Macfarlane* .25
547 *Rich Renteria* .10
548 John Davis .10
549 Floyd Bannister .10
550 Mickey Brantley .10
551 Duane Ward .10
552 Dan Petry .10
553 Mickey Tettleton .10
554 Rick Leach .10
555 Mike Witt .10
556 Sid Bream .10
557 Bobby Witt .10
558 Tommy Herr .10
559 Randy Milligan .10
560 *Jose Cecena* .10
561 Mackey Sasser .10
562 Carney Lansford .10
563 Rick Aguilera .10
564 Ron Hassey .10
565 Dwight Gooden .20
566 Paul Assenmacher .10
567 Neil Allen .10
568 Jim Morrison .10
569 Mike Pagliarulo .10
570 Ted Simmons .10
571 Mark Thurmond .10
572 Fred McGriff .40
573 Wally Joyner .10
574 *Jose Bautista* .10
575 Kelly Gruber .10
576 Cecilio Guante .10
577 Mark Davidson .10
578 Bobby Bonilla .15
579 Mike Stanley .10
580 Gene Larkin .10
581 Stan Javier .10
582 Howard Johnson .10
583a Mike Gallego (photo on card back reversed) 1.00
583b Mike Gallego (correct photo) .10
584 David Cone .50
585 *Doug Jennings* .10
586 Charlie Hudson .10
587 Dion James .10
588 Al Leiter .20
589 Charlie Puleo .10
590 Roberto Kelly .10
591 Thad Bosley .10
592 Pete Stanicek .10
593 *Pat Borders* .25
594 *Bryan Harvey* .15
595 Jeff Ballard .10
596 Jeff Reardon .10
597 Doug Drabek .10
598 Edwin Correa .10
599 Keith Atherton .10
600 Dave LaPoint .10
601 Don Baylor .15
602 Tom Pagnozzi .10
603 Tim Flannery .10
604 Gene Walter .10
605 Dave Parker .15
606 Mike Diaz .10
607 Chris Gwynn .10
608 Odell Jones .10
609 Carlton Fisk .40
610 Jay Howell .10
611 Tim Crews .10
612 Keith Hernandez .10
613 Willie Fraser .10
614 Jim Eppard .10
615 Jeff Hamilton .10
616 Kurt Stillwell .10
617 Tom Browning .10
618 Jeff Montgomery .10
619 Jose Rijo .10
620 Jamie Quirk .10
621 Willie McGee .10
622 Mark Grant .10
623 Bill Swift .10
624 Orlando Mercado .10
625 *John Costello* .10
626 Jose Gonzalez .10
627a Bill Schroeder (putting on shin guards on card back, photo actually Ronn Reynolds) 1.25
627b Bill Schroeder (arms crossed on card back, correct photo) .10
628a Fred Manrique (throwing on card back, photo actually Ozzie Guillen) 1.00
628b Fred Manrique (batting on card back, correct photo) .10
629 Ricky Horton .10
630 Dan Plesac .10
631 Alfredo Griffin .10
632 Chuck Finley .15
633 Kirk Gibson .10
634 Randy Myers .10
635 Greg Minton .10
636 Herm Winningham .10
637 Charlie Leibrandt .10
638 Tim Birtsas .10
639 Bill Buckner .10
640 Danny Jackson .10
641 Greg Booker .10
642 Jim Presley .10
643 Gene Nelson .10
644 Rod Booker .10
645 Dennis Rasmussen .10
646 Juan Nieves .10
647 Bobby Thigpen .10
648 Tim Belcher .10
649 Mike Young .10
650 Ivan Calderon .10
651 *Oswaldo Peraza* .10
652a Pat Sheridan (no position on front) 15.00
652b Pat Sheridan (position on front) .10
653 Mike Morgan .10
654 Mike Heath .10
655 Jay Tibbs .10
656 Fernando Valenzuela .10
657 Lee Mazzilli .10
658 Frank Viola .10
659 Jose Canseco .50
660 Walt Weiss .10
661 Orel Hershiser .10
662 Kirk Gibson .10
663 Chris Sabo .10
664 Dennis Eckersley .10
665 Orel Hershiser .10
666 Kirk Gibson .10
667 Orel Hershiser .10
668 Wally Joyner (TC) .10
669 Nolan Ryan (TC) .60
670 Jose Canseco (TC) .20
671 Fred McGriff (TC) .15
672 Dale Murphy (TC) .10
673 Paul Molitor (TC) .20
674 Ozzie Smith (TC) .20
675 Ryne Sandberg (TC) .30
676 Kirk Gibson (TC) .10
677 Andres Galarraga (TC) .15
678 Will Clark (TC) .20
679 Cory Snyder (TC) .10
680 Alvin Davis (TC) .10
681 Darryl Strawberry (TC) .10
682 Cal Ripken, Jr. (TC) .40
683 Tony Gwynn (TC) .40
684 Mike Schmidt (TC) .25
685 Andy Van Slyke (TC) .10
686 Ruben Sierra (TC) .10
687 Wade Boggs (TC) .20
688 Eric Davis (TC) .10
689 George Brett (TC) .30
690 Alan Trammell (TC) .10
691 Frank Viola (TC) .10
692 Harold Baines (TC) .10
693 Don Mattingly (TC) .30
694 Checklist 1-100 .10
695 Checklist 101-200 .10
696 Checklist 201-300 .10
697 Checklist 301-400 .10
698 Checklist 401-500 .10
699 Checklist 501-600 .10
700 Checklist 601-700 .10
701 Checklist 701-800 .10
702 Jessie Barfield .10
703 Walt Terrell .10
704 Dickie Thon .10
705 Al Leiter .10
706 Dave LaPoint .10
707 *Charlie Hayes* .40
708 Andy Hawkins .10
709 Mickey Hatcher .10
710 Lance McCullers .10
711 Ron Kittle .10
712 Bert Blyleven .10
713 Rick Dempsey .10
714 Ken Williams .10
715 Steve Rosenberg .10
716 Joe Skalski .10
717 Spike Owen .10

718	Todd Burns	.10
719	Kevin Gross	.10
720	Tommy Herr	.10
721	Rob Ducey	.10
722	Gary Green	.10
723	*Gregg Olson*	.25
724	Greg Harris	.10
725	Craig Worthington	.10
726	Tom Howard	.10
727	Dale Mohorcic	.10
728	Rich Yett	.10
729	Mel Hall	.10
730	Floyd Youmans	.10
731	Lonnie Smith	.10
732	Wally Backman	.10
733	Trevor Wilson	.10
734	Jose Alvarez	.10
735	Bob Milacki	.10
736	*Tom Gordon*	.50
737	Wally Whitehurst	.10
738	Mike Aldrete	.10
739	Keith Miller	.10
740	Randy Milligan	.10
741	Jeff Parrett	.10
742	*Steve Finley*	1.50
743	*Junior Felix*	.15
744	*Pete Harnisch*	.25
745	Bill Spiers	.10
746	Hensley Meulens	.10
747	Juan Bell	.10
748	Steve Sax	.10
749	Phil Bradley	.10
750	Rey Quinones	.10
751	Tommy Gregg	.10
752	Kevin Brown	2.00
753	Derek Lilliquist	.10
754	*Todd Zeile*	.75
755	Jim Abbott	.15
756	*Ozzie Canseco*	.10
757	Nick Esasky	.10
758	Mike Moore	.10
759	Rob Murphy	.10
760	Rick Mahler	.10
761	Fred Lynn	.10
762	*Kevin Blankenship*	.10
763	Eddie Murray	.40
764	*Steve Searcy*	.10
765	*Jerome Walton*	.10
766	*Erik Hanson*	.25
767	Bob Boone	.15
768	Edgar Martinez	.60
769	*Jose DeJesus*	.10
770	*Greg Briley*	.10
771	*Steve Peters*	.10
772	Rafael Palmeiro	1.00
773	Jack Clark	.10
774	Nolan Ryan	3.00
775	Lance Parrish	.10
776	*Joe Girardi*	.40
777	Willie Randolph	.10
778	Mitch Williams	.10
779	*Dennis Cook*	.10
780	*Dwight Smith*	.15
781	*Lenny Harris*	.15
782	*Torey Lovullo*	.15
783	*Norm Charlton*	.25
784	Chris Brown	.10
785	Todd Benzinger	.10
786	Shane Rawley	.10
787	*Omar Vizquel*	3.00
788	*LaVel Freeman*	.10
789	Jeffrey Leonard	.10
790	*Eddie Williams*	.15
791	Jamie Moyer	.10
792	Bruce Hurst	.10
793	Julio Franco	.10
794	Claudell Washington	.10
795	Jody Davis	.10
796	Oddibe McDowell	.10
797	Paul Kilgus	.10
798	Tracy Jones	.10
799	Steve Wilson	.20
800	Pete O'Brien	.10

1990 Upper Deck

Following the success of its first issue, Upper Deck released another 800-card set in 1990. The cards feature full-color photos on both sides in the standard 2-1/2" x 3-1/2" format. The artwork of Vernon Wells Sr. is featured on the front of all team checklist cards. The 1990 set also introduces two new Wells illustrations - a tribute to Mike Schmidt upon his retirement and one commemorating Nolan Ryan's 5,000 career strikeouts. The cards are similar in design to the 1989 issue. The high-number series (701-800) was released as a boxed set, in factory sets and in foil packs at mid-season. Cards #101-199 can be found either with or without the copyright line on back; no premium attaches to either.

	MT
Complete Set (800):	25.00
Complete Low Set (700):	20.00
Complete High Set (100):	5.00
Common Player:	.05
Low Foil Pack (15 - Final):	1.00
Low Foil Wax Box (36 - Final):	20.00
High Foil Pack (15 - Final):	1.00
High Foil Wax Box (36- Final):	25.00

1	Star Rookie Checklist	.05
2	*Randy Nosek*	.05
3	*Tom Drees*	.05
4	Curt Young	.05
5	Angels checklist (Devon White)	.05
6	Luis Salazar	.05
7	Phillies checklist (Von Hayes)	.05
8	Jose Bautista	.05
9	*Marquis Grissom*	.50
10	Dodgers checklist (Orel Hershiser)	.05
11	Rick Aguilera	.05
12	Padres checklist (Benito Santiago)	.05
13	Deion Sanders	.50
14	Marvell Wynne	.05
15	David West	.05
16	Pirates checklist (Bobby Bonilla)	.05
17	*Sammy Sosa*	8.00
18	Yankees checklist (Steve Sax)	.05
19	Jack Howell	.05
20	Mike Schmidt Retires (Mike Schmidt)	.50
21	Robin Ventura	.40
22	Brian Meyer	.05
23	*Blaine Beatty*	.05
24	Mariners checklist (Ken Griffey, Jr.)	.75
25	Greg Vaughn	.15
26	*Xavier Hernandez*	.10
27	*Jason Grimsley*	.10
28	*Eric Anthony*	.10
29	Expos checklist (Tim Raines)	.05
30	David Wells	.10
31	Hal Morris	.10
32	Royals checklist (Bo Jackson)	.15
33	*Kelly Mann*	.05
34	Nolan Ryan 5000 Strikeouts (Nolan Ryan)	1.00
35	*Scott Service*	.05
36	Athletics checklist (Mark McGwire)	1.00
37	Tino Martinez	.20
38	Chili Davis	.05
39	Scott Sanderson	.05
40	Giants checklist (Kevin Mitchell)	.05
41	Tigers checklist (Lou Whitaker)	.05
42	*Scott Coolbaugh*	.05
43	*Jose Cano*	.05
44	*Jose Vizcaino*	.25
45	*Bob Hamelin*	.15
46	*Jose Offerman*	.50
47	Kevin Blankenship	.05
48	Twins checklist (Kirby Puckett)	.20
49	*Tommy Greene*	.15
50	N.L. Top Vote Getter (Will Clark)	.10
51	Rob Nelson	.05
52	*Chris Hammond*	.15
53	Indians checklist (Joe Carter)	.05
54a	*Ben McDonald* (Orioles Logo)	1.50
54b	*Ben McDonald* (Star Rookie logo)	.25
55	Andy Benes	.50
56	*John Olerud*	1.00
57	Red Sox checklist (Roger Clemens)	.25
58	Tony Armas	.05
59	*George Canale*	.05
60a	Orioles checklist (Mickey Tettleton) (#683 Jamie Weston)	2.00
60b	Orioles checklist (Mickey Tettleton) (#683 Mickey Weston)	.05
61	*Mike Stanton*	.15
62	Mets checklist (Dwight Gooden)	.05
63	*Kent Mercker*	.10
64	*Francisco Cabrera*	.05
65	Steve Avery	.05
66	Jose Canseco	.40
67	*Matt Merullo*	.05
68	Cardinals checklist (Vince Coleman)	.05
69	Ron Karkovice	.05
70	*Kevin Maas*	.05
71	Dennis Cook	.05
72	*Juan Gonzalez*	3.00
73	Cubs checklist (Andre Dawson)	.05
74	*Dean Palmer*	.75
75	A.L. Top Vote Getter (Bo Jackson)	.15
76	*Rob Richie*	.05
77	*Bobby Rose*	.05
78	*Brian DuBois*	.05
79	White Sox checklist (Ozzie Guillen)	.05
80	Gene Nelson	.05
81	Bob McClure	.05
82	Rangers checklist (Julio Franco)	.05
83	Greg Minton	.05
84	Braves checklist (John Smoltz)	.10
85	Willie Fraser	.05
86	Neal Heaton	.05
87	*Kevin Tapani*	.30
88	Astros checklist (Mike Scott)	.05
89a	Jim Gott (incorrect photo)	2.00
89b	Jim Gott (correct photo)	.05
90	Lance Johnson	.05
91	Brewers checklist (Robin Yount)	.10
92	Jeff Parrett	.05
93	*Julio Machado*	.05
94	Ron Jones	.05
95	Blue Jays checklist (George Bell)	.05
96	Jerry Reuss	.05
97	Brian Fisher	.05
98	*Kevin Ritz*	.10
99	Reds checklist (Barry Larkin)	.10
100	Checklist 1-100	.05
101	Gerald Perry	.05
102	Kevin Appier	.10
103	Julio Franco	.05
104	Craig Biggio	.20
105	Bo Jackson	.20
106	*Junior Felix*	.05
107	Mike Harkey	.05
108	Fred McGriff	.35
109	Rick Sutcliffe	.05
110	Pete O'Brien	.05
111	Kelly Gruber	.05
112	Pat Borders	.05
113	Dwight Evans	.05
114	Dwight Gooden	.10
115	*Kevin Batiste*	.05
116	Eric Davis	.05
117	Kevin Mitchell	.05
118	Ron Oester	.05
119	Brett Butler	.05
120	Danny Jackson	.05
121	Tommy Gregg	.05
122	Ken Caminiti	.25
123	Kevin Brown	.10
124	George Brett	.50
125	Mike Scott	.05
126	Cory Snyder	.05
127	George Bell	.05
128	Mark Grace	.30
129	Devon White	.05
130	Tony Fernandez	.05
131	Don Aase	.05
132	Rance Mulliniks	.05
133	Marty Barrett	.05
134	Nelson Liriano	.05
135	Mark Carreon	.10
136	Candy Maldonado	.05
137	Tim Birtsas	.05
138	Tom Brookens	.05
139	John Franco	.05
140	Mike LaCoss	.05
141	Jeff Treadway	.05
142	Pat Tabler	.05
143	Darrell Evans	.05
144	Rafael Ramirez	.05
145	Oddibe McDowell	.05
146	Brian Downing	.05
147	Curtis Wilkerson	.05
148	Ernie Whitt	.05
149	Bill Schroeder	.05
150	Domingo Ramos	.05
151	Rick Honeycutt	.05
152	Don Slaught	.05
153	Mitch Webster	.05
154	Tony Phillips	.05
155	Paul Kilgus	.05
156	Ken Griffey, Jr.	4.00
157	Gary Sheffield	.35
158	Wally Backman	.05
159	B.J. Surhoff	.05
160	Louie Meadows	.05
161	Paul O'Neill	.10
162	*Jeff McKnight*	.05
163	Alvaro Espinoza	.05
164	*Scott Scudder*	.05
165	Jeff Reed	.05
166	Gregg Jefferies	.20
167	Barry Larkin	.15
168	Gary Carter	.10
169	Robby Thompson	.05
170	Rolando Roomes	.05
171	Mark McGwire	2.50
172	Steve Sax	.05
173	Mark Williamson	.05
174	Mitch Williams	.05
175	Brian Holton	.05
176	Rob Deer	.05
177	Tim Raines	.10
178	Mike Felder	.05
179	Harold Reynolds	.05
180	Terry Francona	.05
181	Chris Sabo	.05
182	Darryl Strawberry	.10
183	Willie Randolph	.05
184	Billy Ripken	.05
185	Mackey Sasser	.05
186	Todd Benzinger	.05
187	Kevin Elster	.05
188	Jose Uribe	.05
189	Tom Browning	.05
190	Keith Miller	.05
191	Don Mattingly	.40
192	Dave Parker	.10
193	Roberto Kelly	.05
194	Phil Bradley	.05
195	Ron Hassey	.05
196	Gerald Young	.05
197	Hubie Brooks	.05
198	Bill Doran	.05

No.	Player	Value
199	Al Newman	.05
200	Checklist 101-200	.05
201	Terry Puhl	.05
202	Frank DiPino	.05
203	Jim Clancy	.05
204	Bob Ojeda	.05
205	Alex Trevino	.05
206	Dave Henderson	.05
207	Henry Cotto	.05
208	Rafael Belliard	.05
209	Stan Javier	.05
210	Jerry Reed	.05
211	Doug Dascenzo	.05
212	Andres Thomas	.05
213	Greg Maddux	1.00
214	Mike Schooler	.05
215	Lonnie Smith	.05
216	Jose Rijo	.05
217	Greg Gagne	.05
218	Jim Gantner	.05
219	Allan Anderson	.05
220	Rick Mahler	.05
221	Jim Deshaies	.05
222	Keith Hernandez	.05
223	Vince Coleman	.05
224	David Cone	.25
225	Ozzie Smith	.35
226	Matt Nokes	.05
227	Barry Bonds	.75
228	Felix Jose	.05
229	Dennis Powell	.05
230	Mike Gallego	.05
231	Shawon Dunston	.05
232	Ron Gant	.15
233	Omar Vizquel	.10
234	Derek Lilliquist	.05
235	Erik Hanson	.05
236	Kirby Puckett	.75
237	Bill Spiers	.05
238	Dan Gladden	.05
239	Bryan Clutterbuck	.05
240	John Moses	.05
241	Ron Darling	.05
242	Joe Magrane	.05
243	Dave Magadan	.05
244	Pedro Guerrero	.05
245	Glenn Davis	.05
246	Terry Steinbach	.05
247	Fred Lynn	.05
248	Gary Redus	.05
249	Kenny Williams	.05
250	Sid Bream	.05
251	Bob Welch	.05
252	Bill Buckner	.05
253	Carney Lansford	.05
254	Paul Molitor	.35
255	Jose DeJesus	.05
256	Orel Hershiser	.05
257	Tom Brunansky	.05
258	Mike Davis	.05
259	Jeff Ballard	.05
260	Scott Terry	.05
261	Sid Fernandez	.05
262	Mike Marshall	.05
263	Howard Johnson	.05
264	Kirk Gibson	.05
265	Kevin McReynolds	.05
266	Cal Ripken, Jr.	1.50
267	Ozzie Guillen	.05
268	Jim Traber	.05
269	Bobby Thigpen	.05
270	Joe Orsulak	.05
271	Bob Boone	.10
272	Dave Stewart	.05
273	Tim Wallach	.05
274	Luis Aquino	.05
275	Mike Moore	.05
276	Tony Pena	.05
277	Eddie Murray	.30
278	Milt Thompson	.05
279	Alejandro Pena	.05
280	Ken Dayley	.05
281	Carmen Castillo	.05
282	Tom Henke	.05
283	Mickey Hatcher	.05
284	Roy Smith	.05
285	Manny Lee	.05
286	Dan Pasqua	.05
287	Larry Sheets	.05
288	Garry Templeton	.05
289	Eddie Williams	.05
290	Brady Anderson	.15
291	Spike Owen	.05
292	Storm Davis	.05
293	Chris Bosio	.05
294	Jim Eisenreich	.05
295	Don August	.05
296	Jeff Hamilton	.05
297	Mickey Tettleton	.05
298	Mike Scioscia	.05
299	Kevin Hickey	.05
300	Checklist 201-300	.05
301	Shawn Abner	.05
302	Kevin Bass	.05
303	Bip Roberts	.05
304	Joe Girardi	.05
305	Danny Darwin	.05
306	Mike Heath	.05
307	Mike Macfarlane	.05
308	Ed Whitson	.05
309	Tracy Jones	.05
310	Scott Fletcher	.05
311	Darnell Coles	.05
312	Mike Brumley	.05
313	Bill Swift	.05
314	Charlie Hough	.05
315	Jim Presley	.05
316	Luis Polonia	.05
317	Mike Morgan	.05
318	Lee Guetterman	.05
319	Jose Oquendo	.05
320	Wayne Tollenson	.05
321	Jody Reed	.05
322	Damon Berryhill	.05
323	Roger Clemens	.75
324	Ryne Sandberg	.40
325	Benito Santiago	.05
326	Bret Saberhagen	.10
327	Lou Whitaker	.05
328	Dave Gallagher	.05
329	Mike Pagliarulo	.05
330	Doyle Alexander	.05
331	Jeffrey Leonard	.05
332	Torey Lovullo	.05
333	Pete Incaviglia	.05
334	Rickey Henderson	.25
335	Rafael Palmeiro	.25
336	Ken Hill	.05
337	Dave Winfield	.30
338	Alfredo Griffin	.05
339	Andy Hawkins	.05
340	Ted Power	.05
341	Steve Wilson	.05
342	Jack Clark	.05
343	Ellis Burks	.10
344	Tony Gwynn	.75
345	Jerome Walton	.05
346	Roberto Alomar	.60
347	*Carlos Martinez*	.05
348	Chet Lemon	.05
349	Willie Wilson	.05
350	Greg Walker	.05
351	Tom Bolton	.05
352	German Gonzalez	.05
353	Harold Baines	.05
354	Mike Greenwell	.05
355	Ruben Sierra	.05
356	Andres Galarraga	.25
357	Andre Dawson	.15
358	*Jeff Brantley*	.15
359	Mike Bielecki	.05
360	Ken Oberkfell	.05
361	Kurt Stillwell	.05
362	Brian Holman	.05
363	Kevin Seitzer	.05
364	Alvin Davis	.05
365	Tom Gordon	.05
366	Bobby Bonilla	.10
367	Carlton Fisk	.20
368	*Steve Carter*	.05
369	Joel Skinner	.05
370	John Cangelosi	.05
371	Cecil Espy	.05
372	*Gary Wayne*	.05
373	Jim Rice	.10
374	*Mike Dyer*	.05
375	Joe Carter	.10
376	Dwight Smith	.05
377	*John Wetteland*	.35
378	Ernie Riles	.05
379	Otis Nixon	.05
380	Vance Law	.05
381	Dave Bergman	.05
382	Frank White	.05
383	Scott Bradley	.05
384	Israel Sanchez	.05
385	Gary Pettis	.05
386	Donn Pall	.05
387	John Smiley	.05
388	Tom Candiotti	.05
389	Junior Ortiz	.05
390	Steve Lyons	.05
391	Brian Harper	.05
392	Fred Manrique	.05
393	Lee Smith	.05
394	Jeff Kunkel	.05
395	Claudell Washington	.05
396	John Tudor	.05
397	Terry Kennedy	.05
398	Lloyd McClendon	.05
399	Craig Lefferts	.05
400	Checklist 301-400	.05
401	Keith Moreland	.05
402	Rich Gedman	.05
403	Jeff Robinson	.05
404	Randy Ready	.05
405	Rick Cerone	.05
406	Jeff Blauser	.05
407	Larry Andersen	.05
408	Joe Boever	.05
409	Felix Fermin	.05
410	Glenn Wilson	.05
411	Rex Hudler	.05
412	Mark Grant	.05
413	Dennis Martinez	.05
414	Darrin Jackson	.05
415	Mike Aldrete	.05
416	Roger McDowell	.05
417	Jeff Reardon	.05
418	Darren Daulton	.05
419	Tim Laudner	.05
420	Don Carman	.05
421	Lloyd Moseby	.05
422	Doug Drabek	.05
423	Lenny Harris	.05
424	Jose Lind	.05
425	*Dave Johnson*	.05
426	Jerry Browne	.05
427	*Eric Yelding*	.05
428	Brad Komminsk	.05
429	Jody Davis	.05
430	Mariano Duncan	.05
431	Mark Davis	.05
432	Nelson Santovenia	.05
433	Bruce Hurst	.05
434	*Jeff Huson*	.05
435	Chris James	.05
436	*Mark Guthrie*	.05
437	Charlie Hayes	.05
438	Shane Rawley	.05
439	Dickie Thon	.05
440	Juan Berenguer	.05
441	Kevin Romine	.05
442	Bill Landrum	.05
443	Todd Frohwirth	.05
444	Craig Worthington	.05
445	Fernando Valenzuela	.05
446	Albert Belle	.50
447	*Ed Whited*	.05
448	Dave Smith	.05
449	Dave Clark	.05
450	Juan Agosto	.05
451	Dave Valle	.05
452	Kent Hrbek	.05
453	Von Hayes	.05
454	Gary Gaetti	.05
455	Greg Briley	.05
456	Glenn Braggs	.05
457	Kirt Manwaring	.05
458	Mel Hall	.05
459	Brook Jacoby	.05
460	Pat Sheridan	.05
461	Rob Murphy	.05
462	Jimmy Key	.10
463	Nick Esasky	.05
464	Rob Ducey	.05
465	Carlos Quintana	.05
466	*Larry Walker*	1.00
467	Todd Worrell	.05
468	Kevin Gross	.05
469	Terry Pendleton	.05
470	Dave Martinez	.05
471	Gene Larkin	.05
472	Len Dykstra	.05
473	Barry Lyons	.05
474	Terry Mulholland	.05
475	*Chip Hale*	.05
476	Jesse Barfield	.05
477	Dan Plesac	.05
478a	Scott Garrelts (Photo actually Bill Bathe)	1.50
478b	Scott Garrelts (Correct photo)	.05
479	Dave Righetti	.05
480	Gus Polidor	.05
481	Mookie Wilson	.05
482	Luis Rivera	.05
483	Mike Flanagan	.05
484	Dennis "Oil Can" Boyd	.05
485	John Cerutti	.05
486	John Costello	.05
487	Pascual Perez	.05
488	Tommy Herr	.05
489	Tom Foley	.05
490	Curt Ford	.05
491	Steve Lake	.05
492	Tim Teufel	.05
493	Randy Bush	.05
494	Mike Jackson	.05
495	Steve Jeltz	.05
496	Paul Gibson	.05
497	Steve Balboni	.05
498	Bud Black	.05
499	Dale Sveum	.05
500	Checklist 401-500	.05
501	Timmy Jones	.05
502	Mark Portugal	.05
503	Ivan Calderon	.05
504	Rick Rhoden	.05
505	Willie McGee	.05
506	Kirk McCaskill	.05
507	Dave LaPoint	.05
508	Jay Howell	.05
509	Johnny Ray	.05
510	Dave Anderson	.05
511	Chuck Crim	.05
512	Joe Hesketh	.05
513	Dennis Eckersley	.05
514	Greg Brock	.05
515	Tim Burke	.05
516	Frank Tanana	.05
517	Jay Bell	.10
518	Guillermo Hernandez	.05
519	Randy Kramer	.05
520	Charles Hudson	.05
521	Jim Corsi	.05
522	Steve Rosenberg	.05
523	Cris Carpenter	.05
524	*Matt Winters*	.05
525	Melido Perez	.05
526	Chris Gwynn	.05
527	Bert Blyleven	.05
528	Chuck Cary	.05
529	Daryl Boston	.05
530	Dale Mohorcic	.05
531	Geronimo Berroa	.05
532	Edgar Martinez	.10
533	Dale Murphy	.15
534	Jay Buhner	.10
535	John Smoltz	.25
536	Andy Van Slyke	.05
537	Mike Henneman	.05
538	Miguel Garcia	.05
539	Frank Williams	.05
540	R.J. Reynolds	.05
541	Shawn Hillegas	.05
542	Walt Weiss	.05
543	*Greg Hibbard*	.10
544	Nolan Ryan	1.50
545	Todd Zeile	.10
546	Hensley Meulens	.05
547	Tim Belcher	.05
548	Mike Witt	.05
549	Greg Cadaret	.05
550	Franklin Stubbs	.05
551	*Tony Castillo*	.05
552	Jeff Robinson	.05
553	*Steve Olin*	.05
554	Alan Trammell	.10
555	Wade Boggs	.30
556	Will Clark	.40
557	Jeff King	.05
558	Mike Fitzgerald	.05
559	Ken Howell	.05
560	Bob Kipper	.05
561	Scott Bankhead	.05
562a	*Jeff Innis* (Photo actually David West)	1.00
562b	*Jeff Innis* (Correct photo)	.05
563	Randy Johnson	.50
564	*Wally Whitehurst*	.05
565	*Gene Harris*	.05
566	Norm Charlton	.05
567	Robin Yount	.50
568	*Joe Oliver*	.05
569	Mark Parent	.05
570	John Farrell	.05
571	Tom Glavine	.40
572	Rod Nichols	.05
573	Jack Morris	.05
574	Greg Swindell	.05
575	Steve Searcy	.05
576	Ricky Jordan	.05
577	Matt Williams	.30
578	Mike LaValliere	.05
579	Bryn Smith	.05
580	Bruce Ruffin	.05
581	Randy Myers	.10
582	*Rick Wrona*	.05
583	Juan Samuel	.05
584	Les Lancaster	.05
585	Jeff Musselman	.05
586	Rob Dibble	.05
587	Eric Show	.05
588	Jesse Orosco	.05
589	Herm Winningham	.05
590	Andy Allanson	.05
591	Dion James	.05

592 Carmelo Martinez .05
593 Luis Quinones .05
594 Dennis Rasmussen .05
595 Rich Yett .05
596 Bob Walk .05
597a Andy McGaffigan (player #48, photo actually Rich Thompson) .75
597b Andy McGaffigan (player #27, correct photo) .05
598 Billy Hatcher .05
599 Bob Knepper .05
600 Checklist 501-600 .05
601 Joey Cora .05
602 *Steve Finley* .20
603 Kal Daniels .05
604 Gregg Olson .05
605 Dave Steib .05
606 *Kenny Rogers* .10
607 Zane Smith .05
608 *Bob Geren* .05
609 Chad Kreuter .05
610 Mike Smithson .05
611 *Jeff Wetherby* .05
612 *Gary Mielke* .05
613 Pete Smith .05
614 *Jack Daugherty* .05
615 Lance McCullers .05
616 Don Robinson .05
617 Jose Guzman .05
618 Steve Bedrosian .05
619 Jamie Moyer .05
620 Atlee Hammaker .05
621 *Rick Luecken* .05
622 Greg W. Harris .05
623 Pete Harnisch .05
624 Jerald Clark .05
625 Jack McDowell .05
626 Frank Viola .05
627 Ted Higuera .05
628 *Marty Pevey* .05
629 Bill Wegman .05
630 Eric Plunk .05
631 Drew Hall .05
632 Doug Jones .05
633 Geno Petralli .05
634 Jose Alvarez .05
635 Bob Milacki .05
636 Bobby Witt .05
637 Trevor Wilson .05
638 Jeff Russell .05
639 Mike Krukow .05
640 Rick Leach .05
641 Dave Schmidt .05
642 Terry Leach .05
643 Calvin Schiraldi .05
644 Bob Melvin .05
645 Jim Abbott .10
646 *Jaime Navarro* .10
647 Mark Langston .05
648 Juan Nieves .05
649 Damaso Garcia .05
650 Charlie O'Brien .05
651 Eric King .05
652 Mike Boddicker .05
653 Duane Ward .05
654 Bob Stanley .05
655 Sandy Alomar, Jr. .10
656 Danny Tartabull .05
657 Randy McCament .05
658 Charlie Leibrandt .05
659 Dan Quisenberry .05
660 Paul Assenmacher .05
661 Walt Terrell .05
662 Tim Leary .05
663 Randy Milligan .05
664 Bo Diaz .05
665 Mark Lemke .05
666 Jose Gonzalez .05
667 Chuck Finley .10
668 John Kruk .05
669 Dick Schofield .05
670 Tim Crews .05
671 John Dopson .05
672 *John Orton* .05
673 Eric Hetzel .05
674 Lance Parrish .05
675 Ramon Martinez .20
676 Mark Gubicza .05
677 Greg Litton .05
678 Greg Mathews .05
679 Dave Dravecky .05
680 Steve Farr .05
681 Mike Devereaux .05
682 Ken Griffey, Sr. .05
683a *Jamie Weston* (first name incorrect) 2.00
683b *Mickey Weston* (corrected) .05
684 Jack Armstrong .05
685 Steve Buechele .05
686 Bryan Harvey .05
687 Lance Blankenship .05
688 Dante Bichette .50
689 Todd Burns .05
690 Dan Petry .05
691 *Kent Anderson* .05
692 Todd Stottlemyre .10
693 Wally Joyner .05
694 Mike Rochford .05
695 Floyd Bannister .05
696 Rick Reuschel .05
697 Jose DeLeon .05
698 Jeff Montgomery .05
699 Kelly Downs .05
700a Checklist 601-700 (#683 Jamie Weston) .05
700b Checklist 601-700 (# 683 Mickey Weston) .05
701 Jim Gott .05
702 "Rookie Threats" (Delino DeShields, Larry Walker, Marquis Grissom) .40
703 Alejandro Pena .05
704 Willie Randolph .05
705 Tim Leary .05
706 Chuck McElroy .05
707 Gerald Perry .05
708 Tom Brunansky .05
709 John Franco .05
710 Mark Davis .05
711 *Dave Justice* 1.50
712 Storm Davis .05
713 Scott Ruskin .05
714 Glenn Braggs .05
715 Kevin Bearse .05
716 Jose Nunez .05
717 Tim Layana .05
718 Greg Myers .05
719 Pete O'Brien .05
720 John Candelaria .05
721 Craig Grebeck .05
722 Shawn Boskie .05
723 Jim Leyritz .10
724 Bill Sampen .05
725 Scott Radinsky .05
726 *Todd Hundley* .40
727 Scott Hemond .05
728 Lenny Webster .05
729 Jeff Reardon .05
730 Mitch Webster .05
731 Brian Bohanon .05
732 Rick Parker .05
733 Terry Shumpert .05
734a Nolan Ryan (300-win stripe on front) 2.00
734b Nolan Ryan (no stripe) 8.00
735 John Burkett .05
736 *Derrick May* .10
737 *Carlos Baerga* .10
738 Greg Smith .05
739 Joe Kraemer .05
740 Scott Sanderson .05
741 Hector Villanueva .05
742 Mike Fetters .05
743 Mark Gardner .10
744 Matt Nokes .05
745 Dave Winfield .25
746 *Delino DeShields* .15
747 Dann Howitt .05
748 Tony Pena .05
749 Oil Can Boyd .05
750 Mike Benjamin .05
751 Alex Cole .05
752 Eric Gunderson .05
753 Howard Farmer .05
754 Joe Carter .10
755 *Ray Lankford* .75
756 Sandy Alomar,Jr. .10
757 Alex Sanchez .05
758 Nick Esasky .05
759 Stan Belinda .05
760 Jim Presley .05
761 Gary DiSarcina .10
762 Wayne Edwards .05
763 Pat Combs .10
764 Mickey Pina .05
765 *Wilson Alvarez* .25
766 Dave Parker .15
767 Mike Blowers .10
768 Tony Phillips .05
769 Pascual Perez .05
770 Gary Pettis .05
771 Fred Lynn .05
772 *Mel Rojas* .10
773 David Segui .40
774 Gary Carter .10
775 Rafael Valdez .05
776 Glenallen Hill .10
777 Keith Hernandez .05
778 Billy Hatcher .05
779 Marty Clary .05
780 Candy Maldonado .05
781 Mike Marshall .05
782 Billy Jo Robidoux .05
783 Mark Langston .10
784 *Paul Sorrento* .25
785 *Dave Hollins* .20
786 Cecil Fielder .10
787 Matt Young .05
788 Jeff Huson .05
789 Lloyd Moseby .05
790 Ron Kittle .05
791 Hubie Brooks .05
792 Craig Lefferts .05
793 Kevin Bass .05
794 Bryn Smith .05
795 Juan Samuel .05
796 Sam Horn .05
797 Randy Myers .10
798 Chris James .05
799 Bill Gullickson .05
800 Checklist 701-800 .05

1990 Upper Deck Reggie Jackson Heroes

This Baseball Heroes set is devoted to Reggie Jackson. The cards, numbered 1-9, are the first in a continuing series of cards issued in subsequent years. An unnumbered cover card that says "Baseball Heroes" was also issued. The Jackson cards were randomly inserted in high number foil packs only. Jackson also autographed 2,500 numbered cards, which were randomly included in high number packs.

	MT
Complete Set (10):	8.00
Common Player:	1.00
Autographed Card:	125.00

1 1969 Emerging Superstar (Reggie Jackson) 1.00
2 1973 An MVP Year (Reggie Jackson) 1.00
3 1977 "Mr. October" (Reggie Jackson) 1.00
4 1978 Jackson vs. Welch (Reggie Jackson) 1.00
5 1982 Under the Halo (Reggie Jackson) 1.00
6 1984 500! (Reggie Jackson) 1.00
7 1986 Moving Up the List (Reggie Jackson) 1.00
8 1987 A Great Career Ends (Reggie Jackson) 1.00
9 Heroes Checklist 1-9 (Reggie Jackson) 1.00
---- Header card 1.00

1991 Upper Deck

More than 110 rookies are included among the first 700 cards in the 1991 Upper Deck set. A 100-card high-number series was released in late summer. Cards feature top quality white stock and color photos on front and back. A nine-card "Baseball Heroes" bonus set honoring Nolan Ryan, is among the many insert specials in the '91 UD set. Others include a card of Chicago Bulls superstar Michael Jordan. Along with the Ryan bonus cards, 2,500 cards personally autographed and numbered by Ryan were randomly inserted. Upper Deck cards are packaged in tamper-proof foil packs. Each pack contains 15 cards and cards and a 3-1/2" x 2-1/2" 3-D team logo hologram sticker.

	MT
Complete Set (800):	20.00
Factory Set (800):	25.00
Complete Low Series (1-700):	15.00
Complete High Series (701-800):	5.00
Common Player:	.05
Low or High Pack (15):	.75
Low or High Wax Box (36):	18.00

1 Star Rookie Checklist .05
2 *Phil Plantier* .10
3 *D.J. Dozier* .05
4 Dave Hansen .05
5 Mo Vaughn .50
6 *Leo Gomez* .10
7 *Scott Aldred* .05
8 *Scott Chiamparino* .05
9 *Lance Dickson* .05
10 *Sean Berry* .15
11 Bernie Williams .50
12 *Brian Barnes* .05
13 *Narciso Elvira* .05
14 *Mike Gardiner* .10
15 *Greg Colbrunn* .15
16 *Bernard Gilkey* .25
17 Mark Lewis .10
18 *Mickey Morandini* .10
19 Charles Nagy .15
20 *Geronimo Pena* .10
21 *Henry Rodriguez* .40
22 Scott Cooper .05
23 *Andujar Cedeno* .05

24 *Eric Karros* .75
25 *Steve Decker* .05
26 *Kevin Belcher* .10
27 *Jeff Conine* .25
28 Oakland Athletics checklist (Dave Stewart) .05
29 Chicago White Sox checklist (Carlton Fisk) .10
30 Texas Rangers checklist (Rafael Palmeiro) .10
31 California Angels checklist (Chuck Finley) .05
32 Seattle Mariners checklist (Harold Reynolds) .05
33 Kansas City Royals checklist (Bret Saberhagen) .05
34 Minnesota Twins checklist (Gary Gaetti) .05
35 Scott Leius .05
36 Neal Heaton .05
37 *Terry Lee* .05
38 Gary Redus .05
39 Barry Jones .05
40 Chuck Knoblauch .40
41 Larry Andersen .05
42 Darryl Hamilton .05
43 Boston Red Sox checklist (Mike Greenwell) .05
44 Toronto Blue Jays checklist (Kelly Gruber) .05
45 Detroit Tigers checklist (Jack Morris) .05
46 Cleveland Indians checklist (Sandy Alomar Jr.) .05
47 Baltimore Orioles checklist (Gregg Olson) .05
48 Milwaukee Brewers checklist (Dave Parker) .05
49 New York Yankees checklist (Roberto Kelly) .05
50 Top Prospect '91 checklist .05
51 *Kyle Abbott* (Top Prospect) .10
52 Jeff Juden (Top Prospect) .15
53 *Todd Van Poppel* (Top Prospect) .15
54 *Steve Karsay* (Top Prospect) .15
55 *Chipper Jones* (Top Prospect) 4.00
56 *Chris Johnson* (Top Prospect) .05
57 *John Ericks* (Top Prospect) .05
58 *Gary Scott* (Top Prospect) .05
59 Kiki Jones (Top Prospect) .05
60 *Wil Cordero* (Top Prospect) .25
61 *Royce Clayton* (Top Prospect) .20
62 *Tim Costo* (Top Prospect) .10
63 Roger Salkeld (Top Prospect) .10
64 *Brook Fordyce* (Top Prospect) .05
65 *Mike Mussina* (Top Prospect) 1.50
66 *Dave Staton* (Top Prospect) .15
67 *Mike Lieberthal* (Top Prospect) .60
68 *Kurt Miller* (Top Prospect) .15
69 *Dan Peltier* (Top Prospect) .05
70 Greg Blosser (Top Prospect) .05
71 *Reggie Sanders* (Top Prospect) .25
72 Brent Mayne (Top Prospect) .10
73 *Rico Brogna* (Top Prospect) .25
74 *Willie Banks* (Top Prospect) .10
75 *Len Brutcher* (Top Prospect) .05
76 *Pat Kelly* (Top Prospect) .10
77 Cincinnati Reds checklist (Chris Sabo) .05
78 Los Angeles Dodgers checklist (Ramon Martinez) .10
79 San Francisco Giants checklist (Matt Williams) .10
80 San Diego Padres checklist (Roberto Alomar) .10
81 Houston Astros checklist (Glenn Davis) .05
82 Atlanta Braves checklist (Ron Gant) .10
83 "Fielder's Feat" (Cecil Fielder) .10
84 *Orlando Merced* .20
85 Domingo Ramos .05
86 Tom Bolton .05
87 *Andres Santana* .05
88 John Dopson .05
89 Kenny Williams .05
90 Marty Barrett .05
91 Tom Pagnozzi .05
92 Carmelo Martinez .05
93 "Save Master" (Bobby Thigpen) .05
94 Pittsburgh Pirates checklist (Barry Bonds) .30
95 New York Mets checklist (Gregg Jefferies) .05
96 Montreal Expos checklist (Tim Wallach) .05
97 Philadelphia Phillies checklist (Lenny Dykstra) .05
98 St. Louis Cardinals checklist (Pedro Guerrero) .05
99 Chicago Cubs checklist (Mark Grace) .10
100 Checklist 1-100 .05
101 Kevin Elster .05
102 Tom Brookens .05
103 Mackey Sasser .05
104 Felix Fermin .05
105 Kevin McReynolds .05
106 Dave Steib .05
107 Jeffrey Leonard .05
108 Dave Henderson .05
109 Sid Bream .05
110 Henry Cotto .05
111 Shawon Dunston .05
112 Mariano Duncan .05
113 Joe Girardi .05
114 Billy Hatcher .05
115 Greg Maddux .75
116 Jerry Browne .05
117 Juan Samuel .05
118 Steve Olin .05
119 Alfredo Griffin .05
120 Mitch Webster .05
121 Joel Skinner .05
122 Frank Viola .05
123 Cory Snyder .05
124 Howard Johnson .05
125 Carlos Baerga .05
126 Tony Fernandez .05
127 Dave Stewart .05
128 Jay Buhner .05
129 Mike LaValliere .05
130 Scott Bradley .05
131 Tony Phillips .05
132 Ryne Sandberg .30
133 Paul O'Neill .20
134 Mark Grace .20
135 Chris Sabo .05
136 Ramon Martinez .15
137 Brook Jacoby .05
138 Candy Maldonado .05
139 Mike Scioscia .05
140 Chris James .05
141 Craig Worthington .05
142 Manny Lee .05
143 Tim Raines .10
144 Sandy Alomar, Jr. .10
145 John Olerud .20
146 *Ozzie Canseco* .10
147 Pat Borders .05
148 Harold Reynolds .05
149 Tom Henke .05
150 R.J. Reynolds .05
151 Mike Gallego .05
152 Bobby Bonilla .05
153 Terry Steinbach .05
154 Barry Bonds .60
155 Jose Canseco .40
156 Gregg Jefferies .10
157 Matt Williams .20
158 Craig Biggio .25
159 Daryl Boston .05
160 Ricky Jordan .05
161 Stan Belinda .05
162 Ozzie Smith .50
163 Tom Brunansky .05
164 Todd Zeile .10
165 Mike Greenwell .05
166 Kal Daniels .05
167 Kent Hrbek .05
168 Franklin Stubbs .05
169 Dick Schofield .05
170 Junior Ortiz .05
171 *Hector Villanueva* .05
172 Dennis Eckersley .05
173 Mitch Williams .05
174 Mark McGwire 2.00
175 Fernando Valenzuela .05
176 Gary Carter .10
177 Dave Magadan .05
178 Robby Thompson .05
179 Bob Ojeda .05
180 Ken Caminiti .15
181 Don Slaught .05
182 Luis Rivera .05
183 Jay Bell .05
184 Jody Reed .05
185 Wally Backman .05
186 Dave Martinez .05
187 Luis Polonia .05
188 Shane Mack .05
189 Spike Owen .05
190 Scott Bailes .05
191 John Russell .05
192 Walt Weiss .05
193 Jose Oquendo .05
194 Carney Lansford .05
195 Jeff Huson .05
196 Keith Miller .05
197 Eric Yelding .05
198 Ron Darling .05
199 John Kruk .05
200 Checklist 101-200 .05
201 John Shelby .05
202 Bob Geren .05
203 Lance McCullers .05
204 Alvaro Espinoza .05
205 Mark Salas .05
206 Mike Pagliarulo .05
207 Jose Uribe .05
208 Jim Deshaies .05
209 Ron Karkovice .05
210 Rafael Ramirez .05
211 Donnie Hill .05
212 Brian Harper .05
213 Jack Howell .05
214 Wes Gardner .05
215 Tim Burke .05
216 Doug Jones .05
217 Hubie Brooks .05
218 Tom Candiotti .05
219 Gerald Perry .05
220 Jose DeLeon .05
221 Wally Whitehurst .05
222 *Alan Mills* .10
223 Alan Trammell .10
224 Dwight Gooden .10
225 Travis Fryman .10
226 Joe Carter .05
227 Julio Franco .05
228 Craig Lefferts .05
229 Gary Pettis .05
230 Dennis Rasmussen .05
231a Brian Downing (no position on front) .50
231b Brian Downing (DH on front) .05
232 Carlos Quintana .05
233 Gary Gaetti .05
234 Mark Langston .05
235 Tim Wallach .05
236 Greg Swindell .05
237 Eddie Murray .25
238 Jeff Manto .05
239 Lenny Harris .05
240 Jesse Orosco .05
241 Scott Lusader .05
242 Sid Fernandez .05
243 *Jim Leyritz* .20
244 Cecil Fielder .10
245 Darryl Strawberry .10
246 Frank Thomas 1.00
247 Kevin Mitchell .05
248 Lance Johnson .05
249 Rick Rueschel .05
250 Mark Portugal .05
251 Derek Lilliquist .05
252 Brian Holman .05
253 Rafael Valdez .05
254 B.J. Surhoff .05
255 Tony Gwynn .60
256 Andy Van Slyke .05
257 Todd Stottlemyre .10
258 Jose Lind .05
259 Greg Myers .05
260 Jeff Ballard .05
261 Bobby Thigpen .05
262 *Jimmy Kremers* .05
263 Robin Ventura .20
264 John Smoltz .15
265 Sammy Sosa 1.00
266 Gary Sheffield .20
267 Len Dykstra .05
268 Bill Spiers .05
269 Charlie Hayes .05
270 Brett Butler .05
271 Bip Roberts .05
272 Rob Deer .05
273 Fred Lynn .05
274 Dave Parker .10
275 Andy Benes .10
276 Glenallen Hill .10
277 *Steve Howard* .10
278 Doug Drabek .05
279 Joe Oliver .05
280 Todd Benzinger .05
281 Eric King .05
282 Jim Presley .05
283 Ken Patterson .05
284 Jack Daugherty .05
285 Ivan Calderon .05
286 *Edgar Diaz* .05
287 Kevin Bass .05
288 Don Carman .05
289 Greg Brock .05
290 John Franco .05
291 Joey Cora .05
292 Bill Wegman .05
293 Eric Show .05
294 Scott Bankhead .05
295 Garry Templeton .05
296 Mickey Tettleton .05
297 Luis Sojo .05
298 Jose Rijo .05
299 Dave Johnson .05
300 Checklist 201-300 .05
301 Mark Grant .05
302 Pete Harnisch .10
303 Greg Olson .05
304 *Anthony Telford* .10
305 Lonnie Smith .05
306 Chris Hoiles .05
307 Bryn Smith .05
308 Mike Devereaux .05
309a Milt Thompson ("86" in stats obscured by "bull's eye") .50
309b Milt Thompson ("86" visible) .05
310 Bob Melvin .05
311 Luis Salazar .05
312 Ed Whitson .05
313 Charlie Hough .05
314 Dave Clark .05
315 *Eric Gunderson* .05
316 Dan Petry .05
317 Dante Bichette .20
318 Mike Heath .05
319 Damon Berryhill .05
320 Walt Terrell .05
321 Scott Fletcher .05
322 Dan Plesac .05
323 Jack McDowell .05
324 Paul Molitor .35
325 Ozzie Guillen .05
326 Gregg Olson .05
327 Pedro Guerrero .05
328 Bob Milacki .05
329 John Tudor .05
330 Steve Finley .05
331 Jack Clark .05
332 Jerome Walton .05
333 Andy Hawkins .05
334 Derrick May .05
335 Roberto Alomar .35
336 Jack Morris .05
337 Dave Winfield .20
338 Steve Searcy .05
339 Chili Davis .05
340 Larry Sheets .05
341 Ted Higuera .05

342 *David Segui* .15
343 Greg Cadaret .05
344 Robin Yount .35
345 Nolan Ryan 1.00
346 Ray Lankford .10
347 Cal Ripken, Jr. 1.00
348 Lee Smith .05
349 Brady Anderson .15
350 Frank DiPino .05
351 Hal Morris .05
352 Deion Sanders .20
353 Barry Larkin .15
354 Don Mattingly .50
355 Eric Davis .05
356 Jose Offerman .05
357 Mel Rojas .05
358 Rudy Seanez .05
359 Oil Can Boyd .05
360 Nelson Liriano .05
361 Ron Gant .10
362 *Howard Farmer* .05
363 Dave Justice .20
364 Delino DeShields .05
365 Steve Avery .05
366 David Cone .10
367 Lou Whitaker .05
368 Von Hayes .05
369 Frank Tanana .05
370 Tim Teufel .05
371 Randy Myers .05
372 Roberto Kelly .05
373 Jack Armstrong .05
374 Kelly Gruber .05
375 Kevin Maas .05
376 Randy Johnson .25
377 David West .05
378 *Brent Knackert* .05
379 Rick Honeycutt .05
380 Kevin Gross .05
381 Tom Foley .05
382 Jeff Blauser .05
383 *Scott Ruskin* .05
384 Andres Thomas .05
385 Dennis Martinez .05
386 Mike Henneman .05
387 Felix Jose .05
388 Alejandro Pena .05
389 Chet Lemon .05
390 *Craig Wilson* .10
391 Chuck Crim .05
392 Mel Hall .05
393 Mark Knudson .05
394 Norm Charlton .05
395 Mike Felder .05
396 *Tim Layana* .05
397 Steve Frey .05
398 Bill Doran .05
399 Dion James .05
400 Checklist 301-400 .05
401 Ron Hassey .05
402 Don Robinson .05
403 Gene Nelson .05
404 Terry Kennedy .05
405 Todd Burns .05
406 Roger McDowell .05
407 Bob Kipper .05
408 Darren Daulton .05
409 Chuck Cary .05
410 Bruce Ruffin .05
411 Juan Berenguer .05
412 Gary Ward .05
413 Al Newman .05
414 Danny Jackson .05
415 Greg Gagne .05
416 Tom Herr .05
417 Jeff Parrett .05
418 Jeff Reardon .05
419 Mark Lemke .05
420 Charlie O'Brien .05
421 Willie Randolph .05
422 Steve Bedrosian .05
423 Mike Moore .05
424 Jeff Brantley .05
425 Bob Welch .05
426 Terry Mulholland .05
427 *Willie Blair* .10
428 Darrin Fletcher .10
429 Mike Witt .05
430 Joe Boever .05
431 Tom Gordon .05
432 *Pedro Munoz* .10
433 Kevin Seitzer .05
434 Kevin Tapani .05
435 Bret Saberhagen .10
436 Ellis Burks .10
437 Chuck Finley .05
438 Mike Boddicker .05
439 Francisco Cabrera .05
440 Todd Hundley .15
441 Kelly Downs .05
442 *Dann Howitt* .05
443 Scott Garrelts .05
444 Rickey Henderson .25
445 Will Clark .30
446 Ben McDonald .05
447 Dale Murphy .10
448 Dave Righetti .05
449 Dickie Thon .05
450 Ted Power .05
451 Scott Coolbaugh .05
452 Dwight Smith .05
453 Pete Incaviglia .05
454 Andre Dawson .10
455 Ruben Sierra .05
456 Andres Galarraga .20
457 Alvin Davis .05
458 Tony Castillo .05
459 Pete O'Brien .05
460 Charlie Leibrandt .05
461 Vince Coleman .05
462 Steve Sax .05
463 *Omar Oliveras* .05
464 *Oscar Azocar* .05
465 Joe Magrane .05
466 *Karl Rhodes* .10
467 Benito Santiago .05
468 *Joe Klink* .05
469 Sil Campusano .05
470 Mark Parent .05
471 *Shawn Boskie* .10
472 Kevin Brown .10
473 Rick Sutcliffe .05
474 Rafael Palmeiro .25
475 Mike Harkey .05
476 Jaime Navarro .05
477 Marquis Grissom .10
478 Marty Clary .05
479 Greg Briley .05
480 Tom Glavine .15
481 Lee Guetterman .05
482 Rex Hudler .05
483 Dave LaPoint .05
484 Terry Pendleton .05
485 Jesse Barfield .05
486 Jose DeJesus .05
487 *Paul Abbott* .05
488 Ken Howell .05
489 Greg W. Harris .05
490 Roy Smith .05
491 Paul Assenmacher .05
492 Geno Petralli .05
493 Steve Wilson .05
494 Kevin Reimer .05
495 Bill Long .05
496 Mike Jackson .05
497 Oddibe McDowell .05
498 Bill Swift .05
499 Jeff Treadway .05
500 Checklist 401-500 .05
501 Gene Larkin .05
502 Bob Boone .05
503 Allan Anderson .05
504 Luis Aquino .05
505 Mark Guthrie .05
506 Joe Orsulak .05
507 *Dana Kiecker* .05
508 Dave Gallagher .05
509 Greg A. Harris .05
510 Mark Williamson .05
511 Casey Candaele .05
512 Mookie Wilson .05
513 Dave Smith .05
514 *Chuck Carr* .05
515 Glenn Wilson .05
516 Mike Fitzgerald .05
517 Devon White .05
518 Dave Hollins .05
519 Mark Eichhorn .05
520 Otis Nixon .05
521 *Terry Shumpert* .05
522 *Scott Erickson* .25
523 Danny Tartabull .05
524 Orel Hershiser .05
525 George Brett .40
526 Greg Vaughn .05
527 Tim Naehring .05
528 Curt Schilling .10
529 Chris Bosio .05
530 Sam Horn .05
531 Mike Scott .05
532 George Bell .05
533 Eric Anthony .05
534 *Julio Valera* .05
535 Glenn Davis .05
536 Larry Walker .25
537 Pat Combs .05
538 *Chris Nabholz* .05
539 Kirk McCaskill .05
540 Randy Ready .05
541 Mark Gubicza .05
542 Rick Aguilera .05
543 *Brian McRae* .25
544 Kirby Puckett .50
545 Bo Jackson .20
546 Wade Boggs .20
547 Tim McIntosh .05
548 Randy Milligan .05
549 Dwight Evans .05
550 Billy Ripken .05
551 Erik Hanson .05
552 Lance Parrish .05
553 Tino Martinez .10
554 Jim Abbott .05
555 Ken Griffey, Jr. 2.00
556 Milt Cuyler .05
557 *Mark Leonard* .05
558 Jay Howell .05
559 Lloyd Moseby .05
560 Chris Gwynn .05
561 *Mark Whiten* .15
562 Harold Baines .05
563 Junior Felix .05
564 Darren Lewis .05
565 Fred McGriff .20
566 Kevin Appier .05
567 *Luis Gonzalez* .50
568 Frank White .05
569 Juan Agosto .05
570 Mike Macfarlane .05
571 Bert Blyleven .05
572 Ken Griffey, Sr. .05
573 Lee Stevens .05
574 Edgar Martinez .05
575 Wally Joyner .05
576 Tim Belcher .05
577 John Burkett .05
578 Mike Morgan .05
579 Paul Gibson .05
580 Jose Vizcaino .05
581 Duane Ward .05
582 Scott Sanderson .05
583 David Wells .10
584 Willie McGee .05
585 John Cerutti .05
586 Danny Darwin .05
587 Kurt Stillwell .05
588 Rich Gedman .05
589 Mark Davis .05
590 Bill Gullickson .05
591 Matt Young .05
592 Bryan Harvey .05
593 Omar Vizquel .05
594 *Scott Lewis* .05
595 Dave Valle .05
596 Tim Crews .05
597 Mike Bielecki .05
598 Mike Sharperson .05
599 Dave Bergman .05
600 Checklist 501-600 .05
601 Steve Lyons .05
602 Bruce Hurst .05
603 Donn Pall .05
604 *Jim Vatcher* .05
605 Dan Pasqua .05
606 Kenny Rogers .05
607 *Jeff Schulz* .05
608 Brad Arnsberg .05
609 Willie Wilson .05
610 Jamie Moyer .05
611 Ron Oester .05
612 Dennis Cook .05
613 Rick Mahler .05
614 Bill Landrum .05
615 Scott Scudder .05
616 *Tom Edens* .05
617 "1917 Revisited" (Chicago White Sox team photo) .10
618 Jim Gantner .05
619 Darrel Akerfelds .05
620 Ron Robinson .05
621 Scott Radinsky .05
622 Pete Smith .05
623 Melido Perez .05
624 Jerald Clark .05
625 Carlos Martinez .05
626 *Wes Chamberlain* .10
627 Bobby Witt .05
628 Ken Dayley .05
629 *John Barfield* .05
630 Bob Tewksbury .05
631 Glenn Braggs .05
632 *Jim Neidlinger* .05
633 Tom Browning .05
634 Kirk Gibson .05
635 Rob Dibble .05
636 "Stolen Base Leaders" (Lou Brock, Rickey Henderson) .15
637 Jeff Montgomery .05
638 Mike Schooler .05
639 Storm Davis .05
640 *Rich Rodriguez* .05
641 Phil Bradley .05
642 Kent Mercker .05
643 Carlton Fisk .25
644 Mike Bell .05
645 *Alex Fernandez* .15
646 Juan Gonzalez .75
647 Ken Hill .05
648 Jeff Russell .05
649 *Chuck Malone* .05
650 Steve Buechele .05
651 Mike Benjamin .05
652 Tony Pena .05
653 Trevor Wilson .05
654 Alex Cole .05
655 Roger Clemens .50
656 "The Bashing Years" (Mark McGwire) .75
657 *Joe Grahe* .05
658 Jim Eisenreich .05
659 Dan Gladden .05
660 Steve Farr .05
661 *Bill Sampen* .05
662 *Dave Rohde* .05
663 Mark Gardner .05
664 *Mike Simms* .05
665 Moises Alou .15
666 Mickey Hatcher .05
667 Jimmy Key .10
668 John Wetteland .05
669 John Smiley .05
670 Jim Acker .05
671 Pascual Perez .05
672 *Reggie Harris* .10
673 Matt Nokes .05
674 *Rafael Novoa* .05
675 Hensley Meulens .05
676 Jeff M. Robinson .05
677 "Ground Breaking" (New Comiskey Park) .15
678 Johnny Ray .05
679 Greg Hibbard .05
680 Paul Sorrento .05
681 Mike Marshall .05
682 Jim Clancy .05
683 Rob Murphy .05
684 Dave Schmidt .05
685 *Jeff Gray* .05
686 Mike Hartley .05
687 Jeff King .05
688 Stan Javier .05
689 Bob Walk .05
690 Jim Gott .05
691 Mike LaCoss .05
692 John Farrell .05
693 Tim Leary .05
694 *Mike Walker* .05
695 Eric Plunk .05
696 Mike Fetters .05
697 Wayne Edwards .05
698 Tim Drummond .05
699 Willie Fraser .05
700 Checklist 601-700 .05
701 Mike Heath .05
702 "Rookie Threats" (Luis Gonzalez, Karl Rhodes, Jeff Bagwell) .60
703 Jose Mesa .05
704 Dave Smith .05
705 Danny Darwin .05
706 Rafael Belliard .05
707 Rob Murphy .05
708 Terry Pendleton .05
709 Mike Pagliarulo .05
710 Sid Bream .05
711 Junior Felix .05
712 Dante Bichette .20
713 Kevin Gross .05
714 Luis Sojo .05
715 Bob Ojeda .05
716 Julio Machado .05
717 Steve Farr .05
718 Franklin Stubbs .05
719 Mike Boddicker .05
720 Willie Randolph .05
721 Willie McGee .05
722 Chili Davis .05
723 Danny Jackson .05
724 Cory Snyder .05
725 "MVP Lineup" (Andre Dawson, George Bell, Ryne Sandberg) .15
726 Rob Deer .05
727 Rich DeLucia .05
728 Mike Perez .05
729 Mickey Tettleton .05
730 Mike Blowers .05
731 Gary Gaetti .05
732 Brett Butler .05

733	Dave Parker	.10
734	Eddie Zosky	.05
735	Jack Clark	.05
736	Jack Morris	.05
737	Kirk Gibson	.05
738	Steve Bedrosian	.05
739	Candy Maldonado	.05
740	Matt Young	.05
741	Rich Garces	.05
742	George Bell	.05
743	Deion Sanders	.20
744	Bo Jackson	.20
745	Luis Mercedes	.05
746	Reggie Jefferson	.05
747	Pete Incaviglia	.05
748	Chris Hammond	.05
749	Mike Stanton	.05
750	Scott Sanderson	.05
751	Paul Faries	.05
752	Al Osuna	.05
753	Steve Chitren	.05
754	Tony Fernandez	.05
755	*Jeff Bagwell*	3.00
756	Kirk Dressendorfer	.05
757	Glenn Davis	.05
758	Gary Carter	.05
759	Zane Smith	.05
760	Vance Law	.05
761	Denis Boucher	.05
762	Turner Ward	.05
763	Roberto Alomar	.30
764	Albert Belle	.40
765	Joe Carter	.10
766	Pete Schourek	.05
767	Heathcliff Slocumb	.05
768	Vince Coleman	.05
769	Mitch Williams	.05
770	Brian Downing	.05
771	Dana Allison	.05
772	Pete Harnisch	.05
773	Tim Raines	.10
774	Darryl Kile	.10
775	Fred McGriff	.20
776	Dwight Evans	.05
777	Joe Slusarski	.05
778	Dave Righetti	.05
779	Jeff Hamilton	.05
780	Ernest Riles	.05
781	Ken Dayley	.05
782	Eric King	.05
783	Devon White	.05
784	Beau Allred	.05
785	Mike Timlin	.10
786	Ivan Calderon	.05
787	Hubie Brooks	.05
788	Juan Agosto	.05
789	Barry Jones	.05
790	Wally Backman	.05
791	Jim Presley	.05
792	Charlie Hough	.05
793	Larry Andersen	.05
794	Steve Finley	.05
795	Shawn Abner	.05
796	Jeff M. Robinson	.05
797	Joe Bitker	.05
798	Eric Show	.05
799	Bud Black	.05
800	Checklist 701-800	.05
SP1	Michael Jordan	15.00
SP2	"A Day to Remember" (Rickey Henderson, Nolan Ryan)	1.50
HH1	Hank Aaron (hologram)	1.50

1991 Upper Deck Final Edition

Upper Deck surprised the hobby with the late-season release of this 100-card boxed set. The cards are numbered with an "F" designation. A special "Minor League Diamond Skills" subset (cards #1-21) features several top prospects. An All-Star subset (cards #79-99) is also included in this set. The cards are styled like the regular 1991 Upper Deck issue Special team hologram cards are included with the set.

		MT
Complete Set (100):		20.00
Common Player:		.05
1	Ryan Klesko, Reggie Sanders (Minor League Diamond Skills Checklist)	.50
2	*Pedro Martinez*	15.00
3	Lance Dickson	.05
4	Royce Clayton	.10
5	Scott Bryant	.05
6	Dan Wilson	.25
7	*Dmitri Young*	.25
8	*Ryan Klesko*	.40
9	Tom Goodwin	.10
10	*Rondell White*	.50
11	Reggie Sanders	.20
12	Todd Van Poppel	.05
13	Arthur Rhodes	.05
14	Eddie Zosky	.05
15	Gerald Williams	.10
16	Robert Eenhoorn	.05
17	*Jim Thome*	1.50
18	*Marc Newfield*	.10
19	Kerwin Moore	.05
20	Jeff McNeely	.05
21	Frankie Rodriguez	.10
22	Andy Mota	.05
23	Chris Haney	.05
24	*Kenny Lofton*	.50
25	Dave Nilsson	.25
26	Derek Bell	.15
27	Frank Castillo	.10
28	Candy Maldonado	.05
29	Chuck McElroy	.05
30	Chito Martinez	.05
31	Steve Howe	.05
32	Freddie Benavides	.05
33	Scott Kamieniecki	.10
34	Denny Neagle	.20
35	Mike Humphreys	.05
36	Mike Remlinger	.05
37	Scott Coolbaugh	.05
38	Darren Lewis	.10
39	Thomas Howard	.10
40	John Candelaria	.05
41	Todd Benzinger	.05
42	Wilson Alvarez	.15
43	Patrick Lennon	.05
44	Rusty Meacham	.05
45	*Ryan Bowen*	.05
46	*Rick Wilkins*	.10
47	*Ed Sprague*	.15
48	*Bob Scanlan*	.05
49	Tom Candiotti	.05
50	Dennis Martinez (Perfecto)	.10
51	Oil Can Boyd	.05
52	Glenallen Hill	.05
53	*Scott Livingstone*	.05
54	*Brian Hunter*	.20
55	*Ivan Rodriguez*	3.00
56	*Keith Mitchell*	.05
57	Roger McDowell	.05
58	Otis Nixon	.05
59	*Juan Bell*	.05
60	Bill Krueger	.05
61	*Chris Donnels*	.05
62	Tommy Greene	.05
63	Doug Simons	.05
64	*Andy Ashby*	.15
65	*Anthony Young*	.05
66	*Kevin Morton*	.05
67	*Bret Barberie*	.10
68	*Scott Servais*	.15
69	Ron Darling	.05
70	Vicente Palacios	.05
71	*Tim Burke*	.05
72	*Gerald Alexander*	.05
73	Reggie Jefferson	.05
74	Dean Palmer	.05
75	Mark Whiten	.05
76	Randy Tomlin	.05
77	*Mark Wohlers*	.25
78	Brook Jacoby	.05
79	Ken Griffey Jr., Ryne Sandberg (All-Star Checklist)	.40
80	Jack Morris (AS)	.05
81	Sandy Alomar, Jr. (AS)	.05
82	Cecil Fielder (AS)	.05
83	Roberto Alomar (AS)	.20
84	Wade Boggs (AS)	.15
85	Cal Ripken, Jr. (AS)	.50
86	Rickey Henderson (AS)	.10
87	Ken Griffey, Jr. (AS)	.75
88	Dave Henderson (AS)	.05
89	Danny Tartabull (AS)	.05
90	Tom Glavine (AS)	.10
91	Benito Santiago (AS)	.05
92	Will Clark (AS)	.15
93	Ryne Sandberg (AS)	.20
94	Chris Sabo (AS)	.05
95	Ozzie Smith (AS)	.20
96	Ivan Calderon (AS)	.05
97	Tony Gwynn (AS)	.25
98	Andre Dawson (AS)	.05
99	Bobby Bonilla (AS)	.05
100	Checklist	.05

1991 Upper Deck Heroes of Baseball

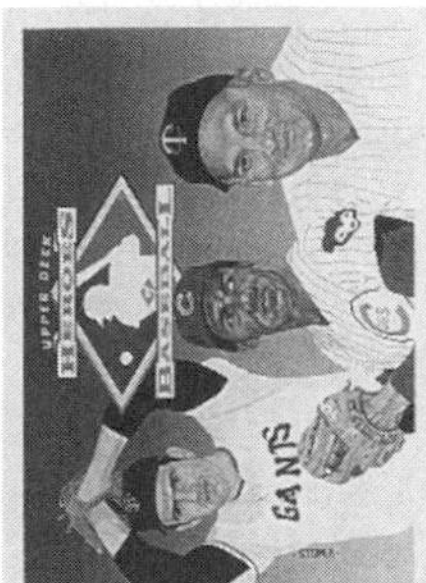

This four-card set features three members of Baseball's Hall of Fame: Harmon Killebrew, Gaylord Perry and Ferguson Jenkins. Each has a card for himself, plus there's a card which features all three players. The cards were found in specially-marked low number foil packs. The cards are numbered H1-H4. Upper Deck also produced 3,000 autographed and numbered cards for each player.

		MT
Complete Set (4):		12.50
Autographed Card:		37.00
1	Harmon Killebrew	4.00
2	Gaylord Perry	4.00
3	Ferguson Jenkins	4.00
4	Gaylord Perry, Ferguson Jenkins, Harmon Killebrew	4.00

1991 Upper Deck Hank Aaron Heroes

This set devoted to Hank Aaron is numbered 19-27 and includes an unnumbered "Baseball Heroes" cover card. The cards are found in foil and jumbo packs of Upper Deck high-number cards.

		MT
Complete Set (10):		6.00
Common Aaron:		.50
Autographed Card:		150.00
Aaron Header:		2.50
19	1954 Rookie Year	.50
20	1957 MVP	.50
21	1966 Move to Atlanta	.50
22	1970 3,000	.50
23	1974 715	.50
24	1975 Return to Milwaukee	.50
25	1976 755	.50
26	1982 Hall of Fame	.50
27	Checklist - Heroes 19-27	.50

1991 Upper Deck Nolan Ryan Heroes

This set devoted to Nolan Ryan is numbered 10-18 and includes an unnumbered "Baseball Heroes" cover card. The cards are found in low-number foil and jumbo boxes.

		MT
Complete Set (10):		6.00
Common Player:		.50
Ryan header Card:		2.50
Autographed Card:		300.00
10	1968 Victory #1	.50

11 1973 A Career Year .50
12 1975 Double Milestone .50
13 1979 Back Home .50
14 1981 All-Time Leader .50
15 1989 5,000 .50
16 1990 The Sixth .50
17 1990 ... and Still Counting .50
18 Checklist - Heroes 10-18 .50

1991 Upper Deck Silver Sluggers

Each year the "Silver Slugger" award is presented to the player at each position with the highest batting average in each league. Upper Deck produced special cards in honor of the 1990 season award winners. The cards were randomly inserted in jumbo packs of Upper Deck cards. The cards feature a "SS" designation along with the card number. The cards are designed like the regular issue Upper Deck cards from 1991, but feature a Silver Slugger bat along the left border of the card.

		MT
Complete Set (18):		15.00
Common Player:		.50
1	Julio Franco	.50
2	Alan Trammell	.50
3	Rickey Henderson	1.00
4	Jose Canseco	2.50
5	Barry Bonds	3.50
6	Eddie Murray	1.00
7	Kelly Gruber	.50
8	Ryne Sandberg	1.50
9	Darryl Strawberry	.50
10	Ellis Burks	.50
11	Lance Parrish	.50
12	Cecil Fielder	.50
13	Matt Williams	.75
14	Dave Parker	.50
15	Bobby Bonilla	.50
16	Don Robinson	.50
17	Benito Santiago	.50
18	Barry Larkin	.75

1992 Upper Deck

Upper Deck introduced a new look in 1992. The baseline style was no longer used. The cards feature full-color action photos on white stock, with the player's name and the Upper Deck logo along the top border. The team name is in the photo's bottom-right corner. Once again a 100-card high number series was released in late summer. Ted Williams autographed 2,500 Baseball Heroes cards which were randomly inserted into packs. Subsets featured in the 1992 issue include Star Rookies and Top Prospects. Cards originating from factory sets have gold-foil holograms on back, rather than silver.

		MT
Complete Set (800):		15.00
Complete Low Series (1-700):		15.00
Complete High Series (701-800):		5.00
Common Player:		.05
Low or Hi Pack (15):		.75
Low or Hi Wax Box (36):		20.00
1	Star Rookie Checklist (Ryan Klesko, Jim Thome)	.40
2	Royce Clayton (Star Rookie)	.15
3	*Brian Jordan* (Star Rookie)	.40
4	*Dave Fleming* (Star Rookie)	.10
5	Jim Thome (Star Rookie)	.50
6	Jeff Juden (Star Rookie)	.10
7	*Roberto Hernandez* (Star Rookie)	.12
8	Kyle Abbott (Star Rookie)	.10
9	*Chris George* (Star Rookie)	.05
10	*Rob Maurer* (Star Rookie)	.05
11	*Donald Harris* (Star Rookie)	.05
12	*Ted Wood* (Star Rookie)	.05
13	*Patrick Lennon* (Star Rookie)	.05
14	Willie Banks (Star Rookie)	.05
15	Roger Salkeld (Star Rookie)	.10
16	Wil Cordero (Star Rookie)	.20
17	*Arthur Rhodes* (Star Rookie)	.10
18	Pedro Martinez (Star Rookie)	1.50
19	*Andy Ashby* (Star Rookie)	.10
20	Tom Goodwin (Star Rookie)	.10
21	*Braulio Castillo* (Star Rookie)	.05
22	Todd Van Poppel (Star Rookie)	.05
23	*Brian Williams* (Star Rookie)	.05
24	Ryan Klesko (Star Rookie)	.25
25	Kenny Lofton (Star Rookie)	.25
26	Derek Bell (Star Rookie)	.15
27	Reggie Sanders (Star Rookie)	.15
28	Dave Winfield (Winfield's 400th)	.10
29	Atlanta Braves Checklist (Dave Justice)	.10
30	Cincinnati Reds Checklist (Rob Dibble)	.05
31	Houston Astros Checklist (Craig Biggio)	.10
32	Los Angeles Dodgers Checklist (Eddie Murray)	.10
33	San Diego Padres Checklist (Fred McGriff)	.10
34	San Francisco Giants Checklist (Willie McGee)	.05
35	Chicago Cubs Checklist (Shawon Dunston)	.05
36	Montreal Expos Checklist (Delino DeShields)	.05
37	New York Mets Checklist (Howard Johnson)	.05
38	Philadelphia Phillies Checklist (John Kruk)	.05
39	Pittsburgh Pirates Checklist (Doug Drabek)	.05
40	St. Louis Cardinals Checklist (Todd Zeile)	.05
41	Steve Avery (Playoff Perfection)	.05
42	*Jeremy Hernandez*	.05
43	*Doug Henry*	.10
44	*Chris Donnels*	.05
45	*Mo Sanford*	.05
46	*Scott Kamieniecki*	.15
47	Mark Lemke	.05
48	Steve Farr	.05
49	Francisco Oliveras	.05
50	*Ced Landrum*	.05
51	Top Prospect Checklist (Rondell White, Marc Newfield)	.20
52	*Eduardo Perez* (Top Prospect)	.10
53	*Tom Nevers* (Top Prospect)	.05
54	*David Zancanaro* (Top Prospect)	.05
55	*Shawn Green* (Top Prospect)	3.00
56	*Mark Wohlers* (Top Prospect)	.05
57	Dave Nilsson (Top Prospect)	.15
58	Dmitri Young (Top Prospect)	.15
59	*Ryan Hawblitzel* (Top Prospect)	.10
60	Raul Mondes i (Top Prospect)	.40
61	Rondell White (Top Prospect)	.15
62	Steve Hosey (Top Prospect)	.05
63	*Manny Ramirez* (Top Prospect)	3.00
64	Marc Newfield (Top Prospect)	.05
65	Jeromy Burnitz (Top Prospect)	.25
66	*Mark Smith* (Top Prospect)	.05
67	*Joey Hamilton* (Top Prospect)	.40
68	*Tyler Green* (Top Prospect)	.10
69	*John Farrell* (Top Prospect)	.05
70	*Kurt Miller* (Top Prospect)	.10
71	*Jeff Plympton* (Top Prospect)	.05
72	Dan Wilson (Top Prospect)	.15
73	*Joe Vitiello* (Top Prospect)	.10
74	Rico Brogna (Top Prospect)	.15
75	*David McCarty* (Top Prospect)	.10
76	*Bob Wickman* (Top Prospect)	.10
77	*Carlos Rodriguez* (Top Prospect)	.10
78	Jim Abbott (Stay in School)	.10
79	Bloodlines (Pedro Martinez, Ramon Martinez)	.40
80	Bloodlines (Kevin Mitchell, Keith Mitchell)	.05
81	Bloodlines (Sandy Jr. & Roberto Alomar, Sandy Jr. & Roberto Alomar)	.15
82	Bloodlines (Cal Jr. & Billy Ripken, Cal Jr. & Billy Ripken)	.40
83	Bloodlines (Tony & Chris Gwynn, Tony & Chris Gwynn)	.20
84	Bloodlines (Dwight Gooden, Gary Sheffield)	.15
85	Bloodlines (Ken, Sr.; Ken, Jr.; & Craig Griffey, Ken, Sr.; Ken, Jr.; & Craig Griffey, Ken, Sr.; Ken, Jr.; & Craig Griffey)	.50
86	California Angels Checklist (Jim Abbott)	.05
87	Chicago White Sox Checklist (Frank Thomas)	.20
88	Kansas City Royals Checklist (Danny Tartabull)	.05
89	Minnesota Twins Checklist (Scott Erickson)	.05
90	Oakland Athletics Checklist (Rickey Henderson)	.10
91	Seattle Mariners Checklist (Edgar Martinez)	.05
92	Texas Rangers Checklist (Nolan Ryan)	.50
93	Baltimore Orioles Checklist (Ben McDonald)	.05
94	Boston Red Sox Checklist (Ellis Burks)	.05
95	Cleveland Indians Checklist (Greg Swindell)	.05
96	Detroit Tigers Checklist (Cecil Fielder)	.05
97	Milwaukee Brewers Checklist (Greg Vaughn)	.05
98	New York Yankees Checklist (Kevin Maas)	.05
99	Toronto Blue Jays Checklist (Dave Steib)	.05
100	Checklist 1-100	.05
101	Joe Oliver	.05
102	Hector Villanueva	.05
103	Ed Whitson	.05
104	Danny Jackson	.05
105	Chris Hammond	.05
106	Ricky Jordan	.05
107	Kevin Bass	.05
108	Darrin Fletcher	.05
109	Junior Ortiz	.05
110	Tom Bolton	.05
111	Jeff King	.05
112	Dave Magadan	.05
113	Mike LaValliere	.05
114	Hubie Brooks	.05
115	Jay Bell	.05
116	David Wells	.05
117	Jim Leyritz	.05
118	Manuel Lee	.05
119	Alvaro Espinoza	.05
120	B.J. Surhoff	.05

No.	Player	Price
121	Hal Morris	.05
122	Shawon Dunston	.05
123	Chris Sabo	.05
124	Andre Dawson	.10
125	Eric Davis	.05
126	Chili Davis	.05
127	Dale Murphy	.10
128	Kirk McCaskill	.05
129	Terry Mulholland	.05
130	Rick Aguilera	.05
131	Vince Coleman	.05
132	Andy Van Slyke	.05
133	Gregg Jefferies	.05
134	Barry Bonds	.40
135	Dwight Gooden	.10
136	Dave Stieb	.05
137	Albert Belle	.30
138	Teddy Higuera	.05
139	Jesse Barfield	.05
140	Pat Borders	.05
141	Bip Roberts	.05
142	Rob Dibble	.05
143	Mark Grace	.20
144	Barry Larkin	.10
145	Ryne Sandberg	.30
146	Scott Erickson	.05
147	Luis Polonia	.05
148	John Burkett	.05
149	Luis Sojo	.05
150	Dickie Thon	.05
151	Walt Weiss	.05
152	Mike Scioscia	.05
153	Mark McGwire	1.50
154	Matt Williams	.10
155	Rickey Henderson	.20
156	Sandy Alomar, Jr.	.10
157	Brian McRae	.05
158	Harold Baines	.05
159	Kevin Appier	.05
160	Felix Fermin	.05
161	Leo Gomez	.05
162	Craig Biggio	.25
163	Ben McDonald	.05
164	Randy Johnson	.30
165	Cal Ripken, Jr.	1.00
166	Frank Thomas	.50
167	Delino DeShields	.05
168	Greg Gagne	.05
169	Ron Karkovice	.05
170	Charlie Leibrandt	.05
171	Dave Righetti	.05
172	Dave Henderson	.05
173	Steve Decker	.05
174	Darryl Strawberry	.10
175	Will Clark	.25
176	Ruben Sierra	.05
177	Ozzie Smith	.25
178	Charles Nagy	.05
179	Gary Pettis	.05
180	Kirk Gibson	.05
181	Randy Milligan	.05
182	Dave Valle	.05
183	Chris Hoiles	.05
184	Tony Phillips	.05
185	Brady Anderson	.10
186	Scott Fletcher	.05
187	Gene Larkin	.05
188	Lance Johnson	.05
189	Greg Olson	.05
190	Melido Perez	.05
191	Lenny Harris	.05
192	Terry Kennedy	.05
193	Mike Gallego	.05
194	Willie McGee	.05
195	Juan Samuel	.05
196	Jeff Huson	.05
197	Alex Cole	.05
198	Ron Robinson	.05
199	Joel Skinner	.05
200	Checklist 101-200	.05
201	Kevin Reimer	.05
202	Stan Belinda	.05
203	Pat Tabler	.05
204	Jose Guzman	.05
205	Jose Lind	.05
206	Spike Owen	.05
207	Joe Orsulak	.05
208	Charlie Hayes	.05
209	Mike Devereaux	.05
210	Mike Fitzgerald	.05
211	Willie Randolph	.05
212	Rod Nichols	.05
213	Mike Boddicker	.05
214	Bill Spiers	.05
215	Steve Olin	.05
216	*David Howard*	.05
217	Gary Varsho	.05
218	Mike Harkey	.05
219	Luis Aquino	.05
220	Chuck McElroy	.05
221	Doug Drabek	.05
222	Dave Winfield	.15
223	Rafael Palmeiro	.25
224	Joe Carter	.05
225	Bobby Bonilla	.05
226	Ivan Calderon	.05
227	Gregg Olson	.05
228	Tim Wallach	.05
229	Terry Pendleton	.05
230	Gilberto Reyes	.05
231	Carlos Baerga	.05
232	Greg Vaughn	.05
233	Bret Saberhagen	.05
234	Gary Sheffield	.15
235	Mark Lewis	.05
236	George Bell	.05
237	Danny Tartabull	.05
238	Willie Wilson	.05
239	Doug Dascenzo	.05
240	Bill Pecota	.05
241	Julio Franco	.05
242	Ed Sprague	.05
243	Juan Gonzalez	.50
244	Chuck Finley	.05
245	Ivan Rodriguez	.50
246	Len Dykstra	.05
247	Deion Sanders	.15
248	Dwight Evans	.05
249	Larry Walker	.25
250	Billy Ripken	.05
251	Mickey Tettleton	.05
252	Tony Pena	.05
253	Benito Santiago	.05
254	Kirby Puckett	.40
255	Cecil Fielder	.05
256	Howard Johnson	.05
257	Andujar Cedeno	.05
258	Jose Rijo	.05
259	Al Osuna	.05
260	Todd Hundley	.10
261	Orel Hershiser	.05
262	Ray Lankford	.05
263	Robin Ventura	.15
264	Felix Jose	.05
265	Eddie Murray	.25
266	Kevin Mitchell	.05
267	Gary Carter	.05
268	Mike Benjamin	.05
269	Dick Schofield	.05
270	Jose Uribe	.05
271	Pete Incaviglia	.05
272	Tony Fernandez	.05
273	Alan Trammell	.10
274	Tony Gwynn	.40
275	Mike Greenwell	.05
276	Jeff Bagwell	.50
277	Frank Viola	.05
278	Randy Myers	.05
279	Ken Caminiti	.15
280	Bill Doran	.05
281	Dan Pasqua	.05
282	Alfredo Griffin	.05
283	Jose Oquendo	.05
284	Kal Daniels	.05
285	Bobby Thigpen	.05
286	Robby Thompson	.05
287	Mark Eichhorn	.05
288	Mike Felder	.05
289	Dave Gallagher	.05
290	Dave Anderson	.05
291	Mel Hall	.05
292	Jerald Clark	.05
293	Al Newman	.05
294	Rob Deer	.05
295	Matt Nokes	.05
296	Jack Armstrong	.05
297	Jim Deshaies	.05
298	Jeff Innis	.05
299	Jeff Reed	.05
300	Checklist 201-300	.05
301	Lonnie Smith	.05
302	Jimmy Key	.05
303	Junior Felix	.05
304	Mike Heath	.05
305	Mark Langston	.05
306	Greg W. Harris	.05
307	Brett Butler	.05
308	Luis Rivera	.05
309	Bruce Ruffin	.05
310	Paul Faries	.05
311	Terry Leach	.05
312	*Scott Brosius*	.25
313	Scott Leius	.05
314	Harold Reynolds	.05
315	Jack Morris	.05
316	David Segui	.05
317	Bill Gullickson	.05
318	Todd Frohwirth	.05
319	*Mark Leiter*	.05
320	Jeff M. Robinson	.05
321	Gary Gaetti	.05
322	John Smoltz	.15
323	Andy Benes	.10
324	Kelly Gruber	.05
325	Jim Abbott	.05
326	John Kruk	.05
327	Kevin Seitzer	.05
328	Darrin Jackson	.05
329	Kurt Stillwell	.05
330	Mike Maddux	.05
331	Dennis Eckersley	.05
332	Dan Gladden	.05
333	Jose Canseco	.25
334	Kent Hrbek	.05
335	Ken Griffey, Sr.	.05
336	Greg Swindell	.05
337	Trevor Wilson	.05
338	Sam Horn	.05
339	Mike Henneman	.05
340	Jerry Browne	.05
341	Glenn Braggs	.05
342	Tom Glavine	.15
343	Wally Joyner	.05
344	Fred McGriff	.15
345	Ron Gant	.10
346	Ramon Martinez	.10
347	Wes Chamberlain	.05
348	Terry Shumpert	.05
349	Tim Teufel	.05
350	Wally Backman	.05
351	Joe Girardi	.05
352	Devon White	.05
353	Greg Maddux	.75
354	*Ryan Bowen*	.10
355	Roberto Alomar	.30
356	Don Mattingly	.50
357	Pedro Guerrero	.05
358	Steve Sax	.05
359	Joey Cora	.05
360	Jim Gantner	.05
361	Brian Barnes	.05
362	Kevin McReynolds	.05
363	*Bret Barberie*	.10
364	David Cone	.10
365	Dennis Martinez	.05
366	*Brian Hunter*	.10
367	Edgar Martinez	.05
368	Steve Finley	.05
369	Greg Briley	.05
370	Jeff Blauser	.05
371	Todd Stottlemyre	.10
372	Luis Gonzalez	.05
373	Rick Wilkins	.05
374	*Darryl Kile*	.10
375	John Olerud	.20
376	Lee Smith	.05
377	Kevin Maas	.05
378	Dante Bichette	.15
379	Tom Pagnozzi	.05
380	Mike Flanagan	.05
381	Charlie O'Brien	.05
382	Dave Martinez	.05
383	Keith Miller	.05
384	Scott Ruskin	.05
385	Kevin Elster	.05
386	Alvin Davis	.05
387	Casey Candaele	.05
388	Pete O'Brien	.05
389	Jeff Treadway	.05
390	Scott Bradley	.05
391	Mookie Wilson	.05
392	Jimmy Jones	.05
393	Candy Maldonado	.05
394	Eric Yelding	.05
395	Tom Henke	.05
396	Franklin Stubbs	.05
397	Milt Thompson	.05
398	Mark Carreon	.05
399	Randy Velarde	.05
400	Checklist 301-400	.05
401	Omar Vizquel	.05
402	Joe Boever	.05
403	Bill Krueger	.05
404	Jody Reed	.05
405	Mike Schooler	.05
406	Jason Grimsley	.05
407	Greg Myers	.05
408	Randy Ready	.05
409	*Mike Timlin*	.15
410	Mitch Williams	.05
411	Garry Templeton	.05
412	Greg Cadaret	.05
413	Donnie Hill	.05
414	Wally Whitehurst	.05
415	Scott Sanderson	.05
416	Thomas Howard	.05
417	Neal Heaton	.05
418	Charlie Hough	.05
419	Jack Howell	.05
420	Greg Hibbard	.05
421	Carlos Quintana	.05
422	*Kim Batiste*	.05
423	Paul Molitor	.30
424	Ken Griffey, Jr.	1.50
425	Phil Plantier	.05
426	Denny Neagle	.05
427	Von Hayes	.05
428	Shane Mack	.05
429	Darren Daulton	.05
430	Dwayne Henry	.05
431	Lance Parrish	.05
432	*Mike Humphreys*	.05
433	Tim Burke	.05
434	Bryan Harvey	.05
435	Pat Kelly	.05
436	Ozzie Guillen	.05
437	Bruce Hurst	.05
438	Sammy Sosa	.75
439	Dennis Rasmussen	.05
440	Ken Patterson	.05
441	Jay Buhner	.05
442	Pat Combs	.05
443	Wade Boggs	.20
444	George Brett	.30
445	Mo Vaughn	.15
446	Chuck Knoblauch	.15
447	Tom Candiotti	.05
448	Mark Portugal	.05
449	Mickey Morandini	.05
450	Duane Ward	.05
451	Otis Nixon	.05
452	Bob Welch	.05
453	Rusty Meacham	.05
454	Keith Mitchell	.05
455	Marquis Grissom	.10
456	Robin Yount	.25
457	*Harvey Pulliam*	.05
458	Jose DeLeon	.05
459	Mark Gubicza	.05
460	Darryl Hamilton	.05
461	Tom Browning	.05
462	Monty Fariss	.05
463	Jerome Walton	.05
464	Paul O'Neill	.15
465	Dean Palmer	.05
466	Travis Fryman	.10
467	John Smiley	.05
468	Lloyd Moseby	.05
469	*John Wehner*	.05
470	Skeeter Barnes	.05
471	Steve Chitren	.05
472	Kent Mercker	.05
473	Terry Steinbach	.05
474	Andres Galarraga	.20
475	Steve Avery	.05
476	Tom Gordon	.05
477	Cal Eldred	.05
478	Omar Olivares	.05
479	Julio Machado	.05
480	Bob Milacki	.05
481	Les Lancaster	.05
482	John Candelaria	.05
483	Brian Downing	.05
484	Roger McDowell	.05
485	Scott Scudder	.05
486	Zane Smith	.05
487	John Cerutti	.05
488	Steve Buechele	.05
489	Paul Gibson	.05
490	Curtis Wilkerson	.05
491	Marvin Freeman	.05
492	Tom Foley	.05
493	Juan Berenguer	.05
494	Ernest Riles	.05
495	Sid Bream	.05
496	Chuck Crim	.05
497	Mike Macfarlane	.05
498	Dale Sveum	.05
499	Storm Davis	.05
500	Checklist 401-500	.05
501	Jeff Reardon	.05
502	Shawn Abner	.05
503	Tony Fossas	.05
504	Cory Snyder	.05
505	Matt Young	.05
506	Allan Anderson	.05
507	Mark Lee	.05
508	Gene Nelson	.05
509	Mike Pagliarulo	.05
510	Rafael Belliard	.05
511	Jay Howell	.05
512	Bob Tewksbury	.05
513	Mike Morgan	.05
514	John Franco	.05
515	Kevin Gross	.05
516	Lou Whitaker	.05
517	Orlando Merced	.05
518	Todd Benzinger	.05
519	Gary Redus	.05
520	Walt Terrell	.05
521	Jack Clark	.05
522	Dave Parker	.10
523	Tim Naehring	.05
524	Mark Whiten	.05

No.	Player	Price
525	Ellis Burks	.05
526	*Frank Castillo*	.10
527	Brian Harper	.05
528	Brook Jacoby	.05
529	Rick Sutcliffe	.05
530	Joe Klink	.05
531	Terry Bross	.05
532	Jose Offerman	.05
533	Todd Zeile	.05
534	Eric Karros	.10
535	*Anthony Young*	.05
536	Milt Cuyler	.05
537	Randy Tomlin	.05
538	*Scott Livingstone*	.05
539	Jim Eisenreich	.05
540	Don Slaught	.05
541	Scott Cooper	.05
542	Joe Grahe	.05
543	Tom Brunansky	.05
544	Eddie Zosky	.05
545	Roger Clemens	.50
546	Dave Justice	.20
547	Dave Stewart	.05
548	David West	.05
549	Dave Smith	.05
550	Dan Plesac	.05
551	Alex Fernandez	.10
552	Bernard Gilkey	.05
553	Jack McDowell	.05
554	Tino Martinez	.10
555	Bo Jackson	.15
556	Bernie Williams	.20
557	Mark Gardner	.05
558	Glenallen Hill	.05
559	Oil Can Boyd	.05
560	Chris James	.05
561	*Scott Servais*	.10
562	*Rey Sanchez*	.15
563	*Paul McClellan*	.05
564	*Andy Mota*	.05
565	Darren Lewis	.05
566	*Jose Melendez*	.05
567	Tommy Greene	.05
568	Rich Rodriguez	.05
569	*Heathcliff Slocumb*	.05
570	Joe Hesketh	.05
571	Carlton Fisk	.20
572	Erik Hanson	.05
573	Wilson Alvarez	.05
574	*Rheal Cormier*	.05
575	Tim Raines	.05
576	Bobby Witt	.05
577	Roberto Kelly	.05
578	Kevin Brown	.10
579	Chris Nabholz	.05
580	Jesse Orosco	.05
581	Jeff Brantley	.05
582	Rafael Ramirez	.05
583	Kelly Downs	.05
584	Mike Simms	.05
585	*Mike Remlinger*	.05
586	Dave Hollins	.05
587	Larry Andersen	.05
588	Mike Gardiner	.05
589	Craig Lefferts	.05
590	Paul Assenmacher	.05
591	Bryn Smith	.05
592	Donn Pall	.05
593	Mike Jackson	.05
594	Scott Radinsky	.05
595	Brian Holman	.05
596	Geronimo Pena	.05
597	Mike Jeffcoat	.05
598	Carlos Martinez	.05
599	Geno Petralli	.05
600	Checklist 501-600	.05
601	Jerry Don Gleaton	.05
602	Adam Peterson	.05
603	Craig Grebeck	.05
604	Mark Guthrie	.05
605	Frank Tanana	.05
606	Hensley Meulens	.05
607	Mark Davis	.05
608	Eric Plunk	.05
609	Mark Williamson	.05
610	Lee Guetterman	.05
611	Bobby Rose	.05
612	Bill Wegman	.05
613	Mike Hartley	.05
614	*Chris Beasley*	.05
615	Chris Bosio	.05
616	Henry Cotto	.05
617	*Chico Walker*	.05
618	Russ Swan	.05
619	Bob Walk	.05
620	Billy Swift	.05
621	*Warren Newson*	.05
622	Steve Bedrosian	.05
623	*Ricky Bones*	.05
624	Kevin Tapani	.05
625	*Juan Guzman*	.10
626	*Jeff Johnson*	.05
627	Jeff Montgomery	.05
628	Ken Hill	.05
629	Gary Thurman	.05
630	Steve Howe	.05
631	Jose DeJesus	.05
632	Bert Blyleven	.05
633	Jaime Navarro	.05
634	Lee Stevens	.05
635	Pete Harnisch	.05
636	Bill Landrum	.05
637	Rich DeLucia	.05
638	Luis Salazar	.05
639	Rob Murphy	.05
640	A.L. Diamond Skills Checklist (Rickey Henderson, Jose Canseco)	.05
641	Roger Clemens (Diamond Skills)	.25
642	Jim Abbott (Diamond Skills)	.05
643	Travis Fryman (Diamond Skills)	.05
644	Jesse Barfield (Diamond Skills)	.05
645	Cal Ripken, Jr. (Diamond Skills)	.50
646	Wade Boggs (Diamond Skills)	.10
647	Cecil Fielder (Diamond Skills)	.05
648	Rickey Henderson (Diamond Skills)	.10
649	Jose Canseco (Diamond Skills)	.20
650	Ken Griffey, Jr. (Diamond Skills)	.50
651	Kenny Rogers	.05
652	*Luis Mercedes*	.05
653	Mike Stanton	.05
654	Glenn Davis	.05
655	Nolan Ryan	1.00
656	Reggie Jefferson	.05
657	*Javier Ortiz*	.05
658	Greg A. Harris	.05
659	Mariano Duncan	.05
660	Jeff Shaw	.05
661	Mike Moore	.05
662	*Chris Haney*	.05
663	*Joe Slusarski*	.05
664	*Wayne Housie*	.05
665	Carlos Garcia	.05
666	Bob Ojeda	.05
667	*Bryan Hickerson*	.05
668	Tim Belcher	.05
669	Ron Darling	.05
670	Rex Hudler	.05
671	Sid Fernandez	.05
672	*Chito Martinez*	.05
673	*Pete Schourek*	.15
674	*Armando Renoso*	.05
675	Mike Mussina	.35
676	Kevin Morton	.05
677	Norm Charlton	.05
678	Danny Darwin	.05
679	Eric King	.05
680	Ted Power	.05
681	Barry Jones	.05
682	Carney Lansford	.05
683	Mel Rojas	.05
684	Rick Honeycutt	.05
685	*Jeff Fassero*	.15
686	Cris Carpenter	.05
687	Tim Crews	.05
688	Scott Terry	.05
689	Chris Gwynn	.05
690	Gerald Perry	.05
691	John Barfield	.05
692	Bob Melvin	.05
693	Juan Agosto	.05
694	Alejandro Pena	.05
695	Jeff Russell	.05
696	Carmelo Martinez	.05
697	Bud Black	.05
698	Dave Otto	.05
699	Billy Hatcher	.05
700	Checklist 601-700	.05
701	Clemente Nunez	.15
702	"Rookie Threats" (Donovan Osborne, Brian Jordan, Mark Clark)	.10
703	Mike Morgan	.05
704	Keith Miller	.05
705	Kurt Stillwell	.05
706	Damon Berryhill	.05
707	Von Hayes	.05
708	Rick Sutcliffe	.05
709	Hubie Brooks	.05
710	Ryan Turner	.05
711	N.L. Diamond Skills Checklist (Barry Bonds, Andy Van Slyke)	.15
712	Jose Rijo (Diamond Skills)	.05
713	Tom Glavine (Diamond Skills)	.05
714	Shawon Dunston (Diamond Skills)	.05
715	Andy Van Slyke (Diamond Skills)	.05
716	Ozzie Smith (Diamond Skills)	.10
717	Tony Gwynn (Diamond Skills)	.20
718	Will Clark (Diamond Skills)	.05
719	Marquis Grissom (Diamond Skills)	.05
720	Howard Johnson (Diamond Skills)	.05
721	Barry Bonds (Diamond Skills)	.20
722	Kirk McCaskill	.05
723	Sammy Sosa	.75
724	George Bell	.05
725	Gregg Jefferies	.05
726	Gary DiSarcina	.05
727	Mike Bordick	.05
728	Eddie Murray (400 Home Run Club)	.15
729	Rene Gonzales	.05
730	Mike Bielecki	.05
731	Calvin Jones	.05
732	Jack Morris	.05
733	Frank Viola	.05
734	Dave Winfield	.15
735	Kevin Mitchell	.05
736	Billy Swift	.05
737	Dan Gladden	.05
738	Mike Jackson	.05
739	Mark Carreon	.05
740	Kirt Manwaring	.05
741	Randy Myers	.05
742	Kevin McReynolds	.05
743	Steve Sax	.05
744	Wally Joyner	.05
745	Gary Sheffield	.15
746	Danny Tartabull	.05
747	Julio Valera	.05
748	Denny Neagle	.10
749	Lance Blankenship	.05
750	Mike Gallego	.05
751	Bret Saberhagen	.05
752	Ruben Amaro	.05
753	Eddie Murray	.15
754	Kyle Abbott	.10
755	Bobby Bonilla	.05
756	Eric Davis	.05
757	Eddie Taubensee	.10
758	Andres Galarraga	.15
759	Pete Incaviglia	.05
760	Tom Candiotti	.05
761	Tim Belcher	.05
762	Ricky Bones	.05
763	Bip Roberts	.05
764	Pedro Munoz	.05
765	Greg Swindell	.05
766	Kenny Lofton	.25
767	Gary Carter	.05
768	Charlie Hayes	.05
769	Dickie Thon	.05
770	Diamond Debuts Checklist (Donovan Osborne)	.05
771	Bret Boone (Diamond Debuts)	.15
772	*Archi Cianfrocco* (Diamond Debuts)	.05
773	*Mark Clark* (Diamond Debuts)	.05
774	*Chad Curtis* (Diamond Debuts)	.20
775	*Pat Listach* (Diamond Debuts)	.05
776	*Pat Mahomes* (Diamond Debuts)	.05
777	*Donovan Osborne* (Diamond Debuts)	.05
778	*John Patterson* (Diamond Debuts)	.05
779	*Andy Stankiewicz* (Diamond Debuts)	.05
780	*Turk Wendel* l (Diamond Debuts)	.05
781	Bill Krueger	.05
782	Rickey Henderson (Grand Theft)	.10
783	Kevin Seitzer	.05
784	Dave Martinez	.05
785	John Smiley	.05
786	Matt Stairs	.20
787	Scott Scudder	.05
788	John Wetteland	.05
789	Jack Armstrong	.05
790	Ken Hill	.05
791	Dick Schofield	.05
792	Mariano Duncan	.05
793	Bill Pecota	.05
794	*Mike Kelly*	.05
795	Willie Randolph	.05
796	*Butch Henry*	.05
797	*Carlos Hernandez*	.05
798	Doug Jones	.05
799	Melido Perez	.05
800	Checklist	.05
SP3	"Prime Time's Two" (Deion Sanders)	1.00
SP4	"Mr. Baseball" (Tom Selleck, Frank Thomas)	2.00
HH2	(Ted Williams) (hologram)	2.00

1992 Upper Deck Bench/Morgan Heroes

This set is devoted to two of the vital cogs in Cincinnati's Big Red Machine: Hall of Famers Johnny Bench and Joe Morgan. Cards, numbered 37-45, were included in high number packs. An unnumbered cover card was also produced. Both players autographed 2,500 of card #45, the painting of the Reds duo by sports artist Vernon Wells.

		MT
Complete Set (10):		8.00
Common Card:		.40
Header Card:		1.50
Autographed Card:		100.00
37	1968 Rookie of the Year (Johnny Bench)	.75
38	1968-77 Ten Straight Gold Gloves (Johnny Bench)	.75
39	1970 & 1972 MVP (Johnny Bench)	.75
40	1965 Rookie Year (Joe Morgan)	.40
41	1975-76 Back-to-Back MVP (Joe Morgan)	.40
42	1980-83 The Golden Years (Joe Morgan)	.40
43	1972-79 Big Red Machine (Johnny Bench, Joe Morgan)	.60
44	1989 & 1990 Hall of Fame (Johnny Bench, Joe Morgan)	.60

45	Checklist - Heroes 37-45 (Johnny Bench, Joe Morgan)	.60

1992 Upper Deck College POY Holograms

This three-card hologram set features the College Player of the Year winners from 1989-91. Cards were randomly inserted in high number foil packs and have a CP prefix for numbering.

		MT
Complete Set (3):		.75
Common Player:		.25
1	David McCarty	.25
2	Mike Kelly	.25
3	Ben McDonald	.25

1992 Upper Deck Hall of Fame Heroes

This set features three top players from the 1970s: Vida Blue, Lou Brock and Rollie Fingers. The cards continue from last year's set by using numbers H5-H8. The three players are each on one card; the fourth card features all three. They were found in low-number foil packs and specially-marked jumbo packs. Both types of packs could also contain autographed cards; each player signed 3,000 cards.

		MT
Complete Set (4):		3.00
Common Player:		4.00
Vida Blue Autograph:		15.00
Lou Brock Autograph:		30.00
Rollie Fingers Autograph:		15.00
5	Vida Blue	.40
6	Lou Brock	2.00
7	Rollie Fingers	.50
8	Vida Blue, Lou Brock, Rollie Fingers	1.00

Player names in *Italic* type indicate a rookie card.

1992 Upper Deck Heroes Highlights

Special packaging of 1992 Upper Deck high numbers produced for sales to dealers at its Heroes of Baseball show series included these cards of former players as inserts. Cards have a Heroes Highlights banner including the player's name and the date of his career highlight beneath the photo. In a tombstone frame on back, the highlight is chronicled. Cards are numbered alphabetically by player name, with the card number carrying an HI prefix.

		MT
Complete Set (10):		15.00
Common Player:		1.00
1	Bobby Bonds	1.00
2	Lou Brock	1.00
3	Rollie Fingers	1.00
4	Bob Gibson	1.25
5	Reggie Jackson	2.00
6	Gaylord Perry	1.00
7	Robin Roberts	1.00
8	Brooks Robinson	1.50
9	Billy Williams	1.00
10	Ted Williams	3.50

1992 Upper Deck Home Run Heroes

This 26-card set features a top home run hitter from each major league team. The cards, numbered HR1-HR26, were found in low-number jumbo packs, one per pack.

		MT
Complete Set (26):		15.00
Common Player:		.40
1	Jose Canseco	1.00
2	Cecil Fielder	.40
3	Howard Johnson	.40
4	Cal Ripken, Jr.	3.00
5	Matt Williams	.75
6	Joe Carter	.40
7	Ron Gant	.40
8	Frank Thomas	1.00
9	Andre Dawson	.40
10	Fred McGriff	.75
11	Danny Tartabull	.40
12	Chili Davis	.40
13	Albert Belle	.75
14	Jack Clark	.40
15	Paul O'Neill	.60
16	Darryl Strawberry	.50
17	Dave Winfield	.65
18	Jay Buhner	.40
19	Juan Gonzalez	1.00
20	Greg Vaughn	.40
21	Barry Bonds	1.00
22	Matt Nokes	.40
23	John Kruk	.40
24	Ivan Calderon	.40
25	Jeff Bagwell	1.00
26	Todd Zeile	.40

1992 Upper Deck Scouting Report

These cards were randomly inserted in Upper Deck high-number jumbo packs. The set is numbered SR1-SR25 and features 25 top prospects, including 1992 Rookies of the Year Pat Listach and Eric Karros. "Scouting Report" is written down the side on the front in silver lettering. The back features a clipboard which shows a photo, a player profile and a major league scouting report.

		MT
Complete Set (25):		12.00
Common Player:		.25
1	Andy Ashby	.35
2	Willie Banks	.25
3	Kim Batiste	.25
4	Derek Bell	.50
5	Archi Cianfrocco	.25
6	Royce Clayton	.25
7	Gary DiSarcina	.25
8	Dave Fleming	.25
9	Butch Henry	.25
10	Todd Hundley	.50
11	Brian Jordan	.50
12	Eric Karros	.50
13	Pat Listach	.25
14	Scott Livingstone	.25
15	Kenny Lofton	3.00
16	Pat Mahomes	.25
17	Denny Neagle	.25
18	Dave Nilsson	.35
19	Donovan Osborne	.25
20	Reggie Sanders	.35
21	Andy Stankiewicz	.25
22	Jim Thome	5.00
23	Julio Valera	.25
24	Mark Wohlers	.25
25	Anthony Young	.25

1992 Upper Deck Ted Williams' Best

Twenty of the best hitters in baseball according to legend Ted Williams are featured in this special insert set from Upper Deck. The cards are styled much like the 1992 FanFest cards and showcase each chosen player. Each card is numbered with a "T" designation.

		MT
Complete Set (20):		20.00
Common Player:		.50
1	Wade Boggs	1.00
2	Barry Bonds	1.50
3	Jose Canseco	1.50
4	Will Clark	.75
5	Cecil Fielder	.50
6	Tony Gwynn	3.00
7	Rickey Henderson	.75
8	Fred McGriff	.75
9	Kirby Puckett	2.00
10	Ruben Sierra	.50
11	Roberto Alomar	1.00
12	Jeff Bagwell	2.00
13	Albert Belle	1.00
14	Juan Gonzalez	2.00
15	Ken Griffey, Jr.	6.00
16	Chris Hoiles	.50
17	Dave Justice	.75
18	Phil Plantier	.50
19	Frank Thomas	2.00
20	Robin Ventura	.65

1992 Upper Deck Ted Williams Heroes

This Baseball Heroes set devoted to Ted Williams continues where previous efforts left off by numbering it from 28-36. An unnumbered "Baseball Heroes" cover card is also included. Cards were found in low-number foil and jumbo packs. Williams also autographed 2,500 cards, which were numbered and randomly inserted in low-number packs.

		MT
Complete Set (10):		6.00
Common Player:		.50
Autographed Card:		400.00
Williams Header:		2.50
28	1939 Rookie Year	.50
29	1941 .406!	.50
30	1942 Triple Crown Year	.50
31	1946 & 1949 MVP	.50
32	1947 Second Triple Crown	.50
33	1950s Player of the Decade	.50
34	1960 500 Home Run Club	.50
35	1966 Hall of Fame	.50
36	Checklist - Heroes 28-36	.50

1993 Upper Deck

Upper Deck introduced its 1993 set in a two-series format to adjust to expansion. Cards 1-420 make up the first series. Special subsets in Series 1 include rookies, teammates and community heroes. Fronts feature color player photos surrounded by a white border. "Upper Deck" appears at the top of the photo and the player ID at the bottom. Backs feature vertical photos, which is a change from the past, and more complete statistics than what Upper Deck has had in the past. The hologram appears in the lower-left corner on the card back.

		MT
Complete Set (840):		35.00
Complete Series 1 (420):		20.00
Complete Series 2 (420):		20.00
Common Player:		.05
Gold Hologram:		4X
Distributed 1:20 in Factory Set form		
Series 1 or 2 Pack (15):		1.00
Series 1 or 2 Wax Box (36):		30.00
1	Tim Salmon (Checklist)	.25
2	Mike Piazza (Star Rookie)	2.00
3	*Rene Arocha* (Star Rookie)	.15
4	*Willie Greene* (Star Rookie)	.15
5	*Manny Alexander* (Star Rookie)	.10
6	Dan Wilson (Star Rookie)	.10
7	*Dan Smith* (Star Rookie)	.05
8	*Kevin Rogers* (Star Rookie)	.05
9	*Nigel Wilson* (Star Rookie)	.05
10	*Joe Vitko* (Star Rookie)	.10
11	Tim Costo (Star Rookie)	.15
12	Alan Embree (Star Rookie)	.15
13	*Jim Tatum* (Star Rookie)	.05
14	*Cris Colon* (Star Rookie)	.10
15	Steve Hosey (Star Rookie)	.10
16	*Sterling Hitchcock* (Star Rookie)	.15
17	*Dave Mlicki* (Star Rookie)	.15
18	*Jessie Hollins* (Star Rookie)	.10
19	*Bobby Jones* (Star Rookie)	.15
20	*Kurt Miller* (Star Rookie)	.15
21	*Melvin Nieves* (Star Rookie)	.15
22	*Billy Ashley* (Star Rookie)	.15
23	*J.T. Snow* (Star Rookie)	.50
24	Chipper Jones (Star Rookie)	1.25
25	Tim Salmon (Star Rookie)	.25
26	*Tim Pugh* (Star Rookie)	.10
27	David Nied (Star Rookie)	.05
28	*Mike Trombley* (Star Rookie)	.10
29	Javier Lopez (Star Rookie)	.25
30	Community Heroes Checklist (Jim Abbott)	.05
31	Jim Abbott (Community Heroes)	.10
32	Dale Murphy (Community Heroes)	.10
33	Tony Pena (Community Heroes)	.05
34	Kirby Puckett (Community Heroes)	.40
35	Harold Reynolds (Community Heroes)	.10
36	Cal Ripken, Jr. (Community Heroes)	.50
37	Nolan Ryan (Community Heroes)	.50
38	Ryne Sandberg (Community Heroes)	.25
39	Dave Stewart (Community Heroes)	.05
40	Dave Winfield (Community Heroes)	.10
41	Teammates Checklist (Joe Carter, Mark McGwire)	1.00
42	Blockbuster Trade (Joe Carter, Roberto Alomar)	.15
43	Brew Crew (Pat Listach, Robin Yount, Paul Molitor)	.15
44	Iron and Steal (Brady Anderson, Cal Ripken, Jr.)	.25
45	Youthful Tribe (Albert Belle, Sandy Alomar Jr., Jim Thome, Carlos Baerga, Kenny Lofton)	.15
46	Motown Mashers (Cecil Fielder, Mickey Tettleton)	.10
47	Yankee Pride (Roberto Kelly, Don Mattingly)	.20
48	Boston Cy Sox (Frank Viola, Roger Clemens)	.25
49	Bash Brothers (Ruben Sierra, Mark McGwire)	1.00
50	Twin Titles (Kent Hrbek, Kirby Puckett)	.20
51	Southside Sluggers (Robin Ventura, Frank Thomas)	.25
52	Latin Stars (Jose Canseco, Ivan Rodriguez, Rafael Palmeiro, Juan Gonzalez)	.25
53	Lethal Lefties (Mark Langston, Jim Abbott, Chuck Finley)	.10
54	Royal Family (Gregg Jefferies, George Brett, Wally Joyner)	.20
55	Pacific Sox Exchange (Kevin Mitchell, Jay Buhner, Ken Griffey, Jr.)	.50
56	George Brett	.50
57	Scott Cooper	.05
58	Mike Maddux	.05
59	*Rusty Meacham*	.05
60	Wil Cordero	.10
61	Tim Teufel	.05
62	Jeff Montgomery	.05
63	Scott Livingstone	.05
64	Doug Dascenzo	.05
65	Bret Boone	.10
66	*Tim Wakefield*	.10
67	Curt Schilling	.10
68	Frank Tanana	.05
69	Len Dykstra	.05
70	Derek Lilliquist	.05
71	Anthony Young	.05
72	*Hipolito Pichardo*	.05
73	Rod Beck	.05
74	Kent Hrbek	.05
75	Tom Glavine	.15
76	Kevin Brown	.10
77	Chuck Finley	.05
78	Bob Walk	.05
79	Rheal Cormier	.05
80	Rick Sutcliffe	.05
81	Harold Baines	.05
82	Lee Smith	.05
83	Geno Petralli	.05
84	Jose Oquendo	.05
85	Mark Gubicza	.05
86	Mickey Tettleton	.05
87	Bobby Witt	.05
88	Mark Lewis	.05
89	Kevin Appier	.10
90	Mike Stanton	.05
91	Rafael Belliard	.05
92	Kenny Rogers	.05
93	Randy Velarde	.05
94	Luis Sojo	.05
95	Mark Leiter	.05
96	Jody Reed	.05
97	Pete Harnisch	.05
98	Tom Candiotti	.05
99	Mark Portugal	.05
100	Dave Valle	.05
101	Shawon Dunston	.05
102	B.J. Surhoff	.05
103	Jay Bell	.05
104	Sid Bream	.05
105	Checklist 1-105 (Frank Thomas)	.20
106	Mike Morgan	.05
107	Bill Doran	.05
108	Lance Blankenship	.05
109	Mark Lemke	.05
110	Brian Harper	.05
111	Brady Anderson	.15
112	Bip Roberts	.05
113	Mitch Williams	.05
114	Craig Biggio	.20
115	Eddie Murray	.20
116	Matt Nokes	.05
117	Lance Parrish	.05
118	Bill Swift	.05
119	Jeff Innis	.05
120	Mike LaValliere	.05
121	Hal Morris	.05
122	Walt Weiss	.05
123	Ivan Rodriguez	.50
124	Andy Van Slyke	.05
125	Roberto Alomar	.30
126	Robby Thompson	.05
127	Sammy Sosa	1.00
128	Mark Langston	.05
129	Jerry Browne	.05
130	Chuck McElroy	.05
131	Frank Viola	.05
132	Leo Gomez	.05
133	Ramon Martinez	.10
134	Don Mattingly	.60
135	Roger Clemens	1.00
136	Rickey Henderson	.35
137	Darren Daulton	.05
138	Ken Hill	.05
139	Ozzie Guillen	.05
140	Jerald Clark	.05
141	Dave Fleming	.05
142	Delino DeShields	.05
143	Matt Williams	.20
144	Larry Walker	.25
145	Ruben Sierra	.05
146	Ozzie Smith	.40
147	Chris Sabo	.05
148	*Carlos Hernandez*	.10
149	Pat Borders	.05
150	Orlando Merced	.05
151	Royce Clayton	.05
152	Kurt Stillwell	.05
153	Dave Hollins	.05
154	Mike Greenwell	.05
155	Nolan Ryan	1.00
156	Felix Jose	.05
157	Junior Felix	.05
158	Derek Bell	.10
159	Steve Buechele	.05
160	John Burkett	.05
161	*Pat Howell*	.05
162	Milt Cuyler	.05
163	Terry Pendleton	.05
164	Jack Morris	.05
165	Tony Gwynn	.75
166	Deion Sanders	.15
167	Mike Devereaux	.05
168	Ron Darling	.05
169	Orel Hershiser	.05
170	Mike Jackson	.05
171	Doug Jones	.05
172	*Dan Walters*	.05
173	Darren Lewis	.05
174	Carlos Baerga	.05
175	Ryne Sandberg	.35
176	Gregg Jefferies	.10
177	John Jaha	.05
178	Luis Polonia	.05
179	Kirt Manwaring	.05
180	Mike Magnante	.05
181	Billy Ripken	.05
182	Mike Moore	.05
183	Eric Anthony	.05
184	Lenny Harris	.05
185	Tony Pena	.05
186	Mike Felder	.05
187	Greg Olson	.05
188	Rene Gonzales	.05
189	Mike Bordick	.05
190	Mel Rojas	.05
191	Todd Frohwirth	.05
192	Darryl Hamilton	.05
193	Mike Fetters	.05
194	Omar Olivares	.05
195	Tony Phillips	.05
196	Paul Sorrento	.05
197	Trevor Wilson	.05
198	Kevin Gross	.05
199	Ron Karkovice	.05
200	Brook Jacoby	.05
201	Mariano Duncan	.05
202	Dennis Cook	.05
203	Daryl Boston	.05
204	Mike Perez	.05
205	Manuel Lee	.05
206	Steve Olin	.05
207	Charlie Hough	.05
208	Scott Scudder	.05
209	Charlie O'Brien	.05
210	Checklist 106-210 (Barry Bonds)	.10
211	Jose Vizcaino	.05

212 Scott Leius .05
213 Kevin Mitchell .05
214 Brian Barnes .05
215 Pat Kelly .05
216 Chris Hammond .05
217 Rob Deer .05
218 Cory Snyder .05
219 Gary Carter .10
220 Danny Darwin .05
221 Tom Gordon .05
222 Gary Sheffield .20
223 Joe Carter .05
224 Jay Buhner .05
225 Jose Offerman .05
226 Jose Rijo .05
227 Mark Whiten .05
228 Randy Milligan .05
229 Bud Black .05
230 Gary DiSarcina .05
231 Steve Finley .05
232 Dennis Martinez .05
233 Mike Mussina .20
234 Joe Oliver .05
235 Chad Curtis .05
236 Shane Mack .05
237 Jaime Navarro .05
238 Brian McRae .05
239 Chili Davis .05
240 Jeff King .05
241 Dean Palmer .05
242 Danny Tartabull .05
243 Charles Nagy .05
244 Ray Lankford .05
245 Barry Larkin .15
246 Steve Avery .05
247 John Kruk .05
248 Derrick May .05
249 Stan Javier .05
250 Roger McDowell .05
251 Dan Gladden .05
252 Wally Joyner .10
253 Pat Listach .05
254 Chuck Knoblauch .20
255 Sandy Alomar Jr. .10
256 Jeff Bagwell .60
257 Andy Stankiewicz .05
258 Darrin Jackson .05
259 Brett Butler .05
260 Joe Orsulak .05
261 Andy Benes .10
262 Kenny Lofton .25
263 Robin Ventura .15
264 Ron Gant .10
265 Ellis Burks .05
266 Juan Guzman .05
267 Wes Chamberlain .05
268 John Smiley .05
269 Franklin Stubbs .05
270 Tom Browning .05
271 Dennis Eckersley .05
272 Carlton Fisk .20
273 Lou Whitaker .05
274 Phil Plantier .05
275 Bobby Bonilla .05
276 Ben McDonald .05
277 Bob Zupcic .05
278 Terry Steinbach .05
279 Terry Mulholland .05
280 Lance Johnson .05
281 Willie McGee .05
282 Bret Saberhagen .10
283 Randy Myers .05
284 Randy Tomlin .05
285 Mickey Morandini .05
286 Brian Williams .05
287 Tino Martinez .10
288 Jose Melendez .05
289 Jeff Huson .05
290 Joe Grahe .05
291 Mel Hall .05
292 Otis Nixon .05
293 Todd Hundley .10
294 Casey Candaele .05
295 Kevin Seitzer .05
296 Eddie Taubensee .05
297 Moises Alou .15
298 Scott Radinsky .05
299 Thomas Howard .05
300 Kyle Abbott .05
301 Omar Vizquel .10
302 Keith Miller .05
303 Rick Aguilera .05
304 Bruce Hurst .05
305 Ken Caminiti .15
306 Mike Pagiarulo .05
307 Frank Seminara .05
308 Andre Dawson .10
309 Jose Lind .05
310 Joe Boever .05
311 Jeff Parrett .05
312 Alan Mills .05
313 Kevin Tapani .05
314 Darryl Kile .05
315 Checklist 211-315 (Will Clark) .05
316 Mike Sharperson .05
317 John Orton .05
318 Bob Tewksbury .05
319 Xavier Hernandez .05
320 Paul Assenmacher .05
321 John Franco .05
322 Mike Timlin .05
323 Jose Guzman .05
324 Pedro Martinez .75
325 Bill Spiers .05
326 Melido Perez .05
327 Mike Macfarlane .05
328 Ricky Bones .05
329 Scott Bankhead .05
330 Rich Rodriguez .05
331 Geronimo Pena .05
332 Bernie Williams .30
333 Paul Molitor .25
334 Roger Mason .05
335 David Cone .15
336 Randy Johnson .30
337 Pat Mahomes .05
338 Erik Hanson .05
339 Duane Ward .05
340 Al Martin .05
341 Pedro Munoz .05
342 Greg Colbrunn .05
343 Julio Valera .05
344 John Olerud .15
345 George Bell .05
346 Devon White .05
347 Donovan Osborne .05
348 Mark Gardner .05
349 Zane Smith .05
350 Wilson Alvarez .05
351 *Kevin Koslofski* .05
352 Roberto Hernandez .05
353 Glenn Davis .05
354 Reggie Sanders .10
355 Ken Griffey, Jr. 2.00
355a Ken Griffey Jr. (promo, 1992-dated hologram on back) 6.00
355b Ken Griffey, Jr. (8-1/2" x 11" limited edition of 1,000) 25.00
356 Marquis Grissom .10
357 Jack McDowell .05
358 Jimmy Key .05
359 Stan Belinda .05
360 Gerald Williams .05
361 Sid Fernandez .05
362 Alex Fernandez .10
363 John Smoltz .15
364 Travis Fryman .10
365 Jose Canseco .50
366 Dave Justice .20
367 *Pedro Astacio* .15
368 Tim Belcher .05
369 Steve Sax .05
370 Gary Gaetti .05
371 Jeff Frye .10
372 Bob Wickman .05
373 *Ryan Thompson* .10
374 *David Hulse* .10
375 Cal Eldred .05
376 Ryan Klesko .20
377 *Damion Easley* .10
378 *John Kiely* .10
379 *Jim Bullinger* .10
380 Brian Bohanon .05
381 Rod Brewer .05
382 *Fernando Ramsey* .05
383 Sam Militello .05
384 Arthur Rhodes .05
385 Eric Karros .10
386 Rico Brogna .05
387 *John Valentin* .25
388 *Kerry Woodson* .05
389 *Ben Rivera* .05
390 *Matt Whiteside* .10
391 Henry Rodriguez .05
392 John Wetteland .05
393 Kent Mercker .05
394 Bernard Gilkey .05
395 Doug Henry .05
396 Mo Vaughn .30
397 Scott Erickson .05
398 Bill Gullickson .05
399 Mark Guthrie .05
400 Dave Martinez .05
401 *Jeff Kent* .15
402 Chris Hoiles .05
403 Mike Henneman .05
404 Chris Nabholz .05
405 Tom Pagnozzi .05
406 Kelly Gruber .05
407 Bob Welch .05
408 Frank Castillo .05
409 John Dopson .05
410 Steve Farr .05
411 Henry Cotto .05
412 Bob Patterson .05
413 Todd Stottlemyre .10
414 Greg A. Harris .05
415 Denny Neagle .05
416 Bill Wegman .05
417 Willie Wilson .05
418 Terry Leach .05
419 Willie Randolph .05
420 Checklist 316-420 (Mark McGwire) 1.00
421 Calvin Murray (Top Prospects Checklist) .10
422 *Pete Janicki* (Top Prospect) .05
423 Todd Jones (Top Prospect) .05
424 Mike Neill (Top Prospect) .05
425 Carlos Delgado (Top Prospect) .50
426 Jose Oliva (Top Prospect) .05
427 Tyrone Hill (Top Prospect) .05
428 Dmitri Young (Top Prospect) .15
429 *Derek Wallace* (Top Prospect) .10
430 *Michael Moore* (Top Prospect) .05
431 Cliff Floyd (Top Prospect) .10
432 Calvin Murray (Top Prospect) .10
433 Manny Ramirez (Top Prospect) 1.00
434 Marc Newfield (Top Prospect) .05
435 Charles Johnson (Top Prospect) .15
436 Butch Huskey (Top Prospect) .10
437 Brad Pennington (Top Prospect) .10
438 *Ray McDavid* (Top Prospect) .10
439 Chad McConnell (Top Prospect) .10
440 *Midre Cummings* (Top Prospect) .15
441 Benji Gil (Top Prospect) .10
442 Frank Rodriguez (Top Prospect) .05
443 *Chad Mottola* (Top Prospect) .10
444 *John Burke* (Top Prospect) .15
445 Michael Tucker (Top Prospect) .10
446 Rick Greene (Top Prospect) .10
447 Rich Becker (Top Prospect) .10
448 Mike Robertson (Top Prospect) .05
449 *Derek Jeter* (Top Prospect) 8.00
450 Checklist 451-470 Inside the Numbers (David McCarty, Ivan Rodriguez) .15
451 Jim Abbott (Inside the Numbers) .05
452 Jeff Bagwell (Inside the Numbers) .25
453 Jason Bere (Inside the Numbers) .05
454 Delino DeShields (Inside the Numbers) .05
455 Travis Fryman (Inside the Numbers) .05
456 Alex Gonzalez (Inside the Numbers) .05
457 Phil Hiatt (Inside the Numbers) .05
458 Dave Hollins (Inside the Numbers) .05
459 Chipper Jones (Inside the Numbers) .40
460 Dave Justice (Inside the Numbers) .15
461 Ray Lankford (Inside the Numbers) .05
462 David McCarty (Inside the Numbers) .05
463 Mike Mussina (Inside the Numbers) .20
464 Jose Offerman (Inside the Numbers) .05
465 Dean Palmer (Inside the Numbers) .05
466 Geronimo Pena (Inside the Numbers) .05
467 Eduardo Perez (Inside the Numbers) .05
468 Ivan Rodriguez (Inside the Numbers) .20
469 Reggie Sanders (Inside the Numbers) .05
470 Bernie Williams (Inside the Numbers) .20
471 Checklist 472-485 Team Stars (Barry Bonds, Matt Williams, Will Clark) .20
472 Strike Force (John Smoltz, Steve Avery, Greg Maddux Tom Glavine) .15
473 Red October (Jose Rijo, Rob Dibble, Roberto Kelly, Reggie Sanders, Barry Larkin) .10
474 Four Corners (Gary Sheffield, Phil Plantier, Tony Gwynn, Fred McGriff) .20
475 Shooting Stars (Doug Drabek, Craig Biggio, Jeff Bagwell) .15
476 Giant Sticks (Will Clark, Barry Bonds, Matt Williams) .20
477 Boyhood Friends (Darryl Strawberry, Eric Davis) .05
478 Rock Solid (Dante Bichette, David Nied, Andres Galarraga) .10
479 Inaugural Catch (Dave Magadan, Orestes Destrade, Bret Barbarie, Jeff Conine) .05
480 Steel City Champions (Tim Wakefield, Andy Van Slyke, Jay Bell) .05
481 “Les Grandes Etoiles” (Marquis Grissom, Delino DeShields, Dennis Martinez, Larry Walker) .10
482 Runnin' Redbirds (Geronimo Pena, Ray Lankford, Ozzie Smith, Bernard Gilkey) .10
483 Ivy Leaguers (Ryne Sandberg, Mark Grace, Randy Myers) .15
484 Big Apple Power Switch (Eddie Murray, Bobby Bonilla, Howard Johnson) .10
485 Hammers & Nails (John Kruk, Dave Hollins, Darren Daulton, Len Dykstra) .05
486 Barry Bonds (Award Winners) .15
487 Dennis Eckersley (Award Winners) .05
488 Greg Maddux (Award Winners) .35
489 Dennis Eckersley (Award Winners) .05
490 Eric Karros (Award Winners) .05
491 Pat Listach (Award Winners) .05
492 Gary Sheffield (Award Winners) .10

No.	Player	Price
493	Mark McGwire (Award Winners)	1.00
494	Gary Sheffield (Award Winners)	.10
495	Edgar Martinez (Award Winners)	.05
496	Fred McGriff (Award Winners)	.15
497	Juan Gonzalez (Award Winners)	.25
498	Darren Daulton (Award Winners)	.05
499	Cecil Fielder (Award Winners)	.05
500	Checklist 501-510 Diamond Debuts (Brent Gates)	.10
501	Tavo Alvarez (Diamond Debuts)	.05
502	Rod Bolton (Diamond Debuts)	.05
503	*John Cummings* (Diamond Debuts)	.10
504	Brent Gates (Diamond Debuts)	.05
505	Tyler Green (Diamond Debuts)	.10
506	*Jose Martinez* (Diamond Debuts)	.10
507	Troy Percival (Diamond Debuts)	.05
508	Kevin Stocker (Diamond Debuts)	.05
509	*Matt Walbeck* (Diamond Debuts)	.15
510	Rondell White (Diamond Debuts)	.20
511	Billy Ripken	.05
512	Mike Moore	.05
513	Jose Lind	.05
514	Chito Martinez	.05
515	Jose Guzman	.05
516	Kim Batiste	.05
517	Jeff Tackett	.05
518	Charlie Hough	.05
519	Marvin Freeman	.05
520	Carlos Martinez	.05
521	Eric Young	.10
522	Pete Incaviglia	.05
523	Scott Fletcher	.05
524	Orestes Destrade	.05
525	Checklist 421-525 (Ken Griffey, Jr.)	.20
526	Ellis Burks	.05
527	Juan Samuel	.05
528	Dave Magadan	.05
529	Jeff Parrett	.05
530	Bill Krueger	.05
531	Frank Bolick	.05
532	Alan Trammell	.10
533	Walt Weiss	.05
534	David Cone	.15
535	Greg Maddux	.75
536	Kevin Young	.05
537	Dave Hansen	.05
538	Alex Cole	.05
539	Greg Hibbard	.05
540	Gene Larkin	.05
541	Jeff Reardon	.05
542	Felix Jose	.05
543	Jimmy Key	.05
544	Reggie Jefferson	.05
545	Gregg Jefferies	.05
546	Dave Stewart	.05
547	Tim Wallach	.05
548	Spike Owen	.05
549	Tommy Greene	.05
550	Fernando Valenzuela	.05
551	Rich Amaral	.05
552	Bret Barberie	.05
553	Edgar Martinez	.05
554	Jim Abbott	.05
555	Frank Thomas	.75
556	Wade Boggs	.20
557	Tom Henke	.05
558	Milt Thompson	.05
559	Lloyd McClendon	.05
560	Vinny Castilla	.25
561	Ricky Jordan	.05
562	Andujar Cedeno	.05
563	Greg Vaughn	.10
564	Cecil Fielder	.05
565	Kirby Puckett	.50
566	Mark McGwire	2.00
567	Barry Bonds	.40
568	Jody Reed	.05
569	Todd Zeile	.05
570	Mark Carreon	.05
571	Joe Girardi	.05
572	Luis Gonzalez	.10
573	Mark Grace	.20
574	Rafael Palmeiro	.20
575	Darryl Strawberry	.10
576	Will Clark	.25
577	Fred McGriff	.20
578	Kevin Reimer	.05
579	Dave Righetti	.05
580	Juan Bell	.05
581	Jeff Brantley	.05
582	Brian Hunter	.05
583	Tim Naehring	.05
584	Glenallen Hill	.05
585	Cal Ripken, Jr.	1.50
586	Albert Belle	.40
587	Robin Yount	.20
588	Chris Bosio	.05
589	Pete Smith	.05
590	Chuck Carr	.05
591	Jeff Blauser	.05
592	Kevin McReynolds	.05
593	Andres Galarraga	.15
594	Kevin Maas	.05
595	Eric Davis	.05
596	Brian Jordan	.10
597	Tim Raines	.05
598	Rick Wilkins	.05
599	Steve Cooke	.05
600	Mike Gallego	.05
601	Mike Munoz	.05
602	Luis Rivera	.05
603	Junior Ortiz	.05
604	Brent Mayne	.05
605	Luis Alicea	.05
606	Damon Berryhill	.05
607	Dave Henderson	.05
608	Kirk McCaskill	.05
609	Jeff Fassero	.05
610	Mike Harkey	.05
611	Francisco Cabrera	.05
612	Rey Sanchez	.05
613	Scott Servais	.05
614	Darrin Fletcher	.05
615	Felix Fermin	.05
616	Kevin Seitzer	.05
617	Bob Scanlan	.05
618	Billy Hatcher	.05
619	John Vander Wal	.05
620	Joe Hesketh	.05
621	Hector Villanueva	.05
622	Randy Milligan	.05
623	*Tony Tarasco*	.10
624	Russ Swan	.05
625	Willie Wilson	.05
626	Frank Tanana	.05
627	Pete O'Brien	.05
628	Lenny Webster	.05
629	Mark Clark	.05
630	Checklist 526-630 (Roger Clemens)	.25
631	Alex Arias	.05
632	Chris Gwynn	.05
633	Tom Bolton	.05
634	Greg Briley	.05
635	Kent Bottenfield	.05
636	Kelly Downs	.05
637	Manuel Lee	.05
638	Al Leiter	.10
639	Jeff Gardner	.05
640	Mike Gardiner	.05
641	Mark Gardner	.05
642	Jeff Branson	.05
643	Paul Wagner	.05
644	Sean Berry	.05
645	Phil Hiatt	.05
646	Kevin Mitchell	.05
647	Charlie Hayes	.05
648	Jim Deshaies	.05
649	Dan Pasqua	.05
650	Mike Maddux	.05
651	*Domingo Martinez*	.10
652	*Greg McMichael*	.05
653	*Eric Wedge*	.05
654	Mark Whiten	.05
655	Bobby Kelly	.05
656	Julio Franco	.05
657	Gene Harris	.05
658	Pete Schourek	.05
659	Mike Bielecki	.05
660	Ricky Gutierrez	.05
661	Chris Hammond	.05
662	Tim Scott	.05
663	Norm Charlton	.05
664	Doug Drabek	.05
665	Dwight Gooden	.10
666	Jim Gott	.05
667	Randy Myers	.05
668	Darren Holmes	.05
669	Tim Spehr	.05
670	Bruce Ruffin	.05
671	Bobby Thigpen	.05
672	Tony Fernandez	.05
673	Darrin Jackson	.05
674	Gregg Olson	.05
675	Rob Dibble	.05
676	Howard Johnson	.05
677	*Mike Lansing*	.15
678	Charlie Leibrandt	.05
679	Kevin Bass	.05
680	Hubie Brooks	.05
681	Scott Brosius	.05
682	Randy Knorr	.05
683	Dante Bichette	.15
684	Bryan Harvey	.05
685	Greg Gohr	.05
686	Willie Banks	.05
687	Robb Nen	.05
688	Mike Scioscia	.05
689	John Farrell	.05
690	John Candelaria	.05
691	Damon Buford	.05
692	Todd Worrell	.05
693	Pat Hentgen	.05
694	John Smiley	.05
695	Greg Swindell	.05
696	Derek Bell	.10
697	Terry Jorgensen	.05
698	Jimmy Jones	.05
699	David Wells	.10
700	Dave Martinez	.05
701	Steve Bedrosian	.05
702	Jeff Russell	.05
703	Joe Magrane	.05
704	Matt Mieske	.05
705	Paul Molitor	.25
706	Dale Murphy	.15
707	Steve Howe	.05
708	Greg Gagne	.05
709	Dave Eiland	.05
710	David West	.05
711	Luis Aquino	.05
712	Joe Orsulak	.05
713	Eric Plunk	.05
714	Mike Felder	.05
715	Joe Klink	.05
716	Lonnie Smith	.05
717	Monty Fariss	.05
718	Craig Lefferts	.05
719	John Habyan	.05
720	Willie Blair	.05
721	Darnell Coles	.05
722	Mark Williamson	.05
723	Bryn Smith	.05
724	Greg W. Harris	.05
725	*Graeme Lloyd*	.10
726	Cris Carpenter	.05
727	Chico Walker	.05
728	Tracy Woodson	.05
729	Jose Uribe	.05
730	Stan Javier	.05
731	Jay Howell	.05
732	Freddie Benavides	.05
733	Jeff Reboulet	.05
734	Scott Sanderson	.05
735	Checklist 631-735 (Ryne Sandberg)	.10
736	Archi Cianfrocco	.05
737	Daryl Boston	.05
738	Craig Grebeck	.05
739	Doug Dascenzo	.05
740	Gerald Young	.05
741	Candy Maldonado	.05
742	Joey Cora	.05
743	Don Slaught	.05
744	Steve Decker	.05
745	Blas Minor	.05
746	Storm Davis	.05
747	Carlos Quintana	.05
748	Vince Coleman	.05
749	Todd Burns	.05
750	Steve Frey	.05
751	Ivan Calderon	.05
752	*Steve Reed*	.10
753	Danny Jackson	.05
754	Jeff Conine	.05
755	Juan Gonzalez	.50
756	Mike Kelly	.05
757	John Doherty	.05
758	Jack Armstrong	.05
759	John Wehner	.05
760	Scott Bankhead	.05
761	Jim Tatum	.05
762	*Scott Pose*	.10
763	Andy Ashby	.05
764	Ed Sprague	.05
765	Harold Baines	.05
766	Kirk Gibson	.05
767	Troy Neel	.05
768	Dick Schofield	.05
769	Dickie Thon	.05
770	Butch Henry	.05
771	Junior Felix	.05
772	*Ken Ryan*	.10
773	Trevor Hoffman	.10
774	Phil Plantier	.05
775	Bo Jackson	.15
776	Benito Santiago	.05
777	Andre Dawson	.10
778	Bryan Hickerson	.05
779	Dennis Moeller	.05
780	Ryan Bowen	.05
781	Eric Fox	.05
782	Joe Kmak	.05
783	Mike Hampton	.05
784	*Darrell Sherman*	.10
785	J.T. Snow	.10
786	Dave Winfield	.20
787	Jim Austin	.05
788	Craig Shipley	.05
789	Greg Myers	.05
790	Todd Benzinger	.05
791	Cory Snyder	.05
792	David Segui	.05
793	Armando Reynoso	.05
794	Chili Davis	.05
795	Dave Nilsson	.05
796	Paul O'Neill	.15
797	Jerald Clark	.05
798	Jose Mesa	.05
799	Brian Holman	.05
800	Jim Eisenreich	.05
801	Mark McLemore	.05
802	Luis Sojo	.05
803	Harold Reynolds	.05
804	Dan Plesac	.05
805	Dave Stieb	.05
806	Tom Brunansky	.05
807	Kelly Gruber	.05
808	Bob Ojeda	.05
809	Dave Burba	.05
810	Joe Boever	.05
811	Jeremy Hernandez	.05
812	Angels Checklist (Tim Salmon)	.10
813	Astros Checklist (Jeff Bagwell)	.25
814	Athletics Checklist (Mark McGwire)	.75
815	Blue Jays Checklist (Roberto Alomar)	.15
816	Braves Checklist (Steve Avery)	.05
817	Brewers Checklist (Pat Listach)	.05
818	Cardinals Checklist (Gregg Jefferies)	.05
819	Cubs Checklist (Sammy Sosa)	.50
820	Dodgers Checklist (Darryl Strawberry)	.05
821	Expos Checklist (Dennis Martinez)	.05
822	Giants Checklist (Robby Thompson)	.05
823	Indians Checklist (Albert Belle)	.20
824	Mariners Checklist (Randy Johnson)	.15
825	Marlins Checklist (Nigel Wilson)	.05
826	Mets Checklist (Bobby Bonilla)	.05
827	Orioles Checklist (Glenn Davis)	.05
828	Padres Checklist (Gary Sheffield)	.10
829	Phillies Checklist (Darren Daulton)	.05
830	Pirates Checklist (Jay Bell)	.05
831	Rangers Checklist (Juan Gonzalez)	.25
832	Red Sox Checklist (Andre Dawson)	.05
833	Reds Checklist (Hal Morris)	.05
834	Rockies Checklist (David Nied)	.05
835	Royals Checklist (Felix Jose)	.05
836	Tigers Checklist (Travis Fryman)	.05
837	Twins Checklist (Shane Mack)	.05
838	White Sox Checklist (Robin Ventura)	.05
839	Yankees Checklist (Danny Tartabull)	.05
840	Checklist 736-840 (Roberto Alomar)	.15
SP5	3,000 Hits (Robin Yount, George Brett)	2.00
SP6	Nolan Ryan	3.00

1993 Upper Deck Clutch Performers

Reggie Jackson has selected the players who perform the best under pressure for this 20-card insert set. Cards were available only in Series II retail packs and use the prefix R for numbering. Fronts have a black bottom panel with "Clutch Performers" printed in dark gray. Jackson's facsimile autograph is overprinted in gold foil. On back, under a second player photo, is Jackson's picture and his assessment of the player. There are a few lines of stats to support the player's selection to this exclusive company.

		MT
Complete Set (20):		15.00
Common Player:		.25
1	Roberto Alomar	1.00
2	Wade Boggs	.40
3	Barry Bonds	1.25
4	Jose Canseco	1.50
5	Joe Carter	.25
6	Will Clark	.75
7	Roger Clemens	2.00
8	Dennis Eckersley	.25
9	Cecil Fielder	.25
10	Juan Gonzalez	1.50
11	Ken Griffey, Jr.	5.00
12	Rickey Henderson	.50
13	Barry Larkin	.40
14	Don Mattingly	1.50
15	Fred McGriff	.50
16	Terry Pendleton	.25
17	Kirby Puckett	1.50
18	Ryne Sandberg	1.00
19	John Smoltz	.25
20	Frank Thomas	1.50

1993 Upper Deck 5th Anniversary

This 15-card insert set replicates 15 of Upper Deck's most popular cards from its first five years. Foil stamping and a fifth-anniversary logo appear on the cards, which are otherwise reproductions of the originals. The prefix A appears before each card number. The cards were available in Series II hobby packs only.

		MT
Complete Set (15):		20.00
Common Player:		.50
1	Ken Griffey, Jr.	6.00
2	Gary Sheffield	.75
3	Roberto Alomar	1.00
4	Jim Abbott	.50
5	Nolan Ryan	4.00
6	Juan Gonzalez	1.50
7	Dave Justice	.75
8	Carlos Baerga	.50
9	Reggie Jackson	.75
10	Eric Karros	.50
11	Chipper Jones	2.50
12	Ivan Rodriguez	1.50
13	Pat Listach	.50
14	Frank Thomas	2.00
15	Tim Salmon	.75

1993 Upper Deck Home Run Heroes

This 28-card insert set features the top home run hitters from each team for 1992. Cards, inserted in Series I jumbo packs, are numbered with an HR prefix. The card fronts have "Home Run Heroes" printed vertically at the left edge and an embossed bat with the player's name and Upper Deck trademark at bottom. Backs have a purple or pink posterized photo and a few words about the player.

		MT
Complete Set (28):		15.00
Common Player:		.25
1	Juan Gonzalez	1.50
2	Mark McGwire	5.00
3	Cecil Fielder	.25
4	Fred McGriff	.50
5	Albert Belle	1.00
6	Barry Bonds	1.50
7	Joe Carter	.25
8	Darren Daulton	.25
9	Ken Griffey, Jr.	5.00
10	Dave Hollins	.25
11	Ryne Sandberg	1.00
12	George Bell	.25
13	Danny Tartabull	.25
14	Mike Devereaux	.25
15	Greg Vaughn	.25
16	Larry Walker	.75
17	Dave Justice	.50
18	Terry Pendleton	.25
19	Eric Karros	.35
20	Ray Lankford	.25
21	Matt Williams	.60
22	Eric Anthony	.25
23	Bobby Bonilla	.25
24	Kirby Puckett	2.00
25	Mike Macfarlane	.25
26	Tom Brunansky	.25
27	Paul O'Neill	.40
28	Gary Gaetti	.25

1993 Upper Deck Highlights

These 20 insert cards commemorate highlights from the 1992 season. Cards, which were randomly inserted in Series II packs, have a '92 Season Highlights logo on the bottom, with the player's name inside a banner trailing from the logo. The date of the significant event is under the player's name. Card backs have the logo at the top and are numbered with an HI prefix. A headline describes what highlight occurred, while the text describes the event.

		MT
Complete Set (20):		100.00
Common Player:		2.00
1	Roberto Alomar	6.00
2	Steve Avery	2.00
3	Harold Baines	2.00
4	Damon Berryhill	2.00
5	Barry Bonds	8.00
6	Bret Boone	2.00
7	George Brett	8.00
8	Francisco Cabrera	2.00
9	Ken Griffey, Jr.	30.00
10	Rickey Henderson	5.00
11	Kenny Lofton	6.00
12	Mickey Morandini	2.00
13	Eddie Murray	4.00
14	David Nied	2.00
15	Jeff Reardon	2.00
16	Bip Roberts	2.00
17	Nolan Ryan	25.00
18	Ed Sprague	2.00
19	Dave Winfield	4.00
20	Robin Yount	5.00

1993 Upper Deck Iooss Collection

Sports photographer Walter Iooss Jr. has captured 26 current players in this insert set featuring their candid portraits. Cards have full-bleed photos and gold foil stamping. Backs have biographical sketches and are numbered using a WI prefix. They are available in Series I retail packs.

		MT
Complete Set (27):		18.00
Common Player:		.50
Header Card:		1.00
1	Tim Salmon	.75
2	Jeff Bagwell	2.00
3	Mark McGwire	5.00
4	Roberto Alomar	1.00
5	Steve Avery	.50
6	Paul Molitor	1.00
7	Ozzie Smith	1.00
8	Mark Grace	.75
9	Eric Karros	.60
10	Delino DeShields	.50
11	Will Clark	.75
12	Albert Belle	1.00
13	Ken Griffey, Jr.	5.00
14	Howard Johnson	.50
15	Cal Ripken, Jr.	4.00
16	Fred McGriff	.75
17	Darren Daulton	.50
18	Andy Van Slyke	.50
19	Nolan Ryan	4.00
20	Wade Boggs	.75
21	Barry Larkin	.60
22	George Brett	1.50
23	Cecil Fielder	.50
24	Kirby Puckett	1.50
25	Frank Thomas	2.00
26	Don Mattingly	1.50

1993 Upper Deck On Deck

These UV-coated cards feature 25 of the game's top players. Each card has a full-bleed photo on the front and questions and answers on the back. Available only in Series II jumbo packs, the cards have a D prefix for numbering.

		MT
Complete Set (25):		24.00
Common Player:		.25
1	Jim Abbott	.25
2	Roberto Alomar	1.00
3	Carlos Baerga	.25
4	Albert Belle	1.00
5	Wade Boggs	.75
6	George Brett	1.50
7	Jose Canseco	1.25
8	Will Clark	.75
9	Roger Clemens	2.00
10	Dennis Eckersley	.25
11	Cecil Fielder	.25
12	Juan Gonzalez	1.50
13	Ken Griffey, Jr.	5.00
14	Tony Gwynn	2.50
15	Bo Jackson	.50
16	Chipper Jones	3.00
17	Eric Karros	.40
18	Mark McGwire	5.00
19	Kirby Puckett	1.50
20	Nolan Ryan	4.00
21	Tim Salmon	.50
22	Ryne Sandberg	1.00
23	Darryl Strawberry	.25
24	Frank Thomas	2.00
25	Andy Van Slyke	.25

1993 Upper Deck Then And Now

This 18-card lithogram set features both Hall of Famers and current players. The cards feature a combination of four-color player photos and a holographic background. They were random inserts in both Series I and Series II packs. Numbering includes the prefix TN. A limited edition of 2,500 supersize 5 by 7 Mickey Mantle Then And Now cards was created for sale through Upper Deck Authenticated.

		MT
Complete Set (18):		50.00
Complete Series 1 (9):		20.00
Complete Series 2 (9):		30.00
Common Player:		.75
1	Wade Boggs	1.50
2	George Brett	2.50
3	Rickey Henderson	1.00
4	Cal Ripken, Jr.	9.00
5	Nolan Ryan	9.00
6	Ryne Sandberg	2.00
7	Ozzie Smith	2.00
8	Darryl Strawberry	.75
9	Dave Winfield	1.00
10	Dennis Eckersley	.75
11	Tony Gwynn	4.00
12	Howard Johnson	.75
13	Don Mattingly	2.50
14	Eddie Murray	1.00
15	Robin Yount	1.50
16	Reggie Jackson	1.50
17	Mickey Mantle	12.00
17a	Mickey Mantle (5" x 7")	40.00
18	Willie Mays	6.00

1993 Upper Deck Triple Crown

These insert cards were available in 1993 Upper Deck Series I foil packs sold by hobby dealers. The set features 10 players who are candidates to win baseball's Triple Crown. Card fronts have a crown and the player's name at the bottom. Backs put that material at the top and explain why the player might lead the league in home runs, batting average and runs batted in.

		MT
Complete Set (10):		15.00
Common Player:		.75
1	Barry Bonds	2.00
2	Jose Canseco	1.50
3	Will Clark	1.00
4	Ken Griffey, Jr.	5.00
5	Fred McGriff	.75
6	Kirby Puckett	2.00
7	Cal Ripken, Jr.	4.00
8	Gary Sheffield	.75
9	Frank Thomas	2.00
10	Larry Walker	1.00

1993 Upper Deck Willie Mays Heroes

This 10-card insert set includes eight individually-titled cards, an illustrated checklist and one header card. The set is a continuation of Upper Deck's previous Heroes efforts, honoring greats such as Hank Aaron, Nolan Ryan and Reggie Jackson, and is numbered 46-54. Cards were randomly inserted into Series 1 foil packs.

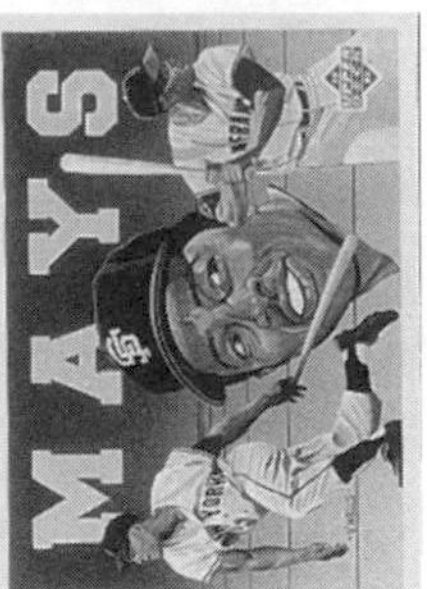

		MT
Complete Set (10):		5.00
Common Mays:		.50
Header Card:		3.00
46	1951 Rookie-of-the-Year	.50
47	1954 The Catch	.50
48	1956-57 30-30 Club	.50
49	1961 Four-Homer Game	.50
50	1965 Most Valuable Player	.50
51	1969 600-Home Run Club	.50
52	1972 New York Homecoming	.50
53	1979 Hall of Fame	.50
54	Checklist - Heroes 46-54	.50

1994 Upper Deck

Upper Deck's 1994 offering was a typical presentation for the company, combining high-quality regular-issue cards with innovative subsets and high-tech chase cards. Series I, besides the standard player cards, features subsets including 30 Star Rookies, with metallic borders, 10 "Fantasy Team" stars who excelled in Rotisserie League stats, 14 Home Field Advantage cards showcasing National League stadiums and hometeam stars, and, 15 stars under the age of 25 in a subset titled, "The Future is Now." Regular issue cards feature a color photo on front and a second, black-and-white version of the same photo at left in a vertically stretched format. The player's name, team and Upper Deck logo appear on front in copper foil. Backs have a color photo, recent and career major league stats and an in-field-shaped hologram. Series II offered, in addition to regular cards, subsets of 14 American League Home Field Advantage cards, a group of "Classic Alumni" minor league players, a selection of "Diamond Debuts" cards and a group of "Top Prospects." Retail packaging contained a special Mickey Mantle/Ken Griffey, Jr. card which could be found bearing either one or both of the players' autographs in an edition of 1,000 each. Series II retail packs offered a chance to find an autographed version of Alex Rodriguez' Classic Alumni card.

		MT
Complete Set (550):		45.00
Complete Series 1 (280):		30.00
Complete Series 2 (270):		18.00
Common Player:		.10
Series 1 E/W Pack (12):		1.50
Series 1 E/W Wax Box (36):		40.00
Series 1 Cen. Pack (12):		2.50
Series 1 Cen. Wax Box (36):		60.00
Series 2 E/W Pack (12):		1.25
Series 2 E/W Wax Box (36):		30.00
Series 2 Cent. Pack (12):		1.50
Series 2 Cent. Wax Box (36):		40.00
1	*Brian Anderson* (Star Rookie)	.40
2	Shane Andrews (Star Rookie)	.25
3	James Baldwin (Star Rookie)	.15
4	Rich Becker (Star Rookie)	.10
5	Greg Blosser (Star Rookie)	.10
6	*Ricky Bottalico* (Star Rookie)	.15
7	Midre Cummings (Star Rookie)	.10
8	Carlos Delgado (Star Rookie)	.75
9	*Steve Dreyer* (Star Rookie)	.10
10	*Joey Eischen* (Star Rookie)	.15
11	Carl Everett (Star Rookie)	.20
12	Cliff Floyd (Star Rookie)	.15
13	Alex Gonzalez (Star Rookie)	.20
14	Jeff Granger (Star Rookie)	.10
15	Shawn Green (Star Rookie)	1.00
16	Brian Hunter (Star Rookie)	.15
17	Butch Huskey (Star Rookie)	.15
18	Mark Hutton (Star Rookie)	.10
19	*Michael Jordan* (Star Rookie)	12.00
20	Steve Karsay (Star Rookie)	.15
21	Jeff McNeely (Star Rookie)	.10
22	Marc Newfield (Star Rookie)	.10
23	Manny Ramirez (Star Rookie)	1.50
24	*Alex Rodriguez* (Star Rookie)	15.00
25	Scott Ruffcorn (Star Rookie)	.10

26 Paul Spoljaric (Star Rookie) .10
27 *Salomon Torres* (Star Rookie) .10
28 Steve Trachsel (Star Rookie) .15
29 *Chris Turner* (Star Rookie) .10
30 Gabe White (Star Rookie) .10
31 Randy Johnson (Fantasy Team) .40
32 John Wetteland (Fantasy Team) .10
33 Mike Piazza (Fantasy Team) 1.00
34 Rafael Palmeiro (Fantasy Team) .20
35 Roberto Alomar (Fantasy Team) .30
36 Matt Williams (Fantasy Team) .20
37 Travis Fryman (Fantasy Team) .10
38 Barry Bonds (Fantasy Team) .40
39 Marquis Grissom (Fantasy Team) .10
40 Albert Belle (Fantasy Team) .30
41 Steve Avery (Future/Now) .10
42 Jason Bere (Future/Now) .10
43 Alex Fernandez (Future/Now) .15
44 Mike Mussina (Future/Now) .30
45 Aaron Sele (Future/Now) .10
46 Rod Beck (Future/Now) .10
47 Mike Piazza (Future/Now) 1.00
48 John Olerud (Future/Now) .15
49 Carlos Baerga (Future/Now) .10
50 Gary Sheffield (Future/Now) .10
51 Travis Fryman (Future/Now) .10
52 Juan Gonzalez (Future/Now) .50
53 Ken Griffey, Jr. (Future/Now) 2.00
54 Tim Salmon (Future/Now) .25
55 Frank Thomas (Future/Now) .50
56 Tony Phillips .10
57 Julio Franco .10
58 Kevin Mitchell .10
59 Raul Mondesi .40
60 Rickey Henderson .40
61 Jay Buhner .10
62 Bill Swift .10
63 Brady Anderson .10
64 Ryan Klesko .20
65 Darren Daulton .10
66 Damion Easley .10
67 Mark McGwire 3.00
68 John Roper .10
69 Dave Telgheder .10
70 Dave Nied .10
71 Mo Vaughn .50
72 Tyler Green .10
73 Dave Magadan .10
74 Chili Davis .10
75 Archi Cianfrocco .10
76 Joe Girardi .10
77 Chris Hoiles .10
78 Ryan Bowen .10
79 Greg Gagne .10
80 Aaron Sele .10
81 Dave Winfield .20
82 Chad Curtis .10
83 Andy Van Slyke .10
84 Kevin Stocker .10
85 Deion Sanders .15
86 Bernie Williams .50
87 John Smoltz .20
88 *Ruben Santana* .10
89 Dave Stewart .10
90 Don Mattingly .75
91 Joe Carter .10
92 Ryne Sandberg .40
93 Chris Gomez .10
94 Tino Martinez .25
95 Terry Pendleton .10
96 Andre Dawson .15

97 Wil Cordero .10
98 Kent Hrbek .10
99 John Olerud .25
100 Kirt Manwaring .10
101 Tim Bogar .10
102 Mike Mussina .40
103 Nigel Wilson .10
104 Ricky Gutierrez .10
105 Roberto Mejia .10
106 Tom Pagnozzi .10
107 Mike Macfarlane .10
108 Jose Bautista .10
109 Luis Ortiz .10
110 Brent Gates .10
111 Tim Salmon .25
112 Wade Boggs .25
113 *Tripp Cromer* .10
114 Denny Hocking .10
115 Carlos Baerga .10
116 *J.R. Phillips* .10
117 Bo Jackson .15
118 Lance Johnson .10
119 Bobby Jones .15
120 Bobby Witt .10
121 Ron Karkovice .10
122 Jose Vizcaino .10
123 Danny Darwin .10
124 Eduardo Perez .10
125 Brian Looney .10
126 Pat Hentgen .10
127 Frank Viola .10
128 Darren Holmes .10
129 Wally Whitehurst .10
130 Matt Walbeck .10
131 Albert Belle .50
132 Steve Cooke .10
133 Kevin Appier .10
134 Joe Oliver .10
135 Benji Gil .10
136 Steve Buechele .10
137 Devon White .10
138 Sterling Hitchcock .10
139 *Phil Leftwich* .10
140 Jose Canseco .50
141 Rick Aguilera .10
142 Rod Beck .10
143 Jose Rijo .10
144 Tom Glavine .20
145 Phil Plantier .10
146 Jason Bere .10
147 Jamie Moyer .10
148 Wes Chamberlain .10
149 Glenallen Hill .10
150 Mark Whiten .10
151 Bret Barberie .10
152 Chuck Knoblauch .20
153 Trevor Hoffman .15
154 Rick Wilkins .10
155 Juan Gonzalez 1.00
156 Ozzie Guillen .10
157 Jim Eisenreich .10
158 Pedro Astacio .10
159 Joe Magrane .10
160 Ryan Thompson .10
161 Jose Lind .10
162 Jeff Conine .10
163 Todd Benzinger .10
164 Roger Salkeld .10
165 Gary DiSarcina .10
166 Kevin Gross .10
167 Charlie Hayes .10
168 Tim Costo .10
169 Wally Joyner .10
170 Johnny Ruffin .10
171 *Kirk Rueter* .10
172 Len Dykstra .10
173 Ken Hill .10
174 Mike Bordick .10
175 Billy Hall .10
176 Rob Butler .10
177 Jay Bell .10
178 Jeff Kent .10
179 David Wells .10
180 Dean Palmer .10
181 Mariano Duncan .10
182 Orlando Merced .10
183 Brett Butler .10
184 Milt Thompson .10
185 Chipper Jones 2.00
186 Paul O'Neill .25
187 Mike Greenwell .10
188 Harold Baines .10
189 Todd Stottlemyre .15
190 Jeromy Burnitz .15
191 Rene Arocha .10
192 Jeff Fassero .10
193 Robby Thompson .10
194 Greg W. Harris .10
195 Todd Van Poppel .10
196 Jose Guzman .10
197 Shane Mack .10

198 Carlos Garcia .10
199 Kevin Roberson .10
200 David McCarty .10
201 Alan Trammell .15
202 Chuck Carr .10
203 Tommy Greene .10
204 Wilson Alvarez .15
205 Dwight Gooden .15
206 *Tony Tarasco* .10
207 Darren Lewis .10
208 Eric Karros .15
209 Chris Hammond .10
210 Jeffrey Hammonds .15
211 Rich Amaral .10
212 Danny Tartabull .10
213 Jeff Russell .10
214 Dave Staton .10
215 Kenny Lofton .50
216 Manuel Lee .10
217 Brian Koelling .10
218 Scott Lydy .10
219 Tony Gwynn 1.50
220 Cecil Fielder .10
221 Royce Clayton .10
222 Reggie Sanders .15
223 Brian Jordan .10
224 Ken Griffey, Jr. 3.00
224a Ken Griffey, Jr. (promo card) 4.00
225 Fred McGriff .20
226 Felix Jose .10
227 Brad Pennington .10
228a Chris Bosio ("ARINERS") .10
228b Chris Bosio ("MARINERS") .10
229 Mike Stanley .10
230 Willie Greene .10
231 Alex Fernandez .15
232 Brad Ausmus .10
233 Darrell Whitmore .10
234 Marcus Moore .10
235 Allen Watson .10
236 Jose Offerman .10
237 Rondell White .20
238 Jeff King .10
239 Luis Alicea .10
240 Dan Wilson .10
241 Ed Sprague .10
242 Todd Hundley .15
243 Al Martin .10
244 Mike Lansing .10
245 Ivan Rodriguez .75
246 Dave Fleming .10
247 John Doherty .10
248 Mark McLemore .10
249 Bob Hamelin .10
250 *Curtis Pride* .20
251 Zane Smith .10
252 Eric Young .20
253 Brian McRae .10
254 Tim Raines .10
255 Javier Lopez .25
256 Melvin Nieves .10
257 Randy Myers .10
258 Willie McGee .10
259 Jimmy Key .10
260 Tom Candiotti .10
261 Eric Davis .10
262 Craig Paquette .10
263 Robin Ventura .20
264 Pat Kelly .10
265 Gregg Jefferies .10
266 Cory Snyder .10
267 Dave Justice (Home Field Advantage) .20
268 Sammy Sosa (Home Field Advantage) 1.50
269 Barry Larkin (Home Field Advantage) .10
270 Andres Galarraga (Home Field Advantage) .10
271 Gary Sheffield (Home Field Advantage) .10
272 Jeff Bagwell (Home Field Advantage) .40
273 Mike Piazza (Home Field Advantage) .75
274 Larry Walker (Home Field Advantage) .25
275 Bobby Bonilla (Home Field Advantage) .10

276 John Kruk (Home Field Advantage) .10
277 Jay Bell (Home Field Advantage) .10
278 Ozzie Smith (Home Field Advantage) .30
279 Tony Gwynn (Home Field Advantage) .75
280 Barry Bonds (Home Field Advantage) .40
281 Cal Ripken, Jr. (Home Field Advantage) 1.00
282 Mo Vaughn (Home Field Advantage) .30
283 Tim Salmon (Home Field Advantage) .25
284 Frank Thomas (Home Field Advantage) .50
285 Albert Belle (Home Field Advantage) .30
286 Cecil Fielder (Home Field Advantage) .10
287 Wally Joyner (Home Field Advantage) .10
288 Greg Vaughn (Home Field Advantage) .10
289 Kirby Puckett (Home Field Advantage) .75
290 Don Mattingly (Home Field Advantage) .75
291 Terry Steinbach (Home Field Advantage) .10
292 Ken Griffey, Jr. (Home Field Advantage) 1.50
293 Juan Gonzalez (Home Field Advantage) .50
294 Paul Molitor (Home Field Advantage) .25
295 Tavo Alvarez (Classic Alumni) .10
296 Matt Brunson (Classic Alumni) .10
297 Shawn Green (Classic Alumni) .40
298 Alex Rodriguez (Classic Alumni) 3.00
299 Shannon Stewart (Classic Alumni) .15
300 Frank Thomas 1.00
301 Mickey Tettleton .10
302 Pedro Munoz .10
303 Jose Valentin .10
304 Orestes Destrade .10
305 Pat Listach .10
306 Scott Brosius .10
307 *Kurt Miller* .10
308 Rob Dibble .10
309 Mike Blowers .10
310 Jim Abbott .10
311 Mike Jackson .10
312 Craig Biggio .40
313 *Kurt Abbott* .20
314 Chuck Finley .10
315 Andres Galarraga .30
316 Mike Moore .10
317 Doug Strange .10
318 Pedro J. Martinez 1.00
319 Kevin McReynolds .10
320 Greg Maddux 1.50
321 Mike Henneman .10
322 Scott Leius .10
323 John Franco .10
324 Jeff Blauser .10
325 Kirby Puckett .75
326 Darryl Hamilton .10
327 John Smiley .10
328 Derrick May .10
329 Jose Vizcaino .10
330 Randy Johnson .75
331 Jack Morris .10
332 Graeme Lloyd .10
333 Dave Valle .10

334 Greg Myers .10
335 John Wetteland .10
336 Jim Gott .10
337 Tim Naehring .10
338 Mike Kelly .10
339 Jeff Montgomery .10
340 Rafael Palmeiro .40
341 Eddie Murray .25
342 Xavier Hernandez .10
343 Bobby Munoz .10
344 Bobby Bonilla .10
345 Travis Fryman .15
346 Steve Finley .10
347 Chris Sabo .10
348 Armando Reynoso .10
349 Ramon Martinez .15
350 Will Clark .35
351 Moises Alou .15
352 Jim Thome .40
353 Bob Tewksbury .10
354 Andujar Cedeno .10
355 Orel Hershiser .10
356 Mike Devereaux .10
357 Mike Perez .10
358 Dennis Martinez .10
359 Dave Nilsson .10
360 Ozzie Smith .50
361 Eric Anthony .10
362 Scott Sanders .10
363 Paul Sorrento .10
364 Tim Belcher .10
365 Dennis Eckersley .10
366 Mel Rojas .10
367 Tom Henke .10
368 Randy Tomlin .10
369 B.J. Surhoff .10
370 Larry Walker .50
371 Joey Cora .10
372 Mike Harkey .10
373 John Valentin .10
374 Doug Jones .10
375 Dave Justice .20
376 Vince Coleman .10
377 David Hulse .10
378 Kevin Seitzer .10
379 Pete Harnisch .10
380 Ruben Sierra .10
381 Mark Lewis .10
382 Bip Roberts .10
383 Paul Wagner .10
384 Stan Javier .10
385 Barry Larkin .15
386 Mark Portugal .10
387 Roberto Kelly .10
388 Andy Benes .15
389 Felix Fermin .10
390 Marquis Grissom .10
391 Troy Neel .10
392 Chad Kreuter .10
393 Gregg Olson .10
394 Charles Nagy .10
395 Jack McDowell .10
396 Luis Gonzalez .10
397 Benito Santiago .10
398 Chris James .10
399 Terry Mulholland .10
400 Barry Bonds .75
401 Joe Grahe .10
402 Duane Ward .10
403 John Burkett .10
404 Scott Servais .10
405 Bryan Harvey .10
406 Bernard Gilkey .10
407 Greg McMichael .10
408 Tim Wallach .10
409 Ken Caminiti .20
410 John Kruk .10
411 Darrin Jackson .10
412 Mike Gallego .10
413 David Cone .20
414 Lou Whitaker .10
415 Sandy Alomar Jr. .15
416 Bill Wegman .10
417 Pat Borders .10
418 Roger Pavlik .10
419 Pete Smith .10
420 Steve Avery .10
421 David Segui .10
422 Rheal Cormier .10
423 Harold Reynolds .10
424 Edgar Martinez .10
425 Cal Ripken, Jr. 2.00
426 Jaime Navarro .10
427 Sean Berry .10
428 Bret Saberhagen .10
429 Bob Welch .10
430 Juan Guzman .10
431 Cal Eldred .10
432 Dave Hollins .10
433 Sid Fernandez .10
434 Willie Banks .10
435 Darryl Kile .10
436 Henry Rodriguez .10
437 Tony Fernandez .10
438 Walt Weiss .10
439 Kevin Tapani .10
440 Mark Grace .20
441 Brian Harper .10
442 Kent Mercker .10
443 Anthony Young .10
444 Todd Zeile .10
445 Greg Vaughn .10
446 Ray Lankford .10
447 David Weathers .10
448 Bret Boone .10
449 Charlie Hough .10
450 Roger Clemens 1.50
451 Mike Morgan .10
452 Doug Drabek .10
453 Danny Jackson .10
454 Dante Bichette .25
455 Roberto Alomar .60
456 Ben McDonald .10
457 Kenny Rogers .10
458 Bill Gullickson .10
459 Darrin Fletcher .10
460 Curt Schilling .15
461 Billy Hatcher .10
462 Howard Johnson .10
463 Mickey Morandini .10
464 Frank Castillo .10
465 Delino DeShields .10
466 Gary Gaetti .10
467 Steve Farr .10
468 Roberto Hernandez .10
469 Jack Armstrong .10
470 Paul Molitor .30
471 Melido Perez .10
472 Greg Hibbard .10
473 Jody Reed .10
474 Tom Gordon .10
475 Gary Sheffield .20
476 John Jaha .10
477 Shawon Dunston .10
478 Reggie Jefferson .10
479 Don Slaught .10
480 Jeff Bagwell .75
481 Tim Pugh .10
482 Kevin Young .10
483 Ellis Burks .10
484 Greg Swindell .10
485 Mark Langston .10
486 Omar Vizquel .10
487 Kevin Brown .15
488 Terry Steinbach .10
489 Mark Lemke .10
490 Matt Williams .30
491 Pete Incaviglia .10
492 Karl Rhodes .10
493 Shawn Green .50
494 Hal Morris .10
495 Derek Bell .10
496 Luis Polonia .10
497 Otis Nixon .10
498 Ron Darling .10
499 Mitch Williams .10
500 Mike Piazza 2.00
501 Pat Meares .10
502 Scott Cooper .10
503 Scott Erickson .15
504 Jeff Juden .10
505 Lee Smith .10
506 Bobby Ayala .10
507 Dave Henderson .10
508 Erik Hanson .10
509 Bob Wickman .10
510 Sammy Sosa 2.00
511 Hector Carrasco (Diamond Debuts) .10
512 Tim Davis (Diamond Debuts) .10
513 Joey Hamilton (Diamond Debuts) .15
514 Robert Eenhoorn (Diamond Debuts) .10
515 Jorge Fabregas (Diamond Debuts) .10
516 Tim Hyers (Diamond Debuts) .10
517 John Hudek (Diamond Debuts) .10
518 *James Mouton* (Diamond Debuts) .10
519 Herbert Perry (Diamond Debuts) .10
520 *Chan Ho Park* (Diamond Debuts) 1.00
521 Bill VanLandingham (Diamond Debuts) .10
522 Paul Shuey (Diamond Debuts) .15
523 *Ryan Hancock* (Top Prospects) .20
524 *Billy Wagner* (Top Prospects) .50
525 Jason Giambi (Top Prospects) .25
526 *Jose Silva* (Top Prospects) .10
527 *Terrell Wade* (Top Prospects) .10
528 Todd Dunn (Top Prospects) .15
529 *Alan Benes* (Top Prospects) .40
530 *Brooks Kieschnick* (Top Prospects) .30
531 Todd Hollandsworth (Top Prospects) .15
532 *Brad Fullmer* (Top Prospects) 1.00
533 *Steve Soderstrom* (Top Prospects) .10
534 Daron Kirkreit (Top Prospects) .10
535 *Arquimedez Pozo* (Top Prospects) .15
536 Charles Johnson (Top Prospects) .20
537 Preston Wilson (Top Prospects) .25
538 Alex Ochoa (Top Prospects) .15
539 *Derrek Lee* (Top Prospects) .50
540 *Wayne Gomes* (Top Prospects) .20
541 *Jermaine Allensworth* (Top Prospects) .50
542 *Mike Bell* (Top Prospects) .30
543 *Trot Nixon* (Top Prospects) 1.50
544 Pokey Reese (Top Prospects) .25
545 *Neifi Perez* (Top Prospects) .75
546 Johnny Damon (Top Prosepcts) .15
547 Matt Brunson (Top Prospects) .15
548 *LaTroy Hawkins* (Top Prospects) .25
549 *Eddie Pearson* (Top Prosepcts) .10
550 Derek Jeter (Top Prospects) 2.00
A298 Alex Rodriguez (autographed) 175.00
MM1 (Mickey Mantle, Ken Griffey Jr.) (Mantle autograph) 450.00
KG1 (Mickey Mantle, Ken Griffey Jr.) (Griffey autograph) 250.00
GM1 (Mickey Mantle, Ken Griffey Jr.) (both autographs) 1000.

1994 Upper Deck Electric Diamond

Each of the regular-issue and subset cards from 1994 Upper Deck was also produced in a limited edition premium insert "Electric Diamond" version. Where the regular cards have the Upper Deck logo, player and team name in copper foil, the Electric Diamond version has those elements in a silver prismatic foil, along with an "Electric Diamond" identification line next to the UD logo. Backs are identical to the regular cards. (Forty-five of the first series cards can be found with player names on back in either silver or copper.) Electric Diamond cards are found, on average, about every other pack.

	MT
Complete Set (550):	100.00
Complete Series 1 (1-280):	60.00
Complete Series 2 (281-550):	40.00
Stars:	2X
Common Player:	.25

(See 1994 Upper Deck for checklist and base card values.)

1994 Upper Deck Diamond Collection

The premium chase cards in 1994 Upper Deck are a series of Diamond Collection cards issued in regional subsets. Ten cards are found unique to each of three geographic areas of distribution. Western region cards carry a "W" prefix to the card number, Central cards have a "C" prefix and Eastern cards have an "E" prefix. The region is also indicated in silver foil printing on the front of the card, with a large "W, C" or "E" in a compass design. The player's name and team are presented in a foil strip at bottom. A "Diamond Collection" logo is shown in embossed-look typography in the background. Diamond Collection cards are inserted only in hobby packs.

		MT
Complete Set (30):		180.00
Common Player:		1.50
Complete Central (10):		65.00
	CENTRAL REGION	
1	Michael Jordan	25.00
2	Jeff Bagwell	10.00
3	Barry Larkin	2.50
4	Kirby Puckett	7.50
5	Manny Ramirez	12.00
6	Ryne Sandberg	7.50
7	Ozzie Smith	7.00
8	Frank Thomas	10.00
9	Andy Van Slyke	1.50
10	Robin Yount	6.00
Complete East (10):		40.00
	EASTERN REGION	
1	Roberto Alomar	4.00
2	Roger Clemens	10.00
3	Len Dykstra	1.50
4	Cecil Fielder	1.50
5	Cliff Floyd	1.50
6	Dwight Gooden	2.00
7	Dave Justice	2.50
8	Don Mattingly	8.00
9	Cal Ripken, Jr.	20.00
10	Gary Sheffield	3.00
Complete West (10):		80.00
	WESTERN REGION	
1	Barry Bonds	8.00
2	Andres Galarraga	3.00
3	Juan Gonzalez	10.00
4	Ken Griffey, Jr.	25.00
5	Tony Gwynn	12.00
6	Rickey Henderson	3.00
7	Bo Jackson	3.00
8	Mark McGwire	25.00
9	Mike Piazza	15.00
10	Tim Salmon	2.50

1994 Upper Deck Jumbo Checklists

Each hobby foil box of 1994 Upper Deck cards contains one jumbo checklist card. Each of the 5" x 7" cards features Ken Griffey, Jr. There is a large color action photo along with a hologram of the player on front, highlighted by copper-foil printing. Backs have one of four checklists and are numbered with a "CL" prefix.

		MT
Complete Set (4):		12.00
Common Card:		3.00
1	Numerical Checklist (Ken Griffey, Jr.)	3.00
2	Alphabetical Checklist (Ken Griffey, Jr.)	3.00
3	Team Checklist (Ken Griffey, Jr.)	3.00
4	Insert Checklist (Ken Griffey, Jr.)	3.00

1994 Upper Deck Mantle Heroes

Mickey Mantle Baseball Hero is a 10-card set that chronicles his career. The cards, which include an unnumbered header card, were randomly inserted into both hobby and retail packs of Series II Upper Deck Baseball. This set starts with his rookie season in 1951 and concludes with his induction into The Hall of Fame. It is numbered 64-72 and was the eighth in the continuing "Baseball Heroes" series, which began in 1990.

		MT
Complete Set (10):		75.00
Common Card:		8.00
64	1951 - The Early Years (Mickey Mantle)	8.00
65	1953 - Tape Measure Home Runs (Mickey Mantle)	8.00
66	1956 - Triple Crown Season (Mickey Mantle)	8.00
67	1957 - 2nd Consecutive MVP (Mickey Mantle)	8.00
68	1961 - Chases The Babe (Mickey Mantle)	8.00
69	1964 - Series Home Run Record (Mickey Mantle)	8.00
70	1967 - 500th Home Run (Mickey Mantle)	8.00
----	Header card (Mickey Mantle)	8.00

1994 Upper Deck Mickey Mantle's Long Shots

Retail packaging was the exclusive venue for this insert set of contemporary long-ball sluggers. Horizontal fronts feature game-action photos with holographic foil rendering of the background. In one of the lower corners appears the logo "1994 Mickey Mantle's Long Shots". Backs have a color player photo at top, with a photo of Mantle beneath and a statement by him about the featured player. Previous season and career stats are included. Cards are numbered with an "MM" prefix. Besides the 20 current player cards there is a Mickey Mantle card and two trade cards which could be redeemed for complete insert card sets.

		MT
Complete Set (21):		45.00
Common Player:		.75
(1)	Mickey Mantle Trade Card (silver): (Redeemable for 21-card Mantle Long Shots set)	4.00
(2)	Mickey Mantle Trade Card (blue): (Redeemable for Electric Diamond version Mantle Long Shots set)	4.00
1	Jeff Bagwell	3.00
2	Albert Belle	2.50
3	Barry Bonds	2.50
4	Jose Canseco	2.00
5	Joe Carter	1.00
6	Carlos Delgado	2.00
7	Cecil Fielder	.75
8	Cliff Floyd	.75
9	Juan Gonzalez	2.50
10	Ken Griffey, Jr.	10.00
11	Dave Justice	1.50
12	Fred McGriff	1.50
13	Mark McGwire	10.00
14	Dean Palmer	.75
15	Mike Piazza	6.00
16	Manny Ramirez	3.00
17	Tim Salmon	1.00
18	Frank Thomas	2.50
19	Mo Vaughn	2.00
20	Matt Williams	1.50
21	Mickey Mantle (Header)	12.00

1994 Upper Deck Next Generation

Next Generation linked 20 of the top current stars with all-time greats, using the HoloView card printing technology. Next Generation trade cards could be redeemed for a complete set matching the cards found in retail packs. This insert set was inserted at a rate of one per 20 packs, while the Trade Card was inserted one per case.

		MT
Complete Set (18):		80.00
Common Player:		1.25
1	Roberto Alomar	3.00
2	Carlos Delgado	2.50
3	Cliff Floyd	1.25
4	Alex Gonzalez	1.25
5	Juan Gonzalez	5.00
6	Ken Griffey, Jr.	16.00
7	Jeffrey Hammonds	1.25
8	Michael Jordan	20.00
9	Dave Justice	2.50
10	Ryan Klesko	1.25
11	Javier Lopez	1.25
12	Raul Mondesi	1.50
13	Mike Piazza	12.00
14	Kirby Puckett	4.00
15	Manny Ramirez	6.50
16	Alex Rodriguez	24.00
17	Tim Salmon	1.50
18	Gary Sheffield	2.00

1994 Upper Deck SP Insert

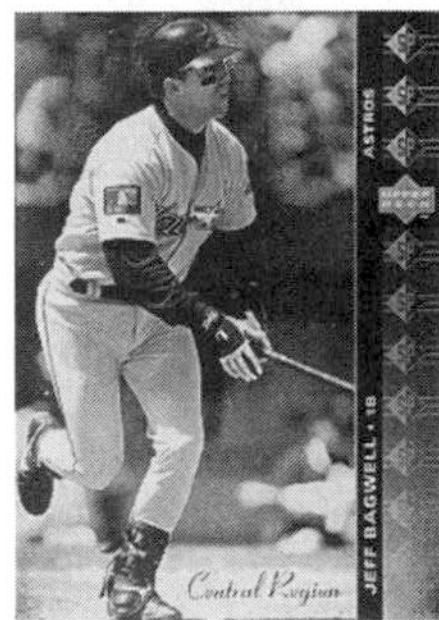

Fifteen SP Preview cards were inserted into Series II packs of Upper Deck baseball. The cards were inserted with regional distribution and gave collectors a chance to see what the SP super-premium cards would look like. There were five cards available in the East, Central and West and were inserted at a rate of about one per 36 packs. Most of the preview inserts have different front and back photos than the regularly issued SPs, along with other differences in typography and graphics elements.

		MT
Complete Set (15):		130.00
Common Player:		.75
EASTERN REGION		
1	Roberto Alomar	4.00
2	Cliff Floyd	.75
3	Javier Lopez	2.00
4	Don Mattingly	10.00
5	Cal Ripken, Jr.	20.00
CENTRAL REGION		
1	Jeff Bagwell	5.00

2 Michael Jordan 25.00
3 Kirby Puckett 7.50
4 Manny Ramirez 5.00
5 Frank Thomas 9.00
WESTERN REGION
1 Barry Bonds 9.00
2 Juan Gonzalez 8.00
3 Ken Griffey, Jr. 25.00
4 Mike Piazza 15.00
5 Tim Salmon 2.50

1995 Upper Deck

Issued in two series of 225 base cards each, with loads of subsets and inserts, the 1995 Upper Deck set was a strong collector favorite from the outset. Basic cards feature a borderless front photo with the player's name and UD logo in bronze foil. Backs have another large color photo, recent stats and career totals and appropriate logos, along with the infield-shaped hologram. Subsets in each series include Star Rookies and Top Prospects, each with special designs highlighting the game's young stars. Series I has a "'90s Midpoint Analysis" subset studying the decade's superstars, and Series II has another hot rookies' subset, Diamond Debuts. The set closes with a five-card "Final Tribute" subset summarizing the careers of five recently retired superstars. Retail and hobby versions were sold with each featuring some unique insert cards. Basic packaging of each type was the 12-card foil pack at $1.99, though several other configurations were also released.

	MT
Complete Set (450):	60.00
Complete Series 1 (225):	30.00
Complete Series 2 (225):	30.00
Common Player:	.10
Series 1 or 2 Pack (12):	2.00
Series 1 or 2 Wax Box (36):	55.00

1 Ruben Rivera (Top Prospect) .15
2 Bill Pulsipher (Top Prospect) .15
3 Ben Grieve (Top Prospect) 1.50
4 Curtis Goodwin (Top Prospect) .15
5 Damon Hollins (Top Prospect) .10
6 Todd Greene (Top Prospect) .15
7 Glenn Williams (Top Prospect) .10
8 Bret Wagner (Top Prospect) .10
9 *Karim Garcia* (Top Prospect) .50
10 Nomar Garciaparra (Top Prospect) 3.00
11 *Raul Casanova* (Top Prospect) .20
12 Matt Smith (Top Prospect) .15
13 Paul Wilson (Top Prospect) .15
14 Jason Isringhausen (Top Prospect) .15
15 Reid Ryan (Top Prospect) .10
16 Lee Smith .10
17 Chili Davis .10
18 Brian Anderson .10
19 Gary DiSarcina .10
20 Bo Jackson .15
21 Chuck Finley .10
22 Darryl Kile .10
23 Shane Reynolds .15
24 Tony Eusebio .10
25 Craig Biggio .40
26 Doug Drabek .10
27 Brian L. Hunter .10
28 James Mouton .10
29 Geronimo Berroa .10
30 Rickey Henderson .40
31 Steve Karsay .10
32 Steve Ontiveros .10
33 Ernie Young .10
34 Dennis Eckersley .10
35 Mark McGwire 3.00
36 Dave Stewart .10
37 Pat Hentgen .10
38 Carlos Delgado .50
39 Joe Carter .10
40 Roberto Alomar .60
41 John Olerud .25
42 Devon White .10
43 Roberto Kelly .10
44 Jeff Blauser .10
45 Fred McGriff .25
46 Tom Glavine .25
47 Mike Kelly .10
48 Javy Lopez .20
49 Greg Maddux 1.50
50 Matt Mieske .10
51 Troy O'Leary .10
52 Jeff Cirillo .15
53 Cal Eldred .10
54 Pat Listach .10
55 Jose Valentin .10
56 John Mabry .10
57 Bob Tewksbury .10
58 Brian Jordan .15
59 Gregg Jefferies .10
60 Ozzie Smith .50
61 Geronimo Pena .10
62 Mark Whiten .10
63 Rey Sanchez .10
64 Willie Banks .10
65 Mark Grace .20
66 Randy Myers .10
67 Steve Trachsel .15
68 Derrick May .10
69 Brett Butler .10
70 Eric Karros .10
71 Tim Wallach .10
72 Delino DeShields .10
73 Darren Dreifort .10
74 Orel Hershiser .10
75 Billy Ashley .10
76 Sean Berry .10
77 Ken Hill .10
78 John Wetteland .10
79 Moises Alou .20
80 Cliff Floyd .10
81 Marquis Grissom .15
82 Larry Walker .50
83 Rondell White .20
84 William VanLandingham .10
85 Matt Williams .30
86 Rod Beck .10
87 Darren Lewis .10
88 Robby Thompson .10
89 Darryl Strawberry .20
90 Kenny Lofton .50
91 Charles Nagy .10
92 Sandy Alomar Jr. .15
93 Mark Clark .10
94 Dennis Martinez .10
95 Dave Winfield .25
96 Jim Thome .30
97 Manny Ramirez 1.00
98 Goose Gossage .10
99 Tino Martinez .15
100 Ken Griffey Jr. 3.00
100a Ken Griffey Jr. (overprinted "For Promotional Use Only") 3.00
101 Greg Maddux (Analysis: '90s Midpoint) 1.00
102 Randy Johnson (Analysis: '90s Midpoint) .15
103 Barry Bonds (Analysis: '90s Midpoint) .30
104 Juan Gonzalez (Analysis: '90s Midpoint) .50
105 Frank Thomas (Analysis: '90s Midpoint) .50
106 Matt Williams (Analysis: '90s Midpoint) .15
107 Paul Molitor (Analysis: '90s Midpoint) .25
108 Fred McGriff (Analysis: '90s Midpoint) .15
109 Carlos Baerga (Analysis: '90s Midpoint) .10
110 Ken Griffey Jr. (Analysis: '90s Midpoint) 1.50
111 Reggie Jefferson .10
112 Randy Johnson .40
113 Marc Newfield .10
114 Robb Nen .10
115 Jeff Conine .10
116 Kurt Abbott .10
117 Charlie Hough .10
118 Dave Weathers .10
119 Juan Castillo .10
120 Bret Saberhagen .10
121 Rico Brogna .10
122 John Franco .10
123 Todd Hundley .10
124 Jason Jacome .10
125 Bobby Jones .10
126 Bret Barberie .10
127 Ben McDonald .10
128 Harold Baines .10
129 Jeffrey Hammonds .10
130 Mike Mussina .40
131 Chris Hoiles .10
132 Brady Anderson .15
133 Eddie Williams .10
134 Andy Benes .15
135 Tony Gwynn 1.50
136 Bip Roberts .10
137 Joey Hamilton .15
138 Luis Lopez .10
139 Ray McDavid .10
140 Lenny Dykstra .10
141 Mariano Duncan .10
142 Fernando Valenzuela .10
143 Bobby Munoz .10
144 Kevin Stocker .10
145 John Kruk .10
146 Jon Lieber .10
147 Zane Smith .10
148 Steve Cooke .10
149 Andy Van Slyke .10
150 Jay Bell .10
151 Carlos Garcia .10
152 John Dettmer .10
153 Darren Oliver .10
154 Dean Palmer .10
155 Otis Nixon .10
156 Rusty Greer .10
157 Rick Helling .10
158 Jose Canseco .75
159 Roger Clemens 1.50
160 Andre Dawson .20
161 Mo Vaughn .60
162 Aaron Sele .10
163 John Valentin .10
164 Brian Hunter .10
165 Bret Boone .10
166 Hector Carrasco .10
167 Pete Schourek .10
168 Willie Greene .10
169 Kevin Mitchell .10
170 Deion Sanders .20
171 John Roper .10
172 Charlie Hayes .10
173 David Nied .10
174 Ellis Burks .10
175 Dante Bichette .25
176 Marvin Freeman .10
177 Eric Young .15
178 David Cone .20
179 Greg Gagne .10
180 Bob Hamelin .10
181 Wally Joyner .10
182 Jeff Montgomery .10
183 Jose Lind .10
184 Chris Gomez .10
185 Travis Fryman .15
186 Kirk Gibson .10
187 Mike Moore .10
188 Lou Whitaker .10
189 Sean Bergman .10
190 Shane Mack .10
191 Rick Aguilera .10
192 Denny Hocking .10
193 Chuck Knoblauch .20
194 Kevin Tapani .10
195 Kent Hrbek .10
196 Ozzie Guillen .10
197 Wilson Alvarez .10
198 Tim Raines .10
199 Scott Ruffcorn .10
200 Michael Jordan 3.00
201 Robin Ventura .25
202 Jason Bere .10
203 Darrin Jackson .10
204 Russ Davis .10
205 Jimmy Key .10
206 Jack McDowell .10
207 Jim Abbott .10
208 Paul O'Neill .25
209 Bernie Williams .40
210 Don Mattingly 1.00
211 Orlando Miller (Star Rookie) .10
212 Alex Gonzalez (Star Rookie) .15
213 Terrell Wade (Star Rookie) .10
214 Jose Oliva (Star Rookie) .10
215 Alex Rodriguez (Star Rookie) 3.00
216 Garret Anderson (Star Rookie) .15
217 Alan Benes (Star Rookie) .10
218 Armando Benitez (Star Rookie) .10
219 Dustin Hermanson (Star Rookie) .10
220 Charles Johnson (Star Rookie) .15
221 Julian Tavarez (Star Rookie) .10
222 Jason Giambi (Star Rookie) .25
223 LaTroy Hawkins (Star Rookie) .10
224 Todd Hollandsworth (Star Rookie) .10
225 Derek Jeter (Star Rookie) 2.00
226 *Hideo Nomo* (Star Rookie) 1.00
227 Tony Clark (Star Rookie) .40
228 Roger Cedeno (Star Rookie) .10
229 Scott Stahoviak (Star Rookie) .10
230 Michael Tucker (Star Rookie) .15
231 Joe Rosselli (Star Rookie) .10
232 Antonio Osuna (Star Rookie) .10
233 *Bobby Higginson* (Star Rookie) 1.00
234 *Mark Grudzielanek* (Star Rookie) .25
235 Ray Durham (Star Rookie) .25
236 Frank Rodriguez (Star Rookie) .10
237 Quilvio Veras (Star Rookie) .10
238 Darren Bragg (Star Rookie) .10
239 Ugueth Urbina (Star Rookie) .10

No.	Player	Value
240	Jason Bates (Star Rookie)	.10
241	David Bell (Diamond Debuts)	.10
242	Ron Villone (Diamond Debuts)	.10
243	Joe Randa (Diamond Debuts)	.10
244	*Carlos Perez* (Diamond Debuts)	.25
245	Brad Clontz (Diamond Debuts)	.10
246	Steve Rodriguez (Diamond Debuts)	.10
247	Joe Vitiello (Diamond Debuts)	.10
248	Ozzie Timmons (Diamond Debuts)	.10
249	Rudy Pemberton (Diamond Debuts)	.10
250	Marty Cordova (Diamond Debuts)	.15
251	Tony Graffanino (Top Prospect)	.10
252	*Mark Johnson* (Top Prospect)	.20
253	*Tomas Perez* (Top Prospect)	.20
254	Jimmy Hurst (Top Prospect)	.10
255	Edgardo Alfonzo (Top Prospect)	.40
256	Jose Malave (Top Prospect)	.10
257	*Brad Radke* (Top Prospect)	.20
258	Jon Nunnally (Top Prospect)	.10
259	Dilson Torres (Top Prospect)	.15
260	Esteban Loaiza (Top Prospect)	.15
261	*Freddy Garcia* (Top Prospect)	.20
262	Don Wengert (Top Prospect)	.10
263	*Robert Person* (Top Prospect)	.10
264	*Tim Unroe* (Top Prospect)	.10
265	Juan Acevedo (Top Prospect)	.10
266	Eduardo Perez	.10
267	Tony Phillips	.10
268	Jim Edmonds	.15
269	Jorge Fabregas	.10
270	Tim Salmon	.20
271	Mark Langston	.10
272	J.T. Snow	.15
273	Phil Plantier	.10
274	Derek Bell	.10
275	Jeff Bagwell	1.00
276	Luis Gonzalez	.15
277	John Hudek	.10
278	Todd Stottlemyre	.15
279	Mark Acre	.10
280	Ruben Sierra	.10
281	Mike Bordick	.10
282	Ron Darling	.10
283	Brent Gates	.10
284	Todd Van Poppel	.10
285	Paul Molitor	.40
286	Ed Sprague	.10
287	Juan Guzman	.10
288	David Cone	.20
289	Shawn Green	.50
290	Marquis Grissom	.15
291	Kent Mercker	.10
292	Steve Avery	.10
293	Chipper Jones	2.00
294	John Smoltz	.20
295	Dave Justice	.20
296	Ryan Klesko	.20
297	Joe Oliver	.10
298	Ricky Bones	.10
299	John Jaha	.10
300	Greg Vaughn	.15
301	Dave Nilsson	.10
302	Kevin Seitzer	.10
303	Bernard Gilkey	.10
304	Allen Battle	.10
305	Ray Lankford	.10
306	Tom Pagnozzi	.10
307	Allen Watson	.10
308	Danny Jackson	.10
309	Ken Hill	.10
310	Todd Zeile	.10
311	Kevin Roberson	.10
312	Steve Buechele	.10
313	Rick Wilkins	.10
314	Kevin Foster	.10
315	Sammy Sosa	2.00
316	Howard Johnson	.10
317	Greg Hansell	.10
318	Pedro Astacio	.10
319	Rafael Bournigal	.10
320	Mike Piazza	2.00
321	Ramon Martinez	.15
322	Raul Mondesi	.25
323	Ismael Valdes	.15
324	Wil Cordero	.10
325	Tony Tarasco	.10
326	Roberto Kelly	.10
327	Jeff Fassero	.10
328	Mike Lansing	.10
329	Pedro J. Martinez	1.00
330	Kirk Rueter	.10
331	Glenallen Hill	.10
332	Kirt Manwaring	.10
333	Royce Clayton	.10
334	J.R. Phillips	.10
335	Barry Bonds	.75
336	Mark Portugal	.10
337	Terry Mulholland	.10
338	Omar Vizquel	.15
339	Carlos Baerga	.10
340	Albert Belle	.60
341	Eddie Murray	.30
342	Wayne Kirby	.10
343	Chad Ogea	.10
344	Tim Davis	.10
345	Jay Buhner	.10
346	Bobby Ayala	.10
347	Mike Blowers	.10
348	Dave Fleming	.10
349	Edgar Martinez	.10
350	Andre Dawson	.15
351	Darrell Whitmore	.10
352	Chuck Carr	.10
353	John Burkett	.10
354	Chris Hammond	.10
355	Gary Sheffield	.40
356	Pat Rapp	.10
357	Greg Colbrunn	.10
358	David Segui	.10
359	Jeff Kent	.10
360	Bobby Bonilla	.10
361	Pete Harnisch	.10
362	Ryan Thompson	.10
363	Jose Vizcaino	.10
364	Brett Butler	.10
365	Cal Ripken Jr.	2.50
366	Rafael Palmeiro	.40
367	Leo Gomez	.10
368	Andy Van Slyke	.10
369	Arthur Rhodes	.10
370	Ken Caminiti	.25
371	Steve Finley	.10
372	Melvin Nieves	.10
373	Andujar Cedeno	.10
374	Trevor Hoffman	.15
375	Fernando Valenzuela	.10
376	Ricky Bottalico	.10
377	Dave Hollins	.10
378	Charlie Hayes	.10
379	Tommy Greene	.10
380	Darren Daulton	.10
381	Curt Schilling	.15
382	Midre Cummings	.10
383	Al Martin	.10
384	Jeff King	.10
385	Orlando Merced	.10
386	Denny Neagle	.10
387	Don Slaught	.10
388	Dave Clark	.10
389	Kevin Gross	.10
390	Will Clark	.30
391	Ivan Rodriguez	.75
392	Benji Gil	.10
393	Jeff Frye	.10
394	Kenny Rogers	.10
395	Juan Gonzalez	1.00
396	Mike Macfarlane	.10
397	Lee Tinsley	.10
398	Tim Naehring	.10
399	Tim Vanegmond	.10
400	Mike Greenwell	.10
401	Ken Ryan	.10
402	John Smiley	.10
403	Tim Pugh	.10
404	Reggie Sanders	.15
405	Barry Larkin	.15
406	Hal Morris	.10
407	Jose Rijo	.10
408	Lance Painter	.10
409	Joe Girardi	.10
410	Andres Galarraga	.25
411	Mike Kingery	.10
412	Roberto Mejia	.10
413	Walt Weiss	.10
414	Bill Swift	.10
415	Larry Walker	.50
416	Billy Brewer	.10
417	Pat Borders	.10
418	Tom Gordon	.10
419	Kevin Appier	.10
420	Gary Gaetti	.10
421	Greg Gohr	.10
422	Felipe Lira	.10
423	John Doherty	.10
424	Chad Curtis	.10
425	Cecil Fielder	.10
426	Alan Trammell	.15
427	David McCarty	.10
428	Scott Erickson	.15
429	Pat Mahomes	.10
430	Kirby Puckett	1.00
431	Dave Stevens	.10
432	Pedro Munoz	.10
433	Chris Sabo	.10
434	Alex Fernandez	.15
435	Frank Thomas	1.00
436	Roberto Hernandez	.10
437	Lance Johnson	.10
438	Jim Abbott	.10
439	John Wetteland	.10
440	Melido Perez	.10
441	Tony Fernandez	.10
442	Pat Kelly	.10
443	Mike Stanley	.10
444	Danny Tartabull	.10
445	Wade Boggs	.20
446	Robin Yount (Final Tribute)	.40
447	Ryne Sandberg (Final Tribute)	.50
448	Nolan Ryan (Final Tribute)	2.00
449	George Brett (Final Tribute)	.75
450	Mike Schmidt (Final Tribute)	.50

1995 Upper Deck Electric Diamond

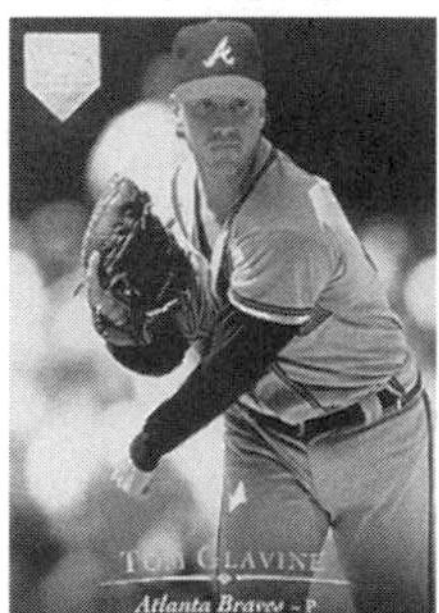

Included as an insert at the rate of one per retail foil pack and two per jumbo pack, this set parallels the regular issue. The only differences are that the Electric Diamond cards utilize silver-foil highlights on front, compared to the copper foil on the regular cards. The Electric Diamond cards also include a home-plate shaped logo printed in silver foil in one of the upper corners.

	MT
Complete Set (1-450):	100.00
Common Player:	.25
Stars/Rookies:	2X

(See 1995 Upper Deck for checklist and base card values.)

1995 Upper Deck Electric Diamond Gold

A parallel set of a parallet set, the Electric Diamond Gold cards were found at an average rate of one per 36 retail packs. They differ from the standard ED inserts in that the home plate-shaped Electric Diamond logo in the upper corner and the player's name at bottom are printed in gold foil, rather than the silver of the ED cards or the copper of the regular-issue UD cards.

	MT
Complete Set (450):	1500.
Common Player:	3.00
Stars/Rookies:	10X

(See 1995 Upper Deck for checklist and base card values.)

1995 Upper Deck Autograph Trade Cards

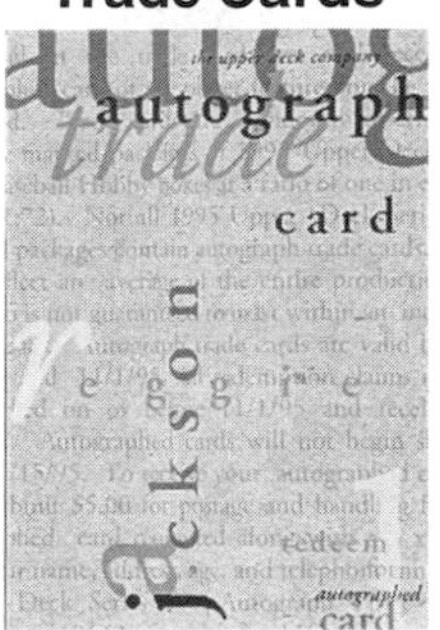

On the average of once every 72 packs (two boxes) of Series II hobby, a trade card good for an autographed player card could be found as an insert. The cards feature the player name, but no picture, on front, while the reverse has instructions for redeeming the card for a $5 fee. The autograph trade cards expired on Nov. 1, 1995.

	MT
Complete Set (5):	10.00
Common Player:	2.00
(1) Roger Clemens	2.00
(2) Reggie Jackson	1.00
(3) Willie Mays	3.00
(4) Raul Mondesi	2.00
(5) Frank Robinson	2.00

1995 Upper Deck Autograph Redemption Cards

These cards were sent to collectors who redeemed Autograph Trade cards found in Series II Upper Deck baseball. A certificate of authenticity with a holographic serial number matching that on the card back was issued with each card.

		MT
Complete Set (5):		180.00
Common Player:		25.00
(1)	Roger Clemens	60.00
(2)	Reggie Jackson	30.00
(3)	Willie Mays	75.00
(4)	Raul Mondesi	25.00
(5)	Frank Robinson	35.00

1995 Upper Deck Autographed Jumbos

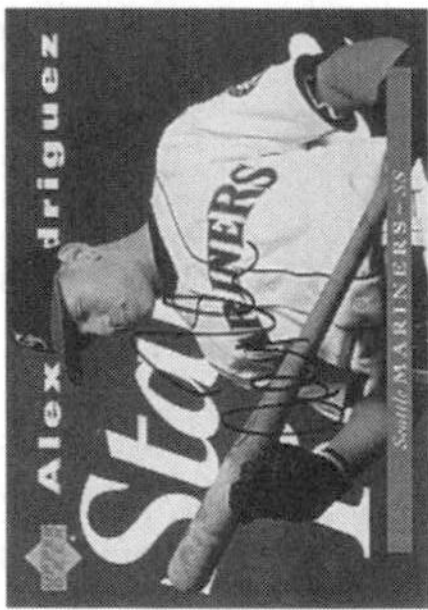

By sending in quantities of foil wrappers from Upper Deck baseball cards, collectors could receive a jumbo 5" x 7" blow-up of a player's card. The offer was limited to 8,000 Roger Clemens cards (Series I) and 6,000 Alex Rodriguez cards (Series II). Each card bears a serial number hologram on back and comes with a matching Upper Deck Authenticated auhtenticity guarantee card.

		MT
Complete Set (2):		150.00
Common Player:		30.00
(1)	Roger Clemens	60.00
(2)	Alex Rodriguez	100.00

Player names in *Italic* type indicate a rookie card.

1995 Upper Deck Babe Ruth Baseball Heroes

In the 100th anniversary year of his birth, Babe Ruth was the featured star in Upper Deck continuing "Heroes" insert set. Ten cards, including an unnumbered header, were issued in Series II packs. The cards featured colorized photos printed on metallic foil on the front. Backs have stats and/or biographical data. On average, one Babe Ruth Heroes card is found per 34 packs.

		MT
Complete Set (10):		100.00
Common Player:		10.00
73	1914-18 Pitching Career (Babe Ruth)	10.00
74	1919 - Move to Outfield (Babe Ruth)	10.00
75	1920 - Renaissance Man (Babe Ruth)	10.00
76	1923 - House That Ruth Built (Babe Ruth)	10.00
77	1927 - 60-Homer Season (Babe Ruth)	10.00
78	1928 - Three-homer Game (Babe Ruth)	10.00
79	1932 - The Called Shot (Babe Ruth)	10.00
80	1930-35 - Milestones (Babe Ruth)	10.00
81	1935 - The Last Hurrah (Babe Ruth)	10.00
---	Header card	3.00

1995 Upper Deck Checklists

Upscale checklists for the 1995 UD set were part of the insert card program, seeded about one per 17 packs, on average. Horizontally formatted fronts are printed on metallic foil and include a career highlight of the pictured player. Backs have the checklist data. Five checklists were issued in each of Series I and Series II.

		MT
Complete Set (10):		15.00
Common Player:		
	Series I	
1	Checklist 1-75 (Montreal Expos)	1.00
2	Checklist 76-150 (Fred McGriff)	1.50
3	Checklist 151-225 (John Valentin) (unassisted triple play)	1.00
4	Special Edition Checklist (Greg Maddux)	3.00
5	Special Edition Checklist 69-135 (Kenny Rogers) (perfect game)	1.00
	Series II	
1	Checklist 226-300 (Cecil Fielder)	1.00
2	Checklist 301-375 (Tony Gwynn)	2.50
3	Checklist 376-450 (Greg Maddux)	3.00
4	Special Edition Checklist 136-203 (Randy Johnson)	1.50
5	Special Edition Checklist 204-270 (Mike Schmidt)	3.00

1995 Upper Deck Award Winners Predictors

Candidates for 1995 MVP and Rookie of the Year in each league are featured in the interactive insert series called Predictors. Twenty potential award winners were released in each of Series I and II at the rate of one per 30 packs on average. Cards feature on front a player photo inside a diamond cutout on a rich looking black and marbled background. In gold foil are his name and team at top, and "PREDICTOR" and the category at bottom. Backs feature game rules and details for redeeming the card if the pictured player wins the specified award. Winners could trade in the card for a foil-enhanced set of Predictor cards. The trade-in offer expired at the end of 1995. Cards are numbered with a "H" prefix.

		MT
Complete Set (40):		45.00
Common Player:		.50
1	Albert Belle	1.00
2	Juan Gonzalez	1.50
3	Ken Griffey Jr.	6.00
4	Kirby Puckett	2.00
5	Frank Thomas	2.00
6	Jeff Bagwell	1.50
7	Barry Bonds	1.50
8	Mike Piazza	4.00
9	Matt Williams	.75
10	1995 MVP Long Shot	.50
11	Armando Benitez	.50
12	Alex Gonzalez	.50
13	Shawn Green	1.50
14	Derek Jeter	4.00
15	Alex Rodriguez	5.00
16	Alan Benes	.50
17	Brian L. Hunter	.50
18	Charles Johnson	.50
19	Jose Oliva	.50
20	1995 ROY Long Shot	.50
21	Cal Ripken Jr.	5.00
22	Don Mattingly	1.50
23	Roberto Alomar	1.00
24	Kenny Lofton	.75
25	Will Clark	1.00
26	Mark McGwire	6.00
27	Greg Maddux	3.00
28	Fred McGriff	.75
29	Andres Galarraga	1.00
30	Jose Canseco	1.50
31	Ray Durham	.50
32	Mark Grudzielanek	.50
33	Scott Ruffcorn	.50
34	Michael Tucker	.50
35	Garret Anderson	.50
36	Darren Bragg	.50
37	Quilvio Veras	.50
38	Hideo Nomo	.75
39	Chipper Jones	4.00
40	Marty Cordova	.50

1995 Upper Deck League Leaders Predictors

Candidates for the Triple Crown categories of league leaders in hits, home runs and RBIs are featured in this retail-only insert set, found at the average rate of one per 30 packs in both Series I and II. If the player pictured on the card front won the category specified on his card, it could be redeemed for a special foil-enhanced version of the subset prior to the Dec. 31, 1995, deadline. Cards are numbered with a "R" prefix.

		MT
Complete Set (60):		70.00
Common Player:		.50
1	Albert Belle	1.00
2	Jose Canseco	1.50
3	Juan Gonzalez	1.50
4	Ken Griffey Jr.	6.00
5	Frank Thomas	2.00
6	Jeff Bagwell	1.50
7	Barry Bonds	1.50
8	Fred McGriff	1.00
9	Matt Williams	.75

10	1995 Home Run Long Shot	.50
11	Albert Belle	1.00
12	Joe Carter	.50
13	Cecil Fielder	.50
14	Kirby Puckett	1.50
15	Frank Thomas	2.00
16	Jeff Bagwell	1.50
17	Barry Bonds	1.50
18	Mike Piazza	4.00
19	Matt Williams	.75
20	1995 RBI Long Shot	.50
21	Wade Boggs	1.00
22	Kenny Lofton	.75
23	Paul Molitor	1.50
24	Paul O'Neill	.75
25	Frank Thomas	2.00
26	Jeff Bagwell	1.50
27	Tony Gwynn	3.00
28	Gregg Jefferies	.50
29	Hal Morris	.50
30	1995 Batting Long Shot	.50
31	Joe Carter	.50
32	Cecil Fielder	.50
33	Rafael Palmeiro	1.00
34	Larry Walker	1.00
35	Manny Ramirez	2.00
36	Tim Salmon	.75
37	Mike Piazza	4.00
38	Andres Galarraga	1.00
39	Dave Justice	.75
40	Gary Sheffield	.75
41	Juan Gonzalez	1.50
42	Jose Canseco	1.50
43	Will Clark	1.00
44	Rafael Palmeiro	1.00
45	Ken Griffey Jr.	6.00
46	Ruben Sierra	.50
47	Larry Walker	1.00
48	Fred McGriff	1.00
49	Dante Bichette	.65
50	Darren Daulton	.50
51	Will Clark	1.00
52	Ken Griffey Jr.	6.00
53	Don Mattingly	1.50
54	John Olerud	1.00
55	Kirby Puckett	1.50
56	Raul Mondesi	.75
57	Moises Alou	.75
58	Bret Boone	.50
59	Albert Belle	1.00
60	Mike Piazza	4.00

1995 Upper Deck Special Edition

Printed on metallic foil on front, and inserted into hobby packs only at the rate of one per pack, this insert series is found in both Series I (#1-135) and Series II (#136-270). A silver stripe at top has the name of the issue and the issuers, while stacked black and silver bars at bottom have the player name, team and position. Backs are conventionally printed and have another color photo, career data and 1994 and lifetime stats.

		MT
Complete Set (270):		150.00
Common Player:		.25
Gold:		4X
1	Cliff Floyd	.25
2	Wil Cordero	.25
3	Pedro Martinez	2.50
4	Larry Walker	1.50
5	Derek Jeter	6.00
6	Mike Stanley	.25
7	Melido Perez	.25
8	Jim Leyritz	.25
9	Danny Tartabull	.25
10	Wade Boggs	1.00
11	Ryan Klesko	.50
12	Steve Avery	.25
13	Damon Hollins	.25
14	Chipper Jones	6.00
15	Dave Justice	.50
16	Glenn Williams	.25
17	Jose Oliva	.25
18	Terrell Wade	.25
19	Alex Fernandez	.25
20	Frank Thomas	3.00
21	Ozzie Guillen	.25
22	Roberto Hernandez	.25
23	Albie Lopez	.25
24	Eddie Murray	.75
25	Albert Belle	2.00
26	Omar Vizquel	.30
27	Carlos Baerga	.25
28	Jose Rijo	.25
29	Hal Morris	.25
30	Reggie Sanders	.25
31	Jack Morris	.25
32	Raul Mondesi	.50
33	Karim Garcia	.25
34	Todd Hollandsworth	.25
35	Mike Piazza	6.00
36	Chan Ho Park	.50
37	Ramon Martinez	.25
38	Kenny Rogers	.25
39	Will Clark	.75
40	Juan Gonzalez	2.50
41	Ivan Rodriguez	2.50
42	Orlando Miller	.25
43	John Hudek	.25
44	Luis Gonzalez	.25
45	Jeff Bagwell	3.00
46	Cal Ripken Jr.	8.00
47	Mike Oquist	.25
48	Armando Benitez	.25
49	Ben McDonald	.25
50	Rafael Palmeiro	1.00
51	Curtis Goodwin	.25
52	Vince Coleman	.25
53	Tom Gordon	.25
54	Mike Macfarlane	.25
55	Brian McRae	.25
56	Matt Smith	.25
57	David Segui	.25
58	Paul Wilson	.25
59	Bill Pulsipher	.25
60	Bobby Bonilla	.25
61	Jeff Kent	.25
62	Ryan Thompson	.25
63	Jason Isringhausen	.25
64	Ed Sprague	.25
65	Paul Molitor	1.50
66	Juan Guzman	.25
67	Alex Gonzalez	.25
68	Shawn Green	1.50
69	Mark Portugal	.25
70	Barry Bonds	2.50
71	Robby Thompson	.25
72	Royce Clayton	.25
73	Ricky Bottalico	.25
74	Doug Jones	.25
75	Darren Daulton	.25
76	Gregg Jefferies	.25
77	Scott Cooper	.25
78	Nomar Garciaparra	6.00
79	Ken Ryan	.25
80	Mike Greenwell	.25
81	LaTroy Hawkins	.25
82	Rich Becker	.25
83	Scott Erickson	.25
84	Pedro Munoz	.25
85	Kirby Puckett	3.00
86	Orlando Merced	.25
87	Jeff King	.25
88	Midre Cummings	.25
89	Bernard Gilkey	.25
90	Ray Lankford	.25
91	Todd Zeile	.25
92	Alan Benes	.25
93	Bret Wagner	.25
94	Rene Arocha	.25
95	Cecil Fielder	.25
96	Alan Trammell	.25
97	Tony Phillips	.25
98	Junior Felix	.25
99	Brian Harper	.25
100	Greg Vaughn	.30
101	Ricky Bones	.25
102	Walt Weiss	.25
103	Lance Painter	.25
104	Roberto Mejia	.25
105	Andres Galarraga	1.00
106	Todd Van Poppel	.25
107	Ben Grieve	1.50
108	Brent Gates	.25
109	Jason Giambi	.50
110	Ruben Sierra	.25
111	Terry Steinbach	.25
112	Chris Hammond	.25
113	Charles Johnson	.25
114	Jesus Tavarez	.25
115	Gary Sheffield	.40
116	Chuck Carr	.25
117	Bobby Ayala	.25
118	Randy Johnson	2.00
119	Edgar Martinez	.25
120	Alex Rodriguez	8.00
121	Kevin Foster	.25
122	Kevin Roberson	.25
123	Sammy Sosa	6.00
124	Steve Trachsel	.25
125	Eduardo Perez	.25
126	Tim Salmon	.40
127	Todd Greene	.25
128	Jorge Fabregas	.25
129	Mark Langston	.25
130	Mitch Williams	.25
131	Raul Casanova	.25
132	Mel Nieves	.25
133	Andy Benes	.25
134	Dustin Hermanson	.25
135	Trevor Hoffman	.25
136	Mark Grudzielanek	.25
137	Ugueth Urbina	.25
138	Moises Alou	.40
139	Roberto Kelly	.25
140	Rondell White	.40
141	Paul O'Neill	.50
142	Jimmy Key	.25
143	Jack McDowell	.25
144	Ruben Rivera	.25
145	Don Mattingly	3.00
146	John Wetteland	.25
147	Tom Glavine	.75
148	Marquis Grissom	.25
149	Javy Lopez	.40
150	Fred McGriff	1.00
151	Greg Maddux	5.00
152	Chris Sabo	.25
153	Ray Durham	.25
154	Robin Ventura	.50
155	Jim Abbott	.25
156	Jimmy Hurst	.25
157	Tim Raines	.25
158	Dennis Martinez	.25
159	Kenny Lofton	2.00
160	Dave Winfield	.40
161	Manny Ramirez	3.00
162	Jim Thome	.60
163	Barry Larkin	.40
164	Bret Boone	.25
165	Deion Sanders	.40
166	Ron Gant	.30
167	Benito Santiago	.25
168	Hideo Nomo	.50
169	Billy Ashley	.25
170	Roger Cedeno	.25
171	Ismael Valdes	.25
172	Eric Karros	.30
173	Rusty Greer	.25
174	Rick Helling	.25
175	Nolan Ryan	8.00
176	Dean Palmer	.25
177	Phil Plantier	.25
178	Darryl Kile	.25
179	Derek Bell	.25
180	Doug Drabek	.25
181	Craig Biggio	1.00
182	Kevin Brown	.40
183	Harold Baines	.25
184	Jeffrey Hammonds	.25
185	Chris Hoiles	.25
186	Mike Mussina	1.50
187	Bob Hamelin	.25
188	Jeff Montgomery	.25
189	Michael Tucker	.25
190	George Brett	2.50
191	Edgardo Alfonzo	.50
192	Brett Butler	.25
193	Bobby Jones	.25
194	Todd Hundley	.25
195	Bret Saberhagen	.25
196	Pat Hentgen	.25
197	Roberto Alomar	2.00
198	David Cone	.40
199	Carlos Delgado	1.50
200	Joe Carter	.25
201	William Van Landingham	.25
202	Rod Beck	.25
203	J.R. Phillips	.25
204	Darren Lewis	.25
205	Matt Williams	.60
206	Lenny Dykstra	.25
207	Dave Hollins	.25
208	Mike Schmidt	1.50
209	Charlie Hayes	.25
210	Mo Vaughn	2.00
211	Jose Malave	.25
212	Roger Clemens	3.00
213	Jose Canseco	2.00
214	Mark Whiten	.25
215	Marty Cordova	.25
216	Rick Aguilera	.25
217	Kevin Tapani	.25
218	Chuck Knoblauch	.50
219	Al Martin	.25
220	Jay Bell	.25
221	Carlos Garcia	.25
222	Freddy Garcia	.25
223	Jon Lieber	.25
224	Danny Jackson	.25
225	Ozzie Smith	1.50
226	Brian Jordan	.25
227	Ken Hill	.25
228	Scott Cooper	.25
229	Chad Curtis	.25
230	Lou Whitaker	.25
231	Kirk Gibson	.25
232	Travis Fryman	.35
233	Jose Valentin	.25
234	Dave Nilsson	.25
235	Cal Eldred	.25
236	Matt Mieske	.25
237	Bill Swift	.25
238	Marvin Freeman	.25
239	Jason Bates	.25
240	Larry Walker	1.50
241	David Nied	.25
242	Dante Bichette	.50
243	Dennis Eckersley	.25
244	Todd Stottlemyre	.25
245	Rickey Henderson	.75
246	Geronimo Berroa	.25
247	Mark McGwire	10.00
248	Quilvio Veras	.25
249	Terry Pendleton	.25
250	Andre Dawson	.40
251	Jeff Conine	.25
252	Kurt Abbott	.25
253	Jay Buhner	.30
254	Darren Bragg	.25
255	Ken Griffey Jr.	10.00
256	Tino Martinez	.50
257	Mark Grace	.50
258	Ryne Sandberg	1.50
259	Randy Myers	.25
260	Howard Johnson	.25
261	Lee Smith	.25
262	J.T. Snow	.35
263	Chili Davis	.25
264	Chuck Finley	.25
265	Eddie Williams	.25
266	Joey Hamilton	.25
267	Ken Caminiti	.75
268	Andujar Cedeno	.25
269	Steve Finley	.25
270	Tony Gwynn	5.00

1995 Upper Deck Special Edition Gold

An insert set within an insert set, gold-foil enhanced versions of the Special Edition cards were seeded into hobby packs at the rate of about one per box. The substitution of gold ink for silver is also carried over onto the background of the card back.

	MT
Complete Set (270):	700.00
Common Player:	2.00
Stars/Rookies:	4X

(See 1995 Upper Deck Special Edition for checklist and base card values.)

1995 Upper Deck Steal of a Deal

A horizontal format with an action photo printed over a green foil background and a large bronze seal indicating how the player was acquired are featured in this 15-card insert set. The front has a terra-cotta border, which is carried over to the back. A large green box on back details the transaction and describes why it can be categorized as a "steal" for the player's new team. These top-of-the-line chase cards were seeded in both hobby and retail packs of Series I at the average rate of one per 34 packs. Cards are numbered with a "SD" prefix.

		MT
Complete Set (15):		80.00
Common Player:		2.00
1	Mike Piazza	15.00
2	Fred McGriff	4.00
3	Kenny Lofton	6.00
4	Jose Oliva	2.00
5	Jeff Bagwell	10.00
6	Roberto Alomar, Joe Carter	4.00
7	Steve Karsay	2.00
8	Ozzie Smith	6.00
9	Dennis Eckersley	2.00
10	Jose Canseco	6.00
11	Carlos Baerga	2.00
12	Cecil Fielder	2.00
13	Don Mattingly	10.00
14	Bret Boone	2.00
15	Michael Jordan	30.00

1995 Upper Deck Update

These 45 cards depicting traded and free agent players in the uniforms of their new 1995 teams were available only by redeeming trade-in cards found in Series II packs. Each trade-in card was good for one nine-card segment of the Update series when sent with $2 prior to the Feb. 1, 1996, deadline. Update cards share the same format as the regular 1995 Upper Deck set. The Updates are sequenced according to team nickname.

		MT
Complete Set (45):		9.00
Common Player:		.15
451	Jim Abbott	.15
452	Danny Tartabull	.15
453	Ariel Prieto	.15
454	Scott Cooper	.15
455	Tom Henke	.15
456	Todd Zeile	.30
457	Brian McRae	.25
458	Luis Gonzalez	.15
459	Jaime Navarro	.15
460	Todd Worrell	.15
461	Roberto Kelly	.15
462	Chad Fonville	.20
463	Shane Andrews	.50
464	David Segui	.15
465	Deion Sanders	.50
466	Orel Hershiser	.25
467	Ken Hill	.15
468	Andy Benes	.25
469	Terry Pendleton	.15
470	Bobby Bonilla	.20
471	Scott Erickson	.25
472	Kevin Brown	.25
473	Glenn Dishman	.15
474	Phil Plantier	.15
475	Gregg Jefferies	.30
476	Tyler Green	.15
477	Heathcliff Slocumb	.15
478	Mark Whiten	.15
479	Mickey Tettleton	.15
480	Tim Wakefield	.15
481	Vaughn Eshelman	.15
482	Rick Aguilera	.15
483	Erik Hanson	.15
484	Willie McGee	.20
485	Troy O'Leary	.15
486	Benito Santiago	.15
487	Darren Lewis	.15
488	Dave Burba	.15
489	Ron Gant	.25
490	Bret Saberhagen	.25
491	Vinny Castilla	.50
492	Frank Rodriguez	.15
493	Andy Pettitte	3.00
494	Ruben Sierra	.15
495	David Cone	.50

1995 Upper Deck Update Trade Cards

Inserted into Series II at the rate of about one per 11 packs was this five-card series of trade cards. Each card could be mailed in with $2 to receive nine cards from a special UD Update set picturing traded or free agent players in the uniforms of their new teams. The front of each trade card pictures one of the traded players in his old uniform against a red and blue background. Backs have instructions for redeeming the trade cards. The mail-in offer expired Feb. 1, 1996. Cards are numbered with a "TC" prefix.

		MT
Complete Set (5):		6.00
Common Player:		1.00
1	Orel Hershiser	1.00
2	Terry Pendleton	1.00
3	Benito Santiago	1.00
4	Kevin Brown	1.00
5	Gregg Jefferies	1.00

1996 Upper Deck

Upper Deck Series I consists of 240 regular-issue cards. There are 187 regular player cards plus subsets of Star Rookies, Young at Heart, Beat the Odds, Milestones, Post-season, checklists and expansion logos. The issue was marketed in 10-card foil packs in hobby and retail versions. Hobby packs feature a Special Edition insert while retail packs offer Electric Diamond parallel cards. Series I insert sets are Blue Chip Prospects, Future Shock and Power Driven. Cal Ripken Jr. Collection cards are inserted in both series, as are Retail Predictor (home runs, batting average and RBIs) and Hobby Predictor (Player of the Month, Pitcher of the Month and rookie hits leaders) cards. Series II has 240 cards, including subsets for Star Rookies, Diamond Debuts, Strange But True, Managerial Salutes and Best of a Generation. Additional insert sets include Hot Commodities, Hideo Nomo Highlights, Run Producers and the Lovero Collection.

		MT
Complete Set (480):		60.00
Complete Series 1 (240):		30.00
Complete Series 2 (240):		30.00
Common Player:		.10
Series 1 Pack (10):		2.00
Series 1 Wax Box (28):		45.00
Series 2 Pack (12):		2.00
Series 2 Wax Box (32):		50.00
1	Cal Ripken Jr. (Milestones)	2.50
2	Eddie Murray (Milestones)	.40
3	Mark Wohlers	.10
4	Dave Justice	.20
5	Chipper Jones	2.00
6	Javier Lopez	.20
7	Mark Lemke	.10
8	Marquis Grissom	.10
9	Tom Glavine	.25
10	Greg Maddux	1.50
11	Manny Alexander	.10
12	Curtis Goodwin	.10
13	Scott Erickson	.10
14	Chris Hoiles	.10
15	Rafael Palmeiro	.40
16	Rick Krivda	.10
17	Jeff Manto	.10
18	Mo Vaughn	.60
19	Tim Wakefield	.10
20	Roger Clemens	1.50
21	Tim Naehring	.10
22	Troy O'Leary	.10
23	Mike Greenwell	.10
24	Stan Belinda	.10
25	John Valentin	.10
26	J.T. Snow	.15
27	Gary DiSarcina	.10
28	Mark Langston	.10
29	Brian Anderson	.10
30	Jim Edmonds	.15
31	Garret Anderson	.10
32	Orlando Palmeiro	.10
33	Brian McRae	.10
34	Kevin Foster	.10
35	Sammy Sosa	2.00
36	Todd Zeile	.10
37	Jim Bullinger	.10
38	Luis Gonzalez	.15
39	Lyle Mouton	.10
40	Ray Durham	.10
41	Ozzie Guillen	.10
42	Alex Fernandez	.10
43	Brian Keyser	.10
44	Robin Ventura	.20
45	Reggie Sanders	.10
46	Pete Schourek	.10
47	John Smiley	.10
48	Jeff Brantley	.10
49	Thomas Howard	.10
50	Bret Boone	.10
51	Kevin Jarvis	.10
52	Jeff Branson	.10
53	Carlos Baerga	.10
54	Jim Thome	.40
55	Manny Ramirez	1.00
56	Omar Vizquel	.15
57	Jose Mesa	.10

No.	Player	Value
58	Julian Tavarez	.10
59	Orel Hershiser	.10
60	Larry Walker	.50
61	Bret Saberhagen	.15
62	Vinny Castilla	.15
63	Eric Young	.15
64	Bryan Rekar	.10
65	Andres Galarraga	.25
66	Steve Reed	.10
67	Chad Curtis	.10
68	Bobby Higginson	.10
69	Phil Nevin	.10
70	Cecil Fielder	.10
71	Felipe Lira	.10
72	Chris Gomez	.10
73	Charles Johnson	.20
74	Quilvio Veras	.10
75	Jeff Conine	.10
76	John Burkett	.10
77	Greg Colbrunn	.10
78	Terry Pendleton	.10
79	Shane Reynolds	.15
80	Jeff Bagwell	1.00
81	Orlando Miller	.10
82	Mike Hampton	.10
83	James Mouton	.10
84	Brian L. Hunter	.10
85	Derek Bell	.10
86	Kevin Appier	.10
87	Joe Vitiello	.10
88	Wally Joyner	.10
89	Michael Tucker	.10
90	Johnny Damon	.15
91	Jon Nunnally	.10
92	Jason Jacome	.10
93	Chad Fonville	.10
94	Chan Ho Park	.20
95	Hideo Nomo	.25
96	Ismael Valdes	.10
97	Greg Gagne	.10
98	Diamondbacks-Devil Rays (Expansion Card)	.25
99	Raul Mondesi	.25
100	Dave Winfield (Young at Heart)	.15
101	Dennis Eckersley (Young at Heart)	.10
102	Andre Dawson (Young at Heart)	.10
103	Dennis Martinez (Young at Heart)	.10
104	Lance Parrish (Young at Heart)	.10
105	Eddie Murray (Young at Heart)	.25
106	Alan Trammell (Young at Heart)	.10
107	Lou Whitaker (Young at Heart)	.10
108	Ozzie Smith (Young at Heart)	.25
109	Paul Molitor (Young at Heart)	.20
110	Rickey Henderson (Young at Heart)	.20
111	Tim Raines (Young at Heart)	.10
112	Harold Baines (Young at Heart)	.10
113	Lee Smith (Young at Heart)	.10
114	Fernando Valenzuela (Young at Heart)	.10
115	Cal Ripken Jr. (Young at Heart)	1.50
116	Tony Gwynn (Young at Heart)	.75
117	Wade Boggs (Young at Heart)	.15
118	Todd Hollandsworth	.15
119	Dave Nilsson	.10
120	*Jose Valentin*	.20
121	Steve Sparks	.10
122	Chuck Carr	.10
123	John Jaha	.10
124	Scott Karl	.10
125	Chuck Knoblauch	.25
126	Brad Radke	.10
127	Pat Meares	.10
128	Ron Coomer	.10
129	Pedro Munoz	.10
130	Kirby Puckett	1.00
131	David Segui	.10
132	Mark Grudzielanek	.10
133	Mike Lansing	.10
134	Sean Berry	.10
135	Rondell White	.15
136	Pedro Martinez	.75
137	Carl Everett	.15
138	Dave Mlicki	.10
139	Bill Pulsipher	.10
140	Jason Isringhausen	.10
141	Rico Brogna	.10
142	Edgardo Alfonzo	.25
143	Jeff Kent	.10
144	Andy Pettitte	.25
145	Mike Piazza (Beat the Odds)	1.00
146	Cliff Floyd (Beat the Odds)	.10
147	Jason Isringhausen (Beat the Odds)	.10
148	Tim Wakefield (Beat the Odds)	.10
149	Chipper Jones (Beat the Odds)	1.00
150	Hideo Nomo (Beat the Odds)	.15
151	Mark McGwire (Beat the Odds)	2.00
152	Ron Gant (Beat the Odds)	.10
153	Gary Gaetti (Beat the Odds)	.10
154	Don Mattingly	1.00
155	Paul O'Neill	.25
156	Derek Jeter	2.50
157	Joe Girardi	.10
158	Ruben Sierra	.10
159	Jorge Posada	.20
160	Geronimo Berroa	.10
161	Steve Ontiveros	.10
162	George Williams	.10
163	Doug Johns	.10
164	Ariel Prieto	.10
165	Scott Brosius	.10
166	Mike Bordick	.10
167	Tyler Green	.10
168	Mickey Morandini	.10
169	Darren Daulton	.10
170	Gregg Jefferies	.10
171	Jim Eisenreich	.10
172	Heathcliff Slocumb	.10
173	Kevin Stocker	.10
174	Esteban Loaiza	.10
175	Jeff King	.10
176	Mark Johnson	.10
177	Denny Neagle	.10
178	Orlando Merced	.10
179	Carlos Garcia	.10
180	Brian Jordan	.10
181	Mike Morgan	.10
182	Mark Petkovsek	.10
183	Bernard Gilkey	.10
184	John Mabry	.10
185	Tom Henke	.10
186	Glenn Dishman	.10
187	Andy Ashby	.10
188	Bip Roberts	.10
189	Melvin Nieves	.10
190	Ken Caminiti	.20
191	Brad Ausmus	.10
192	Deion Sanders	.20
193	Jamie Brewington	.10
194	Glenallen Hill	.10
195	Barry Bonds	.75
196	William VanLandingham	.10
197	Mark Carreon	.10
198	Royce Clayton	.10
199	Joey Cora	.10
200	Ken Griffey Jr.	3.00
201	Jay Buhner	.10
202	Alex Rodriguez	2.50
203	Norm Charlton	.10
204	Andy Benes	.10
205	Edgar Martinez	.10
206	Juan Gonzalez	1.00
207	Will Clark	.25
208	Kevin Gross	.10
209	Roger Pavlik	.10
210	Ivan Rodriguez	.75
211	Rusty Greer	.10
212	Angel Martinez	.10
213	Tomas Perez	.10
214	Alex Gonzalez	.10
215	Joe Carter	.10
216	Shawn Green	.50
217	Edwin Hurtado	.10
218	(Edgar Martinez, Tony Pena) (Post Season Checklist)	.10
219	Chipper Jones, Barry Larkin (Post Season Checklist)	.25
220	Orel Hershiser (Post Season Checklist)	.10
221	Mike Devereaux (Post Season Checklist)	.10
222	Tom Glavine (Post Season Checklist)	.10
223	Karim Garcia (Star Rookies)	.15
224	Arquimedez Pozo (Star Rookies)	.10
225	Billy Wagner (Star Rookies)	.15
226	John Wasdin (Star Rookies)	.10
227	Jeff Suppan (Star Rookies)	.10
228	Steve Gibralter (Star Rookies)	.10
229	Jimmy Haynes (Star Rookies)	.10
230	Ruben Rivera (Star Rookies)	.15
231	Chris Snopek (Star Rookies)	.15
232	Alex Ochoa (Star Rookies)	.10
233	Shannon Stewart (Star Rookies)	.10
234	Quinton McCracken (Star Rookies)	.15
235	Trey Beamon (Star Rookies)	.10
236	Billy McMillon (Star Rookies)	.10
237	Steve Cox (Star Rookies)	.10
238	George Arias (Star Rookies)	.10
239	Yamil Benitez (Star Rookies)	.10
240	Todd Greene (Star Rookies)	.20
241	Jason Kendall (Star Rookie)	.20
242	Brooks Kieschnick (Star Rookie)	.15
243	*Osvaldo Fernandez* (Star Rookie)	.15
244	*Livan Hernandez* (Star Rookie)	.50
245	Rey Ordonez (Star Rookie)	.20
246	*Mike Grace* (Star Rookie)	.10
247	Jay Canizaro (Star Rookie)	.10
248	Bob Wolcott (Star Rookie)	.10
249	Jermaine Dye (Star Rookie)	.15
250	Jason Schmidt (Star Rookie)	.10
251	*Mike Sweeney* (Star Rookie)	2.00
252	Marcus Jensen (Star Rookie)	.10
253	Mendy Lopez (Star Rookie)	.10
254	*Wilton Guerrero* (Star Rookie)	.50
255	Paul Wilson (Star Rookie)	.10
256	Edgar Renteria (Star Rookie)	.20
257	Richard Hidalgo (Star Rookie)	.10
258	Bob Abreu (Star Rookie)	.40
259	*Robert Smith* (Diamond Debuts)	.30
260	Sal Fasano (Diamond Debuts)	.10
261	Enrique Wilson (Diamond Debuts)	.10
262	*Rich Hunter* (Diamond Debuts)	.10
263	Sergio Nunez (Diamond Debuts)	.10
264	Dan Serafini (Diamond Debuts)	.10
265	*David Doster* (Diamond Debuts)	.10
266	Ryan McGuire (Diamond Debuts)	.10
267	Scott Spiezio (Diamond Debuts)	.10
268	Rafael Orellano (Diamond Debuts)	.10
269	Steve Avery	.10
270	Fred McGriff	.30
271	John Smoltz	.20
272	Ryan Klesko	.15
273	Jeff Blauser	.10
274	Brad Clontz	.10
275	Roberto Alomar	.60
276	B.J. Surhoff	.10
277	Jeffrey Hammonds	.10
278	Brady Anderson	.15
279	Bobby Bonilla	.10
280	Cal Ripken Jr.	2.50
281	Mike Mussina	.60
282	Wil Cordero	.10
283	Mike Stanley	.10
284	Aaron Sele	.10
285	Jose Canseco	.60
286	Tom Gordon	.10
287	Heathcliff Slocumb	.10
288	Lee Smith	.10
289	Troy Percival	.10
290	Tim Salmon	.25
291	Chuck Finley	.10
292	Jim Abbott	.10
293	Chili Davis	.10
294	Steve Trachsel	.10
295	Mark Grace	.25
296	Rey Sanchez	.10
297	Scott Servais	.10
298	Jaime Navarro	.10
299	Frank Castillo	.10
300	Frank Thomas	1.50
301	Jason Bere	.10
302	Danny Tartabull	.10
303	Darren Lewis	.10
304	Roberto Hernandez	.10
305	Tony Phillips	.10
306	Wilson Alvarez	.10
307	Jose Rijo (NEW)	.10
308	Hal Morris	.10
309	Mark Portugal	.10
310	Barry Larkin	.15
311	Dave Burba	.10
312	Eddie Taubensee	.10
313	Sandy Alomar Jr.	.15
314	Dennis Martinez	.10
315	Albert Belle	.75
316	Eddie Murray	.40
317	Charles Nagy	.10
318	Chad Ogea	.10
319	Kenny Lofton	.50
320	Dante Bichette	.25
321	Armando Reynoso	.10
322	Walt Weiss	.10
323	Ellis Burks	.10
324	Kevin Ritz	.10
325	Bill Swift	.10
326	Jason Bates	.10
327	Tony Clark	.40
328	Travis Fryman	.15
329	Mark Parent	.10
330	Alan Trammell	.10
331	C.J. Nitkowski	.10
332	Jose Lima	.10
333	Phil Plantier	.10
334	Kurt Abbott	.10
335	Andre Dawson (NEW)	.15
336	Chris Hammond	.10
337	Robb Nen	.10
338	Pat Rapp	.10
339	Al Leiter	.15
340	Gary Sheffield	.20
341	Todd Jones	.10
342	Doug Drabek	.10
343	Greg Swindell (NEW)	.10
344	Tony Eusebio	.10
345	Craig Biggio	.40
346	Darryl Kile	.10
347	Mike Macfarlane	.10
348	Jeff Montgomery	.10
349	Chris Haney	.10
350	Bip Roberts	.10
351	Tom Goodwin	.10
352	Mark Gubicza	.10
353	Joe Randa (NEW)	.10
354	Ramon Martinez	.10
355	Eric Karros	.15
356	Delino DeShields	.10
357	Brett Butler	.10
358	Todd Worrell	.10
359	Mike Blowers	.10
360	Mike Piazza	2.00
361	Ben McDonald	.10
362	Ricky Bones	.10
363	Greg Vaughn	.15
364	Matt Mieske	.10
365	Kevin Seitzer	.10
366	Jeff Cirillo	.10
367	LaTroy Hawkins	.10
368	Frank Rodriguez	.10
369	Rick Aguilera	.10

370	Roberto Alomar (Best of a Generation)	.40
371	Albert Belle (Best of a Generation)	.40
372	Wade Boggs (Best of a Generation)	.15
373	Barry Bonds (Best of a Generation)	.40
374	Roger Clemens (Best of a Generation)	.75
375	Dennis Eckersley (Best of a Generation)	.10
376	Ken Griffey Jr. (Best of a Generation)	2.00
377	Tony Gwynn (Best of a Generation)	.75
378	Rickey Henderson (Best of a Generation)	.20
379	Greg Maddux (Best of a Generation)	.75
380	Fred McGriff (Best of a Generation)	.20
381	Paul Molitor (Best of a Generation)	.20
382	Eddie Murray (Best of a Generation)	.25
383	Mike Piazza (Best of a Generation)	1.00
384	Kirby Puckett (Best of a Generation)	.50
385	Cal Ripken Jr. (Best of a Generation)	1.50
386	Ozzie Smith (Best of a Generation)	.30
387	Frank Thomas (Best of a Generation)	.50
388	Matt Walbeck	.10
389	Dave Stevens	.10
390	Marty Cordova	.10
391	Darrin Fletcher	.10
392	Cliff Floyd	.10
393	Mel Rojas	.10
394	Shane Andrews	.15
395	Moises Alou	.20
396	Carlos Perez	.10
397	Jeff Fassero	.10
398	Bobby Jones	.10
399	Todd Hundley	.15
400	John Franco	.10
401	Jose Vizcaino	.10
402	Bernard Gilkey	.10
403	Pete Harnisch	.10
404	Pat Kelly	.10
405	David Cone	.20
406	Bernie Williams	.40
407	John Wetteland	.10
408	Scott Kamieniecki	.10
409	Tim Raines	.10
410	Wade Boggs	.30
411	Terry Steinbach	.10
412	Jason Giambi	.10
413	Todd Van Poppel	.10
414	Pedro Munoz	.10
415	Eddie Murray-1990 (Strange But True)	.25
416	Dennis Eckersley-1990 (Strange But True)	.10
417	Bip Roberts-1992 (Strange But True)	.10
418	Glenallen Hill-1992 (Strange But True)	.10
419	John Hudek-1994 (Strange But True)	.10
420	Derek Bell-1995 (Strange But True)	.10
421	Larry Walker-1995 (Strange But True)	.25
422	Greg Maddux-1995 (Strange But True)	.75
423	Ken Caminiti-1995 (Strange But True)	.20
424	Brent Gates	.10
425	Mark McGwire	3.00
426	Mark Whiten	.10
427	Sid Fernandez	.10
428	Ricky Bottalico	.10
429	Mike Mimbs	.10
430	Lenny Dykstra	.10
431	Todd Zeile	.10
432	Benito Santiago	.10
433	Danny Miceli	.10
434	Al Martin	.10
435	Jay Bell	.10
436	Charlie Hayes	.10
437	Mike Kingery	.10
438	Paul Wagner	.10
439	Tom Pagnozzi	.10
440	Ozzie Smith	.60
441	Ray Lankford	.10
442	Dennis Eckersley	.10
443	Ron Gant	.10
444	Alan Benes	.10
445	Rickey Henderson	.40
446	Jody Reed	.10
447	Trevor Hoffman	.10
448	Andujar Cedeno	.10
449	Steve Finley	.10
450	Tony Gwynn	1.50
451	Joey Hamilton	.10
452	Mark Leiter	.10
453	Rod Beck	.10
454	Kirt Manwaring	.10
455	Matt Williams	.25
456	Robby Thompson	.10
457	Shawon Dunston	.10
458	Russ Davis	.10
459	Paul Sorrento	.10
460	Randy Johnson	.75
461	Chris Bosio	.10
462	Luis Sojo	.10
463	Sterling Hitchcock	.10
464	Benji Gil	.10
465	Mickey Tettleton	.10
466	Mark McLemore	.10
467	Darryl Hamilton	.10
468	Ken Hill	.10
469	Dean Palmer	.10
470	Carlos Delgado	.50
471	Ed Sprague	.10
472	Otis Nixon	.10
473	Pat Hentgen	.10
474	Juan Guzman	.10
475	John Olerud	.25
476	Checklist (Buck Showalter)	.10
477	Checklist (Bobby Cox)	.10
478	Checklist (Tommy Lasorda)	.25
479	Checklist (Jim Leyland)	.10
480	Checklist (Sparky Anderson)	.15

1996 Upper Deck Blue Chip Prospects

Twenty top young stars who could make a major impact in the major leagues in upcoming seasons are featured in this insert set. Each card is highlighted with blue-foil printing and double die-cut technology, which includes a zig-zag pattern around the top and a die-cut around both bottom corners. The cards are found one per 20 packs in Series 1 foil packs. Cards are numbered with a "BC" prefix.

		MT
Complete Set (20):		150.00
Common Player:		3.00
1	Hideo Nomo	5.00
2	Johnny Damon	4.00
3	Jason Isringhausen	3.00
4	Bill Pulsipher	3.00
5	Marty Cordova	4.00
6	Michael Tucker	4.00
7	John Wasdin	3.00
8	Karim Garcia	4.00
9	Ruben Rivera	4.00
10	Chipper Jones	20.00
11	Billy Wagner	5.00
12	Brooks Kieschnick	3.00
13	Alex Ochoa	4.00
14	Roger Cedeno	4.00
15	Alex Rodriguez	35.00
16	Jason Schmidt	4.00
17	Derek Jeter	35.00
18	Brian L. Hunter	3.00
19	Garret Anderson	4.00
20	Manny Ramirez	10.00

1996 Upper Deck Cal Ripken Collection

Part of a cross-brand insert set, four cards are included as Series I inserts at the rate of one per 24 packs. Five cards are also included in Series II, one per every 23 packs. They chronicle Cal Ripken's career and highlights.

		MT
Complete Set (5-8, 13-17):		45.00
Common Card:		6.00
Header:		6.00
5	Cal Ripken Jr.	6.00
6	Cal Ripken Jr.	6.00
7	Cal Ripken Jr.	6.00
8	Cal Ripken Jr.	6.00
13	Cal Ripken Jr.	6.00
14	Cal Ripken Jr.	6.00
15	Cal Ripken Jr.	6.00
16	Cal Ripken Jr.	6.00
17	Cal Ripken Jr.	6.00

1996 Upper Deck Diamond Destiny

This late-season release is found exclusively in retail foil packs labeled "Upper Deck Tech." They are inserted at a rate of one per pack, sold with eight regular 1996 Upper Deck cards at a suggested retail of around $3. The cards have three versions of the same action photo; in color and black-and-white on front, and in black-and-white on back. A large team logo also appears on front and back. In the upper half of the card is a 1-3/16" diameter round color transparency portrait of the player. The basic version of this chase set had bronze foil highlights. Parallel silver and gold versions are found on average of one per 35 and one per 143 packs, respectively. Cards are numbered with a "DD" prefix.

		MT
Complete Set (Bronze):		75.00
Common Player (Bronze):		.60
Silver:		8X
Gold:		25X
1	Chipper Jones	5.00
2	Fred McGriff	1.25
3	Ryan Klesko	.60
4	John Smoltz	.60
5	Greg Maddux	4.00
6	Cal Ripken Jr.	6.00
7	Roberto Alomar	1.75
8	Eddie Murray	1.25
9	Brady Anderson	.60
10	Mo Vaughn	1.50
11	Roger Clemens	3.00
12	Darin Erstad	3.00
13	Sammy Sosa	5.00
14	Frank Thomas	2.50
15	Barry Larkin	1.00
16	Albert Belle	2.00
17	Manny Ramirez	2.50
18	Kenny Lofton	1.50
19	Dante Bichette	.75
20	Gary Sheffield	.75
21	Jeff Bagwell	2.50
22	Hideo Nomo	.60
23	Mike Piazza	5.00
24	Kirby Puckett	2.00
25	Paul Molitor	2.00
26	Chuck Knoblauch	.75
27	Wade Boggs	1.50
28	Derek Jeter	5.00
29	Rey Ordonez	.60
30	Mark McGwire	8.00
31	Ozzie Smith	2.00
32	Tony Gwynn	4.00
33	Barry Bonds	2.00
34	Matt Williams	1.00
35	Ken Griffey Jr.	8.00
36	Jay Buhner	.60
37	Randy Johnson	1.75
38	Alex Rodriguez	6.00
39	Juan Gonzalez	2.50
40	Joe Carter	.60

1996 Upper Deck Future Stock

Future Stock inserts are found on average of one per six packs of Series 1, highlighting 20 top young stars on a die-cut design. Each card has a blue border, vertical photo and silver-foil stamping on the front. Cards are numbered with a "FS" prefix.

		MT
Complete Set (20):		9.00
Common Player:		.60
1	George Arias	.60
2	Brian Barnes	.60
3	Trey Beamon	.60
4	Yamil Benitez	.60
5	Jamie Brewington	.60
6	Tony Clark	1.00
7	Steve Cox	.60
8	Carlos Delgado	2.00
9	Chad Fonville	.60
10	Steve Gibralter	.60
11	Curtis Goodwin	.60
12	Todd Greene	.60
13	Jimmy Haynes	.60
14	Quinton McCracken	.60
15	Billy McMillon	.60
16	Chan Ho Park	1.00
17	Arquimedez Pozo	.60
18	Chris Snopek	.60
19	Shannon Stewart	.75
20	Jeff Suppan	.60

1996 Upper Deck Gameface

		MT
Complete Set (10):		8.00
Common Player:		.25
1	Ken Griffey Jr.	2.00
2	Frank Thomas	1.00
3	Barry Bonds	.65
4	Albert Belle	.50
5	Cal Ripken Jr.	1.75
6	Mike Piazza	1.50
7	Chipper Jones	1.50
8	Matt Williams	.25
9	Hideo Nomo	.25
10	Greg Maddux	1.00

1996 Upper Deck Hobby Predictor

These inserts depict 60 top players as possible winners in the categories of Player of the Month, Pitcher of the Month and Rookie Hits Leader. If the pictured player won that category any month of the season the card was redeemable for a 10-card set with a different look, action photos and printed on silver-foil stock. Hobby Predictor inserts are found on average once per dozen packs in both series. Winning cards are indicated by (W). Cards are numbered with a "H" prefix.

		MT
Complete Set (60):		55.00
Common Player:		.50
1	Albert Belle	1.00
2	Kenny Lofton	1.00
3	Rafael Palmeiro	1.00
4	Ken Griffey Jr.	5.00
5	Tim Salmon	.75
6	Cal Ripken Jr.	4.00
7	Mark McGwire (W)	5.00
8	Frank Thomas (W)	1.50
9	Mo Vaughn (W)	1.00
10	Player of the Month Long Shot (W)	.50
11	Roger Clemens	2.00
12	David Cone	.75
13	Jose Mesa	.50
14	Randy Johnson	1.00
15	Steve Finley	.50
16	Mike Mussina	1.00
17	Kevin Appier	.50
18	Kenny Rogers	.50
19	Lee Smith	.50
20	Pitcher of the Month Long Shot (W)	.50
21	George Arias	.50
22	Jose Herrera	.50
23	Tony Clark	.75
24	Todd Greene	.50
25	Derek Jeter (W)	4.00
26	Arquimedez Pozo	.50
27	Matt Lawton	.50
28	Shannon Stewart	.75
29	Chris Snopek	.50
30	Rookie Hits Long Shot	.50
31	Jeff Bagwell (W)	1.50
32	Dante Bichette	.75
33	Barry Bonds (W)	1.50
34	Tony Gwynn	2.50
35	Chipper Jones	3.00
36	Eric Karros	.60
37	Barry Larkin	.60
38	Mike Piazza	3.00
39	Matt Williams	.75
40	Player of the Month Long Shot (W)	.50
41	Osvaldo Fernandez	.50
42	Tom Glavine	.75
43	Jason Isringhausen	.50
44	Greg Maddux	2.50
45	Pedro Martinez	1.50
46	Hideo Nomo	1.00
47	Pete Schourek	.50
48	Paul Wilson	.50
49	Mark Wohlers	.50
50	Pitcher of the Month Long Shot	.50
51	Bob Abreu	.75
52	Trey Beamon	.50
53	Yamil Benitez	.50
54	Roger Cedeno (W)	.50
55	Todd Hollandsworth	.50
56	Marvin Benard	.50
57	Jason Kendall	.75
58	Brooks Kieschnick	.50
59	Rey Ordonez (W)	.90
60	Rookie Hits Long Shot (W)	.50

1996 Upper Deck Hobby Predictor Redemption

Persons who redeemed winning cards from UD's interactive Predictor insert series received a 10-card set of the top players in various statistical categories. The redemption cards are similar in format to the Predictor cards, but have fronts printed on silver-foil. In palce of the contest rules found on the backs of Predictor cards, the redemption cards have a career summary.

		MT
Complete Set (30):		12.00
Common Player:		.25
H31	Jeff Bagwell	1.00
H32	Dante Bichette	.40
H33	Barry Bonds	.75
H34	Tony Gwynn	1.00
H35	Chipper Jones	1.50
H36	Eric Karros	.25
H37	Barry Larkin	.25
H38	Mike Piazza	1.50
H39	Matt Williams	.25
H40	Player of the Month Long Shot	.25
H41	Osvaldo Fernandez	.25
H42	Tom Glavine	.40
H43	Jason Isringhausen	.25
H44	Greg Maddux	1.00
H45	Pedro Martinez	.50
H46	Hideo Nomo	.50
H47	Pete Schourek	.25
H48	Paul Wilson	.35
H49	Mark Wohlers	.25
H50	Pitcher of the Month Long Shot	.25
H51	Bob Abreu	.35
H52	Trey Beamon	.25
H53	Yamil Benitez	.25
H54	Roger Cedeno	.25
H55	Todd Hollandsworth	.25
H56	Marvin Benard	.25
H57	Jason Kendall	.35
H58	Brooks Kieschnick	.25
H59	Rey Ordonez	.60
H60	Rookie Hits Long Shot	.25

1996 Upper Deck Retail Predictor

Retail Predictor inserts feature 60 possible winners in the categories of monthly leader in home runs, batting average and RBIs. If the pictured player led a category in any month, his card was redeemable for a 10-card set featuring action photos on silver foil. Retail Predictors are found on average once per 12 packs in each series. Winning cards are indicated by (W). Cards are numbered with a "R" prefix.

		MT
Complete Set (60):		90.00
Common Player:		.75
1	Albert Belle (W)	1.50
2	Jay Buhner (W)	.75
3	Juan Gonzalez	2.50
4	Ken Griffey Jr.	7.50
5	Mark McGwire (W)	7.50
6	Rafael Palmeiro	1.00
7	Tim Salmon	.75
8	Frank Thomas	3.00
9	Mo Vaughn (W)	1.50
10	Home Run Long Shot (W)	.75
11	Albert Belle (W)	1.50
12	Jay Buhner	.75
13	Jim Edmonds	.75
14	Cecil Fielder	.75
15	Ken Griffey Jr.	7.50
16	Edgar Martinez	.75
17	Manny Ramirez	2.00
18	Frank Thomas	3.00
19	Mo Vaughn ((W))	1.50
20	RBI Long Shot (W)	.75
21	Roberto Alomar (W)	1.50
22	Carlos Baerga	.75
23	Wade Boggs	1.00
24	Ken Griffey Jr.	7.50
25	Chuck Knoblauch	.90
26	Kenny Lofton	1.50
27	Edgar Martinez	.75
28	Tim Salmon	.75
29	Frank Thomas	3.00
30	Batting Average Long Shot (W)	.75
31	Dante Bichette	.75
32	Barry Bonds (W)	2.00
33	Ron Gant	.75
34	Chipper Jones	5.00
35	Fred McGriff	1.00
36	Mike Piazza	5.00
37	Sammy Sosa	3.00
38	Larry Walker	1.00
39	Matt Williams	.90
40	Home Run Long Shot	.75
41	Jeff Bagwell (W)	3.00
42	Dante Bichette	.75
43	Barry Bonds (W)	2.00
44	Jeff Conine	.75
45	Andres Galarraga	.75
46	Mike Piazza	5.00
47	Reggie Sanders	.75
48	Sammy Sosa	3.00
49	Matt Williams	.90
50	RBI Long Shot	.75
51	Jeff Bagwell	3.00
52	Derek Bell	.75
53	Dante Bichette	.75
54	Craig Biggio	.90
55	Barry Bonds	2.00

56	Bret Boone	.75
57	Tony Gwynn	3.00
58	Barry Larkin	.90
59	Mike Piazza (W)	5.00
60	AVG Long Shot	.75

1996 Upper Deck Retail Predictor Redemption

Persons who redeemed winning cards from UD's interactive Predictor insert series received a 10-card set of the top players in various statistical categories. The redemption cards are similar in format to the Predictor cards, but have fronts printed on silver-foil. In palce of the contest rules found on the backs of Predictor cards, the redemption cards have a career summary.

		MT
Complete Set (30):		12.00
Common Player:		.25
R31	Dante Bichette	.25
R32	Barry Bonds	.75
R33	Ron Gant	.25
R34	Chipper Jones	1.50
R35	Fred McGriff	.40
R36	Mike Piazza	1.50
R37	Sammy Sosa	1.50
R38	Larry Walker	.35
R39	Matt Williams	.25
R40	Home Run Long Shot	.25
R41	Jeff Bagwell	1.00
R42	Dante Bichette	.25
R43	Barry Bonds	.75
R44	Jeff Conine	.25
R45	Andres Galarraga	.25
R46	Mike Piazza	1.50
R47	Reggie Sanders	.25
R48	Sammy Sosa	1.50
R49	Matt Williams	.25
R50	RBI Long Shot	.25
R51	Jeff Bagwell	1.00
R52	Derek Bell	.25
R53	Dante Bichette	.25
R54	Craig Biggio	.25
R55	Barry Bonds	.75
R56	Bret Boone	.25
R57	Tony Gwynn	1.00
R58	Barry Larkin	.25
R59	Mike Piazza	1.50
R60	AVG Long Shot	.25

1996 Upper Deck Hot Commodities

These 20 die-cut cards were seeded one per every 37 1996 Upper Deck Series II packs. Cards are numbered with a "HC" prefix.

		MT
Complete Set (20):		150.00
Common Player:		3.50
1	Ken Griffey Jr.	25.00
2	Hideo Nomo	3.50
3	Roberto Alomar	5.00
4	Paul Wilson	3.50
5	Albert Belle	5.00
6	Manny Ramirez	9.00
7	Kirby Puckett	7.50
8	Johnny Damon	3.50
9	Randy Johnson	5.00
10	Greg Maddux	12.50
11	Chipper Jones	15.00
12	Barry Bonds	7.50
13	Mo Vaughn	5.00
14	Mike Piazza	15.00
15	Cal Ripken Jr.	20.00
16	Tim Salmon	4.00
17	Sammy Sosa	15.00
18	Kenny Lofton	5.00
19	Tony Gwynn	12.50
20	Frank Thomas	9.00

1996 Upper Deck Lovero Collection

Every sixth pack of 1996 Upper Deck Series II has a V.J. Lovero insert card. This 20-card set features unique shots from Lovero, one of the most well-known photographers in the country. Some of the cards feature Randy Johnson wearing a conehead, Frank Thomas blowing a bubble while throwing the ball, and Jay Buhner and his child both chewing on a bat. Cards are numbered with a "VJ" prefix.

		MT
Complete Set (20):		25.00
Common Player:		.35
1	Rod Carew	.50
2	Hideo Nomo	.75
3	Derek Jeter	3.50
4	Barry Bonds	1.50
5	Greg Maddux	2.75
6	Mark McGwire	5.00
7	Jose Canseco	1.50
8	Ken Caminiti	.35
9	Raul Mondesi	.50
10	Ken Griffey Jr.	5.00
11	Jay Buhner	.35
12	Randy Johnson	.75
13	Roger Clemens	2.25
14	Brady Anderson	.35
15	Frank Thomas	2.50
16	Angels Outfielders	.35
17	Mike Piazza	3.50
18	Dante Bichette	.50
19	Tony Gwynn	2.25
20	Jim Abbott	.35

1996 Upper Deck Nomo Highlights

The 1995 rookie season of Los Angeles Dodgers' pitcher Hideo Nomo is recapped in this five-card 1996 Upper Deck insert set. The cards were seeded one per every 23 Series 2 packs. A 5" x 7" version of each card was also issued as a retail box insert. Values are the same as for small cards.

		MT
Complete Set (5):		10.00
Common Nomo:		2.50
1	Hideo Nomo	2.00
2	Hideo Nomo	2.00
3	Hideo Nomo	2.00
4	Hideo Nomo	2.00
5	Hideo Nomo	2.00

1996 Upper Deck Power Driven

Twenty of the game's top power hitters are analyzed in depth by baseball writer Peter Gammons on these Series 1 insert cards. Found once per 36 packs, on average, the cards are printed on an embossed light F/X design. Cards are numbered with a "PD" prefix.

		MT
Complete Set (20):		125.00
Common Player:		2.50
1	Albert Belle	6.00
2	Barry Bonds	7.50
3	Jay Buhner	2.50
4	Jose Canseco	5.00
5	Cecil Fielder	2.50
6	Juan Gonzalez	8.00
7	Ken Griffey Jr.	25.00
8	Eric Karros	2.50
9	Fred McGriff	4.00
10	Mark McGwire	25.00
11	Rafael Palmeiro	4.00
12	Mike Piazza	17.50
13	Manny Ramirez	9.00
14	Tim Salmon	3.00
15	Reggie Sanders	2.50
16	Sammy Sosa	16.00
17	Frank Thomas	9.00
18	Mo Vaughn	3.00
19	Larry Walker	5.00
20	Matt Williams	3.00

1996 Upper Deck Run Producers

These double die-cut, embossed and color foil-stamped cards feature 20 of the game's top RBI men. The cards were seeded one per every 71 packs of 1996 Upper Deck Series II. Cards are numbered with a "RP" prefix.

		MT
Complete Set (20):		200.00
Common Player:		4.00
1	Albert Belle	8.00
2	Dante Bichette	5.00
3	Barry Bonds	10.00
4	Jay Buhner	4.00
5	Jose Canseco	8.00
6	Juan Gonzalez	10.00
7	Ken Griffey Jr.	40.00
8	Tony Gwynn	20.00
9	Kenny Lofton	6.00
10	Edgar Martinez	4.00
11	Fred McGriff	5.00
12	Mark McGwire	40.00
13	Rafael Palmeiro	6.00
14	Mike Piazza	25.00
15	Manny Ramirez	10.00
16	Tim Salmon	4.00
17	Sammy Sosa	25.00
18	Frank Thomas	15.00
19	Mo Vaughn	6.00
20	Matt Williams	4.00

1997 Upper Deck

The 520-card, regular-sized set was available in 12-card packs. The base card fronts feature a full action shot with the player's name near the bottom edge above a bronze-foil, wood-grain stripe. The player's team logo is in the lower left corner in silver foil. Each card front has the date of the game pictured with a brief description. The card backs contain more detailed game highlight descriptions and statistics, along with a small action shot in the upper left quadrant. Subsets are: Jackie Robinson Tribute (1-9), Strike Force (65-72), Defensive Gems (136-153), Global Impact (181-207), Season Highlights Checklist (214-222) and Star Rookies (223-240). Inserts are: Game Jerseys, Ticket To Stardom, Power Package, Amazing Greats and Rock Solid Foundation. A 30-card update to Series I was released early in the season featuring 1996 post-season highlights and star rookies. The card faces had red or purple borders and were numbered 241 to 270. A second update set of 30 was released near the end of the 1997 season, numbered 521-550 and featuring traded players and rookies in a format identical to Series I and II UD. Both of the update sets were available only via a mail-in redemption offer.

	MT
Complete Set (550):	140.00
Complete Series 1 Set (240):	30.00
Complete Update Set (241-270):	35.00
Common Update (241-270):	.50
Complete Series 2 Set (250):	60.00
Complete Update Set (521-550):	15.00
Common Player:	.10
Series 1 or 2 Pack (12):	3.00
Series 1 or 2 Wax Box (28):	70.00

1	Jackie Robinson	1.00
2	Jackie Robinson	1.00
3	Jackie Robinson	1.00
4	Jackie Robinson	1.00
5	Jackie Robinson	1.00
6	Jackie Robinson	1.00
7	Jackie Robinson	1.00
8	Jackie Robinson	1.00
9	Jackie Robinson	1.00
10	Chipper Jones	2.00
11	Marquis Grissom	.10
12	Jermaine Dye	.10
13	Mark Lemke	.10
14	Terrell Wade	.10
15	Fred McGriff	.30
16	Tom Glavine	.25
17	Mark Wohlers	.10
18	Randy Myers	.10
19	Roberto Alomar	.60
20	Cal Ripken Jr.	3.00
21	Rafael Palmeiro	.30
22	Mike Mussina	.40
23	Brady Anderson	.15
24	Jose Canseco	.50
25	Mo Vaughn	.60
26	Roger Clemens	1.00
27	Tim Naehring	.10
28	Jeff Suppan	.10
29	Troy Percival	.10
30	Sammy Sosa	2.00
31	Amaury Telemaco	.10
32	Rey Sanchez	.10
33	Scott Servais	.10
34	Steve Trachsel	.10
35	Mark Grace	.20
36	Wilson Alvarez	.10
37	Harold Baines	.10
38	Tony Phillips	.10
39	James Baldwin	.10
40	Frank Thomas (wrong (Ken Griffey Jr.'s) vital data)	1.00
41	Lyle Mouton	.10
42	Chris Snopek	.10
43	Hal Morris	.10
44	Eric Davis	.10
45	Barry Larkin	.20
46	Reggie Sanders	.10
47	Pete Schourek	.10
48	Lee Smith	.10
49	Charles Nagy	.10
50	Albert Belle	.75
51	Julio Franco	.10
52	Kenny Lofton	.60
53	Orel Hershiser	.10
54	Omar Vizquel	.10
55	Eric Young	.15
56	Curtis Leskanic	.10
57	Quinton McCracken	.10
58	Kevin Ritz	.10
59	Walt Weiss	.10
60	Dante Bichette	.25
61	Marc Lewis	.10
62	Tony Clark	.40
63	Travis Fryman	.15
64	John Smoltz (Strike Force)	.15
65	Greg Maddux (Strike Force)	.75
66	Tom Glavine (Strike Force)	.15
67	Mike Mussina (Strike Force)	.20
68	Andy Pettitte (Strike Force)	.40
69	Mariano Rivera (Strike Force)	.15
70	Hideo Nomo (Strike Force)	.25
71	Kevin Brown Strike Force)	.10
72	Randy Johnson (Strike Force)	.15
73	Felipe Lira	.10
74	Kimera Bartee	.10
75	Alan Trammell	.10
76	Kevin Brown	.15
77	Edgar Renteria	.15
78	Al Leiter	.15
79	Charles Johnson	.15
80	Andre Dawson	.15
81	Billy Wagner	.15
82	Donne Wall	.10
83	Jeff Bagwell	1.00
84	Keith Lockhart	.10
85	Jeff Montgomery	.10
86	Tom Goodwin	.10
87	Tim Belcher	.10
88	Mike Macfarlane	.10
89	Joe Randa	.10
90	Brett Butler	.10
91	Todd Worrell	.10
92	Todd Hollandsworth	.10
93	Ismael Valdes	.10
94	Hideo Nomo	.25
95	Mike Piazza	2.00
96	Jeff Cirillo	.10
97	Ricky Bones	.10
98	Fernando Vina	.10
99	Ben McDonald	.10
100	John Jaha	.10
101	Mark Loretta	.10
102	Paul Molitor	.50
103	Rick Aguilera	.10
104	Marty Cordova	.10
105	Kirby Puckett	.50
106	Dan Naulty	.10
107	Frank Rodriguez	.10
108	Shane Andrews	.15
109	Henry Rodriguez	.10
110	Mark Grudzielanek	.10
111	Pedro Martinez	.75
112	Ugueth Urbina	.10
113	David Segui	.10
114	Rey Ordonez	.15
115	Bernard Gilkey	.10
116	Butch Huskey	.10
117	Paul Wilson	.10
118	Alex Ochoa	.10
119	John Franco	.10
120	Dwight Gooden	.10
121	Ruben Rivera	.15
122	Andy Pettitte	.75
123	Tino Martinez	.20
124	Bernie Williams	.40
125	Wade Boggs	.25
126	Paul O'Neill	.20
127	Scott Brosius	.10
128	Ernie Young	.10
129	Doug Johns	.10
130	Geronimo Berroa	.10
131	Jason Giambi	.10
132	John Wasdin	.10
133	Jim Eisenreich	.10
134	Ricky Otero	.10
135	Ricky Bottalico	.10
136	Mark Langston (Defensive Gems)	.10
137	Greg Maddux (Defensive Gems)	.75
138	Ivan Rodriguez (Defensive Gems)	.30
139	Charles Johnson (Defensive Gems)	.10
140	J.T. Snow (Defensive Gems)	.10
141	Mark Grace (Defensive Gems)	.15
142	Roberto Alomar (Defensive Gems)	.40
143	Craig Biggio (Defensive Gems)	.15
144	Ken Caminit (Defensive Gems)	.10
145	Matt Williams (Defensive Gems)	.10
146	Omar Vizquel (Defensive Gems)	.10
147	Cal Ripken Jr. (Defensive Gems)	1.50
148	Ozzie Smith (Defensive Gems)	.25
149	Rey Ordonez (Defensive Gems)	.15
150	Ken Griffey Jr. (Defensive Gems)	1.50
151	Devon White (Defensive Gems)	.10
152	Barry Bonds (Defensive Gems)	.50
153	Kenny Lofton (Defensive Gems)	.40
154	Mickey Morandini	.10
155	Gregg Jefferies	.10
156	Curt Schilling	.15
157	Jason Kendall	.10
158	Francisco Cordova	.10
159	Dennis Eckersley	.10
160	Ron Gant	.15
161	Ozzie Smith	.50
162	Brian Jordan	.10
163	John Mabry	.10
164	Andy Ashby	.10
165	Steve Finley	.10
166	Fernando Valenzuela	.10
167	Archi Cianfrocco	.10
168	Wally Joyner	.10
169	Greg Vaughn	.15
170	Barry Bonds	.75
171	William VanLandingham	.10
172	Marvin Benard	.10
173	Rich Aurilla	.10
174	Jay Canizaro	.10
175	Ken Griffey Jr.	4.00
176	Bob Wells	.10
177	Jay Buhner	.10
178	Sterling Hitchcock	.10
179	Edgar Martinez	.10
180	Rusty Greer	.10
181	Dave Nilsson (Global Impact)	.10
182	Larry Walker (Global Impact)	.35
183	Edgar Renteria (Global Impact)	.15
184	Rey Ordonez (Global Impact)	.15
185	Rafael Palmeiro (Global Impact)	.20
186	Osvaldo Fernandez (Global Impact)	.10
187	Raul Mondesi (Global Impact)	.15
188	Manny Ramirez (Global Impact)	.50
189	Sammy Sosa (Global Impact)	1.00
190	Robert Eenhoorn (Global Impact)	.10
191	Devon White (Global Impact)	.10
192	Hideo Nomo (Global Impact)	.25
193	Mac Suzuki (Global Impact)	.10
194	Chan Ho Park (Global Impact)	.10
195	Fernando Valenzuela (Global Impact)	.10
196	Andruw Jones (Global Impact)	.50
197	Vinny Castilla (Global Impact)	.10
198	Dennis Martinez (Global Impact)	.10
199	Ruben Rivera (Global Impact)	.15
200	Juan Gonzalez (Global Impact)	.50
201	Roberto Alomar (Global Impact)	.40
202	Edgar Martinez (Global Impact)	.10
203	Ivan Rodriguez (Global Impact)	.30
204	Carlos Delgado (Global Impact)	.50
205	Andres Galarraga (Global Impact)	.15
206	Ozzie Guillen (Global Impact)	.10
207	Midre Cummings (Global Impact)	.10
208	Roger Pavlik	.10
209	Darren Oliver	.10
210	Dean Palmer	.10
211	Ivan Rodriguez	.75
212	Otis Nixon	.10
213	Pat Hentgen	.10
214	Ozzie Smith, Andre Dawson, Kirby Puckett CL (Season Highlights)	.25
215	Barry Bonds, Gary Sheffield, Brady Anderson CL (Season Highlights)	.25
216	Ken Caminiti CL (Season Highlights)	.10
217	John Smoltz CL (Season Highlights)	.10
218	Eric Young CL (Season Highlights)	.10
219	Juan Gonzalez CL (Season Highlights)	.50
220	Eddie Murray CL (Season Highlights)	.20
221	Tommy Lasorda CL (Season Highlights)	.15
222	Paul Molitor CL (Season Highlights)	.15
223	Luis Castillo	.10
224	Justin Thompson	.10
225	Rocky Coppinger	.10
226	Jermaine Allensworth	.10
227	Jeff D'Amico	.10
228	Jamey Wright	.10
229	Scott Rolen	1.00
230	Darin Erstad	.50
231	Marty Janzen	.10
232	Jacob Cruz	.10
233	Raul Ibanez	.10
234	Nomar Garciaparra	2.00
235	Todd Walker	.10
236	*Brian Giles*	1.50
237	Matt Beech	.10
238	Mike Cameron	.10
239	Jose Paniagua	.10
240	Andruw Jones	1.00
241	Brant Brown (Star Rookies)	.50
242	Robin Jennings (Star Rookies)	.50
243	Willie Adams (Star Rookies)	.50
244	Ken Caminiti (Division Series)	.50
245	Brian Jordan (Division Series)	.50

No.	Card	Price
246	Chipper Jones (Division Series)	6.00
247	Juan Gonzalez (Division Series)	2.50
248	Bernie Williams (Division Series)	1.50
249	Roberto Alomar (Division Series)	1.50
250	Bernie Williams (Post-Season)	1.50
251	David Wells (Post-Season)	.50
252	Cecil Fielder (Post-Season)	.50
253	Darryl Strawberry (Post-Season)	.75
254	Andy Pettitte (Post-Season)	1.00
255	Javier Lopez (Post-Season)	.75
256	Gary Gaetti (Post-Season)	.50
257	Ron Gant (Post-Season)	.75
258	Brian Jordan (Post-Season)	.50
259	John Smoltz (Post-Season)	.50
260	Greg Maddux (Post-Season)	5.00
261	Tom Glavine (Post-Season)	.75
262	Chipper Jones (World Series)	6.00
263	Greg Maddux (World Series)	5.00
264	David Cone (World Series)	.75
265	Jim Leyritz (World Series)	.50
266	Andy Pettitte (World Series)	1.00
267	John Wetteland (World Series)	.50
268	*Dario Veras* (Star Rookie)	.50
269	Neifi Perez (Star Rookie)	.50
270	Bill Mueller (Star Rookie)	.50
271	Vladimir Guerrero (Star Rookie)	1.50
272	Dmitri Young (Star Rookie)	.10
273	*Nerio Rodriguez* (Star Rookie)	.20
274	Kevin Orie (Star Rookie)	.15
275	Felipe Crespo (Star Rookie)	.10
276	Danny Graves (Star Rookie)	.10
277	Roderick Myers (Star Rookie)	.10
278	*Felix Heredia* (Star Rookie)	.25
279	Ralph Milliard (Star Rookie)	.10
280	Greg Norton (Star Rookie)	.10
281	Derek Wallace (Star Rookie)	.10
282	Trot Nixo (Star Rookie)	.15
283	Bobby Chouinard (Star Rookie)	.10
284	Jay Witasick (Star Rookie)	.10
285	Travis Miller (Star Rookie)	.10
286	Brian Bevil (Star Rookie)	.10
287	Bobby Estalella (Star Rookie)	.10
288	Steve Soderstrom (Star Rookie)	.10
289	Mark Langston	.10
290	Tim Salmon	.20
291	Jim Edmonds	.10
292	Garret Anderson	.10
293	George Arias	.10
294	Gary DiSarcina	.10
295	Chuck Finley	.10
296	Todd Greene	.10
297	Randy Velarde	.10
298	David Justice	.25
299	Ryan Klesko	.20
300	John Smoltz	.20
301	Javier Lopez	.15
302	Greg Maddux	1.50
303	Denny Neagle	.10
304	B.J. Surhoff	.10
305	Chris Hoiles	.10
306	Eric Davis	.10
307	Scott Erickson	.10
308	Mike Bordick	.10
309	John Valentin	.10
310	Heathcliff Slocumb	.10
311	Tom Gordon	.10
312	Mike Stanley	.10
313	Reggie Jefferson	.10
314	Darren Bragg	.10
315	Troy O'Leary	.10
316	John Mabry (Season Highlight)	.10
317	Mark Whiten (Season Highlight)	.10
318	Edgar Martinez (Season Highlight)	.10
319	Alex Rodriguez (Season Highlight)	2.50
320	Mark McGwire (Season Highlight)	2.00
321	Hideo Nomo (Season Highlight)	.25
322	Todd Hundley (Season Highlight)	.15
323	Barry Bonds (Season Highlight)	.40
324	Andruw Jones (Season Highlight)	1.00
325	Ryne Sandberg	.75
326	Brian McRae	.10
327	Frank Castillo	.10
328	Shawon Dunston	.10
329	Ray Durham	.10
330	Robin Ventura	.20
331	Ozzie Guillen	.10
332	Roberto Hernandez	.10
333	Albert Belle	.75
334	Dave Martinez	.10
335	Willie Greene	.10
336	Jeff Brantley	.10
337	Kevin Jarvis	.10
338	John Smiley	.10
339	Eddie Taubensee	.10
340	Bret Boone	.10
341	Kevin Seitzer	.10
342	Jack McDowell	.10
343	Sandy Alomar Jr.	.15
344	Chad Curtis	.10
345	Manny Ramirez	1.00
346	Chad Ogea	.10
347	Jim Thome	.40
348	Mark Thompson	.10
349	Ellis Burks	.10
350	Andres Galarraga	.25
351	Vinny Castilla	.15
352	Kirt Manwaring	.10
353	Larry Walker	.50
354	Omar Olivares	.10
355	Bobby Higginson	.10
356	Melvin Nieves	.10
357	Brian Johnson	.10
358	Devon White	.10
359	Jeff Conine	.10
360	Gary Sheffield	.20
361	Robb Nen	.10
362	Mike Hampton	.10
363	Bob Abreu	.10
364	Luis Gonzalez	.15
365	Derek Bell	.10
366	Sean Berry	.10
367	Craig Biggio	.40
368	Darryl Kile	.10
369	Shane Reynolds	.10
370	Jeff Bagwell (Capture the Flag)	.50
371	Ron Gant (Capture the Flag)	.10
372	Andy Benes (Capture the Flag)	.10
373	Gary Gaetti (Capture the Flag)	.10
374a	Ramon Martinez (Capture the Flag (gold back)	.10
374b	Ramon Martinez (Capture the Flag) (white back)	.10
375	Raul Mondesi (Capture the Flag)	.10
376a	Steve Finley (Capture the Flag) (gold back)	.10
376b	Steve Finley (Capture the Flag) (white back)	.10
377	Ken Caminiti (Capture the Flag)	.15
378	Tony Gwynn (Capture the Flag)	.75
379	Dario Veras (Capture the Flag)	.10
380	Andy Pettitte (Capture the Flag)	.40
381	Ruben Rivera (Capture the Flag)	.10
382	David Cone (Capture the Flag)	.10
383	Roberto Alomar (Capture the Flag)	.30
384	Edgar Martinez (Capture the Flag)	.10
385	Ken Griffey Jr. (Capture the Flag)	2.00
386	Mark McGwire (Capture the Flag)	2.00
387	Rusty Greer (Capture the Flag)	.10
388	Jose Rosado	.10
389	Kevin Appier	.10
390	Johnny Damon	.10
391	Jose Offerman	.10
392	Michael Tucker	.10
393	Craig Paquette	.10
394	Bip Roberts	.10
395	Ramon Martinez	.10
396	Greg Gagne	.10
397	Chan Ho Park	.20
398	Karim Garcia	.10
399	Wilton Guerrero	.10
400	Eric Karros	.15
401	Raul Mondesi	.20
402	Matt Mieske	.10
403	Mike Fetters	.10
404	Dave Nilsson	.10
405	Jose Valentin	.10
406	Scott Karl	.10
407	Marc Newfield	.10
408	Cal Eldred	.10
409	Rich Becker	.10
410	Terry Steinbach	.10
411	Chuck Knoblauch	.20
412	Pat Meares	.10
413	Brad Radke	.10
414	not issued	
415a	Kirby Puckett (should be #414)	1.00
415b	Andruw Jones (Griffey Hot List)	3.00
416	Chipper Jones (Griffey Hot List)	6.00
417	Mo Vaughn (Griffey Hot List)	1.50
418	Frank Thomas (Griffey Hot List)	3.00
419	Albert Belle (Griffey Hot List)	1.50
420	Mark McGwire (Griffey Hot List)	12.00
421	Derek Jeter (Griffey Hot List)	8.00
422	Alex Rodriguez (Griffey Hot List)	10.00
423	Juan Gonzalez (Griffey Hot List)	3.00
424	Ken Griffey Jr. (Griffey Hot List)	12.00
425	Rondell White	.15
426	Darrin Fletcher	.10
427	Cliff Floyd	.10
428	Mike Lansing	.10
429	F.P. Santangelo	.10
430	Todd Hundley	.10
431	Mark Clark	.10
432	Pete Harnisch	.10
433	Jason Isringhausen	.10
434	Bobby Jones	.10
435	Lance Johnson	.10
436	Carlos Baerga	.10
437	Mariano Duncan	.10
438	David Cone	.20
439	Mariano Rivera	.20
440	Derek Jeter	2.00
441	Joe Girardi	.10
442	Charlie Hayes	.10
443	Tim Raines	.15
444	Darryl Strawberry	.15
445	Cecil Fielder	.10
446	Ariel Prieto	.10
447	Tony Batista	.15
448	Brent Gates	.10
449	Scott Spiezio	.10
450	Mark McGwire	4.00
451	Don Wengert	.10
452	Mike Lieberthal	.10
453	Lenny Dykstra	.10
454	Rex Hudler	.10
455	Darren Daulton	.10
456	Kevin Stocker	.10
457	Trey Beamon	.10
458	Midre Cummings	.10
459	Mark Johnson	.10
460	Al Martin	.10
461	Kevin Elster	.10
462	Jon Lieber	.10
463	Jason Schmidt	.10
464	Paul Wagner	.10
465	Andy Benes	.10
466	Alan Benes	.10
467	Royce Clayton	.10
468	Gary Gaetti	.10
469	Curt Lyons (Diamond Debuts)	.10
470	Eugene Kingsale (Diamond Debuts)	.10
471	Damian Jackson (Diamond Debuts)	.10
472	Wendell Magee (Diamond Dubuts)	.10
473	Kevin L. Brown (Diamond Debuts)	.10
474	Raul Casanova (Diamond Debuts)	.10
475	*Ramiro Mendoza* (Diamond Debuts)	.75
476	Todd Dunn (Diamond Debuts)	.10
477	Chad Mottola (Diamond Debuts)	.10
478	Andy Larkin (Diamond Debuts)	.10
479	Jaime Bluma (Diamond Debuts)	.10
480	Mac Suzuki (Diamond Debuts)	.10
481	Brian Banks (Diamond Debuts)	.10
482	Desi Wilson (Diamond Debuts)	.10
483	Einar Diaz (Diamond Debuts)	.10
484	Tom Pagnozzi	.10
485	Ray Lankford	.10
486	Todd Stottlemyre	.10
487	Donovan Osborne	.10
488	Trevor Hoffman	.10
489	Chris Gomez	.10
490	Ken Caminiti	.20
491	John Flaherty	.10
492	Tony Gwynn	1.50
493	Joey Hamilton	.10
494	Rickey Henderson	.40
495	Glenallen Hill	.10
496	Rod Beck	.10
497	Osvaldo Fernandez	.10
498	Rick Wilkins	.10
499	Joey Cora	.10
500	Alex Rodriguez	3.00
501	Randy Johnson	.60
502	Paul Sorrento	.10
503	Dan Wilson	.10
504	Jamie Moyer	.10
505	Will Clark	.25
506	Mickey Tettleton	.10
507	John Burkett	.10
508	Ken Hill	.10
509	Mark McLemore	.10
510	Juan Gonzalez	1.00
511	Bobby Witt	.10
512	Carlos Delgado	.50
513	Alex Gonzalez	.10
514	Shawn Green	.50
515	Joe Carter	.10
516	Juan Guzman	.10
517	Charlie O'Brien	.10
518	Ed Sprague	.10
519	Mike Timlin	.10
520	Roger Clemens	1.00
521	Eddie Murray	.25
522	Jason Dickson	.10
523	Jim Leyritz	.10
524	Michael Tucker	.10
525	Kenny Lofton	.60
526	Jimmy Key	.10
527	Mel Rojas	.10
528	Deion Sanders	.25
529	Bartolo Colon	.10
530	Matt Williams	.30
531	Marquis Grissom	.10
532	David Justice	.25
533	*Bubba Trammell*	.25
534	Moises Alou	.15
535	Bobby Bonilla	.10
536	Alex Fernandez	.10
537	Jay Bell	.10
538	Chili Davis	.10
539	Jeff King	.10
540	Todd Zeile	.10
541	John Olerud	.25
542	Jose Guillen	.10
543	Derrek Lee	.10
544	Dante Powell	.10

545	J.T. Snow	.15
546	Jeff Kent	.10
547	*Jose Cruz Jr.*	2.00
548	John Wetteland	.10
549	Orlando Merced	.10
550	*Hideki Irabu*	1.00

1997 Upper Deck Amazing Greats

The 20-card, regular-sized insert set was included every 138 packs of 1997 Upper Deck baseball. The cards include real wood with two player shots imaged on the card front. The team logo appears in the upper right corner of the horizontal card. The cards are numbered with the "AG" prefix.

		MT
Complete Set (20):		320.00
Common Player:		6.00
1	Ken Griffey Jr.	40.00
2	Roberto Alomar	10.00
3	Alex Rodriguez	40.00
4	Paul Molitor	10.00
5	Chipper Jones	25.00
6	Tony Gwynn	20.00
7	Kenny Lofton	8.00
8	Albert Belle	8.00
9	Matt Williams	6.00
10	Frank Thomas	20.00
11	Greg Maddux	25.00
12	Sammy Sosa	25.00
13	Kirby Puckett	15.00
14	Jeff Bagwell	15.00
15	Cal Ripken Jr.	40.00
16	Manny Ramirez	15.00
17	Barry Bonds	15.00
18	Mo Vaughn	8.00
19	Eddie Murray	8.00
20	Mike Piazza	30.00

1997 Upper Deck Blue Chip Prospects

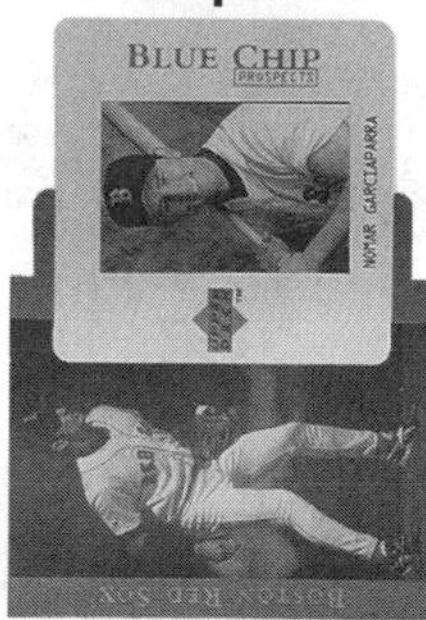

This 20-card insert was found in packs of Series II and features a die-cut design. Cards appear to have a photo slide attached to them featuring a portrait shot of the promising youngster depicted on the card. A total of 500 of each card were produced. Cards are numbered with a "BC" prefix.

	MT
Complete Set (20):	300.00
Common Player:	7.50
1 Andruw Jones	20.00
2 Derek Jeter	50.00
3 Scott Rolen	20.00
4 Manny Ramirez	20.00
5 Todd Walker	7.50
6 Rocky Coppinger	5.00
7 Nomar Garciaparra	50.00
8 Darin Erstad	10.00
9 Jermaine Dye	5.00
10 Vladimir Guerrero	35.00
11 Edgar Renteria	7.50
12 Bob Abreu	7.50
13 Karim Garcia	5.00
14 Jeff D'Amico	5.00
15 Chipper Jones	35.00
16 Todd Hollandsworth	5.00
17 Andy Pettitte	9.00
18 Ruben Rivera	5.00
19 Jason Kendall	7.50
20 Alex Rodriguez	60.00

1997 Upper Deck Game Jersey

The three-card, regular-sized set was inserted every 800 packs of Upper Deck Series I. The cards contained a square of the player's game-used jersey, and carried a "GJ" card number prefix.

		MT
Complete Set (3):		450.00
Common Player:		70.00
GJ1	Ken Griffey Jr.	300.00
GJ2	Tony Gwynn	120.00
GJ3	Rey Ordonez	70.00

1997 Upper Deck Hot Commodities

This 20-card insert from Series II features a flame pattern behind the image of the player depicted on the front of the card. Odds of finding a card were 1:13 packs. Cards are numbered with a "HC" prefix.

		MT
Complete Set (20):		60.00
Common Player:		2.50
1	Alex Rodriguez	8.00
2	Andruw Jones	2.00
3	Derek Jeter	6.00
4	Frank Thomas	3.00
5	Ken Griffey Jr.	8.00
6	Chipper Jones	5.00
7	Juan Gonzalez	2.50
8	Cal Ripken Jr.	8.00
9	John Smoltz	1.00
10	Mark McGwire	10.00
11	Barry Bonds	2.50
12	Albert Belle	1.50
13	Mike Piazza	6.00
14	Manny Ramirez	2.50
15	Mo Vaughn	1.50
16	Tony Gwynn	3.00
17	Vladimir Guerrero	3.00
18	Hideo Nomo	1.50
19	Greg Maddux	5.00
20	Kirby Puckett	2.50

1997 Upper Deck Long Distance Connection

This 20-card insert from Series II features the top home run hitters in the game. Odds of finding a card were 1:35 packs. Cards are numbered with a "LD" prefix.

		MT
Complete Set (20):		100.00
Common Player:		2.00
1	Mark McGwire	20.00
2	Brady Anderson	2.00
3	Ken Griffey Jr.	15.00
4	Albert Belle	3.00
5	Juan Gonzalez	5.00
6	Andres Galarraga	3.00
7	Jay Buhner	2.00
8	Mo Vaughn	3.00
9	Barry Bonds	5.00
10	Gary Sheffield	3.00
11	Todd Hundley	2.00
12	Frank Thomas	6.00
13	Sammy Sosa	10.00
14	Rafael Palmeiro	4.00
15	Alex Rodriguez	15.00
16	Mike Piazza	12.00
17	Ken Caminiti	2.00
18	Chipper Jones	10.00
19	Manny Ramirez	5.00
20	Andruw Jones	5.00

1997 Upper Deck Memorable Moments

This issue was a one per pack insert in special Series 1 and 2 Collector's Choice six-card retail packs. In standard 2-1/2" x 3-1/2", the cards are die-cut at top and bottom in a wave pattern. Fronts, highlighted in matte bronze foil, have action photos and a career highlight. Backs have another photo and a more complete explanation of the Memorable Moment.

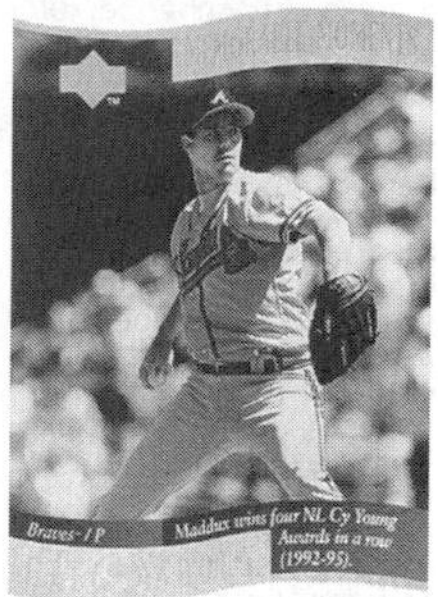

		MT
Complete Set (20):		18.00
Common Player:		.50
		.50
	SERIES 1	
1	Andruw Jones	.75
2	Chipper Jones	2.00
3	Cal Ripken Jr.	2.50
4	Frank Thomas	1.00
5	Manny Ramirez	.75
6	Mike Piazza	2.00
7	Mark McGwire	3.00
8	Ken Griffey Jr.	3.00
9	Barry Bonds	.75
10	Alex Rodriguez	2.50
	SERIES 2	
1	Ken Griffey Jr.	3.00
2	Albert Belle	.60
3	Derek Jeter	2.00
4	Greg Maddux	1.50
5	Tony Gwynn	1.50
6	Ryne Sandberg	.75
7	Juan Gonzalez	.75
8	Roger Clemens	1.50
9	Jose Cruz Jr.	.50
10	Mo Vaughn	.50

1997 Upper Deck Predictor

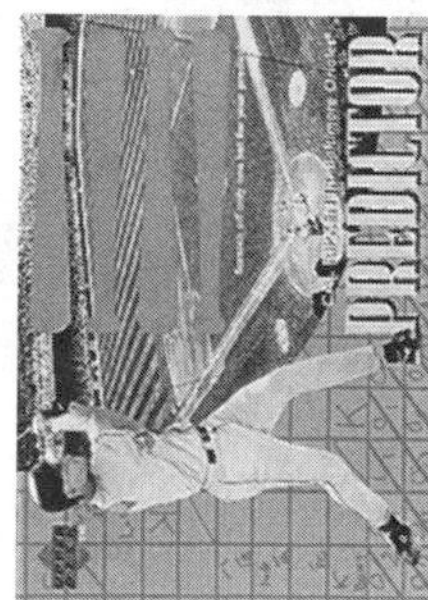

A new concept in interactive cards was UD's Series II Predictor inserts. Each player's card has four scratch-off baseball bats at the top-right. Under each bat is printed a specific accomplishment - hit for cycle, CG shutout, etc. - If the player attained that goal during the '97 season, and if the collector had scratched off the correct bat among the four, the Predictor card could be redeemed (with $2) for a premium TV cel card of the player. Thus if the player made one of his goals, the collector had a 25% chance of choosing the right bat. Two goals gave a 50% chance, etc. The Predictor cards have color action photos of the players at the left end of the horizontal format. The background at left and bottom is a red scorecard motif. Behind the bats is a black-and-white stadium scene. Backs repeat the red scorecard design with contest rules printed in white. A (W) in the checklist here indicates the player won one or more of his goals making his cards eligible for redemption. The redemption period ended Nov. 22, 1997. Values shown are for unscratched cards.

		MT
Complete Set (30):		25.00
Common Player:		.50
Values for Unscratched Cards		
1	Andruw Jones	.50
2	Chipper Jones	1.50
3	Greg Maddux (W)	1.50
4	Fred McGriff (W)	.50
5	John Smoltz (W)	.50
6	Brady Anderson (W)	.50
7	Cal Ripken Jr. (W)	2.50
8	Mo Vaughn (W)	.50
9	Sammy Sosa	2.00
10	Albert Belle (W)	.75
11	Frank Thomas	1.00
12	Kenny Lofton (W)	.50
13	Jim Thome	.50
14	Dante Bichette (W)	.50
15	Andres Galarraga	.50
16	Gary Sheffield	.50
17	Hideo Nomo (W)	.50
18	Mike Piazza (W)	2.00
19	Derek Jeter (W)	2.00
20	Bernie Williams	.50
21	Mark McGwire (W)	3.00
22	Ken Caminiti (W)	.50
23	Tony Gwynn (W)	1.50
24	Barry Bonds (W)	.75
25	Jay Buhner (W)	.50
26	Ken Griffey Jr. (W)	3.00
27	Alex Rodriguez (W)	2.50
28	Juan Gonzalez (W)	1.00
29	Dean Palmer (W)	.50
30	Roger Clemens (W)	1.00

1997 Upper Deck Predictor Prize Cards

Persons who redeemed winning Predictor scratch-off cards prior to the Nov. 22, 1997, deadline received a premium version of that player's card. A $2 per card handling fee was charged. The Predictor prize cards are in a format similar to the scratch-off cards, with a red background on front and back depicting the motif of a baseball score card. The prize cards are printed on plastic in 3-1/2" x 2-1/2" format. Fronts have a player portrait photo at left. At right is a large semi-circular mirrored window with an action photo visible when held to the light. Backs have a few stats, copyright data, logos, etc., with a reverse image in the window. Card fronts were covered with a sheet of peel-off protection plastic. The prize cards are numbered on back with a "P" prefix.

		MT
Complete Set (22):		250.00
Common Player:		3.00
3	Greg Maddux	16.00
4	Fred McGriff	4.50
5	John Smoltz	4.50
6	Brady Anderson	3.00
7	Cal Ripken Jr.	24.00
8	Mo Vaughn	6.00
11	Frank Thomas	15.00
12	Kenny Lofton	6.00
14	Dante Bichette	3.50
17	Hideo Nomo	6.00
18	Mike Piazza	18.00
19	Derek Jeter	16.00
21	Mark McGwire	30.00
22	Ken Caminiti	4.50
23	Tony Gwynn	15.00
24	Barry Bonds	7.50
25	Jay Buhner	3.00
26	Ken Griffey Jr.	30.00
27	Alex Rodriguez	24.00
28	Juan Gonzalez	8.00
29	Dean Palmer	3.00
30	Roger Clemens	12.00

1997 Upper Deck Power Package

The 20-card, regular-sized, die-cut set was inserted every 23 packs of 1997 Upper Deck baseball. The player's name is printed in gold foil along the top border of the card face, which also features Light F/X. The die-cut cards have a silver-foil border and team-color frame with a "Power Package" logo in gold foil centered on the bottom border. The card backs have a short highlight in a brown box bordered by team colors and are numbered with the "PP" prefix.

		MT
Complete Set (20):		100.00
Common Player:		3.00
1	Ken Griffey Jr.	20.00
2	Joe Carter	2.00
3	Rafael Palmeiro	3.00
4	Jay Buhner	2.00
5	Sammy Sosa	12.00
6	Fred McGriff	2.50
7	Jeff Bagwell	5.00
8	Albert Belle	4.00
9	Matt Williams	3.00
10	Mark McGwire	20.00
11	Gary Sheffield	2.00
12	Tim Salmon	3.00
13	Ryan Klesko	2.00
14	Manny Ramirez	5.00
15	Mike Piazza	12.00
16	Barry Bonds	5.00
17	Mo Vaughn	4.00
18	Jose Canseco	5.00
19	Juan Gonzalez	5.00
20	Frank Thomas	6.00

1997 Upper Deck Rock Solid Foundation

The 20-card, regular-sized set was inserted every seven packs of 1997 Upper Deck baseball. The card fronts feature rainbow foil with the player's name in silver foil along the top border. The team logo appears in gold foil in the lower right corner with "Rock Solid Foundation" also printed in gold foil over a marbled background. The card backs have the same marbled background with a close-up shot on the upper half. A short text is also included and the cards are numbered with the "RS" prefix.

		MT
Complete Set (20):		40.00
Common Player:		1.25
1	Alex Rodriguez	12.00
2	Rey Ordonez	1.50
3	Derek Jeter	9.50
4	Darin Erstad	2.50
5	Chipper Jones	8.00
6	Johnny Damon	1.25
7	Ryan Klesko	1.25
8	Charles Johnson	1.25
9	Andy Pettitte	2.00
10	Manny Ramirez	4.00
11	Ivan Rodriguez	3.25
12	Jason Kendall	1.50
13	Rondell White	1.50
14	Alex Ochoa	1.25
15	Javy Lopez	1.50
16	Pedro Martinez	3.25
17	Carlos Delgado	2.50
18	Paul Wilson	1.25
19	Alan Benes	1.25
20	Raul Mondesi	1.25

Modern cards in Near Mint condition are valued at about 75% of the Mint value shown here. Excellent-condition cards are worth 50%. Cards in lower grades are not generally collectible.

1997 Upper Deck Run Producers

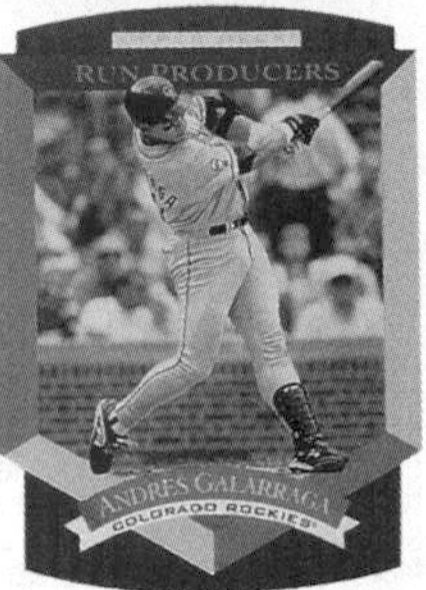

A 24-card insert found in Series II, Run Producers salutes the top offensive players in the game. Cards were inserted 1:69 packs. Die-cut into a shield shape, the cards have an action photo in a home-plate shaped center section and several colors of foil highlights. Backs have recent stats and career highlights. Cards are numbered with a "RP" prefix.

		MT
Complete Set (24):		180.00
Common Player:		3.00
1	Ken Griffey Jr.	25.00
2	Barry Bonds	8.00
3	Albert Belle	5.00
4	Mark McGwire	30.00
5	Frank Thomas	10.00
6	Juan Gonzalez	8.00
7	Brady Anderson	3.00
8	Andres Galarraga	4.00
9	Rafael Palmeiro	6.00
10	Alex Rodriguez	25.00
11	Jay Buhner	3.00
12	Gary Sheffield	5.00
13	Sammy Sosa	15.00
14	Dante Bichette	4.00
15	Mike Piazza	20.00
16	Manny Ramirez	8.00
17	Kenny Lofton	4.00
18	Mo Vaughn	5.00
19	Tim Salmon	4.00
20	Chipper Jones	15.00
21	Jim Thome	5.00
22	Ken Caminiti	3.00
23	Jeff Bagwell	8.00
24	Paul Molitor	6.00

1997 Upper Deck Ticket to Stardom Retail

Double-size "full ticket" versions of Upper Deck's Series 1 Ticket to Stardom inserts were produced as an incentive for collectors to buy a boxed three-pack of Collector's Choice cards in a special retail-only packaging. Unlike the insert Ticket cards which feature only one player and measure 3-1/2" x 2-1/2", the retail version measures 5" x 2-1/2" and features two players. The basic format of the retail cards follows the inserts, with gold-foil background, a vignetted player portrait at one end with an action photo toward center and a league logo at center. Arrangement of graphics on the retail ticket prevent unscrupulous persons from cutting them in half and passing them off as the more valuable insert cards. Backs repeat the player portrait photo and present a career summary. Cards are numbered in the upper-left corner. Seven players were dropped from the original Ticket checklist and replaced in the retail issue with new faces. Cards are numbered with a "TS" prefix.

		MT
Complete Set (10):		55.00
Common Player:		4.00
1	Chipper Jones, Andruw Jones	12.00
2	Rey Ordonez, Kevin Orie	4.00
3	Derek Jeter, Nomar Garciaparra	12.00
4	Billy Wagner, Jason Kendall	4.00
5	Darin Erstad, Alex Rodriguez	15.00
6	Bob Abreu, Jose Guillen	4.00
7	Wilton Guerrero, Vladimir Guerrero	10.00
8	Carlos Delgado, Rocky Coppinger	4.00
9	Jason Dickson, Johnny Damon	4.00
10	Bartolo Colon, Manny Ramirez	8.00

1997 Upper Deck Ticket to Stardom

The 20-card, regular-sized, die-cut set was inserted every 34 packs of 1997 Upper Deck baseball. Card fronts have a gold-foil border on three sides with a portrait and action photo. Half of the player's league emblem appears on either the left or right border of the horizontal cards, as two cards can be placed together to form a "ticket." The card backs feature an in-depth text with the same headshot as the card front and are numbered with the "TS" prefix.

		MT
Complete Set (20):		90.00
Common Player:		2.50
1	Chipper Jones	15.00
2	Jermaine Dye	2.00
3	Rey Ordonez	2.50
4	Alex Ochoa	2.00
5	Derek Jeter	20.00
6	Ruben Rivera	2.00
7	Billy Wagner	2.50
8	Jason Kendall	2.50
9	Darin Erstad	4.00
10	Alex Rodriguez	25.00
11	Bob Abreu	2.50
12	Richard Hidalgo	2.00
13	Karim Garcia	2.00
14	Andruw Jones	4.00
15	Carlos Delgado	3.00
16	Rocky Coppinger	2.00
17	Jeff D'Amico	2.00
18	Johnny Damon	2.00
19	John Wasdin	2.00
20	Manny Ramirez	8.00

1997 Upper Deck UD3

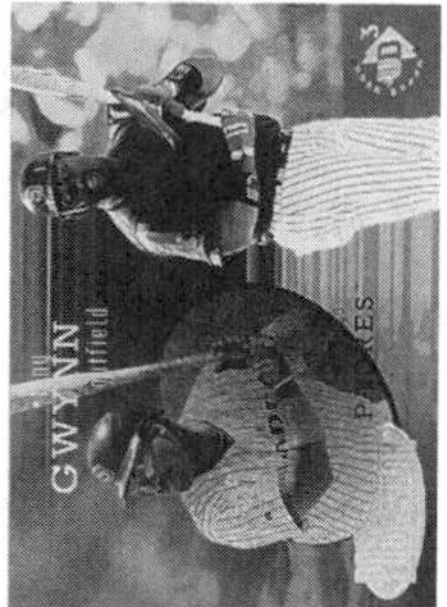

Released in April, this 60-card set is broken down into three different 20-card subsets, each utilizing a different print technology. There are 20 PROmotion cards (Light F/X cards featuring a special foil stock), 20 Future Impact cards (CelChrome cards that feature a 3-D image on transparent chromium), and 20 Homerun Heroes (Electric Wood cards printed on an embossed wood/paper stock). Cards were sold in three-card packs (with one subset card per pack) for $3.99 each. Inserts include Superb Signatures, Generation Next and Marquee Attraction.

		MT
Complete Set (60):		50.00
Common Player:		.40
Pack (3):		4.00
Wax Box (24):		75.00
1	Mark McGwire	6.00
2	Brady Anderson	.50
3	Ken Griffey Jr.	6.00
4	Albert Belle	1.00
5	Andres Galarraga	.75
6	Juan Gonzalez	1.50
7	Jay Buhner	.50
8	Mo Vaughn	1.00
9	Barry Bonds	1.25
10	Gary Sheffield	.75
11	Todd Hundley	.40
12	Ellis Burks	.40
13	Ken Caminiti	.75
14	Vinny Castilla	.40
15	Sammy Sosa	3.00
16	Frank Thomas	2.00
17	Rafael Palmeiro	.75
18	Mike Piazza	3.00
19	Matt Williams	.60
20	Eddie Murray	.75
21	Roger Clemens	2.00
22	Tim Salmon	.50
23	Robin Ventura	.50
24	Ron Gant	.40
25	Cal Ripken Jr.	5.00
26	Bernie Williams	1.00
27	Hideo Nomo	.75
28	Ivan Rodriguez	1.50
29	John Smoltz	.50
30	Paul Molitor	1.00
31	Greg Maddux	2.50
32	Raul Mondesi	.50
33	Roberto Alomar	1.00
34	Barry Larkin	.60
35	Tony Gwynn	2.50
36	Jim Thome	.60
37	Kenny Lofton	1.00
38	Jeff Bagwell	1.50
39	Ozzie Smith	.75
40	Kirby Puckett	1.50
41	Andruw Jones	1.00
42	Vladimir Guerrero	2.50
43	Edgar Renteria	.40
44	Luis Castillo	.40
45	Darin Erstad	.75
46	Nomar Garciaparra	3.00
47	Todd Greene	.40
48	Jason Kendall	.40
49	Rey Ordonez	.40
50	Alex Rodriguez	6.00
51	Manny Ramirez	1.50
52	Todd Walker	.40
53	Ruben Rivera	.40
54	Andy Pettitte	.60
55	Derek Jeter	3.00
56	Todd Hollandsworth	.40
57	Rocky Coppinger	.40
58	Scott Rolen	1.50
59	Jermaine Dye	.40
60	Chipper Jones	3.00

1997 Upper Deck UD3 Generation Next

A 20-card insert saluting the game's up-and-coming stars with two different photos of the player on each card front. Odds of finding these cards were 1:11 packs. Cards are numbered with a "GN" prefix.

		MT
Complete Set (20):		125.00
Common Player:		4.00
1	Alex Rodriguez	25.00
2	Vladimir Guerrero	15.00
3	Luis Castillo	4.00
4	Rey Ordonez	4.00
5	Andruw Jones	5.00
6	Darin Erstad	5.00
7	Edgar Renteria	4.00
8	Jason Kendall	4.00
9	Jermaine Dye	4.00
10	Chipper Jones	20.00
11	Rocky Coppinger	4.00
12	Andy Pettitte	5.00
13	Todd Greene	4.00
14	Todd Hollandsworth	4.00
15	Derek Jeter	20.00
16	Ruben Rivera	4.00
17	Todd Walker	4.00
18	Nomar Garciaparra	15.00
19	Scott Rolen	10.00
20	Manny Ramirez	10.00

1997 Upper Deck UD3 Marquee Attraction

The game's top names are featured in this insert set, inserted 1:144 packs. Cards featured a peel-off protector that would expose a holographic image on the card fronts. Cards are numbered with a "MA" prefix.

		MT
Complete Set (10):		225.00
Common Player:		8.00
1	Ken Griffey Jr.	40.00
2	Mark McGwire	50.00
3	Juan Gonzalez	15.00
4	Barry Bonds	15.00
5	Frank Thomas	20.00
6	Albert Belle	8.00
7	Mike Piazza	30.00
8	Cal Ripken Jr.	40.00
9	Mo Vaughn	8.00
10	Alex Rodriguez	40.00

1997 Upper Deck UD3 Superb Signatures

Autographed cards of Ken Griffey Jr., Ken Caminiti, Vladimir Guerrero and Derek Jeter were inserted 1:1,500 packs.

		MT
Complete Set (4):		550.00
Common Autograph:		40.00
1	Ken Caminiti	40.00
2	Ken Griffey Jr.	250.00
3	Vladimir Guerrero	90.00
4	Derek Jeter	250.00

1998 Upper Deck

Upper Deck Baseball was released in three series. Series One consisted of 270 base cards, with five subsets. Inserts included A Piece of the Action, Amazing Greats, National Pride, Ken Griffey Jr.'s Home Run Chronicles and 10th Anniversary Preview. The 270-card second series also had five subsets. Inserts include Prime Nine, Ken Griffey Jr.'s Home Run Chronicles, Tape Measure Titans, Blue Chip Prospects, Clearly Dominant and A Piece of the Action. The third series, Upper Deck Rookie Edition, had a 210-card base set. Insert sets were Ken Griffey Jr. Game Jersey, Game Jersey Rookie Cards, Unparalleled, Destination Stardom, All-Star Credentials and Retrospectives.

	MT
Complete Set (750):	150.00
Complete Series 1 Set (270):	30.00
Complete Series 2 Set (270):	30.00
Complete Series 3 Set (210):	90.00
Common Emminent Prestige (601-630):	1.00
Common Player:	.10
Series 1 or 2 Pack (12):	2.50
Series 3 Pack (10):	3.00
Series 1 or 2 Wax Box (24):	50.00
Series 3 Wax Box (24):	65.00

1	Tino Martinez (History in the Making)	.10
2	Jimmy Key (History in the Making)	.10
3	Jay Buhner (History in the Making)	.10
4	Mark Gardner (History in the Making)	.10
5	Greg Maddux (History in the Making)	.75
6	Pedro Martinez (History in the Making)	.40
7	Hideo Nomo, Shigetosi Hasegawa (History in the Making)	.20
8	Sammy Sosa (History in the Making)	1.50
9	Mark McGwire (Griffey Hot List)	4.00
10	Ken Griffey Jr. (Griffey Hot List)	4.00
11	Larry Walker (Griffey Hot List)	.40
12	Tino Martinez (Griffey Hot List)	.20
13	Mike Piazza (Griffey Hot List)	2.00
14	Jose Cruz, Jr. (Griffey Hot List)	.50
15	Tony Gwynn (Griffey Hot List)	1.00
16	Greg Maddux (Griffey Hot List)	1.00
17	Roger Clemens (Griffey Hot List)	1.50
18	Alex Rodriguez (Griffey Hot List)	3.00
19	Shigetosi Hasegawa	.10
20	Eddie Murray	.25
21	Jason Dickson	.10
22	Darin Erstad	.40
23	Chuck Finley	.10
24	Dave Hollins	.10
25	Garret Anderson	.10
26	Michael Tucker	.10
27	Kenny Lofton	.30
28	Javier Lopez	.20
29	Fred McGriff	.25
30	Greg Maddux	1.50
31	Jeff Blauser	.10
32	John Smoltz	.20
33	Mark Wohlers	.10
34	Scott Erickson	.10
35	Jimmy Key	.10
36	Harold Baines	.10
37	Randy Myers	.10
38	B.J. Surhoff	.10
39	Eric Davis	.10
40	Rafael Palmeiro	.40
41	Jeffrey Hammonds	.10
42	Mo Vaughn	.40
43	Tom Gordon	.10
44	Tim Naehring	.10
45	Darren Bragg	.10
46	Aaron Sele	.10
47	Troy O'Leary	.10
48	John Valentin	.10
49	Doug Glanville	.10
50	Ryne Sandberg	.75
51	Steve Trachsel	.10
52	Mark Grace	.25
53	Kevin Foster	.10
54	Kevin Tapani	.10
55	Kevin Orie	.10
56	Lyle Mouton	.10
57	Ray Durham	.10
58	Jaime Navarro	.10
59	Mike Cameron	.10
60	Albert Belle	.40
61	Doug Drabek	.10
62	Chris Snopek	.10
63	Eddie Taubensee	.10
64	Terry Pendleton	.10
65	Barry Larkin	.30
66	Willie Greene	.10
67	Deion Sanders	.20
68	Pokey Reese	.10
69	Jeff Shaw	.10
70	Jim Thome	.40
71	Orel Hershiser	.10
72	Omar Vizquel	.20
73	Brian Giles	.20
74	David Justice	.25
75	Bartolo Colon	.20
76	Sandy Alomar Jr.	.20
77	Neifi Perez	.10
78	Eric Young	.15
79	Vinny Castilla	.15
80	Dante Bichette	.20
81	Quinton McCracken	.10
82	Jamey Wright	.10
83	John Thomson	.10
84	Damion Easley	.10
85	Justin Thompson	.10
86	Willie Blair	.10
87	Raul Casanova	.10
88	Bobby Higginson	.10
89	Bubba Trammell	.15
90	Tony Clark	.15
91	Livan Hernandez	.20
92	Charles Johnson	.10
93	Edgar Renteria	.10
94	Alex Fernandez	.10
95	Gary Sheffield	.25
96	Moises Alou	.20
97	Tony Saunders	.20
98	Robb Nen	.10
99	Darryl Kile	.10
100	Craig Biggio	.20
101	Chris Holt	.10
102	Bob Abreu	.10
103	Luis Gonzalez	.20
104	Billy Wagner	.10
105	Brad Ausmus	.10
106	Chili Davis	.10
107	Tim Belcher	.10
108	Dean Palmer	.10
109	Jeff King	.10
110	Jose Rosado	.10
111	Mike Macfarlane	.10
112	Jay Bell	.10
113	Todd Worrell	.10
114	Chan Ho Park	.10
115	Raul Mondesi	.25
116	Brett Butler	.10
117	Greg Gagne	.10
118	Hideo Nomo	.25
119	Todd Zeile	.10
120	Eric Karros	.20
121	Cal Eldred	.10
122	Jeff D'Amico	.10
123	Antone Williamson	.10
124	Doug Jones	.10
125	Dave Nilsson	.10
126	Gerald Williams	.10
127	Fernando Vina	.10
128	Ron Coomer	.10
129	Matt Lawton	.10
130	Paul Molitor	.40
131	Todd Walker	.10
132	Rick Aguilera	.10
133	Brad Radke	.10
134	Bob Tewksbury	.10
135	Vladimir Guerrero	1.00
136	Tony Gwynn (Define The Game)	.50
137	Roger Clemens (Define The Game)	.50
138	Dennis Eckersley (Define The Game)	.10
139	Brady Anderson (Define The Game)	.10
140	Ken Griffey Jr. (Define The Game)	1.50
141	Derek Jeter (Define The Game)	1.50
142	Ken Caminiti (Define The Game)	.15
143	Frank Thomas (Define The Game)	.50
144	Barry Bonds (Define The Game)	.40
145	Cal Ripken Jr. (Define The Game)	1.25
146	Alex Rodriguez (Define The Game)	1.25
147	Greg Maddux (Define The Game)	1.00
148	Kenny Lofton (Define The Game)	.15
149	Mike Piazza (Define The Game)	1.50
150	Mark McGwire (Define The Game)	2.00
151	Andruw Jones (Define The Game)	.50
152	Rusty Greer (Define The Game)	.10
153	F.P. Santangelo (Define The Game)	.10
154	Mike Lansing	.10
155	Lee Smith	.10
156	Carlos Perez	.10
157	Pedro Martinez	.75
158	Ryan McGuire	.10
159	F.P. Santangelo	.10
160	Rondell White	.20
161	*Takashi Kashiwada*	.25
162	Butch Huskey	.10
163	Edgardo Alfonzo	.25
164	John Franco	.10
165	Todd Hundley	.20
166	Rey Ordonez	.10
167	Armando Reynoso	.10
168	John Olerud	.25
169	Bernie Williams	.50
170	Andy Pettitte	.30
171	Wade Boggs	.25
172	Paul O'Neill	.25
173	Cecil Fielder	.10
174	Charlie Hayes	.10
175	David Cone	.20
176	Hideki Irabu	.25
177	Mark Bellhorn	.10
178	Steve Karsay	.10
179	Damon Mashore	.10
180	Jason McDonald	.10
181	Scott Spiezio	.10
182	Ariel Prieto	.10
183	Jason Giambi	.40
184	Wendell Magee	.10
185	Rico Brogna	.10
186	Garrett Stephenson	.10
187	Wayne Gomes	.10
188	Ricky Bottalico	.10
189	Mickey Morandini	.10
190	Mike Lieberthal	.10
191	*Kevin Polcovich*	.25
192	Francisco Cordova	.10
193	Kevin Young	.10
194	Jon Lieber	.10
195	Kevin Elster	.10
196	Tony Womack	.10
197	Lou Collier	.10
198	*Mike Defelice*	.20
199	Gary Gaetti	.10
200	Dennis Eckersley	.10
201	Alan Benes	.10
202	Willie McGee	.10
203	Ron Gant	.15
204	Fernando Valenzuela	.10
205	Mark McGwire	3.00
206	Archi Cianfrocco	.10
207	Andy Ashby	.10
208	Steve Finley	.10
209	Quilvio Veras	.10
210	Ken Caminiti	.15
211	Rickey Henderson	.50
212	Joey Hamilton	.10
213	Derrek Lee	.10
214	Bill Mueller	.10
215	Shawn Estes	.10
216	J.T. Snow	.10
217	Mark Gardner	.10
218	Terry Mulholland	.10
219	Dante Powell	.10
220	Jeff Kent	.10
221	Jamie Moyer	.10
222	Joey Cora	.10
223	Jeff Fassero	.10
224	Dennis Martinez	.10
225	Ken Griffey Jr.	2.50
226	Edgar Martinez	.10
227	Russ Davis	.10
228	Dan Wilson	.10
229	Will Clark	.25
230	Ivan Rodriguez	.75
231	Benji Gil	.10
232	Lee Stevens	.10
233	Mickey Tettleton	.10
234	Julio Santana	.10
235	Rusty Greer	.10
236	Bobby Witt	.10
237	Ed Sprague	.10
238	Pat Hentgen	.10
239	Kevin Escobar	.10
240	Joe Carter	.10
241	Carlos Delgado	.50
242	Shannon Stewart	.10
243	Benito Santiago	.10
244	Tino Martinez (Season Highlights)	.10
245	Ken Griffey Jr. (Season Highlights)	1.00
246	Kevin Brown (Season Highlights)	.15
247	Ryne Sandberg (Season Highlights)	.40
248	Mo Vaughn (Season Highlights)	.20
249	Darryl Hamilton (Season Highlights)	.10
250	Randy Johnson (Season Highlights)	.30

251 Steve Finley (Season Highlights) .10
252 Bobby Higginson (Season Highlights) .10
253 Brett Tomko (Star Rookie) .10
254 Mark Kotsay (Star Rookie) .25
255 Jose Guillen (Star Rookie) .25
256 Elieser Marrero (Star Rookie) .10
257 Dennis Reyes (Star Rookie) .25
258 Richie Sexson (Star Rookie) .15
259 Pat Cline (Star Rookie) .15
260 Todd Helton (Star Rookie) .75
261 Juan Melo (Star Rookie) .10
262 Matt Morris (Star Rookie) .10
263 Jeremi Gonzalez (Star Rookie) .20
264 Jeff Abbott (Star Rookie) .10
265 Aaron Boone (Star Rookie) .10
266 Todd Dunwoody (Star Rookie) .10
267 Jaret Wright (Star Rookie) .25
268 Derrick Gibson (Star Rookie) .10
269 Mario Valdez (Star Rookie) .10
270 Fernando Tatis (Star Rookie) .25
271 Craig Counsell (Star Rookie) .10
272 Brad Rigby (Star Rookie) .10
273 Danny Clyburn (Star Rookie) .10
274 Brian Rose (Star Rookie) .25
275 Miguel Tejada (Star Rookie) .25
276 Jason Varitek (Star Rookie) .20
277 *David Dellucci* (Star Rookie) .50
278 Michael Coleman (Star Rookie) .10
279 Adam Riggs (Star Rookie) .10
280 Ben Grieve (Star Rookie) .25
281 Brad Fullmer (Star Rookie) .10
282 Ken Cloude (Star Rookie) .25
283 Tom Evans (Star Rookie) .10
284 *Kevin Millwood* (Star Rookie) 1.00
285 Paul Konerko (Star Rookie) .25
286 Juan Encarnacion (Star Rookie) .10
287 Chris Carpenter (Star Rookie) .10
288 Tom Fordham (Star Rookie) .10
289 Gary DiSarcina .10
290 Tim Salmon .30
291 Troy Percival .10
292 Todd Greene .10
293 Ken Hill .10
294 Dennis Springer .10
295 Jim Edmonds .20
296 Allen Watson .10
297 Brian Anderson .10
298 Keith Lockhart .10
299 Tom Glavine .25
300 Chipper Jones 1.50
301 Randall Simon .10
302 Mark Lemke .10
303 Ryan Klesko .25
304 Denny Neagle .10
305 Andruw Jones .50
306 Mike Mussina .50
307 Brady Anderson .15
308 Chris Hoiles .10
309 Mike Bordick .10
310 Cal Ripken Jr. 2.50
311 Geronimo Berroa .10
312 Armando Benitez .10
313 Roberto Alomar .50
314 Tim Wakefield .10
315 Reggie Jefferson .10
316 Jeff Frye .10
317 Scott Hatteberg .10
318 Steve Avery .10
319 Robinson Checo .10
320 Nomar Garciaparra 2.00
321 Lance Johnson .10
322 Tyler Houston .10
323 Mark Clark .10
324 Terry Adams .10
325 Sammy Sosa 1.50
326 Scott Servais .10
327 Manny Alexander .10
328 Norberto Martin .10
329 *Scott Eyre* .25
330 Frank Thomas 1.00
331 Robin Ventura .20
332 Matt Karchner .10
333 Keith Foulke .10
334 James Baldwin .10
335 Chris Stynes .10
336 Bret Boone .10
337 Jon Nunnally .10
338 Dave Burba .10
339 Eduardo Perez .10
340 Reggie Sanders .10
341 Mike Remlinger .10
342 Pat Watkins .10
343 Chad Ogea .10
344 John Smiley .10
345 Kenny Lofton .30
346 Jose Mesa .10
347 Charles Nagy .10
348 Bruce Aven .10
349 Enrique Wilson .10
350 Manny Ramirez 1.00
351 Jerry DiPoto .10
352 Ellis Burks .10
353 Kirt Manwaring .10
354 Vinny Castilla .20
355 Larry Walker .50
356 Kevin Ritz .10
357 Pedro Astacio .10
358 Scott Sanders .10
359 Deivi Cruz .10
360 Brian L. Hunter .10
361 Pedro Martinez (History in the Making) .40
362 Tom Glavine (History in the Making) .10
363 Willie McGee (History in the Making) .10
364 J.T. Snow (History in the Making) .10
365 Rusty Greer (History in the Making) .10
366 Mike Grace (History in the Making) .10
367 Tony Clark (History in the Making) .20
368 Ben Grieve (History in the Making) .20
369 Gary Sheffield (History in the Making) .20
370 Joe Oliver .10
371 Todd Jones .10
372 *Frank Catalanotto* .20
373 Brian Moehler .10
374 Cliff Floyd .10
375 Bobby Bonilla .10
376 Al Leiter .15
377 Josh Booty .10
378 Darren Daulton .10
379 Jay Powell .10
380 Felix Heredia .10
381 Jim Eisenreich .10
382 Richard Hidalgo .10
383 Mike Hampton .10
384 Shane Reynolds .10
385 Jeff Bagwell 1.00
386 Derek Bell .10
387 Ricky Gutierrez .10
388 Bill Spiers .10
389 Jose Offerman .10
390 Johnny Damon .10
391 Jermaine Dye .10
392 Jeff Montgomery .10
393 Glendon Rusch .10
394 Mike Sweeney .10
395 Kevin Appier .10
396 Joe Vitiello .10
397 Ramon Martinez .20
398 Darren Dreifort .10
399 Wilton Guerrero .10
400 Mike Piazza 2.00
401 Eddie Murray .25
402 Ismael Valdes .10
403 Todd Hollandsworth .10
404 Mark Loretta .10
405 Jeromy Burnitz .10
406 Jeff Cirillo .10
407 Scott Karl .10
408 Mike Matheny .10
409 Jose Valentin .10
410 John Jaha .10
411 Terry Steinbach .10
412 Torii Hunter .10
413 Pat Meares .10
414 Marty Cordova .10
415 Jaret Wright (Postseason Headliners) .15
416 Mike Mussina (Postseason Headliners) .25
417 John Smoltz (Postseason Headliners) .10
418 Devon White (Postseason Headliners) .10
419 Denny Neagle (Postseason Headliners) .10
420 Livan Hernandez (Postseason Headliners) .20
421 Kevin Brown (Postseason Headliners) .10
422 Marquis Grissom (Postseason Headliners) .10
423 Mike Mussina (Postseason Headliners) .25
424 Eric Davis (Postseason Headliners) .10
425 Tony Fernandez (Postseason Headliners) .10
426 Moises Alou (Postseason Headliners) .10
427 Sandy Alomar Jr (Postseason Headliners) .10
428 Gary Sheffield (Postseason Headliners) .20
429 Jaret Wright (Postseason Headliners) .20
430 Livan Hernandez (Postseason Headliners) .20
431 Chad Ogea (Postseason Headliners) .10
432 Edgar Renteria (Postseason Headliners) .10
433 LaTroy Hawkins .10
434 Rich Robertson .10
435 Chuck Knoblauch .25
436 Jose Vidro .10
437 Dustin Hermanson .10
438 Jim Bullinger .10
439 Orlando Cabrera (Star Rookie) .10
440 Vladimir Guerrero 1.00
441 Ugueth Urbina .10
442 Brian McRae .10
443 Matt Franco .10
444 Bobby Jones .10
445 Bernard Gilkey .10
446 Dave Mlicki .10
447 Brian Bohanon .10
448 Mel Rojas .10
449 Tim Raines .10
450 Derek Jeter 2.00
451 Roger Clemens (Upper Echelon) .50
452 Nomar Garciaparra (Upper Echelon) 1.50
453 Mike Piazza (Upper Echelon) 1.50
454 Mark McGwire (Upper Echelon) 1.50
455 Ken Griffey Jr. (Upper Echelon) 1.50
456 Larry Walker (Upper Echelon) .25
457 Alex Rodriguez (Upper Echelon) 1.50
458 Tony Gwynn (Upper Echelon) 1.00
459 Frank Thomas (Upper Echelon) .50
460 Tino Martinez .25
461 Chad Curtis .10
462 Ramiro Mendoza .10
463 Joe Girardi .10
464 David Wells .10
465 Mariano Rivera .20
466 Willie Adams .10
467 George Williams .10
468 Dave Telgheder .10
469 Dave Magadan .10
470 Matt Stairs .10
471 Billy Taylor .10
472 Jimmy Haynes .10
473 Gregg Jefferies .10
474 Midre Cummings .10
475 Curt Schilling .20
476 Mike Grace .10
477 Mark Leiter .10
478 Matt Beech .10
479 Scott Rolen .50
480 Jason Kendall .20
481 Esteban Loaiza .10
482 Jermaine Allensworth .10
483 Mark Smith .10
484 Jason Schmidt .10
485 Jose Guillen .20
486 Al Martin .10
487 Delino DeShields .10
488 Todd Stottlemyre .10
489 Brian Jordan .10
490 Ray Lankford .10
491 Matt Morris .10
492 Royce Clayton .10
493 John Mabry .10
494 Wally Joyner .10
495 Trevor Hoffman .10
496 Chris Gomez .10
497 Sterling Hitchcock .10
498 Pete Smith .10
499 Greg Vaughn .15
500 Tony Gwynn 1.00
501 Will Cunnane .10
502 Darryl Hamilton .10
503 Brian Johnson .10
504 Kirk Rueter .10
505 Barry Bonds .75
506 Osvaldo Fernandez .10
507 Stan Javier .10
508 Julian Tavarez .10
509 Rich Aurilia .10
510 Alex Rodriguez 2.50
511 David Segui .10
512 Rich Amaral .10
513 Raul Ibanez .10
514 Jay Buhner .10
515 Randy Johnson .50
516 Heathcliff Slocumb .10
517 Tony Saunders .10
518 Kevin Elster .10
519 John Burkett .10
520 Juan Gonzalez .75
521 John Wetteland .10
522 Domingo Cedeno .10
523 Darren Oliver .10
524 Roger Pavlik .10
525 Jose Cruz Jr. .25
526 Woody Williams .10
527 Alex Gonzalez .10
528 Robert Person .10
529 Juan Guzman .10
530 Roger Clemens 1.00
531 Shawn Green .50
532 Cordova, Ricon, Smith (Season Highlights) .10
533 Nomar Garciaparra (Season Highlights) 1.50
534 Roger Clemens (Season Highlights) .50
535 Mark McGwire (Season Highlights) 1.50
536 Larry Walker (Season Highlights) .25
537 Mike Piazza (Season Highlights) 1.50
538 Curt Schilling (Season Highlights) .10
539 Tony Gwynn (Season Highlights) .50
540 Ken Griffey Jr. (Season Highlights) 1.50
541 Carl Pavano (Star Rookies) .10

542 Shane Monahan (Star Rookies) .10
543 *Gabe Kapler* (Star Rookies) 3.00
544 Eric Milton (Star Rookies) .25
545 *Gary Matthews Jr.* (Star Rookies) .50
546 *Mike Kinkade* (Star Rookies) .50
547 *Ryan Christenson* (Star Rookies) .25
548 *Corey Koskie* (Star Rookies) .50
549 Norm Hutchins (Star Rookies) .10
550 Russell Branyan (Star Rookies) .10
551 *Masato Yoshii* (Star Rookies) .50
552 *Jesus Sanchez* (Star Rookies) .30
553 Anthony Sanders (Star Rookies) .20
554 Edwin Diaz (Star Rookies) .10
555 Gabe Alvarez (Star Rookies) .10
556 *Carlos Lee* (Star Rookies) 1.50
557 Mike Darr (Star Rookies) .10
558 Kerry Wood (Star Rookies) .50
559 Carlos Guillen (Star Rookies) .10
560 Sean Casey (Star Rookies) .50
561 *Manny Aybar* (Star Rookies) .40
562 Octavio Dotel (Star Rookies) .15
563 Jarrod Washburn (Star Rookies) .10
564 Mark L. Johnson (Star Rookies) .10
565 Ramon Hernandez (Star Rookies) .10
566 *Rich Butler* (Star Rookies) .50
567 Mike Caruso (Star Rookies) .25
568 Cliff Politte (Star Rookies) .10
569 Scott Elarton (Star Rookies) .10
570 *Magglio Ordonez* (Star Rookies) 4.00
571 *Adam Butler* (Star Rookies) .40
572 Marlon Anderson (Star Rookies) .15
573 *Julio Ramirez* (Star Rookies) .40
574 *Darron Ingram* (Star Rookies) .20
575 Bruce Chen (Star Rookies) .10
576 *Steve Woodard* (Star Rookies) .25
577 Hiram Bocachica (Star Rookies) .10
578 Kevin Witt (Star Rookies) .10
579 Javier Vazquez (Star Rookies) .10
580 Alex Gonzalez (Star Rookies) .15
581 Brian Powell (Star Rookies) .10
582 Wes Helms (Star Rookies) .10
583 Ron Wright (Star Rookies) .10
584 Rafael Medina (Star Rookies) .10
585 Daryle Ward (Star Rookies) .15
586 Geoff Jenkins (Star Rookies) .10
587 Preston Wilson (Star Rookies) .15
588 *Jim Chamblee* (Star Rookies) .25
589 *Mike Lowell* (Star Rookies) .50
590 A.J. Hinch (Star Rookies) .10
591 *Francisco Cordero* (Star Rookies) .25
592 *Rolando Arrojo* (Star Rookies) .50
593 Braden Looper (Star Rookies) .10
594 Sidney Ponson (Star Rookies) .10
595 Matt Clement (Star Rookies) .10
596 Carlton Loewer (Star Rookies) .10
597 Brian Meadows (Star Rookies) .10
598 Danny Klassen (Star Rookies) .20
599 Larry Sutton (Star Rookies) .10
600 Travis Lee (Star Rookies) .10
601 Randy Johnson (Eminent Prestige) 2.50
602 Greg Maddux (Eminent Prestige) 5.00
603 Roger Clemens (Eminent Prestige) 4.00
604 Jaret Wright (Eminent Prestige) 1.00
605 Mike Piazza (Eminent Prestige) 6.00
606 Tino Martinez (Eminent Prestige) 1.00
607 Frank Thomas (Eminent Prestige) 3.00
608 Mo Vaughn (Eminent Prestige) 1.50
609 Todd Helton (Eminent Prestige) 3.00
610 Mark McGwire (Eminent Prestige) 10.00
611 Jeff Bagwell (Eminent Prestige) 3.00
612 Travis Lee (Eminent Prestige) 1.00
613 Scott Rolen (Eminent Prestige) 2.00
614 Cal Ripken Jr. (Eminent Prestige) 8.00
615 Chipper Jones (Eminent Prestige) 6.00
616 Nomar Garciaparra (Eminent Prestige) 6.00
617 Alex Rodriguez (Eminent Prestige) 8.00
618 Derek Jeter (Eminent Prestige) 6.00
619 Tony Gwynn (Eminent Prestige) 3.00
620 Ken Griffey Jr. (Eminent Prestige) 8.00
621 Kenny Lofton (Eminent Prestige) 1.25
622 Juan Gonzalez (Eminent Prestige) 2.50
623 Jose Cruz Jr. (Eminent Prestige) 1.00
624 Larry Walker (Eminent Prestige) 1.50
625 Barry Bonds (Eminent Prestige) 2.50
626 Ben Grieve (Eminent Prestige) 1.50
627 Andruw Jones (Eminent Prestige) 2.00
628 Vladimir Guerrero (Eminent Prestige) 4.00
629 Paul Konerko (Eminent Prestige) 1.00
630 Paul Molitor (Eminent Prestige) 2.00
631 Cecil Fielder .10
632 Jack McDowell .10
633 Mike James .10
634 Brian Anderson .10
635 Jay Bell .10
636 Devon White .10
637 Andy Stankiewicz .10
638 Tony Batista .10
639 Omar Daal .10
640 Matt Williams .25
641 Brent Brede .10
642 Jorge Fabregas .10
643 Karim Garcia .10
644 Felix Rodriguez .10
645 Andy Benes .10
646 Willie Blair .10
647 Jeff Suppan .10
648 Yamil Benitez .10
649 Walt Weiss .10
650 Andres Galarraga .40
651 Doug Drabek .10
652 Ozzie Guillen .10
653 Joe Carter .10
654 Dennis Eckersley .10
655 Pedro Martinez .75
656 Jim Leyritz .10
657 Henry Rodriguez .10
658 Rod Beck .10
659 Mickey Morandini .10
660 Jeff Blauser .10
661 Ruben Sierra .10
662 Mike Sirotka .10
663 Pete Harnisch .10
664 Damian Jackson .10
665 Dmitri Young .10
666 Steve Cooke .10
667 Geronimo Berroa .10
668 Shawon Dunston .10
669 Mike Jackson .10
670 Travis Fryman .20
671 Dwight Gooden .10
672 Paul Assenmacher .10
673 Eric Plunk .10
674 Mike Lansing .10
675 Darryl Kile .10
676 Luis Gonzalez .20
677 Frank Castillo .10
678 Joe Randa .10
679 Bip Roberts .10
680 Derrek Lee .10
681 Mike Piazza 2.00
682 Sean Berry .10
683 Ramon Garcia .10
684 Carl Everett .10
685 Moises Alou .20
686 Hal Morris .10
687 Jeff Conine .10
688 Gary Sheffield LA .25
689 Jose Vizcaino .10
690 Charles Johnson .10
691 Bobby Bonilla LA .15
692 Marquis Grissom .10
693 Alex Ochoa .10
694 Mike Morgan .10
695 Orlando Merced .10
696 David Ortiz .15
697 Brent Gates .10
698 Otis Nixon .10
699 Trey Moore .10
700 Derrick May .10
701 Rich Becker .10
702 Al Leiter .20
703 Chili Davis .10
704 Scott Brosius .10
705 Chuck Knoblauch .30
706 Kenny Rogers .10
707 Mike Blowers .10
708 Mike Fetters .10
709 Tom Candiotti .10
710 Rickey Henderson .50
711 Bob Abreu .10
712 Mark Lewis .10
713 Doug Glanville .10
714 Desi Relaford .10
715 Kent Mercker .10
716 J. Kevin Brown .20
717 James Mouton .10
718 Mark Langston .10
719 Greg Myers .10
720 Orel Hershiser .10
721 Charlie Hayes .10
722 Robb Nen .10
723 Glenallen Hill .10
724 Tony Saunders .10
725 Wade Boggs .40
726 Kevin Stocker .10
727 Wilson Alvarez .10
728 Albie Lopez .10
729 Dave Martinez .10
730 Fred McGriff .25
731 Quinton McCracken .10
732 Bryan Rekar .10
733 Paul Sorrento .10
734 Roberto Hernandez .10
735 Bubba Trammell .10
736 Miguel Cairo .10
737 John Flaherty .10
738 Terrell Wade .10
739 Roberto Kelly .10
740 Mark Mclemore (McLemore) .10
741 Danny Patterson .10
742 Aaron Sele .10
743 Tony Fernandez .10
744 Randy Myers .10
745 Jose Canseco .50
746 Darrin Fletcher .10
747 Mike Stanley .10
748 Marquis Grissom (Season Highlights) .10
749 Fred McGriff (Season Highlights) .20
750 Travis Lee (Season Highlights) .10

1998 Upper Deck A Piece of the Action

A Piece of the Action was inserted in Series One, Two and Three packs. Series One featured 10 cards: five with a piece of game-used jersey and five with a piece of game-used bat. Series Two offered a piece of game-used bat and jersey on four cards. Series Three inserts featured a piece of jersey only. The cards were inserted one per 2,500 packs in Series 1 and 2; the insertion rate in Series 3 was not revealed.

		MT
Complete Set (18):		1600.
Comp. Series 1 Set (10):		1250.
Complete Series 2 Set (4):		350.00
Common Player:		30.00
Inserted 1:2,500		
(1)	Tony Gwynn (Jersey)	125.00
(2)	Tony Gwynn (Bat)	100.00
(3)	Alex Rodriguez (Jersey)	300.00
(4)	Alex Rodriguez (Bat)	200.00
(5)	Gary Sheffield (Jersey)	60.00
(6)	Gary Sheffield (Bat)	50.00
(7)	Todd Hollandsworth (Jersey)	40.00
(8)	Todd Hollandsworth (Bat)	30.00
(9)	Greg Maddux (Jersey)	150.00
(10)	Jay Buhner (Bat)	40.00
RA	Roberto Alomar	150.00
JB	Jay Buhner	40.00
AJ	Andruw Jones	200.00
GS	Gary Sheffield	75.00

1998 Upper Deck Amazing Greats

The 30-card Amazing Greats insert is printed on acetate. The cards are labeled "One of 2,000". A die-cut parallel was sequentially numbered to 250. Amazing Greats was an insert in Upper Deck

Series One packs. Cards carry an "AG" prefix.

		MT
Complete Set (30):		375.00
Common Player:		4.00
Die-Cuts (250):		1.5X
1	Ken Griffey Jr.	30.00
2	Derek Jeter	30.00
3	Alex Rodriguez	30.00
4	Paul Molitor	8.00
5	Jeff Bagwell	10.00
6	Larry Walker	6.00
7	Kenny Lofton	6.00
8	Cal Ripken Jr.	30.00
9	Juan Gonzalez	10.00
10	Chipper Jones	20.00
11	Greg Maddux	20.00
12	Roberto Alomar	8.00
13	Mike Piazza	25.00
14	Andres Galarraga	5.00
15	Barry Bonds	10.00
16	Andy Pettitte	5.00
17	Nomar Garciaparra	25.00
18	Hideki Irabu	4.00
19	Tony Gwynn	15.00
20	Frank Thomas	15.00
21	Roger Clemens	15.00
22	Sammy Sosa	25.00
23	Jose Cruz, Jr.	4.00
24	Manny Ramirez	10.00
25	Mark McGwire	40.00
26	Randy Johnson	10.00
27	Mo Vaughn	6.00
28	Gary Sheffield	6.00
29	Andruw Jones	8.00
30	Albert Belle	6.00

1998 Upper Deck Blue Chip Prospects

Inserted in Series Two packs, Blue Chip Prospects is printed on die-cut acetate. The cards are sequentially numbered to 2,000. They carry a "BC" prefix.

		MT
Complete Set (30):		250.00
Common Player:		3.00
1	Nomar Garciaparra	40.00
2	Scott Rolen	15.00
3	Jason Dickson	3.00
4	Darin Erstad	8.00
5	Brad Fullmer	3.00
6	Jaret Wright	4.00
7	Justin Thompson	3.00
8	Matt Morris	3.00
9	Fernando Tatis	3.00
10	Alex Rodriguez	50.00
11	Todd Helton	15.00
12	Andy Pettitte	6.00
13	Jose Cruz Jr.	3.00
14	Mark Kotsay	3.00
15	Derek Jeter	40.00
16	Paul Konerko	5.00
17	Todd Dunwoody	3.00
18	Vladimir Guerrero	25.00
19	Miguel Tejada	6.00
20	Chipper Jones	35.00
21	Kevin Orie	3.00
22	Juan Encarnacion	3.00
23	Brian Rose	3.00
24	Andruw Jones	10.00
25	Livan Hernandez	3.00
26	Brian Giles	4.00
27	Brett Tomko	3.00
28	Jose Guillen	3.00
29	Aaron Boone	3.00
30	Ben Grieve	8.00

1998 Upper Deck Clearly Dominant

Clearly Dominant was an insert in Series Two. Printed on Light F/X plastic stock, the 30-card set is sequentially numbered to 250. They carry a "CD" prefix.

		MT
Complete Set (30):		750.00
Common Player:		8.00
Production 250 sets		
1	Mark McGwire	80.00
2	Derek Jeter	60.00
3	Alex Rodriguez	60.00
4	Paul Molitor	15.00
5	Jeff Bagwell	20.00
6	Ivan Rodriguez	20.00
7	Kenny Lofton	10.00
8	Cal Ripken Jr.	60.00
9	Albert Belle	10.00
10	Chipper Jones	40.00
11	Gary Sheffield	10.00
12	Roberto Alomar	15.00
13	Mo Vaughn	10.00
14	Andres Galarraga	10.00
15	Nomar Garciaparra	50.00
16	Randy Johnson	20.00
17	Mike Mussina	15.00
18	Greg Maddux	40.00
19	Tony Gwynn	30.00
20	Frank Thomas	30.00
21	Roger Clemens	30.00
22	Dennis Eckersley	8.00
23	Juan Gonzalez	20.00
24	Tino Martinez	8.00
25	Andruw Jones	20.00
26	Larry Walker	10.00
27	Ken Caminiti	10.00
28	Mike Piazza	50.00
29	Barry Bonds	20.00
30	Ken Griffey Jr.	60.00

1998 Upper Deck Ken Griffey Jr.'s HR Chronicles

Griffey's Home Run Chronicles was inserted in both Series 1 and 2 packs. Series 1 had cards spotlighting one of Junior's first 30 home runs of the 1997 season. Series 2 had 26 cards highlighting the rest of his 1997 home run output. In both series, the cards were inserted one per nine packs. Cards are numbered "XX of 56" and printed on silver-metallic foil on front.

		MT
Complete Set (56):		190.00
Common Card:		4.00
Inserted 1:9		
1	Ken Griffey Jr.	5.00
2	Ken Griffey Jr.	5.00
3	Ken Griffey Jr.	5.00
4	Ken Griffey Jr.	5.00
5	Ken Griffey Jr.	5.00
6	Ken Griffey Jr.	5.00
7	Ken Griffey Jr.	5.00
8	Ken Griffey Jr.	5.00
9	Ken Griffey Jr.	5.00
10	Ken Griffey Jr.	5.00
11	Ken Griffey Jr.	5.00
12	Ken Griffey Jr.	5.00
13	Ken Griffey Jr.	5.00
14	Ken Griffey Jr.	5.00
15	Ken Griffey Jr.	5.00
16	Ken Griffey Jr.	5.00
17	Ken Griffey Jr.	5.00
18	Ken Griffey Jr.	5.00
19	Ken Griffey Jr.	5.00
20	Ken Griffey Jr.	5.00
21	Ken Griffey Jr.	5.00
22	Ken Griffey Jr.	5.00
23	Ken Griffey Jr.	5.00
24	Ken Griffey Jr.	5.00
25	Ken Griffey Jr.	5.00
26	Ken Griffey Jr.	5.00
27	Ken Griffey Jr.	5.00
28	Ken Griffey Jr.	5.00
29	Ken Griffey Jr.	5.00
30	Ken Griffey Jr.	5.00

1998 Upper Deck 10th Anniversary Preview

10th Anniversary Preview is a 60-card set. The foil cards have the same design as the 1989 Upper Deck base cards. The set was inserted one per five packs.

		MT
Complete Set (60):		120.00
Common Player:		.75
1	Greg Maddux	8.00
2	Mike Mussina	2.00
3	Roger Clemens	4.00
4	Hideo Nomo	1.50
4	David Cone	.75
6	Tom Glavine	.75
7	Andy Pettitte	2.00
8	Jimmy Key	.75
9	Randy Johnson	2.00
10	Dennis Eckersley	.75
11	Lee Smith	.75
12	John Franco	.75
13	Randy Myers	.75
14	Mike Piazza	8.00
15	Ivan Rodriguez	3.00
16	Todd Hundley	1.00
17	Sandy Alomar Jr.	.75
18	Frank Thomas	5.00
19	Rafael Palmeiro	1.00
20	Mark McGwire	12.00
21	Mo Vaughn	2.00
22	Fred McGriff	1.25
23	Andres Galarraga	1.25
24	Mark Grace	1.25
25	Jeff Bagwell	5.00
26	Roberto Alomar	2.50
27	Chuck Knoblauch	1.50
28	Ryne Sandberg	3.00
29	Eric Young	.75
30	Craig Biggio	1.00
31	Carlos Baerga	.75
32	Robin Ventura	.75
33	Matt Williams	.75
34	Wade Boggs	1.00
35	Dean Palmer	.75
36	Chipper Jones	8.00
37	Vinny Castilla	.75
38	Ken Caminiti	1.25
39	Omar Vizquel	.75
40	Cal Ripken Jr.	10.00
41	Derek Jeter	8.00
42	Alex Rodriguez	10.00
43	Barry Larkin	.75
44	Mark Grudzielanek	.75
45	Albert Belle	2.00
46	Manny Ramirez	4.00
47	Jose Canseco	1.50
48	Ken Griffey Jr.	12.00
49	Juan Gonzalez	4.00
50	Kenny Lofton	2.00
51	Sammy Sosa	5.00
52	Larry Walker	1.50
53	Gary Sheffield	1.50
54	Rickey Henderson	1.00
55	Tony Gwynn	5.00
56	Barry Bonds	3.00
57	Paul Molitor	2.50
58	Edgar Martinez	.75
59	Chili Davis	.75
60	Eddie Murray	1.00

1998 Upper Deck National Pride

National Pride is a 42-card insert printed on die-cut rainbow foil. The set honors the nationality of the player with their country's flag in the background. The cards were inserted one per 24 packs. Cards are numbered with a "NP" prefix.

		MT
Complete Set (42):		250.00
Common Player:		2.25
1	Dave Nilsson	2.25
2	Larry Walker	6.00
3	Edgar Renteria	2.25
4	Jose Canseco	7.50

5	Rey Ordonez	2.25
6	Rafael Palmeiro	5.00
7	Livan Hernandez	2.25
8	Andruw Jones	5.00
9	Manny Ramirez	15.00
10	Sammy Sosa	25.00
11	Raul Mondesi	3.00
12	Moises Alou	3.00
13	Pedro Martinez	12.00
14	Vladimir Guerrero	15.00
15	Chili Davis	2.25
16	Hideo Nomo	3.00
17	Hideki Irabu	2.25
18	Shigetosi Hasegawa	2.25
19	Takashi Kashiwada	2.25
20	Chan Ho Park	2.50
21	Fernando Valenzuela	2.25
22	Vinny Castilla	2.50
23	Armando Reynoso	2.25
24	Karim Garcia	2.25
25	Marvin Benard	2.25
26	Mariano Rivera	2.25
27	Juan Gonzalez	12.00
28	Roberto Alomar	6.00
29	Ivan Rodriguez	9.00
30	Carlos Delgado	4.00
31	Bernie Williams	6.00
32	Edgar Martinez	2.25
33	Frank Thomas	12.00
34	Barry Bonds	9.00
35	Mike Piazza	25.00
36	Chipper Jones	25.00
37	Cal Ripken Jr.	30.00
38	Alex Rodriguez	30.00
39	Ken Griffey Jr.	35.00
40	Andres Galarraga	4.00
41	Omar Vizquel	2.25
42	Ozzie Guillen	2.25

1998 Upper Deck Prime Nine

Nine of the most popular players are featured in this insert set. The cards are printed on silver foil stock and inserted 1:5.

	MT
Complete Set (60):	150.00
Common Griffey (PN1-PN7):	5.00
Common Piazza (PN8-PN14):	3.00
Common Thomas (PN15-PN21):	2.00
Common McGwire (PN22-PN28):	5.00
Common Ripken (PN29-PN35):	4.00
Common Gonzalez (PN36-PN42):	2.00
Common Gwynn (PN43-PN49):	3.00
Common Bonds (PN50-PN55):	2.00
Common Maddux (PN56-PN60):	3.00
Inserted 1:5	

1998 Upper Deck Tape Measure Titans

Tape Measure Titans is a 30-card insert seeded 1:23. The set honors the game's top home run hitters.

		MT
Complete Set (30):		180.00
Common Player:		2.50
Inserted 1:23		
1	Mark McGwire	25.00
2	Andres Galarraga	3.00
3	Jeff Bagwell	6.00
4	Larry Walker	4.00
5	Frank Thomas	8.00
6	Rafael Palmeiro	5.00
7	Nomar Garciaparra	15.00
8	Mo Vaughn	4.00
9	Albert Belle	4.00
10	Ken Griffey Jr.	20.00
11	Manny Ramirez	6.00
12	Jim Thome	4.00
13	Tony Clark	2.50
14	Juan Gonzalez	6.00
15	Mike Piazza	15.00
16	Jose Canseco	5.00
17	Jay Buhner	2.50
18	Alex Rodriguez	20.00
19	Jose Cruz Jr.	3.00
20	Tino Martinez	2.50
21	Carlos Delgado	6.00
22	Andruw Jones	6.00
23	Chipper Jones	12.00
24	Fred McGriff	3.00
25	Matt Williams	3.00
26	Sammy Sosa	12.00
27	Vinny Castilla	2.50
28	Tim Salmon	3.00
29	Ken Caminiti	2.50
30	Barry Bonds	6.00

1998 Upper Deck Rookie Edition A Piece of the Action

A Piece of the Action consists of five Game Jersey cards. Three rookie Game Jersey cards were sequentially numbered to 200, while a Ken Griffey Jr. Game Jersey card was numbered to 300. Griffey also signed and hand-numbered 24 Game Jersey cards.

		MT
Common Card:		75.00
KG	Ken Griffey Jr. (300)	300.00
KGS	Ken Griffey Jr. (24) (Signed)	1500.
BG	Ben Grieve (200)	75.00
JC	Jose Cruz Jr. (200)	50.00
TL	Travis Lee (200)	40.00

1998 Upper Deck Rookie Edition All-Star Credentials

All-Star Credentials is a 30-card insert seeded 1:9. It features the game's top players.

		MT
Complete Set (30):		80.00
Common Player:		.75
Inserted 1:9		
AS1	Ken Griffey Jr.	8.00
AS2	Travis Lee	.75
AS3	Ben Grieve	1.00
AS4	Jose Cruz Jr.	.75
AS5	Andruw Jones	2.00
AS6	Craig Biggio	1.00
AS7	Hideo Nomo	1.50
AS8	Cal Ripken Jr.	8.00
AS9	Jaret Wright	.75
AS10	Mark McGwire	10.00
AS11	Derek Jeter	8.00
AS12	Scott Rolen	2.00
AS13	Jeff Bagwell	2.50
AS14	Manny Ramirez	2.50
AS15	Alex Rodriguez	8.00
AS16	Chipper Jones	5.00
AS17	Larry Walker	1.50
AS18	Barry Bonds	2.50
AS19	Tony Gwynn	3.00
AS20	Mike Piazza	6.00
AS21	Roger Clemens	3.00
AS22	Greg Maddux	5.00
AS23	Jim Thome	1.50
AS24	Tino Martinez	1.00
AS25	Nomar Garciaparra	6.00
AS26	Juan Gonzalez	2.50
AS27	Kenny Lofton	1.50
AS28	Randy Johnson	2.50
AS29	Todd Helton	2.50
AS30	Frank Thomas	3.00

1998 Upper Deck Rookie Edition Destination Stardom

This 60-card insert features top young players. Fronts are printed on a foil background. The insertion rate was one card per five packs.

		MT
Complete Set (60):		75.00
Common Player:		.50
Inserted 1:5		
DS1	Travis Lee	1.50
DS2	Nomar Garciaparra	8.00
DS3	Alex Gonzalez	.75
DS4	Richard Hidalgo	.50
DS5	Jaret Wright	.50
DS6	Mike Kinkade	.50
DS7	Matt Morris	.50
DS8	Gary Mathews Jr.	.50
DS9	Brett Tomko	.50
DS10	Todd Helton	2.50
DS11	Scott Elarton	.50
DS12	Scott Rolen	3.00
DS13	Jose Cruz Jr.	1.00
DS14	Jarrod Washburn	.50
DS15	Sean Casey	4.00
DS16	Magglio Ordonez	6.00
DS17	Gabe Alvarez	.50
DS18	Todd Dunwoody	.50
DS19	Kevin Witt	.50
DS20	Ben Grieve	1.50
DS21	Daryle Ward	.50
DS22	Matt Clement	.50
DS23	Carlton Loewer	.50
DS24	Javier Vazquez	.50
DS25	Paul Konerko	1.00
DS26	Preston Wilson	1.00
DS27	Wes Helms	.50
DS28	Derek Jeter	8.00
DS29	Corey Koskie	.75
DS30	Russell Branyan	.50
DS31	Vladimir Guerrero	6.00
DS32	Ryan Christenson	.50
DS33	Carlos Lee	2.00
DS34	David Dellucci	.50
DS35	Bruce Chen	.50
DS36	Ricky Ledee	1.00
DS37	Ron Wright	.50
DS38	Derrek Lee	.50
DS39	Miguel Tejada	2.50
DS40	Brad Fullmer	1.00
DS41	Rich Butler	.50
DS42	Chris Carpenter	.50
DS43	Alex Rodriguez	12.00
DS44	Darron Ingram	.50
DS45	Kerry Wood	3.00
DS46	Jason Varitek	.50
DS47	Ramon Hernandez	.50
DS48	Aaron Boone	.50
DS49	Juan Encarnacion	.50
DS50	A.J. Hinch	.50
DS51	Mike Lowell	.50
DS52	Fernando Tatis	1.00
DS53	Jose Guillen	.50
DS54	Mike Caruso	.50
DS55	Carl Pavano	.50
DS56	Chris Clemons	.50
DS57	Mark L. Johnson	.50
DS58	Ken Cloude	.50
DS59	Rolando Arrojo	1.00
DS60	Mark Kotsay	1.00

1998 Upper Deck Rookie Edition Retrospectives

Retrospectives is a 30-card insert seeded 1:24. The cards offer a look back at the careers of baseball's top stars.

	MT
Complete Set (30):	180.00
Common Player:	2.00

Inserted 1:24

1	Dennis Eckersley	2.00
2	Rickey Henderson	3.00
3	Harold Baines	2.00
4	Cal Ripken Jr.	20.00
5	Tony Gwynn	8.00
6	Wade Boggs	4.00
7	Orel Hershiser	2.00
8	Joe Carter	2.00
9	Roger Clemens	10.00
10	Barry Bonds	6.00
11	Mark McGwire	25.00
12	Greg Maddux	12.00
13	Fred McGriff	3.00
14	Rafael Palmeiro	5.00
15	Craig Biggio	2.00
16	Brady Anderson	2.00
17	Randy Johnson	6.00
18	Gary Sheffield	4.00
19	Albert Belle	4.00
20	Ken Griffey Jr.	20.00
21	Juan Gonzalez	6.00
22	Larry Walker	4.00
23	Tino Martinez	2.00
24	Frank Thomas	8.00
25	Jeff Bagwell	6.00
26	Kenny Lofton	3.00
27	Mo Vaughn	4.00
28	Mike Piazza	15.00
29	Alex Rodriguez	20.00
30	Chipper Jones	12.00

1998 Upper Deck Rookie Edition Unparalleled

Unparalleled is a 20-card, hobby-only insert. The set consists of holo-pattern foil-stamped cards. They were inserted one per 72 packs.

		MT
Complete Set (20):		375.00
Common Player:		5.00
Inserted 1:72		
1	Ken Griffey Jr.	50.00
2	Travis Lee	8.00
3	Ben Grieve	8.00
4	Jose Cruz Jr.	6.00
5	Nomar Garciaparra	30.00
6	Hideo Nomo	6.00
7	Kenny Lofton	10.00
8	Cal Ripken Jr.	40.00
9	Roger Clemens	20.00
10	Mike Piazza	30.00
11	Jeff Bagwell	15.00
12	Chipper Jones	30.00
13	Greg Maddux	25.00
14	Randy Johnson	10.00
15	Alex Rodriguez	40.00
16	Barry Bonds	12.00
17	Frank Thomas	15.00
18	Juan Gonzalez	12.00
19	Tony Gwynn	25.00
20	Mark McGwire	50.00

1998 Upper Deck UD 3

		MT
Complete Set (270):		700.00
Common Future Impact (1-30):		.50
Inserted 1:12		
Die-Cuts (2,000 sets):		1X
Common Power Corps (31-60):		.25
Inserted 1:1.5		
Die-Cuts (2,000 sets):		3X
Common Establishment (61-90):		.50
Inserted 1:6		
Die-Cuts (2,000 sets):		2X
Common Future Impact Embossed (91-120):		.40
Inserted 1:6		
Die-Cuts (1,000 sets):		3X
Common Power Corps Embossed (121-150):		.25
Inserted 1:4		
Die-Cuts (1,000 sets):		6X
Common Establishment Embossed (151-180):		.25
Inserted 1:1		
Die-Cuts (1,000 sets):		12X
Common Future Impact Rainbow (181-210):		.25
Inserted 1:1		
Die-Cuts (100 sets):		15X
Common Power Corps Rainbow (211-240):		1.50
Inserted 1:12		
Die-Cuts (100 sets):		8X
Common Establishmen Rainbow (241-270):		2.00
Inserted 1:24		
Die-Cuts (100 sets):		5X
Pack (3):		4.00
Wax Box (24):		90.00
1	Travis Lee	6.00
2	A.J. Hinch	.50
3	Mike Caruso	.50
4	Miguel Tejada	1.50
5	Brad Fullmer	1.50
6	Eric Milton	.50
7	Mark Kotsay	2.00
8	Darin Erstad	6.00
9	Magglio Ordonez	2.00
10	Ben Grieve	8.00
11	Brett Tomko	.50
12	*Mike Kinkade*	1.00
13	Rolando Arrojo	5.00
14	Todd Helton	1.50
15	Scott Rolen	4.00
16	Bruce Chen	.50
17	Daryle Ward	.50
18	Jaret Wright	4.00
19	Cliff Politte	.50
20	Paul Konerko	.75
21	Kerry Wood	4.00
22	Russell Branyan	.50
23	Gabe Alvarez	.50
24	Juan Encarnacion	.50
25	Andruw Jones	4.00
26	Vladimir Guerrero	6.00
27	Eli Marrero	.25
28	Matt Clement	.25
29	Gary Matthews Jr.	1.00
30	Derrek Lee	.50
31	Ken Caminiti	.75
32	Gary Sheffield	1.00
33	Jay Buhner	.75
34	Ryan Klesko	.75
35	Nomar Garciaparra	5.00
36	Vinny Castilla	.25
37	Tony Clark	.75
38	Sammy Sosa	5.00
39	Tino Martinez	.75
40	Mike Piazza	5.00
41	Manny Ramirez	3.00
42	Larry Walker	.75
43	Jose Cruz Jr.	1.50
44	Matt Williams	.75
45	Frank Thomas	3.00
46	Jim Edmonds	.25
47	Raul Mondesi	.50
48	Alex Rodriguez	6.00
49	Albert Belle	2.00
50	Mark McGwire	10.00
51	Tim Salmon	.75
52	Andres Galarraga	.75
53	Jeff Bagwell	3.00
54	Jim Thome	1.00
55	Barry Bonds	2.00
56	Carlos Delgado	.75
57	Mo Vaughn	2.00
58	Chipper Jones	4.00
59	Juan Gonzalez	2.00
60	Ken Griffey Jr.	8.00
61	David Cone	.40
62	Hideo Nomo	2.00
63	Edgar Martinez	.25
64	Fred McGriff	1.00
65	Cal Ripken Jr.	10.00
66	Todd Hundley	.25
67	Barry Larkin	.75
68	Dennis Eckersley	.25
69	Randy Johnson	3.00
70	Paul Molitor	3.00
71	Eric Karros	.25
72	Rafael Palmeiro	.75
73	Chuck Knoblauch	2.00
74	Ivan Rodriguez	4.00
75	Greg Maddux	8.00
76	Dante Bichette	1.50
77	Brady Anderson	.25
78	Craig Biggio	.75
79	Derek Jeter	7.00
80	Roger Clemens	6.00
81	Roberto Alomar	2.50
82	Wade Boggs	.75
83	Charles Johnson	.25
84	Mark Grace	.75
85	Kenny Lofton	4.00
86	Mike Mussina	3.00
87	Pedro Martinez	3.00
88	Curt Schilling	.50
89	Bernie Williams	2.50
90	Tony Gwynn	6.00
91	Travis Lee	3.00
92	A.J. Hinch	.50
93	Mike Caruso	.40
94	Miguel Tejada	1.00
95	Brad Fullmer	1.50
96	Eric Milton	.25
97	Mark Kotsay	1.50
98	Darin Erstad	3.00
99	Magglio Ordonez	1.50
100	Ben Grieve	5.00
101	Brett Tomko	.40
102	Mike Kinkade	.40
103	Rolando Arrojo	4.00
104	Todd Helton	2.50
105	Scott Rolen	4.00
106	Bruce Chen	.40
107	Daryle Ward	.40
108	Jaret Wright	3.00
109	Sean Casey	.50
110	Paul Konerko	.75
111	Kerry Wood	4.00
112	Russell Branyan	.40
113	Gabe Alvarez	.40
114	Juan Encarnacion	.40
115	Andruw Jones	3.00
116	Vladimir Guerrero	5.00
117	Eli Marrero	.40
118	Matt Clement	.40
119	Gary Matthews Jr.	1.00
120	Derrek Lee	.25
121	Ken Caminiti	.50
122	Gary Sheffield	.75
123	Jay Buhner	.50
124	Ryan Klesko	.50
125	Nomar Garciaparra	5.00
126	Vinny Castilla	.25
127	Tony Clark	1.00
128	Sammy Sosa	5.00
129	Tino Martinez	1.00
130	Mike Piazza	5.00
131	Manny Ramirez	3.00
132	Larry Walker	1.00
133	Jose Cruz Jr.	1.50
134	Matt Williams	.75
135	Frank Thomas	3.00
136	Jim Edmonds	.25
137	Raul Mondesi	.40
138	Alex Rodriguez	6.00
139	Albert Belle	2.00
140	Mark McGwire	10.00
141	Tim Salmon	.50
142	Andres Galarraga	.75
143	Jeff Bagwell	2.50
144	Jim Thome	.75
145	Barry Bonds	2.00
146	Carlos Delgado	.75
147	Mo Vaughn	2.00
148	Chipper Jones	4.00
149	Juan Gonzalez	2.00
150	Ken Griffey Jr.	8.00
151	David Cone	.40
152	Hideo Nomo	.75
153	Edgar Martinez	.25
154	Fred McGriff	.25
155	Cal Ripken Jr.	3.00
156	Todd Hundley	.25
157	Barry Larkin	.40
158	Dennis Eckersley	.25
159	Randy Johnson	1.00
160	Paul Molitor	1.00
161	Eric Karros	.40
162	Rafael Palmeiro	.40
163	Chuck Knoblauch	.75
164	Ivan Rodriguez	1.25
165	Greg Maddux	2.50
166	Dante Bichette	.50
167	Brady Anderson	.25
168	Craig Biggio	.25
169	Derek Jeter	2.50
170	Roger Clemens	2.00
171	Roberto Alomar	1.00
172	Wade Boggs	.50
173	Charles Johnson	.25
174	Mark Grace	.50
175	Kenny Lofton	1.25
176	Mike Mussina	1.00
177	Pedro Martinez	1.00
178	Curt Schilling	.40
179	Bernie Williams	.75
180	Tony Gwynn	2.00
181	Travis Lee	1.50
182	A.J. Hinch	.25
183	Mike Caruso	.40
184	Miguel Tejada	.75
185	Brad Fullmer	.75
186	Eric Milton	.25
187	Mark Kotsay	.75
188	Darin Erstad	1.50
189	Magglio Ordonez	1.00
190	Ben Grieve	2.00
191	Brett Tomko	.25
192	Mike Kinkade	.25
193	Rolando Arrojo	2.00
194	Todd Helton	1.00
195	Scott Rolen	1.50
196	Bruce Chen	.25
197	Daryle Ward	.25
198	Jaret Wright	1.25
199	Cliff Politte	.25
200	Paul Konerko	.50
201	Kerry Wood	2.00
202	Russell Branyan	.25
203	Gabe Alvarez	.25
204	Juan Encarnacion	.25
205	Andruw Jones	1.00
206	Vladimir Guerrero	2.00
207	Eli Marrero	.25
208	Matt Clement	.25
209	Gary Matthews Jr.	.25
210	Derrek Lee	.25
211	Ken Caminiti	1.50
212	Gary Sheffield	2.50
213	Jay Buhner	2.50
214	Ryan Klesko	2.50
215	Nomar Garciaparra	15.00
216	Vinny Castilla	1.50
217	Tony Clark	4.00
218	Sammy Sosa	15.00
219	Tino Martinez	3.00
220	Mike Piazza	15.00
221	Manny Ramirez	8.00
222	Larry Walker	3.00
223	Jose Cruz Jr.	2.00
224	Matt Williams	2.50
225	Frank Thomas	6.00
226	Jim Edmonds	1.50
227	Raul Mondesi	2.00
228	Alex Rodriguez	20.00
229	Albert Belle	6.00
230	Mark McGwire	30.00
231	Tim Salmon	2.50
232	Andres Galarraga	3.00
233	Jeff Bagwell	8.00

234	Jim Thome	4.00
235	Barry Bonds	6.00
236	Carlos Delgado	3.00
267	Mo Vaughn	6.00
238	Chipper Jones	12.00
239	Juan Gonzalez	6.00
240	Ken Griffey Jr.	25.00
241	David Cone	2.50
242	Hideo Nomo	4.00
243	Edgar Martinez	2.00
244	Fred McGriff	2.50
245	Cal Ripken Jr.	30.00
246	Todd Hundley	2.00
247	Barry Larkin	2.50
248	Dennis Eckersley	2.00
249	Randy Johnson	8.00
250	Paul Molitor	8.00
251	Eric Karros	2.00
252	Rafael Palmeiro	3.00
253	Chuck Knoblauch	4.00
254	Ivan Rodriguez	10.00
255	Greg Maddux	25.00
256	Dante Bichette	3.00
257	Brady Anderson	2.00
258	Craig Biggio	2.00
259	Derek Jeter	25.00
260	Roger Clemens	20.00
261	Roberto Alomar	8.00
262	Wade Boggs	4.00
263	Charles Johnson	2.00
264	Mark Grace	3.00
265	Kenny Lofton	10.00
266	Mike Mussina	8.00
267	Pedro Martinez	8.00
268	Curt Schilling	2.00
269	Bernie Williams	6.00
270	Tony Gwynn	20.00

1998 Upper Deck UD 3 Die-Cut

Die-cut versions of all 270 cards in UD 3 were available and sequentially numbered. FX subset cards (1-90) were numbered to 2,000 sets, Embossed cards (91-180) were numbered to 1,000 and Rainbow foil cards (181-270) were numbered to 100.

	MT
Future Impact (1-30):	1X
Power Corps (31-60):	3X
Establishment (61-90):	2X
Regular Production 2,000 sets each	
Future Impact Embossed (91-120):	3X
Power Corps Embossed (121-150):	6X
Establishment Embossed (151-180):	12X
Embossed Production 1,000 sets each	
Future Impact Rainbow (181-210):	15X
Power Corps Rainbow (211-240):	8X
Establishment Rainbow (241-270):	5X
Rainbow Production 100 sets each	

1998 Upper Deck Special F/X

Special F/X is a retail-only product. The 150-card set consists of 125 regular cards, the 15-card Star Rookies subset and a 10-card subset called Ken Griffey Jr.'s Hot List. The base cards are printed on 20-point stock. The only insert is Power Zone which has four levels: Level One, Level Two - Octoberbest, Level Three - Power Driven and Level Four - Superstar Xcitement.

		MT
Complete Set (150):		50.00
Common Player:		.25
1	Ken Griffey Jr. (Griffey Hot List)	4.00
2	Mark McGwire (Griffey Hot List)	4.00
3	Alex Rodriguez (Griffey Hot List)	4.00
4	Larry Walker (Griffey Hot List)	.75
5	Tino Martinez (Griffey Hot List)	.60
6	Mike Piazza (Griffey Hot List)	3.00
7	Jose Cruz Jr. (Griffey Hot List)	.50
8	Greg Maddux (Griffey Hot List)	3.00
9	Tony Gwynn (Griffey Hot List)	2.50
10	Roger Clemens (Griffey Hot List)	2.50
11	Jason Dickson	.25
12	Darin Erstad	1.50
13	Chuck Finley	.25
14	Dave Hollins	.25
15	Garret Anderson	.25
16	Michael Tucker	.25
17	Javier Lopez	.40
18	John Smoltz	.40
19	Mark Wohlers	.25
20	Greg Maddux	3.00
21	Scott Erickson	.25
22	Jimmy Key	.25
23	B.J. Surhoff	.25
24	Eric Davis	.25
25	Rafael Palmeiro	.50
26	Tim Naehring	.25
27	Darren Bragg	.25
28	Troy O'Leary	.25
29	John Valentin	.25
30	Mo Vaughn	1.00
31	Mark Grace	.75
32	Kevin Foster	.25
33	Kevin Tapani	.25
34	Kevin Orie	.25
35	Albert Belle	1.50
36	Ray Durham	.25
37	Jaime Navarro	.25
38	Mike Cameron	.25
39	Eddie Taubensee	.25
40	Barry Larkin	.50
41	Willie Greene	.25
42	Jeff Shaw	.25
43	Omar Vizquel	.25
44	Brian Giles	.25
45	Jim Thome	1.00
46	David Justice	.75
47	Sandy Alomar Jr.	.50
48	Neifi Perez	.25
49	Dante Bichette	.50
50	Vinny Castilla	.50
51	John Thomson	.25
52	Damion Easley	.25
53	Justin Thompson	.25
54	Bobby Higginson	.25
55	Tony Clark	1.00
56	Charles Johnson	.25
57	Edgar Renteria	.25
58	Alex Fernandez	.25
59	Gary Sheffield	.60
60	Livan Hernandez	.25
61	Craig Biggio	.75
62	Chris Holt	.25
63	Billy Wagner	.25
64	Brad Ausmus	.25
65	Dean Palmer	.25
66	Tim Belcher	.25
67	Jeff King	.25
68	Jose Rosado	.25
69	Chan Ho Park	.75
70	Raul Mondesi	.50
71	Hideo Nomo	.75
72	Todd Zeile	.25
73	Eric Karros	.35
74	Cal Eldred	.25
75	Jeff D'Amico	.25
76	Doug Jones	.25
77	Dave Nilsson	.25
78	Todd Walker	.25
79	Rick Aguilera	.25
80	Paul Molitor	1.00
81	Brad Radke	.25
82	Vladimir Guerrero	2.00
83	Carlos Perez	.25
84	F.P. Santangelo	.25
85	Rondell White	.40
86	Butch Huskey	.25
87	Edgardo Alfonzo	.30
88	John Franco	.25
89	John Olerud	.40
90	Todd Hundley	.25
91	Bernie Williams	.75
92	Andy Pettitte	.75
93	Paul O'Neill	.50
94	David Cone	.40
95	Jason Giambi	.25
96	Damon Mashore	.25
97	Scott Spiezio	.25
98	Ariel Prieto	.25
99	Rico Brogna	.25
100	Mike Lieberthal	.25
101	Garrett Stephenson	.25
102	Ricky Bottalico	.25
103	Kevin Polcovich	.25
104	Jon Lieber	.25
105	Kevin Young	.25
106	Tony Womack	.25
107	Gary Gaetti	.25
108	Alan Benes	.40
109	Willie McGee	.25
110	Mark McGwire	5.00
111	Ron Gant	.35
112	Andy Ashby	.25
113	Steve Finley	.25
114	Quilvio Veras	.25
115	Ken Caminiti	.50
116	Joey Hamilton	.25
117	Bill Mueller	.25
118	Mark Gardner	.25
119	Shawn Estes	.25
120	J.T. Snow	.25
121	Dante Powell	.25
122	Jeff Kent	.25
123	Jamie Moyer	.25
124	Joey Cora	.25
125	Ken Griffey Jr.	5.00
126	Jeff Fassero	.25
127	Edgar Martinez	.25
128	Will Clark	.50
129	Lee Stevens	.25
130	Ivan Rodriguez	1.50
131	Rusty Greer	.35
132	Ed Sprague	.25
133	Pat Hentgen	.25
134	Shannon Stewart	.25
135	Carlos Delgado	.75
136	Brett Tomko (Star Rookie)	.25
137	Jose Guillen (Star Rookie)	.50
138	Elieser Marrero (Star Rookie)	.25
139	Dennis Reyes (Star Rookie)	.25
140	Mark Kotsay (Star Rookie)	.75
141	Richie Sexson (Star Rookie)	.35
142	Todd Helton (Star Rookie)	1.50
143	Jeremi Gonzalez (Star Rookie)	.25
144	Jeff Abbott (Star Rookie)	.25
145	Matt Morris (Star Rookie)	.25
146	Aaron Boone (Star Rookie)	.25
147	Todd Dunwoody (Star Rookie)	.25
148	Mario Valdez (Star Rookie)	.25
149	Fernando Tatis (Star Rookie)	.35
150	Jaret Wright (Star Rookie)	2.00

1998 Upper Deck Special F/X OctoberBest

OctoberBest is Level Two of the Power Zone insert. This 20-card insert is die-cut and printed on silver foil. Inserted one per 34 packs, the set features the postseason exploits of 20 players from Power Zone Level One.

		MT
Complete Set (15):		160.00
Common Player:		3.00
Inserted 1:34		
PZ1	Frank Thomas	12.00
PZ2	Juan Gonzalez	10.00
PZ3	Mike Piazza	20.00
PZ4	Mark McGwire	30.00
PZ5	Jeff Bagwell	12.00
PZ6	Barry Bonds	8.00
PZ7	Ken Griffey Jr.	30.00
PZ8	John Smoltz	3.00
PZ9	Andruw Jones	8.00
PZ10	Greg Maddux	17.50
PZ11	Sandy Alomar Jr.	3.00
PZ12	Roberto Alomar	6.00
PZ13	Chipper Jones	20.00
PZ14	Kenny Lofton	6.00
PZ15	Tom Glavine	3.00

1998 Upper Deck Special F/X Power Driven

Power Driven is Level Three of the Power Zone insert. Inserted 1:69, the set features the top 10 power hitters from Power Zone Level Two. The cards feature gold Light F/X technology.

		MT
Complete Set (10):		150.00
Common Player:		4.00
Inserted 1:69		
PZ1	Frank Thomas	15.00
PZ2	Juan Gonzalez	10.00
PZ3	Mike Piazza	25.00
PZ4	Larry Walker	5.00
PZ5	Mark McGwire	40.00
PZ6	Jeff Bagwell	15.00
PZ7	Mo Vaughn	8.00
PZ8	Barry Bonds	10.00
PZ9	Tino Martinez	4.00
PZ10	Ken Griffey Jr.	40.00

1998 Upper Deck Special F/X Power Zone

Power Zone Level One is a 30-card insert seeded one per seven packs. The cards are printed using silver Light F/X technology.

		MT
Complete Set (20):		50.00
Common Player:		.75
Inserted 1:7		
PZ1	Jose Cruz Jr.	1.00
PZ2	Frank Thomas	4.00
PZ3	Juan Gonzalez	3.00
PZ4	Mike Piazza	6.00
PZ5	Mark McGwire	10.00
PZ6	Barry Bonds	3.00
PZ7	Greg Maddux	6.00
PZ8	Alex Rodriguez	8.00
PZ9	Nomar Garciaparra	6.00
PZ10	Ken Griffey Jr.	10.00
PZ11	John Smoltz	.75
PZ12	Andruw Jones	2.50
PZ13	Sandy Alomar Jr.	.75
PZ14	Roberto Alomar	2.00
PZ15	Chipper Jones	6.00
PZ16	Kenny Lofton	2.00
PZ17	Larry Walker	1.50
PZ18	Jeff Bagwell	4.00
PZ19	Mo Vaughn	2.00
PZ20	Tom Glavine	.75

1998 Upper Deck Special F/X Superstar Xcitement

Printed on Light F/X gold foil, this 10-card set features the same players as the Power Driven insert. This set is Power Zone Level Four and is sequentially numbered to 250.

		MT
Complete Set (10):		450.00
Common Player:		10.00
Production 250 sets		
PZ1	Jose Cruz Jr.	10.00
PZ2	Frank Thomas	30.00
PZ3	Juan Gonzalez	25.00
PZ4	Mike Piazza	60.00
PZ5	Mark McGwire	100.00
PZ6	Barry Bonds	25.00
PZ7	Greg Maddux	50.00
PZ8	Alex Rodriguez	80.00
PZ9	Nomar Garciaparra	60.00
PZ10	Ken Griffey Jr.	80.00

1998 UD Retro

The 129-card set is comprised of 99 regular player cards and 30 Futurama subset cards. Card fronts have a white border encasing the player photo. Retro is packaged in a lunchbox featuring one of six players. Each lunchbox contains 24 six-card packs.

		MT
Complete Set (129):		50.00
Common Player:		.15
Pack (6):		5.00
Wax Box (24):		100.00
1	Jim Edmonds	.25
2	Darin Erstad	.40
3	Tim Salmon	.50
4	Jay Bell	.15
5	Matt Williams	.45
6	Andres Galarraga	.75
7	Andruw Jones	.75
8	Chipper Jones	2.50
9	Greg Maddux	2.00
10	Rafael Palmeiro	.50
11	Cal Ripken Jr.	3.00
12	Brooks Robinson	.50
13	Nomar Garciaparra	3.00
14	Pedro Martinez	1.00
15	Mo Vaughn	.60
16	Ernie Banks	.60
17	Mark Grace	.40
18	Gary Matthews	.15
19	Sammy Sosa	3.00
20	Albert Belle	.75
21	Carlton Fisk	.30
22	Frank Thomas	1.00
23	Ken Griffey Sr.	.15
24	Paul Konerko	.30
25	Barry Larkin	.35
26	Sean Casey	.75
27	Tony Perez	.25
28	Bob Feller	.25
29	Kenny Lofton	.60
30	Manny Ramirez	1.00
31	Jim Thome	.60
32	Omar Vizquel	.15
33	Dante Bichette	.40
34	Larry Walker	.75
35	Tony Clark	.50
36	Damion Easley	.15
37	Cliff Floyd	.15
38	Livan Hernandez	.15
39	Jeff Bagwell	1.00
40	Craig Biggio	.40
41	Al Kaline	.30
42	Johnny Damon	.15
43	Dean Palmer	.15
44	Charles Johnson	.15
45	Eric Karros	.15
46	Gaylord Perry	.15
47	Raul Mondesi	.30
48	Gary Sheffield	.30
49	Eddie Mathews	.50
50	Warren Spahn	.50
51	Jeromy Burnitz	.15
52	Jeff Cirillo	.15
53	Marquis Grissom	.15
54	Paul Molitor	.75
55	Kirby Puckett	1.00
56	Brad Radke	.15
57	Todd Walker	.25
58	Vladimir Guerrero	2.00
59	Brad Fullmer	.40
60	Rondell White	.25
61	Bobby Jones	.15
62	Hideo Nomo	.50
63	Mike Piazza	2.50
64	Tom Seaver	.50
65	Frank J. Thomas	.30
66	Yogi Berra	.60
67	Derek Jeter	2.50
68	Tino Martinez	.30
69	Paul O'Neill	.30
70	Andy Pettitte	.45
71	Rollie Fingers	.15
72	Rickey Henderson	.40
73	Matt Stairs	.15
74	Scott Rolen	1.00
75	Curt Schilling	.25
76	Jose Guillen	.15
77	Jason Kendall	.15
78	Lou Brock	.35
79	Bob Gibson	.50
80	Ray Lankford	.15
81	Mark McGwire	4.00
83	Kevin Brown	.25
84	Ken Caminiti	.25
85	Tony Gwynn	2.00
86	Greg Vaughn	.25
87	Barry Bonds	1.00
88	Willie Stargell	.50
89	Willie McCovey	.40
90	Ken Griffey Jr.	4.00
91	Randy Johnson	.60
92	Alex Rodriguez	3.00
93	Quinton McCracken	.15
94	Fred McGriff	.30
95	Juan Gonzalez	1.00
96	Ivan Rodriguez	1.00
97	Nolan Ryan	3.00
98	Jose Canseco	1.00
99	Roger Clemens	1.50
100	Jose Cruz Jr.	.50
101	*Justin Baughman*	.50
102	*David Dellucci* (Futurama)	.75
103	Travis Lee (Futurama)	.50
104	*Troy Glaus* (Futurama)	5.00
105	Kerry Wood (Futurama)	1.00
106	Mike Caruso (Futurama)	.15
107	*Jim Parque* (Futurama)	.50
108	Brett Tomko (Futurama)	.15
109	Russell Branyan (Futurama)	.15
110	Jaret Wright (Futurama)	.25
111	Todd Helton (Futurama)	1.00
112	Gabe Alvarez (Futurama)	.15
113	*Matt Anderson* (Futurama)	.50
114	Alex Gonzalez (Futurama)	.15
115	Mark Kotsay (Futurama)	.30
116	Derrek Lee (Futurama)	.15
117	Richard Hidalgo (Futurama)	.15
118	Adrian Beltre (Futurama)	1.00
119	Geoff Jenkins (Futurama)	.15
120	Eric Milton (Futurama)	.15
121	Brad Fullmer (Futurama)	.25
122	Vladimir Guerrero (Futurama)	1.50
123	Carl Pavano (Futurama)	.15
124	*Orlando Hernandez* (Futurama)	2.00
125	Ben Grieve (Futurama)	.50
126	A.J. Hinch (Futurama)	.15
127	Matt Clement (Futurama)	.15
128	*Gary Matthews Jr.* (Futurama)	.50
129	Aramis Ramirez (Futurama)	.40
130	Rolando Arrojo (Futurama)	.75

1998 UD Retro Big Boppers

The game's heavy hitters are the focus of this insert set. Cards have a color action photo on a sepia background. Each card is individually serial numbered in red foil in the upper-right, within an edition of 500. Backs repeat part of the front photo, in sepia only, and have recent stats and hitting highlights. Cards are numbered with a "B" prefix.

		MT
Complete Set (30):		325.00
Common Player:		5.00
Production 500 sets		
B1	Darin Erstad	5.00
B2	Rafael Palmeiro	8.00
B3	Cal Ripken Jr.	30.00
B4	Nomar Garciaparra	25.00
B5	Mo Vaughn	6.00
B6	Frank Thomas	15.00
B7	Albert Belle	6.00
B8	Jim Thome	6.00
B9	Manny Ramirez	10.00
B10	Tony Clark	4.00
B11	Tino Martinez	4.00
B12	Ben Grieve	5.00
B13	Ken Griffey Jr.	30.00
B14	Alex Rodriguez	30.00
B15	Jay Buhner	4.00
B16	Juan Gonzalez	10.00
B17	Jose Cruz Jr.	4.00
B18	Jose Canseco	8.00
B19	Travis Lee	4.00
B20	Chipper Jones	20.00
B21	Andres Galarraga	6.00
B22	Andruw Jones	10.00
B23	Sammy Sosa	20.00
B24	Vinny Castilla	4.00
B25	Larry Walker	6.00
B26	Jeff Bagwell	10.00
B27	Gary Sheffield	6.00
B28	Mike Piazza	25.00
B29	Mark McGwire	40.00
B30	Barry Bonds	10.00

1998 UD Retro Groovy Kind of Glove

This 30-card set showcases baseball's top defensive players on a psychadelic, wavy and colorful background. They were inserted 1:7 packs.

		MT
Complete Set (30):		125.00
Common Player:		1.50
Inserted 1:7		
G1	Roberto Alomar	3.00
G2	Cal Ripken Jr.	12.00
G3	Nomar Garciaparra	10.00
G4	Frank Thomas	6.00
G5	Robin Ventura	1.50
G6	Omar Vizquel	1.50
G7	Kenny Lofton	2.00
G8	Ben Grieve	2.50
G9	Alex Rodriguez	12.00
G10	Ken Griffey Jr.	15.00
G11	Ivan Rodriguez	5.00
G12	Travis Lee	2.50
G13	Matt Williams	2.00
G14	Greg Maddux	8.00
G15	Andres Galarraga	3.00
G16	Andruw Jones	4.00
G17	Kerry Wood	4.00
G18	Mark Grace	2.00
G19	Craig Biggio	2.00
G20	Charles Johnson	1.50
G21	Raul Mondesi	2.00
G22	Mike Piazza	10.00
G23	Rey Ordonez	1.50
G24	Derek Jeter	10.00
G25	Scott Rolen	4.00
G26	Mark McGwire	15.00
G27	Ken Caminiti	2.00
G28	Tony Gwynn	8.00
G29	J.T. Snow	1.50
G30	Barry Bonds	4.00

1998 UD Retro Lunchbox

Lunchboxes were the form of packaging for UD Retro. Six different players are featured with each lunchbox containing 24 six-card packs, with a SRP of $4.99.

	MT
Complete Set (6):	55.00
Common Lunchbox:	5.00
Nomar Garciaparra	10.00
Ken Griffey Jr.	12.00
Chipper Jones	8.00
Travis Lee	5.00
Mark McGwire	15.00
Cal Ripken Jr.	12.00

1998 UD Retro New Frontier

This 30-card set spotlights 30 of baseball's top young prospects and is limited to 1,000 sequentially numbered sets.

		MT
Complete Set (30):		80.00
Common Player:		2.00
Production 1,000 sets		
NF1	Justin Baughman	2.00
NF2	David Dellucci	2.00
NF3	Travis Lee	2.00
NF4	Troy Glaus	15.00
NF5	Mike Caruso	2.00
NF6	Jim Parque	2.00
NF7	Kerry Wood	4.00
NF8	Brett Tomko	2.00
NF9	Russell Branyan	3.00
NF10	Jaret Wright	2.00
NF11	Todd Helton	8.00
NF12	Gabe Alvarez	2.00
NF13	Matt Anderson	2.00
NF14	Alex Gonzalez	2.00
NF15	Mark Kotsay	2.00
NF16	Derrek Lee	2.00
NF17	Richard Hidalgo	3.00
NF18	Adrian Beltre	4.00
NF19	Geoff Jenkins	3.00
NF20	Eric Milton	2.00
NF21	Brad Fullmer	3.00
NF22	Vladimir Guerrero	15.00
NF23	Carl Pavano	2.00
NF24	Orlando Hernandez	5.00
NF25	Ben Grieve	3.00
NF26	A.J. Hinch	2.00
NF27	Matt Clement	2.00
NF28	Gary Matthews	2.00
NF29	Aramis Ramirez	2.00
NF30	Rolando Arrojo	2.00

1998 UD Retro Quantum Leap

This 30-card insert set highlights the technology advancements of current Upper Deck products on a horizontal format. A total of 500 serially numbered sets were produced.

		MT
Common Player:		25.00
Production 50 sets		
Q1	Darin Erstad	50.00
Q2	Cal Ripken Jr.	200.00
Q3	Nomar Garciaparra	150.00
Q4	Frank Thomas	100.00
Q5	Kenny Lofton	40.00
Q6	Ben Grieve	30.00
Q7	Ken Griffey Jr.	200.00
Q8	Alex Rodriguez	200.00
Q9	Juan Gonzalez	70.00
Q10	Jose Cruz Jr.	40.00
Q11	Roger Clemens	100.00
Q12	Travis Lee	25.00
Q13	Chipper Jones	125.00
Q14	Greg Maddux	125.00
Q15	Kerry Wood	40.00
Q16	Jeff Bagwell	70.00
Q17	Mike Piazza	150.00
Q18	Scott Rolen	50.00
Q19	Mark McGwire	250.00
Q20	Tony Gwynn	100.00
Q21	Larry Walker	40.00
Q22	Derek Jeter	200.00
Q23	Sammy Sosa	125.00
Q24	Barry Bonds	70.00
Q25	Mo Vaughn	50.00
Q26	Roberto Alomar	60.00
Q27	Todd Helton	75.00
Q28	Ivan Rodriguez	70.00
Q29	Vladimir Guerrero	100.00
Q30	Albert Belle	50.00

1998 UD Retro Sign of the Times

This retor-style autographed set featured both retired legends and current players. They were inserted 1:36 packs.

		MT
Common Autograph:		20.00
Inserted 1:36		
EB	Ernie Banks (300)	65.00
YB	Yogi Berra (150)	100.00
RB	Russell Branyan (750)	20.00
LB	Lou Brock (300)	60.00
JC	Jose Cruz Jr. (300)	30.00
RF	Rollie Fingers (600)	30.00
BF	Bob Feller (600)	40.00
CF	Carlton Fisk (600)	50.00
BGi	Bob Gibson (300)	60.00
BGr	Ben Grieve (300)	40.00
KGj	Ken Griffey Jr. (100)	600.00
KGs	Ken Griffey Sr. (600)	30.00
JG	Jose Guillen	20.00
TG	Tony Gwynn (200)	150.00
AK	Al Kaline (600)	50.00
PK	Paul Konerko (750)	20.00
TLe	Travis Lee (300)	25.00
EM	Eddie Mathews (600)	50.00
GMj	Gary Matthews Jr. (750)	20.00
GMs	Gary Matthews (600)	20.00
WM	Willie McCovey (600)	50.00
TP	Tony Perez (600)	40.00
GP	Gaylord Perry (1,000)	35.00
KP	Kirby Puckett (450)	100.00
BR	Brooks Robinson (300)	60.00
SR	Scott Rolen (300)	60.00
NR	Nolan Ryan (500)	250.00
TS	Tom Seaver (300)	80.00
WS	Warren Spahn (600)	50.00
WiS	Willie Stargell (600)	40.00
FT	Frank Thomas (600)	50.00
KW	Kerry Wood (200)	60.00

1998 UD Retro 1990s Time Capsule

Another retro-styled card that featured current stars who were destined to earn a place in baseball history. They were inserted 1:2 packs.

		MT
Complete Set (50):		75.00
Common Player:		.50
Inserted 1:2		
TC1	Mike Mussina	1.50
TC2	Rafael Palmeiro	1.50
TC3	Cal Ripken Jr.	6.00
TC4	Nomar Garciaparra	5.00
TC5	Pedro Martinez	2.00
TC6	Mo Vaughn	1.00
TC7	Albert Belle	1.00
TC8	Frank Thomas	3.00
TC9	David Justice	1.00
TC10	Kenny Lofton	1.50
TC11	Manny Ramirez	2.00
TC12	Jim Thome	1.50
TC13	Derek Jeter	6.00
TC14	Tino Martinez	.50
TC15	Ben Grieve	.75
TC16	Rickey Henderson	1.00
TC17	Ken Griffey Jr.	6.00
TC18	Randy Johnson	2.00
TC19	Alex Rodriguez	6.00
TC20	Wade Boggs	1.50
TC21	Fred McGriff	.75
TC22	Juan Gonzalez	2.00
TC23	Ivan Rodriguez	2.00
TC24	Nolan Ryan	8.00
TC25	Jose Canseco	1.50
TC26	Roger Clemens	3.00
TC27	Jose Cruz Jr.	.50
TC28	Travis Lee	.50
TC29	Matt Williams	1.00
TC30	Andres Galarraga	1.50
TC31	Andruw Jones	2.00
TC32	Chipper Jones	4.00
TC33	Greg Maddux	4.00
TC34	Kerry Wood	1.00
TC35	Barry Larkin	1.00
TC36	Dante Bichette	.50
TC37	Larry Walker	1.50
TC38	Livan Hernandez	.50
TC39	Jeff Bagwell	2.00
TC40	Craig Biggio	.75
TC41	Charles Johnson	.50
TC42	Gary Sheffield	1.00
TC43	Marquis Grissom	.50

TC44 Mike Piazza 5.00
TC45 Scott Rolen 1.50
TC46 Curt Schilling .50
TC47 Mark McGwire 8.00
TC48 Ken Caminiti .50
TC49 Tony Gwynn 3.00
TC50 Barry Bonds 2.00

1999 Upper Deck

Released in two series, card fronts feature a textured silver border along the left and right sides of the base card. The player name and Upper Deck logo also are stamped with silver foil. Card backs have a small photo, with year by year stats and a brief highlight caption of the player's career. Randomly seeded in packs are 100 Ken Griffey Jr. rookie cards that were bought back by Upper Deck from the hobby and autographed by Griffey Jr. Upper Deck also re-inserted one pack of '89 Upper Deck inside every hobby box. 10-card hobby packs carry a S.R.P. of $2.99.

	MT
Complete Set (525):	90.00
Complete Series 1 (255):	50.00
Complete Series 2 (270):	40.00
Common Player:	.10
Common SR (1-18):	.50
Exclusive Stars/RCs:	20X
Production 100 each	
Pack (10):	3.00
Wax Box (24):	70.00

1 Troy Glaus (Star Rookies) 3.00
2 Adrian Beltre (Star Rookies) 1.00
3 Matt Anderson (Star Rookies) .50
4 Eric Chavez (Star Rookies) 3.00
5 Jin Cho (Star Rookies) .50
6 *Robert Smith* (Star Rookies) .50
7 George Lombard (Star Rookies) 1.00
8 Mike Kinkade (Star Rookies) .75
9 Seth Greisinger (Star Rookies) .50
10 J.D. Drew (Star Rookies) .75
11 Aramis Ramirez (Star Rookies) .75
12 Carlos Guillen (Star Rookies) .50
13 Justin Baughman (Star Rookies) .50
14 Jim Parque (Star Rookies) .50
15 Ryan Jackson (Star Rookies) .50
16 Ramon Martinez (Star Rookies) .50
17 Orlando Hernandez (Star Rookies) 3.00
18 Jeremy Giambi (Star Rookies) 1.00
19 Gary DiSarcina .10
20 Darin Erstad .75
21 Troy Glaus 1.00
22 Chuck Finley .10
23 Dave Hollins .10
24 Troy Percival .10
25 Tim Salmon .25
26 Brian Anderson .10
27 Jay Bell .10
28 Andy Benes .10
29 Brent Brede .10
30 David Dellucci .10
31 Karim Garcia .10
32 Travis Lee .75
33 Andres Galarraga .30
34 Ryan Klesko .25
35 Keith Lockhart .10
36 Kevin Millwood .40
37 Denny Neagle .10
38 John Smoltz .25
39 Michael Tucker .10
40 Walt Weiss .10
41 Dennis Martinez .10
42 Javy Lopez .10
43 Brady Anderson .10
44 Harold Baines .10
45 Mike Bordick .10
46 Roberto Alomar .50
47 Scott Erickson .10
48 Mike Mussina .50
49 Cal Ripken Jr. 2.50
50 Darren Bragg .10
51 Dennis Eckersley .10
52 Nomar Garciaparra 2.00
53 Scott Hatteberg .10
54 Troy O'Leary .10
55 Bret Saberhagen .10
56 John Valentin .10
57 Rod Beck .10
58 Jeff Blauser .10
59 Brant Brown .10
60 Mark Clark .10
61 Mark Grace .25
62 Kevin Tapani .10
63 Henry Rodriguez .10
64 Mike Cameron .10
65 Mike Caruso .10
66 Ray Durham .10
67 Jaime Navarro .10
68 Magglio Ordonez .25
69 Mike Sirotka .10
70 Sean Casey .20
71 Barry Larkin .25
72 Jon Nunnally .10
73 Paul Konerko .25
74 Chris Stynes .10
75 Brett Tomko .10
76 Dmitri Young .10
77 Sandy Alomar .10
78 Bartolo Colon .10
79 Travis Fryman .10
80 Brian Giles .10
81 David Justice .25
82 Omar Vizquel .10
83 Jaret Wright .50
84 Jim Thome .40
85 Charles Nagy .10
86 Pedro Astacio .10
87 Todd Helton .75
88 Darryl Kile .10
89 Mike Lansing .10
90 Neifi Perez .10
91 John Thomson .10
92 Larry Walker .40
93 Tony Clark .40
94 Deivi Cruz .10
95 Damion Easley .10
96 Brian L. Hunter .10
97 Todd Jones .10
98 Brian Moehler .10
99 Gabe Alvarez .10
100 Craig Counsell .10
101 Cliff Floyd .10
102 Livan Hernandez .10
103 Andy Larkin .10
104 Derrek Lee .10
105 Brian Meadows .10
106 Moises Alou .25
107 Sean Berry .10
108 Craig Biggio .25
109 Ricky Gutierrez .10
110 Mike Hampton .10
111 Jose Lima .10
112 Billy Wagner .10
113 Hal Morris .10
114 Johnny Damon .10
115 Jeff King .10
116 Jeff Montgomery .10
117 Glendon Rusch .10
118 Larry Sutton .10
119 Bobby Bonilla .20
120 Jim Eisenreich .10
121 Eric Karros .20
122 Matt Luke .10
123 Ramon Martinez .20
124 Gary Sheffield .25
125 Eric Young .10
126 Charles Johnson .10
127 Jeff Cirillo .10
128 Marquis Grissom .10
129 Jeremy Burnitz .10
130 Bob Wickman .10
131 Scott Karl .10
132 Mark Loretta .10
133 Fernando Vina .10
134 Matt Lawton .10
135 Pat Meares .10
136 Eric Milton .10
137 Paul Molitor .50
138 David Ortiz .10
139 Todd Walker .25
140 Shane Andrews .10
141 Brad Fullmer .25
142 Vladimir Guerrero 1.50
143 Dustin Hermanson .10
144 Ryan McGuire .10
145 Ugueth Urbina .10
146 John Franco .10
147 Butch Huskey .10
148 Bobby Jones .10
149 John Olerud .25
150 Rey Ordonez .10
151 Mike Piazza 2.00
152 Hideo Nomo .40
153 Masato Yoshii .10
154 Derek Jeter 2.00
155 Chuck Knoblauch .25
156 Paul O'Neill .25
157 Andy Pettitte .50
158 Mariano Rivera .20
159 Darryl Strawberry .25
160 David Wells .20
161 Jorge Posada .20
162 Ramiro Mendoza .20
163 Miguel Tejada .25
164 Ryan Christenson .10
165 Rickey Henderson .40
166 A.J. Hinch .10
167 Ben Grieve .75
168 Kenny Rogers .10
169 Matt Stairs .10
170 Bob Abreu .10
171 Rico Brogna .10
172 Doug Glanville .10
173 Mike Grace .10
174 Desi Relaford .10
175 Scott Rolen .75
176 Jose Guillen .20
177 Francisco Cordova .10
178 Al Martin .10
179 Jason Schmidt .10
180 Turner Ward .10
181 Kevin Young .10
182 Mark McGwire 3.00
183 Delino DeShields .10
184 Eli Marrero .10
185 Tom Lampkin .10
186 Ray Lankford .10
187 Willie McGee .10
188 Matt Morris .10
189 Andy Ashby .10
190 Kevin Brown .20
191 Ken Caminiti .20
192 Trevor Hoffman .10
193 Wally Joyner .10
194 Greg Vaughn .20
195 Danny Darwin .10
196 Shawn Estes .10
197 Orel Hershiser .10
198 Jeff Kent .10
199 Bill Mueller .10
200 Robb Nen .10
201 J.T. Snow .10
202 Ken Cloude .10
203 Russ Davis .10
204 Jeff Fassero .10
205 Ken Griffey Jr. 3.00
206 Shane Monahan .10
207 David Segui .10
208 Dan Wilson .10
209 Wilson Alvarez .10
210 Wade Boggs .25
211 Miguel Cairo .10
212 Bubba Trammell .10
213 Quinton McCracken .10
214 Paul Sorrento .10
215 Kevin Stocker .10
216 Will Clark .25
217 Rusty Greer .10
218 Rick Helling .10
219 Mike McLemore .10
220 Ivan Rodriguez .75
221 John Wetteland .10
222 Jose Canseco .60
223 Roger Clemens 1.50
224 Carlos Delgado .75
225 Darrin Fletcher .10
226 Alex Gonzalez .10
227 Jose Cruz Jr. .50
228 Shannon Stewart .10
229 Rolando Arrojo (Foreign Focus) .20
230 Livan Hernandez (Foreign Focus) .10
231 Orlando Hernandez (Foreign Focus) 1.00
232 Raul Mondesi (Foreign Focus) .20
233 Moises Alou (Foreign Focus) .20
234 Pedro Martinez (Foreign Focus) .75
235 Sammy Sosa (Foreign Focus) 1.25
236 Vladimir Guerrero (Foreign Focus) .75
237 Bartolo Colon (Foreign Focus) .10
238 Miguel Tejada (Foreign Focus) .10
239 Ismael Valdes (Foreign Focus) .10
240 Mariano Rivera (Foreign Focus) .10
241 Jose Cruz Jr. (Foreign Focus) .25
242 Juan Gonzalez (Foreign Focus) .50
243 Ivan Rodriguez (Foreign Focus) .40
244 Sandy Alomar (Foreign Focus) .10
245 Roberto Alomar (Foreign Focus) .25
246 Magglio Ordonez (Foreign Focus) .20
247 Kerry Wood (Highlights Checklist) .75
248 Mark McGwire (Highlights Checklist) 2.00
249 David Wells (Highlights Checklist) .10
250 Rolando Arrojo (Highlights Checklist) .20
251 Ken Griffey Jr. (Highlights Checklist) 1.50
252 Trevor Hoffman (Highlights Checklist) .10
253 Travis Lee (Highlights Checklist) .40
254 Roberto Alomar (Highlights Checklist) .25
255 Sammy Sosa (Highlights Checklist) 1.25
266 *Pat Burrell* (Star Rookie) 5.00
267 *Shea Hillenbrand* (Star Rookie) .50
268 Robert Fick (Star Rookie) .10
269 Roy Halladay (Star Rookie) .25
270 Ruben Mateo (Star Rookie) .50
271 Bruce Chen (Star Rookie) .25
272 Angel Pena (Star Angel) .75
273 Michael Barrett (Star Rookie) .50
274 Kevin Witt (Star Rookie) .10
275 Damon Minor (Star Rookie) .10
276 Ryan Minor (Star Rookie) .40
277 A.J. Pierzynski (Star Rookie) .10
278 *A.J. Burnett* (Star Rookie) 2.00

279 Dermal Brown (Star Rookie) .10
280 Joe Lawrence (Star Rookie) .10
281 Derrick Gibson (Star Rookie) .10
282 Carlos Febles (Star Rookie) .75
283 Chris Haas (Star Rookie) .10
284 Cesar King (Star Rookie) .10
285 Calvin Pickering (Star Rookie) .10
286 Mitch Meluskey (Star Rookie) .15
287 Carlos Beltran (Star Rookie) .25
288 Ron Belliard (Star Rookie) .25
289 Jerry Hairston Jr. (Star Rookie) .10
290 Fernando Seguignol (Star Rookie) .50
291 Kris Benson (Star Rookie) .10
292 *Chad Hutchinson* (Star Rookie) 2.50
293 Jarrod Washburn .10
294 Jason Dickson .10
295 Mo Vaughn .75
296 Garrett Anderson .10
297 Jim Edmonds .10
298 Ken Hill .10
299 Shigetosi Hasegawa .10
300 Todd Stottlemyre .10
301 Randy Johnson .50
302 Omar Daal .10
303 Steve Finley .10
304 Matt Williams .25
305 Danny Klassen .10
306 Tony Batista .10
307 Brian Jordan .10
308 Greg Maddux 2.00
309 Chipper Jones 1.50
310 Bret Boone .10
311 Ozzie Guillen .10
312 John Rocker .10
313 Tom Glavine .20
314 Andruw Jones .75
315 Albert Belle .75
316 Charles Johnson .10
317 Will Clark .40
318 B.J. Surhoff .10
319 Delino DeShields .10
320 Heathcliff Slocumb .10
321 Sidney Ponson .10
322 Juan Guzman .10
323 Reggie Jefferson .10
324 Mark Portugal .10
325 Tim Wakefield .10
326 Jason Varitek .10
327 Jose Offerman .10
328 Pedro Martinez .75
329 Trot Nixon .10
330 Kerry Wood .40
331 Sammy Sosa 2.00
332 Glenallen Hill .10
333 Gary Gaetti .10
334 Mickey Morandini .10
335 Benito Santiago .10
336 Jeff Blauser .10
337 Frank Thomas 1.00
338 Paul Konerko .10
339 Jaime Navarro .10
340 Carlos Lee .10
341 Brian Simmons .10
342 Mark Johnson .10
343 Jeff Abbot .10
344 Steve Avery .10
345 Mike Cameron .10
346 Michael Tucker .10
347 Greg Vaughn .10
348 Hal Morris .10
349 Pete Harnisch .10
350 Denny Neagle .10
351 Manny Ramirez 1.00
352 Roberto Alomar .50
353 Dwight Gooden .10
354 Kenny Lofton .75
355 Mike Jackson .10
356 Charles Nagy .10
357 Enrique Wilson .10
358 Russ Branyan .10
359 Richie Sexson .10
360 Vinny Castilla .20
361 Dante Bichette .30
362 Kirt Manwaring .10
363 Darryl Hamilton .10
364 Jamey Wright .10
365 Curt Leskanic .10
366 Jeff Reed .10
367 Bobby Higginson .10
368 Justin Thompson .10
369 Brad Ausmus .10
370 Dean Palmer .10
371 Gabe Kapler 1.50
372 Juan Encarnacion .10
373 Karim Garcia .10
374 Alex Gonzalez .10
375 Braden Looper .10
376 Preston Wilson .10
377 Todd Dunwoody .10
378 Alex Fernandez .10
379 Mark Kotsay .10
380 Mark Mantei .10
381 Ken Caminiti .10
382 Scott Elarton .10
383 Jeff Bagwell .75
384 Derek Bell .10
385 Ricky Gutierrez .10
386 Richard Hildalgo .10
387 Shane Reynolds .10
388 Carl Everett .10
389 Scott Service .10
390 Jeff Suppan .10
391 Joe Randa .10
392 Kevin Appier .10
393 Shane Halter .10
394 Chad Kreuter .10
395 Mike Sweeney .10
396 Kevin Brown .25
397 Devon White .10
398 Todd Hollandsworth .10
399 Todd Hundley .10
400 Chan Ho Park .20
401 Mark Grudzielanek .10
402 Raul Mondesi .25
403 Ismael Valdes .10
404 Rafael Roque .10
405 Sean Berry .10
406 Kevin Barker .10
407 Dave Nilsson .10
408 Geoff Jenkins .10
409 Jim Abbott .10
410 Bobby Hughes .10
411 Corey Koskie .10
412 Rick Aguilera .10
413 LaTroy Hawkins .10
414 Ron Coomer .10
415 Denny Hocking .10
416 Marty Cordova .10
417 Terry Steinbach .10
418 Rondell White .20
419 Wilton Guerrero .10
420 Shane Andrews .10
421 Orlando Cabrerra .10
422 Carl Pavano .10
423 Jeff Vasquez .10
424 Chris Widger .10
425 Robin Ventura .20
426 Rickey Henderson .20
427 Al Leiter .20
428 Bobby Jones .10
429 Brian McRae .10
430 Roger Cedeno .10
431 Bobby Bonilla .10
432 Edgardo Alfonzo .10
433 Bernie Williams .50
434 Ricky Ledee .10
435 Chili Davis .10
436 Tino Martinez .40
437 Scott Brosius .10
438 David Cone .20
439 Joe Girardi .10
440 Roger Clemens 1.00
441 Chad Curtis .10
442 Hideki Irabu .10
443 Jason Giambi .10
444 Scott Spezio .10
445 Tony Phillips .10
446 Ramon Hernandez .10
447 Mike Macfarlane .10
448 Tom Candiotti .10
449 Billy Taylor .10
450 Bobby Estella .10
451 Curt Schilling .20
452 Carlton Loewer .10
453 Marlon Anderson .10
454 Kevin Jordan .10
455 Ron Gant .10
456 Chad Ogea .10
457 Abraham Nunez .10
458 Jason Kendall .20
459 Pat Meares .10
460 Brant Brown .10
461 Brian Giles .10
462 Chad Hermansen .10
463 Freddy Garcia 3.00
464 Edgar Renteria .10
465 Fernando Tatis .10
466 Eric Davis .10
467 Darren Bragg .10
468 Donovan Osborne .10
469 Manny Aybar .10
470 Jose Jimenez .10
471 Kent Mercker .10
472 Reggie Sanders .10
473 Ruben Rivera .10
474 Tony Gwynn 1.50
475 Jim Leyritz .10
476 Chris Gomez .10
477 Matt Clement .10
478 Carlos Hernandez .10
479 Sterling Hitchcock .10
480 Ellis Burks .10
481 Barry Bonds .75
482 Marvin Bernard .10
483 Kirk Rueter .10
484 F.P. Santangelo .10
485 Stan Javier .10
486 Jeff Kent .10
487 Alex Rodriguez 2.50
488 Tom Lampkin .10
489 Jose Mesa .10
490 Jay Buhner .20
491 Edgar Martinez .10
492 Butch Huskey .10
493 John Mabry .10
494 Jamie Moyer .10
495 Roberto Hernandez .10
496 Tony Saunders .10
497 Fred McGriff .25
498 Dave Martinez .10
499 Jose Canseco .60
500 Rolando Arrojo .10
501 Esteban Yan .10
502 Juan Gonzalez 1.00
503 Rafael Palmeiro .40
504 Aaron Sele .10
505 Royce Clayton .10
506 Todd Zeile .10
507 Tom Goodwin .10
508 Lee Stevens .10
509 Esteban Loaiza .10
510 Joey Hamilton .10
511 Homer Bush .10
512 Willie Greene .10
513 Shawn Green .50
514 David Wells .10
515 Kelvim Escobar .10
516 Tony Fernandez .10
517 Pat Hentgen .10
518 Mark McGwire 3.00
519 Ken Griffey Jr. 1.50
520 Sammy Sosa 1.00
521 Juan Gonzalez .50
522 J.D. Drew .30
523 Chipper Jones .75
524 Alex Rodriguez 1.25
525 Mike Piazza 1.00
526 Nomar Garciaparra 1.00
527 Season Highlights Checklist (Mark McGwire) 2.00
528 Season Highlights Checklist (Sammy Sosa) 1.00
529 Season Highlights Checklist (Scott Brosius) .10
530 Season Highlights Checklist (Cal Ripken Jr.) 1.00
531 Season Highlights Checklist (Barry Bonds) .40
532 Season Highlights Checklist (Roger Clemens) .50
533 Season Highlights Checklist (Ken Griffey Jr.) 1.50
534 Season Highlights Checklist (Alex Rodriguez) 1.00
535 Season Highlights Checklist (Curt Schilling) .10

1999 Upper Deck Exclusives

Randomly inserted into hobby packs, this parallel issue is individually serial numbered on back from within an edition of 100 of each card. Besides the serial number, the inserts are readily apparent by the use of copper metallic foil graphic highlights on front. A parallel of this parallel with only one card of each player, was also issued but is not priced here because of rarity. Series 1 Exclusive cards have the serial number on back in gold foil; Series 2 Exclusives have the number ink-jetted in black.

	MT
Common Player:	5.00
Stars:	15X
Rookies:	8X

(See 1999 Upper Deck for checklist, base card values.)

1999 Upper Deck Crowning Glory

These double-sided cards feature players who reached milestones during the '98 season. There are three cards in the set, with four different versions of each card. The regular version is seeded 1:23 packs. Doubles are numbered to 1,000, Triples numbered to 25 and Home Runs are limited to one each.

	MT
Complete Set (3):	60.00
Common Player:	10.00
Inserted 1:23	
Doubles (1,000 sets):	2X
Triples (25 sets):	8X
Home Runs (1 set):	
Values Undetermined	

CG1	Roger Clemens, Kerry Wood	15.00
CG2	Mark McGwire, Barry Bonds	25.00
CG3	Ken Griffey Jr., Mark McGwire	30.00

1999 Upper Deck Game Jersey-Hobby

This six-card set features a swatch of game-used jersey on each card and are available exclusively in hobby packs. The insert ratio is 1:288 packs.

		MT
Common Player:		30.00
Inserted 1:288		
GJKG	Ken Griffey Jr.	250.00
GJAB	Adrian Beltre	40.00
GJBG	Ben Grieve	40.00
GJTL	Travis Lee	30.00
GJIV	Ivan Rodriguez	60.00
GJDE	Darin Erstad	60.00
GJKGs	Ken Griffey Jr. Auto./24 (autographed)	1500.
BF	Brad Fullmer	30.00
BT	Bubba Trammell	30.00
EC	Eric Chavez	30.00
JD	J.D. Drew	50.00
MR	Manny Ramirez	75.00
NRa	Nolan Ryan	200.00
TGw	Tony Gwynn	75.00
CJ	Chipper Jones	75.00
JDs	J.D. Drew (auto, 8)	
NRaS	Nolan Ryan (autographed edition of 34)	1800.
TH	Todd Helton	80.00

1999 Upper Deck Game Jersey

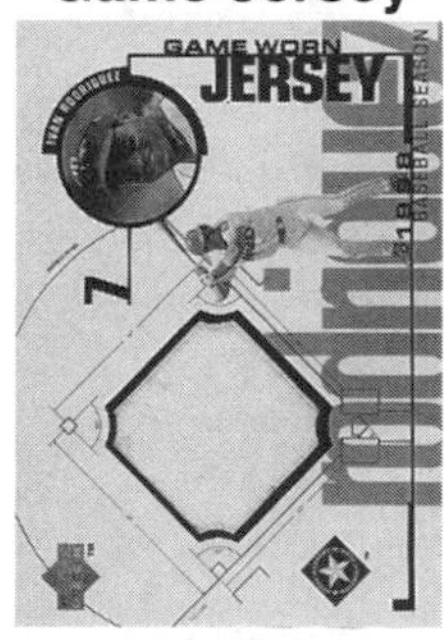

Inserted in both hobby and retail packs, this five-card set features a swatch of game-used jersey on each card. These are seeded 1:2,500 packs.

		MT
Complete Series 1 (5):		850.00
Complete Series 2 (4):		1100.
Common Player:		50.00
Inserted 1:2,500		
GJKW	Kerry Wood	60.00
GJCJ	Charles Johnson	50.00
GJMP	Mike Piazza	150.00
GJAR	Alex Rodriguez	200.00
GJJG	Juan Gonzalez	50.00
GJKWs	Kerry Wood Auto./34 (autographed)	500.00
GJKGs	Ken Griffey Jr. Auto./24	1500.
GM	Greg Maddux	125.00
JR	Ken Griffey Jr.	250.00
NRb	Nolan Ryan	250.00
FT	Frank Thomas	120.00
JRS	Ken Griffey Jr. Auto./24	1500.

1999 Upper Deck Babe Ruth Piece of History Bat

Limited to approximately 400, this unique card has a chip of a bat in it, from an actual game-used Louisville Slugger swung by the Bambino himself. A "signed" version of this card also exists, which incorporates both a cut signature of Ruth along with a piece of his game-used bat; only three exist.

	MT
Babe Ruth Piece of History:	1800.
Babe Ruth Legendary Cut:	27500.

(Production of bat-piece card reported as 400; Legendary Cut - only three.)

1999 Upper Deck Immaculate Perception

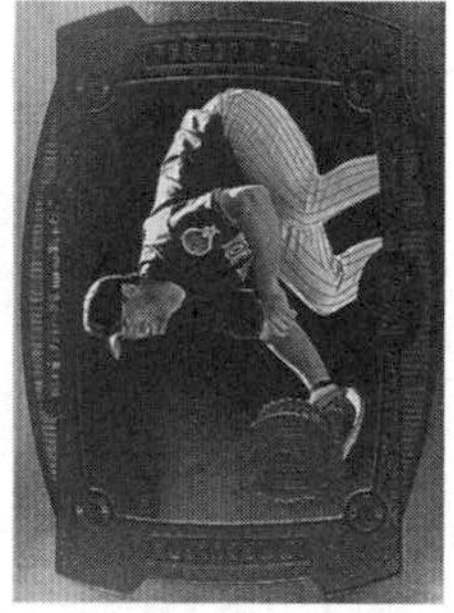

Done in a horizontal format, this 27-card set features baseball's most celebrated players. Card fronts are enhanced with copper and silver foil stamping, encasing the player's image. The cards are numbered with an I prefix and are seeded 1:23 packs. There are also three parallel versions: Doubles numbered to 1,000, Triples numbered to 25 and Home Runs which are limited to one.

		MT
Complete Set (27):		200.00
Common Player:		2.50
Inserted 1:23		
Doubles (1,000 sets):		1.5X
Triples (25 sets): 8X		
Home Runs (1 sets): Values Undetermined		
101	Jeff Bagwell	6.00
102	Craig Biggio	3.00
103	Barry Bonds	6.00
104	Roger Clemens	8.00
105	Jose Cruz Jr.	2.50
106	Nomar Garciaparra	15.00
107	Tony Clark	3.00
108	Ben Grieve	3.00
109	Ken Griffey Jr.	20.00
110	Tony Gwynn	8.00
111	Randy Johnson	5.00
112	Chipper Jones	12.00
113	Travis Lee	3.00
114	Kenny Lofton	4.00
115	Greg Maddux	12.00
116	Mark McGwire	25.00
117	Hideo Nomo	3.00
118	Mike Piazza	15.00
119	Manny Ramirez	6.00
120	Cal Ripken Jr.	20.00
121	Alex Rodriguez	20.00
122	Scott Rolen	5.00
123	Frank Thomas	8.00
124	Kerry Wood	4.00
125	Larry Walker	4.00
126	Vinny Castilla	2.50
127	Derek Jeter	20.00

1999 Upper Deck Wonder Years

These inserts look like a throwback to the groovin' '70s, with its bright, striped, green and pink border. "Wonder Years" is across the top of the card front in yellow lettering. Card backs have the player's three best seasons statistics along with a mention of a milestone. The cards are numbered with a WY prefix and are seeded 1:7 packs. There are three parallel versions: Doubles which are numbered to 1,000, Triples numbered to 25 and Home Runs which are limited to one.

		MT
Complete Set (30):		80.00
Common Player:		1.00
Inserted 1:7		
Doubles (2,000 sets):		2X
Triples (50 sets):		15X
Home Runs (1 set): Values Undetermined		
W01	Kerry Wood	2.00
W02	Travis Lee	1.25
W03	Jeff Bagwell	2.50
W04	Barry Bonds	2.50
W05	Roger Clemens	5.00
W06	Jose Cruz Jr.	1.00
W07	Andres Galarraga	1.25
W08	Nomar Garciaparra	7.50
W09	Juan Gonzalez	3.00
W10	Ken Griffey Jr.	10.00
W11	Tony Gwynn	5.00
W12	Derek Jeter	7.50
W13	Randy Johnson	1.50
W14	Andruw Jones	2.00
W15	Chipper Jones	7.50
W16	Kenny Lofton	1.50
W17	Greg Maddux	5.00
W18	Tino Martinez	1.00
W19	Mark McGwire	10.00
W20	Paul Molitor	1.50
W21	Mike Piazza	7.50
W22	Manny Ramirez	3.50
W23	Cal Ripken Jr.	8.00
W24	Alex Rodriguez	10.00
W25	Sammy Sosa	7.50
W26	Frank Thomas	3.50
W27	Mo Vaughn	1.50
W28	Larry Walker	1.25
W29	Scott Rolen	2.50
W30	Ben Grieve	1.25

1999 Upper Deck Forte

This 30-card set features the top players in the game, highlighted by blue holofoil treatment. Numbers on card backs have a "F" prefix and are seeded 1:23 packs. There are also die-cut parallels to Forte: Double, Triple and Home Run. Doubles are sequentially numbered to 2,000 sets, Triples are limited to 100 numbered sets and Home Runs are limited to 10 numbered sets.

		MT
Complete Set (30):		180.00
Common Player:		2.00
Inserted 1:23		
Doubles (2,000 sets):		2X
Triples (100 sets): 5X		
Quadruples (10 sets): Value Undetermined		
1	Darin Erstad	3.00
2	Troy Glaus	5.00
3	Mo Vaughn	3.00
4	Greg Maddux	10.00
5	Andres Galarraga	3.00
6	Chipper Jones	10.00
7	Cal Ripken Jr.	15.00
8	Albert Belle	3.00
9	Nomar Garciaparra	12.00
10	Sammy Sosa	10.00
11	Kerry Wood	3.00
12	Frank Thomas	6.00
13	Jim Thome	3.00
14	Jeff Bagwell	5.00
15	Vladimir Guerrero	6.00
16	Mike Piazza	12.00
17	Derek Jeter	15.00
18	Ben Grieve	2.00
19	Eric Chavez	3.00
20	Scott Rolen	4.00
21	Mark McGwire	20.00
22	J.D. Drew	3.00
23	Tony Gwynn	6.00
24	Barry Bonds	5.00
25	Alex Rodriguez	15.00
26	Ken Griffey Jr.	15.00
27	Ivan Rodriguez	5.00

28	Juan Gonzalez	5.00
29	Roger Clemens	6.00
30	Andruw Jones	5.00

1999 Upper Deck 10th Anniversary Team

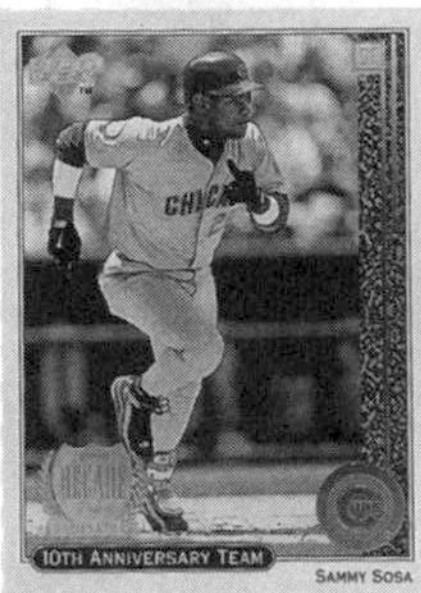

This 30-card set commemorates Upper Deck's 10th Anniversary, as collectors selected their favorite players for this set. Regular versions are seeded 1:4 packs, Doubles numbered to 4,000, Triples numbered to 100 and Home Runs which are limited to one set.

	MT
Complete Set (30):	50.00
Common Player:	.35
Inserted 1:4	
Doubles (4,000 sets):	2X
Triples (100 sets):	20X
Home Runs (1 set): Values Undetermined	

X1	Mike Piazza	4.00
X2	Mark McGwire	6.00
X3	Roberto Alomar	1.00
X4	Chipper Jones	3.00
X5	Cal Ripken Jr.	5.00
X6	Ken Griffey Jr.	5.00
X7	Barry Bonds	1.50
X8	Tony Gwynn	2.00
X9	Nolan Ryan	6.00
X10	Randy Johnson	1.50
X11	Dennis Eckersley	.35
X12	Ivan Rodriguez	1.50
X13	Frank Thomas	2.00
X14	Craig Biggio	.50
X15	Wade Boggs	.50
X16	Alex Rodriguez	5.00
X17	Albert Belle	1.00
X18	Juan Gonzalez	1.50
X19	Rickey Henderson	.50
X20	Greg Maddux	3.00
X21	Tom Glavine	.50
X22	Randy Myers	.35
X23	Sandy Alomar	.50
X24	Jeff Bagwell	1.50
X25	Derek Jeter	4.00
X26	Matt Williams	.35
X27	Kenny Lofton	.75
X28	Sammy Sosa	3.00
X29	Larry Walker	.50
X30	Roger Clemens	2.00

1999 Upper Deck Textbook Excellence

This 30-card set features the game's most fundamentally sound performers. Card fronts have a photo of the featured player with a silver foil stamped grid surrounding the player. The left portion of the insert has the player name, team and his postion on a brown background. These are seeded 1:23 packs. There are three parallels as well: Double, Triple and Home Run. Doubles are hobby exclusive and numbered to 2,000 sets, Triples are hobby-only and limited to 100 numbered sets and Home Runs are hobby-only and limited to 10 numbered sets.

	MT
Complete Set (30):	50.00
Common Player:	.75
Inserted 1:4	
Doubles (2,000 sets):	3X
Triples (100 sets):	15X
Quadruples (10 sets): Value Undetermined	

1	Mo Vaughn	1.00
2	Greg Maddux	3.00
3	Chipper Jones	3.00
4	Andruw Jones	1.50
5	Cal Ripken Jr.	5.00
6	Albert Belle	1.00
7	Roberto Alomar	1.00
8	Nomar Garciaparra	4.00
9	Kerry Wood	1.00
10	Sammy Sosa	3.00
11	Greg Vaughn	.75
12	Jeff Bagwell	1.50
13	Kevin Brown	.75
14	Vladimir Guerrero	2.00
15	Mike Piazza	4.00
16	Bernie Williams	1.00
17	Derek Jeter	5.00
18	Ben Grieve	.75
19	Eric Chavez	.75
20	Scott Rolen	1.00
21	Mark McGwire	6.00
22	David Wells	.75
23	J.D. Drew	1.00
24	Tony Gwynn	2.00
25	Barry Bonds	1.50
26	Alex Rodriguez	5.00
27	Ken Griffey Jr.	5.00
28	Juan Gonzalez	1.50
29	Ivan Rodriguez	1.50
30	Roger Clemens	2.00

1999 Upper Deck View to a Thrill

This 30-card set focuses on baseball's best overall athletes. There are two photos of the featured player on the card front, highlighted by silver foil and some embossing. These are inserted 1:7 packs.

	MT
Complete Set (30):	80.00
Common Player:	1.00
Inserted 1:7	
Doubles (2,000 sets):	2X
Triples (100 sets):	10X
Quadruples (10 sets): Value Undetermined	

1	Mo Vaughn	1.50
2	Darin Erstad	1.50
3	Travis Lee	1.00
4	Chipper Jones	5.00
5	Greg Maddux	5.00
6	Gabe Kapler	1.50
7	Cal Ripken Jr.	8.00
8	Nomar Garciaparra	6.00
9	Kerry Wood	1.50
10	Frank Thomas	3.00
11	Manny Ramirez	2.50
12	Larry Walker	1.50
13	Tony Clark	1.00
14	Jeff Bagwell	2.50
15	Craig Biggio	1.00
16	Vladimir Guerrero	3.00
17	Mike Piazza	6.00
18	Bernie Williams	2.00
19	Derek Jeter	8.00
20	Ben Grieve	1.00
21	Eric Chavez	1.00
22	Scott Rolen	2.00
23	Mark McGwire	10.00
24	Tony Gwynn	3.00
25	Barry Bonds	2.50
26	Ken Griffey Jr.	8.00
27	Alex Rodriguez	8.00
28	J.D. Drew	1.50
29	Juan Gonzalez	2.50
30	Roger Clemens	3.00

1999 Upper Deck Ken Griffey Jr. 1989 UD Autograph

	MT
Complete Set (1):	1200.
Ken Griffey Jr. (100)	1200.

1999 Upper Deck Black Diamond

This 120-card base set features metallic foil fronts, while card backs have the featured player's vital information along with a close-up photo. The Diamond Debut subset (91-120) are short-printed and seeded 1:4 packs.

	MT
Complete Set (120):	120.00
Common Player:	.25
Common Diamond Debut (91-120):	1.00
Inserted 1:4	
Double Diamonds (3,000 each):	3X
Double Diamond Debuts (2,500 each):	1.5X
Triple Diamonds (1,500 each):	6X
Triple Diamond Debuts (1,000 each):	2X
Pack (6):	4.00
Wax Box (30):	100.00

1	Darin Erstad	.75
2	Tim Salmon	.50
3	Jim Edmonds	.25
4	Matt Williams	.40
5	David Dellucci	.25
6	Jay Bell	.25
7	Andres Galarraga	.75
8	Chipper Jones	2.50
9	Greg Maddux	2.50
10	Andruw Jones	.75
11	Cal Ripken Jr.	4.00
12	Rafael Palmeiro	.75
13	Brady Anderson	.25
14	Mike Mussina	1.00
15	Nomar Garciaparra	3.00
16	Mo Vaughn	1.00
17	Pedro Martinez	1.50
18	Sammy Sosa	3.00
19	Henry Rodriguez	.25
20	Frank Thomas	1.50
21	Magglio Ordonez	.75
22	Albert Belle	1.00
23	Paul Konerko	.25
24	Sean Casey	.75
25	Jim Thome	.75
26	Kenny Lofton	1.00
27	Sandy Alomar Jr.	.25
28	Jaret Wright	.25
29	Larry Walker	.75
30	Todd Helton	1.25
31	Vinny Castilla	.25
32	Tony Clark	.50
33	Damion Easley	.25
34	Mark Kotsay	.25
35	Derrek Lee	.25
36	Moises Alou	.40
37	Jeff Bagwell	1.50
38	Craig Biggio	.75
39	Randy Johnson	1.00
40	Dean Palmer	.25
41	Johnny Damon	.25
42	Chan Ho Park	.40
43	Raul Mondesi	.40
44	Gary Sheffield	.40
45	Jeromy Burnitz	.25
46	Marquis Grissom	.25
47	Jeff Cirillo	.25
48	Paul Molitor	1.00
49	Todd Walker	.25
50	Vladimir Guerrero	2.00
51	Brad Fullmer	.25
52	Mike Piazza	3.00
53	Hideo Nomo	.25
54	Carlos Baerga	.25
55	John Olerud	.50
56	Derek Jeter	3.00
57	Hideki Irabu	.40
58	Tino Martinez	.50
59	Bernie Williams	.75
60	Miguel Tejada	.40
61	Ben Grieve	.75
62	Jason Giambi	.25
63	Scott Rolen	1.25

64	Doug Glanville	.25
65	Desi Relaford	.25
66	Tony Womack	.25
67	Jason Kendall	.40
68	Jose Guillen	.25
69	Tony Gwynn	2.50
70	Ken Caminiti	.40
71	Greg Vaughn	.40
72	Kevin Brown	.40
73	Barry Bonds	1.25
74	J.T. Snow	.25
75	Jeff Kent	.25
76	Ken Griffey Jr.	5.00
77	Alex Rodriguez	4.00
78	Edgar Martinez	.25
79	Jay Buhner	.40
80	Mark McGwire	5.00
81	Delino DeShields	.25
82	Brian Jordan	.25
83	Quinton McCracken	.25
84	Fred McGriff	.50
85	Juan Gonzalez	1.25
86	Ivan Rodriguez	1.25
87	Will Clark	.50
88	Roger Clemens	2.00
89	Jose Cruz Jr.	.40
90	Babe Ruth	5.00
91	Troy Glaus (Diamond Debut)	6.00
92	Jarrod Washburn (Diamond Debut)	1.00
93	Travis Lee (Diamond Debut)	2.00
94	Bruce Chen (Diamond Debut)	1.00
95	Mike Caruso (Diamond Debut)	1.00
96	Jim Parque (Diamond Debut)	1.00
97	Kerry Wood (Diamond Debut)	4.00
98	Jeremy Giambi (Diamond Debut)	2.50
99	Matt Anderson (Diamond Debut)	1.00
100	Seth Greisinger (Diamond Debut)	1.00
101	Gabe Alvarez (Diamond Debut)	1.00
102	Rafael Medina (Diamond Debut)	1.00
103	Daryle Ward (Diamond Debut)	1.00
104	Alex Cora (Diamond Debut)	1.00
105	Adrian Beltre (Diamond Debut)	2.00
106	Geoff Jenkins (Diamond Debut)	1.50
107	Eric Milton (Diamond Debut)	1.00
108	Carl Pavano (Diamond Debut)	1.00
109	Eric Chavez (Diamond Debut)	1.50
110	Orlando Hernandez (Diamond Debut)	3.00
111	A.J. Hinch (Diamond Debut)	1.00
112	Carlton Loewer (Diamond Debut)	1.00
113	Aramis Ramirez (Diamond Debut)	1.00
114	Cliff Politte (Diamond Debut)	1.00
115	Matt Clement (Diamond Debut)	1.00
116	Alex Gonzalez (Diamond Debut)	1.00
117	J.D. Drew (Diamond Debut)	2.50
118	Shane Monahan (Diamond Debut)	1.00
119	Rolando Arrojo (Diamond Debut)	1.50
120	George Lombard (Diamond Debut)	1.00

1999 Upper Deck Black Diamond Double Diamond

Double Diamonds are the most common of the parallels to the Black Diamond base cards. The regular player cards (#1-90) feature a red metallic foil background and are serially numbered on back from within an edition of 3,000 each. Diamond Debut cards (#91-120) also feature red foil highlights on front and are individually numbered within an edition of 2,500 each.

	MT
Complete Set (120):	450.00
Common Player (1-90):	1.00
Common Diamond Debut (91-120):	3.00

(See 1999 Upper Deck Black Diamond for checklist, base card values. Stars and rookies #1-90 valued at 3X; #91-120 at 1X.)

1999 Upper Deck Black Diamond Triple Diamond

Triple Diamonds are the second most common of the parallel inserts to the Black Diamond base cards. The regular player cards (#1-90) feature a yellow metallic foil background and are serially numbered on back from within an edition of 1,500 each. Diamond Debut cards (#91-120) also feature yellow foil highlights on front and are individually numbered within an edition of 1,000 each.

	MT
Common Player (1-90):	2.00
Common Diamond Debut (91-120):	3.00

(See 1999 Upper Deck Black Diamond for checklist, base card values. Stars and rookies #1-90 valued at 6X; #91-120 3X.)

1999 Upper Deck Black Diamond Quadruple Diamond

Quadruple Diamonds are the scarcest of the parallel inserts to the Black Diamond base cards. The regular player cards (#1-90) feature a green metallic foil background and are serially numbered on back from within an edition of 150 each. Diamond Debut cards (#91-120) also feature green foil highlights on front and are individually numbered within an edition of 100 each.

		MT
Common Player (1-90):		6.00
Production 150 sets		
Common Diamond Debut (91-120):		8.00
Production 100 sets		
1	Darin Erstad	10.00
2	Tim Salmon	10.00
3	Jim Edmonds	6.00
4	Matt Williams	15.00
5	David Dellucci	6.00
6	Jay Bell	6.00
7	Andres Galarraga	20.00
8	Chipper Jones	90.00
9	Greg Maddux	60.00
10	Andruw Jones	20.00
11	Cal Ripken Jr.	125.00
12	Rafael Palmeiro	25.00
13	Brady Anderson	6.00
14	Mike Mussina	25.00
15	Nomar Garciaparra	100.00
16	Mo Vaughn	25.00
17	Pedro Martinez	40.00
18	Sammy Sosa (66)	100.00
19	Henry Rodriguez	6.00
20	Frank Thomas	35.00
21	Magglio Ordonez	25.00
22	Albert Belle	30.00
23	Paul Konerko	8.00
24	Sean Casey	15.00
25	Jim Thome	20.00
26	Kenny Lofton	25.00
27	Sandy Alomar Jr.	6.00
28	Jaret Wright	6.00
29	Larry Walker	25.00
30	Todd Helton	20.00
31	Vinny Castilla	8.00
32	Tony Clark	15.00
33	Damion Easley	6.00
34	Mark Kotsay	6.00
35	Derrek Lee	6.00
36	Moises Alou	8.00
37	Jeff Bagwell	30.00
38	Craig Biggio	20.00
39	Randy Johnson	25.00
40	Dean Palmer	6.00
41	Johnny Damon	6.00
42	Chan Ho Park	8.00
43	Raul Mondesi	8.00
44	Gary Sheffield	8.00
45	Jeromy Burnitz	6.00
46	Marquis Grissom	6.00
47	Jeff Cirillo	6.00
48	Paul Molitor	25.00
49	Todd Walker	6.00
50	Vladimir Guerrero	40.00
51	Brad Fullmer	6.00
52	Mike Piazza	100.00
53	Hideo Nomo	6.00
54	Carlos Baerga	6.00
55	John Olerud	10.00
56	Derek Jeter	125.00
57	Hideki Irabu	8.00
58	Tino Martinez	15.00
59	Bernie Williams	25.00
60	Miguel Tejada	6.00
61	Ben Grieve	15.00
62	Jason Giambi	6.00
63	Scott Rolen	30.00
64	Doug Glanville	6.00
65	Desi Relaford	6.00
66	Tony Womack	6.00
67	Jason Kendall	8.00
68	Jose Guillen	6.00
69	Tony Gwynn	60.00
70	Ken Caminiti	8.00
71	Greg Vaughn	15.00
72	Kevin Brown	8.00
73	Barry Bonds	30.00
74	J.T. Snow	6.00
75	Jeff Kent	6.00
76	Ken Griffey Jr. (56)	200.00
77	Alex Rodriguez	100.00
78	Edgar Martinez	6.00
79	Jay Buhner	8.00
80	Mark McGwire (70)	200.00
81	Delino DeShields	6.00
82	Brian Jordan	6.00
83	Quinton McCracken	6.00
84	Fred McGriff	8.00
85	Juan Gonzalez	30.00
86	Ivan Rodriguez	30.00
87	Will Clark	15.00
88	Roger Clemens	60.00
89	Jose Cruz Jr.	6.00
90	Babe Ruth	150.00
91	Troy Glaus (Diamond Debut)	40.00
92	Jarrod Washburn (Diamond Debut)	10.00
93	Travis Lee (Diamond Debut)	15.00
94	Bruce Chen (Diamond Debut)	10.00
95	Mike Caruso (Diamond Debut)	10.00
96	Jim Parque (Diamond Debut)	8.00
97	Kerry Wood (Diamond Debut)	40.00
98	Jeremy Giambi (Diamond Debut)	15.00
99	Matt Anderson (Diamond Debut)	10.00
100	Seth Greisinger (Diamond Debut)	8.00
101	Gabe Alvarez (Diamond Debut)	8.00
102	Rafael Medina (Diamond Debut)	8.00
103	Daryle Ward (Diamond Debut)	10.00
104	Alex Cora (Diamond Debut)	8.00
105	Adrian Beltre (Diamond Debut)	15.00
106	Geoff Jenkins (Diamond Debut)	10.00
107	Eric Milton (Diamond Debut)	8.00
108	Carl Pavano (Diamond Debut)	10.00
109	Eric Chavez (Diamond Debut)	12.00
110	Orlando Hernandez (Diamond Debut)	25.00
111	A.J. Hinch (Diamond Debut)	8.00
112	Carlton Loewer (Diamond Debut)	8.00

113	Aramis Ramirez (Diamond Debut)	8.00
114	Cliff Politte (Diamond Debut)	8.00
115	Matt Clement (Diamond Debut)	10.00
116	Alex Gonzalez (Diamond Debut)	10.00
117	J.D. Drew (Diamond Debut)	25.00
118	Shane Monahan (Diamond Debut)	8.00
119	Rolando Arrojo (Diamond Debut)	15.00
120	George Lombard (Diamond Debut)	10.00

1999 Upper Deck Black Diamond A Piece of History

This six-card set features green metallic foil fronts with a diamond-shaped piece of game-used bat from the featured player embedded on the card front. No insertion ratio was released.

		MT
Common Player:		40.00
JG	Juan Gonzalez	75.00
TG	Tony Gwynn	100.00
BW	Bernie Williams	60.00
MM	Mark McGwire	800.00
MV	Mo Vaughn	40.00
SS	Sammy Sosa	200.00

1999 Upper Deck Black Diamond Diamond Dominance

This 30-card set features full-bleed metallic foil fronts and includes the top stars of the game along with Babe Ruth. Each card is numbered with a "D" prefix and is limited to 1,500 sequentially numbered sets.

		MT
Complete Set (30):		400.00
Common Player:		2.00
Production 1,500 sets		
D01	Kerry Wood	10.00
D02	Derek Jeter	25.00
D03	Alex Rodriguez	25.00
D04	Frank Thomas	15.00
D05	Jeff Bagwell	10.00
D06	Mo Vaughn	6.00
D07	Ivan Rodriguez	10.00
D08	Cal Ripken Jr.	30.00
D09	Rolando Arrojo	2.00
D10	Chipper Jones	20.00
D11	Kenny Lofton	6.00
D12	Paul Konerko	2.00
D13	Mike Piazza	25.00
D14	Ben Grieve	6.00
D15	Nomar Garciaparra	25.00
D16	Travis Lee	5.00
D17	Scott Rolen	10.00
D18	Juan Gonzalez	12.00
D19	Tony Gwynn	20.00
D20	Tony Clark	3.00
D21	Roger Clemens	15.00
D22	Sammy Sosa	25.00
D23	Larry Walker	6.00
D24	Ken Griffey Jr.	40.00
D25	Mark McGwire	40.00
D26	Barry Bonds	10.00
D27	Vladimir Guerrero	15.00
D28	Tino Martinez	2.00
D29	Greg Maddux	20.00
D30	Babe Ruth	40.00

1999 Upper Deck Black Diamond Mystery Numbers

The player's card number determines scarcity in this hobby-only insert set. The basic set has an action photo set against a silver-foil background of repated numerals. Backs have a portrait photo and significant stat numbers from the 1998 season. Each base Mystery Numbers card is individually numbered within an edition of 100 cards times the card number within the 30-card set (i.e., card #24 has an edition of 2,400) for a total of 46,500 cards. An emerald version of the Mystery Numbers cards has a total issue of 465 cards, with cards issued to a limit of the player's card number multiplied by 1.

		MT
Complete Set (30):		750.00
Common Player:		3.00
M01	Babe Ruth (100)	150.00
M02	Ken Griffey Jr. (200)	125.00
M03	Kerry Wood (300)	20.00
M04	Mark McGwire (400)	75.00
M05	Alex Rodriguez (500)	50.00
M06	Chipper Jones (600)	30.00
M07	Nomar Garciaparra (700)	35.00
M08	Derek Jeter (800)	35.00
M09	Mike Piazza (900)	30.00
M10	Roger Clemens (1,000)	20.00
M11	Greg Maddux (1,100)	25.00
M12	Scott Rolen (1,200)	12.00
M13	Cal Ripken Jr. (1,300)	30.00
M14	Ben Grieve (1,400)	8.00
M15	Troy Glaus (1,500)	12.00
M16	Sammy Sosa (1,600)	20.00
M17	Darin Erstad (1,700)	6.00
M18	Juan Gonzalez (1,800)	12.00
M19	Pedro Martinez (1,900)	8.00
M20	Larry Walker (2,000)	6.00
M21	Vladimir Guerrero (2,100)	12.00
M22	Jeff Bagwell (2,200)	8.00
M23	Jaret Wright (2,300)	4.00
M24	Travis Lee (2,400)	5.00
M25	Barry Bonds (2,500)	6.00
M26	Orlando Hernandez (2,600)	10.00
M27	Frank Thomas (2,700)	8.00
M28	Tony Gwynn (2,800)	10.00
M29	Andres Galarraga (2,900)	5.00
M30	Craig Biggio (3,000)	4.00

1999 Upper Deck Encore

Encore is essentially a 180-card partial parallel of Upper Deck Series I, that utilizes a special holo-foil treatment on each card. The 180-card base set consists of 90 base cards and three short-printed subsets: 45 Star Rookie (1:4), 30 Homer Odyssey (1:6) and 15 Stroke of Genius (1:8).

		MT
Complete Set (180):		250.00
Common Player (1-90):		.20
Common Player (91-135):		1.00
Inserted 1:4		
Common Player (136-165):		.75
Inserted 1:6		
Common Player (166-180):		1.00
Pack (4):		4.50
Wax Box (24):		100.00
1	Darin Erstad	.40
2	Mo Vaughn	.75
3	Travis Lee	.50
4	Randy Johnson	.75
5	Matt Williams	.40
6	John Smoltz	.20
7	Greg Maddux	2.00
8	Chipper Jones	2.00
9	Tom Glavine	.40
10	Andruw Jones	.75
11	Cal Ripken Jr.	3.00
12	Mike Mussina	.75
13	Albert Belle	.75
14	Nomar Garciaparra	2.50
15	Jose Offerman	.20
16	Pedro J. Martinez	1.00
17	Trot Nixon	.20
18	Kerry Wood	.50
19	Sammy Sosa	2.50
20	Frank Thomas	1.00
21	Paul Konerko	.20
22	Sean Casey	.75
23	Barry Larkin	.50
24	Greg Vaughn	.40
25	Travis Fryman	.40
26	Jaret Wright	.20
27	Jim Thome	.50
28	Manny Ramirez	1.00
29	Roberto Alomar	.75
30	Kenny Lofton	.60
31	Todd Helton	1.00
32	Larry Walker	.75
33	Vinny Castilla	.20
34	Dante Bichette	.40
35	Tony Clark	.50
36	Dean Palmer	.20
37	Gabe Kapler	.50
38	Juan Encarnacion	.20
39	Alex Gonzalez	.20
40	Preston Wilson	.20
41	Mark Kotsay	.20
42	Moises Alou	.40
43	Craig Biggio	.50
44	Ken Caminiti	.30
45	Jeff Bagwell	1.00
46	Johnny Damon	.20
47	Gary Sheffield	.40
48	Kevin Brown	.40
49	Raul Mondesi	.30
50	Jeff Cirillo	.20
51	Jeromy Burnitz	.20
52	Todd Walker	.20
53	Corey Koskie	.20
54	Brad Fullmer	.20
55	Vladimir Guerrero	2.00
56	Mike Piazza	2.50
57	Robin Ventura	.40
58	Rickey Henderson	.60
59	Derek Jeter	2.50
60	Paul O'Neill	.40
61	Bernie Williams	.75
62	Tino Martinez	.40
63	Roger Clemens	1.50
64	Ben Grieve	.50
65	Jason Giambi	.20
66	Bob Abreu	.20
67	Scott Rolen	1.00
68	Curt Schilling	.40
69	Marlon Anderson	.20
70	Kevin Young	.20
71	Jason Kendall	.40
72	Brian Giles	.20
73	Mark McGwire	4.00
74	Fernando Tatis	.40
75	Eric Davis	.20
76	Trevor Hoffman	.20
77	Tony Gwynn	2.00
78	Matt Clement	.20
79	Robb Nen	.20
80	Barry Bonds	1.00
81	Ken Griffey Jr.	4.00
82	Alex Rodriguez	3.00
83	Wade Boggs	.50

84	Fred McGriff	.40
85	Jose Canseco	1.00
86	Ivan Rodriguez	1.00
87	Juan Gonzalez	1.00
88	Rafael Palmeiro	.75
89	Carlos Delgado	.75
90	David Wells	.20
91	Troy Glaus (Star Rookies)	4.00
92	Adrian Beltre (Star Rookies)	1.50
93	Matt Anderson (Star Rookies)	1.00
94	Eric Chavez (Star Rookies)	1.50
95	*Jeff Weaver* (Star Rookies)	5.00
96	Warren Morris (Star Rookies)	1.50
97	George Lombard (Star Rookies)	1.00
98	Mike Kinkade (Star Rookies)	1.00
99	*Kyle Farnsworth* (Star Rookies)	2.00
100	J.D. Drew (Star Rookies)	2.00
101	*Joe McEwing* (Star Rookies)	3.00
102	Carlos Guillen (Star Rookies)	1.00
103	*Kelly Dransfeldt* (Star Rookies)	2.50
104	*Eric Munson* (Star Rookies)	15.00
105	Armando Rios (Star Rookies)	1.00
106	Ramon Martinez (Star Rookies)	1.00
107	Orlando Hernandez (Star Rookies)	2.50
108	Jeremy Giambi (Star Rookies)	2.00
109	*Pat Burrell* (Star Rookies)	12.00
110	Shea Hillenbrand (Star Rookies)	2.50
111	Billy Koch (Star Rookies)	1.00
112	Roy Halladay (Star Rookies)	1.00
113	Ruben Mateo (Star Rookies)	4.00
114	Bruce Chen (Star Rookies)	1.00
115	Angel Pena (Star Rookies)	1.50
116	Michael Barrett (Star Rookies)	1.50
117	Kevin Witt (Star Rookies)	1.00
118	Damon Minor (Star Rookies)	1.00
119	Ryan Minor (Star Rookies)	2.00
120	A.J. Pierzynski (Star Rookies)	1.00
121	*A.J. Burnett* (Star Rookies)	4.00
122	Christian Guzman (Star Rookies)	1.00
123	Joe Lawrence (Star Rookies)	1.00
124	Derrick Gibson (Star Rookies)	1.00
125	Carlos Febles (Star Rookies)	3.00
126	Chris Haas (Star Rookies)	1.00
127	Cesar King (Star Rookies)	1.00
128	Calvin Pickering (Star Rookies)	1.00
129	Mitch Meluskey (Star Rookies)	1.00
130	Carlos Beltran (Star Rookies)	1.00
131	Ron Belliard (Star Rookies)	1.50
132	Jerry Hairston Jr. (Star Rookies)	1.00
133	Fernando Seguignol (Star Rookies)	1.50
134	Kris Benson (Star Rookies)	1.00
135	*Chad Hutchinson* (Star Rookies)	5.00
136	Ken Griffey Jr. (Homer Odyssey)	8.00
137	Mark McGwire (Homer Odyssey)	8.00
138	Sammy Sosa (Homer Odyssey)	5.00
139	Albert Belle (Homer Odyssey)	1.50
140	Mo Vaughn (Homer Odyssey)	1.50
141	Alex Rodriguez (Homer Odyssey)	6.00
142	Manny Ramirez (Homer Odyssey)	2.00
143	J.D. Drew (Homer Odyssey)	1.50
144	Juan Gonzalez (Homer Odyssey)	2.00
145	Vladimir Guerrero (Homer Odyssey)	4.00
146	Fernando Tatis (Homer Odyssey)	.75
147	Mike Piazza (Homer Odyssey)	5.00
148	Barry Bonds (Homer Odyssey)	2.00
149	Ivan Rodriguez (Homer Odyssey)	2.00
150	Jeff Bagwell (Homer Odyssey)	2.00
151	Raul Mondesi (Homer Odyssey)	.75
152	Nomar Garciaparra (Homer Odyssey)	5.00
153	Jose Canseco (Homer Odyssey)	2.00
154	Greg Vaughn (Homer Odyssey)	.75
155	Scott Rolen (Homer Odyssey)	2.00
156	Vinny Castilla (Homer Odyssey)	.75
157	Troy Glaus (Homer Odyssey)	3.00
158	Craig Biggio (Homer Odyssey)	1.50
159	Tino Martinez (Homer Odyssey)	1.00
160	Jim Thome (Homer Odyssey)	1.50
161	Frank Thomas (Homer Odyssey)	2.50
162	Tony Clark (Homer Odyssey)	1.00
163	Ben Grieve (Homer Odyssey)	1.50
164	Matt Williams (Homer Odyssey)	1.00
165	Derek Jeter (Homer Odyssey)	5.00
166	Ken Griffey Jr. (Strokes of Genius)	8.00
167	Tony Gwynn (Strokes of Genius)	4.00
168	Mike Piazza (Strokes of Genius)	5.00
169	Mark McGwire (Strokes of Genius)	8.00
170	Sammy Sosa (Strokes of Genius)	5.00
171	Juan Gonzalez (Strokes of Genius)	2.00
172	Mo Vaughn (Strokes of Genius)	1.50
173	Derek Jeter (Strokes of Genius)	5.00
174	Bernie Williams (Strokes of Genius)	1.50
175	Ivan Rodriguez (Strokes of Genius)	2.00
176	Barry Bonds (Strokes of Genius)	2.00
177	Scott Rolen (Strokes of Genius)	2.00
178	Larry Walker (Strokes of Genius)	1.50
179	Chipper Jones (Strokes of Genius)	4.00
180	Alex Rodriguez (Strokes of Genius)	5.00

1999 Upper Deck Encore Gold

This is a 180-card parallel to the base set featuring gold holo-foil treatment and limited to 125 sequentially numbered sets.

	MT
Gold (1-90):	15X
Gold (91-135):	2X
Gold (136-165):	4X
Gold (166-180):	5X

1999 Upper Deck Encore Driving Forces

This 15-card set is highlighted by holo-foil treatment on the card fronts on a thick card stock. Baseball's top performers are featured in this set and are seeded 1:23 packs. A Gold parallel exists and is limited to 10 sets.

		MT
Complete Set (15):		100.00
Common Player:		1.50
Inserted 1:23		
1	Ken Griffey Jr.	15.00
2	Mark McGwire	15.00
3	Sammy Sosa	10.00
4	Albert Belle	3.00
5	Alex Rodriguez	12.00
6	Mo Vaughn	3.00
7	Juan Gonzalez	4.00
8	Jeff Bagwell	4.00
9	Mike Piazza	10.00
10	Frank Thomas	4.00
11	Barry Bonds	4.00
12	Vladimir Guerrero	6.00
13	Chipper Jones	10.00
14	Tony Gwynn	8.00
15	J.D. Drew	2.00

1999 Upper Deck Encore Pure Excitement

This 30-card set features Light F/X technology and includes the top players in baseball. These are seeded 1:7 packs.

		MT
Complete Set (30):		100.00
Common Player:		1.00
Inserted 1:7		
1	Mo Vaughn	1.50
2	Darin Erstad	1.50
3	Travis Lee	1.50
4	Chipper Jones	6.00
5	Greg Maddux	5.00
6	Gabe Kapler	1.50
7	Cal Ripken Jr.	8.00
8	Nomar Garciaparra	6.00
9	Kerry Wood	1.50
10	Frank Thomas	3.00
11	Manny Ramirez	2.50
12	Larry Walker	2.00
13	Tony Clark	1.00
14	Jeff Bagwell	2.50
15	Craig Biggio	1.50
16	Vladimir Guerrero	4.00
17	Mike Piazza	6.00
18	Bernie Williams	1.50
19	Derek Jeter	6.00
20	Ben Grieve	2.00
21	Eric Chavez	1.00
22	Scott Rolen	2.50
23	Mark McGwire	10.00
24	Tony Gwynn	5.00
25	Barry Bonds	2.50
26	Ken Griffey Jr.	10.00
27	Alex Rodriguez	8.00
28	J.D. Drew	1.50
29	Juan Gonzalez	2.50
30	Roger Clemens	3.00

1999 Upper Deck Encore Rookie Encore

This 10-card set highlights the top rookie prospects in 1999, including J.D. Drew and Gabe Kapler. These are seeded 1:23 packs. A parallel version is also randomly seeded and limited to 500 sequentially numbered sets.

		MT
Complete Set (10):		25.00
Common Player:		1.50
Inserted 1:23		
Parallel:		2X
Production 500 sets		
1	J.D. Drew	2.00
2	Eric Chavez	1.50
3	Gabe Kapler	2.00
4	Bruce Chen	1.50
5	Carlos Beltran	1.50
6	Troy Glaus	5.00
7	Roy Halladay	1.50
8	Adrian Beltre	2.00
9	Michael Barrett	1.50
10	Pat Burrell	10.00

1999 Upper Deck Encore Upper Realm

This 15-card set focuses on the top stars of the game. Card fronts utilize holo-foil treatment, with the initials UR lightly foiled. Card backs are numbered with an "U" prefix and are seeded 1:11 packs.

		MT
Complete Set (15):		60.00
Common Player:		1.00
Inserted 1:11		
1	Ken Griffey Jr.	8.00
2	Mark McGwire	8.00
3	Sammy Sosa	5.00
4	Tony Gwynn	4.00
5	Alex Rodriguez	6.00
6	Juan Gonzalez	2.00
7	J.D. Drew	1.00
8	Roger Clemens	3.00
9	Greg Maddux	4.00
10	Randy Johnson	1.50
11	Mo Vaughn	1.50
12	Derek Jeter	5.00
13	Vladimir Guerrero	4.00
14	Cal Ripken Jr.	6.00
15	Nomar Garciaparra	5.00

1999 Upper Deck Encore 2K Countdown

This set recognizes the countdown to the next century with a salute to baseball's next century of superstars including Derek Jeter and Alex Rodriguez. These are done on a horizontal format and inserted 1:11 packs.

		MT
Complete Set (10):		35.00
Common Player:		1.50
Inserted 1:11		
1	Ken Griffey Jr.	6.00
2	Derek Jeter	4.00
3	Mike Piazza	4.00
4	J.D. Drew	1.50
5	Vladimir Guerrero	2.50
6	Chipper Jones	4.00
7	Alex Rodriguez	5.00
8	Nomar Garciaparra	4.00
9	Mark McGwire	6.00
10	Sammy Sosa	4.00

1999 Upper Deck Encore McGwired!

This 10-card set salutes baseball's reigning single season home run king. These are seeded 1:23 packs. A gold parallel also is randomly seeded and is limited to 500 sequentially numbered sets. A small photo of the pitcher McGwire hit the historic home run off of is pictured as well.

		MT
Complete Set (10):		70.00
Common Card:		8.00
Inserted 1:23		
Parallel:		2X
Production 500 sets		
1	Mark McGwire, Carl Pavano	8.00
2	Mark McGwire, Michael Morgan	8.00
3	Mark McGwire, Steve Trachsel	8.00
4	Mark McGwire	8.00
5	Mark McGwire	8.00
6	Mark McGwire, Scott Elarton	8.00
7	Mark McGwire, Jim Parque	8.00
8	Mark McGwire	8.00
9	Mark McGwire, Rafael Roque	8.00
10	Mark McGwire, Jaret Wright	8.00

1999 Upper Deck Encore UD Authentics

This six-card autographed set features signatures of Griffey Jr. and Nomar Garciaparra. These are seeded 1:288 packs.

		MT
Complete Set (6):		525.00
Common Player:		20.00
Inserted 1:288		
MB	Michael Barrett	20.00
PB	Pat Burrell	50.00
JD	J.D. Drew	40.00
NG	Nomar Garciaparra	125.00
TG	Troy Glaus	40.00
JR	Ken Griffey Jr.	250.00

1999 Upper Deck Encore Batting Practice Caps

This 15-card set features actual swatch pieces of the highlighted players' batting practice cap embedded into each card. These are seeded 1:750 packs.

		MT
Common Player:		25.00
Inserted 1:750		
CB	Carlos Beltran	25.00
BB	Barry Bonds	120.00
VC	Vinny Castilla	50.00
EC	Eric Chavez	40.00
TC	Tony Clark	30.00
JD	J.D. Drew	50.00
VG	Vladimir Guerrero	125.00
TG	Tony Gwynn	100.00
TH	Todd Helton	60.00
GK	Gabe Kapler	50.00
JK	Jason Kendall	40.00
DP	Dean Palmer	40.00
BH	Frank Thomas	150.00
GV	Greg Vaughn	40.00
TW	Todd Walker	25.00

1999 Upper Deck HoloGrFX

HoloGrFX was distributed exclusively to retail and the base set is comprised of 60 base cards, each utilizing holographic technology.

		MT
Complete Set (60):		30.00
Common Player:		.25
AUsome:		3X
Inserted 1:8		
Pack (3):		1.75
Wax Box (36):		40.00
1	Mo Vaughn	.60
2	Troy Glaus	1.00
3	Tim Salmon	.50
4	Randy Johnson	.75
5	Travis Lee	.60
6	Chipper Jones	2.50
7	Greg Maddux	2.00
8	Andruw Jones	.75
9	Tom Glavine	.25
10	Cal Ripken Jr.	3.00
11	Albert Belle	.75
12	Nomar Garciaparra	2.50
13	Pedro J. Martinez	1.00
14	Sammy Sosa	2.50
15	Frank Thomas	1.50
16	Greg Vaughn	.25
17	Kenny Lofton	.60
18	Jim Thome	.50
19	Manny Ramirez	1.00
20	Todd Helton	1.00
21	Larry Walker	.75
22	Tony Clark	.50
23	Juan Encarnacion	.25
24	Mark Kotsay	.25
25	Jeff Bagwell	1.00
26	Craig Biggio	.60
27	Ken Caminiti	.40
28	Carlos Beltran	.30
29	Jeremy Giambi	.25
30	Raul Mondesi	.40
31	Kevin Brown	.25
32	Jeromy Burnitz	.25
33	Corey Koskie	.25
34	Todd Walker	.25
35	Vladimir Guerrero	1.50
36	Mike Piazza	2.50
37	Robin Ventura	.25
38	Derek Jeter	2.50
39	Roger Clemens	1.50
40	Bernie Williams	.60
41	Orlando Hernandez	.50
42	Ben Grieve	.50
43	Eric Chavez	.50
44	Scott Rolen	1.00
45	*Pat Burrell*	4.00
46	Warren Morris	.25
47	Jason Kendall	.25
48	Mark McGwire	4.00
49	J.D. Drew	.40
50	Tony Gwynn	2.00
51	Trevor Hoffman	.25
52	Barry Bonds	1.00
53	Ken Griffey Jr.	4.00
54	Alex Rodriguez	3.00
55	Jose Canseco	.75
56	Juan Gonzalez	1.00
57	Ivan Rodriguez	1.00
58	Rafael Palmeiro	.60
59	David Wells	.25
60	Carlos Delgado	.75

1999 Upper Deck HoloGrFX Launchers

This 15-card set highlights the top home run hitters on holographic patterned foil fronts, including McGwier and Sosa. These are seeded 1:3 packs. A Gold (AU) parallel version is also seeded 1:105 packs.

		MT
Complete Set (15):		40.00
Common Player:		1.00
Inserted 1:3		
Gold:		4X
Inserted 1:105		
1	Mark McGwire	7.50
2	Ken Griffey Jr.	7.50
3	Sammy Sosa	4.00
4	J.D. Drew	1.00
5	Mo Vaughn	1.00
6	Juan Gonzalez	1.50
7	Mike Piazza	4.00
8	Alex Rodriguez	5.00
9	Chipper Jones	4.00
10	Nomar Garciaparra	4.00
11	Vladimir Guerrero	2.50
12	Albert Belle	1.00
13	Barry Bonds	1.50
14	Frank Thomas	2.00
15	Jeff Bagwell	1.50

1999 Upper Deck HoloGrFX StarView

This nine-card set highlights the top players in the game on a rainbow foil, full bleed design. These are seeded 1:17 packs. A Gold parallel version is also randomly seeded 1:210 packs.

		MT
Complete Set (9):		50.00
Common Player:		4.00
Inserted 1:17		
Gold:		3X
Inserted 1:210		
1	Mark McGwire	10.00
2	Ken Griffey Jr.	10.00
3	Sammy Sosa	6.00
4	Nomar Garciaparra	6.00
5	Roger Clemens	4.00
6	Greg Maddux	5.00
7	Mike Piazza	6.00
8	Alex Rodriguez	8.00
9	Chipper Jones	6.00

1999 Upper Deck HoloGrFX Future Fame

This six-card set focuses on players who are destined for Hall of Fame greatness. Card fronts feature a horizontal format on a die-cut design. These are seeded 1:34 packs. A parallel Gold (AU) version is also randomly seeded in every 1:432 packs.

		MT
Complete Set (6):		50.00
Common Player:		8.00
Inserted 1:34		
Gold:		3X
Inserted 1:210		
1	Tony Gwynn	8.00
2	Cal Ripken Jr.	12.00
3	Mark McGwire	15.00
4	Ken Griffey Jr.	15.00
5	Greg Maddux	8.00
6	Roger Clemens	6.00

1999 Upper Deck HoloGrFX UD Authentics

This 12-card autographed set is done on a horizontal format, with the player signature across the front of a shadow image, of the featured player in the background. These are inserted 1:431 packs.

		MT
Common Player:		10.00
Inserted 1:431		
CB	Carlos Beltran	15.00
BC	Bruce Chen	20.00
JD	J.D. Drew	30.00
AG	Alex Gonzalez	15.00
JR	Ken Griffey Jr.	250.00
CJ	Chipper Jones	125.00
GK	Gabe Kapler	30.00
MK	Mike Kinkade	10.00
CK	Corey Koskie	15.00
GL	George Lombard	15.00
RM	Ryan Minor	20.00
SM	Shane Monahan	10.00

1999 UD Ionix

Ionix is a 90-card set that includes a 30-card "Techno" subset that was short-printed (1:4 packs). Packs were sold for $4.99, and contain four cards. The first 60 cards of the set are included in a parallel set in which the photo from the back of the regular card was put on the front of a rainbow-foil Reciprocal card. These cards are sequentially numbered to 750. The remaining 30 cards in the set were also paralleled on a Reciprocal card sequentially numbered to 100. The set also includes 350 Frank Robinson "500 Club Piece of History" bat cards, with a piece of a Robinson game-used bat. Another version of the bat cards includes Robinson's autograph, and are hand-numbered to 20. Insert sets included Hyper, Nitro, Cyber, Warp Zone, and HoloGrFX.

		MT
Complete Set (90):		150.00
Common Player (1-60):		.50
Common Techno (61-90):		1.50
Inserted 1:4		
Reciprocals (1-60):		6x to 8x
Production 750 sets		
Techno Reciprocals (61-90):		6x to 10x
Production 100 sets		
Pack (4):		5.00
Wax Box (20):		80.00
1	Troy Glaus	1.50
2	Darin Erstad	.50
3	Travis Lee	.50
4	Matt Williams	.60
5	Chipper Jones	2.50
6	Greg Maddux	2.50
7	Andruw Jones	1.00
8	Andres Galarraga	1.00
9	Tom Glavine	.75
10	Cal Ripken Jr.	4.00
11	Ryan Minor	.50
12	Nomar Garciaparra	3.00
13	Mo Vaughn	1.00
14	Pedro Martinez	1.50
15	Sammy Sosa	2.50
16	Kerry Wood	1.00
17	Albert Belle	1.00
18	Frank Thomas	1.50
19	Sean Casey	.75
20	Kenny Lofton	1.00
21	Manny Ramirez	1.50
22	Jim Thome	.75
23	Bartolo Colon	.50
24	Jaret Wright	.50
25	Larry Walker	1.00
26	Tony Clark	.75
27	Gabe Kapler	1.00
28	Edgar Renteria	.50
29	Randy Johnson	1.00
30	Craig Biggio	.75
31	Jeff Bagwell	1.50
32	Moises Alou	.50
33	Johnny Damon	.50
34	Adrian Beltre	.75
35	Jeromy Burnitz	.50
36	Todd Walker	.50
37	Corey Koskie	.50
38	Vladimir Guerrero	1.50
39	Mike Piazza	3.00
40	Hideo Nomo	.50
41	Derek Jeter	4.00
42	Tino Martinez	.75
43	Orlando Hernandez	1.00
44	Ben Grieve	.75
45	Rickey Henderson	.75
46	Scott Rolen	1.25
47	Curt Schilling	.75
48	Aramis Ramirez	.50
49	Tony Gwynn	2.50
50	Kevin Brown	.75
51	Barry Bonds	1.50
52	Ken Griffey Jr.	5.00
53	Alex Rodriguez	5.00
54	Mark McGwire	5.00
55	J.D. Drew	.75
56	Rolando Arrojo	.50
57	Ivan Rodriguez	1.50
58	Juan Gonzalez	1.50
59	Roger Clemens	2.00
60	Jose Cruz Jr.	.50
61	Travis Lee (Techno)	1.00
62	Andres Galarraga (Techno)	2.00
63	Andruw Jones (Techno)	2.00
64	Chipper Jones (Techno)	6.00
65	Greg Maddux (Techno)	6.00
66	Cal Ripken Jr. (Techno)	10.00
67	Nomar Garciaparra (Techno)	8.00
68	Mo Vaughn (Techno)	2.00
69	Sammy Sosa (Techno)	6.00
70	Frank Thomas (Techno)	4.00
71	Kerry Wood (Techno)	2.50
72	Kenny Lofton (Techno)	2.00
73	Manny Ramirez (Techno)	3.00
74	Larry Walker (Techno)	2.50
75	Jeff Bagwell (Techno)	3.00
76	Randy Johnson (Techno)	2.50
77	Paul Molitor (Techno)	2.50
78	Derek Jeter (Techno)	8.00
79	Tino Martinez (Techno)	1.50
80	Mike Piazza (Techno)	8.00
81	Ben Grieve (Techno)	2.00
82	Scott Rolen (Techno)	3.00
83	Mark McGwire (Techno)	12.00
84	Tony Gwynn (Techno)	4.00
85	Barry Bonds (Techno)	3.00
86	Ken Griffey Jr. (Techno)	12.00
87	Alex Rodriguez (Techno)	10.00
88	Juan Gonzalez (Techno)	3.00
89	Roger Clemens (Techno)	4.00
90	J.D. Drew (Techno)	1.50 .75
100	Ken Griffey Jr. (SAMPLE)	5.00

1999 UD Ionix HoloGrFX

This insert set consisted of 10-cards, and featured only the best players in the game. The cards in this set were holographically enhanced. These cards were rare with one card inserted every 1,500 packs.

		MT
Complete Set (10):		875.00
Common Player:		40.00
Inserted 1:1,500		
HG01	Ken Griffey Jr.	120.00
HG02	Cal Ripken Jr.	120.00
HG03	Frank Thomas	50.00
HG04	Greg Maddux	75.00
HG05	Mike Piazza	100.00
HG06	Alex Rodriguez	120.00
HG07	Chipper Jones	75.00
HG08	Derek Jeter	120.00
HG09	Mark McGwire	150.00
HG10	Juan Gonzalez	40.00

1999 UD Ionix Hyper

This insert set featured the top players in baseball, and consisted of

20-cards. Hyper cards were inserted one per nine packs.

		MT
Complete Set (20):		120.00
Common Player:		2.00
Inserted 1:9		
H01	Ken Griffey Jr.	12.00
H02	Cal Ripken Jr.	12.00
H03	Frank Thomas	5.00
H04	Greg Maddux	8.00
H05	Mike Piazza	10.00
H06	Alex Rodriguez	12.00
H07	Chipper Jones	8.00
H08	Derek Jeter	10.00
H09	Mark McGwire	15.00
H10	Juan Gonzalez	4.00
H11	Kerry Wood	2.50
H12	Tony Gwynn	5.00
H13	Scott Rolen	4.00
H14	Nomar Garciaparra	10.00
H15	Roger Clemens	5.00
H16	Sammy Sosa	10.00
H17	Travis Lee	2.00
H18	Ben Grieve	2.50
H19	Jeff Bagwell	4.00
H20	J.D. Drew	3.00

1999 UD Ionix Warp Zone

This 15-card insert set contained a special holographic foil enhancement. Warp Zone cards were inserted one per 216 packs.

		MT
Complete Set (15):		550.00
Common Player:		10.00
Inserted 1:216		
WZ01	Ken Griffey Jr.	60.00
WZ02	Cal Ripken Jr.	60.00
WZ03	Frank Thomas	30.00
WZ04	Greg Maddux	40.00
WZ05	Mike Piazza	50.00
WZ06	Alex Rodriguez	60.00
WZ07	Chipper Jones	40.00
WZ08	Derek Jeter	60.00
WZ09	Mark McGwire	80.00
WZ10	Juan Gonzalez	20.00
WZ11	Kerry Wood	10.00
WZ12	Tony Gwynn	30.00
WZ13	Scott Rolen	15.00
WZ14	Nomar Garciaparra	50.00
WZ15	J.D. Drew	15.00

1999 UD Ionix Nitro

Baseball's ten most collectible players are featured in this 10-card insert set. Each card features Ionix technology with rainbow foil and a unique color pattern. Nitro cards were inserted one per 18 packs.

		MT
Complete Set (10):		80.00
Common Player:		3.00
Inserted 1:18		
N01	Ken Griffey Jr.	12.00
N02	Cal Ripken Jr.	12.00
N03	Frank Thomas	5.00
N04	Greg Maddux	8.00
N05	Mike Piazza	10.00
N06	Alex Rodriguez	12.00
N07	Chipper Jones	8.00
N08	Derek Jeter	12.00
N09	Mark McGwire	15.00
N10	J.D. Drew	3.00

1999 UD Ionix Cyber

This insert set consisted of 25-cards of baseball's superstars and red-hot rookies. One card was inserted every 53 packs.

		MT
Complete Set (25):		350.00
Common Player:		5.00
C01	Ken Griffey Jr.	30.00
C02	Cal Ripken Jr.	30.00
C03	Frank Thomas	15.00
C04	Greg Maddux	20.00
C05	Mike Piazza	25.00
C06	Alex Rodriguez	30.00
C07	Chipper Jones	20.00
C08	Derek Jeter	30.00
C09	Mark McGwire	40.00
C10	Juan Gonzalez	10.00
C11	Kerry Wood	6.00
C12	Tony Gwynn	15.00
C13	Scott Rolen	8.00
C14	Nomar Garciaparra	25.00
C15	Roger Clemens	15.00
C16	Sammy Sosa	20.00
C17	Travis Lee	5.00
C18	Ben Grieve	6.00
C19	Jeff Bagwell	10.00
C20	Ivan Rodriguez	10.00
C21	Barry Bonds	10.00
C22	J.D. Drew	8.00
C23	Kenny Lofton	6.00
C24	Andruw Jones	10.00
C25	Vladimir Guerrero	15.00

1999 UD Ionix 500 Club Piece of History

These cards feature an actual piece of game-used bat from one of Hall-of-Famer Frank Robinson's Louisville Sluggers. Approximately 350 were made. Robinson also autographed 20 of his Piece of History inserts.

		MT
FR	Frank Robinson/ 350	200.00
FRA	Frank Robinson Auto./20	750.00

1999 Upper Deck Ovation

Cards 1-60 in the base set have the look and feel of an actual baseball. A player photo is in the foreground with a partial image of a baseball in the background on the card front. Cards 61-90 make up two subsets: World Premiere (61-80) is a 20-card collection consisting of 20 rookie prospects and Superstar Spotlight (81-90) is a 10-card lineup of baseball's biggest stars. Both subsets are short-printed, World Premiere are seeded 1:3.5 packs and Superstar Spotlight 1:6 packs. Five card packs carry a S.R.P. of $3.99 per pack.

		MT
Complete Set (90):		150.00
Common Player:		.40
Common World Premiere:		1.00
Inserted 1:3.5		
Common Superstar Spotlight:		4.00
Inserted 1:6		
Pack (5):		6.00
Wax Box (20):		115.00
1	Ken Griffey Jr.	6.00
2	Rondell White	.40
3	Tony Clark	.75
4	Barry Bonds	1.25
5	Larry Walker	.75
6	Greg Vaughn	.40
7	Mark Grace	.50
8	John Olerud	.50
9	Matt Williams	.60
10	Craig Biggio	.65
11	Quinton McCracken	.40
12	Kerry Wood	1.00
13	Derek Jeter	3.00
14	Frank Thomas	1.50
15	Tino Martinez	.75
16	Albert Belle	.75
17	Ben Grieve	1.25
18	Cal Ripken Jr.	4.00
19	Johnny Damon	.40
20	Jose Cruz Jr.	.75
21	Barry Larkin	.60
22	Jason Giambi	.40
23	Sean Casey	.75
24	Scott Rolen	1.25
25	Jim Thome	.75
26	Curt Schilling	.50
27	Moises Alou	.75
28	Alex Rodriguez	4.00
29	Mark Kotsay	.45
30	Darin Erstad	.75
31	Mike Mussina	.65
32	Todd Walker	.50
33	Nomar Garciaparra	3.00
34	Vladimir Guerrero	2.00
35	Jeff Bagwell	1.25
36	Mark McGwire	6.00
37	Travis Lee	.75
38	Dean Palmer	.40
39	Fred McGriff	.50
40	Sammy Sosa	3.00
41	Mike Piazza	3.00
42	Andres Galarraga	.75
43	Pedro Martinez	1.50
44	Juan Gonzalez	1.50
45	Greg Maddux	2.50
46	Jeromy Burnitz	.40
47	Roger Clemens	2.00
48	Vinny Castilla	.40
49	Kevin Brown	.50
50	Mo Vaughn	.65
51	Raul Mondesi	.50
52	Randy Johnson	.75
53	Ray Lankford	.40
54	Jaret Wright	.40
55	Tony Gwynn	2.50
56	Chipper Jones	3.00
57	Gary Sheffield	.60
58	Ivan Rodriguez	1.25
59	Kenny Lofton	.65
60	Jason Kendall	.40
61	J.D. Drew (World Premiere)	2.00
62	Gabe Kapler (World Premiere)	3.00
63	Adrian Beltre (World Premiere)	2.00
64	Carlos Beltran (World Premiere)	1.50
65	Eric Chavez (World Premiere)	1.50
66	Mike Lowell (World Premiere)	1.00
67	Troy Glaus (World Premiere)	4.00
68	George Lombard (World Premiere)	1.00
69	Alex Gonzalez (World Premiere)	1.00
70	Mike Kinkade (World Premiere)	1.50
71	Jeremy Giambi (World Premiere)	1.50
72	Bruce Chen (World Premiere)	1.50
73	Preston Wilson (World Premiere)	1.25
74	Kevin Witt (World Premiere)	1.00
75	Carlos Guillen (World Premiere)	1.00
76	Ryan Minor (World Premiere)	2.50
77	Corey Koskie (World Premiere)	1.00

78	Robert Fick (World Premiere)	1.00
79	Michael Barrett (World Premiere)	2.00
80	Calvin Pickering (World Premiere)	1.00
81	Ken Griffey Jr. (Superstar Spotlight)	12.00
82	Mark McGwire (Superstar Spotlight)	15.00
83	Cal Ripken Jr. (Superstar Spotlight)	10.00
84	Derek Jeter (Superstar Spotlight)	8.00
85	Chipper Jones (Superstar Spotlight)	6.00
86	Nomar Garciaparra (Superstar Spotlight)	8.00
87	Sammy Sosa (Superstar Spotlight)	8.00
88	Juan Gonzalez (Superstar Spotlight)	4.00
89	Mike Piazza (Superstar Spotlight)	8.00
90	Alex Rodriguez (Superstar Spotlight)	10.00

1999 Upper Deck Ovation Curtain Calls

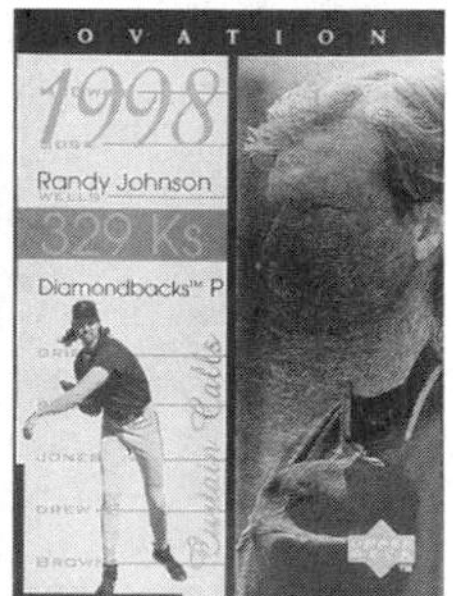

This 20-card set focuses on the most memorable accomplishments posted during the '98 season. Card fronts have two images of the player, one on the right half and a smaller image on the bottom left. Copper foil stamping is used to enhance the card front. These are numbered with a R-prefix and are seeded 1:8 packs.

		MT
Complete Set (20):		70.00
Common Player:		1.00
Inserted 1:8		
R01	Mark McGwire	10.00
R02	Sammy Sosa	5.00
R03	Ken Griffey Jr.	8.00
R04	Alex Rodriguez	8.00
R05	Roger Clemens	3.00
R06	Cal Ripken Jr.	8.00
R07	Barry Bonds	2.50
R08	Kerry Wood	1.50
R09	Nomar Garciaparra	6.00
R10	Derek Jeter	8.00
R11	Juan Gonzalez	2.50
R12	Greg Maddux	5.00
R13	Pedro Martinez	2.50
R14	David Wells	1.00
R15	Moises Alou	1.00
R16	Tony Gwynn	3.00
R17	Albert Belle	1.50
R18	Mike Piazza	6.00
R19	Ivan Rodriguez	2.50
R20	Randy Johnson	2.50

1999 Upper Deck Ovation ReMarkable

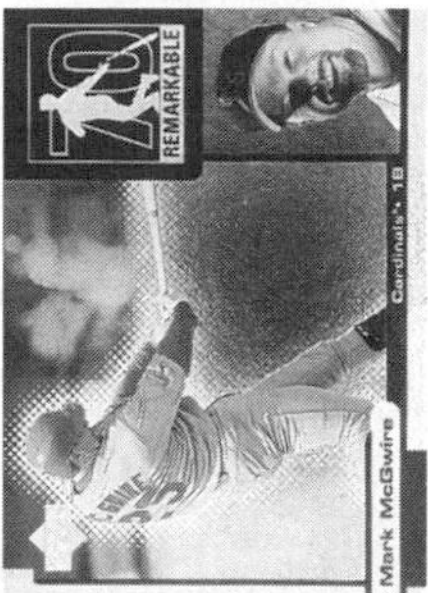

This three-tiered 15-card insert showcases Mark McGwire's historic '98 season. Cards #1-5 are Bronze and inserted 1:9 packs; cards #6-10 are Silver and inserted 1:25 packs; and cards #11-15 are Gold and inserted 1:99 packs.

		MT
Complete Set (15):		150.00
Common #1-5:		6.00
Inserted 1:9		
Common #6-10:		12.00
Inserted 1:25		
Common # 11-15		25.00
Inserted 1:99		
MM01	Mark McGwire	6.00
MM02	Mark McGwire	6.00
MM03	Mark McGwire	6.00
MM04	Mark McGwire	6.00
MM05	Mark McGwire	6.00
MM06	Mark McGwire	12.00
MM07	Mark McGwire	12.00
MM08	Mark McGwire	12.00
MM09	Mark McGwire	12.00
MM10	Mark McGwire	12.00
MM11	Mark McGwire	25.00
MM12	Mark McGwire	25.00
MM13	Mark McGwire	25.00
MM14	Mark McGwire	25.00
MM15	Mark McGwire	25.00

1999 Upper Deck Ovation Major Production

This 20-card set utilizes thermography technology to simulate the look and feel of home plate and highlights some of the game's most productive players. These are inserted 1:45 packs and are numbered with a S prefix.

		MT
Complete Set (20):		200.00
Common Player:		3.00
Inserted 1:45		
S01	Mike Piazza	15.00
S02	Mark McGwire	25.00
S03	Chipper Jones	12.00
S04	Cal Ripken Jr.	20.00
S05	Ken Griffey Jr.	20.00
S06	Barry Bonds	6.00
S07	Tony Gwynn	8.00
S08	Randy Johnson	6.00
S09	Ivan Rodriguez	6.00
S10	Frank Thomas	8.00
S11	Alex Rodriguez	20.00
S12	Albert Belle	4.00
S13	Juan Gonzalez	6.00
S14	Greg Maddux	12.00
S15	Jeff Bagwell	6.00
S16	Derek Jeter	20.00
S17	Matt Williams	3.00
S18	Kenny Lofton	4.00
S19	Sammy Sosa	12.00
S20	Roger Clemens	8.00

1999 Upper Deck Ovation Piece of History

This 14-card set has actual pieces of game-used bat, from the featured player, imbedded into the card. These are inserted 1:247 packs. Ben Grieve autographed 25 versions of his Piece of History insert cards. Although there is no regular Piece of History Kerry Wood card, Upper Deck inserted 25 autographed Piece of History game-used baseball cards. These have a piece of one of Wood's game-hurled baseballs from the 1998 season.

		MT
Common Player:		40.00
Inserted 1:247		
BB	Barry Bonds	80.00
CJ	Chipper Jones	90.00
BW	Bernie Williams	60.00
KGj	Ken Griffey Jr.	200.00
NG	Nomar Garciaparra	200.00
JG	Juan Gonzalez	60.00
DJ	Derek Jeter	200.00
SS	Sammy Sosa	200.00
TG	Tony Gwynn	80.00
AR	Alex Rodriguez	200.00
CR	Cal Ripken Jr.	200.00
BG	Ben Grieve	40.00
VG	Vladimir Guerrero	80.00
MP	Mike Piazza	150.00
BGAU	Ben Grieve (auto, 25)	400.00
KWAU	Kerry Wood (auto, 25)	500.00

1999 Upper Deck Ovation 500 Club Piece of History

Each of these cards actually have a piece of game-used Louisville Slugger, once swung by Mickey Mantle, imbedded in them. Approximately 350 cards exist. There also is one card with a cut signature of Mantle and a piece of his game-used bat on it.

		MT
Production 350 cards		
MIC-P	Mickey Mantle	1200.

1999 Upper Deck Century Legends

The first 47 cards in the 131-card set are taken from the Sporting News' list of Baseball's 100 Greatest Players. Each card bears a Sporting News photo of the featured player and his ranking in silver and copper foil. The next 50 cards tout Upper Deck's rankings of the Top 50 contemporary players. Rounding out the base set are two subsets: "21st Century Phenoms" and "Century Memories".

		MT
Complete Set (131):		50.00
Common Player:		.20
Century Collection:		25X
Production 100 sets		
Pack (5):		5.00
Wax Box (24):		100.00
1a	Babe Ruth (Sporting News Top 50)	4.00
1b	Babe Ruth (SAMPLE overprint on back)	4.00
2	Willie Mays (Sporting New Top 50)	2.00
3	Ty Cobb (Sporting News Top 50)	2.00
4	Walter Johnson (Sporting News Top 50)	.75
5	Hank Aaron (Sporting News Top 50)	1.50
6	Lou Gehrig (Sporting News Top 50)	3.00
7	Christy Mathewson (Sporting News Top 50)	.75
8	Ted Williams (Sporting News Top 50)	2.00

9	Rogers Hornsby (Sporting News Top 50)	.50
10	Stan Musial (Sporting News Top 50)	1.00
12	Grover Alexander (Sporting News Top 50)	.50
13	Honus Wagner (Sporting News Top 50)	.75
14	Cy Young (Sporting News Top 50)	.75
15	Jimmie Foxx (Sporting News Top 50)	.75
16	Johnny Bench (Sporting News Top 50)	.75
17	Mickey Mantle (Sporting News Top 50)	4.00
18	Josh Gibson (Sporting News Top 50)	.75
19	Satchel Paige (Sporting News Top 50)	1.00
20	Roberto Clemente (Sporting News Top 50)	3.00
21	Warren Spahn (Sporting News Top 50)	.50
22	Frank Robinson (Sporting News Top 50)	.50
23	Lefty Grove (Sporting News Top 50)	.50
24	Eddie Collins (Sporting News Top 50)	.50
27	Tris Speaker (Sporting News Top 50)	.50
28	Mike Schmidt (Sporting News Top 50)	.75
29	Napoleon LaJoie (Sporting News Top 50)	.50
30	Steve Carlton (Sporting News Top 50)	.50
31	Bob Gibson (Sporting News Top 50)	.50
32	Tom Seaver (Sporting News Top 50)	.50
33	George Sisler (Sporting News Top 50)	.50
34	Barry Bonds (Sporting News Top 50)	.75
35	Joe Jackson (Sporting News Top 50)	2.00
36	Bob Feller (Sporting News Top 50)	.50
37	Hank Greenberg (Sporting News Top 50)	.50
38	Ernie Banks (Sporting News Top 50)	.75
39	Greg Maddux (Sporting News Top 50)	1.50
40	Yogi Berra (Sporting News Top 50)	.75
41	Nolan Ryan (Sporting News Top 50)	3.00
42	Mel Ott (Sporting News Top 50)	.50
43	Al Simmons (Sporting News Top 50)	.50
44	Jackie Robinson (Sporting News Top 50)	2.50
45	Carl Hubbell (Sporting News Top 50)	.50
46	Charley Gehringer (Sporting News Top 50)	.50
47	Buck Leonard (Sporting News Top 50)	.50
48	Reggie Jackson (Sporting News Top 50)	.75
49	Tony Gwynn (Sporting News Top 50)	1.00
50	Roy Campanella (Sporting News Top 50)	.75
51	Ken Griffey Jr. (Contemporaries)	4.00
52	Barry Bonds (Contemporaries)	.75
53	Roger Clemens (Contemporaries)	1.00
54	Tony Gwynn (Contemporaries)	1.50
55	Cal Ripken Jr. (Contemporaries)	2.50
56	Greg Maddux (Contemporaries)	1.50
57	Frank Thomas (Contemporaries)	1.50
58	Mark McGwire (Contemporaries)	4.00
59	Mike Piazza (Contemporaries)	2.00
60	Wade Boggs (Contemporaries)	.40
61	Alex Rodriguez (Contemporaries)	3.00
62	Juan Gonzalez (Contemporaries)	.75
63	Mo Vaughn (Contemporaries)	.60
64	Albert Belle (Contemporaries)	.75
65	Sammy Sosa (Contemporaries)	2.00
66	Nomar Garciaparra (Contemporaries)	2.00
67	Derek Jeter (Contemporaries)	2.00
68	Kevin Brown (Contemporaries)	.30
69	Jose Canseco (Contemporaries)	.50
70	Randy Johnson (Contemporaries)	.40
71	Tom Glavine (Contemporaries)	.20
72	Barry Larkin (Contemporaries)	.30
73	Curt Schilling (Contemporaries)	.20
74	Moises Alou (Contemporaries)	.20
75	Fred McGriff (Contemporaries)	.20
76	Pedro Martinez (Contemporaries)	.50
77	Andres Galarraga (Contemporaries)	.30
78	Will Clark (Contemporaries)	.30
79	Larry Walker (Contemporaries)	.50
80	Ivan Rodriguez (Contemporaries)	.75
81	Chipper Jones (Contemporaries)	2.00
82	Jeff Bagwell (Contemporaries)	.75
83	Craig Biggio (Contemporaries)	.40
84	Kerry Wood (Contemporaries)	.75
85	Roberto Alomar (Contemporaries)	.50
86	Vinny Castilla (Contemporaries)	.20
87	Kenny Lofton (Contemporaries)	.60
88	Rafael Palmeiro (Contemporaries)	.30
89	Manny Ramirez (Contemporaries)	1.00
90	David Wells (Contemporaries)	.20
91	Mark Grace (Contemporaries)	.30
92	Bernie Williams (Contemporaries)	.25
93	David Cone (Contemporaries)	.20
94	John Olerud (Contemporaries)	.20
95	John Smoltz (Contemporaries)	.20
96	Tino Martinez (Contemporaries)	.25
97	Raul Mondesi (Contemporaries)	.30
98	Gary Sheffield (Contemporaries)	.25
99	Orel Hershiser (Contemporaries)	.20
100	Rickey Henderson (Contemporaries)	.30
101	J.D. Drew (21st Century Phenoms)	.40
102	Troy Glaus (21st Century Phenoms)	1.00
103	Nomar Garciaparra (21st Century Phenoms)	2.00
104	Scott Rolen (21st Century Phenoms)	.75
105	Ryan Minor (21st Century Phenoms)	.20
106	Travis Lee (21st Century Phenoms)	.75
107	Roy Halladay (21st Century Phenoms)	.20
108	Carlos Beltran (21st Century Phenoms)	.25
109	Alex Rodriguez (21st Century Phenoms)	3.00
110	Eric Chavez (21st Century Phenoms)	.75
111	Vladimir Guerrero (21st Century Phenoms)	1.50
112	Ben Grieve (21st Century Phenoms)	.75
113	Kerry Wood (21st Century Phenoms)	.75
114	Alex Gonzalez (21st Century Phenoms)	.20
115	Darin Erstad (21st Century Phenoms)	.75
116	Derek Jeter (21st Century Phenoms)	2.00
117	Jaret Wright (21st Century Phenoms)	.40
118	Jose Cruz Jr. (21st Century Phenoms)	.40
119	Chipper Jones (21st Century Phenoms)	2.00
120	Gabe Kapler (21st Century Phenoms)	1.50
121	Satchel Paige (Century Memories)	1.00
122	Willie Mays (Century Memories)	1.50
123	Roberto Clemente (Century Memories)	3.00
124	Lou Gehrig (Century Memories)	2.50
125	Mark McGwire (Century Memories)	4.00
127	Bob Gibson (Century Memories)	.50
128	Johnny Vander Meer (Century Memories)	.20
129	Walter Johnson (Century Memories)	.50
130	Ty Cobb (Century Memories)	1.50
131	Don Larsen (Century Memories)	.40
132	Jackie Robinson (Century Memories)	2.00
133	Tom Seaver (Century Memories)	.50
134	Johnny Bench (Century Memories)	.50
135	Frank Robinson (Century Memories)	.50

1999 Upper Deck Century Legends Epic Milestones

This nine-card set showcases nine of the most impressive milestones established in major league history. Each card is numbered with a "EM" prefix and are seeded 1:12 packs.

		MT
Complete Set (9):		45.00
Common Player:		2.00
Inserted 1:12		
2	Jackie Robinson	6.00
3	Nolan Ryan	10.00
4	Mark McGwire	12.00
5	Roger Clemens	4.00
6	Sammy Sosa	6.00
7	Cal Ripken Jr.	10.00
8	Rickey Henderson	2.00
9	Hank Aaron	4.00
10	Barry Bonds	3.00

1999 Upper Deck Century Legends Memorable Shots

This 10-card insert set focuses on the most memorable home runs launched during this century. The player's image is framed in an embossed foil, frame-like design. These are seeded 1:12 packs, each card back is numbered with a "HR" prefix.

		MT
Complete Set (10):		40.00
Common Player:		2.00
Inserted 1:12		
1	Babe Ruth	10.00
2	Bobby Thomson	2.00
3	Kirk Gibson	2.00
4	Carlton Fisk	2.00
5	Bill Mazeroski	2.00
6	Bucky Dent	1.00
7	Mark McGwire	10.00
8	Mickey Mantle	12.00
9	Joe Carter	1.00
10	Mark McGwire	10.00

1999 Upper Deck Century Legends All-Century Team

This 10-card set highlights Upper Deck's all-time all-star team. These were seeded 1:23 packs.

		MT
Complete Set (10):		50.00
Common Player:		4.00
Inserted 1:23		
1	Babe Ruth	15.00
2	Ty Cobb	6.00
3	Willie Mays	6.00
4	Lou Gehrig	10.00
5	Jackie Robinson	8.00
6	Mike Schmidt	4.00
7	Ernie Banks	4.00
8	Johnny Bench	4.00
9	Cy Young	4.00
10	Lineup Sheet	1.00

1999 Upper Deck Century Legends Jerseys of the Century

This eight-card set features a swatch of game-worn jersey from the featured player, which includes current and retired players. These are seeded 1:418 packs.

		MT
Common Player:		75.00
Inserted 1:418		
GB	George Brett	175.00
RC	Roger Clemens	125.00
TG	Tony Gwynn	100.00
GM	Greg Maddux	125.00
EM	Eddie Murray	75.00
NR	Nolan Ryan	600.00
MS	Mike Schmidt	150.00
OZ	Ozzie Smith	150.00
DW	Dave Winfield	75.00

1999 Upper Deck Century Legends 500 Club Piece of History

This Jimmie Foxx insert has a piece of of a game-used Louisville Slugger once swung by Foxx, embedded into the card front. An estimated 350 cards of this one exist.

		MT
JF	Jimmie Foxx	300.00

1999 Upper Deck Century Legends Epic Signatures

This 30-card set features autographs from retired and current stars on a horizontal format. A player portrait appears over a ballpark background on front. The portrait is repeated on back with a statement of authenticity. Cards are numbered with player initials. These autographed cards are seeded 1:24 packs.

		MT
Complete Set (30):		2000.
Common Player:		15.00
Inserted 1:24		
EB	Ernie Banks	50.00
JB	Johnny Bench	75.00
YB	Yogi Berra	60.00
BB	Barry Bonds	75.00
SC	Steve Carlton	40.00
BD	Bucky Dent	15.00
BF	Bob Feller	25.00
CF	Carlton Fisk	35.00
BG	Bob Gibson	30.00
JG	Juan Gonzalez	75.00
Jr.	Ken Griffey Jr.	250.00
Sr.	Ken Griffey Sr.	15.00
VG	Vladimir Guerrero	50.00
TG	Tony Gwynn	125.00
RJ	Reggie Jackson	125.00
HK	Harmon Killebrew	40.00
DL	Don Larsen	15.00
GM	Greg Maddux	150.00
EMa	Eddie Mathews	50.00
BM	Bill Mazeroski	15.00
WMc	Willie McCovey	30.00
SM	Stan Musial	80.00
FR	Frank Robinson	50.00
AR	Alex Rodriguez	175.00
NR	Nolan Ryan	350.00
MS	Mike Schmidt	60.00
TS	Tom Seaver	80.00
WS	Warren Spahn	50.00
FT	Frank Thomas	100.00
BT	Bobby Thomson	15.00

Player names in *Italic* type indicate a rookie card.

1999 Upper Deck Century Legends Century Epic Signatures

This 32-card autographed set features signatures from retired and current stars. The cards have a horizontal format and have gold foil stamping. Each card is hand numbered to 100.

		MT
Common Player:		25.00
Production 100 sets		
EB	Ernie Banks	80.00
JB	Johnny Bench	125.00
YB	Yogi Berra	125.00
BB	Barry Bonds	125.00
SC	Steve Carlton	80.00
BD	Bucky Dent	40.00
BF	Bob Feller	50.00
CF	Carlton Fisk	75.00
BG	Bob Gibson	75.00
JG	Juan Gonzalez	150.00
Jr.	Ken Griffey Jr.	400.00
Sr.	Ken Griffey Sr.	35.00
VG	Vladimir Guerrero	80.00
TG	Tony Gwynn	150.00
RJ	Reggie Jackson	175.00
HK	Harmon Killebrew	60.00
DL	Don Larsen	35.00
GM	Greg Maddux	250.00
EMa	Eddie Mathews	60.00
WM	Willie Mays	250.00
BM	Bill Mazeroski	35.00
WMc	Willie McCovey	50.00
SM	Stan Musial	150.00
FR	Frank Robinson	60.00
AR	Alex Rodriguez	300.00
NR	Nolan Ryan	400.00
MS	Mike Schmidt	125.00
TS	Tom Seaver	100.00
WS	Warren Spahn	60.00
FT	Frank Thomas	150.00
BT	Bobby Thomson	35.00
TW	Ted Williams	600.00

1999 Upper Deck MVP

Card fronts of the 220-card set feature silver foil stamping and a white border. Card backs feature year-by-year statistics, a small photo of the featured player and a brief career note. MVP was distributed in 24-pack boxes, with a SRP of $1.59 for 10-card packs.

		MT
Complete Set (220):		30.00
Common Player:		.15
Pack (10):		1.75
Wax Box (28):		40.00
1	Mo Vaughn	.60
2	Tim Belcher	.15
3	Jack McDowell	.15
4	Troy Glaus	.75
5	Darin Erstad	.75
6	Tim Salmon	.30
7	Jim Edmonds	.15
8	Randy Johnson	.50
9	Steve Finley	.15
10	Travis Lee	.75
11	Matt Williams	.25
12	Todd Stottlemyre	.15
13	Jay Bell	.15
14	David Dellucci	.15
15	Chipper Jones	2.00
16	Andruw Jones	.50
17	Greg Maddux	1.50
18	Tom Glavine	.25
19	Javy Lopez	.15
20	Brian Jordan	.15
21	George Lombard	.25
22	John Smoltz	.25
23	Cal Ripken Jr.	2.50
24	Charles Johnson	.15
25	Albert Belle	.75
26	Brady Anderson	.15
27	Mike Mussina	.60
28	Calvin Pickering	.15
29	Ryan Minor	.25
30	Jerry Hairston Jr.	.15
31	Nomar Garciaparra	2.00
32	Pedro Martinez	.60
33	Jason Varitek	.15
34	Troy O'Leary	.15
35	Donnie Sadler	.15
36	Mark Portugal	.15
37	John Valentin	.15
38	Kerry Wood	.75
39	Sammy Sosa	2.00
40	Mark Grace	.25
41	Henry Rodriguez	.15
42	Rod Beck	.15
43	Benito Santiago	.15
44	Kevin Tapani	.15
45	Frank Thomas	1.50
46	Mike Caruso	.15
47	Magglio Ordonez	.25
48	Paul Konerko	.25
49	Ray Durham	.15
50	Jim Parque	.15
51	Carlos Lee	.25
52	Denny Neagle	.15
53	Pete Harnisch	.15
54	Michael Tucker	.15
55	Sean Casey	.30
56	Eddie Taubenese	.15
57	Barry Larkin	.20
58	Pokey Reese	.15
59	Sandy Alomar	.25
60	Roberto Alomar	.60
61	Bartolo Colon	.15
62	Kenny Lofton	.60
63	Omar Vizquel	.15
64	Travis Fryman	.15
65	Jim Thome	.40
66	Manny Ramirez	1.00
67	Jaret Wright	.25
68	Darryl Kile	.15
69	Kirt Manwaring	.15
70	Vinny Castilla	.25
71	Todd Helton	.75
72	Dante Bichette	.25
73	Larry Walker	.50
74	Derrick Gibson	.15
75	Gabe Kapler	.75
76	Dean Palmer	.15
77	Matt Anderson	.15
78	Bobby Higginson	.15
79	Damion Easley	.15
80	Tony Clark	.40
81	Juan Encarnacion	.15
82	Livan Hernandez	.15
83	Alex Gonzalez	.15
84	Preston Wilson	.15
85	Derrek Lee	.15
86	Mark Kotsay	.15
87	Todd Dunwoody	.15
88	Cliff Floyd	.15
89	Ken Caminiti	.15
90	Jeff Bagwell	.75
91	Moises Alou	.25
92	Craig Biggio	.40
93	Billy Wagner	.15
94	Richard Hidalgo	.15
95	Derek Bell	.15
96	Hipolito Pichardo	.15
97	Jeff King	.15
98	Carlos Beltran	.20

99	Jeremy Giambi	.25
100	Larry Sutton	.15
101	Johnny Damon	.15
102	Dee Brown	.15
103	Kevin Brown	.25
104	Chan Ho Park	.25
105	Raul Mondesi	.30
106	Eric Karros	.15
107	Adrian Beltre	.30
108	Devon White	.15
109	Gary Sheffield	.20
110	Sean Berry	.15
111	Alex Ochoa	.15
112	Marquis Grissom	.15
113	Fernando Vina	.15
114	Jeff Cirillo	.15
115	Geoff Jenkins	.15
116	Jeromy Burnitz	.15
117	Brad Radke	.15
118	Eric Milton	.15
119	A.J. Pierzynski	.15
120	Todd Walker	.25
121	David Ortiz	.15
122	Corey Koskie	.15
123	Vladimir Guerrero	1.25
124	Rondell White	.20
125	Brad Fullmer	.20
126	Ugueth Urbina	.15
127	Dustin Hermanson	.15
128	Michael Barrett	.25
129	Fernando Seguignol	.20
130	Mike Piazza	2.00
131	Rickey Henderson	.30
132	Rey Ordonez	.15
133	John Olerud	.25
134	Robin Ventura	.15
135	Hideo Nomo	.25
136	Mike Kinkade	.15
137	Al Leiter	.25
138	Brian McRae	.15
139	Derek Jeter	2.00
140	Bernie Williams	.40
141	Paul O'Neill	.30
142	Scott Brosius	.15
143	Tino Martinez	.30
144	Roger Clemens	1.00
145	Orlando Hernandez	1.00
146	Mariano Rivera	.25
147	Ricky Ledee	.15
148	A.J. Hinch	.15
149	Ben Grieve	.75
150	Eric Chavez	.75
151	Miguel Tejada	.25
152	Matt Stairs	.15
153	Ryan Christenson	.15
154	Jason Giambi	.15
155	Curt Schilling	.25
156	Scott Rolen	.75
157	*Pat Burrell*	2.00
158	Doug Glanville	.15
159	Bobby Abreu	.15
160	Rico Brogna	.15
161	Ron Gant	.15
162	Jason Kendall	.25
163	Aramis Ramirez	.15
164	Jose Guillen	.15
165	Emil Brown	.15
166	Pat Meares	.15
167	Kevin Young	.15
168	Brian Giles	.15
169	Mark McGwire	3.00
170	J.D. Drew	.40
171	Edgar Renteria	.15
172	Fernando Tatis	.20
173	Matt Morris	.15
174	Eli Marrero	.15
175	Ray Lankford	.15
176	Tony Gwynn	1.50
177	Sterling Hitchcock	.15
178	Ruben Rivera	.15
179	Wally Joyner	.15
180	Trevor Hoffman	.15
181	Jim Leyritz	.15
182	Carlos Hernandez	.15
183	Barry Bonds	.75
184	Ellis Burks	.15
185	F.P. Santangelo	.15
186	J.T. Snow	.15
187	Ramon Martinez	.15
188	Jeff Kent	.15
189	Robb Nen	.15
190	Ken Griffey Jr.	3.00
191	Alex Rodriguez	2.50
192	Shane Monahan	.15
193	Carlos Guillen	.15
194	Edgar Martinez	.15
195	David Segui	.15
196	Jose Mesa	.15
197	Jose Canseco	.75
198	Rolando Arrojo	.15
199	Wade Boggs	.25
200	Fred McGriff	.25
201	Quinton McCracken	.15
202	Bobby Smith	.15
203	Bubba Trammell	.15
204	Juan Gonzalez	.75
205	Ivan Rodriguez	.75
206	Rafael Palmeiro	.30
207	Royce Clayton	.15
208	Rick Helling	.15
209	Todd Zeile	.15
210	Rusty Greer	.15
211	David Wells	.15
212	Roy Halladay	.25
213	Carlos Delgado	.40
214	Darrin Fletcher	.15
215	Shawn Green	.50
216	Kevin Witt	.15
217	Jose Cruz Jr.	.20
218	Ken Griffey Jr.	1.50
219	Sammy Sosa	.65
220	Mark McGwire	1.50

1999 Upper Deck MVP Scripts/Super Scripts

Three different parallels of the 220 base cards in MVP are inserted bearing a metallic-foil facsimile autograph on front. Silver Script cards are found about every other pack. Gold Script cards are hobby-only and serially numbered to 100 apiece. Also hobby-only are Super Script versions on which the autograph is in holographic foil and the cards are numbered on the back to 25 apiece.

	MT
Silver Script:	2X
Gold Script:	25X
Super Script:	75X

(See 1999 UD MVP for checklist and base card values.)

1999 Upper Deck MVP Power Surge

This 15-card set features baseball's top home run hitters, utilizing rainbow foil technology. Card backs are numbered with a "P" prefix and are seeded 1:9 packs.

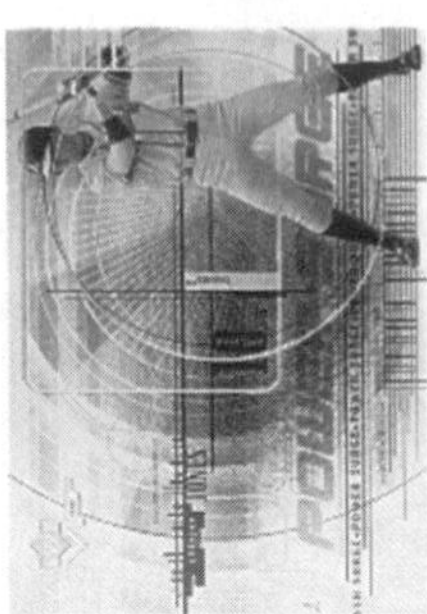

		MT
Complete Set (15):		30.00
Common Player:		.70
Inserted 1:9		
1	Mark McGwire	5.00
2	Sammy Sosa	3.00
3	Ken Griffey Jr.	5.00
4	Alex Rodriguez	4.00
5	Juan Gonzalez	2.50
6	Nomar Garciaparra	3.00
7	Vladimir Guerrero	2.50
8	Chipper Jones	3.00
9	Albert Belle	1.00
10	Frank Thomas	1.50
11	Mike Piazza	3.00
12	Jeff Bagwell	1.25
13	Manny Ramirez	1.25
14	Mo Vaughn	1.25
15	Barry Bonds	1.50

1999 Upper Deck MVP Swing Time

This 12-card set focuses on top hitters in the game and points out three aspects why the featured player is such a successful hitter. Printed on a full foiled front these are seeded 1:6 packs. Card backs are numbered with a "S" prefix.

		MT
Complete Set (12):		20.00
Common Player:		.90
Inserted 1:6		
1	Ken Griffey Jr.	3.50
2	Mark McGwire	3.50
3	Sammy Sosa	2.25
4	Tony Gwynn	1.75
5	Alex Rodriguez	3.00
6	Nomar Garciaparra	2.25
7	Barry Bonds	.90
8	Frank Thomas	1.50
9	Chipper Jones	2.25
10	Ivan Rodriguez	.90
11	Mike Piazza	2.25
12	Derek Jeter	2.25

1999 Upper Deck MVP Scout's Choice

Utilizing Light F/X technology, this 15-card set highlights the top young prospects in the game. Card backs are numbered with a "SC" prefix and are seeded 1:9 packs.

		MT
Complete Set (15):		20.00
Common Player:		.50
Inserted 1:9		
1	J.D. Drew	1.00
2	Ben Grieve	1.25
3	Troy Glaus	2.00
4	Gabe Kapler	1.50
5	Carlos Beltran	.50
6	Aramis Ramirez	.50
7	Pat Burrell	4.00
8	Kerry Wood	1.25
9	Ryan Minor	.50
10	Todd Helton	1.50
11	Eric Chavez	1.25
12	Russ Branyon	.50
13	Travis Lee	1.25
14	Ruben Mateo	1.50
15	Roy Halladay	.50

1999 Upper Deck MVP Dynamics

This 15-card set features holofoil treatment on the card fronts with silver foil stamping. Card backs are numbered with a "D" prefix and are inserted 1:28 packs.

		MT
Complete Set (15):		125.00
Common Player:		3.00
Inserted 1:28		
1	Ken Griffey Jr.	20.00
2	Alex Rodriguez	15.00

3	Nomar Garciaparra	12.00
4	Mike Piazza	12.00
5	Mark McGwire	20.00
6	Sammy Sosa	12.00
7	Chipper Jones	12.00
8	Mo Vaughn	4.00
9	Tony Gwynn	10.00
10	Vladimir Guerrero	8.00
11	Derek Jeter	12.00
12	Jeff Bagwell	5.00
13	Cal Ripken Jr.	15.00
14	Juan Gonzalez	5.00
15	J.D. Drew	3.00

1999 Upper Deck MVP Super Tools

This 15-card insert set focuses on baseball's top stars and utilizes holo foil technology on the card fronts. Card backs are numbered with a "T" prefix and are seeded 1:14 packs.

		MT
Complete Set (15):		60.00
Common Player:		2.00
Inserted 1:14		
1	Ken Griffey Jr.	12.00
2	Alex Rodriguez	10.00
3	Sammy Sosa	8.00
4	Derek Jeter	8.00
5	Vladimir Guerrero	6.00
6	Ben Grieve	2.50
7	Mike Piazza	8.00
8	Kenny Lofton	2.00
9	Barry Bonds	2.50
10	Darin Erstad	2.00
11	Nomar Garciaparra	8.00
12	Cal Ripken Jr.	10.00
13	J.D. Drew	2.00
14	Larry Walker	2.00
15	Chipper Jones	8.00

1999 Upper Deck MVP Game Used Souvenirs

This 10-card set have a piece of game-used bat from the featured player embedded into each card. These are found exclusively in hobby packs at a rate of 1:144 packs.

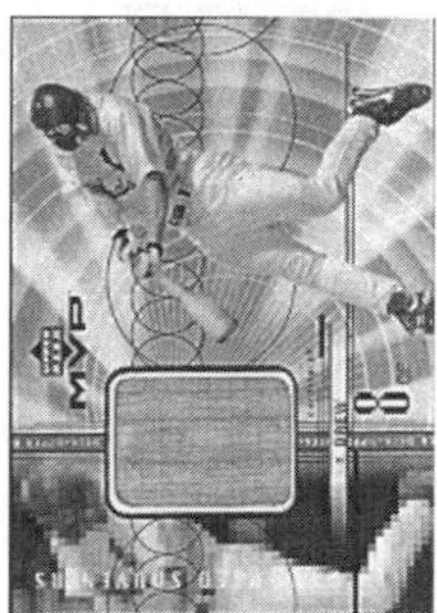

		MT
Complete Set (9):		750.00
Common Player:		50.00
Inserted 1:144		
JB	Jeff Bagwell	60.00
BB	Barry Bonds	50.00
JD	J.D. Drew	40.00
KGj	Ken Griffey Jr.	200.00
CJ	Chipper Jones	125.00
MP	Mike Piazza	125.00
CR	Cal Ripken Jr.	160.00
SR	Scott Rolen	50.00
MV	Mo Vaughn	50.00

1999 Upper Deck MVP Signed Game Used Souvenirs

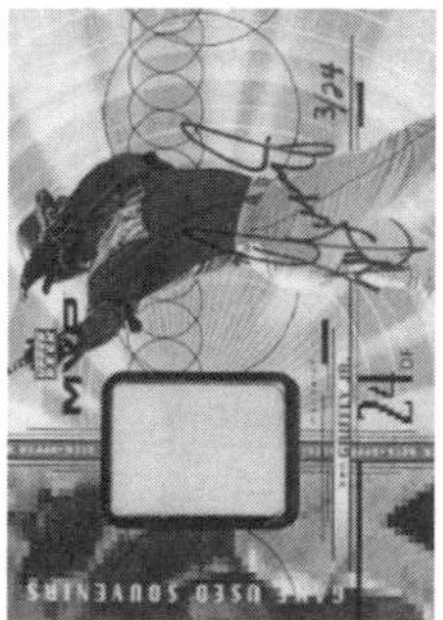

Ken Griffey Jr. and Chipper Jones both signed their Game Used Souvenir inserts to their jersey number, Griffey (24) and Jones (10). These were seeded exclusively in hobby packs.

		MT
Complete Set (2):		1600.
KGj	Ken Griffey Jr.	1200.
CJ	Chipper Jones	500.00

1999 Upper Deck MVP ProSign

This 30-card autographed set is randomly seeded exclusively in retail packs at a rate of 1:216 packs. Card backs are numbered with the featured player's initials.

		MT
Common Player:		10.00
Inserted 1:216 R		
MA	Matt Anderson	15.00
CB	Carlos Beltran	15.00
RB	Russ Branyan	20.00
EC	Eric Chavez	25.00
BC	Bruce Chen	20.00
BF	Brad Fuller	15.00
NG	Nomar Garciaparra	140.00
JG	Jeremy Giambi	20.00
DG	Derrick Gibson	15.00
CG	Chris Gomez	10.00
AG	Alex Gonzalez	15.00
BG	Ben Grieve	40.00
JR.	Ken Griffey Jr.	400.00
RH	Richard Hidalgo	15.00
SH	Shea Hillenbrand	10.00
CJ	Chipper Jones	125.00
GK	Gabe Kapler	40.00
SK	Scott Karl	10.00
CK	Corey Koskie	15.00
RL	Ricky Ledee	15.00
ML	Mike Lincoln	10.00
GL	George Lombard	20.00
MLo	Mike Lowell	20.00
RM	Ryan Minor	20.00
SM	Shane Monahan	10.00
AN	Abraham Nunez	10.00
JP	Jim Parque	10.00
CP	Calvin Pickering	20.00
JRa	Jason Rakers	10.00
RR	Ruben Rivera	10.00
IR	Ivan Rodriguez	80.00
KW	Kevin Witt	10.00

1999 Upper Deck MVP 500 Club Piece of History

This insert has a piece of game-used bat once swung by Mike Schmidt embedded into each card. A total of 350 of this insert was produced. Schmidt also signed 20 of the inserts.

	MT
548HRMike Schmidt	350.00
548HRMike Schmidt Auto./20	1000.

1999 UD Retro

The 110-card base set is comprised of 88 current stars and 22 retired greats. Card fronts have a tan, speckled border while card backs have a year-by-year compilation of the player's stats along with a career note. Retro is packaged in lunchboxes, 24 packs to a box with a SRP of $4.99 per six-card pack.

		MT
Complete Set (110):		30.00
Common Player:		.20
Gold (1-88):		6x to 12x
Gold (89-110):		10x to 20x
Production 250 sets		
Platinum 1/1 issued; values undetermined		
Wax Box:		90.00
1	Mo Vaughn	.75
2	Troy Glaus	1.00
3	Tim Salmon	.40
4	Randy Johnson	.75
5	Travis Lee	.40
6	Matt Williams	.50
7	Greg Maddux	2.00
8	Chipper Jones	2.50
9	Andruw Jones	.75
10	Tom Glavine	.40
11	Javy Lopez	.40
12	Albert Belle	.75
13	Cal Ripken Jr.	3.00
14	Brady Anderson	.20
15	Nomar Garciaparra	2.50
16	Pedro J. Martinez	1.50
17	Sammy Sosa	2.50
18	Mark Grace	.60
19	Frank Thomas	1.50
20	Ray Durham	.20
21	Sean Casey	.50
22	Greg Vaughn	.30
23	Barry Larkin	.30
24	Manny Ramirez	1.00
25	Jim Thome	.50
26	Jaret Wright	.20
27	Kenny Lofton	.75
28	Larry Walker	.75
29	Todd Helton	1.00
30	Vinny Castilla	.40
31	Tony Clark	.40
32	Juan Encarnacion	.20
33	Dean Palmer	.20
34	Mark Kotsay	.20
35	Alex Gonzalez	.20
36	Shane Reynolds	.20
37	Ken Caminiti	.40
38	Jeff Bagwell	1.00
39	Craig Biggio	.50
40	Carlos Febles	.40
41	Carlos Beltran	.40
42	Jeremy Giambi	.20
43	Raul Mondesi	.40
44	Adrian Beltre	.40
45	Kevin Brown	.40
46	Jeromy Burnitz	.30
47	Jeff Cirillo	.20
48	Corey Koskie	.20
49	Todd Walker	.20
50	Vladimir Guerrero	2.00
51	Michael Barrett	.50
52	Mike Piazza	2.50
53	Robin Ventura	.50
54	Edgardo Alfonzo	.50
55	Derek Jeter	2.50
56	Roger Clemens	1.50
57	Tino Martinez	.60
58	Orlando Hernandez	.50
59	Chuck Knoblauch	.50
60	Bernie Williams	.60
61	Eric Chavez	.50
62	Ben Grieve	.50
63	Jason Giambi	.20
64	Scott Rolen	1.00
65	Curt Schilling	.40
66	Bobby Abreu	.20
67	Jason Kendall	.40
68	Kevin Young	.30
69	Mark McGwire	5.00
70	J.D. Drew	.40
71	Eric Davis	.20
72	Tony Gwynn	2.00

73	Trevor Hoffman	.20
74	Barry Bonds	1.00
75	Robb Nen	.20
76	Ken Griffey Jr.	5.00
77	Alex Rodriguez	3.00
78	Jay Buhner	.20
79	Carlos Guillen	.20
80	Jose Canseco	1.00
81	Bobby Smith	.20
82	Juan Gonzalez	1.00
83	Ivan Rodriguez	1.00
84	Rafael Palmeiro	.75
85	Rick Helling	.20
86	Jose Cruz Jr.	.40
87	David Wells	.20
88	Carlos Delgado	.75
89	Nolan Ryan	4.00
90	George Brett	1.50
91	Robin Yount	1.00
92	Paul Molitor	1.00
93	Dave Winfield	.50
94	Steve Garvey	.20
95	Ozzie Smith	1.00
96	Ted Williams	4.00
97	Don Mattingly	1.00
98	Mickey Mantle	4.00
99	Harmon Killebrew	.50
100	Rollie Fingers	.20
101	Kirk Gibson	.20
102	Bucky Dent	.20
103	Willie Mays	2.00
104	Babe Ruth	4.00
105	Gary Carter	.20
106	Reggie Jackson	1.50
107	Frank Robinson	1.00
108	Ernie Banks	1.50
109	Eddie Murray	.50
110	Mike Schmidt	1.50

1999 UD Retro Throwback Attack

This 15-card set has a "Retro" look, borrowing heavily from 1959 Topps. Highlighting top players, the set features card fronts with a circular player photo on a bright orange background. At top in white is, "throwback attack". There is a white border. Backs have a ghosted image of the front photo and career highlights. Cards are attack" across the top and a white border. Card backs are numbered with a "T" prefix and are seeded 1:5 packs. A parallel version is also randomly seeded and limited to 500 numbered sets.

		MT
Complete Set (15):		40.00
Common Player:		1.00
Inserted 1:5		
Level 2:		5x to 10x
Production 500 sets		
1	Ken Griffey Jr.	7.50
2	Mark McGwire	7.50
3	Sammy Sosa	4.00
4	Roger Clemens	2.00
5	J.D. Drew	1.50
6	Alex Rodriguez	5.00
7	Greg Maddux	3.00
8	Mike Piazza	4.00
9	Juan Gonzalez	1.50
10	Mo Vaughn	1.00
11	Cal Ripken Jr.	5.00
12	Frank Thomas	2.00
13	Nomar Garciaparra	4.00
14	Vladimir Guerrero	3.00
15	Tony Gwynn	3.00

1999 UD Retro Distant Replay

This 15-card set recounts the 15 most memorable plays from the 1998 season. Card fronts have a black and white photo of the player and along the bottom of the photo a date of the memorable play and brief description are given. These are seeded 1:8 packs. A parallel version, Level II is also randomly seeded, limited to 100 sequentially numbered sets.

		MT
Complete Set (15):		60.00
Common Player:		2.00
Inserted 1:8		
Level 2:		10x to 20x
Production 100 sets		
1	Ken Griffey Jr.	8.00
2	Mark McGwire	8.00
3	Cal Ripken Jr.	6.00
4	Greg Maddux	4.00
5	Nomar Garciaparra	5.00
6	Roger Clemens	3.00
7	Alex Rodriguez	6.00
8	Frank Thomas	3.00
9	Mike Piazza	5.00
10	Chipper Jones	5.00
11	Juan Gonzalez	2.00
12	Tony Gwynn	4.00
13	Barry Bonds	2.00
14	Ivan Rodriguez	2.00
15	Derek Jeter	5.00

1999 UD Retro Old/New School

This 30-card insert set captures 15 Old School players and 15 New School players. Each card is sequentially numbered to 1,000. A parallel version is also randomly seeded and is limited to 50 sequentially numbered sets. Old School cards are basically black-and-white with color graphic highlights on front and back. New School cards have multiple computer-enhanced color photos and silver-foil highlights.

		MT
Complete Set (30):		300.00
Common Player:		3.00
Production 1,000 sets		
Level 2:		5x to 10x
Production 50 sets		
1	Ken Griffey Jr.	30.00
2	Alex Rodriguez	25.00
3	Frank Thomas	8.00
4	Cal Ripken Jr.	25.00
5	Chipper Jones	20.00
6	Craig Biggio	6.00
7	Greg Maddux	15.00
8	Jeff Bagwell	8.00
9	Juan Gonzalez	8.00
10	Mark McGwire	30.00
11	Mike Piazza	20.00
12	Mo Vaughn	4.00
13	Roger Clemens	10.00
14	Sammy Sosa	20.00
15	Tony Gwynn	15.00
16	Gabe Kapler	5.00
17	J.D. Drew	3.00
18	Pat Burrell	15.00
19	Roy Halladay	3.00
20	Jeff Weaver	3.00
21	Troy Glaus	5.00
22	Vladimir Guerrero	12.00
23	Michael Barrett	3.00
24	Carlos Beltran	3.00
25	Scott Rolen	8.00
26	Nomar Garciaparra	20.00
27	Warren Morris	3.00
28	Alex Gonzalez	3.00
29	Kyle Farnsworth	3.00
30	Derek Jeter	20.00

1999 UD Retro INKredible

INKredible is an autographed insert set that consists of both current players and retired stars. Card fronts have a small photo in the upper left portion of the featured player and a large signing area. These are seeded 1:23 packs.

		MT
Common Player:		12.00
Inserted 1:23		
CBe	Carlos Beltran	15.00
GB	George Brett	125.00
PB	Pat Burrell	40.00
SC	Sean Casey	40.00
TC	Tony Clark	25.00
BD	Bucky Dent	15.00
DE	Darin Erstad	30.00
RF	Rollie Fingers	15.00
SG	Steve Garvey	25.00
KG	Kirk Gibson	25.00
RG	Rusty Greer	15.00
JR	Ken Griffey Jr.	350.00
TG	Tony Gwynn	150.00
CJ	Chipper Jones	125.00
GK	Gabe Kapler	30.00
HK	Harmon Killebrew	35.00
FL	Fred Lynn	20.00
DM	Don Mattingly	100.00
PM	Paul Molitor	50.00
EM	Eddie Murray	50.00
PO	Paul O'Neill	25.00
AP	Angel Pena	12.00
MR	Manny Ramirez	75.00
IR	Ivan Rodriguez	50.00
NR	Nolan Ryan	250.00
OZ	Ozzie Smith	75.00
DWe	David Wells	15.00
BW	Bernie Williams	50.00
DW	Dave Winfield	40.00
RY	Robin Yount	75.00

1999 UD Retro Piece of History 500 Club

Each one of these inserts features a piece of game-used bat swung by Ted Williams embedded into each card. A total of 350 of these were issued. Williams also autographed nine of the 500 Club Piece of History cards.

		MT
TW	Ted Williams (edition of 350)	700.00
TWA	Ted Williams (autographed edition of nine)	

1999 UD Retro Lunchbox

Lunchboxes were the packaging for UD Retro. Each lunchbox contains 24 six-card packs and features 17 different current or retired baseball legends including Babe Ruth.

	MT
Complete Set (17):	300.00
Common lunchbox:	10.00
1 dual player per case	
Roger Clemens	12.00
Ken Griffey Jr.	20.00
Mickey Mantle	20.00
Mark McGwire	20.00
Mike Piazza	15.00
Alex Rodriguez	17.50
Babe Ruth	20.00
Sammy Sosa	15.00
Ted Williams	20.00
Ken Griffey Jr., Mark McGwire	30.00
Ken Griffey Jr., Babe Ruth	30.00
Ken Griffey Jr., Ted Williams	30.00
Mickey Mantle, Babe Ruth	30.00
Mark McGwire, Mickey Mantle	30.00
Mark McGwire, Babe Ruth	30.00
Mark McGwire, Ted Williams	30.00

1999 UD Retro INKredible Level 2

A parallel to INKredible autographed inserts, these are hand-numbered to the featured player's jersey number.

		MT
Common Player:		12.00
Limited to player's jersey #		
CBe	Carlos Beltran (36)	40.00
GB	George Brett (5)	N/A
PB	Pat Burrell (76)	150.00
SC	Sean Casey (21)	175.00
TC	Tony Clark (17)	75.00
BD	Bucky Dent (20)	75.00
DE	Darin Erstad (17)	100.00
RF	Rollie Fingers (34)	60.00
SG	Steve Garvey (6)	N/A
KG	Kirk Gibson (23)	90.00
RG	Rusty Greer (29)	75.00
JR	Ken Griffey Jr. (24)	700.00
TG	Tony Gwynn (19)	500.00
CJ	Chipper Jones (10)	N/A
GK	Gabe Kapler (23)	125.00
HK	Harmon Killebrew (3)	N/A
FL	Fred Lynn (19)	90.00
DM	Don Mattingly (23)	450.00
PM	Paul Molitor (4)	N/A
EM	Eddie Murray (33)	150.00
PO	Paul O'Neill (21)	100.00
AP	Angel Pena (36)	40.00
MR	Manny Ramirez (24)	250.00
IR	Ivan Rodriguez (7)	N/A
NR	Nolan Ryan (34)	800.00
OZ	Ozzie Smith (1)	N/A
DWe	David Wells (33)	75.00
BW	Bernie Williams (51)	100.00
DW	Dave Winfield (31)	125.00
RY	Robin Yount (19)	220.00

1999 Upper Deck PowerDeck

This 25-card set is comprised of 25 digital PowerDeck interactive trading cards, complete with video and audio content. There is also a parallel "paper" version of the base set called Auxiliary Power. Each digital card includes 32 megabytes of information and is compatible with almost any internet ready computer. One PowerDeck digital card comes in every three-card pack.

		MT
Complete Set (25):		80.00
Common Player:		2.00
Pack (3):		5.00
Wax Box (36):		75.00
1	Ken Griffey Jr.	10.00
2	Mark McGwire	10.00
3	Cal Ripken Jr.	8.00
4	Sammy Sosa	6.00
5	Derek Jeter	6.00
6	Mike Piazza	6.00
7	Nomar Garciaparra	6.00
8	Greg Maddux	5.00
9	Tony Gwynn	5.00
10	Roger Clemens	4.00
11	Scott Rolen	2.50
12	Alex Rodriguez	8.00
13	Manny Ramirez	2.50
14	Chipper Jones	6.00
15	Juan Gonzalez	2.50
16	Ivan Rodriguez	2.50
17	Frank Thomas	3.00
18	Mo Vaughn	2.00
19	Barry Bonds	2.50
20	Vladimir Guerrero	4.00
21	Jose Canseco	2.00
22	Jeff Bagwell	2.50
23	Pedro Martinez	2.50
24	Gabe Kapler	2.00
25	J.D. Drew	2.00
	Checklist card	.10

1999 Upper Deck PowerDeck Auxiliary Power

A "paper" parallel version of the 25-card digital set. These have a horizontal format with silver foil stamping. Backs have a close-up photo along with the featured player's past five years of statistics and a brief career highlight.

		MT
Complete Set (25):		25.00
Common Player:		.50
1	Ken Griffey Jr.	4.00
2	Mark McGwire	4.00
3	Cal Ripken Jr.	2.50
4	Sammy Sosa	2.00
5	Derek Jeter	2.00
6	Mike Piazza	2.00
7	Nomar Garciaparra	2.00
8	Greg Maddux	1.50
9	Tony Gwynn	1.50
10	Roger Clemens	1.00
11	Scott Rolen	.75
12	Alex Rodriguez	2.50
13	Manny Ramirez	.75
14	Chipper Jones	2.00
15	Juan Gonzalez	.75
16	Ivan Rodriguez	.75
17	Frank Thomas	1.00
18	Mo Vaughn	.50
19	Barry Bonds	.75
20	Vladimir Guerrero	1.50
21	Jose Canseco	.75
22	Jeff Bagwell	.75
23	Pedro Martinez	.75
24	Gabe Kapler	.50
25	J.D. Drew	.50

1999 Upper Deck PowerDeck Powerful Moments

This six-card digital interactive set has game-action footage pinpointing specific milestones in each of the featured players' careers. These were inserted 1:7 packs.

		MT
Complete Set (6):		60.00
Common Player:		4.00
Inserted 1:7		
1	Mark McGwire	20.00
2	Sammy Sosa	10.00
3	Cal Ripken Jr.	12.00
4	Ken Griffey Jr.	15.00
5	Derek Jeter	10.00
6	Alex Rodriguez	10.00

1999 Upper Deck PowerDeck Powerful Moments-Aux. Power

This "paper" parallel version of the digital set is also inserted 1:7 packs on a horizontal format. Different photos were used from the digital set.

		MT
Complete Set (6):		30.00
Common Player:		4.00
Inserted 1:7		
Gold (one each): Value Undetermined		
1	Mark McGwire	8.00
2	Sammy Sosa	5.00
3	Cal Ripken Jr.	6.00
4	Ken Griffey Jr.	8.00
5	Derek Jeter	5.00
6	Alex Rodriguez	6.00

1999 Upper Deck PowerDeck Most Valuable Performances

This seven-card digital insert set consists of capturing true MVP performances from some of baseball's greatest players, including Ken Griffey Jr. These were seeded 1:287 packs.

		MT
Complete Set (7):		300.00
Common Player:		25.00
Inserted 1:287		
1	Sammy Sosa	50.00
2	Barry Bonds	25.00
3	Cal Ripken Jr.	60.00
4	Juan Gonzalez	25.00
5	Ken Griffey Jr.	80.00
6	Roger Clemens	35.00
7	Mark McGwire, Sammy Sosa	100.00

1999 Upper Deck PowerDeck Most Valuable Performanes-Aux.

A "paper" parallel version of the digital set, these also were inserted 1:287 packs. They have a horizontal format using silver holofoil and also have different photos from the digital version.

		MT
Complete Set (7):		180.00
Common Player:		10.00
Inserted 1:287		
1	Sammy Sosa	30.00
2	Barry Bonds	15.00
3	Cal Ripken Jr.	35.00
4	Juan Gonzalez	15.00
5	Ken Griffey Jr.	50.00
6	Roger Clemens	20.00
7	Mark McGwire, Sammy Sosa	60.00

1999 Upper Deck PowerDeck Time Capsule

Five previous MLB Rookies of the Year are honored in this digital set with the digital content going back to the rookie seasons of the featured players. These were seeded 1:23 packs.

		MT
Complete Set (6):		70.00
Common Player:		6.00
Inserted 1:23		
1	Ken Griffey Jr.	20.00
2	Mike Piazza	12.00
3	Mark McGwire	20.00
4	Derek Jeter	12.00
5	Jose Canseco	6.00
6	Nomar Garciaparra	12.00

1999 Upper Deck PowerDeck Time Capsule-Auxiliary Power

This "paper' parallel set of the digital version utilizes a similar design as the digital insert and uses different photos as well. These were also inserted 1:23 packs.

		MT
Complete Set (6):		45.00
Common Player:		5.00
Inserted 1:23		
Gold (one of each): Values Undetermined		
1	Ken Griffey Jr.	15.00
2	Mike Piazza	8.00
3	Mark McGwire	15.00
4	Derek Jeter	8.00
5	Jose Canseco	5.00
6	Nomar Garciaparra	8.00

1999 Upper Deck Ultimate Victory

The 180-card base set includes two 30-card short-printed (1:4) subsets: McGwire Magic (151-180) and 1999 Rookie (121-150). The base cards have a silver foil border with the featured players' last five seasons of statistics along with a brief career highlight. There are two parallels randomly inserted: Victory Collection and Ultimate Collection. Victory Collection are seeded 1:12 packs with a holographic, prismatic look. Ultimate Collection have a gold holographic, prismatic look and are serially numbered "xxx/100" on the card front.

	MT
Complete Set (180):	300.00
Common Player:	.20
Common SP (121-150):	2.00
Common McGwire Magic (151-180):	2.00
Victory (1-120):	4X
Victory SP (121-150):	1.5X
Inserted 1:12	

Ultimate (1-120):		12X
Ultimate SP (121-150):		2X
Production 100 sets		
Pack:		5.00
Wax Box:		150.00
1	Troy Glaus	1.25
2	Tim Salmon	.40
3	Mo Vaughn	.75
4	Garret Anderson	.20
5	Darin Erstad	.50
6	Randy Johnson	.75
7	Matt Williams	.40
8	Travis Lee	.40
9	Jay Bell	.20
10	Steve Finley	.20
11	Luis Gonzalez	.20
12	Greg Maddux	2.00
13	Chipper Jones	2.50
14	Javy Lopez	.40
15	Tom Glavine	.40
16	John Smoltz	.20
17	Cal Ripken Jr.	3.00
18	Charles Johnson	.20
19	Albert Belle	.75
20	Mike Mussina	.75
21	Pedro Martinez	1.00
22	Nomar Garciaparra	2.50
23	Jose Offerman	.20
24	Sammy Sosa	2.50
25	Mark Grace	.40
26	Kerry Wood	.50
27	Frank Thomas	1.00
28	Ray Durham	.20
29	Paul Konerko	.20
30	Pete Harnisch	.20
31	Greg Vaughn	.25
32	Sean Casey	.50
33	Manny Ramirez	1.00
34	Jim Thome	.40
35	Sandy Alomar	.40
36	Roberto Alomar	.75
37	Travis Fryman	.20
38	Kenny Lofton	.75
39	Omar Vizquel	.20
40	Larry Walker	.75
41	Todd Helton	1.25
42	Vinny Castilla	.40
43	Tony Clark	.40
44	Juan Encarnacion	.20
45	Dean Palmer	.20
46	Damion Easley	.20
47	Mark Kotsay	.20
48	Cliff Floyd	.20
49	Jeff Bagwell	1.00
50	Ken Caminiti	.40
51	Craig Biggio	.75
52	Moises Alou	.40
53	Johnny Damon	.20
54	Larry Sutton	.20
55	Kevin Brown	.40
56	Adrian Beltre	.40
57	Raul Mondesi	.40
58	Gary Sheffield	.40
59	Jeromy Burnitz	.20
60	Sean Berry	.20
61	Jeff Cirillo	.20
62	Brad Radke	.20
63	Todd Walker	.20
64	Matt Lawton	.20
65	Vladimir Guerrero	2.00
66	Rondell White	.40
67	Dustin Hermanson	.20
68	Mike Piazza	2.50
69	Rickey Henderson	.50
70	Robin Ventura	.50
71	John Olerud	.50
72	Derek Jeter	2.50
73	Roger Clemens	1.50
74	Orlando Hernandez	.50
75	Paul O'Neill	.50
76	Bernie Williams	.60
77	Chuck Knoblauch	.40
78	Tino Martinez	.25
79	Jason Giambi	.20
80	Ben Grieve	.50
81	Matt Stairs	.20
82	Scott Rolen	1.00
83	Ron Gant	.20
84	Bobby Abreu	.20
85	Curt Schilling	.40
86	Brian Giles	.20
87	Jason Kendall	.40
88	Kevin Young	.20
89	Mark McGwire	5.00
90	Fernando Tatis	.50
91	Ray Lankford	.20
92	Eric Davis	.20
93	Tony Gwynn	2.00
94	Reggie Sanders	.20
95	Wally Joyner	.20
96	Trevor Hoffman	.20
97	Robb Nen	.20
98	Barry Bonds	1.00
99	Jeff Kent	.20
100	J.T. Snow	.20
101	Ellis Burks	.20
102	Ken Griffey Jr.	5.00
103	Alex Rodriguez	3.00
104	Jay Buhner	.40
105	Edgar Martinez	.20
106	David Bell	.20
107	Bobby Smith	.20
108	Wade Boggs	.50
109	Fred McGriff	.50
110	Rolando Arrojo	.20
111	Jose Canseco	.75
112	Ivan Rodriguez	1.00
113	Juan Gonzalez	1.00
114	Rafael Palmeiro	.75
115	Rusty Greer	.20
116	Todd Zeile	.20
117	Jose Cruz Jr.	.25
118	Carlos Delgado	.75
119	Shawn Green	.50
120	David Wells	.20
121	*Eric Munson* (99 Rookie)	30.00
122	Lance Berkman (99 Rookie)	2.00
123	Ed Yarnall (99 Rookie)	2.00
124	Jacque Jones (99 Rookie)	2.00
125	Kyle Farnsworth (99 Rookie)	3.00
126	Ryan Rupe (99 Rookie)	2.00
127	*Jeff Weaver* (99 Rookie)	5.00
128	Gabe Kapler (99 Rookie)	3.00
129	Alex Gonzalez (99 Rookie)	2.00
130	Randy Wolf (99 Rookie)	2.00
131	Ben Davis (99 Rookie)	2.00
132	Carlos Beltran (99 Rookie)	2.00
133	Jim Morris (99 Rookie)	2.00
134	Jeff Zimmerman (99 Rookie)	4.00
135	Bruce Aven (99 Rookie)	2.00
136	*Alfonso Soriano* (99 Rookie)	15.00
137	*Tim Hudson* (99 Rookie)	10.00
138	*Josh Beckett* (99 Rookie)	25.00
139	Michael Barrett (99 Rookie)	2.00
140	Eric Chavez (99 Rookie)	2.00
141	*Pat Burrell* (99 Rookie)	30.00
142	Kris Benson (99 Rookie)	2.00
143	J.D. Drew (99 Rookie)	3.00
144	Matt Clement (99 Rookie)	2.00
145	*Rick Ankiel* (99 Rookie)	75.00
146	Vernon Wells (99 Rookie)	2.50
147	Ruben Mateo (99 Rookie)	2.00
148	Roy Halladay (99 Rookie)	2.00
149	Joe McEwing (99 Rookie)	4.00
150	Freddy Garcia (99 Rookie)	15.00
151	Mark McGwire (McGwire Magic)	2.00
152	Mark McGwire (McGwire Magic)	2.00
153	Mark McGwire (McGwire Magic)	2.00
154	Mark McGwire (McGwire Magic)	2.00
155	Mark McGwire (McGwire Magic)	2.00
156	Mark McGwire (McGwire Magic)	2.00
157	Mark McGwire (McGwire Magic)	2.00
158	Mark McGwire (McGwire Magic)	2.00
159	Mark McGwire (McGwire Magic)	2.00
160	Mark McGwire (McGwire Magic)	2.00
161	Mark McGwire (McGwire Magic)	2.00
162	Mark McGwire (McGwire Magic)	2.00
163	Mark McGwire (McGwire Magic)	2.00
164	Mark McGwire (McGwire Magic)	2.00
165	Mark McGwire (McGwire Magic)	2.00
166	Mark McGwire (McGwire Magic)	2.00
167	Mark McGwire (McGwire Magic)	2.00
168	Mark McGwire (McGwire Magic)	2.00
169	Mark McGwire (McGwire Magic)	2.00
170	Mark McGwire (McGwire Magic)	2.00
171	Mark McGwire (McGwire Magic)	2.00
172	Mark McGwire (McGwire Magic)	2.00
173	Mark McGwire (McGwire Magic)	2.00
174	Mark McGwire (McGwire Magic)	2.00
175	Mark McGwire (McGwire Magic)	2.00
176	Mark McGwire (McGwire Magic)	2.00
177	Mark McGwire (McGwire Magic)	2.00
178	Mark McGwire (McGwire Magic)	2.00
179	Mark McGwire (McGwire Magic)	2.00
180	Mark McGwire (McGwire Magic)	2.00

1999 Upper Deck Ultimate Victory Bleacher Reachers

This 11-card set focuses on the hitters who were vying for the 1999 home run title. They have a horizontal format with a holographic foil card front. Card backs have a small photo along with his 3-year statistical totals. They are numbered with a "BR" prefix and were inserted 1:23 packs.

		MT
Complete Set (11):		60.00
Common Player:		3.00
Inserted 1:23		
1	Ken Griffey Jr.	12.00
2	Mark McGwire	12.00
3	Sammy Sosa	8.00
4	Barry Bonds	3.00
5	Nomar Garciaparra	8.00
6	Juan Gonzalez	3.00
7	Jose Canseco	3.00
8	Manny Ramirez	4.00
9	Mike Piazza	8.00
10	Jeff Bagwell	4.00
11	Alex Rodriguez	10.00

1999 Upper Deck Ultimate Victory Frozen Ropes

This 10-card set spotlights baseball's top hitters and are seeded 1:23 packs.

		MT
Complete Set (10):		60.00
Common Player:		2.00
Inserted 1:23		
1	Ken Griffey Jr.	12.00
2	Mark McGwire	12.00
3	Sammy Sosa	8.00
4	Derek Jeter	8.00
5	Tony Gwynn	6.00
6	Nomar Garciaparra	8.00
7	Alex Rodriguez	10.00
8	Mike Piazza	8.00
9	Mo Vaughn	2.50
10	Craig Biggio	2.00

1999 Upper Deck Ultimate Victory Fame-Used Memorabilia

This four-card set has a piece of game-used bat embedded into each card, from either George Brett, Robin Yount, Nolan Ryan and Orlando Cepeda. A total of approximately 350 bat cards of each player was produced.

		MT
Complete Set (4):		500.00
Common Player:		50.00
Production 350 cards		
GB	George Brett	125.00
OC	Orlando Cepeda	50.00
NR	Nolan Ryan	250.00
RY	Robin Yount	100.00

Player names in *Italic* type indicate a rookie card.

1999 Upper Deck Ultimate Victory STATure

This 15-card set highlights players with outstanding statistical achievements. The featured stat for the player runs down the right side of the card. Fronts are printed on metallic foil with a textured pattern behind the player photo. Conventionally printed backs repeat the front design numbered with an "S" prefix. These were seeded 1:6 packs.

		MT
Complete Set (15):		25.00
Common Player:		1.00
Inserted 1:6		
1	Ken Griffey Jr.	5.00
2	Mark McGwire	5.00
3	Sammy Sosa	2.50
4	Nomar Garciaparra	2.50
5	Roger Clemens	1.50
6	Greg Maddux	2.00
7	Alex Rodriguez	3.50
8	Derek Jeter	2.50
9	Juan Gonzalez	1.00
10	Manny Ramirez	1.25
11	Mike Piazza	2.50
12	Tony Gwynn	2.00
13	Chipper Jones	2.50
14	Pedro Martinez	1.00
15	Frank Thomas	1.50

1999 Upper Deck Ultimate Victory Tribute 1999

This four-card set is devoted to 1999's Hall of Fame inductees. Card fronts have a horizontal format over a holographic foil design. Card backs have the featured players' year-by-year statistics and are numbered with a "T" prefix.

		MT
Complete Set (4):		15.00
Common Player:		1.50
Inserted 1:11		
1	Nolan Ryan	10.00
2	Robin Yount	3.00
3	George Brett	4.00
4	Orlando Cepeda	1.50

1999 Upper Deck Ultimate Victory Ultimate Competitors

This 12-card set has a close-up photo, along with two miniature action photos in the foreground, all printed on silver foil. Backs repeat the front photos and have a few words about the player's competitive desire. These were seeded 1:23 packs and are numbered with a "U" prefix on the card back.

		MT
Complete Set (12):		60.00
Common Player:		2.00
Inserted 1:23		
1	Ken Griffey Jr.	15.00
2	Roger Clemens	5.00
3	Scott Rolen	3.00
4	Greg Maddux	6.00
5	Mark McGwire	15.00
6	Derek Jeter	8.00
7	Randy Johnson	2.00
8	Cal Ripken Jr.	10.00
9	Craig Biggio	2.00
10	Kevin Brown	2.00
11	Chipper Jones	8.00
12	Vladimir Guerrero	5.00

1999 Upper Deck Ultimate Victory Ultimate Hit Men

This insert set spotlights the eight candidates who competed for the 1999 batting titles. Inserted on the average of 1:23 packs they were numbered with an "H" prefix on the card back.

		MT
Complete Set (8):		30.00
Common Player:		2.00
Inserted 1:23		
1	Tony Gwynn	5.00
2	Cal Ripken Jr.	8.00
3	Wade Boggs	2.00
4	Larry Walker	2.00
5	Alex Rodriguez	8.00
6	Derek Jeter	6.00
7	Ivan Rodriguez	2.50
8	Ken Griffey Jr.	10.00

1999 Upper Deck UD Choice

The 155-card base set consists of 110 regular player cards and two subsets, 27 Star Rookies and 18 Cover Glory subset cards. Card fronts have a white border, with the Upper Deck UD Choice logo on the bottom right of the front. Card backs have complete year-by-year stats along with some vital information. Each pack contains 12 cards. A parallel version also exists, called Prime Choice Reserve and are numbered to 100.

		MT
Complete Set (155):		15.00
Common Player:		.10
Prime Choice Reserve Stars:		60X
Young Stars/RCs:		25X
Production 100 sets		
Pack (12):		1.50
Wax Box (36):		40.00
1	Gabe Kapler (Rookie Class)	.75
2	Jin Ho Cho (Rookie Class)	.15
3	Matt Anderson (Rookie Class)	.20
4	Ricky Ledee (Rookie Class)	.20
5	Bruce Chen (Rookie Class)	.10
6	Alex Gonzalez (Rookie Class)	.10
7	Ryan Minor (Rookie Class)	.25
8	Michael Barrett (Rookie Class)	.10
9	Carlos Beltran (Rookie Class)	.20
10	Ramon Martinez (Rookie Class)	.10
11	Dermal Brown (Rookie Class)	.10
12	Robert Fick (Rookie Class)	.10
13	Preston Wilson (Rookie Class)	.15
14	Orlando Hernandez (Rookie Class)	1.50
15	Troy Glaus (Rookie Class)	1.00
16	Calvin Pickering (Rookie Class)	.10
17	Corey Koskie (Rookie Class)	.10
18	Fernando Seguignol (Rookie Class)	.20
19	Carlos Guillen (Rookie Class)	.10
20	Kevin Witt (Rookie Class)	.10
21	Mike Kinkade (Rookie Class)	.10
22	Eric Chavez (Rookie Class)	.30
23	Mike Lowell (Rookie Class)	.10
24	Adrian Beltre (Rookie Class)	.25
25	George Lombard (Rookie Class)	.10
26	Jeremy Giambi (Rookie Class)	.10
27	J.D. Drew (Rookie Class)	.25
28	Mark McGwire (Cover Glory)	1.25
29	Kerry Wood (Cover Glory)	.40
30	David Wells (Cover Glory)	.10
31	Juan Gonzalez (Cover Glory)	.30
32	Randy Johnson (Cover Glory)	.20
33	Derek Jeter (Cover Glory)	.50
34	Tony Gwynn (Cover Glory)	.50
35	Greg Maddux (Cover Glory)	.60
36	Cal Ripken Jr. (Cover Glory)	.75
37	Ken Griffey Jr. (Cover Glory)	1.25
38	Bartolo Colon (Cover Glory)	.10
39	Troy Glaus (Cover Glory)	.25
40	Ben Grieve (Cover Glory)	.25
41	Roger Clemens (Cover Glory)	.30
42	Chipper Jones (Cover Glory)	.50
43	Scott Rolen (Cover Glory)	.25
44	Nomar Garciaparra (Cover Glory)	.60
45	Sammy Sosa (Cover Glory)	.75
46	Tim Salmon	.20
47	Darin Erstad	.50
48	Chuck Finley	.10
49	Garrett Anderson	.10
50	Matt Williams	.20
51	Jay Bell	.10
52	Travis Lee	.50
53	Andruw Jones	.50
54	Andres Galarraga	.25
55	Chipper Jones	1.25
56	Greg Maddux	1.00
57	Javy Lopez	.15
58	Cal Ripken Jr.	2.00
59	Brady Anderson	.10
60	Rafael Palmeiro	.20
61	B.J. Surhoff	.10
62	Nomar Garciaparra	1.25
63	Troy O'Leary	.10
64	Pedro Martinez	.40
65	Jason Varitek	.10
66	Kerry Wood	.75
67	Sammy Sosa	1.50
68	Mark Grace	.20
69	Mickey Morandini	.10
70	Albert Belle	.50
71	Mike Caruso	.10
72	Frank Thomas	.75
73	Sean Casey	.25
74	Pete Harnisch	.10
75	Dmitri Young	.10
76	Manny Ramirez	.75
77	Omar Vizquel	.10
78	Travis Fryman	.10
79	Jim Thome	.35
80	Kenny Lofton	.35
81	Todd Helton	.50
82	Larry Walker	.35
83	Vinny Castilla	.10
84	Gabe Alvarez	.10
85	Tony Clark	.40
86	Damion Easley	.10
87	Livan Hernandez	.10
88	Mark Kotsay	.20
89	Cliff Floyd	.10
90	Jeff Bagwell	.60
91	Moises Alou	.20
92	Randy Johnson	.35
93	Craig Biggio	.20
94	Larry Sutton	.10
95	Dean Palmer	.10
96	Johnny Damon	.10
97	Charles Johnson	.10
98	Gary Sheffield	.20
99	Raul Mondesi	.20
100	Mark Grudzielanek	.10
101	Jeromy Burnitz	.10
102	Jeff Cirillo	.10
103	Jose Valentin	.10
104	Mark Loretta	.10
105	Todd Walker	.20
106	David Ortiz	.10
107	Brad Radke	.10
108	Brad Fullmer	.20
109	Rondell White	.20
110	Vladimir Guerrero	1.00
111	Mike Piazza	1.25
112	Brian McRae	.10
113	John Olerud	.20
114	Rey Ordonez	.10
115	Derek Jeter	1.50
116	Bernie Williams	.30

117	David Wells	.10
118	Paul O'Neill	.20
119	Tino Martinez	.20
120	A.J. Hinch	.10
121	Jason Giambi	.10
122	Miguel Tejada	.10
123	Ben Grieve	.50
124	Scott Rolen	.50
125	Desi Relaford	.10
126	Bobby Abreu	.10
127	Jose Guillen	.10
128	Jason Kendall	.15
129	Aramis Ramirez	.20
130	Mark McGwire	2.50
131	Ray Lankford	.10
132	Eli Marrero	.10
133	Wally Joyner	.10
134	Greg Vaughn	.10
135	Trevor Hoffman	.10
136	Kevin Brown	.15
137	Tony Gwynn	1.00
138	Bill Mueller	.10
139	Ellis Burks	.10
140	Barry Bonds	.50
141	Robb Nen	.10
142	Ken Griffey Jr.	2.50
143	Alex Rodriguez	2.00
144	Jay Buhner	.10
145	Edgar Martinez	.10
146	Rolando Arrojo	.15
147	Robert Smith	.10
148	Quinton McCracken	.10
149	Ivan Rodriguez	.50
150	Will Clark	.25
151	Mark McLemore	.10
152	Juan Gonzalez	.50
153	Jose Cruz Jr.	.35
154	Carlos Delgado	.25
155	Roger Clemens	.75

1999 Upper Deck UD Choice Prime Choice Reserve

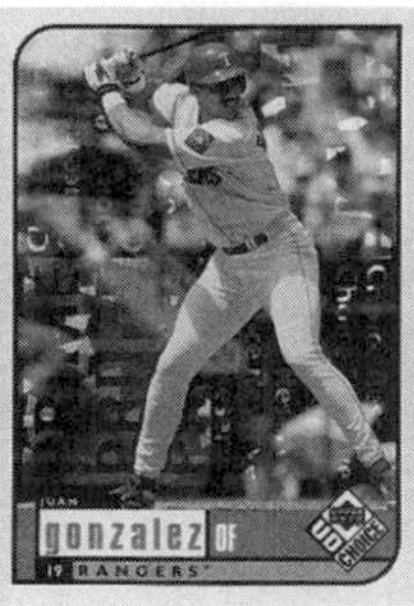

Each card in the UD Choice set is also found in a parallel version with the words "Prime Choice Reserve" repeated in the background of the photo on front in refractive foil. On back, the parallels are individually serial numbered from within an edition of 100 each.

	MT
Common Player:	3.00

(PCR stars valued at 60X regular version; young stars and rookies about 25X. See 1999 UD Choice for base values.)

Player names in *Italic* type indicate a rookie card.

1999 Upper Deck UD Choice Mini Bobbing Head

Inserted 1:5 packs, some of the game's best players can be assembled into a miniature bobbing head figure by following the instructions on the card backs.

		MT
Complete Set (30):		25.00
Common Player:		.40
Inserted 1:5		
B01	Randy Johnson	.60
B02	Troy Glaus	.75
B03	Chipper Jones	2.00
B04	Cal Ripken Jr.	3.00
B05	Nomar Garciaparra	2.00
B06	Pedro Martinez	.60
B07	Kerry Wood	.75
B08	Sammy Sosa	2.50
B09	Frank Thomas	1.00
B10	Paul Konerko	.40
B11	Omar Vizquel	.40
B12	Kenny Lofton	.60
B13	Gabe Kapler	1.50
B14	Adrian Beltre	.40
B15	Orlando Hernandez	1.50
B16	Derek Jeter	2.00
B17	Mike Piazza	2.00
B18	Tino Martinez	.40
B19	Ben Grieve	.75
B20	Rickey Henderson	.50
B21	Scott Rolen	.75
B22	Aramis Ramirez	.40
B23	Greg Vaughn	.40
B24	Tony Gwynn	1.50
B25	Barry Bonds	.75
B26	Alex Rodriguez	3.00
B27	Ken Griffey Jr.	4.00
B28	Mark McGwire	4.00
B29	J.D. Drew	.50
B30	Juan Gonzalez	.75

1999 Upper Deck UD Choice StarQuest

This four-tiered 30-card set features four different colors for each of the levels. Singles are seeded one per pack and have blue foil etching, Doubles (1:8) have green foil etching, Triples (1:23) have red foil etching and Home Runs are limited to 100 numbered sets with gold foil etching.

		MT
Complete Set (30):		18.00
Common Player:		.25
Inserted 1:1		
Green:		2X
Inserted 1:8		
Red:		4X
Inserted 1:23		
Gold:		50X
Production 100 sets		
SQ1	Ken Griffey Jr.	2.50
SQ2	Sammy Sosa	1.50
SQ3	Alex Rodriguez	2.00
SQ4	Derek Jeter	1.25
SQ5	Troy Glaus	.75
SQ6	Mike Piazza	1.25
SQ7	Barry Bonds	.50
SQ8	Tony Gwynn	1.00
SQ9	Juan Gonzalez	.50
SQ10	Chipper Jones	1.25
SQ11	Greg Maddux	1.00
SQ12	Randy Johnson	.40
SQ13	Roger Clemens	.75
SQ14	Ben Grieve	.50
SQ15	Nomar Garciaparra	1.25
SQ16	Travis Lee	.50
SQ17	Frank Thomas	.75
SQ18	Vladimir Guerrero	1.00
SQ19	Scott Rolen	.50
SQ20	Ivan Rodriguez	.50
SQ21	Cal Ripken Jr.	2.00
SQ22	Mark McGwire	2.50
SQ23	Jeff Bagwell	.60
SQ24	Tony Clark	.40
SQ25	Kerry Wood	.50
SQ26	Kenny Lofton	.40
SQ27	Adrian Beltre	.40
SQ28	Larry Walker	.40
SQ29	Curt Schilling	.25
SQ30	Jim Thome	.40

1999 Upper Deck UD Choice Piece of History 500 Club

A piece from a Eddie Murray game-used bat was incorporated into each of these cards, which are limited to 350.

		MT
EM	Eddie Murray (350)	200.00

1999 Upper Deck UD Choice YardWork

This 30-card set showcases the top power hitters in the game. The right side of the card is covered in bronze foil and stamped with YardWork. They are numbered with a Y-prefix and seeded 1:13 packs.

		MT
Complete Set (30):		75.00
Common Player:		1.00
Inserted 1:13		
Y01	Andres Galarraga	2.00
Y02	Chipper Jones	6.00
Y03	Rafael Palmeiro	1.50
Y04	Nomar Garciaparra	6.00
Y05	Sammy Sosa	7.50
Y06	Frank Thomas	4.50
Y07	J.D. Drew	1.50
Y08	Albert Belle	2.00
Y09	Jim Thome	1.50
Y10	Manny Ramirez	3.50
Y11	Larry Walker	1.50
Y12	Vinny Castilla	1.25
Y13	Tony Clark	1.50
Y14	Jeff Bagwell	3.50
Y15	Moises Alou	1.25
Y16	Dean Palmer	1.25
Y17	Gary Sheffield	1.25
Y18	Vladimir Guerrero	5.00
Y19	Mike Piazza	6.00
Y20	Tino Martinez	1.50
Y21	Ben Grieve	2.25
Y22	Greg Vaughn	1.25
Y23	Ken Caminiti	1.25
Y24	Barry Bonds	2.25
Y25	Ken Griffey Jr.	10.00
Y26	Alex Rodriguez	8.00
Y27	Mark McGwire	10.00
Y28	Juan Gonzalez	3.00
Y29	Jose Canseco	1.75
Y30	Jose Cruz Jr.	1.50

1999 Upper Deck Victory

This 470-card base set is printed on 20-point stock and has a white border with UV coating. The set consists of a number of subsets including, 30-card Mark McGwire Magic, 30 team checklist cards, 50 '99 rookies, 15 Power Trip, 20 Rookie

Flashback, 15 Big Play Makers and 10 History in the Making. Twelve-card packs had an SRP of $.99.

	MT
Complete Set (470):	40.00
Common Player:	.05
Pack (12):	1.00
Wax Box (36):	30.00

1 Anaheim Angels (Team Checklist) .05
2 *Mark Harriger* (99 Rookie) .25
3 Mo Vaughn (Power Trip) .20
4 Darin Erstad (Big Play Makers) .15
5 Troy Glaus .40
6 Tim Salmon .20
7 Mo Vaughn .30
8 Darin Erstad .25
9 Garret Anderson .05
10 Todd Greene .05
11 Troy Percival .05
12 Chuck Finley .05
13 Jason Dickson .05
14 Jim Edmonds .05
15 Arizona Diamondbacks (Team Checklist) .05
16 Randy Johnson .30
17 Matt Williams .25
18 Travis Lee .25
19 Jay Bell .05
20 Tony Womack .05
21 Steve Finley .05
22 Bernard Gilkey .05
23 Tony Batista .05
24 Todd Stottlemyre .05
25 Omar Daal .05
26 Atlanta Braves (Team Checklist) .05
27 Bruce Chen (99 Rookie) .15
28 George Lombard (99 Rookie) .05
29 Chipper Jones (Power Trip) .50
30 Chipper Jones (Big Play Makers) .50
31 Greg Maddux 1.00
32 Chipper Jones 1.00
33 Javy Lopez .15
34 Tom Glavine .20
35 John Smoltz .15
36 Andruw Jones .30
37 Brian Jordan .05
38 Walt Weiss .05
39 Bret Boone .05
40 Andres Galarraga .25
41 Baltimore Orioles (Team Checklist) .05
42 Ryan Minor (99 Rookie) .20
43 Jerry Hairston Jr. (99 Rookie) .05
44 Calvin Pickering (99 Rookie) .05
45 Cal Ripken Jr. (History in the Making) .50
46 Cal Ripken Jr. 1.25
47 Charles Johnson .05
48 Albert Belle .40
49 Delino DeShields .05
50 Mike Mussina .30
51 Scott Erickson .05
52 Brady Anderson .10
53 B.J. Surhoff .05
54 Harold Baines .10
55 Will Clark .25
56 Boston Red Sox (Team Checklist) .05
57 Shea Hillenbrand (99 Rookie) .05
58 Trot Nixon (99 Rookie) .05
59 Jin Ho Cho (99 Rookie) .05
60 Nomar Garciaparra (Power Trip) .50
61 Nomar Garciaparra (Big Play Makers) .50
62 Pedro Martinez .40
63 Nomar Garciaparra 1.00
64 Jose Offerman .05
65 Jason Varitek .05
66 Darren Lewis .05
67 Troy O'Leary .05
68 Donnie Sadler .05
69 John Valentin .05
70 Tim Wakefield .05
71 Bret Saberhagen .05
72 Chicago Cubs (Team Checklist) .05
73 *Kyle Farnsworth* (99 Rookie) .20
74 Sammy Sosa (Power Trip) .50
75 Sammy Sosa (Big Play Makers) .50
76 Sammy Sosa (History in the Making) .50
77 Kerry Wood (History in the Making) .15
78 Sammy Sosa 1.00
79 Mark Grace .20
80 Kerry Wood .25
81 Kevin Tapani .05
82 Benito Santiago .05
83 Gary Gaetti .05
84 Mickey Morandini .05
85 Glenallen Hill .05
86 Henry Rodriguez .05
87 Rod Beck .05
88 Chicago White Sox (Team Checklist) .05
89 Carlos Lee (99 Rookie) .15
90 Mark Johnson (99 Rookie) .05
91 Frank Thomas (Power Trip) .25
92 Frank Thomas .50
93 Jim Parque .05
94 Mike Sirotka .05
95 Mike Caruso .05
96 Ray Durham .10
97 Magglio Ordonez .20
98 Paul Konerko .10
99 Bob Howry .05
100 Brian Simmons .05
101 Jaime Navarro .05
102 Cincinnati Reds (Team Checklist) .05
103 Denny Neagle .05
104 Pete Harnisch .05
105 Greg Vaughn .15
106 Brett Tomko .05
107 Mike Cameron .05
108 Sean Casey .25
109 Aaron Boone .05
110 Michael Tucker .05
111 Dmitri Young .05
112 Barry Larkin .25
113 Cleveland Indians (Team Checklist) .05
114 Russ Branyan (99 Rookie) .05
115 Jim Thome (Power Trip) .15
116 Manny Ramirez (Power Trip) .20
117 Manny Ramirez .40
118 Jim Thome .25
119 David Justice .20
120 Sandy Alomar .10
121 Roberto Alomar .30
122 Jaret Wright .10
123 Bartolo Colon .10
124 Travis Fryman .10
125 Kenny Lofton .30
126 Omar Vizquel .10
127 Colorado Rockies (Team Checklist) .05
128 Derrick Gibson (99 Rookie) .05
129 Larry Walker (Big Play Makers) .15
130 Larry Walker .30
131 Dante Bichette .20
132 Todd Helton .40
133 Neifi Perez .05
134 Vinny Castilla .10
135 Darryl Kile .05
136 Pedro Astacio .10
137 Darryl Hamilton .05
138 Mike Lansing .05
139 Kirt Manwaring .05
140 Detroit Tigers (Team Checklist) .05
141 *Jeff Weaver* (99 Rookie) .50
142 Gabe Kapler (99 Rookie) .30
143 Tony Clark (Power Trip) .10
144 Tony Clark .20
145 Juan Encarnacion .05
146 Dean Palmer .10
147 Damion Easley .05
148 Bobby Higginson .05
149 Karim Garcia .05
150 Justin Thompson .05
151 Matt Anderson .05
152 Willie Blair .05
153 Brian Hunter .05
154 Florida Marlins (Team Checklist) .05
155 Alex Gonzalez (99 Rookie) .05
156 Mark Kotsay .05
157 Livan Hernandez .05
158 Cliff Floyd .05
159 Todd Dunwoody .05
160 Alex Fernandez .05
161 Mark Mantei .05
162 Derrek Lee .05
163 Kevin Orie .05
164 Craig Counsell .05
165 Rafael Medina .05
166 Houston Astros (Team Checklist) .05
167 Daryle Ward (99 Rookie) .05
168 Mitch Meluskey (99 Rookie) .10
169 Jeff Bagwell (Power Trip) .25
170 Jeff Bagwell .50
171 Ken Caminiti .15
172 Craig Biggio .25
173 Derek Bell .05
174 Moises Alou .15
175 Billy Wagner .10
176 Shane Reynolds .10
177 Carl Everett .05
178 Scott Elarton .05
179 Richard Hidalgo .05
180 Kansas City Royals (Team Checklist) .05
181 Carlos Beltran (99 Rookie) .10
182 Carlos Febles (99 Rookie) .20
183 Jeremy Giambi (99 Rookie) .15
184 Johnny Damon .05
185 Joe Randa .05
186 Jeff King .05
187 Hipolito Pichardo .05
188 Kevin Appier .05
189 Chad Kreuter .05
190 Rey Sanchez .05
191 Larry Sutton .05
192 Jeff Montgomery .05
193 Jermaine Dye .05
194 Los Angeles Dodgers (Team Checklist) .05
195 Adam Riggs (99 Rookie) .05
196 Angel Pena (99 Rookie) .05
197 Todd Hundley .05
198 Kevin Brown .15
199 Ismael Valdes .10
200 Chan Ho Park .10
201 Adrian Beltre .20
202 Mark Grudzielanek .05
203 Raul Mondesi .15
204 Gary Sheffield .15
205 Eric Karros .15
206 Devon White .05
207 Milwaukee Brewers (Team Checklist) .05
208 Ron Belliard (99 Rookie) .10
209 Rafael Roque (99 Rookie) .05
210 Jeromy Burnitz .10
211 Fernando Vina .05
212 Scott Karl .05
213 Jim Abbott .05
214 Sean Berry .05
215 Marquis Grissom .10
216 Geoff Jenkins .05
217 Jeff Cirillo .05
218 Dave Nilsson .05
219 Jose Valentin .05
220 Minnesota Twins (Team Checklist) .05
221 Corey Koskie (99 Rookie) .05
222 Christian Guzman (99 Rookie) .05
223 A.J. Pierzynski (99 Rookie) .05
224 David Ortiz .05
225 Brad Radke .05
226 Todd Walker .05
227 Matt Lawton .05
228 Rick Aguilera .05
229 Eric Milton .05
230 Marty Cordova .05
231 Torii Hunter .05
232 Ron Coomer .05
233 LaTroy Hawkins .05
234 Montreal Expos (Team Checklist) .05
235 Fernando Seguignol (99 Rookie) .15
236 Michael Barrett (99 Rookie) .25
237 Vladimir Guerrero (Big Play Makers) .25
238 Vladimir Guerrero .50
239 Brad Fullmer .05
240 Rondell White .10
241 Ugueth Urbina .05
242 Dustin Hermanson .10
243 Orlando Cabrerra .05
244 Wilton Guerrero .05
245 Carl Pavano .05
246 Javier Vasquez .05
247 Chris Widger .05
248 New York Mets (Team Checklist) .05
249 Mike Kinkade (99 Rookie) .05
250 Octavio Dotel (99 Rookie) .05
251 Mike Piazza (Power Trip) .50
252 Mike Piazza 1.00
253 Rickey Henderson .10
254 Edgardo Alfonzo .10
255 Robin Ventura .15
256 Al Leiter .15
257 Brian McRae .05
258 Rey Ordonez .10
259 Bobby Bonilla .10
260 Orel Hershiser .10
261 John Olerud .15
262 New York Yankees (Team Checklist) .15
263 Ricky Ledee (99 Rookie) .10
264 Bernie Williams (Big Play Makers) .15
265 Derek Jeter (Big Play Makers) .50
266 Scott Brosius (History in the Making) .05
267 Derek Jeter 1.00
268 Roger Clemens .50
269 Orlando Hernandez .25
270 Scott Brosius .05
271 Paul O'Neill .15
272 Bernie Williams .30
273 Chuck Knoblauch .15
274 Tino Martinez .25
275 Mariano Rivera .15
276 Jorge Posada .10
277 Oakland Athletics (Team Checklist) .05
278 Eric Chavez (99 Rookie) .15
279 Ben Grieve (History in the Making) .20
280 Jason Giambi .05
281 John Jaha .05
282 Miguel Tejada .15
283 Ben Grieve .30
284 Matt Stairs .05
285 Ryan Christenson .05
286 A.J. Hinch .05
287 Kenny Rogers .05
288 Tom Candiotti .05
289 Scott Spezio .05
290 Philadelphia Phillies (Team Checklist) .05
291 *Pat Burrell* (99 Rookie) 2.00
292 Marlon Anderson (99 Rookie) .05
293 Scott Rolen (Big Play Makers) .20
294 Scott Rolen .40
295 Doug Glanville .05
296 Rico Brogna .05
297 Ron Gant .15
298 Bobby Abreu .05
299 Desi Relaford .05
300 Curt Schilling .15
301 Chad Ogea .05
302 Kevin Jordan .05
303 Carlton Loewer .05
304 Pittsburgh Pirates (Team Checklist) .05

305 Kris Benson (99 Rookie) .15
306 Brian Giles .05
307 Jason Kendall .15
308 Jose Guillen .05
309 Pat Meares .05
310 Brant Brown .05
311 Kevin Young .05
312 Ed Sprague .05
313 Francisco Cordova .05
314 Aramis Ramirez .05
315 Freddy Garcia 1.00
316 Saint Louis Cardinals (Team Checklist) .05
317 J.D. Drew (99 Rookie) .40
318 *Chad Hutchinson* (99 Rookie) .40
319 Mark McGwire (Power Trip) 1.00
320 J.D. Drew (Power Trip) .20
321 Mark McGwire (Big Play Makers) 1.00
322 Mark McGwire (History in the Making) 1.00
323 Mark McGwire 1.50
324 Fernando Tatis .15
325 Edgar Renteria .05
326 Ray Lankford .05
327 Willie McGee .05
328 Ricky Bottalico .05
329 Eli Marrero .05
330 Matt Morris .05
331 Eric Davis .15
332 Darren Bragg .05
333 Padres (Team Checklist) .05
334 Matt Clement (99 Rookie) .05
335 Ben Davis (99 Rookie) .15
336 Gary Matthews Jr. (99 Rookie) .05
337 Tony Gwynn (Big Play Makers) .40
338 Tony Gwynn (History in the Making) .40
339 Tony Gwynn .75
340 Reggie Sanders .05
341 Ruben Rivera .05
342 Wally Joyner .05
343 Sterling Hitchcock .05
344 Carlos Hernandez .05
345 Andy Ashby .05
346 Trevor Hoffman .05
347 Chris Gomez .05
348 Jim Leyritz .05
349 San Francisco Giants (Team Checklist) .05
350 Armando Rios (99 Rookie) .15
351 Barry Bonds (Power Trip) .20
352 Barry Bonds (Big Play Makers) .20
353 Barry Bonds (History in the Making) .20
354 Robb Nen .05
355 Bill Mueller .05
356 Barry Bonds .40
357 Jeff Kent .15
358 J.T. Snow .05
359 Ellis Burks .10
360 F.P. Santangelo .05
361 Marvin Benard .05
362 Stan Javier .05
363 Shawn Estes .05
364 Seattle Mariners (Team Checklist) .05
365 Carlos Guillen (99 Rookie) .15
366 Ken Griffey Jr. (Power Trip) .75
367 Alex Rodriguez (Power Trip) .50
368 Ken Griffey Jr. (Big Play Makers) .75
369 Alex Rodriguez (Big Play Makers) .50
370 Ken Griffey Jr. (History in the Making) .75
371 Alex Rodriguez (History in the Making) .75
372 Ken Griffey Jr. 1.50
373 Alex Rodriguez 1.25
374 Jay Buhner .15
375 Edgar Martinez .15
376 Jeff Fassero .05
377 David Bell .05
378 David Segui .05
379 Russ Davis .05
380 Dan Wilson .05
381 Jamie Moyer .05
382 Tampa Bay Devil Rays (Team Checklist) .05
383 Roberto Hernandez .05
384 Bobby Smith .05
385 Wade Boggs .20
386 Fred McGriff .20
387 Rolando Arrojo .05
388 Jose Canseco .40
389 Wilson Alvarez .05
390 Kevin Stocker .05
391 Miguel Cairo .05
392 Quinton McCracken .05
393 Texas Rangers (Team Checklist) .05
394 Ruben Mateo (99 Rookie) .40
395 Cesar King (99 Rookie) .05
396 Juan Gonzalez (Power Trip) .25
397 Juan Gonzalez (Big Play Makers) .25
398 Ivan Rodriguez .40
399 Juan Gonzalez .50
400 Rafael Palmeiro .25
401 Rick Helling .05
402 Aaron Sele .05
403 John Wetteland .10
404 Rusty Greer .10
405 Todd Zeile .10
406 Royce Clayton .05
407 Tom Goodwin .05
408 Toronto Blue Jays (Team Checklist) .05
409 Kevin Witt (99 Rookie) .05
410 Roy Halladay (99 Rookie) .15
411 Jose Cruz Jr. .15
412 Carlos Delgado .25
413 Willie Greene .05
414 Shawn Green .20
415 Homer Bush .05
416 Shannon Stewart .10
417 David Wells .05
418 Kelvim Escobar .05
419 Joey Hamilton .05
420 Alex Gonzalez .05
421 Mark McGwire (McGwire Magic) .40
422 Mark McGwire (McGwire Magic) .40
423 Mark McGwire (McGwire Magic) .40
424 Mark McGwire (McGwire Magic) .40
425 Mark McGwire (McGwire Magic) .40
426 Mark McGwire (McGwire Magic) .40
427 Mark McGwire (McGwire Magic) .40
428 Mark McGwire (McGwire Magic) .40
429 Mark McGwire (McGwire Magic) .40
430 Mark McGwire (McGwire Magic) .40
431 Mark McGwire (McGwire Magic) .40
432 Mark McGwire (McGwire Magic) .40
433 Mark McGwire (McGwire Magic) .40
434 Mark McGwire (McGwire Magic) .40
435 Mark McGwire (McGwire Magic) .40
436 Mark McGwire (McGwire Magic) .40
437 Mark McGwire (McGwire Magic) .40
438 Mark McGwire (McGwire Magic) .40
439 Mark McGwire (McGwire Magic) .40
440 Mark McGwire (McGwire Magic) .40
441 Mark McGwire (McGwire Magic) .40
442 Mark McGwire (McGwire Magic) .40
443 Mark McGwire (McGwire Magic) .40
444 Mark McGwire (McGwire Magic) .40
445 Mark McGwire (McGwire Magic) .40
446 Mark McGwire (McGwire Magic) .40
447 Mark McGwire (McGwire Magic) .40
448 Mark McGwire (McGwire Magic) .40
449 Mark McGwire (McGwire Magic) .40
450 Mark McGwire (McGwire Magic) .40
451 Chipper Jones '93 (Rookie Flashback) .40
452 Cal Ripken Jr. '81 (Rookie Flashback) .50
453 Roger Clemens '84 (Rookie Flashback) .25
454 Wade Boggs '82 (Rookie Flashback) .15
455 Greg Maddux '86 (Rookie Flashback) .50
456 Frank Thomas '90 (Rookie Flashback) .25
457 Jeff Bagwell '91 (Rookie Flashback) .20
458 Mike Piazza '92 (Rookie Flashback) .50
459 Randy Johnson '88 (Rookie Flashback) .15
460 Mo Vaughn '91 (Rookie Flashback) .15
461 Mark McGwire '86 (Rookie Flashback) 1.00
462 Rickey Henderson '79 (Rookie Flashback) .10
463 Barry Bonds '86 (Rookie Flashback) .20
464 Tony Gwynn '82 (Rookie Flashback) .40
465 Ken Griffey Jr. '89 (Rookie Flashback) .75
466 Alex Rodriguez '94 (Rookie Flashback) .50
467 Sammy Sosa '89 (Rookie Flashback) .50
468 Juan Gonzalez '89 (Rookie Flashback) .25
469 Kevin Brown '86 (Rookie Flashback) .05
470 Fred McGriff '86 (Rookie Flashback) .10

1999 Upper Deck Challengers for 70

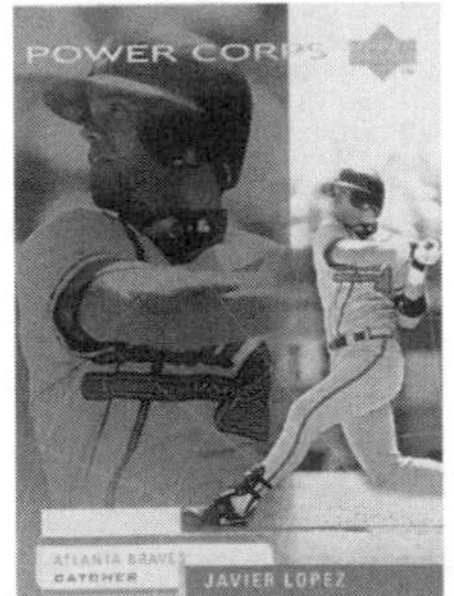

Celebrating Mark McGwire's record-setting season of 1998, and featuring those who would chase his single-season home run crown in 1999, Upper Deck issued this specialty product. The base set of 90 cards is fractured into subsets of Power Elite (#1-10), Power Corps (#11-40), Rookie Power (#41-45), and Home Run Highlights (#46-90). Several styles of inserts and numbered parallels were included in the 5-card foil packs.

	MT
Complete Set (90):	40.00
Common Player:	.15
McGwire (#61-71):	1.50
Pack (5):	3.00
Wax Box (20):	50.00

1 Mark McGwire (Power Elite) 3.00
2 Sammy Sosa (Power Elite) 2.00
3 Ken Griffey Jr. (Power Elite) 3.00
4 Alex Rodriguez (Power Elite) 2.50
5 Albert Belle (Power Elite) .60
6 Mo Vaughn (Power Elite) .50
7 Mike Piazza (Power Elite) 2.00
8 Frank Thomas (Power Elite) 1.00
9 Juan Gonzalez (Power Elite) .75
10 Barry Bonds (Power Elite) .75
11 Rafael Palmeiro (Power Corps) .40
12 Jose Canseco (Power Corps) .75
13 Nomar Garciaparra (Power Corps) 2.00
14 Carlos Delgado (Power Corps) .50
15 Brian Jordan (Power Corps) .15
16 Vladimir Guerrero (Power Corps) 1.50
17 Vinny Castilla (Power Corps) .25
18 Chipper Jones (Power Corps) 2.00
19 Jeff Bagwell (Power Corps) .75
20 Moises Alou (Power Corps) .25
21 Tony Clark (Power Corps) .40
22 Jim Thome (Power Corps) .40
23 Tino Martinez (Power Corps) .25
24 Greg Vaughn (Power Corps) .25
25 Javy Lopez (Power Corps) .15
26 Jeromy Burnitz (Power Corps) .15
27 Cal Ripken Jr. (Power Corps) 2.50
28 Manny Ramirez (Power Corps) .75
29 Darin Erstad (Power Corps) .25
30 Ken Caminiti (Power Corps) .15
31 Edgar Martinez (Power Corps) .15
32 Ivan Rodriguez (Power Corps) .75
33 Larry Walker (Power Corps) .50
34 Todd Helton (Power Corps) .50
35 Andruw Jones (Power Corps) .50
36 Ray Lankford (Power Corps) .15
37 Travis Lee (Power Corps) .25
38 Raul Mondesi (Power Corps) .25
39 Scott Rolen (Power Corps) .75
40 Ben Grieve (Power Corps) .25
41 J.D. Drew (Rookie Power) .25
42 Troy Glaus (Rookie Power) .40
43 Eric Chavez (Rookie Power) .15

44 Gabe Kapler (Rookie Power) .15
45 Michael Barrett (Rookie Power) .15
46 Mark McGwire (Home Run Highlights) 1.50
47 Jose Canseco (Home Run Highlights) .40
48 Greg Vaughn (Home Run Highlights) .15
49 Albert Belle (Home Run Highlights) .30
50 Mark McGwire (Home Run Highlights) 1.50
51 Vinny Castilla (Home Run Highlights) .15
52 Vladimir Guerrero (Home Run Highlights) .75
53 Andres Galarraga (Home Run Highlights) .25
54 Rafael Palmeiro (Home Run Highlights) .25
55 Juan Gonzalez (Home Run Highlights) .50
56 Ken Griffey Jr. (Home Run Highlights) 1.50
57 Barry Bonds (Home Run Highlights) .40
58 Mo Vaughn (Home Run Highlights) .20
59 Nomar Garciaparra (Home Run Highlights) 1.00
60 Tino Martinez (Home Run Highlights) .15
61 Mark McGwire (Home Run Highlights) 1.50
62 Mark McGwire (Home Run Highlights) 1.50
63 Mark McGwire (Home Run Highlights) 1.50
64 Mark McGwire (Home Run Highlights) 1.50
65 Mark McGwire (Home Run Highlights) 1.50
66 Sammy Sosa (Home Run Highlights) 1.00
67 Mark McGwire (Home Run Highlights) 1.50
68 Mark McGwire (Home Run Highlights) 1.50
69 Mark McGwire (Home Run Highlights) 1.50
70 Mark McGwire (Home Run Highlights) 1.50
71 Mark McGwire (Home Run Highlights) 1.50
72 Scott Brosius (Home Run Highlights) .15
73 Tony Gwynn (Home Run Highlights) .75
74 Chipper Jones (Home Run Highlights) 1.00
75 Jeff Bagwell (Home Run Highlights) .40
76 Moises Alou (Home Run Highlights) .15
77 Manny Ramirez (Home Run Highlights) .40
78 Carlos Delgado (Home Run Highlights) .25
79 Kerry Wood (Home Run Highlights) .15
80 Ken Griffey Jr. (Home Run Highlights) 1.50
81 Cal Ripken Jr. (Home Run Highlights) 1.25
82 Alex Rodriguez (Home Run Highlights) 1.25
83 Barry Bonds (Home Run Highlights) .40
84 Ken Griffey Jr. (Home Run Highlights) 1.50
85 Travis Lee (Home Run Highlights) .15
86 George Lombard (Home Run Highlights) .15
87 Michael Barrett (Home Run Highlights) .15
88 Jeremy Giambi (Home Run Highlights) .15
89 Troy Glaus (Home Run Highlights) .40
90 J.D. Drew (Home Run Highlights) .35

1999 Upper Deck Challengers for 70 Challengers for 70

Found one per pack, this insert series identifies 30 of the top contenders for the 1999 home run crown. Action photos on front are highlighted by red graphics and silver-foil. Backs repeat a detail of the front photo and present a capsule of the player's 1998 season. Cards have a "C" prefix to the number. A parallel edition, utilizing refractive foil details on front, is serially numbered within an edition of 70 each.

		MT
Complete Set (30):		40.00
Common Player:		.40
Parallel Edition (# to 70):		6X
1	Mark McGwire	3.00
2	Sammy Sosa	2.00
3	Ken Griffey Jr.	3.00
4	Alex Rodriguez	2.50
5	Albert Belle	.60
6	Mo Vaughn	.50
7	Mike Piazza	2.00
8	Frank Thomas	1.50
9	Juan Gonzalez	1.00
10	Barry Bonds	.75
11	Rafael Palmeiro	.40
12	Nomar Garciaparra	2.00
13	Vladimir Guerrero	1.50
14	Vinny Castilla	.40
15	Chipper Jones	2.00
16	Jeff Bagwell	.75
17	Moises Alou	.40
18	Tony Clark	.40
19	Jim Thome	.40
20	Tino Martinez	.40
21	Greg Vaughn	.40
22	Manny Ramirez	.75
23	Darin Erstad	.40
24	Ken Caminiti	.40
25	Ivan Rodriguez	.75
26	Andruw Jones	.60
27	Travis Lee	.40
28	Scott Rolen	.75
29	Ben Grieve	.40
30	J.D. Drew	.75

1999 Upper Deck Challengers for 70 Mark on History

The details of Mark McGwire successful assault on the single-season home run record are captured in this 25-card insert set, found on average of one per five packs. Cards have action photos set against split red and black backgrounds and are highlighted in red metallic foil. Backs have details of the home run featured on front, a quote from McGwire and another photo. Cards have an "M" prefix to the number. A parallel edition number to 70 was also issued.

		MT
Complete Set (25):		75.00
Common McGwire:		4.00
Parallel:		8X
01	Mark McGwire	4.00
02	Mark McGwire	4.00
03	Mark McGwire	4.00
04	Mark McGwire	4.00
05	Mark McGwire	4.00
06	Mark McGwire	4.00
07	Mark McGwire	4.00
08	Mark McGwire	4.00
09	Mark McGwire	4.00
10	Mark McGwire	4.00
11	Mark McGwire	4.00
12	Mark McGwire	4.00
13	Mark McGwire	4.00
14	Mark McGwire	4.00
15	Mark McGwire	4.00
16	Mark McGwire	4.00
17	Mark McGwire	4.00
18	Mark McGwire	4.00
19	Mark McGwire	4.00
20	Mark McGwire	4.00
21	Mark McGwire	4.00
22	Mark McGwire	4.00
23	Mark McGwire	4.00
24	Mark McGwire	4.00
25	Mark McGwire	4.00

1999 Upper Deck Challengers for 70 Longball Legends

Top home-run threats are featured in this insert series. The action photos on front are repeated in a diffused version on back, where they are joined by a second photo and a bar-graph of the player's home run production in recent seasons. Cards have an "L" prefix to the number. Stated odds of picking a Longball Legends card are one per 39 packs.

		MT
Complete Set (30):		225.00
Common Player:		4.00
1	Ken Griffey Jr.	25.00
2	Mark McGwire	25.00
3	Sammy Sosa	15.00
4	Cal Ripken Jr.	20.00
5	Barry Bonds	6.00
6	Larry Walker	5.00
7	Fred McGriff	4.00
8	Alex Rodriguez	20.00
9	Frank Thomas	12.00
10	Juan Gonzalez	8.00
11	Jeff Bagwell	6.00
12	Mo Vaughn	4.00
13	Albert Belle	5.00
14	Mike Piazza	15.00
15	Vladimir Guerrero	10.00
16	Chipper Jones	15.00
17	Ken Caminiti	4.00
18	Rafael Palmeiro	5.00
19	Nomar Garciaparra	15.00
20	Jim Thome	4.00
21	Edgar Martinez	4.00
22	Ivan Rodriguez	6.00
23	Andres Galarraga	4.00
24	Scott Rolen	6.00
25	Darin Erstad	4.00
26	Moises Alou	4.00
27	J.D. Drew	4.00
28	Andruw Jones	5.00
29	Manny Ramirez	6.00
30	Tino Martinez	4.00

1999 Upper Deck Challengers for 70 Swinging/ Fences

Fifteen top sluggers are included in this insert set. The players' power swing is captured on a muted textured-look background. Back has a color portrait photo and an "S" prefix to the card number. Stated insertion rate is one per 19 packs.

		MT
Complete Set (15):		90.00
Common Player:		3.00
1	Ken Griffey Jr.	15.00
2	Mark McGwire	15.00
3	Sammy Sosa	10.00
4	Alex Rodriguez	12.00
5	Nomar Garciaparra	10.00
6	J.D. Drew	3.00
7	Vladimir Guerrero	8.00
8	Ben Grieve	3.00
9	Chipper Jones	10.00
10	Gabe Kapler	3.00
11	Travis Lee	3.00
12	Todd Helton	3.00
13	Juan Gonzalez	5.00
14	Mike Piazza	10.00
15	Mo Vaughn	3.00

1999 Upper Deck Challengers for 70 Autographed Swinging

A total of 2,700 autographed versions of Swinging for the Fences inserts were featured in the Challengers for 70 issue. Only six of the 15 players' cards were included in this premium version.

		MT
Common Player:		20.00
JR	Ken Griffey Jr.	200.00
VG	Vladimir Guerrero	60.00
TH	Todd Helton	30.00
GK	Gabe Kapler	20.00
TL	Travis Lee	20.00
AR	Alex Rodriguez	200.00

1999 Upper Deck Challengers for 70 Challengers Edition

In this parallel of the 90-card base set, each card is serially numbered within an edition of 600 each.

	MT
Complete Set (90):	375.00
Commons:	4.00
Stars:	6X

(See 1999 Challengers for 70 for checklist and base card values.)

1999 Upper Deck Challengers for 70 Piece/ History 500

A piece of game-used bat from 500-HR club member Harmon Killebrew is featured on these inserts. Only 350 cards were issued, along with three (his uniform number) authentically autographed versions. Backs have an action photo and a congratulatory authentication message from UD CEO Richard McWilliam.

	MT
Harmon Killebrew	300.00
Harmon Killebrew (autographed - value not determined)	

2000 Upper Deck

Released in two 270-card series the base cards feature full-bleed fronts with gold-foil etching and stamping. Card backs have complete year-by-year statistics.

		MT
Complete Set (540):		80.00
Complete Series I (270):		40.00
Complete Series II (270):		40.00
Common Player:		.15
Hobby Pack (10):		3.50
Hobby Box (24):		80.00
1	Rick Ankiel (Star Rookie)	2.00
2	Vernon Wells (Star Rookie)	.50
3	Ryan Anderson (Star Rookie)	.75
4	Ed Yarnall (Star Rookie)	.50
5	Brian McNichol (Star Rookie)	.25
6	Ben Petrick (Star Rookie)	.25
7	Kip Wells (Star Rookie)	.25
8	Eric Munson (Star Rookie)	1.50
9	Matt Riley (Star Rookie)	.40
10	Peter Bergeron (Star Rookie)	.40
11	Eric Gagne (Star Rookie)	.25
12	Ramon Ortiz (Star Rookie)	.25
13	Josh Beckett (Star Rookie)	3.00
14	Alfonso Soriano (Star Rookie)	.50
15	Jorge Toca (Star Rookie)	.25
16	Buddy Carlyle (Star Rookie)	.25
17	Chad Hermansen (Star Rookie)	.25
18	Matt Perisho (Star Rookie)	.40
19	*Tomokazu Ohka* (Star Rookie)	.75
20	Jacque Jones (Star Rookie)	.50
21	Josh Paul (Star Rookie)	.40
22	Dermal Brown (Star Rookie)	.50
23	Adam Kennedy (Star Rookie)	.50
24	Chad Harville (Star Rookie)	.40
25	Calvin Murray (Star Rookie)	.40
26	Chad Meyers (Star Rookie)	.40
27	Brian Cooper (Star Rookie)	.40
28	Troy Glaus	.75
29	Ben Molina	.25
30	Troy Percival	.15
31	Ken Hill	.15
32	Chuck Finley	.15
33	Todd Greene	.15
34	Tim Salmon	.25
35	Gary DiSarcina	.15
36	Luis Gonzalez	.15
37	Tony Womack	.15
38	Omar Daal	.15
39	Randy Johnson	.50
40	Erubiel Durazo	.40
41	Jay Bell	.15
42	Steve Finley	.15
43	Travis Lee	.25
44	Greg Maddux	1.50
45	Bret Boone	.15
46	Brian Jordan	.15
47	Kevin Millwood	.25
48	Odalis Perez	.15
49	Javy Lopez	.25
50	John Smoltz	.25
51	Bruce Chen	.25
52	Albert Belle	.60
53	Jerry Hairston Jr.	.15
54	Will Clark	.40
55	Sidney Ponson	.15
56	Charles Johnson	.15
57	Cal Ripken Jr.	2.50
58	Ryan Minor	.25
59	Mike Mussina	.50
60	Tom Gordon	.15
61	Jose Offerman	.15
62	Trot Nixon	.15
63	Pedro Martinez	1.00
64	John Valentin	.15
65	Jason Varitek	.15
66	Juan Pena	.15
67	Troy O'Leary	.15
68	Sammy Sosa	2.00
69	Henry Rodriguez	.15
70	Kyle Farnsworth	.15
71	Glenallen Hill	.15
72	Lance Johnson	.15
73	Mickey Morandini	.15
74	Jon Lieber	.15
75	Kevin Tapani	.15
76	Carlos Lee	.15
77	Ray Durham	.15
78	Jim Parque	.15
79	Bob Howry	.15
80	Magglio Ordonez	.40
81	Paul Konerko	.25
82	Mike Caruso	.15
83	Chris Singleton	.15
84	Sean Casey	.40
85	Barry Larkin	.40
86	Pokey Reese	.15
87	Eddie Taubensee	.15
88	Scott Williamson	.15
89	Jason LaRue	.15
90	Aaron Boone	.15
91	Jeffrey Hammonds	.15
92	Omar Vizquel	.15
93	Manny Ramirez	.75
94	Kenny Lofton	.60
95	Jaret Wright	.20
96	Einar Diaz	.15
97	Charles Nagy	.15
98	David Justice	.25
99	Richie Sexson	.15
100	Steve Karsay	.15
101	Todd Helton	.75
102	Dante Bichette	.25
103	Larry Walker	.50
104	Pedro Astacio	.15
105	Neifi Perez	.15
106	Brian Bohanon	.15
107	Edgard Clemente	.15
108	Dave Veres	.15
109	Gabe Kapler	.25
110	Juan Encarnacion	.15
111	Jeff Weaver	.25
112	Damion Easley	.15
113	Justin Thompson	.15
114	Brad Ausmus	.15
115	Frank Catalanotto	.15
116	Todd Jones	.15
117	Preston Wilson	.15
118	Cliff Floyd	.15
119	Mike Lowell	.15
120	Jorge Fabregas	.15
121	Alex Gonzalez	.15
122	Braden Looper	.15
123	Bruce Aven	.15
124	Richard Hidalgo	.15
125	Mitch Meluskey	.15
126	Jeff Bagwell	.75
127	Jose Lima	.15
128	Derek Bell	.15
129	Billy Wagner	.15
130	Shane Reynolds	.15
131	Moises Alou	.25

132 Carlos Beltran .25
133 Carlos Febles .15
134 Jermaine Dye .15
135 Jeremy Giambi .15
136 Joe Randa .15
137 Jose Rosado .15
138 Chad Kreuter .15
139 Jose Vizcaino .15
140 Adrian Beltre .25
141 Kevin Brown .25
142 Ismael Valdes .15
143 Angel Pena .15
144 Chan Ho Park .25
145 Mark Grudzielanek .15
146 Jeff Shaw .15
147 Geoff Jenkins .15
148 Jeromy Burnitz .15
149 Hideo Nomo .25
150 Ron Belliard .15
151 Sean Berry .15
152 Mark Loretta .15
153 Steve Woodard .15
154 Joe Mays .15
155 Eric Milton .15
156 Corey Koskie .15
157 Ron Coomer .15
158 Brad Radke .15
159 Terry Steinbach .15
160 Christian Guzman .15
161 Vladimir Guerrero 1.50
162 Wilton Guerrero .15
163 Michael Barrett .25
164 Chris Widger .15
165 Fernando Seguignol .25
166 Ugueth Urbina .15
167 Dustin Hermanson .15
168 Kenny Rogers .15
169 Edgardo Alfonzo .25
170 Orel Hershiser .15
171 Robin Ventura .40
172 Octavio Dotel .15
173 Rickey Henderson .25
174 Roger Cedeno .15
175 John Olerud .30
176 Derek Jeter 2.00
177 Tino Martinez .40
178 Orlando Hernandez .25
179 Chuck Knoblauch .30
180 Bernie Williams .50
181 Chili Davis .15
182 David Cone .25
183 Ricky Ledee .15
184 Paul O'Neill .25
185 Jason Giambi .15
186 Eric Chavez .15
187 Matt Stairs .15
188 Miguel Tejada .15
189 Olmedo Saenz .15
190 Tim Hudson .40
191 John Jaha .15
192 Randy Velarde .15
193 Rico Brogna .15
194 Mike Lieberthal .15
195 Marlon Anderson .15
196 Bobby Abreu .15
197 Ron Gant .15
198 Randy Wolf .15
199 Desi Relaford .15
200 Doug Glanville .15
201 Warren Morris .15
202 Kris Benson .15
203 Kevin Young .15
204 Brian Giles .15
205 Jason Schmidt .15
206 Ed Sprague .15
207 Francisco Cordova .15
208 Mark McGwire 3.00
209 Jose Jimenez .15
210 Fernando Tatis .40
211 Kent Bottenfield .15
212 Eli Marrero .15
213 Edgar Renteria .15
214 Joe McEwing .15
215 J.D. Drew .25
216 Tony Gwynn 1.50
217 Gary Matthews Jr. .15
218 Eric Owens .15
219 Damian Jackson .15
220 Reggie Sanders .15
221 Trevor Hoffman .15
222 Ben Davis .15
223 Shawn Estes .15
224 F.P. Santangelo .15
225 Livan Hernandez .15
226 Ellis Burks .15
227 J.T. Snow .15
228 Jeff Kent .15
229 Robb Nen .15
230 Marvin Benard .15
231 Ken Griffey Jr. 2.50
232 John Halama .15
233 Gil Meche .15
234 David Bell .15
235 Brian L. Hunter .15
236 Jay Buhner .25
237 Edgar Martinez .25
238 Jose Mesa .15
239 Wilson Alvarez .15
240 Wade Boggs .40
241 Fred McGriff .25
242 Jose Canseco .75
243 Kevin Stocker .15
244 Roberto Hernandez .15
245 Bubba Trammell .15
246 John Flaherty .15
247 Ivan Rodriguez .75
248 Rusty Greer .15
249 Rafael Palmeiro .40
250 Jeff Zimmerman .15
251 Royce Clayton .15
252 Todd Zeile .15
253 John Wetteland .15
254 Ruben Mateo .40
255 Kelvim Escobar .15
256 David Wells .15
257 Shawn Green .50
258 Homer Bush .15
259 Shannon Stewart .15
260 Carlos Delgado .50
261 Roy Halladay .15
262 Fernando Tatis CL .25
263 Jose Jimenez CL .15
264 Tony Gwynn CL .75
265 Wade Boggs CL .25
266 Cal Ripken Jr. CL 1.00
267 David Cone CL .15
268 Mark McGwire CL 2.00
269 Pedro Martinez CL .50
270 Nomar Garciaparra CL 1.00
271 Nick Johnson (Star Rookie) .75
272 Mark Quinn (Star Rookie) .15
273 Roosevelt Brown (Star Rookie) .15
274 Adam Everett (Star Rookie) .15
275 Jason Marquis (Star Rookie) .15
276 *Kazuhiro Sasaki* (Star Rookie) 3.00
277 Aaron Myette (Star Rookie) .15
278 *Danys Baez* (Star Rookie) .15
279 Travis Dawkins (Star Rookie) .15
280 Mark Mulder (Star Rookie) .15
281 Chris Haas (Star Rookie) .15
282 Milton Bradley (Star Rookie) .15
283 Brad Penny (Star Rookie) .15
284 Rafael Furcal (Star Rookie) .50
285 *Luis Matos* (Star Rookie) .15
286 Victor Santos (Star Rookie) .15
287 *Rico Washington* (Star Rookie) .15
288 Rob Bell (Star Rookie) .15
289 Joe Crede (Star Rookie) .15
290 Pablo Ozuna (Star Rookie) .15
291 *Wascar Serrano* (Star Rookie) .15
292 Sang-Hoon Lee (Star Rookie) .50
293 Chris Wakeland (Star Rookie) .15
294 Luis Rivera (Star Rookie) .15
295 *Mike Lamb* (Star Rookie) .75
296 Wily Pena (Star Rookie) 1.00
297 Mike Meyers (Star Rookie) .15
298 Mo Vaughn .50
299 Darin Erstad .25
300 Garret Anderson .15
301 Tim Belcher .15
302 Scott Spiezio .15
303 Kent Bottenfield .15
304 Orlando Palmeiro .15
305 Jason Dickson .15
306 Matt Williams .40
307 Brian Anderson .15
308 Hanley Frias .15
309 Todd Stottlemyre .15
310 Matt Mantei .15
311 David Dellucci .15
312 Armando Reynoso .15
313 Bernard Gilkey .15
314 Chipper Jones 1.50
315 Tom Glavine .25
316 Quilvio Veras .15
317 Andruw Jones .50
318 Bobby Bonilla .15
319 Reggie Sanders .15
320 Andres Galarraga .40
321 George Lombard .15
322 John Rocker .15
322 Wally Joyner .15
324 B.J. Surhoff .15
325 Scott Erickson .15
326 Delino DeShields .15
327 Jeff Conine .15
328 Mike Timlin .15
329 Brady Anderson .20
330 Mike Bordick .15
331 Harold Baines .15
332 Nomar Garciaparra 2.00
333 Bret Saberhagen .15
334 Ramon Martinez .15
335 Donnie Sadler .15
336 Wilton Veras .15
337 Mike Stanley .15
338 Brian Rose .15
339 Carl Everett .15
340 Tim Wakefield .15
341 Mark Grace .25
342 Kerry Wood .30
343 Eric Young .15
344 Jose Nieves .15
345 Ismael Valdes .15
346 Joe Girardi .15
347 Damon Buford .15
348 Ricky Gutierrez .15
349 Frank Thomas 1.00
350 Brian Simmons .15
351 James Baldwin .15
352 Brook Fordyce .15
353 Jose Valentin .15
354 Mike Sirotka .15
355 Greg Norton .15
356 Dante Bichette .15
357 Deion Sanders .25
358 Ken Griffey Jr. 2.50
359 Denny Neagle .15
360 Dmitri Young .15
361 Pete Harnisch .15
362 Michael Tucker .15
363 Roberto Alomar .50
364 Dave Roberts .15
365 Jim Thome .40
366 Bartolo Colon .15
367 Travis Fryman .20
368 Chuck Finley .15
369 Russell Branyan .20
370 Alex Ramirez .15
371 Jeff Cirillo .15
372 Jeffrey Hammonds .15
373 Scott Karl .15
374 Brent Mayne .15
375 Tom Goodwin .15
376 Jose Jimenez .15
377 Rolando Arrojo .15
378 Terry Shumpert .15
379 Juan Gonzalez .75
380 Bobby Higginson .15
381 Tony Clark .25
382 Dave Mlicki .15
383 Deivi Cruz .15
384 Brian Moehler .15
385 Dean Palmer .15
386 Luis Castillo .15
387 Mike Redmond .15
388 Alex Fernandez .15
389 Brant Brown .15
390 Dave Berg .15
391 A.J. Burnett .15
392 Mark Kotsay .15
393 Craig Biggio .30
394 Daryle Ward .15
395 Lance Berkman .15
396 Roger Cedeno .15
397 Scott Elarton .15
398 Octavio Dotel .15
399 Ken Caminiti .15
400 Johnny Damon .15
401 Mike Sweeney .15
402 Jeff Suppan .15
403 Rey Sanchez .15
404 Blake Stein .15
405 Ricky Bottalico .15
406 Jay Witasick .15
407 Shawn Green .50
408 Orel Hershiser .15
409 Gary Sheffield .40
410 Todd Hollandsworth .15
411 Terry Adams .15
412 Todd Hundley .15
413 Eric Karros .15
414 F.P. Santangelo .15
415 Alex Cora .15
416 Marquis Grissom .15
417 Henry Blanco .15
418 Jose Hernandez .15
419 Kyle Peterson .15
420 John Snyder .15
421 Bob Wickman .15
422 Jamey Wright .15
423 Chad Allen .15
424 Todd Walker .15
425 J.C. Romero .15
426 Butch Huskey .15
427 Jacque Jones .15
428 Matt Lawton .15
429 Rondell White .25
430 Jose Vidro .15
431 Hideki Irabu .15
432 Javier Vazquez .15
433 Lee Stevens .15
434 Mike Thurman .15
435 Geoff Blum .15
436 Mike Hampton .15
437 Mike Piazza 2.00
438 Al Leiter .15
439 Derek Bell .15
440 Armando Benitez .15
441 Rey Ordonez .15
442 Todd Zeile .15
443 Roger Clemens 1.00
444 Ramiro Mendoza .15
445 Andy Pettite .25
446 Scott Brosius .15
447 Mariano Rivera .25
448 Jim Leyritz .15
449 Jorge Posada .25
450 Omar Olivares .15
451 Ben Grieve .25
452 A.J. Hinch .15
453 Gil Heredia .15
454 Kevin Appier .15
455 Ryan Christenson .15
456 Ramon Hernandez .15
457 Scott Rolen .75
458 Alex Arias .15
459 Andy Ashby .15
460 (Not issued, see #474)
460 .15
461 Robert Person .15
462 Paul Byrd .15
463 Curt Schilling .25
464 Mike Jackson .15
465 Jason Kendall .15
466 Pat Meares .15
467 Bruce Aven .15
468 Todd Ritchie .15
469 Wil Cordero .15
470 Aramis Ramirez .15
471 Andy Benes .15
472 Ray Lankford .15
473 Fernando Vina .15
474a Jim Edmonds .25
474b Kevin Jordan (should be #460) .15
475 Craig Paquette .15
476 Pat Hentgen .15
477 Darryl Kile .15
478 Sterling Hitchcock .15
479 Ruben Rivera .15
480 Ryan Klesko .15
481 Phil Nevin .15
482 Woody Williams .15
483 Carlos Hernandez .15
484 Brian Meadows .15
485 Bret Boone .15
486 Barry Bonds .75
487 Russ Ortiz .15
488 Bobby Estalella .15
489 Rich Aurilia .15
490 Bill Mueller .15
491 Joe Nathan .15
492 Russ Davis .15
493 John Olerud .25
494 Alex Rodriguez 2.50
495 Fred Garcia .15
496 Carlos Guillen .15
497 Aaron Sele .15
498 Brett Tomko .15
499 Jamie Moyer .15
500 Mike Cameron .15
501 Vinny Castilla .15
502 Gerald Williams .15
503 Mike DiFelice .15

504	Ryan Rupe	.15
505	Greg Vaughn	.25
506	Miguel Cairo	.15
507	Juan Guzman	.15
508	Jose Guillen	.15
509	Gabe Kapler	.15
510	Rick Helling	.15
511	David Segui	.15
512	Doug Davis	.15
513	Justin Thompson	.15
514	Chad Curtis	.15
515	Tony Batista	.15
516	Billy Koch	.15
517	Raul Mondesi	.25
518	Joey Hamilton	.15
519	Darrin Fletcher	.15
520	Brad Fullmer	.15
521	Jose Cruz Jr.	.15
522	Kevin Witt	.15
523	Mark McGwire (All-UD Team)	1.50
524	Roberto Alomar (All-UD Team)	.25
525	Chipper Jones (All-UD Team)	.75
526	Derek Jeter (All-UD Team)	1.00
527	Ken Griffey Jr. (All-UD Team)	1.50
528	Sammy Sosa (All-UD Team)	1.00
529	Manny Ramirez (All-UD Team)	.40
530	Ivan Rodriguez (All-UD Team)	.40
531	Pedro J. Martinez (All-UD Team)	.40
532	Mariano Rivera (Season Highlights Checklist)	.15
533	Sammy Sosa (Season Highlights Checklist)	1.00
534	Cal Ripken Jr. (Season Highlights Checklist)	1.00
535	Vladimir Guerrero (Season Highlights Checklist)	.75
536	Tony Gwynn (Season Highlights Checklist)	.50
537	Mark McGwire (Season Highlights Checklist)	1.50
538	Bernie Williams (Season Highlights Checklist)	.25
539	Pedro J. Martinez (Season Highlights Checklist)	.40
540	Ken Griffey Jr. (Season Highlights Checklist)	1.50

2000 Upper Deck Exclusives

Labeled "UD Exclusives," these parallel sets were issued in two versions, silvers numbered to 100 each, and golds which were 1-of-1. Except for the appropriately colored foil highlights on front and dot-matrix serial number, the Exclusives are identical to the regular-issue cards. They were inserted exclusively into hobby packs. Because of their rarity and variable demand, the unique gold cards are not priced.

	MT
Common Silver Exclusive:	5.00
Silver Stars/Rookies:	20X

(See 2000 Upper Deck for checklist and base card values.)

2000 Upper Deck Cooperstown Calling

This 12-card set features players deemed by Upper Deck as future Hall of Famers. Card fronts feature silver holo-foil with gold-foil stamping. Card backs are numbered with a "CC" prefix and are seeded 1:23 packs.

		MT
Complete Set (15):		120.00
Common Player:		3.00
Inserted 1:23		
1	Roger Clemens	8.00
2	Cal Ripken Jr.	15.00
3	Ken Griffey Jr.	20.00
4	Mike Piazza	12.00
5	Tony Gwynn	8.00
6	Sammy Sosa	12.00
7	Jose Canseco	4.00
8	Larry Walker	3.00
9	Barry Bonds	5.00
10	Greg Maddux	10.00
11	Derek Jeter	12.00
12	Mark McGwire	20.00
13	Randy Johnson	5.00
14	Frank Thomas	8.00
15	Jeff Bagwell	5.00

2000 Upper Deck e-Card

Randomly inserted in series 2 packs, each e-Card has an ID number stamped on the card front that can be entered on Upper Deck's Web site. Collectors then find out if that card "evolves" into a signature card, jersey card or a signed jersey card. They are seeded 1:9 packs and are numbered with an "E" prefix on the card back.

		MT
Complete Set (6):		10.00
Common Player:		1.00
Inserted 1:12		
1	Ken Griffey Jr.	4.00
2	Alex Rodriguez	3.00
3	Cal Ripken Jr.	3.00
4	Jeff Bagwell	1.00
5	Barry Bonds	1.00
6	Manny Ramirez	1.00

2000 Upper Deck eVolve Signature

		MT
Complete Set (6):		
Common Player:		50.00
Production 200 sets		
1	Ken Griffey Jr.	250.00
2	Alex Rodriguez	200.00
3	Cal Ripken Jr.	200.00
4	Jeff Bagwell	60.00
5	Barry Bonds	75.00
6	Manny Ramirez	60.00

2000 Upper Deck eVolve Jersey

		MT
Complete Set (6):		
Common Player:		75.00
Production 300 sets		
1	Ken Griffey Jr.	250.00
2	Alex Rodriguez	200.00
3	Cal Ripken Jr.	200.00
4	Jeff Bagwell	75.00
5	Barry Bonds	90.00
6	Manny Ramirez	75.00

2000 Upper Deck eVolve Signed Jersey

		MT
Complete Set (6):		
Common Player:		200.00
Production 50 sets		
1	Ken Griffey Jr.	650.00
2	Alex Rodriguez	600.00
3	Cal Ripken Jr.	600.00
4	Jeff Bagwell	200.00
5	Barry Bonds	275.00
6	Manny Ramirez	200.00

2000 Upper Deck Faces of the Game

Randomly inserted in series 1 at a rate of 1:11 packs card fronts feature a close-up photo of the featured player with bronze-foil etching and stamping. Backs are numbered with an "F" prefix. Two parallel versions are available, Silvers are serially numbered to 100 and golds limited to one set.

		MT
Complete Set (20):		90.00
Common Player:		1.50
Inserted 1:11		
Silver:		6x to 12x
Production 100 sets		
1	Ken Griffey Jr.	12.00
2	Mark McGwire	12.00
3	Sammy Sosa	8.00
4	Alex Rodriguez	10.00
5	Manny Ramirez	3.00
6	Derek Jeter	8.00
7	Jeff Bagwell	3.00
8	Roger Clemens	4.00
9	Scott Rolen	3.00
10	Tony Gwynn	6.00
11	Nomar Garciaparra	8.00
12	Randy Johnson	2.50
13	Greg Maddux	6.00
14	Mike Piazza	8.00
15	Frank Thomas	3.00
16	Cal Ripken Jr.	8.00
17	Ivan Rodriguez	3.00
18	Mo Vaughn	2.50
19	Chipper Jones	8.00
20	Sean Casey	2.00

2000 Upper Deck Five-Tool Talents

Randomly inserted in series 2 at a rate of 1:11 packs, this 15-card set spotlights players who have "five tools." Card fronts have silver holofoil throughout with silver-foil stamping. Card backs are numbered with an "FT" prefix.

		MT
Complete Set (15):		40.00
Common Player:		1.00
Inserted 1:11		
1	Vladimir Guerrero	3.00
2	Barry Bonds	2.50
3	Jason Kendall	1.00
4	Derek Jeter	6.00
5	Ken Griffey Jr.	10.00
6	Andruw Jones	2.00
7	Bernie Williams	2.00
8	Jose Canseco	2.00

9	Scott Rolen	2.50
10	Shawn Green	2.00
11	Nomar Garciaparra	6.00
12	Jeff Bagwell	2.50
13	Larry Walker	1.50
14	Chipper Jones	5.00
15	Alex Rodriguez	8.00

2000 Upper Deck Game-Used Balls

These inserts feature a piece of game-used baseball embedded into the card from the featured player. Card backs are numbered with the featured player's initials and are found on the average of 1:287 series 2 pack.

		MT
Common Player:		30.00
JB	Jeff Bagwell	30.00
RC	Roger Clemens	50.00
KG	Ken Griffey Jr.	100.00
VG	Vladimir Guerrero	60.00
TG	Tony Gwynn	50.00
DJ	Derek Jeter	100.00
CJ	Chipper Jones	60.00
GM	Greg Maddux	60.00
MM	Mark McGwire	200.00
AR	Alex Rodriguez	100.00
BW	Bernie Williams	30.00

2000 Upper Deck Game Jersey

These have a piece of game-used jersey from the featured player embedded into the card. This regular version is found both in hobby and retail packs at a rate of 1:2,500 packs.

		MT
Common Player:		40.00
Inserted 1:2,500		
JC	Jose Canseco	100.00
JG	Juan Gonzalez	75.00
VG	Vladimir Guerrero	100.00
TH	Todd Helton	80.00
CJ	Chipper Jones	120.00
GK	Gabe Kapler	40.00
GM	Greg Maddux	140.00
MR	Manny Ramirez	75.00
CR	Cal Ripken Jr.	200.00
GV	Greg Vaughn	40.00

2000 Upper Deck Game Jersey Hobby

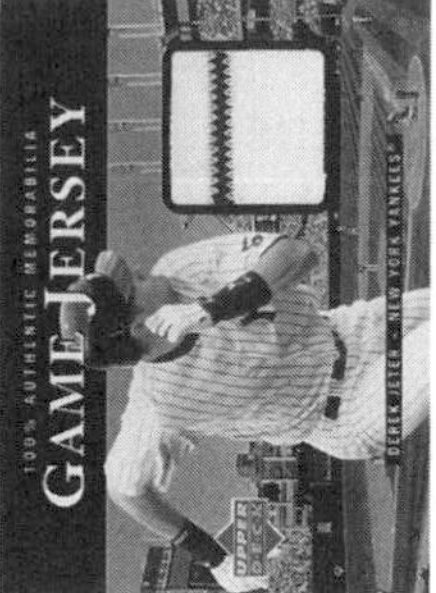

These game-used memorabilia inserts were found exclusively in series 1 packs at a rate of 1:288.

		MT
Common Player:		50.00
Inserted 1:288		50.00
JB	Jeff Bagwell	120.00
TG	Troy Glaus	60.00
CY	Tom Glavine	80.00
Jr.	Ken Griffey Jr.	250.00
DJ	Derek Jeter	275.00
PM	Pedro J. Martinez	150.00
MP	Mike Piazza	200.00
AR	Alex Rodriguez	250.00
FT	Frank Thomas	125.00
LW	Larry Walker	60.00

2000 Upper Deck Game Jersey Patch Series II

Inserted in series 2 packs, these memorabilia inserts have a game-used uniform patch embedded and are seeded 1:7,500 packs. A limited one-of-one Patch insert for each player is also randomly seeded and are not priced due to their limited nature.

		MT
Common Player:		200.00
JB	Jeff Bagwell	500.00
AB	Albert Belle	200.00
CB	Craig Biggio	200.00
BB	Barry Bonds	200.00
JC	Jose Canseco	200.00
EC	Eric Chavez	200.00
DC	David Cone	200.00
TGl	Troy Glaus	200.00
KG	Ken Griffey Jr.	200.00
VG	Vladimir Guerrero	200.00
TG	Tony Gwynn	200.00
DJ	Derek Jeter	200.00
RJ	Randy Johnson	200.00
AJ	Andruw Jones	200.00
CJ	Chipper Jones	200.00
GM	Greg Maddux	200.00
PM	Pedro Martinez	200.00
RP	Rafael Palmeiro	200.00
MR	Manny Ramirez	200.00
CR	Cal Ripken Jr.	200.00
SR	Scott Rolen	200.00
AR	Alex Rodriguez	200.00
IR	Ivan Rodriguez	200.00
FT	Frank Thomas	200.00
JT	Jim Thome	200.00
MV	Mo Vaughn	200.00
BW	Bernie Williams	200.00
MW	Matt Williams	200.00

2000 Upper Deck Game Jersey Patch

Inserted in series 1 packs at a rate of 1:10,000, these memorabilia inserts have a piece of game-used uniform patch embedded.

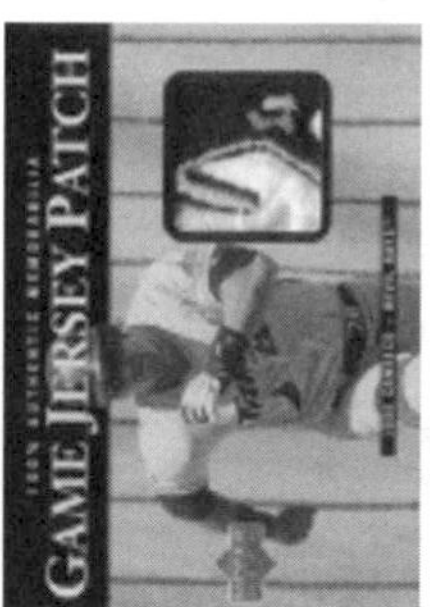

		MT
Common Player:		100.00
Inserted 1:10,000		
JB	Jeff Bagwell	500.00
JC	Jose Canseco	500.00
TG	Troy Glaus	250.00
CY	Tom Glavine	300.00
Jr.	Ken Griffey Jr.	1000.
VG	Vladimir Guerrero	400.00
TH	Todd Helton	180.00
DJ	Derek Jeter	700.00
CJ	Chipper Jones	500.00
GK	Gabe Kapler	100.00
GM	Greg Maddux	500.00
PM	Pedro J. Martinez	500.00
MP	Mike Piazza	500.00
MR	Manny Ramirez	400.00
CR	Cal Ripken Jr.	800.00
AR	Alex Rodriguez	600.00
FT	Frank Thomas	400.00
GV	Greg Vaughn	150.00
LW	Larry Walker	150.00

2000 Upper Deck Game Jersey Auto. Hobby Series 2

Found exclusively in series 2 packs these autographed game-used memorabilia inserts are found only in hobby packs at a rate of 1:287.

		MT
Common Player:		60.00
H-KG	Ken Griffey Jr.	450.00
H-CR	Cal Ripken Jr.	400.00
H-DJ	Derek Jeter	450.00
H-IR	Ivan Rodriguez	120.00
H-AR	Alex Rodriguez	350.00
H-MR	Manny Ramirez	100.00
H-JC	Jose Canseco	100.00
H-BB	Barry Bonds	160.00
H-SR	Scott Rolen	80.00
H-PO	Paul O'Neill	100.00
H-JK	Jason Kendall	60.00
H-VG	Vladimir Guerrero	150.00
H-JB	Jeff Bagwell	120.00

2000 Upper Deck Game Jersey Series 2

These jersey inserts are found in both hobby and retail packs and are seeded 1:287 packs.

		MT
Common Player:		40.00
AR	Alex Rodriguez	225.00
TG	Tony Gwynn	100.00
FT	Frank Thomas	125.00
MW	Matt Williams	50.00
JT	Jim Thome	50.00
MV	Mo Vaughn	50.00
TGl	Tom Glavine	50.00
BG	Ben Grieve	50.00
TrG	Troy Glaus	60.00
RJ	Randy Johnson	80.00
KM	Kevin Millwood	50.00

KG	Ken Griffey Jr.	250.00
AB	Albert Belle	50.00
DC	David Cone	40.00
MH	Mike Hampton	40.00
EC	Eric Chavez	50.00
EM	Edgar Martinez	50.00
PW	Preston Wilson	40.00
RV	Robin Ventura	40.00

2000 Upper Deck Hit Brigade

Fifteen of the game's top hitters are featured on a full foiled front with bronze foil stamping. Card backs are numbered with an "H" prefix and are found in series 1 packs at a rate of 1:8. Two parallels are randomly inserted: Silvers are serially numbered to 100 and Golds are limited to one set.

		MT
Complete Set (15):		35.00
Common Player:		.75
Inserted 1:8		
Silver:		10x to 20x
Production 100 sets		
1	Ken Griffey Jr.	6.00
2	Tony Gwynn	3.00
3	Alex Rodriguez	5.00
4	Derek Jeter	4.00
5	Mike Piazza	4.00
6	Sammy Sosa	4.00
7	Juan Gonzalez	1.50
8	Scott Rolen	1.50
9	Nomar Garciaparra	4.00
10	Barry Bonds	1.50
11	Craig Biggio	.75
12	Chipper Jones	4.00
13	Frank Thomas	1.50
14	Larry Walker	1.25
15	Mark McGwire	6.00

2000 Upper Deck Hot Properties

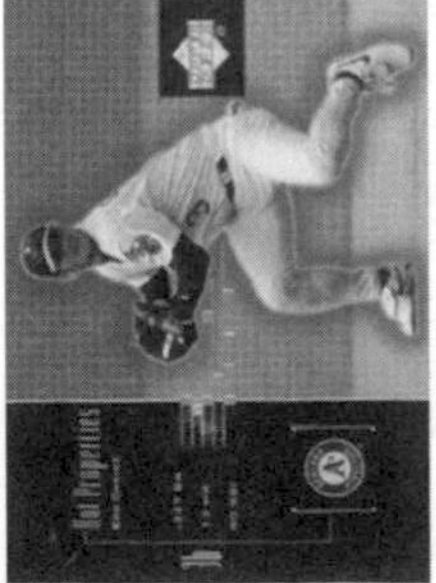

This set spotlights ten rookies and prospects who have a bright future. Card fronts have a horizontal format on a holofoiled stock with silver foil stamping. Card backs are numbered with an "HP" prefix and are found in series 2 packs at a rate of 1:11.

		MT
Complete Set (15):		20.00
Common Player:		1.00
Inserted 1:11		
1	Carlos Beltran	1.00
2	Rick Ankiel	10.00
3	Sean Casey	1.00
4	Preston Wilson	1.00
5	Vernon Wells	1.00
6	Pat Burrell	4.00
7	Eric Chavez	1.00
8	J.D. Drew	1.00
9	Alfonso Soriano	2.00
10	Gabe Kapler	1.00
11	Rafael Furcal	1.50
12	Ruben Mateo	1.00
13	Corey Koskie	1.00
14	Kip Wells	1.00
15	Ramon Ortiz	1.00

2000 Upper Deck Pennant Driven

This 10-card horizontal set has a holofoiled card front with silver-foil stamping. Card backs are numbered with a "PD" prefix and are seeded 1:4 packs.

		MT
Complete Set (10):		10.00
Common Player:		.50
Inserted 1:4		
1	Derek Jeter	2.00
2	Roberto Alomar	.50
3	Chipper Jones	1.50
4	Jeff Bagwell	.75
5	Roger Clemens	1.00
6	Nomar Garciaparra	2.00
7	Manny Ramirez	.75
8	Mike Piazza	2.00
9	Ivan Rodriguez	.75
10	Randy Johnson	.75

2000 Upper Deck Piece of History-500 Club

This card features a piece of a game-used Louisville Slugger once swung by Aaron. Approximately 350 cards were produced. Also randomly inserted are 44 autographed versions.

	MT
755HRHank Aaron	400.00
HAAUHank Aaron Auto./44	1000.

2000 Upper Deck Power Deck

Collectors need access to a CD-ROM in order to enjoy these interactive cards. Found exclusively in hobby packs, cards 1-8 are seeded 1:23 packs and cards 9-11 are found 1:287 packs.

		MT
Complete Set (11):		50.00
Common Player:		2.00
Inserted 1:23		
1	Ken Griffey Jr.	10.00
2	Cal Ripken Jr.	6.00
3	Mark McGwire	10.00
4	Tony Gwynn	5.00
5	Roger Clemens	4.00
6	Alex Rodriguez	8.00
7	Sammy Sosa	6.00
8	Derek Jeter	6.00
9	Ken Griffey Jr.	40.00
10	Mark McGwire	40.00
11	Reggie Jackson	10.00

2000 Upper Deck PowerMARK

		MT
Complete Set (10):		80.00
Common McGwire:		10.00
Inserted 1:23		
Silver:		8x to 15x
Production 100 sets		
1	Mark McGwire	10.00
2	Mark McGwire	10.00
3	Mark McGwire	10.00
4	Mark McGwire	10.00
5	Mark McGwire	10.00
6	Mark McGwire	10.00
7	Mark McGwire	10.00
8	Mark McGwire	10.00
9	Mark McGwire	10.00
10	Mark McGwire	10.00

2000 Upper Deck Power Rally

This 15-card set highlights the top hitters and are numbered with a "P" prefix on the card back. They are found 1:11 packs. Two parallel version are also seeded: Coppers are limited to 100 serially numbered sets and Golds are limited to one set.

		MT
Complete Set (15):		60.00
Common Player:		1.50
Inserted 1:11		
Silver: 8x to 15x		
Production 100 sets		
1	Ken Griffey Jr.	10.00
2	Mark McGwire	10.00
3	Sammy Sosa	6.00
4	Jose Canseco	2.50
5	Juan Gonzalez	2.50
6	Bernie Williams	2.00
7	Jeff Bagwell	2.50
8	Chipper Jones	6.00
9	Vladimir Guerrero	4.00
10	Mo Vaughn	2.00
11	Derek Jeter	6.00
12	Mike Piazza	6.00
13	Barry Bonds	2.50
14	Alex Rodriguez	8.00
15	Nomar Garciaparra	6.00

2000 Upper Deck Prime Performers

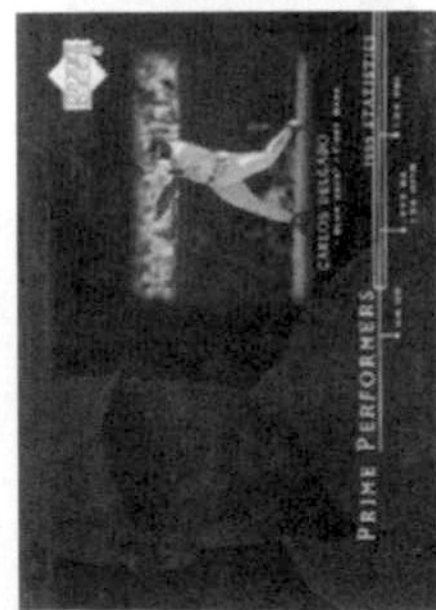

This 10-card set has a horizontal format on a full

holofoiled front, with silver-foil etching and stamping. Card backs are numbered with a "PP" prefix and found 1:8 packs.

		MT
Complete Set (10):		15.00
Common Player:		.75
Inserted 1:8		
1	Manny Ramirez	1.00
2	Pedro Martinez	1.00
3	Carlos Delgado	.75
4	Ken Griffey Jr.	4.00
5	Derek Jeter	2.50
6	Chipper Jones	2.00
7	Sean Casey	.75
8	Shawn Green	.75
9	Sammy Sosa	2.50
10	Alex Rodriguez	3.00

2000 Upper Deck STATitude

This 30-card set spotlights the most statistically dominant players on a horizontal format with silver-foil stamping. Card backs are numbered with an "S" prefix and are inserted 1:4 packs. Two parallel versions are randomly inserted: Coppers are limited to 100 serially numbered sets and Golds are limited to one set.

		MT
Complete Set (30):		50.00
Common Player:		.50
Inserted 1:4		
Silver:		10x to 20x
Production 100 sets		
1	Mo Vaughn	1.00
2	Matt Williams	.75
3	Travis Lee	.50
4	Chipper Jones	4.00
5	Greg Maddux	4.00
6	Gabe Kapler	.75
7	Cal Ripken Jr.	4.00
8	Nomar Garciaparra	4.00
9	Sammy Sosa	4.00
10	Frank Thomas	1.50
11	Manny Ramirez	1.50
12	Larry Walker	1.25
13	Ivan Rodriguez	1.50
14	Jeff Bagwell	1.50
15	Craig Biggio	.75
16	Vladimir Guerrero	3.00
17	Mike Piazza	4.00
18	Bernie Williams	1.00
19	Derek Jeter	4.00
20	Jose Canseco	1.50
21	Eric Chavez	.50
22	Scott Rolen	1.50
23	Mark McGwire	6.00
24	Tony Gwynn	3.00
25	Barry Bonds	1.50
26	Ken Griffey Jr.	6.00
27	Alex Rodriguez	5.00
28	J.D. Drew	.50
29	Juan Gonzalez	1.50
30	Roger Clemens	2.50

2000 Upper Deck 2K Plus

This 12-card set showcases the talents of baseball's next millennium. They are numbered with an "2K" prefix on the card back and are seeded 1:23 packs. Two parallel versions are also randomly inserted: Coppers are limited to 100 serially numbered sets and Golds are limited on one set produced.

		MT
Complete Set (12):		60.00
Common Player:		2.00
Inserted 1:23		
Silver:		5x to 10x
Production 100 sets		
1	Ken Griffey Jr.	15.00
2	J.D. Drew	2.00
3	Derek Jeter	10.00
4	Nomar Garciaparra	10.00
5	Pat Burrell	5.00
6	Ruben Mateo	2.00
7	Carlos Beltran	2.00
8	Vladimir Guerrero	6.00
9	Scott Rolen	4.00
10	Chipper Jones	10.00
11	Alex Rodriguez	12.00
12	Magglio Ordonez	2.00

2000 Upper Deck People's Choice

This 15-card set is printed on a full holo-foiled front with gold-foil stamping. Card backs are numbered with a "PC" prefix and are seeded 1:23 packs.

		MT
Complete Set (15):		120.00
Common Player:		3.00
Inserted 1:23		
1	Mark McGwire	20.00
2	Nomar Garciaparra	12.00
3	Derek Jeter	12.00
4	Shawn Green	4.00
5	Manny Ramirez	5.00
6	Pedro Martinez	5.00
7	Ivan Rodriguez	5.00
8	Alex Rodriguez	15.00
9	Juan Gonzalez	5.00
10	Ken Griffey Jr.	20.00
11	Sammy Sosa	12.00
12	Jeff Bagwell	5.00
13	Chipper Jones	10.00
14	Cal Ripken Jr.	15.00
15	Mike Piazza	12.00

2000 Upper Deck 3,000 Hit Club

This continuing series spotlights Hank Aaron. The series includes a Jersey card (350 produced), Bat card (350 produced), Jersey/Bat combo (100 produced) and Autographed Jersey/Bat combo (44 produced).

		MT
HA-B	Hank Aaron bat/350	300.00
HA-JB	Hank Aaron bat/jersey/100	600.00
HA-J	Hank Aaron jersey/350	350.00
HA	Hank Aaron Auto. bat/jersey/44	1000.

2000 Upper Deck Black Diamond

The base set consists of 120-cards, including a 30-card Diamond Debut (91-120) subset that is seeded 1:4 packs. Card fronts are full foiled with silver etching. Card backs have the player's past five years of statistics, a brief career note and small photo.

		MT
Complete Set (120):		125.00
Common Player:		.20
Common Diamond Debut:		2.00
Pack (6):		4.00
Wax Box (24):		85.00
1	Darin Erstad	.40
2	Tim Salmon	.40
3	Mo Vaughn	.40
4	Matt Williams	.25
5	Travis Lee	.20
6	Randy Johnson	.75
7	Tom Glavine	.40
8	Chipper Jones	1.50
9	Greg Maddux	1.50
10	Andruw Jones	.50
11	Brian Jordan	.20
12	Cal Ripken Jr.	2.50
13	Albert Belle	.40
14	Mike Mussina	.50
15	Nomar Garciaparra	2.00
16	Troy O'Leary	.20
17	Pedro J. Martinez	1.00
18	Sammy Sosa	1.50
19	Henry Rodriguez	.20
20	Frank Thomas	1.00
21	Magglio Ordonez	.40
22	Greg Vaughn	.25
23	Barry Larkin	.40
24	Sean Casey	.30
25	Jim Thome	.40
26	Kenny Lofton	.30
27	Roberto Alomar	.60
28	Manny Ramirez	.75
29	Larry Walker	.30
30	Todd Helton	.75
31	Gabe Kapler	.25
32	Tony Clark	.25
33	Dean Palmer	.20
34	Cliff Floyd	.20
35	Alex Gonzalez	.20
36	Moises Alou	.20
37	Jeff Bagwell	.75
38	Craig Biggio	.30
39	Richard Hidalgo	.20
40	Carlos Beltran	.25
41	Johnny Damon	.20
42	Adrian Beltre	.20
43	Gary Sheffield	.40
44	Kevin Brown	.30
45	Jeromy Burnitz	.20
46	Jeff Cirillo	.20
47	Joe Mays	.20
48	Todd Walker	.20
49	Vladimir Guerrero	1.00
50	Michael Barrett	.20
51	Rickey Henderson	.40
52	Mike Piazza	2.00
53	Robin Ventura	.40
54	John Olerud	.40
55	Edgardo Alfonzo	.40
56	Derek Jeter	2.50
57	Orlando Hernandez	.40
58	Tino Martinez	.30
59	Bernie Williams	.50
60	Roger Clemens	1.00
61	Eric Chavez	.20
62	Ben Grieve	.40
63	Jason Giambi	.40
64	Scott Rolen	.50
65	Bobby Abreu	.20
66	Curt Schilling	.30
67	Mike Lieberthal	.20
68	Warren Morris	.20
69	Brian Giles	.20
70	Eric Owens	.20
71	Tony Gwynn	1.00
72	Reggie Sanders	.20
73	Barry Bonds	.75
74	J.T. Snow	.20
75	Jeff Kent	.20
76	Ken Griffey Jr.	2.50
77	Alex Rodriguez	2.50
78	Edgar Martinez	.20
79	Jay Buhner	.20
80	Mark McGwire	3.00
81	J.D. Drew	.40
82	Eric Davis	.20
83	Fernando Tatis	.20
84	Wade Boggs	.50

85	Fred McGriff	.40
86	Juan Gonzalez	.75
87	Ivan Rodriguez	.75
88	Rafael Palmeiro	.50
89	Shawn Green	.40
90	Carlos Delgado	.60
91	Pat Burrell (Diamond Debut)	5.00
92	Eric Munson (Diamond Debut)	2.50
93	Jorge Toca (Diamond Debut)	2.00
94	Rick Ankiel (Diamond Debut)	8.00
95	Tony Armas, Jr. (Diamond Debut)	2.00
96	Byung-Hyun Kim (Diamond Debut)	2.00
97	Alfonso Soriano (Diamond Debut)	2.00
98	Mark Quinn (Diamond Debut)	2.50
99	Ryan Rupe (Diamond Debut)	2.00
100	Adam Kennedy (Diamond Debut)	2.00
101	Jeff Weaver (Diamond Debut)	2.00
102	Ramon Ortiz (Diamond Debut)	2.00
103	Eugene Kingsale (Diamond Debut)	2.00
104	Josh Beckett (Diamond Debut)	4.00
105	Eric Gagne (Diamond Debut)	2.00
106	Peter Bergeron (Diamond Debut)	2.00
107	Erubiel Durazo (Diamond Debut)	2.00
108	Chad Meyers (Diamond Debut)	2.00
109	Kip Wells (Diamond Debut)	2.00
110	Chad Harville (Diamond Debut)	2.00
111	Matt Riley (Diamond Debut)	2.00
112	Ben Petrick (Diamond Debut)	2.00
113	Ed Yarnall (Diamond Debut)	2.00
114	Calvin Murray (Diamond Debut)	2.00
115	Vernon Wells (Diamond Debut)	2.00
116	A.J. Burnett (Diamond Debut)	2.00
117	Jacque Jones (Diamond Debut)	2.00
118	Francisco Cordero (Diamond Debut)	2.00
119	*Tomokazu Ohka* (Diamond Debut)	3.00
120	Julio Ramirez (Diamond Debut)	2.00

2000 Upper Deck Black Diamond Final Cut

A parallel to the 120-card base set the die-cut design can be used to distinguish them from base cards, the card backs are also numbered with an "F" prefix. Each card is serially numbered within an edition of 100 sets.

	MT
Stars (1-90):	15x to 25x
Diamond Debuts:	3x to 5x
Production 100 sets	

(See 2000 UD Black Diamond for checklist and base card values.)

2000 Upper Deck Black Diamond Reciprocal Cut

A parallel to the 120-card base set, the die-cut design can be used to differentiate them from base cards. Card backs are also numbered with an "R" prefix. Cards 1-90 are found 1:7 packs and Diamond Debuts (91-120) are seeded 1:12 packs.

	MT
Stars (1-90):	2x to 5x
Diamond Debuts	1x to 1.5x
1-90 inserted 1:7	
Diamond Debuts inserted 1:12	

(See 2000 UD Black Diamond for checklist and base card values.)

2000 Upper Deck Black Diamond Diamonation

This 10-card set has a holo-foil background with gold-foil etching and stamping. Card backs are numbered with a "D" prefix and have an insertion ratio of 1:4 packs.

		MT
Complete Set (10):		15.00
Common Player:		1.00
Inserted 1:4		
1	Ken Griffey Jr.	5.00
2	Randy Johnson	1.00
3	Mark McGwire	5.00
4	Manny Ramirez	1.50
5	Scott Rolen	1.50
6	Bernie Williams	1.00
7	Roger Clemens	2.00
8	Mo Vaughn	1.00
9	Frank Thomas	1.50
10	Sean Casey	1.00

2000 Upper Deck Black Diamond Diamonds in the Rough

This 10-card set has a horizontal format utilizing holo-foil and gold-foil stamping. Card backs are numbered with an "R" prefix and seeded 1:9 packs.

		MT
Complete Set (10):		25.00
Common Player:		1.00
Inserted 1:9		
1	Pat Burrell	5.00
2	Eric Munson	5.00
3	Alfonso Soriano	3.00
4	Ruben Mateo	1.00
5	A.J. Burnett	2.00
6	Ben Davis	1.00
7	Lance Berkman	1.00
8	Ed Yarnall	1.00
9	Rick Ankiel	10.00
10	Ryan Bradley	1.00

2000 Upper Deck Black Diamond Diamond Might

DiamondMight's have a horizontal format, utilizing holofoil and gold-foil stamping. Card backs are numbered with an "M" prefix and are seeded 1:14 packs.

		MT
Complete Set (10):		40.00
Common Player:		2.50
Inserted 1:14		
1	Ken Griffey Jr.	10.00
2	Mark McGwire	10.00
3	Sammy Sosa	6.00
4	Manny Ramirez	2.50
5	Jeff Bagwell	2.50
6	Frank Thomas	2.50
7	Mike Piazza	6.00
8	Juan Gonzalez	3.00
9	Barry Bonds	2.50
10	Alex Rodriguez	8.00

2000 Upper Deck Black Diamond Diamond Gallery

This 10-card set spotlights the featured player in a baseball diamond frame with a prismatic background. Gold-foil etching and stamping is also used throughout. Card backs are numbered with a "G" prefix and are seeded 1:14 packs.

		MT
Complete Set (10):		60.00
Common Player:		3.00
Inserted 1:14		
1	Derek Jeter	8.00
2	Alex Rodriguez	8.00
3	Nomar Garciaparra	8.00
4	Cal Ripken Jr.	8.00
5	Sammy Sosa	8.00
6	Tony Gwynn	6.00
7	Mark McGwire	12.00
8	Roger Clemens	5.00
9	Greg Maddux	6.00
10	Pedro Martinez	3.00

Player names in *Italic* type indicate a rookie card.

2000 Upper Deck Black Diamond Constant Threat

A 10-card set spotlighting the top hitters in the game. Card backs are numbered with an "T" prefix and are seeded 1:29 packs.

		MT
Complete Set (10):		70.00
Common Player:		3.00
Inserted 1:29		
1	Ken Griffey Jr.	15.00
2	Vladimir Guerrero	6.00
3	Alex Rodriguez	10.00
4	Sammy Sosa	10.00
5	Juan Gonzalez	4.00
6	Derek Jeter	10.00
7	Nomar Garciaparra	10.00
8	Barry Bonds	4.00
9	Chipper Jones	8.00
10	Mike Piazza	10.00

2000 Upper Deck Black Diamond Barrage

This 10-card set features a prismatic background with silver-foil stamping. Card backs are numbered with a "B" prefix and are seeded 1:29 packs.

		MT
Complete Set (10):		70.00
Common Player:		3.00
Inserted 1:29		
1	Mark McGwire	15.00
2	Ken Griffey Jr.	15.00
3	Sammy Sosa	10.00
4	Jeff Bagwell	4.00
5	Juan Gonzalez	4.00
6	Alex Rodriguez	10.00
7	Manny Ramirez	4.00
8	Ivan Rodriguez	4.00
9	Chipper Jones	8.00
10	Mike Piazza	10.00

2000 Upper Deck Black Diamond A Piece of History Single

These memorabilia inserts have a piece of game-used bat embedded into the card front and are seeded 1:179 packs.

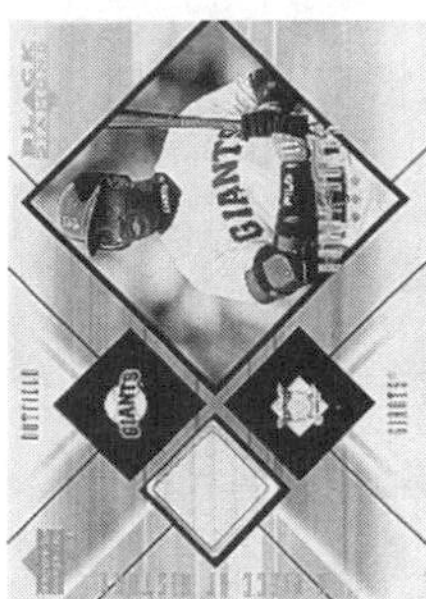

		MT
Common Player:		25.00
Inserted 1:179		
AB	Albert Belle	40.00
BB	Barry Bonds	75.00
JC	Jose Canseco	60.00
DE	Darin Erstad	30.00
JR	Ken Griffey Jr.	175.00
VG	Vladimir Guerrero	75.00
TG	Tony Gwynn	70.00
TH	Todd Helton	50.00
DJ	Derek Jeter	150.00
AJ	Andruw Jones	50.00
CJ	Chipper Jones	75.00
TL	Travis Lee	25.00
RM	Raul Mondesi	30.00
MP	Mike Piazza	90.00
CAL	Cal Ripken Jr.	175.00
AR	Alex Rodriguez	150.00
IR	Ivan Rodriguez	60.00
SR	Scott Rolen	50.00
MV	Mo Vaughn	40.00

2000 Upper Deck Black Diamond A Piece of History Double

These memorabilia inserts have two pieces of game-used bat embedded into the card front and are a parallel to the single set. They are inserted 1:1,079 packs.

		MT
Common Player:		50.00
Inserted 1:1079		
AB	Albert Belle	75.00
BB	Barry Bonds	150.00
JC	Jose Canseco	120.00
DE	Darin Erstad	60.00
JR	Ken Griffey Jr.	300.00
VG	Vladimir Guerrero	150.00
TG	Tony Gwynn	125.00
TH	Todd Helton	100.00
DJ	Derek Jeter	300.00
AJ	Andruw Jones	100.00
CJ	Chipper Jones	150.00
TL	Travis Lee	50.00
RM	Raul Mondesi	60.00
MP	Mike Piazza	180.00
CAL	Cal Ripken Jr.	350.00
AR	Alex Rodriguez	300.00
IR	Ivan Rodriguez	120.00
SR	Scott Rolen	100.00
MV	Mo Vaughn	75.00

2000 Upper Deck Black Diamond 500 Club Piece/History

These Reggie Jackson inserts are part of a cross-brand insert series paying tribute to baseball's 500 Home Run club members. These have a piece of Jackson's game-used bat embedded. An autographed version signed to his jersey number (44) are also randomly inserted.

	MT
Reggie Jackson	300.00
Reggie Jackson Autograph/44	750.00

2000 Upper Deck Black Diamond Rookie Edition

		MT
Complete Set (154):		1000.
Common Player:		.15
Common Rookie Gem (91-120):		8.00
Production 1,000		
Rookie Jersey Gems (121-136):		
Inserted 1:24		
USA Authentics (137-154):		
Inserted 1:96		
Pack (6):		4.00
Box (24):		85.00
1	Troy Glaus	.75
2	Mo Vaughn	.40
3	Darin Erstad	.40
4	Jason Giambi	.40
5	Tim Hudson	.25
6	Ben Grieve	.25
7	Eric Chavez	.25
8	Tony Batista	.15
9	Carlos Delgado	.60
10	David Wells	.15
11	Greg Vaughn	.15
12	Fred McGriff	.25
13	Manny Ramirez	.75
14	Roberto Alomar	.60
15	Jim Thome	.40
16	Alex Rodriguez	2.50
17	Edgar Martinez	.15
18	John Olerud	.20
19	Albert Belle	.40
20	Mike Mussina	.40
21	Cal Ripken Jr.	2.50
22	Ivan Rodriguez	.75
23	Rafael Palmeiro	.40
24	Pedro J. Martinez	.75
25	Nomar Garciaparra	2.00
26	Carl Everett	.15
27	Jermaine Dye	.15
28	Mike Sweeney	.15
29	Juan Gonzalez	.75
30	Bobby Higginson	.15
31	Dean Palmer	.15
32	Jacque Jones	.15
33	Eric Milton	.15
34	Matt Lawton	.15
35	Magglio Ordonez	.25
36	Paul Konerko	.15
37	Frank Thomas	1.00
38	Ray Durham	.15
39	Roger Clemens	1.00
40	Derek Jeter	2.50
41	Bernie Williams	.50
42	Jose Canseco	.40
43	Craig Biggio	.25
44	Richard Hidalgo	.15
45	Jeff Bagwell	.75
46	Greg Maddux	1.50
47	Chipper Jones	1.50
48	Rafael Furcal	1.00
49	Andruw Jones	.50
50	Geoff Jenkins	.25
51	Jeromy Burnitz	.15
52	Mark McGwire	3.00
53	Rick Ankiel	.50
54	Jim Edmonds	.25
55	Kerry Wood	.25
56	Sammy Sosa	2.00
57	Matt Williams	.25
58	Randy Johnson	.75
59	Steve Finley	.15
60	Curt Schilling	.15
61	Kevin Brown	.15
62	Gary Sheffield	.30
63	Shawn Green	.30
64	Jose Vidro	.15
65	Vladimir Guerrero	1.00
66	Jeff Kent	.15
67	Barry Bonds	.75
68	Ryan Dempster	.15
69	Cliff Floyd	.15
70	Preston Wilson	.15
71	Mike Piazza	2.00
72	Al Leiter	.15
73	Edgardo Alfonzo	.25
74	Derek Bell	.15
75	Ryan Klesko	.15
76	Tony Gwynn	1.00
77	Bobby Abreu	.15
78	Pat Burrell	.50
79	Scott Rolen	.50
80	Mike Lieberthal	.15
81	Jason Kendall	.15
82	Brian Giles	.25
83	Ken Griffey Jr.	2.50
84	Pokey Reese	.15
85	Dmitri Young	.15
86	Sean Casey	.15
87	Jeff Cirillo	.15
88	Todd Helton	.75
89	Jeffrey Hammonds	.15
90	Larry Walker	.30
91	*Barry Zito*	70.00
92	*Keith Ginter*	15.00
93	*Dane Sardinha*	10.00
94	*Kenny Kelly*	8.00
95	*Ryan Kohlmeier*	8.00
96	*Leo Estrella*	8.00
97	*Danys Baez*	15.00
98	*Paul Rigdon*	8.00
99	*Mike Lamb*	8.00
100	*Aaron McNeal*	10.00
101	*Juan Pierre*	10.00
102	*Rico Washington*	8.00
103	*Luis Matos*	12.00
104	*Adam Bernero*	10.00
105	*Wascar Serrano*	8.00
106	*Chris Richard*	8.00
107	*Justin Miller*	15.00
108	*Julio Zuleta*	8.00
109	*Alex Cabrera*	10.00
110	*Gene Stechschulte*	10.00
111	*Tony Mota*	8.00
112	*Tomokazu Ohka*	10.00
113	*Geraldo Guzman*	8.00
114	*Scott Downs*	8.00
115	*Timoniel Perez*	15.00
116	*Chad Durbin*	10.00
117	*Sun-Woo Kim*	15.00
118	*Tomas de la Rosa*	8.00
119	*Javier Cardona*	10.00
120	*Kazuhiro Sasaki*	40.00
121	*Brad Cresse* (Rookie Jersey Gems)	50.00
122	*Matt Wheatland* (Rookie Jersey Gems)	30.00
123	*Joe Torres* (Rookie Jersey Gems)	25.00
124	*Dave Krynzel* (Rookie Jersey Gems)	35.00

125	*Ben Diggins* (Rookie Jersey Gems)	20.00
126	*Sean Burnett* (Rookie Jersey Gems)	20.00
127	*David Espinosa* (Rookie Jersey Gems)	25.00
128	*Scott Heard* (Rookie Jersey Gems)	20.00
129	*Daylan Holt* (Rookie Jersey Gems)	20.00
130	*Koyie Hill* (Rookie Jersey Gems)	20.00
131	*Mark Buehrle* (Rookie Jersey Gems)	20.00
132	*Xavier Nady* (Rookie Jersey Gems)	70.00
133	*Mike Tonis* (Rookie Jersey Gems)	40.00
134	*Matt Ginter* (Rookie Jersey Gems)	25.00
135	*Lorenzo Barcelo* (Rookie Jersey Gems)	25.00
136	*Cory Vance* (Rookie Jersey Gems)	15.00
137	Sean Burroughs (USA Authentics)	40.00
138	Todd Williams (USA Authentics)	20.00
139	*Brad Wilkerson* (USA Authentics)	25.00
140	*Ben Sheets* (USA Authentics)	60.00
141	*Kurt Ainsworth* (USA Authentics)	20.00
142	Anthony Sanders (USA Authentics)	15.00
143	Ryan Franklin (USA Authentics)	15.00
144	*Shane Heams* (USA Authentics)	25.00
145	*Roy Oswalt* (USA Authentics)	20.00
146	*Jon Rauch* (USA Authentics)	50.00
147	*Brent Abernathy* (USA Authentics)	20.00
148	Ernie Young (USA Authentics)	15.00
149	Chris George (USA Authentics)	20.00
150	Gookie Dawkins (USA Authentics)	15.00
151	Adam Everett (USA Authentics)	20.00
152	*John Cotton* (USA Authentics)	15.00
153	Pat Borders (USA Authentics)	15.00
154	Doug Mientkiewicz (USA Authentics)	15.00

2000 UD Black Diamond Rookie Edition Diamonation

		MT
Complete Set (9):		30.00
Common Player:		1.50
Inserted 1:12		
1	Pedro J. Martinez	2.50
2	Derek Jeter	8.00
3	Jason Giambi	1.50
4	Todd Helton	2.50
5	Nomar Garciaparra	6.00
6	Randy Johnson	2.50
7	Jeff Bagwell	2.50
8	Cal Ripken Jr.	8.00
9	Ivan Rodriguez	2.50

2000 UD Black Diamond Rookie Edition Diamond Might

		MT
Complete Set (9):		40.00
Common Player:		1.50
Inserted 1:12		
1	Mark McGwire	10.00
2	Mike Piazza	6.00
3	Frank Thomas	3.00
4	Ken Griffey Jr.	8.00
5	Sammy Sosa	6.00
6	Alex Rodriguez	8.00
7	Carlos Delgado	2.00
8	Vladimir Guerrero	3.00
9	Barry Bonds	2.50

2000 UD Black Diamond Rookie Edition Diamond Skills

		MT
Complete Set (6):		25.00
Common Player:		2.50
Inserted 1:20		
1	Alex Rodriguez	8.00
2	Chipper Jones	5.00
3	Ken Griffey Jr.	8.00
4	Pedro J. Martinez	2.50
5	Ivan Rodriguez	2.50
6	Derek Jeter	8.00

2000 UD Black Diamond Rookie Edition Diamond Gallery

		MT
Complete Set (6):		30.00
Common Player:		2.50
Inserted 1:20		
1	Sammy Sosa	6.00
2	Barry Bonds	2.50
3	Vladimir Guerrero	3.00
4	Cal Ripken Jr.	8.00
5	Mike Piazza	6.00
6	Mark McGwire	10.00

2000 UD Black Diamond Rookie Edition Authentics

		MT
Jeter Authentic Pinstripes		
APJ	Derek Jeter jersey/1,000	150.00
APB	Derek Jeter bat/1,000	150.00
APC	Derek Jeter cap/200	250.00
APG	Derek Jeter Glove/200	250.00

2000 Upper Deck Black Diamond Rookie Edition Combos

MT

Random game-used inserts, 25 produced of each combo bat, 100 produced of combo jersey.

DJ-JD	Derek Jeter, Joe DiMaggio bat
DJ-MM	Derek Jeter, Mickey Mantle bat
JDM	Derek Jeter, Joe DiMaggio, Mickey Mantle bat
JWO	Derek Jeter, Bernie Williams, Paul O'Neill jersey

2000 UD Ionix

The base set consists of 90 cards, including a 30-card Futuristics subset that were seeded 1:4 packs. A Reciprocal parallel to the base sets are also randomly inserted. The cards can be distinguished by a holo-foiled front and the number on the back has an "R" prefix. Reciprocals 1-60 are found 1:4 packs, while Futuristics Reciprocals are found on the average of 1:11 packs.

		MT
Complete Set (90):		125.00
Common Player:		.20
Common Futuristic:		2.00
Inserted 1:4		
Reciprocal (1-60):		1.5x-4x
Reciprocal (61-90):		1x-1.5x
Inserted 1:4		
Future Recip. 1:11		
Pack (4):		4.00
Wax Box (24):		85.00
1	Mo Vaughn	.75
2	Troy Glaus	1.00
3	Jeff Bagwell	1.00
4	Craig Biggio	.50
5	Jose Lima	.20
6	Jason Giambi	.20
7	Tim Hudson	.40
8	Shawn Green	.75
9	Carlos Delgado	.75
10	Chipper Jones	2.00
11	Andruw Jones	.75
12	Greg Maddux	2.00
13	Jeromy Burnitz	.20
14	Mark McGwire	4.00
15	J.D. Drew	.40
16	Sammy Sosa	2.50
17	Jose Canseco	1.00
18	Fred McGriff	.50
19	Randy Johnson	.75
20	Matt Williams	.50
21	Kevin Brown	.40
22	Gary Sheffield	.40
23	Vladimir Guerrero	2.00
24	Barry Bonds	1.00
25	Jim Thome	.50
26	Manny Ramirez	1.00
27	Roberto Alomar	.75
28	Kenny Lofton	.75
29	Ken Griffey Jr.	4.00
30	Alex Rodriguez	3.00
31	Alex Gonzalez	.20
32	Preston Wilson	.20
33	Mike Piazza	2.50
34	Robin Ventura	.40
35	Cal Ripken Jr.	2.50
36	Albert Belle	.75
37	Tony Gwynn	2.00
38	Scott Rolen	1.00
39	Curt Schilling	.40
40	Brian Giles	.20
41	Juan Gonzalez	1.00
42	Ivan Rodriguez	1.00
43	Rafael Palmeiro	.60
44	Pedro J. Martinez	1.00
45	Nomar Garciaparra	2.50
46	Sean Casey	.50
47	Aaron Boone	.20
48	Barry Larkin	.50
49	Larry Walker	.75
50	Vinny Castilla	.30
51	Carlos Beltran	.25
52	Gabe Kapler	.40
53	Dean Palmer	.30
54	Eric Milton	.20
55	Corey Koskie	.20
56	Frank Thomas	1.00
57	Magglio Ordonez	.50
58	Roger Clemens	1.50
59	Bernie Williams	.75

60	Derek Jeter	2.50
61	Josh Beckett (Futuristics)	8.00
62	Eric Munson (Futuristics)	8.00
63	Rick Ankiel (Futuristics)	15.00
64	Matt Riley (Futuristics)	5.00
65	Robert Ramsay (Futuristics)	2.00
66	Vernon Wells (Futuristics)	3.00
67	Eric Gagne (Futuristics)	2.00
68	Robert Fick (Futuristics)	2.00
69	Mark Quinn (Futuristics)	4.00
70	Kip Wells (Futuristics)	2.00
71	Peter Bergeron (Futuristics)	2.00
72	Ed Yarnall (Futuristics)	2.00
73	Jorge Luis Toca (Futuristics)	3.00
74	Alfonso Soriano (Futuristics)	4.00
75	Calvin Murray (Futuristics)	2.00
76	Ramon Ortiz (Futuristics)	3.00
77	Chad Meyers (Futuristics)	3.00
78	Jason LaRue (Futuristics)	2.00
79	Pat Burrell (Futuristics)	6.00
80	Chad Hermansen (Futuristics)	2.00
81	Lance Berkman (Futuristics)	2.00
82	Erubiel Durazo (Futuristics)	3.00
83	Juan Pena (Futuristics)	2.00
84	Adam Kennedy (Futuristics)	2.00
85	Ben Petrick (Futuristics)	2.00
86	Kevin Barker (Futuristics)	2.00
87	Bruce Chen (Futuristics)	2.00
88	Jerry Hairston Jr. (Futuristics)	2.00
89	A.J. Burnett (Futuristics)	3.00
90	Gary Matthews Jr. (Futuristics)	2.00

2000 UD Ionix Shockwave

Baseball's top hitters are spotlighted on a holo-foil front. They are found on the average of 1:4 packs and are numbered on the card back with an "S" prefix.

		MT
Complete Set (15):		25.00
Common Player:		.75
Inserted 1:4		
1	Mark McGwire	5.00
2	Sammy Sosa	3.00
3	Manny Ramirez	1.50
4	Ken Griffey Jr.	5.00
5	Vladimir Guerrero	2.50
6	Barry Bonds	1.50
7	Albert Belle	1.00
8	Ivan Rodriguez	1.50
9	Chipper Jones	2.50
10	Mo Vaughn	1.00
11	Jose Canseco	1.50
12	Jeff Bagwell	1.50
13	Matt Williams	.75
14	Alex Rodriguez	4.00
15	Carlos Delgado	.75

2000 UD Ionix Atomic

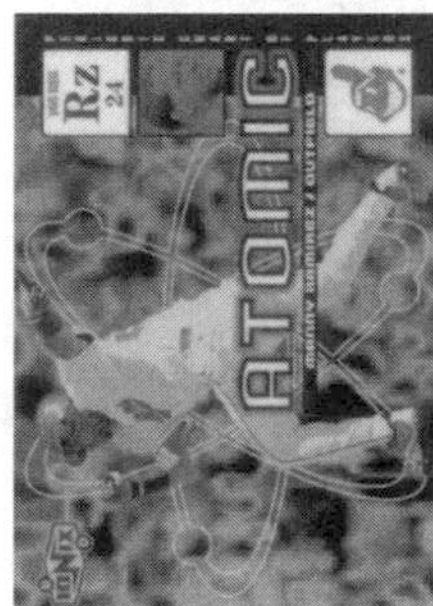

This 15-card insert set has a horizontal format on a holo-foil front. Card backs are numbered with an "A" prefix and are found 1:8 packs.

		MT
Complete Set (15):		60.00
Common Player:		2.00
Inserted 1:8		
1	Pedro J. Martinez	2.50
2	Mark McGwire	10.00
3	Ken Griffey Jr.	10.00
4	Jeff Bagwell	2.50
5	Greg Maddux	5.00
6	Derek Jeter	6.00
7	Cal Ripken Jr.	6.00
8	Manny Ramirez	2.50
9	Randy Johnson	2.00
10	Nomar Garciaparra	6.00
11	Tony Gwynn	5.00
12	Bernie Williams	2.00
13	Mike Piazza	6.00
14	Roger Clemens	4.00
15	Alex Rodriguez	8.00

2000 UD Ionix BIOrhythm

This 15-card set has a holo-foil front and are seeded 1:11 packs. Card backs have a brief career note and are numbered with a "B" prefix.

		MT
Complete Set (15):		75.00
Common Player:		2.00
Inserted 1:11		
1	Randy Johnson	2.50
2	Derek Jeter	8.00
3	Sammy Sosa	8.00
4	Jose Lima	2.00
5	Chipper Jones	6.00
6	Barry Bonds	3.00
7	Ken Griffey Jr.	12.00
8	Nomar Garciaparra	8.00
9	Frank Thomas	3.00
10	Pedro Martinez	3.00
11	Larry Walker	2.50
12	Greg Maddux	6.00
13	Alex Rodriguez	10.00
14	Mark McGwire	12.00
15	Cal Ripken Jr.	8.00

2000 UD Ionix Awesome Powers

A takeoff from the Austin Powers movie which was popular at the time of this release. The cards have a holo-foil front with a "groovin" 70's back-drop. Card backs are numbered with an "AP" prefix and are seeded 1:23 packs.

		MT
Complete Set (15):		150.00
Common Player:		4.00
Inserted 1:23		
1	Ken Griffey Jr.	25.00
2	Mike Piazza	15.00
3	Carlos Delgado	4.00
4	Mark McGwire	25.00
5	Chipper Jones	12.00
6	Scott Rolen	6.00
7	Cal Ripken Jr.	15.00
8	Alex Rodriguez	20.00
9	Larry Walker	5.00
10	Sammy Sosa	15.00
11	Barry Bonds	6.00
12	Nomar Garciaparra	15.00
13	Jose Canseco	6.00
14	Manny Ramirez	6.00
15	Jeff Bagwell	6.00

2000 UD Ionix Pyrotechnics

This 15-card set has a holo-foiled front with an insertion ratio of 1:72 packs. Card backs are numbered with a "P" prefix.

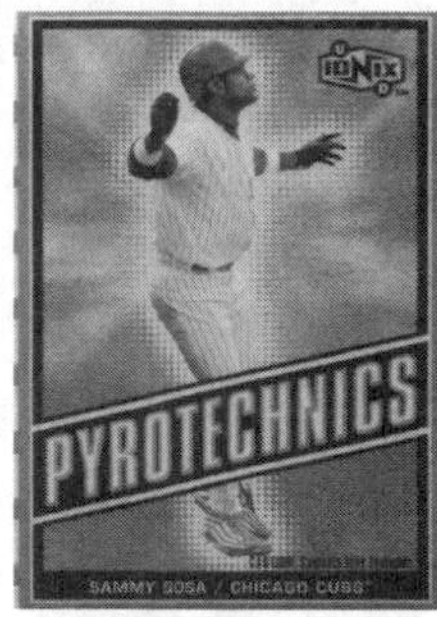

		MT
Complete Set (15):		320.00
Common Player:		12.00
Inserted 1:72		
1	Roger Clemens	20.00
2	Chipper Jones	25.00
3	Alex Rodriguez	40.00
4	Jeff Bagwell	12.00
5	Mark McGwire	50.00
6	Pedro Martinez	12.00
7	Manny Ramirez	12.00
8	Cal Ripken Jr.	30.00
9	Mike Piazza	30.00
10	Derek Jeter	30.00
11	Ken Griffey Jr.	50.00
12	Frank Thomas	12.00
13	Sammy Sosa	30.00
14	Nomar Garciaparra	30.00
15	Greg Maddux	25.00

2000 UD Ionix Warp Zone

This 15-card set has a holo-foiled front with an insertion ratio of 1:288 packs. Card backs are numbered with a "WZ" prefix.

		MT
Complete Set (15):		875.00
Common Player:		25.00
Inserted 1:288		
1	Cal Ripken Jr.	75.00
2	Barry Bonds	30.00
3	Ken Griffey Jr.	120.00
4	Nomar Garciaparra	75.00
5	Chipper Jones	60.00
6	Ivan Rodriguez	30.00
7	Greg Maddux	60.00
8	Derek Jeter	75.00
9	Mike Piazza	75.00
10	Sammy Sosa	75.00
11	Roger Clemens	40.00
12	Alex Rodriguez	90.00
13	Vladimir Guerrero	50.00
14	Pedro Martinez	30.00
15	Mark McGwire	120.00

2000 UD Ionix UD Authentics

These autographed inserts have a horizontal

format and are found on the average of 1:144 packs.

		MT
Common Player:		20.00
Inserted 1:144		
CBE	Carlos Beltran	15.00
AB	Adrian Beltre	25.00
CB	Craig Biggio	50.00
PB	Pat Burrell	50.00
JC	Jose Canseco	100.00
SC	Sean Casey	40.00
BD	Ben Davis	20.00
NG	Nomar Garciaparra	
SG	Shawn Green	75.00
JR	Ken Griffey Jr.	250.00
VG	Vladimir Guerrero	60.00
DJ	Derek Jeter	200.00
CJ	Chipper Jones	125.00
GK	Gabe Kapler	40.00
PM	Pedro Martinez	
RM	Ruben Mateo	25.00
RB	Joe McEwing	30.00
MR	Manny Ramirez	75.00
SR	Scott Rolen	50.00
MW	Matt Williams	50.00

2000 UD Ionix 3,000-Hit Club Piece of History

Upper Deck's cross-brand insert series paying tribute to baseball's 3,000 Hit Club members spotlights Roberto Clemente in UD Ionix. Three versions were randomly inserted: A game-used bat card, bat/cut signature card and a cut signature card.

		MT
RC1	Roberto Clemente	500.00
RC2	Roberto Clemente Bat/Cut/5	
RC3	Roberto Clemente Cut/4	

2000 Upper Deck Hitter's Club

The 90-card base set includes hitters only and features past and current stars. The base set consists of 50 regular cards, 25 Why 3K?, and 15 Hitting the Show subset cards. Card backs of the 50 regular cards have complete year-by-year statistics.

		MT
Complete Set (90):		35.00
Common Player:		.15
Pack (5):		3.00
Wax Box (24):		65.00
1	Mo Vaughn	.50
2	Troy Glaus	.75
3	Jeff Bagwell	.75
4	Craig Biggio	.40
5	Jason Giambi	.15
6	Eric Chavez	.25
7	Carlos Delgado	.50
8	Chipper Jones	1.50
9	Andruw Jones	.50
10	Andres Galarraga	.40
11	Jeromy Burnitz	.15
12	Mark McGwire	3.00
13	Mark Grace	.25
14	Sammy Sosa	2.00
15	Jose Canseco	.75
16	Vinny Castilla	.15
17	Matt Williams	.40
18	Gary Sheffield	.25
19	Shawn Green	.50
20	Vladimir Guerrero	1.50
21	Barry Bonds	.75
22	Manny Ramirez	.75
23	Roberto Alomar	.50
24	Jim Thome	.40
25	Ken Griffey Jr.	3.00
26	Alex Rodriguez	2.50
27	Edgar Martinez	.15
28	Preston Wilson	.15
29	Mike Piazza	2.00
30	Robin Ventura	.25
31	Albert Belle	.50
32	Cal Ripken Jr.	2.50
33	Tony Gwynn	1.50
34	Scott Rolen	.75
35	Bob Abreu	.15
36	Brian Giles	.15
37	Ivan Rodriguez	.75
38	Rafael Palmeiro	.50
39	Nomar Garciaparra	2.00
40	Sean Casey	.40
41	Larry Walker	.50
42	Todd Helton	.75
43	Carlos Beltran	.20
44	Dean Palmer	.15
45	Juan Gonzalez	1.00
46	Corey Koskie	.15
47	Frank Thomas	1.00
48	Magglio Ordonez	.40
49	Derek Jeter	2.00
50	Bernie Williams	.50
51	Paul Waner (Why 3k?)	.40
52	Honus Wagner (Why 3k?)	.50
53	Tris Speaker (Why 3k?)	.40
54	Nap Lajoie (Why 3k?)	.50
55	Eddie Collins (Why 3k?)	.25
56	Roberto Clemente (Why 3k?)	1.50
57	Ty Cobb (Why 3k?)	1.50
58	Cap Anson (Why 3k?)	.50
59	Robin Yount (Why 3k?)	.50
60	Carl Yastrzemski (Why 3k?)	.50
61	Dave Winfield (Why 3k?)	.25
62	Stan Musial (Why 3k?)	1.00
63	Eddie Murray (Why 3k?)	.40
64	Paul Molitor (Why 3k?)	.50
65	Willie Mays (Why 3k?)	2.00
66	Al Kaline (Why 3k?)	.50
67	Tony Gwynn (Why 3k?)	1.50
68	Rod Carew (Why 3k?)	.50
69	Lou Brock (Why 3k?)	.50
70	George Brett (Why 3k?)	1.00
71	Wade Boggs (Why 3k?)	.25
72	Hank Aaron (Why 3k?)	2.00
73	Jorge Luis Toca (Hitting the Show)	.15
74	J.D. Drew (Hitting the Show)	.25
75	Pat Burrell (Hitting the Show)	1.25
76	Vernon Wells (Hitting the Show)	.15
77	Julio Ramirez (Hitting the Show)	.15
78	Gabe Kapler (Hitting the Show)	.25
79	Erubiel Durazo (Hitting the Show)	.25
80	Lance Berkman (Hitting the Show)	.15
81	Peter Bergeron (Hitting the Show)	.15
82	Alfonso Soriano (Hitting the Show)	.50
83	Jacque Jones (Hitting the Show)	.15
84	Ben Petrick (Hitting the Show)	.15
85	Jerry Hairston Jr. (Hitting the Show)	.15
86	Kevin Witt (Hitting the Show)	.15
87	Dermal Brown (Hitting the Show)	.15
88	Chad Hermansen (Hitting the Show)	.15
89	Ruben Mateo (Hitting the Show)	.25
90	Checklist (Ken Griffey Jr.)	1.00

2000 Upper Deck Hitter's Club Epic Performances

This 10-card set showcases some of baseball's top performances on a full-foiled card front with gold-foil stamping. Card backs are numbered with an "EP" prefix and are found 1:3 packs.

		MT
Complete Set (10):		20.00
Common Player:		1.00
Inserted 1:3		
1	Mark McGwire	4.00
2	Sammy Sosa	2.50
3	Ken Griffey Jr.	4.00
4	Carl Yastrzemski	1.00
5	Tony Gwynn	2.00
6	Nomar Garciaparra	2.50
7	Cal Ripken Jr.	3.00
8	George Brett	1.50
9	Hank Aaron	2.50
10	Wade Boggs	1.00

2000 Upper Deck Hitter's Club Generations of Excellence

This 10-card insert set features two players who are linked either by team or position, gold-foil stamping is used throughout. Card backs are numbered with a "GE" prefix and are seeded 1:6 packs.

		MT
Complete Set (10):		25.00
Common Player:		1.50
Inserted 1:6		
1	Cal Ripken Jr., Eddie Murray	4.00
2	Vladimir Guerrero, Roberto Clemente	2.50
3	George Brett, Robin Yount	2.50
4	Barry Bonds, Willie Mays	3.00
5	Chipper Jones, Hank Aaron	3.00
6	Mark McGwire, Sammy Sosa	5.00
7	Tony Gwynn, Wade Boggs	2.50
8	Rickey Henderson, Lou Brock	1.50
9	Derek Jeter, Nomar Garciaparra	4.00
10	Alex Rodriguez, Ken Griffey Jr.	5.00

2000 Upper Deck Hitter's Club Accolades

These inserts have a full-foiled front with gold-foil stamping. Card backs are numbered with an "A" prefix and are seeded 1:11 packs.

		MT
Complete Set (10):		40.00
Common Player:		1.50
Inserted 1:11		
1	Robin Yount	2.00
2	Tony Gwynn	4.00
3	Sammy Sosa	5.00
4	Mike Piazza	5.00
5	Cal Ripken Jr.	6.00
6	Mark McGwire	8.00
7	Barry Bonds	2.00
8	Wade Boggs	1.50
9	Ken Griffey Jr.	8.00
10	Willie Mays	5.00

2000 Upper Deck Hitter's Club On Target

This 10-card set is printed on a full-foiled front with silver-foil stamping. Card backs are numbered with an "OT" prefix and are seeded 1:23 packs.

		MT
Complete Set (10):		35.00
Common Player:		1.00
Inserted 1:23		
1	Nomar Garciaparra	8.00
2	Sean Casey	2.00
3	Alex Rodriguez	8.00
4	Troy Glaus	1.50
5	Ivan Rodriguez	3.00
6	Chipper Jones	6.00
7	Manny Ramirez	3.00
8	Derek Jeter	8.00
9	Vladimir Guerrero	5.00
10	Scott Rolen	3.00

2000 Upper Deck Hitter's Club Eternals

These inserts were printed on a full-foiled front with the word "Eternals" printed a number of times in the background of the player's photo. The player's name and Upper Deck logo are stamped in gold-foil on the bottom portion of the card. Card backs are numbered with an "E" prefix and are seeded 1:23 packs.

		MT
Complete Set (10):		75.00
Common Player:		3.00
Inserted 1:23		
1	Cal Ripken Jr.	12.00
2	Mark McGwire	15.00
3	Ken Griffey Jr.	15.00
4	Nomar Garciaparra	10.00
5	Tony Gwynn	8.00
6	Derek Jeter	10.00
7	Jose Canseco	4.00
8	Mike Piazza	10.00
9	Alex Rodriguez	10.00
10	Barry Bonds	4.00

2000 Upper Deck Hitter's Club The Hitters' Club

These inserts are seeded 1:95 packs and are numbered on the back with an "HC" prefix.

		MT
Complete Set (10):		150.00
Common Player:		8.00
1	Rod Carew	10.00
2	Alex Rodriguez	30.00
3	Willie Mays	25.00
4	George Brett	20.00
5	Tony Gwynn	25.00
6	Stan Musial	15.00
7	Frank Thomas	15.00
8	Wade Boggs	8.00
9	Larry Walker	10.00
10	Nomar Garciaparra	30.00

2000 Upper Deck Hitter's Club Autographs

Former and current players are featured in this signature set, which are seeded 1:215 packs. Card backs are numbered with the featured player's initials.

		MT
Common Player:		40.00
Inserted 1:215		
HA	Hank Aaron #44	250.00
WB	Wade Boggs #12	50.00
GB	George Brett #5	100.00
Lou	Lou Brock #20	40.00
Rod	Rod Carew #29	50.00
TG	Tony Gwynn #19	100.00
Al	Al Kaline #6	50.00
WM	Willie Mays #24	200.00
PM	Paul Molitor #4	50.00
EM	Eddie Murray #33	50.00
Man	Stan Musial #6	90.00
Cal	Cal Ripken Jr. #8	200.00
DW	Dave Winfield #31	40.00
Yaz	Carl Yastrzemski #7	80.00
RY	Robin Yount #19	80.00

2000 Upper Deck Hitter's Club 3,000 Hit Club

Upper Deck's cross-brand series pays tribute to players who have reached 3,000 hits. Hitter's Club features Wade Boggs and Tony Gwynn inserts with Bat, Bat and Cap and Autographed versions randomly inserted.

		MT
Common Player:		125.00
WB	Wade Boggs bat/350	100.00
WB	Wade Boggs bat & cap/50	275.00
WB	Wade Boggs AU/12	N/A
TG	Tony Gwynn bat/350	150.00
TG	Tony Gwynn bat & cap/50	375.00
TG	Tony Gwynn AU/19	N/A
GB	Tony Gwynn, Wade Boggs bat/99	275.00

2000 Upper Deck HoloGrFX

The base set consists of 90-cards on a horizontal format. The cards have a holo-foil front utilizing HoloGrFX technology.

		MT
Complete Set (90):		30.00
Common Player:		.20
Pack (4):		2.00
Wax Box (32):		60.00
1	Mo Vaughn	.75
2	Troy Glaus	.75
3	Daryle Ward	.20
4	Jeff Bagwell	1.00
5	Craig Biggio	.50
6	Jose Lima	.20
7	Jason Giambi	.30
8	Eric Chavez	.30
9	Tim Hudson	.40
10	Raul Mondesi	.40
11	Carlos Delgado	.75
12	David Wells	.20
13	Chipper Jones	2.00
14	Greg Maddux	2.00
15	Andruw Jones	.75
16	Brian Jordan	.20
17	Jeromy Burnitz	.40
18	Ron Belliard	.20
19	Mark McGwire	4.00
20	Fernando Tatis	.40
21	J.D. Drew	.25
22	Sammy Sosa	2.50
23	Mark Grace	.40
24	Greg Vaughn	.40
25	Jose Canseco	1.00
26	Vinny Castilla	.30
27	Fred McGriff	.40
28	Matt Williams	.40
29	Randy Johnson	.75
30	Erubiel Durazo	.40
31	Shawn Green	.75
32	Gary Sheffield	.50
33	Kevin Brown	.40
34	Vladimir Guerrero	2.00
35	Michael Barrett	.20
36	Russ Ortiz	.20
37	Barry Bonds	1.00
38	Jeff Kent	.20
39	Kenny Lofton	.75
40	Manny Ramirez	1.00
41	Roberto Alomar	.75
42	Richie Sexson	.20
43	Edgar Martinez	.30
44	Alex Rodriguez	3.00
45	Fred Garcia	.20
46	Preston Wilson	.20
47	Alex Gonzalez	.20
48	Mike Hampton	.20
49	Mike Piazza	2.50
50	Robin Ventura	.40
51	Edgardo Alfonzo	.40
52	Albert Belle	.75
53	Cal Ripken Jr.	3.00
54	B.J. Surhoff	.20
55	Tony Gwynn	2.00
56	Trevor Hoffman	.20
57	Mike Lieberthal	.20
58	Scott Rolen	1.00
59	Bob Abreu	.40
60	Curt Schilling	.40
61	Jason Kendall	.30
62	Brian Giles	.30
63	Kris Benson	.20
64	Rafael Palmeiro	.50
65	Ivan Rodriguez	1.00
66	Gabe Kapler	.40
67	Nomar Garciaparra	2.50
68	Pedro Martinez	1.00
69	Troy O'Leary	.20
70	Barry Larkin	.50
71	Dante Bichette	.40
72	Sean Casey	.50
73	Ken Griffey Jr.	4.00
74	Jeff Cirillo	.40
75	Todd Helton	1.00
76	Larry Walker	.75
77	Carlos Beltran	.25
78	Jermaine Dye	.20
79	Juan Gonzalez	1.00
80	Juan Encarnacion	.20
81	Dean Palmer	.20
82	Corey Koskie	.20
83	Eric Milton	.20
84	Frank Thomas	1.50
85	Magglio Ordonez	.20
86	Carlos Lee	.20
87	Derek Jeter	2.50
88	Tino Martinez	.50
89	Bernie Williams	.75
90	Roger Clemens	1.50

2000 Upper Deck HoloGrFX Longball Legacy

This 15-card set spotlights the top home run hitters on a horizontal format and completely holo-foiled. Card backs are numbered with an "LL" prefix and seeded 1:6 packs.

		MT
Complete Set (15):		40.00
Common Player:		1.00
Inserted 1:6		
1	Mike Piazza	5.00
2	Ivan Rodriguez	2.00
3	Jeff Bagwell	2.00
4	Alex Rodriguez	6.00
5	Jose Canseco	2.00
6	Mark McGwire	8.00
7	Scott Rolen	2.00
8	Carlos Delgado	1.50
9	Mo Vaughn	1.00
10	Manny Ramirez	2.00
11	Matt Williams	1.00
12	Sammy Sosa	5.00
13	Ken Griffey Jr.	8.00
14	Nomar Garciaparra	5.00
15	Larry Walker	1.50

2000 Upper Deck HoloGrFX Stars of the System

This 10-card set features some of baseball's top prospects on a horizontal format. The fronts are completely holo-foiled with silver foil stamping. Card backs are numbered with an "SS" prefix and seeded 1:8 packs.

		MT
Complete Set (10):		20.00
Common Player:		1.00
Inserted 1:8		
1	Rick Ankiel	8.00
2	Alfonso Soriano	2.50
3	Vernon Wells	1.00
4	Ben Petrick	1.00
5	Francisco Cordero	1.00
6	Matt Riley	2.00
7	A.J. Burnett	1.00
8	Pat Burrell	4.00
9	Ed Yarnall	1.00
10	Dermal Brown	1.00

2000 Upper Deck HoloGrFX StarView

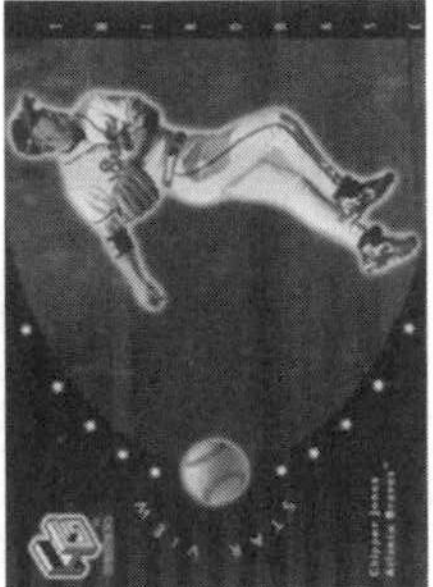

This eight-card set features top stars on a horizontal format. Card backs are numbered with an "SV" prefix and inserted 1:11 packs.

		MT
Complete Set (8):		40.00
Common Player:		2.00
Inserted 1:11		
1	Ken Griffey Jr.	8.00
2	Nomar Garciaparra	5.00
3	Chipper Jones	4.00
4	Mark McGwire	8.00
5	Sammy Sosa	5.00
6	Derek Jeter	5.00
7	Mike Piazza	5.00
8	Alex Rodriguez	6.00

2000 Upper Deck HoloGrFX Future Fame

This six-card set has a horizontal format that is completely holo-foiled with silver-foil stamping. Card backs are numbered with an "FF" prefix and seeded 1:34 packs.

		MT
Complete Set (6):		60.00
Common Player:		5.00
Inserted 1:34		
1	Cal Ripken Jr.	12.00
2	Mark McGwire	15.00
3	Greg Maddux	8.00
4	Tony Gwynn	8.00
5	Ken Griffey Jr.	15.00
6	Roger Clemens	6.00

2000 Upper Deck HoloGrFX Bomb Squad

This six-card set highlights the top home run hitters. They have a horizontal format with complete holo-foiled fronts. Card backs are numbered with a "BS" prefix and are seeded 1:34 packs.

		MT
Complete Set (6):		
Common Player:		4.00
Inserted 1:34		
1	Ken Griffey Jr.	15.00
2	Mark McGwire	15.00
3	Chipper Jones	8.00
4	Alex Rodriguez	12.00
5	Sammy Sosa	10.00
6	Barry Bonds	4.00

2000 Upper Deck HoloGrFX A Piece of the Series

These inserts have a piece of game-used base from a 1999 World Series game embedded. These were inserted at a rate of 1:215 packs.

		MT
Complete Set (12):		500.00
Common Player:		25.00
Inserted 1:215		
1	Derek Jeter	120.00
2	Chipper Jones	80.00
3	Roger Clemens	70.00
4	Greg Maddux	90.00
5	Bernie Williams	50.00
6	Andruw Jones	50.00
7	Tino Martinez	25.00
8	Brian Jordan	25.00
9	Mariano Rivera	40.00
11	Paul O'Neill	40.00
12	Tom Glavine	40.00

2000 Upper Deck HoloGrFX A Piece of the Series Autograph

This is an autographed parallel of the Piece of the Series insert set that is limited to 25 sets.

		MT
Common Player:		150.00
Production 25 sets		
PSA1	Derek Jeter	700.00
PSA2	Chipper Jones	475.00
PSA3	Roger Clemens	350.00
PSA4	Greg Maddux	500.00
PSA6	Andruw Jones	300.00
PSA7	Tino Martinez	150.00
PSA8	Brian Jordan	150.00
PSA11	Paul O'Neill	150.00
PSA12	Tom Glavine	250.00

2000 Upper Deck HoloGrFX 3,000 Hit Club

Upper Deck pays tribute to members of the 3,000 Hit Club with this cross-brand insert series. Robin Yount and George Brett are featured on a game-used bat card (350 produced), game-used jersey card (350 produced), a bat combo of both players (99 produced) and an autographed combo (10 produced).

		MT
Common Card:		100.00
RY	Robin Yount bat/350	125.00
RYJ	Robin Yount jersey/350	150.00
GB	George Brett bat/350	150.00
GBJ	George Brett jersey/350	175.00
BY	George Brett, Robin Yount bat/99	350.00
BYA	George Brett, Robin Yount AU/10	
BYJ	George Brett, Robin Yount jersey/99	300.00

2000 Upper Deck Legends

The 135-card base set consists of 90 regular player cards, 30 20th Century Legends (1:5) and 15 Generation Y2K (1:9). The base cards have a full foiled front with silver-foil stamping. Card backs have complete year-by-year statistics.

	MT
Complete Set (135):	150.00
Common Player:	.15
Common Y2K:	1.50
Inserted 1:9	
Common 20th Century Legend	2.00
Inserted 1:5	
Pack (7):	6.00
Box (24):	125.00

1	Darin Erstad	.25
2	Troy Glaus	.75
3	Mo Vaughn	.50
4	Craig Biggio	.25
5	Jeff Bagwell	.75
6	Reggie Jackson	1.00
7	Tim Hudson	.25
8	Jason Giambi	.25
9	Hank Aaron	2.00
10	Greg Maddux	1.50
11	Chipper Jones	1.50
12	Andres Galarraga	.30
13	Robin Yount	.30
14	Jeromy Burnitz	.15
15	Paul Molitor	.40
16	David Wells	.15
17	Carlos Delgado	.75
18	Ernie Banks	.75
19	Sammy Sosa	2.00
20	Kerry Wood	.40
21	Stan Musial	.75
22	Bob Gibson	.50
23	Mark McGwire	3.00
24	Fernando Tatis	.15
25	Randy Johnson	.75
26	Matt Williams	.40
27	Jackie Robinson	2.00
28	Sandy Koufax	1.50
29	Shawn Green	.50
30	Kevin Brown	.25
31	Gary Sheffield	.40
32	Greg Vaughn	.15
33	Jose Canseco	.50
34	Gary Carter	.15
35	Vladimir Guerrero	1.00
36	Willie Mays	2.00
37	Barry Bonds	.75
38	Jeff Kent	.15
39	Bob Feller	.40
40	Roberto Alomar	.50
41	Jim Thome	.30
42	Manny Ramirez	.75
43	Alex Rodriguez	2.50
44	Preston Wilson	.15
45	Tom Seaver	.75
46	Robin Ventura	.15
47	Mike Piazza	2.00
48	Mike Hampton	.15
49	Brooks Robinson	.75
50	Frank Robinson	.75
51	Cal Ripken Jr.	2.50
52	Albert Belle	.40
53	Eddie Murray	.30
54	Tony Gwynn	1.00
55	Roberto Clemente	2.00
56	Willie Stargell	.15
57	Brian Giles	.15
58	Jason Kendall	.15
59	Mike Schmidt	.75
60	Bob Abreu	.15
61	Scott Rolen	.50
62	Curt Schilling	.15
63	Johnny Bench	.75
64	Sean Casey	.15
65	Barry Larkin	.40
66	Ken Griffey Jr.	3.00
67	George Brett	1.00
68	Carlos Beltran	.15
69	Nolan Ryan	3.00
70	Ivan Rodriguez	.75
71	Rafael Palmeiro	.40
72	Larry Walker	.30
73	Todd Helton	.75
74	Jeff Cirillo	.15
75	Carl Everett	.15
76	Nomar Garciaparra	2.00
77	Pedro Martinez	.75
78	Harmon Killebrew	.40
79	Corey Koskie	.15
80	Ty Cobb	2.00
81	Dean Palmer	.15
82	Juan Gonzalez	.75
83	Carlton Fisk	.15
84	Frank Thomas	1.00
85	Magglio Ordonez	.15
86	Lou Gehrig	2.50
87	Babe Ruth	3.00
88	Derek Jeter	2.00
89	Roger Clemens	1.00
90	Bernie Williams	.50
91	Rick Ankiel (Generation Y2K)	10.00
92	Kip Wells (Generation Y2K)	1.50
93	Pat Burrell (Generation Y2K)	5.00
94	Mark Quinn (Generation Y2K)	3.00
95	Ruben Mateo (Generation Y2K)	2.00
96	Adam Kennedy (Generation Y2K)	2.00
97	Brad Penny (Generation Y2K)	1.50
98	*Kazuhiro Sasaki* (Generation Y2K)	20.00
99	Peter Bergeron (Generation Y2K)	2.00
100	Rafael Furcal (Generation Y2K)	8.00
101	Eric Munson (Generation Y2K)	4.00
102	Nick Johnson (Generation Y2K)	4.00
103	Rob Bell (Generation Y2K)	1.50
104	Vernon Wells (Generation Y2K)	2.00
105	Ben Petrick (Generation Y2K)	2.50
106	Babe Ruth (20th Century Legends)	10.00
107	Mark McGwire (20th Century Legends)	10.00
108	Nolan Ryan (20th Century Legends)	10.00
109	Hank Aaron (20th Century Legends)	6.00
110	Barry Bonds (20th Century Legends)	3.00
111	Nomar Garciaparra (20th Century Legends)	6.00
112	Roger Clemens (20th Century Legends)	4.00
113	Johnny Bench (20th Century Legends)	2.50
114	Alex Rodriguez (20th Century Legends)	8.00
115	Cal Ripken Jr. (20th Century Legends)	8.00
116	Willie Mays (20th Century Legends)	6.00
117	Mike Piazza (20th Century Legends)	6.00
118	Reggie Jackson (20th Century Legends)	3.00
119	Tony Gwynn (20th Century Legends)	4.00
120	Cy Young (20th Century Legends)	3.00
121	George Brett (20th Century Legends)	3.00
122	Greg Maddux (20th Century Legends)	5.00
123	Yogi Berra (20th Century Legends)	3.00
124	Sammy Sosa (20th Century Legends)	6.00
125	Randy Johnson (20th Century Legends)	2.50
126	Bob Gibson (20th Century Legends)	2.00
127	Lou Gehrig (20th Century Legends)	8.00
128	Ken Griffey Jr. (20th Century Legends)	10.00
129	Derek Jeter (20th Century Legends)	6.00
130	Mike Schmidt (20th Century Legends)	3.00
131	Pedro Martinez (20th Century Legends)	2.50
132	Jackie Robinson (20th Century Legends)	6.00
133	Jose Canseco (20th Century Legends)	2.00
134	Ty Cobb (20th Century Legends)	5.00
135	Stan Musial (20th Century Legends)	3.00

2000 Upper Deck Legends Commemorative Collection

A metallized photo background on front distinguishes these 1-of-100 inserts from their base-card parallels. Backs have an ink-jetted serial number from within each card's edition of 100.

	MT
Stars (1-90):	20-35X
Y2K:	2-4X
20th Century Legends:	6-10X
Production 100 sets	

(See 2000 Upper Deck Legends for checklist and base card values.)

2000 Upper Deck Legends Defining Moments

This 10-card set highlights the featured player's greatest baseball moment with a date stamped in gold-foil on the front and a description of the moment on the back. Card backs are numbered with a "DM" prefix and seeded 1:12 packs.

	MT
Complete Set (10):	45.00
Common Player:	1.50
Inserted 1:12	

1	Reggie Jackson	3.00
2	Hank Aaron	6.00
3	Babe Ruth	8.00
4	Cal Ripken Jr.	6.00
5	Carlton Fisk	1.50
6	Ken Griffey Jr.	8.00
7	Nolan Ryan	8.00
8	Roger Clemens	3.00
9	Willie Mays	6.00
10	Mark McGwire	8.00

2000 Upper Deck Legends Eternal Glory

This six-card set has a full holo-foiled front with gold foil stamping. Card backs are numbered with an "EG" prefix and are inserted 1:24 packs.

		MT
Complete Set (7):		35.00
Common Player:		3.00
Inserted 1:24		
1	Nolan Ryan	10.00
2	Ken Griffey Jr.	10.00
4	Sammy Sosa	6.00
5	Derek Jeter	6.00
6	Willie Mays	6.00
7	Roger Clemens	3.00

2000 Upper Deck Legends Legendary Signatures

These autographed inserts are signed in blue Sharpie on the bottom portion and inserted 1:24 packs. A Gold parallel version is also randomly seeded which have gold-foil stamping and individually numbered to 50.

		MT
Common Player:		20.00
Inserted 1:23		
Golds:		1.5-2X
Production 50 sets		
HA	Hank Aaron	300.00
JB	Johnny Bench	90.00
BB	Bobby Bonds	20.00
GB	George Brett	100.00
SC	Sean Casey	20.00
RC	Roger Clemens	90.00
KG	Ken Griffey Jr.	300.00
VG	Vladimir Guerrero	60.00
TG	Tony Gwynn	75.00
RJ	Reggie Jackson	100.00
DJ	Derek Jeter	275.00
RaJ	Randy Johnson	75.00
CJ	Chipper Jones	80.00
SM	Stan Musial	100.00
MP	Mike Piazza	150.00
MR	Manny Ramirez	75.00
CR	Cal Ripken Jr.	250.00
AR	Alex Rodriguez	150.00
IR	Ivan Rodriguez	60.00
NR	Nolan Ryan	225.00
MS	Mike Schmidt	100.00
TS	Tom Seaver	75.00
WS	Willie Stargell	20.00
FT	Frank Thomas	75.00
BW	Matt Williams	25.00

2000 Upper Deck Legends Legendary Jerseys

This game-used memorabilia insert set has a swatch of game-used jersey embedded and were inserted 1:48 packs.

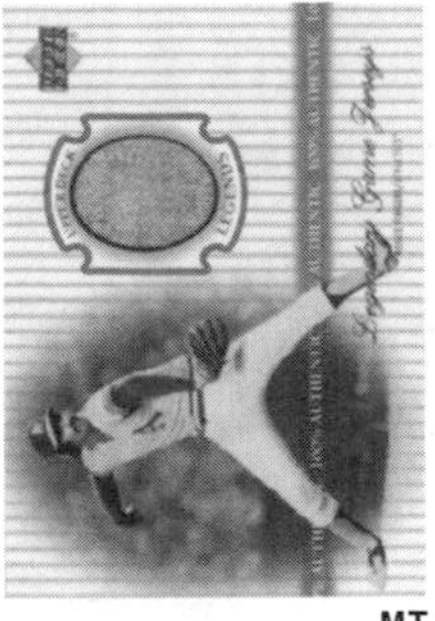

		MT
Common Player:		40.00
Inserted 1:48		
HA	Hank Aaron	300.00
JB	Jeff Bagwell	80.00
JB	Johnny Bench	100.00
WB	Wade Boggs	75.00
BaB	Barry Bonds	80.00
BoB	Bobby Bonds	40.00
GB	George Brett	125.00
LB	Lou Brock	75.00
JC	Jose Canseco	75.00
SC	Steve Carlton	
RC	Roger Clemens	100.00
DC	Dave Concepcion	40.00
DD	Don Drysdale	200.00
RF	Rollie Fingers	40.00
AG	Andres Galarraga	
LG	Lou Gehrig pants	750.00
BG	Bob Gibson pants	80.00
KG	Ken Griffey Jr.	300.00
TG	Tony Gwynn	100.00
RJ	Reggie Jackson	100.00
DJ	Derek Jeter	220.00
RaJ	Randy Johnson	75.00
CJ	Chipper Jones	90.00
SK	Sandy Koufax	500.00
SK	Sandy Koufax auto/32	1000.
GM	Greg Maddux	100.00
MM	Mickey Mantle	500.00
RM	Roger Maris pants	250.00
PM	Pedro J. Martinez	
EM	Eddie Mathews	75.00
WM	Willie Mays	500.00
BM	Bill Mazeroski	50.00
WMc	Willie McCovey	75.00
TM	Thurman Munson	250.00
DM	Dale Murphy	75.00
SM	Stan Musial	400.00
JP	Jim Palmer	70.00
GP	Gaylord Perry	40.00
MR	Manny Ramirez	75.00
CR	Cal Ripken Jr.	250.00
BR	Brooks Robinson	75.00
FR	Frank Robinson	75.00
AR	Alex Rodriguez	150.00
NR	Nolan Ryan	300.00
MS	Mike Schmidt	125.00
TS	Tom Seaver	80.00
OS	Ozzie Smith	90.00
WS	Willie Stargell	40.00
FT	Frank Thomas	90.00
JT	Joe Torre	50.00
EW	Earl Weaver	40.00
MW	Matt Williams	50.00
MW	Maury Wills	50.00
DW	Dave Winfield	90.00

2000 Upper Deck Legends Ones for the Ages

This seven-card set has a holo-foiled front with gold-foil etching and stamping. The player's image is in a classic picture-framed design. Card backs are numbered with an "O" prefix and seeded 1:24 packs.

		MT
Complete Set (7):		40.00
Common Player:		3.00
Inserted 1:24		
01	Ty Cobb	5.00
02	Cal Ripken Jr.	8.00
03	Babe Ruth	10.00
04	Jackie Robinson	6.00
05	Mark McGwire	10.00
06	Alex Rodriguez	8.00
07	Mike Piazza	6.00

2000 Upper Deck Legends Reflections in Time

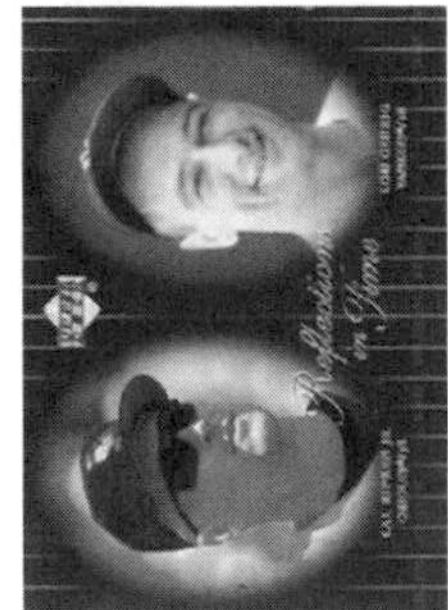

This 10-card horizontal insert set features two players, past and present, linked by significant events or statistics. Card fronts are completely holo-foiled with gold-foil stamping. Card backs are numbered with an "R" prefix and inserted 1:12 packs.

		MT
Complete Set (10):		40.00
Common Player:		2.00
Inserted 1:12		
1	Ken Griffey Jr., Hank Aaron	8.00
2	Sammy Sosa, Roberto Clemente	5.00
3	Roger Clemens, Nolan Ryan	8.00
4	Ivan Rodriguez, Johnny Bench	2.00
5	Alex Rodriguez, Ernie Banks	5.00
6	Tony Gwynn, Stan Musial	3.00
7	Barry Bonds, Willie Mays	5.00
8	Cal Ripken Jr., Lou Gehrig	6.00
9	Chipper Jones, Mike Schmidt	4.00
10	Mark McGwire, Babe Ruth	8.00

2000 Upper Deck Legends UD Millennium Team

This nine-card set has a complete holo-foiled front with silver-foil stamping. The set is Upper Deck's selections for the all-time 20th century team and are inserted 1:4 packs. Card backs are numbered with a "UD" prefix.

		MT
Complete Set (10):		20.00
Common Player:		1.50
Inserted 1:4		
1	Mark McGwire	4.00
2	Jackie Robinson	3.00
3	Mike Schmidt	1.50
4	Cal Ripken Jr.	3.00
5	Babe Ruth	4.00
7	Willie Mays	3.00
8	Johnny Bench	1.50
9	Nolan Ryan	4.00
10	Ken Griffey Jr.	4.00

2000 Upper Deck Legends 3,000 Hit Club

Upper Deck's continuing series pays tribute to Carl Yastrzemski and Paul Molitor. The series includes 350 Bat cards, 350 Jersey cards, 100 Bat/Jersey combo cards and eight autographed Bat/Jersey combo cards from Yastrzemski and 350 Bat cards from Molitor.

		MT
CY	Carl Yastrzemski bat/350	180.00
CY	Carl Yastrzemski jersey/350	180.00
CY	Carl Yastrzemski bat/jersey/100	300.00
CY	Carl Yastrzemski auto/bat/jersey/8	

2000 Upper Deck Gold Reserve

Gold Reserve is primarily a retail distributed product that has virtually the same design as regular 2000 Upper Deck base cards. The base set consists of 300-cards each with the Upper Deck logo and the featured player's last name stamped in gold foil. Above the player's name, "Gold Reserve" is stamped in gold foil. The Fantastic Finds subset (268-297) are serially stamped within an edition of 2,500 for each of the subset cards.

	MT
Complete Set (300):	300.00
Common Player:	.15
Common 268-297:	5.00
Production 2,500 sets	
Pack (10):	4.00
Box (24):	80.00

1	Mo Vaughn	.40
2	Darin Erstad	.40
3	Garret Anderson	.25
4	Troy Glaus	.75
5	Troy Percival	.15
6	Kent Bottenfield	.15
7	Orlando Palmeiro	.15
8	Tim Salmon	.25
9	Jason Giambi	.40
10	Eric Chavez	.15
11	Matt Stairs	.15
12	Miguel Tejada	.15
13	Tim Hudson	.25
14	John Jaha	.15
15	Ben Grieve	.25
16	Kevin Appier	.15
17	David Wells	.15
18	Jose Cruz Jr.	.15
19	Homer Bush	.15
20	Shannon Stewart	.15
21	Carlos Delgado	.75
22	Roy Halladay	.15
23	Tony Batista	.25
24	Raul Mondesi	.25
25	Fred McGriff	.25
26	Jose Canseco	.40
27	Roberto Hernandez	.15
28	Vinny Castilla	.15
29	Gerald Williams	.15
30	Ryan Rupe	.15
31	Greg Vaughn	.25
32	Miguel Cairo	.15
33	Roberto Alomar	.50
34	Jim Thome	.30
35	Bartolo Colon	.15
36	Omar Vizquel	.15
37	Manny Ramirez	.75
38	Chuck Finley	.15
39	Travis Fryman	.25
40	Kenny Lofton	.40
41	Richie Sexson	.15
42	Charles Nagy	.15
43	John Halama	.15
44	David Bell	.15
45	Jay Buhner	.15
46	Edgar Martinez	.15
47	Alex Rodriguez	2.50
48	Fred Garcia	.15
49	Aaron Sele	.15
50	Jamie Moyer	.15
51	Mike Cameron	.15
52	Albert Belle	.40
53	Jerry Hairston Jr.	.15
54	Sidney Ponson	.15
55	Cal Ripken Jr.	2.50
56	Mike Mussina	.40
57	B.J. Surhoff	.15
58	Brady Anderson	.25
59	Mike Bordick	.15
60	Ivan Rodriguez	.75
61	Rusty Greer	.15
62	Rafael Palmeiro	.40
63	John Wetteland	.15
64	Ruben Mateo	.15
65	Gabe Kapler	.25
66	David Segui	.15
67	Justin Thompson	.15
68	Rick Helling	.15
69	Jose Offerman	.15
70	Trot Nixon	.15
71	Pedro Martinez	.75
72	Jason Varitek	.15
73	Troy O'Leary	.15
74	Nomar Garciaparra	2.00
75	Carl Everett	.15
76	Wilton Veras	.15
77	Tim Wakefield	.15
78	Ramon Martinez	.15
79	Johnny Damon	.25
80	Mike Sweeney	.15
81	Rey Sanchez	.15
82	Carlos Beltran	.15
83	Carlos Febles	.15
84	Jermaine Dye	.15
85	Joe Randa	.15
86	Jose Rosado	.15
87	Jeff Suppan	.15
88	Juan Encarnacion	.15
89	Damion Easley	.15
90	Brad Ausmus	.15
91	Todd Jones	.15
92	Juan Gonzalez	.75
93	Bobby Higginson	.15
94	Tony Clark	.15
95	Brian Moehler	.15
96	Dean Palmer	.15
97	Joe Mays	.15
98	Eric Milton	.15
99	Corey Koskie	.15
100	Ron Coomer	.15
101	Brad Radke	.15
102	Todd Walker	.15
103	Butch Huskey	.15
104	Jacque Jones	.15
105	Frank Thomas	1.00
106	Mike Sirotka	.15
107	Carlos Lee	.15
108	Ray Durham	.15
109	Bob Howry	.15
110	Magglio Ordonez	.25
111	Paul Konerko	.15
112	Chris Singleton	.15
113	James Baldwin	.15
114	Derek Jeter	2.00
115	Tino Martinez	.25
116	Orlando Hernandez	.25
117	Chuck Knoblauch	.15
118	Bernie Williams	.50
119	David Cone	.25
120	Paul O'Neill	.25
121	Roger Clemens	1.00
122	Mariano Rivera	.25
123	Ricky Ledee	.15
124	Richard Hidalgo	.25
125	Jeff Bagwell	.75
126	Jose Lima	.15
127	Billy Wagner	.15
128	Shane Reynolds	.15
129	Moises Alou	.15
130	Craig Biggio	.30
131	Roger Cedeno	.15
132	Octavio Dotel	.15
133	Greg Maddux	1.50
134	Brian Jordan	.15
135	Kevin Millwood	.25
136	Javy Lopez	.25
137	Bruce Chen	.15
138	Chipper Jones	1.50
139	Tom Glavine	.40
140	Andruw Jones	.40
141	Andres Galarraga	.40
142	Reggie Sanders	.15
143	Geoff Jenkins	.25
144	Jeromy Burnitz	.15
145	Ron Belliard	.15
146	Mark Loretta	.15
147	Steve Woodard	.15
148	Marquis Grissom	.15
149	Bob Wickman	.15
150	Mark McGwire	3.00
151	Fernando Tatis	.15
152	Edgar Renteria	.15
153	J.D. Drew	.15
154	Ray Lankford	.15
155	Fernando Vina	.15
156	Pat Hentgen	.15
157	Jim Edmonds	.25
158	Mark Grace	.25
159	Kerry Wood	.15
160	Eric Young	.15
161	Ismael Valdes	.15
162	Sammy Sosa	2.00
163	Henry Rodriguez	.15
164	Kyle Farnsworth	.15
165	Glenallen Hill	.15
166	Jon Lieber	.15
167	Luis Gonzalez	.15
168	Tony Womack	.15
169	Omar Daal	.15
170	Randy Johnson	.75
171	Erubiel Durazo	.15
172	Jay Bell	.15
173	Steve Finley	.15
174	Travis Lee	.15
175	Matt Williams	.25
176	Matt Mantei	.15
177	Adrian Beltre	.25
178	Kevin Brown	.25
179	Chan Ho Park	.15
180	Mark Grudzielanek	.15
181	Jeff Shaw	.15
182	Shawn Green	.30
183	Gary Sheffield	.40
184	Todd Hundley	.15
185	Eric Karros	.25
186	Kevin Elster	.15
187	Vladimir Guerrero	1.00
188	Michael Barrett	.15
189	Chris Widger	.15
190	Ugueth Urbina	.15
191	Dustin Hermanson	.15
192	Rondell White	.15
193	Jose Vidro	.15
194	Hideki Irabu	.15
195	Lee Stevens	.15
196	Livan Hernandez	.15
197	Ellis Burks	.15
198	J.T. Snow	.15
199	Jeff Kent	.15
200	Robb Nen	.15
201	Marvin Benard	.15
202	Barry Bonds	.75
203	Russ Ortiz	.15
204	Rich Aurilia	.15
205	Joe Nathan	.15
206	Preston Wilson	.15
207	Cliff Floyd	.15
208	Mike Lowell	.15
209	Ryan Dempster	.15
210	Luis Castillo	.15
211	Alex Fernandez	.15
212	Mark Kotsay	.15
213	Brant Brown	.15
214	Edgardo Alfonzo	.25
215	Robin Ventura	.15
216	Rickey Henderson	.25
217	Mike Hampton	.15
218	Mike Piazza	2.00
219	Al Leiter	.15
220	Derek Bell	.15
221	Armando Benitez	.15
222	Rey Ordonez	.15
223	Todd Zeile	.15
224	Tony Gwynn	1.00
225	Eric Owens	.15
226	Damian Jackson	.15
227	Trevor Hoffman	.15
228	Ben Davis	.15
229	Sterling Hitchcock	.15
230	Ruben Rivera	.15
231	Ryan Klesko	.15
232	Phil Nevin	.15
233	Mike Lieberthal	.15
234	Bobby Abreu	.25
235	Doug Glanville	.15
236	Rico Brogna	.15
237	Scott Rolen	.60
238	Andy Ashby	.15
239	Robert Person	.15
240	Curt Schilling	.25
241	Mike Jackson	.15
242	Warren Morris	.15
243	Kris Benson	.15
244	Kevin Young	.15
245	Brian Giles	.15
246	Jason Schmidt	.15
247	Jason Kendall	.25
248	Todd Ritchie	.15
249	Wil Cordero	.15
250	Aramis Ramirez	.15
251	Sean Casey	.25
252	Barry Larkin	.40
253	Pokey Reese	.15
254	Scott Williamson	.15
255	Aaron Boone	.15
256	Dante Bichette	.25
257	Ken Griffey Jr.	2.50
258	Denny Neagle	.15
259	Dmitri Young	.15
260	Todd Helton	.75
261	Larry Walker	.40
262	Pedro Astacio	.15
263	Neifi Perez	.15
264	Jeff Cirillo	.15
265	Jeffrey Hammonds	.15
266	Tom Goodwin	.15
267	Rolando Arrojo	.15
268	Rick Ankiel (Fantastic Finds)	20.00
269	Pat Burrell (Fantastic Finds)	20.00
270	Eric Munson (Fantastic Finds)	8.00
271	Rafael Furcal (Fantastic Finds)	30.00
272	Brad Penny (Fantastic Finds)	5.00
273	Adam Kennedy (Fantastic Finds)	5.00
274	*Mike Lamb* (Fantastic Finds)	8.00
275	Matt Riley (Fantastic Finds)	5.00
276	Eric Gagne (Fantastic Finds)	5.00
277	*Kazuhiro Sasaki* (Fantastic Finds)	25.00
278	Julio Lugo (Fantastic Finds)	5.00
279	Kip Wells (Fantastic Finds)	5.00
280	*Danys Baez* (Fantastic Finds)	8.00
281	Josh Beckett (Fantastic Finds)	10.00
282	Alfonso Soriano (Fantastic Finds)	6.00
283	Vernon Wells (Fantastic Finds)	5.00
284	Nick Johnson (Fantastic Finds)	6.00
285	Ramon Ortiz (Fantastic Finds)	5.00
286	Peter Bergeron (Fantastic Finds)	6.00
287	*Wascar Serrano* (Fantastic Finds)	6.00
288	Josh Paul (Fantastic Finds)	5.00
289	Mark Quinn (Fantastic Finds)	6.00
290	Jason Marquis (Fantastic Finds)	5.00
291	Rob Bell (Fantastic Finds)	5.00
292	Pablo Ozuna (Fantastic Finds)	5.00
293	Milton Bradley (Fantastic Finds)	6.00
294	Roosevelt Brown (Fantastic Finds)	5.00
295	Terrence Long (Fantastic Finds)	5.00
296	*Chad Durbin* (Fantastic Finds)	5.00
297	Matt LeCroy (Fantastic Finds)	5.00
298	Ken Griffey Jr. (Checklist)	1.25
299	Mark McGwire (Checklist)	1.50
300	Derek Jeter (Checklist)	1.00

2000 Upper Deck Gold Reserve 24-karat Gems

This 15-card set features gold-foil stamping on the front and are numbered on the back with a

"K" prefix. They are found on the average of 1:7 packs.

		MT
Complete Set (15):		20.00
Common Player:		1.00
Inserted 1:7		
1	Pedro Martinez	1.50
2	Scott Rolen	1.25
3	Jason Giambi	1.00
4	Jeromy Burnitz	1.00
5	Rafael Palmeiro	1.00
6	Rick Ankiel	3.00
7	Carlos Beltran	1.00
8	Derek Jeter	4.00
9	Jason Kendall	1.00
10	Chipper Jones	3.00
11	Carlos Delgado	1.50
12	Alex Rodriguez	5.00
13	Randy Johnson	1.50
14	Tony Gwynn	2.50
15	Shawn Green	1.00

2000 Upper Deck Gold Reserve Setting the Standard

This 15-card set spotlights the top hitters and are inserted 1:11 packs. Card fronts feature gold-foil stamping and card backs are numbered with an "S" prefix.

		MT
Complete Set (15):		50.00
Common Player:		1.50
Inserted 1:11		
1	Tony Gwynn	3.00
2	Manny Ramirez	2.00
3	Derek Jeter	5.00
4	Cal Ripken Jr.	6.00
5	Mo Vaughn	1.50
6	Jose Canseco	1.50
7	Barry Bonds	2.00
8	Nomar Garciaparra	5.00
9	Juan Gonzalez	2.00
10	Mark McGwire	8.00
11	Alex Rodriguez	6.00
12	Jeff Bagwell	2.00
13	Ken Griffey Jr.	8.00
14	Frank Thomas	3.00
15	Sammy Sosa	5.00

2000 Upper Deck Gold Reserve Solid Gold Gallery

This 12-card set features close-up shots of the featured player accentuated by gold-foil stamping. Card backs are numbered with a "G" prefix, these were seeded 1:13 packs.

		MT
Complete Set (12):		45.00
Common Player:		1.50
Inserted 1:13		
1	Ken Griffey Jr.	8.00
2	Alex Rodriguez	6.00
3	Mike Piazza	5.00
4	Sammy Sosa	5.00
5	Derek Jeter	5.00
6	Jeff Bagwell	2.00
7	Mark McGwire	8.00
8	Cal Ripken Jr.	6.00
9	Pedro Martinez	2.00
10	Chipper Jones	4.00
11	Ivan Rodriguez	2.00
12	Vladimir Guerrero	3.00

2000 Upper Deck Gold Reserve Game-Used Ball

		MT
Common Player:		30.00
Inserted 1:480		
JB	Jeff Bagwell	80.00
BB	Barry Bonds	80.00
SC	Sean Casey	30.00
RC	Roger Clemens	90.00
NG	Nomar Garciaparra	150.00
SG	Shawn Green	40.00
KG	Ken Griffey Jr.	175.00
TG	Tony Gwynn	80.00
DJ	Derek Jeter	150.00
AJ	Andruw Jones	60.00
CJ	Chipper Jones	100.00
GM	Greg Maddux	120.00
MM	Mark McGwire	200.00
MP	Mike Piazza	120.00
MR	Manny Ramirez	75.00
IR	Ivan Rodriguez	75.00
SR	Scott Rolen	60.00
GS	Gary Sheffield	60.00
SS	Sammy Sosa	100.00
BW	Bernie Williams	50.00

2000 Upper Deck Gold Reserve 3,000 Hit Club

This on-going cross-brand insert series features Al Kaline. Each card features a piece of Kaline's game-used bat, he also signed six cards.

		MT
AK-B	Al Kaline bat/400	275.00
AK-BS	Al Kaline bat/auto/6	

2000 Upper Deck Opening Day 2K

As part of a multi-manufacturer promotion, UD issued eight cards of an "Opening Day 2K" set. Packages containing some of the 32 cards in the issue were distributed by MLB teams early in the season. The cards were also available exclusively as inserts in Upper Deck Victory and Hitter's Club packs sold at K-Mart stores early in the season. The Upper Deck OD2K cards have gold-foil graphic highlights on front. Backs have a monochromatic version of the front photo and are numbered with an "OD" prefix.

		MT
Complete Set (8):		6.00
Common Player:		.50
17	Ken Griffey Jr.	2.00
18	Sammy Sosa	1.00
19	Pedro Martinez	.75
20	Manny Ramirez	.65
21	Shawn Green	.65
22	Carlos Beltran	.40
23	Juan Gonzalez	.50
24	Jeromy Burnitz	.50

2000 Upper Deck MVP

The base set consists of 220-cards with a white-bordered design and bronze-foil stamping. Card backs have a maximum of 10 year-by-year statistics.

		MT
Complete Set (220):		30.00
Common Player:		.10
Pack (10):		1.50
Wax Box (28):		40.00
1	Garret Anderson	.10
2	Mo Vaughn	.30
3	Tim Salmon	.20
4	Ramon Ortiz	.10
5	Darin Erstad	.20
6	Troy Glaus	.50
7	Troy Percival	.10
8	Jeff Bagwell	.50
9	Ken Caminiti	.10
10	Daryle Ward	.10
11	Craig Biggio	.25
12	Jose Lima	.10
13	Moises Alou	.20
14	Octavio Dotel	.10
15	Ben Grieve	.20
16	Jason Giambi	.20
17	Tim Hudson	.20
18	Eric Chavez	.10
19	Matt Stairs	.10
20	Miguel Tejada	.10
21	John Jaha	.10
22	Chipper Jones	1.00
23	Kevin Millwood	.20
24	Brian Jordan	.10
25	Andruw Jones	.25
26	Andres Galarraga	.40
27	Greg Maddux	1.00
28	Reggie Sanders	.10
29	Javy Lopez	.20
30	Jeromy Burnitz	.20
31	Kevin Barker	.10
32	Jose Hernandez	.10
33	Ron Belliard	.10
34	Henry Blanco	.10
35	Marquis Grissom	.10
36	Geoff Jenkins	.20
37	Carlos Delgado	.50
38	Raul Mondesi	.20
39	Roy Halladay	.10
40	Tony Batista	.20
41	David Wells	.10
42	Shannon Stewart	.10
43	Vernon Wells	.10
44	Sammy Sosa	1.25
45	Ismael Valdes	.10
46	Joe Girardi	.10
47	Mark Grace	.20
48	Henry Rodriguez	.10
49	Kerry Wood	.25
50	Eric Young	.10
51	Mark McGwire	2.00
52	Daryle Kile	.10
53	Fernando Vina	.10
54	Ray Lankford	.10
55	J.D. Drew	.25
56	Fernando Tatis	.20
57	Rick Ankiel	3.00
58	Matt Williams	.25
59	Erubiel Durazo	.20
60	Tony Womack	.10
61	Jay Bell	.10
62	Randy Johnson	.50
63	Steve Finley	.10
64	Matt Mantei	.10
65	Luis Gonzalez	.20
66	Gary Sheffield	.25
67	Eric Gagne	.10
68	Adrian Beltre	.20
69	Mark Grudzielanek	.10
70	Kevin Brown	.20
71	Chan Ho Park	.10
72	Shawn Green	.40
73	Vinny Castilla	.20
74	Fred McGriff	.25
75	Wilson Alvarez	.10
76	Greg Vaughn	.20
77	Gerald Williams	.10
78	Ryan Rupe	.10
79	Jose Canseco	.50
80	Vladimir Guerrero	1.00
81	Dustin Hermanson	.10
82	Michael Barrett	.10
83	Rondell White	.20
84	Tony Armas, Jr.	.10
85	Wilton Guerrero	.10
86	Jose Vidro	.10
87	Barry Bonds	.50
88	Russ Ortiz	.10
89	Ellis Burks	.10
90	Jeff Kent	.10
91	Russ Davis	.10
92	J.T. Snow	.10
93	Roberto Alomar	.40
94	Manny Ramirez	.50
95	Chuck Finley	.10

96	Kenny Lofton	.40
97	Jim Thome	.40
98	Bartolo Colon	.20
99	Omar Vizquel	.10
100	Richie Sexson	.10
101	Mike Cameron	.10
102	Brett Tomko	.10
103	Edgar Martinez	.20
104	Alex Rodriguez	1.50
105	John Olerud	.20
106	Fred Garcia	.10
107	*Kazuhiro Sasaki*	1.50
108	Preston Wilson	.10
109	Luis Castillo	.10
110	A.J. Burnett	.10
111	Mike Lowell	.10
112	Cliff Floyd	.10
113	Brad Penny	.10
114	Alex Gonzalez	.10
115	Mike Piazza	1.25
116	Derek Bell	.10
117	Edgardo Alfonzo	.20
118	Rickey Henderson	.20
119	Todd Zeile	.10
120	Mike Hampton	.10
121	Al Leiter	.20
122	Robin Ventura	.20
123	Cal Ripken Jr.	1.50
124	Mike Mussina	.40
125	B.J. Surhoff	.10
126	Jerry Hairston	.10
127	Brady Anderson	.20
128	Albert Belle	.40
129	Sidney Ponson	.10
130	Tony Gwynn	1.00
131	Ryan Klesko	.10
132	Sterling Hitchcock	.10
133	Eric Owens	.10
134	Trevor Hoffman	.10
135	Al Martin	.10
136	Bret Boone	.10
137	Brian Giles	.10
138	Chad Hermansen	.10
139	Kevin Young	.10
140	Kris Benson	.10
141	Warren Morris	.10
142	Jason Kendall	.20
143	Wil Cordero	.10
144	Scott Rolen	.50
145	Curt Schilling	.20
146	Doug Glanville	.10
147	Mike Lieberthal	.10
148	Mike Jackson	.10
149	Rico Brogna	.10
150	Andy Ashby	.10
151	Bob Abreu	.10
152	Sean Casey	.25
153	Pete Harnisch	.10
154	Dante Bichette	.20
155	Pokey Reese	.10
156	Aaron Boone	.10
157	Ken Griffey Jr.	2.00
158	Barry Larkin	.30
159	Scott Williamson	.10
160	Carlos Beltran	.10
161	Jermaine Dye	.10
162	Jose Rosado	.10
163	Joe Randa	.10
164	Johnny Damon	.10
165	Mike Sweeney	.10
166	Mark Quinn	.10
167	Ivan Rodriguez	.50
168	Rusty Greer	.10
169	Ruben Mateo	.10
170	Doug Davis	.10
171	Gabe Kapler	.20
172	Justin Thompson	.10
173	Rafael Palmeiro	.40
174	Larry Walker	.40
175	Neifi Perez	.10
176	Rolando Arrojo	.10
177	Jeffrey Hammonds	.10
178	Todd Helton	.50
179	Pedro Astacio	.10
180	Jeff Cirillo	.10
181	Pedro Martinez	.50
182	Carl Everett	.20
183	Troy O'Leary	.10
184	Nomar Garciaparra	1.25
185	Jose Offerman	.10
186	Bret Saberhagen	.10
187	Trot Nixon	.10
188	Jason Varitek	.10
189	Todd Walker	.10
190	Eric Milton	.10
191	Chad Allen	.10
192	Jacque Jones	.10
193	Brad Radke	.10
194	Corey Koskie	.10
195	Joe Mays	.10
196	Juan Gonzalez	.50
197	Jeff Weaver	.10
198	Juan Encarnacion	.10
199	Deivi Cruz	.10
200	Damion Easley	.10
201	Tony Clark	.10
202	Dean Palmer	.10
203	Frank Thomas	.75
204	Carlos Lee	.10
205	Mike Sirotka	.10
206	Kip Wells	.10
207	Magglio Ordonez	.20
208	Paul Konerko	.20
209	Chris Singleton	.10
210	Derek Jeter	1.25
211	Tino Martinez	.25
212	Mariano Rivera	.20
213	Roger Clemens	.75
214	Nick Johnson	.25
215	Paul O'Neill	.20
216	Bernie Williams	.40
217	David Cone	.20
218	Checklist (Ken Griffey Jr.)	1.00
219	Checklist (Sammy Sosa)	.50
220	Checklist (Mark McGwire)	1.00

2000 Upper Deck MVP Silver

A parallel to the 220-card base set. These 1:2 pack inserts can be distinguished from the base cards by the silver-foil stamping and a silver-foiled facsimile signature of the featured player on the card bottom.

	MT
Stars:	2-3X
Inserted 1:2	

2000 Upper Deck MVP Gold

A parallel to the base set, these can be distinguished from base cards with gold-script stamping. Each card is also serially numbered on the card front within an edition of 50 sets.

	MT
Stars:	60-100X
Production 50 sets	

2000 Upper Deck MVP Super

A parallel to the 220-card base set, these inserts can be distinguished from the base cards by the holo-foil stamping used on the Upper Deck logo and the featured player's facsimile signature on the card bottom. The card fronts are also serially numbered within an edition of 25 sets.

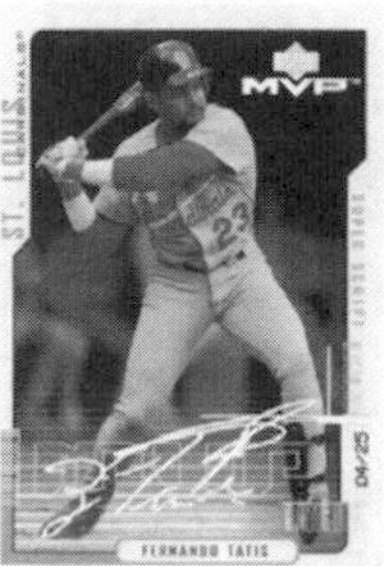

	MT
Stars:	100-150X
Production 25 sets	

2000 Upper Deck MVP Drawing Power

This seven-card set has a holo-foil front with silver foil stamping. Card backs are numbered with a "DP" prefix. They are found on the average of 1:28 packs.

		MT
Complete Set (7):		30.00
Common Player:		2.00
Inserted 1:28		
1	Mark McGwire	8.00
2	Ken Griffey Jr.	8.00
3	Mike Piazza	5.00
4	Chipper Jones	4.00
5	Nomar Garciaparra	5.00
6	Sammy Sosa	5.00
7	Jose Canseco	2.00

2000 Upper Deck MVP Game — Used Souvenirs

These memorabilia inserts feature a game-used piece of glove embedded and are found exclusively in hobby packs at a rate of 1:130 packs.

		MT
Common Player:		15.00
Inserted 1:130		
RA	Roberto Alomar	40.00
JB	Jeff Bagwell	50.00
AB	Albert Belle	40.00
BB	Barry Bonds	50.00
JC	Jose Canseco	50.00
WC	Will Clark	40.00
AF	Alex Fernandez	15.00
JG	Jason Giambi	20.00
TGl	Troy Glaus	25.00
AG	Alex Gonzalez	15.00
BG	Ben Grieve	20.00
KG	Ken Griffey Jr.	175.00
VG	Vladimir Guerrero	60.00
TG	Tony Gwynn	80.00
AJ	Andruw Jones	40.00
CJ	Chipper Jones	80.00
KL	Kenny Lofton	35.00
RM	Raul Mondesi	25.00
PO	Paul O'Neill	25.00
RP	Rafael Palmeiro	50.00
MR	Manny Ramirez	50.00
CR	Cal Ripken Jr.	150.00
AR	Alex Rodriguez	125.00
IR	Ivan Rodriguez	50.00
NR	Nolan Ryan	175.00
TS	Tim Salmon	25.00
LW	Larry Walker	40.00
BW	Bernie Williams	40.00
MW	Matt Williams	35.00

2000 Upper Deck MVP Game Used Souvenirs — Bats

These memorabilia inserts have a piece of game-used bat embedded and are seeded exclusively in hobby packs at a rate of 1:130 packs.

		MT
Complete Set (10):		650.00
Common Player:		15.00
Inserted 1:130		
BB	Barry Bonds	50.00
JC	Jose Canseco	50.00
KG	Ken Griffey Jr.	180.00
VG	Vladimir Guerrero	60.00
TG	Tony Gwynn	80.00
CJ	Chipper Jones	80.00
MR	Manny Ramirez	50.00
AR	Alex Rodriguez	125.00
IR	Ivan Rodriguez	50.00
BW	Bernie Williams	40.00

2000 Upper Deck MVP Prolifics

This seven-card set features a full holo-foiled front with silver-foil stamping and are seeded 1:28 packs. Card backs are numbered with a "P" prefix.

		MT
Complete Set (7):		20.00
Common Player:		1.50
Inserted 1:28		
1	Manny Ramirez	2.00
2	Vladimir Guerrero	4.00
3	Derek Jeter	5.00
4	Pedro Martinez	2.00
5	Shawn Green	1.50
6	Alex Rodriguez	6.00
7	Cal Ripken Jr.	6.00

2000 Upper Deck MVP ProSign

These autographed inserts are found exclusively in retail packs at a rate of 1:216.

		MT
Common Player:		15.00
Inserted 1:216 R		
RA	Rick Ankiel	75.00
MB	Michael Barrett	15.00
RB	Rob Bell	15.00
CB	Carlos Beltran	15.00
LB	Lance Berkman	15.00
RB	Rico Brogna	15.00
SC	Sean Casey	25.00
DD	Doug Davis	15.00
ED	Erubiel Durazo	25.00
RF	Robert Fick	15.00
NG	Nomar Garciaparra	120.00
AG	Alex Gonzalez	15.00
KG	Ken Griffey Jr.	225.00
TG	Tony Gwynn	90.00
TH	Tim Hudson	25.00
DJ	Derek Jeter	150.00
CJ	Chipper Jones	100.00
MM	Mike Meyers	15.00
EM	Eric Milton	20.00
JM	Jim Morris	15.00
WM	Warren Morris	15.00
TN	Trot Nixon	15.00
BP	Ben Petrick	15.00
AP	Adam Piatt	20.00
MP	Mike Piazza	120.00
MQ	Mark Quinn	15.00
MR	Manny Ramirez	50.00
RR	Rob Ramsay	15.00
MRe	Mike Redmond	15.00
MRi	Mariano Rivera	20.00
AR	Alex Rodriguez	120.00
MS	Mike Sweeney	20.00
BT	Bubba Trammell	15.00
JV	Jose Vidro	20.00
DW	Daryle Ward	20.00
KW	Kip Wells	15.00
SW	Scott Williamson	15.00
PW	Preston Wilson	20.00
KW	Kevin Witt	15.00
TW	Tony Womack	20.00
EY	Ed Yarnall	15.00
JZ	Jeff Zimmerman	15.00

2000 Upper Deck MVP Pure Grit

These 1:6 pack inserts have a full holo-foiled front with silver-foil stamping. Card backs are numbered with an "G" prefix.

		MT
Complete Set (10):		12.00
Common Player:		.50
Inserted 1:6		
1	Derek Jeter	2.50
2	Kevin Brown	.50
3	Craig Biggio	.50
4	Ivan Rodriguez	1.00
5	Scott Rolen	1.00
6	Carlos Beltran	.50
7	Ken Griffey Jr.	4.00
8	Cal Ripken Jr.	3.00
9	Nomar Garciaparra	2.50
10	Randy Johnson	1.00

2000 Upper Deck MVP Scout's Choice

This ten-card set spotlights some of the best prospects in 2000. The inserts have a full holo-foiled front with silver-foil stamping. Card backs are numbered with an "SC" prefix and are seeded 1:14 packs.

		MT
Complete Set (10):		20.00
Common Player:		1.00
Inserted 1:14		
1	Rick Ankiel	8.00
2	Vernon Wells	1.50
3	Pat Burrell	4.00
4	Travis Dawkins	1.00
5	Eric Munson	3.00
6	Nick Johnson	3.00
7	Dermal Brown	1.00
8	Alfonso Soriano	2.00
9	Ben Petrick	1.00
10	Adam Everett	1.00

2000 Upper Deck MVP Second Season Standouts

This 10-card set has a full holo-foiled card front with silver-foil stamping. Card backs are numbered with an "SS" prefix and inserted 1:6 packs.

		MT
Complete Set (10):		10.00
Common Player:		.40
Inserted 1:6		
1	Pedro Martinez	1.50
2	Mariano Rivera	.40
3	Orlando Hernandez	.40
4	Ken Caminiti	.40
5	Bernie Williams	.50
6	Jim Thome	.50
7	Nomar Garciaparra	3.00
8	Edgardo Alfonzo	.50
9	Derek Jeter	3.00
10	Kevin Millwood	.50

2000 Upper Deck MVP 3,000 Hit Club

Upper Deck used this cross-brand insert series to salute the players who accomplished 3,000 hits in their career. Stan Musial is featured and offers a Game-used Memorabilia Bat, Jersey, Jjersey/Bat combo and combo Autograph versions.

		MT
Common Player:		
SM	(Stan Musial jersey-350)	220.00
SM	(Stan Musial bat-350)	200.00
SM	Stan Musial jersey/bat-100	400.00
SM	Stan Musial J/B/Auto-6	

2000 Upper Deck Ovation

The base set consists of 90-cards, including a 20-card World Premiere subset and 10-card Superstar Spotlight subset. World Premieres are found 1:3 packs and Superstar Spotlights 1:6 packs. Card fronts are embossed, intended to resemble the feel of a baseball and also has silver-foil stamping.

		MT
Complete Set (89):		125.00
Common Player:		.25
Common World Prem. (61-80):		2.00
Inserted 1:3		
Common Super. Spot (81-90):		3.00
Inserted 1:6		
Pack (5):		4.00
Wax Box (20):		70.00
1	Mo Vaughn	.75
2	Troy Glaus	1.00
3	Jeff Bagwell	1.00
4	Craig Biggio	.50
5	Mike Hampton	.25
6	Jason Giambi	.25
7	Tim Hudson	.50
8	Chipper Jones	2.00
9	Greg Maddux	2.00
10	Kevin Millwood	.50
11	Brian Jordan	.25
12	Jeromy Burnitz	.25
13	David Wells	.25
14	Carlos Delgado	.75
15	Sammy Sosa	2.50
16	Mark McGwire	4.00
17	Matt Williams	.50
18	Randy Johnson	.75
19	Erubiel Durazo	.50
20	Kevin Brown	.25
21	Shawn Green	.75
22	Gary Sheffield	.40
23	Jose Canseco	1.00
24	Vladimir Guerrero	2.00
25	Barry Bonds	1.00
26	Manny Ramirez	1.00
27	Roberto Alomar	.75
28	Richie Sexson	.25
29	Jim Thome	.50

30	Alex Rodriguez	3.00
31	Ken Griffey Jr.	4.00
32	Preston Wilson	.25
33	Mike Piazza	2.50
34	Al Leiter	.25
35	Robin Ventura	.40
36	Cal Ripken Jr.	3.00
37	Albert Belle	.75
38	Tony Gwynn	2.00
39	Brian Giles	.25
40	Jason Kendall	.40
41	Scott Rolen	1.00
42	Bob Abreu	.25
43	Ken Griffey Jr.	8.00
44	Sean Casey	.40
45	Carlos Beltran	.25
46	Gabe Kapler	.40
47	Ivan Rodriguez	1.00
48	Rafael Palmeiro	.50
49	Larry Walker	.75
50	Nomar Garciaparra	2.50
51	Pedro J. Martinez	1.00
52	Eric Milton	.25
53	Juan Gonzalez	1.25
54	Tony Clark	.50
55	Frank Thomas	1.25
56	Magglio Ordonez	.40
57	Roger Clemens	1.50
58	Derek Jeter	2.50
59	Bernie Williams	.75
60	Orlando Hernandez	.50
61	Rick Ankiel (World Premiere)	15.00
62	Josh Beckett (World Premiere)	10.00
63	Vernon Wells (World Premiere)	3.00
64	Alfonso Soriano (World Premiere)	3.00
65	Pat Burrell (World Premiere)	8.00
66	Eric Munson (World Premiere)	8.00
67	Chad Hutchinson (World Premiere)	3.00
68	Eric Gagne (World Premiere)	2.00
69	Peter Bergeron (World Premiere)	2.00
70	Ryan Anderson (Supposed to have been withdrawn, all known cards have embossed UD racing mark.)	300.00
71	A.J. Burnett (World Premiere)	2.00
72	Jorge Luis Toca (World Premiere)	3.00
73	Matt Riley (World Premiere)	5.00
74	Chad Hermansen (World Premiere)	2.00
75	Doug Davis (World Premiere)	2.00
76	Jim Morris (World Premiere)	2.00
77	Ben Petrick (World Premiere)	3.00
78	Mark Quinn (World Premiere)	3.00
79	Ed Yarnall (World Premiere)	3.00
80	Ramon Ortiz (World Premiere)	3.00
81	Ken Griffey Jr. (Superstar Spotlight)	12.00
82	Mark McGwire (Superstar Spotlight)	12.00
83	Derek Jeter (Superstar Spotlight)	8.00
84	Jeff Bagwell (Superstar Spotlight)	3.00
85	Nomar Garciaparra (Superstar Spotlight)	8.00
86	Sammy Sosa (Superstar Spotlight)	8.00
87	Mike Piazza (Superstar Spotlight)	8.00
88	Alex Rodriguez (Superstar Spotlight)	10.00
89	Cal Ripken Jr. (Superstar Spotlight)	10.00
90	Pedro Martinez (Superstar Spotlight)	3.00

2000 Upper Deck Ovation Standing Ovation

A parallel to the 120-card base set, these are identical to the base cards besides the holographic silver stamping on the card front and the backs serially numbered to 50.

	MT
Stars (1-60):	25x-50x
World Prem. (61-80):	3x-6x
Super. Spot. (81-90):	8x-15x
Production 50 sets	

(See 2000 UD Ovation for checklist and base card values.)

2000 Upper Deck Ovation A Piece of History

These memorabilia inserts feature a piece of game-used bat embedded and are limited to 400 sets produced.

		MT
Common Player:		15.00
Production 400 sets		
JB	Jeff Bagwell	60.00
CB	Carlos Beltran	15.00
SC	Sean Casey	40.00
KG	Ken Griffey Jr.	150.00
DJ	Derek Jeter	150.00
TG	Tony Gwynn	60.00
AJ	Andruw Jones	40.00
CJ	Chipper Jones	80.00
RP	Rafael Palmeiro	40.00
MP	Mike Piazza	100.00
MR	Manny Ramirez	60.00
CR	Cal Ripken Jr.	150.00
AR	Alex Rodriguez	125.00
SR	Scott Rolen	40.00
SS	Sammy Sosa	100.00
FT	Frank Thomas	75.00

2000 Upper Deck Ovation Center Stage

Ten of baseball's top performers are highlighted on a card that features gold foil stamping and etching. Card backs are numbered with a "CS" prefix and are seeded 1:9 packs. Two parallels to this insert set are randomly inserted: Golds are found 1:39 packs and Rainbows are seeded 1:99 packs.

		MT
Complete Set (10):		75.00
Common Player:		2.00
Inserted 1:9		
Gold:		2x
Inserted 1:39		
Rainbow:		3x-4x
Inserted 1:99		
1	Jeff Bagwell	3.00
2	Ken Griffey Jr.	12.00
3	Nomar Garciaparra	8.00
4	Mike Piazza	8.00
5	Mark McGwire	12.00
6	Alex Rodriguez	10.00
7	Cal Ripken Jr.	10.00
8	Derek Jeter	8.00
9	Chipper Jones	6.00
10	Sammy Sosa	8.00

2000 Upper Deck Ovation Curtain Call

This 20-card set features gold-foil stamping and highlights some memorable playoff moments. Card backs are numbered with a "CC" prefix and are seeded 1:3 packs.

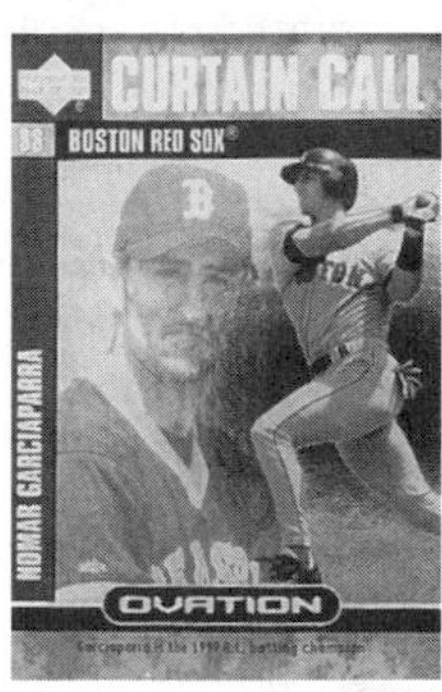

		MT
Complete Set (20):		50.00
Common Player:		1.00
Inserted 1:3		
1	David Cone	1.00
2	Mark McGwire	8.00
3	Sammy Sosa	5.00
4	Eric Milton	1.00
5	Bernie Williams	1.50
6	Tony Gwynn	4.00
7	Nomar Garciaparra	5.00
8	Manny Ramirez	2.00
9	Wade Boggs	1.50
10	Randy Johnson	1.50
11	Cal Ripken Jr.	6.00
12	Pedro J. Martinez	2.00
13	Alex Rodriguez	6.00
14	Fernando Tatis	1.00
15	Vladimir Guerrero	4.00
16	Robin Ventura	1.00
17	Larry Walker	1.50
18	Carlos Beltran	1.00
19	Jose Canseco	2.00
20	Ken Griffey Jr.	8.00

2000 Upper Deck Ovation Diamond Futures

This 10-card set highlights some of baseball's top prospects on a full-foiled front with silver-foil stamping. Card backs are numbered with a "DM" prefix and are seeded 1:6 packs.

		MT
Complete Set (10):		40.00
Common Player:		2.00
Inserted 1:6		
1	J.D. Drew	2.50
2	Alfonso Soriano	3.00
3	Preston Wilson	2.00
4	Erubiel Durazo	3.00
5	Rick Ankiel	20.00
6	Octavio Dotel	2.00
7	A.J. Burnett	2.00

8	Carlos Beltran	2.00
9	Vernon Wells	2.00
10	Troy Glaus	4.00

2000 Upper Deck Ovation Lead Performers

Upper Deck chose 10 players for this set who are thought of as leaders on and off the field. Card fronts have silver-foil stamping and card backs are numbered with an "LP" prefix. These are found on the average of 1:19 packs.

		MT
Complete Set (10):		75.00
Common Player:		3.00
Inserted 1:19		
1	Mark McGwire	15.00
2	Derek Jeter	10.00
3	Vladimir Guerrero	6.00
4	Mike Piazza	10.00
5	Cal Ripken Jr.	12.00
6	Sammy Sosa	10.00
7	Jeff Bagwell	4.00
8	Nomar Garciaparra	10.00
9	Chipper Jones	8.00
10	Ken Griffey Jr.	15.00

2000 Upper Deck Ovation Superstar Theater

This 20-card set is printed on a full-foiled card front enhanced by silver foil stamping and etching. Card backs are numbered with an "ST" prefix and seeded 1:19 packs.

		MT
Complete Set (20):		90.00
Common Player:		3.00
Inserted 1:19		
1	Ivan Rodriguez	6.00
2	Brian Giles	3.00
3	Bernie Williams	5.00
4	Greg Maddux	12.00
5	Frank Thomas	8.00
6	Sean Casey	4.00
7	Mo Vaughn	5.00
8	Carlos Delgado	5.00
9	Tony Gwynn	12.00
10	Pedro Martinez	6.00
11	Scott Rolen	6.00
12	Mark McGwire	25.00
13	Manny Ramirez	6.00
14	Rafael Palmeiro	5.00
15	Jose Canseco	6.00
16	Randy Johnson	5.00
17	Gary Sheffield	3.00
18	Larry Walker	5.00
19	Barry Bonds	6.00
20	Roger Clemens	8.00

2000 Upper Deck Ovation Super Signatures

This two-card insert set features Ken Griffey Jr. and Mike Piazza. Spotlighting the autographs of Griffey and Piazza, Super Signatures is issued in three versions: Silver, numbered to 100; Gold, numbered to 50; and Rainbow, numbered to 10.

		MT
Common Card:		
Jr	Ken Griffey Rainbow/10	
KG	Ken Griffey Gold/50	450.00
KG	Ken Griffey Silver/100	225.00
MP	Mike Piazza Rainbow/10	
MP	Mike Piazza Gold/50	400.00
MP	Mike Piazza Silver/100	200.00

2000 Upper Deck Ovation 3,000 Hit Club

Upper Deck's cross-brand insert series pays tribute to members of the elite 3,000 Hit Club. Ovation features Willie Mays in the series, which has four versions: Bat card, 300 produced; Jersey card, 350 produced; Bat/Jersey combo, 50 produced; and Bat/Jersey autograph, 24 produced.

		MT
1	Willie Mays (Jersey Card/350)	300.00
2	Willie Mays (Bat Card/300)	300.00
3	Willie Mays (Jersey+Bat Card/50)	900.00
4	Willie Mays (Signed Jersey+Bat Card/24)	1500.

2000 Upper Deck PowerDeck

		MT
Complete Set (12):		55.00
Common Card:		3.00
Pack (1):		5.00
Box:		45.00
1	Sammy Sosa	6.00
2	Ken Griffey Jr.	10.00
3	Mark McGwire	10.00
4	Derek Jeter	6.00
5	Alex Rodriguez	8.00
6	Nomar Garciaparra	6.00
7	Mike Piazza	6.00
8	Cal Ripken Jr.	8.00
9	Ivan Rodriguez	3.00
10	Chipper Jones	5.00
11	Pedro Martinez	3.00
12	Manny Ramirez	3.00

2000 Upper Deck PowerDeck Power Trio

		MT
Complete Set (3):		25.00
Common Player:		30.00
Inserted 1:7		
PT1	Derek Jeter	6.00
PT2	Ken Griffey Jr.	10.00
PT3	Mark McGwire	10.00

2000 Upper Deck PowerDeck Magical Moments

		MT
Complete Set (2):		20.00
Inserted 1:10 H		
KG	Ken Griffey Jr.	10.00
CR	Cal Ripken Jr.	10.00

2000 Upper Deck PowerDeck Magical Moments Autograph

		MT
Each signed 50 cards		
KG	Ken Griffey Jr.	275.00
CR	Cal Ripken Jr.	275.00

2000 Upper Deck Pros and Prospects

The 132-card base set consists of 90 regular player cards, a 30-card Prospective Superstars subset and a 12-card Pro-Fame subset. Prospective Superstars are serially numbered to 1,350 and Pro-Fame are serially numbered to 1,000. Card fronts have a white-bordered design with silver foil stamping. Both subsets are serially numbered on the card front.

		MT
Complete Set (132):		800.00
Common Player (1-90):		.15
Common (91-120):		8.00
Production 1,350 sets		
Common (121-132):		8.00
Production 1,000 sets		
Pack (5):		5.00
Box (24):		110.00
1	Darin Erstad	.40
2	Troy Glaus	.75
3	Mo Vaughn	.50
4	Jason Giambi	.40
5	Tim Hudson	.25
6	Ben Grieve	.25
7	Eric Chavez	.25
8	Shannon Stewart	.15
9	Raul Mondesi	.25
10	Carlos Delgado	.75
11	Jose Canseco	.40
12	Fred McGriff	.25
13	Greg Vaughn	.15
14	Manny Ramirez	.75
15	Roberto Alomar	.60
16	Jim Thome	.40
17	Alex Rodriguez	2.50
18	Fred Garcia	.15
19	John Olerud	.15
20	Cal Ripken Jr.	2.50
21	Albert Belle	.40
22	Mike Mussina	.40
23	Ivan Rodriguez	.75
24	Rafael Palmeiro	.40
25	Ruben Mateo	.15
26	Gabe Kapler	.15
27	Pedro Martinez	.75
28	Nomar Garciaparra	2.00
29	Carl Everett	.15
30	Carlos Beltran	.15
31	Jermaine Dye	.15
32	Johnny Damon	.15
33	Juan Gonzalez	.75
34	Juan Encarnacion	.15
35	Dean Palmer	.15
36	Jacque Jones	.15
37	Matt Lawton	.15
38	Frank Thomas	1.00
39	Paul Konerko	.15
40	Magglio Ordonez	.25
41	Derek Jeter	2.00
42	Bernie Williams	.50
43	Mariano Rivera	.25
44	Roger Clemens	1.00
45	Jeff Bagwell	.75

46	Craig Biggio	.25
47	Richard Hidalgo	.25
48	Chipper Jones	1.50
49	Andres Galarraga	.40
50	Andruw Jones	.50
51	Greg Maddux	1.50
52	Jeromy Burnitz	.15
53	Geoff Jenkins	.25
54	Mark McGwire	3.00
55	Jim Edmonds	.25
56	Fernando Tatis	.15
57	J.D. Drew	.15
58	Sammy Sosa	2.00
59	Kerry Wood	.25
60	Randy Johnson	.75
61	Matt Williams	.25
62	Erubiel Durazo	.15
63	Shawn Green	.25
64	Kevin Brown	.25
65	Gary Sheffield	.25
66	Adrian Beltre	.25
67	Vladimir Guerrero	1.00
68	Jose Vidro	.15
69	Barry Bonds	.75
70	Jeff Kent	.15
71	Preston Wilson	.15
72	Ryan Dempster	.15
73	Mike Lowell	.15
74	Mike Piazza	2.00
75	Robin Ventura	.15
76	Edgardo Alfonzo	.25
77	Derek Bell	.15
78	Tony Gwynn	1.50
79	Matt Clement	.15
80	Scott Rolen	.75
81	Bobby Abreu	.15
82	Curt Schilling	.15
83	Brian Giles	.15
84	Jason Kendall	.15
85	Kris Benson	.15
86	Ken Griffey Jr.	2.50
87	Sean Casey	.15
88	Pokey Reese	.15
89	Larry Walker	.25
90	Todd Helton	.75
91	Rick Ankiel (Prospective Superstars)	25.00
92	Milton Bradley (Prospective Superstars)	10.00
93	Vernon Wells (Prospective Superstars)	8.00
94	Rafael Furcal (Prospective Superstars)	35.00
95	*Kazuhiro Sasaki* (Prospective Superstars)	35.00
96	*Joe Torres* (Prospective Superstars)	25.00
97	Adam Kennedy (Prospective Superstars)	8.00
98	Adam Piatt (Prospective Superstars)	15.00
99	*Matt Wheatland* (Prospective Superstars)	25.00
100	*Alex Cabrera* (Prospective Superstars)	20.00
101	*Barry Zito* (Prospective Superstars)	100.00
102	*Mike Lamb* (Prospective Superstars)	15.00
103	*Scott Heard* (Prospective Superstars)	25.00
104	*Danys Baez* (Prospective Superstars)	20.00
105	Matt Riley (Prospective Superstars)	8.00
106	Mark Mulder (Prospective Superstars)	8.00
107	*Wilfredo Rodriguez* (Prospective Superstars)	10.00
108	*Luis Matos* (Prospective Superstars)	20.00
109	Alfonso Soriano (Prospective Superstars)	12.00
110	Pat Burrell (Prospective Superstars)	25.00
111	*Mike Tonis* (Prospective Superstars)	40.00
112	*Aaron McNeal* (Prospective Superstars)	20.00
113	*Dave Krynzel* (Prospective Superstars)	25.00
114	Josh Beckett (Prospective Superstars)	20.00
115	*Sean Burnett* (Prospective Superstars)	20.00
116	Eric Munson (Prospective Superstars)	10.00
117	*Scott Downs* (Prospective Superstars)	8.00
118	*Brian Tollberg* (Prospective Superstars)	15.00
119	Nick Johnson (Prospective Superstars)	10.00
120	*Leo Estrella* (Prospective Superstars)	8.00
121	Ken Griffey Jr. (Pro Fame)	25.00
122	Frank Thomas (Pro Fame)	10.00
123	Cal Ripken Jr. (Pro Fame)	25.00
124	Ivan Rodriguez (Pro Fame)	8.00
125	Derek Jeter (Pro Fame)	20.00
126	Mark McGwire (Pro Fame)	30.00
127	Pedro Martinez (Pro Fame)	8.00
128	Chipper Jones (Pro Fame)	15.00
129	Sammy Sosa (Pro Fame)	20.00
130	Alex Rodriguez (Pro Fame)	25.00
131	Vladimir Guerrero (Pro Fame)	10.00
132	Jeff Bagwell (Pro Fame)	8.00

2000 Upper Deck Pros and Prospects Future Forces

This 10-card set highlights top prosects on a card front featuring gold foil stamping and etching. Card backs are numbered with an "F" prefix and are seeded 1:6 packs.

		MT
Complete Set (10):		10.00
Common Player:		.50
Inserted 1:6		
1	Pat Burrell	2.50
2	Brad Penny	.50
3	Rick Ankiel	4.00
4	Adam Kennedy	.50
5	Eric Munson	1.00
6	Rafael Furcal	4.00
7	Mark Mulder	.50
8	Vernon Wells	.50
9	Matt Riley	.50
10	Nick Johnson	1.00

2000 Upper Deck Pros and Prospects ProMotion

This 10-card set spotlights some of baseball's best all-around talents using gold foil stamping. Card backs are numbered with a "P" prefix and are seeded 1:6 packs.

		MT
Complete Set (10):		20.00
Common Player:		.75
Inserted 1:6		
1	Derek Jeter	3.00
2	Mike Piazza	3.00
3	Mark McGwire	5.00
4	Ivan Rodriguez	1.25
5	Kerry Wood	.75
6	Nomar Garciaparra	3.00
7	Sammy Sosa	3.00
8	Alex Rodriguez	4.00
9	Ken Griffey Jr.	4.00
10	Vladimir Guerrero	1.50

2000 Upper Deck Pros and Prospects Rare Breed

Baseball's top performers are spotlighted in this 12-card set on a full-foiled silver front with gold-foil stamping. Card backs are numbered with an "R" prefix and are inserted 1:12 packs.

		MT
Complete Set (12):		40.00
Common Player:		1.50
Inserted 1:12		
1	Mark McGwire	8.00
2	Frank Thomas	3.00
3	Mike Piazza	5.00
4	Barry Bonds	2.00
5	Manny Ramirez	2.00
6	Ken Griffey Jr.	6.00
7	Nomar Garciaparra	5.00
8	Randy Johnson	2.00
9	Vladimir Guerrero	3.00
10	Jeff Bagwell	2.00
11	Rick Ankiel	2.00
12	Alex Rodriguez	6.00

2000 Upper Deck Pros and Pros. Signed Game-Worn Jerseys

Each of these Game-Worn Jersey cards has a piece of jersey swatch and autograph from the featured player. A Level 2 version is limited to the player's corresponding uniform number.

		MT
Common Player:		40.00
Inserted 1:96		
BB	Barry Bonds	125.00
JC	Jose Canseco	80.00
JD	J.D. Drew	75.00
TG	Tom Glavine	75.00
LG	Luis Gonzalez	40.00
KG	Ken Griffey Jr.	350.00
TG	Tony Gwynn	100.00
DJ	Derek Jeter	400.00
RJ	Randy Johnson	125.00
CJ	Chipper Jones	125.00
KL	Kenny Lofton	70.00
CR	Cal Ripken Jr.	250.00
AR	Alex Rodriguez	250.00
IR	Ivan Rodriguez	100.00
SR	Scott Rolen	80.00
GS	Gary Sheffield	70.00
FT	Frank Thomas	150.00
MV	Mo Vaughn	70.00
RV	Robin Ventura	50.00
MW	Matt Williams	70.00
PW	Preston Wilson	40.00

Player names in *Italic* type indicate a rookie card.

2000 Upper Deck Pros and Prospects The Best in the Bigs

This 10-card set spotlights baseball's best performers on a white-bordered design with gold foil stamping. Card backs are numbered with a "B" prefix and are inserted 1:12 packs.

		MT
Complete Set (10):		40.00
Common Player:		1.50
Inserted 1:12		
1	Sammy Sosa	5.00
2	Tony Gwynn	3.00
3	Pedro Martinez	2.00
4	Mark McGwire	8.00
5	Chipper Jones	4.00
6	Derek Jeter	5.00
7	Ken Griffey Jr.	6.00
8	Cal Ripken Jr.	6.00
9	Greg Maddux	4.00
10	Ivan Rodriguez	2.00

2000 Upper Deck Pros and Prospects 3,000 Hit Club

Upper Deck's continuing series features Lou Brock and Rod Carew. The series features 350 numbered Bat cards, 350 numbered Jersey cards and 100 numbered Bat/Jersey combos. Each player also signed the Bat/Jersey combos to their jersey number, as Brock signed 20 and Carew 29.

	MT
Lou Brock bat/350	150.00
Lou Brock jersey/350	150.00
Lou Brock bat/jersey/100	225.00
Lou Brock auto./bat/jersey/20	N/A
Rod Carew bat/350	150.00
Rod Carew jersey/350	150.00
Rod Carew bat/jersey/100	225.00
Rod Carew auto./bat/jersey/29	N/A

2000 Upper Deck Ultimate Victory

		MT
Complete Set (120):		750.00
Common Player:		.15
Common Ultimate Rookie (91-120):		6.00
Varying production levels		
1	Mo Vaughn	.40
2	Darin Erstad	.40
3	Troy Glaus	.75
4	Adam Kennedy	.15
5	Jason Giambi	.40
6	Ben Grieve	.25
7	Terrence Long	.15
8	Tim Hudson	.25
9	David Wells	.15
10	Carlos Delgado	.60
11	Shannon Stewart	.15
12	Greg Vaughn	.15
13	Gerald Williams	.15
14	Manny Ramirez	.75
15	Roberto Alomar	.60
16	Jim Thome	.40
17	Edgar Martinez	.15
18	Alex Rodriquez	2.50
19	Matt Riley	.15
20	Cal Ripken Jr.	2.50
21	Mike Mussina	.40
22	Albert Belle	.40
23	Ivan Rodriguez	.75
24	Rafael Palmeiro	.40
25	Nomar Garciaparra	2.00
26	Pedro Martinez	.75
27	Carl Everett	.15
28	*Tomokazu Ohka*	.15
29	Jermaine Dye	.15
30	Johnny Damon	.15
31	Dean Palmer	.15
32	Juan Gonzalez	.75
33	Eric Milton	.15
34	Matt Lawton	.15
35	Frank Thomas	1.00
36	Paul Konerko	.15
37	Magglio Ordonez	.25
38	Jon Garland	.15
39	Derek Jeter	2.50
40	Roger Clemens	1.00
41	Bernie Williams	.50
42	Nick Johnson	.15
43	Julio Lugo	.15
44	Jeff Bagwell	.75
45	Richard Hidalgo	.15
46	Chipper Jones	1.50
47	Greg Maddux	1.50
48	Andruw Jones	.50
49	Andres Galarraga	.25
50	Rafael Furcal	1.00
51	Jeromy Burnitz	.15
52	Geoff Jenkins	.25
53	Mark McGwire	3.00
54	Jim Edmonds	.25
55	Rick Ankiel	.50
56	Sammy Sosa	2.00
57	*Julio Zuleta*	.15
58	Kerry Wood	.25
59	Randy Johnson	.75
60	Matt Williams	.25
61	Steve Finley	.15
62	Gary Sheffield	.30
63	Kevin Brown	.15
64	Shawn Green	.25
65	Milton Bradley	.15
66	Vladimir Guerrero	1.00
67	Jose Vidro	.15
68	Barry Bonds	.75
69	Jeff Kent	.15
70	Preston Wilson	.15
71	Mike Lowell	.15
72	Mike Piazza	2.00
73	Robin Ventura	.25
74	Edgardo Alfonzo	.25
75	Jay Payton	.15
76	Tony Gwynn	1.00
77	Adam Eaton	.15
78	Phil Nevin	.15
79	Scott Rolen	.50
80	Bob Abreu	.15
81	Pat Burrell	.50
82	Brian Giles	.25
83	Jason Kendall	.15
84	Kris Benson	.15
85	Gookie Dawkins	.15
86	Ken Griffey Jr.	2.50
87	Barry Larkin	.40
88	Larry Walker	.30
89	Todd Helton	.75
90	Ben Petrick	.15
91	*Alex Cabrera 3,500* (Ultimate Rookie 2000)	10.00
92	*Matt Wheatland 1,000* (Ultimate Rookie 2000)	25.00
93	*Joe Torres 1,000* (Ultimate Rookie 2000)	30.00
94	*Xavier Nady 1,000* (Ultimate Rookie 2000)	75.00
95	Kenny Kelly 3,500 (Ultimate Rookie 2000)	6.00
96	*Matt Ginter 3,500* (Ultimate Rookie 2000)	6.00
97	*Ben Diggins 1,000* (Ultimate Rookie 2000)	30.00
98	*Danys Baez 3,500* (Ultimate Rookie 2000)	10.00
99	*Daylan Holt 2,500* (Ultimate Rookie 2000)	15.00
100	*Kazuhiro Sasaki 3,500* (Ultimate Rookie 2000)	20.00
101	*Dane Artman 2,500* (Ultimate Rookie 2000)	10.00
102	*Mike Tonis 1,000* (Ultimate Rookie 2000)	40.00
103	*Timoniel Perez 2,500* (Ultimate Rookie 2000)	25.00
104	*Barry Zito 2,500* (Ultimate Rookie 2000)	60.00
105	*Koyie Hill 2,500* (Ultimate Rookie 2000)	8.00
106	*Brad Wilkerson 2,500* (Ultimate Rookie 2000)	20.00
107	*Juan Pierre 3,500* (Ultimate Rookie 2000)	10.00
108	*Aaron McNeal 3,500* (Ultimate Rookie 2000)	8.00
109	*Jay Spurgeon 3,500* (Ultimate Rookie 2000)	8.00
110	*Sean Burnett 1,000* (Ultimate Rookie 2000)	25.00
111	*Luis Matos 3,500* (Ultimate Rookie 2000)	8.00
112	*Dave Krynzel 1,000* (Ultimate Rookie 2000)	35.00
113	*Scott Heard 1,000* (Ultimate Rookie 2000)	25.00
114	*Ben Sheets 2,500* (Ultimate Rookie 2000)	60.00
115	*Dane Sardinha 1,000* (Ultimate Rookie 2000)	25.00
116	*David Espinosa 1,000* (Ultimate Rookie 2000)	30.00
117	*Leo Estrella 3,500* (Ultimate Rookie 2000)	6.00
118	*Kurt Ainsworth 2,500* (Ultimate Rookie 2000)	20.00
119	*Jon Rauch 2,500* (Ultimate Rookie 2000)	50.00
120	Ryan Franklin 2,500 (Ultimate Rookie 2000)	10.00

2000 Upper Deck Ultimate Victory Collection

	MT
Parallel 25 Stars:	40-80X
Rookies (91-120):	3-6X
Production 25 sets	
Parallel 100 Stars:	15-30X
Rookies (91-120):	1-3X
Production 100 sets	
Parallel 250 Stars:	5-10X
Rookies (91-120):	1-2X
Production 250 sets	

2000 Upper Deck Ultimate Victory Diamond Dignitaries

		MT
Complete Set (10):		75.00
Common Player:		3.00
Inserted 1:23		
1	Ken Griffey Jr.	12.00
2	Nomar Garciaparra	10.00
3	Chipper Jones	8.00
4	Ivan Rodriguez	4.00
5	Mark McGwire	15.00
6	Cal Ripken Jr.	12.00
7	Vladimir Guerrero	5.00
8	Alex Rodriguez	12.00
9	Sammy Sosa	10.00
10	Derek Jeter	12.00

2000 Upper Deck Ultimate Victory HOF Game Jersey

		MT
Common Card:		40.00
SA	Sparky Anderson	40.00
CF	Carlton Fisk	80.00
TP	Tony Perez	70.00

2000 Upper Deck Ultimate Victory Lasting Impressions

		MT
Complete Set (10):		30.00
Common Player:		2.00
Inserted 1:11		
1	Barry Bonds	2.00
2	Mike Piazza	5.00
3	Manny Ramirez	2.00
4	Pedro J. Martinez	2.00
5	Mark McGwire	8.00
6	Ken Griffey Jr.	6.00
7	Ivan Rodriguez	2.00
8	Jeff Bagwell	2.00
9	Randy Johnson	2.00
10	Alex Rodriguez	6.00

2000 Upper Deck Ultimate Victory Starstruck

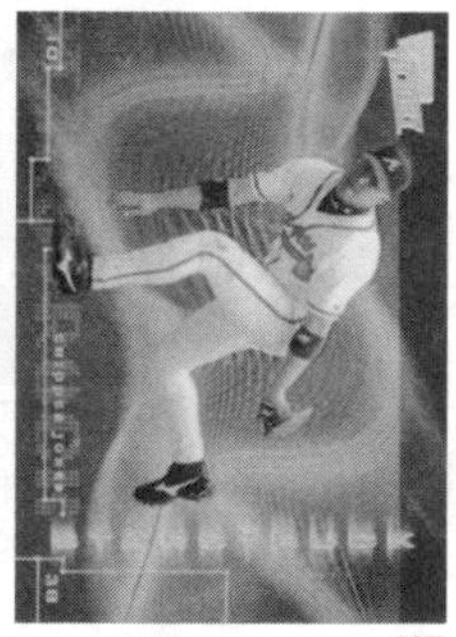

		MT
Complete Set (10):		40.00
Common Player:		2.00
Inserted 1:11		
1	Alex Rodriguez	6.00
2	Frank Thomas	3.00
3	Derek Jeter	6.00
4	Mark McGwire	8.00
5	Nomar Garciaparra	5.00
6	Chipper Jones	4.00
7	Cal Ripken Jr.	6.00
8	Sammy Sosa	5.00
9	Vladimir Guerrero	3.00
10	Ken Griffey Jr.	6.00

2000 Upper Deck Victory

Victory offers no inserts, just your standard 440-card base set that features a white-bordered design with two player images on the card front. The base set includes three subsets: Rookie 2000 (331-370); Big Play Makers (371-390) and JUNIOR Circuit (391-440).

		MT
Complete Set (440):		50.00
Common Player:		.10
Common Griffey (391-440):		.50
Pack (12):		1.00
Wax Box (36):		32.00
1	Mo Vaughn	.30
2	Garret Anderson	.10
3	Tim Salmon	.20
4	Troy Percival	.10
5	Orlando Palmeiro	.10
6	Darin Erstad	.20
7	Ramon Ortiz	.10
8	Ben Molina	.10
9	Troy Glaus	.40
10	Jim Edmonds	.10
11	Mo Vaughn, Troy Percival	.15
12	Craig Biggio	.25
13	Roger Cedeno	.10
14	Shane Reynolds	.10
15	Jeff Bagwell	.50
16	Octavio Dotel	.10
17	Moises Alou	.15
18	Jose Lima	.10
19	Ken Caminiti	.15
20	Richard Hidalgo	.10
21	Billy Wagner	.10
22	Lance Berkman	.10
23	Jeff Bagwell, Jose Lima	.25
24	Jason Giambi	.10
25	Randy Velarde	.10
26	Miguel Tejada	.10
27	Matt Stairs	.10
28	A.J. Hinch	.10
29	Olmedo Saenz	.10
30	Ben Grieve	.20
31	Ryan Christenson	.10
32	Eric Chavez	.10
33	Tim Hudson	.20
34	John Jaha	.10
35	Jason Giambi, Matt Stairs	.10
36	Raul Mondesi	.20
37	Tony Batista	.10
38	David Wells	.10
39	Homer Bush	.10
40	Carlos Delgado	.40
41	Billy Koch	.10
42	Darrin Fletcher	.10
43	Tony Fernandez	.10
44	Shannon Stewart	.20
45	Roy Halladay	.10
46	Chris Carpenter	.10
47	Carlos Delgado, David Wells	.20
48	Chipper Jones	1.00
49	Greg Maddux	1.00
50	Andruw Jones	.40
51	Andres Galarraga	.30
52	Tom Glavine	.20
53	Brian Jordan	.10
54	John Smoltz	.10
55	John Rocker	.10
56	Javy Lopez	.15
57	Eddie Perez	.10
58	Kevin Millwood	.10
59	Chipper Jones, Greg Maddux	.50
60	Jeromy Burnitz	.20
61	Steve Woodard	.10
62	Ron Belliard	.10
63	Geoff Jenkins	.20
64	Bob Wickman	.10
65	Marquis Grissom	.10
66	Henry Blanco	.10
67	Mark Loretta	.10
68	Alex Ochoa	.10
69	Marquis Grissom, Jeromy Burnitz	.10
70	Mark McGwire	2.00
71	Edgar Renteria	.10
72	Dave Veres	.10
73	Eli Marrero	.10
74	Fernando Tatis	.20
75	J.D. Drew	.20
76	Ray Lankford	.10
77	Daryle Kile	.10
78	Kent Bottenfield	.10
79	Joe McEwing	.10
80	Mark McGwire, Ray Lankford	1.00
81	Sammy Sosa	1.25
82	Jose Nieves	.10
83	Jon Lieber	.10
84	Henry Rodriguez	.10
85	Mark Grace	.20
86	Eric Young	.10
87	Kerry Wood	.25
88	Ismael Valdes	.10
89	Glenallen Hill	.10
90	Sammy Sosa, Mark Grace	.60
91	Greg Vaughn	.20
92	Fred McGriff	.20
93	Ryan Rupe	.10
94	Bubba Trammell	.10
95	Miguel Cairo	.10
96	Roberto Hernandez	.10
97	Jose Canseco	.50
98	Wilson Alvarez	.10
99	John Flaherty	.10
100	Vinny Castilla	.15
101	Jose Canseco, Roberto Hernandez	.25
102	Randy Johnson	.40
103	Matt Williams	.20
104	Matt Mantei	.10
105	Steve Finley	.10
106	Luis Gonzalez	.10
107	Travis Lee	.10
108	Omar Daal	.10
109	Jay Bell	.10
110	Erubiel Durazo	.10
111	Tony Womack	.10
112	Todd Stottlemyre	.10
113	Randy Johnson, Matt Williams	.10
114	Gary Sheffield	.25
115	Adrian Beltre	.10
116	Kevin Brown	.20
117	Todd Hundley	.10
118	Eric Karros	.20
119	Shawn Green	.40
120	Chan Ho Park	.10
121	Mark Grudzielanek	.10
122	Todd Hollandsworth	.10
123	Jeff Shaw	.10
124	Darren Dreifort	.10
125	Gary Sheffield, Kevin Brown	.15
126	Vladimir Guerrero	.75
127	Michael Barrett	.10
128	Dustin Hermanson	.10
129	Jose Vidro	.10
130	Chris Widger	.10
131	Mike Thurman	.10
132	Wilton Guerrero	.10
133	Brad Fullmer	.10
134	Rondell White	.20
135	Ugueth Urbina	.10
136	Vladimir Guerrero, Rondell White	.40
137	Barry Bonds	.50
138	Russ Ortiz	.10
139	J.T. Snow	.10
140	Joe Nathan	.10
141	Rich Aurilia	.10
142	Jeff Kent	.10
143	Armando Rios	.10
144	Ellis Burks	.10
145	Robb Nen	.10
146	Marvin Benard	.10
147	Barry Bonds, Russ Ortiz	.25
148	Manny Ramirez	.50
149	Bartolo Colon	.10
150	Kenny Lofton	.35
151	Sandy Alomar Jr.	.15
152	Travis Fryman	.15
153	Omar Vizquel	.10
154	Roberto Alomar	.40
155	Richie Sexson	.10
156	David Justice	.20
157	Jim Thome	.30
158	Manny Ramirez, Roberto Alomar	.25
159	Ken Griffey Jr.	2.00
160	Edgar Martinez	.15
161	Fred Garcia	.10
162	Alex Rodriguez	1.50
163	John Halama	.10
164	Russ Davis	.10
165	David Bell	.10
166	Gil Meche	.10
167	Jamie Moyer	.10
168	John Olerud	.20
169	Ken Griffey Jr., Fred Garcia	1.00
170	Preston Wilson	.10
171	Antonio Alfonseca	.10
172	A.J. Burnett	.10
173	Luis Castillo	.10
174	Mike Lowell	.10
175	Alex Fernandez	.10
176	Mike Redmond	.10
177	Alex Gonzalez	.10
178	Vladimir Nunez	.10
179	Mark Kotsay	.10
180	Preston Wilson, Luis Castillo	.10
181	Mike Piazza	1.25
182	Darryl Hamilton	.10
183	Al Leiter	.20
184	Robin Ventura	.20
185	Rickey Henderson	.20
186	Rey Ordonez	.10
187	Edgardo Alfonzo	.15
188	Derek Bell	.10
189	Mike Hampton	.10
190	Armando Benitez	.10
191	Mike Piazza, Rickey Henderson	.50
192	Cal Ripken Jr.	1.50
193	B.J. Surhoff	.10
194	Mike Mussina	.40
195	Albert Belle	.40
196	Jerry Hairston	.10
197	Will Clark	.20
198	Sidney Ponson	.10
199	Brady Anderson	.15
200	Scott Erickson	.10
201	Ryan Minor	.10
202	Cal Ripken Jr., Albert Belle	.75
203	Tony Gwynn	1.00
204	Bret Boone	.10
205	Ryan Klesko	.10
206	Ben Davis	.10
207	Matt Clement	.10
208	Eric Owens	.10
209	Trevor Hoffman	.10
210	Sterling Hitchcock	.10
211	Phil Nevin	.10
212	Tony Gwynn, Trevor Hoffman	.50
213	Scott Rolen	.50
214	Bob Abreu	.20
215	Curt Schilling	.20
216	Rico Brogna	.10
217	Robert Person	.10
218	Doug Glanville	.10
219	Mike Lieberthal	.10
220	Andy Ashby	.10
221	Randy Wolf	.10
222	Bob Abreu, Curt Schilling	.15
223	Brian Giles	.20
224	Jason Kendall	.20
225	Kris Benson	.10
226	Warren Morris	.10
227	Kevin Young	.10
228	Al Martin	.10
229	Wil Cordero	.10
230	Bruce Aven	.10
231	Todd Ritchie	.10
232	Jason Kendall, Brian Giles	.10
233	Ivan Rodriguez	.50
234	Rusty Greer	.10
235	Ruben Mateo	.10
236	Justin Thompson	.10
237	Rafael Palmeiro	.25
238	Chad Curtis	.10
239	Royce Clayton	.10
240	Gabe Kapler	.20
241	Jeff Zimmerman	.10
242	John Wetteland	.10

No.	Player	Price
243	Ivan Rodriguez, Rafael Palmeiro	.25
244	Nomar Garciaparra	1.25
245	Pedro Martinez	.50
246	Jose Offerman	.10
247	Jason Varitek	.10
248	Troy O'Leary	.10
249	John Valentin	.10
250	Trot Nixon	.10
251	Carl Everett	.10
252	Wilton Veras	.10
253	Bret Saberhagen	.10
254	Nomar Garciaparra, Pedro J. Martinez	.60
255	Sean Casey	.10
256	Barry Larkin	.25
257	Pokey Reese	.10
258	Pete Harnisch	.10
259	Aaron Boone	.10
260	Dante Bichette	.20
261	Scott Williamson	.10
262	Steve Parris	.10
263	Dmitri Young	.10
264	Mike Cameron	.10
265	Sean Casey, Scott Williamson	.10
266	Larry Walker	.40
267	Rolando Arrojo	.10
268	Pedro Astacio	.10
269	Todd Helton	.50
270	Jeff Cirillo	.10
271	Neifi Perez	.10
272	Brian Bohanon	.10
273	Jeffrey Hammonds	.10
274	Tom Goodwin	.10
275	Larry Walker, Todd Helton	.25
276	Carlos Beltran	.15
277	Jermaine Dye	.10
278	Mike Sweeney	.10
279	Joe Randa	.10
280	Jose Rosado	.10
281	Carlos Febles	.10
282	Jeff Suppan	.10
283	Johnny Damon	.10
284	Jeremy Giambi	.10
285	Mike Sweeney, Carlos Beltran	.10
286	Tony Clark	.20
287	Damion Easley	.10
288	Jeff Weaver	.10
289	Dean Palmer	.10
290	Juan Gonzalez	.50
291	Juan Encarnacion	.10
292	Todd Jones	.10
293	Karim Garcia	.10
294	Deivi Cruz	.10
295	Dean Palmer, Juan Encarnacion	.10
296	Corey Koskie	.10
297	Brad Radke	.10
298	Doug Mientkiewicz	.10
299	Ron Coomer	.10
300	Joe Mays	.10
301	Eric Milton	.10
302	Jacque Jones	.10
303	Chad Allen	.10
304	Cristian Guzman	.10
305	Jason Ryan	.10
306	Todd Walker	.10
307	Corey Koskie, Eric Milton	.10
308	Frank Thomas	.75
309	Paul Konerko	.10
310	Mike Sirotka	.10
311	Jim Parque	.10
312	Magglio Ordonez	.10
313	Bob Howry	.10
314	Carlos Lee	.10
315	Ray Durham	.10
316	Chris Singleton	.10
317	Brook Fordyce	.10
318	Frank Thomas, Magglio Ordonez	.25
319	Derek Jeter	1.25
320	Roger Clemens	.75
321	Paul O'Neill	.20
322	Bernie Williams	.40
323	Mariano Rivera	.20
324	Tino Martinez	.20
325	David Cone	.20
326	Chuck Knoblauch	.20
327	Darryl Strawberry	.20
328	Orlando Hernandez	.10
329	Ricky Ledee	.10
330	Derek Jeter, Bernie Williams	.50
331	Pat Burrell (Rookie 2000)	.60
332	Alfonso Soriano (Rookie 2000)	.40
333	Josh Beckett (Rookie 2000)	.75
334	Matt Riley (Rookie 2000)	.50
335	Brian Cooper (Rookie 2000)	.10
336	Eric Munson (Rookie 2000)	.75
337	Vernon Wells (Rookie 2000)	.10
338	Juan Pena (Rookie 2000)	.10
339	Mark DeRosa (Rookie 2000)	.10
340	Kip Wells (Rookie 2000)	.10
341	Roosevelt Brown (Rookie 2000)	.10
342	Jason LaRue (Rookie 2000)	.10
343	Ben Petrick (Rookie 2000)	.10
344	Mark Quinn (Rookie 2000)	.10
345	Julio Ramirez (Rookie 2000)	.10
346	Rod Barajas (Rookie 2000)	.10
347	Robert Fick (Rookie 2000)	.10
348	David Newhan (Rookie 2000)	.10
349	Eric Gagne (Rookie 2000)	.10
350	Jorge Toca (Rookie 2000)	.10
351	Mitch Meluskey (Rookie 2000)	.10
352	Ed Yarnall (Rookie 2000)	.10
353	Chad Hermansen (Rookie 2000)	.10
354	Peter Bergeron (Rookie 2000)	.10
355	Dermal Brown (Rookie 2000)	.10
356	Adam Kennedy (Rookie 2000)	.10
357	Kevin Barker (Rookie 2000)	.10
358	Francisco Cordero (Rookie 2000)	.10
359	Travis Dawkins (Rookie 2000)	.10
360	Jeff Williams (Rookie 2000)	.10
361	Chad Hutchinson (Rookie 2000)	.10
362	D'Angelo Jimenez (Rookie 2000)	.10
363	Derrick Gibson (Rookie 2000)	.10
364	Calvin Murray (Rookie 2000)	.10
365	Doug Davis (Rookie 2000)	.10
366	Rob Ramsay (Rookie 2000)	.10
367	Mark Redman (Rookie 2000)	.10
368	Rick Ankiel (Rookie 2000)	2.00
369	Domingo Guzman (Rookie 2000)	.10
370	Eugene Kingsale (Rookie 2000)	.10
371	Nomar Garciaparra (Big Play Makers)	.60
372	Ken Griffey Jr. (Big Play Makers)	1.00
373	Randy Johnson (Big Play Makers)	.20
374	Jeff Bagwell (Big Play Makers)	.25
375	Ivan Rodriguez (Big Play Makers)	.25
376	Derek Jeter (Big Play Makers)	.60
377	Carlos Beltran (Big Play Makers)	.10
378	Vladimir Guerrero (Big Play Makers)	.40
379	Sammy Sosa (Big Play Makers)	.60
380	Barry Bonds (Big Play Makers)	.25
381	Pedro Martinez (Big Play Makers)	.25
382	Chipper Jones (Big Play Makers)	.50
383	Mo Vaughn (Big Play Makers)	.15
384	Mike Piazza (Big Play Makers)	.60
385	Alex Rodriguez (Big Play Makers)	.60
386	Manny Ramirez (Big Play Makers)	.25
387	Mark McGwire (Big Play Makers)	1.00
388	Tony Gwynn (Big Play Makers)	.50
389	Sean Casey (Big Play Makers)	.10
390	Cal Ripken Jr. (Big Play Makers)	.75
391-440	Ken Griffey Jr.	.50

2000 Upper Deck Yankees Legends

		MT
Complete Set (90):		20.00
Common Player:		.15
Pack (5):		5.00
Box (24):		110.00
1	Babe Ruth	2.00
2	Mickey Mantle	2.00
3	Lou Gehrig	2.00
4	Joe DiMaggio	2.00
5	Yogi Berra	.75
6	Don Mattingly	.75
7	Reggie Jackson	1.00
8	Dave Winfield	.40
9	Bill Skowron	.15
10	Willie Randolph	.15
11	Phil Rizzuto	.50
12	Tony Kubek	.15
13	Thurman Munson	1.00
14	Roger Maris	1.00
15	Billy Martin	.40
16	Elston Howard	.15
17	Graig Nettles	.15
18	Whitey Ford	.50
19	Earl Combes	.15
20	Tony Lazzeri	.15
21	Bob Meusel	.15
22	Joe Gordon	.15
23	Jerry Coleman	.15
24	Joe Torre	.50
25	Bucky Dent	.15
26	Don Larsen	.40
27	Bobby Richardson	.15
28	Ron Guidry	.15
29	Bobby Murcer	.15
30	Tommy Henrich	.15
31	Hank Bauer	.15
32	Joe Pepitone	.15
33	Clete Boyer	.15
34	Chris Chambliss	.15
35	Tommy John	.15
36	Goose Gossage	.15
37	Red Ruffing	.15
38	Charlie Keller	.15
39	Billy Gardner	.15
40	Hector Lopez	.15
41	Cliff Johnson	.15
42	Oscar Gamble	.15
43	Allie Reynolds	.15
44	Mickey Rivers	.15
45	Bill Dickey	.50
46	Dave Righetti	.15
47	Mel Stottlemyre	.15
48	Waite Hoyt	.15
49	Lefty Gomez	.15
50	Wade Boggs	.50
51	Billy Martin (Magic Numbers)	.25
52	Babe Ruth (Magic Numbers)	1.00
53	Lou Gehrig (Magic Numbers)	1.00
54	Joe DiMaggio (Magic Numbers)	1.00
55	Mickey Mantle (Magic Numbers)	1.00
56	Yogi Berra (Magic Numbers)	.40
57	Bill Dickey (Magic Numbers)	.25
58	Roger Maris (Magic Numbers)	.50
59	Phil Rizzuto (Magic Numbers)	.25
60	Thurman Munson (Magic Numbers)	.50
61	Whitey Ford (Magic Numbers)	.25
62	Don Mattingly (Magic Numbers)	.40
63	Elston Howard (Magic Numbers)	.15
64	Casey Stengel (Magic Numbers)	.15
65	Reggie Jackson (Magic Numbers)	.50
66	Babe Ruth (1923) (The Championship Years)	1.00
67	Lou Gehrig (1927) (The Championship Years)	1.00
68	Tony Lazzeri (1928) (The Championship Years)	.15
69	Babe Ruth (1932) (The Championship Years)	1.00
70	Lou Gehrig (1936) (The Championship Years)	1.00
71	Lefty Gomez (1937) (The Championship Years)	.15
72	Bill Dickey (1938) (The Championship Years)	.25
73	Tommy Henrich (1939) (The Championship Years)	.15
74	Joe DiMaggio (1941) (The Championship Years)	1.00
75	Spud Chandler (1943) (The Championship Years)	.15
76	Tommy Henrich (1947) (The Championship Years)	.15
77	Phil Rizzuto (1949) (The Championship Years)	.25
78	Whitey Ford (1950) (The Championship Years)	.25
79	Yogi Berra (1951) (The Championship Years)	.40
80	Casey Stengel (1952) (The Championship Years)	.15
81	Billy Martin (1953) (The Championship Years)	.25
82	Don Larsen (1956) (The Championship Years)	.25
83	Elston Howard (1958) (The Championship Years)	.15
84	Roger Maris (1961) (The Championship Years)	.50
85	Mickey Mantle (1962) (The Championship Years)	1.00
86	Reggie Jackson (1977) (The Championship Years)	.50
87	Bucky Dent (1978) (The Championship Years)	.15

88	Wade Boggs (1996) (The Championship Years)	.25
89	Joe Torre (1998) (The Championship Years)	.25
90	Joe Torre (1999) (The Championship Years)	.25

2000 Upper Deck Yankees Legends Murderer's Row

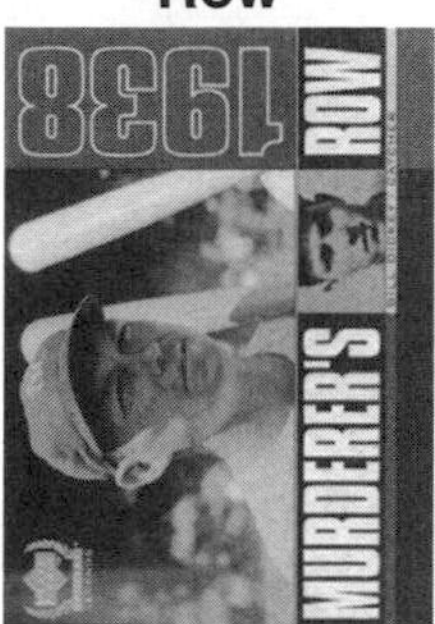

		MT
Complete Set (10):		25.00
Common Player:		1.50
Inserted 1:11		
1	Tony Lazzeri	1.50
2	Babe Ruth	10.00
3	Bob Meusel	1.50
4	Lou Gehrig	10.00
5	Joe Dugan	1.50
6	Bill Dickey	2.50
7	Waite Hoyt	1.50
8	Red Ruffing	1.50
9	Earl Combes	1.50
10	Lefty Gomez	1.50

2000 Upper Deck Yankees Legends Monument Park

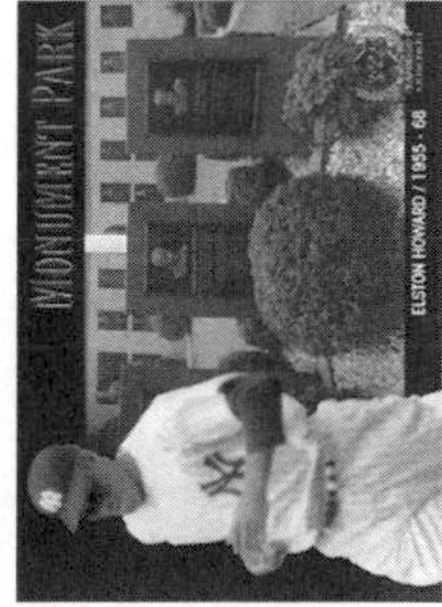

		MT
Complete Set (6):		40.00
Common Player:		
Inserted 1:23		2.50
1	Lou Gehrig	10.00
2	Babe Ruth	10.00
3	Mickey Mantle	10.00
4	Joe DiMaggio	10.00
5	Thurman Munson	5.00
6	Elston Howard	2.50

2000 Upper Deck Yankees Legends Legendary Lumber

		MT
Common Player:		20.00
Inserted 1:23		
HB	Hank Bauer	25.00
YB	Yogi Berra	75.00
PB	Paul Blair	25.00
CB	Clete Boyer	25.00
CC	Chris Chambliss	30.00
JC	Joe Collins	25.00
BD	Bucky Dent	25.00
JD	Joe DiMaggio	600.00
OG	Oscar Gamble	25.00
BG	Billy Gardner	25.00
TH	Tommy Henrich	25.00
RH	Ralph Houk	25.00
EH	Elston Howard	30.00
RJ	Reggie Jackson	75.00
TJ	Tommy John	25.00
CJ	Cliff Johnson	20.00
CK	Charlie Keller	25.00
TK	Tony Kubek	25.00
HL	Hector Lopez	20.00
MM	Mickey Mantle	400.00
RM	Roger Maris	150.00
DM	Don Mattingly	150.00
TM	Thurman Munson	100.00
BM	Bobby Murcer	35.00
GN	Graig Nettles	30.00
JP	Joe Pepitone	25.00
WR	Willie Randolph	25.00
MR	Mickey Rivers	25.00
BR	Babe Ruth	500.00
MS	Moose Skowron	25.00
DW	Dave Winfield	40.00

2000 Upper Deck Yankees Legends Legendary Pinstripes

		MT
Common Player:		40.00
Inserted 1:144		
BD	Bucky Dent	40.00
WF	Whitey Ford	80.00
LG	Lou Gehrig	600.00
GG	Goose Gossage	50.00
RG	Ron Guidry	40.00
TH	Tommy Henrich	40.00
EH	Elston Howard	40.00
RJ	Reggie Jackson	125.00
HL	Hector Lopez	40.00
MM	Mickey Mantle	500.00
RM	Roger Maris	150.00
BM	Billy Martin	100.00
DM	Don Mattingly	150.00
TM	Thurman Munson	150.00
JP	Joe Pepitone	40.00
AR	Allie Reynolds	75.00
BR	Bobby Richardson	50.00
PR	Phil Rizzuto	125.00
DW	Dave Winfield	60.00

2000 Upper Deck Yankees Legends Auto. Legendary Pinstripe

		MT
Common Player:		60.00
BD	Bucky Dent	75.00
WF	Whitey Ford	175.00
GG	Goose Gossage	75.00
RG	Ron Guidry	80.00
TH	Tommy Henrich	100.00
RJ	Reggie Jackson	
HL	Hector Lopez	
GM	Gil MacDougald	75.00
DM	Don Mattingly	275.00
JP	Joe Pepitone	60.00
BR	Bobby Richardson	
PR	Phil Rizzuto	200.00
DW	Dave Winfield	100.00

2000 Upper Deck Yankees Legends Pride of the Pinstripes

		MT
Complete Set (6):		40.00
Common Player:		3.00
Inserted 1:23		
1	Babe Ruth	10.00
2	Mickey Mantle	10.00
3	Joe DiMaggio	10.00
4	Lou Gehrig	10.00
5	Reggie Jackson	5.00
6	Yogi Berra	3.00

Modern cards in Near Mint condition are valued at about 75% of the Mint value shown here. Excellent-condition cards are worth 50%. Cards in lower grades are not generally collectible.

2000 Upper Deck Yankees Legends The Golden Years

		MT
Complete Set (10):		35.00
Common Player:		1.50
Inserted 1:11		
1	Joe DiMaggio	10.00
2	Phil Rizzuto	2.50
3	Yogi Berra	3.00
4	Billy Martin	2.50
5	Whitey Ford	2.50
6	Roger Maris	5.00
7	Mickey Mantle	10.00
8	Elston Howard	1.50
9	Tommy Henrich	1.50
10	Joe Gordon	1.50

2000 Upper Deck Yankees Legends The New Dynasty

		MT
Complete Set (10):		20.00
Common Player:		1.50
Inserted 1:11		
1	Reggie Jackson	5.00
2	Graig Nettles	1.50
3	Don Mattingly	4.00
4	Goose Gossage	1.50
5	Dave Winfield	2.50
6	Chris Chambliss	1.50
7	Thurman Munson	5.00
8	Willie Randolph	1.50
9	Ron Guidry	1.50
10	Bucky Dent	1.50

2000 UD N.Y. Yankees Master Collection

The most popular franchise in sports history

was the subject of this Master Collection limited to just 500 numbered sets. Issued in a serially-numbered mahogany box with pewter team-log inlay, each set includes 25 cards honoring the Yankees' 25 World Championships between 1923-1999. There is also a "Team of the Century" card set with 10 game-used bat cards and a special Gehrig commemorative. Each set also includes a Mystery Pack containing one of 14 autographed memorabilia cards. Retail price at time of issue was around $6,000. Because unopened sets may contain one of the better "Mystery Pack" cards, they maintain a significant premium.

	MT
Complete Boxed Set, Unopened:	5500.
Complete Boxed Set, Opened:	4000.
N.Y. Yankees Master Collection Wood Box	100.00

(See following listings for individual cards and values.)

2000 UD N.Y.Y. Master Collection World Series Champions

Each of the Yankees' 25 World Series Championships between 1923-1999 is marked with one of these "base" cards in the Master Collection. Fronts of the 2 1/2" x 3 1/2" cards have black-and-white or color poses or action photos highlighted with holographic foil. Backs have a portrait photo, a World Series summary and the player's career and Series stats. Each card is serially numbered within an edition of 500.

	MT
Complete Set (25):	950.00
Common Player:	25.00
NYY1Babe Ruth (1923)	100.00
NYY2Lou Gehrig (1927)	75.00
NYY3Tony Lazzeri (1928)	25.00
NYY4Babe Ruth (1932)	100.00
NYY5Lou Gehrig (1936)	75.00
NYY6Lefty Gomez (1937)	50.00
NYY7Bill Dickey (1938)	50.00
NYY8Bill Dickey (1939)	50.00
NYY9Tommy Henrich (1941)	35.00
NYY10Spud Chandler (1943)	25.00
NYY11Tommy Henrich (1947)	35.00
NYY12Phil Rizzuto (1949)	50.00
NYY13Whitey Ford (1950)	50.00
NYY14Yogi Berra (1951)	65.00
NYY15Casey Stengel (1952)	35.00
NYY16Billy Martin (1953)	35.00
NYY17Don Larsen (1956)	45.00
NYY18Elston Howard (1958)	25.00
NYY19Roger Maris (1961)	60.00
NYY20Mickey Mantle (1962)	100.00
NYY21Reggie Jackson (1977)	60.00
NYY22Bucky Dent (1978)	30.00
NYY23Derek Jeter (1996)	50.00
NYY24Derek Jeter (1998)	50.00
NYY25Derek Jeter (1999)	50.00

2000 UD N.Y.Y. Master Collection Team of the Century

An 11-player "Team of the Century" card set within the Yankees Master Collection features game-used bat cards from 10 of the players and a special Lou Gehrig commemorative card (Upper Deck could not get a Gehrig gamer to cut up for the cards). Each card carries an individual serial number from an edition of 500 each.

		MT
Complete Set (11):		3500.
Common Player:		125.00
	GAME-USED BAT CARDS	
(1)	Yogi Berra	300.00
(2)	Whitey Ford	250.00
(3)	Reggie Jackson	300.00
(4)	Derek Jeter	250.00
(5)	Mickey Mantle	1200.
(6)	Billy Martin	200.00
(7)	Don Mattingly	300.00
(8)	Thurman Munson	325.00
(9)	Graig Nettles	125.00
(10)	Babe Ruth	900.00
	COMMEMORATIVE CARD	
(11)	Lou Gehrig	75.00

2000 UD N.Y.Y. Master Collection Mystery Cards

Each Master Collection set contains one foil-pack Mystery Card. The pack may contain one of 14 different types of autographed player memorabilia-cards from cut signatures to bat or jersey cards. The number of each card available is listed parenthetically.

		MT
Unopened Mystery Pack:		600.00
(1)	Yogi Berra (signed bat card) (100))	675.00
(2)	Joe DiMaggio (cut signature card) (5)	2500.
(3)	Joe DiMaggio (bat/cut signature card) (5)	3500.
(4)	Lou Gehrig (cut signature card) (3)	3000.
(5)	Reggie Jackson (signed bat card) (100)	675.00
(6)	Derek Jeter (signed bat card) (100)	675.00
(7)	Derek Jeter (signed jersey card) (100)	750.00
(8)	Tony Lazzeri (cut signature card) (5)	400.00
(9)	Mickey Mantle (cut signature card) (3)	2500.
(10)	Mickey Mantle (bat/cut signature card) (7)	5500.
(11)	Billy Martin (bat/cut signature card) (2)	600.00
(12)	Babe Ruth (cut signature card) (3)	5500.
(13)	Babe Ruth (bat/cut signature card) (3)	9500.
(14)	Bernie Williams (signed jersey card) (100)	375.00

2001 Upper Deck

		MT
Complete Set (270):		40.00
Common Player:		.15
Pack (10):		3.00
Box (24):		65.00
1	Jeff DaVanon (Star Rookie)	.15
2	Aubrey Huff (Star Rookie)	.15
3	Pascual Coco (Star Rookie)	.15
4	Barry Zito (Star Rookie)	1.50
5	Augie Ojeda (Star Rookie)	.15
6	Chris Richard (Star Rookie)	.15
7	Josh Phelps (Star Rookie)	.15
8	Kevin Nicholson (Star Rookie)	.15
9	Juan Guzman (Star Rookie)	.15
10	Brandon Kolb (Star Rookie)	.15
11	Johan Santana (Star Rookie)	.15
12	Josh Kalinowski (Star Rookie)	.15
13	Tike Redman (Star Rookie)	.15
14	Ivanon Coffie (Star Rookie)	.15
15	Chad Durbin (Star Rookie)	.15
16	Derrick Turnbow (Star Rookie)	.15
17	Scott Downs (Star Rookie)	.15
18	Jason Grilli (Star Rookie)	.15
19	Mark Buehrle (Star Rookie)	.15
20	Paxton Crawford (Star Rookie)	.15
21	Bronson Arroyo (Star Rookie)	.15
22	Tomas de la Rosa (Star Rookie)	.15
23	Paul Rigdon (Star Rookie)	.15
24	Rob Ramsay (Star Rookie)	.15
25	Damian Rolls (Star Rookie)	.15
26	Jason Conti (Star Rookie)	.15
27	John Parrish (Star Rookie)	.15
28	Geraldo Guzman (Star Rookie)	.15
29	Tony Mota (Star Rookie)	.15
30	Luis Rivas (Star Rookie)	.15
31	Brian Tollberg (Star Rookie)	.15
32	Adam Bernero (Star Rookie)	.15
33	Michael Cuddyer (Star Rookie)	.15
34	Josue Espada (Star Rookie)	.15
35	Joe Lawrence (Star Rookie)	.15
36	Chad Moeller (Star Rookie)	.15
37	Nick Bierbrodt (Star Rookie)	.15
38	Dewayne Wise (Star Rookie)	.15
39	Javier Cardona (Star Rookie)	.15
40	Hiram Bocachica (Star Rookie)	.15
41	Giuseppe Chiaramonte (Star Rookie)	.15
42	Alex Cabrera (Star Rookie)	.15
43	Jimmy Rollins (Star Rookie)	.15
44	*Pat Flury* (Star Rookie)	.30
45	Leo Estrella (Star Rookie)	.15
46	Darin Erstad	.40
47	Seth Etherton	.15
48	Troy Glaus	.75
49	Brian Cooper	.15
50	Tim Salmon	.25
51	Adam Kennedy	.15
52	Bengie Molina	.15
53	Jason Giambi	.40
54	Miguel Tejada	.15
55	Tim Hudson	.25
56	Eric Chavez	.25
57	Terrence Long	.15
58	Jason Isringhausen	.15
59	Ramon Hernandez	.15
60	Raul Mondesi	.25
61	David Wells	.15
62	Shannon Stewart	.15
63	Tony Batista	.15
64	Brad Fullmer	.15
65	Chris Carpenter	.15
66	Homer Bush	.15
67	Gerald Williams	.15
68	Miguel Cairo	.15
69	Ryan Rupe	.15
70	Greg Vaughn	.25
71	John Flaherty	.15
72	Dan Wheeler	.15
73	Fred McGriff	.30
74	Roberto Alomar	.60
75	Bartolo Colon	.15
76	Kenny Lofton	.40
77	David Segui	.15

78	Omar Vizquel	.15
79	Russ Branyan	.15
80	Chuck Finley	.15
81	Manny Ramirez	.75
82	Alex Rodriguez	2.50
83	John Halama	.15
84	Mike Cameron	.15
85	David Bell	.15
86	Jay Buhner	.15
87	Aaron Sele	.15
88	Rickey Henderson	.30
89	Brook Fordyce	.15
90	Cal Ripken Jr.	2.50
91	Mike Mussina	.40
92	Delino DeShields	.15
93	Melvin Mora	.15
94	Sidney Ponson	.15
95	Brady Anderson	.25
96	Ivan Rodriguez	.75
97	Ricky Ledee	.15
98	Rick Helling	.15
99	Ruben Mateo	.15
100	Luis Alicea	.15
101	John Wetteland	.15
102	Mike Lamb	.15
103	Carl Everett	.15
104	Troy O'Leary	.15
105	Wilton Veras	.15
106	Pedro Martinez	.75
107	Rolando Arrojo	.15
108	Scott Hatteberg	.15
109	Jason Varitek	.15
110	Jose Offerman	.15
111	Carlos Beltran	.15
112	Johnny Damon	.15
113	Mark Quinn	.15
114	Rey Sanchez	.15
115	Mac Suzuki	.15
116	Jermaine Dye	.15
117	Chris Fussell	.15
118	Jeff Weaver	.15
119	Dean Palmer	.15
120	Robert Fick	.15
121	Brian Moehler	.15
122	Damion Easley	.15
123	Juan Encarnacion	.15
124	Tony Clark	.15
125	Cristian Guzman	.15
126	Matt LeCroy	.15
127	Eric Milton	.15
128	Jay Canizaro	.15
129	David Ortiz	.15
130	Brad Radke	.15
131	Jacque Jones	.15
132	Magglio Ordonez	.25
133	Carlos Lee	.15
134	Mike Sirotka	.15
135	Ray Durham	.15
136	Paul Konerko	.15
137	Charles Johnson	.15
138	James Baldwin	.15
139	Jeff Abbott	.15
140	Roger Clemens	1.00
141	Derek Jeter	2.50
142	David Justice	.40
143	Ramiro Mendoza	.15
144	Chuck Knoblauch	.25
145	Orlando Hernandez	.25
146	Alfonso Soriano	.15
147	Jeff Bagwell	.75
148	Julio Lugo	.15
149	Mitch Meluskey	.15
150	Jose Lima	.15
151	Richard Hidalgo	.15
152	Moises Alou	.15
153	Scott Elarton	.15
154	Andruw Jones	.50
155	Quilvio Veras	.15
156	Greg Maddux	1.50
157	Brian Jordan	.15
158	Andres Galarraga	.30
159	Kevin Millwood	.15
160	Rafael Furcal	.50
161	Jeromy Burnitz	.15
162	Jimmy Haynes	.15
163	Mark Loretta	.15
164	Ron Belliard	.15
165	Richie Sexson	.15
166	Kevin Barker	.15
167	Jeff D'Amico	.15
168	Rick Ankiel	.50
169	Mark McGwire	3.00
170	J.D. Drew	.25
171	Eli Marrero	.15
172	Darryl Kile	.15
173	Edgar Renteria	.15
174	Will Clark	.40
175	Eric Young	.15
176	Mark Grace	.30
177	Jon Lieber	.15
178	Damon Buford	.15
179	Kerry Wood	.30
180	Rondell White	.15
181	Joe Girardi	.15
182	Curt Schilling	.15
183	Randy Johnson	.75
184	Steve Finley	.15
185	Kelly Stinnett	.15
186	Jay Bell	.15
187	Matt Mantei	.15
188	Luis Gonzalez	.15
189	Shawn Green	.30
190	Todd Hundley	.15
191	Chan Ho Park	.15
192	Adrian Beltre	.25
193	Mark Grudzielanek	.15
194	Gary Sheffield	.30
195	Tom Goodwin	.15
196	Lee Stevens	.15
197	Javier Vazquez	.15
198	Milton Bradley	.15
199	Vladimir Guerrero	1.00
200	Carl Pavano	.15
201	Orlando Cabrera	.15
202	Tony Armas, Jr.	.15
203	Jeff Kent	.15
204	Calvin Murray	.15
205	Ellis Burks	.15
206	Barry Bonds	.75
207	Russ Ortiz	.15
208	Marvin Benard	.15
209	Joe Nathan	.15
210	Preston Wilson	.15
211	Cliff Floyd	.15
212	Mike Lowell	.15
213	Ryan Dempster	.15
214	Brad Penny	.15
215	Mike Redmond	.15
216	Luis Castillo	.15
217	Derek Bell	.15
218	Mike Hampton	.25
219	Todd Zeile	.15
220	Robin Ventura	.25
221	Mike Piazza	2.00
222	Al Leiter	.25
223	Edgardo Alfonzo	.25
224	Mike Bordick	.15
225	Phil Nevin	.15
226	Ryan Klesko	.25
227	Adam Eaton	.15
228	Eric Owens	.15
229	Tony Gwynn	1.00
230	Matt Clement	.15
231	Wiki Gonzalez	.15
232	Robert Person	.15
233	Doug Glanville	.15
234	Scott Rolen	.40
235	Mike Lieberthal	.15
236	Randy Wolf	.15
237	Bobby Abreu	.25
238	Pat Burrell	.50
239	Bruce Chen	.15
240	Kevin Young	.15
241	Todd Ritchie	.15
242	Adrian Brown	.15
243	Chad Hermansen	.15
244	Warren Morris	.15
245	Kris Benson	.15
246	Jason Kendall	.15
247	Pokey Reese	.15
248	Rob Bell	.15
249	Ken Griffey Jr.	2.50
250	Sean Casey	.15
251	Aaron Boone	.15
252	Pete Harnisch	.15
253	Barry Larkin	.40
254	Dmitri Young	.15
255	Todd Hollandsworth	.15
256	Pedro Astacio	.15
257	Todd Helton	.75
258	Terry Shumpert	.15
259	Neifi Perez	.15
260	Jeffrey Hammonds	.15
261	Ben Petrick	.15
262	Mark McGwire	1.50
263	Derek Jeter	1.25
264	Sammy Sosa	1.00
265	Cal Ripken Jr.	1.25
266	Pedro J. Martinez	.40
267	Barry Bonds	.40
268	Fred McGriff	.20
269	Randy Johnson	.40
270	Darin Erstad	.25

2001 Upper Deck Big League Beat

		MT
Complete Set (20):		20.00
Common Player:		.50
Inserted 1:3		
1	Barry Bonds	.75
2	Nomar Garciaparra	2.00
3	Mark McGwire	3.00
4	Roger Clemens	1.00
5	Chipper Jones	1.50
6	Jeff Bagwell	.75
7	Sammy Sosa	2.00
8	Cal Ripken Jr.	2.50
9	Randy Johnson	.75
10	Carlos Delgado	.75
11	Manny Ramirez	.75
12	Derek Jeter	2.50
13	Tony Gwynn	1.00
14	Pedro J. Martinez	.75
15	Jose Canseco	.50
16	Frank Thomas	1.00
17	Alex Rodriguez	2.50
18	Bernie Williams	.50
19	Greg Maddux	1.50
20	Rafael Palmeiro	.50

2001 Upper Deck e-Card

		MT
Complete Set (6):		10.00
Common Player:		1.00
Inserted 1:12		
1	Andruw Jones	1.00
2	Alex Rodriguez	4.00
3	Frank Thomas	2.00
4	Todd Helton	1.50
5	Troy Glaus	1.50
6	Barry Bonds	1.50

Player names in *Italic* type indicate a rookie card.

2001 Upper Deck Game Jersey

		MT
Common Player:		30.00
Inserted 1:288		
KG	Ken Griffey Jr.	200.00
TG	Tony Gwynn	60.00
TH	Todd Helton	60.00
TiH	Tim Hudson	40.00
DJ	Derek Jeter	200.00
AJ	Andruw Jones	50.00
SK	Sandy Koufax	250.00
PO	Paul O'Neill	50.00
MR	Manny Ramirez	50.00
CR	Cal Ripken Jr.	150.00
AR	Alex Rodriguez	125.00
IR	Ivan Rodriguez	60.00
NRa	Nolan Ryan	200.00
NRr	Nolan Ryan	200.00
FT	Fernando Tatis	40.00
RV	Robin Ventura	30.00
BW	Bernie Williams	50.00
MW	Matt Williams	30.00

2001 Upper Deck Game Jersey Hobby Autograph

		MT
Common Player:		50.00
Inserted 1:288		
RA	Rick Ankiel	60.00
JB	Jeff Bagwell	80.00
BB	Barry Bonds	125.00
JC	Jose Canseco	80.00
SC	Sean Casey	60.00
JD	J.D. Drew	50.00
JG	Jason Giambi	80.00
SG	Shawn Green	60.00
KG	Ken Griffey Jr.	350.00
MH	Mike Hampton	50.00
RJ	Randy Johnson	125.00
JL	Javy Lopez	50.00
GM	Greg Maddux	200.00
RP	Rafael Palmeiro	75.00
AR	Alex Rodriguez	250.00
NRm	Nolan Ryan	400.00
NRa	Nolan Ryan	400.00
FT	Frank Thomas	150.00

2001 Upper Deck Game Jersey Patch

		MT
Common Player:		200.00
Production 25 sets		
RA	Rick Ankiel	
JB	Jeff Bagwell	350.00
BB	Barry Bonds	400.00
JC	Jose Canseco	250.00
JG	Jason Giambi	400.00
KG	Ken Griffey Jr.	750.00
TG	Tony Gwynn	500.00
DJ	Derek Jeter	750.00
RP	Rafael Palmeiro	250.00
CR	Cal Ripken Jr.	750.00
AR	Alex Rodriguez	750.00
IR	Ivan Rodriguez	300.00
NRa	Nolan Ryan	600.00
NRr	Nolan Ryan	600.00
FT	Frank Thomas	400.00

2001 Upper Deck Game-Used Ball

	MT
Common Player:	40.00
Production 100 sets	

RA	Rick Ankiel	50.00
JB	Jeff Bagwell	60.00
BB	Barry Bonds	80.00
JG	Jason Giambi	75.00
SG	Shawn Green	40.00
KG	Ken Griffey Jr.	250.00
ToG	Tony Gwynn	80.00
DJ	Derek Jeter	200.00
RJ	Randy Johnson	60.00
AJ	Andruw Jones	75.00
MM	Mark McGwire	400.00
AR	Alex Rodriguez	225.00
IR	Ivan Rodriguez	60.00
SS	Sammy Sosa	120.00

2001 Upper Deck Home Run Explosion

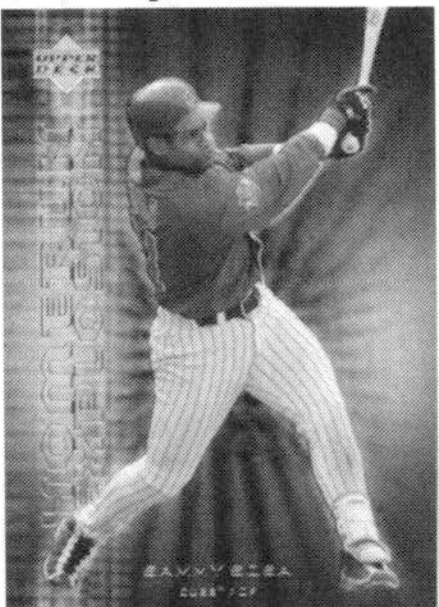

		MT
Complete Set (15):		30.00
Common Player:		.75
Inserted 1:12		
1	Mark McGwire	6.00
2	Chipper Jones	3.00
3	Jeff Bagwell	1.50
4	Carlos Delgado	1.50
5	Barry Bonds	1.50
6	Troy Glaus	1.50
7	Sammy Sosa	4.00
8	Alex Rodriguez	5.00
9	Mike Piazza	4.00
10	Vladimir Guerrero	2.00
11	Ken Griffey Jr.	6.00
12	Frank Thomas	2.00
13	Ivan Rodriguez	1.50
14	Jason Giambi	1.00
15	Carl Everett	.75

2001 Upper Deck Rookie Roundup

		MT
Complete Set (10):		6.00
Common Player:		.50
Inserted 1:6		
1	Rick Ankiel	1.50
2	Adam Kennedy	.50
3	Mike Lamb	.50
4	Adam Eaton	.50
5	Rafael Furcal	2.00
6	Pat Burrell	1.50
7	Adam Piatt	.75
8	Eric Munson	.50
9	Brad Penny	.50
10	Mark Mulder	.50

2001 Upper Deck Superstar Summit

		MT
Complete Set (15):		40.00
Common Player:		1.00
Inserted 1:12		
1	Derek Jeter	5.00
2	Randy Johnson	1.50
3	Barry Bonds	1.50
4	Frank Thomas	2.00
5	Cal Ripken Jr.	5.00
6	Pedro J. Martinez	1.50
7	Ivan Rodriguez	1.50
8	Mike Piazza	4.00
9	Mark McGwire	6.00
10	Manny Ramirez	1.50
11	Ken Griffey Jr.	5.00
12	Sammy Sosa	4.00
13	Alex Rodriguez	5.00
14	Chipper Jones	3.00
15	Nomar Garciaparra	4.00

2001 Upper Deck UD's Most Wanted

		MT
Complete Set (15):		40.00
Common Player:		1.50
Inserted 1:14		
1	Mark McGwire	8.00
2	Cal Ripken Jr.	6.00
3	Ivan Rodriguez	2.00
4	Pedro J. Martinez	2.00
5	Sammy Sosa	5.00
6	Tony Gwynn	2.50
7	Vladimir Guerrero	2.50
8	Derek Jeter	6.00
9	Mike Piazza	5.00
10	Chipper Jones	4.00
11	Alex Rodriguez	6.00
12	Barry Bonds	2.00
13	Jeff Bagwell	2.00
14	Frank Thomas	2.50
15	Nomar Garciaparra	5.00

1995 Zenith

At the top of the pyramid of Pinnacle's baseball card lines for 1995 was Zenith, a super-premium brand utilizing all-foil metallized printing technology on double-thick, 24-point cardboard stock to emphasize the quality look and feel. Six-card packs carried a retail price of $3.99. Two styles comprise the 150-card base set. The 110 veteran player cards are curiously arranged in alphabetical order according to the player's first names (with the exception of card #48, a special Japanese-language card of Hideo Nomo). These cards have a color player action photo on a black and gold background that is a view of a pyramid from its pinnacle. One the horizontal back, a portrait photo of the player in a partly-cloudy blue sky overlooks a playing field which offers his hit location preferences versus righty and lefty pitching. A scoreboard has his 1994 and career stats. The Pinnacle anti-counterfeiting optical-variable bar is in the lower-right corner. The rookie cards which comprise the final 40 cards in the set have a color photo at center with a gold-tone version of the same picture in the background. A large gold "ROOKIE" is vertically at right. Backs are similar to those on the veterans' cards except they have a scouting report in place of the hit-location chart.

		MT
Complete Set (150):		50.00
Common Player:		.25
Pack (6):		2.50
Wax Box (24):		50.00
1	Albert Belle	1.00
2	Alex Fernandez	.25
3	Andy Benes	.25
4	Barry Larkin	.50
5	Barry Bonds	1.00
6	Ben McDonald	.25
7	Bernard Gilkey	.25
8	Billy Ashley	.25
9	Bobby Bonilla	.40
10	Bret Saberhagen	.25
11	Brian Jordan	.25
12	Cal Ripken Jr.	3.50
13	Carlos Baerga	.25
14	Carlos Delgado	.75
15	Cecil Fielder	.40
16	Chili Davis	.25
17	Chuck Knoblauch	.50
18	Craig Biggio	.60
19	Danny Tartabull	.25
20	Dante Bichette	.40
21	Darren Daulton	.25
22	Dave Justice	.40
23	Dave Winfield	.40
24	David Cone	.40
25	Dean Palmer	.25
26	Deion Sanders	.50
27	Dennis Eckersley	.25
28	Derek Bell	.25
29	Don Mattingly	1.50
30	Edgar Martinez	.40
31	Eric Karros	.35
32	Erik Hanson	.25
33	Frank Thomas	1.50
34	Fred McGriff	.50
35	Gary Sheffield	.50
36	Gary Gaetti	.25
37	Greg Maddux	2.50
38	Gregg Jefferies	.25
39	Ivan Rodriguez	1.00
40	Kenny Rogers	.25
41	J.T. Snow	.40
42	Hal Morris	.25
43	Eddie Murray (3,000 hit)	.75
44	Javier Lopez	.40
45	Jay Bell	.25
46	Jeff Conine	.25
47	Jeff Bagwell	1.50
48	*Hideo Nomo*	1.50
49	Jeff Kent	.25
50	Jeff King	.25
51	Jim Thome	.75
52	Jimmy Key	.25
53	Joe Carter	.40
54	John Valentin	.25
55	John Olerud	.50
56	Jose Canseco	1.00
57	Jose Rijo	.25
58	Jose Offerman	.25
59	Juan Gonzalez	1.50
60	Ken Caminiti	.40
61	Ken Griffey Jr.	5.00
62	Kenny Lofton	.75
63	Kevin Appier	.25
64	Kevin Seitzer	.25
65	Kirby Puckett	1.50
66	Kirk Gibson	.25
67	Larry Walker	.75
68	Lenny Dykstra	.25
69	Manny Ramirez	1.00
70	Mark Grace	.40
71	Mark McGwire	5.00
72	Marquis Grissom	.25
73	Jim Edmonds	.25
74	Matt Williams	.50
75	Mike Mussina	.75
76	Mike Piazza	3.00
77	Mo Vaughn	.75
78	Moises Alou	.40
79	Ozzie Smith	.75
80	Paul O'Neill	.50
81	Paul Molitor	.75
82	Rafael Palmeiro	.75
83	Randy Johnson	.75
84	Raul Mondesi	.40
85	Ray Lankford	.25
86	Reggie Sanders	.25
87	Rickey Henderson	.75
88	Rico Brogna	.25
89	Roberto Alomar	.75
90	Robin Ventura	.40
91	Roger Clemens	2.00
92	Ron Gant	.40
93	Rondell White	.40
94	Royce Clayton	.25
95	Ruben Sierra	.25
96	Rusty Greer	.40
97	Ryan Klesko	.40
98	Sammy Sosa	2.50
99	Shawon Dunston	.25
100	Steve Ontiveros	.25
101	Tim Naehring	.25
102	Tim Salmon	.50
103	Tino Martinez	.50
104	Tony Gwynn	2.00
105	Travis Fryman	.40
106	Vinny Castilla	.35

107	Wade Boggs	.75
108	Wally Joyner	.25
109	Wil Cordero	.25
110	Will Clark	.50
111	Chipper Jones	2.50
112	C.J. Nitkowski	.25
113	Curtis Goodwin	.25
114	Tim Unroe	.25
115	Vaughn Eshelman	.25
116	Marty Cordova	.25
117	Dustin Hermanson	.25
118	Rich Becker	.25
119	Ray Durham	.25
120	Shane Andrews	.25
121	Scott Ruffcorn	.25
122	*Mark Grudzielanek*	.75
123	James Baldwin	.25
124	*Carlos Perez*	.50
125	Julian Tavarez	.25
126	Joe Vitiello	.25
127	Jason Bates	.25
128	Edgardo Alfonzo	.50
129	Juan Acevedo	.25
130	Bill Pulsipher	.25
131	*Bob Higginson*	1.50
132	Russ Davis	.25
133	Charles Johnson	.25
134	Derek Jeter	3.00
135	Phil Nevin	.25
136	LaTroy Hawkins	.25
137	Brian Hunter	.25
138	Roberto Petagine	.25
139	Jim Pittsley	.25
140	Garret Anderon	.25
141	Ugueth Urbina	.25
142	Antonio Osuna	.25
143	Michael Tucker	.25
144	Benji Gil	.25
145	Jon Nunnally	.25
146	Alex Rodriguez	4.00
147	Todd Hollandworth	.25
148	Alex Gonzalez	.25
149	*Hideo Nomo*	2.00
150	Shawn Green	1.00
---	Numeric checklist	.25
---	Chase program checklist	.25

1995 Zenith All-Star Salute

The most common of the Zenith inserts is a series of 18 All-Star Salute cards. Fronts have action photos printed on foil. Backs have the 1995 All-Star Game logo and a large photo of the player taken at the game, with a few words about his All-Star history. The Salute cards are seeded at the rate of one per six packs, on average.

		MT
Complete Set (19):		40.00
Common Player:		1.00
1	Cal Ripken Jr.	6.00
2	Frank Thomas	2.50
3	Mike Piazza	5.00
4	Kirby Puckett	2.50
5	Manny Ramirez	2.00
6	Tony Gwynn	4.00
7	Hideo Nomo	1.50
8	Matt Williams	1.50
9	Randy Johnson	1.50
10	Raul Mondesi	1.00
11	Albert Belle	2.00
12	Ivan Rodriguez	2.00
13	Barry Bonds	2.00
14	Carlos Baerga	1.00
15	Ken Griffey Jr.	8.00
16	Jeff Conine	1.00
17	Frank Thomas	2.50
18	Cal Ripken Jr.	6.00
19	Barry Bonds	2.00

1995 Zenith Rookie Roll Call

Dufex foil printing technology on both front and back is featured on this insert set. Fronts have a large and a small player photo on a green background dominated by a large star. Backs have another photo on a green and gold background. A prestigious black and gold box at left in the horizontally formatted design has a few good words about the prospect. Stated odds of finding a Rookie Roll Call card are one per 24 packs, on average.

		MT
Complete Set (18):		110.00
Common Player:		2.50
1	Alex Rodriguez	35.00
2	Derek Jeter	30.00
3	Chipper Jones	20.00
4	Shawn Green	9.00
5	Todd Hollandsworth	2.50
6	Bill Pulsipher	2.50
7	Hideo Nomo	3.00
8	Ray Durham	3.00
9	Curtis Goodwin	2.50
10	Brian Hunter	2.50
11	Julian Tavarez	2.50
12	Marty Cordova	2.50
13	Michael Tucker	2.50
14	Edgardo Alfonzo	4.00
15	LaTroy Hawkins	2.50
16	Carlos Perez	2.50
17	Charles Johnson	4.00
18	Benji Gil	2.50

1995 Zenith Z-Team

The scarcest of the Zenith insert cards are those of 18 "living legends" profiled in the Z-Team series. Found at an average rate of only one per 72 packs, the cards are printed in technology Pinnacle calls 3-D Dufex.

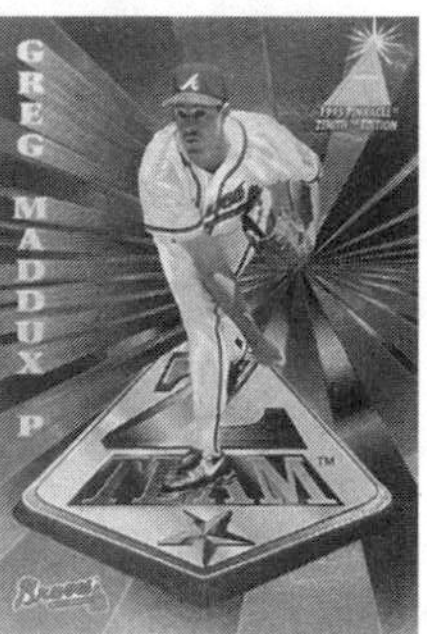

		MT
Complete Set (18):		135.00
Common Player:		2.50
1	Cal Ripken Jr.	20.00
2	Ken Griffey Jr.	25.00
3	Frank Thomas	7.50
4	Matt Williams	5.00
5	Mike Piazza	15.00
6	Barry Bonds	7.50
7	Raul Mondesi	2.50
8	Greg Maddux	12.50
9	Jeff Bagwell	7.50
10	Manny Ramirez	7.50
11	Larry Walker	5.00
12	Tony Gwynn	12.50
13	Will Clark	5.00
14	Albert Belle	6.00
15	Kenny Lofton	6.00
16	Rafael Palmeiro	5.00
17	Don Mattingly	7.50
18	Carlos Baerga	2.50

1996 Zenith

Pinnacle's 1996 Zenith set has 150 cards in the regular set, including 30 Rookies, 20 Honor roll and two checklist cards. Each card in the set has a parallel Artist's Proof version (seeded one per every 35 packs). Insert sets include Z Team, Mozaics and two versions of Diamond Club. Normal Dufex versions of Diamond Club appear one every 24 packs; parallel versions, which have an actual diamond chip incorporated into the card design, were seeded one per every 350 packs.

		MT
Complete Set (150):		40.00
Common Player:		.25
Pack (6):		3.50
Wax Box (24):		70.00
1	Ken Griffey Jr.	4.00
2	Ozzie Smith	.75
3	Greg Maddux	2.00
4	Rondell White	.40
5	Mark McGwire	4.00
6	Jim Thome	.75
7	Ivan Rodriguez	1.00
8	Marc Newfield	.25
9	Travis Fryman	.40
10	Fred McGriff	.40
11	Shawn Green	1.00
12	Mike Piazza	2.50
13	Dante Bichette	.40
14	Tino Martinez	.50
15	Sterling Hitchcock	.25
16	Ryne Sandberg	1.00
17	Rico Brogna	.25
18	Roberto Alomar	.75
19	Barry Larkin	.50
20	Bernie Williams	.75
21	Gary Sheffield	.50
22	Frank Thomas	1.25
23	Gregg Jefferies	.25
24	Jeff Bagwell	1.25
25	Marty Cordova	.25
26	Jim Edmonds	.25
27	Jay Bell	.25
28	Ben McDonald	.25
29	Barry Bonds	1.00
30	Mo Vaughn	.75
31	Johnny Damon	.25
32	Dean Palmer	.25
33	Ismael Valdes	.25
34	Manny Ramirez	1.00
35	Edgar Martinez	.25
36	Cecil Fielder	.35
37	Ryan Klesko	.40
38	Ray Lankford	.25
39	Tim Salmon	.40
40	Joe Carter	.35
41	Jason Isringhausen	.25
42	Rickey Henderson	.75
43	Lenny Dykstra	.25
44	Andre Dawson	.40
45	Paul O'Neill	.50
46	Ray Durham	.25
47	Raul Mondesi	.40
48	Jay Buhner	.40
49	Eddie Murray	.75
50	Henry Rodriguez	.25
51	Hal Morris	.25
52	Mike Mussina	.75
53	Wally Joyner	.25
54	Will Clark	.50
55	Chipper Jones	2.50
56	Brian Jordan	.25
57	Larry Walker	.75
58	Wade Boggs	.75
59	Melvin Nieves	.25
60	Charles Johnson	.25
61	Juan Gonzalez	1.00
62	Carlos Delgado	.75
63	Reggie Sanders	.25
64	Brian Hunter	.25
65	Edgardo Alfonzo	.50
66	Kenny Lofton	.75
67	Paul Molitor	.75
68	Mike Bordick	.25
69	Garret Anderson	.25
70	Orlando Merced	.25
71	Craig Biggio	.60
72	Chuck Knoblauch	.50
73	Mark Grace	.40
74	Jack McDowell	.25
75	Randy Johnson	.75
76	Cal Ripken Jr.	3.00
77	Matt Williams	.50
78	Benji Gil	.25
79	Moises Alou	.40
80	Robin Ventura	.40
81	Greg Vaughn	.40
82	Carlos Baerga	.25
83	Roger Clemens	1.50
84	Hideo Nomo	.50
85	Pedro Martinez	1.00
86	John Valentin	.25
87	Andres Galarraga	.50
88	Andy Pettitte	.75
89	Derek Bell	.25
90	Kirby Puckett	1.25
91	Tony Gwynn	2.00
92	Brady Anderson	.35
93	Derek Jeter	3.00
94	Michael Tucker	.25
95	Albert Belle	.75
96	David Cone	.35
97	J.T. Snow	.25
98	Tom Glavine	.40
99	Alex Rodriguez	3.00
100	Sammy Sosa	2.50
101	Karim Garcia	.25
102	Alan Benes	.25
103	Chad Mottola	.25
104	*Robin Jennings*	.25
105	Bob Abreu	.25
106	Tony Clark	.50

107	George Arias	.25
108	Jermaine Dye	.25
109	Jeff Suppan	.25
110	*Ralph Milliard*	.25
111	Ruben Rivera	.25
112	Billy Wagner	.25
113	Jason Kendall	.25
114	*Mike Grace*	.50
115	Edgar Renteria	.25
116	Jason Schmidt	.25
117	Paul Wilson	.25
118	Rey Ordonez	.40
119	*Rocky Coppinger*	.40
120	*Wilton Guerrero*	.75
121	Brooks Kieschnick	.25
122	Raul Casanova	.25
123	Alex Ochoa	.25
124	Chan Ho Park	.35
125	John Wasdin	.25
126	Eric Owens	.25
127	Justin Thompson	.25
128	Chris Snopek	.25
129	Terrell Wade	.25
130	*Darin Erstad*	6.00
131	Albert Belle (Honor Roll)	.50
132	Cal Ripken Jr. (Honor Roll)	1.50
133	Frank Thomas (Honor Roll)	.60
134	Greg Maddux (Honor Roll)	1.00
135	Ken Griffey Jr. (Honor Roll)	2.00
136	Mo Vaughn (Honor Roll)	.40
137	Chipper Jones (Honor Roll)	1.00
138	Mike Piazza (Honor Roll)	1.25
139	Ryan Klesko (Honor Roll)	.25
140	Hideo Nomo (Honor Roll)	.25
141	Roberto Alomar (Honor Roll)	.40
142	Manny Ramirez (Honor Roll)	.50
143	Gary Sheffield (Honor Roll)	.25
144	Barry Bonds (Honor Roll)	.50
145	Matt Williams (Honor Roll)	.25
146	Jim Edmonds (Honor Roll)	.25
147	Derek Jeter (Honor Roll)	1.50
148	Sammy Sosa (Honor Roll)	1.00
149	Kirby Puckett (Honor Roll)	.75
150	Tony Gwynn (Honor Roll)	1.00

1996 Zenith Artist's Proofs

Each card in the '96 Zenith base set can also be found in a specially marked Artist's Proof version. The AP cards were found on average of once per 35 packs.

	MT
Complete Set (150):	2000.
Common Player:	4.00

1996 Zenith Diamond Club

Twenty different players are featured on these two 1996 Pinnacle Zenith insert cards. Normal Dufex versions are inserted one per every 24 packs. Parallel versions of these cards, containing an actual diamond chip incorporated into the design, were seeded one per every 350 packs.

		MT
Complete Set (20):		125.00
Common Player:		4.00
Diamond Versions:		2x to 4x
1	Albert Belle	5.00
2	Mo Vaughn	4.00
3	Ken Griffey Jr.	20.00
4	Mike Piazza	12.00
5	Cal Ripken Jr.	15.00
6	Jermaine Dye	2.50
7	Jeff Bagwell	5.00
8	Frank Thomas	6.00
9	Alex Rodriguez	15.00
10	Ryan Klesko	3.00
11	Roberto Alomar	4.00
12	Sammy Sosa	12.00
13	Matt Williams	4.00
14	Gary Sheffield	3.00
15	Ruben Rivera	2.50
16	Darin Erstad	5.00
17	Randy Johnson	4.00
18	Greg Maddux	10.00
19	Karim Garcia	2.50
20	Chipper Jones	10.00

1996 Zenith Mozaics

Each of these 1996 Pinnacle Zenith cards contains multiple player images for the team represented on the card. The cards were inserted one per every 10 packs.

		MT
Complete Set (25):		90.00
Common Player:		1.00
1	Greg Maddux, Chipper Jones, Ryan Klesko	8.00
2	Juan Gonzalez, Will Clark, Ivan Rodriguez	4.00
3	Frank Thomas, Robin Ventura, Ray Durham	4.00
4	Matt Williams, Barry Bonds, Osvaldo Fernandez	4.00
5	Ken Griffey Jr., Randy Johnson, Alex Rodriguez	15.00
6	Sammy Sosa, Ryne Sandberg, Mark Grace	10.00
7	Jim Edmonds, Tim Salmon, Garret Anderson	2.00
8	Cal Ripken Jr., Roberto Alomar, Mike Mussina	10.00
9	Mo Vaughn, Roger Clemens, John Valentin	6.00
10	Barry Larkin, Reggie Sanders, Hal Morris	2.00
11	Ray Lankford, Brian Jordan, Ozzie Smith	2.50
12	Dante Bichette, Larry Walker, Andres Galarraga	3.00
13	Mike Piazza, Hideo Nomo, Raul Mondesi	10.00
14	Ben McDonald, Greg Vaughn, Kevin Seitzer	1.50
15	Joe Carter, Carlos Delgado, Alex Gonzalez	1.00
16	Gary Sheffield, Charles Johnson, Jeff Conine	1.50
17	Rondell White, Moises Alou, Henry Rodriguez	1.00
18	Albert Belle, Manny Ramirez, Carlos Baerga	4.00
19	Kirby Puckett, Paul Molitor, Chuck Knoblauch	4.00
20	Tony Gwynn, Rickey Henderson, Wally Joyner	8.00
21	Mark McGwire, Mike Bordick, Scott Brosius	15.00
22	Paul O'Neill, Bernie Williams, Wade Boggs	3.00
23	Jay Bell, Orlando Merced, Jason Kendall	1.00
24	Rico Brogna, Paul Wilson, Jason Isringhausen	1.00
25	Jeff Bagwell, Craig Biggio, Derek Bell	4.00

1996 Zenith Z-Team

Pinnacle's 1996 Zenith baseball continues the Z Team insert concept with a new clear plastic treatment that is micro-etched for a see-through design that allows light to shine through etched highlights and a green baseball field background. The 18 cards were seeded one per every 72 packs.

		MT
Complete Set (18):		135.00
Common Player:		5.00
1	Ken Griffey Jr.	25.00
2	Albert Belle	7.50
3	Cal Ripken Jr.	20.00
4	Frank Thomas	7.50
5	Greg Maddux	12.50
6	Mo Vaughn	4.00
7	Chipper Jones	15.00
8	Mike Piazza	15.00
9	Ryan Klesko	2.50
10	Hideo Nomo	4.00
11	Roberto Alomar	5.00
12	Manny Ramirez	7.50
13	Gary Sheffield	4.00
14	Barry Bonds	7.50
15	Matt Williams	4.00
16	Jim Edmonds	2.50
17	Kirby Puckett	7.50
18	Sammy Sosa	15.00

1997 Zenith

This set combines standard size trading cards with cards in an 8" x 10" format. The standard size set consists of 60 cards. Card fronts feature full-bleed photos and the word "Zenith", but no reference to the player's name or team is found on the fronts. Backs have another player photo, a hit location chart and 1996/career stats. There are four inserts in the set, all of which are printed on the larger size format - 8" x 10", 8" x 10" Dufex, 8" x 10" V-2, and Z-Team. Each sale unit contained one pack of five standard-size cards and two larger size cards for a suggested retail price of $9.99.

		MT
Complete Set (50):		40.00
Common Player:		.25
Pack 5 (cards) 2 (8x10):		3.00
Wax Box (12):		35.00
1	Frank Thomas	1.25
2	Tony Gwynn	2.00
3	Jeff Bagwell	1.00
4	Paul Molitor	.75
5	Roberto Alomar	.75
6	Mike Piazza	2.50
7	Albert Belle	.75
8	Greg Maddux	2.00
9	Barry Larkin	.50
10	Tony Clark	.50
11	Larry Walker	.75
12	Chipper Jones	2.50
13	Juan Gonzalez	1.00
14	Barry Bonds	1.00
15	Ivan Rodriguez	1.00
16	Sammy Sosa	2.50
17	Derek Jeter	2.50
18	Hideo Nomo	.50

19	Roger Clemens	1.50
20	Ken Griffey Jr.	4.00
21	Andy Pettitte	.60
22	Alex Rodriguez	3.00
23	Tino Martinez	.60
24	Bernie Williams	.75
25	Ken Caminiti	.40
26	John Smoltz	.40
27	Javier Lopez	.40
28	Mark McGwire	4.00
29	Gary Sheffield	.50
30	David Justice	.50
30p	David Justice (marked SAMPLE)	2.00
31	Randy Johnson	.75
32	Chuck Knoblauch	.50
33	Mike Mussina	.75
34	Deion Sanders	.50
35	Cal Ripken Jr.	3.00
36	Darin Erstad	.75
37	Kenny Lofton	.60
38	Jay Buhner	.25
39	Brady Anderson	.40
40	Edgar Martinez	.25
41	Mo Vaughn	.60
42	Ryne Sandberg	1.00
43	Andruw Jones	.75
44	Nomar Garciaparra	2.50
45	*Hideki Irabu*	1.00
46	Wilton Guerrero	.25
47	*Jose Cruz Jr.*	.75
48	Vladimir Guerrero	1.50
49	Scott Rolen	1.25
50	Jose Guillen	.25

1997 Zenith V-2

This eight-card die-cut insert utilizes motion technology as well as foil printing to create a very high-tech 8" x 10" card. Cards were inserted 1:47 packs.

		MT
Complete Set (8):		100.00
Common Player:		5.00
1	Ken Griffey Jr.	25.00
2	Andruw Jones	5.00
3	Frank Thomas	7.50
4	Mike Piazza	15.00
5	Alex Rodriguez	25.00
6	Cal Ripken Jr.	20.00
7	Derek Jeter	15.00
8	Vladimir Guerrero	15.00

1997 Zenith Z-Team

This nine-card 8" x 10" insert is printed on a mirror gold mylar foil stock with each card sequentially numbered to 1,000.

		MT
Complete Set (9):		200.00
Common Player:		5.00
1	Ken Griffey Jr.	50.00
2	Larry Walker	8.00
3	Frank Thomas	15.00
4	Alex Rodriguez	40.00
5	Mike Piazza	30.00
6	Cal Ripken Jr.	40.00
7	Derek Jeter	30.00
8	Andruw Jones	5.00
9	Roger Clemens	20.00

1997 Zenith 8x10

This 24-card insert takes select cards from the standard set and blows them up to an 8" x 10" format. Cards were inserted one per pack. A Dufex version of each 8" x 10" insert card was also available at a rate of one per pack (except in packs which contained either a Z-Team or V-2 card).

		MT
Complete Set (24):		45.00
Common Player:		1.00
Dufex versions:		1X
1	Frank Thomas	2.00
2	Tony Gwynn	3.00
3	Jeff Bagwell	1.50
4	Ken Griffey Jr.	6.00
5	Mike Piazza	4.00
6	Greg Maddux	2.50
7	Ken Caminiti	1.00
8	Albert Belle	1.00
9	Ivan Rodriguez	1.50
10	Sammy Sosa	4.00
11	Mark McGwire	6.00
12	Roger Clemens	2.00
13	Alex Rodriguez	5.00
14	Chipper Jones	3.00
15	Juan Gonzalez	1.50
16	Barry Bonds	1.50
17	Derek Jeter	4.00
18	Hideo Nomo	1.00
19	Cal Ripken Jr.	5.00
20	Hideki Irabu	1.00
21	Andruw Jones	1.00
22	Nomar Garciaparra	4.00
23	Vladimir Guerrero	2.50
24	Scott Rolen	1.50

1998 Zenith

Zenith Baseball was part of Pinnacle's "Dare to Tear" program. Sold in three-card packs, the set consisted of 5"-x-7" cards, each with a standard-size card inside. Collectors had to decide whether to keep the large cards or tear them open to get the smaller card inside. Eighty 5"-x-7" cards and 100 regular cards made up the set. The regular, or Z2, cards were paralleled twice - Z-Silver (1:7) and Z-Gold (numbered to 100). The large cards also had two parallels - Impulse (1:7) and Gold Impulse (numbered to 100). Inserts include Raising the Bar, Rookie Thrills, Epix, 5x7 Z Team, Z Team, Gold Z Team, Rookie Z Team and Gold Rookie Z Team.

		MT
Complete Set (100):		60.00
Common Player:		.25
Pack (3):		6.00
Wax Box (18):		90.00
1	Larry Walker	1.00
2	Ken Griffey Jr.	5.00
2s	Ken Griffey Jr. (SAMPLE)	3.00
3	Cal Ripken Jr.	4.00
4	Sammy Sosa	3.00
5	Andruw Jones	1.00
6	Frank Thomas	1.50
7	Tony Gwynn	2.50
8	Rafael Palmeiro	.75
9	Tim Salmon	.50
10	Randy Johnson	1.00
11	Juan Gonzalez	1.50
12	Greg Maddux	2.50
13	Vladimir Guerrero	2.00
14	Mike Piazza	3.00
15	Andres Galarraga	.50
16	Alex Rodriguez	4.00
17	Derek Jeter	4.00
18	Nomar Garciaparra	3.00
19	Ivan Rodriguez	1.50
20	Chipper Jones	3.00
21	Barry Larkin	.75
22	Mo Vaughn	.75
23	Albert Belle	1.00
24	Scott Rolen	1.50
25	Sandy Alomar Jr.	.40
26	Roberto Alomar	.75
27	Andy Pettitte	.50
28	Chuck Knoblauch	.50
29	Jeff Bagwell	1.50
30	Mike Mussina	.75
31	Fred McGriff	.40
32	Roger Clemens	2.00
33	Rusty Greer	.25
34	Edgar Martinez	.25
35	Paul Molitor	1.00
36	Mark Grace	.50
37	Darin Erstad	.50
38	Kenny Lofton	.75
39	Tom Glavine	.40
40	Javier Lopez	.25
41	Will Clark	.75
42	Tino Martinez	.50
43	Raul Mondesi	.40
44	Brady Anderson	.25
45	Chan Ho Park	.40
46	Jason Giambi	.25
47	Manny Ramirez	1.50
48	Jay Buhner	.30
49	Dante Bichette	.35
50	Jose Cruz Jr.	.25
51	Charles Johnson	.25
52	Bernard Gilkey	.25
53	Johnny Damon	.25
54	David Justice	.40
55	Justin Thompson	.25
56	Bobby Higginson	.25
57	Todd Hundley	.25
58	Gary Sheffield	.50
59	Barry Bonds	1.50
60	Mark McGwire	5.00
61	John Smoltz	.40
62	Tony Clark	.50
63	Brian Jordan	.25
64	Jason Kendall	.25
65	Mariano Rivera	.40
66	Pedro Martinez	1.50
67	Jim Thome	.75
68	Neifi Perez	.25
69	Kevin Brown	.40
70	Hideo Nomo	.50
71	Craig Biggio	.75
72	Bernie Williams	.75
73	Jose Guillen	.25
74	Ken Caminiti	.40
75	Livan Hernandez	.25
76	Ray Lankford	.25
77	Jim Edmonds	.25
78	Matt Williams	.75
79	Mark Kotsay	.25
80	Moises Alou	.40
81	Antone Williamson	.25
82	Jaret Wright	.40
83	Jacob Cruz	.25
84	Abraham Nunez	.25
85	Raul Ibanez	.25
86	Miguel Tejada	.25
87	Derek Lee	.25
88	Juan Encarnacion	.25
89	Todd Helton	.75
90	Travis Lee	.50
91	Ben Grieve	.75
92	Ryan McGuire	.25
93	Richard Hidalgo	.25
94	Paul Konerko	.50
95	Shannon Stewart	.25
96	Homer Bush	.25
97	Lou Collier	.25
98	Jeff Abbott	.25
99	Brett Tomko	.25
100	Fernando Tatis	.50

1998 Zenith Silver

This parallel set reprinted all 100 standard sized cards in Zenith on silver foilboard, with a "Z-Silver" logo across the bottom center. Z-Silvers were inserted one per seven packs.

	MT
Veteran Stars:	3X
Young Stars/RCs:	2X
Inserted 1:7	

1998 Zenith Z-Gold

	MT
Common Player:	5.00
Stars/Rookies	20X
Production 100 sets	

1998 Zenith Epix

Epix is a cross-brand insert. The set honors the top Plays, Games, Seasons and Moments in the careers of top baseball players. Epix consisted of 24 cards in Zenith, inserted 1:11. The cards have orange, purple and emerald versions.

		MT
Common Card:		1.50
Purples:		1.5X
Emeralds:		2X
1	Ken Griffey Jr. S	30.00
2	Juan Gonzalez S	8.00
3	Jeff Bagwell S	6.00
4	Ivan Rodriguez S	6.00
5	Nomar Garciaparra S	15.00
6	Ryne Sandberg S	6.00
7	Frank Thomas M	15.00
8	Derek Jeter M	25.00
9	Tony Gwynn M	20.00
10	Albert Belle M	6.00
11	Scott Rolen M	8.00
12	Barry Larkin M	5.00
13	Alex Rodriguez P	6.00
14	Cal Ripken Jr. P	6.00
15	Chipper Jones P	5.00
16	Roger Clemens P	4.00
17	Mo Vaughn P	1.50
18	Mark McGwire P	8.00
19	Mike Piazza G	8.00
20	Andruw Jones G	2.50
21	Greg Maddux G	6.00
22	Barry Bonds G	3.00
23	Paul Molitor G	2.50
24	Eddie Murray G	2.50

1998 Zenith Raising the Bar

Raising the Bar is a 15-card insert seeded 1:25. The set features players who have set high standards for other players to follow.

		MT
Complete Set (15):		150.00
Common Player:		6.00
Inserted 1:25		
1	Ken Griffey Jr.	25.00
2	Frank Thomas	8.00
3	Alex Rodriguez	20.00
4	Tony Gwynn	12.00
5	Mike Piazza	15.00
6	Ivan Rodriguez	6.00
7	Cal Ripken Jr.	20.00
8	Greg Maddux	12.00
9	Hideo Nomo	5.00
10	Mark McGwire	25.00
11	Juan Gonzalez	8.00
12	Andruw Jones	5.00
13	Jeff Bagwell	6.00
14	Chipper Jones	15.00
15	Nomar Garciaparra	15.00

1998 Zenith Rookie Thrills

Rookie Thrills is a 15-card insert seeded 1:25. The set features many of the top rookies of 1998 in action photos printed on a silver-foil background. Backs have a few words about the player's career to that point.

		MT
Complete Set (15):		40.00
Common Player:		3.00
Inserted 1:25		
1	Travis Lee	5.00
2	Juan Encarnacion	3.00
3	Derrek Lee	3.00
4	Raul Ibanez	3.00
5	Ryan McGuire	3.00
6	Todd Helton	6.00
7	Jacob Cruz	3.00
8	Abraham Nunez	3.00
9	Paul Konerko	4.00
10	Ben Grieve	6.00
11	Jeff Abbott	3.00
12	Richard Hidalgo	3.00
13	Jaret Wright	3.00
14	Lou Collier	3.00
15	Miguel Tejada	4.00

1998 Zenith Z-Team

The Z Team insert was created in 5x7 and standard-size versions, each inserted at a 1:35 pack rate. The nine Rookie Z Team cards were seeded 1:58 and gold versions of both were found 1:175.

		MT
Complete Set (18):		200.00
Common Player:		6.00
Golds:		2X
Inserted 1:175		
1	Frank Thomas	10.00
2	Ken Griffey Jr.	30.00
3	Mike Piazza	20.00
4	Cal Ripken Jr.	25.00
5	Alex Rodriguez	25.00
6	Greg Maddux	15.00
7	Derek Jeter	20.00
8	Chipper Jones	20.00
9	Roger Clemens	10.00
10	Ben Grieve	8.00
11	Derrek Lee	6.00
12	Jose Cruz Jr.	6.00
13	Nomar Garciaparra	20.00
14	Travis Lee	8.00
15	Todd Helton	8.00
16	Paul Konerko	6.00
17	Miguel Tejada	8.00
18	Scott Rolen	10.00

1998 Zenith 5x7

The 80 Zenith 5x7 cards all contained a regular-size card. Collectors could tear open the 5x7 to get at the smaller card inside. The set has two parallels: 5x7 Impulse (1:7) and 5x7 Gold Impulse (1:43).

		MT
Complete Set (80):		75.00
Common Player:		.50
1	Nomar Garciaparra	5.00
2	Andres Galarraga	1.00
3	Greg Maddux	4.00
4	Frank Thomas	2.50
5	Mark McGwire	8.00
6	Rafael Palmeiro	1.00
7	John Smoltz	.50
8	Jeff Bagwell	2.00
9	Andruw Jones	1.50
10	Rusty Greer	.50
11	Paul Molitor	1.50
12	Bernie Williams	1.50
13	Kenny Lofton	1.50
14	Alex Rodriguez	6.00
15	Derek Jeter	5.00
16	Scott Rolen	2.00
17	Albert Belle	2.00
18	Mo Vaughn	1.50
19	Chipper Jones	5.00
20	Chuck Knoblauch	.75
21	Mike Piazza	5.00
22	Tony Gwynn	4.00
23	Juan Gonzalez	2.00
24	Andy Pettitte	.75
25	Tim Salmon	.75
26	Brady Anderson	.50
27	Mike Mussina	1.50
28	Edgar Martinez	.50
29	Jose Guillen	.50
30	Hideo Nomo	.50
31	Jim Thome	.75
32	Mark Grace	.50
33	Darin Erstad	.50
34	Bobby Higginson	.50
35	Ivan Rodriguez	2.00
36	Todd Hundley	.50
37	Sandy Alomar Jr.	.50
38	Gary Sheffield	.75
39	David Justice	.75
40	Ken Griffey Jr.	8.00
41	Vladimir Guerrero	3.00
42	Larry Walker	1.00
43	Barry Bonds	2.00
44	Randy Johnson	1.50
45	Roger Clemens	3.00
46	Raul Mondesi	.50
47	Tino Martinez	.75
48	Jason Giambi	.50
49	Matt Williams	.75
50	Cal Ripken Jr.	6.00
51	Barry Larkin	1.00
52	Jim Edmonds	.50
53	Ken Caminiti	.50
54	Sammy Sosa	5.00
55	Tony Clark	.75
56	Manny Ramirez	2.00
57	Bernard Gilkey	.50
58	Jose Cruz Jr.	.50
59	Brian Jordan	.50
60	Kevin Brown	.50
61	Craig Biggio	1.00
62	Javier Lopez	.50
63	Jay Buhner	.75
64	Roberto Alomar	1.50
65	Justin Thompson	.50
66	Todd Helton	1.50
67	Travis Lee	.75
68	Paul Konerko	.50
69	Jaret Wright	.50
70	Ben Grieve	1.50
71	Juan Encarnacion	.50
72	Ryan McGuire	.50
73	Derrek Lee	.50
74	Abraham Nunez	.50
75	Richard Hidalgo	.50
76	Miguel Tejada	.50
77	Jacob Cruz	.50
78	Homer Bush	.50
79	Jeff Abbott	.50
80	Lou Collier	.50
	Checklist	.50

1998 Zenith 5x7 Silver

These silver parallels reprinted each of the 80 cards in the 5" x 7" set. Cards were called Impulse and carried that logo on the front and were inserted one per seven packs. Since these cards contained other cards inside them, they are condition sensitive and only worth full price if left in mint condition and not cut open.

	MT
Veteran Stars:	3X
Young Stars/RCs:	2.5X
Inserted 1:7	

1998 Zenith 5x7 Gold

The 5x7 Gold Impulse set parallels the 80-card 5x7 base set. The cards were inserted one per 43 packs.

		MT
Common Player:		10.00
Semistars:		25.00
Production 100 sets		
1	Nomar Garciaparra	100.00
2	Andres Galarraga	30.00
3	Greg Maddux	100.00
4	Frank Thomas	60.00
5	Mark McGwire	200.00
6	Rafael Palmeiro	30.00
7	John Smoltz	15.00
8	Jeff Bagwell	50.00
9	Andruw Jones	30.00
10	Rusty Greer	20.00
11	Paul Molitor	30.00
12	Bernie Williams	30.00
13	Kenny Lofton	30.00
14	Alex Rodriguez	100.00
15	Derek Jeter	100.00
16	Scott Rolen	50.00
17	Albert Belle	30.00
18	Mo Vaughn	30.00
19	Chipper Jones	100.00
20	Chuck Knoblauch	25.00
21	Mike Piazza	100.00
22	Tony Gwynn	80.00
23	Juan Gonzalez	50.00
24	Andy Pettitte	20.00
25	Tim Salmon	20.00
26	Brady Anderson	15.00
27	Mike Mussina	30.00
28	Edgar Martinez	15.00
29	Jose Guillen	10.00
30	Hideo Nomo	20.00
31	Jim Thome	25.00
32	Mark Grace	20.00
33	Darin Erstad	30.00
34	Bobby Higginson	15.00
35	Ivan Rodriguez	40.00
36	Todd Hundley	10.00
37	Sandy Alomar Jr.	20.00
38	Gary Sheffield	20.00
39	David Justice	20.00
40	Ken Griffey Jr.	160.00
41	Vladimir Guerrero	70.00
42	Larry Walker	30.00
43	Barry Bonds	40.00
44	Randy Johnson	30.00
45	Roger Clemens	75.00
46	Raul Mondesi	15.00
47	Tino Martinez	20.00
48	Jason Giambi	10.00
49	Matt Williams	25.00
50	Cal Ripken Jr.	125.00
51	Barry Larkin	25.00
52	Jim Edmonds	15.00
53	Ken Caminiti	20.00
54	Sammy Sosa	100.00
55	Tony Clark	20.00
56	Manny Ramirez	40.00
57	Bernard Gilkey	10.00
58	Jose Cruz Jr.	20.00
59	Brian Jordan	10.00
60	Kevin Brown	20.00
61	Craig Biggio	30.00
62	Javier Lopez	20.00
63	Jay Buhner	20.00
64	Roberto Alomar	30.00
65	Justin Thompson	15.00
66	Todd Helton	30.00
67	Travis Lee	25.00
68	Paul Konerko	20.00
69	Jaret Wright	20.00
70	Ben Grieve	25.00
71	Juan Encarnacion	20.00
72	Ryan McGuire	15.00
73	Derrek Lee	10.00
74	Abraham Nunez	10.00
75	Richard Hidalgo	10.00
76	Miguel Tejada	20.00
77	Jacob Cruz	10.00
78	Homer Bush	10.00
79	Jeff Abbott	10.00
80	Lou Collier	10.00
	Checklist	10.00

1998 Zenith 5x7 Z-Team

The 5x7 Z Team insert is a nine-card set seeded one per 35 packs.

		MT
Complete Set (9):		250.00
Common Player:		15.00
Inserted 1:35		
1	Frank Thomas	15.00
2	Ken Griffey Jr.	50.00
3	Mike Piazza	30.00
4	Cal Ripken Jr.	40.00
5	Alex Rodriguez	40.00
6	Greg Maddux	25.00
7	Derek Jeter	30.00
8	Chipper Jones	30.00
9	Roger Clemens	20.00